KU-751-934

THE OXFORD THESAURUS

The OXFORD THESAURUS

An A–Z Dictionary of Synonyms

Laurence Urdang

CLARENDON PRESS · OXFORD

Oxford University Press, Walton Street, Oxford OX2 6DP
Oxford New York Toronto
Delhi Bombay Calcutta Madras Karachi
Kuala Lumpur Singapore Hong Kong Tokyo
Nairobi Dar es Salaam Cape Town
Melbourne Auckland Madrid
and associated companies in
Berlin Ibadan

Oxford is a trade mark of Oxford University Press

First published 1991

This edition not available in the USA

British Library Cataloguing in Publication Data
Data available

Plain Edition ISBN 0-19-869151-3
Thumb Index Edition ISBN 0-19-869215-3

5 7 9 10 8 6

Printed in the United States of America

For Irene, Nicole, and Alexa

Foreword

THE biggest problem with a book of this length and complexity is that one's competence and uniformity of judgement improve in the course of its preparation, gaining adequacy in the task only as the deadline for delivery of the manuscript draws nigh. Of course, given all the time in the world one would never complete any project, for each revision would yield not only greater experience but, theoretically, the temptation to achieve perfection, clearly unattainable.

The idea of publishing the *Oxford Thesaurus* was first broached to me in 1986. The book was originally to have been some 300,000 words in length; for various reasons, it was subsequently agreed to increase its size, and the book you are holding contains approximately 650,000 words (not counting the Index). Although Janet Whitcut and Sue Lloyd read the entire text and checked it for conformity to British idiom, the ultimate responsibility for the *Thesaurus* rests with me, not only for errors of omission and commission but for any benefits that I hope might be derived from its use.

LAURENCE URDANG

April 1991
Aylesbury, Buckinghamshire

Introduction

In its narrowest sense, a synonym is a word or phrase that is perfectly substitutable in a context for another word or phrase. People who study language professionally agree that there is no such thing as an ideal synonym, for it is virtually impossible to find two words or phrases that are identical in denotation (meaning), connotation, frequency, familiarity, and appropriateness. Indeed, linguists have long noted the *economy of language*, which suggests that no language permits a perfect fit, in all respects, between any two words or phrases. Many examples of overlapping can be cited; the more obvious ones in English are those that reflect a duplication arising from Germanic and Romance sources, like *motherly* and *maternal*, *farming* and *agriculture*, *teach* and *instruct*. In such pairs the native English form is often the one with an earthier, warmer connotation. In some instances, where a new coinage or a loanword has been adopted inadvertently duplicating an existing term, creating 'true' synonyms, the two will quickly diverge, not necessarily in meaning but in usage, application, connotation, level, or all of these. For example, scientists some years ago expressed dissatisfaction with the term *tidal wave*, for the phenomenon was not caused by tides but, usually, by submarine seismic activity. The word *tsunami* was borrowed from Japanese in an attempt to describe the phenomenon more accurately, but it was later pointed out that *tsunami* means 'tidal wave' in Japanese. Today, the terms exist side by side in English, the older expression still in common use, the newer more frequent in the scientific and technical literature.

Any synonym book must be seen as a compromise that relies on the sensitivity of its users to the idiomatic nuances of the language. In its best applications, it serves to remind users of words, similar in meaning, that might not spring readily to mind, and to offer lists of words and phrases that are alternatives to and compromises for those that might otherwise be overused and therefore redundant, repetitious, and boring. The *Oxford Thesaurus* goes a step further by offering example sentences to illustrate the uses of the headwords and their alternatives in natural, idiomatic contexts. In addition, by marking those synonyms that appear as main entries in the book and by providing a detailed Index of words and expressions, the *Thesaurus* offers an effective, useful networking feature that unifies the language covered into an integrated whole.

1. Selection of headwords

Two criteria have been employed: first, headwords have been selected because of their frequency in the language, on the assumption that synonyms are more likely to be sought for the words that are most used; second, some headwords of lower frequency have been included because it would otherwise be impossible to find a suitable place to group together what are perceived as useful sets of synonyms with their attendant illustrative sentences. Obvious listings have been omitted on the grounds that users of the *Thesaurus* can easily find synonyms for, say, *abdication* by making nouns out of the verbs listed under *abdicate*. This deliberate attempt to avoid duplication is mitigated in the case of very common words. For the convenience of the user, both *shy* and *bashful* are main entries, as are *method*, *manner*, and *mode*, which, though much the same in some respects, differ in detail and application. In this book, however, *mitigate* is a main entry but not *mitigation*, *mistake* and *mistaken* are main entries but not *mistakenly*, etc. Where it is determined that such derivations are neither automatic nor semantically obvious, separate listings have been provided. In all instances, it is wise to consult the Index first to find a word.

2. Index

The Index lists, in alphabetical order, the occurrences of words and phrases that appear among the synonyms in the main text and as main entries, the latter being easily identified by a degree sign. Many Index entries have several references to main entries where the sought-after word or phrase can be found; these references serve as gist-words that pinpoint the particular sense of the word being sought, enabling the user to go directly to the most appropriate main entry. For a fuller description of the principles and layout of the Index, see 'How to use the Index' on p. 559.

3. Illustrative sentences

On the principle that a word is known by the company it keeps, one or more sentences showing the main entry word in context are provided for each sense discrimination. These have been carefully selected to demonstrate the use of the main entry in a context likely to be encountered in familiar written or spoken ordinary English. (See also **8. Substitutability,** below.)

4. Synonym lists

Each main entry is followed by one or more sense groupings, each illustrated by one or more sentences. An effort has been made to group the synonyms semantically as well as syntactically and idiomatically: that is, each synonym listed within a given set should prove to be more or less substitutable for the main entry in the illustrative sentence.

In some instances, idiomatic congruity may, unavoidably, become strained; where it is felt to be stretched too far—though still properly listed among its accompanying synonyms—a semicolon has been inserted to separate sub-groups of synonyms, and, in many cases, additional illustrative sentences have been provided. Such sub-groupings have been confined largely to distinctions between literal uses and figures of speech, between transitive and intransitive verbs, and between synonyms that differ in more subtle aspectual characteristics of meaning or syntax. (See also **8. Substitutability,** below.)

Not all senses of all words are covered for either or both of the following reasons: the sense, though it exists, is relatively rare in ordinary discourse and writing; there are no reasonable synonyms for it. Thus, this sense of *mercy*,

> an affecting or moving of the mind in any way; a mental state brought about by any influence; an emotion or feeling: *Mercy is an affection of the mind.*

is not covered for the first reason, as it is a literary and somewhat archaic usage. The same can be said for the sense,

> a bodily state due to any influence

and for other senses listed in the largest dictionaries but rarely encountered except in literary contexts. Even in such contexts it would be unusual to need a synonym for this word and others like it.

5. Cross references

There are very few cross references between main listings in the *Thesaurus*, for the Index serves as the chief finding mechanism, and it was felt desirable to avoid unnecessary duplications of listings. Where such cross references do occur, they are simple and straightforward:

> **superior** *adj*. . . . 3 See **supercilious,** above.
> —*n*. 4 See **supervisor,** below.

A number of cross references occur within entries, between variant forms of an expression. At the entry for *take*, for example, as one can say either *take* or *take it* in the sense of 'understand' etc., the option is shown in the following way:

> **take** *v*. . . . **19** understand, gather, interpret, perceive, apprehend, deduce, conclude, infer, judge, deem, assume, suppose, imagine, see: *I take him to be a fool. I take it from your expression that you've had bad news.*

> **33 *take it*: a** withstand *or* tolerate *or* survive punishment *or* abuse, survive: *The Marines are extremely tough and can take it.* **b** See **19,** above.

In a few entries, the form 'See also' is used.

A unique feature of the *Thesaurus* is the cross-referencing from synonyms to entries. In this system, a degree sign (°) preceding a synonym indicates that this word also appears as a main entry at which the reader may find further useful synonyms. Thus, users seeking a different aspect or nuance of meaning of a synonym so marked are at once alerted to the fact that it has its own main entry and can look it up directly, without recourse to the Index:

> **locale** *n.* °site, °location, °spot, °place, °setting, venue, °neighbourhood, °situation, locality: *We moved the locale of the film to Spain.*

However, in some cases it would not be helpful to mark a synonym which appears as a main entry, as the reader would not find a useful list of synonyms there. This especially applies where a synonym is a phrase whose elements may mean something very different on their own. So, in this example,

> **overshadow** *v.* ... **2** °spoil, °blight, °ruin, °mar, take (all) the pleasure from, put a damper on, take the edge off, °impair, take the enjoyment out of: *The news from the east overshadowed everyone's spirits at the party.*

'take', 'pleasure', 'put', 'edge', and 'enjoyment' are not marked, even though each appears as a headword, because on their own they are not close in meaning to 'overshadow', and the reader would not find further synonyms of 'overshadow' in these entries.

The degree sign may also appear in front of a plural noun which occurs as a headword in its singular form:

> **pretence** *n.* **1** °show, °display, °pretension, °ostentation, °airs ...
>
> ...
>
> **air** *n.* ... **5** ***airs***: °pretension, °pretence, °show, affectedness ...

6. Labels

A. All words and phrases that are recognized as being typical of a particular variety of English, whether geographical or stylistic, are labelled. It might at first seem that a large number of colloquial, slang, and taboo words have been included, but that is less to provide such alternatives to the main entries than it is to ensure their presence in the Index so that users who need alternatives to them can find them readily. The labels used are those commonly encountered in ordinary dictionaries:

Colloq Colloquial; informal; used in everyday conversation and writing, especially in the popular press and in dramatic dialogue; sometimes avoided where more formal language is felt to be appropriate, as in business correspondence, scholarly works, technical reports, documents, etc.

Slang Belonging to the most informal register and characteristic of spoken English; often originating in the cult language of a particular socio-cultural group. Not sufficiently elevated to be used in most writing (aside from dialogue), although often found in the popular press and frequently heard on popular radio and television programmes.

Taboo Not used in polite society, usually because of the risk of offending sexual, religious, or cultural sensibilities; occasionally encountered on late-night television and radio; often occurring in graffiti and in dialogue in novels, plays, and films.

Archaic Describing an obsolete word or phrase (like *tickety-boo*, *lounge lizard*) that is used deliberately to invoke the feeling of a bygone time.

Old-fashioned Used of a synonym (like *comfit*) that is no longer current but might occasionally be encountered among older speakers and in older writing.

Technical Used of a somewhat specialized word that is not commonly encountered in ordinary, everyday English, like *defalcator*, which appears as a synonym under *swindler*.

Literary Describes a word, like *euchre* 'cheat', that is not usually met with in everyday language, even of the formal genre, but may be found in poetry and other literary works.

Brit, US, Australian, Canadian, New Zealand Marks a word or phrase that occurs mainly in the designated variety.

The meanings of other labels are self-evident.

B. All labels can occur in combination. Usage labels always take precedence over regional labels. For example,

> **pushover** *n.* **1** sure thing, *Colloq* piece of cake, child's play, snap, picnic, walk-over, *US* breeze, *Slang* cinch, *Brit* doddle, *US* lead-pipe cinch.

Here, 'sure thing' is standard universal English. All words and phrases following *Colloq* up to the *Slang* label are colloquial: 'piece of cake, . . . walkover' are universal colloquial English, 'breeze' is US colloquial. All synonyms following the *Slang* label are slang; 'cinch' is universal English slang, 'doddle' is confined to British slang, and 'lead-pipe cinch' is confined to American slang.

> **talented** *adj.* . . . *Colloq* ace, crack, top-notch, *Brit* wizard, whizzo, *US* crackerjack.

In this entry, all synonyms shown are colloquial, 'ace, crack, topnotch' being universal English, 'wizard, whizzo' British, and 'crackerjack' US.

It must be emphasized that such labels are to some extent impressionistic and are based in the *Thesaurus* on a consensus of several sources: that is, there is no implication that 'breeze' is never used in the sense of 'pushover' except in the US, nor should such an inference be made.

C. Comments regarding what might be viewed as 'correct' in contrast to 'incorrect' usage are generally avoided. For example, the non-standard use of *between* in contexts referring to more than two of anything or of *among* in contexts involving fewer than three goes unmarked. However, if the usage question is confined to what can easily be represented in a 'lexical' environment, then suitable treatment is accorded it; thus 'now' and 'at present' are labelled *Non-Standard* under *presently*. To take another example, 'different to', in the typically British usage *His house is different to mine*, is rarely encountered in American English; in American English, purists condemn 'different than', as in *His house is different than mine*, which is increasingly heard in British English; purists on both sides of the Atlantic prefer 'different from'. Such matters are best left to usage books and to usage notes in dictionaries and are not treated in the *Thesaurus*.

D. Main entry words and sub-entries are not labelled, only the synonyms. Thus, under *beat* appears the idiomatic expression, *beat it*, which is not labelled:

> **8** ***beat it:*** depart, leave, abscond, run off *or* away, *Slang US* take it on the lam, lam out of here, hit the road: *You'd better beat it before the cops come.*

The idiom is not labelled because it is assumed that the user has looked it up to find a substitute for it, hence needs no information about it other than a listing of its alternatives (which are labelled, when appropriate) and an illustrative example. Should users need more detailed information about a given word or phrase, they should follow up further references to it in the Index and also resort to a dictionary, the proper repository for such information.

A rare exception to the above rule occurs where a headword has one meaning in British English and quite a different meaning in another regional variety. Thus:

> **subway** *n.* **1** *In US*: underground (railway), tube: *She takes the subway to work.* **2** *In Britain*: tunnel, underpass: *Use the subway to cross the road in safety.*

Here, the two regional labels do not apply to the synonyms (since, for example, 'tunnel' has the same meaning in both British and US English) but to the two definitions of the headword.

E. Synonyms bearing any kind of label appear at the end of the set in which they are listed, except in the case described immediately above.

7. Spelling and other variants

The spellings shown throughout are those preferred by most modern British writers. British variant spellings are shown; if they are variants of the main entry word, they appear as the first word in the set(s) of synonyms following:

> **mousy** *adj.* 1 mousey, . . .
> **movable** *adj.* moveable, . . .

Such variants are also shown when they appear within an entry:

> **movable** *adj.* . . . transferable *or* transferrable, . . .

Common American spelling variants (*humor, traveler, unraveled*) are not shown, but less common ones are listed for convenience. Where both forms are variants in American spelling, they are described by '*or US also*':

> . . . accoutrements *or US also* accouterments, . . .
> . . . phoney *or US also* phony, . . .

This should be understood to mean 'the normal British spelling is *accoutrements* (or *phoney*); this form, together with *accouterments* (or *phony*), occurs in American English'.

8. Substitutability

A. The purpose of a synonym book is to provide the user with a collection of words that are as close as possible in meaning to a designated word. The *Oxford Thesaurus* tries to go to a step further by providing examples that not only illustrate the main entry word in a natural contextual environment but also allow the user to substitute as many of the synonyms as possible into the framework of the context. For example:

> **porous** *adj.* spongy, spongelike, permeable, pervious, penetrable: *The rainwater runs through the porous rock and collects in the pools below.*

It is possible to substitute for *porous* in the sample sentence any of the words given as synonyms without any adjustment of the grammar or phrasing of the example. That is not to suggest that the synonyms are identical: 'permeable' and 'pervious' belong to a different register from that of 'spongy, spongelike', being more common in technical usage. Some might argue that 'penetrable' is not synonymous with the other listed words; but it is the function of this book to provide synonyms for the main entries, not for the other synonyms that might be listed. No claim is made—nor could it be made—that synonyms are identical, either to one another or to another word, merely that they fall well within the criteria of what, for practical purposes, is viewed as synonymy in the language.

It is certainly true that substituting for *porous* any of the five listed synonyms will yield five standard English sentences.

B. Some judgement is required of the user in determining the syntax and idiomaticity with which a given word or expression can be substituted in an illustrative context: words are rarely as readily interchangeable in a context as might be components in a chemical or mathematical formula. Moreover, while such formulae are reflective of science, language offers its users the virtually infinite variety available only in art, with each individual speaker of any language being presented with the opportunity to become an artist.

In the following example, nearly all terms can be substituted for *adjoining* in the first illustrative sentence; to create idiomatic parallels to the second sentence, the parenthetical prepositions must be used:

> **adjoining** *adj*. neighbouring, contiguous (to), adjacent (to), abutting, bordering, next (to): *We have bought the adjoining land and will build our new house there. The land adjoining the supermarket is for sale.*

Interpreting this, the following are all idiomatic: *adjoining land*, *neighbouring land*, *contiguous land*, *adjacent land*, *abutting land*, and *bordering land*. But if the context requires the adjective to come after *land* (with a following noun), then the parenthetical words must be added to yield constructions that are idiomatic, like *land adjoining the supermarket*, *land neighbouring the supermarket*, *land contiguous to the supermarket*, *land adjacent to the supermarket*, *land abutting the supermarket*, *land bordering the supermarket*, and *land next to the supermarket*.

As this is intended as a synonym book and not a work on English collocations, the treatment of idiomaticity cannot be taken further.

C. There are other reasons why direct substitutability is not always possible within a single semantic concept. The following extract demonstrates this:

> **possess** *v*. . . . 3 dominate, control, govern, consume, take control of, preoccupy, obsess; charm, captivate, enchant, cast a spell on *or* over, bewitch, enthral: *What possessed her to think that I could help? He behaves as if he is possessed by the devil.*

Here, two aspects of the same sense have been divided by a semicolon, with the synonyms preceding the semicolon illustrated by the first contextual example and those following it by the second. While it may be argued that in this instance the synonyms following the semicolon, with their illustrative sentence, might better have been listed in a separately numbered set, the close semantic association of the two groups would thereby have been lost.

D. Sometimes, where the sub-sense is familiar enough not to require its own example yet needs to be set off from the other synonyms because of a subtle or aspectual semantic distinction, a semicolon is inserted among the synonyms and only one example is provided:

> **practice** *n*. . . . 2 exercise, discipline, drill, practising, repetition, rehearsal, training, preparation, workout, warm-up; application, study: *She needs more practice on the beginner's slope before going down the main piste.*

The idiomatic usage of this sense of 'study' and 'application' is sufficiently familiar not to require a separate example.

On the other hand, a second example is needed for the next sense of *practice:*

> . . . 3 pursuit, exercise, work, profession, career, vocation, conduct; business, office: *He genuinely enjoys the practice of law. I heard of a veterinary practice for sale in Yorkshire.*

It would be difficult—perhaps impossible—to defend such fine distinctions in every instance: indeed, as a comparison of the different lengths of the entries in any dictionary will quickly reveal, language does not provide the same levels of sense discrimination for all words. The metaphorical focus and diversity of a language provide for polysemy in some semantico-cultural spheres but not in others. The classic observation often cited to demonstrate this linkage is that of the Inuit language that has a large number of distinguishing words for types of snow or of the African language that has an extensive vocabulary to describe the kinship among its speakers. On the grounds that the lexicon of a language is moulded by speakers who, quite naturally, use it to talk (and write) about things that are important to them, one might be tempted to draw conclusions about the voracity of English-speakers by reflecting that the entry for *take* has about twice as many definitions in most dictionaries as that for *give*.

E. Often, the semicolon may be used to separate transitive uses of a verb from intransitive:

> **preach** *v*. . . . **2** moralize, sermonize, advise, counsel, admonish, reprimand, lecture, harangue, pontificate; urge, inculcate, advocate: *Mother used to preach to us about being charitable. Father preached restraint in all things.*

Because of the behaviour of verbs in English, different synonyms may be required depending on what the object of the verb is and, often, whether the object is a word or phrase or a clause:

> **predict** *v*. foretell, prophesy, forecast, foresee, augur, prognosticate, forewarn, presage, vaticinate; portend, foreshadow, foretoken, forebode; intimate, hint, suggest: *My mother predicted that there would be moments like this. If only I could predict the winner of the 2.30!*

F. Wherever possible, the proper prepositional or adverbial particle normally accompanying a verb in a certain sense has been supplied, though it must be emphasized that the one offered is the most frequently used and not, necessarily, the only one acceptable in standard usage. Particles used with some words may vary considerably, owing not only to dialect variation but also to whether the verb is used actively or passively as well as to which nuance of meaning, sometimes far too subtle to be dealt with adequately in a book of this kind, is to be expressed. The following entry illustrates the full treatment that can be accorded to words that occur in a wide variety of grammatical environments:

> **persevere** *v*. Often, ***persevere in*** *or* ***with*** *or* ***at***: persist, resolve, decide, endure, continue, carry on *or* through, keep at *or* on *or* up, be steadfast *or* staunch *or* constant, keep going, stand fast *or* firm, see through, be *or* remain determined *or* resolved *or* resolute *or* stalwart *or* purposeful *or* uncompromising, be tenacious *or* persistent *or* constant *or* pertinacious *or* assiduous *or* sedulous, be tireless *or* untiring *or* indefatigable, show determination *or* pluck *or* grit, be plucky, be patient *or* diligent *or* stubborn *or* inflexible *or* adamant *or* obstinate *or* obdurate, show *or* exhibit *or* demonstrate patience *or* diligence *or* stubbornness *or* inflexibility *or* obstinacy *or* obduracy, remain dogged, pursue doggedly, be intransigent *or* intractable, cling to, stick to, support, stop at nothing, sustain, *Colloq* stick with, stick (it) out: *We must persevere to win. I shall persevere in my loyalty.*

G. In some adjective senses, a split might occur between attributive and predicative uses, though in most such cases, where the syntax is open, only one, usually common, illustration is given. For example, *alone* is used only predicatively or postpositively, not attributively; that is, one cannot say **An alone woman* . . . In this particular case, the normal attributive form would be *lone*, but *lone* is not listed as a synonym for *alone* because they are not mutually substitutable. It is acknowledged that the detailed description of the special syntactic ways in which certain words (like *alone*, *agog*, *galore*) behave lies outside the province of this book.

Although similar cautions must be observed and adjustments made throughout, it is hoped that the illustrative sentences will provide a substantial basis for the user to identify idiomatic contexts and to discriminate senses that are not always carefully distinguished in dictionaries.

A

abandon *v.* **1** °give up *or* over, °yield, °surrender, °leave, °cede, let °go, °deliver (up), °turn over, °relinquish: *I can see no reason why we should abandon the house to thieves and vandals.* **2** °depart from, °leave, °desert, °quit, °go away from: *The order was given to abandon ship.* **3** °desert, °forsake, °jilt, °walk out on: *He even abandoned his fiancée.* **4** °give up, °renounce; °discontinue, °forgo, °drop, desist, abstain from: *She abandoned cigarettes and whisky after the doctor's warning.*
—*n.* **5** recklessness, intemperance, wantonness, lack of restraint, unrestraint: *He behaved with wild abandon after he received the inheritance.*

abandoned *adj.* **1** °left °alone, °forlorn, forsaken, °deserted, neglected; rejected, shunned, °cast off *or* aside, jilted, dropped, °outcast: *An abandoned infant was found on the church steps. Totally alone, she felt abandoned by her friends.* **2** °bad, °immoral, amoral, °wicked, °sinful, °evil, °corrupt, unprincipled, unrestrained, °uninhibited, °reprobate; °loose, °wanton, debauched, °wild, °dissolute, dissipated, °profligate; depraved, °lewd, °lascivious, flagitious: *His abandoned behaviour soon landed him in jail.*

abbreviate *v.* **1** °shorten, compress, °contract, truncate, °trim, °reduce, °curtail: *We abbreviated some of the longer words to save space.* **2** °shorten, °cut, condense, °abridge, °abstract, °digest, epitomize, summarize, *US* synopsize: *The school presented an abbreviated version of* A Midsummer Night's Dream.

abbreviated *adj.* skimpy, °brief, revealing: *The dancers' abbreviated costumes shocked some members of the audience.*

abbreviation *n.* initialism; acronym; shortening, contraction: *UK is one kind of abbreviation, or initialism; NATO, which is pronounced as a word, is another, usually called an acronym.*

abdicate *v.* °give up, °renounce, disclaim, °waive, disown, °surrender, °yield, °relinquish, °abandon, °resign, °quit: *He abdicated all responsibility for care of the children. She abdicated the throne to marry a commoner.*

abduct *v.* °kidnap, °carry off, °make away *or* off with, °seize, *Slang US* °snatch, °grab: *The child that was abducted is safe.*

abet *v.* **1** °encourage, °urge, instigate, °incite, °provoke, egg on, °prod, goad; °aid, °help, °assist: *The jury found that his wife had abetted him in the murder.* **2** countenance, °approve (of), °support, °endorse, °second, °sanction, condone; °further, °advance, °promote, °uphold: *By failing to inform on the terrorists, the neighbours abetted the bombing.*

abeyance *n.* ***in abeyance***: °pending, abeyant, °reserved, in °reserve, shelved, pushed *or* shoved *or* shunted aside, postponed, °put off, suspended, *US* tabled; temporarily °inactive, °dormant; latent; *Colloq* in a holding °pattern, on the back burner; *Slang* on °hold, in the deep-freeze, on the shelf, on ice, hanging °fire: *Legal proceedings were held in abeyance so that talks could take place to reach an out-of-court settlement.*

abhor *v.* °hate, °loathe, °detest, abominate, execrate; regard *or* view with °horror *or* °dread *or* °fright *or* repugnance *or* °loathing *or* °disgust, °shudder at, °recoil *or* °shrink from; be *or* stand aghast at: *He said that he abhorred any violation of human rights.*

abhorrent *adj.* °hateful, detestable, abhorred, °abominable, °contemptible, odious, °loathsome, horrid, heinous, execrable, °repugnant; °repulsive, °repellent, °revolting, °offensive, °disgusting, horrifying, °obnoxious: *The idea of war was totally abhorrent to her.*

abide *v.* **1** °stand, °endure, °suffer, °submit to, °bear, °put up with, °accept, °tolerate, °brook: *How can you abide the company of such a fool?* **2** °live, °stay, reside, °dwell, °sojourn: *Local people believe that the rain god abides in these mountains.* **3** °remain, °stay, °continue, °tarry; °linger, °rest: *He'll abide in my care till he can walk again.* **4** ***abide by***: °consent to, °agree to, °comply with, °observe, °acknowledge, °obey, °follow, °submit to, °conform to, °keep to, °remain °true to, °stand °firm by, adhere to, °hold to: *You must abide by the rules of the club if you become a member.*

abiding *adj.* °lasting, °permanent, °constant, °steadfast, °everlasting, unending, °eternal, °enduring, °indestructible; unchanging, °fast, hard and fast, °fixed, °firm, immutable, °changeless: *Her abiding love is a solace to him.*

ability *n.* **1** adeptness, °aptitude, °facility, °faculty, °capacity, °power, °knack, °proficiency, *Colloq* know-how: *I have perceived your ability to manipulate situations to your own advantage.* **2** °talent, °skill, cleverness, °capacity, °wit, °gift, °genius, °capability: *He has such extraordinary ability it is difficult to see why he doesn't accomplish more.* **3** ***abilities***: °faculty, faculties, °talent(s), °gift(s), °skill(s): *Her abilities have made her one of the finest cellists of our time.*

ablaze *adj.* **1** aflame, afire, °burning, on °fire, alight, blazing: *By the time the firemen arrived, the roof was ablaze.* **2** lit up, alight, brilliantly *or* brightly lit, sparkling, gleaming, aglow, °bright, °brilliant, °luminous, illuminated, °radiant: *The ballroom was ablaze with the light from thousands of candles.*

able *adj.* **1** °capable, °qualified, °competent, °proficient: *I feel quite able to take care of myself, thank you. He is an able tennis player.* **2** °talented, °clever, skilled, °masterful, masterly; °adept, °skilful, °gifted, °superior, °expert, °accomplished: *There is no doubt that Wellington was a very able general.*

abnormal *adj.* **1** °deviant, deviating, °irregular, °unusual, unconventional, aberrant, *Psych jargon* °exceptional: *The wing of a bat is an abnormal structure.* **2** °peculiar, °unusual, °odd, °strange, °queer, freakish, °unnatural, °extraordinary, °weird, °eccentric, °bizarre, anomalous, aberrant, °perverse, °deviant, °irregular, *Colloq* °offbeat, *Slang* oddball, °kinky, °weirdo: *They certainly make the contestants on that TV show do some very abnormal things.*

abnormality *n.* **1** irregularity, unconformity, unusualness, °singularity, °eccentricity, unconventionality, uncommonness, deviation, aberration, idiosyncrasy: *The desire in a man to wear women's clothing is viewed as an abnormality.* **2** distortion, anomaly, malformation, deformity: *The child was born with an abnormality of the right foot.*

abode *n.* °residence, °dwelling, dwelling-place, °house, °home, °domicile, habitation, quarters, °lodging, °accommodation, *Military* billet; *Colloq Brit* digs, diggings: *He was described as being of no fixed abode.*

abolish *v.* °eliminate, °end, put an °end to, °terminate, °destroy, annihilate, annul, °void, make °void, °demolish, do away with, nullify, °repeal, °cancel, °obliterate, liquidate, °stamp out, °quash, °extinguish, °erase, °delete, expunge; eradicate, extirpate, deracinate, °uproot: *The best way to abolish folly is to spread wisdom. Prohibition in the US was abolished in 1933.*

abolition *n.* elimination, °end, °termination, annulment, nullification, repudiation, °cancellation; °destruction, annihilation: *1837 marks the abolition of the slave trade in the British Empire.*

abominable *adj.* **1** °offensive, °repugnant, °repulsive, °vile, °monstrous, °loathsome, odious, execrable, detestable, °despicable, °base, °disgusting, °nauseous, nauseating, °foul, °abhorrent, horrid, °deplorable: *He was accused of crimes too abominable to detail in open court.* **2** °terrible, unpleasant, °disagreeable; °awful, °distasteful, in °bad taste, °horrible, frightful, *Colloq Brit* °beastly: *No one wants to go out in this abominable weather. The décor in this hotel is simply abominable.*

aboriginal *n.* °native, indigene, autochthon; *Colloq Australian* Abo, *Offensive Australian* aborigine, *Slang Australian contemptuous* boong: *Many aboriginals are not assimilated to modern life.*

abound *v.* **1** °prevail, °thrive, °flourish: *Disease abounds among the undernourished peoples of Africa.* **2** ***abound in***: be crowded *or* °packed *or* jammed with, be °abundant *or* °rich in, °proliferate (in *or* with): *The ship abounds in conveniences.* **3** ***abound with***: °teem *or* °swarm *or* °throng with, be filled *or* infested with, overflow with: *The ship abounds with rats.*

about *adv.* **1** °round, around, °close by, °nearby, on every side: *Gather about, for I have something to tell you.* **2** °approximately, around, °nearly, °roughly, more or less, °almost, °close to *or* upon; give or take: *In 1685 London had been, for about half a century, the most populous capital in Europe. Light travels at about 186,000 miles a second.* **3** to and fro, up and down, back and forth, here and there, hither and yon, °far and wide, hither and thither: *He wandered about aimlessly for several days.* **4** here and there, °far and wide, hither and yon, hither and thither, °helter-skelter: *My papers were scattered about as if a tornado had struck.* **5** around, °prevalent, in the air: *There is a lot of flu about this year.* **6** °approximately, °nearly, °close to, not far from, °almost, °just about, °around: *It is about time you telephoned your mother.*
—*prep.* **7** °around, °surrounding, encircling: *There is a railing about the monument.* **8** °round, around, all °round, °everywhere, in all directions, all over: *Please look about the room for my hat.* **9** °near, °nearby, adjacent to, °beside, alongside, °close by, nigh: *There were a lot of trees about the garden.* **10** with, at hand, *Colloq* on: *I am sorry, but I haven't my cheque-book about me.* **11** °touching, °concerning, connected with, involving, in *or* with °reference to, in *or* with °regard to, °regarding, in the °matter of, with °respect to, respecting, °relative to, relating to, apropos, *Formal* anent: *He wrote a book about the Spanish Armada.*

about-turn *n.* °reversal, °reverse, °turn-about, turnround, U-turn, volte-face, *US* about-face: *There has been a complete about-turn in the policy concerning immigration.*

above *adv.* **1** °overhead, on °high, °aloft, in the °sky *or* heavens: *Far above, the clouds scudded swiftly by.* **2** upstairs: *They lived on the ground floor and the landlady lived above.*
—*prep.* **3** on, on (the) °top of, upon, °over, atop: *The plume of smoke remained fixed above the volcano. He hasn't got a roof above his head for the night.* **4** °over, more than, °exceeding, in °excess of, beyond, greater than, °surpassing: *The operations are controlled by gears, of which there are above fifty in number.* **5** insusceptible to, °unaffected by, out of reach of, not susceptible *or* vulnerable *or* exposed to, °superior to: *The judge is above bribery or other influence.* **6** ***above all***: before *or* beyond everything, °first of all, °chiefly, °primarily, in the °first place, °mainly, essentially, at °bottom: *Above all, serve God and country before you serve yourself.*

above-board *adv.* **1** °openly, candidly, °freely, publicly, frankly, straightforwardly, plainly, for all to see, out in the °open, in the °open: *Donald has always dealt completely above-board with everyone.*
—*adj.* **2** °open, °candid, °frank, °straight, °direct, °honourable, straightforward, °forthright, guileless, undeceiving, °artless, °ingenuous, undeceptive, undeceitful, °straight from the °shoulder; °honest, °genuine: *The company's dealings have always been above-board.*

abridge *v.* °shorten, °reduce, condense, °cut, °abbreviate, °cut back, °trim, °curtail, °pare down, °contract, compress, °digest, summarize, epitomize, °abstract, *US* synopsize: *We abridged the original edition of 1000 pages to 480 pages.*

abridgement *n.* **1** shortening, reduction, °abbreviation, condensation, contraction, truncation, trimming: *The abridgement took ten years.* **2** curtailment: *We protested against the abridgement of our right to picket.* **3** °digest, condensation, °epitome, compendium, °concise edition *or* version, °cut edition *or* version; °synopsis, °abstract, °summary, °précis, °outline, résumé: *The one-volume abridgement of the dictionary is easier to use.*

abroad *adv.* **1** °overseas, in °foreign lands *or* parts: *We were abroad on assignment for a few years.* **2** broadly, °widely, at °large, near and °far, °far and wide, °everywhere, extensively, publicly: *Don't spread rumours abroad.* **3** °outside, out of doors, away, out and about: *There are few people abroad this early in the morning.*

abrupt *adj.* **1** °sudden, °hasty, °quick, °precipitate, °snappy; unexpected, unannounced, unplanned, °unforeseen, unanticipated: *The general's abrupt departure has been linked with the disappearance of a great deal of money.* **2** °precipitous, °steep, °sheer, °sudden: *From the ridge there is an abrupt drop of 1000 metres into the valley.* **3** °curt, °short, °brusque, °blunt, °bluff, °gruff, uncivil, °rude, °discourteous, °impolite, unceremonious, °snappish: *My bank manager gave me an abrupt reply when I asked for an increased overdraft.*

absence *n.* **1** non-attendance, non-presence, non-appearance, truancy: *This is Jason's third absence from class in a week. She runs the place in my absence.* **2** °lack, °want, deficiency, non-existence; insufficiency, scantiness, paucity, °scarcity, °dearth: *In the absence of new evidence, the matter must remain undecided.*

absent *adj.* **1** away, °out, °off, °elsewhere, not °present, missing, gone: *Twenty people attended, but Harold was conspicuously absent.* **2** missing, lacking, °wanting, °deficient: *All warmth is absent from her singing.*
—*v.* **3** ***absent (oneself) from***: keep *or* stay away from; °withdraw *or* °retire from: *He absented himself from the court during his father's trial for murder. Absent thee from felicity awhile.*

absent-minded *adj.* °preoccupied, °inattentive, unattentive, °absorbed, unmindful, °absent, °off, °withdrawn, unheeding, °heedless, unheedful, °inadvertent; distracted, abstracted, day-dreaming, in a brown study, in the clouds, °unaware, °oblivious, in a °trance, distrait(e), mooning, (°far) away (somewhere), stargazing, wool-gathering: *The absent-minded professor delivered his lecture to an empty lecture hall.*

absolute *adj.* **1** °perfect, °complete, °total, finished, °thorough, through-and-through, consummate, °flawless, °faultless, unadulterated, °pure, unmixed, unalloyed, °undiluted; °rank: *Alan behaved like an absolute gentleman.* **2** °complete, °outright, °downright, °genuine, °real, °pure, °out-and-out, °transparent, °unmitigated, °categorical, °unqualified, unconditional, utter, °veritable, unconditioned: *Peace is an absolute requirement for prosperity.* **3** unrestricted, unrestrained, unconstrained, °unlimited, °unmitigated, °arbitrary, °despotic, °dictatorial, °totalitarian, °supreme, almighty, autocratic, °tyrannical: *The days of absolute monarchy are numbered.* **4** °positive, °certain, °sure, unambiguous, °unquestionable, °authoritative, verifiable, uncompromised: *Few intelligent people would claim absolute knowledge of anything.*

absolutely *adv.* **1** unqualifiedly, unconditionally, unreservedly, unexceptionally, unequivocally, unquestionably, °positively, °definitely, °really, genuinely, decidedly, °surely, °truly, certainly, categorically: *She is absolutely the best dancer I have ever seen.*

I absolutely refuse to go. **2** °totally, °utterly, °completely, °entirely, fully, °quite, °altogether, °wholly: *It is absolutely necessary that you undergo surgery.* —*interj.* **3** certainly, assuredly, °positively, °definitely, of °course, °naturally, indubitably, yes, to be °sure: *'Are you sure you want to go?' 'Absolutely!'*

absorbed *adj.* engrossed, °lost, wrapped up, occupied, °engaged, immersed, buried, °preoccupied, concentrating, °rapt: *He was absorbed in his reading.*

absorbing *adj.* engrossing, °engaging, °riveting, captivating, fascinating, °spellbinding, gripping: *Maria was watching an absorbing thriller on television.*

abstract *adj.* **1** °theoretical, unapplied, notional, ideational, conceptual, metaphysical, unpractical, °intellectual: *It is difficult to capture abstract ideas on paper.* **2** non-representational, °symbolic, non-realistic: *Museums began buying abstract art in the 1930s.* —*n.* **3** °summary, °epitome, °synopsis, °essence, °digest, condensation, °survey, conspectus, °extract; °outline, °précis, résumé: *By reading the abstracts, you can determine which articles merit reading in full.* —*v.* **4** epitomize, °abbreviate, °digest, summarize, condense, °shorten, °abridge, °cut, °cut down, *US* synopsize: *The service abstracts articles that appear in scientific journals.*

absurd *adj.* **1** °ridiculous, °silly, °nonsensical, °senseless, °outlandish, °preposterous, °farcical, °mad, °stupid, °foolish, idiotic, imbecilic *or* imbecile, moronic, °childish; laughable, °ludicrous, risible, °inane, *Colloq* °crazy, nutty, nuts, *Chiefly Brit* °daft: *The notion that the moon is made of green cheese is absurd.* **2** asinine, °senseless, illogical, irrational, unreasoned, °unreasonable, °incongruous, °paradoxical, °unsound, °meaningless: *Today, most people view it absurd to believe that the earth is flat.*

absurdity *n.* **1** °folly, silliness, ridiculousness, foolishness, ludicrousness, °nonsense, senselessness, meaninglessness, illogicality, irrationality, unreasonableness, incongruity, °stupidity, *Colloq* craziness, nuttiness, *Chiefly Brit* daftness: *Many comics rely on absurdity rather than cleverness for humour.* **2** °paradox, self-contradiction, °error, °fallacy: *No one can abide the man's pretentiousness and other absurdities.*

abundance *n.* overflow, °superfluity, over-abundance, superabundance, °excess, °surplus, oversupply, °glut, °satiety, over-sufficiency; °plenty, plenteousness, plentifulness, plenitude, copiousness, °profusion, *Formal* nimiety: *The days when there was an abundance of fresh drinking-water have come to an end.*

abundant *adj.* **1** °plentiful, overflowing, °ample, copious, over-sufficient, superabundant, plenteous, °profuse, °inexhaustible, °replete, °bountiful, bounteous: *The abundant rainfall fills the reservoirs every day.* **2** abounding (in), °full (of), °rich (in), °luxuriant, °lavish: *We know a stream that is abundant in trout. The abundant vegetation of the rain forest is an ecological wonder.*

abuse *v.* **1** °misuse, misemploy, °pervert, misapply, °exploit: *The officer abused his authority in ordering the forced march at midnight.* **2** maltreat, ill-use, °injure, °wrong, °hurt, °mistreat, °manhandle, °ill-treat; °damage: *I cannot stand by and watch that drunk abuse his wife and family.* **3** malign, revile, censure, °upbraid, assail, objurgate, °lambaste, °berate, °rebuke, °scold, reproach, °disparage, traduce, defame, °insult, °swear at, °curse (at), calumniate, °slander, °libel, decry, deprecate, °vilify, °rail against: *In the report the director was abused in the most virulent terms.* —*n.* **4** °misuse, misusage, misemployment, °perversion, misapplication, misappropriation, *Rhetoric* catachresis: *Beware of imitating his abuse of the language.* **5** addiction, dependence: *They are being treated for drug abuse at the local clinic.* **6** maltreatment, ill-treatment, °ill °use, °fault: *It seemed perfectly natural that he should defend abuses by which he profited.* **7** °self-abuse, self-pollution, masturbation, °violation, defilement; corruption: *The schoolmasters consistently lectured the boys against any abuse of themselves.* **8** revilement, reviling, execration, vituperation, malediction, imprecation, tongue-lashing, calumny, calumniation, vilification, obloquy, scurrility, invective, maligning, upbraiding, berating, objurgation, scolding; billingsgate: *The two parties, after exchanging a good deal of abuse, came to blows.*

abused *adj.* **1** misused: *Permission to use the office copying machine has become an abused privilege.* **2** maltreated, ill-treated, mistreated, °hurt: *It was explained that he had been an abused child.*

abusive *adj.* **1** insulting, °scurrilous, °vituperative, calumnious, calumniatory, offensive, °slanderous, libellous, defamatory, censorious, opprobrious, disparaging, deprecatory, depreciatory, °derogatory, °derisory, derisive, reviling, vilifying, °reproachful; °profane; °rude, °filthy, °dirty, °foul, °vulgar, °obscene, smutty, °vile, thersitical: *The Crown refuses to tolerate abusive satire directed at the king. If I hear another word of abusive language out of you, I'll wash out your mouth with soap!* **2** °perverted, misapplied, °improper, °wrong, °incorrect; exploitive, exploitative, exploitatory; °brutal, °cruel, °injurious, °hurtful, °harmful, °destructive: *Despite the abusive treatment of wives, married women commanded much respect.* **3** °corrupt, °venal, °dishonest, °crooked: *The politicians exercised abusive power over the townspeople.*

abysmal *adj.* **1** °awful, appalling, °dreadful, °terrible, °profound: *The government of Nero presented a spectacle of abysmal degradation.* **2** abyssal, °bottomless, °profound, unfathomable, unfathomed: *The abysmal depths have been plumbed in the diving bell.*

abyss *n.* °deep, abysm, °bottomless °gulf, yawning chasm, gaping °void, unfathomable °cavity, impenetrable °depth(s): *The path led straight down into the abyss. In the scandal the MP was plunged into the abyss of disgrace.*

academic *adj.* **1** scholastic, collegiate; °scholarly, °learned, °lettered, erudite: *Green's academic background qualifies him for the professorship. The university began publishing academic journals in the 19th century.* **2** °theoretical, °hypothetical, conjectural, °speculative, °abstract; ivory-tower, °visionary, °idealistic; °impractical, °unrealistic, unpractical: *The car doesn't run, so the question of miles per gallon is purely academic.*

accent *n.* **1** °emphasis, °stress, °force, °prominence, accentuation; °intensity, inflection; °cadence, °beat: *The accent is on the second syllable in 'reward'.* **2** diacritic, diacritical °mark, °mark, accent °mark: *There is an acute accent on the 'e' in 'cliché'.* **3** °pronunciation, articulation, °intonation, °speech °pattern, inflection: *Even after forty years in the country, he still speaks English with an Italian accent.* —*v.* **4** accentuate, °emphasize, °stress, give °prominence to, °mark, underline, underscore, °distinguish, highlight, °set off *or* °apart: *In her speech, the psychologist accented the 'id' in 'idiot'. Why must he always accent the negative aspect of everything?*

accept *v.* **1** °receive, °take, °allow, °permit: *Sorry, but we cannot accept any more applications.* **2** accede (to), °agree (to), assent (to), °consent (to), °acknowledge, °admit, °allow, °recognize: *We accept your request for a hearing.* **3** °assume, °undertake, °take on *or* up, °agree to °bear: *I'll accept the responsibility for replying.* **4** °reconcile oneself to, °suffer, °undergo, °experience, °stand, °withstand, °stomach, °endure, °bear, °resign oneself to, °brook, °allow, °tolerate, °take: *I think I have accepted enough criticism for one day.*

acceptable *adj.* **1** °satisfactory, °adequate, °tolerable, all °right, °sufficient, admissible, °passable, *Colloq* °OK, okay: *The bread and meat were acceptable, but the beer was awful.* **2** °agreeable, °pleasing, °welcome, °satisfying, °delightful, °pleasant, °pleasing: *Most people find her compliments quite acceptable.*

accessible *adj.* approachable, °open, °available, attainable, obtainable, reachable, °ready, at °hand,

Colloq get-at-able: *The president is always accessible to those seeking help. The mechanism is accessible if the cover is removed.*

accessory *n.* **1** °extra, °addition, adjunct, °attachment, component, °frill, *Slang* bells and whistles, doodah, *US and Canadian* doodad: *My food processor has more accessories than I could ever need.* **2** accessary, °accomplice, helper, °assistant, confederate, °colleague, abettor, °aide, collaborator, co-conspirator, conspirator, fellow-criminal, °associate *or* °partner in crime: *Although he did not rob the bank, he drove the getaway car, which legally makes him an accessory before the fact. A seller of stolen goods is an accessory after the fact.*
—*adj.* **3** °extra, °subordinate, °auxiliary, additional, ancillary, supplemental, °supplementary, °secondary, adventitious, *Formal* adscititious: *For no apparent reason, the salamander grew an accessory limb near its hind leg.*

accident *n.* **1** °mishap, °misfortune, mischance, misadventure, °blunder, °mistake; °casualty, °disaster, °catastrophe, °calamity: *A high percentage of the road accidents were caused by drunken drivers.* **2** °chance, °fortune, °luck, fortuity, °fluke; serendipity: *I came across the gold ring by accident, when cleaning out a disused cupboard.* **3** °non-essential, °accessory *or* accessary, °extra, °addition: *Melancholy is an almost inseparable accident of old age.*

accidental *adj.* °chance, fortuitous, °lucky, unlucky, serendipitous; undesigned, °unpremeditated, uncalculated, unintended, unintentional, unwitting, °inadvertent; unexpected, unplanned, °unforeseen, unanticipated, adventitious; °casual, °random: *Our meeting was entirely accidental.*

accommodate *v.* **1** °fit, °suit, °adapt, °adjust, °modify; customize: *I shall do my best to accommodate the equipment to your needs.* **2** harmonize, make consistent, °reconcile, °adapt: *It is uncertain whether his version of the incident can be accommodated to ours.* **3** °equip, °supply, °provide, °furnish: *Can you accommodate me with five pounds till tomorrow?* **4** °put up, °house, °lodge, °shelter, °quarter, *Military* billet: *The innkeeper is unable to accommodate us tonight.* **5** °suit, °oblige, convenience, °serve: *I was willing to accommodate you by selling your old car.*

accommodating *adj.* **1** °obliging, cooperative, °helpful, °hospitable; °considerate, conciliatory, °easy to deal with, pliant, °yielding, compliant, °polite, °friendly, complaisant, °kind, °kindly: *The lady at the complaints desk in the store was most accommodating.* **2** °pliable, °accessible, corruptible, subornable, get-at-able; bribable: *If you want to get off scot-free, we'll have to find an accommodating judge.*

accommodation *n.* **1** °adaptation, °adjustment, modification, °change, °alteration, conformation, conformity: *Her skilful accommodation to her boss's demands kept the peace in the office.* **2** °settlement, °treaty, compromise: *Negotiations were now opened for an accommodation between the belligerents.* **3** convenience, °favour: *Would you take the mail to the post office as an accommodation to me?* **4** °lodging(s), °room(s), °quarters, °shelter, °housing; °facility, premises, *Brit* digs, *US* accommodations: *We were able to arrange for accommodation at the hotel. Have you seen our new office accommodation?* **5** °loan, (financial) °assistance *or* °aid; °grant, grant-in-aid: *The man was able to obtain an accommodation from his brother-in-law.*

accompany *v.* **1** convoy, °escort, chaperon *or* chaperone, °go (along) with; °attend; usher, °squire: *Allow me to accompany you to your taxi.* **2** °go (along) with, °come with, be associated with, °belong with, °go together with, be linked with: *The roast was accompanied by a bottle of claret.*

accomplice *n.* °accessory *or* accessary, °partner in crime, confederate, °ally, °associate, °colleague, °fellow, °henchman, collaborator, conspirator, co-conspirator, abettor, °assistant, fellow-criminal, *Colloq US* °cohort: *The police arrested the safe-cracker and three accomplices within hours of the robbery.*

accomplish *v.* °fulfil, °perform, °achieve, °carry out, °execute, °carry off, do, °complete, °carry through, °finish, °effect, bring to an °end, conclude, °wind up, °end; attain, °reach, °gain; *Colloq* °bring off, °knock off, °polish off, *Slang* °pull off, *US* °swing, °hack, °cut: *I don't know how she accomplished it, but she sailed around the world single-handed. Has he accomplished his goal yet?*

accomplished *adj.* consummate, °perfect, °expert, °adept, °skilful, °proficient, °practised, °gifted, °talented, skilled, °professional: *Did you know that she is also an accomplished flautist?*

accomplishment *n.* **1** °fulfilment, °consummation, °completion, °realization, attainment, °achievement, conclusion, culmination: *After the accomplishment of the task they were all taken out to celebrate.* **2** coup, °feat, °exploit, °triumph, *tour de force*: *Among her many accomplishments was climbing Mount Everest.* **3** °skill, skilfulness, °talent, °gift, °ability: *Playing the violin is another of his accomplishments.*

accord *v.* **1** °agree, harmonize, concur, be at °one, °correspond, be in °harmony, be °consistent, °go (together), °coincide, °conform: *His principles and practices do not accord with one another.*
—*n.* **2** °agreement, unanimity, concord, °reconciliation, °harmony, °mutual °understanding, conformity, accordance, °rapport, concert: *The countries are in accord on a beneficial trade balance.* **3** °agreement, °treaty, °pact, °contract: *The accords will be signed at the summit meeting in May.* **4** °agreement, °harmony, congruence; correspondence: *The colours of the curtains are in perfect accord with those of the carpet.*

accordingly *adv.* **1** °hence, °therefore, °consequently, °thus, in consequence whereof, (and) so: *Smoking was forbidden; accordingly, we put out our cigars.* **2** suitably, in conformity, in compliance; conformably, °appropriately, compliantly: *Dinner-jackets were required, and the men dressed accordingly.*

according to *adv.phr.* **1** on the °authority of, °consistent with, in conformity *or* °agreement with, as said *or* believed *or* maintained etc. °by: *We are going to play this game according to Hoyle. According to his lawyer, he should never have been acquitted.* **2** conformable to, °consistent with, in conformity with, commensurate with: *The queen greeted them in order, according to rank.*

account *v.* **1** ***account for***: °explain, give a °reason for, give *or* render a °reckoning for, °answer for, °justify, °reckon for: *The treasurer has been able to account for every penny of expense. His desire to conceal his background accounts for his secrecy.*
—*n.* **2** °calculation, accounting, °reckoning, computation, (°financial) °statement; enumeration: *The accounts show that the company has ample funds in reserve. Williams hasn't submitted his expense account for the trip.* **3** °interest, °profit, °advantage, °benefit, °favour; °sake: *Nigel turned his convalescence to good account by writing a best seller. Don't read the book on my account.* **4** °explanation, °statement, °description, °report, °recital, °narrative, °history, °chronicle: *The defendant gave a credible account of his whereabouts at the time of the crime.* **5** °consideration, °use, °worth, °importance, consequence, °note, value, °merit; °standing, °significance, °estimation, °esteem: *The committee decided that length of service is of some account in determining retirement pensions.* **6** °story, °narration, °narrative, °report, °tale, °relation, °description: *Alice's account of the rabbit wearing a waistcoat is unbelievable.* **7** ***take into account*** *or* ***take account of***: °notice, take °note of, °consider, take into °consideration, °allow for: *In passing sentence, the judge took into account the child's poverty and the fact that it was Christmas time.*

accountability *n.* answerability, °responsibility, °liability, culpability, accountableness: *In a democracy, there can be no reducing the accountability of the government to the citizens.*

accountable *adj.* answerable, °responsible, °liable, °obliged, obligated: *I am accountable to no man, but the greatest man in England is accountable to me.*

accumulate *v.* °collect, °gather, °amass, °mass, °pile *or* °heap up, aggregate, cumulate; °assemble, °store, °stock, °hoard, stockpile, °put *or* °lay away: *Overnight, the snow accumulated in six-foot drifts about the house. Ill fares the land, to hast'ning ills a prey,/Where wealth accumulates, and men decay.*

accumulation *n.* **1** collecting, amassing, °gathering, piling *or* heaping up, aggregation: *One effect of the strike was the accumulation of rubbish in the streets.* **2** °growth, °increase, build-up: *The accumulation of wealth has never proved a valid purpose in life.* **3** °heap, °pile, °mass, °collection, °hoard, °store, stockpile, °stock, aggregation; assemblage: *Our gardener made sure that there was an ample accumulation of compost.*

accuracy *n.* exactness, correctness, *Loosely* °precision, preciseness: *The translation from the Greek has been accomplished with great accuracy. Rifling the inside of the barrel of a firearm increases its accuracy.*

accurate *adj.* **1** °exact, °correct, error-free, °precise: *She gave an accurate description of the events. There is a nice distinction between 'accurate' and 'precise'.* **2** °careful, °meticulous, °nice, with an eye to *or* for °detail, °scrupulous, °conscientious: *Marvin is a very accurate typist.* **3** unerring, on °target, *Colloq* on the °mark, spot on (°target): *This rifle is accurate if you allow for the wind.*

accusation *n.* °charge, °allegation, indictment, °charge, citation, arraignment, °complaint; °imputation, incrimination, denunciation, impeachment: *The politician denied the accusation of having accepted a bribe.*

accuse *v.* **1** ***accuse*** **(*of*** *or* ***with*)**: °blame, censure, °hold responsible (for), °charge (with), °denounce (for), point the °finger (at), cite, call to °account: *She accused the Knave of Hearts of lying.* **2** ***accuse*** **(*of*** *or* ***with*)**: °charge, °indict, °impeach, arraign, °incriminate; °attribute, °impute: *The prisoner is accused of assault, criminal damage, and disorderly conduct.*

accustom *v.* °familiarize, °acquaint, habituate, °train, °season; acclimatize *or* acclimate: *Start off by wearing your contact lenses for an hour at a time in order to accustom your eyes to them. She soon accustomed herself to the new surroundings.*

accustomed *adj.* **1** °customary, °habitual, °usual, °traditional, °normal, °regular, °set, °routine, °ordinary, °familiar, wonted, °common, habituated: *The old man took his accustomed place near the fire.* **2** °used: *I've grown accustomed to her face.*

ache *v.* **1** °pain, °hurt, °smart, throb, °pound; °sting: *My jaw has been aching since that tooth was extracted.* **2** °yearn, °long, °hunger, °hanker, pine; crave: *A hostage for a year, he was aching to see his wife and children.*
—*n.* **3** °pain, °pang, throbbing, pounding, smarting, soreness: *I have had this ache in my back, Doctor, and I can't stand up straight.* **4** °pang, °pain; °distress; °longing: *There's been an ache in my heart, my darling, ever since you went away.*

achieve *v.* **1** °accomplish, °carry out, °execute, °succeed in, °complete, °fulfil, °bring off *or* about; °realize, °effect: *When the fund reaches its goal, we shall have achieved our purpose.* **2** °accomplish, attain, °reach, °gain, °get, °acquire, °win, °obtain: *She achieved her ends by cheating and conniving.*

achievement *n.* **1** attainment, °accomplishment, °acquisition, acquirement: *As he was still in his thirties, the achievement of great fame still lay ahead for him.* **2** °accomplishment, attainment, °feat, °deed, °exploit, °victory: *The winning of the Nobel prize was her greatest achievement.* **3** °fulfilment, °realization, °accomplishment, attainment, °completion: *What virtue lies more in achievement than in the desire for it?*

acknowledge *v.* **1** °admit, °confess, °allow, °concede, own, °recognize, °accept, accede, acquiesce; own up to: *We acknowledge that we might have been mistaken. She finally acknowledged my presence by looking up.* **2** °answer, °reply to, °respond to, °react to: *She couldn't possibly acknowledge personally every letter she receives.*

acknowledgement *n.* **1** acknowledging, confessing, admitting, owning, °admission, confession, avowal, affirmation: *His acknowledgement of his involvement in the crime saved the police a great deal of time.* **2** °approval, acceptance, °recognition, °allowance: *By acknowledgement of the parliament, the king was the commander of the army and navy.* **3** °reply, °response, °answer, °recognition: *Our acknowledgement will be in tomorrow's post.*

acme *n.* °peak, apex, °top, °summit, °pinnacle, °zenith; °climax, culmination: *Roger has reached the acme of perfection as a diamond-cutter.*

acquaint *v.* ***acquaint with***: °familiarize with, °inform of *or* about, make °aware of, apprise of, °advise of: *The management requires employees to acquaint themselves with the safety rules.*

acquaintance *n.* **1** °familiarity, °knowledge, acquaintanceship, °understanding, awareness; °experience: *His acquaintance with the works of Coleridge is sparse at best.* **2** °associate, °fellow, °colleague: *She's not a friend of mine, only an acquaintance.*

acquainted *adj.* **1** known to each other *or* one another, °familiar with each other *or* one another, on speaking terms: *I have known Rory for years, but his wife and I are not acquainted.* **2** ***acquainted with***: °familiar with, known to, °aware of, °informed of, °knowledgeable of, conversant with: *I have studied trigonometry, but I am not acquainted with calculus.*

acquire *v.* °get, °obtain, °gain, °win, °earn, °procure, °secure, °come by *or* into; °receive, come into °possession of; °buy, °purchase: *He acquired great wealth by marrying rich old dying widows.*

acquisition *n.* **1** obtaining, getting, acquiring, acquirement, °gain, procurement: *The acquisition of property entails many obligations.* **2** °possession(s), °property, °purchase; °object: *This first edition is a recent acquisition.*

act *n.* **1** °deed, °action, °undertaking, °operation, °step, °move; °feat, °exploit; °accomplishment, °achievement: *The first act of the new commission was to ban smoking in public places.* **2** °performance, °show, °bit, skit, °stand, °routine, °turn, sketch, *Colloq* °thing, *Slang US* shtick: *Stand-up comedians do their acts in nightclubs.* **3** °performance, °pretence, °posture, °stance, feigning, °front, °fake, °dissimulation, °show, °deception, °hoax, °affectation: *She didn't mean what she said—it was just an act.* **4** °bill, law, °decree, edict, statute, °order, ordinance, °command, mandate, °resolution, °measure, enactment: *Are the opening hours of public houses in England regulated by act of Parliament?*
—*v.* **5** °behave (oneself), °carry on, deport oneself, comport oneself, °conduct oneself: *I don't know how she'll act when we're in public.* **6** °perform, °play, do: *She is acting in the West End.* **7** °portray, °represent, impersonate, act out, °personify, take *or* °play the °part *or* °role of, personate: *Reginald acts the fool whenever he has had too much to drink.* **8** feign, °pretend, °counterfeit, °fake, dissemble, °make believe, °sham, simulate, °dissimulate, °posture: *You may think him sincere, but I know he is just acting.* **9** take °effect, °work, °operate, °function, °perform: *This drug will act only if taken with meals.*

action *n.* **1** °activity, °performance, °movement, °motion, °energy, liveliness, vim, °vigour, °spirit, °vitality; °enterprise, °initiative: *Being a man of action, he hates just sitting and reading.* **2** °influence, °effect, °power, °force, °strength: *The action of the moon's gravitational pull causes tides on earth.* **3** °deed, °act, °undertaking, °exertion, °exercise: *The very action of* *breathing caused me pain.* **4** °remedy, °proceeding, °process: *If they don't stop beating their dog we shall take action against them.* **5** fighting, °combat: *We saw action in the Far East.* **6** °fight, °battle, °engagement, °encounter, °clash, °fray, sortie, °skirmish, affray: *How many men were lost in last night's action?* **7** °effect, effectiveness, °activity, °function, °performance, functioning, °reaction: *What is the action of steroids on the lymph system?* **8** ***actions***: °behaviour, °conduct, deportment, demeanour, °ways, °manner, manners: *She must be held responsible for her actions.*

activate *v.* °move, actuate, °set in °motion, get started, °energize, get *or* °set °going, °start, °initiate, °switch *or* °turn on, trigger; °motivate, °rouse, °arouse, °prompt, °stimulate, °stir, °mobilize, °animate, impel, galvanize, *Colloq US* light a fire under: *The sensor in the pavement activates the traffic signal. Her enthusiasm activated him to go into business for himself.*

active *adj.* **1** °strenuous, °vigorous, °full, °dynamic, °physical; °energetic, °lively, °busy, °brisk, bustling, occupied, on the °move, *Colloq* on the °go, °running: *She is healthier for having led a very active life. He always seems to be active.* **2** acting, °effective, °efficacious, °effectual, working, functioning, °operative, °potent, °influential; °powerful: *The active ingredient in her medicine is an antihistamine.* **3** °energetic, °lively, hyperactive, °animated, spry, °nimble, °quick, °agile, °sprightly: *There is no keeping up with an active child.*

activity *n.* **1** °action, °movement, °motion, °vigour, vim, °energy, liveliness, bustle: *Last week there wasn't much activity in the stock market.* **2** °pursuit, °occupation, °vocation, °work, °function, °operation, °job, °labour, °endeavour, °enterprise, °project, °undertaking, °venture, °interest: *What sort of business activity are you engaged in?*

actual *adj.* **1** existing, existent, °real, °genuine, factual, °true, °authentic, verified, verifiable, °true to °life, °manifest, realized, °realistic, *Colloq* °solid: *The actual cost of the project turned out to be double the estimate.* **2** °present, °current, existent, °real, °genuine, °physical, °tangible: *No telescope has detected any actual volcanic eruption on the moon.*

actually *adv.* °really, in °reality, in °fact, in actuality, in point of °fact, in °truth, °absolutely, as a matter of °fact, °indeed, °truly, °literally: *The interest rates actually charged by banks may vary from those quoted publicly.*

acute *adj.* **1** °sharp, °pointed, °narrow: *The two roads meet at an acute angle.* **2** °severe, °intense, °critical, °crucial, °dangerous, °grave, °serious: *This is the ward for patients with acute illnesses.* **3** °sharp, °cutting, °intense, °severe, °violent, °penetrating, °exquisite, °excruciating, °fierce, shooting, stabbing, °piercing, °sudden: *The onset of the disease is marked by acute pains in the abdomen.* **4** °keen, °sharp, °sensitive: *The bloodhound is known for its acute sense of smell.* **5** °keen, sharp-witted, °shrewd, °clever, °ingenious, °astute, °sharp, canny, °incisive, discerning, °perceptive, perspicacious, °intelligent, °penetrating, insightful, percipient, °wise, °sensitive, °discriminating; °alert, °aware, on the qui vive: *Such a circumstance could not be lost upon so acute an observer.*

adapt *v.* **1** °suit, °fit, °make °suitable, °qualify: *The structure of the outer ear is adapted to collect and concentrate the vibrations.* **2** °alter, °modify, °change, remodel, °tailor, reshape, °shape, °fashion; °adjust, °accommodate, °accustom, acclimatize *or* acclimate, habituate: *He adapted the play from an old French comedy. The whale adapts itself to great changes in pressure when it dives thousands of feet.*

adaptable *adj.* °flexible, °pliable, pliant, compliant, accommodative, °tractable, malleable, ductile, °versatile; alterable, °changeable: *Men, in general, are not as adaptable as women.*

adaptation *n.* **1** °fitting, suiting, modifying, adjusting, conversion: *In 1831 electricity was ripe for adaptation to practical purposes.* **2** modification, °change, °adjustment, °accommodation, reworking, customization, °alteration: *She was responsible for the adaptation of her short story to a television play.*

add *v.* **1** °join, °unite, °combine, annex: *5 + 3 denotes that 3 is to be added to 5.* **2** °total, °sum, °sum up, °combine, °count up, °reckon, *Brit* °tot (up), *US* tote (up): *The computer can add all those figures in a few seconds.* **3** °continue, °go on: *'And I won't take no for an answer', she added.* **4** ***add to***: °increase, °enlarge, °amplify, augment, °supplement: *His articles have added greatly to his reputation as a financial analyst.*

addict *n.* **1** (°habitual) °user, *Slang* junkie, dope-fiend, doper, °head, pot-head, acid-head, pill popper, tripper, *Chiefly US* hophead: *His contributions helped set up the halfway houses for addicts.* **2** °devotee, aficionado, °fan, °admirer, °follower, adherent, °supporter, °enthusiast, *Colloq* buff, °hound, °fiend, groupie, *Slang* °freak, °bug, nut, teeny-bopper: *She became a rock 'n' roll addict in the '60s.*

addition *n.* **1** adding, joining, putting together, uniting, combining: *The addition of this paragraph is uncalled for.* **2** totalling, adding up, summing-up, summation, counting up, °reckoning, totting up: *You have made an error in addition.* **3** addendum, appendix, appendage, °supplement, °increment, augmentation, °extension: *This addition contributes nothing to the manuscript.* **4** °extension, ell, *Brit* annexe, *US* annex, wing: *We used our lottery winnings to pay for an addition to the house.*
—*prep.* **5** ***in addition to***: as well as, °besides, beyond, over and above: *In addition to books, the shop sold greetings cards.*
—*adv.phr.* **6** ***in addition***: °moreover, furthermore, additionally, °besides, withal, to °boot, in *or* into the °bargain, too, also, as well: *We were compelled to exercise every morning and in addition we went for a ten-mile run each Saturday.*

address *n.* **1** °speech, °talk, discourse, °oration, °lecture; °sermon: *The Prime Minister's address to the nation was broadcast last night.* **2** °location, °whereabouts: *She couldn't write to me because she didn't have my address.*
—*v.* **3** °speak *or* °talk to; °deliver *or* °give a °speech to; °lecture: *After the coup, the general addressed the crowd in the square.* **4** °greet, °hail, accost, °approach: *She was addressing strangers in the street to ask their views on women's rights.* **5** ***address oneself to***: °devote *or* °direct *or* °apply oneself to: *After the holidays, I again addressed myself to studying for examinations.*

adept *adj.* **1** °versed, °proficient, skilled, well-skilled, °expert, °accomplished, °skilful, adroit, °dexterous *or* dextrous, °able, °masterful, masterly, °polished: *She is an adept pianist, and her husband is adept at carpentry.*
—*n.* **2** °expert, °master, °specialist, authority, *Colloq* dab hand, old hand: *He is an adept at anything that one does with one's hands.*

adequate *adj.* **1** °sufficient, °enough, °ample; °satisfactory, °fitting, °equal, °suitable: *Is there language adequate to describe my feelings?* **2** °passable, °fair, °fair to middling, middling, °average, °tolerable, (°barely) °acceptable, (°barely) °satisfactory, all °right, °competent, not (at all) °bad, so so, *Colloq* °OK *or* okay, up to snuff, not that *or* too °bad, no °great shakes: *The music was good, the band only adequate.* **3** °equal, °suitable, suited, °fitted, up, °proper, °qualified, °competent, °good °enough: *Johnson was unsure that he was adequate to the task at hand.*

adjoining *adj.* °neighbouring, contiguous (to), adjacent (to), abutting, bordering, next (to): *We have bought the adjoining land and will build our new house there. The land adjoining the supermarket is for sale.*

adjust *v.* **1** °set °right, °arrange, °settle, harmonize, °reconcile, °resolve, set *or* °put to °rights; arbitrate, mediate; redress, °rectify, °correct, °patch up: *The labour and management teams have not been able to* *adjust their differences.* **2** °change, °alter, °modify, °regulate, °set: *After he adjusted the pendulum, the clock kept good time.* **3** °adapt (to), °accommodate (oneself) (to), °accustom (oneself) (to); get °used (to), acclimatize *or* acclimate (to), °reconcile (oneself) (to): *If she travels a distance east or west, it takes her a few days to adjust to the local time. Army life was very different, but I was able to adjust quickly.* **4** °put in °order, °arrange, rearrange, °close *or* °fasten *or* zip *or* button (up): *She adjusted the children's coats and did up their shoes.*

adjustment *n.* **1** adjusting, altering, °alteration, °setting, regulating, °regulation, setting *or* putting °right *or* aright *or* to rights, correcting, °correction, calibrating, calibration; tuning: *The adjustment of the clocks is my responsibility.* **2** °arrangement, °balance, coordination, °order, alignment, °harmony, harmonization: *The inspector requires everything to be in perfect adjustment.*

administer *v.* **1** administrate, °manage, °control, °run, °direct, °conduct, superintend, °supervise, °oversee: *The president said that she had administered the department well during her year as its head.* **2** °execute, °carry on, °carry out; °apply, °implement, °prosecute: *It is the responsibility of the police to administer the law, not to make it.* **3** °dispense, °supply, °furnish, °give (out), °provide (with), °mete out, °distribute, °deliver, °deal, °hand out: *Doctors sometimes administer drugs that have side effects.*

administration *n.* **1** °management, °direction, °conduct, supervision, °oversight, superintendence, °regulation, °charge: *Lord Hampden was given administration of her affairs till she came of age.* **2** °authority, °management, *US* °government: *The current administration is in favour of a better health programme.* **3** dispensation, administering, supplying, furnishing, °provision, °delivery, °distribution, °application: *The judge is charged with the administration of justice.*

admirable *adj.* wonderful, awe-inspiring, °excellent, °estimable, °splendid, °marvellous, °superior, °first-rate, first-class, of the first °water, °great, °fine, *Colloq* top-drawer, ripsnorting, A-1, *Brit* smashing, °magic: *His performance in Harper's new play is admirable.*

admiration *n.* °wonder, awe; °delight, °pleasure; °esteem, °regard, °appreciation, °respect: *She is lost in admiration of her mother's latest painting. Randolph was presented with a gold medal as a token of his colleagues' admiration.*

admire *v.* **1** °wonder *or* °marvel (at), °delight in: *Typically, he most admires people who are wealthy.* **2** °esteem, °regard *or* °respect highly, °look up to, °revere, °idolize, °venerate, °worship: *The queen is one of the most admired people in the country.*

admirer *n.* **1** °devotee, aficionado, °fan, °supporter, °enthusiast, adherent, °follower, *Slang* groupie: *Rock stars always seem to be accompanied by a retinue of admirers.* **2** beau, °suitor; °lover, °sweetheart, °darling: *Scarlett was always surrounded by many admirers.*

admission *n.* **1** access, °admittance, entrée, °entry: *The special card gives me admission to the rare book room of the library.* **2** °reception, acceptance, °appointment, °institution, induction, °installation, investiture: *The committee has at last approved the admission of women into the society.* **3** acknowledging, °acknowledgement, allowing, °allowance, admitting, °admittance, conceding, concession: *The court refuses to consider the admission of testimony taken under duress.* **4** °acknowledgement, confession, concession, °profession, °declaration, disclosure, affirmation, divulgence *or* divulgement, °revelation: *The police were able to extract an admission of guilt from the suspect.* **5** ticket, (°entry *or* °entrance) °fee, °tariff: *Admission is free for senior citizens.*

admit *v.* **1** °let in, °allow to °enter, °take *or* °allow in; °accept, °receive: *I opened the window to admit some air. The harbour is too small to admit even one more ship.* **2** °allow, °permit, °grant, °brook, °tolerate: *The governor will admit no delay in the execution of the sentence, and the prisoner will be hanged at dawn.* **3** °accept, °concede, acquiesce, °allow, °grant, °recognize, take °cognizance of: *Descartes' principle admitted nothing but what his own consciousness obliged him to admit.* **4** °confess, own, °concede, divulge, °reveal, °acknowledge, °declare: *She readily admitted to having incited the riot.*

admittance *n.* °leave *or* °permission to °enter, °entry, entering, °entrance, access, entrée: *Admittance to the club is restricted to members.*

adolescent *n.* **1** °teenager, °youth, °juvenile, °minor, °stripling, youngster, *US* teen, *Colloq* kid; *Slang* teeny-bopper: *A group of adolescents volunteered to work at the home for the elderly.*
—*adj.* **2** teenaged, °young, youthful, maturing, pubescent; °immature, °puerile, °juvenile: *Adolescent growth is often dramatic, a gain of two inches in height being not unusual.*

adopt *v.* **1** °take (in), °accept, °take *or* °accept as one's own: *Carol and her husband have adopted two children.* **2** °take, °take up *or* on *or* over, °embrace, espouse; arrogate, °appropriate: *All Hugh's ideas are adopted from others—he's never had one of his own.*

adorable *adj.* °lovable, °beloved, loved, °darling, °sweet, °dear; °delightful, appealing, °attractive, charming, captivating, °fetching: *To look at him now, it is hard to imagine what an adorable child he once was.*

adore *v.* **1** °esteem, °honour, °respect, °admire; °idolize, °dote on: *An entire generation adored the Beatles.* **2** °worship, °venerate, °reverence, °revere, °exalt; °hallow: *O! Come let us adore him—Christ, the Lord!* **3** °love, be in °love with, °cherish, °fancy, °revere, adulate, *Colloq* have a crush on, carry the *or* a torch for: *Katie just adores the captain of the football team at school.*

adult *adj.* **1** °mature, grown (up), full-grown, matured, of °age: *Now that you are adult, you come into a large inheritance.*
—*n.* **2** grown-up: *Tiger cubs are cute, but the adults are very dangerous.*

adulterate *v.* °falsify, °corrupt, °alloy, °debase, °water (down), °weaken, °dilute, bastardize, °contaminate, °pollute, °taint, *Colloq* °doctor; *Slang US* °cut: *Adulterated rape seed oil was found to have caused the deaths of more than 600 people.*

advance *v.* **1** °move *or* °put *or* °push *or* °go forward(s); °approach: *Man has advanced the frontier of physical science. The battalion advanced towards the fort with guns blazing.* **2** °further, °promote, °forward, °help, °aid, °abet, °assist, °benefit, °improve; °contribute to: *The terrorists' dynamiting of the school has done nothing to advance their cause.* **3** °go *or* °move forward, °move (°onward), °go on, °proceed, °get °ahead: *As people advance in life, they acquire what is better than admiration—judgement.* **4** °hasten, accelerate, °speed: *We have advanced the date of our departure from December to October.* **5** °move up, °promote: *In less than a year, Mrs Leland has been advanced from supervisor to manager of the production department.* **6** prepay, °lend: *Could you advance me some money till pay-day?*
—*n.* **7** °progress, °development, forward °movement; °improvement, betterment; °headway: *Who has done more for the advance of knowledge?* **8** °rise, °increase, °appreciation: *Any advance in prices at this time would reduce our sales.* **9** prepayment, °deposit; °loan: *I cannot understand why George is always asking for an advance on his allowance.* **10** ***in advance***: **a** beforehand, °ahead (of °time), °before: *You will have to make reservations well in advance.* **b** °before, in °front (of), °ahead (of), beyond: *The colonel rode in advance of the cavalry.*

advantage *n.* **1** °superiority, °upper hand, dominance, °edge, head °start; °sway; *Colloq US and New Zealand* °drop: *After a year, the advantage was with the Royalists. His height gives him an advantage at basketball.* **2** °gain, °profit, °benefit, °interest; °asset, betterment, °improvement, advancement; °use, °usefulness, utility, °help, °service: *I have information that will be of advantage to her.* **3 *to advantage***: °better, (more) °favourably, advantageously: *The dress sets off her figure to advantage.*

advantageous *adj.* °profitable, °worthwhile, °gainful, °opportune, °beneficial, °favourable, °useful, valuable: *The minister signed an advantageous treaty of commerce with Russia.*

adventure *n.* **1** °exploit, escapade, °danger, °peril; °affair, °undertaking, °feat, °deed; °experience, °incident, °event, °occurrence, °happening, °episode: *We shared many wartime adventures.* **2** °speculation, °hazard, °chance, °risk, °venture, °enterprise: *I lost a fortune in some of his financial adventures.*
—*v.* **3** °venture, °hazard, °risk, imperil, °endanger, °jeopardize, °threaten: *Would you adventure your pension money in such a scheme?* **4** °dare, wager, °bet, °gamble, °stake, °try one's luck, *Brit* °punt: *She adventured a whole week's salary on the pools.*

adventurer *n.* **1** adventuress, °soldier of fortune, swashbuckler, °hero, °heroine, °daredevil; °mercenary: *Errol Flynn often played the role of the adventurer.* **2** adventuress, °cheat, °swindler, charlatan, trickster, °rogue, °scoundrel, knave; cad, bounder, °philanderer, fortune-hunter, opportunist: *That adventurer is just after Nelson's money.*

adventurous *adj.* °daring, °rash, °brash, °reckless, devil-may-care, °bold, °foolhardy, °hazardous, °risky, °daredevil, °venturesome, adventuresome, temerarious, °audacious, °bold, °intrepid, °brave, °courageous: *She was adventurous enough to sail round the world single-handed.*

adversary *n.* **1** foe, °enemy, °opponent, °antagonist, °competitor, °rival: *Before beginning to fight, each adversary sized up the other.*
—*adj.* **2** °opposed, °hostile, antagonistic, competitive: *Why does she always take the adversary position in every argument?*

advertisement *n.* **1** °notice, handbill, blurb, broadside, °bill, °circular, °brochure, °poster, placard, classified, commercial, °spot (°announcement), *US* car-card, *Colloq* ad, °plug, *Brit* advert: *The company has placed advertisements in all major media.* **2** advertising, °promotion; publicity; °propaganda, ballyhoo, hoop-la, *Colloq* hype, beating the drum, *US* puffery: *Advertisement on TV may be very effective, but it is very expensive.*

advice *n.* **1** °counsel, °guidance, °recommendation, °suggestion, °opinion, °view; °warning, admonition, *Technical* parænesis: *His solicitor's advice is to say nothing.* **2** °information, °news, °intelligence, °notice, notification; communication: *Advice has reached the police that a shipment of arms will leave Dover tonight.*

advisable *adj.* recommendable, °expedient, °prudent, °practical, °sensible, °sound, °seemly, °judicious, °wise, °intelligent, °smart, °proper, °politic: *It would be advisable for you to keep out of sight for a few days.*

advise *v.* **1** °counsel, °guide, °recommend, °suggest, commend; °caution, admonish, °warn; °urge, °encourage: *I advised him to be careful driving at night in that area.* **2** °tell, °announce (to), °inform, apprise, °register, °make known (to), °intimate (to), °notify: *We advised her of our disapproval. The police have advised the defendants of their rights.*

adviser *n.* °counsellor, mentor, °guide, cicerone, °counsel, °consultant, confidant(e): *The chairman always consults his advisers before making a decision.*

advisory *adj.* **1** consultive, consultative, counselling, hortatory, monitory, admonitory, *Technical* parænetic(al): *Our firm has been engaged in an advisory capacity on the privatization of the utility companies.*
—*n.* **2** °bulletin, °notice, °warning, admonition, °prediction: *The Weather Office has issued a storm advisory for the weekend.*

advocate *v.* **1** °support, °champion, °back, °endorse, °uphold, °recommend, °stand behind, °second, °favour, °speak *or* °plead *or* °argue for *or* in °favour of: *Don't you advocate the policies of the Party?*
—*n.* **2** °supporter, °champion, °backer, upholder, °second, exponent, °proponent, °patron, defender, apologist: *She is an enthusiastic advocate of free speech.* **3** °lawyer, °counsel; intercessor; *Brit* barrister, °solicitor, *US* attorney, counselor-at-law: *The advocate for the opposition is not in court.*

aesthete *n.* connoisseur, art-lover, lover of °beauty, aesthetician *or* esthetician, *US* tastemaker: *It was the aesthetes who set the standard for the art purchased by the museum.*

aesthetic *adj.* **1** artistic, °tasteful, °beautiful; in good, excellent, etc. °taste: *Daphne always does such aesthetic flower arrangements.* **2** °sensitive, artistic, °refined, °discriminating, °cultivated: *These paintings might be realistic, but they are an aesthetic disaster.*

affair *n.* **1** °matter, °topic, °issue; °business, °concern, °interest, °undertaking, °activity: *These are affairs of state and require the approval of a minister.* **2** °concern, °business, *Slang US* beeswax: *Who wiped the fingerprints off the weapon is none of your affair.* **3** °event, °business, °occurrence, °happening, °proceeding, °incident, °operation: *Last night's farewell party was truly a dull affair.* **4** Also, ***affaire***: °love affair, amour, °romance, °intrigue, °fling, °liaison, °relationship, *affaire d'amour, affaire de cœur*: *Lady Constance is having an affair with the gamekeeper.*

affect[1] *v.* **1** °attack, °act upon, °lay °hold of, °strike: *Arthritis has affected his hands and he can no longer play the piano.* **2** °move, °stir, °impress, °touch, °strike; °perturb, °upset, °trouble, °agitate: *The sportsman was not affected by all the taunts and jeers.* **3** °influence, °sway, °change, °transform, °modify, °alter: *Her sudden fame has affected her view of herself.*

affect[2] *v.* **1** °assume, °adopt, °put on, °pretend (to), feign, °sham, °fake, °counterfeit: *Charles affects a knowledge of high finance.* **2** °choose, °select; °use, °wear, °adopt: *He affected a striped blazer and a boater which he wore at a jaunty angle.*

affectation *n.* **1** affectedness, pretentiousness, artificiality, insincerity, posturing: *She behaves with so much affectation that I never can be sure of her real feelings.* **2** °pretence, simulation, °false °display, °show, °front, °pose, °pretension, façade; °act, °airs: *Some people's charitable concern for others is mere affectation. Using a long cigarette-holder is one of her many affectations.*

affected *adj.* **1** °unnatural, °artificial, °specious, °stilted, °stiff, °studied, °awkward, non-natural, contrived, °mannered: *Dryden found Shakespeare's style stiff and affected.* **2** °pretended, simulated, °hollow, °assumed, feigned, °fake, faked, °false, °counterfeit, °insincere, °spurious, °sham, °bogus, *Colloq* °phoney *or US also* phony: *The heir's affected grief concealed his secret exultation.* **3** °pretentious, °pompous, high-sounding, °mincing, niminy-piminy, *Colloq* la-di-da *or* lah-di-dah *or* la-de-da: *Oliver's affected airs were enough to make his classmates detest him.* **4** attacked, seized, afflicted, °stricken, gripped, touched; °diseased, laid hold of: *Her affected lungs never quite recovered.* **5** afflicted, moved, touched, stirred, distressed, troubled, °upset, °hurt; influenced, swayed, impressed, struck, played *or* worked *or* acted upon: *Many affected theatre-goers enjoyed her performances.*

affection *n.* goodwill, (°high) °regard, °liking, fondness, °attachment, loving °attachment, tenderness, °warmth, °love: *The affection she felt towards her stepchildren was returned many times over.*

affectionate *adj.* °fond, loving, °tender, caring, °devoted, doting, °warm: *She gave her mother an affectionate embrace and boarded the train.*

affiliated *adj.* associated; °attached, connected, combined, °united, joined: *For our members' convenience, the club is now affiliated with one that serves meals.*

affinity *n.* **1** °relationship, °kinship, closeness, °alliance, °connection *or Brit* connexion; °sympathy, °rapport: *He felt an affinity with other redheaded* *people.* **2** friendliness, fondness, °liking, °leaning, °bent, °inclination, °taste, °partiality, attractiveness, °attraction: *I have an affinity for the sea.*

afflict *v.* °affect, °bother, °distress, °oppress, °trouble, °torment: *Last winter's intense cold afflicted everyone, but those in the north especially.*

affliction *n.* **1** °hardship, °misery, °misfortune, °distress, °ordeal, °trial, tribulation, adversity, °suffering, °woe, °pain, °grief, °torment, wretchedness: *Moses saw the affliction of his people in Egypt.* **2** °curse, °disease, °calamity, °catastrophe, °disaster, °plague, °scourge, tribulation, °trouble: *He often observed that greed was the affliction of the middle class.*

afford *v.* **1** have the °means, be °able *or* °rich °enough, °manage, °bear the °expense, °pay, °provide: *We cannot afford to send the children to better schools.* **2** °give, °spare, °give up, °contribute, °donate; °sacrifice: *The loss of a single day's work was more than I could afford.* **3** °yield, °give, °supply, °produce, °provide, °furnish, °grant, °offer; °give forth: *May kind heaven afford him everlasting rest. The poems afford no explanation.*

afoul *adv.* ***afoul of***: entangled with, in °trouble with, in °conflict with, at °odds with: *Barbara fell afoul of the new tax regulations.*

afraid *adj.* **1** °fearful, frightened, °scared, intimidated, apprehensive, lily-livered, white-livered, terrified, °panic-stricken, °faint-hearted, weak-kneed, °timid, timorous, °nervous, °anxious, jittery, on °edge, edgy, °jumpy; °cowardly, pusillanimous, craven, *Colloq* yellow: *Don't be afraid, the dog won't bite you.* **2** °sorry, °unhappy, °regretful, °apologetic, rueful: *I'm afraid I cannot help you find a cheap flat in London.*

age *n.* **1** lifetime, duration, °length of °existence; lifespan: *The age of a stag is judged chiefly by its antlers. She was sixteen years of age.* **2** °maturity, °discretion; °majority, adulthood, seniority: *When he comes of age he will inherit millions.* **3** °period, °stage, °time: *Among these people, both boys and girls undergo rites of passage at the age of puberty. He is a man of middle age.* **4** °long °time, aeon *or esp. US* eon; years: *I haven't seen you for an age! The noise went on for ages.* **5** °era, epoch, °period, °time: *The 18th century was known as the Augustan Age in England.*
—*v.* **6** °grow °old(er), °mature, °ripen: *O, Matilda, I age too fast for my years! You must first age the whisky in the barrel, then bottle it.*

aged *adj.* °old, °elderly, superannuated, °ancient, age-old, °grey, °venerable: *The three aged women crouched in their chairs, each with her own memories.*

agency *n.* °means, °medium, instrumentality; intervention, intercession, °action, intermediation; °operation, °mechanism, °force, °power, °activity, working(s), °energy: *Pollen is carried from flower to flower by the agency of certain insects.*

agent *n.* **1** °representative, °intermediary, °go-between, °proxy, emissary, °delegate, spokesman, spokeswoman, spokesperson, °deputy, °substitute, surrogate, °advocate, legate, °envoy, °factor: *Our agent in Tokyo will look after the matter for you.* **2** °factor, °agency, °cause, °means, °force, °instrument, °power, °vehicle, °ingredient: *The active agent in this cleaner is ammonia.*

aggravate *v.* **1** °worsen, °intensify, exacerbate, °heighten, °magnify, °increase; °inflame: *They introduce new problems and aggravate the old ones.* **2** °exasperate, °frustrate; °anger, incense, °infuriate; °provoke, °irritate, nettle, rile, vex, °annoy, °harass, hector, °bother; embitter, °rankle, *Colloq* peeve, needle, °get on one's °nerves; *Slang Brit* give (someone) aggro: *Threats only serve to aggravate people.*

aggression *n.* **1** aggressiveness, °hostility, belligerence, combativeness, *Slang Brit* aggro: *The mere crossing of the river is an act of aggression.* **2** °attack, °assault, onslaught, °invasion, encroachment: *The conflict had become a war of aggression.*

aggressive *adj.* **1** combative, °warlike, °martial, °belligerent, bellicose, °pugnacious, °quarrelsome, disputatious, litigious; °hostile, unfriendly: *The Germanic tribes were known to the Romans as aggressive and hardened warriors.* **2** °forward, °assertive, °forceful, °bold, *Colloq* °pushy: *Dennis's aggressive nature may yet make him a good salesman.*

aggressor *n.* °assailant, attacker, instigator, initiator, provoker; °belligerent: *You will find that the Nazis were the aggressors in Poland in 1939.*

agile *adj.* **1** °nimble, quick, °brisk, °swift, °active, °lively, lithe, limber, spry, °sprightly: *Sofia is an agile dancer.* **2** °keen, °sharp, °alert, °dexterous *or* dextrous, °resourceful, °acute: *With his agile mind Richard was able to solve the problems in no time at all.*

agitate *v.* **1** °excite, °arouse, °rouse, °move, °perturb, °stir up, disquiet, °fluster, °ruffle, °rattle, disconcert, °discomfit, unsettle, °upset, °rock, °unnerve, °shake (up), *Colloq* discombobulate: *Rachel was agitated to learn of the bank's threat to foreclose on the mortgage.* **2** °push, °press, °campaign; °promote: *The miners have been agitating for better safety measures.* **3** °stir (up), churn, °disturb, °shake, roil: *The calm lake was agitated by the motor boats.*

agitated *adj.* moved, stirred (up), shaken (up), rattled, °disturbed, °upset, °nervous, perturbed, jittery, °jumpy, uneasy, °ill at ease, fidgety, disquieted, discomfited, ruffled, flustered, °unsettled, unnerved, wrought up, discomposed, °disconcerted, aroused, roused, °excited, *Colloq* discombobulated: *The sheriff was in a very agitated state about the mob forming outside the jail.*

agitation *n.* **1** shaking, °disturbance, churning, °stirring, turbulence: *The agitation made the solution become cloudy.* **2** °excitement, arousal, rabble-rousing, °provocation, °stirring up, °incitement, °ferment, stimulation, over-stimulation, commotion: *The organized agitation of the crowds continued for weeks after the coup.*

agitator *n.* activist, °rabble-rouser, incendiary, *agent provocateur*, insurrectionist, °troublemaker, demagogue, firebrand: *The opposition party hires professional agitators to incite the people to riot.*

agog *adj.* °eager, avid, °keen, °enthusiastic, °expectant, °impatient, °breathless: *The children were all agog waiting for Santa Claus to come.*

agonizing *adj.* °painful, distressful, distressing, °harrowing, torturous, racking, °excruciating, tortured, tormented: *We went through an agonizing reappraisal of our policy on immigration.*

agony *n.* °anguish, °trouble, °distress, °suffering, °misery, wretchedness, °pain, °pangs, °woe, °torment, throes, torture, °affliction: *For two days his parents experienced the agony of not knowing whether he was dead or alive.*

agree *v.* **1** concur, °conform, come *or* °go together, °coincide, °correspond, harmonize, °reconcile; °accord, °tally, *Colloq* jibe: *At last my cheque-book agrees with my bank statement!* **2** Often, ***agree to***: °consent to, °favour, acquiesce in *or* to, °approve of, accede to, assent to: *They finally agreed to our offer. We agreed terms with respect to the contract.* **3** °concede, °grant, °consent, °admit, °approve, °allow, °accept, concur; accede (to), acquiesce (in *or* to), assent (to), see eye to eye: *The committee agreed that she should be given time to comply with the request. I objected and they agreed with me.* **4** ***agree with***: °suit: *The climate in England agrees with me, strange to say.*

agreeable *adj.* **1** °pleasing, °pleasant, enjoyable, °pleasurable, °favourable, °delightful, °satisfying, °satisfactory, °good, °nice, °acceptable; to one's °liking *or* °taste: *He found the Caribbean an agreeable place for a holiday.* **2** in °favour, approving, °willing, consenting, acquiescent, complying, compliant, in °agreement *or* °accord, concurring, amenable, °sympathetic, well-disposed; °accommodating, accommodative: *If Anne's agreeable, we can leave tomorrow.*

agreement *n.* **1** °understanding, covenant, °treaty, °pact, °accord, °compact, °settlement, concordat; °contract, °bargain, *Colloq* °deal: *They drew up a ten-year agreement to be signed at the summit in Geneva.* **2** concord, °harmony, compatibility, °unity, concurrence, unanimity: *Agreement in error is far worse than division for the sake of truth.*

ahead *adv.* **1** at the *or* in °front, in °advance, in the °lead *or* vanguard, up ahead, °before, to the fore: *The general rode ahead.* **2** °winning: *At half time, our team was ahead by two points.* **3** °onward(s), forward(s), on: *Please move ahead if you can.*

aid *v.* **1** °help, °support, °assist, °facilitate, °back, °abet, °uphold, °promote; succour, °relieve, °subsidize: *The invasion was aided by Richard's subjects. He salved his conscience by aiding a local charity.*
—*n.* **2** °help, °support, °assistance, °backing, °relief, °benefit, °service, succour, °comfort: *He was convicted of giving aid to the enemy in time of war.* **3** funding, °subsidy, subvention; grant-money, °grant, grant-in-aid, °scholarship: *He could never have gone to university without aid from the endowment.*

aide *n.* aide-de-camp, °assistant, helper, coadjutor; good *or* strong right arm, right hand, right-hand man; °colleague, °partner, °ally, °comrade, comrade-in-arms, *US* cohort, *Colloq* man Friday, girl Friday, *US* gal Friday: *The general's aides are always at his side.*

ail *v.* **1** °trouble, °afflict, °affect, °bother, °distress, °upset, °worry, make °ill *or* °sick, °pain, °hurt: *I cannot imagine what ails him, and the doctor can find nothing wrong.* **2** °suffer, be *or* feel °ill *or* °poorly *or* unwell *or* °indisposed, *US* be °sick: *Granny has been ailing lately.*

ailment *n.* °illness, sickness, °affliction, °disease, °disorder, indisposition, malady; °disability, °infirmity; malaise, queasiness: *Granny's ailment has been diagnosed as influenza.*

aim *v.* **1** °direct, °point, °focus, °train, °level: *The guns of the fort are aimed at the narrow pass.* **2** ***aim at***: °focus on, have designs on, °aspire to, °plan for *or* on, set one's °sights on, °seek, °strive for, °try for, °wish, °want: *Edward aimed at absolute dominion over that kingdom.* **3** °seek, °intend, °plan: *I aim to retire at fifty, if not before.*
—*n.* **4** °direction, pointing, °focus, focusing *or* focussing, sighting: *His aim is so bad that he can't hit the side of a barn with a shotgun.* **5** °purpose, °goal, °ambition, °desire, °aspiration, °object, °end, °objective, °target, °intent, °intention, °plan: *It was never her aim in life to be rich. The aim of the book is set forth in the Foreword.*

aimless *adj.* **1** °purposeless, °pointless, °frivolous: *After receiving the inheritance she led an aimless life of ease and luxury.* **2** undirected, °erratic, °chance, °haphazard, °random, vagrant, wayward; °wanton: *We were annoyed by the tourists' aimless meandering round the village.*

air *n.* **1** °atmosphere, ambience *or* ambiance, °aura, °climate, °feeling, °sense, °mood, °quality: *This restaurant has a delightful air about it.* **2** °breeze, zephyr, °current, °draught; °breath, °puff, °wind: *Light airs sprang up from the south.* **3** °manner, °style, °appearance, °aura, °feeling, °bearing, °quality, °flavour: *Louis has a lugubrious air about him.* **4** °melody, °tune, °song, music: *She was humming airs from some Italian opera.* **5** ***airs***: °pretension, °pretence, °show, affectedness; haughtiness, hauteur, °arrogance, °superiority, superciliousness: *He puts on such airs since he got his knighthood.*
—*v.* **6** ventilate, °freshen, °refresh, aerate: *The chambermaid is airing the room, so you can't go in now.* **7** °show off, °parade, °display, °exhibit; °publish, °broadcast, °circulate, °publicize, make °public *or* known, °reveal, °expose, °disclose, divulge, °tell, °express, °declare: *Once again Andrew is airing his views on modern art.*

akin *adj.* Usually, ***akin to***: °related (to), allied *or* connected *or* °affiliated (to *or* with), associated (with), germane (to), °like, °alike, °similar (to): *Desultoriness is akin to indolence. Their decision not to show the film smacks of something akin to censorship.*

alarm *n.* **1** °warning, °alert, danger- *or* distress-signal; tocsin, bell, gong, °siren, whistle, horn: *At the approach of the storm, the lookouts gave the alarm. The alarm is set to wake me at four o'clock.* **2** °fear, °fright, apprehension, °dismay, trepidation, °terror, °dread, °anxiety, °excitement, °panic, consternation, °distress, nervousness, uneasiness, °discomfort: *He viewed with alarm the arrest of his next-door neighbours.*
—*v.* **3** °frighten, °scare, °daunt, °startle, °terrify, °panic; °unnerve, °dismay, °disturb, °upset: *She was alarmed at the news of the car crash. Don't be alarmed—such delays are quite normal.*

alcohol *n.* spirits, °liquor, the °bottle, the cup that cheers, demon rum, John Barleycorn, *Colloq* °booze, hard stuff, °juice, °moonshine, fire-water, *Slang* rotgut, *US and Canadian* hooch: *Alcohol and driving do not mix.*

alcoholic *adj.* **1** °intoxicating, inebriating: *His doctor has forbidden him any alcoholic beverage.*
—*n.* **2** drunkard, °drunk, dipsomaniac, sot, toper, drinker, winebibber, serious *or* problem drinker, tippler, *Colloq* barfly, °soak, *Slang* boozer, alchy *or* alkie *or* alky, dipso, stew, rummy, *US and Canadian* °lush, booze-hound, wino: *The community runs a centre for rehabilitating alcoholics.*

alert *adj.* **1** °awake, °wide °awake, watchful, °vigilant, °attentive, heedful, °wary, °cautious, on the qui vive, °aware, on guard, on the °lookout, °observant, *Colloq* on the ball, on one's toes: *The sentinels must remain alert throughout the night. Kenneth is alert to the perils of smoking cigarettes.* **2** °active, °nimble, °lively, °agile, °quick, spry, °sprightly, °vivacious: *He is an alert and joyous old soul.*
—*n.* **3** °lookout: *She is always on the alert for new ways of saving money.* **4** °alarm, °warning, °signal, °siren: *Sound the air-raid alert!*
—*v.* **5** °warn, °caution, °advise, °alarm, forewarn, °signal, °notify: *We must alert him to the fact that the man is a vicious killer.*

alibi *n.* **1** °excuse, °explanation: *Your alibi places you very close to the scene of the crime.*
—*v.* **2** °excuse, °explain: *Caught red-handed, she couldn't alibi her way out of it.*

alien *adj.* **1** °foreign, °strange, °exotic, °outlandish, °unfamiliar: *The customs of the country were alien to me.*
—*n.* **2** °foreigner, °stranger, outlander, °outsider, non-native, °immigrant, °newcomer: *Aliens are required to register during January.*

alienate *v.* Usually, ***alienate from***: disabuse (of *or* from), wean away (from), °detach (from), °distance (from): *Gradually the villagers were alienated from their old animistic beliefs.*

alike *adj.* **1** °similar, °akin, resembling *or* °like one another, °akin to *or* °similar to one another, showing *or* exhibiting a °resemblance: *They began to think all religions were alike.*
—*adv.* **2** in °like manner, in the °same manner *or* way, similarly, equally, uniformly, identically: *She believes that all people should be treated alike.*

alive *adj.* **1** living, °live, breathing, among the living, in the land of the living: *My great-grandfather is still alive, in spite of years of defying medical advice.* **2** ***alive to***: °sensitive *or* °alert to, °aware *or* °conscious of, cognizant of: *She is alive to every slight nuance in the poem.* **3** °alert, °active, °lively, °vivacious, quick, °spirited, °animated, °brisk, spry, °sprightly, °vigorous, °energetic: *Look alive, my lads, and hoist away!* **4** astir, teeming, swarming, thronging, crowded, °packed, buzzing, crawling, jumping, bustling, humming, *Colloq* °lousy: *In a few minutes the water around the corpse was alive with deadly piranha.*

allegation *n.* °charge, °accusation, °complaint; °assertion, avowal, asseveration, °claim, °declaration, °statement, deposition: *I resent the allegation that I never do the washing up.*

allege *v.* °declare, aver, °state, assert, °charge, affirm, avow, asseverate, depose, °say: *The guard alleged that he had caught the boy climbing in a basement window.*

alleged *adj.* described, designated; claimed, avowed, stated; purported, °so-called, suspected, °supposed, °assumed, presumed; °hypothetical, conjectural: *The press reported that the alleged assailant had confessed. He is awaiting trial for his alleged involvement in the bombing.*

alliance *n.* **1** °union, confederation, °combination, °federation, °pact, °league, °association, coalition, affiliation, °connection, °bond; °unity, °affinity: *The alliance between the two empires has been faithfully maintained.* **2** °marriage, °affinity: *The alliance between the two families was welded by the children born of it.*

allot *v.* °distribute, apportion, allocate, earmark, °assign, °parcel *or* °dole out, °deal (out), °divide, °share (out), °dispense: *The millionaire allotted an equal share of his fortune to each of his children.*

allotment *n.* **1** °share, apportionment, °ration, °portion, °quota, °allowance, °measure: *Each prisoner was given a daily allotment of four ounces of black bread and a cup of water.* **2** garden °plot, °kitchen garden, °patch, °tract, °plot, *Brit* market garden, *US* truck garden: *If I don't answer the phone, it's because I am digging my allotment.*

allow *v.* **1** °acknowledge, °admit, °grant, °concede, own: *He allowed that he had not been completely truthful about his movements that night.* **2** °agree to, °concede, °cede to, °admit, °permit, °authorize, °entertain, °consent to: *The judge said that he would allow a plea of 'guilty with an explanation'.* **3** °permit, °let, °suffer: *Please allow the children to select their own friends.* **4** °tolerate, °stand (for), °brook, °sanction, countenance, °permit, °consider, °put up with: *The headmaster refuses to allow such goings-on at his school.* **5** °give, °let (someone) have, °appropriate, °grant, budget, earmark, °assign, allocate, °approve: *The company allowed him £100 a day for expenses.* **6** make °allowance *or* concession for, °set °apart *or* aside, put aside, take into °account *or* °consideration; °add; °deduct: *You must allow at least an extra hour for the traffic during rush hour. The shipper allows ten kilos for the weight of the container.*

allowance *n.* **1** °permission, toleration, °tolerance, sufferance, °admission, concession, °sanction; allowing, permitting, tolerating, °suffering, sanctioning, brooking, countenancing: *There were many causes of difference between them, the chief being the allowance of slavery in the south.* **2** °payment, recompense, °remuneration, reimbursement, °remittance: *Allowance will be made for all reasonable expenses.* **3** °stipend, °dole, pin *or* pocket °money, °quota, °ration; °pension, annuity, allocation: *Bill gets a liberal weekly allowance for expenses.* **4** °deduction, °discount, reduction, °rebate; °credit; tret; tare: *You must make allowance for the weight of the crate.* **5** °excuse(s), concession, °consideration: *Allowance must be made for his poor eyesight.*

alloy *n.* **1** °mixture, °mix, °combination, °compound, composite, °blend, °amalgam, admixture; aggregate: *Brass is an alloy of copper and zinc.*
—*v.* **2** °contaminate, °pollute, °adulterate, °debase, °diminish, °impair, °vitiate: *Their external prosperity was not alloyed by troubles from within.* **3** °change, °modify, °temper, °alter, °moderate, allay: *Gentle persons might by their true patience alloy the hardness of the common crowd.*

ally *n.* **1** °comrade, confederate, collaborator, coadjutor; °accessory, °accomplice; °associate, °partner, °friend: *I had hoped to have you as an ally in my proposal for reorganization. The Allies finally defeated the Nazi war machine in 1945.*
—*v.* **2** °league, °combine, °unite, °join (up), °team (up), °side, °band together, °associate, affiliate, °collaborate, confederate: *In their attempt at a take-over of our company, the raiders have allied themselves with two banks. We shall ally the Romans to us and conquer the territory.*

almost *adv.* °nearly, °about, °approximately, °practically, °virtually, wellnigh, bordering on, on the °brink of, verging on, on the °verge of, little short of; not °quite, all but; °barely, °scarcely, °hardly; *Colloq* damn °near: *We are almost ready to go. You almost broke the window!*

aloft *adv.* °above, °overhead, (up) in the °air, in °flight, up (above); on °high; heavenwards, skyward: *The plane was overloaded, but we finally made it aloft. Five women held the banner aloft.*

alone *adj.* **1** °unaccompanied, unescorted, °solitary, by oneself, *tout(e) seul(e)*, °solo, unattended, unassisted; °abandoned, °desolate, °deserted: *I am alone in the world. Leave me alone.* **2** unequalled, °unparalleled, °unique, °singular, unexcelled, unsurpassed, without °equal, °peerless, °matchless: *As a poet, Don stands alone.*
—*adv.* **3** solitarily, by oneself, °solo: *I'll walk alone.* **4** °only, solely, exclusively, °simply, °just, °merely: *You alone can help me.*

aloof *adv.* **1** °apart, away, at a °distance, °separate; at arm's °length: *We invited Martha to join us but she preferred to remain aloof.*
—*adj.* **2** °private, °reticent, °reserved, °withdrawn, °haughty, °supercilious, °standoffish, °formal, unsociable, °unsocial; °distant, °remote: *Deirdre is quite an aloof sort of person—not what you would call a 'mixer'.* **3** °standoffish, °distant, °remote, °cool, °chilly, unresponsive, unfriendly, antisocial, °unapproachable; °unsympathetic, apathetic, °indifferent, undemonstrative: *Roger keeps himself aloof from the needs of those less fortunate than he is.*

alter *v.* °change, °revise, °modify, °vary, °transform; °adjust, °adapt, °convert, remodel: *After the attack, we altered our opinion of the rebels. The dress fits better since being altered.*

alteration *n.* °change, modification, °revision, °transformation; °adjustment, °adaptation, conversion, remodelling: *We found places where alterations had been made in the original document. My new suit needs alteration to fit properly.*

alternate *v.* **1** °rotate, °exchange, °change, interchange, take turns, go *or* take, etc. in °turn, *US* °change off, interexchange: *To help out, we could alternate our days off.* **2** °succeed, be in °succession *or* rotation: *The wallpaper had alternating stripes of pink, grey, and maroon.*
—*adj.* **3** in rotation, °successive; every other, every °second: *The embankment revealed alternate layers of clay and gravel. The nurse visited our district on alternate days.* **4** °alternative, °second, other: *The alternate selection contains only milk chocolate.*
—*n.* **5** °variant, °alternative, (°second) °choice, *US and Canadian* °substitute, °deputy, °stand-in, backup, °understudy; pinch-hitter, *Baseball* designated hitter: *I prefer the alternate to the featured model. My alternate takes over if I am ill.*

alternation *n.* rotation, °succession; °exchange, interchange: *In a temperate climate there is the advantage of the alternation of the seasons.*

alternative *adj.* **1** °alternate, °variant, (an)other, °different, additional; °substitute, surrogate: *Alternative models are available.*
—*n.* **2** °alternate, °variant, °choice, °option, °selection; °possibility; °substitute, surrogate: *The alternative was to remain at home and do nothing. You leave me no alternative. 'Esthetic' is an American spelling alternative.*

altogether *adv.* °entirely, °utterly, °completely, °wholly, °totally, fully, in all respects, °absolutely, °perfectly, °quite; all in all, in all: *I don't altogether agree with you. Altogether, you may be right.*

altruism *n.* selflessness, self-sacrifice, unselfishness, °philanthropy, generosity, °charity, charitableness, humanitarianism, humaneness, °benevolence,

°humanity, public-spiritedness: *Nick does things for others out of altruism, expecting nothing in return.*

always *adv.* **1** at all times, again and again, on all occasions, every *or* each °time, each and every °time, without °exception, unexceptionally; °often, °many times, °usually: *He that indulges hope will always be disappointed. I have always made coffee this way and see no reason for changing.* **2** for ever, continually, °ever, perpetually; unceasingly, unendingly, eternally, evermore, °ever after, everlastingly, till the end of °time, in °perpetuity: *You are a fool, Mike, and you will always be a fool.* **3** in any °case, as a last resort: *You could always refuse to pay.*

amalgam *n.* °mixture, °blend, °combination, °alloy, °mix, composite, admixture, °amalgamation; °compound: *The population was an amalgam of original settlers and new immigrants.*

amalgamate *v.* °blend, °combine, °unite, °mix, °join, consolidate, °compound, °integrate, °merge: *The four sentences of the original are amalgamated into two.*

amalgamation *n.* °blend, fusion, °combination, °mixture, mingling, admixture, composite, °compound, blending, joining, consolidating, consolidation, compounding, commingling, fusing, coalescing, coalescence, °union, uniting, unification, integration, °merger, °association, °composition: *The directors voted for an amalgamation of the two companies that would benefit both.*

amass *v.* °accumulate, °mass, °pile *or* °heap *or* °rack up, °collect, °gather (together), °assemble, aggregate, cumulate, °stock *or* °store up, °hoard, °set aside: *How many points have you amassed? Owing to the bountiful harvest, the farmers amassed huge amounts of grain.*

amateur *n.* **1** layman, non-professional, tiro *or* tyro; dabbler, °dilettante, bungler; *Colloq US* bush-leaguer: *When it comes to repairing cars, I'm a mere amateur.* —*adj.* **2** °lay, non-professional, untrained; °unpaid; °dilettante, amateurish, °unprofessional, unskilled, inexpert, unskilful, °clumsy, °mediocre, °inferior, °crude, bungling, second-rate; *Colloq US* bush-league: *The amateur theatre group's performance received excellent reviews. These paintings are strictly amateur and totally without merit.*

amaze *v.* °astound, °astonish, °surprise, awe, °stun, °stagger, °take aback, °floor, °dumbfound *or* dumfound, confound, °nonplus, stupefy, *Colloq* flabbergast, °dazzle: *Annie Oakley amazed audiences with her fancy shooting. I was amazed that she still cared for me.*

amazement *n.* °astonishment, °surprise, awe, °wonder, stupefaction: *He stared at her in amazement, sure that he had misunderstood what she was saying.*

amazing *adj.* astonishing, astounding, surprising, wonderful, °remarkable, °extraordinary, °marvellous, °fabulous, °stunning, °dazzling, staggering, °awesome: *The Cossacks put on an amazing display of horsemanship.*

ambassador *n.* °envoy, °delegate, legate, emissary, °minister, plenipotentiary, diplomat; °agent, °deputy, °representative, (papal) nuncio, °messenger: *The ambassador must present his credentials to the queen.*

ambiguity *n.* **1** equivocalness, equivocacy, amphibology *or* amphiboly; vagueness, indistinctness, uncertainty, indefiniteness, imprecision, inconclusiveness: *Ambiguity of language must be avoided in legal documents.* **2** equivocation, double-talk, double-speak, equivoque; °pun, *double entendre*, amphibologism: *The minister's speech was full of ambiguities.*

ambiguous *adj.* **1** °equivocal, amphibological, amphibolic *or* amphibolous; misleading: *If one says 'Taylor saw Tyler drunk', which one was drunk is ambiguous.* **2** °doubtful, dubious, °questionable, °obscure, °indistinct, unclear, °indefinite, indeterminate, °uncertain, undefined, °inconclusive, uncertain, °vague, °misty, foggy; °cryptic, Delphic, enigmatic(al), oracular, °mysterious, °puzzling; confusable: *The soothsayer's prophecies were sufficiently ambiguous to allow for several conflicting interpretations.* **3** °unreliable, undependable: *How can the doctor decide on a correct diagnosis when the symptoms are ambiguous?*

ambition *n.* **1** °hunger, °thirst, craving, °appetite, arrivisme: *John's relentless ambition may yet be his undoing.* **2** °drive, °enterprise, °energy, °initiative, °vigour, °enthusiasm, zeal, avidity, *Colloq* get-up-and-go: *The company is seeking young men of ambition. You'll never get anywhere, Stewart, since you are totally lacking in ambition.* **3** °goal, °object, °aim, °aspiration, °hope, °desire, °dream, °objective, °wish, °purpose: *It is Olivia's ambition to marry someone with a title.*

ambitious *adj.* **1** aspiring, °hopeful; °enthusiastic: *My son, I am just as ambitious for you as you are for yourself.* **2** °energetic, °enterprising, °vigorous, zealous, °enthusiastic, °eager: *We prefer ambitious young people to those who are seeking a sinecure.* **3** °greedy, °avaricious, overzealous, overambitious, *Colloq* °pushy, yuppy: *Howard is a trifle too ambitious, expecting to be department head after only one year.*

ambush *n.* **1** °trap, ambuscade *or Archaic* ambuscado: *The company set up an ambush near the crossroads.* —*v.* **2** lie in wait, °trap, °waylay, ensnare, entrap, °lurk, ambuscade, °intercept, *Colloq* lay in wait, *US* bushwhack: *The guerrillas were ready to ambush the soldiers.*

amend *v.* **1** °reform, change for the better, °improve, °better, ameliorate: *The prisoner believes he could amend his ways if given the chance.* **2** °correct, emend, emendate, °rectify, set to °rights, °repair, °fix, °revise: *Take whatever time you need to amend the text.*

amendment *n.* **1** °correction, emendation, reformation, °change, °alteration, rectification, °repair, °reform, °improvement, amelioration, betterment, enhancement: *The committee approved the amendment of the constitution by the addition of the suggested paragraphs.* **2** °attachment, °addition, addendum; clause, paragraph; °alteration: *A two-thirds majority in the Congress is needed to pass the amendment.*

amends *n.* ***make amends***: °compensate, °pay, °repay, make reparation *or* °restitution, recompense, redress, °remedy, °requite: *How can I make amends for the way I've treated you?*

amiable *adj.* °friendly, well-disposed, °kindly, °kind, °amicable, °agreeable, congenial, °genial, °warm, winsome, °winning, affable, °pleasant, °obliging, °tractable, approachable, °benign, °good-natured, good-hearted, kind-hearted; °affectionate: *Melissa is well named for her sweet and amiable disposition.*

amicable *adj.* °friendly, °amiable, congenial, °harmonious, °brotherly, kind-hearted; °warm, °courteous, °cordial, °polite, °civil, °pleasant; °peaceful, °peaceable: *Our countries have always enjoyed the most amicable relations.*

amid *prep.* mid, in *or* into the °middle *or* °midst *or* °centre of, amongst, °among, surrounded by, in the °thick of, *Literary* amidst: *She is sitting in her cottage, Amid the flowers of May. Without further ado, she plunged amid the waves.*

amiss *adj.* **1** °wrong, at °fault, awry, out of °order, °faulty, °defective, °improper, °untoward; astray, °erroneous, fallacious, °confused, °incorrect, °off: *Something is amiss with the ignition. If I am amiss in my thinking, let me know.*
—*adv.* **2** °wrong, awry, °badly, °poorly, imperfectly; inopportunely, unfavourably, unpropitiously: *Everything possible has already gone amiss with the rocket launch.* **3** wrongly, improperly, °badly; incorrectly, inappropriately: *A word of advice might not come amiss here.* **4** ***take*** *or* ***think (it) amiss***: °mistake, °misinterpret, °misunderstand, take °offence (at): *I trust that you will not take amiss what I intended as constructive criticism.*

among *prep.* **1** amongst, °amid, amidst, mid, in the °midst *or* °middle *or* °centre of, surrounded by: *Please take a seat among the people over there. We lay down among the flowers.* **2** amongst, to each *or* all (of): *The* *examination booklets were passed out among the students.*

amount *v.* **1** ***amount to***: **a** °add up to, °total, aggregate, °come (up) to: *Waiter, what does my bill amount to, please?* **b** °become, °develop into: *That son of his will never amount to much.*
—*n.* **2** °quantity, °volume, °mass, °expanse, °bulk, °supply, °lot; °number; °magnitude: *What amount of water is needed to fill the container? She eats a huge amount of chocolates every day.* **3** (°sum) °total, aggregate, °extent, °entirety: *What is the amount of the invoice without the tax?*

ample *adj.* **1** °broad, °wide, °spacious, °extensive, °expansive, °great: *Her ample bosom heaved with sobs.* **2** wide-ranging, °extensive, °broad: *In one ample swoop they snatched up all the land.* **3** °abundant, °extensive, °fruitful: *The event proved a very ample subject for history.* **4** °abundant, °full, °complete, °plentiful, copious, °generous, °substantial; °sufficient, °adequate, °enough: *He had stored ample provision of food for the winter.* **5** °liberal, unsparing, unstinted, unstinting, °generous, °substantial, °large, °lavish: *Steve's contributions have always been ample, especially at Christmas time.* **6** copious, °full, °broad, °detailed, °extensive, extended, °thorough: *The subject deserves more ample treatment.*

amplify *v.* **1** broaden, °widen, °extend, °increase, °expand (on), °enlarge (on), expatiate on, °detail; °add to, augment, °supplement: *Let no man comfort him But amplify his grief with bitter words.* **2** °exaggerate, °overstate, °magnify, °stretch: *The reports have amplified the number of horsemen slain in the encounter.* **3** °enlarge (on), °elaborate (on), °stretch, °lengthen, °detail, °embellish, embroider: *He amplifies every point in microscopic detail.*

amply *adv.* **1** °widely, broadly, extensively, greatly, expansively: *This fabric stretches amply enough to fit over the couch.* **2** to a °great °extent, °largely, fully, abundantly: *My confidence in her was amply recompensed by her success.* **3** abundantly, fully, copiously: *The prophecy was amply fulfilled.* **4** fully, °well, liberally, unstintingly, generously, °richly, °substantially, lavishly; sufficiently: *He has been amply paid for his work.*

amulet *n.* °charm, °talisman, good-luck piece; °fetish: *Whenever the man rubbed the silver amulet, his number would win.*

amuse *v.* **1** °divert, °entertain, °please, °beguile, °interest, °occupy: *Perhaps the crossword puzzle will amuse her while she is waiting.* **2** make °laugh, °delight, °cheer, *Colloq* °tickle: *That form of rowdy slapstick doesn't amuse me.*

amusement *n.* **1** °entertainment, °diversion, °recreation, °pleasure, °relaxation, °distraction, °enjoyment, °fun, °sport, °joke, °lark, beguilement: *The boys in my class used to pull the wings off flies for amusement. They spent their afternoons in the amusement arcade.* **2** °entertainment, °diversion, divertissement, °recreation, °distraction, °pastime; °game, °sport: *During the festival there are concerts, plays, and other amusements.*

anachronism *n.* misdate, misdating, misapplication; antedate, antedating, prochronism; postdate, postdating, parachronism: *The poster showing Cleopatra smoking a cigarette is an anachronism—a prochronism, to be specific.*

analyse *v.* **1** °take °apart *or* to pieces, °separate, dissect, °break down, anatomize: *If we analyse these statistics for England and Wales, we find no pattern. The scientists are analysing the internal constitution of a glacier.* **2** °examine, °investigate, °study, °scrutinize, °interpret; assess, °evaluate, critique, °criticize, °review; °estimate, assay, °test: *We must first explicitly define and analyse the nature of the sample we found.*

analysis *n.* **1** °examination, °investigation, °study, °scrutiny, enquiry *or* °inquiry, dissection, assay, °breakdown, °division: *The analysis has shown the presence of arsenic in her soup.* **2** °interpretation, °opinion, °judgement, °criticism, critique; °review: *She disagrees with our analysis of the poem.*

ancestor *n.* forebear, forefather; °forerunner, °precursor, antecedent, *Formal* °progenitor, primogenitor: *His ancestors were transported to Australia in a prison ship, and he's proud of it. The eohippus, only a foot high, was the ancestor of the horse.*

anchor *n.* **1** mooring: *The ship rode at anchor in the harbour.* **2** °stability, °security, °mainstay, °support, stabilizer, holdfast, sheet anchor: *Marie is an anchor to windward for George, who tends to be a bit irresponsible.*
—*v.* **3** °attach, affix, °secure, °moor, °fix, °fasten; °pin, rivet, °glue: *You must anchor the foundation before adding the walls. She remained anchored to the spot, refusing to move.*

ancient *adj.* **1** °old, °bygone, °past, °former, earlier, *Literary* olden: *In ancient times there were very few books.* **2** °old, °antique, antediluvian, °primitive, °prehistoric, primeval *or Brit also* primaeval, primordial, Noachian, *Literary* Ogygian: *In those ancient days man had only just come down from the trees.* **3** °old, °old-fashioned, archaic, °time-worn, °aged, ageing, °obsolescent, °antiquated, °elderly, °venerable, °grey, hoary, superannuated, °obsolete, fossil, fossilized: *We were accosted by an ancient crone at the mouth of the cave.*

anger *n.* **1** °rage, wrath, ire, °fury, pique, spleen, choler; °antagonism, irritation, vexation, °indignation, °displeasure, °annoyance, irritability, °resentment, °outrage: *Her anger got the better of her, so she simply punched him.*
—*v.* **2** °enrage, °infuriate, °madden, pique, incense, °raise one's hackles, make one's blood °boil, rile, °gall; °annoy, °irritate, vex, nettle, °displease, °exasperate, °provoke: *Father was so angered by the insult that he refused to pay.*

angle[1] *n.* **1** °slant, °oblique, corner, °edge, intersection; °bend, cusp, °point, apex, °projection: *The two walls meet at an angle.* **2** °slant, point of °view, °aspect, °viewpoint, °standpoint, °approach, °position, °side, °perspective: *The managing editor told me he's looking for a new angle on the kidnapping story.*

angle[2] *v.* ***angle for***: fish for; °look for, °seek, be after, °try for, °hunt for: *On holiday we went angling for perch. Fran is angling for compliments on her new dress.*

angry *adj.* **1** enraged, °furious, irate, °resentful, ireful, wrathful, piqued, incensed, infuriated, fuming; irritated, °irritable, annoyed, vexed, irascible, provoked, °indignant, exasperated, splenetic, *Literary* wroth, *Colloq* livid, °hot under the collar, on the warpath, (all) steamed up, up in arms, °mad, *Slang* browned off, *Brit* cheesed off: *Father was angry with me for letting the cat out.* **2** °inflamed, irritated, °sore, smarting: *He has an angry lesion where the fetters rubbed against his ankles.*

anguish *n.* **1** °suffering, °pain, °agony, °torment, torture, °misery: *She endured the anguish of toothache rather than go to the dentist.* **2** °suffering, °grief, °distress, °woe, °anxiety: *He underwent terrible anguish in the waiting-room till the surgeon arrived.*
—*v.* **3** °disturb, °upset, °distress, °afflict, °trouble; °torment, torture: *The anguished cries of prisoners could be heard.*

animal *n.* **1** °creature, being, mammal, °organism: *Scientists are unlikely to employ the popular division of all things into animal, vegetable, or mineral.* **2** °beast, °brute, °savage, °monster: *Think of the poor girl married to that animal!*
—*adj.* **3** zoological, zooid, animalistic: *The sponge is a member of the animal kingdom.* **4** °physical, fleshly, °sensual, °gross, °coarse, °unrefined, uncultured, uncultivated, °rude, °carnal, °crude, bestial, beastlike, subhuman: *His animal appetites occasionally got the better of him.*

animate *v.* **1** °activate, °enliven, invigorate, °stimulate, inspirit, °excite, °stir, °vitalize, °spark, vivify, revitalize, breathe °life into, innervate: *A little*

enthusiasm would have animated their dull relationship. **2** °inspire, inspirit, °stimulate, actuate, °move, °motivate, °incite, °rouse, °arouse, °excite, °fire (up), °encourage, °energize, °vitalize, °spur (on *or* onwards): *He spent the few minutes before the battle in animating his soldiers.*
—*adj.* **3** °lively, °spirited, °vivacious, °animated, quick: *A courser more animate of eye, Of form more faultless never had been seen.* **4** °alive, °moving, breathing, *Archaic* quick: *Although they move, plants are not considered to be animate.*

animated *adj.* **1** °lively, °quick, °spirited, °active, °vivacious, °energetic, °vigorous, °excited, °ebullient, °enthusiastic, °dynamic, vibrant, °ardent, enlivened, °passionate, °impassioned, °fervent: *In the corner, Terence was engaged in an animated conversation with Mary.* **2** °mechanical, automated, °lifelike, °moving: *Each Christmas, the shop has an animated window display.*

animation *n.* **1** °spirit, spiritedness, °vitality, °dash, élan, °zest, °fervour, °verve, liveliness, °fire, °ardour, ardency, exhilaration, °intensity, °energy, °pep, °dynamism, °enthusiasm, °excitement, °vigour, vivacity: *Johnson was in high spirits, talking with great animation.* **2** enlivenment, liveliness, energizing, invigoration, enlivening, innervation: *The scout leader was credited with the animation of the youths in his care.*

animosity *n.* °hostility, °antagonism, antipathy, °ill will, malevolence, enmity, hatred, animus, °loathing, detestation, °contempt; °bad blood, malice, °bitterness, acrimony, °resentment, °rancour: *The animosity he felt for his brother soon disappeared.*

announce *v.* **1** °proclaim, make °public, °make known, °set *or* °put forth, °put out, °publish, advertise, °publicize, promulgate, °broadcast, herald; °circulate; °tell, °reveal, °disclose, divulge, °declare, °propound: *The appointment of a new prime minister has been announced.* **2** °intimate, °suggest, °hint at, °signal: *The sight of a top hat announced Gordon's presence in the club.* **3** °declare, °tell, °state, aver, assert, asseverate; °notify; °confirm: *The president announced that he was resigning because of the scandal.* **4** foretell, betoken, augur, portend, presage, °harbinger, herald, °signal; °precede: *The sighting of the first crocus announces spring.*

announcement *n.* **1** °declaration, °pronouncement, °proclamation, °statement: *Ladies and gentlemen, I wish to make an announcement.* **2** notification, °notice, °word: *We received an announcement of the wedding but no invitation.* **3** commercial, °advertisement, advert, ad, °spot: *The window was filled with announcements of houses for sale.* **4** °report, °bulletin, communiqué, disclosure: *An announcement has just been received from the fire-fighters at the scene.*

announcer *n.* presenter, °master of ceremonies, °master of the revels, MC, emcee, °reporter, anchorman, anchorwoman, °anchor; newsreader, newscaster, sportscaster, weatherman, weathergirl: *The announcer didn't get my name right.*

annoy *v.* **1** °irritate, °bother, °irk, vex, nettle, °get on (someone's) °nerves, °exasperate, °provoke, incense, rile, °madden, *Colloq* °get at: *The anonymous telephone calls were beginning to annoy us.* **2** °pester, °harass, harry, badger, °nag, °plague, °molest, bedevil, *Colloq* °bug, needle, hassle, *Slang* °get up someone's nose: *Stop annoying me with your persistent requests for money.*

annoyance *n.* **1** irritation, °bother, vexation, exasperation, pique, aggravation, *Colloq* botheration: *Must I put up with the annoyance of that constant bickering?* **2** °nuisance, °pest, irritant, °bore, *Colloq* °pain, °pain in the neck *or* arse *or US* ass: *He's such an annoyance, I wish he'd leave.*

answer *n.* **1** °reply, °response; rejoinder, °retort, riposte, *Colloq* comeback: *The boy's answer is unprintable.* **2** *Law* defence, counter-statement, °plea, °explanation; *Technical* °declaration, replication, rejoinder, surrejoinder, rebutter *or* °rebuttal, surrebutter *or* surrebuttal: *Her answer to the charge was 'Not Guilty'.* **3** °solution, °explanation: *Ten points were taken off because I had the wrong answer to question three.*
—*v.* **4** °reply, °respond; °retort, rejoin, riposte: *When I ask you a question, I expect you to answer.* **5** °satisfy, °fulfil, °suffice for, °meet, °suit, °serve, °fit, °fill, °conform to, correlate with: *The bequest answered my needs for the moment.* **6** ***answer back***: °talk back (to): *How dare you answer your father back!* **7** ***answer for***: **a** be °accountable *or* °responsible *or* answerable for, be to °blame for; take *or* undertake responsibility for; °sponsor, °support, °guarantee: *I answer alone to Allah for my motives. So shall my righteousness answer for me.* **b** make °amends for, °atone for, °suffer the consequences of: *Caesar was ambitious and he answered for it with his life.* **c** take *or* accept the blame for: *Andy shouldn't have to answer for his brother's shortcomings.*

antagonism *n.* **1** °opposition, °animosity, enmity, °rancour, °hostility, antipathy: *It is difficult to understand your antagonism towards classical music.* **2** °conflict, °rivalry, °discord, °dissension, °friction, °strife; contention: *Giving jobs only to personal friends has engendered antagonism.*

antagonist *n.* °adversary, °opponent, °enemy, foe; contender, °competitor, °competition, °opposition: *The antagonists prepared to fight.*

anticipate *v.* **1** °forestall, °intercept, °preclude, obviate, °prevent; nullify: *She anticipated her opponent's manoeuvre by moving the queen's bishop one square.* **2** foretell, °forecast, °predict, °prophesy, foretaste, °foresee: *He anticipated that flying would be a future mode of locomotion.* **3** °expect, °look forward to, °prepare for; °count *or* °reckon on: *We eagerly anticipated the arrival of Uncle Robert.*

anticipation *n.* **1** °expectation, expectancy; °hope: *In anticipation of the arrival of Father Christmas, we hung up our stockings.* **2** foreknowledge, precognition; °intuition, presentiment, °feeling; °foreboding, apprehension: *His anticipation of the solar eclipse by a week established him as the foremost scientist of his day.*

antidote *n.* antitoxin, antiserum, antivenin; counteractant, counterirritant; °cure, °remedy, °specific; medication, °medicine, °drug, medicament, *Technical* alexipharmic: *The old prospector says that the best antidote against snakebite is whisky.*

antiquated *adj.* °old, °old-fashioned, outmoded, °passé, out of °date, dated, archaic, °obsolescent, °antique, °obsolete, °quaint, °ancient, antediluvian, medieval *or* mediaeval, °primitive; °extinct; *Colloq* °old hat: *Antiquated laws list penalties for practising witchcraft.*

antique *adj.* **1** °old, °old-fashioned; °antiquated, outmoded, °passé, out of °date, °obsolete: *She wore the antique clothing she had found in the trunk.*
—*n.* **2** collectable *or* collectible, collector's °item, bibelot, objet d'art, objet de vertu, °object *or* article of virtu, heirloom, curio, °rarity: *His hobby is collecting antiques.*

anxiety *n.* **1** °solicitude, °concern, uneasiness, disquiet, nervousness, °worry, °dread, angst, apprehension, °foreboding: *Philip began to feel genuine anxiety over Tanya's safety.* **2** °appetite, °hunger, °thirst, °desire, °eagerness, °longing, °ache, °concern: *It is every person's anxiety to obtain for himself the inestimable pearl of genuine knowledge.*

anxious *adj.* **1** troubled, uneasy, disquieted, °uncertain, apprehensive; °solicitous, °concerned, °worried, distressed, °disturbed, °nervous, °tense, °fretful, on °edge, °restless, edgy, perturbed, °upset; °wary, °cautious, °careful, watchful: *She has been terribly anxious about the diagnosis. We were anxious for her safety.* **2** °desirous, °eager, °keen, °enthusiastic, °ardent, °agog, avid, yearning, °longing, aching, °impatient: *I was anxious to visit the Pitti Palace once again.*

apart *adv.* **1** aside, to one side, by oneself, at a °distance, °separate, °separately: *He stood apart when the* awards were given out. **2** °separately, distinctly, °individually, °singly, °alone, independently: *The provisions of the bill should be seen together as a whole, not viewed apart.* **3** to *or* into pieces, asunder: *At the touch of the button, the building blew apart.* **4** ***apart from***: °except for, excepting, °separately from, aside from, °besides, but for, not including, excluding, not counting: *Apart from the immediate family, no one knows of your indiscretions.*

aperture *n.* °opening, °space, °gap, cleft, °chink, °crevice, °crack, fissure, °hole, chasm: *As much water ran through as the aperture could accommodate.*

apologetic *adj.* °regretful, °sorry, contrite, °remorseful, °penitent, rueful, °repentant, conscience-stricken: *The lad was most apologetic for having broken the window.*

apologize *v.* **1** beg *or* ask pardon, °express °regret(s), feel °sorry *or* °regretful *or* °remorse(ful): *You needn't apologize for sneezing.* **2** make *or* give °excuses *or* °explanation(s), °defend, °justify, °vindicate, espouse: *You don't have to apologize for her.*

appal *v.* °dismay, °shock, °discomfit, °unnerve, °intimidate, °terrify, °frighten, °scare, °horrify, °alarm, °startle, °daunt: *The council were appalled to discover that the police superintendent was accepting bribes.*

apparatus *n.* °equipment, requisites, °tool, °instrument, utensil, °device, °implement, °machine, machinery, °gear, °paraphernalia, °tackle, °outfit; appliance, *Colloq* °contraption, gadgetry, °gadget: *The apparatus needed for the experiment is here.*

apparel *n.* clothing, attire, °clothes, °dress, raiment, °garments, *Colloq* °gear, rags, glad °rags, duds, *Slang US* threads: *The police found various items of apparel strewn about the flat.*

apparent *adj.* **1** °evident, °plain, °clear, °obvious, °patent, unmistakable; °conspicuous, °marked, °manifest, °visible, °discernible: *It was apparent to all of us that she would become a successful opera singer.* **2** appearing, °seeming, °illusory, ostensible, °superficial, °outward: *In an apparent show of strength, he ordered his forces to attack the capital.*

apparently *adv.* **1** °evidently, plainly, °clearly, °obviously, patently, °manifestly: *There is apparently no cure in sight for the disease.* **2** °seemingly, °ostensibly, superficially, °outwardly: *In stop-action photography, the bullet apparently hangs in mid-air.*

appeal *v.* **1** entreat, supplicate, °solicit, °plead, °petition, °apply, °sue; °beseech, °beg, implore, °pray: *She appealed to the king to release her son from the dungeon.* **2** °attract, be °attractive to, allure, °please; invite, °tempt, °beguile, °fascinate, °interest: *He seems to appeal to older women.*
—*n.* **3** °application, °suit; entreaty, °call, °request, °supplication, solicitation, °petition, °plea; °prayer: *Her appeal to the court has been dismissed. I don't know if God heard our appeal.* **4** °attraction, °lure, allurement, °charm, °fascination: *It is not hard to see why his type would have some appeal.*

appear *v.* **1** come forth, become °visible *or* °manifest, put in an °appearance, °materialize, °surface, °emerge, °rise, °arise, °come up, °enter (into) the picture, °show oneself, °turn up, °arrive, °come, *Colloq* crop *or* °show up; *Slang* °show: *Suddenly, a vision appeared before me. His wife appeared after an absence of ten years.* **2** °perform, °act, °play, take the role *or* part of: *She has appeared as Roxanne in dozens of productions of* Cyrano de Bergerac. **3** °occur, °happen, °come up, be included, °figure, °arrive: *That four-letter word does not appear in written form till the 20th century.* **4** °seem, be °clear *or* °evident *or* °plain *or* °manifest; °look: *It appears that the money was taken while the manager was at lunch.* **5** be published, °come out, become °available: *The next issue will appear in March.*

appearance *n.* **1** °arrival, advent; °presence; °publication: *I was awaiting the appearance of the book in the shops.* **2** °aspect, °look(s), °form; mien, °air, demeanour; °bearing, °manner: *The doorman would not let him in because of his shabby appearance.* **3** °display, °show: *Their fine horses with their rich trappings made a splendid appearance.* **4** °semblance, °show, °hint, °suggestion; °illusion: *She gave no appearance of wanting to go.*

appetite *n.* **1** °desire, °inclination, proclivity, °tendency, °disposition, °bent, °preference, °liking, predilection, °zest, fondness, °love, zeal; °enthusiasm; °taste, °relish; *Formal* appetency, appetence: *I have never lost my appetite for chocolate. They tried to suppress their bodily appetites, such as hunger and lust.* **2** craving, °hunger, °thirst, °desire, keenness, hankering, yearning, °longing, °passion, °demand, *Formal* edacity: *She developed an insatiable appetite for reading.*

applaud *v.* **1** °approve, °express °approval, °clap, °cheer, give (someone) a °hand, *Colloq* °root (for): *The audience applauded when the villain was caught.* **2** °express °approval of, °praise, °laud, °hail, commend: *Susan's parents applauded her decision to apply for university.*

applause *n.* clapping, acclamation, acclaim, éclat; cheering, °cheers; °approval, commendation, approbation, °praise, °kudos, plaudit(s): *At the curtain there was applause from the audience.*

applicable *adj.* °fit, °suitable, suited, °appropriate, °proper, apropos, °fitting, °befitting, °pertinent, apt, germane, °right, °seemly, °relevant, apposite: *Are the laws of the mainland applicable to the islands?*

application *n.* **1** °use, °employment, utilization, °practice, °operation: *The committee wants to see a sterner application of the law with respect to mail-order offers.* **2** relevancy, °relevance, °reference, pertinence, germaneness, appositeness; °bearing: *The application of the regulation to present circumstances is somewhat vague.* **3** °attention; diligence, industriousness, °effort, °perseverance, °persistence, assiduity, °devotion, °dedication, commitment, attentiveness, *Colloq* stick-to-it-iveness; °industry: *Her application to her studies leaves little time for recreation. Without application, you will never develop much skill at the piano.* **4** °request, solicitation; °appeal, °petition, °claim: *Gavin made six job applications. The board will consider your application.*

apply *v.* **1** °fasten, °fix, affix, °stick, °cement, °glue: *The signs were applied to the window with a special substance.* **2** °administer, °rub in *or* on, embrocate: *The doctor said to apply this ointment before retiring.* **3** °appropriate, °assign, °allot, °credit; °use, utilize, °employ, put to °use: *He had many skills, but failed to apply them in his daily work. The money raised for food was illegally applied to paying the administrators.* **4** °bear, have °bearing; be °relevant, °refer, °pertain, appertain, °relate, °suit: *I am not sure that the law applies to this situation.* **5** °devote, °dedicate, °commit, °focus, °concentrate, pay °attention, °address; do, °attend, °tend, *Colloq* °buckle down (to): *He stubbornly applies himself to the task at hand.* **6** °seek, °go after; °register, °bid, °try out, °put in; audition, °interview, make °application: *Are you qualified to apply for a job as a nanny?* **7** °petition, °solicit; °appeal, °request: *Geraldine applied to the court for compensation.*

appoint *v.* **1** °fix, °set, °settle, °determine, ordain, °authorize, °establish, °destine, °arrange, °assign, °allot, °prescribe, °decree: *The time appointed for the execution has been delayed.* **2** °name, °designate, °nominate, °elect; °assign, °delegate, commission, deputize; °select, °choose: *I was delighted to have been appointed as chairman.* **3** °equip, °fit out, °furnish, °decorate: *They live comfortably in a well-appointed home in the suburbs.*

appointment *n.* **1** °meeting, °date, rendezvous, °engagement; assignation, tryst: *You are again late for your appointment.* **2** nomination, °election; °assignment, designation; °selection, °choice: *We fully approve of his appointment as chairman.* **3** °job, °position, °post, °situation, °office, °place, °assignment, *Colloq* berth, °slot: *He got the appointment as manager.*

appreciate *v.* **1** value, find °worthwhile *or* valuable; °esteem, °cherish, °enjoy, °admire, °rate *or* °regard °highly, °prize, °treasure, °respect: *I appreciate all you have done for me. Delia's contribution is not really appreciated.* **2** °increase *or* °rise *or* °gain in value *or* °worth: *The property in this area has been appreciating at a rate of about ten per cent a year.* **3** °understand, °comprehend, °recognize, °perceive, °know, be °aware *or* cognizant *or* °conscious of: *Do you appreciate the implications of the new tax law?*

appreciation *n.* **1** °gratitude, thankfulness, gratefulness, thanks; °acknowledgement; °obligation: *She is trying to think of an appropriate way to express her appreciation for all he has done.* **2** °increase, °rise, °advance, °growth, enhancement, °gain; aggrandizement: *The appreciation in the value of the shares made me very wealthy on paper—till the stock-market crash.* **3** °understanding, comprehension, °perception, °recognition, °knowledge, awareness; °realization, °enjoyment; °admiration: *It's fortunate that Richard's appreciation of the finer things in life is supported by his income.*

apprentice *n.* **1** °novice, tiro *or* tyro, °learner, starter, beginner, °greenhorn, *Colloq US* rookie: *Lever served as an apprentice in the soap factory.*
—*v.* **2** indenture, °contract, °bind: *Cartwright was apprenticed to a carpenter before becoming a journeyman cabinet-maker.*

approach *v.* **1** °near, °advance, °draw *or* °come °near *or* nearer *or* °close *or* closer, *Formal* °come nigh: *Claude approached the table. As night approached, the sky darkened. With approaching manhood, you must take on more responsibilities.* **2** °approximate, °nearly equal, °come °close to, °compare with: *The total is beginning to approach your estimate.* **3** °make advances *or* overtures to, °proposition, °propose to, °sound out, make (a) °proposal to, °solicit, *Colloq* °chat up: *Theo makes mincemeat of any man who tries to approach his daughter.*
—*n.* **4** ***approaches***: advances, overtures, proposals, propositions: *Michelle had no intention of discouraging Pierre's approaches.* **5** access, °passage, °way, °path, °course; °entry: *The approach to the house was overgrown with brambles.* **6** °advance, °movement: *Our approach to the gates was being watched very carefully.* **7** °method, °procedure, modus operandi, °way, °technique, °style, °manner, °attitude, *Slang US* MO (= 'modus operandi'): *Our approach in dealing with the problem is different.*

appropriate *adj.* **1** °suitable, apt, °fitting, °fit, °proper, °right, °meet, °becoming, °befitting, °seemly, suited, apropos, °correct, germane, °pertinent, °happy, felicitous: *Will a dinner-jacket be appropriate attire? She has written a poem appropriate to the occasion.*
—*v.* **2** °take, °take over, °seize, expropriate, arrogate, annex, impound; commandeer; °steal, °pilfer, filch, usurp, °make away *or* off with, *Colloq* °pinch, °lift, *Brit* °nick, *US* °boost: *The police appropriated the paintings. Somebody has appropriated my chair.* **3** °set aside *or* °apart, °devote, °assign, earmark, °allot, apportion: *Most of the money has been appropriated for back taxes.*

appropriately *adv.* fittingly, suitably, °properly, correctly, aptly, rightly, becomingly, meetly: *She came down appropriately dressed for dinner.*

approval *n.* °sanction, approbation, °blessing, °consent, °agreement, concurrence; °endorsement, acceptance, imprimatur, affirmation, éclat, confirmation, mandate, authorization; °licence, °leave, °permission, rubber °stamp, *Colloq* °OK, okay, °go-ahead, green light: *I don't think that the plan will meet with the committee's approval. We gave our approval to proceed.*

approve *v.* **1** Often, ***approve of***: °allow, countenance, condone, °permit, °sanction, °authorize, °endorse, put one's imprimatur on, °agree (to), °accept, assent (to), °go along with, *Colloq* °OK *or* okay, give the green light *or* °go-ahead *or* one's °blessing (to), rubber-stamp: *The headmistress would never approve your leaving the building during classes.* **2** °confirm, affirm, °support, °ratify, °uphold, °subscribe to, °second, give the °stamp of °approval to; °favour, commend, °recommend: *Sheila Jones's appointment to the commission has been approved unanimously.* **3** ***approve of***: °sanction, consider °fair *or* °good *or* °right, °accept, °favour, °respect, be °partial to, °like, have °regard for, have a °preference for, °tolerate, °reconcile oneself to: *I always had the feeling that her father didn't quite approve of me.*

approximate *adj.* **1** °rough, °inexact, °loose, °imprecise, estimated, *Colloq* guestimated, ballpark: *The figures are only approximate, not exact.*
—*v.* **2** °near, °approach, come °close to, °verge on: *Your estimates approximate those of the budget committee.* **3** °resemble, °approach, look *or* °seem °like; simulate: *The laboratory tests on rats approximate the way the virus behaves in humans.*

approximately *adv.* approaching; °nearly, °almost, °close to, °about, around, give or take, °roughly, °generally: *I haven't seen Sally for approximately three weeks. There are approximately fifty people in the audience.*

aptitude *n.* **1** °fitness, suitability, appropriateness, °relevance, applicability, suitableness, aptness: *One need only look at an albatross in the air to appreciate its aptitude for flight.* **2** °tendency, propensity, °disposition, predilection, °bent, proclivity; °talent, °gift, °ability, °capability, °facility, °faculty, °flair: *Helen displays a natural aptitude for the violin.* **3** °intelligence, quick-wittedness, °intellect; °capacity, aptness: *The aptitude of that new student sets her apart from the others in the class.*

arbitrary *adj.* **1** °capricious, varying, °erratic, °uncertain, °inconsistent, °doubtful, unpredictable, °whimsical, irrational, °chance, °random, °subjective, unreasoned, *Colloq* chancy, iffy: *The choices are entirely arbitrary, totally at the whim of the council and not based on research or knowledge.* **2** °absolute, °tyrannical, °despotic, °authoritarian, magisterial, °summary, °peremptory, autocratic, °dogmatic, imperious, uncompromising, °inconsiderate, high-handed, °dictatorial, *Rare* thetic(al): *The conduct of the archbishop appears to have been arbitrary and harsh.*

arch *adj.* **1** °chief, °principal, °prime, °primary, °preeminent, °foremost, °first, greatest, consummate, °major: *Moriarty was Holmes's arch-enemy.* **2** °clever, cunning, °crafty, roguish, °tricky, °shrewd, °artful, °sly, °designing: *Brendan loves to play his arch pranks on unsuspecting friends.* **3** waggish, saucy, °mischievous, prankish: *I could tell from the lad's arch expression that he had thrown the snowball.*

ardent *adj.* °eager, °intense, zealous, °keen, °fervent, fervid, °passionate, avid, °fierce, °impassioned, °hot, °warm; °enthusiastic: *Diane was carrying on ardent love affairs with at least three men.*

ardour *n.* °eagerness, °desire, zeal, fervency, °burning °desire, keenness, °fervour, °passion, °heat, °warmth; °enthusiasm: *Bernadette has supported the cause with great ardour.*

arduous *adj.* **1** °laborious, °difficult, °hard, °tough, °strenuous, onerous, °burdensome, back-breaking, °painful, *Formal* operose; tiring, °exhausting, wearisome, fatiguing, taxing, gruelling, °trying, °formidable: *The Sherpas were well equipped for the arduous climb. What an arduous task it is to read the proofs of a dictionary!* **2** °energetic, °strenuous, °vigorous: *Montrose made arduous efforts to reconstruct his army.*

area *n.* **1** °space, °room: *Is there enough floor area here for the carpet?* **2** °extent, °limit, compass, °size, °square footage, acreage: *The area of my greenhouse is thirty by fifteen feet.* **3** °space, °field, °region, °tract, °territory, °district, °zone, °stretch; °section, °quarter, °precinct, arrondissement, °neighbourhood, locality, bailiwick, *US* °block: *An area was set aside for a garden. There has been a lot of crime in that area lately.* **4** °scope, °range, °extent, °breadth, compass, °section: *His studies cover only one area of Scottish history.* **5** court, courtyard, °enclosure, close, yard; °square, °ground, arena, °field, parade-ground, °parade: *The soldiers drill in the area behind the barracks.*

argue *v.* **1** °dispute, °debate, °disagree, °bicker, wrangle, °quarrel, squabble, °spar, °fight, remonstrate, altercate, *Colloq chiefly Brit* °row, °scrap: *The couple next door are continually arguing with each other at the tops of their voices.* **2** °discuss, °reason, °debate, wrangle: *He would argue by the hour, but never for arguing's sake.* **3** make a °case, °talk, °plead, °debate, contend: *I cannot tell whether she's arguing for or against the proposition.* **4** °prove, evince, °indicate, °denote, °demonstrate, °show, °establish, °suggest, °signify, betoken: *The increase in street crime argues that the police are not visible enough.* **5** °say, assert, °hold, °maintain, °reason, °claim, contend: *The defendant argued that he had never met the witness.* **6** ***argue into*** *or* ***out of***: °persuade *or* dissuade, °talk out of *or* into, °prevail (up)on; °convince: *I argued him out of sailing to Bermuda alone. She succeeded in arguing me into going to the tea dance.*

argument *n.* **1** °debate, °dispute, °disagreement, °quarrel, °controversy, polemic, wrangle, squabble, °tiff, spat, altercation; °conflict, °fight, °fracas, affray, °fray, Donnybrook, °feud, *Colloq* °row, falling-out, °scrap, barney: *The argument was about who had invented the wheel. The argument spilt out into the street.* **2** °point, °position, (line of) °reasoning, °logic, °plea, °claim, pleading, °assertion, contention, °case; °defence: *His argument has merit. Arthur's argument falls apart when he brings in the phlogiston theory.*

argumentative *adj.* °quarrelsome, disputatious, °belligerent, combative, contentious, litigious, °disagreeable, °testy: *Evelyn is irritable and argumentative.*

arise *v.* **1** °rise, °get up, °stand up, °get to one's feet; °wake up, °get out of bed, °awake: *We arose when Lady Spencer entered the room. I have arisen before dawn all my life.* **2** °rise, °go up, °come up, ascend, °climb; °mount: *The full moon arose in the eastern sky.* **3** °come up, be brought up, be mentioned, *Colloq* crop up: *The subject never would have arisen if the waiter hadn't spilt the wine on me.* **4** °spring up, °begin, °start (up), °originate, °come up, *Colloq* crop up: *A very unpleasant situation has arisen regarding the missing funds.*

aroma *n.* **1** °smell, °odour, °fragrance, °scent, °perfume, °savour, °bouquet; redolence: *Don't you just love to be awakened by the aroma of fresh coffee?* **2** °smell, °odour, °character, °aura, °atmosphere, °flavour, °hint, °suggestion: *There is an aroma of dishonesty about them that I can't quite identify.*

aromatic *adj.* °fragrant, °spicy, perfumed, °savoury, °pungent: *A most agreeable scent came from a bowl of aromatic herbs.*

around *adv.* **1** °about, °approximately, °nearly, °almost, °roughly; *circa*: *There were around a dozen of us in the place.* **2** °about, °everywhere, in every °direction, on all sides, all over, °throughout: *By this time the rebels were all around and we couldn't move.* **3** °round, °about, for everyone *or* all, *US also* °'round: *I don't think we have enough food to go around.* **4** °round, °about, all about, °everywhere, here and there, hither and thither, hither and yon, °far and wide: *The tinker travelled around selling his wares and repairing pots.*
—*prep.* **5** °round, °about, °surrounding, encompassing, enveloping, encircling, on all sides of, in all directions from, enclosing: *The fields around the castle were cultivated by tenant farmers.* **6** °about, °approximately, °roughly; *circa*: *He was born around the turn of the century.*

arouse *v.* **1** °awaken, °raise (up), °wake up, waken, °rouse, °revive, °stir (up): *I was aroused by the noise and reached for my pistol.* **2** °excite, °stir up, °stimulate, °awaken, °summon up, °spark, *Colloq* °turn on: *My suspicions were aroused because she was carrying my umbrella.* **3** °provoke, °encourage, °quicken, °foster, °call forth, °stir up, °kindle, °foment: *The song aroused feelings of patriotism among the recruits.*

arrange *v.* **1** °order, °dispose, array, °organize, °sort (out), systematize, °group, °set up, °rank, °line up, align, °form, °position: *The teachers arranged the children according to height. The flowers were arranged in a vase so as to conceal the listening device.* **2** °settle, °plan, °set (up), °organize, orchestrate, °manipulate, choreograph; predetermine, °decide, °prepare, °determine, prearrange, °devise, °bring about, contrive; °fix it: *Everything has been arranged—you won't have to lift a finger. For a small fee I can arrange for you to win the first prize.* **3** orchestrate, °score, °adapt: *Flemburgh has arranged music for some of the best-known modern composers.*

arrangement *n.* **1** °order, °disposition, grouping, °organization, array, °display, °structure, structuring, ordering, alignment, line-up, *Colloq* °set-up: *Don't you care for the arrangement of the furniture, Milady?* **2** °structure, °combination, construction, contrivance, °affair, °set-up: *An arrangement of bricks served as a hearth.* **3** °settlement, °agreement, terms, °plan, °contract, covenant, °compact: *The arrangement called for Bosworth to get ten per cent of the gross profits.* **4** orchestration, °score, instrumentation, °adaptation, °interpretation, °version: *I prefer Fats Waller's arrangement of 'Sugar Blues'.* **5** ***arrangements***: preparations, plans; °groundwork, planning: *Arrangements have been made for the limousine to pick you up at five.*

arrest *v.* **1** °stop, °halt, °check, °stall, °forestall, detain, °delay, °hinder, °restrain, °obstruct, °prevent, °block, °interrupt: *The progress of the train has been arrested.* **2** catch, °capture, °seize, apprehend, °take, °take in, °take into °custody, detain, *Colloq* °nab, °pinch, collar, bust, °run in, *Brit* °nick: *Foxworthy was arrested crossing the border.* **3** °slow, °retard, °stop: *I'm afraid that we have here a case of arrested mental development.*
—*n.* **4** °seizure, °capture, apprehension, °detention; °restraint, *Colloq* bust, *US* collar: *The police have made six arrests.* **5** °stop, stoppage, °check, cessation: *The doctor said it was a case of cardiac arrest.* **6** ***under arrest***: in °custody, under °legal °restraint, in the hands of the law, imprisoned, arrested: *You are under arrest for the murder of one Hugh Brown, and anything you say may be used in evidence against you.*

arresting *adj.* °striking, °shocking, °remarkable, °impressive, electrifying, °stunning, °extraordinary, surprising, °dazzling: *It is indeed an experience to be in the presence of such an arresting beauty.*

arrival *n.* **1** coming, advent, °appearance: *We have been awaiting your arrival for weeks.* **2** °newcomer; °immigrant; °traveller, °passenger; °tourist; *Australian* °migrant, new °chum: *The arrivals on flight 422 were questioned about a bearded passenger on the plane.*

arrive *v.* **1** °come, make one's °appearance, °appear, °turn up, *Colloq* °show up; *Slang* °hit (town), °blow in: *She arrived only two minutes before the plane was to take off.* **2** °succeed, °prosper, °get °ahead (in the world), °reach the °top, *Colloq* °make it, °make the °grade, °get somewhere, °get there: *Yuppies believe that once they own a Mercedes, they've arrived.* **3** ***arrive at***: °come *or* °get to, °reach; attain: *I think that Crumley has arrived at the stage in his career where he merits a promotion.*

arrogance *n.* self-assertion, °impertinence, insolence, °presumption, °nerve, °effrontery, °gall, presumptuousness, self-importance, °conceit, egotism, hauteur, haughtiness, loftiness, °pride, hubris, pompousness, pomposity, °pretension, pretentiousness, °bluster, °snobbery, snobbishness, *Colloq* snottiness, *Slang Brit* °side: *He has the arrogance to assume that I wish to see him again.*

arrogant *adj.* **1** °presumptuous, assuming, self-assertive, °conceited, °egotistical, °pompous, °superior, °brazen, bumptious, cavalier: *It would be most arrogant of me to take for myself the glory that rightfully belongs to the whole team.* **2** °haughty, °overbearing, imperious, high-handed, overweening,

°disdainful, °contemptuous, °scornful, °snobbish, °supercilious, °lofty, swaggering, *Brit* toffee-nosed; *Colloq* uppity, on one's °high horse, °high and °mighty, snotty: *Since her husband was made a company director, she's become unbearably arrogant.*

art *n.* **1** °skill, skilfulness, °ingenuity, °aptitude, °talent, artistry, craftsmanship; °knowledge, °expertise; °craft, °technique, adroitness, °dexterity, *Colloq* know-how: *Little art is required to plant turnips.* **2** artistry, artisticness; °taste, tastefulness: *High art differs from low art in possessing an excess of beauty in addition to its truth.* **3** °craft, °technique, °business, °profession, °skill: *The fishermen can't employ their art with much success in so troubled a sea.* **4** °knack, °aptitude, °faculty, °technique, mastery; °dexterity, adroitness: *Conversation may be esteemed a gift, not an art. You have acquired the art of insulting people without their realizing it.* **5** °trickery, craftiness, cunning, wiliness, slyness, guile, °deceit, duplicity, artfulness, cleverness, astuteness: *You have to admire the art with which she wraps him round her little finger.* **6** ***arts***: °wiles, °schemes, °stratagems, °artifices, °subterfuges, °tricks; °manoeuvres: *She was expert in the arts which ladies sometimes condescend to employ for captivation.*

artful *adj.* **1** °scheming, °wily, °sly, cunning, °foxy, °tricky, °crafty, °deceitful, underhand *or* underhanded, double-dealing, guileful, °disingenuous: *That artful fellow managed to sell me a completely useless gadget.* **2** °ingenious, °clever, °astute, °shrewd, °dexterous: *She has practised her artful deceptions so long that nobody believes anything she says.*

artifice *n.* **1** °skill, cunning, °trickery, °craft, craftiness, artfulness, guile, duplicity, °deception, °chicanery, underhandedness, shrewdness, slyness, wiliness, trickiness: *He used artifice to get control of the firm.* **2** °stratagem, °device, °manoeuvre, °trick, contrivance, °wile, °ruse, °subterfuge, °expedient, *Colloq* °dodge: *They were deluded by artifices to cheat them out of their money.*

artificial *adj.* **1** °unnatural, °synthetic, man-made, manufactured, simulated, °imitation, °plastic: *The museum has a strange collection of artificial teeth on display.* **2** made-up, concocted, °bogus, °fake, °sham, °false, °counterfeit, *Colloq* °phoney *or US also* phony: *The figures used in the sample survey are entirely artificial.* **3** °affected, °unnatural, °forced, °pretended, high-sounding, feigned, °assumed, contrived, °factitious; meretricious, °insincere, °sham, faked, *Colloq* °phoney *or US also* phony: *I tell you that Alan's concern for you is entirely artificial.*

artless *adj.* **1** °innocent, °sincere, guileless, °ingenuous, °true, °natural, °open, unartificial, °genuine, °simple, °direct, °candid, °frank, °honest, straightforward, °above-board, uncomplicated, undevious, undeceptive, *Colloq* upfront, on the °level, on the up and up: *Imitation is a kind of artless flattery.* **2** unpretentious, unassuming, °unaffected, °natural, °simple, °naïve, °unsophisticated, °plain, °ordinary, °humble: *The remarks were those of an artless young man who meant nothing sinister.* **3** unskilled, untalented, unskilful, unpractised, °inexperienced, inexpert, °primitive, unproficient, °incompetent, °inept, °clumsy, °crude, °awkward, bungling: *Clogs must be the most artless footwear ever made.*

ashamed *adj.* °embarrassed, abashed, humiliated, chagrined, mortified, blushing, °shamefaced, °sheepish, red-faced: *I was ashamed to have to admit that it was I who had written the nasty letter.*

ask *v.* **1** °question, interrogate, °query, °quiz; °inquire *or* °enquire (of): *Let's ask the policeman for information. Just ask directions of any passer-by. I merely asked if you were going my way.* **2** °demand, °require, °expect, °request: *Doing his laundry is a lot to ask.* **3** °beg, °apply (to), °appeal (to), °seek (from), °solicit (from), °petition, °plead (to), °beg, °beseech, °pray, entreat, implore: *In the streets, thousands of beggars ask passers-by for alms.* **4** invite, °bid, °summon: *Nellie asked me to dinner.* **5** ***ask after*** *or* ***about***: °inquire *or* °enquire after *or* about: *My sister asked after you—wanted to know how you were getting along.* **6** ***ask for***: **a** invite, °attract, °encourage, °provoke: *You're asking for trouble if you walk alone through that neighbourhood after dark.* **b** °request, °seek: *We asked for more time to finish the project.*

aspect *n.* **1** °viewpoint, point of °view, °position, °standpoint, °side: *Looked at from a different aspect, the problem did not seem insurmountable after all.* **2** complexion, °light, °angle, °interpretation, mien, °face: *His conviction for robbery put a different aspect on hiring him as a security guard.* **3** °exposure, °prospect, °outlook, °orientation: *The western aspect of the room made it sunny in the afternoons.* **4** °side, °feature, °attribute, °characteristic, °quality, °detail, °angle, facet, °manifestation, °element, °circumstance: *There are many aspects of Buddhism that you do not understand.*

aspersion *n.* °slander, °libel, false insinuation, calumny, °imputation, °allegation, detraction, °slur, obloquy, defamation, disparagement: *He resented my casting aspersions on the legitimacy of his birth.*

aspiration *n.* °desire, °longing, yearning, craving, hankering, °wish, °dream, °hope; °ambition, °aim, °goal, °objective, °purpose, °intention, °plan, °scheme, °plot: *It was his lifelong aspiration to marry someone with money.*

aspire *v.* ***aspire to***: °desire, °hope, °long, °wish, °aim, °yearn; °dream of: *I'd never aspire to anything higher. He still aspired to being a full professor.*

assailant *n.* attacker, assaulter, mugger: *My assailant threatened me with a knife.*

assault *n.* **1** °attack, onslaught, °onset, °charge, °offensive, blitzkrieg, blitz, °strike, °raid, incursion, sortie; °aggression, °invasion: *At dawn we launched the assault on the fort.* **2** beating, battering, °hold-up, mugging; °rape, °violation, molestation; *Law* battery: *The defendant is accused of assault.*
—*v.* **3** °attack, assail, °set *or* °fall upon, °pounce upon, °storm, °beset, °charge, °rush, °lay into: *The elderly couple were assaulted near their home.* **4** °rape, °violate, °molest: *Three women were assaulted in that neighbourhood last night.* **5** °beat (up), °batter, °bruise, °harm, °hit, °strike, °punch, smite: *She complained that her husband continually assaulted the children.*

assemble *v.* **1** convene, °gather, °call *or* °bring *or* °get together, convoke, °summon, °muster, marshal, °rally, levy, °round up, °collect, congregate, forgather *or* foregather; °meet: *The forces were assembled along the waterfront. A small crowd assembled at the airport.* **2** °accumulate, °gather, °amass, °collect, °bring *or* °group *or* °lump together, °compile, °unite, °join *or* °draw together: *The paintings were assembled from many sources.* **3** °construct, °put together, °erect, °set up, °fit *or* °join *or* °piece together, °connect, °fabricate, °manufacture, °make: *The sculpture was assembled from so-called* objets trouvés, *or 'found' objects.*

assembly *n.* **1** °gathering, °group, °meeting, assemblage, °body, °circle, °company, congregation, °flock, °crowd, °throng, multitude, °host; horde: *A huge assembly of well-wishers greeted the candidate.* **2** convocation, °council, °convention, congress, °association, conclave; °diet, synod: *The assembly voted to re-elect the incumbent officers.* **3** construction, putting together, erection, °connection, °setting up, °set-up, °fitting *or* joining *or* piecing together, °fabrication; °manufacture, making: *Assembly of the bicycle can be completed in an hour.*

assertion *n.* **1** °statement, °declaration, affirmation, contention, asseveration, averment, avowal, °pronouncement; *Law* affidavit, deposition: *He made the assertion that he had never seen the defendant before.* **2** insistence, °proclamation, °representation, affirmation, confirmation: *The kings exercised their jurisdiction in the assertion of their regal power.*

assertive *adj.* declaratory, affirmative, asseverative; °definite, °certain, °sure, °positive, °firm, °emphatic, °bold, °aggressive, °confident, °insistent; °dogmatic, doctrinaire, °domineering, °opinionated, °peremptory,

Colloq °bossy, °pushy: *Harold won't obey unless his mother adopts an assertive tone with him.*

asset *n.* **1** Also, ***assets***: °property, resources, possessions, holdings, °effects, °capital, °means, valuables, °money, °wealth: *We have to pay a tax on the company's assets. Her only liquid asset was some shares in the Suez Canal Company.* **2** °talent, °strength, °advantage, °resource, °benefit: *His main asset is that he speaks fluent Japanese.*

assign *v.* **1** °allot, allocate, apportion, consign, °appropriate, °distribute, °give (out), °grant: *A water ration was assigned to each person.* **2** °fix, °set (apart *or* aside), °settle (on), °determine, °appoint, °authorize, °designate, ordain, °prescribe, °specify: *Have they really assigned Thursday as the day of worship? Please sit in the seats assigned to you.* **3** °appoint, °designate, °order; °name, °delegate, °nominate, °attach; °choose, °select; *Brit* °second: *The men have been assigned to their posts. I assigned David to look after the champagne.* **4** °attribute, ascribe, accredit, °put down; °refer: *To which century did the curator assign this vase?*

assignment *n.* **1** °allotment, allocation, apportionment, giving (out), °distribution: *Assignment of posts in the Cabinet is the responsibility of the Prime Minister.* **2** °task, °obligation, °responsibility, chore, °duty, °position, °post, °charge, °job, °mission, commission; °lesson, homework: *Every agent is expected to carry out his assignment. The school assignment for tomorrow is an essay on Alexander Pope.* **3** °appointment, designation, naming, nomination: *The assignment of Neil Mackay to the post was a stroke of genius.* **4** designation, °specification, ascription: *In ancient medicine, the assignment of the functions of the organs was often wrong.*

assist *v.* **1** °aid, °help, °second, °support: *He could walk only if assisted by the nurse.* **2** °further, °promote, °abet, °support, °benefit, °facilitate: *The rumours will not assist his election.* **3** °help, succour, °serve, °work for *or* with; °relieve: *She has always assisted the poor.*

assistance *n.* °help, °aid, °support, succour, °backing, °reinforcement, °relief, °benefit: *Can you get up without my assistance? The scholarship fund offered financial assistance.*

assistant *n.* **1** helper, helpmate *or* helpmeet, °aid, °aide; aide-de-camp, °second: *These systems make use of rhymes as assistants to the memory.* **2** °deputy, °subordinate, °subsidiary, °auxiliary; underling: *He is now the assistant to the sales manager.*

associate *v.* **1** ***associate (with)***: **a** °ally with, °link, °join *or* °unite (with), °combine *or* confederate (with), °connect (with), conjoin (with): *In the 1930s Abe was associated with Dutch and Louis in Murder, Incorporated. I always associate him with fast cars and hard drinking.* **b** °see, be seen with, °socialize *or* °fraternize (with), °mix *or* °mingle (with), °go (out) with, consort with, have to do with, *Colloq* °hang out with, *Brit* °pal with *or* about, °pal up (with), *US* °pal around (with): *Mother told me not to associate with boys who use that kind of language.*

—*n.* **2** °colleague, °partner; °fellow, fellow-worker: *I'd like you to meet my associate, Ian Lindsay.* **3** confederate, °ally, collaborator; °accomplice, °accessory: *He and his associates have been sent to prison for conspiracy.* **4** °comrade, °companion, °friend, °mate, buddy; confidant(e): *We have been close associates for many years.*

—*adj.* **5** °subsidiary, °secondary: *She is an associate professor at an American university.* **6** allied, affiliate, °affiliated, associated; °accessory: *Publication is under the direction of an associate company.*

association *n.* **1** °society, °organization, confederation, confederacy, °federation, °league, °union, °alliance, guild, coalition, °group; °syndicate, °combine, consortium, cooperative: *The society later became known as the British Association for the Advancement of Science.* **2** °connection, °link, affiliation, °relationship, °bond, °tie, linkage, linking, pairing, joining, conjunction, bonding: *The association between princes and frogs is probably lost on anyone so literal-minded.* **3** °fellowship, intimacy, °friendship, camaraderie, comradeship, °relationship: *There has been a long-standing association between Peter and Wendy.*

assortment *n.* **1** °group, °class, °category, °batch, °set, °lot, classification, grouping: *Which assortment contains only plain chocolates?* **2** °collection, °pot-pourri, °mixture, mélange, array, agglomeration, conglomeration, °medley, farrago, °variety, °miscellany, °jumble, salmagundi, gallimaufry, °mishmash, *Colloq* mixed bag: *That hat looks like something from the assortment at a jumble sale. A bizarre assortment of people attended the meeting.*

assume *v.* **1** °accept, °adopt, °take, °use, °employ; arrogate, °appropriate, °take over *or* up, °undertake: *Who will assume the leadership of the party?* **2** °take on (oneself), °take upon (oneself), °put *or* °try on, don, °adopt; °acquire: *Whenever she delivered the information, she assumed the disguise of an old man. That trivial dispute has assumed gargantuan proportions.* **3** °presume, °suppose, °believe, °fancy, °expect, °think, °presuppose, °take, °take for granted, °surmise, *Chiefly US* °guess: *When I saw the knife in his hand, I assumed the chef was going to slice a lemon. The king assumed he had the cooperation of Parliament.* **4** °pretend to, feign, °sham, °counterfeit, simulate, °affect, °fake: *Though she cared deeply, she assumed a devil-may-care attitude.*

assumed *adj.* **1** appropriated, °taken, usurped, expropriated, pre-empted, seized: *He functions in his assumed capacity as a judge.* **2** °pretended, °put on, °sham, °false, feigned, °affected, °counterfeit, simulated, °spurious, °bogus, °fake; pseudonymous, made-up, *Colloq* °phoney *or US also* phony: *She morosely stared at the floor in assumed contrition. He wrote poetry under an assumed name.* **3** °taken, °taken for granted, presumed, °supposed, accepted, expected, presupposed; °hypothetical, °theoretical, suppositional: *The payment depends materially on the assumed rate of interest.*

assurance *n.* **1** °promise, °pledge, °guarantee *or* guaranty, °warranty, commitment, °bond, surety; °word, °word of honour, °oath, °vow: *You have the bank's assurance that the money will be on deposit.* **2** °insurance, °indemnity: *His life assurance is barely enough to cover the costs of his funeral.* **3** °certainty, °confidence, °trust, °faith, reassurance, surety, assuredness, certitude; °security: *There is no assurance that Herr Kleister will get the job done.* **4** audacity, °impudence, °presumption, boldness, brazenness, °nerve, °effrontery, insolence, *Colloq* °brass, °gall, cheek, chutzpah: *With an air of assurance they quote authors they have never read.* **5** °self-confidence, self-reliance, °confidence, steadiness, intrepidity, self-possession, °poise, aplomb, coolness, °control, °self-control, °resolve, *Colloq* °gumption, guts, gutsiness: *He has the assurance of one born to command.*

assure *v.* **1** °secure, stabilize, °settle, °establish, °confirm, °certify, °warrant, °guarantee, °ensure, be °confident of, make *or* be °sure *or* °certain: *Force, fear, and the multitude of his guard do less to assure the estate of a prince than the good will of his subjects.* **2** °encourage, inspirit, °reassure, hearten: *Your humanity assures us and gives us strength.* **3** °convince, °persuade, °reassure, make (someone) °certain; °ensure: *What can I do to assure you of my love?* **4** assert, °state, asseverate, °promise: *I assure you that we shall do everything possible to find your dog.*

astonish *v.* °amaze, °surprise, °shock, °astound, °stun, °stagger, °dumbfound *or* dumfound, °bowl over, °floor, stupefy, °daze, *Colloq* flabbergast: *She astonished the audience with her gymnastic skill. I was astonished when told my wife had given birth to quintuplets.*

astonishment *n.* °amazement, °surprise, °shock, stupefaction, °wonder, wonderment: *I'll never forget that* *look of astonishment on his face when he learned he had won.*

astound *v.* °surprise, °shock, °astonish, °stun, °stagger, °dumbfound *or* dumfound, °bowl over, °floor, stupefy, °bewilder, °overwhelm, *Colloq* flabbergast: *We were astounded to learn that he had survived all those years on a desert island. The Great MacTavish performs astounding feats of magic and levitation!*

astute *adj.* **1** °shrewd, °subtle, °clever, °ingenious, adroit, °wily, cunning, °calculating, canny, °crafty, °artful, °arch, °sly, °foxy, guileful, underhand, underhanded; *Rare* astucious: *He had the reputation of being an astute businessman.* **2** °sharp, °keen, °perceptive, °observant, °alert, °quick, °quick-witted, °sage, sagacious, °wise, °intelligent, insightful, perspicacious, discerning, °knowledgeable: *That was a very astute comment, Smedley.*

atmosphere *n.* **1** °air, °heaven(s), °sky, aerosphere: *It is gravity that prevents the earth's atmosphere from drifting off into outer space.* **2** °air, ambience *or* ambiance, °environment, °climate, °mood, °feeling, °feel, °spirit, °tone: *There's such a friendly atmosphere in the bar of the Golden Cockerel. The atmosphere became very chilly when she told him she was marrying someone else.*

atone *v.* expiate, make °amends, °pay, °repay, °answer, °compensate; redress, °remedy, propitiate, °redeem: *Nothing can atone for her betrayal of him to the enemy. He has atoned for his sins many times over.*

atonement *n.* °amends, propitiation, reparation, repayment, compensation, °payment, °restitution, recompense, expiation, °penance, °satisfaction: *He sent her flowers in atonement, together with a note apologizing profusely for his actions.*

atrocious *adj.* **1** °cruel, °wicked, iniquitous, °villainous, °fiendish, execrable, appalling, °abominable, °monstrous, °inhuman, °savage, barbaric, °brutal, barbarous, heinous, °dreadful, °flagrant, flagitious, °gruesome, °grisly, °ruthless, °ghastly, unspeakable, horrifying, °horrible, °awful, °infamous, °infernal, °satanic, hellish: *They will never forget the atrocious crimes that took place during the war.* **2** °awful, °terrible, °bad, °rotten, horrid, appalling, °frightful, horrendous, *Colloq* °lousy: *That's the most atrocious book it has ever been my misfortune to review. Priscilla has atrocious taste.*

atrocity *n.* **1** °enormity, wickedness, flagitiousness, iniquity, °infamy, cruelty, heinousness, °horror, °evil, inhumanity, °barbarity, savagery: *The atrocity of the 'Final Solution' was a well-kept secret during the war.* **2** °evil, °outrage, °crime, villainy, °offence: *She could not listen when the prosecutor read a list of the atrocities perpetrated at the camp.*

attach *v.* **1** °fasten, °join, °connect, °secure, °fix, affix; °tack *or* °hook *or* °tie *or* °stick on, °pin, rivet, °cement, °glue, °bond, solder, °weld, braze; °unite; *Nautical* °bend: *The tag is still attached to your dress. Attach this to the wall. How do I attach the sail to the spar?* **2** °connect, °associate, °assign, affiliate, °enlist, °join, °add, subjoin, *Brit* °second: *Her brother-in-law has been attached to my regiment.* **3** endear, °attract: *I won't say that we were in love, but I was very closely attached to her.* **4** °fix, affix, °pin, °apply, ascribe, °assign, °attribute, °put, °place: *Why do you attach so much importance to what Dora says?* **5** adhere, °cleave, °stick: *Many legends have attached themselves to Charlemagne.* **6** °seize, °lay °hold of, °confiscate, °appropriate: *If he cannot meet the mortgage payments the bank will attach his house.*

attached *adj.* **1** connected, joined, *Brit* seconded: *She has been attached to the Foreign Office for many years.* **2** °united, fastened, °fixed: *The knob attached to the outside of the door might come off.* **3** Often, ***attached to***: °devoted (to), °partial (to), °fond (of): *I feel closely attached to her. I became attached to the painting and did not wish to sell it.* **4** °spoken for, married, unavailable, °engaged, betrothed: *I would have asked Suzanne out, but I gather she's attached.*

attachment *n.* **1** °fastening; °connection, °tie, °link, °bond: *The attachment of this fitting is too flimsy. William cannot understand how an attachment could have been formed between his wife and his brother.* **2** attaching, °fastening, linking, joining, affixing, fixing, °connection: *The mode of attachment to the wall is not immediately apparent.* **3** °affection, °regard, fidelity, faithfulness, °devotion, °liking, fondness, °affinity, friendliness, °loyalty, °admiration, tenderness, °partiality, °friendship, °love: *We still feel a deep attachment, despite the divorce.* **4** adjunct, °addition, °accessory, °device, appliance, °extra, accoutrement *or US also* accouterment, appendage, °part; °ornament, °decoration; *Colloq* °gadget: *With this attachment, the film is advanced automatically. Attachments are available at extra cost.*

attack *v.* **1** assail, °assault, °fall *or* °set *or* °pounce upon; °charge, °rush, °raid, °strike (at), °storm; °engage (in battle), °fight; *Colloq* °mug, °jump: *They were attacked on their way home by a gang of boys. Helicopter gunships were sent out to attack the bunker.* **2** °criticize, censure, °berate; °abuse, revile, inveigh against, °denounce, °condemn, malign, denigrate, decry, °disparage, deprecate, °vilify: *His article attacked the minister for his views on housing.* **3** °begin, °start; °approach, °undertake: *We attacked the meal with gusto.* **4** °affect, °seize; infect: *Rheumatism attacks young and old alike.* **5** °waste, °devour, °destroy, °eat; °erode, corrode, °decompose, °dissolve: *Termites have attacked the beams of the house. Watch how the acid attacks the areas on the plate that have not been protected.*
—*n.* **6** °assault, °onset, °offensive, onslaught, incursion, °raid, °strike, °inroad, °invasion: *The enemy responded to our attack with a smokescreen. After capturing the pawn, Karpov launched an attack on the queen.* **7** °criticism, censure; °abuse, denunciation, revilement, denigration, decrial, disparagement, deprecation, vilification: *The quarterly's attack is totally uncalled for.* **8** °seizure, °spell, °spasm, °paroxysm; °fit, °bout: *Preston has had another attack of gout. How do you stop an attack of hiccups?* **9** °destruction, wasting; °erosion, corrosion: *Noting the attack on the planks by shipworm, the surveyor declared the vessel unseaworthy. Aluminium will not withstand the attack of the salt air in this area.*

attempt *v.* **1** °try, °essay, °undertake, °take on, °venture; °endeavour, °strive, *Colloq* have *or* take a crack at, °try on, have a °go *or* °shot at: *It is too stormy to attempt the crossing tonight. Is she going to attempt to dive off the cliff tomorrow?*
—*n.* **2** °endeavour, °try, °essay; °effort, °undertaking, °bid, *Colloq* °crack, °go, °shot: *The weather cleared sufficiently for another attempt at the summit. He made a feeble attempt to wave.* **3** °attack, °assault: *An abortive attempt was made on the life of the vice-president tonight.*

attend *v.* **1** be °present (at), °go to, be at, °appear (at), °put in an appearance (at), °turn up (at), °haunt, °frequent; °sit in (on), *US and Canadian* audit: *Are you attending the concert? She attends Miss Fiennes's elocution class.* **2** °turn to, pay °attention to, °serve, °tend to, take °care of, °deal with, °handle, °heed, °fulfil: *I shall attend to your request as soon as possible, Madam.* **3** Also, ***attend to***: °watch over, °wait on *or* upon, °care for, take °care of, °minister to, °occupy oneself with, °look after, °look out for, °devote oneself to: *Mrs Atterbury attends the patients in the cancer ward on weekdays. The clergyman has his own flock to attend to.* **4** °escort, °accompany, °conduct, convoy, °squire, usher, °wait upon, °follow; chaperon *or* chaperone: *The actress arrived, attended by her entourage of toadies.* **5** °be associated with, °accompany, °result in *or* from, give °rise to: *A departure in the midst of the battle would be attended by great peril, Milord.*

attendance *n.* **1** °presence, °appearance, being: *Your attendance at chapel is required.* **2** audience, °crowd, °assembly, assemblage, °gathering, °turnout, °gate, °house: *The attendance at the fête was greater than we* *expected.* **3** ***in attendance***: waiting upon, attending, serving: *The king always has at least four people in attendance.*

attendant *adj.* **1** waiting upon, accompanying, following; resultant, resulting, °related, consequent, concomitant, depending, °accessory: *The circumstances attendant on your acceptance of the post are immaterial.*
—*n.* **2** °escort, °servant, °menial, helper, usher *or* usherette, chaperon *or* chaperone; °aide, °subordinate, underling, °assistant; °follower, *Derogatory* lackey, °flunkey, °slave; *Colloq US* °cohort: *He dismissed his attendants and entered the church alone.*

attention *n.* **1** °heed, °regard, °notice; concentration: *Please give your attention to the teacher. Pay attention! Don't let your attention wander.* **2** publicity, °notice, °distinction, acclaim, °prominence, *réclame*, °notoriety; limelight: *She seems to have been getting a lot of attention lately.*

attentive *adj.* **1** heedful, °observant, °awake, °alert, °intent, watchful, concentrating, assiduous; °mindful, °considerate: *James is very attentive in class. You really must be more attentive to the needs of others.* **2** °polite, °courteous, courtly, °gallant, °gracious, °accommodating, °considerate, °thoughtful, °solicitous, civil, °respectful, deferential: *He is always very attentive to the ladies.*

attest *v.* bear °witness (to), °bear out, °swear (to), °vow, °testify, °certify, °vouchsafe, °declare, assert, asseverate, aver, affirm, °confirm, °verify, °substantiate, °vouch for, *Law* depose, depose and °say, depone: *I attest to the fact that they left the restaurant together. The merits of château-bottled Bordeaux are attested by most epicures.*

attitude *n.* **1** °posture, °position, °disposition, °stance, °bearing, °carriage, °aspect, demeanour: *The attitude of the figures in the sculpture was one of supplication.* **2** °posture, °position, °disposition, °opinion, °feeling, °view, point of °view, °viewpoint, °approach, °leaning, °thought, °inclination, °bent, °tendency, °orientation: *What is your attitude towards the situation in South Africa?*

attract *v.* °draw, invite; °entice, °lure, allure, °appeal to, °charm, °captivate, °fascinate, *Colloq* °pull: *Our attention was attracted by a slight noise in the cupboard. Melissa attracts men the way flowers attract bees.*

attraction *n.* **1** °draw, °appeal; °magnetism; gravitation, *Colloq* °pull: *David confided to Joan that he felt a strong attraction to her. There is an attraction between the north and south poles of these magnets.* **2** °draw, °lure, °enticement, attractant, °inducement; °show, °entertainment, °presentation, performance, *Colloq* °come-on, crowd-puller, crowd-pleaser: *The presence of the movie stars has been a powerful attraction. The producer has planned to repeat the attraction every evening.*

attractive *adj.* attracting, °drawing, pulling, captivating, °taking, °fetching, appealing, luring, °inviting, enticing, °seductive, °engaging, charming, °interesting, °pleasing, °winning, alluring, good-looking, °pretty, °handsome: *The person I'd like to meet needn't be beautiful or stunning—attractive will do nicely.*

attribute *n.* **1** °quality, °character, °characteristic, °property, °feature, °trait, °virtue: *It is surprising how soon historical personages become invested with romantic attributes.*
—*v.* **2** ascribe, °impute, °assign, °put down to, °trace to, °charge, °credit: *The shrivelled arm of Richard the Third was attributed to witchcraft. To what do you attribute your interest in birds?*

attribution *n.* °assignment, ascription, °credit: *The curator disagreed with the expert's attribution of the painting to Canaletto.*

audacious *adj.* **1** °daring, °bold, °confident, °intrepid, °brave, °courageous, °adventurous, °venturesome, °reckless, °rash, °foolhardy, °daredevil, devil-may-care, °fearless, doughty, mettlesome: *The troop launched an audacious daylight attack. Cranshaw made an audacious bid for the chairmanship.* **2** °presumptuous, °shameless, °bold, °impudent, °pert, saucy, °defiant, °impertinent, °insolent, °brazen, °unabashed, °rude, °disrespectful, °cheeky, °forward: *Charlotte was so audacious as to assume that she could win.*

aura *n.* °air, °atmosphere, °feeling, ambience *or* ambiance, °spirit, °character, °quality, °odour, °aroma, emanation: *There is an aura of elegance about the woman that impresses everyone she meets.*

auspices *n.* aegis, sponsorship, °authority, °protection, °support, °backing, supervision, °guidance, °patronage, °sanction, °approval, °control, °influence: *The competition is under the auspices of the astronomical society.*

authentic *adj.* °genuine, °real, °actual, bona fide, °factual, °accurate, °true, °legitimate, °authoritative, °reliable, °veritable, °trustworthy, °faithful, °undisputed: *This is an authentic Chippendale chair.*

authenticate *v.* °verify, validate, °certify, °substantiate, °endorse, °vouch for, °confirm, corroborate: *You will have to go to the consul to have your passport authenticated.*

author *n.* °creator, originator, inventor, °father, °founder, framer, initiator, maker, °prime mover, architect, °designer; °writer, novelist, *littérateur*: *Adolfo was the author of the plot to kill the governor.*

authoritarian *adj.* °dictatorial, imperious, °totalitarian, autocratic, °arbitrary, °absolute, °dogmatic, °domineering, °strict, °severe, unyielding, °tyrannical, °despotic, *Colloq* °bossy: *Why do people ever elect an authoritarian government?*

authoritative *adj.* **1** °official, valid, °authentic, documented, certified, validated, °legitimate, sanctioned; conclusive: *The second edition is usually considered the authoritative one.* **2** °scholarly, °learned, °authentic, valid, °sound, °veritable, verifiable, °accurate, °factual, °faithful, dependable, °reliable, °trustworthy, °true, °truthful: *There is no more authoritative source than Professor Fitzhugh on early Egyptian history.*

authority *n.* **1** °power, °jurisdiction, °dominion, °right, °control, °prerogative, authorization; hegemony: *Who gave you the authority to tell me what to do? By the authority vested in me, I now pronounce you man and wife.* **2** °word, °testimony, °evidence, *Colloq* °say-so: *Do not accept anything solely on the authority of the* Herald. **3** °expert, °specialist, °scholar, °sage, °judge, arbiter: *Gardner is an authority on Scottish history.* **4** ***authorities***: °government, °establishment, officials, officialdom, °powers that be, °police: *The authorities lowered the speed limit.*

authorize *v.* empower, commission; °sanction, °approve, countenance, °permit, give °leave, °allow, °license, °entitle, °consent *or* °subscribe to, °endorse, *Colloq* °OK *or* okay, give the green light *or* °go-ahead to: *Who authorized you to speak for all of us?*

automatic *adj.* **1** self-acting, self-governing, self-regulating, °mechanical, °robot, automated: *Many modern cars are equipped with an automatic choke.* **2** °mechanical, °involuntary, °unconscious, °instinctive *or* instinctual, °natural, °spontaneous, °impulsive, conditioned, reflex, robot-like, *Slang* knee-jerk: *Flinching is an automatic reaction to a threatening gesture.* **3** °unavoidable, °inevitable, inescapable, ineluctable: *It is automatic for the tax inspector to suspect people of hiding something.*

auxiliary *adj.* **1** °helping, assisting, °supportive, aiding, abetting; °helpful, °accessory, °supplementary: *In a well-balanced mind, imagination and understanding are auxiliary to each other.* **2** °subordinate, additional, °subsidiary, °secondary, ancillary, °extra, °reserve; °accessory: *Larger sailing vessels have an auxiliary motor in case the wind fails.*
—*n.* **3** °help, °assistance, °aid, °support, °accessory: *Knowing another language is a useful auxiliary in the study of your own.* **4** helper, °assistant, °aide, alter ego, °supporter, *Colloq* man Friday, girl Friday: *Let me*

introduce Pat, my auxiliary, who will help you if I am not available.

available *adj.* at *or* to °hand, at one's disposal, °accessible, °handy, °present, °ready, (readily) obtainable, °convenient, °nearby, °close by, within °reach, on °tap, at one's fingertips *or* elbow: *Running water is available. If you need me for anything, I am available.*

avant-garde *adj.* innovative, advanced, °progressive, °experimental, °original, °new, ground-breaking, pioneering, precedent-setting; °revolutionary, °extreme, extremist, *Colloq* far-out, °way-out: *We disapprove of your avant-garde notions of teaching. Some modern art, avant-garde not very long ago, seems quite conventional today.*

avarice *n.* °greed, acquisitiveness, cupidity, craving, covetousness, °desire, greediness, °rapacity, selfishness; stinginess, meanness, miserliness, parsimony, tight-fistedness, close-fistedness, niggardliness, penuriousness: *The classic tale of avarice is that of King Midas, whose touch turned everything to gold.*

avaricious *adj.* °greedy, acquisitive, °grasping, covetous, °mercenary, °selfish; penny-pinching, stingy, °miserly, °mean, parsimonious, tight-fisted, close-fisted, niggardly, °penurious, °tight: *She fell into the clutches of an avaricious lawyer.*

average *n.* **1** °mean, °norm, °usual, °standard: *The Bell Inn is certainly far above average in accommodation, food quality, and service.* **2** ***on average***: in the °main, °generally, normally, °usually, °ordinarily, typically, customarily, as a °rule, for the most °part: *On average, I go abroad twice a year on business.*
—*adj.* **3** °normal, common, °usual, °customary, °general, °typical, °ordinary, °regular: *On an average day, the museum has about 2,000 visitors.* **4** °mediocre, middling, run-of-the-mill, commonplace, °common, °ordinary, °undistinguished, unexceptional, *Colloq* so so: *Boris is only an average violinist, but he's a virtuoso on the harmonica.*

averse *adj.* °disinclined, unwilling, °reluctant, °resistant, °loath, °opposed, anti, antipathetic, ill-disposed, °indisposed: *He does not appear to be averse to your suggestion: in fact, he seems quite keen on it.*

aversion *n.* **1** °dislike, abhorrence, repugnance, antipathy, °antagonism, °animosity, °hostility, °loathing, hatred, odium, °horror; disinclination, unwillingness, °reluctance, °distaste: *Does Anne have an aversion to people who smoke? Your aversion to the theatre might be explained as agoraphobia.* **2** °dislike, hatred, °hate, °loathing: *Turnips are a particular aversion of mine.*

avoid *v.* °shun, °keep (away) from, keep off, leave °alone, keep *or* °steer clear of, °refrain from, °dodge, circumvent, °sidestep, °elude, °escape, °evade: *The doctor suggested that I avoid chocolate. Why does Bennie avoid looking me straight in the eye?*

awake *v.* **1** °wake (up), awaken, °get up, °rouse *or* bestir oneself: *When I awoke, she was standing over me with a pistol.* **2** awaken, °animate, °arouse, °rouse, °stimulate, °revive, °incite, °excite, °activate, °alert, °stir up, °fan, °kindle, ignite, °fire: *Marches awaken my sense of patriotism.* **3** ***awake to***: awaken to, °wake up to, °realize, °understand, become °aware *or* °conscious of: *I finally awoke to the fact that my tax return was overdue.*
—*adj.* **4** up, aroused, roused, wide awake, up and about, °alert, on the °alert, on the qui vive, watchful, on °guard, °attentive, °conscious; heedful, °alive: *I'm always awake a few minutes before the alarm goes off.*

awaken *v.* See **awake, 1, 2,** above.

award *v.* **1** °grant, °give, °confer, °bestow, °present, °accord, °furnish, endow with; °assign, apportion: *Her dog was awarded the blue ribbon in the club show.*
—*n.* **2** °prize, °trophy, °reward: *The award for the tidiest boats has been won by the Bristol Yacht Club.* **3** °grant, bestowal, °presentation, °endowment, awarding: *Before the award of the prizes, we listened to speeches. Profits were up last year despite a large pay award.*

aware *adj.* **1** °informed, apprised, °knowledgeable, °knowing, posted, in the °know, °enlightened, *au fait, au courant*, cognizant, *Slang* °hip, hep, °wise: *She is well aware of the consequences.* **2** °sensitive, °sensible, °conscious: *I became aware that someone was watching us.*

awesome *adj.* awe-inspiring, °awful, °imposing, °amazing, wonderful, breathtaking, °marvellous, wondrous, °moving, °stirring, affecting, °overwhelming, °formidable, daunting, °dreadful, °fearsome, °fearful, °frightening, horrifying, °terrifying, °terrible; °unbelievable, °incredible; alarming, °shocking, °stunning, stupefying, astounding, astonishing: *The eruption of Vesuvius in* AD *67 must have been a truly awesome spectacle.*

awful *adj.* **1** °bad, °terrible, °inferior, °base, °abominable, °rotten, °horrible, horrid; °tasteless, °unsightly, °ugly, °hideous, °grotesque, *Slang* °lousy, *Brit* naff, *Chiefly US* hellacious: *That is an awful piece of sculpture. I feel awful this morning.* **2** °frightful, °shocking, execrable, unpleasant, °grotesque, °nasty, °ghastly, °gruesome, horrendous, horrifying, horrific, °horrible, unspeakable: *That was an awful thing to do.*

awfully *adv.* °very (much), °badly, °terribly, °extremely, greatly, remarkably, in the worst way, dreadfully, extraordinarily, °exceedingly, excessively, °really, °fearfully, inordinately; incomparably: *I get awfully tired running in the marathon. I'm awfully sorry I'm late. Doreen is an awfully good horsewoman.*

awkward *adj.* **1** °clumsy, ungainly, °left-handed, ham-handed, ham-fisted, blundering, bungling, maladroit, uncoordinated, undexterous, inexpert, gauche, unhandy, °inept, oafish, unskilled, unskilful, *Colloq* all °thumbs, butter-fingered, *Brit* cack-handed: *In his awkward attempt at putting the watch back together, Sam left out a few parts.* **2** °ungraceful, ungainly, inelegant, °wooden, gawky: *The ballerina made an awkward, flat-footed pirouette and stumbled off stage.* **3** °embarrassed, °shamefaced, uncomfortable, °ill at ease, uneasy, out of °place, discomfited, °confused: *He felt awkward being the only boy in the class. Terry made an awkward excuse and left the room.* **4** °dangerous, °hazardous, °risky, °precarious, °perilous: *Be careful, there's an awkward step here.* **5** °difficult, °touchy, °sensitive, °embarrassing, °delicate, unpleasant, uncomfortable, °ticklish, °tricky, °trying, °troublesome, *Colloq* °sticky: *He's got himself into a very awkward situation indeed.*

B

babble *v.* **1** °prattle, twaddle, °jabber, gibber, °chatter, °blab, blabber, °gurgle, burble, gabble, *Colloq* °blab, blabber, °gab, ya(c)k, natter, witter, *Brit* rabbit: *The silly fellow kept babbling away, but no one was listening. Madelaine is still too young to talk and just babbles to herself.* **2** divulge, °tell, °disclose, °repeat, °reveal, °tattle, °gossip, °blurt (out), *Colloq* °blab: *Don't tell Nigel about the affair—he'll babble it all over town.*
—*n.* **3** °gibberish, °nonsense, twaddle, °prattle, °chatter(ing), gibber, °jabber, jibber-jabber, °drivel, °rubbish, *bavardage;* °murmur, hubbub: *Ella's conversation about the financial market is just so much babble.*

baby *n.* **1** infant, neonate, newborn, babe, babe in arms, °child, toddler, °tot: *The baby is just beginning to teethe.*
—*v.* **2** cosset, °coddle, °pamper, mollycoddle, °indulge, °spoil, °pet: *He turned out that way because he was babied till he was ten. I know you like to be babied when you're ill.*

back *v.* **1** °invest in, wager *or* °bet on: *She backed a 35-to-2 long shot in the Derby, and she won.* **2** Also, ***back up***: **a** °support, °uphold, °stand behind, °promote, °encourage, °help, °second, °side with, °endorse, °aid,

°abet, °assist; °sponsor, °subsidize, °underwrite, subvene, °finance, *Slang US and Canadian* bankroll: *Your mother and I will back you if you want to start a business.* **b** °reverse, go *or* move in °reverse, °go *or* move °backwards: *He backed into the driveway.* **3** ***back down (from)*** *or* ***off (from)*** *or* ***away (from)*** *or* ***out (of)*** *or* ***up***: °withdraw (from), °retreat (from), °abandon, °retire (from), backtrack (from), °shy away (from), °recoil (from), °turn tail (from): *When Percy stood up to him, the bully backed down. The investment sounded risky, so I backed off. Philippa backed out of singing the leading role. Back up and give me room!*
—*n.* **4** backside, °rear, *Technical* dorsum: *She stood with her back towards me.* **5** ***at the back of*** *or* ***at someone's back***: behind, following, pursuing, chasing, *US* in back of: *Here come the hounds at the back of the fox. You were at my back in the queue a minute ago.* **6** ***behind the back of*** *or* ***behind someone's back***: surreptitiously, °secretly, clandestinely, privately, furtively, sneakily, slyly; treacherously, traitorously, perfidiously, deceitfully, insidiously: *Graham is always telling tales about you behind your back.* **7** ***break the back of***: **a** °overcome, °master: *Now that he's broken the back of that problem he can get on with his work.* **b** *US* crush, °ruin, bankrupt, °destroy, °defeat, vanquish, *Colloq* °break: *The government has tried on many occasions to break the back of the Mafia operation.* **8** ***on (someone's) back***: *US* weighing (down) on *or* upon (someone), burdening (someone), lodged with (someone), resting with (someone): *The responsibility for the decision is on your back.* **9** ***turn one's back on*** *or* ***upon***: °abandon, °forsake, °ignore, °disregard, °repudiate, °reject, °cast off, disown, °deny: *He turned his back on her when she needed him most.* **10** ***with one's back to*** *or* ***against the wall***: hard pressed, struggling (against °odds), without hope, with little *or* no hope, °helpless, in dire straits, in (serious) °trouble: *After the stock-market crash, some brokers found themselves with their backs to the wall.*
—*adj.* **11** °rear; °service, servants': *Both back tyres are flat. Please use the back staircase from now on.* **12** *US and Australian and New Zealand* °outlying, °remote, °isolated, °distant; °undeveloped, °primitive, °raw, °rough, °uncivilized: *They raised three boys in the back country, and all of them became doctors.* **13** in arrears, °overdue, past °due, °late; behindhand: *The tax inspector has advised me that I owe thousands in back taxes.*
—*adv.* **14** to *or* toward(s) the °rear, rearward(s), °backward(s); away: *We beat back the enemy in severe hand-to-hand fighting. I accepted his offer at once, lest he should draw back. Get back from the edge!* **15** in °return *or* repayment *or* °requital *or* retaliation; again: *I'll pay you back when I have the money. She gave him back as good as he had given.* **16** ago, in °time(s) °past: *Two generations back, his was the finest house in the town.* **17** behind, behindhand, in arrears, °overdue: *We are a week back in the rent.* **18** ***go back on***: °renege, °fail; °deny, disavow, °break, °repudiate: *He has gone back on his promise to send the payment on the first of every month.*

backbone *n.* **1** °spine, spinal column: *He's much better since the surgery on his backbone.* **2** °mainstay, °chief *or* °main °support, °buttress, °pillar: *Sheila has been the backbone of the society, but she has now moved away.* **3** resoluteness, sturdiness, firmness, °determination, °strength (of °character), mettle, purposefulness, °resolution, °courage, °fortitude, °resolve, °will, will-power, °stability, °stamina, staying °power, °grit: *Has she the backbone to run the company alone?*

backer *n.* **1** °supporter, °advocate, promoter, °sponsor, °patron: *She has always been an enthusiastic backer of adult education.* **2** investor, °benefactor *or* benefactress, °supporter, underwriter, *Colloq* angel: *The play's backers have made huge profits.* **3** bettor, *Brit* °punter: *His backers are offering odds of 10 to 1.*

background *n.* **1** °history, °experience, qualifications, credentials, grounding, training; °breeding, °upbringing, °family; curriculum vitae, *Colloq* CV: *His background suits him admirably for the post of ambassador.* **2** °distance, offing, °horizon, °obscurity: *I like the way the coastline disappears into the background towards the edge of the painting.* **3** ***in the background***: °inconspicuous, °unnoticed, °unobtrusive, behind the scenes, out of the limelight *or* °spotlight, unseen, out of the °public eye, backstage: *Edward prefers to remain in the background, letting his dealer bid at the auctions.*

backing *n.* **1** °support, °help, °aid, °assistance, succour; °approval, °endorsement, °patronage, sponsorship: *He knows that he can rely on the backing of his local party.* **2** investment, °money, funds, funding, °subsidy, °grant; sponsorship: *How can you launch the company without backing?*

backlash *n.* °reaction, °repercussion, °recoil, counteraction, °rebound, °kickback, backfire; °boomerang: *There was a strong backlash in the USA against giving minorities preferred instead of equal job opportunities.*

backward *adj.* **1** °bashful, °shy, °reticent, diffident, °retiring, °coy, °timid, unwilling, °loath, chary, °reluctant, °averse: *She took him to be a bit backward when he didn't respond to her smile.* **2** °slow, dim-witted, °dull, °stupid, slow-witted, °dumb, °feeble-minded, *Colloq Brit* gormless, °dim: *Some of the more backward students will need extra help.* **3** °slow, °late, behindhand, retarded: *Millie seemed a bit backward in learning to walk.* **4** rearward; to the °rear, behind; to the °past: *She gave him a backward glance. He went on through life with never a backward look.* **5** retrograde, retrogressive, °reverse, regressive: *The ancients were unable to account for the apparently backward motion of the planets.*
—*adv.* **6** °backwards: *Walk backward to the door with your hands up.*

backwards *adv.* **1** rearwards *or* rearward, in °reverse, regressively, retrogressively, °backward; withershins *or* widdershins, *Brit* anticlockwise, *US* counter-clockwise: *The general, who refused to acknowledge defeat, explained that his troops were 'advancing backwards'. Do the clocks run backwards in Australia, Daddy?* **2** in °reverse; °back to °front: *She can even ride sitting backwards on a galloping horse. I think you're wearing your pullover backwards.*

bad *adj.* **1** °poor, °wretched, °inferior, °defective, °awful, °worthless, °miserable, egregious, execrable, substandard, °unsatisfactory, °disappointing, °inadequate, non-standard, *Colloq* °lousy, °rotten, crummy, *Slang Brit* grotty, naff: *Sometimes they would send him a letter, but he was a bad correspondent. We went to see a rather bad play the other night.* **2** °corrupt, polluted, vitiated, debased, °base, °vile, °foul, °rotten, miasmic, noxious, mephitic, °unhealthy, °poisonous, °injurious, °dangerous, °harmful, °hurtful, pernicious, deleterious, °ruinous: *It wasn't healthy to be so near the bad air of the sewer.* **3** °evil, °ill, °immoral, °wicked, °vicious, °vile, °sinful, depraved, °awful, °villainous, °corrupt, amoral, °criminal, °wrong, unspeakable: *The man was thoroughly bad and deserved everything he got.* **4** unpleasant, °offensive, °disagreeable, °inclement, °severe, °awful, unfavourable, adverse, *Colloq* °lousy, °rotten: *Surely you're not going sailing in this bad weather?!* **5** unfavourable, unlucky, unpropitious, °unfortunate, °inauspicious, troubled, °grim, distressing, discouraging, unpleasant: *Agreeing to do that job might yet turn out to have been a bad decision.* **6** °off, tainted, spoilt *or* spoiled, °mouldy, °stale, °rotten, decayed, putrefied, °putrid, contaminated: *The fridge isn't working and all the food has gone bad. She ate a bad egg and felt ill the next day.* **7** irascible, ill-tempered, grouchy, °irritable, °nasty, °peevish, °cross, crotchety, crabby, °cranky, curmudgeonly: *Don't go near the boss—he's been in a bad mood all day.* **8** °sorry, °regretful, °apologetic, contrite, rueful, °sad, conscience-stricken, °remorseful, °upset: *She felt bad about having invited me.* **9** °sad, depressed, °unhappy, °dejected, °downhearted, disconsolate, °melancholy; °inconsolable: *I feel bad about you losing your purse.*

10 °naughty, ill-behaved, misbehaving, °disobedient, °unruly, °wild; °mischievous: *Ronnie isn't a bad boy, he's just bored.* **11** distressing, °severe, °grave, °serious, °terrible, °awful, °painful: *He was laid up with a bad case of the mumps.*

badly *adv.* **1** °poorly, defectively, insufficiently, inadequately, unsatisfactorily, carelessly, ineptly, shoddily, deficiently: *We lived in a badly furnished flat in the East End.* **2** unfortunately, unluckily, unsuccessfully, unfavourably, °poorly: *These are an improvement on the former rules, which worked badly.* **3** incorrectly, faultily, defectively, °poorly, improperly, inaccurately, erroneously, unacceptably; ineptly, inartistically, amateurishly, °awfully: *He speaks English badly. He sings badly.* **4** immorally, wickedly, viciously, mischievously, naughtily, shamefully, improperly, villainously: *The school has had its share of badly behaved pupils.* **5** °dangerously, °severely, gravely, critically, grievously, °seriously: *Her father was badly wounded in the war.* **6** unkindly, cruelly, harshly, °severely, wretchedly, dreadfully, improperly, atrociously, horribly, unspeakably: *The prisoners were treated so badly that few survived.* **7** unfavourably, damagingly, critically: *Even her friends spoke badly of her.* **8** °very much, greatly, °seriously: *Peter is badly in need of extra money.* **9** distressfully, emotionally, °hard: *He took the news badly.*

bag *n.* **1** °sack, shopping bag, reticule, string bag, *Chiefly Brit* carrier bag, *Scots or dialect* °poke, °pocket: *They have helpers at the supermarket who will carry your bags to your car for you.* **2** baggage, °luggage, valise, satchel, °grip, °suitcase, overnight bag, carry-on °luggage *or* bag, Gladstone bag, carpet-bag, portmanteau, toilet kit *or* °case, sponge bag; briefcase, attaché °case, dispatch- *or* despatch-case: *Boarding in London I flew to Buenos Aires while my bag went to Seoul.* **3** °purse, handbag, °evening bag, °wallet, *Highland dress* sporran: *She reached into her bag and felt the gun that the Commander had given her.* **4** crone, °hag, °beast, ogress, gorgon, nightmare, °witch, harridan, *Archaic* beldam, *Slang* °old bat, dog, °monster, *US* two-bagger: *Derek has been romancing some old bag for her money.* **5** °occupation, °hobby, avocation, °business, °vocation, °department, °concern, °affair, *Colloq* °lookout, °worry, *Slang* °thing: *Peter's bag at the moment is learning to play the violin.*
—*v.* **6** catch, °trap, ensnare, °snare, entrap, °capture, °land; °kill, °shoot: *We bagged six pheasants and two partridges this morning.*

balance *v.* **1** °weigh, °estimate, °ponder, °consider, °deliberate, assess, °compare, °evaluate: *We need to balance the advantages and the disadvantages.* **2** °steady, °poise; °equalize, stabilize, °level, °match, °even out *or* up: *The see-saw will balance better if both of you get on the other end.* **3** °compensate (for), °make up for, counterbalance, °offset, °match, °equal; counterpoise: *The column of mercury in the barometer balances the atmospheric pressure on the surface of the bowl. The total of expenses seems to balance the total of income.*
—*n.* **4** °scale(s), steelyard: *According to the balance, the package weighs two pounds.* **5** °control, °command, °authority, °weight, °preponderance: *Britain held the balance of power during those decades.* **6** equilibrium, °stability, steadiness, °footing; equiponderance; °equality, °harmony: *The acrobat almost lost his balance on the high wire. It is important to maintain a balance between presentation and content.* **7** °remainder, °residue, °rest; °excess, °surplus, °difference: *You take these and I'll follow with the balance. My bank balance is down to zero.*

ban *v.* **1** °prohibit, °forbid, °outlaw, proscribe, interdict, °bar, disallow, debar: *They have banned smoking in all public places.*
—*n.* **2** °prohibition, °taboo, proscription, interdiction, interdict; °embargo, °boycott: *They have put a ban on the sale of alcoholic beverages. The ban against importing firearms is strictly enforced.*

banal *adj.* trite, hackneyed, stereotyped, clichéd, stereotypical, commonplace, °old hat, °stock, °common, °everyday, °ordinary, °pedestrian, °humdrum, °tired, unoriginal, unimaginative, platitudinous; trivial, °petty, jejune, *Slang* corny: *The book was blasted as banal and boring. The plot of boy-meets-girl, though banal, still brings in the audiences.*

band[1] *n.* **1** °strip, ribbon, °belt, bandeau, fillet, °tie; °stripe, °line, °border: *He wears a cloth band round his head to keep the sweat out of his eyes. There is a decorative band at the top of each page.*
—*v.* **2** °line, °stripe, °border: *The column is banded at intervals with bas-reliefs depicting scenes from the emperor's life.* **3** °tie, °keep, °bind: *Only those papers that are banded together should be sent off.*

band[2] *n.* **1** °company, troop, °platoon, °corps, °group, °body, °gang, horde, °party, °pack, °bunch: *They were set upon by a band of robbers in the forest.* **2** °group, °ensemble, °combination, orchestra, *Colloq* combo: *A jazz band plays at the Civic Centre every Tuesday evening.*
—*v.* **3** ***band together***: °unite, confederate, °gather *or* °join *or* °league together, °team up, affiliate, °merge, federate: *We must band together if we expect to accomplish anything.*

banish *v.* **1** °exile, expatriate, deport, extradite, °transport, °eject, oust, °expel, rusticate, °drive out *or* away, °dismiss, excommunicate, °outlaw, °ostracize: *After ten years in prison, the thief was released and banished from the kingdom.* **2** °drive (out *or* away), °expel, °cast out, °dismiss, °reject: *He tried to banish suspicion from his mind.*

banner *n.* **1** °standard, °flag, °pennant, ensign, burgee, gonfalon, pennon, °streamer, banderole; °symbol: *The flag of the United States is called the star-spangled banner. He is seeking election under the banner of the Tories.*
—*adj.* **2** °leading, °foremost, °momentous, °memorable, °notable, °important, °noteworthy: *The firm had a banner year, with profits up 25 per cent.*

banquet *n.* **1** °feast, °sumptuous repast *or* °meal, °ceremonial dinner, °lavish dinner: *At the end of the banquet, the guest of honour rose to make a few remarks.*
—*v.* **2** °feast, °indulge, wine and °dine, °regale, °carouse: *The winners of the trophy banqueted night after night on champagne and caviare.*

banter *n.* °raillery, badinage, persiflage, pleasantry, jesting, joking, °repartee; chaffing, teasing, °chaff; *Colloq* kidding, ribbing: *Despite the good-natured banter between them, Ray knew that Stephen really detested him.*

bar *n.* **1** °rod, °shaft, °pole, °stick, °stake: *A heavy iron bar is used to tamp the dynamite into place in the hole.* **2** °strip, °stripe, °band, °belt; °streak, °line: *The company trade mark is a narrow red bar around the barrel of every ball-point pen.* **3** °barrier, °obstacle, °obstruction, barricade, °hindrance, °block, °deterrent, °impediment; °ban, °embargo: *A steel bar was across the entrance. Her pride proved a bar to her success. There is a bar against importing spirits.* **4** sand bar, °shallow, shoal, bank, sandbank: *Because the keel is too deep, the sloop will be unable to cross the bar till high tide.* **5** °tribunal, court, courtroom, lawcourt, bench: *The former mayor was found guilty of corruption at the bar of public opinion.* **6** bar-room, saloon, public house, °café, °lounge, cocktail °lounge, tavern, taproom, canteen, *Brit* °local, wine bar; *Colloq* °pub; *Slang* boozer, gin-mill: *I was at the bar on my third beer when she walked in.* **7** °counter: *We had a quick lunch at the sandwich bar.*
—*v.* **8** °fasten, °close up, °secure, °shut up; °lock, °lock up, padlock: *We tried to get in through the window, but they had barred it.* **9** °block, °obstruct, °stop, °stay, °hinder, °keep (out), °shut out, °exclude, °prevent, °forbid, °prohibit, °set aside; °forestall, °impede, °hamper, °retard, balk, barricade; °ban, °embargo: *After his behaviour, he was barred from the club for a*

year. A huge man in an ill-fitting dinner-jacket barred my way. The regulations bar the import of firearms.
—*prep.* **10** °except (for), excepting, excluding, °barring, °outside (of), °save for, aside from, but: *It's all over now bar the shouting.*

barbarian *n.* **1** °savage, °brute: *The barbarians wore animal skins.* **2** °boor, lowbrow, lout, oaf, °clod, churl, °philistine, ignoramus, yahoo; hooligan, vandal, ruffian, °tough, *Slang Brit* yob, yobbo, skinhead: *Those barbarians ought to be denied admittance to the games.*
—*adj.* **3** °uncivilized, uncultivated, uncultured, °philistine, °savage; barbarous, barbaric, °coarse, °vulgar, uncouth, °rude; °boorish, loutish, oafish, °crude, °rough, insensitive, churlish, uncivil: *One sees a great deal of barbarian behaviour every day.*

barbarity *n.* cruelty, inhumanity, ruthlessness, savagery, brutishness, barbarousness, heartlessness, viciousness, cold-bloodedness, bloodthirstiness: *The barbarity of this mass murderer cannot be overstated.*

bare *adj.* **1** unclothed, °naked, °nude, °stark °naked, unclad, exposed, uncovered, hatless, unshod, undressed, *Brit* starkers; *Colloq* in the altogether, in one's birthday suit, in the buff; *Slang US* bare-ass: *He stood completely bare in the middle of the room.* **2** unconcealed, °undisguised, °open, revealed, °literal, bald, °manifest, °out-and-out, °overt, uncovered, straightforward, °direct, °unvarnished, unembellished, °cold, °hard, °plain, °unadorned, °basic, °simple: *The bare facts point to him as the culprit.* **3** unfurnished, undecorated, °vacant, stripped, °empty: *The landlord entered and found a bare flat—the tenants had done a moonlight flit.* **4** denuded, stripped, leafless, defoliated, shorn, °barren; bared: *After the storm the trees were entirely bare of foliage. The hurricane began blowing in earnest, and the little ketch was driving forward under bare poles.* **5** °plain, °mere, °simple, °minimal, °essential, °absolute, °basic; °meagre, scant, °scanty: *For years we scraped by with only the bare necessities of life.*
—*v.* **6** °expose, °lay bare, uncover, °reveal, °open; undress, °unveil: *The torrential rain had washed away the soil, baring the clay and rock beneath. He tore off his shirt, baring his hairy chest.* **7** °disclose, °reveal, °lay bare, uncover, divulge, °unfold, °tell, °expose, unmask, bring to °light: *Because of the way he had treated her, she decided to bare his secrets to the police. Benson bares his soul in his book.* **8** °strip, °divest, denude; defoliate: *The autumn winds bared all the trees in the arboretum.*

barefaced *adj.* **1** unconcealed, °open, °undisguised, °blatant, °manifest, °unmitigated, °outright, °downright, °out-and-out, °sheer, unalloyed, °undiluted: *His proposal is a barefaced attempt to gain control of the committee.* **2** °audacious, °impudent, °shameless, °insolent, °impertinent, °immodest, °bold, arrant, °unabashed, °forward, °brazen, °brassy, saucy, °pert, unblushing, *Colloq* °cheeky: *She said that he was a barefaced liar and that she would have nothing more to do with him.*

barely *adv.* °scarcely, °only, °just, not °quite, °hardly, only °just, no more than: *I barely had my coat off when she said she'd forgotten to shop for dinner.*

bargain *n.* **1** °agreement, °contract, °understanding, °arrangement, covenant, °pact, °compact, °settlement, °transaction, °deal: *We made a bargain—I would provide the materials and he would do the work.* **2** good °deal, *Colloq* give-away, *US* °steal: *If you paid only £100 for this painting, you got a real bargain.*
—*v.* **3** °negotiate, °trade, °haggle, barter, °dicker, chaffer: *We bargained far into the night, and finally came to an agreement after eight hours of discussion.* **4** ***bargain for***: °expect, °count on, °anticipate, °foresee, take into °account, °allow for, be °prepared for: *Even though the storm had been predicted, it was windier than we had bargained for.*

barren *adj.* **1** °sterile, childless, °infertile: *We won't have any calf from this barren cow.* **2** unproductive, °sterile, °bare, °infertile; °fruitless, °dry, unfruitful, °unprofitable, °poor: *The land was exceedingly stony and barren. The fifteenth century was the most barren period in the history of English literature.*

barrier *n.* **1** °bar, °fence, railing, °wall; ditch, ha-ha: *A barrier was erected at each end of the street. This barrier will keep the dingoes from killing the sheep.* **2** °obstacle, °bar, °obstruction, °block, °impediment, °hindrance: *Neither race, nor creed, nor colour shall be a barrier to success.* **3** °boundary, boundary line, °limit, °frontier: *No mountain barrier lay between France and Flanders.*

barring *prep.* excluding, °exclusive of, °bar, omitting, leaving out, excepting, °except (for), °save for, aside from, °besides, but: *Barring another stock market crash, your money is safe. Nobody else, barring the author, knew the truth of the matter.*

base[1] *n.* **1** °bottom, foot, °support, °stand, °pedestal: *The base of the statue cracked and the whole thing fell down. Have you been able to find a teak base for the new lamp?* **2** °groundwork, °background, °fundamental °principle, °principle, °foundation, underpinning; infrastructure, °basis: *Henry's charter was at once welcomed as a base for the needed reforms.* **3** °root, °theme, °radical, °stem, °core: *In the word* interdigitation *the base is* -digit-. **4** °home, °station, °camp, starting-point, °point of departure, °post, °centre: *Using the Sherpa village as a base of operations, we set up smaller camps as we began to climb the mountain.*
—*v.* **5** °establish, °found, °secure, °build, °ground, °anchor, °fix, hinge, °form; °derive, °draw: *We are basing all our hopes on his ability to do a deal.* **6** °establish, headquarter, °post, °station, °position, °place: *The company is based in Guernsey.*

base[2] *adj.* **1** °low, undignified, °cowardly, °selfish, °mean, °despicable, °contemptible, °filthy, °evil: *He must have had some base motive in revealing to her what Martha had said.* **2** degraded, °degrading, °menial, °inferior, °mean, °unworthy, °lowly, °low, °grovelling, °servile, slavish, subservient, °downtrodden, abject, °miserable, °wretched, °sordid, undignified, ignoble, °dishonourable, °disreputable, °vile, °scurrilous, °wicked, *Colloq* infra dig: *Foolish sinners will submit to the basest servitude, and be attendants of swine.* **3** °mean, °cheap, °sorry, °common, °poor, °shabby, °shoddy: *He cast off his base attire, revealing a splendid suit of armour like burnished gold.* **4** °sordid, °offensive, °lewd, °lascivious, °obscene, °profane, °rude, ribald, °unseemly, °vulgar, °coarse, °dirty, °indecent, °evil-minded, °filthy, °pornographic: *The entertainment in that theatre caters to the basest appetites.* **5** °poor, °shoddy, °cheap, °fake, pinchbeck, °inferior, °counterfeit, °fraudulent, debased, forged, °spurious, °worthless, °bad: *Her jewels look valuable but are, in fact, made of base materials.* **6** °wicked, °evil, °wretched, °corrupt, °shameful, currish, °loathsome, °scurvy, °insufferable, °villainous: *They were labelled as base infidels and treated with contempt and cruelty.*

bashful *adj.* **1** °shy, °retiring, °embarrassed, °meek, abashed, °shamefaced, °sheepish, °timid, diffident, self-effacing, unconfident; °ill at ease, uneasy, uncomfortable, °nervous, °self-conscious, °awkward, °confused, *Colloq* in a tizzy, *US and Canadian* discombobulated: *Henry is so bashful in the presence of women that he blushes merely talking to them.* **2** °modest, °coy, unassuming, unostentatious, demure, °reserved, restrained, *Rare* verecund: *When we first met, she was a bashful young girl of fifteen who had no notion of her own beauty.*

basic *adj.* °fundamental, °essential, °key, °elementary, underlying, °prime, °primary, °root; °principal, °central, °focal, °vital: *He enrolled for a basic course in Sanskrit. We must reconsider the basic facts.*

basis *n.* **1** °foundation, °base, °bottom, °heart, °footing, °principle, underpinning; infrastructure: *The three R's form the basis of elementary education. Do you think our society still rests on the basis of the family?* **2** °essence, main °ingredient *or* constituent, °point of departure: *The basis of the discussion is that the hospitals are understaffed.*

batch *n.* **1** °quantity, °lot; °amount, °volume: *Mother baked a huge batch of bread.* **2** °set, °group, °number, °quantity, °assortment, °bunch, °pack, °collection: *Please sort this batch of cards into alphabetical order.*

batter *v.* **1** °beat, °hit, °strike, clout, °belabour, °pound, pummel *or* pommel, °pelt, bash, smite, thrash, *Colloq* wallop, clobber: *He was battered till he was black and blue.* **2** °bombard, °attack, °assault: *Battering by the cannons finally breached the wall of the fort.* **3** maltreat, °mistreat, °ill-treat, °abuse; maul, °bruise, °harm, °mangle, disfigure: *The police report an increase in complaints about battered wives and children.*

battle *n.* **1** °fight, °conflict, °combat, °action, °encounter, °clash, °engagement, °struggle, Donnybrook, °fray, *Law* affray; °brawl, °fracas, mêlée *or* melee; °contest; duel, hand-to-hand °encounter: *You won the battle, but you lost the war. And now, the battle between the world champion and the challenger!* **2** °argument, °dispute, altercation, °quarrel, °war; °contest, °competition; °struggle, °fight, °crusade, °campaign: *The battle spilt out of the restaurant and into the street. We are not yet winning the battle against AIDS.*
—*v.* **3** Usually, ***battle against***: °fight, contend *or* °struggle *or* °fight with *or* °strive against, °combat: *We must battle against ignorance at every opportunity.*

bauble *n.* °gewgaw, trinket, °ornament, °trifle, °toy, bagatelle, knick-knack, °plaything, kickshaw: *Wear your diamonds to the ball, my dear, not those cheap baubles.*

bawdy *adj.* °lewd, °obscene, °taboo, °vulgar, °dirty, smutty, °filthy, °coarse, °earthy, °gross, scatological, °rude, °lascivious, salacious, indelicate, °indecent, indecorous, °broad, °crude, ribald, °risqué, °suggestive, Rabelaisian, °uninhibited, unrestrained, °lusty, *Literary* lubricious *or* lubricous: *Afterwards, each of us had to recite a bawdy limerick.*

bawl *v.* **1** °shout, °bellow, vociferate, °roar, °yell, trumpet, thunder, *Colloq* holler: *Fishwives bawled out their wares continuously, creating a deafening din.* **2** °cry, wail, °weep, °keen, squall, blubber, whimper; yelp, *Colloq* yammer: *Stop that bawling or I'll really give you something to cry about!* **3** ***bawl out***: °scold, °reprimand, °upbraid: *My father bawled me out because I stayed out past midnight.*

beach *n.* **1** shore, lakeshore, bank, seashore, seaside, lido, strand, °coast, °margin, *Formal* littoral: *The children wanted to go to the beach and build sandcastles.*
—*v.* **2** °ground, run aground, strand; °careen: *Despite the heavy surf, we finally beached the boat safely.*

beacon *n.* °signal, °sign, °fire, °light, bonfire, °flare, signal fire, Very °light, °rocket; lighthouse, pharos: *Beacons blazed at the tops of the hills to spread the news of the victory. The drunkard's nose shone like a beacon.*

beam *n.* **1** °timber, scantling, girder, rafter; °bar, °brace, °plank, °board, stud, trestle: *Are you sure that these beams will support the weight of the upper storeys?* **2** °ray, °gleam; °shaft; pencil: *I could just make out his face in the beam of the electric torch.*
—*v.* **3** °radiate, °shine; °smile radiantly: *The door opened and the firelight beamed forth onto the snowdrifts. 'I'm so happy to meet you at last', she beamed.*

beamy *adj.* °broad, °wide, broad in the beam; °big, °heavy, °chubby, chunky, °fat, °obese: *She's quite a beamy boat, with accommodation for eight below. A beamy gentleman sat on my homburg, squashing it flat.*

bear *v.* **1** °carry, °transport, convey, °move, °take, *Colloq* tote: *She was borne round the stadium on the shoulders of her team-mates.* **2** °carry, °support, °sustain, °shoulder, °hold up, °uphold; °suffer, °undergo, °experience, °endure: *Looking after her invalid mother while working is a heavy burden to bear.* **3** °merit, be °worthy of, °warrant; °provoke, invite: *Gordon's suggestion bears looking into.* **4** °stand, °abide, °tolerate, °brook, °survive, °endure, °stand up to; °reconcile oneself to, °admit of, *Colloq* °put up with: *How can you bear such boring people? His actions will not bear examination. I cannot bear to see you unhappy.* **5** °have, °carry, °show, °exhibit, °display, °sustain: *The getaway car bore German licence plates. The knight bore the scars of many battles. She bears her grandmother's name.* **6** °produce, °yield, °develop, °breed, °generate, engender; °give °birth to, °spawn, °bring forth: *Our apple tree did not bear any fruit this year. She bore thirteen children and still had time to write books.* **7** °entertain, °harbour, °wish: *He bore her no ill will, despite her accusations.* **8** ***bear on*** *or* ***upon***: °relate *or* have °relevance *or* be °relevant to *or* °pertain to, °touch on *or* upon, °affect, °concern, °have a °bearing on *or* upon, °influence: *I don't quite see how your illness bears on which school James attends.* **9** ***bear out***: °confirm, °support, corroborate, °substantiate, °uphold, back up: *The evidence bears out what I said.* **10** ***bear up***: **a** °survive, °hold out, °stand up, °hold up, °withstand: *Can Alex bear up under the strain of keeping two jobs?* **b** °support, °cheer, °encourage: *What hope have you to bear you up?* **11** ***bear with***: °put up with, be °patient with, make °allowance(s) for: *Please bear with me, I'm sure you'll think it was worth waiting when you see the finished result.*

bearable *adj.* °tolerable, °supportable, endurable, °acceptable, °manageable: *The heat last summer was made bearable only by frequent dips in the swimming-pool.*

bearing *n.* **1** °carriage, deportment, °manner, °behaviour, °conduct, °aspect, demeanour, °posture, °stance, °air, °attitude, mien, °presence: *Lewis's noble bearing makes him noticeable, even in a crowd.* **2** sustaining, supporting, °endurance, °enduring: *Thomas Jefferson considered the government of England totally without morality and insolent beyond bearing.* **3** °aspect; °relation, °reference, °relationship, correlation, pertinence, °relevance, °connection, relevancy, applicability, °application, germaneness, °significance: *The legal bearing of the case will become obvious in court. It is unclear exactly what bearing your remarks have on the situation.* **4** Often, ***bearings***: °direction, °orientation, (relative) °position: *The bearing of the lighthouse is now 180°. Which way is north?—I have lost my bearings entirely.*

beast *n.* **1** °animal, °creature, being: *He loves all the beasts of the field, of the sea, and of the air.* **2** °brute, °savage, °animal, °monster: *I've seen that beast hitting his wife in public.*

beastly *adj.* **1** °uncivilized, uncultivated, uncivil, °rude, °crude, °boorish, °unrefined, °coarse; °cruel, °inhuman, °savage, barbaric, barbarous, bestial, °brutal: *Priscilla treats Cyril in a beastly way.* **2** °abominable, intolerable, °offensive, unpleasant, °awful, °terrible, °ghastly, horrid, °disagreeable, °horrible, °hateful, execrable; °foul, °vile, °nasty, °rotten, °dirty, °filthy: *If this beastly weather keeps up, the plane may be delayed.*

beat *v.* **1** °strike, °pound, bash, smite, °batter, pummel *or* pommel, °belabour, °pelt, clout, thrash, give (someone) a °thrashing *or* beating, drub, °manhandle, thump, whack, cane, °scourge, °whip, bludgeon, °club, cudgel, fustigate; °whip, °flog, lash, *Colloq* clobber, wallop, give (someone) a once-over: *At first he refused to tell them, but then they beat it out of him.* **2** °defeat, °best, worst, °win (out) over, vanquish, trounce, °rout, °outdo, °subdue, °overcome, °overwhelm, °pre-empt; °surpass, °conquer, °crush, °master, *US* °beat out: *Can they beat Manchester United for the cup? He first beat the Danes, then the Russians.* **3** throb, °pulsate, palpitate, °pound, thump: *I could feel my heart beating against my ribs.* **4** *Nautical* tack: *Close-hauled, the sloop was beating to windward against the howling gale.* **5** hammer, °forge, °shape, °form, °fashion, °make, °mould: *They shall beat their swords into ploughshares.* **6** °mix, °whip, °stir, °blend: *Beat two eggs, then add the flour and sugar.* **7** tread, °wear, °trample: *The hunters beat a path through the forest.* **8** ***beat it***: °depart, °leave, abscond, °run off *or* away, *Slang US*

°take it on the lam, lam out of here, *US* hit the road: *You'd better beat it before the cops come.* **9** ***beat off***: °drive off *or* away, °rout: *We beat off our attackers, who fled into the forest.*
—*n.* **10** °stroke, °blow: *The signal was to be three beats of a tin cup on the pipes.* **11** °rhythm, °tempo, °measure; °pulse, throb, °stress, pulsation: *In boogie-woogie the beat is eight to the bar.* **12** °course, °round, °tour, °route, °circuit, °run, °path; °area, bailiwick: *In the old days, it was the bobby on the beat who prevented a lot of crime. As a reporter, my beat is the financial news.*
—*adj.* **13** °dead beat, °exhausted, °spent, drained, °worn out, °weary, bone-tired, °fatigued, fagged: *I was really beat after completing the marathon.*

beautiful *adj.* **1** °attractive, charming, °comely, °lovely, good-looking, °fair, °pretty, alluring, appealing, °handsome, °radiant, °gorgeous, *Formal* pulchritudinous, *Scots* °bonny; *Colloq* smashing: *She's not only intelligent, she's beautiful. She entered on the arm of some beautiful youth.* **2** °excellent, °first-rate, unequalled, °skilful, °admirable, °magnificent, °well done; °superb, spectacular, °splendid, °marvellous, wonderful, °incomparable, °superior, °elegant, °exquisite, °pleasant, °pleasing, °delightful, *Colloq* smashing: *The garage did a beautiful job in tuning the engine. Armand's arranged a beautiful wedding reception for us.*

beautifully *adv.* **1** attractively, chicly, fashionably, delightfully, charmingly, splendidly, magnificently, *Colloq* smashingly: *The princess was beautifully dressed in a rose satin ball-gown.* **2** admirably, superbly, excellently, wonderfully, marvellously, splendidly, spectacularly, magnificently, *Colloq* smashingly: *Emily played her solo beautifully.*

beautify *v.* adorn, °embellish, °decorate, °ornament, titivate, °elaborate, garnish, deck (out), bedeck: *The old façade was removed and the building beautified by refacing it with white marble.*

beauty *n.* **1** loveliness, attractiveness, handsomeness, pulchritude: *The beauty of the actress took my breath away.* **2** belle, *Colloq* looker, °knockout, °dream, dreamboat, stunner: *She was one of the great beauties of her day.* **3** °attraction, °strength, °advantage, °asset: *The beauty of the plan lies in its simplicity.*

beckon *v.* °signal, °gesture, °motion; °summon, °bid, °call: *The manager beckoned to me and I went over to see what he wanted.*

become *v.* **1** °turn *or* °change *or* °transform into: *The princess kissed the prince, who immediately became a frog.* **2** °grow *or* °develop *or* evolve into; °mature *or* °ripen into: *It's hard to believe that this dull caterpillar will eventually become a splendid butterfly.* **3** °enhance, °suit, °fit, befit, be °proper *or* °appropriate for, °behove *or US* behoove: *Moonlight becomes you, It goes with your hair.* **4** °grace, adorn: *Walter was a man who became the dignity of his function as a commissionaire.* **5** ***become of***: come of, °happen to: *What will become of you if you don't go to school?*

becoming *adj.* enhancing, beautifying, °seemly; °attractive, °comely, °fetching, °chic, °stylish, °fashionable, °tasteful; °appropriate, °fitting, °fit, °meet, °befitting, °proper, °suitable: *Your new hairdo is most becoming, Frances.*

bedlam *n.* °pandemonium, °uproar, hubbub, commotion, °confusion, °tumult, turmoil, °furore *or US* furor, °chaos; madhouse: *The chancellor's announcement created instant bedlam in the Commons.*

bedraggled *adj.* soiled, °dirty, °muddy, muddied, °untidy, stained, dishevelled, scruffy, messy; °wet, °sloppy, °soaking *or* sopping *or* wringing °wet, soaked, drenched, *Colloq* gungy, *US* grungy: *We took the two bedraggled waifs in out of the pouring rain.*

befitting *adj.* °fitting, °becoming, °due, °suitable *or* suited (to), °appropriate (to), apropos, °proper (to), °seemly (for): *He really ought to behave in a manner befitting his position as chairman. This must be done with a befitting sense of awe.*

before *adv.* **1** °previously, earlier, already, beforehand; °formerly, in the °past; °once: *I have told you before, don't count your chickens.* **2** °ahead, in °advance, in °front, in the forefront, °first, in the vanguard, *Colloq* up °front: *He walked on before, as he knew the way.* **3** °ahead, in the °future, to °come: *Before lie the prospects of surrendering or dying.*
—*prep.* **4** °ahead of, in °advance of, in °front of, forward of: *The king indicated that the page should go before him.* **5** in °front of; in the °presence of: *The entire valley was spread out before me.* **6** °preceding, °previous *or* anterior to, °prior to; on the °eve of: *Before my departure I have to kiss Annie goodbye.* **7** in °preference to, °rather than, sooner than, more °willingly than: *They said they would die before yielding.*
—*conj.* **8** °previous to *or* °preceding the °time when: *This was a nice place before the day-trippers arrived.*

beg *v.* **1** entreat, °beseech, °plead (with), crave, implore, importune, °wheedle, °cajole, supplicate (with), °pray; °ask for, °request: *She begged me to stay.* **2** °solicit, sponge, *Colloq* cadge, °scrounge, *US* panhandle: *When he was an alcoholic, he used to beg drinks off everyone.*

beggar *n.* **1** mendicant, °supplicant, suppliant, almsman, sponger, °tramp, vagrant, °pauper, *Colloq* cadger, scrounger, *US* panhandler: *We were approached by beggars on every street corner.* **2** °fellow, °man, °person, *Colloq* °chap, °guy, bloke: *I feel sorry for the poor beggar who lost his wallet at the station.*
—*v.* **3** impoverish; °want, °challenge, °defy, baffle: *The misery of those people beggars description.*

begin *v.* **1** °start (out *or* off *or* in *or* on), °initiate, °enter on *or* upon, °set out *or* about, °set out on *or* upon, *Rather formal* °commence: *We began the journey full of enthusiasm.* **2** °start (off), °inaugurate, °originate, °open, °launch, °create, °establish, °found, °set up; °go into: *We began the company five years ago.* **3** °arise, °start, °originate, *Rather formal* °commence: *The greatness of the Prussian monarchy begins with Frederick II. The paragraph begins in the middle of the page.*

beginning *n.* **1** °start, commencement, °outset, °onset, inception, °dawn, dawning, °birth, genesis, °origin, °creation, day one; origination, °source, well-spring: *There are several competing theories about the beginning of life on earth. The beginning of the idea can be traced to Galileo.* **2** °opening, °start, inception, commencement: *I have plenty of energy at the beginning of the day. The book is good at the beginning, but then it gets boring.*

begrudge *v.* **1** °resent, °envy, °grudge: *She doesn't begrudge him his success.* **2** give (be)grudgingly *or* unwillingly *or* reluctantly, °deny, °refuse: *He begrudges her the slightest consideration.*

beguile *v.* **1** delude, °deceive, °cheat, °swindle, °dupe, °fool, °mislead, °hoodwink, bamboozle, °take in: *She was easily beguiled by his solicitude.* **2** °defraud (of), °deprive (of), °cheat (out of *or* into), °swindle (out of): *Let no man beguile you of your reward.* **3** °charm, °divert, °amuse, °distract, °fascinate, engross, °engage, allure: *I always meet the most beguiling people at Daphne's parties.*

behalf *n.* ***on*** *or* ***US in behalf of***, *or* ***on*** *or* ***US in one's behalf***: °for, as a °representative of, in °place of, °instead of, in the °name of, on the °part of; in the °interest of, for the °benefit *or* °advantage of: *The lawyer is acting on behalf of the heirs.*

behave *v.* °act, °react, °function, °operate, °perform, °work, °conduct *or* deport *or* comport *or* °bear (oneself); °act obediently, °act °properly, be °good: *The boy behaved with great insolence. I wish the children would behave themselves.*

behaviour *n.* °conduct, demeanour, deportment, °bearing, °manners, comportment; °action(s): *His behaviour in the presence of the royal couple was abominable.*

behead *v.* decapitate, guillotine, *Archaic* decollate: *Criminals and enemies of the state were formerly beheaded.*

behold *v.* °see, °look at, °regard, °set *or* °lay eyes on, descry, °notice, °note, espy, °perceive, discern, °remark, °view: *As we emerged from the gorge, we beheld the mountain looming above us.*

beholden *adj.* °obliged, obligated, °indebted, °grateful, in °debt, under (an) °obligation: *She said that she was beholden to him for everything he had done.*

behove *v.* behoove; be required of, be incumbent on, be proper of, be fitting of *or* for, befit; be advisable for, be worthwhile for, be expeditious for *or* of, be advantageous to *or* for, be useful to *or* for, be beneficial to *or* for: *It behoves you to be respectful to the chairman of the board.*

belabour *v.* thrash, °beat, pummel *or* pommel, buffet, °pelt, °lambaste: *We tried to stop the drover from belabouring the poor horse with a whip.*

belated *adj.* °late; behind °time, behindhand, out of °date; delayed, detained: *I forgot your birthday, so here's a belated gift.*

belief *n.* **1** °trust, dependence, °reliance, °confidence, °faith, °security, °assurance: *He retains his belief in the divine right of kings.* **2** acceptance, credence; assent: *His statements are unworthy of belief.* **3** °tenet, °view, °idea, °sentiment, °conviction, °doctrine, dogma, °principle(s), axiom, °maxim, °creed, °opinion, °persuasion: *The belief that there is no God is as definite a creed as the belief in one God or in many gods.* **4** °intuition, °judgement: *It is her belief that nuclear energy will eventually prove economical.*

believe *v.* **1** °accept, put °faith *or* credence in *or* into, find credible, find creditable; °allow, °think, °hold, °maintain, °feel; °take it, °suppose, °assume: *He still believes that the moon is made of green cheese.* **2** ***believe in***: °trust to *or* in, °rely upon *or* on, have °faith *or* °confidence in, put one's °trust in, be convinced of, °swear by, °credit; have the courage of one's convictions: *Do you believe everything you read in the papers? The chairman believes in your ability to carry out the plan.* **3** ***make believe***: °pretend, °suppose, °imagine, °fancy, conjecture, °assume: *I used to make believe I was a great detective.*

belittle *v.* °diminish, °minimize, °disparage, °slight, decry, °detract from, °depreciate, °trivialize, deprecate, °degrade, denigrate, °downgrade, de-emphasize, °discredit, °criticize, derogate; °reduce, °mitigate, lessen, undervalue, °underestimate, underrate, °minimize, *Colloq* °play down, pooh-pooh: *He belittles the efforts of others but accomplishes nothing himself.*

belligerent *adj.* **1** warring; °warlike, °militant, warmongering, hawkish, jingoistic, bellicose, °martial: *The belligerent nations have agreed to discuss an accord.* **2** °quarrelsome, °pugnacious, contentious, disputatious, °truculent, °aggressive, °hostile, combative, antagonistic, bellicose: *I cannot see why you have to take such a belligerent attitude towards the chairman.*
—*n.* **3** warring party, °antagonist, °contestant; warmonger, hawk, jingoist, °militant: *Our country has refused to sell arms to the belligerents in the conflict.*

bellow *v.* **1** °roar; °yell, °shout, °blare, trumpet, °howl, *Colloq* holler: *Father was bellowing that he couldn't find his pipe. The public-address system bellowed out my name.*
—*n.* **2** °roar; °yell, °shout, *Colloq* holler: *The bull gave a bellow and charged.*

belong *v.* **1** be a °member (of), be °affiliated *or* associated *or* connected (with), be °attached *or* °bound (to), be a °part (of): *Does he belong to the Green party? He didn't want to belong while his wife was a member.* **2** have a (°proper) place (in), be °proper (to): *Do you ever get the feeling that you don't belong here?* **3** ***belong to***: be owned by, be the °property *or* °possession of: *That coat belongs to me.*

belonging *n.* °association, °connection, °alliance, °relationship, °affinity, °relation: *She says the Church gives her a strong sense of belonging.*

belongings *n.* (personal) °property, °effects, °possessions, °goods, °things, chattels: *He returned home to find all his belongings in the street.*

beloved *adj.* **1** loved, cherished, adored, °dear, dearest, °darling, °precious, treasured; admired, worshipped, revered, esteemed, idolized, respected; valued, prized: *He denied nothing to his beloved children. She was their beloved queen.*
—*n.* **2** °sweetheart, °darling, dearest, °love; °lover, °paramour, inamorata *or* inamorato, *Colloq* °flame: *He wrote poems to his beloved.*

below *adv.* **1** °lower down, °further down, farther down: *Please see the explanation given below. The department head could no longer resist the pressures from below.* **2** °beneath, underneath, °under; downstairs, *Nautical* below-decks, *Brit* below-stairs: *Can you hear someone walking about below? They put the captain in irons below.* **3** on °earth, here, in this °world, under the sun: *Man wants but little here below.*
—*prep.* **4** °under, underneath, °beneath: *Below the sea live creatures we have never even seen. Barely discernible below his nose was a tiny moustache. Sign your name below 'Yours truly'.* **5** less *or* °lower *or* cheaper than: *The sale price is below cost.* **6** deeper *or* °further *or* farther down than: *The current is strongest about six feet below the surface.* **7** °under, °beneath, underneath: *Her bright eyes peered at him from below the wide hat.* **8** °lower *or* less than, °under: *The temperature was 20 degrees below zero.* **9** °inferior *or* °subordinate to, °lower than: *He gives orders to the servants below him.* **10** °inferior *or* °secondary to, °under, °beneath, °lower than: *In exports, the USA and UK are below Japan.* **11** °beneath, °unworthy of, unbefitting, not °worth: *Mugging old ladies is below contempt.*

belt *n.* **1** sash; *Literary* girdle, cestus, cincture, °zone: *At her belt she wore a dagger in a golden scabbard.* **2** °zone, °band, °strip, °circuit, °perimeter; °area, °swath, °tract, °region, °district: *The planners ensured that each city would be surrounded by a green belt.*
—*v.* **3** °strike, °hit, °punch; °beat, thrash: *When he insulted her, I simply belted him.* **4** ***belt out***: °sing *or* °perform stridently *or* loudly; °put over *or* across: *Sophie Tucker was there, belting out 'One of These Days'.*

bemoan *v.* °lament, °mourn *or* °grieve *or* °weep *or* °moan for: *She bitterly bemoaned the loss of her sole companion, her canary.*

bemuse *v.* **1** °confuse, °muddle, °mix up, addle, befuddle, °perplex, °bewilder, °puzzle, *Colloq US and Canadian* discombobulate: *The actors were thoroughly bemused by the sudden appearance of a horse on stage.* **2** stupefy, benumb, °numb, °paralyse: *I found him, completely bemused, with the empty bottle beside him.*

bend *n.* **1** curve, °turn, turning, corner; °bow, °angle, crook, °hook, curvature, flexure: *Go left at the bend in the road. If you put a bend in a wire hanger, you can fish out the obstruction.*
—*v.* **2** °arch, °bow, curve, crook: *Soak the branch in water and it will bend easily. Stop bending my arm—it hurts!* **3** °bow; curtsy *or* curtsey; °kowtow, salaam; kneel, genuflect: *The cannibal bent down before a pile of skulls.* **4** °incline, °channel, °focus, °direct, °steer, °set; °fix: *He bent his attention on more important matters. She bent her steps towards the cemetery.* **5** °submit, °bow, °yield, give °way, be pliant *or* subservient *or* °tractable: *The cabinet bends to the will of the prime minister.* **6** °incline, °turn, °deflect: *As you can see, the ray is bent by the lens.*

bender *Colloq n.* °drunk, °spree, °bout, °revel, carousal, °carouse, bacchanal; *Slang* binge, °jag, *US* toot: *He goes off on a bender whenever his wife leaves him.*

beneath *adv.* **1** °low *or* °lower down, °below, °under, underneath: *Please sign beneath if you agree the terms.* **2** °below, underneath, °under; °underground: *The flowers are above the ground, the roots beneath.*
—*prep.* **3** °under, underneath, °below: *Beneath that gruff exterior of his beats a heart of gold.* **4** °below,

°unworthy of, unbefitting, undeserving of, not (even) meriting, °lower than: *Your behaviour is beneath criticism.*

benefactor *n.* °patron, °supporter, °sponsor, °donor, °philanthropist; °backer, investor, *Colloq* angel: *Our benefactor has made a donation that will enable the mission to carry on its work.*

beneficial *adj.* **1** °advantageous, °serviceable, °useful, °profitable, °helpful, °supportive, °favourable, °constructive, °good: *No measures could have been more beneficial to the kingdom.* **2** healthful, °healthy, salutary, salubrious; °efficacious, °effective: *A certain amount of sunshine is quite beneficial.*

benefit *n.* **1** °advantage, °profit, °good, °sake, °gain, °aid, °help, °service: *It would be to their benefit to call off the strike.* **2** Often, ***benefits***: °perquisite(s), emolument(s), °allowance(s), °extra(s), °fringe benefit(s), *Colloq* °perk(s): *We offer one of the best schemes in the industry for employee benefits.*
—*v.* **3** °improve, °aid, °help, °better, °promote, °further, °advance, °forward: *Enrolling on a management course could benefit your chances for advancement.* **4** °profit, °gain: *No one has ever personally benefited a penny from these contributions.*

benevolence *n.* **1** °charity, °kindness, kindliness, °humanity, humanitarianism, beneficence, charitableness, goodness, °altruism, °good will, unselfishness, °philanthropy, generosity, magnanimity: *The poor people in the village used to rely on his benevolence.* **2** °gift, °grant, contribution, °donation, beneficence: *The victims of the famine were recipients of the benevolence of the British people.*

benevolent *adj.* °charitable, well-disposed, °gracious, °good, °kind, °kindly, humane, °humanitarian, well-wishing, °thoughtful, °considerate, °sympathetic, caring, kind-hearted, warm-hearted, compassionate, °benign, benignant; °liberal, °generous, magnanimous, open-handed; °beneficial, °helpful, salutary: *That hypocrite has cast himself in the role of a benevolent despot.*

benighted *adj.* unenlightened, °naïve, °uninformed, °ignorant: *That poor, benighted fool believes that the doctors can cure him.*

benign *adj.* **1** °kindly, °gracious, °good, °kind, kind-hearted, °benevolent, benignant, °warm, warm-hearted, °cordial, °genial, congenial, °tender, tender-hearted, compassionate, °sympathetic, °soft-hearted: *It was Grandad's benign goodwill that kept us together in those hard times.* **2** °bland, °gentle, °mild, °warm: *A benign smile lit the headmaster's face as he announced the awards for scholastic achievement.* **3** °kind, °favourable, °fortunate; salutary, salubrious, °mild, congenial, °propitious: *She recovered rapidly in that most benign climate.* **4** non-fatal, non-malignant, non-virulent, curable, °harmless: *Fortunately, the biopsy showed that the tumour was benign.*

bent *adj.* **1** curved, deflected, bowed, °crooked, distorted: *He complained to the waiter just because the fork was bent.* **2** °strange, °weird, °peculiar, twisted, °deviant, warped, °wry, awry, °corrupt, corrupted; °perverted, °perverse, °abnormal: *You'd be bent, too, if you'd been in prison for fifteen years.* **3** °dishonest, °crooked, °illegal: *That share deal sounds a bit bent to me: I'll pass.* **4** °determined, °intent, °set, resolved, °resolute, °decided: *Garvey is bent on running in the marathon, despite his sprained ankle.*
—*n.* **5** °turn, °inclination, °direction, °disposition, predisposition, °tendency, °bias, °leaning, proclivity, propensity, °partiality, °prejudice; °ability, °aptitude, °talent, °gift: *She wished to follow the bent of her own taste. He has a natural bent for music.*

bequeath *v.* °leave, °make over, °will, °pass on, °hand down *or* on, °transmit, *Law* °devise: *Aunt Margaret has bequeathed her collection of music boxes to the museum.*

bequest *n.* legacy, °inheritance: *A huge bequest was received by the hospital.*

berate *v.* °scold, chide, °rate, °upbraid, revile, °abuse, °rail at, excoriate, °castigate, objurgate; °harangue: *In the square an ancient virago was berating a butcher.*

bereave *v.* °deprive; °strip, °rob, °dispossess: *The accident bereaved him of his child.*

berserk *adj.* amok, °mad, °violent, °wild, crazed, frenzied, °maniacal: *He went berserk, destroying tables and chairs.*

beseech *v.* supplicate, entreat, implore, °plead (with), °beg, importune, obsecrate: *The prisoners beseeched the king to have mercy on them.*

beset *v.* encompass, °surround, °besiege; assail, °attack, °harass, harry, hector, °bother, °afflict, °trouble: *She was beset by all the problems involved in having a job and a family.*

beside *prep.* **1** alongside, °near, next to, with, °close to, hard by, °nearby, °by: *A handsome young man walked up and sat down beside her.* **2** away from, °wide of, °apart from, unconnected with, °off: *The fact that I owe you money is entirely beside the point.* **3** ***beside oneself***: out of one's °mind *or* wits, at the end of one's tether, °overwrought, °agitated, °upset, °crazy, °mad: *She was beside herself with grief when she heard the news.*

besides *adv.* **1** in °addition, additionally, also; °further, furthermore, °moreover, as °well, too; to °boot, on top of everything else, into the °bargain: *Maria is our choice for the post and, besides, she's the only qualified person available. On their anniversary he gave her a diamond ring and a sapphire brooch besides.*
—*prep.* **2** over and above, above and beyond, in °addition to, additionally to, as °well as; aside from, °barring, excepting, °except for, excluding, °exclusive of, not counting *or* including, beyond, °apart from, other than: *St Paul became acquainted with many Christians besides his converts.*

besiege *v.* **1** °lay °siege to, beleaguer: *For ten years Troy was besieged by the Greeks.* **2** blockade, °block, °block off *or* up, hem in, °cut off; °surround, °crowd round: *The strikers have besieged the factory gates, not allowing anyone in or out.* **3** importune, °sue, °petition, assail, pressurize *or US* °pressure, °press, °overwhelm, inundate: *The Home Office has been besieged by requests for leniency in your case.*

best *adj.* **1** °superlative, unexcelled, finest, °pre-eminent, °first, °superb, unsurpassed, °superior, °excellent, °paramount, °first-rate, *Colloq* A-1, A-one: *Henry VIII was the best rider, the best lance, and the best archer in England.* **2** kindest, most beneficent, nicest: *Which of your brothers is the best to you?* **3** °foremost, choicest, °pre-eminent, most °suitable, most °appropriate, most °qualified, most °talented, most °desirable, most °outstanding: *We want the best person to fill the job.* **4** largest, most, greatest: *She had travelled the best part of the way by ship.* **5** richest, wealthiest; first-class, °upper crust, °upper-class: *He associates only with those he considers to be the best people.*
—*n.* **6** finest; °first: *The best is yet to come.* **7** °finery, best °clothes, *Colloq* best bib and tucker: *He was all decked out in his Sunday best.* **8** greatest *or* °maximum effort: *He did his best but it wasn't enough to win.*
—*adv.* **9** most excellently, to the fullest extent, in the most °suitable way, most adroitly, most skilfully, most superbly, most artistically: *All the children performed well, but Alice performed best.* **10** with greatest satisfaction, most successfully: *He who laughs last laughs best.*
—*v.* **11** °win (out) over, °conquer, °beat, °surpass, °overpower, get the °better of, °subdue, °defeat, worst, vanquish, trounce, °rout, °crush, °master, °outdo, °overwhelm, °overcome, °outwit: *He was bested in three falls out of four.*

bestow *v.* °confer; °give, °award, °present, °donate, °grant: *The country has bestowed its highest honours on her.*

bet *n.* **1** wager, °stake, °risk, °venture, *Brit* °punt, *Colloq Brit* °flutter: *He could not afford more than a small bet.*
—*v.* **2** wager, °stake, °gamble, °risk, °hazard, °play, °lay, °put, °chance, °venture, *Brit* °punt: *Every week he bet a small amount on the lottery.*

betray *v.* **1** be *or* prove °false *or* °disloyal to, °sell out, break °faith with, °let down, °fail, °inform on, *Colloq* °sell down the river, *Slang Brit* °shop: *He betrayed her to the enemy.* **2** °reveal, °disclose, divulge, °impart, °tell; °expose, °lay bare: *She betrayed their hide-out to the police. He betrayed an unsuspected streak of cowardice.* **3** lead astray, °mislead, misguide, °deceive, °dupe, °fool, °hoodwink: *He has been betrayed by his own arrogance.*

betrayal *n.* **1** treachery, treason, disloyalty, °perfidy, traitorousness, faithlessness, bad faith, breach of °faith: *His delivery of the country into the hands of an invader was an outright act of betrayal.* **2** °revelation, divulging, disclosure, divulgence: *People should not be led into betrayals of their secret opinions.*

better[1] *adj.* **1** °superior: *You're a better man than I am, Gunga Din. Can you suggest a better investment than the Channel Tunnel? I know of no better invention than the wheel.* **2** more; greater, larger, bigger: *I waited for her the better part of two hours.* **3** wiser, safer, °well-advised, more °intelligent: *It would be better to wait till tomorrow to tell her.* **4** healthier, haler, heartier, less °ill *or US* °sick, improved; cured, recovered: *You will feel better after you have eaten something.*
—*adv.* **5** preferably, °best; more wisely, more advisedly, more safely: *We had better go before the trouble starts.* **6** ***better off***: **a** improved, happier, °well-advised: *You'd be better off attending a technical college.* **b** wealthier, richer: *She is better off than any of us.* **7** ***think better of***: reconsider, °think twice, °change one's °mind: *He was going to fight but thought better of it.*
—*n.* **8** °advantage, mastery, °superiority, °control: *Don't let the obstacle course get the better of you.*
9 ***betters***: superiors: *That young imp should learn how to address his elders and betters!*
—*v.* **10** °improve, ameliorate, °advance, °raise, elevate: *It was impossible in those days for labourers to better their condition.* **11** °surpass, °excel, °outdo, °outstrip, °beat, °improve: *She bettered her record in the 100-metre hurdles by two-tenths of a second.*

better[2] *n.* gambler, speculator, wagerer, gamester, *Brit* °punter, *US* bettor, *Colloq* crap-shooter, °sport: *The betters were gathered round the craps table.*

bewail *v.* °lament, °mourn, °bemoan, °moan *or* °mourn over, °shed tears *or* whimper over, °weep *or* °cry *or* °keen over, beat one's breast over: *Instead of bewailing his condition, why doesn't he do something about it?*

beware *v.* °take °heed, be °careful, be °wary, be °cautious, be on one's °guard, °exercise °caution, °mind, °watch out, °look out, take °care: *There are shoals nearby, so beware. Beware the ides of March!*

bewilder *v.* °confuse, confound, °perplex, °puzzle, °mystify, befuddle, baffle, °bemuse: *I was bewildered by differential calculus.*

bewitch *v.* °enchant, °entrance, spellbind, °charm, °fascinate, °beguile, cast a °spell on *or* over, °captivate, °enrapture: *She easily bewitches men with her sultry good looks and her husky, low voice.*

bias *n.* **1** °prejudice, °partiality; °inclination, °leaning, °bent, °disposition, propensity, °tendency, predilection, predisposition, proclivity: *She shows a marked bias in favour of the Irish.* **2** °angle, °slant, diagonal: *Cut the fabric on the bias.* **3** °influence, impulse, °weight: *If he is under any bias, it is on the side of fairness.*
—*v.* **4** °influence, °affect unduly *or* unfairly, °sway, °incline, °prejudice, °colour, °taint, predispose: *Artists are seldom good critics of art because they have been biased.*

biased *adj.* °prejudiced, °partial; warped, distorted, °jaundiced: *I don't want to listen to your biased opinions about women's rights.*

bicker *v.* °dispute, °quarrel, wrangle, °argue, squabble, °tiff, *Colloq* spat: *The couple next door are always bickering about trifling matters.*

bid *v.* **1** °offer, make an °offer (for), °tender, proffer: *We bid £500 for the painting.* **2** *Archaic or literary* ask, °pray, °press, entreat, °beg, °request, °suggest, invite: *She bade me leave her to mourn alone.* **3** *Formal* command, °demand, °order, °tell, enjoin, °dictate: *Please bid him enter. Custom bade him blow his horn.*

bidding *n.* **1** °invitation, summons: *We attended the ceremony at the bidding of the vice-chancellor.*
2 °command, °order, °dictate, °direction, °instruction, °demand: *The letter was sent to all theatre directors at the bidding of the Arts Minister.*

big *adj.* **1** °large, °great, °grand; °huge, °enormous, °immense, °gigantic, °giant, tremendous, °colossal, Brobdingnagian, °jumbo, *Colloq Brit* socking *or* whacking big *or* °great, *US* humongous: *We live in a big house in the country.* **2** °ample, °hefty, °huge, °bulky, °fat, °obese; °large, °hulking, beefy, °burly, °brawny, strapping, gargantuan, elephantine, °enormous, °gigantic, °immense, °monstrous: *The sumo wrestler was one of the biggest men I'd ever seen.* **3** °tall, grown, °mature, grown-up, °large: *Christopher is certainly big for his age.* **4** °important, °significant, °outstanding, °weighty, consequential, °major, °grave, °momentous, °notable, °noteworthy, °telling: *Changing careers can be one of the biggest decisions of your life.* **5** °important, °prominent, °illustrious, °noteworthy, °notable, °renowned, °eminent, °distinguished, esteemed: *Mr Johnson is a big man in our town.* **6** °generous, magnanimous, °charitable, °unselfish, giving: *It was very big of her to take on the support of the orphanage.* **7** °popular, °famous, °well-known, °successful: *That band is very big with the kids these days.* **8** °capital, °large, °upper case, majuscule: *Always spell* London *with a big* L.
—*adv.* **9** pompously, boastfully, conceitedly, arrogantly, pretentiously: *Alfred talks big at home, but he's very modest when he's with his friends.* **10** successfully, °well, oustandingly, effectively: *I think your speech went over big with those opposed to the new budget.*

bigoted *adj.* °prejudiced, °intolerant, °biased, °jaundiced, °one-sided, °partial: *The judge was bigoted against Blacks, which accounts for the unfair decision.*

bigotry *n.* °prejudice, °intolerance, °bias, °partiality: *No government that practises bigotry can survive long.*

bigwig *n.* **1** °boss, kingpin, °king, °queen, nabob, VIP, *Colloq* °big shot, °big gun, °big cheese, °big wheel, hotshot, °chief, °brass hat, *US* (°chief) honcho, Mr Big: *The bigwig sits here, at the head of the table.*
2 ***bigwigs***: brass, brass hats: *Don't let the bigwigs find out what we've done.*

bilious *adj.* ill-tempered, bad-tempered, ill-natured, °peevish, °testy, °cross, °petulant, tetchy, choleric, dyspeptic, °angry, wrathful: *The director was absolutely bilious when he heard we had lost the account.*

bill[1] *n.* **1** invoice, °account; °tally, °reckoning, tabulation, *US* (restaurant) °check, *Colloq US* °tab: *Have you paid the telephone bill?* **2** *US and Canadian* note, banknote, paper °money, *Colloq* folding °money: *The robbers took only small bills, which they could spend easily.*
—*v.* **3** invoice, °charge: *I haven't got my cheque-book with me, please could you bill me.*

bill[2] *n.* beak, neb, nib, pecker; jaws: *One of the birds had a fish in its bill.*

bind *v.* **1** °tie, °fasten, °secure, make °fast, °tie up: *The thieves bound him hand and foot.* **2** constrain; °hold, °oblige, °obligate: *The contract we signed is equally binding on both parties. The union is bound by an agreement that expires in a month.* **3** gird, °encircle, wreathe, °wrap, °cover, °swathe, bandage: *They were binding his wounded head.* **4** °cement, °stick, cause to

adhere; °attach, °connect: *Ordinary glue will bind these pieces together.*
—*n.* **5** *in the US*: dilemma, °predicament, °tight °spot, (°difficult) °situation, *Colloq* pickle, °fix, °jam: *I'm in a real bind because I've invited two girls to the party.* **6** *in Britain*: annoyance, irritant, °bother, °bore, °trial, °ordeal, irritation, vexation, *Colloq* °pain (in the neck *or* arse): *It was a bit of a bind having to wait three hours at the airport.*

birth *n.* **1** childbirth, °delivery, *Technical* parturition, *Old-fashioned* confinement: *Nicole is expecting the birth of her first baby in early April.* **2** °origin, °creation, °emergence, °beginning, °start, origination: *I believe we may be present at the birth of a powerful idea.* **3** nativity, °origin, °extraction; °parentage, °line, °lineage, ancestry, descent, °family, blood: *She is Scottish by birth. Hortense is of noble birth.*

bisexual *adj.* **1** hermaphrodite *or* hermaphroditic(al), androgynous: *Many of these microscopic animals are bisexual and self-fertilizing.* **2** *Colloq* AC/DC, swinging both ways, *Facetious* ambisextrous: *He was known to have had bisexual relationships.*
—*n.* **3** androgyne, hermaphrodite: *Statistics showed that more women than previously believed were bisexuals.*

bit *n.* **1** °morsel, °piece, °scrap, °fragment, °shred, °particle, °grain, °crumb: *We didn't have a bit of food in the house.* **2** °jot, tittle, whit, scintilla, °trace, °touch, °hint, °suggestion, °suspicion, °particle, iota, °speck, atom: *There's not the slightest bit of evidence to link her with the crime.* **3** °moment, °minute, °second, °flash, *Colloq* two shakes (of a lamb's tail): *I'll be with you in a little bit.* **4** °piece, °share, °equity, °segment, °portion, °part, fraction: *He owns a little bit of the business.*

bitch *n.* **1** °shrew, °nag, termagant, virago, harpy, °fury, spitfire, °scold: *That greedy bitch has the house, and now she's suing me for half my income.* **2** whore, °prostitute, bawd, harlot, call-girl, trollop, strumpet, trull, drab, °tart, floozie *or* floozy *or* floosie, streetwalker, *Colloq* bimbo, pro, *US* hooker, °tramp, hustler: *He roamed the street every night, ending up with some bitch he found in a bar.*
—*v.* **3** °complain, °object, °protest, grumble, *Colloq* °gripe: *Oh, stop your bitching and get on with it!* **4** °bungle, °botch, °ruin, °spoil: *They bitched the job by using too little paint.*

bite *v.* **1** °nip; °chew, °gnaw: *That dog of yours bit a piece out of my ankle.* **2** °sting: *She was bitten by a mosquito.*
—*n.* **3** °mouthful, °morsel, °scrap, °bit, °piece, °taste; °snack, *Slang* nosh: *The survivors hadn't had a bite of food for three days. Come round for a bite on Sunday evening before the concert.* **4** °sting: *These mosquito bites itch horribly.*

biting *adj.* °severe, °harsh, °cutting, °piercing, °penetrating, °keen, °sharp, °bitter; °cold, °wintry, °freezing: *The biting wind went right through his thin coat.*

bitter *adj.* **1** °harsh, acerbic, acrid, °sharp, °caustic, mordant: *I added some cream to the sauce to try and make it taste less bitter.* **2** unappetizing, °distasteful, °unsavoury, unpleasant, hard (to °swallow *or* °take), irritating, °obnoxious, °disagreeable, °nasty, °painful, °unwelcome, °unpalatable: *The demand for additional tax payments was a bitter pill.* **3** °miserable, °grievous, dispiriting, distressing, °cruel, distressful: *Dismissal after all those years in the firm was a bitter experience.* **4** °resentful, °embittered, °rancorous; °hateful: *Andrew felt bitter at not being selected as chairman.* **5** stinging, °cutting, °biting, °harsh, °reproachful, °vicious, acrimonious, °virulent; °cruel, °unkind, unpleasant, °nasty: *His bitter denunciation of other candidates lost him the campaign.* **6** °sharp, °keen, °cutting, °severe, °biting, °cold, °wintry, °freezing: *A bitter gale lashed at the rigging.*

bitterness *n.* **1** harshness, acerbity, acrimony, acrimoniousness, spleen, *Literary* °gall and wormwood: *The bitterness of his opponent's attack was totally uncalled for.* **2** °animosity, hatred, °resentment; °hostility, °antagonism: *She felt bitterness in her heart over the way she had been treated.*

bizarre *adj.* **1** °eccentric, °unusual, unconventional, °extravagant, °whimsical, °strange, °odd, °curious, °peculiar, °queer, °offbeat, °fantastic, °weird, °incongruous, °deviant, °erratic, *Slang* °kinky: *The police thought his behaviour somewhat bizarre and invited him down to the station for questioning.* **2** °grotesque, °irregular, °nonconformist, nonconforming, °outlandish, °outré, °quaint, °fantastic, unconventional: *His house is a bizarre mixture of baroque and modern design.*

blab *v.* °broadcast, °tattle, °babble, °betray, °reveal, °disclose, divulge, °expose: *Don't tell Frieda—she'll blab your secrets all over town.*

blabbermouth *n.* tell-tale, babbler, chatterer, °gossip, *Colloq* °blab, tattle-tale, big-mouth: *Oscar is such a blabbermouth that you can't tell him anything you don't want everyone to know.*

black *adj.* **1** jet, jet-black, coal-black, inky, sooty, swart, °swarthy, raven, ebony, °dusky, *Literary* ebon, hyacinthine: *Her hair was as black as coal.* **2** Negro, Negroid, dark-skinned, *often offensive* coloured: *Most of the Black races originated near or south of the equator.* **3** °dark, °pitch-black, jet-black, coal-black, Stygian; starless, moonless: *He bundled his coat round himself and walked into the black night.* **4** °dark, °sombre, °dusky, °gloomy, °menacing, glowering, louring *or* lowering, °threatening, °funereal: *The sky became black with storm clouds.* **5** °malignant, baleful, baneful, °deadly, deathly, °sinister, °dismal, °hateful, °disastrous: *It was a black day when he came into my life.* **6** °bad, °foul, iniquitous, °wicked, °evil, diabolic(al), °infernal, hellish, °atrocious, °awful, malicious, °abominable, °outrageous, °vicious, °villainous, flagitious, °vile, °disgraceful, °unscrupulous, °unconscionable, unprincipled, blackguardly, knavish, °perfidious, insidious, nefarious, dastardly, treacherous, unspeakable, °shameful, °scurvy, °criminal, felonious: *You have told the blackest lies about me.* **7** °angry, wrathful, °furious, frowning, bad-tempered, sulky, °resentful, clouded, °threatening, glowering: *She gave him a black look and he withered in abject fear.*
—*v.* **8** °boycott, °embargo, blacklist, °ban, interdict: *Because of the dispute over plumbers' wages, the other building-trades unions have blacked every manufacturer in the business.*

blacken *v.* **1** darken, smudge, begrime: *The chimney sweep's face was blackened with soot.* **2** °slander, °libel, asperse, cast aspersions on, traduce, °smear, °sully, °soil, besmirch, °taint, °tarnish, defame, revile, malign, °vilify, °discredit, denigrate: *His article has blackened my reputation.*

blackleg *n.* scab, strikebreaker: *During the strike, the plant was operated by blacklegs.*

blackmail *n.* **1** extortion, °ransom, °tribute, *US* °graft: *Even if you pay the blackmail, that is no guarantee that he won't demand more later.*
—*v.* **2** °extort money from; °force, coerce, compel, °make: *They had discovered his indiscretions and were blackmailing him. He blackmailed her into signing the alimony settlement.*

blade *n.* **1** °knife, cutting °edge: *Don't hold the knife by the blade.* **2** *Literary* sword, rapier, sabre, °dagger, poniard, stiletto, cutlass, bayonet, °knife, penknife, jackknife: *She plunged the blade in up to the hilt.* **3** leaf, °leaflet, frond, °shoot: *The blades of grass were flattened where he had walked.* **4** *Rather old-fashioned* playboy, ladies' °man, man about town, fop, °dandy: *He was quite a gay blade in his youth.*

blame *v.* **1** find °fault with, censure, °criticize, °fault; °accuse, °charge, °indict, °condemn, °point to, °point (the finger) at, °rebuke, °reprimand, recriminate, reproach, °scold, reprehend, °reprove: *Don't blame me if you can't get to school on time.* **2** hold °responsible, fix (the) °responsibility upon *or* on, put *or* place *or* lay

(the) blame on, lay at someone's door, °denounce, °incriminate: *Why blame Carol for the mess?*
—*n.* **3** censure, °criticism, °reproof, °rebuke, °recrimination, °disapproval, disapprobation, reproach, objurgation, condemnation, reprehension: *The cyclist put the blame for the accident on me.* **4** culpability, °responsibility; °guilt, *Slang* °rap: *Why should you take the blame for something that Donald did?*

blameless *adj.* °faultless, guiltless, °innocent, °irreproachable, unimpeachable: *Hugh has led a blameless life.*

bland *adj.* **1** °gentle, °soothing, °smooth, °mild, °suave, urbane, °cool, unruffled, °calm, composed, unemotional, °nonchalant, insouciant: *His reaction to the news of the invasion was bland indifference.* **2** insipid, °boring, °dull, uninteresting, ennuyant, °tasteless, *Colloq US* °plain vanilla; *Slang US* blah: *The play is a bland mixture of clichés embedded in a tired plot.*

blank *adj.* **1** °empty, °plain, °bare: *I stared at the blank paper, unable to write even my name.* **2** unornamented, °unadorned, undecorated, °void: *Whenever Irena sees a blank wall she feels compelled to hang a painting on it.* **3** °vacant, °empty: *The actor's mind went completely blank—he had forgotten his lines.* **4** °passive, °impassive, expressionless, emotionless, vacuous, °mindless, unexpressive: *He gave us a blank look when asked about the missing rare stamps.* **5** °disconcerted, discomfited, nonplussed, °confused, °helpless, resourceless, perplexed, dazed, bewildered: *The two old men looked at each other with blank and horror-stricken faces.* **6** unrelieved, °stark, °sheer, utter, °pure, unmixed, °absolute, °unqualified: *Jack faced the blank prospect of solitary confinement.*
—*n.* **7** °space; °line, °box: *Please fill in the blanks on the form.* **8** °nothing, °zero, °nil; °void, °emptiness: *I asked her when the baby was coming, but I drew a blank.*

blare *v.* **1** °blast, °bellow, trumpet, °ring, °boom, °thunder, °roar, bray; °resound, °echo, reverberate, resonate: *Everyone in the neighbourhood can hear your hi-fi blaring.*
—*n.* **2** °blast, °bellow, °ring, °roar, °boom, °noise, °sound, clamour: *The games began with a blare of trumpets.*

blasé *adj.* **1** bored, °jaded, °weary, unimpressed, ennuyé: *Her blasé attitude does little to endear her at job interviews.* **2** °indifferent, °cool, °superior, °supercilious, °sophisticated, °unmoved, °nonchalant, emotionless, °phlegmatic, apathetic, pococurante, °carefree, light-hearted, insouciant: *His blasé behaviour hides his basic feelings of insecurity.*

blaspheme *v.* **1** °curse, °swear, imprecate, execrate, °profane, °damn: *They were denounced for blaspheming against God.* **2** °abuse, malign, calumniate, defame, °disparage, revile, °put down, decry, deprecate, °depreciate, °belittle: *The ungrateful wretches blaspheme the charitable soul who would help them.*

blasphemous *adj.* °profane, °impious, °irreverent, °disrespectful, °sacrilegious, irreligious, °sinful, °wicked, °evil, iniquitous: *He was excommunicated for his blasphemous writings.*

blast *n.* **1** °blow, °gust, °wind, °gale: *The door opened and a blast of icy air made us shiver.* **2** °blare, °sound, °noise, °racket, °din, °bellow, °roar; °boom: *At the trumpet-blast thousands of Goths descended screaming on the camp.* **3** °explosion, °burst, °eruption, °discharge; detonation: *A blast of dynamite levelled all the houses in the vicinity.* **4** ***(at** or **in) full blast***: fully, at full tilt, at the °maximum, °completely, °thoroughly, °entirely, maximally, *Slang* with no holds barred, *US* to the max: *The factory was going full blast before the strike.*
—*v.* **5** °blow up, °explode, dynamite, °demolish, °destroy, °ruin, °waste, lay °waste, °shatter, °devastate: *The pillbox was blasted out of existence by our guns.* **6** defame, °discredit, °denounce, °criticize, °attack; °ruin, °destroy: *The candidate has been blasted by the press.* **7** °curse, °damn: *The minister continued to blast the proposal till the legislature dropped it.*

blatant *adj.* **1** °obvious, °flagrant, palpable, °obtrusive, arrant, °shameless, unashamed, °brazen, °overt, °glaring: *Those hooligans have shown a blatant disregard for the law.* **2** °noisy, clamorous, °loud, bellowing, °strident, vociferous, °rowdy, °boisterous, °obstreperous, °uproarious: *The blatant radical faction insists on making itself heard.*

blaze *n.* **1** °flame, °fire, °holocaust, inferno, conflagration: *The fuel barrels exploded, feeding the blaze.* **2** °outburst, °eruption, flare-up: *Her speech fanned the Lower House into a blaze of resentment.* **3** °light, brightness, °brilliance, brilliancy, °glow: *The blaze of lamps lit up the whole square.*
—*v.* **4** °burn, °flare up, °flame: *In a few minutes the logs were blazing merrily.* **5** ***blaze away (at)***: °fire, °shoot, open fire, °blast; °bombard, °shell: *The enemy appeared, and we just blazed away at them.*

bleach *v.* **1** whiten, °lighten, °fade, blanch, blench, *Technical* etiolate: *My jeans are all bleached by the sun.*
—*n.* **2** whitener, chlorine: *Add a little bleach to the laundry.*

bleak *adj.* **1** cheerless, °dreary, depressing, °dismal, °gloomy, °sombre, °melancholy, °sad, °unhappy, °mournful: *1940 was one of the bleakest periods in British history.* **2** °cold, °chilly, °raw, °bitter: *The days were getting shorter, and the bleak winter was setting in.* **3** °barren, °bare, exposed, windswept, °desolate: *How depressing the bleak landscape of the Russian steppes can be in winter!*

blemish *v.* **1** °deface, °mar, °scar, °impair, disfigure: *They did nothing to blemish the beauty of the landscape.* **2** °tarnish, °stain, °sully, °spoil, °mar, °flaw, °harm, °damage, °scar, °injure, °bruise, besmirch: *She has blemished my reputation by spreading those stories about me.*
—*n.* **3** disfigurement, °scar, °mark, °impairment, °stain, °smear, °blot; °defect, °flaw, °error, °fault, °imperfection, erratum: *Her complexion was entirely without blemish.*

blend *v.* **1** °mix, °mingle, °combine, meld, commingle, intermingle: *The Latakia is blended with the Virginia to produce a fine smoking tobacco.* **2** °shade, °grade, gradate, °graduate, °merge, coalesce, °fuse, °unite: *Note how the pink sky and the tinted clouds blend in this Turner painting.*
—*n.* **3** °mixture, °mix, °combination, mingling, meld, commingling, intermingling: *His humour is a fine blend of the sardonic with slapstick.*

bless *v.* **1** consecrate, °hallow, °sanctify; °extol, °glorify, °praise, °revere, °adore: *God bless this ship and all who sail in her. Bless the Lord.* **2** °give, make °happy or °fortunate, endow, °favour, °furnish, °provide, °supply, grace: *She is blessed with one of the most beautiful soprano voices that I have ever heard.*

blessing *n.* **1** benediction, °prayer, consecration: *Each spring the vicar officiated at the blessing of the fleet.* **2** °boon, °favour, °advantage, good °fortune, °godsend, °luck, °profit, °gain, °help, °asset, °gift, °bounty: *Hot, sunny days are a blessing for wine growers.*

blight *n.* **1** °affliction, °disease, °plague, infestation, °pestilence, °scourge: *The crops were visited with a blight that lasted seven years.* **2** °misfortune, °curse, °trouble, °woe, °calamity: *Genius may suffer an untimely blight.*
—*v.* **3** °afflict, °infest, °plague, °scourge; wither, °mar, °taint, °blast: *Central Africa has been blighted by famine after famine.*

blind *adj.* **1** sightless, eyeless, unsighted, purblind, stone-blind: *He has been blind from birth.* **2** imperceptive, °slow, insensitive, °thick, °dense, °obtuse, °stupid, weak-minded, dull-witted, slow-witted, dim-witted, *Colloq Brit* gormless: *How blind some parents are! There's another case of the blind leading the blind.* **3** °indiscriminate, undiscriminating, °heedless, °reckless, °rash, °impetuous, °inconsiderate, unreasoning, °mindless, °senseless, °thoughtless, °unthinking, irrational, delusional: *He did her bidding with the blind* *obedience of a dog.* **4** ***blind to***: °unaware *or* °unconscious of, impervious *or* °insensible to, °unaffected *or* untouched *or* °unmoved by: *The critics were blind to her merits as a novelist till many years had passed.* —*v.* **5** °deceive, blindfold, blinker; bamboozle, °hoodwink, °fool: *Wolsey could not blind himself to the true condition of the church. How jealousy blinds people!* **6** °conceal, °hide, °eclipse, °overshadow; °dazzle, blindfold: *The bright lights of the city blinded our view of the airport runway. Her beauty blinded him to her greed.* —*n.* **7** °shade, curtain, °screen, °cover, shutter(s), awning: *The sun is too bright—please draw the blind.* **8** °pretence, °pretext, °front, °cover, smokescreen, °stratagem, °subterfuge, °ruse, °trick, °deception, *Colloq* °dodge; *Slang* scam: *The plumbing service is merely a blind for getting into houses to rob them.*

blindly *adv.* recklessly, heedlessly, deludedly, indiscriminately, rashly, impetuously, irrationally, thoughtlessly, mindlessly, senselessly, unthinkingly: *Despite his parents' warnings, he went blindly on, till one day he was arrested.*

blink *v.* **1** wink, °flicker, *Technical* nictitate: *She blinked in the strong light.* **2** °twinkle, °flicker, °gleam, glimmer, °shimmer, °flash, °sparkle, scintillate, coruscate: *A billion stars blinked in the wintry sky.* **3** °flinch, wince, °shrink, quail, blench, °recoil, °start, °move: *She didn't even blink when she had the injection.* **4** ***blink at***: wink at, °ignore, °overlook, °disregard: *That inspector has been known to blink at health violations.* —*n.* **5** wink, °flicker: *He switched the cards in the blink of an eye.* **6** ***on the blink***: out of order, °broken, in °disrepair, not working *or* operating, not operational, *Slang US* out of whack, on the fritz: *The fridge is on the blink again.*

bliss *n.* °happiness, blitheness, gladness, °joy, blessedness, °delight, felicity, °glee, °enjoyment, °pleasure, joyousness, °cheer, exhilaration, °gaiety, blissfulness, °rapture, °ecstasy: *The bliss of our honeymoon has remained with us throughout our marriage.*

blithe *adj.* **1** blissful, °happy, °cheerful, joyous, °merry, light-hearted, well-pleased, °delighted, °gay, °joyful, °elated, jubilant: *His spirit was blithe and his heart unquenchable.* **2** happy-go-lucky, insouciant, °heedless, °carefree, unconcerned, °blasé, °casual, °detached, °indifferent, uncaring, °careless: *She goes through life with a blithe disregard for the feelings of others.*

bloated *adj.* °swollen, distended, fully, puffy; puffed up, °overgrown, °inflated, °pompous: *He felt bloated after the enormous banquet. That bloated, conceited, self-important petty official had the gall to refuse me a visa.*

blob *n.* °gob, gobbet, globule, °drop, droplet, °bit, gout, °lump, °dab, *Colloq* glob, *Chiefly US and Canadian* smidgen *or* smidgin: *There's a blob of jelly on your tie.*

block *n.* **1** °piece, chunk, hunk, °lump, °slab; °stump; °brick, cube: *The figure is carved out of a solid block of stone.* **2** °bar, °obstacle, °obstruction, °hindrance, °stumbling-block, °deterrent, °impediment, °barrier: *Her arrival should be no block to your leaving.* —*v.* **3** °obstruct, °close off, barricade; °bar, °shut off; °hinder, °hamper, balk, °impede, °prevent: *Entry to the playing field was blocked by the police.* **4** ***block out***: **a** °rough out, °design, °outline, sketch, °lay out, °plan: *The colonel blocked out a strategy for our escape.* **b** °mask, °screen, °blank (out), °erase, °eliminate, °exclude, °blot out, °deny: *She has blocked out that part of her life from her mind.* **5** ***block (up)***: °stuff (up), congest, °clog, *Colloq Brit* bung up: *My nose is all blocked up because of this awful cold.*

bloodshed *n.* °slaughter, °carnage, butchery, °killing, °murder, blood-letting; °violence; genocide: *Let's settle this peaceably and avoid bloodshed.*

bloodsucker *n.* leech, extortionist, extortioner, blackmailer; °parasite, barnacle, *Colloq* sponge, freeloader, °scrounge, scrounger; *Slang US* moocher: *He's nothing but a bloodsucker, always demanding more and more money.*

bloodthirsty *adj.* °murderous, °homicidal, °savage, feral, °cruel, °ruthless, pitiless, °vicious, °brutal, °sadistic, °ferocious, °fierce, *Formal* °sanguinary, *Literary* °fell: *Bloodthirsty pirates had slaughtered the whole crew.*

blot *n.* **1** °stain, °spot, °mark, smudge, blotch, °blemish, disfigurement, °smear, smirch, °scar, *Colloq* splodge *or US also* splotch: *An ink blot covered the date of the document. There are a few blots on his record from his time in the army.* —*v.* **2** °stain, °spot, °spatter, smudge, °mark, °blur: *You have blotted these pages where you wrote with a fountain-pen.* **3** ***blot one's copybook***: °err, °destroy *or* °ruin *or* °mar *or* °spoil one's °reputation, commit an °indiscretion, °transgress, °sin: *She's certainly blotted her copybook by having an affair with that subaltern.* **4** ***blot out***: **a** °obscure, °conceal, °cover (up), °hide, °eclipse, °dim: *The clouds blotted out the sun for a few minutes.* **b** °obliterate, °destroy, °erase, °demolish, efface, annihilate, °delete, °rub *or* °wipe out: *He subconsciously blotted out all memory of the accident.*

blow[1] *v.* **1** °breathe, °puff, °exhale; °expel: *If the crystals turn green when you blow into the tube, it means that you've had too much to drink. Blow some air into the balloon.* **2** °waft, °puff, whistle, whine, °blast: *An icy wind blew through the cracks in the windows.* **3** *Colloq* bungle, °botch, make a °mess of, muff, mismanage, *Colloq* °screw up, °mess up, °fluff, °bugger up, *Taboo* fuck up: *It was my last chance to win and I blew it.* **4** *Colloq* spend, °lavish, squander, °waste, °throw out *or* away: *She blew hundreds on that dress and now she won't wear it.* **5** short-circuit, °burn out: *All the fuses blew when I turned on the electric heater.* **6** ***blow hot and cold***: vacillate, °hesitate, dither, *Colloq* °shilly-shally: *The sales manager has been blowing hot and cold over my proposal for a month now.* **7** ***blow out***: **a** °extinguish: *I blew out all the candles in one breath. The match blew out in the wind.* **b** °explode, °burst: *One of my tyres blew out on the way over here.* **c** short-circuit, °burn out: *The lights blew out during the storm.* **8** ***blow up***: **a** become °furious or °angry or enraged, °flare up, lose one's °temper, *Slang* blow one's top *or US also* °stack, °flip one's lid: *She really blew up when I said I was going to the pub.* **b** °explode, °burst, °shatter, *Colloq* bust; detonate, dynamite, °destroy, °blast: *The bridge blew up with a roar. Demolition experts will blow up the dam.* **c** °enlarge, °inflate, embroider, °magnify, °expand, °exaggerate, °overstate: *The tabloid press has blown up the story out of all proportion.* **d** °enlarge, °magnify, °amplify, °expand, °increase: *Can you blow up just this corner of the photograph?* **e** °inflate; distend, °swell: *We were busy blowing up balloons for the party.* —*n.* **9** °gale, °storm, °tempest, °whirlwind, tornado, cyclone, °hurricane, typhoon, north-easter, nor'easter: *We can expect a big blow tonight—winds of gale force, they say.*

blow[2] *n.* **1** °stroke, °punch, clout, whack, °hit, °knock, thump, thwack, *Colloq* wallop: *He was felled by a blow to the chin in the fourth round.* **2** °shock, °surprise, °bombshell, °jolt, °bolt from the blue, °revelation: *It came as a blow to learn that she was leaving in a month.*

blue *adj.* **1** depressed, low-spirited, dispirited, °sad, °dismal, down, down in the °mouth, °gloomy, °unhappy, °glum, downcast, crestfallen, chap-fallen, °dejected, °melancholy, °despondent, °downhearted, morose: *I've been feeling blue since Kathleen left me.* **2** °obscene, °vulgar, °indecent, titillating, °pornographic, °dirty, °filthy, °lewd, smutty, °risqué, °bawdy, °sexy, X, X-rated, 18, *US* XXX; indelicate, °suggestive, off colour, °erotic, °coarse, °offensive, °improper: *There's a place nearby that shows blue movies.*

bluff[1] *v.* **1** °deceive, °hoodwink, °dupe, °mislead, delude, °trick, cozen, °fool, *Colloq* bamboozle: *I bluffed him into believing that I held four aces.* **2** °pretend,

feign, °bluster, °fool, *Colloq* kid; *Slang* bullshit: *She became frightened, unaware that I was only bluffing.*
—*n.* **3** °bombast, °bravado, boasting, bragging, °bluster, °show, puffery; °deception, °blind; *Literary* rodomontade, gasconade; *Colloq* °hot air: *Roger's ranting is all bluff—he's really very timid.*

bluff[2] *adj.* **1** blustering, °gruff, °rough, °abrupt, °blunt, °curt, °short, °crude: *Fred's bluff manner puts many people off.* **2** °frank, °open, °hearty, straightforward, °plain, plain-spoken, °outspoken, affable, approachable, °good-natured, °friendly: *That comment is typical of his bluff honesty.*
—*n.* **3** °cliff, escarpment, °precipice, scarp, headland, promontory, palisades: *As you sail down the lower Hudson river, the tall bluffs form a natural wall along the western bank.*

blunder *v.* **1** °stumble, °flounder: *I had somehow blundered into a meeting of the local crime syndicate. She blundered upon the truth when she saw them together.*
—*n.* **2** °mistake, °error, gaffe, faux pas, °slip, slip-up, °howler, *Colloq* boo-boo, screw-up, °fluff, boner, *US* goof, goof-up: *I made a stupid blunder in telling him about the plans.*

blunt *adj.* **1** °dull, °worn: *This knife is too blunt to cut bread.* **2** °abrupt, °curt, rough-spoken, plain-spoken, °short, °direct, °candid, °frank, unceremonious, undiplomatic, °inconsiderate, °thoughtless, °brusque, °outspoken, °bluff, °brash, indelicate, °rude, uncivil, °ungracious, °discourteous, °impolite; straightforward, °straight, uncomplicated, uncompromising: *Ralph may be blunt, but at least you know exactly where you stand with him.*
—*v.* **3** °dull, take the edge off: *You've blunted the scissors cutting that cardboard.* **4** °soften, °mitigate, mollify, soothe; efface, °dim, °obscure, °blur, °weaken: *Mother's love is an absorbing delight, blunting all other sensibilities.*

blur *n.* **1** indistinctness, dimness, haziness, cloudiness, fogginess: *We were unable to pick out the star from the blur of the Galaxy.* **2** °fog, haze, *Brit* fuzz: *Without my spectacles, everything is a blur.*
—*v.* **3** °dim, befog, °obscure, bedim; efface: *My vision was momentarily blurred, and I didn't see the oncoming car.* **4** °obscure, °hide, °conceal, °veil, °mask; °weaken: *The Honourable Gentleman has blurred the distinction between the unemployed and the unemployable.*

blurt *v.* Usually, ***blurt out***: °burst out with, utter; °reveal, °disclose, °give away, divulge, *Colloq* °blab: *She blurted out the name of her accomplice.*

blush *v.* be *or* act °ashamed, redden, °flush, °colour: *He blushed when asked if he still loved Belinda.*

bluster *v.* **1** °storm, °rage, °harangue: *It won't do any good to bluster on about the postal service.* **2** °swagger, °strut, °talk °big, °boast, °brag, °blow one's own horn *or* trumpet, °show off, crow: *He's always blustering about his conquests.*
—*n.* **3** swaggering, storming, raging, °raving, haranguing, °tumult; °hot °air, puffery, °bravado, grandiloquence, *Literary* rodomontade: *He's all bluster and will do nothing despite his threats.*

board *n.* **1** °plank, scantling, °timber: *We nailed the last board in place and the house was finished.* **2** table, gaming-table, game table *or* °surface: *I have the chessmen, have you brought the board?* **3** °food, meals, °provisions: *I am moving to the country, where room and board are cheaper.* **4** °council, °committee, directors, directorship, °management, °cabinet, panel, trustees, °advisers: *That issue will be discussed at the meeting of the board.* **5** ***on board***: aboard, on: *Young children are not allowed on board the boat.*
—*v.* **6** °go aboard, °ship aboard; °enter, °embark on: *We all boarded the ship but it didn't leave for an hour.* **7** °feed; °eat, take meals; °accommodate, °lodge, °house, billet, °quarter; °lodge, °stay, °live, °room; *Colloq* °put up: *Mrs O'Brien already boards three gentlemen at her house, but she has agreed to let me board there too.*

boast *n.* **1** °brag, bragging: *They did not make good their boasts of being the fastest in the competition.*
—*v.* **2** °brag, vaunt, crow, °show off, *Colloq US* °blow *or* toot one's (own) horn *or* trumpet; *Slang* °lay it on thick, °talk big: *He boasted that he was the best poker player in the casino.*

boastful *adj.* °ostentatious, °show-off, bragging, vainglorious, °egotistical, °vain, °conceited: *She's boastful about her wealth, but it was all left to her by her mother.*

boat *n.* °vessel, °craft, skiff, small °craft, motor °boat, speedboat, knockabout, runabout, yacht, motor yacht, sailing-yacht, *Brit* rowing-boat, sailing-boat, *US* rowboat, sailboat, *Colloq* °ship: *I bought a 30-foot boat at this year's show. They went off on a slow boat to China.*

bode *v.* portend, °promise, augur, betoken, forebode, presage; °foreshadow: *The weather bodes well for the picnic.*

body *n.* **1** °corpse, °cadaver, remains, carcass, *Slang* °stiff: *A body has been dragged up from the lake.* **2** °trunk, torso: *They found the body, but the arms, legs, and head were missing.* **3** °main °part *or* °portion, °hull, fuselage: *The body of the plane remained intact, though the wings and superstructure broke away.* **4** °substance, essentials, °main °part, °essence, °heart, °centre, °core: *The body of the book is all right, but the index needs work.* **5** °majority, °bulk, °main °part *or* °portion, °mass(es): *Under Henry VIII the main body of the people were prosperous.* **6** °association, °league, °band, °corps, confederation, °fraternity, °society; °committee, °council; °group, assemblage, °assembly, congress, °company: *It is not within the power of this body to do more than vote on the proposal.* **7** richness, °substance, firmness, consistency, solidity, thickness, density, fullness, viscosity: *This wine has excellent body. Add a little cornflour to give the sauce more body.*

bog *n.* **1** °swamp, fen, °marsh, quagmire: *The peat bogs have yielded interesting fossils.* **2** ***bog down***: °impede, °slow, °hamper, °encumber, °stymie, °stick, °handicap, °clog, °check, °set back, °hold back: *Traffic is bogged down owing to roadworks.*

bogus *adj.* °counterfeit, °spurious, °fake, °false, °fraudulent, °sham, °imitation, °fictitious, *Colloq* °phoney *or US also* phony: *The police reported that a gang was trying to pass bogus money to unsuspecting shopkeepers in the area.*

Bohemian *adj.* °nonconformist, unconforming, unconventional, °unorthodox, °casual, °free and easy: *In the '60s she became a flower person and adopted a Bohemian way of life.*

boil[1] *v.* **1** °bubble, °seethe; °simmer, °stew, steam: *A pot of soup was boiling on the kitchen stove.* **2** °seethe, °fume, sizzle, °smoulder, °chafe, fulminate, °ferment, sputter, splutter, °bluster: *When she learned what he had been saying about her, she boiled with furious indignation.*

boil[2] *n.* abscess, carbuncle, pustule, *Technical* furuncle: *The doctor said the boil had to be lanced at once.*

boisterous *adj.* °rowdy, clamorous, °rough, °noisy, °lively, °exuberant, °unruly, °wild, °undisciplined, °tempestuous, °stormy, turbulent, *Colloq* rambunctious: *The boys were sent outside because of their boisterous behaviour.*

bold *adj.* **1** °courageous, °brave, plucky, °confident, stout-hearted, lion-hearted, °daring, °enterprising, °audacious, °fearless, unafraid, °intrepid, °resolute, °dauntless, undaunted, valiant, °stout, valorous, °stalwart, °adventurous, °venturesome; °reckless, °foolhardy, incautious, °daredevil, °rash: *It would take a bold man to enter the ring with the champion.* **2** °audacious, °presumptuous, °forward, °immodest, °brazen, °impudent, temerarious, °impertinent, °shameless: *It was very bold of you to speak your mind to the boss.* **3** °pronounced, °outstanding, °striking, °vigorous,

°clear, °strong, °vivid, °distinct, °conspicuous: *He wrote down their demands in a good, bold hand.*

bolster *v.* °support, °prop (up), °brace, shore up, °buttress, °uphold, back (up), °reinforce, °aid, °help, °assist, °further, °advance: *The miners cited a lack of safety measures to bolster their arguments.*

bolt *n.* **1** arrow, dart, °projectile, °missile, *Historical* °quarrel: *He had only three bolts remaining for the crossbow.* **2** °pin, °bar, °rod, °catch; latch: *We hoped that the bolt would prevent their opening the door.* **3** machine °screw: *Bolts can be tightened or removed, unlike rivets.* **4** °roll, °length: *We sell only full bolts of fabric.* **5** lightning °flash, thunderbolt, *Formal* fulguration: *One bolt travelled down the television aerial and blew out the set.* **6** ***bolt from*** *or* ***out of the blue***: °surprise, °shock, °bombshell, °bomb, °blow, °revelation, eye-opener, *Colloq* shocker: *The news of her resignation came like a bolt from the blue.* **7** ***shoot one's bolt***: °exhaust *or* °use up one's resources, *Slang* °burn out, *US* poop out: *He was fast early in the marathon, but he'd shot his bolt long before the finishing line.*
—*v.* **8** °spring, dart, °shoot off, take °flight, °run (away *or* off), °rush (off *or* away), °break away, °flee, decamp, abscond, °escape, °fly, °dash (off *or* away), *Colloq* skedaddle, scram, *Brit* scarper, do a bunk, do a moonlight °flit, *US* take a (run-out) °powder: *The youths bolted as soon as they saw the police. The couple in room 315 bolted without paying their bill.* **9** °gulp (down), °swallow whole: *When the bell rang, she bolted her breakfast and ran out of the back door.* **10** °fasten, °lock, latch, °secure: *Make sure you bolt your door at night and don't let anyone in.* **11** °fix, °attach, °fasten, °connect, °make °fast to: *The motor must be securely bolted to the workbench.*
—*adv.* **12** ***bolt upright***: °erect, °straight, rigidly, stiffly: *When her name was called, Penny sat bolt upright in her chair.*

bomb *n.* **1** °bombshell, °shell, °explosive: *One of the bombs blew up the school.*
—*v.* **2** °bombard, °shell, °batter, °blow up: *Last night the railway station was bombed.*

bombard *v.* **1** °batter, °bomb, °shell: *The artillery continued to bombard the enemy with everything in their arsenal.* **2** assail, °attack, °assault, °set upon; °besiege: *The Prime Minister was bombarded with requests to amend the law.*

bombast *n.* °pretentious language, flatulence, °bluster, °show, grandiloquence, magniloquence, °hot air, °bravado, °boast, boasting, *Literary* gasconade, rodomontade; *Colloq* puffery: *The speaker continued to bore the audience with his pompous bombast.*

bombastic *adj.* high-flown, °extravagant, °pompous, °grandiose, grandiloquent, magniloquent, °inflated, fustian, flatulent, turgid, *Literary* euphuistic: *The Minister made a bombastic speech full of emotive appeals, but his actual arguments were unconvincing.*

bombshell *n.* °surprise, °shock, eye-opener, °bomb, °blow, °revelation, °bolt from *or* out of the blue, *Colloq* shocker: *Then came the bombshell—she and Tony had been married the week before.*

bona fide *adj.* °genuine, °authentic, attested, °real, °veritable, °legitimate, °true, valid; in °good faith, °sincere, °honest: *The jeweller affirmed that it was a bona fide ruby. I don't believe her reasons are bona fide.*

bond *n.* **1** °tie(s), shackles, chains, fetters, manacles, °handcuffs, °trammels, thongs, °cord(s), °rope(s); °restraint(s), constraint(s), °check(s), °control(s), °rein(s): *The council is hampered by the bonds of the old regulations.* **2** covenant, °pact, °contract, °agreement, °engagement, °compact, °treaty: *To unite the party a bond of confederacy was formed.* **3** °connection, °link, linkage, °union, °tie, °relationship: *The main bond between us was a shared love of the theatre. The bond between the veneer and the board should hold with a little more glue.*
—*v.* **4** °cement, °bind, °hold together, °stick, cohere: *They use mortar to bond the bricks together.*

bondage *n.* °slavery, °servitude, °subjection, subjugation, enslavement, serfdom, thraldom; vassalage, villeinage: *The poor souls were kept in bondage for most of their lives, forced to row in the galleys till they died.*

bonny *adj.* °beautiful, °comely, °attractive, °pretty, °lovely: *She's grown into quite a bonny lass.*

bonus *n.* °reward, °largesse, hand-out, °perquisite, °extra, °honorarium, °tip, gratuity, °remuneration, compensation, *Colloq* °perk: *Employees often receive a Christmas bonus.*

book *n.* **1** °volume, tome, °work, °publication; hardcover, soft-cover, paperback: *Our personal library contains more than 5000 books.* **2** libretto, words, lyrics: *Richard Rodgers wrote the music and Oscar Hammerstein the book for several hit shows.* **3** °rules, °laws, °regulations: *He always insists that we go by the book.*
—*v.* **4** °engage, °reserve; earmark, ticket; °order, °register, °enrol, °list, °enlist, log, °record, °post: *Please phone the restaurant and book a table for four for seven-thirty.*

bookkeeper *n.* clerk; accountant, *Brit* chartered accountant, CA, cashier; *US* CPA, certified public accountant: *The office was haunted by the melancholy ghosts of departed bookkeepers.*

bookworm *n.* bibliophile, book-lover, inveterate *or* °ardent reader, *Formal* bibliophage: *Fiona is such a bookworm, she hardly does anything but read.*

boom *v.* **1** °sound, °resound, resonate, °blast, rumble, °thunder, °roar, bang, °explode: *We heard the cannons booming in the distance.* **2** °prosper, °thrive, °flourish, °progress, °grow, °increase, burgeon *or* bourgeon: *Business is booming in every sector.*
—*n.* **3** °blast, rumble, °explosion: *There was a resounding boom and the car went up in flames.* **4** °prosperity, profitability; °growth, °increase, burgeoning *or* bourgeoning: *In this business it is either boom or bust.*

boomerang *v.* °rebound, °recoil, backfire, °miscarry, redound: *His plan boomeranged.*

boon *n.* °gift, °favour, °award, °reward, gratuity, °present; °blessing, °benefit, °advantage: *The mobile library service is a great boon to the elderly in the area.*

boor *n.* **1** °rustic, °peasant, yokel, (°country) bumpkin, °provincial, backwoodsman, *US* hayseed, hill-billy, Juke, Kallikak, *Slang* hick: *The boor is blind to the beauties of nature.* **2** °barbarian, yahoo, oaf, °clod, clodhopper, °philistine, °clown, Grobian; hoyden, *Colloq* lummox, *Slang* galoot, °slob, *US* goop, slobbovian: *The guests behaved like boors, throwing their food at each other.*

boorish *adj.* °rustic, °barbarian, °rude, °crude, °ill-mannered, uncultured, °coarse, clownish, uncouth, loutish, oafish, gawky, °vulgar, ill-bred: *How can you even think of inviting such a boorish fellow?*

boost *n.* **1** °lift, shove *or* °push up *or* upward(s), *Colloq* °leg up; °rise, °raise: *If you give me a boost up, I can reach the window ledge.* **2** °encouragement, °help, °aid, °assistance, °support: *With a boost from your constituency, Trevor should win the vote.* **3** °increase, °rise, *US* °raise, hike: *He was given a slight boost in salary as an incentive to stay.*
—*v.* **4** °lift, shove *or* °push up *or* upward(s), °raise: *He boosted her over the fence. The second stage is intended to boost the rocket beyond the atmosphere.* **5** °encourage, °promote, °help, °aid, °support, °assist, °improve: *A talk from the manager before the game helped to boost the players' morale.* **6** °increase, °raise: *Her salary was boosted twice in one year.*

boot *n.* **1** ***to boot***: in °addition, into the °bargain, °besides, °moreover, as °well, also, too, additionally: *He's stingy and cruel—and ugly to boot.* **2** shoe, riding-boot, bootee: *I need a new pair of boots for my walking holiday.*
—*v.* **3** °eject, °expel, shove, °propel, °push, *Colloq* °kick: *The landlord booted three rowdies out of the pub.* **4** *Literary* profit, avail, °help, be in °aid of: *What boots it to complain?*

booth *n.* **1** °stall, °stand: *Our company has taken three booths at the book fair.* **2** °compartment, cubicle, °box, kiosk: *We walked across the road to a telephone booth and phoned a garage.*

bootless *adj.* °pointless, unavailing, °vain, °purposeless, °useless, °futile, °worthless, unproductive, °ineffective, °inefficacious, °fruitless, °unprofitable, profitless, unremunerative, unrewarding, °wasteful, time-wasting, Sisyphean: *It's a bootless task trying to persuade him of the importance of a good education.*

booty *n.* °plunder, °gain, °spoil(s), contraband, takings, °loot, *Slang* swag, boodle, (hot) °goods, °take: *The pirates fought over the booty seized from the Spanish galleon.*

booze *n.* **1** °drink, (°hard) °liquor, °spirit(s), °whisk(e)y, °alcohol, *US* demon rum, John Barleycorn, mountain dew, white lightning, white mule; *Slang* rot-gut, poison, fire-water, mother's ruin, *US and Canadian* sauce, juice, hooch, red-eye: *I ordered plenty of booze for the party.*
—*v.* **2** °drink, tipple; *Humorous* bibulate; *Slang* hit the °bottle, *US* hit the sauce: *He has a terrible hangover after boozing all night.*

border *n.* **1** °edge, °margin, hem, binding, trimming, °trim, edging, °periphery, purfle, purfling: *The border of the tablecloth is beautifully embroidered with flowers.* **2** Usually, ***borders***: °limit(s), °bound(s), confines: *Sometimes Tony exceeds the borders of good taste.* **3** °boundary, °frontier: *You won't be able to cross the border without a passport.* **4** °frame, frieze, moulding; dado, wainscot *or* wainscoting *or* wainscotting: *The border of the fresco is in Greek fretwork design.* **5** borderline, °edge, °verge, °brink: *She is just on the border of becoming a born-again Christian.* **6** bed, flowerbed, herbaceous °border: *Hollyhocks are growing in the border.*
—*v.* **7** °edge, °trim, °bind, °fringe, purfle: *The hem of the skirt is bordered with lace.* **8** °resemble (closely), °approach (closely), °verge upon *or* on: *Isabel's attempts at playing the tuba border on the ludicrous.* **9** °lie alongside, adjoin, abut (on *or* upon), °verge upon *or* on, °touch, be adjacent to: *The territory of the Gauls bordered the western lands of the Germans.*

bore[1] *n.* **1** °hole, drill-hole, borehole: *A bore of six inches was carried to a depth of 2086 feet.*
—*v.* **2** °pierce, °perforate, °drill, °penetrate, °puncture, °tap, °punch, °stab, °prick; °sink, °tunnel, °dig (out), °gouge (out); °hollow out: *Bore a hole through this sheet metal. The oil rig is boring through solid rock.*

bore[2] *n.* **1** °annoyance, °nuisance: *Reggie is such a bore—always talking about himself.*
—*v.* **2** °weary, °wear out, °tire, °exhaust, °jade: *The programme so bored me that I fell asleep.*

boredom *n.* dullness, dreariness, ennui, °tedium, monotony: *I have to look forward to the boredom of an evening of chamber music.*

boring *adj.* °dull, °monotonous, °tedious, °humdrum, °tiresome, °dreary, °flat, °dead, uninteresting, unexciting, ennuyant, °stale, °tired, °dry, dry-as-dust, arid; tiring, wearying, wearisome, °exhausting, soporific; °repetitious, °wordy, prolix, unending, long-drawn-out: *Felicity's boring old stories put me to sleep.*

borrow *v.* °take, °appropriate, °draw, °adopt, °refer to, °obtain, *Colloq* sponge, cadge, touch (someone) for, *US* °bum; *Slang* mooch: *Has Fred borrowed my lawnmower again?*

Borstal *n.* °youth °custody °centre, approved °school, *Now chiefly US* °reform °school, reformatory: *He was too young to go to prison, so he was sent to a Borstal.*

bosom *n.* **1** °breast, °chest, bust; *Slang* boobs, knockers, tits, titties, pair, jugs, *Brit* Bristols: *The sex goddess's lack of talent was more than compensated for by her ample bosom.* **2** °midst, °interior, °heart, °core, °centre: *She was welcomed into the bosom of the family as if she had been their own child.* **3** °soul, °heart, °heart of hearts, °bowels, blood, *Colloq* °gut: *I know he loves me, I can feel it in my bosom.*
—*adj.* **4** °close, °intimate, °dear, °beloved, cherished, °boon, °special, °confidential: *We were once bosom companions.*

bosomy *adj.* big-busted, busty, well-endowed: *This tabloid always has a bosomy model on page 3.*

boss *n.* **1** °chief, °supervisor, °head, administrator, °manager, °foreman, °superintendent, °overseer; °employer, °director, °proprietor, °owner, *Brit* managing director, *US* president, *Dialect* himself, *Colloq* supremo, *Brit* governor, gov., gaffer, *US* °super, °leader, kingpin, °big cheese, the °man, *Slang* honcho, °head *or* °chief honcho, Mr Big, prex *or* prexy: *If you have to leave early, check with the boss. The company boss was interviewed on television last night.*
—*v.* **2** °supervise, °head, °manage, °run, °oversee, °overlook, °direct, °control, superintend, °command, take °charge, be in °charge: *Clive has been here only a year and he's already bossing a department.* **3** domineer, °push *or* shove around *or* about, °dominate, °order about, °lord it over: *That slave-driver had better stop bossing me about or I'll quit!*

bossy *adj.* °overbearing, °domineering, °dictatorial, °tyrannical, °despotic, imperious, lordly: *Her boyfriend is awfully bossy—and they're not even married yet.*

botch *v.* °bungle, mismanage, °spoil, *Colloq* °screw *or* louse up, °blow, °mess up, °muck up, make a °mess *or* °hash *or* °muddle of; *Slang* bollocks *or* ballocks *or US* bollix up: *Give Gordon an assignment and he's sure to botch it.*

bother *v.* **1** °annoy, °pester, °worry, °irritate, °trouble, hector, °harass, °hound, dog, °nag, °plague, needle, *Colloq* hassle; *Slang US* °nudge: *I wish they'd stop bothering me about paying the telephone bill.* **2** °trouble (about), °fuss (at), make a °fuss (about), °concern oneself (with), °burden: *Too few people are interested in bothering about the welfare of others.* **3** °confuse, °bewilder, °perplex, °perturb, °upset, disconcert, °discomfit: *She was increasingly bothered by her inability to understand the local language.*
—*n.* **4** °trouble, °inconvenience: *Those pets must be a lot of bother.* **5** °worry, °annoyance, vexation, °nuisance, irritation, °trouble, °effort, °disturbance, °upset, *Slang* hassle: *Painting the lattice will be more bother than it's worth.* **6** dither, °flutter, *Colloq* tizzy, °pet, °stew, °lather, °sweat: *She seems to have worked herself into quite a bother about something quite insignificant.* **7** °pest, irritant, °nag, °nuisance, *Colloq* °pain, °pain in the neck *or Brit taboo* arse or *US taboo* ass; *Slang US* °nudge: *Mother is such a bother, always asking if I wear my galoshes when it rains.* **8** °disturbance, to-do, ado, commotion, °fuss, °trouble, °disorder, °stir, hubbub: *We ran into a bit of bother at the pub last night.*

bottle *n.* **1** flask, container; decanter: *The milkman left two bottles of milk.* **2** °courage, °nerve, manliness, manfulness, °grit, °backbone, °gumption, mettle, °pluck, Dutch °courage, *Slang* guts; *Colloq* °spunk, starch, *US* moxie: *He was going to tell her off but lost his bottle at the last minute.* **3** ***the bottle***: °alcohol, °alcoholic °drink, °spirit(s), °liquor, °booze, sauce: *He's back on the bottle after only two weeks of being on the wagon.*
—*v.* **4** ***bottle up***: **a** °contain, °restrain, °hold back, °control, °suppress, °repress, °hold *or* keep in °check, °stifle: *All the emotions, bottled up for so long, burst upon him at once, and he wept pitiably.* **b** °trap, °cut off, hem in, °box in: *With the help of the posse, we can bottle up the gang in the canyon.*

bottom *n.* **1** °seat, °buttocks, °rear, behind, °rear end, backside, *derrière*, rump, °posterior, hindquarters, breech, fundament, gluteus maximus, *Colloq Brit* °bum, *US* hinie, can, duff, tush *or* tushy *or* tushie, tokus *or* tochis *or* tuchis, keister *or* keester, butt, *Taboo slang Brit* arse, *US* ass: *He just sits there on his bottom, never doing a bit of work.* **2** °base, foot, °foundation, °groundwork, substructure, °footing, underpinning, fundament: *A ditch was dug along the bottom of the wall.* **3** °basis, °foundation, °source, °origin, °cause, °heart, °nub: *We have to get to the bottom of the* *problem.* **4** depths, Davy Jones's locker; bed: *The ship sank to the bottom of the sea.* **5** ***at bottom***: basically, fundamentally, in the °final *or* °last analysis, °really, in °reality, °truly, in °truth, essentially: *Despite her behaviour at the party, at bottom she is very reserved.* **6** ***Bottoms up!*** Prosit!, To your (very good) health!, Cheers!, Here's to —!, Skol!: *Here's to the whole team—Bottoms up!*

bottomless *adj.* unfathomed, unfathomable, abyssal, °abysmal, °inexhaustible, °unlimited, °immeasurable, unplumbable: *The bottomless ignorance of the man is incredible.*

bounce *n.* **1** °bound, °leap, °hop, °recoil, ricochet, °rebound: *The ball took a bad bounce and the infielder missed it.* **2** °vitality, °energy, °verve, °zest, vivacity, liveliness, °animation, °dynamism, °life, *Colloq* °pep, zip, °go, get-up-and-go: *Betty has so much bounce, she is a bit tiring to have around.*
—*v.* **3** °bound, °rebound, °hop; °recoil, ricochet: *The ball bounced over the wall and into the river.*

bound[1] *n.* **1** Usually, ***bounds***: °boundary, boundary line, °limit(s), °extent, °border(s), confines: *Please try to keep the dogs within the bounds of the estate. Carl's plan is beyond the bounds of common sense.*
—*v.* **2** °limit, °restrict, confine, delimit, °define, circumscribe: *The river bounds the property on the east.*

bound[2] *n.* **1** °leap, °jump, vault, °spring; °bounce, °hop: *With a great bound, the dog was upon me.* **2** ***by leaps and bounds***: See **leap, 7,** below.
—*v.* **3** °leap, °jump, °hop, °spring, vault, gambol, °caper, romp, °frolic, °bounce, *Colloq* galumph: *The wolfhound came bounding towards me across the meadow.*

bound[3] *adj.* **1** tied, °fast, °fixed, fastened, confined, secured: *We were bound hand and foot and left in the cave.* **2** °obliged, obligated, required, constrained, °forced, compelled: *In the circumstances, Philippa was bound to do as she was told.* **3** °determined, resolved: *Otto is bound to go to the party if Antonia is going.* **4** °likely, °certain, °sure, °destined, predestined, °fated, °doomed: *He is bound to get the sack if he goes on turning up late.* **5** °destined, scheduled, booked; headed, directed: *We were bound for Cardiff.*

boundary *n.* °border(s), °limit(s), °frontier(s); °bound(s), confines, °perimeter: *If you cross that boundary, you will be safely in Switzerland.*

boundless *adj.* °limitless, unbounded, °unlimited; illimitable, °vast, °endless, unending, °infinite, °immense, °enormous, °immeasurable, incalculable, measureless, unrestricted, unchecked, °inexhaustible, unstoppable, unbridled, °uncontrolled, *Literary* vasty: *How can you keep up with a teenager's boundless energy?*

bountiful *adj.* **1** °generous, beneficent, munificent, °liberal, unsparing, unstinting, °charitable, eleemosynary, magnanimous, *Literary* bounteous: *We are grateful to Sir Roger, our most bountiful patron, for endowing this library.* **2** °ample, °abundant, plenteous, °plentiful, copious, °rich, *Literary* bounteous: *Until the Stock Exchange débâcle, these shares paid bountiful dividends.*

bounty *n.* **1** generosity, liberality, munificence, charitableness, °philanthropy, °charity, unselfishness, beneficence, goodness: *The poor used to be dependent on the bounty of the local gentry.* **2** °gift, °present, °largesse, °grant, °subsidy, °endowment, subvention: *People should be given work and not live off the bounty of the state.* **3** °reward, °award, °premium, °bonus, gratuity: *In America they paid a bounty of $50 for every dead wolf.*

bouquet *n.* **1** nosegay, posy, °bunch, °arrangement, °spray: *I sent her a bouquet of spring flowers for her birthday.* **2** °aroma, °scent, °odour, °fragrance, °perfume: *This '83 burgundy certainly has a fine bouquet.* **3** °compliment(s), °praise, commendation: *Mrs Campbell received many bouquets for her performances.*

bourgeois *adj.* **1** middle-class, °conventional, °philistine, capitalistic, propertied; °materialistic, °greedy, money-grubbing, money-hungry: *The yuppies constitute the modern bourgeois element in society.* **2** working-class, proletarian, °plebeian: *In his bourgeois mind, he had only his labour to offer.*

bout *n.* **1** °turn, °round, °time, °occasion, °spell, °period, °session: *He's just got over a bout of pneumonia.* **2** °chance, °spree, °stint, °opportunity, innings: *We had long planned this bout of shopping.* **3** °contest, °match, boxing-match, prizefight, °meet, set-to, °struggle, °encounter, °engagement; duel: *A bout has been arranged between the heavyweight champion of the world and a challenger from Puerto Rico.*

bow *n.* **1** °nod; curtsy *or* curtsey, salaam, °kowtow, genuflection, °prostration, °obeisance: *We all bowed respectfully before the emperor.*
—*v.* **2** °defer, °yield, °submit, °give in, °bend, °bow down, °capitulate: *I bow to your greater knowledge of the subject.* **3** °bend, °incline, °lower: *The servants bowed their heads when the master entered.* **4** °weigh down, °crush, °overload, °bend down, °burden: *Michael was bowed down by the responsibilities of his new family.* **5** °nod, curtsy *or* curtsey, salaam, °kowtow, genuflect, °prostrate oneself, °make °obeisance: *The natives bowed as the king passed by.*

bowels *n.* °interior, insides, depths; °heart, °centre, °core, intestines, viscera, vitals, belly, °gut, *Colloq* innards, guts: *We descended the shaft into the very bowels of the earth. She hates me, I can feel it in my bowels.*

bowl[1] *v.* °move, trundle, °wheel, °roll, °spin: *We saw him in his car, bowling along at about 40.*

bowl[2] *n.* dish; basin, °pan: *She brought me a bowl of cereal.*

box[1] *n.* **1** °case, °receptacle, crate, carton, container, °casket, coffer, caddy, °chest: *She keeps her valuables in a small tortoise-shell box on the dressing-table.*
—*v.* **2** crate, encase, °package: *The candles are boxed in dozens.* **3** ***box in*** *or* ***up***: °trap, confine, °bottle up, hem in, °enclose, °surround; °pin down: *They have the horses boxed in and are now driving them into the corral.*

box[2] *v.* **1** °fight, °engage in fisticuffs, °spar, °battle: *When he was in the army, he boxed for his regiment.* **2** °strike, buffet, °punch, °hit, *Colloq* slug, sock, whack, thwack, clout, °belt, thump, °lambaste, whomp: *Every time she heard him swear, she'd box his ears.*
—*n.* **3** °blow, buffet, °punch, °hit, °strike, *Colloq* slug, sock, whack, thwack, clout, °belt, thump, whomp: *How would you like a box on the ear, you young rascal!*

boy *n.* **1** °lad, °youth, °young °man, °stripling, youngster, schoolboy, °fellow, urchin, brat, *Colloq* kid, °guy, small fry, little shaver: *There were two girls and five boys in my family.* **2** °servant, house-servant, °attendant; lackey, °slave, *Archaic* knave, varlet, °rogue, °wretch, caitiff: *Here! Boy! Bring me another gin and tonic.* **3** ***old boy***: *Brit* (public) schoolmate; °friend, °chum, °pal, *Archaic* old bean, old egg, old crumpet, dear boy; crony: *I say, old boy, care for a rubber of bridge? Carruthers wouldn't be where he is now if it weren't for the old-boy network.*

boycott *v.* **1** blacklist, °embargo; °avoid, °refuse, °shun, °reject, eschew, °pass over *or* by: *They are boycotting Fern's Dairy because it won't hire women. The US government is still boycotting cigars from Havana.*
—*n.* **2** °embargo, blacklist, blacklisting, °ban: *A boycott of their products soon forced them to change their policies.*

boyish *adj.* **1** °young, youthful, °juvenile, °adolescent: *She liked his boyish good looks.* **2** °childish, °puerile, °juvenile, °immature: *Don't be too hard on them—it was just a boyish prank.*

brace *n.* **1** °bracket, stiffener, °reinforcement, reinforcer, °support, °buttress, °prop, °stay, °strut, truss: *Two steel braces have been installed to steady the columns.* **2** °drill: *He bored three holes in the wood with his brace and auger.* **3** °clasp, °clamp, °buckle, fastener, °clip,

holdfast, °catch, coupler, coupling: *Another brace will be needed here to strengthen the handle.* **4** °pair; °couple, °span, °team (of two): *A brace of duelling pistols was sold at auction last week for £20,000. Her carriage was drawn by a brace of palominos.*
—*v.* **5** °steady, °reinforce, °support, °strengthen, °prop *or* shore up: *Iron bars are used to brace the arches.* **6** ***brace oneself***: °steady *or* gird *or* °prepare oneself; °hold *or* °hang on: *I braced myself against the likelihood that she would refuse.*

bracing *adj.* °invigorating, °tonic, °stimulating, °refreshing, °exhilarating, fortifying, restorative: *I cannot live in the tropics and need the more bracing climate of the north.*

bracket *n.* **1** °support, corbel, °console: *The mantelpiece rests on a pair of stone brackets.* **2** shelf: *Her collection of glass paperweights was arrayed on a bracket in the sitting-room.* **3** °category, °class, °set, °group, grouping, classification, °division, °level; °order, °grade, °rank: *He comes from an altogether different bracket of society.*
—*v.* **4** classify, °rank, °group; °unite, °combine, °join, °link: *I wish you wouldn't bracket her with me—our politics are as different as day and night.*

brag *v.* °boast, crow, trumpet, vaunt, °strut, °swagger, °show off, *Colloq* °talk °big, °blow *or* toot one's own horn *or* trumpet, °go on about: *He's always bragging about what he did in the war.*

braggart *n.* boaster, bragger, braggadocio, windbag, peacock, °show-off, Scaramouch *or* Scaramouche, *Slang* big-mouth, loud-mouth, gasbag: *That braggart William Smith talks about himself incessantly.*

braid *n.* **1** plait: *Katrina wore her blonde hair in a tightly coiled braid on top of her head.* **2** trimming, embroidery, soutache, °lace, fillet, °band, ribbon: *The edges are decorated with narrow braid containing gold thread.*
—*v.* **3** plait, intertwine, interlace, °weave, °twist: *At school we learned how to braid leather laces into a belt.*

brain *n.* **1** brains, °intelligence, °intellect, °understanding, °sense, °thought, °imagination, °capacity, perspicacity, perceptiveness, °perception, percipience; °wisdom, sagacity, °wit, discernment, acumen; °knowledge, cognition: *Although she's not yet ten, she has the brain to become a great mathematician.* **2** °genius, °mastermind, °intellectual; °leader, planner: *Many people regard Einstein as the greatest brain of the 20th century. Ivor was clearly the brains of the operation.*

brake *n.* **1** °curb, °check, °restraint, °restriction, constraint, °control, °rein: *The central bank applied a brake to the upward trend of the dollar by buying Deutschmarks.*
—*v.* **2** °slow, °slow up *or* down, °put on *or* °apply the brakes, °reduce °speed, decelerate, slacken, °hold up: *He braked before the bad curve. She braked the car going down the steep hill.*

branch *n.* **1** °offshoot, arm; limb, bough, °stem, °shoot, °twig, sprig: *The branches of this tree need trimming.* **2** °department, °section, subsection, °division, subdivision, °office, °part, °ramification; affiliate, °subsidiary; spin-off: *What branch of medicine are you going to specialize in? The company maintains branches in New York and Melbourne.*
—*v.* **3** ramify, °divide, subdivide, °diverge; °diversify: *This road branches off in three directions. The company will branch out into electronics this year.*

brand *n.* **1** °kind, °make, °type, °sort, °variety; brand °name, °manufacturer, maker, °trade °name, °trade °mark, °label, °mark, marque, *Chiefly US and Canadian* °name brand: *Which brand of toothpaste do you prefer? Our advertising agency is conducting a survey of brand loyalty.*
—*v.* **2** °mark, °stamp, °identify, °tag, °label, trademark: *We sell only branded merchandise in our shops.* **3** °label, °characterize; °stigmatize, °discredit, °disgrace: *Because his actions at the front were misinterpreted, Corporal Williams was branded as a coward.*

brand-new *adj.* °new, °unused, °fresh, firsthand, °mint, virgin: *We bought a brand-new car last week.*

brash *adj.* **1** °hasty, °rash, °impetuous, °precipitate, °impulsive, headlong, °reckless: *He may be a brash young man, but I think he's going places.* **2** °impudent, °rude, °impertinent, °disrespectful, °insolent, °forward, °audacious, °brassy, °brazen, °bold, °tactless, undiplomatic, °presumptuous, *Colloq* °cheeky, °fresh: *Her brash behaviour has already landed her in trouble with the headmistress.*

brass *n.* °effrontery, °gall, °nerve, temerity, °impudence, insolence, rudeness, *Colloq* cheek, °nerve: *He had the brass to turn down a knighthood.*

brassy *adj.* **1** °impudent, °forward, °insolent, saucy, °brash, °rude, °brazen, °shameless; °coarse, °flashy, florid, °flamboyant; *Colloq* °cheeky, °fresh: *Our landlady was a big brassy blonde.* **2** °harsh, °strident, °tinny, °grating, dissonant, °shrill, °loud: *She has just the right kind of brassy voice for belting out songs like, 'There's No Business Like Show Business'.*

bravado *n.* boldness, °bluster, boasting, braggadocio, °swagger, °front, self-assurance, *Literary* rodomontade, gasconade; °arrogance, pretentiousness, *Colloq* °machismo, *Slang Brit* °side: *With an attempt at bravado, the union leader refused to meet the management representatives.*

brave *adj.* **1** °fearless, °intrepid, °bold, °courageous, °daring, °gallant, °stout, stout-hearted, valiant, valorous, °stalwart, plucky, °staunch, undaunted, °dauntless, unafraid, unfearing, °indomitable, °heroic, *Colloq* °macho; *Slang* gutsy: *Despite her misgivings about her proposal, she put on a brave face in the boardroom. He was brave to face the enemy alone.* **2** °fine, °handsome, °grand, °splendid, °showy, colourful, spectacular, °smart: *The colonel made a brave appearance in full Highland regalia.*
—*v.* **3** °challenge, °defy, °dare; °brazen (out), °face, confront, °encounter, °meet: *We had to brave the elements in the open boat. I had to brave my father at breakfast.*

bravery *n.* °daring, °courage, valour, heroism, °fortitude, fearlessness, intrepidity, intrepidness, °pluck, °determination, staunchness, firmness, resoluteness, °resolution, indomitability, stalwartness, *Colloq* °machismo: *One has to admire the bravery of a woman who supported suffrage in the early 1900s.*

brawl *n.* **1** °fight, mêlée *or* melee, °battle, °battle royal, Donnybrook, °fray, wrangle, °dispute, °disorder, brannigan, °fracas, °row, °quarrel, squabble, *Colloq* punch-up, free-for-all, °scrap, ruckus: *The police had to be brought in to break up the brawl.*
—*v.* **2** °fight, wrangle; °row, °quarrel, squabble, *Colloq* °scrap: *The two brothers always seem to be brawling.*

brawn *n.* muscle(s), °strength, robustness, brawniness, °might, °power, *Colloq* huskiness: *It must take a lot of brawn to lift those weights.*

brawny *adj.* °muscular, °strong, °tough, °robust, °mighty, °powerful, °burly, strapping, beefy, °hefty, °bulky, *Colloq* °husky: *That brawny fellow tossing the caber is my brother.*

brazen *adj.* °brassy, °shameless, °barefaced, °brash, °outspoken, °forward, °immodest, unashamed, °audacious, °candid, °open, °unabashed, brazen-faced; °rude, °impudent, °impertinent, °insolent, saucy, *Colloq* °cheeky, °fresh, *US* sassy: *That's the last time I'll let that brazen hussy near my husband!*

breach *n.* **1** °break, °violation, infraction, disobedience, non-observance, °infringement, contravention: *Their failure to comply with paragraph 3 is a clear breach of our contract.* **2** °break, °rift, °gulf, °split, break-up, °separation, °rupture, severance, °schism, alienation, estrangement: *There seems to be no way to heal the breach between them.* **3** °gap, fissure, °crack, °split, °hole, °opening; chasm: *Their cannon opened a breach in the castle wall.*
—*v.* **4** °rupture; °break through, invade: *The sea has breached the dyke. Someone breached the security measures set up for the missile design.*

breadth *n.* **1** °width, wideness, broadness, °beam, °span, °spread, thickness: *The breadth of the cloth is 54in.* **2** °extent, °magnitude, °degree, °amount, °scope, °expanse, °range, °area, °depth, °detail: *I like the breadth of coverage of the six o'clock news.* **3** liberality, largeness, catholicity, latitude: *Great breadth of vision was exhibited in the conference papers.*

break *v.* **1** break °apart *or* up *or* asunder, °fracture, °rupture, break into bits, °come apart, °shatter, °shiver, °crack, °crash, °splinter, °fragment, °split, °burst, °explode, *Colloq* bust: *The ball flew over the fence and broke my neighbour's window. She fell and broke her wrist.* **2** °reveal, °announce, °disclose, divulge, °tell, make °public: *Break the news to him gently.* **3** °relax, °ease up, °improve, ameliorate, °change for the better: *When will this spell of wet weather break?* **4** °demolish, smash, °destroy, °crush, °ruin, °defeat, °foil, °frustrate: *The power of the dictator was finally broken.* **5** °ruin, bankrupt: *He's the man that broke the bank at Monte Carlo.* **6** °weary, °exhaust, °wear out, °weaken, debilitate: *Twenty years in the chain-gang had broken him completely.* **7** °crush, °overcome; cow, °cripple, °demoralize, °weaken, °undermine, °discourage: *The divorce has broken her spirit.* **8** break in, °tame, °discipline, °train, °condition: *I used to break horses for a living.* **9** °violate, °transgress, °disobey, contravene, °defy, °infringe, fail to observe, °ignore, °disregard, °flout: *If you break the law, you'll regret it. They broke the contract.* **10** break off, °discontinue, °interrupt, °sever, °cut off; °give up, °suspend, °disrupt: *We broke relations with Spain after the incident. It is very difficult to break a habit of a lifetime. The narrative breaks at this point, to be taken up later.* **11** break up, °divide, °disperse, °scatter: *The rain is over and the clouds are breaking.* **12** break °loose *or* away *or* forth, °separate from, break out (of), °escape (from), °depart (from): *The ship broke from its moorings during the storm.* **13** break forth, °burst forth; °emerge *or* °come out °suddenly: *The storm broke in all its fury. After a little while, the sun broke through.* **14** demote, *Colloq* bust: *He was broken from sergeant to private.* **15** ***break away***: °leave, °depart, °separate (oneself): *A small group broke away from the established church to worship as they saw fit.* **16** ***break down***: **a** °demolish, °destroy: *All right, men, let's break down that wall.* **b** °decompose, break up; °analyse: *The carbon dioxide molecules and water are broken down by photosynthesis.* **c** °collapse, give °way, °disintegrate, be crushed, be prostrated: *His health has broken down completely.* **17** ***break ground***: °initiate, °begin, °commence, °found, °set up, °establish, °inaugurate, be innovative, innovate, *Colloq* break the ice, take the °plunge, °start the ball rolling: *Laser printers have broken new ground in the area of computer printout.* **18** ***break in***: **a** °interrupt, interpose, interject, °burst in, °intrude, °intervene, °interfere, °disturb: *If the results of the election become known, we shall break in to keep you informed.* **b** °train, °educate, °prepare; °accustom, °condition, habituate, °wear: *We'll break you in for a week or two on the new machine. Wear your new boots for an hour each day to break them in.* **c** °rob, burgle, burglarize, break and °enter: *Someone broke in and stole my video recorder last night.* **19** ***break off***: **a** °discontinue, °stop, °cease, °end: *Sally broke off in mid sentence. After the Fashoda Incident, Britain broke off relations with France.* **b** °disengage; °sever, °detach, °break: *A large branch broke off from the tree and crashed down, narrowly missing me.* **20** ***break out***: **a** °escape; °emerge, °appear: *She broke out of prison in 1985 and hasn't been seen since.* **b** °erupt, °come out in, break out in *or* into: *He breaks out in a rash from eating strawberries. A war could break out any minute.* **21** ***break the ice***: See **17,** above. **22** ***break through***: °penetrate, °force *or* °get through: *Wit, like beauty, can break through the most unpromising disguise.* **23** ***break up***: See also **11, 16 b,** above. **a** disband, disperse; disintegrate: *Heraclius succeeded in breaking up the Persian power.* **b** °fracture, °fragment, comminute: *In the spring, the ice on the river breaks up.* **c** See **24 a,** below. **24** ***break with***: **a** break up (with), °separate from, °leave, °depart from: *The leader broke with the party and established a new organization. Sally has broken up with Michael.* **b** °renounce, °repudiate, disavow: *They have broken entirely with the traditions we valued so highly.* —*n.* **25** °fracture, °split, °separation, °rupture, °breach, °rift, °schism: *There was a break in a gas pipe. Disagreement over the fishing grounds has resulted in a break in relations.* **26** °gap, °opening, °hole; °crack, °slit: *You can escape through a break in the wall near the bridge.* **27** °interruption, discontinuity, discontinuation, hesitation, °suspension, hiatus, °gap, lacuna, unevenness, irregularity: *There was a five-minute break in transmission from the ship.* **28** °rest, °respite, °rest °period, coffee-break, tea break, °intermission, °interlude, °lull, °pause, playtime, *US* °recess, *Colloq* breather: *We take a break at ten o'clock.* **29** °chance, stroke of luck, °opportunity, °opening: *All he needs is a break to get started.*

breakdown *n.* **1** °collapse, °downfall, °failure, foundering; °destruction, °ruin: *There was a breakdown of our computer system. The arbitrators blamed a breakdown of communication between union and management.* **2** (°mental) °collapse, °nervous breakdown, *Colloq* crack-up: *She had a bad breakdown after her daughter was killed.* **3** °analysis, °run-down, detailing, °review; decomposition, itemization, classification, dissection, distillation, fractionation: *I want a breakdown of these figures by noon. The chemical breakdown of the substance indicated the presence of arsenic.*

breakneck *adj.* °reckless, °dangerous, °daredevil; °excessive, °careless, headlong, °rash, *Colloq* hell for leather: *The car came round the corner at breakneck speed on two wheels.*

breast *n.* **1** °chest, °bosom, bust; teat, *Technical* mamma, *Slang* boob, knocker, tit, titty: *He clasped the child to his breast. On some beaches in Europe, women bare their breasts when sunbathing.* **2** °soul, °core, °heart, °heart of hearts: *I feel in my breast it is the right thing to do.*

breath *n.* **1** °gust, zephyr, °breeze, °puff, whiff, °stirring, °stir: *There wasn't a breath of air in the tent.* **2** °hint, °suggestion, °indication, °touch, °murmur, °whisper, soupçon: *She never allowed the breath of scandal to affect her behaviour.* **3** ***take one's breath away***: °astound, °astonish, °surprise, °amaze, °dazzle, °startle, °shock, °stagger: *The sheer beauty of the waterfall takes your breath away.*

breathe *v.* **1** °live, °exist: *She believes that there never breathed a wiser man than her father.* **2** °inhale and °exhale, respire, suspire: *He was breathing regularly.* **3** °exhale, °expel, °puff, °blow: *The banner depicts a dragon breathing fire.* **4** °whisper, °murmur, °hint (at), °suggest, °tell, °speak, °say: *She told me not to breathe a word of it to anybody.*

breathless *adj.* **1** panting, out of °breath, winded, gasping, °exhausted, °spent, °worn out, °tired out, *Colloq Brit* puffed: *We were breathless after carrying the piano up two flights of stairs.* **2** surprised, amazed, astonished, astounded, awestruck, staggered: *The news of Penny's having given birth to twins left me breathless.* **3** °eager, °agog, °feverish, in °suspense: *We were all breathless with anticipation as the compère opened the envelope.*

breed *n.* **1** °kind, °sort, °type, °variety, species; °race, °lineage, °stock, °family, °strain: *What breed of dog won at Crufts this year?* —*v.* **2** °produce, °generate, °bring forth, °create, engender, °hatch, beget, give °rise to, °develop, °cause: *The cheese is so old it's breeding maggots. Familiarity breeds contempt.* **3** °raise, °rear, °cultivate, °propagate: *Charollais cattle are widely bred in Europe today.* **4** °arise, °originate, °appear; °develop, °grow, °increase, multiply: *The sergeant allowed discontent and jealousy to breed within his platoon.*

breeding *n.* **1** rearing, bringing-up, raising, cultivation, °development, propagation: *The breeding of* *sheepdogs has been Tom's hobby for years.* **2** (good) °upbringing, (good) °manners, °civility, politeness, politesse, gentility, (good) °behaviour: *You can tell from the way she treats people that she has breeding.*

breeze *n.* **1** °breath, °puff, zephyr, °wind, °draught, °gust, *Nautical* cat's-paw: *A breeze sprang up from the north, and the little boat moved forward.* **2** °easy *or* °simple °job *or* °task, °nothing, *Colloq* °snap, *Slang* cinch, *US* lead-pipe cinch: *It ought to be a breeze to find someone at that salary.*

breezy *adj.* **1** airy, °fresh, °windy, draughty, °brisk, gusty: *The afternoon was breezy and warm, ideal for walking.* **2** °casual, °carefree, light-hearted, °cheerful, cheery, airy, °lively, °spirited, blithesome, °buoyant: *The chairman's breezy opening of the annual meeting made everyone feel comfortable.*

brevity *n.* shortness, briefness, conciseness, concision, terseness, succinctness, pithiness, compactness, laconicism *or* laconism, °economy: *Brevity is the soul of wit.*

brew *v.* **1** °ferment, cook, °boil; infuse: *Our beer is brewed using the best hops.* **2** concoct, °devise, °plan, *Colloq* cook up; contrive, °prepare, °bring about, °cause, °produce, °hatch: *They are brewing up a plot to unseat the financial director.* **3** °start, °go on, °hatch, °begin, °form; °stew, °simmer, *Colloq* cook: *A storm is brewing.*
—*n.* **4** beer, ale, stout; tea; beverage, °drink; concoction, °mixture: *She served me some strange brew in which I could detect cinnamon and nutmeg.*

bribe *n.* **1** °graft, °inducement, *Colloq* °kickback, *Chiefly US* payola, *US* plugola: *Some judges were offered bribes for reducing the sentences of convicted felons.*
—*v.* **2** °pay *or* °buy off, °buy; °corrupt, suborn, *Colloq* °fix; *Slang* °oil, grease (someone's) palm, *Brit* nobble: *The guards were bribed to look the other way during the prison break.*

bric-à-brac *n.* bric-a-brac, °curiosities, knick-knacks, collectables *or* collectibles, trinkets, °gewgaws, gimcracks; bibelots, curios, objets d'art, objets de vertu: *On Saturday she went to an antiques fair and bought still more bric-à-brac to clutter up the house.*

brick *n.* **1** °block, cube, chunk, hunk, °slab; stone: *I bought a brick of ice-cream to serve for pudding. A university is not just bricks and mortar.* **2** °pal, °comrade, °friend, *Colloq* °chum, *US and Canadian* buddy: *You're a real brick to watch the children for me till I get back.*

bridal *adj.* °nuptial, °wedding; conjugal, connubial, °marriage: *The bridal gown was white, with lace appliqués.*

bridge *n.* **1** °span: *We could build a bridge over the river here.* **2** °link, connexion *or* °connection, °tie, °bond: *She regarded teaching as a bridge between her studies and a post in school administration.*
—*v.* **3** °span, °cross (over), °go *or* °pass over, °traverse: *The viaduct bridges the swamp.* **4** °connect, °link, °unite, °join, °tie: *The gap between rich and poor is not easily bridged.*

bridle *n.* **1** °restraint, °curb, °check, °control: *Man has need of a bridle on his passions.*
—*v.* **2** °curb, °check, °restrain, °hold in, °control: *You must learn to bridle your temper.* **3** °bristle, draw oneself up, be *or* become °indignant, take °offence *or* °umbrage *or* affront (at), be affronted *or* offended (by): *She bridled at the suggestion that she was responsible for Keith's departure.*

brief *adj.* **1** °short, °momentary, °little, °fleeting; °short-lived, transitory, °transient, evanescent, °passing, °temporary, ephemeral, °fugitive: *The lights went back on after a brief interval. His glory was brief.* **2** °short, °concise, °succinct, to the °point; condensed, shortened, °cut, curtailed, °abbreviated, compressed, abridged, °thumbnail, compendious: *The chairman made a few brief remarks. Here is a brief description of what happened.* **3** °curt, °abrupt, °terse, °short, °blunt, °brusque: *You mustn't be so brief with little children.*
—*n.* **4** °summary, °outline, °digest, °précis, résumé, compendium, °abstract, condensation, °abridgement °synopsis, °extract: *This is merely a brief; the full document will follow.* **5 in brief**: °briefly, concisely, in °sum, in °summary, to °sum up, succinctly, in a °word: *He is a cutthroat, too—in brief, the greatest scoundrel living.*
—*v.* **6** °advise, °inform, °fill in, °coach, °instruct, °enlighten; °explain, °run through *or* down: *Howard will brief you on the details.*

briefly *adv.* **1** concisely, tersely, succinctly, in a °word, in °short; bluntly, curtly, in a nutshell, in a °few words, to °sum up: *Briefly, the plan is a complete non-starter.* **2** momentarily, for a °few moments *or* seconds *or* minutes, fleetingly, hurriedly, °hastily, °quickly: *I stopped briefly at the post office on my way home.*

bright *adj.* **1** °light, shining, gleaming, °radiant, °brilliant, resplendent, glittering, flashing, *Formal* refulgent, effulgent, fulgent, fulgid, fulgorous; alight, aglow, beaming, °dazzling, °glowing, °luminous, lambent, °incandescent, °ablaze with: *We arrived on a bright, sunny day. The water was bright with phosphorescence.* **2** °clear, cloudless, °fair, unclouded: *It certainly is a bright night—you can see every star.* **3** °shiny, °polished, °lustrous, °glossy, sparkling: *I want that brass so bright I can see my face in it.* **4** °hopeful, °optimistic, °favourable, °propitious, auspicious, °promising, °rosy: *Glenys's job prospects are not very bright.* **5** °brilliant, °vivid, °intense, fluorescent, *US trade mark* Day-Glo: *But you said you wanted the room bright orange, Madam.* **6** °intelligent, °clever, °quick-witted, °witty, °brilliant, keen-minded, sharp-witted, °gifted, °astute, °ingenious, °alert, °smart; °precocious; *Colloq* brainy, on the ball: *No one can deny that Alison is a bright young woman.* **7** °illustrious, °glorious, °splendid, °magnificent, °distinguished, °outstanding: *Today has been one of the brightest days in the history of Britain.* **8** °cheerful, °gay, °happy, °exuberant, °lively, °animated, °vivacious, °spirited: *It is a pleasure to see so many bright faces in the audience.*

brighten *v.* **1** °illuminate, °enliven, °lighten, °cheer up, °liven up, *Colloq* °perk up: *Replacing those heavy draperies with thinner curtains ought to brighten the room.* **2** °shine, °polish, burnish: *The silver could use a bit of brightening up.*

brilliance *n.* **1** brightness, °radiance, °lustre, °splendour, magnificence, °sparkle, °dazzle, °glitter, effulgence, °light: *The brilliance of the opening night rivalled that of Hollywood.* **2** °intelligence, °wit, °intellect, keenness, sharpness, acuteness, °genius, °talent, sagacity; precocity: *Her brilliance shows in her books.*

brilliant *adj.* **1** °bright, shining, °lustrous, °radiant, resplendent, °dazzling, °luminous; °incandescent, glittering, sparkling, °scintillating, coruscating, °twinkling, *Formal* effulgent: *At the show I saw the most brilliant display of diamonds.* **2** °splendid, °magnificent, °superb, °beautiful, °distinguished, °striking, °glorious, °remarkable, °exceptional, °outstanding: *The audience rose for a standing ovation after the brilliant last movement of the concerto.* **3** °illustrious, °famous, °noted, °celebrated, °eminent, °prominent, °renowned, °accomplished: *Paul is one of the country's most brilliant chemists.* **4** °intelligent, °clever, °gifted, °bright, °talented, °smart, °expert, °masterful, °accomplished, °ingenious, °imaginative, °creative; °quick-witted, sharp-witted, keen-witted, °enlightened; °resourceful, discerning, °able, °competent: *Goddard's brilliant mind understood principles of practical rocket flight.*

brim *n.* **1** °edge, °margin, lip, °rim; °brink: *I filled the cup to the brim.*
—*v.* **2** be °full *or* filled, overflow: *His cup was brimming with steaming mulled wine. They are brimming over with confidence as they approach the race.*

bring *v.* **1** °carry, °bear, °fetch, °get, °take; °deliver: *Don't forget to bring some wine home for dinner tonight.* **2** °lead, °conduct, convey; °escort, invite, °accompany: *The road brought me to your house. You can bring anyone you like to the party.* **3** °draw,

°attract, °lure, allure: *What brings you to London?* **4** °carry, °bear, convey; °report: *She brought word of the uprising.* **5** bring on, bring about, °occasion, give °rise to, be the °source *or* °cause of, °create, °cause, engender, °produce; °contribute to: *The thought of his mother brought tears to his eyes.* **6** °institute, °advance; invoke: *She is bringing charges against him for slander.* **7** ***bring about***: °occasion, °cause, bring on, °accomplish, °effect, °achieve, °produce: *The government has brought about changes in the health service.* **8** ***bring down***: **a** °overthrow, depose, oust, unseat, dethrone, °overturn, °topple: *A military faction has brought down the government.* **b** °reduce, lessen, °diminish, °cut (back *or* down): *The chancellor promised to bring down taxes in the next budget.* **9** ***bring forth***: **a** °bear, °give °birth to, °produce; °yield: *The kangaroo brings forth young less than an inch in size.* **b** °set forth, bring out *or* in *or* up, °introduce, °present, °produce, °put out, °submit, °offer, °advance: *Mr Hanson has brought forth a new sales plan.* **10** ***bring in***: **a** °earn, °yield, °produce, °realize, °fetch, °return, °sell for: *Advertising brings in more revenue than subscriptions.* **b** See **15,** below. **11** ***bring off***: °succeed (in), °achieve, °accomplish, do, °carry out *or* off, °perform, °pull off; *Colloq* °put over: *Do you really think she'll be able to bring off her masquerade?* **12** ***bring on***: **a** °produce, °put on, °introduce, bring in: *When the children in the audience began to get restless, they brought on the clowns.* **b** °induce, °produce, °occasion, bring about: *Eating strawberries brought on a rash.* **13** ***bring out***: **a** °display, °feature, °focus on, °illuminate, °set off, °make °noticeable *or* °conspicuous, °emphasize, °develop: *The colour of the dress brings out the blue of your eyes.* **b** °publish, °issue, °release, make known *or* °public, °produce; °put on, °stage: *They've brought out a new edition of Dickens's works.* **14** ***bring round*** or ***around***: **a** °revive, resuscitate, bring to; °restore: *The smelling salts brought her round when she fainted.* **b** °persuade, °win over, °convince, °influence: *Can he be brought round to our way of thinking?* **15** ***bring up***: **a** °rear, °raise, °care for, °look after, nurture, °breed; °educate, °teach, °train, °tutor: *She has brought up six children on her own.* **b** °introduce, °broach, bring in, °raise, °pen (up), °set forth, °mention, °touch on, °talk about, °discuss; reintroduce, °recall: *Why bring up irrelevant matters like his age?* **c** °raise, elevate: *So far, they have brought up only three survivors from the mine.* **d** °vomit, °throw up, °regurgitate, disgorge: *He woke up feeling sick and brought up most of the previous night's meal.*

brink *n.* **1** °edge, °brim, °rim, °margin, lip, °border: *He lost his footing and almost went over the brink into the gorge.* **2** °verge, °point: *He was on the brink of telling them everything, but suddenly remembered his promise.*

brisk *adj.* **1** °active, °lively, °busy, °vigorous: *The poachers are doing a brisk trade in rhinoceros horn.* **2** quick, °animated, °sprightly, spry, °energetic, °spirited: *Patrick was a brisk lad, fresh from Oxford.* **3** °strong, °steady, °fresh, °refreshing, °bracing, °invigorating, °stimulating, °crisp, °biting, °bracing, °keen, nippy, °chill, °chilly, °cool, °cold: *A brisk breeze had started up from the north, chilling us through.* **4** °energetic, vibrant, °invigorating, °stimulating: *After a brisk massage, Mariette felt completely revitalized.*

bristle *n.* **1** °hair, whisker, barb, °prickle, °thorn, quill, *Technical* seta: *Shaving brushes are often made from badger bristles.*
—*v.* **2** °prickle, °rise, °stand up, *Formal* horripilate: *He could feel the hair on the back of his neck bristle.* **3** °seethe, °become °angry *or* infuriated *or* °furious *or* maddened, °boil, °flare up, see red, °bridle: *He bristled with enraged frustration.* **4** °teem, °crawl, be °thick, °swarm, be °alive: *The sea urchin was bristling with sharp spines.*

brittle *adj.* **1** °fragile, frangible, breakable; friable: *My fingernails become brittle in the cold and break easily.* **2** °frail, °weak, °delicate, °sensitive, °fragile, °insecure: *She might seem strong, but she has a very brittle nature and is easily upset.*

broach *v.* °introduce, °raise, °open (up), °suggest, °mention, °hint at, °touch on *or* upon, °bring up *or* in, °talk about, °advance: *I didn't dare broach the subject of money.*

broad *adj.* **1** °wide, °expansive, °large, °extensive; °spread out, °ample, °spacious: *The broad highway stretched out for miles before them. Cattle graze in the broad pastures.* **2** °bright, °plain, °open, °full; unshaded: *He had the nerve to kiss me in broad daylight, in front of everyone!* **3** °plain, °clear, °obvious, °emphatic, °explicit, °pronounced, °direct, unconcealed, °undisguised, unsubtle, °evident: *His wink gave a broad hint of what he really had in mind.* **4** °main, °general, generalized, °rough, unspecific, non-specific, °approximate, °sweeping: *Without the details, here is a broad outline of what happened.* **5** plain-spoken, °outspoken, °forthright, °direct, unreserved, °frank, °candid, unrestrained: *When he reached the witness box, he repeated the accusation in broad terms.* **6** °inclusive, °general, °widely applicable, °extensive, wide-ranging, °comprehensive, wholesale; °vague, °imprecise, °indefinite, unfocused, non-specific, unspecified: *We have broad support for these policies. She formulated a broad rule to fit all imaginable cases.* **7** °liberal, °tolerant, °catholic, ecumenical, latitudinarian: *The term 'Broad Church' is said to have been coined by A. H. Clough. The judge feels that he must give the broadest possible interpretation of the law.* **8** °dirty, °blue, °coarse, °rude, °indecent, °vulgar, °improper, indelicate, off colour, °loose, °gross, °obscene, °lewd, °lascivious, °filthy, °pornographic; inelegant, °unrefined, unladylike, ungentlemanly, titillating: *Peter was in the corner telling some of his broad jokes.*
—*n.* **9** °woman, °girl, *Slang* dame, cookie *or* cooky, skirt, bimbo, bird, chick, °number, doll, piece (of baggage): *We picked up a couple of broads at the dance-hall last night.*

broadcast *v.* **1** °air, °transmit, relay; °radio; televise, telecast: *The programme will be broadcast tonight.* **2** °announce, advertise, °publish, °proclaim; disseminate: *It may be a bad idea to broadcast your plans in advance.* **3** °sow, °scatter, °seed: *The farmer broadcasts this seed instead of planting it.*
—*n.* **4** °programme, °show; °transmission, telecast: *I heard the broadcast on my car radio.*

brochure *n.* °pamphlet, booklet; catalogue; folder, °leaflet; °tract: *The brochure advertising the company's products will be ready tomorrow.*

broil *v.* grill, barbecue: *I think hamburgers taste better broiled than fried.*

broke *adj.* penniless, °indigent, down-and-out, poverty-stricken, °penurious, °impoverished, °insolvent, °destitute, °poor, °needy, bankrupt, ruined, *Colloq* on one's beam-ends, on one's uppers, strapped, °flat *or* °dead *or* stony-broke, °hard up, °short, up against it, *US* °flat, on the skids; *Slang Brit* skint: *I was broke after paying the rent—I didn't even have money for food.*

broken *adj.* **1** fragmented, shattered, shivered, splintered, ruptured, cracked, °split, smashed, pulverized, disintegrated, destroyed, demolished: *A broken Ming vase cannot be worth much.* **2** fractured: *With a broken leg, she certainly won't be competing in the slalom.* **3** enfeebled, weakened, crushed, defeated, beaten, ruined; dispirited, °dejected, discouraged, demoralized, °subdued, debilitated, *Colloq* licked: *Rosa's running away with a sailor left Hugh a broken man.* **4** tamed, trained, disciplined, °obedient, docile, domesticated, °subdued; conditioned: *What use is a horse that isn't broken?* **5** violated, transgressed, disobeyed, contravened, defied, flouted, disregarded, ignored, infringed: *The rules of this club are broken too often: we'll have to tighten things up.* **6** interrupted, °disturbed, discontinuous, °disjointed, °disconnected, fragmented, °fragmentary, °intermittent, °erratic, °sporadic: *I couldn't stop worrying about the operation and had a terrible night of broken sleep.* **7** Also, ***broken-down***: out of °order *or* commission, not working *or* functioning, in °disrepair, *Slang* on the °blink, out of kilter, kaput, *US* on the fritz, out of whack: *My watch is broken. Why waste money repairing that broken-down car of yours?*

broken-hearted *adj.* heartbroken, depressed, °downhearted, °dejected, devastated, crushed, overwhelmed, heartsick, downcast, °upset; °forlorn, °sorrowful, disconsolate, °inconsolable, grief-stricken, °miserable, °wretched, °melancholy, heavy-hearted, °sad, °doleful, dolorous, woeful, °woebegone, °gloomy, morose, °glum, cheerless, *Colloq* down: *She was broken-hearted when her puppy was lost.*

broker *n.* stockbroker; °agent, °dealer, middleman, °intermediary, °go-between, *Brit* stockjobber: *I have phoned my broker to tell him to sell all my shares.*

brooch *n.* °clasp, °pin; °fastening: *She was wearing the cameo brooch I had given to her mother.*

brood *n.* **1** °young, °offspring, °progeny; children, °family: *A mallard was tending her brood among the rushes.*
—*v.* **2** °incubate, °hatch, °set, °sit, °cover: *The old hen was brooding three eggs.* **3** Also, ***brood on*** *or* ***over***: °ponder (on *or* over), °meditate (on *or* over), °contemplate, ruminate (on *or* over), °muse (on *or* over): *He just sits there brooding over the subject of his next novel.* **4** mope, °sulk, °pout, pine, eat one's heart out, °fret, °worry, agonize, °despair: *Don't just brood over the problem, do something about solving it!*

brook[1] *n.* °stream, rivulet, °run, runnel, rill, *US and Canadian and Australian and New Zealand* °creek; *No. Eng. dialect* beck, gill *or* ghyll; *Scots* burn: *The river is fed by numerous brooks from every part of the country.*

brook[2] *v.* °endure, °tolerate, °stand, °abide, °put up with, °suffer, °allow: *She runs the business in her own way and brooks no interference from anyone.*

broth *n.* °stock, bouillon, consommé; soup; decoction: *We tossed food scraps into the large, simmering pot to make a broth.*

brothel *n.* bordello, whore-house, °house of °ill fame *or* °ill repute, bawdy-house, bagnio; seraglio, harem, *Obsolete* °stew, *Colloq US* sporting °house, *Slang Brit* knocking-shop, *US* cat-house: *On their first night in Paris, they visited a brothel.*

brother *n.* sibling; °relation, °relative, °kin, kinsman; °fellow, fellow-man, fellow-clansman, fellow-citizen, fellow-countryman, fellow-creature; °associate, °colleague, confrère, °companion, *Colloq* °pal, °chum, *Brit and Australian* °mate, *US* buddy: *Some day, perhaps all men will regard each other as brothers.*

brotherhood *n.* **1** brotherliness, °fellowship, °companionship, °alliance, °friendship, comradeship, camaraderie, °kinship: *We should all live together in harmony and brotherhood.* **2** °fraternity, guild, °society, °association, °order, °league, °union, °organization, °club, community, °circle, °set, °clique: *The tribes fused into a united and enthusiastic brotherhood.*

brotherly *adj.* °fraternal, °kind, °affectionate, °cordial, °friendly, °amicable, °amiable, °neighbourly, °loyal, °devoted: *The boys grew up together and maintained a brotherly relationship throughout their lives.*

browbeat *v.* °bully, °intimidate, °threaten, badger, °dominate, cow, °frighten, °discourage, °tyrannize, hector, °harass, keep after, °nag, *Colloq* hassle: *The foreman constantly browbeat anyone who wasn't one of his drinking cronies.*

browse *v.* °look over *or* through, °skim (through), °scan, °thumb *or* °flip *or* flick through: *I was browsing through some recent acquisitions at the second-hand bookshop.*

bruise *n.* **1** °injury, °hurt, contusion, °bump, °welt, °scrape, abrasion, °scratch, °wound, black-and-blue °mark, blotch, °blemish, °mark, °spot, discoloration, °damage, *Technical* ecchymosis: *I got this bruise from walking into the corner of the table. The price is lower if the fruit has a few bruises.*
—*v.* **2** °injure, contuse, °hurt, °scrape, °harm; °wound, °damage: *I bruised my knee when I fell down. Being arrested certainly bruised his self-esteem.*

bruiser *n.* prizefighter, boxer, fighter; °tough, ruffian, bodyguard, °thug, °hoodlum, bouncer, *Colloq* hooligan, °tough °guy, toughie, *Brit* °minder, *US* roughneck, hood, gorilla, plug-ugly, torpedo, enforcer: *The heavyweight contender is really a big bruiser. Mr Big strode in with two of his bruisers.*

brunt *n.* (full) °force, °burden, onus, °weight, °impact; °shock, °stress, °violence, onslaught: *As the head of the department was on holiday, I had to take the full brunt of the customers' complaints.*

brush[1] *n.* **1** brushwood, shrubs, undergrowth, branches, °scrub, °brush, bracken, brambles, underbrush, underwood: *It took us three days to clear the brush from around the house.* **2** °thicket, °brake, copse, grove, boscage: *The fox disappeared into the brush, which was too dense for the dogs to follow.*

brush[2] *n.* **1** hairbrush, toothbrush, clothes-brush, shoe-brush, nail-brush, paintbrush; broom, dustbroom, besom, *US* °whisk broom: *This brush is too harsh and may damage your teeth.* **2** See **brush-off. 3** °encounter, °engagement, °skirmish, *Colloq Brit* °spot of °bother: *Mark has had several brushes with the law.*
—*v.* **4** °scrub, °clean; °groom, curry; °sweep, °whisk, °gather: *Brush your teeth twice a day. I brushed down the mare before saddling her. Brush the crumbs off the table.* **5** graze, °touch: *He deliberately tried to brush against her in the corridor.* **6** ***brush aside*** *or* ***away***: °disregard, °dismiss, °put aside, shrug off: *Brushing aside the members' objections, he tried to force the committee's acceptance of the new rules.* **7** ***brush off***: °dismiss, °ignore, °rebuff, °send off *or* away *or* packing: *He asked her out, but she brushed him off.* **8** ***brush up*** **(*on*)**: °review, restudy, °go over, °refresh, °study, *Archaic* con: *You should brush up on your geometry before taking trigonometry.*

brush-off *n.* °dismissal, °rebuff, °rejection, snub, *Colloq* cold °shoulder, °put-down, °slap in the face, the (old) heave-ho; *Chiefly US and Canadian* walking papers: *Tanya has given Theo the brush-off—said she never wants to see him again.*

brusque *adj.* °blunt, °rude, °overbearing, °impolite, uncivil, °discourteous, °ungracious, °ill-mannered, unmannerly; churlish, °gruff, °abrupt, °short, °curt, °sharp, °terse, °brash, °bluff: *I could tell that the interviewer had already decided against me by her brusque attitude.*

brutal *adj.* **1** °inhuman, °savage, °cruel, pitiless, °harsh, °severe, barbaric, barbarous, °beastly, bestial, °sadistic, °murderous; inhumane, °heartless, hard-hearted, °unkind, °fierce, stony-hearted, insensitive, unfeeling, °cold-blooded, °unsympathetic, °remorseless, °ruthless, °ferocious, °atrocious, Draconian *or* Draconic, *Literary* °fell: *Few survived the brutal treatment in the concentration camps.* **2** °rude, °ill-mannered, °coarse, °unrefined, °boorish, ill-bred, °rustic, crass, uncouth, uncultured, uncultivated, °rough, °crude: *His brutal behaviour made him unfit to represent the Crown.*

brute *adj.* **1** brutish, °dull, unfeeling, °senseless, °blind, unintelligent, °unthinking, °thoughtless, °mindless, unreasoning, irrational, °instinctive, °physical, °material; insensate, °unconscious: *He was able to lift the safe without help, by sheer brute strength.*
—*n.* **2** °animal, °beast, °savage: *He wrote that man was the middle link between angels and brutes. George behaved like an absolute brute to her.*

bubble *n.* **1** blister, air pocket, globule, droplet: *This painted surface is full of air bubbles.* **2** ***bubbles***: °froth, °foam, suds, °lather, spume; effervescence, carbonation, °fizz: *The cider is full of bubbles.*
—*v.* **3** °foam, °froth, °boil, °seethe, °fizz: *A pot of soup was bubbling on the stove.*

bubbly *adj.* **1** °effervescent, foamy, frothy, fizzy, sparkling: *I could see that the surface was all bubbly.*

2 °effervescent, °merry, °ebullient, bouncy, °animated, °vivacious, °cheerful, cheery, °lively, °excited: *Janet is known for her bubbly personality.*
—*n.* **3** champagne, sparkling wine, sparkling burgundy, Asti spumante, *Colloq Brit* champers: *Let's open a bottle of bubbly and celebrate.*

bucket *n.* pail, scuttle: *Keep this bucket of coal near the hearth.*

buckle *n.* **1** °clasp, fastener, °clip, °fastening, °hook, °catch: *The buckle broke on my belt and my trousers fell down.*
—*v.* **2** °collapse, °cave in, °crumple, °bend, °warp, °distort, °twist, °bulge: *The support gave way and the entire wall buckled.*

bug *n.* **1** insect, beetle, larva, grub, caterpillar, butterfly, mosquito, °fly, spider, *Colloq Brit* creepy-crawly, *US* no-see-em: *There's a bug on your collar.* **2** °microbe, °germ, virus; °disease, °affliction, °illness, sickness, °ailment, °disorder, malady, infection; °condition, °complaint, °infirmity, indisposition: *She's caught some kind of bug and won't be in for a few days.* **3** °obsession, °craze, °fad, °mania, °rage: *Almost everyone in those days succumbed to the hula hoop bug.* **4** °enthusiast, faddist, °fan, °fanatic; hobbyist: *She's turned into a fruit machine bug.* **5** listening °device; microphone, transmitter, electronic eavesdropper, °tap: *They planted a bug in the ambassador's telephone.* **6** °fault, °error, °mistake, °failing, °shortcoming, *Colloq* hang-up, glitch: *There's a bug in the program that's preventing the list from being sorted. They can't market the device till they've ironed out all the bugs.*
—*v.* **7** °annoy, °irritate, °pester, °irk, °harass, °bother: *I wish Mum'd stop bugging me about my homework.* **8** °tap, °spy on: *They bugged her phone and recorded all her conversations.*

bugger *n.* **1** buggerer, sodomite. **2** chap, °fellow, °man; °boy, °lad, °child, °tot; *Slang chiefly Brit* geezer, *US* °jerk; *Colloq* guy, *Brit* bloke, °fool, idiot: *He's a cute little bugger, isn't he? Who's that silly-looking bugger with Christina?*
—*v.* **3** Also, ***bugger up***: °ruin, °destroy, °botch, °bungle, °wreck; make a °mess of, *Colloq* °mess *or* °screw up, *Brit* bollocks *or* ballocks up, balls up, make a balls-up of, cock up, *US* ball up, bollix up; *Taboo* fuck up: *He's buggered the recording, so we'll have to start again at the beginning. Why does she bugger up everything I try to do?* **4** ***bugger about*** *or* ***around***: **a** °fool about, °waste time, °dawdle, *Colloq US* lallygag *or* lollygag; *Taboo* fuck about *or* around: *He buggers about the house all the time instead of looking for a job. Don't bugger about with my hi-fi.* **b** °cause complications for, °create difficulties for: *She pretends to be helping me, but she's just buggering me about.* **5** ***bugger off***: °go away, °depart, °leave, °clear off *or* out, *Colloq* make tracks, skedaddle, °beat it, *Slang* piss off; *Taboo* fuck off: *Oh, bugger off and leave me alone!*

build *v.* **1** °construct, °erect, °raise, °set up, °assemble: *I hope to build my own house in another year or so.* **2** °found, °establish, °base: *The theory is built on the principle that light travels at 186,000 miles per second.* **3** °develop: *She built the company in about five years.* **4** Also, ***build up***: °intensify; °increase, °develop, °enlarge, °strengthen: *The distant hum of voices gradually built to a mighty roar.*
—*n.* **5** °physique, °figure, °body, °shape, *Slang* bod: *He has a good build from working out at the gym.*

building *n.* edifice, °structure, construction, erection: *The building where I work is air-conditioned.*

bulge *n.* **1** °lump, °hump, protuberance, °bump, °swelling, °projection: *This wallet is making a bulge in my jacket.*
—*v.* **2** °protrude, °stick out, °swell (out): *His stomach bulges out over his belt.*

bulk *n.* **1** °volume, °magnitude, °mass, enlargement, largeness, °size: *The sausage-makers add bread just for bulk.* **2** °majority: *The bulk of the people voted for the proposal.*

bulky *adj.* °large, °voluminous, °unwieldy, °awkward, ungainly, cumbersome, *Brit* chunky: *The package, though quite bulky, didn't cost much to post.*

bulletin *n.* °message, °notice, communication, °announcement, communiqué, dispatch *or* despatch, °report, °account, °flash, °news item, newsflash: *And now, here's a bulletin from the centre court at Wimbledon.*

bully *n.* **1** persecutor, intimidator, °tyrant: *That bully Roderick is always beating up the younger boys.*
—*v.* **2** °persecute, °intimidate, °tyrannize, °torment, °browbeat, °daunt, awe, cow, terrorize; hector, °harass, °push around: *Roderick even bullied his best friend into parting with his allowance.*
—*adj.* **3** *Old-fashioned* jolly, °worthy, °admirable: *Ah, there you are, my bully boy!*
—*interj.* **4** Usually, ***Bully for (someone)!*** Bravo!, Great!, Fantastic!, Fabulous!, Marvellous!, Spectacular!; So what?, What of it?; *US* Peachy!, Dandy!, Neat-oh!; *Old-fashioned* Fantabulous!: *'David's won the snooker competition again.' 'Bully for him!'*

bulwark *n.* **1** °defence *or US* defense, °safeguard, redoubt, bastion, buffer, °barrier, °rampart, fortification: *A strong defence is the best bulwark against aggression from outside.*
—*v.* **2** °defend, °protect, °shelter: *Marnie's indifference to others bulwarks her against any feelings of contrition.*

bum *n.* **1** °buttocks, °posterior, hindquarters, fundament, behind, rump, °bottom, *derrière*, °rear °end, backside, °seat, °rear, *Colloq US* fanny, can, hinie, tush *or* tushy *or* tushie, tokus *or* tochis *or* tuchis, keister *or* keester, *Taboo slang Brit* arse, *US* ass: *Why don't you get off your fat bum and go out and get a job?!* **2** °tramp, panhandler, °beggar, vagrant, °loafer, °drifter, °vagabond, hobo, °derelict, gypsy; *Brit* caird, °tinker, °traveller; *US* (shopping-) bag lady: *Along the Bowery the doorways and pavements are strewn with bums.*
—*adj.* **3** °improper, unjustified, °false, trumped up, °untrue, fabricated, made-up, °bogus: *That auto theft charge was a bum rap, but he still served 18 months.* **4** °bad, °awful, unfair, °dishonest, °poor, °rotten, *Slang* °lousy, crummy: *I still think you got a bum deal on that toaster.*
—*v.* **5** °borrow, °beg, sponge, *Colloq* °scrounge, cadge, °touch, put the °touch on, *US* mooch, °hit, °hit up: *Can I bum a cigarette from you?*

bump *n.* **1** °blow, °collision, °thud, °hit, °knock, buffet, clunk, whack: *That bump on the head seems to have affected him.* **2** °lump, protuberance, °welt, °swelling, tumescence, °knob, °bulge: *How did you get that bump on your forehead?*
—*v.* **3** °knock (against), °strike, °hit, °collide (with), °run into, °ram; smash, °crash, *Colloq* wallop: *I bumped into the car in front as I was parking.* **4** ***bump into***: °meet, °encounter, °run into *or* across, °come across, °stumble over: *I bumped into Philippa at the hairdresser's.* **5** ***bump off***: °murder, °kill, °put away, assassinate, do away with, °execute, liquidate, dispatch *or* despatch, *Slang* take for a °ride, °destroy, °eliminate, °rub out, °wipe out, do in, *US* °waste, ice: *They bumped off Wimpy, boss; he was pulled out of the river wearing concrete overshoes.*

bumpy *adj.* °lumpy, °rough, uneven, °irregular, knobby, knobbly, °pitted; potholed, bouncy, jarring, jerky, rutted: *The skin on his forehead is a bit bumpy. This is the bumpiest road in the town.*

bunch *n.* **1** °bundle, °cluster, °batch, °clump; °bouquet, nosegay, posy, °spray: *That's a nice-looking bunch of grapes. Mr Herbert arrived with a bunch of flowers for me.* **2** °crowd, °knot, °collection, °group, °lot, °gathering, °cluster, °clutch, °batch, °assortment, °mass: *A bunch of people stood outside the courtroom, awaiting news of the verdict.*
—*v.* **3** °sort, °class, classify, °categorize, assort, °group together, °bracket: *It would be a mistake to bunch all different kinds of liberals into the same category.* **4** ***bunch up***: °gather; smock; °collect, °crowd, °group,

°cluster: *The fabric is all bunched up at the bottom. Don't let the people bunch up in front of the exits.*

bundle *n.* **1** °bunch, °collection, °package, °parcel, °packet, °pack; bale, sheaf; *Archaic* fardel: *I have to leave this bundle at the laundry today. Bring this bundle of hay for the horse.*
—*v.* **2** °gather (together), °tie up (together), °collect, °pack, °package: *He bundled up all his belongings.* **3** ***bundle off*** *or* ***out***: dispatch *or* despatch, °pack off, °hustle *or* °hurry off *or* away, °send away *or* off; decamp, °scurry off *or* away, *Colloq Brit* do a moonlight °flit: *We bundled Aunt Mary off home as soon as the storm subsided. That couple have bundled out of room 429.*

bungle *v.* °spoil, °botch, mismanage, °stumble, bumble, *Golf* foozle, *Colloq* °foul *or* °screw *or* louse up, °blow, °mess *or* °muck up, make a °mess *or* °hash *or* °muddle of, muff, *Slang Brit* °bugger, *US* snafu, *Taboo* fuck up: *Smith has bungled the job again; we'll have to replace him.*

buoy *n.* **1** (navigational *or* channel) °mark *or* marker, °float; nun (-buoy), can (-buoy), bell buoy, gong (-buoy), °siren, °signal, mooring-buoy, spar-buoy, lollipop: *Returning to port, always leave the red buoys to starboard.*
—*v.* **2** Often, ***buoy up***: °lift, °raise, elevate, °support, hearten, °sustain, °keep up: *We sang songs to buoy up our spirits while the rescuers dug their way towards us.*

buoyant *adj.* **1** afloat, floating, floatable: *The wood was water-logged and no longer buoyant.* **2** °light, resilient, °lively, °vivacious, °bright, °cheerful, °carefree, °blithe, °animated, °jaunty, bouncy, °ebullient, light-hearted, *Colloq* peppy: *One had to admire his buoyant optimism, even under adverse conditions.*

burden *n.* **1** °load, °weight, gravamen; °strain, °pressure, °trouble, onus, millstone, °cross, albatross: *The old man put down his burden. The burden of the evidence is against them. His feeling of guilt over her death in the crash was a terrible burden to bear.*
—*v.* **2** °load, °weigh down, saddle with, °encumber; °tax, °oppress: *The mules were heavily burdened with a month's supply of food. Don't burden me with your problems.*

burdensome *adj.* onerous, cumbersome, °oppressive, °weighty, °troublesome, wearisome, bothersome, distressing, worrying, worrisome, vexatious, °irksome: *A tax on food is burdensome for those on a low income.*

bureau *n.* **1** *Brit* (writing-)desk, *US* °chest of drawers, °chest, dresser, chifferobe, chiffonier: *Simon has a beautiful antique bureau in his office. One of my cuff-links rolled under the bureau.* **2** °office, °agency, °department, °division, °section, subdivision, subsection, desk: *I sent the form to the bureau a month ago, but I still don't have my visa.*

bureaucracy *n.* officialdom, officialism, °government, red tape, °administration, authorities: *The bureaucracy survives because the officials rely on graft for their income.*

burglar *n.* housebreaker, °thief, °robber; sneak-thief, cat °burglar, *US* second-story *or* second-storey man: *The burglars, remarkably, didn't take the most valuable paintings.*

burial *n.* interment, °funeral, entombment, obsequies, sepulture: *His six ex-wives attended the burial.*

burlesque *n.* **1** °caricature, °lampoon, spoof, °parody, °satire, °mockery, travesty, *Colloq* °take-off; (grotesque) °imitation, vulgarization, °exaggeration: *In the mid-19th century, burlesques drove pantomimes off the stage.* **2** *US* striptease, °strip °show, nudie *or* girlie °show: *The old comedians insist that burlesque acts were an art form, but the audience went just for the girls.*
—*v.* **3** °satirize, °take off, °lampoon, spoof, °parody, °caricature, travesty: *Cervantes burlesqued the old romances in* Don Quixote.
—*adj.* **4** °satirical, derisive, mock-heroic, mock-pathetic: *She sang a burlesque opera based on* Hamlet, *called 'Omelette'.*

burly *adj.* °stout, °sturdy, corpulent, °large, °big, °hefty, °stocky, thickset, °brawny, chunky, °heavy, beefy, °muscular, °strong, strapping, °rugged, °tough, *Colloq* °husky: *Two rather burly gentlemen were called in to help me out of the place.*

burn *v.* **1** °blaze, °flame, °flare, °smoulder: *A fire was burning on the hearth.* **2** ignite, set on °fire, °fire, °light, °kindle, incinerate, *Slang* torch: *He burnt the incriminating papers in the fireplace.* **3** °desire, °yearn, °wish, °long, °itch: *He wrote 'Darling, I am burning to be with you tonight'.* **4** °waste, °throw *or* °fritter away, squander: *Don't worry about Norman, he has money to burn.* **5** overcook, °blacken, char, °singe: *If you're not careful, you'll burn the toast again.*

burning *adj.* **1** °flaming, blazing, °fiery; °ablaze, aflame, afire, on °fire: *When we arrived, the entire building was burning.* **2** vehement, °ardent, °excited, °passionate, °fervent, fervid, °intense, °fiery, °enthusiastic: *She had a burning desire to join that illustrious company.* **3** raging, °violent, parching: *His burning fever had finally subsided a little.* **4** °hot, blazing, °scorching, seething, °withering: *She was married on a burning hot day in July.*

burrow *n.* **1** °excavation, °hole, warren, °tunnel: *The rabbit retreated to its burrow under the hedge.*
—*v.* **2** °dig, delve, °tunnel, °bore; °excavate: *The larvae burrow into the wood where the birds can hear them moving about.*

burst *v.* °break (asunder), °rupture, °shatter, °explode, °blow up; °puncture; *Slang* bust: *If it keeps raining the dam will burst and the valley will be flooded.*

bury *n.* **1** inter, inhume, lay to rest: *They buried her next to her husband as she had requested.* **2** °abandon, °forget, consign to °oblivion, eradicate, extirpate: *The residents buried their differences and united to repel the town planners.* **3** °submerge (oneself), °exile (oneself), °plunge, °become engrossed *or* °absorbed: *She buried herself in her book.* **4** °conceal, °obscure, °hide, °cover up: *The real story was by now completely buried beneath the mass of legend.* **5** °overwhelm, °overcome, inundate: *I'm so buried in work I can't take a holiday.*

business *n.* **1** °duty, °function, °occupation, °calling, °vocation, °trade, °profession, °work, °province, °area, °subject, °topic, °concern, °affair, °responsibility, °role, °charge, °obligation: *Her business is supplying models for fashion shows. Mind your own business and don't be such a Nosy Parker.* **2** °matter, °job, °task, °subject, °question, °problem, °issue, °point, °affair: *Gentlemen, let us call the meeting to order and attend to the business at hand.* **3** dealing, °transaction; °trade, °commerce, °traffic: *We've never done any business with that company.* **4** °concern, °establishment, °organization, °company, °firm, °house, °enterprise; corporation, partnership, proprietorship: *Rodney wants to sell the business and retire to Spain.*

busy *adj.* **1** occupied, °engaged, employed, °involved: *I can't talk to you now, I'm busy.* **2** working, °industrious, °active, °diligent; bustling, °hectic, °lively, hustling, °energetic: *Are you very busy at the office these days? The diamond district is certainly a busy place.* **3** °ornate, °elaborate, °detailed, °complicated, complex, (over-)decorated, °intricate, baroque, rococo: *Some of the late Victorian architecture is far too busy for my taste.*
—*v.* **4** °occupy, °involve, °employ, °divert, absorb, engross: *She has busied herself with charity work to get her mind off the tragedy.*

busybody *n.* °pry, °snoop(er), °peep(er), °gossip, meddler, Paul Pry, *Colloq* Nosy Parker, *Slang US* buttinsky: *If he so much as sees us talking together, that busybody will probably cook up some sex scandal.*

butcher *n.* **1** °murderer, slaughterer, °killer, ripper, °cutthroat, executioner, annihilator: *That cold-blooded butcher dismembered his victims after strangling them.*

2 destroyer, bungler, muddler: *Look what that butcher of a tailor has done to my suit!*
—*v.* 3 °slaughter, °massacre, °murder, °cut *or* °hack *or* hew to pieces, dismember, disembowel, °exterminate, annihilate, °kill, liquidate: *The entire crew was butchered by the islanders.* 4 °botch, °bungle, °foul up, *Colloq* °mess up, make a °mess *or* °hash of; *Slang* louse up, °screw up, *Brit* bollocks *or* ballocks up, *US* bollix up; *Taboo* fuck up: *He butchered the restoration of my antique cabinet.*

butt[1] *n.* °target, °end, °object, °prey, °victim, °dupe; gull, *Colloq* pigeon, °sucker; *Brit* Aunt Sally, *Slang US and Canadian* patsy: *He was always the butt of their jokes.*

butt[2] *v.* 1 abut, °join, °meet: *This wall butts up against my garage.* 2 ***butt in*** *or* ***into***: °interfere, °intrude, °interrupt, *Colloq US* kibitz; °meddle: *Please let me finish a sentence without butting in. Don't butt into my affairs.*

buttocks *n.* °bottom, behind, *derrière*, °seat, °rear, °rear °end, backside, °posterior, hindquarters, fundament, *Colloq Brit* °bum, *US* hinie, can, duff, tush *or* tushy *or* tushie, tokus *or* tochis *or* tuchis, keister *or* keester, butt, °tail, prat; *Slang* cheeks, *Taboo slang Brit* arse, *US* ass: *A person with large buttocks should not wear tight shorts.*

buttonhole *v.* 1 corner, detain, accost, importune, °waylay: *A reporter buttonholed one of the senators for details of the new tax bill.*
—*n.* 2 corsage, *US* boutonniere *or* boutonnière: *He wore a rose for a buttonhole.*

buttress *v.* °sustain, °support, °strengthen, °prop (up), °brace, °reinforce, shore up: *Huge beams were needed to buttress the walls after the bombing.*

buxom *adj.* 1 °hearty, °healthy, °vigorous, °lusty, °attractive, °comely, °plump, *Colloq* °hefty: *Sylvia was a buxom serving-wench at the Bugle Horn.* 2 busty, °bosomy, chesty, well-endowed, big-busted: *The centrefolds in this magazine usually show quite buxom women.*

buy *v.* 1 °purchase; °acquire, °obtain, °get, °procure, °gain, °come by, °secure: *Where did you buy that hat?* 2 °accept, °allow, °take, °believe, °swallow, °go for: *Did you buy his story about having his car stolen?* 3 °bribe, suborn, °pay off, °buy off, °corrupt: *That customs man must have been bought or he wouldn't have let the package through.*
—*n.* 4 °purchase, °acquisition: *We made a bad buy at the last auction.* 5 Also, ***good buy***: °bargain, *Colloq US and Canadian* °steal: *If you paid only £2,000, that was a real buy.*

buyer *n.* °customer, consumer, °client, purchaser: *Is it likely that you will find many buyers of Basque dictionaries in this country?*

buzz *n.* 1 °hum, °murmur, drone: *I lay and listened to the buzz of the bees.* 2 °stir, °ferment, °talk, °undercurrent: *A ringing could be heard above the buzz of conversation.* 3 phone °call, °ring: *I think I'll give him a buzz to see if our appointment is still on.* 4 °thrill, feeling of °excitement, °sensation, stimulation, °kick, *Colloq* °high: *I got quite a pleasant buzz from that drink.*
—*v.* 5 °hum, °murmur, drone: *The flies were buzzing around the dead squirrel.* 6 °fly down on, zoom on to: *The pilot was grounded for a month for buzzing the airfield.* 7 °telephone, °ring (up), °call (up), phone; °summon, °signal, buzz *or* °ring for: *She said she'd buzz me if she needed anything.*

by *prep.* 1 °near, °beside, next to, °close to, alongside: *I park my car by my house.* 2 via, by °way of, °through; °past: *I go home by High Wycombe.* 3 by °means of, on: *I often travel by train.* 4 °before, not later than, sooner than: *I have to leave by Monday.* 5 during, at: *We travel only by night.*
—*adv.* 6 Often, ***close by***: °near, °nearby, at °hand, °close, °about, around, *Literary* nigh: *When she is close by I get a tingling sensation.* 7 °past, °nearby: *When he walked by I nearly died.* 8 away, aside: *We put by a little for a rainy day.*

bygone *adj.* °past, °former, olden; of °old, of yore: *In bygone times, the fashion was for high-button shoes.*

bypass *v.* 1 °avoid, °evade, circumvent, °sidestep, skirt, °go *or* °get °round, °detour; °ignore, *Slang* give the go-by: *I shall bypass many problems if I take that route.*
—*n.* 2 °detour, alternative (°way, °route, etc.), alternate °way *or* °route: *Take the bypass and avoid the town traffic.*

bystander *n.* °spectator, °onlooker, °observer, °witness, non-participant, passer-by, °eyewitness: *He has always claimed he was an innocent bystander, but I'm not so sure.*

byword *n.* °proverb, °proverbial saying, °parable, °maxim, adage, °motto, °slogan, apophthegm *or* apothegm, aphorism, catchword, catch-phrase: *My byword has always been, Honesty is the best policy.*

C

cab *n.* °taxi, taxi-cab, *Obsolete* (horse-drawn) hackney, hansom (cab); *Old-fashioned US* °hack: *A cab picked me up and dropped me at the hotel.*

cabal *n.* 1 °intrigue, °plot, °conspiracy, °scheme: *The cabal against Washington found supporters exclusively in the north.* 2 °junta *or* junto, °clique, °set, coterie, °faction, °band, °league; °unit, °party, caucus, °club; °ring, °gang: *A cabal of artists was formed.*
—*v.* 3 °intrigue, °plot, conspire, connive, machinate: *The barons began to sow dissension and to cabal against his succession.*

cabaret *n.* 1 nightclub, °club, nightspot: *The ever-popular entertainer Mimi opened at the Golden Palm cabaret last night.* 2 floor °show, °show, °entertainment, °amusement: *The dinner was poor, but the cabaret was marvellous.*

cabin *n.* 1 °hut, °shack, °cottage, °cot, shanty; bungalow, °lodge, chalet; *Scots* bothy: *The old trapper lives in a cabin in the forest. You are welcome to come skiing with us and stay in our cabin.* 2 stateroom, °compartment, berth: *We had a cabin on the starboard side.*

cabinet *n.* 1 cupboard, °bureau, chifferobe, commode, chiffonier, °chest (of drawers), chest-on-chest, tallboy, *US* highboy, lowboy: *The aspirin is in the medicine cabinet. Our china cabinet is, unfortunately, not a genuine Chippendale.* 2 °council, °ministry, °committee, °advisers, senate: *At the age of thirty, he became the youngest member of the cabinet.*

cable *n.* 1 wire, °line, °rope, hawser, °chain, mooring, strand, °guy: *The cable broke and we were set adrift.* 2 °telegram, wire, cablegram, radiogram, *US* Mailgram: *Send a cable to Jones about the meeting.*
—*v.* 3 telegraph, wire; °radio: *Cable Jones to come at once.*

cache *n.* 1 hiding-place, °hole, vault, repository: *There was a small cache concealed by the panelling in the library.* 2 °store, °hoard, °supply, °reserve, °nest egg, stockpile, *Colloq US and Canadian* stash: *The wise hunter keeps a cache of supplies buried along his route.*
—*v.* 3 °hide, °store, °conceal, squirrel away, °secrete, °bury, *Colloq* stash (away): *I cached the money in a biscuit tin.*

cachet *n.* 1 °stamp, °feature, distinguishing °mark, °identification: *The cachet of good taste is simplicity of design.* 2 °distinction, °prominence, °importance, °prestige, °dignity: *Her new job doesn't pay much, but it has a certain cachet.*

cadaver *n.* °corpse, (°dead) °body, remains, *Slang* °stiff: *The medical students and doctors once paid to have cadavers exhumed for anatomical study.*

cadence *n.* °measure, °beat, °rhythm, °tempo, °accent, °pulse, metre, lilt, °swing: *The snare drum marked the cadence for the marching band.*

café *n.* coffee-house, coffee °bar, coffee-shop, bistro, °snack °bar, brasserie; tearoom, lunch-room, restaurant, eating-house, canteen; cafeteria, *US* diner, *Colloq* eatery; *Slang Brit* caff, *US* greasy spoon: *We stopped at a café for refreshment.*

cage *n.* **1** crate, °enclosure, °pen, °pound, coop, hutch: *He keeps rooks in a cage.*
—*v.* **2** Also, ***cage up*** *or* ***in***: confine, °enclose, °pen, impound, °shut up *or* in, coop (up), °imprison; °restrict, °restrain, hem in: *They keep the kitten caged like a wild animal. I don't like to stay caged up in my office all day.*

cajole *v.* °wheedle, °coax, °beguile, °jolly (along), °cosy along, °seduce, inveigle, °persuade, *Colloq* soft-soap, butter (up), °stroke, sweet-talk: *Robert's wife always has to cajole him to go and visit her mother.*

cajolery *n.* wheedling, coaxing, blandishment, beguilement, jollying, °persuasion, seduction, inveigling, inveiglement, *Colloq* soft soap, buttering-up, °sweet talk: *She uses cajolery rather than threats to get what she wants.*

cake *n.* **1** pastry, bun, *Brit* gateau: *Right now, I should like to have a glass of milk and a piece of chocolate cake.* **2** °piece, chunk, °bar, °block, cube, °lump, °loaf, °slab: *Barbara gave me a cake of fancy perfumed soap for my birthday.*
—*v.* **3** °harden, °solidify, °thicken, congeal, °dry, °coagulate, encrust, consolidate: *You can see where the paint has caked.*

calamitous *adj.* distressful, dire, °tragic, °disastrous, °destructive, °awful, °devastating, °fatal, °deadly, pernicious, cataclysmic, catastrophic, °ruinous, °dreadful, °terrible: *They seemed unaware of the calamitous consequences of what they were doing to the environment.*

calamity *n.* **1** °disaster, °destruction, °ruin, °catastrophe, cataclysm, devastation, °tragedy, misadventure, mischance, °mishap: *Calamity befell the town when it was engulfed in a landslide.* **2** °distress, °affliction, °trouble, °hardship, °misery, °tragedy, °misfortune, adversity, °reverse, °ruin, ruination, °desolation, wretchedness: *So full is the world of calamity that every source of pleasure is polluted.*

calculate *v.* °compute, °reckon, °add up, assess, °evaluate, °count, °figure (out), °estimate, °gauge, °determine, ascertain, °work out: *Bradley was able to calculate the velocity of light. They calculated where the sun would come up at the equinox and built their temple accordingly.*

calculated *adj.* **1** arranged, designed, planned, °prepared, adjusted, adapted, °fit, °fitted, intended, suited: *The coach was calculated to carry six regular passengers.* **2** °deliberate, °purposeful, °intentional, °premeditated, planned: *The so-called accident was really a calculated attempt to kill me.*

calculating *adj.* °shrewd, conniving, °crafty, °sly, °scheming, °designing, Machiavellian, manipulative, canny, contriving: *She is a calculating woman, who knows what she wants and manoeuvres people to help her get it.*

calculation *n.* **1** computation, °reckoning, counting, °estimation, figuring, determining: *We needn't number them one by one, for the total can be arrived at by calculation.* **2** °answer, °product, °result, °figure, °count, °estimate, °amount: *This calculation is wrong, so please do it again.* **3** °estimate, °forecast, °expectation, °prediction, deliberation; circumspection, cautiousness, wariness, °caution, °prudence, °forethought, °discretion: *His attack was not the inspiration of courage but the result of calculation.*

calculator *n.* computer, adding °machine; abacus: *According to my calculator, the answer should be 7.1592.*

calendar *n.* **1** °appointment book, °schedule, slate, *Brit* °diary, *US* date-book, *US law* docket: *I have next week's lunch date in my calendar.* **2** almanac, °chronology, °chronicle, annal(s): *The ecclesiastical calendar lists today as St David's Day.*

calibrate *v.* °adjust, °graduate; °standardize: *This balance has been dropped on the floor, and you'll have to calibrate it again.*

calibre *n.* **1** diameter, °size, °bore, °gauge: *You need a .38 calibre bullet to fit a .38 calibre pistol.* **2** °merit, °ability, °talent, °capability, competence, °capacity, °quality, °strength, stature: *They should be playing against a team of their own calibre.* **3** °degree, °measure, °stamp, °quality: *I doubt that you will find anyone of equal calibre to Julia in artistic sensibility.*

call *v.* **1** °shout, °cry (out), °hail, °yell, °roar, °bellow, call out, *Colloq* holler: *I heard someone calling my name.* **2** °name, °designate, °denote, denominate, °term, °style, °nickname, °label, °title, °entitle, °tag, °identify, dub, °christen, baptize: *My real name is Angus, but they call me Scotty. A person from Glasgow is called a Glaswegian.* **3** call up, °telephone, phone, °ring (up), dial, *Colloq* °buzz: *As it's her birthday, I must call my mother in Australia. Don't call us, we'll call you.* **4** °summon, invite, °assemble, convoke, convene, °bid, °gather, °collect, °muster, °rally: *From the minaret, the muezzin was calling the faithful to prayer. Many are called but few are chosen.* **5** °visit, °attend; call in; call on: *My great aunt Frederica came to call last Sunday.* **6** °awake, °awaken, °wake up, °rouse, *Colloq Brit* °knock up: *Please call me at six.* **7** ***call down***: **a** °appeal to, invoke, °petition, °request, entreat, supplicate: *He called down the wrath of God on the Philistines.* **b** °reprimand, °chastise, °castigate, °upbraid, °scold, °reprove, °rebuke: *He was called down for having left the house after curfew.* **8** ***call for***: **a** °demand, °request, °ask for, °order, °require, °claim: *The people in room 429 have called for clean towels. The problem calls for your urgent attention.* **b** °pick up, °fetch, °come for, °get, °accompany, *Colloq* °collect: *I'll call for you at seven o'clock.* **9** ***call forth***: °summon, invoke, °draw on *or* upon, °evoke; °elicit, °inspire: *Susan called forth all her courage and faced her accusers. He failed to call forth much enthusiasm in his listeners.* **10** ***call on*** *or* ***upon***: **a** °request of, entreat, °ask, °address; apostrophize: *The teacher called on me today to recite Hamlet's soliloquy.* **b** supplicate, apostrophize, °appeal to: *He called on Æolus, god of the winds, for a fair breeze to carry his ship home.* **c** °visit: *The vicar called on us when we first moved in.* **11** ***call off***: °cancel; °discontinue; °postpone: *The picnic has been called off because of rain.* **12** ***call up***: **a** °summon, °enlist, °recruit, conscript, *US* °draft: *Father was called up as soon as war was declared.* **b** call, °telephone, phone, °ring (up): *Call me up sometime.*
—*n.* **13** °shout, °cry, °yell, °whoop, *Colloq* holler: *I'll be out in the garden, so give me a call if you want me.* **14** summons, °invitation, °bidding, °notice, notification, °order, °request, °demand, °command; °telephone call, phone call, *Brit* °ring; *Colloq* tinkle: *She received a call to report at once for duty.* **15** °reason, justification, °cause, °need, °occasion, °right, °excuse; °requirement: *You have no call to be abusive, regardless of what you think about him.* **16** ***on call***: °ready, on °duty, °standing by, on °stand-by, awaiting orders: *They had to remain on call from midnight till eight o'clock.* **17** ***within call***: within earshot *or* hearing *or* (easy) °reach: *Please stay within call in case I need you.*

calling *n.* °vocation, °occupation, °profession, °business, °trade, °employment, °work, °line, °job, métier, °pursuit, °career, °area, °province, (°area of) °expertise, *Brit* °speciality *or US* specialty, *Colloq* °racket: *He found his calling as a veterinary surgeon very satisfying.*

callous *adj.* hardened, °thick-skinned, unfeeling, uncaring, °insensible, insensitive, °hard, hard-hearted, °tough, hardbitten, °cold, °cold-hearted, °heartless, °indifferent, °unsympathetic, apathetic, *Colloq* hard-boiled, hard-nosed: *It was callous of Gerry to go off to the snooker club right after the funeral.*

callow *adj.* °inexperienced, °immature, °juvenile, °naïve, °green, guileless, °unsophisticated, °innocent, °raw, °unfledged, °untried, *Colloq* (still) °wet behind the ears: *It was a mistake to let a callow youth take out the boat alone.*

calm *n.* **1** °quiet, stillness, tranquillity, °serenity, °hush, °peace, peacefulness: *A storm raged outside, but in the harbour was a breathless calm.* **2** calmness, composure, placidity, placidness, °peace, °repose, °sang-froid, coolness, °self-control, equanimity, self-possession: *The calm exhibited by the passengers during the hijacking was admirable.*
—*adj.* **3** °quiet, °still, °tranquil, °serene, °peaceful, balmy, halcyon, °mild, undisturbed, unagitated, placid, pacific; motionless, °smooth, °even; windless: *The sea is never calm in the same sense as a mountain lake.* **4** composed, °cool, cool-headed, self-controlled, °impassive, °dispassionate, °unmoved, unruffled, °serene, °tranquil, °sedate, °staid, °stoical, *Colloq* together: *She remained calm while the others panicked.*
—*v.* **5** Also, ***calm down***: °quiet, °quieten, °still, soothe, °hush, °lull, pacify; mollify, appease, placate, become *or* make °quiet *or* pacified *or* less °agitated, *Colloq* °cool off *or* down: *The arbitrator did his best to calm the two litigants by suggesting a compromise. After everyone had calmed down, the speaker continued.*

camouflage *n.* **1** °disguise, concealment, cover-up, °cover, °guise, °cloak, °mask, °screen, °blind, (false) °front, °show, façade, °pretence, °trickery, °deception; °protective colouring *or* coloration, *Technical* apatetic *or* aposematic *or* °cryptic colouring *or* coloration: *Camouflage prevented the enemy from seeing our tanks.*
—*v.* **2** °disguise, °cloak, °mask, °cover (up), °hide, °conceal, °screen, °veil; °misrepresent, °falsify: *We camouflaged our movements by fastening twigs and leaves to our helmets.*

camp[1] *n.* **1** camping-ground, camp-ground, bivouac, encampment, camp-site; °settlement; camping-site, *Brit* caravan °site: *The name 'Chester' derives from Latin* castrum, *meaning 'camp', for the city was originally the site of a Roman camp. Is there a camp where we can stay overnight?* **2** °faction, °set, coterie, °clique, °group, °party, °body: *On this issue, the politicians are divided into two camps.*
—*v.* **3** encamp, °pitch camp, tent: *Our family likes to go camping in the mountains during the summer.* **4** °lodge, bivouac, °settle: *The platoon camped by the river.* **5** ***camp out***: *Slang* crash: *Mind if I camp out in your pad tonight?*

camp[2] *adj.* **1** °outré, °outrageous, exaggerated, °artless, °affected, inartistic, °extravagant, °artificial, Dadaistic, °theatrical, °mannered, °flamboyant, °showy, °ostentatious, °effeminate, *Colloq* campy: *Some of the kitsch produced in the 1930s was the epitome of camp. His manner is a bit too camp for my taste.*
—*v.* **2** °exaggerate, °show off, °strut, °flaunt, °flounce, °prance, °posture, *Colloq* ham: *Clarence just loves to camp it up whenever there are women around.*

campaign *n.* **1** °operation(s), °manoeuvre(s), °crusade, °action; °drive, °offensive, °push, °effort; °struggle: *Napoleon's Russian campaign ended in disaster. Our next sales campaign will be aimed at teenagers.* **2** °competition, °contest, °rivalry, °race: *Presidential campaigns last for more than a year.*
—*v.* **3** °run, °electioneer, °compete, *Brit* °stand; *US and Canadian* °stump; *Colloq* throw *or* toss one's hat in the ring: *Next week the Labour candidate will campaign in Yorkshire.*

cancel *v.* **1** °void, annul, invalidate, nullify, °quash; °revoke, rescind, °redeem, °repeal, °abolish, °retract, °withdraw, °recall, °repudiate, abrogate, countermand, °deny: *The bonds have been cancelled and are worthless. She cancelled the incorrect cheque.* **2** °delete, °obliterate, °cross *or* °strike *or* °blot out, dele, °rub out, °erase, expunge, efface, eradicate, °quash, deracinate; °eliminate, do away with: *I was forced to cancel the chapter of my book that dealt with M.I.5 activities.* **3** Sometimes, ***cancel out***: °neutralize, nullify, counterbalance, countervail, °compensate (for), °make up for, °offset, °counteract: *His later kindnesses cancel his previous injustices.*

cancellation *n.* **1** cancelling, annulment, nullification, rescinding, voiding, rescission, revocation, °abolition, abandonment, withdrawal, abrogation; °repeal: *We found a hotel room in the end because of a late cancellation.* **2** invalidation, revocation, °abolition, discontinuance, °termination, °suppression: *If you fail to pay the premium, the policy is subject to cancellation.* **3** elimination, °abolition; stoppage, cessation: *Owing to the storm, some trains are subject to cancellation.*

candid *adj.* **1** °frank, °open, °plain, °sincere, °ingenuous, °straight, straightforward, °truthful, °forthright, °direct, unequivocal, plain-spoken, plain-speaking, °outspoken, °honest, °artless, °blunt, guileless, open-hearted, °above-board, undeceitful, undeceiving, undeliberative, uncalculating, uncalculated, °unpremeditated, uncontrived, *Colloq* upfront: *Henry offered a very candid account of his feelings. Let us be candid and speak our minds.* **2** °just, °impartial, °objective, °fair, °equitable, unbiased, °unprejudiced, even-handed; unbigoted: *The speaker expressed a candid view of all of the proposals.* **3** unposed, °informal, impromptu: *Here is a candid photo of the two of us in Rome.*

candidate *n.* aspirant, seeker, office-seeker, °runner, °nominee; applicant, entrant; °prospect, °possibility: *There are quite a few candidates for the post.*

candour *n.* **1** openness, frankness, ingenuousness, °simplicity, °naïvety, outspokenness, unreservedness, forthrightness, °honesty, °sincerity, directness, straightforwardness, unequivocalness: *I admire her candour, but the truth sometimes hurts.* **2** impartiality, fairness, °justice, °objectivity, open-mindedness: *In criticism candour is as rare as bigotry is frequent.*

candy *n.* °sweet(s), bon-bon(s), sweetmeat(s), confectionery: *Eating candy can be bad for your teeth.*

cannibal *n.* anthropophagite, man-eater: *They were said to have been captured by cannibals living in remote regions.*

cant *n.* **1** °hypocrisy, insincerity, °sham, °pretence, humbug, sanctimony, sanctimoniousness, lip-service, affectedness, °pretension: *He wasn't really enthusiastic—all that talk was just cant.* **2** °jargon, °shop, shop-talk, argot, °vernacular, slang, °dialect, patois, Creole, pidgin, °gobbledegook *or* gobbledygook, *Colloq* °lingo: *The criminals use a cant not understood by those outside their fraternity.*

cantankerous *adj.* ill-natured, °quarrelsome, °perverse, °cross, choleric, cross-grained, crabby, curmudgeonly, crusty, grumpy, °surly, irascible, °snappish, bad-tempered, ill-tempered, bearish, °bilious, °peevish, °testy, °irritable, °touchy, °disagreeable, tetchy, °contrary, *Colloq* crotchety, grouchy, *US* °cranky: *Simon used to be so friendly, but he's become a cantankerous old codger.*

canvass *v.* **1** °solicit, °electioneer, °campaign, °poll, *US and Canadian* °stump: *The candidates will be canvassing in farming areas next week.* **2** °survey, °poll, °study, °analyse, °examine, °investigate, °interview, °question: *The statisticians are not satisfied that enough women were canvassed to provide an accurate sample.*
—*n.* **3** solicitation, °campaign: *The party's canvass of rural areas for new supporters was not very successful.* **4** °survey, °study, °investigation, °poll, °examination, °tally: *A canvass of editors shows they have a conservative view of the language.*

canyon *n.* °gorge, °ravine, °gully *or* gulley, °pass, defile, *Brit dialect* gill or ghyll, *US and Canadian* coulée, gulch; *US* °gap, arroyo: *The canyon created by the river is more than a thousand feet deep.*

cap *n.* **1** hat, °head covering: *The plumber took off his cap and scratched his head.* **2** lid, °top, °cover: *Screw the cap on tight.* **3** ***cap in hand***: humbly, meekly, servilely, submissively, subserviently, docilely, respectfully: *He went cap in hand to ask for a pay rise.* —*v.* **4** °surpass, °outdo, °outstrip, °better, °beat, °exceed, °top, °excel: *Betty capped her earlier triumphs by winning the semifinals.* **5** °cover, °protect: *As it's begun to rain, you'd best cap the camera lens.*

capability *n.* °ability, °power, °potential, °capacity, °means, °faculty, wherewithal; °talent, °proficiency, °aptitude, adeptness, °skill, competence: *Deirdre has the capability to be first in her form.*

capable *adj.* **1** °able, °competent, °efficient, °proficient, °qualified, °talented, °gifted, skilled, °skilful, °accomplished, apt, °adept, °clever, °effective, °effectual; °expert, masterly, °masterful: *Halliwell is quite capable of speaking for himself. He is a capable violinist, but scarcely a virtuoso.* **2** ***capable of***: °disposed to, °inclined to, predisposed to: *Though violent, he is not capable of murder.*

capacity *n.* **1** °volume, °content, °size, dimensions; °room, °space: *What is the capacity of this bottle in litres? The car is of sufficient capacity to hold only four adults.* **2** °potential, °ability, °capability, competence, °intelligence, °wit, °brain(s), °talent, °aptitude, acumen, °understanding, °sense, °judgement, perspicacity, perceptiveness, °perception, mother °wit, °intellect, °genius, °skill, °gift, °faculty, °power, *Colloq chiefly US* right °stuff, the goods: *They don't yet have the capacity to absorb advanced theory.* **3** °position, °condition, °character, °place, °post, °role, °job, °office, °duty, °responsibility, °province, °sphere, °function; *Law* competency, °qualification: *She has every right to sign cheques in her capacity as director.*

cape[1] *n.* headland, promontory, peninsula, neck, °point, *Archaic* ness: *We sailed round the cape and made for the harbour.*

cape[2] *n.* °mantle, shawl, °stole, °cloak: *His black cape reached to the floor.*

caper *n.* **1** °skip, °leap, °spring, °frolic, °hop, gambol, °frisk, curvet, gambado: *He can dance, though he does not cut capers.* **2** escapade, °stunt, °mischief, °prank, °high jinks, *US* °crime, burglary, °robbery, *Colloq* shenanigan, dido, °lark, *Slang US and Canadian* °job: *The capers we used to get up to after lights-out in the dormitory!*
—*v.* **3** °skip, °hop, °frolic, °leap, °jump, °frisk, romp, gambol, °prance, °cavort, curvet: *She capered about like a lamb in a meadow.*

capital *n.* **1** °head, °top, °crown, °cap: *The column was surmounted by a finely carved capital.* **2** °seat (of °government): *Winnipeg is the capital of Manitoba.* **3** °money, assets, funds, °finance(s), °cash, wherewithal; °wealth, °means, °property, resources, savings, °principal: *My capital is invested in land at the moment.* **4** majuscule, °upper case, large °letter, °initial, *Colloq* °cap: *The chapter titles should be set in capitals.*
—*adj.* **5** °chief, °main, °major, °important, °cardinal, °central, °principal, °prime, °primary, °paramount, °pre-eminent, °foremost, °leading: *Our capital responsibility is to ensure the passengers' safety.* **6** first-class, °first-rate, °excellent, °superior, °matchless, °peerless, °choice, °select, °outstanding, °fine, °superb, °splendid, °marvellous, °extraordinary, *Colloq* smashing, °great, °super, *Brit* brill, *Old-fashioned* topping, top-hole, °ripping, ripsnorting: *Eating out tonight was a capital idea.*

capitulate *v.* **1** °surrender, °yield, °give up, °submit, °succumb: *Want of provisions quickly obliged the fortress to capitulate.* **2** acquiesce, °concede, °relent, °give in, °yield: *He begged so piteously that the king finally capitulated and allowed him to live.*

capricious *adj.* °whimsical, °erratic, °flighty, °fickle, mercurial, unsteady, °variable, °unstable, wayward, unpredictable, undependable, °changeable, °impulsive, crotchety, quirky, °unreliable, °inconstant, °fanciful, °wanton: *His decisions are capricious and not based on sound judgement. The weather in March is capricious: as Mark Twain said, if you don't like it, just wait five minutes.*

capsize *v.* °upset, °overturn, °turn turtle *or* upside down, °tip (over), keel over, invert: *When the wind capsized the boat, we lost all our gear overboard.*

captivate *v.* enthral *or US* enthrall, °enslave, °fascinate, °hypnotize, °entrance, °beguile, °charm, enamour, °enchant, °bewitch, °enrapture, °dazzle, infatuate, °attract, allure, °seduce, °win: *Her beauty captivated film-goers everywhere.*

captive *n.* **1** °prisoner, °convict, °hostage, detainee, internee; °slave, bondman *or* bondsman, bondservant: *The captives were kept in a wretched hole.*
—*adj.* **2** imprisoned, incarcerated, confined, caged, locked up, under lock and key: *Captive animals lose their free spirit.*

captivity *n.* confinement, °imprisonment, internment, °detention, °custody, incarceration, °restraint; °bondage, °slavery, thraldom *or US also* thralldom, enslavement, °servitude; *Archaic* durance: *Some wild creatures do not survive in captivity. Entire populations of conquered territories were taken into captivity in ancient times.*

capture *n.* **1** °seizure, °taking, °catching, °arrest, apprehension, *Slang* °pinch, collar: *They celebrated the capture of the Spanish galleon. The State has offered a reward for the capture of the bank robbers.*
—*v.* **2** °seize, °take, °catch, °lay *or* °take °hold of, °grab, apprehend, °arrest, *Slang* °pinch, collar, °nab, *Brit* °nick: *Eventually, they captured the thief on the roof.*

car *n.* **1** (motor) °vehicle, motor car, automobile, passenger car, *Old-fashioned or slang* motor; *Chiefly US* auto; *Colloq* jalopy, heap, pile, crate, °machine, buggy, °transport; *Slang* wheels: *Borrow a car and drive down for the weekend.* **2** (railway) °carriage: *The body was found in a sleeping car of the Orient Express.*

card *n.* **1** playing-card, *Slang* pasteboard: *The winning card was the ten of diamonds.* **2** calling-card, visiting-card, *carte de visite*, °business card: *Visitors used to leave their cards on the silver tray at the front door.* **3** greetings card, Christmas card, birthday card, anniversary card, condolence card, Easter card, New Year card: *I sent Jacquelyn a card for her birthday last year.* **4** postcard, *US* postal card: *Drop me a card when you get there, just so I'll know you're all right.* **5** °index card, °file card: *The names and addresses of our members, formerly held on cards, are now stored in the computer.* **6** membership card; °press card; °union card: *I showed my card at the door and they let me in without any problem.* **7** dance-card: *She told me that her dance-card was full—and was likely to be for the next ten years.* **8** *US* car-card, window-card, show-card: *At the cost of a card on the New York buses, we'd never get our money back.* **9** °credit card; bank card: *You may pay by card or cheque. They won't accept your cheque without a card.* **10** °identity *or* °identification card, I.D. (card): *The police asked to see my card.* **11** °joker, prankster, practical °joker, °wag, humorist, °comedian, comedienne, °funny man *or* woman: *That Oscar—he's quite a card, isn't he?* **12** ***on*** *or esp US* ***in the cards:*** °destined, °fated, slated, in the offing; °likely, °probable, °possible, °liable: *I doubt that a change of government is on the cards for some time to come.* **13** ***play one's cards right, well, badly, etc.***: °act, °behave, take °action; °plan, use °strategy: *If Francis plays his cards right, he may be made head of department when Mark leaves.* **14** ***put*** *or* ***lay one's cards on the table*** *or* ***show one's cards***: act °openly, °reveal all, be °forthright, be °direct, be °open, be °honest, be unsecretive, *Colloq* come °clean: *I'm going to put my cards on the table, and let you know all my plans.*

cardinal *adj.* °important, °chief, °key, °special, °main, °central, °principal, °prime, °primary, °essential, °necessary, °fundamental; °supreme, °paramount, highest, °first, °foremost, °leading, °pre-eminent: *The cardinal virtues are justice, prudence, temperance, and* *fortitude, to which some writers add faith, hope, and charity.*

care *n.* **1** °anxiety, °worry, °trouble, °anguish, disquiet, °distress, °grief, °sorrow, dolour, °sadness, °suffering, °misery, °woe, tribulation: *His haggard look reflected a life of care.* **2** °concern, °regard, °vigilance, mindfulness, °heed, °solicitude; heedfulness, °attention, pains, carefulness, meticulousness, punctiliousness; °caution, circumspection: *The essence of public-spiritedness is care for the common good. He looks after his moustache and beard with great care. Open with care.* **3** °responsibility, °charge, °protection, guardianship, °custody, keeping, °safe keeping; °control, °direction, supervision: *The child has been released into our care.* **4** ***take care of***: °look after, °attend to, be °responsible for, take °charge of, take °responsibility for; °tend, °nurse: *You should take care of your money. Does she have enough experience to take care of someone who is ill?*
—*v.* **5** be °concerned, °trouble oneself, feel °interest, °worry, °fret, °trouble, *Brit* °mind: *Do you care whether Arnold gets the job he wants? I don't care who you are, you can't come in here!* **6** ***care for***: **a** °look after, °tend, °attend (to), °watch over, °protect, take care of, °provide for; °nurse: *He cared for his ailing parents for about twenty years.* **b** °like, °fancy, be attracted to, be °fond of, °love, be °keen on, be enamoured of: *Jennifer admitted last night how much she cares for David.*

careen *v.* °heel over, keel over; *US loosely* °career, °sway, °tip, °pitch, veer, °swerve, °lurch: *We hauled out the boat, careened her, and proceeded to caulk her seams.*

career *n.* **1** °employment, °occupation, °calling, °vocation, °pursuit, (life's) °work, °job, °business, livelihood; °profession, °trade, °craft, métier: *She has made a career out of helping others. He is undecided whether to pursue a career in accountancy.*
—*v.* **2** °speed, °race, °rush, °dash, °fly, °tear, °hurtle, °bolt, °shoot, *Colloq* zoom: *A bicycle came careering around the corner and knocked him down.*

carefree *adj.* °nonchalant, °easy, °easygoing, insouciant, light-hearted, °blithe, happy-go-lucky, °breezy, airy; °blasé, °indifferent, unconcerned, unworried, trouble-free, worry-free, contented, °happy: *Till he graduated from university, he had lived an entirely carefree life.*

careful *adj.* **1** °cautious, °wary, circumspect, chary, °prudent, watchful, °aware, °alert, °vigilant: *These days one cannot be too careful about walking in the city at night.* **2** °meticulous, °painstaking, °attentive, punctilious, (well-)organized, °systematic, °precise, °fastidious, °thorough, °scrupulous, °conscientious, °particular, °finicky, finical, °fussy: *The police conducted a careful search for weapons.*

careless *adj.* **1** unconcerned, untroubled, unworried, °casual, °indifferent, °heedless, °thoughtless, °inconsiderate, uncaring, devil-may-care, °irresponsible, °cursory, °lackadaisical, °perfunctory: *No one could approve of the careless way he treats his family.* **2** °inattentive, negligent, °thoughtless, °absent-minded, neglectful, °remiss; unobservant, °unthinking, °imprudent, unmindful, incautious, °unwary, °reckless, slapdash, °rash: *Many of the errors come from being careless.* **3** °inaccurate, °imprecise, °inexact, °incorrect, °wrong, error-ridden, °erroneous, *Colloq* °sloppy: *You won't get a good mark for such a careless paper.* **4** unstudied, °ingenuous, °artless, °casual, °nonchalant: *I dislike his careless way of dressing, but it does show some style.*

caress *n.* **1** °pat, °stroke, fondling, blandishment; °cuddle, °embrace, °hug; nuzzle, °kiss: *He submitted willingly to her caresses.*
—*v.* **2** °touch, °pat, °pet, °fondle, °stroke; °cuddle, °embrace, °hug; nuzzle, °kiss: *The kitten approached warily and Isabella caressed it.*

cargo *n.* shipment, consignment, shipload, truckload, wagon-load *or* waggon-load, °load, trainload, *US* carload; °freight, goods, °merchandise: *The cargo of rifles was delivered to the warehouse. The ship was lost with all its cargo.*

caricature *n.* **1** cartoon, °parody, °burlesque, °lampoon, °satire, pasquinade, *Colloq* °take-off, spoof, *Brit* send-up: *The cartoon in the newspaper showed a caricature of the Prime Minister.*
—*v.* **2** °parody, °satirize, °lampoon, °burlesque, °ridicule, °mock, °distort, *Colloq* °take off, *Brit* °send up: *Hogarth caricatured Churchill in the form of a bear.*

carnage *n.* °slaughter, butchery, °massacre, blood bath, °holocaust, °killing, *Shoah*, *Churban* or *Hurban*: *The battle was fought with much carnage on both sides.*

carnal *adj.* fleshly, °sensual, °animal, bodily, °lustful, °voluptuous, libidinous, °lecherous, concupiscent, °sexual, °erotic, °lascivious, licentious, °lewd, °prurient: *She is intent on satisfying her carnal desires.*

carouse *v.* **1** make °merry, °revel, *Colloq* °party, pub-crawl, make whoopee, go on a °bender *or* tear *or* binge *or* toot, °paint the town red, binge, °booze: *After the cup final, we all caroused till the wee hours.*
—*n.* **2** °revel, °spree, °fling, wassail, carousal, °drunk, bacchanal, *Colloq* binge, °bender, °booze, boozer, *Brit* knees-up, *US* °tear, toot: *They go on a carouse on Burns Night every year, then need a day to sleep it off.*

carp *v.* find °fault, °criticize, °cavil, °complain, °nag, °pick at, °pick on, °bully, bullyrag *or* ballyrag, *Colloq* °knock, °pick holes (in), °gripe, *Brit* whinge: *She said that she would leave him if he kept on carping at her about her cooking.*

carriage *n.* **1** (°railway) °coach, *US* °car: *We moved our belongings into the next carriage.* **2** °bearing, mien, °air, °manner, deportment, °conduct, demeanour, °attitude, °posture, °stance, °presence, °behaviour, comportment: *His upright carriage immediately identified him as a military man.* **3** °freight, freightage, transportation, cartage, shipping; postage: *Carriage is free within mainland Britain.*

carrier *n.* **1** bearer, °porter; transporter, drayman, shipper, haulier *or US* hauler; carter: *The company we use as a carrier is expensive.* **2** transmitter, *Immunology* vector, *US* Typhoid Mary: *She couldn't have caught the disease directly, only through some carrier.*

carry *v.* **1** °transport, convey, °bear, °lug, °drag, °cart, °move, *Colloq* tote, *Slang US* schlep: *He shouldn't carry such heavy packages at his age.* **2** °conduct, convey, °lead, °take, °transport, °transfer, °transmit: *This cable carries the power to the town.* **3** °drive, impel, °conduct, convey, °take, °move: *He travelled aimlessly, wherever the wind carried his ship.* **4** °support, °maintain, °finance: *I had a wife and four children and was unable to carry my brother's family as well.* **5** °bear, °hold up, °uphold, °maintain: *Despite her troubles, she carried her head high.* **6** °win, °take, °sweep, °capture, °gain, °secure: *She carried the election easily.* **7** °stock, °sell, °offer; °display: *We don't carry purple shoes in this shop, Madam.* **8** °broadcast, disseminate, °offer, °release; °communicate, °present, °read, °report, °announce; °give: *The news is carried on this station every night at nine.* **9** ***carry away***: °transport, °excite, °enrapture, °delight: *He was quite carried away by her attentions.* **10** ***carry off***: **a** °win, °gain, °capture, °secure: *She managed to carry off the first prize for the third year running.* **b** abscond with, °kidnap, °take, purloin, *Colloq Brit* °pinch, °nick: *I'm afraid that some of your chickens have been carried off by a fox.* **c** °accomplish, °perform, °effect, do, °succeed, °handle *or* °manage successfully, °bring off, °carry out: *We carried off the raid without loss of a single man.* **d** °kill, be *or* °cause the °death of, °cause to °die: *He was carried off by yellow fever in his eightieth year.* **11** ***carry on***: **a** °continue, °proceed, °go on, °persist, °keep on *or* at, °persevere: *Don't stop—just carry on with what you were doing.* **b** °manage, °conduct, °operate: *Despite the fire, we are carrying on our business as usual.* **c** °misbehave, *Colloq* °act up, °fool around, *Brit* °play up: *The children are carrying on so, I can't get any work done.* **12** ***carry out*** *or* ***through***: °perform, °effect, °implement, °complete, °execute,

°accomplish, °continue, conclude: *Henry is carrying out his father's wishes according to the terms of his will.*

cart *n.* **1** handcart, pushcart, trolley, barrow, wagon *or Brit also* waggon: *You'll need a cart to carry all these things to the car.*
—*v.* **2** °carry, convey, °move, °lug, °drag, tote, °transport, °bring, °haul, *Colloq US* schlep: *Why do you cart that heavy bag everywhere you go?*

carte blanche *n.* °licence, °permission, °sanction, free rein, °authority, °discretion: *She was given* carte blanche *to spend the money any way she wished.*

carve *v.* **1** hew, °cut, sculpt, °sculpture, °shape, °chisel, °model, °fashion, °engrave, incise, °grave, °whittle, °chip: *The bust is carved out of solid marble.* **2** Often, ***carve up*** *or* ***out***: °divide (up), °cut (up), subdivide, apportion, °parcel out, °allot, °partition: *The gang-leaders carved up the territory, and the killings stopped for a while.*

case[1] *n.* **1** °instance, °example, °event, °occurrence; °happening, °occasion, °circumstance, °state, °situation: *In a recent case a farmer was attacked by a man-eating tiger. Holmes is investigating a case of a missing necklace.* **2** °action, °suit, lawsuit, °dispute; °cause: *I lost my case.* **3** °patient, °invalid, °victim: *Four new cases were admitted to the hospital yesterday.* **4** °specimen, °instance, °example: *Howard is an odd case, isn't he?* **5** ***in any case***: in any °event, come what may, at all events, anyhow, anyway: *In any case, your decision won't affect me.* **6** ***in case***: **a** lest, for °fear that: *He was worried in case his wife found out where he had been.* **b** if, in the °event that, if it happens *or* proves *or* turns out that, if it should °happen *or* °prove *or* °turn out that: *In case you were thinking of leaving, remember that we have your car keys.* **7** ***in case of***: in the °event of; for °fear of: *In case of fire, you must use the staircase. We insured the house in case of fire.* **8** ***the case***: the °fact, the actuality, the °truth, the °reality, what °really happened *or* took °place: *She said he was drunk, but that's not the case.*

case[2] *n.* **1** °box, container, carton, crate; °chest, holder, °receptacle; °trunk, °suitcase, °casket: *Please order two cases of paper for the copying machine. The cosmetics came in a fitted case lined in velvet.* **2** covering, °cover, °protection, casing, envelope, °wrapper: *The engraving was on the inside of the watch-case. The book came in a case of fine calfskin.*
—*v.* **3** encase, °box, crate, °pack, °package, containerize: *The computer arrived, completely cased in rigid foam.*

cash *n.* **1** °money, currency, bills, notes, banknotes, °change, hard cash *or* °money, specie, °coin of the realm, legal °tender, *Slang* moolah, dough, bread, °loot, spondulicks *or* spondulix, *Brit* lolly, °ready, °readies, *US* scratch, gelt, mazuma: *The shop accepts only cash, no charge cards.*
—*v.* **2** Also, ***cash in***: °change, °sell, liquidate, °exchange; °realize: *She cashed some bonds to pay off the overdraft.*

casket *n.* **1** °chest, °box, container, °case, coffer, °receptacle: *She keeps her jewels in a leather casket on the dressing-table.* **2** °coffin; sarcophagus: *After the funeral, the pallbearers carried the casket from the church.*

cast *n.* **1** °throw, °toss, °pitch, °shy, °lob, °thrust, chuck: *In his next cast, the bowler lightly struck the jack.* **2** dramatis personae, actors and actresses, °players, °performers, troupe, °company: *We invited the cast to a party after the show.* **3** °form, °shape, °mould; °formation, formulation, °arrangement: *She can appreciate the turn of the phrase, the happy cast and flow of the sentence.* **4** °model, casting, °mould; °stamp, °type: *The Ming vase was copied from a cast. There are not many men of the cast of Crocker.* **5** °twist, °turn, irregularity, °warp; squint: *The mare had a cast in her gallop. The pirate had a cast in his left eye.* **6** °turn, °inclination, °bent, °hint, °touch; tinge, °tint, colouring: *He has a melancholy cast of mind.*
—*v.* **7** °throw, °toss, °pitch, °fling, °sling, °hurl, °dash, °send, *Colloq* chuck, °shy: *She tore off the gold necklace and cast it into the lake.* **8** °assign, °delegate, °appoint, °designate, °name, °nominate, °choose, °pick, °select: *He has cast me as the villain in his little drama.* **9** °form, °mould, °found: *The king's death-mask, cast in plaster, was on the floor of the tomb.* **10** ***cast about for***: °search for, °look for, °seek: *He was casting about for an excuse to avoid going to the Fordyces' for dinner.* **11** ***cast aside***: °reject, °discard, cast *or* °throw away *or* out, get °rid of: *The expensive toys had been cast aside and the children were playing with the boxes and wrappings.* **12** ***cast away***: °maroon, shipwreck: *Jim O'Shea was cast away upon an Indian isle.* **13** ***cast off***: °throw off, °shed, doff: *One's upbringing cannot be cast off like an old overcoat.* **14** ***cast out***: °expel, °drive out, °throw out, °evict, °eject, oust, °exile, °remove, cast aside: *She was cast out of the house by her mother, who had married a biker.*

castaway *n.* °reject, cast-off, °outcast, pariah, °exile: *She always looked after the moral well-being of the castaways of society.*

caste *n.* (social) °class, °rank, °order, °level, °stratum, °standing, °position, °station, °status, °estate: *The women of her caste practised suttee.*

castigate *v.* °chastise, °punish, °correct, °penalize, °discipline, °rebuke, °reprimand, read (someone) the riot act, keelhaul, °chasten, °criticize, *Colloq* tell off, °dress down, *Chiefly Brit* tick off, *Brit* carpet, haul over the coals, *US and Canadian* °chew out, rake over the coals, put *or* call on *or* on to the carpet: *They were castigated in the press for their extravagant lifestyle.*

castle *n.* **1** fortress, °stronghold, citadel: *The king moved to Windsor Castle during the winter.* **2** mansion, °palace, manor-house, °hall, château: *Mr Mooney lives alone in his castle and has nothing to do with his neighbours.*

casual *adj.* **1** °accidental, °chance, °random, fortuitous, unexpected, °unforeseen, °unpremeditated, unplanned, unforeseeable, unpredictable, serendipitous: *It was only a casual remark, but it was taken very seriously. We interviewed casual passers-by.* **2** °uncertain, unsure, °haphazard, °occasional, °random, °irregular, unsystematic, °sporadic, °erratic: *The budget includes provision for both certain and casual revenues.* **3** °indifferent, °nonchalant, °offhand, insouciant, apathetic, °cool, unconcerned, uninterested, pococurante, °dispassionate, °blasé, °relaxed, °lackadaisical: *He may seem casual, but he is genuinely concerned about the patients.* **4** °informal; lounge: *Dinner dress is not required: you may come in casual clothes.* **5** °offhand, happy-go-lucky, °natural, °easy, °easygoing, devil-may-care, unconcerned, °relaxed, *dégagé*, unconstrained: *Phil is quite casual about losing money at roulette.*

casualty *n.* **1** °disaster, °catastrophe, °calamity, °accident, mischance, misadventure, °mishap: *The company insures against casualties at sea.* **2** **a** victim, fatality, *Colloq* statistic: *I'm afraid that Jeff was a casualty of last year's cut in personnel. She was only one of thousands of casualties of the earthquake.* **b** Usually, ***casualties***: *Chiefly military* wounded, injured, missing, missing in °action, °dead, °fatalities, *US* MIA(s), body count: *The casualties were mounting.*

catastrophe *n.* **1** °disaster, °calamity, cataclysm: *The eruption of Vesuvius was one of the major catastrophes in recorded history.* **2** °misfortune, bad °luck, °shock, °blow, °tragedy, °disaster; °mishap, mischance, misadventure, °accident, °fiasco, °failure: *Cook reported a catastrophe with the layer cake.*

catch *v.* **1** °capture, °seize, apprehend, °take *or* °get (°hold of), °grab, °grip, °grasp, °take °captive, °hold, °arrest, °take °prisoner, *Colloq* °nab, °pinch, collar, *Brit* °nick: *The police caught him when he returned to the scene of the crime.* **2** °trap, ensnare, entrap, °snare, °net, °bag, °hook, °round up, corral: *We caught three trout this morning. I caught all the horses that had broken through the fence.* **3** take, °get on *or* on to,

°board: *You can catch the London train at Aylesbury.* **4** °surprise, °discover, °find: *They fired him after catching him with his hand in the till.* **5** be seized *or* °taken °hold of by *or* with, °come down with, be afflicted by *or* with, °contract, °get, °suffer from: *You'll catch a cold if you don't wear a hat.* **6** °strike, °hit, °deliver, °fetch, °box: *She caught him a great blow on the ear and he went down.* **7** °tangle, become entangled *or* stuck *or* trapped *or* hooked: *His foot caught in the stirrup when he fell, and he was dragged along.* **8** °restrain, °stop, °check, °curb: *She caught herself before telling the police where the thief was hiding.* **9** °intercept, °grab, °seize, °snatch: *He caught the ball before it touched the ground.* **10** °understand, °see, °comprehend, °grasp, apprehend, °fathom, °perceive, discern, °follow, °take in, °gather, *Colloq* °figure out, °get, catch on (to), get the °drift (of), *Brit* °twig: *I didn't quite catch what you said—please can you repeat it?* **11** °captivate, °charm, °bewitch, °enchant, °fascinate, °seduce, °attract, °entice, allure: *She knows how to use her charms to catch a man.* **12** °attract, °draw: *A very slight movement caught my eye.* **13** ***catch on***: **a** °understand, °grasp, °see (through), °comprehend, °get (it), *Brit* °twig: *I didn't catch on to what she planned to do it till it was too late. The joke's on you and you still don't catch on, do you?* **b** °take °hold, °succeed, become °popular *or* °fashionable: *Do you think the hula hoop will catch on again?* **14** ***catch up***: **a** absorb, °involve, enthral, °immerse: *He was completely caught up in the plot of the new novel.* **b** °reach, °overtake, °overhaul: *I finally caught up with her as she neared the house.*
—*n.* **15** °capture, °take, °bag, °prize, °trophy: *The catch of the day was a 20-pound pike.* **16** °acquisition; °conquest: *She was considered quite a catch.* **17** °clasp, °hook, °pin, °clip, °fastening, fastener: *The catch on the necklace opened and pearls spilt all over the floor.* **18** °trick, °disadvantage, °hitch, °snag, °fly in the ointment, catch-22, °trap, °problem, drawback, *Colloq US* hooker: *The first book is free, but the catch is that you have to buy four more at the regular price.*

catching *adj.* **1** contagious, °infectious, transmissible, transmittable, communicable: *The doctor said that what I have is not catching.* **2** °attractive, captivating, fascinating, °enchanting, bewitching, entrancing, °winning, enticing, alluring, °fetching: *The strange object in the shop window was most catching to the eye of a passer-by.*

categorical *adj.* °direct, °explicit, °express, unconditional, °firm, °positive, unreserved, unrestricted, °absolute, °outright, °downright, unequivocal, unambiguous, °specific; °emphatic, °unqualified, °authoritative, °dogmatic, *Technical* apodeictic *or* apodictic: *His denial was clear and categorical.*

categorize *v.* classify, °class, °sort, °organize, assort, °rank, °order, °section, departmentalize, °group, °arrange: *Should plankton be categorized under zoology or botany?*

category *n.* °class, classification, °type, °sort, °kind, °variety, °group, grouping, listing, °rank, ranking, °list, °grade, °department, °division, °section, sector, °area, °sphere; °head, heading: *Into which category would you put the partially disabled?*

cater *v.* **1** °provision, victual; purvey, °provide: *We cater exclusively for housebound gourmets.* **2** ***cater for or to***: °indulge, °humour, °serve, dance °attendance on, °pamper, °baby, °coddle, °minister to, °spoil, mollycoddle, cosset, °pander to: *She caters for him night and day. Our music group caters for all levels of ability.*

catholic *adj.* °universal, °general, °inclusive, all-inclusive, °broad, °wide, °comprehensive, widespread, all-embracing, eclectic, °liberal: *Her musical tastes are catholic—they range from Bach to Berry (Chuck, that is).*

cattle *n.* livestock, °stock, beef; cows, bulls, bullocks, steers, bovines, oxen: *He spent 20 years as a cowboy, herding cattle in Texas.*

cause *n.* **1** °origin, °occasion, °source, °root, genesis, °agent, °prime mover, well-spring: *The cause of the train crash is not yet known.* **2** originator, °creator, °producer, °agent, °agency: *His indecision was the cause of many of our problems.* **3** °ground *or* °grounds, justification, °reason, °basis, °call, °motive: *You have no cause to be dissatisfied.* **4** °case, °matter, °issue, °concern; °movement, °undertaking; °ideal, °belief: *We appealed the miners' cause to the high court.*
—*v.* **5** °make, °induce: *What causes hot air to rise?* **6** °effect, °bring on *or* about, give °rise to, °result in, °produce, °create, °precipitate, °occasion, °lead to, °induce, °generate, °provoke, °promote; engender; °motivate, compel: *Overeating causes indigestion.*

caustic *adj.* **1** °burning, corrosive, °destructive, mordant, astringent: *Sulphuric acid is the caustic agent that eats away the metal.* **2** °sarcastic, °biting, acrimonious, °sharp, °bitter, °sardonic, °cutting, °trenchant, °critical, °scathing, acid, °harsh, °pungent, °virulent: *His caustic remarks do not earn him many friends.*

caution *n.* **1** °warning, admonition, admonishment, caveat, monition, °advice, °counsel, °injunction: *A word of caution is needed before you go ahead.* **2** wariness, °prudence, °care, °vigilance, °forethought, °heed, watchfulness, alertness, circumspection, °discretion: *Drivers should exercise extra caution in bad weather.*
—*v.* **3** °warn, admonish, forewarn, °tip (off); °advise, °counsel: *Some employees had to be cautioned about arriving on time.*

cautious *adj.* °wary, heedful, °careful, °prudent, circumspect, watchful, °vigilant, °alert, °discreet, °guarded: *They were very cautious about letting their children go out on their own.*

cave *n.* **1** cavern, grotto, °hollow, °hole, °cavity, den: *In the cave were prehistoric wall paintings.*
—*v.* **2** ***cave in***: **a** °collapse, °break down, give °way, °subside, °fall in *or* inwards: *The earthquake caused the walls of the house to cave in.* **b** °yield, °submit, give °way; °surrender; *Colloq* °buckle, knuckle under: *After eight hours of questioning, he caved in and told them everything.*

cavil *n.* **1** °quibble, °complaint: *There is a minor cavil at the wording of the statutes.*
—*v.* **2** °carp, °quibble, split hairs, °complain, find °fault, censure, °criticize, °dispute, °object, demur, *Colloq* nit-pick: *They cavilled at a mere misspelling.*

cavity *n.* °pit, °hole, °hollow, °opening, crater, °gap; °space: *The limestone is marked with a pattern of cavities. Vowel sounds resonate in the oral cavity.*

cavort *v.* curvet, °prance, °caper, °frisk, °bound, gambol, romp, °skip, °leap, °jump, °dance: *Stop cavorting about and settle down.*

cease *v.* **1** °stop, °end, °finish, °leave off, °terminate, °halt, °discontinue, desist (from), °break off (from), °refrain (from): *Will that noise never cease?*
—*n.* **2** ***without cease***: ceaselessly, endlessly, unendingly, incessantly, interminably, continuously, continually, constantly, ad infinitum, infinitely, perpetually, for ever, eternally, everlastingly, °nonstop, unremittingly: *Sisyphus was condemned to roll his burden uphill without cease.*

cede *v.* °yield, give °way, °give up, °grant, °give, °surrender, °deliver up, °turn *or* °make *or* °hand over, convey, °transfer, °relinquish, °abandon, °renounce, °abdicate: *Let private concerns always cede to the common good. The territory was ceded to our government in 1792.*

celebrant *n.* officiant, °official; °priest: *The celebrant at High Mass was the archbishop.*

celebrate *v.* **1** °hold, °perform, solemnize, ritualize, °observe, °keep, °honour, °officiate at; °sanctify, °hallow, consecrate, °dedicate: *The archbishop himself celebrated holy communion.* **2** °rejoice (in *or* at), °memorialize; have a °party, °revel, make °merry, wassail, *Colloq* °party, °paint the town red, whoop it up: *The entire town celebrated the opening of the bridge with a huge party.* **3** °extol, °praise, °exalt, °glorify, °laud, °eulogize, °honour; lionize: *She was widely celebrated for her achievements.* **4** °publicize, advertise,

°broadcast: *The stones themselves would find a Voice, To celebrate his Praise.*

celebrated *adj.* °famous, °renowned, °well-known, famed, °prominent, °noted, °eminent, °noteworthy, °distinguished, °illustrious, acclaimed: *Their son became a celebrated brain surgeon.*

celebration *n.* **1** °observance, °observation, °performance, solemnization, hallowing, sanctification, memorialization, commemoration: *The celebration of the Eucharist was delayed because the vicar had been called to a sickbed.* **2** praising, extolling, honouring: *The ceremony was a celebration of their achievements in space exploration.* **3** °party, °fête, *or* fete, °gala, °festivities, °frolic, °revelry, merrymaking: *The New Year's celebration is planned at Jill's house this year.*

celebrity *n.* **1** °renown, °fame, repute, °reputation, °prominence, eminence, °distinction, °prestige, famousness, °popularity, notability, stardom; °notoriety: *Dr Johnson was not enriched in proportion to his celebrity.* **2** °notable, °dignitary, °star, luminary, °toast of the town, °personage, °name, °personality, superstar: *The hotel lobby was packed with celebrities from show business.*

celestial *adj.* **1** °heavenly, °divine, °spiritual, °godly, paradisiac(al) *or* paradisaic, °sublime, empyrean, Elysian, ethereal, °immortal, °supernatural: *They worshipped Jupiter and other celestial beings.* **2** astronomical, astral: *We studied celestial navigation and how to use a sextant.*

celibacy *n.* **1** bachelorhood, spinsterhood, singleness: *People who say they enjoy celibacy may simply have not met the right partner.* **2** °chastity, virginity, continence, (self-)°restraint, abstinence, °purity: *They have to take a vow of celibacy before entering the priesthood.*

celibate *adj.* **1** °unmarried, °single, unwed: *Both brother and sister remained celibate all their lives.* **2** abstinent, abstemious, continent, ascetic; virgin(al), °pure, °chaste, unsullied, undefiled, °virtuous, °immaculate: *He led the celibate life of a monk for twenty years.*
—*n.* **3** bachelor, spinster: *She belonged to an order of female celibates.*

cell *n.* °chamber, °room, apartment, cubicle; °stall: *As a friar, he lived in a small, plain cell for most of his life.*

cellar *n.* basement, vault: *She led me down to the cellar to show me her wine collection.*

cement *n.* **1** mortar, °bond, °glue, gum, paste, solder; adhesive: *You'll need a special kind of cement to stick metal to glass.*
—*v.* **2** °stick, °glue, paste, solder, °weld, braze, °bond; °join, °bind, °combine, °unite; cohere, °hold, °cling, adhere: *First cement the tiles to the wall. The ashes and cinders cement readily into a compact mass.*

central *adj.* **1** °middle, medial, median; inner, °inside: *The central reservation between the carriageways will be planted with bushes.* **2** °main, °principal, °important, °chief, °key, °leading, °dominant, °prime, °primary, °pre-eminent, °cardinal, °significant, °essential: *Odysseus is the central figure of the poem.*

centre *n.* **1** °middle, °core, °heart; °nucleus, °focal °point, °hub, °pivot, nave; mid-point: *He stood in the centre of the road. We journeyed to the centre of the earth. The tower is at the centre of the market square. The amount to be paid was at the centre of the controversy. Mark the centre of the line.*
—*v.* **2** °focus, °converge, °meet, °concentrate, °cluster: *The business of the meeting centred on the nomination of a chairperson. All my hopes were centred on getting the job as supervisor.*

ceremonial *adj.* **1** °ritual, celebratory, commemorative: *We followed the ceremonial procession.* **2** °formal, °solemn, °stately, °dignified; °ceremonious, august: *The ceremonial robes of his office were white. The ceremonial rites of passage involve many participants.*
—*n.* **3** °rite, °ritual, °formality, °ceremony, °service, °observance: *These are the ceremonials prescribed in the Anglican service.*

ceremonious *adj.* **1** °ceremonial, °formal, °dignified, °solemn, *Colloq* °stuffy, °stiff, starchy: *There are many ceremonious procedures involved in a coronation.* **2** courtly, °courteous, °polite, °civil, °correct, °proper, °conventional, punctilious, °careful: *He entered the room and made a ceremonious bow.*

ceremony *n.* **1** °rite, °observance, °solemnity, °service, °ceremonial, °ritual, °formality, °function; obsequies: *I had to attend my grandmother's funeral ceremony and was absent from school.* **2** motions, °formalities *or* °formality, °conventions *or* °convention, niceties, °proprieties, °form, °protocol; lip-service, appearances, pro formas, °etiquette, °decorum: *Going through the ceremony is all they want—they don't care what you believe. Please sign even if only for ceremony's sake.*

certain *adj.* **1** °determined, °set, °fixed, °predetermined, °decided, settled, °firm, °stable, °invariable, established, °standard, °constant, unchanging, °steady, unfluctuating, non-fluctuating, °traditional: *He agreed to pay a certain yearly rent. She met him there every day at a certain time.* **2** °sure, unerring, °definite, dependable, °trustworthy, unfailing, °infallible, °reliable, assured, guaranteed: *How do you know that the dividend is certain?* **3** °sure, °inevitable, inescapable, °destined, predestined, ineluctable, inexorable, °unavoidable, °definite, °firm; unchanging, °changeless, °infallible, °permanent, *Colloq* on the cards, a °sure thing, *US* in the cards: *It is not always certain that justice will triumph. Nothing is certain but death and taxes.* **4** indubitable, °indisputable, °undisputed, undoubted, °sure, °doubtless, unequivocal, incontestable, undeniable, °incontrovertible, °absolute, irrefutable, °unquestionable, unquestioned, unarguable, valid: *It is certain only that we exist, according to Descartes.* **5** °confident; assured, °sure, °positive, °definite: *I am certain that she did not steal the money.* **6** °specific, °particular, °definite; unnamed, unspecified, non-specified, non-specific: *He gave us certain information which we now have reason to doubt.*

certainty *n.* **1** °fact, actuality, °reality, °truth, *Colloq* °sure thing: *I would not advise you to neglect a certainty for something doubtful.* **2** °assurance, self-assurance, definiteness, °confidence, °conviction, °faith, authoritativeness, positiveness, certitude: *The certainty with which he played the card showed he expected it to be a winner.* **3** ***for a certainty***: assuredly, °definitely, certainly, °surely, °positively; °undoubtedly, indubitably, without (a) °doubt, undeniably, unquestionably, °absolutely, *Colloq* for °sure: *I know for a certainty that I cannot fly.*

certify *v.* **1** °confirm, °attest (to), °verify, °testify (to), affirm, aver, asseverate, corroborate, °substantiate, °endorse, °guarantee, °warrant; °swear (to), °bear °witness (to), °vouchsafe, °vouch (for): *I will certify the accuracy of the report. She certified that she was the owner of the car.* **2** °declare, classify, °establish, °confirm: *The magistrate certified the man insane.*

chafe *v.* **1** °rub, °warm (up), °heat (up): *I took the chill off my hands by chafing them a bit.* **2** °rub, abrade, °fret, °gall, °irritate, make °sore: *The skin is very tender where it was chafed.* **3** °fume, °rage, °seethe; °ruffle, vex, °fret, °irritate: *I chafed in impotent rage and exasperation at the ridiculous regulations. To chafe and vex me is a part of her nature.*
—*n.* **4** °sore, abrasion, °bruise, soreness, irritation: *The saddle caused a chafe on the inside of my thigh.*

chaff *n.* **1** °banter, °raillery, °ridicule, badinage, joking, teasing, twitting, *Colloq* kidding, ragging, *Chiefly US and Canadian* joshing: *After the speech, he had to put up with a lot of good-natured chaff from the audience.*
—*v.* **2** °banter, °tease, °twit, °rail at, *Colloq* kid, °rag, *Chiefly US and Canadian* josh: *When he was in the navy, his family chaffed him for having a girl in every port.*

chain *n.* **1** °string, series, °combination; °sequence, °succession, °train, °course, °set, concatenation: *He*

owns a chain of bookshops. Interruption of the food chain can cause serious ecological consequences. A curious chain of circumstances led me to a small hotel at Torquay in February. **2** °restraint, °check, °trammel, °control, confinement, fetter, °bond, °manacle, °shackle, gyve: *The family finally threw off the chains of poverty.*
—*v.* **3** °shackle, °secure, °fasten, °bind, gyve; confine, fetter, °restrain, °restrict, °tie, °limit: *Prometheus was chained to a rock as punishment for having brought fire to man. Marguerite felt chained after twenty years of marriage.*

chair *n.* **1** °seat, armchair, stool, bench, easy chair, rocking-chair: *He offered me a chair so I sat down.* **2** throne, bench, °position, cathedra, °authority; professorship, directorship: *Sue has been offered a chair on the board.* **3** chairperson, chairman, chairwoman, presiding °officer, °leader, °moderator: *The chair ruled on the matter after due consideration.*
—*v.* **4** °preside, °lead, °govern, °moderate, °run, °direct, °manage, °oversee: *Katherine will chair the meetings during the absence of the president.*

challenge *v.* **1** °question, °dispute, °defy, °object to, take °exception to, °contest, °doubt, call into °doubt, call into °question, impugn: *I challenge the validity of your accusation.* **2** invite, °dare, °summon, °call out, °provoke: *The duke was challenged to a duel.* **3** °brave, °dare, confront, °defy, °contest: *We could challenge criticism with an easy confidence.*
—*n.* **4** °question, °dispute, °doubt: *His opinions are open to challenge.* **5** °invitation, °dare, summons, °provocation, confrontation, defiance; °ultimatum: *An older opponent might not have issued such a challenge.* **6** °problem, °demand, stimulation, °trial, °test: *Are you sure that Mr Wilson will be able to meet the challenge of the new position?*

chamber *n.* **1** °assembly, °body, legislature, judicature, °house, congress, judiciary, senate, °diet; consortium: *She is entitled to sit in the Upper Chamber.* **2** meeting-hall, °reception °room, °assembly °room: *The council chamber was packed with people.* **3** °compartment, °niche, °nook, °cavity: *We hid the gold in a small chamber in the cave.* **4** °room, apartment; bedroom, bedchamber: *On the first floor are the magnificent royal chambers.*

champion *n.* **1** °victor, °winner, conqueror, titleholder, prizewinner, titleist: *She is the women's singles champion for the fourth year in a row.* **2** defender, °guardian, °protector, °hero, °supporter, °backer, °protagonist, °advocate: *He acquired a reputation as champion of the low-paid.* **3** fighter, combatant, °hero, warrior, campaigner, °veteran: *A stouter champion never handled a sword. The boar is often regarded as the champion among beasts.*
—*v.* **4** °defend, °protect, °guard; °support, °back, °stand up for, °fight for, °maintain, °sustain, °uphold; espouse, °forward, °promote, °advocate: *He has always championed the cause of the underdog.*

chance *n.* **1** °fortune, °luck, °fate: *We met, as chance would have it, at the supermarket. Life is but a game of chance for those who cannot control their destiny.* **2** °opportunity, °time, °turn; °occasion: *You have had your chance to return the money, now it is too late.* **3** Also, ***chances***: °likelihood, °probability, °prospect, °odds, °certainty, predictability; conceivability, °possibility: *Chances are that he'll be late. The chance of winning the lottery is pretty remote.* **4** Also, ***chances***: °risk, °speculation, °gamble: *You are taking a chance going out there without a weapon. I'll take my chances.* **5** ***by chance***: **a** accidentally, unintentionally, inadvertently: *By chance the witness saw him talking to the suspect.* **b** °perhaps, °maybe, °possibly, conceivably: *Have you by chance a match?*
—*adj.* **6** °casual, °incidental, °accidental, unintentional, °inadvertent; unplanned, °unpremeditated, unexpected, °unforeseen; unlooked-for: *The affair began with a chance meeting at a pub.*
—*v.* **7** °happen; °occur, come to °pass, take °place, °come about; befall, betide: *We chanced to see him jogging in the park. It chanced that a passer-by called the police.* **8** °risk, °hazard; imperil, °endanger, °jeopardize, °stake, °bet, wager: *Few would chance severe penalties or jail by lying on a tax return. Don't chance everything you've worked for!*

change *n.* **1** °substitution, replacement, °exchange, interchange, °switch: *You have five minutes for a change of costume. This sunny weather is certainly a change for the better.* **2** °variation, °difference, °switch, °variety, °novelty: *We prefer to live where there is a change of the seasons, not in the tropics.* **3** °variation, °alteration, change-over, °mutation, °shift, modulation, modification, °transformation, metamorphosis, °revolution: *I can't believe the change that has come over Betty since the divorce.* **4** °coin(s), coppers, °silver; (hard) °cash: *I need some change for the coffee machine.*
—*v.* **5** °exchange, interchange, °switch, °trade; °replace (with), °substitute, *Colloq* swap or swop: *I won't be a minute, I just want to change my shoes. I'd like to change this shirt for a larger size.* **6** °modify, °alter, °modulate; mutate, °transform, metamorphose: *Antoinette has changed since her marriage. I never thought anyone would be able to make her change her mind.* **7** °fluctuate, °shift, °vary; vacillate: *The temperature often changes very rapidly here.* **8** ***change to*** or ***into***: °turn into, °become, °transform, mutate, transmute, °convert, metamorphose: *The alchemists tried to change base metal into gold. Every winter changes into spring—sooner or later.*

changeable *adj.* **1** °variable, mutable, °protean, °inconstant, °unstable, °unsettled, shifting, °uncertain, °irregular, uneven, unpredictable, labile, °capricious, °erratic, °fickle, °unreliable, undependable, mercurial, °volatile: *The weather has been changeable for the past week.* **2** alterable, modifiable, transformable, convertible: *Their meeting-places were changeable and known only to them.*

changeless *adj.* **1** unchanging, unvaried, °eternal, °permanent, °fixed, °stable; unchangeable, immutable, unalterable, °inevitable, °uniform: *We studied photographs of the changeless Martian landscape. The fundamental truths of the Gospel are changeless.* **2** °abiding, °permanent, °constant, °perpetual, °everlasting, °steadfast, unvarying, unchanging: *Nothing could alter my changeless love for you.*

channel *n.* **1** watercourse, canal, waterway, ditch, aqueduct, sluice, trench, trough, gutter, moat; riverbed, stream-bed: *The engineers dug a channel to drain the swamp.* **2** °strait, narrows, neck: *The English Channel connects the North Sea with the Atlantic Ocean.* **3** °furrow, °groove, flute: *The channels cut into this column are not straight.* **4** °course, °means, °way, °approach, avenue, °medium, °path, artery, conduit: *We have to open a new channel of communication with the terrorists.*
—*v.* **5** °direct, convey, °pass, °guide, °lead, °conduct: *Their grievances are being channelled through the information officer.*

chant *n.* **1** °song, psalm, hymn, canticle, plainsong, plainchant, mantra, paean, dirge, monody, descant, carol; singsong: *The war chant of the natives, echoing over the water, struck fear into their enemies.*
—*v.* **2** °sing, intone, descant, carol: *The choir chanted the verses of a lugubrious threnody.*

chaos *n.* formlessness, °disorder, °confusion; °pandemonium, °bedlam, turmoil, °tumult; entropy: *The universe arose out of chaos. If you want to see chaos, look in any teenager's bedroom. There was chaos as the bank closed its doors and ceased trading.*

chaotic *adj.* **1** formless, °shapeless, °incoherent, disordered, °disorderly, disorganized, unorganized, unsystematic, unsystematized, unmethodical, °haphazard, °irregular, °helter-skelter, °confused, °topsy-turvy, jumbled, higgledy-piggledy, *Brit* shambolic: *The present solar system is thought to have condensed from a chaotic mass of nebulous matter. The rules may seem chaotic at first sight.* **2** °tumultuous, °noisy, clamorous, °uproarious, °wild, °riotous, frenzied, °hectic, turbulent, unstuck: *The press conference became chaotic when the president announced his resignation.*

chap *n.* °fellow, °lad, °man, °boy, *Colloq* °guy, geezer, °customer, gink, *Brit* bloke, *Australian* cove, *US* buddy, gazabo *or* gazebo; *Old-fashioned Brit* (old) egg, (old) bean, (old) crumpet, (old) °boy; *Slang US* bozo: *I went with some of the chaps from the club.*

character *n.* **1** °brand, °stamp, °mark, °symbol, monogram, insigne, badge, °emblem, °sign, °seal, °label; °letter, °number, °figure, °type, °sort, °arbitrary, °peculiar, rune, hieroglyphic *or* hieroglyph: *They used to brand the character of a horse on the forehead of their slaves. We shall need to obtain a set of Cyrillic characters if we are going to print Russian texts.* **2** °characteristic, °quality, °distinction, °trait, °feature, °mark; °sort, °kind, °type, °nature, °description, °attribute; idiosyncrasy, °peculiarity: *He now tried to give the war the character of a crusade. It is the character of some people to be curious.* **3** °morality, °honesty, °integrity, respectability, °rectitude, °honour, °courage, goodness: *Everyone agrees that she is a person of outstanding character.* **4** °person, °personage, °personality, °individual: *Cobbett had more sagacity and foresight than any other public character of his time.* **5** °role, °part, °personality, characterization, dramatis °persona: *He played the character of Caesar.* **6** °eccentric, °card, *Colloq* oddball, nut, nutter, loony, bat, °weirdo, nutcase, screwball, crackpot, fruit cake, *Australian and old-fashioned Brit* cove: *She was regarded as quite a character because of her many strange habits.* **7** °role, °position, °status, °capacity: *He assumes the character of a Dutch uncle when he speaks to me.* **8** ***in character***: °fitting, °proper, °suitable, in keeping, °typical, °normal, expected, °characteristic: *It is completely in character for Len to criticize everything he encounters.* **9** ***out of character***: untypical, atypical, uncharacteristic, °abnormal, unexpected, unfitting: *It would be out of character for Janet to refuse help to someone in need.*

characteristic *adj.* **1** °typical, °representative; °emblematic, °symbolic, °distinctive, idiosyncratic, °symptomatic: *How characteristic it is of them to refuse to go to the dance! These subjects are characteristic of the early Impressionists.*
—*n.* **2** °mark, °trait, °attribute, °feature, °quality, °property, °peculiarity, idiosyncrasy, °character, earmark: *It is a characteristic of bees to swarm.*

characterize *v.* delineate, °describe, °portray, depict, °represent, °define, °brand, °label, °mark, °note, °identify: *She has consistently characterized him as a buffoon. 'Virago' is the term that would best characterize Felicity.*

charade *n.* travesty, °absurdity, °mockery, farce, °parody: *He has made a charade of what could have been a serious relationship.*

charge *n.* **1** °load, °burden, °weight, onus, °impediment; °care, °concern, °obligation: *She feared that she would become a charge on her children.* **2** °price, °fee, °cost: *What is the charge for admission?* **3** °debt, debit, °expense, assessment, °liability: *Any charge against the estate of the deceased will be paid in full.* **4** °care, °custody, °protection, guardianship, wardship, supervision, °jurisdiction, °control, °responsibility, °safe keeping: *We left the children in the charge of Nanny and Nanny in charge of the children.* **5** °order, mandate, °injunction, °precept, °command, °dictate, °direction, °instruction, °demand, exhortation: *The judge's charge to the jury was to ignore the evidence given by the caretaker.* **6** °accusation, °imputation, indictment, °allegation: *The charge is murder. The police decided to drop the charges against him.* **7** °attack, °onset, °action, °assault, sally, °raid, foray, sortie: *At the signal the cavalry began their charge.*
—*v.* **8** °fill, imbue, °load, °instil, pervade, °permeate, °saturate, °suffuse: *The air was highly charged with a stench from the kitchen.* **9** °burden, °entrust, commission, °assign; °afflict, °tax: *He was charged with the supervision of all the military schools.* **10** °command, °order, °bid, enjoin, exhort, °urge, °require, °instruct, °direct: *I charge you not to speak of this matter to anyone.* **11** °blame, censure, °accuse; °indict, cite, °name; °allege, assert: *She charged him with being a hypocrite. He has been charged with assault. It is charged that she was present at the commission of the crime.* **12** °bill, invoice, assess, debit: *Please charge these items to my account. Do not charge me for merchandise not shipped.* **13** °ask, °demand, °claim, °require, °expect: *How much do they charge for asparagus at the supermarket?* **14** °attack, °assault, °storm, assail, do °battle (with): *Four thousand horsemen stood ready to charge the enemy.*

charitable *adj.* **1** °generous, °liberal, °bountiful, munificent, °unselfish, open-handed, magnanimous, °philanthropic, public-spirited, unsparing, eleemosynary: *Despite her income, Irena has always been most charitable when it comes to worthwhile causes.* **2** well-disposed, °kindly, °kind, beneficent, °benevolent, well-wishing, °lenient, °tolerant, °forgiving, °indulgent, °understanding, compassionate, humane, °sympathetic, °considerate, well-meaning, °good: *They took a charitable view of the matter and decided not to press charges.*

charity *n.* **1** generosity, alms-giving, munificence, liberality, open-handedness, magnanimity, beneficence, °philanthropy, unselfishness, °humanity, humanitarianism, good will: *Your charity towards this hospital has been unequalled by any other donor, Sir Keith.* **2** leniency, big-heartedness, large-heartedness, °benevolence, magnanimity, °indulgence, considerateness, °consideration, compassion, °understanding, °sympathy, kind-heartedness: *We are all urged to show charity towards those who wrong us.* **3** alms, °donation, contribution, °largesse, *Colloq Brit* °dole, *US* °welfare, °relief: *I want the opportunity to work, not the government's charity.*

charm *n.* **1** °amulet, °talisman, °fetish, rabbit's foot, good-luck piece: *She wears a charm to ward off evil spirits.* **2** attractiveness, °appeal, °fascination, allure, °magnetism, desirability, °elegance, urbanity, °sophistication, sophisticatedness, suavity, grace, °refinement, cultivatedness, cultivation, °culture, °polish; °magic, °enchantment, °spell, °sorcery: *To Diderot we go not for charm of style but for a store of fertile ideas. To get ahead Colin relies more on his charm than on his ability.* **3** ***charms***: °beauty, attractiveness, pulchritude, prettiness, handsomeness, °appeal, allure, °magnetism, °pull, °draw: *For all her charms, I would not trust her one inch.* **4** ***like a charm***: successfully, °perfectly, miraculously, marvellously, extraordinarily, especially °well: *His appeal to their egos worked like a charm.*
—*v.* **5** °influence, °control, °subdue, °bind, put a °spell on, °bewitch, °enchant, °seduce, °hypnotize, mesmerize, enthral *or US* enthrall, °captivate, °delight, °fascinate, *Literary* °enrapture: *He charmed them with some tale and they gave him their money.* **6** °overcome, °subdue, °calm, soothe, allay, assuage, °hypnotize, mesmerize: *Music is said to have qualities capable of charming savages.*

charmed *adj.* **1** bewitched, spellbound, °enchanted, magical: *Apollonius considered the use of charmed rings essential to quackery.* **2** fortified, protected: *He must lead a charmed life to have survived all those battles.* **3** °pleased, °delighted, °enchanted, °happy: *I am charmed to meet you at last, Madam President.*

charmer *n.* enchanter, enchantress, °sorcerer, sorceress, °magician; vamp, °siren, Circe, Cleopatra, Lorelei, °temptress, °seductress; °seducer, Romeo, Valentino, Don Juan, Lothario, Casanova, lady-killer, ladies' man; °flatterer; °smooth talker, *Colloq* (big-time) °operator, con artist *or* man, *Old-fashioned* smoothie, wolf: *Charlotte has run off with some charmer she met at a party.*

chart *n.* **1** sea-chart, map: *According to the chart, we are fifty miles west of the Lizard.* **2** map, °table, tabulation, graph, diagram; blueprint: *A weather chart*

appears on page 23. Here is a chart of the highest-yielding unit trusts. She drew up a genealogical chart of the descendants of Queen Victoria.
—*v.* **3** °plot, °plan, map (out), °design: *He charted a course of action for the company. Have you charted the shortest route between Gibraltar and Cyprus?*

charter *n.* **1** °document, °contract, °compact, °agreement, covenant: *This year we again commemorate the signing of the United Nations charter.* **2** °permit, °permission, °licence *or US* °license, °authority, franchise, °right, °privilege, concession: *He was given an exclusive charter to export furs in 1679.* **3** °lease, °contract: *We have the yacht under charter for the summer.*
—*v.* **4** °license, °authorize, °document, commission, °approve, °certify, franchise, °qualify; °recognize: *He is a chartered accountant, she a chartered surveyor.* **5** °let, °lease, °rent, °hire, °engage, °contract: *I chartered the sloop for three weeks.*

chase *n.* **1** hunting, °hunt, °pursuit: *Police dogs entered the chase and the prisoner was finally caught.* **2** °run after, °follow, °pursue, °track, °go (out) after; court, woo: *The police were chasing a man down the street. Stop chasing women and settle down.* **3** ***chase away, off, out, etc.***: °rout, put to °flight, °hound; °drive away, °off, °out, etc.: *I chased the cat away from the birdcage.*

chaste *adj.* **1** °pure, virginal, virgin, °celibate, abstinent, continent, °virtuous, undefiled, stainless, unstained, unsullied, unblemished, °decent, °clean, °good, °wholesome, °moral: *Only a knight who was wholly chaste would find the Grail.* **2** °subdued, °severe, restrained, °unadorned, austere, unembellished, °simple, °pure, undecorated, °clean: *In some respects, modern architecture emulates the chaste style of the ancient Egyptians.*

chasten *v.* **1** °discipline, °correct, °chastise, °punish, °castigate: *He used every means to chasten the unruly and disobedient.* **2** °moderate, °temper, °subdue, °curb, °restrain, °repress, °tame, °suppress: *I am not as sanguine as I was—time and experience have chastened me.*

chastise *v.* °punish, °beat, thrash, °belabour, °spank, °whip, °flog, °scourge, birch, cane; °discipline, °chasten, °correct, censure, °berate, °scold: *Pupils are not being chastised as in the old days.*

chastity *n.* °purity, continence, virginity, maidenhood, maidenhead, °virtue, °celibacy, abstinence, abstention, abstemiousness, °restraint, self-restraint, forbearance: *She was a nun and had taken a vow of chastity.*

chat *n.* **1** °conversation, colloquy, °talk, small °talk, °gossip, °palaver, chit-chat, °tête-à-tête, heart-to-heart, *Colloq* °gab, *Chiefly Brit* chin-wag, confab, *Brit* witter, natter, *US and Canadian* °rap, gabfest, bull °session: *We'd get together for a chat every now and then.*
—*v.* **2** °converse, °gossip, °talk, chit-chat, *Colloq* °gab, °chew the fat *or* the rag, jaw, *Brit* witter, natter; *Slang US and Canadian* °rap, bullshit: *We were just chatting when I smelt something burning.* **3** *Brit* ***chat up:*** flirt *or* dally with, °persuade, °induce, °prevail (up)on, °tempt, °lure, °entice, inveigle, °seduce, °proposition: *Rick chats up every girl he meets.*

chatter *v.* **1** °prattle, gabble, °jabber, prate, °patter, gibber, cackle, jibber-jabber, *Brit* chaffer, *Colloq* °gab, jaw, *Brit* natter, witter, rabbit on *or* away, °waffle: *He just kept chattering on about nothing.* **2** clatter, °rattle: *It was so cold my teeth were chattering.*
—*n.* **3** °prattle, prate, °patter, °gossip, cackle, jabbering, chattering: *I don't want to hear any more chatter in the library.*

cheap *adj.* **1** °inexpensive, low-priced, bargain-priced, low-cost, sale-priced, cut-price, °reasonable; °economy, budget(-priced): *He was chewing on a cheap cigar. Everything used to be a lot cheaper when I was younger.* **2** °economical; reduced: *Eggs are cheaper by the dozen.* **3** °shoddy, °base, °shabby, °tawdry, °sleazy, tatty, °seedy; °inferior, low-grade, °poor, second-rate, trashy, °worthless, *Brit* twopenny *or* tuppenny; *Colloq* °tacky, *Brit* tinpot, *Slang US* two-bit, °lousy, chintzy: *Those cheap pictures ruin the look of the place.* **4** stingy, °miserly, °penurious, niggardly, penny-pinching, cheese-paring, °frugal, °tight, tight-fisted, Scrooge-like, skinflinty: *That cheap brother of yours wouldn't give even a penny to a beggar.*
—*adv.* **5** inexpensively, cheaply, for a °song, *Brit* for twopence *or* tuppence: *You can buy those cheap from any street vendor.* **6** cheaply, °easily, reasonably, for a °song, *Brit* for twopence *or* tuppence: *She has sold cheap that which she holds most dear.*
—*n.* **7** ***on the cheap***: inexpensively, reasonably, cheaply, at *or* below °cost, for a °song, *Brit* for twopence *or* tuppence; *Slang* for peanuts: *We buy these watches on the cheap and sell them to tourists.*

cheat *n.* **1** °swindler, deceiver, °impostor, °fraud, faker, °fake, trickster, confidence man, con man, °operator, charlatan, mountebank, °rogue, shark, *Colloq* °phoney *or US also* phony, *US* snake-oil artist: *It is amazing how many cheats are out there waiting to take advantage of you.*
—*v.* **2** °swindle, °deceive, bilk, °trick, °take, °fleece, °defraud, euchre, °hoax, °hoodwink, *Colloq* con, °take in, rook, flimflam, finagle, diddle, °fiddle, move the goalposts, bamboozle, take for a °ride; *Slang* °rip off: *His own solicitor cheated him out of his inheritance. If you paid ten pounds for that painting, you were cheated.*

check *v.* **1** °stop, °arrest, °stay, °halt, °obstruct, °block, °limit; °retard, °slow, °brake, °curb, °hinder, °hamper, °impede, °thwart: *They are trying to check the spread of the disease in West Africa.* **2** °restrain, °control, °repress, °stay, °inhibit, °contain, °curb, °restrict: *The animal population is checked only by availability of food.* **3** °authenticate, °verify, °confirm, °substantiate, validate, corroborate, check into, check out, check up on: *Please check his story to make sure he's not lying.* **4** °enquire about *or* after *or* into, check into, check (up) on, °examine, °investigate, °inspect, make sure of, °verify, °monitor, °test, °study, °scrutinize: *You'd best check the temperature in the kiln.* **5** °correspond, °coincide, °agree, jibe, °tally, °conform, check out, °fit, °mesh; °compare: *His alibi doesn't check with the witness's statement.* **6** ***check in***: °arrive, °report: *We check in for work at 0800.* **7** ***check in*** *or* ***into***: °register, °sign in *or* on, °enrol, log in: *We checked into the hotel.* **8** ***check into***: °investigate, check out, check up on, °verify, check: *The detective checked into the backgrounds of all applicants.* **9** ***check off***: tick (off), °mark, check: *Check off the names in red.* **10** ***check out***: **a** °depart, °leave; °go: *He checked out of the hotel and took a taxi to the airport.* **b** °investigate, °research, °explore, °enquire into, °look into *or* at *or* over, °scrutinize, °examine, °inspect, °probe, °survey, check up on, check, check into, check over: *You had best check out her references before hiring her.* **c** °pass, °pass °muster *or* °scrutiny, meet °approval, be verified, check: *According to our records, his story checks out.* **d** *Slang* cash in one's checks *or* chips, kick the bucket, croak: *Sam checked out last week—heart attack, I think.* **11** ***check over*** *or* ***out***: °review, °verify, °authenticate, check: *Please check over my figures before I submit them to the accountant.* **12** ***check up (on)***: **a** °investigate, do °research, °probe, °explore, check: *I don't know her name, but I'll check up and let you know.* **b** °determine, °discover, °find out, °look into, check: *I want you to check up on where they eat lunch.*
—*n.* **13** °stop, stopping, °cease, surcease, hesitation, cessation, stoppage, °interruption, °break, °pause, balk *or* baulk, discontinuity, discontinuation, discontinuance, °suspension: *The visitors continued to arrive without check, far into the night.* **14** °restraint, °repression, °inhibition, limitation, °curb, °restriction, °control, constraint, °hindrance, °obstruction, °impediment, damper: *He keeps a good check on the foreman. This tax will serve as a check against free trade.* **15** °control, °test, inspection, °examination, °scrutiny, verification, substantiation, authentication, confirmation, validation, corroboration: *We do a thorough check on the quality of every product.* **16** *US* tick,

°mark, °dash, X: *Place a check in the box alongside your choice.* **17** °token, °receipt, counterfoil, °stub; voucher, chit, certificate: *Don't lose your baggage check.* **18** °chip, °counter: *Let's cash in our checks and go home.* **19** *Chiefly US* bill, °tab, °charge(s): *In the USA, people generally add 15 per cent to the check for a tip.*

cheeky *adj.* °impudent, °impertinent, °insolent, °audacious, °disrespectful, °rude, uncivil, °forward, °brazen, °pert, saucy: *That cheeky little brat told me to get lost!*

cheer *n.* **1** °disposition, °frame of mind, °spirit: *They were of good cheer, considering their predicament.* **2** cheerfulness, gladness, °mirth, °joy, °gaiety, blitheness, °happiness, buoyancy, light-heartedness, merrymaking: *There wasn't much cheer at the pub when we learnt of what had befallen poor Grover.* **3** °comfort, °solace, °encouragement, consolation: *She brought in a little breath of cheer from the outside world.* **4** °shout, °cry, hurrah, rah, huzzah, hurray *or* hooray: *Three cheers for Penelope!*
—*v.* **5** °comfort, °console, °solace, °encourage, inspirit, °warm, *Colloq* buck up: *Your friendly note cheered me considerably.* **6** °gladden, °enliven, cheer up, hearten, °buoy up, °brighten, elate, uplift, °lift up: *Let thy heart cheer thee in the days of thy youth.* **7** °applaud, °shout, hurrah, °clap, °yell; *Colloq Brit and Australian and New Zealand* barrack for: *The crowd cheered for five minutes when Mr Flews stood to speak.*

cheerful *adj.* **1** joyous, °glad, gladsome, blithesome, °blithe, °happy, cheery, of good °cheer, °joyful, °jolly, °exuberant, jubilant, °gleeful, °gay, light-hearted, °merry: *I am pleased to see that Agatha is so cheerful. Why do you cry at weddings, which are supposed to be such cheerful occasions?* **2** cheering, gladdening, animating, °bright, enlivening, cheery, °gay, °buoyant, °invigorating: *She has redecorated the bedroom in more cheerful colours.*

chequered *adj.* **1** chequer-board, checked; °patchwork; plaid, tartan: *You cannot use a chequered tablecloth for a formal dinner.* **2** °variegated, diversified, alternating, °variable, good and bad, varying, fluctuating, up and down; °uncertain: *David Williams had a rather chequered career in the army.*

cherish *v.* **1** °treasure, hold *or* keep °dear, °prize: *I know that she cherishes every moment you were together.* **2** °foster, °tend, °cultivate, °preserve, °sustain, nurture, °nourish, °nurse, cosset: *For their sweetness gillyflowers are cherished in gardens. We cherish little Edward and probably spoil him a bit too much.*

chest *n.* **1** °box, coffer, °trunk, strongbox, caddy, °casket, °case: *It took four men to carry the chest outside, where we could open it. Martha kept her jewels in a small chest on the dresser.* **2** °breast; thorax: *The wrestler was pounding his chest and shouting 'I am the greatest!'*

chew *v.* **1** masticate, °grind, °munch; °bite, °gnaw: *Make sure to chew each mouthful thoroughly. The puppy chewed up my slipper.* **2** ***chew the fat*** *or* ***rag***: °gossip, °palaver, °chat, °converse, °talk, *Slang US and Canadian* bullshit: *We sat round the fire and chewed the fat all evening.* **3** ***chew out***: °scold, °rebuke, °reprimand: *The sergeant chewed out the recruit because his boots were dirty.* **4** ***chew over***: °think about *or* on *or* over, °consider, °review, °ponder, ruminate on, °meditate on *or* over: *I'll chew over your proposal and let you know.*

chic *adj.* **1** °stylish, °fashionable, à la °mode, modish, °smart, °tasteful, °elegant; °sophisticated; *Colloq* °trendy: *Susanna was always a chic dresser.*
—*n.* **2** °style, °fashion, °good °taste, tastefulness, °elegance, stylishness, modishness: *There is an air of chic about him that repels many men but attracts many women.*

chicanery *n.* °trickery, sophistry, °deception, quibbling, sharp practice, cheating, deviousness, duplicity, pettifoggery, double-dealing, °artifice, skulduggery: *They lost the case because of the chicanery of their lawyers.*

chief *n.* **1** °head, °leader, °principal, °superior, °supervisor, °superintendent, °manager, °overseer, captain, °master, ringleader, chieftain, *Dialect* himself, *Colloq* °boss, bossman, *Brit* governor, gov., supremo, *US* °man, kingpin, (°head *or* °chief) honcho, number one, numero uno, headman, °big White Chief, °big Chief, Great White Father, °big Daddy, °super; *Slang* °big cheese, *Brit* gaffer, *Chiefly US* Mr Big: *You'd best ask the chief for permission to fly to Rome.*
—*adj.* **2** °head, °leading, ranking, °superior, °supreme, °foremost, °premier, °first, greatest, °outstanding: *Terry is your chief competition for the singles trophy.* **3** °principal, most °important, °essential, °key, °paramount, (°first and) °foremost, °primary, °prime, °main: *The chief reason I came was to see you. Here is a list of the chief crimes committed in the area last year.*

chiefly *adv.* °mainly, in °particular, °especially, °particularly, above all, most of all, °pre-eminently, °principally, °primarily, mostly, predominantly, °largely, by and °large, on the °whole, in the °main, °generally, in °general, °usually, as a °rule: *Inflation affected chiefly the price of food.* The Anatomy of Melancholy *consists chiefly of quotations.*

child *n.* **1** °offspring, °descendant, son *or* daughter, °little one, youngster, *Formal* °progeny, °issue, *Colloq* kid, nipper, *Slang Brit* sprog: *How many children do you have?* **2** foetus, newborn, neonate, infant, °baby, babe, toddler, °boy *or* °girl, °lad *or* °lass, °stripling, youngster, °youth, °juvenile, °adolescent, °teenager, °young man *or* woman, °young gentleman *or* lady, *Chiefly Scots* laddie *or* lassie: *No children were born in the village for five years. These miscreants are mere children, who should not be punished as adults.*

childhood *n.* °infancy, babyhood, boyhood *or* girlhood, °youth, °puberty, minority, adolescence, teens: *During her childhood the family moved to Kent. She spent most of her childhood dreaming about travelling to the moon.*

childish *adj.* °childlike, °juvenile, °puerile, °infantile, babyish; °immature, °inexperienced, °naïve, °undeveloped, underdeveloped, retarded; °silly, *US* sophomoric: *They thought his reaction to their criticism was childish and petulant.*

childlike *adj.* youthful, °young, °innocent, trustful, °ingenuous, °unsophisticated, °naïve, °trusting, credulous, °open, undissembling, unassuming, guileless, °artless: *There is a childlike simplicity to some primitive paintings.*

chill *n.* **1** coldness, °cold, coolness, sharpness, °nip: *We put on our jackets to ward off the chill of the evening.* **2** °cold, flu, influenza, (la *or* the) grippe, ague, *Technical* coryza, *Colloq* (the) sniffles, sneezles and wheezles: *Take off those wet clothes before you catch a chill.* **3** coolness, iciness, frigidity, aloofness; unfriendliness, °hostility: *Mrs Marlow felt the chill in the stare of her husband's ex-wife.*
—*adj.* **4** °cold, °cool, numbing, chilling, °chilly, °raw, °penetrating, °icy, °frigid, °wintry, frosty, arctic, °polar, glacial: *A chill easterly wind made me shiver.* **5** shivering, chilled (through), °numb, numbed, numbing, benumbed: *She kissed me with a lip more chill than stone.* **6** °cold, °cold-blooded, °aloof, °indifferent, insensitive, unemotional, °unsympathetic; °chilly: *The prison commandant viewed the corpses with chill detachment.*
—*v.* **7** °cool, °freeze, °refrigerate, ice: *The fruit tastes better if it has been chilled.* **8** °dampen, dispirit, °depress, deject, dishearten, °distress: *The news of mother's illness chilled us all.*

chilly *adj.* **1** °cool, coldish, °cold, °frigid, nippy, frosty, °icy, °crisp, °chill: *The weather has been quite chilly for May.* **2** °chill, °unenthusiastic, unresponsive, unreceptive, frosty, unwelcoming, °crisp, °cool, °cold, unfriendly, °hostile; °distant, °aloof: *The suggestion that the charity fair be held in her garden met with a chilly response from Lady Griffiths.*

chime *n.* **1** bell, set of bells, carillon, °ring, °peal: *Our church has a full chime of eight bells.* **2** ringing, °peal, chiming, tolling, tintinnabulation, clanging, ding-dong, °striking; tinkle, °jingle, °jangle: *We could hear the chimes of Big Ben from our hotel room.*
—*v.* **3** °ring, °peal, °toll, °sound, tintinnabulate, clang, °strike: *The clock chimed on the hour.* **4** °mark, °denote, °indicate, °announce: *The carillon chimed the hour at noon.* **5** ***chime in***: **a** °join in, °blend, harmonize: *When singing this round, chime in at the third bar.* **b** °interrupt, intercede, °intrude, °interfere, °break in, *Colloq* °chip in; *Slang* °butt in: *I was about to speak when he chimed in with some silly remark.*

chink *n.* fissure, °rift, °crack, °crevice, °gap, °opening, cleft, °slit, °aperture, °cranny: *We could see daylight through a chink in the fence.*

chip *n.* **1** °fragment, °piece, shard *or* sherd, °splinter, °flake, °sliver, °scrap, °morsel, °bit: *A chip of slate rattled down off the roof.* **2** °counter, marker, °token; °plaque, *US* °check: *He put his chip on number 14.*
—*v.* **3** °chisel, °whittle, hew: *He chipped away at the stone till it fitted perfectly into the hole.* **4** ***chip in***: **a** °contribute; °participate: *All the neighbours chipped in to pay for the street decorations.* **b** °interrupt, °break in, °intrude, °interfere, intercede, interpose, *Colloq* °chime in: *Clive chipped in with his usual silly comment.*

chirp *v.* **1** tweet, °peep, °twitter, chirrup, warble, trill, cheep, chitter, chirr, °pipe: *I was awakened by the birds, chirping away in the forest.*
—*n.* **2** tweet, °peep, °twitter, chirrup, warble, trill, cheep, chitter, chirr: *The canary gave two chirps and jumped onto its perch.*

chisel *v.* **1** °carve, °cut, °pare, °groove, °shape, °engrave, °grave: *He was chiselling the figure of an eagle out of the board.* **2** °cheat, °defraud, °swindle, bilk, °trick, °fool, °dupe, gull, *Colloq* bamboozle: *The gamblers chiselled him out of a week's wages.*

chivalrous *adj.* courtly, °gracious, °courteous, °polite, °gallant, °noble, knightly, gentlemanly, °considerate, °kind, °charitable, magnanimous: *It was quite chivalrous of you to drive me home.*

chivalry *n.* knight-errantry; °honour, °bravery, °courage, °courtesy, politeness, courtliness, gallantry, °nobility, virtuousness, righteousness, justness, fairness, impartiality, equitableness: *All the noble sentiments blended together constitute chivalry.*

choice *n.* **1** °selection, °election, °preference, choosing, °pick, acceptance: *I don't care for his choice of language.* **2** °option, realm of possibilities; °alternative, °voice, °determination: *She was given no choice in selecting her husband.* **3** °pick, °élite, °flower, °best, °select, cream, *crème de la crème*: *The king's guard is made up from the choice of the kingdom.*
—*adj.* **4** °select, °exquisite, °special, °superior, °prime, high-quality, °excellent, °pre-eminent, °best, °prize, °first-rate, °exceptional, preferred, °desirable, °ideal, °rare, *Colloq Brit* plummy: *She has the choicest wines in her cellar.* **5** selected, °select, hand-picked, well-chosen, °fit, °appropriate, °fitting: *The eulogy was disposed of in a few choice words.*

choke *v.* **1** suffocate, asphyxiate, °smother, °stifle, strangle, throttle, garrotte *or* garrote *or* garotte, burke: *He choked his elderly victims, then stole their money.* **2** °stop, °fill (up), °block (up), °obstruct, congest, °clog, dam (up), constrict: *The channel is completely choked with weeds.* **3** Also, ***choke off***: °smother, °suppress, °stifle, °prohibit, °frustrate, °deny, obviate, °cut off, °stop, put a °stop to; dissuade, °discourage: *His policies choked off any chance for innovation.* **4** ***choke back*** *or* ***down***: °suppress, °repress, °stifle, °restrain: *He choked back the tears when he saw the gravestone.*

choose *v.* °select, °elect, °pick (out), °determine, °judge; °decide, °prefer, opt, °settle upon *or* on: *She had the right to choose the course that seemed the best to her. Given the options, I chose to stay.*

choosy *adj.* °selective, °discriminating, discerning, °fastidious, °finicky *or* finical, °particular, °fussy, °demanding, °exacting, °difficult, °hard to please, *Colloq* picky: *If you weren't so choosy, you wouldn't have to pay so much.*

chop *v.* **1** Also, ***chop away*** *or* ***down*** *or* ***off***: °cut, °hack, hew, °lop, crop, °cleave, °sever: *Chop away that underbrush. I tried to chop off the end. Don't chop down that tree!* **2** Also, ***chop up***: mince; dice, cube; °hash: *Chop up the parsley very fine before adding it to the sauce.*
—*n.* **3** °cut, °blow, °stroke: *With a quick chop of the axe, the branch was severed.*

christen *v.* **1** baptize, anoint: *They are going to christen the baby next week.* **2** °name, °call, dub: *The child was christened Madelaine. The highest peak in Wales is christened Snowdon.*

chronic *adj.* **1** long-lasting, long-standing, °lingering, inveterate, °persistent, continuing, °lasting, long-lived: *The doctor said that the condition, for which there is no cure, is chronic.* **2** inveterate, °persistent, dyed in the wool, confirmed, °habitual, hardened: *Abby is a chronic liar.*

chronicle *n.* **1** °record, °history, °diary, °chronology, °account, °narrative, °description, °report, °register, annal(s), archive: *She has written a chronicle of the events leading up to the War of Jenkins' Ear.*
—*v.* **2** °record, °register, °list, °enter, archive, °document, °describe; °tell, °recount, °narrate, °report, °relate, retail: *In the* Iliad *Homer chronicled the legends of the Trojan War.*

chronology *n.* °account, °record, °calendar, almanac, °journal, log; °sequence: *Describe the chronology of events preceding your discovery of the body.*

chubby *adj.* podgy *or US* pudgy; stumpy, stubby, chunky, tubby, °plump, °dumpy, thickset, heavy-set, °heavy, °ample, overweight: *She was a bit chubby when a teenager but became a professional model when she was 21.*

chuckle *v.* **1** °laugh, chortle, crow, snigger, °giggle, °titter: *Robin always chuckled when the subject of embezzlement came up.*
—*n.* **2** chuckling, °laugh, chortle, crowing, °giggle; °laughter, snigger, sniggering: *It was hard to resist a chuckle when we saw the looks on their faces.*

chum *n.* **1** °friend, °comrade, °companion; confidant(e), °familiar; °fellow, °colleague, *Colloq* °pal, sidekick, *Chiefly Brit and Australian and New Zealand* °mate, *Chiefly US and Canadian* buddy: *I invited a chum of mine for the weekend.*
—*v.* **2** Often, ***chum around***: °associate, *Colloq* °pal (around): *Yes, we used to chum around together in the army.* **3** ***chum up with***: °ally (oneself) with, be °friendly with, °go with, °associate with, *Colloq* °pal (up *or* about *or* around) with, *US* °team up with: *Lionel chummed up with Ashley to go swimming.*

chummy *adj.* °friendly, °sociable, °intimate, °close, °thick, *Colloq* pally, *US* palsy-walsy, buddy-buddy: *You were very chummy with Peter once, weren't you?*

chute *n.* **1** °waterfall, °rapid: *The canoe skimmed down the chute with lightning speed.* **2** °slide, °shaft, °channel, °ramp, runway, trough, °incline: *The parcels come down this chute and you have to sort them by postcode.*

circle *n.* **1** disc *or chiefly US* disk, °ring, hoop, °loop, °band, °wheel, annulus, ringlet; cordon: *Using a compass, he carefully drew a circle. We formed a circle around the speaker.* **2** °set, coterie, °clique, °class, °division, °group, °crowd; °society, °fellowship, °fraternity, °company: *John and I don't move in the same circles.*
—*v.* **3** °encircle, circumambulate, °go °round *or* around, °tour; circumnavigate: *For exercise, I circle the lake in the park every morning.* **4** °encircle, °surround, gird, °enclose, circumscribe: *Twenty small diamonds circle each star sapphire.*

circuit *n.* **1** compass, circumference, °perimeter, °periphery, °girth, °border, °boundary, °edge, °limit, ambit, °margin, °outline, confine(s), °bound, °pale: *The circuit* *of the area amounts to 72 miles.* **2** °round, °tour, ambit, °circle, °orbit, °course, °lap: *The rider completed the circuit of the ranch, mending the fence as he went.*

circular *adj.* **1** °round, disc-shaped *or chiefly US* disk-shaped, disc-like *or chiefly US* disk-like, discoid; ring-shaped, ring-like, annular: *Notice the circular pattern of growth of this ivy.* **2** °roundabout, °indirect, circuitous, °tortuous, twisting, twisted, anfractuous; periphrastic, circumlocutory; °devious: *We had to take a circular route because the road was closed. Why can't she say what she means instead of being so circular?* **3** illogical, °inconsistent, °redundant, fallacious, irrational, *Formal* °sophistic *or* sophistical: *To say that you exist because you think and that you think because you exist is an example of circular reasoning.*

circulate *v.* **1** °move *or* °go about *or* °round *or* around, °orbit, °flow, °course, °run, °circle: *The blood circulates from the heart through the arteries and veins and back to the heart.* **2** °spread, °distribute, disseminate, °issue, °publish, °air, °announce, °proclaim, make known, °noise °abroad, bruit about, °report, °broadcast, °reveal, divulge, advertise, °publicize, promulgate, °put about, °bring *or* °put out, °pass out *or* °round *or* around: *He has been circulating the story that his ex-wife cheated on her income tax.* **3** °spread, °go round *or* around, be bruited about, °come out: *A rumour has been circulating about your behaviour at the office party.*

circulation *n.* **1** °circuit, °course, °orbit, °flow, flowing, °motion: *It was Harvey who discovered the circulation of the blood.* **2** °spread, spreading, dissemination, °transmission, °passage, °distribution, diffusion, °publication, °advertisement, °announcement, issuance, issuing, °pronouncement, °proclamation, promulgation, °broadcast, broadcasting: *The state has again forbidden the free circulation of information.*

circumstance *n.* **1** Often, ***circumstances***: °situation, °condition(s), °state (of affairs); °status, °station, resources, °income, finances: *In the circumstances, all leave is cancelled. Each person will be helped according to the individual circumstance.* **2** °event, °incident, °episode, °occurrence, °affair, °happening, °occasion: *Any unforeseen circumstance could set off a shooting war.*

circumstantial *adj.* **1** °indirect, °presumptive, evidential *or* evidentiary, interpretive, deduced, presumed, presumable, implicative, implied, inferred, inferential: *Some circumstantial evidence is very strong, as when you find a gun in the suspect's house.* **2** °accidental, °incidental, hearsay, °indirect, unimportant, adventitious, °provisional, °secondary, unessential, °non-essential, fortuitous, °chance, °extraneous: *Such circumstantial trivia have no bearing on the case.* **3** °detailed, °particular, °precise, °explicit, °specific: *We cannot believe that he invented so circumstantial a narrative.*

citizen *n.* **1** voter; °native; householder, °resident, °inhabitant, °denizen, dweller, freeman; *Brit* patrial, ratepayer; *US* taxpayer: *All citizens are entitled to certain rights.* **2** city-dweller, town-dweller, townsman, townswoman, villager, burgess, oppidan: *She considers herself a citizen of Oxford.*

city *n.* °metropolis, °municipality, borough, burgh; conurbation, megalopolis; *Brit* urban °district; °see, diocese, bishopric; *New Zealand* urban °area; *Colloq* °town, *US* burg, big apple: *We gave up our flat in the city and moved to the country.*

civil *adj.* **1** civilian, non-military, °lay, laic, laical, °secular: *There is a distinction between civil law and canon law.* **2** °domestic, °internal; °public: *The economic conditions have led to civil strife.* **3** °polite, °courteous, °respectful, well-mannered, °proper, civilized, °cordial, °formal, courtly, urbane, °polished, °refined: *They are civil enough, but I always have the feeling they really despise tourists.*

civility *n.* °courtesy, politeness, °respect, comity, urbanity, amiability, °consideration, courteousness, cordiality, °propriety, °tact, °diplomacy, politesse, °protocol: *Despite his rude behaviour at her dinner-party, she treats him with great civility.*

civilization *n.* **1** °culture, °refinement, cultivation, enlightenment, °edification, °sophistication, °polish: *The Romans brought civilization to many peoples who had been quite barbarous.* **2** °culture, mores, °custom(s): *He has studied Egyptian civilization all his life.*

civilize *v.* **1** °enlighten, °refine, °polish, edify, °educate, acculturate: *Civilized people do not behave in such a boorish way.* **2** °tame, domesticate; broaden, elevate, acculturate: *The claim that they civilized the Aborigines means only that they forced them to conform to the White man's notion of civilization.*

claim *n.* **1** °demand, °assertion, °request, °requisition, °petition, °application; °requirement: *As far as the land is concerned, his claim has been denied.* **2** °right(s), °call, °title: *What possible claim could the Miss Dashwoods have on his generosity?*
—*v.* **3** °demand, °seek, °ask *or* °call (for), °exact, °insist (on *or* upon), °require, °command, be entitled to: *She has every right to claim a share in the estate.* **4** °declare, assert, °allege, °state, °put *or* °set forth, affirm, contend, °maintain: *These measurements lack the degree of accuracy claimed for them. She claims that she was the first person to ring the police.*

clammy *adj.* **1** °moist, °sticky, gummy, °pasty, viscous, °slimy: *In the swamp the police found a clammy pistol that they believe to be the weapon.* **2** °moist, °damp, °humid, °close, °muggy, °wet, °misty, foggy: *It was the kind of clammy summer's day when your shirt sticks to your back.*

clamp *n.* **1** °clasp, °vice, °brace, °clip, fastener: *Use a clamp to hold the pieces together till the glue dries.*
—*v.* **2** °fasten (together), °clip (together), °bracket, make °fast, °clasp: *You should clamp the planks together and plane the edges of both.*

clan *n.* **1** °tribe, °family, °dynasty, °line, °house: *There had been a feud of long standing between the two clans, which culminated in the massacre of Glencoe.* **2** °fraternity, °brotherhood, °party, °set, °clique, coterie, °circle, °crowd, °group, °fellowship, °society, °faction, °family, °tribe; °band, °ring, °gang: *He regards social scientists as a clan quite separate from other scientists.*

clap *v.* **1** °applaud; °cheer, acclaim: *Everyone clapped when the boxer climbed into the ring.* **2** °slap, °strike, °pat: *He clapped me on the shoulder in the friendliest way.* **3** °put, °place, °slap, °fling, °toss, cast, *Colloq* °stick: *He had no sooner set foot in the town when he was clapped in jail.* **4** °impose, °lay, °apply: *The magistrate clapped a severe fine on me for speeding.*
—*n.* **5** °crack, °slap, °report, °crash, bang, °snap: *There was a loud clap of thunder, making the house shake.*

clapper *n.* °tongue: *We attached a rope to the clapper of the bell.*

clarify *v.* **1** elucidate, make °clear, °simplify, make °plain, °clear up, °explain, shed *or* throw °light on *or* upon, °illuminate, explicate: *She offered to clarify any points about which we had questions.* **2** °clear, °purify, °clean: *The trout should be lightly basted with clarified butter.*

clarity *n.* **1** clearness, transparency, limpidity, pellucidity: *The clarity of the sea in the tropics is owing to a lack of plankton.* **2** lucidity, °definition, definiteness, distinctness; comprehensibility, understandability, intelligibility, unambiguousness: *One cannot argue with the clarity of her explanation of Hegelianism.*

clash *n.* **1** °crash, clang, clank, clangour: *The concerto ends with a clash of cymbals.* **2** °collision, smash, (°hostile) °encounter, °conflict, °engagement, °fight, °battle, °disagreement, °difference, °argument, °dispute, altercation, °quarrel, squabble: *He has witnessed many a clash between the prime minister and parliament.*
—*v.* **3** °conflict, °fight, °battle, °disagree, °differ, °argue, °dispute, °quarrel, squabble, °feud, wrangle, °cross swords: *My brother and I always clash on the question of who should pay our father's hospital bills.*

4 °conflict, disharmonize, °jar, be at °odds *or* out of keeping: *The pink of the blouse and the fuchsia of the skirt clash badly.*

clasp *n.* 1 fastener, °fastening, °hook, catch, °clip, °pin, °brooch: *The ends were fastened together with a diamond clasp.* 2 °embrace, °hug, °hold, °grasp, °grip: *He held her tight in his clasp.*
—*v.* 3 °fasten, °secure, °close, °hold, °hook, °clip, °pin, °clamp: *The robe was clasped by an emerald pin.*
4 °hold, °embrace, take °hold of, °hug, °enclose, °envelop: *The beggar clasped my hand, his eyes seeking mine in piteous supplication.* 5 °grab, °grasp, °seize, °clutch, °grip: *They clasped hands in friendship.*

class *n.* 1 °rank, °grade, °level, °order, °stratum; °caste, °lineage, °birth, °pedigree, °stock, °extraction, descent: *He was born in the 1940s into a family of the middle class.* 2 °category, °division, classification, °group, °genre, °league, °realm, °domain; °kind, °sort, °type: *As a dancer, she in a class by herself.* 3 °excellence, °merit, °refinement, °elegance, °prestige, °importance, °taste, discernment, °distinction, °bearing, °presence, savoir faire, savoir vivre, °breeding: *He may be a good drinking companion, but he has no class whatsoever.* 4 year, °form, *US* °grade: *We were in the same class at school.*
—*v.* 5 classify, °group, °arrange, assort, °type, °categorize, °rank, °grade, °rate, °order: *They are classed as self-employed for these purposes.*

classic *adj.* 1 °standard, °leading, °outstanding, prototypic(al), °definitive, °model, °ideal, archetypal, paradigmatic: *His military career is a classic example of what family connections can achieve.* 2 °legendary, °immortal, °enduring, °deathless, ageless, °timeless, undying, °venerable, °time-honoured; °outstanding, °first-rate, °superior, °excellent, °noteworthy, °notable, °exemplary: *By the time she was ten, she had read most of the classic works of English literature. He collects classic cars.*
—*n.* 3 °paragon, °epitome, °outstanding example, exemplar, °model, paradigm, °prototype: *When it comes to comedians, Ronnie is a classic.* 4 °masterpiece, master-work: *The Rolls-Royce Silver Ghost is regarded as a classic by collectors.*

classical *adj.* 1 °standard, °model, °exemplary, °traditional, established, °influential, °authoritative, °serious, °weighty: *Classical authors are those who are regarded as being of good credit and authority in the schools. Montaigne is the earliest classical writer in the French language.* 2 Greek, Latin, Roman: *Architectural styles of the 18th century harked back to Classical designs.*

claw *n.* 1 talon, °nail: *The cat had scratched her badly with its claws.*
—*v.* 2 °scratch, °tear, °scrape, °rake, °slash: *She clawed at his face to break his grip on her throat.* 3 °grapple, °grab, °catch, °scrape, scrabble: *He tried to climb up the embankment, clawing at the steep wall.*

clean *adj.* 1 °pure, undefiled, unsullied, unmixed, unadulterated, uncontaminated, unpolluted, uninfected, °unspoiled *or* unspoilt, °sanitary, disinfected; antiseptic, decontaminated, purified, °sterile: *The laboratory reports that our well water is absolutely clean. You must use a clean bandage.* 2 unsoiled, untainted, unstained; unsullied; cleansed, cleanly, (freshly) laundered *or* washed, scrubbed; °spotless, °immaculate: *She puts on clean underwear every day in case she's involved in an accident.* 3 clean-cut, °neat, °simple, °definite, uncomplicated, °smooth, °even, °straight, °trim, °tidy: *The edges of the fracture are clean and will mend quickly.* 4 °innocent, °blameless, °inoffensive, °respectable; °decent, °chaste, °pure, °honourable, °good, undefiled, °virtuous, °moral: *The suspect was completely clean—he was out of town at the time of the robbery.* 5 non-radioactive: *They say they've produced a clean bomb, but I don't believe it.*
6 °unarmed, weaponless: *Frisk that suspect and make sure he's clean.*
—*adv.* 7 °completely, °entirely, °thoroughly, fully, °totally, °wholly, °altogether, °quite, °utterly, °absolutely: *Geoff's clean out of his mind if he believes that. With one blow he cut the orange clean through.* 8 ***come clean***: °confess, °acknowledge, make a clean breast, °admit, °make a °revelation, °reveal, *Colloq* own up, °spill the beans; *US dialect* fess up; *Slang* °sing: *In the end he saw that he was trapped and decided to come clean.*
—*v.* 9 °cleanse, °wash, lave, (take a) °shower, sponge, mop, °scrub, °scour, °sweep, dust, vacuum, °polish, °launder, dry-clean, *Brit* hoover; °tidy, °neaten, do up, °straighten up *or* out, unclutter; *Brit* bath; *US and Canadian* bathe: *When we cleaned the urn, we could read the inscription. I have told Richard a thousand times to clean his room.* 10 ***clean out***: **a** °exhaust, deplete: *The gambler cleaned her out of every penny she had in the world.* **b** °empty, leave °bare, °clear out, °evacuate: *We must clean out the larder before it can be painted.* 11 ***clean up***: **a** clean, °cleanse, °wash, (take a) °shower, *Brit* bath; *US* take a bath, bathe, °wash up: *Clean up, please, dinner is almost ready. It took us a week to clean up the stables.* **b** °purge, °purify, °disinfect, depollute, decontaminate, °clear, sanitize: *The council has led the way towards cleaning up the wetlands of chemical waste.*

cleanse *v.* 1 °clean, absterge, deterge, °wash, °scour, °scrub: *You need a scrubbing brush to cleanse the tub.* 2 °purify, depurate; °purge, °wash away, expiate: *Each prayer repeated has a certain value in cleansing away sin.*

clear *adj.* 1 unclouded, cloudless, °sunny, °fair, sunlit, °fine: *On a clear day, you can see the lighthouse several miles away.* 2 °transparent, limpid, crystalline; translucent, uncloudy, unclouded, pellucid: *The water was clear enough to see the bottom.* 3 °bright, °lustrous, shining, °shiny, sparkling, *Formal* nitid: *We painted the bathroom a lovely clear blue.* 4 °bright, °fresh, unblemished, unscarred: *She has a lovely clear complexion.* 5 °distinct, °sharp, well-defined, °definite; °legible, °readable; °acute, °vivid: *The notes were written in a large clear hand.* 6 understandable, °intelligible, perspicuous, lucid, comprehensible, apprehensible, °discernible, °plain, °obvious, unambiguous, unequivocal, °explicit, °definite, unmistakable, °indisputable, °undisputed, °unquestionable, °incontrovertible: *He has made himself very clear on that point.*
7 °distinct, unclouded, unconfused, °explicit, °plain, °definite, clear-cut, palpable: *I have a clear recollection of her words.* 8 °evident, °plain, °obvious, °patent, °manifest, °apparent: *It became clear that someone was trying to compromise her.* 9 °perceptive, °acute, °sensitive, perspicacious, discerning, °keen: *It was only his clear vision of the situation that saved us all.*
10 °certain, °sure, convinced, °confident, °positive, °determined, °definite, assured: *I am not clear that the subject was a good one.* 11 °pure, unwavering, well-defined, °distinct, clarion, bell-like: *We heard father's clear voice calling from below.* 12 °pure, guileless, °unsophisticated, °innocent, °blameless, °faultless; not °guilty: *I still cannot look her in the eye with a clear conscience.* 13 unencumbered, °free, °net: *In our first year we made a clear profit of 25 per cent.* 14 °unlimited, °unqualified, unquestioned, °unquestionable, °absolute, °complete, °entire; °pure, °sheer, °perfect: *You must allow three clear days for the ascent.* 15 disengaged, disentangled, unentangled, °free, freed, °rid, °quit, °loose, unencumbered, released: *When the line is clear of any obstruction, hoist sail and let's be off.*
16 °open, unencumbered, °free, unblocked, unobstructed, °unimpeded, °direct: *There is a clear view of the park from here.*
—*adv.* 17 brightly, effulgently, radiantly, luminously, lambently: *The stars were shining clear in the night sky.* 18 distinctly, °clearly, starkly, perceptibly, discernibly, understandably, prominently: *When you see the reef, sing out loud and clear.* 19 °completely, °utterly, °entirely, cleanly, °clean, °wholly, °totally: *The thief got clear away in the confusion.*
—*v.* 20 °clarify, °cleanse, °clean, °purify: *The chemical soon cleared the water of all sediment.* 21 exonerate, absolve, acquit; °excuse, °forgive: *He has been cleared*

of all charges and released. **22** Also, ***clear up***: °explain, elucidate, explicate, °clarify, make °plain *or* clear, disambiguate: *We should be able to clear up the mystery by this evening.* **23** Also, ***clear up***: become °fair *or* cloudless *or* °sunny: *I hope the weather clears in time for the game.* **24** °open (up), °free; unblock, unclog, unstop; disencumber, dislodge: *We were able to clear a path through the jungle. He cleared his throat and began to speak.* **25** °empty: *Clear the land of trees before farming it.* **26** Also, ***clear away*** *or* ***out***: °remove, °eliminate, °take; °cut away *or* down: *Clear those branches from the paths.* **27** disburden, unburden, °purge, °free, °rid: *He has cleared his conscience of any responsibility in the matter.* **28** °leap *or* °jump over, vault: *She cleared the fence easily.* **29** Also, ***clear up***: °settle, °discharge, °pay, °square, °defray, °satisfy: *The company has cleared all its debts.* **30** ***clear off*** *or* ***out***: °leave, °depart, decamp, °go *or* °run off, °get out, °withdraw, *Slang* °beat it, scram, *Taboo Brit* sod off, *Chiefly Australian* °shoot through, *US and Canadian* take a (run-out) °powder: *I told them to clear off and stop bothering me.* **31** ***clear up***: **a** °eliminate, °remove, °settle; °clarify: *I hope we can clear up any misunderstanding between us.* **b** °tidy (up), °neaten (up), put *or* set in °order, clear: *I'll clear up after dinner.*
—*n.* **32** ***in the clear***: °innocent, not guilty; exonerated, forgiven, absolved; unburdened, disburdened, unencumbered, °free: *The other chap confessed, leaving me in the clear.*

clearance *n.* **1** °space, °gap, °hole, °interval, °separation, °room, °margin, °leeway, °allowance: *You must allow a clearance of 2 millimetres.* **2** °approval, °endorsement, authorization, °consent; °licence, °leave, °permission: *He cannot get security clearance with his prison record.*

clearly *adv.* **1** distinctly; starkly, plainly: *With spectacles, I can see everything more clearly.* **2** °evidently, °apparently, °manifestly, °obviously, certainly, °definitely, °positively, unequivocally, unquestionably, incontestably, without °doubt, °undoubtedly, indubitably, demonstrably, °absolutely, °utterly: *His statement is clearly untrue.* **3** audibly, distinctly, understandably: *I wish she would speak more clearly.*

cleave *v.* °split, °divide, °cut, °cut *or* °chop *or* hew in two *or* asunder, bisect, halve, °separate, °slit, rive: *With a mighty blow the log was cleaved cleanly in two.*

clergyman *n.* **1** ecclesiastic, churchman, cleric, reverend, °divine, man of the °cloth, °holy man, °priest, °minister, chaplain, °father, rabbi, °pastor, parson, rector, vicar, dean, canon, presbyter, prebendary *or* prebend, deacon, sexton, sacristan, guru, ayatollah, imam: *In his black frock coat he looked like a clergyman.* **2** °monk, friar, °brother, monastic, °religious: *A clergyman was responsible for his religious education.* **3** °preacher, gospeller, evangelist, revivalist, °missionary, sermonizer: *She was moved by the clergyman's sermon.*

clerical *adj.* **1** ecclesiastical, churchly, °pastoral, sacerdotal, °priestly, hieratic, rabbinical, ministerial, monastic, apostolic, prelatic, papal, pontifical, episcopal, canonical: *He was wearing his clerical vestments.* **2** white-collar, °office, °professional, secretarial, stenographic, accounting, bookkeeping: *He runs the shop and his wife has the clerical responsibilities.*

clever *adj.* **1** skilled, °talented, °skilful, adroit, °dexterous, °gifted, °agile, °quick-witted, °intelligent, °perceptive, discerning, °sharp, sharp-witted, °adept, °able, *Colloq* brainy: *She was very clever at mathematics.* **2** °shrewd, cunning, guileful, canny, °artful, °crafty, °sly, °wily, °foxy: *It was a clever move to sound out the chairman before the meeting.* **3** °intelligent, °wise, °sage, sagacious; °ingenious, °original, °resourceful, Daedalian, inventive, °creative, °smart, °imaginative: *It was very clever of her to memorize the record-book for the competition.* **4** deft, adroit, nimble-fingered, °dexterous, °handy, °skilful: *The old woman is clever with her hands.*

cliché *n.* stereotype, bromide, trite saying, old °saw *or* °maxim, °truism, platitude, commonplace, banality, *Colloq* chestnut: *The report was full of clichés and convinced no one.*

client *n.* °customer, °patron, shopper; °patient: *She opened a law practice and already has a number of clients.*

clientele *n.* °clients, °patrons, °customers; °custom, °business, °trade, °patronage, following: *What sort of clientele do you expect to attract?*

cliff *n.* °precipice, °bluff, escarpment, scarp, °crag, rock-face, cuesta, °scar *or Scots* scaur: *The commandos are trained to scale a 100-foot cliff.*

climate *n.* **1** °weather, *Literary* clime: *We are retiring to the Maldives because we like a sunny climate.* **2** °atmosphere, ambience *or* ambiance, °air; °feeling, °mood, °aura, °milieu, °feel: *In the present climate of opinion, we'd best delay introducing the bill.*

climax *n.* **1** culmination, °height, °acme, apex, °summit, °zenith, apogee, °peak, °high °point, °maximum, °supreme moment: *The war reached its climax at the battle of Arbela.* **2** turning-point, °crisis, crossroads: *The climax of the play occurs in the third act.* **3** orgasm: *She told her psychiatrist that she had never reached a climax with her husband.*
—*v.* **4** culminate, °peak, °crest, come to a °head: *The week's events climaxed with the presentation of the gold medal.*

climb *v.* **1** Also, ***climb up***: °mount, ascend, °go up, °scale, °shin (up), clamber up, *US* shinny (up): *In one of the games we had to climb a greased pole. Two Japanese teams have climbed Mount Everest.* **2** °creep, °trail, °twine; °grow: *The ivy has climbed all over the garden wall.* **3** °rise, °arise, ascend, °go up, °mount; °advance: *Watch the smoke climb into the sky.* **4** ***climb along***: °creep, °edge, clamber, °crawl, inch: *The cat burglar climbed along the ledge till he reached the window.* **5** ***climb down***: **a** °descend, °go down: *We shall need a rope to climb down from here.* **b** Usually, ***climb down from***: °retreat (from), °withdraw (from), back away (from), °give up, °abandon, °renounce: *He has climbed down from his earlier position regarding women in the priesthood.*
—*n.* **6** °grade, °incline, °route, °pitch; ascent; descent: *It was a steep climb to Camp Four.*

clinch *v.* **1** °secure, °settle, °confirm, °determine, conclude, °dispose of, °complete, °wind up, °finalize, *Colloq* °sew up: *He clinched the argument by resigning.*
—*n.* **2** °close quarters, °hug, °clasp, °embrace; °cuddle: *The boxers went into a clinch to regain their breath.*

clincher *n.* finishing °touch, °pay-off, punch-line, *coup de grâce*, °final *or* crowning °blow: *The point about saving costs proved to be a clincher, and we were given the go-ahead.*

cling *v.* **1** °stick, adhere, °attach, °fasten, °fix: *The detectives found that one of the victim's hairs had clung to the suspect's lapel.* **2** °favour, be *or* °remain °devoted *or* °attached to, °embrace, °hang on to, °retain, °keep, °cherish: *He still clung to his old-fashioned notions of honour.* **3** ***cling together*** *or* ***to one another***: °embrace, °hug, °cleave to one another, °clasp one another, °clutch one another, °hold (°fast) to one another, °grasp one another: *The children clung together in the darkness.*

clip[1] *v.* **1** °clasp, °fasten, °fix, °attach, °hold, °clinch; °staple: *Please clip these papers together.*
—*n.* **2** °clasp, fastener: *That clip isn't strong enough to hold all these papers.*

clip[2] *v.* **1** °trim (off), °lop (off), °cut (off), crop, bob, °snip: *The barber clipped my hair short. Roger has clipped two seconds off the record.* **2** °shorten, °reduce, °abbreviate, °diminish, °cut (°short): *The film was clipped by fifteen minutes for television. In her rapid-fire way of speaking, she clipped each word.* **3** °strike, °hit, °punch, smack, °box, cuff, whack, *Colloq* wallop, clout; *Slang* sock: *He was clipped on the jaw and knocked out.* **4** °cheat, °swindle, bilk, overcharge,

Slang rook: *They clipped him out of a week's wages. She was clipped for a ten per cent 'service fee'.*
—*n.* **5** °segment, °interval, °section, °part, °portion, °extract, °cutting, °excerpt, °bit, snippet, °scrap, °fragment: *We were shown a film clip of the cheese-making process.* **6** °blow, cuff, °punch, °hit, °strike, smack, whack, °box, *Colloq* wallop, clout; *Slang* sock: *She gave him a clip at the side of the head and he went down.* **7** °pace, °rate, °speed: *I was riding along at a good clip when my horse shied and I was thrown off.*

clique *n.* °set, coterie, °crowd, °circle, °group: *There was the usual clique from the Sales Department standing round the bar.*

cloak *n.* **1** °mantle, °cape, °robe, °wrap, poncho; °coat, overcoat: *She pulled her cloak around her in the chill night air.* **2** °mantle, concealment, °cover, °screen, °shroud, °veil: *He stole away under the cloak of darkness.*
—*v.* **3** °conceal, °hide, °mask, °screen, °veil, °shroud, °cover up; °disguise: *All of the spies' activities were cloaked in secrecy.*

clod *n.* **1** °lump, °mass, °gob, °wad, hunk, chunk; °piece of sod *or* °turf; *Colloq* glob: *A clod of earth was stuck between the spikes of my golf shoes.* **2** idiot, °fool, °dolt, blockhead, simpleton, dunce, °dope, oaf, Neanderthal, lout, ass, °boor, °clown, ninny, ninny-hammer, bumpkin, clodhopper, *Slang* vegetable, *US and Canadian* °jerk: *He felt a bit of a clod standing there with no idea which way to go.*

clog *v.* °hamper, °encumber, °impede; °obstruct, °choke (up), °block, congest, °jam: *The road was clogged with returning holiday-makers. A piece of orange peel had clogged the sink drain.*

close *v.* **1** °shut, close up, °seal; close off, °lock, padlock, °secure, °fasten: *I closed my eyes. Please close the door behind you.* **2** make °inaccessible, °shut, *Chiefly US* place off limits: *The Bodleian Library will be closed for a week.* **3** conclude, °end, °finish, °complete, bring to a close *or* an °end, °terminate, °climax, *Colloq* °wind up: *A brilliant flourish closes the first movement of the symphony.* **4** conclude, °sign, °seal, °make, °settle, °clinch, °agree, °arrange, °work out, °establish: *Union and management closed a deal, and the strike was called off.* **5** Also, ***close down***: °discontinue, °terminate, °stop, °suspend, °shut down, go out of business, °cease operations, close (up), *Colloq* °wind up, °shut up shop, put up the shutters: *Competition from the supermarket forced the greengrocer to close down.* **6** Also, ***close off***: °seal, make °inaccessible, °shut (off), °obstruct, obturate: *This wing of the museum has been closed off temporarily.* **7** ***close one's eyes to***: °ignore, °overlook, °disregard: *You have always closed your eyes to his faults.* **8** ***close up***: **a** close (down), °shut (up), °lock up: *It's time to close up for the night.* **b** close, °come *or* °draw *or* °bring together, °unite, °join; °connect: *We closed up ranks and stood at attention.*
—*adj.* **9** °near; adjacent, proximate, proximal: *He claims to have had a close encounter with an extraterrestrial. There certainly is a close resemblance between Kathy and her daughter.* **10** closed, °shut (up), °fixed, °fast, °secure, °tight: *The hostages spent a month in close confinement.* **11** °dense, °compact, °tight, °cramped, compressed, °tiny, minuscule, °minute: *I could hardly read the close writing on the matchbox.* **12** °stuffy, °musty, °stale, fusty, confining, °oppressive, airless, unventilated, confined, stifling, suffocating: *They locked me in a room that was so close I could hardly breathe.* **13** °nearly °equal *or* °even, close-matched, neck and neck, °tight: *It was a close race, but Flanagan won by a hair.* **14** °careful, assiduous, °precise, °detailed, concentrated, °strict, rigorous, °minute, searching, °attentive, °alert, °intent, °intense, °thorough, °painstaking: *Close analysis has revealed that the handwriting is that of a left-handed adult.* **15** °attached, °intimate, °devoted, °familiar, inseparable, close-knit, °solid, °confidential; °fast; *Colloq* °thick, °thick as thieves, pally, *US and Canadian* palsy-walsy, buddy-buddy: *They are a very close family. She and her father are very close.* **16** °private, °privy, °secret, °guarded, closely °guarded, °confidential: *Although it should have been a close secret, the press managed to get hold of it.* **17** °secretive, °reticent, °taciturn, °reserved, close-mouthed, °tight-lipped, °silent: *She is very close about the whereabouts of her husband.* **18** stingy, °mean, °miserly, niggardly, tight-fisted, close-fisted, parsimonious, °penurious, penny-pinching, cheese-paring, Scrooge-like, skinflinty, *Colloq* near, *Brit* mingy: *He's so close he charges his own mother rent.* **19** °secluded, concealed, °shut up *or* away, °hidden: *The fugitives decided to lie close till nightfall.*
—*adv.* **20** °near, in the °neighbourhood (of), not °far (from), adjacent (to); alongside; at °hand, °nearby, close by: *The murder took place close to my house. I'm frightened, so please stay close by.* **21** ***close to*** *or* ***on*** *or* ***onto***: °nearly, °almost, °about, °practically, °approximately, nigh unto, approaching: *For close to two thousand years the site lay untouched.*
—*n.* **22** °end, °termination, conclusion, °finish, °completion, cessation; culmination: *By the close of trading, share prices had risen again.*

cloth *n.* **1** °fabric, °material, textile, *Chiefly Brit* °stuff: *The curtains are made of cloth, not plastic.* **2** ***the cloth***: the clergy, the (°religious) °ministry, the priesthood: *He is a man of the cloth.*

clothe *v.* **1** °dress, attire, garb, °apparel, °outfit, °fit out *or* up, accoutre *or US also* accouter, *Brit* °kit out *or* up, *Colloq* tog up *or* out: *He earns barely enough to clothe and feed his family.* **2** endow, °invest, caparison, endue: *They tried to clothe their transactions with the raiment of honesty.*

clothes *n.pl.* clothing, °apparel, attire, °wear, °dress, °garments, raiment, °wardrobe, °outfit, °ensemble, vestment(s), *Old-fashioned* duds, *Colloq* togs, °gear, °get-up, *Slang* glad °rags, *Brit* clobber; *Slang US* (set of) threads: *Put on some old clothes and make yourself comfortable.*

clown *n.* **1** jester, °fool, °zany, °comic, °comedian, comedienne, funny man *or* woman: *Of all the performers at the circus, I like the clowns best.* **2** buffoon, °boor, °rustic, yahoo, oaf, lout, °clod, °dolt, bumpkin, clodhopper, °provincial, °peasant, yokel, *Colloq* lummox; *Slang chiefly US* °jerk; *Old-fashioned* galoot *or* galloot; *Slang chiefly US and Canadian* hick: *That's the kind of language we expect to hear only from the most ignorant clowns.*
—*v.* **3** Often, ***clown around*** *or* ***about***: °fool (around), play the °fool, horse around *or* about, °caper, cut a °caper *or* capers, engage in °high jinks *or* hijinks, *US* cut up, cut didos: *Stop clowning around with that hose and help water the garden.*

club *n.* **1** cudgel, bat, bludgeon, mace, billy, truncheon, baton, °staff, °stick; cosh, *Chiefly US and Canadian* blackjack: *The blow from the club required six stitches.* **2** °association, °society, °organization, °fraternity, sorority, °fellowship, °brotherhood, sisterhood, °federation, °union, guild, °lodge, °alliance, °league, °order, consortium, °company: *Our sailing club holds an annual race.* **3** clubhouse: *The society's club is near Pall Mall.* **4** nightclub, °cabaret, *Colloq* nightspot: *After the theatre, we stopped at Oscar's club for a nightcap.*
—*v.* **5** °beat, cudgel, bludgeon, bat, °belabour; °lambaste, baste, thrash, trounce: *The guerrillas caught the traitor and clubbed him to death.* **6** Often, ***club together***: °band *or* °join *or* °league (together), °team (up), °join forces, °combine, °ally, °associate, confederate, °cooperate: *We clubbed together to purchase the antique clock.*

clue *n.* **1** °hint, °suspicion, °trace, intimation, °suggestion, °inkling, °indication, °pointer, °lead, °tip, tip-off, °evidence, °information, °advice; °key, °answer, °indicator: *There is no clue pointing to anyone in particular. Any clue to the solution of the mystery disappeared in the fire.*

—*v.* **2** ***clue someone in*** *or Brit also* ***up***: °hint, °suggest, °imply, °intimate, °inform, °advise, °indicate: *She clued us in as to who might have sent the letter.*

clump *n.* **1** °lump, °mass, °clod, chunk, hunk, °wad, °gob, *Colloq* glob: *As the soup cooled, clumps of fat formed on its surface.* **2** °bunch, °cluster; °thicket, copse; wood, *Chiefly Brit* spinney: *The deer disappeared into a clump of trees. That clump will provide good cover for us.*
—*v.* **3** °lump, °mass, °heap, °collect, °gather, °bunch, °pile: *She wore her hair clumped on top her head.*

clumsy *adj.* °awkward, ungainly, °unwieldy, °ungraceful, gawky, maladroit, unhandy, unskilful, °inept, bungling, bumbling, cloddish, ox-like, bovine, uncoordinated, lubberly, oafish; gauche, *Colloq* butter-fingered, ham-fisted, ham-handed, cack-handed: *He made a clumsy attempt to put the key in the lock. She gave a clumsy excuse for being in the bank after hours.*

cluster *n.* **1** °collection, °bunch, °clutch, tuft, °bundle: *Notice that cluster of flowers near the top of the plant.* **2** °collection, °bunch, °group, °knot, °body, °band, °company, °gathering, °crowd, °assembly, congregation, °throng, °flock, assemblage, °swarm: *A cluster of well-wishers stood talking with the minister.*
—*v.* **3** °collect, °bunch, °group, °band, °gather, °crowd, congregate, °throng, °assemble, °accumulate, °mass, aggregate: *A number of people clustered round the new sculpture. Why do these flowers cluster at this tree?*

clutch *v.* **1** °seize, °snatch, °grab, °grasp, °take *or* °lay °hold of; °hold; *US* °snag: *She clutched feebly at the rope before losing her grip and plunging into the abyss below. He clutched the child to his bosom.*
—*n.* **2** ***clutches***: **a** °grasp, °hold; °embrace: *We watched as the gazelle deftly eluded the cheetah's clutches.* **b** °influence, °control, °power, °domination, dominance, °possession: *He fell into the clutches of the Triads.*

clutter *n.* **1** °mess, °litter, °jumble; °mishmash, olla podrida, °confusion, °hash, gallimaufry, °hotchpotch *or US also* hodgepodge, °muddle, farrago, °medley: *I must insist that you clear up the clutter in your room at once. That philosophy is a clutter of competing ideas.* **2** °confusion, °tangle, °chaos, disarray: *The town was a clutter of narrow, crooked, dark, and dirty lanes.*
—*v.* **3** Often, ***clutter up***: °mess up, °litter, °strew, make a °shambles of: *Please don't clutter up my desk with newspaper cuttings.*

coach *n.* **1** °carriage, bus, omnibus, motor °coach: *The sightseeing coach broke down near Exeter.* **2** °tutor, trainer, °instructor, °teacher, mentor, *Brit* crammer: *Her voice coach says she's not yet ready for grand opera.*
—*v.* **3** °tutor, °train, °instruct, °guide, °direct, °drill, °prepare, °prompt, °school, °exercise, *Brit* °cram: *Her lawyers have coached her in what to say in court.*

coagulate *v.* congeal, gel, °jell, clot, curdle, °set: *The white of the egg had coagulated, but the yolk was still runny.*

coarse *adj.* **1** °rough, uneven, °scratchy, °prickly, bristly; °crude, rough-hewn, unfinished, °unrefined: *He has a three-day coarse growth of beard. The surface on the furniture is still too coarse.* **2** °rude, °boorish, loutish, °crude, °ill-mannered, unpolished, °rough, uncouth, °impolite, uncivil, °unrefined: *Nigel's behaviour is coarse, and he spits when he talks.* **3** °rude, °indecent, °improper, indelicate, °obscene, °lewd, °vulgar, °gross, smutty, °dirty, °filthy, °foul, °offensive, °lascivious, ribald, °bawdy; foul-mouthed: *Don't use that kind of coarse language with me.* **4** °inferior, low-quality, second-rate, °shoddy, °tawdry, trashy; kitschy: *That shop stocks only the coarsest merchandise.*

coast *n.* **1** seaside, seashore, shore, °sea-coast, strand, °beach, littoral, coastline, seaboard: *Be careful of rocks if you sail near the coast.*
—*v.* **2** °glide, °skim, °slide, °sail: *The children coasted down the hill on the toboggan.*

coat *n.* **1** overcoat, greatcoat; jacket, anorak, parka, *Brit* cagoule, *Colloq Brit* cag: *Put on your coat, it's cold out.* **2** coating, layer, covering, overlay; °film: *Two coats of paint ought to be enough. There was a coat of dust on everything.*
—*v.* **3** °cover, °paint, °spread: *We coated the floor with three layers of varnish.*

coax *v.* °persuade, °urge, °wheedle, °cajole, °beguile, °charm, inveigle, °jolly, °manipulate: *She coaxed me into spending a weekend with her at Blackpool.*

cocky *adj.* °overconfident, °arrogant, °haughty, °conceited, °self-important, °egotistical, °proud, °vain, prideful, cocksure, saucy, °cheeky, °brash: *Since she won the beauty contest, Claire has been entirely too cocky.*

coddle *v.* °pamper, °baby, cosset, mollycoddle, °indulge, °humour, °spoil, *Brit* cocker: *Give him a cold bath and don't coddle him so much.*

code *n.* **1** law(s), °regulation(s), °rule(s), jurisprudence, jus canonicum 'canon law', jus civile 'civil law', jus divinum 'divine law', jus gentium 'universal law', jus naturale 'natural law', corpus juris, pandect, lex non scripta 'common law, unwritten law', lex scripta 'statute law': *In the present code there is no statute that forbids keeping a pet gnu.* **2** cipher *or* cypher, cryptogram: *Our agents send all their messages in code.* **3** °system, °practice(s), °convention(s), °standard(s), criterion (criteria), °principle(s), °rule(s), °maxim(s), °custom(s), °pattern(s), °structure, °tradition(s), °organization, °protocol, orthodoxy: *Our code of behaviour is completely foreign to the islanders.*
—*v.* **4** encode, encipher *or* encypher, encrypt: *It took an hour to code the information.*

coffin *n.* °casket, °pall, (pine) °box; sarcophagus: *The coffin was slowly lowered into the grave.*

cog *n.* **1** tooth, gear-tooth, sprocket, ratchet: *Stripping the gears means breaking the cogs off them.* **2** underling, °pawn, °subordinate, nonentity, °zero, cipher *or* cypher, °nothing, °nobody, °small fry: *He's only a small cog in the organization—we're after the big wheel himself.*

cognizance *n.* °knowledge, awareness, °perception, °notice, consciousness, mindfulness: *They ran the gambling den with the full cognizance of the police.*

coherent *adj.* **1** °consistent, °orderly, organized, well-organized, °logical, °rational, °reasonable, well-ordered: *The MP set forth a coherent argument against an excise tax.* **2** understandable, °sensible, comprehensible, °intelligible, articulate, lucid, °clear: *He was so frightened and hysterical that he was unable to tell a coherent story.*

cohort *n.* **1** troop, °squad, squadron, °platoon, brigade, °unit, cadre, wing, legion, °detachment, contingent: *Ten select Roman cohorts were sent against the Mitanni.* **2** °company, °band, °group, °faction, °set, °body, °corps: *She was a member of a small cohort of suffragettes.* **3** °companion, confederate, °accomplice, °associate, °fellow, °comrade, °friend, confrère: *Gerald then arrived with a few of his cohorts.*

coil *v.* **1** °wind, °twist, °snake, °wrap, enwrap, °spiral, *Nautical* °fake *or* °flake (down): *The rope is coiled round a capstan.*
—*n.* **2** winding(s), °circle(s), °loop, whorl, °spiral, helix, °twist: *His foot caught in the coil of rope and he was carried overboard.*

coin *n.* **1** specie, °money, currency; °change, °cash, °silver: *I have only a few coins in my pocket. As he had no notes he had to pay in coin.*
—*v.* **2** °mint, °stamp: *The US government has stopped coining silver dollars.* **3** °invent, °create, °conceive, °originate, °start, °make up, °fabricate, °frame, concoct, °think *or* °dream up: *James Joyce coined the word 'quark'.* **4** ***coin it in*** *or US only* ***coin money***: °earn *or* make °money, become °wealthy, °enrich oneself, *Colloq* °rake it in: *Those rock stars really coin it in from their record sales.*

coincide *v.* °fall *or* °come *or* °go together, °line up, co-occur, °correspond, synchronize, °match, °tally, °agree, (be in) °accord, °equal, jibe: *This year, Easter* *and Passover coincide. The southern boundary coincides with the Thames.*

coincidence *n.* **1** co-occurrence, simultaneity, correspondence, concurrence, consistency, contemporaneity, synchronism, synchrony, coextension, coevality, coinstantaneity: *The coincidence of twelve by the clock with noon by the sundial is exact only four times in the year.* **2** congruence, °matching, jibing, °agreement, concord, °accord, °harmony, accordance, conformity, congruity, consonance, concomitance: *Fortunately there was a coincidence of views on the main issues.* **3** °chance °occurrence, °fluke, °chance, °accident, °luck, fortuity, fortuitousness, *US and Canadian* happenstance: *By sheer coincidence, I met my next-door neighbour on the train from Glasgow.*

coincidental *adj.* °chance, °lucky *or* unlucky, fortuitous, °accidental, unexpected, unpredicted, unpredictable, °unforeseen: *It was entirely coincidental that we were on the same train.*

cold *adj.* **1** °chill, °chilly, frosty, °icy, °keen, nippy, °freezing, °frigid, ice-cold, stone-cold, °bitter, bitter cold, °raw, °biting, biting-cold, numbing, gelid; °wintry, hibernal, brumal; arctic, glacial, °polar, hyperborean *or* hyperboreal, Siberian: *It was so cold that the canal had completely frozen over.* **2** °chilly, chilled; unheated, heatless: *The room is cold; we'd better put the heating on.* **3** °indifferent, apathetic, °chilly, chilling, °cool, °icy, °dispassionate, °unsympathetic, °aloof, unresponsive, spiritless, °frigid, unfriendly, uncordial, °lukewarm; °cold-blooded, insensitive, uncaring, unemotional, undemonstrative, °reserved, °unmoved, °callous, °remote, °distant, °standoffish, °unapproachable, stony-hearted, emotionless, unfeeling, °cold-hearted: *My ideas received rather a cold reception. Because she had offended him, he was quite cold to her.* **4** depressing, cheerless, chilling, °gloomy, dispiriting, deadening, disheartening, °bleak, °dismal, discouraging: *The sweat stood out on his brow in cold apprehension.* **5** unmoving, °stale, trite, stereotyped; °dead: *The coldest word was once a glowing new metaphor.* **6** °weak, °faint, °stale, °old, °dead: *The trail of the tiger had grown cold.* **7** °unprepared, unready: *She hadn't studied and went into the exam cold.* **8** Often, ***getting cold***: °far, °distant, °remote, off the °track: *As I searched for the weapon, I felt I was getting cold the further I went from the kitchen.*
—*n.* **9** coldness, frigidity, iciness: *Last winter, the cold killed off many of our shrubs.* **10** head *or* chest *or* common cold, influenza, ague, (la *or* the) grippe, *Technical* coryza, gravedo, *Colloq* sniffles, the flu, °bug, sneezles and wheezles: *I caught a cold waiting for you in the rain.*
—*adv.* **11** °completely, °thoroughly, °entirely, °absolutely, unhesitatingly, °promptly, °immediately, unreservedly, abruptly: *His application to join the police was turned down cold.*

cold-blooded *adj.* **1** *Technical* poikilothermic *or* poikilothermal: *Reptiles are cold-blooded.* **2** unexcited, unemotional, °cool, unimpassioned, unfeeling, °callous, °thick-skinned, insensitive, °heartless, uncaring, °stony, °steely, stony-hearted, °cold-hearted, imperturbable, °unmoved, °indifferent, unresponsive, °unsympathetic, apathetic, °dispassionate: *The murder appeared to be the act of a cold-blooded killer.* **3** °cruel, °brutal, °savage, °inhuman, barbarous, °vicious, barbaric, °merciless, pitiless, °ruthless: *They were victims of a cold-blooded policy of repatriation.*

cold-hearted *adj.* insensitive, °unsympathetic, apathetic, °indifferent, unfeeling, uncaring, °callous, °thick-skinned, °cold, °cool, °frigid, hard-hearted, °heartless, °unkind, °thoughtless, unthoughtful, uncharitable, °ruthless, pitiless, °unmerciful, °cruel, °merciless, °mean: *Putting that kitten out on a snowy night is the most cold-hearted thing you ever did.*

collaborate *v.* °cooperate, °join (forces), °work together, °team up: *We collaborated in writing both the lyrics and music.*

collapse *v.* **1** °fall (down *or* in *or* °apart), °crumple, °cave in, deflate, °crumble, °tumble down, °break down, °go: *When he opened the valve, the balloon collapsed. Hundreds of buildings collapsed in the earthquake.* **2** °fail, (come to an) °end, °fall through, peter out, °disintegrate, °dissolve, °fall flat, °founder, come to nothing *or* naught *or* nought, °break up *or* down; °decline, °diminish; °disappear, °evaporate, go up in smoke, go bankrupt, °go under, *Brit* go to the °wall, *Colloq* °fizzle out: *After the imprisonment of their leader, the entire movement collapsed. Owing to the recession, many businesses collapsed.* **3** °pass out, °faint, °drop, *Colloq* keel over; *Old-fashioned or literary* swoon: *He collapsed on-stage and they took him to his dressing-room.* **4** °break down (mentally), have a (nervous) °breakdown, go to °pieces, °come *or* °fall apart, *Colloq* °crack up, *US also* °crack: *She finally collapsed from overwork and is now in a sanatorium.*
—*n.* **5** cave-in, °breakdown: *The collapse of the house was attributed to termites.* **6** °failure, °downfall, °ruin; disappearance, disintegration, °dissolution, bankruptcy: *Will he be able to survive the collapse of his financial empire?* **7** (°mental) °breakdown, °prostration, *Colloq* crack-up: *He suffered a mental collapse when his family was killed in a car crash.*

colleague *n.* team-mate, fellow-worker, co-worker; °associate, °comrade, °ally, confrère, °mate, consociate, *Chiefly Brit and Australian* °mate, *US* buddy: *I have asked some of my colleagues from the office to join us for dinner.*

collect *v.* **1** °gather (together), °get *or* °bring *or* °come together, °amass, °accumulate, °assemble, °compile, °pile up, °heap up, °rack up; convene, congregate, °converge, °rally, °meet: *A crowd had collected outside the mayor's home. They were collecting evidence for their case.* **2** °summon (up), °draw (up), °muster, °gather (up), °concentrate: *She collected all her courage to ask for an increase in salary.*

collected *adj.* °calm, °serene, controlled, °cool, °sedate, composed, °nonchalant, °poised, unruffled, unperturbed, at °ease, °comfortable, °tranquil, unexcited; imperturbable; °confident: *Considering what she's just gone through, Tanya seems quite collected.*

collection *n.* **1** collecting, °gathering, solicitation, garnering, gleaning, °accumulation, amassment, aggregation, *Colloq Brit* whip-round: *The collection of donations in this neighbourhood is going well.* **2** °accumulation, °hoard, °store, assemblage, omnium gatherum; anthology, chrestomathy: *Would you like to come up to see my collection of etchings? They have published some very interesting collections.*

collector *n.* gatherer, accumulator; connoisseur, art-lover: *The rent collector is coming tomorrow. We are collectors of paintings by unknown artists.*

collide *v.* **1** °crash, °strike *or* °dash together: *The cars collided at the bridge.* **2** ***collide with***: °crash into, smash into, °run into, °bump into, smack into: *The car collided with the bus at the crossing.*

collision *n.* smash-up, smash, °crash, °wreck, °pile-up, *Colloq Brit* prang; *US* crack-up: *There has been a major collision on the Tring road.*

colossal *adj.* **1** °huge, °vast, °enormous, °gigantic, °giant, mammoth, °massive, gargantuan, Cyclopean, Brobdingnagian, °immense, °monumental, titanic, Herculean, elephantine, °jumbo: *Mystery surrounds the exact methods used in moving the colossal stones used in the pyramids.* **2** spectacular, stupendous, wonderful, awe-inspiring, staggering, °extraordinary, °incredible, °overwhelming, °unbelievable: *The old Hollywood extravaganzas were described by press agents as 'colossal'. I think you have made a colossal mistake in failing to hire Cynthia.*

colour *n.* **1** °hue, °tint, tincture, °shade, °tone, °cast, tinge, pigmentation; pigment, dye: *The colours of the curtains don't match the wall.* **2** ***colours***: **a** °flag, ensign, °standard, °pennant, °banner, burgee: *The sloop hoisted the British colours.* **b** °device, badge,

°emblem, insigne *or pl* insignia, °symbol(s), °identification; °identity, °appearance, °face; loyalties: *The investigators found he'd been operating under false colours. She has shown her true colours at last.*
—*v.* **3** °tint, dye, °stain, °paint, crayon, tincture, tinge; pigment: *These sections will stand out better if you colour them red.* **4** °influence, °affect, °distort, °falsify, °taint, °warp, °twist, °slant, °pervert, °bias: *Jealousy colours his opinion of his supervisor.* **5** °blush, redden, °flush: *After their affair, she visibly coloured whenever they met.* **6** °falsify, °distort, °misrepresent, °disguise, °mask, °conceal: *He feigns confusion when he wishes to colour his true feelings.*

colourless *adj.* **1** °pale, pallid, blanched, °white; °wan, ashen, sallow, waxen, °sickly, washed out: *You could see from his colourless complexion that he had not been outside for months.* **2** °dull, °drab, uninteresting, vacuous, °vapid, °lifeless, °boring, °tedious, spiritless, °dry, dry-as-dust, °dreary, characterless, insipid, °bland, namby-pamby, °lacklustre, uninspiring, uninspired: *She has led a colourless life. Few people have so colourless a personality as he.*

combat *n.* **1** °fight, °encounter, °engagement, duel, °battle, °conflict, °war, warfare; °skirmish: *The two men were locked in single combat.* **2** °struggle, °contest, °strife, °controversy, °dispute, °quarrel, °disagreement, altercation, °vendetta, °feud: *There was endless combat between father and son.* **3** °opposition, °difference, confrontation: *The combat between good and evil can never end.* **4** °action, fighting, °battle, °war: *He was in combat on three occasions. Have you seen any combat?*
—*v.* **5** °fight, (do) °battle, °war, °clash, contend, duel, joust, °wrestle, come to blows, °spar, °grapple (with): *The soldiers are combating hand to hand in the trenches.* **6** °fight, °struggle *or* °strive against, °contest, °oppose, °defy, enter the lists against, °withstand: *There was broad support for measures to combat crime and pollution.*

combination *n.* **1** °union, conjunction, °mixture, °mix, grouping, °set, array: *They always serve the same combination of foods.* **2** °association, °alliance, coalition, °union, °federation, confederation, °combine, syndication, °syndicate, consortium, °trust, bloc, cartel, °party, °society, °organization, °league, °cabal, °conspiracy, °clique; claque: *When they get together they form an unbeatable combination.* **3** °mixture, °amalgam, °compound, compounding, °mix, °alloy, conglomerate, conglomeration, aggregate, aggregation, °amalgamation, °blend, emulsion, °suspension, colloid °solution, °composition, *Technical* parasynthesis, parathesis; mosaic, °patchwork: *From a combination of ingredients the witch made a slimy love potion. A combination of every colour of the rainbow covered the walls.*

combine *v.* **1** °unite, °unify, °join, °connect, °relate, °link, conjoin, °band, °ally, °associate, °integrate, °merge, °pool: *Combine forces, and we'll win.* **2** °blend, °mix, °amalgamate, °mingle, consolidate, °compound, °incorporate, °put together: *Combine the water, butter, and salt in a saucepan.* **3** °blend, °fuse, synthesize, °bind, °bond, °compound, °unite, coalesce, °come together, commingle, °mingle: *When heated, the silver combines with the chlorine.*

come *v.* **1** °approach, °advance, (draw) °near, °move, *Archaic or literary* draw nigh: *The car came towards us. She has come to me for comforting words. Winter is coming.* **2** °arrive, °appear, make *or* put in an appearance, *Colloq* °blow in, °report (in), °turn *or* °show up, °check in, °sign in, clock on *or* in, °roll in: *Winter has come. When Cora comes, we'll ask her.* **3** °enter: *Come into the light, where I can see you.* **4** ***come about***: **a** °occur, °happen, take °place, come up; befall, *Loosely* °transpire: *I cannot imagine how this state of affairs came about.* **b** *Nautical* tack, °go about: *After the marker, come about and hoist the spinnaker.* **5** ***come across***: **a** °find, °discover, °encounter, °meet (up *or* up with), °run across *or* into, °happen *or* °chance upon *or* on, °hit *or* °light on *or* upon, °stumble upon *or* on, *Colloq* °bump into: *I came across some information about Charles.* **b** °pay (up), °settle; °yield, °give up, °submit: *Frank owes me money but refuses to come across.* **c** be communicated *or* understandable, °penetrate, °sink in: *I am not sure that my points came across.* **6** ***come along***: °fare, do, °progress, °move along: *How is William coming along at his new school?* **7** ***come apart***: °disintegrate, °crumble, °fall *or* fly to °pieces, °separate, °break (°apart *or* up *or* down): *The carburettor came apart in my hands.* **8** ***come at***: °attack, °assault, °charge, °rush (at), °fly at, °descend upon *or* on, *Colloq* °go *or* °make for: *She came at me waving her umbrella.* **9** ***come by***: **a** °acquire, °obtain, °get, °procure, °secure, °find, °take *or* °get °possession of, °get *or* °lay °hold of, °get *or* °lay *or* °put (one's) hands *or US also* °fingers on; be given: *The tax inspector wondered how she came by such valuable property.* **b** °win, °earn, attain; be awarded: *I came by that trophy fair and square.* **10** ***come clean***: See **clean, 8,** above. **11** ***come down on*** *or* ***upon***: °pounce on *or* upon, °rebuke, °criticize, revile, °reprimand, °bear down on, °blame: *Mother really came down on us when she discovered who had taken the pie.* **12** ***come down with***: °succumb to, °contract, °catch, be °stricken *or* afflicted with, °acquire: *He's come down with pneumonia.* **13** ***come in***: **a** °win, °succeed; *Colloq* °finish (in the money): *My horse came in.* **b** be, °prove, °turn out *or* °prove to be: *Knowing someone on the council can come in handy.* **c** °finish, °end up, °arrive: *Donald came in first in the backstroke.* **d** °enter: *Don't come in, I'm dressing.* **14** ***come off***: **a** °occur, °happen, come to °pass, take °place, *Loosely* °transpire: *I doubt that the performance will ever come off.* **b** °emerge, °result as: *We came off the winners in Saturday's game.* **15** ***come out***: **a** be revealed, become °public *or* known *or* common knowledge, °get about *or* around, °get *or* °leak out, °emerge: *The story has come out that he tried to bribe the inspector.* **b** be published *or* issued *or* produced *or* distributed, be shown, be in °print, °première *or* premiere: *The new edition of the dictionary has just come out.* **c** °end, conclude, °turn out, °terminate, °finish: *How did the chess match come out?* **16** ***come over***: **a** °go over, °communicate, come across, be communicated, °succeed, be received: *How did my speech come over?* **b** °affect, °influence, °possess: *I can't imagine what's come over Louis.* **c** °visit, °drop *or* °stop by *or* in: *Quentin and his wife came over for dinner last night.* **17** ***come through***: **a** °recover (from), °recuperate (from), get °well *or* °better: *He came through his operation with flying colours.* **b** conclude *or* °end (up) *or* °finish *or* °wind up successfully *or* satisfactorily, °succeed, °arrive, not °fail *or* °disappoint: *I knew he'd come through.* **18** ***come to***: **a** °amount to, °add up to, °total, aggregate: *My bill came to more than I had with me.* **b** regain *or* °recover consciousness, °awake(n), °revive, °wake up, come (a)round: *When I came to, I was on the floor with a terrific headache.* **c** °regard, °concern, °relate to, be a °question of, °involve, be °relevant to, be °involved: *When it comes to real ale, Mario is the expert.* **19** ***come up***: **a** °arise, °surface, °present itself, be brought up, be broached, come about, °turn up, °rise, *Colloq* crop up: *The question of religion never came up.* **b** °grow, °thrive, °appear: *None of my tulips came up this year.* **c** °rise, °arise: *The moon came up just as the sun was setting.*

comedian *n.* comedienne, humorist, °comic, °wit, °wag, jokesmith; °clown, buffoon, °funny man *or* woman, funster, jester, °fool, °zany, °merry andrew: *The new comedian at the variety show is very funny.*

comely *adj.* good-looking, °pretty, °bonny, °lovely, °fair, °beautiful, °handsome, °attractive, appealing, °wholesome, winsome, °buxom: *She is a comely woman who has had no shortage of suitors.*

come-on *n.* °lure, °attraction, °enticement, °inducement, °temptation, bait; loss-leader: *The free glassware is a come-on to buy a tankful of petrol.*

comfort *v.* **1** °console, °solace, soothe, assuage, °reassure, °relieve, hearten, °cheer, °gladden: *It might*

comfort you to know that Roderick has recovered completely. He comforted her when the pain became unbearable.
—*n.* **2** consolation, °solace, °relief, °cheer: *I derived some comfort from knowing that my attacker had been caught.* **3** °ease, °luxury, °security, °abundance, °plenty, opulence: *Cordelia lived out her days in comfort after inheriting a fortune from her aunt.*

comfortable *adj.* **1** at °ease, °easy, °tranquil, °serene, °relaxed, contented, untroubled, undisturbed: *After the operation, the nurses did everything they could to make me comfortable.* **2** °well off, °carefree, insouciant, contented, satisfied; self-satisfied, complacent, °smug: *They don't have a lot of money, but they're comfortable enough.* **3** °likeable, °easy, congenial, °amiable, °cordial, °warm, °pleasant, °agreeable, enjoyable, relaxing: *Daphne is a very comfortable sort of person to be with.* **4** °suitable, °acceptable, °adequate, °satisfactory, °reasonable: *The radio was on very loud, so I turned down the volume to a more comfortable level.*

comic *adj.* **1** °funny, droll, comical, °humorous, °hilarious, side-splitting, mirthful, jocose, jocular, °witty, waggish, °clever, facetious, amusing: *Barry's comic routines have made him a popular performer for years.*
—*n.* **2** See **comedian**, above.

command *v.* **1** °order, °direct, °bid, enjoin, °charge, °request, °require, °demand, °instruct; °say, °prescribe, °decree: *What the Queen commands must be done.* **2** °control, °dominate, °have *or* °maintain *or* °wield °authority *or* °control *or* °sway *or* °influence over, °hold °sway over; °lead, °rule, °govern, have under one's °thumb, call the tune; °head (up): *Whoever commands the sea commands the town. He commanded a battalion during the war.* **3** °master, °draw upon *or* on, °control, °summon: *The work required all the skill the sculptor could command.* **4** °attract, °earn; °exact, compel, °demand: *Gunga Din's bravery commanded the respect of the entire regiment.* **5** °dominate, °control, °overlook, °look down on; °have, °enjoy, °possess: *The tower commands a view of the entire valley.*
—*n.* **6** °order, °direction, behest, mandate, °charge, °bidding, °instruction: *Your wish is my command.* **7** °control, °authority, °power, °sovereignty, °dominion, °regulation, °direction, °management, °government, °oversight, °leadership, °charge, °sway, stewardship, °jurisdiction: *The unit is under the command of the colonel.* **8** mastery, °control, (thorough) °grasp *or* °knowledge: *He has a good command of three languages.*

commemorate *v.* °memorialize, °remember, °celebrate, °observe, °dedicate, consecrate, solemnize, °sanctify, °hallow, °reverence, °revere, °honour, °venerate, pay °tribute *or* °homage to, °salute; °immortalize: *We are here to commemorate deeds of valour and the men who performed them.*

commence *v.* **1** °begin, °enter upon, °start, °initiate, °launch, °embark on *or* upon: *Tomorrow morning, we commence the ascent of Mont Blanc.* **2** °begin, °start, °open: *The ceremonies are about to commence.* **3** °begin, °start, °initiate, °launch, °inaugurate, °establish: *We commenced operations at this plant last year.*

comment *n.* **1** °remark, °reference, animadversion, °note, annotation, °criticism, °exposition, °explanation, °expansion, elucidation, clarification, footnote: *The author's comments on his sources appear in the appendix.* **2** commentary, °opinion, °remark, °view, °observation, °reaction: *The judge's comments are not for publication.*
—*v.* **3** °remark, °observe, opine, °say: *He commented that he knew nothing about the minister's private life.* **4** ***comment on*** *or* ***about***: °discuss, °talk about, °remark on; °reveal, °expose: *She declined to comment on what had happened the previous night.*

commerce *n.* °trade, °business, mercantilism, marketing, merchandising, °traffic, trafficking: *All commerce consists in the exchange of commodities of equal value. My husband is in commerce.*

commit *v.* **1** °entrust, consign, °transfer, °assign, °delegate, °hand over, °deliver, °give; °allot, °pledge, allocate: *They committed the goods to traders with strong distribution facilities.* **2** °sentence, °send (away), confine, °shut up, intern, °put away, °imprison, incarcerate: *The judge committed her to prison. You can be committed for such behaviour.* **3** °perpetrate, do, °perform, °carry out: *They committed murder for money.* **4** ***commit oneself***: °pledge, °promise, covenant, °agree, °assure, °swear, give one's °word, °vow, °vouchsafe, °engage, °undertake, °guarantee, °bind oneself: *He committed himself to buying the company after seeing the books.*

committee *n.* °council, °board, °cabinet, panel, °body, commission: *They have set up a committee to oversee park planning.*

common *adj.* **1** °ordinary, °everyday, commonplace, °prosaic, °usual, °familiar, °customary, °prevalent, °frequent, run-of-the-mill, °general, °normal, °standard, °conventional, °regular, °routine, °stock, °average, °proverbial; °plain, °simple, garden-variety, common or garden, workaday, °undistinguished, unexceptional: *Intermarriage is a common occurrence among the members of the sect. We planted a common variety of carrot.* **2** °mutual, °reciprocal, °joint, shared: *Our common heritage must be protected.* **3** low-class, °ordinary, °plain, °simple, °plebeian, °bourgeois, proletarian, run-of-the-mill, °vulgar, °unrefined: *Kings avoid dealing with the common people.* **4** °inferior, low-grade, °mean, °cheap, °base: *He was smoking a cigar of the commonest type.* **5** °public, °general, community, communal, collective, non-private, °universal; °well-known: *The contents of the library are the common property of everyone. Their romance is common knowledge in the village.* **6** trite, °stale, hackneyed, °worn out, °banal, °tired, overused, stereotyped, clichéd, stereotypical: *The term 'yuppie' has become too common to have much impact any longer.*

communicate *v.* **1** make known, °impart, °confer, °transmit, °transfer, °hand on *or* down, °share, °pass on *or* along, °send on, °spread; °tell, divulge, °disclose, °reveal, °announce, promulgate, proffer, °tender, °offer, convey, °deliver, °present, °give, °yield, °supply: *Moral qualities are sometimes thought to be communicated by descent. I communicated to them the information that I had about the missiles.* **2** Also, ***communicate with***: be in communication (with), °converse (with), °talk (with), °chat (with); °correspond (with); °associate (with), be in °contact *or* °touch (with), °reach: *Donald and I haven't communicated in years. Instead of communicating with him by telephone, she did so via personal notices in the newspaper.* **3** °get *or* °put across, make understandable; °get through to, °reach, be of one °mind, be in °tune, °relate, be in *or* en °rapport, make oneself understood, *Slang* be *or* vibrate on the same frequency *or* wavelength: *He has difficulty in communicating his ideas to his students. We might talk, but are we communicating?*

compact *adj.* **1** °packed, compacted, closely-knit, condensed, concentrated, consolidated, compressed; °dense, °solid, °firm, °thick: *The sesame seeds are mixed with honey and pressed into a compact block.* **2** °tight, °small, °snug, °little: *The table folds up into a compact unit for storage.* **3** condensed, °terse, laconic, °close, pithy, °succinct, °concise, °brief, compendious, °epigrammatic, aphoristic: *The information is given in a compact form with many abbreviations and symbols.*

companion *n.* **1** °fellow, °associate, °comrade, °colleague, confrère, *Colloq chiefly Brit and Australian* °mate, *US and Canadian* buddy: *For ten years they had been constant companions.* **2** °vade-mecum, °manual, handbook, °guide, °reference °book, enchiridion: *They publish a pocket companion listing the month's events.* **3** °escort, chaperon(e), °attendant, *in Spain, Portugal*: duenna: *Aunt Dinah is too old to be alone, so we have engaged a companion for her.*

companionship *n.* °fellowship, camaraderie, comradeship, °company, °society, amity, °friendship, °fraternity: *I often enjoy the companionship of an older person.*

company *n.* **1** °companionship, °society, °fellowship; °attendance, °presence; associates, friends, companions, °comrades: *It was a stormy night, and I was only too glad to have his company. A man is known by the company he keeps.* **2** assemblage, °party, °band, °group, °retinue, entourage, °suite, °train, coterie, °ensemble, troop, followers, following, °flock; °circle, °assembly, °gathering, °convention, °body, °crowd, °throng, *Theatre* troupe, °cast, °players, actors and actresses, °performers: *The king arrived with his company at the gate of the city. The speaker addressed the assembled company. The company leaves today for a month on the road.* **3** °guest(s); °visitor(s), caller(s): *Are you having company for dinner tonight?* **4** °firm, °business, °house, °concern, °institution, °establishment, °enterprise; proprietorship, partnership, corporation, *Brit* public limited company, plc, *Australian and New Zealand and South African* proprietary limited company, Pty: *The company was founded in 1867.*

compare *v.* **1** °liken, °associate, make (an) analogy (with), °refer, analogize: *How can you compare your collection to mine?* **2** ***compare with***: °resemble, be *or* °look °like, be on a °par with, be in a °class *or* the same °class with, °correspond, °match, °parallel, °approach, °approximate, °bear *or* °merit °comparison (with); °rival, °compete with *or* against, be a °match for: *Your paintings compare well with Picasso's. The new recordings don't begin to compare with the old ones.* **3** °contrast, °measure against, °weigh, juxtapose, °set °side by °side, °relate, correlate: *We need to compare the results of the two surveys.*

comparison *n.* **1** contrasting, °contrast, juxtaposing, juxtaposition, balancing, °balance, weighing: *His comparison of the candidates is prejudiced.* **2** °match, similarity, °resemblance, °likeness, comparability, °relation, °relationship, commensurability, °kinship, °point of °agreement *or* correspondence: *There is no comparison between a racing car and a family car.*

compartment *n.* °division, °section, °partition, °part, °space, °chamber, bay, alcove, °cell, pigeon-hole, locker, cubby-hole, °niche, cubicle, °slot: *Each specimen is in its own separate compartment.*

compensate *v.* **1** recompense, °make up (for), make °restitution *or* reparation, °offset, °make good, indemnify, °repay, °reimburse, redress, °requite; expiate, °atone, make °amends (for): *The company compensated us for the loss of the car. Arriving at school early today, Gerard, does not compensate for having been late yesterday.* **2** °balance, counterpoise, counterbalance, °equalize, °neutralize, °even (up), °square, °offset: *Deduct six ounces to compensate for the weight of the container.* **3** °pay, remunerate, °reward, °repay, recompense: *Two pounds does not compensate me adequately for an hour's work.*

compensatory *adj.* compensative, remunerative, restitutive *or* restitutory, expiatory, reparative *or* reparatory, piacular: *His huge donation to the church was a compensatory offering for his past sins.*

compete *v.* contend, °vie, °struggle, °strive, °conflict, joust, °fence; °fight, °battle, °clash, °collide: *They are competing to see who will become chairman of the company. These two designs compete with one another for the viewer's attention.*

competent *adj.* **1** °adequate, °suitable, °sufficient, °satisfactory, °acceptable, all °right, *Colloq* °OK *or* okay: *Colquhon will make a competent bureau chief.* **2** °qualified, °fit, °capable, °proficient, °able, °prepared: *Do you really think that fellow Johnson competent to write a dictionary?*

competition *n.* **1** °rivalry, contention, striving, °struggle: *The competition for newspaper circulation becomes keener every day.* **2** °contest, °match, °meet, °game, °tournament, °event; championship: *We entered the competition as underdogs.* **3** See **competitor,** below.

competitor *n.* °rival, °opponent, °competition, °opposition, °adversary; °antagonist, °contestant, contender: *Our main competitor has just announced a new product.*

compile *v.* °collect, °put together, °gather, °accumulate, °assemble, °amass, collate, °organize, °order, systematize; anthologize, °compose: *He has compiled a large butterfly collection. Every year she compiles a volume of the best stories.*

complain *v.* grumble, °moan, °groan, wail, grouse, °carp (at), whimper, °cry, °lament, °bemoan, *Colloq* °gripe, °squawk, grouch, *Brit* whinge, *Slang* °bitch, beef, *US* kick: *What are you complaining about now?*

complaint *n.* grumble, °grievance, grouse, *Colloq* °gripe, squawk, *Slang* beef, *US* kick: *I have no complaints about my treatment while I was in hospital.*

complement *v.* **1** °completion, °perfection, confirmation, finishing °touch, °consummation: *The grand tour was considered the necessary complement of an English education in the 18th century.* **2** °crew, °team, °company, °band, °outfit; °quota, °allowance, quorum: *The regiment's full complement was attained by selecting from among the recruits.*
—*v.* **3** °complete, °perfect, °round out *or* off, °set off, °top off; °flesh out: *The setting was complemented by a huge floral arrangement. His argument was complemented by evidence from rare documents.* **4** °supplement, °enhance, °add to: *These are facts that complement but do not contradict her story.*

complete *adj.* **1** °entire, °whole, °intact, uncut, unbroken, °undivided, °unabridged, °full, undiminished, unabated, unreduced: *The complete works of Dickens are available in paperback. They performed the complete opera, a six-hour marathon.* **2** finished, ended, concluded, °over, done, °accomplished, terminated; settled, executed, performed: *The company's figures are not yet complete. When will your building plan be complete?* **3** °entire, °total, °thorough, °absolute, utter, °unqualified, unmixed, unalloyed, °pure, °unmitigated, °rank: *I attribute the disaster to a complete breakdown of communication, together with the complete incompetence of the site manager.* **4** °perfect, consummate, °exemplary, °ideal, °model, °superior, °superlative, °superb, °faultless, °flawless: *Her dissertation is a work of complete scholarship.*
—*v.* **5** conclude, °finish, °end, °bring to an °end, °accomplish, °achieve, do, *Colloq* °wrap up; °finalize: *He stopped after completing ten ciruits of the track. Have you completed the prospectus?* **6** °round out, °round off, °perfect; °crown, culminate: *The unit was completed by the addition of five platoons. A golden cupola completed the top of the dome.*

completely *adv.* **1** °entirely, fully, °quite, °wholly, °totally, °altogether, in toto, °thoroughly, °perfectly, °exactly, °precisely, down to the ground, from °start to °finish, from °beginning to °end, from A to Z, from the word go, in °full; lock, stock, and barrel; °hook, line, and sinker; heart and soul; °root and branch; en masse: *The currency does not completely represent the wealth of the country.* **2** unqualifiedly, unconditionally, °thoroughly, °utterly, °totally, °absolutely, °quite, °altogether, unreservedly: *He's completely mad if he thinks that thing will fly.* **3** °clearly, °expressly, explicitly, unambiguously, °entirely, fully, °totally, °wholly, °altogether, unequivocally, °truly, categorically, flatly: *I am completely in agreement with your policy.*

completion *n.* **1** conclusion, °end, °close, °termination, °fulfilment, culmination, °realization, °accomplishment, °finish: *The completion of the building phase is scheduled for next July.* **2** finishing, finalization, wind-up, finishing-off, completing: *The completion of the house is scheduled for next October.*

complexity *n.* **1** °complication, convolution: *We are finding it difficult to understand the complexities of the agreement.* **2** intricacy, involvement, complicatedness;

inscrutability: *The complexity of her theory makes it difficult to interpret.*

complicate *v.* **1** °mix up, °entangle, °snarl, °tangle, confound, °muddle, °confuse: *You only complicate matters by bringing up the question of religion in a discussion of money.* **2** °make °complicated *or* complex, make °involved *or* °intricate, make a °shambles *or* °mess *or* °muddle of, °mess up, *Colloq* °screw up: *The phenomena of tides and currents greatly complicate coastwise navigation.*

complicated *adj.* °involved, °intricate, complex, °compound, °elaborate; °ornate, Byzantine, Daedalian, tangled, knotty, °confused, °labyrinthine: *In birds the eye is a more complicated organ than in our own species. His plan is too complicated to understand.*

complication *n.* **1** °complexity, involvement, intricacy, convolution: *The complications of the diagram make it almost impossible to understand.* **2** °difficulty, °problem, °predicament, °dilemma, °obstacle, °obstruction, °snag, °drawback: *Asking for more money might create complications.*

compliment *n.* **1** °praise, °homage, commendation, °honour, °tribute, °flattery, °bouquet, °favour: *The greatest compliment given to my work has been its success.* **2** Usually, ***compliments***: °respects, °regards, good *or* best wishes, felicitations, salutations, °greetings: *I stopped by to pay my compliments to your mother.*

—*v.* **3** °honour, °praise, pay °homage *or* °tribute to, commend, °laud, °congratulate, felicitate; °flatter: *She came backstage to compliment me on my performance.*

complimentary *adj.* **1** °laudatory, commendatory, encomiastic, panegyrical, eulogistic, congratulatory, °flattering: *The duke was most complimentary about my sculpture.* **2** °free, gratis, on the °house: *The shoehorn is complimentary when you buy a pair of shoes.*

comply *v.* °agree, °obey, °conform, °consent, acquiesce, concur, °submit, °yield, accede; °accord: *They require your signature and I hope you'll comply.*

compose *v.* **1** constitute, °form, °make (up), be a constituent *or* °ingredient *or* component *or* °element of, be a °part of: *Clouds are composed of countless particles of water.* **2** °write, °create, °imagine, °think up, °originate, °frame, °formulate, °make (up), °author, °devise; contrive; °set to music, °arrange: *He composed the poem while travelling on the Flying Scotsman. That symphony was composed in 1873.* **3** ***be composed of***: consist of *or* in, comprise, be formed *or* made (up) of, be constituted of: *The new government is composed of a coalition of three parties.* **4** ***compose oneself***: °calm (down), °quiet *or* °quieten (down), pacify, °control oneself, get °control of *or* over oneself: *They stopped crying and composed themselves.*

composition *n.* **1** °theme, °essay, article, °paper, °story: *The teacher required each of us to write a thousand-word composition every week.* **2** °combination, °make-up, °structure, °form, °assembly, °set-up, °organization, layout, °arrangement, configuration, shaping; °balance, °harmony, °proportion, °placement, placing, construction: *Notice the composition of the various elements in this painting.* **3** °combination, aggregate, °mixture, °compound, compounding, °mix, formulation, °formula, composite, °amalgam, °alloy, mélange, °medley: *The medication was a composition of several odd ingredients.* **4** °creation, origination, formulation, fashioning: *The composition of the opera was begun in 1837.* **5** °make-up, constitution: *What goes into the composition of brass?*

compound *v.* **1** °put together, °combine, °mix, concoct, °compose, °make (up), °formulate, °blend: *They compound curry powder from different spices.* **2** °blend, °merge, coalesce, °combine, °unite, °fuse °come *or* °go together: *Sometimes two words compound to form one, as in 'ingrown', 'outgrow', and 'uptake'.* **3** °aggravate, °intensify, exacerbate, °heighten, augment, °add to, °worsen, °increase; °enhance, multiply: *Demanding your money back now will only compound the problem.*

—*adj.* **4** °intricate, complex, °involved, °complicated; composite, multiple, multiform, multifaceted, *Technical* parasynthetic, parathetic: *The compound eye of the fly | Lets it see far better than I. A compound sentence is composed of two or more clauses joined by one or more coordinating conjunctions, express or understood.*

—*n.* **5** composite, °blend, °synthesis, °combination, consolidation, *Technical* parasynthesis, parathesis; °mixture, °amalgam, °alloy, merging, °merger, °mix: *Table salt is a compound of the metallic element sodium and the gaseous element chlorine. 'Slithy' is a compound of 'slimy' and 'writhe'.*

comprehend *v.* °understand, °see, °grasp, °conceive, °take in, apprehend, °realize, °fathom, °perceive, discern, absorb, assimilate, °appreciate: *Do you comprehend how serious the matter has become?*

comprehensive *adj.* °inclusive, encompassing, °thorough, °extensive, °full, °exhaustive, °complete, °sweeping, °wide, °broad, °encyclopedic *or* encyclopaedic: *We hope to give comprehensive coverage to all aspects of the subject in our new book.*

compulsive *adj.* compelling, °obsessive, coercive, °urgent, °forceful, °overwhelming, constrained: *She is such a compulsive workaholic that she double-checks everything done by her staff.*

compunction *n.* **1** °remorse, contrition, °regret, uneasiness of °mind, °pang *or* pricking of °conscience, self-reproach: *He has no compunction about hurting your feelings.* **2** hesitation, °reluctance, °reserve, disinclination, °qualm, °misgiving, unwillingness, °fear: *She has no compunction about speaking her mind.*

compute *v.* °calculate, °reckon, °figure (out), °work out, °determine, ascertain, °estimate: *My accountant computed my income tax for this year and told me that I was entitled to a refund.*

comrade *n.* °colleague, °associate, °friend, °companion, crony, confrère, *Colloq* °pal, °chum, *Chiefly Brit and Australian* °mate, *Australian* cobber, *US* buddy: *None of my comrades from the old regiment attended the reunion this year.*

conceal *v.* **1** °hide, °secrete, °bury, °cover, °disguise, °camouflage: *Packets of a white powdery substance were concealed inside each doll.* **2** °keep °secret *or* °hidden, °keep °quiet about, °disguise, not °reveal; dissemble: *He concealed his true identity even from his wife.*

concede *v.* **1** °admit, °allow, °grant, °acknowledge, °confess, own (up *or* to *or* up to), °accept: *I conceded that I had no business in the bank after closing.* **2** °grant, °yield, °surrender, °cede, °give up, °submit, °resign, °relinquish, °abandon, °waive: *In chess, upon the loss of a queen, many players will concede. She has conceded any right to the estate of her uncle.*

conceit *n.* **1** °vanity, °pride, egotism, °self-esteem, self-admiration, self-love, narcissism, vainglory, *amour propre*; °arrogance: *His conceit is matched only by his incompetence.* **2** °fancy, whim, caprice: *Some have a conceit their drink tastes better | In an outlandish cup than their own.* **3** elaborate figure (of speech), °affectation, strained *or* far-fetched °metaphor: *A conceit would be calling the waves 'nodding hearse-plumes'.*

conceited *adj.* °vain, °egotistical, self-centred, egocentric, self-admiring, narcissistic, prideful, °proud, °arrogant, self-involved, °self-important, self-satisfied, °smug, complacent, vainglorious, °snobbish, *Colloq* stuck-up; *Slang* snotty: *That conceited ass really thinks the world of himself.*

conceive *v.* **1** °have, °bear, beget, sire, °father, give °birth to; become °pregnant (with): *After the twins, they conceived three boys.* **2** °formulate, °devise, °plan, contrive, °create, °plot, °hatch, °develop, evolve, °fabricate, °think *or* °make up, °form, °frame, °design: *He conceived a scheme for swindling that poor woman out of her life savings.* **3** °think (up), °imagine, °speculate (on), °perceive, °see, °understand, °realize, °comprehend, °envision, °envisage, conjure up, °dream up, hypothesize, postulate, °posit, °suggest, °suppose:

I cannot conceive of any reason why she shouldn't be allowed to take part.

concentrate *v.* **1** °focus, °direct, °centre, centralize, °converge, consolidate: *The council concentrated its efforts on refurbishing the schools.* **2** condense, °reduce, distil, °intensify, °refine, °strengthen: *The sap of the sugar maple is concentrated by boiling.* **3** °gather, °collect, congregate, °draw *or* °bring together, °crowd, °cluster, °group: *Much of the population is concentrated around the large cities.* **4** °think, °focus one's thoughts *or* °attention, °apply oneself: *I cannot concentrate with the radio on.*

conception *n.* **1** °birth, °beginning, genesis, inception, commencement, °emergence, °start, inauguration, °initiation, °launch, launching, °origin, origination, °formation, formulation, introduction: *We were excited to be in at the conception of the scheme.* **2** °idea, °notion, °inkling, °clue, concept; *idée reçu;* °understanding, °knowledge, °appreciation, comprehension: *He has no conception of what is involved in maintaining a yacht.* **3** °design, °plan, °scheme, °proposal, °outline: *Transporting a building from another site instead of constructing one was a bold conception.*

concern *v.* **1** °refer *or* °relate to, have °relation *or* °reference to, be about, °pertain *or* appertain to, be °pertinent *or* °relevant to, °regard, °apply to, be connected *or* °involved with, °bear on, be germane to, °involve, °touch (on): *The matter concerns your inheritance, Cosgrove.* **2** °affect, °have (a) °bearing *or* (an) °influence on, °involve, °touch; °interest, be of °importance *or* °interest to: *This war concerns us all.* **3** °worry, °trouble, °disturb, °bother, °perturb, unsettle, °upset, °distress: *He doesn't let anything concern him.*
—*n.* **4** °business, °affair, °problem; °responsibility, °duty, °charge, °task, involvement, *Colloq* °thing; *Slang* bag, shtick: *What she does is no concern of yours. The safety of the passengers is his concern.* **5** °interest, °regard, °consideration, °care, °thought, awareness, °attention: *You should show more concern for those less fortunate than you.* **6** °anxiety, °worry, °solicitude, apprehension, °distress, apprehensiveness, uneasiness, malaise, disquiet, disquietude: *It's only a cold, and no cause for concern.* **7** °business, °firm, °company, °house, °establishment, °enterprise, °organization: *The business is being sold as a going concern.* **8** °matter, °affair, °issue: *The preservation of wildlife is an international concern.*

concerned *adj.* **1** °involved, °responsible, °interested, °active; caring, °solicitous: *The best governments are run by a concerned citizenry.* **2** troubled, vexed, °anxious, °worried, distressed, uneasy, perturbed, bothered, °upset, °disturbed: *They were not at all concerned about the state of my health.*

concerning *prep.* °about, °regarding, °relative *or* relating to, referring to, with *or* in °reference to, as regards, in *or* with °regard to, with an °eye to, with °respect to, respecting, apropos (of), as to *or* for, in the °matter of, on the °subject of, re, *Formal* anent: *Concerning your recent application, please phone this office.*

concise *adj.* °brief, °terse, laconic, °compact, °direct, °succinct, °epigrammatic, cogent, pithy, compendious, °summary, °trenchant, compressed, condensed, °short; shortened, abridged, curtailed, °abbreviated: *He gave a concise summary of the findings. This is a concise edition of the dictionary.*

concrete *adj.* °real, °actual, °literal, °realistic, °authentic, valid, °genuine, bona fide, °reliable; °specific, °particular, °definite, °definitive, clear-cut, °material, °physical, °tangible, °substantial: *Have you any concrete evidence for the existence of UFOs?*

condemn *v.* **1** censure, °blame, °criticize, remonstrate with *or* against, °denounce, °disparage, reproach, °rebuke, °reprove, °scold, °reprimand, °upbraid: *The council was condemned for failing to provide adequate health care.* **2** °convict, °find °guilty; °sentence, °doom: *The judge condemned them to twenty years' imprisonment.* **3** ***condemned***: °doomed, damned, °destined, °fated, ordained, foreordained; consigned: *He has been condemned to wander forever.*

condescend *v.* °stoop, °deign, °lower *or* °humble *or* demean oneself, come down off one's high horse: *She wouldn't condescend to talk to the stable-boy directly.*

condescending *adj.* patronizing, belittling, °disdainful, °contemptuous, °pompous, °overbearing, high-handed, imperious, °snobbish, °haughty, *Colloq* snooty, *Brit* toffee-nosed; *Slang* snotty: *He thinks he's better than everyone, and I can't stand his condescending manner.*

condition *n.* **1** °state; °circumstance(s), °shape: *What condition is the house in? My bank account is in a poor condition.* **2** °stipulation, °proviso, °demand, °requirement, °term, °qualification, contingency, requisite, °prerequisite: *The terrorists have announced their conditions for releasing the hostages.* **3** working °order, °fitness, °shape, °form, fettle; °health: *He's in good condition, but his car isn't.* **4** ***conditions***: circumstances; °quarters; °environment: *The ship's crew live in very crowded conditions.*
—*v.* **5** °ready, get *or* make °ready, °prepare, °equip, °outfit, °fit (out *or* up), °adapt, °modify: *The mechanics are conditioning the plane for high-altitude flights.* **6** °train, °educate, °teach; brainwash; °influence, °mould, °persuade: *The children were conditioned to avoid talking to strangers.* **7** °accustom, inure, °adapt, acclimate, acclimatize: *At this training base, we condition the commandos to all kinds of hardships.*

conduct *n.* **1** °behaviour, actions, demeanour, manners, deportment, comportment, °attitude: *Such conduct will not be tolerated in this school.* **2** °guidance, °direction, °management, supervision, °leadership, °administration, °government, °running, handling, °control, °command, °regulation, °operation: *Had the conduct of the war been left up to him, we should have lost.*
—*v.* **3** °guide, °direct, °supervise, °manage, °carry on, °run, °control, °administer, °regulate, °operate: *They conduct a remarkably successful business.* **4** °lead, °guide, °escort, °show (in *or* out), usher: *We were conducted through the gallery by the curator herself.* **5** °channel, °carry, °transmit, convey; °direct: *Electrical power is conducted by the cable.* **6** ***conduct oneself***: °behave, °act, demean, deport, comport, acquit: *For a six-year-old, he conducted himself very well.*

confer *v.* **1** °converse, °consult, °deliberate, °talk (over), °discuss, °take °counsel: *I shall have to confer with my colleagues on that matter.* **2** *When transitive:* °confer on, °give, °grant, °present, °award; °bestow (on): *The prizes will be conferred after the dinner. He was bewildered by the honours conferred on him.*

conference *n.* °meeting, °convention, symposium, congress, seminar, forum, colloquium; °discussion, °talk, colloquy, *US* bull °session: *In 1988, the conference was held in Budapest.*

confess *v.* °disclose, °acknowledge, °admit, own (up *or* to *or* up to), °declare, avow, make a °clean breast (of); °reveal, divulge, °confirm, °concede, affirm, aver, °testify; disbosom oneself, *Colloq* come °clean: *She confessed her part in the swindle. Confronted with the evidence, he confessed.*

confidence *n.* **1** °trust, °reliance, °faith; °belief: *Your parents have a great deal of confidence in you.* **2** °assurance, °self-confidence, self-assurance, self-reliance, °poise, aplomb, coolness; °conviction, certitude, boldness, °courage, °nerve: *We admire the confidence she shows in her daring plan.* **3** ***in confidence***: in °secrecy, in °privacy, privately, confidentially, intimately, *Colloq* on the q.t. *or* Q.T.: *I am telling you this in confidence.*

confident *adj.* **1** °secure, °sure, °certain, assured, °positive, convinced: *I feel confident that we shall get the contract.* **2** °self-confident, self-assured, °self-possessed, reliant, self-reliant, °dauntless, °bold, °cool, cocksure, °fearless, °courageous, *Colloq* °cocky: *He strode into the room with a confident air.*

confidential *adj.* °private, °secret, °intimate; classified; *Colloq* hush-hush: *These confidential papers must never be out of your possession.*

confirm *v.* **1** °ratify, °sanction, °authorize, °endorse, °support, °sustain, °approve, °uphold, back up, validate, °verify, °recognize; °authenticate, accredit: *By-laws shall not take effect unless confirmed by the local authority.* **2** °establish, °settle, affirm, °ensure, °clinch, °substantiate, °guarantee, °bind, °seal: *The king thereby confirmed his control over the islands.* **3** °strengthen, °encourage, °fortify, °reinforce, corroborate, °substantiate, °buttress, °prove: *Later events confirmed his opinion.*

confiscate *v.* °appropriate, °seize, impound, sequester, sequestrate, expropriate, °take (away), commandeer: *The police confiscated my car to use as evidence.*

conflict *n.* **1** °fight, °battle, °combat, °engagement, °struggle, °war, °fray, °fracas, affray, °brawl, Donnybrook: *Gurkha troops entered the conflict.* **2** °dispute, °argument, °controversy, wrangle, contention, °disagreement, altercation, °feud, °quarrel, °row; squabble, °tiff, *Colloq* spat: *The counsellor was unable to resolve the conflict between the sisters regarding the will.* **3** °clash, °antagonism, °difference, °opposition, °disagreement, °variance, °discord: *There is a basic conflict between the interests of labour and of management.* —*v.* **4** °clash, °disagree, °differ, be °incompatible *or* at °odds *or* at °variance, be in °opposition (to): *The plans conflict on only one point.*

conform *v.* **1** °comply (with), °follow, °observe, °obey, °respect, °abide by, °adapt *or* °adjust (to): *We agree to conform to the rules of the club.* **2** °accord (with), °agree (with), concur (with), °coincide (with), °correspond (with), harmonize (with), °square (with), °match, °tally (with), °fit (in with), be °consistent (with), be in °accord *or* in accordance (with): *Their behaviour did not conform with what is expected in such circles. The two plans do not conform.*

confuse *v.* **1** disconcert, °perplex, °puzzle, °bewilder, °mystify, baffle, °bemuse, befuddle, °discomfit, confound, °fluster, °flummox, °upset, disorient, °embarrass, abash, °shame, °dismay, *Colloq* °rattle, °throw, *Chiefly US* discombobulate, *US and Canadian* buffalo: *She was completely confused by his offer to help.* **2** °disorder, confound, disorganize, °throw into disarray, °muddle, °mix up, °snarl (up), ensnarl, °tangle (up), °entangle, °botch, *Colloq* °mess up, make a °mess of, °screw up, *Brit* make a balls-up of, *US* ball up: *He has done more to confuse the situation than to clear it up.* **3** °mix up, confound, °muddle, °jumble, °snarl (up), ensnarl; °blur: *The identities of the children were confused at birth.*

confused *adj.* **1** °mixed up, jumbled, disordered, disorganized, °disorderly, muddled, muddle-headed, snarled (up), messy, baffling, confusing, mystifying, °puzzling, °perplexing; °contradictory, °ambiguous, misleading, °inconsistent, °mixed up, botched (up), *Colloq* higgledy-piggledy: *The accountants have provided a confused set of figures.* **2** bewildered, perplexed, puzzled, baffled, (be)fuddled, mystified, disoriented, discomposed, at °sea, flummoxed, dazed, muddled, bemused, °mixed up, nonplussed, °disconcerted, abashed, °put off, °put out, °disturbed, flustered, °ill at ease, °upset, at sixes and sevens, at a loss, *Rare* metagrobolized, *Colloq* screwed-up, muzzy, out of it, not with it, *Chiefly US* discombobulated, fouled up; *Slang* (all) balled up, *Brit* (all) bollocksed *or* ballocksed (up), *US* (all) bollixed (up), *US and Canadian* snafu: *I have never seen anyone so confused about a simple question of astrophysics.* **3** jumbled, °mixed up, muddled, °disorderly, confusing, messy, disorganized, °topsy-turvy; °miscellaneous, motley, *Brit* shambolic: *The books lay in a confused heap on the floor.*

confusion *n.* **1** °disorder, °mix-up, °mess, °jumble, °muddle, disarray, disarrangement, °chaos, °shambles: *The files are in complete confusion.* **2** °tumult, commotion, °disorder, turmoil, °pandemonium, °bedlam, °chaos: *Untold confusion resulted from sounding the alarm.* **3** °mix-up, confounding; °ambiguity, ambiguousness, °misunderstanding, contradiction, inconsistency: *There is often some confusion between the name of a thing and the thing itself.* **4** mixing, combining, mixing up, intermingling: *The removal firm is responsible for the confusion of your books with mine.* **5** °assortment, °mixture, °pot-pourri, gallimaufry, °hotchpotch *or US and Canadian also* hodgepodge: *A confusion of products lines the shelves.* **6** °embarrassment, discomfiture, mortification, abashment, shamefacedness, chagrin: *He felt terrible confusion when confronted with the evidence.*

congested *adj.* (over)crowded, blocked (up), jammed, crammed, plugged, stopped *or* stuffed (up), choked: *The police are trying to deal with traffic at congested intersections.*

congratulate *v.* felicitate, °compliment: *Her friends congratulated her on winning the award.*

congratulations *interjection.* Felicitations!, Best wishes!, Well done!, Many happy returns!, *Colloq* Nice going!, Good show!: *Heartiest congratulations! You've come in first!*

connect *v.* **1** °join *or* °link *or* °tie (together), °unite: *An old road connects the two towns.* **2** °associate, affiliate, °link, °relate, °league, °tie (in): *The police connected him with the break-in. The institute is connected with a pharmaceuticals company.* **3** °fasten, °bind, °unite, °tie, °link, °join, °attach, °couple, °put together, °secure, °fit, °fix, affix, °stick, °anchor, °lock; rivet, °weld, braze, solder, °screw, °nail, stitch, °sew, °pin, °hook, °staple, °tack, °glue, °cement, °fuse, °seal, °buckle, strap, °bolt, °lash, °chain, °moor: *Connect the parts to the frame.*

connection *n.* **1** uniting, joining, linking, connecting, coupling; °union, °bond, °joint, °link: *The US constitution forbids a formal connection between Church and State. The connection between the fittings has broken.* **2** °link, °tie, (inter)relation(ship), interplay, °bearing, °reference, °relevance, appropriateness, correlation, °tie-in; coherence, consistency, °association: *Your answer had no connection with the question.* **3** Often, ***connections***: °contact, °ally, °acquaintance, °friend (at court); °influence, *Colloq* °pull; *Slang US* drag: *With their connections, they can get away with anything.* **4** ***connections***: relatives, relations, °family, °kin, kith and °kin: *They have connections in Australia.*

conquer *v.* **1** °overcome, vanquish, °beat, °defeat, °subdue, °crush, °subjugate: *The Moors conquered most of Spain.* **2** °capture, °seize, °win, °gain, °acquire, °obtain; °occupy, annex, °overrun: *They conquered the territory by force of arms.* **3** °overcome, °triumph *or* °prevail over, °beat, surmount, °master, °win out (over): *He has finally conquered the habit of biting his fingernails.*

conquest *n.* **1** vanquishment, subjugation, °defeat, °domination, °subjection: *Hernando Cortés is famous for his conquest of Mexico.* **2** °victory, °triumph, mastery, °win: *He is credited with the conquest of a number of diseases by means of this drug.*

conscience *n.* °morality, morals, °judgement, fairness, sense of right and wrong, ethics, °honour, °standards, °principles, °scruples: *In such matters, your conscience must be your guide.*

conscientious *adj.* **1** °scrupulous, °principled, °fair, °moral, °ethical, °strict, °righteous, right-minded, upstanding, °upright, °honourable, °just, °responsible, high-minded; incorruptible: *Fetherby is a conscientious arbitrator.* **2** °cautious, °careful, °scrupulous, °exacting, °meticulous, punctilious, °painstaking, °diligent, °particular, rigorous, °thorough: *A conscientious effort was made to restore the painting to its original condition.* **3** °prudent, °discreet, °politic, °careful, circumspect, heedful, °attentive, °serious: *Fred is conscientious about keeping secrets.*

conscious *adj.* **1** °aware, °awake, °alert: *I was conscious of an eerie presence. The victim of the attack is now conscious.* **2** °deliberate, °intentional, purposive, °purposeful, °wilful, °studied: *Lydia has been making a conscious effort to be friendlier to me.*

consent *v.* **1** °agree, °comply, concur, accede, acquiesce, °concede, °yield, °submit, °cede, °conform, °give in: *He asked for payment in advance and I consented.* **2** ***consent to***: °permit, °allow, °agree to, °give in to, °approve, °authorize: *Richard's parents consented to his going on the outing.*
—*n.* **3** °approval, assent, °permission, °sanction, authorization, imprimatur, °seal of °approval, *Colloq* °OK, okay, °go-ahead: *Have Richard's parents given their consent?* **4** °agreement, acceptance, acquiescence, compliance, °approval, concurrence: *Taxes cannot be raised without the consent of Parliament.*

consequently *adv.* so, °therefore, as a °result *or* consequence, °accordingly, ergo, °hence, °thus: *He was found guilty and, consequently, sentenced to death.*

conservation *n.* °preservation, °protection, °safe keeping, °maintenance, °upkeep, °management, safeguarding; husbandry, °economy: *The conservation of natural resources must be a priority.*

conservative *adj.* **1** °reactionary, °right, right-wing, rightist, Tory: *In his conservative view, no change is ever for the better.* **2** °cautious, °careful, °prudent, °moderate, °temperate, middle-of-the-road, °sober, °stable; unprogressive, °orthodox, °traditional, conformist, °hidebound, °conventional, °standard, fundamentalist, true-blue, dyed in the wool: *The conservative approach would be to study the problem before making a change. The conservative members voted against electing certain members to the club.*
—*n.* **3** °reactionary, rightist, right-winger, Tory, fundamentalist; °moderate, middle-of-the-roader: *He's a conservative and favours a classical education.*

conserve *v.* **1** °keep, °preserve, °hold on to, °save, °spare, °reserve: *Conserve your energy for later, when we get near the top.* **2** °preserve, °maintain, °keep up, take °care of: *These buildings should be conserved for later generations.*

consider *v.* **1** °think about *or* over, take into *or* under consideration, °deliberate (over *or* about), °contemplate (on *or* over), °weigh, °ponder, °mull over, cogitate on, °meditate (on *or* upon *or* over), °reflect (on *or* upon), ruminate (on *or* over), °chew over, °study, °examine: *The council will consider your proposal.* **2** °heed, °mark, take into °account *or* consideration, °reckon with, bear in °mind, °note, °observe, make °allowance for; °esteem, °respect, have °regard for: *Consider your mother's feelings in the matter.* **3** °regard, °look upon; °judge, deem, °take to be, °think, °believe, °gauge, °rate, °estimate, °reckon: *Consider yourself under arrest. I don't consider Simon the best person for the job.*

considerable *adj.* **1** sizeable, °substantial, °large, °big, °great; appreciable, °respectable, °noticeable, largish, biggish, °goodly, °decent, °fair, *Colloq* °tidy: *A considerable crowd were gathered outside.* **2** °important, °worthy, of consequence, of °distinction, °distinguished, °illustrious, °noteworthy, °notable, °remarkable, °estimable, °influential, °respectable: *Some of the most considerable citizens were banished.*

considerate *adj.* °thoughtful, °kind, °kindly, kindhearted, good-hearted, °helpful, °friendly, °neighbourly, °gracious, °obliging, °accommodating, °charitable, °generous, °unselfish; °sympathetic, compassionate, °sensitive; °attentive; °solicitous: *It was very considerate of you to offer your car.*

consideration *n.* **1** °regard, °concern, attentiveness, °solicitude, thoughtfulness, compassion, °kindness, kindliness, kind-heartedness, considerateness, °respect, caring, °care: *Out of consideration for your father, you should complete your studies.* **2** °reward, compensation, °remuneration, °fee, °payment, recompense, emolument, °tip, gratuity, *pourboire*, baksheesh *or* backsheesh; °honorarium: *The boy will look after your luggage for a small consideration, madam.* **3** °thought, deliberation, °reflection, contemplation, rumination, cogitation, °study, °examination: *After some consideration, we have decided that we will finance the project.*

considering *prep.* in °view of, in (the) °light of, bearing in °mind, making °allowance for, taking into consideration *or* °account, looking at, all in all, all things *or* everything considered, inasmuch as, insomuch as: *Considering your background, I doubt that you are qualified.*

consistent *adj.* **1** agreeing, in °agreement, in °harmony, in keeping, °harmonious, in concordance, conforming, in conformance, accordant, compatible, in °accord *or* accordance, consonant: *Her story is not consistent with the facts.* **2** dependable, °regular, °predictable, undeviating, °steady, °steadfast, unchanging, °uniform, unswerving, °constant: *His behaviour, even under pressure, has been quite consistent.*

consistently *adv.* **1** steadily, constantly, regularly, uniformly, °daily, day by day: *Her piano technique is improving consistently.* **2** dependably, unswervingly, staunchly, devotedly, °firmly, resolutely, faithfully, uniformly, unfailingly: *The courts have consistently upheld her claim to custody of the children.*

console *v.* °comfort, soothe, °calm, assuage, °solace, °cheer (up): *Ivan made an effort to console the grieving widow.*

conspicuous *adj.* **1** °obvious, °clear, °evident, °plain, palpable, °perceptible, °patent, °prominent, °apparent, clear-cut, °unquestionable, incontestable, °incontrovertible: *The sultan played a conspicuous role in the kidnapping of the envoy.* **2** °obvious, unmistakable, °prominent, °outstanding, °noticeable, °impressive, °vivid, °obtrusive; °striking, °showy, °garish, °gaudy, °loud, °tawdry, °blatant, °lurid, °vulgar, °flashy, °ostentatious: *The silhouette of the castle was conspicuous against the sky. Fingal was again conspicuous, this time in a green wig and bowler.* **3** °notable, °noteworthy, °exceptional, °outstanding, °eminent, °unusual, °marked, °extraordinary, °remarkable, °distinguished, °impressive, °awesome, awe-inspiring, °glorious: *The medal is awarded for conspicuous bravery.*

conspiracy *n.* °plot, °scheme, °stratagem, °intrigue, collusion, °cabal, connivance, foul play, °dirty work: *He suspected them of a conspiracy to defraud their clients.*

constable *n.* policeman, policewoman, (°police) °officer, *US* patrolman, *Colloq* cop, copper, *Brit* bobby; *Slang* flatfoot, fuzz: *A constable was standing on the corner, and we asked him the way.*

constant *adj.* **1** °resolute, °immovable, °steadfast, °firm, dependable, unshakeable *or* unshakable, °determined, unswerving, undeviating, persevering, unwearying, unwearied, °untiring, indefatigable, °tireless, unflagging, unwavering, unfailing, unfaltering, °persistent; °loyal, °true, tried and °true, °devoted, °staunch, trusty, °faithful: *He was her constant companion during her troubles.* **2** incessant, unceasing, ceaseless, °perpetual, °persistent, uninterrupted, °steady, °regular, °invariable, unremitting, unvarying, °relentless, unrelenting, °continuous, °continual; unending, °endless, never-ending, °non-stop, °perennial, °eternal, °everlasting, *Literary* sempiternal: *The constant pain almost made me cry out. Their constant bickering is getting on my nerves.* **3** unchanging, unchanged, °invariable, unvarying, °fixed, °uniform, unalterable, immutable, °changeless, °persistent: *The numbers might change, but the ratio is constant.*

construct *v.* **1** °build, °erect, °make, °put together, °frame, °set up, °put up, °assemble: *We constructed a summer-house in the garden.* **2** °fabricate, °devise, °create, °forge, °invent, °formulate, °compose, °shape, °set up, °fashion: *He has constructed a complex argument to support his theory.*

constructive *adj.* **1** °helpful, °useful, °practicable, °advantageous, °practical, °productive, °beneficial, °positive: *She provided much constructive advice on how to design the factory.* **2** °virtual, inferential, °implicit, inferred, derived, deduced: *As it turned out, the shareholders were the constructive victims of the fraud.*

consult *v.* **1** Often, ***consult with***: °confer (with), °discuss (with), °deliberate (with), °talk over (with), °inquire *or* °enquire of, °seek °advice from, °ask (of), °question, interrogate, take °counsel (with *or* of): *I shall have to consult a doctor about my headaches. You should consult with your lawyer.* **2** °refer to, °look up, °seek °information from: *If in doubt, consult the dictionary.*

consultant *n.* **1** °physician, °doctor, °specialist, °expert: *You ought to get the opinion of another consultant.* **2** °adviser *or* advisor, °expert, °counsellor *or US* counselor: *Our financial consultant tells us how to handle the company funds.*

consume *v.* **1** °devour, °eat (up), °gulp (down), °swallow, °drink (up), °put away, gobble (up); °digest: *When those teenagers come home, they consume everything in sight.* **2** °use up, °exhaust, deplete, °drain, °expend, °diminish, °reduce: *The new car has consumed all our savings.* **3** °waste, °occupy, squander, °fritter away, °dissipate, absorb, °lose, °throw away, °lavish, *Slang* °blow: *Too much of your time has already been consumed by that problem.* **4** °destroy, °ruin, (lay) °waste, °demolish, °wreck, °gut, °raze, *Slang US and Canadian* total: *Fire consumed the entire house.* **5** °overcome, °overwhelm, °devastate, °destroy, annihilate, °ravage, (lay) °waste, °wear out, °ruin, °eat up, °devour, do in; preoccupy, °obsess: *He is consumed by jealousy.*

consummation *n.* **1** °completion, °accomplishment, °fulfilment, °finish, °end, °realization, attainment, °achievement, °success; completing, accomplishing, fulfilling, finishing, ending, realizing, attaining, achieving: *Owning a Rolls Royce was the consummation of her dreams.* **2** °acme, °perfection, °peak, culmination, finishing °touch, conclusion, °grand finale, °climax: *The Nobel prize was the consummation of an arduous life of research.*

contact *n.* **1** °junction, conjunction, °connection: *If the wires make contact, the fuse will blow.* **2** °acquaintance, °friend, °connection, *Colloq US* in: *I have a contact on the board of directors.* **3** °touch, communication, °association: *Are you still in contact with Georgina?* —*v.* **4** get in °touch with, °communicate with, °reach, get °hold of; phone, °ring (up), °telephone, °speak to *or* with, °write to, °correspond with: *Try to contact the manager at his home.*

contain *v.* **1** °hold, °have in it; °bear, °carry: *The capsule contained a deadly poison.* **2** °hold, have the °capacity for, °accommodate, °admit, °carry; °seat: *This bottle contains no more than a quart. The theatre can contain 200.* **3** °restrain, °restrict, confine, °repress, °control, °hold back *or* in, °curb, °bridle, keep under control, °suppress, °check, °stifle: *He could hardly contain himself when he learnt he had passed the examination.*

contaminate *v.* defile, °sully, °pollute, °corrupt, °rot, °stain, °soil, °taint, infect, °poison, °foul, °spoil, befoul; °debase, °adulterate, °vitiate: *The river has been contaminated by effluent from a nearby factory.*

contemplate *v.* **1** °look *or* °gaze at *or* on *or* upon, °behold, °view, °survey, °observe, °regard, °eye; °scan, °scrutinize, °inspect: *I contemplated the scene of the Grand Canal from my hotel room.* **2** ruminate (over), °ponder (on *or* over), °deliberate (over), °muse (on *or* over), °meditate *or* °reflect (on), °think (about *or* over), °mull over, cogitate (over), °turn over in one's mind, °brood on *or* over, °chew on *or* over, °consider, °study, °examine: *She was contemplating the events of the past night. Give me a moment to contemplate.* **3** °plan, °intend, °think of *or* about, °consider, °entertain the idea *or* notion of: *After we broke up, I contemplated emigrating to Australia.*

contemporary *adj.* **1** of the °time, contemporaneous, coeval, coexistent, concurrent, concomitant, °parallel, synchronous, synchronic, °coincidental, coetaneous: *We examined some of the documents contemporary with his reign.* **2** °modern, °current, present-day, °new, up to °date, °stylish, °fashionable, modish, à la °mode, °latest, in; °novel, newfangled, *Colloq* °trendy: *She always keeps up with contemporary fads in dress and make-up. I find much of the contemporary metal-and-glass architecture rather boring.*

contempt *n.* °loathing, abhorrence, hatred, odium, °hate; °scorn, disdain, contumely, °disgust: *She has nothing but contempt for cowards.*

contemptible *adj.* °despicable, °loathsome, detestable, °scurvy, °low, °mean, °base, °inferior, currish, °wretched, °vile, abject, ignominious, °unworthy, °shabby, °shameful: *It was contemptible of you to give away my secret.*

contemptuous *adj.* °scornful, °disdainful, sneering, derisive, insulting, contumelious, °insolent: *The maestro was contemptuous of my piano-playing.*

content[1] *n.* **1** °capacity, °volume, °size, °measure: *The content of the barrel is exactly 55 gallons.* **2** Usually, ***contents***: ingredients, components, constituents; °load: *The bottle broke and its contents spilt on the floor.* **3** °substance, subject-matter; °significance, purport, °import, °essence, °text, °theme, °topic, °thesis: *The book is amusing but its content is quite trivial.*

content[2] *n.* **1** °pleasure, °satisfaction, °gratification, °happiness, contentment, contentedness, felicity, °delight: *He kept on singing to his heart's content.* **2** °ease, °comfort, tranquillity, °serenity, °peace, peacefulness, contentedness: *I have a feeling of such content merely being with you.* —*adj.* **3** °pleased, satisfied, °happy, °delighted, contented, gratified, °glad, °cheerful; °comfortable, fulfilled: *I was quite content to be home once more.* —*v.* **4** °satisfy, °please, °gratify, soothe, °cheer, °gladden, °delight: *It contented him to be near her.*

contest *n.* **1** °competition, °match, °tournament, championship, tourney, °meet, °game, °rivalry, °trial: *The contest was won by a woman from Shropshire.* **2** °strife, °controversy, °dispute, contention, °debate, altercation, °argument, velitation; °conflict, °struggle, °fight, °battle, °combat, °war: *The contest is between those for and those against capital punishment.* —*v.* **3** contend, °argue, °dispute, °debate; °challenge, (call into) °question, °oppose, °counter, confute, °object to, refute: *David has decided to contest his father's will.*

contestant *n.* contender, °competitor, °opponent, °rival, °adversary, entrant, °player, °participant: *The winner is the contestant from Chearsley.*

context *n.* °structure, framework, °environment, °situation, °circumstance(s); ambience *or* ambiance, °surround, °surroundings, °frame (of °reference), °setting, °background: *It is often hard to understand something taken out of its context.*

continual *adj.* °constant, incessant, °perpetual, °non-stop, °persistent, uninterrupted, °regular, °steady, unbroken, unceasing, ceaseless, °eternal, unremitting, interminable, °endless, unending; *Loosely* °continuous: *She has this continual ringing in her ears.*

continue *v.* **1** °carry on, °proceed (with), °keep up *or* on *or* at, °go on (with), °pursue, °persist (in), °persevere (in): *Please continue whatever it was you were doing.* **2** °endure, °last, °go on, °persist, be prolonged, °remain: *How long will the curfew continue?* **3** °maintain, °keep (on), °prolong, °perpetuate, °carry on (with), °persist in *or* with, °sustain, °extend: *My mother continued her career throughout my childhood.* **4** °resume, °pick up, °take up, °carry on (with): *Allow me to continue my story and don't interrupt again.* **5** °proceed, °go (on), °extend: *The road continues for about a mile, ending at the sea.*

continuous *adj.* **1** connected, unbroken, uninterrupted: *The wall is continuous except for one gate.* **2** incessant, °persistent, °perpetual, °non-stop, unceasing, ceaseless, °constant, unremitting, interminable, °endless, unending; *Loosely* °continual: *A continuous stream of refugees passed through the camp.*

contract *n.* **1** °agreement, °understanding, °deal, °bargain, °arrangement, °pact, commitment, °obligation, °compact: *We have just signed a contract to supply office equipment to a new electronics company.*
—*v.* **2** °engage, °agree, °promise, covenant, °undertake: *Our company contracted to maintain the roads in this area.* **3** °catch, °acquire, °get, °come down with, °develop, °become infected with, *Brit* °go down with: *Eunice contracted diphtheria.* **4** °diminish, °shrink, °draw together, °roll (oneself), °narrow, °squeeze, constrict, compress, condense, °decrease, °reduce: *When disturbed, the animal contracts itself into a ball.* **5** °wrinkle, °knit, crease, corrugate, °pucker: *His brow contracted into a frown.*

contradict *v.* **1** °deny, gainsay, °dispute, controvert, °argue against; °oppose: *He is very opinionated, and doesn't like to be contradicted.* **2** contravene, belie, refute, disallow, °forbid, disaffirm, °counter, abrogate, nullify, annul, °reverse, °counteract: *The evidence yields nothing that contradicts my argument.*

contradictory *adj.* °inconsistent, °paradoxical, °incongruous, conflicting, °incompatible, discrepant; °ambiguous, ambivalent: *The witnesses' descriptions of the robbers are contradictory.*

contraption *n.* contrivance, °device, °gadget, °mechanism, °apparatus, *Colloq* widget, thingumabob *or* thingamabob, thingumajig *or* thingamajig, thingummy, whatsit, doodah, thingy, *US* gizmo *or* gismo, Rube Goldberg (°invention), whatchamacallit, *Colloq Brit* gubbins: *People began to build all sorts of contraptions that they hoped might fly.*

contrary *adj.* **1** °opposite, °opposing, °opposed, °different, °contradictory, conflicting, antagonistic: *Set aside enough time to hear the contrary side of the argument.* **2** antagonistic, °perverse, contrarious, °hostile, unfriendly, inimical, cross-grained, refractory, contumacious, °self-willed, °argumentative, unaccommodating, antipathetic, *Literary* froward: *He can disagree, but why must he be so contrary?* **3** adverse, unfavourable, °inauspicious, unlucky, °unfortunate, unpropitious, °untoward, °inopportune, °bad, °foul: *We ran into contrary winds and were delayed.*
—*n.* **4** °opposite, °reverse: *Her present position is the direct contrary of the one she took yesterday.*
—*adv.* **5** perversely, oppositely, contrariwise, contrarily, in °opposition to: *The rat in the maze acted contrary to the expected pattern.*

contrast *v.* **1** juxtapose, °oppose, °compare, °distinguish, °differentiate, °discriminate, °set *or* °place against; °set off: *Contrast life in the 18th century with life today.* **2** °conflict, °differ *or* °diverge *or* °deviate (from): *The two styles contrast sharply. Australian speech contrasts with that of Canada in many respects.*
—*n.* **3** °comparison; °difference, °distinction, °disparity, °dissimilarity: *The author emphasizes the contrasts between the two economic policies.*

contribute *v.* **1** °give, °furnish, °donate, °bestow, °grant, °present, °provide, °supply: *He contributed three paintings by Longchamp to the museum. They contributed generously to the restoration fund.* **2** ***contribute to***: °add to, °promote, °advance, °help, °aid, °support, °forward, have a hand in, play a °part *or* °role in: *They believe that poor parental supervision contributes to juvenile delinquency.*

control *v.* **1** °command, °dominate, °direct, °steer, °pilot, hold °sway over, °rule, °exercise °power *or* °authority over, °govern, °manage, °lead, °conduct, be in control (of), call the tune, °guide, °oversee, °supervise: *Does she really control the future of the company?* **2** °check, °hold back *or* in °check, °curb, °repress, °contain: *Try to control yourself.* **3** °suppress, °put down, °master, °subdue, °restrain, °curb, °manage: *They were totally unable to control the unruly teenagers.*
—*n.* **4** °command, °direction, °power, °authority, °leadership, °management, °guidance, supervision, °oversight, °charge; °sway, °rule, °jurisdiction: *Turn control of the mission over to Mrs Beale. The court is under the control of the State.* **5** °restraint, °check, °curb, mastery, °command, dominance, °domination: *You must get better control over your emotions.* **6** °knob, button, dial, °handle, lever, °switch; °device, °mechanism: *This control opens the door to the safe.*

controversial *adj.* **1** °debatable, °disputable, °questionable, °moot, °doubtful, °unsettled: *Who will run the department is a controversial matter.* **2** polemical, dialectic, litigious, °factious: *She has studied the controversial writings of the 19th-century feminists.* **3** disputatious, °argumentative, contentious; °provocative: *Race relations have remained a controversial issue for centuries.*

controversy *n.* **1** °dispute, °debate, contention, °argument, argumentation, disputation, wrangling, confrontation, questioning, °disagreement: *The inquest went ahead without controversy.* **2** °argument, °dispute, °disagreement, °quarrel; squabble, °tiff, *Colloq* spat: *Controversy still rages over the theory of natural selection.*

convalesce *v.* °recover, °improve, get °better, °recuperate: *The doctor said I needed only a week to convalesce after the operation.*

convenient *n.* **1** °suitable, commodious, °useful, °helpful, °handy, °serviceable, °expedient, °opportune, °advantageous: *The bus is quite convenient for getting to and from the airport.* **2** °handy, °nearby, within (easy) °reach, at one's fingertips, close at °hand, °available, °accessible; (at the) °ready: *There's a convenient post office round the corner.*

convention *n.* **1** °assembly, °meeting, °gathering, congregation, congress, °conference, symposium, °council, conclave, °diet, synod, seminar: *The annual convention of cat fanciers will take place in June.* **2** °rule, °practice, °custom, °tradition, °usage, °formality, conventionalism: *According to convention, this year's vice-president becomes president next year.*

conventional *adj.* °customary, °habitual, °usual, °normal, °regular, °standard, °orthodox, °traditional, established, °ordinary, °everyday, °common, commonplace, °accustomed, received, agreed; °reactionary, °old-fashioned, °stodgy, °stuffy, °old hat: *Conventional methods of teaching mathematics are being criticized.*

converge *v.* °come *or* °go together, °meet, °join, °unite, °merge, °coincide; °blend: *The roads converge in the valley.*

conversation *n.* °discussion, °talk, °chat, °dialogue, colloquy, °parley; chit-chat, °gossip, discourse, °palaver, *Colloq chiefly Brit* chin-wag: *The conversation about the situation in the Middle East ended abruptly. I want action, not conversation.*

conversationalist *n.* deipnosophist: *It was a pleasure to have dinner with an intelligent conversationalist for a change.*

converse *v.* °discuss, °talk, °speak, °chat, °parley, discourse, °gossip, °chatter: *The men were conversing about her over dinner.*

convert *v.* **1** °change, °modify, °alter, °transform, transmute, mutate, transfigure, transmogrify, remodel, remake, metamorphose: *We converted our rowing-boat into a sailing dinghy.* **2** proselytize, °switch, °change (over): *To avoid the horrors of the Inquisition, many Spanish Jews converted to Catholicism.*
—*n.* **3** proselyte; neophyte, catechumen, °disciple: *Converts are often the most passionate believers.*

convict *v.* **1** find *or* prove °guilty: *She was convicted of theft.*
—*n.* **2** °prisoner, °captive, *Slang* con, jailbird *or Brit also* gaolbird, *Brit* lag: *The rioting convicts burnt down two prison buildings.*

conviction *n.* **1** °proof of °guilt: *After his conviction, he was sentenced to life imprisonment.* **2** °belief, °opinion, °view, °persuasion, °position: *It is her conviction that the painting is by Titian.* **3** °certainty, sureness, positiveness, °confidence, °assurance, certitude: *He doesn't have the courage to back up his convictions.*

convince *v.* °win over, °talk into, °persuade, °bring (a)round, °sway: *I have at last convinced them of the need for more resources.*

cool *adj.* **1** °chilly, °chill, chilling, cooling, unheated; chilled, °cold, °refreshing, °fresh: *It's rather cool outside today. I'd prefer some cool lemonade.* **2** °calm, °serene, °collected, °level-headed, °quiet, unexcited, unemotional, undisturbed, unexcitable, unruffled, unflappable, cool-headed, °relaxed, controlled, under °control, °self-possessed, self-controlled, unperturbed, °phlegmatic, composed, imperturbable: *He remains cool even in a crisis.* **3** °dispassionate, °cold, °cold-blooded, emotionless, °deliberate, °cold-hearted, °calculated, °wilful, °premeditated, °purposeful, purposive: *It was clearly the cool act of a professional criminal.* **4** uninvolved, °distant, °remote, °aloof, °detached, removed, uninterested, unconcerned, °unsympathetic, apathetic, °cold, °cold-hearted, °cold-blooded: *How can you be so cool where human lives are concerned?* **5** °lukewarm, °distant, uncordial, unfriendly, unsociable, °unapproachable, °standoffish, °forbidding, unwelcoming, °cold, °frigid: *After the affair, she was distinctly cool towards him.* **6** °bold, °audacious, °brazen, °overconfident, °presumptuous, °shameless, °unabashed, °impertinent, °impudent, °insolent: *I cannot account for the cool way he insulted his host.*
—*n.* **7** coolness, °chill, chilliness, *Colloq* coolth: *I shall have a sherry to ward off the cool of the evening.* **8** aplomb, °poise, sedateness, °control, °self-control, composure, °sang-froid: *He really lost his cool when she told him he was a lousy driver.*
—*v.* **9** °chill, °refrigerate, ice: *Cool the pudding before serving.* **10** °diminish, °reduce, lessen, abate, °moderate: *Her interest quickly cooled when she discovered he was married.*

cooperate *v.* **1** °collaborate, °work together, °join, °unite, interact, °team up, °join forces, °act jointly *or* in concert: *If we cooperate, the work will be done in half the time.* **2** °participate, °contribute, lend a °hand, °help, °assist: *You must learn to cooperate and not just sit there.*

cooperation *n.* **1** collaboration, teamwork, interaction, synergism *or* synergy: *Only through cooperation will we be able to achieve success.* **2** °support, °help, °aid, °assistance, °patronage, °backing, advocacy, °favour, °helping °hand, °friendship, °blessing, sponsorship, °auspices, backup: *We needed the cooperation of people like you to mount the exhibition.*

coordinate *v.* **1** °organize, classify, °order, °arrange, systemize, systematize, codify, °categorize, °group, °match (up), °dispose, °rate, °rank, °grade: *Coordinate the information before preparing the report.* **2** harmonize, correlate, °unify, °mesh, synchronize, °integrate, *Colloq* °pull together: *We must coordinate our efforts for the best results.*
—*adj.* **3** °equivalent, °parallel, °correspondent, complementary, correlative, °equal, °reciprocal, coordinating, coordinative, *Technical* paratactic: *The two systems are coordinate and operate in parallel.*

cope *v.* **1** °manage, °get along *or* by, °make do, °survive, subsist, °come through: *Even with seven children to care for, she copes very well.* **2** ***cope with***: be a °match for, °withstand, contend with *or* against, °handle, °deal with, °dispose of: *I cannot cope with all the work I have been given to do.*

copy *n.* **1** °reproduction, °replica, °facsimile, °likeness, °imitation, °double, °twin, duplication, °duplicate, °transcript, replication, carbon (°copy), photocopy, °print: *She found a copy of the lost manuscript.* **2** °example, °sample, °specimen: *How many copies of the book have been sold?* **3** °text, °writing: *The copy is ready; we are waiting for the illustrations.*
—*v.* **4** °reproduce, °duplicate, replicate, °transcribe: *Don't copy others' work—they might be wrong.* **5** °imitate, °mimic, impersonate, emulate, ape, °parrot, °echo: *Ted copies the rock stars in every possible detail of their dress and behaviour.*

cord *n.* °string, °line, °twine; °rope: *Tie the cord around the parcel twice.*

cordial *adj.* °friendly, °warm, affable, °amiable, °kindly, °genial, °gracious, welcoming, °pleasant, °good-natured, °nice; °courteous, °polite: *After a cordial greeting at the door, the guests were served champagne.*

core *n.* **1** °centre, °heart, °middle, °nucleus, °inside(s): *Remove the core of the apple first.* **2** °essence, marrow, °heart, °pith, °gist, °quintessence, °sum and substance: *The core of the problem is her refusal to consider any alternative.*
—*v.* **3** °pit, °seed: *The pie might have tasted better if you'd cored the apples first.*

corps *n.* °body of men *or* women, troop, cadre, °unit, °detachment, °cohort, °division, battalion, brigade, °platoon, °squad, column, squadron: *We delivered supplies to the medical corps.*

corpse *n.* °body, remains, °cadaver, *Slang* °stiff; *of an animal* carcass: *The corpses were buried in a mass grave.*

correct *v.* **1** °right, set *or* put °right, °amend, redress, °rectify, °remedy, °repair, °fix; °cure: *A good mechanic will be able to correct the faults in the engine.* **2** °scold, admonish, °rebuke, °reprimand, °berate, chide, °reprove; censure, °blame: *You mustn't correct people for their bad manners.* **3** °punish, °chastise, °chasten, °discipline, °castigate: *The boys were corrected for swearing at the teacher.* **4** °reverse, °offset, °counteract, counterbalance, °neutralize, nullify, °make up for, annul, °cancel; °adjust, °change, °modify: *Adding this fertilizer should correct the acid content of the soil.* **5** °mark, °grade: *The exam papers haven't yet been corrected.*
—*adj.* **6** °proper, °decorous, °decent, °appropriate, °suitable, °fit, °right, °meet, °fitting, °befitting, apt, *de rigueur, comme il faut, Old-fashioned Brit* tickety-boo: *I have found her behaviour correct at all times.* **7** °conventional, established, °set, °standard, °normal, °orthodox, approved, in °order, *de rigueur, comme il faut,* °usual, natural, °customary, °traditional, done, °right, *Old-fashioned Brit* tickety-boo: *Sending flowers to the funeral parlour would be the correct thing to do.* **8** °accurate, °right, °precise, °exact, °factual, valid, °true, °proper, °fitting, apt, °suitable, °appropriate; °faultless, °perfect, unimpeachable: *Joanna gave the correct answer.*

correction *n.* **1** °improvement, emendation, rectification, redress, °remedy, reparation, °amendment; corrigendum: *With these corrections, the work will be vastly better.* **2** °punishment, castigation, chastisement: *He resented her continual correction of him for trivial things.*

correspond *v.* **1** °agree, °conform, °tally, °comply, °accord, harmonize, be congruous, °match, °coincide: *The results of the surveys correspond.* **2** °write, °communicate, be in °touch *or* °contact: *We have been corresponding for years.*

correspondent *n.* newspaperman, newspaperwoman, pressman, presswoman, °journalist, °reporter, stringer, newsman, newsperson: *Here is a report from our correspondent in Sydney.*

corridor *n.* °hall, hallway, °passage, passageway: *We met in the corridor outside my room.*

corrupt *adj.* **1** °dishonest, untrustworthy, °dishonourable, underhand(ed), °venal, *Colloq* °crooked: *He got off by bribing a corrupt judge.* **2** debased, depraved, °perverted, subverted, °evil, °wicked, °degenerate, degraded: *The inhabitants practised a corrupt form of Christianity.*
—*v.* **3** °debase, °pervert, °subvert, °degrade, deprave, °warp: *A funds manager could easily be corrupted by all that money.* **4** °adulterate, °contaminate, °pollute, °taint, defile, infect, °spoil, °poison: *Drainage from the site has corrupted the purity of the water.* **5** °bribe, suborn, °buy (off): *He thought he knew a juror who might be corrupted.*

cost *n.* **1** °price, °outlay, °payment, °charge, °expense, °expenditure, °rate, °tariff: *The gold strap will double the cost of the watch. If the cost increases, the selling price must go up.*
—*v.* **2** °sell for, °get, °fetch, °bring in, *Colloq* set (someone) back: *This would cost twice as much in London.*

costume *n.* °dress, clothing, attire, °clothes, garb, °apparel, raiment, °garments, °outfit, vestment, livery, °uniform, °kit, *Colloq* °gear, togs, °get-up; *Slang* °rags, *US* threads: *What kind of costume is Celia wearing to the fancy-dress ball?*

cosy *adj.* **1** °comfortable, °snug, °warm, °restful, °secure, relaxing, °easy, *US* cozy, *Colloq* comfy: *They bought a cosy little rose-covered cottage in the Cotswolds.* **2** °convenient, °expedient, self-serving, underhand(ed): *He has a cosy arrangement with the planning board.*

cot *n.* bed, crib; cradle, bunk: *The baby is asleep in his cot.*

cottage *n.* °hut, °shack, °cabin, bungalow, shanty, *Literary* °cot; *US and Canadian* °lodge, chalet: *She's going to stay at our cottage for a week.*

couch *n.* **1** sofa, settee, settle, divan, love-seat, *chaise (longue)*; day-bed; °tête-à-tête, vis-à-vis, siamoise; *US* Davenport: *Come and sit by me on the couch.*
—*v.* **2** embed, °frame, °style, °express, °phrase: *Her warning was couched in friendly words.*

council *n.* **1** °assembly, °meeting, conclave, °conference, synod, consistory, °convention, congress, congregation, °gathering, convocation, *US* caucus: *The council voted to ban nuclear arms.* **2** °board, °ministry, directors, °cabinet, panel, °committee, °body, directorate, directory, caucus: *She was elected to the council last year.*

counsel *n.* **1** °advice, °judgement, °direction, °opinion, °guidance, °instruction, °recommendation, exhortation, *Technical* parænesis: *Your counsel has always been wise in the past.* **2** consultation, °discussion, deliberation, °consideration: *We took counsel with the cabinet on the matter.* **3** °adviser *or* advisor, °guide, °counsellor; °lawyer, *Brit* barrister; *US* attorney: *My counsel suggests we settle out of court.*
—*v.* **4** °advise, °recommend to, °suggest to, °instruct; °guide: *I have counselled her to pursue the matter.*

counsellor *n.* °adviser *or* advisor, °counsel, °lawyer, *Brit* counsellor-at-law, barrister, *US* counselor, counselor-at-law, attorney: *We have retained Vestley and Stock as our counsellors.*

count *v.* **1** count up *or* off, °enumerate, °number, °calculate, °add up, °total, °reckon, °compute, °tally, °figure up, quantify, *Colloq* °figure out: *Maddie counted the number of pencils in the box.* **2** °include, °consider, °regard, deem, °judge, °look on *or* upon: *You can count me among those who favour the idea.* **3** ***count on*** *or* ***upon***: °rely on *or* upon, °depend on *or* upon, be °sure of, °trust, bank on, be °confident of, *Chiefly Brit or US dialect* °reckon on *or* upon, *Chiefly US* °figure on *or* upon: *I knew I could count on Moira to do the right thing.*

counter *n.* **1** °token, disc, °chip, °piece, marker: *She placed three counters on the number 14.* **2** °table, °bar: *We do not serve beer at this counter.*

counteract *v.* counterbalance, °neutralize, °correct, annul, nullify, °cancel, °oppose, °mitigate: *The coffee counteracted the effect of the sleeping-pill.*

counterfeit *adj.* **1** forged, °fake, °fraudulent, °imitation, °bogus, °spurious, *Colloq* °phoney *or US also* phony: *The bank reported the counterfeit money to the police.* **2** make-believe, °sham, °pretended, °pretend, feigned, °insincere, °fake, faked, °false, °artificial, meretricious, pseudo, °factitious, °synthetic, °unreal, simulated: *You were warned about his counterfeit sincerity.*
—*n.* **3** °fake, °imitation, °forgery, °reproduction, *Colloq* °phoney *or US also* phony: *This is the original deed, that one is a counterfeit.*
—*v.* **4** °forge, °copy, °reproduce, °falsify, °imitate; *Slang* hang paper: *He made a living counterfeiting passports.* **5** feign, °pretend, simulate, °put on, °fake: *The suspects have shown signs of wealth that are difficult to counterfeit.*

counterfeiter *n. Slang* paper-hanger: *The counterfeiter, who forged only five-pound notes, was arrested today.*

country *n.* **1** °nation, °state, °power; °territory, °realm: *How many countries belong to the British Commonwealth?* **2** (°native) °land, homeland, °fatherland, motherland, mother country: *I would gladly fight for my country.* **3** countryside, °rural area *or* surroundings, provinces, hinterlands; mountains, woods, wilderness, outback, *Colloq* sticks, *US* boondocks, boonies: *We are spending our holiday in the country.*

couple *n.* **1** °pair, duo, twosome; °brace, °span, yoke, °team: *They certainly make a nice couple.* **2** ***a couple of***: a °few, °several, a °handful (of), one or two, three or four: *I'll be with you in a couple of minutes.*
—*v.* **3** °join, °link, yoke, °combine, °unite, °match up, °connect: *The two carriages are easily coupled together.*

courage *n.* °bravery, valour, boldness, intrepidity, gallantry, dauntlessness, °daring, fearlessness, heroism, °nerve, *Colloq* °grit, guts, °pluck, °spunk, *US* moxie, sand, *Slang Brit* °bottle: *She had the courage to face the two of them alone.*

courageous *adj.* °brave, valiant, valorous, °bold, °intrepid, °gallant, °dauntless, °daring, °fearless, °heroic, *Colloq* plucky: *The soldiers were very courageous and fought against tremendous odds.*

course *n.* **1** °path, °way, °orbit, °route, °run, °track, ambit, °line, °circuit, °passage: *We continued on our course. The sun pursued its fiery course across the heavens.* **2** °movement, °progress, °headway, °advance, °progression; °speed: *The driver slackens his course at the curves.* **3** °procedure, °process, °performance, °routine, °conduct, °order, °practice, dispatch *or* despatch, °execution: *In the course of her duties, she handles a great deal of money.* **4** °direction, °tack: *If we stay on this course we'll run aground.* **5** °class, °lecture, seminar, °programme: *You should sign up for a course in English grammar.* **6** ***of course***: °naturally, °surely, certainly, °positively, °obviously, °definitely, assuredly, by all °means; °undoubtedly, indubitably, without (a) °doubt, no °doubt, *Colloq US* °sure: *Of course I'll go to the theatre with you!*

courteous *adj.* °polite, well-mannered, well-behaved, gentlemanly, °ladylike, °well-bred, °polished, urbane, civilized, °respectful, °civil, courtly, °proper, °decorous, °tactful, °considerate, °diplomatic: *He might have been rude to you, but he was always quite courteous to me.*

courtesy *n.* politeness, °elegance, courtliness, politesse, courteousness, °respect, respectfulness, °good manners, °formality, °civility, °ceremony: *I much appreciated the courtesy with which they treated me.*

cover *v.* **1** °protect, °shelter, °shield, °screen; °guard, °defend, °command: *The guns covered the approaches to the town.* **2** Also, ***cover up*** *or* ***over***: °conceal, °hide, °bury, °mask, °shroud, °obscure; dissemble; °enclose, °envelop: *I was unable to cover my embarrassment. Her face was covered by the hood of the cloak.* **3** overlie, °spread over, overspread, °lie on, layer, °coat, blanket: *Oil covers the surface of the lake.* **4** °wrap, swaddle: *Mother covered us with warm blankets.* **5** °dress, °clothe, garb, attire, °robe, sheathe: *She was covered in silk from neck to ankle.* **6** °extend *or* °stretch over, °occupy, engulf, inundate, °submerge: *A lake has covered the original site of Abu Simbel.* **7** °include, °comprehend, °provide for, comprise, °extend over, °contain, °embody, °incorporate, °account for, take into °account, °take in, °deal with: *This report covers our activities over the past year.* **8** °act, take °responsibility *or* °charge, °stand *or* °sit in, °substitute, °take over, °run things, °double: *Go and get some coffee—I'll cover for you.* **9** °traverse, °complete, °pass *or* °travel over, °travel, °cross: *With frequent stops, we could not*

cover more than 50 miles a day. **10** °compensate for, °defray, be °enough *or* °sufficient for, °counter, °offset, counterbalance, °make up for, insure *or* °protect against: *The policy covers losses of up to a million.*
—*n.* **11** lid, °top, °cap, covering: *I can't find the cover for this pot.* **12** binding, boards, °wrapper, dust-jacket, jacket: *You can't tell a book by its cover.* **13** Often, ***covers***: blanket, quilt, eiderdown, duvet, bedclothes, bedding, (bed) °linen; coverlet, counterpane; *US* comforter: *I crept into bed and pulled the covers over my head.* **14** °shelter, °protection, concealment, hiding-place, hide-out, °retreat, °refuge; °hide, *US and Canadian* blind; *Colloq Brit* hidey-hole: *We tried to find some sort of cover till the sun went down.* **15** °cloak, °screen, °disguise, concealment, °pretence, °front, °camouflage, smokescreen, cover-up, °mask, covering: *His bluster and bullying were only a cover for his cowardice.*

coward *n.* poltroon, craven, dastard, °sissy *or* cissy, °baby, mouse, °milksop; Scaramouch *or* Scaramouche; *Colloq* chicken, *Slang* yellow-belly; *US and Canadian* milquetoast: *He's such a coward that he's afraid of his own shadow.*

cowardice *n.* cowardliness, chicken-heartedness, faint-heartedness, timidity, timorousness, pusillanimity: *Owing to the cowardice of the lieutenant, the troop surrendered without a shot being fired.*

cowardly *adj.* °timid, °fearful, frightened, °afraid, °scared, °faint-hearted, timorous, chicken-hearted, chicken-livered, lily-livered, white-livered, craven, namby-pamby, dastardly, pusillanimous, vitelline, *Slang* yellow, yellow-bellied: *The cowardly rascals ran from the battle.*

coy *adj.* °shy, °modest, diffident, demure, °timid, °bashful, °self-conscious, °sheepish, timorous, unassuming, unpretentious; °reserved, °self-effacing, °retiring, °evasive, °reluctant, °recalcitrant: *She was so coy she would disappear whenever we had guests.*

crack *n.* **1** °break, °fracture, °chink, °crevice, °rift, °gap, °flaw, °split, fissure, °slit, cleft, check, °rupture, °breach: *The crack in the dam was caused by an earthquake.* **2** °snap, °report, bang, °clap, °shot: *I ducked when I heard the crack of the rifle.* **3** °moment, °instant, °time, °second: *She gets up at the crack of dawn.*
—*v.* **4** °snap: *He cracks the whip and the horses start up.* **5** °break, °fracture, °rupture; °shiver, °shatter, smash: *He fell backwards on the pavement and cracked his skull.* **6** fissure, craze, crackle, *US* alligator: *The heat of the sun caused the paint to crack.*

craft *n.* **1** °skill, °ability, artisanship, handiwork, °ingenuity, skilfulness, °art, °talent, °dexterity, cleverness, mastery, expertness, °expertise, °flair, genius, *Colloq* know-how: *Considerable craft is required to make that kind of jewellery.* **2** °deceit, guile, cunning, °fraud, °trickery, wiliness, foxiness, artfulness, craftiness, duplicity: *He exhibits that crooked wisdom called craft.* **3** °trade, °occupation, °calling, °vocation, métier; °profession: *He was a member of one of the medieval craft guilds.* **4** °vessel, °ship, °boat; hovercraft; aircraft, aeroplane, °plane; spaceship, spacecraft, °rocket: *One day there will be at least as many craft in space as there now are in the air.*
—*v.* **5** °make, °fashion, °fabricate: *She crafted the figures out of solid wood.*

crafty *adj.* °artful, cunning, °clever, °shrewd, °foxy, canny, °wily, °sly, °scheming, °calculating, °designing, plotting, °tricky, °sneaky, °deceitful, °shifty, °dodgy, guileful, insidious, double-dealing, °two-faced, duplicitous, treacherous: *That crafty beggar has made off with my life's savings.*

crag *n.* °cliff, °bluff, tor, °peak, °rock, escarpment, scarp, °precipice, *US* palisade: *Soaring above us was a huge crag that we still had to climb.*

cram *v.* **1** °pack, °stuff, overstuff, overcrowd, °jam, °fill: *The car was crammed to the top with suitcases.* **2** °study, burn the midnight oil, *Literary* lucubrate, *Colloq* °grind, *Brit* swot: *Bob can't go out because he's cramming for an exam.*

cramped *adj.* °tight, crowded, incommodious, uncomfortable, °close: *The tiny cabin was too cramped to hold all of us at once.*

crank *n.* **1** °eccentric, °character, °oddity, *Colloq* nut; *Slang Brit* nutter, nutcase: *Pay no attention to Jason, he's just a crank.* **2** monomaniac, °zealot, °fanatic: *The restaurant is patronized mainly by health-food cranks.*

cranky *adj.* **1** °eccentric, °odd, °weird, °strange, °queer, °peculiar, quirky, °capricious, °whimsical: *He's a cranky old bird who hardly goes out at all.* **2** °testy, grouchy, crabby, °short-tempered, °surly, irascible, °waspish, churlish, °gruff, curmudgeonly, °cantankerous, choleric, °snappish, °petulant, °peevish, contentious, °querulous, °irritable, splenetic, *Colloq* crotchety: *He's always cranky before breakfast.*

cranny *n.* °chink, °crevice, °crack, fissure, check, °fracture, °break, °furrow, °split, cleft: *Flowers grew from the crannies in the ancient wall.*

crash *v.* **1** °fall, °topple: *The vase crashed onto the stone floor.* **2** °force, °drive, °run, smash: *He crashed the car into a wall.* **3** bang, °boom, °explode: *The thunder crashed all around us.*
—*n.* **4** °boom, bang, smash, °explosion, °blast: *We heard a great crash as the building collapsed.* **5** °disaster, °collapse, °failure: *The stock-market crash has had a devastating effect.*

crawl *v.* **1** °creep, worm, °wriggle, wiggle, °squirm; °edge: *A spider is crawling on your collar.* **2** inch, °creep, °drag: *For a solid hour the cars just crawled along at a snail's pace.* **3** cower, °cringe, grovel, toady, fawn: *Don't worry, he'll soon come crawling, begging you to take him back.* **4** °teem, °abound, °swarm, be °overrun *or* swamped: *The scene of the crime crawled with police.*

craze *n.* °fad, °fashion, °trend, °enthusiasm, °rage, °mania, °thing, °obsession; last word, *dernier cri*: *The craze for printed T-shirts goes on and on.*

crazy *adj.* **1** °mad, °insane, demented, °deranged, °unbalanced, unhinged, lunatic, *non compos mentis*, °daft, certifiable, °mental, touched (in the head), out of one's °mind *or* °head, °mad as a March hare *or* hatter, maddened, crazed, *Colloq* barmy *or* balmy, cuckoo, cracked, crackers, crack-brained, dotty, daffy, dippy, gaga, goofy, crackpot, loony, off one's rocker, have a screw loose, screwy, batty, bats, bats in the belfry, *Brit* barmy (in the crumpet), potty, bonkers, round the bend *or* °twist, off one's chump, doolally, *US* off one's trolley, out of one's gourd, screwball, nuts, nutty (as a fruit cake); *Slang* bananas, *US* out to lunch, meshuga, flaky, flaked-out, (plumb) loco: *His wife thinks he's crazy to want to walk around the world.* **2** °silly, °absurd, °foolish, °nonsensical, °inane, °ridiculous, °preposterous, laughable, risible, °ludicrous, asinine, °stupid, moronic, imbecile *or* imbecilic, idiotic, °feeble-minded, °hare-brained, *Colloq* crackpot: *Someone came up with a crazy idea of a square tennis ball to slow down the game.* **3** °impractical, °impracticable, unworkable, °unsound, °pointless, °imprudent, °rash, °reckless, ill-considered: *Columbus' plan to sail round the world was thought to be crazy at the time.* **4** °enthusiastic, °eager, avid, zealous, °keen, °excited: *I'm really crazy about windsurfing.* **5** °infatuated, °keen on *or* about, °wild, °mad, *Colloq* dotty, *US* nuts, nutty; *Slang US* ape: *Marjorie, I'm absolutely crazy about you.*

create *v.* **1** °make, °produce, °form, °bring into being, °originate, °conceive; sire, °father: *The question remains whether God created Man or vice versa.* **2** engender, beget, °spawn, °generate, °invent, °imagine, °think up, °frame, °forge, °fashion, °fabricate, °manufacture, °develop, °design, contrive, °devise, °produce, °dream up, °initiate: *Here is where they create many of the most successful television advertisements.*

creation *n.* **1** °beginning, °origin, °birth, °start, inception, genesis, making, °formation: *The creation of the lake began with the damming of the stream.* **2** the °world, the °universe, the cosmos: *He was the most wicked man in the history of all creation.*

creative *adj.* °imaginative, inventive, originative, artistic, °original, °ingenious, °resourceful: *A truly creative artist seldom lacks for inspiration.*

creator *n.* **1** originator, °author, initiator, °founder, °father, inventor, architect, °designer, framer, maker, °prime mover: *The creator of this painting must have been a genius.* **2** God, Supreme Being, the Deity: *Some day you will have to answer to your Creator for your sins.*

creature *n.* **1** being, °organism, °entity, living °thing: *The hound had the saddest face I have ever seen on any creature.* **2** ***creature comforts***: (°physical *or* bodily *or* °material *or* mundane *or* °superficial *or* non-spiritual) luxuries: *He has the money to enjoy all the creature comforts.*

credit *n.* **1** °belief, °faith, °trust, credence: *I don't give much credit to what they say.* **2** creditation, °acknowledgement *or* acknowledgment, °attribution, ascription: *Credit for inventing the telegraph goes to Guglielmo Marconi.* **3** °trust, °confidence, faithfulness, reliability, trustworthiness, °honesty, °probity, dependability; solvency: *Her credit rating at the bank is excellent.* **4** °honour, commendation, °praise, °tribute, acclaim, °esteem, °recognition, °merit: *The team's victory in the finals has brought credit to the school.*
—*v.* **5** °believe, °trust, hold °accountable, put *or* place one's °faith *or* °confidence in, have °faith *or* °confidence in, °rely on, °accept, °depend on *or* upon: *If you credit the Bible, the world was created in six days.* **6** ascribe, °acknowledge, °attribute, °assign; °impute: *The goal was credited to Barnes.*

creed *n.* °tenet, dogma, °doctrine, credo, teaching, principles, °belief, set of °beliefs: *She adheres to the creed of the Golden Rule.*

creek *n.* **1** *in Britain*: inlet, bay, cove, °harbour: *Overnight we moored in a little creek, sheltered from the sea.* **2** *in the US and Canada*: stream, streamlet, °brook, rivulet, rill, runnel, °run, °burn: *We used to fish in the creek behind the house.*

creep *v.* **1** °crawl, °slither, inch, °squirm, °wriggle, wiggle: *A tiny lizard was creeping up the wall.* **2** °crawl, °drag: *The hours creep by slowly when you have nothing to do.* **3** °steal, °sneak; °slink, skulk, tiptoe, *Colloq* °pussyfoot: *The thief must have crept in through the kitchen window. Someone is creeping about out there in the dark.*

crescent *n.* **1** demi-lune, semi-lune, lune, lunette: *The moon's crescent hung low in the western sky.*
—*adj.* **2** crescent-shaped, demi-lune, semi-lune, biconcave, concavo-concave: *For chopping, the chef uses a crescent blade that just fits into a curved wooden bowl.*

crest *n.* **1** °top, °summit, °pinnacle, °peak, °head, °ridge: *The surfers rode in on the crest of a wave.* **2** °seal, °device, °figure, badge, °emblem, insigne, °symbol, °design: *The school crest shows an inkpot and a scroll.*
—*v.* **3** °top, °crown, surmount, °cap: *The ancient walls were crested with ivy.* **4** culminate, °reach, °top, *US* °top out: *The flood-waters crested at nine feet.*

crevasse *n.* °gorge, chasm, °abyss, °ravine, fissure, °crack, °furrow: *One of the climbers fell into a crevasse in the glacier.*

crevice *n.* °crack, fissure, °chink, cleft, °cranny, °groove, °furrow, °break, °split, °rift: *Water ran down the crevices in the rocks.*

crew *n.* °group, °company, °band, troupe, °party, °gang, °team, °corps, °body: *We shall need a crew of twenty for tomorrow's job.*

crime *n.* °offence, °violation, °misdeed, °wrong; felony, misdemeanour; lawlessness: *The number of crimes of violence is increasing.*

criminal *adj.* **1** °illegal, °unlawful, °illicit, °lawless, °dishonest, *Colloq* °crooked: *Arson is a criminal act. We have to weed out the criminal element.* **2** °wicked, °evil, °bad, °wrong, °corrupt, °vile, °black, °immoral, amoral, °sinful, °villainous, iniquitous, flagitious, depraved; °disgraceful, reprehensible: *The way they treat their children is absolutely criminal.*
—*n.* **3** °felon, °convict, lawbreaker, °outlaw, °culprit, °offender, °miscreant, malefactor, wrongdoer, °villain, °scoundrel, knave, blackguard; °gangster, Mafioso, desperado, °racketeer; °hoodlum, °thug, hooligan, °tough, ruffian, °terrorist, *Colloq* roughneck, °bad °guy, °black hat, °bad hat, baddie *or* baddy, crook; *Slang* hood, *US* mobster: *He was arrested for consorting with known criminals.*

cringe *v.* **1** cower, wince, °flinch, quail, °recoil, blench, °tremble, °quiver, °quake *or* °shake in one's boots *or* shoes, °shrink: *That dirty little coward cringed even when they called his name.* **2** °defer, °kowtow, grovel, °crawl, fawn, boot-lick, *US* apple-polish; *Slang* °kiss someone's arse *or US and Canadian* ass, *Taboo slang* brown-nose: *The man cringed before the magistrate, his eyes downcast, tugging his forelock.*

cripple *n.* **1** amputee, paralytic: *He has been a cripple since the accident.*
—*v.* **2** disable, °lame, °incapacitate, °handicap, maim; °impair, °damage, °weaken, debilitate, emasculate, °enervate: *She was crippled when a child. The dictator's power was crippled by the revolt.*

crippled *adj.* **1** °disabled, °lame, handicapped, incapacitated; weakened, °weak, debilitated: *He takes care of his crippled mother. The crippled party platform succumbed to attack from the far left.* **2** damaged, immobilized, inoperative: *The crew stayed with the crippled vessel.*

crisis *n.* **1** turning-point, °critical time *or* °moment: *She has passed the crisis and will be better tomorrow.* **2** °disaster, °emergency, °calamity, °catastrophe, °danger: *The storm has created a crisis and the residents are being evacuated.*

crisp *adj.* **1** °brittle, crunchy, friable, breakable, crumbly, frangible: *Keep the biscuits crisp in this special jar.* **2** curly, crispy, crinkly, frizzy, frizzled: *His hair is brown and crisp, just like his father's.* **3** *US* chip: *I'll bet you can't eat just one potato crisp.*

critical *adj.* **1** carping, °fault-finding, censorious, disparaging, depreciatory *or* depreciative, depreciating, deprecatory *or* deprecative, deprecating, judgemental: *The article was highly critical of the council.* **2** °crucial, °important, °essential, °basic, °key, decisive, °pivotal, °vital, °momentous: *The meeting at the bank will be critical for us.* **3** °grave, °serious, °dangerous, °uncertain, °perilous, °severe, touch-and-go, °ticklish, °sensitive, °touchy, *Colloq* °parlous: *His illness has reached the critical stage.*

criticism *n.* **1** °judgement, °evaluation, appraisal, °analysis, assessment, °estimation, valuation: *Their criticism was generally favourable.* **2** censure, °disapproval, condemnation, disparagement: *I was very upset by her criticism of my behaviour.* **3** critique, °review, commentary: *My sister writes the theatre criticisms for the local paper.*

criticize *v.* **1** °judge, °evaluate, value, assess, appraise, °estimate; °discuss, °analyse: *He criticizes books for the quarterly.* **2** censure, find °fault (with), °carp (at), °cavil (at), °condemn, °attack, °denounce, °disapprove (of), °put down, impugn, °blast, °lambaste, *Colloq* °pan, °knock, *Brit* slate: *His book was criticized because of its poor scholarship. Why must he constantly criticize, even when there's nothing wrong?*

crooked *adj.* **1** °criminal, °dishonest, °illegal, °unlawful, °illicit, °wrong, °perverse, *Slang Brit* °bent: *Selling a stolen painting is crooked.* **2** °bent, bowed, askew, awry, °deformed, distorted, contorted, °lopsided, twisted, °misshapen, °disfigured, warped, °gnarled: *Because of the constant west wind, the trees are all crooked.*

cross *n.* **1** crucifix, rood: *In ancient times, it was common to execute certain criminals by nailing them to a cross.* **2** °hybrid, cross-breed, °mongrel; °blend, °combination: *This fruit is a cross between a plum and a pear.*

—*v.* **3** ***cross off*** *or* ***out***: °strike out, °erase, °cancel, °rub out, °delete, °wipe out: *After that remark, I'm crossing you off my list.* **4** °meet, intersect, °join: *The roads cross further on.* **5** °cross over, °go across, °pass over, °span, °traverse: *The bridge crosses the river here.*
—*adj.* **6** °peevish, irritated, annoyed, piqued, °irritable, °testy, °snappish, irascible, °surly, choleric, splenetic, grouchy, huffish *or* huffy, pettish, °cranky, grumpy, °touchy, °moody, fractious, vexed, curmudgeonly, °petulant, °waspish, °querulous, °cantankerous, crusty, °short-tempered, on a short fuse, *Colloq* crotchety, *Slang Brit* shirty: *He's cross because he has a headache.* **7** annoyed, irritated, °angry, irate, °furious: *I was very cross that you took the car without permission.*

crouch *v.* °bend (down), squat (down), hunker down, °stoop (down): *If you crouch down, no one will see you in the bushes.*

crowd *n.* **1** °throng, multitude, horde, °swarm, °mass, °press, °flood, °mob, °flock, °pack: *A huge crowd descended on the village square.* **2** °company, °set, °circle, °lot, °bunch, °group, coterie, °clique, claque, °faction: *She doesn't associate with our crowd any longer.*
—*v.* **3** °throng, °swarm, °herd, °pour, °pile, °press, °cluster, °gather, °get together, °flood, °flock, °assemble, congregate: *People crowded into the stadium.* **4** °push, °press, °drive, shove, °thrust, °force, °load, °pack, °cram, °jam, corral: *The police crowded the hooligans into vans.* **5** compress, °squeeze, °pack, °jam, °cram, °collect; °stuff: *We were so crowded in the cabin we could hardly breathe.*

crown *n.* **1** coronet, diadem, wreath, fillet, circlet, tiara: *The princess wore a golden crown set with jewels.* **2** °sovereignty, °rule, °dominion, °authority, °government, °realm, rulership, °jurisdiction: *They discovered many lands and annexed them to the Crown.* **3** °monarch, ruler, °sovereign, potentate; °king, °queen, emperor, empress, His *or* Her Majesty, His *or* Her Highness: *The Crown has very little real power these days.*
—*v.* **4** enthrone, *Colloq US* coronate: *He was crowned on the death of his father.* **5** °cap, °top, surmount, culminate, °climax, consummate, °fulfil, °reward: *All her years of practising the violin were finally crowned with success.*

crucial *adj.* °critical, decisive, °pivotal, °vital, °momentous, °major, °important, °essential: *It is crucial that you press the right button.*

crude *adj.* **1** °unrefined, °raw, °natural, °original, unprocessed: *Those are the prices of crude oil, not the petrol used in cars.* **2** °rough, unpolished, °rudimentary, °immature, °undeveloped, °primitive, °unrefined, unfinished: *At this stage, she has only a crude idea of the design.* **3** °rough, °coarse, °rude, °unrefined, uncouth, crass, °gross, °rustic, uncivil: *Don't you despise his crude manners?* **4** °blunt, °brusque, °unsophisticated, °inconsiderate, °tasteless, indelicate, °offensive, °improper, °vulgar: *How crude of him to ask her how long since her husband had 'croaked'!*

cruel *adj.* **1** °merciless, pitiless, hard-hearted, °harsh, stony-hearted, °heartless, unsparing, °callous, °beastly, °cold-blooded, °ruthless, °unkind, °hard: *It was cruel of you to refuse to help.* **2** °ferocious, °inhuman, barbaric, barbarous, °brutal, °savage, °bloodthirsty, °vicious, °sadistic, °fiendish, diabolic(al), hellish, °atrocious, Neronian *or* Neronic *or* Neroic: *His captors subjected him to the cruellest tortures.*

cruise *v.* **1** °sail, °coast, °travel, °journey, voyage; yacht: *We cruise in the Caribbean during the winter.*
—*n.* **2** °sail, voyage, °journey, °boat *or* yachting °trip: *I took a three-day cruise around the Isle of Wight.*

crumb *n.* °fragment, °morsel, °bite, °scrap, °particle, °shred, snippet, °sliver, °bit, °speck, scintilla, mote, molecule, atom: *There isn't a crumb of food in the house.*

crumble *v.* °disintegrate, °fragment, break apart, °break up, °shiver, °come to pieces: *Acid rain has caused the stone façade to crumble. In the face of the attack, his resolve crumbled.*

crumple *v.* °wrinkle, °crush, crease, °rumple, °mangle, crinkle: *Your jacket is all crumpled.*

crunch *v.* **1** °chew, °bite, °crush, °grind, °munch: *He crunched the nuts between his teeth.*
—*n.* **2** moment of truth, °decision °time, °crisis, °critical °moment, °showdown, crux, °juncture: *You can count on me when it comes to the crunch.*

crusade *n.* **1** °campaign, °expedition, °holy °war; jihad *or* jehad: *He joined the crusade against the Saracens.*
—*v.* **2** °campaign, °war, °battle; °take up a °cause, °lobby, °fight: *She is crusading for equal rights for women.*

crush *n.* **1** °break, smash, °crunch, °pulverize, °shiver, °splinter, °pound, °grind: *The vandals crushed the statue to bits with hammers.* **2** °crumple, °wrinkle, crease, crinkle, °rumple, °mangle: *The shirts came back crushed from the laundry.* **3** squash, °pulp, mash, °squeeze, compress, °press: *The machine crushes the oranges and extracts the juice.* **4** °overcome, °defeat, °conquer, vanquish, °beat, thrash; °subdue, °put down, °quash, °quell, °overwhelm, °squelch, °suppress, °repress: *The title-holder crushed the challenger. The junta crushed the uprising without bloodshed.* **5** abash, °embarrass, °shame, °mortify, °depress, °devastate, °humiliate, °disgrace: *She was really crushed when he refused to see her.*
—*n.* **6** °press, °pressure, °crowd: *When the fire alarm sounded, I was almost caught in the crush of the people trying to escape.*

cry *v.* **1** °weep, °sob, wail, °keen, °bawl, °shed tears: *Paul cried when they took his mother away.* **2** whimper, °snivel, pule, mewl, whine, °moan, °groan, °fret, *Colloq* turn on the waterworks, *Brit* grizzle: *Don't cry over spilt milk.* **3** ***cry out for***: °demand, °need, °call for, °beg for, °plead for: *Her hair is so untidy it cries out for trimming. Wanton murder cries out for vengeance.*
—*n.* **4** °scream, °shriek, wail, °howl, yowl: *I heard the mournful cries of those being tortured.* **5** °shout, °whoop, °yell, °howl: *Uttering blood-curdling cries, the rebels attacked.* **6** °call, °sound, °note: *The noise was the cry of the lesser grebe to its mate.* **7** °war cry, battle-cry, °slogan, watchword: *'Down with the king!' was the cry used to rally the rabble.* **8** ***a far cry***: a long °way, °quite a °distance, °remote, °distant, not, not °quite, °very °different (from): *This report is a far cry from what I had expected.*

crypt *n.* °tomb, vault, mausoleum, °sepulchre, °grave, catacomb; °cellar, basement: *He is buried in the crypt of St Paul's.*

cryptic *adj.* **1** °secret, °occult, °mystical, °hidden, esoteric, mystic, cabbalistic: *The sarcophagus was covered with cryptic symbols.* **2** °obscure, °mysterious, unclear, °nebulous, °vague, inscrutable, °recondite, arcane, enigmatic, °puzzling: *I cannot make head or tail of her cryptic remarks.*

cuddle *v.* **1** °snuggle up (to), °nestle *or* °huddle (against): *She cuddled the baby closer to her.* **2** °caress, °embrace, °fondle, °hug, °pet, bill and coo, make °love (to), *Colloq* neck, smooch, *Australian and New Zealand* smoodge *or* smooge, *Slang US* °make out (with), watch the submarine races: *The couple were cuddling in the back seat.*
—*n.* **3** °hug, °embrace, °snuggle: *Give us a cuddle, Janie.*

cue *n.* **1** °prompt, °hint, °reminder, °signal, °sign: *Give her the cue to start singing.*
—*v.* **2** °signal, °prompt, °remind: *She was cueing me to begin, but I'd lost my voice.*

culprit *n.* **1** accused, °prisoner: *How does the culprit plead?* **2** °offender, °criminal, malefactor, wrongdoer: *They caught the culprit red-handed.*

cultivate *v.* **1** °till, °plough, °farm, °work: *These lands have been cultivated since time immemorial.* **2** °grow,

°raise, °tend, °produce: *What crops can be cultivated in this climate?* **3** °develop, °promote, °further, °encourage, °foster, °advance: *She's been cultivating a friendship with her boss.* **4** woo, make advances to, ingratiate oneself with, court, pay court to, curry °favour with, *Colloq* °work on, *Slang* suck up to, butter up, *US* shine up to; *Taboo slang* brown-nose: *He is cultivating Trevor only because he wants something from him.*

cultivated *adj.* °sophisticated, cultured, °educated, °refined, °elegant, soigné(e), civilized, °polished, aristocratic, urbane, °suave, cosmopolitan: *She prefers to go out with cultivated older men.*

culture *n.* **1** cultivation, °refinement, °sophistication, urbanity, suavity, °elegance, (good) °breeding, °background, erudition, °education, enlightenment, °learning, °taste, °discrimination, savoir faire, savoir vivre, discernment: *She is a lady of considerable culture as well as beauty.* **2** °civilization, mores, °customs, lifestyle, °way of °life, (sense of) values: *In their culture, women make the important decisions.*

curb *n.* **1** °check, °restraint, °control: *You should put a curb on your tongue.*
—*v.* **2** °check, °restrain, °bridle, °control, °contain, °repress, °subdue, °suppress: *Try to curb your exuberance.*

cure *n.* **1** course of °treatment, °therapy, °remedy, medication, medicament, °medicine, °drug, °prescription; cure-all, nostrum, panacea: *The doctor said there was no cure for her illness.*
—*v.* **2** °heal, °mend, °restore to °health *or* working °order, °remedy, °rectify, °correct, °repair, °fix: *What can't be cured must be endured.* **3** smoke, pickle, °dry, °salt, °preserve, corn, marinate: *That cured ox tongue is simply delicious!*

curiosity *n.* **1** inquisitiveness, °interest: *His insatiable curiosity next led him to study astronomy.* **2** snooping, prying, peeping, intrusiveness, meddlesomeness, °interference, *Colloq* nosiness, Nosy Parkerism: *Curiosity killed the cat.* **3** curio, °oddity, °rarity, conversation piece, *objet de virtu* or *vertu*, *objet d'art*, found °object; bric-à-brac *or* bric-a-brac, knick-knack, °bauble, trinket, °gewgaw: *The shop sells curiosities, like goblets made from ostrich eggs. In those days, every house had a curiosity cabinet.*

curious *adj.* **1** °inquisitive, inquiring, °interested: *I am curious to know what you were doing in there all night.* **2** snooping, prying, °intrusive, meddlesome, interfering, *Colloq* °nosy: *Our neighbours are entirely too curious about our activities.* **3** °odd, °peculiar, °eccentric, °strange, °outré, °queer, °unusual, °outrageous, °offbeat, °weird, °bizarre, unconventional, freakish, °exotic, °singular, out of the °ordinary, °extraordinary, °erratic, pixilated, °quaint, °outlandish, °grotesque, aberrant, °abnormal, °irregular, °deviant, °deviate, *Colloq* °kinky, nuts, nutty; *Slang Brit* barmy: *How do you explain Frieda's curious behaviour?*

current *adj.* **1** °contemporary, °ongoing, °present, contemporaneous, °simultaneous, coeval: *The current issue of the magazine came out last week.* **2** °prevalent, °prevailing, °common, °popular, accepted, known, widespread, reported, in °circulation, going °round *or* around, bruited about, °widely known, in the °air, present-day: *The current theories reject those of a decade ago.* **3** °fashionable, °stylish, à la °mode, modish, in °vogue, °latest, up to °date, *Colloq* °trendy: *The current trend is towards shorter skirts.* **4** *US* up to date, in the °know, °informed, advised, in °touch, °aware, posted, *au courant*, *au fait*, on the qui vive: *The* Financial Journal *keeps me current on stock prices.*
—*n.* **5** °stream, °flow, °undercurrent: *The canoe was caught in the current and carried away.* **6** °course, °progress, °tendency, °tenor, °drift, °trend, °inclination, mainstream: *The current of public opinion is turning in favour of policies that are more environmentally responsible.*

curse *n.* **1** malediction, imprecation, denunciation, damnation, execration, °oath: *He heaped curses on all those who opposed him.* **2** °evil, bane, °misfortune, °affliction, °torment, °harm, °scourge, cross to °bear: *The curse of our generation is that so few of us deeply believe anything.* **3** °profanity, °oath, blasphemy, obscenity, bad °language, °dirty °word, swear-word, curse-word: *A stream of curses issued from the bathroom when Joe cut himself shaving.*
—*v.* **4** °damn, execrate, °blast, °denounce, anathematize, excommunicate: *He was cursed by the priests and forbidden ever to enter a temple again.* **5** °swear at, °blaspheme at: *The muleteer was cursing his team.* **6** °burden, saddle, °weigh down, °handicap: *She was cursed with bad eyesight and had to wear thick glasses.*

cursory *adj.* °superficial, °hasty, °hurried, °passing, quick, slapdash, °perfunctory, °rapid, °summary: *She gave the note a cursory glance and threw it away.*

curt *adj.* °abrupt, °short, °terse, °brief, laconic, °concise; °blunt, °gruff, °harsh, °brusque, unceremonious, °snappish, crusty, °rude: *His answer was a curt 'No', without any explanation.*

curtail *v.* °shorten, °abbreviate, °cut °short, °abridge, °diminish, °reduce, °cut, °cut back, °cut down: *Both our working week and our salaries were curtailed.*

cushion *n.* **1** pillow, °bolster, °pad: *The women of the harem sat on cushions on the floor.*
—*v.* **2** °soften, absorb, °mitigate, °reduce, buffer, °insulate, mollify, lessen: *They offered me a month's paid holiday to help cushion the blow of being transferred.*

custody *n.* **1** °care, custodianship, °safe keeping, °protection, °charge, guardianship, keeping: *She was granted custody of the children.* **2** °imprisonment, °detention, incarceration, confinement: *The police took three troublemakers into custody.*

custom *n.* **1** °practice, °habit, °usage, °fashion, °way, wont, °tradition, °routine, °convention, °form: *According to custom, the warriors of the tribe paint their bodies.* **2** ***customs***: °toll, °duty, impost, °tax, excise, levy, °dues, °tariff: *He was assigned to collect customs and port duties.* **3** °patronage, °support, °business, °trade: *The new butcher needs as much custom as possible.*
—*adv.* **4** °specially, °especially, °expressly, exclusively, °particularly; to °order: *All her clothes are custom-made.*

customary *adj.* **1** °usual, °normal, °conventional, °routine, °everyday, °common, commonplace, °ordinary: *Is it customary for them to eat lunch on the premises?* **2** °accustomed, °habitual, °regular, °traditional, wonted: *I took the customary way home.*

customer *n.* **1** °client, °patron, °buyer, purchaser; consumer: *Mrs Morris is one of our regular customers.* **2** °chap, °fellow, °character, °person, °guy, *Colloq Brit* bloke: *She would never go out with an ugly customer like that.*

cut *v.* **1** °gash, °slash, °slit; °open: *I cut my finger on the glass.* **2** °slice, °cut off, °carve: *Please cut me a thick piece of steak.* **3** Often, ***cut up***: °hurt, °wound, °pain, °upset, °grieve, °distress, aggrieve, °slight, °insult, °offend, affront: *I was really all cut up by her nasty remarks.* **4** °trim, °snip, °lop, °clip, crop, °shorten, shear, °chop off; °mow; °dock: *The barber has cut too much off the sides.* **5** °abbreviate, °shorten, crop, condense, °abridge, °edit, cut back, °reduce, cut down; epitomize, °abstract, °digest, summarize, °curtail: *Cut this script to make it fit into the allotted time.* **6** °dilute, °thin, °water (down), °weaken; °degrade, °adulterate: *They cut the rum with water to make grog.* **7** °avoid, °fail to °attend, eschew: *Cynthia cut classes three days this week.* **8** °lower, °reduce, lessen, cut back (on), cut down (on), °slash, °diminish, °decrease, retrench (on), °curtail: *We shall have to cut expenses if the company is to survive.* **9** conclude, °settle, °agree: *Once the deal was cut, there was no going back on it.* **10** °prepare, °draw, °write, °sign: *We'll have accounting cut your cheque and send it at once.* **11** ***cut back***: **a** See 5, above. **b** See **8,** above. **12** Often, ***cut dead***: snub, °slight, °spurn, °shun, °ignore, give the cold °shoulder (to): *Cornelia had the gall to cut Jason dead at his own party.* **13** ***cut down***: **a** °fell, °chop *or* hew down: *Don't cut down that tree!* **b** °kill, cut off, °murder, assassinate: *He was cut down in his prime.* **14** ***cut in***: °interrupt, °intrude, °interfere, *Colloq* °butt in: *Please don't cut in on our conversation.* **15** ***cut off***: **a** °cleave, °sever, °chop *or* °lop *or* °hack off: *Cut the branch off near the trunk.* **b** °intercept, °interrupt, °discontinue, °end, °stop, °terminate, °break off: *There was a click and our phone conversation was cut off.* **c** °separate, °sever, °split, estrange: *He's been cut off from the family for years.* **d** disinherit, disown, °reject: *She was cut off with a shilling.* **16** ***cut out***: **a** °delete, °remove, excise, °strike *or* °cross out, °edit out, °omit, cut, °kill, *Technical* dele: *The publishers made me cut out parts of the book that they were advised might be libellous.* **b** °extract, excise, °remove, resect: *My appendix was cut out years ago.* **c** °stop, °cease, desist (from), °quit: *Whenever it rains the engine cuts out. Cut out the clowning around.* **d** °suit, °equip, °fit: *I don't think Cyril's cut out to be a lumberjack.* **e** °plan, °prepare, °ready, °organize, °destine: *He certainly has his work cut out for him!* **17** ***cut up***: **a** °chop (up), dice, cube, mince, cut, °divide (up), °carve (up): *Cut the celery up very small.* **b** °misbehave: *The football supporters began to cut up rough.* **18** ***cut up rough***: get °angry, lose one's °temper, °show °resentment: *The driver began to cut up rough when I refused to pay.*

—*n.* **19** °gash, °slash, °incision, °nick, °wound: *I got a nasty cut from that razor.* **20** °share, °portion, °percentage, °piece, dividend, commission: *Blatchley gets a cut on every car we sell.* **21** reduction, cut-back, curtailment, °decrease: *The government's cuts in spending affect us all.* **22** deletion, excision, °omission: *The author refuses to approve the cuts in the script.* **23** affront, °insult, °offence, °slight, snub, °dig, jibe, °slap in the face, cold °shoulder: *The unkindest cut was the accusation of cheating.* **24** °engraving, °plate: *This cut is too badly worn for use now.* **25** artwork, °picture, °illustration, °plate, °drawing, line cut, line °engraving, half-tone: *The book has 300 cuts and only 20 pages of text.*

—*adj.* **26** separated, °detached, severed: *I prefer cut flowers to a plant.* **27** abridged, °abbreviated, cut-down, shortened, edited, curtailed: *The magazine published a cut version of the novel.* **28** reduced, diminished, lowered, discounted: *This shop sells everything at cut prices.* **29** ***cut and dried***: **a** clear-cut, settled, arranged, °decided, °predetermined, prearranged: *Unfortunately, the solution to this problem is not cut and dried.* **b** °stale, unoriginal, trite, hackneyed, °old; °dull, °boring: *His suggestions for improvement are always cut and dried.* **c** manufactured, °automatic, unchanging, unchanged: *Mr Mackay will again present his old cut and dried plan.*

cute *adj.* **1** °pretty, °attractive, °adorable, °dainty, °lovely, °beautiful, *Colloq US* cunning: *There were a lot of cute children at the beauty competition.* **2** °clever, °shrewd, °ingenious, adroit, °crafty, cunning: *It was very cute of him to suggest his brother for the job.*

cutthroat *n.* **1** °murderer, °pirate, °killer, °thug, hatchet man, gunman, assassin, *Slang US* gunsel, torpedo, hit man: *Those streets are frequented by thieves and cutthroats.*

—*adj.* **2** °merciless, °ruthless, °unmerciful, unprincipled, °relentless, pitiless, °brutal, °cold-blooded, °cold-hearted: *Her cutthroat tactics call for dismissing all executives.* **3** °murderous, °homicidal, °lethal, °deadly, barbaric, °fierce, °cruel, barbarous, °savage, °inhuman, °brutal, brutish, °violent, °ferocious, °bloodthirsty, °sanguinary, bloody, feral, °vicious, °truculent: *He was once a member of a gang of cutthroat hoodlums.*

cutting *adj.* **1** °severe, °biting, °chill, °cold, °icy, °frigid, °freezing, °raw, °piercing, °penetrating: *A cutting wind seemed to go right through me.* **2** °sarcastic, °sardonic, °bitter, °scornful, sneering, acid, °scathing, acerb(ic), wounding, °stern, °harsh, °caustic, mordant, acrimonious, °contemptuous; malevolent, malicious, invidious, °vicious, °venomous: *Her cutting remarks completely devastated me.*

—*n.* **3** scion, °slip, clipping: *Mrs Galloway allowed me to take a cutting from her rose bush.*

cycle *n.* **1** °round, rotation, °circle, °course; series, °sequence, °run, °succession, °pattern: *We must learn to break the continuous cycles of war and peace.*

—*v.* **2** °recur, °return, °rotate, recycle, °circle: *The water from the fountain is cycled back to the reservoir.*

D

dab *v.* **1** daub, °pat, °tap, tamp, °touch: *Dab a little more paint into the crevices.*

—*n.* **2** °touch, °drop, °trace, °bit, mite, °hint, °suggestion, °pinch, °dash, °spot, tinge, *Colloq* dollop, smidgen *or* smidgin: *Add just a dab of mustard to the sauce.* **3** daub, °poke, °pat, °tap, °touch: *Wipe it away with a dab of a damp cloth.*

dabble *v.* **1** °dip, °splash, °spatter, sprinkle, bespatter, besprinkle, bedabble: *I sat on the rock, dabbling my toes in the pool.* **2** ***dabble in*** *or* ***with*** *or* ***at***: °tinker, °trifle (with), °potter *or US* putter, dally, *Colloq* °fool (around *or* about *or* with *or* about with): *She's not seriously interested in music—she just dabbles in it.*

dab hand *n.phr.* past °master, °expert, °master, °adept, °authority, wizard, *Colloq* ace: *Oscar is a dab hand at wood-carving.*

daft *adj.* **1** °foolish, °silly, °giddy, °senseless, °absurd, °ridiculous, °stupid, °nonsensical, fatuous, fatuitous, imbecile *or* imbecilic, idiotic, moronic, °obtuse, cretinous, boneheaded, fat-headed, dim-witted, witless, asinine, attocerebral, weak-minded, simple-minded, brainless, °feeble-minded, feather-brained, rattle-brained, °hare-brained, slow-witted, °halfwitted, fat-witted, addle-pated, addle-brained, *Brit* gormless; *Colloq* °dumb, dopey *or* dopy, daffy; *Slang* cock-eyed, *US* cockamamie *or* cockamamy, running on 'Empty': *He has the daft idea that he will be appointed managing director.* **2** See **crazy, 1,** above. **3** ***daft about***: °mad about, °infatuated with, besotted by *or* with, °sweet on, *Colloq* nuts about, °crazy about: *Those two are daft about each other.*

dagger *n.* °knife, poniard, skean, °short sword, stiletto, dirk, °blade, kris, bowie °knife, bayonet: *It was his dagger that was sticking out of the man's back.*

daily *adj.* **1** °diurnal, circadian, °everyday, quotidian: *The daily papers reported nothing about the fire.* **2** °ordinary, °common, commonplace, °everyday, °routine, °regular: *Her trip to the market has become a daily occurrence.*

—*adv.* **3** constantly, °always, habitually, day after day, regularly, every day, continually, continuously: *The trains run daily between here and London.*

dainty *adj.* **1** °delicate, °graceful, °fine, °elegant, °exquisite, °neat: *The value lies in this dainty border painted round the edge of the cup.* **2** °fastidious, °sensitive, °squeamish, °finicky *or* finical, over-nice, over-refined, °genteel, °mincing: *He seems somewhat dainty in his choice of words.* **3** °choice, °delicious, delectable, °tasty, appetizing, palatable, toothsome: *They were given a few dainty morsels to nibble while waiting.*

—*n.* **4** °delicacy, sweetmeat, °treat, comfit, °titbit *or US* tidbit, °morsel: *A plate of dainties was placed beside the bed each night.*

damage *n.* **1** °harm, °injury, °hurt, °impairment, mutilation, °destruction, devastation: *Fortunately, there was little damage from the storm.* **2** °expense, °price, °cost; °bill, invoice, *US* °check: *At the restaurant, the damage came to £50.* **3** ***damages***: compensation, reparation, °indemnity: *We won the suit and were awarded damages of £10,000 for defamation of character.*

—*v.* **4** °harm, °hurt, °injure; °wound; °mutilate, disfigure, °mar, °deface; °wreck, °ruin, °spoil, °impair: *Although the car was badly damaged, the passengers escaped unharmed. Will this news damage your chances of a promotion?*

damn *v.* **1** °condemn, °criticize, find °fault with, °berate, °castigate, °upbraid, °attack, °blast, °reprimand, °reprove, remonstrate, °denounce; °blame: *Some would damn him for saving the murderer from drowning, others would damn him if he didn't.* **2** °doom, °condemn, °sentence: *Sisyphus was damned for all eternity to roll a heavy stone up a hill.* **3** °curse (at), °swear (at), execrate: *I damned the day I first set foot in that house.*
—*n.* **4** °jot or tittle, brass farthing, *Slang* hoot, two hoots (in hell), *Slang* tinker's damn *or* cuss: *His opinion isn't worth a damn.* **5** ***give a damn***: °care, °mind, be °concerned, °worry, *Slang* give a hoot: *Why should he give a damn if the critics panned his play?*

damnable *adj.* °awful, °terrible, °horrible, horrid, °atrocious, °abominable, °dreadful, °hideous, execrable, accursed, cursed, detestable, °hateful, °abhorrent, °despicable, °loathsome, °wicked, °sinful, °offensive, heinous, pernicious, °infernal, malicious, malevolent, °outrageous, °foul, °rotten, °base, °vile, odious: *He has been telling the most damnable lies about her since they broke up.*

damp *adj.* **1** °clammy, °moist, wettish; °humid, dank, °misty, dewy, °steamy, °muggy: *Wipe off the table with a damp cloth. Nothing dries out in this damp weather.*
—*n.* **2** moistness, moisture, dampness, clamminess, humidity: *The mould on the walls is the result of the damp.*

dampen *v.* **1** °damp, moisten, sprinkle, bedew: *Dampen the clothes before ironing them.* **2** °stifle, °deaden, °damp, °check, °chill, °cool, °restrain, °retard, lessen, °diminish, °reduce, °suppress, abate, °moderate, allay, °subdue, °temper, °dull, °discourage: *His constant chattering on about himself dampened her ardour.*

dance *v.* **1** °cavort, gambol, °caper, °skip, °leap, romp, trip the light fantastic (toe), *US* cut a rug, sashay, *Colloq* bop, hoof it: *We danced for joy when we heard the news. Would you care to dance?*
—*n.* **2** ball, social, dancing °party, *thé dansant*, *US* tea dance, °promenade, *Colloq* shindig *or* shindy, hop, bop, *US and Canadian* prom: *I have invited her to the dance on Saturday evening.*

dandy *n.* **1** fop, coxcomb, (°gay) °blade, beau, °gallant, lady-killer, ladies' °man, °rake, *Colloq* °swell, clotheshorse, *Brit* toff, blood, *US* °dude: *He was a great dandy, and spent hours dressing every day.*
—*adj.* **2** °fine, °splendid, °first-rate, °great, °marvellous, °neat, spectacular: *Penny's father bought her a dandy new car.*

danger *n.* **1** °peril, °risk, °threat, °hazard, °jeopardy: *The danger of an avalanche is too great to go skiing.* **2** ***in danger of***: °likely (to be), °liable (to be): *If you drink and drive, you are in danger of causing a road accident.*

dangerous *adj.* **1** °risky, °perilous, °hazardous, unsafe, °precarious, °rickety, *Colloq* chancy, iffy: *Rock-climbing is very dangerous.* **2** °threatening, °menacing, °harmful, treacherous: *He is a dangerous criminal, wanted for murder.*

dangerously *adv.* **1** perilously, hazardously, unsafely, precariously, recklessly: *He's a mountain-climber who likes to live dangerously.* **2** ominously, alarmingly: *She is standing dangerously close to the edge.*

dangle *v.* **1** °hang (down), °droop, °depend, °swing, °sway: *The rope dangled from the top of the flag-pole.* **2** °flaunt, brandish, °wave, °flourish: *Competitors often dangle big salary increases in front of those who agree to leave our company.* **3** °wait, *Slang* cool one's heels: *They have kept me dangling for weeks for their decision.*

dapper *adj.* °neat, °spruce, °smart, °trim, well-dressed, °well turned out, °stylish, °fashionable, °elegant, °chic, °dressy; *Colloq* got up *or* dressed to the nines, dressed to kill, °swanky *or* swank, ritzy; *Slang* snazzy, °nifty, spiffy, °sharp, °swell, classy: *Tony looks very dapper in his new Savile Row suit.*

dapple *adj.* **1** spotted, dotted, °mottled, °speckled, °flecked, dappled; brindled; pied, piebald, skewbald, °paint, flea-bitten, *US* pinto: *Take the chestnut mare—I'll ride the dapple grey.*
—*v.* **2** °spot, °dot, mottle, speckle, bespeckle, stipple: *Dapple paint on the wall with a sponge to get a mottled effect.*

dare *v.* **1** °challenge, °defy, °provoke; throw down the gauntlet: *She dared me to jump, so I jumped.* **2** °risk, °hazard, °gamble, °venture, °face, make °bold, be so °bold as: *I would never dare to talk to my father that way.*
—*n.* **3** °challenge, °provocation, °taunt; °ultimatum: *She took the dare and swam across the lake.*

daredevil *n.* **1** exhibitionist, °showman, °stunt man, °stunt woman; °adventurer, soldier of fortune, *Colloq* °show-off: *William finally got a job as a daredevil in the circus.*
—*adj.* **2** °reckless, °rash, death-defying, °impulsive, °daring, °dashing, °impetuous, incautious, °imprudent, °wild, °foolhardy, madcap, devil-may-care; °audacious, °bold, °brave, °fearless, °gallant, °courageous, °intrepid: *Do you consider ski-jumping a sport or an example of daredevil madness?*

daring *n.* **1** °courage, boldness, °bravery, valour, intrepidity, fearlessness, °grit, °pluck, °spirit, mettle, adventurousness, derring-do, *Colloq* guts, °spunk, °nerve; *Slang Brit* °bottle: *Diving from a cliff into the sea takes a lot of daring.*
—*adj.* **2** °bold, °audacious, °courageous, °brave, valorous, °intrepid, °fearless, unafraid, plucky, mettlesome, °adventurous, °venturesome, °hardy; °rash, °reckless, *Colloq* gutsy, *US* nervy: *In the 19th century, a few daring explorers penetrated the jungles of Africa.*

dark *adj.* **1** unlit, unlighted, unilluminated, ill-lighted, ill-lit, °sunless; °black, Stygian, pitch-dark, inky, jet-black: *We cowered in a recess in the dark cave.* **2** °dim, °murky, tenebrous, °shady, °shadowy: *I could scarcely see ahead of me in the dark forest.* **3** °gloomy, °dismal, °dreary, °dull, °drab, subfuscous, subfusc, °bleak, cheerless, °mournful, °dour, °pessimistic, °sombre, °doleful, °joyless, °grim, °sad, °melancholy, °sorrowful: *Why do you always look at the dark side of things?* **4** °evil, °wicked, °vile, °base, °foul, iniquitous, nefarious, black-hearted, °villainous, °sinister, °satanic, °devilish, hellish: *Nostradamus predicted that dark forces would overrun the world.* **5** °murky, °overcast, cloudy, °threatening, °black, °dusky, louring *or* lowering; foggy, °misty; *US* glowering: *Another dark day on the moor and I thought I'd go mad.* **6** °mysterious, °deep, °profound, °incomprehensible, enigmatic, °puzzling, impenetrable, unfathomable, abstruse, °recondite, arcane, °obscure: *She took her dark secret to the grave.* **7** °hidden, concealed, °secret, °occult, mystic(al), °cryptic: *The true reason for his leaving was always kept dark in the family.* **8** brunette; °black, °swarthy, brown; (sun)tanned, *Old-fashioned* swart: *One is fair with dark hair, the other has dark skin.* **9** °ignorant, unenlightened, °benighted: *Our culture passed through a dark phase before the Renaissance.*
—*n.* **10** °night, night-time, nightfall: *We waited till dark to make good our escape.* **11** darkness, blackness, °gloom, gloominess, murk, murkiness: *At fifty, isn't he a bit old to be afraid of the dark?* **12** °obscurity, °ignorance: *She was always kept in the dark about his true identity.*

darling *n.* **1** °sweetheart, °beloved, °love, °dear, dearest, true-love: *She insists on buying all her darling's clothes.* **2** °pet, °favourite, apple of one's eye, *Brit* blue-eyed boy *or* girl; *US* fair-haired boy *or* girl: *Frank might have been the black sheep of the family, but he was always his mother's darling.*

—*adj.* **3** °beloved, loved, cherished, adored, °dear, °precious, treasured: *He travelled everywhere with his darling niece.* **4** °pleasing, °fetching, °attractive, °adorable, °enchanting, °lovely, alluring, °engaging, bewitching, charming: *Josephine was wearing a darling frock she'd just bought at the Corner Boutique.*

dash *v.* **1** °crash, smash, °shatter, °break, °shiver, °fragment, °split; °destroy, °ruin, °spoil, °frustrate, °obliterate: *The mirror was dashed to smithereens when it fell. The ship didn't see our raft, and our hopes of rescue were dashed.* **2** °hurl, °toss, °throw, °fling, °cast, °pitch, *Colloq* chuck: *We drank a toast, then dashed our glasses into the fireplace.* **3** °rush, °run, dart, °spring, °bolt, °bound, °race, sprint; °hasten, °fly, °hurry, °speed: *I'll have to dash to catch my train.* **4** ***dash off***: scribble: *I've just dashed off a note to mother.*
—*n.* **5** dart, °bolt, °rush, °run, °spurt, °spring, °bound, sprint: *He made a dash for the door but it was too late.* **6** °flourish, élan, °flair, liveliness, °style, °panache, °spirit, brio, °verve, °zest, °spice; °ardour, °fervour, °vigour, °energy: *She is known for her beauty as well as her dash and courage.* **7** °bit, °pinch, soupçon, °hint, °suggestion, °touch, °trace, tinge, °taste, °drop, °piece, *Colloq* smidgen *or* smidgin, *US* tad: *Add a dash of nutmeg at the end.*

dashing *adj.* **1** °spirited, °lively, °impetuous, °energetic, °vigorous, °dynamic, °animated, *Colloq* peppy: *She is now going out with a dashing young fellow from the City.* **2** °fashionable, °stylish, °chic, à la °mode, modish, °smart, °elegant, °dapper, *Colloq Brit* °swish: *That's a dashing coat, Felicia.* **3** °flamboyant, °showy, °ostentatious, °pretentious: *George Hutton was a bit too dashing for her taste.*

data *n.* facts, °information, statistics, °figures, °details, °matter, observations, °material(s); °text; °evidence: *We shall process the data on the computer and print out the results.*

date *n.* **1** °time, year, °season, °period, °day; °age, °era, epoch, °stage, °phase: *These artefacts are from an earlier date than was first supposed.* **2** °appointment, °meeting, °engagement, rendezvous, assignation, tryst; °fixture: *She already has a date for Saturday night.* **3** °escort, °companion, °friend, boyfriend, girlfriend, °girl, °woman, °boy, °man, swain, beau, °lover, *Colloq* steady: *Bob is Sally's date for the dance.* **4** ***out of date***: °old-fashioned, °old, °ancient, archaic, °antiquated, dated, °passé, outmoded, °obsolete, °obsolescent, *Colloq* °old hat: *This timetable is out of date. Why do you wear those out of date clothes?* **5** ***up to date***: °modern, °latest, °current, °contemporary, à la °mode, °fashionable, *Colloq* °trendy: *Her taste in music is quite up to date. Use this up-to-date edition of the encyclopedia.*
—*v.* **6** show one's °age, make °obsolete *or* °obsolescent *or* °old-fashioned: *That pompadour hair-do really dates her.* **7** °entertain, °escort, °go out (with), °go steady (with): *Does Michael still date Patsy? Those two are still dating.*

daunt *v.* °intimidate, cow, °discourage, dishearten, dispirit, °unnerve, °shake, °upset, disconcert, °discomfit, °put off, awe, °overawe, °appal, °alarm, °threaten, °frighten, °terrify, °scare, terrorize: *He was daunted by the prospect of facing the entire council.*

dauntless *adj.* °fearless, undaunted, unafraid, unflinching, °stalwart, °brave, °courageous, °bold, °audacious, °intrepid, valorous, °daring, °gallant, °heroic, °venturesome, plucky, stout-hearted, valiant: *Dauntless, the knight rode into the thick of the fray.*

dawdle *v.* °linger, loiter, °straggle, °delay, °procrastinate, dally, °lounge, laze, °idle, °lag, °lie about, °waste °time, *Colloq* dilly-dally, °shilly-shally: *We have to catch the next train, so stop dawdling.*

dawn *n.* **1** daybreak, sunrise, break of °day, °crack of dawn, °first °light, dawning, cock crow, *Literary* aurora, day-spring, *US* sun-up: *We shall attack the castle at dawn.* **2** dawning, °beginning, commencement, °start, °birth, awakening, inception, genesis, °outset, °onset, °origin, °appearance, °arrival, advent, °emergence, inauguration, °rise, °first °occurrence: *The dawn of western civilization has been placed in Anatolia.*
—*v.* **3** °gleam, °break, °brighten, °lighten: *The day dawned on the deserted beach.* **4** °begin, °originate, °commence, °arise, °appear, °emerge, °start, °arrive, °develop, °unfold: *The day of the computer had not yet dawned when I was a child.* **5** ***dawn on*** *or* ***upon***: °occur to, °come to °mind, become °apparent *or* °evident to: *It slowly dawned on me that he had been lying all along.*

day *n.* **1** daytime, °daylight, broad °daylight, °light of day: *Sunrise quickly turned night into day.* **2** °time, hour, °age, °period, °era, epoch, °date, °prime, heyday; lifetime: *Her day will come. In his day, there was no telephone.*

day-dream *n.* **1** °reverie, wool-gathering, °fantasy, °fancy, °dream, musing, °castle in the air *or* in Spain, pipedream: *The realities of life have cured me of many day-dreams.*
—*v.* **2** °fantasize, °imagine, °fancy, °envisage, °envision, °dream: *She still day-dreams that a knight in shining armour will come and carry her away.*

daylight *n.* **1** sunlight, °sun, sunshine, °light: *Coming from the cave, we were blinded by the daylight.* **2** °open, broad daylight, °light of day, full °view, full °knowledge, °clarity: *We must bring his treachery out into the daylight.*

daze *v.* **1** °stun, stupefy, °blind, °dazzle, bedazzle, °shock, °stagger, °startle, °astonish, °astound, °amaze, °surprise, °overcome, °overpower, °dumbfound, benumb, °paralyse, *Colloq* °bowl over, °floor, flabbergast; *Slang* blow one's mind: *She was dazed to learn her husband was still alive.* **2** befuddle, °confuse, °bemuse, °bewilder, °puzzle, °mystify, baffle, °perplex, °nonplus, °blind: *He was dazed by the difficulty of the examination.*
—*n.* **3** °confusion, °flurry, °spin, whirl: *The entire week was a continuous daze of cocktail parties and dinner parties.* **4** ***in a daze***: stupefied, in a °trance, bewildered, °confused, perplexed, disoriented, °dizzy, dazzled, bedazzled, °overcome, overpowered, nonplussed, befuddled, flustered; startled, surprised, shocked, stunned, astonished, astounded, amazed, staggered; bemused, baffled, puzzled, mystified, *Colloq* flabbergasted, bowled over, floored: *Arthur was in a daze to find himself the centre of attention.*

dazzle *v.* **1** °impress, °bewitch, °enchant, °charm, °beguile, °intrigue, °captivate, °fascinate, spellbind, °entrance, °hypnotize, mesmerize: *Every man in the room was dazzled by Mrs d'Arcy's brilliant wit and good looks.* **2** See **daze, 1,** above.
—*n.* **3** °brilliance, °splendour, magnificence, °sparkle, °glitter, *Slang* razzle-dazzle, razzmatazz: *Many actors are lured to New York by the dazzle of Broadway.*

dazzling *adj.* °bright, °brilliant, resplendent, blinding, bedazzling, °radiant, °splendid, °magnificent, °glorious, sparkling, °scintillating; °stunning, °overwhelming, °overpowering, stupefying, dizzying; °gorgeous; *Colloq* splendiferous, mind-boggling: *In the chest was a dazzling collection of the finest jewels.*

dead *adj.* **1** deceased, °defunct, °extinct, gone, departed, °late, °lifeless, no more, *Colloq* done for, *Slang Brit* gone for a burton: *Both his parents are dead, and his only brother lives in Australia. Lycidas is dead, dead ere his prime.* **2** insensate, °insensible, °numb, paralysed, benumbed, unfeeling: *After the accident, my left thumb was completely dead.* **3** °insensible, °unconscious, °out, dead to the world, deathlike, deathly: *At the news of her son, she fell in a dead faint.* **4** insensitive, unemotional, unfeeling, emotionless, apathetic, °lukewarm, °cool, °cold, °frigid, unresponsive, °unsympathetic, °indifferent, unconcerned, uninterested; °numb, °wooden, °callous, hardened, impervious, inured, °inert: *He has always been dead to others' problems.* **5** °out, smothered, extinguished: *The fire is dead.* **6** °inanimate, °lifeless, °inert, inorganic: *Dead*

stones speak volumes to the geologist. **7** °extinct, °obsolete, perished, °past, outmoded, °disused, expired, °passé: *Latin is a dead language.* **8** °barren, unfruitful, °infertile, unproductive: *That area off the coast is dead as far as fishing goes.* **9** °tired (out), °exhausted, °worn out, °fatigued, °spent, collapsing, in a °state of °collapse, *Slang* bushed, °beat, *Brit* knackered, *US and Canadian* pooped: *We were completely dead after the hike into town.* **10** °dull, lustreless, °flat, °neutral, °vapid, °empty, °bland, °colourless, °grey, beige, °dun: *The walls of the prison were painted a dead white.* **11** °stagnant, motionless, °still, °standing, °static, °inert, unmoving, °inactive, °quiet, °calm: *There were small pools of dead water covered with a green slime. Without a breath of air stirring, the boat was dead in the water.* **12** °boring, °dull, °tedious, °tiresome, °monotonous, °prosaic, uninteresting, run-of-the-mill, °ordinary, commonplace, °dry, insipid, °bland, °flat, two-dimensional, °lifeless, °stiff, °rigid, °stony: *The play was bad, the performance dead.* **13** °dull, muffled, deadened, anechoic, unresounding, non-resonant: *One room in the laboratory was built to be dead to all sound.* **14** °complete, °entire, °total, °absolute, °downright, °thorough, through and through, utter, all-out, °out-and-out, °unqualified, unrelieved, unbroken, °categorical, °outright: *My investment in the anti-gravity pill has so far been a dead loss.* **15** °profound, °deep: *I fell into a dead sleep.* **16** °sudden, °abrupt, °complete, °full: *The train came to a dead stop.* **17** °certain, °sure, unerring, °exact, °precise, °accurate, crack: *According to the records, Calamity Jane was a dead shot.*
—*adv.* **18** °completely, °entirely, °absolutely, °totally, °utterly, categorically, °thoroughly, unconditionally, unqualifiedly: *You are dead right about Pontefract.* **19** °completely, °entirely, °absolutely, °totally; abruptly, °suddenly: *He stopped dead in his tracks and stared at me.* **20** °directly, °exactly, °precisely: *An enormous maelstrom lay dead ahead of the fragile craft.*
—*n.* **21** °depth(s), °extreme, °midst, °middle: *She used to visit his room in the dead of night.*

deaden *v.* **1** °numb, benumb, °paralyse, anaesthetize, desensitize, °dull; °damp: *This injection will deaden your hand and you'll feel no pain.* **2** °weaken, °moderate, soothe, °mitigate, assuage, °reduce, lessen, °diminish, alleviate, °cushion, °soften, mollify, °blunt, °dull: *He took to drink to deaden the shock of losing his only son.*

deadlock *n.* **1** °standstill, °impasse, °stalemate, stand-off, °draw, stoppage, *Colloq US* Mexican stand-off: *Union and management negotiators have reached a deadlock on the pension issue.*
—*v.* **2** bring *or* come to a °standstill *or* °impasse, °stall, °stop, °halt: *The Congress is likely to deadlock on the question of expanding national health benefits.*

deadly *adj.* **1** °lethal, °fatal; °dangerous, pernicious, °poisonous, noxious, toxic; baleful, °harmful, nocuous: *This drug is deadly if taken in large doses.* **2** °mortal, °implacable, °ruthless, °savage: *They were deadly enemies long after the war was over.* **3** °murderous, °homicidal, °bloodthirsty, °brutal, °vicious, °ferocious, barbarous, barbaric, °savage, °inhuman, °cold-blooded, °heartless, °ruthless, pitiless, °merciless: *Two deadly killers have escaped from Dartmoor prison.* **4** deathly, deathlike, °pale, pallid, °ghostly, cadaverous, °ghastly, °wan, °white, livid, ashen: *He turned a deadly hue, as if he had seen a ghost.* **5** °boring, °excruciating, °dull, °tiresome, °tedious, °dreary, °humdrum, °lacklustre, wearying, wearisome: *It was a deadly play put on by deadly actors.* **6** °exact, °precise, °accurate, °true, unerring, unfailing: *Each arrow hit the bull's-eye with deadly accuracy.*

deaf *adj.* **1** hard of hearing, stone-deaf: *Sean is slightly deaf in his left ear.* **2** unhearing, unheedful, °heedless, °insensible, insensitive, impervious, °indifferent, °oblivious, unresponsive, °unmoved, unconcerned, unyielding: *The judge was deaf to all appeals for clemency.*

deal *v.* **1** °distribute, °dole out, °give out, °parcel out, °mete out, °allot, apportion, °administer, °dispense: *Deal thirteen cards to each of the four players. She dealt out her own brand of justice to criminals.* **2** °buy and °sell, °handle, °stock, do °business, °trade, °traffic: *This shop deals only in the most expensive linens.* **3** °behave, °act, °conduct oneself: *Simon has never dealt openly, so you mustn't trust him.* **4** ***deal with***: °treat, °handle, take °care of, have to do with, °attend to, °see to, °reckon with, °grapple with, °act on; °practise, °administer, °engage in: *I shall deal with the matter tomorrow.*
—*n.* **5** °transaction, °arrangement, °negotiation, °agreement, °contract, °bargain, °understanding: *The deal to sell the textbook division is off.* **6** Often, ***great deal***: (°large *or* °great) °amount, °lot, (°large *or* °huge) °quantity; extent: *There's been a great deal of crime in that neighbourhood.*

dealer *n.* °trader, businessman, businesswoman, °merchant, °tradesman, retailer, shopkeeper, vendor, merchandiser; wholesaler, jobber, distributor, stockist, supplier; °broker, °agent, salesman, *US* storekeeper: *He has been a dealer in precious gems for years.*

dealings *n.pl.* °business, °commerce, °exchange, °trade, °traffic, °transactions, °negotiations; °relations, relationships, °affairs: *All his business dealings are reviewed by his solicitor.*

dear *adj.* **1** °beloved, loved, adored, °darling, °precious, cherished, prized, valued, treasured, °favoured, °favourite, °pet, esteemed, admired, venerated, honoured: *He was my nearest and dearest friend.* **2** °expensive, costly, high-priced, °highly priced, *Colloq* °pricey *or* pricy: *Tomatoes are much too dear at this time of the year.*
—*n.* **3** °darling, °sweetheart, °beloved, °love, true-love, °sweet, honey, °precious, °pet, °favourite, °treasure, *Colloq* sweetie, sweetie-pie, *Slang* °baby: *My dear, I hope we'll be together always.*
—*adv.* **4** °dearly; at great °cost *or* °expense, at a high *or* excessive °price: *That little error will cost you dear, my friend.*

dearly *adv.* **1** greatly, °very much, °indeed, °sincerely: *I should dearly like to go, but I cannot.* **2** affectionately, °fondly, lovingly, tenderly: *He loves his mother very dearly.* **3** expensively, °dear, at °great °cost *or* °expense, at a °high *or* °excessive °price, punitively: *The victory at Thalamos was dearly bought.*

dearth *n.* °scarcity, °want, °need, °lack, deficiency, sparseness *or* sparsity, scantiness, insufficiency, inadequacy, °shortage, paucity, exiguity, °poverty, exiguousness; °absence: *There is a dearth of major roles for black actors.*

death *n.* **1** demise, decease, °passing, °dying, °end: *She was overcome with grief at the news of his death.* **2** °end, °termination, cessation, °expiration, expiry: *Nobody mourned the death of the bill in the lower house.* **3** °end, °finish, °termination; extinction, °destruction, extermination, annihilation, eradication, obliteration, extirpation, liquidation, °ruin, °downfall, °undoing: *The invasion marked the death of the Roman Empire.*

deathless *adj.* °eternal, °everlasting, °immortal, undying, imperishable, °permanent, unending, °timeless, never-ending: *In his opinion, his novel was another example of his deathless prose.*

debase *v.* **1** °lower, °degrade, devalue, °depreciate, °depress, demote, deprecate, °belittle, °diminish, °reduce, °disparage: *Words which denote fine qualities are in time debased.* **2** °adulterate, °contaminate, °taint, °pollute, °corrupt, °mar, °spoil, °impair, °vitiate, abase, defile, bastardize; °poison: *To increase profits, the manufacturer has debased the traditional formula.*

debatable *adj.* °controversial, arguable, °questionable, °doubtful, dubious, °problematic *or* problematical, °disputable, open *or* subject to °dispute *or* °doubt *or* °question, in °dispute *or* °doubt *or* °question, °moot, polemic *or* polemical, unsure, °uncertain, °unsettled, undecided: *Whether he is the best person for the job is debatable.*

debate *n.* **1** °discussion, °argument, °dispute, altercation, °controversy, wrangle, contention, polemic; argumentation: *I refuse to take sides in the debate over social services.* **2** deliberation, °consideration, (careful) °thought, °reflection, cogitation, meditation, contemplation: *Payment of reparations to the victims of the disaster is a matter for debate.*
—*v.* **3** °argue, wrangle, °dispute, °contest, contend; °discuss, °moot, °question: *We debated only the most important issues.* **4** °deliberate, °consider, °reflect (on), °mull over, °ponder (over), °weigh, ruminate (over), °meditate (on *or* over), °think (over *or* on), °think through: *I have often debated in my own mind the question of capital punishment.*

debonair *adj.* **1** °suave, soigné(e), °elegant, urbane, °refined, °dapper, °genteel, °well-bred, °courteous, °civil, mannerly, °gracious, °polite, affable, °obliging, °pleasant, *Colloq* °smooth: *Despite his vicious temper, he was most debonair in company.* **2** °carefree, insouciant, °gay, °nonchalant, light-hearted, °dashing, charming, °cheerful, °buoyant, °jaunty, °sprightly: *Being handsome and debonair, he was much sought after by hostesses.*

debt *n.* **1** °obligation; °due, indebtedness, °liability, °responsibility, °accountability, °encumbrance: *He owes a debt of gratitude to his wife for her moral support. The company takes care of all debts promptly.* **2** ***in debt***: under °obligation, owing, °accountable, °beholden, °indebted, °responsible, answerable for, °liable, encumbered, in arrears, °straitened, in dire straits, in (financial) °difficulty *or* °difficulties, in the red, *Colloq US and Canadian* in hock: *I shall always be in debt to you for your help. The London branch is in debt for ten million pounds.*

début *n.* **1** °première *or* premiere, introduction, °initiation, inauguration, °launch *or* launching, coming out: *The young soprano's début at La Scala was a triumph.*
—*v.* **2** °launch, °come out, °enter, °appear: *His plan is to début with a zither accompaniment.*

decadent *adj.* **1** declining, decaying, deteriorating, debased, degenerating, falling off, on the °wane, °withering, degenerative: *The decadent literature of the period was a reflection of the decline in moral standards.* **2** °corrupt, °dissolute, °immoral, debauched, dissipated, °self-indulgent, °degenerate: *His decadent behaviour brought him to the attention of the police.*

decay *v.* **1 a** °decline, °wane, °ebb, °dwindle, °diminish, °decrease: *The magnetic field rapidly decays when the power is removed.* **b** °decline, °waste away, atrophy, °weaken, wither, °degenerate, °deteriorate, °disintegrate; °crumble: *Her great beauty decayed quickly.* **2** °rot, °decompose, moulder, °putrefy, °spoil; °turn, go °bad, °go off: *The flesh has decayed and only a skeleton remains.*
—*n.* **3** °decline, weakening, °failing, fading, deterioration, decadence, degeneration, wasting, atrophy, dilapidation, disintegration, °collapse; °downfall: *The buildings were in an advanced state of decay.* **4** °rot, rotting, decomposition, °mould, putrefaction, mortification: *The decay has weakened the timbers supporting the bridge.*

deceit *n.* **1** °deception, deceitfulness, °fraud, fraudulence, cheating, °trickery, °chicanery *or* chicane, °dissimulation, dishonesty, misrepresentation, double-dealing, duplicity, °hypocrisy, treachery, underhandedness, guile, °craft, slyness, craftiness, cunning, knavery, funny business, *Colloq* °hanky-panky, monkey business: *Inside traders on the Stock Exchange profit enormously from deceit.* **2** °trick, °subterfuge, °stratagem, ploy, °ruse, °manoeuvre, °artifice, °wile, °hoax, °swindle, °double-cross, misrepresentation, °pretence, °sham, contrivance, °shift, confidence °trick, subreption, gloze, *Brit dialect or colloq US* flam; *Colloq* flimflam; *Slang* scam, con, con °trick, con °game: *She was sick of all his lies and deceits.*

deceitful *adj.* °dishonest, underhand(ed), untrustworthy, misleading, °crooked, °insincere, °false, °fraudulent, °counterfeit, °disingenuous, °lying, mendacious, untruthful; °wily, °crafty, °sly, cunning, °scheming, guileful, °artful, °sneaky, double-dealing, °two-faced, °hypocritical, duplicitous, *Colloq* °phoney *or US also* phony: *It was deceitful of you to pretend you loved her when all you wanted was her money.*

deceive *v.* °mislead, delude, °impose on *or* upon, °fool, °hoax, °trick, °cheat, °swindle, °betray, °double-cross, °lead on, °lead up *or* down the garden °path, °lead astray, pull the wool over (someone's) eyes, inveigle, °cajole, *Archaic* cozen; *Colloq* con, bamboozle, °take in, take for a °ride, two-time, move the goalposts; *Slang US* °take: *He deceived even his friends and family into believing he had been a war hero.*

decent *adj.* **1** °becoming, °suitable, °appropriate, °proper, °seemly, °fitting: *Despite the life she led, the woman should have a decent burial.* **2** °seemly, °decorous, °tasteful, °dignified, mannerly, °nice, °clean, °respectable, °polite, °modest, °presentable, °acceptable: *Hereafter, you will use only decent language when speaking to me!* **3** °adequate, °acceptable, °passable, °fair, °competent, °mediocre, middling, °fair to middling, °moderate, °respectable, not °bad, °ordinary, so so, not °outstanding, unimpressive, °average, neither here nor there, all °right, °reasonable, °tolerable, °satisfactory, °good enough, *Colloq* °OK *or* okay: *Sales in the first quarter were decent but hardly outstanding.* **4** °courteous, °proper, °right, °fair, °honest, °honourable, °friendly, °considerate, °gracious, °nice, °thoughtful, °obliging, °kind, °generous, °accommodating: *You can count on David to do the decent thing.* **5** °chaste, °pure, °virtuous, °modest, °well-bred, °decorous, °well brought up, °nice, °respectable: *Caroline is a decent girl, but no great brain or beauty.*

deception *n.* **1** duplicity, °deceit, °intrigue, °hypocrisy, °fraud, cheating, °trickery, °chicanery *or* chicane, °dissimulation, double-dealing, °subterfuge, sophistry, treachery, knavery, tergiversation; see also **deceit 1,** above: *He practised deception even in his family relationships.* **2** °trick, °ruse, °artifice, °stratagem, °subterfuge, °manoeuvre, °wile, imposture, °hoax, °sham, °pretence; see also **deceit 2,** above: *He tried every deception in the book to separate her from her money.*

deceptive *adj.* **1** misleading, °false, °illusory, deceiving, °unreliable: *He has the look of an athlete, but appearances can be deceptive.* **2** °fraudulent, °deceitful, °dishonest, untruthful, °fake, °false, °shifty, fallacious, °specious, °spurious, °bogus, °counterfeit, pseudo, sophistical; °tricky, °dodgy, °evasive, °elusive, °slippery, *Colloq* °phoney *or US also* phony: *The bank is being deceptive about his credit rating.*

decide *v.* **1** °determine, °settle, °resolve, conclude, take *or* reach *or* come to a °decision *or* conclusion, make up one's °mind, arbitrate, °judge, adjudicate, referee, °umpire: *She decided that you were right. They decided the case in my favour.* **2** ***decide on*** *or* ***upon***: °fix *or* °fasten *or* °settle on *or* upon, °choose, °select, °pick (out), °elect, opt (for), °commit oneself (to): *I have decided on a British-made car.*

decided *adj.* **1** °definite, °pronounced, °marked, unmistakable, unambiguous, unequivocal, °certain, °sure, °absolute, °obvious, °clear, °evident, °unquestionable, unquestioned, °indisputable, °undisputed, undeniable, irrefutable, incontestable, °unqualified, unconditional, °incontrovertible, °solid: *The party was a decided success.* **2** °fixed, °firm, °resolute, °determined, adamant, °stony, °unhesitating, decisive, °definite, unfaltering, °assertive, asseverative, unswerving, unwavering: *They are decided in their approval of her plan.*

decipher *v.* **1** decode, decrypt; unravel, unscramble, disentangle, °translate, °work out, °explain, °solve, *Colloq* °figure out: *It was Champollion who deciphered the Rosetta Stone.* **2** °read, °interpret, °make out, *Colloq* °figure out: *I can't decipher Theresa's handwriting or what she's trying to say.*

decision *n.* **1** °settlement, °determination, °resolution, settling, resolving, arbitration: *The decision is the* *umpire's responsibility.* **2** °judgement, conclusion, °resolution, verdict, °sentence, ruling, °finding, °decree, °settlement, °outcome: *According to the decision, the victims will receive compensatory damages.* **3** °determination, firmness, decidedness, °resolve, decisiveness, conclusiveness, steadfastness, °purpose, purposefulness: *She asserted her position with decision.*

declaration *n.* **1** °statement, °assertion, attestation, deposition, asseveration, affirmation, avowal, °announcement, °proclamation, °pronouncement, °profession: *Henrietta desperately wanted to believe Henry's declaration of love.* **2** °proclamation, °announcement, °pronouncement, promulgation, pronunciamento, edict, ukase, manifesto, °notice: *The colonists issued a declaration of independence.*

declare *v.* **1** assert, °say, °offer, °submit, affirm, °state, aver, asseverate, avow, avouch, °profess, °protest, °swear, °claim, °proclaim; °confirm, °certify, °ratify: *I solemnly declare that the testimony I am to give is true, so help me God.* **2** °announce, °make known, °pronounce, °decree, °rule, °proclaim, herald, promulgate, °publish, °broadcast, trumpet (forth): *Robert has declared his intention to make Marianne his wife.*

decline *v.* **1** °refuse, °turn down, °deny, °reject, demur, °forgo, °veto, °avoid, abstain from: *She declined help with the packages. Roger was offered a professorship at the university but he declined.* **2** °diminish, lessen, °decrease, °wane, °flag, °go down, °fall *or* °taper off, °subside, °ebb, abate, °dwindle, °shrink, °fade, *Colloq* peter out, °run out of steam, *US* °run out of gas: *Demand for hula hoops declined.* **3** °slope *or* °slant (downwards), °descend, °drop *or* °fall off, °dip, °sink: *The meadow declines towards the river.* **4** °deteriorate, °degenerate, °worsen, °fail: *My health has declined over the last year.* **5** °go *or* °drop down, °settle, °dip, °sink, °set: *The sun was declining as I went home.*
—*n.* **6** diminution, °decrease, lessening, °ebb, downturn, fall-off, reduction, abatement, °slump, descent: *There has been a steady decline in the value of the pound.* **7** degeneration, deterioration, °loss, diminution, weakening, debility, °weakness, worsening, °decay, °failing: *We noted a decline in the physical condition of those living nearby.* **8** declivity, (°downward) °slope *or* °slant, descent, °downgrade, °incline: *The path led down a steep decline towards the pond.*

decompose *v.* **1** °disintegrate, °separate, °fall *or* °come °apart, °break up *or* down, take °apart, dissect, anatomize, atomize, °resolve, decompound, °analyse: *By absorption the scientists decomposed the green light into yellow and blue.* **2** °rot, °disintegrate, °decay, moulder, °putrefy; °spoil, °go off *or* °bad, °turn °sour: *The meat will decompose if it is left outside the fridge.*

decorate *v.* **1** °embellish, adorn, °ornament, garnish, embroider, °elaborate, bedeck, deck (out), °trim, °dress (up), °spruce *or* smarten up, °beautify, *Literary* caparison, *Colloq Brit* °tart up: *We decorated the pub for the Christmas holidays.* **2** *Brit* paint, wallpaper, redecorate, furbish, °refurbish, °renovate, °fix up, °restore: *All the bedrooms have been decorated.*

decoration *n.* **1** garnish, °trim, trimming, adornment, °embellishment, °ornament, ornamentation, garnishment: *There's a bit too much decoration on the cake.* **2** medal, laurel, °award, badge, colours, °order, ribbon, °star, garter: *Captain Harder won many decorations in the war.*

decorous *adj.* °becoming, °dignified, °decent, °correct, mannerly, °seemly, °refined, °elegant, °polite, well-behaved, °genteel, demure, °polished, gentlemanly, °ladylike: *Your behaviour was less than decorous at last night's party.*

decorum *n.* **1** °etiquette, °proper °behaviour, °propriety, °good °form, mannerliness, politeness, °dignity, gentility, °good °manners, respectability, courtliness, deportment: *The decorum of the meeting was disturbed by rabble-rousers.* **2** correctness, °propriety, °protocol, punctilio, conformity: *Please observe proper decorum when visiting the embassy.*

decoy *n.* **1** bait, °lure, °trap, °attraction, °enticement, °inducement, stool-pigeon: *The hunters set out their decoys and waited for the ducks.*
—*v.* **2** °lure, entrap, °entice, °attract, °induce, °seduce, bait, °trick, °tempt, ensnare, inveigle, allure: *He was decoyed into a dark alley and robbed.*

decrease *v.* **1** °diminish, °reduce, °decline, lessen, °lower, abate, °fall off, °shrink, °shrivel (up), °contract, °dwindle, °ebb, °subside, °wane, °taper off, de-escalate, slacken, °let up, °ease (off *or* up), °curtail, °cut (down *or* back), *Colloq* °run out of steam, *US* °run out of gas: *Demand for tickets to rock concerts has decreased over the years. The number of applicants for work is decreasing.*
—*n.* **2** diminution, reduction, °decline, lessening, lowering, abatement, falling off, shrinking, shrivelling, contraction, decrement, dwindling, °ebb, subsidence, tapering off, °wane, de-escalation, slackening, easing (off *or* up), curtailment, °cut, cut-back: *There has been no noticeable decrease in the price of houses in the south-east. Have you noticed the decrease in arrests for dangerous driving?*

decree *n.* **1** °order, mandate, directive, ordinance, edict, law, statute, °regulation, enactment, °act, ruling, dictum, °dictate, °injunction, °sanction, manifesto, °proclamation, promulgation, °determination, °decision, °judgement, rescript, °prescription, pronunciamento, firman, ukase, *Rom Cath Ch* decretal: *The star chamber issued a decree restricting the freedom of the press.*
—*v.* **2** °order, °command, °direct, °rule, mandate, ordain, °dictate, °charge, enjoin, °proclaim, °pronounce, °prescribe, °decide, °determine, adjudge, *Scots law* decern: *The council has decreed that no spirits can be sold on Sundays.*

decrepit *adj.* **1** °feeble, enfeebled, °weak, weakened, °frail, °infirm, wasted, °worn out, unfit, debilitated, enervated, °disabled, incapacitated, °crippled, °doddering; out of °shape, in °bad °shape; °aged, °old, °elderly, °ancient, superannuated, senescent, °senile, *Colloq* gaga: *The old man was so decrepit he was unable to lift the cup to his lips.* **2** °dilapidated, deteriorated, crumbling, decayed, decaying, withered, wasted, °antiquated, °tumbledown, broken-down, °rickety, °unstable, °shaky, °ramshackle, °derelict, creaking, creaky, °run-down: *The barn was so decrepit we had to tear it down.*

decrepitude *n.* **1** feebleness, °weakness, °infirmity, debilitation, enervation, incapacity, °old °age, superannuation, senescence, °senility, caducity, dotage: *Her decrepitude was so extreme that she could neither walk nor understand what was said to her.* **2** dilapidation, deterioration, °decay, °ruin: *The house is in an advanced state of decrepitude.*

dedicate *v.* **1** °devote, consecrate, °give (up *or* over), °yield, °offer, °surrender, °commit, °pledge, °assign: *She dedicated her life to helping the poor.* **2** consecrate, °bless, °sanctify, °hallow: *There stands the temple dedicated to Apollo.* **3** inscribe; °address, °assign: *This book has been dedicated to you.*

dedication *n.* **1** °devotion, °assignment, °pledge, commitment, allegiance, adherence, faithfulness, fidelity, °loyalty, devotedness, wholeheartedness, single-mindedness, fixedness, fealty: *I admire Rudolph's dedication to duty.* **2** inscription, °address; °message: *The dedication reads, 'To my mother and father'.* **3** consecration, sanctification, hallowing: *The ceremony for the dedication of the youth centre will be held tomorrow.*

deduce *v.* conclude, °infer, °understand, °gather, °assume, °presume, °derive, °draw, °work out, °divine, glean, °take it, °suppose, °surmise, °suspect, *Slang Brit* suss out: *From the tone of his letter she deduced that he was going to change his mind.*

deduct *v.* °subtract, °take away *or* out *or* off, °take from, °remove, °withdraw, *Colloq* °knock off: *Deduct six from ten and you're left with four.*

deduction *n.* **1** subtraction, diminution, °decrease, reduction, withdrawal, °removal, abstraction: *After deductions for expenses, you'll be left with nothing.* **2** conclusion, °inference, °finding, °reasoning, °result: *After considering the evidence, my deduction is that the butler didn't do it.*

deed *n.* **1** °act, °action; °performance: *Their deeds did not match their promises.* **2** °exploit, °feat, °achievement, °accomplishment: *We are here to honour her for her many deeds, both on and off the tennis court.* **3** °title(-deed), °document, °instrument, indenture, °contract, °agreement: *The bank holds the title-deed until the mortgage is paid off.*

deep *adj.* **1** °extensive, °bottomless, abyssal, unfathomable, °profound; °wide, °broad, yawning, chasmal *or* chasmic: *All our supplies were lost in a deep crevasse in the glacier.* **2** °profound, arcane, °recondite, °difficult, abstruse, °obscure, esoteric, °incomprehensible, beyond *or* °past comprehension, impenetrable, unfathomable, inscrutable, °mysterious, mystic(al), °occult, °weighty, °serious, *Colloq* °heavy: *Religious philosophy is too deep a subject to discuss at breakfast.* **3** °wise, °learned, °sage, sagacious, °astute, perspicacious, °profound, discerning, °acute, °intense, °penetrating, °knowledgeable, °knowing: *Margaret is one of the deepest thinkers on the subject.* **4** °rapt, °absorbed, engrossed, occupied, °preoccupied, °intent, °intense, °involved, °engaged, immersed, °lost, *Colloq* into: *Don't disturb him when he's deep in thought.* **5** °devious, cunning, °shrewd, °crafty, canny, °clever, °knowing, °scheming, °artful, °designing: *He thinks there is a deep plot against him.* **6** °profound, °intense, °sincere, °serious, °heartfelt, °earnest, °ardent, °fervent, °poignant, deep-rooted: *I know of your deep concern for her.* **7** °low, °resonant, booming, resounding, sonorous, rumbling: *The deep sound of thunder rolled across the valley.* **8** °rich, °dark, °intense, °strong: *The sky was a deep blue.*
—*n.* **9** ***the deep***: the °ocean, the °main, the °sea, the waters, the high °seas, the briny (deep), the °wave(s), Davy Jones's locker, Neptune's *or* Poseidon's kingdom *or* domain: *It was midnight on the waters and a storm was on the deep.*
—*adv.* **10** °deeply, °far down, °profoundly, intensely, earnestly, heavily: *We drank deep of the cooling liquid.*

deepen *v.* **1** °dig out, °burrow, °sink, dredge, °excavate, °scoop (out): *We'll have to deepen the hole to support the flag-pole.* **2** °intensify, °increase, °concentrate, °strengthen, °expand, °magnify: *The programme reflects a deepening interest in education.*

deeply *adv.* **1** °deep, (far) °downwards *or* inwards, °way down, °deep down: *The glacier was deeply fissured. She swam to the surface and inhaled deeply.* **2** °profoundly, intensely, strongly, powerfully, °very much, acutely, keenly, gravely, greatly, to a °great °extent, °extremely, °thoroughly, °completely, °entirely, °seriously, °severely, irrevocably, unreservedly; passionately, heavily, emotionally: *She is deeply involved with a man from Kent. They were deeply committed to the labour movement.*

deface *v.* °mar, disfigure, °spoil, °ruin, deform, °blemish, °damage, °mutilate, °harm, °impair, °injure, °destroy: *Nothing should be allowed to deface the beauty of these buildings.*

default *n.* **1** °failure, °fault, °defect, °neglect, °negligence, dereliction, °lapse, °oversight, non-performance, non-fulfilment, inaction: *We won the case because of their default on the contract. The other contestant failed to appear, so Gordon won the match by default.* **2** non-payment, delinquency: *Default in the rent may result in eviction.*
—*v.* **3** °fail, °neglect, °dishonour, °lapse, fall °short, come (up) °short: *He has defaulted on a car payment.*

defeat *v.* **1** °overcome, °conquer, vanquish, be °victorious over, get the °better of, °beat, °subdue, °overwhelm, °overpower, °prevail over, °triumph over, °bring down, worst, thrash, °rout, °repulse, °overthrow, trounce, °whip, °crush, °destroy, do in, °best: *The champion defeated the contender in a ten-round match.* **2** °thwart, °frustrate, °disappoint, °check, balk, °stop, °terminate, °end, °finish, °foil: *He never let his handicap defeat his hopes of winning.*
—*n.* **3** °conquest, °overthrow, beating, °repulse, trouncing, °rout, vanquishment: *The defeat of our team must be charged to lack of training.* **4** frustration, °undoing, °failure, °miscarriage, °set-back; Waterloo: *The stock market crash spelled the defeat of the company's plan for a share issue.*

defecate *v.* °void (excrement), °move the °bowels, excrete, °eliminate, °evacuate (the °bowels), have a (°bowel) °movement *or* bm, °open the °bowels, °relieve oneself, *Babytalk* do number two, *Euphemistic* °go to the men's *or* ladies' (room), °go to the °toilet *or* bathroom *or* °lavatory, °excuse (oneself), wash (one's) hands, °go to the powder-room; *Mincing* °go to the little boys' *or* girls' room; *Colloq Brit* °spend a penny, *Colloq Brit* °go to the loo, °pass a °motion, *Taboo slang* (take a) crap *or* shit: *The first symptoms of bowel disease are problems when defecating.*

defect *n.* **1** °shortcoming, deficiency, °lack, °want, inadequacy, insufficiency, shortfall, °failure, °weakness, °frailty, °weak point, °imperfection, irregularity, °liability: *See the doctor about that hearing defect.* **2** °blemish, °imperfection, °failing, °weakness, °flaw, °fault, °mark, °stain, irregularity, °mistake, °error: *The products should be inspected for defects before shipping.*
—*v.* **3** °desert, °change sides *or* loyalties, °turn °traitor, °go over; °escape: *Ropovich tried to defect, but the Albanians sent him back.*

defective *adj.* **1** °imperfect, °faulty, °flawed, °deficient, °broken, out of °order, impaired, marred, *Colloq* on the °blink, *US* on the fritz: *The brakes on his car were defective.* **2** retarded, °simple, °feeble-minded, (mentally) °deficient *or* °incompetent, °backward, subnormal, *Brit education* ESN ('educationally subnormal'), *US education* °exceptional: *Found to be defective, he could not stand trial.*

defector *n.* °deserter, apostate, °turncoat, °traitor, °renegade, *Colloq* rat: *Some political defectors were suspected of being spies.*

defence *n.* **1** °shelter, °protection, °cover, °guard, °safeguard, °shield: *There is no defence against certain illnesses.* **2** fortification, armour, barricade, °screen, °bulwark, °rampart: *Shore defences were set up, including barbed wire entanglements and concrete pillboxes.* **3** °excuse, apology, °reason, apologia, °explanation; justification, vindication, °argument, °plea, advocacy, °support: *His defence for decreasing welfare payments was inadequate. She spoke in defence of nationalizing industry.*

defenceless *adj.* unprotected, exposed, °vulnerable, °unguarded; °helpless, °weak, °powerless, °impotent: *Would you take advantage of a poor, defenceless creature?*

defend *v.* **1** °protect, °watch over, °guard, °safeguard, °keep (°safe), °shelter, °shield, °screen, °preserve; °fight for: *We must defend our civil rights.* **2** °fortify, arm, °secure; °fend *or* °ward off, parry: *Can you defend your position from attack?* **3** °plead for, °speak *or* °stand up for, °stick up for, go to bat for, °support, °uphold, °stand by, °champion, °stand with *or* behind *or* beside, °argue on *or* for *or* in °behalf of, hold a °brief for, espouse: *The lawyers defended her right to free speech.*

defer[1] *v.* °put off, °postpone, °delay, °shelve, °lay *or* °put aside, adjourn, *US* °table; *Colloq Brit* kick into touch: *The judge has deferred his decision.*

defer[2] *v.* Often, ***defer to***: °give in (to), °give ground *or* °way (to), °yield (to), °submit (to), °bow (to), °capitulate (to), °cede (to), accede (to), acquiesce (to); °comply (with), °agree (to): *I'll defer to your decision in the matter.*

deference *n.* **1** °respect, °regard, politeness, °civility, °courtesy, °consideration, °esteem: *They treated him with deference owing to his age.* **2** °obeisance, °submission, acquiescence, °obedience, compliance:

Considering her accomplishments, she is paid little deference.

defiant *adj.* challenging, °bold, °brazen, °audacious, °daring; °rebellious, °disobedient, °stubborn, °recalcitrant, °obstinate, refractory, unyielding, °insubordinate, °mutinous, °unruly, °self-willed, °aggressive, headstrong, contumacious, °pugnacious, °hostile, °belligerent, antagonistic, *Slang* gutsy, spunky: *His defiant attitude towards authority often gets him into trouble.*

deficient *adj.* **1** °wanting, lacking, °defective, °incomplete, unfinished, °short, °insufficient, °inadequate, °sketchy, skimpy, °scarce: *Some foods are deficient in vitamins.* **2** °faulty, impaired, °flawed, °imperfect, °incomplete, °defective, °inferior, °unsatisfactory: *Many have a deficient knowledge of their legal rights.*

deficit *n.* °loss, deficiency, shortfall, °shortage, °default: *At the end of the year there was a considerable deficit.*

define *v.* **1** °determine, °establish, °fix, demarcate, °mark off *or* out, delimit, °limit, °lay *or* °set down, circumscribe, °specify, °identify, delineate, °describe: *You must first define the subjects to be covered.* **2** °describe, °explain, °interpret, °spell out, °detail, °clarify, delineate, °expand on, expatiate on *or* upon; °characterize, °state, °name: *No one dictionary defines all the words of a language. Please define exactly what you want me to do.*

definite *adj.* **1** °specific, °particular, °exact, °pronounced, °explicit, °express, °precise: *She came here with a definite purpose.* **2** °sure, °positive, °certain, assured, °fixed, settled, confirmed: *Then we have a definite appointment for two o'clock?* **3** °clear, °plain, well-defined, unambiguous, unequivocal, °distinct, clear-cut, °obvious: *The plans for revision are definite.*

definitely *adv.* °positively, °absolutely, °surely, to be °sure, assuredly, certainly, indubitably, °undoubtedly, categorically, unequivocally, unquestionably, decidedly, °finally, once and for all; plainly, °clearly, °obviously, patently: *Then you're definitely not going to the dance with Waldo? That was definitely the worst movie of the year.*

definition *n.* **1** delineation, delimitation, demarcation, outlining; acutance, °resolution, distinctness, °clarity, sharpness, °focus, °precision: *The definition at the edge of the photograph is fuzzy.* **2** °description, °explanation, explication, clarification, °statement (of °meaning), °sense, °meaning: *How many definitions are there for the word 'good'?*

definitive *adj.* **1** decisive, °final, conclusive, °ultimate: *My definitive answer will be given tomorrow.* **2** °thorough, through and through, °exhaustive, °ultimate, consummate, °complete, °authoritative, °reliable: *She has written the definitive work on the axolotl.* **3** clarifying, unambiguous, °categorical, °absolute, °unqualified, °accurate, °exact, °precise: *We expect a definitive statement from the union regarding their claims.*

deflect *v.* avert, °turn away *or* aside, °deviate, °change, °swerve, °switch, °divert, °shy, veer, °sidetrack; °fend off: *The trajectory of a bullet is deflected by gravity. By deflecting a bit to their left, they managed to regain their original course.*

deformed *adj.* **1** °misshapen, malformed, distorted, twisted, °grotesque, °gnarled, °crooked, contorted, awry, warped, °bent: *This tree is deformed because of the constant wind.* **2** °disfigured, °crippled, °lame, °misshapen; °abnormal: *He was born with a deformed foot.* **3** distorted, warped, °bent, °perverted, twisted, °grotesque; °abnormal: *The deformed personalities of his patients are the subject of my book.*

defraud *v.* °cheat, °swindle, °trick, °beguile, cozen, °dupe, delude, °fool, bilk, °fleece, °victimize, °take in, °deceive, humbug, °hoodwink, flimflam, *Colloq* do, diddle, con, slip one over on, °put (something) over on, pull a fast one on, fast-talk, °rope in, *US* °take; *Slang* take for a °ride, gyp, °rob, °rip off, rook; *Dialect* flam: *Shareholders are defrauded by insider trading schemes.*

defray *v.* °pay, °settle, °meet, °discharge, liquidate, °clear, °cover, °reimburse, *Colloq* pick up the °bill *or* °tab *or US* °check (for), foot the °bill (for): *The company defrays the cost of all travelling expenses.*

defunct *adj.* **1** °dead, deceased, °extinct: *The dinosaurs have been defunct for millions of years.* **2** inoperative, °inapplicable, °unused, unusable, °invalid, expired, °obsolete, °passé, °dead, °non-existent, outmoded, °out: *Although still on the books, that law is defunct.*

defy *v.* **1** °challenge, °dare, °face, confront, °brave, °stand up to, °flout, °brazen out, °thumb one's nose at, *Colloq Brit* cock a snook at: *The defendant defied the prosecutor to prove the allegations.* **2** °frustrate, °thwart, baffle, °resist, °withstand, °repel, °disobey, °repulse: *Her feats of legerdemain defy the imagination. Copeley has invented a device that defies the law of gravity.*

degenerate *adj.* **1** debased, degraded, °corrupt, corrupted, vitiated, °decadent, depraved, °reprobate, °dissolute, ignoble, °base, °low, °inferior, °vile: *He was a degenerate descendant of a once noble lineage. Ben sank into the depths of a degenerate existence after Penelope left him.*
—*v.* **2** °decline, °deteriorate, °decay, °sink, °worsen; backslide, regress, retrogress, °weaken, go to the dogs, go to °rack and °ruin, *Colloq* go to pot: *He felt that art had degenerated since the days of Rembrandt.*
—*n.* **3** °reprobate, debauchee, °wastrel, °profligate, °rake, rakehell, °roué; °pervert, °deviate: *The detective said that only a degenerate could have committed such a crime.*

degradation *n.* **1** degeneracy, degeneration, deterioration, corruptness, corruption, vitiation, baseness, depravity, turpitude: *History records the moral degradation of a whole society.* **2** disrepute, °discredit, °shame, °humiliation, ignominy, °dishonour, °disgrace, abasement, debasement: *He had to face the degradation of an accusation of child molestation.*

degrade *v.* **1** °downgrade, demote, °break, *Military* cashier, *Ecclesiastical* unfrock, *Law* disbar; depose, unseat; disfranchise *or* disenfranchise; *Military* drum out (of the corps), *Chiefly naval* disrate; *US military* bust: *They degraded him from captain to lieutenant.* **2** °disgrace, °dishonour, °humble, °shame, °discredit, °debase, demean, abase; °humiliate, °mortify, °belittle, deprecate, °depreciate, cheapen, °reduce, °lower: *He has been degraded to mopping the floor.* **3** °dilute, °adulterate, °weaken, °thin, °water (down), °alloy: *Cologne is, essentially, degraded perfume.*

degrading *adj.* demeaning, humiliating, °shameful, shaming, debasing, lowering, discreditable: *Why should you deem selling a degrading occupation?*

degree *n.* **1** °grade, °level, °stage, °class, °caste, °rank, °order, °scale, °standing, °status, °station, °position, °situation, °estate, °condition: *He is entertaining a lady of high degree.* **2** °measure, °magnitude, °extent, °limit, °point; lengths, °step: *All our needs, desires, and goals are biologically determined to some degree.* **3** ***by degrees***: little by little, °bit by bit, °step by step, inch by inch, inchmeal, °gradually, slowly, (almost) imperceptibly: *By degrees, her health has improved.* **4** ***to a degree***: **a** °rather, °somewhat, °quite: *She is to a degree a better dancer than he.* **b** °substantially, considerably, °highly, decidedly, °exceedingly, to a °considerable °extent: *She must be stupid to a degree if she believes in levitation.*

deign *v.* °condescend, °stoop, °vouchsafe, °concede; °yield, °agree: *Lord Worthington deigned to say good morning to us.*

deity *n.* °god, goddess, Supreme Being, °creator, demiurge: *Deities in various religions are represented as men, women, or animals.*

dejected *adj.* downcast, °downhearted, depressed, dispirited, discouraged, °despondent, down, °low, chapfallen, crestfallen, °melancholy, °sad, °unhappy,

°gloomy, °glum, °miserable, °blue, low-spirited, in °low spirits, °forlorn, °woebegone, disconsolate, °sorrowful, morose, °heartbroken, heavy-hearted, in the doldrums, *Colloq* down in the dumps, down in the °mouth: *She was bound to feel dejected when she couldn't find a job.*

delay *v.* **1** °postpone, °put off *or* aside, °defer, temporize, °suspend, °shelve, °put on °hold, °hold in °abeyance, put *or* °keep in a holding pattern, pigeon-hole, put on ice, put in *or* into the deep-freeze, *Colloq* put on the back burner, *Brit* kick into touch, *US* °hold off *or* up (on), °table: *We shall delay our decision till next month.* **2** °hold up *or* back, detain, °impede, °hinder, °retard, °keep, °bog down, °set back, °slow (up *or* down); °stop, °arrest, °halt, °check; °obstruct: *Delivery of the mail has been delayed by the strike. We were delayed by traffic.* **3** loiter, °procrastinate, °hesitate, °poke *or* °drag (along), °tarry, °wait, °lag (behind), °dawdle, °hang back, °stall, °linger, dally, mark time, °potter *or US* putter; vacillate; *Colloq* dilly-dally, °shilly-shally, °drag one's feet: *Stop delaying and get to work.*
—*n.* **4** °postponement, deferral, deferment, °wait, °hold-up; °set-back: *There will be a ten-day delay in paying the rent.* **5** °lull, °interlude, hiatus, °interruption, °gap, °interval, lacuna, °stop, stoppage, °wait, waiting, °hold-up, °suspension: *After an hour's delay, service was resumed.* **6** tarrying, loitering, dawdling, *Colloq* dilly-dallying, shilly-shallying: *There should be no further delay in shipping the order.*

delectation *n.* °delight, °enjoyment, °amusement, °entertainment, °diversion, °pleasure, °satisfaction: *For your delectation, Le Moulin Rouge presents La Goulue!*

delegate *n.* **1** °envoy, °agent, legate, °representative, °ambassador, plenipotentiary, °minister, emissary, commissioner, (papal) nuncio, (papal) internuncio, spokesperson, spokesman, spokeswoman, °go-between: *They kowtowed to the delegate from His Imperial Highness.*
—*v.* **2** depute, commission, °appoint, °designate, °assign, °name, °nominate, accredit, °authorize, empower, mandate: *The president delegated Ambassador Foxley to represent him at the meeting.* **3** °assign, °give, °hand over *or* on, °pass over *or* on, depute, °transfer, °entrust, °relegate, *Colloq* °pass the buck for, *US* buck: *She has delegated the responsibility to one of the directors.*

delete *v.* °erase, °cancel, °rub *or* °cross out *or* off, °remove, °blot out, expunge, efface, °eliminate, °obliterate, °wipe out, eradicate, °strike out, °cut *or* °edit (out), *Publishing* blue-pencil; *Printing* dele: *Delete the old address and insert the new one.*

deliberate *adj.* **1** °intentional, planned, °studied, °wilful, intended, °premeditated, °calculated, °conscious, prearranged, °purposeful, °preconceived, considered; °cold-blooded: *The insult was deliberate, not a slip.* **2** °slow, °methodical, °careful, °unhurried, paced, °measured, °regular, °even, °steady, °sure, °unhesitating, unfaltering, °confident: *He moved across the room with a deliberate step and tore the medals from the general's tunic.* **3** °careful, °prudent, °cautious, °painstaking, °discreet, considered, °considerate, °thoughtful, well-thought-out, °thorough, °methodical, °systematic, °fastidious, °orderly, punctilious, °dispassionate, °cool, composed, °collected, °calm, °serene, unruffled: *A deliberate speaker, he chose his words with care.*
—*v.* **4** °consider, °ponder, °think (about *or* over), °weigh, °debate, °meditate (on *or* over), °reflect (on *or* over), cogitate (on *or* over), °study: *I shall need a few days to deliberate on that question.*

deliberately *adv.* intentionally, on °purpose, purposely, wilfully *or US* willfully, consciously, wittingly, calculatedly, calculatingly, knowingly, pointedly, resolutely, of one's (own) free °will, on one's own, with one's eyes (wide) open: *She did that deliberately, not by accident.*

delicacy *n.* **1** fineness, exquisiteness, gracefulness, °beauty, lightness, daintiness: *Notice the delicacy of the tracery in the rose window.* **2** fragility, fragileness, °frailty, frailness, °weakness, °infirmity, feebleness, tenderness; susceptibility: *Because of the delicacy of his constitution, even a cold might be fatal.* **3** °sensitivity, °difficulty, ticklishness, °finesse, nicety, °sensibility: *The delicacy of the situation demands the utmost diplomacy.* **4** °luxury, sweetmeat, °dainty, °titbit *or US* tidbit, °savoury: *The table was laden with delicacies from all over the world.*

delicate *adj.* **1** °fragile, breakable, °frail, °tender, frangible, °dainty; perishable, °flimsy: *This filament is extremely delicate, so be careful.* **2** °fine, °exquisite, °dainty, °graceful, °elegant, °subtle: *A delicate border of lace sets off the collar.* **3** °feeble, °weak, °sickly, °frail, debilitated, weakened, enfeebled, °unhealthy: *Her condition is too delicate for her to be moved.* **4** °critical, °ticklish, °sensitive, °dangerous, °tricky, °precarious, °touchy, *Slang* °hairy; *Colloq* °sticky: *Rescuing the survivors of the avalanche was a delicate operation.* **5** °dainty, °squeamish, °queasy, °fastidious, °prudish, Victorian, °finicky, finical, °refined, °discriminating, discerning, °sensitive, puristic, °proper, °coy, °modest, demure: *In those days ladies were thought to be too delicate to mention such matters.* **6** °gradual, °subtle, °nice, °precise, muted, °soft, °faint, °subdued: *The delicate shading at the horizon is characteristic of this artist.*

delicious *adj.* **1** delectable, °luscious, ambrosial, °savoury, mouth-watering, toothsome; °choice, flavourful, °tasty, appetizing, palatable, *Colloq* scrumptious; *Slang* °yummy: *Larry's fried chicken is quite delicious.* **2** enjoyable, °delightful, °pleasurable, °pleasing, °pleasant, °choice, °enchanting, fascinating; °agreeable, charming, °engaging; amusing, °entertaining: *I heard the most delicious bit of gossip about the Browns.*

delight *v.* **1** °please, °gratify, °satisfy, °gladden, °cheer, °tickle, °amuse, °entertain, °divert, °excite, °thrill, °captivate, °entrance, °fascinate: *We were delighted to hear the Mighty Allen Art Players once again.* **2** ***delight in***: °enjoy, °appreciate, °like, °relish (in), °savour, °revel in, °glory in; °love, °adore; *Colloq* get a kick from *or* out of; *Slang* °get off on: *She delights in any kind of jazz.*
—*n.* **3** °pleasure, °gratification, °joy, °satisfaction, °enjoyment, °delectation; °bliss, °ecstasy, °rapture: *She takes great delight in playing practical jokes on her guests. In his dreams he visited the garden of earthly delights.*

delighted *adj.* °pleased, °happy, °charmed, thrilled, °enchanted, *enchanté(e)*: *I am delighted to meet you. 'Miss Smith, meet Mr Brown.' 'Delighted!'*

delightful *adj.* **1** °pleasing, °agreeable, °pleasurable, enjoyable, °joyful, °pleasant, °lovely, amusing, °entertaining, diverting, °exciting, °thrilling: *We spent a delightful evening together.* **2** °attractive, congenial, °winning, winsome, charming, °engaging, °exciting; captivating, °ravishing, fascinating, °enchanting: *Georgina is one of the most delightful people I have met in a long time.*

delinquent *n.* **1** malefactor, (young *or* youthful) °offender, wrongdoer, lawbreaker, °culprit, °criminal, °miscreant; hooligan, ruffian, roughneck: *The police rounded up six juvenile delinquents and charged them with rowdyism.*
—*adj.* **2** neglectful, negligent, °derelict, °remiss, °failing, defaulting: *I have been delinquent in my obligations to my mother.* **3** °overdue, °past °due, in arrears, °late, °unpaid: *All these delinquent accounts should be collected as soon as possible.*

delirious *adj.* **1** °wild, °hysterical, distracted, °incoherent, °rambling, irrational, °raving, ranting, frenzied, °frantic, °disturbed, demented, °deranged, unhinged, °mad, °insane, °crazy, lunatic: *He is still delirious and doesn't know what he's saying.* **2** °wild, °excited, crazed, thrilled, °ecstatic: *She was delirious with joy that Ken was coming home.*

deliver *v.* **1** °carry, °bring, convey, °distribute, °give *or* °hand out; purvey, °take °round; °cart, °transport: *Only in a few places in the world do they still deliver milk to the door.* **2** °hand over, °give, °surrender, °cede, °yield, °make over, °relinquish, °give up *or* over, °commit, °transfer, °turn over, °resign: *We were forced to deliver our children to the enemy as hostages.* **3** set °free, °liberate, enfranchise, °extricate, °release, °save, °rescue; °emancipate, manumit, °redeem; disencumber, disburden, °ransom: *They were delivered from certain death by the arrival of the helicopter. Modern appliances have delivered millions of women from the drudgery of housework.* **4** °give, °present, utter, °read, °broadcast; °proclaim, °announce, °declare, °set forth, °communicate, °make known, °express, °publish, °hand over, °hand out, promulgate, °pronounce, °enunciate: *He has to deliver a speech tonight. The police delivered an ultimatum to the terrorists.* **5** °give, °administer, °inflict, °deal, °direct, °send, °launch, °impart, °throw; °cast, °hurl, °shoot, °discharge, °fire: *He delivered a blow on the chin that knocked me out. The ball was delivered with enormous speed.* **6** °bring forth, °bear, °give °birth to, °bring into the °world: *In the next three years, she delivered three more girls.* **7** °produce, °perform, put one's money where one's mouth is: *Roger had better deliver, or we shall have to take drastic measures.*

delivery *n.* **1** °distribution, delivering, deliverance, conveyance, transportation, °transport: *The strikers have caused delivery of newspapers to stop.* **2** °liberation, °release, deliverance, emancipation: *His delivery from poverty was still a few years away.* **3** childbirth, parturition; confinement: *Many women find that their second child is an easier delivery.* **4** °presentation, °performance; utterance, enunciation, articulation, °pronunciation, °expression, °execution: *He is an accomplished orator, with a spellbinding delivery.*

delusion *n.* **1** °deception, °trick, °stratagem, °artifice, °ruse, °pretence: *It was a snare and a delusion to represent the painting as genuine.* **2** °false *or* °mistaken °impression, °fallacy, °illusion, °mistake, °error, °misconception, misbelief, °hallucination: *He suffers under the delusion that he is a great pianist.*

demand *v.* **1** °require, °order, °bid, °call (for); °insist, °command: *I demand that you retract that remark! She demanded to know where he was going.* **2** °claim, °ask (for), °require, °insist on; °exact: *They had paid for tickets and demanded entrance.* **3** °require, °call for, °need, °want, necessitate, °cry out for: *This superb dish demands an excellent claret.* **4** °ask (for), °inquire *or* °enquire, °request; °requisition: *We demanded help from the police.*
—*n.* **5** °request, °bid, behest, °requisition, °order, insistence; °outcry: *Our demand for service went unheeded.* **6** °want, °need, °requirement, °desire; °market (°demand), marketability; consumer *or* °customer acceptance: *The demand for our products is low at the moment.* **7** ***in demand***: wanted, needed, requested, coveted, °popular, sought after, desired, °desirable, *Brit* in °request, *US* on °request: *Bright graduates are always in demand.* **8** ***on demand***: on °call, on °request, on °presentation, when requested *or* required; at °once, °immediately, without °delay: *These notes are payable on demand.*

demanding *adj.* **1** °difficult, °hard, exigent, °tough, °exacting, °trying, taxing: *Edwards is a demanding boss. Diamond cutting is demanding work.* **2** °insistent, clamorous, °urgent, °nagging, °persistent: *Your demanding fans want another encore.*

democratic *adj.* egalitarian, classless; republican, °representative, °popular, self-governing, autonomous: *The colonists voted for a democratic form of government.*

demolish *v.* **1** °tear *or* °pull down, dismantle, °reduce to °ruin(s), smash, °pull to °pieces, °knock down, °raze, °topple, °destroy, °level: *This building will have to be demolished to make room for the new shopping mall.* **2** °destroy, °end, bring to an °end, make an °end of, put an °end to, °devastate, °terminate, annihilate, °overturn, °overthrow, °crush, °defeat, refute, °disprove, °dispose of, °suppress, °squelch, °quash: *With just one phrase he demolished their entire argument.*

demon *n.* **1** °devil, °evil °spirit, °fiend, cacodemon; °monster, ghoul, °ogre, harpy, vampire: *Medieval demons are generally depicted as having horns, hoofs, and tails.* **2** °fanatic, °fiend, °enthusiast, °addict, *Colloq* °freak: *He's a real speed demon when he gets onto the motorway.*

demonstrable *adj.* provable, confirmable, attestable, verifiable; °evident, °self-evident, °obvious, undeniable, °apparent, °manifest, °indisputable, °unquestionable, °positive, °certain, conclusive: *The judge showed a demonstrable bias against my client.*

demonstrate *v.* **1** °show, °prove, make °evident, °establish, evince, °evidence, °exhibit, °manifest: *The increase in arrests demonstrates the efficiency of the police.* **2** °display, °explain, °expose, °describe, °present; °illustrate: *The salesman demonstrated the new camera for us.* **3** °picket, °march, °parade, °rally, °protest: *More than 5000 people demonstrated against the fraudulent election.*

demonstration *n.* **1** °proof, °evidence, °testimony, confirmation, verification, substantiation; °manifestation, °exhibition, °display, °illustration, °indication: *I have seen sufficient demonstration of her ineptitude.* **2** °presentation, °display, °show, °explanation, °description, clarification, elucidation, °exposition, *Colloq* demo: *The student gave an excellent demonstration of how a computer works.* **3** picketing, °march, °parade, °protest, °rally, sit-in, *Colloq Brit* demo: *There have been numerous demonstrations against the government's policies.*

demonstrative *adj.* **1** °open, unrestrained, unconstrained, unreserved, °expansive, °effusive, °emotional, °warm, °tender, °affectionate, loving: *Pat is quite demonstrative, often causing me to blush.* **2** illustrative, indicative, °representative, probative, evidential; provable, °evident: *Her point was proved by several demonstrative arguments. The hostility of these few is demonstrative of what to expect of the entire group.*

demoralize *v.* **1** dispirit, °daunt, dishearten, °discourage, °defeat; °weaken, °cripple, °enervate, devitalize, °depress, °subdue, °crush: *The party's crushing defeat in the election thoroughly demoralized its supporters.* **2** °corrupt, °pervert, deprave, °vitiate, °debase, debauch: *The committee consider him a demoralizing influence and insist he should resign.* **3** °bewilder, °discomfit, °unnerve, °shake (up), °confuse, °fluster, disconcert, °perturb, °disturb, °upset, *Colloq* °rattle: *The demonstrators were completely demoralized when arrested for loitering.*

denial *n.* **1** contradiction, negation, repudiation, refutation, disavowal, disclaimer, disaffirmation: *Her denials notwithstanding, she was found guilty.* **2** retraction, recantation, renunciation, withdrawal: *The arbitrary denial of civil rights to some is unconscionable.* **3** °refusal, °rejection, negation; °veto: *The boy's persistent denial of authority went into his record.*

denizen *n.* °inhabitant, dweller, °occupant, frequenter, °resident; °citizen: *The depths of the seas harbour some strange denizens. Carl is a denizen of The Bottle and Glass.*

denomination *n.* **1** °sect, °persuasion, °school, church, °order: *He is a member of the Mormon denomination.* **2** °sort, °kind, °type, °nature, °variety, °unit, °size, value; °grade, °class, genus, species, °order, classification: *The kidnappers demanded the ransom money in used notes of small denomination.* **3** designation, appellation, °name, °identification, °style, °title, °tag, °term; designating, naming, identifying, styling, classifying, titling, entitling, tagging, terming, denominating: *The denomination of people by race, creed, colour, or sex is discriminatory.*

denote *v.* **1** °indicate, °specify, °designate, °distinguish, °signify, °mark, °note: *Hypothetical linguistic* *forms are denoted by an asterisk.* **2** °mean, °name, °symbolize, °represent, betoken: *The word* mother *denotes 'female parent', but its connotations are far more extensive.*

denounce *v.* **1** °accuse, °brand, °stigmatize, °charge, °blame, °incriminate, °implicate, °complain about: *He has been denounced for the blackguard he is.* **2** °betray, °inform against, °report, °reveal: *He denounced his own son to the authorities.* **3** °criticize, °condemn, decry, denunciate, °attack, assail, censure, impugn, declaim *or* °rail (against), °vituperate, revile, °vilify, inveigh against; °ridicule, (hold up to) °shame, pillory, (heap) °scorn (upon), cast a °slur on: *The playwright was denounced as a neo-Nazi.*

dense *adj.* **1** °compact, °thick, compressed, condensed, °close, °solid, °heavy, impenetrable: *The fox escaped into a dense thicket.* **2** crowded, °packed, °tight, impenetrable, impassable: *There was a dense crowd blocking the exit.* **3** °stupid, °slow, slow-witted, thickheaded, °dull, thick-witted, °obtuse, °stolid, °dim, dim-witted, °foolish, *Colloq* °thick, °dumb: *He may be a gifted artist but he is dense when it comes to money matters.*

deny *v.* **1** °contradict, gainsay, refute, controvert, disaffirm, disclaim, confute, negate, °dispute: *She denies ever having met the defendant.* **2** °reject, °refuse, °withhold, °forbid, °turn down, °decline, disallow; °recall, °revoke, °recant: *He asserts that his right to counsel was denied.* **3** disavow, °repudiate, °renounce, disown, forswear, disclaim: *The witch-doctor demanded sacrifices, saying that the angry gods would not be denied.*

depart *v.* **1** °go, °go away *or* out *or* from *or* off, °leave, °quit, °retire (from), °retreat (from), °withdraw (from), °exit (from), °set out *or* forth *or* off, decamp, abscond, °fly, cut and °run, °skip (out), °run off *or* away *or* out, take to the road, take one's °leave, °check out, °disappear, vanish, °evaporate, *Jocular* toddle off, *Imperative* Begone!, *Colloq* °beat it, scram, shove off, make oneself scarce, *Brit* scarper, *US* hit the road, be out of (someplace), *Slang* °split, *Imperative* get lost, *US* cut (on) out, vamoose, take a (run-out) °powder, lam (on) out, take it on the lam, *Brit* do a moonlight °flit, *Usually imperative* °bugger off, °buzz off, *Taboo, imperative* fuck off: *Our bags are packed and we depart at noon.* **2** Often, ***depart from***: °deviate (from), °change, °diverge (from), °turn (aside *or* away) (from), °differ (from), °vary (from), °break away (from), °leave, °abandon, °stray (from), veer (from): *She refused to depart from established practices.*

department *n.* **1** °division, subdivision, °branch, °office, °bureau, °section, °segment, °unit, °part: *Some departments are in another building.* **2** °responsibility, °concern, °worry, °sphere, bailiwick, °jurisdiction, °domain, °control, °area *or* °sphere of °influence *or* °activity: *He was only responsible for the launch of the missiles — where they came down was not his department.*

depend *v.* **1** ***depend (on*** or ***upon)***: be contingent *or* dependent *or* conditional on, °turn on, hinge on, °pivot on, °hang on, be °subject to, °rest on, be influenced *or* °determined *or* conditioned by: *The plans for our picnic depend on the weather.* **2** ***depend on*** or ***upon***: °trust (in), °rely on, °count on, °reckon on, bank on, be °sure of, put one's °faith *or* °trust in: *I knew we could depend on you, Giles, to do the right thing.*

deplorable *adj.* **1** °lamentable, °regrettable, °sad, woeful, °grievous, °wretched, °miserable, °unfortunate, °awful, distressing, °disturbing, troubling, upsetting, °grave, °serious, °oppressive, °difficult, °desperate, °hopeless, °tragic, °disastrous: *Orphaned at six, he had a deplorable childhood.* **2** °shameful, °disgraceful, °scandalous, °disreputable, °awful, °bad, appalling, °dreadful, °abominable, execrable, °terrible, reprehensible: *What did you think of Annie's deplorable behaviour at last week's dance? That's a deplorable painting.*

deposit *v.* **1** °place, °leave, °set *or* °put *or* °lay (down), °drop, *Colloq US* plunk down: *You are requested to deposit litter in the bin.* **2** °entrust, °leave, °lodge, consign, °keep, °place, °put; °store, °save, °set aside, bank, °lay *or* °put away, *Brit* °pay in, *Colloq* stash away: *Each morning she deposits the children at the day nursery and goes to work. He deposits money every week in a pension fund.*
—*n.* **3** down °payment, part *or* partial °payment, °advance °payment: *A small deposit will hold your purchase until you are ready to pay for it in full.* **4** °precipitate, °sediment, °silt, alluvium, °dregs, lees, °accumulation, deposition: *There is a dark deposit at the bottom of the coffee-pot.*

depreciate *v.* **1** devalue, devaluate, °decrease, °diminish, lessen, °reduce, °lower, °depress, cheapen, °mark down: *The abundant harvest has depreciated the price of commodities.* **2** °disparage, °diminish, °deride, decry, underrate, undervalue, °underestimate, °minimize, °belittle, °slight, derogate, deprecate, °discredit, denigrate, °run down, vilipend, *Colloq* °play down, *US* °talk down: *When he depreciates another's work he adds nothing to the value of his own.*

depredation *n.* °plunder, plundering, °pillage, pillaging, despoliation, despoiling, ravaging, sacking, laying °waste, devastation, °destruction; ransacking, °robbery, looting; °ravages: *The depredation caused by ten years of war is unimaginable.*

depress *v.* **1** deject, dispirit, °oppress, °sadden, °grieve, °cast down, dishearten, °discourage, °dampen, °cast a °gloom *or* °pall over, °burden, °weigh down: *He's very depressed right now because he failed to get a promotion.* **2** °weaken, °dull, debilitate, °enervate, °sap; °depreciate, cheapen, devalue, devaluate; °diminish, °lower, °bring down, °reduce: *The news about a new oil field depressed the market today.* **3** °press (down), °push (down) (on), °lower: *If the pressure gets too high, just depress this lever.*

depression *n.* **1** °indentation, dent, dimple, °impression, °pit, °hollow, °recess, °cavity, concavity, °dip: *When the box fell, its corner left a small depression in the top of the metal cabinet.* **2** dejection, °despair, °gloom, downheartedness, °sadness, °melancholy, discouragement, despondency, gloominess, glumness, the blues, unhappiness; *Colloq* the dumps: *A general feeling of depression came over us at the doctor's words.* **3** °recession, °slump, (°economic) °decline, downturn, *US and Canadian* bust: *The analysts are unable to predict accurately either booms or depressions.*

deprive *v.* °withhold, °deny, °refuse; °withdraw, °remove, °strip, °dispossess, °take away, expropriate, °divest; mulct: *They deprived him of the right to have visitors.*

deprived *adj.* °needy, in °want, in °need, °impoverished, °badly off, °destitute, °poor, poverty-stricken, *Euphemistic* underprivileged, disadvantaged: *As a deprived family, they are entitled to a number of benefits.*

depth *n.* **1** deepness, °extent, °measure, °profundity, profoundness: *The depth of the cavern was at least three miles.* **2** °profundity, profoundness, abstruseness, °obscurity, reconditeness, °complexity, intricacy: *There is great depth of meaning in many proverbs.* **3** °profundity, °wisdom, sagacity, sageness, °understanding, °perception, astuteness, perspicacity, perspicaciousness, °insight, °intuition, acumen, °penetration: *One would scarcely characterize Mickey Mouse as possessed of great depth.* **4** °intensity, °profundity, °strength; vividness, °brilliance, brilliancy, brightness, richness: *It is hard for me to express the depth of my feeling for you. The depth of colour is much better in this picture.* **5** ***depths***: °deep(s), °abyss, abysm, chasm, °bowels of the earth, (°bottomless) °pit, nethermost reaches *or* regions, nadir: *As we descended into the depths the temperature increased. She is in the depths of despair and needs your moral support.* **6** ***in depth***: °thoroughly, comprehensively, in °detail, °profoundly, °deeply, extensively, intensively, concentratedly, probingly: *The specialists have looked into the problem in depth and have no answer yet.*

deputy *n.* °substitute, replacement, surrogate, °stand-in, °reserve, °proxy; °agent, °operative, °representative, °go-between, °intermediary, spokesperson, spokesman, spokeswoman, °delegate, °ambassador, °minister, emissary, °envoy, legate, (papal) nuncio; *Chiefly US* °alternate: *She excused herself from the meeting, leaving her deputy in charge.*

deranged *adj.* °mad, °insane, demented, lunatic, unhinged, °unbalanced, °berserk, °crazy, crazed, °psychotic, irrational, *non compos mentis*, out of one's °mind *or* senses *or* °head, not all there, of °unsound °mind, crack-brained, °mad as a hatter *or* March hare, off the rails, *Colloq* touched, dotty, °daft, cracked, bats, cuckoo, *Brit* potty, *US* have nobody home (upstairs), out to lunch, off-the-wall; *Slang* bonkers, dippy, barmy *or* balmy, batty, screwy, loony, nuts, nutty, wacky, bananas, off one's rocker, off one's trolley, °mental, missing a few marbles, not having all one's marbles, kooky, with a screw loose, *Chiefly Brit* off one's chump, *Chiefly US* (plumb) loco, meshuga: *Police said that the killer was completely deranged and should be approached with caution.*

derelict *adj.* **1** °deserted, °abandoned, forsaken, neglected; ruined, °dilapidated, °run-down, °tumbledown: *The council has a scheme for the renovation of derelict buildings in the inner city.* **2** negligent, °remiss, neglectful, °delinquent, dilatory, °careless, °heedless, °lax, °slack, °irresponsible, °slipshod, slovenly, *Colloq* °sloppy: *He was accused of having been derelict in his duty.*
—*n.* **3** vagrant, °tramp, °outcast, pariah, °loafer, °wastrel, °good-for-nothing, ne'er-do-well, malingerer, °vagabond, °slacker, down-and-out, *US and Canadian* hobo, *Colloq US* °bum: *Because of alcohol, he ended up as a derelict.*

deride *v.* °mock, °ridicule, °scoff (at), °jeer (at), °laugh (at), make °fun *or* °sport (of), °tease, °taunt, °twit, °poke °fun (at), make a laughing-stock (of), °sneer (at), °scorn, °flout, disdain, pooh-pooh, °belittle, °diminish, °disparage, °laugh off, *Brit* °rally, *Colloq* °knock, *Brit* take the mickey *or* micky out of: *His classmates had always derided his attempts at getting anywhere with the girls.*

derision *n.* °ridicule, °mockery, °raillery, °laughter, °sarcasm, scoffing, °contempt, °scorn, contumely, °disrespect; °satire, °lampoon, pasquinade, °burlesque, °caricature, travesty: *Her suggestion was greeted with derision.*

derisory *adj.* mocking, ridiculing, °scornful, derisive, °disdainful, °contemptuous, taunting, insulting, contumelious, jeering; °sardonic, °sarcastic, ironic(al), °satirical: *He felt crushed by their derisory laughter.*

derivation *n.* °origin, descent, °extraction, °source, °beginning, °foundation, ancestry, genealogy, etymology, °root: *The derivations of many words are unknown.*

derivative *adj.* **1** derived, borrowed, procured, obtained, acquired; unoriginal, °second-hand, copied, imitative, plagiarized, plagiaristic: *He created nothing of his own — all his compositions were highly derivative.*
—*n.* **2** °derivation, °offshoot, °development, spin-off, by-product: *French, Italian, and other Romance languages are derivatives from Latin.*

derive *v.* **1** °draw, °extract, °get, °obtain, °acquire, °procure, °receive, °secure, °gain, °elicit, °deduce, educe, °infer, °gather, °collect, °harvest, glean, cull, winnow: *I derive no pleasure from punishing you. I derived from her remark that she didn't like the play.* **2** ***derive from***: °arise from *or* out of, °originate in *or* with *or* from, °emerge from *or* out of, °come (forth) from *or* out of, °arrive from, °issue from, °proceed from, °develop from, °spring from, °flow from, °emanate from, °stem from, be traceable *or* traced to: *The word* delicate *derives from Latin. All our knowledge is derived from experience.*

derogatory *adj.* depreciatory, depreciating, depreciative, disparaging, abasing, debasing, lowering, denigrating, belittling, diminishing, demeaning, detracting, deflating, minimizing, °mitigating; uncomplimentary, °offensive, insulting: *The family took a somewhat derogatory attitude towards commerce. He said something derogatory about my wife, so I punched him.*

descend *v.* **1** °come *or* °go down, °move down, °climb down, °get down: *The sun was setting as he descended from the mountain.* **2** °decline, °incline (°downwards), °slope, °slant, °dip, °drop, °fall, °plunge, °plummet: *Beyond the curve, the road descends suddenly for a mile.* **3** °stoop, °condescend, °sink, °lower oneself: *If you start shouting, you're just descending to Basil's level.* **4** ***descend on***: °attack, °assault, invade, °pounce on *or* upon, °swoop down on *or* upon: *Fighter planes descended in droves and destroyed the base entirely.*

descendant *n.* °offspring, °progeny, °issue, °heir, °posterity, °family; °child, son, daughter, grandchild, scion; °offshoot: *They claim to be descendants of Tsar Nicholas.*

describe *v.* **1** °tell (of), °recount, °relate, give an °account (of), °narrate, °recite, °report, °chronicle; retail: *He described his adventures in Rio.* **2** °detail, °define, °explain, °specify, delineate: *Please describe exactly where you found the body.* **3** °characterize, °portray, °paint, depict, °identify, °label, °style; °represent: *I would describe her as careless rather than uncaring.* **4** °trace, °mark out, °outline, °traverse, °draw: *The trail of the comet described a perfect arc in the black sky.*

description *n.* **1** portrayal, characterization, depiction, (°thumbnail) sketch, °portrait: *Her description of her boss was far from flattering.* **2** °account, °narrative, °story, °report, °representation, °statement, °definition; °explanation, commentary; °chronicle, °history, °record, °narration; °memoir: *I want your detailed description of what led up to the argument.* **3** °sort, °kind, °nature, °character, °type, °variety, °brand, °breed, species, °category, genus, ilk, °genre, °class; °stripe, kidney, feather: *Carstairs is a roué of the worst description.*

desecrate *v.* °profane, defile, °blaspheme (against), °dishonour, °degrade, °debase, befoul, °contaminate, °pollute, °corrupt, °violate, °pervert, °vitiate: *Vandals desecrated the temple of Minerva.*

desert[1] *n.* **1** °waste, wilderness, wasteland, dust bowl: *The nearest oasis was fifty miles away across the desert.*
—*adj.* **2** °barren, °desolate, °uninhabited, unpeopled, °lonely, °deserted; arid, °bare, °vacant, °empty, °wild, uncultivated: *I was marooned on a desert island.*
—*v.* **3** °forsake, °leave, °abandon; °jilt, °throw over; °maroon, strand, °leave to twist (slowly) in the wind; *Colloq* °run *or* °walk out on, °leave flat *or* in the °lurch, leave high and dry: *His courage deserted him when he saw the child's eyes. He has deserted his wife for some floozie.* **4** abscond, °quit, °run away (from), °defect, °abandon; *Military slang* go over the hill: *He deserted and will be court-martialled.*

desert[2] *n.* Often, ***deserts***: °payment, recompense, °requital, compensation, °due, °right; °retribution, °justice, *Slang* comeuppance, what's coming to one: *She'll get her just deserts one of these days.*

deserted *adj.* °abandoned, °desolate, forsaken, neglected, °uninhabited, unpeopled, °vacant, vacated, unfrequented, unvisited, unoccupied, °empty; stranded, rejected, God-forsaken, °isolated, °solitary, °lonely, friendless: *At that hour the streets are completely deserted.*

deserter *n.* °runaway, °fugitive, escapee, absconder, °defector, °renegade, °outlaw; °traitor, °turncoat, *Colloq* rat: *Deserters are shot when caught.*

deserve *v.* °merit, °earn, be entitled to, be °worthy of, °rate, °warrant, °justify: *You ought to be nicer to him — he really doesn't deserve such unkind treatment.*

deserved *adj.* merited, earned, °just, °rightful, °suitable, °fitting, °fit, °appropriate, °proper, °right, °fair,

°equitable, °meet, warranted, condign: *Carla was never given her deserved credit for catching the thief.*

deserving *adj.* °meritorious, °worthy, merited, commendable, °laudable, °praiseworthy, creditable, °estimable: *Perhaps you should leave your money to a deserving charity.*

design *v.* **1** °plan, °draw up, °think of, °conceive of, °contemplate, °devise, °lay out, visualize, °envisage, °envision, sketch (out), °pattern, °set up: *The building was originally designed as the centre-piece for a whole new development.* **2** °plan, sketch (out), delineate, °outline, °draft, °work *or* map *or* °block out, °lay out, °devise, °invent, contrive, °create, °conceive, °originate, °think up, °develop, °organize, °frame, °shape, °mould, °forge, °make, °construct, °form, °fashion: *John Smithers has designed a new sales strategy for the company.* **3** sketch, °draft, °lay out, °draw; °form, °devise: *Who designed the company's new logo?* **4** °intend, °mean, °plan; °purpose, °destine; °scheme, °plot: *The building was originally designed to be a school. The book was designed for children.*
—*n.* **5** °plan, °scheme, °conception, °study, °project, °proposal, °undertaking, °enterprise; blueprint, °pattern, °chart, diagram, layout, map, °drawing, °draft, sketch, °model, °prototype: *The grand design for rebuilding the city was not approved.* **6** °form, °shape, configuration, °pattern, °style, °motif, °format, layout, °make-up, delineation, °arrangement, °organization, °composition, °structure, construction: *I don't much care for her new design of my monogram.* **7** °aim, °purpose, °intention, °objective, °object, °goal, °point, °target, °intent: *My design had been to go at once to London.* **8** ***designs***: °plot, °intrigue, °stratagem, °cabal, °conspiracy, conniving, manipulation, connivance, °evil °intent *or* °intentions: *His designs against me have borne bitter fruit.*

designate *v.* **1** °indicate, °specify, pinpoint, particularize, delineate, °point out, °identify, °state, °set forth, °write *or* °put down, °name: *You should designate your heirs in your will.* **2** °appoint, °nominate, °name, °identify, denominate, °select, °pick, °choose, °elect, °assign, °appropriate, °delegate, depute: *She has not yet designated her successor.* **3** °mean, °stand for, °symbolize, °denote, °represent: *The Greek letter* pi *designates the ratio of the circumference of a circle to its diameter.* **4** °call, °name, °style, °term, °label, °christen, dub, °nickname, °entitle: *Elvis was publicly designated 'The King of Rock 'n' Roll'.*

designer *n.* **1** °creator, originator, architect, artificer, °author, deviser, inventor; (°interior) decorator, artist; draughtsman: *Raymond Loewy was a designer of locomotives and fountain pens. Lady Mendl was the best-known interior designer of the 1920s.* **2** intriguer, schemer, conniver, plotter, conspirator: *He is a cunning designer who has wormed his way into favour with the management.*

designing *adj.* °scheming, plotting, conniving, conspiring, intriguing, °calculating, °wily, °tricky, cunning, °sly, underhand(ed), °crafty, °artful, °shrewd, Machiavellian, guileful, °deceitful, double-dealing, °devious, treacherous, *Colloq* °crooked: *The prince has fallen prey to designing courtiers.*

desirable *adj.* **1** sought-after, wanted, coveted, longed-for, looked-for, desired: *Few things are more desirable than security in old age.* **2** °attractive, °pleasant, °pleasing, °agreeable, °winning, winsome, captivating, °seductive, alluring, °fetching: *Their daughter had grown up into a most desirable young lady.* **3** °good, °goodly, °excellent, °choice, °fine, °superior, °superb, *Colloq Brit* plummy: *The company has produced some very desirable motor cars.* **4** °profitable, °worthwhile, °beneficial, °advantageous, valuable, °worthy, °estimable, commendable, °admirable: *Lady Chelm's plan possesses many desirable attributes.*

desire *v.* **1** crave, °want, °fancy, covet, °wish for, °hope for, °long *or* °yearn for, pine *or* °sigh for, °hanker after, have an °eye *or* °taste for, °hunger *or* °thirst for *or* after, °die for, have one's heart set on, give one's eye-teeth for, *Colloq* have a yen for, *Slang US* have the hots for: *I desire nothing but your happiness. He desired her more than anything else in the world.* **2** °ask for, °request, °order, °demand, °solicit, importune, °summon, °require: *Do you desire anything further, sir?*
—*n.* **3** °longing, craving, yearning, hankering, °hunger, °thirst, °appetite; °passion, °lust, libido, lustfulness, concupiscence, lecherousness, lechery, lasciviousness, salaciousness, prurience, *Slang* °hot pants, *US* the hots; *Colloq* yen: *He felt desire rising in him like a fever.* **4** °wish, °request, °urge, °requirement, °order, °requisition, °demand, desideratum; °appeal, entreaty, °petition: *He fulfils her every desire.*

desirous *adj.* wishful, desiring, °longing, yearning, °hopeful, hoping: *I was desirous to learn more about his whereabouts.*

desolate *adj.* **1** °solitary, °lonely, °isolated, °deserted, °forlorn, forsaken, friendless, °alone, °abandoned, neglected; °desert, °uninhabited, °empty, unfrequented, °bare, °barren, °bleak, °remote: *He felt desolate after his wife's death. Tristan da Cunha is a group of four desolate islands in the Atlantic.* **2** laid °waste, ruined, devastated, ravaged, destroyed: *The explosion left the surrounding countryside desolate.* **3** °dreary, °dismal, °wretched, °joyless, cheerless, comfortless, °miserable, °unhappy, down, disconsolate, °sad, °melancholy, °sorrowful, °forlorn, °mournful, °woebegone, °gloomy, °broken-hearted, heavy-hearted, °inconsolable, °dejected, downcast, °downhearted, dispirited, low-spirited, depressed, °melancholy, spiritless, °despondent, distressed, discouraged, °hopeless: *He has brought some happiness into her desolate existence.*
—*v.* **4** depopulate: *The country was desolated by famine.* **5** °destroy, °devastate, °ruin, lay °waste, despoil, °ravage, °demolish, °obliterate, annihilate, °raze, °gut: *Invaders desolated the countryside.* **6** °dismay, dishearten, °depress, °daunt, dispirit, °sadden, deject, °discourage: *He was either buoyed up by renewed hope or desolated by despair.*

desolation *n.* **1** °destruction, °ruin, devastation, °waste, spoliation, despoliation, °sack, °depredation, extirpation, obliteration, ravagement, barrenness, °havoc, °chaos: *We had to shape a new life from the desolation left by the war.* **2** °grief, °sorrow, dreariness, °despair, °gloom, °distress, °melancholy, °sadness, °misery, °woe, °anguish, wretchedness, dolour, dolefulness, unhappiness: *She felt the desolation of loneliness after her husband's death.*

despair *n.* **1** hopelessness, °desperation, discouragement, disheartenment, despondency, dejection, °depression, °gloom, gloominess, °misery, °melancholy, wretchedness, °distress, miserableness, °anguish; °resignation: *The despair of the prisoners was evident in their ravaged faces.*
—*v.* **2** °give up *or* lose °hope; °surrender, °quit: *We despaired of ever seeing our children again.*

desperate *adj.* **1** °reckless, °foolhardy, °rash, °impetuous, °frantic, frenzied, °panic-stricken: *Desperate measures are required in such a desperate situation.* **2** °careless, °hasty, devil-may-care, °wild, °mad, frenetic, °furious: *They made a last desperate attack on the fort.* **3** °anxious (for), craving, °hungry (for), °thirsty (for), needful (of), °desirous (of), covetous (of), °eager (for), °longing *or* yearning (for), wishing (for), hoping (for), aching (for), pining (for): *She is desperate for attention.* **4** °urgent, °pressing, compelling, °serious, °grave, °acute, °critical, °crucial, °great: *There is a desperate need for medicines at the disaster site.* **5** °precarious, °perilous, life-threatening, °hazardous, °dangerous, °tenuous, °hopeless, beyond hope *or* help: *Avalanches are making the climbers' situation even more desperate.* **6** at one's wits' °end, °forlorn, despairing, °despondent, °wretched, at the °end of one's tether, °frantic: *With no one to turn to for help, he was truly desperate.*

desperation *n.* **1** recklessness, impetuosity, rashness, foolhardiness, imprudence, heedlessness: *Penniless and half-starved, he was driven to desperation and stole a loaf of bread.* **2** °despair, °anxiety,

°anguish, anxiousness, despondency, °depression, dejection, discouragement, defeatism, pessimism, hopelessness, °distress, °misery, °melancholy, wretchedness, °gloom, °sorrow: *In a final act of desperation, he attempted suicide.*

despicable *adj.* °contemptible, below *or* beneath *or* beyond °contempt *or* °scorn *or* disdain, °mean, detestable, °base, °low, °scurvy, °vile, °sordid, °wretched, °miserable, ignoble, ignominious, °shabby; °shameful, °shameless, reprehensible: *He is a thoroughly despicable person and you should have nothing more to do with him.*

despise *v.* disdain, °scorn, °look down on *or* upon, be °contemptuous of, °sneer at, °spurn, contemn; °hate, °loathe, °detest, °abhor: *She despised her servants and treated them badly. He despised anyone who had not been to university.*

despite *prep.* in °spite of, °notwithstanding, undeterred by, °regardless of, in the °face *or* teeth of, in defiance of, without °considering, without °thought *or* °consideration *or* °regard for, ignoring: *We went sailing despite the fact that gales had been forecast.*

despondent *adj.* °dejected, °sad, °sorrowful, °unhappy, °melancholy, °blue, depressed, down, downcast, °downhearted, °low, morose, °miserable, disheartened, discouraged, dispirited, low-spirited, down in the °mouth, *Colloq* down in the dumps: *He's been despondent since she went away.*

despot *n.* °absolute ruler, °dictator, °tyrant, °oppressor, autocrat: *History has painted Ivan the Terrible as one of the cruellest despots of all time.*

despotic *adj.* °dictatorial, °tyrannical, °oppressive, °authoritarian, imperious, °domineering, °totalitarian, °absolute, autocratic, °arbitrary: *The country was under the despotic rule of a callous tyrant.*

despotism *n.* autocracy, monocracy, autarchy, totalitarianism, absolutism, dictatorship, °tyranny, °oppression, °suppression, °repression: *She denounced the new laws as another instance of the brutal despotism of the regime.*

dessert *n.* °sweet, *Brit* pudding, *Colloq Brit* pud, afters: *For dessert, I had ice-cream and she had a fruit tart.*

destination *n.* journey's °end, terminus, °stop, stopping-place; °goal, °end, °objective, °target: *Our destination is Bristol.*

destine *v.* **1** °fate, predetermine, predestine, ordain, foreordain, preordain; °doom: *His only ambition was to be a successful farmer, but the gods destined him for greater things.* **2** °design, °intend, °mean, °devote, °assign, °appoint, °designate, °purpose, °mark, earmark, °set aside: *He beheld the chariot destined to carry him heavenwards.*

destined *adj.* **1** meant, intended, designed, °predetermined, foreordained, predestined, °fated; °doomed, written; *US* in *or* on the cards: *His destined end was to be shot while escaping. Oliver was destined to fail at everything he tried. It was destined that the boy would become king.* **2** °certain, °sure, °bound, ineluctable, °unavoidable, °inevitable, inescapable: *Being devoured by monsters is the destined demise of all who dare to enter there.*

destiny *n.* °fate, °doom, °fortune, °lot, kismet, karma: *It is my destiny to be ignored when living and forgotten when dead.*

destitute *adj.* **1** in °want, °impoverished, poverty-stricken, °poor, °indigent, down and out, °needy, on one's uppers, °badly off, penniless, °penurious, impecunious, °insolvent, bankrupt, *Colloq* °hard up, °broke, *US* on skid row: *Why distribute food to destitute families only at Christmas?* **2** Usually, ***destitute of***: bereft of, °deficient in, °deprived of, devoid of, lacking (in), °wanting (in), in °need, needful (of), without: *The landscape was entirely destitute of trees.*

destroy *v.* **1** °demolish, °tear *or* °pull down, °raze, °wipe out, °ravage, °wreck, smash, °ruin, °break up *or* down, annihilate, °crush, eradicate, extirpate, °exterminate, °devastate, commit °mayhem, lay °waste, vandalize, *Slang US* °trash: *The invading hordes destroyed everything, leaving desolation in their wake. The storm destroyed fifty houses.* **2** °ruin, do away with, °end, make an °end of, bring to an °end, bring *or* put an °end to, °terminate, °finish, °kill: *Realizing what he had done, he destroyed himself. The trial destroyed his career.* **3** °counteract, °neutralize, nullify, annul, °cancel (out), °reverse; °stop, °interfere with: *Caught embezzling, Martin destroyed everything he had worked for. Sunspot activity destroyed radio transmission this week.* **4** °disprove, refute, confute, °deny, °contradict, negate, °overturn, °overthrow, °ruin, °spoil, °undermine, °weaken, enfeeble, devitalize, °exhaust, disable, °cripple: *By pointing out just one flaw, she destroyed his entire argument.*

destruction *n.* **1** demolition, razing, wrecking, °ruin, ruining, ruination, breaking up *or* down, °mayhem, °havoc, annihilation, devastation, tearing *or* knocking down, laying °waste, ravagement; rack and °ruin, *Colloq* wiping out: *The destruction of the city took place in 1942.* **2** °slaughter, annihilation, °killing, eradication, °murder, extermination, °holocaust, liquidation, °massacre, extinction, genocide, assassination, slaying, putting to °death, putting an °end to, making an °end of, doing away with, putting away, *Colloq* doing in, wiping out; *Slang US* rubbing out, rub-out: *They were bent on the destruction of an entire people.* **3** °undoing, °end, °ruin, ruination, °downfall, °termination, breakup, °breakdown, °collapse: *The imprisonment of the bosses spelt the destruction of the entire crime network.*

destructive *adj.* **1** °harmful, °injurious, baneful, pernicious, °dangerous, °hurtful, toxic, °poisonous, °virulent, noxious, °bad, °malignant, baleful, °unwholesome, damaging, °detrimental, deleterious, °devastating; °deadly, °fatal, °lethal, °fell, °killing, internecine: *The spray keeps away insects but is destructive of the plant life.* **2** °negative, adverse, °opposing, °opposed, °contrary, °contradictory, antithetical, conflicting, unfavourable, condemnatory, °derogatory, disparaging, disapproving, °critical: *The playwrights feared and disliked him because of his destructive criticism.*

desultory *adj.* shifting, °devious, unsteady, °irregular, wavering, °inconstant, °fitful, °spasmodic, unmethodical, °disconnected, unsystematic, °disorderly, disordered, unorganized, disorganized, °inconsistent, °random, °haphazard, °chaotic, °erratic, °shifty: *He made no more than a desultory effort to stop smoking. The countries engaged in intermittent, desultory warfare for decades.*

detach *v.* °separate, uncouple, °part, disjoin, °disengage, disunite, °disconnect, disentangle, °free, unfasten, °undo, °cut off, °remove: *She carefully detached the printer lead from the back of the computer.*

detached *adj.* **1** °disconnected, °unattached, °separate(d), °free, °isolated, disentangled, unfastened, removed, °cut off, divided, disjoined: *He suffered from a detached retina. Their new house is detached.* **2** °disinterested, °aloof, uninvolved, unemotional, °dispassionate, *dégagé(e)*, °reserved, °impersonal, °impartial, °neutral, °objective, unbiased, °unprejudiced: *She seemed rather detached and did not get involved in the discussion.*

detachment *n.* **1** separating, unfastening, disconnecting, detaching, disengaging; °separation, disconnection, disengagement: *Most young birds cannot survive a prolonged period of detachment from their parents.* **2** aloofness, unconcern, °indifference, coolness, inattention, insouciance: *He viewed the carnage of the battle with regal detachment.* **3** See **detail, 3,** below.

detail *n.* **1** °particular, °element, °factor, °point, °fact, °specific, technicality, component, °item, °feature; °aspect, °respect, °count: *He gave us a general idea of the plan but not a single detail.* **2** ***details***: °particulars, minutiae, niceties, °fine °points, specifics, technicalities: *Must we go into all the details of his dismissal?* **3** °detachment, °squad, °party, cadre, °duty, °fatigue,

°group: *The sergeant appointed a detail to police the area.* **4** ***in detail***: specifically, °particularly, °thoroughly, in °depth, °item by °item, °point by °point, exhaustively, comprehensively, °inside out, °perfectly: *We examined the report in detail.*
—*v.* **5** °specify, °spell out, °itemize, delineate, catalogue, °list, °tabulate, °enumerate, particularize, °recount, cite (chapter and verse): *She detailed every little move I was to make.* **6** °assign, °appoint, °charge, °delegate, °name, °specify, °send: *We have been detailed to act as your bodyguard during your visit.*

detailed *adj.* **1** itemized, °exhaustive, °comprehensive, °thorough, °full, °complete, °inclusive, particularized, °precise, °exact, °minute, blow-by-blow, °circumstantial: *He kept a detailed report of everything that happened on D-Day.* **2** °intricate, complex, °complicated, °elaborate, °ornate: *Note the detailed scroll-work on this screen.*

detect *v.* **1** uncover, °find (out), °discover, °locate, °learn of, ascertain, °determine, °dig up, °unearth: *The pathologist detected the presence of prussic acid in the victim's bloodstream.* **2** °perceive, °note, °notice, °identify, °spot, °observe, °sense, °read, °scent, °smell, discern, °feel, catch, °find: *Did I detect a tone of sarcasm in your reply, young man?*

detective *n.* investigator, private investigator, CID man, policeman, °constable, *Colloq* private eye, °sleuth, Sherlock, °snoop, snooper, *Brit* tec, *US* P.I., dick, hawkshaw; *Slang* cop, copper, *US and Canadian* gumshoe, peeper: *Detectives have at last solved the case of the missing weapon.*

detention *n.* °custody, confinement, °imprisonment, °captivity, internment, incarceration, °restraint, *Archaic or literary* durance: *The culprit was kept in detention for a week.*

deter *v.* dissuade, °discourage, °inhibit, °intimidate, °daunt, °frighten off *or* from *or* away, °scare off *or* from; °prevent, °stop, °obstruct, °check, °hinder, °impede: *I was deterred from entering by three large dogs. Regular spraying of plants helps to deter aphid infestation.*

detergent *n.* **1** cleaner, cleanser, soap (powder *or* flakes *or* liquid); surfactant, surface-active agent, detersive: *You put too much detergent into the washing machine and it overflowed.*
—*adj.* **2** cleaning, cleansing, washing, purifying, detersive: *The detergent effect is reduced if too much soap is used.*

deteriorate *v.* **1** °worsen, °decline, °degenerate, °degrade, °spoil, get worse, °depreciate, °slip, °slide, *Colloq* °go to pot, °go to the dogs, °go downhill: *We have watched their relationship deteriorate over the years.* **2** °decay, °decline, °disintegrate, °fall apart, °decompose, °crumble, °erode: *The building slowly deteriorated and is now uninhabitable.*

determination *n.* **1** resoluteness, °resolution, firmness, °resolve, steadfastness, °tenacity, °perseverance, °fortitude, doggedness, °persistence, constancy, single-mindedness, °will(-power), *Colloq* °grit, guts: *The idea is a good one, if only she has the determination to see it through.* **2** °settlement, °resolution, resolving, °decision, °solution, °judgement, verdict, °outcome, °result, °upshot, conclusion, °end, °termination: *None of us could live in peace till the determination of the border dispute.* **3** fixing, settling, ascertainment, ascertaining, delimitation, °definition: *The determination of our position is critical in setting our course.*

determine *v.* **1** °settle, °decide, °clinch, arbitrate, °judge, adjudge, conclude, °terminate, °end: *The ambiguity must be determined one way or the other.* **2** ascertain, °find out, °discover, conclude, °infer, °draw, °learn, °detect; °verify: *From the evidence, they determined the identity of the intruder.* **3** °decide, °choose, °select, °resolve, make up one's °mind, °settle on *or* upon, °fix on *or* upon: *You alone can determine which candidate you want to vote for.* **4** °affect, °influence, °act on, °shape, °condition, °govern, °regulate, °dictate: *There were many factors determining my choice.*

determined *adj.* **1** °decided, °resolute, resolved, °purposeful, dogged, strong-willed, °strong-minded, °single-minded, °tenacious, °intent, °firm, unflinching, unwavering, °fixed, °constant, °persistent, persevering, °steady, unfaltering, °unhesitating, unyielding, °stubborn, °obstinate, adamant: *He was determined not to go. We made a determined effort to locate the wreck.* **2** °fixed, determinate, °definite, °exact, °precise, °distinct, °predetermined, ascertained, identified: *They worked to a previously determined plan. They agreed to pay a percentage of the determined price.*

deterrent *n.* °hindrance, °impediment, discouragement, disincentive, dissuasion, °check, °hitch, °obstacle, °obstruction, °stumbling-block; °catch, °snag, °rub, °fly in the ointment, °bar, °drawback: *Some experts hold that the death penalty is no deterrent to murder. The only deterrent to your plan is that we are likely to be caught.*

detest *v.* °despise, °loathe, °hate, °abhor, execrate, abominate: *They served turnips, which I detest, and sat me next to Ida, whom I also detest.*

detour *n.* **1** °diversion, deviation, circuitous °route *or* °way, °roundabout °way, °bypass: *The detour took us five miles out of our way.*
—*v.* **2** °deviate, °turn (away) from, °divert, °bypass: *I detoured from the main road and took a short cut.*

detract *v.* ***detract from***: °diminish, °reduce, °take away from, °subtract from, lessen, °depreciate, °disparage: *Once you are in the public eye, your slightest fault detracts from your reputation.*

detriment *n.* °disadvantage, °drawback, °liability; °damage, °harm, °ill, °impairment, °injury, °hurt, °loss: *He has a tendency to support lost causes, to his own detriment. Seeds survive without detriment where their plants would perish.*

detrimental *adj.* disadvantageous, °harmful, °injurious, °hurtful, damaging, deleterious, °destructive, °prejudicial, adverse, unfavourable, inimical, pernicious: *I know nothing detrimental about either one of them.*

devastate *v.* **1** lay °waste, °ravage, °destroy, °waste, °sack, °raze, °ruin, °desolate, °spoil, °wreck, °demolish, °level, °flatten, °gut, °obliterate: *The island was completely devastated by the tidal wave that followed the typhoon.* **2** disconcert, confound, °discomfit, take aback, °nonplus, °shatter, °overwhelm, abash, °shock; °humiliate, °mortify, °embarrass, chagrin, *Colloq* °floor, *US* discombobulate: *She was devastated by the news of Bertie's expulsion from college.*

devastating *adj.* **1** °keen, °incisive, mordant, °penetrating, °trenchant, °telling; °sardonic, °sarcastic, °bitter, acid, °caustic, °savage, °satirical, °virulent, vitriolic: *Because of his bland manner, his devastating wit often caught people by surprise.* **2** °ravishing, captivating, °enthralling, °stunning, °overpowering, bewitching, °spellbinding; spectacular: *Kathy was wearing a devastating black silk dress.*

develop *v.* **1** °bring out *or* forth, °advance, °expand (on *or* upon), broaden, °enlarge (on *or* upon), °amplify, evolve, expatiate (on *or* upon), °elaborate (on *or* upon), °reveal, lay °open, °expose, °unfold, °disclose, °bare, (°cause to) °grow, °realize the °potential (of); °cultivate, °improve, °promote, °exploit, °strengthen: *The plot is fine, but the characters need to be developed more fully. It is the aim of the school to develop the students' natural abilities.* **2** (make) °grow, °mature, °ripen, °age, °expand; °flower, blossom, bloom, °increase: *You can't develop that idea without financial backing. These shrubs will be fully developed next year.* **3** °exhibit, °display, °show, °demonstrate, °manifest: *She has recently developed an interest in cooking.* **4** °emerge, °arise, °appear, °come out, °come to °light, evolve, °originate, °begin, °commence, °happen, °occur, °come about; °come forth, °result: *A serious fault has developed in the rocket's fuel line. His natural* *talent for music developed when he joined the school band.*

development *n.* **1** °occurrence, °happening, °event, °incident, °circumstance, °situation, °condition, °phenomenon: *William Nye will report new developments from the scene.* **2** °evolution, °growth, evolvement, maturation, unfolding, maturing, °maturity, °increase, °expansion, enlargement, °increment; °advance, advancement, °progress; °improvement: *She has studied the region's economic development.*

deviant *adj.* **1** deviating, °divergent, °different, °abnormal, °strange, uncommon, °unusual, °odd, °peculiar, °curious, aberrant, °eccentric, idiosyncratic, °deviate, °queer, quirky, °weird, °bizarre, °offbeat, °singular, *Slang* °kinky, freaky, *Chiefly Brit* °bent: *They have been observing his deviant behaviour for some time.* **2** See **homosexual, 2,** below.
—*n.* **3** See **homosexual, 1,** below.

deviate *v.* **1** °turn aside *or* away, °swerve, veer, °wander, °stray, °drift, digress, °diverge; °divert: *He has chosen a path that deviates from the straight and narrow.*
—*adj., n.* **2** See **deviant, 1, 3,** above.

device *n.* **1** contrivance, °mechanism, °machine, machinery, °implement, utensil, °apparatus, °instrument, appliance, °tool, °gadget, °gimmick, *Colloq* °contraption, widget, thingumajig *or* thingamajig, *Brit* gubbins: *She has patented a device for peeling hard-boiled eggs.* **2** °stratagem, °scheme, °trick, °artifice, °ruse, °plot, ploy, gambit, °strategy, °manoeuvre, °machination; machinery, °apparatus, °mechanism, contrivance, °gimmick, °tool, weapon: *They resorted to a variety of devices in order to achieve their ends. That lawyer used every device he could think of to separate Cornelia from her inheritance.* **3** °design, °emblem, °figure, (heraldic) °bearing, insigne, cadency °mark, °mark of cadency, °hallmark, trade °mark, °symbol, badge, coat of arms, °seal, °crest, colophon, logotype, logo, monogram, °charge, °cognizance, signet; °motto, °slogan, °legend: *The family silver bore their device, a lion rampant.* **4** ***devices***: °pleasure, °disposition, °will, °inclination, °fancy, °desire, whim: *Left to his own devices, he'll survive very well indeed.*

devil *n.* **1** Satan, Lucifer, Mephistopheles, Beelzebub, Asmodeus, Abaddon, Apollyon, Belial, Lord of the Flies, prince of darkness, °spirit of °evil, °evil °spirit, cacodemon, °evil one, °wicked one, archfiend, Fiend, deuce, *Scots* Clootie; *Colloq* Old Harry, (Old) Nick, *US* (Old) Scratch: *In medieval times the devil was given horns, a tail, and cloven hooves.* **2** °brute, °fiend, °demon, °beast, °ogre, °monster, °rogue, °scoundrel, °rake, knave, rakehell, °villain, ghoul, hell-hound, vampire, °barbarian; °witch, hell-cat, °shrew, termagant, vixen, virago, ogress, harpy, °hag, Xanthippe *or* Xantippe, crone: *If you hit me again I'll phone the police, you devil!* **3** °fellow, °person, °chap, °wretch, bloke, °guy, °beggar, °unfortunate, *Colloq* °bugger, *Brit* sod: *The poor devil lost an arm at Gallipoli.* **4** °imp, scamp, °rascal, fox, slyboots, °sly dog, rapscallion, confidence man, trickster, *Colloq* °operator, smoothie, °smooth *or* °slick °operator, con man, con artist: *The little devil has stolen our hearts. The devil wormed his way into our confidence and then made off with our money.* **5** ***like the devil***: °exceedingly, °extremely, excessively, violently, speedily, confoundedly, deucedly: *The car was going like the devil when it hit the tree. She fought like the devil to protect the house.* **6** — ***the devil***: in heaven's name, the dickens, in the °world, on God's green earth, in °hell: *What the devil do you think you are doing? Who the devil is she? Where the devil have you put my trousers?*

devilish *adj.* °diabolic(al), °satanic, Mephistophelian, °fiendish, demonic, cacodemonic, demoniac(al), °infernal, hellish, °villainous, °sinister, °wicked, °evil, iniquitous, °sinful, flagitious, heinous, malign, malevolent, °malignant, °cruel, maleficent; impish, °mischievous, prankish, °naughty, °crazy, madcap: *He has come up with a devilish plan for stealing the secret formula.*

devilry *n.* **1** deviltry, °mischief, mischievousness, roguery, naughtiness, rascality, roguishness, diablerie, archness, knavery, knavishness: *His latest bit of devilry is hiding father's bedroom slippers.* **2** deviltry, devilishness, wickedness, °evil, fiendishness, diablerie, cruelty, malice, malevolence, viciousness, perversity, iniquity, hellishness, villainy: *That traitor is up to some devilry.*

devious *adj.* **1** °deceitful, underhand(ed), °insincere, °deceptive, misleading, subreptitious, °sneaky, °furtive, °surreptitious, °secretive, double-dealing, treacherous, °dishonest, °shifty, °smooth, °slick, °slippery, °scheming, plotting, °designing, °foxy, vulpine, °wily, °sly, °crafty, °tricky, *Colloq* °crooked: *The plot to poison the queen was the product of a devious mind.* **2** °indirect, °roundabout, zigzag, °evasive, circuitous, °crooked, °rambling, °serpentine, °tortuous, sinuous, anfractuous: *That is about the most devious bit of reasoning I have ever heard!*

devise *v.* **1** concoct, °make up, °conceive, °scheme, contrive, °dream up, °design, °draft, °frame, °form, °formulate, °plan, °arrange, °work out, °think up, °originate, °invent, °create, *Colloq* cook up: *He devised a method for making sandals out of leather scraps.* **2** °bequeath, °will, convey, °hand down, °give, °assign, °dispose of, °transfer, °bestow: *I devise to my nephew, Ian Ferguson, my property in Yorkshire.*

devote *v.* **1** °apply, °appropriate, °assign, °allot, °commit, allocate, °set aside *or* °apart, °put away *or* aside, °dedicate, consecrate: *Each of the chapels was devoted to a separate sect.* **2** °apply, °pledge, °dedicate, °commit, °give up: *She has devoted her life to helping others.*

devoted *adj.* °faithful, °true, dedicated, committed, °devout, °loyal, loving, doting, °staunch, °tender, °steadfast, °constant; °ardent, caring, °fond, °earnest, zealous, °enthusiastic: *Your brother was my most devoted friend throughout his life.*

devotee *n.* °fan, aficionado, adherent, votary, °enthusiast, °addict, *Colloq* buff, °fiend, *US* hound; *Slang* °bug, nut, °freak, *US* head, junkie, groupie: *The band was followed about on tour by scores of screaming devotees of rock music.*

devotion *n.* **1** devotedness, devoutness, °reverence; earnestness, religiousness, °piety, religiosity, pietism, godliness, holiness, spirituality, °sanctity; °worship, °prayer, °observance, °ritual: *The sect was noted for its devotion to martyrs and their relics. It is gratifying to see such devotion amongst the younger members of the congregation. They interrupted the holy man at his devotions.* **2** °dedication, consecration, °attachment, °loyalty, devotedness: *His devotion to duty will be remembered by his fellow soldiers.* **3** zeal, °ardour, °fervour, ardency, °intensity, °fanaticism, °eagerness, °enthusiasm, earnestness, °readiness, willingness; °love, °passion, infatuation, fondness, °affection, °attachment, adherence, °loyalty, allegiance: *They would dedicate themselves with slavish devotion to some brutal master.*

devour *v.* **1** wolf (down), °gulp (down), °bolt, °swallow (up), °gorge, gobble (up), gormandize, °cram, °stuff, °eat (up) greedily, *Archaic* gluttonize; *Colloq Brit* pig, *US and Canadian* pig out (on): *He was so hungry when he came in that he devoured two whole pies and a plate of chips.* **2** °consume, °waste, °destroy, °wipe out, °ravage, annihilate, °demolish, °ruin, wreak °havoc (up)on, °devastate, °obliterate, eradicate: *A quarter of Europe was already devoured by the plague.* **3** °relish, °revel in, absorb, be °absorbed by; engulf, °consume, °drink in, °eat up, °swallow up, °take in; °swamp, °overcome, °overwhelm: *He eagerly devoured all of Dickens's novels. The sea devoured its victims silently.*

devout *adj.* **1** °devoted, °pious, °religious, reverent, worshipful, °faithful, dedicated, °staunch, churchgoing; °holy, °godly, °saintly, °pure: *When I last saw him, he had become a devout Christian.* **2** devotional, reverential, °religious, °solemn: *Through devout prayer one might see the kingdom of heaven.* **3** °earnest,

°sincere, °genuine, °hearty, °heartfelt, °devoted, °ardent, zealous: *You have my devout best wishes for your happiness.*

dexterity *n.* **1** °touch, nimbleness, adroitness, deftness, °facility, °knack, °skill, °proficiency; sleight of hand: *Much fine rug-weaving is done by little children because of the dexterity of their small fingers.* **2** cleverness, °ingenuity, ingeniousness, °tact, astuteness, keenness, sharpness, shrewdness, cunning, guile, canniness, artfulness: *I admire his dexterity in arguing the case in court. He exercised great dexterity in eluding capture.*

dexterous *adj.* **1** dextrous, deft, lithe, °nimble, °supple, °agile, °quick, °skilful: *He was a dexterous archer.* **2** °clever, °ingenious, °astute, °keen, °sharp, °shrewd, cunning, guileful, canny, °artful, °crafty, °slick: *She was devout in religion, decorous in conduct, and dexterous in business. He was the most dexterous of our political leaders.*

diabolic *adj.* **1** diabolical, °devilish, °satanic, Mephistophelian, demonic, demoniac(al), °fiendish, hellish, °infernal: *His interest in the supernatural included participation in diabolic rituals of the most repulsive kind.* **2** diabolical, °cruel, °wicked, iniquitous, °evil, °fiendish, appalling, °dreadful, °inhuman, °atrocious, execrable, °abominable, °awful, °terrible, °damnable, accursed, horrid, °horrible, °hideous, °monstrous, odious, °vile, °base, °corrupt, °foul, depraved, flagitious, heinous, malicious, malevolent, malign, maleficent, °sinister, °sinful, °impious, °bad: *The prisoners suffered the most diabolic treatment.*

diagnose *v.* °identify, °name, °determine, °recognize, °distinguish, pinpoint, °interpret; °analyse: *The doctor diagnosed the symptoms as those of rheumatoid arthritis.*

dialect *n.* °speech (pattern), phraseology, °idiom, °accent, °pronunciation, patois, °vernacular; °jargon, °cant, slang, argot, °language, °tongue, Creole, pidgin; brogue, burr, *Colloq* °lingo: *Some of the regional dialects are hard to understand.*

dialogue *n.* **1** duologue, °conversation, °discussion, °conference, °talk, °chat, colloquy, communication: *I wrote down that dialogue — it was hilarious!* **2** °parley, °conference, °meeting, °huddle, °tête-à-tête, colloquy, *Colloq US and Canadian* °rap session: *A meaningful dialogue between labour and management could easily settle the question.*

diary *n.* °appointment book, date-book, °calendar, °engagement book; °journal, °chronicle, log, °record, annal(s): *According to my diary, the date we dined was the 1st.*

dicey *n.* °risky, °tricky, °dangerous, °difficult, °ticklish, unpredictable, °uncertain, unsure, °doubtful, *Colloq* iffy, chancy, °hairy: *Asking for another pay rise could be pretty dicey, Daniel.*

dicker *v.* **1** °bargain, °trade, barter, °deal, °haggle, °negotiate: *If I dicker with him, he may drop his price.* —*n.* **2** °bargain, °deal, °haggle, °negotiation: *We had a bit of a dicker but finally settled on a figure.*

dicky *adj.* dickey, °shaky, °unreliable, unsteady, °unsound, °faulty, *Colloq* °dodgy: *The engine sounds a bit dicky to me — you'd better have it seen to.*

dictate *v.* **1** °say, °prescribe, ordain, °decree, °demand, °command, °lay down (the law), °order, °direct, °pronounce, °impose: *It is our leader who dictates what we may say and do.*
—*n.* **2** °decree, °demand, °command, °order, °direction, °instruction, °charge, °pronouncement, edict, fiat, ukase, mandate, caveat, °injunction, °requirement, °bidding, behest: *Each must act in accord with the dictates of his conscience.*

dictator *n.* autocrat, °absolute ruler *or* °monarch, °despot, overlord, °oppressor, tsar *or* czar, °tyrant, Fuehrer *or* Führer: *Among monarchs, Henry VIII certainly could have been characterized as a dictator.*

dictatorial *adj.* **1** °absolute, °arbitrary, °totalitarian, °authoritarian, autocratic, all-powerful, omnipotent, °unlimited: *The peoples of some countries often confer dictatorial powers on their leaders.* **2** °despotic, °tyrannical, °authoritarian, iron-handed, °domineering, imperious, °overbearing, *Colloq* °bossy: *The dictatorial way she runs the department makes those who work there miserable.*

diction *n.* **1** °language, °wording, (°verbal *or* °writing) °style, °expression, °usage, expressiveness, °terminology, °word choice, vocabulary, phraseology, phrasing, °rhetoric: *Please go over my paper and correct the diction.* **2** articulation, °pronunciation, enunciation, °delivery, elocution, °oratory, °presentation, °speech, °intonation, inflection: *That course in public speaking improved Brian's diction enormously.*

dictionary *n.* lexicon, °glossary, wordbook; °thesaurus: *My dictionary gives the pronunciation, etymology, and meanings of hundreds of thousands of words.*

die *v.* **1** lose one's life, lay down one's life, °perish, °expire, decease, °suffer °death, *Euphemistic* °depart, give up the ghost, be no more, (go to) meet one's Maker, °breathe one's last, go to the °happy hunting-grounds, go to one's reward, go to one's °final *or* °last resting-place, go west, pay the debt of nature, pay one's debt to nature, °pass through the pearly gates, °pass away *or* on, join the majority, go the way of all flesh; *Slang* pop off, bite the dust, kick the bucket, croak, *Brit* snuff it, go for a burton, pop one's clogs, *US* turn up one's toes, cash in one's chips *or* checks: *He died of tuberculosis, a rare affliction these days.* **2** Often, ***die down** or **out** or **away***: °dwindle, lessen, °diminish, °decrease, °ebb, °decline, °wane, °subside, wither (away), °wilt, °melt (away), °dissolve, peter out, °fail, °weaken, °deteriorate, °disintegrate, °degenerate, °fade (away), °droop, moulder, °sink, vanish, °disappear: *We lost the race because the breeze died down. After the third try, her enthusiasm died. The sound of the flute died away among its echoes.* **3** °expire, °end, °stop, °cease: *Your secret will die with me.* **4** Usually, ***die off** or **out***: become °extinct, °perish: *By about 200 million years ago, all the dinosaurs had died out.* **5** °long, pine, °yearn, crave, °hanker, °want, °desire, °hunger, °ache: *He said he was dying to meet a real movie star.*

diet[1] *n.* **1** °fare, °food, °nourishment, nutriment, °sustenance, °subsistence, victuals, intake, aliment: *A well-balanced diet is very important.* **2** regimen, °regime: *She is on a diet of bread and water.*
—*v.* **3** °fast, abstain; °slim; °reduce: *I am dieting to lose weight.*

diet[2] *n.* °council, congress, °parliament, senate, legislature, °house, °chamber, °assembly: *In Japan, the legislature is called a* diet.

differ *v.* **1** °diverge, °deviate, be °separate *or* °distinct, be °dissimilar *or* °different, °contrast; °depart: *Even the leaves of the same tree differ from one another. These substances differ in their magnetic properties.* **2** °disagree, °conflict, °contradict, be °contradictory, °vary, be at °variance, take °issue, °part company, °fall out, °quarrel, °argue: *Opinions differ as to the best way to bring up children. She differed with me on many subjects.*

difference *n.* **1** °distinction, °dissimilarity, °discrepancy, unlikeness, °disagreement, inconsistency, °diversity, °variation, imbalance; °inequality, dissimilitude, incongruity, °contrast, contradistinction, contrariety: *Difference of opinion can be constructive in a business partnership. Being colour-blind, he cannot tell the difference between red and green.* **2** Often, ***differences***: °dispute, °quarrel, °argument, °disagreement, °dissension, °conflict: *We were able to settle our differences amicably.* **3** °change, °alteration, metamorphosis, reformation, °transformation, conversion, °adjustment, modification: *Since her operation, the difference in Philippa is surprising.* **4** idiosyncrasy, °peculiarity, °characteristic, °character, °nature: *There are important differences between socialism and communism.* **5** °rest, °remainder, °leftovers, °balance: *After each had taken his share, the difference was 12, which we divided equally among the four of us.*

different *adj.* **1** °unlike, unalike, °dissimilar, conflicting; °contrary, °discrete, contrastive, contrasting, disparate, °divergent, °diverse, °distinct, °opposite, °separate, distinguishable; another *or* other: *We both enjoy boating but in different ways. When modelling, she assumes a different pose every few seconds.* **2** °unique, °unusual, °peculiar, °odd, °singular, °particular, °distinctive, °personal, °extraordinary, °special, °remarkable, °bizarre, °rare, °weird, °strange, unconventional, °original, out of the °ordinary; °new, °novel, °exceptional, °unheard-of: *And now, for something completely different, we present a juggling trick cyclist.* **3** assorted, °manifold, multifarious, numerous, °abundant, °sundry, °various, °varied, °divers, °many, °several: *Different kinds of breakfast cereal are now available.*

differentiate *v.* **1** °distinguish, °discriminate, contradistinguish, °separate, °contrast, °oppose, °set off *or* °apart, °tell apart: *They must learn how to differentiate one species from another.* **2** °modify, specialize, °change, °alter, °transform, transmute, °convert, °adapt, °adjust: *All organisms possess the power to differentiate special organs to meet special needs.*

difficult *adj.* **1** °hard, °arduous, °toilsome, °strenuous, °tough, °laborious, °burdensome, onerous, °demanding: *He found it difficult to work the longer hours. The first birth is sometimes difficult.* **2** °puzzling, °perplexing, baffling, enigmatic(al), °profound, abstruse, °obscure, °recondite, complex; °thorny, °intricate, °sensitive, knotty, °problematic(al), °ticklish, scabrous: *Some of the questions in the exam were very difficult. The analyst raised a lot of difficult issues which I had to confront.* **3** intractable, °recalcitrant, obstructive, °stubborn, unmanageable, °obstinate, °contrary, unaccommodating, refractory, unyielding, uncompromising; °naughty, ill-behaved; *Colloq Brit* bloody-minded: *Tessa has three difficult teenagers in the house these days.* **4** troubled, troubling, °tough, °burdensome, onerous, °demanding, °trying, °hard, °grim, °dark, unfavourable, straitening: *We have been through some difficult times together.* **5** °fussy, °particular, °demanding, °finicky, finical, °fastidious, °critical, °troublesome, *difficile*, °awkward, *Colloq* nit-picking: *I'll go wherever you like; I don't want to be difficult about it. Sharon can be a very difficult person to be with.*

difficulty *n.* **1** °strain, °hardship, arduousness, laboriousness, formidableness, tribulation, painfulness: *Despite much difficulty she succeeded.* **2** °hardship, °obstacle, °problem, °distress, °pitfall, °dilemma, °predicament, °snag, °hindrance; Gordian °knot: *He has encountered difficulties during his career.* **3** Often, ***difficulties***: °embarrassment, °plight, °predicament, °mess, °strait(s), °trouble, °scrape, *Colloq* hot water, °jam, pickle, °fix; hot potato: *She always seems to be in financial difficulties.*

diffuse *adj.* **1** °spread (out *or* about *or* around), scattered, dispersed, widespread; °sparse, °meagre, °thin (on the ground): *A few diffuse clouds could be seen on the horizon.* **2** °wordy, verbose, prolix, long-winded, loquacious, °discursive, digressive, °rambling, circumlocutory, °meandering, °roundabout, circuitous, periphrastic, ambagious, diffusive, pleonastic: *The style of the book is very diffuse, being extravagantly uneconomic of expression.*
—*v.* **3** °spread, °circulate, °distribute, °dispense, °disperse; dispel, °scatter, °broadcast, °sow, disseminate; °dissipate: *The colour rapidly diffused, turning the liquid crimson. She has successfully diffused her ideas of female equality throughout the community.*

dig *v.* **1** °excavate, °burrow, °gouge, °scoop, °hollow out; °tunnel: *He dug a hole in which to set the post.* **2** °nudge, °thrust, °stab, °jab, °plunge, °force, °prod, °poke: *I dug my spurs into my horse and rode off. He kept digging me in the ribs with his finger.* **3** °appreciate, °enjoy, °like, °understand: *They really dig the jazz of the big-band era.* **4** °notice, °note, °look at, °regard: *Hey, man, dig that crazy gear!* **5** ***dig into***: °probe (into), delve into, °go °deeply into, °explore, °look into, °research, °study: *We dug into many books of forgotten lore to find the words of the magic spell.* **6** ***dig out*** *or* ***up***: °unearth, disinter, exhume, °bring up, °find, °obtain, °extract, ferret out, winkle out, °discover, bring to °light, °expose, dredge up, °extricate, °come up with, *Australian* fossick: *I dug out an old book on witchcraft. She has dug up some interesting information about your friend Glover.*
—*n.* **7** °thrust, °poke, °jab, °stab, °nudge: *She playfully gave him a dig in the ribs.* **8** °insult, insinuation, °gibe, °slur; °taunt, °jeer; *Colloq* °slap (in the face), °wisecrack, °crack, *US* low °blow: *Referring to him as a Dartmoor graduate was a nasty dig.*

digest *v.* **1** assimilate: *She has trouble digesting milk.* **2** °bear, °stand, °endure, °survive, assimilate, °accept, °tolerate, °brook, °swallow, °stomach: *The attack was too much for even him to digest.* **3** °comprehend, assimilate, °understand, °take in, °consider, °grasp, °study, °ponder, °meditate (on *or* over), °reflect on, °think over, °weigh: *I need a little time to digest the new regulations.* **4** °abbreviate, °cut, condense, °abridge, compress, epitomize, summarize, °reduce, °shorten: *Her assistant had digested the report into four pages by noon.*
—*n.* **5** condensation, °abridgement, °abstract, °précis, résumé, °synopsis, °summary, conspectus, °abbreviation: *I never did read the original novel, only a digest.*

dignified *adj.* °stately, °noble, °majestic, °formal, °solemn, °serious, °sober, °grave, °distinguished, °honourable, *distingué*, °elegant, august, °sedate, °reserved; °regal, courtly, lordly, °lofty, °exalted, °grand: *Despite the abuse, he maintained a dignified demeanour.*

dignify *v.* °distinguish, ennoble, elevate, °raise, °exalt, °glorify, upraise, °lift, uplift, °enhance, °improve, °better, upgrade: *The critic wrote that he wouldn't deign to dignify the book by calling it a novel.*

dignitary *n.* °personage, °official, °notable, °worthy, magnate, °power, higher-up; °celebrity, lion, luminary, °star, superstar, *Colloq* VIP, °bigwig, °big shot, °big wheel, °big °name, °big gun, hotshot, hot stuff, °big noise, °big White Chief, °big Chief, °big Daddy, *Brit* Lord *or* Lady Muck, high-muck-a-muck, *Slang* °big cheese, *Chiefly US* Mr Big, biggie, °fat cat: *Anyone with a lot of money is treated today as a dignitary.*

dignity *n.* **1** °nobility, majesty, °gravity, gravitas, °solemnity, courtliness, °distinction, stateliness, °formality, °grandeur, eminence; hauteur, loftiness: *She entered and walked with dignity to the throne.* **2** °worth, worthiness, °nobility, nobleness, °excellence, °honour, honourableness, respectability, respectableness, °standing, °importance, greatness, °glory, °station, °status, °rank, °level, °position: *The real dignity of a man lies not in what he has but in what he is.* **3** °self-respect, self-regard, *amour propre*, °self-confidence, °self-esteem, °pride, self-importance: *It was beneath her dignity to speak directly to a footman.*

digression *n.* **1** aside, departure, deviation, °detour, obiter dictum, parenthesis, apostrophe, excursus: *His numerous digressions made it difficult to focus on the main points of the speech.* **2** digressing, deviating, divergence, °going off at a tangent, °rambling, °meandering, straying, wandering, deviation: *Digression from the main theme of his speech only diluted his argument.*

dilapidated *adj.* ruined, broken-down, in ruins, gone to rack and °ruin, wrecked, destroyed, falling °apart, °decrepit, °derelict, battered, °tumbledown, °rundown, °ramshackle, crumbling, decayed, decaying, °rickety, °shaky, °shabby, *Brit* raddled: *We shall have to fix up that dilapidated barn if we expect to use it.*

dilemma *n.* °predicament, °quandary, double °bind, catch-22, °impasse, °deadlock, °stalemate; °plight, °difficulty, °trouble; °stymie, snooker; *Colloq* °bind, °box, °fix, °jam, °spot, pickle, °squeeze: *He was faced with the dilemma of killing the injured animal or allowing it to die in agony.*

dilettante *n.* dabbler, trifler, °aesthete, °amateur: *You know art like a curator; I am a mere dilettante.*

diligent *adj.* persevering, °persistent, °industrious, assiduous, sedulous, °intent, °steady, °steadfast, focused, concentrated, °earnest, °attentive, °conscientious, hard-working, indefatigable, °tireless, °constant, °painstaking, °careful, °thorough, °scrupulous, °meticulous, punctilious: *Only through diligent application was she able to get through law school.*

dilute *v.* °water (down), °thin (down *or* out), °cut, °weaken, °doctor, °adulterate; °mitigate, lessen, °diminish, °decrease: *For the table, wine was often diluted with water. He dilutes his argument by citing irrelevancies.*

dim *adj.* **1** °obscure, obscured, °vague, °faint, °weak, weakened, °pale, °imperceptible, °fuzzy, °indistinct, ill-defined, indiscernible, undefined, °indistinguishable, foggy, clouded, cloudy, °nebulous, blurred, blurry, unclear, °dull, °hazy, °misty, °dark, °shadowy, °murky, tenebrous, °gloomy, °sombre, °dusky, crepuscular: *Her beauty made The bright world dim. We could barely see in the dim light of the cave.* **2** °stupid, °obtuse, doltish, °dull, dull-witted, °foolish, slow-witted, dim-witted, °dense, *Colloq* °thick, °dumb: *Anyone who can't understand that is really quite dim.*
—*v.* **3** °obscure, °dull, becloud: *His natural feelings of compassion had been dimmed by neglect.* **4** darken, bedim, °shroud, °shade: *Twilight dims the sky above. The stage-lights dimmed and the curtain fell.*

diminish *v.* **1** °decrease, °decline, abate, lessen, °reduce, °lower, °shrink, °curtail, °contract, °lop, crop, °dock, °clip, °prune, °cut, truncate, °cut down, °abbreviate, °shorten, °abridge, compress, condense, °pare (down), °scale down, °boil down: *As the height increases, the pressure diminishes. The need for police patrols was diminished when we hired security guards.* **2** °belittle, °disparage, °degrade, °downgrade, °discredit, °detract (from), °vitiate, °debase, deprecate, demean, derogate, °depreciate, vilipend, devalue, cheapen, °put down, °dismiss, °humiliate, °reject: *His abuse by the authorities did not diminish him in her eyes.* **3** °wane, °fade, °dwindle, °ebb, °die out *or* away, peter out, °recede, °subside; slacken, °let up, °wind down, °slow (down), °ease (off), *Colloq* °run out of steam: *Soaking in the hot water, I felt the tensions of mind and body gradually diminishing. The campaign finally diminished to a negligible effort.*

diminutive *adj.* °small, °tiny, °little, °miniature, °petite, °minute, minuscule, mini, °compact, °undersized, °pocket, pocket-sized, pygmy, °elfin, Lilliputian, midget, °wee, microscopic; micro, infinitesimal; *US* vest-pocket, vest-pocket-sized, *Colloq* teeny, teeny-weeny *or* teensy-weensy: *The bride and groom appeared with their diminutive page-boys and bridesmaids behind them.*

din *n.* **1** °noise, clamour, °uproar, shouting, screaming, yelling, babel, clangour, clatter, commotion, °racket, °row, hullabaloo, hubbub, hurly-burly, °rumpus, hollering, °blare, blaring, bray, braying, °bellow, bellowing, °roar, °blast, roaring, °pandemonium, °tumult: *We couldn't hear the speech above the din of the crowd.*
—*v.* **2** °instil, drum, hammer: *The names and dates of the British monarchs were dinned into me in childhood.*

dine *v.* °eat, °banquet, °feast, sup, break bread, breakfast, lunch, have a °bite *or* °snack, nibble, *Colloq* °feed, *Slang* nosh: *We'll dine at 8.00, so don't be late.*

dingy *adj.* °dark, °dull, °gloomy, °dim, °lacklustre, faded, discoloured, °dusky, °drab, °dreary, °dismal, cheerless, depressing, °shadowy, tenebrous, smoky, sooty, grey-brown, smudgy, grimy, °dirty, soiled: *He was a dingy man, in dingy clothes, who lived in a dingy house.*

dip *v.* **1** °immerse, °plunge, °duck, dunk, douse, bathe, °submerge: *He dipped each dish into the soapy water.* **2** °decline, °go down, °fall, °descend, °sag, °sink, °subside, °slump: *The road dips after the next curve. The price of shares has dipped again.* **3** ***dip in*** *or* ***into***: °dabble in, °play at; °skim, °scan: *I haven't had time to read it, but I dipped into it here and there.*
—*n.* **4** swim, °plunge; immersion; *Brit* bathe: *We are going for a dip in the pool before dinner.* **5** lowering, °sinking, °depression, °drop, °slump, °decline: *This dip in the price of oil means nothing.*

diplomacy *n.* **1** °tact, tactfulness, adroitness, °discretion: *She was able to get rid of that rude boor with her customary diplomacy.* **2** statecraft, statesmanship, °negotiation; °intrigue, Machiavellianism, °machination, manoeuvring *or* maneuvering: *Cardinal Richelieu is considered the founder of modern diplomacy.*

diplomatic *adj.* °tactful, °discreet, °prudent, °wise, °sensitive, °politic, °courteous, °polite, discerning, °perceptive, perspicacious, °thoughtful: *How diplomatic it was of you to have invited Frances's husband!*

direct *v.* **1** °manage, °handle, °run, °administer, °govern, °regulate, °control, °operate, superintend, °supervise, °command, °head up, °rule; *Colloq* °call the shots: *She directs the company with an iron hand.* **2** °guide, °lead, °conduct, °pilot, °steer, °show *or* °point (the °way), be at the °helm; °advise, °counsel, °instruct, °mastermind; usher, °escort: *He has directed the company for 40 years, through good times and bad. Can you direct me to the post office?* **3** °rule, °command, °order, °require, °bid, °tell, °instruct, °charge, °dictate, enjoin; °appoint, ordain: *He directed that the attack be launched at dawn.* **4** °aim, °focus, °level, °point, °train; °turn: *That bullet was directed at my heart. Direct your attention to the front of the room.* **5** °send, °address, °post, °mail: *Please direct the letter to my home.*
—*adj.* **6** °straight, unswerving, shortest, undeviating, through: *We turned off the direct road to take in the view.* **7** uninterrupted, unreflected, unrefracted, without °interference, unobstructed: *She cannot remain in direct sunlight for very long.* **8** unbroken, lineal: *He claims to be a direct descendant of Oliver Cromwell's.* **9** straightforward, °unmitigated, °outright, °matter-of-fact, °categorical, °plain, °clear, unambiguous, unmistakable, to the °point, without *or* with no beating about the bush, °unqualified, unequivocal, °point-blank, °explicit, °express: *I expect a direct answer to my direct question. Have you direct evidence of his guilt? That was a gross insult and a direct lie!* **10** straightforward, °frank, °candid, °outspoken, plain-spoken, °honest, °blunt, °open, °uninhibited, unreserved, °forthright, °sincere, unequivocal; undiplomatic, °tactless: *She is very direct in commenting about people she dislikes.*

direction *n.* **1** directing, aiming, pointing, guiding, °guidance, conducting, °conduct, instructing, °instruction, managing, °management, administering, °administration, governing, °government, supervising, supervision, operating, °operation, °running, °leadership, directorship, directorate, °control, captaincy, handling, manipulation, °regulation, °rule, °charge: *The Freedom Party's direction of the country has led to many reforms.* **2** Often, ***directions***: °instruction(s), °information; °bearing, °road, °way, °route, avenue, °course: *To assemble the appliance, follow the directions printed in the leaflet. Can you give me directions to the nearest filling-station?*

directly *adv.* **1** °straight, in a beeline, unswervingly, undeviatingly, as the crow flies: *This road should take me directly to the beach.* **2** °immediately, at °once, °straight away, °right away, °quickly, °promptly, without °delay, speedily, instantly, *Colloq US and Canadian* momentarily: *She called and I went directly.* **3** °soon, later (on), anon, °presently, in a (little) while, °shortly: *The doctor will be here directly.* **4** °exactly, °precisely, °just; °completely, °entirely: *My garage is directly opposite. The cricket pitch is directly at the centre of the park.*
—*conj.* **5** as °soon as, when: *The police arrested him directly he entered the building.*

director *n.* **1** °executive, administrator, °official, °principal; chairman, chairperson, chairwoman, president, vice-president; governor; °head, °chief, °boss, °manager, °superintendent, °supervisor, °overseer, °foreman, headman, *Colloq* kingpin, number one, numero uno, Mr Big, the man; *Slang* °top dog, °top banana, *Brit* gaffer, *US* °big cheese, °head *or* °chief honcho: *The sale of the company was announced at the meeting of the board of directors.* **2** °guide, °leader; steersman, helmsman, °pilot, °skipper, commander, commandant, captain; cicerone; maestro, concert-master, conductor; impresario: *We were lucky to have a director who really knew what he was doing.*

dirt *n.* **1** °soil, °mud, °muck, °mire, °grime, slime, °sludge, °ooze, slop; dust, soot; excrement, ordure; °filth, °waste, °refuse, °trash, °garbage, °rubbish, offal, °junk, dross, sweepings; leavings, °scrap, orts; *Slang Brit* gunge, *US* grunge: *This vacuum cleaner is guaranteed to pick up any kind of dirt.* **2** °soil, °earth, loam, °ground, clay: *Hydroponics is the technique of farming without dirt, using only liquid nutrients.* **3** indecency, obscenity, smut, °pornography, foulness, corruption, °filth, vileness: *Customs confiscated much of the dirt before it could enter the country.* **4** °gossip, °scandal, °talk, °rumour, °inside information, *Colloq* °low-down, °dope, *Slang US* scuttlebutt: *I got the dirt from David about what really happened at the party.*

dirty *adj.* **1** °foul, unclean, befouled, soiled, begrimed, sooty, grimy, °filthy, mucky, besmeared, besmirched, polluted, squalid, sullied, stained, spotted, smudged, slovenly, °unwashed, °bedraggled, slatternly, °untidy, *Slang Brit* gungy, *US* grungy: *If you think his shirt was dirty, you should have seen his body!* **2** smutty, °indecent, °obscene, ribald, off colour, °prurient, °risqué, salacious, °lewd, °lascivious, °pornographic, °coarse, licentious, °rude, °blue, scabrous: *His parents were shocked to hear him telling dirty jokes.* **3** unfair, °unscrupulous, unsporting, °dishonest, °mean, underhand(ed), unsportsmanlike, °dishonourable, °deceitful, °corrupt, treacherous, °perfidious, °villainous, °disloyal; malicious, malevolent, °rotten, °filthy: *It was a dirty trick of Sue's to tell the teacher.* **4** °bad, °foul, °nasty, °stormy, rainy, °windy, blowy, blowing, squally, °sloppy: *We're in for some dirty weather, Mr Christian, so you'd best reduce sail.* **5** °bitter, °resentful, °angry, °furious, wrathful, smouldering: *She gave me a dirty look when I said anything about her sister.* **6** °sordid, °base, °mean, °despicable, °contemptible, ignoble, °scurvy, °low, °low-down, ignominious, °vile, °nasty, °infamous: *That villain has done his dirty work and now we must all suffer. He's nothing but a dirty coward!*
—*v.* **7** °stain, °sully, befoul, °soil, begrime, besmirch, °pollute, °muddy, °smear, defile; °blacken, °tarnish: *She refused to so much as dirty her hands to help us. Are you afraid it will dirty your reputation to be seen with me?*

disability *n.* **1** °handicap, °impairment, °defect, °infirmity, disablement: *James is unable to play tennis owing to his disability.* **2** °inability, incapacity, unfitness, °impotence, powerlessness, helplessness: *The teacher helped her to overcome her disability.*

disabled *adj.* incapacitated, °crippled, °lame; damaged, ruined, impaired, harmed, non-functioning, inoperative, *Slang Brit* scuppered: *Disabled ex-servicemen ought to receive compensation. No parts could be found for the disabled machines.*

disadvantage *n.* **1** deprivation, °set-back, °drawback, °liability, °handicap, °defect, °flaw, °shortcoming, °weakness, °weak spot, °fault: *Being colour-blind has not been a disadvantage in his kind of work.* **2** °detriment, °harm, °loss, °injury, °damage; °prejudice, °disservice: *Failure to send in a tax return will be to your distinct disadvantage.*

disagree *v.* **1** °differ, dissent, °diverge: *She disagrees with most of my ideas. I said the painting was by Hockney, but he disagreed.* **2** °conflict, °dispute, °quarrel, °argue, contend, °contest, °bicker, °fight, °fall out, squabble, wrangle, °debate: *Those who agree on major principles often disagree about trifles, and vice versa.*

disagreeable *adj.* **1** unpleasant, unpleasing, °offensive, °distasteful, °repugnant, °obnoxious, °repellent, °repulsive, objectionable, °revolting, odious: *He found the heat and humidity in the tropics most disagreeable.* **2** °offensive, noxious, °unsavoury, °unpalatable, nauseating, °nauseous, °nasty, sickening, °disgusting, °revolting, °repellent, °abominable, objectionable: *A disagreeable odour arose from the beggar on the doorstep.* **3** bad-tempered, ill-tempered, disobliging, uncooperative, unfriendly, uncivil, °abrupt, °blunt, °curt, °brusque, °short, uncourtly, °impolite, bad-mannered, °ill-mannered, °discourteous, °rude, °testy, grouchy, splenetic, °cross, ill-humoured, °peevish, morose, sulky, °sullen: *Brian became quite disagreeable, and I did not see him again.*

disagreement *n.* **1** °difference, °discrepancy, °discord, discordance, discordancy, °dissimilarity, disaccord, °diversity, incongruity, nonconformity, incompatibility: *Can you resolve the disagreement between the results of these experiments?* **2** dissent, °opposition, °conflict, contradiction, °difference, °disparity: *The problem arises from a basic disagreement in their principles.* **3** °quarrel, °strife, °argument, °dispute, velitation, altercation, °controversy, contention, °dissension, °debate, °clash, *Colloq US* rhubarb: *Their mother had to settle the disagreement between the brothers.*

disappear *v.* **1** vanish, °evaporate, vaporize, °fade (away *or* out), evanesce, *Poetic* evanish: *After granting my wish, the genie disappeared, laughing diabolically.* **2** °die (out *or* off), become °extinct, °cease (to exist), °perish (without a trace): *The dinosaurs, though enormously successful as a species, suddenly disappeared from the earth.*

disappoint *v.* **1** °let down, °fail, dissatisfy: *Miss Sheila disappointed her public by refusing to sing.* **2** °mislead, °deceive, disenchant, *Colloq* °stand up: *She disappointed me by saying she would be there and then not arriving.* **3** °undo, °frustrate, °foil, °thwart, balk, °defeat: *How can I answer you truthfully without disappointing your expectations?*

disappointed *adj.* **1** frustrated, unsatisfied, °dissatisfied, disillusioned, °disenchanted, discouraged, °downhearted, disheartened, downcast, saddened, °unhappy, °dejected, °discontented, °let down: *There will be a lot of disappointed children at Christmas this year.* **2** foiled, thwarted, balked, defeated, °undone, failed, °let down: *Though she campaigned energetically, Theodora was among the disappointed candidates.*

disappointing *adj.* discouraging, dissatisfying, °unsatisfactory, unsatisfying, °disconcerting; °poor, second-rate, °sorry, °inadequate, °insufficient, °inferior, °pathetic, °sad: *The former champion turned in a disappointing performance yesterday evening.*

disappointment *n.* **1** frustration, non-fulfilment, unfulfilment, unsatisfaction, °dissatisfaction, °set-back, °failure, °let-down, °defeat, °blow, °fiasco, °calamity, °disaster, °fizzle, *Brit* damp squib, *Colloq* washout: *Recently he has had one disappointment after another.* **2** dejection, °depression, discouragement, disenchantment, °distress, °regret, mortification, chagrin: *I cannot tell you the disappointment your father and I felt when you failed to get into university.*

disapproval *n.* disapprobation, condemnation, censure, °criticism, °reproof, reproach, °objection, °exception, °disfavour, °displeasure, °dissatisfaction: *The council voiced their disapproval of holding a carnival in the village square.*

disapprove *v.* °condemn, °criticize, censure, °object to, decry, °denounce, °put *or* °run down, deplore, deprecate, °belittle, °look down on, °frown on *or* upon, *Colloq* °knock, °look down one's nose at, tut-tut: *I don't care if you disapprove of my marrying Eustace. The monopolies commission has disapproved the merger.*

disarm *v.* **1** unarm; demilitarize, demobilize, °disband, deactivate: *After the war, most—but not all—European countries disarmed.* **2** °win over, put *or* set at °ease, mollify, appease, placate, pacify, °reconcile, conciliate, propitiate, °charm: *I was completely disarmed by her friendly disposition. Many people found his naïvety disarming.*

disaster *n.* °catastrophe, °calamity, cataclysm, °tragedy, °misfortune, débâcle, °accident, °mishap, °blow, act of God, adversity, °trouble, °reverse: *The flooding of the river was as much of a disaster as the earlier drought.*

disastrous *adj.* **1** °calamitous, catastrophic, catalysmic, °tragic, °destructive, °ruinous, °devastating, appalling, °harrowing, °awful, °terrible, dire, horrendous, °horrible, horrifying, °dreadful, °fatal: *There has been a disastrous earthquake which killed thousands.* **2** °awful, °terrible, unlucky, °unfortunate, °detrimental, °grievous, °harmful: *The postal strike has had disastrous effects on the mail-order business.*

disband *v.* °disperse, disorganize, °scatter, °break up, °dissolve, demobilize, deactivate, °retire: *After the war, the special spy force was disbanded.*

discard *v.* **1** get °rid of, °dispense with, °dispose of, °throw away *or* out, °toss out *or* away, °abandon, jettison, °scrap, *Colloq* °trash, °dump, *Slang* ditch: *We discarded boxes of old photographs when we moved house.*
—*n.* **2** °reject, cast-off: *I felt like a discard from the lonely hearts club.*

discernible *adj.* **1** °perceptible, °visible, seeable, perceivable, °apparent, °clear, °observable, °plain, detectable; °conspicuous, °noticeable: *A small sailing-boat was discernible on the horizon.* **2** distinguishable, recognizable, identifiable, °distinct: *To me there is a discernible difference between puce and burgundy.*

discharge *v.* **1** °release, °let out, °dismiss, let go, °send away; °pardon, exonerate, °liberate, (set) °free, acquit, °let off, absolve: *She was discharged from hospital yesterday. He was discharged from police custody last week.* **2** °expel, oust, °dismiss, cashier, °eject, give °notice, *Colloq* °sack, give (someone) the °sack, °fire, °kick out: *He was discharged from his job yesterday.* **3** °shoot, °fire (off); °set *or* °let off, detonate, °explode: *It is illegal to discharge a firearm or other explosive device in this area.* **4** °emit, °send out *or* forth, °pour out *or* forth, °gush; disembogue; °ooze, °leak, exude; excrete, °void: *The sore in his leg continued to discharge pus. We can ill afford to discharge those effluents into the sea.* **5** °carry out, °perform, °fulfil, °accomplish, do, °execute: *He faithfully discharges the duties of his office.* **6** °pay, °settle, liquidate, °clear, °honour, °meet, °square (up): *Before going off on holiday, we discharged all our financial obligations.* **7** °unload, offload, disburden, °empty: *After discharging its cargo, the vessel rode high in the water.*
—*n.* **8** °release, °dismissal: *What is the date of his discharge from the clinic?* **9** °expulsion, ouster, °dismissal, °ejection, °notice, *Colloq* the axe, the °sack, the boot, *Chiefly US and Canadian* walking papers, *Slang US and Canadian* the bounce, the gate: *Her discharge from the firm was rather ignominious.* **10** shooting, firing (off), °report, °shot; salvo, fusillade, °volley; detonation, °explosion, °burst: *The discharge of a pistol could not be heard at that distance. I heard the discharge from the guns of the firing squad in the courtyard below. The discharge of the bomb maimed three children.* **11** emission, °release, °void, voiding, excretion, excreting, emptying, °flow; °ooze, oozing, pus, suppuration, °secretion, seepage: *The discharge of blood from the wound continued.* **12** °performance, °fulfilment, °accomplishment, °execution, °observance, °achievement: *The discharge of my family responsibilities will have to await my return from the front.* **13** °payment, °settlement, liquidation, squaring (up), °clearance: *The bank expects full discharge of all debts before they lend any money.* **14** unloading, disburdening, off-loading, emptying: *The customer will pay in full after the discharge of his cargo.*

disciple *n.* **1** °apprentice, °pupil, °student, proselyte, °learner, °scholar: *Pietro Zampollini was a disciple of the great artist Ravelli.* **2** °follower, adherent, °devotee, °admirer, votary; °partisan, °fan, aficionado: *She is a disciple of Louis Armstrong's.*

disciplinarian *n.* taskmaster, taskmistress, martinet, drill-sergeant; °tyrant, °despot, °dictator: *The headmaster at Briarcliffe was a stern disciplinarian who regularly used to beat us.*

discipline *n.* **1** training, drilling, regimen, °exercise, °practice, °drill, inculcation, indoctrination, °instruction, °schooling: *Strict discipline is good for young people, according to my father.* **2** °punishment, °penalty, chastisement, castigation, °correction: *The discipline meted out to senior students was very harsh.* **3** °order, °routine, (°proper) °behaviour, °decorum: *The sergeant is there to maintain discipline among the recruits.* **4** °direction, °rule, °regulation, °government, °control, °subjection, °restriction, °check, °curb, °restraint: *There was far too much discipline during my childhood, both at school and at home.* **5** °subject, °course, °branch of knowledge, °area, °field, °speciality *or chiefly US and Canadian* specialty: *Latin is a discipline which is fast disappearing from our schools.*
—*v.* **6** °train, °break in, °condition, °drill, °exercise, °instruct, °coach, °teach, °school, °indoctrinate, inculcate; edify, °enlighten, °inform: *The aim of his education is to discipline him to respond to orders.* **7** °check, °curb, °restrain, °bridle, °control, °govern, °direct, °run, °supervise, °manage, °regulate, hold *or* keep in °check, *US* ride herd on: *You have to discipline those children or they will always misbehave.* **8** °punish, °chastise, °castigate, °correct, °penalize, °reprove, °criticize, °reprimand, °rebuke: *Discipline that boy or he will just do it again.*

disclose *v.* **1** °reveal, °impart, divulge, °betray, °release, °tell, °blurt out, °blab, °leak, let °slip, °report, °inform, *Colloq* °spill the beans, °blow the gaff, *Slang* squeal, snitch, squeak, rat, peach, *US* fink: *To get a shorter sentence, he disclosed all to the police.* **2** °bare, °reveal, °expose, uncover, °show, °unveil: *When the pie was opened, twenty-four blackbirds were disclosed.*

discomfit *v.* **1** °embarrass, abash, disconcert, °disturb, °confuse, make uneasy *or* uncomfortable, discompose, °fluster, °ruffle, confound, °perturb, °upset, °worry, unsettle, °unnerve, *Colloq* °rattle, *US* faze, discombobulate: *Being short, she was discomfited by references to her height.* **2** °frustrate, °foil, °thwart, baffle, °check, °defeat, trump, °outdo, °outwit, °overcome: *Discomfited by her violent reaction, her attacker fled.*

discomfort *n.* **1** uneasiness, °hardship, °difficulty, °trouble, °care, °worry, °distress, vexation: *She hasn't known the discomfort of being the wife of a miner.* **2** °ache, °pain, °twinge, soreness, irritation; °bother, °inconvenience, °nuisance: *Some discomfort persisted in my legs long after the accident.*

disconcerted *adj.* discomposed, discomfited, ruffled, uneasy, °put out *or* off, uncomfortable, °queasy, flustered, °agitated, °upset, shaken, °unsettled, perturbed, °confused, bewildered, perplexed, baffled, puzzled, *US* thrown off, *Colloq* rattled, *US* fazed, discombobulated; *Slang* (all) shook (up): *They were really disconcerted by the arrival of the police.*

disconcerting *adj.* °awkward, discomfiting, off-putting, upsetting, unnerving, °unsettling, °disturbing, confusing, confounding, bewildering, °perplexing, baffling, °puzzling: *I found his persistence quite disconcerting.*

disconnect *v.* °separate, disjoin, disunite, uncouple, °detach, unhook, °undo, °disengage, unhitch; °cut *or* °break off; °cut *or* °pull °apart, °part, °divide, °sever: *They disconnected the engine after pushing the carriages onto a siding. Disconnect the power before changing the light-bulb.*

disconnected *adj.* **1** unconnected, °separate, °apart, °unattached; °split, separated: *A totally disconnected thought suddenly occurred to me.* **2** °incoherent, irrational, °confused, illogical, garbled, °disjointed, °rambling, mixed-up, unintelligible, uncoordinated, °random: *He lost the debate because his argument was disconnected and lacked cogency.*

discontent *n.* °displeasure, unhappiness, °dissatisfaction, discontentment, °distaste, uneasiness; malaise: *He felt discontent at being barred from the club.*

discontented *adj.* displeased, °dissatisfied, °discontent, annoyed, vexed, °fretful, irritated, °testy, piqued, °petulant, °disgruntled, exasperated, *Colloq* fed up, *Slang* browned off, pissed off, *Brit* cheesed *or* brassed off: *The umpire's decision made many fans quite discontented.*

discontinue *v.* °cease, °break off, °give up, °stop, °terminate, put an °end to, °quit, °leave off, °drop; °interrupt, °suspend: *Please discontinue newspaper delivery until further notice.*

discord *n.* °strife, °dissension, °disagreement, °conflict, disharmony, contention, disunity, discordance, °division, incompatibility: *The seeds of discord between the families were sown generations before.*

discordant *adj.* **1** °contrary, disagreeing, °divergent, °opposite, °opposed, adverse, °contradictory, °incompatible, differing, °different, conflicting, at °odds, °incongruous, in °conflict, in °disagreement, at °variance, °dissimilar: *The testimony of the fossils is discordant with the evidence in the legend.* **2** inharmonious, dissonant, jarring, cacophonous, unmelodious, unmusical, °harsh, °strident, jangling, °grating: *He struck some discordant notes on his zither.*

discount *v.* **1** °reduce, °mark down, °deduct, °lower, take *or* knock off: *As I was buying a dozen, he discounted the price by ten per cent.* **2** °diminish, lessen, °minimize, °detract from: *One must discount what she says when she's angry.* **3** °disregard, °omit, °ignore, °pass *or* °gloss over, °overlook, °brush off, °dismiss: *Those statistics are old and can be discounted.*
—*n.* **4** reduction, mark-down, °deduction, °rebate, °allowance: *The shop overstocked the item and is offering it at a big discount.*

discourage *v.* **1** dispirit, dishearten, °daunt, unman, °dismay, cow, °intimidate, awe, °overawe, °unnerve: *We were discouraged by the arrival of more enemy troops.* **2** °deter, °put off, dissuade, advise *or* hint against, °talk out of, °divert from; °oppose, °disapprove (of), *Colloq* throw cold water on: *They discouraged me from applying again.* **3** °prevent, °inhibit, °hinder, °stop, °slow, °suppress, obviate: *This paint is supposed to discourage corrosion.*

discourteous *adj.* uncivil, °impolite, °rude, unmannerly, °ill-mannered, bad-mannered, °disrespectful, misbehaved, °boorish, °abrupt, °curt, °brusque, °short, ungentlemanly, unladylike, °insolent, °impertinent, °ungracious: *He had been discourteous and would not be invited again.*

discover *v.* **1** °find (out), °learn, °perceive, °unearth, uncover, bring to °light, °turn *or* °dig up, smoke *or* °search out, °root *or* ferret out; °determine, ascertain, °track down, °identify; °locate: *He discovered the ninth moon of Saturn. We discovered why the tyre had gone flat.* **2** °see, °spot, catch °sight *or* a glimpse of, lay eyes on, °behold, °view, °encounter, °meet (with); °notice, espy, descry, °detect, discern: *He discovered Madagascar lying right on their course.* **3** °originate, °conceive (of), °devise, contrive, °invent, °make up, °design, °pioneer; °come *or* °chance *or* °stumble upon: *She discovered a method for tin-plating gold.*

discovery *n.* **1** °finding, °recognition, uncovering, determining, ascertaining, unearthing; origination, °invention, °conception, °idea; °development: *Who is credited with the discovery of Christmas Island? That year marks the discovery of a vaccine against smallpox.* **2** °exploration, disclosure, detection, °revelation: *He's off on a voyage of discovery.*

discredit *v.* **1** °detract, °disparage, defame, °dishonour, °disgrace, °degrade, bring into °disfavour *or* disrepute, deprecate, demean, °lower, devalue, °depreciate, devaluate, °belittle, °diminish, °reduce; °slur, °slander, °vilify, calumniate, °sully, °smear, °blacken, °taint, °tarnish, besmirch, smirch, °stigmatize, asperse, malign, °libel: *Both of them were thoroughly discredited by the scandal.* **2** disbelieve, °deny, °dispute, °doubt, °question, raise °doubts about, °distrust, °mistrust, give no credit *or* credence to: *As he's a known liar, you can discredit whatever he tells you.* **3** °disprove, °reject, refute, invalidate; °mock, °ridicule: *The phlogiston theory is generally discredited by most modern chemists.*
—*n.* **4** °dishonour, °degradation, °disfavour, disrepute, °ill repute, °disgrace, ignominy, °infamy, odium, °stigma, °shame, °smear, °slur, °scandal, obloquy, opprobrium, °humiliation: *Her performance has brought discredit to all female saxophonists.* **5** °damage, °harm, °reflection, °slur, °aspersion, °slander, defamation, °blot, °brand, °tarnish, °blemish, °taint: *The discredit to her reputation is irreparable.* **6** °doubt, °scepticism, dubiousness, doubtfulness, °qualm, °scruple, °question, incredulity, °suspicion, °distrust, °mistrust: *The new evidence throws discredit on the validity of the previous testimony.*

discreet *adj.* °careful, °cautious, °prudent, °judicious, °considerate, °guarded, °tactful, °diplomatic, circumspect, °wary, chary, heedful, watchful: *She has always been very discreet in her business dealings with me.*

discrepancy *n.* °gap, °disparity, lacuna, °difference, °dissimilarity, deviation, divergence, °disagreement, incongruity, incompatibility, inconsistency, °variance; °conflict, discordance, contrariety: *There is a great discrepancy between what he says and what he means.*

discrete *adj.* °separate, °distinct, °individual, °disconnected, °unattached, discontinuous: *These items must be treated as discrete entities and not taken together.*

discretion *n.* **1** °tact, °diplomacy, °prudence, °care, discernment, °sound °judgement, circumspection, sagacity, common °sense, good °sense, °wisdom, °discrimination: *You can rely on my discretion not to reveal the club's secrets.* **2** °choice, °option, °judgement, °preference, °pleasure, °disposition, °volition; °wish, °will, °liking, °inclination: *Buyers may subscribe to insurance cover at their own discretion.*

discriminate *v.* **1** °distinguish, °separate, °differentiate, discern, draw a °distinction, °tell the °difference: *He cannot discriminate between good art and bad.* **2** °favour, °disfavour, °segregate, show °favour *or* °prejudice *or* °bias for *or* against, be °intolerant: *It is illegal here to discriminate against people on the basis of race, creed, or colour.*

discriminating *adj.* discerning, °perceptive, °critical, °keen, °fastidious, °selective, °particular, °fussy, °refined, °cultivated: *From the wine you chose, I see you are a lady of discriminating tastes.*

discrimination *n.* **1** °bigotry, °prejudice, °bias, °intolerance, °favouritism, one-sidedness, unfairness, inequity: *In Nazi Germany discrimination was practised against everyone except the Nazis.* **2** °taste, °perception, perceptiveness, discernment, °refinement, acumen, °insight, °penetration, keenness, °judgement, °sensitivity; connoisseurship, aestheticism: *He exercises excellent discrimination in his choice of paintings.*

discursive *adj.* wandering, °meandering, digressing, digressive, °rambling, circuitous, °roundabout, °diffuse, long-winded, verbose, °wordy, prolix, °windy: *Frobisher was again boring everyone with his discursive description of life in an igloo.*

discuss *v.* °converse about, °talk over *or* about, °chat about, °deliberate (over), °review, °examine, °consult on; °debate, °argue, thrash out: *We discussed the problem but came to no conclusion.*

discussion *n.* °conversation, °talk, °chat, °dialogue, colloquy, °exchange, deliberation, °examination, °scrutiny, °analysis, °review; confabulation, °conference, powwow; °debate, °argument; *Colloq chiefly Brit* chin-wag, *US and Canadian* bull °session: *The subject of your dismissal came up for discussion yesterday.*

disdainful *adj.* °contemptuous, °scornful, contumelious, derisive, sneering, °superior, °supercilious, °pompous, °proud, prideful, °arrogant, °haughty, °snobbish, lordly, °regal; jeering, mocking, °insolent, insulting, *Colloq* °hoity-toity, high and mighty, stuck-up, highfalutin *or* hifalutin; *Slang* snotty: *She was most disdainful of our efforts to enter the cosmetics market.*

disease *n.* **1** sickness, °affliction, °ailment, malady, °illness, infection, °complaint, °disorder, °condition, °infirmity, °disability, *Archaic* murrain, *Colloq* °bug: *The colonel contracted the disease while in Malaysia.* **2** °blight, cancer, virus, °plague; contagion: *Panic spread through the Exchange like an infectious disease.*

diseased *adj.* °unhealthy, unwell, °ill, °sick, ailing, °unsound, °infirm, out of sorts, abed, infected, contaminated; afflicted, °abnormal: *We must care for the diseased patients before those with broken bones.*

disembark *v.* °land, alight, go *or* put ashore, °get *or* °step off *or* out, °leave; debark, detrain, deplane: *Tomorrow we disembark at Tunis.*

disembodied *adj.* incorporeal, bodiless; °intangible, °immaterial, °insubstantial *or* unsubstantial, impalpable, °unreal; °spiritual, °ghostly, °spectral, °phantom, wraithlike: *She wafted before his eyes, a disembodied spirit.*

disenchanted *adj.* disillusioned, disabused, undeceived, °disappointed; °blasé, °indifferent, °jaundiced, °sour(ed), cynical: *I'm afraid she's now thoroughly disenchanted with her job.*

disengage *v.* °loose, °loosen, unloose, °detach, unfasten, °release, °disconnect, disjoin, °undo, disunite, °divide, °cleave (from), °separate, uncouple, °part, disinvolve, °extricate, °get out (of), °get away (from), °cut °loose, °throw off, °shake (off), get °rid of, °break (with *or* from), °break (up) (with); unbuckle, unhitch, unclasp, unlatch, unbolt, unlock, unleash, unfetter, unchain, unlace, unhook, unbind, untie; (set) °free, °liberate, disentangle: *She was holding on to me so tenaciously that I could hardly disengage myself.*

disfavour *n.* **1** °disapproval, °dislike, °displeasure, disapprobation, unhappiness: *Katerina regards your decision with disfavour.* **2** disesteem, °discredit, °dishonour, °disgrace, disrepute: *After last night's events, we are really in disfavour with the management.*
—*v.* **3** °disapprove (of), °dislike, discountenance, °frown on *or* upon: *We strongly disfavour the merger.*

disfigured *adj.* marred, damaged, scarred, defaced, mutilated, injured, impaired, blemished, disfeatured, °deformed, distorted, spoilt *or* spoiled, ruined: *Plastic surgery has repaired her disfigured face.*

disgrace *n.* **1** ignominy, °shame, °humiliation, °embarrassment, °degradation, debasement, °dishonour, °discredit, °disfavour, disrepute, vitiation, °infamy; disesteem, °contempt, odium, obloquy, opprobrium: *His conduct has brought disgrace on his family.* **2** °blemish, °harm, °aspersion, °blot, °scandal, °slur, °stigma, vilification, smirch, °smear, °stain, °taint, °black mark: *The way she has been treated by the company is a disgrace.*
—*v.* **3** °shame, °humiliate, °embarrass, °mortify: *He has been disgraced by his son's cowardice.* **4** °degrade, °debase, °dishonour, °discredit, °disfavour, °vitiate, defame, °disparage, °scandalize, °slur, °stain, °taint, °stigmatize, °sully, besmirch, smirch, °tarnish, °smear, asperse, °vilify, °blacken, drag through the mud, reflect (adversely) on: *Once again his actions have disgraced the family name.*

disgraceful *adj.* **1** °shameful, humiliating, °embarrassing, °dishonourable, °disreputable, °infamous, ignominious, °degrading, debasing, degraded, debased, °base, °low, °vile, °corrupt, °bad, °wrong, °sinful, °evil, °mean, °despicable, °contemptible, opprobrious: *He was forced to submit to the most disgraceful punishment.* **2** °shameless, °outrageous, °notorious, °shocking, °scandalous, °improper, °unseemly, °unworthy; °indecent, °rude, °flagrant, °lewd, °lascivious, °delinquent, objectionable: *Your drunken behaviour at the party last night was a disgraceful performance.*

disgruntled *adj.* displeased, °dissatisfied, irritated, peeved, vexed, °cross, exasperated, annoyed, °unhappy, °disappointed, °discontented, °put out; malcontent, °discontent, °testy, °cranky, °peevish, grouchy, grumpy, °moody, °sullen, sulky, ill-humoured, bad-tempered, ill-tempered, *Colloq* fed up, *Slang* browned off, *Brit* cheesed off: *He was disgruntled at the thought of having to go shopping in the pouring rain.*

disguise *v.* **1** °camouflage, °cover up, °conceal, °hide, °mask: *The van was disguised as a hay wagon.* **2** °misrepresent, °falsify, °counterfeit, °fake, °deceive: *They have disguised the true profits to avoid paying taxes.*
—*n.* **3** °guise, °identity, cover-up, °camouflage, °appearance, °semblance, °form, °outfit, °costume: *She appeared in the disguise of a policewoman.* **4** °pretence, °deception, °dissimulation, façade, °semblance, *Colloq* °front: *Disguise is seldom resorted to by spies these days.*

disgust *v.* **1** °sicken, °offend, °nauseate, °repel, °revolt, °put off, °outrage, °appal, *Slang* °gross out: *His patronizing attitude disgusts those who work for him.*
—*n.* **2** °revulsion, nausea, sickness, repugnance, fulsomeness, °outrage, °distaste, °aversion: *One look at the food filled me with disgust.* **3** °loathing, °contempt, hatred, abhorrence, odium, animus, °animosity, enmity, °antagonism, antipathy, °dislike: *Some feel disgust at the thought of eating insects.*

disgusted *adj.* °nauseated, sickened, °nauseous, °queasy; offended, outraged, *Colloq* fed up (with), °sick (of), °sick and °tired (of); *Slang US* grossed out: *Disgusted customers complain about delays in service.*

disgusting *adj.* nauseating, sickening, °offensive, °outrageous, sick-making, fulsome, °repulsive, °revolting, °repugnant, off-putting, °repellent, °obnoxious, °loathsome, °gross, °vile, °foul, °nasty; unappetizing, °unsavoury, objectionable, °distasteful: *Spitting in public is now considered a disgusting way to behave.*

dishonest *adj.* untrustworthy, underhand(ed), °dishonourable, °fraudulent, °fake, °counterfeit, deceiving, °deceptive, unfair, double-dealing, thieving, thievish, knavish, cheating, °deceitful, °lying, untruthful, mendacious, treacherous, °perfidious, °corrupt, °unscrupulous, unprincipled; °two-faced, °hypocritical; *Colloq* °crooked, °shady; *Chiefly Brit slang* °bent: *He was so dishonest he stole from his mother's purse.*

dishonour *v.* **1** °insult, °abuse, affront, °outrage, °slight, °offend, °injure: *His slaughter of the prisoners has dishonoured our flag.* **2** °disgrace, °degrade, °shame, °debase, °humiliate, °mortify, abase, °vitiate, °humble: *We were all dishonoured by our colleague's defection.* **3** defile, °violate, °ravish, °rape, °seduce, deflower, debauch: *The general learned that his wife had been dishonoured by one of his adjutants.*
—*n.* **4** disesteem, °disrespect, irreverence, °slight, °indignity, ignominy, °disgrace, °shame, disrepute, °discredit, °insult, °offence, affront, loss of °face, depreciation, belittlement, disparagement, detraction, derogation, obloquy: *You cannot retreat without dishonour.* **5** °aspersion, defamation, °libel, °slander, °blot, °slur, °smear, smirch, °black mark, °blemish, denigration: *His actions have brought us dishonour.*

dishonourable *adj.* **1** °disgraceful, °degrading, inglorious, ignominious, °shameful, shaming, °base, debased: *After the court martial, he received a dishonourable discharge.* **2** unprincipled, °shameless, °corrupt, °unscrupulous, untrustworthy, treacherous, °traitorous, °perfidious, °dishonest, °hypocritical, °two-faced, duplicitous, °disreputable, discreditable, °base, °despicable; °disloyal, unfaithful, °faithless: *A double agent is considered dishonourable by both governments.* **3** °improper, °unseemly, °unbecoming, °unworthy, °outrageous, objectionable, reprehensible, °flagrant, °bad, °evil, °vile, °low, °mean, °contemptible, below *or* beneath criticism, °foul, heinous, °dirty, °filthy: *Informing on your classmates is the most dishonourable thing you can do.*

disillusion *v.* disabuse, °disappoint, disenchant, break the spell, °enlighten, set straight, disentrance, disenthral, undeceive: *When I saw her without make-up, I was thoroughly disillusioned.*

disinclined *adj.* °averse, °indisposed, °reluctant, unwilling, °loath, °opposed, unwilling; °hesitant: *I was disinclined to try skydiving.*

disinfect *v.* °clean, °cleanse, °purify, °purge, sanitize, °fumigate, decontaminate, °sterilize: *The bedding will have to be disinfected before it can be used.*

disinfectant *n.* germicide, antiseptic, sterilizer, bactericide, sanitizer, fumigant, decontaminant, decontaminator, purifier, cleaner, cleanser: *Most disinfectants are poisonous.*

disingenuous *adj.* °clever, °artful, °crafty, °sly, on the qui vive, cunning, insidious, °foxy, °wily, °slick, °smooth; °insincere, °false, °dishonest, °tricky, °devious, °deceitful, underhand(ed), guileful, °shifty; double-dealing, °two-faced, duplicitous, °hypocritical, °scheming, plotting, °calculating, °designing, contriving: *It is disingenuous to ask for advice when what you want is assistance.*

disintegrate *v.* °break up *or* °apart, °shatter, °come *or* °fall °apart, come *or* go *or* °fall to °pieces, °crumble; °decompose, °rot, °decay, moulder: *The fossil disintegrated in my hands.*

disinterested *n.* unbiased, °impartial, °unprejudiced, altruistic, °objective, °fair, °neutral, open-minded, °equitable, °just, °dispassionate, °detached, even-handed, °impersonal, uninvolved: *The judge is supposed to be a disinterested party.*

disjointed *adj.* **1** disjoined, °separate(d), °disconnected, unconnected, dismembered, disunited, divided, °split (up): *The disjointed parts of the building were kept in a warehouse.* **2** ununified, °loose, °incoherent, °confused, °aimless, directionless, °rambling, muddled, jumbled, °mixed up, °fitful, discontinuous, disorganized, unorganized, °disorderly: *His speech was disjointed—total gibberish.*

dislike *v.* **1** be °averse to, °mind, °turn from, °disfavour, disesteem, be °put *or* turned off by; °hate, °loathe, °scorn, °despise, contemn, °detest, abominate, execrate: *I no longer dislike spinach.*
—*n.* **2** °aversion, °displeasure, °distaste, °disfavour, disesteem, disrelish, disaffection, disinclination; °loathing, hatred, animus, °animosity, antipathy, detestation, °contempt, execration, °ill will; °disgust, repugnance; °hostility, °antagonism: *I took an instant dislike to the fellow. She feels an intense dislike for her father.*

disloyal *adj.* unfaithful, °faithless, °untrue, °false, untrustworthy, recreant; treasonable *or* treasonous, treacherous, °traitorous, unpatriotic, °subversive, °perfidious, °deceitful; °renegade, apostate, °heretical: *It would be disloyal of you not to vote along party lines.*

dismal *adj.* depressing, °gloomy, cheerless, °melancholy, °sombre, °dreary, °sad, °bleak, °funereal, lugubrious, °forlorn, morose, °solemn, °dark, °grim, °wretched, °woebegone, woeful, °black, °blue, °joyless, °doleful, dolorous, °unhappy, °miserable, lowering; °pessimistic: *She was alone, alone on the dismal moor. The prospects for the company looked very dismal.*

dismay *v.* **1** °alarm, °frighten, °scare, °terrify, °appal, °panic, °horrify, °petrify, °intimidate, cow, disconcert, °unnerve: *We were dismayed when the motor-cycle gang came to the house.* **2** unsettle, discompose, °upset, °discourage, °take aback, °startle, °shock, °put off, dishearten: *I was dismayed to hear she was still married to Grimsby.*
—*n.* **3** consternation, °alarm, °anxiety, °agitation, °terror, °panic, °horror, °shock, °fright, °fear, trepidation, apprehension, °dread, awe: *The thought of the children alone in the boat filled me with dismay.*

dismiss *v.* **1** °discharge, oust, °release, give °notice (to), °let °go, °lay off, °throw out, °toss out, °remove, *Chiefly military* cashier, *Old-fashioned military* drum out, *Brit politics* deselect, *Colloq* °fire, °send packing, °kick out, *Brit* °sack, give (someone) the °sack, °boot (out), turn off, *US* give (someone) his *or* her walking papers, give (someone) a pink slip, can; *Slang* give (someone) the (old) heave-ho: *Gabney has been dismissed without notice.* **2** °reject, °set aside, °repudiate, °spurn, °discount, °disregard, °lay aside, °put out of one's mind, think no more of, °write off, °banish, have *or* be done with, °scorn, °discard, °ignore, shrug off; °belittle, °diminish, pooh-pooh: *She dismissed the story as just so much gossip.* **3** °disperse, °release, °disband, °send away: *After returning from the mission, the commando unit was dismissed.*

dismissal *n.* **1** °discharge, °expulsion, °notice, *Colloq* firing, bounce, marching orders, *Chiefly US and Canadian* walking papers, *Brit* °sack, sacking, one's cards, *US* pink slip; *Slang* the (old) heave-ho, *Brit* the boot: *Cholmondley got his dismissal yesterday.* **2** °cancellation, adjournment, °discharge, °end, °release; *congé: The judge ordered dismissal of the charge of murder.*

disobedient *adj.* **1** °insubordinate, °unruly, °naughty, °mischievous, °bad, ill-behaved, °badly behaved, °obstreperous, unmanageable, refractory, fractious, °ungovernable, uncomplying, unsubmissive, wayward, non-compliant, incompliant, intractable, °defiant; °delinquent, °derelict, disregardful, °remiss, undutiful: *Disobedient children will be kept in after school.* **2** °contrary, °perverse, °wilful, headstrong, °stubborn, °recalcitrant, obdurate, °obstinate, contumacious, wayward, cross-grained, °opposed, °mutinous, °rebellious, °revolting, anarchic(al), *Colloq* pigheaded: *We cannot tolerate disobedient recruits.*

disobey *v.* °defy, °break, contravene, °flout, °disregard, °ignore, °resist, °oppose, °violate, °transgress, °overstep, go counter to, °fly in the face of, °infringe, °thumb one's nose at, °snap one's fingers at, *Brit* cock a snook at; °mutiny, °rebel, °revolt, °strike: *You cannot play because you disobeyed the rules. If anyone disobeys, throw him in irons.*

disorder *n.* **1** disarray, °confusion, °chaos, disorderliness, disorganization, untidiness, °mess, °muddle, °jumble, °hash, °mishmash, °tangle, °hotchpotch *or US and Canadian also* hodgepodge, derangement, °shambles, °clutter: *After the party, the place was in terrible disorder.* **2** °tumult, °riot, °disturbance, °pandemonium, °upheaval, °ferment, °fuss, °unrest, °uproar, hubbub, hullabaloo, commotion, clamour, turbulence, turmoil, °violence, °bedlam, free-for-all, °rumpus, brouhaha, °fracas, affray, °fray, °brawl, Donnybrook, scuffle, °fight, mêlée *or* melee, battle royal, °battle, civil disorder, °breach of the peace, *Colloq Brit* kerfuffle *or* carfuffle *or* kurfuffle, *Slang Brit* bovver: *The army had to be called out to quell the disorder.* **3** °ailment, °illness, sickness, °affliction, malady, °affection, °complaint, °disease: *The doctors diagnosed it as a liver disorder.*
—*v.* **4** °upset, disarrange, °muddle, °confuse, confound, unsettle, disorganize, discompose, °shake up, °disturb, °mix (up), befuddle, °jumble, °scramble, °tangle, °snarl: *You obscure the sense when you disorder the words.*

disorderly *adj.* **1** °confused, °chaotic, scrambled, muddled, disordered, °irregular, °untidy, messy, messed-up, disarranged, disorganized, unorganized, jumbled, cluttered, °haphazard, in disarray, °pell-mell, °helter-skelter, *Colloq* °topsy-turvy, higgledy-piggledy: *The books lay about in disorderly array.* **2** °unruly, °uncontrolled, °undisciplined, ungoverned, °disobedient, °mutinous, °rebellious, °lawless, °obstreperous, refractory, turbulent, °violent, °tumultuous, unrestrained, °boisterous, °noisy, °rowdy, °wild; unmanageable, °ungovernable, uncontrollable, intractable: *He was charged with being drunk and disorderly.*

disorientated *n.* °confused, bewildered, °lost, adrift, (all) at °sea, °mixed up, °uncertain, unsure, °insecure, disoriented, *Colloq* out of it, in a °fog, *Brit* off (the) beam, *US* off the beam: *I left by another door and was completely disorientated for a moment.*

disparage *v.* **1** °belittle, °diminish, °depreciate, devalue *or* devaluate, cheapen, °talk down, °discredit, °dishonour, decry, demean, °criticize, denigrate, deprecate, derogate, underrate, undervalue, °downgrade, °reduce, °minimize: *She keeps making remarks that disparage her husband.* **2** °run down, °slander, °libel, defame, traduce, malign, backbite, °vilify,

°insult, °stab in the back, *US* back-stab; *Colloq* poor mouth; *Slang US and Canadian* bad-mouth: *A loving person never disparages others.*

disparity *n.* °difference, °discrepancy, °gap, °inequality, unevenness, imbalance, °dissimilarity, °contrast, imparity, inconsistency, incongruity: *Our interests differ owing to the disparity in our ages.*

dispassionate *adj.* **1** °cool, °calm, composed, °self-possessed, unemotional, unexcited, unexcitable, unflappable, °level-headed, °sober, self-controlled, even-tempered, unruffled, °unmoved, °tranquil, °equable, placid, °peaceful, °serene: *You can count on Henry for a dispassionate treatment of the subject.* **2** °fair, °impartial, °neutral, °disinterested, °detached, °equitable, even-handed, unbiased, °just, °objective, °unprejudiced, open-minded, °candid, °frank, °open: *The judge is known to be completely dispassionate in his decisions.*

dispatch *v.* **1** °send off *or* away *or* out, °send on one's way: *We dispatched a messenger with the parcel.* **2** °send, °mail, °post, °transmit, °forward, °ship, °express, °remit, convey, *Chiefly US and Canadian* °freight: *Please dispatch this letter as quickly as possible.* **3** °kill, °murder, slay, °dispose of, put to °death, °execute, do away with, do in, assassinate, liquidate, °finish (off), put an °end to, °put away (for good), *Slang* °polish off, °bump off, °eliminate, gun down, °silence, °get, °erase, °rub out, °knock off, °bury, *US* ice, °hit, take for a °ride, °waste, °zap: *The gang soon dispatched all their rivals.* **4** °hasten, °hurry, °speed up, accelerate, get done, °accomplish, °get through, conclude, °finish off, °complete, °execute, do: *The task was dispatched in just two days.*
—*n.* **5** °haste, °speed, promptness, quickness, °expedition, expeditiousness, celerity, alacrity, swiftness, °hurry, °rapidity: *She concluded the interview with dispatch and sent me away.* **6** communiqué, °report, °bulletin, °story, °news (°item), communication, °message, °piece: document, instruction, missive: *Here is a dispatch from our correspondent on Pitcairn Island.* **7** °execution, °killing, °murder, disposal, assassination, dispatching, slaying: *The dispatch of the consul left us without a representative.*

dispensable *adj.* °disposable, °non-essential, unessential, inessential, °unnecessary, unneeded, °expendable, °superfluous, °needless, °useless: *He said that a dishwasher was a luxury and entirely dispensable.*

dispense *v.* **1** °distribute, °give out, °hand *or* °pass out, °furnish, °supply, °provide, °give away, °deal (out), °dole out, °parcel out, disburse, °mete out, °share (out), °issue, apportion, allocate, °allot, °assign, *Colloq* dish out: *The Red Cross dispensed medicines to the stricken villagers.* **2** °administer, °conduct, °direct, °operate, superintend, °supervise, °carry out, °execute, °discharge, °apply, °implement, °enforce: *It is the governor who dispenses justice in these islands.* **3** ***dispense with***: **a** do without, °forgo, °give up, eschew, °relinquish, °refuse, °waive, forswear, abstain (from), °renounce, °reject: *Can we dispense with the jokes and get to work?* **b** do away with, get °rid of, °eliminate, °dispose of, °abolish, °manage *or* do without, °remove, °cancel, °ignore, render °unnecessary *or* °superfluous: *Building on solid rock will dispense with the need for a foundation.*

disperse *v.* **1** °spread (out), °scatter, °broadcast, °distribute, °circulate, °diffuse, disseminate: *The practice is now widely dispersed throughout Asia.* **2** °disband, °spread out, °scatter, °dissipate, °break up; °disappear, vanish; dispel, °dismiss, °rout, °send off *or* away: *The crowd dispersed quietly.*

displace *v.* **1** °move, °transfer, °shift, relocate, dislocate, misplace, °disturb, disarrange, °disorder, unsettle: *The entire population of the village was displaced when the dam was built.* **2** °expel, unseat, °eject, °evict, °exile, °banish, depose, °remove, oust, °dismiss, °discharge, cashier, *Colloq* °fire, °kick *or* °throw out, *Brit* °sack: *The voters displaced the corrupt council.* **3** take the place of, °supplant, °replace, °supersede, °succeed: *Watching television has displaced reading in many modern homes.*

display *v.* **1** °show, °exhibit, °air, °put *or* °set forth, make °visible, °expose, evince, °manifest, °demonstrate, °betray, °reveal, °unveil, °disclose; advertise, °publicize: *Her paintings are being displayed at the gallery today.* **2** unfurl, °unfold, °spread *or* °stretch *or* °open out, °present: *The ship suddenly displayed the Jolly Roger.* **3** °show off, °flaunt, °parade, °flourish, vaunt, *Colloq* flash: *He goes on those quiz programmes only to display his knowledge.*
—*n.* **4** °show, °exhibition, °exhibit, °presentation, array; °demonstration; °exposition, °manifestation, °revelation: *We visited a display of weapons at the armoury. I have seldom seen such a display of ignorance.* **5** °ostentation, °spectacle, °flourish, °show, °parade, °ceremony, °pageantry, °pageant, °splendour, array, panoply, magnificence, °grandeur, °pomp, °splash, éclat, élan, °dash: *The display put on for Queen Victoria's jubilee was truly lavish.*

displease *v.* °offend, °put out, dissatisfy, °upset, °provoke, °exasperate, °worry, °trouble, vex, °annoy, °irritate, pique, °irk, nettle, peeve, °chafe, rile, °ruffle, °anger, °infuriate, °frustrate, get (someone's) goat, *Colloq* miff; *Slang US* °bug: *Having to listen to rock 'n' roll on your damned hi-fi is what displeases me most.*

displeasure *n.* **1** °dissatisfaction, °disapproval, °disfavour, discontentment, °distaste, °dislike, discountenance: *Your parents view your giving up college with displeasure and disappointment.* **2** °annoyance, irritation, vexation, chagrin, °indignation, dudgeon, ire, °anger, exasperation: *He incurred the king's displeasure and was banished from the land.*

disposable *adj.* **1** discardable, throw-away, non-returnable, °paper, °plastic, biodegradable: *The new product is packaged in a disposable container.* **2** °available, °liquid, spendable, usable, °expendable, obtainable: *Her disposable assets include valuable government bonds.*

dispose *v.* **1** °place, °arrange, °move, °adjust, °order, array, °organize, °set up, °situate, °group, °distribute, °put: *She is planning how to dispose the furniture in the room.* **2** °incline, °influence, °persuade, °induce, °bend, °tempt, °move, °motivate, °lead, °prompt, °urge: *Her actions disposed me to cut her out of my will.* **3** ***dispose of***: **a** °deal with, °settle, °decide, °determine, conclude, °finish (with): *I hope we can dispose of these matters quickly.* **b** °throw away *or* out, °discard, get °rid of, jettison, °scrap, *Colloq* °dump, °junk, *US* °trash: *Dispose of the remains of the broken chair.* **c** °distribute, °give out, °deal out, °give (away), °dispense, apportion, °parcel out, °allot, °part with, °transfer, °make over, °bestow, °sell: *My grandfather disposed of his wealth before he died.* **d** do away with, °finish off, °put away, °demolish, °destroy, °consume, °devour, °eat, *Slang* °kill (off), °knock off, °polish off: *She could dispose of four hamburgers at one sitting. The boys disposed of Louie because he knew too much.*

disposed *adj.* °likely, °inclined, apt, °liable, °given, tending *or* °leaning °towards, °prone, °subject, of a °mind to, minded, °willing, °ready, predisposed: *She was still awake when he got home and seemed disposed to talk.*

disposition *n.* **1** °character, °temper, °attitude, temperament, °nature, °personality, °bent, °frame of mind, °humour, °make-up, °spirit: *Alan's son David has a cheerful disposition.* **2** °arrangement, °organization, °placement, disposal, ordering, grouping, °set, placing: *I don't care much for the disposition of the furniture.* **3** °transfer, transference, dispensation, disposal, °assignment, °settlement, °determination, bestowal, parcelling out, °distribution: *The disposition of father's assets is not your affair.* **4** °determination, °choice, disposal, °power, °command, °control, °management, °discretion, °decision, °regulation: *Distribution of favours is at the disposition of the crown.*

dispossess *v.* °evict, °expel, oust, °eject, °turn *or* °drive out, dislodge, *Colloq* °kick *or* °throw out, *Brit*

°boot out, *US* bounce: *The landlord dispossessed them for non-payment of rent.*

disproportion *n.* °inequality, unevenness, °disparity, imbalance, asymmetry, irregularity, lopsidedness, °dissimilarity, inconsistency, incongruity: *Now that we're older, there isn't such a disproportion in our ages.*

disproportionate *adj.* °unbalanced, out of proportion, asymmetrical, °irregular, °lopsided, °dissimilar, °inconsistent, incommensurate, °incongruous; unfair, unequal, uneven, disparate: *The windows are disproportionate to the size of the house. The contractor was paid a disproportionate amount for his work.*

disprove *v.* refute, confute, invalidate, °contradict, negate, °rebut, °discredit, controvert, °puncture, °demolish, °destroy, *Colloq* shoot *or* poke full of holes: *Modern science has disproved the phlogiston theory.*

disputable *n.* °debatable, °moot, °doubtful, °uncertain, dubious, °questionable, undecided, °unsettled, °controversial; arguable: *His claim to ownership of the property is disputable.*

dispute *v.* **1** °argue with *or* against, °question, °debate, °challenge, impugn, gainsay, °deny, °oppose, °fight (against), °object to, take °exception to, °disagree with, °contest, confute, °quarrel with, °doubt, °raise doubts about, dissent (from): *The council dispute his right to build a hotel on that land.* **2** °argue (about), °debate, °discuss, °quarrel about, wrangle over, °differ (on *or* about): *A bill of rights has occasionally been disputed in Parliament.*
—*n.* **3** °argument, °debate, °disagreement, °difference (of opinion), °controversy, polemic, °conflict, °quarrel, wrangle, velitation; °discussion; *Colloq Brit* argy-bargy *or* argie-bargie *or* argle-bargle: *There is a dispute about the runner's eligibility for the race.* **4** °conflict, °disturbance, °fight, altercation, °row, °disagreement, °brawl, Donnybrook, °feud, °rumpus, °fracas; °strife, °discord; °tiff, velitation, *US* spat: *Four people have been injured in the dispute.*

disqualify *v.* declare °ineligible *or* °unqualified, °turn down *or* away, °reject, °exclude, °bar, debar, °rule out: *He was disqualified from voting because of his age.*

disregard *v.* **1** °ignore, °overlook, pay little *or* no °heed *or* °attention to, take little *or* no °notice *or* °account of, °dismiss from one's mind *or* thoughts, turn a blind eye *or* deaf ear to, °brush aside, °pass up, wink *or* °blink at, make °light of, let °go by, °gloss over, *Rare* pretermit: *I shall disregard those insulting remarks.* **2** snub, °slight, turn up one's nose at, °disparage, °despise, contemn, disdain, °scorn, (give the) cold °shoulder (to), °cut; underrate, °underestimate, take little *or* no °account of, undervalue, °minimize, °dismiss, °sneeze at, *Slang* °brush off, give the go-by: *Visitors often disregard the cultural attractions of Las Vegas.*
—*n.* **3** °disrespect, °contempt, °indifference, inattention, non-observance, °neglect, heedlessness, *Rare* pretermission; disdain, low °regard, disesteem: *Some drive with a profound disregard for the law.*

disrepair *n.* °decay, °ruin, °collapse, dilapidation, deterioration, ruination: *The house is in a terrible state of disrepair.*

disreputable *adj.* **1** °low, °base, abject, °contemptuous, unrespectable, disrespectable, untrustworthy, discreditable, °dishonourable, °disgraceful, reprehensible, °shameful, °despicable, ignominious, °bad, °wicked, heinous, °vicious, iniquitous, °vile, opprobrious, °scandalous, louche, °questionable, dubious, *Colloq* °shady: *She keeps disreputable company.* **2** dishevelled, °unkempt, slovenly, °untidy, °shabby, disordered, messy, °dirty, °bedraggled, scruffy, °seedy, °threadbare, °tattered, *Brit* down at °heel, raddled, *US* down at the °heel(s), *Colloq* °sloppy, *Slang Brit* grotty: *That disreputable beggar is your brother?*

disrespect *n.* rudeness, impoliteness, discourtesy, °incivility, unmannerliness, irreverence, °impudence, °impertinence, insolence, indecorum, *Colloq* cheek: *I meant no disrespect by keeping my hat on, ma'am.*

disrespectful *adj.* °impolite, °rude, °discourteous, uncivil, unmannerly, °ill-mannered, bad-mannered, °irreverent, °impudent, °insolent, indecorous, °pert, saucy, °forward, *Colloq* °fresh, °cheeky: *Sara is sometimes disrespectful to her elders.*

disrobe *v.* undress, °strip, °bare oneself: *She disrobed and put on a swimsuit.*

disrupt *v.* **1** °disorder, °upset, disorganize, °disturb, unsettle, °shake up, disconcert, °agitate: *You've disrupted my plan completely.* **2** °interrupt, °break in *or* into, °interfere (with): *They disrupted the meeting with their loud outbursts.*

dissatisfaction *n.* **1** °discontent, discontentment, unhappiness, °displeasure, non-fulfilment, °disappointment, frustration, °discomfort, uneasiness, disquiet, malaise: *I was left with a feeling of dissatisfaction at the end of the play.* **2** °annoyance, irritation, °dismay, °displeasure: *Complaints concerning dissatisfaction with the food plagued the hospital administrators.*

dissatisfied *adj.* °discontented, displeased, °disappointed, unsatisfied, °discontent, °disgruntled, °unhappy, unfulfilled, ungratified, frustrated: *We return the full purchase price to any dissatisfied customer.*

dissension *n.* °disagreement, dissent, °discord, contention, °strife, °conflict, discordance, °friction: *The issue has sown dissension among the members.*

disservice *n.* °harm, °damage, °injury, °wrong, unkindness, °bad °turn, °disfavour, °injustice: *It was a disservice to tell my boss about my expense account.*

dissident *n.* **1** dissenter, °nonconformist, protester *or* protestor, heretic, °rebel, apostate, recusant; °revolutionary: *Many dissidents were released and allowed to leave the country.*
—*adj.* **2** disagreeing, °nonconformist, nonconforming, dissenting, dissentient, apostate, non-compliant, heterodox, °discordant, conflicting, contentious: *The couple spent ten years in Siberia for promoting their dissident philosophy.*

dissimilar *adj.* °different, °unlike, unalike, °distinct, °separate, contrasting, °diverse, °unrelated, heterogeneous: *The styles are entirely dissimilar.*

dissimilarity *n.* °difference, dissimilitude, unlikeness, °disparity; °discrepancy: *The dissimilarities between art deco and art nouveau are too numerous to mention.*

dissimulate *v.* °pretend, dissemble, feign, °disguise, °camouflage, °cover up, °conceal, °deceive, °misrepresent, °fake, °counterfeit: *She's dissimulating her real attitude towards the wealthy.*

dissimulation *n.* °deception, misrepresentation, dissembling, °deceit, °hypocrisy, °sham, °pretence, duplicity, double-dealing: *There can be no dissimulation between honest people.*

dissipate *v.* **1** °scatter, °spread (out), °disperse, be dispelled, °diffuse; disseminate, °sow, °distribute; °break up: *The crowd had dissipated by noon.* **2** °spread thin, °evaporate, vanish, °disappear, vaporize, peter out, °diminish: *By the time we were ready to go, the clouds had dissipated.* **3** squander, °waste, °fritter away, °throw away, °burn up, °use up, °exhaust, °run through: *By the time he was twenty, he had dissipated a huge fortune.* **4** °revel, °carouse, °party, sow one's wild oats, burn the candle at both ends, roister, make °merry, debauch, go on a °spree: *Before their marriage, he was seen dissipating in the fleshpots of Europe.*

dissipation *n.* **1** squandering, °waste, wastefulness, °profligacy, °abandon, abandonment, self-indulgence, self-gratification, over-indulgence, intemperance, hedonism, °fast *or* °high living, *dolce vita*, voluptuousness, sensualism, sybaritism, dissoluteness, °dissolution, °excess(es), wantonness, debauchery, carousing, °prodigality, recklessness, °extravagance, rakishness: *Owing to my dissipation, I had become an alcoholic vagrant.* **2** disappearance, dispersion, dispersal, diffusion, °scattering, vanishing: *The dissipation of the tear-gas was rapid in the strong breeze.* **3** °distraction,

°amusement, °diversion, °entertainment: *Reading, once a dissipation, had become an obsession.*

dissociate *v.* °separate, °cut off, °sever, disassociate, disjoin, °disconnect, °abstract, °disengage, °detach, °isolate, °distance, °break off (from), °break up (with), °divorce, °set °apart, °segregate: *I have carefully dissociated myself from any political party.*

dissolute *adj.* dissipated, debauched, °abandoned, °corrupt, °degenerate, °rakish, °profligate, °wanton, rakehell, intemperate, °incontinent, °loose, licentious, over-indulgent, carousing, °self-indulgent, hedonistic, pleasure-bound, °immoral, amoral, libidinous, unrestrained, depraved: *He has paid dearly for his dissolute life.*

dissolution *n.* **1** disintegration, °separation, breakup, °breakdown, breaking up, breaking down, °collapse, °undoing: *Much ill will attended the dissolution of our marriage.* **2** °destruction, decomposition, °decay, °ruin, °overthrow, dissolving, disbandment, °dismissal, dispersal, disorganization, discontinuation; adjournment, ending, °end, °termination, conclusion, °finish: *A vote of no confidence led to the dissolution of Parliament.*

dissolve *v.* **1** °melt (away), liquefy, °disperse, °disintegrate, °diffuse, °decompose, °thaw (out), °fuse, deliquesce; °sublime; vanish, °disappear, °fade (away), °diminish, °decline, peter out: *Dissolve one tablet in water. The sugar dissolved in the tea.* **2** °collapse, °break into, °melt into: *She dissolved into tears whenever he shouted at her.* **3** °break up, °disperse, °dismiss, °terminate, °finish, conclude, adjourn, °recess, °disband, °wind up; liquidate: *We took a vote and dissolved the meeting.*

distance *n.* **1** remoteness, °space, °gap, °interval, mileage, footage, °stretch: *What is the distance from here to your house?* **2** aloofness, °detachment, °reserve, coolness, haughtiness, hauteur, stiffness, rigidity: *He maintains a distance between himself and the servants.* —*v.* **3** °separate, °detach, °dissociate, disassociate: *She distanced herself from her students.*

distant *adj.* **1** °far, far-off, °remote, °far-away, long-way-off; removed: *The creature said he had come from a distant star.* **2** away, °off: *The ship is ten miles distant.* **3** °aloof, °detached, °reserved, °cool, °cold, °haughty, °standoffish, °unapproachable, °inaccessible, °withdrawn, °reticent, °ceremonious, °formal, °stiff, °rigid, °frigid, unfriendly: *You find him warm, but I think him very distant.*

distaste *n.* **1** °dislike, °disfavour, antipathy, disrelish, disinclination; °dissatisfaction, °displeasure, discontentment: *You know of my distaste for cocktail parties.* **2** °aversion, °revulsion, °disgust, nausea, abhorrence, °loathing, repugnance, °horror: *She has a distinct distaste for avocado pears.*

distasteful *adj.* °disgusting, °revolting, sick-making, nauseating, °nauseous, °repugnant, °repulsive, °loathsome, fulsome, °nasty, °disagreeable, °foul, off-putting, °unpalatable, °obnoxious, objectionable, °offensive, unpleasing, unpleasant, displeasing: *I found their children's table manners quite distasteful.*

distinct *adj.* **1** °clear, °perceptible, °plain, understandable, °vivid, °definite, well-defined, °precise, °exact, unmistakable, °noticeable, recognizable, °obvious, °patent, °marked, °manifest, °evident, °apparent, °explicit, unambiguous, clear-cut, palpable, unequivocal, lucid, °sharp, pellucid, limpid, °transparent: *There is a distinct outline of a figure on the Turin shroud.* **2** °separate, °detached, °discrete, °different, °dissimilar, distinguishable, °distinguished; °individual, sui generis, °unique, °special, °singular; °peculiar, °unusual, uncommon, contrasting: *The government of Puerto Rico is distinct from that of the US. He has been charged with three distinct offences.*

distinction *n.* **1** differentiation, °discrimination, °difference, °contrast, °separation, °division, dividing °line; distinctiveness: *Any distinction between them is difficult to discern.* **2** °honour, °credit, °prominence, eminence, °pre-eminence, °superiority, uniqueness, greatness, °excellence, °quality, °merit, °worth, value, °prestige, °note, °importance, °significance, consequence, °renown, °fame, repute, °reputation, °celebrity, °glory, °account: *We all know her as a scholar of distinction.*

distinctive *adj.* distinguishing, °characteristic, °unique, °singular, °distinct, °individual, °typical, idiosyncratic, °peculiar: *She has developed a distinctive style of her own.*

distinguish *v.* **1** °differentiate, °discriminate, °tell the °difference, °tell °apart, °determine, °judge, °decide, °tell who's who *or* what's what: *He is still unable to distinguish between his own twin daughters.* **2** classify, °categorize, °characterize, individualize, °mark, °identify, °define, °designate, °denote, °indicate, °separate, °single out, °set °apart; °grade, °group: *The male is distinguished by his brighter colouring.* **3** °sense, °make out, °perceive, discern, °pick out, °recognize, °identify, °detect, °notice; °see, espy, descry; °hear; °smell; °taste; °feel: *I could distinguish two people in the dark.* **4** call °attention to, °identify, °mark, °set °apart, °separate, °segregate, °indicate, particularize: *She distinguished herself by her great beauty and her awful voice.*

distinguished *adj.* **1** °celebrated, °famous, °illustrious, °noted, °renowned, °notable, °noteworthy, °pre-eminent, °eminent, °prominent, honoured, respected, °honourable: *Churchill was one of the most distinguished men of his day.* **2** °dignified, °noble, °grand, °stately, *distingué*, °royal, °regal, aristocratic: *What is he doing in this distinguished gathering?*

distort *v.* **1** °twist, °warp, deform, misshape, contort, gnarl, °bend, disfigure, °wrench: *The car was completely distorted in the crash.* **2** °twist, °warp, °slant, °tamper with, °colour, varnish, torture, °pervert, °misrepresent, °fabricate, °falsify, misstate, °alter, °change, °bend, °garble, °violate: *She distorted the facts if she said it was Bill who had a gun.*

distract *v.* **1** °divert, °deflect, °sidetrack, °turn aside, °draw away: *Sorry, I was distracted for a moment—where were we?* **2** °divert, °amuse, °entertain, °gratify, °delight, °occupy, °interest, absorb, engross: *We found the belly-dancers quite distracting.* **3** °bewilder, °confuse, confound, °perplex, °puzzle, discompose, befuddle, °mystify, disconcert, °fluster, °rattle, °bemuse, °daze, °disturb, °agitate, °trouble, °bother: *I am distracted with doubts about whether to phone the police.*

distraction *n.* **1** bewilderment, befuddlement, °disorder, °disturbance, °upset, °confusion, °agitation: *The princess loves you to distraction.* **2** °diversion, °entertainment, °amusement: *I was never really interested in him, he was merely a temporary distraction.*

distraught *adj.* distracted, °agitated, troubled, °disturbed, °upset, perturbed, wrought *or* worked up, °excited, °frantic, at (one's) wits' end, °overwrought, frenetic, °nervous, frenzied, °feverish, °wild, °hysterical, °delirious, irrational, °crazy, °mad, °insane, °berserk, run(ning) amok *or* amuck: *He is distraught with grief.*

distress *n.* **1** °anguish, °anxiety, °affliction, angst, °grief, °misery, °torment, °ache, °pain, °suffering, °agony, torture, °woe, woefulness, wretchedness; unhappiness, °sorrow, °sadness, °depression, heartache, °desolation: *It is impossible to imagine the distress of a bereaved parent.* **2** °calamity, °trouble, adversity, °catastrophe, °tragedy, °misfortune, °difficulty, °hardship, straits, °trial, °disaster: *Has he no sympathy for the distresses that have beset his people?* —*v.* **3** °bother, °disturb, °perturb, °upset, °trouble, °worry, harrow, harry, vex, °harass, °plague, °oppress, °grieve, °torment, torture, °afflict: *The thought of Miss Camberley as a hostage distressed us all.*

distribute *v.* **1** °deal *or* °dole out, °parcel out, °give (out), °mete out, °dispense, apportion, °allot, °share (out), °partition, °divide up, °assign, °issue, °circulate, °pass out, °pass °round *or* around, °hand out, °deliver, convey, *Colloq* dish *or* spoon out: *Emergency rations* *were distributed to the flood victims.* **2** °disperse, °scatter, °strew, °spread (°round *or* around *or* about), °diffuse, disseminate: *Mammals are uniformly distributed over the globe.* **3** °sort, classify, °class, °categorize, assort, °arrange, °group, °file, °order: *Distribute the packages according to their size.*

distribution *n.* **1** apportionment, °allotment, allocation, °assignment, parcelling out, sharing; deployment: *She supervised the distribution of the prizes.* **2** issuance, °circulation, dissemination, giving (out), dispersal, dispensation; deployment: *The distribution of food parcels is being handled by charities.* **3** °arrangement, °disposition, grouping, classification, °order, ordering, °division, cataloguing, codification; deployment: *What is the distribution of scientists among the population?*

district *n.* °territory, °region, °section, sector, °division, °partition, °part, °precinct, locality, °area, °locale, °department, °province, community, °quarter, °neighbourhood, °ward: *We need a new hospital in our district.*

distrust *v.* **1** °mistrust, °doubt, °question, be °sceptical of, be circumspect *or* °cautious about, °suspect, be °suspicious *or* °wary of, °discredit, disbelieve, *Colloq* smell a rat; *Colloq* be °leery of: *I distrusted her motives from the very beginning.*
—*n.* **2** °mistrust, °doubt, doubtfulness, uncertainty, °misgiving(s), °scepticism, °suspicion, disbelief, incredulity, incredulousness, hesitation, °caution, wariness, °qualm, hesitancy: *His claims were greeted with distrust.*

distrustful *adj.* distrusting, untrusting, mistrustful, doubting, chary, °wary, °cautious, °suspicious, °sceptical, °doubtful, dubious, cynical, disbelieving, °unbelieving, uneasy, °nervous, °hesitant, hesitating, unsure, °uncertain, *Colloq* °leery: *She is distrustful of men who bring her flowers.*

disturb *v.* **1** °interrupt, °disrupt, °intrude (on), °inconvenience, °put out, °interfere (with); °bother, °pester, °annoy, °irritate, °irk, °upset, °plague, hector, harry, °harass, °worry, vex, °provoke, pique, peeve, get on (someone's) nerves, *Colloq* °bug, miff, get under (someone's) skin, get in (someone's) hair, drive nuts *or* °crazy *or* bats *or* batty *or* bananas *or* up the wall, hassle: *The sound of dripping water disturbed me. Please do not disturb the animals.* **2** °agitate, °stir *or* churn (up), °shake (up), unsettle, roil, °disorder: *The lake's surface was violently disturbed by an enormous creature.* **3** unsettle, °affect, °upset, °damage, °harm, °destroy: *We put the delicate mechanism where it wouldn't be disturbed by curious visitors.* **4** °trouble, disconcert, °discomfit, °perturb, °ruffle, °fluster, °upset, °agitate, °put off, °bother, discommode, °put out, unsettle, °distress; °alarm, *Colloq* °shake (up): *He was greatly disturbed by the death of his father.* **5** °affect, °upset, confound, °confuse, °change, °put off, °ruin, °destroy, °cancel, make °ineffectual *or* °ineffective, negate: *Any change in temperature will disturb the results of the experiment.*

disturbance *n.* **1** disruption, °disorder, disorganization, disarrangement, disarray; °upheaval, °interruption, °upset, intrusion, °interference: *She won't tolerate any disturbance to her schedule.* **2** commotion, °disorder, °upset, °outburst, °tumult, turmoil, turbulence, °violence, hubbub, hullabaloo, hurly-burly, °uproar, brouhaha, °rumpus, °brawl, mêlée *or* melee, °breach of the peace, Donnybrook, °fray, affray, °fracas, °trouble, *Colloq* ruckus, *Brit* spot of °bother, *Slang Brit* spot of bovver: *There was a disturbance at the pub yesterday.*

disturbed *adj.* **1** °upset, uneasy, uncomfortable, discomfited, troubled, °worried, bothered, °agitated, °anxious, °concerned, apprehensive, °nervous: *He's disturbed that Marie didn't come home last night.* **2** psychoneurotic, °neurotic, °unbalanced, psychopathic, °psychotic, maladjusted, °mad, °insane, out of one's °mind, depressed, *Colloq* °crazy, unable to cope, *Brit* bonkers, *Slang* nuts, screwy, batty, off one's rocker, off the deep end, messed-up, screwed-up: *She looks after her sister, who is disturbed.*

disturbing *adj.* upsetting, off-putting, perturbing, troubling, °unsettling, worrying, °disconcerting, disquieting, alarming, distressing: *There is disturbing news from the front.*

disused *adj.* °abandoned, neglected, °unused; discontinued, °obsolete, archaic: *We had to sleep in a disused railway carriage.*

diurnal *adj.* °daily, circadian; day-to-day, °regular, °everyday, quotidian; daytime: *Jet lag is a disturbance of the body's diurnal rhythms. Are these animals nocturnal or diurnal?*

dive *v.* **1** °plunge, nosedive, °sound, °descend, °dip, °submerge, °go under, °sink; °jump, °leap, °duck; °swoop, °plummet: *The submarine dived at once.*
—*n.* **2** °plunge, nosedive: *The plane went into a dive.* **3** °bar, saloon, nightclub, bistro, °club, *Colloq* nightspot, *Slang* °joint, *US* °dump, honky-tonk, juke-joint: *He met the woman in a dive in Limehouse.*

diverge *v.* **1** °separate, °radiate, °spread (°apart), °divide, subdivide, fork, °branch (off *or* out), ramify, °split: *The roads diverge further on.* **2** °deviate, °turn aside *or* away, °wander, digress, °stray, °depart, °drift, divagate: *Our policy diverges from that set up by the committee.*

divergent *adj.* differing, °different, °dissimilar, disparate, °variant, °separate, diverging, disagreeing, conflicting, discrepant: *There are divergent theories about the origin of the universe.*

divers *adj.* °various, °several, °sundry; °miscellaneous, multifarious, °manifold, °varied, assorted, °variegated, differing, °different; some, numerous, °many: *We have the divers statements of the witnesses.*

diverse *adj.* divers, °different, °varied, diversified, multiform, °various, assorted, °mixed, °miscellaneous; °distinctive, °distinct, °separate, varying, °discrete, °dissimilar, differing, °divergent, heterogeneous: *Diverse subjects are available for study.*

diversify *v.* °vary, variegate, °change, °mix; °spread, °distribute, °divide, °break up, °separate; °branch out: *We must diversify our investments to hedge against losses. Perhaps this is not a good time to diversify into other areas.*

diversion *n.* **1** °digression, deviation, departure, °distraction: *George created a diversion, while we robbed the safe.* **2** °detour, °sidetrack, deviation, °bypass: *Owing to roadworks, we had to take a diversion off the main road.* **3** °amusement, °distraction, °entertainment, °pastime, °recreation, divertissement, °game, °play, °relaxation: *She prefers chess for diversion.*

diversity *n.* **1** °difference, °dissimilarity, dissimilitude, unlikeness, °disparity, deviation, divergence, departure, distinctiveness, diverseness, °variation, °variety, individuality, inconsistency, contrariety, °discrepancy, °contrast: *Flowers are impressive in their diversity.* **2** °variety, °range, °extent, heterogeneity, multiplicity, multifariousness, variegation, multiformity: *Democracy encourages diversity of opinion.*

divert *v.* **1** °switch, rechannel, redirect; °change, °alter, °deflect: *Funds for the new civic centre have been diverted to housing. We must divert the course of the river.* **2** °turn away, °turn aside, avert, re-route, °deflect; °change course, °swerve (off *or* away), °shift, °sidetrack, °depart, °deviate: *Cars were diverted to avoid flooded areas. We diverted from our route because of the roadworks.* **3** °entertain, °amuse, °distract, °interest, °beguile, °engage, °occupy, absorb: *We found the stand-up comedian mildly diverting but not really funny.*

divest *v.* **1** °strip, denude, °rid, get °rid, °relieve, disencumber, °deprive, °dispossess; despoil, mulct: *The company has been divested of all its assets.* **2 divest oneself of**: °take *or* °put off, doff, °remove; °disrobe, unclothe, undress: *She divested herself of her fur coat.*

divide *v.* **1** °separate, °split (up), °break up, °cleave, °cut up *or* asunder, °partition, °segregate, subdivide; °disconnect, disjoin, °detach, °sever, sunder, °part: *Argyle divided his mountaineers into three regiments. A divided nation cannot stand. Some would like to see*

Britain divided from continental Europe. **2** Sometimes, ***divide up***: °distribute, °share (out), °measure out, °parcel out, °partition, °dole (out), °deal (out), °mete out, allocate, °allot, apportion, °dispense, °give (out): *The remaining food was divided among us.* **3** °separate, °split, cause to °disagree, °alienate, disunite, °set at °odds, sow °dissension (among), °pit *or* °set against one another, disaffect: *Racial issues still divide the people.* **4** °branch (out), ramify, °split, °separate: *The road divides there and passes on each side of that huge rock.* **5** °categorize, classify, °sort, assort, °grade, °group, (put in) °order, °rank, °organize, °arrange: *You have to divide the books into several piles according to size.*

divine *adj.* **1** °godlike, °godly, °holy, deiform, deific, angelic, °seraphic, °saintly; °heavenly, °celestial; °sacred, sanctified, hallowed, consecrated, °religious, °spiritual: *They believe in the divine right of kings. He receives divine inspiration at divine services.* **2** °superhuman, °supernatural, °gifted, °pre-eminent, °superior, °excellent, °supreme, °exalted, °transcendent, °extraordinary: *Even the divine Homer nods.* **3** °great, °marvellous, °splendid, °superlative, °glorious, °superb, °admirable, wonderful, °awesome, °perfect, °excellent, °beautiful, *Colloq* °super, °terrific, smashing, °fantastic, splendiferous, *Colloq Brit* ace, °magic: *They say that the new musical is simply divine.*
—*v.* **4** intuit, °imagine, conjecture, °guess, °assume, °presume, °infer, °suppose, hypothesize, °surmise, °suspect, °understand, °perceive, °speculate, °theorize, °predict, foretell, have foreknowledge of; °determine, °discover: *He had divined that she might be there.*
—*n.* **5** °holy man, °priest, °clergyman, cleric, ecclesiastic, °minister, °pastor, reverend, churchman, prelate: *At his club, he enjoys the company of bishops, archbishops, and other divines.*

division *n.* **1** dividing, °split, splitting (up), breaking up, °partition, partitioning, partitionment, °separation, separating, diremption, segmentation, segmenting, compartmentation, sectioning, apportioning, apportionment, °allotment: *In England a division between Church and State is not recognized.* **2** °section, °compartment, °segment; °partition, °separation: *Egg crates have 144 divisions.* **3** °branch, °department, sector, °section, °unit, °group, arm; °part, °set, °category, °class, classification: *The textile division of the company lost money last year.* **4** °boundary (°line), °border, borderline, °frontier, °margin, °line, dividing °line: *Where is the division between good and evil?* **5** °discord, °disagreement, °upset, °conflict, °strife, disunity, disunion: *The issue of equal rights has led to much division within the movement.*

divorce *n.* **1** °separation, °split, split-up, °dissolution, severance, disunion, break-up: *Their divorce after twenty years surprised everyone.*
—*v.* **2** °separate, °divide, °split (up), °part, °sever, °detach, °dissociate, disassociate; °dissolve: *A splinter group has divorced itself from the main party. We were divorced last year.*

dizzy *adj.* **1** °giddy, vertiginous, light-headed, °faint, dazed, tottering, unsteady, reeling, tipsy, *Colloq* woozy: *I felt dizzy after going down the helter-skelter.* **2** °confused, °silly, °giddy, empty-headed, °scatter-brained, muddled, befuddled, °flighty, feather-headed, feather-brained, rattle-brained, °hare-brained, °frivolous: *He is dizzy with power.*

dock *n.* **1** wharf, °pier, berth, jetty, quay: *We went to the dock to see them off.*
—*v.* **2** (drop) °anchor, berth, °tie up, °moor, °land, °put in: *The ship docks at noon.*

doctor *n.* **1** °physician, medical practitioner, M.D., general practitioner, G.P., *Colloq* medic, medico, doc, sawbones, bones: *You ought to see a doctor about that cough.*
—*v.* **2** °treat, °attend, medicate; °cure, °heal; °practise °medicine: *She knows very little about doctoring children, in spite of having worked as a general practitioner.* **3** °mend, °repair, °patch (up), °fix: *We doctored the tyre as best we could.* **4** °falsify, °tamper with, °adulterate, °disguise, °change, °modify, °alter; °cut, °dilute, °water (down); °spike; °drug, °poison: *This sauce has been doctored.*

doctrine *n.* teaching, body of °instruction, °precept; °principle, °tenet, dogma, article of °faith, canon, °conviction, °creed, °belief, credo, °opinion, °idea, concept, theory, °proposition, °thesis, postulate: *Few believe the doctrine that all men are created equal.*

document *n.* **1** °paper, certificate, °instrument, °report, °chronicle, °record: *All the legal documents are at my lawyer's office.*
—*v.* **2** °record, °chronicle, particularize, °detail, °describe; °verify, validate, °certify, °authenticate, corroborate, °substantiate: *Detectives have documented every move you made since the murder.*

doddering *adj.* shaking, quaking, palsied, trembling, trembly, quivering, quavering, reeling, unsteady, °shaky, staggering, °shambling, °decrepit, faltering; °feeble, °weak, °frail, °infirm; °aged, °old, superannuated, °senile, anile: *Once a vigorous sportsman, his illness has reduced him to a doddering octogenarian.*

dodge *v.* **1** dart, °shift, °move aside, °sidestep, °duck, bob, °weave, °swerve, veer: *He dodged here and there across the traffic.* **2** °avoid, °elude, °evade, °escape from: *He neatly dodged the punches of his opponent.* **3** °escape from answering, °sidestep, °duck, °evade, hedge; °quibble, tergiversate, double-talk, *Colloq* °waffle: *She dodged the questions put to her by the interviewer.*
—*n.* **4** °trick, °subterfuge, ploy, °scheme, °ruse, °device, °stratagem, °plan, °plot, °machination, chicane, °deception, prevarication, contrivance, °evasion, *Slang* wheeze, °racket: *Crenshaw worked out a new dodge to avoid paying tax.*

dodgy *adj.* °tricky, °dangerous, °perilous, °risky, °difficult, °ticklish, °sensitive, °delicate, °touchy; °uncertain, °unreliable; °rickety, *Colloq* chancy, °hairy, *Brit* °dicky, °dicey: *Climbing up the sheer face of that rock could be a bit dodgy. You shouldn't be exerting yourself with your dodgy ticker.*

dogmatic *adj.* °arbitrary, °categorical, °dictatorial, imperious, °peremptory, °overbearing, doctrinaire, °authoritarian, °emphatic, °insistent, °assertive, °arrogant, °domineering; obdurate, °stubborn; °opinionated, °positive, °certain, *Rare* thetic(al), *Colloq* °pushy: *Patrick tends to be quite dogmatic when he is sure of his ground.*

dole *n.* **1** °portion, °allotment, °share, °quota, °lot, °allowance, °parcel; compensation, °benefit, °grant, °award, °donation, °gift, °largesse, alms, gratuity; *Slang* hand-out: *The prisoners received a daily dole of bread. If you've lost your job, are you eligible for the dole?* **2** °distribution, apportionment, allocation, dispensation: *The money was given to the disaster victims by dole.*
—*v.* **3** °give (out), °deal (out), °distribute, °hand out, °mete out, °share (out), °dispense, °allot, allocate, apportion, *Colloq* dish out: *They dole out the reparations on the basis of need.*

doleful *adj.* °sad, °sorrowful, °melancholy, °gloomy, °mournful, cheerless, °joyless, °sombre, depressed, disconsolate, °blue, down, distressed, °dejected, °downhearted, °forlorn, °unhappy, lugubrious, dolorous, °wretched, °miserable, °woebegone, °dreary, woeful, *Colloq* down in the °mouth, down in the dumps; distressing, °funereal, depressing, °grievous, °harrowing: *From his doleful expression I thought he would cry any minute. She lives in the most doleful surroundings.*

dolt *n.* °fool, ass, blockhead, dunce, dullard, idiot, nitwit, ignoramus, numskull *or* numbskull, donkey, nincompoop, ninny, ninny-hammer, simpleton, dunderpate, dunderhead, bonehead, °twit, fat-head, goon, moron, imbecile, *Colloq* °dope, dumb-bell, dimwit, chump, °dummy, °halfwit, birdbrain, pinhead, clot, °clod, chucklehead, *Brit* muggins, *US* thimble-wit, °jerk, knuckle-head, lunkhead, meat-head, lame-brain, dingbat, ding-a-ling, °flake: *The dolt actually tried to buy striped paint!*

domain *n.* **1** °realm, °dominion, °territory, °property, °land(s), °province, °kingdom, empire: *At one time his domain included most of Europe.* **2** °province, °realm, °territory, °field, bailiwick, °area, °department, °sphere, °discipline, °speciality *or US* specialty, specialization, °concern: *As a dentist, he considered diseases of the throat outside his domain.*

domestic *adj.* **1** °home, °private, °family, familial; residential, household: *Her domestic life is a shambles. This toaster is for domestic use.* **2** °tame, domesticated, house-trained, house-broken: *Tenants are forbidden to keep domestic animals.* **3** °home, °native, °indigenous, °internal, autochthonous: *The domestic market accounts for most of the company's income.*
—*n.* **4** °servant, (hired) °help, housekeeper, majordomo, steward: *Her domestics left and she now does the cleaning herself.*

domicile *n.* **1** °dwelling (-place), °residence, °abode, °home, habitation, (living) quarters, °housing, °accommodation(s), °lodging(s), *Colloq Brit* digs, diggings, *Slang* °pad: *Domiciles in south-east England have increased enormously in value.*
—*v.* **2** °locate, °quarter, °lodge, °settle, °establish, °situate, domiciliate: *She is domiciled abroad, hence pays no income tax here.*

dominant *adj.* **1** commanding, °authoritative, controlling, governing, ruling, °leading, reigning, °influential, °assertive, °supreme, °superior, ascendant: *He has taken a dominant role in promoting foreign language teaching.* **2** °predominant, °chief, °main, °principal, °primary, °prevailing, °outstanding, °pre-eminent, °paramount: *A large nose is a dominant characteristic in their family.*

dominate *v.* **1** °command, °control, °govern, °rule, °direct, °lead, °reign (over), exercise °command *or* °authority *or* °control *or* °rule over, have the whip *or* °upper hand (over), °run (things), be in *or* have under °control, °rule the roost *or* roast, *Colloq* call the shots *or* the tune, wear the trousers *or US* the pants, be in the driver's seat, °rule with an iron hand, have under one's °thumb: *She clearly dominates the board of directors.* **2** °overlook, °look (out) over, °tower over *or* above, °rise above, °overshadow; °predominate: *The Eiffel Tower dominates the Parisian skyline.*

domination *n.* **1** °authority, °control, °rule, °power, °command, °influence, °sway, °supremacy, ascendancy, hegemony, the whip *or* °upper hand, °pre-eminence, mastery: *The tsar's domination lasted for more than thirty years.* **2** °oppression, °subjection, °repression, °suppression, subordination, enslavement, enthralment; dictatorship, °despotism, °tyranny: *The Allies finally brought to an end the Fascist domination of Europe.*

domineering *adj.* °overbearing, imperious, °officious, °arrogant, autocratic, °authoritarian, high-handed, high and mighty, °masterful, °arbitrary, °peremptory, °dictatorial, °despotic, °tyrannical, °oppressive, °strict, °hard, °harsh, °tough, *Colloq* °bossy, °pushy: *A classic character in humorous writing is the domineering spouse.*

dominion *n.* **1** °rule, °authority, °control, dominance, °domination, °grasp, mastery, °grip, °command, °jurisdiction, °power, °sovereignty, °sway, ascendancy, °pre-eminence, primacy, °supremacy, hegemony: *The magician claimed dominion over the entire universe.* **2** °domain, °realm, °territory, °region, °area, °country, °kingdom: *For six generations the dynasty ruled over its dominions on five continents.*

donate *v.* °give, °provide, °supply, °present, °contribute, °subscribe (to *or* for), °pledge, °award, °bestow, °confer, °grant, °vouchsafe, °will, °bequeath: *Lady Crayford donated two silver candlesticks to our charity drive.*

donation *n.* **1** °gift, contribution, °largesse, °present, °grant, °award, alms, °offering, °bequest: *Donations have exceeded our expectations.* **2** giving, contribution, bestowal, °allotment, °provision, °offer: *We are seeking the donation of a piano for our theatre group.*

donor *n.* giver, provider, supplier, °benefactor *or* benefactress, contributor, °supporter, °backer: *Blood donors receive a suitably inscribed certificate.*

doom *n.* °fate, karma, °destiny, °fortune, °lot, kismet; °downfall, °destruction, °death, °ruin, extinction, annihilation, °end, °termination, terminus: *The warrior had defied the Snake God, and his doom was sealed.*

doomed *adj.* **1** °fated, cursed, condemned, damned, °destined, ordained, foreordained, predestined: *She was doomed to live for ever.* **2** accursed, bedevilled, ill-fated, luckless, star-crossed, bewitched, condemned: *The doomed ship sank to the bottom of the sea.*

dope *n.* **1** See **dolt,** above. **2** °narcotic, °drug, opiate, hallucinogen, psychedelic, *Slang* upper, downer: *He was caught trying to smuggle dope past customs.*
3 °information, °data, facts, °news, details, °story, °scoop, *Slang* info, °low-down, °score, *Brit* gen, *US and Canadian* poop: *The real dope on the minister is sensational!*

dormant *adj.* **1** asleep, sleeping, slumbering, resting, at °rest, °quiet, °inactive, °still, °inert, unmoving, motionless, stationary, immobile, quiescent, comatose, °torpid, hibernating, slumberous, somnolent, °sleepy, °lethargic, °dull, sluggish: *The bears are dormant during much of the winter.* **2** latent, °potential, °hidden, concealed, undisclosed, unrevealed, unexpressed: *The theory lay dormant for centuries and has only recently been revived.*

dose *n.* **1** °portion, °quantity, °amount, °measure, dosage: *How big a dose of the medication did the doctor prescribe?*
—*v.* **2** °dispense, °administer, °prescribe: *I was dosed with medicine and slept all day.*

dot *n.* **1** °spot, °speck, °point, °jot, °mark, iota, fleck, °dab; decimal °point, *Brit* full °stop, *US* °period: *Use three dots to denote text omissions.* **2** ***on the dot***: °exactly, °precisely, punctually, to the minute *or* second, on °time, *Colloq* on the button: *She arrived at noon on the dot.*
—*v.* **3** °spot, fleck, speckle, stipple, bespeckle: *The wallpaper is dotted with tiny squares of colour.*

dote *v.* Often, ***dote on*** *or* ***upon***: be °fond of, be °infatuated with, °love, °idolize, hold °dear, °adore, °make much of; °coddle, °pamper, °spoil, °indulge: *I think she dotes on her husband at the expense of the children. What we need is a doting grandmother to babysit when we want to go out.*

double *adj.* **1** twofold, paired, coupled, °duplicate(d), doubled: *The forms* banned *and* banning *are spelt with a double* n. **2** folded *or* doubled *or* °bent over, overlapped, two-ply: *This wound needs a double bandage.* **3** dual, twofold, °ambiguous, double-barrelled: *He pronounced it 'de-seat', giving* deceit *a double meaning.* **4** twice: *The plant had grown to double its size.* **5** °deceitful, °dishonest, treacherous, °traitorous, °insincere, °hypocritical, double-dealing, °false: *It was Maria who exposed Fernando as a double agent.*
—*v.* **6** °duplicate, replicate; °copy; °increase, °enlarge; °magnify: *We'll have to double our milk order.*
—*n.* **7** °twin, °duplicate, °copy, °replica, °facsimile, clone, counterpart, *doppelgänger*, °look-alike, °stand-in, °understudy, *Slang* (dead) ringer, spitting °image *or* °spit and °image: *He could be Clint Eastwood's double.* **8** ***at*** *or* ***on the double***: °quickly, on the °run, at full °speed *or* tilt, briskly, °immediately, at °once, without delay, *Slang* p.d.q. (= 'pretty damned quick'): *Put down that book and come over here on the double!*

double-cross *v.* °cheat, °defraud, °swindle, °hoodwink, °trick, °betray, °deceive, °mislead, play °false with, *Colloq* two-time: *He swore he'd give me the money but he double-crossed me and kept it himself.*

doubt *v.* **1** disbelieve, °discredit, °mistrust, °distrust, have °misgivings (about), °question, °suspect: *I doubted his ability to beat the record.* **2** °hesitate, waver, vacillate, °fluctuate, °scruple, be °uncertain, entertain doubts, have reservations: *Who ever doubted her honesty?*

—*n.* **3** uncertainty, hesitation, °misgiving, °reservation(s), °qualm, °anxiety, °worry, apprehension, disquiet, °fear: *He has harboured doubts about the success of the enterprise.* **4** °distrust, °mistrust, °suspicion, incredulity, °scepticism, dubiousness, dubiety *or* dubiosity, lack of °faith *or* °conviction, irresolution: *Her doubts about his intentions have evaporated.* **5** ***in doubt***: See **doubtful,** below.

doubtful *adj.* **1** in °doubt, dubious, °questionable, open to °question, °problematic, °debatable, °disputable, °uncertain, unpredictable, indeterminate, °unsettled, °unresolved, conjectural, °indefinite, unclear, °obscure, °vague, anybody's guess, *Colloq* up in the air: *The result is very doubtful.* **2** °sceptical, unconvinced, °distrustful, mistrustful, °suspicious, °uncertain, unsure, °hesitant, hesitating, vacillating, °indecisive: *I am doubtful whether an investigation will yield anything.* **3** dubious, °questionable, °shady, louche, °disreputable, °controversial: *Those are people of doubtful reputation.*

doubtless *adv.* **1** doubtlessly, °undoubtedly, no °doubt, indubitably, indisputably, unquestionably, °surely, for °sure, certainly, for °certain, °naturally, without (a) °doubt, beyond *or* without (a shadow of) a °doubt, °truly, °positively, °absolutely, *Colloq* absotively-posolutely, *US* make no mistake: *You doubtless remember my aunt?* **2** °probably, most *or* very °likely, in all °probability, °supposedly, °presumably: *He will doubtless be refused entry into the country.*

dour *adj.* **1** °sullen, °sour, unfriendly, °cold, °gloomy, morose, °dreary, °grim, cheerless, °dismal, °forbidding: *We went to Spain, away from the dour northern climate.* **2** °hard, °tough, austere, °severe, °hardy, °inflexible, °obstinate, °stubborn, unyielding, uncompromising, °strict, °rigid, obdurate, °stern, °harsh, adamant, *Colloq* hard-nosed: *Her father was a dour Scot who wouldn't let me in the house.*

dowdy *adj.* frowzy *or* frouzy *or* frowsy, frumpy, frumpish, °drab, °dull, °seedy, °shabby, °unseemly, °unbecoming; slovenly, °sloppy, messy, °unkempt; °old-fashioned, unfashionable, *Colloq US* °tacky: *Aunt Patience looked particularly dowdy in her dressing-gown and slippers.*

down and out *adj.* **1** °indigent, poverty-stricken, °poor, penniless, °destitute, °impoverished, *Colloq* °broke, *US* on the skids, on skid row, on the °bum, *Slang Brit* skint: *Those vagrants are down and out and need help, not pity.*
—*n.* **2** ***down-and-out***: °derelict, °beggar, °outcast, °tramp, vagrant, °vagabond, *US* °bum: *He took to drink and ended up a complete down-and-out.*

downfall *n.* °ruin, °undoing, débâcle, °collapse, °degradation, °defeat, °overthrow, °breakdown: *Selling the company to the conglomerate spelt its downfall.*

downgrade *v.* **1** demote, dethrone, °humble, °lower, °reduce, °displace, depose, °dispossess, disfranchise *or* disenfranchise, *US military* bust; *Colloq* bring *or* take down a °peg: *He was downgraded from supervisor to foreman.* **2** °belittle, °minimize, °play down, °disparage, decry, denigrate, °run down, *US and Canadian* downplay: *How could she downgrade her own sister?*
—*n.* **3** descent, °decline, declension, (°downward) °slope, gradient, °grade, °inclination: *Apply the brake as you approach the downgrade.* **4** ***on the downgrade***: on the °wane, waning, declining, falling, slipping, falling off, losing ground, going downhill, *US and Canadian* on the skids: *After the drug scandal, her popularity was on the downgrade.*

downhearted *adj.* discouraged, depressed, low-spirited, °miserable, °blue, °sad, downcast, °dejected: *Don't be so downhearted, we know you can win the gold medal.*

downpour *n.* rainstorm, deluge, inundation, cloudburst, thunder-shower, thunderstorm, °torrential °rain, °torrent; monsoon: *We got caught in that downpour without an umbrella.*

downright *adj.* **1** °direct, straightforward, °plain, °frank, °open, °candid, plain-spoken, °explicit, °blunt, °brash, °bluff, not roundabout *or* circuitous, unambiguous, °out-and-out, °outright, °categorical, °flat, unequivocal, °outspoken, unreserved, °unabashed, unrestrained, unconstrained, °bold: *She speaks with a downright honesty you have to admire.*
—*adv.* **2** °completely, °entirely, °totally, °thoroughly, certainly, °surely, (most) assuredly, °definitely, °absolutely, unconditionally, unequivocally; °very, °extremely, unqualifiedly, °perfectly, uncompromisingly, unmitigatedly, °utterly, unquestionably, °profoundly, °undoubtedly, indubitably: *It's downright stupid of you to leave in this weather.*

downtrodden *adj.* subjugated, oppressed, burdened, plagued, afflicted, exploited, overwhelmed, cowed, °overcome, beaten, °abused, mistreated, maltreated, tyrannized, *Colloq* °beat: *This poor, downtrodden wreck of a man had once been on top.*

downward *adj.* declining, sliding, slipping, spiralling, descending, going *or* heading *or* moving down: *This downward trend in the market will soon be reversed.*

downwards *adv.* down, °downward, °below, °lower: *We moved downwards, towards the centre of the earth.*

doze *v.* **1** Often, ***doze off***: (take *or* have a) °nap, catnap, drowse, °sleep, slumber, *Colloq* snooze, have forty winks, °drop *or* °nod off, grab some shut-eye, *Chiefly Brit* (have *or* take a) zizz, *Brit* kip, *US* catch *or* log a few zees (Z's): *I was dozing in the sun when the phone rang.*
—*n.* **2** °nap, catnap, siesta, °sleep; °rest; *Colloq* snooze, forty winks, shut-eye, *Brit* zizz, kip, lie-down: *I'll have a short doze before dinner.*

drab *adj.* °dull, °colourless, °dreary, °dingy, °lacklustre, lustreless, °dismal, cheerless, °grey, °sombre: *She wore drab clothes and no make-up.*

draft *n.* **1** °plan, sketch, °drawing, °outline, °rough (sketch), blueprint, diagram, °prospectus: *We must have the draft of the new design by morning.* **2** °bill of exchange, cheque, °money order, postal order; letter of credit: *Our customer issued a draft in full payment.*
—*v.* **3** sketch, delineate, °outline, °design, °plan, °frame, °block out, °compose, diagram, °draw (up): *The art department has drafted the layout for the new encyclopedia.*

drag *v.* **1** °pull, °draw, °haul, °tow, °tug, °trail, °lug: *It took the two of us to drag the desk into the other office.* **2** °pull, °distract, °draw; °induce, °persuade, °coax, °wheedle: *She's been unable to drag him away from the TV.* **3** trudge, slog, °crawl, °creep, inch, °shuffle, shamble: *He's looking for a job and just drags along from one employment agency to another.* **4** °trail (behind), °linger, °dawdle, °lag (behind), °straggle, draggle, °potter *or US* putter, loiter, poke (along), dilly-dally, *US* lallygag: *She just drags along after us wherever we go.* **5** (be) °prolong(ed), (be) °extend(ed), (be) °draw(n) out, (be) protract(ed), (be) °stretch(ed) out, °spin out *or* be spun out: *Why drag out the agony of uncertainty any longer? His speech dragged on for another hour.* **6** ***drag one's feet*** *or* ***heels***: °delay, °procrastinate, °hang back; °obstruct, °block, °stall: *The committee is dragging its feet on the housing issue.*
—*n.* **7** °bore, °nuisance, °annoyance; °pest; *Colloq* °drip, °pain (in the neck), °headache: *That course in botany is a real drag.*

drain *n.* **1** ditch, °channel, trench, culvert, conduit, °pipe, gutter, °outlet, watercourse, sewer, cloaca: *The storm drains have overflowed.* **2** depletion, reduction, sapping, °sap, °exhaustion, °strain, °drag; outgo, outflow, withdrawal, disbursement, °expenditure: *The cost of the new roof was a drain on our resources.* **3** ***down the drain***: wasted, gone, thrown away, °lost, *Slang* up the °spout: *All that money spent on his education went down the drain.*
—*v.* **4** °draw off, °tap, °extract, °remove, °take away, °withdraw, °pump off *or* out; °empty, °evacuate, °drink up *or* down, quaff, °swallow, °finish: *After washing the lettuce, drain off the water. He drained the glass in one gulp.* **5** °consume, °use up, °exhaust, °sap, deplete,

bleed, °strain, °tax, °spend; °weaken, debilitate, °impair, °cripple: *The car repairs drained my bank account. After climbing to the top of the mountain, we were completely drained.* **6** seep, °trickle, °ooze, °drip, °leave, °go *or* °flow from *or* out of, °disappear (from), °ebb: *Let the pus drain from the boil. The blood drained from his face when he saw her.*

drama *n.* **1** °play, °stage °play, photoplay, screenplay, (°stage) °show, (°theatrical) °piece, (°stage) °production; °scenario: *He plays only in dramas, never in musicals.* **2** dramaturgy, stagecraft, °theatre °art(s), °Thespian *or* histrionic °art(s), acting, °theatre, °dramatic °art(s): *She has studied drama at RADA.* **3** histrionics, dramatics, theatrics, theatricalism, play-acting: *There's always a drama over who's going to wash up.*

dramatic *adj.* **1** theatric(al), dramaturgic(al), °Thespian, histrionic, °stage: *She was studying the dramatic works of Shakespeare. There will be a festival of dramatic arts at the centre next week.* **2** °vivid, °sensational, °startling, breathtaking, °sudden, °striking, °noticeable, °extraordinary, °impressive, °marked, °shocking, °expressive, °graphic, °effective; °complete, °considerable, °radical, °major: *A dramatic change has come over him since meeting her.* **3** °flamboyant, °melodramatic, colourful, °showy, °stirring, spectacular; °theatrical, histrionic, exaggerated, overdone: *His presentation was quite dramatic, well staged and with much arm-waving.*

dramatist *n.* °playwright, dramaturge, screenwriter, scriptwriter, scenarist, tragedian, melodramatist: *The actors failed to carry out the dramatist's intentions.*

dramatize *v.* °exaggerate, overplay, °overstate, °overdo, make a production *or* °show (out) of, *Colloq* °lay it on (thick), °pile it on, ham (something *or* it) up: *He always dramatizes everything way out of proportion.*

drape *v.* **1** °hang, festoon, °swathe, deck, array, bedeck, adorn, °ornament, °decorate: *The coffin was draped with the national flag.*
—*n.* **2** °drapery, curtain; hanging, tapestry: *The drapes match neither the carpet nor the wallpaper.*

drapery *n.* °drape, curtain; hanging, valance, pelmet, tapestry, arras, *portière*, lambrequin, °drop: *Which colour will you choose for the drapery?*

drastic *adj.* °violent, °severe, °extreme, °strong, °powerful, °potent, puissant, °fierce, °forceful, °vigorous, rigorous, °harsh, °radical, Draconian, °desperate, dire: *I shall have to take drastic measures if this misbehaviour continues.*

draught *n.* **1** °breeze, °breath (of °air), (light) °wind, °current (of °air), °puff (of °air *or* °wind): *You'll get a cold sitting in the draught.* **2** °dose, °portion, °measure, °quantity, °drink, °swallow, °sip, °nip, °tot, potation, dram, °gulp, *Colloq* swig, tipple: *The doctor recommended a draught of this tonic before meals.*

draw *v.* **1** °pull, °tug, °tow, °drag, °haul, °lug: *The gypsy caravan was drawn by two horses.* **2** °pull *or* °take out, °extract; unsheathe, unholster: *The cowboy drew his gun and began firing.* **3** draw off; °pour; °drain off *or* out: *She drew two pails of water for the horses.* **4** °attract, °gather, allure, °lure, °bring out *or* forth, °elicit, *Colloq* °pull: *Anything will draw a crowd in New York.* **5** depict, sketch, °portray, °outline, delineate, °design, limn, °paint: *The artist was drawing pictures in chalk on the pavement.* **6** °devise, draw up, °draft, °create, contrive, °frame, °compose, °prepare: *The plans for the new civic centre have not yet been drawn.* **7** °inhale, °breathe (in), °inspire; suck in: *She's very ill and may draw her last breath any minute.* **8** draw out, °withdraw, °take, °receive, °get, °acquire, °obtain, °secure, °procure, °extract, °remove: *I have to draw some money from my bank account for groceries.* **9** °choose, °pick, °select, °take: *It is your turn to draw a card.* **10** ***draw back***: °retreat, °recoil, °shrink (from), °withdraw: *He drew back quickly when he saw the snake.* **11** ***draw in***: °arrive, °pull in: *The train drew in to the station.* **12** ***draw off***: **a** °tap, °pour: *The barmaid drew off two large beers from the keg.* **b** °withdraw, draw *or* °go away, °depart, °leave: *The Indians drew off and waited to see what we would do.* **13** ***draw on***: **a** °employ, °use, make °use of, °exploit, have °resort *or* °recourse to, °resort to, °fall back on, °rely *or* °depend on: *She drew on her years of experience as a doctor.* **b** °come °close *or* °near, °near, draw nigh, °approach, °advance: *With the cold season drawing on, we had to get in the crops.* **14** ***draw out***: **a** °extend, °drag out, °prolong, protract, °lengthen, °stretch, °spin out: *Her visit has been drawn out to a week.* **b** °elicit, °evoke, °induce to talk: *I drew him out on his feelings about social security.* **c** See **8**, above. **15** ***draw up***: **a** °halt, °stop, °pull up *or* over: *A taxi drew up and I got in.* **b** °draft, °compose, °prepare, °put down (in °writing), °frame, °compile, °put together, °formulate: *We drew up the agreement only yesterday.* **c** °arrange, deploy, °position, °order, °rank, marshal: *The troops were drawn up in full battle array.*
—*n.* **16** °magnetism, °attraction, °lure, °enticement, *Colloq* °pull, drawing °power: *The draw of the rock concert was extraordinary.* **17** °tie, °stalemate, dead heat, °deadlock: *The race ended in a draw for second place.*

drawback *n.* °disadvantage, °hindrance, °stumbling-block, °obstacle, °impediment, °hurdle, °obstruction, °snag, °problem, °difficulty, °hitch, °catch, °handicap, °liability, °flaw, °defect, °detriment, *Colloq* °fly in the ointment: *Lack of education is a serious drawback to getting a good job.*

drawing *n.* °picture, depiction, °representation, sketch, °plan, °outline, °design, °composition, black-and-white, monochrome: *The book is illustrated by some delightful pen-and-ink drawings.*

drawn *adj.* °haggard, °worn out, °tired, °fatigued, °strained, pinched, °tense, °exhausted: *Sidonia looks a bit drawn after her ordeal.*

dread *v.* **1** °fear, be °afraid of, apprehend, °anticipate, °flinch, °shrink *or* °recoil from, °cringe *or* quail *or* blench *or* wince at, view with °horror *or* °alarm: *She dreads any kind of surgery.*
—*n.* **2** °fear, °fright, fearfulness, trepidation, apprehension, apprehensiveness, uneasiness, °anticipation, °alarm, nervousness, °qualm, queasiness, °misgiving, °dismay, °worry, °anxiety, consternation, °concern, °distress, perturbation, disquiet, °aversion, °horror, °terror, °panic, *Colloq* cold feet, butterflies (in the stomach), the °jitters; *Slang* the heebie-jeebies, the willies, the collywobbles: *I regarded the history exam with dread.*
—*adj.* **3** feared, dreaded, °dreadful, °terrifying, °terrible: *Before us, breathing fire, was the dread dragon of the Druids.*

dreadful *adj.* **1** °bad, °awful, °terrible, *Colloq* °rotten, *Slang* °lousy: *That TV soap opera is simply dreadful.* **2** °grievous, dire, °horrible, horrendous, horrifying, horrid, °monstrous, °fearful, feared, °frightful, °dread, °frightening, °shocking, alarming, appalling, °fearsome, °hideous, °ghastly, °atrocious, heinous, °wicked, °evil, iniquitous, °villainous, flagitious, °fiendish, diabolic(al), °devilish, demonic, malevolent, maleficent, malefic, *Colloq* °scary: *They did the most dreadful things to political prisoners.*

dream *n.* **1** °reverie, °day-dream, °delusion, °fantasy, °hallucination, °illusion, °vision, mirage, pipedream, (flight of) °fancy, °speculation: *When I awoke I realized that my winning the lottery had just been a dream.*
—*v.* **2** °imagine, °fancy, conjure up, hallucinate: *I dreamt I dwelt in marble halls.*

dreamer *n.* fantasizer, °visionary, idealist, °romantic, romanticist, idealizer, Utopian; day-dreamer, escapist, star-gazer: *If you think people change, you're a dreamer.*

dreamlike *adj.* °unreal, °fantastic, °unbelievable, phantasmagoric(al), hallucinatory *or* hallucinative *or* hallucinational, surreal, delusionary *or* delusional, illusionary *or* illusional, delusive *or* delusory, °illusory *or* illusive, °insubstantial *or* unsubstantial, °imaginary, chimerical, °fanciful, °fancied, °visionary: *His plans have a dreamlike quality about them that make them impractical.*

dreamy *adj.* **1** °dreamlike, °vague, °indefinite, °indistinct, undefined, °intangible, °misty, °shadowy, °faint: *He has a dreamy recollection of being awakened in the middle of the night.* **2** °absent-minded, °absent, °faraway, abstracted, °pensive, °thoughtful; daydreaming, musing, occupied, in a °reverie, in a brown study, in the clouds; *Colloq* off somewhere: *I was in a dreamy mood, my mind wandering through old memories.* **3** relaxing, °soothing, calming, lulling, °gentle, °tranquil, °peaceful, °peaceable, °quiet; °lazy, °sleepy, °drowsy: *It was one of those dreamy, hot midsummer days.*

dreary *adj.* **1** °dismal, °joyless, cheerless, °gloomy, °bleak, drear, °sombre, °doleful, depressing, °wretched; °sad, °melancholy, downcast, depressed, °funereal, °glum, °unhappy, °forlorn, °mournful, morose, °blue, °miserable: *One more day on these dreary moors and I shall go mad. Caroline was again in a dreary mood.* **2** °boring, °lifeless, °colourless, ennuyant, °drab, °dull, arid, °dry, uninteresting, °dead, °monotonous, °prosaic, °tedious, °tiresome, tiring, wearisome, wearying, °humdrum, °ordinary, °vapid, run-of-the-mill, unstimulating, unexciting: *Do you mean to tell me that that dreary book is a best seller!*

dregs *n.pl.* **1** °sediment, °grounds, lees, °deposit, °residue, solids, °remains; °precipitate: *Filter the coffee to remove the dregs.* **2** °outcasts, pariahs, °rabble, °riffraff, scum, °tramps, °down-and-outs, °losers: *That park is frequented by the dregs of society.*

drench *v.* °soak, °saturate, °wet, °flood, inundate, °immerse, °drown: *She had no coat or umbrella and got completely drenched in the storm.*

dress *v.* **1** °clothe, °put on (clothing *or* °clothes), attire, °apparel, °outfit, °fit out, garb, accoutre *or US also* accouter; array, bedeck, deck out, °rig out, smarten up: *They dressed him to look like a prince.* **2** array, °equip, adorn, °decorate, deck out, °arrange: *He has a job dressing shop windows.* **3** bandage, °treat, medicate, °doctor: *After dressing my wound they gave me a sedative.* **4** ***dress down***: °reprimand, °scold, °berate, °castigate, °rebuke, °reprove, °upbraid, *Colloq* °tell off, haul (someone) over the coals, *Brit* tear (someone) off a strip, *US and Canadian* °chew out, *US* rake (someone) over the coals, tee off on (someone): *The colonel dressed us down and cancelled all leave.*
5 ***dress up***: **a** °put on dinner *or* °formal °clothes, °put on one's (Sunday) °best (°clothes), *Colloq* °put on one's °best bib and tucker *or* one's glad °rags: *On the cruise, we dressed up in our dinner-jackets every night.* **b** (°put on a) °costume, °disguise, °masquerade, °camouflage, °put on °fancy °dress: *The children dressed up as goblins for Hallowe'en.*
—*n.* **6** frock, gown, °outfit, °costume, *Colloq* °get-up: *Why not wear your new dress to the dance tonight?*

dressmaker *n.* seamstress, °tailor, couturier *or* couturière, modiste: *She's at the dressmaker's having a ball gown fitted.*

dressy *adj.* **1** °formal, dressed-up, °elegant, °fancy, °chic: *A black suit is too dressy to wear tonight—it's not a dressy party.* **2** °elegant, °smart, °stylish, *Colloq* classy, ritzy, *Brit* °swish: *That's a very dressy outfit, I must say!*

drift *v.* **1** °coast, °float, °waft: *A log drifted by on the tide.* **2** °wander, °roam, °meander, °stray, rove, °ramble, *Colloq* mosey: *He seems just to drift through life, without a purpose.*
—*n.* **3** °trend, °tendency, °direction, °course, °current, °bias, °inclination, °flow, °sweep, °bent: *The drift of the conversation seemed to be towards politics.* **4** °intention, °meaning, purport, °purpose, °aim, °object, °tenor, °tone, °spirit, °colour, °essence, °gist, °significance, °import: *Offended by the drift of her remarks, I excused myself.* **5** °accumulation, °pile, °heap, °mass, bank, °mound, dune: *After the snowstorm, a huge drift blocked the door.*

drifter *n.* vagrant, °tramp, °vagabond, beachcomber, rambler, wanderer, *Colloq* knight of the road, *US* °bum, hobo: *A drifter, he had no place to call home.*

drill *v.* **1** °bore, °penetrate, °pierce, °cut a °hole: *The thieves drilled into the safe.* **2** °rehearse, °train, °practise, °exercise, °teach, °instruct, °school, °tutor, °coach, °indoctrinate; °discipline: *We were thoroughly drilled in the Latin conjugations and declensions.*
—*n.* **3** auger, (°brace and) bit, gimlet: *The bit for this drill is no longer sharp.* **4** °practice, training, °repetition, °exercise, °rehearsal; °discipline: *Tomorrow there will be a complete drill of the parts of speech.*

drink *v.* **1** quaff, imbibe, °sip, °gulp, °swallow, °swill, guzzle, °toss off, °lap (up), *Colloq* wet one's whistle, swig, °knock back, *US* belt: *She prefers not to drink beer.* **2** tipple, °nip, °indulge, tope, chug-a-lug, °carouse, *Colloq* °booze, bend the elbow, hit the °bottle, go on a binge *or* °bender, drown one's sorrows, *US and Canadian* go on a toot, *Chiefly Brit* pub-crawl: *He threatened to leave her if she continued to drink.* **3** ***drink to***: °toast, °salute, °celebrate, °pledge: *Let's drink to friendship!*
—*n.* **4** beverage, potation, °liquid °refreshment, °liquid, potable, °draught: *After the match I was dying for a drink.* **5** °alcohol, spirits, °liquor, the cup that cheers; stirrup-cup; *Colloq* °booze, the °bottle, °hard stuff, mother's °ruin, eye-opener, nightcap, *US* hooch; *Slang* rot-gut, *US* the sauce, red-eye: *After the accident, he took to drink.* **6** °tot, °nip, °draught *or US also* °draft, schooner, pint, bumper, jigger, snifter, °sip, °taste, °glass, °gulp, °swallow, *Scots* (wee) deoch an doris *or* doch an dorris, (wee) dram, *Brit* sundowner; *Colloq* snort, slug, swig: *Granny likes a drink before retiring.* **7** ***the drink***: the °sea, the °ocean, the main, the °deep, *Nautical* Davy Jones's locker, *Colloq* the briny: *The canoe tipped and our picnic went right into the drink!*

drip *v.* **1** dribble, °trickle, °drop; drizzle, sprinkle: *The tap began to drip and kept me awake all night.*
—*n.* **2** dribble, °trickle, °drop, dripping: *Yes, it was the drip from the tap that kept me awake.* **3** °milksop, °bore, wet blanket, °killjoy, damper, *Colloq Brit* °wet, weed, *Colloq* wimp, *Slang* °pill, °drag, *US and Canadian* milquetoast: *Must you invite that drip George?*

drive *v.* **1** °push, °propel, impel, °urge, °press, °thrust, °move, °motivate, actuate, °prod, °spur, goad, °force, °make, compel, coerce, constrain, °oblige, °pressure *or Brit* pressurize, high-pressure, °induce, °require; °demand: *What drove you to become a traitor?*
2 °operate, °conduct, °manoeuvre, °manipulate, °handle, °steer, °control; °pilot: *Have you a valid licence to drive this car?* **3** °ride, °travel, motor, °go, °move, °proceed, °journey, °tour, *Colloq* °tool along: *Luckily, when the tyre blew out, we were driving at only 20 m.p.h.* **4** °stab, °plunge, °thrust, °sink, °push, °send, °dig, °ram: *He has driven the dagger deep into the monster's heart.* **5** °herd, drove, °shepherd, °ride °herd (on): *We used to drive the cattle up the old Chisholm Trail to market in Abilene.* **6** ***drive at***: °hint (at), °suggest, °imply, °intimate, allude *or* °refer to, °intend, °mean, have in °mind, °indicate, *Colloq* °get at: *He was so naïve he had no idea what she was driving at.*
—*n.* **7** °ride, °trip, °outing, °journey, °run, °tour, °excursion, *Colloq* °spin, whirl: *On Sundays we would go for a drive in the country.* **8** °energy, °effort, °impetus, °vigour, vim, °spunk, °enterprise, °industry, °initiative, °ambition, ambitiousness, °determination, °persistence, °urgency, zeal, °enthusiasm, keenness, aggressiveness, *Colloq* get-up-and-go, °pep, zip, °push, °hustle: *She owes her success to her drive as well as her talent.* **9** driveway, °approach, (private) °road *or* °street, lane, byway, (scenic) °route: *The drive up to the house is lined with trees.* **10** °campaign, °effort, °appeal, °crusade: *The club has had a successful membership drive this year.*

drivel *v.* **1** dribble, drool, slobber, °slaver: *You're drivelling all over the front of your shirt!* **2** °babble, prate, °prattle, gibber, °jabber, burble, gabble, °chatter, blether *or US* blather, *Colloq* jibber-jabber, °gab, *Brit*

rabbit *or* witter *or* natter on, *US* run off at the mouth: *She keeps drivelling on about her family.*
—*n.* **3** °gibberish, °rubbish, (°stuff and) °nonsense, twaddle, balderdash, hogwash, *Colloq* eyewash, tripe, °garbage, malarkey, hooey, °hot air, bosh, boloney *or* baloney, *Slang* crap, bull, bilge (water), codswallop, *US* horse feathers, *Taboo* bullshit, balls, *Brit* (load of old) cobblers: *I've never heard so much drivel from a candidate in my entire life!*

droop *v.* **1** °sag, °hang (down), °wilt, °dangle: *Flags drooped in the windless heat.* **2** languish, °weaken, °flag, °wilt, wither, be °limp, °slump, °sag: *Halfway through the marathon she began to droop a bit.*

drop *n.* **1** globule, bead, °drip, droplet, °tear: *A drop of sweat hung from his nose.* **2** °bit, °spot, °particle, °taste, dram, °sip, °nip, °pinch, °dash, °dab, *Colloq* smidgen *or* smidgin: *Add a drop of milk before kneading the dough.* **3** descent, °fall: *There was a sheer drop of a thousand feet from the ledge into the chasm below.* **4** °decline, °slope, fall-off, drop-off, declivity, °incline: *The drop is about 15 feet in 100.*
—*v.* **5** °drip, °trickle, dribble: *As the water drops, filling the tube, the float rises.* **6** °fall, °descend, °sink, drop away *or* down *or* off, °dive, °plunge, °plummet, °decline, °collapse: *The barometer dropped 10 millibars in 10 minutes. Near that rock, the road drops to the beach. At the first shot, we dropped to the ground.* **7** °desert, °forsake, °give up, °abandon, °leave, °quit, °throw over, °jilt, °discard, °reject, °repudiate, °renounce, *Colloq* chuck, ditch, °dump; °relinquish, °let °go, °discontinue, °stop, °cease, °end: *After what he said, she dropped him like a hot potato. I wish you'd drop the subject of my disability.* **8** °release, °let °go of, °shed, °cast off, °discard, doff: *Deciduous trees drop their leaves in winter.* **9** °omit, °leave out, °exclude, °eliminate: *To avoid confusion with his father, he dropped his middle initial.* **10** °dismiss, °let °go, °fire, °discharge, oust, *Colloq chiefly Brit* °sack, give (someone) the °sack: *They dropped her after a week's trial.* **11** °decline, °decrease, drop *or* °fall off, °diminish, slacken, °slack *or* °taper off, °subside, lessen: *Demand for swimsuits drops during the winter.* **12** ***drop in (on)***: °visit, °call (on), °pop in (on), °come by, °stop in: *Viola dropped in for tea yesterday.* **13** ***drop out***: °withdraw (from), °leave; rusticate, °depart, decamp, °go away *or* off, °take off, °turn off: *She dropped out of school. After winning the award, Crater dropped out and hasn't been seen since.*

drown *v.* **1** °flood, inundate, °swamp, deluge, °drench, °immerse, °submerge, engulf: *The village was completely drowned in the tidal wave.* **2** °overwhelm, °overcome, °overpower, engulf, °swamp, deluge, inundate: *We were almost drowned by the responses to our advertisement.*

drowsy *adj.* °sleepy, heavy-lidded, °groggy, somnolent, dozy, oscitant; °nodding, yawning; °torpid, sluggish, °tired, °weary, °listless, °lethargic, °lazy: *We all felt a bit drowsy after that big dinner.*

drudgery *n.* toil, °labour, moil, travail, (°hack) °work, donkey-work, chore, slog, slogging, °slavery, *Colloq* °grind, °sweat, *Brit* skivvying, °fag: *She wanted some relief from the sheer drudgery of housework.*

drug *n.* **1** medication, °medicine, medicament, pharmaceutical, °remedy, °cure, °treatment; cure-all, panacea: *My doctor prescribes too many drugs.* **2** opiate, °narcotic, °stimulant, °tranquillizer, antidepressant, hallucinogen(ic), psychedelic, hypnotic, soporific, °sedative, analgesic, °painkiller, *Slang* °dope, downer, upper: *Can they control the traffic in drugs?*
—*v.* **3** °dose, medicate, °treat: *I was drugged with antihistamines and unable to drive.* **4** anaesthetize, °dope, °deaden, °knock out, °sedate, stupefy, °numb, benumb, °dull, narcotize; °poison, *Slang* slip (someone) a Mickey (Finn): *The victim had been drugged and kidnapped.*

druggist *n.* °pharmacist, apothecary, *Brit* chemist: *Only a druggist is qualified to dispense this medication.*

drunk *adj.* **1** drunken, intoxicated, inebriated, besotted, tipsy, °groggy, sotted, crapulent *or* crapulous, in one's cups, under the weather, under the influence, °maudlin, ebriate, ebriose, ebrious, *Colloq* soused, pickled, °high (as a kite), °tight, boozed, boozy, lit (up), half-seas-over, three *or* four sheets to the wind, out (cold), under the table, *Brit* squiffy; *Slang* pie-eyed, °loaded, stoned, stewed (to the gills), (well-)oiled, bombed (out of one's mind), crocked, plastered, tanked, sloshed, polluted, stinko, smashed, blotto, pissed: *He was so drunk he tried to fly.* **2** exhilarated, °excited, °exuberant, invigorated, inspirited, °animated, °ecstatic; flushed, °feverish, °inflamed, aflame, °fervent, fervid, °delirious: *Since he became a director, he's been drunk with power.*
—*n.* **3** drunkard, drinker, toper, tippler, sot, °soak, bibber, winebibber; dipsomaniac, °alcoholic, problem drinker; *Colloq* guzzler, swiller, sponge, *Slang* wino, boozer, dipso, °lush, souse, alchy *or* alkic *or* alky, *US* juicer, juice-head, rummy: *The drunks who volunteered were registered for treatment.* **4** °carouse, bacchanal, carousal, bacchanalia, °revel, *Slang* °bender, °tear, °jag, bat, *US and Canadian* toot, *Chiefly Brit* pub-crawl: *I went off on a wild drunk the night before my wedding.*

drunkenness *n.* intoxication, insobriety, intemperance, sottishness, bibulousness, inebriety, crapulence, crapulousness, tipsiness, ebriety; dipsomania, alcoholism, ebriosity; *Colloq* boozing, *Slang* hitting the °bottle *or US* the sauce: *Only a psychiatrist could help cure his drunkenness.*

dry *adj.* **1** dehydrated, desiccated, arid, sear, parched, waterless, moistureless; °barren, °bare, °fruitless: *With no rain for a month, the dry earth yielded no crops.* **2** °dreary, °boring, °tedious, °tiresome, wearisome, wearying, tiring, °dull, uninteresting, °monotonous, °prosaic, commonplace, °stale, uninspired; °plain, °unadorned, unembellished: *The minister's speech was as dry as could be, a litany of dry statistics.* **3** °witty, droll, °wry, cynical, °biting, °sarcastic, °cutting, °keen, °sly, ironic: *Oscar Wilde was known for his dry witticisms.*
—*v.* **4** dehydrate, desiccate, °parch: *As the rainfall subsided, the land dried and changed into a desert.* **5** dry up *or* out, wither, °shrivel, °shrink, °wilt: *The plants dried because they weren't watered.*

duck *v.* **1** bob, °dodge, °dip, °dive, °stoop, °bow, °bend, °crouch: *I ducked to avoid hitting my head on the beam.* **2** °plunge, °submerge, °immerse, dunk: *In the pool, she ducked me when I least expected it.* **3** °avoid, °sidestep, °evade, °dodge, °elude, °shun, °steer clear of, °shy away from; °shirk: *He is known for ducking his responsibilities.*

dud *n.* **1** °failure, *Colloq* °flop, lead balloon, lemon, washout, *Colloq US and Canadian* dog, clinker: *Her second novel certainly proved a dud—it sold only ten copies.*
—*adj.* **2** °worthless, valueless, °broken, unusable, °useless, inoperative, non-functioning, malfunctioning, *Colloq* kaput, bust(ed), *Brit* °duff: *They deliberately supplied us with dud ammunition.*

dude *n.* **1** °dandy, fop, °fancy dresser, Beau Brummell, popinjay, boulevardier, man about town, *Archaic* coxcomb, macaroni; *Slang* °swell, *Brit* toff: *He dressed like a real dude—zoot suit and all.* **2** °man, °fellow, °chap, *Colloq* °guy: *Hey, man, who's that dude in the tartan suit?*

due *adj.* **1** °payable, owed, owing, °unpaid, °outstanding, in arrears: *The rent is due tomorrow.* **2** °fitting, °right, °rightful, °correct, °proper, °appropriate, apropos, apposite, °suitable, apt, °meet; °deserved, (well-)earned, merited, °just, justified: *Was she treated with due respect?* **3** °necessary, needed, °adequate, °sufficient, °enough, °satisfactory; °ample, °plenty of: *I do not think my case was given due consideration.* **4** expected, scheduled, anticipated: *He was due on the two o'clock plane.*
—*adv.* **5** °directly, °exactly, °precisely, °straight: *Go due east to the river, then turn north.*

dues *n.pl.* (membership) °fee, °charge(s): *If you have not paid your dues, you may not use the club's facilities.*

duff *adj.* °bad, °useless, °worthless, unworkable, inoperable, inoperative, °broken; °fake, °false, °counterfeit, *Colloq* °dud, °phoney *or US also* phony: *We couldn't get that duff radio to work. We were provided with duff papers for crossing the border.*

duffer *n.* °incompetent, blunderer, bungler, oaf, *Colloq* ox, lummox: *He may be an expert at computers but he's a duffer at golf.*

dull *adj.* **1** °stupid, slow-witted, °dense, °stolid, bovine, cloddish, clod-like, °backward, °obtuse, doltish, crass, °dumb, *Colloq* °thick, °dim, dim-witted, *Brit* °dim as a Toc H lamp: *He might be a dull student but he's a brilliant artist.* **2** insensitive, °numb, °insensible, imperceptive *or* impercipient, unresponsive, °indifferent, unfeeling, °unsympathetic, °callous, hardened, °hard, inured, obtundent: *He knew that he could expect only a dull response to his pleading.* **3** °lifeless, °indifferent, unresponsive, sluggish, °slow, °listless, °inactive, °torpid: *The market for luxury cars is a little dull now.* **4** °boring, °tiresome, °tedious, °monotonous, uninspired, uninspiring, unoriginal, uninteresting, °humdrum: *All work and no play make Jack a dull boy.* **5** °dismal, °dreary, depressing, °sombre, °grey, °dark, °murky, °gloomy, cloudy, clouded, °overcast, °sunless: *If the day is dull, the photographs will show it.* **6** blunted, °blunt; °obtuse: *I nicked myself with that dull razor.* **7** °hazy, blurry, °opaque, °drab: *Rub the dull film off that silver goblet.* **8** muffled, numbing, deadened, muted, °indistinct: *I've had a dull pain in my arm all day.*
—*v.* **9** allay, assuage, °relieve, °mitigate, lessen, °reduce: *Weeping dulls the inner pain.* **10** °dim, °tarnish, °obscure, bedim, °blur, cloud, becloud: *A mist dulled the rich colours of the glen.* **11** stupefy, narcotize, °numb, benumb, desensitize, °deaden, °blunt, obtund: *His war experiences had dulled his feelings towards others.*

duly *adv.* **1** °properly, fittingly, deservedly, °appropriately, suitably, befittingly, rightly, correctly, °accordingly: *Those elected were duly installed in office.* **2** punctually, on °time: *The train duly arrived.*

dumb *adj.* **1** °mute, °speechless, voiceless; °silent, °quiet, °taciturn, °mum, wordless; °inarticulate: *She was struck dumb with astonishment.* **2** °dull, °stupid, *Colloq* °thick: *He's too dumb to understand what you are saying.*

dumbfound *v.* dumfound, °amaze, °shock, °surprise, °startle, °astonish, °astound, °bewilder, °stagger, °stun, °floor, °nonplus, °confuse, confound, *Colloq* flabbergast, °bowl over: *Their offer for the house dumbfounded us.*

dumbfounded *adj.* dumfounded, amazed, shocked, surprised, startled, astonished, astounded, bewildered, staggered, floored, nonplussed, overwhelmed, °speechless, stunned, °thunderstruck, dazzled, dazed, dumbstruck, taken aback, °confused, confounded, bemused, perplexed, baffled, °disconcerted, *Colloq* bowled over, flabbergasted, knocked out, thrown (off), *US* thrown for a loss, *Brit* knocked for six, knocked sideways: *She is dumbfounded that he proposed marriage.*

dummy *n.* **1** mannequin, manikin *or* mannikin, °model, °figure: *I saw the coat on a dummy in the shop window.* **2** °sample, °copy, reprint, °reproduction, °likeness, °substitution, °imitation, °sham, mock-up, simulation, *Colloq* °phoney *or US also* phony: *Those aren't the real crown jewels, they're just dummies.* **3** °fool, idiot, dunce, blockhead, ninny, ass, °dolt, numskull *or* numbskull, simpleton, *Colloq* dim-wit, *US* thimble-wit: *They're such dummies they don't know that you're joking.* **4** *US* pacifier: *Give the baby the dummy to suck.*

dump *v.* **1** °unload, offload, °empty, °drop, °deposit, °throw *or* °fling down, °tip: *They dumped the topsoil all over the path.* **2** get °rid of, °throw away, °scrap, °discard, ditch, jettison, °dispose of, °reject, °tip, °toss out *or* away, *Colloq* °junk, chuck out *or* away: *We dumped all the food when the fridge broke down.*
—*n.* **3** junk-yard, °rubbish °heap *or Brit* °tip, *US* °garbage dump: *You'll have to take this garden refuse to the dump.*

dumpy *adj.* °stocky, pudgy, squat, chunky, °chubby, tubby, °stout, °plump, portly, °fat: *No one with a dumpy figure looks good in shorts.*

dun *v.* °press, importune, °solicit, °plague, °nag, °pester, *Slang US* °bug: *The gas company has been dunning me to pay the bill.*

dung *n.* manure, °muck, droppings, cow-pats, fertilizer, guano, excrement, faeces *or US* feces, *US* cow *or* buffalo-chips, horse-apples, *Taboo* shit: *The dung is spread on the fields.*

dungeon *n.* donjon, °keep, °cell, °prison, lock-up, oubliette, black °hole, °stronghold: *Throw the infidels into the dungeon and give them twenty lashes!*

dupe *n.* **1** °fool, gull, °victim, fair °game, *Colloq* chump, *Chiefly US and Canadian* fall guy; *Slang* °sucker, °sap, boob, °pushover, pigeon, mark, *Brit* °mug, *Chiefly US and Canadian* patsy: *Swindlers often choose tourists as likely dupes.* **2** cat's-paw, °pawn, °tool, °puppet, *Slang* stooge: *I'm not going to be the dupe in your little game!*
—*v.* **3** °deceive, °fool, °outwit, °cheat, °trick, °take in, °defraud, humbug, °hoax, °swindle, °hoodwink, bilk, gull, cozen, delude, °mislead, snooker, °victimize, *Colloq* bamboozle, flimflam, °put one over on, pull a fast one on; *Slang* con, °rip off, °take, *US and Canadian* snow, do a snow job on: *She was duped into believing she had won the lottery.*

duplicate *adj.* **1** °identical; °twin, °matching: *They sent me duplicate tickets by mistake.*
—*n.* **2** (°exact *or* carbon) °copy, photocopy, machine °copy, °double, clone, (perfect) °match, °facsimile, °twin, °reproduction, °replica, replication, °look-alike, *Trade Mark* Xerox (°copy), *Slang* (°dead) ringer: *This painting looks like a duplicate of the one you bought.*
—*v.* **3** °copy, photocopy, clone, °match, replicate, °imitate, °reproduce, °double, *Trade Mark* Xerox; °repeat, °equal: *Would you please duplicate this letter for me? Can he duplicate his performance in the Commonwealth Games?*

durable *adj.* °enduring, long-lasting, °stable, wear-resistant, heavy-duty, hard-wearing, long-wearing, °lasting, °persistent, °indestructible, °substantial, °sturdy, °tough, °stout, °strong, °firm, °sound, °fixed, °fast, °permanent, dependable, °reliable: *The product is durable, guaranteed to last a lifetime.*

duress *n.* **1** coercion, °threat, °pressure, constraint, compulsion; °force, °power: *The boys wash the dishes only under duress.* **2** confinement, °imprisonment, incarceration, °captivity, °restraint, *Literary* durance: *There were workhouses, prisons, and other forms of duress.*

dusk *n.* °twilight, sundown, nightfall, °evening, sunset, °dark, eventide: *The workers came in from the fields at dusk.*

dusky *adj.* **1** °dark, °black, ebony, sable, jet-black; °swarthy, swart, dark-complected, dark-complexioned: *'Dusky diamonds' is another name for coal. A dusky gentleman offered to see her home safely.* **2** °shadowy, °shady, °dim, °dark, unilluminated, unlit, °murky, subfusc, subfuscous, °gloomy, °obscure: *An ominous figure was lurking in the dusky area under the stairs.*

dutiful *adj.* °obedient, compliant, °willing, °obliging, filial, °faithful, °conscientious, °reliable, °responsible, °diligent, °attentive, punctilious, °respectful, °polite, °considerate, deferential, °submissive, °yielding, acquiescent, malleable, °flexible, pliant, °accommodating, *Formal or archaic* duteous: *A dutiful son, he visits his parents weekly.*

duty *n.* **1** °responsibility, °obligation, °burden, onus, devoir, °office, °work, °task, °assignment, °job, °stint, chore, °occupation, °calling, °function, °role, °part, °bit, °charge: *Every man is expected to do his duty.*

2 °respect, °deference, °loyalty, fealty, fidelity, faithfulness, allegiance: *I think she did it out of a sense of duty to her family.* 3 °tax, excise, °tariff, impost, levy, customs: *You will have to pay duty on that whisky.*

dwarf *v.* °overshadow, °dominate, °diminish, °minimize: *The new tower dwarfs the older buildings.*

dwell *v.* 1 reside, °abide, °live, °lodge, °stay, °remain, °rest, *Formal* °domicile: *After the father's death, the mother dwelt with her daughter.* 2 ***dwell on*** *or* ***upon***: harp on, °persist in, °emphasize, °stress, °focus on, °linger *or* °tarry over, °elaborate (on); °labour: *Why must you always dwell on a person's shortcomings?*

dwelling *n.* °abode, habitation, dwelling-place, °house, °domicile, °lodging, quarters, °home, °residence, homestead: *His dwelling is a shanty in old shanty town.*

dwindle *v.* °diminish, °decrease, °shrink, lessen, °wane, °fade, °contract, condense, °reduce, peter out, °waste away, °die out *or* down *or* away, °ebb, °decline, °subside, °taper off, °shrivel (up *or* away): *The last days of summer dwindled away. His funds have dwindled until today he has nothing.*

dying *adj.* expiring; °sinking, slipping away, °going, °failing, fading (fast), at death's door, on one's deathbed, with one foot in the °grave, *in extremis;* °moribund: *The doctor said the dying man was in no pain.*

dynamic *adj.* dynamical, °vigorous, °active, °forceful, °energetic, °potent, °powerful, high-powered, °lively, spry, °vital, °electric, °spirited, zealous, °eager, °emphatic: *We are seeking a dynamic salesman for our Reading office.*

dynamism *n.* °energy, °vigour, °pep, °vitality, liveliness, °spirit, spiritedness, forcefulness, °power, °drive, °initiative, °enterprise, *Colloq* get-up-and-go, zip, °push: *That woman has the dynamism needed to get ahead in this organization.*

dynasty *n.* °line, °family, °heritage, °house: *The Ming dynasty ruled China for more than 300 years.*

E

eager *adj.* avid, zealous, °ardent, °earnest, °keen, °enthusiastic, °hot, °hungry, °fervent, fervid, °passionate, °spirited, inspirited, °energetic, energized, vehement, °animated, °excited, vitalized, stimulated; °desirous, yearning, desiring, craving, °wanting, °longing, itchy, °impatient; °anxious; *Colloq* dying, *Slang US* °hot to trot: *We were particularly eager to spend our holiday in Spain.*

eagerness *n.* 1 avidity, zeal, earnestness, keenness, °enthusiasm, °fervour, °hunger, vehemence, °animation, °vitality, °appetite, °zest, °relish, °spirit, spiritedness, °gusto, °verve, °dash, élan, vim, °vigour, °energy, *Colloq* get-up-and-go, zip, go: *Such eagerness for learning is rare. In his eagerness to please everyone he satisfies no one.* 2 °desire, °longing, wishing, yearning: *He observed the eagerness, the open hunger, with which she now waited for Mr Browning.*

eagle-eyed *adj.* °sharp-eyed, sharp-sighted, keen-eyed, keen-sighted, lynx-eyed, hawk-eyed; °perceptive, perspicacious, discerning, °sharp, watchful, °alert: *It would be impossible to deceive our eagle-eyed supervisor.*

ear *n.* 1 °attention, °heed, °notice, °regard, °consideration: *See if you can get his ear for a moment between meetings.* 2 °sensitivity, °appreciation, °taste, °discrimination: *She has an excellent ear for the right expression.*

early *adv.* 1 beforehand, ahead (of °time), °prematurely: *I arrived too early and had to wait.* 2 anciently, initially, °originally, at *or* near the °start *or* °beginning: *Plants appeared early in the development of life forms on earth.* 3 betimes, at cock crow *or* cock's-crow, at (the crack *or* break of) °dawn, at daybreak: *You're up early this morning!*
—*adj.* 4 untimely, °premature; °inopportune, °inappropriate: *The early fruit isn't as sweet.* 5 °initial, °beginning, °original, °first, °pioneer, advanced: *He was one of the earliest writers on the subject.* 6 primeval *or Brit also* primaeval, °primitive, primordial, °ancient, °old, °prehistoric, antediluvian, °original; °antique, °antiquated: *The Olduvai Gorge has yielded up many early humanoid fossils.*

earn *v.* 1 °merit, °deserve, be °worthy of, be °entitled to, °win, °warrant, °rate, °qualify for, have a °claim *or* °right to: *Peter has earned everyone's respect.* 2 °make, °pocket, °gross, °net, °clear, °realize, °receive, °get, °procure, °collect, °reap, °bring in, °take home; °draw, *Colloq US* °pull down: *It is still the case that most men earn more than their wives.*

earnest *adj.* 1 °serious, °solemn, °grave, °sober, °intense, °steady, °resolute, resolved, °firm, °determined, assiduous, °sincere, dedicated, committed, °devoted, °thoughtful: *He made an earnest promise to do his best.* 2 zealous, °ardent, °diligent, assiduous, °industrious, hard-working, °devoted, °eager, °conscientious, °keen, °fervent, fervid, °enthusiastic, °passionate: *Burbridge is an earnest pupil.* 3 ***earnest-money***: °deposit, down °payment, binder, handsel, °guarantee, °security, °pledge: *The company paid £10,000 earnest-money to secure the bid.*
—*n.* 4 ***in earnest***: °serious, °sincere: *She said she would come, but I doubt whether she was in earnest.*

earnings *n.pl.* °wages, °salary, °income, compensation, °pay, °stipend, emolument, °proceeds, °return, °revenue, °yield, takings, *Slang* °take: *The interest from tax-free bonds was not included in my earnings.*

earth *n.* 1 °globe, mother earth, planet, °world, blue planet, Terra: *Ozone depletion in the upper atmosphere may be threatening life on earth.* 2 °soil, °dirt, loam, sod, clay, °turf, °ground, °mould: *Pack the earth firmly around the roots.*

earthly *adj.* 1 °terrestrial, terrene, telluric: *Extraterrestrial beings might be unable to survive in our earthly atmosphere.* 2 °worldly, mundane, °material, °materialistic, °physical, non-spiritual, °sensual, °carnal, fleshly, corporeal, °base, °natural: *He has forsaken earthly pleasures in favour of spiritual pursuits.* 3 °human, °temporal, °secular, °profane, °mortal, °physical, non-spiritual, °material: *His earthly remains were committed to the sea.* 4 conceivable, imaginable, °feasible, °possible: *What earthly reason could she have had for kissing me?*

earthy *adj.* ribald, °bawdy, °unrefined, °coarse, °crude, °shameless, °wanton, °uninhibited, °abandoned, °vulgar, °lusty, °rough, °dirty, °indecent, °obscene: *She found Henry Miller's books a bit too earthy for her tastes.*

ease *n.* 1 °comfort, °repose, well-being, °relaxation, °leisure, °rest, contentment, calmness, tranquillity, °serenity, peacefulness, °peace, °peace and °quiet: *After 50 years of hard work, she felt entitled to a few years of ease.* 2 easiness, °simplicity, °facility, effortlessness, adeptness: *He passed the other runners with ease.* 3 affluence, °wealth, °prosperity, °luxury, opulence, °abundance, °plenty: *He has always led a life of ease, never having had to work.* 4 naturalness, informality, unaffectedness, ingenuousness, casualness, artlessness, insouciance, nonchalance, aplomb; unconcern: *I admire the ease with which she converses with complete strangers.*
—*v.* 5 °comfort, °relax, °calm, °tranquillize, °quiet(en), °still, pacify, soothe, disburden: *It eased his mind to learn that there was a reserve budget for emergencies.* 6 lessen, °diminish, abate, °mitigate, °reduce, °decrease, allay, alleviate, assuage, mollify, appease, palliate, °quiet(en), °relieve: *Her anxiety was considerably eased by the news that John would not need an operation after all.* 7 °manoeuvre, °manipulate, inch, °guide, °steer, °slip: *The helmsman eased the ship into dock.* 8 °facilitate, °expedite, °simplify, °smooth,

°further, °clear, °assist, °aid, °advance, °forward, °help: *Having a wealthy father eased her way in life.*

easily *adv.* **1** smoothly, effortlessly, °readily, °simply, °handily, without a hitch, °hands down, without even trying, comfortably, with no *or* without difficulty, *Colloq* °easy as pie: *You can easily tackle the job yourself.* **2** by °far, beyond *or* without doubt *or* question, indisputably, indubitably, °undoubtedly, °doubtless(ly), unquestionably, °clearly, °far and away, °definitely, definitively, conclusively, certainly, °surely, undeniably, °obviously, patently: *He is easily the best lawyer in the firm.* **3** °probably, most *or* very °likely, °well, almost certainly: *We may easily be the first in Hampton to have plaster flamingos on the lawn.*

easy *adj.* **1** °simple, °effortless, °plain, °clear, straightforward, °hands down, uncomplicated, °elementary, °foolproof; easy as pie, easy as can be: *Feeding goldfish is an easy job that children can undertake for themselves.* **2** °carefree, °easygoing, °casual, °lenient, undemanding, °relaxed, °quiet, °serene, °restful, °tranquil, °peaceful, untroubled, undisturbed, unoppressive, °gentle, °mild, °calm, °comfortable, °cosy, °unhurried, leisurely: *He has a pretty easy life now that he's retired.* **3** °light, °lenient, undemanding, °mild, °flexible, °indulgent, °tolerant: *You really should be easy on him after what he's been through.* **4** °tractable, pliant, docile, compliant, °submissive, acquiescent, amenable, °accommodating, °soft, °suggestible, credulous, °trusting, °weak, °easygoing: *He was an easy victim for confidence tricksters. She has the reputation of being a woman of easy virtue.* **5** unstrained, °gentle, °moderate, °unhurried, leisurely, °even, °steady, undemanding, °comfortable, unexacting: *They kept up an easy pace of about five miles an hour.* **6** affable, °friendly, °amiable, °amicable, °agreeable, °outgoing, °informal, unceremonious, down-to-earth, unreserved, relaxing, °natural, °relaxed, °easygoing: *We found them easy to be with.*
—*adv.* **7** effortlessly; calmly, unexcitedly, temperately, peacefully, tranquilly, serenely, nonchalantly, casually: *Take it easy and don't get so worked up about things.*

easygoing *adj.* °relaxed, °casual, °mellow, °carefree, undemanding, °easy, even-tempered, forbearing, °lenient, °tolerant, °permissive, over-tolerant, overpermissive, °lax, °weak, *Colloq* °wishy-washy, laid-back: *He's an easygoing sort of person.*

eat *v.* °dine, lunch, breakfast, sup, break bread, °snack, have a °bite; °consume, °devour, take (in) °nourishment, *Colloq* °put *or* pack away, *Slang* nosh, put *or* tie on the nosebag *or US and Canadian* feed-bag: *I'm not hungry, thank you: I've already eaten.*

eavesdrop *v.* °listen in, °tap, overhear, °snoop; °spy, °pry: *They were eavesdropping on our conversation, that's how they knew about Martha.*

ebb *v.* **1** °recede, °flow back, °subside, °go out, °go down; °fall back *or* away, °retreat, retrocede, °retire: *The tide ebbed, leaving the boat stranded.* **2** °decline, °flag, °decay, °wane, °diminish, °decrease, °drop, slacken, °fade (away), °drain (away), °dwindle, peter out, °waste (away), °deteriorate: *His enthusiasm for exercise is beginning to ebb.*
—*n.* **3** °low tide, °low water, ebb tide, °low point: *The rocks appear when the sea is at its ebb.* **4** °decline, °decay, °decrease, diminution, °wane, °drop, slackening(off), dwindling, lessening, deterioration, degeneration: *She was no longer willing to contend with the ebb and flow of his temper.*

ebullient *adj.* bubbling, overflowing, °effervescent, °excited, °effusive, exhilarated, °elated, °buoyant, °exuberant, °enthusiastic, zestful: *The crowd was ebullient at the news from Mafeking.*

eccentric *adj.* **1** unconventional, °unusual, uncommon, idiosyncratic, anomalous, °unorthodox, out of the ordinary, °irregular, atypical, °incongruous, errant, aberrant, °exceptional, °individual, °singular, °unique; °abnormal, °odd, °peculiar, °strange, °curious, °bizarre, °outlandish, °queer, °quaint, quirky, °weird, °offbeat, *Colloq* far-out, °kinky, °cranky: *Yes, I would agree that walking a canary is a bit eccentric.*
—*n.* **2** °original, °individualist, °nonconformist, °queer fellow, °odd fish, *Colloq* °character, °card, °freak, (nut) °case, °crank, oddball, °weirdo *or* weirdie, *US* oner: *In today's conformist society, anyone who isn't a carbon copy of his neighbour is regarded as an eccentric.*

eccentricity *n.* **1** unconventionality, unusualness, uncommonness, irregularity, nonconformity, individuality, individualism, °singularity, uniqueness, strangeness, oddness, bizarreness, distinctiveness, capriciousness, weirdness: *Why should someone be criticized for eccentricity?* **2** idiosyncrasy, °quirk, °peculiarity, °mannerism, crotchet, aberration, anomaly, °oddity, °curiosity, caprice: *Eating crackers in bed is only one of her eccentricities.*

echo *n.* **1** reverberation, °repercussion, °repetition, iteration, reiteration: *The echo of the church bells could be heard throughout the valley.* **2** °imitation, °copy, °replica *or* replication, duplication, °reproduction, simulation, °facsimile; °reflection, °mirror °image, °repetition: *Modern Rome is but a feeble echo of its glorious past.*
—*v.* **3** °resound, reverberate, °ring: *The hall echoed with children's laughter.* **4** °imitate, ape, °parrot, °mimic, °copy, °duplicate, °reproduce, simulate, °repeat, emulate, °mirror, °reflect: *The poems are unoriginal and merely echo the works of others.*

eclipse *v.* **1** °conceal, °hide, °blot out, °obscure, °block, °veil, °shroud, °cover, darken: *A black cloud eclipsed the moon.* **2** °overshadow, °obscure, °surpass, °top, outshine: *His career was eclipsed by his wife's brilliant successes.*
—*n.* **3** concealment, covering, hiding, blocking, blockage, occultation, obscuring, obscuration, darkening, shading, dimming: *Though good may suffer an eclipse, it can never be extinguished.* **4** °decline, downturn, °slump; °recession: *After the scandal, her career went into eclipse.*

economic *adj.* **1** °financial, °fiscal, pecuniary, °monetary, budgetary; commercial, °mercantile, °trade: *The economic indicators for July affected the markets.* **2** °profitable, cost-effective, money-making, remunerative, °productive; °solvent: *Increased demand for our products has made the company economic.*

economical *adj.* **1** cost-effective, money-saving, °thrifty, unwasteful; °cheap, °inexpensive, °reasonable; °economic: *This car is very economical to run.* **2** °provident, °thrifty, °sparing, economizing, °prudent, °conservative, °frugal; parsimonious, °penurious, stingy, °cheap, °miserly, niggardly, °tight, close-fisted, tight-fisted, °mean, penny-pinching, scrimping: *Aunt Gertrude was always a very economical housekeeper.*

economize *v.* °save, °cut back, °husband, retrench; tighten one's belt, °cut corners *or* costs, scrimp, skimp, °pinch pennies: *Without the extra income, we'll have to economize on something.*

economy *n.* **1** °thrift, husbandry, thriftiness, °conservation, conservatism, °saving, °restraint, °control, frugality: *We'll have to exercise economy to get through the winter.* **2** °brevity, briefness, succinctness, terseness, conciseness, concision, compactness, °restraint, curtness: *He manages to get his ideas across with an admirable economy of language.*

ecstasy *n.* **1** °delight, °joy, °rapture, °bliss, °transport, nympholepsy *or* nympholepsia, °happiness, gladness, elation, °pleasure, °enjoyment, °gratification; °heaven on earth: *The prospect of being with her again filled me with ecstasy.* **2** exaltation, °frenzy, °thrill, elation, °paroxysm, °excitement: *The ecstasy of space flight is impossible to describe.*

ecstatic *adj.* exhilarated, thrilled, °exultant, blissful, euphoric, °rapturous, enraptured, nympholeptic, °enchanted, transported, °rhapsodic, °excited, °elated, °delighted, °joyful, °gleeful, °overjoyed, °happy, °glad, beside oneself, °delirious, orgasmic, *Colloq* on cloud nine, *Brit* over the moon, in the seventh °heaven, cock-a-hoop, *US* in seventh °heaven, flying: *Our team had won an Olympic gold medal, and we were truly ecstatic.*

eddy *n.* **1** °swirl, whirl, vortex, gurgitation; °whirlpool, maelstrom, Charybdis; dust devil, °whirlwind, °twister, tornado, cyclone, typhoon, °hurricane; waterspout: *These treacherous eddies are caused by tidal changes.*
—*v.* **2** °swirl, whirl, °turn, °spin: *The wind eddied round us, driving the dinghy this way and that.*

edge *n.* **1** °brink, °verge, °border, °side, °rim, lip, °brim; °fringe, °margin, °boundary, °bound, °limit, bourn, °perimeter, °periphery: *I was hanging on to the very edge of the cliff. The edge of the handkerchief was trimmed with lace.* **2** acuteness, sharpness, keenness: *That hunting knife has quite an edge.* **3** harshness, sharpness, acrimony, pungency, °force, °urgency, effectiveness, incisiveness, causticity, °virulence, vehemence: *There was an edge to her voice when she told me not to bother her.* **4** °advantage, head °start, °superiority, °lead, °upper hand: *You're holding the gun, so I guess you have the edge on me.* **5** ***on edge***: on tenterhooks, °nervous, °touchy, °sensitive, °prickly, itchy, °tense, irascible, crabbed, °irritable, °peevish, apprehensive, with one's heart in one's mouth, edgy, °anxious, °ill at ease, °restive, °restless, fidgety, *Colloq* uptight, like a cat on a hot tin roof: *She was on edge waiting for the exam results.*
—*v.* **6** inch, °move, °sidle, °crawl, °creep, °steal, worm, °work (one's way): *The burglar was edging along the wall, 30 storeys above the street.*

edible *adj.* eatable, esculent, palatable, °good *or* °fit (to °eat), °wholesome, *Rare* comestible: *After the sell-by date, fresh food is no longer considered edible.*

edification *n.* enlightenment, °improvement, uplifting, enlightening, °guidance, °education, °information, °tuition, teaching, °schooling, °instruction: *The exhibition is designed for both edification and enjoyment.*

edit *v.* **1** redact, copy-edit, rewrite, rephrase, °modify, °alter, °adapt, °change, °revise, °correct, emend, °style, restyle, °polish, °touch up: *His job is to edit the stories into idiomatic English.* **2** Often, ***edit out***: blue-pencil, °cut (out), °delete, censor, °erase, bleep, blip; bowdlerize, expurgate, °clean up: *They edited out all his slanderous asides before broadcasting the interview.* **3** °cut, condense, compress, °shorten, crop, °reduce: *The story has to be edited so that it fits on one page.* **4** °prepare, °compile, °assemble, °select, °arrange, °organize, °order, reorganize, reorder: *Margoliouth edited the collected letters of Andrew Marvell.*

edition *n.* °number, °issue, printing, °print °run; °copy; °version: *The first Monday edition carried the news of the break-in, and a later edition reported the detention of a suspect.*

editor *n.* rewrite man *or* woman, rewriter, °copy editor, redactor, reviser; °writer, columnist, °journalist, °editorial °writer, *Brit* leader-writer; editor-in-chief, managing editor, senior editor; compiler, °collector: *The editor sent the reporter out to check the facts of the story.*

editorial *n.* op-ed article, think-piece, opinion piece, position statement; essay, article, column; *Brit* leader, leading article: *Did you see the editorial about the Middle East situation in today's paper?*

educate *v.* °teach, °train, °instruct, edify, °tutor, °school, °inform, °enlighten, °indoctrinate, inculcate, °coach, °drill, °prepare, °ready, °rear, °bring up, °cultivate, °develop, °civilize: *It is the responsibility of the state to educate the people.*

educated *adj.* **1** °cultivated, cultured, erudite, well-read, °lettered, °literary, °scholarly, °learned; (°well-) °informed, °knowledgeable, °enlightened: *There is no real evidence that educated people enjoy greater job satisfaction than those who leave school at 16. I haven't got the answer, but I could make an educated guess.*
2 °refined, °polished, °cultivated, civilized; discerning, °critical, °sensitive: *She has an educated palate and really knows her wines.*

education *n.* **1** teaching, °schooling, training, °instruction, °tuition, tutelage, °edification, tutoring, cultivation, °upbringing, indoctrination, drilling: *His education was in the hands of monks until he was twelve.* **2** °learning, °lore, °knowledge, °information, erudition: *Education is gained from the experience of others.* **3** °lesson, °course (of °study): *The inhabitants gave her an education in how to survive in the forest.*

educational *adj.* **1** °academic, scholastic, pedagogical, instructional: *This is one of the best educational centres in the world.* **2** °informative, °instructive, enlightening, edifying, eye-opening, revelatory, educative: *A year spent abroad is always educational.*

eerie *adj.* °frightening, °weird, °strange, uncanny, °ghostly, °spectral, °dreadful, °unearthly, °frightful *Poetic or Scots* eldritch, *Scots* °mysterious, *Colloq* °scary, creepy, spooky: *I had the eeriest feeling I was being watched.*

effect *n.* **1** °result, consequence, °outcome, conclusion, °upshot, aftermath, °impact: *The effects of the storm could be seen everywhere.* **2** effectiveness, efficacy, °force, °power, °capacity, potency, °influence, °impression, °impact, *Colloq* clout, °punch: *His threats had no effect.* **3** °significance, °meaning, signification, purport, °sense, °essence, °drift, °implication, °import, °tenor, °purpose, °intent, °intention, °object, °objective: *She said 'Get lost', or words to that effect.* **4** °impact, °impression, °form, °sensation: *He didn't mean that, he just said it for effect.* **5** ***in effect***: effectively, °virtually, for (all) practical purposes, so to °speak, more or less; °actually, in (point of) °fact, °really, essentially, basically, at °bottom, in °truth, °truly, to all intents and purposes, at the end of the day, any way you look at it: *She always spoke of him as her adopted son and this, in effect, was what he was.* **6** ***take effect***: become °operative *or* operational, come into °force, °begin *or* °start to °work *or* °function *or* °operate: *The regulation doesn't take effect till next week.*
—*v.* **7** °bring about, °cause, °make °happen *or* take °place, °effectuate, °achieve, °accomplish, °secure, °obtain, °make, °execute, °carry out, °produce, °create: *The opposition was unable to effect any change in the law.*

effective *adj.* **1** °effectual, °efficacious, °productive; °capable, °useful, °serviceable, °competent, °operative, °able, °functional, °efficient: *The effective life of the battery is six months.* **2** °impressive, °remarkable, °noticeable, °conspicuous, °outstanding, °striking, °powerful, compelling, °moving, °telling, °effectual: *The stage setting was very effective.* **3** °operative, operational, in °operation, functioning, °real, °actual, °essential, °basic, °true: *The monthly interest may seem low, but the effective annual rate is much higher.*

effects *n.pl.* °belongings, (personal) °property, °gear, °possessions, °stuff, things, °paraphernalia, chattels, °goods, *Colloq* °junk, crap, *Brit* clobber, *Taboo slang US* shit: *His personal effects were left scattered around the house.*

effectual *adj.* **1** °effective, °efficacious, °efficient, °functional, °productive, °useful, °telling, °influential, °powerful, °forcible, °forceful; °capable, °adequate: *What is the most effectual way of stopping a take-over of the company?* **2** °effective, in °force, °legal, °lawful, binding, °sound, valid: *You must register the agreement for it to be effectual.*

effectuate *v.* °bring about, °effect, °carry out, °implement, °accomplish, do, °execute, °realize, °achieve; °cause, °make °happen: *It is unclear just how she will effectuate her escape.*

effeminate *adj.* unmanly, womanish, womanly; °gay, °homosexual; *All the following are offensive and derogatory* °sissy, °weak, campy; *Slang Brit* °bent, poncey, *US* limp-wristed, faggy, faggoty: *He's too effeminate to play the part of Othello.*

effervescent *n.* **1** bubbling, fizzy, carbonated, sparkling, fizzing, gassy; foaming, foamy, frothing, frothy, °bubbly: *I prefer effervescent mineral water to still.*

2 bubbling, °bubbly, high-spirited, °vivacious, °ebullient, °lively, °exuberant, °buoyant, °animated, °lively, exhilarated, °excited, °enthusiastic, °irrepressible: *Jeanette's effervescent personality endeared her to everyone who met her.*

efficacious *adj.* °effective, °effectual, °productive, °competent, °successful, °efficient, °useful, °serviceable; °capable: *He was not very efficacious in getting the council to change their policy.*

efficiency *n.* **1** effectiveness, efficacy, competence, °capability, adeptness, °proficiency, expertness, °expertise, know-how, °experience, °skill, skilfulness, °dexterity, adroitness: *The efficiency of the staff has been greatly improved.* **2** productivity, effectiveness, efficaciousness: *How does the efficiency of a diesel compare with that of other engines?*

efficient *adj.* unwasteful, °economic, °thrifty; °effective, °efficacious, °effectual, °competent, °productive, °proficient, °operative: *The technique for producing electrical power from tidal action has not yet proved efficient.*

effort *n.* **1** °exertion, striving, °struggle, °strain, °labour, °pains, °energy, toil, °application, °trouble, travail, °work, *Colloq* elbow-grease: *He's gone to a lot of effort to please her. Getting the place cleaned up took a great deal of effort.* **2** °attempt, °endeavour, °essay, °try, °venture, *Colloq* °stab, crack: *Her efforts to be pleasant met with a stony response.* **3** °achievement, °accomplishment, °creation, °feat, °deed, attainment, °exploit: *Last year's fund-raising fair was a superb effort.*

effortless *adj.* °easy (as pie *or* as A, B, C, *or* as 1, 2, 3), °simple, °painless, °smooth, trouble-free, uncomplicated: *She admired the apparently effortless grace of the dancer.*

effrontery *n.* °impertinence, °impudence, audacity, °nerve, °presumption, presumptuousness, brazenness, boldness, insolence, temerity, brashness, rashness, °arrogance, °front, °indiscretion, *Archaic* frowardness, *Colloq* °gall, °brass, °nerve, cheek, lip, °mouth, *Slang Brit* °side: *He had the effrontery to call her 'Queenie'!*

effusive *adj.* °demonstrative, gushing, (over)enthusiastic, unrestrained, unchecked, unreserved, °expansive, °emotional, °exuberant, °rhapsodic, °ebullient, °lavish, °voluble, °profuse; fulsome: *Her aunt greeted her with an effusive outpouring of affection.*

egoistic *adj.* egoistical, self-centred, egocentric, narcissistic, self-seeking, self-absorbed, °selfish, self-serving, °self-indulgent, °self-important: *She is too egoistic to consider anyone but herself.*

egotistical *adj.* egotistic, °conceited, °proud, overweening, bragging, °boastful, boasting, swelled-headed *or* swell-headed *or* swollen-headed, °vain, vainglorious, self-worshipping, self-admiring, vaunting, crowing: *Considering his poor track record, he has nothing to be so egotistical about.*

eject *v.* **1** °force *or* °drive out, °expel, oust, °remove, get °rid of, °evict, *Colloq* °throw *or* °kick *or* °boot out: *They were ejected for causing a disturbance.* **2** °expel, °emit, °throw up *or* out, °spew (forth), °discharge, °spout, disgorge, °vomit (up *or* forth), °send out *or* forth; °ooze, exude, extravasate: *The volcano ejected boulders the size of houses.* **3** °discharge, °dismiss, cashier, drum out, °lay off, °declare *or* make °redundant, *Colloq* °fire, °sack, °boot out, axe, give the °sack *or* boot *or* axe, give (someone) his *or* her marching orders *or US also* walking papers, °send packing: *He was ejected for stealing paper clips.*

ejection *n.* **1** °expulsion, casting out *or* up, disgorgement, vomiting forth, throwing out *or* up, °discharge, emission, disgorging: *The ejection of lava was preceded by loud rumblings.* **2** °exile, °expulsion, banishment, deportation, ouster, °removal; °eviction, dispossession: *His ejection from the meeting angered his supporters. My ejection by the landlord was illegal.* **3** °dismissal, °discharge, *congé*, cashiering, lay-off, *Colloq* firing, sacking, *Slang* the °sack, the boot, the axe, the (old) heave-ho, *US* the bounce: *Business was bad, and the entire staff was faced with ejection.*

elaborate *adj.* **1** °detailed, °painstaking, °meticulous, punctilious, °comprehensive, °thorough, °complete, °exhaustive, °intricate, °involved, °minute, °precise, °exact: *The escape had been worked out in elaborate detail.* **2** °complicated, complex, convoluted, °ornate, °fancy, Byzantine, °laborious, °laboured, °extravagant, °showy; ornamented, decorated, baroque, rococo, °busy, °fussy, gingerbread: *We marvelled at the elaborate mosaics. His plan is too elaborate and should be simplified.*
—*v.* **3** °ornament, °decorate, °complicate, °embellish, garnish, adorn: *Later craftsmen elaborated the earlier Greek motifs.* **4** °enlarge, °expand (upon *or* on), expatiate, °develop, °cultivate, °flesh out, °enhance, °refine, °enrich, °improve, °better, ameliorate, emend, °polish: *Later on, I shall elaborate on the recruitment methods we used.*

elaboration *n.* **1** enhancement, °refinement, enrichment, °improvement, amelioration, melioration, betterment; °embellishment, adornment, garnish, garnishment, °decoration, over-decoration, gingerbread, *Slang* bells and whistles: *The customers always welcome elaboration of the equipment.* **2** enlargement, °development, amplification, °expansion: *The argument requires further elaboration.*

elapse *v.* °pass (by), °go (by), °slip by *or* away, °pass away, °slide by, °glide by, °transpire: *Three weeks have elapsed since I last saw her.*

elastic *adj.* **1** °flexible, stretchable, stretchy, °stretch, bendable, °pliable, springy, °plastic, extensile, extensible, expansible, expandable, contractile, resilient, bouncy, compressible: *Is it elastic enough to stretch round that box?* **2** adjustable, °adaptable, °accommodating, °flexible: *The schedule for our main project is elastic, so we can fit in additional tasks at very short notice.*

elasticity *n.* **1** °flexibility, °resilience, rubberiness, plasticity, ductility, springiness, stretchability, stretchiness, °stretch, suppleness, pliancy, *Colloq* °give: *Dry hair has no elasticity: it's brittle and breaks easily when brushed or combed.* **2** °flexibility, adjustability, adaptability, °tolerance, suppleness: *Their plan lacks the elasticity needed to accommodate changes.*

elated *adj.* exhilarated, uplifted, °elevated, °gleeful, °joyful, jubilant, joyous, °exultant, °ecstatic, blissful, °happy, °delighted, euphoric, °overjoyed, °excited, thrilled, transported, °pleased (as Punch), on °top of the world, on cloud nine, *Colloq* tickled, tickled °pink, *Brit* chuffed, over the moon, in the seventh °heaven, *US* in seventh °heaven: *We were elated to learn that our daughter had won first prize.*

elder *adj.* **1** older, °senior: *My elder brother was born in 1930.* **2** °venerable, respected, (pre-)°eminent; °experienced, °veteran: *Clemenceau was an elder statesman at the Geneva Convention.*
—*n.* **3** °senior, °superior; patriarch, elder statesman, dean, doyen *or* doyenne: *Everyone paid great respect to the elders of the tribe.*

elderly *adj.* **1** °old, past middle age, oldish, advanced in years, of advanced age, along in years, °grey, ageing, °aged, °venerable; hoary, °ancient, senescent, °decrepit, superannuated; °senile, anile; *Colloq* over the hill, past it, long in the tooth, having one foot in the grave, old-fogyish *or* old-fogeyish: *Today, a person isn't considered elderly till he's past 65.*
—*n.* **2** ***the elderly***: the retired, the °old, °senior citizens, pensioners, O.A.P.'s, old-age pensioners, golden-agers, *Colloq* old-timers, (°old) geezers, (°old) fogies *or* fogeys, *Brit* wrinklies: *The elderly constitute an increasingly large body of voters.*

elect *v.* **1** °choose, °select, °pick, °vote (for), °determine, °designate: *We must elect a new chairperson at the next meeting.*
—*adj.* **2** chosen, elected, selected, picked out: *The president-elect takes office next month.* **3** °select,

°choice, °first-rate, first-class: *An elect few make up the executive committee.*

election *n.* °poll, °vote, referendum, °plebiscite; °selection, °choice, choosing, nomination, designation, °appointment; voting, electing: *They held an election and Michael lost. The election of a new social secretary is required.*

electioneer *v.* °campaign, °canvass, °support, °back, °promote: *They are busy electioneering for their candidate.*

electric *adj.* charged, °tense, energized, °stimulating, °exciting, °thrilling, galvanizing, electrifying, °moving, °stirring: *As the jury filed in, the atmosphere in the courtroom was electric.*

electricity *n.* °excitement, °verve, °energy, °tension, tenseness, fervency, °intensity, °ardour; vibrations: *I could feel the electricity between us.*

electrify *v.* **1** °startle, °shock, °stun, °jolt, °stagger, °astound, °jar, °astonish, °amaze: *We were electrified by the news of the disaster.* **2** °excite, galvanize, °animate, °move, °rouse, °stir, °stimulate, °vitalize, °fire, °thrill, °arouse: *His fiery oratory electrified the audience.*

elegance *n.* **1** °refinement, grace, tastefulness, good °taste, gentility, °polish, courtliness, °culture, politeness, politesse, °propriety, °dignity: *Where but in 18th-century France could one find such elegance?* **2** °luxury, °grandeur, luxuriousness, sumptuousness, exquisiteness, °splendour, °beauty: *The overwhelming elegance of the palace took our breath away.*

elegant *adj.* **1** °tasteful, °exquisite, °handsome, °beautiful, °comely, °dapper, °smart, °well turned out; °graceful, °choice, °superior, °fine, °select, °refined, °delicate, discerning, artistic; °dignified, °genteel, °sophisticated, °cultivated, °polished, urbane, Chesterfieldian, °suave, soigné(e), °debonair, courtly, to the manner born, °well-bred, well-born, high-born: *Desmond and Elizabeth are such an elegant couple!* **2** artistic, °stylish, modish, à la °mode, °chic, °fashionable, *Colloq* in, with it: *The newly refurbished rooms are very elegant.* **3** °luxurious, °sumptuous, °grand, °opulent, °plush, *Colloq* °posh, swank, °swanky, ritzy, °fancy: *We stayed in a very elegant West End hotel.* **4** apt, °clever, °ingenious, °neat: *What is needed is a more elegant solution to the problem.*

element *n.* **1** component, constituent, °ingredient, °essential, °fundamental, °part, °unit, °piece, °segment, °feature, °factor, °detail, °particular: *Each element was carefully designed with a view to its place in the whole.* **2** °environment, °atmosphere, °situation, °locale, °territory, °sphere, °habitat, °medium, °domain: *Ordway is really in his element at a party.* **3** ***elements***: **a** (adverse *or* unfavourable) °weather, climatic conditions: *Stay here tonight—there's no need to brave the elements.* **b** °rudiments, basics, °fundamentals, °foundations, essentials, °principles: *It was she who taught me the elements of flying a helicopter.*

elemental *adj.* °basic, °fundamental, primal, °original, primordial, °primitive: *Elemental religion focused on worship of the sun and fertility.*

elementary *adj.* **1** °simple, °rudimentary, °easy, straightforward, uncomplicated, °clear, understandable, °plain: *This is an elementary mistake which most beginners make.* **2** °basic, °fundamental, °primary, °introductory, °initial, °beginning; °elemental: *She received her elementary education in France.*

elevated *adj.* **1** raised, upraised, uplifted, lifted (up): *Only three hands were elevated in opposition and the motion was carried.* **2** uplifted, °noble, °lofty, °high, °grand, °exalted, °dignified, °eminent, °pre-eminent, ennobled, °prominent, °notable, °illustrious, °distinguished, °imposing, °impressive, °sublime: *He has rather elevated notions of morality.* **3** °elated, °cheerful, °happy, exhilarated, °animated, °joyful, °glad: *Her elevated spirits and pleasant countenance make her a welcome guest.*

elevation *n.* **1** altitude, °height: *The elevation of Denver, Colorado, is one mile above sea level.* **2** °swelling, °lump, wen, eminence, °prominence; °hill, °height, °rise: *From this elevation, you can see seven counties. The doctor noticed a slight elevation in the skin near the eye.* **3** advancement, °promotion, uplifting, enhancement, °advance: *Since her elevation to the peerage, she has had less time for local community work.* **4** °grandeur, nobleness, loftiness, exaltation, sublimity, °distinction, °dignity, °refinement, cultivation: *The elevation of his style means that his work is not accessible to a mass readership.*

elfin *adj.* **1** elvish, elfish, elf-like, impish, puckish, °frolicsome, °sprightly, °arch, °playful, °mischievous, °tricky: *I suppose she has a certain elfin charm, but I don't like her.* **2** °small, °wee, °diminutive, °tiny, °little, °dainty, Lilliputian: *This is a delightful tale of elfin folk and magic birds.*

elicit *v.* °draw out, °call forth, °evoke, °bring out *or* forth, bring to °light, °extract, wring, wrest, °wrench: *They finally elicited the fact that she had been lying about his whereabouts.*

eligible *adj.* **1** °fit, °worthy, °qualified, °proper, °suitable, °appropriate, °fitting: *Is he an eligible candidate for the post?* **2** °single, °unmarried, unwed, °available: *He is one of the few eligible bachelors in the town.*

eliminate *v.* **1** °remove, °exclude, °rule out, °reject, °drop, °leave out, °omit: *Police have eliminated him from their enquiries.* **2** °take out *or* away, °omit, get °rid of, °dispose of, °expel, °knock out: *He was eliminated in the first heat of the 100-metre run.* **3** °erase, eradicate, expunge, °obliterate, °strike (out), °cross out *or* off, °cut (out), excise, °delete, °throw out, °edit (out), blue-pencil, °cancel: *The censors have eliminated all references to sex.* **4** °kill, °murder, assassinate, slay, °terminate, °exterminate, °dispose of, liquidate, °finish off, annihilate, °stamp out, °destroy, *Slang* °bump off, °polish off, *US* °rub out, take for a °ride, °bury, ice, °waste: *They used a sub-machine gun to eliminate the competition.*

élite *n.* **1** elite, °gentry, aristocracy, aristocrats, °elect, °upper °class, °nobility, °privileged °class, °blue bloods, *crème de la crème, haut monde,* jet °set, jet-setters, *US* Four Hundred, F.F.V., First Families of Virginia, *Colloq* °upper crust, beautiful people, *Brit* nobs: *The economic collapse had barely touched the wealthy élite.*
—*adj.* **2** elite, aristocratic, °elect, °upper-class, °privileged, blue-blooded, °noble, °exclusive, °choice, °best, °top: *She socializes with rather an élite group of people.*

elixir *n.* **1** panacea, cure-all, nostrum, wonder °drug, miracle °drug, sovereign °remedy: *In the Middle Ages alchemists sought a universal cure, an elixir.* **2** °essence, °potion, °extract, tincture, °compound, °mixture: *Ophidia's Elixir was the name of a patent snake-oil medicine.* **3** °pith, °core, °kernel, °heart, °essence, °quintessence, °principle, °extract, °base, °basis, °soul: *The elixir of life is wisdom and its mystic ingredient is not knowledge but understanding.*

eloquent *adj.* **1** °expressive, articulate, silver-tongued, °fluent, well-spoken, °effective, °persuasive, convincing, cogent, °trenchant, °incisive, °graphic, °vivid, °striking, facile, °smooth, °glib, oratorical, °rhetorical: *He was an eloquent speaker. He rose and gave an eloquent speech.* **2** °suggestive, °meaningful, °pregnant: *His eyebrow was raised in eloquent scepticism.*

elsewhere *adv.* somewhere else, to another °place; in another °place, °abroad, °absent, away: *She's not in the office so I assume she's gone elsewhere. Elsewhere, winds have died down and temperatures are slowly rising.*

elude *v.* **1** °evade, °escape, °avoid, °dodge, °slip away from, *Colloq* °duck, give the °slip, °shake off: *The suspect has eluded the police for a year.* **2** °evade, °escape; baffle, °puzzle, °confuse, °bewilder, confound; °frustrate, °stump, °thwart: *The point of your argument eludes me.*

elusive *adj.* **1** °evasive, °slippery, °tricky, °shifty: *One of the world's most elusive guerrilla leaders was spotted in public yesterday.* **2** °evasive, evanescent, °fleeting,

°fugitive, transitory, indefinable, elusory, °intangible, impalpable: *The notion of truth is always elusive.*

emaciated *adj.* emaciate, atrophied, shrivelled, °wizened, shrunken, °haggard, °gaunt, °drawn, pinched, bony, skeletal, cadaverous, withered, wasted, consumptive, phthisic, anorexic *or* anorectic, wasting (away), °scrawny, °skinny, °thin, °lean, °spare, undernourished, underfed, °starved, half-starved: *The inmates of the camp were so emaciated they could scarcely stand.*

emanate *v.* **1** °issue, °come (out), °emerge, °proceed, °flow, °ooze, exude; °radiate: *Black smoke emanated from the mouth of the idol.* **2** °radiate, °give off *or* out, °send out *or* forth, disseminate, °discharge, °put out, °emit; °exhale, °ooze, exude: *The idol's eyes emanated a blue light.*

emancipate *v.* °release, set °free, °liberate, enfranchise, manumit, °loose, °let °loose, °let go, disenthral, unfetter, unchain, unshackle; °deliver: *Britain emancipated the slaves almost 50 years before Lincoln's Emancipation Proclamation.*

embargo *n.* **1** °restraint, °block, blockage, °bar, °ban, stoppage, cessation, proscription, °prohibition, interdiction, °check, °restriction, °barrier; °hindrance, °impediment: *The government placed an embargo on the export of oil.*
—*v.* **2** °restrain, °block, °bar, °ban, °stop, °cease, proscribe, °prohibit, interdict, °check, °restrict, °hold back, °prevent; °hinder, °impede, °retard, °hold up: *They may embargo oil shipments in case of war.*

embark *v.* **1** °board, go aboard; entrain; emplane *or* enplane: *We embarked and the ship sailed.* **2** Often, ***embark on***: °commence, °begin, °enter (upon), °initiate, °launch, °start, °go into, °set about, °take up *or* on, °engage in, °assume, °tackle: *He will embark on the new enterprise next month.*

embarrass *v.* disconcert, °discomfit, chagrin, abash, °shame, °mortify, °humble, °humiliate, discountenance, discompose, °fluster, °upset, °distress, °disgrace, *Colloq* °show up: *He embarrassed his colleagues by his bad manners.*

embarrassed *adj.* **1** °ashamed, shamefaced, blushing, °disconcerted, discomfited, chagrined, abashed, shamed, mortified, humiliated, discountenanced, discomposed, flustered, distressed, red-faced, uncomfortable, °self-conscious, °sheepish, red in the face; humbled, disgraced: *She was extremely embarrassed by all the attention.* **2** in °debt, in the red, °straitened, °insolvent, *Colloq* °short, °hard up, °broke, *Brit* skint: *I'm financially embarrassed now but I'll pay you later.*

embarrassing *adj.* °awkward, humiliating, mortifying, shaming, °shameful, uncomfortable, discomfiting, °disconcerting, °touchy, distressing, worrying: *I had an embarrassing moment when I forgot the client's name.*

embarrassment *n.* **1** bashfulness, awkwardness, clumsiness, discomposure, abashment, uneasiness, °discomfort, self-consciousness, mortification, chagrin: *My embarrassment made me blush.* **2** °difficulty, °mess, °predicament, °dilemma, °problem, °trouble, *Colloq* hot water, pickle, °fix, °scrape, °bind: *Finding them together presented me with a real embarrassment.* **3** °excess, °superfluity, superabundance, over-abundance, *embarras de richesse, embarras de choix*, oversupply, °surplus, °profusion: *An embarrassment of options was open to me.*

embellish *v.* **1** °beautify, °improve, titivate *or* tittivate, °dress (up), °trick out *or* up, °enhance, °elaborate, °enrich, embroider, gild, furbish (up), garnish, °decorate, adorn, °ornament, deck, bedeck, °trim, caparison, rubricate, varnish; gild refined gold, paint the lily, *Misquote* gild the lily: *The saddles are embellished with silver studs.* **2** °elaborate, °exaggerate, °overdo, embroider, °enhance, °dress up: *His reports are so embellished that you cannot separate fact from fiction.*

embellishment *n.* **1** °decoration, ornamentation, °ornament, °elaboration, adornment, embroidery: *The basic design, which is shoddy, is unimproved by embellishment. Good pasta needs minimal embellishment.* **2** °exaggeration, enhancement, tinsel, garnish, gilding, °frill: *All the embellishments make her story totally unbelievable.*

embers *n.pl.* live coals; cinders, ashes; °remains, °remnants: *The dying embers of the fire symbolized her waning love for Darrin.*

embezzle *v.* °misappropriate, peculate, misapply, °misuse, °steal, °make off *or* away with, filch, °pilfer, purloin, *Law* defalcate; *Colloq* have one's hand in the till: *The treasurer had embezzled half a million from the company.*

embezzlement *n.* misappropriation, peculation, misapplication, °misuse, misusing, abstraction, °stealing, °theft, thievery, larceny, filching, purloining, pilferage, pilfering, *Law* defalcation: *Wanted for embezzlement, he fled to Brazil.*

embittered *adj.* °bitter, °resentful, °sour, soured, °caustic, acrimonious, acid, envenomed; °angry, choleric, °rancorous: *His conviction for fraud left him an embittered man.*

emblem *n.* badge, insigne, °symbol, °representation, °device, °seal, °crest, °token, °sign; trade °mark, logotype *or* logo: *The white knight's emblem was a pair of crossed flaming swords.*

emblematic *adj.* emblematical, °symbolical, °representative, representational: *The white dove is emblematic of peace.*

embodiment *n.* **1** incarnation, °realization, concretization, °manifestation, °expression, personification, materialization, actualization, reification, substantiation: *The golden section is the embodiment of an ancient principle of proportion.* **2** consolidation, °collection, unification, incorporation, °inclusion, integration, °combination, concentration, systematization, °organization, codification, °synthesis, °epitome: *This book is the embodiment of Arnolfo's theories of aesthetics.*

embody *v.* **1** concretize, °realize, °manifest, °express, °personify, °materialize, reify, actualize, externalize, incarnate: *Her feminist convictions are embodied in her lifestyle.* **2** °exemplify, °typify, °represent, °symbolize, °stand for: *Note how this painting embodies Longchamp's unique notions of form.* **3** consolidate, °collect, °unite, °unify, °incorporate, °include, °integrate, °combine, °concentrate, systematize, °organize, comprise, codify, epitomize, synthesize: *The teachings of the sect are embodied in their scriptures.*

embrace *v.* **1** °hug, °clasp, °grasp, °hold, enfold, °cuddle, °cleave together, *Archaic* °clip: *She embraced him warmly when they met again.* **2** °adopt, espouse, °take up *or* in, avail oneself of, °use, make °use of, °employ, °accept, °receive, °welcome: *They embraced Christian ideals.* **3** °include, comprise, °embody, °incorporate, °comprehend, encompass: *Their tribal territory embraces all areas south of the mountains.*
—*n.* **4** °hug, °squeeze, °clutch, *Slang* °clinch: *He gave her a tender embrace and left.*

emerge *v.* **1** °appear, °come out, °come forth, °come up, °rise; °arise, °surface, °come into °view *or* °notice, come to °light, be °revealed, crop up, °turn out, °develop, become known, become °apparent, °transpire, °happen, evolve: *It emerged that she had bought a pistol that morning.* **2** °issue, °emanate, °come forth, °proceed: *The train emerged from the tunnel.*

emergence *n.* °rise, surfacing, °appearance; °development, materialization, °manifestation: *They were surprised by his emergence as leader.*

emergency *n.* °crisis, exigency, °danger, °predicament, °difficulty, °pinch: *In an emergency, put on lifebelts.*

emigrant *n.* émigré, expatriate, displaced person, DP, °refugee, boat person; colonist, °settler: *For millions of European emigrants, their first sight of the promised land was the Statue of Liberty in New York harbour.*

emigrate *v.* °migrate, °move, relocate, resettle; °leave, °quit, °depart, °forsake: *Her parents emigrated from Turkey and settled in Scotland.*

eminent *adj.* **1** °distinguished, esteemed, °exalted, respected, revered, honoured, °dignified, °notable, °noteworthy, °important, °noted, °outstanding, °prominent, °pre-eminent, °conspicuous, °superior, °great, °illustrious, °famous, °renowned, °well-known, °celebrated: *McLeod is an eminent meteorologist.* **2** °conspicuous, °outstanding, °marked: *His suggestion made eminent good sense.*

eminently *adv.* °very, °exceedingly, °extremely, exceptionally, remarkably, singularly, °notably, signally: *This man is eminently well suited for his job.*

emit *v.* °discharge, °eject, °expel, °emanate, °send out *or* forth, °pour out *or* forth, °give off *or* out, °issue, °vent, °radiate; °exhale; exude, °ooze: *The factory has been emitting toxic gases into the atmosphere.*

emotion *n.* °feeling, °passion, °sentiment, °sensation: *They say there is a fine line between the emotions of love and hate.*

emotional *adj.* **1** °passionate, °impassioned, °ardent, °enthusiastic, °heated, zealous, °heartfelt, °excited, °fervent, fervid: *She reacted in a very emotional way to the suggestions.* **2** °tense, °nervous, °excitable, highly-strung, high-strung, °temperamental, °volatile, °hot-headed, °demonstrative: *He is a very emotional person, who should not be driving a bus.* **3** °sensitive, °warm, °sentimental, °tender, °moving, °poignant, °stirring, emotive, affective, °touching: *Their meeting after 50 years was certainly emotional.* **4** °frantic, °agitated, irrational, °hysterical, °wild, ranting: *She became very emotional when the police took away her son.*

emphasis *n.* °importance, °stress, °significance, °prominence, °attention, °weight, °gravity, °force, °moment, °pre-eminence, °priority, underscoring, underlining, *Technical* paralipsis: *They place too much emphasis on the social aspects of school.*

emphasize *v.* °stress, accentuate, °accent, underscore, °point up, underline, call *or* draw °attention to, °mark, highlight, °play up, °spotlight, °feature: *The new procedures emphasize safety.*

emphatic *adj.* °firm, uncompromising, °determined, °decided, °resolute, dogged; °earnest, °definite, unequivocal, unambiguous, °distinct, °dogmatic, °categorical, °peremptory, °explicit, °incisive, °insistent, affirmative, °positive, °sure, °certain, unmistakable, °specific, °definitive, °direct; °forceful, °vigorous, °energetic, °assertive, °intense; °express, °pronounced, °strong: *She was emphatic about leaving then and there.*

empirical *adj.* empiric, experiential, °practical, observed, pragmatic, °experimental: *He has been there and has empirical knowledge of the system.*

employ *v.* **1** °hire, °engage, °enlist, °recruit, °enrol, °sign (up), °take on, °retain, commission: *I have employed a solicitor to look after my affairs while I am away. The company employed 120 engineers.* **2** °use, make °use of, utilize, °apply: *We plan to employ the most modern equipment.* **3** °occupy, °take (up), °engage, °involve: *He is employed with his stamp collection.*

employee *n.* °worker, °staff °member, wage-earner; °hand: *The employees are on strike.*

employer *n.* **1** °proprietor, °owner, °patron, °manager, °director, °chief, °head, *Colloq* °boss, *Brit* gaffer, governor, guv'nor, guv: *My employer comes in late every day.* **2** °company, °firm, corporation, °business, °establishment, °organization, *Colloq* °outfit: *She took her employer to court for unfair dismissal.*

employment *n.* **1** °occupation, °job, °trade, °work, °business, °profession, °vocation, °calling, livelihood, °pursuit, *métier*, °skill, °craft, *Colloq* °line, *Slang* °racket: *My employment for many years has been restoring antique furniture.* **2** °hire, hiring, °engagement, engaging, employing, taking on, retaining, enlistment, enlisting: *The employment of 50 people by the new firm will help the town.* **3** °use, utilization, °application, °operation, implementation: *The job involves the employment of specialized techniques.*

emptiness *n.* **1** voidness, hollowness, vacantness, °vacancy, vacuity, blankness, bareness, barrenness, °desolation, desertedness, vacuum, °void: *He was again alone in the vast emptiness of space. After she left, I felt a terrible emptiness.* **2** senselessness, meaninglessness, pointlessness, aimlessness, purposelessness, futility, uselessness, worthlessness, hollowness: *The emptiness of the candidate's words was apparent to all.* **3** vacuity, vacuousness, vacantness, blankness, expressionlessness, emotionlessness: *The emptiness of her facial expression told me that she hadn't understood a word.*

empty *adj.* **1** °void, unfilled, °hollow, °bare, °barren, °vacant, unfurnished, °unadorned, undecorated; emptied, drained, °spent, °exhausted: *That empty space on the wall needs a painting.* **2** °vacant, unoccupied, °uninhabited, untenanted: *He finally found an empty flat with two bedrooms.* **3** °deserted, °desolate, °uninhabited, °wild, °waste, °bare, °barren; forsaken: *He wandered for days on the empty moor.* **4** trivial, °insincere, °hypocritical, °hollow, °cheap, °worthless, valueless, °meaningless, °insignificant, °insubstantial, unsatisfying, °idle: *His promises were merely words, empty words.* **5** °vacant, °blank, deadpan, expressionless, poker-faced; vacuous, fatuous, °stupid, °foolish, °inane: *He looked at me with that empty expression of his.* **6** °blank, °clean, °new, °unused, °clear: *On an empty page write your name and the date.* **7 *empty of*:** devoid of, lacking (in), °wanting, in °want of, °deficient in, °destitute of, without, sans: *Their hearts are empty of compassion.*
—*v.* **8** °clear, °remove, °take out *or* away, °put out, °cast *or* °throw out, °eject; °vacate, °evacuate; °dump, °drain, °exhaust, °pour out, °void, °discharge, °unload: *Thieves emptied everything from the house. The police are emptying the building because of a bomb scare. Empty these bottles outside.*

enable *v.* **1** °qualify, °authorize, °entitle, °permit, °allow, °sanction, °approve, empower, °license, commission, °entrust, depute, °delegate, °assign, °charter, franchise: *An act was passed to enable them to build the railway.* **2** capacitate, °facilitate, °expedite, °help, °aid, °assist: *The grant enabled me to continue my studies.* **3** °permit, °allow, °approve, assent to, °go along with, °agree to, give the °go-ahead *or* green light, *Colloq* °OK *or* okay: *Her press pass enables her to get through police lines.*

enact *v.* **1** °pass, legislate, °ratify; ordain, °decree, °rule, °command, °order, °authorize: *The law was enacted to protect consumers.* **2** °act (out), °represent, °play, °portray, depict, °perform, °appear as: *She enacted the role of a modern Lady Macbeth.*

enchant *v.* **1** °bewitch, cast a °spell on, ensorcell *or* ensorcel, spellbind, °hypnotize, mesmerize, voodoo, *Brit* °magic, *US* hex, *Colloq* hoodoo: *Circe enchanted Ulysses' men and turned them into swine.* **2** °charm, °fascinate, °beguile, °captivate, enthral, °enrapture, °attract, allure, °delight, °entrance: *With her sultry looks she has enchanted the most cynical of men.*

enchanted *adj.* °pleased, °delighted, °happy, thrilled, French *enchanté(e)*: *I am enchanted to meet you at last, Mrs Thompson.*

enchanting *adj.* beguiling, bewitching, entrancing, °spellbinding, charming, fascinating, captivating, intriguing, °enthralling, alluring, °delightful, hypnotic, °attractive, appealing, winsome, °ravishing, °seductive: *Caesar found Cleopatra utterly enchanting.*

enchantment *n.* **1** witchcraft, °sorcery, °magic, wizardry, thaumaturgy, conjuration *or* conjury; °spell, °charm, °jinx, *US* hex: *Stories of enchantment and magic fail to interest today's sceptical five-year-old. When she worked her enchantment on me, I succumbed completely.* **2** °charm, beguilement, allure, °fascination, °rapture, mesmerism, °bliss: *She was completely carried away by the enchantment of the moment.*

encircle *v.* °surround, gird, °circle, °enclose, °ring, encompass, compass, confine, hem *or* °hold in; wreathe: *When the horde encircled the castle we thought we were doomed.*

enclose *v.* **1** inclose, confine, °shut in, °close *or* hem in, °surround, °pen, °encircle, encompass, °bound, °envelop, hedge in, °wall in, immure, °fence in *or* off, *US and Canadian* corral: *A high wall encloses the garden.* **2** °insert, °include, °contain; °wrap: *The cheque was enclosed in the same envelope.*

enclosure *n.* **1** °fold, °pen, cote, °run, sty, yard, farmyard, barnyard, courtyard, quadrangle *or* quad, °square, °compound, *Brit* °close, *US and Canadian* corral: *We had trouble keeping the dogs in the enclosure.* **2** °fence, °wall, °rail, railing, °barrier, hedge, barricade, °boundary: *The buildings serve as an enclosure.*

encounter *v.* **1** °meet, °come upon, °run into *or* across, °happen upon, °chance upon, °hit upon, °light upon, °stumble upon, *Colloq* °bump into: *She encountered him again in the supermarket.* **2** °face, °experience, °meet with, contend with, be °faced with, come into °contact with, °wrestle with: *She encounters such problems every day.* **3** come into °conflict with, contend with, assail, cross swords (with), °grapple with, °engage, joust with, do °battle with, confront, °clash with, °join, °meet: *The ballad tells how he encountered the black knight in single combat.*
—*n.* **4** °meeting: *It was a chance encounter that brought us together.* **5** confrontation, °brush, °quarrel, °disagreement, °dispute, altercation, °engagement, °action, °battle, °fight, °clash, °conflict, °skirmish, °contest, °competition, duel, contention, °struggle, °war, *Colloq* dust-up, °scrap, °run-in, set-to: *My uncle took part in the bloody encounter in the Ardennes.*

encourage *v.* **1** hearten, embolden, °reassure, °buoy (up), °stimulate, °animate, °support, inspirit, °inspire, °cheer (up), °urge *or* °spur on *or* onward(s), °incite, *Colloq* egg on, °pep up: *She encouraged him in his study of medicine.* **2** °promote, °advance, °aid, °support, °help, °assist, °abet, °foster, °forward, °boost, *Colloq* give a °shot in the arm: *The continued success of the team encouraged attendance at the games.*

encouragement *n.* **1** heartening, reassuring, reassurance, buoying up, °stimulating, stimulation, stimulus, animating, °animation, supporting, °support, promoting, °promotion, inspiring, °inspiration, cheering, urging, °spur, spurring, exhorting, exhortation, prodding, urging, innervation, inciting, °incitement: *Without her encouragement, I could never have won.* **2** °boost, stimulus, °help, °aid, °support, *Colloq* °pep talk: *The team gets a lot of encouragement from local merchants.*

encroach *v.* Often, ***encroach on*** *or* ***upon***: °intrude, trespass, °infringe, invade, make inroads: *When you mention arctophily, you're encroaching on my territory.*

encumber *v.* **1** °burden, °weigh down, °load (up *or* down), °overload, overburden, °strain, °oppress, saddle, °tax, overtax: *Encumbered with intolerable taxes, the people revolted. She almost drowned because she was encumbered with her numerous petticoats.* **2** °hamper, °impede, °hinder, °handicap, °inconvenience, °trammel, °retard, °slow down: *Though encumbered by an invalid husband, she managed to qualify as a barrister.*

encumbrance *n.* °weight, °burden, onus, cross (to bear), albatross, millstone, °handicap, °impediment, °hindrance, °obstacle, °obstruction, °liability, °disadvantage, °drag: *The children were regarded merely as an encumbrance.*

encyclopedic *adj.* encyclopaedic, °comprehensive, °inclusive, °broad, °extensive, °universal, °thorough, °exhaustive, wide-ranging, °complete: *She has an encyclopedic knowledge of Chinese art.*

end *n.* **1** °extremity, °extreme, °extent, °bound, °boundary, °tip, °limit, terminus: *That fence marks the southern end of the property. At the end of the garden was a large shed.* **2** °close, °termination, conclusion, cessation, °expiration, °finish, °completion, finale, ending, wind-up; denouement *or* dénouement: *At the end of the film, the lights came on.* **3** °aim, °purpose, °intention, °intent, °objective, °object, °goal, °point, °reason, *raison d'être*, °destination, °motive, motivation, °aspiration: *To what end does she persist so vehemently?* **4** consequence, °result, °outcome, °effect, °upshot: *The end of the affair was that he had to leave town.* **5** °destruction, °death, °ruin, extermination, annihilation, °termination, conclusion: *That would spell the end to all life on earth.* **6** ***at a loose end*** *or US and Canadian* ***at loose ends***: °unsettled, unoccupied, °unemployed, uncommitted, undecided, °indecisive, ambivalent, vacillating, °purposeless, °aimless, adrift, drifting, betwixt and between, neither here nor there: *My wife has gone off to visit her mother and I'm at a loose end.* **7** ***on end***: **a** °upright, °erect, °standing: *He can balance a ruler on end.* **b** continuously, uninterruptedly, unceasingly, incessantly, consecutively: *It rained for days on end.* **8** ***the end***: **a** the worst, the °last straw, the °final blow, *Colloq* the °limit, too much: *Brian's winning first prize is the absolute end.* **b** the °best, the greatest: *That disc by The What is the living end.*
—*v.* **9** °terminate, conclude, bring to an end, °stop, °halt, °cease, °wind up *or* down, °settle, put an end to, °discontinue, °break off, °cut off, °close, °finish, culminate, end up, *Brit* put paid to; °die (out), °expire, °climax, peter out, vanish: *We have ended our relationship. The book ends with her returning to him. The year ends on December 31st.* **10** °kill, put to °death, annihilate, °exterminate, °terminate, °extinguish; °destroy, °ruin: *He ended his life last night with a bullet.* **11** °surpass, °outdo, outclass, outshine, °outstrip, °supersede: *It is a disaster film to end all disaster films.*

endanger *v.* imperil, °threaten, °jeopardize, °risk, put at °risk, °hazard, expose (to °danger), put in °jeopardy, tempt fate: *She endangered her life while trying to save his.*

endangered *adj.* imperilled, threatened, near extinction: *Every effort must be made to protect endangered species.*

endearing *adj.* °attractive, °engaging, °likeable, appealing, winsome, captivating, °winning: *He has a few endearing qualities, I suppose.*

endeavour *v.* **1** °try, °attempt, °strive, make an °effort, do one's °best, °struggle, °exert oneself, °undertake; °aim, °aspire; *Colloq* take a °stab at, have a °go *or* crack *or* whack *or* °shot at: *For years he's endeavoured to see her.*
—*n.* **2** °effort, pains, °attempt, °try, striving, °struggle, °venture, °enterprise, *Colloq* °stab, crack, whack, °shot: *Her endeavours to be published have come to naught.*

endless *adj.* **1** °limitless, °unlimited, °boundless, unbounded, °infinite, °immeasurable, °eternal, unending: *They found themselves in the endless reaches of outer space.* **2** ceaseless, uninterrupted, incessant, unceasing, unending, °constant, °perpetual, interminable, unremitting, °non-stop, °continuous, °continual, °everlasting: *I wish you two would stop your endless bickering.*

endorse *v.* **1** indorse, °approve, °sanction, °authorize, °advocate, °support, °back, °subscribe to, °sustain, °confirm, countenance, put one's °stamp *or* °seal (of °approval) on, set one's °seal (of °approval) to, give (something) one's imprimatur, *Colloq* °OK, okay: *The council endorsed our application for planning permission.* **2** indorse, countersign: *Endorse the cheque to cash it.*

endorsement *n.* **1** indorsement, °approval, affirmation, °sanction, authorization, confirmation, ratification, °support, °backing, approbation, °seal *or* °stamp of °approval, imprimatur, *Colloq* °OK, okay: *He is acting with the full endorsement of his union.* **2** counter-signature: *His endorsement is on the back of the cheque.*

endowment *n.* **1** °grant, (°financial) °aid, °subsidy, subvention, °allowance, °allotment, contribution,

°donation, °gift, °present, °award; °bequest, °inheritance, dowry: *The endowment was enough to support me for a year.* **2** °gift, °presentation, bestowal, °award, awarding, °settlement: *The endowment of the grant was approved by the college.* **3** ***endowments***: °qualities, talents, °gifts, °abilities, °aptitudes, °capabilities, °capacities, °qualifications, °strengths; °attributes, °properties, °characteristics: *She is a woman of considerable endowments.*

endurance *n.* **1** °stamina, staying °power, °perseverance, °persistence, °resolution, °fortitude, °tenacity, °patience, °tolerance, *Colloq US* stick-to-it-iveness: *He showed remarkable endurance in the pentathlon trials.* **2** °lasting quality, durability, longevity, lifetime, continuation: *In this film, he uses the river as a symbol of endurance and timelessness.*

endure *v.* **1** °last, °persist, °stay, °remain, °abide, °prevail, °survive, °continue, °hold, °live (on), *Colloq* go the distance: *Her fame as a poet will endure.* **2** °stand, °abide, °tolerate, °face, °survive, °withstand, °bear, °weather, °take (it), °suffer, °stomach, °undergo, °hold out (against), *Colloq* °hang in (there), °stick *or* °sweat (it *or* something) out: *He endured the pressure of his job as long as he could.* **3** °suffer, °undergo, °bear, °face, °stand, °put up with, °stomach, °take: *Consider the tyranny that Europe endured under Hitler.*

enduring *adj.* °lasting, long-lasting, °durable, °abiding, continuing, long-standing, persisting, °persistent, °remaining, °steady, °steadfast; °eternal, °immortal, °permanent: *Their enduring faith carried them through the ordeal.*

enemy *n.* foe, °antagonist, °adversary, °opponent, °rival, °competitor, °contestant, contender; the °opposition, the other side: *His enemies were running a smear campaign against him.*

energetic *adj.* °lively, °active, °vigorous, invigorated, °dynamic, °animated, °spirited, °untiring, °tireless, indefatigable, °sprightly, spry, °vital, high-powered, °brisk, vibrant, zesty, zestful, *Colloq* °hot, peppy, full of °pep, full of get-up-and-go, zippy, on one's toes, zingy, full of beans: *I feel most energetic at the start of the day.*

energize *v.* °enliven, °liven up, °stimulate, °animate, invigorate, °activate, actuate, °move, °motivate, galvanize, °electrify, °inspire, inspirit, °pep up, waken, °rouse, °stir, arouse, °excite, egg on, °urge: *Max's enthusiasm energized the whole of the research team.*

energy *n.* °vitality, forcefulness, vivacity, liveliness, °vigour, °animation, °spirit, °force, °dynamism, °drive, °verve, °dash, élan, °intensity, °power, °determination, puissance, °strength, °might, *Colloq* °pep, vim and °vigour, *US* stick-to-it-iveness, get-up-and-go, zip, zing: *At seventy, she just couldn't put as much energy into her performance as she once did.*

enervate *v.* °weaken, °tire, °strain, enfeeble, debilitate, °fatigue, °exhaust, °drain, °sap, °wear out, devitalize, °break, °defeat: *I have always found the tropics quite enervating.*

enforce *v.* **1** °insist upon *or* on, °stress, °require, °impose, °support, put into °effect, °apply, °administer, °carry out, °inflict, bring to bear, °implement, °prosecute, °discharge; °reinforce; *Colloq* °crack *or* °clamp down: *The police will enforce the curfew tonight.* **2** °force, compel, °pressure *or Brit* pressurize, °press, coerce, lay °stress upon *or* on, °impose upon *or* on, °impress upon *or* on, °insist upon *or* on, °demand, °require; °intimidate, °browbeat, °bully, °railroad; *Colloq* °lean on, °twist (someone's) arm: *They hired thugs to enforce their claim.*

engage *v.* **1** °employ, °hire, °enrol *or US also* enroll, °enlist, °retain, °sign (up), °contract with *or* for, indenture; °rent, °book, °reserve, °secure, bespeak: *She was engaged on a part-time basis. We engaged rooms for the night.* **2** °occupy, engross, °busy, absorb, °involve, °tie up, preoccupy, °employ: *This task will engage all available resources until the end of next month.* **3** °pledge, °undertake, °bargain, °agree, covenant, °promise, °guarantee, °contract: *I engaged to complete the work by Tuesday.* **4** °attract, °hold, °capture, catch, °draw: *The museum has many exhibits that will engage the interest of children.* **5** °join (in) °combat *or* °battle with, °meet, °encounter, °fight, °combat, °attack, °battle, °clash with, °grapple with: *The enemy was engaged at dawn.* **6** ***engage in***: °participate (in), °partake in, take °part (in), °enter (into), °undertake, °embark on: *She engages in many out-of-school activities.*

engaged *adj.* **1** betrothed, affianced, plighted, pledged, promised; °spoken for: *They got engaged on St Valentine's Day.* **2** °busy, occupied, tied up, °involved, employed, °absorbed, °preoccupied, wrapped up: *He is otherwise engaged and cannot meet me today.*

engagement *n.* **1** °appointment, °meeting, °date, rendezvous, °arrangement, commitment: *I'm sorry, I have a previous engagement.* **2** betrothal: *Their engagement was announced in all the papers.* **3** °agreement, °bargain, °obligation, °promise, °pledge, covenant, °contract: *The company undertook an engagement to provide the steel.* **4** °job, °position, °post, commission, booking; °employment, °work; *Colloq* °spot, *Slang* (of a musician) gig: *He has an engagement with the newspaper.* **5** °fight, °battle, °conflict, °encounter, °combat: *The naval engagement lasted three days and nights.*

engaging *adj.* charming, °pleasant, °attractive, winsome, °winning, appealing, °agreeable, °delightful, °pleasing, °likeable, °friendly, °open: *With her engaging personality, it is no wonder she has so many friends.*

engine *n.* motor, °machine, °mechanism, appliance, °apparatus; locomotive: *The invention of the internal combustion engine revolutionized modern transport.*

engineer *n.* **1** °designer, originator, inventor, contriver, architect, planner, °mastermind: *The engineer of this scheme was one David Jones.* **2** (°engine-) driver, conductor, °operator: *He was the engineer on the afternoon train out of Washington.* **3** mechanic, technician, repairman: *The telephone engineers will be here on Monday to install a new phone system.*
—*v.* **4** °devise, °plan, °develop, °originate, contrive, °invent, °mastermind, °construct, °build, °make: *It is said that Daedalus engineered the first man-made wings.* **5** °manipulate, °scheme, °plot, machinate, °intrigue, connive, conspire, °manoeuvre, °rig, °set up, °organize, °arrange, °put over, *Colloq* finagle, °wangle, °swing: *She tried to engineer the laundering of the money, but was caught.*

engrave *v.* **1** °cut, °carve, °chisel, inscribe; °etch: *The ring was a plain gold band, engraved with daisies.* **2** °impress, °stamp, °set, °lodge, °fix, embed, imprint, ingrain: *The horror of that night was forever engraved in his mind.*

engraving *n.* **1** intaglio, cameo, etching, dry-point, woodcut, linocut, wood *or* steel engraving, anaglyph, °block *or US also* °cut: *She uses a burin to make these engravings.* **2** °print, °impression, etching, dry-point: *The exhibition of Dürer engravings closes tomorrow.*

enhance *v.* °improve, °better, augment, °boost, °raise, elevate, °lift, °heighten, °exalt, °enlarge, °swell, °magnify, °increase, °add to, °amplify, °intensify, °enrich, °embellish, °complement, °reinforce, °strengthen: *His public image was greatly enhanced by his support of charities.*

enigma *n.* °puzzle, conundrum, °mystery, °riddle, poser, °problem: *How he escaped is an enigma to the police.*

enjoy *v.* **1** °delight in, °appreciate, °like, take *or* derive °pleasure *or* °satisfaction in *or* from, °relish (in), °fancy, °take to, *Slang* °dig, get a °kick *or* °lift *or* °charge out of, get °high on, °get off on: *Bernard really enjoys Wagner.* **2** °benefit *or* °profit from, take °advantage of, °use, utilize, make °use of, °use to °advantage, °have, °possess: *He cannot be charged because he enjoys diplomatic immunity.* **3** ***enjoy oneself***: have a good time, make °merry, *Colloq* have a ball *or* the time of one's life: *I enjoyed myself at your party.*

enjoyment *n.* **1** °pleasure, °delight, °joy, °gratification, °satisfaction, °relish, °zest, °delectation, °recreation, °entertainment, °diversion, °amusement: *The public has derived much enjoyment from Shaw's plays.* **2** °use, utilization, °exercise, °possession; °benefit, °advantage: *As a member, you are entitled to the enjoyment of all club privileges.*

enlarge *v.* **1** °increase, °expand, °magnify, °amplify, °extend, °swell, dilate, °spread, wax, °widen, broaden, °lengthen, elongate, °stretch, distend; °add to, °supplement, augment; °inflate; *Colloq* °blow up: *The government will enlarge the area devoted to public parks. Enlarge the photographs and details appear.*
2 ***enlarge on*** *or* ***upon***: °expand on, expatiate on, °amplify, expound; °detail, °elaborate (on): *The speaker was asked to enlarge on her plans for building new hospitals.*

enlighten *v.* °inform, edify, °instruct, °teach, °tutor, °educate, °coach, apprise, make °aware, °advise, °counsel: *You must enlighten George on how to behave in public.*

enlightened *adj.* °well-informed, °informed, °educated, °aware, °knowledgeable, literate, °rational, °reasonable, °sensible, common-sense, commonsensical, broad-minded, open-minded, °liberal; °cultivated, civilized, °sophisticated, *Colloq* in the know: *In a democracy, the press serves an enlightened public.*

enlist *v.* **1** °enrol, °register, °join (up), volunteer, °sign up *or* on; °engage, °recruit, °induct, °muster, conscript, °impress, °call up, *US* °draft: *He enlisted in the navy at 17.* **2** °employ, °hire, °engage, °retain, make °available, °secure, °obtain, °get, °procure, °gather, drum up, °mobilize, *Colloq* °organize: *We must enlist all the help we can.*

enliven *v.* **1** invigorate, inspirit, °animate, °pep up, °stimulate, °energize, vivify, °vitalize, °quicken, exhilarate, arouse, °rouse, awaken, °wake up, °spark (off), °kindle, enkindle, °fire (up), °inspire: *Enlivened by the coach's talk, we were determined to win.* **2** °brighten, °cheer (up), °buoy (up), °gladden, uplift: *The room was considerably enlivened by the new curtains.*

enormity *n.* outrageousness, °outrage, atrociousness, °atrocity, wickedness, heinousness, flagitiousness, horribleness, °horror, °barbarity, savagery, monstrousness, horridness, °evil, viciousness: *The enormity of the crime shocked us all.*

enormous *adj.* °huge, °immense, °gigantic, elephantine, gargantuan, mammoth, titanic, °colossal, tremendous, °vast, °massive, stupendous, Brobdingnagian, °gross, °monstrous, °prodigious: *An enormous dragon blocked their way out of the cave.*

enormousness *n.* immensity, hugeness: *I was staggered by the sheer enormousness of the building.*

enough *adj.* **1** °sufficient, °adequate, °ample: *There isn't enough food to go round.*
—*n.* **2** sufficiency, adequacy, °ample °supply, °plenty: *I have enough for myself.*
—*adv.* **3** sufficiently, adequately, reasonably, satisfactorily, tolerably, passably: *Your word is good enough for me.*

enquire *v.* **1** °inquire, °ask, °question, °query: *The police enquired whether we had noticed any strange goings-on next door.* **2** See **inquire,** below.

enrage *v.* °anger, °infuriate, °madden, incense, °provoke, °inflame, make (someone's) blood boil, *Colloq* get (someone's) back *or* Irish *or* hackles *or* dander up, make (someone) see red, wave a red flag before (someone), *US* burn (someone) up, *Slang Brit* put (someone's) monkey up, *US* tick (someone) off, tee (someone) off, *Taboo slang US* piss (someone) off: *Lord Thimble was enraged at being made to wait his turn.*

enrapture *v.* °enchant, °entrance, °transport, °thrill, °bewitch, spellbind, °fascinate, °charm, enthral, °captivate, °beguile, °delight: *The soprano quite enraptured her audience.*

enrich *v.* **1** endow, °enhance, °improve, upgrade, °better, ameliorate, °refine, °add to: *His novels have enriched our literature.* **2** °ornament, adorn, °decorate, °embellish; °beautify, °grace: *Before us rose a lofty dome enriched with precious stones.*

enrol *v.* **1** °enlist, °register, °sign up *or* on (for), °join; volunteer; °recruit; *Colloq* °join up: *He enrolled at the university.* **2** °record, °register, °chronicle, °put down, °list, °note, inscribe, catalogue: *Their names will be enrolled forever in the Book of Heroes.*

ensemble *n.* **1** °outfit, °costume, clothing, °clothes, attire, °apparel, garb, °garments, coordinates, *Colloq* °get-up: *A black hat, gloves, and shoes completed the ensemble.* **2** °band, °combination, orchestra, °group; chorus, choir; *Colloq* combo: *A new chamber music ensemble is performing tonight at the town hall.*
3 assemblage, composite, aggregate, °collection, °set, °whole, °entirety, °totality; agglomeration, conglomeration: *A strange ensemble of objects was on display.*

enslave *v.* °subjugate, yoke, fetter, enchain, °shackle, °trammel, °dominate; °bind, indenture, *Archaic* enthral: *The enslaved masses rose and overcame their masters.*

ensure *v.* **1** insure, °assure, make °sure *or* °certain, °confirm, °certify, °guarantee; °secure, °effect: *He must ensure that there is no leak.* **2** insure, °protect, make °safe, °safeguard, °guard, °secure: *The captain is responsible for ensuring the safety of the passengers.*

entail *v.* °involve, °require, °call for, necessitate, °demand, °occasion, give °rise to, °impose; °lead to, °cause: *The post has entailed working an average 60-70 hours a week.*

entangle *v.* **1** °tangle, ensnarl, °snarl, enmesh, catch (up), entrap, °snag, °foul, °implicate, °knot (up), °twist; °impede; °involve, embroil: *The propeller became entangled in the seaweed so that the boat couldn't move.* **2** °confuse, °mix (up), °twist, °snarl, ensnarl, ensnare, °hamper, °complicate, confound, °bewilder, °perplex, °embarrass: *He became entangled in a web of social and business liaisons.*

enter *v.* **1** °go *or* °come (in *or* into), °pass (into): *Please enter at the left.* **2** °penetrate, °pierce, °stick (into), °stab (into), °puncture; invade, infiltrate: *The nail entered the tyre here. The iron entered into his soul.* **3** °insert, inscribe, °write, °set *or* °write *or* °put down, °note, °record, °take *or* °jot down, °register; log, °document, °minute: *Enter your name on the dotted line.* **4** enter on *or* upon, °begin, °start, °commence, °undertake, °set out on, °take up: *I didn't want to enter the marathon if I couldn't finish.* **5** °enrol, °enlist, °sign on *or* up, °join, become a member of: *He has entered the ranks of the unemployed.* **6** °present, °offer, proffer, °tender, °submit: *More than 100 poems were entered in the competition.* **7** °file, °register, °record, °submit: *The defendant entered a plea of 'Not guilty'.* **8** ***enter into***: °engage *or* °participate in, °sign, be (a) party to, co-sign, countersign: *We entered into an agreement to buy the house.*

enterprise *n.* **1** °undertaking, °project, °venture, °adventure, °effort, °programme, °plan, °scheme: *His latest enterprise involves establishing a chain of pizza shops.* **2** boldness, °daring, °courage, mettle, adventurousness, audacity, °enthusiasm, zeal, °energy, °spirit, °drive, °vigour, °ambition, °initiative, °push, °eagerness, °determination, °resolve, purposefulness, °purpose; aggressiveness; *Colloq* get-up-and-go, zip, °pep, °gumption, °guts, *US* starch: *It takes a lot of enterprise to start your own business.* **3** °business, °operation, °firm, °company, °concern, °establishment: *We began this enterprise on a shoestring.*

enterprising *adj.* °resourceful, °venturesome, °adventurous, °daring, °courageous, °bold, °brave, mettlesome, °audacious, °enthusiastic, °eager, °keen, zealous, °energetic, °spirited, °vigorous, °ambitious, °determined, resolved, °resolute, °earnest, °purposeful, purposive, goal-oriented; °aggressive, hard-working, indefatigable, °tireless, °diligent, assiduous, °industrious, persevering; *Colloq* °pushy, °go-ahead: *She is an enterprising young lawyer with her own practice.*

entertain *v.* **1** °amuse, °divert; °delight, °please; °occupy: *While we waited the boy entertained us with his juggling.* **2** °receive, °accommodate, °treat, be °host (to), °cater (for *or* to); have *or* see people *or* guests *or* visitors *or* company; *Colloq* °host: *We entertain on Tuesdays only.* **3** °contemplate, °consider, °have, °hold, °harbour, °foster, °tolerate, °allow, °maintain, °sustain, °support: *They felt that they could not entertain the idea of their daughter marrying the gardener's son.*

entertaining *adj.* amusing, diverting, °delightful, enjoyable, °pleasant, °fun, °pleasing, °pleasurable, °interesting, °engaging; °funny, °comic, °humorous, °witty: *We find Laurel and Hardy films entertaining.*

entertainment *n.* **1** °amusement, °diversion, °distraction, °pastime, °recreation, °sport, °play, °fun, °pleasure, °enjoyment, °relaxation, °relief: *What do you do for entertainment?* **2** °performance, °presentation, °diversion, °amusement, divertissement, °exhibition, °pageant, °spectacle, °show, °production, spectacular, °extravaganza: *They put on a lavish entertainment for the queen.*

enthralling *adj.* captivating, entrancing, °spellbinding, °enchanting, bewitching, beguiling, fascinating, gripping, °absorbing, intriguing, hypnotizing, mesmerizing, °riveting: *There was an enthralling melodrama on TV last night.*

enthusiasm *n.* **1** °eagerness, keenness, earnestness, °fervour, avidity, zeal, °excitement, °passion, °ardour, °interest, °relish, °devotion, devotedness, °gusto, °exuberance, °zest; °fanaticism, °mania, °rage: *No one matches her enthusiasm for grand opera.* **2** °rage, °passion, °craze; °hobby, °interest, °pastime, °diversion, °amusement; *Colloq* °fad: *His current enthusiasm is acid rock.*

enthusiast *n.* °fan, °devotee, aficionado, °lover, °admirer, °zealot, °addict, °fanatic, promoter, °supporter, °champion, °follower, °disciple, adherent, *US* booster, *Colloq* teeny-bopper, °bug, °hound, buff, °fiend, *Slang* nut, °freak, groupie, *US* °head: *They are model railway enthusiasts.*

enthusiastic *adj.* °eager, °keen, °fervent, fervid, °hearty, °ardent, avid, °energetic, °vigorous, °devoted, °earnest, °passionate, °spirited, °exuberant, zealous, °fanatic(al), °unqualified, unstinting, °irrepressible: *He's an enthusiastic supporter of the prime minister's policies.*

entice *v.* °lure, allure, °tempt, °attract, °draw, °seduce, °coax, °persuade, °prevail (up)on, °beguile, °cajole, blandish, °wheedle; °decoy, °lead on, inveigle, *Colloq* sweet-talk, soft-soap, *Slang* suck in: *The prospectus enticed 3.15 million people to buy shares in the company.*

enticement *n.* **1** °temptation, allurement, beguilement, seduction, °cajolery, wheedling, blandishment, coaxing, °persuasion: *Do you approve of the system of enticement used to get you to buy time-share holidays?* **2** °lure, bait, °decoy, °trap, °inducement, °attraction, °temptation, *Colloq* °come-on, soft soap: *Among the enticements offered was a free weekend in Paris.*

entire *adj.* **1** °complete, °whole, °total, °full, °undivided, °absolute, °thorough, unreserved, unrestricted, undiminished, unconditional, °express, unexceptional, unmixed, unalloyed: *That problem has occupied my entire attention all week.* **2** °intact, °whole, °sound, unbroken, undamaged, unimpaired, inviolate, without a scratch, °unscathed, in °one piece: *Twelve amphorae were recovered entire from the wreck.* **3** °continuous, °full, °whole, °complete, uninterrupted: *She has lasted an entire year in her new job.*

entirely *adv.* **1** °completely, °wholly, °altogether, fully, °totally, °utterly, unreservedly, unqualifiedly, unexceptionally, in every respect, in all respects, °thoroughly, to a T, *in toto*, exhaustively, all out, from head to toe *or* foot, (right) down to the ground, from A to Z, lock, stock and barrel, root and branch, without exception *or* reservation: *She was entirely satisfied. I agree with that entirely.* **2** solely, exclusively, °only, unambiguously, unequivocally; °positively, °definitely, °clearly: *It was entirely my fault.*

entirety *n.* **1** completeness, °unity, °totality, wholeness, fullness, °integrity, °perfection: *Any chance of completing his mission in its entirety had vanished.* **2** °whole, °sum °total, °everything, all: *The entirety of the bequest amounted to a million francs.*

entitle *v.* **1** °allow, °permit, °qualify, make °eligible, °authorize, °fit; enfranchise, °license, empower: *This document entitles her to half of the estate.* **2** °name, °title, °call, °label, °nickname, dub, °designate, °term; °christen, baptize: *His first novel was entitled* Out of the Depths.

entity *n.* **1** °thing, °object, being, °existence, °quantity, article, °individual, °organism: *The emergence of the youth movement as a separate entity posed problems for the party leadership.* **2** °essence, °real °nature, quiddity, °quintessence, *Metaphysics* ens: *Every living creature has a distinct entity.*

entrance[1] *n.* **1** (right of) °entry, access, °admission, °admittance, entrée, introduction: *You need security clearance to gain entrance.* **2** °entry, entry-way, access, door, °gate, °passage, °way (in); ingress: *The entrance is locked after midnight.* **3** °arrival, °appearance; coming, °entry, coming *or* °going in: *Her entrances were accompanied by cheers. He opposed our entrance into the war.* **4** °beginning, °start, commencement: *Today marks his entrance into his new duties.*

entrance[2] *v.* °enchant, °enrapture, °fascinate, °bewitch, spellbind, °transport, °delight, °charm, °captivate, enthral, °overpower, mesmerize, °hypnotize: *He was entranced by her beauty.*

entrenched *adj.* °rooted, deep-rooted, embedded, °fixed, (firmly) planted, established, °set, deep-seated, unshakeable *or* unshakable, ineradicable, °ingrained: *We were unable to combat their entrenched opposition to the proposals.*

entrust *v.* intrust, °trust, °charge, °assign, °delegate, confide: *I entrusted her with my secret.*

entry *n.* **1** access, °entrance, entrée, °admittance, °admission: *The burglar gained entry through the skylight.* **2** access, °entrance, entry-way, door, inlet, °passage, °way in: *Both entries were blocked.* **3** °entrance, °arrival, coming *or* °going in: *His entry was met with jeers.* **4** °record, °item, °memorandum, °note, °account, listing; registration; *Colloq* memo: *There is no entry in his diary for the 15th of April.* **5** °competitor, °contestant, °player, entrant, °participant, °candidate; °rival, °adversary, °opponent: *Dennis was a late entry in the marathon.*

entwine *v.* intwine, interlace, °braid, interweave, intertwine, °weave, °knit, plait, °twist, °coil, °twine, °splice; °entangle, °tangle: *Her hair was entwined with wild flowers.*

enumerate *v.* **1** °list, °name, °itemize, °specify, °detail, °spell out, catalogue, tick off, take °stock of, cite, °quote, °recite, °recount, °relate, narrate, *US* °check off: *I shall enumerate the reasons why you may not go.* **2** °count, °calculate, °compute, °reckon, °tally, °add, °number: *The researcher could enumerate only seven different species.*

enunciate *v.* **1** articulate, °pronounce, utter, °voice, °say, °speak, vocalize, °express, °deliver, °present, *Formal* enounce: *Foreign names should be enunciated clearly.* **2** °state, °proclaim, °declare, promulgate, °announce, °broadcast, °pronounce, °propound: *The party platform was enunciated in last night's speech.*

envelop *v.* **1** °wrap, °enclose, enfold, enwrap, °cover, engulf, °swathe, °shroud, enshroud, swaddle: *The body was enveloped in a white robe.* **2** °shroud, enshroud, °cover, °conceal, °hide, °screen, °shield, °obscure, °veil, °cloak: *The motive for the murder was enveloped in a mass of misleading clues.*

enviable *adj.* °desirable, wanted, desired, sought-after, covetable, in °demand: *He is in an enviable financial position.*

envious *adj.* °jealous, covetous, °resentful, begrudging, green-eyed, green (with °envy), °desirous: *He is envious of his wife because she has a better job.*

environment *n.* surroundings, environs, °atmosphere, ecosystem, conditions, °habitat, circumstances, °medium, °milieu; °territory, °locale, °setting, *mise en scène*, °situation: *Car exhaust fumes are ruining our environment.*

environmentalist *n.* ecologist, conservationist, naturalist, preservationist, nature-lover, °green *or* Green: *We have environmentalists to thank for clean-air laws.*

envisage *v.* **1** visualize, °contemplate, °imagine, °picture, °conceive (of), °fancy, °think *or* °dream *or* conjure up, *Chiefly US* °envision: *Envisage a city built entirely of glass.* **2** °foresee, °see, °predict, °forecast, °anticipate: *I envisage a time when all people will be free.*

envision *v.* °envisage, visualize, °imagine, °conceive of, °foresee, °anticipate, °predict, °forecast, °prophesy: *I envision great success for you.*

envoy *n.* °delegate, legate, °ambassador, diplomat, °minister, (papal) nuncio, attaché; °representative, emissary, °agent; *Formal* envoy extraordinary, °minister plenipotentiary: *The government sent an envoy to discuss trade.*

envy *n.* **1** jealousy, enviousness, °resentment: *She was consumed with envy of anyone who had more money than she did.* **2** covetousness, °desire, °longing: *Success excites my envy.*
—*v.* **3** covet, °begrudge, °resent: *He envies his brother and his new car.*

epicure *n.* °gourmet, connoisseur, °aesthete, °epicurean, °sybarite, hedonist, gastronome, *bon viveur*, *bon vivant*, Lucullus; gourmand: *An epicure, he refuses to eat any food not prepared by his own chef.*

epicurean *adj.* **1** °sensual, sybaritic, °luxurious, °voluptuous, °carnal, °self-indulgent, pleasure-seeking, pleasure-oriented, hedonistic, °gluttonous, intemperate, overindulgent, crapulent *or* crapulous, swinish, porcine, piggish, °immoderate, orgiastic, libidinous, °wild, unrestrained, unconfined, °dissolute, dissipated, Bacchanalian, Saturnalian: *The king's epicurean lifestyle contrasted with that of his starving subjects.* **2** Lucullan, °gourmet: *That was truly an epicurean repast.*
—*n.* **3** °epicure: *It was a meal that would have won the approval of the greatest epicureans.*

epidemic *adj.* **1** widespread, °universal, °prevalent, °prevailing, °rampant, °general, wide-ranging, pandemic: *The disease has reached epidemic proportions.*
—*n.* **2** °plague, °pestilence, °scourge, °rash, °growth, upsurge, outbreak, °spread: *An epidemic of anthrax has affected the cattle.*

epigram *n.* **1** °witticism, bon mot, °quip, mot, turn of °phrase, *jeu d'esprit*, Atticism; °pun, °double entendre, *jeu de mots*, °play on words, equivoque; paronomasia: *His epigram characterizing Eskimos as 'God's frozen people' was widely quoted.* **2** °proverb, aphorism, °maxim, °saw, saying, adage, apophthegm *or* apothegm: *'Nothing succeeds like success' is his favourite epigram.*

epigrammatic *adj.* pithy, °terse, laconic, °concise, °succinct, compendious, piquant, °pungent, °trenchant, sententious, °witty, °pointed, °proverbial, aphoristic, apophthegmatic *or* apothegmatic, *Colloq* °snappy, punchy: *Oscar Wilde is known for his epigrammatic sayings.*

episode *n.* **1** °event, °incident, °occurrence, °happening, °experience, °adventure, °affair, °matter: *Please do not remind me of the episode with the chicken.* **2** chapter, °scene, instalment, °part: *Don't miss tonight's episode of your favourite soap opera.*

epitome *n.* **1** °essence, °quintessence, °embodiment, personification, archetype, exemplar, (°typical) °example, °model, °prototype: *My secretary is the epitome of laziness.* **2** °summary, °abstract, condensation, °synopsis, °digest, compendium, °abridgement, °abbreviation, conspectus, résumé, contraction; °outline, °précis, syllabus: *The chairman wants an epitome of the report by lunch-time.*

equable *adj.* **1** even-tempered, °easygoing, °serene, °calm, placid, composed, °cool, imperturbable, °collected, unruffled, °tranquil, °peaceful, °level-headed, *Colloq* unflappable: *With his equable temperament, Edgar is the man for the job.* **2** °uniform, unvarying, unvaried, °consistent, °stable, °steady, °regular, °even, unchanging, °invariable, °constant: *We moved to the Caribbean because of its equable climate.*

equal *adj.* **1** °identical, the °same (as), interchangeable, °one and the °same, coequal, selfsame; °like, °alike, tantamount, °similar (to), °equivalent, commensurate: *This year's sales figures are equal to last year's.* **2** °uniform, °regular, corresponding, °correspondent, congruent, congruous, (evenly) balanced, (evenly) matched, °matching; °equivalent, °even; commensurate, comparable, proportionate, (evenly) proportioned, °harmonious, °symmetrical; *Colloq* fifty-fifty, *Brit* °level pegging, *US* even Steven: *Women are entitled to equal employment opportunities. The scores are equal.* **3** ***equal to***: up to, °capable of, °fit(ted) *or* suited *or* °suitable for, °adequate for, *Archaic or literary* °sufficient unto: *Are you sure that Renwick is equal to the responsibility?*
—*n.* **4** °peer, °colleague, °fellow, °brother, °mate, counterpart, °equivalent, °alter ego, compeer: *Constance is certainly anyone's equal in intelligence.*
—*v.* **5** °match, °meet, °even, °correspond (to), °square (with), °tally (with), °tie (with), °parallel, °come up to; °rival: *He will never be able to equal the world record.*

equality *n.* **1** °parity, sameness, °identity, coequality, °uniformity: *The equality of the two bids was very suspicious.* **2** similarity, °likeness, °resemblance, equivalence, correspondence, conformity, congruence, similitude, analogy, comparability, °comparison, °coincidence: *The equality between their performances is surprising.* **3** impartiality, fairness, °justice; egalitarianism: *Surely we all deserve equality of treatment under the law.*

equalize *v.* regularize, °even up, °square, °balance, equate, °match, °standardize, (make) °equal: *Equalize the amounts of liquid in all the containers.*

equip *v.* °furnish, °provide, °supply, °stock, °outfit, °fit (out *or* up), °rig (out *or* up), accoutre *or US also* accouter, array, attire, °dress, deck (out), caparison, °clothe, *Chiefly Brit* °kit out *or* up: *We can equip you with any scuba gear you may require.*

equipment *n.* °gear, °apparatus, furnishings, accoutrements *or US also* accouterments, appurtenances, °paraphernalia, °kit, materiel *or matériel*, °tackle, °outfit, °trappings, °tack, equipage, *Colloq Brit* clobber: *They spent a fortune on mountain-climbing equipment.*

equitable *adj.* °fair, even-handed, °just, °impartial, °objective, unbiased, °unprejudiced, °square, fair-minded, open-minded, °disinterested, °dispassionate, °neutral, °tolerant, unbigoted, °reasonable, °judicious, °ethical, °principled, °moral, °proper, right-minded, *Colloq* °fair and °square: *Suspects have the right to equitable treatment.*

equity *n.* fairness, impartiality, even-handedness, °justice, °fair play, °objectivity, disinterest, fair-mindedness, equitableness, open-mindedness, disinterestedness, neutrality, °tolerance, judiciousness, right-mindedness, high-mindedness: *This court recognizes the equity of your claim.*

equivalent *adj.* **1** tantamount, commensurate, °alike, °similar, °close, comparable, corresponding, interchangeable, °equal, °synonymous, of a °piece *or* a kind: *He didn't really believe that women's rights should be equivalent to men's.*
—*n.* **2** °match, °equal, °peer, counterpart, °twin: *The garage could not supply the same part but they offered an equivalent.*

equivocal *adj.* **1** °evasive, misleading, °roundabout, hedging, °suspicious, duplicitous, °questionable,

°oblique, circumlocutory, °ambiguous, ambivalent, amphibolic *or* amphibolous, *Colloq* waffling, °wishy-washy: *When asked about the guarantee, they gave an equivocal answer.* **2** °ambiguous, °vague, °hazy, °indefinite, unclear, °indistinct, enigmatic(al), °puzzling, °perplexing, indeterminate, °uncertain, *Colloq* waffling: *Just say Yes or No—none of your equivocal responses.*

equivocate *v.* °evade, °mislead, hedge, °deceive, °quibble, °dodge, weasel out (of), double-talk, °fence, °sidestep, skirt, °avoid, tergiversate, prevaricate, *Colloq* °waffle, beat about the bush, °pussyfoot: *I wish she'd confirm or deny it and stop equivocating.*

era *n.* °age, °period, °time(s), °day(s), epoch, °stage; °generation, °cycle, °date: *They lived in an era of peace.*

erase *v.* **1** expunge, °rub *or* °scratch *or* °blot *or* °wipe out, °delete, °cancel, efface, °scratch, °cross *or* °strike out *or* off, °obliterate: *The scribe erased one line and substituted another.* **2** °abolish, °destroy, °obliterate, °remove, °eliminate, (get) °rid of, eradicate, efface: *We erased every trace of evidence that we had been there.*

erect *adj.* **1** °upright, °standing, upstanding, °straight, vertical, °perpendicular, °plumb: *There was a slight stoop now in what had previously been a notably erect body.*
—*v.* **2** °build, °construct, °put up, °raise; °pitch: *I could swear that they erected that building overnight!* **3** °establish, °found, °set up, °form, °institute, °organize, °create: *Their religion was erected on the principles of utilitarianism.*

erode *v.* °wear (down *or* away), °eat away, °grind down, abrade, °gnaw away (at), °consume, corrode, °wash away; °deteriorate, °destroy, deplete, °reduce, °diminish: *Water has eroded the rock. Their continued lying has eroded my confidence in their honesty.*

erosion *n.* °wear (and tear), wearing (down *or* away), wasting away, washing *or* grinding *or* rubbing away, corroding, corrosion, abrading, abrasion, eating *or* gnawing away, chafing, fraying, weathering, attrition: *Erosion by rainwater has washed away the topsoil.*

erotic *adj.* **1** °sensual, °stimulating, °suggestive, titillating, °risqué, °bawdy, ribald, °seductive, °voluptuous, °lustful, *Colloq* °sexy: *Some insist that there is a difference between pornographic and erotic literature.* **2** amatory, °venereal, amorous, anacreontic: *Many classical poets wrote erotic verse.* **3** erogenous, °naughty, °carnal, arousing, °rousing, aphrodisiac, libidinous, lubricious *or* lubricous, °prurient, °lascivious, °lewd, concupiscent, salacious, °obscene, °pornographic, °dirty, °filthy, °nasty, *Colloq* °blue: *He has a collection of photos that he calls erotic art.*

err *v.* **1** be °wrong, be in °error, be °mistaken, be °inaccurate, be °incorrect, be in the °wrong, go °wrong, go astray, make a °mistake, °miscalculate, (make a) °blunder, °bungle, °botch, °fumble, muff, make a °mess of, make a faux pas, °mess up, *US* bobble; *Colloq* goof (up), °slip (up), drop a clanger, °foul up, *Brit* drop a brick, °blot one's copybook, *Slang* °screw up, *Brit* boob, *Taboo slang* fuck up: *The referee erred in ruling that the ball was out.* **2** °misbehave, °sin, °transgress, trespass, °lapse, °fall, do °wrong: *She has erred many times in her long life.*

errand *n.* **1** °trip, °journey: *She was on an errand of mercy.* **2** °mission, °charge, °assignment, commission, °task, °duty: *Francis is out running some errands for me.*

erratic *adj.* **1** °irregular, unpredictable, °inconsistent, °unreliable, °capricious, °changeable, °variable; wayward, °unstable, aberrant, °flighty: *The buses run on an erratic schedule.* **2** °peculiar, °abnormal, wayward, °odd, °eccentric, °outlandish, °strange, °unusual, °unorthodox, °extraordinary, °queer, °quaint, °bizarre, °weird, unconventional: *He thinks that his erratic behaviour marks him as an individualist.* **3** wandering, °meandering, directionless, planetary, °aimless, °haphazard, °discursive, errant, divagatory: *Their course was erratic, following the loss of their compass.*

erroneous *adj.* °wrong, °mistaken, °incorrect, °inaccurate, °inexact, °imprecise, °amiss, awry, °false, °faulty, misleading, °flawed, botched, bungled, °unsound, °invalid, °untrue, fallacious, °spurious, °counterfeit, *Colloq* off the mark, off course, *Brit* off beam, *US* off the beam: *He gives the erroneous impression of being intelligent. 'Seperate' is an erroneous spelling of 'separate'.*

error *n.* **1** °mistake, inaccuracy, °fault, °flaw, °blunder, °slip, gaffe; °misprint, typographical error, erratum, °solecism; *Brit* literal, *Colloq* slip-up, goof, clanger, °fluff, boo-boo, °howler, *Brit* bloomer, *Slang* foul-up, boner, *Brit* boob: *I cannot accept a report so full of errors.* **2** °sin, °transgression, trespass, °offence, °indiscretion, wrongdoing, misconduct, iniquity, °evil, wickedness, flagitiousness: *He seems to have seen the error of his ways.* **3** ***in error***: **a** °wrong, °mistaken, °incorrect, at °fault: *She was in error about the date of the conference.* **b** mistakenly, incorrectly, by °mistake, erroneously: *I caught the earlier train in error.*

erupt *v.* **1** °eject, °discharge, °expel, °emit, °burst forth *or* out, °blow up, °explode, °spew forth *or* out, °break out, °spout, °vomit (up *or* forth), °throw up *or* off, °spit out *or* up, belch (forth), °gush: *The volcano erupted ash and lava.* **2** °appear, °come out, °break out: *A boil erupted on his chin.*

eruption *n.* **1** outbreak, °outburst, °discharge, °expulsion, emission, bursting forth, °explosion, spouting, vomiting (up *or* forth), belching forth: *The eruption of Vesuvius killed thousands in Pompeii.* **2** outbreak, °rash: *The doctor said the eruption would disappear in a day.*

escape *v.* **1** °get away, °break out *or* °free, °bolt, °flee, °fly, °run away *or* off, elope, decamp, abscond, °steal *or* °slip off *or* away, take to one's heels, take French °leave, °disappear, vanish, *Brit* levant, *Colloq* °take off, °clear out, cut and °run, °duck out, make oneself °scarce, do a disappearing act, *Brit* do a moonlight °flit, *US* vamoose, hightail it, skedaddle, *US and Canadian* °skip (town), °fly the coop, cut out; *Brit* do a bunk, °bugger off, mizzle off, *US and Canadian* scram, blow, lam out, take it on the lam, take a (run-out) powder, *Chiefly Australian* °shoot through: *They escaped when I wasn't looking.* **2** °evade, °elude, °avoid, °dodge: *They escaped detection for years by hiding in a deserted monastery.* **3** °drain, °leak, °issue, seep, °discharge, °emanate: *Steam was escaping through a hole.* **4** °elude, °evade, baffle, °stump, °mystify, °puzzle, be °forgotten by, be beyond (someone): *How the thing started escapes me for the moment.*
—*n.* **5** °flight, °getaway, departure, decampment, °bolt, jailbreak, prison-break, *Colloq* °break, break-out: *The escape was planned for midnight.* **6** °distraction, °relief, °diversion, °recreation: *He watches westerns as an escape.* **7** leakage, leaking, seepage, seeping, drainage, draining, °leak, °discharge, °outpouring, outflow, effluence, efflux, effluxion: *An escape of radioactive waste from the nuclear power station had been reported earlier.*

escort *n.* **1** °guard, convoy, bodyguard, °protection, °guardian, °protector, chaperon, cortege *or* cortège, °retinue, entourage, safe °conduct, usher, °companion: *The king rode in with his armed escort.* **2** °guide, °attendant, conductor, °leader, cicerone: *The curator acted as our escort through the museum.* **3** °companion; °date, boyfriend, beau: *Donald is Thea's escort to the ball.*
—*v.* **4** °accompany, °shepherd, °squire, usher, °conduct, °guide, °attend: *Would you please escort Denise in to dinner?* **5** °guard, convoy, °protect, °watch over: *The oil tankers were escorted by destroyers.*

especially *adv.* **1** °particularly, °specially, specifically, exceptionally, conspicuously, singularly, remarkably, extraordinarily, unusually, uncommonly, peculiarly, outstandingly, uniquely, °notably, strikingly, noticeably, markedly, signally: *She was especially good at mathematics.* **2** °chiefly, °mainly, predominantly, °primarily, °principally, °first, firstly,

°first of all, above all: *He is especially interested in music.*

essay *n.* **1** article, °composition, °paper, °theme, °piece; °thesis, dissertation, disquisition, °tract: *Her essay is on the life cycle of the flea.* **2** °attempt, °effort, °try, °endeavour, °venture; *Colloq* °shot, °go: *This is his first essay into the financial world.*
—*v.* **3** °try, °attempt, °endeavour, °strive, make an °effort, °undertake, °venture, °tackle, °test, °go about, *Colloq* take a crack *or* whack *or* °stab at, *Slang* give (it *or* something) a °shot, have a °go *or* bash (at): *Let him essay to do better.*

essence *n.* **1** °quintessence, quiddity, (°essential) °nature, °substance, °spirit, being, °heart, °core, °pith, °kernel, marrow, °soul, °significance, (active) °principle, crux, cornerstone, foundation-stone, *Colloq* °bottom line: *The essence of her argument is that animals have the same rights as people.* **2** °extract, °concentrate, distillate, °elixir, tincture: *The room smelled faintly of essence of roses.* **3** ***in essence***: essentially, basically, fundamentally, °materially, °substantially, at °bottom, in the final analysis, *au fond;* in °effect, °virtually: *In essence, there is little to choose between Trotskyism and Stalinism.* **4** ***of the essence***: °essential, °critical, °crucial, °vital, °indispensable, requisite, °important: *In this job, time is of the essence.*

essential *adj.* **1** °indispensable, °necessary, requisite, required, °important, °imperative, °vital, °material, quintessential: *A strong defence is essential to peace.* **2** °fundamental, °basic, °intrinsic, °elemental, °elementary, °principal, °primary, °key, °main, °leading, °chief: *Yeast or baking powder is an essential ingredient of bread.*

establish *v.* **1** °found, °create, °institute, °set up, °start, °begin, °inaugurate, °organize, °form, constitute; °decree, °enact, ordain, °introduce: *The company was established in 1796. A new law was established to protect consumers.* **2** °secure, °settle, °fix, entrench, °install *or* instal, °seat, ensconce; °lodge, °locate; °station: *Hitler became established as dictator in 1933. Are you established in your new house?* **3** °prove, °confirm, °certify, °verify, affirm, °determine, °authenticate, °demonstrate, °show, °substantiate, corroborate, validate, °support, back (up): *It will be difficult to establish exactly how the crime was committed.*

establishment *n.* **1** °foundation, founding, °formation, °organization, construction, °creation, °origin, origination, °institution, inauguration, setting up: *We look forward to the establishment of a democratic government.* **2** °business, °concern, °firm, °company, °enterprise, °institution, °organization; °office; °shop, °store, °market: *He works for a retail establishment.* **3** ***the Establishment***: the °system, the °government, the authorities, the °administration, the °power structure, the ruling class, the (established) °order, the conservatives, the powers that be; the Church: *The press must not be under the control of the Establishment.*

estate *n.* **1** °property, holdings, °domain, demesne, °land, landed estate, manor, mansion: *They live on a large estate in the south of France.* **2** °property, holdings, °assets, °capital, resources, °wealth, °fortune; °belongings, °possessions, chattels: *The estate was divided among the heirs.* **3** estate of the °realm, °class, °caste, °order, °standing, °position, (social) °status, °state, °station, °place, °situation, °stratum, °level, °rank: *By virtue of her high estate, she is entitled to certain privileges.* **4** °development, *Brit* °housing *or* industrial *or* trading estate: *They live in a council house on an estate near Reading.*

esteem *v.* **1** °respect, value, °treasure, °prize, °cherish, °hold °dear, °appreciate, °admire, °look up to, °regard °highly, °venerate, °revere, °reverence, °honour, °defer to; °like, °love, °adore: *The novels of Virginia Woolf were greatly esteemed by a small intellectual group.* **2** °consider, °judge, deem, °view, °regard, °hold, °estimate, °account, °believe, °think, °rate, °rank, °reckon, °evaluate: *The Duke was esteemed throughout Europe as 'the perfect knight'.*
—*n.* **3** °estimation, (°high) °regard, °respect, (°high) °opinion, °favour, °admiration, °appreciation, °approval, approbation: *He holds her talents in very high esteem. My esteem for your father's accomplishments is undiminished.*

estimable *adj.* esteemed, °respectable, respected, °admirable, admired, valuable, valued, creditable, °worthy, °meritorious, °reputable, honoured, °honourable, °laudable, °praiseworthy, commendable, °excellent, °good: *I want you to meet my estimable friend, Esterhazy.*

estimate *v.* **1** °approximate, °gauge, °determine, °judge, °guess; assess, appraise, value, °evaluate, °reckon, °calculate, °work out, *Colloq* guestimate *or* guesstimate: *Experts estimated the cost of restoration at £10,000.* **2** °consider, °think, °believe, °guess, conjecture, °judge: *I estimate our chances of success as very low.*
—*n.* **3** approximation, °gauge, °guess, conjecture, assessment, appraisal, °evaluation, °reckoning, °calculation, *Colloq* guestimate *or* guesstimate: *What is your estimate of the company's value?* **4** °estimation, °belief, °opinion, °judgement, °thinking, °feeling, °sentiment, °sense, (point of) °view, °viewpoint: *My estimate of his abilities is that he is not the man for the job.*

estimation *n.* **1** °opinion, °judgement, °view, (way of) °thinking, °mind: *In my estimation, the scheme will fail.* **2** °esteem, °regard, °respect, °admiration: *Her estimation of his talent is unflagging.* **3** °estimate, approximation, °guess, °gauge: *You must make an estimation of the value for insurance purposes.*

estranged *adj.* alienated, divided, separated, °withdrawn, disaffected, driven °apart, dissociated, disassociated: *Iain has had a lot of trouble with his estranged wife.*

etch *v.* **1** °engrave, incise, °carve, inscribe, °grave, °cut, °score, °scratch, corrode, °eat into: *After the design has been painted on, acid is used to etch the metal plate.* **2** °impress, imprint, °engrave, ingrain: *The scene will be etched into my memory forever.*

eternal *adj.* **1** °everlasting, °timeless, °infinite, °endless, °immortal, °limitless: *They pledged eternal love for one another.* **2** unending, °endless, ceaseless, unceasing, incessant, °perpetual, °constant, °continuous, interminable, uninterrupted, °non-stop, unremitting, °persistent, °relentless; °continual, °recurrent: *I'm sick and tired of my neighbours' eternal arguing.* **3** unchanged, unchanging, immutable, °invariable, unvarying, unalterable, °permanent, °fixed, °constant, °everlasting, °enduring, °lasting, undiminished, unfaltering, unwavering: *To the north there was only the eternal silence of the greatest desolation.*

eternity *n.* endlessness, everlastingness, unendingness, boundlessness, °perpetuity, timelessness, infinity: *Many religions believe in the eternity of the soul.*

ethical *adj.* °moral, °upright, °righteous, °right, °just, °principled, °correct, °honest, °proper, °open, °decent, °fair, °good, °virtuous, straightforward, high-minded, °noble: *It wasn't ethical of him to disclose details of the report.*

etiquette *n.* °code (of °behaviour), °form, °convention, °ceremony, formalities, °protocol, °rules, °custom(s), °decorum, °propriety, politesse, politeness, °courtesy, (good) °manners, °civility, seemliness: *Etiquette requires that you address me as 'Sir'.*

eulogize *v.* °praise, °extol, °laud, °applaud, °compliment, sound *or* sing the °praises of, acclaim; °appreciate, °honour; °flatter: *Kirk was eulogized for his contribution to space travel.*

eulogy *n.* °praise, commendation, acclaim, acclamation, °tribute, °compliment, °applause, °homage, plaudits, encomium, accolade, paean, panegyric: *The eulogy listed Wotton's many achievements.*

euphemism *n.* amelioration, mollification, mitigation, cushioning, *Technical* paradiastole: *Euphemism is saying 'not too good' when you mean 'bad' or 'awful'.*

evacuate *v.* **1** °empty, °clear (out), °exhaust, °drain, deplete, °purge, get °rid of, °void, °discharge, °vent; °divest, °deprive: *In cases of poisoning, they first evacuate the stomach.* **2** °vacate, °desert, °leave, °depart (from), °withdraw *or* °retire (from), °go away (from), °quit, °relinquish, °abandon, decamp (from), °move *or* °pull out (of *or* from): *When the enemy approached, the troops evacuated the area.* **3** relocate, °move: *Thousands were evacuated to a safe distance when the bomb was discovered.*

evade *v.* **1** °avoid, °elude, °dodge, °sidestep, °escape (from); °get away (from), °get out of, °duck, circumvent, °shirk, *Colloq chiefly US and Canadian* weasel out (of): *The prisoner evaded capture. Don't evade your responsibilities.* **2** °quibble, °equivocate, tergiversate, °manoeuvre, hedge, °shuffle, fudge, °fence, parry, *Colloq* °waffle, *Slang* cop out: *The witness continued to evade the barrister's questions.*

evaluate *v.* **1** value, appraise, assess: *You must be an expert to evaluate netsuke.* **2** °judge, °rank, °rate, °gauge, °estimate, °approximate, °calculate, °reckon, °compute, °figure, quantify, °determine, ascertain: *How can they evaluate your importance to the project?*

evaluation *n.* **1** appraisal, valuation, assessment: *The insurance company refused to accept a higher evaluation on my house.* **2** °estimate, °estimation, approximation, rating, °opinion, ranking, °judgement, °reckoning, figuring, °calculation, computation, °determination: *The committee meets annually to discuss the evaluation of each employee's contribution.*

evaporate *v.* **1** vaporize; °boil off *or* out; dehydrate, desiccate: *Much of the surplus liquid will evaporate during cooking.* **2** °disappear, °disperse, °dissipate, vanish, evanesce, evanish, dispel; °fade (away), °melt away, °dissolve: *Opposition to his appointment seems to have evaporated.*

evaporation *n.* **1** vaporization, drying (up *or* out), dehydration, desiccation, exsiccation, parching, searing: *Clouds are formed by the evaporation of terrestrial water.* **2** disappearance, dispersion, dispelling, °dissipation, evanescence, dematerialization, °dissolution, fading (away), melting (away): *He was pleased to note the evaporation of all serious opposition.*

evasion *n.* **1** °escape, avoidance, shirking, dodging: *They disapproved of his evasion of his civic duties.* **2** °subterfuge, °deception, °deceit, chicane *or* °chicanery, °artifice, cunning, °trickery, sophistry, °excuse, dodging, prevarication, °lying, fudging, evasiveness, quibbling, equivocation, double-talk: *All the interviewers' questions were met with evasion.*

evasive *adj.* °devious, °indirect, equivocating, °equivocal, misleading, °oblique, °ambiguous, sophistical, casuistic, °shifty, dissembling, cunning, °tricky, °deceitful, *Colloq* cagey, Jesuitical: *When asked if he had visited her, he gave an evasive reply. She too was evasive about how she had spent the evening.*

eve *n.* **1** °evening *or* °day *or* °night before, °time *or* °period before; vigil: *It was Christmas Eve, and we went out carolling.* **2** °verge, °threshold, °brink: *We met on the eve of my departure for Hungary.*

even *adj.* **1** °smooth, °flat, °plane, °level, °regular, °uniform, °flush, °straight, °true: *Sand the edges till they are even.* **2** Sometimes, ***even with***: °level *or* °uniform (with), coextensive (with), °flush (with), °parallel (with *or* to): *Make sure that the lines at the bottom of the columns are even. Is that board even with the others?* **3** °steady, °regular, °consistent, °constant, °uniform, unvaried, unvarying, °methodical, unchanging, °set, °equable, °stable, °measured, metrical, rhythmic(al), °orderly, ordered, °monotonous, unbroken, uninterrupted: *We walked along at an even pace.* **4** even-tempered, °calm, °equable, composed, placid, °serene, °peaceful, °cool, °tranquil, unruffled, imperturbable, undisturbed, °impassive, °steady, °temperate, equanimous, °self-possessed, °sober, °staid, °sedate, sober-sided: *People of even disposition are unexcited, unexcitable, and unexciting.* **5** balanced, °equal, the °same, °identical, coequal, °level, °drawn, on a °par, tied, neck and neck; °equivalent, *Colloq* fifty-fifty, *Brit* °level pegging, *US* even Steven: *At half-time the scores were even. I have an even chance of getting the job.* **6** °square, quits, °equal: *If I pay for this round, we'll be even.* **7** °fair (and °square), °square, °impartial, °disinterested, °neutral, °just, even-handed, °equitable, straightforward, on the °level, °honest, °upright, unbiased, °unprejudiced: *See that you make an even distribution of the food parcels.* **8** °exact, °precise, °round, rounded off *or* out *or* up *or* down: *The bill came to an even fifty pounds.* **9** ***get even (with)***: °repay, °revenge oneself (on), even *or* °settle accounts *or* the score (with), °requite, °reciprocate, °retaliate, be °revenged: *I'll get even with her for telling my mother. Whenever he feels that he's been insulted, he wants to get even.*

—*adv.* **10** °still, °yet; all the more, °indeed, (more) than ever: *He is even dumber than I thought. He is in debt to everyone, even his daughter.* **11** Sometimes, ***even with*** *or* ***though***: °notwithstanding, °despite, in °spite of, disregarding: *Even with delays, we arrived on time.* **12** ***even so***: °nevertheless, °nonetheless, °still, °yet, °notwithstanding, all the °same, in °spite of that, °despite that: *He refused to attend; even so, we sent him an invitation.*

—*v.* **13** Usually, ***even up*** *or* ***out***: °smooth, °flatten, °level, °equalize; align: *This road will be fine when they even out the bumps.* **14** ***even out*** *or* ***up***: °equalize, °balance (out), °settle; °compensate: *Unfortunately, our profits and our expenses evened out.*

evening *n.* nightfall, eventide, °dusk, sunset, sundown, p.m., *Literary* gloaming: *The Klincks will join us for dinner this evening.*

event *n.* **1** °occurrence, °happening, °incident, °episode, °occasion, °circumstance, °affair, °experience: *An event then took place that changed the course of his life.* **2** °issue, °outcome, consequence, °result, conclusion, °upshot, °end, °effect: *There is no merit in preparing for a disaster after the event.* **3** ***at all events*** *or* ***in any event***: come what may, in any °case, at any °rate, °regardless, anyhow, anyway: *At all events, we were ready and waiting when the raid started.* **4** ***in the event***: in the °reality *or* actuality, as it *or* things turned out, at the °time, when it happened: *In the event, we left as soon as we could.*

eventful *adj.* °busy, °full, °active, °lively, °exciting, °interesting; °important, °significant, °signal, consequential, °notable, °noteworthy, °momentous, °memorable: *What with your wedding and the birth of your son, it certainly has been an eventful week.*

eventual *adj.* **1** °ultimate, °final, °last, concluding, resulting: *The eventual cost is impossible to forecast.* **2** °due, expected, anticipated, °inevitable, °likely, consequent, resulting, resultant, foreordained, preordained, °unavoidable, °destined, predestined, ineluctable, °probable: *As they cannot afford the mortgage payments, they are faced with the eventual loss of their home.*

eventuality *n.* °circumstance, contingency, °event, °occurrence, °happening, °case; °likelihood, °chance, °possibility, °probability: *We must prepare for the eventuality of war.*

eventually *adv.* °ultimately, °finally, at °last, in the °end *or* long run, at the °end of the day, sooner or later, when all is said and done, in the °final analysis, in due course, in (the course of) °time, after all: *We must all die eventually.*

ever *adv.* **1** at all, (at) any °time, at any °point *or* °period, on any °occasion, in any °case, by any °chance: *Do you ever visit London?* **2** °always, °for ever, °yet, °still, °even, at all times, in all cases, eternally, perpetually, endlessly, everlastingly, constantly, continuously, continually, for ever and a day, till the end of time, till the cows come home, till doomsday; all the °time: *He is ever the one to make us laugh. Literacy is becoming ever more important.*

everlasting *adj.* °eternal, °deathless, undying, °immortal, °infinite, °timeless; never-ending, °perpetual, °constant, °continual, °continuous, °permanent, unceasing, incessant, interminable, °endless: *They believed in everlasting punishment after death. I wish that dog would stop its everlasting barking.*

everyday *adj.* **1** °daily, day-to-day, quotidian, °diurnal; circadian: *In our family a big breakfast was an everyday occurrence.* **2** commonplace, °common, °ordinary, °customary, °regular, °habitual, °routine, °usual, run-of-the-mill, unexceptional, °accustomed, °conventional, °familiar: *She found herself unable to cope with everyday tasks that she used to take in her stride.* **3** °prosaic, mundane, °dull, unimaginative, unexciting, °mediocre, °inferior: *These are very everyday paintings of little value.*

everyone *pron.* everybody, all (and °sundry), °one and all, each and every °one *or* °person, the °whole °world, everybody under the sun, every Tom, Dick, and Harry: *Everyone will want to come to my party.*

everything *pron.* all, all things, the aggregate, the (°whole *or* °entire) °lot, the °total, the °entirety, *Colloq* the °whole kit and caboodle, the °whole shooting match, *Chiefly US and Canadian* the °whole shebang: *Everything was destroyed in the earthquake.*

everywhere *adv.* in all places, in *or* to each *or* every °place *or* °part, in every nook and cranny, high and low, °far and wide, near and °far; ubiquitously, °universally, globally; °throughout: *She went everywhere searching for clues. The smell of jasmine was everywhere. Errors occur everywhere in his writings.*

evict *v.* oust, dislodge, °turn out (of house and home), °expel, °eject, °remove, °dispossess, °put out, *Law* disseise *or* disseize, *Colloq* °toss *or* °throw *or* °kick *or* °boot out, *Brit* °turf out: *The landlord evicted us for non-payment of rent.*

eviction *n.* ouster, dispossession, dislodgement, °expulsion, °ejection, °removal, *Law* disseisin *or* disseizin, *Colloq* the boot: *His eviction from the club was for refusing to wear a tie.*

evidence *n.* **1** °proof, °ground(s), °fact(s), °data, °basis, °support, verification, attestation, affirmation, confirmation, validation, corroboration, substantiation, documentation, certification: *Have we enough evidence to convict the suspects?* **2** °testimony, °statement, deposition, affidavit, averment, °assertion: *The prosecution will present its evidence tomorrow.* **3** °indication, °sign, °mark, °token, °manifestation, °demonstration, °hint, °suggestion, °clue, °trace, smoking gun: *There is evidence that there are mice in the house.* —*v.* **4** °demonstrate, °show, °display, °manifest, °signify, °exhibit, °reveal, °denote, °attest, °prove, evince, °testify, (bear) °witness: *The destruction of the forests is evidenced by the open plains.*

evident *adj.* °clear, °obvious, °plain, °apparent, °manifest, °patent, palpable, °conspicuous, clear-cut, °express, unmistakable, °incontrovertible, understandable, comprehensible, recognizable, °perceptible, perceivable, °discernible, °noticeable: *It was evident that someone had been tampering with the mechanism.*

evidently *adv.* **1** °clearly, °obviously, plainly, °manifestly, palpably, °apparently, patently, indubitably, °undoubtedly, °doubtless(ly), without a doubt, indisputably, incontestably, incontrovertibly, undeniably, unquestionably, °surely, certainly, to be °sure: *He is evidently the culprit.* **2** °apparently, °outwardly, °seemingly, it would °seem, so it °seems, as far as one can see *or* tell, to all appearances, °ostensibly: *Evidently, there were two people here, not just one.*

evil *adj.* **1** °bad, °awful, °wrong, °immoral, °wicked, °sinful, nefarious, iniquitous, °base, °corrupt, °vile, accursed, °damnable, °villainous, heinous, °infamous, flagitious, °foul, °nasty, °abominable, °atrocious, °horrible, horrid, °ghastly, °grisly, °dreadful, depraved, °vicious, malevolent, maleficent, malefic, black-hearted, °evil-minded: *He was an evil tyrant who killed anyone who opposed him.* **2** treacherous, °traitorous, °perfidious, insidious, °unscrupulous, unprincipled, °dishonest, °dishonourable, °crooked, °criminal, felonious, knavish, °sinister, underhand(ed), °dirty, °corrupt: *He thought up an evil plan for getting rid of his wife.* **3** °harmful, °destructive, °hurtful, °injurious, °mischievous, °detrimental, °ruinous, deleterious, °disastrous, catastrophic, pernicious, noxious, °malignant, malign, °virulent, toxic, °poisonous, °deadly, °lethal: *Evil policies were promulgated against minority groups, and racist attacks abounded.* **4** °unfortunate, unlucky, °ominous, °inauspicious, dire, unpropitious, °calamitous, infelicitous, woeful: *Their business had fallen on evil times.* **5** °bad, °offensive, °disgusting, °repulsive, °awful, °nasty, mephitic, noxious, °foul, pestilential, °putrid, °vile; °disagreeable, unpleasant: *An evil odour permeated the crypt.* —*n.* **6** badness, °sin, °vice, wickedness, iniquity, turpitude, immorality, °profligacy, depravity, degeneracy, corruption, °degradation, °devilry *or* deviltry, villainy, nefariousness, viciousness, vileness, heinousness, flagitiousness, baseness, foulness: *The evil that men do lives after them, the good is oft interred with their bones.* **7** °harm, °hurt, °injury, °mischief, °damage, °ruin, °calamity, °misfortune, °catastrophe, °destruction, °disaster, cataclysm; °ill, °misery, °suffering, °pain, °sorrow, °woe, °agony, °anguish: *Evil befell the residents of Pompeii.*

evil-minded *adj.* **1** °dirty(-minded), smutty, °obscene, depraved, °lewd, °lascivious, °lecherous, salacious, licentious, °filthy, °nasty; foul-mouthed: *Those anonymous phone calls were made by some evil-minded degenerate.* **2** °wicked, °sinful, flagitious, °vicious, °hateful, malicious, °spiteful, malevolent, °evil, °bad: *The evil-minded old witch grabbed Hansel and Gretel.*

evoke *v.* °summon (up), °call up *or* forth, °elicit, conjure up, invoke, °recall, reawake(n), awake, °wake(n), (a)rouse, °raise: *Seeing her again evoked fond memories.*

evolution *n.* °development, °advance, °growth, °progress, °progression, phylogeny, evolvement, developing, growing, evolving, °formation, maturation, °production: *This book traces the evolution of the aeroplane. His treatise is on the evolution of insects.*

exact *adj.* **1** °precise, °accurate, °correct, °faithful, °true, °faultless, °identical, °literal, °perfect, consummate: *This is an exact copy of the original. Were those her exact words?* **2** °careful, °meticulous, °strict, rigorous, °accurate, °exacting, °severe, °fastidious, °scrupulous, °thorough, °painstaking, °rigid, punctilious: *He has conducted the most exact experiments.* —*v.* **3** °demand, °extort, °require, °enforce, °insist on *or* upon, °extract, °impose, wrest, compel, enjoin, °call for, °requisition, °claim: *The chief exacted tribute before releasing the prisoners.*

exacting *adj.* °demanding, rigorous, °difficult, °rigid, °stern, °hard, °tough, °severe, °harsh, °burdensome, taxing, stringent, °imperative, unsparing, °oppressive, °tyrannical: *I know of no more exacting job than that of air traffic controller.*

exactly *adv.* **1** accurately, °precisely, strictly, °perfectly, correctly, unerringly, faultlessly, faithfully, scrupulously, °literally, to the °letter, word for word, °verbatim, closely; methodically, systematically: *She translated the passage exactly, with no errors.* **2** °definitely, °absolutely, °positively, undeniably, °surely, certainly, unequivocally, °completely, in every respect, in all respects, °particularly, specifically, explicitly, °just, °quite, °expressly, °precisely, accurately, °truly, *Colloq Brit* bang on: *This is exactly the kind of house we want.*

exaggerate *v.* °overstate, °magnify, °inflate, overdraw, embroider, °embellish, °elaborate, °enlarge, °stretch, °romance, overemphasize, overstress, overplay, °overdo, °exalt, hyperbolize, °paint, *Colloq* °lay it on thick, °play up, °pile it on: *She exaggerates when she claims to be the best actress in the world. He believes the health risks are exaggerated.*

exaggeration *n.* overstatement, °magnification, inflation, embroidery, °embellishment, °elaboration, enlargement, °stretch, romanticization, °extravagance, overemphasis, °excess, exaltation, enhancement, hyperbole; °empty °talk, °bombast, bragging, boasting, boastfulness, magniloquence, *Literary* gasconade, rodomontade, *Colloq* fish °story, puffery, *Slang* bull(shit), °hot air: *It was a press agent's exaggeration to call the movie a 'colossal epic'.*

exalt *v.* **1** elevate, °raise *or* °lift (up *or* on high), upraise, uplift, upgrade, °boost, °promote, °advance: *The goalkeeper was exalted to heroic status by the fans.* **2** °praise, °honour, °extol, °glorify, °idolize, °dignify, ennoble, °revere, °reverence, °venerate, pay °homage *or* °tribute to, °celebrate; lionize: *O magnify the Lord with me, and let us exalt His name together.* **3** °stimulate, °excite, °animate, (a)rouse, °fire, °inspire, °electrify, awaken, °spur, °stir (up), inspirit: *Certain drugs have the effect of exalting the imagination.*

exalted *adj.* **1** °elevated, °lofty, °high, °eminent, °notable, °noted, °prominent, °famous, famed, °celebrated, °distinguished, °dignified, honoured, °prestigious, °glorified, °sublime, °grand: *During his later life he enjoyed an exalted reputation.* **2** °elevated, °noble, °lofty, °superior, uplifting, heightened, high-flown; exaggerated, °pretentious, overblown, °inflated: *His writing is euphuistic, that is, flowery or exalted. She has an exalted notion of her importance.* **3** °elated, °excited, °exultant, °ecstatic, jubilant, °overjoyed, °joyful, °rapturous, transported, blissful, °happy, joyous, in seventh °heaven, uplifted, *Colloq* on cloud nine, *Brit* over the moon: *They were in too exalted a mood to be interested in such mundane matters.*

examination *n.* **1** °investigation, °scrutiny, °study, °analysis, inspection, °inquiry *or* enquiry, °probe, °search, °exploration, °research, °survey, going-over, check-up, °check(out), appraisal, assessment: *Examination of the finances revealed a secret Swiss bank account.* **2** testing, °test, °quiz, exam: *There will be a written examination on Friday.* **3** °interrogation, inquisition, °inquiry *or* enquiry, catechism, cross-examination, *Colloq* third degree, grill(ing): *Examination of the prisoners is left to intelligence officers.*

examine *v.* **1** °investigate, °scrutinize, °study, °peruse, °scan, °pore over, °analyse, °sift, °inspect, °inquire *or* °enquire into, °go over *or* through *or* into, °look over *or* into, °probe, °search, °explore, °research, °survey, °check up on, °check (out), appraise, assess, °weigh, *Brit* °vet, *Slang* °case: *The theory will be examined thoroughly.* **2** °test; interrogate, °quiz, catechize, cross-examine, °question, °sound out, *Colloq* grill, °pump: *The director closely examined all applicants for the position.*

example *n.* **1** °instance, °case, °sample, °specimen, °illustration: *If this is an example of your work, I'm afraid we aren't interested.* **2** °model, °prototype, °standard, archetype, exemplar, °pattern, benchmark, °norm, criterion: *You should set an example to the children.* **3** °warning, admonition, °lesson: *The judge made an example of him by giving him the maximum sentence.* **4** ***for example***: for °instance, as a °case in point, as an °illustration *or* example, by way of °illustration, to °illustrate, e.g. *or* eg, *exempli gratia*: *Consider, for example, the following poem by Wordsworth.*

exasperate *v.* **1** °anger, °infuriate, °enrage, incense, °madden, rile, drive °mad; embitter; °inflame; *Colloq* drive °crazy, drive up the °wall: *Dealing with a bureaucracy can be exasperating for anyone.* **2** °irritate, °irk, °annoy, °bother, °harass, pique, °gall, nettle, °rankle, °provoke, vex, °pester, °torment, °plague; hector, badger, *Colloq* °bug, needle, peeve, °get, °get under (someone's) skin, °rub (up) the wrong way, °aggravate, *Slang* °get (someone's) goat, piss (someone) off: *The child's constant questions were beginning to exasperate me.*

excavate *v.* **1** °dig (out *or* up), °hollow *or* °gouge (out), °scoop out, °burrow *or* °cut (out): *They are excavating a great hole in the centre of the site.* **2** °unearth, uncover, expose, °clear, °lay °bare, °dig up, disinter, °bring up, exhume: *A large part of Pompeii has been excavated.*

excavation *n.* °cavity, °hole, °pit, crater, °cut, ditch, trench, trough, °burrow, °hollow, °shaft, °tunnel; °mine, °quarry: *Concrete for the foundations will be poured into the excavation.*

exceed *v.* **1** °surpass, °top, °excel, be °superior to, °go beyond, °beat, °overwhelm, °better, outdistance, °pass, °overtake, °outstrip, outrank, outrun, °outdo, outpace, °transcend, outshine, outreach, °overshadow, °eclipse: *The success of the new product exceeded our expectations.* **2** °overstep, °go beyond, overextend: *His behaviour exceeded the bounds of decency.*

exceeding *adj.* °great, °huge, °enormous, °extraordinary, °excessive, °exceptional, °surpassing: *The exceeding poverty of the people is heart-rending.*

exceedingly *adv.* °very, °extremely, °especially, exceptionally, considerably, incomparably, immeasurably, extraordinarily, remarkably; excessively, greatly, hugely, enormously: *She plays the violin exceedingly well. Even for a dog, that is an exceedingly ugly dog.*

excel *v.* °surpass, be °superior (to), °dominate, °top, °exceed, °go beyond, °beat, °outstrip, outrank, °outdo, outpace, outshine, °overshadow, °eclipse; °shine, be °pre-eminent: *Few places excel the Caribbean islands for beauty. He really excels when it comes to swimming.*

excellence *n.* °superiority, °merit, (°high) °quality, goodness, fineness, greatness, °prominence, eminence, °pre-eminence, °distinction, value, °worth, °supremacy: *Those who attain excellence often devote their lives to one pursuit.*

excellent *adj.* °superb, °outstanding, °exceptional, °superior, °matchless, °peerless, unequalled, without equal, °nonpareil, °supreme, °superlative, °sterling, °capital, first-class, °first-rate, °prime, °choice, °select, °distinguished, °noteworthy, °notable, °worthy, the °best, tiptop, °admirable, °splendid, °remarkable, °marvellous, °extraordinary, *Colloq* A-1 *or* A-one, °great, smashing, °super, °terrific, °fantastic, *Brit* °magic, *Dialectal* °champion, *Old-fashioned* top-hole, °ripping, tickety-boo, *US* A number 1, °major, *Australian* bonzer, *Slang* °cool, ripsnorting: *Thank you for an excellent dinner. He is an excellent pianist.*

except *prep.* **1** Sometimes ***except for***: excepting, °save, but, excluding, °exclusive of, °barring, °bar, with the °exception of, omitting, not counting, °apart from, but for, other than, °saving: *There was no one there except us. Except for us, no one came.*
—*conj.* **2** ***except that***: except *or* but (for the fact) that, but, °save that: *He would have gone except that he has no car.*
—*v.* **3** °exclude, °omit, °leave out, °excuse: *As usual, the wealthy were excepted from the tax increase.*

exception *n.* **1** °exclusion, °omission: *With the exception of those who are absent, all members are entitled to a free T-shirt.* **2** debarment, blockage, lockout, shutout: *His wife was deeply offended by his exception from membership of the country club.* **3** departure, anomaly, irregularity, °special case; °oddity, °freak, °rarity, °peculiarity, °quirk: *The exception proves the rule. Why does Viv always have to be an exception?* **4** ***take exception (to)***: make *or* raise (an) °objection (to *or* against), raise °objections (to *or* against) °object (to), demur (at), find °fault (with), take °offence *or* °umbrage (at), be offended (at); (call into) °question, °cavil, °quibble, °challenge, °oppose, °disagree (with): *She takes exception to everything I suggest. If you propose to ban smoking at the meeting, will some people take exception?*

exceptionable *adj.* objectionable, °disputable, °questionable, criticizable, °unacceptable, °unsatisfactory: *We found nothing exceptionable about the service.*

exceptional *adj.* **1** °special, °unusual, especial, out of the ordinary, °extraordinary, uncommon, °rare, °singular; °strange, °irregular, aberrant, °odd, °peculiar, anomalous: *The candlesticks turned out to be of exceptional value. He insisted that rainstorms in the Sahara were not exceptional.* **2** °gifted, °talented, °superior, °outstanding, above °average, °excellent, °prodigious,

°extraordinary: *Your child is exceptional, Mrs Einstein.* **3** handicapped, below average, °deficient, *Brit* ESN (='educationally subnormal'): *The boy attends a school for exceptional children.*

excerpt *n.* **1** °extract, °selection, °quotation, citation, °passage, pericope: *The speaker read excerpts from well-known writers.*
—*v.* **2** °extract, °select, °quote, cite, cull (out), °pick (out), °take: *Parts of this book were excerpted from his earlier writings.*

excess *n.* **1** °surplus, over-abundance, overflow, superabundance, nimiety, °superfluity, °surfeit, plethora, °glut, redundancy, over-sufficiency, supererogation, leftovers; overkill: *The excess of income over expenses constitutes profit. There is an excess of water on the road after a rainstorm.* **2** Often, ***excesses***: debauchery, °extravagance, immoderation, °prodigality, overindulgence, intemperance, °dissipation, dissoluteness: *Because of their excesses they have been shunned by their friends.*
—*adj.* **3** °surplus, °extra, °superfluous, °excessive, °leftover, °residual, °remaining: *After paying the bills, any excess money goes into savings.*

excessive *adj.* **1** °immoderate, °inordinate, °disproportionate, °extravagant, °exorbitant, °superfluous, °excess, undue, °enormous, °extreme, °unreasonable, °unwarranted, unjustifiable, °outrageous, °unconscionable: *This job is making excessive demands on my time.* **2** overdone, fulsome, cloying, nauseating, °disgusting: *I was sickened by her excessive sweetness.*

exchange *v.* **1** °trade, barter, °switch, °change, interchange, °reciprocate, °return, *Colloq* swap *or* swop: *We exchange gifts every Christmas.*
—*n.* **2** °trade, barter, °change, °traffic, °commerce, dealing, °truck, °transfer, interchange, reciprocity, reciprocation, °switch, quid pro quo, tit for tat, *Colloq* swap *or* swop: *An exchange of prisoners was negotiated. What can I do for you in exchange?* **3** altercation, °argument, °quarrel, °disagreement, unpleasantness: *We had a brief exchange, then he struck me.* **4** °market, stock °market, Stock Exchange, securities exchange, the Market, the Board, the Big Board, the Exchange, the Bourse, Wall Street, *US* the Street: *The exchange reported little activity in anticipation of the finance minister's speech.*

excitable *adj.* °volatile, °jumpy, apprehensive, °nervous, °restive, °restless, fidgety, edgy, °touchy, highly-strung, high-strung, mercurial, °emotional, °quick-tempered, °testy, hot-blooded, °feverish, °hysterical, *US* on a short string: *The director becomes very excitable before each performance.*

excite *v.* **1** (a)rouse, °spur (on), °stir (up), °move, °animate, °enliven, °activate, °motivate, invigorate, °energize, °stimulate, °cause, °provoke, °prod, °agitate, °incite, °quicken, °urge, (a)wake, (a)waken, °call forth, °summon (up), °elicit, °inspire, inspirit, °rally, galvanize, °electrify, °foment, °fire (up), °inflame, °kindle, ignite, °initiate, instigate, °generate, °occasion, °begin, °start, °bring about, °effect, set in motion, *Colloq* get going, °spark, °wind up, get (someone) (all) steamed up, °hop up, *US* kick-start, light a fire under: *The speech excited the crowd's patriotic fervour.* **2** °agitate, °disturb, °perturb, °stir up, discompose, °fluster, °ruffle, °upset, disconcert: *Don't excite the horses.* **3** °thrill, °stir up, titillate, °work up, arouse, °inflame: *Risqué films are intended to excite viewers.*

excited *adj.* **1** (a)roused, stirred (up), stimulated, °agitated, °disturbed, perturbed, °upset, worked up, wrought up, °wound up, keyed up, °overwrought, discomposed, °disconcerted, discomfited, °nervous, edgy, on °edge, uneasy, flustered, ruffled, fidgety, °frantic, frenetic, aflame, °feverish, frenzied, °hysterical, beside oneself, *Colloq* itchy, (all) °hot and bothered, °high, on a °high, off the deep end, out of one's °mind: *Turner was in a very excited state by the time the police arrived. Don't get so excited just because he called you a name.* **2** °ardent, zealous, °impassioned, °passionate, °eager, energized, °energetic, °active, °brisk, °animated, °lively, °spirited, fervid, °fervent, vehement, stimulated, °enthusiastic, galvanized, electrified, intoxicated, *Colloq* turned on: *The excited children scrambled into the boat. She becomes excited listening to rock 'n' roll.*

excitement *n.* **1** restlessness, disquiet, disquietude, °tension, °agitation, °unrest, malaise, °discomfort, jumpiness, nervousness, freneticness, excitation: *He had to give the patient an injection to quell her excitement.* **2** perturbation, °upset, °action, ado, °activity, °ferment, °furore *or US* furor, turmoil, °tumult, to-do, °stir, commotion, hubbub, brouhaha, °fuss, hurly-burly, *Colloq* fireworks: *The robbery caused a lot of excitement at the bank.* **3** °animation, °eagerness, °enthusiasm, exhilaration, ebullience: *She could hardly contain her excitement at winning the lottery.*

exciting *adj.* **1** °stimulating, °intoxicating, heady, °thrilling, °stirring, °moving, inspiring, °rousing, °exhilarating, electrifying, galvanizing, energizing, °invigorating; °overwhelming, °overpowering, astounding, astonishing, °amazing, mind-boggling, *Colloq* far-out, rip-roaring, mind-blowing: *Orbiting the world in the space shuttle was the most exciting experience of my life.* **2** °seductive, °sensuous, °voluptuous, °ravishing, captivating, charming, °tempting, enticing, alluring, °provocative, titillating, *Colloq* °sexy: *Fenella is truly an exciting young woman.*

exclaim *v.* °call *or* °cry (out), °proclaim, vociferate, utter, °declare, ejaculate, °shout, °yell, °bawl, °bellow, °burst out (with), °blurt out, *Colloq* holler: *'It's a girl!' he exclaimed.*

exclamation *n.* °outcry, °call, °cry, utterance, ejaculation, °interjection, vociferation, °shout, °yell, °bellow, *Colloq* holler: *She gave an exclamation of surprise at seeing me there.*

exclude *v.* **1** Often, ***exclude from***: °keep out *or* away, °lock *or* °shut out, °ban, °bar, debar, °prohibit, interdict, °forbid, proscribe, °deny, °refuse, disallow: *Women are excluded from participating in certain religious ceremonies. Must we exclude Maria, too?* **2** °eliminate, °leave out, °reject, °omit, °except, °preclude, °repudiate, °count out: *Exclude them from consideration as candidates.* **3** °eject, °evict, °expel, oust, get °rid of, °remove, °throw out, *Colloq* °toss out, *Slang* bounce: *He was excluded from the club because of his behaviour.*

exclusion *n.* **1** lockout, shut-out, °ban, °bar, °prohibition, interdiction, forbiddance, °denial, °refusal, disallowance, proscription: *He would not join a club that supported the exclusion of women members.* **2** elimination, °rejection, °omission, repudiation, °exception, preclusion: *We must ensure the exclusion of unqualified candidates.* **3** °ejection, °eviction, °expulsion, ouster, °removal, riddance: *The exclusion of rowdies and hooligans is in the club's best interests.*

exclusive *adj.* **1** °incompatible, inimical; unshared, °unique, °absolute, restricted, °limited: *Exclusive concepts, like 'animal' and 'vegetable', do not coincide save in their both being 'alive'. Our newspaper printed the exclusive story of the disaster.* **2** °chic, clannish, °choice, °upper-class, aristocratic, closed, restricted, restrictive, °private, °snobbish, °fashionable, °elegant, °stylish, °select, *Colloq* °trendy, *Slang* classy: *They are seen in the most exclusive nightclubs.* **3** °only, °single, °one, °sole, °singular, °unique: *Boats are the exclusive means of transport here.* **4** Usually, ***exclusive of***: excluding, excepting, °except for, omitting, ignoring, leaving aside, °apart from, (de)barring, not counting, eliminating: *Charges range from $220 to $350 a night, exclusive of meals.*

excruciating *adj.* tormenting, torturing, torturous, °agonizing, °painful, racking, °intense, °extreme, °unbearable, unendurable, °severe, °acute, °exquisite, °harrowing, distressful, distressing, °piercing, °insufferable: *She was racked with excruciating pain.*

excursion *n.* **1** °trip, °tour, °outing, airing, °expedition, voyage, °cruise, °journey, junket, jaunt; °ramble, °stroll, °walk, hike, trek, °drive, °ride, °sail: *We left the* *city and took an excursion into the mountains.* **2** °detour, deviation, side-trip, °diversion, °digression, excursus: *Forgive the excursion, but I'll return to the subject in a minute.*

excuse *v.* **1** °forgive, °pardon, °overlook, absolve, °clear, exonerate, acquit, exculpate, °pass over, °disregard, wink at, °ignore, be °blind to, look the other way, pay no °attention *or* °heed (to), find *or* prove °innocent (of): *Please excuse my tardiness.* **2** °release, °let go *or* off, °liberate, °free, °relieve, °exempt, absolve; °dismiss, *Colloq* °let off the °hook: *She was excused from attending class today. You may be excused.* **3** condone, °allow, °permit, °defend, °apologize for, °justify, °warrant, °explain, °vindicate, °rationalize, °mitigate, extenuate, palliate: *Poverty does not excuse your stealing.* —*n.* **4** apology, °explanation, °story, °reason, justification, °defence, °plea, vindication, condonation, rationalization, extenuation, mitigation, palliation; °basis, °grounds, °foundation, °cause: *Can you think of any excuse for your behaviour?* **5** °forgiveness, °remission, °pardon, °indulgence, °reprieve, clearing, exculpation, absolution, exoneration, acquittal, °disregard, heedlessness, vindication, °clearance, acquittance: *Ignorance of the law is not an excuse.* **6** °evasion, °subterfuge, °pretence, °pretext, °makeshift, °escape, °loophole, °way out, *Colloq* °alibi, °stall, *Slang* cop-out: *He always uses his grandmother's illness as an excuse for missing school.*

execute *v.* **1** °accomplish, do, °carry out *or* off *or* through, °perform, °discharge, °dispatch *or* despatch, °bring about *or* off, °implement, °engineer, °cause, *Colloq* °pull off, °put over, *Slang US* °swing, °cut, °hack (out): *She executes her duties satisfactorily.* **2** °complete, °finish, °deliver; °achieve, consummate, °fulfil, °effect, °effectuate; °sign, °seal, validate, countersign: *He executed the portrait in an hour. The contract was executed yesterday.* **3** put to °death, °kill, put to the sword, °butcher; liquidate, assassinate, °murder, °remove, slay, *Slang* °bump off, °rub *or* °wipe out, snuff (out), °knock off, *US* °waste, ice: *Convicted murderers are no longer executed in this country. The mob executed the rival gangleaders.*

execution *n.* **1** °accomplishment, °performance, carrying out, doing, °discharge, °dispatch *or* despatch, implementation, prosecution, °realization, enactment: *His drinking interferes with the execution of his responsibilities.* **2** °completion, °fulfilment, °consummation, °achievement, attainment, implementation, bringing about, °administration, pursuance: *The company will pay ten thousand dollars upon execution of the agreement.* **3** °killing, capital °punishment; assassination, °murder, °removal, liquidation, slaying: *The traitor's execution is tomorrow. There has been another gangland style execution.* **4** °skill, °art, mastery, °technique, °style, °manner, °mode, °touch, °approach, °delivery, °rendering, °rendition, °production: *The cellist's execution was superb.*

executive *n.* **1** chairman (of the °board), chairperson, chairwoman, °director, managing °director, °chief executive, president, °chief (executive °officer), CEO, °manager, °head, °leader, °principal, administrator, °official; °supervisor, °foreman, °superintendent, °overseer, °boss, °master, *Colloq* Mr Big, (°chief *or* °head) honcho, number one, kingpin, *Slang* °top banana, °big cheese, numero uno, °top dog: *She is an executive in the local power company.* **2** °administration, °management, directorship, directorate, °government, °leadership, supervision: *Five people form the executive of the society.* —*adj.* **3** administrative, managerial, °supervisory, °official, governing, governmental, gubernatorial, regulatory: *He works in the executive department of the government.*

exemplary *adj.* **1** illustrative, °typical, °characteristic, °representative, archetypal; paradigmatic: *The text contains passages exemplary of good writing.* **2** °model, °meritorious, °outstanding, °noteworthy, °admirable, commendable, °praiseworthy, °excellent, °superior: *Private Jones is an exemplary soldier.* **3** cautionary, admonitory, °warning, monitory: *In addition to payment for the damage, we were awarded exemplary damages.*

exemplify *v.* **1** °illustrate, °typify, °represent, epitomize, °instance; °embody, °personify: *This painting exemplifies Picasso's blue period.* **2** °demonstrate, °display, °show, °exhibit, °model, depict: *Early Mediterranean civilization is exemplified at Knossos.*

exempt *v.* **1** Often, ***exempt from***: °free *or* °liberate *or* °release from, °excuse *or* °relieve from, °spare from, °let off, absolve, °except, *Colloq* °let off the °hook: *The doctor exempted Becker from strenuous activity.* —*adj.* **2** exempted, °free, liberated, released, excused, relieved, spared, °let off, excepted, °immune, *Colloq* off the °hook: *It seems that Becker is now exempt from doing any work.*

exemption *n.* °exception, °immunity, °freedom, °release, impunity, dispensation, °exclusion: *This document confirms his exemption from jury service.*

exercise *v.* **1** °employ, °use, °apply, °practise, bring to bear, put to °use *or* °effect; °discharge, °exert, °wield, °execute; utilize, °effect: *Try to exercise better judgement next time. The chairman exercises too much authority.* **2** °work out, limber up, °warm up, °train, °drill: *She exercises for an hour every day.* **3** °harass, °annoy, °irritate, vex, harry, °distress, °worry, °concern, °burden, °try, °trouble, °perturb, °disturb, °agitate, make °nervous, *Colloq* drive °crazy, drive up the °wall: *We have been much exercised over the issue of acid rain.* —*n.* **4** °activity, workout, working-out, warm-up, warming up, callisthenics, aerobics, isometrics, gymnastics; training, °drill, drilling: *Exercise is good for the heart.* **5** °action, °application, °practice, °performance, °discharge, °use, utilization, °employment, °execution, °operation: *We expect the exercise of your best endeavours.*

exert *v.* **1** °exercise, °use, utilize, put to °use *or* °work *or* °effect, °employ, °wield, bring to bear, bring into play, °expend: *Please exert your influence to have his conviction quashed.* **2** ***exert oneself***: °attempt, °try, °endeavour, make an °effort, °apply oneself, °strive, do one's °best, °work, °strain, °struggle, toil, °push, °drive (oneself), go all out, °give one's all, *Colloq* knock oneself out, cudgel one's brains, beat one's brains out, do one's damnedest, *Slang* bust a gut: *If Peter exerted himself a bit more, we might see some results.*

exertion *n.* °action, °effort, striving, °strain, °work, °struggle, toil, °drive, °push, diligence, °industry, assiduity, assiduousness, sedulousness, sedulity, *Colloq US* stick-to-it-iveness: *By considerable exertion, we finished on time. He was tired after all his exertions.*

exhalation *n.* **1** °expiration, exhaling, °breath, respiration, suspiration: *The doctor could detect the wheezing only on exhalation.* **2** °vapour, °breath, °air, °puff, whiff, °exhaust, emission, steam, °mist, gas, °fog, °fume, emanation, effluvium, °evaporation: *Poisonous exhalations from vents on the side of the volcano had destroyed all vegetation.*

exhale *v.* °breathe (out), °blow, °puff, °huff, °gasp, °evaporate, °pass off, °discharge, °emit, °emanate, °issue (forth), respire, suspire, °give forth, °blow off, °eject, °expel, exsufflate: *Please exhale into this balloon. The volcano continued to exhale noxious fumes.*

exhaust *v.* **1** °use (up), °expend, °consume, °finish, deplete, °spend, °dissipate, °run through, squander, °waste, °fritter away, *Slang* °blow: *In less than a year, he had exhausted all his funds.* **2** °tire (out), °fatigue, °weary, °wear out, °enervate, °fag, overtire, °sap, °strain, °tax, °weaken, °prostrate, debilitate, disable, *Colloq* frazzle: *Working sixty hours a week would exhaust anyone.* **3** °empty, °drain, °evacuate, °void, °clean *or* °clear out: *The pump is used to exhaust the chamber of air.* **4** °overdo, °overwork, treat thoroughly, deplete, °drain, °empty: *I think we've exhausted that topic.* **5** °empty (out), °drain (off *or* out),

°vent, °issue, °escape, °discharge, °run out: *The fumes exhaust through this tube.*
—*n.* **6** emanation, effluent, emission, fumes, gas: *Car exhausts are polluting the atmosphere.*

exhausted *adj.* **1** (°dead) °tired, °fatigued, °weary, wearied, °worn out, enervated, debilitated, overtired, °weak, weakened, °prostrate, °worn *or* fagged *or* played *or* burnt-out, °spent, all in, out on one's feet, *Colloq* dog-tired, °dead (on one's feet), wiped out, drained, knocked out, done in, frazzled, *Slang* (°dead) °beat, *Brit* knackered, *US and Canadian* pooped: *I must sleep: I'm exhausted.* **2** °empty, emptied, °bare; depleted, consumed, done, gone, at an °end, finished: *Our supply of paper-clips is exhausted.* **3** °spent, °worn out, depleted, °impoverished, °poor, °infertile, °barren: *It is impossible to grow anything in this exhausted soil.*

exhausting *adj.* **1** tiring, fatiguing, wearying, enervating, wearing, debilitating: *Proofreading these figures can be exhausting.* **2** °arduous, °laborious, back-breaking, °strenuous, °hard, gruelling, crippling, °difficult, °burdensome, onerous: *Harvesting sugar is exhausting work.*

exhaustion *n.* **1** emptying, drawing out *or* forth, °discharge, draining, evacuation, voiding, depletion, consumption, °finish(ing): *The exhaustion of air from the cylinder is accomplished by a powerful pump.* **2** tiredness, °fatigue, enervation, debilitation, weariness, lassitude: *The survivors were suffering from exposure and exhaustion.*

exhaustive *adj.* °complete, °comprehensive, all-inclusive, °thorough, all-encompassing, °encyclopedic *or* encyclopaedic, °extensive, thoroughgoing, far-reaching, °sweeping, full-scale, in-depth, maximal, °maximum, *Colloq* all-out: *The police conducted an exhaustive investigation of the company's finances.*

exhibit *v.* °show, °display, °present, °offer, expose; °show off, °parade, brandish, °flaunt; °demonstrate, °reveal, °betray, °manifest, °exemplify, evince, °evidence, °disclose, °express: *Her paintings are widely exhibited. Such behaviour exhibits poor judgement.*

exhibition *n.* °exposition, °fair, °show(ing), °display, °demonstration, °presentation, °offering, *US* °exhibit, *Colloq* expo, demo: *The craft exhibition will be held at the civic centre.*

exhilarating *adj.* **1** °invigorating, °bracing, °stimulating, vivifying, enlivening, rejuvenating, °refreshing, vitalizing, fortifying, restorative, °tonic: *We took an exhilarating walk round the lake.* **2** cheering, uplifting, gladdening, elating, inspiriting, heartening, comforting, reassuring; °happy, °good, °delightful: *We received the exhilarating news of Phoebe's complete recovery.*

exile *n.* **1** expatriation, banishment, °expulsion, deportation, transportation; °separation: *Napoleon was sentenced to exile on Elba.* **2** expatriate, émigré(e), °emigrant, °outcast, deportee, pariah, displaced person, DP; °alien, °foreigner, °outsider: *Many of the exiles from Nazi Germany settled in Britain.*
—*v.* **3** deport, °expel, °alienate, °banish, expatriate, oust, °eject, °displace, °transport, °drive *or* °run *or* °cast out, °outlaw, °exclude, oust, °evict, °bar, °ban; extradite; °maroon: *Many criminals were exiled to Australia.*

exist *v.* **1** be, °continue, °prevail, °endure, °abide; °live, °breathe: *Some believe that the universe exists only in our imagination.* **2** °survive, subsist, eke out a living *or* an °existence, °stay °alive, °get by *or* along: *How can the family exist only on his pension?* **3** °occur, °happen, be °found, be °present, °remain, °persist; °obtain, °prevail: *A two-foot gap exists between the wall and the roof. 'Status quo' refers to the circumstances that exist.*

existence *n.* **1** being, °presence, actuality, °fact: *Most cultures believe in the existence of one god or more.* **2** °life, living; continuance, continuation, °persistence, °permanence, duration, °endurance: *The early settlers had to struggle for existence.* **3** °entity, being, °creature; ens, quiddity, °essence: *In Hindu philosophy, there is no limit to the number of existences.*

exit *n.* **1** °way out, egress, door, °gate; °outlet, °vent: *Everyone left by the emergency exit when the alarm rang. This is the exit for the smoke.* **2** departure, leave-taking, withdrawal, leaving, °retreat, retirement; °flight, exodus, evacuation, °escape: *Terribly embarrassed, they made their exit. The villain's exit from the stage was marked by catcalls.*
—*v.* **3** °go (out *or* away), (take one's) °leave, °depart, take *or* make one's departure, °retire, (beat a) °retreat, bid adieu, °withdraw, °run, (take a) °walk, °walk out (on), °quit, °escape, take to one's heels, show a clean pair of heels, vanish, °disappear, *Colloq* °take off, skedaddle, °kiss °goodbye, *US* °cut out; *Slang* °beat it, *US and Canadian* take it on the lam, lam (on) out of *or* from, take a (run-out) powder: *He exited from the party as soon as he could.*

exorbitant *adj.* °extraordinary, °excessive, °extravagant, °outrageous, °immoderate, extortionate, °extreme, °unreasonable, °inordinate, °disproportionate, °unconscionable, °preposterous, undue, °unwarranted, unjustifiable, unjustified: *The price of petrol in Britain is exorbitant.*

exotic *adj.* **1** °foreign, °alien, non-native, imported: *She raises exotic plants.* **2** °strange, °unfamiliar, °unusual, °bizarre, °odd, °peculiar, °unique, °singular, °extraordinary, °remarkable, out of the ordinary, °different, °outlandish, °weird, °crazy: *His exotic clothes make him stand out in a crowd.* **3** striptease, belly, go-go, topless, bottomless, °nude: *Her daughter is an exotic dancer at the new disco.*

expand *v.* **1** °enlarge, °spread (out), °extend, °increase, °open (out *or* up), °swell, °inflate, distend; °unfold: *His waistline began to expand as he approached middle age.* **2** °prolong, °lengthen, °stretch, dilate: *An elastic valve expands easily.* **3** °increase, °extend, °amplify, °magnify, broaden, °widen, augment, °heighten, °develop: *The minister sought to expand his influence.* **4** Often, ***expand on***: °detail, °enlarge on, °embellish, °develop, °amplify, expatiate on *or* upon, °elaborate (on); °flesh out: *The speaker expanded on the topic of health insurance.*

expanse *n.* °stretch, °extent, °area, °space, °range, °sweep, °reach, °length and °breadth, °spread: *The vast expanses of space are yet to be explored.*

expansion *n.* **1** °increase, augmentation, °development, enlargement, °extension, burgeoning *or* bourgeoning, flourishing, °growth, °spread: *How will the company finance its expansion in other markets?* **2** dilatation *or* dilation, stretching, distension *or* distention, inflation, °swelling: *The animal moves by the alternate expansion and contraction of the muscle.*

expansive *adj.* **1** expansible *or* expandable *or* expandible, inflatable, dilatable, extensible *or* extendible *or* extendable; extending, expanding, enlarging, spreading, °opening *or* stretching (out): *Increased temperature causes the enlargement of expansive materials.* **2** °effusive, °open, °free, °easy, °genial, °amiable, °friendly, °warm, affable, °sociable, °outgoing, communicative, °outspoken, extrovert(ed) *or* extravert(ed), °talkative, loquacious, garrulous, °frank, unreserved: *William became relaxed, almost expansive over the meal.* **3** °broad, °extensive, far-reaching, wide-ranging; °comprehensive, widespread, all-embracing, (all-) °inclusive: *We stood on the edge of an expansive desert. The company has expansive interests in Europe.*

expect *v.* **1** °anticipate, °look forward *or* °ahead to, have *or* keep in view, await, °envisage, °watch *or* °look for, °wait for, °contemplate, °foresee, *US* °envision: *She expects to leave. He was expecting her at noon.* **2** °assume, °presume, °suppose, °imagine, °believe, °think, °trust, °surmise, conjecture; °foresee, *US and Canadian* °guess: *I expect you will be hungry when you return.* **3** °look for, °want, °require, °wish, °need, °demand, °reckon on *or* upon, °hope for, °calculate *or* °count on *or* upon: *What did you expect me to do?*

expectant *adj.* °expecting, (a)waiting, °ready, °eager, apprehensive, °anxious, with bated breath, °hopeful, looking, watchful, anticipating: *The understudy waited, expectant, in the wings.*

expectation *n.* **1** °anticipation, °confidence, hopefulness, watchfulness, apprehension, apprehensiveness, expectancy, °suspense: *There was an air of expectation in the room.* **2** °hope, assumption, °presumption, °surmise, °supposition, °belief, conjecture, *US and Canadian* °guess: *Our expectation is that he will come on the next train.* **3** °demand, °requirement, °wish, °desire, °want, insistence, °reliance: *I think your expectations might be too optimistic.* **4** °prospects, °outlook: *He had great expectations from his rich uncle.*

expecting *adj.* °pregnant, gravid, with child, enceinte, *Brit* in the family way, *US* in a family way, *Colloq* in the club, *Brit* preggers, *Slang US* with a bun in the oven: *Monica is expecting and will give birth any day.*

expedient *adj.* **1** °suitable, °appropriate, °fitting, °fit, °befitting, °proper, apropos, °right, °correct, °meet, °pertinent, °applicable, °practical, pragmatic, °worthwhile, °politic: *To cross the river, a bridge would prove expedient.* **2** °advantageous, °beneficial, °advisable, °desirable, recommended, °useful, °practical, utilitarian, °prudent, °wise, °propitious, °opportune, °helpful, °effective: *Count on him to do what is expedient and ignore what is honest.*
—*n.* **3** °device, °resource, °means, °measure, contrivance, °resort, °recourse: *Life jackets are a useful expedient if the boat sinks.*

expedite *v.* **1** °hasten, °rush, °hurry, °speed *or* °step up, accelerate; °dispatch *or* despatch: *The shipment has been expedited and should reach you tomorrow.* **2** °advance, °facilitate, °promote, °forward, °ease, °enable: *The growing process can be expedited by adding this chemical.*

expedition *n.* **1** °exploration, °journey, voyage, field (trip), °tour, °excursion; °enterprise, °undertaking, °mission, °quest: *She went on an expedition up the Amazon to research herbal medicines.* **2** °speed, promptness, celerity, alacrity, °dispatch *or* despatch, °haste, °rapidity, swiftness, quickness: *He was ordered to complete his chores with expedition.*

expeditious *adj.* °ready, quick, °rapid, °swift, °fast, °brisk, °speedy, °fleet, °efficient, °diligent: *We made an expeditious passage round Cape Horn. The problem requires an expeditious solution.*

expel *v.* **1** °eject, dislodge, °throw *or* °cast out, °drive *or* °force out, °evict, °put *or* °push out, °remove, °run (someone) off *or* out, °displace, °dispossess, show the door, °suspend, °dismiss, °let °go, *Colloq* °fire, *Brit* °sack, °turf out: *They will expel the tenant at the earliest opportunity.* **2** °banish, deport, °exile, expatriate, °outlaw, °maroon; proscribe, °ban, °bar, debar, °dismiss, °exclude, blackball, drum out, cashier, °discharge, oust: *The leader of the opposition was expelled from the country. The committee voted to expel Horace from the club.*

expend *v.* **1** °pay out, °spend, disburse, °use, °employ, *Slang* °lay *or* dish out, fork *or* °shell out: *Reduce the money expended on entertainment.* **2** °use up, °consume, °exhaust, deplete, °finish (off), °dissipate, °sap, °drain: *I expended all my energies eking out a bare living.*

expendable *adj.* °dispensable, °disposable, °nonessential, inessential *or* unessential, °unnecessary, replaceable; unimportant, °insignificant: *In terms of military strategy, the commando unit was expendable.*

expenditure *n.* °outlay, outgoings, disbursement, spending, °payment, °expense, °cost; °price, °charge, °fee: *The financial director must closely examine all expenditures. I cannot justify that kind of expenditure for a car.*

expense *n.* **1** Often, ***expenses***: °payment, °cost(s), °outlay, outgoings, disbursement, °expenditure, spending, out-of-pocket (expenses); °price, °charge, °fee, °rate: *Keep your expenses to a minimum. Expenses for travel and entertainment will be reimbursed by the company.* **2** °detriment, °sacrifice, °cost, °loss, °impairment, °ruin, °destruction: *They continue to smoke at the expense of their health.*

expensive *adj.* costly, °dear, high-priced, up-market, valuable, °precious, °priceless, °extravagant; overpriced: *Richard and Elizabeth flew off for an expensive holiday in the sun.*

experience *n.* **1** °knowledge, °contact, involvement, °practice, °familiarity, °acquaintance, °exposure; participation, °observation: *Her book on nursing is based on personal experience.* **2** °incident, °event, °happening, °affair, °episode, °occurrence, °circumstance, °adventure, °encounter; °trial, °test, °ordeal: *He has lived through some harrowing experiences.* **3** common °sense, °wisdom, sagacity, °knowledge, know-how, savoir faire, savoir vivre, °sophistication, °skill, °judgement, *Slang* savvy: *She is a woman of experience.*
—*v.* **4** °undergo, °live *or* °go through, °suffer, °endure, °sustain, °face, °encounter, °meet (with), °feel, °sense, °taste, °sample, be °familiar with, °know: *Your problem is that you have never experienced genuine hunger.*

experienced *adj.* **1** °adept, skilled, °skilful, °accomplished, °practised, °proficient, °knowledgeable, °knowing, °wise, °sage, sagacious, °shrewd, °prepared, (°well-)°informed, trained, (well-)°versed, °expert, °master, masterly, °qualified, °professional, °competent, °efficient, °capable, *au fait; Slang* on the ball, *US* savvy: *She is an experienced surgeon.* **2** °mature, °seasoned, °sophisticated, battle-scarred, °seasoned, °veteran; *Slang* in the know, *US* savvy: *We need an experienced leader.*

experiment *n.* **1** °test, °trial, °investigation, °inquiry *or* enquiry, °examination, experimentation, °research, °proof: *Experiment has shown that the ointment cures many minor skin ailments.* **2** °procedure, °policy: *Totalitarianism seems to have failed as a political experiment.*
—*v.* **3** ***experiment on*** *or* ***with***: °test, °try, °examine, °investigate, °research, °probe: *The time has come to experiment on human subjects. Artists now experiment with many media, from canvas to computers.*

experimental *adj.* **1** °hypothetical, °theoretical, °tentative, °speculative, conjectural, exploratory: *Man's first attempts at flying were purely experimental.* **2** °empirical, experiential: *She has profound experimental knowledge of what is involved.*

expert *n.* **1** °authority, °professional, °specialist, °scholar, °master, connoisseur, pundit, *Colloq* wizard, whiz, pro, ace, *Brit* °dab hand, boffin, *Slang US* maven *or* mavin: *We rely on experts to verify the age of works of art.*
—*adj.* **2** °skilful, skilled, trained, °knowledgeable, °learned, °experienced, °practised, °qualified, °adept, °proficient, °accomplished, *au fait*, adroit, °dexterous, °polished, finished, °masterful, masterly, °first-rate, °excellent, °superb, wonderful, °superior, °champion(ship), A-one, A-1, °virtuoso, *Colloq* top-notch, *Brit* whizzo, wizard, *US* crackerjack, °crack: *Davis is an expert snooker player.*

expertise *n.* expertness, °skill, °knowledge, know-how, °judgement, mastery; °dexterity, adroitness, *Slang* savvy: *You need a great deal of expertise to be a museum curator.*

expiration *n.* expiry, °finish, (coming to an) °end, °termination, running out, ending, conclusion, concluding, °close, closing, discontinuance, discontinuation: *The expiration of the option is in March.*

expire *v.* **1** °cease, (come to an) °end, °close, °finish, °terminate, °run out, conclude, °discontinue: *Your subscription expires with the next issue.* **2** °die, breathe one's last, decease, °perish, °pass away: *His grandmother expired only last year, at the age of 110.* **3** °exhale, °breathe out, °expel: *In the daytime we expire more carbon dioxide than during the night.*

explain *v.* **1** °interpret, °define, explicate, °detail, delineate, make °plain, °simplify, °spell out, °resolve,

°get across, °clarify, °clear up, elucidate, °illustrate, expound, °describe, °disclose, °unfold, unravel, untangle: *The teacher explained the theory so that even I could understand it.* **2** Also, ***explain away***: °justify, °account for, °excuse, °rationalize, °legitimate, legitimatize, extenuate, palliate: *You will be required to explain your absence.*

explanation *n.* **1** °interpretation, °definition, explication, delineation, simplification, °resolution, clarification, elucidation, °description, °illustration, °exposition, °account, disclosure; exegesis, commentary, °criticism, °analysis: *The encyclopedia contains detailed explanations of how machines work.* **2** °excuse, rationalization, justification, vindication: *What is your explanation for such outrageous behaviour?* **3** °cause, °motive, °reason, °key, signification, °solution: *The explanation for aberrant behaviour often lies in hormonal imbalance.*

explanatory *adj.* explanative, elucidative, revelatory, interpretive *or* interpretative, expository, descriptive; °critical, exegetic(al): *Please read the explanatory notes below.*

expletive *adj.* **1** °wordy, verbose, prolix, °repetitious, °redundant, tautological, iterative, reiterative, pleonastic; °unnecessary, unneeded, °needless, unessential, °non-essential, °gratuitous, °superfluous: *Her speech is punctuated by expletive words and phrases, like 'like, you know', and so forth.*
—*n.* **2** °oath, swear-word, °curse, obscenity, epithet, *Colloq* cuss-word, °dirty word, four-letter word: *Expletives sometimes lend an air of naturalness to written dialogue.* **3** filler, padding, redundancy, °tautology, pleonasm: *Some grammarians term the 'It' in 'It is raining' an expletive.*

explicit *adj.* **1** °specific, °categorical, (crystal-)°clear, °definite, well-defined, °distinct, unambiguous, °precise, °exact, unequivocal, °express, stated, °plain, °manifest, unmistakable, °positive, °absolute, °final, °peremptory, °unqualified, unconditional: *The children had explicit instructions to keep away from the canal.* **2** °open, °outspoken, unreserved, unrestrained, °candid, °frank, °direct, °forthright, straightforward, °definite: *She was explicit in her orders.*

explode *v.* **1** °blow up, °burst, °blast, °fly °apart, °go off, °erupt, fulminate; °set off, detonate: *Police exploded the bomb after clearing the area. Rockets exploded in the night sky.* **2** °reject, °discredit, refute, °repudiate, °disprove, debunk, belie, give the lie to, *Slang* pick holes in, poke *or* shoot full of holes: *Ptolemy's geocentric theory has been thoroughly exploded.* **3** lose one's °temper, °rant, °rave, °rage, °storm, throw a °tantrum, *Colloq* get into a tizzy, °blow one's top, °fly off the handle, go through *or* hit the roof, hit the ceiling; *Slang* °lose one's °cool, go up the °wall, *US* blow one's °stack *or* °cool, °flip (one's lid), freak out: *He exploded when he learned his car had been smashed up.*

exploit *n.* **1** °achievement, °deed, °feat, attainment, °accomplishment: *The speaker regaled them with tales of his exploits as an explorer.*
—*v.* **2** °use, take °advantage of, °manipulate, make °capital out of, °profit from, utilize, turn to °account, °manoeuvre, °work: *Far from being your friends, they are exploiting you for their own purposes. They need capital to exploit the country's natural resources.*

exploration *n.* °examination, °investigation, °search, °probe, °inquiry *or* enquiry, °study, °research, °analysis, °review, °scrutiny, inspection, °survey, °reconnaissance, °observation; °expedition: *Exploration of the intestine revealed the presence of polyps. He is noted for his exploration of the sources of the Nile.*

explore *v.* **1** °survey, °tour, °travel, °reconnoitre, °traverse: *They are on safari, exploring the Congo.* **2** °investigate, °scrutinize, °examine, °inquire *or* °enquire into, °inspect, °probe, °search, °research, °look into, °study, °analyse, °review, °observe: *We ought to explore the possibility of your working for us.*

explosion *n.* **1** °blast, bang, °report, °burst, °boom, °clap, °crack, °eruption, °crash, °outburst, fulmination; detonation: *The explosion shook the entire house.* **2** °outburst, outbreak, °paroxysm, °upheaval, flare-up, °eruption, °burst, °fit, °spasm, °tantrum, *Colloq Brit* °paddy *or* paddywhack *or* paddywack, wax: *The unrest among the people is building up to an explosion.* **3** °increase, burgeoning *or* bourgeoning, °expansion, welling up, mushrooming: *The population explosion has caused a housing shortage.*

explosive *adj.* **1** °volatile, °sensitive, °delicate, °tense, °anxious, °fraught, touch-and-go, °touchy, °inflammable, (highly) charged, °unstable, °uncertain, °unsound, °shaky, °hazardous, chancy, unpredictable, °precarious, °dangerous, °perilous, °critical, °nasty, °ugly, *Colloq* °dicey, iffy: *The explosive situation between the strikers and management may lead to bloodshed.*
—*n.* **2** dynamite, TNT, gunpowder, gelignite, °plastic, plastique: *The car was blown up by a powerful charge of explosive.*

expose *v.* **1** (lay) °bare, °reveal, uncover, °show, °exhibit, °present, °display, °disclose; divulge, °unveil, unmask, °discover, °air, ventilate, °let out, °leak, °betray, bring to °light, °make known: *He unbuttoned his shirt, exposing his hairy chest. The facts of the case will be exposed tomorrow. Will he expose the names of his accomplices?* **2** °risk, imperil, °endanger, °jeopardize, °hazard: *Do not expose your house to danger of flooding by building it so close to the river.* **3** ***expose to***: °subject to, °introduce to, °acquaint with, bring into °contact with: *Today children are not taught, but 'exposed to education'.*

exposition *n.* **1** °exhibition, °show(ing), °presentation, °display, °demonstration, *US* exhibit, *Colloq* expo: *There is a special exposition of medieval farming implements in the museum.* **2** °description, °declaration, °statement, °explanation, explication, clarification, °interpretation, exegesis: *The exposition of his argument was remarkably lucid.* **3** °paper, °theme, article, °essay, °thesis, dissertation, treatise, disquisition, °study, critique, commentary: *She received high marks for her exposition on Zoroastrianism.*

exposure *n.* **1** baring, uncovering, laying °open, unveiling, disclosure, disclosing, unmasking, revealing, °revelation, exposé, airing, °publication, publishing, communicating, communication, leaking, °leak, divulging: *The exposure of the spy was part of the plan.* **2** °jeopardy, °risk, °hazard, endangerment, vulnerability, imperilment; °danger, °peril: *By diversifying your investments, you reduce your exposure to a loss in just one.* **3** °familiarity, °knowledge, °acquaintance, °experience, °contact, conversancy: *My exposure to Chinese philosophy has been negligible.* **4** °aspect, °view, °outlook, °orientation, frontage; °setting, °location, °direction: *She said that she preferred a bedroom with an easterly exposure.*

express *v.* **1** articulate, verbalize, °phrase, utter, °voice, °state, °word, °put (into words), °set *or* °put forth, °put *or* °get across, °communicate, depict, °portray; °say, °speak, °tell: *She expressed her thoughts on the subject very clearly.* **2** °show, °indicate, °demonstrate, °manifest, °exhibit, evince, °evidence, °reveal, expose, °disclose, divulge, °make known, °intimate, betoken, °signify, °embody, depict, °designate, °denote, convey: *His tone of voice expressed his resentment.* **3** °symbolize, °represent, °signify, °stand for, °denote, °designate: *The ratio can be expressed in the form of a fraction.* **4** °press *or* °squeeze *or* wring *or* °force out, °expel, °extract: *The oil is expressed from ripe olives.*
—*adj.* **5** °explicit, °clear, °plain, unambiguous, unmistakable, °unqualified, °outright, °definite, °out-and-out, °downright, straightforward, °categorical, °direct, °specific, well-defined, °distinct, °precise, °accurate, °exact, °positive: *We had an express understanding not to enter into competition with one another.* **6** °specific, °special, °particular, clear-cut; °true: *Our express purpose in coming was to see you.* **7** quick, °speedy,

°swift, °fast, °rapid, °prompt, °immediate; °direct, °nonstop: *The documents must be sent by express delivery.*

expression *n.* **1** verbalization, airing, °representation, °declaration, utterance, °assertion, enunciation, asseveration, °pronouncement, communication, voicing, °announcement: *Any expression of criticism of government is forbidden in many countries.* **2** °representation, °manifestation, °sign, °token, °symbol, °show, °demonstration, °indication, °evidence: *A curled lip is an expression of scorn.* **3** °look, mien, °air, °appearance, °face, °aspect, countenance: *He had long straight hair and a completely blank expression. Her smile twisted into an expression of frustration.* **4** °tone, °note, nuance, °intonation, °accent, °touch, shading, loudness, softness; expressiveness, °emotion, °feeling, °sensitivity, °passion, °spirit, °depth, °ardour, °intensity, pathos: *There was much expression in her playing of the fugue.* **5** °word, °term, °phrase, °idiom, turn of °phrase, locution, saying: *Some find the expression 'Have a nice day' to be irritating.* **6** °wording, phrasing, phraseology, °language, °style, °diction, °usage, °speech, °delivery: *Writers are not the only ones who should study effective expression.*

expressive *adj.* **1** indicative, °suggestive, allusive, °eloquent, revealing, °meaningful, °significant, denotative: *Her frown is expressive of her disapproval.* **2** °pointed, pithy, °explicit: *Leave it to him to make some expressive remark about Frieda's hat.* **3** °striking, °vivid, °telling, °pregnant, °loaded, °forceful, °moving, °emotional, °poignant, °provocative, thought-provoking: *His poetry contains much expressive language.*

expressly *adv.* **1** distinctly, °definitely, categorically, explicitly, °absolutely, °positively, °directly, unambiguously, unequivocally, unmistakably, plainly, pointedly, °exactly, °clearly: *He expressly denied the rumour.* **2** purposely, °especially, purposefully, °particularly, specifically, °specially; on °purpose: *The gift was intended expressly for you.*

expulsion *n.* expelling, °ejection, °eviction, repudiation, ouster, °removal, °dismissal, °discharge; *Colloq* the (old) heave-ho, *Brit* the boot, the °sack, sacking, *US* the bounce: *His expulsion from the pub was accompanied by cheers from the patrons.*

exquisite *adj.* **1** °delicate, °fine, °elegant, °graceful, °excellent, °choice, well-crafted, well-made, well-executed, °refined, °elaborate: *They have a collection of exquisite miniature portraits.* **2** °ingenious, °detailed, recherché, °rare, °subtle, °deep, abstruse; °far-fetched: *He is expert in the exquisite points of seduction.* **3** °beautiful, °perfect, °lovely, °attractive, °handsome, °comely, good-looking; °smart, °chic, °elegant, °striking: *In her youth, she was an exquisite blonde goddess. He wore an exquisite silk costume.* **4** °acute, °sharp, °keen, °excruciating, °agonizing, °intense; °elaborate: *The most exquisite pain I have known is occasioned by gout. Spies, subjected to exquisite torture, usually revealed their secrets.* **5** °superb, °superior, °peerless, °matchless, °incomparable, unequalled, °rare, °precious, °choice, consummate, °outstanding, °superlative, °excellent, °select, °flawless, °perfect, wonderful, °splendid, °marvellous: *She wore a tiara of exquisite diamonds.*

extemporaneous *adj.* unstudied, °unpremeditated, extempore, extemporary, impromptu, improvised, °spontaneous, unrehearsed, extemporized, °unprepared, unplanned, unscripted, °offhand, ad lib, *Colloq* off the cuff: *Though extraordinarily well-organized, Charlotte's speech was entirely extemporaneous.*

extend *v.* **1** °stretch *or* °spread (out), outstretch, outspread, °open (out), unroll, °unfold; °reach, °range; °carry on, °draw out, °continue, °develop: *The carpet extends from wall to wall. Her reputation extends worldwide. The city walls extended to the river.* **2** °lengthen, elongate, °widen, °continue; broaden, °enlarge, °add to, augment; °increase, °stretch (out), °supplement: *We are planning to extend the sitting-room. They asked the mortgage company to extend the repayment period.* **3** °last, °stretch, °continue, °go *or* °carry on; °perpetuate, °drag on *or* out, °keep up *or* on, °prolong: *Their visit extended until the following week.* **4** °offer, proffer, °give, °present, °hold out, °stretch forth, °tender; °bestow; °grant, °impart, °confer, °accord, °advance: *She extended her hand. The store does not extend credit to any customers.*

extension *n.* **1** stretching, °expansion, °increase, enlargement, augmentation, °development, amplification, broadening, widening, lengthening, °spread, spreading: *The extension of the plan is scheduled for next year.* **2** °range, extensiveness, °scope, °extent, °magnitude, °gauge, compass, °sweep, °reach, °size, °volume, dimension(s), °proportions, °capacity, °span; °breadth, °width, °height, °length, °spread, °stretch: *The extension of the mind seems almost limitless.* **3** addendum, °addition, annexe, wing, adjunct, ell, appendage; appendix, °supplement: *We have built an extension to the house.*

extensive *adj.* **1** °broad, °wide, °expansive, far-reaching, far-ranging, wide-ranging, far-flung, °sweeping, widespread, °comprehensive, all-embracing; °national, nationwide, °international, intercontinental, cosmopolitan, worldwide, °global, °universal, °vast; cosmic; °catholic: *The storm is responsible for extensive crop damage. He has extensive business connections.* **2** °large, °big, °great, °huge, °substantial, °considerable, sizeable, °immense, °enormous, °vast, °gigantic, °massive; °voluminous, °spacious, commodious, capacious: *The extensive gold deposits were soon depleted. The cave contains several extensive chambers.*

extent *n.* **1** °magnitude, dimensions, compass, °size, °range, °scale, °sweep, °scope, °expanse, immensity, °enormousness, capaciousness, spaciousness, °space, amplitude: *The extent of space is unimaginably vast.* **2** °limit, bounds, limitation, °lengths; °range, °scope: *To what extent will he go to see justice done?* **3** °area, °region, °tract, °territory, compass: *In the whole extent of Europe you could find no better mushroom.*

extenuating *adj.* °mitigating, lessening, tempering, palliating, moderating, diminishing, qualifying: *Owing to extenuating circumstances, he could not be tried for murder.*

exterior *adj.* **1** outer, °outside, °external, °outward, °superficial, °surface: *The exterior covering of the capsule becomes very hot on re-entry into the earth's atmosphere.* **2** °external, °extrinsic, °extraneous, °foreign, °alien, °exotic, °outside: *The problem can be overcome without exterior help.*
—*n.* **3** °outside, °surface, covering, coating, °facing, °face, °front, °skin, °shell, façade: *The exterior is of pink stucco.*

exterminate *v.* °destroy, °root out, eradicate, extirpate, annihilate, °eliminate, weed out, get °rid of, °wipe out, °obliterate, put an °end to, °terminate, liquidate, °massacre, °murder, °kill (off), °butcher, °slaughter, *Slang* °bump off, *US* °rub out, °waste: *It is his avowed intention to exterminate all the vermin of the criminal fraternity.*

external *adj.* **1** outer, °outside, °outward, °exterior: *This medication is for external use only.* **2** °outside, °exterior, °extrinsic, °extraneous, °alien, °foreign, °exotic: *Do not ignore the external influences on the nation's economy.* **3** °apparent, °visible, °perceptible, °superficial, °surface: *The external features of the planet barely suggest what lies within.*

extinct *adj.* **1** °defunct, °dead, died out, gone, departed, vanished: *These are the bones of an extinct species of flying mammal.* **2** dated, outmoded, °old-fashioned, °antiquated, °obsolete, archaic, out of °date, antediluvian, °ancient, °old hat, °passé, *démodé*: *High-button shoes and bustles have been extinct for almost a century.* **3** °out, extinguished, quenched, burnt- *or* °put *or* snuffed out; °inactive, °dormant: *The lake is in the caldera of an extinct volcano.*

extinguish *v.* **1** °put *or* snuff *or* °blow out, °quench; °turn off *or* out: *We are landing shortly, so please extinguish all smoking materials. Extinguish the lights before leaving.* **2** °kill (off), annihilate, °destroy, °obliterate, °abolish, °exterminate, °eliminate, do away with, nullify, eradicate, °remove, °banish, °wipe *or* °blot out: *The potion contained a drug that extinguished all memory of unhappiness.* **3** °obscure, °eclipse, °dim, °outdo, put in the °shade, °overshadow, adumbrate, *Colloq* °show up: *His personality is completely extinguished by the dazzle of his wife.*

extol *v.* °exalt, elevate, uplift, °glorify, °praise, °laud, °applaud, commend, acclaim, °cheer, °celebrate, pay °tribute *or* °homage to, sing the °praises of, °make much of, °honour, °congratulate, °compliment: *William is always extolling the talents of some dancer or other.*

extort *v.* °exact, °extract, °blackmail, °bully, coerce, °force, wring, wrest, *Colloq* °milk, bleed, put the arm on (someone): *Threatening to swear that it was my fault, she extorted a promise from me to keep silent about the body.*

extra *adj.* **1** additional, added, °auxiliary, °accessory, °supplementary, supplemental, °further, ancillary, °subsidiary, collateral, adventitious: *We had an extra person for dinner.* **2** °leftover, °excess, °spare, °surplus, °unused, °superfluous, supernumerary, °reserve: *After all were served, we had two extra desserts.*
—*n.* **3** °addition, addendum, °accessory, appurtenance, °supplement, °bonus, °premium, dividend: *As an extra, each customer receives a free ball-point pen.* **4** °supplement, *US* mark-up, surcharge, *Slang US and Canadian* kicker: *There is an extra if you want bread and butter.* **5** supernumerary, walk-on, *Colloq* °super, spear-carrier: *One could scarcely call being an extra a 'Hollywood career'.*
—*adv.* **6** uncommonly, unusually, exceptionally, unexpectedly, extraordinarily, remarkably, °notably, surprisingly, amazingly, °very, °particularly, °especially, °extremely, strikingly: *Teacher said that Philip was extra good today.* **7** additionally, again, more, in °addition: *They charge extra for room service.*

extract *v.* **1** °draw *or* °pull (out), °remove, °withdraw, °pluck *or* °take out, °draw forth, °extricate: *The dentist extracted two teeth. I extracted some important papers from your waste-paper basket.* **2** °draw, °derive, °deduce, °develop, glean, °extricate, distil, °get, °obtain: *I could extract little sense from her ramblings.* **3** °wrench, wring, wrest, °extort, °draw (forth), °evoke, °elicit, °extricate, winkle out, worm (out), prise (out), °force (out): *Using torture, they finally extracted a confession from him. She extracted money from her victims by threatening to tell their wives.* **4** °copy, °quote, cite, °abstract, °select, °choose, glean, cull: *We extracted useful material from some old encyclopedias.*
—*n.* **5** °concentrate, distillate, °essence, distillation, °quintessence, concentration, °extraction, decoction: *We boiled off the water and used the extract as a salve.* **6** °excerpt, °abstract, °quotation, citation, clipping, °cutting, °passage, °selection: *Extracts from other works are printed in smaller type.*

extraction *n.* **1** °removal, extrication, withdrawal, uprooting, eradication, extirpation, deracination: *The extraction of my tooth was completely painless.* **2** °extract, °concentrate, distillate, °essence, distillation, °quintessence, concentration, decoction, °separation, °derivation: *This syrup is an extraction from coffee beans.* **3** °origin, °birth, ancestry, descent, °lineage, °derivation, blood, °parentage, °breed, °strain, °race, °stock, °pedigree: *The family is of Scandinavian extraction.*

extraneous *adj.* **1** unessential, °non-essential, inessential, °peripheral, °superfluous, °unnecessary, unneeded, °extra, added, additional, adventitious, supernumerary, °incidental, °needless: *Filter out all the extraneous substances.* **2** not pertinent, °impertinent, °inapplicable, inapt, unapt, unfitting, °inappropriate, °unrelated, °irrelevant, inapposite, unconnected, °remote, °alien, °foreign, °exotic, °strange, °outlandish, °external, °extrinsic, out of place, off the mark *or* point *or* subject, beside the point *or* mark: *Why must you constantly bring up extraneous matters?*

extraordinary *adj.* **1** °unusual, uncommon, °remarkable, °exceptional, °particular, °outstanding, °special, °rare, °unique, °singular, °signal, °unheard-of, °curious, °peculiar, °odd, °bizarre, °queer, °strange, °abnormal, unprecedented, °unparalleled: *She showed extraordinary courage in coming here.* **2** °amazing, surprising, astonishing, astounding, °remarkable, °notable, °noteworthy, °marvellous, °fantastic, °incredible, °unbelievable, °impressive, °fabulous, °miraculous, °unparalleled, *Colloq* °super, smashing, °lovely, °gorgeous, *Slang* far-out, °unreal: *This is an extraordinary example of the bookbinder's art.*

extravagance *n.* **1** wastefulness, °waste, lavishness, °profligacy, °prodigality, squandering, °dissipation, improvidence, exorbitance, recklessness, overspending, °excess: *Our present debts are the result of extravagance.* **2** immoderation, immoderateness, excessiveness, outrageousness, unrestraint, °superfluity, superfluousness, over-sufficiency, preposterousness, unreasonableness, irrationality, °absurdity; capriciousness, whim, °fantasy, flightiness: *His tawdry life belied the extravagance of his dreams.*

extravagant *adj.* **1** °wasteful, °lavish, °profligate, °prodigal, °improvident, °reckless, °excessive, °spendthrift, °profuse, °extreme, °immoderate: *She cannot afford to maintain her extravagant way of life for long.* **2** unrestrained, uncontained, °wild, °outrageous, °preposterous, °immoderate, °ridiculous, °foolish, °fanciful, °unreasonable, °absurd, °impractical; undeserved, unjustified, unjustifiable: *The speaker lavished extravagant praise on the award winners.* **3** °expensive, costly, extortionate, °unreasonable, overpriced, °exorbitant, °high; °dear; *Colloq* °steep: *That trip to Istanbul by private jet was extravagant to say the least.* **4** °gaudy, °garish, °ostentatious, °showy, °ornate, °flashy, °loud, °flamboyant; exaggerated, high-sounding: *She appears at parties wearing the most extravagant costumes.*

extravaganza *n.* spectacular, °spectacle, °pageant, °production, °show, °exposition: *An extravaganza was staged to celebrate the opening of the World's Fair.*

extreme *adj.* **1** °unusual, uncommon, °exceptional, °outstanding, °notable, °noteworthy, °abnormal, °different, °extraordinary, °remarkable: *We experienced extreme difficulty driving home.* **2** °immoderate, °excessive, °severe, °intense, °acute, °maximum, worst: *This equipment is made to withstand extreme arctic conditions.* **3** outermost, endmost, farthest, °ultimate, utmost, uttermost, remotest, °last, far-off, far-away, °distant, °very: *She walked to the extreme end of the pier.* **4** °rigid, °stern, °severe, °strict, °conservative, °hidebound, °stiff, stringent, restrictive, constrictive, uncompromising, Draconian, °harsh, °drastic: *Grandfather favoured taking extreme measures against terrorists.* **5** unconventional, °radical, °outrageous, °wild, °weird, °bizarre, °queer, °outrageous, °offbeat, °exotic, °eccentric, °different, outré, Slang far-out, °way-out, *US and Canadian* kooky: *I find your outfit too extreme to wear in public.* **6** beyond the pale *or* limits *or* bounds, °extravagant, °inordinate, °excessive, °disproportionate, °outrageous: *Because of your extreme behaviour, you will be confined to the house for a week.*
—*n.* **7** Often, ***extremes***: °limit(s), °bounds, utmost, °maximum, *Colloq* °swing: *Try to be more moderate and to avoid extremes.* **8** Often, ***go to extremes***: °limit(s), °bounds, °maximum, °acme, °zenith, °pinnacle, °summit, °height, apex, apogee, °peak, °extremity; °depth, nadir: *Thea's moods varied between the extremes of joy and grief.* **9** ***in the extreme***: °extremely, °very, exceptionally, °exceedingly, extraordinarily, unusually: *His table manners are rude in the extreme.*

extremely *adv.* °very, °exceedingly, outrageously, extraordinarily, unusually, uncommonly, exceptionally, damned, hellishly, to the nth degree, *Colloq Brit* bloody, *US* darned: *The service was extremely bad. They are extremely stupid.*

extremity *n.* **1** °end, °termination, °limit, °edge, °boundary, °bound, °border, °margin; °periphery; °frontier: *A fence marks the eastern extremity of our land.* **2** ***extremities***: °fingers, fingertips, toes; °hands, feet; arms, °legs, limbs; paws, trotters, hooves, wings: *His extremities were numb with frostbite.* **3** °extreme, utmost, °maximum, °limit(s), °bounds: *The situation tested the extremity of my patience. They were driven to extremities in their search for food.*

extricate *v.* unravel, disentangle, untangle, °disengage, (set) °free, turn °loose, °release, °liberate, °rescue, °save, °deliver: *You helped extricate me from a terrible predicament.*

extrinsic *adj.* °external, °extraneous, °irrelevant, °exterior, °unrelated, °outside; outer, °outward: *Such extrinsic factors may be excluded from the discussion.*

exuberance *n.* **1** cheerfulness, °joy, joyfulness, ebullience, effervescence, exhilaration, buoyancy, °animation, °spirit, spiritedness, sprightliness, liveliness, °vitality, vivacity, °enthusiasm, °excitement, zeal, °zest, °energy, °vigour: *It is hard to imagine the dog's exuberance when he saw his master.* **2** °abundance, lavishness, effusiveness, flamboyance, copiousness, superabundance, °superfluity, °excess, °profusion, °prodigality, bounteousness, bountifulness: *Everything attests to the exuberance of the author's genius.*

exuberant *adj.* **1** °cheerful, °joyful, °ebullient, °effervescent, °buoyant, °animated, °spirited, spry, °sprightly, °lively, °vivacious, °enthusiastic, zealous, °energetic, °vigorous: *She enjoys exuberant good health.* **2** °happy, °glad, °delighted, °overjoyed, °joyful, °ecstatic, *Brit* in the seventh °heaven, *US* in seventh °heaven, *Colloq* on cloud nine: *She was exuberant at the news of Lyle's return.*

exult *v.* °rejoice, °revel, °glory (in), jump for °joy, °delight, °celebrate, make °merry: *We exulted in our new-found freedom.*

exultant *adj.* °delighted, jubilant, °overjoyed, °elated, °joyful, °gleeful, °glad, °ecstatic, °exuberant, in seventh °heaven, cock-a-hoop, *Colloq* on cloud nine, *Brit* over the moon: *We were exultant to learn that the war was over.*

eye *n.* **1** eyeball, °orb, *Colloq* optic: *The eye of the eagle is nearly as large as that of an elephant.* **2** °vision, (eye) sight, visual acuity, °perception: *Her eyes are weakened by so much reading.* **3** discernment, °perception, °taste, °judgement, °discrimination, percipience, perspicacity, °appreciation, °sensitivity; °knowledge, °recognition, comprehension: *Shirley has a good eye for Chinese antiques. Walmsley has the eye of an artist.* **4** °liking, °affection, fondness, °partiality, °appreciation; lustfulness: *Old Bisley still has an eye for the girls.* **5** °ogle, °leer, °look, wink, glad eye, sidelong °glance: *The barmaid gave me the eye as soon as I walked in.* **6** °view, °respect, °regard, °aim, °intention, °purpose, °design, °plan, °idea, °notion: *He lent me the money with an eye to asking a favour in return.* **7** °attention, °regard, °look, °scrutiny, °view, °examination, °observation; supervision: *All our comings and goings were under the watchful eye of Scotland Yard.* **8** °guard, °lookout, °watch, vigil: *The class monitor is expected to keep an eye on the younger children.* —*v.* **9** °examine, °scrutinize, °look at, °regard: *My future mother-in-law eyed me up and down.* **10** °behold, °gaze *or* °look *or* °peer at *or* upon, °contemplate, °study, °regard, °view, °inspect; °watch, °observe: *The doctor eyed the wound with concern.*

eyewitness *n.* °witness, °observer, °spectator, viewer, watcher; °bystander, °onlooker, passer-by: *The police sought eyewitnesses to the accident.*

F

fabric *n.* **1** °cloth, textile, °material, °stuff: *The chair is upholstered in traditional floral fabric.* **2** construction, constitution, °core, °heart, °foundation, °structure, framework, °organization, configuration, °make-up: *Extensive strikes threatened the very fabric of our society.*

fabricate *v.* **1** °erect, °build, °construct, °frame, °raise, °put *or* °set up, °assemble, °fashion, °form, °make, °manufacture, °produce: *The basic structure was fabricated of steel.* **2** °invent, °create, °originate, °make up, °manufacture, concoct, °think up, °imagine, °hatch, °devise, °design: *Numerous lies, fabricated by politicians, were already in circulation.* **3** °forge, °falsify, °counterfeit, °fake, feign, °manufacture; trump up, *Colloq* cook up, *Brit* cook: *He admitted to having fabricated the data in his application.*

fabrication *n.* **1** construction, °assembly, assemblage, making, fashioning, °production, °manufacture, putting together, °building, erection, °formation, formulation, structuring, constructing, °organization, forming, framing, architecture: *The fabrication of thousands of parts took only a month.* **2** °invention, °creation, origination, °make-up, °manufacture, hatching, concoction, contrivance, °design: *Only Vanessa could have been responsible for the fabrication of such a diabolical plot.* **3** °falsehood, °lie, °fib, prevarication, °story, °tale, untruth, fiction, °yarn, fable; falsification, °forgery, °fake, °sham, *Colloq* cock-and-bull °story, *Brit* fairy °story, fairy °tale: *His war record is a complete fabrication.*

fabulous *adj.* **1** fabled, mythic(al), °celebrated, °legendary, storied, °fictitious, °fictional, °unreal, °fanciful, °imaginary, story-book, fairy-tale: *Greek mythology tells us of a fabulous winged horse called Pegasus.* **2** °fantastic, °marvellous, °incredible, °unbelievable, °inconceivable, wonderful, astounding, astonishing, °amazing, wondrous, °extraordinary, °miraculous, °phenomenal: *Houses in London were selling at fabulous prices.* **3** °superb, °marvellous, °terrific, wonderful, *Colloq* °great, °super, smashing, °thumping, °whopping, thundering, rattling, howling, *US* °neat, °keen, *Slang* fab, °hot, far-out, °cool, *Old-fashioned* fantabulous, in the groove, groovy, ace, *Brit* °magic, *US and Canadian* copacetic: *I saw an absolutely fabulous new film the other night.*

face *n.* **1** visage, countenance, physiognomy, °features, lineaments, *Slang* °mug, mush, kisser, °pan, puss, *Brit* phiz, phizog, dial, clock: *I don't like the expression on your face.* **2** °look, °appearance, °aspect, °expression, mien: *He has the face of someone who is very proud of himself. Modern farming has changed the face of the countryside.* **3** °mask, °veneer, façade, °front, °camouflage, °pretence, °disguise, (°false) °impression, °semblance, °masquerade: *She puts on a bold face, but we know she was deeply hurt by your remarks.* **4** °dignity, °image, °self-respect, °standing, °reputation, repute, °name, °honour, °status: *You might lose face if you admit you were wrong.* **5** boldness, °daring, audacity, °effrontery, °impudence, °impertinence, °presumption, brashness, *Colloq* °gall, °brass, °nerve, cheek, °guts, gutsiness, *Brit* °brass neck, *Slang US* balls: *Who would have the face to name such a hotel 'The Palace'?* **6** °surface, °exterior, °front, °outside, °cover, °facing, façade, °skin: *The building will have a face of white marble.* **7** right °side, obverse, °front; dial: *The card landed face up. The face of the clock is enamelled.* **8** ***face to face***: confronting, facing, °opposite, *en face*, vis-à-vis, °tête-à-tête, *à deux*, eye to eye, head to head, *Colloq* eyeball to eyeball: *We met face to face for the first time in the courtroom.* **9** ***in the face of***: in defiance of, °notwithstanding, °despite, in °spite of, confronting, in °opposition to: *Some experts attacked the report for flying in the face of received wisdom.* **10** ***make a face***:

change one's °expression, murgeon: *When I said I would be there, she made a face.* **11 *on the face of it*:** to all *or* outward appearances, °seemingly, °apparently, superficially, °evidently: *On the face of it, he seemed guilty.* **12 *show one's face*:** °put in *or* make an °appearance, °appear, °arrive, be seen, °turn up, *Colloq* °show up: *I suppose I ought to show my face at the office party.* **13 *to one's face*:** °directly, brazenly, eye to eye, face to face, candidly, °openly, frankly: *I told him to his face that he was a liar.*
—*v.* **14** confront, °brave, °meet (with), °encounter, °experience, °deal *or* °cope with, °come *or* °go up against; °appear before: *In the jungle we faced grave danger from man-eating tigers. She faces her first audience tonight.* **15** °give (out) *or* °front on *or* on to, °front °towards, °overlook, °look out on *or* over; be °opposite: *Our rooms face the lake. Facing page 22 is a map of the area.* **16** °coat, °surface, °cover, clad, °dress, sheathe, overlay, °finish; °veneer: *The collar is faced with velvet.* **17 *face down*:** confront, °intimidate, cow, °subdue, °overawe, °browbeat: *I'll not be faced down by that impudent clerk.* **18 *face up to*:** **a** °admit, °accept, °acknowledge, °allow, °confess: *We must all face up to our own shortcomings.* **b** confront, °deal *or* °cope with, °come *or* °go up against, °brave, come to °terms with; °brazen through *or* out, bite (on) the bullet, grasp the nettle: *You wouldn't be able to face up to your wife if you'd forgotten her birthday.*

facilitate *v.* °ease, °expedite, °smooth, °further, °promote, °advance; °assist, °aid, °help: *It would facilitate transport if you would bring your own car.*

facility *n.* **1** °ease, smoothness, °fluency, effortlessness, °readiness, easiness, °skill, skilfulness, deftness, °dexterity, adroitness, °ability, °aptitude, °expertise, expertness, °proficiency, mastery, masterfulness, masterliness, °efficiency; quickness, alacrity, celerity, swiftness, °speed: *They praised her new-found facility with the Italian language.* **2** Often, ***facilities*:** **a** °plant, °system, °building(s), °structure, complex: *The company is building a new facility in France.* **b** convenience(s), °privy, °equipment, °lavatory, °toilet, powder-room, *Nautical* head, *Brit* water-closet, WC, loo, *US and Canadian* °rest room, men's room, ladies' room, *Colloq* the Gents, the Ladies('), *Slang Brit* bog, karzy, *US and Canadian* john: *An American asked where he could find the facilities.*

facing *n.* façade, °front, cladding, °surface, overlay, °skin; coating: *The houses all have a colourful stucco facing.*

facsimile *n.* °copy, °reproduction, °print, carbon (°copy), °replica, °duplicate, photocopy, fax, *Trade Mark* Xerox (°copy), Photostat, *Colloq US* dupe: *Send a facsimile of the report to each field office.*

fact *n.* **1** °reality, actuality, °truth, °certainty: *The fact of the matter is that she didn't do it. Is there a basis in fact for your allegations?* **2** °accomplishment, *fait accompli;* °occurrence, °event, °happening, °incident, °episode, °experience, °act, °deed: *Supersonic travel has been a fact for many years.* **3** Often, ***facts*:** °data, °information, °particular(s), °detail(s), °point(s), °item(s), °factor(s), *Colloq* °low-down, (°inside) info, the °score, *Brit* the gen, *US and Canadian* the poop: *If I am going to defend you, I need all the facts of the case.* **4 *in fact*:** °indeed, to be °sure, as a matter of (°actual) fact, in °truth, °truly, truthfully, °actually, °really, in °reality, in point of fact, factually: *He didn't come; in fact, he had gone abroad the week before.*

faction *n.* **1** °group, °cabal, bloc, cadre, °camp, °splinter °group, °circle, camarilla, °clique, °set, coterie, °lobby, °pressure °group, °junta *or* junto, °ring, °gang, *Brit* ginger °group, *Colloq* °crowd: *There is a small faction plotting to assassinate the finance minister.* **2** °dissension, °intrigue, °strife, °sedition, disharmony, °discord, °disagreement, quarrelling, contention, °controversy, infighting, °rupture, °split, °rift, °schism, °clash: *Faction within the party has no regard for national interests.*

factious *adj.* contentious, disputatious, litigious, refractory, divisive, conflicting, °discordant, °argumentative, at °odds, at loggerheads, °quarrelsome, °seditious, °mutinous, °rebellious: *A factious Congress spells trouble for the President.*

factitious *adj.* °fake(d), °bogus, °false, °mock, falsified, °artificial, °insincere, °unreal, °synthetic, fabricated, engineered, manufactured, °spurious, °counterfeit, °sham, simulated, °imitation, unauthentic, °set *or* got up, rigged, *Colloq* °phoney *or US also* phony: *We are all victims of factitious desires by which luxuries have become necessities.*

factor *n.* **1** constituent, °ingredient, °element, °part, °particular, °piece, component; °circumstance, °consideration, °aspect, °fact, °influence, determinant, °cause: *Which factors contributed to the decline of Mayan civilization?* **2** °agent, °representative, °proxy, middleman, °intermediary, °deputy, °go-between: *Our company has a factor handling all our exports.* **3** banker, °financier, °backer, moneylender, lender: *The factors lent us money to buy the stock needed to fill the orders.*

factory *n.* °works, °mill, °plant: *She has a job at the piano factory.*

factual *adj.* **1** °actual, °real, °true, °authentic, verifiable, °realistic, °true to life, °genuine, valid, bona fide: *The report is a forgery, but the letters are factual.* **2** °accurate, °correct, °true, °faithful, °precise, unbiased, undistorted, °unvarnished, unexaggerated, °objective, °unprejudiced, straightforward: *This is a factual account of the Battle of Marathon.*

faculty *n.* **1** °ability, °capacity, °skill, °aptitude, °potential, °talent, °flair, °knack, °gift, °genius; °dexterity, adroitness, cleverness, °capability: *She has a faculty for making people feel at home.* **2** °school, °department, °discipline: *Her graduate studies were in the Faculty of Philosophy.* **3** °staff, personnel, °members, *Brit* dons: *Each member of the faculty has a doctorate.* **4** °power, authorization, dispensation, °sanction, °licence, °prerogative, °privilege, °right, °permission, °liberty: *The government has the faculty to judge treasonable acts.*

fad *n.* °craze, °mania, °rage, °fashion, °trend, °fancy, °vogue: *Do you remember the hula-hoop fad?*

fade *v.* **1** (grow) °dim *or* °pale, grow °faint, cloud (over), °dull; °bleach, whiten, etiolate, °wash out, blanch *or* blench, discolour: *The scene faded in the distance. Look how the sun has faded the curtains!* **2** °droop, wither, °decline, °die out *or* away, °perish, °ebb, °flag, °wane, °wilt, °waste away, °sag, °diminish, °dwindle, languish, °deteriorate, °decay, °shrivel, peter out *or* away: *As he aged, his lust for life faded.*

fag *v.* **1** Often, ***fag out*:** °exhaust, °weary, °tire (out), °fatigue, °wear out, °jade, *Colloq Brit* knacker, *US* poop: *I am completely fagged out from studying all night.*
—*n.* **2** *Brit* bore, °nuisance, °drag, chore, °pain: *It's a bit of a fag having to fetch water from the garden.* **3** °servant, °menial, °flunkey, drudge, lackey, underling: *The seniors used to have fags to clean their shoes.* **4** See **homosexual, 1,** below. **5** cigarette, smoke, *Colloq* °butt, cig(gy), weed, coffin-nail, cancer stick, *Old-fashioned* gasper: *Got a fag?*

fail *v.* **1** not succeed, be °unsuccessful, °miss, °miscarry, °misfire, °fall short (of), °fall flat, °fall through, falter, be (found) lacking *or* °wanting, be °defective, be °deficient, be *or* prove °inadequate, come to °grief *or* °naught *or* °nothing, °go °wrong, abort, °meet with °disaster, °founder, °run aground, *Colloq* °flop, °fizzle (out), go up in smoke, flunk: *Guy Fawkes's plot failed utterly. Gloria failed her history examination.* **2** °let down, °disappoint, °forsake, °desert, °abandon, °neglect, °ignore, °slight: *I was really counting on Mary, but she failed me.* **3** °decline, peter out, °dwindle, °diminish, °wane, °deteriorate, °weaken, °decay, °fade *or* °die (out *or* away), °disappear, °flag, °ebb, °sink, languish, °give out; gutter, °go out: *His health is failing. The light failed, leaving us in darkness.* **4** go bankrupt, go out of business, °go under, go into receivership, become °insolvent, °close up shop, °close up *or* down, °cease operation(s), *Brit* go to the °wall, *US* file for Chapter Eleven, *Colloq* °fold (up), go bust *or* °broke, *US* °drown in red ink: *According to the statistics, hundreds of businesses fail every week.*

failing *n.* **1** °weakness, °shortcoming, °foible, °flaw, °fault, °defect, °weak spot, °blind spot, °blemish, °imperfection: *Bigotry and prejudice are her most serious failings.*
—*prep.* **2** lacking, °wanting, in °default of, without, sans, in the °absence of: *Failing a favourable decision, we shall lodge an appeal.*

failure *n.* **1** °failing, °default, non-performance, remissness; °neglect, °omission, dereliction, deficiency: *His failure to do his duty resulted in a court martial.* **2** °breakdown, °collapse, discontinuance, °miscarriage, °loss; °decline, °decay, deterioration: *Power disruptions are caused by the failure of the national grid.* **3** °loser, non-starter, °incompetent, also-ran, nonentity, *Colloq* °flop, °fizzle, damp squib, °dud, lemon, °washout, dead duck, *US* lead balloon: *He was an utter failure as a violinist.* **4** bankruptcy, °ruin, insolvency, °downfall, °crash, *Colloq* folding: *Bank failures increased owing to bad loans and other poor investments.*

faint *adj.* **1** °dim, °dull, °pale, faded, °indistinct, °vague, °hazy, °imperceptible, indiscernible, unclear, blurred, blurry, muzzy, wavering, faltering, ill-defined, °weak, °feeble, flickering, °subdued; °low, °soft, °slight, hushed, muffled, muted, °inaudible, stifled: *A faint light burned in the corridor. I heard a faint noise.* **2** °dizzy, light-headed, unsteady, vertiginous, °giddy, *Colloq* woozy: *I felt faint after climbing the stairs.*
—*v.* **3** °black out, °pass out, °lose consciousness, swoon, °drop, °collapse, *Colloq* keel over: *She fainted when they told her the news.*
—*n.* **4** °loss of consciousness, blackout, unconsciousness, °collapse, swoon, *Medicine* syncope: *He dropped in a dead faint.*

faint-hearted *adj.* **1** °cowardly, timorous, °afraid, frightened, °scared, °faint, lily-livered, white-livered, pusillanimous; °timid, °shy, diffident; *Colloq* yellow (-bellied), chicken-hearted, chicken-livered, chicken: *He's too faint-hearted to ask her to marry him.* **2** °irresolute, °weak, °ineffectual, °feeble, °puny, feckless: *She made only a faint-hearted attempt at reconciliation.*

fair[1] *adj.* **1** °impartial, even-handed, °disinterested, °equitable, °just, °unprejudiced, unbiased, °objective, *Colloq* °square: *Judge Leaver is known for his fair decisions. We are counting on your sense of fair play.* **2** °honest, °above-board, °honourable, °lawful, °trustworthy, °legitimate, °proper, °upright, straightforward: *He won the trophy in a fair fight.* **3** °light, blond(e), fair-haired, flaxen-haired, tow-headed, tow-haired; light-complexioned, peaches and cream, °rosy; unblemished, °clear, °spotless, °immaculate: *She has fair hair and fair skin.* **4** °satisfactory, °adequate, °respectable, pretty °good, °tolerable, °passable, all °right, °average, °decent, middling, °reasonable, *comme ci, comme ça*, not bad; °mediocre, °indifferent, *Colloq* so so, °OK *or* okay: *The performance was fair but not outstanding.* **5** °favourable, °clear, °sunny, °fine, °dry, °bright, cloudless, °pleasant, halcyon, °benign: *Fair weather is promised for tomorrow's picnic.* **6** unobstructed, °open, °clear, °free: *Every spectator has a fair view of the football field.* **7** °attractive, good-looking, °handsome, °comely, pretty, °beautiful, pulchritudinous, °lovely, beauteous: *Faint heart never won fair lady.* **8** °civil, °courteous, °polite, °gracious, °agreeable: *She was not deceived by his fair words.*

fair[2] *n.* °fête *or* fete, °festival, kermis *or* kirmess, °exhibition, °exposition, °show; °market, bazaar, mart, *US* °exhibit: *Ashby will judge the sheep at the annual fair.*

fairly *adv.* **1** °quite, °rather, pretty, °somewhat, tolerably, adequately, sufficiently, passably, °moderately, *Colloq* °sort of, °kind of: *I thought that the singing was fairly good.* **2** equitably, impartially, justly, °properly, °honestly, objectively: *Please make certain that everyone is treated fairly.* **3** °absolutely, °totally, °utterly, °completely, °positively, °really, °actually, veritably, °virtually: *The crowd fairly cheered themselves hoarse.*

fairyland *n.* dreamland, wonderland, never-never land, happy valley, °paradise, cloud-land, °enchanted forest, cloud-cuckoo-land, Nephelococcygia, Shangri-La: *Zuleika's thoughts are always off somewhere in fairyland.*

faith *n.* **1** °belief, credence, °confidence, °conviction, °trust, °certainty, certitude, °assurance, assuredness, sureness, °reliance, dependence: *His faith in God is unassailable. I have great faith in her ability.* **2** °belief, °religion, °creed, °persuasion, dogma, teaching, °doctrine, °denomination, °sect: *To which faith do you belong? She is of the Jewish faith.* **3** °duty, allegiance, °obligation, °promise, faithfulness, °loyalty, fidelity, °devotion, consecration, °dedication, fealty, °obedience: *Don't break faith with your electorate by supporting the bill.*

faithful *adj.* **1** °true, °loyal, °devoted, °steadfast, dedicated, °attached, unswerving, °firm, °staunch, unwavering, °constant: *He has always remained faithful to his wife.* **2** °close, °exact, °accurate, °true, °correct, °precise, °perfect, valid; °literal: *Jowett's is a faithful translation from the Greek.* **3** °conscientious, °dutiful, °scrupulous, °careful, °meticulous, °thorough, punctilious, °finicky *or* finical, °detailed, °fastidious, rigorous, °rigid, °severe, °particular: *He received a gold watch for fifty years of faithful attendance to his duties.* **4** °reliable, dependable, trusted, °trustworthy, trusty, °honest, °true, °truthful, °righteous, °right, °moral, °virtuous, °upright, veracious: *He has remained my faithful friend for many years.*

faithless *adj.* **1** °sceptical, doubting, °unbelieving, disbelieving, agnostic, atheistic, freethinking: *Faithless wretches are called Doubting Thomases.* **2** unfaithful, °disloyal, treacherous, °traitorous, °perfidious, shifting, °shifty, °fickle, °inconstant, untrustworthy, °unreliable, °false, °hypocritical, °insincere, °dishonest, °crooked, °unscrupulous, conscienceless, recreant: *With faithless friends like her, who needs enemies?*

fake *v.* **1** °falsify, °doctor, °alter, °modify, °counterfeit, °fabricate, °manufacture, °forge: *He faked the evidence in order to implicate his own sister.* **2** °pretend, make a °pretence of, dissemble, feign, °sham, °make believe, simulate, °affect: *She faked a headache to avoid gym classes.*
—*n.* **3** °hoax, °counterfeit, °sham, °forgery, °imitation, *Colloq* °phoney *or US also* phony: *The experts agree that the painting is a fake.* **4** faker, °impostor, charlatan, °fraud, hoaxer, mountebank, °cheat, humbug, °quack, °pretender, *Colloq* °phoney *or US also* phony: *He isn't a doctor—he's a fake!*
—*adj.* **5** °false, °counterfeit, forged, °sham, °fraudulent, °imitation, pinchbeck, °bogus, °spurious, °factitious, *Colloq* °phoney *or US also* phony: *He escaped the country using a fake passport.*

fall *v.* **1** °descend, °sink, °subside, °settle, °drop *or* °come (down), °plummet, °plunge, °dive, (take a) nose-dive; cascade: *The bucket fell to the bottom of the well. A meteorite fell on my house. The water falls 100 metres over the cliff at this point.* **2** °tumble, °trip, °stumble, °slump, °collapse, keel over, °topple, °crumple: *Mother fell in the kitchen and hurt her knee.* **3** °diminish, (become) °lower, °sink, °decline, fall *or* °drop off, °drop, °decrease, °dwindle, °subside, °come *or* °go down: *The price of oil fell today to a new low.* **4** °slope, fall away, °decline: *Beyond the spinney, the meadow falls towards the river.* **5** °succumb, °surrender, °yield, °give up *or* in, °capitulate, be °defeated *or* °conquered, be °captured, be taken (°captive *or* °prisoner), be °overthrown, come *or* go to °ruin, be °destroyed, be °lost: *The castle fell after a year's siege.* **6** °die, °perish, °drop °dead, be slain *or* °killed: *His grandfather fell at the Battle of the Marne.* **7** ***fall apart***: °disintegrate, °crumble, °collapse, fall *or* come *or* go to °pieces, °break up, be °destroyed; °break °apart, °fragment,

°shatter: *I knew she would fall apart on the witness stand. The gadget fell apart as soon as we used it.* **8 *fall back***: °retreat, °retire, °withdraw, °draw back; °recede: *As the enemy advanced, we fell back.* **9 *fall back on*** or ***upon***: have °recourse to, °rely *or* °depend on *or* upon, °return to, °count on *or* upon, °resort to, °call on *or* upon, make °use of, °use, °employ: *All the ready ammunition was gone and we had to fall back on our reserves.* **10 *fall behind***: °drop back, °trail, °lag; be in arrears: *If you fall behind, I'll wait for you. We fell behind in our mortgage payments.* **11 *fall down***: **a** °collapse, °drop: *She hit me so hard that I fell down.* **b** °fail, be (found) °wanting *or* lacking, be °unsuccessful, be *or* prove °inadequate *or* °disappointing: *He had to be replaced because he fell down on the job.* **12 *fall flat***: °collapse, °fail, *Colloq* °flop, *US* °bomb (out), lay an egg, go over like a lead balloon: *A hit in London might fall flat in New York.* **13 *fall for***: **a** fall in °love with, be °infatuated with: *Some people will fall for anyone who tells them the right time.* **b** be °fooled *or* °duped *or* °taken in *or* °deceived by, °accept, °swallow, °succumb to, *Slang* be a °sucker for, *US and Canadian* be a patsy for: *Did Beaseley really fall for that old confidence trick?* **14 *fall in***: °cave in, °collapse, °sink inwards: *The walls were about to fall in on us.* **15 *fall in with***: °join, °associate with, become associated *or* °allied with, befriend; °cooperate with, °go along with, concur with, °support, °accept: *He fell in with a gang of thieves and spent the next few years avoiding the police. She agreed to fall in with my plan.* **16 *fall off***: °diminish, °decrease, °decline, °deteriorate: *Business falls off immediately after Christmas.* **17 *fall on*** or ***upon***: °attack, °assault, assail, °set upon: *Three muggers fell on me and stole my wallet.* **18 *fall out***: °disagree, °differ, °quarrel, °clash, squabble, wrangle, °dispute, °fight: *We fell out over politics.* **19 *fall short***: prove *or* (turn out to) be °inadequate *or* °insufficient *or* °deficient *or* lacking *or* °wanting *or* °disappointing, °miss, °fail, °disappoint: *The results of the sales campaign fell short of expectations.* **20 *fall through***: °fail, come to °nothing *or* °naught, °miscarry, °die, *Colloq* °fizzle (out), °flop: *The deal to buy the company fell through.* **21 *fall to***: °start, °begin, °commence, °set *or* °go about, get under °way, °undertake, °tackle, °take on; get moving, °attack, *Colloq* get the show on the road, get cracking, *US* get a wiggle on, °move it: *The washing-up had to be done so I fell to.*

—*n.* **22** °drop, descent, °dive, nosedive, °plunge, °tumble, dropping, falling: *How could he have survived a fall from such a height?* **23** *Chiefly in the US and Canada*: autumn: *They turn the clocks back one hour in the fall.* **24** °decline, °decay, °collapse, °downfall, °failure, °destruction, °ruin, deterioration, °eclipse: *Have you read Poe's classic* Fall of the House of Usher? **25** Usually, ***falls***: cascade, cataract, °waterfall; rapids: *How many falls are there along the Limpopo River?* **26** depreciation, °sinking, diminution, °decrease, °decline, °lapse, downturn, down-swing, °drop, drop-off, lowering, abatement, °slump, °collapse: *On the Stock Exchange today, investors experienced sharp falls in share prices.* **27** °slope, declivity, descent, °decline, °drop, downhill, *Chiefly US and Canadian* °downgrade: *Note the smooth rise and fall of the land.* **28** °surrender, capitulation, °submission, °taking, °seizure, °capture, °overthrow, °defeat, °conquest, °downfall: *The fall of Khartoum in 1898 marked the re-establishment of British rule in the Anglo-Egyptian Sudan.*

fallacy *n.* °misconception, miscalculation, misjudgement, °mistake, °error, *non sequitur*, °solecism, °delusion; paralogism; sophism: *It is a fallacy to think that you could ever learn to play the violin as well as Susannah.*

false *adj.* **1** °untrue, unfactual, untruthful, °wrong, °amiss, °mistaken, °erroneous, °incorrect, °inaccurate, °inexact, °imprecise, °faulty, °flawed, °invalid, °unsound, °unreal, °imaginary, °fictitious, °spurious: *The explorers gave a completely false picture of the local inhabitants.* **2** °untrue, untruthful, °lying, misleading, fallacious, fabricated, made-up, concocted, mendacious, untrustworthy, °fraudulent, meretricious, °deceptive, °deceitful, treacherous, *Colloq* °phoney *or US also* phony: *The testimony of this witness is completely false.* **3** °counterfeit, °imitation, simulated, °sham, forged, °fraudulent, °fake, °artificial, °synthetic, manufactured, °unnatural, °spurious, °bogus, ersatz, °factitious, °mock, pseudo, *Colloq* °phoney *or US also* phony: *Your false teeth look almost real.* **4** °sham, feigned, °affected, °insincere, faked, manufactured, °counterfeit(ed): *Don't shed any false tears over me when I'm gone.* **5** illogical, fallacious, °unsound, °invalid, °flawed, °faulty: *That conclusion could come only from false reasoning.*

falsehood *n.* °lie, °fib, prevarication, untruth, °fabrication, °misstatement, fiction, (fairy) °tale, °story, distortion, *Colloq* cock-and-bull °story, *Slang Brit* °load of codswallop: *That was a complete falsehood about the goings-on in the attic, wasn't it?*

falsify *v.* °fake, °alter, °distort, misstate, °misrepresent, °twist, *Colloq* fudge, trump up, *Brit* cook: *The tax inspector found that the accounts had been falsified.*

falsity *n.* untruthfulness, mendacity, mendaciousness, fraudulence, deceptiveness, °deceit, deceitfulness, dishonesty, spuriousness, speciousness, casuistry, °hypocrisy, insincerity, falseness: *The prosecution was unable to prove the falsity of her statement.*

fame *n.* °renown, repute, °reputation, °celebrity, illustriousness, °superiority, °pre-eminence, stardom, °prominence, eminence, °glory, °name, °notoriety, acclaim: *Randolph's fame has spread far and wide.*

familiar *adj.* **1** °well-known, °common, commonplace, °everyday, °ordinary, °current: *That's a familiar melody.* **2** °frequent, °usual, °customary, °habitual, °routine, °traditional: *He strolled along his familiar route through the trees.* **3** °friendly, affable, °close, °intimate, °sociable, °social, °free, °free and °easy, °relaxed; over-friendly, overfree, overfamiliar, °bold, °forward, °insolent, °impudent, °presumptuous, presuming, °disrespectful, unreserved, unrestrained; °informal, °casual, °cordial, unceremonious; *Colloq* °chummy, *Slang US and Canadian* buddy-buddy, palsy-walsy: *She began to get entirely too familiar.* **4 *familiar with***: °aware *or* °conscious *or* cognizant of, °knowledgeable about *or* of *or* in, conversant *or* °acquainted with, no stranger to, on speaking terms with, up on *or* in, (well-)°versed in, °informed of *or* about, °privy to, in the know about, *au courant, au fait*: *Are you familiar with the latest theories in particle physics?*

familiarity *n.* **1** °knowledge, °acquaintance(ship), °grasp, °understanding, comprehension, °cognizance, awareness, conversance, °experience: *I have no familiarity at all with particle physics.* **2** friendliness, affability, sociability, neighbourliness, °fellowship, intimacy, intimateness, closeness, openness, naturalness, °ease, informality, unceremoniousness: *He prided himself on his familiarity with celebrities.* **3** boldness, presumptuousness, overfamiliarity, °presumption, °impudence, insolence, °impertinence, °impropriety: *He put his arm round her waist with offensive familiarity.*

familiarize *v.* Usually, ***familiarize with***: °accustom (to), make °familiar *or* °acquaint (with), °initiate (in), °inform (about *or* on), °enlighten (about *or* as to), °teach (about), °educate *or* °instruct *or* °tutor (in): *I am trying to familiarize myself with the music of John Cage.*

family *n.* **1** (kith and) °kin, kinsmen, °kindred, kinsfolk *or US and Canadian* kinfolk, next of °kin, °relatives, °relations, household, °people, one's own °flesh and blood, one's nearest and dearest, ménage, *Colloq* folks: *We usually spend the holidays with my family.* **2** children, °offspring, °progeny, °issue, °brood, *Colloq* kids: *Large families were much more common in the 19th century.* **3** °ancestors, forebears, forefathers, °progenitors; ancestry, °parentage, descent, °extraction, °derivation, °lineage, °pedigree, genealogy, family tree, °house, °line, bloodline, °dynasty; blood, °stock, °strain: *He came from an old family of German bankers.* **4** °group, °set, °division, subdivision, classification, °type, °kind, °class, °genre, °order, species, genus: *English belongs to the Indo-European family of languages.*

famine *n.* starvation; °shortage, °dearth, °scarcity, deficiency, paucity, exiguity, barrenness, °lack: *In days of abundance, no one should die of famine.*

famished *adj.* starving, °starved, °voracious, °ravenous, ravening, craving, °hungry: *The survivors were famished after a fortnight in the lifeboat.*

famous *adj.* °renowned, °celebrated, °popular, famed, °well-known, °noted, °eminent, °pre-eminent, °conspicuous, °prominent, °illustrious, °notable, acclaimed, °venerable, °legendary, °distinguished, °praiseworthy, honoured, lionized: *A famous architect has been invited to address the convention.*

famously *adv.* excellently, (very) °well, superbly, marvellously, splendidly, capitally, spectacularly, superlatively: *The prince and I get on famously.*

fan *n.* °admirer, °enthusiast, adherent, °devotee, aficionado, °follower, °supporter, °lover, °zealot, *Colloq* buff, °fiend, °hound, °bug, °addict, nut, *US* booster, *Slang* junkie, °freak, groupie: *Avid fans of Ascot United, we go to all the matches.*

fanatic *n.* °maniac, extremist, °zealot, *Colloq* °fiend, nut, *Slang* °freak: *Religious fanatics killed 'heathens' or 'infidels' by the thousand.*

fanatical *adj.* °fanatic, °extreme, distracted, °maniacal, °mad, °rabid, zealous, frenzied, °feverish, °burning, °frantic, frenetic, °obsessive, °fervent, °compulsive, monomaniacal, fervid, perfervid, °passionate, °enthusiastic, °agog, °immoderate, °excessive: *The entire family are fanatical in their fundamentalism.*

fanaticism *n.* **1** °devotion, °dedication, devotedness; infatuation, °enthusiasm, °fervour, zeal, obsessiveness, franticness, °frenzy, hysteria: *Her fanaticism for rock musicians is getting a bit out of hand.* **2** monomania, single-mindedness, °mania, °madness, extremism, °intolerance, °bigotry, °bias, °partiality, °prejudice, narrow-mindedness, close-mindedness: *Some religious sects are characterized by virulent fanaticism.*

fancied *adj.* °imaginary, °unreal, °fanciful, imagined, °illusory, make-believe, °mythical, fairy-tale: *They support their king in the pursuit of his fancied rights.*

fanciful *adj.* **1** °whimsical, °capricious, °impulsive, °inconstant, °fickle, °changeable, °variable: *Those graffiti are products of a fanciful mind.* **2** °extravagant, chimerical, °fantastic, °fabulous, °mythical, fairy-tale, °imaginative, °fancied, make-believe, °unreal, °illusory, imagined, °visionary, °imaginary: *Some of the more fanciful ideas of science fiction have become realities.* **3** °curious, °odd, °peculiar, °bizarre, °unusual, °original: *The chalice was decorated with fanciful curlicues.*

fancy *adj.* **1** °ornate, decorative, decorated, °ornamental, ornamented, °elaborate, embellished, embroidered, °fanciful, °extravagant, rococo, baroque, gingerbread, Byzantine, °complicated, °intricate, complex: *The modern trend has been away from fancy architecture.* **2** °illusory, °capricious, °fanciful, °extravagant, °fantastic, °far-fetched, delusive, °whimsical, °visionary, °unrealistic, °grandiose: *He has some fancy ideas about building an undersea city.* **3** de luxe, °luxury, °luxurious, °choice, °select, °prime, °special, °elegant, °superior, °quality, °high-class; °posh: *They stock only fancy fruits and vegetables. She has a fancy suite at the Cardigan Hotel.* **4** °high, °exorbitant, °inflated, °outrageous: *One has to pay very fancy prices for haute couture.*
—*n.* **5** °imagination, °creation, °conception, inventiveness, creativeness, creativity: *These chimeras are entirely a product of his fancy.* **6** °imagination, °fantasy, °hallucination, °delusion, °illusion, unreality, make-believe, °dream, day-dream, pipedream, mirage, phantasm, °phantom, figment (of the °imagination), °impression: *Our plans for the future must be based on fact, not fancy.* **7** °liking, °inclination, fondness, °taste, °penchant, °attraction, °preference, °partiality, predilection, yearning, craving, hankering, °wish, °desire, °longing: *Miss Crow's fancy for younger men often causes her some embarrassment.* **8** °idea, whim, caprice, whimsy, °urge, impulse, °notion, vagary, °quirk, crotchet, °peculiarity: *His fancy today is that he invented electricity.*
—*v.* **9** °imagine, °conceive, °picture, visualize, °envisage, °think *or* °make up, conjure up, *US* °envision, *Colloq* °dream up: *He fancies himself on a big yacht in the Mediterranean.* **10** °think, °imagine, °understand, °believe, °suspect, °guess, conjecture, °presume, °surmise, °assume, °take it, °suppose, °infer, °reckon: *From his costume I fancy he must be Superman. Fancy Kim winning the Nobel prize!* **11** °like, be °attracted to, take (a °liking) to, °desire, °want, crave, °long *or* pine for, have a yen *or* craving for, have an °eye for, °wish for, °hunger for, °favour, °prefer, °lust after: *Terry has always fancied tall women. I wouldn't fancy being 40 feet up a swaying ladder like that.*

fanfare *n.* **1** °flourish, fanfaron, fanfaronade, (trumpet-)°blast *or* °blare: *Following a loud fanfare, the toreador strutted into the ring.* **2** hullabaloo, hubbub, brouhaha, commotion, °stir, ado, °show, °fuss, *Colloq* to-do, ballyhoo: *Despite the enormous fanfare, the film was a failure.*

fantasize *v.* °dream, °imagine, day-dream, °muse, °mull (over), build castles in the air *or* in Spain, °speculate, °envisage, star-gaze; hallucinate, *US* °envision: *She often fantasized about the kind of man she would marry.*

fantastic *adj.* **1** °fanciful, °strange, °weird, °peculiar, °odd, °eccentric, °queer, °bizarre, °quaint, °outlandish, °exotic, °extravagant, °grotesque, °nightmarish, °alien, °remarkable: *She wore the most fantastic costume to the fancy-dress ball.* **2** °imaginary, °illusory, illusive, °unreal, °visionary, °fanciful, °unrealistic, imagined, irrational: *His books are inhabited by fantastic creatures.* **3** °unbelievable, °incredible, °preposterous, °extraordinary, °implausible, °absurd, °unlikely: *At 85, he made the fantastic decision to enter the marathon.* **4** °marvellous, spectacular, °splendid, wonderful, tremendous, °overwhelming, *Colloq* °great, °fabulous, °terrific: *The Picasso exhibition is simply fantastic.*

fantasy *n.* **1** °imagination, °fancy, creativity, inventiveness, °originality: *We encourage the children to give free rein to their fantasy.* **2** °vision, °hallucination, °illusion, mirage, °delusion, chimera, °dream, day-dream, (flight of) °fancy, pipedream: *Her fantasy is to become prime minister.* **3** make-believe, °invention, fabrication, fiction, °masquerade, fable, concoction, °pretence: *His story about being an orphan is pure fantasy.*

far *adv.* **1** afar, far-away *or* -off, a good *or* great *or* °long °way *or* °distance off *or* away: *We caught sight of a sail far to the south.* **2** (very) much, considerably, decidedly, incomparably: *She is a far better swimmer than George.* **3** ***by far***: (very) much, considerably, decidedly, incomparably, (im)measurably, by a long °shot, far and away, °clearly, plainly, °obviously, °doubtless(ly), indubitably, °undoubtedly, °definitely, beyond (the shadow of a) °doubt, without a °doubt, *Colloq Brit* by a long chalk: *She's a better swimmer than George by far. He is by far the wealthiest person I know.* **4** ***far and wide***: °everywhere, near and far *or* far and near, extensively, °widely, °high and low; here, there, and °everywhere: *We searched far and wide to find these specimens.* **5** ***far gone***: **a** beyond *or* past help, advanced, deteriorated, °worn out, °dilapidated, near the °end: *That shirt is too far gone to send to the laundry. My house is so far gone it's beyond repair.* **b** °drunk, besotted, *Slang* °loaded, pissed, paralytic, paralysed: *He's too far gone to walk.* **6** ***go far***: **a** °progress, °advance, °succeed, go places, °get ahead, °rise (in the world), make a name for oneself, become °successful, set the world on fire, *Brit* set the Thames on fire, *US* cut a swath: *He is a very bright youngster and*

I'm sure he will go far in whatever profession he chooses. **b** °help, °aid, °contribute, play a part: *The new law will go far towards inhibiting child abuse.* **7** ***go too far***: °go overboard *or* over the top, not know when to stop, °go to extremes; °exceed, °overdo, °overstep, °transcend, °go beyond: *Ambition is one thing, but he went too far when he tried to get his boss's job.* **8** ***so far***: **a** thus far, (up) to *or* till *or* until °now *or* the °present *or* this °point, to °date, to this °point in time: *So far, we have been able to keep up with the mortgage payments.* **b** to a certain °extent *or* °limit *or* °point: *She said she would go just so far and no further.*
—*adj.* **9** (more) °remote *or* °distant, °far-away, far-off; °extreme, °further, farther, farthest: *She claimed the ability to see into the far future. He kicked the ball to the far end of the field.*

far-away *adj.* **1** faraway, °distant, °remote, far-off, °outlying, far-flung: *People came from far-away places as news of the miracle spread.* **2** faraway, °dreamy, °detached, °absent, °absent-minded, abstracted: *When you have that far-away expression, I know you don't hear a word I say.*

farcical *adj.* °ludicrous, laughable, risible, °funny, °nonsensical, °ridiculous, °silly, °preposterous, °absurd, °foolish; comical, °humorous, droll, amusing: *His farcical attempts at surfing fully dressed had us in hysterics.*

fare *n.* **1** °passenger, °traveller: *The taxi-driver deposited his fare at the hotel.* **2** °charge, °price, °cost: *What is the fare from Oxford to London?* **3** °food, °diet, victuals, °meals, viands, eatables, °provisions: *Prison fare consisted of bread and water.*
—*v.* **4** do, make one's way, °manage, °get on *or* along, °make out, °survive: *The children didn't fare very well on their own.*

farewell *n.* **1** adieu, °goodbye: *We said our farewells and left.* **2** departure, leave-taking, *congé*, °parting, *Colloq* send-off: *I want to avoid a tearful farewell.*
—*interjection.* **3** Adieu!, Goodbye!, So long!, Godspeed!, Adios!, Hasta luego!, Hasta la vista!, Auf Wiedersehen!, Ciao!, Sayonara!, Aloha!, Vaya con Dios!, *Colloq Brit* God bless!, *Old-fashioned* Toodle-oo!, Pip! Pip!, Ta-ta!, *US old-fashioned* See you later (alligator)!, Don't take any wooden nickels!: *I said farewell and we went our separate ways.*

far-fetched *adj.* °strained, stretched, °improbable, °implausible, °unlikely, °doubtful, dubious, °questionable, °forced, unconvincing, °unrealistic, °fantastic, °preposterous, hard to °believe, °unbelievable, °incredible, *Colloq* hard to °swallow, °fishy: *They told some far-fetched tale about being robbed by a gang of midgets.*

farm *n.* **1** farmstead, farmhouse, grange, homestead, holding; °land, farmland, acreage, arable; *Brit* steading, smallholding, °allotment, *Scots* farm-toun, croft: *My grandfather owns a farm in Yorkshire.* **2** ***buy the farm***: °die, be °killed: *A MIG caught Johnson and he bought the farm.*
—*v.* **3** °cultivate, °work the °land, °till the °soil: *His family has been farming this land for centuries.* **4** ***farm out***: °contract, subcontract, °lease, °delegate, °let (out): *They cut staff and now farm out much of the work.*

farmer *n.* husbandman, agriculturist, agronomist, yeoman, *Brit* smallholder, *US dialect* granger: *The farmers here were hard hit by the drought.*

farming *n.* agriculture, agronomy, husbandry, agribusiness, cultivation: *Less than 8,000 years ago man turned from hunting and gathering to farming.*

far-sighted *adj.* **1** far-seeing, foresighted, prescient, °provident, °prudent, °shrewd, °perceptive, discerning, insightful, °wise, sagacious, °acute, °sharp, °astute, °sensible, °imaginative: *The committee drew up a far-sighted plan for the redevelopment of the town centre.* **2** long-sighted, hyperopic *or* hypermetropic, presbyopic: *I'm far-sighted, so I wear glasses only for reading.*

fascinate *v.* °bewitch, °enchant, cast a °spell on *or* over, ensorcell, spellbind, °hold spellbound, put *or* have under a °spell, °charm, °captivate, °intrigue, °beguile, °hypnotize, mesmerize, °transfix, °entrance, engross, enthral, °enrapture, absorb, allure, °attract: *Desmond is utterly fascinated by Elizabeth.*

fascination *n.* °enchantment, °sorcery, °magic, attractiveness, °attraction, °draw, °pull, (animal) °magnetism, °charm, allure, captivation, °influence, witchcraft, entrancement: *Blondes always held a strange fascination for him.*

fashion *n.* **1** °style, °mode, °vogue, °trend, °look, °taste: *That year there was a fashion for stiletto heels.* **2** the °fad, °mania, the °craze, the °rage, the °latest (°thing), *dernier cri*, *Colloq Brit* the go: *He remembers when upswept hair-dos were the fashion.* **3** °manner, °mode, °way, °approach, °attitude: *I'll always be true to you, darling, in my fashion.* **4** ***in fashion***: See **fashionable,** below.
—*v.* **5** °make, °model, °style, °shape, °form, °frame, °mould, °create, °construct, °forge, °work, °manufacture: *She fashions the most beautiful vases out of shapeless lumps of clay.*

fashionable *adj.* in °fashion, °chic, à la °mode, modish, °stylish, °smart, in °vogue, up to the °minute, up to °date, *Colloq* °trendy, in, with it, *Colloq Brit* all the go: *The couturiers insist that black will be fashionable this year.*

fast[1] *adj.* **1** quick, °swift, °fleet, °speedy, °brisk; °brief, °hurried, °hasty, high-speed, accelerated, °expeditious, °rapid, °express: *She is very fast on her feet. We need a fast turn-round on this job.* **2** °loose, °profligate, °wild, °extravagant, dissipated, intemperate, °irresponsible, sybaritic, °self-indulgent, °dissolute, unrestrained, indecorous, °rakish, licentious, °promiscuous, °immoral, °wanton, °lecherous, °lustful: *They led quite a fast life till their divorce.* **3** °firm, fastened, °secure(d), °fixed, tied, °bound, connected, °attached: *The boat was fast to the pier.* **4** °firm, °fixed, settled, °stable, °solid, °immovable, unshakable *or* unshakeable, °tight: *The sword was fast in the stone.* **5** °firm, °stable, °steadfast, °staunch, unwavering, °constant, °lasting, °close, °loyal, °devoted, °faithful, °permanent: *We maintained a fast friendship over the years.*
—*adv.* **6** °quickly, °swiftly, °rapidly, speedily, briskly, presto, °hastily, hurriedly, with all °speed *or* °haste, expeditiously, apace, °post-haste, like a °flash, in the blink of an eye, in a wink, before you can say 'Jack Robinson', in no °time (at all), *Colloq* like a bat out of hell, like a °shot, p.d.q. (='pretty damned quick'), *Brit* like the clappers (of hell), *US and Canadian* quick like a bunny *or* rabbit, lickety-split: *Don't talk so fast. He ran out of there very fast. I'll be back very fast.*
7 °firmly, fixedly, immovably, solidly, unshakeably *or* unshakably, °tightly, securely, soundly: *The rope held fast. He is fast asleep.* **8** closely, °close to, °immediately, °near, (°close) on, °right: *Fast on the heels of the fugitive came the police.* **9** loosely, wildly, recklessly, intemperately, irresponsibly, fecklessly, extravagantly, intemperately, sybaritically, self-indulgently, dissolutely, unrestrainedly, indecorously, rakishly, licentiously, promiscuously, immorally, wantonly, lecherously, lustfully: *He's been living fast since inheriting that fortune.*

fast[2] *v.* **1** abstain, go °hungry, °deny oneself, °diet, starve (oneself): *Do you fast during Lent?*
—*n.* **2** abstention, abstinence, fasting, °self-denial, °diet; °hunger °strike: *She went on a two-week fast.*

fasten *v.* **1** °attach, °tie, °bind, °bond, °stick, affix, °anchor, °fix, °lock, °hook (up), °secure, °join, °connect, °link, °fuse, °cement, °clamp: *Fasten your seat belts. The mussels fasten themselves by their byssi to underwater piles.* **2** °fix, rivet, °focus, °concentrate, °direct, °aim, °point: *He fastened his gaze on Kitty. She fastened her attention on the ceiling.*

fastening *n.* fastener, catch, °clasp, latch, °lock, °tie, °bond: *Can you see what kind of fastening is holding the cover?*

fastidious *adj.* °squeamish, °delicate, over-nice, °fussy, °meticulous, °finicky, finical, pernickety *or US also* persnickety, °particular, °difficult, °critical, hypercritical, supercritical, over-precise, punctilious, *Colloq* nit-picking, picky: *The Prioress was too fastidious to allow a morsel drop from her lip.*

fat *adj.* **1** °obese, °stout, overweight, °heavy, °plump, °rotund, corpulent, portly, °well-fed, °chubby, podgy *or chiefly US* pudgy, roly-poly, tubby, °bulky, fleshy, paunchy, pot-bellied, overfed, °flabby, elephantine, *Colloq* °broad in the beam, °beamy, beefy, *Slang US* five-by-five: *A fat man squeezed in beside me.* **2** °oily, oleaginous, unctuous, °greasy, fatty, pinguid, sebaceous, adipose: *His complexion is bad because he eats too much fat food.* **3** °rich, °wealthy, °prosperous, affluent, well-to-do, well off, *Colloq* well-heeled, °loaded: *They grew fat on their profits from the black market.* **4** °profitable, lucrative, °fruitful, remunerative, *Slang* cushy: *He has a fat job as a purchasing agent for the government.*
—*n.* **5** °obesity, corpulence, stoutness, overweight, heaviness, plumpness, rotundity, portliness, chubbiness, podginess *or chiefly US* pudginess, tubbiness, fleshiness, paunchiness, flabbiness: *He leans a little towards fat because of lack of exercise.* **6** °riches, °wealth, °prosperity, fertility, °yield, °abundance, °plenty, plenteousness: *He's living off the fat of the land.*

fatal *adj.* **1** °fateful, °deadly, °murderous, °lethal, °mortal, toxic, °terminal, °final; baneful, °poisonous: *She drank the fatal potion without a word. Who dealt the fatal blow?* **2** °destructive, °fateful, °ruinous, °calamitous, °dreadful, °disastrous, °devastating, cataclysmic, catastrophic, °harmful, °mischievous, damaging: *Discovery by the police would prove fatal to our plan.* **3** °fateful, °fated, °destined, predestined, decreed, ordained, foreordained, preordained, °predetermined, °inevitable, °unavoidable, °necessary, °essential, inescapable, ineluctable: *The events fell into their fatal sequence.*

fatality *n.* **1** °catastrophe, °disaster, °calamity, cataclysm: *The eruption of Vesuvius was a relatively recent fatality.* **2** °death, °casualty: *Traffic fatalities are on the increase.*

fate *n.* **1** °fortune, °lot, °luck, °chance, °life, °destiny, God's °will, °providence *or* Providence, °doom, karma, kismet, toss *or* throw of the dice, *Colloq US and Canadian* the breaks, the way the cookie crumbles, the way the ball bounces: *Fate has brought us together. Our meeting this way was just fate.* **2** °doom, °destruction, °downfall, °undoing, °ruin, °disaster, °collapse, °death, nemesis, °end, °finish: *The defenders of Masada met their fate bravely.* **3** °end, °outcome, °future, °destination, °disposition: *There was no trace of the fate of the explorers. What is to be the fate of this obsolete equipment?*

fated *adj.* **1** °destined, predestined, °predetermined, decreed, °doomed, °fateful, ordained, foreordained, preordained, °decided: *The fated day of my trial arrived.* **2** °sure, °certain, °doomed, damned, cursed: *Was I fated to spend the rest of my life in this fetid dungeon?* **3** °fatal, °fateful, °unavoidable, inescapable, °inevitable, ineluctable: *Their fated punishment was to bail out the sea using sieves.*

fateful *adj.* **1** °significant, °momentous, °ominous, °major, consequential, °important, °critical, °crucial, decisive, °weighty, °portentous, earth-shaking, °pivotal: *The minister is faced with having to make a fateful decision.* **2** °deadly, °lethal, °fatal, °destructive, °ruinous, °disastrous, catastrophic, cataclysmic: *Failure to preserve the environment could have fateful consequences.*

father *n.* **1** sire, paterfamilias, *Colloq* dad, daddy, pa, papa, °pop, old man, old boy, *Brit* governor, pater: *His father is a chemist.* **2** forebear, °ancestor, forefather, °progenitor, primogenitor: *The father of the dynasty fought at Hastings.* **3** °creator, °founder, originator, inventor, °author, architect, framer, initiator: *He regards Lavoisier as the father of modern chemistry.* **4** °priest, confessor, curé, abbé, °minister, °pastor, °shepherd, parson, °clergyman, chaplain, *Colloq* padre, *Military slang* sky pilot: *We should see the Father about the funeral service.*
—*v.* **5** sire, beget, °get, engender, procreate, °generate: *He had fathered more than forty children in his harem.* **6** °originate, °establish, °found, °invent, °author, °frame, °initiate, °institute, °create: *Galileo fathered modern astronomy by inventing the telescope.*

fatherland *n.* motherland, °native °land, °mother °country, homeland, (old) °country, birthplace: *They return to their fatherland for an annual visit.*

fatherly *adj.* °paternal, °kindly, °kind, °warm, °friendly, °affectionate, °protective, °amiable, °benevolent, well-meaning, °benign, caring, °sympathetic, °indulgent, °understanding; parental: *My nephew used to come to me for fatherly advice.*

fathom *v.* °probe, °sound, °plumb, °penetrate, °search (out), °investigate, °measure, °gauge, °determine, ascertain, °work out, get to the °bottom of, delve into, °understand, °grasp, °divine: *I never quite fathomed the purpose of this device.*

fatigue *n.* **1** weariness, tiredness, °weakness, °exhaustion, lassitude, listlessness, °lethargy, languor, °sluggishness, enervation: *She kept on tending the wounded till fatigue finally overcame her.*
—*v.* **2** °weary, °tire, °weaken, °exhaust, °drain, °enervate, *Colloq* °fag (out): *My morning's work had fatigued me.*

fatigued *adj.* °weary, wearied, °tired, overtired, °dead °tired, °weak, weakened, °exhausted, °listless, °lethargic, languorous, sluggish, enervated, °strained, wasted, *Colloq* whacked (out), knocked out, °dead, °beat, dead beat, all in, *Brit* knackered, jiggered, buggered, *US and Canadian* pooped, bushed: *The firemen were fatigued after being on duty round the clock.*

fatness *n.* °obesity, stoutness, corpulence, *embonpoint*, portliness, plumpness, chubbiness, rotundity, podginess *or chiefly US* pudginess: *His fatness is owing to a glandular condition, not overeating.*

fault *n.* **1** °imperfection, °flaw, °defect, °blemish, deficiency, °shortcoming, °failing, °weakness; °frailty, °foible, °peccadillo: *The fault lies in this circuit. Using filthy language is only one of his faults.* **2** °mistake, °error, °blunder, °lapse, °failure, °offence, °oversight, °slip(-up), °indiscretion, gaffe, gaucherie, faux pas, *Slang* boner, °howler, goof, boo-boo, *Brit* boob: *People should be responsible for their faults. There are many faults in this manuscript.* **3** °responsibility, °liability, culpability; °blame, °accountability, answerability: *It wasn't my fault that the tree fell down. The fault lies with you, James.* **4** °sin, °transgression, trespass, °misdeed, °offence, misdemeanour, °vice, °indiscretion, misconduct, °misbehaviour: *He will confess his faults to anyone who will listen.* **5** ***at fault***: to °blame, blameable, blameworthy, in the °wrong, °responsible, answerable, °accountable, °liable, culpable, °guilty: *You were at fault for failing to report the crime.* **6** ***find fault***: °criticize, censure, take °exception (to), °carp (at), °cavil (at), °pick at, °pick on, °pick apart, °pick holes in, °niggle, °fuss, *Colloq* nit-pick, °knock: *She constantly finds fault with everything I do.* **7** ***to a fault***: excessively, °extremely, to an °extreme, in the °extreme, unreasonably, °exceedingly, °unduly, disproportionately, immoderately, irrationally, *US* °overly: *She is modest to a fault.*
—*v.* **8** find fault with, censure, °blame, °criticize, call to °account, impugn, call into °question, hold (someone) °responsible *or* °accountable *or* to °blame, lay at (someone's) door, °accuse: *You cannot be faulted for not knowing the fuel tank was empty.*

fault-finding *n.* **1** °criticism, censure, carping, cavilling, captiousness, hypercriticism, quibbling, fussiness, °hair-splitting, pettifogging, *Colloq* nit-picking, pickiness: *Why continue to put up with the foreman's fault-finding?*

—*adj.* **2** °critical, censorious, carping, cavilling, captious, hypercritical, °fussy, °hair-splitting, pettifogging, °niggling, contentious, °querulous, quibbling, *Colloq* nit-picking, picky: *She could no longer abide his fault-finding attitude.*

faultless *adj.* °perfect, °flawless, °immaculate, °ideal, °exemplary, °correct, °accurate, °foolproof, °irreproachable, unimpeachable, *Colloq Brit* bang on, °spot on: *Their performance was faultless.*

faulty *adj.* °defective, °unsound, °imperfect, °flawed, impaired, out of °order, malfunctioning, °broken, °bad; damaged; *Slang* on the °blink, *Chiefly US* on the fritz: *The carburettor is faulty.*

favour *n.* **1** °good °will, °approval, °support, approbation: *Father looked with favour on my marriage to Leslie.* **2** °courtesy, °good *or* °kind °deed, °good °turn, °kindness, °gesture, *beau geste;* °service: *As a favour, I'll walk your dog while you're away.* **3** °favouritism, °partiality, °prejudice, °bias, °preference, °patronage: *They show favour in repeatedly giving the contract to the same company.* **4** °grace, °esteem, °consideration, °view, °regard, °opinion, °account, (good *or* bad) books; °disposition, °taste, predisposition: *How does Rochester stand in the favour of the king?* **5** ***in favour (of)***: °for, pro, on the °side of, in °support (of), at the back of, °backing, behind, on *or US and Canadian* in °behalf (of), in back of: *Please vote in favour of the resolution. Are you in favour or against?*
—*v.* **6** °approve, °prefer, °like, have a °liking *or* °preference for, be °partial to, °advocate, espouse, °back, °endorse, °support, °champion, °recommend, °incline to *or* towards, °side with, take the °side *or* °part of, °go for, opt for, °fancy, °select, °choose, °elect, °single out, °sponsor, °adopt, °go in for: *Which candidate do you favour?* **7** °pamper, °coddle, °baby, °protect, °indulge, be °partial to: *Notice how Billie favours his left leg when walking?* **8** °advance, °forward, °promote, °facilitate, °expedite, °help, °benefit, °assist, °aid, °encourage, °accommodate, °smile upon: *The warm, moist climate favours the growth of mould.* **9** °resemble, °look °like, °take after: *Little Jimmy favours his father, I think.*

favourable *adj.* **1** °advantageous, °promising, auspicious, °fair, °beneficial, °suitable, °fitting, °appropriate, encouraging, facilitative, °helpful, °helping, °supportive, supporting, °convenient, °useful, °opportune, °propitious, °accommodating, accommodative; facultative: *A favourable breeze sent our craft towards Cyprus.* **2** °good, °promising, °positive, encouraging, reassuring, affirmative, well-disposed, °sympathetic; commendatory, °laudatory, °enthusiastic, °eager, °ardent, zealous: *They concluded a very favourable deal to supply the army with boots. My latest book received favourable reviews.*

favourably *adv.* **1** graciously, indulgently, sympathetically, genially, °positively, agreeably, enthusiastically, with °favour: *They reacted favourably to my suggestion.* **2** advantageously, affirmatively, °positively, in °favourable terms: *Your application has been considered favourably.*

favoured *adj.* **1** preferred, chosen, °choice, selected, °popular, °favourite, °pet: *The favoured explanation is that he is the boss's son.* **2** advantaged, °privileged, blessed, °prosperous, °wealthy, °rich, affluent, well off: *She is one of the favoured few who can afford to travel.*

favourite *n.* **1** °choice, °pick, °preference, preferred, esteemed, °darling, °pet, °ideal, apple of (someone's) eye, *Colloq Brit* blue-eyed boy *or* girl, flavour of the month, *US* white-haired *or* white-headed boy *or* girl, fair-haired boy *or* girl: *Raising interest rates doesn't exactly make the chancellor everyone's favourite.*
—*adj.* **2** °beloved, chosen, picked, selected, preferred, best-liked, most-liked, °favoured, °choice, °pet, °ideal: *Which is your favourite flavour?*

favouritism *n.* °partiality, °bias, predisposition, prepossession, °prejudice, °bent, partisanship, nepotism, preferment; °preference, °leaning, °inclination, proclivity: *He openly admits to favouritism in selecting employees.*

fear *n.* **1** °dread, °terror, °fright, °panic, °horror, °alarm, trepidation, apprehension, fearfulness, apprehensiveness, °dismay, consternation, hesitation, qualms, diffidence, timidity, cravenness, °cowardice, °second thoughts: *His fear of going into the jungle alone is understandable.* **2** awe, °respect, °reverence, °veneration: *That'll put the fear of God into him!* **3** °horror, °spectre, nightmare, bogey *or* bogy, °phobia, bugbear, *bête noire,* °misgiving(s), °foreboding(s): *When they came to break the news, her worst fears were realized.* **4** °solicitude, °anxiety, angst, °foreboding(s), °distress, °misgiving(s), °concern, apprehension, °worry, uneasiness, unease: *Fear for her safety is shared by all of us.*
—*v.* **5** be °afraid *or* °scared *or* °fearful *or* °frightened (of), °dread, quail *or* °tremble *or* °quake at, °shudder at, °shrink from, °quiver: *What man cannot understand he often fears.* **6** °revere, °respect, °venerate, be *or* stand in awe of: *If you fear the Lord as I do, you won't take his name in vain.* **7** °expect, °anticipate, °imagine, °suspect, °foresee: *I fear we are too late for dinner.*

fearful *adj.* **1** °afraid, °scared, frightened, terrified, alarmed, °panic-stricken, terror-stricken *or* terror-struck: *Of all disasters, I am most fearful of fire.* **2** °hesitant, °timid, timorous, °shy, diffident, unwilling, intimidated, °jumpy, °nervous, edgy, panicky, °anxious, apprehensive, °cowardly, pusillanimous, *Colloq* yellow, jittery: *Why is she so fearful of meeting her prospective in-laws?* **3** °awful, dire, °dreadful, °frightful, °frightening, °terrifying, °terrible, appalling, °ghastly, °atrocious, °horrible, horrifying, horrendous, horrific, °hideous, °gruesome, °grisly, °grim, baleful, °monstrous, unspeakable, °loathsome, heinous, °repugnant, °repulsive, °revolting, °disgusting, nauseating, °nauseous: *The fearful monster blocked our only way out.*

fearfully *adv.* **1** hesitantly, timidly, timorously, shyly, diffidently, unwillingly, nervously, edgily, anxiously, apprehensively: *Fearfully, she approached the altar.* **2** °very, °awfully, °terribly, °extremely, °exceedingly, °frightfully, tremendously: *It was fearfully considerate of you to come.*

fearless *adj.* °brave, °bold, °intrepid, valorous, °dauntless, °courageous, valiant, plucky, °daring, °audacious, °heroic, °venturesome, °gallant, °chivalrous: *These fearless commandos cared nothing for their personal safety.*

fearsome *adj.* °dreadful, °awesome, appalling, °formidable, daunting, °frightening, °frightful, awe-inspiring, °menacing, °terrible, °terrifying, intimidating: *Last week's typhoon was the most fearsome storm of the century.*

feasibility *n.* practicability, workability, applicability, viability, practicality: *The feasibility of the scheme has yet to be assessed.*

feasible *adj.* °practicable, workable, doable, °applicable, °viable, °practical, °possible, realizable, achievable, attainable, °sensible, usable, °realistic: *The world needs a feasible method for disposing of nuclear waste.*

feast *n.* **1** °banquet, (°lavish) dinner, (°sumptuous) repast, (Lucullan *or* Epicurean) °treat, *Colloq* °spread, *Brit* beanfeast; *Slang* blow-out, *Brit* beano: *Dinner at Patrick's is no mere meal—it is a feast.* **2** °observance, °celebration, °rite, °ritual, solemnization, commemoration, memorialization, anniversary, birthday, jubilee, feast-day, °festival, °fête *or* fete, holy day, °holiday, red-letter day, °occasion, °event, °gala: *Church calendars list both movable and immovable feasts.* **3** °treat, °delight, °pleasure, °gratification: *Seeing you again was a feast for the eyes.*
—*v.* **4** °dine, wine (and °dine), °fare well *or* sumptuously, (over)indulge, °gorge (oneself), gormandize, °eat one's °fill: *We feasted on roast turkey with all the trimmings.* **5** °entertain, °feed, wine and °dine, °treat,

°regale: *Visitors to Arthur's court were feasted with the finest viands available.* **6** °delight, °gratify, °please, °cheer, °gladden: *Ali Baba feasted his eyes on the vast treasure in the cave.*

feat *n.* °exploit, °deed, °act, attainment, °achievement, °accomplishment, *tour de force*: *Persuading your wife to let you go fishing was quite a feat.*

feature *n.* **1** °characteristic, °attribute, °trait, °mark, °hallmark, earmark, °property, °character, °quality, °aspect, facet, °peculiarity, °quirk, idiosyncrasy: *What are the identifying features of traditional Chinese architecture?* **2** (main) °attraction, °draw, °special °attraction, high °point *or* °spot, best *or* °memorable °part; °main °film; *US and Canadian* drawing card; column, °piece, article, °item: *The feature of the show was the appearance of Gracie Fields. He writes the gardening feature for a Sunday newspaper.* **3** ***features***: °face, visage, physiognomy, countenance, °looks, *Slang* °mug, kisser, chips and plaice: *Her features twisted into a frown.*
—*v.* **4** °present, °promote, °publicize, advertise, highlight, °spotlight, put into the limelight, °star, °stress, °emphasize, call °attention to, °play up, °puff up, *Colloq* headline, hype: *He was featured in many films.* **5** be, °act, °perform, take *or* have a °role *or* °part, °participate, be °involved *or* drawn in: *Novels feature prominently in our publishing programme.*

federation *n.* °combination, confederacy, confederation, °amalgamation, coalition, °league, °alliance, °union, °association, *Bund*, °society: *The central government consists of a federation of states.*

fee *n.* **1** °charge, °price, °cost, °fare, °bill, °tariff, °toll, *Colloq* °damage(s): *The membership fee is £25.* **2** °pay, °payment, emolument, compensation, recompense, °honorarium, °remuneration, °rate, °wage(s), °stipend, °salary: *What is your fee per hour for proofreading?*

feeble *adj.* **1** °weak, °infirm, °frail, °puny, °slight, feckless; debilitated, enervated, °decrepit, enfeebled, °exhausted, weakened; effete, °delicate, °fragile, °powerless, °impotent, impuissant, languid, spiritless, °sickly, ailing, °unsound, °faint, °dizzy; *Colloq* woozy, *Brit* wonky: *The survivors were suffering from exposure and too feeble to walk.* **2** °flimsy, °weak, °ineffectual, °ineffective, namby-pamby, half-baked, °lame, unconvincing, °shoddy, °thin, °insubstantial, °poor, °unsatisfactory, °insufficient, °inadequate, unavailing, °meagre, °paltry, °insignificant, *Colloq* °wishy-washy, *Brit* °wet: *She gave her usual feeble excuse for being late.* **3** °weak, °obscure, °dim, °imperceptible, °faint, °distant, °indistinct, unclear: *He could see little in the feeble light from the one candle. We heard a feeble cry from under the rubble.*

feeble-minded *adj.* °stupid, °dull(-witted), witless, moronic, idiotic, imbecilic, °simple, °slow (on the uptake), slow-witted, weak-minded, dim-witted, addlepated, °halfwitted, °deficient, subnormal, mentally °defective, retarded, attocerebral, *Brit* ESN (= 'educationally subnormal'), *Colloq* °dumb, °thick, °soft in the head, boneheaded, empty-headed, °vacant, *Brit* gormless, *US* °exceptional: *Why do you spend so much time with that feeble-minded twit?*

feed *v.* **1** °provision, °cater *or* °provide (for), victual, purvey, °provender, °supply, °maintain, nurture, °nourish, °board, °support, °sustain, wine and °dine: *Is there enough to feed everyone?* **2** °eat, °devour, graze, °pasture: *Cattle feed most of the day.* **3** ***feed on*** *or* ***upon***: subsist *or* °survive *or* °depend *or* °thrive on *or* upon, be °nourished *or* °gratified *or* °supported by: *Swindlers feed on others' gullibility.*
—*n.* **4** fodder, forage, pasturage, silage, °food, °provender: *What kind of feed are you giving the sheep?*

feel *v.* **1** °touch, °see, °note, °sense, °perceive, °experience, °determine; °handle, °manipulate, °finger: *Feel how rough the skin is at this spot.* **2** °stroke, °caress, °pet, °fondle: *I like to feel a bare carpet with my toes.* **3** °sense, be °conscious of, °perceive, be °aware *or* °sensible of, °experience: *I could feel the heat of the fire across the room.* **4** °sense, °believe, °think, °perceive, °judge, °consider, deem, °know, discern, intuit, *Colloq* get *or* have the °impression, have a °hunch, °guess, have a (funny) °feeling, feel in one's bones: *I feel I have outstayed my welcome.* **5** °undergo, °sense, °suffer, °bear, °endure, °withstand, °stand, °abide, °brook, °tolerate, °go through: *Let the other team feel the agony of defeat for a change.* **6** °seem, °appear, °strike one, give the °impression, have a *or* the °feeling: *It felt as if a great weight has been lifted from me. It feels like old times. That feels silky.* **7** °seem to be, be, °regard *or* °characterize oneself as, °take oneself to be: *I feel certain that we've met before. I felt a perfect fool.* **8** ***feel for***: °sympathize *or* empathize with, commiserate with, bleed for, be °sorry for, °pity, have compassion for: *She feels for all mothers whose sons have died.* **9** ***feel like***: °incline *or* °lean to *or* °towards, °prefer, °fancy, °want, °desire, crave: *I feel like a cup of hot tea.*
—*n.* **10** °texture, °surface, °sensation, °touch, °finish: *This wood has the feel of satin.* **11** °feeling, °air, °atmosphere, °climate, ambience *or* ambiance, °sense, °note, °tone, °quality: *It's so cosy here—it has the feel of home.*

feeler *n.* **1** antenna, tentacle, palp, sensor: *Those moths have long, feathery feelers.* **2** °overture, °hint, °suggestion, foretaste, °probe, tester, sensor: *The questionnaire is a feeler put out to test public opinion.*

feeling *n.* **1** (°sense of) °touch, °sensitivity, °sense, °perception, °sensation, °sensibility: *I had no feeling in my left side.* **2** °intuition, °idea, °notion, °inkling, °suspicion, °belief, °hunch, theory, °sense; °premonition, °hint, presentiment, °sense of °foreboding, °sensation, °impression, °opinion, °view; °instinct, consciousness, awareness: *I have a feeling you're fooling. Do you ever have the feeling of being watched?* **3** °regard, °sympathy, empathy, °identification, compassion, tenderness, °appreciation, °concern, °understanding, °sensitivity, °sensibility: *He has a genuine feeling for animals.* **4** °ardour, °warmth, °passion, fervency, °fervour, ardency, °intensity, °heat, °sentiment, °emotion, vehemence: *She said she loved me with so much feeling that I thought she meant it.* **5** ***feelings***: °emotions, °sensitivity, °sympathies, °sensibilities, susceptibilities: *She hurt my feelings.* **6** °feel, °mood, °atmosphere, °climate, °sense, °air, ambience *or* ambiance: *There is a feeling of impending doom about this place.*
—*adj.* **7** sentient, °sensitive, °tender, tender-hearted, compassionate, °sympathetic: *Their behaviour did the soldiers honour as feeling men.*

feint *n.* °distraction, °mock °attack, °bluff, °dodge, °manoeuvre, °false °move, °pretence, °ruse, ploy, °subterfuge, °deception, °tactic, °stratagem, gambit, °artifice: *The attack on the flanks is merely a feint—the main thrust will be at the centre.*

fell *v.* °cut *or* °knock *or* °strike down, °floor, °prostrate, °level, hew (down), °flatten, °demolish, °mow (down); °kill: *He felled his opponent with one blow. All the trees in this area must be felled.*

fellow *n.* **1** °man, °boy, °person, °individual, gentleman, °one, *Colloq* °guy, °chap, °customer, kid, *Brit* bloke, *Slang* geezer, gink, *US old-fashioned* gazabo: *There was a fellow here asking for you today.* **2** °colleague, °associate, °comrade, °companion, °ally, °peer, compeer: *He is going to meet some of his fellows at the club.* **3** °mate, °match, counterpart, °partner, °complement, concomitant, °accessory: *I lost one glove last week and now have lost its fellow.* **4** boyfriend, °man, °sweetheart, °love, young °man; °lover, °paramour, *Formal* °suitor, *Old-fashioned* beau, *Archaic* swain, *Slang* °guy: *Bailey has been Sue's fellow for years.*
—*adj.* **5** °associate(d), affiliate(d), allied, °auxiliary, °related: *Ladies, not accorded membership in the men's club, belonged to a fellow organization. She shared her sandwiches with a fellow passenger.*

fellowship *n.* **1** °companionship, camaraderie, comradeship, amity, °brotherhood, fraternization, togetherness, °association, °friendship, companionability, sociability, intimacy: *I have always enjoyed the fellowship of my university colleagues.* **2** °society, °club,

°association, °alliance, guild, °league, °union, sisterhood, sorority, °brotherhood, °fraternity, congregation, °circle, community, °order, °organization, consortium, partnership; °lodge, °clan, °company, coterie, °set, °clique, coalition, bloc, cartel, °trust: *They belong to the worldwide fellowship of artists.* **3** friendliness, clubbiness, sociability, intimacy, amicability, affability, kindliness, cordiality, °familiarity, °affinity, °belonging, congeniality, °warmth, °hospitality: *Being a club member gives him a feeling of fellowship.*

felon *n.* °criminal, °outlaw, lawbreaker, °offender, °culprit, °miscreant, malefactor, wrongdoer: *Only if convicted of a certain class of crime is a person technically a felon.*

feminine *adj.* **1** female, womanlike, womanly, °ladylike, °submissive, deferential, amenable, °gentle, docile, °tender, °soft, °delicate: *She is much more feminine than her sister.* **2** °effeminate, womanish, unmanly, unmasculine, °sissy *or Brit* cissy, sissified *or Brit* cissified, effete, °affected: *Barry's manner and behaviour seem to become more feminine every day.*

fence *n.* **1** °barrier, °enclosure, barricade, confine, °wall, °rampart; railing(s), palisade: *Maurice had a fence put up round his house.* **2** ***on the fence***: undecided, °indecisive, vacillating, uncommitted, °uncertain, °irresolute; °impartial, °neutral, °non-partisan, unbiased, °unprejudiced, unaligned, °non-aligned, °independent: *She is on the fence with regard to the issue of capital punishment.*
—*v.* **3** °enclose, °encircle, °surround, circumscribe, °bound, coop, °restrict, hedge, confine, °fortify, °protect, °separate: *The pasture is fenced both to keep the sheep in and the wolves out. Fence off this area for a garden.* **4** parry, °avoid, °fend off, °sidestep, °dodge, °evade, hedge, stonewall, °equivocate, palter, tergiversate, vacillate, °shilly-shally, °quibble, °cavil, °beat about the bush, °qualify, prevaricate, *Colloq Brit* °waffle: *Awkward questions were adroitly fenced by the chairman. Give a straight answer and stop fencing.*

fend *v.* **1** ***fend for oneself***: °get *or* °scrape along (on one's own), °make out, °get by, °make do, °shift for oneself, take °care of *or* °provide for *or* °support oneself: *Mother didn't believe I could fend for myself.* **2** ***fend off***: °discourage, parry, °keep *or* °hold at bay, °resist, °repel, stave *or* °ward *or* °fight off, °deflect, °turn aside, avert, °divert: *We fended off our attackers for three days.*

ferment *v.* **1** °boil, effervesce, °seethe, °bubble, °foam, °froth, °brew; °rise, °raise, °work, leaven: *A rebellion is fermenting in the northern counties. Adding yeast causes the bread to ferment.* **2** °excite, °stir up, °incite, instigate, °agitate, °foment, °inflame, °rouse, °provoke: *He helped to ferment a riot.*

ferocious *adj.* °fierce, °savage, °cruel, °vicious, feral, °fell, °brutal, bestial, °merciless, °ruthless, pitiless, °inhuman, barbaric, barbarous, °violent, °destructive, °murderous, °bloodthirsty, °sanguinary, °predatory, °fiendish, diabolic(al), °devilish, hellish, °monstrous: *Cerberus, a ferocious beast with three heads, guards the gates of hell.*

fertile *adj.* °fruitful, °prolific, fecund, °productive, bounteous, °profuse, °abundant, copious, fructuous, plenteous, generative, teeming, °rich, °luxuriant: *The land was fertile enough to grow anything. This book is a fertile source of ideas.*

fertilize *v.* **1** °impregnate, inseminate, pollinate, fecundate, fructify: *The flower should be fertilized by pollen from a different stock.* **2** manure, mulch, °feed, °nourish, °enrich, °dress, compost: *The earth can be fertilized at any time.*

fervent *adj.* **1** fervid, °fiery, °burning, °glowing, °hot, °intense, °passionate, °impassioned, °ardent, °hot-headed, °inflamed, °fanatic(al), °excited, °frantic, frenzied: *Only the most fervent acolytes were ordained as ministers of the faith.* **2** °eager, °earnest, °enthusiastic, zealous, °animated, °intense, °heartfelt, °emotional: *It is my fervent desire to see you happy.* **3** °ecstatic, transported, °rapturous, °rapt, enrapt, enraptured, captivated: *The fervent crowds cheered wildly when Caesar arrived.*

fervour *n.* fervency, °ardour, °warmth, °passion, vehemence, °glow, °intensity, zeal, °eagerness, earnestness, °enthusiasm, °animation, °gusto, ebullience, °spirit, °verve: *She went about her studies with a fervour we had not seen before.*

fester *v.* **1** ulcerate, suppurate, °run, °ooze, °putrefy, putresce, necrose, °mortify, °rot, °decay, °decompose: *His entire body was covered with festering sores.* **2** °rankle, °smoulder, °gall, °chafe, °inflame: *Bitterness over the way he had been treated festered inside him for years.*

festival *n.* **1** °holiday, holy day, fête *or* fete, °feast, commemoration, anniversary: *He wanted to be with his family for the Christmas festival.* **2** °celebration, °fête, festivities, carnival, °entertainment, red-letter day, gala day, anniversary, birthday: *The town organizes a festival every autumn.*

festivity *n.* **1** rejoicing, °gaiety, °mirth, jubilation, conviviality, joyfulness, °merriment, °revelry, merrymaking, °glee, jollity, jollification, felicity, *Colloq Brit* mafficking: *There were laughter and festivity in the air.* **2** ***festivities***: °celebration(s), °festival, °party, °fun and games, °entertainment, °amusement, °hilarity, boisterousness, frivolity: *Come along and join the festivities at our house tonight.*

fetch *v.* **1** °get, °go after *or* for, °bring (back), °retrieve, °deliver, °obtain, °carry *or* convey (back): *Would you please fetch my slippers?* **2** °summon, °bring *or* °draw forth, °call, °elicit: *The doorbell fetched me from my bath.* **3** °sell for, °bring (in), °go for, °yield, °earn, °make, °cost, °realize: *These days a house near London fetches a high price.*
—*n.* **4** °reach, °stretch, °range, °span, °extent: *It is quite a long fetch across the bay.*

fetching *adj.* °attractive, alluring, °taking, winsome, °winning, °cute, °enchanting, charming, captivating, intriguing: *Fingal's sister is a fetching young lass.*

fête *n.* **1** fete, °festival, °entertainment, °reception, levee, °gala, rejoicing, °celebration, °party, °festivities, °get-together, °social, °amusement, °revel, °fair, ball, °frolic, °spree, °jamboree, carnival, °event, °occasion, *Colloq* blow-out, shindig, bash, do, bust, *Slang US and Canadian* wingding, °blast: *You are invited to our annual fête on New Year's Eve.*
—*v.* **2** °entertain, °feast, roll *or* bring out the red carpet for, wine and °dine, °celebrate, °honour, lionize, °fuss over, kill the fatted calf for: *Fiona's book was a great success and she was fêted all over Europe.*

fetish *n.* **1** °charm, °amulet, °talisman, totem, *Rare* periapt: *Round his neck he wore the dreaded fetish of the fish god.* **2** °obsession, compulsion, °fixation, °mania, *idée fixe*: *It's a fetish of hers to kiss only under the mistletoe.*

feud *n.* **1** °dispute, °conflict, °vendetta, °hostility, °strife, enmity, °animosity, hatred, °antagonism, °rivalry, °ill will, bad blood, °hard feelings, contention, °discord, °grudge, °dissension, °disagreement, °argument, °quarrel, bickering, squabble, falling out, estrangement: *A silly feud broke out over whose turn it was to bring the Christmas goose.*
—*v.* **2** °dispute, °quarrel, °bicker, °disagree, °conflict, °row, °fight, °fall out, °clash, be at °odds, be at daggers drawn: *The Hatfields and McCoys feuded for decades.*

feverish *adj.* °inflamed, flushed, °burning, °fiery, °hot, °ardent, °fervent, hot-blooded, °passionate, frenzied, °frantic, °excited, frenetic, zealous; *Pathology* febrile, pyretic, pyrexic: *I was looking forward to our rendezvous with feverish excitement.*

few *adj.* **1** °hardly *or* °scarcely any, not °many, °insufficient; infrequent, °occasional: *Few people came to my party. He is a man of few words.*
—*n.* **2** °handful, some, °scattering: *I invited a lot of people, but only a few came.*

—*pron.* **3** (only) one or two, not °many: *Many apply but few are chosen.*

fiancé(e) *n.* betrothed, wife- *or* bride- *or* husband-to-be, intended: *He went out to buy a ring for his fiancée.*

fiasco *n.* °failure, °disaster, °muddle, °mess, abortion, °botch, *Colloq* °fizzle, °flop: *My effort to help Donald with his maths homework was a complete fiasco.*

fib *n.* **1** °falsehood, (little) white °lie, untruth, prevarication, °fabrication, °invention, misrepresentation, °story, (fairy) °tale, fiction; °lie; *Colloq* °tall °story, *US* °tall °tale, cock-and-bull °story, whopper: *I told a little fib when I said my grandmother was ill.*
—*v.* **2** prevaricate, °misrepresent, fudge, °falsify, palter; °lie; *Colloq* °waffle: *They admitted they had fibbed about who had thrown the egg.*

fibre *n.* **1** filament, °thread, strand, fibril, tendril: *This fabric is woven from cotton fibre.* **2** °texture, °structure, °material, °fabric: *The fibre of this rock is granular.* **3** °essence, °character, °nature, °mould, °composition, constitution, °substance, °quality, °stripe, °cast, °make-up: *Love for him is wrapped up in the very fibre of her being.*

fickle *adj.* °flighty, °capricious, °frivolous, unpredictable, °moody, °giddy, °fanciful, °whimsical, °fitful, mercurial, °volatile, °unstable, °changeable, mutable, °inconstant, changeful, unsteady, unsteadfast, °indecisive, undecided, vacillating *or rarely* vacillant, unsure, °uncertain, °irresolute, wavering, °erratic, °unreliable, undependable, °irresponsible, untrustworthy, °faithless, unfaithful, °disloyal, *Colloq* °wishy-washy: *That fickle woman has already taken up with someone else. You should know how fickle the tastes of the public are.*

fictional *adj.* °unreal, °imaginary, invented, made-up, °mythical, °fanciful; °legendary, °fabulous: *The newspaper article was a hoax—completely fictional. Lorna Doone is Janet's favourite fictional heroine.*

fictitious *adj.* **1** imagined, °imaginary, °non-existent, °unreal, made-up, invented, fabricated, °mythical, °fancied, °fanciful, fictive, °untrue, apocryphal: *The claim that an article had appeared was completely fictitious.* **2** °false, °counterfeit, °bogus, °artificial, °spurious; °assumed, improvised, made-up, invented, make-believe, °imaginary, *Colloq* °phoney *or US also* phony: *When arrested they gave fictitious names.*

fiddle *v.* **1** Often, ***fiddle with***: °meddle (with), °tamper (with), °interfere (with), °alter, °falsify, °fix; °cheat, °swindle, flimflam; *Colloq* finagle, *Brit* cook: *The treasurer had been fiddling the accounts for years.* **2** Often, ***fiddle with*** or ***about*** or ***around***: °toy *or* °trifle *or* °fidget (with), °twiddle *or* °play *or* °tinker (with), °fool *or* °fuss (with), *Colloq* °mess *or* °muck (about *or* around) (with), frivol (away), °monkey (around) (with): *He sat there nervously fiddling with his ear. Stop fiddling about and get on with your work.*
—*n.* **3** *Brit* swindle, °fraud, °racket, thimblerig, *US* shell-game, *Slang* skin °game, °funny business, °monkey business: *The tax inspector caught him in some fiddle with his business expenses.* **4** violin, viola, viol, cello, violoncello, kit: *He played fiddle for the tsar.*

fiddlesticks *interj.* °Nonsense!, °Rubbish!, *Colloq* Fiddle-de-dee!, Balderdash!, °Stuff and Nonsense!, Poppycock!, Pish and tush!, Tommy-rot!, Hogwash!, Eyewash!, Boloney!, Bilge-water!, °Moonshine!, Humbug!, Bosh!, Fiddle-faddle!, Bull!, Rot!, *Brit* Codswallop!, *Taboo slang* Bullshit!, Balls!, Crap!, Horseshit!, *Brit* Bollocks! *or* Ballocks!: *When he said he'd pay what he owed, I just said, 'Fiddlesticks!'*

fidget *v.* **1** °squirm, twitch, °shuffle, °wriggle, wiggle, °fiddle, °fuss; °fret, °chafe: *Stop fidgeting and tell me the truth!*
—*n.* **2** fusspot, fuss-budget, cat on hot bricks, *US* cat on a hot tin roof, *Colloq US* °nervous Nellie: *If her conscience is clear, why is she such a fidget?* **3** ***the fidgets***: restlessness, fidgetiness, dither, uneasiness, the °jitters, nervousness, itchiness, *Colloq* heebie-jeebies, jim-jams, ants in one's pants: *Whenever he tells a lie he gets a bad case of the fidgets.*

field *n.* **1** °ground, °land, arable, °pasture, grassland, °meadow, °green, °lawn, °common, clearing, °tract, °area, acreage, *Literary* greensward, lea, sward; *Archaic* mead: *The house looks out over the fields.* **2** battlefield, battleground, airfield; (cricket) °pitch, football *or* hockey *or* soccer field, *American football* gridiron: *We marched onto the field prepared for anything.* **3** °competition, competitors, players, entrants, contestants, participants, candidates, possibilities, applicants: *Who can match you among today's field?* **4** °area, °domain, °realm, °department, °territory, °province, °sphere, °scope, °division, °interest, °line, métier, °discipline, bailiwick, °speciality *or US* specialty, specialization, °expertise, °forte, °strength: *She is certainly the leading expert in her field. My field is biochemistry.*
—*v.* **5** catch, °stop, °return, °retrieve, °pick up: *Did you see how Border fielded that ball?* **6** °answer, °reply to, °respond to, °handle, °manipulate, °deal with, °react to, °cope with: *The candidate adroitly fielded questions from the press.*

fiend *n.* **1** See **devil,** above. **2** °addict, °maniac, °fanatic; °fan, aficionado, °enthusiast, °devotee, °hound, °follower, *Colloq* buff, nut, *Slang* °freak: *He's a Welsh rarebit fiend.*

fiendish *adj.* °cruel, °savage, °inhuman, °monstrous, °ghoulish, °malignant, malevolent, malicious, °wicked, °evil, °bad, black-hearted, °satanic, °devilish, Mephistophelian, demonic, demoniac(al), °diabolic(al), cacodemonic, hellish, °infernal: *He sniggered with fiendish glee as he tightened the thumbscrew.*

fierce *adj.* **1** °ferocious, °savage, °wild, °truculent, brutish, feral, bestial, tigerish, °brutal, °cruel, °fell, °murderous, bloodthirsty, °sanguinary, °homicidal, barbaric, barbarous, °inhuman, °dangerous: *The fierce beasts will tear you limb from limb.* **2** intractable, °angry, °furious, °hostile, °aggressive, vehement, frenzied, °stormy, °violent, turbulent, °wild, °tempestuous, °tumultuous, raging, °merciless, uncontrollable: *The old curmudgeon is in a fierce mood again today. A fierce storm raged for three days.* **3** °severe, °awful, °dreadful, °intense, °keen, dire, °bitter, °biting, racking: *Wear warm clothes to protect you from the fierce cold.*

fiercely *adv.* °very, °extremely, °exceedingly, vehemently, intensely, impetuously, violently, furiously, ferociously, viciously, savagely: *She refuses to deal with anyone who is so fiercely competitive.*

fiery *adj.* **1** °burning, °flaming, blazing, °hot, red-hot, white-hot, overheated; afire, on °fire, in flames, °ablaze: *Fiery lava burst from the volcano.* **2** °glowing, red, °incandescent, °brilliant, °luminous, °glaring, gleaming, °radiant; aglow, afire: *We watched the fiery sunset fade into azure hues.* **3** °ardent, °eager, °spirited, °passionate, °excited, °excitable, peppery, irascible, °touchy, °irritable, edgy, °hotheaded, °fierce: *I had best not be late as my boss has a fiery temper.*

fight *v.* **1** contend (with), °battle, °conflict (with), °encounter, °war (against), °engage, °clash, °feud (with), °combat, bear *or* take up arms (against), °brawl, °struggle *or* °strive (with *or* against), cross swords (with), °close (with), °come to *or* °exchange blows (with), go to *or* °wage °war (with *or* against), joust (with), °grapple *or* °wrestle (with), °skirmish (with), tussle *or* scuffle (with *or* against); °box, °spar; *Old-fashioned* °broil: *He offered to fight anyone in the place. Why are the boys always fighting?* **2** °dispute, °question, confront, °contest, °oppose, °contradict, °defy, confute, °protest, °resist, °rail *or* °struggle against, °withstand, refute, oppugn, make *or* take a °stand against, contravene, confound: *He has sworn to fight prejudice wherever he finds it.* **3** °rise up, make *or* take a °stand, °struggle, take up arms: *It is better to fight for the good than to rail at the ill.* **4** °argue, °dispute, °bicker, °quarrel, wrangle, squabble, spat, °tiff, °fall out (over), have words, °disagree, °row, altercate, °debate: *I hear the neighbours fight every night.* **5** ***fight off***: °repel, °repulse: *Prepare to fight off anyone trying to come over the side!* **6** ***fight shy of***: °avoid,

keep *or* remain °aloof from *or* of, keep away from: *She usually fights shy of going to cocktail parties.*
—*n.* **7** °battle, °conflict, °bout, duel, (single) °combat, monomachy, one-on-one, °action, warfare, °clash, hostilities, °war, °match, °struggle, °engagement, °meeting, °encounter, °contest, fighting, °brawl, Donnybrook, affray, °fray, °fracas, °disturbance, °riot, °row, mêlée *or* melee, tussle, scuffle, °scrimmage, °skirmish, °brush, *Colloq* free-for-all, set-to, °scrap, *Brit* scrum, bovver, *Slang US* rumble, *Old-fashioned* °broil: *Three policeman were injured in the hour-long fight.* **8** altercation, °argument, °quarrel, °feud, °dispute, °run-in, °disagreement, °dissension, dissidence, dissent, °difference (of opinion), squabble, bickering, spat, °misunderstanding, °row, °discord, *Colloq* ruckus: *Such fights between husband and wife happen all the time.* **9** pugnacity, mettle, militancy, belligerence, truculence, °spirit, °pluck, zeal, °enthusiasm, °zest: *She had enough fight left in her to go on to win.*

figure *n.* **1** °physique, °build, °shape, °form, configuration, conformation, °body, °outline, °silhouette; °cut, °cast; *Slang* bod, chassis: *It's exercise that gives Kathy such a fine figure.* **2** °appearance, °image, °likeness, °representation, °semblance: *The vision came to him in the figure of a dragon.* **3** °person, °individual, °human (being): *A burly figure loomed up out of the fog.* **4** °statue, effigy, °sculpture, bust, °mould, °cast, °image, °representation, °idol, icon: *Hundreds of figures are carved into the stone of the temple façade.* **5** °picture, °illustration, diagram, °drawing, sketch, °plate: *See Figure 12 for a graph showing the rate of inflation for the past decade.* **6** °personality, °celebrity, °somebody, °leader, °personage, °worthy, °notable, °individual, °presence, °force, °character: *Chaplin looms large as a figure in the history of comedy.* **7** °number, numeral, cipher, digit; °character, °symbol, °device, °sign; °design, °pattern, °motif, °emblem: *His salary is in six figures.*
—*v.* **8** Often, ***figure up***: °calculate, °compute, °reckon, °work out; °count, °enumerate, numerate, °total, °tot up, °tally, °sum: *Please figure up how much I owe you.* **9** °picture, °imagine, °think, °take, °reckon, °consider, °calculate, °judge, °believe; °assume, °presume, °suppose; °accept, °acknowledge, °concede: *I never figured her to be the guilty one.* **10** °act, °participate, take *or* play a °part *or* °role, °appear, °feature, have a °place; be included *or* mentioned, be featured *or* °conspicuous: *He does not figure in my plans.* **11** ***figure on*** *or* ***upon***: **a** °rely *or* °depend on *or* upon, °count on *or* upon, °trust in, put °faith in: *You mustn't figure on his help.* **b** °plan on *or* upon, take into °consideration *or* °account, °consider, make °allowance for: *They were figuring on consumer demand for a better mousetrap.* **12** ***figure out***: **a** °calculate, °reckon, °compute, °work out: *I haven't yet figured out last year's profits and losses.* **b** °decipher, °translate, °understand, °interpret, °solve, °grasp, °get, °fathom, °see, °perceive, *Colloq* °dig, make head(s) or tail(s) of, °get through one's head, °get the hang *or* °drift of, catch on (to), get a fix on, *Brit* °twig, suss out: *Can you figure out what this article is trying to say?*

figurehead *n.* °puppet, °dummy, marionette, °mouthpiece, *Brit* man of straw, *US and Canadian* straw man, *Colloq* °front man, *Chiefly US* °front: *The king is a mere figurehead with no power at all.*

file *n.* **1** °document, documentation, dossier, °case, °data, folder, portfolio, °information: *Interpol has files on Cowdery's activities going back ten years.* **2** °line, °queue, column, °row, °rank: *The file of armoured vehicles stretched for miles.*
—*v.* **3** classify, °organize, systematize, °categorize, alphabetize, chronologize, °order, °arrange, pigeonhole, interfile, °put *or* °place in °order, °register, °record, °enter: *Must all this correspondence be filed today?* **4** °submit, °send in, °complete, °fill in *or US and Canadian also* °fill out, °enter: *I have already filed my application for a transfer.* **5** °walk, °march, troop, °parade: *Please file into the classroom and take your seats.*

fill *v.* **1** °crowd, °stuff, °cram, °jam, °load, °burden, °pack, °squeeze: *A huge number of people filled the stadium.* **2** °top (off), °top up, fill up, make °full; °inflate, °swell, °stretch, °blow up, distend, °expand: *Pour in just enough to fill the bottle. See if you can fill the balloon. Wind filled the sails.* **3** Sometimes, ***fill up***: °supply, °provide, °furnish: *Irena has filled her house with paintings.* **4** °meet, °satisfy, °fulfil, °answer: *Will a dozen fill your needs for a while?* **5** °satisfy, °satiate, bloat, sate, °gorge, °stuff; °stock: *The guests filled themselves with choice foods at the reception.* **6** °abound in, overflow, be °abundant *or* °plentiful in: *Trout filled the lake.* **7** °close, °stop (up), °block, °stuff, °plug, caulk, °seal: *The dentist had to fill two cavities.* **8** °occupy, °take over, °discharge, °carry out, do, °execute: *Can you fill her job while she's away?* **9** ***fill in*** *or US and Canadian also* ***out***: **a** °make out, °complete, °answer: *Please fill in this application.* **b** take the °place, °stand in, °substitute: *Could you fill in during my secretary's absence?* **c** °inform, °tell, °advise, °let in on, °notify, bring up to °date, °share, °let in on: *Don will fill you in on the details later.* **10** ***fill out***: **a** °swell, °expand, °grow, distend, °stretch; fatten, °increase: *The sails filled out in the freshening breeze.* **b** *US* fill in. See **9a.**
—*n.* **11** ***one's fill***: °plenty, °enough; °surfeit, sufficiency: *We ate our fill and left.*

filling *n.* filler, stuffing, padding, wadding; °contents, components, *Colloq* innards: *What kind of filling do you like in a pie?*

film *n.* **1** coating, °skin, °coat, membrane, °peel, integument, layer, overlay, covering, °cover, °sheet, dusting, °veil, *Technical* pellicle: *There is a film of grease over everything.* **2** motion °picture, °movie, °picture; videotape; *Colloq* flick, pic; video: *Why do they show the same films every Christmas?* **3** °veil, °screen, murkiness, °blur, smokescreen, haze, °mist, haziness, mistiness, cloud, °vapour, °fog, steam: *I could barely make out the road through the film on the windscreen.*
—*v.* **4** film over, °coat, °cover, °dim, °obscure, °fade (away), °veil, °screen, °blur, blear, °mist, cloud, °glaze: *The pond filmed over with bacteria. Her eyes filmed with tears.* **5** °photograph, °shoot, °take, (video)tape: *If the director insists, then the scene must be filmed again.*

filmy *adj.* **1** gauzy, gossamer(-like), °sheer, °delicate, diaphanous, °transparent, translucent, °flimsy, °light, cobwebby, °insubstantial, °see-through, peekaboo: *Phoebe looked very seductive in her filmy negligee.* **2** °murky, blurry, cloudy, °hazy, °misty, bleary, blurred, °dim, clouded, beclouded, milky, °pearly, °opalescent: *We inched down the cliff in the filmy light of the moon.*

filter *n.* **1** sieve, colander, °riddle, °screen, strainer, gauze, °cloth, cheesecloth, membrane: *To allow the liquid to pass through, a clean filter must be used.*
—*v.* **2** Sometimes, ***filter out***: °strain, °screen, °sift, winnow, °clarify, °refine, °purify, °clean; °separate, weed out, °exclude, °eliminate: *Some people filter tap water to improve its taste. This company would be improved if we could filter out the undesirable elements.* **3** leach, °percolate, °drip, seep, dribble, °trickle, °drain, °run *or* °pass through, °ooze: *The rainwater is filtered through fine sand to purify it.*

filth *n.* **1** sewage *or* sewerage, °dirt, slime, °muck, °sludge, sullage, effluent, °pollution, °trash, °rubbish, °garbage, °refuse, ordure, (night-)°soil, excrement, faeces, excreta, manure, droppings, guano, °dung, °foul °matter, filthiness, offal, leavings, carrion, °decay, putrescence, putrefaction, *Slang* crud, *Brit* gunge, *US* grunge, *Taboo slang* shit: *Cleaning the filth from the Augean stables was the fifth labour of Hercules.* **2** corruption, vileness, baseness, foulness, rottenness, debasement, defilement, °taint, °pollution, adulteration, °perversion, °degradation; sullying, besmirchment: *Sodom and Gomorrah were destroyed along with their filth.* **3** indecency, obscenity, smut, °pornography, corruption, nastiness, °vulgarity, grossness: *The censors forbade the showing of films with any hint of filth.*

filthy *adj.* **1** defiled, polluted, tainted, °foul, °nasty, °dirty, unclean, °vile, °putrid, °rotten, fetid *or* foetid, maggoty, fly-blown, purulent, feculent, faecal, scummy, °slimy, mucky, *Slang* cruddy, *Brit* gungy, *US* grungy: *That city's public lavatories are the filthiest I have ever seen.* **2** °dirty, °unwashed, begrimed, squalid, °sordid, °shabby, soiled, °low, stained, grimy, °bedraggled, °unkempt, slovenly, °sloppy, °mean, °scurvy, °disgusting, °miserable, °wretched, *Slang Brit* gungy, *US* grungy: *The filthy beggar turned out to be Holmes in disguise.* **3** °immoral, °taboo *or* tabu, °indecent, °impure, °obscene, smutty, °pornographic, X-rated, depraved, °corrupt, °dirty, °lewd, °lascivious, licentious, °gross, °offensive, °coarse, °bawdy, ribald, °blue, °suggestive, foul-mouthed, dirty-minded, filthy-minded: *Customs officers confiscated thousands of filthy books, magazines, films, and videos.*

final *adj.* **1** ending, concluding, terminating, finishing, closing, °last, °terminal, °ultimate, °end: *The final sentence needs rewriting.* **2** conclusive, decisive, unalterable, °irreversible, °irrevocable, °incontrovertible, irrefutable, °indisputable, unchangeable, immutable, °definitive; settled, °fixed, °absolute, °certain, °sure: *Those are my final words on the subject. We made a final series of measurements.*

finality *n.* conclusiveness, decisiveness, unalterability, irreversibility, irrevocableness, incontrovertibility, irrefutability, indisputability, unchangeability, immutability, definitiveness, °certainty, certitude, sureness, fixedness: *There is an air of finality in the way she gives orders.*

finalize *v.* conclude, °settle, °complete, °decide, *Colloq* °wrap up, °clinch, °sew up: *We finalized the agreement yesterday by signing the contract.*

finally *adv.* **1** at (long) °last, lastly, °eventually, in the °end, °ultimately, at °length, when all is said and done, in the long °run, at the °end of the day, at the °last °moment: *We finally arrived in port.* **2** conclusively, °once and for all, decisively, irrevocably, in °fine, °completely, inexorably, °absolutely, definitively, °definitely, for °good, °for °ever, for all °time: *I didn't want to commit myself finally till I'd seen the plans.*

finance *n.* **1** °resource(s), banking, accounting, economics, °money (°management), °business, °commerce, (°financial) affairs, investment: *Bendick is the officer in charge of finance for the company.* **2** ***finances***: °capital, °money, °cash, °funds, °resources, °assets, holdings, °wealth, wherewithal: *Have you the finances needed to buy the house?*
—*v.* **3** °fund, subvene, °invest in, °back, capitalize, °underwrite, °subsidize, °pay for, *Colloq US* bankroll: *The new enterprise is being financed entirely by small investors.*

financial *adj.* °monetary, pecuniary, °fiscal, °economic: *We must get the financial affairs of the country in order.*

financier *n.* capitalist, banker, plutocrat, investor, °backer, *US* money-man, *Colloq* angel: *The financiers suggest switching investment from shares to bonds.*

find *v.* **1** °discover, °come across, °happen *or* °come on *or* upon, °hit upon *or* on, °chance *or* °stumble on *or* upon; °encounter, °bump into: *We've found a tiny bistro on the Left Bank where we like to go.* **2** Often, ***find out***: uncover, °discover, °unearth, °lay one's hand(s) on, °turn up, °come up with, °reveal, bring to °light, °light upon *or* on, °catch °sight of, °see, espy, descry, °detect, °learn, °spot, °locate, °track down; °identify, °become °aware of, °determine, ascertain, put one's °finger on, °point to, *Colloq* °tumble to, *Brit* °twig; *Slang* °finger, rumble, *Brit* suss out: *The police are trying to find the murderer. Can you find who did it?* **3** °discover, °perceive, °see, °understand, °notice, °mark, °remark, °note, °distinguish, discern; °realize: *I find nothing odd about her attire.* **4** °consider, °think, °regard, °view, °feel *or* °discover to be: *I have always found Lady Sharpless exceedingly dull. He finds it impossible to refuse her demands.* **5** °get, °obtain, °procure, °secure, °acquire, °win, °gain; °experience: *We despair of finding customers for our services in these hard times. He found relief only in painkillers.* **6** °recover, °locate, °get back; repossess, °recoup: *I hope you find the earring you lost.* **7** °summon (up), °call up, °command, °gather (up), °muster (up), °rouse, arouse, awaken: *I tried to find the courage to ask her to marry me.* **8** °set aside, °allot, °assign, °manage, °get: *Have you found the time to read Connie's new book?* **9** °judge, °decide *or* °determine to be, °pronounce, °declare: *A jury found her guilty. The judge found in favour of the plaintiff.*
—*n.* **10** °discovery, °catch, °bargain, °deal; °boon, °windfall: *The gold doubloon was the find of a lifetime.*

finding *n.* **1** °discovery, °find: *The findings from Pompeii are in the Museum of Portici.* **2** °judgement, °decree, verdict, °decision, °determination, °pronouncement, °declaration, conclusion: *The findings of the Law Lords are final.*

fine[1] *adj.* **1** °superior, °excellent, °superb, °magnificent, °supreme, °marvellous, °exceptional, °splendid, °exquisite, °elegant, first-class, °first-rate, °prime, °choice, °select, top-grade, high-grade, top-drawer, °quality, °admirable, °good, °satisfactory, *Colloq* out of this °world, °great, °OK *or* okay, peachy, °keen, *Brit* tickety-boo, *US* °neat, *Australian* bonzer, *Slang* °swell, °cool, *Brit old-fashioned* °ripping, *Dialectal* °champion: *He is a connoisseur of fine paintings. She turned in a fine performance.* **2** °sunny, °fair, °bright, °clear, cloudless, balmy, °pleasant, °dry, °nice: *It was a fine day for a picnic.* **3** enjoyable, °satisfying, °entertaining, amusing, °good, °interesting, °pleasant, °nice: *Thank you for inviting us to such a fine party.* **4** °accomplished, °skilful, consummate, °outstanding, masterly, °brilliant, °virtuoso: *Ann-Sofie is a fine pianist.* **5** °delicate, °subtle, °exquisite, well-made, °dainty, °elegant; °superior, °excellent, °outstanding: *What a fine example of miniature-painting!* **6** °delicate, °dainty, °thin, gossamer, diaphanous, gauzy, °sheer, °slender, °frail, °flimsy, filamentous, threadlike: *The sword hung over Damocles' head by a fine thread.* **7** powdered, powdery, pulverized, comminuted, crushed, fine-grained: *As soon as they touched the papyrus, it disintegrated into a fine powder.* **8** °sharp, °keen, keen-edged, razor-sharp, °pointed, °acute: *The points of the sea urchin's spines are so fine you don't feel them enter.* **9** °subtle, °delicate, °refined, °acute, °keen, °discriminating, °critical, °precise, °nice, °hair-splitting: *There is sometimes a fine distinction between pleasure and pain.* **10** good-looking, °handsome, °attractive, °striking, °beautiful, pretty, °lovely, °seemly, °fair, °comely, *Colloq US* °cute, *Scots* °bonny: *Jeanette married a fine young man.* **11** °meritorious, °worthy, commendable, °admirable, °excellent, °superb, °splendid, °good, *Colloq* °great: *She has displayed fine courage in the face of terrible family problems.* **12** °healthy, °well, healthful, °robust, all °right, *Colloq* °OK *or* okay: *I told the doctor that I was feeling fine.* **13** °close: *Arriving at the airport with only minutes to spare is cutting it pretty fine.*

fine[2] *n.* **1** °penalty, °charge, °fee, mulct, °forfeit, amercement; forfeiture: *He was unable to pay the parking fine.*
—*v.* **2** °penalize, °charge, mulct, amerce: *She was fined for parking at a bus stop.*

finery *n.* °decoration(s), °ornaments, °trappings, trinkets, frippery, °showy °dress, *Colloq* °best bib and tucker, Sunday °best, Sunday °clothes, °gear, glad rags: *They were all dressed in their finery at the reception.*

finesse *n.* **1** artfulness, °subtlety, cunning, craftiness, cleverness, °strategy, shrewdness, °skill, °style, °dash, élan, °panache, °knack, skilfulness, °talent, adroitness, expertness, °expertise, adeptness, °proficiency, °ability, °facility: *I admire the finesse with which she persuaded him to give the painting to the museum.* **2** °trick, °artifice, °stratagem, °wile, °ruse, °scheme, °machination, °intrigue, °device, °expedient, °manoeuvre, °deception, °deceit: *He used every finesse in the book to get her to work for him.* **3** °tact, °diplomacy,

°discretion, °grace, °taste, °delicacy, °polish, °refinement, °elegance: *With infinite finesse, Lord Lacey suggested that the duchess might like to stay the night.* —*v.* **4** °manoeuvre, °manipulate, °bluff, °trick, delude, °deceive, °fool, °outwit, °hoodwink, *Colloq* finagle, *Slang* con: *She was finessed into making him heir to her fortune.*

finger *n.* **1** digit: *How many fingers am I holding up?* **2** ***have a finger in***: be *or* become *or* get °involved in, °figure in, have a hand in, °influence, °interfere in, °tamper *or* °meddle *or* °tinker *or* °monkey with: *I knew that Lightfoot must have had a finger in the deal.* **3** ***keep one's fingers crossed***: °hope *or* °pray for the best, touch *or esp. US* knock wood: *I'm sure you'll win, but I'll keep my fingers crossed just the same.* **4** ***lay*** *or* ***put a finger on***: (so much as) °touch, °strike, °hit, °punch: *If you lay a finger on her, you'll have to answer to me!* **5** ***lay*** *or* ***put one's finger on***: **a** °recall, °remember, °recollect, bring *or* call to °mind, °think of, °pin down: *I can't quite put my finger on the date when we met.* **b** °locate, °find, °discover, °unearth, °lay *or* °put one's hands on, °track down, °get °hold of, °come by, °acquire; °buy, °purchase: *I was finally able to put my finger on the book you asked for.* **c** °indicate, °identify, °point to, °pin down, *Colloq* °zero (in) on: *Frank put his finger on the problem at once.* **6** ***(not) lift*** *or* ***raise (even) a (little) finger***: make an °attempt *or* °effort, °offer, make a °move, °contribute, do one's °part, do anything *or* something: *She didn't so much as lift a finger when I needed her.* **7** ***pull*** *or* ***get one's finger out***: °get on with it, stop delaying *or* procrastinating, *Colloq* °get cracking: *He should have finished by now, and I wish he'd pull his finger out.* **8** ***put the finger on***: °accuse, °inform on *or* against, °tell *or* °tattle on, °betray, bear °witness, *Slang* snitch *or* squeal on, peach on: *After Louise put the finger on the kingpin, the cops arrested him.* **9** ***slip through one's fingers***: °elude, °escape, °get away, vanish, °disappear: *Despite the cordon round the house, the fugitive slipped through our fingers.* **10** ***twist*** *or* ***wrap around one's little finger***: °control, °dominate, °lord it over, have under °control, °manipulate, °manoeuvre, °wield °power *or* °authority over, have under one's °thumb, have the upper hand over, be °master of, °influence, make subservient: *She has her father twisted around her little finger, and can do no wrong in his eyes.* —*v.* **11** °touch, °handle, °feel; °toy *or* °play *or* °fiddle with: *He was quite nervous and kept fingering his tie.* **12** °identify, °point out, °put the finger on: *It was too late, the mob had already fingered Slats for assassination.*

finicky *adj.* **1** finical, °fussy, °fastidious, °critical, °difficult, °meticulous, °hard to °please, (over-) °delicate, (over-)°dainty, (over-)°particular, over-nice, over-precise, niminy-piminy, punctilious, (over-) °scrupulous, *Colloq* pernickety *or US also* persnickety, °choosy, nit-picking, picky: *No one can work for him—he's too finicky.* **2** °fussy, °elaborate, °detailed, °fine, °delicate: *Notice the tiny, finicky engraving on this watch-case.*

finish *v.* **1** °stop, conclude, °end, °cease: *When you have finished eating, please clear the table.* **2** °complete, °accomplish, °perfect, °achieve, °carry out, °fulfil, consummate, °clinch, write 'finis' to, *Colloq* °wrap up: *We finished the work on time.* **3** Sometimes, ***finish off***: °dispose of, °dispatch *or* despatch, °exhaust, °consume, °eat *or* °drink (up), °use (up), °devour, °drain, *Colloq* °polish off: *We finished the last of the beer last night.* **4** Sometimes, ***finish off***: °kill, °exterminate, annihilate, °destroy, get °rid of, °dispose of, °dispatch *or* despatch, put an °end to, administer *or* deliver *or* give the *coup de grâce*, bring down, °overcome, °beat, °defeat, °conquer, °best, worst, *Colloq* °polish off, °terminate, *Slang* °bump off, °rub out, *US* °waste, ice: *The cavalry finished off the last of the enemy. The contender was finished in the third round.* **5** Sometimes, ***finish up***: conclude, °close, °terminate, °wind up, °end, culminate: *He goes straight home when he finishes work. When will you finish?* **6** Sometimes, ***finish up***: °end up, °settle: *Where did you finish up after the party?* **7** Sometimes, ***finish off***: °perfect, put the °final touches on, °polish, put a finish on: *He finishes fine furniture for a living.* **8** ***finish with***: °release, °let °go, have *or* be done with, °let °loose, set °free: *I'll finish with you later, young man!* —*n.* **9** conclusion, °termination, °end, °close, closing, °completion, culmination, ending, finale, *Colloq* winding up, *US* wind-up: *Tomorrow is the finish of the hunting season.* **10** °death, °killing, annihilation, extermination, °downfall, °destruction, °defeat: *A major catastrophe spelt the finish of the dinosaurs.* **11** °polish, °surface, °texture: *Just feel the finish on this gunstock!*

finite *adj.* °limited, bounded, °bound, restricted, delimited, numerable, countable: *It has been shown that there are a finite number of grains of sand in the universe.*

fire *n.* **1** °flame(s), °blaze; conflagration, °holocaust, inferno: *We gathered round the roaring fire.* **2** °feeling, °passion, °ardour, ardency, °fervour, fervency, °intensity, °vigour, °spirit, °energy, vim, vivacity, °sparkle, °animation, liveliness, °verve, °pep, élan, éclat, °dash, °vitality, °eagerness, °enthusiasm, fever, feverishness: *I have never seen the role of Carmen performed with such fire.* **3** firing, fusillade, °volley, barrage, bombardment, salvo, cannonade, shelling, broadside, °flak: *The fire from the guns shook the house.* **4** ***hang fire***: °delay, be delayed, be in °abeyance, be suspended, be shelved, be °put off, be postponed, be up in the °air, *Colloq* be put on °hold, be (put) on the back burner: *The decision is hanging fire till tomorrow.* **5** ***on fire***: afire, °burning, blazing, alight, aflame, °flaming; °ardent, °passionate, °fervent, fervid, hot-blooded, °intense, aroused, stirred, stimulated, °enthusiastic, fired up, °eager, inspired, °excited: *The building is on fire: you must leave at once. My very soul is on fire when I think of you.* **6** ***play with fire***: undertake a °risk *or* °hazard *or* °peril, run a °risk, °risk (something *or* everything), imperil *or* °endanger (something), tempt °fate, live °dangerously: *He warned people not to play with fire by stirring up racial hatred.* **7** ***set fire to***: See **8**, below. —*v.* **8 a** set fire to, set afire, set on fire, ignite, set alight, kindle, spark (off), put to the torch, °burn, *Slang US* torch: *Arsonists fired our headquarters last night.* **b** Sometimes, ***fire up***: °inflame, impassion, °incite, °excite, °provoke, °foment, °whip up, arouse, °rouse, °work up, enkindle, °light a fire under, °stimulate, inspirit, °motivate, °move, °stir, °animate, °inspire, °awaken, °energize, °vitalize, vivify: *She fired the crowd's emotions with her impassioned speech.* **9** °discharge, °shoot, °let °go (with), °launch, °propel, °throw, catapult, °hurl: *He fired the missile towards the enemy.* **10** detonate, °set off, ignite, °set fire to, °light, °let off: *It is against the law to fire any explosives in this area.* **11** °discharge, °dismiss, oust, °let °go, cashier, give (someone) °notice, *Brit* make *or* declare °redundant, *Colloq Brit* ask for *or* get (someone's) cards, *US* give (someone) a pink slip; *Slang* bounce, give (someone) the bounce, axe, give (someone) the axe, show (someone) the door, can, give (someone) the (old) heave-ho, °give (someone) his *or* her (*Brit*) marching orders *or* (*US*) walking papers, *Brit* °sack, give (someone) the °sack, °boot (someone) out, give (someone) the boot: *They fired me last month and I can't find work.*

firm *adj.* **1** °compact, °solid, °dense, compressed, condensed, concentrated, °rigid, °stiff, °hard, unyielding, °inflexible, inelastic: *I prefer a firm mattress.* **2** °stable, °fixed, °fast, °secure, °steady, °solid, stationary, anchored, moored, unmovable, °immovable: *This pole is firmer than that one.* **3** °steady, °strong, °sturdy, °tight, unwavering, unshakable *or* unshakeable, unswerving: *What we need is a firm hand at the controls.* **4** °resolute, °determined, dogged, °definite, resolved, °positive, decisive, °decided, °set on *or* upon, °steadfast, °constant, unflinching, °staunch, unshaken, unshakeable *or* unshakable, °immovable, °inflexible,

°rigid, unwavering, undeviating, unchanging, unchangeable, °obstinate, obdurate, °stubborn, °strict, unyielding, unbending, unalterable: *Father was firm about my not staying out past midnight.*
—*v.* **5** Often, ***firm up***: consolidate, °establish, °settle (down), °solidify, °resolve, °determine, °set up: *We firmed up the terms of the contract. Sugar prices firmed today.*
—*n.* **6** °company, °organization, corporation, °limited °company, °public °limited °company, plc, partnership, proprietorship, °business, °enterprise, °concern, °house, conglomerate, multinational (°company), cartel, *Colloq* °outfit; *US jargon* CIA, Central Intelligence Agency: *He works for a firm in the City.*

firmament *n.* °heaven, the °heavens, °sky, the °skies, vault (of °heaven), *Literary* welkin, empyrean: *Sirius is one of the brightest stars in the firmament.*

firmly *adv.* **1** solidly, strongly, securely, °tightly, rigidly, °fast, immovably: *The column is set firmly into the concrete.* **2** resolutely, steadfastly, determinedly, staunchly, unwaveringly, decisively, unhesitatingly, constantly: *Jacquelyn firmly supports John in anything he says.*

first *adj.* **1** °foremost, °leading, °chief, °head, °premier, °prime, °primary, °principal, °pre-eminent: *The Kennedys were regarded as among 'the first people of Boston'. I heard that your son is now first violinist in the Philharmonic.* **2** earliest, °original, °senior, oldest; °initial, °beginning, °maiden, °opening: *The first clock in England was made about 1288. The first assault resulted in great loss of life.* **3** °fundamental, °elementary, °basic, °primary, °cardinal, °key, °essential: *It is necessary to return to first principles.*
—*adv.* **4** °before, in °front, earliest, beforehand, °ahead, sooner, °foremost: *Bannister came in first.* **5** in the first °place, firstly, before all *or* anything else, initially, at the °outset *or* °beginning, to °begin *or* °start with, from the °start, *Colloq* first off: *First, I want to thank you all for coming to my party.*
—*n.* **6** °beginning, °start, inception, commencement, °outset, *Colloq* word go: *I knew you'd win from the first.* **7** first °place, blue ribbon, gold (medal), °triumph, °victory; °win: *Britain achieved three firsts in yesterday's athletics meeting.* **8** ***at first***: initially, in the °beginning, at the °start *or* °outset, *Colloq* from the word go: *I didn't believe him at first.*

first-rate *adj.* first-class, high-grade, °prime, °excellent, °superior, °superb, °great, °remarkable, °admirable, °fine, °exceptional, °outstanding, °extraordinary, °unparalleled, °matchless, unsurpassed, *Colloq* A-1 *or* A-one, top-notch, tiptop, °crack, °top, ace, *Brit* whizbang *or* whizz-bang, wizard: *Sarah is a first-rate pianist.*

fiscal *adj.* °financial, °economic, budgetary, pecuniary, °monetary: *It is against our fiscal policy to deal in off-shore securities.*

fishy *adj.* **1** piscine, fishlike, piscatory, piscatorial: *On the fishmonger's slab lay an array of fishy offerings, only a few of which I could recognize.* **2** dubious, °doubtful, °questionable, °unlikely, °far-fetched, °suspicious, not kosher, °peculiar, °odd, °queer, °strange, °suspect, °improbable, °implausible, *Colloq* °shady, °funny: *There is something fishy about this deal.*

fit[1] *adj.* **1** °fitting, °appropriate, °fitted, °suitable, suited, adapted, apt, °meet, apropos, °applicable; °befitting, °becoming, °convenient, °proper, °right, °correct: *Those books are not fit for children. It's not a fit night out for man or beast.* **2** °prepared, °ready, °able, °capable, °qualified, °worthy, °right, °adequate: *The question is, is such a man fit to lead men into battle?* **3** °healthy, °well, °hale, °hearty, °stalwart, °vigorous, °strong, °sturdy, °robust, strapping, able-bodied, in °good °shape *or* °trim *or* °condition, in °fine fettle: *Is she fit enough to run in the marathon?* **4** °ready, °angry, troubled, °upset, °inclined, °disposed, °ready *or* °likely *or* about to, °exhausted °enough: *I worked till I was fit to drop. Mr Barrett was coughing fit to burst.*
—*v.* **5** befit, °suit, °become, be suited to, be °suitable *or* °appropriate for, °answer, °satisfy: *This computer program does not fit my needs.* **6** °join, °conform, °go (together), °match, °correspond, dovetail, °tally: *I cannot make the parts fit.* **7** °adjust, °modify, °change, °adapt, °alter, °accommodate, °shape, °fashion: *You will just have to fit your schedule to conform to ours.* **8** °equip, °supply, °furnish, °provide, °outfit, fit out *or* up, °install *or* instal, °rig out, °gear up: *I am having my boat fitted with radar.*

fit[2] *n.* **1** °attack, °seizure, convulsion, °spasm, °spell, °paroxysm, °bout, °throe: *She has periodic fits of severe depression.* **2** °outburst, outbreak, °paroxysm, °spell, °period: *Occasionally, Gurning would go into a fit of hysterical laughter.* **3** °tantrum; °eruption, °explosion: *She throws a fit if I so much as mention Maria's name.* **4** ***by fits and starts***: sporadically, °occasionally, fitfully, spasmodically, intermittently, erratically, haphazardly, °now and then, irregularly, unsystematically; unreliably: *The fridge works only by fits and starts.*

fitful *adj.* °irregular, °sporadic, °intermittent, °occasional, °periodic, °erratic, °spasmodic, °haphazard, unsystematic, °changeable, °unstable, °capricious, varying, fluctuating, °variable, uneven: *The dying torch emitted a fitful light. No true patriot pays merely fitful allegiance to his country.*

fitness *n.* **1** aptness, appropriateness, suitability, suitableness, competence, pertinence, seemliness; eligibility, adequacy, °qualification(s): *There is some doubt about Henryson's fitness as a leader.* **2** °health, healthiness, (°good) (°physical) °condition, °vigour, well-being, (°good) °shape, (°fine) fettle, °tone, wholesomeness, salubriousness *or* salubrity: *Tony is a fanatic about physical fitness and exercises daily.*

fitted *adj.* custom-made, °tailor-made; tailored, bespoke: *The house boasts a fully fitted kitchen.*

fitting *adj.* **1** °fit, °befitting, °suitable, °appropriate, °meet, °becoming, °proper, *comme il faut*, °seemly, apt, apropos, apposite, germane, °relevant: *Is it fitting to send flowers? It was a fitting end to the story.*
—*n.* **2** ***fittings***: fitments, °attachments, °accessories, °elements, °pieces, °parts, °units, °fixtures; appointments, °extras, installations, furnishings, °trappings, °furniture, °equipment, accoutrements *or US also* accouterments, °paraphernalia, trimmings: *Gold-plated bathroom fittings are available at extra cost.*

fix *v.* **1** affix, °pin, °fasten, make °fast, °attach, °secure, °stick, °connect, °link, °tie, °couple, °clasp, °clamp, rivet, °cement, °weld, °fuse: *Fix this sign to the door.* **2** °establish, °set, °settle, °agree to, °determine, °organize, stabilize, °firm up, °solidify, °decide, conclude, °arrive at, °define, °specify, °resolve, °arrange, °install *or* instal, °institute: *The new limits must be fixed by tomorrow.* **3** °repair, °mend, fix up, °remedy, °rectify, °correct, emend, °adjust, °patch (up), °regulate, °put *or* °set to rights, °doctor, °straighten out: *My watch is at the jeweller's being fixed.* **4** °hold, °fasten, °focus, °direct, °level, rivet, °concentrate, °freeze; fixate: *He fixed his attention on the ice-cream.* **5** °hold, rivet, spellbind, mesmerize, °hypnotize, °fascinate, °freeze, immobilize: *She fixed him with a baleful stare.* **6** °concentrate, °focus: *Fix your thoughts on how we're going to get out of here.* **7** °harden, congeal, °thicken, °set, consolidate, °solidify, rigidify, become °rigid, °stiffen, °freeze: *Mould the clay before it becomes fixed.* **8** °establish, °set, °settle, °organize, °install *or* instal, °situate, °locate, °position, °place: *Her family is comfortably fixed.* **9** °impose, °assign, allocate, °attribute, ascribe, °specify, °pin, °attach, °fasten, °establish: *They tried to fix the responsibility for the accident.* **10** °settle, °set, stabilize, °freeze, °solidify: *The introduction and spread of printing fixed many spellings.* **11** °bribe, suborn, °buy (off), °corrupt, °influence, °manipulate, *Colloq* grease (someone's) palm: *He attempted to fix a judge.* **12** °arrange, prearrange, predetermine, °set up, contrive, *Colloq* °fiddle, °pull strings, °rig: *We knew the winner as they had fixed the race.* **13** desexualize, desex, °alter, °cut; castrate, emasculate, see to, eunuchize, geld, caponize; spay, oophorectomize, ovariectomize: *Animals that have been fixed are* *usually more tractable.* **14** °retaliate against, °wreak °vengeance on, °hit *or* °strike *or* °get back at, °get °even with, °even the °score with, make °reprisal against, avenge oneself against, take °revenge *or* °retribution on *or* against, °repay, °pay back, *Colloq* °settle (someone's) hash, cook (someone's) goose, °sort (some) out: *I'll fix him for tattling to the teacher!* **15** ***fix on*** *or* ***upon***: °decide (on *or* upon), °set, °agree (on *or* upon), °choose, °select, °settle (on), °determine, °finalize: *We can't fix on a date till we know David's schedule.* **16** ***fix up***: **a** °furnish, °supply, °provide, °accommodate, °set up, *Brit* °lay on: *Her mother fixed her up with a nice young man. Can you fix me up with a room for the night?* **b** (re)decorate, °furnish, °renovate, °restore, furbish, °refurbish; °straighten out *or* up, °organize, do up, °set up: *I like the way you've fixed up the basement. Please fix up your room before the guests arrive.* **c** °clear up, °resolve, °reconcile, °sort out, °settle: *Have they fixed up their differences yet?* **d** °repair, °patch (up): *Fix up my car so it will run at least till I get home.*

—*n.* **17** °dilemma, °predicament, °difficulty, corner, double °bind, catch-22, °quandary, °mess, (°bad) °situation, °strait(s), *Colloq* pickle, °jam, °hole, (°tight *or* °tough) °spot, °pinch, *US* °bind: *You could help me get out of a terrible fix.* **18** °arrangement, prearrangement, °fiddle; bribery, subornation; *Slang chiefly US and Canadian* °set-up: *The fix is on for her to win at roulette.*

fixation *n.* °mania, °obsession, compulsion, °fixed °idea, *idée fixe*, °fetish, monomania, preoccupation, infatuation, *Colloq* hang-up, °thing, °kick: *He has a health-food fixation.*

fixed *adj.* **1** fastened, °attached, anchored, °set, °secure(d), °firm, °stable, settled, °immovable, immobile, stationary, °rigid, °rooted, °solid; immobilized, stuck: *While this part rolls, the other remains fixed. There was a fixed smile on her face.* **2** established, °secure, unalterable, °steadfast, °set, °firm, unchangeable, unchanging, °persistent, unfluctuating, unflagging, unwavering, °inflexible, undeviating, unflinching, unblinking, °rigid, °rooted, immutable, °definite, °resolute, resolved, °determined, °intent; °obstinate, °stubborn: *I admire Philip's fixed determination to persevere.* **3** settled, resolved, agreed, °regular, °habitual, °decided, arranged, prearranged, °definite, established: *We have a fixed date on which we meet each month.* **4** arranged, prearranged, °set-up, framed; °crooked, °dishonest, °bent, *Colloq* rigged, °put-up: *He lost everything in a fixed poker game.*

fixture *n.* **1** °meet, °meeting, °event, °match, °occasion, °occurrence: *The Davis Cup tennis championship is an annual fixture.* **2** appliance, °accessory, °fitting, °equipment, °apparatus, °device, °instrument, °tool, °gadget, contrivance, appendage, fitment: *The landlord forbids the removal of any fixture.*

fizz *v.* **1** °bubble, effervesce, °sparkle, °froth, °fizzle; °hiss, sputter, sizzle: *The champagne fizzed in my glass.*

—*n.* **2** effervescence, °sparkle, carbonation, bubbling, °froth, °fizzle, fizziness: *All the fizz is gone from my drink!* **3** °hiss, hissing, sibilance: *The steam escaped with a loud fizz.* **4** *US* soda, soda °water, °club soda, seltzer, *Dialect* plain; °soft °drink, °tonic: *May I have a little fizz with my scotch?* **5** champagne, *Colloq Brit* champers: *We celebrated with oysters and a bottle of fizz.*

fizzle *v.* **1** °fizz: *This headache powder makes the water fizzle.* **2** Often, ***fizzle out***: °die (out *or* away), °fizz out, °expire, peter out, come to °nothing *or* °naught, °fail, °fall through, °miscarry, abort, come to °grief, °misfire, °collapse, °cave in: *Her grandiose plans for staging an extravaganza quickly fizzled out.*

flabby *adj.* **1** °limp, °loose, °lax, flaccid, °slack, floppy, sagging, drooping, baggy, °pendulous, quaggy, °soft: *After forty, he began to get a bit flabby around the middle.* **2** °weak, °spineless, °feeble, °impotent, °ineffective, °ineffectual: *The critics found the characterizations flabby and the plot non-existent.*

flag[1] *n.* **1** °banner, ensign, °standard, °pennant, banneret, pennon, °streamer, bunting, jack, gonfalon, vexillum: *Our flag was raised over the fort.*

—*v.* **2** Often ***flag down***: °warn, °signal, °hail, °inform, °stop: *A workman flagged us down because the bridge was out.* **3** °mark, °tag, °label, °tab, °identify, *Brit* tick (off), *US and Canadian* °check (off): *Flag the supplies you need that are listed here.*

flag[2] *v.* **1** °droop, °sag, °dangle, °hang down, swag, festoon: *In the doldrums the sails flagged soggily about the masts.* **2** °weaken, languish, falter, °fail, °dwindle, °fade, °deteriorate, °waste away, °degenerate, °die, °decline, °diminish, °decrease, lessen, abate, peter out, °taper off, °let up, °ease (up), °subside, °slump, °fall off, °wane, °ebb, °sink, °lag: *As she approached the finish line she was alarmed to feel her energy flagging.*

flagrant *adj.* °blatant, °brazen, °bold, °barefaced, °audacious, arrant, °glaring, °outrageous, °shocking, °shameless, °scandalous, °atrocious, °infamous, °notorious, °defiant, egregious, °obvious, °conspicuous, °open, °complete, °out-and-out, utter, flagitious, °monstrous, heinous, °cruel, °villainous, treacherous, nefarious, °awful, °gross, °rank, °inconsiderate, °scornful, °contemptuous; reprehensible; °contemptible: *Speeding shows a flagrant disregard for the safety of others.*

flair *n.* **1** °talent, °ability, °aptitude, °feel, °knack, °genius, °skill, °mind, °gift, °faculty, propensity, °bent, proclivity, °facility: *He showed a flair for music at an early age.* **2** °chic, °panache, °dash, élan, éclat, °style, stylishness, °glamour, °verve, °sparkle, °vitality, °elegance, °taste, *Colloq* savvy, pizazz *or* pizzazz, *Old-fashioned* oomph: *She dresses with great flair.*

flak *n.* flack, °criticism, °disapproval, censure, °abuse, °blame, °aspersion, °complaint(s), disapprobation, condemnation, *Colloq* brickbats: *He took a lot of flak from the press for his comments.*

flake *n.* **1** snowflake; °scale, °chip, °bit, °piece, °scrap, °particle, tuft, °flock, scurf, °fragment, shaving, °sliver; wafer, lamina, *Technical* squama: *A flake of slate caught him in the eye.*

—*v.* **2** Often, ***flake off***: °scale, °chip, °fragment; *Technical* desquamate, exfoliate: *The paint is flaking off on this side.* **3** ***flake out***: **a** °collapse, °go to °sleep, °fall asleep, °drop off (to °sleep), °pass out, keel over: *After the game, I flaked out on the couch for ten hours.* **b** become flaky, act °crazy: *He flaked out when he heard the new record.*

flamboyant *adj.* **1** °elaborate, ornamented, °ornate, decorated, embellished, baroque, rococo, florid: *We chose a flamboyant wallpaper with purple peacocks.* **2** °extravagant, °ostentatious, °showy, °gaudy, °flashy, °dazzling, °brilliant, °splendid, °dashing, °rakish, °swashbuckling, °jaunty; high, wide, and °handsome: *With a flamboyant display of swordsmanship, d'Artagnan dispatched his attacker.*

flame *n.* **1** °fire, °blaze; conflagration: *The flame began to lick about my feet.* **2** °passion, °fervour, °ardour, °intensity, °warmth, °fire, zeal, feverishness, °enthusiasm, °eagerness: *The flame of love is still burning.* **3** boyfriend, girlfriend, °lover, heartthrob, °sweetheart, beau: *Linda is an old flame of Trevor's.*

—*v.* **4** °burn, °blaze, °glow, °flare: *Flaming embers from the chimney set fire to the roof. Here and there civil unrest flamed up in the countryside.*

flaming *adj.* °obvious, °conspicuous, °blatant, °flagrant, egregious, °extravagant, *Slang* bloody, bleeding, blasted, damned, blooming: *That flaming idiot was appointed to the Ministry of Defence!*

flammable *adj.* °inflammable, combustible, burnable: *The warning on the tin says the contents are flammable.*

flank *n.* **1** °side, °quarter; loin, haunch: *The enemy was about to attack our flank. The pony drew back with trembling flanks.*

—*v.* **2** °edge, °border, °line: *Armed guards flanked the entrance.* **3** skirt, outmanoeuvre, outflank, °circle, °go (a)round: *They have enough troops to flank our forces to the east.*

flannel *n.* **1** °flattery, humbug, °nonsense, blarney, °rubbish, prevarication, *Colloq* eyewash, hogwash, boloney, °soft soap, weasel words, sweet talk, bull, crap, *Brit* °waffle, cock, *US* bushwa; *Taboo slang* bullshit, horseshit, (load of) shit, *Brit* codswallop, bollocks *or* ballocks: *Don't believe a thing Fordyce says—it's all flannel.*
—*v.* **2** °flatter, hedge, °mislead, pull the wool over (someone's) eyes, *Colloq* soft-soap, sweet-talk, *Taboo slang* bullshit, horseshit, shit: *They aren't sincere—they're just flannelling you.*

flap *v.* **1** °slap, slat, °beat, flail, °wave, °wag, waggle, °flutter, thresh, thrash, °oscillate, °vibrate: *An ornithopter is an aeroplane that flaps its wings like a bird. The Union Jack was flapping in the breeze.*
—*n.* **2** flapping, °beat, °wave, °wag, waggle, °flutter, oscillation: *With a flap of its wings, the bird flew away.* **3** °fold, °fly, lappet, °lap, °tail, °tab: *Leave a flap of cloth to cover the pocket.* **4** °upset, °agitation, to-do, ado, commotion, °panic, °flurry, °fuss, °distress, *Colloq* °state, tizzy, °sweat, *Brit* kerfuffle: *She's in a flap about what to wear to the dance.* **5** °quarrel, °argument, °dispute: *There was a big flap over which car model to buy.*

flare *v.* **1** Often, ***flare up***: °blaze *or* °flame (up), °flash, °erupt, °break out; °dazzle, °flicker, glimmer, °shimmer, °flutter: *The fire flared up briefly when he tossed the paper onto it.* **2** Often, ***flare out***: °spread (out *or* outwards), °widen, broaden, °expand, °increase, °enlarge, °bulge, °swell: *The sides of the vase flare out near the top.* **3** Often, ***flare up***: °anger, lose one's °temper, °chafe, °seethe, °fume, °rage, throw a °tantrum, become incensed *or* °angry (etc.); °blow up, °burst forth, °erupt, °explode; *Colloq* get one's back up, get one's Irish *or* dander up, see red, °get worked up, °fly off the handle, lose one's °cool, go out of *or* lose °control, get °hot under the collar, blow one's top: *He flares up at the very mention of her name. Tempers flared when we touched on the subject of politics.*
—*n.* **4** °blaze, °flame, °burst, °outburst, °flash, °glare, °dazzle, incandescence, °brilliance, luminosity: *A bright orange flare erupted from the mouth of the cave.* **5** °beacon, °light, °signal, torch, flambeau, °link: *We prayed that the rescue party would see our flares.* **6** °spread, broadening, widening, °expansion, °swelling, °bulge, °increase, enlargement: *I like that slight flare at the hem of the skirt.*

flash *n.* **1** °blaze, °flame, °flare, °burst, °dazzle, °spark, °sparkle, coruscation, fulguration, °glitter, °twinkle, °twinkling, °flicker, flickering, scintilla, scintillation, glint, °shimmer, glimmer, °gleam, °beam, °ray, °shaft: *There was a blinding flash of blue light and the little man was gone.* **2** (sudden *or* momentary) °display, °stroke, °show, °manifestation, °outburst, outbreak, °sign, °indication, °exhibition; °touch, °hint, °suggestion: *She has occasional flashes of insight bordering on genius.* **3** °moment, (split) °second, °instant, °twinkling (of an eye), trice, °minute, *Colloq* two shakes (of a lamb's tail), jiffy, °shake, before you can say 'Jack Robinson': *In a flash he was at her side.*
—*v.* **4** °burn, °blaze, °flame, °flare, °burst (out), °dazzle, °spark, °sparkle, coruscate, fulgurate, °glitter, °twinkle, °flicker, scintillate, °shimmer, glimmer, °gleam, °beam, °glare, °shine: *The light flashed every eight seconds.* **5** °race, °speed, °dash, °streak, flick, °tear, °rush, °hurry, °hasten, °fly, zoom, °shoot, °bolt, whistle; °run, sprint, dart, scuttle, scamper, *Colloq* scoot, skedaddle, °take off, whiz *or* whizz: *The train flashed by, doing about 100.*
—*adj.* **6** °dazzling, °showy, °ostentatious, °smart, °chic, *Colloq* °swish, classy, ritzy, snazzy: *Barbara's new car looks very flash.* **7** See **flashy, 1,** below.

flashy *adj.* **1** °flash, °gaudy, °flamboyant, °glaring, fulgurous, °showy, °ostentatious, °loud, °garish, °vulgar, °cheap, meretricious, °pretentious, °tawdry, °tasteless, *Colloq* °tacky, *Slang* jazzy, *US* glitzy: *He was attracted by her flashy appearance.* **2** °superficial, cosmetic, °skin-deep, °surface, °shallow, °glib, °slick, facile, °insubstantial, °thin: *The reviewer called it a flashy interpretation of the Bard.*

flat *adj.* **1** °level, °horizontal, °even, °smooth, °plane, unbroken, uninterrupted: *I looked out over the flat surface of the frozen bay.* **2** °prostrate, °prone, °supine, °lying (down), stretched out, °recumbent, outstretched, reclining, spread-eagle(d), °spread out, outspread: *I lay flat on my back staring up at the sky.* **3** collapsed, levelled, overthrown, laid °low: *The air raid had left all the buildings completely flat.* **4** °downright, °outright, °unqualified, unreserved, unconditional, °absolute, °categorical, °explicit, °definite, °firm, °positive, °out-and-out, unequivocal, °peremptory, unambiguous, unmistakable, °direct, °complete, °total: *The request for clemency was met with the judge's flat refusal.* **5** featureless, °monotonous, °dull, °dead, uninteresting, unexciting, °vapid, °bland, °empty, two-dimensional, insipid, °boring, °tiresome, °lifeless, spiritless, °lacklustre, °prosaic, °stale, °tired, °dry, jejune: *The critics wrote that she turned in a very flat performance.* **6** deflated, collapsed, punctured, ruptured, blown out: *We had a flat tyre on the way.* **7** unchangeable, unchanging, °invariable, unvaried, unvarying, °standard, °fixed, unmodified, unmodifiable, *Colloq US* cookie-cutter: *They charge the same flat rate for children, the elderly, and all between.* **8** °dead, insipid, °stale, °tasteless, flavourless, °unpalatable; decarbonated, non-effervescent: *My beer has gone flat.* **9** °exact, °precise: *It's a flat ten minutes from here to the railway station.* **10** °definite, °certain, °sure, °irrevocable: *I said I'm not going, and that's flat.* **11** °dull, °slow, sluggish, °inactive, depressed: *Business has been a bit flat since Christmas.* **12** °dull, mat *or* matt, unshiny, non-gloss(y), non-reflective, non-glare, unpolished: *The table looks better with a flat finish.* **13** lacking perspective, two-dimensional, °lifeless, °unrealistic: *Some of his paintings seem pretty flat to me.*
—*n.* **14** Often, ***flats***: **a** *US* low shoes, loafers, sandals, *Colloq* flatties: *Cynthia said that wearing flats makes her feet hurt.* **b** lowland(s), °plain(s), tundra, steppe(s), prairie(s), savannah *or* savanna, heath, °moor, pampas; mud-flat(s); °shallow(s), shoal, strand; °marsh, °bog, fen, °swamp: *Before us was a large flat of barren ground.* **15** °rooms, °suite, apartment: *How can you afford to keep a flat in London?*
—*adv.* **16** °absolutely, °completely, categorically, °utterly, °wholly, uncompromisingly, irrevocably, °positively, °definitely, °directly; °exactly, °precisely, flatly: *He has come out flat in favour of the status quo. When he started drinking, she left him flat.* **17** ***flat out***: **a** at °maximum *or* °top *or* °full *or* °breakneck °speed, speedily, °quickly, apace, on the °run, °rapidly, °swiftly, at °full °speed *or* gallop, °post-haste, hell for leather, like a bat out of hell, like a °shot, like (greased) lightning, like the wind: *Someone shouted 'Fire!' and we headed flat out for the exits.* **b** flatly, unhesitatingly, °directly, at °once, °immediately, forthwith, without °delay; plainly, °openly, baldly, brazenly, brashly: *He asked to borrow some money and she told him 'No', flat out.*
—*n.* **18** °room(s), °suite (of rooms), chambers, tenement; garden °flat, maisonette, penthouse, studio, *Brit* bedsitter, bedsit; °accommodation, living quarters, *Colloq Brit* digs, *US and Canadian* apartment, furnished °room, walk-up, duplex, triplex, garden apartment: *We rented a two-bedroom flat in a good neighbourhood.*

flatten *v.* **1** °level *or* °even (off *or* out); °smooth (out), °press *or* iron (out), °roll: *The children's noses were flattened against the window of the toy shop. You will have to flatten the lawn if you want to play croquet on it.* **2** °knock down *or* over, °knock out, °floor, °prostrate: *Menges flattened the champion in the first round.* **3** °raze, °tear down, °demolish, °level: *The bomb flattened every house in the area.*

flatter *v.* **1** butter up, °play up to, °compliment, °praise, fawn (on *or* upon), toady to, °truckle to, court, curry °favour with, *Colloq* °flannel, soft-soap, °oil;

Slang °shine *or* suck up to, boot-lick, *Taboo* °kiss (someone's) arse *or US* ass, brown-nose: *Flattering the boss won't get you a salary increase.* **2** °enhance, °complement, °suit, °show to °advantage: *That colour flatters her complexion.* **3** °cajole, °wheedle, °coax, inveigle, °beguile, sweet-talk: *He was flattered into signing that contract.*

flatterer *n.* toady, sycophant, fawner, wheedler, timeserver, courtier, backscratcher, sponge, °parasite, leech, °hanger-on, sweet-talker, backslapper, truckler, lickspittle, *Colloq* °yes-man; *Slang* bootlicker, *Taboo* brown-noser, *Brit* arse-kisser, arse-licker, bumsucker, *US* ass-kisser, ass-licker: *Don't believe anything that flatterer tells you.*

flattering *adj.* **1** °complimentary, °becoming, °kind, enhancing: *That is quite a flattering portrait of Dorian.* **2** adulatory, °laudatory, gratifying, fulsome, honeyed, sugary, fawning, °ingratiating, unctuous, °slimy, *Chiefly Brit* smarmy: *Authors once wrote the most flattering dedications to their patrons.*

flattery *n.* adulation, °cajolery, blandishment, sweet talk, beguilement, wheedling, gloze, *Colloq* soft soap, *Slang* boot-licking, *Taboo* brown-nosing, *Brit* arse-kissing, arse-licking, bum-sucking, *US* ass-kissing, ass-licking: *A judicious use of flattery moved him up the corporate ladder.*

flaunt *v.* °display, °show (off), °parade, °flourish, °exhibit, °sport, disport, °spotlight: *They were like all the other nouveaux riches who flaunt their wealth in the stylish continental resorts.*

flavour *n.* **1** °taste, °savour, °tang, piquancy, °zest; tastiness, savouriness; °essence, °extract, °seasoning, flavouring, °seasoning, °spice; °aroma, °odour, °scent; *Rare* sapor: *Overcooking destroys the flavour of food. This sweet has a minty flavour.* **2** °character, °spirit, °nature, °quality, °property, °mark, °stamp, °essence, °characteristic, °style, °taste, °feel, °feeling, ambience *or* ambiance, °sense, tinge, °aroma, °air, °atmosphere, °hint, °suggestion, °touch, soupçon: *We all agreed that the new play has a Shavian flavour.*
—*v.* **3** °season, °spice: *She flavours her teacakes with ginger.*

flaw *n.* **1** °fault, °defect, °imperfection, °error, °mistake, °blemish, °blot, °stain, °taint, (°black) °mark, °damage, disfigurement, °failing, °weakness, °weak °spot; °loophole: *Flaws in the casting give this bell a dull sound. I can see flaws in your argument.* **2** °crack, °break, °breach, °chink, °chip, °fracture, °rupture, fissure, cleft, °split, °slit, °cut, °gash, °rent, °rift, °tear, °rip, °puncture, °hole, perforation: *The tiniest flaw may reduce the value of a pot to a collector.*
—*v.* **3** °damage, °harm, °spoil, °ruin, °mark, °weaken, disfigure: *Careless workmanship has flawed many of the objects they produced.* **4** °discredit, °stigmatize, °damage, °hurt, °harm; °taint, °mar, °stain, °blot: *Her reputation has already been flawed.*

flawed *adj.* damaged, harmed, marred, weakened, tainted, stained, tarnished, °defective, °imperfect, °unsound, °faulty: *His flawed record prevented him from getting work.*

flawless *adj.* **1** °perfect, °pristine, °pure, uncorrupted, °chaste, virgin, °intact, °whole, °clean, °immaculate, unsullied, unspoiled *or* unspoilt, unsoiled, °impeccable, unblemished, °faultless, undamaged, unimpaired, °spotless, °untarnished: *Two flawless artefacts were found in the tomb. Many envied her flawless reputation.* **2** undeniable, unassailable, unimpeachable, °unquestionable, irrefutable, °foolproof, °sound, °demonstrable: *The prosecutor's evidence appears to be flawless.*

flecked *adj.* spotted, dappled, pied, (be)speckled, (be)sprinkled, dotted, °marked, stippled, dusted, specked, spattered, freckled: *His lank brown hair was flecked with grey.*

flee *v.* **1** °quit, °run away *or* off, °escape, °get away, °fly, °take °flight, °bolt, °go (away), decamp, abscond, seek safety, °avoid, °make off, make an °exit, °make (good) one's °escape, °make a (clean) °getaway, °beat a (hasty) °retreat, °take to one's heels, show a clean pair of heels, turn tail, °make tracks, make a °run for it, °cut and °run, vanish, °disappear, *Brit* levant, *Colloq* °take off, scoot, °make oneself °scarce, °beat it, °clear out, °fly the coop, skedaddle, scram, *Brit* scarper, *Australian and New Zealand* °shoot through, *US and Canadian* take a (run-out) powder, °skip (town), °cut out, hightail it, *Old-fashioned* skiddoo; *Slang* °split, *Brit* °bugger off, do a moonlight flit, do a bunk, *US and Canadian* vamoose, lam out, take it on the lam, °blow, bail out: *He fled the town and was never seen again. When they saw what they had done, they fled. She fled to Brazil to avoid the tax authorities.* **2** °avoid, °evade, °shun, °escape from, eschew: *She fled the responsibilities of caring for her children.*

fleece *v.* °cheat, overcharge, °swindle, bilk, °defraud, °victimize, °plunder, °strip, °milk, °rob, *Colloq* °take, flimflam, gyp, diddle, bleed, take for a °ride *or* to the cleaners, *Slang* °rip off, °chisel, °pluck, rook, °clip, °soak: *The gang stole credit cards and fleeced the companies out of millions.*

fleet[1] *n.* armada, flotilla, °navy, (naval) (task) °force, squadron, convoy, °division: *A fleet of submarines was sent to harass shipping in the Atlantic.*

fleet[2] *adj.* °swift, °rapid, °fast, °speedy, °quick, °nimble, °expeditious, °agile: *Nowadays, the fleetest transportation in a large city is by bicycle.*

fleeting *adj.* transitory, °fugitive, °transient, °temporary, °passing, ephemeral, fugacious, evanescent, °momentary, °short-lived, °fly-by-night, °short, °brief: *I caught only a fleeting glimpse of the car as it sped by.*

flesh *n.* **1** °meat; °tissue, muscle: *We ate the flesh and threw away the fat, bones, and skin.* **2** °body, corporeality, flesh and blood, °human °nature, physicality; mortality: *The spirit is willing but the flesh is weak.* **3** ***flesh and blood***: °real, °physical, corporeal, °human, °natural: *He pointed out that he was flesh and blood, not a robot.* **4** ***in the flesh***: °personally, in °person, °really, physically, bodily, °alive, living, in °life: *She stood before me, in the flesh.* **5** ***one's (own) flesh and blood***: °kin, kinsfolk *or US and Canadian* kinfolk, °family, °stock, blood, kith and °kin, relatives, relations: *How could she treat her own flesh and blood that way?*
—*v.* **6** ***flesh out***: °substantiate, °fill (in *or* out), give *or* °lend °substance *or* dimension to, °incorporate, °embody, °colour: *The idea is good, but it needs fleshing out.*

flex *n.* **1** wire, °lead, °cord, °cable, °extension: *Replace this flex before you have a short circuit.*
—*v.* **2** °bend, °give, °stretch, curve: *The plastic tube can be flexed many times without breaking.* **3** °exercise, °tense, °tighten, °contract: *He flexed his muscles before lifting the weight.*

flexibility *n.* **1** pliability, pliancy *or* pliantness, °elasticity, °resilience *or* resiliency, suppleness, flexibleness, bendability, limberness, °stretch, °give, °spring, springiness, ductility: *Chemists improved the flexibility of the substance by adding more plasticizer.* **2** conformability *or* conformableness, adaptability, versatility, adjustability *or* adjustableness, compliance *or* compliancy, manageability, tractability *or* tractableness, malleability, °obedience, submissiveness, docility, agreeableness, conformity: *Fletcher has the flexibility needed to move from one department to another.*

flexible *adj.* **1** °pliable, pliant, °elastic, resilient, °supple, bendable, limber, lithe, stretchy, stretchable, springy, extensible *or* extensile, ductile, flexile, tensile, °yielding, °willowy: *The foil is a thin, flexible duelling sword.* **2** modifiable, °adaptable, conformable, compliant, malleable, °obedient, °tractable, °manageable, cooperative, amenable, persuadable *or* persuasible: *English seems to be an infinitely flexible language. Nicole is flexible in her attitude towards politics.* **3** °easy, facile, °submissive, complaisant, docile: *Discipline at the school might be a little too flexible.*

flicker *v.* **1** °twinkle, °blink, waver, glimmer, glint, °sparkle, °shimmer, °flare, gutter: *A slight draught* *made the candles flicker.* **2** °flap, °flutter, °quiver, °twitter, °fluctuate, °oscillate, °shake, °tremble, °vibrate: *Dozens of tiny flags flickered in the wind.* —*n.* **3** glimmer, glint, glimmering, °sparkle, °spark, °twinkle, °twinkling, °gleam, °flare, °glare: *With a dying flicker the torch went out.* **4** °hint, °suggestion, °trace, glimmer, °vestige, scintilla, °spark: *I thought I detected a flicker of recognition when our eyes met.*

flight[1] *n.* **1** flying, soaring, winging, °excursion: *The flight above the mountains was exhilarating. He is subject to wild flights of the imagination.* **2** (°air) voyage *or* °journey *or* °trip: *We had a fine flight from New Delhi.* **3** aeroplane, airliner, °plane, aircraft: *Our flight was delayed in Istanbul.* **4** °flock, °swarm, cloud, covey (of grouse *or* partridge), bevy (of quail), skein (of geese), exaltation (of larks): *A flight of migrating birds passed overhead.* **5** feather: *The flights on this dart are broken.*

flight[2] *n.* **1** °escape, °retreat, departure, °exit, exodus, °getaway, fleeing, bolting, *Slang* °split: *Mohammed's flight from Mecca to Medina in 622 is called a 'hegira'.* **2** ***put to flight***: °chase *or* °drive (off *or* away), °disperse, °send off *or* away, °send packing, °dismiss, °rout, °stampede: *They put the Saracens to flight in a decisive battle.* **3** ***take flight***: °flee, °go *or* °run away *or* off, abscond, °desert, °depart, (°beat a) °retreat, °exit, °bolt, decamp, °withdraw, take to one's heels, show a clean pair of heels, *Colloq* °light out, shove off, *Brit* scarper, *US* take a (run-out) °powder, °take it on the lam, lam out; *Slang* °split, *Brit* do a bunk, do a moonlight flit, °bugger off: *The constable blew his whistle and the thief took flight.*

flighty *adj.* **1** °fickle, °frivolous, °inconstant, °capricious, °fanciful, °changeable, °variable, mercurial, skittish, °volatile, °unstable, unsteady, °giddy, °wild: *These flighty girls never stay in a job more than a month.* **2** °irresponsible, light-headed, rattle-brained, °silly, °hare-brained, °dizzy, °crazy, °mad, °reckless, °thoughtless, *Colloq* nutty, screwy, dotty, dippy: *It was flighty of Caroline to pour the brandy into the well.*

flimsy *adj.* **1** °slight, °frail, °weak, °insubstantial *or* unsubstantial, °feeble, °makeshift, °fragile, frangible, breakable, °rickety, °ramshackle, °dilapidated, jerry-built, gimcrack, °delicate: *That flimsy ladder will never support me. He lives in a flimsy shack near the railway.* **2** °slight, trivial, °paltry, °feeble, unconvincing, °weak, °makeshift, °implausible, °unbelievable, °unsatisfactory, °insubstantial *or* unsubstantial, °poor, °inadequate: *Her flimsy excuse was that she had a headache.* **3** °sheer, °light, gauzy, °transparent, °thin, °filmy, diaphanous, gossamer, °delicate: *She was wearing a flimsy pink blouse.*

flinch *v.* wince, °draw back, °withdraw, cower, °cringe, °recoil, °start, quail, blench, °shrink (from), °shy (away) (from), °dodge, °duck: *Each time he raised the whip, I flinched.*

fling *v.* **1** °toss, °pitch, °throw, °cast, °hurl, °heave, °sling, °propel, °fire, °let °fly, °send, *Colloq* °lob, chuck: *The smugglers had flung the contraband into the sea.* —*n.* **2** °indulgence, debauch, binge, °spree, °party, *Colloq* blow-off: *This will be my last fling before going into the army.* **3** °gamble, °risk, °venture, °attempt, °try, °go, °shot, *Colloq* °crack, whirl, bash: *Her brief fling at an acting career was unsuccessful.*

flip *v.* **1** °toss, flick, °snap, °flop, °turn, °twist, °spin: *Flip a coin to see who goes first.* **2** °anger, become °angry *or* °furious, °go °mad, °go °crazy, °go °berserk, *US also* °flip out, *Colloq* °go off the deep end, °lose one's °cool, *Slang* °flip one's lid *or Brit* °top, *Brit* freak, *US* freak out, °lose it: *Father flipped when I said I was quitting college.*

flippancy *n.* **1** frivolousness, facetiousness, °levity, light-heartedness, frivolity, jocularity, offhandedness, unseriousness: *I was chagrined that she should treat my proposal of marriage with such flippancy.* **2** °disrespect, disrespectfulness, °impudence, °impertinence, irreverence, sauciness, rudeness, discourtesy, brazenness, brashness, pertness, insolence, *Colloq* cheek, cheekiness, lip, °mouth, *Slang Brit* °side: *The headmaster will not tolerate flippancy on serious subjects such as religion and race relations.*

flippant *adj.* **1** °frivolous, facetious, light-hearted, jocular, °offhand(ed), unserious, °shallow, °thoughtless, °superficial; °supercilious, belittling, °scornful, dismissive: *I don't appreciate your flippant remarks when I'm trying to be serious.* **2** °disrespectful, °impudent, °impertinent, °irreverent, saucy, °rude, °pert, °discourteous, °brazen, °brash, °insolent, *Colloq* °cheeky, °flip: *He disapproves of Charles's flippant attitude towards the royal family.*

flirt *v.* **1** coquette, °play *or* °act the coquette, °tease, °tantalize, °toy, °lead on, dally, philander, *Colloq Brit* °chat up; *Slang US* °come on to: *Amanda enjoys flirting with the boys.* **2** ***flirt with***: °trifle *or* °toy *or* °play *or* °tinker with, °contemplate, °consider, °entertain, give a thought to, °think about *or* of, *Colloq Brit* °try on: *Many teenagers flirt with the idea of leaving home.* —*n.* **3** coquette, °tease, vamp, hussy, playgirl, minx; °philanderer, °playboy, *Slang* lady-killer, *Old-fashioned* wolf, sheik, masher, lounge lizard, *Taboo slang* cock-teaser, prick-teaser: *They are both such flirts, I can't tell if their advances are genuine.*

flirtatious *adj.* coquettish, vampish, °seductive, flirty, °coy, philandering, °provocative, enticing, alluring, amorous, come-hither: *They exchanged many flirtatious looks across the table.*

flit *v.* °move, °go, °fly, °flee, dart, °skip, °skim, flick, °hop, °whisk, °flutter, °flash: *As a bee flits from flower to flower, she flits from man to man.*

float *v.* **1** °hover, °poise, bob, °waft, be suspended, °hang; °sail, °drift, °glide, swim: *In the clear Caribbean waters, the boat seemed to float in mid-air.* **2** °launch, °establish, °set up, °organize, °found, °initiate, °get °going *or* °moving: *The financiers are trying to float a new company.* **3** °negotiate, °arrange, °transact, °bring *or* °carry off, °get, °effect, consummate, *Colloq* °pull off, °swing: *Were you able to float a loan on your house?* —*n.* **4** raft, *Brit* °platform: *I can swim out to the float.* **5** °buoy; pontoon: *The bridge is supported by floats.* **6** (°parade) °exhibit *or* °display: *Our parade float won first prize.*

flock *n.* **1** °body, °company, °group, °band, °pack, °bunch, troop, °set, °collection, °assembly, convoy, °gathering, congregation, °crowd, °mass, °mob, °throng, °gang, multitude, °number, °quantity, °host, horde, °swarm, drove; °herd, °flight, troupe, °fleet, °school; bevy: *A huge flock of buyers sought bargains in the post-Christmas sales.* —*v.* **2** °assemble, °meet, °collect, °gather, °come *or* °go together, congregate, °crowd, °mass, °mob, °throng, °pour, °flood, °swarm, °herd (together), °band together, °go: *People flocked around the speaker.*

flog *v.* **1** °whip, °lash, horsewhip, strap, flagellate, flay, °scourge, thrash, thresh, °beat; °chastise, °castigate, °punish: *He will be flogged, then drawn and quartered. He was flogged for stealing a loaf of bread.* **2** °sell; °promote, °publicize: *Her latest job is flogging encyclopedias door-to-door.*

flood *n.* **1** inundation, deluge, overflow(ing), débâcle: *The hurricane was accompanied by a devastating flood.* **2** °torrent, cataract, freshet, overflow, °stream, °spate: *A flood of lava poured down the mountain.* **3** °abundance, deluge, overflowing, °surge, °outpouring, °torrent, tide, tidal °wave, °stream, °rush, °flow, °glut, °surfeit, °satiety, °profusion, over-abundance, superabundance, nimiety, plethora, °excess, °surplus, °superfluity: *A flood of invective poured from her lips.* —*v.* **4** inundate, °submerge, overflow, °swamp, °immerse, deluge, °pour over, °drown: *The water flooded everything in the basement.* **5** °overwhelm, °glut, oversupply, °saturate, °choke: *The market is being flooded with cheap imitations.* **6** °sweep, °flow, °swarm, °surge, °rush, °crowd, °pour: *As soon as the doors opened, the people flooded in.* **7** °permeate, °fill, engulf, °cover, °pour into *or* °throughout *or* over: *I open the curtain and sunlight floods the room.*

floor *n.* **1** flooring, parquet, boarding, planking, *Nautical or colloq* deck: *The floor is mopped once a week.* **2** °storey, °level; deck: *On which floor is your flat?* **3** °minimum, °bottom, °base, lower limit, lowest (°level): *Owing to inflation, the wage floor was raised. Share prices went through the floor in today's trading.*
—*v.* **4** °knock over *or* down, °bowl over, °prostrate, °fell, °overthrow, °bring down, (make) °fall; °beat, °defeat, °conquer, °destroy, °rout, °overwhelm, °crush, °whip, trounce, thrash, drub, °best, worst: *The champion was floored by a blow to the head.* **5** °stump, °bewilder, baffle, °dumbfound *or* dumfound, °confuse, confound, disconcert, °nonplus, °perplex, °puzzle, °astound, °astonish, °amaze, °surprise, °shock: *Alexandra was floored when she received a gift from her ex-husband.*

flop *v.* **1** °collapse, °drop (down), °fall (down), °tumble, °topple, °plump down, plop down, °flounce down: *I was so exhausted that I flopped into bed at once.* **2** °flap, °wave, °swing: *The door, unfastened, flopped back and forth in the wind.* **3** °fail, °fall °flat, come to °naught *or* °nothing, °founder, *Colloq* °fold, *US* °bomb: *The musical flopped on the first night.*
—*n.* **4** °failure, °fiasco, °disaster, non-starter, débâcle, *US* °fizzle, *Colloq* °dud, °washout, clanger, *US* lead balloon, °bomb; *Slang* lemon, *Brit* cock-up, damp squib: *His idea for a new corkscrew was a complete flop.*

flounce *n.* **1** °frill, furbelow, peplum, °ruffle, °ornament, valance, trimming: *The dress has decorative flounces round the skirt.*
—*v.* **2** °fling, °toss, °bounce, °twist, °strut, °parade, °march, °storm, °stamp, *US* sashay: *She flounced out of the room in high dudgeon.*

flounder *v.* °grope, °blunder, °stumble, °tumble, °struggle, °stagger, °plunge about: *We floundered about in the dark till someone found the light switch.*

flourish *v.* **1** °prosper, °thrive, °grow, °develop, °luxuriate, bloom, blossom, °flower, °bear fruit, fructify, °boom, burgeon *or* bourgeon, °mature, °ripen, °increase, °succeed, °get °ahead, do *or* °fare °well, °make °good; °go up *or* °rise in the world; *Slang* °go °great guns: *We understand that Amy's medical practice has flourished.* **2** °wave, °wield, brandish, °wag, °swing, °twirl, °flaunt, vaunt, °swagger, °swish, °shake: *The band-leader flourished his baton.*
—*n.* **3** °decoration, °embellishment, floridness, floweriness, ornamentation, °elaboration, adornment, °frill, embroidery, curlicue, furbelow: *His signature is characterized by all these flourishes.* **4** °fanfare, °display, °show, showiness, °dash, gesturing, °wave: *With a flourish of his hand, the king signalled the tourney to begin.*

flourishing *adj.* °luxuriant, °lush, thriving, prospering, blooming, blossoming, °fruitful, flowering, burgeoning *or* bourgeoning, °successful, °prosperous, booming, growing, increasing: *Patel runs a flourishing flower shop in Bicester.*

flout *v.* °deride, °scorn, disdain, contemn, °spurn, decry, °denounce, misprize, °blaspheme, °depreciate, °degrade, abase, °belittle, °minimize, deprecate, °disparage, denigrate, °mock, °jeer, °guy, °ridicule, °scoff, °sneer, °gibe *or* jibe (at), °taunt, °twit, °insult, affront, *Archaic* fleer; *Colloq* °put down, °chaff, °rag, °knock: *When introduced in the sixties, miniskirts brazenly flouted convention.*

flow *v.* **1** °stream, °pour, °run, °rush, °course, °surge, °move, °go, °proceed, °progress, °drift; °gush, °glide, purl, °roll, °ripple, °trickle, °gurgle, °bubble; °swirl, whirl, °circulate: *People continue to flow past the window. The Thames flows silently to the sea.* **2** °rush, °gush, °surge, °well (forth), °stream, °spring, °issue, °spout, °spurt, squirt, °spew, °flood, cascade, °fall, °rain; °brim, overflow, °spill, °teem: *Open the gates to allow water to flow into the lock. A stream of insults flowed from his lips. Her tears flowed like wine.* **3** °issue, °originate, °come, °emanate, °rise, °begin: *With the dam repaired, water will once again flow from the reservoir. The authority of the state constitutions does not flow from Congress.* **4** °spread, overspread, °cover: *The paint flowed effortlessly onto the canvas.*
—*n.* **5** °rush, °gush, °surge; °current, °course, °stream, °run, °movement, °drift: *A dam blocks the flow of water here. The sound of a shot interrupted the flow of conversation.* **6** °abundance, superabundance, °flood, plethora, °excess, overflow(ing), deluge, tide, °supply; °plenty: *London experiences an unending flow of tourists.*

flower *n.* **1** blossom, bloom, floret *or* floweret, bud, *Technical* efflorescence: *He brought me flowers for my birthday.* **2** cream, °best, °pick, élite, *crème de la crème*, finest, choicest: *The flower of the city's youth were put to death by the wicked caliph.*
—*v.* **3** blossom, bloom, bud, burgeon *or* bourgeon, °come out, °open, °unfold, *Technical* effloresce: *The century plant was so called because it was thought to flower only once every hundred years.*

flowery *adj.* florid, °ornate, °fancy, °elaborate(d), decorated, ornamented, °overwrought, embellished, rococo, baroque, arabesque, euphuistic, Gongoristic, Ossianic, grandiloquent, °bombastic, °inflated, °pompous, °affected, °artificial, high-flown, °showy: *Many find his flowery style of writing difficult to stomach.*

fluctuate *v.* °vary, °change, °alternate, °see-saw, °swing, vacillate, undulate, waver, °oscillate, °shift: *Prices fluctuate according to supply and demand.*

fluctuation *n.* Sometimes, ***fluctuations***: °variation(s), °change(s), °alternation(s), °swing(s), vacillation(s), wavering(s), oscillation(s), undulation(s), ups and downs, instability, unsteadiness, °inconstancy: *We can expect fluctuation in temperatures during the coming week.*

fluency *n.* articulateness, eloquence, °control, °command, °ease, °grace, effortlessness, °facility, felicity, smoothness, °polish, slickness, glibness, volubility: *His extemporaneous speeches are marked by an enviable fluency.*

fluent *adj.* articulate, °eloquent, well-spoken, felicitous, °graceful, facile, °easy, °natural, °effortless, °ready, °smooth, °polished, flowing, °voluble, °glib, °slick; °expressive: *She is a fluent speaker of Spanish.*

fluff *n.* **1** down, fuzz, feather(s), thistledown, floss, lint, dust, dust-ball, fuzz ball: *Be sure you clean the fluff from under the beds.* **2** ***bit of fluff***: poppet, °girl (°friend), °mistress, *Slang* bit of all right, (bit of) crumpet, (bit of) skirt *or* stuff, *Old-fashioned Brit* popsy: *Bickerley keeps a bit of fluff on the side.* **3** °blunder, °error, °slip, °mistake, *Colloq* °howler, *Brit* bloomer, *US and Canadian* blooper: *They showed a video of the fluffs actors make during recordings.*
—*v.* **4** °muddle, °spoil, °ruin, make a °mess of, °bungle, °botch, *Colloq* °foul up, °screw up, °mess up, *US* snafu, *Slang Brit* cock up, balls up, *US* ball up, *Taboo* fuck up: *I have a funny story about how Barrymore fluffed Hamlet's soliloquy.* **5** ***fluff up***: °puff up, °shake out *or* up, aerate: *He doesn't like the pillows on his bed fluffed up.*

fluffy *adj.* **1** °soft, downy, puffy, whipped up, °light, airy, feathery, wispy: *Beat the egg whites till they are fluffy.* **2** °frivolous, °superficial, trivial, unimportant, airy, °thin, lightweight, °light, °insubstantial, gossamer, *Brit* airy-fairy: *Mr Piffle is too fluffy-headed to offer anything useful.*

fluid *n.* **1** °liquid, °solution, °liquor, ichor; gas, °vapour: *It might surprise some to learn that physicists consider gases to be fluids.*
—*adj.* **2** °liquid, flowing, °running, runny, °watery, aqueous: *Once the metal has become fluid, it is poured into the moulds.* **3** °changeable, mutable, °flexible, adjustable, °variable, pliant, unformed, formless, unfixed, unstatic *or* non-static, °plastic, °protean, mercurial, °mobile, °unstable, shifting, °uncertain, °indefinite, °unsettled: *The situation is fluid and the decision could go either way.*

fluke *n.* °lucky *or* °successful °stroke, °stroke of (°good) °luck, °lucky *or* °big °break, (°happy) °accident, °quirk *or* °twist of °fate, °windfall, fortuity, serendipity: *If he won first prize, it was by a fluke.*

flummox *v.* °confuse, baffle, °perplex, °bewilder, confound, °throw into °confusion, °stymie, °stump, °puzzle, °mystify, fox, °deceive, °hoodwink, °nonplus: *We were completely flummoxed by the licensing requirements.*

flunkey *n.* **1** °servant, retainer, lackey, footman, °menial, minion, hireling, underling, °subordinate, °inferior; °slave; *Colloq* dogsbody, *Slang US and Canadian* gofer: *A company flunkey drove me to the airport.* **2** toady, °hanger-on, °yes-man, jackal, doormat, stooge, lickspittle, sycophant, *Colloq US and Canadian* apple-polisher, *Taboo* brown-noser: *He has a collection of flunkeys waiting about for hand-outs.*

flurry *n.* **1** °activity, commotion, ado, to-do, °fuss, °upset, hubbub, pother, °stir, °excitement, °disturbance, °agitation, °tumult, whirl, °furore *or US* furor, bustle, °hurry, °hustle, °flutter, °fluster; °burst, °outburst; *Colloq* tizzy: *I was happy to leave the worry and flurry of the city. There was a brief flurry of activity at the Stock Exchange today.*
—*v.* **2** °confuse, °bewilder, °agitate, °put out, °disturb, °excite, °fluster, disconcert, °upset, °perturb, unsettle, °shake (up), *Colloq* °rattle: *He was quite flurried by the arrival of the police.*

flush[1] *v.* **1** °blush, redden, crimson, °glow, °burn, °colour (up): *When he told her she was pretty she flushed a bit.* **2** Often, ***flush out***: °rinse, °wash (out *or* away), douse, douche, hose down, °flood, °drench, °clean out, °cleanse, °purge, °discharge, °empty: *Oil tankers are flushed out far from shore.* **3** °animate, °stir, °inflame, impassion, °quicken, arouse, °excite, elate, °encourage, °cheer, °delight, °thrill, °gladden: *Suzie was flushed with the success of having got the job.*
—*n.* **4** °blush, redness, bloom, rosiness, °colour, blood, °glow, °radiance: *When he was asked what had happened to the money, a flush rose to his cheek.* **5** °flood, deluge, drenching, °soaking, overflow, inundation, °rush, °gush, °surge, °stream, °flow: *The flush of water washed away all the debris.* **6** °thrill, °excitement, °passion, quickening, arousal, °stir, °stirring, °animation, elation, euphoria, °delight, °encouragement, tingle: *In the first flush of success, they were overwhelmed with orders. He felt a flush come over him when he won the race.*

flush[2] *adj.* **1** (on the °same) °plane *or* °level (with), °even, °smooth, °flat, °square, °true, °continuous; adjacent, next to: *See that the tabletop is flush with the countertop. The mirror should be flush against the wall.* **2** °full, overflowing, °replete, °abundant: *Turn off the water when it is flush with the top of the basin.* **3** °solvent, well supplied, °comfortable; well-to-do, well off, well-found, °wealthy, °rich, °prosperous, affluent, moneyed, *Colloq* well-heeled, on Easy Street, in the °money, *US* in the chips; *Slang* °loaded, rolling (in °money *or* it): *He's flush enough to take us all out to dinner.*
—*adv.* **4** °even(ly), °square(ly), levelly, °plumb, °directly: *Cut this branch off flush.*

fluster *v.* **1** °agitate, °stir (up), discompose, °discomfit, °discomfort, disconcert, °shake (up), °upset, disquiet, discommode, °bother, °put out *or* off, °disturb, °perturb, °flurry, °flutter, make °nervous, °throw off, °distract, °confuse, baffle, confound, °puzzle, °perplex, befuddle, °bewilder, °daze, °dazzle, *Colloq* °rattle, °throw, discombobulate, hassle, faze: *Don't be flustered by her rude manner.*
—*n.* **2** °agitation, °upset, °discomfort, disquiet, °bother, °disturbance, commotion, perturbation, dither, °flurry, °flutter, nervousness, °distraction, °confusion, bafflement, befuddlement, °perplexity, bewilderment: *All this fluster came about through the absence of a coherent plan.*

flutter *v.* **1** °flap, °flop, °fluctuate, vacillate, °wave, waver, °oscillate: *The paper streamers fluttered in the breeze.* **2** °flit, °flicker, flitter, °hover, °dance; °fuss: *We shall never get done if you keep fluttering about.* **3** °tremble, °shake, °quiver, dither, °jump, °vibrate, twitch: *She is fluttering with anticipation waiting for the postman.*
—*n.* **4** fluttering, flapping, flopping, °fluctuation, fluctuating, vacillation, vacillating, °wave, waving, oscillation, oscillating, trembling, °quiver, quivering: *The slightest flutter of her fan communicates volumes.* **5** See **fluster, 2,** above.

flux *n.* instability, °change, °mutation, modification, °fluctuation, °unrest, °swing, °swinging, wavering, °movement, °motion, oscillation, °indecision, indecisiveness: *The economic indicators are in a constant state of flux.*

fly *v.* **1** take wing, take °flight, take to the °air, wing, °soar, °sail, °hover; °flutter, °flit, °flap: *A stork flew overhead. Daedalus taught Icarus to fly.* **2** Also, ***fly away or off***: take °flight, °depart, °leave, °flee, decamp, °bolt, °run away *or* off, °escape, make (good) one's °escape, take to one's heels, show a clean pair of heels, °rush *or* °nip off *or* out *or* away, (make a) °run (for it), °go *or* °get away *or* off, abscond, make a °getaway, °cut and °run, °beat a (hasty) °retreat, °take off, scoot, *Colloq* °light out, °beat it, °clear out *or* off, skedaddle, scram, *US* °cut out, hightail (it), take it on the lam, take a (run-out) powder, lam out, take to the hills, take to the woods; *Slang Brit* scarper, °bugger off, *US* vamoose, °blow: *She flew off before I could get her telephone number.* **3** °hasten, °hurry, °rush, °run, °race, °dash, sprint, °tear, scamper, scoot, *Colloq* make tracks: *I must fly if I'm to catch the train.* **4** °pass (by), °elapse, °go (by), °expire, °run its course, °slip *or* °slide by *or* away: *Time flies quickly when you're having fun.* **5** aviate, °pilot; jet: *Parker flies his own plane. I flew down to Paris with him.* **6** ***fly in the face of***: °flout, °defy, °go against, contemn, °scorn, °scoff at, °oppose, °go *or* °run °counter to, °counter, °counteract, countervail, countermine, °contradict, contravene, °thumb one's nose at, *Colloq Brit* cock a snook at: *His actions fly in the face of conventional behaviour.* **7** ***fly off the handle***: fly into a °rage *or* °fury *or* °temper *or* °passion, lose one's °temper, have a °fit *or* °tantrum, be fit to be tied, °go °berserk, °go °crazy *or* °mad, °explode, *Colloq* lose *or* °blow one's °cool, °blow one's top, hit *or* °go through the roof, *US* hit the ceiling, °blow one's stack, get worked up (over); *Slang* °blow a fuse *or* a gasket, °flip (one's lid), have a haemorrhage, *Brit* °flip one's top: *Rudolf flies off the handle at the slightest provocation.* **8** ***let fly***: **a** °throw, °toss, °cast, °hurl, °fling, °heave, °pitch, °lob, °sling, chuck, °shoot, °fire (off), °let °rip, °discharge, °launch, °propel, °let °go *or* off: *They let fly a volley of arrows.* **b** °let °go with, °let (someone) have it, °lash out, °vent one's spleen, lose one's °temper, °burst out *or* forth, °burst into, *Colloq* pull no punches, °tear into: *That was the last straw, and she really let fly at him.*
—*n.* **9** Often, *Brit* ***flies***: °flap, fly °front, *Brit* zip, *US* zipper: *He was embarrassed to find his flies were open.* **10** ***fly in the ointment***: °hitch, °snag, °impediment, °obstacle, °obstruction, °problem, °difficulty, °drawback, detraction, °rub, °hindrance, bugbear, bogey *or* bogy, bugaboo: *The one fly in the ointment is that my mother won't give me permission to go.*

fly-by-night *adj.* **1** °temporary, °short-lived, transitory, °fugitive, ephemeral, °transient, °fleeting, °passing, °brief, impermanent, here today, gone tomorrow: *That fly-by-night operation was in business for less than a month.* **2** °unreliable, untrustworthy, °disreputable, °irresponsible, dubious, °questionable; °shifty, °dishonest, °sharp, °crooked, *Colloq* °shady, *Brit* cowboy: *Guarantees on double glazing are worthless if installed by some fly-by-night company.*

foam *n.* **1** bubbles, °froth, spume, °lather, suds; effervescence, °sparkle, carbonation, °fizz: *The foam leaves spots when it dries.*
—*v.* **2** °bubble, °froth, spume, °lather, suds, soap up: *Watch the solution foam when I drop this tablet into it.*

focal *adj.* °central, focused, concentrated, convergent, centred, centralized: *The light rays come together at this focal point. Harris's address was the focal point of the conference.*

focus *n.* **1** °centre, concentration, °focal °point, °heart, °core, °target, convergence, °hub, nave; cynosure: *Why should Anita always be the focus of attention?* **2** ***in focus***: °clear, °distinct, well- *or* °sharply defined: *With the telescope in focus, you feel as if you can almost touch the distant shore.* **3** ***out of focus***: unclear, °indistinct, blurred, blurry, °fuzzy, °woolly: *The photos are so out of focus that I can't tell who's who.*
—*v.* **4** °concentrate, °centre, °converge, °meet, pinpoint, °spotlight; bring into focus; *Colloq* °zero in: *Without distractions, we can focus on the problem at hand.*

fog *n.* **1** °mist, haze, smog, °vapour, cloud, *Colloq* pea-souper: *Our flight was grounded because of fog.* **2** °trance, °daze, °stupor, brown study, °confused state; coma: *He's in a fog and didn't hear a word you said.*
—*v.* **3** °dim, °obscure, cloud, bedim, becloud, °blind, °stifle: *The purpose of all that verbiage is merely to fog the issue.* **4** Usually, ***befog***: °bewilder, °mystify, °perplex, °confuse, °muddle, °puzzle, °nonplus: *I was completely befogged by the technical language he used.* **5** Also, ***fog up*** *or* ***over***: °mist over *or* up, cloud up *or* over, °shroud: *My bathroom mirror fogs when I take a hot shower.*

fogy *n.* Usually, ***old fogy*** *or* ***fogey***: fogey, °conservative, °relic, *Colloq* fuddy-duddy, fossil, °antique, °stick-in-the-mud, back number, °square: *That old fogy still dances the foxtrot.*

foible *n.* °weakness, °imperfection, °weak point, °fault, °frailty, °shortcoming, °flaw, °defect, °failing, °blemish, °infirmity; °peculiarity, idiosyncrasy, °quirk, crotchet, °eccentricity, preoccupation, °kink, *Colloq* hang-up, °bug: *One of her foibles is that she loves junk food.*

foil[1] *v.* °thwart, °offset, °defeat, baffle, balk, parry, °frustrate, °counter, °check, °impede, °hamper, °outwit, circumvent, checkmate, °daunt, disconcert, °discomfit, °disappoint, pull the rug out from under (someone), cut the ground from under someone's feet, nullify, °nip in the bud, countervail (against), *Brit* put a spoke in (someone's) wheel, *Colloq* clip (someone's) wings, cut (someone) down to size, °spoil (someone's) game, *Chiefly US and Canadian* faze: *The villain and his evil plan were again foiled by the arrival of the sheriff.*

foil[2] *n.* layer, lamina, lamination, °sheet, membrane, °film, coating, °flake, °scale, wafer: *Cigarettes once came packaged in tin foil.*

foist *v.* palm *or* °pass off, °impose, °unload, °put (off), °push (off), *Colloq* °lay (off), *Brit* fob off: *Don't try to foist those fake paintings on me!*

fold *v.* **1** °bend, °ply, °double (over *or* up), °overlap, crease, pleat, °gather, crimp: *Fold the letter before putting it into the envelope.* **2** °enclose, °envelop, enfold, °wrap, enwrap, °clasp, °clip, °embrace, °hug, °gather: *He folded her in his arms.* **3** °give °way, °collapse, °fail, °close (up *or* down), °shut down, °go out of business, °go bankrupt, *Colloq* °go under, °go °broke, °go bust, *Brit* go to the °wall: *The company folded and ten employees were made redundant.*
—*n.* **4** crease, °wrinkle, crinkle, °pucker, pleat, °gather, crimp, °overlap, °lap: *The folds will remain crisp if you use starch when ironing.*

folk *n.* °people, °tribe, (ethnic) °group, °clan, °race; °society, °nation, (°general) °public, °populace, °population, citizenry: *Archaeologists refer to these people as the 'Beaker Folk'. Some folks disliked the performance.*

follow *v.* **1** °go *or* °come after *or* next; °go *or* °walk *or* tread *or* °move behind, bring up the rear, *Colloq* °string *or* °tag along: *You go on ahead and I'll follow shortly. Please see the comments that follow.* **2** adhere to, °cleave to, °support, °believe in, °accept, °adopt, °conform to, °comply with, °obey, be guided by, be modelled after *or* on, °observe, °heed, °mind, °go along with, °reflect, °mirror, °echo, °imitate, °copy, °mimic, ape: *This newspaper follows strict party policy.* **3** °attend, °accompany, °escort, °go (along) with; °serve: *Mary's little lamb followed her everywhere.* **4** °chase, °pursue, dog, °hunt (down), °stalk, °run down, °track, °trail, °tail, °trace, °shadow: *The detective swore to follow him to the ends of the earth.* **5** °succeed, °supersede, °step into the shoes of, take the °place of, °replace, °supplant: *Who followed Henry VIII on the throne?* **6** °practise, °pursue, °engage in, °carry on, °occupy oneself with, °apply *or* °dedicate *or* °devote oneself to, °cultivate: *After the war he followed a career as a teacher.* **7** °result from, ensue, °issue, °flow, °arise, °develop: *The conclusion follows logically from the premise.* **8** °understand, °fathom, °comprehend, °get, °grasp, °see, °catch, °appreciate, °take in, °keep up with, *Colloq* °dig: *Were you able to follow everything in that lecture?* **9** °watch, be a °fan *or* aficionado of, °pursue, take an °interest in, °keep up with, °keep abreast of, °cheer *or* °root for, °admire: *He follows international yacht racing.* **10** ***follow through (on)***: °persist *or* °persevere, °continue, °perform, conclude, °realize, consummate, °pursue, °carry out, °see through, °make good, °discharge, adhere to, °keep: *I only hope she follows this through and delivers the goods.* **11** ***follow up (on)***: **a** °pursue, °go after, °track, °investigate, °check (out), °check up (on), °inquire, make inquiries, °look into: *MacGregor is very good at following up on the most obscure references.* **b** °pursue, °prosecute, °reinforce, consolidate, °support, °buttress, augment, °bolster, °ensure: *The Romans followed up their success with an attack on Olbia.*

follower *n.* **1** °disciple, adherent, °student, °pupil, °apprentice, °protégé(e): *They were followers of Buddha.* **2** °attendant, °henchman, °servant, retainer, bodyguard, myrmidon: *Louie walked in with two of his followers.* **3** °supporter, °devotee, °fan, aficionado, promoter, °enthusiast, booster, °advocate, °proponent, *US* rooter, *Colloq* groupie: *She is a faithful follower of The Dirty Knees, a rock group.*

follow-through *n.* °perseverance, diligence, °persistence, steadfastness, °endurance, °stamina, indefatigableness, sedulousness, sedulity, pursuance, °tenacity, °resolve, °determination, *Colloq US* stick-to-it-iveness: *One needs imagination for new ideas but follow-through to make them succeed.*

follow-up *n.* °reinforcement, °support, backup, bolstering; consolidation: *The failure of the sales campaign was attributed to lack of follow-up.*

folly *n.* **1** foolishness, °nonsense, °absurdity, daftness, silliness, preposterousness, absurdness, senselessness, fatuousness, fatuity, rashness, °stupidity, asininity, inanity, nonsensicalness, idiocy, imbecility, irrationality, °lunacy, °insanity, °madness, craziness, °eccentricity, weak-mindedness, feeble-mindedness, simple-mindedness, muddle-headedness, thickheadedness, stolidity, stolidness, obtuseness, brainlessness, *Colloq* dumbness, dopiness, nuttiness, *US and Canadian* kookiness: *They saw the folly of fighting against such enormous odds. It would be folly to leave in this storm.* **2** °absurdity, °mistake, °blunder, °error, faux pas, gaffe, *Colloq* goof, °fluff: *What follies have been committed in the name of honour!*

foment *v.* °rouse, °stir *or* °whip up, °awaken, waken, °provoke, °incite, instigate, °initiate, °prompt, °start, °motivate, °inspire, °work up, °inflame, °fan the flames (of), °kindle, galvanize, °rally, °excite, °stimulate, °encourage, °promote, °foster, °forward, °further, °advance, °cultivate, °sow the seeds of, °spur, goad, egg on, °urge: *He is always fomenting ill will against the management.*

fond *adj.* **1** °tender, loving, °affectionate, °warm, adoring, caring: *She clasped him in a fond embrace.* **2** °foolish, °bootless, °empty, °vain, °naïve: *She had fond hopes of his being elected.* **3** ***fond of***: °partial to, (having a) °liking (for), °soft on *or* about, °affectionate towards, °attached to, having a °fancy *or* °taste for, fancying, predisposed *or* °inclined to *or* towards; addicted to, *Colloq* hooked on: *She is inordinately fond of chocolate.*

fondle *v.* °caress, °stroke, °pet, °pat, °touch, °cuddle, °snuggle; °handle: *See that couple over there fondling one another? He fondled his dagger.*

fondly *adv.* affectionately, lovingly, tenderly, °warmly, adoringly, caressingly: *Martin regarded his wife fondly.*

food *n.* °nourishment, nutriment, aliment, °sustenance, °subsistence; foodstuffs, edibles, eatables, viands, bread, victuals, °rations, °provisions, comestibles, *Brit* commons, *Colloq* grub, eats, chow, *Brit* °scoff, prog: *Without any food for days, the survivors were near starvation.*

fool *n.* **1** simpleton, ninny, ninny-hammer, nincompoop, ass, jackass, dunce, °dolt, °halfwit, numskull *or* numbskull, blockhead, bonehead, pinhead, °silly, feather-brain, loon, goose, booby, jay, goon, mooncalf, idiot, ignoramus, dim-wit, nitwit, imbecile, moron, °clod, clodpole, clodpoll, clodpate, oaf, *Psychology* retardate, *Scots* gomerel, *Colloq* birdbrain, dumb-bell, fat-head, chump, °twit, knuckle-head, chucklehead, nit, twerp *or* twirp, *Brit* pillock, *US and Canadian* °jerk, °retard; *Slang* °sap, °dope, *Brit* git, *Australian* boofhead: *He's such a fool he'll believe anything.* **2** (court) jester, °clown, °comic, °comedian *or* comedienne, entertainer, °zany, buffoon, °merry andrew, *farceur*, *farceuse*, °joker, jokester, droll, Punch, Punchinello, pierrot, harlequin: *In Shakespeare's plays, the fool is often the wisest character.* **3** °butt, °dupe, gull, °victim, cat's-paw, *Colloq* chump, °greenhorn, (easy) mark, *US* fall guy; *Slang* pigeon, °sucker, stooge, *Brit* °mug: *His co-workers liked to make a fool out of him.*
—*v.* **4** °trick, °deceive, °take in, °swindle, °defraud, °hoax, °cheat, °fleece, cozen, °hoodwink, °bluff, °dupe, gull, humbug, delude, °mislead, make a fool of; pull the wool over (someone's) eyes, °have (someone) on, °pull (someone's) °leg, °tease, °twit, *Archaic* chouse; *Colloq* kid, con, snow, do a snow job on, bamboozle, °put one *or* something over on, pull something *or* a fast one on, *Brit* °twist, *Chiefly US and Canadian* josh; *Slang* °pluck, *Brit* nobble: *When he said the diamond was fake, he certainly fooled me. I think she was fooling when she said she'd inherited millions.* **5** °joke, jest, °banter, °tease, °twit, feign, °fake, °pretend, °make °believe, *Colloq* kid: *She insists that she is not fooling but dead serious.* **6** ***fool with*** *or* ***around*** *or* ***about (with)***: °play (around *or* about) (with), °toy *or* °trifle (with), °mess *or* °fiddle (around *or* about) (with), °monkey (around *or* about) with, °meddle (with), °tamper with, fribble (with): *Please stop fooling with the dials on the radio.* **7** ***fool around*** *or* ***about***: **a** °play *or* °mess around *or* about, gambol, °frolic, romp, °cavort: *Stop fooling around and get serious.* **b** °waste *or* °fritter away *or* squander *or* kill time, fribble, loiter, °dawdle, °idle, *Brit* °potter (about), °lark *or* °muck about *or* around, *US* putter around *or* about, *Colloq* footle: *She's always fooling around instead of getting on with her work.*

foolhardy *adj.* °rash, °imprudent, °impetuous, °reckless, °brash, °venturesome, °bold, °cheeky, °daring, °audacious, temerarious, °adventurous, °daredevil, incautious, °hotheaded, °careless, °heedless, devil-may-care, °hasty, °thoughtless, °unthinking, °irresponsible, °wild, madcap, *Colloq US and Canadian* nervy, *Slang* gutsy: *It is foolhardy to go scuba diving without a companion.*

foolish *adj.* **1** °senseless, incautious, °imprudent, impolitic, °indiscreet, unwise, injudicious, ill-considered, °ill-advised, °misguided, °short-sighted, °impetuous, headlong, °rash, °brash, °reckless, °hasty, °heedless, °unwary, °foolhardy, °thoughtless, °mindless: *Standing under a tree in a thunderstorm is foolish.* **2** °nonsensical, °stupid, asinine, °inane, °silly, fatuous, fatuitous, dim-witted, °scatterbrained, °harebrained, °crazy, °mad, °insane, demented, irrational, °erratic, °unstable, crack-brained, feather-brained, bird-brained, simple-minded, light-headed, muddle-headed, numskulled *or* numbskulled, addle-pated, rattle-brained, bemused, °confused, °feeble-minded, moronic, idiotic, imbecilic, °halfwitted, dull-witted, slow-witted, witless, brainless, empty-headed, block-headed, boneheaded, thickheaded, °obtuse, °stolid, *Colloq* °dumb, balmy *or Brit* barmy, loony, nuts, nutty, batty, dopey *or* dopy, °soft (in the head), °dim, °thick, dippy, dotty, °dizzy, *Brit* potty, °daft, *Slang* cuckoo, goofy, screwy, wacky: *Tracy was foolish to believe him when he said he loved her.* **3** °preposterous, °ridiculous, °absurd, irrational, illogical, °unreasonable, °ludicrous, °wild: *They have some foolish idea about building a hotel in Antarctica.*

foolproof *adj.* °safe, °certain, °sure, °trustworthy, dependable, °reliable, °infallible, unfailing, guaranteed, warranted, *Colloq* sure-fire: *She claims to have a foolproof way of preventing unwanted pregnancies.*

footing *n.* **1** °foundation, °basis, °base, °ground(s): *The events put our entire relationship on a new footing.* **2** °standing, °status, °level, °condition, °position, terms, °state, °rank: *The two departments are on an equal footing as far as funding is concerned.* **3** foothold, toe-hold; °balance, °stability: *She lost her footing on the icy pavement and down she went.*

footstep *n.* **1** °step, footfall, tread: *I recognized her footstep.* **2** Usually, ***footsteps***: footprint(s), °track, °trail, °trace, spoor, footmark(s); °tradition, °example, °way of life: *He followed in his master's footsteps.*

for *prep.* **1** representing, championing; in °favour of, *Brit* on *or US and Canadian also* in °behalf of, on the °side of, in °support of, in the °service of, as a °service to, for the °benefit of, pro: *Are you for or against the candidate? She did it for herself.* **2** in °search *or* °quest of, seeking, looking for *or* after, after, with a °view *or* an °eye to: *We're just here for the beer.* **3** °instead of, in °place of, representing, as a replacement for, *Brit* on *or US and Canadian* in °behalf of; in °return *or* °exchange for, in compensation *or* recompense *or* °payment *or* repayment for, in °requital for: *I am acting for my father. This cheque is for the toaster. Will you accept nothing for your pains?* **4** for the °treatment of, as a °remedy for, against; for the °purpose *or* °object of: *This medication is for skin infections only. It's for your own good.* **5** for the °sake of, *Brit* on *or US and Canadian also* in °behalf of, in the °interest of: *Would you really do that for me?* **6** in the °direction of, to, °towards, into: *Head for the hills!* **7** to °save, in the °interest *or* °benefit of, for the °sake *or* °benefit of, conducive to; because of, on °account of, by °reason of: *Every summer, they went to Carlsbad for their health. She hated him for what he represented.* **8** to °go to, °destined for: *I am leaving for Tierra del Fuego tomorrow.* **9** °suitable *or* suited for, °fit *or* °fitted *or* °fitting for, °appropriate for, °proper for: *I am not sure that this colour is for you. Is it right for me to speak out now?* **10** for the duration of; over (the °extent of), during, in the °course of, °throughout, °through: *She stayed for a week.* **11** °despite, in °spite of, °notwithstanding, allowing for: *For all his complaining, he seemed satisfied.* **12** ***as for***: °regarding, in °regard to, as regards, respecting, °concerning, as °far as (something *or* someone) is °concerned: *As for Betty, let her do as she likes.*
—*conj.* **13** because, since, as, inasmuch as, °seeing that, owing *or* °due to the °fact that: *I was unable to see him, for he was out of the office.*

forbid *v.* °prohibit, °ban, °hinder, °stop, °exclude, debar, °preclude, °prevent; °outlaw, interdict, disallow, proscribe, °taboo; °veto: *I was forbidden from entering. They forbid smoking in the classrooms.*

forbidding *adj.* **1** °repellent, °repulsive, °offensive, odious, °abhorrent: *In his long cloak and mask, he presented a forbidding appearance.* **2** °hostile, unfriendly, °stern, °harsh, °menacing, °threatening, °ominous, °dangerous, °bad, °nasty, °ugly, unpleasant: *The coast here is rocky and forbidding. The old crone gave him a forbidding look and we cringed.*

force *n.* **1** °power, °might, °energy, °strength, potency, °vigour, °intensity, °violence, °impact; °dynamism, °pressure: *The force of the blow knocked me down.* **2** coercion, °pressure, constraint, °duress, compulsion, arm-twisting: *When persuasion failed, the guards resorted to force.* **3** troops, °soldiers, army: *NATO*

forces are on manoeuvres. **4** °weight, persuasiveness, °persistence, cogency, effectiveness, efficacy, °strength, validity, °significance, value: *The force of his argument was sufficient to convince us.* **5** °meaning, °import, °significance: *Are they able to cope with the full force of the word 'God'?* **6** ***in force***: in °effect, °effective, in °operation, °operative, valid, binding, °current: *The ancient customs still remain in force. The law came into force at midnight.*
—*v.* **7** °make, °oblige, °require, compel, coerce, °exact, constrain, °enforce, impel, °intimidate, °pressure *or Brit also* pressurize, °press, dragoon, °twist (someone's) arm, *Colloq* bulldoze, put the °squeeze on (someone): *Each of us was forced to dig his own grave.* **8** °push, °drive, °thrust, °propel; prise *or* °prize, °break, °wrench, °crack, jemmy, *US* °pry: *The tornado forced the chair through the wall. He forced open the safe and took the money.* **9** °exact, °extort, °extract, wrest, wring, °drag: *The CIA tried to force a confession from her.*

forced *adj.* °artificial, °unnatural, contrived, °stilted, °calculated, °studied, °laboured, °strained, °stiff, °false, feigned, °fake(d), °mannered, °affected, °self-conscious, *Colloq* °phoney *or US also* phony: *Her forced joviality failed to conceal her contempt for those present.*

forceful *adj.* **1** °vigorous, °energetic, compelling, °dynamic, °intense, °potent, °strong, °mighty, °powerful, °aggressive, °weighty, °effective, convincing, °persuasive: *The colonel was known as a forceful leader of men.* **2** °effective, °efficacious, cogent, °logical, °impressive, °telling, convincing, °persuasive, °strong, °mighty, °forcible, °powerful, compelling, °irresistible; pithy, meaty: *The most forceful arguments came from Catherine towards the end of the discussion.*

forcible *adj.* **1** See **forceful, 2,** above. **2** °drastic, °forceful, °violent, °aggressive, coercive, °severe, stringent: *The plan involves the forcible repatriation of refugees.*

foreboding *n.* **1** apprehension, apprehensiveness, °feeling, °sense, °misgiving, °dread, °suspicion, °intuition, °anxiety, °fear: *An atmosphere of foreboding filled the crypt.* **2** °premonition, augury, °prophecy, °prediction, prognostication, °warning, foretoken, foreshadowing, presentiment, °omen, °sign, portent, intimation, forewarning, presage, °advance word: *I had a strange foreboding of horror as I entered the room.*

forecast *v.* **1** °predict, foretell, °prophesy, °prognosticate, °foresee, augur, presage, vaticinate, °anticipate; forewarn, °calculate: *Seers forecast coming events; meteorologists forecast the weather.*
—*n.* **2** °prediction, °prophecy, °prognosis, prognostication, °foresight, augury, vaticination, °anticipation; forewarning, °calculation: *Have you heard the weather forecast for tomorrow?*

foregoing *adj.* °preceding, °above, °former, °previous, °precedent, °prior, antecedent; earlier, °preliminary, anterior; aforementioned, aforesaid: *The foregoing paragraph set forth the principles.*

foregone *adj.* Usually in ***foregone conclusion***: °assumed, established, pre-established, °predetermined, °fixed, °inevitable, °set, accepted, °cut and dried: *His incarceration for the crime was a foregone conclusion.*

foreign *adj.* **1** °alien, imported, non-native; °overseas, °distant, tramontane, transalpine, transatlantic, transpacific: *Duty is payable on foreign goods. We holiday in a different foreign country each year.* **2** °strange, °outlandish, °exotic, °unfamiliar, °peculiar, °odd, °curious: *She regards anything except beans and toast as foreign food.* **3** °unknown, °unfamiliar, °strange, °inappropriate, °unrelated, unconnected, unassimilable, °remote, °extrinsic, °extraneous: *Their philosophy is completely foreign to my way of thinking.*

foreigner *n.* °alien, non-native, °immigrant, °newcomer, °new °arrival, °outsider, outlander, °stranger: *The word* xenophobia *means 'dread of foreigners'.*

foreman *n.* °superintendent, °manager, °boss, °supervisor, °overseer, *Brit* shopwalker, *US* floor-walker, *Colloq* °super, *Brit* gaffer, *US* straw °boss: *The foreman insists we use the time clocks.*

foremost *adj.* **1** °first, °primary, °prime, °leading, °pre-eminent, °supreme; °prominent, °notable, °noteworthy, °noted, °chief, °paramount, °main, °best, °superior: *She is one of the foremost eye surgeons in her country.*
—*adv.* **2** °first, firstly, °primarily, in (the) °first place, before anything else: *First and foremost, we must consider the matter of safety.*

forerunner *n.* **1** °predecessor, °precursor, foregoer; herald, °harbinger, °envoy; forebear, °ancestor, forefather, °progenitor: *This dishwasher is better designed than its forerunners. The cuckoo is thought by many to be the forerunner of spring.* **2** °omen, portent, foretoken, °premonition, °sign, augury, °token: *A drop in the barometer is a forerunner of bad weather.*

foresee *v.* presage, foretell, °envisage, °picture, °forecast, °predict, °prophesy, augur, *US* °envision: *I don't foresee any problems.*

foreshadow *v.* presage, foretoken, portend, augur, °indicate, °prophesy, °predict, °bode, °signal, °signify, betoken: *The surrender of Ghent foreshadowed the fate of Flanders.*

foresight *n.* **1** °providence, °prudence, °care, far-sightedness, watchfulness, °caution, °precaution, long-sightedness, perspicacity, °wisdom, sagacity, °insight, circumspection: *The commander demonstrated foresight in ordering a retreat.* **2** prevision, °perception, °prospect, °vision, foreknowledge, prescience; °expectation: *A little foresight could have prevented the calamity.*

forestall *v.* °anticipate, °prevent, °obstruct, °hinder, obviate, °thwart, °preclude, °frustrate, avert, °ward *or* stave *or* °fend off, °intercept, parry, °stop, °delay: *The frigate effectively forestalled our plan to sail away secretly.*

forethought *n.* premeditation, planning, plotting, far-sightedness, long-sightedness: *Much forethought went into the assassination scheme.*

for ever *adv.* **1** forever, °always, for good, °ever, (for) evermore, forevermore, eternally, everlastingly, for °ever and a day, undyingly, for °eternity, till doomsday, till the °end of °time, *Colloq* till the cows come home, till hell freezes over: *They swore to be true for ever.* **2** forever, constantly, continually, continuously, all the °time, unceasingly, incessantly, without °cease *or* surcease, endlessly, °consistently, persistently, interminably, perpetually: *She was for ever watching soap operas on the telly.*

foreword *n.* °preface, prologue, prelude, prolegomenon, °preamble, *Literary* proem; introduction: *He set forth the purpose of the book in the foreword.*

forfeit *n.* **1** °penalty, °fine, °fee, °charge, damages, forfeiture, sequestration, amercement, mulct: *You will have to give me a kiss as a forfeit.*
—*v.* **2** °lose, °yield (up), °give up *or* over, °relinquish, °surrender, be °stripped *or* °deprived of, °forgo, °renounce, °waive: *You have forfeited your right to trial and you will be hanged at dawn.*
—*adj.* **3** surrendered, °lost, yielded, relinquished, forgone, waived, renounced: *His life was forfeit the moment he volunteered to defuse the bomb.*

forge *v.* **1** °make, °construct, °fashion, °fabricate, °manufacture, °shape, °mould, °cast, hammer out: *This plant forges heavy steel tools. He forged a new life for himself in the American West.* **2** °create, °invent, °conceive (of), °coin, °devise, °think up, °frame: *I have forged a new plan of escape.* **3** °counterfeit, °copy, °reproduce, °imitate, °falsify, °fake, *Slang US* hang paper: *She forged her employer's name on the cheque. The gang was caught because they forged three-pound notes.*

forgery *n.* **1** counterfeiting, falsification, °fraud, fraudulence: *He was sent to prison for ten years for forgery.* **2** °counterfeit, °fake, °sham, °imitation, *Colloq* °phoney *or US also* phony: *The police have found three forgeries of Dali paintings.*

forget *v.* **1** °fail *or* °cease to °remember *or* °recall *or* °think of, °lose, draw a °blank: *I forgot what I was supposed to buy at the market.* **2** °leave (behind), °omit *or* °neglect (doing *or* taking): *I forgot my umbrella this morning.* **3** °ignore, °dismiss from (one's) °mind *or* thoughts, °disregard, °overlook, consign to °oblivion: *Forget the fact that you ever met me.*

forgetful *adj.* amnesiac; °absent-minded, distracted, abstracted, °inattentive, °preoccupied, neglectful, negligent, °careless, °lax, °dreamy, dreaming, in dreamland, in the clouds, in cloud-cuckoo-land *or* cloud-land *or* Nephelococcygia, °remote, distrait(e), *Colloq* not turned on, turned off, out of it: *Franklin is so forgetful he'd lose his head if it weren't stitched on.*

forgive *v.* **1** °pardon, °excuse, °allow, make °allowance(s) for, °indulge, condone, °vindicate; °overlook, °ignore, °disregard, pay no °attention to, °pass over, *US* slough over: *Please forgive my curiosity, but where did you get that hat?* **2** °clear, acquit, absolve, exculpate, exonerate; °spare; *Colloq* °let off: *Father, forgive them, for they know not what they do.* **3** °cancel, °waive, °abolish, °void, nullify, °erase, °delete; *Colloq* °let off (the °hook): *Her dream was to awake one day and find all her debts forgiven.*

forgiveness *n.* **1** °pardon, °reprieve, absolution, °remission, acquittal, acquittance, amnesty, °allowance, vindication, exculpation, exoneration, *Archaic* shrift: *Oh, Lord, I ask forgiveness for my sins.* **2** °mercy, mercifulness, compassion, °grace, leniency, clemency, °indulgence, °tolerance: *He begged her forgiveness for the way he had treated her.*

forgiving *adj.* °tolerant, °lenient, °sparing, forbearing, °merciful, compassionate, conciliatory, magnanimous, humane, °soft-hearted, clement: *In a forgiving mood, the judge gave her a light sentence.*

forgo *v.* **1** °give up, °renounce, forswear, °forsake, °abandon, do *or* °go without, °sacrifice, °eliminate, °omit, °leave out *or* °alone, °cede, °waive; °avoid, °shun, eschew, abstain from, °turn down, °pass up, °deny (oneself): *His new diet requires him to forgo all dairy produce.* **2** °resign, °give up, °yield, °surrender, °relinquish, °cede, °waive, °renounce, forswear, °abdicate, °abandon: *Did he not forgo all right to the throne by marrying a commoner?*

forlorn *adj.* **1** °miserable, °wretched, °desolate, °woebegone, °lost, °pitiable, °pitiful, °pathetic, woeful, cheerless, °joyless, °unhappy, depressed, °sad, disconsolate, °gloomy, lugubrious, °glum, °despondent, °dismal, °dejected, dispirited, low-spirited, comfortless, down, °melancholy, dolorous, °sorrowful, °mournful, °inconsolable: *She looked so fragile and forlorn as she struggled to hold back her tears.* **2** °abandoned, forsaken, °deserted, neglected, shunned, °outcast, °alone, °lonely, °lonesome, friendless, bereft: *We came upon a forlorn little village.*

form *n.* **1** °shape, configuration, conformation, °order, °organization, °arrangement, °formation, construction, °structure, °construct, °frame, °cut, °cast, °mould, °pattern, °appearance; °manifestation: *The equipment in the playground was in a variety of geometric forms. In what form will the jinnee appear next?* **2** °figure, °body, °build, °shape, °physique, anatomy; °silhouette, °aspect, °look, °appearance, °profile, contour; °carriage, °bearing, °attitude, °pose, *Slang US* bod, built: *She has the form of a wrestler.* **3** °type, °kind, °variety, °sort, °breed, species, genus, °genre, °character, °make, °brand, °colour, °tone, °tint, °texture, °fabric, °material, feather, °description, °manner, °way, °nature, °style, °stamp, °manifestation: *What forms of life are not of divine origin? He revelled in music in all its forms.* **4** °blank; °model, °format, °frame, framework, °course, °procedure, °order, regimen, °method, °system, °ritual, °formula, °rule(s), °practice, °technique, °way, °means, °approach, °mode, °fashion, °manner, °style: *Fill in the application form in ink. Please follow the proper form when submitting articles.* **5** °condition, °state, °shape, °trim, fettle: *He seems in unusually good form tonight.* **6** °decorum, °behaviour, deportment, °formality, °ceremony, °convention, °etiquette, manners, °conduct, °custom, °protocol, °propriety, °ritual: *Follow correct form when writing to the king. Spitting is considered bad form.*
—*v.* **7** °make, °fabricate, °forge, °shape, °mould, °fashion, °produce, °turn out, °manufacture, °construct, °assemble, °put together, °set up, °put up, °build, °erect, elevate, °raise; °organize, codify; °develop: *The architect takes the many elements and forms them into a coherent whole. Have you formed an opinion of the book?* **8** °create, °originate, °devise, °invent, °compose, °formulate, give form *or* °shape, °coin, concoct, °conceive, contrive, °dream up, °imagine, visualize, °envisage, *US* °envision: *His ideas of religion were formed when he was very young. A picture of the battle was formed in my mind.* **9** °make up, constitute, be made up of, comprise, be composed of; °serve as: *This compound is formed of many elements. Six fugues formed the main part of the programme.* **10** °acquire, °develop, °cultivate, °contract; °get: *In prison I formed the habit of rolling my own cigarettes. We formed a lasting friendship.* **11** °develop, °grow, °arise, °appear, °materialize, °show up, take °shape *or* form, °accumulate: *When the yeast is added, a barm forms on the surface.*

formal *adj.* **1** °standard, °conventional, °customary, established, prescribed, °regular, °normal, °correct, °proper; °strict, formulaic, °inflexible, punctilious, °exacting, unchanging, °methodical, °orderly, °systematic, °set, pro forma, °ritual, ritualistic, °ceremonial, °proper, °official, °routine, °fixed, °rigid, °stiff, °stilted, °stately, starched, unbending, °solemn; confining, °straitened, °limited; *Colloq* °straight, °square: *Formal rules of behaviour are observed.* **2** °explicit, °express, °definite, spelt *or* spelled out, formalized, authorized, °official, °solemn, °legal, °lawful: *Formal demands have been made for the withdrawal of our ambassador.* **3** prim, °ceremonious, °dignified, °stuffy, °strait-laced, °stiff, °precise, °exact: *He made a formal bow and left our company.*

formality *n.* **1** Often, ***the formalities***: °form, °convention, conventionality, °practice, °procedure, °custom, wont, °observance, °protocol, °ceremony, °rite, °ritual: *Observe the legal formalities by having this document witnessed. Formality requires that you walk backwards out of the room.* **2** strictness, punctilio, exactness, °precision, correctness, rigidity, stiffness, inflexibility: *We must maintain the formality of Sunday service.* **3** °etiquette, politesse, °decorum, punctilio, conformity, °propriety: *Formality prohibits casual conversation.*

format *n.* **1** °appearance, °look(s), °aspect, layout, °plan, °design, °style, °form, dimension(s), °shape, °size: *In its present format, the magazine resembles an academic journal.* **2** °composition, °content(s), °make-up, constitution, °arrangement, °plan, °organization, °order, °set-up: *Her TV programme has the format of a chat show.*

formation *n.* **1** °development, °appearance, materialization, °shape, °accumulation, °generation, °creation, crystallization, forming, genesis, °production: *The formation of bubbles indicates that the acid is working.* **2** °establishment, °institution, °creation, founding, °set-up, organizing, °organization, °development, °composition: *We met to discuss the formation of a new company.* **3** array, °display, °pattern, °arrangement, °structure, grouping, °organization, configuration, °disposition: *The vast military formation covered the entire valley.*

former *adj.* **1** °previous, earlier, °prior, ex-, one-time, °preceding, erstwhile, °late, °latest, °last, °recent, *ci-devant*, quondam, *Archaic* whilom: *I ran into a former girl-friend at the art show.* **2** °old, °past, °bygone; °ancient, (pre)historic, departed, antediluvian: *In former times, one could demand—and get—decent service.*

formerly *adv.* °once, °before, °previously, hitherto, °long ago, at °one °time, in the °old days, °once upon a °time, in days gone by, in days *or* °time °past, °time was, back then, when the world was young(er), *Colloq* °way back *or US also* °way back when: *Formerly, there were no tall buildings to block one's view.*

formidable *adj.* **1** alarming, appalling, °dreadful, °frightful, °awesome, awe-inspiring, °menacing, horrifying, °frightening, intimidating, daunting, petrifying, °terrifying: *A formidable, fire-breathing dragon blocked our exit.* **2** °terrific, °fantastic, °unbelievable, °incredible, °impressive, °prodigious, mind-boggling, °awesome, *Colloq* mind-blowing, freaky: *They are a formidable talent and will sell a million records this year.* **3** °arduous, °indomitable, °overwhelming, staggering, °powerful, °mighty, °difficult, challenging, °burdensome, onerous: *She has formidable obstacles to overcome before becoming a doctor.*

formula *n.* °recipe, rubric, formulary; °rule(s), °prescription, °directions, °instructions, blueprint, °method, °technique, °means, °way, °pattern, °procedure, modus operandi, *Colloq US* MO: *Ali Baba uttered the formula, 'Open sesame!', and the rock opened. Alchemists sought to discover a formula for making gold from lead.*

formulate *v.* **1** systematize, codify, °define, °specify, articulate, particularize, °denote: *You must try to formulate your ideas more clearly.* **2** °devise, °originate, °create, °think up *or* of, °dream up, °conceive, concoct, °invent, °improvise, *Colloq* cook up: *I have formulated a plan in my mind to deal with the problem.* **3** °develop, °forge, evolve, °work out, °design, map out, °block out, °draw up: *You have three days to formulate a workable procedure.*

forsake *v.* **1** °abandon, °desert, °quit, °leave, °flee, °depart, °vacate: *He forsook balmy California to dig for gold in the Klondike.* **2** °abandon, °desert, °leave, °jilt, °reject, °throw over, jettison, °cast off: *She has forsaken Michael for another man.* **3** °give up, °yield, °renounce, °repudiate, °relinquish, °forgo, forswear, °surrender, °resign, °abdicate, °recant, °deny, have *or* be done with, °turn one's back on: *Would you forsake a throne for the love of a woman?*

forte *n.* °talent, strong point, °gift, °speciality *or US* specialty, °strength, °aptitude, °genius, *Colloq* long suit: *His forte is carving ivory miniatures.*

forthcoming *adj.* **1** approaching, nearing, °impending, °imminent, coming, upcoming; °near *or* °close (by), (°near *or* °close) at °hand, in the offing, on the °horizon, *Colloq Brit* on the °cards, *US* in the °cards: *The forthcoming tax increase will affect everyone. A new regulation is forthcoming.* **2** awaited, expected, anticipated, looked-for, watched for, °prospective, foreseen: *The forthcoming payment will be be a little late.* **3** °outgoing, °friendly, °amiable, affable, °sociable, °accessible, °expansive, chatty, °talkative, communicative, °informative, °open, °free, revealing, unreserved: *Barry was most forthcoming when questioned about his finances.*

forthright *adj.* straightforward, °direct, °blunt, °candid, °frank, °above-board, unambiguous, unequivocal, °open, °outspoken, °uninhibited, unreserved, unconstrained, unrestrained: *She has always been forthright and honest in her dealings with me.*

fortify *v.* **1** °strengthen, °reinforce, shore up, °buttress, °brace, °bolster, °secure: *Steel plates were used to fortify the walls.* **2** °cheer, °encourage, hearten, °buoy, invigorate, °energize, embolden, °reassure, °brace: *Her enthusiasm fortified him to face what was coming.* **3** °supplement, °enhance, °enrich, °boost, augment: *The drink was fortified by the addition of whisky.*

fortitude *n.* °strength, mettle, °backbone, °courage, °nerve, °resolution, resoluteness, °perseverance, °endurance, °tenacity, pertinacity, °grit, °determination, will-power, *Colloq* °guts: *His encouragement gave me the fortitude to carry on.*

fortunate *adj.* **1** °lucky, in °luck, fortuitous, blessed: *You were fortunate to have survived the crash.* **2** °favoured, °advantageous, °propitious, auspicious, °providential, °favourable, °opportune, °timely, °well-timed: *It was a fortunate time to be buying a house.*

fortune *n.* **1** °position, °worth, °means, °assets, holdings, °wealth, °property, °estate, °possessions; °riches, affluence, opulence, °treasure, °money, °prosperity: *Each member is liable to the full extent of his fortune. He acquired his fortune from oil.* **2** °luck, °chance, fortuity; °lot, °fate, kismet, °destiny, karma; °future; *US* happenstance: *It was just fortune that put me in the right place at the right time. She'll tell your fortune if you cross her palm with silver.* **3** Usually, ***fortunes***: °circumstance(s), °experience(s), °adventures, °expectation(s), °lot: *My fortunes of late have been poor.*

fortune-teller *n.* °oracle, soothsayer, °prophet, diviner, augur, °seer, clairvoyant, prognosticator, sibyl, haruspex, crystal-gazer, tea-leaf reader, palmist, palm reader, star-gazer; futurologist: *The fortune-teller said to beware the Ides of March.*

forward *adj.* **1** °advance, °leading, °foremost, °front, °head, °first: *The forward contingents of the army moved into the town.* **2** °bold, °pert, °impudent, °brash, °insolent, °impertinent, °disrespectful, °brazen, °audacious, °rash, unashamed, °unabashed, saucy, °flippant, °presumptuous, °cheeky, *Colloq* °flip, °fresh, °pushy: *It was a bit forward of you to call the chairman by his nickname.* **3** (well-)advanced, (°well-)developed, °progressive, °precocious, forward-looking: *She was quite a forward girl at fifteen.*

—*adv.* **4** forwards, °ahead, °onward, along; clockwise, deasil: *I moved forward to the head of the queue. Set the clock forward an hour tonight.* **5** up, °out, forth, to the fore, into °consideration, into °view, into the °open, to the surface, on to the °table: *Cooper brought forward an interesting proposal.*

—*v.* **6** °advance, °further, °promote, °back, °foster, °support, °aid, °assist, °help; °patronize, °encourage, °nourish, °nurse along: *He did his best to forward her career.* **7** °dispatch *or* despatch, °send, °ship, °deliver, °transmit, °express, °post, °mail, consign, °remit; °send on: *The shipment will be forwarded as soon as payment is received. The post office will forward mail to my new address.* **8** °speed (up), accelerate, °advance, °hasten, °expedite, °hurry, °quicken, °step up: *This mixture is said to forward the flowering of plants.*

foster *v.* **1** °promote, °encourage, °stimulate, °further, °forward, °advance, °cultivate, nurture, °nourish, °support, °back, °assist, °help, °aid, succour, °patronize: *Cutting back these offshoots fosters growth of the main stem. Representatives have fostered acceptance of our products throughout Europe.* **2** °bring up, °rear, °raise, take °care of, °maintain, °care for: *The Cartwrights have fostered eight orphans in their home.*

foul *adj.* **1** °offensive, °loathsome, °disgusting, °obnoxious, °revolting, °repulsive, °repellent, °repugnant, sickening, °nauseous, nauseating, °nasty, °beastly, *Archaic* fulsome: *The bartender makes a foul concoction he swears will cure a hangover.* **2** °filthy, unclean, °nasty, polluted, °putrid, putrescent, putrefactive *or* putrefacient, defiled, soiled, spoiled, °rotten, decayed, decomposed, °rancid, soured, turned, tainted, °mouldy, °impure, adulterated, contaminated, °stale, °bad, *Brit* off: *The hamburger place was closed when public health inspectors found foul food in the freezer.* **3** °smelly, °stinking, noisome, fetid *or* foetid, °rank, evil-smelling, foul-smelling, malodorous, °musty, mephitic, graveolent: *A foul odour emanated from the cabinet.* **4** °wicked, °vile, °bad, °base, °abominable, °low, °sordid, iniquitous, °evil, flagitious, °atrocious, °monstrous, nefarious, °sinful, °immoral, amoral, °vicious, °villainous, °scandalous, °infamous, °dishonourable, °shameful, °disgraceful, ignominious; detestable: *They were finally brought to justice for their foul deeds.* **5** °dirty, °obscene, °filthy, °profane, scatological, °gross, smutty, foul-mouthed, °blue, licentious, salacious, °lewd, °indecent, °improper, °coarse, uncouth, °vulgar, °rude, °scurrilous, °rough, indelicate, °immodest, °risqué, off colour, °suggestive, °bawdy, ribald, Rabelaisian, Fescennine, *US* °raw, *Slang* raunchy: *My mother forbids my reading books containing foul language.* **6** °abusive, °offensive, affronting, insulting, disparaging, maligning, thersitical, calumnious *or* calumniatory, aspersive, °slanderous, defamatory, libellous, denigrating, °derogatory, deprecatory *or* deprecative, depreciatory *or* depreciative, denunciatory *or* denunciative, °derisory, derisive, °scornful, belittling, fulminous, objurgatory *or* objurgative, °vituperative, invective: *Keep your foul tongue to yourself.* **7** °dishonest, unfair, unjust, unsportsmanlike, °dishonourable, °fraudulent, underhand(ed), double-dealing, °two-faced, °corrupt, °venal, °dirty, treacherous, °perfidious, °traitorous, °unscrupulous, *Colloq* °crooked, °shady, *Slang chiefly Brit* °bent: *Thrupp will get his way by fair means or foul.* **8** °nasty, °dangerous, °rough, °disagreeable, unfavourable, °sloppy, °stormy, adverse; °windy, blustery; snowy, sleety, °wet, rainy: *We ran into a spot of foul weather at Dover.* **9** obstructed, blocked, choked, stopped (up), plugged (up), clogged (up): *The drain is foul with all that rubbish.* **10** tangled, entangled, caught, ensnared, enmeshed, snarled: *A foul anchor is a common nautical symbol.* **11** °illegal, prohibited, forbidden, interdicted, not °fair; °dirty: *In boxing a hit below the belt is a foul blow.*

—*v.* **12** °dirty, °pollute, °sully, befoul, defile, °soil, °contaminate, °adulterate, °taint: *Effluent from the factory was fouling the river.* **13** °tangle, °entangle, catch, °snare, ensnare, enmesh, °snag, °snarl, °jam, °twist: *We can't hoist the mainsail because the halyard is fouled.* **14** °disgrace, °dishonour, °sully, °taint, besmirch, defile, °soil, °stain, °smear, °tarnish, °blacken, denigrate, °debase, °degrade, abase, demean, °disparage, defame, derogate, asperse, devaluate, devalue, °depreciate, °vitiate, °belittle, °discredit, bring *or* call into disrepute: *That act of treachery will foul the family name for generations.* **15** °obstruct, °block, °choke, °stop *or* °plug *or* °clog (up): *Dead leaves fouled the downpipe.* **16** ***foul up***: **a** See **13**, above. **b** mismanage, °mishandle, °botch, °bungle, make a °mess (of), °mess up, °spoil, °ruin, *Colloq* muff, *Brit* throw a spanner in(to) (the works), *US* throw a monkey wrench into (the machinery); *Slang* °muck up, goof (up), °blow, °screw up, louse up, *Chiefly Brit* °bugger (up), *US and Canadian* snafu: *Give him a chance and he's sure to foul up. She fouled up my hi-fi.*

—*n.* **17** °violation, °infringement, infraction, illegality: *The Rangers' forward has already been charged with two fouls.*

—*adv.* **18** °afoul, in °conflict, in °trouble, in °violation: *Curshaw has fallen foul of the law again.*

foul play *n.* treachery, °chicanery, °perfidy, perfidiousness, duplicity, double-dealing, °deception, guile, °crime, °sharp °practice, skulduggery, °dirty work *or* business, °dirty trick(s); °murder, homicide, manslaughter; *Colloq* °hanky-panky: *The travellers suspected foul play when the aeroplane failed to arrive. The hacked up corpse suggested foul play to Detective Lemaître.*

found *v.* **1** °establish, °originate, °institute, °set up, °organize, °inaugurate, °start, °initiate, °create, °bring about, °develop: *The society was founded a hundred years ago.* **2** °base, °ground, °establish, °set, °build; °rest: *This charity was founded on love and concern for children.*

foundation *n.* **1** °basis, °base, substructure, understructure, underpinning, °bottom, foot, basement, °cellar: *This foundation is of stone.* **2** °basis, °base, °fundamental, (underlying *or* °fundamental) °principle, °grounds, °groundwork, °rationale, *raison d'être*, °purpose: *Their morality finds its foundations in Judaeo-Christian culture.* **3** founding, °establishment, instituting, °institution, °creation, origination, °setting up, organizing, °organization, inauguration, °endowment: *We voted for the foundation of an institute to study the English language.*

founder[1] *n.* originator, °creator, °progenitor, °author, framer, °father, architect, °designer, builder, initiator, establisher, institutor: *Today we honour the founder of this great university.*

founder[2] *v.* **1** °sink, °go down *or* under, °go to Davy Jones's locker, be wrecked *or* destroyed: *Many a proud vessel has foundered on this rock.* **2** °fail, °miscarry, °collapse, come to nothing *or* naught, °fall through, abort, falter, °break down, come to °grief, °die: *After Alice left to get married, the business foundered.* **3** °trip, °stumble, °stagger, °lurch, °fall, °topple (over *or* down), °collapse; go °lame: *He drove the horse too hard and caused it to founder.*

foundling *n.* orphan, waif; °stray, °outcast: *We are trying to raise money for a hospital for foundlings.*

fountain *n.* **1** fount, °spring, font, jet, °spout, °spray, well, well-spring, well-head, fountain-head: *Bathing in the city fountains is forbidden.* **2** °source, °origin, genesis: *Miss Corbell was a fountain of wisdom on the subject of basket-weaving.*

foxy *adj.* **1** °clever, °sly, cunning, °wily, °crafty, °tricky, guileful, °shifty, °devious, °slippery, °smooth, °slick, °artful, °resourceful, °ingenious, °calculating, °designing, plotting, °scheming, °disingenuous, °knowing, °shrewd, °sharp, °astute, °wise; foxlike, vulpine; *Colloq* cagey *or* cagy: *Be careful dealing with him, for he can be foxy.* **2** °attractive, alluring, °seductive, vampish, *Colloq* °sexy: *Margo is a very foxy lady.*

fracas *n.* **1** °trouble, °disturbance, commotion, °rumpus, °fuss, hubbub, °pandemonium, hullabaloo, °uproar, °disorder, °scramble, scuffle, °brawl, °roughhouse, rough-and-tumble, turmoil, °tumult, free-for-all, °riot, °fray, brouhaha, mêlée *or* melee, *Law* affray; *Brit* scrum, *US* brannigan; *Colloq* ruckus, punch-up, *Slang Brit* bovver: *It was football hooligans who caused the fracas after the game.* **2** °argument, °disagreement, °quarrel, °dispute, °discord, wrangle, altercation, squabble, spat, °tiff, °fight, °row, tussle, Donnybrook, °brawl, *Colloq* barney, °scrap: *After the referee's ruling, a fracas broke out.*

fracture *n.* **1** °break, breakage, breaking: *An old fracture makes him walk with a limp.* **2** °break, °crack, °split, °rupture, °breach, °separation, cleavage, °division, °rift: *We can permit no fracture in the united front we present to the voters.*

—*v.* **3** °break, °rupture, °crack, °split, °breach, °separate, °cleave: *He fractured three vertebrae in the accident.*

fragile *adj.* °frail, breakable, °brittle, frangible, °delicate, °dainty, °thin, °light, °slight, °weak, °feeble, °infirm, °decrepit; °tenuous, °shaky, °flimsy, °rickety, unsubstantial *or* °insubstantial: *Because of her great age, her bones had become fragile. The argument in favour of acquittal is very fragile, indeed.*

fragment *n.* **1** °piece, °portion, °part, °chip, shard *or* sherd, °splinter, °sliver, °scrap, °bit, °speck, snippet, °morsel, °crumb, °particle, °remnant, °shred, °snatch: *A fragment of the airliner was found twenty miles from the crash.* **2** ***fragments***: smithereens; debris, *Literary disjecta membra*: *The car was blown into thousands of fragments. I tried to pick up the fragments of my former life.*

—*v.* **3** °shatter, °splinter, °break *or* °split (up), °explode, °disintegrate, °come *or* °go to °pieces, °come °apart: *I picked up the skull and it fragmented in my fingers.*

fragmentary *adj.* °disconnected, °piecemeal, °incomplete, scattered, °disjointed, °incoherent, °sketchy: *Accounts of the disaster are still fragmentary.*

fragrance *n.* fragrancy, °scent, °aroma, °smell, °odour, redolence, °perfume, °bouquet, balm: *The fragrance of orange blossom filled the room.*

fragrant *adj.* °aromatic, odorous, °redolent, perfumed, balmy, odoriferous, ambrosial, sweet-scented, sweet-smelling: *A fragrant breeze wafted over the meadow.*

frail *adj.* **1** See **fragile,** above. **2** ailing, unwell, °ill, °sick, °sickly, °poorly, °thin, °skinny, °slight, °puny, °scrawny, wasting *or* fading away, languishing, °infirm, °feeble; °crippled, consumptive, phthisic: *She is too frail to see visitors.*

frailty *n.* **1** °weakness, °infirmity, °delicate °condition, feebleness, fragility, °delicacy: *The doctors are concerned about his frailty.* **2** susceptibility, °liability, suggestibility, impressionability, vulnerability; fallibility, °foible, °flaw, °defect, °imperfection, °fault: *You just said that to take advantage of my frailty. Her vanity is her greatest frailty.*

frame *n.* **1** framework, °shell, °form, skeleton, °support, chassis, framing, °structure, °fabric, scaffolding, construction: *We made a frame of sticks over which the canvas was stretched.* **2** °border, casing, case-mounting, °mount, °edge, edging; °setting: *This picture would look best in a gold frame.* **3** °system, °form, °pattern, °scheme, schema, °plan, °order, °organization, framework, °structure, °construct, construction, °arrangement, blueprint, °design, layout, °composition, °context, °make-up, configuration: *The proposed new department does not fit into the present frame of the company.* **4** °physique, °build, bone °structure, °body, skeleton, °figure: *He has an unusually large frame for a dancer.* **5** ***frame of mind***: °mood, °humour, °state, °condition, °attitude, °bent, °disposition: *I am not in the right frame of mind to put up with your nonsense at the moment.*
—*v.* **6** °construct, °build, °put together, °assemble, °set up, °put up, °erect, °raise, elevate: *We framed the entire house in two days.* **7** °make, °fashion, °form, °mould, °carve out, °forge, °originate, °create, °devise, °compose, °formulate, °put together, °conceive, °draw up, °draft, °shape, °block out, give °form *or* °shape to; contrive: *The founding fathers met to frame a new constitution.* **8** °enclose, °box (in); °set off: *I like the way you've framed that painting.* **9** °set up, °incriminate (fraudulently), °trap, entrap: *Did Dr Crippen kill his wife or was he framed?*

frank *adj.* **1** °open, °free, °candid, °direct, °outspoken, unreserved, °uninhibited, °honest, °sincere, °genuine, °truthful, plain-spoken, °forthright, °downright, °explicit, unrestrained, unchecked, unconstrained, unrestricted, °unabashed: *I asked for a frank appraisal of my work and, unfortunately, he gave it.* **2** °candid, °naïve, guileless, °artless, °ingenuous, °innocent, (°open and) °above-board, on the up and up, *Colloq* upfront, on the °level: *The boy's description of the events was completely frank.*

frantic *adj.* frenzied, °excited, frenetic, °nervous, °overwrought, °excitable, wrought up, distracted, °distraught, beside oneself, °hysterical, °wild, °berserk, °mad, running amok *or* amuck; °upset, °agitated, perturbed, at one's wit's end, °disconcerted, °confused; °hectic; *Colloq* in a °state, in a tizzy, up the °wall, in a dither, out of one's °mind, *Chiefly US and Canadian* discombobulated: *They are frantic because they haven't heard from Edmund in a week.*

fraternal *adj.* °brotherly, °platonic, °friendly, comradely, °idealistic, °intellectual: *He insists that his interest in her is purely fraternal.*

fraternity *n.* **1** community, °brotherhood, °crowd, °set, °clique, coterie, °circle, °society, *US* °club: *Rumours have been circulating in the academic fraternity for months.* **2** brotherliness, °kinship, °fellowship, camaraderie, sodality, comradeship, °friendship, °companionship, relatedness, closeness, °association, affiliation, °solidarity, °unity, esprit de corps, clannishness: *A sense of fraternity prevents them from betraying one another.* **3** °company, guild, °clan, °league, °club, °union, °society, °association: *She has joined the fraternity of legal clerks.*

fraternize *v.* consort (with), °associate (with), °socialize (with), °go (around *or* round) with *or* together, spend time with *or* together, keep °company (with), °hobnob with, °mingle (with), °mix (with), °take up with *or* together, keep up (with), °fall in with, °rub shoulders (with), *Colloq* °hang out (with *or* together), °hang about *or* around with *or* together: *Soldiers are forbidden to fraternize, which means they are not allowed to fraternize with local people.*

fraud *n.* **1** °deception, °trickery, cheating, °sharp practice, °chicanery, °deceit, swindling, double-dealing, duplicity, °artifice, °craft, guile, humbug, humbuggery, treachery, *Colloq* monkey business, funny business, °hanky-panky: *The company directors have been convicted of fraud.* **2** °trick, °hoax, °swindle, °deception, °cheat, °wile, °stratagem, °dodge, bilk, °ruse, °sham, °fake, °subterfuge, *Colloq* flimflam, *Slang* gyp, °rip-off, scam: *The investigation exposed extensive fraud in the handling of local government funds.* **3** deceiver, trickster, °cheat(er), °impostor, °swindler, charlatan, humbug, sharper, shark, bilk(er), °quack, mountebank, °fake(r), °pretender, °bluff(er), confidence man, inveigler, defrauder; °scoundrel, °rogue, *Archaic* knave; *Colloq* con man *or* artist, °phoney *or US also* phony, flimflam man *or* artist, flimflammer, *US and Canadian* four-flusher; *Slang US* barracuda: *He is a fraud who extracts protection money from the elderly.*

fraudulent *n.* **1** °fake, °counterfeit, forged, °false, falsified, °spurious, °imitation, °sham, pinchbeck, *Colloq* °phoney *or US also* phony: *These banknotes are fraudulent.* **2** °deceitful, °dishonest, °criminal, °deceptive, °tricky, °artful, °crafty, double-dealing, duplicitous, °shifty, guileful, °sharp, *Colloq* °shady, °crooked, °bent: *Substituting paste for diamonds is a fraudulent act.*

fraught *adj.* **1** Usually, ***fraught with***: filled *or* charged *or* °packed with, °loaded with, teeming *or* °replete *or* overflowing with, oversupplied with, abounding *or* °abundant in, attended *or* accompanied by: *The scene was fraught with emotion.* **2** °tense, °taut, stressful, °trying, °anxious, distressing, distressful, upsetting, °nerve-racking *or* nerve-wracking, °fretful, °strained, °traumatic: *Relations between the two countries became even more fraught following the incident.*

fray[1] *n.* °disturbance, °skirmish, °fight, °battle, °brawl, tussle, scuffle, °fracas, mêlée *or* melee, Donnybrook, wrangle, °rumpus, °row, °quarrel, °dispute, altercation, *Law* affray, *Colloq* ruckus, punch-up: *He leapt into the fray and fought like a tiger.*

fray[2] *v.* °shred, °wear (°thin *or* °threadbare), °wear out, °rub, abrade, °chafe, ravel, unravel, frazzle: *He saves his frayed shirts to wear at home.*

freak *n.* **1** °monstrosity, °monster, mutant, deformity: *The show features freaks such as a two-headed calf and a bearded lady.* **2** anomaly, °rarity, °abnormality, irregularity, °oddity, °curiosity, *rara avis*, °rare bird, *Brit* one-off, *Colloq* one-shot: *Biologists regard the albino giraffe as a freak of nature.* **3** whim, caprice, vagary, crotchet, °quirk, °eccentricity, °fancy, idiosyncrasy, °peculiarity: *The snow in New York in July was a freak.* **4** °enthusiast, °fan, °devotee, aficionado; °fanatic, °addict; *Colloq* buff, °fiend, nut: *She's been a jazz freak for years.*
—*adj.* **5** freakish, freaky, °abnormal, anomalous, °extraordinary, °unique, °rare, atypical, °unusual, °odd, °queer, °strange, °exceptional, °bizarre, °weird, °unparalleled, °unforeseen, unexpected, unpredicted, unpredictable, *Brit* one-off, *Colloq* one-shot: *He claims he had a freak experience with a lion that had a thorn in its foot.*

free *adj.* **1** at °liberty, unfettered, unchained, unshackled, unconfined, untrammelled, unencumbered, unrestrained, unrestricted, unconstrained, °uncontrolled, free-born, °independent, self-governing, self-governed, self-ruling, autonomous, °democratic, °sovereign: *These people want to be free. It's a free country.* **2** liberated, at °large, °let °go, °let off, emancipated, delivered, manumitted, set free, unshackled, unfettered, released, freed, °loose, °out, *Colloq* sprung, on the °loose: *After ten years he was free at last.* **3** unoccupied, unengaged, at °liberty, not °busy, °available, °accessible; °unused, °vacant, °empty, °spare, °extra, °uninhabited, untenanted: *Are you free for dinner tonight? Here is a free room we can use for the meeting.* **4** cost-free, free of °charge, °complimentary, gratis, for °nothing, without °cost (or °obligation), unencumbered, *Colloq* for free, on the °house: *The food was free but we paid for our drinks.* **5** °unattached, unfastened, untied, °loose: *Tie the free end of the rope*

round your waist. **6** °unasked for, °unsolicited, °gratuitous, unbidden, °voluntary, °spontaneous, unconditioned, unconditional: *Let me give you some free advice.* **7** °generous, °lavish, °open, °liberal, munificent, unstinting, °bountiful, open-handed, unsparing; °charitable: *Fred is quite free with his donations to good causes.* **8** °relaxed, °casual, °informal, free and °easy, °easy, °natural, unceremonious, *Colloq* laid-back: *He is quite free about letting me use his car.* **9** °open, °aboveboard, °honest, °direct, °outspoken, °uninhibited, unconstrained, unrestrained, °relaxed: *You can be free in your criticism.* **10** unhindered, °unimpeded, unencumbered, unhampered, unobstructed, allowed, permitted, °able, °clear, unrestricted, unregulated: *She's free to do as she pleases. The two countries have signed a free-trade agreement.* **11** ***free of***: °rid of, °exempt(ed) from, relieved of, °safe from, not °liable *or* °subject to, °immune from, °unaffected by, °above, without, untouched by: *He thinks he is free of her influence.*
—*adv.* **12** °freely, °openly, at °will, unrestrictedly, °loose; loosely: *Our dog runs free on the farm. Let the rope hang free.* **13** gratis, at no °cost, free of °charge, without °charge: *They give new businesses advice free.*
—*v.* **14** set free, set at °liberty, enfranchise, °release, °let °go, °liberate, °let out, °let °loose, unloose, unchain, unfetter, uncage; °emancipate, disenthral, manumit; °pardon, parole, furlough: *Bail was paid and we were freed. Lincoln freed the slaves. He was freed after six years in prison.* **15** °disengage, untie, unbind, °loose, unfasten, °undo, unshackle, unlock, °open, °release, disentangle, °loosen, °detach, °extricate: *Free the end of that rope.* **16** °relieve, °rid, unburden, disburden, disencumber, unbosom; °rescue, °redeem: *Free yourself of any preconceived notions on the subject.*

freedom *n.* **1** °liberty, °independence, °self-government, self-determination, self-direction, autonomy: *Democracy is based on the freedom of the individual.* **2** °release, deliverance, °liberation, emancipation, manumission: *Will these people ever get their freedom?* **3** °exemption, °immunity, deliverance, °liberation, °relief: *All citizens should enjoy freedom from want.* **4** °range, latitude, °scope, °play, deregulation, noninterference, °discretion, °margin, °free hand, °facility, °ease, °licence, °permission, °right, °privilege, °authority, authorization, °power, *carte blanche*: *He must have the freedom to make decisions. I have the freedom to do as I wish.* **5** °free °time, °leisure, °spare °time: *I like a lot of freedom to do things in my own time.* **6** °candour, °honesty, openness, frankness, candidness, unrestraint, unconstraint, naturalness: *Freedom of speech is practised here.* **7** boldness, overfamiliarity, audacity, audaciousness, forwardness, brazenness, °brass, °impertinence, °impudence, °disrespect, °arrogance, °presumption, presumptuousness, °nerve, °gall: *Where does she get the freedom to talk to you that way?*

freely *adv.* **1** candidly, frankly, °openly, unreservedly, without °reserve, unrestrainedly, without °restraint, unconstrainedly, without constraint, unceremoniously, plainly: *Please speak freely.* **2** °willingly, spontaneously, °readily, °voluntarily, on (one's) own, independently, of (one's) own °accord, of (one's) own °volition *or* °free °will: *I didn't send for her—she came to me freely.* **3** unrestrainedly, unrestrictedly, without °restriction, without °let or °hindrance, without °interference: *He was allowed to move freely about the island.* **4** liberally, lavishly, unreservedly, generously, unstintingly, open-handedly, ungrudgingly, munificently, °amply, plentifully, abundantly: *He has no money to donate but he gives freely of his time.* **5** °readily, °easily, smoothly, cleanly, unobstructedly: *With the obstacle removed, the water ran freely through the pipes.*

freeze *v.* **1** °chill, °refrigerate, ice, deep-freeze, flash-freeze, frost: *If you freeze the leftovers, they keep better.* **2** °solidify, congeal, °harden, °stiffen, ice up *or* over: *When the lake freezes, we can go skating.* **3** °fix, immobilize, °paralyse, °stop (dead *or* dead in one's tracks), °stay, °pin, °transfix, gorgonize; become °fixed, °stand (stock-)°still *or* motionless; °peg, °stick, °set: *She froze him with an icy stare. He froze to the spot in horror. Rates of exchange are no longer frozen.* **4** ***freeze out***: °exclude, debar, °ban, °reject, °ostracize; °eject, °drive away *or* out, °expel, °force out: *When he tried to join the club, he was frozen out.*
—*n.* **5** frost, *Brit* freeze-up, *US* ice-up, deep-freeze: *There will be a freeze tonight in northern counties.* **6** °fix, immobilization: *The government has put a freeze on wages.*

freezing *adj.* °frigid, °icy, arctic, frosty, boreal, hyperboreal, numbing, Siberian, °polar, glacial, (ice-) cold, °wintry, bone-chilling, °bitter, °biting, °bitter(ly) °cold, perishing, °chill, tooth-chattering; chilled to the bone, frozen, shivering, *Archaic* frore: *The rescue was performed under freezing conditions. We were freezing in our thin jackets.*

freight *n.* **1** °transport, transportation, °carriage, conveyance, shipping, shipment, freightage, °delivery: *The charges for freight are included.* **2** °goods, °cargo, tonnage, freightage; °load, boatload, shipload, lorry °load, °haul, consignment, payload: *How much freight passes through here?*

frenzy *n.* **1** °excitement, °agitation, °fury, fever, *Brit* °furore *or US* furor, °passion, turmoil, °transport: *The crowd was whipped into a frenzy at the match.* **2** °distraction, °paroxysm, °seizure, °outburst, °bout, °fit: *She went into a frenzy of despair after the death of her family.*

frequent *adj.* **1** °recurrent, recurring, °habitual, °regular, °familiar, °everyday, °customary, °usual, °ordinary, °normal, °common, repeated, iterative, reiterative, °persistent, continuing, °continual, °constant; °many, numerous, countless, innumerable: *She was a frequent visitor at our house. She paid us frequent visits.*
—*v.* **2** °haunt, °patronize, °visit, °resort to, °go to *or* °attend regularly, *Colloq* °hang out *or* around at: *Yes, Inspector, I used to frequent the pub called The Saracen's Head.*

frequently *adv.* **1** °often, regularly, continually, °repeatedly, over and over (again), again and again, a °lot, °many times, °many a °time, °time after time, °time and (time) again, *Archaic* oftentimes, oft-times: *She has visited me frequently during the past weeks.* **2** °often, habitually, customarily, regularly, °usually, °ordinarily, °generally, commonly, every so °often, °many a °time, as °often as not, *Archaic* oftentimes, oft-times: *He frequently stops at The Golden Hind after work.*

fresh *adj.* **1** °new, today's, °brand-new; (most) °recent, °late(st): *Don't you love the smell of fresh bread? This is the product of fresh research.* **2** °new, °modern, up to °date, °novel, °original, newfangled, °unusual, unconventional, °different, °alternative, °unorthodox: *We are seeking a fresh approach.* **3** °raw, °inexperienced, untested, °unsophisticated, °green, °untried, °unfledged, °immature, untrained, °naïve, °callow, (still) wet behind the ears, *Brit* still in nappies; *US* still in diapers: *These troops are too fresh to send into battle.* **4** additional, °new, °further, renewed, °extra, °supplementary: *We need a fresh supply of paper towels.* **5** °alert, refreshed, °vigorous, °energetic, invigorated, spry, °lively, full of vim and °vigour, fresh as a daisy, °keen, °bright, °brisk, °active, *Colloq* bright-eyed and bushy-tailed: *Put the horses through the dressage while they are fresh.* **6** °wholesome, °healthy, well, refreshed, °glowing, °fair, °rosy, ruddy, blooming, °flourishing: *She came back to work fresh from a week's rest.* **7** °moderate, °brisk, °strong; °cool, °clean, °pure, °clear, unpolluted: *Sailing conditions were ideal: a fresh breeze and good visibility. Open the window for some fresh air.* **8** °bold, °impudent, °impertinent, °brazen, °brassy, °forward, °disrespectful, saucy, °pert, °cheeky, °presumptuous, °insolent, °rude, *Colloq* smart-alecky *or* smart-aleck, *US* sassy, flip: *That fresh kid called her an old bag.*

freshen *v.* **1** °strengthen, °increase, °blow harder: *The wind began to freshen as we sailed past the headland.* **2** Sometimes, ***freshen up***: invigorate, °revive,

°refresh, °enliven, (re)vitalize, °stimulate, titivate, °rouse, °liven up: *I'll just freshen up before dinner. Freshen these flowers by changing the water.* **3** ventilate, °air out, deodorize, °purify: *We freshen the rooms by opening all the windows.* **4** °strengthen, °spike, °lace, °fortify: *May I freshen your drink?*

fret *v.* **1** °worry, be °concerned, agonize, lose sleep, be °upset *or* distressed *or* °anxious *or* °disturbed, °grieve, °brood, whine, °fuss, °complain, *Colloq* °stew, tear one's hair: *Your kitten is safe now, so stop fretting.* **2** °worry, °concern, °distress, vex, °annoy, °irritate, °torment, °provoke, *US* °rankle: *She fretted herself about Henry's health.*

fretful *adj.* °irritable, vexed, ill-tempered, bad-tempered, °peevish, edgy, °cross, °petulant, °testy, °touchy, tetchy, splenetic, irascible, choleric, crabby, fractious, °short-tempered, grumpy, sulky, °moody, °fault-finding, carping, °querulous, whining, complaining, captious, ill-natured, °disagreeable, °impatient, °snappish, °waspish, °short, °abrupt, °curt, *US and Canadian* °cranky: *Are you always so fretful before breakfast?*

friction *n.* **1** abrasion, rubbing, abrading, chafing, fretting, attrition, scraping, °grating, °erosion: *Friction is always accompanied by heat.* **2** °disagreement, °discord, °conflict, contention, °dispute, °dissension, disharmony, °controversy, dissent, bickering, °argument, wrangling, °ill feeling, °ill will, bad blood, °animosity, °rivalry, °hostility, °antagonism, °strife: *Politics have always been a source of friction between them.*

friend *n.* **1** (boon) °companion, °partner, °comrade, crony, °familiar, confidant(e), °intimate, Achates, alter ego, °ally, compeer; °acquaintance, °playmate, pen-pal *or Brit also* pen-friend; *Colloq* °chum, °pal, *Brit* cocker, *Chiefly Brit and Australian and New Zealand* °mate, *Australian* cobber, *US and Canadian* (°bosom) buddy, *SW US* compadre; *Slang Brit* (old) china: *She is spending the weekend with some friends.* **2** °ally, °associate, °fellow, confederate, °colleague, co-worker, confrère, compatriot, consociate, *US* °cohort: *A friend from the office is coming to dinner.* **3** room-mate, bunk-mate, flatmate, soul °mate, bedfellow, °lover, °sweetheart, °escort; °girl, °woman, girlfriend, concubine, °mistress, *Old-fashioned* doxy; °man, boyfriend, *Old-fashioned* beau; *Colloq US* alternative other, POSSLQ (= 'Person of the Opposite Sex Sharing Living Quarters'), roomie; *Slang* °baby, moll, sugar-daddy, *US* °squeeze, twist, *Chiefly Brit* bird: *Chris, why don't you introduce us to your new friend?* **4** °benefactor *or* benefactress, °patron, °supporter, °advocate, adherent, °backer, °financier, Maecenas; angel, investor: *He has long been associated with the Friends of the Library.*

friendly *adj.* **1** °amicable, congenial, °sociable, companionable, comradely, convivial, °familiar, well-disposed, °close, on °good terms, *simpatico*, °comfortable, at home, °neighbourly, clubby, °fraternal, °brotherly, sisterly, *Colloq* °chummy, pally, °thick, *Brit* matey, *US* palsy-walsy, buddy-buddy: *We've always been friendly with the people next door.* **2** °amiable, °affectionate, loving, °demonstrative, °cordial, warm-hearted, °warm, °genial, °agreeable, °good-natured, °pleasant, °kind, °kindly, kind-hearted, affable, approachable, °accessible, unreserved, °open, *Brit* clubbable: *Clare can be very friendly when she wants to be.*

friendship *n.* **1** amity, congeniality, sociability, companionability, comradeship, °fellowship, conviviality, °familiarity, closeness, neighbourliness, °harmony, clubbiness, °fraternity, °brotherhood, sisterhood, °alliance: *I hope that this affair will not affect the friendship between our countries.* **2** friendliness, amiability, amicability, °esteem, °warmth, °devotion, °affection, fondness, °attachment, (deep) °regard, °rapport, intimacy, °love: *What can I do to regain your friendship?*

fright *n.* **1** °fear, °alarm, °terror, °dread, °horror, °panic, trepidation, °dismay, consternation, apprehension, *Colloq* (blue) funk: *He almost dies of fright at the sight of blood.* **2** °scare, °shock: *Here, sip this brandy; you've had a terrible fright.* **3** °spectre, °monster, eyesore, *Colloq* °sight, °mess: *He looked a perfect fright when I saw him after the accident.*

frighten *v.* °terrify, °scare, °alarm, °panic, °startle, °shock, °petrify, °horrify, °dismay, °appal, °unnerve, °distress, °daunt, cow, °intimidate, *Colloq* °scare out of one's wits, make one's hair stand on end, °scare the (living) daylights (*etc.*) out of, °scare °stiff, *Brit* put the °wind up (someone), put the frighteners on (someone): *She was frightened by the neighbours' vicious dog. Are you frightened of aeroplanes?*

frightening *adj.* °terrifying, alarming, °startling, °shocking, petrifying, horrifying, dismaying, appalling, unnerving, dire, distressing, daunting, intimidating, °formidable, °frightful, °fearful, hair-raising, °harrowing, °dreadful, *Colloq* °scary, spooky: *Skydiving can be a frightening experience. The sight of their mangled bodies was frightening.*

frightful *adj.* **1** See **frightening,** above. **2** °awful, °dreadful, °terrible, °disagreeable, °atrocious, °abhorrent, °loathsome, °grisly, °ghastly, °lurid, °macabre, °horrible, horrifying, horrid, horrendous, °nasty, °hideous, °vile, unspeakable, nauseating, °nauseous, °repugnant, °repulsive, °shocking, °revolting, °abominable, °offensive, °ugly: *Brixton police report a frightful crime of decapitation.*

frightfully *adv.* °awfully, °very, °extremely; amazingly, surprisingly: *We saw a frightfully good play last night.*

frigid *adj.* **1** °cold, arctic, frosty, frozen, glacial, °icy, hyperboreal, °polar, bone-chilling, boreal, Siberian, °freezing, °wintry, °chilly, °chill, *Archaic* frore: *We were huddled in that frigid alpine hut for two days.* **2** °cold, °cool, °cold-hearted, °forbidding, austere, unemotional, unfeeling, °stiff, °rigid, prim, °strait-laced, °stony, °callous, °steely, obdurate, °thick-skinned, impervious, °inaccessible, °remote, °unapproachable, unfriendly, °standoffish, °haughty, °aloof, °reserved: *His behaviour to his ex-wife has always been frigid.* **3** °unapproachable, unresponsive, °impassive, °passive, °indifferent, °cold; °impotent: *She says he's impotent and he insists that she's frigid.*

frill *n.* **1** trimming, °decoration, °ornament, furbelow, °flounce, °ruffle: *This dress would be suitable without the frill.* **2** ornamentation, frippery, falderal *or* fal de rol *or* folderol, frou-frou, showiness, °ostentation, °embellishment, °luxury, trimming, °extra, °addition, °superfluity, °gewgaw, (bit of) °paraphernalia, *Colloq US* foofaraw, bells and whistles, *Slang* jazz: *They ordered a computer system that has every imaginable frill.*

fringe *n.* **1** trimming, °edge, edging, °border, °frill, °flounce, °ruffle, purfle, purfling, ruff, ruche *or* rouche, ricrac *or* rickrack, °ornament, °decoration, furbelow: *The curtains would look better without that pink fringe.* **2** °border, °perimeter, °edge, °boundary, °bounds, °periphery, °limits, °margin, °outskirts, march(es); *Technical* fimbria: *We live on the fringes of Oxford.*

—*v.* **3** °edge, °border, °trim, °surround: *The grounds are fringed with trees.*

frisk *v.* **1** °caper, gambol, °cavort, °frolic, °skip, °trip, romp, curvet, °leap, °dance, °prance, °play, rollick: *She was frisking about like a lamb.* **2** °search, °inspect, °examine, °check (out), °go over: *At the airport, we were frisked for weapons.*

frisky *adj.* °lively, °frolicsome, rollicking, °playful, °active, °animated, (°high-)°spirited, coltish: *Tell Frances to calm down—she's getting a bit too frisky.*

fritter *v.* ***fritter away***: squander, °waste, °idle away, misspend, °dissipate: *Stop frittering away your time watching television. She frittered away every penny of her inheritance.*

frivolous *adj.* **1** °trifling, °inconsequential, unimportant, trivial, nugatory, °insignificant, °minor, °petty, °paltry, °niggling, °peripheral, °superficial, °worthless, *Colloq* °small-time, *Brit* twopenny, two a penny, *US* two-bit, penny-ante, nitty-gritty: *Don't waste my time with frivolous details.* **2** °scatterbrained, bird-brained, °silly, feather-brained, °irresponsible, °flippant, °casual, °flighty, °giddy, °foolish, °childish, °puerile; airy, °light, °slight, *Brit* airy-fairy, *Colloq* °flip: *Try to be serious and less frivolous about such important matters.*

frolic *n.* **1** °merriment, merrymaking, °gaiety, °sport, °fun (and games), °high jinks, jollity, °mirth, jollification, °festivity, °celebration, °revelry, °play, horseplay, *Colloq* skylarking, partying: *After we won the cup there was great frolic in the town.* **2** romp, °party, °spree, °revel, gambol, °caper, gambado, antic; escapade, °prank: *The noise of our frolics echoed across the square.*
—*v.* **3** °frisk, °cavort, °caper, skylark, gambol, rollick, romp, cut capers, curvet, °play, °skip, °sport, have °fun, *Colloq* °party, make whoopee, horse around *or* about: *Gregory frolics about instead of getting on with his work.*

frolicsome *adj.* °playful, °merry, °frisky, °sportive, °gay, °lively, °sprightly, °animated, °spirited, coltish: *Irene may seem frolicsome but she has her sober side as well.*

front *n.* **1** °face, façade, °facing, fore-part, anterior; obverse: *The front of the door has a painting on it. This dress buttons up the front.* **2** frontage, forefront: *The front of the property measures only 40 feet.* **3** °beginning, °head, fore, vanguard, forefront, van: *At the front of the parade marched the mayor.* **4** °bearing, demeanour, mien, °air, °face, countenance, façade, °mask, °expression, °show, °appearance, °aspect, °look, °exterior: *Despite her grief, she put on a brave front at the wake.* **5** °disguise, °cover, °guise, °mask, cover-up, °show, °pretext, façade: *The restaurant was merely a front for a narcotics operation.* **6** °movement, °organization, °league, bloc, °party, °group, °faction, wing: *A new popular front was formed out of a coalition of several opposition groups.* **7** haughtiness, overconfidence, °effrontery: *He frightens away potential clients by showing so much front.* **8** ***in front***: °first, °leading, °ahead, to the fore, in the forefront, in the vanguard *or* van, in °advance, in the °lead, °before; °winning: *In this picture the man in front is my father. My horse was in front all the way.* **9** ***upfront***: **a** See **8,** above. **b** open, straightforward, °honest, °direct, °forthright, °frank, °candid: *Why can't you be upfront instead of conspiring against me?*
—*adj.* **10** °first, °advance, °foremost, °leading, °head; °main: *The front carriage was smashed in the train wreck. Enter by the front door.*
—*v.* **11** °overlook, °face, °look out on *or* °towards, be °opposite: *Our house fronts the river. The flat fronts on the street.* **12** ***front for***: °act for, °represent; °substitute for, °replace: *I hate formal affairs and hoped that you might front for me.*

frontier *n.* °front °line; °border, °boundary, °bound(s), marches, (°far) reaches, °limit(s), °pale, °extreme(s), bourn: *We'll need our passports to cross the frontier into Italy.*

froth *n.* **1** °foam, spume, suds, °lather, bubbles; °head: *The froth tickles my nose.* **2** trivia, °rubbish, °nonsense, twaddle, °babble, °gibberish, °drivel, *Colloq* °hot air, gas, °gab, piffle: *His sermons were just so much froth.*
—*v.* **3** °foam, spume, °bubble, °fizz, effervesce, aerate: *You are supposed to drink the medicine while it is frothing.* **4** °foam, salivate; °lather: *He was so angry he began to froth at the mouth.*

frown *v.* **1** °scowl, glower, °glare, °knit one's brows, grimace, give a dirty °look, *Brit* °lour *or US also* °lower: *Don't frown so much or you'll get wrinkles.* **2** ***frown on*** *or* ***upon***: °disapprove (of), (°look on *or* °regard *or* °view with) °disfavour, discountenance, °look down on *or* upon, °look askance at, not take kindly to, not think much of, °look disapprovingly upon, *Colloq* take a dim °view of, be turned off by: *My parents frown on my seeing you.*
—*n.* **3** °scowl, glower, °glare, grimace, dirty °look, *Brit* °lour *or US also* °lower: *Her forehead is always furrowed by a frown.*

frugal *adj.* **1** °thrifty, °sparing, °economic(al), °careful, °prudent, °provident, °saving, °conservative, conservational, °moderate: *Mother had to become quite frugal when father fell ill.* **2** parsimonious, °penurious, penny-pinching, cheese-paring, °mean, °miserly, stingy, niggardly, °tight(-fisted), °close(-fisted), hand to mouth: *He led a frugal existence on his earnings as an artist.* **3** °meagre, °paltry, °poor, skimpy, scant(y), °small, °negligible, piddling: *His frugal meal consisted entirely of bread and water.*

fruit *n.* Often, ***fruits***: °product(s), °result(s), °revenue(s), outgrowth, °outcome, consequence(s), °return(s), °advantage(s), °benefit(s), °profit(s), emolument, °payment, °income, compensation, recompense, °desert(s): *He didn't live to enjoy the fruit of his work.*

fruitful *adj.* **1** °productive, °fertile, °prolific, fecund; fructiferous, frugiferous, fructuous: *The soil in this valley is extremely fruitful.* **2** °effective, °worthwhile, well-spent, °profitable, °successful, °useful, °rewarding, °advantageous, °beneficial, °productive, °fertile: *We had a fruitful meeting and accomplished a great deal.* **3** °plentiful, °abundant, bounteous, °bountiful, °prolific, plenteous, copious, °luxurious, °rich, °flourishing: *We expect another fruitful harvest this year.*

fruition *n.* °realization, °fulfilment, °consummation, °achievement, °success, materialization, °maturity, ripeness, maturation, °completion; °perfection: *I saw my plans for the town brought to fruition.*

fruitless *adj.* °barren, unfruitful, unproductive, °worthless, °bootless, °futile, °pointless, °useless, °vain, °idle, unavailing, °ineffectual, °ineffective, °unprofitable, for °naught, to no avail, °unsuccessful, unrewarding, abortive: *Our search for a new manager has so far been fruitless.*

frustrate *v.* **1** °thwart, °foil, °stymie, °block, baffle, °check, balk *or* baulk, °disappoint, °discourage, °forestall, °prevent, °stop, °halt, °cripple, °hinder, °hamper, °impede, hamstring, °defeat, °counteract, °neutralize, nullify, °counter, °fight off, °repel, °repulse: *So far, we have been able to frustrate take-over bids for the company.* **2** °discourage, °disappoint, °upset, °exasperate: *I feel frustrated because mother won't let me help with the bills.*

fuel *n.* **1** tinder, combustible, kindling; fossil *or* °nuclear °fuel: *You must pay a lot for fuel to heat that big house.* **2** ammunition, °encouragement, stimulus, °incitement, °provocation: *Her teasing him only provided more fuel for his passion.* **3** °nourishment, nutriment, °sustenance, °food, nutrition: *The body needs more fuel on a cold day.*
—*v.* **4** °nourish, °feed, °sustain; °stimulate, °encourage, °incite, °provoke, °inflame, exacerbate, °excite: *U-235 is used to fuel the reactor. Frustration fuels the flame of desire.*

fugitive *n.* **1** °runaway, escapee, °deserter, °refugee, *Archaic* runagate: *Many fugitives from political oppression seek asylum in the UK.*
—*adj.* **2** fleeing, escaped, °running away, °runaway: *They police are able to devote little time to tracing fugitive children.* **3** °fleeting, °passing, °brief, °short-lived, transitory, °transient, ephemeral, evanescent, °momentary, °volatile, fugacious: *She once entertained the fugitive notion of becoming an opera singer.*

fulfil *v.* **1** °bring about, °achieve, °accomplish, °bring *or* °carry to °completion, °carry out, °complete, consummate, °discharge, °live up to, °abide by, °observe, °realize, °effect, °bring *or* °carry off, °carry through, °keep, °satisfy, do, °perform, °execute, °effectuate: *I trust that you will fulfil all your obligations. Will she ever fulfil her ambition to be a virtuoso pianist?* **2** °answer, °satisfy, °meet, °implement, °look *or* °see to, °conform to *or* with, °comply with, °obey: *This hammer will fulfil my needs for the moment. Will your new assistant be able to fulfil your requirements?*

fulfilment *n.* °completion, °consummation, °performance, carrying out *or* through, °discharge, °realization, implementation, °execution, °accomplishment, compliance, conformity *or* conformance, making °good,

°meeting, °satisfaction, answering, °achievement: *You will be paid upon fulfilment of the contract.*

full *adj.* **1** filled, °replete, brimming, brim-full, °packed, jam-packed, °congested, °loaded, bursting, chock-a-block, chock-full *or* choke-full *or* chuck-full, jammed, crammed, °solid, well supplied, crowded, stuffed; gorged, saturated, sated, satiated: *The tank is full of petrol. Her Christmas stocking was full of toys. I'm full; I couldn't manage another bite.* **2** °complete, °thorough, °detailed, °comprehensive, °total, all-inclusive, °broad, °extensive, all-encompassing, °exhaustive, plenary: *The police are demanding a full investigation.* **3** °complete, °entire, °whole: *The recipe calls for a full dozen egg yolks.* **4** utmost, greatest, °maximum, highest, °top; °extreme: *Full speed ahead.* **5** °wide, °ample, °generous, °broad, copious, °loose (-fitting): *The tight bolero jacket is offset by a full skirt.* **6** occupied, engrossed, °absorbed, immersed, °preoccupied, obsessed, consumed, °engaged, °concerned: *She's entirely too full of herself to pay any attention to us.* **7** filled *or* rounded out, °round(ish), well-rounded, °plump; °robust, °shapely, well-shaped, curvaceous, °buxom, busty, °voluptuous, full-bodied, well-proportioned, well-built, *Slang* stacked, *Brit* well-stacked, *US* zaftig, built: *His face is rather full, so wrinkles don't show. Her figure is what I'd call full.* **8** unrestricted, non-restricted, unconditional, °unqualified: *Payment of dues entitles you to full membership privileges.* **9** °sentimental, °emotional, overflowing: *His heart was so full he could say no more.* **10** unobscured, unshaded, undimmed, °open, °broad, °bright, shining, °brilliant, °dazzling, °glaring, °intense, blazing, blinding; °harsh, °vivid, revealing: *We emerged into full daylight. In the full light of day, the plan seems unworkable.* **11** °powerful, °resonant, °rich, °deep, °loud: *His full bass voice was unmistakable.* **12** °complete, °whole, °entire; °comprehensive, uncut, °unabridged, °intact, unshortened, unbowdlerized, uncensored: *We were to receive full pay for a half day's work. Is this a full deck of cards? I have a full set of the original engravings.*
—*adv.* **13** fully, °completely, °entirely, °wholly, °thoroughly, °altogether: *That is not a full-grown horse.* **14** squarely, °directly, °right, °precisely, °exactly, bang, *Colloq* °slap, smack: *The ball hit him full in the eye.* **15** °very, °perfectly, °exceedingly, °quite, *Slang* damned: *You know full well why I am here.*
—*n.* **16** °maximum, greatest °degree, fullest: *The moon is at its full tonight.* **17** ***in full***: °completely, fully, °entirely, °wholly, °thoroughly, in its °entirety, °totally, *in toto*: *Copy this report in full.* **18** ***to the full*** *or* ***fullest***: °completely, fully, °quite, °thoroughly, to the utmost, to the greatest *or* fullest °extent; a °great °deal, greatly, hugely, enormously: *We enjoyed our visit to the full.*

fumble *v.* **1** °grope, °feel, °stumble: *She fumbled about for the light switch.* **2** °mishandle, °drop, muff, °bungle, °botch, *Colloq US* bobble, flub: *Bosworth fumbled the ball and Fernpath scored again.*

fume *v.* **1** °seethe, °smoulder, °chafe, °boil, °rage, °storm, °rant, °flare up, °bluster, °lose one's °temper, °explode, *Colloq* get steamed (up) (over *or* about), °lose one's °cool, °flip one's lid, °flip (out), °fly off the handle, hit the roof, °raise the roof, blow one's top *or* stack, °get °hot under the collar, blow a gasket, °go off the deep end: *She was fuming because I was five minutes late.* **2** smoke: *The mixture fumes if you add these ingredients.*
—*n.* **3** Usually, ***fumes***: smoke, °vapour, effluvium, gas, °exhalation, °exhaust; °smell, °odour, °aroma, °fragrance, °stench, stink, miasma; °pollution, smog: *The fumes from O. C. Cabot's cigar spread through the building.*

fumigate *v.* °disinfect, °cleanse, °purify, sanitize, °sterilize, decontaminate: *There have been no insects since the kitchen was fumigated.*

fun *n.* **1** °merriment, merrymaking, °gaiety, °glee, jollity, °mirth, °cheer, °high °spirits, °delight, °frolic, °festivity, °high jinks; °amusement, °diversion, °sport, °enjoyment, °recreation, °entertainment, °pastime, °joy, °pleasure, *Colloq* (making) whoopee: *Your party was great fun. We always have fun when we're together. Want to have some fun?* **2** tomfoolery, horseplay, joking, playfulness, clowning, °pranks, °sport, jesting, jocularity, °nonsense, fooling around *or* about, *Colloq* skylarking: *This is no time for fun—we have to catch a train.* **3** ***in*** *or* ***for fun***: jokingly, teasingly, in jest, facetiously, with °tongue in cheek, playfully, as a °lark, for a °joke *or* °gag; not °seriously: *In fun, we told him that he had missed the last ferry.* **4** ***Like fun!*** Under no circumstances!, No way!, *Colloq* Like hell!, *US* No way, Jose!: *Like fun will I go swimming in the nude!* **5** ***make fun of***: poke fun at, °tease, °deride, (hold up to) °ridicule, °scoff at, °lampoon, °parody, °satirize, make °sport *or* °game of, °taunt, °gibe, °rag, *Colloq* kid, rib, *Brit* °send up: *Kevin is always making fun of people by imitating them.*

function *n.* **1** °purpose, °aim, °use, °role *or* rôle, *raison d'être*, °responsibility, °mission, °charge, °concern, °business, °province, °duty, °job, °occupation, °work, °office, °task, chore, °assignment, commission, °activity: *A knife's function is to cut; a guard's is to stand watch.* **2** °reception, °gathering, °affair, °party, dinner, °banquet, °gala, °ceremony, °formality, °rite, °ritual; °occasion, °event: *We are attending a function at the embassy tonight.*
—*v.* **3** °act, °operate, °perform, °behave, °work, °go, °run: *Are you sure the engine is functioning properly?* **4** °serve, take the °role *or* rôle of, °act the °part of, °act as, °work as: *Dunmow will function as host in my absence.*

functional *adj.* **1** utilitarian, °useful, °serviceable, °practical, °practicable, functioning, working; °essential, °important, °effective: *This gear is a functional part, not mere decoration.* **2** working, operating, operational, °running, °going: *Is this telephone functional?*

functionary *n.* °official, commissioner, bureaucrat, office-holder, °officer: *She is some sort of functionary at the Ministry of Information.*

fund *n.* **1** °supply, °stock, °reserve, °store, °pool, °cache, reservoir, repository, °mine: *Alison is a veritable fund of information about art.* **2** Often, ***funds***: °money, (hard) °cash, °ready °money, °assets, °means, °wealth, resources, wherewithal, savings, °capital, nest egg, °endowment, *Colloq* °loot, lucre, pelf, °green, bread, dough, *Brit* °ready, readies, lolly, *US* bucks, °scratch: *He has the funds to buy out his partners. Have you contributed to the fund for indigent lexicographers?*
—*v.* **3** °finance, °back, capitalize, °stake, °support, °pay for, endow, °grant, °subsidize: *The company has funded a number of new businesses.*

fundamental *adj.* **1** °basic, °rudimentary, °elementary, °primary, °main, °prime, °first, °principal, underlying, °cardinal, °central, °essential, quintessential, constitutional, °inherent, °intrinsic, °important, °crucial, °critical, °organic, °vital: *Our fundamental aim is to provide employment.*
—*n.* **2** °principle, °law, °rule, axiom, °essential, °element, *sine qua non*, cornerstone, °keystone: *Freedom of speech is a fundamental in a democracy.*

funeral *n.* obsequies, exequies; °burial, interment, sepulture, entombment, inhumation; cremation: *It is fitting to wear black when attending a funeral.*

funereal *adj.* °grave, °solemn, °sad, °unhappy, morose, °sombre, °mournful, °doleful, °sorrowful, °melancholy, °gloomy, lugubrious, °dismal, °grievous, depressing, °dreary, woeful, °dark, sepulchral: *Why are you in such a funereal mood?*

funny *adj.* **1** comical, °humorous, °comic, °ludicrous, laughable, °ridiculous, risible, waggish, side-splitting, °hilarious, °uproarious, jocular, jocose, °merry, droll, facetious, °witty, °farcical, slapstick, °zany; amusing, °entertaining, diverting, *Colloq* °hysterical: *A comedian's material may be funny but he relies on timing for much of his effect.* **2** °peculiar, °odd, °unusual, °curious, °strange, °mysterious, mystifying, °puzzling, °queer, °weird, °bizarre, °remarkable, unconventional,

°eccentric, *Slang* off-the-wall: *She had a funny expression on her face. If you do love me, you have a funny way of showing it.*

furious *adj.* **1** °angry, enraged, raging, infuriated, fuming, incensed, irate, maddened, °mad, boiling, wrathful, provoked, beside oneself, up in arms, in high dudgeon, on the warpath, foaming at the °mouth, *Literary* wroth, *Colloq* steaming, livid, in a tizzy, *Slang* up the °wall, pissed off, browned off, *Brit* cheesed off: *Mark was furious at Betty for leaving without him.* **2** °fierce, °wild, °violent, °savage, °intense, unrestrained, °frantic, frenzied: *A few made a furious attempt to jump off the burning ship.*

furnish *v.* **1** °supply, °provide, °afford, °equip, °outfit, °fit (out *or* up), °rig (out *or* up), °provision, °give, °stock up, *Colloq Brit* °kit out *or* up: *The trading post furnished what we needed for a month in the wilderness. Can you furnish me with a blanket?* **2** °decorate, °equip: *She received a commission to furnish a ten-room house.*

furniture *n.* **1** furnishings, household (°goods); movables, chattels, °paraphernalia, °effects, °possessions, °belongings, *Colloq* °gear, °things, °stuff, *Slang* shit: *There wasn't any furniture in the room, not even a chair.* **2** °fittings, fitments, °equipment, °fixtures, °apparatus, °devices, °tackle, °tack, °trappings, °gear, accoutrements *or US also* accouterments, °accessories, appliances, *Colloq Brit* clobber: *The front door has some fine brass furniture.*

furore *n.* **1** furor, °uproar, °outburst, °tumult, commotion, turmoil, brouhaha, ado, hurly-burly, to-do, hubbub, °stir, °fuss, °disturbance, °excitement: *The deportation of the student caused a furore among his supporters.* **2** °rage, °craze, °mania, °vogue, °enthusiasm, °obsession, °fad: *The furore for antiques has driven up prices enormously.*

furrow *n.* **1** °groove, °channel, °rut, trench, °track, ditch, gutter, trough, fosse, fissure, sulcus, sulcation, flute, °score, °cut, °gash, °scratch, °line; °wrinkle, crease, corrugation, crow's-feet, *Technical* sulcus: *He can't even plough a straight furrow. The furrows in his brow come from worry.*
—*v.* **2** °groove, °channel, flute, °score, °cut, °gash, °scratch; °plough, harrow: *This rock was furrowed by glacial action.* **3** °wrinkle, crease, corrugate, °knit, °pucker, crinkle: *A frown furrowed his forehead.*

further *adj.* **1** more, additional, another, other, °new, supplemental, °supplementary, °accessory, °auxiliary, °extra, °spare, °fresh: *Further investment by our group is out of the question.* **2** farther, more °distant *or* °remote: *Some day, we may travel to the further reaches of the galaxy.*
—*adv.* **3** furthermore, °besides, °moreover, too, also, additionally, in °addition, over and above, beyond, °above, what is more, to °boot, °yet, then (again), again: *She told him he was rude and, further, ugly as well.* **4** farther, at *or* to a greater °distance *or* °depth: *She has looked into the matter much further than I.*
—*v.* **5** °advance, °promote, °favour, °push *or* °urge °onward(s) *or* forward(s), °forward, °foster, °back, °patronize, °support, °help, °assist, °aid: *What can I do to further your efforts?*

furtherance *n.* °promotion, advancement, °pursuit, °backing, boosting, °boost, fostering, championing, championship, advocating, advocacy, °patronage, °support, °help, °aid, °assistance, succour: *The furtherance of anti-pollution laws is all to the good.*

furtive *adj.* **1** °secret, °private, °secretive, clandestine, °surreptitious, °stealthy, underhand(ed), covert, °hidden, conspiratorial, skulking, °deceitful, under the table, under the counter, hugger-mugger, *Colloq* °sneaky: *She gave me a furtive look to let me know she was on to me.* **2** °sly, °foxy, cunning, °crafty, °wily, °shifty, untrustworthy, *Colloq* °sneaky: *His furtive manoeuvres mark him as one not to be trusted.*

fury *n.* **1** °anger, °rage, wrath, °indignation, ire, choler, °rancour: *Hell hath no fury like a woman scorned.* **2** impetuosity, ferocity, savagery, vehemence, fierceness, tempestuousness, turbulence, °violence: *How can we stem the fury of his attack?* **3** virago, °shrew, spitfire, hell-cat, termagant, vixen, she-devil, °hag, °witch,*offensive slang* °bitch, *Archaic* beldam: *She is a fury when provoked.*

fuse *v.* °blend, °merge, °unite, °combine, °compound, °mix, commingle, coalesce, °flow *or* °come together, consolidate, °amalgamate; °melt: *The metals fuse at a relatively low temperature.*

fuss *n.* **1** °bother, pother, dither, °fluster, °flurry, °fret, commotion, ado, bustle, to-do, °excitement, °furore *or US* furor, °unrest, (deal of) °trouble, disquiet, °upset, °stir, °uproar, °disturbance, hubbub, °agitation, brouhaha, *Colloq* hoo-ha, °flap, stink, *Brit* kerfuffle, *Slang US* hoop-la: *Stop making such a big fuss over nothing.*
—*v.* **2** make a fuss, °rush about *or* around, °flutter, *Colloq* kick up a fuss: *I do wish she'd stop fussing—the party is going very well.*

fussy *adj.* **1** °particular, °finicky, finical, °dainty, °discriminating, °difficult, °fastidious, °exacting, °demanding, *Colloq* picky, °choosy, nit-picking, pernickety *or US also* persnickety: *He's so fussy that he'll wear only custom-made shoes.* **2** °fancy, °elaborate, over-decorated, gingerbread, rococo, °ornate, °detailed, Byzantine: *The style is a bit too fussy for my taste.*

futile *adj.* °unsuccessful, unavailing, °useless, °unprofitable, °vain, abortive, profitless, °bootless, °worthless, °empty, °sterile, °barren, unproductive, °impotent, °ineffective, °ineffectual; *Chiefly literary* sleeveless: *After several futile attempts to get in touch with you, I gave up.*

future *n.* **1** days *or* °time to °come; tomorrow: *Who knows what the future may bring?*
—*adj.* **2** coming, tomorrow's, later, °prospective, following, unborn, °subsequent, expected, approaching; to be to °come: *Future generations will appreciate what we have done here.*

fuzzy *adj.* **1** °woolly, downy, linty, fleecy, furry, °fluffy, frizzy, flossy, flocculent, floccose, floccus; feathery: *Tiny bits from her fuzzy pullover kept coming off on my suit.* **2** °dim, °faint, °hazy, foggy, °misty, blurred, blurry, °indistinct, unclear, °vague, °shadowy, °indefinite, °obscure, ill-defined, °woolly, distorted: *The picture was too fuzzy to make out any details.*

G

gab *v.* **1** °jabber, gabble, °chatter, gibber, blather *or* blether, prate, °prattle, °blab, °gossip, *Colloq Brit* natter, witter, *Slang* jaw, ya(c)k, *US* run off at the mouth: *Stop gabbing and get on with your work!*
—*n.* **2** °chatter, chit-chat, °prattle, jibber-jabber, °jabber, °gossip, blarney, blather *or* blether, tittle-tattle; cackle, °moonshine, °nonsense, °drivel, twaddle, °rubbish, °gobbledegook *or* gobbledygook, °mumbo-jumbo, poppycock, bunk *or* bunkum, balderdash, °stuff and °nonsense, hogwash, eyewash, *Colloq* piffle, flummery, °rot, bull, codswallop, *Slang* bullshit, horseshit, shit, crap, °garbage, *Chiefly Brit* tosh, balls: *He had nothing important to say—just a lot of gab.*

gad *v.* Usually, ***gad about*** *or* ***around***: gallivant, °run around, °flit about, traipse: *He's never home, always gadding about from one party to another.*

gadget *n.* contrivance, °device, appliance, °creation, °invention, °machine, °tool, utensil, °implement, °instrument, °mechanism, °apparatus, *Colloq* °contraption, widget, thingumabob *or* thingamabob *or* thingumbob, thingumajig *or* thingamajig *or* thingummy, whatchamacallit, what's-its-name, *Brit* doodah, *US* hickey, doodad, doohickey, whosis, whatsis, dingus, *Chiefly US and Canadian* gismo *or* gizmo: *He invented a gadget for resealing fizzy drink bottles.*

gag[1] *v.* **1** °silence, °stifle, °still, °muffle, °stop (up), muzzle, °quiet(en), °curb, °suppress, °repress, °restrain, throttle, strangle, °check, °inhibit, °discourage: *The department gagged him, forbidding any press interviews.* **2** retch, °choke, °heave; °gasp for air, °struggle for breath; *US* keck: *That drink made me gag.*
—*n.* **3** °restraint, °curb, muzzle, °check: *MI5 tried to put a gag on the revelations of the former spy.*

gag[2] *n.* **1** °joke, °witticism, jest, °quip, °pun, °gibe, *Colloq* °wisecrack, *Slang* °crack: *He told some gags but nobody found them funny.* **2** practical °joke, °hoax, °prank, °trick, *Colloq* fast one: *For a gag, we put a snake in the sergeant's bed.*

gaiety *n.* **1** cheerfulness, exhilaration, elation, °glee, *joie de vivre*, buoyancy, light-heartedness, blitheness, °happiness, felicity, °pleasure, °delight, °joy, joyfulness, joyousness, exultation, °merriment, °mirth, mirthfulness, jubilation, °good *or* °high spirits, sprightliness, liveliness, joviality, jollity, °hilarity: *The gaiety of the celebration was becoming infectious.* **2** °Often, ***gaieties***: merrymaking, °festivity, festivities, °celebration, °revelry, °revels, rejoicing, conviviality, *Old-fashioned Brit* mafficking: *We all joined in the gaiety of Mardi Gras.* **3** °colourfulness, brightness, gaudiness, garishness, °brilliance, brightness, cheeriness: *The gaiety of her costume was offset by her lugubrious expression.*

gaily *adv.* **1** °showily, gaudily, brightly, splendidly, brilliantly, colourfully, flashily, flamboyantly, garishly: *The dancers appeared in their gaily coloured dresses.* **2** °happily, cheerfully, cheerily, gleefully, joyously, joyfully, jubilantly, merrily, blithely, light-heartedly, airily, jauntily, insouciantly: *The revellers came cavorting gaily down the street.*

gain *v.* **1** °get, °obtain, °acquire, °procure, attain, °achieve, °secure, °earn, °win, °capture, °bag, °net, °harvest, °reap, °garner, glean, °collect, °gather, °come by, °pick up: *Any advantage we gain today may be lost tomorrow.* **2** °make, °get, °profit, gain ground, °earn, °benefit, °realize, °clear, °bring in, °produce, °yield: *Have you gained from the transaction?* **3** °improve, °recuperate, °progress, °rally, °get °better, °advance, gain ground: *Her health has gained steadily since the cyst was removed.* **4** °catch up (to *or* on *or* with), °approach, °get nearer (to), °overtake, °close with, °close in (on), °narrow the gap, gain ground: *As we came to the finish line, Tom was gaining on me. Though he kept gaining, I won.* **5** °leave behind, outdistance, °draw *or* °pull away (from), widen the gap, °get *or* °go *or* °move °further *or* farther °ahead, °get °further *or* farther away (from), °increase the °lead: *I kept gaining on him till I was a mile ahead.* **6** °reach, °arrive at, °get to, °come to: *After paddling for hours, we finally gained the shore.* **7** °increase, °move °ahead, °improve, °advance, °progress, gain ground: *Shares gained again on the exchange.*
—*n.* **8** °profit, °advantage, °margin, °yield, °return, °revenue, °income, dividend, °benefit, emolument, °payment, °pay, °money; proceeds, °earnings, winnings; *Colloq chiefly US* °take, payout, °pay-off: *What was your gain on the sale of the house? He has seen gains of 20 per cent on his investment.* **9** °increase, °increment, °improvement, °rise, °addition, enhancement, °elevation, augmentation, upward *or* forward °movement, °advance, °progress: *Each month has seen a gain in share prices.* **10** °acquisition, °achievement, attainment: *My gain was at the expense of their sacrifice.*

gainful *adj.* °advantageous, °profitable, °productive, °fruitful, °beneficial, °useful, valuable, °worthwhile, °rewarding, remunerative, lucrative, moneymaking: *Your father thinks it about time you sought gainful employment.*

gala *n.* **1** °fête *or* fete, °festival, °festivity, °feast, °celebration, °event, red-letter day, °holiday, holy day, carnival, °occasion, °happening, pageant, °party, ball; field-day: *The annual gala is planned for Midsummer's Eve.*
—*adj.* **2** °merry, festive, °joyful, joyous, °gleeful, jovial, °gay, celebratory, °jolly, convivial, °happy, °cheerful, cheery: *Her home-coming was a gala occasion.*

gale *n.* **1** wind-storm, °strong °wind, (big *or* hard) °blow, °blast, turbulence, °storm, °tempest: *I refuse to take the boat out in that gale.* **2** °outburst, °burst, °explosion, °eruption; °peal, °roar, °scream, °shout, °howl, °shriek: *Bea Lillie needed merely to raise an eyebrow to send her audience into gales of laughter.*

gall[1] *n.* **1** °bitterness, acerbity, acrimony, harshness, vitriol, asperity, bile, spleen, causticness *or* causticity, °bite, mordacity *or* mordaciousness, sharpness, rancidness *or* rancidity; °venom, °poison, °rancour: *Once more he experienced the gall of disappointment.* **2** °impudence, insolence, °impertinence, audacity, brashness, brazenness, sauciness, °effrontery, temerity, overconfidence, °front, *Colloq* °brass, °nerve, °guts, cheek, lip, crust, °sauce, *US and Canadian* chutzpah, moxie; *Slang* balls: *One student had the gall to suggest that he would be a better teacher than I am.*

gall[2] *n.* **1** °sore (°spot), abrasion, °scrape, graze, °scratch, °chafe: *This gall on my leg is from the saddle.* **2** °irritation, °annoyance, °nuisance, °bother, exasperation, vexation, *Colloq* aggravation: *One has to tolerate a lot of gall in this job.*
—*v.* **3** °irritate, °chafe, abrade, °fret, °scrape, °rub, °grate, °scratch: *His shoe was galling his heel.* **4** °irritate, °annoy, °bother, vex, °irk, °exasperate, °harass, harry, °plague, °provoke, goad, °nag, °pester, hector, badger, nettle, needle, °ruffle, °fret, °anger, °enrage, °inflame, °infuriate, incense, arouse, *US* °rankle: *It galls me to think of all the animals killed just to make fur coats.*

gallant *adj.* **1** °brave, °courageous, °bold, valiant, °daring, °dauntless, °intrepid, plucky, °fearless, valorous, unafraid, undaunted, °manly, manful, plucky, mettlesome, stout-hearted, lion-hearted, °heroic, °dashing, (high-)°spirited: *Three gallant soldiers held off the enemy attack.* **2** °chivalrous, courtly, °courteous, °polite, °attentive, gentlemanly, °noble, °gracious, °considerate, °thoughtful, °well-bred, mannerly: *What man is so gallant today as to give up his seat on a bus to a lady?* **3** °dignified, °elegant, °imposing, °grand, °noble, °glorious, °fine, °splendid, °majestic, °stately, °magnificent: *Overwhelmed by four enemy men o' war, the gallant ship sank beneath the waves.*
—*n.* **4** °champion, °hero, knight, cavalier, paladin: *Which gallant wears her scarf on his sleeve in today's jousts?* **5** °lover, Romeo, °sweetheart, °beloved, °paramour, boyfriend, beau, °escort, °suitor, °admirer, *Literary* swain: *In those days, gallants continually sent their ladies gifts and flowers.*

gallows *n.* gibbet: *Another name for gallows was 'Tyburn tree', after that at Tyburn, in London.*

galore *adv.* in °abundance, in °large °quantity *or* numbers *or* amounts, in °excess, °everywhere, aplenty, in °profusion: *There were prizes galore for everything from swimming to skittles.*

gamble *v.* **1** °risk, °venture, °hazard, °bet, wager, °stake, °chance, °speculate; °play, °game, *Brit* °punt: *I wouldn't gamble that he'll be on time. I go to Monte Carlo to gamble.* **2** ***gamble on***: °back, °bet *or* wager on, °stake *or* put °money on, take a °chance *or* flier on, °try one's °luck *or* °fortune on, lay *or* place *or* make a wager *or* °bet on; °count on, °rely on: *We gambled on the horse to win. I was gambling on his having forgotten the debt.*
—*n.* **3** °chance, °risk, °venture; uncertainty, °speculation, *Colloq US* crap-shoot: *I had to take the gamble that the rope would hold. All of life is just a gamble.* **4** °bet, wager, °stake, *Brit* °punt: *She took a gamble on number 14.*

game *n.* **1** °amusement, °pastime, °diversion, °distraction, °recreation, °play; °sport: *She regards love as just a game.* **2** °contest, °competition, °meeting *or US also* °meet, °tournament *or US also* tourney, °match, °encounter, °engagement, °event, °round; regatta:

Would you like to see a football game? The games are held annually. **3** °scheme, °plan, °plot, °design, °stratagem, °strategy, °tactic, °artifice, °trick, °device(s), ploy: *Aha! I am on to your little game!* **4** °occupation, °line (of °work), °job, °position, °field, °business, °trade, °profession, *Slang* °racket: *She is in the advertising game.* **5** °quarry, °prey; °victim, °target: *Game has been plentiful this year, especially pheasant and quail. He is fair game for any unscrupulous swindler.* **6** ***play games***: dissemble, °dissimulate, be °deceitful *or* underhand, °misrepresent, °pretend, °practise °deceit *or* °deception, °fake, feign: *She wasn't serious about selling, she was just playing games.*
—*adj.* **7** °ready, °willing, °prepared; plucky *or* °spirited *or* °daring *or* °adventurous enough: *She's game for anything: I'm sure she'll jump at the chance of scuba-diving lessons.* **8** °plucky, °spirited, high-spirited, °daring, devil-may-care, °adventurous, unflinching, °courageous, °brave, °bold, °heroic, *Colloq* nervy, gutsy: *Entering the cave to rescue the dog was a game thing for him to do.*
—*v.* **9** °gamble: *He has taken up gaming as a hobby.*

gamut *n.* °range, °scale, spectrum, compass, °spread, °sweep, °field, series: *Parker said that Hepburn's acting ran the whole gamut of emotions from A to B.*

gang *n.* **1** °group, °band, °crowd, °company, °pack, °mob, °ring: *The police are looking for the gang that robbed the mail train.* **2** °clique, °set, coterie, °circle, °party, °company, °team, troupe: *A whole gang of my friends came over yesterday evening.*
—*v.* **3** ***gang up (on*** *or* ***against)***: conspire *or* °plot against, °combine *or* °unite *or* °unify *or* °join (against), °league *or* °ally *or* °club *or* °band (against), °join forces (against), °overwhelm: *When they all ganged up on me, I decided to change my mind.*

gangster *n.* °criminal, °gang °member, °racketeer, Mafioso, °soldier, hooligan, gunman, °thug, mugger, °robber, °tough, ruffian, desperado, brigand, bandit, *Brit* skinhead, *Australian and New Zealand* larrikin, *Chiefly US and Canadian* °hoodlum, gunslinger, *Colloq* crook; *Slang* hood, hit man, *US* gunsel, torpedo, mobster, goon: *The gangsters were arrested for smuggling cocaine.*

gap *n.* **1** °opening, °space, °aperture, °distance, °hole, °void, °gulf, °cavity, °break, °breach, °crevice, °chink, °crack, °split, °division, cleft, °rift, °rip, °tear, °rent; °interruption, °interval, lacuna, hiatus, discontinuity, disruption; °lull, °pause, °rest, °recess, °halt, °stop, °suspension, °delay, °wait, °intermission, °respite: *The gap between the walls is just big enough for a child. I can see through a gap in the curtain. There is a gap in his payment record.* **2** °difference, divergence, °disparity, °disagreement, inconsistency, °discrepancy; °division, °distinction: *A gap exists between your ideas of justice and mine.*

gape *v.* **1** °stare, °gawk, goggle, *Slang* °rubberneck, *Brit* gawp *or* gaup: *She gaped when they brought in the boar's head.* **2** yawn, °open °wide, °part; °split: *The jaws of the huge shark gaped to swallow the diver.*

garbage *n.* °rubbish, °refuse, °waste, °muck, offal, sweepings, °swill, °filth, slops, dross, scraps, °junk, °litter, debris, detritus, *Chiefly US and Canadian* °trash, *Slang* crap: *The garbage in the river is a health hazard.*

garble *v.* **1** °warp, °distort, °twist, °corrupt, °adulterate, °slant, °colour, °mangle, °mutilate, °pervert, °doctor, °falsify, °misrepresent, belie, misstate, misquote, misreport, mistranslate, misrender; °misunderstand, misconstrue, misread: *She has garbled the story and it makes no sense. I've garbled your message completely.* **2** °confuse, °mix up, °jumble, °mumble, °mutter: *He garbles his words so badly that I cannot understand him.*

garish *adj.* °gaudy, °flashy, °glaring, °cheap, °tawdry, florid, raffish, °vulgar, °harsh, °loud, meretricious, Brummagem, °showy, °crude, °tasteless, *Colloq* °flash, *Slang US* glitzy: *Their flat is filled with the most garish decorations.*

garland *n.* **1** wreath, festoon, °crown, chaplet, circlet: *Diana crowned the sleeping Endymion with a garland of flowers.*
—*v.* **2** °wreathe, festoon, °crown, °decorate, °coil, °spiral, °encircle, °ring, °circle: *The columns were all garlanded with brightly coloured paper decorations.*

garments *n.pl.* garb, °clothes, clothing, raiment, °dress, attire, °apparel, °costume, °outfit, °habit, vestments, habiliment; °wardrobe; °uniform, livery; *Colloq* duds, °rig, togs, *Slang* rags, threads, °gear: *All his garments are custom-made in Savile Row.*

garner *v.* °gather, °collect, °accumulate, °assemble, °amass, °store (up), °stock (up), °husband, °lay in *or* up *or* down *or* by, °heap *or* °pile up, °put away *or* by, °stow (away), °cache, °store, °save, °reserve: *He garnered what he could from the family estate.*

gash *n.* **1** °cut, °slash, °wound, °score, cleft, °incision, laceration, °slit, °groove, °split: *The chisel slipped, cutting a deep gash in the table.*
—*v.* **2** °cut, °slash, °wound, °score, °cleave, incise, °lacerate, °slit, °groove, °split: *I've gashed my hand on a rusty nail.*

gasp *v.* **1** °pant, °gulp for air, fight for air *or* breath; catch one's breath, snort, °huff, °puff: *I gasped when I saw the condition of the room.*
—*n.* **2** °snort, °puff, °blow, °gulp, wheeze: *He gave a gasp of horror.*

gate *n.* **1** gateway, °barrier, doorway, door, access, °entrance, °exit, °passage, °opening: *The garden gate sagged on its hinges.* **2** °admissions, °attendance, °crowd, audience, assemblage: *We had the biggest gate of the year at yesterday's game.*

gather *v.* **1** °collect, °assemble, °accumulate, °amass, °muster, °heap *or* °pile (up), °garner, °pick, °harvest, glean, °get *or* °bring together, stockpile, °stock: *I gathered all the firewood I could find.* **2** °collect, °assemble, convene, °meet, °huddle, forgather *or* foregather, °get *or* °come together, congregate, °turn out, °flock *or* °herd (together), °group, °cluster, °throng, °crowd, °swarm, °rally: *We gathered round the old man's bed.* **3** °purse, shirr, °pucker, tuck, °ruffle, pleat, °draw *or* °pull together, °contract, constrict: *The fabric is gathered at the waist.* **4** °draw, conclude, °infer, °assume, °deduce, °understand, °learn, °hear, be led to °believe: *I gather that you'd prefer not to collect the award in person.* **5** °increase, °grow, °enlarge, °expand, °extend, wax, °heighten, °deepen, °intensify, °build, °rise: *He stood, menacingly, in the gathering shadows.*

gathering *n.* °assembly, convocation, °convention, congress, assemblage, °meeting, °get-together, °turnout, conclave, °rally, aggregation: *There is a gathering of the clan once a year.*

gaudy *adj.* °garish, °flashy, °glaring, °tawdry, °loud, °cheap, florid, °showy, °ostentatious, raffish, °vulgar, °crude, °tasteless, Brummagem, meretricious, tinselly, gimcrack, °shoddy, trashy, *Brit* tatty, *US and Canadian* honky-tonk, *Colloq US* °tacky, chintzy: *The carnival stands were painted pink, purple, and other gaudy colours.*

gauge *v.* **1** °measure, °determine, °weigh, °calculate, °compute, °reckon, °figure, *US technical also* gage: *Try to gauge the height of that building.* **2** °judge, °evaluate, appraise, assess, °rate, °estimate, °guess, *US technical also* gage: *How can we gauge the strength of the opposition?*
—*n.* **3** °standard, °yardstick, criterion, benchmark, °basis, °measure, °norm, °model, °example, °pattern, °rule, °touchstone, °test, °guide, guideline, *US* litmus °test, *Technical also* gage: *You cannot use your compulsive work habits as a gauge for others.* **4** °scope, °capacity, °amount, °extent, °measure, °size, dimension(s), °magnitude, °degree, °limit: *There are a number of narrow-gauge railways in Wales. What will be the gauge of your involvement in the enterprise?*

gaunt *adj.* **1** °emaciated, °scrawny, °raw-boned, bony, angular, °haggard, skeletal, wasted, starved-looking, cadaverous, scraggy, spindly, °meagre, hollow-cheeked, °spare, °skinny, lank(y), pinched, °thin, underweight: *We were shocked by the gaunt faces of the famine victims.* **2** °dreary, °dismal, °bleak, °bare, °barren, °deserted, °desolate, °harsh, °hostile, unfriendly, inimical, °stern, °forbidding, °stark, °grim, °forlorn: *Under the low cloud, the moor looked even more gaunt than usual.*

gawk *n.* **1** °oaf, lout, bumpkin, °clod, °boor, churl, °dolt, dunderhead *or* dunderpate, ninny, ninnyhammer, ignoramus, °fool, simpleton, ass, bungler, bumbler, *Colloq* clodhopper, lummox, *Slang chiefly US old-fashioned* galoot *or* galloot, °lug: *You big gawk, get out of my way!*
—*v.* **2** °stare, goggle, °gape, *Colloq* °rubberneck, *Slang Brit* gawp *or* gaup: *Stop gawking and help me get him to a hospital.*

gay *adj.* **1** See **homosexual, 1,** below. **2** °happy, °blithe, jovial, light-hearted, °carefree, °debonair, °cheerful, °gleeful, °bright, °joyful, joyous, jubilant, high-spirited, °merry, °lively, °vivacious, °buoyant, °effervescent, °bubbly, bubbling, sparkling, *US* chipper: *In those days our hearts were young and gay.* **3** °garish, °gaudy, °flashy, °bright, °brilliant, °vivid, many-coloured: *The gay decorations added to the atmosphere to the party.*
—*n.* **4** See **homosexual, 2,** below.

gaze *v.* **1** °look at *or* on *or* upon *or* over, °view, °regard, °contemplate, °stare; °wonder, °gape: *She stood gazing out to sea. I gazed at the screen in disbelief.*
—*n.* **2** °fixed *or* °steady *or* °intent °look, °stare, °look: *His gaze faltered and he averted his eyes.*

gear *n.* **1** °cog, cog-wheel; gearbox, °mechanism, machinery; °works: *This gear operates the automatic doors.* **2** °equipment, °apparatus, appliances, °implements, °tools, °tackle, utensils, supplies, °material(s), accessories, accoutrements *or US also* accouterments, appurtenances, °paraphernalia, panoply, °outfit, °trappings, °fixtures, materiel *or matériel: Have you taken all the camping gear?* **3** clothing, °apparel, attire, °clothes, °garments, °habit, habiliments, vestments, raiment, °regalia, °uniform, livery, *Colloq* duds, togs, *Brit* clobber: *You should keep your gear in your locker.* **4** °belongings, °things, °stuff, °effects, °kit, chattels, °goods, impedimenta, (°bag and) baggage, accoutrements *or US also* accouterments, *Colloq* °junk, *Slang* shit: *Get your gear together and get out of here!*
—*v.* **5** °adjust, °adapt, °fit, °suit, °tailor, °accommodate: *You will have to gear your schedule according to our plans.*

gem *n.* **1** gemstone, °jewel, stone, °precious *or* semiprecious stone: *The crown was set with rubies and other precious gems.* **2** °ideal, °quintessence, °perfect °example; °pearl (of °great price), °marvel, °flower, élite, cream, *crème de la crème*, °pick, °nonpareil, °treasure, °prize, °masterpiece, *chef-d'œuvre*: *This is a perfect gem of a painting. The vale of Grasmere is a gem in the diadem of the Lake District.*

general *adj.* **1** °common, °prevailing, accepted, °popular, °public, communal, community, widespread, shared, °extensive, °prevalent, °universal, worldwide, °global; °comprehensive, °inclusive, all-inclusive, non-exclusive, °overall, unrestricted: *The general feeling is that she should resign. We demanded a general revision of the law.* **2** °ordinary, °common, °normal, °customary, °habitual, °regular, °usual, run-of-the-mill, °everyday, °familiar, °accustomed; non-specialized, unspecialized, non-specific, unspecific: *Indoor plumbing became general only in the twentieth century. Within the general area of ceramics there are scores of specialities.* **3** °mixed, assorted, °miscellaneous, heterogeneous, °encyclopedic *or* encyclopaedic, diversified, extended, °broad, °comprehensive, °inclusive, all-inclusive, non-exclusive, °overall, blanket, across the °board, °sweeping, °panoramic, °catholic, composite, combined, blended, °hybrid, °mongrel: *The plan is to prepare a general work of reference.* **4** °vague, °indefinite, °broad, ill-defined, °loose, °inexact, °imprecise, undetailed, non-specific, unspecific, generalized, °overall; °approximate: *This kind of general report fails to pinpoint problems.*

generality *n.* **1** generalization, abstraction, °abstract, °vague *or* °loose *or* °sweeping *or* °indefinite °statement, °imprecise *or* °vague notion: *His talks are characterized by empty generality, without detailed facts.* **2** °Often, ***generalities***: °principle(s), °law(s), abstraction(s), generalization(s), universality *or* universalities: *You have given us the generalities, now we want the particulars.*

generally *adv.* **1** °usually, commonly, °ordinarily, in °general, customarily, habitually, conventionally, normally, typically, on °average, as a °rule, by and °large, for the most °part, mostly, °mainly, on the °whole, predominantly: *Generally, people do not have a healthy diet. He is generally in the office at noon.* **2** superficially, non-specifically, unspecifically, °roughly, broadly, in a °general way, loosely, °approximately, °largely, in the °main, °mainly, °principally: *He covered the subject generally, not dwelling on details.*

generate *v.* **1** °produce, °create, °originate, °make, °manufacture: *At these stations we can generate 1000 megawatts of electricity.* **2** °spawn, °father, sire, °bring into being, procreate, °breed, beget, engender, °propagate: *This one fish would generate millions of offspring if all survived.* **3** °produce, °create, °give °rise to, °inspire, °whip up, °cause, °initiate: *Her good fortune generated in him a feeling of envy.* **4** °produce, °create, °invent, °coin, °make up, °fabricate, °fashion, °devise, °develop, °form, °forge, °mould, contrive, °construct, °put together: *We must generate a new theory to account for these phenomena.*

generation *n.* **1** °production, °reproduction, propagation, procreation, begetting, fathering, siring: *In the lower animals, the generation of offspring is asexual.* **2** °time(s), °day(s), °age, °period, °era, epoch: *The trait did not appear till later generations. The 1950s and '60s spawned the yuppie generation of the '80s.* **3** °origination, °creation, genesis, inception, °initiation, °start, °beginning, °institution, °establishment, °formation, formulation: *The generation of legal systems can be traced to the oldest civilizations.* **4** °crop; °age (°group); contemporaries: *This generation of Americans has a rendezvous with destiny. He prefers to be with people of his own generation.*

generous *adj.* **1** °bounteous, °bountiful, magnanimous, °charitable, eleemosynary, °philanthropic, °lavish, open-handed, °free, °liberal, unstinting, ungrudging, beneficent, °benevolent, big-hearted, munificent: *Not everyone who has money is generous with it.* **2** °magnanimous, °benevolent, °charitable, °unselfish, °humanitarian, humane, °kindly, °noble, high-minded, °lofty, °good, °disinterested, °unprejudiced: *He was too generous in acknowledging the accomplishments of his political foes.* **3** °plentiful, °full, °lavish, overflowing, °abundant, bounteous, °handsome, copious, °ample: *They certainly serve generous portions at that restaurant.*

genial *adj.* affable, °amiable, °cordial, °warm, °friendly, congenial, °agreeable, °good-natured, good-humoured, well-disposed, °neighbourly, °sociable, °kindly, °kind, °hospitable, °easygoing, °relaxed, °pleasant, °nice, °cheerful, cheery, convivial: *And here is your genial host, Sonny Gegenschein!*

genitals *n.pl.* genitalia, °sexual *or* reproductive organs, °sex organs, organs of procreation *or* °generation, °private parts, privates: *They wore loincloths to cover their genitals.*

genius *n.* **1** °mastermind, °master, °virtuoso, °intellect; maestro, °expert, °adept; *Colloq* °brain, Einstein: *At the age of nine, this genius entered university.* **2** °intelligence, °brilliance, °wit, °ingenuity, brains, °ability, °aptitude: *She is a woman of incredible genius.* **3** °talent, °gift, °knack, °faculty, °flair, °aptitude, °forte, °capacity, °ability, °capability: *He has a genius for saying the wrong thing.*

genre *n.* °kind, °sort, °type, °class, °style, °brand, °character, °category, genus, species, °variety, °fashion: *Her paintings are in the classicist genre.*

genteel *adj.* **1** over-polite, °unnatural, °pretentious, °affected, °mannered, putting on airs, °pompous, overdone, *Colloq* °posh, la-di-da *or* lah-di-dah *or* la-de-da, °phoney *or US also* phony, *Brit* county: *The Brumfits are a bit too genteel for my taste.* **2** °courtly, °polite, °civil, well-mannered, °well-bred, °courteous, mannerly, °gracious, °proper, °respectable, °decorous, °ladylike, gentlemanly, °chivalrous, cavalier, °debonair, °suave, patrician, °high-class, °upper-class, aristocratic, thoroughbred, blue-blooded, °noble, °royal, *Colloq* classy, tony, °upper crust, *US* silk-stocking: *His son married a woman from an ancient, genteel house.* **3** °refined, °polished, °sophisticated, °debonair, °suave, urbane, cosmopolitan, °cultivated, cultured, °elegant, *Colloq* ritzy: *Why small feet are considered genteel, I cannot say.*

gentle *adj.* **1** °kind, °kindly, °mild, °tender, °benign, °moderate, °easy, °quiet, °calm, °still, °temperate, unruffled, untroubled, undisturbed, °tranquil, °restful, °peaceful, pacific, placid, °smooth, °lenient, °patient, °indulgent, °soothing, °thoughtful, °gracious, compassionate, humane, tender-hearted, °merciful; °soft, °light, balmy: *Amy is very gentle with the patients. A gentle breeze barely stirred the leaves. The gentle waves belied the terror that lurked below.* **2** °tame, °tractable, docile, °manageable, controllable; °broken: *As he's a beginner, he's been given a gentle mare to ride.* **3** °gradual, °easy, °moderate: *The car rolled down the gentle slope and stopped.*

gentry *n.* ladies and gentlemen, élite, aristocracy, landed gentry, gentlefolk, °upper °class(es) *or* strata, cream, *crème de la crème;* landowners, *Brit* squirearchy, *Colloq* °upper crust *or* strata: *He thinks he is privileged because he belongs to the gentry.*

genuine *adj.* **1** °authentic, °real, bona fide, °veritable, °legitimate, °true, °original, °proper, not °counterfeit *or* °fake; °pukka *or* pukkah *or* pucka: *Is that a genuine diamond? I know his feelings for her are genuine. Armstrong is a genuine leader of men.* **2** °candid, °frank, °open, °sincere, °earnest, °honest, unfeigned: *His art is much more genuine than the pretentious output of his contemporaries.*

germ *n.* **1** °micro-organism, °microbe, bacterium, virus, *Colloq* °bug: *Germs were not conceived of before Leeuwenhoek's invention of the microscope.* **2** °source, °origin, fount, embryo, °seed, °root, rudiment, °beginning, °start, °base, °basis: *The germ of romantic literature lies in folk-tales.*

gesture *n.* **1** °movement, °motion, gesticulation, °signal, °indication, °action, *Colloq US* high °sign: *She made a gesture of dismissal.* **2** °formality, °move; gambit, ploy; °token, °indication, °symbol: *Sending her flowers was a friendly gesture. Their burning the flag was a gesture of defiance.*
—*v.* **3** °motion, gesticulate, °signal, °sign, °indicate, *Colloq US* give (someone) the high °sign: *He gestured for me to step forward.*

get *v.* **1** °obtain, °secure, °acquire, °come by *or* into (the) °possession of, °procure, °pick up; °collect; °buy, °purchase, °book, °retain, °hire, °engage, °rent, °lease; accede to, °inherit, °fall °heir to, °succeed to: *Where did you get these beautiful prints? You had better get yourself a good lawyer. They got the furniture from his mother's estate.* **2** °receive; be °given, °come by: *He got a bicycle from his grandma. I got a job at the carwash.* **3** °earn, °receive, °realize, °make, °take, °gross, °clear, °net, °pocket, be paid; °win, *Colloq* °take home, °pull down: *He gets a lot of money for just standing there and answering questions.* **4** °fetch, °go (to *or* and) get, °go for *or* after, °pick up; °bring (back), °retrieve: *Please get me a cup of tea.* **5** °catch, °contract, °have, °suffer from, °come down with, °fall °ill *or* °sick with, be afflicted with, °become infected with, °acquire: *You'll get pneumonia if you go out without your coat.* **6** °become, °fall: *We got ill from eating too much chocolate.* **7** °become, °turn, °grow: *It got very cold last night. He got rich almost overnight.* **8** °capture, °seize, °arrest, °take, apprehend, °grab, °pick up, °lay °hold of, °bag, *Colloq* collar, °nab, °pinch: *Are the police sure that they got the right person?* **9** °manage, °arrange, °come, °succeed; contrive, °fix it, °manoeuvre, °manipulate, *Colloq* °wangle: *How did you get to be chairman?* **10** °reach, °arrive (at), °come, °go, °travel, °journey: *She got home by taxi.* **11** °catch, °take, °enter, °make, °come *or* °go by, °travel *or* °journey by: *He got the midnight train.* **12** °reach, get in °touch with, °communicate with, get onto *or* through to, *Colloq* °contact: *We finally got him just before he left for the day.* **13** °receive, °pick up, °tune in to *or* on, °listen to *or* °watch: *I cannot get that programme.* **14** °persuade, °prevail (up)on, °coax, °induce, °influence, °cajole, °wheedle, °talk (someone) into, °sway, °bring (someone) round, °make, °cause: *How did you ever get them to let you go?* **15** °put, °place, °set, °fit, °manoeuvre, °manipulate, wiggle, °wriggle: *I can't get this knob back on.* **16** °affect, °stir, °move, °touch, arouse, °stimulate, °excite, °have an °impact *or* °effect on, °make an °impression on, °impress, °leave a °mark on, get to, *Colloq* °turn (someone) on: *Those old romantic songs really get me.* **17** get at, °irritate, °annoy, vex, °irk, nettle, pique, °provoke, °anger, °exasperate, °bother, °perturb, rile, *Colloq* °bug, get (someone's) goat, °rub (someone) (up) the wrong way, *Sometimes non-standard* °aggravate: *Doesn't it get you to see people going unpunished for their crimes?* **18** baffle, °confuse, confound, °puzzle, °perplex, °bewilder: *You've got me! I don't know where it is!* **19** °understand, °appreciate, °fathom, °see, °grasp, apprehend, °perceive, °follow, °comprehend, °take in, °work out, make head(s) or tail(s) of: *You just don't get the joke, do you?* **20** °catch, °hear: *I didn't get the name; please repeat it.* **21** °derive, °learn, glean, absorb, °take in: *Did you get anything from yesterday's lecture?* **22** °have, °place, °put, °fix, pinpoint: *Eventually, I'll get him where I want him!* **23** get °even with, °revenge oneself on, °take °vengeance on, °pay (someone) back, °settle *or* °even the °score with, get back at: *I'll get him for betraying me if it's the last thing I do!* **24** °strike, °hit, °punch, smack; °shoot; °hurt, °harm, °damage, °injure; *Slang* sock, slug: *She got him right between the eyes.* **25** ***get about*** *or* ***around***: **a** °spread, become known, °leak (out), °circulate, be bruited about *or* around, be noised °abroad, °go about *or* around: *He let the news get about that he needed a secretary.* **b** be socially °active, °socialize, °go *or* get out; °run about *or* around, °gad about: *Since his accident, he doesn't get around much any more.* **26** ***get across***: get *or* °put over, °put across, get through, °communicate, make °clear, °impart: *She is trying to get across to you the fact that she despises television.* **27** ***get ahead***: °succeed, °prosper, be *or* become °successful, do well, °flourish, °thrive, °make good, °progress, °rise (up) in the world, *Colloq* °go places: *With his contacts, he's bound to get ahead.* **28** ***get along***: **a** be °friendly *or* compatible (with), °associate (with), °agree (with), be °agreeable, get on (with), *Colloq* °hit it off (with): *She gets along with most people quite well. Do you think they'll get along?* **b** °manage, °cope, °shift, °fare, °survive, make both ends meet, keep the wolf from the door, keep one's head above water, get on, *Colloq* get by, °make out, °make do: *How are you getting along with your new novel?* **c** °leave, °depart, °go *or* °move away, get °going, get on, °go along, °proceed: *I have to get along now or I'll miss my train.* **d** °progress, °proceed, get on, °advance, °move °ahead *or* along *or* on: *How are you getting along with your new novel?* **e** get on, °age, get *or* become *or* °grow older, °advance: *They are getting along but you wouldn't guess that they're eighty.* **29** ***get around***: **a** See **25**, above. **b** See **46**, below. **30** ***get at***: **a** °gain access to, access, °reach, °put *or* °lay one's hands on, get to: *I can't get at the lock from here.* **b** °intend, °mean, °suggest, °hint (at), °insinuate, °imply, have in °mind *or* °view, °contemplate: *She just didn't understand what I was getting at.* **c** get, °tease, °taunt, °criticize, find °fault with, °carp, °nag, °pick on, *US* get to: *She is really beginning to get at me with her* *persistent criticism.* **d** get to, °influence, °intimidate, °corrupt, °bribe, °undermine, °subvert, suborn: *They tried to get at the judge.* **e** °learn, °find out, ascertain, °determine: *The police said they were only trying to get at the facts.* **31** ***get away***: **a** °escape, °leave, °break out *or* away, °flee, °depart, make good one's °escape, °elude one's captors, °break °free, °disappear: *He will never be able to get away now!* **b** °escape, take a °holiday *or US also* vacation, get *or* take a °rest *or* °respite: *I must get away for a few days.* **c** °start, get *or* °take off: *Black Flash got away from the starting gate at top speed.* **32** ***get back***: **a** °return, °come *or* °go back: *I'll try to get back before midnight.* **b** reacquire, °recover, regain, °retrieve, °recoup, repossess: *Can you get your money back for that hat?* **33** ***get back at***: See **23,** above. **34** ***get behind***: °back, °support, °promote, °finance, °fund, °push, *Colloq* °plug, hype: *If you get behind the enterprise, I know it will succeed.* **35** ***get by***: See **28 b,** above. **36** ***get down***: **a** dismount, alight, °descend, °come *or* °go down, °climb *or* °step down, get off: *He got down from his horse and drew his gun.* **b** °write (down), °note (down), °record, make a °note of: *She wasn't able to get down everything Shaw said.* **c** °depress, dispirit, °sadden, dishearten, °discourage, deject: *Don't let a little thing like that get you down.* **d** °swallow, °eat: *No sooner does he get some food down than it comes right back up again.* **37** ***get down to***: °concentrate *or* °focus on, °turn °attention to, °attend to: *Let's get down to business.* **38** ***get in***: **a** °enter, get into *or* on *or* onto, °embark, entrain, emplane *or* enplane, get *or* °go aboard: *We got in the car and were driven away. You can get in here.* **b** °enter, °arrive, °return, °come *or* °go in: *I got in at eight today.* **c** °fit *or* °squeeze in, °insert, °slip in, °include: *He got in my comment. The doctor got me in before anyone else.* **d** °arrive, °come in, °land: *My flight got in at dawn.* **39** ***get into***: **a** put on, don, °dress in, get dressed in: *Here, get into this uniform.* **b** °go into, °discuss, become °involved in, °pursue, °treat, °describe, delineate, °detail, °follow up on, °penetrate: *Do you really want me to get into the nasty details?* **c** be into, be *or* become °involved in, °take up, °pursue; °enjoy, °like, become °enthusiastic about, *Slang* get off on, get *or* become °high on: *I could really get into farming.* **d** See **38 a,** above. **40** ***get off***: **a** alight, °disembark, get down from, get out of, dismount, °descend (from), °climb *or* °step down off *or* from, deplane, detrain: *She got off her bike and came towards me.* **b** °leave, °depart, °go (off), °set out *or* off: *I hope to get off tomorrow morning.* **c** °remove, °take off, °shed, doff: *Can you get those boots off easily?* **d** cause to be °set *or* °go °free, be *or* cause to be acquitted *or* liberated *or* released *or* °set °free: *A clever lawyer could have got him off. He got off on a technicality.* **41** ***get off on***: See **39 c,** above. **42** ***get on***: **a** See **28,** above. **b** See **38 a,** above. **c** See **39 a,** above. **d** grow *or* become °late: *It's getting on and they'll be waiting.* **43** ***get onto***: **a** See **12,** above. **b** See **38 a,** above. **c** °discover, °learn about, become °aware of, °find out about, *Colloq Brit* °twig, *US* cotton (on) to: *If they get onto the missing stores we're in for it.* **44** ***get out (of)***: **a** °leave, °depart, °go out *or* away, be off, °retire: *We got out as quickly as we could.* **b** °escape, °extricate oneself; be released: *She thought she'd never get out alive.* **c** °extract, °draw, wrest, °force, °drag *or* °pry out, wring *or* get from: *They'll never get anything out of me!* **d** °gain, °profit: *Ask yourself what you will get out of the deal.* **e** °avoid, °evade, °sidestep, °escape: *Gabriela was somehow always able to get out of PE class.* **f** See **25 b,** above. **45** ***get over***: **a** surmount, °cross, °climb, °pass, °traverse: *A dog can't get over a fence that high.* **b** °recover *or* °recuperate from, °survive: *Which takes longer, getting over a love affair or the measles?* **c** °finish, °complete, bring to an °end: *Let's get this over with as soon as possible.* **d** See **26,** above. **46** ***get round*** *or* ***around***: **a** °bypass, circumvent, skirt, °avoid, °evade, °elude, °outsmart, °outwit, outmanoeuvre, outflank, steal a march on, *Colloq* give (someone) the °run-around: *Chris is always trying to get round the parking restrictions.* **b** °cajole, °wheedle, °flatter, °persuade, °coax, °win over: *I didn't want to propose, but she managed to get round me.* **c** See **25 b,** above. **47** ***get round*** *or* ***around to***: get *or* °come to, °reach, °arrive at (°finally), °find °time for: *He said he would do the repairs if he got round to it.* **48** ***get through***: **a** (°help to) °succeed *or* °complete: *She got me through the ordeal. Without her help, I never could have got through.* **b** °reach, °contact: *The line is engaged and I cannot get through to mother.* **c** °finish, conclude: *When you get through, please put away the dishes.* **d** °communicate (with): *Parents sometimes have trouble getting through to their children.* **49** ***get (to)***: **a** °arrive at, °come to; °near, °approach: *What time did you get to the office? How did you get home?* **b** See **28 c, d,** above. **50** ***get together***: **a** °gather, °accumulate, °collect, °assemble: *Get your things together and leave at once!* **b** °assemble, convene, °gather, °meet, congregate, °socialize: *Have you time to get together on Friday?* **c** °arrive at *or* °reach an °agreement *or* °settlement, °come to terms, °come to an °understanding: *I think we can get together on the question of wages.* **51** ***get up***: **a** °arise, °awaken, °wake (up): *I get up at dawn.* **b** °stand (up): *Get up and you'll be able to reach it.* **c** °mount, °climb (up), ascend: *Can we get up the next hill? She got up on the table and started to dance.* **d** °create, °devise, °organize, °arrange, °prepare: *We got up a cabaret for the after-dinner entertainment.* **e** °dress, °clothe, °apparel, °outfit, attire, °turn out, deck out, °rig out, °dress up, °fit out *or* up: *She got herself up as a cabaret dancer.* **f** °study, °learn, *US* get up on: *You'd best get up your history before the exam.* **52** ***get up to***: become *or* be °involved in, be up to: *If you don't watch her, she'll get up to no good.*

getaway *n.* °escape, °flight, °retreat: *The prisoners made their getaway in a van. Lady Fenella was so boring I couldn't wait to make my getaway.*

get-together *n.* °gathering; °meeting, °conference, °convention: *We had a get-together at my house. Can we arrange a get-together for all the members?*

get-up *n.* **1** °costume, °outfit; °rig: *He came in a diver's get-up.* **2** °format, layout, °arrangement, °structure, °look, °style: *Who is responsible for the magazine's new get-up?*

gewgaw *n.* trinket, °bauble, gimcrack, °trifle, knick-knack, bagatelle, kickshaw, °toy, °novelty, bijou, °vanity; °bric-à-brac *or* bric-a-brac: *She has a huge collection of worthless gewgaws.*

ghastly *adj.* **1** °dreadful, °awful, °terrible, °terrifying, °frightful, °hideous, °horrible, horrendous, horrid, horrifying, °grim, °grisly, °loathsome, °gruesome, °ugly, °repellent, °repulsive, °shocking, appalling, *Colloq* °gross, °scary: *He was involved in a ghastly accident.* **2** °grim, cadaverous, °haggard, ashen, °wan, °pale, pallid, °pasty(-faced), °drawn, livid, °ghostly, °spectral, °macabre: *She looked ghastly after the surgery.* **3** °awful, °bad, °terrible, °ill, ailing, °sick: *We felt ghastly after eating the undercooked chicken.*

ghost *n.* **1** apparition, °phantom, °spectre, phantasm, °shade, °spirit, wraith, poltergeist, banshee, doubleganger, *doppelgänger*, ghoul, manes, *No. Eng. dialect* boggart; °hallucination, °illusion, °vision; *Colloq* spook: *The ghost of his uncle appeared before him.* **2** °hint, °suggestion, °shadow, °trace, scintilla, glimmer: *Vera hasn't the ghost of a chance of meeting anyone suitable at the office.*

ghostly *adj.* **1** °spectral, ghostlike, wraithlike, phantasmal, °phantom, °eerie, °unreal, °unnatural, °supernatural, preternatural, °unearthly, °sinister, °strange, uncanny, °weird, *Colloq* spooky, °scary, creepy: *I heard a ghostly voice calling my name.* **2** See **ghastly, 2,** above.

ghoulish *adj.* **1** °devilish, demonic, °satanic, °diabolic(al), °fiendish, demoniac(al), cacodemonic, Mephistophelian; °infernal, hellish, malign: *The coven engage in the most ghoulish practices.* **2** °macabre, °grisly, °morbid, °gruesome, °disgusting, °monstrous, °abominable, °hideous, horrendous, °horrible, horrifying, horrid, °brutal, barbaric, °savage, °ruthless, pitiless,

°merciless, °cruel, °vicious, feral, °inhuman, bloodthirsty, °ferocious, *Colloq* °sick: *She has some ghoulish notions about being eaten alive by rats.*

giant *n.* **1** °superhuman, titan, colossus, Goliath; giantess, amazon, °ogre; behemoth, °monster, leviathan, mammoth: *Blocking the road in front of Jack was a giant nearly thirty feet tall.*
—*adj.* **2** See **gigantic,** below.

gibberish *n.* °drivel, °nonsense, °rubbish, gibber, °prattle, twaddle, gabble, °jabber, balderdash, jibber-jabber, blather *or* blether, Jabberwocky, °gobbledegook *or* gobbledygook, °mumbo-jumbo, rodomontade, Gongorism, cackle, °chatter, °patter, °jargon, °babble, claptrap, poppycock, *Colloq* tripe, codswallop, crap, bunk, piffle, *US* °garbage, horse feathers; *Taboo slang* balls, bull(shit), *US* crock (of shit): *If one listens to such gibberish long enough, one begins to believe it.*

gibe *v.* **1** jibe (at), °jeer (at), °scoff (at), °flout, °mock, °deride, make °fun of, °poke °fun at, °ridicule, °twit, °taunt, °sneer (at), °chaff, °tease, °rag, °heckle, *No. Eng. dialect* gird, *Colloq* kid, rib, *US and Canadian* razz: *All of us at school used to gibe at David because he wore fancy clothes.*
—*n.* **2** jibe, °jeer, °taunt, °sneer, °dig, °cutting °remark, °thrust, °chaff, °raillery, scoffing, °derision, °ridicule, °mockery, *Rare* mycterism, *Slang* °crack, °wisecrack: *David paid no attention to his classmates' gibes.*

giddy *adj.* **1** °dizzy, °faint, unsteady, light-headed, vertiginous, reeling, *Colloq* woozy: *This medication may make you feel a bit giddy.* **2** °silly, °frivolous, °scatterbrained, °flighty, °capricious, °irresponsible, °erratic, °fickle, °volatile, °impulsive, °reckless, °whimsical: *You can't marry a giddy young girl like Peggy.*

gift *n.* **1** °present, °donation, °favour, °grant, °largesse, °bounty, benefaction, °offering, °honorarium, contribution, give-away, °premium, °bonus, °prize; alms, hand-out, °dole, °charity, °benefit; °tip, gratuity, baksheesh *or* backsheesh, *pourboire*, cumshaw: *Before we left, our neighbours made a gift to us of some local pottery.* **2** °talent, °ability, °aptitude, °genius, °flair, °knack, °facility, °forte, °strength, strong point, °bent, °capability, °capacity, °power: *Her family never recognized her special gifts.*

gifted *adj.* °talented, °able, skilled, °capable, °skilful, °outstanding, °excellent, °superior, °superb, °brilliant, °expert, °master, °masterful, masterly, °virtuoso, first-class, °first-rate, top-drawer, top-flight, °good, *Colloq* top-notch, ace, crackerjack, °crack: *Grants are available for gifted, indigent artists.*

gigantic *adj.* °big, °large, °huge, °enormous, °massive, °giant, °colossal, °immense, mammoth, tremendous, stupendous, °towering, staggering, °vast, titanic, gargantuan, elephantine, Cyclopean, Herculean, Brobdingnagian; king-size, extra-large, *Colloq* °jumbo, walloping, °whopping, °thumping, thundering, strapping, super-duper, *US* humongous: *The gigantic tower, reaching to the heavens, appeared before us.*

giggle *v.* **1** °titter, °snicker, snigger, °chuckle, °laugh, chortle, cackle, °twitter: *Stop that giggling at the rear of the classroom!*
—*n.* **2** °titter, °snicker, snigger, °chuckle, °laugh, chortle, cackle, °twitter: *Did I hear a giggle?* **3** °joke, °prank, °laugh: *Just for a giggle, we tied his shoelaces together.*

gimmick *n.* **1** °device, °strategy, °stratagem, ploy, °trick, °ruse, °wile, °subterfuge, °manoeuvre, °artifice, °deception, °trap, °snare, *US* °hook, *Colloq* °dodge: *We need some sort of gimmick to attract buyers.* **2** °device, contrivance, °gadget, °invention, *Colloq* °contraption, widget, thingumbob *or* thingumabob *or* thingamabob, thingumajig *or* thingamajig *or* thingummy, whatchamacallit, what's-its-name, *Brit* doodah, *US* doohickey, doodad, hickey, whosis, whatsis, dingus, Rube Goldberg (°invention), *Chiefly US and Canadian* gismo *or* gizmo: *He uses some kind of gimmick to break into cars.*

gingerly *adv.* **1** warily, cautiously, charily, carefully, delicately, °fastidious, daintily, squeamishly, tentatively, nervously, cannily, circumspectly, guardedly, watchfully, timidly, timorously, shyly: *Handle that nitroglycerine very gingerly.*
—*adj.* **2** °wary, °cautious, chary, °careful, °fastidious, °delicate, °dainty, °squeamish, °tentative, °nervous, canny, circumspect, °guarded, watchful, °timid, timorous, °shy: *Note the gingerly way he handles the nitroglycerine.*

girl *n.* **1** female, °woman, °lass, (°young) lady, °miss, mademoiselle, wench, *Fräulein*, °maid, °maiden, damsel, demoiselle, *Irish* colleen, *Australian and New Zealand* sheila, *Colloq* chick, filly, gal, *Slang* bird, frail, skirt, piece, mouse, *Brit* crumpet, bit of skirt *or* stuff, *Old-fashioned Brit* popsy, *US* dame, °broad, (bit of) San Quentin quail *or* jail-bait: *His mother wants to introduce him to a nice girl.* **2** girlfriend, °sweetheart; betrothed, fiancée; °mistress, °lover, °friend, live-in °lover, inamorata, tally, *US* POSSLQ (= 'Person of the Opposite Sex Sharing Living Quarters'), *Colloq Brit* popsy, *Slang* moll, *US* twist, °squeeze: *She's his girl and she'll stick by him.*

girth *n.* **1** circumference, °perimeter, ambit, °periphery, °circuit: *His girth steadily expanded as he approached fifty.* **2** °belt, girdle, °border, cincture, waistband, cestus, cummerbund, *Archaic* zone, *US and Canadian* cinch: *Tighten that girth or the saddle will come off.*

gist *n.* °essence, °core, °heart, °substance, °point, °theme, °quintessence, °pith, °meat, marrow, °focus, °nub, °significance, (°main *or* °basic) °idea; °direction, °drift: *It will save time if I tell you the gist of the argument.*

give *v.* **1** °present, °deliver, °pass (over), °turn *or* °hand over, °confer, °vouchsafe, °provide, °supply, °furnish, °bestow, °donate, °accord, °afford, °award, °hand out, °contribute, °distribute, °grant, °allow, °transfer, °make over, °entrust: *Please give me the envelope. I have given the files to the tax inspector. Give freely to charity.* **2** °exchange, °pay, °transfer, °trade, barter, swap *or* swop: *Philippa gave a week's salary for that dress.* **3** °impart, °pass on, °communicate, °transmit, °send, convey, °express: *Give my regards to Broadway.* **4** °afflict with, °cause, °occasion: *Rock music gives me a headache.* **5** °sacrifice, °devote, °dedicate, °yield (up), °surrender, give up, °cede, °concede, consign, °apply (oneself) to: *Those monks have given their lives to the study of Scripture.* **6** °present, °offer; °announce, °introduce: *Ladies and gentlemen, I give you Madja Kiziamainska, the Polish Nightingale!* **7** °present, °announce, °offer, °recite, °sing, °act, °perform, °read, °put on: *We were asked to give a performance for charity.* **8** utter, °emit, give out (with), °issue: *He gave a shout to warn us.* **9** °yield, °relax, give way, °fail, °collapse, °buckle, °break down, °fall *or* °come °apart: *If that pillar gives, the balcony will come down.* **10** °cause, °lead, °induce, °persuade, °make, °prompt, °move, °dispose: *I was given to understand that I was not welcome.* **11** °cede, °relinquish, °concede, °allow, °surrender, °yield: *He gave me the first game but I lost the second.* **12** ***give away***: **a** See **1,** above. **b** °reveal, °betray, °let out, divulge, °disclose, expose, °inform on, uncover, °leak, °let °slip; °let the cat out of the bag; *Colloq* blow the whistle on, *Slang* rat on, *US* fink on: *The traitor gave me away, and I was arrested.* **13** ***give in***: °yield, °submit, give up, give ground, back away (from), back off, °capitulate, °surrender, °admit °defeat: *After trying for hours to make him change his mind, he finally gave in.* **14** ***give off***: give out, °emit, exude, °exhale, °discharge, °send *or* °throw out, °release, °smell of: *Her clothing gave off a scent of lavender.* **15** ***give out***: **a** See **14,** above. **b** °distribute, °hand out, give, °deal (out), °pass out *or* around, disseminate, °dispense, °allot, apportion, allocate, °assign, °distribute, °issue, °mete out, °ration (out), °dole (out), °pay, *Colloq* dish *or* fork out, °shell out: *The prizes will be given out to the winners at a special ceremony. She was giving out handbills to passers-by.*

c °publish, °announce, °make known, °broadcast, °impart, °issue, make °public, °reveal: *You shouldn't give out that kind of information.* **d** become °exhausted, be reduced *or* depleted, °fail, °run out: *What will we do when the food gives out?* **e** See **8,** above. **16** ***give over***: °assign, °resign, °hand over, °surrender, °relinquish, °pass over, give up; °entrust: *We gave our dog over to Lambert's for training.* **17** ***give up***: **a** °abandon, °stop, °cease, °quit, °leave off, °forgo, °forsake, °renounce, desist from, °swear off, abstain from; °reject; *Colloq* °cut out, chuck: *I am trying to give up smoking.* **b** °surrender, °capitulate, °yield, °cede, °concede, give in (to °defeat), °throw in the towel *or* sponge; °despair: *I've tried to convince him but finally gave up.* **c** See **4,** above. **d** See **13,** above. **e** See **16,** above.

—*n.* **18** °slack, °play, °leeway, °excess; °flexibility, °stretch: *There is very little give in the rules governing working hours. Nylon is used for boat anchor ropes because it has some give.*

give and take *n.* compromise, °cooperation, reciprocity, interaction, °fair °exchange, teamwork, °joint °effort, synergy: *There is a lot of give and take in our relationship—I give and she takes.*

given *adj.* **1** stated, accepted, agreed(-upon), delineated, confirmed, °noted, affirmed, specified, settled, °set, (pre)arranged, preordained, foreordained: *You must solve the problem using the given information.* **2** presupposed, °assumed, °understood, postulated, premised, conceded, acknowledged, allowed: *I think we can take her honesty as given.* **3** °prone, °accustomed, dedicated, addicted, °inclined, °disposed: *Our headmaster is not exactly given to flights of fancy.*

—*n.* **4** assumption, donnée; °fact, °certainty, °reality, actuality, °gospel, the °truth: *Can we accept her interest in the job as a given?*

glad *adj.* **1** °happy, °pleased, contented, gratified, satisfied; °delighted, thrilled, °joyful, °overjoyed, tickled, *Colloq* tickled pink *or* to death, °pleased as Punch, *Slang Brit* chuffed: *I am genuinely glad to see you.* **2** (°ready and) °willing, °happy, °keen, °eager, (well-) °disposed, °inclined, °ready: *I would be glad to help you, madam.*

gladden *v.* °cheer, °enliven, °brighten, °delight, hearten, exhilarate, elate, °buoy (up), °animate: *It certainly gladdened me to be home again.*

gladly *adv.* cheerfully, °happily, °readily, °willingly, with °pleasure: *I'd go with you gladly if I had the time.*

glamorous *adj.* **1** alluring, fascinating, charming, °attractive, °magnetic, captivating, °enthralling, °desirable, appealing, °enchanting, entrancing, intriguing, beguiling, bewitching, magical: *Esmé designs clothes for the most glamorous women in the world.* **2** °chic, °smart, °stylish, °fashionable, *Colloq* °trendy: *She always wears the most glamorous clothes.*

glamour *n.* allure, °fascination, °charm, attractiveness, °brilliance, °glitter, °attraction, °magnetism, charisma, captivation, desirability, °appeal, °enchantment, bewitchment, witchcraft, °sorcery, °magic: *Who today can match the glamour of the movie stars of the '30s?*

glance *v.* **1** glimpse, °peek, °peep, °scan, °look, *Colloq Brit* have a shufti *or* shufty at, take a dekko at: *I've only had time to glance at the report.* **2** °reflect, glint, °glisten, °shimmer, °twinkle, °gleam, °flicker, glimmer, °sparkle, scintillate, °glitter, °flash: *A ray of sunlight glanced off the windows opposite.* **3** °bounce (off), °reflect, ricochet, °rebound, carom: *The stone glanced off the pavement and struck my leg.*

—*n.* **4** glimpse, °peek, °peep, °look, *coup d'œil, Colloq* gander, *Brit* shufti *or* shufty, dekko: *She turned and gave him a questioning glance, As he fingered the tip of his fer-de-lance.* **5** °gleam, glint, glimmer, °shimmer, °twinkle, °sparkle, scintillation, °glitter, °flicker, °flash: *The silver light, with quivering glance, Played on the water's still expanse.*

glare *n.* **1** °dazzle, °brilliance, brightness, °splendour, resplendence, °radiance, effulgence, °lustre, °shine, °flame, °flare, °blaze: *We had to shade our eyes from the glare.* **2** °frown, °dirty *or* °nasty *or* °black °look, °scowl, °stare, glower, °lower *or Brit also* °lour: *She shrank from his fierce glare.* **3** garishness, gaudiness, floridity *or* floridness, flashiness, tawdriness, showiness, °ostentation, meretriciousness: *His writing is filled with the pomp and glare of rhetoric.*

—*v.* **4** °frown, give a °dirty *or* °nasty *or* °black °look, °scowl, °stare, glower, °lower *or Brit also* °lour, °look daggers (at): *She simply glared at him and he withered.*

glaring *adj.* **1** °blatant, °flagrant, egregious, °conspicuous, °obtrusive, °prominent, °evident, °obvious, °manifest, °patent, °overt, °clear, °visible, unconcealed, °outrageous, °gross, flagitious, °atrocious, heinous, °shameless, °disgraceful, °shocking, °scandalous: *They pointed out a glaring omission in the proposals.* **2** °garish, °dazzling, °brilliant, blinding, blazing, °vivid, °harsh, °strong: *I was blinded when we first walked out into the glaring sunlight.*

glass *n.* **1** glassware, crystal: *Use the best glass for the party.* **2** °mirror, looking-glass: *He constantly looks at himself in the glass.* **3** window, °pane, window-pane, plate glass: *The children pressed their noses against the glass of the toy shop.* **4** tumbler, drinking-glass, beaker, goblet: *May I have a glass of beer?* **5** barometer: *The glass fell as the storm approached.* **6** lens, magnifying glass, °telescope, spyglass, microscope: *Look at this drop of water through the glass.* **7** ***glasses***: spectacles, eyeglasses, lorgnon, lorgnette, opera-glasses, binoculars, field-glasses, bifocals, trifocals, goggles, sun-glasses, *Colloq* specs: *These are my reading glasses.*

glassy *adj.* **1** shining, °shiny, gleaming, °smooth, °slippery, °glossy, °icy, mirror-like, *US* °slick: *We skidded on the glassy surface and crashed into a wall.* **2** °fixed, staring, trancelike, hypnotic, °vacant, °empty, expressionless, °blank, °void, vacuous, dazed, °dull, glazed, °cold, °lifeless: *His glassy stare made me very uncomfortable.*

glaze *v.* **1** varnish, lacquer, shellac, enamel, °coat, °cover; °polish, burnish, °shine, °gloss: *Many of the works of art had been glazed for protection.*

—*n.* **2** varnish, lacquer, shellac, enamel, coating, covering; °polish, °shine, °gloss, °lustre, patina: *The glaze distorts the design beneath.*

gleam *n.* **1** °light, glimmer, glint, °glow, °flicker, °shine, °shimmer, °glitter, °twinkle, °spark, °flare, °glare, °flash; °beam, °ray, °shaft: *I could just make out the faint gleam of a candle.* **2** °hint, °suggestion, °indication, °vestige, °trace, scintilla, °inkling, glimmer, °ray, °spark, °flicker: *There wasn't a gleam of hope of rescue.* **3** °look, glint: *He got a strange gleam in his eye when he talked about his inventions.*

—*v.* **4** glimmer, glint, °shimmer, °shine, °twinkle, °glitter, °glisten, °beam, °sparkle: *I could see the beast's eyes, gleaming in the dark. The shore was dotted with gleaming white houses.*

glee *n.* °delight, °exuberance, cheerfulness, °high *or* °good °spirits, °cheer, exhilaration, elation, exultation, °joy, °happiness, °rapture, gladness, felicity, °pleasure, joyfulness, °merriment, jubilation, joyousness, joviality, jollity, °gaiety, mirthfulness; °enjoyment, °satisfaction, *Schadenfreude*: *We watched with great glee as the villain was thwarted.*

gleeful *adj.* °happy, °merry, °joyful, °delighted, °exuberant, °ecstatic, °cheerful, in °high *or* °good °spirits, exhilarated, °elated, °exultant, °rapturous, °overjoyed, °pleased, jubilant, joyous, jovial, °jolly, °gay, mirthful: *He wrote a gleeful report of the chairman's conviction for insider trading.*

glib *adj.* °ready, °fluent, °smooth, °slick, facile, smooth-spoken, smooth-tongued, smooth-talking, fast-talking, °fluid, °easy, unctuous, °suave, °nonchalant, °superficial: *Why must obituary notices always be so glib?*

glide *v.* °slide, °slip, °coast, skate, °soar, °float, °sail, glissade, °stream, °flow: *The skiff glided peacefully down the river.*

glisten *v.* °shine, °reflect, glint, glimmer, °gleam, °sparkle, °glitter, wink, °blink; °glow, °twinkle: *The lamplight glistened on his wet coat. A tear glistened on her cheek.*

glitter *v.* **1** See **glisten,** above.
—*n.* **2** See **gleam, 1,** above. **3** See **glamour,** above. **4** showiness, gaudiness, garishness, °flash, flashiness, °ostentation, floridity *or* floridness, °spectacle, °pageantry, °splendour, refulgence, °brilliance, *Colloq* pizazz *or* pizzazz, razzle-dazzle, razzmatazz, *Slang US* glitz: *In those days, Hollywood was all glitter.*

gloat *v.* Often, ***gloat over***: °exult (in), °glory (in), °relish (in), °revel (in), crow (over *or* about), °delight (in): *He is still gloating over the misery he caused her.*

global *adj.* worldwide, °international, °broad, °extensive, wide-ranging, far-reaching, °epidemic, pandemic, °universal: *Protection of the atmosphere is a global responsibility.*

globe *n.* **1** °earth, °world, planet, Terra: *Our family is scattered all round the globe.* **2** °sphere, ball, °orb; globule: *On the table was a lamp with a green glass globe.*

gloom *n.* **1** shadowiness, gloominess, °shade, °shadow, murkiness, murk, dimness, °dusk, dullness, °dark, darkness, cloudiness, blackness, °obscurity: *We arose in the gloom of a midwinter's morning.* **2** despondency, °depression, °sadness, dejection, downheartedness, °melancholy, °woe, °sorrow, moroseness, °desolation, °low spirits, blues, doldrums, °despair, dolour, °misery, *Colloq* dumps: *The team suffered the gloom of defeat.*

gloomy *adj.* **1** °shadowy, shaded, °shady, °murky, °dim, °dusky, °dull, °dark, cloudy, °overcast, °obscure, °black, inky, *Literary* Stygian: *It is too gloomy a day to have a picnic.* **2** depressed, °melancholy, °sad, °dejected, morose, °glum, lugubrious, °unhappy, cheerless, °dismal, °moody, down, downcast, °desolate, °doleful, °sorrowful, crestfallen, chap-fallen, °downhearted, °forlorn, °despondent, °miserable, °joyless, dispirited, despairing, °dreary, °sullen, °blue, distressed, down in the °mouth, in the doldrums, saturnine, *Colloq* (down) in the dumps: *Both of them have been very gloomy since the divorce.* **3** depressing, cheerless, °dreary, °dismal, dispiriting, °sad, disheartening: *The décor is much too gloomy for a doctor's waiting-room.*

glorified *adj.* **1** overrated, °pretentious, overdone, high-flown, high-sounding, °affected, °pompous, °exalted, *Colloq* jumped-up: *You say he is a scholar, but he behaves more like a glorified schoolboy.* **2** °sham, °pretend, °imitation, °counterfeit, °fake, °substitute, ersatz, *Colloq* °phoney *or US also* phony: *In that outfit, she looks like a glorified chorus girl.*

glorify *v.* **1** elevate, °exalt, °raise (up), upgrade, °promote, °advance, °boost, °enhance, °dignify, ennoble, °immortalize: *Winning first prize glorified his reputation considerably. In her book she glorifies motherhood. These men are glorified by their heroism.* **2** canonize, deify, °idolize, °revere, °venerate, °sanctify, °worship, pay °tribute *or* °homage to, ennoble, °idealize, apotheosize, °eulogize, panegyrize, °adore, °honour, °look up to, °celebrate, °extol, °praise, °laud, commend, °hail, lionize, °applaud, acclaim: *The world glorified Lindbergh for the first solo flight across the Atlantic.*

glorious *adj.* **1** °illustrious, famed, °famous, °renowned, °celebrated, °distinguished, honoured, °eminent, °excellent: *England may be proud of her glorious literary heritage.* **2** °outstanding, °splendid, °magnificent, °marvellous, wonderful, spectacular, °fabulous, °dazzling: *They announced another glorious victory over enemy forces.* **3** enjoyable, °delightful, °fine, °great, °excellent, °pleasurable, °superb, *Colloq* °heavenly: *We had a glorious holiday in the Greek islands.* **4** °beautiful, °splendid, °brilliant, °gorgeous, resplendent, °admirable, °superior, °excellent, °estimable: *The walls are covered with frescos in glorious colour.*

glory *n.* **1** °honour, °fame, repute, °reputation, exaltation, °celebrity, °renown, eminence, °distinction, illustriousness, °prestige, °dignity, immortality: *Our soldiers fought for glory not for gain. Even today we sense the glory that was Rome.* **2** °honour, °veneration, °reverence, °homage, °gratitude, glorification, exaltation, °worship, adoration, °praise, laudation, thanksgiving; benediction, °blessing: *Glory be to God in the highest.* **3** °splendour, °pomp, magnificence, °grandeur, °beauty, °brilliance, °radiance, effulgence, refulgence, °excellence, °pageantry, °nobility, °triumph, greatness: *Her photographs depict the Amazonian rain forest in all its glory.* **4** aureole, nimbus, °halo; °crown, circlet, corona: *A glory surrounds the saint's head in the painting.*
—*v.* **5** °revel, °relish, °delight, °exult, °pride oneself, crow, °rejoice, °gloat; °show off, °boast: *She sat by the window, glorying in the magnificence of the scenery.*

gloss[1] *n.* **1** °sheen, °lustre, °polish, °glow, °glaze, °shine, °gleam, burnish, brightness: *I prefer a dull gloss to a high polish on furniture.* **2** °show, façade, °mask, °front, °surface, °veneer, °disguise, °camouflage, °false °appearance, °semblance: *She soon saw through the gloss, and the honeymoon was over.*
—*v.* **3** °glaze, °polish, burnish, °shine: *Gloss up your shoes a bit.* **4** Usually, ***gloss over***: °veil, °cover up, °smooth over, °conceal, °hide, °disguise, °camouflage, °mask, *Colloq* °whitewash: *He tried to gloss over his voting record.*

gloss[2] *n.* **1** °explanation, °interpretation, exegesis, explication, °definition, elucidation, °comment, commentary, annotation, critique, °criticism, °analysis, footnote; °translation: *Some editions of Shakespeare give glosses of difficult words and phrases at the foot of each page.*
—*v.* **2** °comment on *or* upon, °explain, °interpret, explicate, °define, elucidate, annotate, °criticize, °analyse, °review, *US* critique; °translate: *Johnson was not the first to gloss the word 'pastern'.* **3** See **gloss**[1]**, 4,** above.

glossary *n.* °gloss, (specialized *or* special-subject) °dictionary, wordbook, word-list: *There is a useful glossary of terms at the end of the book.*

glossy *adj.* **1** shining, °shiny, °smooth, °polished, glazed, °lustrous, burnished, °sleek, waxed, °glassy, glistening: *Our magazine is printed on glossy paper.* **2** °slick, °specious, °put-on, °artificial, meretricious, contrived, °pretended, simulated, feigned, °insincere, pseudo, °false, °unreal; °bogus, °counterfeit, °fraudulent, °imitation, *Colloq* °phoney *or US also* phony: *It is only a glossy remake of the original film.*

glow *n.* **1** luminosity, phosphorescence, incandescence, °light, lambency, °lustre: *The surface of the flying saucer emitted a faint green glow.* **2** °light, brightness, °gleam, luminousness, °brilliance, °radiance, resplendence, °splendour, effulgence: *The glow in the east is from a forest fire.* **3** °flush, °blush, redness, ruddiness, °burning, °excitement, °warmth, °fervour, fervency, °enthusiasm, feverishness, °thrill, *Colloq* °rush: *I can feel a glow just thinking of you.*
—*v.* **4** °shine, °radiate, incandesce, phosphoresce, glimmer, °gleam, °light up: *The numerals on the clock were glowing in the dark.* **5** °heat, overheat, °burn; ablate: *The spaceship began to glow as it entered the atmosphere.* **6** °flush, bloom, °colour, °blush: *As you can see from her complexion, she simply glows with good health.* **7** °blush, °flush, redden, °colour, turn red *or* scarlet: *My cheeks glowed with embarrassment.*

glowing *adj.* **1** aglow, °incandescent, °burning, lambent, °luminous, candent; smouldering: *I stirred the glowing embers.* **2** °rich, °warm, vibrant, °bright, °brilliant: *Banners in glowing colours enlivened the hall. He is in glowing health.* **3** °laudatory, °complimentary, °enthusiastic, eulogistic, °rhapsodic, °favourable, encomiastic, panegyrical: *The critics described her performance in glowing terms.*

glue *n.* **1** °cement, adhesive, mucilage, gum, paste: *You need a specialist glue to mend a break like that.*

—*v.* **2** °cement, paste, °stick, affix, °fix, °seal: *Let's glue this picture into the album.*

glum *adj.* °gloomy, °sullen, morose, dispirited, °woebegone, °dismal, °sad, sulky, °dour, °moody, °sour, crestfallen, °doleful, down, °low, °pessimistic, lugubrious, saturnine: *After Irena left, I was feeling rather glum.*

glut *n.* **1** °excess, °surplus, over-abundance, superabundance, °surfeit, oversupply, overflow, °superfluity, nimiety: *The glut of razor-blades in the market is due to increased production.* **2** saturation, glutting, satiation: *Glut leads to a lowering of prices.*
—*v.* **3** oversupply, °flood, °saturate, °swamp, inundate, deluge, °overload, overstock, °clog, °stuff, °gorge: *The markets will soon be glutted with mobile telephones.* **4** °satiate, sate, °choke, °cram, °overload, overfeed, °gorge, °surfeit, °pall, cloy, °jade, °sicken, °weary: *Everyone was thoroughly glutted before the wedding reception was over.*

glutton *n.* trencherman, gormandizer, gourmand *or* gormand, overeater, hog, pig, *Grangousier*, *Colloq* greedy-guts, *Slang Brit* gannet, *US* chowhound: *Like the glutton that he is, he asked for more after eating an enormous meal.*

gluttonous *adj.* °voracious, gormandizing, edacious, °greedy, °ravenous, insatiable, esurient, piggish, °hoggish, swinish: *She was so gluttonous that she ate my dinner after finishing her own.*

gluttony *n.* overeating, gormandizing, gormandism *or* gourmandism, °greed, hoggishness, piggishness, °rapacity, voraciousness, greediness, voracity, insatiability, edacity, crapulence, crapulousness, intemperance, immoderation, *Archaic* gulosity: *The Bible categorizes gluttony among the seven deadly sins.*

gnarled *adj.* twisted, knotty, °lumpy, °bumpy, knotted, °bent, °crooked, distorted, contorted, warped; arthritic: *I concealed myself in the gnarled branches of the old oak. The beggar reached out to me with her gnarled hand.*

gnaw *v.* **1** °chew, nibble, °eat, °bite, champ: *The marks were made by deer gnawing the bark.* **2** °erode, °eat away, corrode, °wear down *or* away, °fret, °consume, °devour: *The acid continues to gnaw away at the metal till it is gone.* **3** °fret, °irritate, harry, hector, °pester, °worry, °bother, °plague, °trouble, °torment, torture, °distress, badger, °harass, °haunt, °nag, vex, °gall, nettle, °irk, peeve, °annoy: *The feeling that something was very wrong continued to gnaw at her.*

go *v.* **1** °move (°ahead *or* forward *or* °onwards), °proceed, °advance, °pass, make °headway, °travel, voyage, °set off, °tour, trek, wend, °stir, budge: *Would you go to the market for me?* **2** °leave, °depart, go out, °move (out *or* away), decamp, °make off, °withdraw, °repair, °retire, °retreat, *Colloq* °take off: *I wish he would go at once. She went to her country cottage for the weekend.* **3** °function, °operate, °work, °run, °perform: *I cannot get the engine to go properly.* **4** °lead, °open to, °give access to, °communicate to *or* with, °connect with *or* to: *Where does this door go?* **5** °lead, °communicate with, °run: *Does this road go to Oxford?* **6** °fit, °belong (together), °agree *or* °conform (with each other), harmonize, °blend, °match, be °appropriate *or* °suitable (for *or* to), °complement each other: *These colours don't go.* **7** °become: *He went mad when he learnt about the accident.* **8** °fit, °extend, °reach, °span, °stretch: *My belt would never go round your waist!* **9** be °disposed of *or* discarded *or* thrown away, be dismissed, be got °rid of *or* abolished, be °given up, be °cast *or* °set *or* °put aside, be done with: *That out-dated computer has to go.* **10** °disappear (without a trace), vanish (into thin air), °evaporate: *Where has all the money gone?* **11** °pass, °elapse, °slip *or* tick away, °fly: *Time goes quickly when you're having fun.* **12** °fail, °fade, °decline, °flag, °weaken, °degenerate, °wear out, °give (out); °give °way, °collapse, °fall *or* °come *or* go to pieces, °disintegrate, °crack: *I'm afraid the tyres are going. When that last support goes, the roof will come down.* **13** °die, °expire, be gone, meet one's Maker, °pass on *or* away, shuffle off this mortal coil, go to one's reward, go to the happy hunting-grounds, go to that great cricket-pitch in the sky, *Slang* kick the bucket, snuff it: *By the time the doctor arrived, Graham had gone.* **14** °sound, °pronounce, °enunciate, articulate, °say, utter: *And this little pig goes 'Wee, wee, wee', all the way home.* **15** °survive, °last (out), °endure, °live, °continue: *How long can we go without water?* **16** be used up *or* consumed *or* finished: *The last of our food was gone.* **17** go to the °toilet *or* the °lavatory *or* the bathroom, °move (one's) °bowels, °urinate, °defecate, *Slang* pee, take a °leak *or* a crap, *Chiefly Brit* go to the loo, *Chiefly US* go to the john, *Taboo slang* (take a) piss *or* shit: *We stopped at a motorway filling station because Jane had to go.* **18** ***go about***: °approach, °tackle, °set about, °undertake, °begin, °start: *I don't like the way she goes about her work. How does one go about establishing a business?* **19** ***go ahead***: °proceed, °continue, °move *or* go forward, °advance, °progress, go on: *She told me I could go ahead with the scheme. The policeman motioned to go ahead.* **20** ***go along (with)***: **a** °escort, °accompany: *We asked if we could go along with them to the cinema.* **b** °agree (to), concur (with), acquiesce (to), assent (to), °support: *Beverly would never go along with a plan like yours.* **21** ***go around*** *or* ***about*** *or* ***round (with)***: **a** °move around, °circulate: *I wish he'd stop going round telling everyone about me. There's a lot of flu going around.* **b** °socialize (with), °frequent *or* °seek the °company of, °spend °time with, °associate with, *Colloq* °hang around *or* about (with), °hang out (with): *The boy is going around with that Collins girl.* **c** °wander *or* °move around: *He goes about picking through rubbish bins.* **22** ***go at***: °attack, °assault, assail: *We went at the enemy with all the fire power we could muster.* **23** ***go away***: go (off), °leave, °depart, °withdraw, °exit; °retreat, °recede, decamp: *The clouds went away and the sun came out. We are going away for the weekend.* **24** ***go back (to)***: **a** °return (to); °revert (to), °change back (to): *He went back to his old job after the war. Can we go back to the way things were before we were married?* **b** °originate (in), °begin *or* °start (with), °date back (to): *Our friendship goes back to our childhood.* **25** ***go back on***: °renege (on), °break, °retract, °repudiate, °forsake: *She's gone back on our agreement.* **26** ***go by***: **a** °pass (by), go °past, °move by; °elapse: *We used to watch the goods trains go by. The months went by quickly since our last meeting.* **b** °rely *or* °count *or* °depend *or* bank on, °put °faith in(to), be guided by, °judge from: *You cannot go by what Atherton tells you.* **27** ***go down***: **a** °sink, go under, °founder, °submerge: *The ship went down within minutes of striking the mine.* **b** °decrease, °decline, °drop, °sink: *The Nikkei Index went down 200 points.* **c** °fall, be defeated *or* beaten, °suffer °defeat, °lose, °collapse: *Our forces went down under an onslaught from the attacking armies.* **d** be remembered *or* memorialized *or* recalled *or* commemorated *or* recorded: *That day of infamy will go down in history.* **e** find °favour *or* acceptance *or* °approval, be accepted: *His ideas have not gone down well with the council.* **28** ***go for***: **a** °fetch, °obtain, °get: *Please go for help.* **b** °apply *or* °relate to, °concern, °involve: *The rule against smoking goes for you, too, Smedley.* **c** °fancy, °favour, °like, °admire, be attracted to, °prefer, °choose, *Slang* °dig: *I can tell that Peter really goes for Maria. I could go for a pint of beer right now.* **d** °attack, °assault, assail, °set upon: *The dog went for him as soon as he opened the gate.* **e** °set one's sights on, °aim for, °focus °attention *or* °effort(s) on: *I decided to risk all and go for Drogheda Boy at 100–8.* **29** ***go in for***: **a** °enter, °enrol, °start, °begin, °embark on, °pursue, °take up, °embrace, espouse, °undertake, °follow, °adopt, go into, *US* go out for: *He is going in for a career in boxing.* **b** °like, °fancy, °favour, °practise, do, °engage in: *I don't go in for mountain-climbing.* **30** ***go into***: **a** See **28 a**, above. **b** delve into, °examine, °pursue, °investigate, °analyse, °probe, °scrutinize, °inquire into, °study: *I want to go into the subject of your absences with you, Fanshawe.* **c** °touch on, °discuss, °mention: *I should avoid going into the subject of money with Pauline if I were you.* **31** ***go off***:

a go out, °cease to function: *I saw the lights go off at nine.* b °explode, °blow up, detonate, °erupt; °fire, be discharged: *The bomb is set to go off in an hour. The gun went off, killing the mouse.* c °occur, °happen, °take °place: *The conference went off as planned.* d °depart, °leave, go (away), °set out, °exit, decamp, °quit: *She went off without another word.* e *Brit* deteriorate, °rot, moulder, go °stale, go °bad, °spoil, °sour, °turn: *After two days the milk goes off.* f Usually, ***go off into***: °start *or* °break into *or* out in: *He goes off into gales of laughter whenever I mention your name.* **32** ***go on***: a °continue, °proceed, °keep on, °carry on; °persist, °last, °endure, °persevere: *He went on coughing all night long. The party went on into the small hours.* b °happen, °occur, take place, °come about, *Colloq* °come off: *I have always wondered what went on in there.* c °come on, °begin *or* resume functioning: *The lights went on at midnight.* d °enter, make an °entrance: *She doesn't go on till the third act.* e going on. approaching, nearing, °nearly, °almost, not quite: *He's six going on seven. It's going on eight o'clock.* f gabble, °chatter, drone on, *Brit* natter, *Colloq Brit* witter (on), rabbit on: *He goes on endlessly about his cars.* g °rely *or* °depend on, °use: *The detective had very little to go on.* **33** ***go out***: a °fade *or* °die (out), °expire, °cease functioning, go off, be extinguished: *The lights went out, throwing the room into Stygian blackness.* b °depart, °leave, °exit: *He went out at six and has not been seen since.* c °socialize, °associate; court, go together, *Brit* °walk out, *US* °date: *Harry is going out with Annabel.* **34** ***go over***: a °review, °skim (through *or* over), go through, °scan, °look at, °read, °study; °inspect, °examine, °scrutinize, °investigate: *I went over your report last night. They are going over everyone's luggage with a fine-tooth comb.* b be received: *The first song went over very well.* c °clean, °tidy *or* °neaten (up): *I've just gone over the entire flat.* d °rehearse, °repeat, °reiterate, °review, go through: *We keep going over the same things, again and again.* **35** ***go round*** *or US also* ***around***: a °revolve, °rotate, °spin, whirl, °twirl: *The earth takes a year to go round the sun.* b °suffice, be °sufficient *or* °adequate *or* °enough, °satisfy: *Are there enough life jackets to go around?* c See **21,** above. **36** ***go through***: a °experience, °suffer, °undergo, °bear, °take, °stand, °tolerate, °put up with, °brook, °submit to, °endure, °live through, °brave: *I don't think I could go through another war.* b be accepted *or* approved, °pass (°muster): *The bill went through without a hitch.* c See **34 a,** above. **37** ***go together***: a harmonize, °accord, °agree, °fit, go, °suit each other, °belong (with each other): *I don't think that puce and vermilion go together.* b See **33 c,** above. **38** ***go under***: a See **27 a,** above. b °fail, °collapse, °subside, go bankrupt, °succumb, *Brit* go to the °wall, *Colloq* °fold, *US* go belly up: *Statistics show that more than 500 companies go under every week in the USA.* **39** ***go up***: a °rise, °increase: *If inflation goes up, the Chancellor will raise interest rates.* b °explode, °blow up: *The munitions factory went up, showering debris over the whole neighbourhood.* **40** ***go with***: a go together with, harmonize with, °blend with, be °suitable *or* suited for, °fit (in) with, °accord *or* °agree with: *That scarf does not go with the dress.* b °socialize with, °associate with, °accompany, court, *Old-fashioned Brit* °walk out with, *US* °date: *I hear that Connie is going with Don.* **41** ***go without***: do *or* °manage *or* °get by without, °lack, be °deprived of, °need; abstain from, °survive *or* °live *or* °continue without: *In the old days, if you could not afford something, you went without. She cannot go without a cigarette for more than an hour.*
—*n.* **42** °chance, °turn, °opportunity, °try, °attempt, *Colloq* whack, crack, whirl, °shot, °stab: *I don't expect much, but I'll have a go anyway.*

go-ahead *n.* **1** °permission, °approval, °leave, authorization, °sanction, *Colloq* °say-so, okay *or* °OK, green light, *US* the °nod: *I have the go-ahead to proceed with the project.*
—*adj.* **2** °ambitious, °enterprising, °progressive, forward-looking, °resourceful: *The directors, all under thirty, make it a real go-ahead company.*

goal *n.* °object, °aim, °purpose, °end, °objective, °target, °ambition, °ideal, °aspiration: *Fletcher's goal is to be head of the company.*

gob *n.* chunk, °piece, °blob, °lump, gobbet, °morsel, °fragment, °bite: *She took a gob of peanut butter and spread it on the bread.*

gobbledegook *n.* **1** gobbledygook, °jargon, °nonsense, °gibberish, °moonshine, °rubbish, tommy-rot, °mumbo-jumbo, humbug, balderdash, eyewash, hogwash, poppycock, °drivel, *Colloq* bunk, °rot, °garbage, bosh, pish and tush, piffle, bilge (water), *Slang* crap, malarkey, bull, bullshit, *Brit* (load of old) cobblers *or* codswallop: *Can you make sense out of all that computer gobbledegook?* **2** gobbledygook, equivocation, double-talk, °deception, deceptiveness, vagueness, quibbling, circumlocution, obscurantism, obfuscation, ambagiousness, shiftiness: *Ordinary people are often confused by the gobbledegook of official pronouncements.*

go-between *n.* °intermediary, °agent, middleman, °medium, °mediator, °negotiator, °messenger, internuncio, °liaison; intercessor, interceder: *David served as go-between in our negotiations with the rebels.*

goblin *n.* elf, gnome, hobgoblin, °imp, kobold, leprechaun, °demon, brownie, pixie *or* pixy, nix *or* nixie: *On Hallowe'en the ghouls and goblins will get you if you don't watch out!*

god *n.* °deity, demigod, demiurge, divinity, °spirit, °immortal, °genius, °power, tutelary, numen: *Throughout man's sojourn on earth he has worshipped many gods.*

godless *adj.* **1** °wicked, °evil, iniquitous, °sinful, unrighteous, unholy, hellish; °impious, °blasphemous, °profane, °sacrilegious, °ungodly: *The prison was a godless place, where one was murdered for a crust of bread.* **2** atheistic, nullifidian, agnostic, °unbelieving, °sceptical: *In theory, communism is a godless ideology.*

godlike *adj.* **1** °divine, °godly, °sacred, °holy, °saintly, angelic, °seraphic, blest, blessed, sainted: *The tribe thought her a goddess and treated her with godlike reverence.* **2** °heavenly, °celestial, blissful, °rapturous, °ecstatic, beatific, ethereal: *For a decade, she lived a godlike existence with the tribe.*

godly *adj.* °religious, °pious, °devout, God-fearing, °good, °righteous, °holy, °virtuous, °moral, °pure, °saintly, reverent, pietistic, °devoted, °faithful: *The monks pursue a godly life in their mountain fastness.*

godsend *n.* °gift, °blessing, benediction, °boon, °windfall, bonanza, stroke of (°good) °fortune, piece *or* bit of (°good) °luck: *The Red Cross parcels were a godsend to the prisoners of war.*

goggle-eyed *adj.* °agog, awestruck, wide-eyed, thunderstruck, agape, open-mouthed, gawking, staring, °dumbfounded *or* dumfounded, astonished, astounded, amazed, stupefied, dazed, surprised: *His first time in the city, Eugene stood goggle-eyed at the skyscrapers.*

going *adj.* **1** thriving, °successful, succeeding, °prosperous, °wealthy, affluent, booming, prospering, °flourishing, growing: *The Davises took over a failing business and turned it into a going concern.* **2** °current, °present, °contemporary, °active, °effective, accepted, °prevailing, °prevalent, °universal, °common, °usual, °customary: *What is the going rate for a skilled cabinet-maker?*

golden *adj.* **1** yellow, yellowish, gold, blond *or* blonde, flaxen, aureate; tow(-haired): *Her golden tresses fell about her shoulders.* **2** gold, auriferous; gilded, gilt, aureate; *Technical* auric, aurous: *They drank together from a golden bowl.* **3** °bright, shining, °brilliant, °sunny, gleaming, °lustrous, °shiny, glittering, °dazzling, resplendent, °radiant, °glowing, sparkling: *We emerged from the black tunnel into golden sunshine.* **4** °happy, blissful, °delightful, °joyful, °glorious, joyous, °exuberant: *We can never recapture the golden days of our youth.* **5** °flourishing, halcyon, °prosperous, thriving, °favourable, °excellent, °outstanding, °productive, °fertile, blessed, blest, °good, °successful, palmy: *After the golden age of Greece and Rome, Europe was plunged into the dismal gloom of the Dark Ages.* **6** °gifted, °talented, °favoured, °special, °exceptional, °favourite, cherished, °pet, *Brit* blue-eyed, white-headed, white-haired, *US* fair-haired: *As long as the company's profits were increasing, Hamilton was the golden boy.* **7** °advantageous, °propitious, auspicious, °promising, °rosy, °opportune, °optimistic, °favourable: *She missed a golden opportunity by turning down the job.*

good *adj.* **1** °agreeable, °satisfactory, commendable, °acceptable, °fair, °adequate, admissible, °tolerable, all right, °passable, *Colloq* okay *or* °OK: *According to the reviews, the new opera is good but not great.* **2** °admirable, °outstanding, °first-rate, first-class, °fine, °superb, °superior, tiptop, °extraordinary, °exemplary, °choice, °excellent, °capital, °marvellous, wonderful, °splendid, °sterling, *Colloq* °super(-duper), °great, smashing, A-1 *or* A-one, *Brit* cracking, °brilliant, °amazing, ace, °knockout, brill, °fantastic, °terrific, °unbelievable, groovy, fab, °fabulous, °crucial, °serious, *Slang US* °bad, *Old-fashioned Brit* tickety-boo, *No. Eng.* °champion, *Chiefly US* A-OK: *I thought that was a really good dinner.* **3** °correct, °proper, °decorous, °orderly, °right, °seemly, °fit, °fitting, °suitable, °meet, °appropriate, allowable, °permissible, admissible, °passable, °satisfactory, °tolerable: *He should get time off for good behaviour.* **4** °obedient, well-behaved, °proper, well-mannered: *Why can't you be a good boy when we go out?* **5** °moral, high-minded, °righteous, °noble, °wholesome, °chaste, °pure, °honourable, °ethical, upstanding, °upright, °virtuous, °worthy, °lofty, °elevated, °saintly, angelic, °godly, °godlike: *Think only good thoughts and still you may not get to heaven.* **6** °kind, °benevolent, beneficent, °gracious, °gentle, °kindly, °nice, °considerate, °friendly, °solicitous, good-hearted, °sympathetic, °benign, °charitable, humane, kind-hearted, well-disposed: *Her parents have always been good to me.* **7** °fresh, unspoiled *or* unspoilt, °edible, consumable, palatable: *These eggs are good but the milk has gone off.* **8** °genuine, valid, °legitimate, °authentic, °proper, °reliable, °secure, dependable, °safe, creditable, °sound, °solid, °substantial, well-founded, °trustworthy, °honest, °actual, °real; credible, believable, convincing, compelling, cogent: *Have you a good reason for saying that?* **9** °honourable, esteemed, respected, °respectable, °well-thought-of, °reputable, established, °solid: *They say that he comes from a good family.* **10** well-proportioned, °shapely, °attractive: *Yes, I'd say that Marilyn has a good figure.* **11** °thorough, °complete, °penetrating, °careful: *Has she had a good look at the defendant?* **12** °gifted, °talented, °competent, °capable, °skilful, °clever, °accomplished, °proficient, °adept, adroit, skilled: *Am I a good enough actor to audition for the part?* **13** °advantageous, °propitious, °opportune, °beneficial, °profitable, °favourable; °safe, °secure, °reliable, °sound, °sensible: *Are utilities a good investment? Is this a good time to buy shares?* **14** °healthy, salubrious, salutary, °beneficial, °wholesome: *We'll have to put you on a good diet.* **15** °best, company, Sunday, special-occasion, most °luxurious: *Should we use the good glasses tonight?* **16** °ample, °sufficient, °adequate, °considerable, °full, °extensive, sizeable, °large, °substantial: *We have a good supply of food available.* **17** approving, °complimentary, °flattering, °positive, °favourable, °enthusiastic, °laudatory, eulogistic, encomiastic: *His book received a very good review in the Sunday supplement.* **18** °great, °considerable, sizeable, °substantial, °fair: *We are still a good distance away from land.*
—*n.* **19** °benefit, °advantage, °profit, °use, °usefulness, °gain, °worth, avail: *What good does it do to complain?* **20** goodness, °morality, °virtue, °merit, righteousness, °right, °rectitude, °worth, °probity, virtuousness, °integrity, °nobility, high-mindedness, honourableness, °honesty: *The evil that men do lives after them, The good is oft interred with their bones.* **21** ***goods***: **a** °possessions, (personal) °property, chattels, °things, °gear, °belongings, °effects, °paraphernalia, movables, °stuff: *He's gone and he's taken all his goods with him.* **b** °merchandise, commodities, °wares, °stock, °produce, tangibles, °assets: *We shall pay on delivery of the goods.* **c** *US and Canadian* (incriminating) °evidence *or* °proof *or* °information *or* documentation *or* °facts *or* °data: *The police have the goods on the murderer.* **d** °fabric, °cloth, textile, °material, yard goods, piece-goods: *My tailor said he had made it from the best goods available.* **e** °freight: *A goods train had broken down on the line between Oxford and Banbury.*

goodbye *interj.* Farewell!, *Hawaiian* Aloha!; *Italian* Arrivederci!, Ciao!; *German* Auf Wiedersehen!; *French* Au revoir!, Adieu!; *Japanese* Sayonara!; *Spanish* Adios!, Hasta la vista!, Hasta luego!; *Latin* Vale!; *Colloq* Bye! *or* 'Bye!, Bye-bye!, Toodle-oo!, So long!, *Brit* Ta-ta!, Cheers!, cheerio, *Old-fashioned* Pip! Pip!, *US* See you later (alligator)!: *We said our goodbyes and went on our way.*

good-for-nothing *adj.* **1** °worthless, °useless: *'You are asking too much for that good-for-nothing old lamp', Aladdin told the pedlar.*
—*n.* **2** ne'er-do-well, °wastrel, waster, °idler, °loafer, layabout, lazybones, slugabed, sluggard, black sheep, *Colloq US* gold brick, goof-off: *Why doesn't that lazy good-for-nothing get a job?*

goodly *adj.* °considerable, sizeable, °substantial, °ample, °great, °large, °significant, consequential: *The museum attracts a goodly number of visitors each year.*

good-natured *adj.* good-humoured, °friendly, °agreeable, °genial, °gracious, good-hearted, °pleasant, °mellow, °easygoing, °considerate, °nice, °kind, °kindly, kind-hearted, tender-hearted, °charitable, °tolerant, °generous, °courteous, °cordial, °warm, warm-hearted, °amiable, °amicable, cooperative: *He seems a good-natured fellow, but not too bright.*

goody-goody *adj.* °smug, °sanctimonious, °self-righteous, °priggish, prim, holier-than-thou, Pecksniffian, °hypocritical: *She's one of those goody-goody people who never do anything wrong.*

gooey *adj.* **1** gluey, °sticky, °tacky, glutinous, mucilaginous, gummy: *The pudding was accompanied by an unpleasantly gooey sauce.* **2** °sweet, sugary, saccharine, °sentimental, unctuous, cloying, syrupy, mawkish, °maudlin, *Colloq* °mushy, slushy, °sloppy: *They like to watch those gooey soap operas.*

gore[1] *n.* blood, °carnage, butchery, °slaughter, °bloodshed: *The current crop of horror films have too much gore for my taste.*

gore[2] *v.* °pierce, °stab, °poke, horn, °penetrate, °puncture, spear, °gouge, °spit, °stick, °impale, disembowel: *The matador, severely gored by the bull, was carried away.*

gorge *n.* **1** °ravine, °canyon, defile, °pass, chasm, fissure, °crevasse, °gully *or* gulley, wadi *or* wady, °gap, *Brit* gill *or* ghyll, *US and Canadian* notch: *Water runs in this gorge only during the rainy season.* **2** °vomit, vomitus: *Injustice makes my gorge rise.*
—*v.* **3** °fill, °stuff, °glut, °cram; °gulp, gobble (down), °devour, °bolt (down), wolf (down), gormandize, °swallow: *She acquired the habit of gorging on cream cakes.*

gorgeous *adj.* **1** resplendent, °splendid, °magnificent, °glorious, °exquisite, °sumptuous, °dazzling, °grand, °beautiful, splendorous, breathtaking, °radiant, refulgent, °brilliant, °showy, colourful, *Colloq* splendiferous: *The males are known for their gorgeous plumage.* **2** °great, °terrific, °fantastic, wonderful, °marvellous, °glorious, spectacular, °superb, °excellent, *Colloq* fantabulous, marvy, smashing, °super, °nifty, °neat, °swell: *He married a gorgeous fashion model.*

gory *adj.* bloody, °sanguinary, blood-soaked, blood-stained; °gruesome, °grisly, horrific, blood-curdling: *The scene was so gory as to turn the strongest stomach.*

gospel *n.* °truth, °fact, °certainty: *He swears that his story is gospel.*

gossip *n.* **1** °chat, °conversation, °talk, chit-chat, small °talk, °palaver; tittle-tattle, °prattle; *Scots* clishmaclaver; gup; *Colloq Brit* natter, chin-wag: *I was just having a little gossip with my neighbour.* **2** °rumour, °scandal, hearsay, °information, *on dit*, °word, *Colloq* °grapevine, (inside) info, tittle-tattle, *Slang* °dope, *Chiefly US* scuttlebutt, *US and Canadian* poop: *The latest gossip is that she left him for another woman.* **3** rumour-mill, rumour-monger, scandalmonger, gossip-monger, newsmonger, °busybody, tattle-tale, quidnunc, blabber, blatherskite, tell-tale, °talebearer, flibbertigibbet, *Colloq* big-mouth, chatterbox, °blabbermouth, Nosy Parker: *That old gossip will tell everybody your business.*
—*v.* **4** Sometimes, ***gossip about***: bruit, °tattle, °rumour, °whisper, blether *or US* blather, gabble, *Colloq* °blab, *Brit* natter, *Slang* jaw: *I was just gossiping to my friend about your new job.*

gouge *v.* **1** °chisel, °gash, incise, °scratch, °groove, °dig; °scoop *or* °hollow (out): *The screwdriver slipped and gouged a piece out of the table. She's so mad she wants to gouge out your eyes.* **2** °extort, °extract, bilk, °defraud, wrest, °wrench, °squeeze, °blackmail, *Colloq* °milk, bleed, °skin, °fleece, °cheat, °swindle: *The gang gouged money from Alice by threatening to tell the teacher she had cheated on her French exam.*
—*n.* **3** °groove, °furrow, °scratch, °gash, °hollow; trench, ditch: *The retreating glacier cut a deep gouge in the landscape.*

gourmet *n.* °epicure, connoisseur, Lucullus, gastronome, gourmand, *bon vivant*, bon viveur: *My dear, that was a dinner fit for a gourmet!*

govern *v.* **1** °rule, °control, °direct, °reign, hold °sway (over), °lead, °conduct, °guide, °manage, °regulate, °run, °supervise, superintend, °oversee, °steer, captain, °pilot, °command, °head (up), °look after, sit on the throne, wield the sceptre, wear the crown, °run the show, be in °power, be in °charge (of), exercise *or* wield °power *or* °control (over), have *or* hold the whip hand, *Colloq* wear the pants, be in the saddle *or* driver's °seat: *Catherine governed with an iron hand.* **2** °control, °check, °bridle, °curb, °master, °subdue, °restrain, °contain, °hold in, °suppress, °repress: *You must govern the urge to scream out.*

government *n.* **1** °rule, °command, °authority, °regulation, °control, °management, °direction, °administration, °sway, superintendence, supervision, °oversight, °guidance, °domination: *His government of the island has led to disorder.* **2** °administration, °ministry, °regime: *The government intends to ban smoking in public places.*

grab *v.* **1** °snatch, °lay *or* °catch °hold of, °fasten upon, °grasp, °seize; °catch, °grip, °clutch; *Colloq* latch on to, °get one's hands *or* fingers on, °nab, *US* °snag: *The thief grabbed my purse and ran. She grabbed the railing to break her fall.* **2** °appropriate, expropriate, °seize, commandeer, °take over, usurp, arrogate: *The general grabbed the reins of government in the coup.* **3** °arrest, °capture, °catch, *Colloq* °nab, °pinch, collar: *The police grabbed him as he was leaving the scene of the crime.*
—*n.* **4** °snatch, °clutch; °grasp, °grip: *I made a grab for the rope.*

grace *n.* **1** °elegance, gracefulness, suppleness, °finesse, °refinement, °ease, °polish, °poise: *She rides well, with an unconscious grace.* **2** tastefulness, (good) °taste, cultivation, suavity *or* suaveness, °culture, savoir faire, discernment, °discrimination, (good) manners, politeness, °breeding, °consideration, decency, °etiquette, °tact, °propriety, °decorum, mannerliness: *They had the grace to ignore my rough attire.* **3** °indulgence, °forgiveness, °mercy, mercifulness, leniency, compassion, clemency, °charity, goodwill, goodness: *We survived the fire only by the grace of God. The company gives you 30 days' grace to pay the bill.* **4** °kindness, °favour, kindliness, °benevolence, generosity, goodness, graciousness, becomingness, seemliness; °excellence, °virtue, strength of °character, considerateness: *At least he had the good grace to admit being wrong.* **5** °blessing, thanksgiving, °prayer, benediction: *Grace was said before each meal.*
—*v.* **6** adorn, °embellish, °set off, °decorate, °ornament, °beautify, °enhance, garnish: *The table was graced by a huge silver candelabrum.* **7** °dignify, °enhance, °distinguish, °enrich, °honour, °favour: *The dinner-party is graced by your presence.*

graceful *adj.* **1** °fluid, flowing, °supple, lissom *or* lissome, lithe, facile, °smooth, °nimble, °agile, deft: *How graceful a dancer she is!* **2** °tactful, well-mannered, °polite, °courteous, mannerly, °refined, °tasteful, °elegant, courtly, urbane, °polished, °refined, °suave: *In return for certain concessions, the chief was graceful enough to release the hostages.*

gracious *adj.* °kind, °courteous, °polite, well-mannered, °kindly, °benevolent, beneficent, °indulgent, kind-hearted, warm-hearted, °cordial, °warm, °friendly, °sociable, °good-natured, °amiable, affable, °benign, °accommodating, °obliging, °agreeable, °considerate: *It was gracious of you to grant me an audience.*

grade *n.* **1** °degree, °position, °rank, °status, °stage, °standing, °station, gradation, echelon, °class, °level, °category, °condition, °state, °estate, °situation, rung: *She is a singer of the first grade.* **2** rating, °mark, °score: *What grade did you get in physics?* **3** °class, °form, year: *My daughter is in the third grade.* **4** °hill, °slope, °rise, gradient, acclivity, declivity, °incline, °decline, ascent, descent, upgrade, °downgrade: *The car coasted down a gentle grade into the lake.* **5** ***make the grade***: °pass, °measure up, °succeed, °qualify, *Colloq US* °make it, *Slang US and Canadian and NZ* °hack *or* °cut it: *Do you think that Simpson can make the grade?*
—*v.* **6** classify, °class, °order, °organize, °rank, °sort, °size, °group, °categorize, °rate: *Her job is to grade pearls according to their size.* **7** °mark, °rate, °correct, °evaluate: *My teacher was up late grading our exams.*

gradual *adj.* °easy, °gentle, °even, °moderate, °slow, °piecemeal, inchmeal, °regular, °steady: *There is a gradual slope down to the garden wall. The acceleration was gradual. He became aware of a gradual erosion of his authority.*

gradually *adv.* slowly, evenly, °piecemeal, inchmeal, °drop by drop, °step by step, °bit by bit, °little by little, °piece by piece, *gradatim*: *The water gradually seeped through the filter. We advanced gradually through the forest.*

graduate *n.* **1** bachelor, postgraduate, *US* alumnus (*pl.* alumni) *or* alumna (*pl.* alumnae): *Even university graduates found it difficult to get a job.*
—*v.* **2** gradate, °mark, °calibrate, °grade, °scale: *This thermometer is graduated in increments of one tenth of a degree.*

graft[1] *n.* **1** bud, scion, °shoot, °splice, implantation *or* °implant, °transplant: *New varieties were created by the implantation of grafts that have desirable qualities.*
—*v.* **2** °implant, °splice, °insert, °join: *Fruit-bearing stems are grafted onto a sturdy rootstock.*

graft[2] *n.* corruption, jobbery; bribery, extortion, *Colloq* payola, °kickback: *After only five years, he retired on the takings from graft.*

grain *n.* **1** °seed, °kernel, stone, pip, °pit: *Grains from each crop are stored ready for sowing.* **2** cereal, corn, grist: *The grain harvest was sparse this year.* **3** °particle, °bit, °fragment, °crumb, °speck, granule, °morsel, mote, molecule, atom, fleck, iota, ounce, °scrap, °trace, scintilla, °hint, °suggestion, whit, °jot (or tittle), °dab, soupçon, °taste, *Colloq US and Canadian* smidgen *or* smidgin: *There's not a grain of truth in anything that's been said.* **4** °texture, °pattern, °fibre, °weave, °nap: *Use a different kind of saw for cutting across the grain.*

grand *adj.* **1** °large, °great, °huge, °immense, °enormous, °impressive, °imposing, °splendid, °fine, °majestic, °stately, °lofty, °monumental, °lavish, °magnificent, °opulent, °luxurious, °palatial, °sumptuous, *Colloq* °posh: *We were led into a grand hall where thousands awaited the emperor.* **2** °dignified, °distinguished, august, respected, °eminent, °pre-eminent, °outstanding, °celebrated, °illustrious, °renowned, °notable, °legendary, °exalted, revered, °venerable, °immortal: *He is regarded as the grand old man of chemistry.* **3** °flamboyant, overdone, histrionic, °ostentatious, °pretentious, °grandiose, lordly: *The abysmal performance was punctuated by the actors' grand strutting and gesturing.* **4** °complete, °total, °sum, °comprehensive, (all-)°inclusive; bottom-line: *The grand total of expenses came to £12,467.22.* **5** °marvellous, wonderful, °outstanding, first-class, °first-rate, °splendid, °excellent, °superb, °admirable, *Colloq* °great, marvy, smashing, °terrific, °fantastic, °fabulous, fantabulous, °super: *Isn't it grand that Freda will be able to go!* **6** °principal, °chief, °main, °head, °leading, °foremost, highest: *The grand vizier was second only to the caliph.*

grandeur *n.* **1** °splendour, magnificence, majesty, sublimity, luxuriousness, °pomp: *The grandeur of the French court was never to be equalled.* **2** °nobility, augustness, nobleness, eminence, majesty: *The emperor received us with a grandeur befitting his station.*

grandiose *adj.* **1** °pretentious, °ostentatious, °showy, °flamboyant, °bombastic, histrionic, °extravagant, °pompous, fustian, high-flown, high-flying, overambitious, overdone, over-dramatic, °melodramatic, Ossianic, °inflated, °affected, florid, °flashy, *Colloq* highfalutin *or* hifalutin, °flash: *The council is unimpressed by your grandiose plans to redevelop the area, Mr Wren.* **2** °imposing, °impressive, °ambitious, °grand, °monumental, °magnificent, °lofty: *She has some grandiose ideas for a national symphony orchestra.*

grant *v.* **1** °give, °confer, °bestow, °present, °award, °offer; °supply, °furnish, °distribute, °donate; allocate, °assign: *She has been granted a sum that will enable her to complete the book.* **2** °concede, accede (to), °cede, °give (up), °agree (to), °consent (to), °allow, °permit, °admit; °let: *They granted my request for clemency.*
—*n.* **3** °gift, °present, °endowment, °bequest, subvention, °subsidy, °award, grant-in-aid, °donation, contribution, concession, °allowance: *He received a government grant to study abroad.*

granular *adj.* grainy, granulated, particulate, comminuted, gravelly, sandy, °gritty: *The sauce was somewhat granular and tasted too strongly of nutmeg.*

grapevine *n.* rumour-mill, jungle telegraph, grapevine telegraph; °rumour, °gossip: *According to the grapevine, you two are going to be married.*

graphic *adj.* **1** °vivid, °distinct, well-defined, °detailed, °explicit, °particular, °clear, lucid, °plain, °manifest, crystal °clear, unmistakable, unambiguous, °accurate, °precise, well-drawn, °photographic, descriptive, °telling, °picturesque, °pictorial, °realistic, °lifelike, °true to °life, *Colloq* °gory: *He described his injuries in graphic detail.* **2** written, drawn, diagrammatic, delineated, °visible: *The magazine won a prize for graphic design.*

grapple *v.* **1** °grasp, °grab, °grip, °seize, °clasp, catch, °wrestle; °hold, °clutch, °snatch: *They grappled each other at the edge of the Reichenbach Falls.* **2** ***grapple with***: come to grips with, °cope with, contend with, °deal with, °struggle with, °tackle, °face, °take on: *The government is grappling with the problem of unemployment.*

grasp *v.* **1** °grip, °grab, °seize, °clasp, °clutch, °snatch, °hold, °take *or* °lay *or* °catch °hold of, *Colloq* °nab: *I grasped the rope and was pulled to safety.* **2** °understand, °comprehend, °appreciate, °catch (on), °get, get the °drift *or* °point of, °follow, °see, °realize, apprehend, °learn, *Colloq* °make head(s) or tail(s) of, *Slang* °dig: *I am trying to grasp the full import of what you are saying.*
—*n.* **3** °hold, °grip, clutches, °clasp, °embrace, °lock: *He loosened his grasp on my throat and I could breathe again.* **4** °possession, °control, °power, mastery, °sovereignty, suzerainty, °hold: *By then, even the outer islands had fallen within his grasp.* **5** °understanding, comprehension, apprehension, awareness, °perception, °sense: *He has a poor grasp of the basics of the subject.*

grasping *adj.* °greedy, °avaricious, acquisitive, °rapacious, °mean, °miserly, stingy, °penurious, parsimonious, niggardly, °tight, tight-fisted, penny-pinching, close-fisted, °mercenary: *If the company weren't so grasping, they'd have less difficulty hiring staff.*

grass *v.* **1** °inform, °betray, °give away, *Slang* peach, squeal, snitch, squeak, °tattle, rat on, °sell out, *Brit* °blow the gaff, nark: *He received a shorter sentence for grassing on his accomplices.*
—*n.* **2** °traitor, °informer, *Slang* stool-pigeon, stoolie, squealer, snitch, squeaker, rat, *Brit* nark: *A grass is treated roughly by fellow inmates.*

grate *v.* **1** °shred, °rasp, °scrape, °rub, triturate: *Peel six raw potatoes and grate them fine.* **2** °scrape, °rasp, °rub, °grind, °scratch, screech, stridulate: *The cricket grates its legs against its wing covers to produce the 'singing' sound.* **3** Often, ***grate on*** *or* ***upon***: °annoy, vex, °irk, °irritate, °pester, set one's teeth on edge, °jar, °fret, °chafe, °rub (someone) (up) the wrong way, go against the grain, *Colloq* °get on one's nerves: *Her voice just grates on me.*

grateful *adj.* °thankful, appreciative: *I am grateful for any help I can get.*

gratification *n.* °satisfaction, °fulfilment, °enjoyment, °pleasure, °delight, compensation, recompense, °reward, °return, °requital: *She does it only for the gratification she gets from making the children happier.*

gratify *v.* °please, °satisfy, °fulfil, °delight, °compensate, recompense, °reward, °requite, °cheer, °gladden, °favour: *Albert would be gratified to see the good coming from his charitable bequests.*

grating *adj.* **1** jarring, °strident, °raucous, °harsh, °discordant, dissonant, unharmonious, °offensive, irritating, °irksome, annoying, vexatious, galling: *I find the noise of chalk squeaking on the blackboard very grating.* **2** grinding, °gritty, squeaky, jangling, screeching, creaking, °shrill, °piercing, squawking, croaking, rasping: *The grating noise you hear is my fridge motor.*
—*n.* **3** °grate, grid, reticle *or* reticule, grille, lattice, trellis, °screen, °network, reticulation: *When a beam of light is directed through the fine grating, odd patterns are formed.*

gratitude *n.* thankfulness, °appreciation, gratefulness; °thanks, °return, compensation, thanksgiving: *Here is a box of chocolates in gratitude for looking after my cat.*

gratuitous *adj.* **1** gratis, °free, °complimentary, °spontaneous: *The earth is a machine which has, till now, yielded gratuitous service.* **2** °unasked for, unrequested, unsought for, °wanton, unprovoked, °unsolicited, unlooked-for, uncalled-for, °unwelcome, unjustified, °unwarranted, baseless, °groundless, °needless, °unfounded, ungrounded, unjustifiable, irrational: *He seems to derive some twisted pleasure from spreading gratuitous lies about me.*

grave[1] *n.* °crypt, °sepulchre, °tomb, vault, mausoleum, °last *or* °final resting-place, eternal °rest: *She began to sob as the coffin was slowly lowered into the grave.*

grave[2] *adj.* **1** °serious, °sombre, °solemn, °earnest, unsmiling, °staid, °sedate, °sober, °dour, °gloomy, °grim, grim-faced, grim-visaged, *Brit* °po-faced: *The doctor, looking very grave, said that he had done all he could.* **2** °serious, °critical, °vital, °dangerous, life and death, °crucial, °urgent, °weighty, °important, °pressing, °pivotal, °perilous: *Fenwick is in intensive care in a grave condition.*

graveyard *n.* burial-ground, churchyard, cemetery, God's acre, necropolis, potter's °field, *W US* Boot Hill, *Rare* Golgotha, *Slang* bone-yard: *Uncle Valentine is buried in the graveyard on the hill.*

gravity *n.* **1** gravitation; °attraction: *After middle age, the body obeys the laws of gravity but not of mutual attraction.* **2** seriousness, acuteness, immediacy,

°importance, °significance, °weight, °magnitude, °severity, °urgency, exigency, momentousness, weightiness: *When I saw mother's expression I realized the gravity of the situation.* **3** °solemnity, °dignity, sombreness, staidness, sedateness, °sobriety, gravitas, soberness, °reserve; gloominess, grimness: *The ceremony was conducted with suitable gravity.*

greasy *adj.* **1** °oily, sebaceous, fatty, °fat, buttery, lardy, soapy, oleaginous, pinguid, butyraceous, saponaceous, waxy: *Before curing, the hide is greasy with natural oils.* **2** unctuous, °oily, °slippery, slithery, °smooth, °glib, fawning, °slick, toadying, sycophantic, *Slang Brit* smarmy: *Edna is so greasy, always trying to manoeuvre you into doing something for her.*

great *adj.* **1** °big, °large, °huge, °immense, °enormous, °gigantic, °giant, °grand, °extensive, °prodigious, °colossal, °massive, °vast, tremendous; °spacious, capacious, mammoth, gargantuan, °monstrous, titanic, Cyclopean, Brobdingnagian: *Europe was covered by a great forest. A great castle loomed before me.* **2** °large, °huge, °immense, °enormous, °gigantic, °prodigious, °vast, tremendous, °abundant, countless: *Plague killed a great number of people.* **3** °extreme, °considerable, °marked, °pronounced, °inordinate, °extraordinary, °significant; °excess, °excessive: *I have something of great importance to tell you. Your news created great confusion.* **4** °critical, °important, °crucial, °momentous, °significant, °serious, °weighty, consequential: *Those were great days for the history of England.* **5** °important, °prominent, °major, °eminent, °celebrated, °distinguished, °famous, famed, °renowned, °notable, °noteworthy, °illustrious, °outstanding, °well-known, °weighty, °influential, *Rare* eximious: *What of the great universities, like Oxford and Cambridge? Our mayor thinks of himself as a great man.* **6** °talented, °gifted, °excellent, °outstanding, °exceptional, °major, °superlative, °superior, °leading, °best, °incomparable, °matchless, °peerless, °skilful, artistic, °brilliant, °first-rate, °remarkable, °top, °accomplished: *Flaubert was one of the greatest writers of his age. Tamara is a good dancer, but not a great dancer.* **7** °lofty, °elevated, °exalted, °noble, high-minded, °grand: *Great thoughts come from great minds.* **8** °talented, skilled, °skilful, adroit, °clever, °adept, °able, °proficient, °expert: *Daphne is really great at playing bridge.* **9** °keen, zealous, °eager, °active, °enthusiastic, °devoted, °ardent, °passionate: *Frank is a great stamp collector.* **10** °close, °devoted, dedicated, °fast, °faithful, °true, °loyal, °intimate, loving: *Graham and Pembroke quickly became great friends.* **11** °terrible, °bad, °awful, unforgivable, horrendous, heinous, °grievous, horrific, °horrible, °terrific, °huge, °colossal, °enormous, °gigantic, °significant, °cardinal, egregious, °basic, °profound, °flagrant, °glaring, arrant, consummate, °out-and-out: *Inviting her at the same time as her ex-husband was a great mistake.* **12** spectacular, °marvellous, °outstanding, °excellent, °superb, °grand, wonderful, °fine *Colloq* °fantastic, °terrific, stupendous, marvy, smashing, fantabulous, *Old-fashioned Brit* tickety-boo: *He says that we missed a truly great show.*

greed *n.* **1** greediness, °avarice, avariciousness, covetousness, acquisitiveness, cupidity, avidity, craving, yearning: *Greed accounts for most of man's dishonesty.* **2** meanness, stinginess, miserliness, selfishness, niggardliness, penuriousness, parsimony, close-fistedness, penny-pinching, tight-fistedness: *From a life of greed he had accumulated enormous wealth.* **3** °gluttony, voraciousness, edacity, esurience, voracity, overeating, gormandizing, ravenousness, insatiableness: *Obesity owes more to greed than to glandular disorder.*

greedy *adj.* **1** °ravenous, °voracious, °gluttonous, piggish, °hoggish, swinish, cormorant, edacious, esurient, insatiable, °unquenchable: *I'd love another slice, but I mustn't be greedy.* **2** °avaricious, acquisitive, covetous, °grasping, craving; °materialistic, money-hungry: *If some people were less greedy, there would be plenty for everyone.* **3** stingy, °miserly, °mean, °selfish, niggardly, parsimonious, °penurious, penny-pinching, °mercenary, close-fisted, tight-fisted, °close, *Colloq* near, °tight, *Brit* mingy: *He's so greedy that he asks beggars for receipts.*

green *adj.* **1** verdant, grassy, °fresh, °leafy; °rural, country-like: *Plans call for a green belt to be created around every major city.* **2** °immature, unripe, unripened; °naïve, °callow, untested, untrained, unversed, °inexperienced, °new, °raw, unseasoned, °unsophisticated, °gullible, °amateur, unskilled, unskilful, amateurish, non-professional, inexpert, *Colloq* wet behind the ears: *This banana is still too green to eat. Isn't Piers a bit green to be given so much responsibility?* **3** environmental, conservationist: *The green activists appear to be gaining influence in governmental circles.*
—*n.* **4** °lawn, sward, °common, grassland: *Let us meet on the village green at noon.* **5** °environmentalist, conservationist, preservationist: *The greens are opposed to draining the marshes.*

greenhorn *n.* °newcomer, beginner, °novice, tiro *or* tyro, neophyte, °initiate, °learner, tenderfoot, *Colloq* rookie: *They send all the greenhorns off to fetch a bucket of steam and a can of striped paint.*

greet *v.* **1** °welcome, °receive, usher in, °meet: *We were greeted warmly by the family.* **2** °hail, accost, °address, °salute: *People greeted him in the street with a wave and a smile.*

greeting *n.* **1** salutation, °hail, hello, °welcome, °reception: *She had a smile and a greeting for every passer-by.* **2** greetings °card, °card, °message, °note: *The Queen sent me a greeting on my 100th birthday.* **3** ***greetings***: °regards, °respects, best *or* °good wishes, devoirs, °compliments: *I sent you greetings from Barbados, where I took my holiday.*

grey *adj.* **1** ashen, °leaden, °colourless, °pale, pallid, °wan, livid, °pearly, griseous, smoky, sooty, bloodless: *The cadaver's skin was a dead, whitish grey.* **2** °gloomy, °dismal, °dull, depressing, °glum, °dreary, °sombre, °drab, cheerless, °dark, °murky, foggy, °misty, cloudy, °overcast, °sunless: *As if to mould her temperament, Kathleen was born on a grey December day in 1791.* **3** °aged, °elderly, hoary, °old, °venerable, °ancient: *A stooped, grey crone inched along, muttering to herself.* **4** °mature, °wise, °experienced: *Seventy years have spread their grey experience over his hoary head.*

grief *n.* **1** °anguish, °suffering, °agony, °misery, wretchedness, °pain, °hurt, °sadness, °sorrow, dejection, °depression, despondency, °melancholy, unhappiness, °woe, °torment, °desolation, heartbreak, °remorse, °regret, ruth, heartache: *Nothing equalled the grief I felt at the death of my dog, Whiffler.* **2** °distress, °trouble, °difficulty, tribulation, °trial, °burden, °load, onus, °ordeal, travail, °affliction, °worry, °bitterness, °curse; adversity, °misfortune, °evil days, °bad *or* °ill °fortune *or* °luck, °calamity, °disaster, °catastrophe, trauma: *The death of her only child was a lasting grief to Millie.* **3** ***come to grief***: °fail, go to °rack and °ruin, meet with °disaster, °miscarry, °fall *or* °come °apart, *Colloq* °come unstuck: *Our plans for retirement came to grief when my husband went bankrupt.*

grievance *adj.* **1** °wrong, °ill, °injustice, °disservice, unfairness, °injury, °damage, °harm, °outrage, affront, °indignity, °hardship, °calamity: *I had to listen to details of every grievance she had ever suffered.* **2** °complaint, °objection, °charge, plaint, °allegation, °grudge, *Colloq* °gripe, bone to pick, *Brit* crow to pluck, *Slang* beef: *Please register all your grievances at the office next door.*

grieve *v.* **1** °mourn, °bemoan, °lament, °regret, rue, deplore, °bewail, mope, eat one's heart out: *Sylvia is still grieving over the loss of her husband.* **2** °weep, °cry, °mourn, °moan, °keen, °suffer, °sorrow; °shed tears, °complain: *Go in and try to comfort the grieving widow.*

grievous *adj.* **1** °severe, °heavy, °painful, °grave, °serious, distressing, °harmful; damaging, °hurtful, °acute, wounding: *The church buildings suffered grievous damage from the storm. He was charged with causing grievous bodily harm.* **2** egregious, °awful, °flagrant, °terrible, °outrageous, heinous, °dreadful, °atrocious, °monstrous, appalling, °shocking, °deplorable, °calamitous, °lamentable, intolerable, °shameful, °unbearable: *Missing that catch was a grievous error.*

grim *adj.* **1** °stern, °severe, unrelenting, °resolute, uncompromising, unyielding, °inflexible, adamant, °stony, iron, unbending, °firm, intractable, unflinching, unmoving, °unmoved, °implacable, inexorable, °determined, °steadfast, (dead) set, °fixed, °decided, °obstinate, headstrong, °stubborn, obdurate, dogged, unwavering: *By controlling the purse strings, she kept a grim hold over the family.* **2** °forbidding, °formidable, °harsh, °ferocious, °fierce, °cruel, °savage, °merciless, °heartless, °ruthless, pitiless, °vicious, °brutal, brutish, feral, °inhuman, °fiendish, °violent, °bloodthirsty, °murderous, °homicidal, °fell: *A grim pack of howling wolves loped after our sledge.* **3** dire, °dreadful, °ghastly, °awful, °frightful, °frightening, °sinister, °hideous, horrid, horrific, °horrible, horrendous, °terrible, °terrifying, °terrific, °harrowing, °dread, alarming, appalling, °grotesque, °gruesome, °eerie, °macabre, flagitious, heinous, °evil, °wicked, iniquitous, °atrocious, °monstrous: *Before me appeared the ghostly apparition of the Grim Reaper.*

grime *n.* °dirt, °filth, soot, °mud, °muck, slime, scum: *The lad began to rub the grime from the old oil lamp.*

grind *v.* **1** °pound, °powder, °pulverize, abrade, °crush, granulate, °mill, °grate, °rasp, °crumble, kibble, mash, triturate, bray, comminute: *The rock was soon ground to a fine powder.* **2** °sharpen, °whet; °file, °smooth, °polish: *He is grinding the edge to be razor sharp.* **3** gnash, °grit, °grate: *He grinds his teeth when he's angry.* **4** Also, ***grind away***: °labour, toil, °slave (away); °study, lucubrate, burn the midnight oil, *Colloq* °cram, *Brit* swot: *George has been grinding away at the same job all his life. Languages came easily, but he had to grind away at the sciences.* **5** ***grind down***: °wear down *or* away, °crush, °oppress, °subdue, °suppress, °tyrannize, °persecute, maltreat, °ill-treat, harry, °harass, °hound, hector, °plague, badger: *Dictators first grind down all opposition, then destroy it.* **6** ***grind out***: °produce, °generate, °crank out, churn out, °turn out: *For 20 years he has been grinding out the daily gossip column.*
—*n.* **7** toil, °labour, °drudgery, travail, °exertion, °task, chore: *Working at the checkout counter hour after hour is a terrible grind.*

grip *n.* **1** °hold, °grasp, °clutch, handgrip, °clasp, handclasp: *Losing his grip on the rope, he plummeted into the abyss.* **2** °control, °command, °hold, mastery; °authority, °influence, °power, °rule, °domination, °sovereignty, °tenure, °dominion, suzerainty, °custody: *Peter is losing his grip on reality. The dictator kept a tight grip on the people right up to his death.* **3** °grasp, °understanding, apprehension, comprehension, °sense, °sensitivity, °feel, °feeling, awareness, °perception, °view, *Slang US* °handle: *Skerry is having trouble getting a grip on what you plan to do.* **4** handgrip, valise, (travelling *or* overnight) °bag, °case, satchel, °suitcase, *Brit* holdall, *US and Canadian* carry-all: *I got off the plane in New York, but my grip went on to Detroit.* **5** ***come*** or ***get to grips with***: °tackle, confront, °approach, °handle, °meet (head on), °undertake, °grapple *or* contend with, °cope *or* °deal with, °face: *We must come to grips with the problem of Cassandra.*
—*v.* **6** °grasp, °clutch, °clasp, °hold, °seize: *He gripped the handle of the revolver more tightly.* **7** engross, °engage, °hold, °fascinate, enthral, °entrance, absorb, mesmerize, °hypnotize, spellbind, rivet: *Just at the gripping climax, the reel broke and the film stopped.*

gripe *v.* **1** °complain, °moan, grumble, whimper, whine, bleat, °nag, °cavil, °carp, grouse, *Colloq* beef, *Brit* whinge, *Slang* °bitch, bellyache: *It's natural to gripe about the food in the army.*
—*n.* **2** °complaint, °grievance, °objection, °protest; complaining, moaning, grumbling, whimpering, whining, °nagging, cavilling, carping, grousing, *Colloq* beef, *Brit* whinging, *Slang* bitching, bellyaching: *I don't want to hear any more gripes about the food!* **3** Usually, ***gripes***: cramp, °twinge, °pang, °pain, °ache, colic, °distress, *Colloq* bellyache: *The gripes became so painful that he was sure he had appendicitis.*

grisly *adj.* °gruesome, °gory, °abhorrent, °abominable, °awful, appalling, °hideous, °shocking, °nasty, °dreadful, °repulsive, °repellent, °repugnant, °disgusting, sickening, nauseating, horrific, horrid, horrendous, horrifying, °terrible, °terrifying, °terrific: *A grisly scene greeted the soldiers who liberated the concentration camp.*

grit *n.* °courage, courageousness, valour, °bravery, °fortitude, °resolution, resoluteness, °resolve, toughness, mettle, °pluck, °spirit, °backbone, °nerve, gameness, intrepidity *or* intrepidness, dauntlessness, °tenacity, °determination, firmness, hardiness, hardihood, staunchness, stalwartness, doughtiness, fearlessness, *Colloq* °guts, gutsiness, °spunk, spunkiness, starch, *Brit* °bottle, *US and Canadian* chutzpah, moxie, stick-to-it-iveness: *Mountain-climbing requires more grit than you might think.*

gritty *adj.* **1** sandy, gravelly, °granular, grainy, °rough, abrasive, rasping, arenose: *The texture of the mud-pack felt somewhat gritty on her face.* **2** °courageous, valorous, °brave, °resolute, °tough, mettlesome, plucky, °spirited, °game, °intrepid, °dauntless, °tenacious, °determined, °persistent, °firm, °hardy, °staunch, °stalwart, doughty, °fearless, *Colloq* gutsy, spunky: *The band of gritty frontiersmen was led by Sheriff Boswell.*

groan *v.* **1** °moan, °sigh, °murmur, wail, whimper, whine: *Unattended patients were lying there, groaning in agony.* **2** °complain, grumble, grouse, °object, °protest, *Colloq* °gripe, beef, yammer, *Brit* whinge, *Slang* °bitch: *Now that he's rich, he's groaning about taxes.*
—*n.* **3** °moan, °sigh, °murmur, wail, whimper, whine: *I thought I heard a groan coming from the attic.* **4** °complaint, grumble, grousing, muttering, *Colloq* °gripe, griping, beef, yammering, *Slang* bitching: *His announcement that the whole class would be punished was met by groans.*

groggy *adj.* unsteady, °shaky, wobbly, weak-kneed, °weak, staggering, stupefied, dazed, stunned, reeling, punch-drunk, °numb, numbed, benumbed, °faint, in a °trance *or* °stupor, muddled, addled, °confused, bewildered, confounded, puzzled, baffled, befuddled, *Colloq* dopey, punchy, woozy, *Brit* muzzy: *I was still groggy from the blow on the head.*

groom *n.* **1** stable-boy, stableman, *Brit* stable-lad, *Archaic* ostler *or* hostler, equerry: *The groom unsaddled the horses and began to curry them.* **2** bridegroom: *Let's drink to the bride and groom!*
—*v.* **3** °spruce up, °dress, °tidy *or* °neaten up, smarten up, titivate *or* tittivate, °preen, °primp, °refresh: *Every time she passes a mirror Vivian stops to groom herself.* **4** °fit, °train, °prepare, °coach, °tutor, °brief, °drill, °prime, (get *or* make) °ready, °adapt, °shape: *McCusker is being groomed for a directorship.*

groove *n.* °slot, °cut, °channel, °furrow, °gouge, trough; flute, °scratch, striation *or* stria, rifling, °rifle, *Architecture* glyph, *Technical* sulcus: *The door slides in these grooves at the sides.*

grope *v.* °feel, °fumble, fish, °probe: *I groped for the switch in the dark.*

gross *adj.* **1** °fat, °obese, corpulent, overweight, °big, °large, °bulky, °great, °heavy, °ponderous, °massive, cumbersome, °unwieldy: *The gross detective eased his bulk onto a tiny chair.* **2** °total, aggregate, °entire, pre-tax, (all-)°inclusive, °overall, °whole: *The gross profit was up by 15 per cent this year.* **3** °coarse, °vulgar, °crude, °unsophisticated, uncultured, uncultivated,

°earthy, crass, indelicate, °indecent, °inappropriate, °unseemly, °improper, °unrefined, °bawdy, ribald, Rabelaisian, °raw, °rude, °offensive, °obscene, °lewd, °dirty, smutty, °pornographic, °filthy: *That was too gross a story for mixed company.* **4** °outrageous, °flagrant, °obvious, °plain, °glaring, °shameful, °blatant, °monstrous, heinous, °manifest, °evident: *Her conviction was a gross miscarriage of justice.* **5** °disgusting, °repulsive, °repellent, °revolting, nauseating: *His table manners are truly gross.*
—*v.* **6** °earn, °bring *or* °take in, °make: *We grossed over a million but netted only 50,000 after expenses.*
—*n.* **7** (°overall) °total, °take, intake, takings, °receipts, °gate: *As I said, the gross was over a million.*

grotesque *adj.* **1** distorted, °bizarre, freakish, twisted, °misshapen, malformed, °deformed, °gruesome, °gnarled: *Victor Hugo created the character of Quasimodo, the grotesque bell-ringer of Notre Dame.* **2** °absurd, °incongruous, °weird, °odd, °fantastic, °strange, °queer, °peculiar, °curious, °outlandish, °offbeat, °abnormal, aberrant, anomalous, °ludicrous, °ridiculous, °preposterous: *The idea of marrying Leonard is too grotesque for even Gladys to contemplate.*

ground *n.* **1** °earth, °soil, °turf, sod, °dirt, loam, clay; °land, °terrain: *There is a great hole in the ground behind my house.* **2** °territory, °area, °range, °scope, compass: *We covered the ground quite thoroughly at our meeting.* **3** Often, ***grounds***: °basis, °foundation, °base, °reason, °footing, justification, °rationale, °argument, °cause, °motive, °excuse: *What are her grounds for suing for divorce?* **4** ***grounds***: °sediment, °dregs, lees, °deposit, settlings, *Brit* grouts: *Filter out the grounds before drinking the coffee.*
—*v.* **5** °base, °establish, °organize, °found; °settle, °set: *The school's philosophy is grounded on the principles of Maria Montessori.* **6** °instruct, °teach, °train, °coach, °tutor, °inform, °prepare, °initiate: *The purpose of the course is to ground students in basic mathematics.*

groundless *adj.* baseless, without °foundation, °unsound, °unfounded, unsupported, unjustified, unjustifiable, °unwarranted, uncalled-for, °gratuitous, unreasoned, °unreasonable, °speculative, suppositional, °hypothetical, °tenuous, °flimsy, °illusory, °imaginary, chimerical: *Assumptions that the boy is guilty are entirely groundless.*

groundwork *n.* °basis, spadework, °preparation(s), °base, °foundation, underpinning(s), cornerstone: *The report provided the groundwork for the research.*

group *n.* **1** °assembly, assemblage, °gathering, congregation, °company, °number, °alliance, °union, °association, °organization, °league, °society, coterie, °clique, °set, °band, °circle, °club, °party, °body, °faction, °crowd, °team, °corps, guild, troupe, °unit, troop, °platoon, °squad, °gang: *A group of revolutionaries meets nightly in a basement in Krakowskaya Street.* **2** °batch, aggregation, °set, grouping, °collection, assemblage, °bunch, °accumulation, conglomeration, agglomeration, °assortment, series; °pile, °heap, °bundle: *The entire group of abstract paintings was auctioned at double their estimated value.*
—*v.* **3** classify, °class, °sort, °bracket, °organize, °order, °rank, assort, °categorize, catalogue: *Books are grouped according to subject.* **4** °collect, °assemble, °arrange, °place, °dispose, °gather, °organize, °bring *or* °put together, °set °apart: *Group oversized books together on the lowest shelves.*

grovelling *adj.* °obsequious, fawning, toadying, toadeating, sycophantish, subservient, slavish, °servile, °submissive, kowtowing, cringing, cowering, truckling, snivelling, scraping, tugging the forelock, abject, crawling, °base, °low, °mean, °sordid, *Colloq* bootlicking, *US* apple-polishing; *Slang* brown-nosing, *Brit* arse-kissing, arse-licking, *US* ass-kissing, ass-licking: *The grovelling coward threw himself to the ground, begging forgiveness.*

grow *v.* **1** °flourish, °develop, °increase, become larger *or* greater, °enlarge, wax, °swell, °expand, broaden, °thicken, °spread, °lengthen, multiply, burgeon *or* bourgeon, °thrive, °luxuriate, °prosper, °mature, °ripen, bloom, °flower, blossom, fructify, bear *or* yield °fruit: *The seeds he had planted grew abundantly. The population continues to grow.* **2** °develop, evolve, °arise, °issue, °stem, °spring (up), °originate: *A great friendship grew out of their association.* **3** °plant, °cultivate, °breed, nurture, °raise, °propagate, °produce; °sow: *Cathcart grows sorghum where he used to grow alfalfa.* **4** °become, °get: *I am growing fonder of you every day, Abbie.* **5** ***grow on***: °get *or* °become accepted by, °come *or* °begin to be liked by, gain *or* °increase in °interest *or* °attraction to, become more °pleasing to: *I didn't like her at first, but she grows on you.* **6** ***grow up***: °mature, °reach *or* attain °maturity *or* adulthood, °come of °age, °reach one's °majority: *Those who grew up in the Great Depression knew real poverty.*

growth *n.* **1** °development, °evolution, evolvement, cultivation, nurturing, °increase, °expansion, broadening, °extension, enlargement, °spread, °proliferation, flowering: *The growth of education was a slow and painful process.* **2** vegetation, crop: *The area is covered with a dense growth of timber.* **3** °advance, advancement, °success, °improvement, °expansion, °rise, °progress: *The growth of the economy has slowed down in the last quarter.* **4** wen, excrescence, wart, °lump, °tumour, °swelling, intumescence: *He developed an ugly growth on his nose.*

grudge *n.* **1** °bitterness, °resentment, °rancour, °ill will, °hard feelings, °spite, °grievance, pique, °dislike, °aversion, antipathy, animus, °animosity, enmity, °venom, malice, malevolence, hatred: *He had harboured a grudge against her ever since she was promoted.*
—*v.* **2** °begrudge, °resent, °envy, °mind, covet: *She grudges other people their simple pleasures.*

gruesome *adj.* °ghastly, °repugnant, °horrible, horrid, horrific, horrendous, °grisly, °hideous, °revolting, °repellent, °repulsive, °loathsome, °grim, °grotesque, °macabre, °abominable, °frightful, °frightening, °fearsome, °shocking, °terrible, °awful: *She told a tale too gruesome to repeat here.*

gruff *adj.* **1** °surly, crusty, grumpy, curmudgeonly, °cantankerous, °sour, °peevish, churlish, °rude, uncivil, bearish, °testy, °querulous, °irritable, °cross, °petulant, crabbed, irascible, °sullen, sulky, °bluff, °abrupt, °curt, °blunt, °brusque, °short, °short-tempered, ill-humoured, ill-natured, bad-tempered, stinging, °cutting, °biting, acerb, acrimonious, acid, °caustic, *Colloq* grouchy, crotchety: *It is difficult to work for someone as gruff as he is.* **2** throaty, °deep, °rough, guttural, rasping, °low, °husky, hoarse, °harsh(-sounding): *Instantly I recognized father's gruff voice on the telephone.*

guarantee *n.* **1** guaranty, °warranty, °assurance, °pledge, °bond, °obligation, °promise; °word (of °honour), °oath, °undertaking: *The guarantee expires one month from the sell-by date. Have I your guarantee that this battery will last a year?*
—*v.* **2** guaranty, °warranty, °assure, °ensure, °pledge, °promise, °undertake, °stand behind, °vouch for, °certify, make °sure *or* °certain, °swear to, °attest to: *The manufacturer guarantees every car for three years or 50,000 miles.*

guard *v.* **1** °protect, °shield, °safeguard, (°keep *or* °stand) °watch (over), °defend, convoy, °escort, °police, °look after, °tend, °mind: *Only three men will be guarding the bullion when we make our move.* **2** °control, °mind: *Guard your tongue—the walls have ears.*
—*n.* **3** °sentinel, °watchman, sentry, °security guard, custodian, °guardian, °protector, °picket, °watch, bodyguard; evzone, bashibazouk; *Brit* warder, wardress, *Slang* screw, *Brit* °minder: *The guards go to eat at noon.* **4** °protection, convoy, °escort, °patrol: *A guard of six men will accompany the van along this route.* **5** °defence, °protection, °safety, °safeguard, °security, °shield: *This bandage will serve as a guard against infection.*

guarded *adj.* °careful, °cautious, heedful, °prudent, circumspect, °wary, °noncommittal, restrained,

°mindful, °suspicious, °leery *or Brit also* leary, apprehensive; °loath *or* loth, °reticent, °reluctant, *Colloq* cagey: *He became very guarded under close questioning. When I asked where she had been, she gave a guarded answer.*

guardian *n.* °protector, defender, paladin, °champion; trustee, custodian, °keeper, preserver: *She fancies him her guardian, her knight in shining armour. Do we really need guardians of the 'purity' of the language?*

guerrilla *n.* guerilla, °partisan *or* partizan, °resistance *or* °freedom *or* °underground fighter, °irregular; insurgent, saboteur, °terrorist; *US history* Jayhawker, *French history* Maquis: *The guerrillas continue to attack the government's supply convoys.*

guess *v.* **1** conjecture, °estimate, hypothesize, °speculate, postulate, *Slang* guestimate *or* guesstimate: *We guessed that he might try to come in through the window.* **2** °think, °suppose, conclude, °assume, °believe, °dare °say, °surmise, °judge, deem, °reckon, °imagine, °fancy, °feel, °suspect, °divine: *I guess you were right about her.*
—*n.* **3** conjecture, °estimate, °hypothesis, °speculation, °surmise, assumption, °judgement, °feeling, °suspicion, °supposition, postulate, theory; guesswork; *Colloq* °shot in the dark, *Slang* guestimate *or* guesstimate: *My guess as to which card would turn up was wrong.*

guest *n.* °visitor, °company, caller; °patron, °customer, lodger, boarder, roomer: *Our guests get clean linen daily.*

guidance *n.* **1** °leadership, °direction, °management, °government, °conduct, °control, °regulation, °charge, handling, °rule, °auspices: *The company prospered under her guidance.* **2** °counsel, °advice, counselling, advisement, °instruction, teaching: *I have turned to you for guidance in the matter.*

guide *v.* **1** °lead, °show *or* °lead the way, °conduct, °shepherd, °direct, usher, °steer, °orient *or Brit* orientate: *She guided me to the proper office. What will guide your judgement in dealing with this situation?* **2** °steer, °pilot, °manoeuvre, °navigate, °direct: *He carefully guided the boat between the shoals.* **3** °counsel, °advise, °influence, °sway; °supervise, °oversee, °handle, °manage, superintend, °direct, °control, °regulate, °govern: *Mr Thrall guided my artistic development from the beginning.* **4** °instruct, °teach, °tutor, °train: *From early youth we were guided by the elders of the community.*
—*n.* **5** °leader, conductor, °director, cicerone, chaperon, mentor, °counsel, °counsellor, °adviser *or* advisor, guru, °master: *He served as my guide through the financial jungle. Let your conscience be your guide.* **6** °model, criterion, exemplar, °standard, °ideal, °example, °inspiration: *She looked upon the life of Mother Theresa as a guide.* **7** °beacon, °light, °signal, guiding °light, °landmark, lodestar, °sign, marker: *The Southern Cross was our constant guide sailing round the Horn.* **8** handbook, °manual, enchiridion, °vademecum, guidebook, Baedeker: *Can you recommend a good guide to English usage?*

guilt *n.* **1** culpability, guiltiness, criminality, °blame, °responsibility, blameworthiness; °crime, sinfulness, feloniousness, wrongdoing, misconduct: *Confronted by the evidence, Shillingworth admitted his guilt.* **2** °remorse, self-reproach, °regret, °sorrow, contrition, repentance, °shame, contriteness, self-condemnation, °bad °conscience: *That feeling of guilt would plague me for the rest of my life.*

guilty *adj.* **1** °responsible, culpable, answerable, blameworthy, at °fault, °delinquent, °wrong; offending, reprehensible: *Whoever was guilty will be prosecuted. First we must find the guilty party.* **2** °remorseful, contrite, °regretful, °sorry, °apologetic, °repentant, °sorrowful, conscience-stricken, rueful, °penitent; °ashamed, shamefaced, °sheepish, °embarrassed, red-faced: *Gavin felt terribly guilty for having insulted Tina.*

guise *n.* **1** °appearance, °aspect, °semblance, °look, °image, °likeness, mien; °air, °behaviour, °conduct, deportment, comportment, °bearing, demeanour: *This is nothing but an old political concept in a new guise.* **2** °semblance, °disguise, façade, °front, °pretence: *The treacherous Lothario assumed the guise of a knight in shining armour.*

gulf *n.* **1** bay, bight, cove, inlet, °sound, loch *or* °sea loch, firth *or* frith, fiord *or* fjord, *Irish* lough, *Brit* °creek: *We sailed into the gulf to shelter from the wind behind the cliffs.* **2** chasm, °deep, °depth, °abyss, abysm, °void, °space, °opening, °rift, °breach, °gap, °separation, °split: *After the divorce, the gulf between us widened even further.*

gullible *adj.* °innocent, °green, °simple, credulous, °unsophisticated, °naïve, °unsuspecting, °unwary, unsuspicious, wide-eyed, born yesterday, °inexperienced, °immature: *He was gullible enough to fall for the old con game, three-card monte.*

gully *n.* gulley, °channel, river-bed, watercourse, °gorge, °ravine, °canyon, °notch, °cut, °pass, defile, °valley, °corridor, wadi *or* wady, *Brit* gill *or* ghyll, *W US* arroyo, *US and Canadian* gulch: *We rode along in the gully so as not to be seen.*

gulp *v.* **1** °bolt, gobble, wolf (down), °devour, °gorge, °swallow, °throw down, °toss off, quaff, guzzle, °swill, *Colloq* °knock back, swig, *US* chug-a-lug: *The boy gulped his dinner and ran out to play.* **2** °swallow, °suppress, °stifle, °choke (back), °smother, strangle: *She gulped back her tears as the coffin was lowered.*
—*n.* **3** °mouthful, °swallow, °draught, °swill, *Colloq* swig: *He took a gulp of his drink before making another bid.*

gumption *n.* **1** resourcefulness, shrewdness, cleverness, (mother) °wit, (common) °sense, astuteness, °judgement, *Colloq* horse °sense, brains, *Slang Brit* nous: *It takes a lot of gumption to run a good cattle auction.* **2** °backbone, °grit, °pluck, mettle, °enterprise, °initiative, °courage, °spirit, gameness, °nerve, °daring, °vigour, °energy, boldness, audacity, °stamina, *Colloq* °spunk, °guts, get-up-and-go, *US* moxie, *Slang Brit* °bottle, *Taboo slang* balls: *He hasn't the gumption to go into business for himself.*

gurgle *v.* **1** °bubble, burble, °babble, °ripple, °splash, plash, °lap, °murmur, purl: *The cool brook gurgled merrily through the meadow.*
—*n.* **2** °babble, burble, bubbling, babbling, burbling, °splash, gurgling, splashing, plashing, murmuring, purl, purling: *I lay back, listening to the gurgle of the spring among the rocks.*

gush *v.* **1** cascade, °rush, °flood, °stream, °spurt, jet, °spout, °burst; °run, °flow: *The water gushed out of the pipe, soaking us all.* **2** °bubble over, overflow, be °ebullient *or* °effusive *or* °effervescent, effervesce, °make much of, °fuss over, °prattle, °chatter, °babble, °jabber, blather *or* blether, *Colloq Brit* natter, witter: *It was impossible to stop them from gushing on about the performance.*
—*n.* **3** cascade, °rush, °flood, °flow, °stream, °spurt, jet, °spout, °burst, °torrent: *A gush of water hit me right in the face.* **4** °exuberance, effusion, bubbling over, °outburst: *After the first gush of enthusiasm, everything quieted down.*

gushy *adj.* gushing, fulsome, cloying, mawkish, °excessive, °effusive, overdone, (over-)°sentimental, (over) °enthusiastic, *Colloq* °sloppy, slushy: *It's another gushy film about a little girl and a lost kitten.*

gust *n.* **1** °puff, °blow, °wind, °breeze, °blast: *A gust of wind blew my hat off.*
—*v.* **2** °puff, °blow, °blast, °surge, °increase: *The wind gusted up to gale force overnight.*

gusto *n.* °enthusiasm, °relish, °zest, °appetite, zeal, zealousness, avidity, °eagerness, °enjoyment, °appreciation, °pleasure, °delight, °satisfaction: *We attacked the meal with great gusto and soon dispatched every scrap.*

gut *n.* **1** Often, ***guts***: °bowels, intestines, entrails, viscera, °stomach, offal, vitals, °vital parts, gurry, *Brit* (of a deer) gralloch, *Colloq* insides, innards *or*

inwards: *As soon as the game is killed, the guts must be removed.* **2** °stomach, abdomen, belly; beer-belly, bay window, corporation: *His enormous gut hung over his belt.* **3** ***guts***: **a** °backbone, °bravery, boldness, audacity, °pluck, °courage, °determination, °daring, °spirit, °grit, mettle, °gumption, °nerve, intestinal °fortitude, *Colloq* °spunk, gutsiness, *Slang Brit* °bottle, *Taboo* balls: *He hasn't the guts to tell the boss what he thinks of him.* **b** °integrity, will-power, °stamina, °endurance, forcefulness, °dynamism: *It takes real guts to stand up for your rights.*
—*v.* **4** disembowel, eviscerate, °draw, °dress, °clean: *It will take hours to gut all these fish.* **5** °ransack, °pillage, °plunder, °sack, despoil, °strip, °ravage, °loot, °rifle, *Rare* depredate; °clean out, °devastate, °empty: *The building was completely gutted by the fire.*
—*adj.* **6** °basic, °heartfelt, °instinctive, instinctual, intuitive, visceral, deep-seated, deep-rooted, °emotional: *My gut reaction is to refuse the offer.*

guttersnipe *n.* waif, (street) Arab, (street) urchin, °ragamuffin, brat, gamin, °rogue, *Colloq Brit rare* mudlark: *That little guttersnipe stole my wallet!*

guy *n.* **1** °man, °lad, °youth, °boy, °fellow, °person, *Colloq* °chap, geezer, *Brit* bloke, *Slang* gink, cat, °customer, *US* °dude, *Old-fashioned* gazabo *or* gazebo: *Clarence is a pretty nice guy.*
—*v.* **2** °mock, °ridicule, make °fun of, °caricature, °satirize, °poke °fun at, °lampoon, *Colloq* rib, °take off, *Brit* °send up: *We put on a show at school in which we guyed the teachers.*

gyrate *v.* °rotate, °spin, °revolve, °turn (°round *or* about), whirl, °twirl, °swirl, °pirouette; °swivel: *The dancers were gyrating to the deafening music.*

H

habit *n.* **1** °custom, °routine, °practice, °convention, °policy, °pattern, °usage, °mode, °rule, wont, praxis: *Jogging every morning had become a habit. She is a creature of habit.* **2** °tendency, °disposition, °manner, °practice, °way, °custom, °inclination, °bent, predisposition, second nature, °frame of mind, °attitude, °penchant, propensity, proclivity; addiction, compulsion: *This kettle has a habit of leaking. Try to control your bad habits.* **3** attire, clothing, °dress, °apparel, °clothes, garb, °costume, °garments, vestments, °uniform, raiment, livery, °regalia, habiliment(s), *Colloq* °gear: *She was disguised in a monk's habit.*

habitable *adj.* liveable, inhabitable: *With some effort, two rooms were made habitable.*

habitat *n.* °abode, °home, °haunt, °domain, °range, °territory, bailiwick, °realm, °terrain, °element, °environment, surroundings, *Colloq* stamping-ground: *The winter habitat of the monarch butterfly is in northern Mexico. Curtis doesn't function well outside his natural habitat.*

habitual *adj.* **1** settled, °fixed, °customary, °usual, °conventional, °accustomed, °set, °rooted, established, °traditional, °standard, °routine, °ritual, °regular, °normal, wonted, °common, °ordinary, °natural: *He follows his habitual practice of rising at dawn.* **2** inveterate, established, °chronic, confirmed, hardened, °ingrained, °frequent, °persistent, °constant, °continual, °perpetual: *Many English people are habitual tea-drinkers.*

habitué *n.* frequenter, °patron, °regular °customer, *Colloq* °regular: *Larry has been a habitué of The Bell Inn for 20 years.*

hack[1] *v.* **1** °chop, hew, °lacerate, °gash, °slash, °cut; °mangle, °butcher, °mutilate, °ruin, °destroy, smash, °batter, °damage, °deface: *He hacked the furniture to pieces with an axe.* **2** bark, cough: *She was disgusted by the man's hacking and spitting.*
—*n.* **3** °cut, °gash, °slash, °chop: *He took a hack at the log with his hatchet.*

hack[2] *n.* **1** drudge, penny-a-liner, scribbler, Grub Street °writer: *We made a mistake hiring that hack as a feature writer.* **2** plodder, drudge, toiler, °menial, °flunkey, lackey, °slave, *Brit* °fag, *Slang* °grind, *Brit* swot: *Fergus gets good grades because he's such a hack.* **3** saddle-horse, riding-horse, hackney, *Archaic* palfrey: *The hack was a fine bay mare.*
—*adj.* **4** hackneyed, trite, °banal, overdone, commonplace, °routine, stereotyped, °stock, °tired, °tedious, °mediocre, overworked, °stale, unoriginal, run-of-the-mill, °humdrum, moth-eaten, °mouldy, *Colloq* old hat: *Haverstock keeps publishing hack romances.*

hag *n.* crone, °fury, °witch, ogress, gorgon, harpy, fishwife, harridan, °shrew, virago, termagant, vixen, hell-cat, maenad *or* menad, Xanthippe, *Archaic* beldam; dog, °beast, °monster; *Colloq* battleaxe, *Slang* °bitch, °bag, *US* two-bagger: *Perseus met the Graeae, three old hags with one eye that they passed among them.*

haggard *adj.* °gaunt, °drawn, wasted, °emaciated, hollow-eyed, hollow-cheeked, °scrawny, scraggy, °ghastly, cadaverous, °run-down, wearied, °weary, careworn, °spent, played out, °exhausted, toil-worn, °worn, shrunken, withered: *She looked haggard, as if she hadn't slept for a week.*

haggle *v.* wrangle, °bargain, higgle, °bicker, chaffer, palter, °dispute, squabble, °quibble, °negotiate; barter, °deal; *Colloq US* °dicker: *However little you ask for the lamp, she's sure to haggle over the price.*

hail[1] *v.* **1** °greet, accost, °address, °signal, °call: *Robert hailed us from across the road.* **2** °cheer, °salute, °applaud, °approve, °glorify, °praise, °laud, °honour, acclaim, °congratulate, felicitate, °acknowledge: *He was hailed by all for his charitable work.*

hail[2] *v.* **1** °rain *or* °beat *or* °shower (down) on, °bombard, °pelt, °volley, barrage: *Rocks and debris hailed down on us from the cliffs above.*
—*n.* **2** °volley, °storm, °shower, °torrent, bombardment, barrage: *They were greeted by a hail of abuse when they entered the meeting hall.*

hair *n.* **1** tresses, locks, mane, curls, ringlets; braids, plaits: *You will recognize her by her red hair.* **2** hair's breadth, whisker, °trifle, fraction, skin of one's teeth: *He won the race by a hair.*

hairdo *n.* coiffure, hairstyle, °cut, coif: *Your hairdo is very becoming.*

hairless *adj.* bald, bald-headed, bald-pated, glabrous, calvous: *She finds hairless men rather sexy.*

hair-splitting *adj.* quibbling, (over-)°fussy, hypercritical, °petty, captious, carping, °fault-finding, °finicky, (over) °nice, °fastidious, cavilling, °niggling, *Colloq* nit-picking: *His hair-splitting attention to detail gets on my nerves.*

hairy *adj.* **1** hirsute, °shaggy, downy, fleecy, °fluffy, °woolly, lanate *or* lanose, lanuginous *or* lanuginose, bristly, setaceous, setal, hispid, comate *or* comose, fringy, crinite, trichoid, strigose *or* strigous, strigillose; whiskered, bewhiskered, bearded, barbate, unshaven: *The creature had a very hairy face.* **2** °tricky, °dangerous, °perilous, °risky, °uncertain, °precarious, °hazardous, °frightening, worrying, °nerve-racking *or* nerve-wracking, *Colloq* °scary: *The situation at the office has become very hairy.* **3** tangled, °intricate, knotty, complex, °complicated, °difficult, °problematic, °confused, confusing: *The exam contained some hairy questions.*

hale *adj.* °healthy, °hearty, °fit (as a fiddle), °sound, able-bodied, °hardy, °wholesome, °robust, °flourishing, in °good *or* °fine fettle, in the pink: *Her grandmother was as hale and hearty as ever.*

half-hearted *adj.* °indifferent, uncaring, unconcerned, °lukewarm, uninterested, °dispassionate, °cool, °unenthusiastic, half-baked, °nonchalant, °phlegmatic, °lackadaisical, insouciant: *The council has made only a half-hearted effort to solve the problem.*

halfwit *n.* dunce, °fool, idiot, simpleton, ninny, ass, ninny-hammer, moron, imbecile, °dolt, dunderhead *or* dunderpate, rattle-brain, nincompoop, dullard, *Colloq* numskull *or* numbskull, nitwit, dim-wit, birdbrain, *Brit* nit, °twit: *He's such a halfwit, he can hardly expect me to give him a job!*

halfwitted *adj.* °stupid, °foolish, °silly, °simple, °inane, asinine, moronic, imbecilic, doltish, rattle-brained, °feeble-minded, attocerebral, cretinous, °thick, *non compos mentis*, dim-witted, weak-minded, *Colloq* °dumb, *Brit* dotty, barmy (in the crumpet): *She had some halfwitted idea that she would win the lottery.*

hall *n.* **1** °corridor, hallway, passageway, °passage; foyer, °entry, entry-way, °lobby, vestibule: *Let us step out into the hall for a brief word.* **2** auditorium, °assembly *or* meeting *or* convention °hall, °theatre, amphitheatre, hired hall; lecture-room, lecture-hall, classroom: *We hired a hall for the wedding reception.*

hallmark *n.* **1** authentication, verification, °seal *or* °stamp (of authenticity *or* approval), °mark, °device, °sign, °symbol; plate-mark; assay-mark: *From this hallmark we know when and where the piece was made, by whom, and its degree of purity. Surprise endings are the hallmark of O. Henry's short stories.* **2** °feature, °stamp, °mark, earmark, trade °mark, °characteristic, °identification: *From his hallmark, a tiny axe, you can tell that the painting is a genuine Fellworthy.*

hallow *v.* **1** consecrate, °bless, °sanctify, °dedicate, °honour, enshrine, °glorify: *Englishmen look upon this battlefield as hallowed ground.* **2** °venerate, °worship, °revere, °reverence, °respect, °honour, pay °homage *or* °respect *or* °honour to, °exalt: *We must observe the hallowed traditions of the university.*

hallucination *n.* °fantasy, mirage, day-dream, °illusion, °delusion, °vision, °dream, aberration, chimera, phantasm, °phantom, figment of the °imagination, apparition, °spectre, °ghost; paræsthesia: *Alone at sea for a fortnight, I began having hallucinations.*

halo *n.* nimbus, °aura, aureole *or* aureola, corona, °radiance, *Painting* vesica, mandorla; °ring, disc, °circle, annulation, annulus: *The saints can be identified by the golden halos round their heads.*

halt *n.* **1** °stop, °standstill, °end, °termination, °close, stoppage, cessation: *We must call a halt to absenteeism in the factory.*
—*v.* **2** °stop, °quit, °end, °terminate, °cease, °check, °curb, °stem, °discontinue, desist, bring *or* come *or* °draw to an °end *or* °close, put an °end *or* °stop to, conclude, °shut *or* °close down *or* up: *We halted when we came to the river. The guerrillas halted the armoured column at the pass.*

halting *adj.* °hesitant, hesitating, wavering, shifting, uneven, faltering, stumbling, °faulty, unsteady, °awkward, stammering, stuttering: *He told her in halting English that there was no news of her friend.*

hamper[1] *v.* °slow, balk *or* baulk, °delay, °hold up, °retard, °inhibit, °encumber, °hinder, °obstruct, °block, °impede, °prevent, °interfere with, °frustrate, °restrict, °curb, °limit, °handicap, °restrain, °trammel, °bar, barricade, °shackle, °clog, °curtail, lessen, °reduce, °diminish: *Ice floes hampered their further progress.*

hamper[2] *n.* basket, pannier, creel, *Brit* punnet; hanaper, *Dialectal* skep: *A hamper arrived from Fortnum's, packed full of delicacies such as foie gras and peaches in brandy.*

hand *n.* **1** *Slang* mitt, paw, *US* lunch-hook: *Keep your hands off me, you oaf!* **2** °help, °aid, °assistance, °helping hand, °relief, °boost; °leg up: *Please give me a hand with this trunk.* **3** °influence, °agency, participation, involvement, °part, °share: *Did you have a hand in my getting the appointment?* **4** (manual) °labourer, °worker, workman, °man, °help, °employee: *It's getting harder to find hands for the farm.* **5** °pointer, °indicator, °index: *The minute hand covers the hour hand at noon and midnight.* **6** (round of) °applause, °ovation, °clap: *Give the lad a hand for trying.* **7** handwriting, °penmanship, °script; calligraphy: *The writing was in a hand that she could not recognize.* **8** Often, ***hands***: °control, °hold, °grasp, °possession, °custody, clutches, keeping, °power, disposal, °jurisdiction, °authority, supervision, °management, guardianship, °care: *At last, the government is in the hands of the people.* **9** ***at hand***: °nearby, °close, °near, °close by, °handy, (°readily) °available, to *or* on hand, at one's fingertips, °convenient, within (arm's) °reach, °accessible, °present; approaching, °imminent, around the corner: *He always kept a pistol at hand. The Day of Judgement is at hand.* **10** ***hand in glove***: hand in hand, in °league, together, in collusion, collusively, connivingly, conspiringly, intimately, closely, jointly, *Colloq* in cahoots: *An informer is working hand in glove with the police.* **11** ***hand in hand***: together, °side by side, hand in glove: *They walked hand in hand down the road.* **12** ***hand-over-fist***: °quickly, speedily, °rapidly, °swiftly, steadily, like mad: *He makes money hand-over-fist in the stock market.* **13** ***hands down***: °easily, °readily, effortlessly: *He can win the marathon hands down.*
—*v.* **14** °give, °pass, °deliver, °present to *or* with: *Please hand me the hammer.* **15** ***hand down*** *or* ***on*** *or* ***over***: **a** °bequeath, °will, °pass on; °transfer, °turn over: *The farm has been handed down from father to son for seven generations.* **b** See **18 a,** below. **16** ***hand in***: °submit, °give in, °tender, proffer, °offer: *I handed in my resignation.* **17** ***hand out***: °distribute, disseminate, °pass out *or* round *or* around, °give out, °deal (out), °mete *or* °dole out, °dispense; disburse: *She was handing out leaflets to passers-by.* **18** ***hand over***: **a** °deliver, °submit, °yield, °give up, °surrender, °turn over; °transfer: *The man produced a gun and told the cashier to hand over the money.* **b** See **15 a,** above.

handcuffs *n.pl.* manacles, shackles, *Colloq* cuffs, bracelets, *Slang Brit* darbies: *The police put handcuffs on them all.*

handful *n.* **1** °few, °couple, sprinkling, °small °number; fistful: *Only a handful of restaurants are open that late. He gave the beggar a handful of change.* **2** (°behaviour *or* disciplinary) °problem, °bother, mischief-maker, °troublemaker, °nuisance: *Timothy was a real handful when he was five.*

handicap *n.* **1** °hindrance, °restraint, °encumbrance, °restriction, limitation, °impediment, °barrier, °bar, °obstacle, (stumbling) °block, constraint, °check, °curb, °trammel, °disability, °disadvantage: *Did Douglas Bader view the loss of his legs as a handicap?*
—*v.* **2** °hinder, °hamper, °restrain, °encumber, °restrict, °limit, °impede, °bar, °block, °check, °curb, °trammel, disable, °disadvantage: *He was severely handicapped by the loss of his sword.*

handily *adv.* **1** °readily, °easily, effortlessly, without °strain, comfortably, with both hands tied (behind one's back): *Donald handily won the first prize in the poetry competition.* **2** skilfully, capably, deftly, cleverly, dexterously, adroitly, expertly, proficiently, masterfully: *I could never do that intricate work as handily as she.*

handle *n.* **1** °grip, hilt, handgrip, haft, helve: *Hold it by the handle, not the blade.*
—*v.* **2** °feel, °touch, °finger, °hold; °caress, °fondle, °pat: *Be careful how you handle that knife.* **3** °manage, °run, °operate, °direct, °administer, °supervise, °oversee, °control, °command, °guide: *At the age of 26, she was handling all foreign business for the company.* **4** °steer, °control, °manage, °cope with, °manoeuvre, °manipulate: *Are you sure he can handle that horse?* **5** °deal *or* °trade *or* °traffic in, (°buy and) °sell, °market: *The gang was found to be handling stolen goods worth millions every month.* **6** °treat, °control, °deal with, °cope with: *She handled the customers with the utmost tact and respect.* **7** °treat, °employ, °use, utilize; °deal with, °wield, °tackle, °manipulate: *Don't you admire how she handled the perspective in this painting?*

handsome *adj.* **1** good-looking, fine-looking, °attractive, °fair, °comely: *He's handsome enough to be a movie star.* **2** °generous, sizeable, °large, °big, °substantial, °considerable, °good, °goodly, °ample, °abundant: *She has made a handsome profit on the painting.*

handy *adj.* **1** °nearby, °accessible, °available, at *or* on *or* to °hand, °close (by), °convenient, at one's fingertips, within (easy) reach, (at the) °ready: *Because of the* *recent break-ins, she keeps a pistol handy.* **2** usable, °serviceable, manoeuvrable, °clever, °useful, °helpful, °practical: *A pair of pliers and a screwdriver are the handiest tools.* **3** deft, °clever, °dexterous, adroit, °adept, skilled, °skilful, °proficient, °expert: *Aunt Sara is very handy with a needle and thread.*

hang *v.* **1** °suspend, °depend, °dangle; be °poised *or* suspended, °hover, °swing: *Hang the lantern from this branch. The laundry was hanging on the line.* **2** gibbet, send to the °gallows, lynch, °execute, °kill, *Colloq* °string up, °stretch: *They hanged two murderers this morning.* **3** °drape, °fall: *The skirt isn't hanging straight.* **4** ***hang about*** or ***around***: **a** loiter, °wait, °linger, dally, °idle, tarry, *Colloq* hang out: *He hangs about after school every day, waiting for Susan.* **b** Also, ***hang about*** or ***around (with)***: °frequent, °haunt, °visit, °spend °time at; °associate with, °socialize with, °hobnob with, °rub elbows with, consort with, °fraternize with, °mix *or* °mingle with, *Colloq* hang out (with): *He hangs about the Golden Crown. I saw him hanging around with some pretty unsavoury characters.* **5** ***hang back (from)***: be °reluctant, °recoil (from), °shrink (from), °hesitate, falter, °stay away (from): *Move to the front of the queue and don't hang back.* **6** ***hang fire***: be delayed, °remain °unsettled *or* unfinished, be in °suspense *or* °abeyance; °stall, °hold up, °delay: *The decision will hang fire till after the election.* **7** ***hang on***: **a** Also, ***hang on to***: °hold on (to), °cling (to), °clutch, °grip, °grasp, °grab: *Hang on to me when we're crossing the street.* **b** °wait, °stay, °stop: *Hang on a minute—what did you call me?* **c** °wait, °persist, °remain, °carry on, °persevere, °go on, °hold out, °endure, °hold the phone, *Colloq US* hang in there: *Hang on a minute, I have to put down the phone to get a pencil.* **d** Also, ***hang on to*** or ***upon***: °listen carefully *or* attentively, give one's undivided °attention, be °rapt: *She hung on every word the guru uttered.* **e** °depend *or* °rely (on), be dependent *or* contingent (on), be °subject (to), be conditioned *or* conditional (on): *The entire project now hangs on their approval of the budget.* **8** ***hang one's head***: be °ashamed *or* humiliated *or* abashed *or* humbled *or* °embarrassed: *She hung her head as the store detective confronted her with the stolen goods.* **9** ***hang out***: See **5 a**, above. **10** ***hang over***: be °put off *or* postponed *or* delayed: *We must first deal with matters hanging over from our last meeting.* **11** ***hang together***: **a** °unite, be °united, be as °one, °stick together, °join forces, °cooperate, act in concert *or* °harmony: *We must hang together or we shall hang separately.* **b** make sense, be °logical, be °consistent, °correspond, °match (up), cohere, be °coherent: *The statements issued yesterday and today just don't hang together.* **12** ***hang up***: °break the connection, °disconnect, °cut off, put down the receiver: *Whenever a salesman phones, I simply hang up.*

hanger-on *n.* °follower, dependant, leech, °parasite, toady, sycophant, °yes-man, *Colloq* scrounger, *US* freeloader, *Slang* groupie, sponger *or* sponge: *The rock star came in, surrounded by his hangers-on.*

hangman *n.* executioner, *Archaic Brit* Jack Ketch: *The hangman, a black hood concealing his identity, slipped the noose over the prisoner's head.*

hanker *v.* Usually, ***hanker after*** *or* ***for***: °yearn for, °long for, °thirst after *or* for, °hunger after *or* for, °itch for, pine for, °lust after *or* for, covet, crave, have a hankering for, °want, °desire, °fancy, *Colloq* have a yen for: *She hankered after a big box of chocolates.*

hanky-panky *n.* °mischief, °trickery, double-dealing, legerdemain, °deception, duplicity, °chicanery, naughtiness, foolishness, tomfoolery, *Colloq* °funny business, jiggery-pokery, °monkey business, shenanigans, goings-on, antics: *He'd best not try any of his hanky-panky with the tax inspector.*

haphazard *adj.* **1** °random, °arbitrary, °chance, fortuitous, aleatory, °accidental, °unforeseen, unlooked-for, unexpected, adventitious, serendipitous: *Her fate was to be decided by a haphazard throw of the dice.* **2** °casual, °offhand, hit-or-miss, unsystematic, slapdash, °slipshod, °careless, disorganized, °disorderly: *He took some haphazard shots at the target.*

happen *v.* **1** °occur, take place, °come about, °go on, come to °pass, °develop; betide, °chance, °prove, °materialize, *Colloq* °transpire, °come off, *Slang* cook: *What is happening? As it happens, everyone has already left.* **2** befall, °become of: *What will happen to me if I refuse?* **3** ***happen on*** *or* ***upon***: °come upon, °chance *or* °hit on *or* upon, °stumble on *or* upon, °find, °turn up, °encounter, °meet with: *It was then that I happened on an old letter of his.*

happening *n.* °event, °incident, °occurrence, °occasion, taking place, °circumstance, °chance, °episode, °phenomenon: *Such a conjunction of the planets is a very rare happening.*

happily *adv.* **1** fortunately, luckily, propitiously, providentially, opportunely: *Happily, she made a full recovery and was soon back at work.* **2** joyfully, joyously, delightedly, gleefully, cheerily, cheerfully, °gaily, merrily, blithely; enthusiastically, heartily: *She waved happily as they drove off.* **3** °gladly, with °pleasure, agreeably, contentedly, °willingly, peaceably: *And they both lived happily ever after.*

happiness *n.* °pleasure, °delight, felicity, °enjoyment, °joy, joyousness, joyfulness, jubilation, cheerfulness, cheeriness, °cheer, blithesomeness, gladness, lightheartedness, exhilaration, elation, °exuberance, high spirits, °glee, °ecstasy: *My happiness at seeing you again was unbounded.*

happy *adj.* **1** °pleased, °delighted, °glad, joyous, °joyful, °overjoyed, jubilant, °cheerful, cheery, °blithe, blithesome, light-hearted, contented, exhilarated, °exultant, cock-a-hoop, °elated, °exuberant, thrilled, °gleeful, euphoric, °ecstatic, satisfied, gratified, *Colloq* on top of the world, on cloud nine, °pleased as Punch, tickled pink, *Brit* in the seventh °heaven, over the moon, *US* in seventh °heaven: *Her parents were happy that Georgina was married at last.* **2** °lucky, fortuitous, °propitious, °fortunate, auspicious, °advantageous, °beneficial, °favourable, felicitous, °opportune, °timely, °well-timed, apt, °appropriate: *By a happy chance, we were in Bermuda at the same time.*

harangue *n.* **1** diatribe, °tirade, °oration, peroration, declamation, philippic, screed, exhortation, vituperation, rodomontade, °speech, °address, *Colloq* spiel: *This morning he delivered a ten-minute harangue on the weakness of the coffee.*
—*v.* **2** declaim, °hold forth, °preach, °lecture, sermonize, pontificate, °vituperate, °rant and °rave: *Our neighbour is always haranguing her husband about trimming the hedges.*

harass *v.* badger, harry, hector, °trouble, °torment, °bother, °exasperate, °hound, °plague, °persecute, vex, °annoy, °irritate, °pester, °worry, °beset, bait, °nag, °pick on *or* at, °tease, torture, *Brit* chivvy *or* chivy *or* chevy: *The police harass me by turning up at all hours for 'help with their inquiries'.*

harbinger *n.* °forerunner, herald, °precursor, °omen, foretoken, °sign, portent, augury: *The crowing cock is the harbinger of dawn.*

harbour *n.* **1** °port, (°safe) haven, anchorage, mooring: *We sailed into the harbour just as the storm broke.*
—*v.* **2** °shelter, °keep °safe, °protect, °shield, °guard, °safeguard, °conceal, °hide: *They were found guilty of harbouring a known fugitive.* **3** °cherish, °foster, nurture, °nurse, °keep, °retain, °maintain, °hold, °cling to: *She harbours a grudge against whoever set the fire.*

hard *adj.* **1** °rigid, °stiff, °solid, °inflexible, °firm, °dense, condensed, compressed, °close, solidified, hardened; °stony, rocklike, °concrete, °petrified, granite(-like), flinty, °steely; °tough, °rugged, leathery, °callous; unyielding, adamant(ine), impenetrable, obdurate, impervious, °impregnable: *The cement gets hard in an hour. This steak is as hard as shoe-leather. The metal was so hard that I broke three drills trying to make a hole in it.* **2** °difficult, °laborious, °arduous,

back-breaking, °burdensome, onerous, fatiguing, tiring, °exhausting, wearying, °strenuous, °tough, °toilsome: *Laying track for the railway is a very hard job.* **3** °difficult, °perplexing, knotty, °puzzling, baffling, enigmatic, °intricate, °complicated, complex, tangled, °involved, °thorny, °incomprehensible, inscrutable, unsolvable, insoluble, *Colloq* °tough: *There were a lot of hard questions in the exam.* **4** °stern, °cold, °callous, intractable, °exacting, °strict, °demanding, hard-hearted, stony-hearted, °severe, °tyrannical, °despotic, °dictatorial, magisterial, °oppressive, °cruel, °ruthless, pitiless, °merciless, °savage, °brutal, brutish, °inhuman, °heartless, °harsh, °unkind, °implacable, °unsympathetic, °dispassionate, uncompassionate, unfeeling, obdurate, indurate; unsentimental, insensitive, °thick-skinned, °tough, hard-boiled, °stony, hardbitten, unfeeling, unsparing: *Hemel is a hard taskmaster. Of the prison warders, each was harder than the next. He advocates taking a hard line against white-collar crime.* **5** °bad, °difficult, °grievous, °calamitous, racking, °disastrous, °dark, °grim, distressing, °devastating, °agonizing, °painful, unpleasant, °severe, austere, *Colloq* °tough, °rough: *The years of the Great Depression were hard for everyone.* **6** °cool, unemotional, °calculating, uncompromising, °methodical, °critical, °systematic, °practical, pragmatic, businesslike, °realistic, °penetrating, searching, hard-headed, *Colloq* °tough, hard-nosed: *Shareholders should take a hard look at the annual report. Chapelle drives a hard bargain.* **7** sedulous, assiduous, °devoted, °conscientious, °industrious, indefatigable, °untiring, °persistent, dogged, °intent, °eager, zealous, °ardent, °energetic, °keen, avid: *Galpin is a very hard worker who gets a lot done.* **8** °cold, °bare, °plain, °straight, straightforward, °blunt, °unvarnished, °unquestionable, verifiable, °real, °indisputable, undeniable, incontestable, °incontrovertible, °strict, inescapable, ineluctable, °unavoidable, unalterable, immutable: *The hard fact is that the bill has never been paid.* **9** °angry, °bitter, acrimonious, °hostile, antagonistic, °harsh, unpleasant, unfriendly: *I'm afraid there were some hard words between us.* **10** spirituous, °alcoholic, °strong: *She won't touch hard liquor.* **11** addictive, habit-forming: *He later changed from marijuana to hard drugs.* **12** °sharp, well-defined, °clear, °distinct, °stark, °definite: *Note the hard edges of objects in Realist paintings.*
—*adv.* **13** °vigorously, forcefully, forcibly, energetically, mightily, arduously, laboriously, strenuously, earnestly, actively, dynamically, eagerly, intensely, ardently, heartily, zealously, °intently, spiritedly, diligently, assiduously, sedulously, studiously, determinedly, steadfastly, conscientiously, industriously, devotedly, urgently, persistently, untiringly, indefatigably, perseveringly, unfalteringly, relentlessly, doggedly: *They always had to work very hard just to scrape by. He's hard at work writing his new book.* **14** violently, °deeply, intensely, °badly, distressingly, °painfully, °severely, agonizingly: *Failing the examination hit him quite hard.* **15** °intently, carefully, earnestly: *The judge thought long and hard before passing sentence.* **16** harshly, °severely, °badly, °ill: *It's going to go hard with her if she doesn't change her ways.* **17** ***hard up***: °poor, °indigent, poverty-stricken, °impoverished, penniless, impecunious, bankrupt, *Colloq* in the red, °broke, bust(ed), on one's uppers, *Slang Brit* skint: *He's so hard up he can't afford a decent meal.*

harden *v.* **1** °set, °solidify, °stiffen, °freeze: *The concrete will harden overnight.* **2** °intensify, °strengthen, °brace, °fortify, toughen, °reinforce, °stiffen: *The opposition have hardened their stand against privatization.*

hardly *adv.* °scarcely, °barely, °only, °just, °only °just; not quite, by no °means; °seldom, °rarely: *I hardly knew her. There was hardly enough to eat. He hardly ever visits his old mum any more.*

hardship *n.* °want, °privation, deprivation, °suffering, °misery, °distress, °affliction, adversity, austerity, °misfortune, unhappiness, ill fortune, bad luck, °difficulty, °trouble: *The hardship of frontier life has never been fully described.*

hardware *n.* **1** °tools, metal goods, *Brit* ironmongery: *Go down to the hardware shop for some nails.* **2** (computer) °equipment, components, °devices, machinery; arms, munitions, armament(s), *matériel: We need the personnel to operate the hardware.*

hardy *adj.* **1** °robust, °sturdy, °strong, °rugged, °tough, °durable, °sound, °stalwart, °stout, °vigorous, able-bodied, red-blooded, °fit, °hale, °healthy, *Colloq* °husky: *The pioneers were hardy souls.* **2** °bold, °courageous, °daring, valorous, valiant, °brave, °manly, °intrepid, °fearless, °heroic, plucky: *He was among the hardy sailors who went with Magellan.*

hare-brained *adj.* **1** °rash, °foolhardy, °wild, madcap, °reckless, °heedless, °improvident, °visionary, °fanciful, airy, *Colloq* crackpot: *Don't put money into any of Zenobia's hare-brained schemes.* **2** °foolish, °silly, °inane, asinine, °flighty, witless, brainless, °mindless, °giddy, °frivolous, °scatterbrained: *Such hare-brained behaviour is not expected in two sober adults.*

harm *n.* **1** °injury, °damage, °mischief, °hurt, °abuse, °misfortune: *A bodyguard was hired to see that no harm would come to her.* **2** °evil, wrongdoing, wickedness, iniquity, °wrong, badness: *I meant no harm when I told Phoebe that her husband was having dinner with Kathy.*
—*v.* **3** °hurt, °damage, °injure, °abuse, maltreat, °wound: *She insists that her pet viper would never harm her.*

harmful *adj.* °dangerous, pernicious, deleterious, °destructive, damaging, °bad, °detrimental, °injurious; °unhealthy, noxious, baleful, toxic, °poisonous, °venomous, *Archaic* baneful: *Do you really think that Barbara has had a harmful influence on him? That substance can be harmful if swallowed.*

harmless *adj.* °benign, innocuous, °inoffensive, °gentle, °mild, °innocent, °safe; non-toxic, non-poisonous, non-venomous: *Pay no attention to such harmless gossip. It is impossible to identify harmless snakes by sight.*

harmonious *adj.* °agreeable, compatible, congruous, consonant, in °accord, congenial, complementary, °sympathetic, concordant, Colloq *simpatico: Our careers have always been harmonious.*

harmony *n.* **1** °agreement, °accord, concord, compatibility, °rapport, unanimity, °unity: *The purpose is to promote harmony among the warring factions.* **2** consonance, congruity, °balance, orderliness, closeness, togetherness, consistency, °fitness, parallelism: *A sense of harmony can be felt among the European nations.* **3** melodiousness, euphony, tunefulness: *Their voices are in perfect harmony.*

harrowing *adj.* distressing, vexing, alarming, unnerving, °frightening, °terrifying, horrifying, °horrible, torturous, chilling, °heart-rending, °nerve-racking *or* nerve-wracking, °traumatic, °agonizing, °painful; °disturbing, upsetting, worrying, worrisome, °disconcerting, daunting, dismaying, disquieting: *Waiting for the rescue team to release me was a harrowing experience.*

harsh *adj.* **1** °rough, °coarse, bristly, °scratchy, °hairy, °crude; hoarse, °grating, °raucous, rasping, °husky, guttural; clashing, inharmonious *or* unharmonious, °discordant, atonal, dissonant, cacophonous, °strident, °shrill, grinding, °sour; °bitter, acrid: *He found harsh the sights, sounds, tastes, and smells of the Casbah.* **2** °stern, austere, °bleak, °dour, °unkind, unfeeling, comfortless, uncompassionate, unfriendly, °grim, °hard, °Spartan, stringent, over-exacting, Draconian, °tyrannical, °stark, °severe, °cruel, °abusive, °punishing, °punitive, °brutal, brutish, °inhuman, °merciless, °ruthless, pitiless: *Simon is a very harsh taskmaster.* **3** unpleasant, °disagreeable, °impolite, °discourteous, uncivil, °rude, °nasty, °curt, °abrupt, °brusque, °bluff, °gruff, curmudgeonly, choleric, splenetic, °surly,

°sullen, irascible, °short-tempered, °petulant, °peevish, °waspish, grouchy, °bilious, °cross, acrimonious, °sarcastic, acerbic: *Why is Maria so harsh to Alan?*

harvest *n.* **1** crop, °yield, °produce, °output, °fruit; °vintage: *If we get enough rain, the harvest should be good this year.*
—*v.* **2** °reap, °gather, °pick, glean, °collect: *The oranges are harvested while they are still greenish.* **3** °earn, °make, °take in, °collect, °garner, °get, °receive, °obtain, °procure, °net: *They harvest huge profits from slot machines.*

hash *n.* **1** °mixture, °confusion, °hotchpotch *or US and Canadian* hodgepodge, °pot-pourri, gallimaufry, farrago, °mishmash, °jumble, °mess, °shambles, olla podrida, mélange, °medley: *The building is a hash of a dozen architectural styles.* **2** °fiasco, °disaster, °botch, °mess, *Slang Brit* balls-up, *US* snafu: *The council really made a hash of its housing policy.*
—*v.* **3** Often, ***hash up***: °mangle, °mess *or* °mix up, make a hash *or* °mess *or* °jumble of, °muddle, °bungle, °botch, °mishandle, mismanage, °ruin, °spoil, °butcher, *Colloq* °foul *or* louse up, °screw up, muff, *Brit* °bugger up: *Our plans for a holiday have been all hashed up.*

haste *n.* **1** swiftness, °rapidity, quickness, °speed, °velocity, °expedition, °urgency, °dispatch *or* despatch, alacrity, celerity, briskness: *We must return to Baker Street with all haste, Watson.* **2** °hurry, °rush, rashness, hastiness, °hustle, bustle, impetuousness *or* impetuosity, recklessness, precipitancy: *Haste makes waste.*

hasten *v.* **1** °hurry, °rush, make °haste, °fly, °run, sprint, °race, °bolt, °dash, °scurry, scamper, scuttle, °speed: *He hastened forward to greet her.* **2** °hurry (up), °speed (up), °dispatch *or* despatch, °send, °move, °quicken, accelerate, °expedite, °rush, impel, °urge: *Is there any way to hasten delivery of the mail?*

hastily *adv.* **1** °quickly, speedily, °swiftly, °rapidly, at °once, °immediately, °instantaneously, °promptly, without °delay, °right away, °straight away, °post-haste, hurriedly, °directly, °suddenly, in °haste, precipitately, on the °spur of the moment, in a °flash *or* wink, before you can say 'Jack Robinson', *Colloq* pronto, like a °shot, like greased lightning, *US* lickety-split, *Slang* p.d.q. (= 'pretty damned quick'): *She left hastily when I asked for the return of the loan.* **2** impetuously, impulsively, rashly, recklessly, unthinkingly, thoughtlessly, heedlessly, incautiously: *This is a trick question, so don't answer hastily.*

hasty *adj.* **1** quick, °speedy, °swift, °rapid, °fast, °brisk, °prompt, °immediate, instantaneous: *He made a hasty departure so as not to be late.* **2** °careless, °rash, °precipitate, °impetuous, °impulsive, °reckless, °thoughtless, °unthinking, incautious, °heedless, ill-considered, °inconsiderate: *His was a hasty decision.* **3** °quick, °speedy, °cursory, °superficial, °fleeting, °passing, slapdash, °perfunctory, °momentary, °brief: *I had a hasty look at the contract, which seemed all right.* **4** °irritable, °quick-tempered, irascible, °testy, °passionate, °impatient, hot-tempered, °petulant, °waspish, °volatile, contentious, choleric, splenetic, bearish, °short-tempered, *US and Canadian and Irish* °cranky: *Grandfather needn't have been so hasty with the poor child.*

hatch *v.* **1** °breed, °brood, °incubate, °bring forth: *The normal clutch of three eggs is hatched in a fortnight.* **2** °devise, contrive, concoct, °design, °formulate, °originate, °invent, °dream up, *Colloq* cook up: *Two of them hatched a scheme to discredit me.*

hate *v.* **1** °loathe, °abhor, °detest, have an °aversion to, be °averse to, abominate, °dislike, execrate, °despise, °scorn: *I hate the smell of petrol, it really turns my stomach.* **2** be °loath, be °reluctant *or* unwilling *or* °disinclined; °resist, °shrink *or* °flinch from, °dislike: *I hate to tell you what I really think. She hated revealing Bill's affair to his wife.*
—*n.* **3** hatred, abhorrence, °loathing, odium, °animosity, animus, antipathy, °aversion, °hostility, °antagonism, malice, enmity, detestation: *He didn't believe he could feel so much hate for one person.*

hateful *adj.* **1** °loathsome, detestable, °abhorrent, horrid, °horrible, °abominable, odious, execrable, °despicable, °scurvy, °obnoxious, heinous, °foul, °contemptible, °repugnant, °repulsive, °repellent, °revolting, °vile: *No vice is universally so hateful as ingratitude.* **2** °malignant, malefic, malevolent, malicious, °evil, °mean, °spiteful, °contemptuous: *She gave me a hateful glance.*

haughty *adj.* °arrogant, °proud, °superior, °self-important, °smug, self-satisfied, complacent, °pretentious, °conceited, °egotistical, °snobbish, °overbearing, °lofty, °presumptuous, overweening, patronizing, °supercilious, °vain, °condescending, °contemptuous, belittling, derisive, °disdainful, °scornful, *Colloq* highfalutin *or* hifalutin, °hoity-toity, stuck-up, swell-headed *or* swelled-headed *or* swollen-headed, °high and °mighty, on (his *or* her) high horse, snooty, la-di-da *or* lah-di-dah *or* la-de-da, *Slang* snotty, °uppish, uppity: *She's too haughty to have made any friends here.*

haul *v.* **1** °drag, °pull, °tug, °tow, °trail, °lug, °heave, °draw: *Are you sure that one horse can haul that load?* **2** °cart, °transport, °carry, convey, °truck, °move: *The new vehicles are equipped to haul bulk dry goods.*
—*n.* **3** °pull, °tug, °drag, °draw; °heave; °attraction: *The tides are greater under the haul of both sun and moon.* **4** catch, °take, °yield, °harvest, °bag: *We returned with quite a good haul of cod.*

haunt *v.* **1** °visit, °frequent, °hang about *or* around, °spend °time at, *US* habituate: *She haunts the yacht club, waiting for her ship to come in.* **2** °beset, °obsess, °plague, °torment, °trouble, °possess, °prey on: *He is haunted by the fear that she told the police everything.*
—*n.* **3** gathering-place, meeting-place, stamping-ground, *Colloq* hang-out: *She returned to Abergavenny to visit the haunts of her youth.*

have *v.* **1** °possess, own, °keep; °maintain: *Imelda had more shoes than you could count.* **2** °receive, °take, °accept, °get, °obtain, °acquire, °procure, °secure: *How many gifts did you say she had from him?* **3** °entertain, be struck by: *I have an idea!* **4** °possess, °bear, °contain, °include, comprise: *The night has a thousand eyes.* **5** °suffer with *or* from, be °suffering with *or* from, be experiencing, be undergoing, be °enduring, be subjected to: *My daughter was really ill when she had measles.* **6** °arrange, °organize, °set up, °prepare; °hold: *If I have a party, will you come? We shall have our next meeting on Saturday.* **7** °partake of, °participate in, °experience, °enjoy; °eat; °drink: *I hope you have a good time.* **8** give birth to, °bear, °deliver, °bring into the world; beget, sire, °father: *She had three children in as many years. How many children has he had?* **9** °make, °demand; °force, °oblige, °cause, °induce, °press, °require, compel: *We'll have the caterers come at noon.* **10** ***had better*** *or* ***best***: ought to, °must, should: *I had better not drink as I'm driving.* **11** ***had rather*** *or* ***sooner***: °prefer to, would °rather *or* sooner: *I'd rather be with you.* **12** ***have on***: **a** be wearing, be dressed *or* clothed *or* attired in: *I'll have on the silk nightgown you like so much.* **b** be committed to, have planned, have in the offing, have on the agenda: *I have something on next Tuesday evening.* **c** °trick, °tease, °deceive, °pull (someone's) °leg, play a °joke on, °fool: *Do you really love me or are you having me on?*

havoc *n.* **1** °ruin, devastation, °destruction, °desolation, °rack *or* wrack and °ruin, despoliation, spoliation, °damage: *Gales of more than 80 m.p.h. wreaked havoc right across the British Isles.* **2** °confusion, °chaos, °upset, °disorder, °mayhem, °shambles, disruption: *The railway slow-down created havoc with commuter schedules.*

hazard *n.* **1** °peril, °danger, °risk, endangerment, °threat, °jeopardy: *The greatest hazard in sailing single-handed round the world is the loneliness.*

2 °chance, °gamble, uncertainty, °luck, °fortune: *They banned all games that depended on hazard.* —*v.* **3** °venture, °dare; °gamble, °risk, °jeopardize, °endanger, °threaten, imperil, °stake: *May I hazard a guess as to the origin of the word? He hazarded his entire fortune on the turn of a card.*

hazardous *adj.* unsafe, °risky, °fraught with °danger, °questionable, °shaky, °dangerous, °precarious, °uncertain, unpredictable, °parlous, °ticklish, °tricky, *Colloq chiefly Brit* °dicey, °dicky *or* dickey, *Slang* °hairy: *It took three months to make the hazardous overland journey in those days.*

hazy *adj.* **1** °misty, foggy, smoggy, cloudy, °overcast: *It was so hazy that we couldn't see the town a mile away.* **2** °indistinct, blurred, blurry, °dull, °dim, °faint, °nebulous, °vague, unclear, °fuzzy, °indefinite, muddled: *He has only a hazy idea of the plot.*

head *n.* **1** skull, pate, cranium, *Colloq* dome, *Slang* coco(nut), belfry, noggin, bean, nut, rocker, noodle, gourd, *Brit* conk, crumpet, noddle, °loaf: *She laid her head on the pillow and fell sound asleep.* **2** °chief, °leader, administrator, °chief °executive °officer, CEO, (managing) °director, MD, president, chairman, chairwoman, chairperson, °chair, °employer, °principal, °superintendent, °supervisor, governor, °prime °minister, headmaster, headmistress, *Colloq* °boss, headman, the °man, *Brit* guv'nor, guv, *US* (°chief) honcho; *Slang* °big cheese, *US* Mr Big: *The new head has called a meeting of the board of directors.* **3** °front, vanguard, forefront, van, fore-part: *At the head of the column marched the general himself.* **4** °aptitude, °intellect, °intelligence, °talent, °perception, perceptiveness, °mentality, °faculty, °flair, °genius, °brain, °mind, °wit, *Colloq* °brains, grey matter: *I have no head for figures.* **5** °crisis, apex, (°critical *or* turning) °point, °peak, °crest, (fever) °pitch, °climax, culmination, conclusion, crescendo: *Matters have been brought to a head because of the coming elections.* **6** °source, °origin, fount, font, fountain-head, well-spring: *We were trying to reach the head of the stream before nightfall.* **7** °top, °first place, °leading °position, °leadership, forefront: *Albert is at the head of his class in mathematics.* **8** ***head over heels***: °completely, °entirely, °deeply, °utterly, °wholly, fully, *Colloq* °madly, wildly: *The two of them are head over heels in love.* —*adj.* **9** °first, °chief, °main, °principal, °leading, °premier, °foremost, °prime, °pre-eminent, °cardinal, °paramount, °supreme, °superior, °senior: *Alphonse is our new head chef.* —*v.* **10** °go, °move, °proceed, °turn, °steer, °aim, °point, head for, °make a beeline for: *I shall head home when I leave here.* **11** head up, be in *or* take charge (of), °direct, °supervise, °oversee, °control, °govern, °run, (take the) °lead, °guide, °manage, °command, °rule, °administer, °conduct: *Who will head the organization if you resign?* **12** °lead, °precede, °top: *Charlotte heads the list of candidates.* **13** ***head off***: **a** °intercept, °divert; °cut off, °stop, °block: *The cavalry will head them off at the pass.* **b** °stop, °forestall, °prevent, °inhibit, avert, °ward *or* °fend off: *What can we do to head off inflation?*

headache *n.* **1** migraine, *Technical* cephalalgia: *Hazel says she has a headache and cannot come to work today.* **2** °worry, °bother, vexation, °inconvenience, °nuisance, °annoyance, °problem, °difficulty, °trouble, bane, *Colloq* °pain (in the neck), *Slang* °pain in the *Brit* arse *or US* ass: *The balance of payments deficit is a perpetual headache.*

headway *n.* **1** °progress, forward °motion, °improvement: *Headway against that current was almost impossible. Any headway to report?* **2** ***make headway***: °advance, °progress, °move forward, °go, °gain (ground), get *or* go °ahead, °proceed, get going: *I tried to persuade her but haven't made much headway.*

heal *v.* **1** cure, °repair, °renew, revitalize, °rejuvenate, °restore; °mend, °recuperate, °recover, °improve: *The wounds have healed. The ointment healed his wounds. I heal quickly.* **2** °reconcile, °settle, °patch up, °put *or* set straight *or* °right, °remedy, °repair, °mend: *His only wish was to heal the rift with his brother.*

health *n.* **1** °condition, °fitness, °trim, fettle, °form, constitution: *My health has improved enough for me to return to work.* **2** healthiness, haleness, healthfulness, robustness, °vigour, vigorousness, salubrity, salubriousness, well-being, °strength: *The health of the economy is good.*

healthy *adj.* **1** °well, °fit, °trim, in °good *or* °fine fettle *or* °shape, in °good °health, °robust, °hale (and °hearty), °sturdy, °strong, °vigorous, thriving, °flourishing, *Colloq* in the pink: *How come he is so healthy if he smokes?* **2** °wholesome, healthful, salubrious, salutary, °beneficial, nourishing, °nutritious, °tonic, °bracing: *The answer lies in eating healthy food and living in a healthy climate.*

heap *n.* **1** °collection, °pile, °mound, °stack, °accumulation, aggregation, agglomeration, congeries, conglomeration, °hoard, °mass, °store, °mountain, stockpile, °supply, *Colloq US and Canadian* stash: *Donors contributed a huge heap of clothing for the sale.* **2** Often, ***heaps***: °abundance, plethora, superabundance, °lot(s), °plenty, °great °deal, scores, peck, °sea, *Colloq* lashings, °load(s), °piles, ton(s), raft(s), pots, oodles, scad(s), *US and Canadian* slew: *It was served with heaps of chocolate sauce. Heaps of people bought your record. You're in for a heap of trouble.* —*v.* **3** °collect, °gather, °harvest, °reap, glean, °garner, °pile (up), °accumulate, cumulate, aggregate, °amass, stockpile, °save (up), bank, °lay by *or* up *or* in, °set aside, *Colloq* stash (away): *In autumn, squirrels heap up their supplies of nuts for the winter.* **4** °shower, °load, °bestow, °give, °provide, °burden: *The grateful prince heaped us with treasure beyond imagination.*

hear *v.* **1** °perceive, °understand, °listen (to), °attend (to), pay °attention (to), °catch, °heed, hark (to): *Please hear what I have to say first.* **2** °understand, °learn, °discover, °find out, °gather, °get wind of, °pick up, ascertain, be told *or* advised *or* °informed: *I hear you're thinking of resigning.* **3** ***hear of***: °entertain, °consider; °approve (of), °sanction, condone, °agree *or* °consent *or* assent to: *I won't hear of your leaving.*

heart *n.* **1** *Colloq* ticker, °pump: *The doctor says I have a dicky heart.* **2** °stomach, °nerve, °courage, °bravery, mettle, °will, boldness, °pluck, °resolution, °determination; callousness, insensitivity, heartlessness; *Colloq* °guts, °spunk: *I haven't the heart to tell him that his hamster died.* **3** (basic) °nature, °core, °centre, °focus, °hub, °middle, marrow, °pith, °essence, °quintessence, °nucleus, °nub, crux, basics, fundamentals, *Colloq* nitty-gritty: *Let's get down to the heart of the matter.* **4** °sincerity, °sentiment(s), °feeling(s), °spirit, °verve, °enthusiasm: *She's going through the motions, but her heart isn't in her work.* **5** °humanity, humanitarianism, °sympathy, °understanding, °kindness, kindliness, compassion, empathy, goodness, °consideration, °concern, °soul, tenderness, magnanimity, generosity, °sensitivity, °sensibility, °sentiment, °pity, (brotherly) °love, °affection: *Mother Theresa is known for having a lot of heart. Have you no heart, Genghis?*

heartbroken *adj.* °broken-hearted, °downhearted, dispirited, °unhappy, °miserable, grief-stricken, °upset, °dejected, heartsick, crestfallen, °despondent, depressed, disconsolate, distressed, °woebegone, °doleful, °sorrowful, °mournful, morose, disheartened, °disappointed, crushed: *Lucy was heartbroken over the loss of her locket.*

heartfelt *adj.* °sincere, °honest, °genuine, unfeigned, °earnest, °serious, °wholehearted, °deep, °profound, dedicated, °devoted, °ardent, committed, °fervent, fervid, °hearty, °passionate: *It is my heartfelt wish that you should succeed.*

heartless *adj.* °cruel, hard-hearted, °callous, unconcerned, °inhuman, inhumane, °unkind, unfeeling, °unsympathetic, °brutal, °cold, °merciless, pitiless, °ruthless, °cold-blooded: *Taking away the child's toys was a heartless thing to do.*

heart-rending *adj.* °agonizing, distressing, °excruciating, °bitter, °painful, heartbreaking, °harrowing, °piteous, °tragic, depressing, °poignant: *Her distress was heart-rending to behold.*

heart-warming *adj.* **1** °moving, °touching, warming, affecting, uplifting, inspiriting, cheering, encouraging: *I heard the heart-warming news about Alan's recovery.* **2** °satisfying, gratifying, °pleasing, comforting, °pleasurable, °rewarding: *It was heart-warming to see the family together at Christmas.*

hearty *adj.* **1** °genial, °warm, kind-hearted, °affectionate, °amiable, °amicable, °friendly, affable, °cordial, °open, convivial: *I was greeted by a hearty welcome when I returned.* **2** °genuine, unfeigned, °authentic, °sincere, °heartfelt, °warm, °wholehearted, °honest, °earnest, °devout, °stalwart, °stout: *Please give Desmond my hearty congratulations.* **3** °enthusiastic, °vigorous, °energetic, °eager, zealous, °exuberant, °robust, °active, °animated, °strong: *They are hearty supporters of our cause.* **4** °abundant, °ample, °substantial, °solid, sizeable, °satisfying, °square; nourishing, °invigorating, strengthening: *On Sundays, we had a hearty meal at midday when we could afford it.* **5** °healthy, °hale, °vigorous, °robust, °strong, °sound: *Well, Eric, now that you're over your malaria you appear to be quite hearty.*

heat *n.* **1** °warmth, warmness, hotness, fever, fieriness, torridity *or* torridness: *The heat of the sun feels good after that cold swim.* **2** °passion, °ardour, °fervour, fervidness, °intensity, °fury, zeal, zealousness, earnestness, vehemence, °eagerness, °enthusiasm, °excitement, tenseness, °tension, °stress, °agitation, arousal, impetuosity, stimulation, exhilaration: *If I shouted at you in the heat of the moment, I apologize.* —*v.* **3** °warm (up): *It costs a lot to heat this house.* **4** Often, ***heat up***: °excite, °intensify, impassion, °inflame, °kindle, ignite, °quicken, inspirit, °rouse, awaken *or* waken, °stir, °animate, °stimulate, °warm (up), °activate, *Colloq Brit* °hot up: *It took a while for the debate to heat up.*

heated *adj.* °impassioned, °excited, intensified, aroused, quickened, stimulated, °inflamed, vehement, °fiery, frenzied, °frantic, frenetic, °passionate, °fervent, fervid, °ardent, °intense, °furious, °stormy, °tempestuous, °violent; °angry, °bitter: *There was a heated dispute over animal rights, which finally led to blows.*

heathen *n.* **1** unbeliever, °infidel, °pagan, idolater *or* idolatress, polytheist, atheist, nullifidian, °sceptic, agnostic, heretic: *One often finds more mercy in a heathen than in a brother Christian.* —*adj.* **2** °infidel, °pagan, atheist(ic), °godless, nullifidian, °sceptic(al), doubting, agnostic, °heretical, irreligious: *After the missionaries left, the tribe returned to their heathen practices.* **3** °savage, °barbarian, barbaric, °uncivilized, °primitive, unenlightened, uncultured, Philistine; polytheistic, pantheistic: *Each of these tribesmen carries with him a tiny sculptured image of the heathen god.*

heave *v.* **1** °raise, °lift, °hoist, °haul, °pull, °draw, °tug; °move: *We heaved in the anchor and made sail.* **2** °throw, °toss, °hurl, °fling, °cast, °sling, °pitch, let °fly, °send, °launch, *Colloq* °peg, chuck: *When he heaved the sword into the lake a hand rose from the waters and caught it.* **3** °breathe, utter, °sigh, °groan, °moan, °gasp: *We heaved a sigh of relief when we heard that they had been found.* **4** °gag, retch, °vomit, be °sick, °regurgitate, disgorge, *Colloq* °throw up, *Slang* puke, lose one's lunch, return one's dinner, *US* upchuck, spiff one's biscuits: *The smell of petrol always makes me heave.*

heaven *n.* **1** °paradise, °bliss, hereafter, nirvana, Abraham's °bosom, Elysian Fields *or* Elysium, Valhalla, Zion, °happy hunting-grounds, Avalon, Isles of the Blessed, the Blessed *or* Fortunate *or* Happy Isles *or* Islands: *Will I go to heaven when I die?* **2** ***heavens***: °sky, skies, °firmament, *Literary* welkin, empyrean: *The heavens opened and the rain started to pour down.* **3** °happiness, °bliss, °joy, °rapture, °ecstasy, °paradise, contentment, seventh heaven, Eden, Garden of Eden, °Utopia, heaven on earth, °paradise on earth: *Darby said that his years with Joan had been sheer heaven.*

heavenly *adj.* **1** °divine, angelic, °seraphic, °celestial, °holy, °immortal, blessed, beatific, beatified, °spiritual, °saintly; supernal, °unearthly, other-worldly, ultramundane, extramundane, extraterrestrial: *Alone on the mountain, she heard a heavenly voice calling her name.* **2** °delightful, wonderful, °marvellous, °sublime, paradisiac(al) *or* paradisaic(al), °glorious, °splendid, °superb, °exquisite, °perfect, °ideal, °excellent, °fantastic, °rapturous, entrancing, blissful, *Colloq* °gorgeous, °divine, smashing, °great: *André's serves a perfectly heavenly lobster thermidor.*

heavy *adj.* **1** °weighty, °ponderous, °massive, *Literary* massy; °compact, °dense: *This box is much too heavy for me to lift.* **2** °abundant, overflowing, °excessive, copious, °profuse, °prodigious, °ample, unmanageable: *We just crawled along in the heavy traffic.* **3** °serious, °grave, °important, °crucial, °critical, °acute: *You always bring up heavy topics at the end of the meeting.* **4** °burdensome, onerous, °oppressive, °weighty, °unbearable, °severe, °grievous, distressful, °sore, intolerable, insupportable *or* unsupportable, °awful: *Teenagers often feel that they are weighed down with heavy responsibilities.* **5** °sad, °sorrowful, distressing, °grievous, upsetting, depressing, °gloomy, °sombre, °melancholy: *Some heavy news has been received from the front.* **6** °unhappy, °miserable, depressed, °melancholy, grieving, °sad, °dejected, °downhearted, disconsolate, downcast, °despondent, °gloomy, heavy-hearted, morose, crestfallen, cheerless: *Heavy at heart, he returned to his cheerless home.* **7** °ponderous, °tedious, °monotonous, °boring, uninteresting, °leaden, °dull, °prosaic, °dry, dry-as-dust, °stodgy, °staid, °stuffy, stifling, stultifying: *The critics found the style much too heavy for the subject being treated.* **8** °thick, °coarse, °broad, °blunt, °clumsy, °ungraceful: *These heavy brush-strokes prove that the painting is not a Turner.* **9** °gloomy, cloudy, °overcast, °bleak, °dismal, °dreary, °leaden, °grey, °dark, louring *or* lowering, °threatening: *it was another of Scotland's heavy February days.* **10** °intense, concentrated, °severe, °forceful, °violent, °torrential: *The snowfall was the heaviest of the year.* **11** overweight, °fat, °obese, °stout, °chubby, °plump, corpulent, portly, paunchy, tubby, *Brit* podgy *or US* pudgy, *Colloq* beer-bellied: *The doctor did not say I was too heavy, only that I ought to be six inches taller.* **12** °weighty, °difficult, complex, °recondite, arcane, °deep, °profound, esoteric, °incomprehensible, impenetrable, unfathomable: *He specializes in some heavy subject like micro-palaeontology.* **13** burdened, laden, encumbered, °loaded, overloaded, weighed down: *We spied two Indiamen, heavy with cargoes of spices, sailing towards us.*

heavy-handed *adj.* **1** °awkward, °clumsy, °inept, maladroit, unskilful, °ungraceful, graceless, bungling: *She made a heavy-handed attempt to apologize.* **2** autocratic, imperious, magisterial, °overbearing, °despotic, °dictatorial, °tyrannical, °oppressive, °domineering, iron-handed, °harsh, °severe: *For more than 30 years he exercised heavy-handed control over the country.*

heckle *v.* badger, °pester, °annoy, °irritate, °bother, nettle, bait, °harass, harry, °plague, hector, °taunt, °jeer, *Colloq* hassle, °bug, *Brit and Australian and New Zealand* barrack: *One man kept heckling the speaker with persistent interruptions.*

hectic *adj.* °feverish, °excited, °agitated, °busy, bustling, rushed, hyperactive, over-active, frenzied, °frantic, °chaotic, °wild, °mad, frenetic, °riotous: *What with the new baby and everyone else having the flu, I've had a pretty hectic week.*

heed *v.* **1** pay °attention to, °attend, (take *or* make) °note (of), °listen to, °mark, °consider, bear in °mind; °take, °follow, °obey, °mind, °respect, °accept, °abide by: *I wish I had heeded her suggestions for redecorating the house. Heeding his advice, I joined the army.* —*n.* **2** °attention, °notice, °ear, °mind, °respect, °consideration, °thought: *Let us give heed to the speaker's admonitions.*

heedless *adj.* °inattentive, uncaring, unmindful, neglectful, unobservant, °regardless; °oblivious, °deaf, °blind: *Heedless of tradition, they replaced the older buildings with council housing.*

heel[1] *n.* **1** °end, °butt *or* °tail *or* °fag(-°end), °stump, °remainder, °remnant, °rind, crust: *You can always freeze the heel of a loaf to use at some later date for breadcrumbs.* **2** cad, °scoundrel, swine, °rogue, scamp, °philanderer, *Old-fashioned* worm, knave, *Chiefly Brit* blackguard, *Colloq Brit* rotter, *Old-fashioned* bounder, *Slang* bastard, *Brit* sod: *He's an absolute heel—he got her pregnant and then left her.* **3** ***down at heel***: *US also* down at the heels; °poor, °destitute, °impoverished, down and out, on (one's) uppers, in °straitened circumstances; °shabby, °seedy, °dowdy, °run-down, slovenly, *Brit* out at elbows, *US* out at the elbows, *Colloq* °broke, strapped: *Farrington looked down at heel, so I slipped him a fiver.* **4** ***take to (one's) heels***: take °flight, °flee, °escape, °run off *or* away, show a clean pair of heels, *Colloq* °split, *Brit* do a moonlight °flit, *US* take a (run-out) powder, °fly the coop, *Australian and New Zealand* °shoot through: *When I mentioned payment, she took to her heels.*
—*v.* **5** dog, °follow (closely), °shadow, °chase, °pursue: *We have taught our puppy to heel.*

heel[2] *v.* °list, °lean (over), °tilt, °tip, °incline: *The boat heeled as we turned to beat into the wind.*

hefty *adj.* **1** °big, °large, °bulky, cumbersome, °awkward, °unwieldy, °clumsy, °substantial, °massive: *That's a pretty hefty box for one person to carry.* **2** °brawny, °strong, °powerful, °burly, °muscular, strapping, °rugged, °robust, *Colloq* °husky, beefy: *That hefty man over there is the Olympic weight-lifting champion.* **3** °substantial, °considerable, sizeable, °impressive, °enormous, °huge, *Colloq* °thumping *or Brit* socking °great: *I've just received a hefty increase in salary.*

height *n.* **1** altitude, °elevation, °level; tallness: *At what height is the second camp on Mount Everest? The height of the skyscrapers impressed me.* **2** °acme, °crest, °pinnacle, °top, °zenith, apogee, °peak, apex, °maximum, °high °point, °summit, °climax, culmination, °extreme: *Popularity of that style reached its height in the 1930s. His remark reflected the height of arrogance.* **3** Often, ***heights***: °elevation, °mound, °hill, eminence, °prominence, °mountain, °peak, °crag, °summit; tor, °cliff, °bluff, promontory, escarpment, scarp, headland, *No. Eng. and Scots* fell: *As we gazed down from the heights, the villages seemed tiny.*

heighten *v.* **1** °raise, elevate, °build up, °increase, °lift (up), upraise: *A white ceiling gives the effect of heightening a room.* **2** °intensify, °deepen, °strengthen, °reinforce, °amplify, °magnify, °increase, °enhance, augment, °add to, °supplement: *Adding some blue heightens the effect. The bribery scandal has only heightened distrust of the ruling party.*

heir *n.* heiress, beneficiary, inheritor, legatee, successor: *What if you are not the rightful heir to the estate?*

hell *n.* **1** Erebus, Hades, Acheron, Tartarus, Gehenna, Tophet, Abaddon, Pandemonium, Dis, Sheol, Avernus, °underworld, °infernal regions, °abyss, abode of the damned, inferno, hell-fire, lower world, nether regions, bottomless °pit, other place: *For his sins he was condemned to everlasting hell.* **2** °chaos, °misery, °torment, °agony, torture, °ordeal, nightmare, °trial: *The office has been an absolute hell since you left.* **3** °anguish, °pain, °agony, °torment, torture, °misery, °suffering, °affliction: *We have been through hell since Grenville's heart attack.* **4** °criticism, censure; scolding, castigation, °reprimand, upbraiding: *My mother gave me hell for getting home late.*

helm *n.* **1** tiller, °wheel, rudder, steering gear *or* apparatus: *I had to put the helm over hard to avoid hitting the pier.* **2** directorship, presidency, chairmanship, °leadership, °control, °rule, °command, *Colloq* driver's seat, saddle: *Arthur remained at the helm of the company for 40 years.*

help *v.* **1** °aid, °assist, °lend a hand, °support, °serve; succour: *Let me help you carry that package, Mrs Smith. His charitable efforts have long helped the poor.* **2** °relieve, alleviate, °mitigate, °improve, °facilitate, °ease, °better, °remedy, °cure: *Complaining about it won't help the situation.* **3** °stop, °refrain from, °avoid, eschew, °resist, °keep from, forbear, °escape: *I know it was a secret but I couldn't help telling Sam.* **4** °assist, °serve, °advise, °inform: *May I help you, sir?* **5** ***help oneself***: °appropriate, °take, arrogate, commandeer, expropriate; °steal, purloin, usurp, plagiarize, °pirate, *Colloq* °pinch, °lift, *Brit* °nick, *US* °boost: *She helped herself to some money from the till.*
—*n.* **6** °aid, °support, succour, °assistance: *I need help in solving this problem.* **7** °employee(s), °worker(s), °staff, helper(s), °hand(s), °assistant(s), °labourer(s), °domestic(s), °servant(s), *Brit* °daily (help): *We have to hire more help to finish on time.* **8** °supporter, °aide, °assistant, helper: *You have been a great help to me.* **9** °relief, °remedy, °cure, balm: *This ointment has been a great help in stopping the itching.*

helpful *adj.* °useful, °serviceable, °practical, pragmatic, utilitarian, °beneficial, valuable, °profitable, °advantageous, °constructive, °productive; °supportive, reassuring, °sympathetic, °considerate, caring, °accommodating, °kind, cooperative, °neighbourly, °friendly, °benevolent: *A reference book might be helpful in answering that question. Mrs Carlyle gave me such helpful advice.*

helping *n.* serving, °portion, °ration, plateful, *Brit* help, *Colloq* dollop: *He has already asked for a third helping of potatoes.*

helpless *adj.* **1** dependent, °vulnerable, °weak, °helpless, °feeble, °infirm, °lame, °crippled, °disabled: *The disease has left him completely helpless.* **2** °confused, baffled, mystified, bewildered, perplexed, at °sea, confounded, muddled, nonplussed: *I am completely helpless when it comes to balancing my accounts.* **3** weakened, °weak, debilitated, °faint, enfeebled, °feeble, °worn out, °spent, °exhausted, °prostrate, enervated: *All of us were simply helpless from laughing so much.* **4** °worthless, °incapable, °incompetent, °useless, unavailing, °inefficient, °inept, unfit, °unqualified: *Dali was said to be helpless without Gala to manage his affairs.*

helter-skelter *adj.* **1** °disorderly, disorganized, °confused, muddled, °haphazard, °careless, jumbled, °random, °topsy-turvy, *Colloq* higgledy-piggledy: *How can one find anything in this helter-skelter mess?*
—*adv.* **2** confusedly, °pell-mell, in all directions, recklessly, unsystematically, chaotically, erratically, aimlessly, *US* every which way, *Colloq* higgledy-piggledy: *When the giant appeared, the children ran away, helter-skelter.*

hence *adv.* **1** °therefore, °consequently, °thus, °accordingly, ergo, as a °result, for that *or* this °reason: *She has homework to do, hence cannot go to the cinema.* **2** away, from here *or* this place: *Get thee hence, you wicked witch!* **3** from °now, in the °future: *Where will I be two years hence?*

henceforth *adv.* hereafter, henceforward, from °now on, *Colloq US* from here on out: *Henceforth, make no more personal remarks.*

henchman *n.* (fellow-) mobster *or* °gangster *or* °hoodlum, °gangster, bodyguard, myrmidon, right-hand man, °associate, °attendant, °follower, °supporter, confidant, crony, *Colloq* sidekick, hooligan, *Brit* °minder, *US* buddy, °cohort; *Slang* °heavy, *US* torpedo, gunsel, goon: *Mr Big strutted in with his henchmen and wrecked the place.*

henpeck *v.* °nag, °harass, hector, °pester, °torment, °bully, °carp, °cavil: *She henpecked him so much that he finally left her.*

herd *n.* **1** °group, °pack, °bunch, °cluster, °flock, °crowd, multitude, °host, horde, °throng, °mass, °swarm, °press, °crush; assemblage, °collection: *A herd of protesters gathered before the embassy.* **2** °common °herd, °rabble, hoi polloi, great °unwashed, °riff-raff,

°masses: *How can you expect the herd to understand these principles?*
—*v.* **3** °gather, congregate, °flock, °assemble, °collect: *The reporters herded round to interview the minister.* **4** °round up, °gather (together), °shepherd, °drive, *W US and Canadian* wrangle, corral: *Herd those cattle into the pen.*

hereditary *adj.* **1** heritable, inheritable, transmissible, transferable *or* transferrable, inherited, genetic, congenital, °inborn, innate; atavistic: *Green eyes and red hair are hereditary in our family.* **2** °traditional, handed down, inherited, bequeathed, willed; ancestral: *Priesthood was hereditary among Aaron's descendants. These are the hereditary lands that go with the castle.*

heretical *adj.* °unorthodox, heterodox, °impious, freethinking, heretic, apostate *or* apostatical, iconoclastic, °schismatic, °sceptic, agnostic, atheist(ic), idolatrous, °heathen, °pagan, °infidel, °godless: *The purpose of the Inquisition was to discover and suppress heretical views.*

heritage *n.* **1** °estate, °inheritance, legacy, patrimony, birthright: *The manor-house was included in the heritage that was passed on to me.* **2** °tradition: *The documentary examines our cultural heritage.*

hermetic *adj.* hermetical, airtight, sealed; impervious: *If the hermetic seal is broken, sterility is not guaranteed.*

hermit *n.* °recluse, eremite, anchorite *or* anchoret *or* anchoress, °solitary, stylite: *He has retired from the world to become a hermit.*

hero *n.* **1** °heroine, °champion, exemplar, °star, superstar, °idol, °ideal, man of the hour, luminary, °notable, °celebrity; knight, paladin, warrior: *She was a hero to every aspiring woman lawyer. She expects a hero in shining armour on a white horse to sweep her off her feet.* **2** °protagonist, (male) °lead *or* °star, °leading man *or* actor, °principal: *Gérard Depardieu plays the hero in this lavishly produced film.*

heroic *adj.* **1** °brave, °courageous, °bold, valiant, valorous, undaunted, °dauntless, stout-hearted, °noble, °intrepid, °gallant, °chivalrous, °daring, plucky, °audacious, °fearless, °manly, virile, manful: *We published a book about Aylesworthy's heroic exploits.* **2** °noble, altruistic, magnanimous, °generous, upstanding, °honourable, °virtuous, °staunch, °steadfast, °stalwart, °determined: *This plaque commemorates Manzanilla's heroic work in curbing religious persecution.* **3** °desperate, °drastic, °extreme: *Despite heroic efforts, it was impossible to rescue the entire crew.* **4** °grand, larger than life, exaggerated, magniloquent, °grandiose, °extravagant; °giant, °gigantic, °enormous, °huge, titanic, °colossal, stupendous: *The heroic phrases of the demagogue still ring in my ears. Statues of heroic proportions have been moved from Abu Simbel.* **5** mythological, epic, Homeric, °legendary, °classical, °fabulous, wonderful, °miraculous: *He enjoyed tales of heroic demigods like Hercules.* **6** °majestic, °lofty, °elevated, °grand, august, °towering, °eminent, °distinguished, °prominent: *The entire court was silent as the heroic figure of the emperor entered.*

heroine *n.* (female) °lead, °leading actress *or* lady, prima donna *or* ballerina, *première danseuse*, diva: *The heroine was played by Mme Kropeczka.*

hesitant *adj.* **1** hesitating, undecided, °uncertain, °unsettled, °irresolute, vacillating, shilly-shallying, dithering, fluctuating, wavering, °unresolved, ambivalent, in *or* of two minds, °indefinite, *Brit* havering: *He was hesitant about whether to buy the blue or the green model.* **2** °halting, stammering, stuttering, faltering: *From her hesitant speech I'd say she was nervous.*

hesitate *v.* **1** °delay, °hold *or* °hang back, °pause, dilly-dally, °wait, temporize, think twice, balk, boggle at, °shrink from, demur, °scruple, *Brit* haver, jib, *Colloq* °stall: *He who hesitates is lost.* **2** °fumble, °equivocate, tergiversate, °fluctuate, °alternate, waver, dither, vacillate, °shilly-shally: *He hesitated between the doors—did this one conceal the lady or the tiger?* **3** °stammer, stutter, falter, sputter, splutter, °stumble, hem and haw: *She hesitated throughout the speech purely from stage fright.*

hidden *adj.* concealed, °secret, °obscure(d), °occult, °veiled, °cryptic, °recondite, arcane, covert, esoteric, unseen, °private: *Was this an ordinary shopping list or did it have some hidden meaning?*

hide[1] *v.* **1** °conceal, °secrete, °cache, squirrel away; °go °underground, take °cover, °lie low, go into hiding, °lurk, go to ground, drop out of °sight, hibernate, latibulize, *Colloq* °hide out, °hole up, °lie low, *Brit* °lie doggo: *Hide the sweets where the children won't find them. I found a place to hide under the stair.* **2** °conceal, °cover, °mask, °camouflage, °disguise, °veil, °shroud, °screen, °cover up, keep °secret: *He managed to hide his embarrassment.* **3** °eclipse, °blot out, °obscure, °block: *The clouds hid the moon as we made good our escape.* **4** °suppress, °hush (up), °repress, °silence, keep quiet *or* °secret: *She hid all knowledge of the crime.*

hide[2] *n.* **1** °pelt, °skin, °fell, leather, fur, °fleece: *Once tanned and dyed, the hide was made into clothing.*
—*v.* **2** °flog, °whip, °lash, flail, °beat, thrash: *The masters took great satisfaction in hiding the boys.*

hideaway *n.* °refuge, °retreat, °sanctuary, hide-out, hiding-place, °lair, (°safe) haven, *Colloq* °hole, *Brit* hidey-hole *or* hidy-hole: *My brother and I would crawl into our hideaway and pretend we were being held prisoner by pirates.*

hidebound *adj.* °strait-laced, °conventional, ultra-conventional, °conservative, °reactionary, °rigid, °set (in one's ways), °narrow-minded, close-minded, °inflexible, intractable, uncompromising, restricted, °cramped, °bigoted, °intolerant: *She's too much of a hidebound disciplinarian to rescind the punishment.*

hideous *adj.* **1** °grotesque, °ugly, °repulsive, °revolting, °repellent, °monstrous, °beastly, gorgonian, °unsightly, °ghastly, °disgusting, °grisly, nauseating, °nauseous, sickening, °gruesome: *Suddenly, a hideous face appeared at the kitchen window.* **2** °foul, °abhorrent, heinous, horrifying, appalling, °outrageous, °abominable, °vile, °shocking, °loathsome, °contemptible, °hateful, odious, °atrocious, horrific, °beastly, °damnable, execrable: *Two hideous crimes were committed here last night.*

high *adj.* **1** °tall, °lofty, °elevated, °towering: *High mountains surround the valley.* **2** °extreme, °excessive, °extraordinary, °exorbitant, °outrageous, *Colloq* °steep, °stiff: *Houses in that district are fetching high prices.* **3** costly, °dear, °expensive, high-priced: *Shares are not as high as they were before the crash.* **4** °great, °huge, °enormous, °considerable, °strong; °violent, turbulent: *These wires carry high voltages. The high winds blew down trees.* **5** °exalted, °elevated, °lofty, °superior, °high-class: *With insider trading, theft became a high art in the financial world.* **6** consequential, °important, °grave, °serious, °weighty, °momentous, heinous; °capital: *His activities constitute high treason.* **7** high-pitched, high-frequency, squeaky, °acute, treble, soprano; °shrill, °strident, °sharp, °penetrating, °piercing, ear-splitting: *The higher notes make my radio speaker vibrate. She has an irritatingly high voice.* **8** °cheerful, °exuberant, °elated, °boisterous, exhilarated, °hilarious, °merry, °excited: *I find his persistent high spirits rather depressing.* **9** euphoric, intoxicated, inebriated, °drunk, drugged, *Colloq* °loaded, tipsy, turned on, on a °trip, *Slang* stoned, spaced out, *Brit* squiffy, *US* spacy, squiffed: *They got high sniffing glue.* **10** gamy, tainted, °aged, °ripe, *Slang Brit* pongy: *He likes to hang venison till it is quite high.* **11** °chief, °leading, °important, °principal, °foremost: *He regards himself as the high priest of women's fashion.* **12** °elaborate, °luxurious, °grand, °extravagant, °lavish, °rich, °prodigal, sybaritic: *With her millions she can now enjoy the high life.* **13** °considerable, °favourable, °great: *She is held in high esteem by her colleagues.*
—*adv.* **14** °far up; °great in °extent: *Daedalus warned Icarus not to fly so high. I was willing to go as high as 20,000 for the painting.*

—*n.* **15** °peak, °record, °height, °maximum, °acme, apex: *Employment is expected to reach a high next summer.* **16** intoxication, altered consciousness: *The high lasts till the drug wears off.* **17** anticyclone: *The high passing over the country will bring fair weather.*

highbrow *n.* **1** °scholar, °intellectual, savant, °sage, °mastermind, °genius; °aesthete, connoisseur, *Colloq* egghead, °brain: *Many who pretend to deride highbrows secretly envy them.*
—*adj.* **2** °scholarly, °intellectual, °learned, erudite, °deep, bookish, cultured, °sophisticated, °cultivated, °aesthetic, *Colloq* brainy: *Books on philosophy are too highbrow for the market we cater to.*

high-class *adj.* **1** °first-rate, °superior, °better, top-drawer, *Colloq* tops, tiptop, A-one *or* A-1, °super, °great: *He has had the benefit of a high-class education.* **2** aristocratic, °upper-class, élite, °select, °exclusive; °upper crust, °fancy, *Brit* county, *US and Canadian* tony, *Slang* classy: *She says she comes from a high-class family.*

highly *adv.* **1** greatly, much, tremendously, well, enthusiastically, °warmly, immensely, hugely: *Her play was highly praised by all the critics.* **2** °very, °extremely, °quite, exceptionally, extraordinarily, incomparably, decidedly: *It is highly unlikely that I shall come to your party.* **3** °favourably, well, enthusiastically, approvingly, °warmly, praisefully: *They seem to think highly of him at the office.* **4** °well, influentially, powerfully, strongly, authoritatively, effectively, importantly: *I have the information from a highly placed government official.*

hilarious *adj.* °funny, side-splitting, °humorous, comical, amusing, °entertaining, mirthful; °merry, °gay, °jolly, jovial, °cheerful, cheery, joyous, °joyful, rollicking, °uproarious; *Colloq* °hysterical: *Binky told me a hilarious story about his aunt's pet boa constrictor. We had a hilarious time at your party.*

hilarity *n.* °laughter, °gaiety, joviality, jollity, °merriment, °mirth, °exuberance, °glee, boisterousness, cheerfulness, joyfulness, jubilation, elation, °revelry, conviviality, °high spirits, vivacity, exhilaration: *Thurgood did not join in the hilarity of his retirement party.*

hill *n.* **1** °elevation, °rise, highland, °mound, °prominence, promontory, eminence, °knoll, hillock, hummock, °height, foothill, tor, °mount, upland, downs *or* downland, *Scots* brae, *No. Eng. and Scots* fell, *W Eng.* tump, *US and Canadian* butte: *The house is on a hill overlooking the valley.* **2** °heap, °pile, °mound, °stack; °mountain: *By the autumn, the hill of compost had reached six feet in height.* **3** °slope, °incline *or* °decline, acclivity *or* declivity, gradient *or esp. US* °grade, *US* upgrade *or* °downgrade: *Are you sure this car can make it up the next hill?*

hinder *v.* **1** °hamper, °delay, °interrupt, °impede, °interfere with, °foil, °thwart, °frustrate, °forestall, °bar, °stymie, °check, balk *or* baulk, °encumber, °obstruct, °handicap, °set *or* °keep *or* °put *or* °hold back, °defer, °retard, °restrain, °slow, °postpone: *The difficulty of the task should not hinder the attempt.* **2** °stop, °prevent, °check, °preclude, °arrest; °discourage, °deter, °inhibit, obviate: *Does the threat of capital punishment hinder people from committing murder?*

hindrance *n.* **1** °obstruction, °impediment, °snag, °check, °obstruction, °barrier, °obstacle, °restraint, °drawback, °hitch, °stumbling-block, °deterrent, °encumbrance: *The only hindrance to the plan is Phyllis's disapproval of it.* **2** °prevention, °curb, limitation: *The presence of police cars serves as a hindrance to speeding motorists.*

hint *n.* **1** °suggestion, °clue, °implication, °inkling, °indication, °tip, tip-off, intimation, allusion, °innuendo, insinuation; °pointer, °help, °advice: *The quizmaster gave me a hint and I got the answer at once.* **2** °trace, °suggestion, °touch, °taste, °breath, °dash, soupçon, whiff, undertone, tinge, °whisper: *Which government has ever served without any hint of scandal?*
—*v.* **3** °suggest, °imply, °indicate, °tip (off), °intimate, allude, °insinuate, °mention, °clue, °cue, °signal, °refer, advert: *She hinted that I might appeal to her sister.*

hip *adj.* °informed, °aware, °knowledgeable, °knowing, °perceptive, °alert, in *or* up on, onto, *Colloq* °wise (to), with it, °cool, *Old-fashioned* hep: *He's not hip to what they're saying about him and Carrie.*

hippie *n.* bohemian, *Old-fashioned* drop-out, beatnik, °beat, longhair, flower child *or* person, hipster: *A few hippies were playing their guitars at the street corner.*

hire *v.* **1** °engage, °employ, °take on, °appoint, °enlist, °sign on: *Alexandra had to hire more people to get all the work done.* **2** °rent, °lease, °engage, °charter: *We hired a car for the day.* **3** ***hire out***: °rent (out), °lease (out), °let (out), °charter (out): *I hire out my boat by the day.*
—*n.* **4** °rent, °lease, °charter, letting: *Do you have bicycles for hire by the day?* **5** (hire) °charge, °cost, °fee, °price, °rate, °rent, rental: *How much is the hire of a horse by the hour?*

hiss *n.* **1** hissing, sibilance: *Serpents and geese make a sound like a hiss.* **2** catcall, °jeer, boo, hoot, *Slang* raspberry, *US* Bronx cheer: *The villain was greeted by hisses from the audience.*
—*v.* **3** boo, hoot, °jeer, °deride, °mock, °taunt, decry, °disparage: *The workers hissed and booed the speaker.*

historic *adj.* °momentous, °important, °noteworthy, °significant, red-letter, °notable, °celebrated, °distinguished, °prominent, °great, consequential, °signal, unforgettable, °memorable: *We are gathered here to commemorate a historic event.*

historical *adj.* °factual, °true, verifiable, °reliable, °real, °authentic, recorded, documented: *The historical truth of what actually happened on that day has been obscured by legends.*

history *n.* **1** °account, °story, °record, °description, depiction, portrayal, °representation, °telling, retelling, °recital, °narration, °narrative, °relation, retailing: *Washington Irving's* Knickerbocker's History of New York *begins with the creation of the world.* **2** °news, °summary, recapitulation, °report, °intelligence, °information: *The history of these events is recounted in a book by Robinson.* **3** °past, °background, °life; °experiences, °adventures, °story, biography: *This woman appears to have had a rather curious history. The history of your years in Polynesia would make an interesting book.* **4** °record, °experience, °information, biography, CV *or* curriculum vitae, *US* résumé: *Your entire work history should be included in your application.* **5** °chronicle, annals, °record, °account: *The history of Parliamentary debate can be traced through Hansard.* **6** °ancient history, the °past, yesterday, the (good °old) days, days of yore, olden days, yesteryear, antiquity: *What can history tell us about the future?* **7** °dead letter, yesterday's news, old hat: *Any animosity I might have felt towards him is now history.*

hit *v.* **1** °strike, cuff, smack, °knock, whack, bash, bang, thump, thwack, °punch, buffet, °slap, swat, bludgeon, °club, smite; °spank, thrash, °beat, pummel, °batter, °flog, °scourge, birch, cane, °lash, °belabour, flagellate, °whip, horsewhip, cudgel, *Archaic* fustigate; *Colloq* °belt, wallop, clobber, clout, sock, °clip, °crown, bop, conk, paste, °lambaste, °zap: *She hit him on the jaw and he went down.* **2** °strike, bat, swat, °knock, °drive, °propel: *He hit the ball over the heads of the fielders.* **3** °strike, °collide *or* °impact with, °run *or* smash *or* °crash into, °bump *or* bang into: *The car went off the road and hit a tree.* **4** °affect, °touch, °stir, °move, °wound, °hurt, °strike *or* hit home, make *or* leave an °impression *or* a °mark on, (make an) °impact (on): *The new taxes hit the wealthy more than the poor.* **5** °dawn on, enter one's mind, °occur to, °strike: *It finally hit Graham that he had been insulted.* **6** °reach, attain, °arrive at, °gain, °achieve: *Those who have hit eighty know the meaning of old age. She hit the jackpot this week.* **7** °experience, °encounter, °meet (with): *It was at that point that we hit a snag in the negotiations.* **8** Also, ***hit up***: importune, °beseech, °petition, °beg, implore, entreat, °ask for: *As usual, Guthrie hit me for a loan as soon as we met.* **9** ***hit on*** or ***upon***: **a** °come *or* °happen *or* °chance *or* °light on *or* upon, °discover, °find, uncover, °unearth, °stumble *or* °blunder on *or* upon, °arrive at: *After years of experimentation, the Curies hit upon pitchblende as a source of radium.* **b** °devise, °think of *or* up, °invent, °dream up, °come up with, °work out, °see, °perceive, °detect, discern, °find: *I have hit upon a way to counteract the force of gravity.* —*n.* **10** °impact, °collision; °blow, °punch, °knock, °strike, swat, °shot, smack, °bump, bang, *Colloq* whack, thwack, conk, bop, sock: *The weakness of the hit caused only a slight dent in my car door. The boxer reeled after a hard hit to the midriff.* **11** °success, °triumph, coup, °winner, °sensation, *Colloq* smash (hit), sell-out: *After opening in the West End the musical became a hit on Broadway.* **12** °kick, °jolt, °thrill, *Slang* charge, *US* °rush, bang: *Give me a hit off that reefer.*

hitch *v.* **1** °connect, °couple, °fasten, °attach, °join, harness, °tie, °unite, °hook (up), °link, °fix: *When I arrived, she was hitching the horses to the wagon.* **2** Often, ***hitch up***: °raise, °pull up, hike (up), °tug (up), °hoist, °yank, °jerk, *Brit* hoick: *He hitched up his trousers, tucked in his shirt, and tightened his belt.* **3** hitchhike, °thumb a lift *or* ride, *Colloq US* °bum a ride: *I had no money and no car, so I hitched here from Newcastle.* —*n.* **4** °snag, catch, °difficulty, °trouble, °problem, °mishap, °handicap, entanglement, °interference, °impediment, °hindrance, °obstruction, °obstacle: *The entire plan went off without any hitch.*

hoard *n.* **1** °supply, °stock, °store, stockpile, °reserve, °fund, reservoir, °accumulation, °collection, °cache: *They kept a hoard of food in the shelter in case of attack. Occasionally, farmers turn up a hoard of gold coins buried by the ancient Romans.* —*v.* **2** °amass, °collect, °accumulate, °pile (up), °assemble, °gather, °put away, stockpile, °store, °reserve, °set aside, °save (up), squirrel away, °lay in *or* away *or* aside *or* up, *Colloq* stash away: *Hoarding food was against the law during rationing.*

hoax *n.* **1** °deception, °fraud, °swindle, °trick, flam *or* flimflam, imposture, °cheat, humbug, *Slang* con (°game), gyp, scam, °game, *US* snow job: *They perpetrated a hoax on you, and I am afraid there is no way of getting your money back.* —*v.* **2** °deceive, °defraud, °swindle, °trick, °fool, °dupe, °take in, cozen, °hoodwink, gull, °bluff, *Slang* con, gyp, bamboozle: *She was hoaxed into investing in Sicilian gold-mines.*

hobble *v.* **1** °limp, falter, dodder, °totter, °stagger, °reel, °weave, °stumble, °shuffle, shamble: *I hobbled about on crutches for weeks.* **2** °shackle, fetter, °restrain, °restrict, °hamper, °hinder, °impede, °trammel: *As hobbled horses do not stray, she tried to think of some way to hobble Clarence's errant ways.* —*n.* **3** °limp, °shuffle, shamble, claudication, °stagger: *With the leg-irons on, I could walk only with a jerking hobble.*

hobby *n.* °pastime, avocation, sideline, °recreation, °diversion, °relaxation: *Her hobby is collecting wedding rings.*

hobnob *v.* °associate, °fraternize, °socialize, consort, °mingle, °rub elbows *or* shoulders, °mix, °hang about *or* around, keep company: *He hobnobs with the aristocrats.*

hocus-pocus *n.* **1** °trickery, °chicanery, °deceit, °deception, °artifice, °cheat, duplicity, °mischief, °hoax, humbug, °trick, °swindle, °pretence, *Colloq* con (°game), jiggery-pokery, flimflam, °hanky-panky: *He tried some hocus-pocus on the company books but was caught.* **2** °mumbo-jumbo, abracadabra, incantation, °nonsense, °rigmarole, °gibberish, *Colloq* °gobbledegook: *The medicine man muttered some hocus-pocus over the body, which began to rise into the air.* **3** sleight of hand, legerdemain, prestidigitation, °magic, conjuring, jugglery: *From the earliest days religion has had its share of hocus-pocus.*

hoggish *adj.* piggish, °greedy, °avaricious, insatiable, °gluttonous, °voracious, edacious, acquisitive, °possessive, self-seeking, °selfish: *Don't be so hoggish; share the cake with the others.*

hoi polloi *n.* °riff-raff, °rabble, °mob, °common °herd, proletariat, °populace, °common °people, °crowd, masses, multitude, °rank and file, plebeians, bourgeoisie, °man in the street, *Brit* admass, °man on the Clapham omnibus, *US* John Q. Public, *Colloq* great °unwashed, proles, plebs, *US* silent °majority: *Much of what goes on in government is incomprehensible to hoi polloi.*

hoist *v.* **1** °lift (up), elevate, °raise, °heave, uplift, winch: *The lifeboat with the survivors aboard is now being hoisted onto the rescue vessel.* —*n.* **2** crane, °lift, elevator, davit, winch, °tackle: *The cable of the hoist broke, and the container dropped onto the pier.*

hoity-toity *adj.* °haughty, °arrogant, overweening, °snobbish, °disdainful, °supercilious, °conceited, °lofty, °superior, °self-important, *Colloq* °high and mighty, stuck-up, snooty, uppity *or chiefly Brit* °uppish, *Brit* toffee-nosed, *Slang* snotty: *Eleanor became very hoity-toity after her husband got his knighthood.*

hold *v.* **1** °grasp, °grip, °clasp, °seize, °clutch, °keep; °carry, *Colloq* °hang on to: *She asked me to hold the baby for just a minute while she bought her railway ticket.* **2** °hug, °embrace, °clasp, cradle, clench, °clutch, enfold: *He held me in his arms briefly before the guards led him into the quad.* **3** °maintain, °keep, °put: *Hold up your hands and kick the gun over here to me.* **4** °maintain, °keep, °sustain, absorb, °occupy, °engage, °involve, engross, °monopolize: *You hold his attention while I try to get round behind him.* **5** confine, °restrain, detain, °contain, coop up: *Even a strait-jacket and chains couldn't hold Houdini.* **6** °imprison, detain, confine, place into °custody, put behind bars, °jail: *He is being held overnight for questioning.* **7** °believe, deem, °judge, °consider, °regard, °look on *or* upon, °maintain, °think, °esteem, °take, °assume: *What do you hold to be important in life? Father holds me responsible for every little dent in his car.* **8** °accommodate, °support, °carry: *That little nail won't hold this picture.* **9** °contain, °include, comprise: *This suitcase holds everything I own in the world.* **10** °call, convene, °assemble, convoke; °run, °conduct, °engage in, °participate in, °have, °carry on, °preside over, °officiate at: *The next meeting will be held on Tuesday, at noon.* **11** °apply, hold good, be in °effect *or* in °force, °stand *or* hold up, hold *or* °prove *or* be °true, be the °case, °function, °operate, be *or* °remain *or* °prove valid *or* °relevant *or* °applicable *or* °operative, *Colloq* hold °water, °wash: *What may be in order for Manchester may not necessarily hold for another city.* **12** °have, °possess: *She holds two engineering degrees. He was holding four aces.* **13** °remain *or* °keep (°fast), °stay, °stick: *Screws are needed here—nails won't hold.* **14** ***hold back***: **a** °restrain, °repress, °suppress, °curb, °inhibit, °control, °check, °keep back, °hinder: *Many reasons hold me back from telling you what I think.* **b** °withhold, °reserve, °deny, °keep back, °refuse: *We ought to hold back payment till the work is completed.* **15** ***hold down***: **a** °control, °restrain, °check; °reduce, °diminish: *We must hold down inflation.* **b** °keep, °maintain, °manage: *He has to hold down two jobs to pay all the bills.* **16** ***hold forth***: **a** Often, ***hold forth on*** or ***upon***: °lecture (on), declaim, °harangue, °preach (on *or* about), orate, sermonize (on), discourse (on), speechify (on *or* about), expatiate *or* °expand on *or* upon, *Colloq* °go on (about), *Brit* rabbit *or* natter *or* witter on (about): *As usual, Pinckley endlessly held forth on his pet subject, fishing.* **b** hold out, °offer, proffer, °tender, °submit, °advance, °propose, °propound, °extend: *The company has held forth a profit-sharing plan that we cannot refuse.* **17** ***hold in***: **a** °control, °curb, °check, hold back, °restrain, °contain: *I could hold myself in no longer and a scream escaped my lips.* **b** °conceal, °hide, °suppress: *How can I hold in my feelings for you?* **18** ***hold off***: **a** °delay, °defer, °put

off, °refrain from, °postpone, °avoid: *We held off buying till we had the money saved up.* **b** °repel, °keep off, °repulse, °fend off, °rebuff, °resist, °withstand: *We held off the attackers till help came.* **19 *hold on*:** **a** °grip, °grasp, hold, °clutch, °cling: *Hold on to the rope and I'll pull you up.* **b** °keep, °maintain, °cling, °hang on, °retain: *Don't try to hold on to yesterday's dreams.* **c** °stop, °wait, hold off, *Colloq* °hang on: *Hold on a minute! I'm not finished.* **20 *hold out*:** **a** °last, °carry on, °persist, °persevere, °continue, °hang on, °stand °firm *or chiefly US* °pat, °endure: *I hope that the good weather holds out for our trip. Can we hold out till reinforcements arrive?* **b** °offer, proffer, °extend, hold forth, °present: *I grasped the hand he held out.* **21 *hold over*:** **a** °postpone, °delay, °defer, °put off, hold off, °suspend: *The decision is to be held over till next year.* **b** °continue, °retain, °extend, °prolong: *The singer was popular enough to be held over a month.* **22 *hold up*:** **a** °rob, °waylay, *Colloq* °mug, °stick up; °knock off *or US* over: *Two men held up the bank courier last night.* **b** °delay, °impede, °hinder, °slow (down *or* up), °set back, detain: *I was held up by the infernal traffic again.* **c** °last, °survive, °fare, °bear up, °endure: *I am not sure that my car will hold up through another winter.* **d** °present, °show, °exhibit, °display: *Gibbons has been held up to ridicule since the scandal.* **23 *hold with*:** °support, °sustain, °agree to *or* with, °favour, countenance, °approve (of), °subscribe to, condone, concur with: *Being married to her doesn't mean you have to hold with all her ideas.*
—*n.* **24** °grasp, °grip, °clasp, °clutch: *Take hold of the rope!* **25** foothold, toe-hold, °purchase: *She lost her hold and fell. He has a good hold on the subject.* **26** °power, dominance, mastery, °control, ascendancy, °authority, °influence, leverage, °sway, *Colloq* °pull, clout: *She has a hold over him that makes him do her bidding.*

hold-up *n.* **1** (armed) °robbery, *Colloq* stick-up, mugging, *US* heist: *The robbers escaped with my gold watch in the hold-up.* **2** °delay, °set-back, °hitch, °snag, °interruption, lacuna, °gap, hiatus, °break, stoppage: *The cause of the hold-up was an overturned van.*

hole *n.* **1** °cavity, °pit, °hollow, °excavation, °burrow, crater, cavern, °cave, °recess, °niche, °nook, °pocket, °depression, °indentation, dent, °impression: *The snake disappeared into a hole in the rock.* **2** °opening, °aperture, orifice, perforation, °puncture, °slit, °slot, °breach, °rip, °tear, °rent, °break, °crack, fissure: *The water poured through a hole in the pipe.* **3** hole in the wall, °shack, °hut, shanty, °slum, °hovel; *Slang* °dump, °dive, °joint: *How can anyone live in such a hole? She finally got a job dancing in some hole downtown.* **4** °cell, °prison, °dungeon, donjon, °keep, °jail, oubliette, brig, °cage: *When he refused to talk, they put him in the hole for a week.* **5** °difficulty, °trouble, °dilemma, °predicament, °situation, °fix, corner, *Colloq* (tight) °spot, hot water, °scrape, box, °bind, pickle, catch-22, °mess, °muddle: *She really got herself into a hole with the tax man.* **6** °flaw, °shortcoming, inconsistency, °fault, °error, °mistake, °fallacy, °discrepancy, °loophole: *He never offers anything original but is always ready to pick holes in any suggestion you make.*
—*v.* **7** °puncture, °pierce, °perforate: *A floating log holed the hull and the boat went down with all aboard.*

holiday *n.* **1** °time off, °break, °recess, °respite, °leave (of °absence), furlough, sabbatical, *Chiefly US* vacation: *We spent our holiday in Ibiza this year.* **2** °festival, °feast, °celebration, °fête *or* fete; °gala, °fair, red-letter day, °event: *Where are you going over the Christmas holiday?*

hollow *adj.* **1** °vacant, °empty, °void, unfilled: *A hollow space in the wall concealed a secret passage.* **2** °sunken, concave, indented, dented, recessed, depressed: *Dust gathers in the hollow places of the floor.* **3** °hungry, °ravenous, °starved, °empty, °famished: *I'm feeling hollow and should prefer to eat now, not later.* **4** °insincere, °false, °hypocritical, °sham, °artificial, °counterfeit, feigned, °fraudulent, °spurious, °deceitful, mendacious, °deceptive, cynical: *Politicians campaigning for office often make hollow promises they do not intend to keep.* **5** °empty, °futile, costly, Pyrrhic, °worthless, °vain, unavailing, °bootless, °fruitless, profitless, °unprofitable, valueless, °ineffective, °pointless, °senseless, °meaningless: *Winning the lawsuit was a hollow victory, for the man was bankrupt.* **6** muffled, °dull, °flat, °low, sepulchral, toneless: *His voice sounded hollow, as if he were speaking into a metal bowl.*
—*n.* **7** °hole, °cavity, cavern, crater, basin, °depression, °excavation, °pit, trough, °furrow, °indentation, dent, °impression; °valley, dale, dell, glen, °dip: *We hid ourselves in a hollow in the ground hoping not to be seen. The dog herded the sheep into the hollow near the stream.*
—*v.* **8** °excavate, °dig (out *or* up), °gouge, °scoop, °furrow, dredge: *Huskies hollow out places for themselves to sleep in the snow.*

holocaust *n.* **1** conflagration, fire-storm, inferno, °fire; °destruction, devastation: *When the volcano exploded, few escaped the holocaust.* **2** genocide, mass °murder, °massacre, blood bath, pogrom, butchery, °carnage, annihilation, extinction, extermination, eradication, elimination: *Survivors of the Nazi holocaust hold periodic memorial services.*

holy *adj.* **1** °sacred, °religious, consecrated, sanctified, blessed, hallowed, venerated, °divine, °heavenly, supernal, °celestial: *The holy relics are kept in a silver casket.* **2** °godly, °godlike, °saintly, saintlike, °pious, °devout, reverent, reverential, °faithful, God-fearing, °chaste, °pure, unsullied, °clean, sinless, °spotless, °immaculate, undefiled, uncorrupted, untainted: *The holy men, in their saffron robes, sat in a circle, contemplating the master of the universe.*

homage *n.* °obeisance, °respect, °deference, °honour, °esteem, °admiration; °loyalty, allegiance, fidelity, °tribute: *Today we pay homage to those who fought and died so that we might be free.*

home *n.* **1** dwelling-place, °residence, °domicile, °abode, °dwelling, °house, (living) quarters, habitation, °lodging(s), *Brit* °accommodation *or US* accommodations, *Colloq* °place, *Chiefly Brit* digs, diggings: *He has been a guest in my home on many occasions.* **2** (home) °base, residency, °territory, °haunt, home °ground, bailiwick, *Colloq* stamping-ground: *As you travel so much, what do you call home these days?* **3** hospice, °retreat, nursing home, old folks' *or* people's home, retirement community, almshouse, poorhouse, °refuge, haven, °institution, °shelter, rest-home, *US* snug harbor: *His parents, who are very old and indigent, have been sent to a home.* **4 *at home*:** **a** °comfortable, at °ease, °relaxed, °cosy, composed, °tranquil, placid, °peaceful, °serene, untroubled: *The Harrises certainly do make one feel at home.* **b** in, °accessible, °available, welcoming: *You know that we are always at home to you, Frances.* **5 *at home with* or *in*:** °comfortable with, conversant with, °knowledgeable in *or* about, °familiar with, well-versed in, °competent in, °expert in, °proficient in, skilled in, up on, °current in, °adept in, adroit in, °qualified in, (°well-) °informed in *or* on *or* about: *Widely read, she is at home in almost any subject you can name.*
—*adj.* **6** °domestic, °native, °national, °internal: *Buying more foreign than home goods upsets the balance of trade.* **7** °domestic, household: *She now sells home appliances for a big manufacturer.* **8** °family, °domestic: *What kind of home life has he had?*
—*adv.* **9** homeward(s): *When will you come home?* **10** to the °heart *or* °core, to the quick; effectively, tellingly, °profoundly, °deeply, stingingly, cuttingly, harshly, °severely, *Colloq* where it hurts, where one lives: *That remark really hit home.* **11 *bring or drive home*:** °stress, °emphasize, °impress upon, make clear: *I am trying to bring home to you the hardships people suffered during the war.*

homeless *adj.* **1** dispossessed, °outcast, exiled, °vagabond, °derelict, °unsettled; unhoused: *Their houses destroyed in the war, homeless people wandered everywhere.*

—*n.* **2** ***the homeless***: knights of the road, vagrants, vagabonds, tramps, *US* bums, hoboes: *There are not enough shelters for the homeless.*

homely *adj.* **1** homey, homelike, unpretentious, °modest, unassuming, °simple, °unaffected, °informal, °plain, °natural, °everyday, °unsophisticated, °homespun, commonplace, °ordinary, °familiar, °friendly, °amiable, °neighbourly, affable, congenial, *Colloq chiefly US* folksy: *Her success as a doctor is traceable in part to her homely approach.* **2** homey, homelike, °warm, °cosy, °snug, °domestic, °comfortable, °easy, °serene, °peaceful, °restful, °tranquil: *I like staying here for the homely atmosphere.* **3** °ugly, °plain, uncomely, unattractive, unlovely, ill-favoured: *Peggy-Jo's rather homely face is redeemed by her good-humoured nature.*

homesick *adj.* nostalgic, °longing, pining, °lonely, °lonesome; °wistful, °reminiscent: *I was homesick for the smell and taste of a good haggis.*

homespun *adj.* °rustic, °plain, °simple, °unrefined, unpolished, °unsophisticated, down-to-earth, °coarse, °rough, °rude, °crude, inelegant, °amateur, amateurish, non-professional, °unprofessional; handmade: *The furniture is not of museum standard, but it has a homespun quality.*

homicidal *adj.* °murderous, °lethal, °deadly, death-dealing, °mortal, bloodthirsty, °sanguinary, °ferocious, °maniacal, °berserk, amok *or* amuck, °mad, °insane: *The doctors say he is homicidal and should be institutionalized.*

homogeneous *adj.* °uniform, °consistent, unvarying, °identical, °constant; °similar, comparable, °alike, °akin: *The rock is ground up to make homogeneous powder.*

homosexual *n.* **1** °gay, homophile; lesbian, tribade, sapphist; *All the following are offensive and derogatory* °pervert, invert, *Slang* °queer, fairy, pansy, nancy *or* nancy boy, nance, °queen, drag °queen, homo; butch, (bull) dyke; *Brit* poof, poofter, ginger (beer), *US* °fruit, auntie, °fag, faggot: *Homosexuals prefer to be called 'gay'.*
—*adj.* **2** (*of either sex*) °gay, homoerotic, homophile; (*of a female*) lesbian, tribadic, sapphic; (*of a male*) °effeminate; *All the following are offensive and derogatory* °perverted, inverted, *Colloq chiefly Brit* °bent, *Slang* °queer, °camp, campy, °kinky, *Chiefly US* fruity, limp-wristed, faggy, °swish, swishy: *We never knew of her homosexual tendencies.*

honest *adj.* **1** °trustworthy, °truthful, veracious, trusty, °honourable, creditable, °decent, law-abiding, uncorrupted, uncorrupt, incorruptible, °ethical, °moral, °virtuous, °principled, °upright, high-minded, dependable, °reliable, °reputable, on the up and up: *How often does one meet an honest person in politics?* **2** °above-board, °straight, °square, square-dealing, °fair, °just, on the up and up, straightforward, °proper, °genuine, bona fide, °real, °authentic, *Colloq* on the °level, *US* square-shooting: *I write because I cannot earn an honest living. Would Felix give me an honest deal on a used car?* **3** °candid, °frank, °open, °plain, straightforward, °forthright, °direct, °sincere, °ingenuous, °explicit, °uninhibited, unreserved, unrestrained, unconstrained, °above-board, plain-spoken, unambiguous, unequivocal, *Colloq* upfront: *To be completely honest, I cannot stand the sight of you.* **4** °fair, °just, °equitable, °legitimate, valid, °rightful, °sound, °proper: *He gets an honest day's pay for an honest day's work.*

honestly *adv.* **1** truthfully, honourably, creditably, decently, ethically, morally, uprightly, dependably, reliably, in good °faith, justly, °fairly, equitably, even-handedly, disinterestedly, objectively, impartially: *In general, the police deal honestly with suspects.* **2** candidly, frankly, °openly, straightforwardly, forthrightly, °sincerely, °truly, ingenuously, unreservedly, °above-board, unambiguously, unequivocally, plainly, °simply, °straight (out), to one's face, in °plain words *or* English, bluntly: *I tell you honestly that I have never heard of the man.*

honesty *n.* **1** trustworthiness, uprightness, °rectitude, °probity, °integrity, °virtue, virtuousness, °honour: *As he will deal with large amounts of money, his honesty cannot be in question.* **2** truthfulness, veracity, °candour, openness, frankness, forthrightness, directness, straightforwardness, outspokenness, °sincerity, guilelessness, ingenuousness, bluntness: *You might not like what he says, but you have to admire his honesty.* **3** fairness, °equity, equitableness, even-handedness, °objectivity, impartiality, disinterestedness, justness, °justice: *We rely on the honesty of judges in meting out punishment to convicted felons.*

honorarium *n.* (token) °fee, compensation, recompense, °pay, °payment, °remuneration, emolument: *Would you be willing to accept an honorarium in lieu of your usual fee?*

honorary *adj.* °nominal, °titular, in °name *or* °title only, ex officio: *She has several honorary doctoral degrees, which is not bad for someone who never went to university.*

honour *n.* **1** °integrity, °honesty, fairness, justness, °probity, uprightness, decency, goodness, righteousness, °rectitude, °justice, °morality, °principles, virtuousness, °virtue: *Doing the right thing is a matter of honour.* **2** °respect, °esteem, °reverence, °veneration, approbation, °deference, °admiration, °homage, °regard, accolade, °praise, °kudos, °fame, °glory, °celebrity, °distinction, °prestige, illustriousness: *Great honour accompanies the award of a Nobel prize.* **3** °privilege, °distinction, °pleasure, °joy, °delight; °credit, °blessing: *I have the honour to introduce tonight's speaker. It has been an honour to serve under you, Admiral.* **4** virginity, °chastity, °virtue, °purity, innocence: *How did she manage to preserve her honour when fighting with the partisans?*
—*v.* **5** °respect, °esteem, °revere, °venerate, adulate, °adore, °worship, °approve, °prize, value, °defer to, °admire, pay °homage to: *Albert Schweitzer was much honoured in the latter part of his life.* **6** °praise, °laud, °glorify, °celebrate, °eulogize, °salute, °hail, acclaim, ennoble, °dignify, °exalt: *We have come together to honour those who have died for their country.* **7** °keep, °maintain, °carry out, °live up to, °discharge, °fulfil, °observe, °meet: *She has done her best to honour her obligations.* **8** °pay, °redeem, °accept, °clear, °cash: *The bank refused to honour his cheque because of 'insufficient funds'.*

honourable *adj.* **1** °upright, upstanding, °trustworthy, trusty, °honest, °just, °fair, °moral, °principled, uncorrupt, uncorrupted, incorruptible, high-minded, °noble, °virtuous: *Mark Antony referred to Caesar as an honourable man.* **2** °right, °correct, °proper, °fitting, °appropriate, °virtuous, °ethical, °worthy, °respectable, °reputable, °decent, °square: *I think you can count on Cedric to do the honourable thing.* **3** °fair (and °square), °impartial, °equitable, °just, °honest, unbiased, °unprejudiced, non-prejudicial, even-handed, °straight, °disinterested, guileless, °ingenuous, °artless, °open, °sincere, °above-board, on the up and up, undeceiving, undeceitful, *Colloq* upfront, on the °level: *Eleanor is too honourable to accept payment for work she did not do.* **4** °distinguished, °prestigious, °eminent, °notable, °noteworthy, °noted, °illustrious, °famous, famed, honoured, °exalted, respected, °celebrated, °renowned, acclaimed, °well-thought-of: *Ian enjoys an honourable reputation as a publisher.*

hoodlum *n.* °gangster, °thug, °racketeer, mobster, desperado, °terrorist, ruffian, °tough, °rowdy, knave, *Colloq* hooligan, baddy, crook, *US* plug-ugly, *Slang* goon, *Brit* yob, yobbo, *US* mug, bad actor, roughneck, hood, gunsel, hit man, torpedo, *French* apache, *Australian* larrikin: *He has a few hoodlums on the payroll who do the dirty work.*

hoodwink *v.* °fool, °trick, °deceive, delude, °dupe, gull, °hoax, °defraud, °mislead, humbug, °outwit, *Colloq* bamboozle, pull the wool over (someone's) eyes, pull a fast one on, °lead (someone) up *or* down the garden path, °put one over on (someone), throw dust in (someone's) eyes, take (someone) for a °ride, °string (someone) along, *Slang* rook, con, suck in, *US* °sucker in, snow: *They are trying to hoodwink the voters into believing that the recession is over.*

hook *n.* **1** hanger, °peg, holder; fastener, catch, °clasp, °clip, °pin: *Hang your hat on that hook. I'm using a safety pin because the hook on my dress is gone.* **2** °snare, °trap; fish-hook: *What can we use as a hook to catch the fish?* **3** ***by hook or by crook***: °somehow (or other), someway, come what may, by fair means or foul, (by) one way or another: *I have to get out of this place by hook or by crook.* **4** ***hook, line, and sinker***: °completely, °entirely, all the way, through and through, °thoroughly, °totally, °utterly, °wholly: *She actually fell for that old routine hook, line, and sinker.* **5** ***off the hook***: (set) °free, (in the) °clear, out of it; out of °trouble, acquitted, exonerated, cleared, °let off, vindicated, °off: *After paying them the extortion money, he still wasn't off the hook.*
—*v.* **6** °catch, °trap, entrap, °snare, ensnare; °grab, °capture, collar, °nab, °seize; *Chiefly US and Canadian* °snag, *Colloq* °pinch: *The petty crooks have been caught but we now want to hook the big fish himself.* **7** °steal, °pilfer, filch, palm, shoplift, °rob, *Slang* snitch, °rip off, *Euphemistic* °liberate, °remove, °borrow, °appropriate, *Brit* °nick, *Chiefly Brit* °pinch: *They used to hook sweets from Woolies'.*

hop *v.* **1** °jump, °leap, °bound, °spring, vault; °skip, °caper, gambol, °dance: *Here comes Peter Cottontail, Hopping down the bunny trail.* **2** take a (short) °trip *or* voyage, °travel, °come, °go, °proceed; °fly: *Those yuppies think nothing of hopping over to Paris just for dinner.*
—*n.* **3** °jump, °leap, °bound, °spring, vault; °skip, °caper, °dance: *In a few hops the bird was off the branch and onto my finger.* **4** (short) °trip *or* °flight *or* °journey *or* voyage: *The Bahamas are just a hop from Miami.*

hope *n.* **1** °desire, °wish, °expectation, yearning, hankering, craving, °longing, °fancy; °ambition, (day-) dream: *It was always my hope that you would go to university.* **2** °prospect, °promise, °expectation, expectancy, °confidence, °anticipation, assumption, °security, °faith, °conviction, °belief, °trust: *We had given up hope of being rescued.*
—*v.* **3** °aspire, °count *or* °rely on *or* upon, °anticipate, °contemplate, °foresee, °look forward to, °expect, await, °wait: *After all these years, he is still hoping to meet the girl of his dreams.* **4** °trust; °wish, °want, °desire; *Dialect* °expect: *I hope my ship will come in soon. I hope to see the last of her tomorrow.*

hopeful *adj.* **1** °expectant, anticipating, °optimistic, °sanguine, °confident, assured: *We are hopeful of victory in the forthcoming election.* **2** °promising, °bright, °rosy, reassuring, heartening, encouraging, auspicious, °propitious, inspiriting: *Today was a disaster, but tomorrow looks more hopeful.*

hopefully *adv.* **1** expectantly, optimistically, sanguinely, confidently: *Jocelyn set off hopefully for the party.* **2** with (any) °luck, if things go well, all being well, it is hoped, expectedly: *Hopefully, we shall arrive in time to catch the train.*

hopeless *adj.* **1** °desperate, beyond hope *or* saving, irreparable, beyond repair, irremediable, °lost, gone, °irretrievable; °incurable, °terminal, °deadly, °fatal, °lethal: *As their ship drifted into the intergalactic void, they saw that their situation was hopeless. They told me that her condition was hopeless.* **2** °bad, °poor, °incompetent, °inferior, °inadequate, °inept, °unqualified, unfit, unskilful, °deficient: *You might make a good surgeon, but as a judge of human nature you're hopeless.* **3** despairing, °despondent, °forlorn, °woebegone, disconsolate, °inconsolable, depressed, °dejected, °melancholy, downcast, °gloomy, °miserable, discouraged, °wretched, lugubrious, °funereal, °sorrowful, °sad, °unhappy: *Utterly hopeless after his script was rejected by Hollywood, he moped in his room.* **4** °futile, °vain, °bootless, unavailing, °impossible, °impracticable, unworkable, °pointless, °worthless, °useless: *It would be hopeless to try to send out a lifeboat in this storm.*

horizon *n.* °view, purview, °range, °scope, vista, compass, °perspective, °prospect, ken, field of °vision, °limit(s): *This is something that lies beyond the horizon of present-day knowledge.*

horizontal *adj.* °level, °flat, °plane; °prone, °supine: *Make sure that the plank is horizontal before fastening it down. They say that dancing is merely a vertical expression of a horizontal desire.*

horrible *adj.* **1** °awful, horrendous, horrid, horrifying, horrific, °terrible, °terrifying, °dreadful, °abominable, °abhorrent, appalling, °frightening, °frightful, °ghastly, °grim, °grisly, °ghoulish, °gruesome, °loathsome, °hideous, °repulsive, °revolting, °disgusting, sickening, nauseating, °nauseous, °harrowing, bloodcurdling, °macabre, unspeakable, °shocking: *The horrible sight of her father's mangled body haunted her for the rest of her days.* **2** °awful, °nasty, unpleasant, °disagreeable, horrid, °terrible, °dreadful, °obnoxious, °offensive, °atrocious, °monstrous, °contemptible, detestable, °despicable, *Colloq Brit* °beastly: *The food was perfectly horrible at our hotel. Take that horrible little dog away.*

horrify *v.* **1** °terrify, °frighten, °scare, °alarm, °intimidate, °panic, °scare *or* °frighten to death, °petrify, *Colloq* °scare *or* °frighten the living daylights out of, °scare stiff, make (someone's) hair stand on end, °make (someone's *or* the) blood run cold, curl (someone's) hair, °scare the pants off: *I was horrified to see the attack dogs racing towards me.* **2** °shock, °startle, °upset, °put off, °outrage, °dismay, °appal, °distress, discountenance, disconcert: *I was horrified to hear that you weren't coming to my party.*

horror *n.* **1** °fear and °loathing, repugnance, °terror, °dread, hatred, °revulsion, detestation, abhorrence, °distaste, °dislike; °aversion, antipathy, °hostility, °animosity, animus, °rancour; odium, execration: *She has a horror of bats.* **2** °fear, °dismay, °distress, °dread, °fright, °alarm, °upset, perturbation, °panic, °terror, °fear and trembling, trepidation, °anxiety, angst, apprehension, uneasiness, queasiness, nervousness, awe: *The doctor helped me overcome my horror of flying.*

hors-d'œuvre *n.* appetizer, apéritif, antipasto, smorgasbord *or* smörgåsbord, °relish; *Chiefly Brit* starter; *Archaic* warner: *A Sauvignon was served with the hors-d'œuvre, which was gravadlax.*

hospitable *adj.* **1** welcoming, °gracious, °courteous, °genial, °friendly, °agreeable, °amicable, °cordial, °warm, congenial, °sociable, °generous: *It was most hospitable of you to invite me.* **2** open-minded, °receptive, amenable, approachable, °tolerant: *The director is always hospitable to suggestions for improving sales.*

hospital *n.* medical °centre, °health °centre, °infirmary, clinic, polyclinic, dispensary, sickbay; asylum, °sanatorium, nursing °home, convalescent °home *or* °facility, *US* sanitarium: *With that wound, you ought to be in a hospital.*

hospitality *n.* graciousness, °courtesy, courteousness, friendliness, amicability, cordiality, °warmth, congeniality, sociability, generosity: *I am grateful for the hospitality you showed my sister during her visit.*

host[1] *n.* **1** hostess, innkeeper, hotelier, hotel-keeper, hotelman, °landlord *or* °landlady, °manager *or* manageress, °proprietor *or* proprietress, *Brit* publican: *As host, it is my responsibility to greet the guests.* **2** entertainer, °master *or* °mistress of ceremonies, emcee, MC, °announcer, *Brit* presenter, compère, *US* tummler: *For twenty years he has been the host of popular TV quiz shows.*
—*v.* **3** °entertain, act *or* play the host *or* hostess, °have: *She hosts a dinner-party for close friends every Wednesday.*

host[2] *n.* army, °swarm, °crowd, horde, multitude, °throng, °mob, °pack, °herd, troop, legion, °body,

°assembly, assemblage, drove: *The rock group turned up with a host of followers, their so-called groupies.*

hostage *n.* °pledge, °security, surety, °pawn, °captive, °prisoner, gage: *The terrorists threatened that if their demands were not met they would kill the hostages.*

hostile *adj.* **1** °opposed, antagonistic, °contrary, against, anti, adverse; °averse, °loath: *The government is hostile to curbs on business.* **2** unfriendly, inimical, °unsympathetic, °cold, °inhospitable; unfavourable: *Why do many social workers seem hostile to the people they are supposed to help? The polar regions are very hostile environments to man.* **3** warring, °belligerent, bellicose, °warlike, combative, °militant, °aggressive: *The UN units function as a buffer between the hostile forces.*

hostility *n.* **1** °antagonism, °opposition, enmity, °animosity, antipathy, animus, °ill will, malevolence, malice, °aversion, unfriendliness: *Do you still harbour the feelings of hostility towards them that you had during the war? The petty quarrels broke out into open hostility.* **2** ***hostilities***: °war, warfare, fighting, °combat, °action, state of °war, °bloodshed: *Hostilities ceased when the factions agreed to parley.*

hot *adj.* **1** °fiery, white-hot, red-hot, piping hot, °burning, blistering, °scorching, roasting, frying, sizzling, searing, boiling, scalding, steaming, simmering, °torrid, °sweltering, °sultry, °heated: *The hot, molten steel is cast into ingots here. During the day it is hot, but it cools down at night.* **2** °spicy, peppery, °sharp, piquant, °pungent, °biting, acrid: *She likes very hot food, with plenty of chilli.* **3** °intense, °fervent, zealous, °ardent, °enthusiastic, °passionate, fervid, vehement, °excited, °animated; °impetuous, °fiery, °fierce, °inflamed, °sharp, °violent: *He had some hot words with the foreman who had dismissed him.* **4** °eager, °keen, avid, °anxious, °burning; °intense, °fervent, zealous, °ardent, °enthusiastic, °passionate, fervid, vehement, °excited, °animated, °earnest, *Slang US* gung-ho: *Desmond set out in hot pursuit of the thief.* **5** °recent, °fresh, °new, °latest, °brand-new: *The hottest gossip is that she is marrying for the seventh time.* **6** °popular, sought-after, commercial, saleable, marketable: *The publisher believes* Zenobia's Memoirs *to be the hot property of the year.* **7** °lustful, °lecherous, libidinous, lubricous *or* lubricious, °sensual, concupiscent, °prurient, licentious, oversexed, sex-crazed, sex-mad, *Archaic* lickerish, horn-mad, *Slang* horny, *Chiefly Brit* °randy, *US* °hard up: *They were really hot, not having been with anyone of the opposite sex for months.* **8** °intense, °vivid, °striking, °bright, °brilliant, °dazzling, °loud: *That hot pink lipstick looks good with your suntan.* **9** electrified, °live, charged, powered: *The hot wire connects to the other terminal—I think.* **10** °dangerous, °precarious, °risky, °sensitive, °delicate, °unstable, °touchy, unpredictable: *The situation is getting a bit too hot to handle.*
—*v.* **11** ***hot up***: °intensify, °build up, °heighten, °increase, °worsen, °warm up, °heat up: *The environment is hotting up as a political issue.*

hot air *n.* blather *or* blether, bunkum, verbiage, °talk, °wind, pretentiousness, pomposity, °bombast, grandiloquence, magniloquence, flatulence, gasconade, rodomontade, *Colloq* claptrap, bosh, gas, guff: *Management's promises of pay increases were nothing but hot air.*

hotbed *n.* breeding ground, fertile source: *Slums are a hotbed of crime.*

hotchpotch *n.* °miscellany, °mixture, gallimaufry, °jumble, farrago, mélange, °mishmash, °mess, °tangle, °medley, °hash, conglomeration, agglomeration, olio, olla podrida, °pot-pourri, rag-bag, °welter, *US and Canadian* hodgepodge, *Colloq* omnium gatherum, mixed bag: *That hotchpotch of junk is scarcely what I should call an 'antiques collection'.*

hotel *n.* hostelry, inn, °lodging, caravanserai; motel, motor hotel, bed and breakfast *or* B & B, guest-house, °pension, *Australian and New Zealand* °pub, *US* tourist °house: *We are staying at a small hotel just outside of town.*

hotheaded *adj.* °impetuous, headlong, hot-tempered, °quick-tempered, °volatile, °rash, °hasty, °wild, °foolhardy, °reckless, °precipitate, °thoughtless, °heedless, madcap, °daredevil, devil-may-care: *He is too hotheaded to succeed in the diplomatic corps.*

hothouse *n.* **1** °hotbed, greenhouse, glasshouse, conservatory: *These tomatoes were grown during the winter in our hothouse.*
—*adj.* **2** °dainty, °delicate, °sensitive, °fragile, °frail, pampered, overprotected, sheltered, shielded, spoiled, coddled, babied: *She was glad to exchange the hothouse atmosphere of the university for the real world.*

hotly *adv.* intensively, energetically, doggedly, persistently, zealously, fervently, fervidly, ardently, °warmly, enthusiastically: *Hotly pursued by the police, I managed to hide in a culvert.*

hound *v.* °bully, °browbeat, °persecute, °nag, °harass, °annoy, °pester, harry, badger: *Although he was found innocent, his neighbours hounded him so much that he had to leave town.*

house *n.* **1** °residence, °dwelling, dwelling-place, °home, °abode, household, homestead, °domicile, °lodging(s), quarters, °building, edifice: *We are playing bridge at my house next Saturday.* **2** °family, °line, °lineage, °dynasty, °clan, ancestry, °strain, °race, blood, descendants, forebears: *She is a member of the royal house of Sweden.* **3** legislature, legislative °body, congress, °parliament, °assembly, °council, °diet: *Both houses of the legislature passed the bill.* **4** °establishment, °firm, °concern, °company, °business, °organization, °enterprise, °undertaking, *Colloq* °outfit: *He has gone from one publishing house to another with his manuscript.* **5** auditorium, °theatre, concert-hall: *The house is sold out.* **6** house of °ill repute *or* °ill fame *or* prostitution, °brothel, whore-house, bagnio, bordello, *Archaic* bawdy-house, *Colloq* sporting house, crib, *Slang US* cat-house: *She used to run a house in Lambeth.* **7** ***on the house***: °free, gratis, for °nothing, as a °gift: *Drinks will be on the house tonight to celebrate the tenth anniversary of our opening.*
—*v.* **8** °shelter, °accommodate, °domicile, °lodge, °quarter, °put up, °take in, °board, billet, °harbour: *We have housed as many as ten people at a time in the cottage.* **9** °contain, °accommodate, °quarter: *This building houses our computer operations.*

housing *n.* **1** °homes, °houses, °lodging(s), quarters, °accommodation, habitation, °dwelling; °shelter, °protection: *The Council is trying to provide housing for the elderly.* **2** °case, casing, °cover, covering, °enclosure, container, °box, °shield: *We keep the sensitive equipment in a dust-proof housing.*

hovel *n.* °hole, °shack, shanty, (pig)sty, pigpen, coop, crib, °hut, *Colloq US* °dump: *The beggar lives in a hovel near the railway station.*

hover *v.* **1** °drift, °poise, °float, °hang, be *or* °hang suspended, °hang in the air: *The humming bird hovers over a flower, drinking its nectar.* **2** °linger, loiter, °wait, °hang about *or* around: *The waiter's constant hovering about is making me nervous.*

however *adv.* **1** °notwithstanding, °regardless, °nevertheless, °nonetheless, °despite that, in °spite of that, °still, but, °though, °yet, °even so, be that as it may, come what may, no matter what; at any °rate, anyway, anyhow, on the other hand, in all events, in any °event, in any °case, after all: *He insisted the council should give their approval; however, that is not their responsibility. I was ready to move to Cardiff; she didn't offer me the job, however.* **2** to whatever °manner *or* °extent *or* °degree, howsoever, no matter how, in any °way *or* °manner *or* °respect, anyhow, how, in whatever °way *or* °manner: *However you view it, he is still the boss. Spend the money however you see fit.*
—*conj.* **3** how, how on earth, how in the world, in what °way *or* °manner: *However do you manage with only three to help, you poor thing?* **4** no matter how,

°regardless how, putting *or* °setting aside how, °notwithstanding how: *However much she earns, she is always short of money.*

howl *v.* **1** yowl, °cry, wail, ululate, bay; °shout, °yell, °bellow, °scream, °roar, *Colloq* holler: *The wolves were howling at the moon last night. He howled with pain when he caught his finger in the door.*
—*n.* **2** yowl, yowling, ululation, ululating, wail, wailing, yelp, yelping, °cry; °shout, °yell, °bellow, °scream, °roar, *Colloq* holler: *The wolf's howl is an eerie, chilling sound. I kicked him and he let out a howl.*

howler *n.* °blunder, °mistake, °error, gaffe; malapropism, Irish bull; *Brit* bloomer, *US* clinker, *Colloq Brit* clanger, *US* boner: *One paper contained the howler, 'Money is the route of all evil', which the author explained should be corrected to, 'The* love *of money is the* root *of all evil'.*

hub *n.* °centre, °focus, °focal °point, °pivot, °heart, °core, °nucleus, nave: *This is the hub of the city, around which everything else moves.*

huddle *n.* **1** °cluster, °group, °bunch, °clump, °pack, °herd, °crowd, °throng, °mass: *Everyone got into a huddle, trying to keep warm.* **2** °meeting, °conference, °discussion, consultation: *They were in a huddle, deciding what to do next.*
—*v.* **3** °cluster, °gather, °crowd *or* °press together, °throng *or* °flock together, °nestle, °jam *or* °cram together, °squeeze together: *We huddled in basements during air raids.* **4** °meet, °discuss, °confer, °consult: *Let's huddle on this question of the advertising schedule.*

hue *n.* °colour, °tint, °shade, tinge, °tone, °cast, tincture, *Technical* chroma: *The dust in the atmosphere gives the sunsets a reddish hue.*

huff *n.* **1** ***in a huff***: piqued, peeved, °testy, irritated, angered, vexed, annoyed, in high dudgeon, provoked, exasperated, °petulant, in a °pet, *Colloq* (all) het up: *She went off in a huff because I didn't praise her painting.*
—*v.* **2** °puff, °blow, °bluster: *When I complained about the food, the manager simply huffed and puffed and walked away.*

hug *v.* **1** °embrace, °clasp, °squeeze, °cuddle, °snuggle, *Archaic or literary* °clip: *They hugged each other warmly, then kissed goodbye.* **2** °follow closely, °cling to, stay *or* keep °near *or* °close to: *We hugged the ground as the bullets whizzed by overhead.*
—*n.* **3** °embrace, °clasp, °squeeze, *Colloq* °clinch: *She saw me, ran over, and gave me a big hug.*

huge *adj.* °large, °great, °enormous, °gigantic, °giant, °immense, °massive, tremendous, gargantuan, °prodigious, mammoth, °colossal, °monumental, Brobdingnagian, titanic, stupendous, elephantine, leviathan, °mountainous, °vast, *Colloq* °jumbo, °whopping: *The red spot on Jupiter is so huge it could swallow the earth several times over.*

hulk *n.* **1** shipwreck, °wreck, °derelict, °shell, skeleton: *The rusting hulk of the once-proud ship is tied up at the dock.* **2** oaf, °clod, lout, ox, *Slang US* galoot *or* galloot, klutz: *Don't tell me that hulk of a man painted these delicate miniatures!*

hulking *adj.* °clumsy, °awkward, ungainly, lubberly, oafish, loutish; °unwieldy, cumbersome, °bulky, °ponderous, °massive, °ungraceful, inelegant: *Their great hulking son could no longer fit into his clothes. That hulking monolith of an office building dominates the entire neighbourhood.*

hull *n.* **1** framework, skeleton, °frame, °structure, °body: *The hull of the ship completed, we added the superstructure.* **2** °shell, pod, °case, husk, °skin, °peel, °rind, *US* shuck: *Squirrels carefully nibble through the hull of the nut to get at the kernel inside.*
—*v.* **3** °shell, °peel, °skin, husk, *US* shuck: *We hulled all the nuts and they are now ready for the fruit cake.*

hum *v.* **1** °buzz, drone, thrum, °murmur, whirr, purr, °vibrate, *Technical* bombinate *or* bombilate: *I want to smell the wild flowers and hear the bees hum once again.* **2** bustle, °stir, be °active, °move briskly, *Colloq* tick (over): *Within three months of completion, the new plant was humming.* **3** intone: *I said, 'Do you know your rock guitar is keeping me awake?', and he replied, 'No, man, but if you hum it I'll try to play it.'*
—*n.* **4** °buzz, buzzing, drone, droning, thrum, thrumming, °murmur, murmuring, murmuration, whirr, whirring, purr, purring, vibration: *From the other room came the hum of conversation.*

human *adj.* **1** °mortal, anthropoid, hominoid, android; hominid; *Possibly offensive* manlike: *The aliens from the spaceship had few human characteristics. It is human nature to think.* **2** °sensitive, °defenceless, °weak, fallible, °vulnerable: *She is human, too, and can be easily hurt.* **3** °kind, °kindly, kind-hearted, °considerate, °charitable, compassionate, °merciful, °benign, benignant, °tender, °gentle, °forgiving, °lenient, °benevolent, beneficent, °generous, magnanimous, °humanitarian, °understanding, °accommodating, °sympathetic, °good-natured, humane, °sensitive: *Human concern for others is in short supply these days.*
—*n.* **4** human being, °person, °individual, °woman, °man, °child, °mortal, °one, °soul, someone, °somebody: *Humans have long maltreated many of the animals on which they depend.*

humanitarian *adj.* **1** See **human, 3,** above.
—*n.* **2** Good Samaritan, °benefactor *or* benefactress, °philanthropist, altruist: *Because of her charitable works, Lady Pendleton is thought of as a great humanitarian.*

humanity *n.* **1** °human °race, °people, °society, humankind, Homo sapiens; the °public, the masses, community; *Possibly offensive* °man, mankind: *From what we are told, humanity took millions of years to evolve.* **2** humanness, °human °nature, mortality: *On his first voyage to Mars, Kollworth began to doubt his own humanity.* **3** °kindness, kindliness, kind-heartedness, °consideration, helpfulness, charitableness, open-heartedness, warm-heartedness, °good °will, °benevolence, compassion, mercifulness, °mercy, benignity, tenderness, °warmth, gentleness, leniency *or* lenience *or* lenity, beneficence, generosity, unselfishness, magnanimity, °understanding, °sympathy, °sensitivity: *It was owing to the humanity of our neighbours that we survived the bombing.*

humble *adj.* **1** °modest, °reserved, unpretentious, unostentatious, self-effacing, unassuming, unpresuming: *For someone who has accomplished so much, she is quite humble.* **2** °submissive, °meek, °servile, °obsequious, deferential, °mild, °respectful, subservient, °subdued: *Usually pompous, Nigel became humble in the presence of the chairman.* **3** °lowly, °low, °inferior, °mean, ignoble, °ordinary, °plebeian, °common, °simple, °obscure, unprepossessing, unimportant, °undistinguished, °insignificant; low-born, °base, baseborn: *He lives in a humble cottage. Though she came from a humble background, she rose to become prime minister.*
—*v.* **4** °chasten, °bring *or* °pull down, °subdue, abase, °debase, demean, °lower, °degrade, °downgrade, °reduce, make (someone) eat humble pie, lose °face, °shame, °humiliate, °crush, °break, °mortify, chagrin, *Colloq* °put down, °take (someone) down a peg *or* notch: *He found army discipline a humbling experience.*

humdrum *adj.* °dull, °boring, °tedious, °tiresome, wearisome, °monotonous, unvaried, unvarying, °routine, undiversified, unchanging, °repetitious, uneventful, unexciting, uninteresting, °prosaic, mundane, °ordinary, commonplace, °common, °banal, °dry, insipid, jejune: *They saw no way of escaping from their humdrum lives.*

humid *adj.* °damp, °moist, °muggy, °clammy, °sticky, °steamy, soggy, °sultry, °wet: *The weather has been oppressively hot and humid all week.*

humiliate *v.* See **humble, 4,** above.

humiliation *n.* °disgrace, °shame, mortification, °dishonour, ignominy, °indignity, °discredit, loss of °face, obloquy, abasement, depreciation, detraction,

°degradation, derogation, belittlement, disparagement, shaming, °embarrassment, humbling: *He had to suffer the humiliation of being drummed out of the corps.*

humility *n.* modesty, meekness, self-effacement, shyness, diffidence, timidity, timorousness, meekness, bashfulness, mildness, unpretentiousness, submissiveness, °servility, self-abasement, lowliness: *She sees humility as dissatisfaction with oneself on account of some defect or infirmity.*

humorous *adj.* °funny, comical, facetious, laughable, risible, °ludicrous, °farcical, side-splitting, °hilarious, °merry; droll, °whimsical, amusing, °witty, waggish, jocular, jocose, °playful, °pleasant, *Colloq* °hysterical: *The humorous parts of the play sent the audience into gales of laughter.*

humour *n.* **1** funniness, comedy, °wit, facetiousness, ludicrousness, drollery, jocoseness *or* jocosity, jocularity, waggishness, °raillery, °banter: *One writer defined humour as 'the happy compound of pathos and playfulness', another referred to the sense of humour as a 'modulating and restraining balance-wheel'.* **2** comedy, farce °jokes, jests, witticisms, °wit, *Slang* wisecracks, gags: *Milton was scarcely known as a writer of humour.* **3** °mood, °frame of mind, °temper; °spirit(s); °disposition, °nature, temperament: *She is in a bad humour till after breakfast.*
—*v.* **4** soothe, °gratify, placate, °please, mollify, °indulge, appease, °pamper, cosset, °coddle, mollycoddle, °jolly, °baby, °spoil: *They are trying to humour him because he's in a bad mood.*

hump *n.* **1** °bulge, °lump, °bump, protuberance, °protrusion, °projection, °knob, node, °mass, °hunch, enlargement, °swelling, °growth, excrescence, tumefaction, tumescence; °mound, barrow, °tell, hummock, hillock, tumulus, *Brit dialect* tump: *Digging into the hump near the trees, we uncovered an ancient burial-ground.*
—*v.* **2** °hunch, °arch, curve, crook, °bend: *Sulking in the corner, he humped his back and refused to speak to anyone.* **3** °drag, °lug, °haul, °carry, °heave: *She had to hump two heavy suitcases all the way from the railway station.*

hunch *n.* **1** (intuitive) °guess, °intuition, °feeling, °impression, °suspicion, °premonition, presentiment: *I had a hunch they would be late.* **2** See **hump, 1,** above.
—*v.* **3** See **hump, 2,** above.

hunger *n.* **1** hungriness, °emptiness, °appetite, ravenousness, voraciousness, voracity; °famine, starvation: *We ate leaves to stave off the pangs of hunger. Some optimists hope to eliminate hunger from the planet by the year 2000.* **2** yearning, °desire, craving, °itch, °thirst, °longing, hankering, °mania, cupidity, *Formal* cacoethes, *Colloq* yen: *She felt an insatiable hunger for intellectual companionship.*
—*v.* **3** Usually, ***hunger for*** *or* ***after***: crave, °yearn, °desire, °thirst, °want, °hanker, *Colloq* yen, have a yen: *Blessed are they who hunger and thirst after righteousness.*

hungry *adj.* **1** °famished, °starved, starving, °ravenous, °voracious, °empty, °hollow, *Colloq chiefly Brit* peckish: *I'm hungry enough to eat a horse.* **2** craving, covetous, °eager, avid, °greedy, °keen, yearning, °desirous, °longing, hungering, thirsting, starving, °dying, *Colloq* hankering: *Marooned for years, Crusoe was hungry for the sight of another human being.* **3** acquisitive, °greedy, °thirsty, insatiable, °deprived: *The parched, hungry earth drank up the rain.*

hunt *v.* **1** °chase, °pursue, dog, °hound, °stalk, °trail, °track (down), °trace; °course: *The jewel thieves were hunted across three continents.* **2** Also, ***hunt for*** *or* ***up*** *or* ***out*** *or* ***through***: °seek (out), °search (for), go in °search of *or* for, °look (high and low) for, °quest after, go in °quest of, °scour, °ransack, °investigate, °pry into, go over *or* through with a fine-tooth comb, °examine, °explore, *Colloq US* °check out: *Detectives hunted the carpet for clues. She is hunting a job in publishing. I have hunted for the ring but cannot find it. Can you hunt up someone to fill the vacancy? Hunt through your pockets again for the key.*
—*n.* **3** °chase, °pursuit, tracking (down), stalking, hunting; °course: *The ten-year hunt for the thieves continues.* **4** °search, °quest: *My hunt ended when I found the ring.*

hunter *n.* huntsman, huntswoman, stalker, tracker, Nimrod, Orion; huntress: *An expert hunter, she bagged three tigers last year.*

hurdle *n.* **1** °barrier, °obstacle, °impediment, °hindrance, °obstruction, °bar, °handicap, °restraint, °snag, (stumbling) °block, °check, °difficulty, °complication, °interference: *Can she overcome the hurdle of prejudice against women?*
—*v.* **2** °leap (over), vault (over), °jump (over): *The fugitive easily hurdled the fence around the compound.*

hurl *v.* °throw, °toss, °shy, °sling, °fling, °pitch, °cast, °send, °fire, °heave, °propel, let °fly, *Colloq* chuck: *The fast bowler hurled the ball past the batsman.*

hurricane *n.* cyclone, tornado, typhoon, °whirlwind, °twister, wind-storm, °storm, °gale, °blow: *The 1985 hurricane destroyed millions of trees.*

hurried *adj.* **1** °hasty, °feverish, °frantic, °hectic, °breakneck, frenetic, °impetuous, rushed, °precipitate, °swift, quick, °speedy; °brief, °short: *We ate a hurried lunch before leaving to catch the train.* **2** °superficial, °cursory, °offhand, °perfunctory, slapdash: *Airport security guards made only a hurried examination of the hand luggage.*

hurry *v.* **1** °rush, °hasten, °make °haste, °speed, °race, °dash, °hustle, °scurry, °tear, °fly, °run, °shoot, scoot, scamper, scuttle, hotfoot (it), *Colloq* shake a leg, get cracking, get a °move on, go hell for leather, skedaddle, °step on it, °step on the gas, *Chiefly US* hightail (it), go like greased lightning, get a wiggle on: *You'll have to hurry to catch your bus.* **2** °speed up, accelerate, °hasten, °rush, °push, °press, °expedite; °urge, egg: *Such changes take time and can't be hurried. She hurried the children along so that they wouldn't miss the bus.*
—*n.* **3** °haste, °rush, °urgency, °eagerness; °agitation, disquiet, °upset, dither, °fuss, bustle, ado, to-do, °furore *or US* furor, commotion, turmoil, °stir, pother; *Colloq* °stew, °sweat: *Why all the hurry to finish before dark? He's in an awful hurry to get home.*

hurt *v.* **1** °harm, °injure, °wound; °damage, °impair, °mar, °spoil, °vitiate, °ruin: *She's so gentle she wouldn't hurt a fly. The scandal hurt the candidate's chances of election.* **2** °ache, °smart, °pain, °pinch, °sting, °burn, °torment, °gripe: *My elbow really hurts where I hit it.* **3** °distress, °grieve, °affect, °afflict, aggrieve, °depress, °upset, °disappoint, °pain, °cut to the quick, affront, °offend: *Sticks and stones may break my bones but names will never hurt me. You always hurt the one you love.* **4** °injure, °maim, °wound, °cripple, °lame, disable, °incapacitate, °damage, °mutilate, °mangle: *Three people have been badly hurt in a car crash on the motorway.*
—*n.* **5** °harm, °injury, °damage, °detriment, °disadvantage: *How much more hurt can you cause beyond what you have done already?* **6** °ache, °pain, °pang, °distress, °discomfort, °suffering, °torment, torture, °agony; °anguish, °misery, °woe, dolour, °sadness, °depression: *If you rub on this ointment, the hurt will go away. You cannot imagine the hurt we felt when he failed his examinations.*
—*adj.* **7** injured, wronged, pained, rueful, grieved, °unhappy, aggrieved, °sad, °wretched, °woebegone, °sorrowful, °mournful, depressed, °dejected, °dismal, °gloomy, °melancholy: *Whenever I mention getting a job she gets that hurt expression on her face.* **8** damaged, °defective, marred, impaired, °broken, °worn, °dilapidated, shop-worn, scratched, bruised, scarred: *They are holding a sale of hurt merchandise at the warehouse tomorrow.*

hurtful *adj.* **1** °harmful, °injurious, °detrimental, pernicious, °prejudicial, disadvantageous, damaging, deleterious, °destructive, noisome, noxious, baneful, °mischievous: *Efficient government is advantageous to many and hurtful to none.* **2** °nasty, °cruel, °cutting, malicious, °mean, °unkind, wounding, °spiteful: *He made some hurtful accusations about the librarian's efficiency.*

hurtle *v.* °rush (headlong), °tear, °shoot, °race, °speed; °plunge: *The car hurtled round the corner and crashed into a tree. Two bodies hurtled past me into the abyss below.*

husband *n.* **1** °mate, spouse, °groom, bridegroom, °partner, *Colloq* old °man, hubby: *My husband and I take turns cleaning the house.*
—*v.* **2** °save, °keep, °retain, °hoard, °conserve, °preserve, °store; budget, °economize (on), °manage: *If we husband our resources, we shall have enough for a rainy day.*

hush *interj.* **1** Shush!, Quiet!, Be *or* Keep °quiet *or* °silent *or* °still!, Hold your °tongue!, Mum's the word!, *Slang* Shut up!, Clam up!, Shut your °trap!, Button your lip!, Shut your °gob!, *Brit* Belt up!, *US* Hush up!, Shut your °face!, *US dialect* Hush your °mouth!: *Hush! You're in a library.*
—*v.* **2** shush, °silence, °still, °quiet(en): *I wish she'd hush the child's wailing.* **3** °suppress, °mute, °soften, soft-pedal, °whisper: *They spoke in hushed tones.* **4** Usually, ***hush up***: °suppress, °repress, °quash, °cover up, °hide, °conceal, °keep °quiet, *Colloq* °squelch: *They tried to hush up the news about his extramarital affairs.* **5** soothe, allay, °calm, °quiet(en), mollify, pacify, placate, °tranquillize: *Our worst fears were hushed by father's comforting words.*
—*n.* **6** °silence, °quiet, stillness, °peace, tranquillity: *A hush came over the crowd as she rose to speak.*

husky *adj.* **1** °brawny, strapping, °sturdy, °burly, well-built, °robust, °hefty, °rugged, °powerful, °strong, °stout, thickset, °muscular, °tough, *Colloq* beefy: *Two husky men arrived to move the piano.* **2** hoarse, °gruff, °dry, °harsh, rasping, °rough, °raucous: *She has a deep, husky voice I would recognize anywhere.*

hustle *v.* **1** °rush, °push, °hurry, °hasten, °run, °dash, scamper, scuttle, °scurry, sprint: *Mrs Grumble hustles off to the market every morning. He said that one must really hustle to make a living these days.* **2** shove, °push, °drive, °force, °hasten, °expedite, °press: *The bill was hustled through the legislature in just one day.* **3** shove, °crowd, °push, jostle, elbow, °thrust, °force: *She tried to hustle her way to the front of the queue.* **4** °push, °eject, °force, coerce, °drive, *Colloq* °bounce: *He was hustled out the back door.*
—*n.* **5** pushing, jostling, buffeting, jarring, elbowing, shoving, nudging: *We always take taxis to avoid the hustle in the underground.* **6** °activity, °action, °stir, °movement: *I can't concentrate with all the hustle and bustle going on in the office.*

hut *n.* °cabin, °shack, shanty, °shed, lean-to, °shelter, cote, *Literary* cot, *Australian* gunyah: *We found a tiny hut where we could keep out of the storm.*

hybrid *n.* °mixture, cross-breed, half-breed, °mongrel, °cross, composite, °combination, °compound: *The best wheat for this region is a hybrid developed in our laboratory.*

hygienic *adj.* °clean, °sanitary, °sterile, disinfected, germ-free, aseptic, °pure: *It is essential that hygienic surroundings be maintained in hospitals.*

hypnotize *v.* °fascinate, mesmerize, °entrance, °cast a °spell over *or* on, °captivate, °enchant, °charm, spellbind, °bewitch, °enrapture, ensorcell, °transport: *Greg is completely hypnotized by that singer at Felipe's nightclub.*

hypocrisy *n.* °deceit, deceitfulness, duplicity, double-dealing, °deception, °chicanery, guile, quackery, charlatanism *or* charlatanry, falseness, fakery, °lying, mendacity, Pharisaism *or* Phariseeism, Tartuffery, insincerity, two-facedness, sanctimony, sanctimoniousness, *Colloq* phoneyness *or US also* phoniness: *I loath hypocrisy and double standards.*

hypocrite *n.* deceiver, double-dealer, °quack, charlatan, °impostor *or* imposter, mountebank, °confidence man *or* trickster, faker, °pretender, °liar, °Pharisee, whited sepulchre, Tartuffe, flimflammer, *Colloq* °phoney *or US also* phony, con man, flimflam man *or* artist, two-face: *It is incredible that so many were duped by that hypocrite.*

hypocritical *adj.* °deceptive, °deceitful, deceiving, °insincere, dissembling, feigning, dissimulating, double-dealing, °false, °fake, faking, °two-faced, pretending, °lying, mendacious, °Pharisaic(al), °sanctimonious, °dishonest, underhand, treacherous, °perfidious, untrustworthy: *He regards the Victorians as nothing but smug prudes and hypocritical moralizers.*

hypothesis *n.* theory, °theorem, postulate, °premise *or* premiss, °proposition, assumption, °supposition, °speculation: *Cadwallader's Hypothesis is that television sets watch viewers while viewers are watching them.*

hypothetical *adj.* °assumed, °supposed, conjectural, conjectured, hypothesized, putative, surmised, °assumed, presumed, suspected, imagined, guessed, °speculative, speculated, °theoretical, suppositional, suppositious *or* supposititious: *Let us take the hypothetical case of someone, for example, who refuses to pay income tax.*

hysterical *adj.* **1** °raving, °mad, beside oneself, crazed, irrational, distracted, °rabid, °frantic, frenzied, °wild, °berserk, °uncontrolled, uncontrollable, unrestrained, unrestrainable: *They are subject to violent, hysterical outbursts.* **2** °hilarious, side-splitting, °uproarious, °farcical, comical, °funny: *The show we saw last night was absolutely hysterical.*

I

icing *n.* **1** frosting, glaze, coating: *Our favourite treat was chocolate cake with chocolate icing.* **2** °bonus, fringe) °benefit, (°extra) added °attraction, °extra, °reward, dividend: *He clinched a seventh victory with his partner, putting the icing on the cake of their shared world championship.*

icy *adj.* **1** ice-cold, °frigid, arctic, °bitter, glacial, °freezing, frozen, °chill, hyperborean *or* hyperboreal, °polar, Siberian, °wintry, °raw, °cold, chilling, °chilly: *The icy wind cut through to the marrow of my bones.* **2** °cool, °chill, °chilly, °frigid, °distant, °aloof, °remote, °freezing, ice-cold, unemotional, unimpassioned, °stony, °steely, °callous, flinty, °formal, °reserved, °forbidding, unfriendly, °hostile: *She fixed him with an icy stare.*

idea *n.* **1** concept, °conception, °construct, °thought, °notion, °plan, °design, °scheme, °suggestion, °recommendation: *Is that your idea of a good singing voice? Peter has an excellent idea for increasing sales.* **2** °notion, °fancy, °impression, °picture, (°mental) °image, concept, °conception, °perception, °understanding, awareness, apprehension, °inkling, °suspicion, °hint, °suggestion, approximation, °clue, intimation, °guess, °estimate, °estimation: *I haven't the slightest idea what you are talking about. Can you give us any idea of the cause of the delay?* **3** °belief, °opinion, °sentiment, °feeling, teaching(s), °doctrine, °tenet, °principle, °philosophy, °view, °viewpoint, °outlook, °notion, °conviction, °position, °stance: *Western and Eastern ideas differ as to the role of women in society.* **4** °aim, °goal, °purpose, °objective, °object, °end, °point, °reason, *raison d'être*: *What was the idea of telling the teacher? The idea behind the scheme was to boost sales. The idea of the game is to capture your opponent's king.* **5** °hypothesis, theory, °notion, °dream, °fantasy *or* phantasy: *His invention is based on the idea of an anti-gravity device.*

ideal *n.* **1** °model, °paragon, °standard, criterion, paradigm, exemplar, °pattern, °example, °epitome: *She regarded Florence Nightingale as her ideal.* **2** °acme, (°standard of) °perfection, °nonpareil: *The ideal can rarely be achieved, so you had better settle for reality.* **3** ***ideals***: °principles, °morals, °standards: *Everyone's ideals are compromised sooner or later.*
—*adj.* **4** °perfect, °excellent, °supreme, consummate, °complete, °model, °idyllic: *This is an ideal home for a young couple.* **5** conceptual, imagined, °imaginary, °unreal, °visionary, °idealistic, °fictitious, Utopian, notional, °mythical *or* mythic, °fantasy, °dream, °romantic, chimeric(al), °illusory, °fanciful, °fancied: *In his ideal world there is no crime, so there is no need for police.*

idealistic *adj.* °visionary, °romantic, romanticized, °optimistic, starry-eyed, °quixotic, Panglossian, °impractical, °unrealistic: *He is idealistic enough to believe that people are basically good.*

idealize *v.* °exalt, elevate, °glorify, °worship, ennoble, deify, apotheosize, put on a °pedestal, romanticize: *Because she idealizes him, she cannot see his true nature.*

ideally *adv.* **1** under *or* in the °best of circumstances, at °best, in a °perfect world, all things being °equal: *Ideally, February is the time to holiday in the Caribbean.* **2** theoretically, in theory, in °principle: *Ideally, people ought to have money before they are too old to enjoy it.* **3** °perfectly: *John and Marsha are ideally suited to each other.*

identical *adj.* **1** °same, °twin, °duplicate, °indistinguishable, interchangeable; selfsame: *The two leaves look identical to me. The duchess and I had the identical suite at the hotel, but a week apart.* **2** °similar, °matching, °like, °alike, comparable, °equal, °equivalent, corresponding: *The children are dressed in identical clothing.*

identification *n.* **1** °connection, °recognition, distinguishing, °indication, °perception, detection, °selection, naming, labelling, pinpointing, designation, characterization, °denomination; authentication, verification, °establishment, certification, substantiation, corroboration, *Colloq* fingering: *Her identification of him as her attacker is not sufficient to convict him.* **2** classification, classifying, cataloguing, categorization, categorizing, pigeon-holing: *How much time is needed for the identification of the minerals in the moon rocks?* **3** ID, ID card, °identity card, badge, credentials: *Only up-to-date identification will be accepted as proof of ownership.* **4** °connection, °association, affiliation, empathy, °sympathy, °rapport, °relationship: *His continued identification with comic-book heroes is immature.*

identify *v.* **1** classify, °categorize, catalogue, pigeonhole, °sort (out), °specify, pinpoint, home (in) on, °name, °label, °tag, °recognize, °place, °mark, pinpoint, °single out, °point out, *Colloq* °put one's °finger on: *We are unable to identify the butterfly you caught.* **2** °connect, °associate, °relate, °ally: *She is closely identified with the success of the enterprise.* **3** °diagnose, °specify, °name, °recognize: *From the symptoms, the doctor identified the disease as bubonic plague.* **4** Usually, ***identify with***: empathize (with), °sympathize (with), °relate (to), *Colloq* °dig: *His problem is that he identifies too closely with his dog.*

identity *n.* **1** sameness, oneness, unanimity, indistinguishability, °agreement, °accord, congruence: *Identity of purpose held them together under stress.* **2** °personality, individuality, distinctiveness, uniqueness, particularity, °singularity: *Many who join the army lose their identity.*

ideology *n.* °belief(s), °convictions, tenets, credo, °philosophy, °principles, °creed, dogma, teachings, °doctrine: *Buddhism had a great influence on his ideology.*

idiom *n.* **1** °language, °tongue, °speech, °vernacular, °dialect, argot, patois, °jargon, °cant, idiolect, °parlance, *façon de parler*, phraseology: *The play is written in a rather old-fashioned idiom.* **2** °expression, (°set) °phrase, phrasing, locution, °cliché: *The term* red herring, *an idiom meaning 'false trail', is used of something which is neither red nor a herring.*

idle *adj.* **1** °unused, °inactive, unoccupied, non-operative, stationary: *The looms were idle for months. The devil finds work for idle hands.* **2** °unemployed, out of °work, °redundant, jobless, workless, *Colloq* at °leisure, at °liberty, between assignments, resting, *US* on the beach: *Unable to find work, Gilbert has been idle for a year.* **3** °indolent, °lazy, °listless, °lethargic, loafing, °slothful, °shiftless, °lackadaisical, loitering, fainéant: *Since winning the lottery, Crouch has become one of the idle rich.* **4** °bootless, °fruitless, unproductive, abortive, unfruitful, °pointless, °vain, °trifling, trivial, °shallow, nugatory, °superficial, °insignificant, °meaningless, °senseless, unimportant, °frivolous, °worthless, °useless, otiose, unavailing, °futile: *We were passing the time at the pub in idle chatter when Michael walked in. He had no factual information to offer, only idle speculation.*
—*v.* **5** Often, ***idle away***: °waste, °fritter away, while away, °kill: *They idle away the hours lying by the swimming-pool.* **6** laze (about), loiter, °kill time, °loaf, loll, °lounge, take it °easy, *Brit* °potter *or US* putter about *or* away, °mess around *or* about, °fool away, °fool around *or* about, *Colloq Brit* °muck around *or* about, °bugger around *or* about, *US* lallygag *or* lollygag, goof off *or* around, *Military slang US* gold-brick: *Stop idling and get down to work.*

idleness *n.* **1** °inactivity, inaction, °lethargy, °torpor, °indolence, laziness, °sluggishness, °sloth, slothfulness, shiftlessness, °inertia, lassitude, *flânerie, dolce far niente*; unemployment, *Colloq US* lallygagging *or* lollygagging, *Military slang US* gold-bricking: *The strike created enforced idleness for non-union workers as well.* **2** shirking, malingering, dawdling, loafing, time-wasting, lazing, *Colloq* dilly-dallying, shilly-shallying, *Brit* skiving: *The foreman warned that he would not tolerate idleness.*

idler *n.* °loafer, layabout, °slacker, shirker, sluggard, lazybones, slugabed, °laggard, dawdler, clock-watcher, drone, °slouch, ne'er-do-well, fainéant, *Colloq* lounge lizard, *Military slang US* gold brick *or* gold-bricker: *To fill out a crew we often recruited men from among waterfront idlers.*

idly *adv.* **1** unproductively, lazily, indolently: *She wanders about the shops, idly whiling away the hours.* **2** offhandedly, unconsciously, mechanically, thoughtlessly, unthinkingly, obliviously, insensibly, indifferently: *He sat quietly, his fingers idly drumming on the tabletop.*

idol *n.* **1** (graven) °image, icon *or* ikon, effigy, °fetish, tiki, °symbol: *Nebuchadnezzar's people worshipped golden idols.* **2** °hero *or* °heroine, superstar, °celebrity, luminary, matinée °idol, °favourite, °pet, °darling: *When he was a lad his idol was Quatermain, from the Rider Haggard novels.*

idolize *v.* °adore, °admire, adulate, °worship, °revere, °reverence, °venerate, put on a °pedestal, °exalt, °glorify, deify, lionize, °look up to, apotheosize: *She had always idolized her father, and his death came as a terrible blow to her.*

idyllic *adj.* Arcadian, paradisaic(al) *or* paradisiac(al), °heavenly, Edenic, halcyon, °ideal, idealized, °pastoral, °rustic, bucolic, °picturesque, charming, unspoilt *or* °unspoiled, °peaceful, pacific: *He returned to the island to live out his life in idyllic repose.*

ignorance *n.* unfamiliarity, unawareness, unconsciousness, benightedness, unenlightenment, °inexperience, greenness: *Ignorance of the law is no excuse. Mistakes are often caused by ignorance rather than stupidity.*

ignorant *adj.* **1** unknowing, °uninformed, untaught, °uneducated, unschooled, unread, unlearned, unlettered, °illiterate: *Is there anyone so ignorant as not to know who Julius Caesar was?* **2** °unaware, °unfamiliar, °unconscious, °benighted, unenlightened, unwitting, in the °dark, °oblivious, *Formal* nescient: *She knows many things about which we are ignorant.* **3** °inexperienced, °green, °naïve, °innocent, °unsophisticated: *They used to tease ignorant young apprentices by sending them to find a left-handed hammer.* **4** uncouth, °ill-mannered, °discourteous, °impolite, uncivil, °boorish: *Don't be so ignorant and open the door for the lady!*

ignore *v.* **1** °disregard, °overlook, °pass over *or* by, turn a °blind eye to, be °blind to, turn one's back on, turn a °deaf ear to, wink at, °brush off *or* aside: *If you are over 65, you may ignore this paragraph.* **2** snub, give (someone) the cold °shoulder, °reject, °send to Coventry, °turn one's back on, *Colloq* give (someone) the °brush-off *or* go-by, °cut, °turn one's nose up at: *I don't care if you are cruel to me, just don't ignore me.*

ill *adj.* **1** ailing, °unsound, °sick, °indisposed, °infirm, °unhealthy, in a °bad °way, °diseased, afflicted, in °bad °health, °sickly, unwell, not well, out of commission; invalided, valetudinarian; *Colloq* under the °weather, in a °bad °way, °poorly, not up to snuff, out of sorts, on the sick-list, off one's feed, *Slang Brit* °dicky, °seedy: *Call a doctor—this man is ill. I was rather ill last night after eating that fish mousse.* **2** °bad, °wicked, °sinful, °evil, iniquitous, °immoral, depraved, °vicious, °vile, °wrong, °corrupt: *Police raided several houses of ill repute.* **3** °hostile, unfriendly, antagonistic, °belligerent, malevolent, malicious, ill-wishing, °unkind(ly), °harsh, °cruel: *The reading of the bequests sparked ill will amongst the heirs.* **4** °harmful, °hurtful, °injurious, °detrimental, damaging, pernicious, °dangerous, adverse, deleterious, baleful, °bad, unfavourable, °destructive, °disastrous, catastrophic, °ruinous, cataclysmic: *He suffered no lasting ill effects from the accident.* **5** °bad, °miserable, °wretched, °disastrous, unfavourable, unpropitious, °untoward, °disturbing, °unfortunate, unlucky, °inauspicious, °ominous, °unpromising, °sinister, °unwholesome: *Ill fortune led Ulysses to our isle. It is an ill wind that blows nobody good.* **6** ***ill at ease***: uncomfortable, discomfited, uneasy, edgy, on °edge, fidgety, °nervous, °anxious, °disturbed, distressed, troubled, °awkward, unsure, °uncertain: *I felt ill at ease in the presence of so august a personage.*
—*n.* **7** °evil, °abuse: *Speak no ill of her in my home!* **8** °harm, °damage, °injury, °hurt, °mischief, °trouble, °misfortune, °misery, °affliction, °pain, °distress, °woe, woefulness, °discomfort, unpleasantness, °disaster, °catastrophe, cataclysm, °calamity, adversity, °suffering, °ruin, °destruction: *You will be held responsible if any ill befalls the children.* **9** °injustice, inequity, °wrong, °evil, °sin, °transgression, °abuse, °mistreatment, maltreatment: *He entered politics hoping to cure some of society's ills.*
—*adv.* **10** °badly, adversely, unfavourably, °poorly, inauspiciously, unfortunately, unluckily: *Don't speak ill of the dead.* **11** °badly, adversely, unfavourably, critically, harshly, unkindly: *Please don't think ill of me for failing to attend your wedding.* **12** unkindly, harshly, unfairly, unjustly, improperly, °badly, wrongly, wrongfully, unsatisfactorily, °poorly, malevolently, maliciously: *He insists that he was ill-treated when in prison.* **13** °scarcely, °hardly, by no °means, in no °way: *It ill behoves you to criticize other people's English.*

ill-advised *adj.* **1** inadvisable, ill-judged, injudicious, ill-considered, °misguided, unwise, °imprudent, °inappropriate, unpropitious, inexpedient, impolitic, wrong-headed, °thoughtless; °indiscreet: *It would be ill-advised to sell your house at this time.* **2** °hasty, °rash, °reckless, °impetuous, °rash, °foolhardy, incautious, °short-sighted, °improvident: *Driving without a seat belt is ill-advised.*

illegal *adj.* °unlawful, °illegitimate, °criminal, felonious, outlawed, prohibited, interdicted, forbidden, proscribed, wrongful, °unauthorized, *verboten*, °illicit, *Law* actionable: *The bookkeeper was prosecuted for illegal appropriation of funds.*

illegible *adj.* unreadable, unintelligible, indecipherable *or* undecipherable, °incomprehensible: *An illegible message was scrawled on the wall.*

illegitimate *adj.* **1** See **illegal,** above. **2** bastard, °natural, fatherless, born out of wedlock, born on the wrong side of the blanket, misbegotten: *Illegitimate children were often offered for adoption in those days.* **3** °irregular, °improper, °incorrect, non-standard, °invalid, °unauthorized, °spurious: *Purists consider* the reason is because *an illegitimate usage.*

ill-founded *adj.* °groundless, baseless, without °foundation, unsupported, unsubstantiated, °empty, unjustified, unproven, uncorroborated, °unsound, °erroneous: *He wasted a great deal of time refuting her ill-founded accusations.*

illicit *adj.* **1** See **illegal,** above. **2** °wrong, °improper, underhand(ed), °secret, °furtive, clandestine, backdoor, *Colloq US* °sneaky: *They grew rich on the proceeds of illicit liquor.*

illiterate *adj.* unlettered, analphabetic; unschooled, untaught, °uneducated, °benighted, °ignorant, unenlightened: *She teaches illiterate people to read.*

ill-mannered *adj.* °rude, °discourteous, °impolite, ill-bred, uncivil, °disrespectful, uncourtly, ungallant, °ungracious, indecorous, ungentlemanly, unladylike, °impudent, °insolent, insulting, °impertinent, °brazen: *That ill-mannered oaf didn't even apologize for knocking me down.*

illness *n.* sickness, °disease, °disorder, °affliction, °ailment, malady, °complaint, °infirmity, °disability, indisposition, °affection, *Colloq* °bug: *His illness is serious but not contagious.*

ill-treat *v.* °mistreat, maltreat, °abuse, °misuse, °harm, °hurt, °injure, °persecute, °mishandle: *He is at last being punished for those years he ill-treated his wife.*

illuminate *v.* **1** °light (up), °brighten, °lighten, °throw *or* °cast *or* °shed °light on *or* upon: *She had only a single candle to illuminate her sewing.* **2** °clarify, °throw *or* °cast *or* °shed °light on *or* upon, °enlighten, °clear up, elucidate, °explain, explicate, °reveal: *The lectures on Heidegger illuminated his philosophy to some extent.* **3** rubricate, °decorate, adorn, °embellish, °ornament: *The museum has the best collection of illuminated manuscripts.*

illumination *n.* **1** lighting, °light, brightness, °radiance, luminosity, incandescence, fluorescence, phosphorescence: *The illumination from the fire was barely enough to read by.* **2** enlightenment, °insight, °information, °learning, °revelation, °edification, °instruction, awareness, °understanding, clarification: *It is astonishing what illumination his lectures brought to his audiences.*

illusion *n.* **1** °deception, °delusion, °fancy, °misconception, misapprehension, °fallacy, °error, °mistake, °mistaken *or* °false °impression: *He is labouring under the illusion that he is a great pianist.* **2** °fantasy, daydream, °hallucination, phantasm, °phantom, chimera, phantasmagoria, mirage, aberration, °vision, °spectre, figment of the °imagination, will-o'-the-wisp, ignis fatuus: *For years after he died, she had the illusion of seeing her father everywhere.*

illusory *adj.* illusive, °imaginary, °fictional, °unreal, °untrue, fallacious, °false, °mistaken, imagined, °fanciful, °fancied, hallucinatory, °deceptive, misleading, °apparent: *Any financial gains that you perceive in the scheme are purely illusory.*

illustrate *v.* **1** °instance, °exemplify, °demonstrate: *Let me illustrate my point with the following example.* **2** °picture, °illuminate, grangerize; °decorate, °embellish, emblazon, °ornament, adorn: *We are looking for an artist to illustrate the book.*

illustration *n.* **1** °example, °case (in point), °instance, °sample, °specimen, exemplar, *Colloq* for °instance: *This film is an illustration of the* film noir *genre.*

2 °picture, depiction, °representation, °figure: *An illustration of a jet engine appears on page 32.*

illustrious *adj.* °distinguished, °famous, °noted, °renowned, famed, °eminent, °well-known, °prominent, °important, °notable, respected, esteemed, °venerable, honoured, acclaimed, °celebrated, °great: *He belongs in the same category as other illustrious generals, like Kitchener.*

ill will *n.* °dislike, °animosity, hatred, °hate, °loathing, abhorrence, detestation, malevolence, malice, °hostility, enmity, animus, antipathy, °aversion, °rancour, acrimony, °spite, °venom, vitriol, acerbity: *I bear her no ill will for the way she treated me. She incurred his ill will by refusing him access to the children.*

image *n.* 1 °likeness, °representation, °picture, °sculpture, °statue, effigy, °figure, °portrait, simulacrum; icon *or* ikon, °idol, graven °image, °fetish, tiki: *Images of Bolivar can be seen in every town square in Venezuela. The tribesmen still worshipped golden images of their gods.* 2 °epitome, °duplicate, °copy, counterpart, °facsimile, °replica, °double, °twin, doppelgänger, clone, *Colloq* °spitting image *or* °spit and image, (°dead) ringer: *He's the image of father. He stared at his image in the mirror.* 3 °impression, concept, °conception, °perception, °idea, °perception, °notion, °mental °picture: *You are quite different from my image of you.* 4 °epitome, °representative, °model, (°typical) °example, °essence, archetype, °embodiment, incarnation, personification, materialization, reification, corporealization: *For us, she was the very image of what a leader should be.* 5 °figure (of °speech), trope, °metaphor, allusion, simile, °symbol: *The poem contains images that are obscure unless you know Greek myths.* 6 °form, °appearance, °likeness, °guise, °semblance, °aspect, °mould, °cast: *Man claims to be created in God's image.*

imagery *n.* figurativeness, allusion, symbolism: *Constance's poems are filled with ornate imagery.*

imaginary *adj.* °fictitious, °fanciful, °fancied, chimerical, imagined, fictive, °illusory *or* illusive, °visionary, made-up, °unreal, °untrue, °mythical *or* mythic, notional, °abstract; °legendary, mythological: *When he was a boy, he had an imaginary friend called Carbonario.*

imagination *n.* 1 mind's eye, °fancy; creativity, inventiveness, °ingenuity, °insight, °inspiration, °vision, imaginativeness, °creative °power(s): *His fertile imagination conjured up all kinds of terrifying pictures.* 2 °thought, °thinking, (°mental) acuity, °intelligence, °wit: *It doesn't take much imagination to see why you don't want to go to school this morning.*

imaginative *adj.* 1 °creative, °original, °clever, °ingenious, inventive, innovative, inspired, inspiring, °enterprising, °resourceful: *Richard is a highly imaginative computer programmer.* 2 °fanciful, °fantastic, °visionary, °poetic(al), °whimsical, contrived, °fictitious, °fictional: *The imaginative tale of Don Quixote sprang from the mind of Cervantes.*

imagine *v.* 1 °think of, °contemplate, °picture, °envisage, °consider, °ponder, °meditate on, °envision, visualize, °conceive (of), conceptualize, °create, °think up, concoct, °devise, *Colloq* °dream up, cook up: *I cannot imagine what you are referring to. Imagine, if you can, a world without conflict.* 2 °suppose, °guess, conjecture, °assume, °presume, °take it, °infer, °take (it) for granted, °take it as °given, °think, °fancy, °believe, °gather, °surmise, °suspect, °judge, deem: *I imagine that you won't want a drink if you are driving. You are imagining things if you think she is trying to undermine your authority.*

imitate *v.* 1 °mimic, °copy, ape, °parrot, °monkey, emulate, impersonate, do an °impression of; °echo, simulate: *Cruikshank was imitating the boss, who walked in at that very moment. His style imitates that of Carlyle.* 2 °copy, °mimic, °mock, °parody, °satirize, °burlesque, °caricature, travesty, *Colloq* spoof, °take off, *Brit* °send up: *In* Hudibras, *Samuel Butler imitated the style of the heroic epic.*

imitation *n.* 1 copying, mimicking, mimicry, aping, parroting, emulating, emulation, impersonating, impersonation, °impression: *Imitation is the sincerest form of flattery.* 2 impersonation, °parody, satirization, °burlesque, °caricature, °mockery, travesty, *Colloq* °take-off, *Brit* send-up: *In his nightclub act, he does scathing imitations of celebrities.* 3 °copy, °fake, °counterfeit, °forgery: *These are modern imitations of ancient coins.* 4 °copy, °replica, replication, °reproduction, simulation, °facsimile, °duplicate, duplication, simulacrum: *We keep the original in a safe place and put the imitations on display.*
—*adj.* 5 °fake, °synthetic, °artificial, simulated, °sham, ersatz, °mock, °factitious, °reproduction, man-made, *Colloq* °phoney *or US also* phony: *It doesn't take an expert to see that this is an imitation diamond.*

immaculate *adj.* 1 °spotless, stainless, unblemished, °pure, °clean, °untarnished, unsullied, unsoiled, snow-white, spick and °span, °dapper, °spruce; °tidy, °neat: *Each morning he donned an immaculate uniform.* 2 °pure, °chaste, °innocent, virginal, °virtuous, vestal, °pristine, undefiled, untainted, °unspoiled *or* unspoilt, unblemished, stainless, unadulterated: *He remained convinced of his wife's immaculate reputation.* 3 °faultless, °flawless, °perfect, errorless, °impeccable: *His essay on Gibbon is an example of immaculate scholarship.*

immaterial *adj.* 1 unimportant, °inconsequential, nugatory, trivial, °trifling, °petty, °slight, °insignificant, °flimsy, °light, unessential, °non-essential, of °little °account *or* value: *Whether he stays or goes is immaterial to me.* 2 airy, incorporeal, °disembodied, ethereal, ephemeral, evanescent, unsubstantial: *The concept of immaterial matter, such as a gas, is difficult to comprehend.*

immature *adj.* 1 °premature, °undeveloped, unripe, °rudimentary, half-grown, unformed, °unfledged, fledgling *or Brit also* fledgeling, unfinished, °young, °new, °fresh, °incomplete: *The immature growth in the spring is not hardy enough to survive a frost.* 2 °green, °callow, °unsophisticated, °naïve, jejune, °inexperienced, babyish, °childish, °childlike, °puerile, °juvenile, °raw, *Colloq* wet behind the ears: *She is a bit immature to assume so many responsibilities.*

immeasurable *adj.* °vast, °infinite, °immense, °huge, °great, °limitless, °boundless, °endless, interminable, unbounded, °unlimited, measureless, °inestimable, unfathomable; innumerable, °numberless, uncountable, uncounted, incalculable: *The tiny ship hurtled through the immeasurable vastness of space. An immeasurable quantity of angels can dance on the head of a pin. He accomplished immeasurable good during his lifetime.*

immediate *adj.* 1 instantaneous, °instant, °abrupt, °sudden, °swift; °spontaneous, °instinctive, triggered, °unhesitating, °unthinking, °automatic, reflex, knee-jerk: *Why is your immediate reaction always to say 'It cannot be done'?* 2 °direct, nearest, next, closest, adjacent, proximate; °nearby: *Although he had cancer, the immediate cause of death was pneumonia. Is there a phone box in the immediate vicinity?* 3 existing, °present, °current, °actual, °pressing, °urgent: *The immediate problem is to find a way of getting out of here.*

immediately *adv.* 1 at °once, instantly, °instantaneously, °promptly, °right away, °right °now, without °delay, unhesitatingly, without hesitation, forthwith, this °instant, °directly, in a wink, in a °second, in a °minute, *tout de suite*, instanter, *Chiefly Brit* °straight away, *Colloq* pronto, in a jiffy, in two shakes of a lamb's tail, before you can say 'Jack Robinson', at the drop of a hat: *Come here immediately. I shall be there immediately.* 2 °directly, closely, intimately: *These reactions are immediately concerned with the temperature.*
—*conj.* 3 when, as °soon as, the °moment (that), *Brit* °directly: *Immediately he heard the news, he hurried to her side.*

immense *adj.* °enormous, °gigantic, °extensive, °vast, °huge, °massive, °voluminous, tremendous, staggering, stupendous, mammoth, °colossal, °giant, titanic, Cyclopean, °jumbo, elephantine, Brobdingnagian, *Slang US* humongous: *Our exit from the cave was blocked by an immense boulder.*

immerse *v.* **1** °plunge, °sink, °submerge, °dip, dunk, °duck, inundate: *Immerse the device in the water before switching it on.* **2** °plunge, °sink, °submerge, °bury, absorb, engross, °engage, °occupy, °involve: *I immersed myself in my work and never noticed the time.*

immigrant *n.* °newcomer, °arrival, °settler, *Australian* °migrant; °alien, °foreigner, outlander, °outsider: *Her parents were immigrants from the Ukraine.*

imminent *adj.* °impending, looming, °threatening, °menacing, at °hand, nigh, °immediate, °close (by *or* at °hand), (forth)coming, drawing °near *or* °close *or* nigh, °momentary: *We face imminent disaster if steps are not taken now.*

immoderate *adj.* °excessive, °extreme, °exorbitant, °unreasonable, °inordinate, °extravagant, intemperate; °outrageous, °preposterous, exaggerated, unrestrained, undue: *Their immoderate demands for reparations cannot be met.*

immodest *adj.* **1** °indecent, °shameless, °shameful, indecorous, titillating, revealing; indelicate, °improper, °wanton, °loose, unrestrained, °provocative, °obscene, °lewd, smutty, °dirty, °lascivious, °bawdy, °coarse, *Colloq* °sexy: *The striptease was, to say the least, immodest. The streakers will be punished for their immodest behaviour.* **2** °brazen, °forward, °bold, °impudent, °impertinent, °brash, °arrogant, °insolent, °presumptuous, °disrespectful, *Colloq* °fresh, °cheeky: *Carl's immodest demand for a private office was ignored.*

immoral *adj.* **1** °corrupt, °bad, °wicked, °evil, iniquitous, °sinful, °impure, unethical, unprincipled, °abandoned, °base, °wrong, °vile, depraved, °dissolute, °degenerate, °reprobate, unregenerate, nefarious, flagitious, °villainous, treacherous, °unscrupulous, °dishonest: *Is it immoral to avoid paying one's taxes?* **2** °immodest, debauched, °indecent, °wanton, °libertine, °lecherous, °lustful, libidinous, °carnal, concupiscent, salacious, licentious, °lascivious, °lewd, °obscene, °pornographic, °dirty, smutty, °filthy: *He was convicted for living off immoral earnings.*

immortal *adj.* **1** undying, °eternal, °deathless, °everlasting, imperishable, sempiternal, never-ending, °endless, ceaseless, °perpetual, °timeless, °constant, °permanent, °indestructible: *Did the Egyptian pharaohs believe themselves immortal?* **2** °divine, °heavenly, °godlike: *The immortal wisdom of God guides man.* **3** remembered, °celebrated, unfading, °famous, °renowned, °classic, lauded, praised, honoured, °timeless: *The immortal writings of Shakespeare inspire us still.*
—*n.* **4** Olympian, °god *or* goddess; °hero *or* °heroine, °legend, °genius, °great: *To be sure, we must consider Bach as one of the immortals.*

immortalize *v.* °celebrate, °honour, °glorify, °memorialize, °commemorate, apotheosize, canonize, beatify, °exalt, ennoble, °extol: *Dickens's father was immortalized as Mr Micawber.*

immovable *adj.* **1** unmovable, °fixed, °fast, °rooted, °set, immobile, stationary, motionless, °stable, riveted, anchored, frozen: *What happens when an irresistible force meets an immovable object?* **2** immutable, unchangeable, unalterable, settled, °set, unmovable, °fixed, °inflexible; unshakeable *or* unshakable, unswerving, °firm, °determined, °steadfast, °staunch, °rigid, dogged, obdurate, unyielding, unwavering, °resolute, unflinching, adamant(ine), °stony, °impassive, unbending, emotionless, °unmoved: *Christmas day, which always falls on December 25th, is an immovable feast. Despite pleas for mercy, the judge was immovable and she was hanged the next day.*

immune *adj.* inoculated, vaccinated; °exempt, °safe, protected, insusceptible *or* unsusceptible, invulnerable, untouched, °unaffected: *She never caught smallpox because a mild case of cowpox had made her immune. Rick mistakenly thought himself immune to Sally's charms.*

immunity *n.* **1** °exemption, non-liability, invulnerability, °protection, °excuse, °release, °exclusion, °privilege, °freedom, °indemnity, amnesty, exoneration, absolution: *In return for his testimony he was granted immunity from prosecution.* **2** insusceptibility *or* unsusceptibility, °protection, inoculation, vaccination: *Immunity to a number of diseases is conferred by this one injection.*

imp *n.* °devil(kin), °demon, sprite, °evil °spirit, hobgoblin, °goblin, elf, pixie *or* pixy, leprechaun, puck, brownie, fairy; scamp, urchin, gamin, °rogue, °rascal, mischief-maker, brat: *Sitting on my shoulder as I write is a tiny imp that inserts the misspellings. Give me a hug, you little imp!*

impact *n.* **1** °collision, °contact, °striking, °crash, smash, °bump, colliding, crashing, smashing, bumping: *The impact of the car against the stone wall was heard a mile away.* **2** °effect, °impression, °influence, °import, °meaning, °bearing, °force, °thrust, °weight, °burden, °brunt, repercussions, results, consequences: *It is becoming clear that technology is having an adverse impact on the environment.*
—*v.* **3** °strike, °hit, °collide with: *When its orbit decays, the satellite will impact the surface of the moon.* **4** °affect, °modify, °change: *I wonder how the news of the bankruptcy will impact share prices.*

impair *v.* °weaken, °cripple, °damage, °harm, °mar, °injure, °spoil, °ruin: *Standing too close to the speakers at a disco can impair your hearing.*

impairment *n.* lessening, weakening, °damage, °harm, °injury, °flaw, °imperfection, reduction, vitiation, deterioration, °decrease, diminution, enfeeblement, debilitation, undermining, worsening, marring: *The impairment to my eyesight was caused by reading in the dark.*

impale *v.* spear, °stab, °pierce, skewer, °spit, °stick, °transfix, °spike: *They impaled the heads of their enemies on poles as a warning.*

impart *v.* **1** °give, °cede, °lend, °bestow, convey, °confer, °grant, °afford, °accord, °contribute: *The dyes impart different colours to the ink.* **2** °communicate, °tell, °relate, °transmit, °reveal, divulge, °disclose, °pass on, °intimate, confide: *I've had a hard week imparting knowledge to bored schoolchildren.*

impartial *adj.* °fair, °just, even-handed, °disinterested, °neutral, °unprejudiced, unbiased, °objective, °equitable: *Judge Leaver can be relied on to render an impartial verdict.*

impasse *n.* °deadlock, °dead °end, °stalemate, stand-off, °block, blockage, *Colloq* °blind alley: *Negotiations reached an impasse and the meeting broke up.*

impassioned *adj.* °passionate, inspired, °spirited, °stirring, °fervent, °emotional, fervid, °ardent, °heated, °warm, °rousing, aroused, vehement, zealous, °eager, °earnest, °enthusiastic, °vigorous, °animated, °fiery, °inflamed, °glowing: *The barrister made an impassioned plea for the accused.*

impassive *adj.* °cool, apathetic, °calm, °serene, composed, °unmoved, °cold, °cold-blooded, °reserved, imperturbable, unimpressionable, unruffled, controlled, contained, °phlegmatic, °lackadaisical, °stoical, unemotional, °taciturn, unfeeling, °stolid, emotionless, uncaring, °indifferent, undisturbed, °callous, °unsympathetic, °stony, °dispassionate, °detached, °nonchalant, unconcerned, insouciant, °remote: *I could see nothing in the judge's impassive expression to hint at his decision.*

impatient *adj.* **1** uneasy, °nervous, fidgety, °agitated, °restless, °restive, unquiet, °eager, °fretful, °agog, chafing, °impetuous, athirst, *Slang* itchy, *US* antsy: *There is a short wait for seats, so please don't get impatient.* **2** °irritable, irascible, °testy, °short-tempered,

°querulous, °waspish, °brusque, °curt, °short, hot-tempered, °snappish, °indignant, °demanding: *I don't mean to be impatient, but I have been waiting for three hours.*

impeach *v.* **1** °charge, °accuse, arraign, °indict, °incriminate, °implicate, inculpate, °blame, censure: *They were impeached for crimes against the state.* **2** (call into) °question, °challenge, °attack, °disparage, °discredit, impugn, deprecate, °belittle, asperse, cast aspersions on, declaim, °slander, malign, °vilify: *My daughter's character had been impeached by the witness.*

impeccable *adj.* °faultless, °flawless, °perfect, °ideal, °pure, °correct, °proper, °spotless, °immaculate, unblemished, unimpeachable, °blameless: *His lectures, though impeccable in content and style, lacked fire.*

impede *v.* °bar, °obstruct, °block, °thwart, °check, °hinder, °hamper, °slow, °retard, °restrain, °brake, °hold up, °delay, °foil, confound, °inhibit, °curb, °spike, °stop: *You can do nothing to impede the relentless march of time.*

impediment *n.* °bar, °barrier, °obstruction, °block, °check, °hindrance, °encumbrance, °restraint, °hold-up, °hitch, °snag, °restriction, °stricture, bottleneck, °delay, hang-up, °inhibition, °curb: *What are the impediments to a happy marriage?*

impending *adj.* °imminent, approaching, (°close *or* °near) at °hand, °close, nearing, forthcoming, brewing, to °come, in °view, in °prospect, in °store, in the offing, on the °horizon, in the air; looming, °threatening, °menacing; *Colloq Brit* on the cards, *US* in the cards: *The impending deadline made us work all the faster. We had a feeling of impending doom.*

imperative *adj.* **1** °mandatory, compulsory, °necessary, required, requisite, demanded, °obligatory, °indispensable, °essential, °crucial, °vital, °urgent, °pressing, exigent: *It is imperative that we catch the 5.04 to London.* **2** imperious, commanding, °authoritarian, °overbearing, °peremptory, autocratic, °domineering, magisterial, lordly, °arbitrary, °dictatorial, °dogmatic, °tyrannical, °despotic, *Colloq* °bossy: *We were all shaken into obedience by her imperative tone.*

imperceptible *adj.* **1** °invisible, indiscernible, °indistinguishable, undetectable, °obscure, °vague, ill-defined; °inaudible: *The differences between the twins are imperceptible.* **2** °indistinct, unclear, unnoticeable, °slight, °subtle, inconsiderable, inappreciable, °minute, °tiny, minuscule, infinitesimal, microscopic: *Her only response was an imperceptible flicker of her eyelid.*

imperfect *adj.* °wanting, unfinished, °undeveloped, °incomplete, °deficient, °defective, °faulty, °flawed, patchy: *This is an imperfect translation of the poem.*

imperfection *n.* °flaw, °failing, °fault, °error, °defect, °blemish, °damage; inadequacy, insufficiency, deficiency, °frailty, °weakness, °foible, °shortcoming, °peccadillo, shortfall, fallibility, °infirmity: *We have reduced the price because of tiny imperfections in the weave. Imperfections in her character make her unsuitable for the job.*

imperial *adj.* **1** kingly, kinglike, queenly, queenlike, °princely, princelike, °regal, °royal, °sovereign: *The imperial court was rich and splendid.* **2** °majestic, °royal, °regal, °lofty, °exalted, °supreme, august, °noble, °superior, °imposing, °splendid, °magnificent, °grand, °excellent: *Her imperial presence outshone all at the ball.*

impermeable *adj.* impenetrable, impassable, impervious, closed, sealed, °hermetic: *The floor has been damp-proofed by the insertion of an impermeable membrane under the concrete.*

impersonal *adj.* **1** °detached, °objective, °disinterested, °fair, °equitable, °dispassionate, °unprejudiced, unbiased: *The enforcement of the law should be entirely impersonal.* **2** °formal, °stiff, °strait-laced, °wooden, °rigid, prim, °stuffy, °cool, °detached, unfriendly, °cold, °mechanical: *Why does my bank manager have to be so impersonal?*

impertinence *n.* insolence, boldness, brazenness, °impudence, °presumption, presumptuousness, brashness, sauciness, pertness, °incivility, forwardness, impoliteness, discourtesy, °disrespect, audacity, rudeness, °effrontery, *Colloq* cheek, °brass, brassiness, °nerve, °gall, *Slang* chutzpah: *Why, the impertinence of that waitress to call you by your Christian name!*

impertinent *adj.* °presumptuous, °insolent, °bold, °brazen, °impudent, °brash, saucy, °pert, uncivil, °forward, °impolite, °discourteous, °disrespectful, °audacious, °rude, *Colloq* °cheeky, °fresh, °brassy, *US* nervy: *That impertinent little upstart had the nerve to ask the lady's age!*

impetuous *adj.* °spontaneous, °unpremeditated, °impulsive, unplanned, °hasty, °abrupt, °precipitate, quick, °unthinking, unreasoned, °offhand, °rash, °reckless, spur-of-the-moment, unreflective, headlong: *Don't be impetuous and accept the first offer that comes along.*

impetus *n.* °drive, stimulus, °push, impulse, goad, °thrust, °energy, °momentum, stimulation, °incentive, motivation, °encouragement, °inspiration: *Roger's innovative ideas provided the impetus to develop new products.*

impious *adj.* irreligious, °irreverent, °ungodly, °sacrilegious, °blasphemous, °profane, unholy, °wicked, °sinful, iniquitous: *The priest said that he would be punished for his impious remarks.*

implacable *adj.* unappeasable, unmollifiable, unpacifiable, unforgiving, intractable, uncompromising, °inflexible, inexorable, unyielding, unrelenting, °ruthless, °cruel, pitiless, °merciless, °hard, °rigid, °unsympathetic, uncompassionate: *Ever since that incident at school he has been my implacable enemy.*

implant *v.* **1** °introduce, °instil, °insinuate, °inject; °indoctrinate, inculcate, °teach, °impress, imprint: *They spent months implanting that notion in his mind.* **2** °graft, °root, embed, inlay: *You must implant the scion nearer the main stem.*
—*n.* **3** °graft, scion, ingraft; °insert: *Are they really experimenting with brain implants to improve the memory?*

implausible *adj.* °improbable, °unlikely, °doubtful, dubious, °questionable, °unbelievable, °incredible, °far-fetched, unconvincing, °debatable, °unreasonable: *He told an implausible tale of having been raised by apes.*

implement *n.* **1** utensil, °tool, °instrument, °apparatus, °device, appliance, contrivance, °mechanism, (°piece of) °equipment, *Colloq* °gadget, °contraption: *You need the proper implement for measuring inside diameters.*
—*v.* **2** °carry out, °execute, °accomplish, °perform, °achieve, (°put into) °effect, °bring about, °cause, °fulfil, °realize: *You will need our help to implement the plan.*

implicate *v.* **1** °involve, °include, °associate, embroil, ensnare, entrap, enmesh, °entangle: *Don't implicate me in your hare-brained schemes!* **2** °incriminate, inculpate, °connect, °involve, °associate, °suspect, °concern: *Wasn't he implicated in that fraud case last year?*

implication *n.* **1** involvement, °connection, °inclusion, °association, entanglement: *My implication in that affair was minimal.* **2** °suggestion, °hint, insinuation, °innuendo, intimation: *I resent the implication that I had anything to do with the murder.* **3** °significance, purport, °drift, °meaning, denotation, conclusion, °inference, °import, connotation, °sense, °burden, °substance, °essence, °pith: *The implication of the article is that the government knew about the illegal exports all along.*

implicit *adj.* **1** implied, °indirect, inferable, °understood, unspoken, undeclared, °tacit, °inherent, inferential, latent: *Certain provisions are implicit in every legal contract and need not be expressed.* **2** °absolute, unquestioning, unquestioned, °unqualified, °total,

°sheer, °complete, °unmitigated, unalloyed, °undiluted, °unlimited, unconditional, unreserved, utter, °full, °wholehearted: *I have implicit faith in Nicole's judgement.*

imply *v.* **1** °suggest, °hint (at), °intimate, °insinuate: *Are you implying that I don't know what I'm talking about?* **2** connote, allude to, °refer to, advert to, °signify, °signal, betoken, °denote, °indicate, °mean, °express; °involve, °include, °evidence, °assume, °presume, °entail: *Silence sometimes implies consent. Discovery of the tools implies a more advanced culture.*

impolite *adj.* °discourteous, °ill-mannered, uncivil, °rude, °ungracious, ungentlemanly, unladylike, °pert, °disrespectful, saucy, °boorish, churlish, °crude, indecorous, indelicate, °unrefined, ill-bred, °vulgar, °coarse: *The waiter was so impolite that I refused him a tip.*

imponderable *adj.* unmeasurable, °inestimable, °inconceivable, °incomprehensible, °subtle: *There are too many imponderable questions to give you a definite answer.*

import *v.* **1** °introduce, °bring in: *We import the raw materials and export the finished product.* **2** convey, °mean, °signify, °denote, °imply, betoken: *He was a dictator, in all the senses that word imports.* —*n.* **3** °meaning, °sense, denotation, signification, °gist, °drift, °thrust, °intention, °implication, purport, connotation, °suggestion, allusion, intimation: *It was difficult for me to catch the import of her words.* **4** °importance, °significance, °weight, consequence, °moment, °substance: *One could see at once that she was a personage of some import.*

importance *n.* **1** °significance, consequence, °import, value, °worth, °weight, °account, °concern, °moment, °substance, °matter: *How chemicals affect the ozone layer is of great importance to everyone.* **2** eminence, °distinction, °esteem, °standing, °status, °position, °rank, °prominence, °pre-eminence, °prestige, °power, °influence, °note: *His family is of considerable importance in the community.*

important *adj.* **1** °significant, consequential, °critical, °material, °vital, °urgent, °portentous, °weighty, °grave, °substantial, °momentous, °signal: *If it is important, put it in writing.* **2** °leading, °prominent, °notable, °noted, °noteworthy, °worthy, °eminent, °distinguished, respected, high-ranking, top-level, high-level, °superior, °outstanding, °foremost, °conspicuous, °impressive: *She is the most important member of the committee.* **3** °influential, °effective, well-connected, °powerful, °formidable, °mighty, °impressive: *With those important politicians supporting him, he might win.*

impose *v.* **1** °inflict, °force, °foist: *Stop imposing your standards on others.* **2** °interrupt, °interfere, °intrude, interpose, °insinuate: *I hope I am not imposing?* **3** levy, °place, °put, °exact: *A tax has been imposed on entertainment.* **4** ***impose on*** *or* ***upon***: **a** saddle, °burden: *He imposes on everyone with his demands for charity.* **b** °exploit, take °advantage (of), °misuse: *I hope I am not imposing on your good will in what I ask.*

imposing *adj.* °grand, °magnificent, °impressive, °stately, august, °majestic, °effective, commanding: *In his dress uniform, the general was an imposing presence at the reception.*

imposition *n.* **1** inflicting, infliction; applying, °application, enforcing, enforcement, levy, levying, promulgating, promulgation, introducing, introduction, placing, °placement, laying on: *People resent the imposition of a curfew.* **2** °burden, onus, °weight; intrusion, °misuse: *A flat-rate tax is a terrible imposition on the poor. Walking the dog is an imposition on my time.*

impossible *adj.* **1** °hopeless, °impracticable, °inconceivable, unimaginable, °unthinkable, unattainable, unsuitable, out of the °question, unachievable, unrealizable, unworkable, unresolvable, unsolvable: *Reading of the cipher is impossible without a key.* **2** °absurd, °ludicrous, °preposterous, °ridiculous, illogical, unworkable, °outrageous, °farcical, °outlandish, °crazy, °weird: *Inventors came up with the most impossible designs for aeroplanes.*

impostor *n.* imposter, impersonator, °pretender, deceiver, °cheat, °fraud, °swindler, trickster, °confidence man, shark, charlatan, mountebank, °hypocrite, *Colloq* con man, °phoney *or US also* phony, °tricky Dick, flimflam man *or* artist, *US* four-flusher: *It wasn't the bank manager but an impostor.*

impotence *n.* **1** °weakness, powerlessness, helplessness, °frailty, feebleness, enervation, debilitation: *The doctor said that his impotence was caused by exhaustion.* **2** impotency, inadequacy, inefficacy, ineffectualness, ineffectiveness, ineptness, °incompetence: *Georgiana was frustrated by her impotence in dealing with the situation.* **3** sterility, infertility: *Eating raw eggs and oysters does not cure impotence.*

impotent *adj.* **1** °weak, °powerless, °helpless, °frail, °feeble, enervated, debilitated, °infirm: *When it came to political influence, I was impotent.* **2** °inadequate, °ineffective, °ineffectual, °inept, °incompetent: *The attempted robbery was a half-hearted, impotent effort.* **3** °sterile, °barren, °infertile, infecund: *They never had any children because Dixon was impotent.*

impoverished *adj.* **1** °destitute, °poor, poverty-stricken, °penurious, beggared, °needy, necessitous, impecunious, in sore *or* bad °straits, °straitened, in °distress, °badly off, bankrupt, °insolvent, ruined, *Colloq* (°dead *or* °flat) °broke, stony-broke, °bad off, pinched, up against it, on one's uppers, °short, *US* strapped, wiped out, *Slang Brit* skint: *A series of failed harvests left many farmers impoverished.* **2** stripped, °barren, °desolate, wasted, °empty, depleted, denuded, drained, °exhausted: *Two years of drought left the land impoverished.*

impracticable *adj.* **1** unworkable, infeasible *or* unfeasible, °impossible, unattainable, unachievable: *The new engine design proved impracticable because of its high fuel consumption.* **2** unsuitable, unfit, unusable, °useless, °inapplicable: *As we have no electricity, air conditioners are impracticable.*

impractical *adj.* **1** °visionary, starry-eyed, °unrealistic, °romantic, °quixotic, °wild: *Laura's solutions are very creative but quite impractical.* **2** °useless, °ineffective, °ineffectual, unworkable, unavailing, °impracticable: *The idea looked good on paper but proved impractical when we tried it.*

imprecise *adj.* °inexact, °inaccurate, °wrong, inexplicit, °indefinite, ill-defined, °indistinct, °vague, °hazy, cloudy, blurred, °fuzzy, °woolly, °ambiguous: *The readings are imprecise because the needle wavers so much.*

impregnable *adj.* invulnerable, impenetrable, inviolable, unconquerable, °invincible, °unbeatable, °indomitable, °secure, °safe, °mighty, well-fortified: *The walls of the castle, sixteen feet thick, were impregnable.*

impregnate *v.* **1** °fertilize, inseminate, fecundate, make °pregnant: *The female can be impregnated only during one ten-day interval each year.* **2** imbue, °suffuse, °permeate, °penetrate, pervade, infuse, °saturate, °drench, °soak, °steep, °fill: *The preservative must be allowed to impregnate the wood.*

impress *v.* **1** °affect, °touch, °move, °reach, °stir, °strike, °sway, °influence, °persuade, *Colloq* °grab, get under one's skin: *She was genuinely impressed by his sincerity.* **2** °print, imprint, °stamp, °mark, °engrave, emboss: *Before the bowl was placed in the kiln, the potter's seal was impressed in its underside.* **3** Often, ***impress on*** *or* ***upon***: °stress, °emphasize, °urge, bring °home (to): *They tried to impress on him the gravity of the situation.*

impression *n.* **1** °sensation, °feeling, °sense, °suspicion, awareness, consciousness, °idea, °belief, °fancy, °notion: *I have the impression that I have been here before. She gave me the impression that she didn't like me.* **2** °impact, °effect, °influence: *Are you concerned about the impression of his speech on the crowd?* **3** dent, °indentation, °depression, °hollow, °mark; °stamp,

°impress, °brand: *Look here, where the chair has made an impression in the carpet.* **4** printing, °issue, °print, °copy, °run: *This is the third impression from the original plates.* **5** impersonation, °imitation; °parody, °satire, *Colloq* °take-off, *Brit* send-up: *After dinner, Gerry did his impression of Churchill.*

impressionable *adj.* °suggestible, °susceptible, persuadable *or* persuasible, impressible, °receptive, °responsive: *They seek to enrol students who are at an impressionable age.*

impressive *adj.* evocative, °moving, affecting, °stimulating, °exciting, °stirring, °powerful, °provocative, arousing, awe-inspiring, °awesome, °imposing, °formidable, °portentous, redoubtable: *She has many impressive talents.*

imprison *v.* incarcerate, confine, detain, remand, °jail *or Brit also* gaol, °lock up, intern, °shut up, put behind bars, °put in *or* °throw into irons, °put away, *Colloq Brit* °send down, *US* °send up (the °river): *He was imprisoned for a crime he didn't commit.*

imprisonment *n.* incarceration, confinement, °detention, remand, °custody, *Literary* durance (vile): *The sentence is imprisonment for not less than one year.*

improbable *adj.* °doubtful, dubious, °unlikely, °questionable, °unrealistic, °far-fetched, °remote, °implausible, °unthinkable, °hard to °believe *or* °imagine, °inconceivable, °unbelievable, °fanciful, °incredible, °ridiculous, °ludicrous, °absurd, °crazy, °mad, °insane, °wild, °weird, °peculiar, °strange; °impossible; *Colloq* °fishy: *It is improbable that they will marry. He gave the most improbable excuses.*

improper *adj.* **1** °wrong, °mistaken, °erroneous, °false, °incorrect, °inaccurate, °inexact, °imprecise, °amiss, °faulty, °untrue, °irregular, °abnormal: *Sloppy research had led to improper conclusions.* **2** unfit, unsuitable, °inappropriate, inapt, °inapplicable, infelicitous, °incongruous, unsuited, °unseemly, unbefitting, unfitting, uncalled-for, inapposite, malapropos, out of keeping, out of °place, °incompatible, °inopportune: *Do you think it improper for shops to open on Sundays? His wedding was an improper occasion for comments about his philandering.* **3** indecorous, °indecent, indelicate, °immodest, °unseemly, °untoward, °unbecoming, °impolite, °suggestive, °risqué, off colour, °obscene, °corrupt, °immoral, °sinful, °wicked, °lewd, °lascivious: *Do you see anything improper in sex education for children?*

impropriety *n.* **1** improperness, erroneousness, incorrectness, °falsity, falseness, inaccuracy, inaccurateness, inexactitude, inexactness, imprecision, impreciseness, irregularity, °abnormality: *I fail to see the impropriety in refusing to support capital punishment.* **2** unfitness, unsuitableness, inappropriateness, inaptness, inapplicability, infelicity, infelicitousness, incongruity, incongruousness, unseemliness, incompatibility, inopportuneness: *The judge criticized the impropriety of allowing the child to testify.* **3** indecorousness, °bad *or* °poor °taste, indecency, °indelicacy, immodesty, unseemliness, suggestiveness, immorality, sinfulness, wickedness, lewdness, lasciviousness: *In those days, the impropriety in wearing a brief bathing costume was thought shocking.* **4** °slip, °blunder, °mistake, °error, gaffe, gaucherie, faux pas: *She admitted to many improprieties during her term of office.*

improve *v.* **1** °better, ameliorate, upgrade, uplift, °amend, °enhance, °fix up, °reform, °redeem, °rehabilitate, redress, °repair, °correct, °rectify, °put *or* °set °right, emend; °modernize, update, °refurbish, recondition, °renovate, °repair, °overhaul, remodel: *We must improve procedures for dealing with small claims. The landlord refuses to spend any money to improve the property.* **2** °develop, °increase, °advance, °promote, °further, °benefit; °look up, °recover, °pick up, *Colloq* give a new lease of *or US* on life, take a °turn for the °better, *US* take a new lease on life: *How can I improve my chances of winning at snooker? Business has improved considerably.* **3** °convalesce, °recuperate, °recover, get °better, °mend, °rally, (make) °progress, °gain (strength *or* ground), °revive: *Mrs Costello is out of intensive care and improving daily.*

improvement *n.* **1** betterment, amelioration; °reform, rehabilitation, upgrading, enhancement, °repair: *The committee is working for the improvement of the neighbourhood.* **2** °recovery, °rise, °increase, °gain, °advance, upswing, °progress; recuperation, convalescence: *There was an improvement in share prices after release of the trade figures. The patient shows considerable improvement.* **3** °advance, °change for the °better: *This year's crop is an improvement over last year's.*

improvident *adj.* **1** °short-sighted, °imprudent, °wasteful, °profligate, °prodigal, °spendthrift, °extravagant, °lavish, °profuse, happy-go-lucky, penny wise and pound foolish, uneconomic(al), thriftless: *He who is improvident in his youth plans for a short life.* **2** incautious, °unwary, °rash, °reckless, °impulsive, °impetuous, headlong, °heedless, °careless, °unthinking, unthoughtful, unmindful: *The club's present financial straits are the result of having an improvident treasurer.*

improvise *n.* **1** ad lib, extemporize, *Colloq* °play (it) by ear, °fake it, wing it: *I like a comedian who improvises as he goes along.* **2** °invent, concoct, °devise, contrive, jury-rig; °make do: *We had to improvise a mast from parts of the boom. When you have nothing to work with, you have to improvise.*

imprudent *adj.* °indiscreet, °impulsive, °rash, °reckless, °hasty, incautious, °impetuous, °improvident, °careless, °heedless, °foolhardy, °irresponsible, injudicious, ill-judged, °thoughtless, ill-considered, °ill-advised, inadvisable, unwise, inexpedient, °foolish, °mad, °crazy, °insane, °inane, °silly, °perverse, °wrong, wrong-headed: *It would be imprudent to go out during the storm.*

impudence *n.* °impertinence, °effrontery, insolence, °disrespect, °presumption, presumptuousness, audacity, shamelessness, pertness, sauciness, boldness, brazenness, °incivility, rudeness, impoliteness, *Colloq* lip, °gall, guff, °sauce, °mouth, *Brit* backchat, side, *US* back talk, *Slang* chutzpah: *He had the impudence to suggest that I was too old for the job!*

impudent *adj.* °shameless, °impertinent, °insolent, °disrespectful, °forward, °presumptuous, °audacious, °pert, saucy, °bold, °brazen, °cocky, cocksure, °arrogant, uncivil, °ill-mannered, °rude, °impolite, *Colloq* °fresh, °brassy, °cheeky: *Asked the simplest question, she is always ready with an impudent response.*

impulsive *n.* °impetuous, °emotional, unpredictable, °unpremeditated, unplanned, spur-of-the-moment, °extemporaneous, unconsidered, °offhand, °instinctive, °involuntary, °spontaneous, quick, °sudden, °precipitate, °immediate, °snap, °rash, headlong, °rash, °reckless, devil-may-care, °foolhardy, madcap, °wild: *You may say that it was impulsive of me to give her all that money, but I love her.*

impure *adj.* **1** °dirty, soiled, unclean, sullied, tainted, polluted, defiled, °foul, °filthy, feculent, infected, scummy, °putrid, putrescent, °rotten: *The water is impure and not fit to drink.* **2** °mixed, alloyed, contaminated, adulterated, debased, °unrefined: *Impure ore contains other substances which are removed during processing.* **3** unclean, unhallowed, forbidden, disallowed, *Judaism* tref *or* treif *or* treifa: *Certain foods are considered impure in some religions.* **4** °unchaste, °immoral, °sinful, °wicked, °evil, °vile, unvirtuous, unvirginal, corrupted, defiled, debased, vitiated, °degenerate, depraved, °loose, °wanton, °lustful, °promiscuous, libidinous, °dissolute, licentious, °obscene, °prurient, °dirty, °filthy, lubricious *or* lubricous, salacious, °lascivious, °lewd, °lecherous: *The book was condemned as 'likely to encourage impure thoughts'.*

impurity *n.* **1** °pollution, contamination, defilement, adulteration, dirtiness, uncleanness, foulness: *The impurity of the water in our rivers is a cause for* *concern.* **2** Often, ***impurities***: °dirt, contaminant, pollutant, °pollution, smut, °filth, °foreign °matter *or* °body: *This filter is guaranteed to remove impurities from the water.* **3** unchastity, immorality, sinfulness, wickedness, °evil, vileness, corruption, degeneration, depravity, looseness, wantonness, °lust, lustfulness, promiscuity, promiscuousness, libidinousness, dissoluteness, licentiousness, obscenity, prurience, dirtiness, filthiness, lubricity, salaciousness, lasciviousness, lewdness, lecherousness: *Children ought not be exposed to the impurity encountered on everyday television.*

imputation *n.* °charge, indictment, °accusation, °allegation, °challenge, censure, °blame, reproach, °slur, °aspersion, °attribution, ascription, insinuation, °implication, °innuendo: *I resent the imputation that I broke the vase on purpose.*

impute *v.* ascribe, °assign, °attribute, °credit, °charge, °put *or* °set down to; °insinuate, °imply, °suggest, °hint at: *The critic imputed meanings to the book that the author had never intended.*

inability *n.* incapacity, incapability, °incompetence, unfitness, ineptness, °ineptitude, unqualifiedness, °impotence: *The inability of many school-leavers to perform simple arithmetical tasks is deeply worrying.*

inaccessible *adj.* **1** unavailable, unobtainable, unattainable, unreachable, °unapproachable: *The minister has made himself inaccessible for interviews.* **2** impenetrable, impassable, °out-of-the-way: *The tomb lies in a part of the jungle inaccessible except by air.*

inaccurate *adj.* °wrong, °incorrect, °erroneous, °mistaken, °inexact, °imprecise, °faulty, °flawed, °imperfect, °amiss, awry, °false, fallacious, illogical, °unsound, *Colloq* off the °mark, off the beam, °cold, *Chiefly US* all wet, *US* (way) off base *Slang* cock-eyed, full of °hot air: *Reports of my death were obviously inaccurate.*

inactive *adj.* **1** °passive, placid, °quiet, °tranquil, quiescent, °serene, °peaceful, pacific, resting, unmoving, motionless, immobile, immobilized, °still, °inert, °lifeless, °inanimate, sluggish, °listless, °lethargic, °lackadaisical, languid, °indolent, °lazy, °torpid, somnolent, °idle, °slothful, °supine: *Although there was plenty to do round the house, he remained inactive all summer.* **2** non-functioning, inoperative, °dormant; unoccupied, °idle, °unemployed, jobless, out of °work, out of a °job: *The volcano was inactive for a thousand years. These miners have been inactive for six months.*

inactivity *n.* **1** passiveness *or* passivity, placidity *or* placidness, °quiet, tranquillity, °serenity, °peace, peacefulness; motionlessness, immobility, stillness, °inertia, inertness, lifelessness, °sluggishness, listlessness, °lethargy, languidness, °indolence, laziness, °torpor, somnolence, °idleness, slothfulness, °sloth: *She alternates between periods of activity and inactivity.* **2** inaction, quiescence; hibernation, aestivation: *During repairs, the reactor will be in a state of inactivity. Some animals have a period of inactivity during certain times of the year.*

inadequate *adj.* **1** °insufficient, °deficient, not °enough, too °little, °scarce, °meagre, °scanty, skimpy, °sparse, (in) °short (supply); °unsatisfactory, °imperfect, °incomplete, °defective, unsuitable, °disappointing, °flawed, °faulty: *Funds are inadequate to meet her expenses. The terms of the agreement are inadequate.* **2** ***inadequate to***: unsuited to *or* for, unfit for, °unqualified for, not up to, unequal to, °unworthy of, inapt for, °inept for, °incapable of: *He proved inadequate to the demands of the job.*

inadmissible *adj.* disallowed, unallowable, unallowed, forbidden, °unacceptable, prohibited, unsuitable, unsuited, °unqualified, °inappropriate, °inapplicable, °improper, objectionable, °exceptionable, °incorrect, °wrong: *Such evidence is inadmissible in court.*

inadvertent *adj.* **1** unintentional, unintended, °unpremeditated, °accidental, °unthinking, unwitting, °chance; °unconscious, unplanned, unstudied, undesigned, uncalculated: *She was an inadvertent witness to the murder. I assure you that the error was entirely inadvertent.* **2** °careless, °inattentive, negligent, °heedless, unobservant: *Inadvertent commentators failed to see the significance of her words.*

inalienable *adj.* untransferable, intransferable, °absolute, °inherent, unconsignable, sacrosanct, inviolable, non-negotiable, unnegotiable, unchallengeable, *Law* imprescriptible, entailed, indefeasible: *People have an inalienable right to life, liberty, and the pursuit of happiness.*

inane *adj.* °silly, asinine, °vapid, °vacant, vacuous, °absurd, fatuous, °foolish, °senseless, °nonsensical, °unreasonable, °preposterous, °ludicrous, °ridiculous, laughable, risible, °mad, lunatic, °crazy, °stupid, °dumb, idiotic, moronic, imbecilic, *Colloq* nutty, nuts, °daft, daffy, screwy, batty, dippy, wacky, cuckoo, loony, goofy, *Brit* bonkers, dotty: *Students seem especially prone to inane behaviour.*

inanimate *adj.* °lifeless, motionless, immobile, unmoving, °inactive, °inert, °still, spiritless, soulless, °cold, °dead, °defunct: *He just sits there, like an inanimate piece of furniture.*

inapplicable *adj.* °inappropriate, unsuitable, unsuited, inapt, °irrelevant, °unrelated, unconnected, inapposite, beside the °point *or* °question, °extraneous, off the °mark, *Colloq US* off base: *That law is inapplicable in your case.*

inappropriate *adj.* °improper, unfitting, unfit, unsuitable, unsuited, unbefitting, °incompatible, malapropos, ungermane, inapt, inapposite, out of keeping, °incongruous, infelicitous, °inopportune, untimely, °irrelevant, °inapplicable: *Your facetiousness was quite inappropriate to such a solemn occasion.*

inarticulate *adj.* **1** °disjointed, unconnected, °incoherent, °incomprehensible, jumbled, unintelligible, unclear, illogical, °discursive, °rambling, scrambled, °wild, irrational, muddled, mixed-up, °confused, digressive: *She sat through an inarticulate lecture on Joyce's use of the subjunctive.* **2** mumbled, garbled, blurred, muffled, muttered, faltering, °halting, °indistinct, unclear, unintelligible: *They communicate with each other in inarticulate grunts.* **3** °speechless, °tongue-tied, (struck) °dumb, °mute, voiceless: *Ed is inarticulate when it comes to describing Vera.*

inattentive *n.* unobservant, °heedless, °careless, negligent, neglectful, °indifferent, uncaring, apathetic, °slack, °remiss, unconcerned, °detached, unmindful, distracted, distrait(e), °absent-minded, abstracted, in a brown study, day-dreaming, oscitant, wool-gathering, musing, °oblivious, (with one's head) in the clouds, in a world of one's own: *It was late and the children were getting restless and inattentive.*

inaudible *adj.* unheard, °imperceptible, °indistinct, °low, °faint, muted, °quiet, °soft, muffled, stifled: *The film was good, although some of the dialogue was inaudible.*

inaugurate *v.* **1** °initiate, °begin, °commence, °enter upon, °start, °introduce, usher in, °institute, °launch, °originate, °set up, °get under °way, °get °going: *A new programme of health services has been inaugurated.* **2** °install *or* instal, °induct, °invest, °establish, instate: *The President was inaugurated last week.*

inauspicious *adj.* °unpromising, unlucky, °unfortunate, unfavourable, unpropitious, °untoward, ill-starred, °ominous, ill-omened, ill-fated, °portentous, °menacing, °doomed, °sinister, °dark, °gloomy, cloudy, clouded, °black: *The middle of a recession is an inauspicious time to set up a business.*

inborn *adj.* innate, congenital, °inherent, inherited, °hereditary, inbred, °natural, °native, constitutional, deep-seated, deep-rooted, °ingrained, °instinctive *or* instinctual, *Technical* connate: *A gift for music is inborn.*

incandescent *adj.* °glowing, red-hot, white-hot, alight, aflame, °flaming, °burning, °fiery, candent, flaring: *Light-bulbs contain an incandescent filament.*

incapable *adj.* **1** Often, ***incapable of***: °unable (to), °powerless (to), °incompetent (to), unfit (to), °unqualified (to), °impotent (to), unequal to, not up to: *He seems incapable of completing his assignment.* **2** ***incapable of***: insusceptible to, °resistant to, impervious to, ill-disposed to, °disinclined to, not open to: *He is incapable of dishonesty.*

incapacitate *v.* disable, °cripple, °paralyse, °lame, °wound, °maim, °impair, °weaken, enfeeble, °enervate, °exhaust, devitalize; immobilize, inactivate, deactivate, put out of °action, indispose: *Severely incapacitated in the crash, John cannot walk without the aid of crutches. The power plant was incapacitated by one well-placed grenade.*

incentive *n.* °incitement, °impetus, °encouragement, goad, °prod, °provocation, °spur, impulse, °enticement, °lure, °inducement, stimulus, motivation, *Colloq* carrot: *The discount is offered as an incentive to buy a new car.*

incidence *n.* frequency, °rate, °degree, °extent, °occurrence, °prevalence; °quantity, °amount, °number: *The incidence of heart disease is high in Britain.*

incident *n.* **1** °event, °occasion, °occurrence, °proceeding, °circumstance, °fact, °happening, °experience, °episode: *A curious incident led to the discovery.* **2** °disturbance, °scene, °affair, °upset, commotion, °fracas, °skirmish, set-to, *Colloq* to-do, do: *The police were called because of an incident at the pub next door.*

incidental *adj.* **1** °casual, °chance, fortuitous, aleatory, °random, °haphazard, serendipitous, unpredictable, °accidental, adventitious, unplanned, unlooked-for, *Colloq* fluky: *Any good that came from the war was incidental.* **2** °subordinate, °secondary, ancillary, °minor, lesser, °non-essential, unimportant, trivial, °negligible, °inconsequential, °insignificant, °petty, °trifling, °paltry: *The incidental events were not covered by the press.*

incidentally *adv.* **1** by the °way, by the by, apropos (of), parenthetically: *Incidentally, I won't be able to go the party tonight.* **2** casually, as °luck would have it, accidentally, by °chance, perchance: *In addition to being held for murder, he was incidentally charged with possession of an illegal weapon.*

incision *n.* °cut, °gash, °slit, °slash: *The surgeon made an incision in the abdominal wall.*

incisive *adj.* **1** °keen, °sharp, °acute, °piercing, perspicacious, °perceptive, percipient, °penetrating, °trenchant, canny, °shrewd: *Shirley offered some incisive observations on the matter.* **2** °sarcastic, °biting, mordant, °cutting, °caustic, °sardonic, ironic(al), °sharp, acid, °tart, acrid, acrimonious, °bitter, acerbic, cynical, stinging, °critical: *Your incisive comments are not really appreciated, George.*

incite *v.* °stimulate, °inspire, °prompt, °move, °stir, °stir *or* °whip *or* °work up, bestir, °excite, °fire, exhort, °agitate, °foment, °inflame, °provoke, °rally, goad, °spur, °prick, °prod, °drive, °push, egg on, °encourage, °urge, °influence, °wake, waken, awaken, °rouse, °arouse: *Who was it that incited the crowd to violence?*

incitement *n.* **1** stimulation, instigating, spurring, urging, influencing, awakening, wakening, arousing, prodding, prompting, °stirring, °whipping, °exciting, firing, exhorting, agitating, fomenting, inflaming, provoking, rallying, goading, pricking, needling: *Certain rabble-rousers have been accused of incitement of the crowds at the football stadiums.* **2** stimulus, °incentive, °inducement, °enticement, °temptation, impulse, motivation, °influence, instigation, °provocation, °inspiration, °persuasion, exhortation, °agitation, fomentation, °inflammation, arousal, °encouragement, °excitement: *Greed is a powerful incitement to dishonesty.*

incivility *n.* rudeness, boorishness, coarseness, discourtesy, uncourtliness, unmannerliness, indecorum, indecorousness, discourteousness, impoliteness, tactlessness, ungentlemanliness, bad °breeding, ill °breeding, bad °manners, °misbehaviour: *The incivility with which the ambassador was treated is unforgivable.*

inclement *adj.* °extreme, intemperate, °severe, °harsh, rigorous; °stormy, °violent, rainy, squally, blustery, °raw, °bad, °tempestuous: *We are expecting inclement weather for the weekend.*

inclination *n.* **1** °bow, bowing, °bend, bending, °nod, °nodding, °tilt, tilting: *His tacit sign of recognition was an inclination of his head.* **2** °slope, °slant, °angle, °bend, °incline, °tilt: *The inclination of the track is far too steep for such a vehicle.* **3** °disposition, predisposition, °tendency, °bent, °bias, °leaning, °preference, °turn, °cast, proclivity, propensity, °attitude, proneness, susceptibility, predilection, °partiality, °affection, °taste, °liking, °desire, velleity: *His inclination in favour of the offer is largely instinctive.* **4** °desire, °longing, craving, °appetite, °taste, °stomach, °sympathy, predilection, °penchant, °fancy, °eagerness, °enthusiasm, zeal, °fervour, °ardour: *I have no inclination to watch open-heart surgery.*

incline *v.* **1** °tend, °lean, °bend, °bow, °slant, °tilt, °angle, bank, °slope, ascend, °rise, °descend: *The road inclines to the horizontal after a curve.* **2** °dispose, °influence, °persuade, predispose, °make, °lead, °prejudice, °bias: *Their accents might incline you to think of them as foreigners.* **3** °tend, °lean, gravitate, °show °favour *or* °preference, be attracted to, be °biased *or* °prejudiced, have a °mind; be °disposed *or* predisposed, °lean: *I incline towards the other candidate. He inclines towards corpulence.*
—*n.* **4** °slope, °pitch, °grade, gradient, °slant, °ramp, °hill, °dip, descent, declivity, °rise, ascent, acclivity: *The car picked up speed going down one incline and slowed going up the next.*

inclined *adj.* **1** tending, °disposed, predisposed, °prone, °willing, °keen, °eager, *Colloq* of a °mind: *Though she is inclined to believe she has doubts.* **2** °likely, apt, °liable, minded, °prone: *He is equally inclined to kiss you as kill you.* **3** sloping, slanting, °leaning, bending, tilting, gravitating, °bearing, verging: *This wall is slightly inclined towards the river.*

include *v.* **1** °incorporate, °embody, comprise, °embrace, °cover, encompass, °take in, subsume, °comprehend, °contain: *Staff changes are included in the plan for reorganization.* **2** classify, °categorize, °group, °file, °list, catalogue, °tabulate, °register: *Did you include psychology among the social sciences?* **3** °involve, °count, °number, °allow for: *Please don't forget to include me in the invitation list.*

inclusion *n.* incorporation, involvement, counting, numbering, grouping, classification: *The inclusion of her name among the culprits was an error.*

inclusive *adj.* **1** °comprehensive, °general, all-encompassing, °wide, °broad, °extensive, °full, °umbrella, blanket, across the °board, all-in-one, unified: *We have an inclusive insurance policy that covers the entire family.* **2** ***inclusive of***: including, embracing, comprising, °taking in, covering, incorporating, embodying: *Is this bill inclusive of service?*

incognito *adj.* **1** °unknown, disguised, concealed, °unidentified, in °disguise, unrecognizable, unrecognized: *I did not tell them who I was; I wanted to remain incognito.*
—*adv.* **2** unrecognizably, in °disguise, °secretly, on the °sly, under °cover, clandestinely: *Why travel incognito if no one knows or cares who you really are?*

incoherent *adj.* °confused, garbled, °mixed up, disordered, jumbled, muddled, scrambled, °rambling, illogical, irrational, °wild, unstructured, disjoined, °disconnected, °disjointed, °loose, unconnected, uncoordinated, unintelligible, °inarticulate: *He arrived late with an incoherent excuse involving measles, his car, and a policeman.*

incombustible *adj.* °non-flammable, non-inflammable, fireproof, non-combustible; flame-proof: *She has to wear incombustible clothing at her job.*

income *n.* °return, °revenue(s), °receipts, proceeds, °profit(s), °gain(s), takings: *Most of his income is from investments.*

incoming *adj.* **1** arriving, entering: *Incoming passengers must pass through customs.* **2** °new, entering: *They are trying to predict the likely policies of the incoming government.*

incomparable *adj.* beyond °compare, unequalled, °matchless, °peerless, inimitable, °unparalleled, unrivalled, °nonpareil, °transcendent, °surpassing, °supreme, °superior, °superlative, unsurpassed, unsurpassable: *Her performance as Lady Macbeth was incomparable.*

incompatible *adj.* °mismatched, unsuited, °discordant, clashing, jarring, °inconsistent, °contradictory, conflicting, uncongenial, irreconcilable, °incongruous; antithetic, °opposed, °opposite, °contrary, antipathetic, antagonistic, °hostile: *The colours in the carpet are incompatible with those in the curtains. My sister and I are totally incompatible and can never meet without arguing.*

incompetence *n.* °inability, incapacity, inadequacy, insufficiency, deficiency, °ineptitude, inefficiency, uselessness, faultiness: *The students' failure to perform well is often attributable to the incompetence of their teachers.*

incompetent *adj.* °unqualified, unfit, °unable, °incapable, unskilled, unskilful, °inept, maladroit, inexpert, °awkward, floundering, °clumsy, bungling, gauche, °useless, °inadequate, °insufficient, °ineffective, °ineffectual, °inefficient: *Incompetent managers need competent secretaries in order to survive.*

incomplete *adj.* unfinished, °undone, °imperfect, °undeveloped, °deficient, °defective, unaccomplished, °partial, °sketchy, °crude, °rough, °fragmentary, fragmented, °piecemeal: *An incomplete manuscript of a new novel was found in his desk.*

incomprehensible *adj.* unintelligible, unfathomable, impenetrable, °deep, abstruse, arcane, °recondite, indecipherable, undecipherable, inscrutable, °cryptic, °obscure, °opaque, °dark, °occult, °perplexing, °mysterious, mystifying, enigmatic, °puzzling, over (someone's) head, baffling, unimaginable, °inconceivable: *They spoke in Swahili, an incomprehensible language to me.*

inconceivable *adj.* °incredible, °unbelievable, °unthinkable, unimaginable, °incomprehensible, °unheard-of, undreamed of *or* undreamt of, unthought of, °impossible, °overwhelming, staggering, *Colloq* mind-boggling: *Putting a man on Mars before 2000 is inconceivable.*

inconclusive *adj.* °indecisive, °unresolved, °indefinite, °unsettled, °open, indeterminate, in °limbo, *Colloq* up in the air: *The test results are inconclusive, so we must continue our investigations.*

incongruous *adj.* °inconsistent, inharmonious, disharmonious, °discordant, dissonant, disconsonant, °incoherent, °incompatible, incongruent, conflicting, °unbecoming, °unseemly, unsuited, unsuitable, unapt, °inappropriate, misallied, unfitting, unfit, °improper, malapropos, unmeet, °absurd, discrepant, disparate, °different, °divergent, disagreeing, °contrary, °contradictory, °paradoxical, out of °step, out of keeping, out of °line: *That jacket looks incongruous with those trousers. It was incongruous to see two octogenarians dancing at the disco.*

inconsequential *adj.* unimportant, °insignificant, trivial, °trifling, nugatory, inconsiderable, inappreciable, °negligible, °minor, °paltry, °petty, °immaterial, °slight, lightweight, °worthless, *Colloq* piddling: *Why dwell on inconsequential details?*

inconsiderate *adj.* °thoughtless, unthoughtful, °unthinking, unconcerned, uncaring, unmindful, °heedless, unheeding, insensitive, °unsympathetic, °tactless, °intolerant, °rude, °ungracious: *How could you be so inconsiderate as to work late on my birthday?*

inconsistent *adj.* **1** See **incongruous,** above. **2** °irregular, °capricious, °fickle, °erratic, °inconstant, uneven, unpredictable, °unreliable, undependable, °unstable, unsteady, °changeable, °variable: *Their behaviour is so inconsistent that I can't tell what they'll do next.*

inconsolable *adj.* disconsolate, °broken-hearted, heartbroken, °desolate, °forlorn, despairing, °miserable, °wretched, grief-stricken: *They are inconsolable over the death of their dog.*

inconspicuous *adj.* unnoticeable, °unnoticed, °unobtrusive, unostentatious, °insignificant, °indefinite, °indistinguishable, °undistinguished; °modest, unassuming, °discreet: *Wearing a grey coat and hat, he was quite inconspicuous in the crowd. He played an inconspicuous role in the entire affair.*

inconstancy *n.* changeableness, fickleness, irregularity, mutability, variability, unsteadiness, unsteadfastness, capriciousness, volatility, mercurialness *or* mercuriality, inconsistency, unreliability; faithlessness, unfaithfulness, changeability: *How do you deal with inconstancy in one you thought a friend?*

inconstant *adj.* °changeable, mutable, °fickle, °capricious, mercurial, °volatile, vacillating, unsteady, unsteadfast, °irresolute, °unreliable, undependable, fluctuating, wavering, °erratic, °inconsistent, °flighty, °unstable, °unsettled, °fitful, °vague, °indefinite, °variable, °moody: *His supporters proved inconstant, and he fell from power. The inconstant wind blew their craft hither and thither.*

incontinent *adj.* **1** unrestrained, unconstrained, unrestricted, °uncontrolled, uncontrollable, ungoverned, °ungovernable, unbridled, uncurbed: *She must learn to suppress her incontinent tongue.* **2** °lecherous, libidinous, °lascivious, °libertine, °lustful, °lewd, debauched, °wanton, °dissolute, °loose, lubricious *or* lubricous, salacious, °profligate, °obscene, °dirty, °filthy: *Members of the Hell-Fire Club were well known for their incontinent behaviour.* **3** self-soiling, bedwetting, *Medicine* enuretic: *Some old people lose control and become incontinent.*

incontrovertible *adj.* irrefutable, °indisputable, indubitable, undeniable, incontestable, °unquestionable, °sure, °certain, °definite, °definitive, established, °absolute, °positive: *The fingerprint was incontrovertible evidence that he had been there.*

inconvenience *n.* **1** °disadvantage, °discomfort, °pain, °trouble, °bother, °annoyance, °nuisance, awkwardness, °disturbance, disruption, °burden, °drawback, °hindrance, °impediment, °difficulty, °upset: *How are you coping with the inconvenience of walking with crutches?* **2** cumbersomeness, unwieldiness, burdensomeness, onerousness, troublesomeness, disadvantageousness, awkwardness, inappropriateness, untimeliness: *The delay has led to considerable public inconvenience.*
—*v.* **3** discommode, °trouble, incommode, °disturb, °disrupt, °upset, °put out, °bother, °annoy, °irritate, °irk: *Would it inconvenience you to meet me at the station?*

inconvenient *adj.* cumbersome, °unwieldy, °burdensome, onerous, °troublesome, bothersome, annoying, irritating, °irksome, °unsettling, °disturbing, upsetting, disrupting, disadvantageous, °awkward, °inappropriate; inexpedient, °inopportune, untimely, ill-timed: *Those large boxes of washing-powder are inconvenient because they're so heavy. It is inconvenient for me to go to the door now.*

incorporate *v.* °embody, °include, °combine, comprise, °embrace, °integrate, consolidate, °unite, °amalgamate, assimilate, coalesce, °unify; °merge, °mix, °blend: *The university incorporates several independent colleges. Gently fold in the egg whites, incorporating them into the mixture.*

incorrect *adj.* °wrong, °mistaken, °inaccurate, °untrue, °imprecise, °inexact, °erroneous, fallacious, °specious; °improper, °false, °faulty: *Your method is right but the answer is incorrect. That is the incorrect key for this lock.*

incorrigible *adj.* °bad, °naughty, °villainous, °wicked, °sinful, °hopeless; intractable, unchangeable, unalterable, °habitual, inveterate, °incurable, °stubborn, hardened, obdurate, °inflexible, uncontrollable: *When a teenager, Giles was absolutely incorrigible. Among other things, he was an incorrigible liar.*

incorrupt *adj.* **1** °moral, °upright, °righteous, °pure, upstanding, °honourable, °good, °virtuous, °honest, straightforward, °straight, unimpeachable, incorruptible, undefiled, °impeccable, °spotless, °immaculate, °faultless, °flawless: *Show me one nation run by a totally incorrupt government.* **2** error-free, °correct, uncorrupted: *He possesses the only incorrupt manuscript of the play.*

increase *v.* **1** °grow, °swell, °enlarge, dilate, wax, °expand, °extend, distend, °inflate, augment, snowball, °enhance, °heighten, °raise, °develop, multiply, burgeon *or* bourgeon, °flourish, °proliferate, °spread, broaden, °widen, °lengthen: *Since you left, my work has increased threefold.* **2** °prolong, °advance, °further, °improve, °better, °strengthen: *The more lottery tickets you buy, the more you increase your chances of winning.*
—*n.* **3** °growth, enlargement, °expansion, °extension, augmentation, enhancement, °development, multiplication, °proliferation, °spread: *The increase in scientific knowledge has been phenomenal.* **4** °addition, °increment, escalation, inflation, °gain, °rise, °boost: *Increases in costs are reflected in increases in prices.* **5** ***on the increase***: waxing, developing, growing, expanding, increasing, escalating, on the °rise, proliferating, spreading: *Trade with the Far East will be on the increase next year.*

incredible *adj.* **1** °unbelievable, beyond °belief, °inconceivable, unimaginable, °unthinkable, °improbable, °implausible, °far-fetched, °absurd, °preposterous, °ridiculous, °unlikely, °impossible, °unrealistic, °unreal, °fictitious, mythic(al): *Incredible as it may appear, continents move a few inches a year.* **2** °extraordinary, astounding, astonishing, °amazing, wonderful, awe-inspiring, °awesome, tremendous, °marvellous, °prodigious, *Colloq* far-out, *US* humongous: *The incredible amounts spent on arms could be better spent on medical research.*

incredulous *adj.* disbelieving, °unbelieving, dubious, °doubtful, °sceptical, mistrustful, °distrustful, °suspicious: *We were incredulous when we learnt who had won the award.*

increment *n.* °increase, °addition, °gain, accrual *or chiefly Brit* accrument, augmentation: *The increment last year barely compensated for inflation.*

incriminate *v.* °accuse, °charge, °blame, °implicate, inculpate, °indict, °impeach, °involve, °entangle, *Colloq* °point the °finger at, *Chiefly US* put the °finger on, *Slang US* °finger: *The suspect confessed and incriminated two others.*

incubate *v.* °hatch, °brood; °nurse, nurture, °develop: *How long have you been incubating this plan?*

incumbent *adj.* **1** °obligatory, °necessary, required, °mandatory, compulsory, binding, °demanding, commanding, prescribed: *As their father, you ought to feel it incumbent on you to talk to the children's teachers.* **2** office-holding: *The incumbent chairman is not responsible for his predecessor's mistakes.*
—*n.* **3** office-holder, °official, °occupant: *As the incumbent, you have a better chance of being re-elected.*

incur *v.* °bring upon *or* on (oneself), °draw, °attract, °arouse, °provoke, invite, expose (oneself) to, lay (oneself) °open to: *For some reason he incurred the displeasure of his manager.*

incurable *adj.* **1** irremediable, °terminal, inoperable, °fatal, °hopeless: *The doctor told me yesterday that the condition is incurable.* **2** °hopeless, inveterate, °habitual, °incorrigible, dyed in the wool, unflagging, °relentless, irredeemable; irreparable, unrectifiable: *You are an incurable optimist if you think you will complete this book by the deadline.*

indebted *adj.* obligated, owing, °obliged, °beholden, °bound, °liable, °responsible: *I am indebted to the Salvation Army for their help.*

indecent *adj.* **1** indecorous, indelicate, °immodest, °improper, °unbecoming, unsuitable, unfit, °inappropriate; in °bad °taste: *When he proposed marriage she accepted with indecent haste.* **2** °unseemly, °shameless, °shameful, °offensive, °outrageous, °repellent, °repulsive, °distasteful, °ill-mannered, °rude, °suggestive, °coarse, °risqué, °vulgar, °blue, °obscene, °gross, °rank, °prurient, °dirty, °foul, °filthy, °pornographic, ithyphallic, scatological, salacious, °lascivious, licentious, °lewd, lubricious *or* lubricous, smutty, °vile, °degenerate, debauched: *There are always a lot of complaints about indecent language on television.*

indecision *n.* hesitation, wavering, indecisiveness, vacillation, irresolution, uncertainty, ambivalence, °shilly-shally *or* shilly-shallying, °fluctuation, tergiversation: *Her indecision stems from caution, not ignorance of the issues.*

indecisive *adj.* **1** hesitating, °hesitant, wavering, °doubtful, vacillating, undecided, °irresolute, °uncertain, of two minds, ambivalent, shilly-shallying, °wishy-washy, namby-pamby, fluctuating, tergiversating: *Why are you so assertive at the office yet so indecisive at home?* **2** °indefinite, indeterminate, undecided, °inconclusive, °open, °unsettled, °moot, °doubtful: *The battle was indecisive, with both sides incurring heavy losses.*

indeed *adv.* **1** certainly, °surely, to be °sure, °doubtless(ly), °undoubtedly, undeniably, °definitely, °positively, °absolutely, °exactly, °just so, °actually, °truly, truthfully, °seriously, (all) joking aside, in (point of) °fact, of °course, °really, in °reality, to be °realistic, °naturally, upon my °word, on my °honour, on my °oath, *Brit* °rather, *Colloq* no kidding: *Indeed, that is the news he has been expecting.* **2** what is more, °still, not to say, as a matter of °fact, if the °truth be known, to say the least: *His had been a depressing, indeed miserable childhood.*
—*interj.* **3** Is that so!, You don't say!, Really!, By George!, By Jove!, (Upon) my word!, My goodness!, Goodness!, Gracious!, Mercy!, Good Lord!, Good heavens!, My stars!, Fancy that!, Imagine (that)!, Well, I'll be (damned)!, *Colloq Brit* Blimey!, Cor!, Crikey!: *'I've torn up the winning lottery ticket.' 'Indeed!'*

indefinite *adj.* **1** °uncertain, undetermined, undefined, °imprecise, °inexact, inexplicit, unspecified, °unsettled, unfixed, unspecific, non-specific, °vague, °general, indeterminate, undecided, *sub judice*: *The time of the meeting was indefinite.* **2** °vague, unclear, °obscure, °confused, confusing, °puzzling, baffling, °cryptic, bewildering, mystifying, °equivocal, °ambiguous, unspecific, non-specific, inexplicit, °inexact, °imprecise: *Your directions for getting here were too indefinite.* **3** ill-defined, undefined, blurred, blurry, °hazy, °indistinct, °obscure, °dim, °fuzzy, unrecognizable, °indistinguishable: *Indefinite shapes loomed in the fog.* **4** °unlimited, °unknown, uncounted, uncountable, undefinable, indeterminate, indeterminable, unbounded, °boundless, °immeasurable, incalculable, °limitless, °endless, °infinite: *He pondered the indefinite capacities of the mind.* **5** °hesitant, °vague, shilly-shallying, vacillating, °indecisive, undecided, °inconstant, wavering, unsure, °uncertain, *Colloq* °wishy-washy: *She is still indefinite about going to the party.*

indelible *adj.* ineradicable *or* uneradicable *or* non-eradicable, inerasable *or* unerasable *or* non-erasable, ineffaceable, inexpungible, °indestructible, uncancellable *or* non-cancellable, °enduring, °permanent, °lasting, °fixed, °ingrained, inextirpable: *The laundry marks are in indelible ink. Irena makes an indelible impression on everyone she meets.*

indelicacy *n.* coarseness, crudeness, roughness, °vulgarity, boorishness, churlishness, offensiveness, rudeness, immodesty, indecency, shamelessness; °incivility, indecorum, inelegance, uncourtliness, unmannerliness, impoliteness, unrefinement, unseemliness, tastelessness, °bad *or* °poor °taste, grossness: *She refuses to comment on the indelicacy of his proposal.*

indemnity *n.* **1** compensation, repayment, reimbursement, °remuneration, recompense, °consideration, °restitution, reparation(s), redress, indemnification, °return, quid pro quo, °restoration, °award, °reward, °payment, disbursement, °amends, °requital, °atonement, °reckoning, quittance: *The victors demanded indemnity for the losses they had suffered.* **2** °insurance, °protection, °security, °safety, °guarantee, °assurance, underwriting, °warrant, °endorsement, certification; °exemption, impunity, °privilege: *Am I covered for indemnity against third-party claims?*

indentation *n.* °notch, dent, °nick, °cut, °score, °mark, °depression, °impression, °hollow, dimple, °pit; *Typography* indention: *The chair legs had left small indentations in the parquet floor. The indentation of each paragraph should be five spaces.*

independence *n.* **1** °freedom, °liberty, autonomy, °sovereignty, self-rule, home °rule, self-determination, °self-government, self-direction, autarchy: *The colony gained independence from Portugal.* **2** °confidence, °self-confidence, self-sufficiency, self-reliance, self-assurance: *Edwina asserted her independence by taking over the company herself.*

independent *adj.* **1** °free, self-governing, autonomous, °sovereign: *In 1829 Greece was acknowledged as an independent state.* **2** unrestrained, unrestricted, unfettered, untrammelled, unregulated, °uncontrolled, °separate(d), unconnected, °disconnected, °unrelated, °distinct: *Air is made up of independent particles.* **3** self-reliant, °self-sufficient, self-assured, (self-)°confident, °bold, individualistic, °competent: *For a six-year-old, he is very independent.* **4** °voluntary, °non-partisan, °spontaneous, °unsolicited, unbidden, °unprejudiced, unbiased, °non-aligned, unaligned, °disinterested, °neutral: *Four independent witnesses testified to seeing him at the scene of the crime.* **5** °unlimited, unrestricted, affluent, °self-sufficient; unearned: *She is a woman of independent means.* **6** unallied, unaffiliated, uncommitted, individualistic, undecided: *Independent candidates outnumber those of the two main parties in this election.* **7** °outside, °external, unaffiliated, non-affiliated, unconnected, °disinterested: *An independent auditor was engaged to go over the company's books.* **8** ***independent of***: irrespective of, disregarding, °notwithstanding, ignoring, excluding; °exclusive of, °except for, °barring, °apart from, °besides, beyond, *US* aside from: *He insists on doing things his way, independent of others' feelings. Independent of you and me, no one cares what he does.* —*n.* **9** °individual, °nonconformist, maverick, *Colloq* loner: *He is an independent, not affiliated to any political party.*

indestructible *adj.* °durable, long-lasting, °everlasting, °eternal, °endless, °perennial, °permanent, °fixed, unchanging, °changeless, unchangeable, °indelible, ineradicable, inextirpable, immutable, unalterable, °constant, undying, non-perishable, imperishable; unbreakable, non-breakable, shatter-proof: *The problem is that many plastics are virtually indestructible.*

index *n.* **1** °guide, directory, °list, listing, °table of contents, catalogue, °key, °thesaurus: *To find synonyms for a word in this book, look first in the index.* **2** °mark, °sign, °clue, °token, °hint, °pointer, °indicator, °indication, °guide: *An index to his feelings can be seen in the way he treats people.* **3** index °finger, forefinger, first °finger; °pointer, marker, needle, *Chiefly Brit typography* hand, *Chiefly US typography* fist: *Use an index to emphasize important paragraphs.* **4** °ratio, °measure, °formula, °factor: *The cephalic index is the ratio of the width of a skull to its length multiplied by 100.*

indicate *v.* **1** °point out, °point to, °mark, °specify, °designate; call *or* direct °attention to, °show: *The thermometer indicated that the temperature was 22°C. Sally indicated the place where the dam would be built.* **2** °imply, °suggest, betoken, °manifest, °signify, bespeak, °reveal, evince, °evidence, °denote: *Measles is indicated by the presence of Koplik's spots.* **3** °suggest, °hint, °imply, °intimate; °say, °express, °state, °disclose, °tell, °make known, °make °clear, °register, °show, °display, °exhibit: *His frown indicated his doubts. She indicated her displeasure in a few, well-chosen words.* **4** °call for, °require, °demand, °need, °recommend: *The doctor advised that a surgical procedure is indicated in such cases.*

indication *n.* **1** °sign, °signal, °token, °suggestion, °hint, intimation, °inkling, °clue, °implication, °symptom: *A bullet-riddled corpse, said the detective, is usually a good indication of foul play.* **2** reading, °measure, °degree: *The indication on the pressure gauge is reaching the danger point.* **3** °omen, portent, forewarning, °warning, augury, foreshadowing, foretoken: *Those black clouds are an indication that a storm is brewing. Can't you give us any indication of what will become of us?* **4** ***indications***: °evidence, °data, °clues, °signs: *Indications are that she left on the last train.*

indicative of *adj.* signifying, indicating, indicatory of, suggesting, °suggestive of, hinting (at), °symptomatic of, denotative of, °characteristic of, °typical of, typifying: *Repeated stalling is indicative of some fault in the fuel.*

indicator *n.* °pointer, needle; °gauge, meter, °display: *The indicator reads exactly 67°C.*

indict *v.* Often, ***indict for***: °charge (with), °accuse (with *or* of), arraign (for), °incriminate (in *or* for), inculpate (in *or* for), cite (for *or* with), °denounce (for), °blame (for *or* with); °summon, summons, subpoena: *She has been indicted for murder in the first degree.*

indifference *n.* **1** unconcern, apathy, listlessness, disinterest, coolness, nonchalance, insouciance, aloofness, °detachment, °disregard, inattention, pococuranteism *or* pococurantism, coldness, phlegm, stolidity, callousness, insensibility, impassiveness *or* impassivity: *I cannot believe the indifference she showed on learning about the tragedy.* **2** unimportance, insignificance, irrelevance, unconcern, inconsequence, °triviality: *Whether I go or stay is a matter of indifference to me.* **3** dispassion, disinterestedness, impartiality, neutrality, °objectivity, fairness, equitableness, even-handedness: *The judges demonstrated their indifference by awarding first prize to a novice.*

indifferent *adj.* **1** unconcerned, apathetic, uncaring, °listless, °disinterested, uninterested, °cool, °nonchalant, °lukewarm, °lackadaisical, Laodicean, °dispassionate, insouciant, °aloof, °detached, °distant, removed, °inattentive, pococurante, °cold, °phlegmatic, °stolid, °callous, unemotional, uncompassionate, insensitive, unfeeling, °inconsiderate, °unsympathetic, °insensible, °impassive: *Joan remained totally indifferent to Charles's attentions.* **2** °impartial, °neutral, °just, even-handed, °objective, °fair, °equitable, unbiased, °unprejudiced, °non-partisan, non-discriminatory, °dispassionate, °disinterested: *The problem is in reaching an indifferent judgement.* **3** °neutral, °average, °mediocre, °fair, °undistinguished, uninspired, lightweight, °passable, middling, °ordinary, commonplace, °everyday, so so, not bad; °poor, °inferior, not very *or* particularly *or* especially °good, *Slang Brit* naff: *He is a writer of indifferent quality. I held indifferent cards but lost little money.* **4** unimportant, °insignificant, trivial, °trifling, nugatory, °immaterial, °inconsequential, °minor, inappreciable, °slight, neither here nor there: *It is indifferent to him where she spends her money.*

indigenous *adj.* **1** °native, °local, autochthonous, endemic, °natural, °aboriginal, °original: *The indigenous inhabitants were displaced by marauding tribes.* **2** innate, °inborn, inbred, °inherent: *It is often difficult to distinguish between man's indigenous and his acquired characteristics.*

indigent *adj.* °needy, °poor, °destitute, poverty-stricken, in °want, penniless, °impoverished, °penurious, impecunious, necessitous, *Colloq* (dead *or* flat) °broke, stony-broke, °hard up, °short, on one's uppers, *Brit* skint, *US* strapped: *The two brothers made certain that their indigent parents were well looked after.*

indigestion *n.* dyspepsia, °upset °stomach, °stomach °distress; stomach-ache, gastralgia: *A bit of bicarbonate of soda cured my indigestion at once.*

indignant *adj.* provoked, exasperated, °disgruntled, piqued, irked, irritated, annoyed, vexed, °angry, °furious, irate, angered, enraged, incensed, wrathful, in high dudgeon, in a °temper, in a °rage, in a °pet, *Literary* wroth, *Colloq* peeved, riled, in a °huff, huffy, miffed, °mad, livid, °sore, *US* teed off, *Slang* pissed off: *Peter was quite indignant to learn that the publisher had lost his manuscript.*

indignation *n.* °anger, °fury, °rage, wrath, exasperation, irritation, °annoyance, vexation, °resentment, *Literary* ire, choler: *She was filled with righteous indignation at the treatment she received.*

indignity *n.* °insult, affront, °outrage, °injury, °offence, °humiliation, °disrespect, °slight, °dishonour, snub, obloquy, contumely, °scorn, reproach, °abuse, discourtesy, °aspersion, *Colloq* °slap (in the face): *The duchess had to suffer the indignity of arrest for shoplifting.*

indirect *adj.* **1** °roundabout, circuitous, circumambient, °devious, °tortuous, zigzag, winding, °rambling, roving, wandering, °erratic, °meandering, ambiguous, °crooked, °oblique, twisted, twisting; circumlocutory, periphrastic: *In an indirect way she told me that I was fired.* **2** °secondary, °incidental, ancillary, collateral, °accidental, °side, °subordinate, °subsidiary, °accessory, additional, adscititious, adventitious: *An indirect effect of winning the prize was an offer of more work.*

indiscreet *adj.* °imprudent, °tactless, incautious, impolitic, undiplomatic, °improvident, injudicious, °ill-advised, ill-judged, ill-considered, °rash, °reckless, °audacious, °bold, temerarious, °impulsive, °hasty, °impetuous, °thoughtless, insensitive, °heedless, °careless, °unthinking, °mindless, unwise, °naïve, °foolish, °foolhardy: *Your reference to her plastic surgery was indiscreet to say the least.*

indiscretion *n.* **1** imprudence, tactlessness, improvidence, injudiciousness, rashness, recklessness, audacity, boldness, temerity, impulsiveness, hastiness, °haste, impetuousness, impetuosity, thoughtlessness, insensitivity, heedlessness, carelessness, °naïvety, foolishness, foolhardiness, °folly: *He was guilty of indiscretion in talking to the press about the confidential report.* **2** °blunder, °error, °mistake, °slip, °lapse, °misstep, gaffe, faux pas, °peccadillo, *Colloq* boner, *Brit* bloomer: *He spent much of his adult life paying for the indiscretions of his youth.*

indiscriminate *adj.* **1** undiscriminating, unselective, unparticular, uncritical, undiscerning, °careless, °promiscuous, °random: *Viola seems indiscriminate in her choice of companions.* **2** °confused, °haphazard, unorganized, °chaotic, disorganized, jumbled, disordered, disarranged, scrambled, mixed-up, °casual, °random, unsystematic, unsystematized, uncoordinated, unmethodical, wholesale, °erratic, *Colloq* higgledy-piggledy: *The Aztecs were victims of indiscriminate slaughter at the hands of the conquistadors.*

indispensable *adj.* **1** °crucial, °vital, °essential, °urgent, °imperative, °necessary, needed, needful, required, requisite, demanded, in °demand, called-for, of the °essence, °important, compelling: *A good television manner is indispensable in a national leader these days.* **2** °key, °unavoidable, inescapable, ineluctable, compulsory, °mandatory, *sine qua non*, °obligatory: *Are a black bowler and tightly furled umbrella still indispensable to doing business in the City?*

indisposed *adj.* **1** °ill, ailing, unwell, °sick, °sickly, °unsound, °unhealthy, in °bad °health, valetudinarian, out of commission, *Colloq* on the sick-list, (doing) °poorly, laid up, in a °bad °way, not up to snuff, off one's feed *or Brit also* grub, under the °weather: *Madam is indisposed and cannot have tea with you.* **2** °averse, °disinclined, °loath, unwilling, °reluctant, °resistant, °hesitant: *The judge was indisposed to leniency in such a serious case.*

indisputable *adj.* °unquestionable, °incontrovertible, incontestable, irrefutable, undeniable, indubitable, beyond °doubt, °sure, °certain, °positive, °definite, °definitive, °absolute, °fixed: *It was indisputable that the outlook was grim. The show was an indisputable success.*

indistinct *adj.* **1** °faint, °dim, °obscure, °vague, blurred, blurry, °filmy, °hazy, °misty, bleary, °shadowy, °fuzzy, foggy, °murky, °muddy, unclear, indiscernible, °illegible, muffled, unintelligible, °indistinguishable, indeterminate, °confused, °indefinite: *I could barely make out an indistinct figure in the dark. The writing on the matchbox was indistinct.* **2** °indistinguishable, °ambiguous, not °distinct, °equivocal, inseparable, ill-defined, undefined, °nebulous, °vague, °confused: *The identity of the three brothers is indistinct in my mind.*

indistinguishable *adj.* **1** Often, ***indistinguishable from***: undifferentiated (from), °identical (to), °alike, °like two peas in a pod, °twin, inseparable: *He is indistinguishable from his brother. Her fingerprints and those found on the dagger are indistinguishable.* **2** indiscernible, °imperceptible, °indefinite, unclear, °indistinct: *His good qualities were indistinguishable to me.*

individual *adj.* **1** °single, °sole, °particular, °separate, °distinct, °discrete, °solitary, lone: *Consider the entire utterance, not just the individual words.* **2** °singular, °special, °specific, idiosyncratic, own, °characteristic, °distinctive, individualistic, °unique, °peculiar, °personal, °proper; unitary: *She has her individual style of dressing.*

—*n.* **3** °person, °human (being), (living) °soul, °mortal; °one, °party: *In a democracy each individual is entitled to one vote.*

individualist *n.* °independent, freethinker, °nonconformist, maverick, loner, lone wolf: *Nick is an individualist and seldom agrees with the majority.*

individually *adv.* °one at a time, °singly, °one by one, °separately, severally, °apart: *We must study each of these specimens individually.*

indoctrinate *v.* °train, °teach, °instruct, °school, °discipline, °drill, brainwash, propagandize; inculcate, imbue, °instil, °implant: *The children were indoctrinated to believe that they were members of the master race. He indoctrinated them with the idea that they were capable of anything.*

indolence *n.* laziness, slothfulness, °sloth, °sluggishness, °idleness, °lethargy, shiftlessness, languor, languidness, lassitude, listlessness, °torpor, torpidity, °inertia, inaction, °inactivity, fainéance, *dolce far niente*, oscitancy: *After winning the lottery, he spent his days in indolence.*

indolent *adj.* °lazy, °slothful, sluggish, °idle, °lethargic, °shiftless, languorous, languid, °torpid, °inert, °inactive, °stagnant, fainéant, °listless: *'Peel me a grape', she said in her most indolent manner.*

indomitable *adj.* °resolute, resolved, °determined, °steadfast, °staunch, °persistent, unstoppable, °irrepressible, indefatigable, °untiring, °tireless, unflagging, unyielding, unswerving, unwavering, unflinching, undaunted, °dauntless, °fearless, unafraid, °intrepid, °brave, °courageous, plucky, mettlesome; unconquerable, °unbeatable, °invincible: *She survived the prison camp by dint of indomitable strength of character.*

induce *v.* **1** °lead, °persuade, °influence, °prevail on *or* upon, °sway, °move, °convince, °get, °talk into, °prompt, °incite, instigate, actuate, °motivate, impel, °encourage, °inspire, °stimulate, °nudge, °push, °press, °urge, °prod, goad, °spur, egg on, °coax, °cajole, °lure, °entice, inveigle, °seduce: *He was induced to sell the* *secret plans to the enemy for a large sum.* **2** °cause, °bring about *or* on, °produce, give °rise to, engender, °create, °generate, °lead to; °effect, °occasion, °set in °motion: *Some drugs induce a state of euphoria.*

inducement *n.* °attraction, °lure, °incentive, stimulus, °enticement, bait, °encouragement, °incitement, °provocation, °spur, °premium, °consideration, °reward, *Colloq* carrot, *Chiefly US* °come-on: *What inducement were you offered to take out that subscription?*

induct *v.* **1** °install *or* instal, °inaugurate, °invest, instate, °establish, °swear in: *Crocker was inducted as president of the lodge last night.* **2** °call up, °enlist, conscript, °enrol, °register, *US* °draft: *He was inducted into the army at 18.*

indulge *v.* **1** Often, ***indulge in***: °yield (to), °succumb (to), °favour, °gratify, °humour, °oblige (with), °comply (with), °minister to, °cater to, °pander to, °treat (to), °pamper (with): *When it comes to chocolates, I indulge myself to the fullest. We indulge in an occasional beer. She indulges his every whim.* **2** °coddle, °baby, °pamper, cosset, mollycoddle, °spoil: *He doesn't believe in indulging children.*

indulgence *n.* **1** °tolerance, sufferance, °understanding, °patience, °good °will, °allowance, forbearance; acceptance, overlooking: *Genevieve's behaviour is testing the limits of Tom's indulgence.* **2** self-indulgence, °luxury, °extravagance, °profligacy, self-gratification, self-satisfaction: *A notorious pleasure-seeker, his capacity for indulgence is legendary.* **3** °treat, °luxury, °extravagance: *My sole indulgence is vintage port.*

indulgent *adj.* °tolerant, °permissive, °patient, °understanding, forbearing, °lenient, °easygoing, °relaxed, °liberal, °lax, °kind, °kindly, well-disposed, °agreeable: *Tony and Hazel are extremely indulgent parents.*

industrious *adj.* sedulous, assiduous, hard-working, °diligent, °intense, °conscientious, °energetic, °dynamic, °aggressive, °vigorous, °untiring, °tireless, indefatigable, unflagging, °persistent, pertinacious, dogged, °tenacious, *US* hustling: *The business was built up only because she was so industrious.*

industry *n.* **1** °production, °manufacture, °trade, °commerce, °business: *Competition in the car industry helps keep prices lower.* **2** diligence, assiduity, sedulousness, °energy, °exertion, °effort, °application, °perseverance, °persistence, °work, °labour, toil: *We were complimented on our industry by the teacher.* **3** industriousness, °energy, °activity, °vigour, °hustle, bustle, °dynamism, °enterprise, earnestness, °determination: *The sales office is a hive of industry.*

ineffable *adj.* **1** unutterable, unspeakable, °unmentionable, °taboo: *In certain religions, the name of the deity is ineffable.* **2** °inexpressible, indefinable *or* undefinable, indescribable *or* undescribable, beyond °description, beyond words: *The Royal Hotel had an ineffable air of serene affluence.*

ineffective *adj.* **1** unproductive, unfruitful, °bootless, °idle, °vain, °useless, °ineffectual, °inefficacious, inoperative, non-functioning, °inadequate, °insufficient, °worthless: *The anti-crime measures appear to have been ineffective.* **2** °inefficient, °incompetent, °incapable, unskilled, unskilful, °inept, unfit, unproficient: *The new office manager is totally ineffective.*

ineffectual *adj.* **1** °unsuccessful, unavailing, °futile, °bootless, °sterile, °barren, °fruitless, unproductive, °ineffective, °inefficacious, inoperative: *Our efforts to deal with pollution have been largely ineffectual.* **2** °weak, °feeble, effete, °impotent, °tame, °lame, °powerless, °inefficient, °incompetent, °inadequate: *We tried to read the inscription by the ineffectual light of a match.*

inefficacious *adj.* See **ineffectual** and **ineffective,** above.

inefficient *adj.* **1** °ineffective, °incompetent, °incapable, °unqualified, inexpert, unskilled, unskilful, unfit, °inept, °ineffectual, °deficient: *Poorly paid labour is inefficient labour.* **2** uneconomic(al), °wasteful, disorganized, °slipshod: *For our purposes, the layout of the factory is quite inefficient.*

ineligible *adj.* °unqualified, °unacceptable, unfit, unsuited, unsuitable, °inappropriate, °improper: *He is ineligible for benefit as he left his job voluntarily.*

inept *adj.* **1** °clumsy, °awkward, bungling, maladroit, ungainly, bumbling, gauche, inexpert, unskilled, unskilful, °incompetent, °inefficient: *If he is inept at sailing, he'd better become proficient.* **2** °inappropriate, inapt, °unseemly, °improper, unfitting, unfit, unsuitable, impolitic, undiplomatic, injudicious, °imprudent, °indiscreet, ill-considered, ill-judged, °ill-advised, unadvised, unadvisable *or* inadvised, °misguided, inexpedient, out of °place, unwise: *She made some inept comment and blushed furiously.*

ineptitude *n.* **1** ineptness, clumsiness, awkwardness, maladroitness, ungainliness, gaucherie, °incompetence, inefficiency, unfitness, unsuitableness: *He displays a remarkable ineptitude for the pronunciation of French.* **2** inappropriateness, inaptness, °absurdity, unsuitability, unseemliness: *The ineptitude of her comments embarrasses everyone.*

inequality *n.* **1** °disparity, °difference, °discrepancy, unevenness, nonconformity, incongruence, incongruity, inconsistency, °dissimilarity, imbalance: *The inequality between their incomes made him resentful.* **2** °bias, °prejudice, °partiality, unfairness, °injustice, inequity: *Why should they have to tolerate any inequality of treatment?*

inert *adj.* **1** °inactive, unreactive, unresponsive, °neutral: *Argon, xenon, and neon are inert gases.* **2** motionless, immobile, °inanimate, °lifeless, °still, °quiet, quiescent, stationary, °static: *He was mute and inert: it was like talking to a zombie.* **3** sluggish, °slow, °torpid, °dull, °inactive, °idle, °indolent, °lazy, °slothful, °leaden, °slack, °passive, °supine, °dormant, otiose, °listless, languid *or* languorous: *I contemplated the inert bodies sunbathing around the swimming-pool.*

inertia *n.* inertness, °inactivity, °sloth, °sluggishness, °torpor, dullness, °idleness, °indolence, laziness, slothfulness, passivity, apathy, lassitude, dormancy, listlessness, languor, immobility, motionlessness: *Adele finds it difficult to overcome her feeling of inertia in the morning.*

inestimable *adj.* **1** incalculable, °immeasurable, measureless, °untold, incomputable; °priceless, °invaluable, °precious: *You have been of inestimable help in completing the project on time.* **2** countless, innumerable, °vast, °immense, °prodigious, °boundless, unfathomable, °infinite, incalculable, °immeasurable, measureless, °untold, incomputable: *An inestimable number of organisms have inhabited the earth.*

inevitable *adj.* °unavoidable, inescapable, ineluctable, unpreventable, °certain, °sure, °destined, °fated, assured, inexorable, °irrevocable, unchangeable, °absolute, ordained, decreed, °authoritative, incontestable: *The inevitable outcome of war is misery for all participants.*

inexact *adj.* °imprecise, °inaccurate, °erroneous, °incorrect, °wrong, °false, °faulty, °indefinite, fallacious, °fuzzy, muddled: *This gauge is giving an inexact reading.*

inexcusable *adj.* unjustifiable, unjustified, indefensible, unpardonable, unforgivable, intolerable, inexpiable: *Insulting your hostess was inexcusable.*

inexhaustible *adj.* **1** °limitless, °boundless, °unlimited, unbounded, unrestricted, °endless, measureless, indeterminate, °infinite, incalculable: *The supply of tasteless television programmes seems virtually inexhaustible.* **2** °untiring, °tireless, indefatigable, unflagging, unfailing, unfaltering, unwearying, unwearied: *Bartell is an inexhaustible practical joker.*

inexpensive *adj.* °cheap, °economical, low-priced, low-cost, °reasonable, budget-priced: *What might seem inexpensive to you is very costly for me.*

inexperience *n.* immaturity, innocence, °naïvety, greenness, callowness, unsophistication: *I attribute his mistakes to inexperience.*

inexperienced *adj.* °immature, °innocent, °naïve, °green, °callow, °unsophisticated, unworldly, °unfledged, °raw, uninitiated, untrained, unschooled, °uninformed, unseasoned, *Colloq* (still) wet behind the ears, born yesterday: *Isn't she too inexperienced to take on such a great responsibility?*

inexplicable *adj.* unexplainable, °unaccountable, unintelligible, inscrutable, °puzzling, enigmatic, mystifying, °perplexing, confounding, baffling, bewildering, °incomprehensible: *I find inexplicable their refusal to allow freedom of religion.*

inexpressible *adj.* unutterable, °ineffable, unspeakable, indescribable, indefinable: *I felt inexpressible joy at seeing my children again.*

inextinguishable *adj.* °unquenchable, °irrepressible, unsuppressible; °enduring, undying, imperishable, °eternal, °everlasting: *The teacher had to cope with inextinguishable giggling. Our hopes for freedom were inextinguishable.*

inextricably *adv.* inescapably, ineluctably, unavoidably, irretrievably, °completely, inseparably, indissolubly, °totally, complicatedly, intricately: *I found myself inextricably caught up in her emotional problems.*

infallible *adj.* **1** unerring, °faultless, °flawless, °perfect, oracular, unmistaken: *The infallible logic of computers sometimes defeats their users.* **2** unfailing, dependable, °sure, °secure, °certain, °reliable, °foolproof: *The vaccination provides infallible protection against the virus.*

infamous *adj.* **1** °notorious, °disreputable, ill-famed, stigmatized, °scandalous, discreditable, °dishonourable, ignominious: *So this is the infamous house where the murders took place!* **2** °bad, °awful, °wicked, °evil, iniquitous, °villainous, heinous, °vile, °abominable, °outrageous, execrable, °abhorrent, opprobrious, °despicable, °loathsome, detestable, odious, °foul, °scurvy, °rotten, °atrocious, flagitious, °revolting, °monstrous, egregious, °base, °low, °shameful, °disgraceful: *A number of infamous criminals are portrayed in the Chamber of Horrors.*

infamy *n.* **1** °notoriety, °ill repute, °ill °fame, disrepute, °shame, ignominy, obloquy, °disgrace, °dishonour, °stigma, °discredit: *She has to suffer the infamy of her husband's treachery.* **2** wickedness, °evil, iniquity, villainy, heinousness, vileness, abomination, °outrage, abhorrence, opprobrium, loathsomeness, detestation, hatred, odium, °atrocity, °revulsion, °monstrosity, egregiousness, °shame, shamefulness, °disgrace, disgracefulness: *The infamy of his profligate behaviour is widely known.*

infancy *n.* **1** babyhood, early °childhood: *His limp was the result of polio, which he had contracted in infancy.* **2** °beginning(s), inception, °early *or* °initial °stage(s), commencement, °start, °emergence, °dawn, °rise: *When psychiatry was in its infancy it was marked by a notable lack of success.*

infantile *adj.* °childish, °immature, °puerile, babyish, °juvenile: *Ben behaves in the most infantile way whenever there are girls about.*

infatuated *adj.* fascinated, beguiled, °enchanted, bewitched, spellbound, °charmed, ensorcelled, enraptured, °possessed, hypnotized, mesmerized, captivated, besotted, °taken with, obsessed, °smitten, enamoured, °fond: *Francis is completely infatuated with the girl who moved in next door.*

infectious *adj.* contagious, °catching, communicable, transmissible: *There is also a highly infectious variety of the disease.*

infer *v.* °deduce, °derive, °draw, conclude, °understand, °gather, °surmise, °guess, °assume: *From the evidence, I infer that you were not at home last night.*

inference *n.* °deduction, conclusion, °understanding, °surmise, assumption, °presumption: *If this man's father is my father's son, the inference is that this man is my nephew.*

inferior *adj.* **1** °lower, nether: *We descended into the inferior regions of the cavern. The numeral in H_2O is called an inferior character.* **2** lesser, °lower, °subordinate, °secondary, °junior, °minor, unimportant, °insignificant, °lowly, subservient, °humble, °servile: *He occupies an inferior position in the company.* **3** °poor, °bad, low-quality, °mediocre, °indifferent, °imperfect, °defective, second-rate, second-class, substandard, low-grade, °shoddy, gimcrack, *Colloq* grotty, junky, crummy *or* crumby, °lousy, *Slang* crappy, *Brit* naff: *They tried to market an inferior product, but it was rejected by consumers.*
—*n.* **4** °subordinate, underling, °junior, °menial, lackey, °flunkey, dogsbody, cat's-paw, doormat, stooge, °yes-man, lickspittle, bootlicker: *She is tired of being treated as an inferior.*

inferiority *n.* **1** unimportance, insignificance, lowliness: *The inferiority of his position rankled with him.* **2** inadequacy, deficiency, insignificance, unimportance, worthlessness: *Do not confuse modesty with a sense of inferiority.* **3** shoddiness, °imperfection, mediocrity: *Consumers are not fooled by the inferiority of a product for long.*

infernal *adj.* **1** hellish, °underworld, nether, Hadean: *Virgil was Dante's guide in the infernal regions.* **2** °devilish, °diabolic(al), demonic(al), demoniac(al), °fiendish, °satanic, Mephistophelian; °damnable, damned, execrable, malicious, malevolent, maleficent, °wicked, °evil, iniquitous, flagitious, °villainous, heinous, dire, °sinister, °dreadful: *She tells everyone that there is an infernal plot against her.*

infertile *adj.* °sterile, °barren, infecund, unproductive, unfruitful, °non-productive: *The stony, infertile earth yielded only cactus and scrub grass.*

infest *v.* invade, °plague, °beset, °overrun, overspread, °flood, °swarm over, inundate, pervade, °permeate, °penetrate, infiltrate: *Mosquitoes infested this area before the swamp was drained.*

infidel *n.* unbeliever, °heathen, disbeliever, heretic, °pagan, agnostic, atheist, nullifidian, freethinker: *Thousands of the fanatics swarmed over the infidels, slaughtering them mercilessly.*

infidelity *n.* **1** unfaithfulness, faithlessness, treachery, traitorousness, disloyalty, °perfidy, falseness, apostasy, heresy: *The infidelity of his supporters brought about his downfall.* **2** adultery, cuckoldry; °affair, °liaison, amour, *Colloq* cheating: *Infidelity is a common cause of marriage break-up. She forgave him his many infidelities.*

infinite *adj.* **1** °boundless, °vast, °limitless, °unlimited, illimitable, °endless, interminable, indeterminable, indeterminate, °inestimable, astronomical, °numberless, multitudinous, uncountable, uncounted, innumerable, incalculable, °inexhaustible, °immense, °enormous, °immeasurable, measureless, °bottomless, unfathomable: *They hurtled through infinite space at the speed of light. We do what we can, but our resources are not infinite. In his infinite wisdom, God made the garden slug.* **2** °eternal, °everlasting, °perpetual, °endless, unending, °inexhaustible, undying, never-ending: *It is difficult to conceive of time as being anything but infinite, without beginning or end. With infinite patience she reassembled the pieces of the vase.*

infirm *adj.* **1** °ill, °indisposed, debilitated, °frail, °fragile, °weak, °feeble, weakened, ailing, °decrepit, enfeebled, °failing, wasted, on the °decline, °sick, °sickly, unwell, °lame, °crippled: *Campbell is infirm and unable to travel.* **2** °shaky, °flimsy, wobbly, wobbling, °doddering, °unstable, faltering, vacillating, wavering, unsteady, unsteadfast, °inconstant, °changeable, °irresolute: *We must find stalwart recruits, recruits who are not infirm of purpose.*

infirmary *n.* clinic, °hospital, sickbay, first-aid °station; dispensary, *Brit* nursing °home, surgery: *The infirmary is able to deal only with emergencies, not with long-term care.*

infirmity *n.* **1** °weakness, feebleness, frailness, °frailty, debility, °decrepitude, sickliness: *At 100, she finally succumbed to infirmity, and ceased going out altogether.* **2** sickness, °ailment, °disease, malady, °affliction, °disorder, °defect, °complaint: *What infirmity struck him down?*

inflame *v.* **1** °arouse, °incite, °touch off, ignite, enkindle, °provoke, °rouse, °excite, impassion, °foment, incense, °agitate, °stir (up), °fire (up), °heat, °anger, °enrage, °madden, °infuriate, °whip *or* °lash up, °work up, rile, °exasperate, °stimulate, °animate, °move, °motivate, °urge, °prod, goad, °spur (on), °rally, °drive: *The speakers inflamed the crowd to riot against the police.* **2** °aggravate, °intensify, °deepen, °heighten, °fan, exacerbate, °increase, augment, °fuel: *She inflamed his dislike of his brother into hatred.*

inflamed *adj.* irritated, °sore, °angry, chafing, chafed, red, °swollen, °heated, °hot, fevered, °feverish, infected, septic: *The wound became inflamed and we had no medicine to reduce the infection.*

inflammable *adj.* burnable, combustible, °flammable: *The plastic foam formerly used to stuff furniture is highly inflammable.*

inflammation *n.* irritation, redness, °swelling, °sore, infection: *The inflammation subsided as the injection took effect.*

inflammatory *adj.* incendiary, °fiery, inflaming, °explosive, °rousing, °provocative, °rabid, rabble-rousing, °passionate, °fervent, fervid, °frantic, frenzied, fomenting, demagogic, insurgent, °riotous, °mutinous, °seditious, °rebellious, °revolutionary, °traitorous, treacherous: *His inflammatory speeches at the university created tension between the students and the administration.*

inflate *v.* **1** °blow up, balloon, °expand, dilate, °enlarge, °swell, °pump up, °puff up *or* out, distend: *We inflated two plastic bags to use as floats.* **2** °boost, °increase: *The price of the company's shares was inflated by rumours of a take-over bid.* **3** °exaggerate, °amplify, °magnify, °blow up: *He tends to inflate to huge proportions the small contribution he made to the project.*

inflated *adj.* **1** exaggerated, °conceited, overblown, °grandiose, puffed up, overstated, magnified, amplified, overdrawn, °smug, egotistic(al), °immodest, °cocky, °vain, °self-important, *Colloq Brit* swelled-headed *or* swollen-headed, *US* swell-headed: *He has an inflated idea of the importance of his work.* **2** grandiloquent, °bombastic, orotund, high-flown, °pompous, °pretentious, °extravagant, magniloquent: *She always talks about her husband in such inflated terms.*

inflexible *adj.* unbending, °stiff, °rigid, °firm, rigorous, unyielding, adamant, °severe, Rhadamanthine, inelastic, °hard (and °fast), °determined, °fixed, obdurate, °immovable, intractable, unvaried, unvarying, °invariable, unchangeable, immutable, °obstinate, °stubborn, pigheaded, mulish, dyed in the wool, headstrong, refractory, °steely, °stony, °resolute, resolved, unadaptable, unaccommodating, uncompliant, uncompromising, unshakeable *or* unshakable: *The committee remain inflexible about changing the rules of the club to admit women.*

inflict *v.* °impose, °apply, °visit, °administer, levy, °force on *or* upon; °trouble, °afflict: *The new government is seeking ways of inflicting more taxes on us. You ought not to inflict punishment on such small children.*

influence *n.* **1** °power, °pressure, °weight, °sway, °impact, °force, °effect, leverage, potency; °hold, °control, mastery, ascendancy, *Colloq* °pull, clout: *Would you use your influence to see if you can get me a job? The boy is under the influence of his tutor.* **2** connections, °favour, °favouritism, *Colloq* °pull: *He got his position through influence, not merit.*
—*v.* **3** °affect, °move, °change, °modify, °alter, °bias, °sway, °persuade, °induce, °work on, °impress (upon), °play *or* °act upon *or* on, °incline; bring °pressure to bear on *or* upon, °motivate, °manipulate, *Brit* pressurize, *US* °pressure, *Colloq* pull strings *or US also* wires: *She was able to influence the minister to drop the scheme.*

influential *adj.* °powerful, °weighty, °strong, °forceful, °effective, °effectual, °efficacious, °instrumental, °telling, °significant, °persuasive, °dominant, °leading, guiding, °authoritative, °predominant, °important, °substantial, °prestigious, controlling: *He comes from an influential family. What factors were influential in reaching your decision?*

inform *v.* **1** °tell, apprise, °advise, °communicate, °enlighten, °notify, °acquaint, °brief; °impart, °disclose, divulge, °reveal, °report, *Colloq* °tip (off): *I have informed everyone about the storm warning.* **2** Usually, ***inform against*** *or* ***on***: °betray, °incriminate, °implicate, °identify, *Colloq* °tell (on), °blab (on), rat (on), *US* °blow the whistle (on); *Slang* peach (on), snitch (on), squeal (on), put the °finger on, °sing, °name names, *Brit* nark (on), °grass (on), °split on, *US* °finger: *He informed on his accomplices in return for a lighter sentence.*

informal *adj.* **1** unceremonious, °casual, °natural, unstilted, °familiar, °ordinary, °everyday, °unaffected, unassuming, unpretentious, °simple, °relaxed, °free, °free and °easy, *Brit* °common or garden, *US* garden-variety: *We had an informal dinner in the kitchen.* **2** °unofficial, unconventional, unconstrained, °casual, °everyday, °simple: *On duty he wore informal clothes—blue jeans and a denim jacket.* **3** °vernacular, colloquial, °simple, °unaffected, °ordinary, unpretentious, °everyday: *He uses informal language devoid of scientific jargon.*

information *n.* °knowledge, °data, °facts, °intelligence, °message, °word, °advice, °news, tidings, °report, communication, *Colloq* info, °low-down, *Slang* °dirt, °dope, *Brit* gen, bumf, *US* poop: *I have little information regarding her divorce.*

informative *adj.* communicative, °instructive, °educational, edifying, revealing, illuminating: *We found his report about the missiles very informative.*

informed *adj.* **1** °intelligent, °knowledgeable, °enlightened, °educated, °learned, cultured, °cultivated: *An informed public is democracy's greatest asset.* **2** °alert (to), °aware (of), advised, in touch, *au fait*, briefed, conversant (with), (well-)°versed, up (on), up to °date, *Colloq* in the °know, °wise: *Keep me informed as to your whereabouts.*

informer *n.* °traitor, betrayer, tattle-tale, taleteller, informant, *Slang* stool-pigeon, snitch, squealer, weasel, *Brit* °grass, *Chiefly US* rat, *US* stoolie, canary, shoo-fly: *According to the informer, the secret meeting is scheduled for tonight.*

infrequently *adv.* °rarely, °seldom, sporadically, °occasionally, °now and then, irregularly, exceptionally: *They were only infrequently seen in public in later years.*

infringe *v.* **1** °violate, contravene, °break, °disobey, °transgress, °overstep: *Publication of this article has infringed her right to a fair trial.* **2** ***infringe on*** *or* ***upon***: °intrude on, impinge on, trespass on, °encroach on, invade: *Never let pleasure infringe on the domain of duty.*

infringement *n.* °violation, °breach, contravention, infraction, disobedience, °non-compliance, breaking, °transgression: *Publication without permission constitutes infringement of copyright. The inventor sued the company for patent infringement.*

infuriate *v.* °enrage, °anger, °madden, incense, make (someone's) blood °boil, °provoke, °inflame, °work *or* °stir *or* °fire up, rile, arouse, vex, pique, °gall, °annoy, °irritate, °bother, °chafe, °agitate, °irk, nettle, °exasperate, raise (someone's) hackles, make (someone's) hackles rise, *Brit* have *or* get (someone's) blood up, *Colloq* miff, °bug, peeve, get under (someone's) skin, get *or Brit also* put (someone's) back up, make (someone) see red, *Chiefly US* get (someone's) Irish *or* dander up, *US* °burn up, *Slang* piss (someone) off, brown (someone) off, *Brit* cheese (someone) off: *It really infuriated him to see injustice done to anyone.*

ingenious *adj.* °clever, °skilful, skilled, °shrewd, cunning, °crafty, canny, °dexterous, adroit, °acute, °sharp, °keen, °resourceful, °adept, apt, °smart, °gifted, °bright, °brilliant, °talented, deft, °handy, inventive, Daedalian, °creative, °imaginative, °original, *Colloq* °neat, °keen, *US* crackerjack, *Slang* on the ball: *My friend here has come up with an ingenious solution to our problem.*

ingenuity *n.* ingeniousness, °genius, °brilliance, cleverness, °skill, shrewdness, cunning, °craft, °art, °knack, °flair, °dexterity, dexterousness, adroitness, acuteness, sharpness, keenness, resourcefulness, adeptness, aptness, smartness, canniness, °gift, °talent, °ability, °capability, °faculty, deftness, handiness, inventiveness, creativity, creativeness, °imagination, imaginativeness, °originality: *She displayed extraordinary ingenuity in preparing the case against the plaintiff.*

ingenuous *adj.* **1** °naïve, °simple, °innocent, °unsophisticated, °childlike, °suggestible, °artless, °sincere, °genuine, °trusting, guileless, °natural, °straight, uncomplicated, (°fair and) °square, °honest, °fair, °just, °open, undeceitful, °unaffected, undeceptive, undissembling, unfeigning, (°open and) °above-board, *Colloq* on the °level: *What ideas have you been implanting into the mind of this ingenuous young girl?* **2** °frank, °candid, °open, °trustworthy, °honourable, °forthright, °direct, straightforward, four-square, °honest, °outspoken, °blunt, °bluff, °bold, unreserved, °free, °uninhibited, °unabashed: *I shall be ingenuous enough to confess that what you heard about me is true.*

ingrained *adj.* engrained, deep-rooted, °fixed, inveterate, deep-seated, °fundamental, °basic, °essential, °inherent, °inborn, innate, inbred, inherited, °hereditary, °organic, °intrinsic, °native, °natural: *He has an ingrained fear of heights.*

ingratiating *adj.* fawning, °grovelling, sycophantic, toadying, toad-eating, °servile, °obsequious, °flattering, °time-serving, wheedling, cajoling, unctuous, °oily, buttery, sweet-talking, sugary, saccharine, *US* blandiloquent, *Colloq* boot-licking, °slimy, *Brit* smarmy, *US* apple-polishing, *Slang US* brown-nosing: *It is Crawley's ingratiating manner that none of us can abide.*

ingratitude *n.* unthankfulness, ungratefulness, thanklessness, unappreciativeness, non-recognition: *Despite the favours they had received, they showed their ingratitude by refusing to contribute to the fund drive.*

ingredient *n.* constituent, °element, °part, component, °factor; (*pl.*) makings: *Humour is a necessary ingredient in any working relationship.*

inhabit *v.* °dwell in, reside in, °live in, °abide in, °occupy, °settle; °locate in, °populate, °people; colonize: *This bird inhabits northern Africa. North America was inhabited by emigrants from Europe.*

inhabitant *n.* °resident, dweller, °denizen, °citizen, °tenant, °occupant, occupier: *The inhabitants of the village refused to pay taxes.*

inhale *v.* °breathe in, °inspire, °draw *or* suck in: *I stepped outside and inhaled the fresh spring air.*

inherent *adj.* °intrinsic, indwelling, °essential, °basic, innate, connate, °ingrained *or* engrained, °native, congenital, inherited, °hereditary, °inborn, inbred, °indigenous, immanent, built-in: *It is difficult to tell which characteristics are derived and which are inherent.*

inherit *v.* °come into, fall *or* be *or* become °heir to, be bequeathed, °succeed to, be left, °receive, °acquire, *Colloq* °come by: *She inherited the property when her father died.*

inheritance *n.* patrimony, °heritage, legacy, °bequest, birthright; °property: *He came into his inheritance when he was 21.*

inhibit *v.* °discourage, °repress, °frustrate, °hold back, °bridle, °curb, °control, °govern, °hinder, °restrain, °impede, °obstruct, °interfere with, °check, °prevent, °bar, °stop: *Her sad look inhibited my expression of delight at seeing her again.*

inhibited *adj.* °reticent, restrained, repressed, °reserved, °self-conscious, °shy, abashed, °embarrassed, *Colloq* uptight: *He is much too inhibited to appear on television.*

inhibition *n.* self-consciousness, °restraint, constraint, °impediment, °hindrance, °bar, °barrier, °defence, °defence °mechanism, blockage, °interference, °check, °curb, °stricture: *Geoff overcame his inhibitions and went over to talk with Anne. She had no inhibitions about singing in public.*

inhospitable *adj.* **1** unwelcoming, unreceptive, °uninviting, unsociable, °unsocial, °aloof, °cold, °cool, °standoffish, unfriendly, inimical, antisocial, °hostile, xenophobic: *They were most inhospitable and refused to let me in.* **2** unfavourable, °forbidding, °hostile, °barren, °desert, °uninviting, uninhabitable: *They were marooned on an inhospitable reef in the middle of the Pacific.*

inhuman *adj.* **1** inhumane, °merciless, °cruel, pitiless, °ruthless, °heartless, °severe, °unsympathetic, unfeeling, °unkind, unkindly, uncompassionate, °cold-blooded, °vicious, stony-hearted, hard-hearted, °callous, insensitive, barbaric, barbarous, °savage: *Many refugees have suffered torture and other inhuman treatment.* **2** °animal, bestial, °brutal, brutish, °fiendish, diabolic(al), demonic: *The spectre, assuming an inhuman form, loomed over them.*

initial *adj.* **1** °original, °primary, °first; °prime, °beginning, incipient, inaugural, °opening, °introductory, commencing: *His initial plan, to take the children, was vetoed by his wife. It is best to tread cautiously during the initial stages of the programme.*
—*v.* **2** °sign, °approve, °endorse: *Please initial the clauses of the contract that we have changed.*
—*n.* **3** monogram: *The initial 'M' is on all their towels.*

initiate *v.* **1** °begin, °commence, °enter upon *or* on, °originate, °introduce, °set in °motion, °start, °give °rise to, °get under °way, °launch, °get *or* °set °going, trigger, °set off, actuate, °activate, instigate, °institute, °inaugurate: *The programme was initiated last spring with much fanfare.* **2** °admit, °accept, °introduce: *The new members were initiated last night, with due ceremony.* **3** °teach, °instruct, °train, °tutor, °drill, °coach: *His responsibility is to initiate recruits in the rudiments of jungle warfare.*
—*n.* **4** °novice, beginner, °new boy *or* girl, °greenhorn, rookie, neophyte, tiro *or* tyro, °newcomer, tenderfoot, fledgling, °apprentice, (°raw) °recruit, abecedarian, noviciate *or* novitiate, catechumen, *Brit* fresher *or US* freshman, *Australian* °new °chum: *In the first weeks, initiates are drilled in the basics.*

initiation *n.* **1** °beginning, commencement, inauguration, origination, début, introduction, inception, °establishment: *April the first is the date for initiation of the new system.* **2** °admittance, °admission, °entrance, induction, enrolment, instatement, investiture, ordination, °installation; °ceremony, °rite, °ritual: *The initiation of new members is scheduled for tomorrow at midnight.*

initiative *n.* **1** °first °move *or* °step, °lead, °opening °move: *Hogan took the initiative by winning the first set.* **2** °enterprise, aggressiveness, °drive, °ambition, ambitiousness, resourcefulness, °leadership, °dynamism, °energy, °vigour, °hustle, élan, *Colloq* get-up-and-go, °pep, °snap, zip, zing: *At least she had the initiative to get the company back on a profitable basis.*

inject *v.* **1** °introduce, °insert, °drive *or* °force (in), °shoot (in), intromit; inoculate: *The serum is injected into the upper arm. The doctor injected me with antibiotics.* **2** °introduce, °insert, imbue, °instil, °bring in, interject, °throw in: *Can't you inject a little more enthusiasm into your work?*

injunction *n.* **1** °prohibition, interdict, interdiction, °restriction, °restraint, *US law* restraining °order: *There is an injunction against picketing.* **2** °order, mandate, directive, °command, °direction, °instruction, ruling, °dictate, exhortation; °warning, admonition: *Mother's parting injunction was always to dress warmly.*

injure *v.* **1** °harm, °wound, °hurt, °damage, °impair: *He's sure to injure himself if he's allowed to play with a knife.* **2** °wrong, °offend, °abuse, °hurt, °wound, °outrage, °slight, °insult, affront, °mistreat, °misuse, °ill-treat, maltreat: *She starts the arguments yet she invariably takes the role of the injured party.*

injurious *adj.* **1** damaging, °harmful, °hurtful, °bad, deleterious, unfavourable, °detrimental, °unhealthy, insalubrious, pernicious, °destructive; adverse, °ruinous: *Smoking is said to be injurious to health.* **2** °abusive, insulting, °scornful, °slanderous, libellous, defamatory, °scandalous, °scurrilous, °harsh, calumnious, calumniatory, disparaging, °derogatory, deprecatory, °contemptuous, denigrating, °offensive: *She speaks of her ex-husband in the most injurious terms.*

injury *n.* °damage, °hurt, °harm, °wound, °impairment; °wrong, °abuse, maltreatment, °mistreatment, °mischief, °offence, °outrage; °mayhem: *The injury was less painful to his foot than to his self-esteem.*

injustice *n.* **1** unfairness, °favouritism, °discrimination, °bias, °inequality, °partiality, partisanship, °prejudice, °bigotry, one-sidedness, unjustness, inequity: *Class privilege has always condoned injustice.* **2** °wrong, °injury: *You do me an injustice if you think me capable of dishonesty.*

inkling *n.* °hint, °suggestion, glimmering, °suspicion, °whisper, intimation, °indication, soupçon, °clue, °notion, (faintest *or* foggiest) °idea, °tip, tip-off: *Can you give me an inkling of what you are getting at?*

inmate *n.* °prisoner, °convict, °captive, jailbird *or Brit also* gaolbird, *Slang Brit* lag; °patient, °case; °inhabitant, °occupant, °resident: *The inmates were fed on bread and water in those days. Inmates at the sanatorium are well treated.*

innocent *adj.* **1** not °guilty, guiltless, °blameless, °honest, (in the) °clear, unimpeachable, above °suspicion, above reproach, °faultless: *We all believe her innocent of extortion.* **2** °pure, sinless, °virtuous, °chaste, virgin(al), undefiled, untainted, unstained, unsullied, °pristine, °incorrupt, uncorrupted, °immaculate, °spotless, unblemished, unpolluted: *She is still a sweet child, innocent as the day she was born.* **3** °harmless, well-intentioned, °safe, innocuous, °inoffensive, unobjectionable: *What began as an innocent stroll became a dangerous expedition.* **4** °naïve, °unsuspecting, unsuspicious, °ingenuous, °unsophisticated, °trusting, trustful, °gullible, credulous, °green, °inexperienced, °childlike, unworldly, guileless, °artless, °simple, °open, unartificial, °sincere: *Youngsters would arrive in London directly from the farm, entirely innocent and unaware of the perils of city life.*
—*n.* **5** infant, babe (in arms *or* in the wood(s)), °child; ingénue, °novice, beginner, °newcomer, *Colloq* °greenhorn: *She's certainly no innocent when it comes to men.*

innovation *n.* **1** °novelty; °invention: *The flush toilet was a 19th-century innovation.* **2** modernization, °alteration: *Consumer product development is marked by a spirit of tireless innovation.*

innuendo *n.* insinuation, °imputation, °suggestion, °hint, intimation, °implication, allusion, °overtone; °reference, animadversion: *I resent your innuendo that I know more about the affair than I am letting on.*

inoffensive *adj.* °harmless, unobjectionable, innocuous, unoffending, °neutral, °retiring, °mild, °tame: *Bligh is so inoffensive, how could he possibly have upset you?*

inopportune *adj.* °inappropriate, malapropos, ill-timed, untimely, °inconvenient, unsuited, unsuitable, out of °place, unpropitious, unfavourable, °inauspicious, ill-chosen, °unseasonable, °unseemly, °untoward, °unfortunate: *Your call came at a most inopportune moment, as we were just sitting down to dinner.*

inordinate *adj.* **1** °immoderate, unrestrained, intemperate, °excessive, °disproportionate, °extravagant, overdone, °extreme, °exorbitant, °outrageous, °preposterous, °unconscionable, °unreasonable, undue, uncalled-for, °unwarranted: *Her inordinate appetite for scandal has made her a successful gossip columnist.* **2** °irregular, °disorderly, disordered, °uncontrolled, °unlimited, unregulated, unsystematic, °erratic, °haphazard: *Laws have been passed to limit the inordinate hunting of deer.*

inquire *v.* **1** Usually, ***inquire into***: °search, °investigate, °probe, °examine, °research, °look into, °inspect, °study, °explore, °survey, °scrutinize: *Scientists are inquiring into the causes of the greenhouse effect.* **2** See **enquire,** above.

inquiry *n.* **1** enquiry, °investigation, °probe, °examination, °research, °search, inspection, °study, °exploration, °survey, °scrutiny, inquest; questioning, querying, °interrogation, cross-examination, inquisition: *The police have asked me to help them with their inquiry. They are conducting an inquiry into the cause of the accident.* **2** enquiry, °question, °query, °interrogation: *Would you please repeat the inquiry?*

inquisitive *adj.* **1** inquiring, °curious, probing, questioning, °interested, investigative, searching, exploring, analytical: *Children have a naturally inquisitive nature.* **2** prying, °intrusive, *Colloq* snooping, snoopy, °nosy *or* nosey: *Don't be so inquisitive about things that don't concern you!*

inroad *n.* **1** incursion, °raid, °attack, °invasion, °penetration, foray, encroachment, forced °entry, intrusion: *Our armoured units have made an inroad into enemy territory.* **2** Often, ***inroads***: °advance(s), °progress, breakthrough: *Have researchers made significant inroads into the problem of AIDS?*

insane *adj.* **1** °mad, demented, °psychotic, schizophrenic, schizoid, *non compos mentis*, manic, °maniacal, lunatic, °deranged, °unbalanced, psychoneurotic, °neurotic, °eccentric, °crazy, of °unsound °mind, crazed, unhinged, out of one's °mind *or* °head, °mad as a hatter *or* a March hare, quirky, *Colloq* round the bend *or* °twist, off one's rocker *or* chump, loopy, loony, certifiable, °mental, screwy, dotty, cuckoo, not all there, not have all one's marbles, off-the-wall, out of it, *Brit* potty, *Slang* °daft, nutty (as a fruit cake), nuts, spaced out, spacy, batty, have bats in one's belfry, not right upstairs, barmy (in the crumpet), crackers, have a screw loose, schizo, *Brit* bonkers, *US* bugs, bughouse, loco, °crazy as a bedbug, (gone) off the deep end, kooky, °kinky, out to lunch: *Witney was certified insane and institutionalized. You're insane if you think I am going out on that ledge.* **2** °stupid, °dumb, °dull, °silly, asinine, °ridiculous, idiotic, irrational, °absurd, fatuous, °ludicrous, °foolish, °nonsensical, °irresponsible, °reckless, °wild, imbecilic, moronic, °feeble-minded, °hare-brained, addle-pated, addle-brained, °scatterbrained, thimble-witted, attocerebral, *Brit* gormless, *Colloq* nutty, screwy, °crazy: *People in love sometimes do insane things.*

insanity *n.* **1** °madness, °lunacy, °mental °illness *or* °disorder, dementia (praecox), psychosis, schizophrenia, (°mental) derangement, °mania; psychoneurosis, neurosis: *Because of the plea of temporary insanity he never stood trial for the murders.* **2** °folly, foolishness, °stupidity, idiocy, imbecility, °lunacy, °absurdity, fatuity, fatuousness, °nonsense, senselessness, irresponsibility, irrationality, inanity: *What insanity it was to think I could win the lottery!*

insecure *adj.* **1** °uncertain, °afraid, unsure, unconfident, °nervous, °worried, °anxious, °disconcerted, apprehensive, uncomfortable, °shaky, °jumpy, unnerved, °fearful: *Harry is beginning to feel insecure about his job.* **2** unsafe, °dangerous, unprotected, °vulnerable, °unguarded, °defenceless, undefended, exposed, °open: *The machine-gun position is insecure and will soon be taken.* **3** °unstable, °shaky, wobbly, °precarious, °infirm, °weak, °flimsy, °frail, °rickety, unsubstantial, °rocky, °unsound, unsteady, °unreliable, °uncertain: *The structure collapsed because the footings were insecure.*

insensible *adj.* **1** insensate, °unconscious, insentient, °numb, benumbed, °senseless, °torpid, anaesthetized, *Colloq* out, out of it: *She was totally insensible for an hour after the blow on the head.* **2** Often, ***insensible to or of***: insensitive, °callous, °indifferent, impervious, °impassive, apathetic, °cool, unsusceptible; °unaffected, °unmoved, untouched; °unaware, °deaf, °inconsiderate; hard-hearted, °thick-skinned, unfeeling, emotionless, °dispassionate, °thoughtless, *Colloq* cloth-eared: *He remained wholly insensible to her desires and needs.*

insert *v.* **1** °introduce, °place *or* °put *or* °stick in, intercalate; interpolate, interject, interpose: *Please do not insert comments of your own.*
—*n.* **2** insertion, °addition, addendum, °supplement, °advertisement, broadside, °brochure, tip-in, handbill, °circular, *Colloq Brit* advert, *US* ad, flier *or* flyer; outsert, wraparound *or* wrapround: *The postage will be higher with this eight-page insert.*

inside *n.* **1** °interior, °centre, °core, °middle, °heart; contents; lining, °backing: *From the outside one could never guess what the inside looks like. Please paint the inside of the cabinet blue.* **2** Usually, ***insides***: °bowels, entrails, viscera, °gut(s), °stomach, *Colloq* innards: *He has had trouble with his insides for years.* **3** ***inside out***: everted, reversed; °backwards: *He is wearing his pullover inside out.*
—*adj.* **4** °favoured, °advantageous, °favourable, advantaged, °privileged, preferred, °preferential, °propitious, °exclusive; °internal, °private, °secret, °confidential, °privy, clandestine: *She has an inside track to the chairman. He claims to have inside information about the successful bidder.* **5** °internal, °interior; arranged, prearranged: *The police think it was an inside job.*
—*adv.* **6** fundamentally, basically, at °bottom, by °nature: *Despite her gruff exterior, inside she is quite sentimental.* **7** in °prison, in °jail *or Brit also* gaol, imprisoned, incarcerated, *Slang Brit* in quod, *US* up the river: *He'll be inside for another five years.*
—*prep.* **8** within, *US* inside of: *Because of rain, the party was held inside the building.*

insight *n.* °perception, percipience, °sensitivity, perspicacity, perceptiveness, perspicaciousness, discernment, acuteness, acuity, acumen, sharpness, °understanding, °judgement, comprehension, °vision: *Chambers has brought his considerable insight to bear on this complex problem.*

insignificant *adj.* °paltry, °trifling, °petty, inconsiderable, °inconsequential, trivial, unimportant, °nonessential, °minor, °negligible, nugatory, unessential, °niggling, °puny, °insubstantial, unsubstantial, *Colloq* piddling: *These insignificant differences can be ignored. What you and I might do with our lives is, in the larger sense, insignificant.*

insincere *adj.* °hypocritical, °dishonest, dissembling, °deceptive, °disingenuous, °deceitful, untruthful, °false, °artificial, ungenuine, treacherous, °perfidious, °faithless, double-dealing, duplicitous, °two-faced, Janus-faced, °lying, mendacious, °sly, Machiavellian, cunning, °crafty, °slick, °foxy, vulpine, °wily, °artful, °evasive, °shifty, °time-serving, unctuous, °slimy, °slippery, °tricky, underhanded, °crooked, *Colloq* °phoney *or US also* phony: *From the first act I thought Iago insincere.*

insinuate *v.* **1** °impute, °suggest, °hint, °intimate, °imply, °whisper, °indicate; convey, °signify: *They insinuated that she married me for my money.* **2** °insert (oneself), °inject (oneself), worm *or* °work *or* inveigle *or* °manoeuvre (oneself *or* one's way); infiltrate, °intrude: *She insinuated herself into our group uninvited.* **3** °inject, infuse, °instil, °introduce: *Wild imaginings began to insinuate themselves into my mind.*

insist *v.* **1** °demand, °require, °call for, °command, importune, °urge, exhort, °argue, remonstrate, expostulate: *The chairman insisted that proper parliamentary procedure be followed.* **2** assert, °state, °declare, °emphasize, °stress, °maintain, °persist, °hold, °dwell on, °vow, avow, aver, asseverate: *He insisted that he wanted to see the last act but she insisted on leaving.*

insistent *adj.* °firm, dogged, °emphatic, °persistent, °tenacious, °resolute, °determined, °assertive, uncompromising, unfaltering, unwavering, persevering, perseverant, unrelenting, inexorable, °stubborn, °obstinate, unyielding, compelling, °urgent, importunate: *The judges were insistent that we should follow the rules to the letter.*

insolent *adj.* °impertinent, °impudent, °pert, saucy, °bold, °presumptuous, °brazen, °brash, °disrespectful, insulting, °contemptuous, °offensive, °rude, °crude, uncivil, °insubordinate, *Colloq* °fresh, °brassy, °cheeky, *Slang Brit* smart-arsed *or US* smart-ass(ed), *US* wise: *That insolent boor had the gall to call her 'Queenie'!*

insolvent *adj.* bankrupt, ruined, in receivership, penniless, °impoverished, °destitute, *US* in Chapter Eleven, *Colloq* °broke, wiped out, in the red, on the rocks, (gone) bust, gone to the °wall, *Brit* in Queer Street, skint: *A business is insolvent if its liabilities exceed its assets.*

inspect *v.* °examine, °scrutinize, °study, °scan, °survey, °vet, °check (up (on) *or* out), °investigate, °pore over; °peruse: *The customs man inspected every last inch of our luggage.*

inspiration *n.* **1** awakening, arousal, stimulus, °revelation, impulse, °feeling, afflatus, enlightenment, °insight, °spur, °incitement, °incentive; °spirit, °energy, élan, °passion, °ardour, zeal, °enthusiasm, °vigour, °gusto, ebullience, °sparkle: *Her extraordinary eyes gave me the inspiration I needed and I finished writing the song in an hour.* **2** °influence, stimulus, stimulation, °encouragement, °provocation, °suggestion, °guide, °education: *Kitchener's life was an inspiration to many a career soldier.*

inspire *v.* **1** °animate, °activate, actuate, °stimulate, invigorate, °stir, °move, waken, °awaken, arouse, °rouse, instigate, °prompt, °rally, °energize, °enliven, °vitalize, vivify, galvanize, inspirit, °excite, °spark (off), °quicken, °kindle, °fire, °provoke: *It was the inflammatory speeches that inspired the crowd to riot. His enthusiasm inspired her to take up writing as a profession.* **2** °encourage, °strengthen, °support, °reinforce, °buoy (up), uplift, °boost, affirm, °confirm, °fortify, °buttress: *Your example has inspired many young people.*

install *v.* **1** instal, °invest, instate, °initiate, °establish, °inaugurate, °induct, °institute; °place, °put, °position, °introduce, °settle: *The new bishop will be installed in office next week.* **2** instal, °fit, °set up, °connect, °fix (in °place): *I installed our new air conditioner myself.*

installation *n.* **1** investiture, instatement, °initiation, °establishment, inauguration, induction, °institution, °placement, introduction, solemnization, swearing-in, consecration, *Ecclesiastical* ordination; crowning, coronation: *Will you attend the installation of the new vice-chancellor?* **2** °fitting, °placement, °connection, positioning: *The plumber will supervise the installation of the new heating system.* **3** °base, °post, °station, depot, °camp, °establishment: *Military installations all over the country are being picketed.*

instance *n.* **1** °case (in point), °example, exemplar, °illustration, °precedent, exemplification, °occurrence, °event: *The damage to the bus shelter is yet one more instance of hooliganism.* **2** ***for instance***: for °example, as an °example, e.g., °say; in the °event, as it happens *or* happened: *Consider her, for instance: she managed to work and raise a family.*

instant *n.* **1** °moment, °point, °second, °time: *I was thinking of you at the very instant the phone rang.* **2** °moment, °second, °minute, °flash, °twinkling (of an eye), trice, *Colloq* jiffy: *I'll be with you in an instant, sir.*

—*adj.* **3** instantaneous, °immediate, on the °spot, overnight: *His novel was an instant best seller.* **4** °urgent, crying, °pressing, °earnest, °imperative, °critical, exigent; split-second, °direct: *We have an instant need for a computer specialist.* **5** °ready-made, ready-mixed, °prepared, ready-to-serve, precooked: *This is an instant soup—just add hot water to the powder.*

instantaneously *adv.* instantly, °immediately, at °once, (°right) °now, °directly, forthwith, °promptly, this °minute *or* °second *or* °instant, without °delay, *tout de suite*, instanter, *Brit* °straight away *or US* °right away; *Colloq* pronto, *US* momentarily: *The results will be beamed instantaneously to 176 million people around the world.*

instead *adv.* **1** as an °alternative *or* a °substitute: *She wanted me to go but I stayed instead.* **2** ***instead of***: alternatively, preferably, in °preference to, in °place of, in lieu of, °rather than, as a °substitute for; as contrasted with, as °opposed to: *Instead of going to the cinema we went to the theatre.*

instil *v.* instill, imbue, inculcate, infuse, ingrain *or* engrain, °implant; °insinuate, °impart: *From childhood a sense of justice was instilled in us.*

instinct *n.* °intuition, °feel, °feeling, empathy, °sensitivity, °tendency, propensity, °leaning, °bent, °skill, °talent, °faculty, sixth °sense, °knack, predisposition, °capacity, °aptitude; °subconscious: *She has an uncanny instinct for finding the most interesting person in a crowd.*

instinctive *adj.* **1** instinctual, intuitive, °natural, innate, °native, °inborn, inbred, congenital, constitutional, reflex, visceral, intestinal, °intrinsic, intuitional, °subconscious, *Colloq* °gut: *She has an instinctive flair for design.* **2** °immediate, °involuntary, irrational, °mechanical, °automatic, °spontaneous: *Harvey took an instinctive dislike to Percy when they met.*

institute *n.* **1** °society, °organization, °association, °league, °alliance, guild: *They tried to establish an institute for research on badgers.* **2** See **institution, 2,** below.

—*v.* **3** °establish, °found, °launch, °organize: *The principles of sportsmanship were instituted on the playing fields of England.* **4** °inaugurate, °introduce, °initiate, °set up, °start, °begin, °originate, °commence, °pioneer: *If you do not pay, we shall be obliged to institute proceedings against you.*

institution *n.* **1** establishing, °establishment, forming, °formation, origination, founding, °foundation, °installation, introduction, °creation, °organization: *Who was responsible for the institution of cricket as a national pastime?* **2** °establishment, °institute, academy, °foundation, university, college, °school: *He attended an institution of higher learning after leaving the army.* **3** °hospital, medical centre, °sanatorium *or US also* sanitarium, °home, asylum: *They spent their last days in an institution.* **4** °custom, °tradition, °habit, °practice, °routine, °rule, °order (of the day), °code (of °practice); °doctrine, dogma: *Throwing the coxswain into the river after the race has become an institution.*

instruct *v.* **1** °teach, °train, °tutor, °drill, °educate, °coach, °inform, °guide, edify, °prepare, °indoctrinate, inculcate: *My parents employed a tutor to instruct me in Latin.* **2** °direct, °order, °bid, °require, °tell, enjoin, °command, importune, °charge: *We were instructed to tell no one where we were going.*

instruction *n.* **1** Often, ***instructions***: °order, °direction, °brief, briefing, directive, guideline, °advice, °recommendation, °rule; °information; *Colloq* °drill: *The next instruction is to insert the plug into the back of the receiver. Follow the instructions carefully.* **2** teaching, °education, °schooling, training, °drill, drilling, °tuition, °guidance, indoctrination, °preparation, lessons, classes, coaching, tutelage; tutorial: *Where did you receive instruction in first aid?*

instructive *adj.* °informative, informational, informatory, °educational, instructional, °helpful, revealing, edifying, enlightening, illuminating: *Studying the mistakes of others can be highly instructive.*

instructor *n.* °teacher, trainer, °tutor, °coach, mentor, °adviser, educator, pedagogue, scholastic, academe, academician, °doctor, docent, lecturer, professor, *Brit* °master, °mistress, don, preceptor, *US* docent: *Charlotte was not spending time with the tennis instructor just to improve her backhand.*

instrument *n.* **1** °implement, °tool, °device, °apparatus, utensil, appliance, contrivance, °mechanism, °gadget, *Colloq* °contraption, thingumabob, thingumajig, thingummy, thingy, whatsit, what's-its-name, whatnot, what-d'you-call-it, *Brit* gubbins, *US* gismo *or* gizmo: *Which instrument should I use to loosen this bolt? The doctor extracted the splinter with some sort of instrument.* **2** °agency, °means, °way, °factor, °mechanism, instrumentality, wherewithal, (°prime) mover, catalyst, °agent: *Summers refused to be the instrument of bringing free people into slavery.* **3** °contract, (°legal) °document, (written) °agreement, °pact, °compact, °paper: *After the signing, copies of the instruments were exchanged.*

instrumental *adj.* °helpful, °useful, utilitarian, contributory, of °service, °supportive, supporting, °advantageous, catalytic, conducive, °beneficial, valuable, °significant, °important; °accessory, ancillary: *Your presence will be instrumental in effecting a favourable settlement.*

insubordinate *adj.* °disobedient, °rebellious, °defiant, refractory, °mutinous, insurgent, insurrectional, insurrectionist, °revolutionary, °seditious, incompliant *or* uncompliant, uncooperative, °recalcitrant, contumacious, fractious, °unruly, °perverse, °contrary, °obstreperous, *Colloq Brit* stroppy: *The insubordinate officers have been court-martialled.*

insubstantial *adj.* **1** unsubstantial, °insignificant, °meagre, diaphanous, °small, °flimsy, °frail, °weak, °feeble, °paltry, °puny, °slight, °thin, °tenuous, °fragile, °light, gossamer, wispy, wisp-like, °fine: *Though the spider's thread appears insubstantial, for its weight it is enormously strong.* **2** °illusory, °unreal, illusive, °imaginary, imagined, °fanciful, °fancied, °visionary, °immaterial, °intangible, impalpable, incorporeal, airy, ethereal, °spiritual, chimerical, °phantom, phantasmal, phantasmagorical, hallucinatory, °fantastic; °false: *Through the mist London seemed insubstantial, a dream city of vapours rising from the Thames.*

insufferable *adj.* °unbearable, insupportable *or* unsupportable, intolerable, unendurable, °impossible: *The babysitter said she refused ever again to look after such an insufferable brat.*

insufficient *adj.* °inadequate, °deficient, °unsatisfactory, °meagre, °scanty, scant, °scarce; too °little, not °enough: *This light is insufficient for me to read by. We have insufficient skill to play the Brahms concerto.*

insulate *v.* **1** °detach, °separate, °isolate, °segregate, °shelter, °preserve, °set *or* °keep °apart, sequester, sequestrate, quarantine: *The rock star's aides did their best to insulate her from her screaming fans.* **2** °lag, °protect, °shield, °cushion, °wrap, °cover: *Insulate the pipes to prevent heat loss. Insulate the wire with this tape. Nitroglycerine must be insulated from shock.*

insult *v.* **1** °offend, affront, °slight, °outrage; °abuse, °dishonour, defame, °injure; asperse, °slander, °libel: *Don't be insulted if I arrive late and leave early. You insult her by suggesting that she has never heard of Keats.*

—*n.* **2** °offence, affront, °indignity, °slight, °outrage, barb, °dig, °slur, °dishonour, °abuse, defamation, discourtesy; °aspersion, °slander, °libel; *Colloq* °slap (in the face), °put-down: *Refusing to bow at a Japanese funeral is taken as an insult.*

insurance *n.* °assurance, surety, °indemnity, indemnification, °guarantee *or* guaranty, °warranty, °bond,

°security, °protection, °cover: *The cost of insurance is higher owing to the increase in crime.*

intact *adj.* °whole, °entire, °perfect, °complete, °integral, °sound, unbroken, °solid, (all) in °one °piece, °undivided, uncut, together, untouched, unreduced, undiminished, unimpaired, inviolate, unblemished, °unscathed, uninjured, unharmed, undamaged, unsullied, undefiled, untainted: *The ancient city has been preserved virtually intact.*

intangible *adj.* impalpable, unperceivable, °imperceptible, incorporeal, unsubstantial, °insubstantial, °imponderable, °immaterial, ethereal, vaporous, airy, evanescent, °vague, °obscure, °dim, °imprecise, °indefinite, °shadowy, °fleeting, °elusive: *The architect must deal with intangible ideas of design, how people work and live, etc.*

integral *adj.* **1** °basic, °elementary, °elemental, °fundamental, °essential, °intrinsic: *The rhythm is an integral part of the music.* **2** See **intact,** above.

integrate *v.* °combine, °unite, °blend, °bring *or* °put together, °assemble, °merge, °amalgamate, °join, °knit, °mesh, consolidate, coalesce, °fuse; *US* desegregate: *We must integrate all the parts into a coherent whole. Several cultures have been well integrated into our community.*

integrity *n.* **1** °honesty, °probity, veracity, uprightness, °honour, °rectitude, °principle, °morality, goodness, trustworthiness, decency, °virtue, incorruptibility, righteousness: *He is a person of unimpeachable integrity.* **2** wholeness, °entirety, °unity, togetherness, soundness, completeness, coherence, oneness, °totality: *Care should be taken not to disturb the integrity of the protective film.*

intellect *n.* **1** rationality, °reason, reasonableness, (common) °sense, °understanding, °judgement, cleverness, °intelligence, °mind, *Colloq* brains: *You have the intellect, my boy, but it wants developing.* **2** See **intellectual, 3,** below.

intellectual *adj.* **1** °mental, cerebral: *The greatest minds have brought their intellectual powers to bear on the problem.* **2** °thoughtful, thought-provoking, °highbrow, °academic, bookish, °scholarly, *Colloq* brainy: *The professor did not find the subject intellectual enough for a dissertation.*
—*n.* **3** °thinker, °intellect, °highbrow, °mastermind, °genius, *Colloq* °brain, egghead: *He enjoys associating with intellectuals at the university.* **4** °scholar, academician, professor, savant, °sage, °wise man, guru, polymath, pundit, °authority: *The editor of the journal is an intellectual who leaves the details of administration to her deputy.*

intelligence *n.* **1** °intellect, °understanding, °aptitude, °capacity, brainpower, cleverness, astuteness, quickness, alertness, keenness, brightness, shrewdness, °wit, °mother °wit, (common) °sense, °insight, perspicacity, °perception, discernment, °discretion, percipience, perspicaciousness, °wisdom, sagacity, *Colloq* brains, savvy, grey matter, *Slang Brit* nous: *He may not know anything about computer programming but he has the intelligence to learn how to do it.* **2** °information, °knowledge, °word, °data, °facts, °advice, °news, tidings, findings, *Colloq* °dope, °low-down, info, *Brit* gen, *US* °inside, poop: *Our agents are trying to gather intelligence on the Bulgarian situation.*

intelligent *adj.* °bright, °smart, °clever, discerning, perspicacious, °perceptive, percipient, °understanding, °rational, apt, °astute, quick, °quick-witted, °keen, °sharp, °alert, °shrewd, canny, insightful, °gifted, °sensible, °wise, °sage, sagacious, °enlightened, °knowing, °aware, °knowledgeable, erudite, *au fait*, *Colloq* brainy, *Chiefly US* savvy: *She is certainly intelligent enough to be first in her class, if only she would study harder.*

intelligentsia *n.pl.* °intellectuals, literati, savants, illuminati, masterminds, highbrows, *Colloq* °brains, eggheads, brains trust: *The government stifled free speech and persecuted the intelligentsia.*

intelligible *adj.* understandable, comprehensible, fathomable, decipherable, °legible, °clear, °plain, lucid, unambiguous: *Crowther's notes are barely intelligible.*

intend *v.* °mean, have in °mind *or* in °view, °propose, °contemplate, °design, °plan, °aim, °purpose, °resolve, °determine: *I intend to give him a piece of my mind. She is intending to go, but I don't know if she will be able to.*

intense *adj.* **1** °extreme, °excessive, °severe, °strong, °great, °fierce, °harsh, °acute, °powerful, °profound, °deep: *The intense heat kept the firemen at bay.* **2** °eager, °enthusiastic, °keen, °earnest, °sincere, °heartfelt, °deep, °passionate, °impassioned, °ardent, zealous, °animated, °burning, consuming, °fervent, fervid, perfervid, vehement, °frantic, °fanatical, frenzied: *I had an intense desire to see the culprit brought to justice.* **3** highly-strung *or chiefly US* high-strung, °emotional, °temperamental, °tense, °touchy, °testy, °volatile, °hysterical, °hotheaded, °feverish, °nervous, (°high-)°spirited, °impetuous, °impulsive, *Colloq* uptight: *I appreciate his enthusiasm, but I wish Henshawe were a bit less intense about his politics.*

intensify *v.* °concentrate, °focus, °sharpen, °whet, °strengthen, °reinforce, °heighten, escalate, °deepen, °quicken, °emphasize, °magnify, °increase, augment, °double, redouble, °heat up, *Colloq* °step up, *Brit* °hot up: *We must intensify our efforts to effect a settlement of the crisis. The war is intensifying.*

intensity *n.* concentration, °focus, °strength, forcefulness, °force, °power; °vigour, °energy, vehemence, °fervour, zeal, °ardour, °passion, °sincerity: *The storm is diminishing in intensity. Political partisanship is often attended by great intensity of emotion.*

intensive *adj.* concentrated, focused, intensified, °comprehensive, °exhaustive, °thorough(-going), all-out: *The police have launched an intensive manhunt.*

intent *n.* **1** °intention, °aim, °goal, °target, °purpose, °object, °objective, °end, °design, °plan, °idea: *Was it your intent that I should go with you? The charge is assault with intent to kill.* **2** °inclination, °tendency, °desire, intending: *The mere intent to commit treason is often tantamount to treason.* **3** ***to all intents and purposes***: °virtually, °practically, for all °practical purposes, (°almost) as good as, (°almost) the °same as, more or less, in °effect: *Telling you that the position was being discontinued is, to all intents and purposes, the same as firing you.*
—*adj.* **4** concentrated, focused, °fixed, °steady, °intense, °determined, °earnest, engrossed, °absorbed, °rapt, °steadfast, °resolute, °attentive: *Her intent stare unnerved many of her lecturers.* **5** °bent, °set, °resolute, committed, °decided, °firm, °keen; resolved, °eager, °determined, zealous, avid, °enthusiastic: *If you're intent on going, we won't try to change your mind.*

intention *n.* °aim, °purpose, °intent, °design, °goal, °end, °object, °objective, °target, °ambition: *Was it your intention to stay till the fat lady sings?*

intentional *adj.* °deliberate, intended, °premeditated, meant, °wilful, designed, planned, °preconceived, °studied, considered, contrived; °purposeful, on °purpose: *That slur was intentional and not just a slip of the tongue.*

intently *adv.* closely, attentively, concentratedly, earnestly, fixedly, unflinchingly, determinedly, °searchingly, steadily, steadfastly, continuously, assiduously, doggedly, unremittingly, eagerly, keenly, studiously: *They regarded one another intently across the table.*

intercept *v.* °interrupt, °deflect, °stop, °arrest, °check, °interfere (with), °head off, °block, °impede, °cut off, °seize, °grab, °catch, °trap: *He was intercepted as he was about to board a plane with the documents. Keeler intercepted the ball, preventing a goal.*

intercourse *n.* **1** °commerce, °traffic, °trade, °dealings, °exchange, communication, °contact, interaction: *In normal business intercourse our paths often cross.*

2 °sexual intercourse, coitus, coition, °sexual congress *or* °union, mating, copulation, °sexual relations, °carnal °knowledge, making °love, lovemaking, intimacy, °sexual °connection, *Colloq* °sex: *The plaintiff admits engaging in intercourse with the defendant.*

interest *n.* **1** °attention, attentiveness, °concern, °regard, °curiosity, °scrutiny, °notice, °engagement: *The way the puzzle fitted together drew my interest. She examined the books with interest. She shows interest in taking a writing course.* **2** °concern, °significance, °importance, °weight, °moment, °note, consequence: *Of what interest is a newly found painting by Tiepolo?* **3** Often, ***interests***: °profit, °advantage, °benefit, °good, avail, °worth, value, °consideration, °behalf, behoof: *Is it in our interest to sell the business?* **4** °share, °portion, °stake, investment, °piece, °cut, °percentage, participation, involvement: *I have a small interest in an emerald mine.* **5** Often, ***interests***: °business, °concern, °affair, °property; °hobby, °pastime, °diversion, avocation, °amusement, °entertainment, °pursuit, °relaxation, °occupation: *She travels abroad to look after her interests. Caroline has many interests besides business.* **6** (lending) °fee *or* °charge, °percentage, °rate, *Slang US* vigorish: *How much interest would the bank charge on a £40,000 mortgage?*
—*v.* **7** °engage, absorb, engross, °attract, °draw, °catch, °capture, °captivate, °hold, °fascinate, °intrigue, °excite, °incite, °provoke, arouse, °affect, °quicken, infect, °animate, °kindle, °fire: *At that time, our daughter was interested only in boys. There is something about astronomy that interests me.* **8** °influence, °induce, °persuade, °move, °tempt, °involve, °enrol, °enlist, °dispose, °incline, °prevail (up)on, °talk into, °concern: *Could I interest you in investing in my company?*

interested *adj.* **1** Also, ***interested in***: °engaged, °absorbed, engrossed, °drawn (to), attracted (by), °involved (in), °curious (about), fascinated (by), °keen (on), stimulated (by), °responsive (to), °concerned (about): *We talked about investing in my plastics company, and he seemed interested. She has become interested in designing jewellery.* **2** °concerned, °involved, non-objective, °partial, °biased, °prejudiced, °prejudicial, °partisan, predisposed: *You cannot get an honest appraisal of the painting's value from an interested party.*

interesting *adj.* °absorbing, °engaging, gripping, °riveting, engrossing, °attractive, compelling, intriguing, °provocative, °stimulating, °exciting, °inviting, fascinating, °enchanting, °spellbinding, captivating: *Nick has just told me the most interesting story about Tony.*

interfere *v.* **1** °meddle, °intrude, °butt in, °intervene, intercede, interpose, °interrupt, *Colloq* horn in, put *or* °stick in one's oar *or* one's oar in, °poke one's nose in, *US* kibitz: *Stop interfering in things that do not concern you.* **2** °hinder, °impede, °hamper, °block, °obstruct, °encumber, °slow, °retard, °handicap, °set back, get in the °way of, °frustrate, °conflict, °inhibit, °trammel, °subvert, °sabotage: *Allow nothing to interfere with the course of true love.*

interference *n.* **1** meddling, intrusion, intruding, intervention, interceding, intercession: *This interference in our personal affairs has gone far enough.* **2** °hindrance, °impediment, °block, °obstruction, °encumbrance, impedance, °difficulty, °snag, °hitch, °handicap, °set-back; frustration, °inhibition, °conflict, °opposition: *The lawsuit became an unwelcome interference in the smooth flow of our lives.*

interior *adj.* **1** °inside, °internal, inner, inward: *The interior surfaces are to be painted white.* **2** °internal, °domestic, °civil, °national, °local, °home: *We will not accept the interference of foreign governments in our interior affairs.* **3** inner, °private, °intimate, °personal, °individual, °secret, °hidden, °veiled: *Some of Hamlet's great speeches are in the form of interior monologues, or soliloquies.* **4** upland, inland, up-country, landlocked: *The most beautiful scenery is in the interior part of the country, away from the marshy coast.*
—*n.* **5** °inside: *The interior is coated with Teflon.* **6** °heart, °centre, °middle, °core, depths: *This is the story of a journey to the interior of the earth.* **7** uplands, up-country, heartland, hinterland: *The interior is covered with rocks and scrub pine.*

interjection *n.* °exclamation, ejaculation, °cry, interpolation, utterance: *Grammarians regard expressions like 'Hello' and 'Goodbye' as interjections.*

interlude *n.* °interval, entr'acte, °intermission, °pause, °stop, stoppage, °respite, °interruption, °break, hiatus, lacuna, °gap, °halt, °wait, breathing-space, °recess, °rest, °spell, °lull, *Colloq* °let-up: *There is a ten-minute interlude between the acts.*

intermediary *n.* °go-between, middleman, °agent, °representative, °broker, °intermediate, third °party, °mediator, arbitrator, arbiter, referee, °umpire, °judge: *Donaldson acted as intermediary and arranged the deal.*

intermediate *adj.* **1** °middle, in-between, medial, midway, halfway, transitional, intervening, °intermediary: *Middle schools cater for the age-range intermediate between primary and secondary schooling. In sublimation a substance changes from a gas to a solid (or vice versa), skipping the intermediate liquid state.* **2** See **intermediary,** above.

intermission *n.* See **interlude,** above.

intermittent *adj.* °irregular, discontinuous, °disconnected, °sporadic, °occasional, °random, °spasmodic, °fitful, °broken, °periodic, alternating, cyclic(al), °rhythmic(al), pulsating, seasonal, on-and-off, on-again-off-again, stop-and-go, stop-go: *Tomorrow, intermittent showers in the morning will yield to sunshine.*

internal *adj.* See **interior, 1, 2, 3,** above.

international *adj.* supranational, °global, worldwide, °universal, intercontinental, cosmopolitan, ecumenic(al) *or* oecumenic(al); °foreign: *An international conference is being held on disarmament. My father is engaged in international trade.*

interpret *v.* **1** °explain, explicate, °clear up, °clarify, elucidate, °illuminate, °throw *or* °shed °light on, °simplify, °decipher, decode, °define, °spell out, make °sense (out) of, °translate, °paraphrase: *Would you interpret this clause of the agreement for me?* **2** °understand, construe, °take (to °mean), °read, °figure *or* °work out, °sort out, unravel: *I haven't any idea how to interpret this poem.*

interpretation *n.* **1** °explanation, clarification, elucidation, simplification, decipherment, °solution, working-out, unravelling, sorting out, decoding, °definition, °illustration, °translation, paraphrasing: *Sharon's detailed interpretation of the data is quite easy to understand.* **2** °analysis, diagnosis, °examination, exegesis, explication, reading, construal, °inference, °understanding: *These figures are subject to individual interpretation.*

interrogation *n.* questioning, °examination, cross-examination, inquisition, °investigation, *Colloq* third degree, grilling: *Caught by the rebels, we were subjected to hours of interrogation.*

interrupt *v.* **1** °break in, °cut in, °intrude in, °butt in, °interfere in, °punctuate, °disturb, *Colloq* barge in, °chime in, horn in: *He keeps interrupting the discussion with his silly remarks.* **2** °discontinue, °break off, °cut off, °cut °short, °interfere with, °disrupt, °suspend, °hold up, °halt, °stop, °end, °terminate, °cease: *We interrupt this programme to bring you a news bulletin.*

interruption *n.* **1** °break, intrusion, °disturbance, °interference, disruption: *Please forgive this interruption, but you're wanted on the phone.* **2** °break, °gap, °interval, lacuna, hiatus, °respite, °rest, °pause, pausing, °intermission, stopping, °stop, °suspension, cessation, °cease, ceasing, surcease, hesitation, *Prosody* caesura, *Colloq* °let-up: *She talked for an hour without interruption.*

interval *n.* **1** °intermission, °interlude, entr'acte, °break, °pause; °recess, °rest (°period), °period, °time, °wait, °spell, °delay, °lapse: *The play was so bad we left in the interval. After a brief interval, the lights came on* *again.* **2** °meanwhile, °meantime, interim: *He returned later but found that in the interval she had changed her mind.* **3** °gap, °opening, °space, °hole, °void, lacuna, °distance, interstice, *Architecture* intercolumniation: *The interval between the columns is exactly three metres.*

intervene *v.* **1** °interfere, °intrude, °break in, °interrupt, intercede, °meddle, interpose, °butt in, *Colloq* °poke one's nose in, horn in, put in one's oar, °step in: *If I had not intervened you might have been killed. She intervened on my behalf.* **2** °come *or* °go (between), °pass, °elapse: *A week intervened before we saw each other again.*

interview *n.* **1** °meeting, (°press) °conference, °discussion, °conversation, °talk, °question °period, audience: *The reporter phoned to ask for an interview.* **2** °evaluation, appraisal, vetting, assessment: *I have a job interview scheduled for tomorrow.*
—*v.* **3** °question, °examine, interrogate, °sound out, °talk with *or* to: *She interviewed the Prime Minister on television last night.* **4** appraise, °evaluate, °check (out), °vet: *The headmaster himself interviews the teachers.*

intimate[1] *adj.* **1** °close, °personal, °warm, °affectionate, loving, °dear, °bosom, cherished, °familiar, *intime*: *She had a party for intimate friends.* **2** °secret, °confidential, °private, °personal, °privy, °hidden, *intime*; °detailed, °penetrating, °deep, °profound, °thorough, °exhaustive: *In his autobiography he reveals intimate particulars of his marriage.* **3** °sexual; °carnal: *It is well known that Millie was on intimate terms with her chauffeur.* **4** °cosy, °informal, °snug, °friendly, °warm, °comfortable; *intime, à deux*, °tête-à-tête, *Colloq* comfy: *The two of us had an intimate dinner at home last night.*
—*n.* **5** °friend, °associate, °comrade, crony, °familiar, confidant(e), (°constant) °companion, Achates, alter ego, °colleague, confrère, *Colloq* sidekick, °chum, °pal, *Brit and Australian* °mate, *US* buddy, *Slang Brit* china (plate), mucker: *He and a few of his intimates like to get together now and then for a game of snooker.*

intimate[2] *v.* °hint, °imply, °suggest, °insinuate, °indicate, °refer to, allude to, °communicate, °make known, °give (someone) to °understand, °warn, °caution, *Colloq* °tip (off): *He intimates that my wife will be a widow if I tell the police.*

intimidate *v.* °frighten, °scare, °alarm, cow, °daunt, °dismay, abash, °appal, awe, °overawe, °browbeat, °menace, °threaten, °terrify, °petrify, terrorize, °tyrannize; *Slang* have *or* get (someone) by the short and curlies: *You can't intimidate me with your threats!*

intolerance *n.* °bias, °prejudice, °bigotry, °discrimination, °partiality, illiberality, narrow-mindedness, dogmatism; racism, racialism, sexism, classism, ageism, xenophobia: *The government has legislated against intolerance of minorities.*

intolerant *adj.* **1** °unsympathetic, unforbearing, unindulgent, °impatient, °inconsiderate, °inhospitable, uncharitable: *The present system seems intolerant of the aged.* **2** °biased, °prejudiced, °bigoted, discriminatory, °partial, illiberal, °narrow-minded, °parochial, °provincial, °jaundiced, warped, twisted, °one-sided, °opinionated, close-minded; racist, racialist, sexist, classist, ageist, xenophobic: *How can some religions be so intolerant of other people's beliefs?*

intonation *n.* °accent, accentuation, °speech *or* °sound °pattern, °delivery, modulation, articulation, °pronunciation, vocalization, °pitch, °tone, inflection: *You can tell the speaker's mood by his intonation.*

intoxicate *v.* **1** inebriate, make °drunk, addle, stupefy, °muddle, befuddle: *He tried to intoxicate me with his home-made brew.* **2** °stimulate, °excite, °overwhelm, elate, exhilarate, °animate, °enliven, invigorate, inspirit, °thrill, galvanize, °electrify, make one's head °spin, take one's °breath away, infatuate, °entrance, °enchant, °enrapture, °fascinate, °bewitch, cast a °spell on, ensorcell: *She was intoxicated by the atmosphere of the place.*

intoxicating *adj.* **1** °alcoholic, spirituous, inebriant: *Do not drink intoxicating beverages if you plan to drive.* **2** °exhilarating, °invigorating, °thrilling, °exciting, heady, °stimulating, electrifying, entrancing, fascinating: *Making a film of the life of Lola Montez is an intoxicating idea.*

intrepid *adj.* °fearless, °brave, °bold, °daring, °dauntless, undaunted, °steadfast, °resolute, °courageous, unafraid, plucky, °gallant, valiant, valorous, doughty, °audacious, °heroic, °manly, manful, °dashing, °adventurous, °venturesome, stout-hearted, lion-hearted, °game: *Quatermain was known to the enemy as an intrepid soldier.*

intricate *adj.* **1** °involved, °complicated, convoluted, entangled, tangled, knotty, complex, twisted, winding, °tortuous, sinuous, anfractuous, °labyrinthine, °elaborate, Byzantine, °fancy, °ornate, rococo, Daedalian *or* Daedalean *or* Daedalic, *Literary* daedal *or* dedal: *The plot was far too intricate and I became confused.* **2** °perplexing, °puzzling, mystifying, enigmatic: *The code was so intricate that even the computer needed hours to decipher the message.*

intrigue *v.* **1** °fascinate, °beguile, °captivate, °attract, absorb, °charm, pique, °interest, titillate, arouse *or* °excite the °curiosity (of): *It intrigues me to watch them put those ships into bottles.* **2** conspire, °plot, connive, °scheme, °manoeuvre: *She was sure that everyone was intriguing against her.*
—*n.* **3** °conspiracy, °plot, °scheme, °manoeuvre, collusion, °stratagem, °trickery, °chicanery, double-dealing, guile, °subterfuge, °artifice, °machination, °deception: *Many of those close to the government are engaged in intrigue of some kind.* **4** °affair, °liaison, amour, °romance, intimacy; adultery: *We all knew about the intrigue he was carrying on with the duke's wife.*

intrinsic *adj.* °inherent, °basic, °fundamental, °essential, °proper, °elemental, °organic, °natural, °native, inbred, congenital, inherited, °hereditary, innate, °inborn, immanent, indwelling, underlying, constitutional; °real, °true, °actual, °genuine: *As no painting has intrinsic worth, its value is arbitrary.*

introduce *v.* **1** °acquaint, °present, °make known: *Sandy introduced Gerald and Daphne to each other.* **2** °bring in *or* up, °advance, °present, °broach, °put *or* °set forth, °put forward, °suggest, °offer, °propose, °mention: *It was she who introduced the issue of bacteria in canned goods.* **3** °announce, °present: *Please introduce the next speaker.* **4** °start, °begin, °originate, °launch, °establish, °set up, °pioneer, °initiate, usher in, °institute, °bring out *or* in, °organize: *When was paper money first introduced?* **5** °insert, °add, interpose, °inject, °put in, interpolate: *Why introduce irrelevant matters into the discussion?*

introductory *adj.* **1** °opening, °prefatory, °preliminary, °preparatory, °beginning, inaugural, °initial: *His 'introductory' remarks lasted longer than the speeches!* **2** °primary, °basic, °fundamental, °elementary, °first, °rudimentary: *Take an introductory course before enrolling for more advanced study.*

intrude *v.* °interfere, °break in, °interrupt, °intervene, °push in, interpose, °butt in, °infringe, °encroach, °obtrude, *Colloq* horn in, barge in: *They want to be alone and you are intruding. Forgive me for intruding into your conversation.*

intruder *n.* **1** interloper, gatecrasher, uninvited °guest, °unwelcome °visitor; trespasser, encroacher, invader, infiltrator, squatter; °burglar, °thief: *The intruders were quickly expelled by the guards.* **2** meddler, °busybody, *Colloq* °snoop(er), Nosy Parker, *US* kibitzer: *You are an intruder into my private affairs.*

intrusive *adj.* intruding, interfering, meddlesome, invasive, meddling, prying, °inquisitive, °obtrusive, importunate, °officious, °presumptuous, °forward; °unwelcome, uncalled-for, unwanted, unsought, *Colloq* °nosy, °pushy, snoopy: *He said he apologized if he was being intrusive.*

intuition *n.* °instinct, °insight, °hunch, sixth °sense, presentiment, °premonition, °foreboding; °perception, perceptiveness, percipience, perspicacity, common °sense, mother °wit: *Intuition told me I should find the answer here.*

invalid[1] *adj.* **1** ailing, °sick, °sickly, °ill, °infirm, valetudinarian, °disabled: *His invalid sister is confined to a wheelchair.*
—*n.* **2** °patient, valetudinarian, °victim, sufferer, °incurable, °cripple, *Chiefly US and Canadian* shut-in: *Many invalids have claimed complete recovery after a visit to Lourdes.*

invalid[2] *adj.* °void, null (and °void), nullified, annulled, repudiated, °untrue, °false, °faulty, °erroneous, °wrong, °spurious; °incorrect, °imperfect, impaired, °unsound, °untenable, °ineffective: *He was driving with an invalid licence. Your reasons for quitting school are invalid.*

invaluable *adj.* °priceless, valuable, °precious, of °inestimable *or* incalculable value; irreplaceable, irredeemable; costly, °expensive, high-priced, °dear: *The thieves made off with several invaluable paintings.*

invariable *adj.* **1** unchanging, °changeless, unvarying, invariant, unwavering, °constant, °steady, °stable, °regular; °fixed, °fast, °set, °rigid, °uniform, unfailing, unexceptional: *She is invariable in her opinion of a woman's right to abortion. His invariable routine calls for a dawn swim, regardless of the weather.* **2** immutable, unchangeable, unalterable, unmodifiable: *The law of supply and demand is invariable.* **3** °permanent, °fixed, °enduring, °abiding, °eternal, unaltered, unvarying, unchanged, unvaried, unmodified: *The positions of the stars appear to be invariable.*

invasion *n.* **1** incursion, °raid, foray, intrusion, °inroad, encroachment, trespass, infiltration; °infringement, infraction, °transgression, °violation: *The poachers were charged with invasion of private property. Unauthorized publication of that material is an invasion of your rights.* **2** °attack, °assault, onslaught, °aggression, °offensive, °drive, storming, blitzkrieg: *The armoured divisions succeeded in stopping the invasion.*

invent *v.* **1** °create, °devise, contrive, °originate, °think up, °dream up, °conceive, concoct, °make up, °imagine, °formulate, °improvise, °design, °hit upon; °coin: *He claims to have invented the toothpaste tube.* **2** °fabricate, °make up, concoct, *Colloq* cook up: *She invented that story about having been a lion-tamer.*

invention *n.* **1** °creation, origination, contriving, devising, °conception, contrivance, introduction, °development: *The invention of the screwdriver has spared many a broken fingernail.* **2** °creation, contrivance, °device, °gadget, *Colloq* °contraption, *US* gismo *or* gizmo: *Thomas Edison held patents on a huge number of inventions.* **3** fiction, figment, °story, °fantasy, °fabrication, °tale, fable, °yarn, °fib, °tall °story *or* °tale, falsification, °fake, °sham, °falsehood, °lie, prevarication: *Her claim that the accident was my fault is a flagrant invention.*

invest *v.* **1** °venture, °lay out, °put in, °sink: *She was persuaded to invest her life savings in unit trusts.* **2** °devote, °allot, °spend, °contribute, °supply, °provide: *We have invested a lot of time in cleaning up local government.* **3** °install *or* instal, °inaugurate, °induct, °initiate, instate, °establish, ordain, °swear in, °seat: *He will be invested with the Order of Merit on Tuesday.*

investigate *v.* °enquire *or* °inquire into, °examine, °study, °consider, °explore, °probe, °look into, °research, °scrutinize, °analyse, °sift (through), winnow: *The laboratory is investigating the nature of the strange phenomenon.*

investigation *n.* enquiry *or* °inquiry, °examination, °study, °review, °exploration, °quest, °search, °probe, °research, °discovery °procedure, °scrutiny, °analysis, inquest, inquisition, °interrogation, questioning: *Has the investigation turned up any evidence of collusion?*

invigorating *adj.* °stimulating, °bracing, rejuvenating, °tonic, vitalizing, restorative, energizing, vivifying, enlivening, °exhilarating; °fresh, healthful, °healthy, salubrious, salutary: *Each morning I go for an invigorating walk. The doctor recommended the invigorating mountain air.*

invincible *adj.* **1** unconquerable, °unbeatable, °indomitable, insuperable, undefeated, unstoppable: *United look invincible, and are likely to retain the cup for a fourth successive season.* **2** °impregnable, invulnerable, impenetrable, °indestructible, unassailable: *The Romans believed the fortress to be invincible.*

invisible *adj.* **1** unseeable, °imperceptible, undetectable, imperceivable; unseen: *The air we breathe is invisible.* **2** concealed, °hidden, disguised, camouflaged, masked, covered, unperceived, °veiled, indiscernible: *Once the part has been painted, the damage will be invisible.*

invitation *n.* **1** summons, °request, °call, °bidding, *Colloq* invite: *I am still waiting for my invitation to their wedding.* **2** °attraction, °inducement, allure, allurement, °enticement, °temptation, °magnetism, bait, °lure, °draw, °pull: *The possibility of going where no man had gone before was too great an invitation to ignore.*

inviting *adj.* alluring, °tempting, enticing, °attractive, beckoning, appealing, captivating, °engaging, intriguing, °irresistible, winsome, beguiling, bewitching, entrancing, fascinating, tantalizing, °seductive: *She gave him an inviting smile but he still approached cautiously.*

involuntary *adj.* °unconscious, unintentional, °unthinking, °impulsive, °spontaneous, °unpremeditated, °instinctive, instinctual, unwitting; °automatic, reflex, °mechanical, conditioned, °uncontrolled, uncontrollable: *When I was struck, my involuntary reaction was to strike back at once. At the mention of his name she gave an involuntary start.*

involve *v.* **1** °include, °contain, comprise, °cover, °embrace, °incorporate, encompass, °take in, subsume, °embody, °comprehend, °number among, °count in: *The survey involved many people from all walks of life.* **2** °imply, °entail, °suggest, °mean, betoken, °require, necessitate, °presuppose: *Enrolling for a course involves doing homework as well as attending classes.* **3** Often, ***involve in*** *or* ***with***: °implicate, °concern, °affect, °touch, °entangle, °draw in; °incriminate, inculpate; °associate with, °connect with, °catch (up) in: *I didn't know that Annette was involved. Are you involved in that murder investigation?*

involved *adj.* **1** implicated, °concerned, °affected, °interested, °active: *The public enquiry was attended by all involved members of the community.* **2** tangled, °complicated, complex, twisted, snarled, convoluted, °confused, confusing, °intricate, °tortuous, °elaborate, knotty, Byzantine, °labyrinthine: *The plot is too involved to be followed easily. The involved problems of adolescence cannot be treated in a one-day conference.* **3** ***involved with***: associated with, entangled with, embroiled with, enmeshed with, *Colloq* °mixed up in *or* with: *Dennis is still very much involved with that singer from the Green Dragon.*

irk *v.* °irritate, °annoy, vex, °pester, °provoke, °chafe, nettle, °exasperate, *Colloq* needle, miff, °aggravate, °bug, peeve, °rub (someone) (up) the wrong way, °put out: *It really irks me to know that we lost because we didn't practise.*

irksome *adj.* irritating, annoying, vexing, vexatious, chafing, nettling, exasperating, bothersome, °troublesome, °burdensome, °tiresome, °tedious, °boring, wearisome, uninteresting, *Colloq* aggravating, pestiferous: *The mosquitoes are particularly irksome on muggy, windless evenings.*

irregular *adj.* **1** uneven, °bumpy, °lumpy, °coarse, °rough, unequal, unsymmetric(al), asymmetric(al), °pitted, potholed, °jagged, craggy, °lopsided: *The irregular surface of the road bounced us about in the car.* **2** °sporadic, uneven, °random, °erratic, unequal,

°fitful, °haphazard, unsystematic, unsystematized, °disorderly, °uncertain, unmethodical; °occasional, °casual: *In the distance I could hear the staccato of irregular machine-gun fire.* **3** °extraordinary, °unusual, °eccentric, °abnormal, anomalous, aberrant, °unnatural, °peculiar, °queer, °odd, °weird, °bizarre, °strange, °singular, nonconforming, °nonconformist, °exceptional, unconventional, °offbeat, uncommon, freakish, *Colloq* freaky: *Don't you think that keeping a Komodo dragon as a pet is somewhat irregular?*

irrelevant *adj.* °inappropriate, °inapplicable, °impertinent, °unrelated, °alien, inapposite, malapropos, beside the °point, inapt, non-germane, unconnected, °extraneous, neither here nor there, out of °place, °gratuitous, uncalled-for, *Colloq* out of the blue, off the beam, *Slang* off-the-wall: *The name of the person who asked the question is entirely irrelevant.*

irrepressible *adj.* unrestrainable, irrestrainable, uncontainable, uncontrollable, unmanageable, insuppressible *or* unsuppressible, unstoppable, °ebullient, °buoyant, °effervescent, bubbling, °boisterous: *Nothing could dampen our irrepressible high spirits after winning the game.*

irreproachable *adj.* °blameless, unimpeachable, beyond reproach, unreprovable, °faultless, °innocent, above °suspicion, °impeccable, inculpable, °honest, °pure: *Till now, Forsyth's record in the army has been irreproachable.*

irresistible *adj.* **1** °irrepressible, unconquerable, °indomitable, °overpowering, °unbearable, °overwhelming, °overriding, unmanageable, °ungovernable, uncontrollable: *I had an irresistible desire to punch him in the nose.* **2** unstoppable, inexorable, °relentless, °unavoidable, ineluctable, inescapable: *What happens when an irresistible force meets an immovable object?*

irresolute *adj.* vacillating, wavering, faltering, °indecisive, °infirm of purpose, in *or US only* of two minds, undecided, °hesitant, hesitating, shifting, changing, °erratic, °uncertain, unsure, undetermined, °unresolved, °half-hearted, *Colloq* °wishy-washy: *You must act; this is no time to be irresolute.*

irrespective of *prep.* °regardless of, °notwithstanding, °despite, °apart from, in °spite of, without °regard to, ignoring, discounting: *We shall carry on irrespective of public opinion.*

irresponsible *adj.* °careless, °reckless, devil-may-care, unanswerable, °unaccountable, non-liable, °rash, °unruly, °wild; °unreliable, undependable, untrustworthy, °weak, feckless, °ineffectual: *Cyril is too irresponsible to take care of the children by himself.*

irretrievable *adj.* **1** non-retrievable, unretrievable, unrecoverable, irrecoverable, unsalvageable, unsavable, °lost, irreclaimable: *The data that was deleted is now irretrievable.* **2** irreparable, irremediable, uncorrectable, unrectifiable, irredeemable, °irreversible, °irrevocable: *The radiation from the atomic blast did irretrievable damage.*

irreverent *adj.* **1** °blasphemous, °impious, °profane, °sacrilegious, unholy, °ungodly, irreligious: *She was reprimanded for her irreverent attitude to morning prayers.* **2** °disrespectful, insulting, °insolent, °rude, °discourteous, uncivil, derisive, °impudent, °impertinent, saucy, °flippant, mocking, tongue-in-cheek, *Colloq* °flip, °cheeky: *The prince did not appreciate being the butt of the irreverent skit.*

irreversible *adj.* unreversible, non-reversible, °irrevocable, unchangeable, unalterable, °permanent, °fixed, °final, unrepealable, irredeemable, °irretrievable: *Burning, essentially the chemical process of rapid oxidation, is irreversible.*

irrevocable *adj.* °irreversible, unchangeable, immutable, °changeless, °fixed, unalterable, settled, unrecallable, °irretrievable, irrepealable, not undoable; irreparable, °permanent, °enduring, °everlasting: *The colonel says that his was an irrevocable order. That speech did you irrevocable harm.*

irritable *adj.* °impatient, °excitable, °testy, °touchy, °quarrelsome, grouchy, °fretful, °peevish, °cross, crabby, crusty, °short-tempered, °petulant, °prickly, irascible, °moody, °temperamental, °gruff, °cantankerous, curmudgeonly, dyspeptic, bad-tempered, ill-tempered, ill-humoured, °snappy *or* °snappish, grumpy *or Brit also* grumpish, *Colloq* crotchety, *US and Canadian and Irish* °cranky: *Why are you always so irritable before breakfast?*

irritate *v.* °annoy, vex, nettle, °pester, °provoke, °bother, °anger, °enrage, °chafe, pique, °exasperate, °ruffle, hector, °harass, harry, °nag, °plague, °worry, °fret, °fluster, °trouble, °pick at *or* on, *Colloq* needle, °get under (someone's) skin, °get in (someone's) hair, hassle, peeve, °get on (someone's) nerves, drive (someone) up the °wall, °get (someone's) hackles up, °get (someone's) back up, drive (someone) °crazy *or* °mad, °rub (someone) (up) the wrong way, *Brit* °get up (someone's) nose, *US* °burn (someone) up: *All these stupid questions are beginning to irritate me.*

island *n.* isle, islet, ait, cay, key; atoll; archipelago; *Brit dialect* eyot, holm: *There are actually about 1,500 islands in the Thousand Islands in the St Lawrence river.*

isolate *v.* °separate, °segregate, sequester, cloister, °detach, °cut off, send to Coventry, °ostracize, °maroon, °exclude, °shut out, °bar, debar, °banish, deport, °transport, °exile, °reject, °eject, °throw out, °expel, °shun, °spurn, °avoid, °ignore, snub; quarantine; *Colloq* cut, give (someone) the cold °shoulder: *You cannot isolate a child from the pressures of modern society.*

isolated *adj.* **1** lone, °solitary, °single, °singular, °unique, anomalous, °separate, °special, °particular, °individual, °exceptional, °unrelated: *In one isolated case they recommended a suspended sentence.* **2** °alone, separated, segregated, °secluded, sequestered, cloistered, unconnected, °detached, (set) °apart, removed, °cut off, excluded; °forlorn, °lonely, hermitic(al), eremitic(al), anchoretic(al), troglodytic(al), monastic: *Away from his friends and family, he felt totally isolated. After his wife died, he led an isolated existence.* **3** °secluded, °remote, °out-of-the-way, off the beaten track, unfrequented, °lonely; °secret, °hidden: *For twenty years we lived in that isolated shack in the wilderness.*

issue *n.* **1** outflow, °outgoing, °exit, egress, issuance, emanation, efflux, debouchment, °emergence, °outlet: *The river's colour changed abruptly at its point of issue into the sea.* **2** °outcome, conclusion, consequence, culmination, °result, °end, °effect, °consummation, °event, °climax, *Colloq* °pay-off: *Whatever the issue, it has been a brave effort.* **3** °point, °topic, °subject, °matter, °affair, °problem, °question: *That is an issue you should take up with the mayor.* **4** Usually, ***major issue***: (°major *or* °big) °problem *or* °difficulty, °controversy, °fight, °dispute, *cause célèbre*: *He turns even walking the dog into a major issue.* **5** printing, °edition, °version; °copy, °number: *I have a copy of the Sunday issue. See if you can buy an issue of today's paper.* **6** °publication, promulgation, issuance, issuing, °distribution, °delivery, dissemination, broadcasting, °proclamation, °circulation: *There will be a special issue of stamps to commemorate his death.* **7** °offspring, °child *or* children, °descendant(s), °progeny, °young, scion(s), son(s), daughter(s): *According to the records, your uncle died without issue, making you his sole heir.* **8** ***at issue***: in contention, in °dispute, °unresolved, °unsettled, °uncertain, up in the air, to be °decided: *The point at issue is which system will be the most efficient.* **9** ***take issue***: °disagree, °argue, contend, °dispute, °oppose, take °exception: *I feel that I must take issue with your conclusion.*

—*v.* **10** °proclaim, promulgate, °declare, °publish, °put out, °put *or* °set forth, °announce, °circulate, °distribute, °release, °deliver, °broadcast, disseminate, °get out: *The kidnappers have issued an ultimatum.* **11** °emerge, °come *or* °go forth, °exit, °emanate, °discharge, °stream, °flow, °pour; °appear, °originate,

°spring, °stem, °arise: *The play ended, and people issued from the theatre. Where Pegasus stamped his foot the Pierian spring issued forth.*

itch *v.* **1** °tickle, tingle, °prickle: *These mosquito bites itch terribly.* **2** °desire, crave, °hanker, °hunger, °thirst, °yearn, pine, °wish, °want, °die: *I am itching to get my hands on whoever told you that I was dead.*
—*n.* **3** °tickle, tickling, tingle, tingling, °prickle, prickling, irritation: *My frustration is like having an itch I can't scratch.* **4** °desire, craving, hankering, °hunger, °thirst, yearning, °longing, *Colloq* yen: *I have a sudden itch to visit mother for the weekend.*

item *n.* **1** °detail, article, °point, °particular, °matter, °thing, °element, component, °ingredient: *There's one item I'd like you to keep in mind.* **2** °piece, °mention, °notice, °note, °memorandum, memo, filler, jotting: *We often publish short items to fill out a column.*

itemize *v.* °enumerate, °list, °specify, particularize, °detail, °document, °number, °record, °count, °tabulate: *Must I itemize every single book in the inventory?*

J

jab *v.* **1** °stab, °thrust, °poke, °dig, °prod; °plunge; °nudge; °tap: *The doctor jabbed a needle into my arm.* **2** °punch, °hit, °strike, °belt, smack, °rap, whack, thwack, cuff, thump, wallop; elbow; *Colloq* °clip, sock, slug, biff: *I jabbed him in the jaw with a quick left.*
—*n.* **3** °stab, °thrust, °poke, °dig, °prod, °nudge: *I felt the jab of her elbow signalling me to be quiet.* **4** °punch, °belt, smack, °rap, whack, thwack, cuff, thump, wallop, *Colloq* °clip, sock, slug, biff: *A hard jab in the stomach made the bully turn to pudding.*

jabber *v.* **1** blether *or US only* blather, °chatter, °babble, gibber, gabble, prate, °prattle, °patter, °drivel, °rattle, *Brit* natter, *Scots* yatter, *Colloq* °gab, gas, °yap, witter: *The couple behind me jabbered throughout the entire film.*
—*n.* **2** See **jargon, 2,** below.

jade *n.* **1** °nag, °hack, *Slang Brit* screw, *US* plug: *That old jade hasn't won a race in his last ten times out.* **2** °shrew, harridan, °nag, °hag, °drab, °witch, crone, hussy, minx, vixen, virago, termagant, beldam, slut, °slattern, trull, trollop, baggage, °tart, *Slang* battle-axe, °broad, °bitch, old °bag, floozie *or* floozy *or* floosie: *He was married to an expensive jade of a wife.*

jaded *adj.* **1** °exhausted, °weary, °tired, °dead °tired, bone-tired, bone-weary, dog-tired, °fatigued, enervated, °spent, *Colloq* (°dead) °beat, °dead, bushed, fagged, *US and Canadian* pooped: *The nightspot was full of jaded businessmen, who had gone there to relax after a heavy day at the office.* **2** sated, satiated, cloyed, °surfeited, glutted, gorged, fed up, °sick (and °tired) of, slaked; °dull, bored: *You need a little champagne and caviar to reawaken your jaded palate.*

jag *n.* °spree, °carouse, °orgy, °bout, *Colloq* binge, *US and Canadian* toot: *She was terribly hung-over after last night's jag.*

jagged *adj.* °rough, uneven, °notched, sawtooth(ed), °ragged, toothed, spiked, indented, denticulate, °serrated, chipped: *I cut myself on the jagged edge of that broken window.*

jail *n.* **1** gaol, °prison, lock-up, reformatory, *Brit* °Borstal, *US* penitentiary, °reform school, *Nautical* brig, *Slang* cooler, clink, can, °jug, °stir, slammer, *Brit* °nick, quod, choky *or* chokey, *US* calaboose, big house, °pen, coop, hoosegow, poky *or* pokey: *They were sent to jail for life.*
—*v.* **2** °imprison, °lock up, incarcerate, detain, confine, *Brit* °send down, *US* °send up (the river): *He was jailed for 30 days.*

jailer *n.* gaoler, turnkey, guard, *Brit* warder, governor, *US* warden, *Slang* screw: *The jailers let us out for exercise for an hour each day.*

jam *v.* **1** °cram, °force, °push, °wedge, °stuff, °press, °ram, °squeeze, shove, °pack, °crowd: *We were jammed in so tightly that we couldn't move.* **2** °block, °obstruct, congest, °fill up, °clog, °plug, °stop up: *The toilet is jammed with paper again.* **3** °slam, °activate, actuate: *I jammed on the brakes.*
—*n.* **4** °obstruction, blockage, blocking, °block, congestion, °tie-up, bottleneck, stoppage: *She was stuck in a traffic jam for an hour.* **5** °crush, °squeeze, °crowd, °mob, °swarm, multitude, °throng, °mass, horde, °pack, °press: *You wouldn't believe the jam of football fans at the cup final!* **6** °trouble, °difficulty, °predicament, °quandary, °dilemma, *Colloq* °bind, °fix, °hole, pickle, hot water, (tight) °spot, °scrape: *Harry helped me out of a jam once, and I won't forget it.*

jamboree *n.* °gathering, °get-together, °party, °celebration, °fête, °festival, °festivity, carnival, °frolic, °revelry, °spree, °carouse, jubilee, revels, charivari: *Everyone is invited to the annual jamboree in the village square.*

jangle *v.* **1** clatter, °clash, °rattle, clang, clank, °crash, °ring, °jingle: *The chains jangled as the prisoners marched to their cells.* **2** °jar, °upset, °irritate: *The continuous screaming of the sirens jangled my nerves.*
—*n.* **3** jangling, clatter, °clash, °rattle, jarring, clang, clanging, clank, clanking, °crash, clangour, °noise, °din, °racket, clamour, dissonance, cacophony, reverberation, *Literary* stridor: *I heard the jangle of the rag-and-bone man's cart in the next street.*

jar[1] *n.* crock; °receptacle, °vessel, container, urn, °pot, vase; °jug, pitcher, ewer, flagon, carafe, °bottle, amphora: *We always keep some small change in that blue jar.*

jar[2] *v.* **1** °shake, °agitate, °disturb, °stir, °shock, °jolt, jounce, °bounce, °jog, °jerk, °jiggle, joggle: *Don't jar the oven or the cake will collapse.* **2** °disagree, °conflict, °clash, °bicker, °quarrel, wrangle, °oppose, °discord: *She finds that her emotions about her ex-husband are jarring.* **3** °disturb, °upset, disconcert, unsettle, disquiet, °bother, °trouble, vex, °gall, °offend, °take aback, °irritate, °grate, °irk, nettle, °annoy: *It jars me to think that they got off with light sentences.*
—*n.* **4** °shock, °start, °jolt, °surprise: *Seeing Sam after all those years gave me quite a jar.*

jargon *n.* **1** °cant, argot, °parlance, °idiom, °vernacular, slang; patois, Creole, °dialect, pidgin; *Colloq* °lingo: *In the jargon of philately, this is known as a 'first day cover'.* **2** blether *or US also* blather, °chatter, °babble, °gibberish, °jabber, gabble, °gobbledegook *or* gobbledygook, °prattle, °patter, °drivel, cackle, jabberwocky, twaddle, (°stuff and) °nonsense, °rubbish, codswallop, balderdash, bunk, humbug, °palaver, *bavardage*, *Colloq* °rot, °garbage, hogwash, bosh, piffle, flapdoodle, chit-chat, °gab, claptrap, *Slang* bull, crap: *When I questioned my bank manager about the fee, he just gave me a lot of jargon.*

jaundiced *adj.* **1** coloured, tainted, distorted, twisted, °prejudiced, °opinionated, °biased, °preconceived, untrustworthy, °bigoted, °partial, unfair, °perverted; °dishonest, °corrupt: *Even the most jaundiced view must acknowledge the merits of the plan.* **2** splenetic, cynical, °bitter, °envious, °resentful, °jealous, °hostile, °spiteful, unfriendly, disapproving, °critical, unfavourable, disparaging, denigrating: *I can't say that I agree with Cartwright's jaundiced review of the play.*

jaunty *adj.* **1** °spirited, °lively, high-spirited, °buoyant, °brisk, °frisky, °sprightly, °free (and °easy), °blithe, jovial, °happy, jubilant, °jolly, °merry, °cheerful, °gay: *It is heartening to see those pensioners in such a jaunty mood.* **2** °chic, °smart, °stylish, °dashing, °debonair, °elegant, colourful, °spruce, °flashy, °flash, °showy, °flamboyant, *Colloq* °sporty, natty: *Tipping his hat at a jaunty angle, the old boulevardier strolled off, twirling his walking-stick.*

jealous *adj.* **1** °resentful, °bitter, grudging, °envious, covetous, °green with °envy, green-eyed: *Brian is* *jealous of attention paid to anyone but himself.* **2** °distrustful, distrusting, mistrustful, mistrusting, °suspicious; °anxious, °insecure, threatened, imperilled, °vulnerable: *Ken is very jealous of Kathleen. If anyone so much as looks at her, he feels jealous.*

jealously *adv.* watchfully, carefully, guardedly, protectively, warily, vigilantly, scrupulously, zealously, eagerly, attentively, anxiously, suspiciously: *Victor jealously keeps all details of his business to himself.*

jeer *v.* **1** Often, ***jeer at***: °mock, °laugh *or* °scoff *or* °sneer (at), °flout, °deride, °ridicule, make °fun of, °thumb one's nose at, °gibe *or* jibe, °chaff, decry, °twit, °taunt, *Colloq* °rag, bullyrag, roast, *Brit* cock a snook at, *Brit and Australian* barrack, *Slang* °knock: *Don't jeer at aromatherapy till you've tried it.*
—*n.* **2** °taunt, °gibe *or* jibe, °aspersion, hoot, °hiss, boo, catcall; °derision, °ridicule, obloquy: *Just because he was fat, Christopher had to suffer the jeers of his classmates.*

jell *v.* **1** °set, congeal, °solidify, °harden, °coagulate, °thicken, °stiffen, gelatinize: *The mixture won't jell till you add hot water.* **2** (°take) °form, °take °shape, crystallize, °materialize, °come together, be °set: *Their plans for the shopping centre have not yet jelled.*

jeopardize *v.* °endanger, imperil, °threaten, °menace, °risk, °hazard, °venture: *You may jeopardize your freedom if you stand up for your rights.*

jeopardy *n.* Usually ***in*** (sometimes ***at***) ***jeopardy***: °danger, °peril; °threat, °menace, °risk, °hazard, °chance, uncertainty, vulnerability, °exposure, °liability: *She put her life in jeopardy by going into the lion's cage.*

jerk *v.* **1** °yank, °wrench, °pluck, °nip, °tug, °twist, °tweak: *I jerked the dagger out of his hand, leaving him defenceless.* **2** twitch, °lurch, °jolt, °jump, °start, jig, °jiggle, °wriggle, wiggle: *The creature jerked about convulsively, screaming, then lay still.*
—*n.* **3** °yank, °pull, °wrench, °tug, °twist, °tweak: *With a sharp jerk, he pulled the plaster from the child's leg.* **4** °lurch, °jolt, °start, °bump: *The train stopped with a jerk, throwing me off balance.* **5** idiot, °fool, moron, imbecile, *Slang US* °dope, °creep, yo-yo, nerd, dweeb: *Why would she want to go out with a jerk like that?*

jewel *n.* **1** °gem, gemstone, °brilliant, °ornament, bijou, *Colloq* °rock, sparkler: *Thieves stole a diamond necklace and an heirloom brooch set with precious jewels.* **2** °treasure, °marvel, °find, °godsend, °gem, °pearl, °prize, °boon, *Colloq* °catch: *What would you do without your secretary—she's an absolute jewel!*

jewellery *n.* gems, °precious stones, °jewels, ornaments, °finery, bijouterie: *Alexandra keeps her jewellery in a bank vault.*

jiggle *v.* **1** °jog, joggle, jig, °shake, °agitate, wiggle, °wriggle, °jerk: *It's odd to see grown people jiggling about on the dance floor like that. Jiggle the key up and down—maybe then you can turn it.*
—*n.* **2** °jog, joggle, jig, °shake, wiggle, °jerk: *I gave the line a few jiggles, hoping to attract a fish.*

jilt *v.* °throw over, °reject, °dismiss, °drop, °discard, °desert, °break (up) with, °forsake, °abandon, *Colloq* ditch, °dump, °brush off *or* give (someone) the °brush-off, *Chiefly US and Canadian* give (someone) his *or* her walking papers: *Angela met Tony and promptly jilted Mike.*

jingle *v.* **1** tinkle, °ring, tintinnabulate, clink, °chink, °chime: *She wore a dozen bracelets, which jingled when she walked.*
—*n.* **2** tinkle, tinkling, °ring, ringing, tintinnabulation, clink, clinking, °chink, chinking, °chime, chiming: *I like to feel the jingle of change in my pocket.* **3** °tune, ditty, °melody, °song, °rhyme, verse, doggerel: *The only thing he ever wrote was a jingle for a dog-food commercial.*

jingoism *n.* chauvinism, flag-waving, superpatriotism, nationalism; hawkishness, warmongering, belligerence, bellicosity: *'Might makes right' is a basic tenet of jingoism.*

jinx *n.* **1** (°evil) °spell, °curse, evil eye, malediction, voodoo, *US and Canadian* hex: *I felt I had lost at roulette because she had put a jinx on me.* **2** nemesis, Jonah: *If we don't throw that jinx overboard we shall all die.*
—*v.* **3** °curse, °bewitch, °damn, °doom, °sabotage, °condemn, *US and Canadian* hex: *My career was jinxed from the start.*

jitters *n.pl.* °shakes, °fidgets, °nerves, uneasiness, queasiness, nervousness, skittishness, restlessness, apprehension, apprehensiveness, *Slang* heebie-jeebies, willies, *US* whim-whams: *He always gets an attack of the jitters before an exam.*

job *n.* **1** °work, °employment, °position, berth, livelihood; °career, °occupation, °calling, °vocation, °appointment, °pursuit, °field, °trade, °craft, °profession, métier, °area: *What kind of job is she looking for? Harry has a new job.* **2** °assignment, °responsibility, °concern, chore, °task, °undertaking, °function, °duty, °role, °mission, °province, contribution, °charge: *It is my job to see that the machines run properly.* **3** °task, °undertaking, °procedure, °proceeding, °affair, °operation, °project, °activity, °business, °matter, chore: *The job of changing the gasket will take only a few minutes.* **4** °problem, °difficulty, °burden, °nuisance, °bother; toil, °grind, °drudgery; *Colloq* °headache, °pain (in the neck), hassle, *Slang* °pain in the *Brit* arse *or US* ass: *It was a real job getting them to pay for the damage.* **5** °crime, felony; °robbery, burglary, *Slang US and Canadian* °caper: *From the modus operandi, I'd say that the same gang did that job in Manchester.*
—*v.* **6** Often, ***job out***: °let out, °assign, apportion, °allot, °share out, °contract, °hire, °employ, subcontract, °farm out, consign, commission: *They undertake to do the work, but then they job it out to others.*

jog *v.* **1** °trot, lope, dogtrot, °run: *I jog around the reservoir every morning for exercise.* **2** °jar, °prod, °nudge, arouse, °stir, °stimulate, °prompt, °activate, °shake: *I jogged his memory by referring to the time the dog bit him.* **3** °bounce, °shake, °jolt, joggle, jounce, °jerk: *I was being jogged about in the back of the van as we sped over the rocky terrain.*

join *v.* **1** °unite, °connect, °couple, °link, °marry, yoke, °combine, °fasten *or* °tie *or* °glue *or* °weld *or* solder (together), °unify: *These two pieces should be joined for greater strength.* **2** °ally *or* °league with, °associate (oneself) with, °team up with, throw (one's lot) in with, °enlist (in), °sign (up) (with), °enrol (in), °enter: *She was invited to join the bridge club.* **3** °go *or* be with, °associate with, °accompany, °attach (oneself) to, °participate with: *Would you care to join us for a game of bridge?* **4** °border (on *or* upon), °meet, °touch, abut, °butt, adjoin, be adjacent (to), °extend to, °verge on, °coincide (with), juxtapose, be contiguous *or* conterminous (with), be coextensive (with): *The two properties join at the top of the ridge.*

joint *n.* **1** °seam, °union, °juncture, °connection, °junction, intersection: *The joint won't show after the whole thing's been painted.* **2** *Slang* dive, °dump, *US and Canadian* honky-tonk: *We went into a joint in Soho, looking for some action.* **3** roast: *Who carves the Sunday joint at your house?*
—*adj.* **4** shared, °mutual, combined, collective, cooperative, °common, communal, collaborative: *Our aims can only be achieved by joint effort.*

jointed *v.* articulated, segmented, sectioned, sectionalized, hinged: *The stick is jointed so that it can be folded for carrying in the pocket.*

joke *n.* **1** jest, °witticism, °quip, *bon mot*, °laugh, wordplay, °pun, °story, anecdote, *Colloq* °gag, °wisecrack, one-liner, °crack: *Ronnie comes up with the funniest jokes I have ever heard.* **2** laughing-stock, °butt, (fair) °game, buffoon: *After that incident, he became the joke of the regiment.* **3** farce, °mockery, °absurdity, travesty, °caricature: *My efforts to play the piano became a joke.*
—*v.* **4** jest, °quip, °pun, °frolic, °wisecrack, °tease, °taunt, °banter, °chaff, °fool, *Colloq* kid, *US* °crack

°wise: *They joked about our predicament. You must be joking if you think I'm going to go out with him!*

joker *n.* **1** jokester, °comedian, comedienne, °funny man *or* woman, humorist, jester, °comic, °clown, °wag, °wit, punster, droll, °zany, °merry andrew, buffoon, trickster, prankster, *Colloq* °card, gagster, °gag man, kidder: *Give him a drink and a funny hat and Roger thinks he's the greatest joker in the world.* **2** *US* catch, °hitch, °snag, °drawback, °trap, °twist, °pitfall, fine *or* small print, *Colloq* catch-22, no-win °situation: *The joker is that whoever treats the patients catches the disease.*

jolly *adj.* **1** °merry, °cheerful, °frolicsome, °gay, jovial, °joyful, °sportive, convivial, jocund, jocose, jocular, °frisky, coltish, °playful, festive, jubilant, cheery, °exuberant, high-spirited, °animated: *Everyone was in a jolly mood at her birthday party.*
—*v.* **2** Often, ***jolly along***: °humour, appease, °deceive, °string along, °fool, °hoax: *They're just jollying him along because they want him to invest in their scheme.*

jolt *v.* **1** °jar, °shake (up), jostle, °bump, °bounce, °jerk: *The cart jolted over the rough terrain.* **2** °butt, °strike, °hit, °push, °nudge, elbow, °knock, °jab: *He jolted me so hard he actually cracked a rib.* **3** °shock, °astonish, °astound, °amaze, °surprise, °startle, °stun, °dumbfound *or* dumfound, stupefy, °strike °dumb, °daze, °shake (up): *I was jolted to learn that my husband had been arrested for murder.*
—*n.* **4** °lurch, °jar, °jerk, °bump, °jump, °bounce, °start: *The train started with a jolt that almost knocked me over.* **5** °blow, °shock, °surprise, °bolt from the blue, °bombshell: *It was certainly a jolt to discover that she had left me.*

jot *v.* **1** Usually, ***jot down***: make a °note of, °write *or* °note (down), °put *or* °set *or* °take down, °record: *Jot down this telephone number.*
—*n.* **2** °scrap, °grain, (°wee) °bit, °speck, mite, iota, whit, °particle, tittle, *Colloq* slightest, *US and Canadian* tad, smidgen *or* smidgin: *I don't care a jot what she thinks about the situation in Central America.*

journal *n.* **1** °periodical, °magazine, gazette, newspaper, °paper, newsletter, °review, tabloid; °daily, weekly, monthly, fortnightly, °quarterly, annual: *The journal contains information about every building permit awarded in the entire country.* **2** °diary, °chronicle, dossier, °record, °register, log, logbook, minutebook, minutes, documentation, album, °scrapbook, °memoir, almanac, annal, °history, yearbook, °record °book; °roll, catalogue, °list: *He kept a detailed journal of every event in his twenty-year exile.*

journalist *n.* °reporter, newspaperman, newspaperwoman, °correspondent, newsman, newswoman, °member of the fourth estate, gentleman *or* lady of the °press, stringer; columnist; °hack; newscaster, anchorman, anchorwoman, commentator, broadcaster, *Brit* pressman, paragraphist; newsreader, *Colloq* °scribe, newsmonger, *US and Canadian* legman, news-hawk, news-hound, news-hen: *Journalists crowded round the minister, urging her to make a statement.*

journey *n.* **1** °trip, voyage, °excursion, °tour, °travel, °outing, °expedition, junket, °cruise, jaunt, °pilgrimage, peregrination, odyssey, trek: *Did your wife accompany you on your journey to Tierra del Fuego?* **2** °way, °passage, °passing, °transit, °transition, °progress, °course, °trip, °route, °career: *On your journey through this life, Whatever be your goal, Keep your eye upon the doughnut, And not upon the hole.*
—*v.* **3** °travel, °tour, voyage, °go (°abroad *or* °overseas), make *or* take a °trip, make *or* wend one's °way, make a °pilgrimage, peregrinate, trek, rove, °range, °wander, °roam, °cruise, °gad (about), gallivant *or* galivant *or* galavant: *He journeyed to the far corners of the earth seeking an answer to life's mysteries.*

joy *n.* **1** °pleasure, °gratification, °satisfaction, °happiness, contentment, °enjoyment, gladness, °delight, felicity, elation, exaltation, °ecstasy, °bliss, exhilaration, exultation, °rapture: *We felt indescribable joy at seeing the children safe and sound.* **2** °gaiety, cheerfulness, °cheer, °glee, buoyancy, joviality, jollity, jocundity, joyfulness, joyousness, jubilation, °merriment, light-heartedness, blithesomeness: *Let me wish you joy in this holiday season.* **3** °delight, °pleasure, °treat, °blessing, °gratification, °satisfaction, °prize: *A thing of beauty is a joy forever.*

joyful *adj.* **1** °cheerful, °happy, °buoyant, °gleeful, °merry, jovial, °jolly, jocund, joyous, jubilant, °gay, light-hearted, °blithe, blithesome, °sunny: *We are delighted that you have all come to help us celebrate this joyful occasion.* **2** °glad, °pleased, gratified, °delighted, °happy, °elated, °ecstatic, exhilarated, °exultant, °overjoyed, jubilant, in °heaven, *Brit* in the seventh °heaven, *US* in seventh °heaven, *Colloq* on cloud nine, tickled (pink), *Brit* over the moon: *Mark was joyful at the news that he was father of a boy.*

joyless *adj.* **1** °sad, °unhappy, °miserable, depressed, °dejected, °mournful, °downhearted, downcast, down, °despondent, dispirited, °melancholy, heavy-hearted, cheerless, °doleful, grief-stricken, disheartened, saddened, crestfallen, °wretched, disconsolate, °inconsolable, morose, heartsick, °sorrowful, woeful, °woebegone: *It was a joyless company that stood at the grave side. The cat died, the dog died, and my husband was ill—all in all, a joyless time.* **2** °gloomy, depressing, dispiriting, disheartening, °dreary, lugubrious, cheerless, °dismal, °bleak, °inhospitable, °desolate, °grim, austere, °severe: *The shuttered, joyless house loomed out of the misty moor ahead.*

judge *n.* **1** °justice, magistrate, jurist, *Isle of Man* deemster *or* dempster, *Slang Brit* beak: *The judge demanded order in the court.* **2** arbitrator, arbiter, °umpire, referee, adjudicator, judicator, °mediator, °moderator: *She served as a judge at Cruft's dog show last year.* **3** connoisseur, °expert, °authority, arbiter, appraiser, evaluator, reviewer, critic, *arbiter elegantiarum* or *elegantiae*: *Let me be the judge of which work I do best.*
—*v.* **4** adjudicate, adjudge, arbitrate, °decide, °find, conclude, °settle, °determine, °decree, °pass °judgement, deem, °rule, °pronounce *or* °pass °sentence: *Do you think the jury will judge in Claus's favour?* **5** assess, °evaluate, appraise, °estimate, °rate, value, °weigh, °measure, °review, °consider, °size up, °appreciate: *A ballistics expert is required to judge this evidence.* **6** referee, °umpire, mediate, °moderate, arbitrate: *Mr Farnsworth agreed to judge the essay competition.* **7** °believe, °suspect, °think, °consider, °suppose, °guess, conjecture, °surmise, conclude, °infer: *Palaeontologists judge the age of the specimens to be 400 million years.*

judgement *n.* **1** °discretion, discernment, °discrimination, judiciousness, °prudence, °wisdom, °wit, sagacity, perspicacity, clear-headedness, °perception, perspicuousness, percipience, acumen, °intelligence, (°good) °sense, °common °sense, level-headedness, °understanding, shrewdness: *Charlotte's judgement is often sought in such matters.* **2** °decision, ruling, verdict, conclusion, °determination, °opinion, adjudication, °finding, °decree, °order; °outcome, °result, °upshot: *The judgement of the court is final. It was the judgement of Paris to award the golden apple to Aphrodite.* **3** °criticism, censure, °disapproval, °reproof, condemnation: *They offered a moral, not a legal judgement.* **4** °opinion, °view, °belief, (way of) °thinking, °mind, °perception; °sentiment: *In my judgement, she is innocent.* **5** °evaluation, valuation, appraisal, °estimation, assessment: *One critic's unfavourable judgement of a play can spell its doom.*

judicial *adj.* **1** °legal, judiciary, judicatory, juridic(al); °official: forensic: *A formal judicial procedure can be quite costly.* **2** °critical, analytical, °discriminating, distinguishing, discerning, °keen, °sharp, °perceptive, percipient, perspicacious, differentiating, discriminatory, discriminative, °judicious: *Her decisions have always been judicial.* **3** judgelike, magisterial, °impartial, °fair: *He brought judicial procedures to bear on the handling of the problem.*

judicious *adj.* °sensible, commonsensical, °sound, °sober, °intelligent, °aware, °enlightened, °wise, °sage, sapient, °thoughtful, °reasonable, °rational, °sane, °logical, discerning, °discriminating, discriminative, °astute, °perceptive, percipient, perspicacious, °well-advised, (well-)°informed, °prudent, °discreet, °tactful, °diplomatic, °politic, °careful, considered, circumspect: *The treasurer was considered not to have made judicious use of the club's funds.*

jug *n.* pitcher, ewer, urn, carafe, °bottle, flask, decanter, °jar: *She came in from the barn carrying a jug of fresh milk.*

juggle *v.* °manipulate, °tamper with, °falsify, °fix, °rig, °distort, misstate, °misrepresent, °alter, °arrange, *Colloq* °doctor, cook: *The accountant refused a bribe to juggle the company's books.*

juice *n.* **1** °extract, °liquid, °fluid: *The recipe calls for the juice of one lemon.* **2** °essence, °pith, °extract, °vigour, °force, °vitality, °spirit, °strength, °power: *He really squeezed the juice out of my argument.*

juicy *adj.* **1** °succulent, °moist, °lush: *This is a very juicy pear.* **2** °interesting, °sensational, °lurid, colourful, °vivid, °exciting, °stirring, °thrilling, intriguing, fascinating, °provocative, °suggestive, °racy, °spicy, °risqué: *I've got such a juicy piece of gossip for you!*

jumble *v.* **1** °disorder, °mix (up), °mingle, °confuse, confound, °muddle, °shuffle, disarrange, disorganize, °tangle, °entangle: *I found my belongings all jumbled together.*
—*n.* **2** °muddle, °tangle, °medley, °mess; °disorder, °confusion, disarray, °chaos, °clutter: *My clothes were in a jumble on the bed.*

jumbo *adj.* °huge, °gigantic, °enormous, elephantine, °immense, oversized, king-sized, *Colloq US* humongous: *Grandad brought us a jumbo box of chocolates.*

jump *v.* **1** °leap, °bound, °spring, °pounce, °hurdle, vault, °hop, °skip; °caper, °cavort, gambol: *Jack, jump over the candlestick! Lambs were jumping about in the meadow.* **2** °start, °jerk, wince, °flinch, °recoil: *The sudden noise made me jump.* **3** Sometimes, ***jump over***: °skip (over), °omit, °pass over *or* by, °bypass, °avoid, °leave out, °ignore, °disregard, °overlook, °gloss over: *Jump the boring parts and read me the sexy bits.* **4** °pass, °move, °leap, °skip: *She jumped from one subject to another so quickly that I couldn't keep track.* **5** °advance, °increase, °rise, °gain, °surge, escalate: *The cost of living jumped again this month, causing fear of inflation.* **6** ***jump at***: °accept, °grab, °snatch, °swoop up, °leap at, °pounce on: *Most people would jump at the chance to better themselves.* **7** ***jump on***: °attack, °swoop down on *or* upon; °reprimand, °rebuke: *She jumps on anyone who suggests that she used influence to get her job.*
—*n.* **8** °leap, °bound, °spring, °pounce, °hurdle, vault, °hop, °skip: *With one jump the cheetah was upon the gazelle.* **9** °rise, °increase, °boost, hike, °advance, °gain, °surge, escalation, upsurge, °increment, °elevation: *A jump in the Retail Price Index drove share prices lower again yesterday.* **10** barricade, °obstacle, °hurdle, °fence, °rail, °obstruction: *My horse cleared the first jump easily.* **11** °start, °jerk, °spasm, twitch, °recoil, °lurch, °jolt: *When they called his name, he gave a little jump.* **12** °break, °gap, hiatus, lacuna, °space, °hole, °breach, °rift, °interruption: *There's a jump in continuity at the end of the fourth chapter.*

jumpy *adj.* °nervous, °agitated, °anxious, jittery, fidgety, °restless, edgy, on °edge, °tense, °shaky, skittish, °fretful, uneasy, °queasy, °restive, panicky: *Do you think he was jumpy because we were approaching Count Dracula's castle?*

junction *n.* °juncture, °union, °combination, joining, conjunction, °meeting, linking, °connection, conjoining, intersection, confluence; crossroads, interchange: *The train robbery took place at the junction of the two railways.*

juncture *n.* **1** See **junction,** above. **2** °point, °time, °moment, °stage, °period: *At this juncture, suggesting a merger seems premature.*

junior *adj.* °secondary, lesser, °lower, °minor, °subordinate, °inferior; younger: *Thompson has been offered a junior partnership in his firm.*

junk *n.* **1** °rubbish, °waste, °refuse, °litter, debris, °scrap; *US* °garbage, °trash: *A man came to cart away the junk that we had cleared out of the garage.*
—*v.* **2** *Colloq* discard, °throw away, °scrap, °cast aside, jettison, *US* °trash: *We bought a new washing-machine and junked the old one.*

junta *n.* junto, °cabal, °clique, °faction, °gang, coterie, °band, °set, camarilla: *After the coup, the country was run by a military junta.*

jurisdiction *n.* °authority, °power, °prerogative, °dominion, °sovereignty, °say, °control, °rule, ascendancy, hegemony, °influence; °province, °district, °area, bailiwick, compass, °realm, °sphere (of °influence), °reach, clutches, °range, °orbit: *Tierra del Fuego seems a bit far to go just to be outside the jurisdiction of the Inland Revenue.*

just *adj.* **1** °fair, °equitable, °impartial, unbiased, °unprejudiced, °reasonable, fair-minded, even-handed, °neutral, °objective: *Do you think you can expect a just trial after all that publicity?* **2** °upright, °righteous, right-minded, °honourable, °honest, °ethical, °moral, °principled, °straight, °decent, °good, upstanding, °virtuous, °lawful: *In our system of law, one must believe that juries are basically just.* **3** justified, justifiable, well-founded, well-grounded, °legitimate, valid, °reasonable, °rightful, (well-)°deserved, °due, °fitting, °proper; condign: *She has a just claim to her father's estate. His punishment was just.*
—*adv.* **4** °only, °merely, °nothing but, solely, °simply, at °best, at most, no more than: *She said just that and nothing else.* **5** °exactly, °precisely, °perfectly; °barely, °only just, °hardly, °scarcely, by a hair's breadth, *Colloq* by the °skin of one's teeth: *My new car just fits into the garage, with only inches to spare.* **6** (only *or* just) °now, a °moment ago, (very) recently, °lately: *We have just returned from a holiday in Tenerife.*

justice *n.* **1** fairness, impartiality, °objectivity, objectiveness, °equity, equitableness, fair-mindedness, justness, even-handedness, neutrality, °fair play: *Justice triumphed on this occasion, and he was convicted of fraud.* **2** the °law, the °police; °punishment, °prison, °imprisonment, incarceration, °detention: *He is a fugitive from justice.* **3** °law, °right, °morality, lawfulness, rightfulness, legitimacy, judiciousness: *His conviction was a miscarriage of justice.* **4** See **judge, 1,** above.

justify *v.* °vindicate, °legitimate, legitimatize *or* legitimize, legalize, °rationalize, °substantiate, °defend, °support, °uphold, °sustain, validate, °warrant, °confirm; °excuse, °explain, absolve, acquit, exculpate: *My worst fears were justified. How can you justify owning three cars?*

jut *v.* °extend, °overhang, °project, °protrude, °stick out, beetle: *The balcony juts out over the lake.*

juvenile *adj.* **1** °young, youthful, under °age, °minor, teenage(d), °immature, °adolescent, °childish, °infantile, babyish, °puerile, °unsophisticated: *What could be more juvenile than painting graffiti on public buildings.*
—*n.* **2** °youth, °boy, °girl, °adolescent, °minor, *Law* infant: *The police have arrested two juveniles for attacking an old lady in her own home.*

K

keen[1] *adj.* **1** °enthusiastic, avid, zealous, °devoted, °ardent, °fervent, fervid, °earnest, °impassioned, °passionate, °intense, °active; °agog, °eager, itching, °anxious: *They are keen fans of TV soap operas. I was keen to go swimming.* **2** °sharp, sharpened, razor-sharp, razor-like, knife-edged; °trenchant, °incisive, °cutting, rapier-like, °pointed, mordant, acid, vitriolic, acerbic, astringent, °biting, acrid, acrimonious, stinging, °scorching, °caustic, searing, °withering, °virulent, °pungent, °sarcastic, °sardonic: *This axe is very keen, so be careful. With his keen wit, the playwright answered his severest critics. His play is a keen satire on the government.* **3** °painful, °bitter, °acute, °poignant, °fierce, °grievous, °severe, distressing, distressful, °strong, °deep, °profound, °intense, °extreme, °heartfelt: *She felt keen resentment at the way she had been treated.* **4** °vivid, °detailed, °specific, unmistaken, unmistakable, °distinct: *He has a keen recollection of seeing the suspect on the bus.* **5** °sharp, °acute, °sensitive, °penetrating, °discriminating, °fine: *The bloodhound has an extremely keen sense of smell.* **6** °intelligent, °sharp, °acute, °perceptive, perspicacious, percipient, °sensitive, discerning, °astute, °smart, °bright, °discriminating, discriminative, °quick(-witted), °shrewd, °clever, canny, cunning, °crafty, °wise: *Philip has a keen understanding of what is required of him.* **7** ***keen on** or **about***: °fond of, enamoured of, °devoted to, °interested in: *Alan is almost as keen on Mary as on his stamp collection.*

keen[2] *v.* **1** °weep, wail, °moan, °lament, °mourn, °grieve; °bewail, °bemoan: *Finnegan's widow still keens over him.*
—*n.* **2** dirge, elegy, knell, °lament, °lamentation, Requiem, monody, threnody, thanatopsis, epicedium, *Scots and Irish* coronach: *The keens could be heard throughout the neighbourhood.*

keep *v.* **1** °retain, °hold, °hang on to, °preserve, °conserve, °have, °save, °maintain, °control: *The difficulty is not in making money but in keeping it.* **2** °hold, °have, take °care *or* °charge of, °mind, °tend, °care for, °look after, °guard, keep an °eye on, °watch over, °protect, °safeguard; °maintain, °feed, °nourish, victual, °board, nurture, °provide for, °provision: *Would you keep this parcel for me until I return? They keep chickens and ducks.* **3** °accumulate, °save (up), °amass, °hoard (up), °husband, °retain, °preserve, °put *or* °stow away: *My brother has kept all the toys he ever had.* **4** °maintain, °store, °preserve: *I keep woollen things in a cedar chest.* **5** Often, ***keep on** or **at***: °continue, °carry on, °persist (in), °persevere (in); °prolong, °sustain: *How did you keep going after Elsa's death? She kept at it all night long. Keep on working till I tell you to stop.* **6** keep to, °abide by, °follow, °obey, °mind, adhere to, °attend to, pay °attention to, °heed, °regard, °observe, °respect, °acknowledge, °defer to, accede (to), °agree (to): *Only a stickler would keep the letter of such a law.* **7** °stay, °remain: *Keep off the grass. Keep to the left.* **8** °support, °finance, °provide for, °subsidize, °maintain: *He kept a mistress in Chelsea.* **9** confine, detain; °imprison, incarcerate, °jail *or Brit also* gaol: *The police have kept him overnight.* **10** °celebrate, °observe, solemnize, °memorialize, °commemorate: *We always kept Easter at my mother's house in the country.* **11** °last, be preserved, °survive, °stand up, °stay °fresh: *Eggs keep longer in the refrigerator.* **12** °harbour, °maintain, °safeguard, keep °dark: *Can you keep a secret?* **13** ***keep from***: °prevent, keep *or* °hold back, °restrain, (hold in) °check, °restrict, °prohibit, °forbid, °inhibit, disallow, °block, °obstruct, °deny, °curb, °deter, °discourage: *How can I keep my plants from dying while I'm away?* **14** ***keep in***: **a** keep *or* °hold back, °repress, °suppress, °stifle, °smother, muzzle, °bottle up, °withhold, °conceal, °hide, °shroud, °mask, °camouflage: *She keeps in her true feelings. He could hardly keep in the tears.* **b** confine, °shut in *or* up, coop up, detain; °fence in: *Keith thought the teacher kept him in after school because she liked him.*
—*n.* **15** °upkeep, °maintenance, °support, °room and °board, °subsistence, °food, °sustenance, living: *He works hard to earn his keep.* **16** donjon, °tower, °dungeon: *He was imprisoned in the keep of the castle for twenty years.*

keeper *n.* custodian, °guardian, °guard, warden, caretaker; warder, °nurse, °attendant, *Brit* °minder: *The keepers are very strict about not letting people feed the animals. How come they let you out without your keeper?*

keepsake *n.* °memento, souvenir, °token, °reminder, °remembrance, °relic: *The locket is a keepsake from those happy days in Antibes.*

keg *n.* cask, barrel, °butt, hogshead, tun, puncheon: *We bought a keg of beer for the party.*

kernel *n.* **1** °grain, °seed, pip, stone; nut, °meat, *US* nut-meat: *Try to extract the walnut kernel without breaking it.* **2** °centre, °core, °nucleus, °heart, °essence, °quintessence, °substance, °gist, °pith, °nub, quiddity: *Let's get down to the kernel of the problem.*

key *n.* **1** latchkey, skeleton °key, passkey, opener: *Have you lost your car keys again? You will need a key to open the air valve on the radiator.* **2** °clue, °cue, °guide, °indication, °indicator, °explanation: *The key to his behaviour can probably be found in the way his mother treated him in his childhood.* **3** °pitch, °tone, °timbre, °level, tonality, frequency: *The song was originally written in the key of C.* **4** °legend, °explanation, °description, explication, clarification, °translation: *A key to the symbols appears on every other page.* **5** °mood, °tenor, °tone, °humour, °style: *In this passage there is a change to a more sombre key.*
—*adj.* **6** °important, °essential, °vital, °necessary, °crucial, °critical, °main, °pivotal: *Automatic reversal is a key feature of this cassette player. Roderick is a key man in the company.*

keystone *n.* °necessity, crux, linchpin, °basis, °principle, °foundation, cornerstone: *Predestination was the keystone of his religion.*

kick *v.* **1** °boot, °punt: *The basic aim in soccer is to kick the ball into the back of the net.* **2** °recoil, °backlash, °rebound: *The shotgun kicked when I fired it.*
—*n.* **3** °punt, drop-kick: *His kick sent the ball down the field.* **4** °recoil, °backlash, °rebound: *That gun has quite a kick!*

kickback *n.* °rebate, refund, °share, compensation, commission, °percentage, °reward; °bribe, °pay-off, *Colloq chiefly US* payola, *US* plugola: *We get a kickback on every computer sold. Some disc jockeys were accepting kickbacks for playing particular records.*

kidnap *v.* °abduct, °capture, °seize, °carry off, *Slang* °snatch: *He was kidnapped by guerrillas and held prisoner for over two years.*

kill *v.* **1** °execute, slay, °murder, assassinate, do away with, put to death, cause the death of, liquidate, °dispatch *or* despatch, take (someone's) life, °finish (off), put an end to, write 'finis' to, °silence, kill off, administer the *coup de grâce*, °eliminate, put (someone) out of (his *or* her) misery, °exterminate, °extinguish, °obliterate, eradicate, °destroy, annihilate, °massacre, °slaughter, decimate, °butcher, (of animals) °put down, put to sleep, *Slang* do in, °bump *or* °knock off, °hit, °polish off, snuff (out), take for a °ride, *US* °waste, °rub out, ice, fit with concrete overshoes *or* a wooden kimono: *He was the third police officer to be killed this year.* **2** °destroy, °ruin, °devastate, °ravage, °wreak *or* °work °havoc (up)on, °kill off: *The entire orange crop was killed by the sudden frost.* **3** °muffle, °neutralize, °deaden, °damp, °silence, nullify, °dull, absorb, °smother, °stifle, °suppress, °still: *This padding should kill the noise of the motor.* **4** °exhaust, °tire (out), °fatigue, °weary, *Colloq* °fag (out): *Pushing that mower all day nearly killed me.* **5** °hurt, °pain, °torment, torture: *These shoes are killing me.* **6** °quash, °suppress, °defeat, °veto, °cancel: *The tobacco interests campaigned to kill the bill to ban smoking in public places.* **7** °consume, °use up, °spend, while away, °occupy, °fill, °pass, °idle: *While waiting, I killed time doing a crossword puzzle.*
—*n.* **8** °game, °prey; °quarry: *The lioness allowed her cubs to eat part of the kill.* **9** °death, °killing, °end, °finish, deathblow, *coup de grâce;* °termination, denouement *or* dénouement, conclusion: *She wants to be in at the kill.*

killer *n.* **1** °murderer, assassin, slayer, °cutthroat, °butcher, exterminator, Bluebeard, (Jack the) ripper,

Slang US torpedo, hit man, triggerman, gunsel, hooligan, gunfighter, iceman, hatchet man: *What are the statistics on the number of killers who are not caught?* **2** *Slang old-fashioned* bee's knees, *US* humdinger, doozy, killer-diller (from Manila), lallapalooza *or* lollapalooza, lulu, daisy, dilly: *The new show at the Odeon is a killer.*

killing *n.* **1** °murder, °carnage, butchery, °execution, °slaughter, °bloodshed, °death, °massacre, genocide, liquidation, mass °murder *or* °destruction, decimation, extermination, blood bath, manslaughter; slaying, homicide, °fatality: *The killing of dissidents must stop. There has been another killing in the park.* **2** coup, bonanza, °success, °windfall, stroke of °luck, °gain, °profit, *Colloq Brit* °bomb: *They've made a killing on the Stock Exchange.*
—*adj.* **3** °devastating, °ruinous, °destructive, °punishing, °exhausting, debilitating, fatiguing, tiring, enervating, °difficult, °arduous: *How can you keep up the killing pace of having two jobs?*

killjoy *n.* °spoilsport, damper, dampener, grouch, grump, malcontent, pessimist, cynic, prophet of °doom, Cassandra, *Colloq* °wet blanket, sourpuss, *US* party pooper, °gloomy Gus, picklepuss: *Go to the dance and stop being such a killjoy!*

kin *n.* **1** °family, °relative(s), °relation(s), °kindred, kinsfolk *or US and Canadian* kinfolk, kinsman, kinswoman, °stock, °clan, blood-relation(s), blood-relative(s): *We might have the same name, but he's no kin of mine. Grandmother says that too many people are thoughtless of their kin these days.*
—*adj.* **2** °related, °akin (to), °kindred, consanguineous, consanguine, cognate, agnate: *One often forgets that all men are kin.*

kind[1] *adj.* °friendly, °kindly, °nice, congenial, affable, approachable, °amiable, °obliging, °accommodating, °amicable, well-disposed, °courteous, °good, °good-natured, °benevolent, well-meaning, well-wishing, °thoughtful, well-intentioned, °generous, big-hearted, °humanitarian, °charitable, °philanthropic, °gentle, °understanding, °sympathetic, °considerate, °lenient, °tolerant, °indulgent, compassionate, kind-hearted, °gracious, °warm, warm-hearted, °cordial, tender-hearted, °affectionate: *It was kind of you to stop and help us. I never thought of him as a kind man.*

kind[2] *n.* **1** °sort, °type, °variety, °style, °genre, species, °class, °breed; °brand, °make: *What kind of tree is the cypress? Do we always have to have the same kind of breakfast cereal?* **2** °nature, °character, °manner, °description, °sort, °persuasion, °stripe, feather, kidney: *What kind of person is she? Today's students are of a totally different kind.*

kindle *v.* ignite, °light, set alight, set °fire to, set afire, °inflame, °fire, °foment, °incite, instigate, °provoke, °prompt, °prick, goad, °spur, °whip up, °stir (up), °work up, °excite, °agitate, °shake up, °jolt, arouse, °rouse, (a)waken, °inspire, inspirit, °stimulate, °animate, °enliven, °energize, innervate, galvanize: *Kindling a fire in the rain is not easy. The wholesale pillaging kindled a feeling of deep resentment among the native population.*

kindly *adj.* **1** See **kind,** above.
—*adv.* **2** cordially, graciously, obligingly, amiably, amicably, politely, genially, courteously, thoughtfully, considerately, hospitably, agreeably, pleasantly: *He very kindly invited me in for a cup of tea.* **3** °please, be so °kind as to, be °good enough to: *Would you kindly pass the salt?*

kindness *n.* **1** friendliness, kind-heartedness, warm-heartedness, graciousness, goodness, good-naturedness, good-heartedness, °good °will, °benevolence, benignity, humaneness, °humanity, decency, tenderness, gentleness, kindliness, °charity, charitableness, generosity, °philanthropy, beneficence, compassion, °sympathy, °understanding, thoughtfulness, °consideration, cordiality, °hospitality, °warmth, geniality, °indulgence, °tolerance, °patience: *We shall always appreciate the kindness shown to us by our hosts during our visit.* **2** °favour, °good deed *or* turn, °service, act of kindness; generosity, °assistance, °aid: *She did me a great kindness in introducing me to you. How can I repay your kindness?*

kindred *adj.* **1** °close, associated, °united, allied, analogous, °like, °similar, °matching, °parallel, °common, °related; °akin: *Because we both like sports, Samantha's interests are kindred to mine.* **2** °related, consanguineous, consanguine, cognate, agnate: *Linguists regard the Romance languages as kindred tongues.*
—*n.* **3** See **kin, 1**, above.

king *n.* prince, crowned °head, majesty, °sovereign, °monarch, ruler, regent, *Colloq Brit* °royal: *In former times, the king had power of life and death over his subjects.*

kingdom *n.* **1** °realm, empire, °sovereignty, principality, °monarchy: *He sought a suitable wife throughout the kingdom.* **2** °field, °area, °domain, °province, °sphere (of °influence), °territory, bailiwick, *Colloq* °turf: *The operating theatre is the surgeon's kingdom.*

kink *n.* **1** °twist, crimp, °tangle, °knot, °wrinkle, curl, °coil, curlicue, crinkle: *Those kinks wouldn't occur if you had coiled the rope properly.* **2** °pang, °twinge, °stab, °spasm, cramp, stitch, °tweak, crick: *I have a kink in my neck from constantly looking down.* **3** °difficulty, °complication, °flaw, °hitch, °snag, °defect, °imperfection, distortion, deformity: *There were several kinks that had to be ironed out before the plan was presented to the board.* **4** crotchet, °quirk, whim, caprice, °fancy, vagary, °eccentricity, idiosyncrasy: *He would win more support if he rid himself of certain kinks in his thinking.*

kinky *adj.* **1** °outlandish, °peculiar, °odd, °queer, quirky, °bizarre, crotchety, °eccentric, °strange, idiosyncratic, °different, °offbeat, °unorthodox, °capricious, °irregular, °erratic, unconventional, °unique, freakish, °weird, °fantastic, °whimsical: *This school is not interested in kinky notions of education.* **2** °perverted, °unnatural, °deviant, °degenerate, warped, °abnormal, depraved: *There is a rumour that they engage in kinky sex.* **3** °crisp, frizzy, frizzed, frizzled, curly, crimped, °wiry; knotted, tangled, twisted: *He has kinky red hair.*

kinship *n.* **1** consanguinity, (blood) °relationship, (°family) ties, (°common) descent, °lineage, one's (own) flesh and blood: *At that time, several of the royal houses of Europe were connected by kinship.* **2** °connection, correspondence, parallelism, °relationship, similarity, °association, °agreement, °alliance; °affinity: *There is a clear kinship among the Germanic languages. She felt a kinship with other adopted children.*

kiss *v.* **1** osculate, peck, *Colloq* smack, smooch, neck, *Old-fashioned* spoon, canoodle: *I kissed her on the cheek. A young couple were kissing on the park bench.* **2** °touch, °brush, graze: *The cue-ball barely kissed the black, toppling it into the pocket.* **3** ***kiss goodbye***: °bid adieu, say °farewell to, °give up, °relinquish, °abandon, °forsake, °desert, °renounce, °repudiate, °forget (about), °dismiss, °disregard, °ignore: *With those marks, you can kiss goodbye to any thought of winning a scholarship.*
—*n.* **4** osculation, peck, *Colloq* smack, smooch, *US and Canadian* buss, *Slang Brit* smacker: *He ran over and gave me a big hug and a kiss.*

kit *n.* °apparatus, °gear, °equipment, °paraphernalia, appurtenances, °rig, accoutrements *or US also* accouterments, °tackle, °trappings, °supplies, furnishings; °instruments, °tools, utensils, °implements: *Did you bring your tennis kit? The model aeroplanes were built from kits. The plumber left his tool kit behind.*

kitchen *n.* kitchenette, cookhouse; scullery, pantry, larder; *Nautical* galley, *Brit* caboose: *He was in the kitchen getting dinner ready.*

kittenish *adj.* °coy, °seductive, °flirtatious, coquettish, °sportive, °playful: *Barbara tends to get a bit kittenish when she's with men.*

kitty *n.* °pot, °pool, °collection: *Has he contributed anything to the kitty?*

knack *n.* °genius, °intuition, °talent, °gift, °facility, °skill, °aptitude, °bent; °ability, °flair, °dexterity, °capacity, adroitness, °proficiency, skilfulness: *He has an uncanny knack for saying the wrong thing. When it comes to gourmet cooking, Peggy certainly has the knack.*

knife *n.* **1** °blade: *This knife couldn't cut through warm butter.*
—*v.* **2** °stab, °pierce, °slash, °cut, °wound: *There was a struggle, and one youth was knifed in the chest.*

knit *v.* **1** °join *or* °fasten *or* °weave (together), interweave, interlace, interconnect, intertwine, °link, °bind, °unite, °tie (up *or* together), consolidate, °combine, °compact: *He was the first king to succeed in knitting together the diverse elements of the empire.* **2** °grow (together), °heal, °mend, °join: *The broken bones will knit in about a month.* **3** °furrow, °contract, °wrinkle, °knot, crease: *He knit his brow and sighed.*

knob *n.* boss, stud, protuberance, °projection, °protrusion, °handle: *Turn the knob, then pull the drawer open.*

knock *v.* **1** °strike, °hit, °rap, thwack, whack, thump, bang, °tap: *Knock on the door. He knocked the man on the head with his walking-stick.* **2** criticize, deprecate, °carp *or* °cavil at, °disparage, °put down, °run down: *Don't knock something till you've tried it.* **3** ***knock about*** or ***around***: **a** °wander, °roam, °ramble, rove, °travel, °gad about: *She's going to knock about the world for a bit before settling down.* **b** °associate with, consort with: *He was only knocking about with some of the boys.* **c** °discuss, °debate, °talk over, *Colloq* °kick about *or* around: *I have a business proposition that I want to knock around with you.* **d** °beat (up), maltreat, °mistreat, maul, °manhandle, °batter, °abuse, °hit, °strike: *He's been known to knock his wife about.* **4** ***knock down***: **a** °raze, °demolish, °destroy, °level, °wreck, lay in ruins, °throw *or* °pull down: *They knocked down those beautiful old houses and erected an ugly office block in their place.* **b** °fell, °floor, °cut down: *As soon as he got up, McCloskey knocked him down again.* **5** ***knock off***: **a** stop °work(ing), °quit, °go home, clock off *or* out, °terminate, °lock up, °close down: *I think I'll knock off for a few hours' rest.* **b** °steal, °pilfer, thieve, °rob, *Colloq* °lift, *Brit* °pinch, *Slang Brit* °nick, *US* knock over: *Two men in balaclavas knocked off the bank in the High Street.* **c** See **kill, 1,** above. **d** make quick *or* short work of, complete, finish, bring to an end, *Colloq* polish off: *He knocked off that book in a week.* **e** *US* copy, °imitate: *They knock off expensive items, then sell them for much less than the originals.* **6** ***knock out***: **a** knock *or* °render °unconscious, °floor, °prostrate, trounce, °whip, *Slang* °flatten, K.O. *or* kayo: *The smart money says that the challenger will knock out the champion in the third round.* **b** °overwhelm, °overcome, °daze, °stagger, °astound, °astonish, °bewilder, °stun, *Colloq* °bowl over, blow (someone's) mind, *Slang Brit* knock for six: *She'll really knock them out in that dress!* **7** ***knock up***: **a** knock *or* °put together, °improvise: *I think I can knock up something quickly that will pass muster.* **b** arouse, (a)waken, °wake up: *They knocked me up at dawn to go to work.* **c** impregnate, get with child, make °pregnant: *Her boyfriend knocked her up and then refused to marry her.*
—*n.* **8** °blow, °rap, °tap, thump, pounding, hammering: *I was woken by a knock on the wall from my neighbour.* **9** °blow, °punch, °jab, smack, thwack, whack, right, left, cuff, *Colloq* clout, bop, biff, conk: *He gave me a knock on the nose, and it started to bleed.* **10** °slap (in the face), censure, °criticism, condemnation, °slur, °insult: *My latest novel took quite a few knocks from the reviewers.*

knock-off *n.* imitation, copy, simulation, replica, facsimile, duplication: *This cheap knock-off of a £1,000 watch is selling for £50.*

knockout *n.* **1** *coup de grâce, Slang* K.O., kayo: *Carnera won by a knockout in the first round.* **2** °success, °sensation, °triumph, *Colloq* °hit, °winner, smash, smash °hit, stunner: *She looks a knockout with her new hairstyle.*

knoll *n.* hillock, hummock, °mound, barrow, °hill, °elevation, °rise: *We climbed to the top of the knoll where we had a better view of the house.*

knot *n.* **1** °snarl, gnarl, °tangle; °tie, °bond: *I cannot loosen this knot.* **2** °collection, assemblage, aggregation, congregation, °crowd, °cluster, °bunch, °gathering, °company, °band, °gang, °crowd, °throng: *A small knot of people were standing in front of my painting.*
—*v.* **3** °fasten, °tie, °bind, °secure, °lash, °tether, affix, °fix, °attach: *I knotted the rope around his neck.*

know *v.* **1** °understand, °comprehend, be °familiar with, °grasp, be °acquainted with, be °versed *or* skilled in: *Do you know anything about nuclear physics? I know Italian fairly well. She knows how to dance the tango.* **2** °recognize, °identify, °recall, °remember, °recollect: *I know him from somewhere.* **3** be °sure *or* °certain *or* °positive: *I knew I was right! I just know I'm going to win the first prize.* **4** °distinguish, °separate, discern, °differentiate, °recognize, °identify: *Charles doesn't know right from wrong.* **5** be °aware *or* °conscious *or* cognizant of, be °informed *or* advised of, have °knowledge of: *He knows that he cannot fire her because she knows too much.*

knowing *adj.* **1** conspiratorial *or* conspiratory, °secret, °private; °significant, °meaningful, °eloquent, °expressive; °shrewd, canny, °artful, °sly, °wily, °crafty: *She gave him a knowing wink.* **2** °wise, °clever, °shrewd, (well-)°informed, °knowledgeable *or* knowledgable, °aware, °expert, °qualified, °astute, °perceptive, °intelligent, sagacious: *Harold is quite knowing about horses, why not ask him?*

knowledge *n.* **1** °knowing, awareness, apprehension, cognition, °grasp, °understanding, discernment, consciousness, °conception, °insight: *Miles's knowledge of history is extensive.* **2** facts, °information, °data, °intelligence: *They had no knowledge of any defections to the enemy.* **3** °acquaintance, acquaintanceship, °familiarity, °appreciation, conversance, °expertise, °experience, adeptness, °proficiency: *Has he any knowledge of their work on the DNA molecule?* **4** °schooling, °education, °scholarship, °instruction, °learning, erudition: *A little knowledge is a dangerous thing.*

knowledgeable *adj.* **1** °aware, *au fait, au courant,* up to °date, (well-)°informed, (well-)°acquainted, cognizant, °familiar, °enlightened, °expert, °knowing, *Colloq* in the °know: *She is knowledgeable about events in eastern Europe.* **2** well-educated, erudite, °learned, cultured, well-read, °intelligent, °sophisticated, °worldly, °wise, °sage, sagacious: *Professor Evans is one of the most knowledgeable people I have ever met.*

kowtow *v.* Often, ***kowtow to***: genuflect (before), salaam (to), °prostrate oneself (before), °bow (down) (to *or* before), pay court to, °scrape before, °cringe before, fawn (before), grovel (before), toady ((up) to), °pander to, °truckle ((up) to), dance attendance on, *Colloq* butter up, *Slang* suck up to, °play up to, shine up to, *Taboo slang US* brown-nose: *He kowtows to anyone who he thinks may be of use to him.*

kudos *n.* °praise, acclaim, °glory, °fame, °renown, °honour, plaudits, °applause, laudation, acclamation, accolade: *They got a lot of kudos out of funding a new opera-house.*

L

label *n.* **1** °identification, identifier, ID, °mark, marker, earmark, °tag, ticket, sticker, °stamp, imprint, °hallmark, °brand, *Brit* docket: *The label shows the weight, composition, and price of the contents. A proper shipping label should show both source and destination.*

2 °name, °denomination, designation, appellation, °nickname, epithet, sobriquet, classification, characterization, °description: *It is difficult to give a label to the kind of novels she writes.* 3 trade °mark, trade °name, °brand, logo, °mark: *Many supermarket chains market products under their own label.*
—*v.* 4 °identify (as), °mark, °tag, earmark, ticket, °stamp, °hallmark, imprint, °brand, *Brit* docket: *In those days, every liberal was labelled a communist. Prepared food packages must be labelled with their ingredients.* 5 °name, denominate, °designate, °call, °term, dub, classify, °categorize, pigeon-hole, °class, °characterize, °describe, °portray, °identify, *Colloq US* peg: *We cannot label Voltaire either spiritualist or materialist.*

laborious *adj.* 1 °arduous, °burdensome, onerous, °strenuous, gruelling, back-breaking, Herculean, °exhausting, taxing, tiring, fatiguing, wearying, wearisome, °toilsome, °difficult, °tough, °hard, uphill, °stiff: *Few realize how laborious farm work can be.* 2 °painstaking, °detailed, °careful, °thorough, °diligent, °scrupulous, °exhaustive, °steady, °steadfast, °relentless, unrelenting, dogged, assiduous, sedulous, persevering, °persistent, °untiring, °tireless, indefatigable, unremitting: *After laborious research the virus was finally identified.* 3 °industrious, hard-working, dogged, °determined, unwavering, °obstinate, °stubborn, unflagging, obdurate: *He made a laborious effort to get ahead.* 4 °laboured, °strained, °forced, °ponderous, overworked: *The book contains some of the most laborious prose ever written.*

labour *n.* 1 toil, (°hard) °work, travail, °exertion, °effort, laboriousness, °strain, °drudgery, °pains, °industry, °slavery, donkey-work, *Colloq* °sweat, °grind, elbow-grease, *Brit* swot: *They know the labour involved in building a road.* 2 °employees, °workers, wage-earners, °labourers: *A meeting between labour and management is scheduled for today.* 3 °effort, °task, °job, chore, °undertaking: *Raising funds for the museum was a labour of love.* 4 travail, childbirth, parturition, labour pains, contractions, °delivery: *She went into labour at midnight, and the twins were born just after four.*
—*v.* 5 °work, toil, travail, drudge, °strain, °strive, °struggle, °slave, *Colloq* °sweat, °grind, *Brit* °peg away (at), swot: *We laboured hard to get where we are today.* 6 °dwell on, °overdo, overemphasize, harp on, overstress, °strain, *Colloq* °belabour: *I heard you the first time, so don't labour the point.* 7 ***labour under***: be burdened *or* troubled *or* distressed by, be deluded *or* deceived by, be disadvantaged by, °suffer, °endure: *He is labouring under a misapprehension. She labours under the impression that she will not be affected by a lack of education.*

laboured *adj.* 1 °strained, °forced, °difficult, °hard, °laborious, °heavy: *His breathing became laboured.* 2 overdone, °excessive, °overwrought, °ornate, °elaborate, overworked, over-embellished, contrived, °affected, °artificial, °unnatural: *Her writing style is very laboured and much too stiff.*

labourer *n.* °worker, workman, °hand, blue-collar °worker, working man, °manual °worker, drudge, *Colloq Brit* navvy: *Get some labourers to clear away that rubble.*

labyrinthine *adj.* labyrinthian, maze-like, mazy, °tortuous, sinuous, winding, convoluted, °complicated, confusing, °perplexing, °puzzling, enigmatic, baffling, confounding, complex, Daedalian *or* Daedalean *or* Daedalic, daedal, °intricate, Byzantine, twisted, °gnarled, snarled, tangled, knotted, knotty, Gordian: *The plot was so labyrinthine that the audience was unable to follow it.*

lace *n.* 1 lace-work, tatting, openwork, filigree, °mesh, °web, webbing, °net, netting, °network: *She wore a collar of handmade lace.* 2 shoelace, shoestring, bootlace, °cord, °string, thong, °tie, lacing: *They made me remove my belt, tie, and laces before locking me in a cell.*
—*v.* 3 °thread, °weave, °string, °twine, interweave, intertwine: *First lace the cord through the eyelets, then draw it tight.* 4 °spike, °fortify, °strengthen: *I saw her lace my punch with vodka, so I didn't drink it.* 5 ***lace into***: **a** °attack, °assault, °beat, assail, thrash, °belabour, °fall on *or* upon, °set upon, °pounce on *or* upon, °lay into, *Colloq* °light into: *The brothers laced into one another with a fury.* **b** °berate, °scold, revile, °attack, °upbraid, °castigate, °rant *or* °rave at: *She really laced into me for being an hour late for dinner.*

lacerate *v.* °gash, °cut, °slash, °tear, °rip, °claw, °mangle; °wound, °rend, °hurt: *My feet were lacerated by the sharp stones. She suffered a lacerating attack from him for forgetting to pass on the message.*

lack *n.* 1 °want, deficiency, °dearth, °absence, °scarcity, °shortage, °need, insufficiency, paucity, °deficit, inadequacy: *We suffered from a severe lack of water. The orchestra is experiencing a serious lack of talent at the moment.*
—*v.* 2 °want, °need, °require, be °deficient in, be *or* fall °short of, be without: *He lacks the votes needed to win. Simon lacks the ability to paint any better.*

lackadaisical *adj.* 1 °lethargic, languorous, languid, °listless, °lazy, sluggish, spiritless, °idle, °indolent, °inactive, °slothful, fainéant: *She's much too lackadaisical to go out and get a job.* 2 °unenthusiastic, °dull, apathetic, insouciant, uncaring, unconcerned, °indifferent, °blasé, °cold, °cool, °lukewarm, °tepid, unexcited, °phlegmatic, unemotional, unexcitable, uninterested, unimpressed, uninspired, °unmoved, pococurante: *How can you explain the government's lackadaisical attitude towards the greenhouse effect?*

lacklustre *adj.* °drab, °dull, lustreless, °flat, °dingy, °colourless, °dismal, °dreary, unexciting, °boring, °prosaic, °tiresome, °tedious, wearisome, uninteresting, two-dimensional, insipid, °vapid, °bland, unimaginative, °thick, °slow, °dense, *Colloq* °wishy-washy, blah: *He gave a very lacklustre performance as Shylock. She has been leading a lacklustre life since John left.*

lad *n.* °boy, °young °man, °fellow, schoolboy, °youth, °juvenile, youngster, hobbledehoy, °stripling, (street) urchin, (street) Arab, gamin, *Colloq* °guy, (little) shaver, kid, *US* sprout: *Round up a few of the lads for a game of football.*

ladylike *adj.* °well-bred, well-born, aristocratic, °noble; °refined, °respectable, cultured, °polished, °elegant, mannerly, °gracious, °genteel, °courteous, °polite, courtly, °dignified, °proper, °correct, °decorous: *I cannot believe that Mrs Gibson did not behave in a ladylike way.*

lag *v.* 1 °fall behind, °linger, loiter, °delay, °straggle, °trail, °hang back, dally, °dawdle, inch *or* poke along: *If you lag behind too far, you'll never catch up.* 2 °diminish, °decrease, slacken, abate, °slow (down *or* up), °flag, °wane, °ebb, falter, °fail, °let up, °fall (off *or* away), °ease (up), °lighten: *Contributions to the fund are lagging. Military preparations are lagging.*

laggard *n.* straggler, °idler, dawdler, loiterer, °slouch, sluggard, °loafer, snail, loller, *Colloq Brit* slowcoach, *US* slowpoke: *As a young boy he was always the laggard, dragging along behind everyone else.*

lair *n.* 1 den, °burrow, °hole, °nest, °tunnel, °cave, °hollow, covert: *We cautiously approached the lair of the man-eating tiger.* 2 hide-out, °hideaway, °retreat, hiding-place, °refuge, asylum, °sanctuary, *Colloq* hidey-hole *or* hidy-hole: *Oliver will not emerge from his lair before tea-time.*

laissez-faire *n.* laisser-faire, laissez-faireism, °free °enterprise, non-intervention, non-interference, °freedom, °free °trade, individualism, laissez-aller *or* laisser-aller, deregulation, decontrol, laxness: *The government's policy of laissez-faire has spurred business on.*

lambaste *v.* 1 °beat, °whip, °scourge, °flog, °lash, maul, horsewhip, cane, birch, thrash, bludgeon, trounce, drub, pummel, °batter, °belabour, cudgel: *Terry threatened to lambaste anyone who interfered.*

2 censure, °rebuke, °scold, °reprimand, chide, admonish, °reprove, °upbraid, °berate, °scold, revile, °attack, °castigate, flay, *Colloq* °dress down, get on (someone's) back, rake *or* haul over the coals, *US* °call down, *Slang* °chew *or* °bawl out: *The press lambasted the company for its unfair employment policies.*

lame *adj.* **1** °crippled, °disabled, handicapped, hobbled, limping, incapacitated, impaired, °halting, °halt, spavined, *Colloq US* gimpy: *The mare was found to be lame after the previous day's hunting.* **2** °feeble, °weak, °flimsy, °thin, unconvincing, unpersuasive, °awkward, °clumsy, °poor, °ineffective, *Colloq* half-baked: *Refusing to go because you have a headache sounds like a pretty lame excuse to me.*

lament *v.* **1** °mourn, °bemoan, °bewail, wail, °weep (over), °grieve (for *or* over), °keen (over), °sorrow (for *or* over): *A year later, and she is still lamenting the death of her hamster?!*
—*n.* **2** °lamentation, moaning, °mourning; °keen, dirge, elegy, knell, Requiem, monody, threnody, thanatopsis, epicedium, *Scots and Irish* coronach: *Laments for Kitty's late husband were heard throughout the village.*

lamentable *adj.* °deplorable, °wretched, °miserable, °terrible, distressing, °awful, °regrettable, °pitiful, °despicable, intolerable, °unfortunate: *The hall was left in a lamentable state after the party. His death was presaged by a lamentable series of events.*

lamentation *n.* °mourning, grieving, moaning, weeping, wailing, crying, sobbing, lamenting: *The lamentation went on far into the night.*

lampoon *n.* **1** °burlesque, °caricature, °satire, °parody, pasquinade *or* pasquil, squib, *Colloq* °take-off, *Brit* send-up: *The students published a hilarious lampoon of the teaching staff.*
—*v.* **2** °burlesque, °caricature, °satirize, °parody, pasquinade *or* pasquil, °mock, °ridicule, squib, *US* skewer, *Colloq* °take off, °put *or* °run down, *Brit* °send up: *The cows we hold most sacred are often lampooned by irreverent cartoonists.*

lance *n.* **1** spear, pike, javelin, assegai; lancet: *He transfixed the knight with his lance, and claimed victory in the joust.*
—*v.* **2** °pierce, °stab, °puncture, °prick, incise, °open, °slit: *The boil must be lanced at once to draw out the poison.*

land *n.* **1** °earth, (solid) °ground, terra firma: *After weeks in an open boat, Captain Bligh was relieved to have land under his feet again.* **2** °dirt, °earth, °soil, °turf, sod, loam, °mould: *Trumble tilled the land as his ancestors had done for generations.* **3** °property, grounds, real °property *or* realty *or US and Canadian also* real °estate, acreage; °estate: *How much land goes with the house?* **4** °fatherland, motherland, °nation, °country, homeland, °native land: *The land of our fathers flowed with milk and honey.*
—*v.* **5** °arrive, alight, °light, °touch *or* °come *or* °go down, splash down, °settle on *or* upon, come to °rest, berth, °dock, °disembark, debark, go ashore, deplane, dismount: *The plane was forced to land on the water. We land at dawn.* **6** catch, °capture, take °captive, *Colloq* °bag: *He was unable to land the shark unaided.* **7** get, °secure, °obtain, °win, °acquire: *He finally landed a job with his father-in-law. Sadie finally landed a millionaire!*

landing *n.* **1** touchdown, alighting, splashdown, docking: *The fog made landing quite dangerous.* **2** disembarkation, deplaning, °arrival: *After landing, passengers proceed through passport control.* **3** landing-place, °dock, °pier, jetty, wharf, quay: *We walked on to the landing to watch the ship come in.*

landlady *n.* **1** °proprietor *or* proprietress, lady of the house, mistress, °manager *or Brit* manageress, hostess: *My landlady owns three bed and breakfasts.* **2** See **landlord, 2,** below.

landlord *n.* **1** °host, publican, °proprietor, innkeeper, hotelier, °manager, restaurateur, Boniface: *Landlord! Two pints of your best bitter!* **2** °landlady, landowner, householder, (property) °owner, lessor, *Brit* freeholder: *My landlord has raised my rent claiming that his expenses have increased.*

landmark *n.* **1** °feature, °guide, guidepost; °identification: *The tower serves as a landmark for those seeking the castle.* **2** turning-point, watershed, milestone, °monument: *His essay remains a landmark in philosophical thought.*
—*attributive* **3** °critical, °crucial, °pivotal, °important, °historic, °significant, precedent-setting, °momentous, °notable, °noteworthy, °major: *This stands out as a landmark decision in the annals of criminal law.*

landscape *n.* °prospect, °view, °scene, °aspect, vista, countryside: *Here and there the landscape is dotted with spinneys.*

language *n.* **1** °speech, °tongue, °idiom, °parlance, °dialect, idiolect, patois, °jargon, °cant, argot, °vernacular, *Colloq* °lingo: *How many languages do you speak?* **2** communication, °intercourse, interaction: *Karl von Frisch studied the language of the bees.* **3** °jargon, lingua franca, vocabulary, °terminology, °vernacular, *Colloq* °lingo: *In medical language, a head cold is called 'coryza'.* **4** °wording, °words, phrasing, phraseology, °style, °diction: *Guarantees, insurance policies, and other such things should be written in simple language.*

lanky *adj.* °thin, loose-jointed, lank, °lean, °gaunt, gangling, rangy, long-legged: *They recruited three tall, lanky youths for the basketball team.*

lap[1] *v.* **1** Often, ***lap up***: lick up, °tongue; °sip, °drink: *In a moment, the cat had lapped all the cream from the saucer.* **2** °wash, °splash, °ripple, plash, purl: *The water rose till it was lapping at the doorstep.* **3** ***lap up***: **a** °consume, °drink, °eat: *The dog lapped up every last scrap of food.* **b** °accept, °believe, °credit, °fall for, *Colloq* °swallow (whole), °buy: *She lapped up Felix's sob story and invited him in at once.*

lap[2] *n.* **1** °circuit, °orbit, ambit, °circle, °tour, °trip, °revolution: *She runs four laps round the track every day for exercise.* **2** °flap, °fold, lappet, °projection, lapel, °overlap: *This lap hides the zip.*
—*v.* **3** °overlap, °fold, enfold, °envelop, °wrap: *Lap the fabric so as to cover the seam.*

lapse *n.* **1** °slip, °error, °mistake, °fault, °failing, °oversight, °blunder, °shortcoming, °omission, *Formal* lapsus, *Colloq* slip-up, °fluff, goof: *Apart from a brief lapse, the child behaved very well. Owing to a lapse, your payment was not credited.* **2** °gap, °break, °interval, °intermission, °interruption, °pause, lacuna, hiatus, *Prosody* caesura, *Colloq* °hold-up: *Listeners in Scotland experienced a lapse in transmission, for which we apologize.* **3** °decline, lowering, °fall, deterioration, °drop, diminution, descent: *There has been a serious lapse in church attendance.*
—*v.* **4** °decline, °lower, °fall, °drop, °diminish, °sink, °slip, °slump, °subside, °deteriorate: *Despite the doctor's best efforts, he lapsed into a coma.* **5** °run out, °expire, be discontinued, become °void, °terminate, °end, °cease, °stop: *Your option to sell the shares at the offering price lapses on Friday.* **6** °pass, °elapse, °go by, °slip away: *Three months had lapsed since she last saw him.*

large *adj.* **1** °big, °great, °broad, °stout, °heavy, thickset, chunky, °stocky, heavy-set, °brawny, °husky, °sturdy, °hefty, °muscular, strapping, °burly, °solid, °weighty, corpulent, °fat, °obese, °rotund, portly, adipose, °beamy, overweight: *Two large gentlemen came up and offered to help me find the door.* **2** °big, °generous, °bountiful, °charitable, eleemosynary, °philanthropic, open-handed, magnanimous, munificent, °unselfish, big-hearted, large-hearted, °substantial, °considerable, °ample, beneficent, °liberal; °goodly, °kind, °good; *Colloq* °tidy: *We have to thank Mr Wilson for large donations to our Christmas fund.* **3** °big, °huge, °ample, °enormous, °gigantic, °immense, °colossal, °monumental, °massive, mammoth, Brobdingnagian, gargantuan, elephantine, °monstrous,

staggering, sizeable, °substantial, °wide, °broad, capacious, °extensive, *Colloq* °jumbo, *US* humongous, ginormous: *The house has a large dining room. Supertankers are the largest ships afloat.*
—*adv.* **4** °big, prominently, overwhelmingly, imposingly, °eminently, °pre-eminently: *The problem looms large in the history of biology.*
—*n.* **5** ***at large***: **a** °free, unfettered, at °liberty, on the °loose, unconfined, unrestrained: *One of the robbers is still at large.* **b** °generally, °mainly, in °general, °chiefly, as a °whole, in a body, °altogether, in the °main: *The people at large support reductions in taxes.*

largely *adv.* °chiefly, °mainly, as a °rule, by and °large, °generally, in °general, to a °great extent, mostly, in °great part, in °great measure, in the °main, on the °whole, °pretty much, essentially, at °bottom, basically, fundamentally: *The voters are largely in favour of keeping the present government.*

largesse *n.* largess, °gifts, alms, °grants, °bonuses, endowments, °presents, contributions, °donations, hand-outs; °support, subvention, °aid, °subsidy, °charity, °philanthropy, generosity, munificence, °bounty, liberality, open-handedness: *The church depends on the largesse of its members.*

lark *n.* **1** °frolic, °spree, escapade, °caper, °fling, romp, °adventure, °revel, jape, °game, antic, horseplay, shenanigans, °mischief, °prank, practical °joke: *The boys say they took the horse just as a lark.*
—*v.* **2** Often, ***lark about***: °frolic, °caper, romp, °revel, °play, °sport, °cavort, gambol, *Colloq* skylark: *We spent a lot of time larking about after our exams.*

lascivious *adj.* **1** °lustful, °randy, °lecherous, licentious, °lewd, °prurient, salacious, libidinous, °erotic, °sensual, lubricious *or* lubricous, ruttish, goatish, hircine, satyr-like, °wanton, Cyprian, debauched, *Slang* horny, °hot: *I wouldn't let that lascivious old man near my daughter.* **2** °pornographic, °obscene, °blue, °lurid, °indecent, smutty, °dirty, Fescennine, °filthy, °vile, ribald, °bawdy, °gross, °coarse, °offensive: *He said that such lascivious novels should be banned and certainly not read in schools.*

lash[1] *n.* **1** °whip, °scourge, cat-o'-nine-tails, cat, quirt, knout, bull-whip, thong; rope's end: *The bosun gave him twenty of the best with his lash.* **2** °stroke, °blow, °strike, °slash, °cut: *Few could stand up after five lashes with his whip.*
—*v.* **3** °flog, °beat, thrash, °switch, °whip, °scourge, horsewhip, °lambaste, flail, smite, thwack, *Colloq* whack: *Any boy was liable to be lashed for the most trivial misdemeanour.* **4** ***lash out***: °attack, flay, °lambaste, °belabour, °punish; °criticize, °berate, °scold: *She often lashes out at her critics quite virulently.*

lash[2] *v.* °fasten, °tie, °bind, °secure, °rope, °fix, strap, make °fast: *His crew lashed Odysseus to the mast as they sailed past the land of the Sirens.*

lass *n.* °girl, °young °woman, °miss, mademoiselle, schoolgirl, *Old-fashioned* °maiden, °maid, damsel, demoiselle; *Scots* lassie, *Irish* colleen: *He has married a young lass from Arbroath.*

lasso *n.* **1** lariat, °rope, *SW US* reata *or* riata: *The cowboy tossed the lasso round the calf's neck.*
—*v.* **2** °rope: *He lassoed steers to practise for the rodeo.*

last[1] *adj.* **1** hindmost, rearmost, aftermost; °final: *I was the last person to board the plane.* **2** °latest, newest, most °recent *or* up to °date: *What was the subject of his last novel? During the last week I have seen seven films.* **3** °final, concluding, °terminal, °ultimate, terminating: *The last train to London leaves at eleven. She was the last speaker of Cornish.* **4** °definitive, conclusive, decisive, closing: *That is my last word on the subject.*
—*adv.* **5** behind, at *or* in the °end, in *or* at the °rear, after: *My horse always seems to come in last.*
—*n.* **6** °end, °termination, °finish: *That was the last we ever saw of Charlie.* **7** ***at last***: °finally, °eventually, °ultimately, at °length: *At last we shall see the results of our work.*

last[2] *v.* **1** °continue, °endure, °survive, °keep on, °persist, °remain, °stay, °abide, °carry on, °hold out, *Colloq* go the distance: *He wouldn't last a day in my job.* **2** °wear, °stand up, °endure, °survive: *This shirt has lasted through innumerable washings.*

last[3] *n.* °mould, matrix, °form, °model, °pattern: *These shoes were not made on the same last as those.*

lasting *adj.* °permanent, °enduring, °durable, °everlasting, long-term, undying, °eternal: *She made a lasting contribution to ophthalmology.*

late *adj.* **1** °tardy, delayed, °overdue, behindhand, dilatory, unpunctual; °belated, *US* °past due: *He was even late for his own wedding. Better late than never. Your mortgage payment is late again.* **2** °recent, °last, °new, °fresh, °current, up to °date: *Have you got a copy of a late edition of today's newspaper?* **3** deceased, departed, °dead; °former, °past, ex-, °recent, °previous, °preceding, °old (see also **5,** below): *Here is a song by the late, great Bing Crosby. He has a meeting with Lord Pamby, late chairman of United Oxidation.* **4** ***of late***: See **5,** below.
—*adv.* **5** recently, °lately, °previously, °formerly, °once, heretofore, in °recent *or* °former °time(s), of late, latterly (see also **3,** above): *They are dining tonight with Sir Keith, late of Scotland Yard.* **6** °till *or* at an advanced hour *or* °time: *I was up late last night. She married late.* **7** tardily, unpunctually, belatedly: *We arrived too late for the first act.* **8** recently, °lately: *As late as a week ago they were still holding the job open for her.*

lately *adv.* See **late, 5,** above.

latest *adj.* **1** See **last**[1]**, 2,** above. **2** °fashionable, °current, °modern, up to the °minute, *Colloq* in: *She drives the latest model.*
—*n.* **3** most °recent *or* up-to-date *or* °modern development *or* news *or* example: *What's the latest? Have you seen the latest in scuba gear?*

lather *n.* **1** suds, °froth, °foam: *He spread lather on his face and began to shave.* **2** °sweat; dither, °fuss, pother, °flutter, *Colloq* tizzy, °state, °flap: *He got into a real lather when he missed the train.*
—*v.* **3** soap (up); °foam, °froth: *The barber lathered my chin thoroughly.* **4** thrash, °beat, °belabour, maul, drub, °flog, whack, pummel, buffet, °whip, flail, °lash: *If he dared to swear, his father would lather him.*

laud *v.* °praise, commend, °celebrate, sing *or* speak *or* sound the praises of, °honour, acclaim, °extol, °glorify, °promote, °advance, °recommend, °exalt: *Bramble's paintings have been lauded by leading art critics the world over.*

laudable *adj.* °praiseworthy, °meritorious, creditable, °admirable, °outstanding, °excellent, °noteworthy, °notable, commendable, °estimable: *He has made a laudable effort to keep up in his work.*

laudatory *adj.* laudative, praiseful, eulogistic, panegyric(al), encomiastic(al), °complimentary, °favourable: *None of the laudatory comments made in the introduction was true.*

laugh *v.* **1** °titter, °giggle, snigger, °snicker, °chuckle, chortle, guffaw, split one's sides, *Colloq* break *or* crack up, roll on the floor, go into hysterics, °roar with °laughter, hoot: *Whenever he wore his hat, they couldn't stop laughing.* **2** Often, ***laugh at***: **a** °deride, °ridicule, °mock (at), °jeer (at), make a °mockery of, poke °fun (at), make °fun *or* °sport (of), make an ass *or* a °fool (out) of, °tease, °taunt, pull (someone's) °leg, °satirize, pasquinade *or* pasquil, °parody, °lampoon, jest (at), °joke (about), °scoff (at), °scorn, *Colloq Brit* take the mickey out of, *US* roast: *They laughed when I sat down—I didn't know the chair was broken. Why did the other children laugh at you?* **b** laugh away *or* off, °spurn, °dismiss, °brush aside, °minimize, shrug off, °reject, °ignore, °disregard, °deny, °belittle, *Colloq* pooh-pooh: *He laughed off his injury and insisted on continuing to work.*
—*n.* **3** °titter, °giggle, snigger, °snicker, °chuckle, chortle, guffaw, horse laugh: *She would do anything for a laugh.*

laughter *n.* laughing, tittering, giggling, sniggering, snickering, chuckling, chortling, guffawing: *Children's laughter filled the air.*

launch *v.* **1** °start (off), °set in °motion, °set *or* °get °going, °begin, °embark upon *or* on, °initiate, °inaugurate: *The council is about to launch a scheme for dockside development. The attack was launched at dawn.* **2** °originate, °establish, °organize, °set up, °found, °open, °start: *Robson is talking about launching a new company.* **3** °shoot, °fire, °discharge, °hurl, °throw, °sling, °pitch, °fling, catapult, °send, °dispatch *or* despatch: *The enemy launched ground-to-air missiles against our planes.* **4** °float, °set afloat: *Two frigates will be launched today.*
—*n.* **5** inauguration, °start, °initiation, °opening: *The launch of the offensive is scheduled for noon tomorrow.* **6** °boat, skiff, °tender, motor °boat, runabout, gig, dinghy: *The launch will shuttle passengers between the pier and the cruise ship.*

launder *v.* **1** °wash, °clean, °scrub, °cleanse: *The chambermaid laundered three shirts for me.* **2** legitimize, legitimatize, °legitimate, legalize: *The money from heroin was being laundered through several car dealerships.*

laurels *n.pl.* °honour(s), °distinction(s), °fame, °awards, °tributes, °rewards, acclaim, acclamation, °glory, °renown, °celebrity, °popularity, °reputation; °successes, °accomplishments: *With no new fields to conquer, he is resting on his laurels.*

lavatory *n.* water-closet, WC, °toilet, bathroom, *Colloq Brit* the Gents('), the Ladies('), Men's (Room), rest room, °privy, *Chiefly military or institutional* latrine; *Nautical* head; *Brit* (public) convenience, *US* equipment, outhouse; *Colloq* (little) boys' *or* girls' room, powder-room, *Brit* loo, lav, *US* can; *Slang Brit* bog: *Our new house has two upstairs bathrooms and a downstairs lavatory.*

lavish *adj.* **1** °profuse, °abundant, °liberal, copious, °plentiful, °prolific, °opulent: *He wore a silk tunic with lavish gold embroidery.* **2** °generous, °liberal, openhanded, unstinting, °bountiful, unsparing, °unselfish, °effusive, °free: *She showered the most lavish gifts on her children.* **3** °extravagant, °wasteful, exaggerated, °prodigal, °improvident, °excessive, °unreasonable, °immoderate, °profligate, uncurbed, unrestrained, intemperate: *The council was accused of lavish overspending on the civic centre.*
—*v.* **4** squander, °waste, °throw away, °dissipate, °spend, °expend, °sink: *We lavished a fortune on the gardens.* **5** °shower, °bestow, °thrust, °heap, °pour: *Granny always lavished gifts on us.*

law *n.* **1** °rule, °regulation, ordinance, statute, °act, enactment, by(e)-law, °measure, edict, °decree, °order, directive, °injunction, °command, commandment, canon, mandate, ukase: *They have a law that forbids smoking on aeroplanes.* **2** corpus juris, (°legal) °code, constitution, °rules and °regulations, °charter, *Law* °equity: *The law must be applied equally to all citizens.* **3** °principle, °proposition, theory, °theorem, °formula, axiom, °deduction, corollary, postulate, conclusion, °inference: *Not every observable phenomenon obeys the laws of physics.*

lawful *adj.* **1** °legal, licit, °legitimate, de jure, constitutional, °just, °rightful, valid, °proper: *I am the lawful heir.* **2** °permissible, allowable, justifiable, authorized, allowed, permitted: *It is not lawful to let your dog foul the footpath.*

lawless *adj.* **1** anarchic(al), anarchist(ic), °chaotic, °unruly, unregulated: *There was a lawless period between the revolution and the establishment of government.* **2** °illegal, °illicit, °unlawful, °criminal, felonious, larcenous, °dishonest, °corrupt, °venal, *Colloq* °crooked: *Holding a demonstration without a permit is a lawless act.* **3** °villainous, nefarious, °wicked, °sinful, flagitious, iniquitous, treacherous: *He was once a member of a lawless motor-cycle gang.*

lawn *n.* sward, greensward, °turf, sod, °green: *I lay back on the lawn and gazed at the sky.*

lawyer *n.* °counsel, °advocate, member of the °bar, °legal practitioner, *Brit* °solicitor, barrister, Queen's *or* King's °counsel, bencher, *US* attorney(-at-law), counselor(-at-law), *Slang US* °mouthpiece: *We have turned the case over to a lawyer.*

lax *adj.* **1** °loose, °slack, °casual, °slipshod, °easygoing, °careless, negligent, °permissive, °weak, °indulgent, °flexible, °relaxed: *Law enforcement has always been lax in that city.* **2** °imprecise, undefined, °indefinite, non-specific, unspecific, °vague, °shapeless, amorphous, °general, °broad, °inexact, hit-or-miss, °careless, °untidy, *Colloq* °sloppy: *His ideas about tactics are too lax for a military man.*

lay[1] *v.* **1** °place, °put (down), °set (down), °position, °deposit; °spread: *Lay the cloth on the table, then lay the book on top of it.* **2** °set, °arrange: *The table was laid for four.* **3** Often, ***lay down***: °establish, °build, °construct: *Before I can argue my case, I must lay a firm foundation of trust.* **4** °stake, °bet, wager, °gamble, °hazard, °risk: *I'll lay ten to one that you won't be able to move that crate.* **5** °destroy, °suppress, exorcize: *Did Edward ever succeed in laying that ghost of a rumour that haunted his career for so long?* **6** °present, °offer, °submit, °set *or* °put forth, °advance, °bring *or* °put forward, °set out: *We have laid our proposal before the board.* **7** charge, °impute, °direct, °lodge, °prefer, °aim, °attribute, ascribe: *There is no justification for laying the blame on Leonard.* **8** copulate (with), couple (with), have (°sexual) °intercourse (with), °sleep (with), °lie (with), bed, go to bed (with), °mate (with), have °sex (with), go all the way (with), service, *Slang* °screw, °shack up (with), *Brit* roger, *Taboo* fuck. **9** ***lay bare***: expose, °reveal, uncover, °disclose, divulge, bring to °light, °show, °unveil, lift the °veil from: *She laid bare the most intimate details of their relationship.* **10** ***lay down***: °stipulate, °require, °demand, °insist on, °dictate: *She laid down the conditions on which he could return home.* **11** ***lay hold of***: °seize, °grab, °snatch, °nab, catch *or* °get °hold of, °get: *I have been trying to lay hold of that book for weeks.* **12** ***lay in***: See **19 a,** below. **13** ***lay into***: °attack, °assault, °set about, assail, °lambaste, °belabour: *We laid into the gang and gave them a sound drubbing.* **14** ***lay it on***: °exaggerate, °overstate, embroider: *Don't believe what Frank tells you—he really lays it on pretty thick sometimes.* **15** ***lay low***: See **18 c,** below. **16** ***lay off***: **a** °suspend; °dismiss, °discharge, °fire, °let go, cashier, drum out of the corps, *Colloq* (give the) °sack, (give the) axe, °kick out, (give the) °boot, °boot out, give (someone) his *or* her walking papers: *Fifty workers were laid off because business was slack.* **b** °let up, °quit (it), °stop (it), °cease, desist, °leave off, °leave °alone, *Colloq* °knock (it) off, °cut (it) out, come off (it): *I wish you'd lay off for a while and stop bothering me. You must lay off phoning your mother twice a day.* **17** ***lay on***: **a** °provide, °cater (for), °supply: *The company laid on quite a Christmas party.* **b** °impose, °charge, assess; °demand, °require: *In addition to enforcing payment of back taxes, they laid on a penalty of 20 per cent.* **18** ***lay out***: **a** °design, °plan, °outline, sketch, °arrange, °set up: *The art department laid out the advertisements for the new campaign.* **b** °advance, disburse, °spend, °expend, °pay, °give, °contribute, *Colloq* °shell out, ante up, kick in with, fork out: *The salesmen often lay out the money for their expenses and are then reimbursed.* **c** lay low, °floor, °prostrate, °knock down *or* out, °strike *or* °cut down, °flatten, °fell, *Colloq* °knock for six, kayo *or* K.O.: *He laid out the challenger with a blow to the solar plexus.* **19** ***lay up***: **a** lay in, °amass, °accumulate, °save (up), °hoard, °preserve, °store, °keep, °put away, °put by: *We laid up a supply of canned goods for the winter.* **b** hospitalize, °incapacitate, disable, confine to bed, keep indoors: *She has been laid up with a virus all week.*

lay[2] *adj.* **1** °secular, non-clerical, laic, non-ecclesiastical: *He served as a lay preacher for many years.* **2** °amateur, non-professional, non-specialist: *Members of the lay public did not immediately understand the dangers of the greenhouse effect.*

lay[3] *n.* ballad, °song, °air, °refrain, °strain, °melody; °poem, ode, °lyric, °rhyme, ballade: *Macaulay wrote a book entitled* Lays of Ancient Rome.

lazy *adj.* **1** °indolent, °slothful, dilatory, °idle, °shiftless, °inactive, °listless, fainéant, otiose, °slack, °lax, °lethargic: *He's so lazy and so rich that he pays someone just to walk his dog.* **2** °slow, languid, °easy, °easygoing, sluggish, slow-moving, languorous: *The hot lazy summer days were whiled away fishing.*

lead *v.* **1** °conduct, °escort, usher, °guide, °show the °way, °pilot, °steer: *If you lead, I'll follow.* **2** °cause, °influence, °prompt, °bring, °incline, °induce, °persuade, °move, °dispose, °convince: *What led you to suspect the butler?* **3** °head (up), °direct, °govern, °command, °supervise, superintend, °preside (over), take the lead, take *or* assume °command (of), °manage, captain, *Colloq* °skipper: *The orchestra would like you to lead. Who is going to lead the men into battle? Nicole leads a weekly discussion group on alcoholism.* **4** come *or* be *or* go °first, °excel, °surpass, °exceed, °precede, be °ahead (of), °outstrip, °distance, outrun, °outdo: *They lead the world in the production of sugar.* **5** °live, °experience, °spend, °pass; while away: *He is leading a life of ease on the French Riviera.* **6** be conducive to, °create, engender, °cause, °contribute to, °result in, °bring on *or* about, °produce: *Your stubbornness can lead only to frustration.* **7** ***lead astray***: lead on, °mislead, misguide, °misdirect, °deceive; °fool, °decoy, °hoodwink, *Colloq* bamboozle: *She might have been led astray by that wolf in sheep's clothing.* **8** ***lead off***: °start (off *or* in *or* out *or* up), °begin, °commence, get °going *or* °moving, get under °way, °initiate, °inaugurate, *Colloq* kick off: *The proceedings will lead off with the national anthem. Who is going to lead off the singing?* **9** ***lead on***: **a** See **7**, above. **b** °lure, °entice, °seduce, °beguile, inveigle, °tempt: *They led me on with offers of a huge salary.* **10** ***lead up to***: **a** °prepare *or* °pave *or* °clear (the °way), do the °groundwork *or* spadework, °precede: *The events leading up to the overthrow of the government may never be known.* **b** °approach, °broach, °bring up, °present, °introduce, °work up *or* °round *or* around to, get (up) to: *I should lead up to the subject delicately, if I were you.*
—*n.* **11** °front, vanguard, van, lead *or* °leading °position *or* °place, °advance *or* advanced °position *or* °place: *The horse that he had bet on was in the lead coming down the home straight.* **12** °advantage, °edge, °advance, °supremacy, °margin, °priority, primacy, °pre-eminence: *She has the lead over all her competitors. Our team had a two-point lead at half-time.* **13** °direction, °guidance, °leadership, °precedent, °example, °model, exemplar, °pattern, °standard: *We decided to follow his lead.* **14** °tip, °clue, °hint, °suggestion, °cue, intimation; °prospect, °possibility, °potential; *Colloq* tip-off: *Barry is following up some leads for a new job. The advertisement produced some new sales leads.* **15** leash, °tether, °restraint, °cord, °chain: *The dog fetches his lead himself when he wants to go out.* **16** °protagonist, °hero *or* °heroine, °leading *or* starring °role *or* °part, °leading *or* lead actor *or* actress, °leading lady *or* man, male *or* female lead, °principal; prima donna, diva, prima ballerina, *première danseuse*, °*premier danseur*: *She has the lead in the new production of* Giselle. **17** wire, °cable, *Brit* °flex: *Connect this lead to the power source.*
—*adj.* **18** °leading, °foremost, °first; °main, °chief, °principal, °premier, °paramount: *The lead climber fell when the rope broke. The lead story in today's paper is about an American take-over bid for the longest-standing British car-manufacturing company.*

leaden *adj.* **1** °heavy, onerous, °ponderous, °dense, °burdensome: *Exhausted, he dragged his leaden feet to the next meeting.* **2** °heavy, °dull, numbing, °oppressive: *I was happy to escape the leaden atmosphere of the theatre.* **3** °grey, °dull, °dingy, °gloomy, glowering, lowering, °dreary, °dismal, °oppressive, °dark, °sullen, °sombre: *The leaden sky seemed to forebode disaster as he fled across the moor.* **4** °inert, °lifeless, °listless, sluggish, °inanimate, °inactive, °lethargic, languid, languorous, °torpid, spiritless, °stagnant, °static, °dormant, soporific, °sleepy: *The refugees trudged along at a leaden pace.*

leader *n.* **1** °chief, °head, commander, ruler, °superior, °director, chairman, chairwoman, chairperson, chieftain, captain, commandant, °principal, *Colloq* °boss, bossman, kingpin, °big cheese, number one, numero uno, *Brit* gaffer, *Chiefly US* Mr Big, *Slang US* the man: *The police can identify the leader of the gang. The leader of the assembly is elected for a year.* **2** bandmaster, °band leader, °director, *US and Canadian* conductor, bandleader, concert-master: *The leader tapped his baton for silence.*

leadership *n.* °direction, °guidance, °management, directorship, °administration, supervision, °command, °regulation, °control, °operation, °influence, °initiative; governorship, superintendence, °running: *The company made huge profits under Katherine's leadership. The leadership of the country at this time was in the hands of the privileged class.*

leading *adj.* **1** °important, °influential, °chief, °prime, °cardinal, °foremost, °paramount, °primary: *A leading politician hinted today that interest rates might go down soon.* **2** °best, °outstanding, °pre-eminent, greatest, °supreme, °peerless, °matchless, unequalled, unrivalled, unsurpassed: *He was the leading writer of his time.*

leaflet *n.* folder, °circular, °brochure, handbill, bill, booklet, °advertisement, *US and Canadian* throwaway, flier *or* flyer, *Colloq Brit* advert: *The candidate gave out leaflets urging us to vote for him.*

leafy *adj.* °green, verdant, bosky, woody, °shady, shaded, arborescent: *We lay beneath the leafy bowers and dreamed of summers past.*

league *n.* **1** confederation, °association, °alliance, °combination, coalition, °federation, confederacy, guild, °society, °fraternity, °union, °band, °fellowship, °club: *The teams in the south favour forming a football league of their own.* **2** ***in league (with)***: allied (with), °united (with), associated (with), leagued (with), federated (with), collaborating (with), conspiring (with), in collusion (with), *Colloq* in cahoots (with): *The suspects are said to be in league with saboteurs.*
—*v.* **3** °ally, °unite, °associate, °band, °combine, °collaborate, °join (forces), conspire, collude: *Did most people league with the rebels or the official government?*

leak *n.* **1** leakage, leaking, °discharge, °trickle, °escape, seepage, seeping, oozing, exudation: *We have to stop leaks of radioactive waste from power plants.* **2** °hole, fissure, °crack, °chink, °crevice, °aperture, °opening, °puncture, °cut, °break, °split, °gash, °rent, °tear, °gap, °flaw: *There was a leak in the balloon and it began to descend.* **3** disclosure, °revelation: *The press knew about his defection because of a security leak.*
—*v.* **4** °escape, °discharge, °spill, °trickle, °drip, seep, °ooze, exude, extravasate: *Oil was leaking out through a hole in the container.* **5** °disclose, divulge, let °slip, °release, °give away (the game), °make known *or* °public, let (something *or* it) be known, *Colloq* °spill the beans (about); let the cat out of the bag: *Someone as yet unidentified leaked the scandal to a reporter.* **6** ***leak out***: °transpire, become known, °come out, be revealed: *Their secret relationship has leaked out.*

lean[1] *adj.* **1** °thin, °slim, °slender, rangy, °spare, °wiry, °lanky, lank, °skinny, angular, bony, °raw-boned, °gaunt, gangling, gangly, °meagre, skeletal, scraggy, °scrawny, °haggard, °emaciated, pinched, wasted, shrunken, macilent: *He has the lean leggy build typical of a runner.* **2** unfruitful, unproductive, °barren, °infertile, °poor, °meagre, °scanty, °bare, arid, °sparse, °impoverished: *The Kanes tried for years to eke a living from the lean soil.* **3** °impoverished, °destitute, °needy, poverty-stricken, °penurious, °indigent, necessitous, °hard, °bad, °difficult: *The Depression was a lean period for most people.*

lean[2] *v.* **1** °rest (against *or* on *or* upon), be held up *or* supported by: *She leant her head on his shoulder.* **2** °incline, °slant, °tilt, °bend, °tip: *Isn't that pole leaning over too much?* **3** Often, ***lean towards***: °favour, gravitate towards, °tend towards, be °disposed towards, °prefer, show a °preference for, °incline towards, be *or* lean on the °side of, be °biased towards, be (°prejudiced) in °favour of: *She leans towards conservatism when it comes to morality.* **4** ***lean on***: **a** °rely on, °depend on, °count on, °believe *or* °trust in, °pin one's hopes *or* °faith on *or* upon: *You can lean on me if you need help.* **b** °pressure, bring °pressure to bear on, °intimidate, °threaten, cow, terrorize, °terrify, °scare, °frighten, °warn, °menace, °endanger, imperil, *Brit* pressurize: *Sometimes the gang would lean on a shopkeeper who refused to pay for 'protection'.*

leaning *n.* °bent, °inclination, °bias, °prejudice, °favouritism, °partiality, predilection, °liking, °taste, °preference, °penchant, °sympathy, °tendency, tendentiousness: *The judges' leanings in favour of short-haired dogs are well known.*

leap *n.* **1** °spring, °bound, °jump, vault (into); °hurdle, °clear, °hop over, °skip over, °negotiate: *He leapt into the saddle. Superman leaps tall buildings at a single bound.* **2** °jump, °cavort, gambol, °dance, °frisk, °caper, °frolic, romp, °prance, curvet: *He leapt for joy at the news that he had won first prize.* **3** °jump, °rush, °hasten, °form °hastily, accept (prematurely *or* without question): *The speaker kept leaping from one subject to another. Don't leap to conclusions about her strange behaviour.* **4** ***leap at***: °jump at, °accept, be °eager for, move °quickly, °take: *I leapt at the chance to apply for a scholarship.*
—*n.* **5** °spring, °bound, °jump, vault, °hurdle, °hop, °skip: *With one leap I was on the other side.* **6** °jump, °increase, (up)surge, °rise, upswing, °growth, escalation: *The figures show a leap in inflation for the month.* **7** ***by leaps and bounds***: °rapidly, °quickly, °swiftly, speedily: *The plans for the new theatre are progressing by leaps and bounds.*

learn *v.* **1** Often, ***learn of***: °find out, °discover, °hear (of), °chance *or* °hit upon, °understand, °gather, have revealed to one; °determine, ascertain, uncover: *I learned today that you are leaving. I learned of your plans yesterday.* **2** be taught, be instructed in, °master, become °proficient (in), °acquire °knowledge (of): *I learned German at school.* **3** °understand, see the °light, °get the picture, *Colloq* catch on, °get the idea, °get it, *Brit* °twig: *No matter how often they are told, some people never learn.* **4** °memorize, commit to memory, learn by heart: *Bolton was told to learn his part by the next day.*

learned *adj.* (°well-)°informed, erudite, °knowledgeable, *au fait*, cultured, °intellectual, °highbrow, (well-)°educated, °scholarly, °academic, scholastic, °lettered, °experienced, skilled, °practised, °accomplished, °expert, literate, well-read, (well-)°versed, (well-)trained, (well-)grounded: *The consultants to the encyclopedia are all learned people.*

learner *n.* °student, °pupil, °scholar, trainee, °apprentice, °novice, tiro *or* tyro, abecedarian, beginner, °initiate, neophyte: *Learners of English as a second language will benefit from this book.*

learning *n.* °knowledge, erudition, °culture, °scholarship, °lore, °information, °wisdom: *You have the advantage of being able to draw on centuries of learning.*

lease *n.* **1** rental °agreement *or* °contract, sublease, sublet: *A new ten-year lease will be signed tomorrow.*
—*v.* **2** °rent (out), °let (out), sublet (out), sublease (out), °charter (out), °hire (out): *They leased their home to us for the summer. We arranged to lease their boat for the weekend.*

leave[1] *v.* **1** °go (away *or* off), °depart, °set off, be off, °get away *or* off, °retire, °retreat, °withdraw, decamp, (make an) °exit, °run, be gone, bid (someone *or* something) °goodbye, say °goodbye *or* adieu (to), take (one's) leave (of), °quit, °desert, °pull out, °check out, °fly, *Colloq* °push *or* shove off, °take off, skedaddle, °flit, °disappear, do a disappearing act, pull up stakes, up-anchor, *Slang* °beat it, scram, vamoose, °split, *Brit* beetle off, do a bunk, do a moonlight flit, °hop it, *Taboo slang Brit* °bugger off: *Please leave at once. May I leave the room? She left him alone.* **2** °go *or* °run off, °deviate from: *The car left the road and hit a tree.* **3** °forget, °mislay, °lose: *I left my car keys somewhere in the house.* **4** °abandon, °desert, take leave of, °wash one's hands of, °turn one's back on; °quit, °resign from, °give up, °renounce, °drop (out of): *She left him because he mistreated her. I left school at sixteen.* **5** °make, °render, °cause to be *or* become *or* remain: *The beauty of the place left me speechless.* **6** °bequeath, °will, °hand down, °devise, demise, °transfer: *Her aunt left some valuable paintings to my wife.* **7** °entrust, °commit, °assign, °cede, °relinquish, °give over *or* up, consign, °resign: *They are leaving all the responsibility to me.* **8** °cause *or* °allow to °remain, have as a °remainder, °yield, °give: *Seven from eleven leaves four.* **9** ***leave off***: °stop, °cease, desist, forbear, °give up, °refrain from, °discontinue, abstain (from), °renounce: *He won't leave off gossiping about her.* **10** ***leave out***: °omit, °disregard, °ignore, °neglect; °count out, °reject, °exclude, °eliminate, °bar, °except: *You left out the best part. Don't leave me out of the fun!*

leave[2] *n.* **1** °permission, authorization, °consent, °freedom, °liberty, °licence, °sanction, dispensation: *Who gave you leave to borrow my car?* **2** furlough, leave of °absence, °time off, sabbatical, °recess, °holiday, vacation: *I am overworked and badly in need of some leave.* **3** departure: *He took his leave of us at last.*

lecherous *adj.* °lewd, °lascivious, salacious, libidinous, °sensual, lubricious *or* lubricous, °lustful, concupiscent, licentious, °prurient, dirty-minded, filthy-minded, °carnal, goatish, hircine, °randy, °libertine, °wanton, °profligate, depraved, °degenerate, °decadent, °dissolute, *Slang* horny: *The lecherous villain dared to proposition my wife.*

lecture *n.* **1** °speech, °address, °talk, discourse, disquisition, treatise, dissertation, °paper, °lesson, °instruction, °sermon, declamation, °harangue, diatribe, philippic, screed: *The preacher delivered a lecture on the evils of drink.* **2** °reproof, °reprimand, °rebuke, °criticism, censure, reproach, scolding, upbraiding, chiding, berating, °tongue-lashing, remonstration, *Colloq* dressing-down, telling-off, *Slang Brit* wigging, *US and Canadian* chewing-out: *I had to listen to another lecture about staying out late.*
—*v.* **3** °make *or* °deliver *or* °give a °speech *or* °address *or* °talk, discourse; sermonize, °hold forth, moralize, pontificate, orate, °preach, declaim, expound, °go on about, °harangue: *She lectures on Chinese art of the 18th century. He insists on lecturing to everyone he meets.* **4** °reprove, °reprimand, °rebuke, reproach, °scold, °upbraid, °berate, chide, tongue-lash, remonstrate with, °rail at, fulminate against; admonish, °warn; *Colloq* °dress down, °tell off, °send (someone) away *or* off with a flea in his *or* her ear, *Slang Brit* wig, *US and Canadian* °chew out: *She is always lecturing me about keeping my room tidy.*

ledge *n.* shelf, °projection, °step, mantel *or* °mantle, mantelpiece *or* mantlepiece, °overhang, sill: *We stood on a small ledge of rock unable to move.*

leer *v.* **1** °ogle, °eye: *He leers at every pretty girl.*
—*n.* **2** °ogle, the °eye, *Colloq* once-over, *Slang* glad °eye: *She was repelled when he gave her a leer.*

leery *adj.* °suspicious, °sceptical, dubious, °doubtful, doubting, °distrustful, °wary, °cautious, chary, °careful: *I was very leery of his story.*

leeway *n.* °space, elbow-room, °room, °play, °scope, °slack, latitude, °wide berth; °freedom: *We allowed him some leeway to make changes in the manuscript.*

left *adj.* **1** left-hand, sinistral, *Nautical* °port, *Formerly* larboard, *Heraldry* °sinister: *In most countries,*

the driver sits on the left side. **2** leftist, left-wing, °progressive, °liberal, socialist(ic), °pink; °radical, communist(ic), red: *The party's platform has become a bit too left for my taste.*
—*n.* **3** left side *or* hand *or* fist, *Nautical* °port, °port side, *Formerly* larboard: *The fort is on the left as you enter the bay. The champion has a powerful left.*

left-handed *adj.* **1** °clumsy, °awkward, gauche, fumbling, maladroit, cack-handed: *He has a left-handed way of doing things.* **2** insulting, disparaging, derisive, uncomplimentary, °paradoxical, °ambiguous, °questionable, dubious, °doubtful: *Calling her piano-playing 'not bad' was a left-handed compliment.*

leftover *n.* **1** Usually, ***leftovers***: °remainder(s), °remnant(s), °rest, °residue, residuum, °balance, °surplus, °excess, °superfluity, overage; °scrap(s), leavings, crumbs, °odds and ends, debris, °refuse, °waste, °rubbish, rubble, detritus, *Archaic* orts: *I'm just having leftovers for dinner tonight.*
—*adj.* **2** °remaining, °residual, °extra, °excess, °unused, uneaten: *Save some of the leftover ice-cream for later.*

leg *n.* **1** limb, °member, *Colloq* pin, peg, stump, *Slang* gam: *I have a touch of arthritis in my left leg.* **2** °support, °brace, °prop, °upright, °standard, column, °pillar: *One of the legs of this table is about to collapse.* **3** °part, °portion, °segment, °stretch, °stage, °section, °length, °lap: *The first leg of my journey passed without incident.* **4** ***a leg up***: °boost, °assistance, °push, °help, °helping °hand, °advance, °support, *US and Canadian* °assist: *Let me give you a leg up over the wall. Gordon might give you a leg up in getting a job.* **5** ***leg it***: °run, °hurry, °hasten, °scurry, *Colloq* scoot, skedaddle: *He legged it down the street to catch the bus.* **6** ***not a leg to stand on***: °defenceless, unsupported, insupportable *or* unsupportable, indefensible, unjustifiable, °untenable, °invalid: *She insists she's right, but she hasn't got a leg to stand on.* **7** ***on one's*** *or* ***its last legs***: °decrepit, °failing, °exhausted, °dying, °worn out, °run-down, falling °apart *or* to °pieces, broken-down, the worse for °wear; °dilapidated, °rickety, °shabby, °ramshackle, crumbling, °tumbledown: *George looked as if he was on his last legs. My car is on its last legs.* **8** ***pull someone's leg***: °tease, °mock, °jeer at, °taunt, °gibe, make °fun of, °chaff, °guy, °fool, °deceive, *Chiefly Brit* °twit, *Colloq* rib, kid, °rag: *We were just pulling his leg, but he took it seriously.* **9** ***shake a leg***: **a** °hurry (up), °hasten, °rush, *Colloq* get °going *or* °moving *or* cracking, look alive *or* lively: *You'll have to shake a leg to catch that train.* **b** °dance, °trip the light fantastic (toe), *Slang* hoof it, *US* cut a rug: *What do you say we go out and shake a leg tonight?* **10** ***stretch one's legs***: (take *or* go for a) °walk, (take some) °exercise: *After sitting for so long, I have to stretch my legs.*

legal *adj.* **1** °lawful, licit, statutory, °acceptable, °permissible, permitted, admissible, authorized: *The police officer was found to have exceeded his legal authority.* **2** °legitimate, °proper, °right, °rightful, °sound, constitutional, authorized, *Slang* legit: *I question whether his business is legal. Who is the legal heir?* **3** °judicial, juridical, judiciary, forensic: *The case is without legal precedent.*

legalistic *adj.* °narrow(-minded), disputatious, contentious, litigious, °literal, °strict, °niggling, °hair-splitting, cavilling, quibbling, Jesuitical, pettifogging, °nice, °fine, °subtle, *Colloq* nit-picking: *Her argument is legalistic and ignores the spirit of the law.*

legend *n.* **1** epic, °saga, °myth, °story, (°folk) °tale, °romance, °narrative, fable, °tradition, fiction, *Scandinavian* Edda: *There are scores of legends woven into the cultural fabric of our lives.* **2** °celebrity, °phenomenon, °tradition, °wonder, luminary, °personage, °somebody: *Someone said that Rudolph had become a legend in his own mind.* **3** °key, °table of symbols, °code, °explanatory °note: *Refer to the legend for explanations of symbols used in the map.* **4** °motto, °slogan, inscription, caption, °title: *The legend reads, 'Dieu et mon droit'.*

legendary *adj.* **1** fabled, storied, °traditional; °heroic, epic, mythic: *Legendary tales have been identified in every culture.* **2** °fanciful, °imaginary, °fabulous, °mythical, °romantic, °fictional: *Was King Arthur a real person or a legendary figure?* **3** °famous, °celebrated, °noted, famed, °well-known, °renowned, °illustrious, °immortal, °prominent, °eminent, °great, acclaimed, °noteworthy: *Irena became known for her legendary dinner parties.*

legible *adj.* °readable, decipherable, °clear, understandable, °plain, °distinct: *The handwriting is legible, but I don't know what language it's in.*

legitimate *adj.* **1** valid, °proper, °right, °rightful, authorized, °legal, °genuine, °real, °true, °authentic: *Which one of them was the legitimate Anastasia?* **2** °lawful, licit, °legal, by °law, *de jure*, statutory: *Bonnie Prince Charlie claimed to be the legitimate ruler of Scotland.* **3** commonsensical, °sensible, °reasonable, °proper, °correct, °acceptable, valid, °logical, justifiable, °just, °fair: *The question is perfectly legitimate and deserves a proper answer.*
—*v.* **4** legitimize, legitimatize, legalize, °authorize, °sanction, °warrant, validate, °certify: *By signing before two witnesses, she legitimated her will.*

leisure *n.* **1** °spare *or* °free °time, °time (off), °liberty, °freedom, °opportunity: *How many people these days have the leisure to do what they like?* **2** °holiday, vacation, °respite, °relief, °rest, °recreation, °relaxation, °ease, breathing-space, °quiet, tranquillity, °repose, *US military* °rest and °recreation, R and R: *Everyone needs a few days of leisure now and then.* **3** ***at leisure***: **a** unoccupied, °inactive, retired, resting, °free, on °holiday *or chiefly US and Canadian* vacation; at °liberty, °available, °unemployed: *I have been at leisure for a year now.* **b** Often, ***at one's leisure***: at one's convenience, when °convenient, unhurriedly, in one's own °time: *I shall mow the lawn at my leisure.*
—*adj.* **4** recreational: *The 'leisure industry' is booming with theme parks opening throughout the country.* **5** °free, unoccupied, non-working, unencumbered, °idle, °holiday, vacation: *How do you usually spend your leisure time?*

leisured *adj.* °wealthy, °rich, affluent, °prosperous, moneyed *or* monied, well-to-do: *Yachts of that size are strictly for the leisured classes.*

lend *v.* **1** make a °loan of, °loan, °advance: *The bank agreed to lend me the money for a boat.* **2** °impart, °furnish, °bestow, °give, °confer, °contribute, °add: *The silk scarf lends cachet to the whole outfit.* **3** ***lend itself to***: °suit, °fit, be °fitted *or* °appropriate *or* °suitable (to *or* for), be °applicable *or* °adaptable (to *or* for): *The book lends itself well to film adaptation.*

length *n.* **1** °extent, °measure, °span, °reach, °size, °magnitude, dimension, °measurement: *What is the length of a piece of string? The pool is 25 metres in length and 15 metres in width.* **2** duration, °stretch, °term, °period, °space: *What length of time did he spend in prison?* **3** ***at full length***: fully, °completely, to the fullest °extent: *They were stretched out at full length on the floor.* **4** ***at length***: **a** °finally, at (°long) °last, °eventually, after a (°long) °time *or* while, °ultimately; in the °long °run: *At length, the doctor emerged from his office.* **b** for a °long °time, interminably, for ages: *He read to her at length, till she dozed off.* **c** in °depth, °thoroughly, °completely, exhaustively, extensively, to the fullest *or* greatest °extent, in °detail: *I haven't the time to go into the story at length just now.*

lengthen *v.* make longer, °extend, elongate; °stretch, °drag out, °draw out, °prolong, protract, °expand, °continue: *I need to lengthen the skirt an inch. The ten-minute interview lengthened into an hour. They lengthened the playing field.*

lengthy *adj.* °long, over-long, long-drawn(-out), °protracted; °endless, interminable, prolonged, long-winded, °wordy, prolix, verbose, garrulous, °talkative, loquacious, °boring, °dull, °tedious: *He underwent a lengthy operation for removal of the clot. She launched into a lengthy description of the life cycle of a frog.*

lenient *adj.* °gentle, °kind, °kindly, °easy, °sparing, °merciful, °tender, humane, tender-hearted, kind-hearted, °indulgent, °permissive, °forgiving, °easy-going, °tolerant, °patient, compassionate, forbearing, °understanding, magnanimous, °generous, °charitable: *Do you think they were lenient in their treatment of prisoners caught while escaping?*

lesson *n.* **1** °exercise, °drill, reading, °lecture, °recitation; °assignment, homework, °task: *The pupils are having an English lesson at the moment. You must finish your lessons before you can go out and play.* **2** °class, °session; °instruction, teaching, tutoring, °schooling; °practice: *I take piano lessons on Tuesday afternoons.* **3** °example, exemplar, °model, °guide, °maxim, °paragon, °message, °deterrent, discouragement; °warning, admonition; °moral, °precept: *Norman's punishment should be a lesson to you.* **4** °punishment, chastisement, chastening, castigation, scolding, chiding, °rebuke, °reprimand, °reproof: *If she does that again, I'll give her a lesson she won't forget in a hurry!*

let[1] *v.* **1** °allow (to), °permit (to), °sanction (to), give °permission *or* °leave (to), °authorize (to), °license (to), °suffer (to): *Don't let him go alone. Let George do it.* **2** °cause (to), °arrange for, °enable (to): *Let me know if you have any difficulty. Let me help you. Let the police know of any crime.* **3** Sometimes, ***let out***: °rent (out), °hire (out), °lease (out), °charter (out); °contract (out), subcontract (out), °farm (out), °job (out): *Mrs Finney lets rooms by the week. Much of the work is let out to people who work at home.* **4** ***let down***: °disappoint, °fail, °frustrate; disenchant, dissatisfy, °disillusion: *He promised to be here at nine, but he let me down.* **5** ***let in***: °admit, °allow in; °include, °take in, °receive, °welcome, °induct, °install *or* instal: *I'll just open a window and let in some fresh air. I wouldn't want to be a member of a club that would let in someone like me.* **6** ***let off***: **a** °pardon, °forgive, °excuse, °release, °discharge, let go: *They let him off with only a severe reprimand.* **b** exonerate, absolve, °clear, acquit, °vindicate, *Slang* let off the °hook: *When the real culprit confessed, she was let off.* **c** detonate, °explode, °discharge, °fire, °set off: *Don't let off those fireworks so near the haystack.* **d** °emit, °give out *or* off, °release, °throw off *or* out, let °loose, exude: *Some plastics let off an awful smell when they burn.* **7** ***let on***: **a** °confess, °admit, °disclose, divulge, °reveal, expose, let it be known, let out, °say, °tell, °give away, let °slip, °betray; °leak: *I'll never let on that you are to blame.* **b** feign, °affect, °pretend, °fake, (°put on an) °act, simulate, dissemble, °dissimulate: *He let on that he had a bad leg and couldn't play in the match, when in fact he just wanted to go away for the weekend.* **8** ***let out***: **a** See **7 a,** above. **b** (let) °loose, °liberate, (°set) °free, °release, let go, °discharge: *He served three years before being let out. Let the cat out, will you.* **c** °emit, give °vent to, °produce: *She let out a scream that could have woken the dead.* **d** °end, °stop, °break up, °finish, °close, °terminate: *When does school let out for the Christmas holidays?* **9** ***let up***: °decrease, abate, °ease (up), slacken, °diminish, lessen, °mitigate, °subside, °moderate: *Perhaps we can still go if the rain lets up soon.* **10** ***let up on***: °ease up on, °slack off on: *He didn't let up on haranguing us for an hour.*

let[2] *n.* °hindrance, °impediment, °obstruction, °obstacle: *People can now cross the border without let or hindrance.*

let-down *n.* °disappointment, disillusionment, disenchantment: *She had practised so hard that losing was all the more of a let-down.*

lethal *adj.* °deadly, °fatal, °mortal: *The lethal blow was delivered by a blunt instrument.*

lethargic *adj.* **1** lethargical, sluggish, °slow, °dull, °heavy, °lazy, °indolent, °phlegmatic, °slothful, °idle, languid, languorous, °listless, fainéant, °inactive, °torpid, stuporous, comatose; °indifferent, apathetic: *They were so lethargic that they did absolutely nothing about it.* **2** °weary, °tired, fagged out, °fatigued, enervated, °weak, °exhausted, °drowsy, °sleepy, somnolent: *I have a bad cold and feel very lethargic.*

lethargy *n.* **1** °sluggishness, °sloth, dullness, heaviness, laziness, °indolence, phlegm, °idleness, languidness, languor, listlessness, *dolce far niente*, °inactivity, °inertia, °torpor, °stupor; °indifference, apathy: *After taking the medicine, a feeling of lethargy overtook me.* **2** weariness, tiredness, °fatigue, °weakness, °exhaustion, drowsiness, sleepiness, somnolence: *The strident persistence of my alarm clock dragged me out of my lethargy.*

letter *n.* **1** °character, °symbol, °sign: *Epsilon is a letter in the Greek alphabet.* **2** °missive, epistle, communication, °note, °line, °message, °dispatch *or* despatch; correspondence: *Write me a letter when you get there.* **3** ***letters***: °literature, the humanities, belles-lettres, the classics; erudition, °culture, the world of letters, °learning, °scholarship: *He is a widely known man of letters.* **4** ***to the letter***: °precisely, °literally, °exactly, accurately, strictly, *sic*, °thus, letter for letter, *literatim*, °word for word, °verbatim: *The document has been copied to the letter.*
—*v.* **5** inscribe, °write, °spell (out): *She carefully lettered the caption under the picture.*

lettered *adj.* literate, °literary, (well-)°educated, erudite, °scholarly, °learned, °well-informed, °enlightened, °knowledgeable, (well-)°versed, well-read, cultured, °cultivated: *He was greatly influenced by the lettered men of his time.*

let-up *n.* °cease, °stop, stopping, ceasing, cessation, surcease, °break, °interruption, °pause, °intermission, °suspension, °time out *or* off; moderation, lessening, abatement, diminution, °relief, hesitation, °respite, °relaxation: *I was nagged without let-up about getting the work done by the end of the month.*

level *adj.* **1** °even, °smooth, °plane, °uniform, °plain, °flat, °flush, °straight, °true: *The plaster is not level enough to apply the wallpaper.* **2** °horizontal; °prone, °supine: *Make sure the playing field is level. Try to keep the body level when doing this exercise.* **3** °uniform, °constant, °steady, °consistent, °invariable, unvarying, unalterable, unchanging, unfluctuating; °very: *I did my level best to warn him, but he wouldn't listen.* **4** °parallel, °even, °equal, °equivalent, °consistent: *The top floor of my house is level with the roof of the one across the street. The problem arises because wages are not level with inflation.* **5** up (on), °informed (about *or* on), up to °date (on *or* with), *au fait* (with), *au courant* (with): *He does his best to keep level with what is going on in the world.* **6** °even, tied, °equal, neck and neck: *The scores are level. So at half-time, it's level pegging between Arsenal and Liverpool.* **7** See **level-headed,** below.
—*v.* **8** level off, °even, °smooth (out), °flatten (out): *The concrete is levelled by dragging a straight-edge over it.* **9** °destroy, °demolish, °raze, lay °waste, °devastate, °knock down, °tear down, °pull down, °wreck, bulldoze: *The building was levelled in a matter of minutes.* **10** °aim, °point, draw a bead, °direct, °train, °focus: *He levelled his gun at her and she screamed.* **11** ***level with***: be *or* play °fair with, be °honest *or* °straight with, be °open *or* °frank *or* straightforward with, *Colloq* be upfront with: *I am going to level with you—I find you very difficult to work with.*
—*n.* **12** °plane, °horizontal, °elevation, °height; altitude: *The windows are at the same level.* **13** °floor, °storey: *On which level is Mr Stone's office?* **14** °plane, °position, °status, °standing, °rank, °stage: *She functions at a higher level, both administratively and intellectually.* **15** ***on the level***: °straight, straightforward, °honest, °direct, °sincere, °square, °open, °aboveboard, *Colloq* upfront, on the up and up, *US* straight-shooting: *You haven't been on the level with me about your plans for the company.*

level-headed *adj.* (well-)balanced, °sensible, °sane, °reasonable, commonsensical, °level, unruffled, undisturbed, unperturbed, imperturbable, even-tempered, composed, °calm, °cool, °collected, °tranquil, °serene, unflappable, °poised, °relaxed, °self-possessed: *Even when she was a teenager, Fran was quite level-headed.*

levity *n.* light-heartedness, lightness, frivolity, frivolousness, °flippancy, trivialization, °triviality, facetiousness: *Politics is a weighty business and should not be treated with levity.*

lewd *adj.* °lascivious, salacious, °lecherous, °lustful, licentious, °carnal, goatish, hircine, satyric(al), ruttish, concupiscent, libidinous, lubricious *or* lubricous, °indecent, °offensive, °wild, debauched, °obscene, smutty, °crude, °dirty, °foul, °filthy, °rude, °pornographic, °prurient, °gross, °dissolute, Fescennine, °bawdy, ribald, °scurrilous, °raw, °blue, °erotic, °suggestive, °unchaste, unvirtuous, *Colloq* °randy, *Slang* °hot, horny: *He is said to have chronicled the lewd goings-on at the Hellfire Club.*

liability *n.* **1** answerability, °responsibility, °burden, onus, °accountability: *Who bears the liability for the company's losses?* **2** °obligation, °debt, indebtedness, arrear(s), debit: *Outstanding shares are treated as a liability of the corporation.* **3** °disadvantage, °drawback, °hindrance, °impediment, °encumbrance, °snag, °hitch, °barrier, °obstacle, °obstruction, °burden, onus: *Her biggest liability is her inability to read.* **4** °exposure, susceptibility, vulnerability: *The insurer's liability is spread amongst many underwriters.*

liable *adj.* **1** °likely, apt, °prone, °inclined, °disposed: *She is liable to want payment for her contribution.* **2** answerable, °responsible, °accountable, obligated, blameable, blameworthy, *Law* actionable: *An owner is liable for damage done by his dog.* **3** exposed, °susceptible, °vulnerable, °open, °subject: *Certain kinds of plants are more liable to disease.*

liaison *n.* **1** °connection, communication, °contact, linkage, affiliation, °relationship, relations: *Liaison between the ministries is improving.* **2** °contact, °intermediary, °link, °tie, °medium, °go-between, °agent: *She acts as liaison between the heads of research and manufacturing.* **3** (°love) °affair, amour, °relationship, *affaire d'amour*, *affaire de cœur*, °intrigue, °romance, entanglement, flirtation: *David's wife soon found out about his liaison with the girl in the typing pool.*

liar *n.* fabricator, prevaricator, perjurer, falsifier, teller of tales, °false witness, Ananias, Baron von Münchhausen, *Colloq* fibber: *He's a liar if he says he saw me that night—I was ill in bed.*

libel *n.* **1** defamation, vilification, denigration, denunciation, deprecation, depreciation, belittlement, disparagement, derogation, °disgrace, °ill repute, °dishonour, obloquy, °shame, °humiliation, mortification: *His entire conversation is a perpetual libel on his acquaintances.* **2** °slander, calumny, °lie, °falsehood, prevarication, untruth, misrepresentation, °aspersion, °innuendo, insinuation, °slur, °smear, °blot, °stain, smirch, °stigma: *For years he suffered the libels circulated by his ex-mistress.*
—*v.* **3** defame, °vilify, denigrate, °denounce, deprecate, °depreciate, °belittle, °disparage, derogate, °disgrace, °dishonour, °shame, °humiliate, °mortify: *He claims to have been libelled by an article in the newspaper.* **4** °slander, calumniate, °lie about, °misrepresent, asperse, °insinuate, °slur, °smear, malign, °stain, °blacken, °discredit, besmirch, °stigmatize, traduce, °vilify, *Rare* vilipend, *Colloq chiefly US* bad-mouth: *There is often a fine line between libelling a person and exercising freedom of speech.*

liberal *adj.* **1** °generous, °bountiful, °free, open-hearted, °open, open-handed, bounteous, °charitable, °philanthropic, munificent, magnanimous, °big, big-hearted, unstinting, °unselfish, unsparing; °lavish, °abundant, °ample, °large, °handsome, °plentiful, copious: *Lady Browning is a liberal benefactor of our cause. Thank you for your liberal contributions.* **2** °progressive, libertarian, reformist, humanistic, °left (of centre), latitudinarian, °non-partisan, unaligned *or* °non-aligned, individualistic, *South African* verligte: *The liberal voters found little to attract them in the latest election.* **3** °free, not literal, °flexible, °lenient, °loose, °broad, °open, °disinterested, °impartial, °dispassionate, °fair, broad-minded, open-minded, °unprejudiced, unbigoted, unjaundiced, unopinionated, °tolerant: *That judge is known for his liberal interpretation of the law.*
—*n.* **4** °progressive, libertarian, reformer, progressivist, latitudinarian, °independent, freethinker, leftist, left-winger, *South African* verligte: *They think of themselves as liberals, not as conservatives.*

liberalize *v.* **1** broaden, °widen, °extend, °expand, °stretch, °enlarge: *The purpose of the law is to liberalize the functions of solicitors.* **2** °loosen, °ease, slacken, °relax, °modify, °change, °moderate, °soften: *The police really ought to liberalize the parking regulations in this area.*

liberate *v.* **1** (set) °free, °release, set at °liberty, disenthral, °emancipate, manumit, °deliver, enfranchise, (°let) °loose, °let go, °let out, °let off: *When the enemy retreated, the army liberated the prisoners of war. After her divorce, she felt like a liberated woman.* **2** °steal, °pilfer, purloin, °take, °appropriate: *She was caught liberating some books from the library.*

liberation *n.* freeing, liberating, deliverance, emancipation, enfranchisement, enfranchising, °delivery, °rescue, rescuing, °release, releasing, loosing, unfettering, unshackling, unchaining: *The liberation of the prisoners occurred on May Day, 1945.*

libertine *n.* **1** lecher, °reprobate, °profligate, °rake, rakehell, °roué, debaucher, womanizer, °seducer, fornicator, adulterer, debauchee, whoremonger, °philanderer, Don Juan, Lothario, Casanova, *Colloq* wolf, lady-killer, (old) goat, dirty old man: *He fancied himself a libertine, but women shunned him like the plague.*
—*adj.* **2** licentious, °lecherous, °reprobate, °profligate, °rakish, rakehell, philandering, °dissolute, °immoral, °degenerate, depraved, debauched, °decadent, °dirty, °filthy, amoral, °wanton, °lewd, °lascivious, °prurient, lubricious *or* lubricous, salacious, Paphian, libidinous, ruttish, goatish, hircine, satyric(al), °carnal, bestial, *Colloq* °randy, *Slang* horny: *A paragon of prudery to his family, Viscount Guarnier secretly led a life of wild, libertine abandon.*

liberty *n.* **1** °freedom, °independence, self-determination, autonomy, self-rule, °self-government, self-direction, °sovereignty: *People have always been willing to die for their liberty.* **2** °right, °freedom, franchise, *carte blanche*, °privilege, °prerogative, °licence, °leave, °permission, authorization: *I was given the liberty to go where I pleased.* **3** °freedom, °licence, °initiative, °exemption, °exception, °privilege: *On a strict diet, she allowed herself no liberties whatever.* **4** ***at liberty***: °free, °uninhibited, unfettered, unconstrained, unrestricted, unrestrained, liberated: *I was at liberty to do as I pleased.* **5** ***take a liberty*** *or* ***the liberty*** *or often* ***liberties***: be unrestrained *or* °presumptuous *or* °bold *or* °uninhibited *or* overfamiliar *or* forward *or* °aggressive *or* °impudent *or* °impertinent *or* °audacious *or* °improper; display *or* exercise boldness *or* °impropriety *or* °presumption *or* presumptuousness *or* indecorum *or* unseemliness *or* boldness *or* °arrogance: *She thought he was taking liberties in asking her to dance. I took the liberty of asking her to accompany me.*

licence *n.* **1** °leave, °permission, °liberty, authorization, °authority, entitlement, dispensation, °right, *carte blanche*, °freedom, latitude, °free °choice, °privilege, °charter: *Merely being eighteen does not give you licence to do exactly as you please.* **2** °permit, certificate, credential(s), °paper(s): *Bring along your driving licence.* **3** °disregard, deviation, departure, nonconformity, °non-compliance, divergence: *Such grammatical abnormalities are an exercise of poetic licence.*

license *v.* **1** °authorize, °allow, °permit, °certify, °sanction, °approve, commission: *The government once had the power to license books for publication.* **2** °certify, °document, accredit, °entitle, validate, °enable, empower: *Whoever licensed him to drive a car made a grave mistake.*

lie[1] *v.* **1** prevaricate, °fabricate, °misrepresent, °invent, commit °perjury, perjure *or* forswear oneself, *Colloq* °fib: *If he says that I ate the last cake, he's lying.* —*n.* **2** °falsehood, untruth, falsification, misrepresentation, fiction, °invention, prevarication, °fib, °fabrication, *Colloq* °story, cock-and-bull °story, (tall) °tale, whopper, *US* fish °story, fish °tale: *His claim of having been attacked was found to be a lie.*

lie[2] *v.* **1** °recline, °stretch out, be °prostrate *or* °recumbent *or* °prone *or* °supine: *I'm going to lie down for a nap before dinner.* **2** °rest, °repose; can be found, be, be situated: *The book is lying on the table. The land lies on the Berkshire–Surrey border.* **3** °rest, °repose, be, reside, °dwell, °abide, °remain, °belong: *The responsibility lies with you.* **4** °press, °burden, °weigh, °rest, be: *The onus for the crime lies heavily on him.* **5** ***lie low***: °hide, remain concealed *or* in hiding, keep out of sight, *Colloq Brit* lie doggo: *You'd better lie low till the affair is forgotten.* —*n.* **6** ***lie of the land***: °state, °status, °condition, °situation, °atmosphere, °mood, °spirit, °temper, °character: *You ought to determine the lie of the land before submitting your proposal.*

life *n.* **1** °existence, entity, being; sentience, viability: *Who can imagine the possible forms of life in the universe?* **2** °existence, survival, living, °subsistence, °sustenance: *Certain nutriments are necessary to life on earth.* **3** °existence, living, °way of life, lifestyle: *What kind of life does he lead? I enjoy country life.* **4** °existence, lifetime, °time; duration: *She did much during her short life. The life of a light-bulb depends on how often it is switched off and on.* **5** °person, °mortal, °human (being), °individual, °soul: *The new drug might save millions of lives.* **6** biography, autobiography, °memoir(s), (life) °story: *He has written a life of Mozart.* **7** °soul, °spirit, °spark of life, °vital °spark, °moving °spirit, life-force, *élan vital*; lifeblood; °animation, °vitality, liveliness, sprightliness, vivacity, °sparkle, °dazzle, °dash, élan, °vigour, °verve, °zest, °flavour, pungency, freshness, effervescence, brio, °flair, vim, °energy, °exuberance, °enthusiasm, *Colloq* °pep, zing, get-up-and-go: *We must breathe some life into these people. Eva is always the life of the party.* **8** °obsession, preoccupation, °passion, °fixation, compulsion: *Model railways are his life.* **9** °bounce, °resilience, °spring, °elasticity: *There's no life in this old tennis ball.*

lifeless *adj.* **1** °dead: *I stared at the lifeless body of the man.* **2** °unconscious, °inanimate, insensate, °inert, unmoving, °dead, °insensible: *At the news of the accident, she sank, lifeless, to the floor.* **3** °dull, °boring, °tiresome, °heavy, °lacklustre, °torpid, °tedious, °flat, °stale, uninteresting, °colourless, uninspiring, °vapid, °wooden: *The production was a success apart from Ellen's lifeless performance as Portia.* **4** °barren, °desert, °desolate, °bare, °sterile, °bleak, °empty, °uninhabited, unoccupied, °dreary, °waste: *We gazed at the lifeless landscape of the moon.*

lifelike *adj.* °authentic, °realistic, °natural, °true to life, °real, °faithful, °graphic, °vivid: *She painted a very lifelike picture of her cat.*

lift *v.* **1** °raise, elevate; °hoist, °heave (up): *She lifted her eyes to the heavens. The pallbearers lifted the coffin to their shoulders.* **2** Often, ***lift up***: °exalt, °raise, elevate, uplift, °boost, upgrade, °promote, °advance; °improve, ameliorate, °better, °dignify, °enhance, ennoble, enshrine, deify, °immortalize: *His unusual talents lifted him up from the ranks of ordinary mortals.* **3** °discontinue, °end, °terminate, °stop: *The siege was lifted after six months.* **4** °withdraw, °cancel, °confiscate, °take away, rescind, °void, annul: *They charged him with driving while intoxicated and lifted his licence.* **5** °rise, °disappear, °dissipate, vanish: *When the fog lifted, I saw that we were about to run aground.* **6** °steal, °appropriate, °pilfer, °pocket, thieve, °take, purloin; plagiarize, °copy, *Colloq* °pinch, crib, °liberate, *Slang Brit* °nick, *Old-fashioned* half-inch: *He went into the supermarket and lifted a bottle of scotch. This passage was lifted from my book in its entirety.* —*n.* **7** °ride: *She looked tired so I gave her a lift home.* **8** *In US and Canada*: elevator: *Take the lift to the tenth floor.* **9** °encouragement, °boost, stimulus, °inducement, °inspiration, reassurance, cheering up, *Colloq* °shot in the arm: *Winning first prize has given Susan the lift she needed to continue with her writing.*

light[1] *n.* **1** °illumination, brightness, °daylight, lamplight, candlelight, firelight, gaslight, torchlight, starlight, moonlight, sunlight; gegenschein, counterglow: *There is just enough light for me to read the label.* **2** lamp, light-bulb, torch, °beacon, lantern, candle, °flare, headlight *or* headlamp, street-light *or* street lamp, *US and Canadian* flashlight: *I saw a light in the distance. Someone turned off the lights.* **3** °radiance, °radiation, luminescence, °glare, °gleam, °glow, °reflection, luminosity, °shine, °sparkle, scintillation, incandescence, phosphorescence, fluorescence: *The light of the full moon shone through the window.* **4** daybreak, °dawn, sunrise, *US* sun-up: *We leave at first light.* **5** clarification, enlightenment, °insight, °understanding, elucidation, simplification, °explanation: *After an hour's talk with his lawyer, he finally saw the light and confessed. Can you shed a little light on this problem, Robyn?* **6** window, window-pane: *The west wall has three windows of six lights each.* **7** match, lighter, spill, taper, fire, flame, ignition: *Can you give me a light for my cigarette?* **8** highlight: *Note the chiaroscuro effect from the lights and shadows in the drawing.* **9** ***bring to light***: °reveal, °unearth, °find, uncover, °unveil, °discover, expose, °disclose, °make known: *A vital fact has recently been brought to light.* **10** ***come to light***: be revealed, be unearthed, be uncovered, be unveiled, be discovered, be exposed, be disclosed, °appear, °come out, °turn up, °transpire, °develop, evolve, °emerge: *The truth about her parents has finally come to light.* **11** *Brit* ***in the light of*** *or US* ***in light of***: considering, in view of, in consideration of, taking into account, keeping *or* bearing in °mind: *In the light of his condition, he has decided to pull out of the competition.* **12** ***shed*** *or* ***throw (some, a little) light on***: °explain, elucidate, °simplify, °clarify: *Perhaps you could throw some light on the reason why she refuses to leave the house.* —*adj.* **13** (well-)illuminated, °bright, alight, (well-)lit, (well-)lighted, shining, °luminous, effulgent, °brilliant, beaming, °incandescent, phosphorescent, fluorescent: *The lightest room in the house is the kitchen.* **14** °pale, light-hued: *Put the light blue chair over here.* —*v.* **15** ignite, set alight, set *or* put a match to, °kindle; °burn, °touch off, set °fire to, °fire: *It's getting chilly, so you'd better light the fire. When the bomb was in place, they lit the fuse.* **16** °illuminate, °light up, °lighten, °brighten: *Take this candle to light your way to the bedroom.* **17** °turn on, °switch on, °put on: *Light the lamps.* **18** ***light up***: °lighten, °brighten, °cheer up, °liven up: *The moment she walked in, the whole room lit up. Her face lit up when she saw him.*

light[2] *adj.* **1** lightweight, °portable: *I bought some light garden furniture.* **2** underweight, °skinny, °slight: *Isn't Ted a bit light for his height?* **3** °faint, °dim, °obscure, °indistinct, unclear, faded, °imperceptible: *There is a very light pencil mark on the paper.* **4** °faint, °gentle, °mild, °slight, °delicate, °insignificant: *A light breeze rippled the surface of the pool.* **5** °dainty, °graceful, °delicate, °gentle, °slight: *He felt the light brush of her lips on his.* **6** not °weighty, °frivolous, unimportant, °insignificant, °inconsequential, inconsiderable, trivial, °trifling, evanescent, unsubstantial, °slight, °superficial: *The party was a very light affair.* **7** °nimble, °agile, °active, °swift, spry, lithe, °sprightly, lightsome, light-footed, limber, lissom *or* lissome: *When dancing, he may be light on his feet, but he's not very light on mine.* **8** simple-minded, light-headed, °scatterbrained, rattle-brained, bird-brained, feather-brained, °hare-brained, °flighty, °giddy, °dizzy, °silly, °inane, °foolish, °frivolous, empty-headed, °vacant, vacuous, °shallow, °superficial: *Featherstone is a bit too light in the head to be a good manager.* **9** °cheerful, °happy, °gay, °sunny, °merry, light-hearted, happy-go-lucky, °easygoing, °joyful, jovial, °jolly: *Noël has written another light drawing-room comedy.* **10** °easy, not °burdensome, endurable, °bearable, °tolerable, °supportable, undemanding, °effortless, untaxing, °moderate: *After my surgery, I was able to resume light duties at the office. The tax on such a small income is very light. You should take some light exercise every day.* **11** amusing, °entertaining, °witty, diverting: *The book hasn't much substance, but it makes good light reading.* **12** ***make light of***: °dismiss, °write off, shrug off; °trivialize; °ridicule: *The teacher made light of my attempts to play the concerto.*

—*v.* **13** alight, °land, °come *or* °go down, °descend, °settle; deplane, °disembark *or* debark, detrain, dismount: *The bird was so tame it lighted on my finger.* **14** ***light into***: °attack, assail, °lambaste, °assault, °pounce *or* °fall on *or* upon, °beat, °belabour; °abuse, tongue-lash, °harangue, °upbraid, °scold, °berate, *Colloq* °lace into; *Slang* clobber: *He really lit into the challenger in the third round. Her mother lit into her for not doing her homework.* **15** ***light on*** or ***upon***: °chance *or* °happen *or* °stumble *or* °hit on *or* upon, °come across, °encounter, °find, °meet up with: *She claimed she lit upon the formula when reading some ancient hieroglyphics.*

lighten[1] *v.* **1** °illuminate, °brighten, °light up: *Opening the curtains would lighten up the room.* **2** °cheer (up), °brighten, °gladden, °shine; °smile: *Her face lightened when he said he would be home for the holidays.*

lighten[2] *v.* disencumber, disburden, °relieve, alleviate, °reduce, lessen, °mitigate: *To lighten my load, I had left my suitcase at the hotel.*

like[1] *adj., adv.* **1** °similar (to), °akin (to), allied (to), °parallel (to *or* with), comparable (to *or* with), °equivalent (to), °equal (to), °identical (to), cognate (with), analogous (to), corresponding (to), °correspondent (to), °close (to), homologous (to *or* with), of a piece (with), (much) the °same (as), along the °same lines (as), not °unlike: *We hold like opinions. Her opinions are like mine. Her pies are like the ones my mother used to bake. Problems like this give me a headache. Opposite charges attract, like charges repel.* **2** in the °mood for, °disposed to: *Do you feel like a walk in the park? He felt like going with me.*

—*adv.* **3** as if, as °though: *He ran like mad.*

—*prep.* **4** °similar to, °identical to *or* with: *Her daughter looks like her. He makes her feel like a perfect fool.* **5** in the °same °way as, in the °manner of, similarly to: *Sometimes she acts like a maniac. The jacket fits him like a glove. He laughed like a drain. He treats his mother like a child.* **6** such as, for °example, for °instance, e.g., that is (to say), i.e., in other words, °namely, to wit, viz.: *Mistletoe grows on various trees, like oaks and birches.*

—*n.* **7** °match, °equal, °peer, °fellow, °opposite °number, counterpart, °twin: *It is doubtful that we shall see his like again.* **8** °same *or* °similar °kind *or* °sort *or* ilk *or* °type *or* kidney *or* °breed *or* °mould *or* °cast *or* °strain: *The book deals with music, literature, theatre, painting, and the like.*

like[2] *v.* **1** be °fond of, °approve of, °appreciate, be °partial to, °have a fondness *or* °liking for, have a °weakness for, °take to, °delight in, °take °pleasure in, °derive *or* get °pleasure from, find °agreeable *or* congenial, feel attracted to, be *or* feel °favourably impressed by, °relish, °love, °adore, adulate, *Colloq* take a °shine to, *Slang* °go for, °dig, get a kick out of, *US* °get off on, °groove on, get a bang *or* a charge out of: *She likes a day at the seaside. He likes chocolate ice-cream. I think she likes me.* **2** Usually, ***would*** or ***should like***: °prefer, °want, °wish, °ask: *I would like you to try to get to work on time in future. I'd like a drink.*

—*n.* **3** Usually, ***likes***: °preference, °partiality, predilection, °liking: *We all have our different likes and dislikes.*

likeable *adj.* °likeable, °genial, °amiable, congenial, °pleasant, *simpatico*, °agreeable, °pleasing, °attractive, appealing, °nice, °friendly, °winning, charming, °engaging, °good-natured, winsome: *He is likeable enough, but not my ideal son-in-law.*

likelihood *n.* °probability, strong *or* distinct °possibility, good °chance: *We must consider the likelihood that she will refuse to go.*

likely *adj.* **1** °probable, °liable, expected: *Three o'clock is the likely arrival time.* **2** °probable, conceivable, °reasonable, credible, °plausible, °tenable: *It seemed likely that Holmes would solve the case.* **3** °fitting, °able, °suitable, °probable, °seemly, °meet, °right, °proper, °qualified, °acceptable, °appropriate, apposite; °favourite, odds-on, °favoured, °promising: *Peters is the likely man for the job.* **4** °disposed to, apt to, °inclined to, °liable to: *It's likely to rain. You're likely to think me mad, but I have my reasons for going.*

—*adv.* **5** °probably, °undoubtedly, indubitably, no °doubt, in all °probability, *Colloq* like as not: *You would most likely say that I am wrong. He will very likely win the election.*

liken *v.* °compare, equate, °match, juxtapose: *How can you liken him to Mahatma Gandhi?*

likeness *n.* **1** similarity, °resemblance, correspondence, analogy, °agreement, parallelism: *The artist has caught her likeness in the second painting.* **2** °copy, °replica, °facsimile, °duplicate, °reproduction, °model, °representation, °portrait, painting, °picture, °drawing, °photograph, °sculpture, °statue, statuette, °image, simulacrum, icon *or* ikon: *He sells miniature likenesses of the Eiffel Tower to tourists.* **3** °appearance, °face, °figure, °image: *The premier's likeness appears on posters throughout the country.*

likewise *adv.* **1** similarly, in the °same *or* °like °manner *or* °way: *Penny is sitting quietly and you should do likewise.* **2** as well, too, also, furthermore, °further, °besides, in °addition, °moreover, to °boot: *There are many ways to take exercise and, likewise, many ways to avoid it.*

liking *n.* **1** °affinity, fondness, °affection, °love, °partiality, °bias, °preference, °bent, predilection, predisposition, °inclination, °appreciation, °penchant; °eye, °appetite, soft spot, °weakness: *He has a liking for good claret and beautiful women.* **2** °taste, °pleasure, °fancy, °preference: *The chef will prepare the steak to your liking.*

limbo *n.* ***in limbo***: up in the air, consigned to °oblivion, in °abeyance, suspended, hanging (°fire), neither here nor there, *Colloq* on hold, treading water, holding one's breath, *US* in a holding pattern, on the shelf, on the back burner: *My career is in limbo till I learn the result of the interview.*

limit *n.* **1** Sometimes, ***limits***: °extent, °bound(s), °end, limitation, °check, °curb, °restriction, °restraint: *Is there no limit to how far you will go to get your own way?* **2** Often, ***limits***: °border, °edge, °end, °extent, °boundary, °bound(s), (°boundary *or* °border *or* °partition) °line, °frontier, °perimeter, °periphery: *That row of poplars marks the limit of the property to the east.* **3** Often, ***limits***: °area, °territory, confines, °zone, °region, °quarter, °district, °precinct(s): *Stay outside the three-mile limit. We have jurisdiction only within city limits.* **4** ***the limit***: **a** the °end, the °last straw, the straw that broke the camel's back, all (that) one can °take, °enough, too much, *Colloq* it: *Your presumption is the absolute limit—you can't seriously expect me to lend you money.* **b** °outrage, °joke, °surprise, *Colloq* caution: *Wasn't Nigel the limit in that hat!?*

—*v.* **5** °check, °curb, °bridle, °restrict, °restrain, °hold in °check: *We must limit spending on arms. The shackles limited my movements.* **6** °restrict, confine, delimit, °narrow, °focus, °guide, °channel: *Please limit your questions to the subject at hand.* **7** °set, °define, °determine, °fix: *The bank manager has limited my overdraft to half what it was.*

limited *adj.* **1** circumscribed, restricted, °fixed, °predetermined; °small, °little, reduced, °minimal: *The theatre seats a limited number of people. She was awarded limited access to the children.* **2** °narrow, restricted, restrictive, °meagre: *Few original ideas presented themselves to his limited imagination.*

limitless *adj.* unrestricted, unrestrained, unconfined, unbounded, °boundless, °extensive, °vast, °immense, °enormous, °unlimited, illimitable; interminable, unceasing, incessant, undefined, °immeasurable, innumerable, °numberless, countless, myriad, unending, °perpetual, °everlasting, °eternal: *Dickens possessed a seemingly limitless capacity for characterization. In the depths of space exist limitless numbers of stars. God's love is limitless.*

limp[1] *v.* **1** °hobble, °stagger, °totter, dodder, falter: *He limped slowly along the road.*
—*n.* **2** °hobble, hobbling, °stagger, staggering, °totter, tottering, dodder, °doddering, falter, faltering, claudication, *Slang US* gimp: *He was easy to recognize at a distance because of his limp.*

limp[2] *adj.* **1** flaccid, °flabby, °lax, °slack, °soft, drooping, °relaxed, unstarched, unstiffened, °flexible, °pliable, floppy, °loose: *The banners hung limp in the still, sultry air.* **2** °exhausted, °tired, °fatigued, °worn out, °spent, enervated, wasted, debilitated, °weak, °feeble, °frail: *He felt limp with exhaustion after the day's hiking.* **3** °weak, °feeble, °ineffective, °ineffectual, °flimsy, °half-hearted, °lukewarm, °spineless, thewless, namby-pamby, *Colloq* °wishy-washy, *Slang* gutless: *Having to visit her grandmother seemed a pretty limp excuse to me.*

line[1] *n.* **1** °mark, pencil-mark, pen-mark, °rule, °score; °stroke, underline, underscore; diagonal, °slash, virgule, shilling-mark, solidus, separatrix, °oblique: *The lines on this paper are very faint. Draw a red line under your name. A line separates the numerator from the denominator.* **2** °strip, °belt, °stripe, °band, °border, °edge, edging: *Do you see that line of trees? Put a heavy black line round the obituary notices.* **3** °wrinkle, crease, crinkle, °furrow, crow's-foot: *He has many lines on his face. The palmist said I have a long lifeline.* **4** °border, borderline, °frontier, °limit, °boundary; demarcation, °threshold: *We crossed the line into Italy. I don't mind cooking dinner, but I draw the line at washing the dishes. There is a fine line between genius and insanity.* **5** °outline, °silhouette, contour, °figure, °profile: *The line of the skirt is too straight.* **6** °row, °rank, column, °file, °train, °parade, cortege *or* cortège, °procession, *Brit* °queue, *Colloq Brit* crocodile, tailback: *I stood in line for six hours for tickets. The line wound all the way round the block.* **7** °field, °area, °activity, °forte, °speciality *or chiefly US and Canadian also* specialty, specialization, °business, °profession, °occupation, (line of) °work, °job, °vocation, °pursuit, °trade, °calling, °employment, *Colloq* °racket, °game: *Saying that he was a computer programmer, he asked me my line.* **8** °note, °word, °card, postcard, °letter, *US* postal °card: *Drop me a line when you get there.* **9** °course, °direction, °path, °way, °route, °road, °track, °procedure, °tack, °policy, °strategy, °tactic(s), °approach, °plan: *What line will our competitors take to win the account? I adopted the line of least resistance.* **10** °information, °data, °word, °lead, °clue, °hint: *Interpol is trying to get a line on where he might be found.* **11** °cord, °string, °thread, °twine, °yarn, strand, filament, °rope, °cable, hawser: *The anchor line became entangled. Hang the clothes out on the line.* **12** °track, °railway *or US and Canadian also* °railroad: *The accident on the southern line is delaying all the trains.* **13** telephone, wire, °cable: *We have three lines at the office. He tried all day to get you on the line.* **14** °front (line), vanguard, °formation: *These men have been in the line for weeks. Captain Hughes was given command of a ship of the line.* **15** ancestry, descent, °stock, °lineage, °succession, °family, °parentage, °extraction, °heritage, genealogy: *She comes from a long line of horsewomen.* **16** °assortment, °stock, °merchandise, offerings, °goods, °brand, °make, °type, °kind, °variety: *What line of lawnmower do you distribute?* **17** Often, ***lines***: °part, °role, °speech, °script, °words, *Theatre US* sides: *I know my lines by heart for the school play. She has one line in the third act.* **18** °story, (sales) pitch, blarney, *Colloq* spiel, °song and dance, *Slang* con: *He handed her a line about being lonely, but she soon found out why.* **19** ***in*** *or* ***into line***: **a** aligned, in alignment, °true, °straight, in a °row, °plumb: *Bring the balusters for the railing in line.* **b** in °agreement, in °accord, in accordance, in conformity, in °step, in °harmony, *US* lined up: *We are bringing the staffing requirements into line with the council's recommendations.* **c** Usually, ***into line***: under *or* in °control: *Were you able to bring the other board members into line?* **20** ***in line for***: °ready for, short-listed for, on the short list for, up for, being considered for, under °consideration for, a °candidate for, in the °running for: *We all think she's in line for a promotion.*
—*v.* **21** °rule, inscribe, °score, underline, underscore: *If you use lined paper, your writing won't be so wavy.* **22** °edge, °border, °fringe: *Millions lined the streets for the parade.* **23** ***line up***: **a** °organize, °prepare, °ready, °assemble, °set up, °put *or* °set in °place, °develop, °formulate, °arrange (for), °coordinate: *Everything is all lined up for the big event.* **b** °arrange for, °secure, °get (°hold of), °obtain, °contract for; uncover, °dig up, °acquire, °engage, °hire, °sign (up), °contract with, °employ: *We lined up an excellent after-dinner speaker.* **c** °queue (up), °form a line, °get in line, °form ranks *or* columns: *Hundreds of us lined up for meals three times a day.* **d** align, array, °straighten, °order: *These paragraphs should line up. Line up the troops for inspection at 0600.*

line[2] *v.* **1** interline, °cover, °face; ceil: *The coat is lined with fur.* **2** ***line one's pockets***: accept °bribes, °graft, *US* °sell out, *Colloq US* be on the take: *He was secretly lining his pockets during his years on the council.*

lineage *n.* **1** °extraction, ancestry, °family tree, °pedigree, descent, °stock, bloodline, °parentage, genealogy: *She has spent a lot of time tracing the lineage of the village's families.* **2** forebears, forefathers, foremothers, °family, °people, °clan; descendants, °succession, °progeny, °offspring: *Does Debrett list his lineage? Peerages were confined to the lineage of the person ennobled.*

linen *n.* Often, ***linens***: bedclothes, bed linen(s), °sheets and pillowcases; table linen(s), napery, tablecloths and napkins; bath linen(s), towels and wash-cloths: *The soiled linen is sent to the laundry.*

linger *v.* **1** Sometimes, ***linger on***: °stay (behind), °remain, °tarry, loiter, °persist, °hang on, °endure, °persevere, °survive, *Colloq* °hang *or* °stick about *or* around: *The smell of tobacco lingered for hours after he had gone. He lingered on for a day, then died from his wounds.* **2** °pause, °dawdle, dally, °lag, °idle: *She lingered for a moment at the jeweller's window.* **3** Often, ***linger on*** *or* ***over***: °dwell on, °elaborate, harp on, °labour: *I shall not linger over the details of the crime.* **4** °procrastinate, dither, °shilly-shally, temporize: *You must stop lingering and decide today.*

lingering *adj.* **1** °long, °persistent, °protracted, °remaining: *I was left with the lingering feeling that I had forgotten to tell her something.* **2** °slow, long-drawn-out, °gradual: *She died a lingering, painful death.*

lingo *n.* °jargon, argot, °cant, patois, pidgin, Creole, °parlance, °vernacular, °dialect, °idiom, °language, °talk, °speech; °gobbledegook *or* gobbledygook, °gibberish, °mumbo-jumbo: *In medical lingo, he is suffering from coryza—in other words, a cold.*

link *n.* **1** °tie, °bond, coupling, connector, vinculum; °element, constituent, component: *A chain is no stronger than its weakest link.* **2** °connection, °tie-up, °tie-in, °relation, °relationship, °association, affiliation, interdependence: *What is the link between her arrival and his sudden departure? He thinks he's identified the missing link.*
—*v.* **3** Often, ***link up***: °couple, °join, °fasten (together), °unite; concatenate: *They linked arms to form a barrier.* **4** °connect, °tie (up *or* in *or* together), °associate, °relate, °identify with: *I cannot help feeling that this murder links up with the others.*

liquid *n.* **1** °fluid, °liquor, °juice, °solution: *Mixing these two liquids could be dangerous.*
—*adj.* **2** °fluid, flowing, °running, runny, °fluent, liquefied, °watery, molten, melted: *The Saturn V was the first space vehicle to be fuelled by liquid hydrogen and liquid oxygen.* **3** °bright, shining, °brilliant, °clear, °transparent, translucent, limpid: *The surface of the lake gleamed like liquid sunshine.* **4** convertible; °solvent, °profitable: *Government bonds are regarded as liquid assets. The company remains liquid despite losses.*

liquor *n.* **1** spirits, °alcohol, (strong) °drink, intoxicants, John Barleycorn, schnapps, °whisky *or US and Irish* whiskey, demon rum, °moonshine, *US* white lightning, white mule; *Colloq* °booze, pick-me-up, hard stuff, fire-water, juice, mother's ruin (= 'gin'), *US* Kickapoo mountain joy juice; *Slang* rot-gut, *Chiefly US and Canadian* hooch *or* hootch, *US* sauce, red-eye, mountain dew: *I don't drink liquor, but I will have some tea.* **2** °liquid, °fluid, °extract, °broth, °stock, distillate, °concentrate, infusion: *After poaching the fish, pour off the liquor and save it.*

list[1] *n.* **1** listing, roster, °roll, rota, catalogue, directory, °register, °index, °record, °schedule, °muster, slate, beadroll, laundry list, shopping list, inventory, °file, tabulation; bibliography, *liber veritatis, catalogue raisonné: Select what you need from this list.*
—*v.* **2** catalogue, °register, °index, °record, °note, °itemize, °enumerate, °schedule, °tabulate, °chronicle, °book, °enter, °enrol: *Those eligible to vote are listed in this computer printout.*

list[2] *v.* **1** °lean (over), °tilt, °slant, °heel (over), °tip, °careen, °cant, °incline: *The ship suddenly listed to starboard and I was thrown onto the deck.*
—*n.* **2** °lean, °tilt, °slant, °heel, °tip, °cant, °slope, °inclination: *The leak caused a severe list to port.*

listen *v.* **1** °hear, pay °attention (to), °attend, lend an ear (to), prick up one's ears, keep one's ears open, *Archaic* hark (to), hearken *or US also* harken (to): *I was listening to the radio when you phoned.* **2** °obey, °heed, °mind, pay °attention (to), do as one is told: *You wouldn't be in this trouble if you'd listened to me.*

listless *adj.* sluggish, °lethargic, °weary, °weak, enervated, °spent, languid, °lifeless, °heavy, °phlegmatic, unemotional, °impassive; °unenthusiastic, °indifferent, apathetic, unconcerned, °lukewarm, °tepid, °cool, uncaring, insouciant; pococurante, Laodicean: *She was just over an illness and feeling quite listless.*

litany *n.* **1** °prayer, invocation, °supplication, °petition: *The monks trudged through the streets, chanting their litany.* **2** °recitation, °recital, enumeration, listing, °list, cataloguing, catalogue, inventorying, inventory: *We had to sit through an interminable litany of the names of contributors to the fund.*

literal *adj.* **1** word-for-word, °verbatim, line-for-line, letter-for-letter, *literatim*, °exact, °precise, °faithful, °strict: *In a literal translation the spirit of the original is often lost.* **2** denotative, etymological, semantic, dictionary, lexical, °basic, °essential, °pure, °simple, simplistic, °real, °objective, °true, °genuine, bona fide, °unvarnished, unadulterated, unembellished, simple-minded, uncomplicated, unbiased, °unprejudiced, *Colloq* honest-to-goodness, honest-to-God: *'Female parent' may be the literal definition of* mother, *but it doesn't convey the emotional and connotative senses of the word.* **3** °prosaic, °matter-of-fact, °colourless, °dull, down-to-earth, literal-minded, unimaginative, °humdrum, °boring, °tedious: *His literal approach to everything spoils the conversation for those who have any spirit.*

literally *adv.* **1** word for word, °verbatim, line for line, letter for letter, *literatim*, faithfully, strictly, °exactly, °precisely, closely; °thus, *sic: Generally* cordon sanitaire *means 'buffer zone', but literally it means 'sanitary line'.* **2** °actually, °truly, in °fact, °really: *When I said he'd spilled the beans, I meant it figuratively, not literally.*

literary *adj.* **1** erudite, well-read, cultured, °learned, bookish, °scholarly, °lettered, °cultivated, °refined, °educated; literate: *Her latest book has been scorned by the literary élite.* **2** written, °formal, °scholarly, °pedantic, °learned, °academic, scholastic, schoolmarmish: *His writing contains literary words rarely heard in ordinary conversation.*

literature *n.* **1** °writing(s), °letters, belles-lettres, °creative °writing(s): *These works are representative of the literature of the period.* **2** °information, °facts, °data, publicity; °propaganda; °brochures, °pamphlets, handouts, handbills, °leaflets, circulars: *As a member, you will be sent literature about future events. They print subversive literature.*

litigant *n.* litigator, °party, plaintiff, appellant, °suitor, petitioner, suer, defendant, appellee, accused: *The judge suggested that the litigants settle out of court.*

litigation *n.* lawsuit, °suit, °action, °case, °legal °remedy: *The costs of litigation are extremely high.*

litter *n.* **1** °rubbish, debris, °refuse, fragments, °odds and ends, *US and Canadian* °trash, *Colloq* °junk: *The room was strewn with food wrappers, cigarette butts, and other litter.* **2** °brood, °issue, °offspring, °young: *Note the differences in the young of the same litter.* **3** stretcher, palanquin *or* palankeen, sedan °chair: *The potentate was borne in on a litter carried by four huge slaves.*
—*v.* **4** °clutter, °strew, °scatter: *The streets were littered with bricks and broken glass.*

little *adj.* **1** °small, °short, °slight, °tiny, °minute, °diminutive, °miniature, mini, °baby, doll-sized, °undersized, °dwarf, midget, pygmy, °elfin, °toy, bantam, °petite, °wee, infinitesimal, minuscule, Lilliputian, teeny, teeny-weeny, teensy-weensy, itty-bitty, itsy-bitsy, microscopic: *I live in a little house. A little red-faced man suddenly appeared. They sat drinking coffee out of little white cups.* **2** °young, °small, youthful: *You are asking a lot from a little boy.* **3** °small, °sparse, skimpy, °meagre, scant, °insufficient, °inadequate, not enough, °scanty, °barely *or* °hardly any: *A little crowd gathered round us. You will get little help from her. There's too little milk for us to make custard.* **4** °short, °brief: *We had only a little time together before he was sent overseas.* **5** °trifling, trivial, °small, °minor, °petty, °paltry, °insignificant, inconsiderable, unimportant, °inconsequential, °negligible: *He seemed to consider my safety of little importance. He does a little business on the side. You are too concerned about little things.* **6** °small(-minded), °petty, picayune, °mean, ungenerous, illiberal, °cheap, °narrow(-minded), unimaginative, °shallow: *What is going on in his cunning little brain?*
—*adv.* **7** °seldom, °rarely, °hardly ever, °scarcely: *I travel very little these days.* **8** (but *or* only) °slightly, °barely, °hardly, °scarcely, no, not any, not much: *She arrived with little more than what she was wearing.* **9** °scarcely, °hardly: *Little does he care whether he wins his wager.*
—*pron.* **10** °bit, °dab, dollop, °particle, spoonful, °taste, thimbleful, °speck, °spot, °scrap, °crumb, °particle, *Colloq* smidgen *or* smidgin: *If you could spare me a little of your time, I'd be grateful.*

live *adj.* **1** living, breathing, °animate, °viable, existent; °material, °physical, °tangible, °real, °actual, palpable: *She said she'd rather be a live beggar than a dead countess. My cat brought a live mouse into the house the other day.* **2** °energetic, °lively, °spirited, °vigorous, °active, °dynamic, °busy; °current, °contemporary: *Our new advertising agency seems to have some live ideas. The other party made nuclear disarmament a live issue in the election.* **3** °burning, °glowing, °flaming, alight, red-hot, white-hot: *A live coal popped out of the grate onto the carpet.* **4** °loaded, °explosive, unexploded, combustible: *Builders have dug up a live bomb in London.* **5** charged, electrified: *Don't touch a live wire or you'll get a shock.*
—*v.* **6** °breathe, °exist; °function: *There has never lived a more gifted scholar. She lives as a recluse.* **7** °survive, °persist, °last, °persevere, °endure; °spend, °continue,

°live out, °complete, °end, conclude, °finish: *He lived out his days happily in Torquay.* **8** reside, °dwell, be; °abide, °stay, °remain, °lodge, °room: *He normally lives in Acton, but at the moment he's living with his mother in Kent.* **9** subsist, °get along, °survive, °fare: *Many old-age pensioners complain that they have barely enough to live on.*

lively *adj.* **1** full of °life, °vigorous, °energetic, °vivacious, °spirited, °brisk, spry, °active, °animated, °frisky, °sprightly, °agile, °nimble, °perky, chirpy, bouncy, °buoyant, °gay, cheery, °cheerful, *Colloq* chipper, full of °pep, peppy: *His speech sparked off a lively discussion. The carriage was drawn by a pair of lively horses.* **2** °strong, °intense, °vivid, °keen, °pointed, °eager, °energetic, °active: *She takes a lively interest in current affairs.* **3** °active, °busy, bustling, °stirring, °eventful, swarming, teeming; astir, °alive: *We joined the lively crowd at the antiques fair. The streets near the square were lively with people rushing to and fro.* **4** °vivid, °bright, °gay, °cheerful, °glowing, °brilliant, °gorgeous, °rich: *Some lively colours in the upholstery and curtains would brighten up the sitting-room.*

liven *v.* Often, ***liven up***: **1** °brighten, °cheer, °enliven, °perk up: *You need some fresh paint to liven up the outside of the house.* **2** invigorate, °stimulate, °energize, inspirit, °activate, °animate, °fire, °stir (up), put (some) °life into, °enliven, °perk up, *Colloq* °pep up: *We need a good dance band to liven up the place in the evenings.*

load *n.* **1** °weight, °burden; onus, °pressure, °encumbrance, millstone, °cross, albatross, °responsibility, °care, °anxiety, °worry, °trouble: *He put down his load and rested. Seeing her safe is a load off my mind.* **2** shipment, consignment, °cargo, °weight: *That load is too heavy for the van.*
—*v.* **3** °pack, °pile, °stack, °heap, °fill, lade, °stuff, °cram, °jam, °squeeze: *Load all the boxes you can in the truck.* **4** Often, ***load down***: °weigh down, °burden, °encumber, saddle with, °overwhelm: *I was loaded down with too many responsibilities.*

loaded *adj.* **1** overloaded, overwhelmed, burdened, laden, weighted (down), filled (up), chock-full, chock-a-block, stuffed, jammed, °packed, crowded, brimming, brim-full, crammed: *A fully loaded lorry has overturned near exit 5. The train was loaded with commuters.* **2** charged, primed, °ready: *Be careful—the gun is loaded.* **3** charged, °tricky, manipulative, insidious, °prejudiced, °prejudicial, °trap, °devious: *'When did you stop beating your wife?' is what anybody would call a loaded question.* **4** °rich, °wealthy, affluent, moneyed, well-to-do, °well off, *Colloq* °flush, well-heeled, *US* in the chips, *Slang* rolling in it: *I hear that her new husband is really loaded.* **5** °drunk: *He was loaded before he even went to the party.*

loaf[1] *n.* **1** °brick, °cake, °block, chunk; °lump, cube: *We could do with an extra loaf of bread.* **2** °head, °sense, brains, *Colloq* noggin, noodle, block, bean, *Brit* noddle, *Slang Brit* chump: *Use your loaf!*

loaf[2] *v.* **1** °lounge (about *or* around), loiter, °idle, laze, °lie about *or* around, take it °easy, vegetate, watch the grass grow, *Colloq US* lallygag *or* lollygag, *Slang Brit* skive, *Military* scrimshank, *US* goof around *or* off, *US military* gold-brick, *Taboo slang US* fuck off, fuck the dog: *There are always some youngsters loafing about in the park.* **2** ***loaf away***: °waste, °fritter away, °idle away: *He loafs away all his time watching the telly.*

loafer *n.* °idler, layabout, °wastrel, shirker, *flâneur*, ne'er-do-well, °tramp, vagrant, *Old-fashioned* °lounge lizard, slugabed, *Colloq* lazybones, *Brit* drone, *US* °bum, (ski *or* tennis *or* surf) °bum, *Slang Brit* skiver, *Military* scrimshanker, *US military* gold brick *or* gold-bricker, *Taboo slang US* fuck-off: *Why did she marry that good-for-nothing loafer?*

loan *n.* **1** °advance, °allowance, °credit, °accommodation: *We needed a loan to pay for Melissa's education.*
—*v.* **2** °lend, °advance, °allow, °credit: *The bank loaned us enough money to buy a car.*

loath *adj.* loth, unwilling, °reluctant, °averse, °disinclined, °indisposed: *I was loath to tell my wife where I had been.*

loathe *v.* °detest, °hate, °despise, °abhor, abominate, execrate, °shrink *or* °recoil from, °shudder at: *I love broccoli but loathe cauliflower.*

loathing *n.* hatred, abhorrence, °aversion, °hate, odium, detestation, antipathy, repugnance, °horror, °revulsion: *She treated her critics with loathing.*

loathsome *adj.* detestable, °abhorrent, odious, °hateful, °disgusting, execrable, °abominable, °despicable, °contemptible, noisome, °offensive, °horrible, °repulsive, °repugnant, nauseating, sickening, °revolting, °nasty, °vile: *Without warning, the loathsome beast attacked me. She died shortly of a loathsome disease.*

lob *v.* **1** loft, °toss, °pitch, °shy, °heave, °fling, chuck, °hurl, °throw: *She lobbed the ball high in the air over the net.*
—*n.* **2** °toss, °throw, °bowl, °pitch, °hit, *US* °fly: *I misjudged the slow lob and swung too soon.*

lobby *n.* **1** foyer, entrance-hall, vestibule, °entry, *US* entry-way; °reception (room *or* area), waiting-room, °corridor, °hall, hallway: *We were to meet in the main lobby of the arts centre.* **2** special-interest °group, °pressure °group, lobbyist: *A powerful lobby has been formed to influence farming legislation.*
—*v.* **3** (bring) °pressure (to bear), (exert) °influence, °persuade, °pull strings *or* wires, put one's weight behind, °sway, °press, °push, °promote, °urge, *Brit* pressurize: *Environmentalists are lobbying for a ban on chlorofluorocarbons.*

local *adj.* **1** °neighbourhood, °neighbouring, °nearby, °close by; °adjoining: *She works for a local butcher. The law affects only the local area.* **2** °provincial, regional, °district, °state, county, shire, °municipal, °city, °town, village, °neighbourhood; restricted, °limited, °specific, °particular, °peculiar: *Clean water is a general, not a local problem.*
—*n.* **3** °resident, °native, townsman, townswoman, townsperson: *The locals all voted against the proposition.* **4** neighbourhood °pub: *He stopped in at his local on the way home.*

locale *n.* °site, °location, °spot, °place, °setting, venue, °neighbourhood, °situation, locality: *We moved the locale of the film to Spain.*

locate *v.* **1** °situate, °place, °site, °position, °set (up), °fix, pinpoint, °establish, °settle, °base: *Where is your office located? We located our warehouse close to the railway.* **2** °find, °come across, °discover, °unearth, lay *or* put *or* get one's hand(s) *or* °finger(s) on, °chance *or* °hit upon, °turn up, °track down: *Where can I locate a good piano player?*

location *n.* **1** °site, °place, °locale, °spot, °setting, °situation, °position: *We have just moved to a new location.* **2** °finding, °discovery, laying *or* putting *or* getting one's hand(s) *or* °finger(s) on, unearthing, turning up, tracking down: *The location of the other half of the coin became an obsession with him.*

lock[1] *n.* **1** padlock, hasp, °bolt, latch, °bar, °hook, °clasp, catch: *Why put a lock on the door if there is nothing worth stealing inside?* **2** °hold; °control, °power, °sway, °authority, °command, supervision: *The bureau has a complete lock on the issue of licences.*
—*v.* **3** Often, ***lock up***: padlock, °bolt, latch, °bar, °secure, °seal: *Lock the doors before leaving for the day.* **4** °clasp, °entangle, °engage, °join, °entwine, °close; °clutch, °grasp, °grapple: *For six hours the knights were locked in battle.* **5** ***lock away***: See **9,** below. **6** ***lock in***: **a** °secure, °retain, °fix, °plant, °implant, stabilize: *What does the maker mean by 'the flavour is locked in'?* **b** °commit, °oblige, constrain, °bind: *We are locked in to the promises we made to our employees.* **c** lock up *or* away, confine, °restrain, coop up: *You'd better lock in the dogs before you leave.* **7** ***lock on***: °fix on *or* upon, °track, °follow, °pursue, keep °track of: *Our sights are locked on the target.* **8** ***lock out***: °exclude, °shut out, °close out, °keep out, °bar, debar:

During the strike, the management locked out all employees. **9** ***lock up*** *or* ***away***: confine, °jail *or Brit also* gaol, °imprison, coop up, incarcerate, detain, impound, put behind bars, °restrict, °cage: *They threatened to lock him up and throw away the key.*

lock[2] *n.* tress, curl, ringlet: *As a love token, she sent him a lock of her hair.*

lodge *n.* **1** hunting-lodge, °cabin, chalet, °cottage, °house; gatehouse, °shelter, °hut: *I have a small lodge in the mountains.* **2** °branch, chapter: *He belongs to the Manchester lodge of the Masons.*
—*v.* **3** reside, °live, °dwell, °abide, °stay, °stop, °room, °occupy rooms: *For years they lodged together at 221B Baker Street.* **4** °accommodate, °board, °put up, billet, °quarter, °house, °take in; °shelter, °harbour: *Mrs Mulrooney is lodging a student in her spare room. Her house cannot lodge more than three.* **5** °stick, °wedge, catch, °deposit, become stuck *or* wedged *or* °fixed *or* caught *or* deposited, embed itself, become embedded: *I've got an apple pip lodged in one of my back teeth.* **6** °register, °enter, °record, °submit, °bring forward, °set forth *or* out, °file: *We lodged a complaint against our neighbours because of the noise.*

lodging *n.* Often, ***lodgings***: °accommodation(s), °shelter, °quarters, °rooms, apartment, °housing, °house, °dwelling, dwelling-place, °residence: *I found a night's lodging in Cranberry Street.*

lofty *adj.* **1** °tall, °high, °elevated, °towering, soaring: *The lofty skyscrapers of New York always impress visitors on first sight.* **2** °exalted, °majestic, °imposing, °grand, °magnificent, °noble, °regal, °imperial, blue-blooded, thoroughbred, aristocratic, magisterial, august, °stately, °venerable, °distinguished, °dignified, °elevated, °eminent, °celebrated, honoured, °honourable, respected, °renowned, °famous, °prominent, °illustrious, °notable, °leading, °pre-eminent, °sublime, °immortal: *He is heir to one of England's loftiest peerages.* **3** °elevated, °honourable, °superior, °exalted, °noble: *Public servants should adhere to lofty principles of morality.* **4** °grand, °grandiose, °haughty, °arrogant, °disdainful, °condescending, °contemptuous, °scornful, °supercilious, contumelious, patronizing, °superior, overweening, vainglorious, °pompous, °snobbish, *Colloq* °high and °mighty, snooty, uppity, *Brit* °uppish, *Slang* snotty, *Brit* toffee-nosed: *Her lofty attitude made her unpopular with the voters.*

logic *n.* **1** °reasoning, °deduction, dialectics, ratiocination, inferential *or* °scientific °reasoning: *Mill defined logic as the science of proof, or evidence.* **2** (good *or* common) °sense, °sound °judgement, °wisdom, °presence of mind: *According to Disraeli, England was not governed by logic.* **3** reasonableness, °intelligence, judiciousness, practicality, rationality: *Your logic is valid, but you are forgetting the human factor.*

logical *adj.* **1** syllogistic(al), inferential, deductive, inductive: *Her argument follows basic logical criteria.* **2** °reasonable, °plausible, °sensible, °sound, valid, °intelligent, °judicious, °practical, °rational, °wise, °proper: *Is it logical to assume that people will believe you?* **3** well-organized, °sound, °coherent, °consistent, °sensible, °rational, °reasonable, well-reasoned, well-thought-out: *The proposal is set forth in a logical fashion, from premise to conclusion.*

lonely *adj.* **1** °single, °solitary, °sole, lone, °one; °unaccompanied, °alone: *The lonely survivor of the crash struggled out of the jungle. She walked for miles, lonely and desolate.* **2** °desolate, °uninhabited, °deserted, °barren: *Robinson Crusoe's world was a lonely place.* **3** friendless, °lonesome, °abandoned, °outcast, forsaken; °solo, hermit-like, eremitic(al), °reclusive, °secluded, °retiring, °withdrawn, °unsocial: *He felt lonely in the strange city. She leads a lonely existence with only her cat for company.*

lonesome *adj.* **1** °alone, forsaken, friendless, rejected, °unpopular, °unwelcome, °outcast, °deserted, °abandoned, °estranged: *She was terribly lonesome and homesick before meeting Patrick.* **2** See **lonely, 2,** above.

long[1] *adj.* **1** °extensive, extended, elongate(d), °large, °great, °big: *That is a very long snake!* **2** °lengthy, prolonged, °protracted; °extensive, extended, °sustained: *I waited for a long time.*

long[2] *v.* °wish, crave, °want, °yearn, °desire, °hunger, °fancy, covet, °dream of, °hanker, eat one's heart out: *I am longing for a good roast beef dinner. I long to see you once more.*

longing *n.* craving, °wish, yearning, °hunger, °fancy, °desire, hankering, *Colloq* yen: *I have a longing to be home again.*

look *v.* **1** Usually, ***look at***: °see, °observe, °consider, °contemplate, °regard, °view, °survey, °inspect, °scrutinize, °study, °scan; pay °attention, °attend, °notice, °watch, °witness; *Literary* °behold, *Slang US* eyeball: *Look at what you've done! Look at the way I do it.* **2** °seem (to be), °appear (to be): *That looks like a useful utensil. You certainly look healthy.* **3** °face, °front (on), °overlook, look out on: *The house looks over the sea at the back.* **4** ***look after***: °care for, take °care of, be °responsible for, °attend, °mind, °watch, °serve, °wait on, °nurse, °protect: *Rose will look after your house while you're away. I need someone to look after me.* **5** ***look down on*** *or* ***upon*** *or* ***US at***: disdain, °despise, contemn, °scorn, °disparage, derogate, °spurn, °sneer, misprize, *Colloq* turn one's nose up at, look down one's nose at: *They look down on anyone with less money.* **6** ***look for***: **a** °seek, °demand, °require: *We aren't looking for the same things in a person.* **b** °hunt for, forage for, °search for: *I am looking for a cup to match my set.* **c** °expect, °hope, °anticipate, °count on, °reckon on: *I am looking for a better school report next term.* **7** ***look forward to***: **a** °anticipate, await, °wait for: *I am looking forward to Sunday's match.* **b** °expect, °count *or* °rely on *or* upon: *We were looking forward to your help.* **8** ***look into***: °examine, °study, °investigate, °inspect, delve into, °dig into, °probe, °scrutinize, °explore, °go into, °research, °check (out), °check into: *I shall have to look into the matter.* **9** ***look out***: be °careful, be °alert, be °vigilant, be on the qui vive, be watchful, °watch out, °beware, pay °attention, be on °guard: *If you don't look out, you'll bang your head.* **10** ***look over***: look at, °examine, °read, °scan, °study, °check (out *or* over), *Slang US* eyeball: *I haven't had a chance to look over the material you gave me.* **11** ***look up***: **a** °seek, °search for, °hunt for, try to find, °track *or* °run down: *I meant to look up the etymology of 'picnic'.* **b** get in touch with, (tele)phone, °ring (up), °visit, °call on, °call up, look *or* °drop in on, go to °see: *I looked up a friend of mine when I was in Chicago.* **c** °improve, get °better, °pick up, show °improvement, °progress, °gain, make °headway *or* °progress: *He was pleased to see that business was looking up.* **12** ***look up to***: °admire, °regard °highly, °respect, °esteem, °honour, °revere, °extol, °worship, °idolize, °venerate: *The boy really looks up to you.*
—*n.* **13** °gaze, °glance: *Her look was inviting. He gave me a dirty look. Let me have a look at you.* **14** looks, °appearance, °aspect, °bearing, °manner, °air, demeanour; °expression, countenance, °face, mien: *I just didn't like the look of the man. He had a nasty look.*

look-alike *n.* °twin, °double, °exact *or* °perfect °likeness *or* °match, clone, *Colloq* spitting °image *or* °spit and °image; *doppelgänger*; *Slang* (°dead) ringer: *She is such a perfect look-alike of Princess Di's that people follow her in the street.*

lookout *n.* **1** °guard, sentry, °sentinel, °watchman: *The lookout reported that the fort was surrounded by Cochise's braves.* **2** °alert, qui vive; °guard, °watch: *Be on the lookout for shoplifters.* **3** °responsibility, °worry, °concern, °problem, °difficulty, *Colloq* °headache: *How he wastes his free time is his lookout, how he spends his working time is ours.*

loom *v.* **1** °appear, °emerge, take °shape *or* °form, °materialize, °surface, °arise: *A huge figure loomed out of the fog.* **2** °menace, impend, °threaten, °overshadow,

°tower, °dominate, °hang *or* °hover over: *Count Dracula's dark castle loomed over us.* **3** ***loom large***: °dominate, °predominate, play a big *or* an important role *or* part: *Sales to children loom large in your predictions.*

loop *n.* **1** hoop, noose, °ring, °circle, °bow, eye, eyelet, °coil, whorl, *Nautical* bend: *I caught my toe in a loop of rope and fell on the deck.*
—*v.* **2** °twist, °coil, °wind, °tie, °circle, curl, °entwine, °turn, °ring, *Nautical* bend: *Loop the thread round the crochet hook and pull it through.*

loophole *n.* °outlet, °way out, means of °escape, °escape, °subterfuge, °pretext, °evasion, °quibble, *Colloq* °dodge: *They couldn't prosecute him because he found a loophole in the law.*

loose *adj.* **1** °unattached, unconnected, °disconnected, °detached, °free, unsecured, unfastened, °movable: *I have a loose tooth. The vacuum cleaner will pick up any loose bits.* **2** unconfined, untied, unfettered, released, freed, unshackled, unchained; °free, at °liberty, at °large, on the loose, untrammelled: *In Pamplona, they allow loose bulls to run through the streets to the arena.* **3** unconfining, free-flowing, flowing, baggy, °slack, hanging: *That skirt is loose on you since you lost weight.* **4** disordered, disorganized, unbound, untied, messy; strewn *or* °spread *or* tossed *or* thrown about *or* around, scattered (about *or* around), in °disorder, in disarray, dispersed: *On the desk was a loose pile of papers.* **5** °rambling, °disconnected, unstructured, unconnected, discontinuous, non-specific, unspecific, °indefinite, °imprecise, °inexact, °inaccurate, °free, °broad, °rough, °offhand, °casual, °careless, °untidy, °sloppy, slapdash, °general, °vague: *He gave a loose description of his assailant. A loose translation does not convey the flavour of the original.* **6** °lax, °relaxed, negligent, °careless, °sloppy: *Discipline has been quite loose around here lately.* **7** °wanton, °dissolute, debauched, °immoral, °promiscuous, °abandoned, °fast, °libertine, °profligate, licentious, °lewd, °perverted, °corrupt: *She was quickly gaining a reputation for being a loose woman.*
—*adv.* **8** ***break loose***: °escape, °flee: *The boy broke loose from my grasp and ran to greet his mother.* **9** ***hang*** *or* ***stay loose***: °relax, stay *or* keep °calm *or* °cool, °cool off *or* down, °sit back, take it °easy: *Hang loose and everything will be all right.* **10** ***let*** *or* ***set*** *or* ***turn loose***: °discharge, let go (with); °emit, °give out (with), °fire: *They let him loose after questioning. She let loose a stream of invective like a fishwife.*
—*v.* **11** let go, (set) °free, °release, let *or* set *or* turn loose; °liberate, °deliver: *Ten thousand balloons were loosed in the celebration.* **12** untie, °undo, unfasten, let go, °disengage, °relax, °ease, °loosen, slacken; cast off: *Loose these ropes, please.* **13** let go, let °fly, °fire, °discharge, °shoot, unleash, °deliver: *We loosed a devastating barrage at the enemy.*

loosen *v.* **1** °loose; °undo, unfasten, unhook, unbutton, unlace, untie, unbind, unbuckle; unscrew: *Quick! Loosen his collar!* **2** °weaken, °detach, °separate, °sever, °break *or* °cut (°apart): *The vibration has loosened the rivets.*

loot *n.* **1** °booty, spoils, °plunder, °prize, °haul, *Slang* swag, boodle: *They divided up the loot amongst the gang.*
—*v.* **2** °plunder, °sack, °ransack, °rob, °pillage, despoil, °raid, °ravage, maraud, *Rare* depredate: *The soldiers looted every house in the city.*

lop *v.* Often, ***lop off***: °chop off, °trim, °top, °head, crop, °prune, °dock, °clip, °snip off, shear off, °cut off, °pare, °shorten, °hack off, amputate: *Lop the lower branches off close to the trunk.*

lopsided *adj.* **1** uneven, askew, °one-sided, awry, unsymmetric(al), asymmetric(al), unequal, °crooked, °unbalanced, °irregular, *Colloq* cock-eyed: *That lopsided bookcase is the sole product of Ed's cabinet-making class.* **2** uneven, unequal, °one-sided, °biased, °disproportionate, unfair, warped, twisted: *Four against two—I'd call that lopsided, wouldn't you?*

lord *n.* **1** °master, °monarch, ruler, °sovereign: *Harry considers himself lord of all he surveys.* **2** °noble, nobleman, °peer, aristocrat; earl, duke, °count, viscount, baron: *He was made a lord in recognition of his achievements.* **3** ***The*** *or* ***Our Lord***: God, the Almighty, God Almighty, the Creator, the Supreme Being, Christ, Jesus, Jehovah: *The Lord moves in mysterious ways his miracles to perform.*
—*v.* ***lord it over***: domineer, °swagger, be °overbearing, *Colloq* °boss (around), act °big, pull °rank: *He lords it over everyone in the office.*

lore *n.* **1** folklore, °beliefs, °culture, °tradition(s), °mythology, °myths, mythos, ethos, teaching(s), °doctrine, °wisdom: *According to their lore, the American Indians go to the Happy Hunting Ground when they die.* **2** °knowledge, °learning, erudition: *He was acquainted with medical lore through his reading.*

lose *v.* **1** °mislay, misplace, °displace, °part with; suffer the °loss of, be °deprived of: *I lost my pen. He lost a leg in the war.* **2** °forfeit, °yield: *He says he lost the rent money gambling.* **3** °give up, °yield, °capitulate, °admit °defeat, °succumb, °bow to, be defeated *or* conquered, °suffer °defeat, be beaten *or* °overcome *or* worsted *or* bested, *Colloq* lose out: *It was a good game, but we lost.* **4** °waste, let °slip, squander, °dissipate, °fritter *or* °trifle away, °run out of; °consume, °use (up), °expend, °spend: *We lost a lot of time waiting for him to decide.* **5** °elude, °evade, °escape, °throw *or* °shake off, give the °slip: *I managed to lose the sinister-looking man who was shadowing me.*

loser *n.* also-ran, °misfit, °failure, °fiasco, non-starter, *Colloq* °flop, °dud, °washout, bummer, lead balloon, lemon, born loser, *Brit* damp squib, *Brit and Australian* no-hoper, *US* clinker, nebbish, schlemiel *or* schlemihl *or* shlemiel, schlimazel *or* shlimazel *or* shlimazl, schnook, sad sack: *Dick is a real loser and will never amount to anything. His idea for a company newsletter was a loser.*

loss *n.* **1** deprivation, bereavement, °privation, °denial, °sacrifice, forfeiture, disappearance: *We must be constantly vigilant to watch for any loss of our liberty.* **2** diminution, °erosion, reduction, impoverishment, depletion, shrinkage: *New policies are in place to stem the loss of parkland.* **3** °disadvantage, °detriment, °harm, °impairment, °injury, °damage: *I don't regard Wentworth's resignation as any great loss.* **4** °waste, wastage, wasting, squandering: *The loss of time was owing to a train delay.* **5** °defeat, °set-back, °disadvantage, °disappointment, °failure, °downfall, °collapse, °breakdown, °ruin; drubbing, trouncing: *His loss is my gain.* **6** Often, ***losses***: debit(s), °liability (liabilities), negative cash flow: *The company wrote off the losses.* **7** Often, ***losses***: °death, °dying, °passing, demise, °destruction, extermination, extinction, annihilation: *The loss from disease was overwhelming. What losses did they suffer in the battle?*

lost *adj.* **1** gone, departed, vanished, strayed; missing, mislaid, misplaced, irrecoverable: *They found my lost dog. The airline told me that my bag was lost.* **2** wasted, °misspent, gone by the board, squandered, down the °drain, °spent, °exhausted, *Colloq* out of the window: *The new arrangement is resulting in a lot of time lost. I watched another lost opportunity slip by.* **3** °confused, baffled, perplexed, puzzled, mystified, bewildered, confounded, adrift, °helpless, disoriented, at °sea, astray: *I am totally lost when it comes to high finance.* **4** forgotten, °bygone, °extinct, °past, °obsolete, vanished, buried: *Good writing needn't be a lost art.* **5** °dead, °extinct, departed, fallen, °late: *We held a memorial service for our lost comrades.* **6** destroyed, demolished, devastated, ruined, wrecked, irreparable, unsalvageable, irreclaimable, irremediable: *After the exposé in the newspaper, his name was consigned to the limbo of lost reputations.* **7** damned, cursed, accursed, °abandoned, °corrupt, fallen, °wanton, °unchaste, °dissolute: *Unrepentant sinners are lost souls.* **8** °hopeless, °distraught, distracted, °desperate, °frantic, frenzied: *He had the lost look of a cornered fugitive.*

lot *n.* **1** °collection, °batch, consignment, °assortment, °group, °portion, °set, °quantity, grouping, apportionment: *They are expecting a new lot of furniture this afternoon.* **2** °luck, °fortune, °destiny, °fate, kismet, °plight, °doom, °end: *It seems to be my lot to stay in the same place all my life.* **3** °lottery, °drawing, °raffle, drawing lots *or* straws: *The winner will be decided by lot.* **4** °share, °portion, °division, °interest, °part, °allotment, °assignment, apportionment, °ration, °allowance: *Marguerite was bequeathed the house, while my lot included the paintings.* **5** ***a lot*** *or* ***lots***: **a** a good *or* great °deal: *You have a lot of nerve! I'd give a lot to be able to paint like you. He got into a lot of trouble.* **b** much, loads *or* a °load, mountains *or* a °mountain, tons *or* a ton, barrels *or* a barrel, stacks *or* a °stack, °piles *or* a °pile, heaps *or* a °heap, masses *or* a °mass, °oceans, *Colloq* oodles, scads, *US* gobs: *She has lots of money.* **c** °many, myriad, numerous, countless, reams, °infinite *or* an infinity, quantities *or* a °quantity, °enormous numbers *or* an °enormous °number, *Colloq* oodles, scads, °loads, tons, °masses: *There are lots of fish in the sea.* **6** ***the lot***: °everything, *Colloq* the whole kit and caboodle, all: *I'll give you a fiver for the lot.*

lotion *n.* cream, liniment, balm, °salve, °ointment, embrocation, unguent, pomade: *The doctor said to rub in some of this lotion twice a day.*

lottery *n.* °raffle, sweepstake, drawing, °pool, *Brit* tombola: *I've never known anyone who won anything in the national lottery.*

loud *adj.* **1** deafening, ear-splitting, booming, blaring, stentorian, thundering, °thunderous, sonorous, °noisy, clamorous, °piercing, fortissimo: *The hi-fi is so loud I can't hear myself think. A loud crash came from the kitchen.* **2** °tawdry, °garish, °flashy, °gaudy, °tasteless, °extravagant, °showy, °ostentatious, *Colloq* splashy, snazzy, jazzy: *He was wearing a check suit and the loudest shirt and tie I had ever seen.*

lounge *v.* **1** °idle, °loaf, laze, loll, languish, vegetate: *After dinner, we lounged till midnight, sipping port.* —*n.* **2** sitting-room, salon, front room, °parlour: *Mother insisted that we entertain visitors in the lounge.* **3** °lobby, foyer, waiting-room, °reception (room), vestibule: *I was waiting in the lounge when the doctor returned.* **4** cocktail lounge, (lounge *or* saloon) °bar: *We went into the lounge and ordered a drink.* **5** sofa, °couch, divan, studio °couch, day-bed, settee, settle, love-seat, *chaise longue*; causeuse, tête-à-tête; *US and Canadian* Davenport: *The psychoanalyst has a lounge on which you lie while talking to him.*

lour *v.* **1** lower, darken, °threaten, °menace, °loom: *The clouds loured: she suddenly began to feel afraid.* **2** lower, °frown, °scowl, glower; °sulk, °pout, mope: *He said nothing, but loured at me from beneath his beetled brow.*

lousy *adj.* **1** °awful, °terrible, °mean, °contemptible, °low, °base, °hateful, detestable, °despicable, °vile, °wretched, °miserable, °scurvy, °dirty, °vicious, *Colloq* °rotten: *Telling tales to the teacher was a lousy thing to do.* **2** °bad, °poor, °awful, °terrible, °inferior; low-quality, °shoddy, °shabby, °miserable, second-rate, °wretched: *We had lousy seats for the theatre last week. The dealer seems to have sold you a really lousy car.* **3** pedicular, pediculous, *Brit* lice-infested, lice-ridden, *US* louse-infested, louse-ridden: *Even lice are lousy—they have their own parasites.* **4** ***lousy with***: °alive with, overloaded with, swarming with, teeming with, *Colloq* crawling with, knee-deep in: *In five minutes the place was lousy with cops.*

lovable *adj.* loveable, °adorable, °darling, °dear, cherished, °likeable, °attractive, °engaging, °cute, °fetching, °taking, alluring, °endearing, appealing, winsome, °sweet, °tender, cuddly, °affectionate, charming, °enchanting: *She has the most lovable little baby boy.*

love *n.* **1** °warmth, °affection, °attachment, fondness, tenderness, °devotion, °attraction, °friendship, amity, °regard, °admiration, °fancy, adoration, adulation, °ardour, °passion, °fervour, °rapture, infatuation: *Her love for him grew over the years.* **2** °liking, °delight, °enjoyment, °pleasure, fondness, °attraction, predilection, °bent, °leaning, proclivity, °inclination, °disposition, °weakness, °partiality, °preference, °taste, °relish, °passion: *In his retirement, Charles has developed a love for golf.* **3** °darling, °beloved, °sweetheart, sweetie, °sweet, honey, °dear one, dearest, angel, turtle-dove, true-love, light of one's life, °lover, °paramour, °mate, intended, betrothed; girlfriend, inamorata, lady-love, young lady, fiancée; boyfriend, beau, inamorato, °suitor, swain, young man, fiancé, *Archaic* leman, tally, *US* POSSLQ (= 'Person of the Opposite Sex Sharing Living Quarters'), *Colloq* girl, woman, guy, man: *Let me tell you something, my love. Come live with me and be my love.* **4** °sympathy, tenderness, °concern, °charity, °care, °solicitude, °affinity, °rapport, °harmony, °brotherhood, sisterhood, fellow-feeling: *He has great love for his fellow human beings.* **5** ***love affair***: **a** amour, °liaison, °affair, °romance, °relationship, *affaire de cœur*, °intrigue: *He's been having a love affair with his secretary.* **b** °passion, °mania, *Colloq* °thing: *George allows nothing to interfere with his love affair with tennis.* **6** ***make love (to)*** *or* ***(with)***: °embrace, °cuddle, °caress, °fondle, have °sexual °intercourse, *Archaic* take, know, *Colloq* neck, °pet, canoodle, °romance, have °sex, make the beast with two backs, *US and Canadian* make out; *Taboo slang* °screw, fuck, hump, bang, *Brit* roger, bonk: *He still makes love to his wife even though they are both in their eighties.*
—*v.* **7** °cherish, °admire, °adore, be in love with, lose one's heart to, °worship, °idolize, °dote on, °treasure, be °infatuated with, think the world of, adulate, hold °dear, °like, *Colloq* be hung up on, be °crazy *or* nuts *or* °wild *or* °mad about, have a crush on: *Only after ten years of friendship did she discover that she loved him.* **8** °delight in, take °pleasure in, derive °pleasure *or* °enjoyment from, °relish, be °partial to, have a °passion *or* °preference *or* °taste for, be attracted to, be captivated by, be °fond of, °like, °enjoy, °appreciate, value, *Colloq* get a kick from *or* out of, be °wild about, be thrilled by, *US* get a bang *or* charge from *or* out of: *She loves chocolates. I just love your new dress! Love me, love my dog.*

love-letter *n.* billet-doux, *Archaic* mash °note: *She saved all his love letters.*

lovely *adj.* **1** good-looking, °pretty, °handsome, °attractive, °comely, °fair, °fetching, °engaging, captivating, alluring, enticing, bewitching, °ravishing, °gorgeous, °beautiful, beauteous, pulchritudinous: *Larry has two lovely daughters. The house has a lovely view of Lake Windermere.* **2** °satisfying, °satisfactory, °agreeable, enjoyable, gratifying, °nice, °pleasing, °pleasant, °pleasurable, °engaging, °delightful: *What a lovely way to spend an evening!*

lover *n.* See **love, 3,** above.

low[1] *adj.* **1** °short, squat, °little, °small, stubby, stumpy, °stunted; low-lying: *The terrain has many low shrubs, not more than two feet tall.* **2** °inadequate, °insufficient, °deficient, down, °short, °sparse, °scanty, scant, °limited: *The air in the tyres is a bit low. Our water supply ran low.* **3** °coarse, °unrefined, indelicate, °improper, °naughty, °risqué, °indecent, °unseemly, °vulgar, °crude, °common, °rude, °offensive, °gross, ill-bred, °lewd, °obscene, ribald, °bawdy, °scurrilous, smutty, °pornographic, °dirty: *The old burlesque acts were characterized by their low humour.* **4** °weak, °frail, °feeble, debilitated, enervated, °sickly, °unhealthy, °infirm, °shaky, °decrepit, °ill, °sick: *He's very low and sinking fast.* **5** °ineffectual, °ineffective, °weak: *Her resistance to disease is low. I have a low pain threshold.* **6** °miserable, °dismal, °wretched, °abysmal, °sorry, abject, °destitute: *I seem to have reached a low point in my career.* **7** °humble, °poor, low-born, °lowly, °base, °inferior, base-born, °plebeian, proletariat, ignoble: *He rose from those low beginnings to a peerage.* **8** °unhappy, depressed, °dejected, °sad, °gloomy, °melancholy, °miserable, °despondent, disconsolate, °blue, downcast, down, °glum, °wretched, morose, crestfallen, °broken-hearted, heartbroken,

°tearful, lachrymose, °sorrowful, °mournful, heavy-hearted: *I felt low for weeks after the death of my kitten.* **9** °inferior, second-rate, °poor, °bad, not up to °par, °worthless, °shoddy, °shabby, °mediocre, substandard: *Their products are of low quality.* **10** °inferior, °lower, lesser, °small, smaller: *Play a low card.* **11** low-cut, décolleté, revealing, *Colloq US* low and behold in the front and vie de Bohème in the back: *Gilda wore a low, strapless black satin evening gown.* **12** °base, °vile, abject, °contemptible, °despicable, °mean, °menial, °servile, ignoble, degraded, °vulgar, °foul, dastardly, depraved, °nasty, °sordid: *That was a low trick he played telling on his friends. I didn't know that anyone could sink to such a low level.* **13** °quiet, hushed, °soft, °subdued, °gentle, muted, muffled, stifled, °indistinct, whispered, murmured, murmurous: *Her low voice was sweet.* **14** unfavourable, °critical, adverse: *She has a rather low opinion of his singing.*

low[2] *v.* moo, °bellow; °bawl: *The lowing herd moved slowly into the pasture.*

low-down *n.* °information, °intelligence, °data, the °facts, °inside story, *Colloq* info, °dope, °dirt, *Brit* bumf: *I have the low-down on the scandal.*

lower[1] *v.* **1** °drop, °reduce, °decrease, °mark down, °discount, lessen, °diminish, °downgrade, °cut, °slash: *Prices on all goods have been lowered.* **2** °let *or* °move *or* °bring *or* °put down, °drop: *The drawbridge was lowered and the knights rode across. They lowered the coffin into the grave.* **3** °cut *or* °lop off, °cut *or* °take down, °reduce, °diminish, crop, °trim: *We lowered the hedge by a foot.* **4** abase, °debase, °degrade, °discredit, °shame, °disgrace, demean, °belittle, °humble, °humiliate; °stoop, °deign, °condescend: *I wouldn't lower myself to so much as speak to him.* **5** °turn down, °quieten, °moderate, °modulate, °soften, °tone down: *He lowered his voice to a whisper.*
—*adj.* **6** °further *or* farther down: *My mother has a flat on a lower floor of the building.* **7** earlier: *These primitive amphibians are from the Lower Carboniferous.* **8** ***lower case***: °small, minuscule: *Use capitals for the first letters and lower case for the rest in these names.*

lower[2] *v.* See **lour,** above.

lowly *adj.* See **low**[1]**, 7,** above.

loyal *adj.* °faithful, °true, dependable, °devoted, °trustworthy, trusty, °steady, °steadfast, °staunch, trusted, °reliable, °stable, unswerving, unwavering, dedicated, °constant, °patriotic: *Give me twelve men loyal and true and we shall rout the enemy.*

loyalty *n.* faithfulness, fidelity, dependability, devotedness, °devotion, allegiance, patriotism, trustworthiness, steadfastness, staunchness, firmness, °resolution, °resolve, reliability, °stability, °dedication, constancy: *I hope that we can rely on the loyalty of everyone in your unit, Colonel.*

luck *n.* **1** °fortune, °chance, °destiny, °fate, °accident, fortuity, serendipity; °fluke, stroke of luck, *US* happenstance: *Luck brought us together.* **2** good °fortune, (good) °break: *It takes a lot of luck to get the kinds of roles you want as an actor.* **3** °chance(s), °success rate, °fortune(s): *I hope that my luck improves soon.*

lucky *adj.* **1** °fortunate, blessed, °favoured, °charmed: *She was very lucky to get the job.* **2** °providential, °timely, °opportune, °propitious, °favourable, auspicious, °advantageous, °convenient, fortuitous: *It was lucky that you were at the swimming pool to save her.*

ludicrous *adj.* °ridiculous, laughable, °absurd, °farcical, °nonsensical, °preposterous, °incongruous, asinine, °foolish, °silly, °zany, °crazy, comical, risible; °funny, facetious, droll, waggish, jocular, °witty, jocose: *The explanations of the new tax laws have been carried to ludicrous extremes. You can count on Billy to come up with some ludicrous prank on All Fools' Day.*

lug *v.* °drag, °tug, °tow, °haul, °heave; °carry, tote, °transport: *You're mistaken if you think I'm going to lug that case round everywhere.*

luggage *n.* baggage, °bags, °gear, impedimenta, °paraphernalia, °things, °belongings: *When I arrived in Torremolinos, I found my luggage was missing.*

lukewarm *adj.* **1** °tepid, room temperature, °warm: *I like my bath-water lukewarm.* **2** °cool, °indifferent, °half-hearted, °chill, °chilly, °phlegmatic, unresponsive, °unenthusiastic, °nonchalant, °lackadaisical, apathetic, insouciant, Laodicean, °unmoved, *US* half-baked, *Colloq* laid-back: *My ideas for improving efficiency continued to receive a lukewarm reception from the board.*

lull *n.* **1** °pause, °respite, °interlude, °intermission, °interval, °break, hiatus, °interruption, °stop, °halt, °lapse, °delay, *Literary* caesura, *Colloq* °let-up: *After a brief lull, the hurricane resumed in all its ferocity.* **2** °quiet, quiescence, °hush, °calm, calmness, stillness, °silence, °peace, peacefulness, tranquillity: *There was a lull, then the noise of the artillery again shattered the night.*
—*v.* **3** soothe, °calm, °quiet, °hush, pacify, mollify, °tranquillize: *Do not let her sweet words lull you into a sense of false security. I was lulled to sleep by the crickets and the bees.*

lumber *n.* **1** °odds and ends, °junk, °clutter, °jumble, °rejects, white elephants; °rubbish, °litter, *Chiefly US* °trash: *The small room off the kitchen is for lumber.* **2** °timber, wood, °beams, °planks, °boards: *I have ordered the lumber for building the garage.*
—*v.* **3** °encumber, °burden, °load, °overload, saddle, °impose upon, land: *We have been lumbered with looking after our neighbours' six cats.*

luminous *adj.* **1** °shiny, shining, °bright, °brilliant, lighted (up), lit (up), illuminated, °radiant, alight, resplendent, °lustrous, gleaming, shimmering, glistening, sparkling, °dazzling, refulgent, effulgent: *The moon shone with a luminous beauty.* **2** °glowing, aglow, luminescent, °incandescent, phosphorescent, fluorescent: *He had a watch with luminous hands.* **3** °clear, lucid, perspicuous, percipient, perspicacious, °penetrating, discerning, °perceptive, clear-eyed, clear-headed, °keen, °acute, °sharp, °explicit, °incisive, °specific, °express; understandable, °intelligible: *His latest novel provides another example of his luminous style.*

lump[1] *n.* **1** °mass, °piece, °gob, gobbet, °clod, chunk, clot, °wad, °clump, hunk, nugget; cube, °wedge, °cake: *There was a lump of earth clogging the drain. May I have two lumps of sugar, please?* **2** °bump, °growth, °swelling, protuberance, °protrusion, °prominence, °bulge, excrescence, tumescence, nodule, °knob; wen, cyst, °boil, carbuncle, blister, wart, corn: *You ought to see a doctor about that lump on your foot.*
—*v.* **3** Often, ***lump together***: °combine, °join, consolidate, °collect, °bunch, °group, °unite, °mass, aggregate, °blend, °mix, °throw *or* °put together: *Don't lump me together with everyone else, without even asking my opinion.*

lump[2] *v.* Usually, ***lump it***: °allow, °tolerate, °suffer, °put up with, °bear, °stand, °brook, °endure: *I'm afraid you'll just have to lump it, whether you like it or not.*

lumpy *adj.* chunky, °bumpy, uneven, °granular, grainy: *Mix the batter till it is no longer lumpy.*

lunacy *n.* **1** °madness, °insanity, dementia, craziness, derangement, psychosis, °mania: *Formerly, it was believed that lunacy fluctuated in accordance with the phases of the moon.* **2** °folly, foolishness, bad *or* poor °judgement, illogicality, illogic, senselessness, ridiculousness, irrationality, foolhardiness, °stupidity: *It would be sheer lunacy to confess to something you did not do.*

lunge *n.* **1** °thrust, °jab, °strike: *He was impaled by the first lunge of the sword.* **2** °dive, °plunge, °rush, °leap, °jump, °spring, °pounce: *I made a lunge for the knife but missed.*
—*v.* **3** °dive, °plunge, °charge, °pounce, °dash, °bound, °jump; °thrust, °stab, °strike, °hit, °jab, °cut: *He lunged at her with his machete.*

lurch[1] *n.* ***leave in the lurch***: °desert, °abandon, °forsake; °drop, °jilt: *He left her in the lurch, waiting at the church.*

lurch[2] *n.* **1** °stagger, °sway, °pitch; °list, °tilt, °toss: *The man gave a sudden lurch, knocking the vase from my hands.*
—*v.* **2** °stagger, °sway, °stumble; °roll, °tilt, veer, °pitch, °list, °heel, °wallow: *He lurched into the room, a dagger protruding from his back. The ship lurched dangerously in a heavy sea.*

lure *v.* **1** °tempt, °attract, °induce, °coax, inveigle, °seduce, °draw in, °entice, °lead on, °decoy, °charm, °persuade, allure, catch: *She lured me into the trap of believing that she loved me.*
—*n.* **2** bait, °decoy, °attraction, °temptation, °inducement, magnet, °siren song, °charm, *US* drawing card, *Slang* °come-on: *Too many naïve people fall for the lure of easy money.*

lurid *adj.* **1** °sensational, °vivid, °shocking, °startling, °graphic, °melodramatic: *The tabloids delight in a lurid scandal.* **2** °ghastly, horrid, horrifying, horrendous, °gory, °grisly, °gruesome, °macabre, °revolting, °disgusting, appalling, °frightful, °terrible, °awful: *Every lurid detail of the massacre was shown on TV.* **3** °pale, ashen, sallow, °wan, pallid, °ghastly, baleful: *From the lurid shade of his skin, I could see he had some horrible affliction.* **4** °glaring, °fiery, °flaming, °burning, aglow, °glowing, glowering: *The burning city cast a lurid light in the sky.*

lurk *v.* skulk, °slink, °prowl, °steal, °sneak, °hide, (°lie in) wait, °lie low: *The muggers were lurking in the shadows, waiting for a victim.*

luscious *adj.* delectable, °delicious, mouth-watering, °tasty, toothsome, °savoury, appetizing, °rich, °sweet, °epicurean, ambrosial, palatable, °pleasant; °succulent, °juicy, *Colloq* scrumptious, °yummy: *My grandmother used to make the most luscious pies and tarts.*

lush *adj.* **1** °luxuriant, °thick, °lavish, °flourishing, verdant, °green, °dense, °overgrown, °exuberant: *The walls were covered with a lush growth of ivy.* **2** °juicy, °succulent, mouth-watering, °fresh, °moist, °ripe: *We ate lush pears that we picked straight from the tree.* **3** °palatial, °extravagant, °elaborate, °luxurious, °opulent, °sumptuous, *Colloq* ritzy, °plush: *The bridal suite is the lushest accommodation they offer.*

lust *n.* **1** sensuality, libido, libidinousness, sexuality, lustfulness, concupiscence, °sexual °appetite, *Slang* horniness: *The nouveaux riches spend much of their time and money satisfying their lust.* **2** °desire, °drive, °energy, voracity, avidity, avidness, °ambition, ravenousness: *Henry has an infectious enthusiasm and lust for life.*
—*v.* **3** ***lust after***: °desire, crave, °hunger *or* °thirst *or* °hanker for *or* after, °ache for: *Barney was lusting after the barmaid at The Two Magpies.*

lustful *adj.* libidinous, °carnal, concupiscent, licentious, °lewd, °prurient, °lascivious, salacious, *Colloq* horny, °randy: *On her way to work she was forced to endure daily the lustful calls of the construction workers.*

lustre *n.* **1** °sheen, °gleam, °glow, °gloss, luminosity, luminousness, °radiance: *A good waxing should restore the lustre to the table.* **2** °glory, °renown, °brilliance, °celebrity, °honour, °distinction, °fame, illustriousness: *Winning first prize lent a little lustre to his tarnished reputation.*

lustrous *adj.* °glossy, °shiny, shined, °polished, burnished: *French polishing gives the furniture a lustrous finish.*

lusty *adj.* **1** °vigorous, °healthy, °strong, °energetic, °robust, °hale and °hearty, °lively; °buxom: *The sailors were accompanied by a couple of lusty young women.* **2** °vigorous, °substantial, °strong, °husky, °powerful: *He sang in a lusty voice.*

luxuriant *adj.* **1** °abundant, °profuse, copious, °lush, °rich, bounteous, overflowing, full, °luxurious: *Her luxuriant hair hung down to her waist.* **2** °lavish, full, °rank, °prolific, thriving, rife, °exuberant, °lush, abounding, plenteous, °abundant, superabundant, °dense, °fruitful, teeming: *The luxuriant orange groves are yielding a bumper crop this year.* **3** °ornate, °elaborate, decorated, °fancy, rococo, baroque, °flowery, frilly, florid, overdone, °flamboyant, °showy, °ostentatious, °gaudy, °garish, *Colloq* °flashy: *The elders disapproved of the luxuriant ornamentation of the churches.*

luxuriate *v.* **1** Often, ***luxuriate in***: °wallow in, swim in, bask in, °indulge in, °delight in, °relish, °revel in, °enjoy oneself, °savour, °appreciate, °like, °love: *She luxuriates in her new-found wealth.* **2** live in °luxury *or* °comfort, be in the lap of °luxury, have a good *or* great *or* marvellous time, take it °easy, °enjoy oneself, live the life of Riley, live off the °fat of the land, *Colloq* have the time of one's life, have a ball, *US* live high off the hog: *Their postcard says that they are luxuriating on Capri for a week.*

luxurious *adj.* **1** °opulent, °sumptuous, °grand, °extravagant, °lavish, °magnificent, °splendid, de luxe, °fancy; °epicurean, °gourmet; *Colloq* °swanky, swank, ritzy, °plush, °posh: *We had a luxurious room overlooking the sea and ate the most luxurious meals.* **2** °self-indulgent, °voluptuous, voluptuary, sybaritic, hedonistic, pampered: *We lived a truly luxurious life for two years till the money ran out.*

luxury *n.* **1** opulence, °splendour, sumptuousness, °grandeur, °extravagance, magnificence, richness, luxuriousness: *I cannot describe the overwhelming luxury of the maharaja's palace.* **2** °indulgence, self-indulgence, hedonism, sybaritism, voluptuousness: *He had been living a life of luxury in Tahiti.* **3** °security, °confidence; °gratification, °satisfaction, °enjoyment, °pleasure, °delight, °comfort: *He has the luxury of knowing that his dog will be well looked after.* **4** °frill, °extravagance, °extra, °indulgence, °non-essential, °expendable, °treat: *He showered her with luxuries from the finest shops.*

lying *n.* **1** prevarication, fibbing, mendacity, mendaciousness, falsification, untruthfulness, °perjury; dishonesty, °deceit, duplicity: *She was accused of lying while under oath.*
—*adj.* **2** untruthful, °false, mendacious, °hypocritical, °dishonest, °deceitful, °deceptive, duplicitous, treacherous, °perfidious: *Whoever told you they had found the solution is a lying scoundrel.*

lyric *adj.* **1** melodic, song-like, °musical, °melodious, °lyrical: *Lyric drama is no longer fashionable.* **2** °personal, °subjective, °individual, idiosyncratic; °sentimental, °rhapsodic: *He expresses his own feelings in the lyric poems.* **3** °sweet, dulcet, °graceful, silvery, lilting, mellifluous, °mellow, °light: *This song sounds best when sung by a lyric tenor.*
—*n.* **4** ***lyrics***: libretto, °book, °words: *Ira Gershwin wrote the lyrics for much of George Gershwin's music.*

lyrical *adj.* **1** See **lyric, 1,** above. **2** °enthusiastic, °ecstatic, encomiastic, °rapturous, °rhapsodic, °effusive, °impassioned, °emotional, °ebullient, °exuberant, panegyrical: *He waxed lyrical whenever he spoke of his children.*

M

macabre *adj.* °grim, °ghastly, °grisly, °gory, °gruesome, °grotesque, °ghoulish, °fiendish, °dread, °eerie, °fearsome, °frightful, °frightening, °terrifying, °terrible, °dreadful, dire, °morbid; deathly, °deadly, deathlike, °ghostly, cadaverous: *He told a macabre story of how they survived by resorting to cannibalism. The crypt had a macabre eeriness about it.*

Machiavellian *adj.* °deceitful, cunning, °shrewd, °crafty, °wily, °foxy, °scheming, °tricky, °perfidious, nefarious, treacherous, °sneaky: *Mr Williams has concocted a truly Machiavellian plan for getting the pensioners to move out.*

machination *n.* plotting, °scheming, intriguing, manoeuvring, °designing, manipulating; °plot, °scheme, °intrigue, °manoeuvre, °design, °stratagem,

°ruse, °trick, °trickery, °artifice, °dirty °trick(s), °wile, manipulation, ploy, °tactic(s), °move, gambit: *He escaped from the machinations of his enemies. Must you resort to such machinations merely to get them to listen?*

machine *n.* **1** °mechanism, °device, °apparatus, contrivance, appliance, °instrument, °implement, °tool, utensil, °gadget, *Colloq* °contraption, *US* gismo *or* gizmo: *What kind of machine is used to make a corkscrew?* **2** °engine, motor, prime mover, °vehicle; °car, automobile, motor °car, *US* auto: *We used to get into the machine and go for Sunday picnics.* **3** °organization, °system, °ring, °gang, °cabal, °clique, °party, °faction: *The entire council is run by a political machine.*
—*v.* **4** °shape, °make, °manufacture: *In this department we machine the castings to a tolerance of one ten-thousandth of an inch.*

machismo *n.* masculine °pride *or* °arrogance, manliness, virility, masculinity, °grit, *Colloq* guts, *Slang* balls: *He is just trying to impress you with his machismo.*

macho *adj.* °manly, masculine, virile, °proud, °arrogant: *He's afraid his macho image will be destroyed if he admits to enjoying ballet.*

mad *adj.* **1** °insane, °deranged, °crazy, crazed, demented, lunatic, unhinged, °delirious, out of one's °mind, °psychotic, °maniacal, (mentally) °unbalanced, mentally °ill, of °unsound °mind, *non compos mentis, Chiefly Brit* °daft, *Colloq* out of one's head, touched (in the head), screwy, cuckoo, °mental, certifiable, having a screw loose, dotty, cracked, mad as a March hare, mad as a hatter, not all there, off-the-wall, stark °raving mad, *Chiefly Brit* potty, *US* nutty as a fruit cake; *Slang* nuts, loony, goofy, loopy, crackers, batty, off one's rocker *or* trolley, bananas, *Brit* round the bend *or* twist, twisted, off one's chump, barmy *or* balmy, bonkers, *US* out to lunch, bughouse, bugs, °crazy as a bedbug *or* a coot, loco, wacky, out of one's tree, meshuga: *You're mad if you think I'm going in there with that lion.* **2** °foolish, °silly, °childish, °immature, °puerile, °wild, °nonsensical, °foolhardy, madcap, °heedless, °senseless, °absurd, °imprudent, unwise, °indiscreet, °rash, °ill-advised, ill-considered, °reckless, °extravagant, irrational, fatuous: *I did many mad things when I was a student. Hitching to Inverness is a mad idea.* **3** °wild, °ferocious; °rabid: *Have they caught that mad dog yet?* **4** °furious, °angry, infuriated, incensed, enraged, irate, fuming, °berserk, irritated, provoked, wrathful, exasperated, *Literary* wroth: *Will you get mad if I ask you a question? Please don't be mad with me—I wrecked your car.* **5** ***like mad***: °madly, feverishly, in a °frenzy, frenziedly, desperately, excitedly, violently, wildly, hysterically, furiously; enthusiastically, fervently, ardently; *Colloq* like °crazy: *He's been running about like mad trying to find her.* **6** ***mad (about*** *or* ***for)***: °crazy, °infatuated, °ardent, °enthusiastic, °eager, avid, zealous, °passionate, °fervent, fervid, °keen, °fanatical, °wild, *Colloq* hooked, *Brit* dotty, *Slang* nuts: *She's absolutely mad about cricket.*

madden *v.* **1** °infuriate, °anger, °enrage, incense, °provoke, °inflame, °excite (someone) to (a) °frenzy *or* °rage, make (someone's) blood °boil, raise (someone's) hackles, make (someone) see red, get (someone's) back up, drive (someone) °crazy, *Literary* raise (someone's) ire, *Colloq* drive (someone) up the °wall, *Brit* drive (someone) round the bend *or* twist, *US* tick (someone) off, burn (someone) up, tee (someone) off, °bug: *Their getting away with something like that maddened us all.* **2** °irk, vex, pique, °exasperate, °irritate: *He has the maddening habit of affecting a lisp.* **3** bait, badger, °torment, °plague, bedevil, *US* rile, hassle: *The dog was maddened into attacking anything that moved.*

madly *adv.* **1** insanely, hysterically, dementedly, wildly, distractedly, frenziedly: *The patient keeps screaming madly, day and night.* **2** foolishly, stupidly, inanely, ridiculously, ludicrously, idiotically, absurdly, irrationally, senselessly: *The king madly spurned the proffered aid and was soundly defeated.* **3** furiously, wildly, ferociously, °fiercely, energetically, desperately, like °mad, vehemently, feverishly, excitedly, fanatically, violently, impetuously: *He dashed about madly trying to get help.* **4** excessively, °extremely, desperately, intensely, passionately, wildly, ardently, fervently, fervidly, °exceedingly: *She was madly in love with George.*

madman *n.* madwoman; lunatic, psychopath, °psychotic, °maniac, *Colloq* crackpot, psycho, loony, screwball, *US* kook, *Slang* nut, nutcase, *Brit* nutter: *I am working like a madman to finish the book by the deadline.*

madness *n.* **1** °insanity, °lunacy, °mania, dementia, psychosis, °mental °illness: *That form of madness is called schizophrenia.* **2** craziness, °lunacy, °folly, foolishness, °nonsense, senselessness, ridiculousness, pointlessness, illogicality, illogic, illogicalness, impracticality, preposterousness, futility: *He soon realized the madness of trying to stem the tide of public opinion.*

magazine *n.* **1** °periodical, °journal, °publication: *We publish a quarterly magazine about language.* **2** arsenal, ammunition *or* munitions dump, armoury: *Saboteurs infiltrated the camp and blew up the magazine.*

magic *n.* **1** witchcraft, °sorcery, wizardry, °black magic, necromancy, °black °art, voodoo, obeahism, °devilry *or* deviltry, diabolism, demonolatry, occultism; sortilege, theurgy, white magic; °spell: *As the magic began to work, he slowly changed into a horrible ghoul.* **2** legerdemain, conjuring, prestidigitation, sleight of hand, °illusion, °hocus-pocus, °trickery: *He performs tricks of magic, including sawing a woman in half.* **3** °enchantment, allure, allurement, °charm, bewitchment, °spell, witchery, witchcraft, wizardry, °glamour, °fascination, °magnetism, ensorcellment: *She worked her magic on every man she met.*
—*adj.* **4** magical, °miraculous: *The magic ointment made her young again.* **5** necromantic, °occult, mystic, shamanistic, theurgical: *Using a magic spell, she turned him into a toad.* **6** magical, °enchanting, entrancing, bewitching, fascinating, hypnotic, mesmerizing, °spellbinding, charming, °magnetic, ensorcelling: *The music had a magic effect on them.*

magician *n.* **1** conjuror *or* conjurer, illusionist, wizard, °sorcerer, sorceress, magus, necromancer, enchanter, enchantress, Merlin, Houdini, Circe, °witch, warlock; thaumaturge, theurgist: *The court magician changed the pebbles into precious stones by a wave of his wand.* **2** °marvel, miracle-worker, °virtuoso, wizard, °genius, °master, *Colloq* whiz: *Mary Lou Williams is a magician on the boogie-woogie piano.*

magnetic *adj.* °attractive, attracting, °engaging, captivating, °enthralling, °seductive, alluring, entrancing, bewitching, beguiling, °arresting, °spellbinding, °irresistible, charismatic, °winning, winsome, °inviting: *Because of Amy's magnetic personality, men flock about her.*

magnetism *n.* °attraction, °draw, °appeal, allure, °magic, °lure, attractiveness, °charm, °pull, seductiveness, irresistibility, °drawing °power, charisma, *duende*, likeableness, °sex °appeal: *JFK's personal magnetism won him millions of votes.*

magnification *n.* enlargement, amplification; build-up, strengthening, enhancement, aggrandizement, raising, °elevation, °increase, °expansion, heightening, glorification, ennoblement: *The microdot can be read only at a magnification of X260. The advertising agency worked on the magnification of the candidate's record of achievement.*

magnificent *adj.* °great, °excellent, °splendid, °superior, °superb, °marvellous, °glorious, °grand, °fine, °impressive, °imposing, awe-inspiring, °brilliant, commanding, august, °noble, °majestic, °regal, °distinguished, °elegant, °exalted, °sublime, °outstanding; °sumptuous, resplendent, °opulent, °rich, °luxurious, °lavish: *She lives in a magnificent country house.*

magnify *v.* **1** °enlarge, °expand, °amplify, °inflate, °increase, augment, °exaggerate, °heighten, °build up, °boost, °dramatize, °aggravate, °worsen, exacerbate; °overstate, *Colloq* °blow up, make a mountain out of a molehill: *Tiny errors in the beginning are magnified later on. I fear that he has magnified its importance out of all proportion.* **2** °enlarge, °blow up: *They had to magnify the photograph to read the registration number of the stolen car.*

magnitude *n.* **1** greatness, °size, °extent, bigness, immensity, °enormousness, dimensions: *You cannot imagine the magnitude of the unemployment problem in our area.* **2** °importance, °significance, consequence, °note: *This is a matter of sufficient magnitude to warrant a board meeting.*

maid *n.* **1** °girl, °maiden, °lass, °miss, nymphet, nymph, wench, damsel, mademoiselle, demoiselle, *Scots* lassie; virgin, *virgo intacta*: *A lovely young maid was milking the cow.* **2** housemaid, maidservant, °domestic, chambermaid, lady's maid, *Archaic or literary* abigail, *Brit* daily, *Archaic colloq Brit* tweeny: *When she rang, the maid brought in the tea.* **3** ***old maid***: spinster, bachelor girl: *She never married and now is an old maid.*

maiden *n.* **1** See **maid, 1,** above.
—*adj.* **2** virgin, virginal, undefiled, °intact, °chaste, (*virgo*) *intacta*; °unmarried, unwed: *His maiden aunt was visiting for the weekend.* **3** inaugural, °first, °initial, *Colloq US* shakedown: *The* Titanic *sank on her maiden voyage.*

mail *n.* **1** °post, correspondence; °letters: *Has the mail arrived?*
—*v.* **2** °post, °send, °dispatch *or* despatch: *Please mail this letter tonight.*

maim *v.* °cripple, °mutilate, °lame, disable, °incapacitate, °wound, wing, °impair, hamstring, put out of action *or* commission; °injure, °harm, °damage: *Their daughter was badly maimed in the fire.*

main *adj.* **1** °chief, °primary, °prime, (most) °important, °principal, °cardinal, °paramount, °first, °foremost, °leading, °pre-eminent, °predominant, predominating, °dominant, ranking, °major; °outstanding: *The main cause of traffic deaths is drunken driving. In Britain, the main street of a town is called 'the High Street'. We arrived late and missed the main entertainment.* **2** largest, biggest, greatest, strongest: *The main part of the strike force landed in Normandy.* **3** °necessary, °essential, °basic, °particular, °fundamental, °critical, °crucial, °vital: *Economic recovery is the main thrust of our programme for reform.* **4** °sheer, °brute, utter, °pure, °out-and-out, °absolute, °mere, °plain: *He lifted that block by main force!*
—*n.* **5** °pipe, duct, °channel, °line, °pipeline, water *or* gas main, *Brit* (electric) °cable, mains, power (°supply), conduit: *Water reaches the city through a huge underground main.* **6** °strength, °power, °might, °effort, °energy, °vigour: *With all his might and main he tried to move the stone blocking the cave.* **7** ***in the main***: See **mainly,** below.

mainly *adv.* in the °main, °chiefly, °principally, predominantly, °generally, above all, on the °whole, in °general, mostly, most of all, effectively, essentially, at °bottom, °first and °foremost, for the most part, °largely, by and °large, °primarily, as a °rule, °usually, all in all, on °balance, for all practical purposes, in the long °run: *We are concerned mainly with safety. The tourists are mainly from Italy.*

mainstay *n.* °main *or* °chief *or* °principal °support, °anchor (to windward), sheet °anchor, °bulwark, °buttress, linchpin, °main *or* greatest °strength: *David remains the mainstay of the sales force.*

maintain *v.* **1** °continue, °preserve, °persevere in, °keep going, °persist in, °keep (up), °carry on, °retain, °perpetuate, °prolong, °sustain, °uphold: *Sarah maintained friendly relations with her ex-husband. Try to maintain your composure.* **2** °look after, take °care of, °care for, °preserve, (°keep in) °service, °keep up, °keep in °repair; nurture, °support: *It is expensive to maintain a vintage car. Allison maintains an ancient aunt in Piddlington.* **3** °hold, °state, °say, °declare, °claim, assert, °allege, °testify, contend, aver, avow, °announce, °proclaim, °vouchsafe, °profess, °insist (on), affirm: *Despite evidence to the contrary, he maintains that he is innocent.* **4** °defend, °stand by, °keep, °fight for; take up the cudgels for, make a case for, °advocate, °champion, take *or* make a °stand for, °plead for, back (up), °support, °vindicate, °justify, *Colloq* go to bat for: *He maintained his ground in the face of virulent attacks.*

maintenance *n.* **1** °upkeep, °care, °preservation, °conservation, °support, sustention, sustentation: *I can no longer afford the maintenance of a large country estate.* **2** continuation, continuance, perpetuation, prolongation, °persistence, maintaining: *His maintenance of an untenable position will lose him votes.* **3** °upkeep, livelihood, °subsistence, °support, °allowance, living, °sustenance, °stipend, subvention, contribution, alimony, °keep: *How much maintenance does he pay to his ex-wife and children?*

majestic *adj.* **1** °regal, °dignified, °grand, °imperial, °royal, °noble, lordly, °lofty, °elevated, °exalted, °glorious, °magnificent, °monumental, °impressive, °striking, °imposing, °awesome, °splendid, °marvellous, kingly, queenly, °princely: *With majestic ceremony, the procession entered the cathedral.* **2** °pompous, °supercilious, °disdainful, °superior, °arrogant, °haughty, magisterial, imperious, °grandiose, °affected: *She dismissed him with a majestic wave of her hand.*

major *adj.* **1** larger, greater, bigger, °main, °chief, °important: *Henderson grabbed the major portion of the credit.* **2** °vital, °important, °critical, °crucial, °principal, °foremost, °paramount, °primary, °prime, °main, °big, biggest, °pre-eminent, °notable, °noteworthy, °significant, °outstanding, °dominant, dominating; °serious, °grave, worst: *The major problem in commercial kitchens is sanitation.*

majority *n.* **1** °bulk, °preponderance, °mass, more than half, the °better *or* °best °part, the greater °part *or* °number, lion's °share: *The majority of shares were bought by existing shareholders.* **2** adulthood, °maturity, seniority, womanhood, °manhood: *They reach their majority in 1997.*

make *v.* **1** °build, °assemble, °construct, °erect, °put together, °set up, °fashion, °form, °mould, °shape, °frame, °create, °originate, °fabricate, °manufacture, °produce, °put out, °forge, contrive, °devise: *She makes her own dresses. They make TV sets here. The Colossus of Rhodes was said to be made of bronze.* **2** °cause, compel, °force, impel, coerce, °provoke, °urge, exhort, °press, °pressure, °require, °command, °order, °induce, °persuade, °prevail (up)on, °insist (up)on, °oblige, *Brit* pressurize: *The devil made me do it.* **3** °bring about, °occasion, °cause, give rise to: *The new regulation is going to make trouble for you.* **4** make out *or* up, °draw (up), °create, °write, °sign, °frame: *I made a new will leaving everything to my children.* **5** °produce, °cause, °create, °generate: *The engine made a funny noise, then died.* **6** °enact, °pass, °frame, °establish, °institute: *He thinks that laws were made to be broken.* **7** °earn, °return, °reap, °garner, °take in, °get, °procure, °gather, °clear, °realize, °gross, °net, °pocket, °acquire, °obtain, °receive; °win, °gain, *Slang US* °pull down: *Has her invention made money? He makes a good living out of his shop. He made £25 playing poker.* **8** °amount to, constitute, °represent, °add up to, °total, °come to: *He knows how many beans make five. Three and two do not make four. One singer does not make an opera.* **9** °change, °turn, °alter, °modify, °transform, °convert; transmute, mutate, metamorphose: *He made her into a star. The alchemists tried to make base metal into gold.* **10** °become, be, °change *or* °turn *or* °grow into, °perform as: *I think Quentin will make a brilliant surgeon one day.* **11** °serve as *or* for, be °suitable for, be, °prove to be, °turn out to be, °turn into, °become: *This cut of meat will not make a good roast.* **12** °fetch, °realize, °earn, °return: *The locket made £1,000 at the* *auction.* **13** °score, °earn, °secure: *The West Indies made 654 in their first innings.* **14** °reach, °arrive at, attain, °get (to), °win, °achieve, °accomplish; °come in, *Brit* be placed, *US* °place: *Fran might make first place in the marathon.* **15** °prepare, °arrange, rearrange, °tidy (up), °neaten (up): *You have made your bed, now you will have to lie on it.* **16** °record, °arrange, °fix, °decide (on *or* upon), °agree (to): *I made an appointment to see the doctor.* **17** °prepare, °fix, cook: *I made what you like for dinner.* **18** °deliver, °present: *Janet made a good speech.* **19** °traverse, °cover, do, °travel, °navigate: *We cannot make more than 100 miles a day over this terrain.* **20** do, °go, °travel *or* °move at, °move: *His old banger could hardly make 40 m.p.h.* **21** °judge, °think, °calculate, °estimate, °reckon, °gauge, °suppose: *What do you make of Sidney's new book?* **22** °establish, °set up, °organize: *We made our headquarters in the farmhouse.* **23** °appoint, °name, °select, °choose, °elect, °vote (in as), °designate, °authorize, commission, °delegate, depute, deputize, °assign, °sanction, °approve, affirm, °certify, °confirm: *They made him their leader.* **24** °seduce, make it with: *Kenneth tried to make Sharon last night.* **25** ***make as if** or **as though***: °pretend, feign, °act as if *or* as °though, °affect, make a °show *or* °pretence of, give the °impression of: *He made as if to strike me.* **26** ***make away***: °run off *or* away, °flee, °fly, make off, abscond, take to one's °heels, decamp, °beat a (hasty) °retreat, *Colloq* °run for it, make a °run for it, °beat it, °clear out, °cut and °run, skedaddle, °take off, °cut out, °skip (town), make tracks, *US* °fly the coop, *Slang* scram, vamoose, *US* hightail it, take a (run-out) °powder: *Taking the jewels, he made away as fast as he could run.* **27** ***make away with***: °steal, °rob, filch, °pilfer, purloin, °walk away *or* off with, *Colloq* °borrow, °liberate, *Slang* °pinch, °hook, °swipe, °rip off, °lift, *US* boost: *That boy has made away with my cherry tarts!* **28** ***make believe***: °pretend, °fancy, play-act, °dream, °fantasize, °imagine, °act as if: *We used to make believe we were grown-ups.* **29** ***make do***: °get by *or* along, °cope, °scrape by *or* along, °manage, °muddle through, °survive, *Colloq* make out: *We have to make do on the pittance Randolph gets from the university.* **30** ***make for***: **a** °head for *or* towards, °aim for, °steer (a course) for, °proceed towards, be °bound for: *After this is done, I am making for the nearest pub.* **b** °assault, °attack, °set upon, °charge, °rush (at), °pounce upon, °fall upon *or* on, °go for, °lunge at, °storm, assail: *The big fellow was making for me with a knife when the lights went out.* **c** °promote, °contribute to, be conducive to, °favour, °facilitate: *Good fences make for good neighbours.* **31** ***make good***: **a** make up (for), °pay (for), °compensate for, recompense (for), °repay, °offset, make °restitution for, °settle, °square, °rectify, put to rights, set °right, °remedy, °correct, °restore: *He agreed to make good any losses.* **b** °succeed, °prosper, °flourish, °thrive, *Colloq* make it: *In later life he made good as a property developer.* **c** °fulfil, °carry out, *Colloq* °deliver (the goods): *She made good on her promise to return my book.* **32** ***make it***: **a** °succeed, °prosper, °triumph, °win, make good, *Colloq* make the °grade: *Do you think she will make it as a doctor?* **b** °arrive, °get (somewhere), °show up, °appear, °turn up: *They are hoping to catch the 5:03 to Ipswich but I doubt if they will make it.* **33** ***make known***: °tell of, °impart, °disclose, °reveal, divulge, °mention, °communicate, °announce, °declare, promulgate, °publish, let °slip, *Colloq* °tip off: *She made known her demands.* **34** ***make much of***: **a** °exaggerate, °overstate, °colour, hyperbolize, *Colloq* make a big deal of, °blow up: *He made much of his new title.* **b** °coddle, cosset, °baby, °pamper, °dote on, °flatter, toady (up) to, °cajole, °humour, °indulge, *Colloq* butter up: *Henry makes much of his grandchildren.* **35** ***make off***: See **make, 26,** above. **36** ***make off with***: See **make, 27,** above. **37** ***make out***: **a** °see, discern, descry, espy, °detect, °discover, °distinguish, °perceive: *I made out a dim figure in the gloom.* **b** °complete, °fill in, *Brit* °fill up, *US and Canadian* °fill out: *I made out an application for the job.* **c** °draw (up), °write (out *or* down), °record, *Colloq US* cut: *Please make out a list of your complaints. Make out the cheque to me, personally.* **d** °understand, °fathom, °comprehend, °figure out, °perceive, °follow, °grasp, °see, °decipher, °read: *She mumbles so, I cannot make out what she's saying. Can you make out this name?* **e** °suggest, °imply, °hint, °insinuate, °indicate, °impute, °intimate, make to °appear, °pretend, make as if *or* as °though, °represent; °present, °show, °demonstrate, °establish: *She tried to make out that I was a fool. He made out a strong case for dog licensing.* **f** °get on, °survive, °manage, °fare, °thrive, °succeed: *How are you making out in your new house?* **38** ***make over***: **a** do over, remodel, redecorate, °alter: *We are making over our kitchen.* **b** °transfer, °hand over, °sign over, convey, °assign, °turn over: *The property has been made over to me.* **39** ***make up***: **a** °complete, °fill out, °finish (out), °flesh out: *We need another player to make up the team.* **b** °compose, °form, constitute, be comprised of: *The gang is made up of ex-convicts.* **c** °hatch, °invent, concoct, °devise, °create, °construct, °dream up, °originate, °coin, °compose, *Colloq* cook up: *He made up that story about the murder.* **d** be reconciled, make °peace, °settle amicably, come to °terms, bury the hatchet: *The litigants have kissed and made up.* **e** °construct, °build: *The shack is made up of scrap boards.* **40** ***make up for***: °compensate, redress, make good, atone, make °amends: *How can I make up for all the bad things I said about you?* **41** ***make way***: °move aside, °clear the °way, allow to pass, make °room *or* °space: *Make way for the Lord High Executioner!*

—*n.* **42** °kind, °brand, °style, °sort, °type, °mark: *Foreign makes of car currently dominate the marketplace.* **43** ***on the make***: °aggressive, °assertive, °go-ahead, °enterprising, °vigorous, °energetic, *Colloq* °pushy: *The book is about a young man on the make in today's financial world.*

makeshift *adj.* **1** °temporary, °stopgap, °expedient, °emergency, jury-rigged, improvised, °tentative, °stand-by, slapdash: *We were able to fashion a makeshift rudder out of an oar.*

—*n.* **2** °stopgap, °expedient, improvisation, °substitute: *The heater broke down and we had to get along with a makeshift.*

make-up *n.* **1** cosmetics, *maquillage*, greasepaint, *Colloq* warpaint: *Do you think I am wearing too much make-up?* **2** constitution, °character, °cast, °disposition, °personality: *There is not an ounce of sympathy in Janet's make-up.* **3** constitution, °arrangement, construction, °composition, °format, configuration, °build, °form: *What is the chemical make-up of the plastic?*

male *adj.* masculine, man's; virile, °manly, manful; *Archaic* spear: *His is bound to be a male point of view.*

malignant *adj.* **1** °virulent, pernicious, °deadly, °fatal, toxic, °poisonous, °harmful, life-threatening: *The tumour proved to be malignant.* **2** malign, malevolent, °evil, malicious, pernicious, °vicious, invidious, °spiteful, °bitter, °hateful, °venomous: *The exposé was full of malignant insinuations.*

man *n.* **1** gentleman, °male, °fellow, *Colloq* °guy, °chap, *Brit* bloke, °squire, *Slang* gink, geezer, *US* gazabo: *Have you met the man she is going to marry?* **2** °people, °human beings, mankind, °mortals, *Homo sapiens*, °humanity, humankind, the °human °race: *Man wants but little here below.* **3** valet, manservant, gentleman's gentleman, °servant, retainer, houseboy, houseman: *Humberson sent his man round with a note.*

—*v.* **4** °staff, °people, °crew; °cover: *Who will man the office while I am away?*

manacle *n.* **1** ***manacles***: shackles, fetters, °handcuffs, gyves, °chains, irons, *Colloq* cuffs, *Slang* bracelets, *Brit* darbies: *The manacles are cutting into his wrists.*

—*v.* **2** °shackle, fetter, handcuff, °restrain, put *or* throw *or* °clap in irons, °chain, *Colloq US* cuff: *The manacled prisoner was led away.* **3** confine, °inhibit, °restrain, °curb, °check, °control, °hamper: *They felt manacled by the nine o'clock curfew.*

manage *v.* **1** °handle, °administer, °run, °supervise, °look after, °watch over, °direct, °head, °oversee, superintend, °preside over, be in charge (of), take °care of, °control; °rule (over), °govern, °regulate: *Mr Grant manages the glove department.* **2** °handle, °cope *or* °deal with, °control, °govern, °manipulate: *Will you be able to manage such a frisky horse?* **3** °conduct, °carry on, °carry out, °bring off, °control, °undertake, take °care of, °look after, °handle: *Is she old enough to manage her own affairs?* **4** °succeed, °function, °make do, °make it, °shift (for oneself), °get along *or* by *or* on, °make out, °muddle through, °survive: *Will you be able to manage from here on?*

manageable *adj.* controllable; °tractable, compliant, amenable, docile, tameable, °tame, trainable, teachable, manipulable, °submissive: *Keep your spending within manageable limits. The dog is quite manageable.*

management *n.* **1** managing, °control, supervision, manipulation, handling, °direction, directing, directorship, °administration, °government, °conduct, governance, °operation, °running, superintendence, °command, °guidance, stewardship: *The management of the company is in your hands.* **2** °administration, °executive(s), °bosses, °directors, °board (of °directors), directorate, *Colloq* (°top) brass: *The management believes that you are the right person for the job.*

manager *n.* °supervisor, °superintendent, °director, °executive, °head, °proprietor, °overseer, °foreman, forewoman, administrator, *Chiefly Brit* manageress, *US* straw °boss, *Colloq* °boss, °chief: *The position of manager entails a lot of responsibility.*

mandatory *adj.* compulsory, °obligatory, requisite, required; °essential, commanded, demanded, °necessary, needed: *The wearing of safety belts in cars is mandatory.*

mangle *v.* °destroy, °mutilate, °butcher, deform, disfigure, °spoil, °mar, °ruin, °wreck; °cut, °hack, °lacerate, °chop (up), °crush, °damage, °cripple, °maim: *Don't you hate the way they mangle the English language? His hand was badly mangled in the accident.*

mangy *adj.* scruffy, °dirty, °sleazy, °wretched, °miserable, °repulsive, °sorry, squalid, slovenly, °unkempt, °filthy, °dingy, °seedy, °poor, °shabby, °mean, °low, ignominious, °base, abject, odious, °disreputable, moth-eaten, °contemptible, °despicable, °nasty, °scurvy: *That mangy beggar was once a top athlete.*

manhandle *v.* maul, paw, °rough up, °batter, °beat (up), pummel, °abuse, °mistreat, maltreat, °ill-treat, trounce, °belabour, *Slang* °knock about *or* around, clobber: *His captors manhandled him into a car and drove off.*

man-hater *n.* °misanthrope, misanthropist: *He says he prefers to live alone because he's a man-hater.*

manhood *n.* **1** masculinity, manliness, manfulness, virility, *Colloq* °machismo: *He felt that looking after the children at home somehow compromised his manhood.* **2** °bravery, °pluck, boldness, °determination, °resolution, °fortitude, °grit, °spirit, °force, *US* intestinal °fortitude, *Colloq* guts: *He joined the army to test his manhood.*

mania *n.* **1** °rage, °craze, °passion, °obsession, compulsion, °urge, °fascination, preoccupation, °furore *or US* furor, yearning, craving, °desire, cacoethes, *Colloq* °fad, yen: *By that time, the hula hoop mania had died down. She has a mania for collecting apostle spoons.* **2** °madness, °lunacy, °insanity, dementia, derangement, hysteria, *Technical* manic °disorder: *The psychiatrists diagnosed his problem as a mania.*

maniac *n.* **1** °madman, madwoman, lunatic, psychopath, °psychotic, *Colloq* crackpot, *Slang* nut, *Brit* nutter, loony, *US* kook: *In former times, maniacs were scorned and maltreated.* **2** °fanatic, °fan, °enthusiast, °zealot, *Slang* °freak, °fiend: *Since his retirement, he has become a golf maniac.*

maniacal *adj.* **1** manic, °maniac, °insane, lunatic, °mad, demented, °deranged, °hysterical, mentally °ill, of °unsound °mind, *non compos mentis*, °psychotic: *He had to be hospitalized because of his maniacal behaviour.* **2** °hysterical, °berserk, °wild, °crazy, *Slang* loony: *His maniacal outbursts frightened us.*

manifest *adj.* **1** °apparent, °clear, °evident, °obvious, °plain, °patent, °blatant, °conspicuous, unmistakable, °discernible, recognizable, comprehensible, °distinct, palpable, °definite, °explicit, unambiguous, °unquestionable, indubitable, °indisputable: *He lost his job because of his manifest dishonesty.*
—*v.* **2** °show, °demonstrate, °exhibit, evince, °reveal, °disclose, °display, °betray; °express, °declare: *Fitzsimmons had been manifesting signs of dissatisfaction with his assignment.* **3** °prove, corroborate, °substantiate, °attest: *His distaste for cauliflower was manifested by the look on his face.*

manifestation *n.* °display, °exhibition, °demonstration, °show, disclosure, °appearance, °exposure, °presentation, °sign, °indication, °mark, °expression, °example, °instance; °declaration, avowal, °publication, °announcement: *The police feared that the crime wave was a manifestation of civil unrest. The first manifestation of thought is speech.*

manifestly *adv.* °evidently, °clearly, °obviously, plainly, °apparently, patently, unmistakably, palpably, unquestionably, indubitably, °undoubtedly, indisputably: *The treaty is manifestly to England's advantage.*

manifold *adj.* °diverse, diversified, multifarious, °varied, °various, assorted, multiplex, °miscellaneous, °sundry, many-sided, °many °different, *Literary* °divers; °many, numerous, multitudinous: *I have manifold reasons for wishing you to stay.*

manipulate *v.* **1** °manage, °handle, °control, °manoeuvre, orchestrate, choreograph, °influence, °use, °exploit, °play on, utilize: *He knows how to manipulate people to make them do what he wants.* **2** °handle, °control, °operate, °direct, °work, °use, °employ, °negotiate: *The controls can be manipulated to make the robot imitate human motion.* **3** °rig, °falsify, °juggle, °tamper with, °doctor, *Colloq* cook, *Chiefly Brit* °fiddle: *He's been manipulating his expense account for years.*

manly *adj.* manful, virile, °courageous, °bold, °brave, °intrepid, valorous, valiant, °dauntless, °fearless, plucky, °daring, °venturesome, stout-hearted, °resolute, °stable, °steadfast, unflinching, unwavering, unshrinking, °chivalrous, °gallant, °noble, °heroic; masculine, °male, *Colloq* °macho, red-blooded: *Emerson characterized the English as manly rather than warlike.*

manner *n.* **1** °way, °mode, °style, °technique, °procedure, °method, °fashion; °means, °approach: *Her incisive manner of reporting is widely admired.* **2** °air, °behaviour, mien, demeanour, °bearing, deportment, comportment, °conduct, °attitude, °aspect: *His manner is overbearing and dictatorial.* **3** ***manners***: °etiquette, °decorum, (°good) °form, politeness, proprieties, °protocol, politesse, °civility, °ceremony, °social °code, °social graces, °formalities, niceties, amenities, °social °conventions; °behaviour, °conduct: *Can't you teach him some manners?*

mannered *adj.* °artificial, contrived, °stilted, °stiff, °affected, °insincere, °pompous, °pretentious, posed, °unnatural, °hypocritical, *Colloq* °phoney *or US also* phony, pseudo, highfalutin *or* hifalutin, la-di-da *or* lah-di-dah *or* la-de-da, °hoity-toity, on one's high horse, high-hat, uppity *or Brit* °uppish: *Alice's speech is too mannered for anyone to feel close to her.*

mannerism *n.* °quirk, °peculiarity, idiosyncrasy, °trait, °characteristic, °habit: *She has the irritating mannerism of pulling on her ear lobe.*

manoeuvre *n.* **1** °move, °stratagem, °tactic, °trick, gambit, ploy, °subterfuge, °ruse, °dodge, °artifice, °device, °wile, *démarche;* °strategy, °plan, °plot, °scheme, °intrigue, °machination: *That manoeuvre will never work on a clever woman.* **2** °exercise, °operation, °drill, war-game, kriegspiel, training: *We were out on manoeuvres for a week.*

—*v.* **3** °manipulate, contrive, °plot, °scheme, machinate, °intrigue, °trick, °devise, °engineer, °finesse, °manage, *Colloq* finagle, °wangle: *His manoeuvred his way out of going on that mission.* **4** °manipulate, °operate, °run, °drive, °guide, °navigate, jockey: *She manoeuvred the car into a surprisingly tiny space.*

mantle *n.* **1** °cloak, °cape, °wrap, shawl, pelisse, pelerine: *Over his armour he wore a mantle embroidered with his bearing.* **2** covering, °cover, °sheet, °veil, blanket, °screen, °cloak, °shroud, °pall, canopy, curtain: *A mantle of snow lay on the ground.*
—*v.* **3** °cover, °clothe, °envelop, °surround, °encircle, °shroud, °veil, °screen, °obscure, °cloak, °conceal, °hide, °mask, °wrap, °disguise: *The mountains were brilliantly mantled and capped with snow.*

manual *n.* handbook, °vade-mecum, enchiridion; directions, instructions, °guide: *Follow the manual carefully to avoid mistakes.*

manufacture *v.* **1** °make, (°mass-)°produce, °construct, °build, °assemble, °fabricate, °put together, °turn out, °create, °originate: *The company manufactures windscreen wipers.* **2** concoct, °create, contrive, °invent, °make up, °fabricate, °think up, *US and Canadian* °create out of *or* from whole cloth, *Colloq* cook up: *She manufactured that tale about being an orphan.*
—*n.* **3** making, (°mass) °production, construction, °building, °assembly, °fabrication, turning *or* putting out, putting together, °creation, origination: *The manufacture of durable goods increased 0.02% in the last quarter.*

manufacturer *n.* maker, °producer, industrialist, fabricator: *Manufacturers of computers usually buy components from specialized firms.*

many *adj.* **1** numerous, multitudinous, myriad, °profuse, innumerable, °numberless, uncountable: *Many people have an irrational fear of spiders.* **2** °diverse, multifarious, °varied, °various, assorted, °sundry, *Literary* °divers: *There are many kinds of courage.*
—*n.* **3** horde(s), °crowd(s), °lot(s), °swarm(s), °throng(s), °mass(es), °profusion, multitude(s), °abundance, °plenty, shoal(s), °flock(s), drove(s), °torrent(s), °flood(s), °number(s), °score(s), hundred(s), (thousand(s), etc.); *Colloq* ton(s), scads: *A great many will turn out to vote next week. Many are picked but few are chosen.*

mar *v.* **1** °damage, °ruin, °mutilate, °deface, °spoil, °scar, disfigure: *The surface of the table was marred by a deep scratch.* **2** °damage, °wreck, °ruin, °impair, °harm, °hurt, °blight, °blot, °taint, °stain, °tarnish: *She claims that her reputation was marred by the article.*

march *v.* **1** °parade, °step, stride, °strut, tread, °pace, °walk: *They marched from Baxter Street to the Town Hall.*
—*n.* **2** °parade, °procession, °demonstration, cortege *or* cortège, °walk: *The march was organized to protest against the government's nuclear arms policy.* **3** °walk, trek, slog, hike: *We had a long march ahead of us to get to Hastings.*

margin *n.* **1** °edge, °border, °perimeter, °periphery; °rim, lip, °side, °brink, °verge: *Leave a one-inch margin at the left side of the page. Trees grew at the margin of the pond.* **2** °limit(s), °bound(s), °boundary (°line), °border, °frontier, °line, °partition °line: *These streets form the margin of the inner city.* **3** °allowance, °play, °leeway, latitude, °scope, °freedom, °room, °space; compass: *These calculations do not provide much of a margin for error.*

marginal *adj.* **1** borderline, °minimal, °small, °slight, °negligible, °insignificant, °tiny, infinitesimal: *There are marginal differences in policy on this issue.* **2** borderline, on the °edge, °disputable, °questionable, °doubtful, dubious: *His qualifications for the job are marginal.*

marine *adj.* **1** maritime, °nautical, naval, °seafaring, seagoing, ocean-going, °sea: *Marine commerce has declined during recent decades.* **2** maritime, °sea, °oceanic, aquatic, salt-water, pelagic, thalassic: *Many groups are concerned about the conservation of marine life.*

mark *n.* **1** °spot, °stain, °blemish, °smear, smudge, °trace, °impression, dent, °nick, °scratch, pock-mark *or* pock, °streak, °line, *Brit* splodge, *US* splotch: *One of the children had made a mark on the newly painted wall.* **2** °sign, °symbol, insigne, °emblem, °device, °hallmark, earmark, fingerprint, badge, °characteristic, °token, °brand, °stamp, °label, °identification, °indication, °feature, °attribute, °trait, °quality, °property: *This work bears the mark of true genius.* **3** °standard, criterion, °norm, °yardstick, °level, °measure: *I'm afraid your son's work has not come up to the mark.* **4** rating, °grade, grading: *I'd give her a low mark for originality but high marks for technique.* **5** °influence, °impression, °effect: *Her innovations have left their mark on all music composed since 1900.* **6** °target, °goal, °objective, °aim, °purpose, °end, °object: *Her criticisms fell wide of the mark.* **7** marker, °indicator, °guide, signpost, °landmark: *The next mark, a bell-buoy, should be left to port.* **8** consequence, °importance, °note, noteworthiness, notability, °distinction, eminence, °dignity, °prestige, °standing, °account: *Granada was a place of little mark as compared with Cordova.* **9** ***make one's mark***: °succeed, get °ahead, °triumph, °distinguish oneself, attain °distinction, bring °honour upon oneself, acquit oneself, bring °credit to oneself, have an °effect, *Colloq* °make it °big, make the °grade: *Randolph has made his mark in the world of scholarship.*
—*v.* **10** Sometimes, ***mark up***: °spot, °stain, °blemish, °smear, smudge, °streak, dent, °trace, pock-mark, °nick, °scratch, °cut, °chip, °pit, °bruise: *That glass has marked the finish on the table.* **11** °signify, °specify, °indicate, °designate, °identify, tick, °label: *Mark your choice with an 'X' next to the candidate's name.* **12** pay °attention to, °attend (to), pay °heed to, °note, °notice, take °notice of, °watch, °see, °look at, °observe; °respect, °mind, °heed, °obey: *Mark the way she swings the golf club. Mark my words or you'll be sorry.* **13** °brand, °stamp, °identify, °characterize, °distinguish: *His music is marked by long atonal passages.* **14** °correct; °grade, °evaluate, assess, appraise: *The teachers are busy marking exam papers.* **15** ***mark down***: **a** °write (down), °record, °register, make (a) °note of, °note (down): *Mark down these numbers in your book.* **b** °decrease, °reduce, devalue, devaluate, °cut, °slash, °discount: *We marked down the prices for a quick sale.* **16** ***mark up***: **a** See **10,** above. **b** °increase, °raise, hike, up: *Prices were marked up to keep pace with inflation.*

marked *adj.* °noticeable, °conspicuous, °decided, °pronounced, °considerable, °remarkable, °significant, °signal, unmistakable, °prominent, °obvious, °patent, °evident, °apparent: *There is a marked improvement in your work.*

market *n.* **1** market-place, °exchange, Stock Exchange: *There are some excellent buys on the market.* **2** °shop, °store, bazaar, supermarket, *Chiefly US* superstore: *If you are going to the market, please buy some milk.* **3** °demand, °customer °base, °call: *The market for computers is still growing rapidly.*
—*v.* **4** °sell, °merchandise, retail, vend, °peddle, hawk, make available, °furnish; °trade (in), °buy and °sell, °deal in: *We market these computers worldwide.*

maroon *v.* °abandon, °cast away, °desert, strand, °forsake; °isolate, seclude: *They were marooned on a desert island.*

marriage *n.* **1** matrimony, wedlock: *Their marriage has lasted over forty years.* **2** nuptials, °wedding: *The marriage took place at noon.* **3** °association, °alliance, confederation, °federation, affiliation, °connection, coupling, °union, °merger, °amalgamation, integration, *Colloq* hook-up: *Would a marriage of the companies benefit the shareholders?*

marry *v.* **1** °wed, °join in matrimony *or* wedlock, become man and wife, *Colloq* get hitched *or* spliced, tie the knot: *They married and lived happily ever after.* **2** °match (up), go *or* °fit together, °fit; °unite, °unify,

°bond, °weld, °fuse, °put together, °couple, °join, °link; °league, affiliate, °ally, °amalgamate, °combine: *The marble head, found in London, married perfectly with the torso, found in Crete. The best qualities of each earlier model are married in this new product.*

marsh *n.* °swamp, °bog, fen, slough, quagmire: *The marsh teems with new life in the spring.*

martial *adj.* **1** °warlike, °belligerent, bellicose, °pugnacious, °militant: *We had no suspicion of their martial intentions. He is an expert in the martial arts.* **2** °military, soldierly, °courageous, °brave, valorous, valiant, °stalwart, °staunch, stout-hearted: *The speech was intended to rouse the soldiers' martial spirit.*

marvel *v.* **1** °wonder (at), °gape (at), be awed *or* amazed (by), be °agog *or* astonished (at): *We marvelled at the way the homing pigeons found their way home.*
—*n.* **2** °wonder, miracle, °phenomenon: *Tammy was a marvel at fixing electrical equipment.*

marvellous *adj.* wonderful, astonishing, °amazing, astounding, surprising, °remarkable, °extraordinary, °phenomenal, °glorious, °splendid, °superb, °excellent, spectacular, breathtaking, °miraculous, °unbelievable, °incredible, °sensational, mind-boggling, °unparalleled, *Colloq* °terrific, °great, °fantastic, °fabulous, smashing, *Slang* far-out, °crazy, °wild, groovy, °super, out of this °world, fantabulous, *Brit* spot *or* bang on, *US* marvy: *It was a marvellous show, and Renfrew is a marvellous actor.*

mask *n.* **1** °false °face, domino: *She wore a mask, and I don't know who she was.* **2** °disguise, °guise, °camouflage, °show, °semblance, °pretence, °cover, cover-up, °false colours, °false flag, concealment, °cloak, façade, °veil: *He wormed his way into her confidence under the mask of friendship.*
—*v.* **3** °disguise, °camouflage, °cover (up), °conceal, °hide, °obscure, °veil, °screen, °shroud: *She was unable to mask her true feelings for him.*

masquerade *n.* **1** masked ball, masquerade ball, °costume °party, *ballo in maschera, bal masqué*: *He went to the masquerade as Lorenzo di Medici.* **2** °disguise, °deception, °pose, °dissimulation, °bluff, °subterfuge, °false °show, °outward °show, fakery, imposture, play-acting, °false °front, cover-up, °camouflage, *Colloq* °act, °front, *Slang* °put-on: *How long will she continue her masquerade as a wealthy widow?*
—*v.* **3** Usually, ***masquerade as***: °pretend (to be), °pass oneself off (as), impersonate, simulate, °pose (as), °imitate, °mimic: *He is a conservative masquerading as a liberal to garner votes.*

mass *n.* **1** °pile, °heap, °mountain, °load, °stack, °mound, °bunch, °bundle, °lot, °batch, °quantity, °hoard, °store, °collection, °accumulation, aggregation, agglomeration, congeries, °assortment, °miscellany, assemblage, conglomeration: *There was a mass of boulders at the bottom of the cliff.* **2** °abundance, °quantity, °profusion, °volume, multitude, horde, °host, °mob, °crowd, °throng, drove(s), °herd(s), °swarm(s), legion(s), °score(s), °number(s), *Colloq* °bunch(es), ton(s), °mountain, °piles, bags, barrels, oodles, °lots, °oceans, loads, scads, *US* °mess, slew(s): *A mass of bills awaited my return from a trip abroad. Masses of people greeted us at the airport.* **3** °block, concretion, chunk, °lump, hunk, nugget: *A mass of sludge was clogging the valve.* **4** °majority, °best *or* °better *or* greater °part, °bulk, °body, °preponderance, almost all, lion's °share: *The great mass of the votes was still uncounted.* **5** dimension, °size, °magnitude, °bulk, bigness, massiveness, °enormousness, immensity: *The very mass of the elephant made it a hard target to miss.* **6** ***the masses***: the °common °people, the (°common) °herd, the proletariat, the plebeians, *hoi polloi*, the °lower °class(es), the man *or* woman in the street, *Brit* the man *or* woman on the Clapham omnibus, A. N. Other, *US* John Q. Public, John *or* Jane Doe *or* Roe: *The taxes became burdensome and the masses rebelled.*
—*v.* **7** °amass, °pile *or* °heap up, °gather: *Thunderclouds began to mass over the mountains.* **8** aggregate, °accumulate, °collect, °assemble, congregate, °meet, °get *or* °come together, °gather, forgather *or* foregather, °throng, convene, °flock together, °rally, °group, °cluster, marshal, °muster, °mobilize: *Thousands of people massed in front of the embassy. The massed bands made a tremendous noise.*

massacre *n.* **1** °slaughter, slaughtering, °carnage, annihilation, annihilating, blood bath, °killing, °execution, extermination, exterminating, butchery, butchering, (°mass) °murder, murdering, slaying, liquidation, pogrom, genocide: *The massacre of millions of innocent people followed the coup.*
—*v.* **2** °slaughter, annihilate, °kill, °execute, °exterminate, °butcher, °murder, slay, liquidate, °destroy, °eliminate, °obliterate, eradicate, put to the sword, decimate, *Colloq* °mow down, *Slang* °bump off: *It was their policy to massacre all the men and take captive all the women and children.*

massage *n.* **1** rub-down, °rub, manipulation, kneading: *I felt really relaxed after the massage and steam bath.*
—*v.* **2** °rub down, °manipulate, knead, palpate: *She gently massaged my temples with her fingertips.* **3** °manipulate, °handle, °manoeuvre, *Colloq* finagle, *Brit* °fiddle: *He massaged the figures to make it look as if the company was solvent.*

massive *adj.* °big, °large, oversized, °huge, °bulky, °enormous, °hulking, °immense, °gigantic, °towering, mammoth, °colossal, titanic, °vast, tremendous, °prodigious, °mountainous, gargantuan, Brobdingnagian, Cyclopean, elephantine, °jumbo, stupendous, °mighty, °weighty, °ponderous, *Literary* massy, *Colloq* walloping, °whopping, °monster, *Brit* whacking (°great), *US* ginormous, humongous: *They built a massive wall round the city. Massive beams support the roof.*

master *n.* **1** °owner, °head, °chief, °leader, chieftain, commander, °lord, governor, °director, controller, °employer, °manager, °overseer, °supervisor, °superintendent, taskmaster, slave-driver, °principal, °sovereign, °monarch, ruler, *Colloq* °lord high muck-a-muck, Pooh Bah, kingpin, °boss, °skipper, *Brit* gaffer, *US* king-fish, the man, °big fish, °big °boss, bossman; *Slang US* °big cheese, °big wheel, Mr Big, °chief *or* °head honcho: *He is master of all he surveys. Decisions about punishment are referred to the master.* **2** °expert, °authority, °genius, craftsman, °adept, maestro, °mastermind, past master, old hand, °virtuoso, ace, °professional, *Colloq* pro, wizard, *Chiefly Brit* dab hand, *US* crackerjack; *Slang US* maven *or* mavin: *He is a master in the art of chicanery.* **3** °teacher, °tutor, °instructor, °guide, °leader, guru, swami: *She studied under the master for years.*
—*adj.* **4** °adept, °ingenious, °expert, °masterful, masterly, °skilful, skilled, °proficient: *After twenty years, he became a master craftsman.* **5** °overall, controlling, °principal, °main, °prime, °basic, °chief: *Only the leader knows the master plan for conquering the planet. This is the master switch that turns off all the power.* **6** °main, biggest, °principal, owner's: *The master bedroom had a bathroom en suite.*
—*v.* **7** °learn, °grasp, become °expert in, °know inside out and backwards, °know, °understand: *He claims to have mastered the art of levitation.* **8** °control, °overcome, °repress, °suppress, °subdue, °bridle, °check, °quell, get the better of, *Colloq* get a °grip on: *You must learn to master your emotions.*

masterful *adj.* **1** masterly, °adept, °expert, °excellent, °superior, °superb, adroit, °exquisite, °superlative, °supreme, consummate, °accomplished, °peerless, °matchless, °first-rate, °proficient, °dexterous, deft, °skilful, skilled, *Colloq* crack: *She gave a masterful performance of Bruch's violin concerto.* **2** °authoritarian, °dictatorial, °tyrannical, °despotic, °arbitrary, °domineering, imperious, °overbearing, °arrogant, dominating, autocratic, high-handed, magisterial, overweening, °self-willed, *Colloq* °bossy: *I dislike Ian's masterful attitude, always telling everyone what to do.*

mastermind *v.* **1** °plan, °devise, °conceive, °think up, °engineer, °design, °generate, °create, °manage,

°organize, °develop, °work up *or* out: *It was probably Fu Manchu who masterminded this diabolical plot.* —*n.* **2** planner, contriver, conceiver, °creator, architect, °genius, °mind, °intellect, *Colloq* °brain(s): *it would take a mastermind to get even a pass mark on that exam.*

masterpiece *n.* master-work, *magnum* °*opus, chef-d'œuvre, tour de force,* °jewel, °work of °art, °work of °genius, *pièce de résistance*: *Among his many fine paintings, I consider this his masterpiece.*

match *n.* **1** °equal, °equivalent, °peer, °fellow, °mate; °parallel, °replica, °copy, °double, °twin, °look-alike, °facsimile, counterpart: *When it comes to punning, Crosby has finally met his match.* **2** °contest, °competition, °game, °meet, tourney, °tournament, °bout, duel, °rivalry, °trial: *The match was between the top-seeded players.* **3** °marriage, betrothal, °alliance, °combination, °compact, °contract, partnership, °union, affiliation: *It was a match made in heaven.* **4** °prospect, °candidate: *With his inheritance, he's considered a good match.*
—*v.* **5** match up, °join, °marry, °unite, °link, °combine, °put together, °pair up *or* off, juxtapose, conjoin: *However did you manage to match names and faces? Glynis matched them up at the dinner table.* **6** °equal, be °equivalent (to), °resemble, °compare (with), °tie, °measure up (to), °compete (with), °vie (with), °rival: *His skill on the flute will never match hers.* **7** °fit, °go with, °suit, °accord, °agree, harmonize, °go (together), °coordinate, °blend, °correspond: *Who will notice that your socks match your tie? Your eyes don't match.*

matching *adj.* **1** corresponding, homologous, comparable, °equivalent, complementary: *Birds' wings and fishes' fins are matching parts.* **2** analogous, °like, corresponding, °identical: *He wore a pink jacket and matching shoes. She bought a set of matching luggage.*

matchless *adj.* °unique, °original, °peerless, unequalled, without °equal, inimitable, unmatched, °incomparable, °unparalleled, beyond °compare: *Stefania has a contralto voice of matchless quality.*

mate *n.* **1** °companion, °associate, °colleague, °fellow, °chap, co-worker, °comrade, crony, °ally, °friend, alter ego, *Colloq* °chum, °pal, *US* buddy, °cohort, *Slang Brit* cully, china: *After work, my mates and I stop off for a beer or two (or three).* **2** spouse, °partner, helpmeet, helpmate, consort, °husband *or* wife, better half, *Colloq* hubby, old man *or* lady *or* woman, lord and master, *US* bride, *Slang* trouble and strife (= 'wife'): *He scarcely seems a worthy mate for the winner of a Miss World contest.* **3** °fellow, °twin, counterpart, °parallel, one of a °pair: *Have you seen the mate to this sock anywhere?*
—*v.* **4** °pair (up), °match (up), °marry, °wed, °join, °unite, °couple, °link (up): *People should be free to mate with whom they wish.* **5** °breed, °couple, copulate, °pair (up): *The zoo was able to get the rhinoceroses to mate. A lion was mated with a tiger to produce a tigon.* **6** °match (up), °fit (together), synchronize, °join: *I cannot get these gears to mate.*

material *n.* **1** °substance, °matter, °stuff, °fabric: *It is hard to tell what material this is made of.* **2** °cloth, °fabric, textile, °stuff: *This material is too sheer for a dress.* **3** constituents, °elements, components: *We import the raw materials and make the finished product here.* **4** °information, °data, °facts, statistics, figures, °documents, documentation, °papers, °notes, °resources, °means, °research, °apparatus, °supplies: *I have not yet gathered enough material for the article.*
—*adj.* **5** °physical, °tangible, °concrete, °solid, °real, substantive, °substantial, palpable, corporeal, bodily: *It was many years before scientists could persuade people that air is a material substance.* **6** consequential, °important, °significant, °serious, °substantial: *How could one horseshoe nail be material in the outcome of a battle?* **7** °worldly, °earthly, mundane, °temporal, non-spiritual, °secular, °lay, °materialistic: *He ponders the abstract, not the base, material things of everyday life.*

materialistic *adj.* °expedient, money-oriented, possession-oriented, °greedy, *Slang* yuppy: *He's very materialistic and only married her for her money.*

materialize *v.* **1** °appear, °turn up, become °visible, become °manifest, be revealed, take °shape *or* °form, °form, °emerge: *A hulking shape began to materialize out of the fog.* **2** °happen, come to pass, take place, °occur, become °manifest *or* °real, be realized, become an actuality, be actualized: *The dream of a united Europe is finally materializing.*

materially *adv.* °substantially, palpably, significantly, °seriously, essentially, basically, considerably, greatly, much, in the long °run, at °bottom: *I doubt that his criticism will materially affect the success of the play.*

maternal *adj.* motherly, °warm, nurturing, caring, °understanding, °affectionate, °tender, °kind, °kindly, °devoted, °fond, doting; maternalistic: *Her interest in him is strictly maternal.*

maternity *n.* **1** motherhood, parenthood, pregnancy: *Maternity brings about great changes in a woman's life.* **2** parenthood, motherhood: *The maternity of the child was not questioned until the hospital revealed that there had been a mix-up in the nursery.*

mathematical *adj.* arithmetical; °precise, °exact, rigorous: *He went about his plans with mathematical precision.*

matrimonial *adj.* marital, °marriage, °wedding, conjugal, °nuptial; married, °wedded, connubial: *She obtained a court injunction banning him from the matrimonial home. They enjoy matrimonial bliss.*

matter *n.* **1** °material, °substance, °stuff, °sum and °substance: *Some yellowish matter oozed out of the wound. It is a question of mind over matter.* **2** °situation, °issue, °question, °affair, °business, °subject, °topic, °condition, °thing, °fact, °concern; °occurrence, °episode, °incident, °event, °occasion, °proceeding: *It was a matter of life and death. His loss of face is not a matter that need involve you.* **3** °problem, °difficulty, °trouble, °complication, °worry, °upset, °dilemma, °quandary, °enigma, °puzzle: *What is the matter?* **4** °content, °essentials, °pith, °context, °theme, °argument, purport, °implication; signification, °meaning, meaningfulness, °import, °importance, °significance, °moment, °weight, consequence: *Pay attention to the matter in his speech, not his manner. It is of little matter to me whether you go or not.* **5** °amount, °sum, °quantity, °question: *It was only a matter of a few pennies' difference.*
—*v.* **6** be °important *or* of °importance, °count, be of consequence, make a °difference, °mean something: *What you think matters a great deal.*

matter-of-fact *adj.* straightforward, °direct, °forthright, °sober, °factual, unimaginative, unartistic, °prosaic, unpoetic, °dry, dry-as-dust, °dull, °boring, °tiresome, °flat, mundane, °lifeless, featureless, °unvarnished, °colourless, unembellished, °unadorned: *The report contained a matter-of-fact description of the events.*

mature *adj.* **1** °adult, grown (up), full-grown, fully grown, of °age, fully fledged, full-fledged, fully developed, matured, °experienced, °knowledgeable, °sophisticated: *At twenty-two, she is mature enough to be on her own.* **2** °ripe, °ready, ripened, °mellow, °aged, °seasoned: *A good wine, like fruit, should not be consumed till it is mature.* **3** °complete, matured, °perfect, perfected, °polished, °refined, °ready, fully developed, consummated: *Our plans are not yet mature.*
—*v.* **4** °grow up, °age, °develop, come of °age; *Brit* be one's °age, *US* °act one's °age: *Has he matured sufficiently to be trusted alone in the house for the weekend? I wish he'd mature a bit more.* **5** °ripen, °mellow, °age, °season; maturate: *Fruit that has matured on the plant tastes best.* **6** °develop, °perfect, °refine, °polish, maturate, °bring to °fruition: *Their plans for major changes in company structure have not yet fully matured.*

maturity *n.* **1** adulthood, °majority, full °growth *or* °development: *Maturity is as much a state of mind as a* *matter of age.* **2** ripeness, °readiness, mellowness; maturation: *Different wines need ageing for different periods to attain maturity.* **3** °readiness, °perfection, °completion, fullness, °consummation, operability, applicability; maturation: *Their plans were brought to maturity.*

maudlin *adj.* °sentimental, (over)emotional, mawkish, °romantic; °tearful, lachrymose, weepy, teary(-eyed); *Colloq* °mushy, slushy, *Brit* soppy, *US* soupy: *He gets maudlin thinking about his childhood in the countryside.*

maxim *n.* saying, °proverb, axiom, aphorism, adage, °byword, °saw, apophthegm *or* apothegm, °epigram, °motto, °slogan; mot, °witticism; °cliché, °truism: *Her maxim is, 'What you don't know, can't hurt you'.*

maximize *n.* **1** °increase, broaden, °improve, °magnify, augment, °add to, °expand, °build up, °enlarge: *He maximizes his chances for winning by betting on several numbers. To compete, you must maximize your productivity.* **2** °inflate, overplay, °overdo, °overstate, °exaggerate, oversell, make much of, overstress, (over)colour, °enhance, embroider (on), °embellish, °elaborate, °magnify: *Roland tends to maximize his role while minimizing others'.*

maximum *n.* **1** most, utmost, uttermost, greatest, °peak, °extreme, °extremity, °pinnacle, °top, highest, (°upper) °limit: *Turn the volume up to the maximum.* **2** °zenith, °pinnacle, °peak, °limit, apex, °acme, apogee, °climax, °crest, °high(est) °point, °top, °summit: *Her career reached its maximum in the 1930s.*
—*adj.* **3** maximal, greatest, most, utmost, uttermost, °superlative, °supreme, °paramount, °extreme, highest, °top, topmost, climactic, crowning: *The maximum amount that I can afford for a car is £2,000.*

maybe *adv.* °perhaps, °possibly, *Literary* perchance, *Archaic or dialect* mayhap, *Archaic* peradventure: *We could go and see a film tonight, or maybe have a meal somewhere.*

mayhem *n.* maihem, °violence, °havoc, °destruction, °disorder, devastation, °chaos; °fracas, commotion, °confusion: *Someone screamed 'Fire!', and the ensuing mayhem was unbelievable.*

maze *n.* labyrinth, complex, intricacy, twistings and turnings, convolutions: *His application has been lost in the maze of bureaucratic bungling.*

meadow *n.* °field, meadow-land, °pasture, °pasture °land, *Archaic or literary* lea, mead: *The entire meadow was dotted with little puffy clouds of white sheep.*

meagre *adj.* **1** °scanty, scant, °poor, °paltry, °inadequate, skimpy, scrimpy, °sparse, °spare, °insufficient, °bare, °puny, piddling, °trifling, °pathetic, exiguous, *Colloq* °measly: *Angela scraped out a meagre living as a shop assistant. The meagre supplies wouldn't last another day.* **2** °spare, °skinny, °scrawny, bony, °emaciated, °gaunt, °thin, °lean, bare-boned, (half-)°starved, underfed, undernourished, starving: *The meagre faces of the survivors told of their ordeal.* **3** °spare, °plain, bare-boned, °unadorned, unembellished, unelaborate, unelaborated, °simple, simplified, oversimplified, °bare, °inadequate, °deficient, undetailed, °indefinite, non-specific, °general, °broad, °loose, °vague: *The police have only a meagre description to go on.*
4 unfruitful, °infertile, °barren, °deficient, °poor, unproductive: *This land is too meagre to provide the people with a living.*

meal *n.* **1** °food, repast, victuals, °nourishment, °spread, collation, refection; dinner, supper, breakfast, lunch, luncheon, *Brit* tea: *Meals will be served in the main dining room.* **2** ***make a meal of***: °overdo, overplay, go overboard, go *or* carry to °extremes, carry *or* go too °far, do to °excess: *Perkins is bound to make a meal of the slightest thing.*

mealy-mouthed *adj.* °mincing, °reticent, °reluctant, °hesitant, °equivocal, equivocating, °ambiguous, °indirect, unwilling to call a spade a spade, euphemistic, °roundabout, °vague, circumlocutory, periphrastic, °hypocritical, °deceitful, °artful, °slick, °oily, unctuous: *All you'll get from that mealy-mouthed hypocrite is platitudinous twaddle.*

mean[1] *v.* **1** °intend, °design, °purpose, °plan, °aim, have in °mind, °contemplate, have in °view; °want, °wish, °expect, °hope; be motivated by, have as justification: *I did mean to phone you but had no time. I am sure she meant nothing by her remark.* **2** °denote, °signify, °indicate, °note, °specify, °designate, °represent, betoken, °signal, °carry, convey, °drive at, °refer to, allude to, °communicate, °express, °bring out, °get over *or* across; °imply, °suggest, connote, °intimate, °hint (at): *What does 'canicular' mean? It depends on what you mean by 'liberty'. The footprints meant that someone had already been here.* **3** portend, °show, foretell, °foreshadow, °promise, presage, augur, herald: *Those clouds mean that it will soon rain.* **4** carry *or* have the °weight *or* °significance *or* °importance of: *Money means little to someone in her circumstances.*

mean[2] *adj.* **1** stingy, °miserly, °tight, °close, °cheap, parsimonious, °penurious, stinting, niggardly, penny-pinching, tight-fisted, close-fisted, °mercenary, uncharitable, ungenerous, mean-spirited, unaccommodating, °small, °petty, *Colloq* near, money-grubbing, °measly, *Brit* mingy: *He is far too mean to buy anyone a Christmas present. It seems rather a mean contribution to the fund, given his wealth.* **2** °lowly, °low, °base, °inferior, abject, °menial, °servile, degraded, °degenerate, undignified, ignoble, °plebeian, proletarian, °modest, °humble, °common: *He rose to a position of great power in spite of his mean background.* **3** °disgraceful, °run-down, °poor, °sorry, °miserable, scruffy, °seedy, °scurvy, °shabby, squalid, °wretched, °vile, °mangy, °sordid, °contemptible, °dismal, °dreary, °abysmal: *They live in very mean circumstances.* **4** °unkind, malicious, °cruel, unaccommodating, disobliging: *It was very mean of you to steal that toy from the baby.* **5** °cantankerous, churlish, °nasty, °hostile, ill-tempered, bad-tempered, °sour, unpleasant: *That mean old lady would never even talk to us.* **6** °excellent, wonderful, °marvellous, °great, °exceptional, °effective, °skilful, skilled, *Slang* far-out, *US* bad: *The saxophonist in that combo is one mean cat.*

mean[3] *n.* **1** °average, °middle, °norm, (happy) °medium: *We are attempting to achieve the mean between the two extremes.* **2** ***by all means***: **a** °absolutely, °definitely, certainly, °surely, assuredly, of °course, °positively: *By all means, do tell us what you think is wrong.* **b** in any °event, at all events, no matter what, without °fail, at any °cost, in any °case: *By all means, you must do what you think is right.* **3** ***by means of***: by dint of, via, °through, by °way of, with the °help *or* °aid of, employing, using, utilizing: *She gained access to her victims by means of the telephone directory. We entered by means of the front door.*
4 ***means***: **a** °instrument, °agency, °method, °process, °technique, °mode, °manner, °way(s), °approach, °course, °procedure, avenue, °medium, °vehicle: *If you can find the means, then get the job done at once.* **b** °resources, °funds, °money, wherewithal, °capital, °finances, °backing, °support: *I wanted to go to Australia to see my brother, but I simply didn't have the means.* **c** °substance, °wealth, °property, °position, °financial °stability: *She is a woman of considerable means.* **5** ***by no means***: by no manner of means, in no °way, not at all, °definitely *or* °absolutely not, on no °account, not conceivably, not in one's wildest dreams *or* fantasies, not by any stretch of the imagination, *Colloq* no way, *US* no way José: *This is sometimes but by no means always the case. He is by no means a great artist.*
—*adj.* **6** °middle, °centre, °intermediate, medial, °medium, median, °average, middling: *The mean temperature for the year has increased.*

meander *v.* **1** °wander, °ramble, zigzag, °snake, °wind, °twist, °turn; °stroll, amble, rove, *Colloq* mosey, *Brit* swan around *or* about: *The river meandered with a mazy motion through the meadows. We meandered through the forest.*

—*n.* **2** Often, ***meanders***: °meandering(s), °turn(s), turning(s), °twist(s), twisting(s), winding(s), curve(s), curving(s), °loop(s), looping(s), °bend(s), °coil(s), zigzag(s), convolutions; tortuosities, flexuosities, anfractuosities: *We followed the river's meanders till we came to the ruined church.*

meandering *adj.* wandering, °roundabout, circuitous, sinuous, °tortuous, winding, °serpentine, °indirect, flexuous, curvy, °crooked, convoluted, °labyrinthine, mazy, anfractuous: *The meandering road followed the river through the valley.*

meaning *n.* **1** °sense, °import, °content, signification, denotation, °message, °substance, °gist: *The meaning of the word 'lucid' is clear.* **2** purport, °implication, °drift, °spirit, connotation, °significance, °intention: *You understand my meaning, so I need not explain.* **3** °interpretation, °explanation: *What is the meaning of my dream about being attacked by my philodendron?*

meaningful *adj.* **1** °significant, °important, consequential, °serious, °sober, °deep, °substantial, pithy, substantive, °telling, °weighty, valid, °relevant: *Tired of casual encounters, he was ready for a meaningful relationship.* **2** °suggestive, °pregnant, tell-tale, °pointed, sententious, °significant, °expressive, °eloquent: *She gave him a meaningful look.*

meaningless *adj.* **1** °empty, °hollow, vacuous, unsubstantial, °absurd, °silly, °foolish, fatuous, asinine, °ridiculous, °preposterous, °nonsensical: *He gave some meaningless excuse for having forgotten the appointment. This gibberish is entirely meaningless to me.* **2** °ineffective, °ineffectual, °inefficacious, °bootless, unavailing, to no avail, trivial, nugatory, °trifling, °puny, °paltry, °worthless, not °worth anything *or* a straw *or* a rap, valueless, °inconsequential, unimportant, of no °moment, °insubstantial, °vain, °pointless, °senseless, °purposeless, undirected, °irrelevant, °insignificant: *Considering the enemy forces, anything we could do would be meaningless.*

means *n.* See **mean**[3], **4,** above.

meantime *n., adv.* See **meanwhile,** below.

meanwhile *n.* **1** interim, °meantime, °interval: *In the meanwhile, you could study for the exam.*
—*adv.* **2** in the meanwhile, °meantime, in the °meantime, in the interim, for the °moment, °temporarily, for °now, for the °time being, during the °interval, in the intervening °time: *Ruth was watching TV; meanwhile George was washing up.*

measly *adj.* °sparse, scant, °scanty, °meagre, °paltry, °pathetic, skimpy, °puny, piddling, °miserly, niggardly, °miserable, beggarly, stingy, *Colloq Brit* mingy: *'Nouvelle cuisine' is the name given to a restaurateur's design to serve decorative, but measly, portions.*

measure *n.* **1** °amount, °quantity, °magnitude, amplitude, °size, °bulk, °mass, °extent, °reach, dimension, °scope, proportions, °range, °spread; °capacity, °volume; °width, °length, °breadth, °height; °weight: *It is difficult to calculate the measure of an irregularly shaped object.* **2** °scale, °gauge *or technical* gage, °yardstick, °rule, *US* litmus °test: *I cannot determine the length without a proper measure.* **3** °system, °standard, criterion, °rule, °method; barometer, Richter °scale: *The measure by which ice-cream is sold ought to be weight, not volume. What sort of measure do you apply when judging character?* **4** assessment, °evaluation, valuation, appraisal, value, °gauge *or US* gage, °rank, rating, °measurement, °stamp, °estimation: *It is not easy to get the measure of a man who wants to marry your daughter.* **5** °quota, °allotment, °ration, °share, °amount, °degree, °proportion, °quantity, °allowance; °portion, °part: *He was accorded a measure of freedom in choosing the method for getting the job done. She has had her measure of praise.* **6** Often, ***measures***: °step(s), °procedure, °proceeding, °action, °course (of °action), °plan, °method, °means, avenue, °tactic(s), °way, °direction, °approach, °technique: *They took measures to ensure that it never happens again.* **7** °bill, °resolution, legislation, °act, statute, °law; °plan, °proposal: *A measure to change the speed limit is before the council.* **8** °bound, °limit, °end, °extreme, °extent, limitation, moderation, °control, constraint, °restraint: *Drug trafficking has gone beyond all measure in some countries.* **9** °beat, °rhythm, °cadence, metre, °time; °melody, °tune, °bar, °theme, °motif: *The ambassador entered, and the band played in stately measures.* **10** ***for good measure***: to °boot, in °addition, additionally, as a dividend, into the °bargain, °besides, as *or* for a °bonus, °moreover, furthermore: *The job includes a company car and, for good measure, free medical insurance.*
—*v.* **11** °rank, °rate, °gauge *or US* gage, meter, °weigh, °calculate, °reckon, °compute, °calibrate, °determine, ascertain, °figure out *or* up, assess, appraise, °estimate, °evaluate, °judge, value; °survey, °find out: *We must measure the effect of the new safety regulations on our equipment budget. Public acceptance of the new product may be difficult to measure.* **12** °proportion, °pace, °adapt, °gauge *or US* gage, relate, °tailor, °fit, °adjust, °regulate, °control: *Teachers should measure homework assignments according to pupils' available time. Measure your words when speaking to young children.* **13** ***measure off*** *or* ***out***: °mark off *or* out, °limit, delimit, °fix, °pace off *or* out, °lay off: *Now measure off exactly 122.5 metres due north.* **14** ***measure out***: °mete out, °dole out, °ration (out), °parcel out, apportion, °allot, °share out, °assign, allocate; °give out, °deal out, °distribute, °issue, °pass out, °hand out, °dispense, °disperse, °spread around *or* about: *The relief workers measured out food and water to the victims of the famine.* **15** ***measure up (to)***: **a** °meet, °equal, °fulfil, °match, °reach, attain: *The first eleven have not measured up to their coach's expectations. Will they ever measure up?* **b** °qualify (for), be °suitable (for), be °equal to, be °fit *or* °fitted for, be °adequate (to), be up to, *Colloq* °make the °grade, come up to °scratch, be up to snuff, *US* cut the mustard: *If Clive gets the assignment, are you sure that he'll measure up? No one else measures up to the job.*

measured *adj.* **1** °slow, regulated, °unhurried, leisurely, °stately, °majestic, °dignified, °sedate, °solemn: *The silent procession moved through the streets at a measured pace.* **2** °careful, °cautious, °prudent, °calculated, °studied, considered, °deliberate, °systematic, °sober, °intentional, planned, regulated, °premeditated, well-thought-out, reasoned: *He planned the murder with the same measured deliberation he used in writing computer programs.* **3** °rhythmic(al), °regular, cadenced, °steady, °uniform, °even, °monotonous: *The measured marching of the soldiers echoed through the night.* **4** °precise, regulated, °exact, °predetermined, modulated, quantified; clockwork: *A measured amount of each ingredient is automatically added at each stage of the manufacturing process.*

measurement *n.* **1** measuring, °reckoning, gauging *or US* gaging, ascertainment, °determination, assessment, °estimation, appraisal, °evaluation, valuation, °judgement, °calculation, computation, mensuration, commensuration; metage: *The measurement of astronomical distances can only be approximate.* **2** dimension, °extent, °size, °amount, °magnitude, amplitude; °length, °breadth, °height, °width, °depth; °area; °volume, °capacity; °weight, tonnage; (elapsed) time, period; (square *or* cubic) footage, (square) yardage, mileage, acreage: *I need the measurements of the room to order the fitted carpet.*

meat *n.* **1** °flesh; °food, °nourishment, °sustenance, viands, victuals, nutriment, °provisions, °provender, comestibles, edibles, eatables, *Colloq* eats, chow, grub: *She's turned vegetarian and won't touch meat in any form.* **2** °pith, °core, °heart, marrow, °kernel, °vital °part, °essence, °gist, °substance, °basics, °essentials, crux: *The sub-plot seems to swamp the real meat of the play.*

mechanical *adj.* **1** °automatic, automated, machine-driven; machine-made: *Early mechanical toys are sometimes quite intricate. This is a mechanical, not a hand-crafted device.* **2** °automatic, reflex, °involuntary,

°instinctive, °routine, °habitual, °unconscious, °perfunctory, machine-like, robot-like: *Good manners ought to be mechanical. Blinking is a mechanical reaction to bright light.* **3** °impersonal, °distant, °cold, °matter-of-fact, unfeeling, °insensible, ritualistic, °lifeless, spiritless, °dead, °inanimate, unanimated, unemotional, unartistic, mechanistic, °colourless, uninspired, businesslike: *The girl at the check-out gave us a mechanical smile.*

mechanism *n.* **1** °device, appliance, contrivance, °apparatus, °instrument, °machine: *This mechanism will detonate the bomb at the right moment.* **2** machinery, workings, °works, °structure, °system, °organization, °arrangement: *Astrophysicists can offer only an imperfect account of the mechanism of the universe.* **3** °way, °means, °method, °procedure, °approach, °technique, °medium, °process, °agency: *We shall use every mechanism at our disposal to have the case heard by a different judge.* **4** materialism, mechanicalism, physicalism, °logical positivism, °identity theory, monism: *His notions of mechanism reject the idea of free-thinking individualism.*

meddle *v.* °interfere, °intrude, °butt in, °pry, °intervene, interlope, °tamper, °snoop, *Rare* intermeddle, *Colloq* °stick *or* °poke one's nose in, have a *or* one's °finger in the pie, kibitz: *Why are you always meddling in things that don't concern you?*

mediator *n.* arbitrator, arbiter, referee, °umpire, °judge, °negotiator, °intermediary, °go-between, middleman, °moderator, °liaison, intercessor, interceder, conciliator, appeaser, °peacemaker: *To avoid a lawsuit, they agreed to allow a mediator to settle their differences.*

medicinal *adj.* healing, remedial, °therapeutic, curative, restorative, sanative; medical, iatric(al), *Medicine* roborant, analeptic, alexipharmic: *The doctor prescribed a medicinal ointment for the rash.*

medicine *n.* medication, medicament, °remedy, °drug, pharmaceutical, °prescription, *Archaic* physic; nostrum, panacea, cure-all: *There is no medicine that can cure your affliction.*

mediocre *adj.* middling, °indifferent, °ordinary, commonplace, °average, °medium, °everyday, run-of-the-mill, °pedestrian, °undistinguished, uninspired, unimaginative, unexceptional, °tolerable, °fair, not (that *or* too) good, not bad, second-rate, third-rate, °inferior, °poor, *Brit* common-or-garden variety, *US* garden-variety, *Colloq* °so so, °fair to middling, nothing to brag *or* to write home about, no °great shakes: *It was a mediocre play, and we couldn't be bothered to sit through it.*

meditate *v.* **1** °reflect, °think, °muse, °ponder, °study, ruminate, cogitate, °contemplate, cerebrate, be °lost in °thought, be in a brown study: *Please don't interrupt me while I'm meditating.* **2** Often, ***meditate on*** *or* ***upon***: °consider, °contemplate, °mull over, °reflect on *or* upon, °ponder on *or* over, °chew over, °plan, °scheme, °devise, °design, °conceive, °frame, °think up, have in °mind: *She was meditating revenge, while I was meditating on how to discourage her.*

meditative *adj.* °thoughtful, °pensive, contemplative, °reflective, °studious, cogitative, excogitative, abstracted, °rapt, engrossed, °lost *or* °deep in °thought, ruminative, brooding: *She suddenly stopped talking and became meditative, looking at me with a curious expression.*

medium *adj.* **1** °average, °middle, mid, medial, median, °normal, °standard, °usual, °everyday, °ordinary; mid-sized: *His wife has an estate car of medium size—nothing extravagant.* **2** See **mediocre,** above. —*n.* **3** °average, °middle, mid-point, compromise, °centre, °mean, °norm, mediocrity: *Instead of going to extremes, try for the happy medium.* **4** °atmosphere, °environment, ambience *or* ambiance, °milieu: *The air serves as a medium of sound. The light is refracted as it passes into a denser medium.* **5** °means, °method, °mode, °approach, instrumentality, °device, °mechanism, intermediation, °technique, contrivance, °agency, °expedient, °way, °course, °route, °road, avenue, °channel, conveyance, °vehicle: *Latin and Greek were the media of the scholarship, the science, and the theology of the Middle Ages. Television is a powerful advertising medium.*

medley *n.* °mixture, °assortment, °combination, °miscellany, mélange, °collection, conglomeration, agglomeration, °hotchpotch *or US and Canadian* hodgepodge, olio, °blend, gallimaufry, omnium gatherum, °pastiche, °pot-pourri, salmagundi, olla podrida, °mishmash, °jumble, °mess, farrago, °stew, goulash, *Colloq* °mixed bag: *The programme consisted of a medley of show tunes.*

meek *adj.* **1** °modest, °humble, °submissive, unassuming, unambitious, unpretentious, °mild, °bland, °patient, deferential, °shy, °retiring, °lowly: *The meek shall inherit the earth.* **2** °tame, °timid, °weak, docile, compliant, °submissive, °yielding, acquiescent, unaggressive, non-militant, °tractable, °manageable, °subdued, repressed, spiritless, suppressed, °broken, *Colloq* wimpish: *The people are meek and will not offer any resistance to such dictatorial government.*

meet[1] *v.* **1** °encounter, °come across, °chance on *or* upon, °happen on *or* upon, °stumble on *or* into, °see, *Colloq* °run across *or* into, °bump into: *Guess who I met in the park this morning!* **2** Often, ***meet with***: rendezvous (with), °get together (with); convene, °assemble, °gather, °collect, forgather *or* foregather, congregate: *I met with the mysterious stranger as arranged. The board meets at 9.00 a.m.* **3** make the °acquaintance of, be introduced to, first °encounter, °come across, °find: *Where did you meet your wife?* **4** °link up, °join, °come together, °unite, adjoin, abut, °touch, intersect: *The horizon is where the sky meets earth.* **5** °answer, °deal with, °handle, °satisfy, °fulfil, take °care of, °dispose of, °heed, °observe, °carry out; °gratify, °pay, °settle, °defray, liquidate: *Will these precautions meet the requirements of the Department of the Environment? The police advised the parents not to meet the kidnapper's demands.* **6** ***meet with***: °encounter, be met by, °experience; °undergo, °endure, °suffer, °have, °go through: *All our efforts met with little or no response. Gary met with an accident yesterday.* —*n.* **7** °competition, °contest, °meeting, °match, tourney, °tournament; °muster, °rally: *The track meet was won by our team.*

meet[2] *adj.* °fitting, °suitable, °appropriate, °proper, °fit, congruous: *It is meet to offer praises to God.*

meeting *n.* **1** °appointment, °engagement, rendezvous, °encounter, assignation, tryst, *Slang US* meet: *She arranged a meeting with her ex-husband.* **2** °assembly, °convention, °conference, °gathering, congress, conclave, °session, congregation, convocation, *US* caucus, *Colloq* °get-together: *Nominations for next year's officers will be presented at the next meeting.* **3** convergence, converging, confluence, joining, °union, °junction, conjunction, intersection: *The earliest settlement was at the meeting of the two rivers.* **4** See **meet, 7,** above.

melancholy *adj.* **1** °sad, morose, depressed, °unhappy, °dejected, °despondent, °blue, °downhearted, °glum, °gloomy, woeful, °woebegone, lugubrious, disconsolate, downcast, dispirited, low-spirited, cheerless, crestfallen, chap-fallen, °forlorn, °heartbroken, °mournful, °sorrowful, °miserable, °dismal, *Colloq* down in the °mouth, (down) in the dumps, °low: *Harold has been melancholy ever since Lucy left.* —*n.* **2** °sadness, °sorrow, °misery, °woe, °gloom, unhappiness, blues, moroseness, °depression, dejection, dejectedness, despondence, despondency, downheartedness, glumness, gloominess, woefulness, lugubriousness, disconsolateness, dispiritedness, cheerlessness, mournfulness, sorrowfulness, miserableness, dolour, °anguish: *Getting Harold's mind off his problems may relieve his melancholy.*

mellow *adj.* **1** °soft, °juicy, °luscious, °delicious, °rich, °sweet, flavourful, full-flavoured, °ready, °ripe, °mature, ripened, °aged: *She set before us a dish of mellow peaches. Amontillado sherry is noted for its*

mellow taste. **2** °musical, °melodious, °full, °pure, °rich, °sweet, dulcet, mellifluous, euphonious, vibrant: *Her voice was low, mellow, and suggestive.* **3** °soft, softened, °subtle, muted, pastel: *The mellow shades of this painting would fit well into the décor.* **4** °easygoing, °genial, °gentle, °good-natured, °easy, °cordial, °friendly, °warm, °amiable, °agreeable, °pleasant, °cheerful, °happy, jovial, felicitous: *Patrick seems to have become more mellow with age.*
—*v.* **5** °mature, °ripen, °age, °season, °sweeten, °develop, °improve (with °age), °soften: *Frank has mellowed since taking up golf.*

melodious *adj.* °sweet(-sounding), dulcet, °tuneful, euphonious, °harmonious, melodic, °lyrical, °musical, mellifluous, mellisonant, silvery, °golden: *I agreed with her father that Sylvia has a most melodious voice.*

melodramatic *adj.* °sensational, sensationalistic, °dramatic, stagy, °theatrical, emotionalistic, (over-)°sentimental, (over-)sentimentalized, overdrawn, overworked, °overwrought, overdone, exaggerated, blood-and-thunder, histrionic, *Colloq* hammy, *US* schmaltzy, hokey: *The slightest thing that happened to him he blew up with melodramatic effect to elicit Maria's sympathy.*

melody *n.* **1** °song, °tune, °air, °strain, °measure, °theme, °refrain: *Isn't that the melody from Mimi's aria in* La Bohème? **2** tunefulness, melodiousness, euphoniousness, euphony, °harmony, musicality, sweetness: *The older music seems to be marked by so much more melody than rock 'n' roll.*

melt *v.* **1** °soften, °thaw, liquefy, °fuse, °dissolve, liquidize, deliquesce: *You'd better eat that ice-cream before it melts.* **2** °soften, °thaw, mollify, assuage, °touch, °move, °disarm, °mellow: *The look on the child's face melted his icy reserve.* **3** Usually, ***melt into***: °blend, °fade, °merge, °disappear, °dissolve, °shrink: *As soon as the police arrived, Phyllis tried to melt into the background.* **4** ***melt away***: °disappear, °dissolve, vanish, °evaporate, °go away, °fade, °pass, °decline, °decrease, °shrink, °dwindle, °diminish: *When the company began to make a profit, all his previous reservations melted away.*

member *n.* °colleague, °associate, °fellow: *I am going to propose Fred as a member of the club.*

memento *n.* **1** souvenir, °keepsake, °remembrance, °relic, °trophy, °token: *I kept his medals as a memento of our time together.* **2** ***mementos***: memorabilia: *There will be an auction of war mementos next week.*

memoir *n.* **1** °account, °report, reportage, °narrative, °essay, dissertation, disquisition, °paper, °journal, °record, biography, °life: *They found her memoir about life in the jungle very exciting.* **2** ***memoirs***: autobiography, °reminiscences, °recollections, °memories, °diary, confessions, °letters, °life °story; annals, °history, °account(s), °record(s), °chronology: *She was reading the memoirs of Henry Kissinger.*

memorable *adj.* unforgettable, catchy, never-to-be-forgotten, °noteworthy, °notable, °remarkable, °significant, °important, °worthy, °momentous, °eventful, °historic, °illustrious, °celebrated, °great: *His first book contains many memorable and quotable passages.*

memorandum *n.* °note, °record, °minute, °reminder, °message, *Brit* chit *or* chitty, *Colloq* memo: *Send a memorandum reminding them of the meeting.*

memorial *adj.* **1** commemorative: *A memorial plaque will be dedicated to him tomorrow.*
—*n.* **2** °monument, marker, °plaque, cenotaph, °statue, °memento, °remembrance, °reminder, souvenir: *Let this serve as a memorial to those who died in the wars. Wreaths were laid at the foot of the memorial.*

memorialize *v.* °honour, °commemorate, pay °homage *or* °respect *or* °tribute to, °remember, °eulogize, °celebrate, °mark: *His life, devoted to botany, is memorialized in these beautiful gardens.*

memorize *v.* °learn by heart *or* rote, °commit to °memory, °learn word for word, °retain; °remember: *He memorized the entire* Rime of the Ancient Mariner.

memory *n.* **1** °recall, °recollection, retention: *My memory of the incident is very vivid. She has a poor memory for faces.* **2** °recollection, °reminiscence, °thought: *The interviewer was drawing on grandfather's memories of the 1920s.* **3** °remembrance, °honour, °homage, °respect, °tribute, °celebration: *He wrote a sequence of poems in memory of a dear friend.*

menace *v.* **1** °threaten, °intimidate, °daunt, terrorize, °terrify, cow, °bully, °frighten, °scare, °alarm: *The loan sharks menaced him when he refused to pay.*
—*n.* **2** °threat, °danger, °peril, °hazard, °risk: *The sunken wreck is a menace to navigation.* **3** intimidation, °scare, °threat, °warning, commination: *According to law, a menace alone does not constitute an injury.*

menacing *adj.* °threatening, looming, °impending, °ominous, °frightening, °terrifying, intimidating, minacious, minatory *or* minatorial, louring *or* lowering; °dangerous, °perilous, °hazardous, °risky, chancy: *Menacing storm clouds scudded across the darkening sky.*

mend *v.* **1** °repair, °fix, °patch (up), °rectify, °correct, °remedy, °restore, °rehabilitate; °heal: *When will you get round to mending the roof?* **2** °correct, °improve, °better, ameliorate, °reform, °revise, °rectify, set *or* put °right, emend: *When are you going to mend your ways?* **3** °heal, °improve, °recover, °convalesce, °recuperate, get °better: *It took me a few months to mend after the accident.*
—*n.* **4** °repair, °patch: *You can hardly see where the mend is.* **5** ***on the mend***: recovering, recuperating, convalescing, convalescent, improving: *The good news is that father is on the mend after his attack.*

menial *adj.* **1** °lowly, °servile, °humble, subservient, °base, °low, °mean, slavish, demeaning, °degrading, ignoble; °routine, unskilled: *He took a number of menial jobs to pay for his daughter's wedding.* **2** °servile, fawning, °grovelling, toadying, sycophantic, °obsequious, cringing, °time-serving, °flattering, snivelling, *Colloq* boot-licking, *Taboo slang* brown-nosing: *His insecurity makes him surround himself with menial hangers-on.*
—*n.* **3** lackey, °flunkey, serf, °slave, underling, minion, *Brit* °fag, *Colloq Brit* dogsbody, skivvy, *US* gofer: *He works as one of the menials in the hotel kitchen.* **4** toady, sycophant, °yes-man, lickspittle, leech, °parasite, time-server, *Colloq* bootlicker, *Taboo slang* brown-nose(r): *The film star was attended by a retinue of menials, all anxious to keep in her favour.*

mental *adj.* **1** °intellectual, cognitive, cerebral, perceptual, °rational, conceptual, °theoretical, noetic, °abstract: *The boy staggered us with his ability to perform rapid mental arithmetical calculations.* **2** lunatic, °mad, °crazy, °psychotic, demented, mentally °ill, °unstable, °unbalanced, °deranged, °disturbed, °daft, certifiable, *Slang* off one's rocker, nutty, batty, balmy *or* barmy, loony, screwy, bonkers, crackers, nuts, bananas, loco: *My great-aunt has gone a bit mental in her old age.*

mentality *n.* **1** °intelligence, °brain, °capacity, °intellect, °wit, °sense, °judgement, acuity, acumen, I.Q., rationality, °understanding: *I'd say that Frank is a man of average mentality.* **2** °inclination, °attitude, °bent, mind-set, °disposition, °frame of °mind, temperament, °outlook, °view: *The news betrays little about what is actually happening, but much about the mentality of the leadership. They criticized Britain's 'island mentality'.*

mention *v.* **1** °speak *or* °write about, °refer to, allude to, °touch on *or* upon, make mention (of), °bring up *or* in, °introduce, °broach, call *or* direct attention to, °note, °name, cite, °acknowledge; °point out, °indicate, °make known, adduce, °report, °quote: *Sergeant Payne was mentioned in dispatches from the front. He mentions the works of Conrad in support of his thesis.* **2** divulge, °reveal, °intimate, °disclose, °impart, °suggest, animadvert on *or* upon, °hint (at), °imply, °insinuate: *Did he mention that Liz was present?*
—*n.* **3** °reference, allusion, °note, naming, citation, mentioning, *Colloq* cite: *There was a mention of you in*

the newspaper today. **4** °recognition, °tribute, °acknowledgement, °kudos, °praise: *She won no prize but came in for an honourable mention.* **5** °announcement, °reference, referral, °remark: *The speaker's mention of the conference reminded me of something.*

mercantile *adj.* commercial, °business, °trade, marketing, °market: *The book dealt with the mercantile affairs of the Hanseatic League.*

mercenary *adj.* **1** money-oriented, °grasping, °greedy, acquisitive, covetous, °predatory, °avaricious, °venal, *Colloq* money-grubbing: *She objected that the 'financial world' ought to be renamed the 'mercenary world'.* **2** °venal, bribable, °corrupt, bought, *Colloq US* on the take: *They found themselves a mercenary judge and the indictment was quashed.*
—*n.* **3** hireling, legionnaire, °soldier of fortune: *The highly trained task force was made up entirely of mercenaries.*

merchandise *n.* **1** °goods, commodities, °products, °stock, °staples, °produce: *The merchandise you ordered was shipped yesterday.*
—*v.* **2** °trade, °deal in, °traffic in, °market, °distribute, retail, (°buy and) °sell, °promote, advertise: *We are merchandising the new product line via direct mail.*

merchant *n.* **1** °dealer, retailer, °seller, shopkeeper, °store °owner, °trader, °tradesman *or* tradeswoman, vendor: *High Street merchants are complaining about a decline in sales.* **2** °pedlar, hawker; (travelling) salesman, (sales) °representative, commercial traveller, huckster, door-to-door salesman, *US old-fashioned* drummer, *Colloq* (sales) rep: *His work as an itinerant merchant took him away from home most of the week.* **3** distributor, wholesaler, jobber, °broker, °agent, forwarder; businessman *or* businesswoman, merchant prince, °mogul, °tycoon, magnate, industrialist, *US* baron: *She comes from a family of steel merchants.*

merciful *adj.* compassionate, °sympathetic, °forgiving, °kind, °kindly, clement, kind-hearted, forbearing, °sparing, °lenient, °tender, humane, °liberal, °mild, tender-hearted, °soft-hearted, °gracious, °generous, magnanimous, benignant, beneficent, °charitable, °thoughtful, °considerate, °indulgent, °big: *She begged the governor to be merciful and to spare her life.*

merciless *adj.* °cruel, pitiless, °ruthless, °heartless, °unmerciful, inhumane, °inhuman, °brutal, °savage, barbarous, barbaric, °barbarian, °crude, °rude, °rough, °harsh, °tough, °callous, °hard, hard-hearted, illiberal, °tyrannical, stony-hearted, °cold, °severe, unsparing, insensitive, °indifferent, °unsympathetic, unforgiving, °ungracious, malevolent, °thoughtless, uncharitable, °inconsiderate, °unmoved, unbending, °inflexible, °relentless, unrelenting, inexorable: *Their captors proved to be utterly merciless. The merciless sun beat down on the desert outpost.*

mercy *n.* compassion, °pity, forbearance, °quarter, °tolerance, °sympathy, °favour, °forgiveness, °kindness, kindliness, leniency, tenderness, °humanity, humaneness, liberality, kind-heartedness, tender-heartedness, soft-heartedness, graciousness, generosity, magnanimity, benignity, beneficence, °charity, thoughtfulness, °consideration, °indulgence: *May the Lord have mercy on your soul. We could expect no mercy from that slave-driver.*

mere *adj.* °bare, °basic, scant, °stark, °sheer; °absolute, unmixed, °only, °just, °nothing but, °pure (and °simple), °unmitigated, °undiluted: *She was a mere slip of a girl. We need something more to go on than mere hearsay evidence.*

merely *adv.* **1** °only, °simply; basically, purely, essentially, fundamentally, at °bottom: *I was merely going to ask if you'd like to go to the cinema.* **2** °only, no more than; °barely, °scarcely, °simply, solely, °entirely: *She was merely the scullery-maid. We can't unlock the safe merely on your authority.*

merge *v.* °combine, coalesce, °unite, °join, °amalgamate, consolidate, °pool, °blend, °mix, °mingle, commingle, °fuse: *If we merge our companies, we shall save on overhead costs.*

merger *n.* °combination, coalescence, °union, merging, °amalgamation, consolidation, coalition, pooling, blending, mixing, mingling, commingling, fusing, fusion: *A merger of the two firms might result in a monopoly.*

merit *n.* **1** °worth, worthiness, value, °excellence, °quality, °virtue, °good, goodness: *Philip's plan has a good deal of merit.* **2** Often, ***merits***: °assets, strong point, °advantage, rights and wrongs: *What exactly are the merits of his approach over mine? The case should be tried on its own merits.*
—*v.* **3** °earn, °deserve, °warrant, °rate, have a °right *or* °claim to, be entitled to, be °qualified for, be °worthy of: *What gave you the idea that you merited any special consideration?*

meritorious *adj.* °honourable, °laudable, °praiseworthy, commendable, creditable, °admirable, °estimable, °excellent, °exemplary, °outstanding: *Penny has won the company award for meritorious service five months in a row.*

merriment *n.* jollity, joviality, merrymaking, °revelry, °gaiety, °high *or* °good spirits, °mirth, mirthfulness, joyfulness, felicity, jubilation, °festivity, exhilaration, buoyancy, °exuberance, °cheer, cheerfulness, °glee, °fun, °hilarity, °enjoyment, °happiness, blithefulness, blithesomeness, frolicking: *Everyone joined in the merriment at the office party.*

merry *adj.* **1** °cheerful, °happy, °gay, cheery, °jolly, jovial, in °high *or* °good spirits, mirthful, °joyful, joyous, °hilarious, jubilant, rejoicing, festive, °exhilarating, °exuberant, °vivacious, convivial, °buoyant, °gleeful, °blithe, blithesome, °carefree, light-hearted, °delighted: *Didn't we have a merry old time at the Christmas party!* **2** ***make merry***: °revel, °celebrate, °carouse, °frolic: *The guests made merry till the wee hours of the morning.*

mesh *n.* **1** mesh-work, °network, netting, °net, °web, webbing, lattice, lattice-work, °screen, screening, interlacing, lace-work, grid, °grate, °grating, grater, sieve, strainer, trellis, trellis-work, decussation, *Technical* rete, reticle *or* reticule *or* graticule, reticulation, plexus, plexure, reticulum; interstice: *The mesh of the hammock broke and I fell to the ground.* **2** Often, ***meshes***: °grip, °clutches, °grasp, toils, °web, °trap, entanglement, °tangle, complex, °complexity, intricacy: *Her papers were lost in the meshes of the filing system.*
—*v.* **3** catch, °entangle, enmesh, °grab, °trap, entrap, °snare, ensnare, °involve: *I became meshed inextricably in the complexities of her life.* **4** °engage, °fit (together), dovetail, °knit, enmesh, °match, interlock: *After they were aligned, the gears meshed perfectly.*

mess *n.* **1** °chaos, °disorder, disarray, disorganization, °shambles, °muddle, disarrangement, °clutter, °hotchpotch *or US also* hodgepodge, °litter, °tangle, °jumble, °confusion, °mishmash; untidiness: *Would you help me clean up this mess? Drugs have made a mess of her life.* **2** concoction, °mixture, °medley, °miscellany, °hash, gallimaufry, farrago, olio, olla podrida, °pot-pourri, smorgasbord *or* smörgåsbord, kedgeree: *They presented us with a huge mess of things from which we must select what we want.* **3** °predicament, °difficulty, °plight, °pinch, °trouble, °dilemma, °quandary, imbroglio, *Colloq* foul-up, °stew, °fix, hot water, (pretty *or* fine) kettle of fish, pickle, °jam, *Slang* screw-up, *Brit* balls-up, can of worms, *US* snafu: *You have got yourself into a fine mess this time!*
—*v.* **4** ***mess about*** *or* ***around (with)***: **a** °potter *or US* putter, °fool (around), dally, °busy oneself, °fiddle about *or* around, °play: *He enjoys messing about in boats.* **b** philander, °trifle, °toy, °flirt, °seduce, °sleep around, °fool around, °run around: *She doesn't want him to mess about with other women.* **5** ***mess up***: **a** disarrange, disarray, dishevel, °tousle, *Colloq US* muss (up): *He always messes up my hair when he kisses me.* **b** °ruin, °destroy, make a °shambles of, °wreck, °bungle, °botch, °foul up, *Colloq* make a °hash of, *Slang* °muck up: *Making that one little mistake messed up his whole career.* **c** °dirty, °clutter up, make °untidy,

turn upside down, °pull to °pieces, °upset: *The police messed up my whole house looking for the pistol.* **6** ***mess with***: °interfere in *or* with, °intervene, °meddle with *or* in, °intrude in, °butt in *or* into, °tinker with, °tamper with, get °involved in *or* with: *They ought to learn not to mess with things that don't concern them.*

message *n.* **1** communication, °bulletin, °report, communiqué, °news, °dispatch *or* despatch, °information, °word, °intelligence, tidings; °note, °missive, °letter, °memorandum: *The message reached us by carrier pigeon.* **2** °speech, °address, °presentation, °statement, °declaration: *His message was delivered via television to people everywhere.* **3** °idea, °point, °import, °meaning, °essence, °implication: *The message that he isn't liked around here still hasn't penetrated his thick skull.*

messenger *n.* °envoy, emissary, legate, nuncio, °intermediary, °go-between; °page, errand-boy, errand-girl, messenger-boy, messenger-girl, courier, °runner, dispatch-rider, Pheidippides, Mercury, Hermes; herald, °harbinger; *Colloq US* gofer: *If you don't like the message, don't take it out on the messenger.*

Messiah *n.* deliverer, liberator, emancipator, °saviour, rescuer: *They believe in a Messiah who will release them from earthly bondage.*

metaphor *n.* figure (of °speech), allusion, analogy, analogue, °reference, °image, trope, °symbol; simile, parabole; metonymy, symbolism, °imagery: *When she said she was blue, she was using 'blue' as a metaphor. Poetry is rife with metaphor.*

metaphoric *adj.* metaphorical, non-literal, allusive, analogic(al), analogous, figurative, °symbolic, referential, parabolic(al), metonymic, metonymous, tropological: *I meant 'filthy' in a metaphoric, not a literal, sense.*

mete *v.* Usually, ***mete out***: °deal (out), apportion, °distribute, °dole (out), °allot, °assign, allocate, °parcel out, °share (out), °ration (out), °measure out, °dispense, °hand out, °give out, °pass out, *Colloq* dish out: *Punishment was meted out to those who deserved it.*

meteoric *adj.* **1** °brief, °short-lived, °temporary, transitory, °transient, ephemeral, evanescent, impermanent, °fleeting, °momentary, °swift, overnight: *She enjoyed a meteoric rise as a singer, but after two years at the top she disappeared without a trace.* **2** °brilliant, °dazzling, flashing, spectacular, °sensational: *His meteoric career was launched in 1974.*

method *n.* **1** °way, °means, °procedure, °approach, °route, avenue, °road, °mode, °manner, °technique, °process, °routine, *modus operandi*; °plan, °scheme, °programme, °course, °practice, °pattern, °system, methodology; *Colloq US* M.O.: *What method was used to arrive at the answer?* **2** °arrangement, °order, °system, °structure, °organization, °design, °pattern, orderliness, neatness, °regularity, °discipline: *There is a discernible, underlying method to what seems superficially chaotic.*

methodical *adj.* organized, ordered, °systematic, structured, businesslike, °orderly, °neat, °tidy, °regular, °routine, balanced, disciplined, °painstaking, °meticulous, °deliberate, paced, °laborious, plodding, °laboured: *The weaver resumed his methodical throwing of the shuttle, back and forth, back and forth.*

meticulous *adj.* °careful, °precise, °accurate, °exact, °fastidious, °scrupulous, °thorough, °particular, °painstaking, punctilious, °fussy, °finicky, °demanding, °strict, °critical, °exacting, °perfectionist: *His work is noted for its meticulous attention to detail.*

metropolis *n.* °capital, (°capital) °city; metropolitan °area, urban °sprawl, megalopolis, °municipality: *Street crime has become a problem in every major metropolis.*

microbe *n.* micro-organism, microzoon, °germ; bacterium, virus, *Colloq* °bug: *Only recently has science learnt that diseases are caused by microbes.*

midday *n.* °noon, noontime, twelve (o'clock) °noon, *US* high °noon: *By midday, the temperature had reached 34° Celsius.*

middle *adj.* **1** °central, °centre, halfway, mid, midway, °mean, medial, *Technical* mesial: *We had reached the middle stage of our journey. Her index finger and middle finger are almost exactly the same length.* —*n.* **2** °centre, mid-point, °midst, halfway °point; °heart, bull's-eye: *He lives in the middle of the city. The arrow found the very middle of the target.* **3** midriff, waist, mid-section, °stomach: *She wore a red sash round her middle.*

midst *n.* °middle, °centre, mid-point, halfway °point: *In the midst of life we are in death. They live in a fairy-tale château in the midst of beautiful Breton countryside. This proved a welcome boost in the midst of a difficult election campaign.*

midwife *n.* accoucheur *or* accoucheuse: *Most babies in the world are delivered by midwives.*

might *n.* **1** °strength, °power, °energy, °force, muscle, potency, *Literary* puissance: *I hit my attacker with all my might. Might doesn't always make right.* **2** °influence, °authority, °weight, °sway, °dominion, ascendancy, °superiority, mightiness, °capability, °capacity, °power, °effect, effectiveness, *Colloq* clout: *It was not till the 20th century that the might of the United States was felt outside its borders.*

mighty *adj.* **1** °powerful, °strong, °potent, °influential, °dominant, °predominant, ascendant, °weighty, doughty, °authoritarian, autocratic, °indomitable: *The pen is mightier than the sword. He should have thought twice before challenging such a mighty opponent.* **2** °strong, °muscular, °powerful, °robust, strapping, °sturdy, °brawny, °burly, well-built, able-bodied, °hardy, *Colloq* °husky, °hefty: *The smith a mighty man was he, With large and sinewy hands.* **3** °big, °large, °huge, °grand, °great, °enormous, °gigantic, tremendous, °towering, °monumental, °prodigious, °massive, °bulky: *The giant plucked a mighty tree from the earth and flung it across the sea.* —*adv.* **4** °very, °extremely: *It was mighty nice of you to visit me here in the Ozarks.*

migrant *n.* **1** wanderer, °rover, °drifter, gypsy, nomad, itinerant, °transient, migrator, wayfarer, bird of °passage, peregrinator, °traveller; vagrant; *Colloq US* wetback: *The townspeople were having difficulty finding accommodation for the migrants.* —*adj.* **2** °transient, migratory, itinerant, peripatetic, drifting, nomadic, °travelling, gypsy, floating; vagrant: *The farmers depend on migrant workers to bring in the harvest.*

migrate *v.* **1** °go, °move, °travel, °settle, resettle, relocate, °move °house; °emigrate, immigrate, expatriate: *During the potato famine, many migrated from Ireland to America.* **2** °wander, °roam, voyage, rove, °drift, °range: *Some say that the American Indians migrated across the Bering land bridge from Asia.*

mild *adj.* **1** placid, °peaceful, °calm, °tranquil, °bland, °mellow, °inoffensive, °gentle, °serene, °good-natured, affable, °amiable, °kind, °kindly, °equable, °easygoing, °temperate, non-violent, conciliatory, °indulgent, °merciful, °forgiving, compassionate, °lenient, forbearing, °peaceable, pacific, °passive, °submissive, °yielding, °tractable, °meek, unassuming, °modest, °quiet, °subdued: *Judge Leaver is known for his mild disposition.* **2** clement, balmy, °warm, °fair, °pleasant, °temperate, placid, °moderate: *We've had a succession of mild winters here.* **3** °bland, °soothing, lenitive, mollifying, demulcent, emollient, °gentle, calming, softening: *The doctor recommended a mild laxative.*

milieu *n.* °environment, °climate, surroundings, environs, °background, ambience *or* ambiance, °sphere, °setting, °atmosphere, °medium, °element, °precincts: *The British Library was the perfect milieu in which to pursue his research and writing.*

militant *adj.* **1** °aggressive, combative, °pugnacious, °belligerent, °hostile, contentious, antagonistic,

°offensive, °truculent, °fierce, °ferocious, °warlike, bellicose, °martial, jingoistic, hawkish: *Those who have experienced war are not likely to be militant.* **2** warring, fighting, combatant, combating, embattled; at °war, up in arms: *The militant members of the council refused to discuss terms.*
—*n.* **3** fighter, °aggressor, combatant, °belligerent, warrior, °soldier: *Anyone who experiences the hardships of a long strike may think twice before being a militant.*

military *adj.* **1** °martial, soldierly, naval, army, fighting, °service: *The military machine was poised to strike.*
—*n.* **2** (armed) °services *or* °forces, army, °navy, air °force, military establishment, soldiery: *The military will oppose any reductions in spending for arms.*

militate *v.* **1** Usually, ***militate against***: °discourage, °work *or* °go *or* °operate against, °foil, °counter, countervail, °cancel (out), °reduce (possibility of), °prevent, °hinder, °resist, °oppose: *His poor prison record militates against his early parole.* **2** Usually, ***militate for*** *or* ***in favour of***: be on the °side of, °favour, °further, °promote, °help, °aid: *The same reasoning that militated in favour of lower taxes then persists today.*

milk *v.* °drain, bleed, °extract, °tap, °exploit, wring, °draw off *or* out, °withdraw: *The comic milked the joke for yet another laugh. The taxman is milking me dry.*

milksop *n.* °sissy *or Brit also* cissy, °coward, °weakling, namby-pamby, mollycoddle, cry-baby, nancy (boy), nance, dastard, poltroon, caitiff, (little) Lord Fauntleroy, *Archaic* caitiff, *US* milquetoast, *Colloq* chinless wonder, *Brit* mother's *or* mummy's boy, *US* mama's boy, pantywaist, *Slang* pansy: *We want men, not milksops, in the Marines.*

mill *n.* **1** grinder, quern, crusher, °roller: *In many parts of the world, corn is still ground by hand in a stone mill.* **2** °plant, °factory, °works, workshop, °shop, foundry: *This mill turns out rolled steel.* **3** ***been through the mill***: °experienced, °knowledgeable, °sophisticated, toughened, hardened, °seasoned, battle-scarred, *Colloq* been through the wringer, in the know: *He's been through the mill and knows what to expect.* **4** ***run-of-the-mill***: °average, unexceptional, °ordinary, °common, unremarkable, °everyday, °basic, °simple, *Brit* common-or-garden variety, *US* garden-variety: *Critics found her voice pleasant but rather run-of-the-mill.*
—*v.* **5** °grind, °crush, comminute, °powder, °pulverize, °grate, granulate, °pound, triturate, masticate, bray; °crunch, mince: *Flour milled to a very fine consistency is more suitable for pastries than for breads.* **6** ***mill about*** *or* ***around***: °meander, °wander, °walk, °stroll, amble, °move about *or* around, °crowd, °throng, °swarm: *There were quite a few people milling about our stand at the trade fair.*

mimic *v.* **1** °imitate, ape, °copy, simulate, °mirror, °echo: *The image in the mirror mimicked every move I made.* **2** °reproduce, °duplicate, °copy: *This frieze mimics one on the Parthenon.* **3** °mock, °ridicule, °satirize, °caricature, °parody, make °fun of, °lampoon, impersonate, *Colloq* °take off: *It is rude to mimic your elders.*
—*n.* **4** impersonator, imitator, impressionist, caricaturist, parodist, *Colloq* copycat: *Professor Eidolon, the greatest mimic in the world, is here to entertain you!*
—*adj.* **5** imitative, °imitation, °mock, simulated, mimetic, °sham, make-believe, °pretend(ed); °fake, °counterfeit, feigned: *Naumachia is the name given to the mimic sea battle staged in ancient Rome.*

mincing *adj.* °effeminate, °dainty, °delicate, niminy-piminy, foppish, dandyish, over-dainty, °affected, °put-on, °pretentious, °precious, *Brit* °twee, *Colloq* la-di-da *or* lah-di-dah *or* la-de-da: *His mincing speech sets my teeth on edge.*

mind *n.* **1** °intelligence, °intellect, °wit(s), °mentality, °brain, brains, brainpower, °sense, sagacity, °wisdom, °perception, percipience, °reason, astuteness, °insight, shrewdness, sapience, *Colloq* grey matter: *There is nothing wrong with your son's mind, Mr Field; he just doesn't want to apply it to school work.* **2** °memory, °recollection; °remembrance: *Keep in mind what I am about to tell you.* **3** °aptitude, °head, °perception, °capacity, °brain: *She has a great mind for dates—for figures of all kinds.* **4** °intellect, °intellectual, °sage, °genius, °thinker, *Colloq* °brain: *There is no doubt that your daughter is one of the great minds of all time.* **5** °intention, °disposition, °temper, temperament, °humour, °fancy, °tendency, °bent, °inclination, °bias, °persuasion: *I was of a mind to let him have his own way.* **6** °opinion, °sentiment, °attitude, (°point of) °view, °feeling, °judgement, °belief, °viewpoint, °position: *She has a mind of her own. To my mind, the process could be greatly speeded up.* **7** °feeling, °position, °will, °wish, °desire, °plan(s): *Won't you change your mind and stay to dinner?* **8** °attention, °thoughts, concentration, °thinking: *Try to keep your mind on your work.* **9** ***bear*** *or* ***keep in mind***: °remember, do not forget *or* overlook, °recall, °retain, be °aware *or* cognizant *or* °mindful of, °consider: *Bear in mind that the post office is closed tomorrow.* **10** ***give someone a piece of one's mind***: °castigate, °scold, °rebuke, °reprimand, °rail at, °reprove, reproach, °chastise, °upbraid, °berate, read (someone) the riot act, *Colloq* °tell off, °dress down, haul *or* rake over the coals, °skin alive, *US* °bawl out; *Slang* give someone °hell, *US* °chew out: *This time my father really gave the maître d'hôtel a piece of his mind.* **11** ***in*** *or* ***of two minds***: vacillating, undecided, ambivalent, °uncertain, shilly-shallying, unsure, wavering: *Sam was in two minds about ordering a new computer.* **12** ***know one's (own) mind***: be °decided *or* resolved, be °firm *or* °resolute, be °sure *or* °certain *or* °positive, be (self-)assured *or* (self-) °confident, be in touch with oneself: *He knows his own mind when it comes to his career.* **13** ***make up one's (own) mind***: °decide, °choose, conclude, form an °opinion; °determine, °consider, °weigh, °judge, deem: *Sally hasn't yet made up her mind about marrying Jim. Let her make up her own mind.* **14** ***out of one's mind***: °insane, °mad, °crazy: *You're out of your mind if you think I'll go swimming in that shark-infested bay!*
—*v.* **15** °object to, °resent, take °offence at, be offended by, °dislike, be troubled *or* annoyed by, °care, have any °objection to, °disapprove of, be bothered *or* affronted by: *Do you mind not smoking? Yes, I mind very much. Would you mind moving your car, you're blocking the drive.* **16** °heed, °attend to, pay °attention to, °obey, °listen to, make *or* take °note of, °mark, °note: *Please mind what your mother says.* **17** °watch, be °careful of, take °care with, be °cautious of: *Mind your head at that low doorway!* **18** °watch over, take °care of, °care for, °look after, °sit with, babysit, °guard, keep an eye on *or* out for, have *or* take °charge of, °attend: *Suzie is minding the children so that we can get some work done.* **19** ***never mind***: °ignore, °disregard, °forget, pay no °attention to, do not °think twice about, do not give a second °thought to, °erase *or* °obliterate *or* °cancel from the mind, slough off: *Never mind what that naughty boy calls you!*

minder *n.* **1** child-minder, babysitter, sitter, nanny, °nurse, governess: *The minder will put the children to bed.* **2** bodyguard, °escort, °protector: *Arthur hired an ex-fighter as his minder.*

mindful *adj.* Often, ***mindful of***: °aware, °alert, °attentive to, °alive, °conscious, heedful, °conscientious, watchful, °vigilant, on the qui vive, on the °lookout, circumspect, °cautious: *I am ever mindful of the way you like things done. She was always mindful of keeping the plants well watered.*

mindless *adj.* **1** °stupid, asinine, °thick, thickheaded, °obtuse, idiotic, imbecilic, moronic, °thoughtless, witless, °senseless, brainless, °feeble-minded, fatuous, addle-brained, addle-pated, feather-brained, *Colloq* *Brit* gormless: *Many of the programmes on television* *are mindless twaddle.* **2** °inattentive, °unthinking, °thoughtless, °unaware: *He plunged into the pool, mindless of any of the perils that awaited him.*

mine *n.* **1** °pit, °excavation, lode, °vein; colliery, coal-field: *My father worked in a mine from the age of 14.* **2** °source, mother-lode, °vein, °store, °storehouse, °supply, °deposit, depository *or* depositary, repository, °reserve, °hoard, °treasure trove, reservoir, well-spring; °abundance, °fund, gold-mine, °wealth, °treasury: *This encyclopedia is a rich mine of information.* —*v.* **3** °excavate, °dig, °quarry, °extract, °scoop out *or* up, °remove, °unearth; °derive, °extract, °draw: *He claims to have mined coal in Wales and gold in South Africa. Analysis shows this ore was mined in Pennsylvania.* **4** °ransack, °search, °rake through, °scour, °scan, °read, °survey, °look through, °probe: *Several directories were mined to compile our list of sales prospects.*

mingle *v.* **1** °mix, °blend, intermingle, commingle, intermix, °combine, °amalgamate, °merge, °compound, °marry, °join, °unite: *The stories cleverly mingle gravity and levity, the mundane and the magical. There was loud applause, mingled with a few chuckles and gasps.* **2** °mix, °socialize, °associate, °join, °circulate, °fraternize, °hobnob, consort, °go, °spend time, *Colloq* °hang about *or* around *or* out, °rub shoulders, *Brit* °pal up, *US* °pal around: *I asked Fred to mingle with the guests and make them feel at home.*

miniature *adj.* °small, small-scale, °little, °tiny, °diminutive, °minute, °wee, minuscule, mini, microscopic, micro, midget, °dwarf, bantam, °baby, pygmy, °pocket, Lilliputian, *US* vest-pocket, *Colloq* °minimal: *This miniature TV fits in the palm of your hand.*

minimal *adj.* least, smallest, minutest, littlest, tiniest, slightest; °minimum, °nominal, °token: *As a house plant, the cactus requires minimal attention. There is a minimal charge for service.*

minimize *v.* **1** °reduce, °shrink, lessen, °diminish, °prune, °abbreviate, °pare (down), °cut (down), °curtail, °abridge, °shorten, °decrease, minify: *Our stringent safety measures minimize the chance of an accident.* **2** °belittle, de-emphasize, downplay, °play down, make °little *or* °light of, °disparage, decry, deprecate, °depreciate, misprize, devalue, devaluate, undervalue, underrate, °underestimate, *US* °talk down: *Being modest, she minimizes her role in the organization.*

minimum *n.* **1** least, lowest, nadir: *The hotel offered the minimum of comfort for the maximum price.* —*adj.* **2** °minimal, °nominal, reduced, minutest, littlest, least, slightest, lowest: *What is the minimum deposit the travel agent will accept? He refused to make even the minimum effort needed to save himself.*

minister *n.* **1** cleric, °clergyman, clergywoman, ecclesiastic, °pastor, vicar, °priest, °father, reverend, churchman, °divine, parson, °preacher, man *or* woman of the °cloth, evangelist, °missionary, dean, curate, curé, abbé, chaplain, *Colloq* padre, *Slang US military* sky pilot, Holy Joe: *The marriage was performed by a visiting minister.* **2** °envoy, °delegate, legate, diplomat, °ambassador, emissary, plenipotentiary, minister plenipotentiary, °envoy °extraordinary, minister °resident, consul, °agent, chargé d'affaires, *Brit* °cabinet °officer *or* °member: *The minister himself signed the treaty.* —*v.* **3** Usually, ***minister to***: °attend (to *or* on *or* upon), °wait on, °care for, °look after, °see to, °accommodate; °serve, °supply, °aid, °help, °assist, °support: *In his last days, she ministered to him in every way.*

ministry *n.* **1** priesthood, °sacred °calling, the church, the pulpit, the °cloth; °religion, °holy orders: *Burt retired from the ministry to write tracts.* **2** clergy, clergymen *or* clergywomen, clericals, the °cloth, church elders *or* elders of the church: *During his regime, the ministry exercised great influence on the government.* **3** °department, °office, °bureau, °agency: *Military affairs are the responsibility of the Ministry of Defence.*

minor *adj.* **1** lesser, smaller, °secondary, °subordinate, °subsidiary: *The minor planets are bodies orbiting the sun in the asteroid belt.* **2** °insignificant, °obscure, °inconsequential, unimportant, °trifling, trivial, °negligible, inconsiderable, °slight, °petty, °paltry, °small, *Colloq* °small-time, one-horse, *Brit* two a penny, *US* minor-league, bush-league, penny-ante, two-bit, picayune: *It is a minor matter to me whether you stay or go. She is only a minor player in this game.* —*n.* **3** °child, youngster, °youth, °stripling, °teenager, °adolescent, schoolboy, schoolgirl, °boy, °girl, °lad, laddie, °lass, lassie, *Law* °ward, infant: *At your age, you are still a minor in the eyes of the law.*

minstrel *n.* bard, troubadour, balladeer, jongleur, skald *or* scald, minnesinger, Meistersinger: *The medieval minstrels wandered the countryside, entertaining as they went.*

mint *n.* **1** (small) °fortune, °lot, king's ransom, millions, billions, *Colloq* °bundle, °pile, °heap, °wad(s), °packet, °pot(s), loads, ton, *Slang Brit* bomb, *US* (big) bucks: *He lost a mint at roulette last night. She made a mint on her inventions.* —*v.* **2** °make, °coin, °produce, °earn: *Special commemorative coins were minted to celebrate the Coronation.*

minute[1] *n.* **1** °instant, °second, split °second, °flash, °moment, before you can say 'Jack Robinson', °blink *or* wink *or* °twinkling of an eye, *coup d'œil*, trice, *Colloq* °one sec, two secs, bat of an eye, shake, jiffy, tick, *Brit* half a mo, two shakes (of a lamb's tail): *I'll be with you in a minute.* **2** ***minutes***: log, °record, °journal, °transcript, °notes, °summary, résumé, °proceedings, °transactions, °memorandum: *Have you the minutes of the last meeting?* **3** ***up to the minute***: °latest, newest, °modern, up to °date, °trendy, °fashionable, °smart, all the °rage, in °vogue, °stylish, in °style, in °fashion, à la °mode, *Colloq* in, with it, hep *or* °hip, °hot, °cool, *US* °now: *She always wears the most up-to-the-minute clothes.* —*v.* **4** °record, °transcribe, °take down, °write down, °note, °make (a) °note of, °document, log: *We need someone to minute the meeting.*

minute[2] *adj.* **1** °small, °little, °tiny, tiniest, minuscule, °miniature, °wee, infinitesimal, microscopic, micro, °diminutive, mini, °baby, pint-sized, bantam, Lilliputian, *Colloq* teeny, teensy-weensy, itty-bitty, itsy-bitsy: *The minute furniture in the doll's house was made entirely by hand.* **2** unimportant, °petty, °insignificant, least, °slight, °mere, °meagre, °trifling, trivial, °minor, °small, °little, *Colloq* piddling, *US* picayune: *The painting was a perfect copy, down to the minutest detail.*

miraculous *adj.* °marvellous, wonderful, wondrous, °incredible, °unbelievable, °inexplicable, unexplainable, °extraordinary, spectacular, °amazing, astounding, astonishing, mind-boggling, °remarkable, °phenomenal, °fantastic, °fabulous; magical, °supernatural, preternatural, °superhuman, *Colloq* out of this °world, *Slang* far-out, °crazy: *Langley has made a miraculous recovery from yellow fever.*

mire *n.* **1** °swamp, °bog, fen, °marsh, quagmire, °morass, slough, *Brit dialect* sump: *The horse stumbled into the mire and began to flounder.* **2** °mud, °ooze, °muck, slime, °dirt: *I had to wade through muck and mire to get to your front door.* —*v.* **3** enmire, °bog down, become entangled *or* tangled, become enmeshed *or* meshed, become °involved: *Sorry I'm late; I got mired in a problem at the office.* **4** °dirty, °soil, begrime, °muddy, befoul, besmirch, °sully, °tarnish, °smear, °blacken, defile, smudge: *My boots were badly mired. The scandal badly mired his reputation.*

mirror *n.* **1** looking-glass, °glass, speculum, reflector: *She stared at her reflection in the mirror, wondering whether she should grow her hair.* **2** °reflection, °reproduction, °picture, °representation, replication, (mirror) °image: *Language is the mirror of society, reflecting every social change.* —*v.* **3** °reflect, °reproduce, °represent, depict, °repeat, °echo, °send back: *The calm lake mirrored the moonlight. The people's misery was mirrored in their faces.*

mirth *n.* °merriment, merrymaking, jollity, °gaiety, °fun, °laughter, °amusement, °frolic, frolicking, joviality, joyousness, °revelry, rejoicing, °glee, high spirits, mirthfulness, °hilarity, buoyancy, *Formal* jocundity: *Life without mirth is a lamp without oil. Christmas is a time for mirth.*

misalliance *n.* mésalliance, mismarriage, mismatch, mismatchment, bad match, mismating: *No one is surprised that John and Marsha's misalliance has ended in divorce.*

misanthrope *n.* misanthropist, mankind-hater; °man-hater, woman-hater, misogynist; loner, °hermit, °recluse, anchorite *or* anchoret, *Colloq* lone wolf: *The longer he lived and the more he learned of his fellowman, the more of a misanthrope he became.*

misanthropic *adj.* man-hating; antisocial, °unsocial, unfriendly, egocentric, °egoistic: *In his misanthropic moods, Joel disdains human company.*

misappropriate *v.* **1** °embezzle, °steal, filch, expropriate, °pocket, *Formal* peculate, defalcate: *He was found guilty of misappropriating club funds.* **2** misapply, °misuse, °pervert, misemploy: *The money intended for the health service was misappropriated for the war effort.*

misbehave *v.* °disobey, behave °badly *or* improperly, be °bad *or* °naughty *or* °mischievous, *Colloq* °carry on, act up, *Slang* raise hell, raise Cain: *The teacher sent for me because Robyn misbehaved in class.*

misbehaviour *n.* naughtiness, badness, misconduct, misdemeanour(s), disorderliness, disobedience, delinquency, °disorderly °conduct, °rowdyism: *She was severely reprimanded for persistent misbehaviour in class.*

miscalculate *v.* misjudge, °err, misevaluate, misestimate, misreckon, miscompute, miscount, misappreciate, misread; °underestimate, undervalue, underrate; overestimate, overvalue, °overrate: *She miscalculated the effect of her resignation.*

miscarriage *n.* °failure, abortion, °collapse, °breakdown, °failing, mismanagement, non-fulfilment, °defeat, non-success, frustration: *Her acquittal was a miscarriage of justice.*

miscarry *v.* abort, °fail, °fall through, °break down, go °wrong, °founder, °come to nothing *or* naught *or* nought, go awry, come to °grief, go °amiss, °misfire, go up *or* end up in smoke, °perish, °die: *The plan to steal the crown jewels miscarried.*

miscellaneous *adj.* °varied, heterogeneous, °diverse, °mixed, diversified, °divers, motley, °sundry, assorted, °various, varying, multifarious, multiform, many-sided, multiplex, °manifold: *A large part of the exhibition is devoted to miscellaneous paintings and prints from his early period.*

miscellany *n.* °mixture, °assortment, °variety, °medley, °diversity, °mixed bag, job °lot, rag-bag, mélange, °pot-pourri, gallimaufry, motley, °hotchpotch *or US and Canadian* hodgepodge, salmagundi, olio, olla podrida, smorgasbord *or* smörgåsbord, °odds and ends, omnium gatherum, °hash, °mess, *Brit* lucky dip, °jumble, *US* grab-bag: *A miscellany of household goods was contributed for the jumble sale.*

mischief *n.* **1** °misbehaviour, naughtiness, impishness, elfishness *or* elvishness, roguishness, rascality, °devilry *or* deviltry, mischievousness, playfulness, devilment, badness, *Colloq* °monkey business, shenanigans, *Brit* °monkey tricks *or US* monkeyshines: *That boy is always up to some mischief.* **2** °harm, °injury, °damage, °detriment, °trouble, °hurt, °wrong, °difficulty, disruption, °destruction, °misfortune, °evil: *He didn't realize the mischief a casual remark could do. She was accused of malicious mischief when she punctured his car tyres.*

mischievous *adj.* **1** °naughty, impish, roguish, rascally, °devilish, elfish *or* elvish, puckish, scampish, °frolicsome, °playful, °sportive: *Tying his cousin's shoelaces together was a mischievous prank and not malicious.* **2** °harmful, °injurious, °hurtful, damaging, pernicious, °detrimental, °destructive, deleterious, °dangerous, °spiteful, malicious, °vicious, malign, baleful, baneful, noxious, °wicked, °evil, °bad: *The government regards as mischievous the detention of any Foreign Office personnel.*

misconceive *v.* °misunderstand, misconstrue, misjudge, °mistake, misapprehend, °misinterpret, misread, get *or* have the wrong idea, get *or* have (hold of) the wrong end of the °stick: *He has misconceived the purpose in banning firearms.*

misconception *n.* °false *or* °wrong °notion *or* °idea, °misunderstanding, misconstruction, misconstrual, misjudgement, miscalculation, misapprehension, °mistaken °belief, °error, °mistake, °delusion: *The confused wording of the warranty could result in a misconception of one's rights.*

miscreant *n.* **1** °villain, °wretch, mischief-maker, scamp, °rascal, °criminal, evil-doer, °felon, malefactor, °rogue, °reprobate, °scoundrel, wrongdoer, °good-for-nothing, ne'er-do-well, blackguard, hooligan, ruffian, °hoodlum, °thug, °rowdy, *Archaic* knave, caitiff, varlet, rapscallion, *Colloq* crook, roughneck, scallywag *or* scalawag, *Slang* hood, *Brit* °mug, °rough, *Australian* larrikin, *US* baddy, bad actor: *The police have apprehended the miscreant who had been attacking passers-by.*

—*adj.* **2** °villainous, °wretched, °mischievous, rascally, °criminal, felonious, °corrupt, malefic, malevolent, °evil, depraved, °base, nefarious, iniquitous, °vicious, unprincipled, ne'er-do-well, °reprobate, scoundrelly, °wicked: *The miscreant terrorists may be hiding in Greece.*

misdeed *n.* Often, ***misdeeds***: °offence, °crime, felony, wrongdoing, misdoing, °transgression, misdemeanour, °fault, misconduct, °sin, trespass, °wrong, °peccadillo: *Who will punish him for his misdeeds now that he is safe in Argentina?*

misdirect *v.* misguide, misadvise; misaddress: *He misdirected us by saying the lavatory was downstairs. The letter, misdirected, was returned.*

miser *n.* skinflint, hoarder, niggard, penny-pincher, pinchpenny, cheese-parer, Scrooge, *Colloq* cheapskate, *US* tightwad: *For that old miser, charity begins and ends at home.*

miserable *adj.* **1** °wretched, °unhappy, depressed, woeful, °woebegone, °sad, °dejected, °forlorn, disconsolate, °despondent, °heartbroken, °sorrowful, °broken-hearted, °mournful, °desolate, °desperate, despairing, °downhearted, °melancholy, °glum, low-spirited, °gloomy, °dismal, lachrymose, °tearful, *Colloq Brit* °cut up: *Tanya is miserable because no one invited her to go to the dance.* **2** unpleasant, °inclement, °inconvenient, °untoward, °bad, unfavourable, °awful, °terrible, adverse, *Colloq* °rotten, °lousy: *The weather was miserable throughout the weekend.* **3** °inadequate, °unworthy, °poor, °deplorable, °contemptible, °bad, °despicable, °sorry, °pitiful, °pathetic, °lamentable, *Colloq* °rotten, °lousy: *That was the most miserable play I have ever had the misfortune to sit through.* **4** squalid, °wretched, °bad, abject, °deplorable, °shabby, °mean, °vile, °shameful, °scurvy, °awful, °disgraceful, °contemptible: *He lives in a cellar in the most miserable conditions.*

miserly *adj.* stingy, °penurious, niggardly, penny-pinching, parsimonious, °mean, °cheap, cheese-paring, °tight, tight-fisted, °close, close-fisted, °mercenary, °avaricious, °greedy, covetous, *Colloq* money-grubbing, *Brit* mingy, *US* chintzy: *Flynn is too miserly to lend you a penny.*

misery *n.* **1** unhappiness, °distress, °discomfort, wretchedness, °woe, °sadness, °melancholy, °sorrow, dolour, heartache, °grief, °anguish, °anxiety, angst, °depression, °despair, °desperation, °desolation, despondency, °gloom: *Worn out by grief and misery, she collapsed into a chair.* **2** squalor, °poverty, destitution, °privation, indigence, penury, wretchedness, sordidness: *The misery of those slums is unbelievable.* **3** °hardship, °suffering, °calamity, °disaster, °curse, °misfortune, °ordeal, °woe, °trouble, °catastrophe,

°trial, tribulation, adversity, °burden, °affliction: *She cannot bear the twin miseries of illness and poverty.* **4** °spoilsport, damper, °killjoy, dampener, Job's comforter, grouch, grump, malcontent, pessimist, cynic, °prophet of doom, Cassandra, *Colloq* wet blanket, sourpuss, *US* party pooper, °gloomy Gus, picklepuss: *How can you stand living with such a misery?*

misfire *v.* **1** °fail, abort, °miscarry, go °wrong, °fizzle (out), °fall through, *Colloq* °flop, come a cropper, *Brit* go phut, *US* go pfft *or* phft: *The plan to take over the conglomerate misfired when the shares soared in price.* —*n.* **2** °miscarriage, °failure, °fizzle, °dud, *Colloq* abort, °flop: *After two misfires, we gave up trying to buy a time-share in the Algarve.*

misfit *n.* oner, °eccentric, °individual, °nonconformist, maverick, square peg in a round hole: *People regard him as one of society's misfits and tend to steer clear.*

misfortune *n.* **1** °bad °luck, °ill °luck, °ill °fortune, °hard °luck, infelicity, adversity, °loss: *He had the misfortune to marry the wrong woman.* **2** °accident, misadventure, °mishap, °calamity, °catastrophe, mischance, °disaster, contretemps, °tragedy, °blow, °shock; °reverse, stroke of °bad °luck, *Colloq* °bad news: *With the death of his father, then his illness, then the loss of his business, one misfortune followed another.*

misgiving *n.* apprehension, °mistrust, °worry, °concern, °anxiety, °qualm, °scruple, disquiet, hesitation, °doubt, °question, uncertainty, °suspicion, unease, uneasiness, °discomfort; °dread, °premonition, °foreboding, *Colloq* °funny °feeling: *I had grave misgivings about driving all that way on my own.*

misguided *adj.* misled, °wrong, misdirected, °foolish, °unreasonable, °erroneous, °mistaken, misplaced, °imprudent, unwise, impolitic, °ill-advised, fallacious, uncalled-for, labouring under a misapprehension, °wide of the mark, *Colloq* off (the mark), barking up the °wrong tree: *Her helpfulness is often misguided, ending in disaster for all concerned.*

mishandle *v.* **1** °abuse, °mistreat, maltreat, °ill-treat, °beat (up), brutalize, maul, °molest, °injure, °hurt, °harm, °handle *or* °treat °roughly, °manhandle, *Colloq* °knock about *or* around: *The poor child was mishandled by her parents.* **2** mismanage, °bungle, °botch, misconduct, °mangle, °mess up, °muddle, °wreck, °ruin, °destroy, *Colloq* muff, make a °mess *or* °hash of, *Slang* °screw up, °bugger up, *Taboo* fuck up: *Forster mishandled the deal so badly that it cost the company millions.*

mishap *n.* See **misfortune, 2,** above.

mishmash *n.* °mess, °medley, °hash, gallimaufry, farrago, °pot-pourri, °jumble, °pastiche, °mixture, salmagundi, °hotchpotch *or US and Canadian* hodgepodge, °tangle, omnium gatherum, *mélange*, olio, olla podrida, goulash, °stew: *His paper is nothing more than a mishmash of other people's ideas.*

misinform *v.* misguide, °mislead, misadvise, °misdirect, delude, °deceive, °dupe, °defraud, °fool, gull, °lead astray, throw someone off the scent, *Colloq* con, slip *or* put something over on someone, pull a fast one on, *US* give (someone) a bum °steer, throw someone a curve: *If you think you have a right to compensation, you've been misinformed.*

misinformation *n.* disinformation, misintelligence; red herring, °false trail, °false °scent: *When we uncover an enemy agent in our midst, we allow him to collect misinformation.*

misinterpret *v.* °misunderstand, °mistake, misconstrue, °misconceive, misread, misjudge, misapprehend, *Slang* °screw up, °bugger up: *He misinterpreted what I said and stepped off the ledge.*

mislay *v.* misplace, °lose, mislocate; misfile: *I have mislaid my reading spectacles.*

mislead *v.* °misinform, °lead astray, misguide, °misdirect, throw off the scent *or* track, pull the wool over someone's eyes, °fool, °outwit, °bluff, °hoodwink, °trick, humbug, bamboozle, °deceive, °dupe, gull, cozen, *Colloq* con, °take in, lead up the garden path, flimflam, slip *or* put *or* pass one over on, *Slang* °take, *US* give someone a bum °steer: *I was misled into believing that she loved only me. He is misleading you if he says that the shares will soon increase in value.*

mismatched *adj.* mismated, ill-matched, ill-mated, °incompatible, unfit, °inappropriate, unsuited, unsuitable, °incongruous, misallied, disparate, uncongenial, °inconsistent, inharmonious, °discordant: *With her interest in art and his in football, they made a mismatched pair.*

misprint *n.* °error, °mistake, erratum, typographical °error, printer's *or* printing °error, *Brit* literal, *Colloq* typo: *We cannot publish a book containing so many misprints.*

misrepresent *v.* °distort, °twist, °pervert, °garble, misstate, °mangle, °falsify, belie, °disguise, °colour: *In his report, he misrepresented everything I said.*

miss[1] *v.* **1** °skip, °forgo, °absent oneself from, be °absent from, fail to keep; °avoid, °evade, °escape, °dodge, *Colloq* °pass up: *I missed my dentist's appointment. I missed school because my grandmother was ill.* **2** °long for, °yearn for, pine for, °feel nostalgia for, be nostalgic for *or* about, °want, °need, °wish for: *I miss those long summer evenings by the lake.* **3** °misunderstand, °misinterpret, misconstrue, misapprehend, fail to understand *or* perceive, °mistake: *You have completely missed the point.* **4** Sometimes, **miss out (on)**: °pass up, °omit, °leave out, °slip up (on), °overlook, let °slip (by), let °pass, °pass over, °disregard, °ignore: *You can be sure that Frobisher would never miss a free meal.*
—*n.* **5** °omission, °oversight, °slip, °failure, °mistake, °error, °blunder, *Colloq* slip-up: *A miss is as good as a mile.*

miss[2] *n.* Ms, °girl, °lass, lassie, °maid, °maiden, young lady, young °woman, schoolgirl, mademoiselle, nymphet, °teenager, virgin, spinster, old °maid, *Brit* bachelor °girl, *Irish English* colleen, *Literary* nymph, *Archaic* demoiselle, damsel, *Colloq old-fashioned* gal, *US* coed, Valley °girl, bachelorette, *Slang* teenybopper, groupie, *Chiefly Brit* bird, *Old-fashioned US* bobby-soxer: *She's a pretty young miss, isn't she?*

misshapen *adj.* distorted, twisted, contorted, °crooked, °deformed, °crippled, malformed, °grotesque, awry, warped, °gnarled, ill-proportioned, ill-made, °monstrous, *Technical* acromegalic: *The misshapen bell-ringer in* The Hunchback of Notre Dame *was named Quasimodo.*

missile *n.* °projectile, brickbat; guided missile, ballistic missile: *Bottles, stones, and other missiles were thrown at the police during the riot.*

mission *n.* **1** °task, °duty, °function, °purpose, °job, °office, °work, °assignment, °errand, °charge, °business, commission, °undertaking, °pursuit, °activity, °aim, °objective: *He accepted the mission to convert the natives to Christianity.* **2** °calling, °occupation, °vocation, °trade, °line (of °work), °profession, métier: *It has become my mission in life to see that you learn how to do sums.* **3** delegation, legation, deputation, commission, °committee, °group, °ministry: *She has been sent on a governmental trade mission to Botswana.*

missionary *n.* evangelist, °preacher, °minister, proselytizer: *During the 19th century, many missionaries were dispatched to spread the faith in Africa.*

missive *n.* °letter, communication, °message, °dispatch, °note, °line, postcard, °card, epistle: *I have just received a missive from great-aunt Cecilia that took me an hour to read.*

misspent *adj.* wasted, squandered, °idle, dissipated, thrown away, profitless, °prodigal: *Proficiency at billiards is a sign of a misspent youth.*

misstatement *n.* **1** falsification, misreport, misquotation, miscitation, distortion, misrepresentation, misconstruction, misinterpretation, °perversion, °lie, °falsehood, untruth, °fabrication: *The prosecutor's indictment is a misstatement of the charges against the defendant.* **2** °solecism, °error, °mistake, gaffe, faux pas, °slip of the °tongue, *lapsus linguae*, °blunder, *Slang* °howler, *Brit* bloomer, *US and Canadian* blooper: *For an educated man his speech is sprinkled with too many grammatical misstatements.*

misstep *n.* **1** °false °step, °blunder, °mistake, °error, °bad *or* °wrong *or* °false °move, °trip, °stumble, °slip: *One misstep meant a fall into the abyss.* **2** °indiscretion, °mistake, °lapse, faux pas, °oversight, °error, gaffe, *Colloq* slip-up, *Slang* °howler, *Brit* bloomer, *US and Canadian* blooper, goof: *Her misstep was telling her fiancé's mother that she had formerly been an artist's model.*

mist *n.* **1** °fog, haze, smog, (low-hanging) cloud, °vapour; drizzle, *Brit dialect* mizzle: *I could scarcely make out the road in the mist.*
—*v.* **2** Usually, ***mist up*** *or* ***over***: cloud (up *or* over), becloud, °fog, befog, °dim, °blur, °film, steam up: *The mirror in the bathroom had misted up when I was having a shower.*

mistake *n.* **1** °misconception, misapprehension, °error, °fault, miscalculation, misjudgement, °blunder, °botch, °fumble, °bad °move, °misstep, °slip, erratum, gaffe, faux pas, *Colloq* boo-boo, clanger, muff, °howler, *Brit* boob, bloomer, *US* blooper, goof, goof-up, flub: *Giving Aston a salary rise was a mistake.* **2** °indiscretion, °misstep, °false °step, °wrong °move: *It was a mistake not to stand up when she entered.*
—*v.* **3** °misunderstand, °misinterpret, misjudge, misconstrue, °take the °wrong way, get °wrong, misread, misapprehend: *The fool mistook my remark as a compliment.* **4** ***mistake for***: °mix up in *or* with, misidentify as, °confuse with, °take for: *In the dark, she mistook him for her husband.*

mistaken *adj.* **1** (all *or* completely) °wrong, °amiss, incorrect, in °error, °wide of the mark, in the °wrong, °inaccurate, out of °order, *Colloq* barking up the °wrong tree, °off, (way) off the beam, on the °wrong track, *US* full of °hot air, *Slang* full of it (= *Taboo* 'full of shit'), *US* all wet: *I may be mistaken, but I thought I saw your wife with your squash partner.* **2** °erroneous, °faulty, °false, fallacious, misinformed, °incorrect, °wrong, °inaccurate, °flawed, warped, distorted, twisted, °misguided, *Slang* cock-eyed: *You have a mistaken impression of me.*

mistreat *v.* °abuse, maltreat, ill-use, °ill-treat, °misuse, °damage, °manhandle, °harm; °hurt, °injure, °molest, maul, °rough up, brutalize: *He was found guilty of mistreating his dogs. She was mistreated by her husband for years.*

mistreatment *n.* °abuse, maltreatment, °ill °use, ill-treatment, brutalization, °misuse; manhandling, molestation, mauling, roughing-up, °rough handling, battery, °assault: *This mistreatment of employees must stop at once. The children complained of their parents' mistreatment.*

mistress *n.* **1** °lover, girlfriend, live-in °lover, kept °woman, concubine, inamorata, °paramour, *Literary* odalisque, *Archaic* doxy, *Colloq US* alternative other, POSSLQ (= 'Person of the Opposite Sex Sharing Living Quarters'): *She was the mistress of a leading politician.* **2** schoolmistress, instructress, governess; headmistress: *She had a rewarding career as a mistress in a girls' school in Lancashire.*

mistrust *v.* **1** °suspect, °distrust, be °suspicious of, °doubt, be *or* feel °wary *or* °suspicious *or* °doubtful of *or* about, have (one's) doubts about, °question, have reservations; °beware; *Slang* be *or* feel °leery of *or* about: *He has not done anything specifically bad, but I mistrust his motives.*
—*n.* **2** °suspicion, °distrust, °doubt, °scepticism, wariness, °reservation, chariness, °misgiving(s), uncertainty, unsureness, apprehension, apprehensiveness: *Is there nothing I can say to dispel your mistrust of me?*

misty *adj.* cloudy, foggy, °hazy, °murky; °fuzzy, °dim, blurred, blurry, unclear, °indistinct, °vague, °dark, °opaque, °shadowy, °obscure, unintelligible: *It is very misty, so drive carefully. I have only the mistiest idea of what you mean.*

misunderstand *v.* °misconceive, misconstrue, °misinterpret, misapprehend, get (it *or* it all) wrong, get the wrong idea (about), misread, misjudge, °miscalculate, °miss the point (of): *He understood your words but misunderstood your meaning.*

misunderstanding *n.* **1** °misconception, misconstruction, misinterpretation, misapprehension, misreading, misjudgement, miscalculation, °wrong °idea, °wrong *or* °false °impression, mistaking, *Technical* parasynesis: *Misunderstanding of the law is no excuse for flouting it.* **2** °disagreement, °discord, °dispute, °argument, °difference, °dissension, °controversy, °quarrel, °rift, *Colloq* falling out: *We had a slight misunderstanding about who was to pay the restaurant bill.*

misuse *n.* **1** misapplication, misusage, misappropriation, misemployment, diverting, °diversion, perverting, °perversion: *He was accused of the misuse of public funds for his personal gain.* **2** misusage, °abuse, corruption, °solecism, malapropism, barbarism, catachresis, ungrammaticality, infelicity: *His misuses of English have made him a laughing-stock.* **3** See **mistreatment,** above.
—*v.* **4** °abuse, misapply, misemploy, °misappropriate; °pervert: *I broke the knife blade misusing it as a screwdriver. He was accused of misusing the courts to his own ends.* **5** See **mistreat,** above.

mitigate *v.* °moderate, °temper, °reduce, abate, lessen, °decrease, °relieve, °ease, °ease up (on), °relax, alleviate, °remit, assuage, allay, °let up (on), slacken, slacken up (on), °tone down, °lighten, appease, palliate, mollify, °calm, °tranquillize, soothe, placate, °quiet *or chiefly Brit* °quieten, °still, °soften, °dull, °blunt, take the edge off, *US* °lighten up (on): *The pain was mitigated by taking aspirin. The relief organizations did their best to mitigate the effects of the disaster.*

mitigating *adj.* °extenuating, justifying, excusatory, palliating, vindicating, qualifying: *Were there mitigating circumstances in her taking the money?*

mix *v.* **1** °mingle, °combine, intermingle, °blend, °incorporate, °put together, °merge, °unite, °alloy, commingle, °amalgamate, coalesce: *Mix the ingredients to a creamy consistency.* **2** °socialize, °fraternize, consort, °hobnob, °go round *or* around *or* about (together), °get together, keep °company, °join (with), °associate (with), *Colloq* °hang out *or* about *or* round *or* around (with): *The Hatfields and the McCoys do not mix very well, so you'd best invite them separately.* **3** ***mix in***: °add, °stir in, °combine, °fold in: *Mix in the chocolate at the very end.* **4** ***mix up***: **a** See **1,** above. **b** °confuse, confound, °bewilder, °muddle, °perplex, °puzzle, °fluster, °upset; addle, °disturb; *Colloq US and Canadian* discombobulate: *She mixed me up so that I cannot decide what to do.* **c** °snarl, ensnarl, °tangle, °entangle, °scramble, °jumble: *The treasures were all mixed up with the rubbish at the church sale.* **d** °confuse, interchange, °exchange: *Have they mixed up our room keys again?* **5** ***mix up in***: °involve, °implicate, °include, °connect, °draw *or* °drag into: *Wasn't Wilcox mixed up in that scandal last year?* **6** ***mix up with***: °confuse, °mistake, misidentify, confound; interchange, °exchange: *I think you must have me mixed up with somebody else. The porter mixed up my bag with someone else's.*
—*n.* **7** °mixture, °blend, °compound; °amalgam, °combination, °alloy, °assortment, °distribution: *Was this cake made from a mix or from scratch? The centre party has a good mix of liberals and conservatives.*

mixed *adj.* **1** °hybrid, half-bred, °mongrel, interbred, cross-bred; °impure, tainted, adulterated: *This horse has mixed blood.* **2** °confused, muddled; °varied, °various, °diverse; conflicting, °contradictory, °opposing, clashing, °opposite: *He had mixed feelings about ending his relationship with her.* **3** ***mixed up in*** *or* ***with***: °involved, connected, associated: *Wasn't she mixed up in that scandal last year? He doesn't want his children mixed up with people who take drugs.*

mixture *n.* **1** °assortment, °amalgam, °amalgamation, °medley, °combination, mingling, intermingling, composite, °blend, °jumble, °mix, °miscellany, *mélange*, °mess, °mishmash, °hotchpotch *or US and Canadian* hodgepodge, gallimaufry, farrago, olio, olla podrida, °hash, °pot-pourri, ragout, goulash, omnium gatherum, salmagundi: *The design is an unfortunate mixture of many incompatible styles.* **2** mixing, °amalgamation, amalgamating, combining, mingling, intermingling, °combination, °blend, blending, °association, associating, °compound, compounding, °synthesis, interweaving, merging, °merger, fusion, fusing, °alloy, alloying: *The mixture of household ammonia and bleach creates noxious fumes.*

mix-up *n.* °confusion, °mess, °muddle, °hotchpotch *or US also* hodgepodge, °tangle, °jumble, *Colloq* °botch, °mishmash, foul-up, *Slang US* screw-up, snafu, *Taboo slang Brit* balls-up: *The mix-up in the files is due to a computer malfunction.*

moan *n.* **1** °complaint, °lament, °lamentation, °groan, wail, moaning, °grievance: *Disregard his moans about money—he has plenty.*
—*v.* **2** °complain, °lament, °groan, wail, °bewail, grumble, °bemoan, deplore, whine, whimper, *Colloq* grouse, °gripe, beef, °bitch, *Brit* whinge: *She's always moaning about the way people take advantage of her.* **3** °sigh, °mourn, °weep, °sorrow, °cry, wail, °keen, °grieve, °sob, °snivel, °bawl, mewl, pule, ululate: *The women, all in black, moaned and tore their hair as they neared the coffin.*

mob *n.* **1** horde, °host, °press, °throng, °crowd, °pack, °herd, °swarm, °crush, °jam, multitude, °mass, °body, assemblage, °collection, °group: *The mob surged forward, hurling sticks and stones at anyone in uniform.* **2** °rabble, °riff-raff, proletariat, °populace, the masses, great °unwashed, *hoi polloi*, canaille, bourgeoisie, °lower classes, scum (of the earth), °dregs of society: *The mob cheered when the king was beheaded.*
—*v.* **3** °crowd (round *or* around), jostle, °throng, °surround, °beset, clamour over, °swoop down on *or* upon: *Thousands of screaming teenagers mobbed the singer.*

mobbed *adj.* crowded, °packed, thronged, °congested, teeming, swarming, full, filled: *They tried to leave by the emergency exit, but that was mobbed, too.*

mobile *adj.* **1** °movable, non-stationary, unstationary, unfixed, °travelling, °portable, transportable: *A mobile display was designed for industrial fairs.* **2** motorized, °mechanical, transportable, °movable: *They live in a mobile home. The mobile library comes round every Wednesday.* **3** °expressive, °sensitive, °animated, °plastic, °flexible, *US* facile: *Her mobile face at once reflected her thoughts.* **4** °agile, °versatile, °nimble, quick, °alert, °active, °responsive: *You need your wits about you to keep up with Randolph's mobile mind.* **5** ambulatory, ambulant: *After the artificial joint surgery, Keith was once again completely mobile.*

mobilize *v.* °assemble, marshal, conscript, °enrol, °enlist, °organize, °muster, levy, °rally, °activate, °call up, °prepare, °ready, *US* °draft: *A huge army was mobilized, virtually overnight.*

mock *v.* **1** °deride, °ridicule, make °fun of, °tease, °taunt, °tantalize, °jeer (at), °gibe (at), °thumb one's nose at, °chaff, °laugh at, °poke °fun at, make °sport of, °guy, °scorn, °flout, °abuse, °defy, °scoff (at), °sneer (at), disdain, °disparage, decry, *Archaic* fleer (at), *Colloq* °rag, rib, kid, °put (someone) on, *Brit* take the mickey out of, cock a snook at: *He was taken in for questioning only because he mocked a police officer. Jealousy is the green-eyed monster that mocks the meat it feeds on.* **2** ape, °mimic, °imitate, °caricature, °lampoon, °satirize, °parody, °burlesque, travesty, *Colloq* spoof, °take off, *Brit* °send up: *The political cartoonist mocks governments daily on the pillory of his pen.*
—*adj.* **3** °substitute, °artificial, simulated, °fake, °synthetic, °imitation, °false, forged, ersatz, °sham, feigned, °counterfeit, °fraudulent, °bogus, make-believe, °pretend, *Colloq* °phoney *or US also* phony, pseudo: *By means of a mock car accident they demonstrated how to rescue victims. Mock turtle soup, though good, does not taste like real turtle soup.*

mockery *n.* **1** °ridicule, °derision, disdain, taunting, disparagement, °abuse, °scorn, °contempt, contumely, decrial: *John was expelled for his mockery of the headmaster.* **2** °semblance, °imitation, impersonation; °caricature, °parody, °burlesque, travesty, °lampoon, °satire, pasquinade, farce; °miscarriage; *Colloq* spoof, °take-off, *Brit* send-up: *That wasn't a trial, it was a mockery of justice.* **3** °disappointment, °joke, °laugh, °absurdity: *It is a mockery to speak of that wretched sadist and humanity in the same breath.*

mode[1] *n.* **1** °way, °manner, °method, °approach, °form, °course, °fashion, °procedure, °technique, °system, °wise, *modus operandi*, methodology, standard operating °procedure, SOP: *What mode of teaching foreign languages do you use?* **2** °status, °condition, °state, configuration, °set-up: *The computer is now in printing mode.*

mode[2] *n.* °fashion, °style, °look, °vogue; °trend, °rage, °craze, *Colloq* °fad: *We went to the ball dressed in the mode of the 1920s.*

model *n.* **1** °representation, °replica, mock-up, maquette, scale model, working model, °miniature, °dummy, °image, °likeness, °facsimile, °copy: *This is a model of the house he is planning.* **2** °original, °mould, archetype, °prototype, °pattern, °paragon, °ideal, exemplar, °example, °standard: *When the wax model is finished, we cast it in bronze using the cire perdue* process. Their government was established after the Roman model. **3** °ideal, °paragon, exemplar, °epitome, *beau idéal*, cream, *crème de la crème, ne plus ultra*, °nonpareil, nonsuch *or* nonesuch: *He is the very model of what a father should be.* **4** °subject, sitter, poser: *Dali's wife served as his model for many paintings.* **5** mannequin; °dummy: *She is tall and thin enough to be a fashion model. May I see the hat that is on that model in the window?* **6** °design, °kind, °type, °style, °version; °variety, °sort, °form, °fashion, configuration; °brand, °mark: *I'm intending to trade my car in for a newer model.*
—*v.* **7** °fashion, °mould, °shape, °form, sculpt, °carve (out), °make, °fabricate, °produce: *She modelled these figures out of fine clay.* **8** °pose in, °display, °show (off), °wear, *Colloq* °sport: *She makes a fortune modelling swimwear.* **9** ***model after*** *or* ***on***: °imitate, °copy, °pattern on *or* after, emulate, °follow: *Architects often used to model public buildings after the temples on the Acropolis.*
—*adj.* **10** °copy, °imitation, °facsimile, °representative, °miniature: *He enjoys building model aeroplanes.* **11** °ideal, °exemplary, °perfect, archetypal, unequalled, consummate, inimitable: *Oliver has been a model student.*

moderate *adj.* **1** °temperate, °calm, °reasonable, °cool, °judicious, °rational, balanced, unexcessive, °modest, °sober, °sensible, commonsensical, controlled, °deliberate, °steady: *In view of the conflicting interests expressed, the council has adopted a moderate policy regarding parking.* **2** °centre, middle-of-the-road, nonradical, non-reactionary: *Bella's political outlook is said by some to be moderate.* **3** °fair, middling, °average, °ordinary, °medium, °middle, °modest, °mediocre, unexceptional, *Colloq* °fair to middling: *They have a good range of clothing, all sold at very moderate prices.*
—*n.* **4** middle-of-the-roader, non-radical, non-reactionary, centrist: *Where do the moderates stand on the issue of constitutional reform?*
—*v.* **5** abate, °calm, mollify, soothe, °ease, °relax, alleviate, °mitigate, °soften, °dull, °blunt, °cushion, °relieve, °reduce, lessen, °remit, slacken, °diminish, °decrease, defuse, °temper, *Colloq* °let up (on): *He would get along better if he moderated the violence of his reactions and learned to relax.* **6** mediate, arbitrate, referee, °judge, °chair, °supervise, °preside (over), °coordinate, °run, °regulate, °manage, °direct: *Professor Gill will moderate the panel discussion.*

moderately *adv.* °somewhat, °rather, °quite, °fairly, °pretty, comparatively, °slightly, passably, more or less; to some °extent, within °reason, to a certain

°extent, to a °degree, to some °degree, in some °measure, in moderation, within limits; temperately; *Colloq* °sort of, kind of: *Clifford is moderately well off. It was a moderately hot day.*

moderator *n.* °mediator, arbiter, arbitrator, °judge, referee, °umpire; *Chiefly US* °chair, chairperson, chairman, chairwoman, presiding °officer, president, coordinator, (discussion) °leader; anchorman, anchorwoman; °master of ceremonies, toastmaster, *Brit* compère, *Colloq* emcee, MC: *Lady Felicia was chosen as the moderator of next year's panel.*

modern *adj.* up to °date, °current, °contemporary, today's, °new, °fresh, °novel, °brand-new, up to the °minute, present-day, °latest, new-fashioned, newfangled; à la °mode, modish, in °vogue, °fashionable, in °fashion, °stylish, in °style, °chic, *Chiefly Brit* flavour of the month, *Slang* °trendy, in, with it, mod, °hip, °hot: *Elaine has little patience with modern electronic gadgets.*

modernize *v.* °renovate, streamline, redo, redecorate, °refurbish, refurnish, update, do over, °rejuvenate, °refresh, °revamp, redesign, remodel, refashion, remake: *We installed air conditioning when we modernized our offices.*

modest *adj.* **1** unassuming, unpresuming, °humble, unpretentious, °unobtrusive, °reserved, °retiring, diffident, °shy, °bashful, demure, °coy, shamefaced, self-effacing, °self-conscious, °reticent, °reluctant, °timid, °meek, timorous, *Rare* verecund: *Caroline is quite modest about her accomplishments.* **2** °humble, °simple, °plain, °ordinary, unpretentious, °homely, °lowly, unexceptional, unostentatious; °inconspicuous, °unobtrusive: *They live in a modest little cottage.* **3** °moderate, °limited, °understated, unimportunate, unexaggerated, °reasonable, °sensible, constrained, restricted, restrained: *The workers' demands seem modest enough.*

modicum *n.* °bit, °trifle, °jot, °jot *or* tittle, atom, scintilla, °spark, °particle, iota, °speck, °grain, whit, °scrap, °shred, snippet, °sliver, °fragment, °splinter, °morsel, °crumb, ounce, dram, °drop, °dash, °spot, °touch, tinge, °hint, °suggestion, *Colloq* smidgen *or* smidgin: *One must exercise a modicum of judgement in affairs of the heart.*

modify *v.* **1** °adjust, °adapt, °change, °transform, °alter, °revise, °amend, redo, remake, remould, reshape, reconstruct, °reform, °revamp, refashion, remodel, rework, °reword, reorient, reorganize: *They are modifying the car to increase its performance. He should modify his views on censorship.* **2** °reduce, °decrease, °diminish, lessen, °moderate, °temper, °soften, °lower, abate, °tone down, °modulate; °qualify, °limit, °restrict: *The severity of the winter is modified by our proximity to the sea. We shall have to modify our demands.*

modulate *v.* °adjust, °regulate, °set, °tune, °balance, °temper, °moderate, °modify; °lower, °tune *or* °tone *or* °turn down, °soften: *Modulate the volume to suit the size of the auditorium. Please modulate your voice—everyone can hear you!*

mogul *n.* magnate, °tycoon, baron, mandarin, *Colloq* °big shot, °big gun, °big cheese, Pooh Bah, °bigwig, °big wheel, °big (White) Chief, °big Daddy, hotshot, VIP, °big noise, nabob, *Slang US* Mr Big: *In the old days, he was one of the moguls in Hollywood.*

moist *adj.* **1** °damp, wettish, dampish, dewy, dank, °humid, °clammy, °muggy, °steamy, °misty, foggy: *During the monsoon everything becomes so moist that your clothes never seem to dry.* **2** °damp, °wet, rainy, drizzly, soggy, moisture-laden: *The moist climate keeps Ireland green.* **3** °tearful, teary, °misty, lachrymose: *Every eye in the theatre was moist at the end of that scene.*

molest *v.* **1** °annoy, °irritate, vex, °disturb, °pester, badger, needle, °provoke, nettle, °tease, °harass, harry, °worry, hector, °irk, °bother, °gall, °chafe, roil, °torment, °plague, beleaguer: *For weeks people on the beach have been molested by green flies.* **2** accost, °meddle with, °interfere with, °annoy, °abuse, °bother, °attack, °ill-treat, maltreat, °manhandle; paw: *The police are looking for a man who has been molesting girls in the park.*

moment *n.* **1** °instant, °second, °minute, half a °second, two seconds, °flash, °twinkling, °blink *or* wink of an eye, °twinkling of an eye, trice, *Colloq* jiffy, shake, two shakes (of a lamb's tail), before you can say 'Jack Robinson', *Brit* mo, half a mo, tick: *I'll be with you in a moment, Madam.* **2** °instant, °time, °second, °minute, hour, °point (in time), °juncture, °stage: *At that very moment, the phone rang.* **3** °importance, °weight, consequence, °significance, °import, °gravity, seriousness, °prominence, °concern, °note, °interest, °consideration: *What you decide to do is of no great moment.*

momentary *adj.* °fleeting, °temporary, ephemeral, evanescent, impermanent, °fugitive, °passing, transitory, °brief, °short-lived, quick, °short, °hasty: *The medicine afforded only momentary relief from the pain.*

momentous *adj.* °important, °weighty, consequential, °significant, °grave, °serious, decisive, °crucial, °critical, °vital, °pivotal, °portentous, charged, laden, °fraught, of °concern: *The Augustan Age was a momentous period in Latin literature.*

momentum *n.* °energy, °force, °drive, °strength, °impetus, °power, °inertia, impulse, °thrust, °push: *The car's momentum carried it over the cliff. Her encouragement has given me the momentum needed to carry on.*

monarch *n.* **1** ruler, °sovereign, potentate, crowned °head; °queen, °king, empress, emperor, tsar *or* czar: *Mary was the monarch of Scotland from 1542 to 1567.* **2** ruler, °sovereign, °chief, °lord, °master, °owner, *Colloq* °boss: *He is monarch of all he surveys.*

monarchy *n.* **1** °kingdom, empire, °domain, °dominion, principality; °state, °nation, °country: *According to Gibbon, a hereditary monarchy presents the fairest scope for ridicule.* **2** monocracy, autocracy, absolutism, royalism, monarchism, °sovereignty, totalitarianism, authoritarianism; °despotism, °tyranny: *Those who are discontented with monarchy call it tyranny.*

monastery *n.* abbey, cloister, priory, friary, charterhouse, hospice, *Buddhism* vihara, *Hinduism* ashram, *Tibetan Buddhism* lamasery: *In later life he retired to a monastery to contemplate the world.*

monetary *adj.* pecuniary, °cash, °money, °fiscal, °financial, °capital; numismatic, *Technical* nummular, nummary: *Monetary shortages result from the government's tightening its hold on the economy by raising interest rates.*

money *n.* **1** currency, legal °tender, medium of °exchange, specie, (hard) °cash, °ready money, banknotes, paper money, *Brit* notes, *US* °bills, °coin(s), °change, small °change, *Derogatory* (filthy) lucre, pelf, *Colloq* shekels, *Brit* dosh, lolly, *US* folding money, cold (hard) °cash, *US and Canadian and Australian* shinplasters; *Slang* °loot, dough, bread, spondulicks *or* spondulix, boodle, readies *or* the °ready, moolah, *Brit* rhino, *US* (long) green, greenbacks, mazuma, wampum, simoleons, bucks, scratch, gelt, kale, cabbage, lettuce, spinach: *He makes daily rounds to collect the money from the launderettes he owns.* **2** °resources, °wealth, °fortune, °funds, °capital, wherewithal, affluence, °means, (liquid) °assets, °riches; *Slang* bundle: *All the family money is invested in long-term bonds.* **3** °gain, °profit, °net, *Colloq* °take, °percentage, *Slang* °rake-off: *How much money does the shop take in at the end of the day?* **4** ***in the money***: °rich, °wealthy, affluent, moneyed *or* monied, °well off, well-to-do, °prosperous, *Colloq* °flush, in clover, in *or* on Easy Street, *Slang* °loaded, well-heeled, rolling in it *or* in money *or* in dough, filthy °rich, stinking °rich, °fat: *They have been in the money since their uncle died.*

mongrel *n.* cur, mutt, cross-breed, °mixed °breed, °hybrid, half-breed, *Technical* bigener; lurcher: *There is little chance of that mongrel winning a prize in the dog show.*

monitor *n.* **1** watchdog, °supervisor, °sentinel, °guard, °guardian, custodian; *Brit* invigilator, prefect, *Rare* prepositor *or* praepostor; *US* proctor: *The government has appointed a committee to monitor oil prices.* **2** (°television) °screen, cathode-ray tube °screen, CRT, °display, *Chiefly Brit* visual display unit, VDU: *Do you prefer an amber, green, or black-and-white monitor?* —*v.* **3** °watch, °oversee, °observe, °check (out *or* up on), audit, °supervise, superintend, °scan, °examine, °study, °follow, °keep an °eye on, °survey, keep °track of, °track, °trace, °record, *Brit* °vet: *Before a drug is approved, it must be monitored through thousands of tests.*

monk *n.* °brother, °religious, coenobite, monastic, *Loosely* friar: *He was accepted into the Benedictine order, also called the black monks.*

monkey *n.* **1** simian, ape, primate, *Colloq* monk: *The monkeys' antics forever delight the children.* **2** °fool, ass, laughing-stock, °butt, °victim, °target, (fair) game, *Colloq* goat, *Slang* °sucker: *The teacher should not have made a monkey out of Hubert in front of his classmates.* **3** °imp, °devil, mischief-maker, °rascal, scamp, rapscallion: *She's a real little monkey: you wouldn't believe what she got up to this morning.* —*v.* **4** °mimic, mime, °imitate, impersonate, °copy, ape, °duplicate: *He monkeys everything you do.* **5** Usually, ***monkey around*** *or* ***about (with)***: °fool around (with), °play (with), °fiddle (about *or* around) with, °meddle (with *or* in), °interfere (with *or* in), °mess (about *or* around) (with), °tinker (with), °tamper (with), *Colloq US* °screw around (with): *Stop monkeying around with that switch or the light will fuse. Colin is always monkeying around in class.*

monograph *n.* treatise, dissertation, disquisition, °essay, °paper: *Entwhistle's monograph is the definitive work on Hawthorne.*

monolithic *adj.* °massive, °huge, °enormous, °monumental, °imposing, °colossal, °gigantic, °giant; featureless, °uniform, undifferentiated, characterless; °rigid, impenetrable, invulnerable, unbending, °inflexible, °solid, °stolid, intractable, °immovable: *These monolithic international conglomerates, assembled with the aid of junk bonds, staffed by yuppies, and controlling markets worth hundreds of billions, resemble the monolithic glass towers that house them.*

monopolize *v.* corner (the °market in), °control, °dominate, own, *Slang* hog: *Till recently, one company monopolized the telephone business in the US.*

monotonous *adj.* °boring, °tedious, °dull, °tiresome, °humdrum, sleep-inducing, soporific, wearisome, wearying, tiring, monotonic, °repetitious, °prosaic, °banal, °dry, dry-as-dust, uninteresting, °dreary, °colourless, unexciting, run-of-the-mill, °ordinary, commonplace, °routine, uneventful, °everyday, °mechanical, banausic, *Colloq* ho-hum: *Working in an assembly line became monotonous, so I took a job in advertising.*

monster *n.* **1** °beast, °fiend, °ogre, °giant, dragon, °brute, °demon, troll, bog(e)yman: *Why are so many children's fairy tales populated by monsters?* **2** °monstrosity, (living) abortion, mutant, °mutation, °freak, deformity, *lusus naturae*, eyesore, °horror, miscreation, missing link: *Monsters of every description were the main features of circus sideshows for centuries.* —*adj.* **3** See **monstrous, 3,** below.

monstrosity *n.* **1** See **monster, 2,** above. **2** monstrousness, heinousness, horribleness, horridness, hideousness, awfulness, nightmarishness, dreadfulness, frightfulness, °horror, hellishness, ghoulishness, fiendishness, °barbarity: *The monstrosity of the concentration camps was not widely known till after the war.*

monstrous *adj.* **1** °awful, °horrible, horrid, horrific, horrendous, horrifying, °hideous, °ugly, °nightmarish, °dreadful, heinous, °grisly, °gruesome, °disgusting, °nauseous, nauseating, °repulsive, °repellent, °revolting, °frightful, °grotesque, hellish, °ghoulish, freakish, °fiendish, barbaric, barbarous, °savage, °inhuman, °merciless, °ruthless, °brutal, brutish, °beastly: *How could anyone treat another human being with such monstrous cruelty!* **2** °outrageous, °shocking, °scandalous, °atrocious, appalling, °wicked, °villainous, °evil, °vile, insensitive, °cruel, °base, debased, °shameful, °shameless, °infamous, °disgraceful, nefarious, egregious, °foul, °vicious, flagitious, °loathsome, depraved: *It is monstrous to suggest that money could compensate for the loss of a child. It was a monstrous trick to make him think he had failed the exam when he'd got the top mark.* **3** °gigantic, °giant, °huge, °vast, °enormous, °colossal, °monster, gargantuan, °jumbo, °immense, tremendous, titanic, °prodigious, °massive, °towering, elephantine, mammoth: *They are planning to build a monstrous shopping mall in the town centre.*

monument *n.* **1** marker, cairn, °memorial, °tablet, shrine, commemoration; °sepulchre, gravestone, °tombstone, headstone, °tomb, mausoleum, cenotaph: *Many monuments have been established in memory of those who died in the war.* **2** °testimony, °testimonial, testament, °token, °witness, °record, °evidence, °example, exemplar: *The book will survive as a lasting monument to her scholarship.*

monumental *adj.* **1** staggering, awe-inspiring, °outstanding, °prominent, stupendous, °vast, °awesome, epoch-making, °historic, history-making, °memorable, °lasting, °permanent, unforgettable, °significant, °notable, °noteworthy, °impressive, °marvellous, °prodigious, wonderful, wondrous, spectacular, °magnificent, °grand, °striking, °glorious, °enduring, °classic: *This work is a monumental contribution to linguistic theory.* **2** °massive, °huge, °gigantic, °enormous, °prodigious, °colossal, °immense, °vast, tremendous: *These monumental stones, each as big as a house, were dragged from a quarry hundreds of miles away.* **3** commemorative, °memorial: *A monumental obelisk will be raised to mark the battle.* **4** egregious, catastrophic, °calamitous, °huge, °enormous, °awful, abject, °terrible, unforgivable, °unbelievable, °monstrous, *Colloq* °whopping: *Announcing our plans in advance could prove to be a monumental blunder.*

mood *n.* **1** °humour, °attitude, °inclination, °disposition, °nature, °temper, °frame of °mind, °spirit, °atmosphere, °sense, °feeling: *The mood of the people is rebellious. She's in a bad mood.* **2** **in the mood**: °ready, °willing, °eager, °keen, (well-)°disposed, °inclined, °sympathetic, minded: *I'm not in the mood for a film tonight, but I am in the mood to go dancing.*

moody *adj.* **1** °sullen, °melancholy, °blue, °sad, °unhappy, °dejected, depressed, crestfallen, downcast, °despondent, chap-fallen, in the doldrums, °downhearted, °gloomy, °glum, moping, mopy, mopish, sulky, sulking, morose, brooding, broody, heavy-hearted, °dour, cheerless, °dismal, °desolate, disconsolate, lugubrious, disheartened, saturnine, *Colloq* down in the °mouth, (down) in the dumps, out of sorts, *US* off (one's) feed: *He's been moody the past few days, and I don't know how to cheer him up.* **2** °testy, crotchety, °short-tempered, °abrupt, °short, °curt, °impatient, crabby, crusty, huffy, huffish, crabbed, °cantankerous, curmudgeonly, ill-humoured, ill-tempered, °cranky, °petulant, °waspish, °temperamental, °snappish, °snappy, °irritable, °peevish, °touchy, piqued; in a (fit of) pique, in high dudgeon: *If I were you, I shouldn't ask her for a favour today as she's very moody.* **3** °fickle, °volatile, °capricious, mercurial, °unstable, °fitful, °flighty, unsteady, °changeable, °erratic, uneven, °inconstant, undependable, °unreliable, unpredictable: *Being artists, they are moody, and there's no telling if they will want to be interviewed today.*

moonshine *n.* **1** moonlight, moonbeams: *Her hair reflected silver in the moonshine.* **2** (stuff and) °nonsense, °rubbish, taradiddle, humbug, °drivel, twaddle, balderdash, blather *or* blether, *Colloq* °hot air, claptrap, pack of lies, con, bosh, gas, eyewash, hogwash, bunk, guff, piffle, hokum, °rot, malarkey, bilge (water), tripe, (the old) °song and dance, °line, *Brit* tommy-rot, *US* apple-sauce, razzmatazz, jive, *Slang* crap, bull, hooey, *Brit* tosh, *US* °garbage, BS, *Taboo slang* horseshit, bullshit: *He fed her a load of moonshine about owning a big yacht.* **3** poteen, *Colloq chiefly US and Canadian* hooch *or* hootch, white lightning, white mule, home-brew, bootleg: *Government agents raided a still that produced 100 gallons of moonshine a day.*

moor[1] *n.* heath, moorland, wasteland, *No. Eng. and Scots* fell: *The police pursued the escaped prisoner across the moor, but they lost him.*

moor[2] *v.* °secure, °tie up, make °fast, °dock, berth, (drop) °anchor; °fix: *The vessel was soon moored and the passengers disembarked. The huge aerial is moored by cables.*

moot *adj.* **1** °debatable, arguable, undecided, undetermined, °controversial, °doubtful, °disputable, °open to °debate, at °issue, °indefinite, °problematic(al), °questionable, °open (to °question *or* to °discussion), confutable, confuted, contestable, contested, °unsettled, °unresolved, up in the air, unconcluded: *Whether he would be found innocent was still a moot point.*

—*v.* **2** °bring up *or* forward, °introduce, °broach, °put forward, proffer, °posit, °propound, °advance, °submit, °suggest: *It has been mooted that she was with the victim just before the murder.*

moral *adj.* **1** °ethical; °right, °good, °pure, °honest, °proper, °upright, °honourable, °decent, moralistic, °respectable, high-minded, °virtuous, upstanding, °righteous, °principled, °scrupulous, incorruptible, °noble, °just: *She is one of the most moral people I have ever met.* **2** °ethical, moralizing, moralistic: *Questions of right and wrong are a subject for moral philosophy. It is a moral, not a legal, issue.*

—*n.* **3** °lesson, homily, teaching, °point, °message; aphorism, °maxim, °precept, apophthegm *or* apothegm, adage, °saw, °proverb, °epigram, °motto, °slogan: *The moral of the story is, 'Do unto others before they do unto you'.* **4** ***morals***: °behaviour, °conduct, mores, °belief, °habit(s), °custom(s), °practice(s), °principle(s), °scruples, ethics, °ideals, °standards; °probity, °morality, °rectitude, °integrity: *For this appointment, we require a person of the highest morals.*

morale *n.* °dedication, °spirit(s), °unity, *esprit de corps*, °disposition, °attitude, °confidence, °self-confidence, °self-esteem: *The team's morale improved after they won their first game in five weeks.*

morality *n.* **1** ethics, °morals, ethicalness, moralness, °principle(s), mores, °integrity, °propriety, standards, °ideals; °honesty, °right, rightness, righteousness, °rectitude, °justice, °fair play, fairness, decency, uprightness: *Morality should not be conditioned by expediency.* **2** °behaviour, °conduct, °habit(s), °custom(s): *Are you suggesting that utilitarianism is a guide for morality?*

morass *n.* **1** °bog, °marsh, °swamp, fen, quagmire, slough, marshland, moorland, *No. Eng. and Scots* moss: *The land not under cultivation was morass or forest.* **2** entanglement, °confusion, °muddle, °mess, quagmire, °tangle, quicksand: *It took years to extricate the company from the legal morass of the bankruptcy courts.*

moratorium *n.* °halt, hiatus, °suspension, °stay, °respite, °freeze, °delay, waiting-period, °postponement: *The arts commission requests a six-month moratorium on sales to foreign purchasers.*

morbid *adj.* **1** °unhealthy, °unwholesome, disordered, °unsound, °sick, pathological, pathogenic: *Inhalation of fumes containing lead has caused this morbid condition.* **2** °grim, °ghoulish, °macabre, °monstrous, °ghastly, °grotesque, °grisly, °gruesome: *At an early age, Glynis exhibited a morbid interest in cadavers. Spare me the morbid details—please!* **3** °gloomy, lugubrious, °glum, morose, °sombre, °blue, °sad, °melancholy, °despondent, depressed, °dejected, downcast: *With Charley again in one of his morbid moods, we can anticipate another cheerless visit.*

moreover *adv.* furthermore, °further, °besides, not °only that, more than that, what is more; to °boot, into the °bargain, in °addition, additionally, as well, too: *She was pleased that I had brought some wine—it was, moreover, her favourite burgundy.*

moribund *adj.* **1** °dying, *in extremis*, at death's door, °failing, fading, with one foot in the °grave, half-dead, breathing one's last, expiring, on one's last legs, on one's deathbed: *Apparently moribund for weeks, he suddenly revived when he saw her.* **2** ending, declining, °obsolescent, °weak, on the way out, waning, on the °wane, °dying out; stagnating, °stagnant: *At the time, the Ottoman Empire was already moribund.*

morning *n.* **1** forenoon, a.m., °dawn, daybreak, sunrise, *Literary* morn, *Archaic* cock crow, day-spring, morrow, *Chiefly US* sun-up: *The meeting will be at nine o'clock in the morning.*

—*adj.* **2** matutinal, matinal, a.m., forenoon: *I prefer a morning meeting.*

morsel *n.* **1** °mouthful, °bite, gobbet, spoonful, forkful, °chew, °taste, °sample, nibble, °bit, °drop, dollop, soupçon: *She delicately ate tiny morsels of the banana.* **2** °bit, °crumb, °fragment, °scrap, °sliver, °splinter, shard *or* sherd, °shred, °remnant, °particle, atom, °speck, whit, fraction, °grain, granule, °pinch, °piece, *Colloq* smidgen *or* smidgin: *There wasn't the slightest morsel of evidence to connect me with the crime.*

mortal *adj.* **1** °human; transitory, °temporal, °transient, ephemeral: *It finally dawned on him that the king was mortal, like other men.* **2** °physical, bodily, corporeal, corporal, fleshly, °earthly, °worldly, perishable: *Her mortal remains are buried at Bognor Regis.* **3** °deadly, °fatal, °lethal, °terminal, °destructive, °disastrous: *The admiral lay dying from a mortal wound.* **4** °relentless, °implacable, unrelenting, °bitter, sworn, °deadly, unremitting, unappeasable, unceasing: *Halifax was the mortal enemy of despotism.* **5** abject, °extreme, °awful, °great, °enormous, °intense, °terrible, °inordinate, dire: *Giles lived in mortal fear of offending his mother.*

—*n.* **6** °human (being), °man, °woman, °person, °soul, °individual, °creature, earthling: *The novel depicts a lifestyle far removed from that of ordinary mortals. We mortals have nothing to fear from intergalactic aliens.*

mortify *v.* **1** °humiliate, °shame, °humble, °embarrass, abash, chagrin, °rebuff, °crush, °discomfit, deflate, °bring down, °degrade, °downgrade, °reduce, °chasten, °subdue, °suppress, make someone eat °humble pie, teach someone his *or* her °place, *Colloq* °put down: *She was mortified to learn that she had been disqualified.* **2** °punish, °castigate, °discipline, °control, °subdue, °subjugate: *Repentance was considered insufficient penance, so the flagellants mortified the flesh with scourges.* **3** gangrene, °fester, necrose, °putrefy, °rot, °decompose, °decay, putresce: *After a fortnight, the flesh mortifies and falls away.*

mother *n.* **1** dam, materfamilias, (female) °parent, *Old-fashioned or formal or jocular* mater, *Formal* progenitrix; matriarch, *Colloq* ma, old lady, old °woman, *Brit* mummy, mum, *US* mom, mommy, mama, mamma, maw, mammy, mam: *He runs crying to his mother whenever anyone teases him.* **2** °source, °origin, genesis: *Necessity is the mother of invention.* **3** nourisher, nurturer, °nurse: *Poverty was the mother of anarchy.*

—*adj.* **4** °native, °natural, innate: *She has the mother wit to know better.*

—*v.* **5** nurture, °nourish, °nurse, °care for, °look after, °protect, °shelter, °watch over, take °care of: *She mothered me when I needed her, and I won't desert her now.* **6** °pamper, °baby, °coddle, °spoil, °indulge, °fuss over, overprotect: *You mother the child too much.*

motif *n.* °theme, °idea, °topic, °subject, concept, leitmotif; °pattern, °figure, °refrain, °device, °ornament, °decoration, °element, °convention: *The painter repeats the motif throughout his pictures in much the same way that a composer repeats a bar of music.*

motion *n.* **1** °movement, °moving, °change, °shift, shifting, °action, °going, °travelling, °travel, °progress,

°passage, °transit; °activity, commotion, °stir, °agitation, turmoil, turbulence: *One could barely sense the slow motion of the train. The leaves of the aspen appear to be in constant motion.* **2** mobility, movability, motility: *I could feel the motion gradually returning to my numbed limbs.* **3** gait, °bearing, °carriage, tread, °walk, °step: *The machine works with alternate upward and downward motions.* **4** °gesture, gesticulation, °signal, °sign: *She made a motion for me to come nearer.* **5** °proposal, °suggestion, °proposition, °recommendation, °offering, °submission: *A motion must be seconded by a member in good standing.*
—*v.* **6** °gesture, gesticulate, °beckon, °signal, °sign, °wave: *The cashier motioned to me and I went over to the window.*

motivate *v.* °prompt, °activate, °move, °inspire, °incite, °induce, actuate, °stimulate, °provoke, °influence, °encourage, °occasion, °bring about, °cause; °excite, egg (on), °urge, °prod, °spur, galvanize, goad, °rouse, °arouse, °stir (up), °wheedle, °coax, °persuade, °cajole, °tempt, °push, impel, °drive, instigate: *The biggest problem is motivating students to apply themselves to academic subjects.*

motive *n.* **1** °inducement, °incentive, motivation, stimulus, motivating °force, stimulation, °incitement, °influence, °cause, °reason, °rationale, grounds; °attraction, °lure, °enticement, goad, °spur, °urge, °prod: *It is thought that jealousy was his motive for murder.* **2** °purpose, °aim, °intention, °intent, °object, °objective, °goal, °end, *arrière pensée* (= 'hidden motive'); °ambition, °desire; *Colloq* °angle: *I asked the chairman what his motive was in trying to expand the company.*
—*adj.* **3** driving, impelling, propelling, propulsive, °moving, kinetic, activating, °operative: *The motive power used in the ultra-light aircraft is provided entirely by the pilot's pedalling.*

mottled *adj.* dappled, brindled, marbled, streaked, splodgy *or US* splotchy, blotched, blotchy, freckled, spotted, °spotty, patchy, °speckled, °flecked, sprinkled, spattered, splashed, streaky, stippled, pied, piebald; multicoloured, °variegated, particoloured, *Colloq* splodged *or US* splotched: *Do you like that mottled effect on the wallpaper?*

motto *n.* °maxim, °proverb, saying, adage, °saw, aphorism, apophthegm *or* apothegm, gnome, °slogan, °byword, catchword, battle-cry, °guide, °moral, °principle, °rule, °precept: *The motto of the Order of the Garter is* Honi soit qui mal y pense, *'Shame on whoever thinks ill of it'.*

mould[1] *n.* **1** °form, °cast, matrix, °die; °template *or* templet, °pattern, °form: *He broke the mould to prevent the casting of a duplicate statuette.* **2** °form, °shape, °pattern, °format, °structure, °build, construction, °design, °arrangement, °organization, configuration, °kind, °brand, °make, °line, °type, °stamp, °cut: *Was man made in the same mould as his God, or vice versa?* **3** °character, °nature, °stamp, °type, °kind, kidney, ilk, °sort: *Grandpa said that he wouldn't want someone of her mould in the family.*
—*v.* **4** °shape, °form, °make, °work, °fashion, configure, °sculpture *or* sculpt, °model, knead, °construct: carve, cut: *The artist moulded the original design in clay.* **5** °forge, °cast, °stamp, die-cast: *These beads are moulded from solid gold.* **6** °influence, °shape, °form, °affect, °make, °control, °direct, °guide, °lead: *The speech-writer's job is to mould the language to fit his client's ideas. The candidate is trying to mould public opinion in his favour.*

mould[2] *n.* mildew, fungus, °blight, smut: *A mild solution of bleach will clean that mould off the bathroom tiles.*

mould[3] *n.* °soil, °earth, loam, topsoil, °dirt, humus: *Add some rich mould to the house-plants periodically and they will flourish.*

mouldy *adj.* °aged, °ancient, out-dated, °old-fashioned, antediluvian, °unused, °stale, decayed, decaying, carious, mildewed, mouldering, °musty; spoilt *or* spoiled, °rotten, rotting, °putrid, putrescent, putrefying, °rancid, °rank, decomposed, decomposing, mucid: *Digging about in the files, he unearthed some mouldy old plans of the house. All the food in the fridge had gone mouldy while they were away.*

mound *n.* **1** hillock, °rise, hummock, °hill, °hump, bank, °elevation, °knoll, °knob, °swell, dune, °slope, tor, *Chiefly W US and Canadian* butte: *We stood on a high mound from which we could see for miles.* **2** °heap, °pile, °stack, *Archaeology* tumulus, °tell, barrow, (kitchen) midden: *Excavation of the mound yielded scores of Iron Age artefacts.*

mount *n.* **1** See **mountain, 1,** below.
—*v.* **2** °climb (up), °go up, ascend, °scale, clamber up, make one's way up: *We mounted the ladder to the roof. The speaker mounted the dais.* **3** °rise (up), °arise, °soar, °fly (up), °rocket (upwards): *With the salmon in its grasp, the eagle mounted to the sky.* **4** °climb *or* °get *or* clamber up on, bestride, straddle, bestraddle: *The gunfighter mounted his horse and rode off.* **5** (put on) °display, (put on) °exhibit, put on °exhibition, °present, °install *or* instal, °stage, °prepare, °ready, °put on, put in °place, °set up; °arrange, °coordinate, °compose, °organize, set in °motion, °launch: *The gallery will mount a show of John's sculpture next spring. They have mounted a major advertising campaign for their face cream.* **6** °frame, mat *or* matt, °set off: *This print should be mounted using an olive green paper.* **7** °increase, wax, °rise, escalate, °intensify, °swell, °expand, °grow, °mount up, multiply, °pile up, °build up, °accumulate: *Complaints have been mounting against the vulgar language heard on prime-time TV.*
—*n.* **8** °backing, °setting, °support, mounting, °background, °set, °arrangement, backdrop, °scene: *This style of mount sets off the ruby to its best advantage.* **9** horse, steed, charger, palfrey: *Her mount was a grey mare.*

mountain *n.* **1** °height, °elevation, °mount, eminence, °prominence, °peak, alp, tor, °summit, *No. Eng. and Scots* fell, *Scots and Irish English* ben: *Her favourite sport is climbing mountains.* **2** °heap, °pile, °stack, °mound, °accumulation, °abundance, °mass, *Colloq* ton(s), °heaps, °piles, °stacks: *I have a mountain of laundry to do.*

mountainous *adj.* **1** craggy, alpine, Himalayan: *It was very slow going through the mountainous parts of the country.* **2** °huge, °towering, °high, °steep, °enormous, °immense, °formidable, °mighty, °monumental, °prodigious, staggering: *Their tiny craft was almost engulfed by the mountainous seas.*

mourn *v.* °grieve (over), °lament, °sorrow (over), °bemoan, °bewail, °keen, °weep for *or* over, °regret, rue, deplore: *We all mourned the loss of a great leader. After his death, the nation mourned for a month.*

mournful *adj.* **1** °sad, °sorrowful, °dismal, °melancholy, °blue, afflicted, °doleful, dolorous, grief-stricken, rueful, °forlorn, °woebegone, °sombre, lugubrious, °funereal, °joyless, dispirited, cheerless, °unhappy, °downhearted, heavy-hearted, disconsolate, °heartbroken, °inconsolable, °despondent, °desolate, despairing, heartsick, °overcome, °prostrate: *The mournful crowd filed past the bier to pay their last respects.* **2** °deplorable, °sorrowful, °grievous, distressing, upsetting, °tragic, saddening, disheartening, depressing, °lamentable, catastrophic, °calamitous, °disastrous: *The mournful news of the great loss of life in the explosion was broadcast round the world.*

mourning *n.* **1** °grief, °lament, grieving, °lamentation, sorrowing, keening, weeping, wailing: *The Highlanders are wont to mingle a degree of solemn mirth with their mourning.* **2** bereavement, °loss, °anguish, °sorrow, °misery, °grief, °sadness, °woe, woefulness, °melancholy, heartache, despondency, °despair, °desolation: *In China people wear white as a sign of mourning.* **3** °black, widow's weeds, sackcloth and ashes: *It was customary at that time to spend at least one month in mourning.*

mousy *adj.* **1** mousey, mouse-coloured, °dun, °grey, greyish-brown, brownish-grey, brownish, brown, °dull, lustreless, °lacklustre, °drab, °flat, °plain, °colourless: *Her lank, mousy hair hung down over her shoulders.* **2** °timid, cowering, timorous, °shy, self-effacing, diffident: *Adrian is far too mousy to ask for an increase in salary.*

mouth *n.* **1** lips; maw, jaws, °oral °cavity, *Technical* stoma, *Slang* °trap, kisser, muzzle, °gob, chops, °yap, *US* bazoo: *I want to hear that you don't love me from your own mouth.* **2** °opening, °aperture, doorway, door, gateway, °gate, access, °entrance, inlet, °entry, entryway, °way in, entrée; °passage, passageway, °way, orifice; °exit, °way out, °vent, °outlet, outfall, *Technical* debouchment *or* debouchure, debouch *or* débouché, embouchure: *We stood at the mouth of the cave. An enormous delta formed at the mouth of the river.* **3** bragging, boasting, braggadocio, empty *or* idle °talk, °bombast, rodomontade, fustian, *Slang* claptrap, °hot air, gas: *The fellow is all mouth and no action.* **4** °disrespect, °impudence, insolence, sauciness, rudeness, °impertinence, pertness, boldness, audacity, presumptuousness, brashness, °flippancy, *Colloq* lip, cheek, backchat, °sauce, freshness, *US* sass, back °talk: *He'd better not give me any of his mouth or I'll have his guts for garters.* **5** grimace, °pout, *moue*, °face: *She made a mouth when I said she couldn't go.* **6** ***down in*** *or* ***at the mouth***: °dejected, °despondent, °sad, °sorrowful, °unhappy, °melancholy, °blue, crestfallen, dispirited, disheartened, downcast, *Colloq* (down) in the dumps, °broken up: *He was very down in the mouth after seeing the results of the laboratory tests.*
—*v.* **7** utter, °say, °speak, °pronounce, °announce, °enunciate, articulate, °voice, °sound, °express, vocalize; declaim, orate: *He mouthed each word with excruciating care. Who wants to hear some pompous fool mouthing platitudes?*

mouthful *n.* °morsel, °bite, spoonful, forkful, °lump, chunk, °gob, hunk: *He took a mouthful of food.*

mouthpiece *n.* **1** embouchure; bit: *I need a new mouthpiece for my clarinet.* **2** spokesman, spokeswoman, spokesperson, °agent, °representative, intermediator, °mediator, °delegate: *He is always quoted through his mouthpiece, never directly.* **3** °lawyer, attorney, *Slang US* shyster: *A good mouthpiece could get me out of this fix.*

movable *adj.* moveable, floating, °variable, °changeable, unfixed; °portable, transportable, transferable *or* transferrable: *Easter Sunday is a movable feast and has no fixed date on the calendar. Recent developments have produced computers that are smaller than an attaché case and easily movable.*

move *v.* **1** °shift, °stir, budge, make a move, °go; °proceed, °advance, °progress: *It is difficult to move in a strait-jacket. The train is moving at a rate of sixty miles an hour. Don't move—I have a gun.* **2** move house, move out, °remove, move away, relocate, decamp, °depart, °change residence, °emigrate, °go *or* °make off, °transfer, *Colloq* °take off (for), pull up °stakes, *Brit* up sticks, *Slang US* °split (for): *When did you say you were moving to London?* **3** °shake (up), °disturb, °stir (up), °agitate, °affect, °touch: *We moved heaven and earth to find a proper place for her to stay.* **4** °affect, °touch, °stir, °shake up, °agitate, °hit (hard), °upset, °strike, smite, °disturb, °ruffle, disquiet, have an (*or* a profound) °effect (on), make a (deep) °impression (on): *The pictures of starving children moved everyone.* **5** °provoke, °arouse, °excite, °stir up, °lead, °rouse, °stimulate: *At the end of the film, when she died, I was moved to tears.* **6** °arouse, °rouse, °provoke, actuate, °lead, °prompt, °spur, °motivate, °influence, impel, °prod, °remind, °inspire, °make: *His mention of families moved me to ask when he had last seen his father.* **7** °propose, °put forward *or* forth, °forward, °advance, °submit, °suggest, °advocate, °propound: *The question of budget was moved at the last meeting.*
—*n.* **8** °change, change-over, relocation, °transfer, °shift, °removal: *My supervisor suggested a move to a different department.* **9** °manoeuvre, °device, °trick, °caper, °dodge, ploy, °stratagem, °artifice, °ruse, °action, °act, °deed, *Colloq* °gimmick: *Getting Diana to invite Colin was a very good move.* **10** °turn, °time, °opportunity: *I have had my turn, now it's your move.* **11** °gesture, gesticulation, °action, °motion, °stirring: *One move and you're a dead man!* **12** ***get a move on***: **a** get °moving, °begin, °start, °commence, get °going, get under °way, get started, °stir *or* bestir oneself, *Colloq* get *or* °start the ball rolling, get the show on the road, °break the ice, get cracking, °step on it *or* the gas: *He doesn't usually get a move on till noon.* **b** °hurry, °hasten, °make °haste, °rush, °run: *Get a move on down to the supermarket before it closes.* **13** ***on the move***: **a** °travelling, in °transit, on the °way, on one's °way, on the °road, on the °go, °moving: *She is always on the move and it is difficult to catch her.* **b** on the go, working, on the °run, °busy, occupied: *I have been on the move since six this morning.* **c** °proceeding, progressing, advancing, °moving °ahead, succeeding, on the go: *It looks as if the industry is again on the move after a brief decline.*

movement *n.* **1** repositioning, °move, °motion, relocation, °moving, migration, °shift, °transfer, °flow, displacement: *Population movement increased dramatically in the Middle Ages.* **2** °action, °activity, °move, °moving, °stir, °stirring: *There was a sudden movement in the bushes.* **3** °gesture, gesticulation, °move, °flicker, °sign, °signal; °manoeuvre, change of attitude *or* position: *Only the slightest upward movement of his eyebrow indicated his surprise. Every little movement has a meaning all its own.* **4** °mechanism, °works, workings, °moving parts, machinery, °action, gears, *Colloq* innards: *Technically, the movement of a watch does not include the escapement.* **5** °campaign, °crusade, °drive; °front, °faction, °party, °group, wing: *The 1960s saw many successes for the civil rights' movement in America.* **6** °change, °activity, °action, °shift, °advance *or* °decline, °increase *or* °decrease, upward *or* °downward movement, stirring; °development, °progress: *Shares displayed little movement in today's trading.* **7** °drift, °trend, °tendency, °course, °swing: *They have noted a growing movement towards religious fundamentalism.*

movie *n.* **1** motion picture, °film, moving picture, silent (picture), talking picture, *Colloq* talkie, flick: *Her grandfather was one of the first actors in silent movies.* **2** Usually, ***movies***: picture °show, cinema, flicks, *Colloq* big *or* large °screen, silver °screen: *Why don't we go to the movies instead of watching television tonight?*

moving *adj.* **1** °touching, °poignant, emotive, affecting, °stirring, °heart-rending, °emotional, °telling, °effective, °impressive, °striking, compelling; °pathetic, °exciting, °thrilling, inspiring, inspirational, impelling, °persuasive: *He related a moving story of his years in various concentration camps.* **2** °active, °mobile, unfixed, unstationary, motile, going, operating, working, in °motion, on the °move: *Be careful not to touch any of the moving parts inside the clock.*

mow *v.* **1** °cut (down), scythe, °trim, shear: *You don't need to mow the lawn so much during a dry spell.* **2** ***mow down***: annihilate, °kill, °massacre, °butcher, °slaughter, °exterminate, liquidate, eradicate, °wipe out, °cut down, °cut to °pieces, °destroy, decimate: *The first platoon was mowed down by machine-gun fire.*

muck *n.* **1** ordure, manure, °dung, excrement, faeces, droppings; guano: *The muck is saved for use as fertilizer.* **2** °dirt, °filth, bilge, slime, °sludge, °ooze, scum, sewage, °mire, °mud, feculence, *Colloq* gunge, gunk, *US* grunge: *Give me a chance to get the muck off my shoes.*
—*v.* **3** ***muck about***: °fool around, °waste time, °idle, loiter, °mess around *or* about: *She told me to stop mucking about and get a job.* **4** ***muck up***: °ruin, °wreck, °destroy, make a °mess of, °botch, °mess up, °bungle, *Colloq* °screw up, *Slang* °bugger up, make a muck of: *She's mucked up her own life, and, given the chance, she'll muck up mine.*

mud *n.* °muck, °ooze, slime, °mire, clay, °sludge, °silt, °dirt, *US and Canadian* gumbo *or* gombo: *The mud came up to my ankles.*

muddle *v.* **1** °bewilder, °confuse, confound, °mystify, baffle, °mix up, disorient, befuddle, °perplex, °bemuse, °puzzle, befog: *I am totally muddled by your explanation of differential calculus.* **2** °confuse, °mix up, °jumble, °scramble, °entangle, °tangle, °mess up, °disorder, disarrange, disorganize, °bungle, mismanage, *Colloq* muff: *My financial affairs got hopelessly muddled when I changed banks.* **3** ***muddle through***: (barely) °manage, °cope, °make it, °scrape through *or* along, contrive, °make do, °get by, °get along: *We were just muddling through when James was offered this wonderful job.*
—*n.* **4** °mess, °confusion, °mix-up, °jumble, °tangle, °disorder, °hotchpotch *or US also* hodgepodge, °mishmash, °chaos, °disaster, *Colloq* °stew, *Slang US* screw-up, snafu, *Taboo slang Brit* balls-up: *A lot of muddles, mix-ups, and misunderstandings ensued.*

muddy *adj.* **1** fouled, befouled, muddied, mud-spattered, °dirty, grubby, grimy, soiled, mud-caked, °slimy, mucky, miry; oozy, squelchy, squashy, boggy, fenny, marshy, swampy; *Formal* feculent; *Colloq* squishy, squushy, squooshy: *Take off those muddy boots before you come into the house. The walk up to the house has become all muddy in the rain.* **2** °confused, unclear, °vague, °obscure, °dull, °dim, °fuzzy, muddled, addled, mixed-up: *Greg has only a muddy idea of what you're talking about.* **3** °drab, °subdued, blurred, °dingy, °flat, °murky, mat *or* matt, washed out: *The colours in her paintings look very muddy to me.*
—*v.* **4** °obscure, °dull, °dim, °confuse, °mix up, befog, cloud: *His explanation muddied the issue rather than clarifying it.* **5** °dirty, °soil, begrime, smirch, besmirch, °spatter, bespatter: *A passing car muddied my new skirt.*

muffle *v.* **1** Often, ***muffle up***: °wrap, °swathe, swaddle, °cloak, °envelop, °cover (up), enfold, °shroud, enshroud, °conceal, °protect: *Make sure your neck is muffled when you're out in that icy wind.* **2** °deaden, °silence, °suppress, °stifle, °subdue, °damp, °dampen, °mute, °hush, °quiet(en), °tone down, °still: *A few more thicknesses of flannel will muffle the noise of the motor.*

muffler *n.* scarf, boa; shawl, °wrap: *Wrap this muffler round your neck for added warmth.*

mug *n.* **1** °jug, tankard, stein, toby (°jug), °pot, beaker, cup: *The relief workers passed round mugs of hot coffee to the homeless.* **2** °face, visage, features, countenance, *Slang* puss, kisser, mush, *Brit* clock, dial, *Archaic* phiz *or* phizog, *US* °pan: *The ex-boxer has a mug that only a mother could love.* **3** °fool, °duffer, simpleton, °dupe, gull, °innocent, *Colloq* chump, °mark, soft *or* easy touch, *Brit* muggins, *Slang* °sucker: *The mug thought he had found a full wallet.*
—*v.* **4** make a °face *or* faces, grimace: *Here are some pictures of the twins mugging for the camera.* **5** °attack, °set upon, °rob, °assault; garrotte, throttle: *Anyone who walks through the park at night risks getting mugged.* **6** ***mug up (on)***: °study, *Formal* lucubrate, *Colloq* °cram, burn the midnight oil, °get up (on), *Brit* swot, bone up (on): *I have to mug up on my Latin for tomorrow's examination.*

muggy *adj.* °humid, °damp, °sticky, °sultry, °oppressive, °clammy, °steamy, °close, °stuffy, °moist, soggy: *It was so muggy that every night the bedlinen was completely soaked.*

mull *v.* Usually, ***mull over***: °ponder, °consider, °study, °think (over *or* about), cogitate (on *or* over *or* about), con, °evaluate, °turn over, °weigh, °deliberate (on *or* over), °reflect (on), °muse (on), °review, °examine, °contemplate, °meditate (on), °chew over, ruminate (on *or* over),: *I have been mulling over your suggestion that I should join the navy.*

mum *adj.* **1** °silent, °mute, close-mouthed, °quiet, °tight-lipped: *She swore she would keep mum about where the money was hidden.*
—*n.* **2** ***Mum's the word***: Don't tell a soul, Keep °silent, Keep °secret, Keep °quiet, Keep (something) to oneself, Keep (something) under one's hat, Say nothing, Tell no-one, Play dumb: *He told who stole the bell, but mum's the word.*

mumble *v.* °murmur, °mutter, °say inarticulately, utter indistinctly, swallow one's words: *He mumbled the name of the person who had shot him, but she didn't catch it.*

mumbo-jumbo *n.* **1** °gibberish, °nonsense, °rubbish, °gobbledegook *or* gobbledygook, °drivel, humbug, bunkum, double-talk, °rigmarole *or* rigamarole, jabberwocky, blather *or* blether, poppycock, *Colloq* eyewash, °rot, tommy-rot, hogwash, bilge, bosh, bull, malarkey, claptrap, piffle, *US* hooey, °moonshine, bunk *Slang* crap, *Brit* tosh, *Taboo slang* bullshit: *Before he would give me the cheque, the lawyer made me sign something full of legal mumbo-jumbo.* **2** °spell, incantation, °chant, °formula, °charm, abracadabra, °hocus-pocus, °rite, °ritual, conjuration, °magic: *She had to sit through all the mumbo-jumbo of her husband's investiture.*

munch *v.* °chew, °crunch, masticate, champ, chomp, scrunch: *He just sat there munching peanuts.*

municipal *adj.* civic, °civil, metropolitan, urban, °city, °town, village, borough, parish, *Brit* °council: *Voting takes place in the municipal elections next week.*

municipality *n.* °city, °metropolis, °town, village, borough, °district, township; suburb, exurb: *The recreational facilities offered by the municipality are in need of refurbishing.*

murder *n.* **1** homicide, manslaughter, regicide, patricide, matricide, parricide, fratricide, sororicide, uxoricide, infanticide; °killing, slaying, assassination: *In many countries, murder is a crime punishable by death.* **2** °slaughter, butchery, genocide, °massacre, liquidation, decimation, extermination, eradication, wiping out, murdering, slaying, °killing, °bloodshed, °carnage: *Their wanton murder of thousands of prisoners of war has been proven.*
—*v.* **3** °kill, slay, assassinate, put to °death, °end the life of, °put away *or* down, °put out of one's misery, °wipe out, °destroy, °butcher, °massacre, liquidate, °exterminate, eradicate, annihilate, °extinguish, °slaughter, lay low, *Slang* °eliminate, °bump off, °knock off, do in, °polish off, °blow away, *US* °rub out, °waste, ice, take for a ride, fit with a concrete overcoat *or* with concrete overshoes, snuff(out): the drug dealers were murdered, one by one, by a rival gang. **4** °spoil, °ruin, °mar, °destroy, °wreck, °kill, °mangle, °butcher, °mutilate: *She murdered the song by singing it far too fast.*

murderer *n.* murderess, °killer, slayer, assassin, homicide, °cutthroat, liquidator, executioner, °butcher, *Slang* hit man: *The police have arrested someone they are certain is the murderer.*

murderous *adj.* **1** °fatal, °lethal, °deadly, deathly, °mortal, °destructive, °devastating, °sanguinary, bloody, °brutal, °savage, °bloodthirsty, barbarous, °fell, °cruel, °inhuman: *The tolling of the bell signalled that the murderous deed had been done.* **2** °killing, °strenuous, stressful, °difficult, °arduous, °exhausting, hellish, °harrowing, rigorous, intolerable, °unbearable: *You cannot keep up such a murderous pace, without any rest, and remain healthy.*

murky *adj.* °dark, °gloomy, °threatening, °dim, clouded, cloudy, °overcast, °grey, °dismal, °dreary, °bleak, °sombre, °grim, °funereal, °shady, °shadowy: *I could barely make out her face in the murky corner of the chapel.*

murmur *n.* **1** °undercurrent, undertone, background °noise *or* °sound, rumble, rumbling, °mumble, mumbling, drone, droning, °buzz, buzzing, murmuration, murmuring, °hum, humming, whispering, *Formal* susurration *or* susurrus: *They spoke in low voices, barely audible above the murmur of the mourning doves.* **2** muttering, complaining, °complaint, grumble, grumbling, *Colloq* grousing, grouse: *We have heard not a murmur since everyone had an increase in salary.* —*v.* **3** °mumble, °mutter, °whisper: *He murmured into her ear something about being pleased to see her.* **4** °complain, grumble, °mutter, °moan, °lament, wail, *Colloq* grouse: *Employees will always find something to murmur about.*

muscular *adj.* °sinewy, °brawny, °burly, °powerful, powerfully built, strapping, °rugged, °husky, °robust, athletic, °sturdy, well-muscled, broad-shouldered: *We all envied Nick's muscular physique.*

muse *v.* cogitate, °meditate, °reflect, °contemplate, ruminate, °think over, °think about, °consider, °chew over, °deliberate, °revolve, °weigh, °evaluate, °study, °mull over, °brood (over), °ponder; be °absorbed (in °thought), be in a brown °study, °dream, °day-dream, be in a °trance *or* °reverie: *Asked for a decision, Michael mused for a while before answering.*

mushy *adj.* **1** °soft, pulpy, doughy, squidgy, spongy; swampy, boggy, miry; *Colloq* squishy, squushy, squashy, squooshy: *The peach was overripe and mushy. The bottom of the pond is all mushy and feels awful when you stand up.* **2** mawkish, °maudlin, °sentimental, °romantic, saccharine, sugary, syrupy, *Colloq* corny, °sloppy, °gooey, slushy, *Brit* wet, *Slang* schmaltzy: *She cried three handkerchiefs-full over the mushy parts of* Gone With The Wind.

musical *adj.* °tuneful, melodic, °harmonious, lilting, °lyrical, °melodious, mellifluous, dulcet, euphonious: *Many modern compositions, while technically competent, are not as musical as the old-fashioned pieces.*

must *v.* **1** ought (to), should, °have to, be °obliged *or* obligated to, be compelled *or* °forced to, be required to: *I must get this work done before lunch-time. Must you go? Yes, I must.*
—*n.* **2** °necessity, requisite, °requirement, °obligation, *sine qua non*, °essential: *Patience is an absolute must in this job.*

muster *v.* **1** °call *or* °come together, °assemble, convoke, convene, °collect, °mobilize, °rally, °round up, °gather, marshal, °summon (up): *Within a month he had mustered a force of thousands to fight the invaders. I mustered up enough courage to ask Joan out to dinner.*
—*n.* **2** °rally, °assembly, assemblage, convocation, °meet, °meeting, °convention, congress, °round-up, °turnout, °gathering, congregation, aggregation, aggregate: *We attended the annual muster of bagpipe marching bands.* **3** ***pass muster***: come up to °scratch, make the °grade, °measure up, be °acceptable, *Colloq* come *or* be up to snuff: *Are you sure that your new design will pass muster with the art director?*

musty *adj.* **1** °mouldy, °damp, mildewed, mildewy, °sour, °rancid, spoilt, decayed, °rotten, °putrid, fetid *or* foetid, fusty, °stale: *Open the windows to get rid of that musty odour.* **2** °stale, °old-fashioned, °antiquated, antediluvian, °ancient, out of °date, °bygone, °passé, °old hat, °obsolete, archaic, °tired, hoary, °worn out, trite, clichéd, stereotypical: *I've heard all those musty jokes of his a thousand times before.*

mutation *n.* **1** °change, changing, °alteration, altering, modification, modifying, °transformation, transforming, metamorphosis, transmutation, transmuting, transfiguration, transfiguring, °evolution, evolving, °variation, varying: *For years he studied the mutation of the sweet pea.* **2** °variant, °variation, deviation, °deviant, mutant, anomaly, departure: *The mutations exhibited marked differences over the generations.*

mute *adj.* **1** °silent, °dumb, °speechless, voiceless, wordless, °tight-lipped, °taciturn, °tacit, °reserved, °quiet, *Colloq* °mum: *Though I persisted in asking his name, he remained mute.* **2** unspoken, unsaid, °tacit, °silent: *The stain on the floor was a mute reminder of the crime.*
—*v.* **3** °deaden, °silence, °muffle, °stifle, °dampen, °damp, °subdue, °suppress, °quiet *or Brit also* °quieten, °hush, soft-pedal, °turn down, °tone down: *The carpet muted her footsteps as she crept up behind him.*

mutilate *v.* **1** °maim, disfigure, °mangle, °cripple, °lame, °butcher, disable; dismember, amputate, °hack off, °cut off, °lop off, °tear off, °rip off: *Formerly, the hands of thieves were mutilated as an example to others.* **2** °spoil, °mar, °ruin, °damage, °deface, vandalize, °destroy: *As the book had been mutilated, he had to buy the library a replacement.*

mutinous *adj.* **1** °rebellious, °revolutionary, °subversive, °seditious, insurgent, insurrectionary: *The mutinous crew was finally subdued and clapped in irons.* **2** °recalcitrant, refractory, contumacious, °obstinate, °defiant, °insubordinate, °disobedient, °unruly, unmanageable, °ungovernable, uncontrollable: *Whenever we told Clare to work harder at school she became mutinous.*

mutiny *n.* **1** °revolt, °rebellion, °revolution, °subversion, subversiveness, insurgency, insurgence, insurrection, °uprising: *The crew are threatening a mutiny.* —*v.* **2** °rebel, °rise up (against), °strike, °revolt; °disobey, °subvert, °agitate (against): *The crew of the* Bounty *mutinied and set Captain Bligh adrift.*

mutter *v.* **1** °mumble, °murmur, grunt: *He was muttering something to himself that I didn't catch.* **2** grumble, °complain, *Colloq* grouch, grouse, *Brit* chunter: *She has been muttering about cuts in the postal service ever since I can remember.*

mutual *adj.* **1** °reciprocal, reciprocated, requited, interactive, complementary: *I love her and I hope that the feeling is mutual.* **2** °common, communal, °joint, shared: *Gerald is our mutual friend.*

mysterious *adj.* **1** °puzzling, enigmatic, baffling, insoluble, unsolvable, bewildering, confounding, confusing, °perplexing, mystifying, °weird, °bizarre, °strange, uncanny, °curious: *A mysterious force makes the saucer rise off the ground and fly at incredible speeds.* **2** °cryptic, arcane, °secret, inscrutable, covert, hidden, °furtive, unclear, °dark, concealed, °occult, °inexplicable, °incomprehensible, mystic(al), °unknown, unfathomable, °mystical, °recondite, abstruse: *It is mysterious how the agency accomplishes its ends.*

mystery *n.* **1** °puzzle, °enigma, conundrum, °riddle, °question: *How he escaped from the locked room is a mystery.* **2** °obscurity, °secrecy, indefiniteness, vagueness, nebulousness, °ambiguity, ambiguousness, inscrutability, inscrutableness: *The identity of the beautiful lady in the green dress is shrouded in mystery.* **3** detective story *or* novel, murder (story), *Colloq* whodunit: *Joel, who once fancied himself an intellectual, now reads nothing but mysteries.*

mystical *adj.* **1** allegorical, °symbolic(al), mystic, cabbalistic, arcane, unrevealed, °secret, °occult, °supernatural, esoteric, other-worldly, preternatural, °cryptic, concealed, hidden, clandestine, °private, °veiled, °ineffable, °mysterious: *A mystical spirit dwells in the raven that sits on his shoulder.* **2** See **mysterious, 2,** above.

mystify *v.* °fool, °hoax, humbug, °confuse, confound, °mix up, °bewilder, °stump, °puzzle, baffle, *Colloq* bamboozle, °flummox, *Slang* °beat: *We were totally mystified by the unfamiliar symbols on the wall.*

mystique *n.* °mystery, °magic, charisma, °aura, inscrutability, supernaturalism, preternaturalism, strangeness: *She has a certain mystique about her.*

myth *n.* **1** °legend, fable, allegory, °parable, °tradition, °saga, epic, (°folk) °tale, °story, mythos; °history: *The ancient myths have provided sources for much of modern literature.* **2** fable, °lie, (tall) °tale, °fib, prevarication, fiction, untruth, °falsehood, °fabrication, cock-and-bull °story, *Colloq* whopper: *He told her some myth about his being a multimillionaire and she believed it.*

mythical *adj.* **1** mythic, mythological, fabled, °legendary, °traditional, folkloric, storied, °romantic, fairy-tale, story-book; allegorical, °symbolic, parabolic(al): *Campbell has demonstrated astounding similarities amongst the mythical tales of unrelated cultures.*

2 mythic, °fanciful, °imaginary, °fictitious, make-believe, made-up, chimerical, °untrue: *When she was about seven, my daughter had a mythical friend named Theodosia.*

mythology *n.* (body of) °myths, folklore, °tradition, °lore, °stories, mythos: *After only one generation, an extraordinary mythology has been created about Marilyn Monroe.*

N

nab *v.* catch, °capture, °arrest, put *or* place under °arrest, °seize, apprehend, °pick up, °bring in, take into °custody, *Colloq* °pinch, collar, °run in, °nail, *Brit* °nick: *They finally nabbed that cat burglar in Hampstead.*

nag[1] *v.* **1** Sometimes, ***nag at***: °annoy, °irritate, °irk, °pester, °criticize, °ride, °scold, °carp (at), °upbraid, badger, °harass, harry, vex, °henpeck, °torment, hector, °pick at, goad, °pick on, find °fault with, °berate, nettle, °bully, °provoke, °plague, °worry, °bother, *Brit* chivvy *or* chivy *or* chevy, *Colloq* needle: *He nags her day and night about going on a diet.*
—*n.* **2** °scold, harpy, °pest, °shrew, virago, termagant, fishwife: *You certainly can be a terrible nag, can't you?*

nag[2] *n.* °jade, Rosinante; horse, °hack, pony, dobbin, racehorse, thoroughbred, *Slang* gee-gee, *US* hay-burner, plug, bangtail, gee-gee: *That old nag wouldn't be able to clear the fence.*

nagging *adj.* distressing, °chronic, °continuous, °continual, °persistent, unrelenting, °relentless, recurring: *He complains of a nagging pain in his shoulder. I have a nagging feeling that I have an appointment to be somewhere.*

nail *n.* **1** fastener, °fastening, °spike, °pin: *The pieces were held together by several nails.* **2** fingernail, toenail, °claw, talon: *The detective found some fibres under the victim's nails.* **3** ***bite one's nails***: °worry, agonize, °fret, lose sleep (over), °chafe, °suffer, *Colloq* °stew (over *or* about): *Carl is biting his nails over the result of his cholesterol test.* **4** ***hard*** *or* ***tough as nails***: **a** °tough, °vigorous, °hardy: *After years of mountain-climbing, René is as hard as nails.* **b** °cold, unsentimental, °unsympathetic, unfeeling: *The boss, as hard as nails, doesn't care what you sacrifice to get the job done.* **5** ***hit the nail on the head***: be °accurate, be °correct, be °precise, be °right, put (one's) °finger on it: *When you said they were fools, you really hit the nail on the head.* **6** ***on the nail***: °immediately, at °once, °straight *or* °right away, °promptly, without °delay, on the spot, *Colloq US* on the barrel-head: *He has always paid his bills right on the nail.*
—*v.* **7** °attach, °secure, °join, °pin, °tack, °clinch *or* clench; °fasten, °fix, °focus, rivet, °glue: *The door to the mysterious room was nailed shut. His eyes were nailed to the pressure gauge.* **8** See **nab,** above. **9** °hit, °strike; °punch; °shoot: *She nailed him with a left hook and he sank like a stone.* **10** ***nail down***: °settle, °secure, °resolve, °complete, conclude, make °final; °finalize: *Let's celebrate: I nailed down the order for 10,000 air-conditioning units.*

naïve *adj.* naive *or* naïf, °ingenuous, °innocent, credulous, °childlike, born yesterday, °unaffected, °unsophisticated, °inexperienced, °green, unworldly, °unsuspecting, unenlightened, unsuspicious, °trusting, trustful, °gullible, °artless, guileless, °simple, simplistic, simple-minded, unpretentious, unpretending, °candid, °natural: *Is Chatterley naïve enough to believe that the gamekeeper's meetings with his wife were to discuss fox-hunting?*

naïvety *n.* naïveté, ingenuousness, innocence, credulity, credulousness, °inexperience, (blind) °trust, gullibility, artlessness, callowness, guilelessness, °simplicity, unpretentiousness, °candour, naturalness, frankness, openness, °sincerity: *I hope that no one takes advantage of her naïvety.*

naked *adj.* **1** stark naked, unclothed, undraped, °bare, exposed, stripped, undressed, unclad, uncovered, bared, °nude, in the °nude, *Colloq* in the altogether, in one's birthday suit, in the buff, in the raw, *au naturel*, in a state of nature, *Brit* starkers, in the nuddy: *The two of them stood there, completely naked.* **2** unaided, unassisted: *Stars of the seventh magnitude or brighter are visible to the naked eye.* **3** °plain, °unadorned, unembellished, °stark, °overt, °patent, °obvious, °conspicuous, °manifest, °sheer, °undisguised, °unvarnished, °unmitigated, °evident, palpable, unconcealed, in °plain sight *or* view, °blatant, °barefaced, undeniable, °glaring, °flagrant, unmistakable, unalloyed, unmixed, °blunt, unadulterated, °pure: *He told her the naked truth about how he felt.* **4** unsheathed, unprotected, °bare, exposed: *How dare he show a naked sword in the presence of the Emperor?!*

name *n.* **1** designation, °label, appellation, °term, °tag, °style, *Colloq* moniker *or* monicker, handle: *His name is Chauncy but they call him Rusty.* **2** °reputation; repute, °honour, °esteem, (high) °regard, °respect, °rank, °standing, rating, °pre-eminence, °superiority, eminence, notability, °prominence, °prestige, °favour, °distinction, °renown, °fame, °popularity, °celebrity: *She has made a name for herself as a clever business executive. He thinks he has to protect his name as a ladies' man.* **3** °personage, °somebody, °celebrity, °star, superstar, °hero, VIP, °dignitary, luminary, *Colloq* °big shot, °bigwig, °big cheese, °big name: *The programme included some well-known names in the entertainment world.*
—*v.* **4** °label, °tag, °style, °entitle; °call, dub, °christen, baptize: *They named their book 'The Alien Tongue'. Why would people want to name their child 'Quercus'?* **5** °choose, °elect, °select, °delegate, °nominate, °designate, °appoint; °identify, denominate, pinpoint, °specify: *She has been named 'Woman of the Year'. I asked her to name our wedding day. She refuses to name her attacker.* **6** ***name names***: °identify, °specify, °mention, cite: *In exchange for a lighter sentence, the witness agreed to name names.*

nameless *adj.* **1** unnamed, innominate, °unidentified, anonymous, pseudonymous, °incognito, °unknown, °unheard-of, °unsung: *How much we owe the nameless inventor of the wheel!* **2** °inexpressible, indefinable, unidentifiable, unspecified, unspecifiable: *A nameless dread seized him as he entered the cave.* **3** °ineffable, unutterable, unspeakable, °unmentionable, °abominable, °horrible, indescribable, °repulsive: *Paganism allowed man to sink beneath a flood of nameless sensualities.*

namely *adv.* specifically, to °wit, that is (to say), *id est*, i.e., *videlicet*, viz., *scilicet*, sc.; for °example, for °instance, *exempli gratia*, e.g. *or* eg: *We visited three countries, namely, France, Italy, and Switzerland.*

nap[1] *v.* **1** °doze, °nod (off), catnap, *Colloq* catch forty winks, °drop off (to °sleep), get some shut-eye, snooze, zizz, *US* catch *or* log a few zees (Z's): *I nap every afternoon.*
—*adv.* **2** ***napping***: °unawares, off °guard, unexpectedly, in an °unguarded moment: *The ball, hit to his backhand, caught him napping.*
—*n.* **3** °doze, catnap, siesta, *Colloq* forty winks, shut-eye, snooze, zizz, *Brit* lie-down: *Take a short nap before dinner.*

nap[2] *n.* °pile, °fibre, °texture, °weave, down, shag: *Choose a carpet with a short nap for areas of heavy wear.*

narcotic *adj.* **1** soporific, stuporific, hypnotic, °sedative, somnolent, sleep-inducing, opiate, dulling, numbing, anaesthetic, stupefacient, stupefying, stupefactive, tranquillizing, Lethean: *Most narcotic drugs may be sold only with a doctor's prescription.*
—*n.* **2** °drug, soporific, stuporific, hypnotic, °sedative, opiate, anaesthetic, stupefacient, °tranquillizer: *Many doctors are reluctant to prescribe narcotics.*

narrate *v.* °relate, °tell, °recount, °report, give an °account (of), °recite, °rehearse, °repeat, °review, °unfold, °chronicle, °describe, °detail, °reveal, retail: *She narrated a bone-chilling story of intrigue and murder. Please narrate the events leading up to your finding the body, Mrs Easton.*

narration *n.* **1** °telling, relating, unfolding, recounting, chronicling, recording, describing; °report, °recital, °recitation, °rehearsal, °relation, °chronicle, °description, portrayal, detailing, °revelation, °story, °tale, °narrative: *His narration was accompanied by nervous gestures. Her narration disagrees with her husband's in certain essential respects.* **2** reading, voice-over: *The narration did not seem to be coordinated with the pictures on the screen.*

narrative *n.* **1** °story, °tale, °chronicle, °description, °revelation, portrayal, °account, °report, °record, °history, °recital, °statement: *The characterizations were poor, but the narrative was fascinating.* —*adj.* **2** storytelling, chronicling, anecdotal: *One of her long, narrative poems has been published in a collection.*

narrator *n.* °reporter, storyteller, °raconteur, taleteller, teller of °tales, anecdotist *or* anecdotalist, relator, annalist, chronicler, describer, °author; voice-over: *We sat spellbound waiting for the narrator to continue.*

narrow *adj.* **1** constricted, °slender, °slim, °thin, restricted, °straitened, attenuated, narrowed; narrowing, tapering: *We squeezed through the narrow passage to freedom.* **2** confined, confining, °limited, °cramped, °close, °meagre, pinched, °tight, incommodious: *I awoke in a cell so narrow I could scarcely move.* **3** °strict, °careful, °close, °precise, °exact, °exacting, °demanding, °finicky, finical, °sharp, °meticulous, °scrupulous, °fussy, °rigid, searching, °critical: *The suspected forgeries were submitted to the narrow scrutiny of several experts.* **4** restricted, °limited, circumscribed, proscribed, denotative: *I learnt the meaning of charity in its narrowest sense.* **5** See **narrow-minded,** below. **6** °close, hairbreadth, °lucky: *I'd had a very narrow escape, for the bullet just grazed my scalp.* **7** stingy, niggardly, parsimonious, °miserly, °tight, °sparing, tight-fisted, °mean, °mercenary *Brit* mingy, *Dialectal* near, *Colloq* °close: *He was so narrow he barely allowed himself the essentials.* —*v.* **8** constrict, °limit, °qualify, °reduce, lessen, °diminish, °decrease: *She narrowed her chances of winning by buying only one lottery ticket.* **9** °limit, °restrict, °focus, confine, °concentrate, °narrow down: *They have narrowed the search for the boy to the area near Chester.* —*n.* **10** ***narrows***: °strait(s), °channel, °passage: *The vessel approached the narrows at dead slow speed.*

narrowly *adv.* **1** °barely, (only) °just, °scarcely, °hardly, by a hair's breadth; by the °skin of one's teeth, *Colloq* by a whisker: *The speeding lorry narrowly missed those children.* **2** closely, carefully, meticulously, scrupulously, °searchingly, critically: *She regarded him narrowly before speaking.*

narrow-minded *adj.* °bigoted, °prejudiced, illiberal, °narrow, °biased, °opinionated, °one-sided, °intolerant, non-objective, °conservative, °reactionary, °parochial, ultra-conservative, stiff-necked, °conventional, °hidebound, fundamentalist, literal-minded, narrow-spirited, mean-minded, mean-spirited, °petty, pettifogging, °small-minded, puritanical, unprogressive, °old-fashioned, old-fogyish *or* old-fogeyish, °strait-laced, *Colloq* °stuffy, *US* close-minded, °square, screed-bound, red-necked: *The vote reflected a reasonable balance between broad-minded and narrow-minded factions.*

nasty *adj.* **1** °foul, °filthy, °dirty, unclean, °offensive, °disgusting, nauseating, °revolting, °horrible, °loathsome, °repugnant, °repellent, °vile, odious, °obnoxious, objectionable, °nauseous, sickening, vomit-provoking, fetid *or* foetid, noisome, mephitic, °rank, malodorous, °rancid, noxious: *The nasty stench of rotting vegetation assailed our nostrils.* **2** unpleasant, °disagreeable, °unsavoury, °painful, objectionable, annoying, °untoward, °awkward, °difficult, °bad, °serious: *He had some very nasty experiences in the war.* **3** °obscene, °dirty, °pornographic, °blue, smutty, °lewd, °vulgar, °sordid, °indecent, licentious, °gross, °coarse, °crude, °rude, ribald, °bawdy, °risqué, °off colour, °suggestive, *Colloq* X-rated, raunchy: *The shops are selling some rather nasty videos that I don't want the children to watch.* **4** unpleasant, °disagreeable, °ugly, bad-tempered, °vicious, currish, °surly, °abusive, °spiteful, irascible, ill-natured, ill-tempered, °cruel, °inconsiderate, °rude, churlish, °obnoxious, crotchety, curmudgeonly, °cantankerous, crabbed, °cranky, *US and Canadian* °mean: *Why is your father so nasty to everyone who wants to go out with you?* **5** °bad, °severe, °acute, °painful, °serious; °dangerous, °critical: *I got a nasty shock when I opened the cupboard door. That's a nasty wound you have there.*

nation *n.* °country, °state, °land, °political entity, polity, °domain, °realm: *The countries of Europe are unlikely to become one nation.*

national *adj.* **1** nationwide, country-wide, °state, governmental, °civil; °public, °popular, *US* federal: *It took years to enact national clean-air laws.* **2** °nationalistic, nationalist, °patriotic, jingoistic, chauvinistic: *During the war, national feelings ran high.* —*n.* **3** °citizen, °subject, °inhabitant, °resident; °native: *Stephenson left England years ago and is now an Australian national.*

nationalistic *adj.* nationalist, °patriotic, jingoist(ic), chauvinist(ic), xenophobic, isolationist: *As communications improved, nationalistic feelings were eroded.*

nationality *n.* **1** citizenship: *Some countries allow their citizens dual nationality.* **2** °race, °nation, ethnic °group, ethnos, °clan, °tribe; °strain, °stock, °pedigree, °heritage, °roots, °extraction, bloodline, °breed: *The country became a melting-pot of myriad nationalities.*

native *adj.* **1** innate, natal, °inborn, °natural, °inherent, congenital, indwelling, inherited, °hereditary, in the blood, °intrinsic, constitutional: *Early in life, Carla demonstrated a native ability for music.* **2** °domestic, °local, home-grown; °indigenous, autochthonous, °aboriginal: *The native oysters in this area are superb.* **3** °basic, °first, °best, °original, °exclusive: *Can you tell that my native language is Hungarian?* **4** °national, ethnic, °clan, tribal: *We visited a Dutch town where the people wear traditional native dress.* **5** °aboriginal, °provincial, °local: *We soon fell in with the native custom of taking a siesta.* **6** born; by °birth: *Are you a native Glaswegian?* —*n.* **7** aborigine, indigene, autochthon; °national, °citizen, °resident, °inhabitant: *It is not difficult to distinguish the natives from the tourists in London.*

natural *adj.* **1** °ordinary, °common, commonplace, °normal, °standard, °regular, °usual, °customary, unexceptional, °routine, °habitual, °typical, °everyday; °reasonable, °logical, °sensible, accepted: *They say that Count Dracula could not die a natural death. The natural thing to do in case of attack is to defend oneself.* **2** °normal, °ordinary, °regular, expected; °spontaneous: *The natural motion of the waves carried the bottle out to sea.* **3** °simple, °basic, °fundamental, °real, unartificial, °genuine, unembellished, °unadorned, unpretentious: *She has great natural beauty and needs no cosmetics.* **4** unstudied, unconstrained, °candid, °frank, °spontaneous, °unaffected, °easy, °honest, °straight, straightforward, °artless, guileless, °impulsive, °unpremeditated, °ingenuous, °unsophisticated, unsophistic(al): *His kindness is quite natural.* **5** See **native, 1,** above: *She has a natural gift for painting.* **6** °true, °real, °genuine, °actual, °authentic, bona fide: *That, believe it or not, is his natural hair.* **7** °lifelike, °true to life, °realistic: *Note the natural colours of the sea in this painting by Whistler.* **8** °illegitimate, bastard: *He was the duke's natural son and had no claim on the estate.* **9** °consistent, consonant, consequent, °logical, °reasonable, °fitting, °appropriate, °proper, expected, not °incongruous, understandable: *In the circumstances, it would have been natural for her*

to despise Jonathan. **10** °organic, organically grown, non-chemical, °health: *They eat only natural foods, which they grow themselves.*
—*n.* **11** °genius, artist, °talent: *When it comes to chess, Boris is a natural.* **12** *Archaic* idiot, imbecile, simpleton, °fool, °halfwit: *One would have to be a natural to give money to that crook.*

naturally *adv.* **1** (as a matter) of °course, °needless to say, to be °sure, certainly, °surely, not unexpectedly, as expected *or* anticipated, °obviously, °clearly, logically, °consequently, as a consequence *or* °result: *He treated her badly, so, naturally, she refuses to see him again.* **2** normally, by °nature, by °character, °really, °actually, genuinely; inherently, instinctively, innately, congenitally: *My hair is naturally curly. He is not aloof, just naturally shy.* **3** unaffectedly, unpretentiously, °easily, candidly, °openly, °simply, plainly, °honestly, straightforwardly, uncomplicatedly: *If only politicians expressed themselves naturally and not pompously.*

nature *n.* **1** °quality, properties, features, °character, °personality, °make-up, °essence, constitution, °identity, attributes, °disposition, temperament, complexion: *Only detailed analysis will reveal the nature of this compound. It is not in his nature to be envious.* **2** °universe, cosmos, °world, °creation, °environment: *Science fiction deals with phenomena and contrivances that defy the laws of nature.* **3** scenery, countryside, wildness, primitiveness, °simplicity: *I often enjoyed sitting by the river, communing with nature.* **4** °kind, °variety, °description, °sort, °class, °category, °type, °genre, species; °stamp, °cast, °mould, feather, kidney, °colour, °stripe: *The duties of the position are largely of a ceremonial nature.* **5** ***by nature***: See **naturally, 2,** above.

naught *n.* nought, °nothing, °nil, °zero, aught *or* ought; °ruin, °destruction, °disaster, °collapse, °failure: *All my efforts had come to naught.*

naughty *adj.* **1** °mischievous, impish, puckish, roguish, scampish, °devilish; °frolicsome, °playful: *The children would get naughty the minute the teacher turned her back to the class.* **2** °disobedient, refractory, °insubordinate, °bad, °perverse, °wicked, fractious, °unruly, wayward, unmanageable, °ungovernable, °undisciplined, °defiant, °obstreperous: *Naughty pupils in this school are birched.* **3** °improper, °offensive, °vulgar, °indecent, °immoral, °risqué, °off colour, ribald, °bawdy, °blue, °pornographic, smutty, °lewd, °obscene, °dirty, *Colloq* X-rated, raunchy: *The teacher caught Keith reading a naughty book.*

nauseate *v.* °sicken, °disgust, °repel, °revolt, °offend: *Your hypocrisy nauseates me. When you get used to it, eating snails no longer seems nauseating.*

nauseated *adj.* sickened, °disgusted, repelled, revolted, offended, °sick (to one's stomach), °queasy, °squeamish; seasick, carsick, airsick: *They were nauseated when they saw the cadavers. I became nauseated by the rocking of the boat.*

nauseous *adj.* nauseating, °loathsome, sickening, °disgusting, °repellent, vomit-provoking, °offensive, °revolting, °repugnant, °repulsive, °abhorrent, °nasty, °foul, unpleasant, stomach-turning, *Technical* emetic: *A nauseous odour emanated from the crypt.*

nautical *adj.* maritime, °marine, °seafaring, seagoing; naval; boating, yachting, sailing; navigational: *Britain has always been a nautical nation. One must observe the nautical rules of the road.*

navel *n. Technical* umbilicus, omphalos, *Colloq* belly button: *The dancer wore a ruby in her navel.*

navigable *adj.* **1** °passable, traversable, negotiable, unblocked, unobstructed, °clear: *The Thames is not navigable above Lechlade.* **2** manoeuvrable, sailable, controllable, steerable, yare: *My boat is navigable when under way at about four knots.*

navigate *v.* **1** °sail, voyage, °cruise, °journey; °cross, °traverse: *After navigating the Indian Ocean for a month, we reached the Seychelles.* **2** °manoeuvre, °handle, °sail, °guide, °pilot, °steer, °direct, °skipper, captain, *Nautical* con: *It was tricky navigating through the shoals. Richard has navigated the company through rough waters over the years.*

navigation *n.* pilotage, helmsmanship, seamanship, steersmanship, steering, sailing: *The navigation of a small vessel in such a storm is no mean task.*

navigator *n.* °pilot, helmsman, seaman, tillerman, wheelman, steersman, °skipper: *The navigator without knowledge of local waterways must engage a pilot.*

navy *n.* °fleet, flotilla, naval °force(s), armada, *Literary* argosy: *The entire navy sailed across the Channel to Le Havre.*

naysayer *n.* denier, refuser, disdainer, rejecter *or* rejector; °prophet of doom, pessimist, °sceptic, dissenter, defeatist: *Don't expect any encouragement from a naysayer like Raymond.*

near *adv.* **1** °close (by *or* at °hand), not °far (off *or* away), °nearby, nigh, in *or* into the °vicinity *or* °neighbourhood, within (easy) °reach: *Draw near and listen to my tale.* **2** °close to, next to: *Don't go near the edge!* **3** °nearly, °almost, °just about, wellnigh, °close to being; not °quite, °virtually: *She was damn near killed in the car crash.*
—*adj.* **4** °close, °imminent, °immediate, °impending, looming, coming, approaching, °forthcoming; in the offing, at °hand: *We hope to settle the pollution problem in the near future. The time is near for me to go.* **5** °nearby, °close (by), adjacent, next-door, °adjoining, abutting, °neighbouring, contiguous: *My nearest neighbours live a mile away.* **6** stingy, °mean, niggardly, °miserly, parsimonious, °penurious, °cheap, penny-pinching, cheese-paring, °selfish, °close, tight-fisted, close-fisted: *He is so near he begrudged me even a cup of tea.* **7** °close, °intimate, connected, °related, °attached: *In case of emergency, list the name and address of a near relative.* **8** °close, °narrow, hair-breadth: *Although I escaped, it was a near thing.*
—*prep.* **9** °close to, in the °vicinity *or* °neighbourhood of, next to, adjacent to, within °reach of, within a mile of; a stone's throw from, not °far (away) from: *She wouldn't allow the doctor to come near her. I live near the railway.*
—*v.* **10** °approach, °draw near *or* nigh, come °close *or* closer, °verge on, °approximate on, °lean °towards: *As summer nears, I think of going on holiday. The ship neared port. His estimate is beginning to near mine.*

nearby *adv.* **1** °close by, °close at °hand, not far-off *or* -away, in the °vicinity *or* °neighbourhood, within (easy) °reach, °about, °around: *Hyenas loitered nearby waiting for the lions to leave the kill.*
—*adj.* **2** °close, within °reach, °handy, °accessible, at *or* to °hand, adjacent: *Nearby villagers helped put out the fire. We always kept a gun nearby because of pirates.*

nearly *adv.* **1** °almost, not quite, °about, °approximately, all but, °just about, °virtually, wellnigh, °practically, as good as, more or less; °around, approaching, nearing, °barely, °hardly, °scarcely, °close to: *We were nearly there but couldn't make it. She was nearly ninety when her first book was published.* **2** closely, identically, °exactly, °precisely: *Her opinions agree most nearly with his. His painting most nearly resembles Picasso's.*

near-sighted *adj.* **1** myopic, °short-sighted: *Being near-sighted, I must wear spectacles for driving.* **2** *Chiefly US* short-sighted, °narrow-minded, blinkered, °narrow, close-minded, illiberal, °unthinking, °heedless, insular, °partial, °one-sided, °parochial, °unsophisticated, unimaginative, °biased, unobjective, °opinionated, °dogmatic, °prejudiced, °intolerant, °bigoted: *They maintain a near-sighted attitude towards associating with anyone outside their immediate clique.*

neat *adj.* **1** °tidy, °orderly, °clean, uncluttered, °trim, °spruce, natty, °fastidious, spick and span, °shipshape (and Bristol fashion), organized, well-organized, well-ordered, °systematic, *Brit dialect* trig, *Colloq* neat as a pin, *Brit* dinky: *His room was always neat—very odd for a teenager.* **2** °straight, unadulterated, unmixed, °undiluted, uncut, unblended, °pure: *He drinks his whisky neat.* **3** unembellished, °unadorned, unornamented, °simple, °elegant, °graceful, °smart, uncomplicated, °regular, °precise, copperplate; calligraphic: *An invitation in her neat handwriting awaited my return from abroad.* **4** deft, adroit, °clever, °efficient, °ingenious, °expert, °practised, °skilful, °dexterous: *He contrived a neat plan to avoid paying taxes.* **5** °fine, wonderful, °marvellous, °great, °splendid, °excellent, °exceptional, °capital, °grand, first-class, *Colloq* cool, smashing, keen, °nifty, top-notch, A-1 *or* A-one, *Brit* top-hole, *Chiefly US* A-OK *or* A-okay, *Slang* °swell, far-out, boss, *Brit* topping, *US and Canadian* spiffy: *She found a really neat way to get boys to ask her out. Gordon has a neat new car.*

neaten *v.* Often, ***neaten up***: °tidy (up), °straighten (up *or* out), °clean (up), °spruce up, (put in) °order, *Brit dialect* trig: *If you don't neaten up your room, Mandy, you may not borrow the car.*

nebulous *adj.* °vague, °hazy, clouded, unclear, °obscure, °indistinct, °fuzzy, °muddy, ill-defined, °shapeless, amorphous, blurred, indeterminate, °murky, °opaque, turbid, °dim, foggy, °faint, °pale: *He has only the most nebulous idea of what the lecture was about.*

necessarily *adv.* inevitably, unavoidably, inescapably, axiomatically, inexorably, ineluctably, irresistibly, incontrovertibly, automatically, °naturally, (as a matter) of °course, as a °result, certainly, °surely, to be °sure, like it or not, °willy-nilly, perforce, of °necessity, by definition: *If you accept his premise, then you must, necessarily, accept his conclusion. You don't necessarily need to be rich to be happy.*

necessary *adj.* **1** °indispensable, °essential, required, needed, compulsory, requisite, °vital, demanded, °imperative, °obligatory, needful, of the °essence, °important, of the utmost °importance, top-priority, high-priority, °urgent, exigent, compelling, life-and-death *or* life-or-death: *A good diet is necessary for good health. It is necessary that you come at once. Take the necessary steps to get the job done.* **2** °inevitable, °unavoidable, inescapable, ineluctable: *In the circumstances, we find it necessary to ask for your resignation.* **3** °sure, °certain, °predetermined, predestined, °fated, inexorable; resulting, resultant: *The necessary outcome of the affair was that the child was returned to her natural parents.*
—*n.* **4** See **necessity, 1,** below.

necessity *n.* **1** °requirement, °essential, °necessary, requisite, °need, °prerequisite, °basic, °fundamental, *sine qua non*, desideratum, constraint: *I was marooned for a year with only the bare necessities of life. We regard honesty as a necessity in a bank manager.* **2** indispensability, unavoidability, needfulness, inexorability: *The necessity for exercise is often met by private health clubs.* **3** °poverty, °want, indigence, °need, destitution, penury, straits, °difficulty, °difficulties, pauperism, neediness: *The extreme necessity of the unemployed demands that the government act quickly.* **4** °urgency, °emergency, °crisis, °misfortune, exigency, °pinch, °extreme, matter of life and death: *She has made a virtue of necessity. Electric power is no longer a matter of choice but of necessity.*

need *v.* **1** °require, °demand, °want, be in °want of, °call for, have need of *or* for; °lack, °miss, have °occasion for: *This room needs a coat of paint. Although she may want more money, she doesn't need it. Do you need anything to make you more comfortable?*
—*n.* **2** °necessity, °requirement; °call, °demand, constraint: *There's no need to shout—I can hear you. There is a need to keep this matter confidential. This facility will meet our electricity needs for decades.* **3** °essential, °necessary, requisite, °prerequisite, °necessity, °basic, °fundamental, *sine qua non*, °necessary, desideratum: *I am perfectly capable of taking care of my family's needs.* **4** °distress, °difficulty, °trouble, (dire *or* °desperate) straits, °stress, °emergency, exigency, °extremity, neediness, needfulness; °poverty, penury, impecuniousness, destitution, °privation, deprivation, indigence, beggary: *She was very supportive in his hour of need. The need of the people in that district is heart-rending.* **5** °want, °lack, °dearth, °shortage, paucity, °scarcity, insufficiency, desideratum: *The need for medical supplies was most sharply felt in areas that were already ravaged by famine.*

needless *adj.* **1** °unnecessary, °non-essential, unessential, unneeded, unwanted, °useless, uncalled-for, °gratuitous, °superfluous, °redundant, °excess, °excessive, tautological, °dispensable, °expendable, supererogatory, *de trop*, pleonastic: *He went to a lot of needless trouble to change the tyre. It is needless to raise further questions.* **2** ***needless to say***: °naturally, (as a matter) of °course, °obviously, it goes without saying: *Needless to say, he will have to resign when this comes to light.*

needy *adj.* °poor, °indigent, poverty-stricken, °destitute, °impoverished, penniless, impecunious, necessitous, underprivileged, °deprived, disadvantaged, below the °poverty level, in dire straits, in *or* on the way to the poorhouse, in reduced circumstances, down-and-out, °insolvent, *Colloq* on one's uppers, °dead *or* °flat *or* stony-broke, °hard up, strapped, pinched, on the breadline, up against it, *Brit* on the °dole, *US* °dead °broke, on welfare, on °relief: *It is not enough to look after needy families only at Christmas time.*

negative *adj.* **1** °contradictory, anti, °contrary, dissenting, dissentious, disputing, disputatious, °argumentative, adversarial, adversative, antagonistic, antipathetic, adverse, *US* °adversary: *He has adopted a very negative attitude towards his job. Few negative voices were heard on the issue.* **2** °pessimistic, °unenthusiastic, °cool, °cold, uninterested, unresponsive: *The reaction to our offer has been largely negative.* **3** nullifying, annulling, neutralizing, voiding, cancelling: *The laws are mainly negative, listing only things one must not do.* **4** negating, refusing, denying, gainsaying, °opposing: *The judge came to a negative decision regarding bail.* **5** ***in the negative***: negatively, 'No': *Asked if she wanted to go, she replied in the negative.*

neglect *v.* **1** °disregard, °ignore, °slight, pay no °attention to, be °inattentive to, °overlook, °pass by, °spurn, °rebuff, °scorn, disdain, contemn, *Colloq* cold-shoulder: *Scholars neglected his work for years.* **2** °fail (in), °omit; °disregard, let °slide *or* °pass, be °remiss (about *or* in *or* regarding), °abandon, °lose sight of, °forget, °shirk: *Have I neglected telling you how much I love you? Sybil has neglected her obligations.*
—*n.* **3** °disregard, °disrespect, inattention, °indifference, slighting, unconcern, °oversight, heedlessness, neglectfulness, carelessness, inadvertence: *We lost business to our competitor through simple neglect.* **4** °negligence, laxity, laxness, slackness, neglectfulness, passivity, passiveness, °inactivity, inaction, dereliction, °default, °failure, °failing, remissness: *She has been accused of neglect in not looking after her children properly.*

negligence *n.* inattention, inattentiveness, °indifference, carelessness, unconcern, dereliction, °failure, °failing, heedlessness, laxity, laxness, °disregard, °oversight, °omission, inadvertence, °neglect, remissness, forgetfulness, oscitancy *or* oscitance: *The car crash was attributed to the lorry driver's negligence.*

negligible *adj.* °insignificant, °minor, unimportant, °trifling, trivial, °inconsequential, piddling, inappreciable, °small, °slight, °paltry, nugatory, °worthless, °petty, °niggling, not worth mentioning *or* talking about: *The differences between the two plans are negligible.*

negotiate *v.* **1** °deal, °bargain, °dicker, °haggle, chaffer, palter; °discuss, °debate, mediate, °consult, °parley, °speak, °talk, °transact, come to °terms: *A conglomerate is negotiating to buy our company. The company asked me to negotiate on our behalf.* **2** °arrange (for), °organize, orchestrate, °conduct, °handle, °manoeuvre, °manage, °engineer, °work out,

°settle, °get, °obtain, °bring off *or* about, °carry off, °accomplish, do, °execute, °effect, °complete, conclude, *Colloq* °pull off: *Will you be able to negotiate a loan for the car?* **3** °manoeuvre, °clear, °get through *or* past *or* round *or* over, °pass, °cross, *Colloq* °make (it (through *or* past *or* round *or* over)): *Will you be able to negotiate the barbed-wire fence?*

negotiation *n.* **1** °discussion, mediation, arbitration, bargaining, °parley, parleying, °talk, coming to °terms: *The disarmament negotiations have dragged on for years.* **2** °deal, °bargain, °transaction, °agreement, °arrangement, °understanding, °determination, °decision, °settlement; °contract, °pact, °compact, covenant, concordat, °treaty: *All parties seem pleased with the final negotiation.*

negotiator *n.* arbitrator, arbiter, °mediator, °moderator, diplomat, °ambassador, °go-between, middleman, intercessor, interceder, intervener, °agent, °broker: *An independent negotiator was invited to the bargaining table with the union and management representatives.*

neighbourhood *n.* **1** locality, °area, °region, °vicinity, vicinage, environs, °quarter, °district, °precinct(s), purlieus, °locale; surroundings, confines: *Houses in the neighbourhood of the blast were levelled.* **2** ***in the neighbourhood of***: °approximately, °about, °around, °nearly, °practically, °close to, °almost, more or less, *Colloq* in the ballpark of, in the °region of, *Brit* getting on for, not far off, *US* within an eyelash of, *Slang* as °near as dammit to: *The playground will cost in the neighbourhood of £5,000.*

neighbouring *adj.* °nearby, °near, °around, adjacent (to), °surrounding, °adjoining, contiguous (to), °touching, bordering (on), next (to), nearest: *Owners of properties neighbouring the nuclear power plant worry about radiation. The neighbouring villages will participate in the fête at Long Norton.*

neighbourly *adj.* °friendly, °cordial, °warm, °amiable, °agreeable, affable, companionable, well-disposed, °kindly, °kind, well-wishing, °genial, °sociable, °social, °harmonious, °considerate, °thoughtful, °helpful, °gracious, °courteous, °civil: *It was quite neighbourly of the Constables to look after our cat.*

neologism *n.* neoterism, coinage, neology, nonce-word; °blend, portmanteau °word: *Lexicographers must decide the neologisms to be added to their dictionaries.*

nerve *n.* **1** °courage, coolness, boldness, °bravery, intrepidity, °determination, valour, °daring, fearlessness, dauntlessness, °pluck, mettle, °spirit, °fortitude, °will, °tenacity, steadfastness, staunchness, firmness, doughtiness, resoluteness, *Colloq* guts, °grit, °gumption, °spunk, *US* sand, *Brit* °bottle, *US* moxie, *Taboo slang* balls: *It took a lot of nerve to go back into that burning building.* **2** °effrontery, brazenness, °gall, °impertinence, °brass, °impudence, insolence, audacity, brashness, °presumption, presumptuousness, temerity, *Colloq* cheek, °sauce, chutzpah, *Slang* crust: *You have a lot of nerve, talking to your mother that way!* **3** ***get on someone's nerves***: °annoy, °irritate, °upset: *That loud rock music gets on my nerves.* **4** ***nerves***: °tension, nervousness, hysteria, °anxiety, fretfulness, °stress, °worry, apprehension, °fright, *Colloq* the °jitters, *Slang* the willies, the heebie-jeebies, *US* the whim-whams: *I had a bad case of nerves before learning the doctor's diagnosis.*

nerve-racking *adj.* nerve-wracking, °harrowing, °agonizing, distressing, °trying, vexing, vexatious, °troublesome, worrisome, °irksome, irritating: *Waiting for the names of the survivors was the most nerve-racking experience of my life.*

nervous *adj.* **1** highly-strung, °excitable, °sensitive, °tense, °agitated, wrought up, worked up, °upset, flustered, ruffled, °disturbed, perturbed, distressed, °worried, °anxious, troubled, °concerned, disquieted, edgy, on °edge, on tenterhooks, fidgety, °fretful, uneasy, apprehensive, frightened, °fearful, °shaky, °scared, skittish, *US* on a tightrope, *Colloq* °jumpy, jittery, flappable, in a °stew, in a dither, in a °sweat, in a tizzy, in a °flap, uptight, *Brit* nervy, *US* on pins and needles, *Slang* strung out: *Thomas is nervous because he has to give a speech.* **2** °difficult, °tense, °critical: *There were a few nervous moments before we knew if the rope would hold.*

nest *n.* **1** roost, °perch, eyrie *or US also* aerie, den, °lair: *The birds, which mate for life, return to the same nest each year.* **2** snuggery, °retreat, °refuge, °haunt, °hideaway, hide-out; °resort: *We have a little nest in the country which we escape to at weekends.*

nestle *v.* °cuddle (up), °snuggle (up), °huddle, curl up, nuzzle (up): *They nestled close together to keep warm.*

net[1] *n.* **1** °network, netting, °mesh, mesh-work, °web, webbing, openwork, lattice, lattice-work, trellis, trellis-work, lace-work, reticulum, reticle, rete, plexus, grid, grid-work, grille, °grate, °grating, fretwork; sieve, °screen, strainer, sifter: *They watched the fishermen mending their nets.*
—*v.* **2** °catch, °capture, °trap, entrap, °snare, ensnare, °bag: *As I bring the fish close to the boat, you net it with this.*

net[2] *n.* **1** nett, (net) °profit, °gain, °earnings, °return(s), *Colloq US* °take: *The net for the first quarter was 15 per cent higher than last year's.*
—*adj.* **2** °clear, after deductions, after taxes, take-home, °final, bottom-line: *The tax increase was greater than my salary increase, so my net income was lower this year.* **3** °final, °end, closing, concluding, conclusive, °effective, °ultimate: *The net result of the advertising campaign was a sales increase of 18 per cent.*
—*v.* **4** °make, °realize, °clear, take home, °bring in, °earn, °pocket, °take in, °get: *How much did you net last year—after taxes, that is.*

network *n.* **1** See **net**[1], **1**, above. **2** °system, °arrangement, °structure, °organization, complex, grid, criss-cross, °web, plexus; °maze, labyrinth, jungle, °tangle: *She has developed a worldwide network of contacts for her business. Before transistors, the back of a radio was a network of multicoloured wires.*

neurotic *adj.* psychoneurotic, °unstable, °disturbed, °confused, irrational, disordered, maladjusted, °distraught, °overwrought, °anxious, °nervous, °obsessive, °deviant, °abnormal: *Many people are neurotic about something.*

neuter *adj.* **1** asexual, sexless, epicene: *Worker bees are neuter, neither male nor female.*
—*v.* **2** desex *or* desexualize, °doctor; castrate, emasculate, geld, capon *or* caponize, eunuchize; spay, ovariectomize, oophorectomize; *Colloq* °fix, cut, *US* alter: *We had our cat neutered after her first litter.*

neutral *adj.* **1** non-belligerent, non-combatant, unaligned, °non-aligned, unaffiliated, uninvolved, unallied, non-allied, °non-partisan, °impartial, °disinterested, °indifferent, °dispassionate, unbiased, uncommitted, °noncommittal, °aloof, °withdrawn, °detached, °remote, removed: *Switzerland has remained neutral during both world wars.* **2** °dull, °drab, °colourless, achromatic, toneless, washed out, °pale, °indefinite, °indistinct, °indistinguishable, indeterminate, °vague, beige, ecru: *A neutral wallpaper colour won't clash with the paintings.*

neutralize *v.* °void, annul, °cancel (out), nullify, invalidate, negate, °delete, °undo, make *or* render °ineffective, counterbalance, °counteract, °offset, °equalize, °even, °square, °compensate for, °make up for: *The forces on both sides of the sail, being equal, neutralize each other.*

never *adv.* **1** at no °time, not °ever, not at any °time, on no °occasion, under no °circumstances *or* condition(s), on no account, not at all, *Colloq* not in a million years, not till hell freezes over: *You are never to use such language again!* **2** in no way, not in any way, not in the least, not in any °degree, not under any condition, not: *Never fear, for I am near.*

nevertheless *adv.* °still, °notwithstanding, °yet, in °spite of that, °despite that, °nonetheless, °regardless, be that as it may, for all that, °even so, but, °however,

°just *or* all the °same, °everything considered, at any °rate, anyway, in any °case, in any °event, at all events, *Literary* withal: *He said he dislikes sweets; nevertheless, he ate a whole bar of chocolate.*

new *adj.* **1** °novel, °original, °unique, °unusual, °different, °fresh, °creative, °imaginative, °brand-new: *Ruth has a new idea for the sales campaign.* **2** °latest, °late, °modern, °contemporary, modish, °stylish, °fashionable, °chic, °recent, advanced, up to °date, °brand-new, late-model, *Colloq* °trendy, *Slang* mod, °hip: *MacGregor buys a new car every year: it has to be equipped with the newest gadgets.* **3** °fresh, °further, additional, supplemental, °supplementary: *Has the new issue of* Verbatim *come out yet?* **4** °unfamiliar, °unknown, °strange, °different; °unique, unheard-of: *I hear there's a new girl in your office. I want to introduce my new friend, Dan Hammond. Every year they discover a new virus.* **5** revitalized, reborn, renewed, rejuvenated, changed, altered, redone, restored, redesigned, remodelled: *I saw before me a new Marie. They published a new version of the Bible.* **6** °inexperienced, °green, °fresh, °callow, °unfledged, budding, °immature, unripe, untrained: *Let us look over the new recruits, Sergeant.* **7** °late, °young, °recent: *We found newer fossils at higher levels.* **8** °uncharted, unexplored, untrodden, °unknown, °experimental: *Astronomers are breaking new ground in the analysis of pulsars.*

newcomer *n.* **1** °alien, °immigrant, °foreigner, outlander, °stranger, °settler, colonist, °outsider: *The newcomers quickly established themselves and became self-sufficient.* **2** beginner, °amateur, °novice, proselyte, neophyte, tiro *or* tyro, °initiate, trainee, °learner, fledgling *or Brit also* fledgeling, *Brit* fresher *or US* freshman, *Colloq* °greenhorn: *Though experienced in book publishing, he was a newcomer to magazine publishing.*

news *n.* **1** tidings, °word, °information, °advice, °intelligence; °rumour, °talk, °gossip, hearsay, °dirt, °scandal, exposé, *Colloq* info, °low-down, °scoop, *US* scuttlebutt, *Slang* °dope: *What's the latest news about the situation in the Middle East?* **2** °dispatch *or* despatch, °report, °account, °story, communication, °bulletin, communiqué, °announcement, °information, °message, °word, °statement, (°press) °release, (news)-flash: *The news from our correspondent contains no mention of finding a cache of arms.* **3** newscast, news °broadcast *or* telecast, news °programme; newsflash: *Please be quiet so that I can listen to the news.* **4** (good) °copy, front-page news, (hot) item: *The royal family is always news.*

nice *adj.* **1** °pleasant, °agreeable, °amiable, °amicable, °friendly, °cordial, °warm, °gracious, warm-hearted, °kind, °kindly, °outgoing, charming, °genial, °delightful, °courteous, °polite, °refined, gentlemanly, °ladylike, winsome, °likeable, °attractive: *They are one of the nicest couples I have ever met.* **2** °good, °satisfactory, commendable, °worthy, °worthwhile: *The manager said that I had done a nice job in preparing the specifications.* **3** °good, °fine, °superb, °superior, °attentive, °sharp, °acute, °keen, °careful, °exact, °exacting, rigorous; °precise, °accurate, unerring, °scrupulous, °meticulous, punctilious, °discriminating, discriminative, °perceptive, °delicate, °fastidious, °flawless, °faultless, °subtle, °strict, °close, °small, °slight, °minute, complex, °complicated, °intricate: *A diamond cutter must have a nice eye for detail. It is difficult to maintain nice distinctions of meaning among certain words, given that people are so careless with their speech these days.* **4** °delicate, °subtle, °sensitive, °exquisite, °hair-splitting, over-nice, °fine, °critical, °ticklish, °dangerous, °precarious, °perilous, *Colloq* °hairy: *The matter of Hong Kong requires some nice political negotiations.* **5** °trim, °well turned out, °tidy, °neat, °fine: *Don't you want to look nice for your birthday party?* **6** ***nice and —***: pleasantly, delightfully, pleasingly, agreeably, enjoyably, gratifyingly, satisfyingly, comfortably: *It's nice and warm by the fire.*

niche *n.* **1** °recess, °hollow, alcove, °nook: *A small statue of Buddha stood in a niche in the wall.* **2** °place, °position, *Colloq* °slot, pigeon-hole: *Humphrey has finally found a niche for himself working as a tax inspector.*

nick *n.* **1** °cut, °notch, °chip, °gouge, °gash, °scratch, dent, °indentation, °flaw, °mark, °blemish, °defect: *Be careful of that nick in the rim of the glass.* **2** °jail *or Brit also* gaol; police station: *The police took him to the nick to help them with their inquiries.*
—*v.* **3** °steal, purloin, °take, °appropriate, °make off with, *Colloq* °pinch: *Who nicked my biro?* **4** °arrest, °nab, °take in, *Colloq* collar: *Alan was nicked for possession of marijuana.* **5** ***nick off***: °depart, °go *or* °run off *or* away, °take off, take to one's °heels, show a clean pair of °heels, beat a (hasty) °retreat, *Colloq* scarper, make tracks, °beat it: *The cops were coming so I nicked off.*

nickname *n.* **1** °pet °name, sobriquet, epithet, agnomen, *Colloq* moniker *or* monicker, handle: *Her real name is Josephine, but her nickname is Dusty.* **2** °diminutive: *A common nickname for Terence is Terry.*

nifty *adj.* **1** °smart, °stylish, modish, °chic, °spruce: *I borrowed a nifty outfit from Grandma for the flapper's costume ball.* **2** °healthy, in °good °form, spry, °energetic, °agile, quick: *I'm not as nifty as I was in 1950.* **3** °excellent, °neat, °great, °splendid, °fine, °clever, °skilful, apt, °suitable: *Having a picnic was a nifty idea. That was as nifty a bit of bargaining as I've ever seen.* **4** °satisfactory, °satisfying, °good, °profitable, °substantial, °considerable: *He made a nifty profit on the sale of his house in Chelsea.*

niggle *v.* °find °fault, °nag, °carp, °fuss, °cavil, °criticize; °complain, *Colloq* grouse, *Slang* °bitch, *US* kvetch: *I do wish she would stop niggling when we cannot do anything about the situation.*

niggling *adj.* **1** irritating, worrying, worrisome, °irksome, vexing, vexatious, annoying, °troublesome: *There are a few niggling matters that I must see my accountant about.* **2** °petty, nugatory, °trifling, trivial, °fussy, °insignificant, unimportant, °inconsequential, °frivolous, *Colloq* piddling, nit-picking, *US and Canadian* picayune: *Bill always ignores the core of a problem and occupies himself with the niggling details.*

night *n.* **1** (Stygian *or* Cimmerian) °dark *or* darkness *or* blackness *or* °gloom; night-time, shades of night, *Formal* tenebrosity *or* tenebrousness *or* tenebriousness: *The strange creature slunk off into the night.* **2** nightfall, gloaming, °twilight, °dusk, eventide, °evening, evensong, edge of night, sunset, sundown, end of day, vespers: *When night comes, one can hear the frogs calling from the pond.* **3** ***night and day***: all the °time, continually, incessantly, unceasingly, continuously, unendingly, endlessly, round-the-clock, ceaselessly, °non-stop: *Those animals keep up their caterwauling night and day.*

nightly *adj.* **1** every °night, each °night, each and every °night, °night after °night: *The watchman does his nightly rounds.* **2** night-time, nocturnal, bedtime: *A nightly glass of warm milk promotes sound sleep.*
—*adv.* **3** every °night, each °night, nights, after °dark, after sunset; nocturnally: *The bird sings nightly outside my window.*

nightmarish *adj.* °frightening, °terrifying, alarming, horrific, °horrible, °dreadful, °awful, °ghastly, dismaying, °agonizing, worrisome, exasperating, frustrating, Kafkaesque, *Colloq* creepy, °scary: *Dealing with officialdom can be a nightmarish experience when abroad.*

nil *n.* °nothing, °zero, nought *or* °naught, aught *or* ought, *Tennis, table tennis, etc.* love, *Cricket* duck, *US* goose-egg, *Slang US* zip: *Oxford United: 4; Queens Park Rangers: Nil.*

nimble *adj.* **1** °agile, °lively, °active, °light, lithe, limber, spry, °sprightly, °brisk, °smart, °energetic, °rapid, quick, °swift, adroit, deft, °dexterous; nimble-fingered; nimble-footed: *She's as nimble as a cat on a hot tin roof.* **2** °agile, °alert, °acute, nimble-witted,

°quick-witted, ready-witted, °intelligent, °keen, °sharp; °smart, °brilliant, sparkling, °scintillating, coruscating: *Despite his inability to make decisions, Desmond has quite a nimble mind.*

nip[1] *v.* **1** °bite, nibble; °pinch, °snip, °clip, °cut, °snap, °tweak, twitch, °trim, °lop, crop, shear; °grip, °squeeze: *The dog nipped the postman's ankle. Nip off the suckers to promote healthy growth of the tomatoes.* **2** ***nip in the bud***: °stop, °arrest, °check, °thwart, °frustrate, °stymie, °forestall; °quash, °squelch, °suppress, °extinguish, °put down: *The revolt of the army officers was nipped in the bud.*

—*n.* **3** °bite, nibble, °morsel, °pinch, °snip: *The deer had taken nips off the tips of the shrubbery.* **4** °chill, coldness, iciness, sharpness, °tang, °bite: *There's a definite wintry nip in the air tonight.*

nip[2] *n.* °taste, °drop, °sip, soupçon, °portion, °swallow, °gulp, °mouthful, °finger, *Brit* peg, °tot, °draught, *Scots* dram, *US* draft, *Colloq* snort, °shot: *I had a few nips of brandy to ward off the cold.*

nobility *n.* **1** nobleness, °dignity, °grandeur, illustriousness, greatness, °glory, °influence, °authority, °leadership, °distinction, °probity, °integrity, °excellence, goodness, °character, °rectitude, righteousness, ethics, °honesty, honourableness, decency, justness, high-mindedness, magnanimity, °prestige, loftiness, primacy, °significance: *The man's nobility was evident from his mien and bearing.* **2** °rank, °position, °class, °birth, blue blood: *Their nobility is recognized only at court and in fashionable society.* **3** ***the nobility***: the °gentry, the °élite, the aristocracy, *Colloq* the °upper crust, the ruling °class(es), the Establishment, *US* the Four Hundred: *With a name like Hohenzollern, her family must be from the European nobility.*

noble *n.* **1** nobleman, noblewoman, aristocrat, patrician, °lord, lady, °peer; gentleman, gentlewoman, *Colloq* blue blood: *The nobles united and forced King John to sign the Magna Carta.*

—*adj.* **2** high-born, °high-class, °upper-class, aristocratic, titled, high-ranking, lordly, patrician, *Colloq* blue-blood(ed): *She came from a noble Austrian family.* **3** °dignified, °eminent, °distinguished, august, °grand, °lofty, °elevated, °illustrious, °prestigious, °pre-eminent, °noted, honoured, esteemed, °celebrated, °renowned, acclaimed, respected, venerated: *The noble Knights of the Round Table have become legend throughout the world.* **4** °upright, °righteous, °honourable, °honest, °virtuous, incorruptible, °chivalrous, °staunch, °steadfast, °true, °loyal, °faithful, °trustworthy, °true, °principled, °moral, °good, °decent, self-sacrificing, magnanimous, °generous: *The qualities that make a noble friend make a formidable enemy.* **5** °splendid, °magnificent, °imposing, °impressive, °stately, °exquisite, °sublime, °grand, °striking, °stunning, °superb, °admirable, °elegant, °rich, °sumptuous, °luxurious: *The Taj Mahal is probably one of the noblest works of man.*

nobody *pron.* **1** no one, not anyone, no person: *We had to wait because nobody was in the shop when we entered.*

—*n.* **2** nonentity, °unknown, °zero, cipher, *Colloq* °nothing: *Overnight, Tony went from being a celebrity to being a nobody.*

nod *v.* **1** °greet, °acknowledge, °recognize: *The maître d'hôtel nodded to me as I entered the restaurant.* **2** say yes; °consent, assent, °agree, concur, acquiesce: *Asked if she had seen Nick, the barmaid nodded. I asked permission to leave the room and the teacher nodded.* **3** °doze (off), °nap, drowse, °drop off, °fall asleep: *Exhausted travellers nodded in their chairs waiting for their flights to be announced.* **4** °slip (up), °err, make a °mistake, be °mistaken *or* °wrong; be °careless *or* negligent *or* °lax *or* °inattentive: *Sometimes, even Homer nods.*

—*n.* **5** °signal, °sign, °cue, °indication, °gesture: *I saw him give a nod to the barber, who suddenly held a cut-throat razor to my throat.* **6** °approval; °consent, acquiescence, concurrence, assent, °agreement, *Colloq* OK *or* okay: *The company has given me the nod to open an office in Acapulco.*

nodding *adj.* °casual, °slight, °superficial, °distant; °incomplete: *I know Graham slightly—he's a nodding acquaintance. It was clear that the violinist had only a nodding acquaintance with Mozart's concerto.*

noise *n.* **1** °sound, clamour, °crash, °clap, °clash, clangour, °din, °thunder, thundering, rumble, rumbling, °outcry, hubbub, °uproar, hullabaloo, °racket, charivari *or US and Canadian also* shivaree, °rattle, caterwauling, °rumpus, °blare, °blast, blasting, bawling, babel; commotion, °bedlam, °fracas, °tumult, °pandemonium, turmoil; discordance, dissonance, cacophony; *Archaic* alarms *or* alarums and excursions, *Colloq* ruckus, ruction, ballyhoo: *I couldn't sleep because of the unbearable noise from the party next door. You may call acid rock music, but she calls it noise.* **2** °sound, °disturbance: *Did you just hear that strange noise? It's only the noise of the crickets.*

—*v.* **3** Often, ***noise about*** *or* ***around***: °circulate, °spread, °rumour, bruit (about): *It is being noised about that John and Marsha are getting a divorce.*

noiseless *adj.* muted, °quiet, °soft, hushed, muffled, deadened, dampened, damped; °silent, °mute, °still, °inaudible, soundless: *We watched the noiseless boats gliding past.*

noisy *adj.* °loud, deafening, ear-splitting, jarring, °grating, °harsh, °piercing, °shrill, °discordant, unmusical, dissonant, cacophonous, resounding, clarion, clamorous, clangorous, °thunderous, °uproarious, blaring, blasting, °obstreperous, vociferous, °boisterous, °tumultuous, °riotous: *I could hear nothing over the noisy aeroplane engines. When she arose to speak, the noisy crowd fell silent.*

nominal *adj.* **1** °titular, in °name only, °formal, °pretended, °so-called, °self-styled, *soi-disant*, °professed, purported, °supposed, would-be, representational, represented, supposititious; proposed, propositional; °puppet: *Elliot is the nominal chairman, but Foster actually runs the company.* **2** °insignificant, trivial, °trifling, °minor, minuscule, °tiny, °small, °insubstantial, °minimal, inconsiderable, °token: *We charge a nominal fee for the analysis if you refuse our recommendation.*

nominate *v.* °choose, °select, °name, °appoint, °designate, °suggest, °offer, °submit, °recommend, °propose, °present, °put up *or* forward; °forward; *Formal* put forth: *Baker has been nominated for the presidency.*

nominee *n.* °candidate, office-seeker, designee, selectee, appointee, assignee: *We must choose a nominee to run in the next election.*

non-aligned *adj.* uncommitted, non-allied, non-affiliated, unaligned, unaffiliated, unallied; °neutral, °impartial: *There are several non-aligned nations that remain independent of the influence of the superpowers.*

non-believer *n.* unbeliever, disbeliever, cynic, doubting Thomas, doubter, °sceptic, freethinker, agnostic, atheist, nullifidian; °infidel, °heathen, °pagan: *During his reign, thousands of non-believers were put to the sword.*

nonchalant *adj.* °cool, unexcited, unexcitable, unperturbed, imperturbable, undisturbed, untroubled, unflappable, unruffled, °dispassionate, unemotional, °detached, °distant, unconcerned, °indifferent, pococurante, insouciant, uninterested, °aloof, °blasé, °offhand, °calm, °collected, composed, °easygoing, °free and °easy, happy-go-lucky, °casual, °relaxed, at °ease; °unenthusiastic, apathetic; *Colloq* laid-back, together: *How can you be so nonchalant about important issues that affect all our lives?!*

noncommittal *adj.* °wary, °cautious, °careful, °gingerly, °guarded, (playing it) °safe, circumspect, watchful, °prudent, canny, °tentative, on °guard, °reserved, °cool; precautionary *or* precautional, precautious; *Colloq* playing it °cool, playing it °safe, playing it *or* one's cards close to the chest: *The company is still noncommittal about the take-over of the American company.*

non-completion *n.* non-fulfilment, unfulfilment, non-performance, incompleteness, deficiency: *We regret the non-completion of the work on your house and will refund in full the amount already paid.*

non-compliance *n.* disobedience, nonconformity, non-observance, °disregard, disregarding, °failure, non-cooperation, uncooperativeness, unresponsiveness, °rejection, °refusal, °denial: *If you fail to provide the records requested by the tax inspector, you can be charged with non-compliance.*

nonconformist *n.* **1** nonconformer, °renegade, maverick, °rebel, °radical, °individualist, heretic, dissenter, °dissident, iconoclast, loner, °exception, anomaly: *In the 1960s, Alastair counted himself among the nonconformists who wore unconventional clothes and flouted conventional behaviour.*
—*adj.* **2** nonconforming, °renegade, maverick, °rebellious, °radical, °individualist(ic), °heretical, dissentient, °dissident, iconoclastic: *Suffragists were ridiculed for their nonconformist ideas.*

nondescript *adj.* indescribable, unclassifiable, unclassified, °ordinary, common-or-garden variety, °common, commonplace, unremarkable, °colourless, °drab, °everyday, °bland, uninteresting, insipid, characterless, undistinctive, unexceptional: *He was wearing nondescript clothing and blended into the crowd.*

none *pron.* no one, not anyone, °nobody, no person; not one; not any; °nil: *Of all the people I met, none impressed me more than Kathy. I'd give you a sweet if I had one, but I have none. I'd even give you money, but I have none.*

non-essential *adj.* **1** non-vital, unessential, unneeded, °unnecessary, °needless, °inconsequential, °insignificant, unimportant, °superfluous, °dispensable, °expendable, °gratuitous, uncalled-for, °extraneous, °peripheral, °extra, *de trop*, adventitious, additional, supplemental, adscititious, °redundant, °accessory, °subordinate, °secondary, °subsidiary: *The non-essential industries were converted to the war effort during the 1940s.*
—*n.* **2** unessential, inessential, nonentity, cipher, °zero, °nobody; °extra, supernumerary, spear-carrier, *Colloq* °nothing, *Slang US* nebbish: *She used him as a lackey, a non-essential whom she could dispose of at will.*

nonetheless *adv.* See **nevertheless,** above.

non-event *n.* anticlimax, *Colloq* non-starter, lead balloon, °dud, *Brit* damp squib: *Jeremy's party turned out to be the non-event of the year.*

non-existent *adj.* °unreal, °imaginary, imagined, °fictional, fictive, °fanciful, °fancied, °mythical, °fabulous, fabled, °illusory, chimerical, delusive: *Although the entire Graeco-Roman pantheon became non-existent overnight, its gods and goddesses continue to pervade our culture.*

non-flammable *adj.* non-combustible, °incombustible, non-inflammable, unburnable; fire-retardant: *The government recently passed regulations requiring that non-flammable materials be used in upholstered furniture.*

no-nonsense *adj.* °serious, unfrivolous, businesslike, °practical, non-trivial, untrivial: *Customs officials take a no-nonsense approach to drug trafficking.*

nonpareil *n.* °paragon, °model, °standard, *ne plus ultra*, exemplar, °ideal, *Literary* nonsuch *or* nonesuch, *Colloq* oner, one in a million, *Brit* one-off: *Annabelle was a nonpareil among the artists of her day.*

non-partisan *adj.* **1** non-partizan, °non-aligned, unaligned, unaffiliated, °independent, non-committed, uncommitted, °neutral, uninvolved, °free, (sitting) on the °fence: *Choose between non-partisan and coalition candidates.* **2** °impartial, even-handed, °fair, °just, °objective, unbiased, °unprejudiced, °equitable, °dispassionate, °disinterested: *One could not find a more non-partisan judge than Sir Ronald.*
—*n.* **3** °independent, °neutral, mugwump: *I am a non-partisan on the subject of privatization of public utilities.*

nonplus *v.* confound, °perplex, °puzzle, °confuse, °dismay, baffle, °stop, °check, °stun, °shock, °dumbfound *or* dumfound, °take aback, °astonish, °astound, *US* faze, *Colloq* bring up short, °flummox, °stump: *She was nonplussed to learn that Simpson had been arrested.*

non-productive *adj.* **1** unproductive, °barren, °sterile, °infertile, unfertile, unfruitful, infecund: *Non-productive land was left uncultivated.* **2** °ineffectual, °bootless, °ineffective, °impractical, unavailing, °pointless, °useless, °worthless, °wasteful, time-consuming, time-wasting: *Executives should spend more time working and less in non-productive meetings discussing the work to be done.*

nonsense *n.* **1** °rubbish, °drivel, °gibberish, °gobbledegook *or* gobbledygook, twaddle, °trash, °babble, balderdash, °moonshine, °bombast, fustian, rodomontade, puffery, flummery, blather *or* blether, bunkum, poppycock, stuff and nonsense, double-talk, °jargon, °mumbo-jumbo, jabberwocky, cackle, gas, °palaver, *Colloq* bunk, piffle, °rot, bosh, eyewash, hogwash, malarkey, bilge (water), boloney *or* baloney, claptrap, °hot air, *Brit* tosh, *Old-fashioned Brit* gammon, °waffle, *US* apple-sauce, horse feathers, °garbage, bushwa; *Slang* crap, tripe, bull, hooey, double Dutch, *Taboo slang* bullshit, horseshit, *Brit* (a load of old) cobblers: *Watson's speech on the benefits of tobacco was unmitigated nonsense.* **2** °mischief, clowning, antics, capering, horseplay, pranks, °tricks, °jokes, silliness, foolishness, inanity, frivolity, tomfoolery, joking, jesting, waggishness, buffoonery, shenanigans, *Colloq* °monkey business, *Brit* °monkey tricks, *US* monkeyshines: *Keep up this nonsense and you'll get into a lot of trouble!*

nonsensical *adj.* °senseless, °meaningless, °absurd, °ridiculous, °ludicrous, laughable, °preposterous, irrational, warped, askew, °crazy, °mad, °silly, °foolish, °hare-brained, asinine, idiotic, moronic, imbecilic, °stupid, °dumb, *Colloq* nutty, screwy, cock-eyed, °fool, screwball, *Slang* loony: *What is your nonsensical excuse for being late this time?*

non-stop *adj.* **1** uninterrupted, °continuous, unbroken, °direct: *Is this a non-stop flight to New York?* **2** unending, °endless, interminable, unceasing, ceaseless, °continual, °continuous, uninterrupted, unbroken, °persistent, °relentless, °constant, unremitting, °steady, round-the-clock, ongoing, continuing, °unhesitating, unfaltering, °tireless; °regular, °habitual: *I told my neighbour that his non-stop rock 'n' roll music was driving me mad.*
—*adv.* **3** unendingly, endlessly, interminably, unceasingly, ceaselessly, continually, continuously, uninterruptedly, persistently, relentlessly, constantly, unremittingly, steadily, round-the-clock, day in and day out, tirelessly; regularly, habitually: *He continues to play his hi-fi non-stop.*

nook *n.* **1** °cranny, °recess, °niche, alcove, corner, °cavity, °crevice, °crack, °opening: *Flowers grew from the nooks in the wall.* **2** °retreat, hide-out, °hideaway, °nest; inglenook: *I curled up with a book in my nook next to the fireplace.*

noon *n.* twelve o'clock (noon), °midday, 1200 hours, noontime, high noon, *Archaic* noontide; noonday: *We sit down to lunch promptly at noon. The noon sun is terribly hot in the tropics.*

norm *n.* **1** °usual, °average, °mean, °normal: *The norm for the day is 12 degrees Celsius.* **2** °model, °standard, °type, °pattern, criterion, °rule, °measure, °gauge, °yardstick, benchmark: *That style of window became the norm for many years.*

normal *adj.* **1** °standard, °regular, °average, °conventional, °usual, run-of-the-mill, °ordinary, °routine, °universal, °general, °common, °customary, °natural, °typical, conformist, °orthodox; °healthy: *If living in this mess seems normal to you, we clearly have different* *standards. His temperature and pulse are normal.* **2** °sane, °stable, °rational, °reasonable, well-adjusted: *After he had set fire to his school, Julian's parents began to wonder if he was quite normal.*

normalize *v.* regularize, °standardize, °regulate, °control; °conform: *The program is directed at normalizing the codes used in keyboarding text.*

nosy *adj.* nosey, °curious, °inquisitive, prying, meddlesome, °spying, peeping, eavesdropping, *Colloq* snooping, snoopy: *Mind your own business and don't be so nosy.*

notable *adj.* **1** °noteworthy, °noted, °famous, famed, °well-known, °renowned, °illustrious, °important, °prominent, °eminent, °outstanding, °great, °distinguished, °celebrated, acclaimed: *Many notable people attended my college.* **2** °remarkable, °different, °distinctive, °singular, °unusual, uncommon, °pre-eminent, °peerless, °matchless, unmatched, unequalled, °unparalleled, °extraordinary, °conspicuous, °outstanding, °memorable, unforgettable, °striking: *She enjoyed a notable reputation as a cellist. Last night's notable performance was enjoyed by a capacity audience.*
—*n.* **3** °dignitary, °personage, °worthy, VIP; °celebrity, luminary, *Colloq* (°big) °name, °big shot: *Many notables attended the charity ball.*

notably *adv.* **1** °particularly, °especially, markedly, noticeably, signally, distinctly, remarkably, unusually, uncommonly, outstandingly, conspicuously, °clearly, °obviously, °evidently, °manifestly, specifically, curiously, oddly, uniquely, strangely, strikingly, shockingly, surprisingly, stunningly: *In the temperate zones, the seasons vary notably in length.* **2** meaningfully, significantly, importantly, prominently: *The viruses changed in notably different ways.*

notation *n.* **1** °note, °memorandum, jotting, °record, °reminder, °minute(s), °abstract, *Colloq* memo: *I shall make a notation of that in my diary.* **2** symbols, signs, °code, characters, symbolism: *In musical notation, a minim represents two crotchets.*

notch *n.* **1** °nick, °cut, dent, °indentation, °groove, cleft, °score, °mark, °gouge, °gash: *For every man he killed, the gunfighter cut a notch in the barrel of his gun.* **2** °step, °grade, °level, rung, °peg, °degree, °stage, gradation: *Gillian's promotion moves her up another notch towards the chairmanship.*
—*v.* **3** °nick, °cut, dent, indent, °groove, °score, °mark, °gash, °gouge: *You notch the end of the arrow to admit the bowstring.* **4** ***notch up***: °gain, °win, °accomplish, °achieve, °score, °register, °mark (up): *The All-India cricket team has notched up another win.*

notched *adj.* serrate(d), sawtooth(ed), crenellate(d), crenate, serriform, pinked, scalloped, zigzag, toothed, dentate, denticulate(d), dentiform: *The flower has notched yellow petals. The vase was decorated with a notched pattern.*

note *n.* **1** See **notation, 1,** above. **2** °message, °letter, communication, (piece of) correspondence, °memorandum, epistle, postcard *or* (postal) °card, fan °letter, love-letter, billet doux, bread-and-butter °letter, °word, °line, thank-you note, *Colloq* memo, *US old-fashioned* mash note: *She sent Rob a note only last week asking him to attend the meeting.* **3** °comment, commentary, °remark, °observation, °explanation, annotation, footnote, side-note, marginalia (*pl.*), °gloss, critique, °criticism, *Literary* scholium, exegesis, eisegesis, *Technical* shoulder-note: *Her notes on insect behaviour are of great interest.* **4** banknote, °money, °bill, currency, °treasury note; promissory note, °demand note, °bill of °exchange, °letter of °credit, (bank) °draft, note of hand; *Colloq* folding °money: *I found a packet of notes dropped by the bank robbers. The bank is holding my note for £10,000.* **5** °theme, °characteristic, °motif, °element, °quality, °mood, °tone, °tenor: *There is a note of angry frustration that runs through her writing.* **6** °signal, °cue, intimation, °hint, °inkling, °suspicion, °clue, °suggestion, °idea, °tip, *Slang* tip-off: *Her greeting, though warm, contained a note of suspicion. On that note, I decided to leave.* **7** °heed, °attention, °notice, °regard, °respect, °thought, *Colloq US* °mind: *Note of the prosecutor's objection to that line of questioning has been taken.* **8** °mark, consequence, °substance, °importance, °moment, °weight, °distinction, °merit, °prestige, (°high) °rank *or* °standing, eminence, °prominence, repute, °reputation, °renown: *People of note have been entertained at our table.* **9** °tone, °sound; °key: *He knows the music but gets the notes wrong.* **10** ***notes***: jottings, impressions, °record(s), °report, (°thumbnail) sketch, (°rough) °draft, °outline, °synopsis: *The entire account is based on the notes she made during the trial.*
—*v.* **11** °notice, °observe, °perceive, °see, °mark, °think about, give °thought to, °consider, °contemplate, °study, pay °attention to, °attend to; °look into, °investigate, °check out: *Have you ever noted how people try to avoid you because of your bad temper? Note how quickly the days seem to grow shorter towards the end of summer. A detective has been assigned to note every move the suspect makes.* **12** °record, °register, °write down, °put *or* °set down, put on °record, °jot down, put in °writing, °chronicle: *The traffic warden noted down the number-plate of the car.* **13** call °attention to, °remark on *or* about, °mention, °report, °touch on, °comment on *or* about: *The report failed to note the disappearance of the murder weapon.*

noted *adj.* respected, °eminent, °distinguished, °illustrious, esteemed, acclaimed; °well-known, °famous, famed, °prominent, °celebrated, °notable, °popular; °notorious: *We are pleased to welcome the noted violinist, David Popov. Was it his aunt or his mother who ran the noted house of ill repute near Brighton?*

noteworthy *adj.* °notable, °exceptional, °extraordinary, out of the °ordinary, °unusual, °rare, uncommon, °singular, °unique, °different: *Miss Byrne has made many a noteworthy contribution to our knowledge of local Roman sites.*

nothing *n.* **1** °naught *or* nought, °nothing at all *or* whatsoever, no thing, not anything, *Taboo slang Brit* bugger-all, (sweet) Fanny Adams *or* F.A., SFA: *Nothing that you tell me can be held against you in court. You may think it important, but I tell you it is nothing.* **2** cipher, °zero, °nobody, nonentity: *If it weren't for her, he would be nothing.* **3** °trifle, bagatelle, *Colloq* peanuts: *A million is nothing to him.*

notice *v.* **1** °note, take *or* make °note (of), take notice (of), pay *or* give °attention to, °attend (to), °heed, take °heed (of), give °heed to, °mark, °remark, °mind, °observe, °perceive, °see: *Notice how quickly he retracted his remarks when challenged. I waved to them, but they didn't notice me.* **2** °mind, °observe, °perceive, discern, °see, °detect, °make out, °identify, °recognize, *Colloq* °spot: *I noticed signs of illness when I visited her.*
—*n.* **3** °attention, awareness, consciousness, °perception, °observation, °cognizance: *Let me bring to your notice the second paragraph on page six.* **4** °regard, °consideration, °respect, °observation, °attention, °note, °heed: *They have published many books worthy of notice. He considers matters of money beneath his notice.* **5** notification, °announcement, °information, °advice; °warning, intimation: *A notice showing the currency exchange rates is posted in the bank. The company let Corbett go without notice.* **6** °criticism, critique, °review, °comment, commentary: *The play has enjoyed excellent notices in the London newspapers.* **7** ***give notice***: °warn, admonish, °notify, °announce, °advise, °inform: *British Rail gave notice of a curtailment of service to this station. Barry gave notice today of his resignation.*

noticeable *adj.* **1** °discernible, perceivable, °observable, °perceptible, recognizable, distinguishable, °visible, palpable, °manifest, °distinct, °evident, °clear, clear-cut, °conspicuous, °obvious; °patent, unmistakable, °undisguised, unconcealed: *Is the scratch noticeable? Wrinkles around the eyes are one of the first noticeable signs of ageing.* **2** °noteworthy, °notable, °significant, °signal, °remarkable, °important, °singular, °exceptional, °pronounced, °distinct, especial,

°considerable, °major: *After the reprimand, there was a noticeable improvement in his work.*

notify *v.* **1** °inform, °tell, °advise, °alert, apprise, °warn: *She notified us that she might come in late today. They wrote to notify shareholders of the new share offer.* **2** °announce, °publish, °declare, °proclaim, give °notice of; °intimate, °hint: *The arrival of the first salmon notified to us the change of season.*

notion *n.* **1** °idea, °thought, concept, °conception, °image, °impression, general °idea, (°mental) °picture, °inkling: *She has a pretty good notion of who did it. I haven't the slightest notion of what you are talking about.* **2** °fancy, whim, crotchet, whimsy, caprice, impulse, °inclination, vagary, °conceit, °quirk, °kink: *She suddenly took a notion to fly to New York and left.*

notoriety *n.* notoriousness, disrepute, °dishonour, °disgrace, °infamy, °shame, °discredit, °scandal, °stain, °blot, obloquy, ignominy, opprobrium: *The notoriety attending his latest escapades displeased the prime minister.*

notorious *adj.* **1** °disreputable, °dishonourable, °disgraceful, °infamous, °shameful, shaming, °embarrassing, discreditable, °scandalous, °naughty, °flagrant, ignominious, opprobrious: *Charles was yet again seen in public with a notorious arms dealer.* **2** °celebrated, °renowned, °famous, °well-known, fabled, °legendary, °memorable: *Annie was notorious for riding her horse to victory in every event.*

notwithstanding *adv.* **1** °nevertheless, °nonetheless, °despite that, in °spite of that, °yet, anyway: *He was refused permission to go but he left notwithstanding.*
—*prep.* **2** °despite, in °spite of, °regardless of, in the °face of, against: *Notwithstanding his mother's objections, George married Marsha.*
—*conj.* **3** although, °though, °even °though, °despite the fact that: *The product was almost totally unknown, notwithstanding it had been on the market for years.*

nourish *v.* **1** °feed, °sustain, °support, °maintain, °keep, °provide for, °care for, take °care of, °look after, nurture, °nurse: *The child seems to be thriving and well nourished.* **2** °foster, °cherish, °nurse, °maintain, °harbour, °keep, nurture, °sustain: *Iago nourished a terrible hatred for Othello.* **3** °strengthen, °fortify, °encourage, °promote, °stimulate, °cultivate, °help, °advance, °aid: *These malcontents continue to nourish trouble in the party ranks.*

nourishment *n.* °food, °sustenance, nutriment, nutrition, victuals: *You must take nourishment to maintain your strength.*

novel *adj.* **1** °new, °unusual, °unfamiliar, unconventional, °fresh, °different, °original, °creative; untested, °untried: *I have a novel idea for the design of an ultralight aircraft.*
—*n.* **2** °story, °tale, °narrative, °romance; novella, novelette, best-seller, *Colloq* blockbuster: *The members of our company board behave like characters out of a novel.*

novelty *n.* **1** °originality, newness, uniqueness, freshness, innovativeness: *We are enthusiastic about the novelty of the new sales campaign.* **2** °gimmick, gimcrack, °trifle, °gewgaw, °bauble, knick-knack, °toy, trinket, °ornament, °plaything, Brummagem, kickshaw: *New subscribers receive as a premium some novelty, like a ball-point pen or a cheap clock.*

novice *n.* beginner, neophyte, °newcomer, proselyte, tiro *or* tyro, noviciate *or* novitiate, °learner, °amateur, °initiate, °apprentice, trainee, probationer, fledgling *or Brit also* fledgeling, *Brit* fresher *or US* freshman, *Colloq* °greenhorn, rookie: *She is a mere novice at parachuting.*

now *adv.* **1** at °present, °just now, °right now, at the °present °time *or* °moment, at this (°very) °moment *or* °minute *or* °second *or* °instant: *He's in the shower and cannot come to the phone now.* **2** these days, °nowadays, today, in these times, at the °moment, in this day and age, under *or* in the °present circumstances *or* conditions, in the °present °climate, things being what they are, contemporarily, any more, any longer; for the °time being, for the nonce: *What makes you say that the minimum wage is enough to live on now? Selling now might bring the highest price.* **3** at °once, °immediately, °right away, without °delay, instantly, °promptly, *Chiefly law* instanter, *Chiefly Brit* °straight away: *I want you here now—not in five minutes, but now!* **4** ***now and then*** *or* ***again***: °occasionally, from time to time, at times, on °occasion, °sometimes, sporadically, °once in a while, every now and then *or* again, randomly, intermittently; °infrequently, °seldom, °rarely, °once in a blue moon: *There was a power cut now and then. He visits his mother only now and then.*
—*adj.* **5** °contemporary, up to °date, °modern, °stylish, °fashionable, °trendy, *Colloq* in, with it: *Advertisers must appeal to the yuppies of the now generation.*

nowadays *adv.* See **now, 2,** above.

nub *n.* **1** °projection, protuberance, °knob, boss, °lump, °bump, knop, °protrusion, °bulge, node, °knot; excrescence, °swelling, tumescence: *Press the small nub on the side to open the door.* **2** °essence, °core, °heart, °nucleus, crux, °point, °gist, °pith, °kernel, °nucleus, °meat, (°sum and) °substance, °main °issue, gravamen: *Let's get to the nub of the argument.*

nuclear *adj.* atomic: *He joined the protest march against nuclear weapons.*

nucleus *n.* °core, °heart, °centre, °kernel, °pith, °focus, °nub: *We already have the nucleus of a very good team. The market square was the nucleus around which many towns were built.*

nude *adj.* unclothed, undressed, uncovered, *au naturel,* °bare, °naked, in the nude, stark °naked, undraped, without a stitch (on), *Colloq* in the buff, in the altogether, in one's birthday suit, *Brit* starkers, *Brit and Australian* in the nuddy: *A nude man streaked across the football pitch.*

nudge *v.* **1** °jog, °poke, elbow, °jab, °dig, °bump, °prompt, shove; °prod, °push, *US* °encourage: *I had to nudge him to stay awake for the film's thrilling climax.*
—*n.* **2** °jog, °poke, elbow, °jab, °dig, °bump, shove; °prod, °push, °encouragement: *Nigel just needs a nudge in the right direction.*

nuisance *n.* **1** °annoyance, °inconvenience, °trial, °ordeal, °burden, irritation, irritant, °thorn in the flesh *or* side, °difficulty, °bother, *US* bur(r) under the saddle, *Colloq* °pain (in the neck *or* rear), °headache, hassle, *Slang US and Canadian* °pain in the butt, *Taboo slang* °pain in the *Brit* arse, *or US* ass: *Having to paint the room again was a terrible nuisance.* **2** °bore, °pest, °nag, °tease, tormentor *or* tormenter: *James has made a nuisance of himself by telephoning every fifteen minutes.*

numb *adj.* **1** numbed, benumbed, °insensible, insensate, °dead, deadened, without °feeling, sensationless, °senseless; asleep: *My feet are numb from the cold.*
—*v.* **2** benumb, anaesthetize, °drug, °deaden, °dull, °freeze, °paralyse, immobilize, °stun: *The doctor numbed my hand before removing the wart. Fear numbed her, and she felt nothing as the monster approached.*

number *n.* **1** numeral, integer, °figure, digit: *The columns of numbers were entered in a neat hand.* **2** °few, °handful, °crowd, slew, °gang, °bunch, °party, bevy, covey, troop, °company, °platoon, °swarm, horde, multitude, °mob, °host, army, °mass, hundred, thousand, million, billion; °several, °many, numbers, legions, *US and Canadian* slew(s), *Colloq* loads, tons: *A number of people attended the meeting. An enormous number of viruses could fit on the head of a pin.* **3** °issue; °edition, °copy: *The fourth number of the quarterly is published at the end of the year.*
—*v.* **4** °count, °enumerate, °compute, °calculate, °tally, °figure (up), °add (up), °include, °total, tot (up), °reckon, °sum (up): *Who can number the stars?*

numberless *adj.* uncountable, uncounted, countless, innumerable, incalculable, °immeasurable, numerous, °untold, myriad, °infinite: *Although seemingly* *numberless, the number of grains of sand in the universe is calculable.*

nuptial *adj.* °bridal, °matrimonial, °wedding, spousal, °wedded, marital; connubial, conjugal, *Literary* hymeneal: *The nuptial arrangements have been made.*

nurse *n.* **1** angel of mercy, Florence Nightingale, *Brit* sister: *I awoke to see two nurses bending over me.* —*v.* **2** °care for, °look after, °tend, °attend, °minister to, °treat; nurture, °foster, °coddle, °baby, °pamper, °cherish, °preserve, °keep alive, °cultivate, °develop: *During his illness, she nursed him night and day. We nursed the company along through the first year.* **3** wet-nurse, suckle, breast-feed, °nourish: *Nursing mothers must be careful about what they eat.* **4** °preserve, °harbour, °keep alive, nurture, °foster: *She has nursed a grudge against him for ten years.*

nutritious *adj.* healthful, °healthy, nutritive, °wholesome, life-giving, °beneficial, salutary, nourishing, alimentary, nutrimental: *Be sure you eat a nutritious breakfast every day.*

O

oar *n.* **1** °paddle, scull: *The ancient galleys sometimes had six men on each oar.* **2** oarsman, oarswoman, bencher, sculler, rower, paddler: *With Hanson out because of his back, we'll need a new oar for tomorrow's race.*

oasis *n.* **1** °fertile °patch, watering hole: *In the desert, you cannot always be sure whether you are looking at an oasis or a mirage.* **2** haven, °refuge, (°safe) °harbour, °sanctuary, °retreat, asylum, °resort, °sanctum: *We escaped to the cottage, a tiny oasis away from the city's frenetic activity.*

oath *n.* **1** °vow, avowal, °pledge, °promise, °word (of °honour), °promise, °plight, °guarantee *or* guaranty, °warrant *or* °warranty, (sworn) °statement, *Archaic* troth: *She has taken an oath to tell the whole truth.* **2** °curse, °profanity, °blasphemous language *or* expression *or* word, imprecation, malediction, swear-word, °expletive, four-letter word, obscenity, °dirty word: *The door slammed on his finger and he muttered a foul oath.*

obedience *n.* compliance, dutifulness, °observance, °respect, respectfulness, tractability, conformity *or* conformance, °yielding, conformability, adaptability, °agreement, agreeability, agreeableness, acquiescence, submissiveness, °submission, subservience, docility, passiveness, passivity: *The abbot demanded unquestioning obedience with regard to every rule of the monastic order.*

obedient *adj.* compliant, °dutiful, duteous, °observant, °respectful, °tractable, °yielding, conformable, °adaptable, °agreeable, amenable, acquiescent, °submissive, subservient, docile, °passive, °timid, biddable, pliant: *Prunella was always an obedient child. All matter and energy is obedient to the laws of physics.*

obeisance *n.* °deference, °respect, respectfulness, °homage, °submission, °reverence, °honour: *As she entered the chamber, she made obeisance to the king.*

obese *adj.* °fat, overweight, °stout, fleshy, °gross, corpulent, °heavy, °plump, portly, tubby, pudgy, °chubby, paunchy, °rotund, pot-bellied, *Rare* abdominous: *I sat down next to an obese person who occupied nearly two chairs.*

obesity *n.* corpulence, plumpness, tubbiness, chubbiness, grossness, *embonpoint*, rotundity, portliness, paunchiness, °size, °bulk, °weight, avoirdupois: *Risk factors with respect to heart disease include smoking, bad diet, obesity, and family history of heart disease.*

obey *v.* **1** °comply (with), °agree (to), °consent (to), °submit (to), °abide (by), °observe, °respect, adhere to, °follow, °conform (to *or* with), acquiesce (to *or* in), °mind, °accept, °heed, °defer to, °yield (to), knuckle under (to), give °way (to), °surrender (to), °succumb (to), °give in (to), °truckle to, °bow to, °bend to, take *or* °accept orders from: *Unfortunately, Ogilvy has obeyed his baser instincts in making the punishment fit the crime. Everything must obey the laws of nature. Harold obeys Millie's slightest whim.* **2** °discharge, °execute, °effect, °carry out, °fulfil, °meet, °satisfy, do, °perform; °serve, °act: *We obeyed the colonel's orders to the letter. It is your function to command, mine to obey.*

obituary *n.* necrology, °death notice, °eulogy, necrologue, *Colloq* obit: *Mark Twain is one of the few people ever to have read his own obituary.*

object *n.* **1** °thing, °tangible, °item; °reality, °entity, °fact, °phenomenon: *A number of objects lay on the table. Thoughts may be considered as objects of the imagination.* **2** °focus, °target, °butt, °aim, °destination, °quarry, °goal: *The object of my affection has married someone else.* **3** °purpose, °end, °intention, °objective, °reason, °intent, °idea, °goal: *The object of our visit is to ask you a few questions.* —*v.* **4** °protest (to *or* against), °interfere (with), °raise °objection(s) (to), °argue (against), °oppose, be against, take °exception (to), °disapprove (of), draw the line (at), °complain (about), remonstrate (over *or* about), take a °stand (against), °refuse: *I won't object if you want to bring the wine. Would you object to rereading that passage? If they ask me, I cannot object.*

objection *n.* °protest, °opposition, °exception, °argument, °challenge, °interference, demur *or* demurral *or* demurrer, °question, °doubt, °disapproval, °interference, °complaint, remonstration, remonstrance, °stand, °refusal, °dislike, antipathy: *The meeting proceeded without further objection from the audience. If you have no objection, I'd like to leave now. The secretary has raised an objection to the method of procedure.*

objective *adj.* **1** °fair, °impartial, °just, °judicious, °equitable, °neutral, °disinterested, °dispassionate, open-handed, open-minded, °detached, unbiased, °unprejudiced, unbigoted, even-handed, uncoloured, unjaundiced: *How can you be objective about the guilt or innocence of your own child?* —*n.* **2** °target, °goal, °object, °aim, °purpose, °end (in view), °intent, °intention, °design, °aspiration, °ambition, °hope: *If we capture the flag, we shall have gained our objective. My objective is to win the pentathlon.*

objectivity *n.* impartiality, fairness, fair-mindedness, equitableness, equitability, even-handedness, neutrality, disinterest, °detachment, °indifference, dispassion: *The jury's objectivity was never in doubt.*

obligate *n.* °oblige, °pledge, °commit, °bind; °require, compel, constrain, °force: *I feel deeply obligated to her for her kindness to our children. We are obligated to do what we are told.*

obligation *n.* **1** °responsibility, °duty, charge, °burden, onus; °accountability, °liability, °trust; °demand, °requirement, compulsion, *Literary* devoir: *It was Frank's obligation to get the children home safely. Civil servants have an obligation to serve the people. I could never fulfil all my obligations.* **2** constraint, °requirement, °contract, °promise, °pledge, °bond, °agreement, covenant: *The company is under no obligation to replace a product because the customer dislikes its colour. I am under an obligation to her for introducing us.* **3** °debt, °liability: *Denby may be unable to meet all his obligations.*

obligatory *adj.* required, demanded, °necessary, requisite, compulsory, °mandatory; °incumbent; °indispensable, °essential: *Has she been able to meet all the obligatory qualifications?*

oblige *v.* **1** °accommodate, °indulge, °favour, °serve, °please, °cater to, °gratify: *The hotelier obliged us with every luxury he had to offer. Please oblige us by keeping your dog on a lead.* **2** °make, °require, °demand, °force, compel, coerce, °bind, °obligate: *What hold has she over you that obliges you to do her housework?*

obliged *adj.* **1** °thankful, °grateful, appreciative, °beholden, °indebted, obligated: *We are deeply obliged to you for lending us your car.* **2** °bound, required, compelled, °forced, made, obligated: *Under the terms of the agreement, I am obliged to repay the debt by May.*

obliging *adj.* °accommodating, °willing, °indulgent, °gracious, °courteous, °civil, °considerate, °polite, °agreeable, amenable, °kind, °kindly, °helpful, °friendly, °amiable, °neighbourly, °supportive: *It was very obliging of you to look after my cat while I was gone.*

oblique *adj.* **1** slanting, slanted, sloping, aslant, °inclined, diagonal, inclining, angled, angling, canted, canting, banked, banking, cambered, °crooked, askew, °divergent, diverging, tilted, atilt, tilting: *The roof joins the wall at an oblique angle.* **2** awry, °devious, °roundabout, °indirect, circuitous, circumlocutionary, °evasive, °sly, °sidelong, °offhand, °surreptitious, °furtive, implied, clandestine, underhand(ed), °deceitful, °deceptive, °false: *She made some oblique comments about the candidate's wife.*

obliterate *v.* **1** °erase, expunge, °rub out, efface, eradicate, °wipe out, °delete, dele, °strike off *or* out, °strike from, °rule out, °eliminate, °write off: *After the scandal, that name was obliterated from the roll of honour.* **2** annihilate, °destroy, °kill, °exterminate, °wipe out, °eliminate, °blot out, eradicate, extirpate: *The entrance to the cave was completely obliterated by the explosion.*

oblivion *n.* **1** blankness, blackness, darkness, °obscurity, nothingness, nihility, anonymity, extinction, non-existence, °void, °limbo: *The rock band enjoyed brief fame, then sank into oblivion.* **2** unawareness, obliviousness, forgetfulness, heedlessness, °disregard, unconsciousness, insensibility: *I sank back into the sweet oblivion of deep sleep.*

oblivious *adj.* °unaware, °unconscious, unmindful, disregardful, °insensible, insensitive, °distant, unconcerned, °detached, removed, unfeeling, abstracted, °absent-minded, °forgetful, Lethean: *Many are completely oblivious to the plight of the starving millions in Africa.*

obnoxious *adj.* °revolting, °repulsive, °repugnant, °disgusting, °offensive, objectionable, fulsome, noisome, °vile, °repellent, °nauseous, nauseating, sickening, °foul, noxious, mephitic, °unsavoury, execrable, °abominable, °abhorrent, °loathsome, detestable, °hateful, odious, °scurvy, °base, °obscene, °despicable, °awful, °terrible, °unpalatable, °distasteful, unlikeable, unpleasant, °nasty, *Colloq chiefly Brit* °beastly: *Mary's obnoxious sister even has obnoxious table manners.*

obscene *adj.* **1** inelegant, °improper, °rude, °impure, °unchaste, °shameless, °shameful, °indecent, °immodest, °off colour, indecorous, indelicate, °risqué, °vulgar, °immoral, °degenerate, amoral, °dissolute, °broad, °suggestive, °erotic, °sensual, ribald, debauched, °wanton, °loose, °libertine, °bawdy, °blue, scabrous, °coarse, °dirty, °filthy, smutty, °pornographic, libidinous, °lewd, licentious, °lecherous, °lustful, goatish, °carnal, ruttish, °lascivious, salacious, °prurient, °disgusting, °offensive, °repulsive, °foul, °abominable, °vile, °loathsome, °gross, foul-mouthed, °scurrilous, scatological, *Literary* Cyprian, Paphian, Fescennine, thersitical: *In the cinema business, 'adult' and 'obscene' seem to be synonyms.* **2** °evil, °wicked, heinous, °atrocious, °awful, °outrageous, °repulsive, °shocking, °repellent, °obnoxious, off-putting, objectionable, °beastly, intolerable, °insufferable, °unpalatable, °distasteful, °nauseous, nauseating, sickening, execrable, °despicable, °nasty: *The obscene monster dashed the brave warriors to the rocks far below.*

obscure *adj.* **1** °dark, unlit, °gloomy, °sombre, °dismal, °murky, °dusky, °black, Cimmerian, tenebrous, °dim, °faint, blurred, °veiled, °shadowy, subfusc, subfuscous, umbral, °shady, °hazy, foggy, befogged, clouded, °nebulous, °overcast, cloudy: *The traveller's lantern was barely seen in the obscure reaches of the wood.* **2** unclear, °uncertain, °ambiguous, °vague, °hazy, °doubtful, dubious, °equivocal, °indefinite, °indistinct, °fuzzy, blurred, °confused, confusing, Delphic, °puzzling, enigmatic, °perplexing, baffling, mystifying, °mysterious, °cryptic, °incomprehensible, °unfamiliar, °foreign, °strange: *The sorcerer muttered some obscure words, and a golden horse stood prancing before them.* **3** °secret, concealed, hidden, °remote, °out-of-the-way, °inconspicuous, unnoticeable, °secluded, °unnoticed: *The caped figure scurried down the alley and disappeared into some obscure doorway.* **4** °unknown, °unheard-of, anonymous, unnamed, °insignificant, unimportant, °inconsequential, °humble, °lowly, °mean, inglorious, °inconspicuous, °undistinguished, °unnoticed, °unsung, °minor, little-known: *Though extremely popular, the song was written by an obscure composer.* **5** abstruse, arcane, °recondite, esoteric, °intricate, complex, °occult, out of the ordinary, °unfamiliar, *Colloq* far-out: *He is an authority on some obscure subject like Coptic calligraphy.*
—*v.* **6** °cover, °conceal, °hide, °veil, °shroud, °cloak, °mask, °screen, °disguise, °keep from: *Her link with military intelligence was obscured from her family.* **7** °dim, bedim, cloud, becloud, °dull, °shroud, °shade, adumbrate, °overshadow, darken, obfuscate, °block, °eclipse: *The street lamp was obscured by trees.*

obscurity *n.* **1** dimness, darkness, °gloom, murk, murkiness, duskiness, °dusk, blackness, faintness, blurriness, °shade, °shadow, haze, °fog, cloudiness, nebulousness: *The two of them vanished into the obscurity of the night.* **2** abstruseness, ambiguousness, intricacy, °complexity, unintelligibility; °mystery, arcanum, °secret, esoterica (*pl.*): *Can he truly believe that he has fathomed all the obscurities of Scripture?* **3** insignificance, unimportance, ingloriousness, inconspicuousness, anonymity, namelessness, °limbo: *After a fleeting surge of popularity, punk rock sank into obscurity.*

obsequious *adj.* °low, cringing, toadying, toadyish, sycophantic, sycophantish, unctuous, truckling, °grovelling, crawling, fawning, deferential, °ingratiating, °menial, °flattering, °servile, slavish, subservient, °submissive, abject, °mealy-mouthed, °slimy, *Colloq* boot-licking, *Chiefly Brit* smarmy, *Taboo slang* brown-nosing, *Brit* arse-kissing, arse-licking, *US* ass-licking, ass-kissing: *He is surrounded with obsequious followers who cater to his every whim.*

observable *adj.* °perceptible, perceivable, °noticeable, °discernible, recognizable, detectable, °visible, °apparent, °distinct, °evident, °manifest, °plain, °obvious, °clear, °explicit, °transparent, °patent, °tangible, unmistakable: *A marked change in public sentiment became at once observable.*

observance *n.* **1** °observation, observing, °obedience, obeying, compliance, complying, conformity, conforming, adherence, adhering, keeping, accordance, °regard, °recognition, recognizing, °respect, respecting, °heed, heeding, °attention: *Observance of the rules by everyone makes for a happier community.* **2** °ceremony, °celebration, °ceremonial, °practice, °rite, °ritual, °service, °performance, °form, °custom, °convention, °tradition, °formality, °usage, °habit, wont, °institution: *Almost all the fine arts derived their origin from religious observances.* **3** °observation, °examination, inspection, °scrutiny, looking, watching: *His observance of the passing scene was chronicled in his diary.*

observant *adj.* **1** watchful, °alert, °attentive, °vigilant, on the °lookout, on the qui vive, on °guard, wide °awake, regardful, °mindful, °aware, °keen, keen-eyed, °sharp-eyed, °eagle-eyed, °perceptive, °sharp, °shrewd: *Hannay was observant of all who passed him on the way to the train. How very observant of you to spot the man in the crowd!* **2** Usually, ***observant of***: °obedient (to), compliant (with), °respectful (of), heedful (of), °attentive (to *or* of), conformist (to), adherent (to): *One must be always be observant of the rules of the road.*

observation *n.* **1** watching, °examination, °scrutiny, inspection, viewing, °survey, °surveillance; °notice, °discovery, °attention, awareness: *The police put the house under 24-hour observation. The smuggled* *weapon escaped the guard's observation.* **2** °comment, °remark, °note, °reflection, °opinion, °sentiment, point of °view, °impression, °feeling, commentary, °criticism; utterance, °word, °announcement, °pronouncement, °proclamation, °declaration: *She made a number of trenchant observations concerning life in Britain today.*

observe *v.* **1** °obey, °abide by, °comply with, be heedful of, °attend to, °conform to, °regard, °keep, °follow, adhere to, °respect, pay °attention to: *We observed the prohibition against swimming.* **2** °watch, °look at, °examine, °monitor, °scrutinize, °study, °regard, °view, °inspect, °pore over, °contemplate, consider, *Colloq* °check (out *or* up on), °check over, °size up, *Slang* case: *The naturalists went to the Arctic to observe the polar bears.* **3** °see, °mark, °notice, °look, °perceive: *Observe how swiftly the skin forms pustules when this substance is applied.* **4** Sometimes, ***observe on*** *or* ***upon***: °comment (on *or* upon), °remark (on *or* upon), °mention, °say, °note, °refer (to), make °reference to, animadvert on *or* upon *or* to; °state, °declare: *It is impolite to observe on others' manners. He couldn't help observing to his cell-mate how easy it would be to escape.* **5** °celebrate, °keep, solemnize, °respect, °keep holy, °mark, °commemorate, °memorialize, °remember, °recognize: *We always observe the sabbath.*

observer *n.* °witness, °eyewitness, °spectator, viewer, °onlooker, beholder, watcher, looker-on; non-participant: *UN observers reported that the battle was over.*

obsess *v.* °haunt, °harass, °plague, bedevil, °torment, °take over, preoccupy, °dominate, °control, °grip, °possess, °hold: *He was obsessed by the conviction that he could design a successful flying machine.*

obsession *n.* °fixed °idea, *idée fixe,* °fixation, °conviction, preoccupation, prepossession, °passion, °mania, °phobia, *Colloq* hang-up, °thing: *Thoughts of death became his constant obsession.*

obsessive *adj.* haunting, harassing, tormenting, dominating, controlling, possessing, all-encompassing, °passionate, unshakeable *or* unshakable: *She has an obsessive fear of heights.*

obsolescent *adj.* fading, waning, on the °wane, declining, °dying, on the way out, on the °decline, going *or* passing out of °use *or* °fashion *or* °style: *Much of yesterday's newest slang is obsolescent today.*

obsolete *adj.* out of °date, out of °fashion, out-dated, °*passé,* °out, °dead, outmoded, °old, °antiquated, antediluvian, °ancient, superannuated, dated, archaic, °old-fashioned, *démodé;* °unused, °disused, discarded, superseded, °extinct, *Colloq* °old hat: *The expression 'tickety-boo' is obsolete. He plays his 78-rpm records on an obsolete gramophone.*

obstacle *n.* °impediment, °hindrance, °obstruction, °hurdle, °hitch, catch, °snag, °stumbling-block, °barrier, °bar, °check: *The obstacles in the road prevented our proceeding further. One must often overcome many obstacles before achieving success.*

obstinacy *n.* obstinateness, stubbornness, doggedness, °tenacity, °persistence *or* persistency, mulishness, pigheadedness, wilfulness, contrariness, perverseness, perversity, cantankerousness, recalcitrance, uncooperativeness, rebelliousness, contumacy, contumaciousness, refractoriness, intractability, intransigence, pertinacity, pertinaciousness, obduracy, fixedness, stolidity, inflexibility, firmness, *Archaic* frowardness, *Colloq Brit* bloody-mindedness: *His obstinacy and narrow-mindedness made it impossible to work with him in any cooperative way.*

obstinate *adj.* °stubborn, dogged, °tenacious, °persistent, mulish, °perverse, headstrong, pigheaded, °single-minded, °wilful, strong-willed, °self-willed, °contrary, °recalcitrant, uncooperative, °rebellious, contumacious, refractory, intransigent, pertinacious, obdurate, °fixed, °inflexible, °stony, adamant, °set, unmoving, °immovable, inexorable, intractable, unchangeable, °resolute, °steadfast, unyielding, persevering, °stiff, °rigid, °hard, *Archaic* froward, *Colloq Brit* bloody-minded: *The obstinate man does not hold opinions—they hold him.*

obstreperous *adj.* vociferous, clamorous, °noisy, °loud, °raucous, °riotous, °uproarious, °tumultuous, °boisterous, °rowdy, rumbustious, °tempestuous, °unruly, °disorderly, unmanageable, uncontrollable, °uncontrolled, unrestrained, °irrepressible, out of control, °undisciplined, roisterous, °wild, turbulent, *Colloq* rambunctious, *Brit* mafficking: *The party was getting rough and some of the guests a bit too obstreperous.*

obstruct *v.* **1** °block, °bar, °check, °prevent, °stop (up), °arrest, °halt, °clog, make impassable; bring to a °standstill: *The vein is obstructed by a large blood clot. A clogged drain is obstructing the water.* **2** °hamper, °slow, °impede, °interfere with, °retard, °hinder, °interrupt, °delay, °stay, °stall: *An overturned truck obstructed traffic on the motorway.* **3** °preclude, °prevent, debar, °block, °prohibit, °forbid, °stop, °stand in the °way of: *They are manoeuvring to obstruct her from taking over the company.*

obstruction *n.* **1** °obstacle, °barrier, °bar, °check, °stumbling-block, °hindrance, °impediment, °hurdle, °hitch, °snag, catch, bottleneck, limitation, constraint, °restriction: *The fallen trees created an almost impassable obstruction.* **2** checking, stopping, cessation, proscription, °forbidding, forbiddance; hindering, impeding, limiting, °halting, slowing: *The obstruction of the bill's passage can be blamed on the Tories.*

obtain *v.* **1** °get, °procure, °acquire, °come by, °come into (the) °possession of, °secure, °get hold of *or* one's °hands on, °grasp, °capture, take °possession of, °seize; °buy, °purchase: *She has been unable to obtain the job she wants. You can obtain that kind of soap at the supermarket.* **2** °earn, °gain: *We talked to the manager about obtaining an increase in wages.* **3** °prevail, be in °force, be in °vogue, °exist, subsist, have (a) place, be °prevalent, be established, be °customary, °apply, be °relevant, °relate: *A different set of regulations obtains here.*

obtrude *v.* °thrust (oneself) forward *or* forth, °intrude, °impose (oneself), °force (oneself): *The best writers never obtrude between the reader and the story.*

obtrusive *adj.* interfering, °intrusive, meddling, °officious, meddlesome, importunate, °forward, °presumptuous, °forceful, *Colloq* °pushy: *She found him somewhat obtrusive—always giving advice when she least needed it.*

obtuse *adj.* **1** rounded, unpointed, °blunt: *When mature, the leaves become more obtuse.* **2** °dull, insensitive, unfeeling, imperceptive, °thick-skinned, °stolid, °thick, °dense, doltish, cloddish, thickheaded, dull-witted, dim-witted, slow-witted, (mentally) retarded, boneheaded, lumpish, loutish, oafish, °simple, simple-minded: *Luke is a bit too obtuse to get the point of the story.*

obvious *adj.* °clear, °plain, °apparent, °patent, °perceptible, °evident, °self-evident, clear-cut, °manifest, palpable, (much) in °evidence, °conspicuous, °open, °visible, °overt, ostensible, °pronounced, °prominent, °glaring, undeniable, unconcealed, unhidden, unsubtle, °distinct, °simple, bald, bald-faced, straightforward, °direct, self-explanatory, °indisputable, unmistakable: *There are obvious flaws in the fabric. The reason you were refused seemed obvious to me.*

obviously *adv.* °clearly, plainly, °apparently, patently, °evidently, °simply, certainly, of °course, undeniable, unmistakably, indubitably, °doubtless(ly): *You are obviously the right person for the assignment.*

occasion *n.* **1** °time, °moment, °circumstance, °incident, °occurrence, °opportunity, °chance, °opening, °advantage: *I took the occasion of the inquiry to leave town.* **2** °reason, °cause, °call, justification, °ground(s), °warrant, °provocation, prompting, impulse, stimulus, °incitement, °inducement: *Tom gave David no occasion to doubt his honesty.* **3** °event, °function, °happening, °affair, °observance, commemoration, °ceremony, °celebration, °gala, °party: *Grandpapa's ninetieth birthday* *was a great occasion. This hall is saved for important occasions.* **4 *on occasion***: See **occasionally,** below. —*v.* **5** give °rise to, °bring about, °cause, °bring on, °effect, °prompt, °provoke, °evoke, °call forth, °elicit, °call up, °induce, impel, °create, °generate, engender, °produce, °make (for): *An increase in the inflation rate occasions a decrease in the value of money.*

occasional *adj.* **1** °intermittent, °irregular, °periodic, °random, °sporadic, infrequent, °casual, °incidental: *They staged occasional raids on the arsenal. He works as an occasional farm hand.* **2** additional, °extra, °spare, °supplementary, °incidental, °auxiliary, °accessory: *We bought a few occasional chairs in case we have company.* **3** °special, °particular, °ceremonial, °ritual: *She writes occasional verses for memorial services.*

occasionally *adv.* °sometimes, on °occasion, (every) °now and then, from time to time, at times, (every) °now and again, °once in a while, every so often, periodically, intermittently, sporadically, irregularly, off and on: *We go up to the Lake District for a weekend occasionally. Trevor occasionally drops in at the local pub for a beer.*

occult *adj.* **1** °secret, °dark, concealed, °private, °privy, hidden, °obscure, °veiled, obscured, shrouded, °vague, abstruse, °shadowy, °mystical, °mysterious, cabbalistic, esoteric, °recondite, arcane: *Printing was kept an occult art for generations.* **2** magical, °mystical, alchemic(al), unexplained, unexplainable, °inexplicable, °puzzling, baffling, °perplexing, mystifying, °mysterious, °incomprehensible, inscrutable, indecipherable, impenetrable, unfathomable, transcendental, °supernatural, preternatural, mystic: *They dress in odd clothes and participate in occult rituals at peculiar times of the day and night.*
—*n.* **3** Usually, ***the occult***: the °supernatural, the °unknown, the °black arts; arcana, cabbala *or* kabbala; cabbalism *or* kabbalism, occultism, °sorcery, witchcraft, °black °magic: *Keith has studied the occult for many years.*

occupant *n.* °resident, °inhabitant, occupier, °tenant, lessee, leaseholder, renter, °owner, householder, indweller, dweller, °denizen, lodger, roomer, boarder; addressee; °incumbent: *The occupant of the flat upstairs is rarely home.*

occupation *n.* **1** °job, °position, °post, °situation, °appointment, °employment, °vocation, °line (of °work), °career, °field, °calling, °trade, *métier*, °craft, °skill, °profession, °business, °work: *Claverton pursued his occupation as a miniaturist for some fifty years.* **2** °possession, °tenure, occupancy, °rule, °control, suzerainty, subjugation, °subjection, °oppression, °bondage: *Terrible atrocities were committed while the land was under the occupation of the Mongols.* **3** °conquest, °seizure, appropriation, take-over: *Francisco Pizarro was responsible for the occupation of Peru.*

occupy *v.* **1** °capture, °seize, °take °possession of, °conquer, invade, °take over, °overrun, garrison, °dominate, °hold: *Rebel forces had occupied the capital and toppled the governor.* **2** °live *or* reside *or* °dwell in, °tenant, be established *or* ensconced *or* situated in, °establish *or* ensconce *or* °situate oneself in, °inhabit, be settled in *or* into, °settle in *or* into, °take up residence in, make one's °home in, °move in *or* into; be located in: *She occupies a luxurious flat in Belgravia.* **3** °engage, °busy, absorb, °monopolize, °hold, °take up *or* over, catch, °grab, °seize, °grip; °divert, °amuse, °entertain, °distract, °beguile, preoccupy, °hold (someone's) °attention, °interest, engross, °involve: *Other matters occupied my attention last Sunday. While one man was keeping the shopkeeper occupied, the other man was robbing the till.* **4** °fill (in *or* up), °take up, °cover, °extend over, °consume, °use (up), *Colloq* °eat up: *The car occupies more garage space than I thought it would. Housework occupies very little of my time.*

occur *v.* **1** °happen, take place, °arise, °come about, befall, come to pass, °chance, °appear, °surface, °materialize, °develop, become °manifest, °manifest itself, *Colloq* °transpire, crop up, °come off, °turn up: *We reported to the police all that had occurred. What occurred to make you late this time?* **2 *occur to***: °dawn on, °strike, °hit, °come to, °suggest itself to, cross (someone's) mind, enter (someone's) head, be brought to (someone's) °attention: *Has it occurred to you that she might not like opera?*

occurrence *n.* **1** °happening, °event, °incident, °phenomenon, °affair, °matter, °experience: *Earthquakes are frequent occurrences in California.* **2** °existence, °instance, °manifestation, materialization, °appearance, °development: *The occurrence of mutations diversifies the species.* **3** frequency, °incidence, °rate; °likelihood, °chance: *What is the recorded occurrence of typhoons in the South China Sea?*

ocean *n.* **1** (deep blue) °sea, (bounding) main, high °seas, the °deep, Davy Jones's locker, the depths, *Colloq* the briny, the °drink: *The sails filled, and our tiny craft was swept out into the open ocean.* **2** Often, ***oceans***: °flood, °abundance, multitude, °profusion, plethora, *Colloq* scads, loads, tons, °lots, oodles, gobs, zillions: *The direct mail campaign yielded oceans of responses.*

oceanic *adj.* °marine, pelagic, thalassic; salt-water, deep-water, aquatic, maritime, °sea, °ocean: *These creatures are chiefly oceanic, coming ashore only to breed.*

odd *adj.* **1** °strange, °peculiar, °unusual, uncommon, °different, unexpected, °unfamiliar, °extraordinary, °remarkable, atypical, untypical, °exotic, out of the ordinary, °unparalleled, unconventional, °exceptional, °unique, °singular, °individual, anomalous, idiosyncratic, °rare, °deviant, °outlandish, uncanny, °queer, °curious, °bizarre, °weird, °eccentric, °funny, °quaint, °fantastic, °freak, °abnormal, freakish, *Colloq* °offbeat, screwy, °kinky, freaky, *Slang Brit* barmy, °bent, rum, *US and Canadian* kooky: *Ebenezer is an odd name for a dog. Where did you get that odd hat? I cannot account for his odd behaviour.* **2** °occasional, °casual, part-time, °irregular, °random, °sporadic, discontinuous, °disconnected, °various, °varied, °miscellaneous, °sundry, °incidental: *After being made redundant, he worked at odd jobs for a year or so. The odd shower can be expected during the afternoon.* **3** °leftover, °surplus, °remaining, °unused, °spare, °superfluous, °extra: *After the patterns were cut, we were allowed to take the odd scraps of fabric.* **4** uneven, unmatched, unpaired: *This gallery has an odd number of columns.*

oddity *n.* **1** °peculiarity, strangeness, unnaturalness, curiousness, incongruity, incongruousness, °eccentricity, outlandishness, extraordinariness, unconventionality, bizarreness, weirdness, queerness, oddness, unusualness, individuality, °singularity, distinctiveness, anomalousness, anomaly, *Colloq* kinkiness, *US and Canadian* kookiness: *What caught my attention was the oddity of the clothes worn by the students.* **2** °peculiarity, °curiosity, °rarity, °freak, °original, °phenomenon, °character, °eccentric, °nonconformist, fish out of water, odd bird, *rara avis*, °misfit, square peg in a round hole, maverick, *Colloq* °card, °crank, weirdie *or* °weirdo, oner, *Brit* odd fish, *US and Canadian* kook, oddball, screwball: *The townspeople thought Albert an oddity, but we knew he was a genius.* **3** °peculiarity, irregularity, anomaly, idiosyncrasy, °eccentricity, deviation, °quirk, °mannerism, °twist, °kink, crotchet: *I suppose people all have their own oddities when it comes to food.*

odds *n.pl.* **1** chances, °likelihood, °probability: *The odds are that Janet will finish the job in time.* **2** °edge, °advantage, °lead, °superiority: *We have won before against greater odds.* **3** °difference, °inequality, °disparity, unevenness, °discrepancy, °dissimilarity, °distinction: *It makes no odds who you are, you may not go in there.* **4 *at odds***: at °variance, at loggerheads, at daggers drawn, at sixes and sevens, at cross purposes, at each other's throats, in °disagreement, in °opposition, on bad terms, not in keeping, out of line, inharmonious, conflicting, clashing, disagreeing, differing: *Teenagers have been at odds with their parents since* *time immemorial.* **5** ***odds and ends***: oddments, °fragments, debris, °leftovers, leavings, °remnants, °bits (and pieces), °particles, °shreds, snippets, scraps, °rubbish, °litter, *Colloq Brit* odds and sods: *We managed to pack everything into boxes except for a few odds and ends.*

odour *n.* **1** °smell, °scent, °aroma, °bouquet, °fragrance, °perfume, redolence; °stench, stink, fetor *or* foetor: *The air was filled with the odour of orange blossoms. The odour of rotting vegetation assailed our noses.* **2** °air, °breath, °hint, °suggestion, °atmosphere, °spirit, °quality, °flavour, °savour, °aura, °tone: *She would never allow the odour of scandal to touch her family.*

off *adv.* **1** away, °out, °elsewhere: *His secretary said that he'd gone off for the weekend.* **2** °distant, away, afar, far-off: *The U-boat was a mile off. Christmas is only a month off.*
—*adj.* **3** °incorrect, °wrong, °inaccurate, in °error, °mistaken, °misguided, misled, off the mark: *I'm afraid you're off on the question of the best way to approach him.* **4** °mad, °insane, °crazy, °eccentric, touched (in the head), *Colloq* dotty, dippy, nutty, potty: *Underwood's aunt is slightly off.* **5** °remote, °distant, °improbable, °unlikely: *He went to the station on the off chance that she would be on the midday train.* **6** off work, at °leisure, °idle, °free, °open; on °holiday: *Can you get the day off tomorrow to go on a picnic with me?* **7** °sour, °mouldy, °bad, °rotten, °rancid, turned, °high: *The cream smells a bit off.* **8** °bad, unpropitious, °disappointing, °unsatisfactory, disheartening, displeasing, °slack, °slow, substandard, below °par, below °average, °quiet: *It has been an off year for the local football team.* **9** cancelled, postponed: *The meeting is off till next week.* **10** situated, °fixed, supplied: *Is he really that well off? She was much worse off when they were married.*

offbeat *adj.* °strange, °eccentric, °bizarre, °weird, °peculiar, °odd, °queer, unconventional, °unorthodox, °Bohemian, idiosyncratic, °unusual, unexpected, °*outré*, °outlandish, °deviant, °novel, innovative, *Colloq* °kinky, °way-out, far-out, off-the-wall, freaky, °weirdo: *Jasper's offbeat, satirical humour has made him a popular comedian.*

off colour *adj.* **1** unwell, °ill, off °form, out of sorts, °queasy, °sick, °run down, °awful, °seedy, *Colloq* under the °weather, °poorly, *Slang* °lousy, °rotten: *I have been feeling off colour since eating that fish.* **2** indelicate, °risqué, ribald, °bawdy, °indecent, °suggestive, °broad, inelegant, °improper, °inappropriate, °unseemly, °blue: *My mother does not tolerate off-colour remarks at the dinner table.*

offence *n.* **1** °violation, °breach, °crime, felony, misdemeanour, infraction, °transgression, trespass, °wrong, wrongdoing, °sin, °peccadillo, °misdeed, °fault, °infringement, malefaction; dereliction, °lapse, °slip, °error: *He was accused of offences against the rights of others. Some regard the splitting of an infinitive an offence against the Queen's English.* **2** ***give offence***: incur °displeasure, create °annoyance *or* irritation *or* °resentment *or* pique, evoke °indignation *or* °anger; °slight, °injure, °hurt, °harm, °offend, °insult, °outrage, *Colloq* °put (someone) down: *He denied that he meant to give offence in his criticism of the play.* **3** ***take offence***: take °umbrage, feel °displeasure *or* °annoyance *or* °resentment *or* pique *or* °indignation, be angered *or* enraged: *Why should you take offence at what a fool says?*

offend *v.* **1** °hurt (someone's) feelings, affront, °insult, °slight, snub, give °offence, °hurt, °pain, °displease, disgruntle, chagrin, °humiliate, °embarrass; pique, °fret, °gall, vex, °annoy, °irritate, nettle, needle, °rankle, °provoke, °ruffle, °outrage, rile, anger, *Colloq* miff, put (someone's) back up, put (someone's) nose out of joint, tread *or* step on (someone's) toes, °put (someone) out, °rattle: *I hope you weren't offended by my saying that you could do with losing some weight.* **2** °disgust, °sicken, turn (someone's) stomach, °nauseate, °repel, °repulse, °revolt, *Colloq* °turn (someone) off: *I, for one, am offended by seeing explicit sex on television.*

offender *n.* °criminal, malefactor, lawbreaker, °outlaw, wrongdoer, °culprit, °miscreant, °transgressor, °sinner, evil-doer, *Slang* crook: *I don't know if they apprehended the offender.*

offensive *adj.* **1** antagonistic, °hostile, contentious, °quarrelsome, attacking, °aggressive, °threatening, °provocative, combative, °martial, °belligerent, °warlike, bellicose: *The minute the enemy made an offensive move, we attacked.* **2** insulting, °rude, °disrespectful, uncivil, °insolent, °discourteous, °impolite, unmannerly, °impertinent, °impudent, objectionable, displeasing: *Nigel has been asked to leave because of his offensive behaviour.* **3** °disgusting, °unsavoury, °unpalatable, nauseating, °nauseous, noisome, noxious, °obnoxious, °repugnant, °repulsive, °repellent, °revolting, °abominable, °foul, °loathsome, °vile, sickening, fetid *or* foetid, °rank, malodorous, mephitic, °putrid, putrescent, putrefying, °rancid, °rotten: *An offensive stench emanated from the stagnant pond.*
—*n.* **4** °attack, °offence: *At last, our team was on the offensive.* **5** °attack, onslaught, °drive, °assault, °offence, °push: *The offensive to capture the arsenal will be launched at dawn tomorrow.*

offer *v.* **1** proffer, °propose, °tender, °bid: *They offered twice what I had paid for it. She offered to buy my old car.* **2** make °available, °present, °tender, put on the °market, °sell, put up for °sale, °put up, °furnish: *The supermarket is offering lettuce at half price.* **3** proffer, °provide, °submit, °put forward *or* forth, °advance, °tender, °extend, °make; °suggest: *Can you offer a suggestion for improving office efficiency? He offered to forget the whole thing if I paid him £1,000.* **4** volunteer, °present oneself, °step *or* °come forward: *I offered to help with her luggage.*
—*n.* **5** °proposal, °bid, °tender, °offering: *She said she would double any offer we have already had for the painting.* **6** °proposal, °presentation, proffer, °proposition: *The company said they could entertain no offers past the deadline. My offer to lend the money was contingent on being repaid.*

offering *n.* °sacrifice, oblation, contribution, °donation, °gift, °present: *They made offerings to the gods in order to propitiate them.*

offhand *adj.* **1** offhanded, °casual, °informal, °nonchalant, °cool, °distant, °aloof, °easygoing, °blasé, unceremonious, °relaxed, °easy, °smooth, unconcerned, insouciant, light-hearted, uninterested, °superficial, °cursory, cavalier, °careless: *His offhand reaction shows that he doesn't care as much about her as we thought.* **2** °curt, °brusque, °abrupt, °perfunctory, °ungracious, °glib, °smooth: *When asked when he expected to pay, he gave an offhand reply.* **3** extempore, impromptu, °unpremeditated, unstudied, °extemporaneous, °informal, off the cuff, ad lib: *She rose to make some offhand comments about the accomplishments of the guest of honour.*
—*adv.* **4** extempore, impromptu, extemporaneously, informally, off the cuff, ad lib, on the °spur of the moment, at the drop of a hat: *That was a pretty good speech considering it was made offhand.* **5** casually, informally, °incidentally, by the °way, offhandedly, by the by, parenthetically, in °passing, *en passant*, cursorily, superficially: *Offhand, I'd say that the two of them deserve each other.*

office *n.* **1** °business, °organization, °department, °firm, °house, °establishment, °company, corporation: *Whenever I'm travelling, I always try to phone the office once a day.* **2** commission, °department, °branch; °section, °division: *He was with the overseas office for years.* **3** workplace, offices; °room, °area: *Our new office is completely air-conditioned. My office is next to the board room.* **4** °duty, °obligation, °responsibility, °charge, commission, °service, °employment, °occupation, °position, °post, °appointment, °assignment, chore, °task, °job, °place, berth, °work, °role, °function, °purpose, °part, bit, *Colloq* °thing, *Slang* shtick: *He was appointed to the office of Minister of Health. In her* *office as Minister of Finance, she wields great power.* **5** ***offices***: °indulgence, intermediation, °auspices, °support, advocacy, aegis, °help, °aid, intercession, mediation, °patronage, °favour, °backing, backup: *She appealed to the police chief's good offices to allow her to visit her son.*

officer *n.* **1** (°public) °official, °dignitary, office-holder, °public °servant, office-bearer, (°political) appointee, (°government) °agent, bureaucrat, °functionary, commissioner, administrator, °manager, °director; apparatchik: *He was stopped by customs officers who demanded to search his baggage. The bailiff is an officer of the court.* **2** policeman, policewoman, °police officer, officer of the law, °constable, *Old-fashioned* catchpole, *US* lawman, peace officer, G-man, T-Man, *Colloq* gendarme, *Slang* cop, copper, fuzz, *US* dick, narc, *Brit* Old Bill, tec: *The officer standing at the door was there to serve a writ.*

official *adj.* **1** authorized, °legitimate, °lawful, °legal, °authentic, bona fide, °proper, °true, accredited, valid, documented, licensed, sanctioned, endorsed, certified, verified, recognized, accepted: *I won't believe I've won till I hold the official notification in my own hands.* **2** °ceremonial, °formal, °solemn, ritualistic, °ceremonious, °pompous, °stiff, °proper, °seemly, °decorous: *She has to make an acceptance speech at the official dinner.*
—*n.* **3** See **officer, 1,** above.

officiate *v.* °preside, °direct, °manage, °chair, °conduct, °oversee, °head (up), °run, °lead, °supervise, superintend; °umpire, referee, °judge, adjudicate, °moderate, mediate: *Who will officiate at the annual meeting? Dennis has been invited to officiate at the football match on Saturday.*

officious *adj.* °dictatorial, °intrusive, intruding, meddlesome, meddling, °obtrusive, °forward, °bold, interfering, °aggressive, °insistent, °persistent, °demanding, importunate: *Hamish is one of those officious little men who are always ready to give unasked-for advice.*

offset *v.* **1** °compensate, counterbalance, countervail, counterpoise, °counteract, °balance (out), °equalize, °even (out *or* up), °square, °cancel (out), °neutralize, nullify, °make up (for), °atone (for), redress; recompense, °repay, °make °amends *or* °restitution, °make good, °reimburse, indemnify: *The votes from the Centre offset those lost to the Far Left. How are you going to offset losses resulting from pilferage by shop assistants?*
—*n.* **2** compensation, counterbalance, counteraction, °check, equalizer, neutralizer: *The bank manager considered the money owed to the company as sufficient offset for the money owed by it.*

offshoot *n.* **1** °branch, °spur; °shoot, limb, bough, °twig, °stem, appendage, °sucker, °sprout, sprig, tendril, scion: *There is an offshoot of this road that goes up the hill. The offshoots are trained to grow along the arms of the espalier.* **2** °descendant, °relation, °relative, °kin, °kindred, °offspring, scion, °heir: *One offshoot of the family later emigrated to the United States.* **3** outgrowth, °development, °branch, spin-off; by-product, °derivative: *An offshoot of the company manufactures optical instruments. The sale of gravel for concrete is an offshoot of our mining operations.*

offspring *n. Often used as plural*: °child, °progeny, °issue, °seed, youngster, °brood, °young, successor, °heir: *None of the earl's offspring ever amounted to much.*

often *adv.* °frequently, regularly, much, °many times, °usually, habitually, commonly; °ordinarily, again and again, over and over again, °time after °time, °repeatedly, °time and (°time) again, in °many cases *or* instances, on numerous occasions, day in (and) day out, continually, *Literary* oftentimes, oft: *How often do you visit your mother? We often went to the seaside for our summer holiday. She was often warned not to go too near the edge.*

ogle *v.* **1** °leer, °eye, make °eyes at, *Colloq* give (someone) the glad °eye, give (someone) the once-over, make sheep's eyes at: *The old lecher is always ogling the pretty young secretaries.* **2** °gape, °gaze, goggle, °gawk, °stare, *Slang Brit* gawp *or* gaup: *We took turns ogling the rings of Saturn through the telescope.*
—*n.* **3** °leer, °stare, °gape, goggle, oeillade, *Colloq* once-over, glad °eye: *They all crowded round the paper for an ogle at the pin-ups.*

ogre *n.* ogress, °monster, °giant, °fiend, °demon, troll, man-eater, bogey *or* bogy, bogeyman *or* bogyman, bugbear, °spectre, Minotaur, Cyclops, gorgon, Caliban; °brute, sadist, °villain, cad, °scoundrel: *The ogre chased Jack to the beanstalk. The persistent ogre of poverty threatened him all his life.*

oil *n.* **1** lubricant, grease, lubricator, unguent: *A little oil will stop that squeak.* **2** °fuel: *Miraculously, the lamp burned for eight days with only one day's supply of oil.*
—*v.* **3** lubricate, grease: *Oil the bearings or they will burn out.*

oily *adj.* **1** °greasy, oleaginous, °fat, fatty, adipose, pinguid, sebaceous, soapy, saponaceous, buttery, butyraceous, lardaceous; °slippery, °slimy, slithery, °smooth, unctuous: *The cars slid about as the tyres failed to grip the oily surface.* **2** °glib, °smooth, unctuous, °servile, °obsequious, sycophantic, °ingratiating, °flattering, °hypocritical; °suave, urbane, °sophisticated, *Colloq* smarmy: *Sarah found Curtis's approach sickeningly oily.*

ointment *n.* unguent, balm, °salve, emollient, embrocation, demulcent, pomade, pomatum, petrolatum; °lotion, cream: *A little ointment will keep the sore moist till it heals.*

OK *interj.* **1** O.K.!, Okay!, Fine!, Yes!, Definitely!, Agreed!, Very °well!, All right!: *'Would you have dinner with me?' 'OK!' 'I think you ought to leave.' 'OK!'*
—*adj.* **2** °satisfactory, °acceptable, °correct, °suitable, all °right, °fine, °good, in °order: *Is it OK if I go the cinema tonight? That dress is OK to wear to the dance.* **3** °adequate, °mediocre, °fair, middling, °passable, °tolerable, *Colloq* °so so, °pretty good, not bad, not great: *The film was OK, I suppose.* **4** °well, °healthy; °sound, in °good °condition, in °fine fettle, °fine, all °right: *Now that he's on the proper medication, Sam is OK. The mechanic assured me that my car would be OK.*
—*v.* **5** °approve, °sanction, °ratify, °authorize, °endorse, °support, °agree to, °allow, °consent to, °agree to, *Colloq* give the °go-ahead *or* green light to, give the thumbs up *or* the °nod to, rubber-stamp: *A department head must OK your expense account before you can be reimbursed.*
—*n.* **6** °approval, °sanction, ratification, authorization, °endorsement, °agreement, °support, °permission, °consent: *You need an OK from the security guard to enter the restricted area.*
—*adv.* **7** all °right, satisfactorily, °well (enough), adequately: *She can get along OK without me.*

old *adj.* **1** °elderly, ageing, °aged, advanced in years *or* °age, long-lived, past one's °prime, °grey, full of years, getting on (in years), hoary, superannuated, *Colloq* over the hill, °past it: *Bill is too old to continue working in the mine.* **2** °ancient, °antiquated, antediluvian, fossil, °prehistoric, Noachian, °obsolete, °antique, out-dated, out of °date, old-time, dated, archaic, °stale, out-moded, °*passé*, *Literary* Ogygian: *The archaeological dig has turned up some interesting old artefacts.* **3** °time-worn, decayed, °dilapidated, °ramshackle, disintegrated, crumbling, °shabby, °worn out, dusty, broken-down, °tumbledown, °disused, °unused, °cast off, °cast aside: *They have torn down the old mill near the river.* **4** long-standing, °well-established, °enduring, °lasting, age-old, °time-honoured: *It is hard to see an old friendship die.* **5** °former, olden, °bygone, °early, primordial, °primitive: *In the old days, it took a week to travel from London to Edinburgh.* **6** °previous, °preceding, °prior, °former, quondam, erstwhile, one-time, ex-: *The West End was my old stamping-ground when I lived in London.* **7** °experienced, °veteran, °practised, (well-)°versed, °knowledgeable, °proficient, °accomplished, °adept, skilled, °expert, old-time: *Charles is an* *old hand at steam engines.* **8** °dear, °beloved, loved, esteemed, valued, °precious, °well-known, °intimate, °close, °familiar: *Penelope is an old friend of the family's.*

old-fashioned *adj.* °antiquated, °antique, °*passé*, outmoded, out-dated, unfashionable, °stale, dated, out of °date, °tired, old-time, °obsolete, °obsolescent, °dead, superseded, replaced, °disused, °out, old-fangled, °old hat: *Whoever thought we would see the day when mini-skirts were old-fashioned?*

omen *n.* portent, augury, °sign, °token, foretoken, °indication, °harbinger, forewarning, °premonition, foreshadowing, writing on the wall, prognostic, presage: *Solar eclipses were once regarded as omens, sometimes good, sometimes bad.*

ominous *adj.* **1** °foreboding, °threatening, °fateful, °dark, °black, °gloomy, lowering *or* louring, °menacing, °sinister; unpropitious, unfavourable, ill-omened, ill-starred, °unpromising, star-crossed, °inauspicious: *With ominous solemnity, the judge placed a black cloth square on his head before passing the death sentence.* **2** minatory, °warning, admonitory, cautionary: *The whispering had taken on ominous overtones.* **3** °portentous, °prophetic, oracular, vaticinal, predictive, prognostic, augural, mantic, sibyllic, °meaningful, premonitory, foreshadowing, foretelling, foretokening, indicative: *Virtually everything was regarded as ominous in ancient times.*

omission *n.* **1** non-inclusion, omitting, leaving out *or* off, excluding, eliminating, dropping, skipping; °exclusion, °exception, deletion, elimination, excision: *The omission of your name from the list was a mistake. Allowing for inadvertent omissions, the inventory is complete.* **2** °failure, °default, °neglect, dereliction, °oversight, °shortcoming, °negligence: *She is being punished for her innocent omission in failing to notify the police, while he is at liberty despite his deliberate commission of a crime.*

omit *v.* **1** °leave out, °exclude, °skip, °except, °pass over; °delete, °erase, °cancel, eradicate, °edit out, °strike (out), dele, °cut (out), °cross out, °obliterate: *She was offended because he omitted any mention of all that she had contributed.* **2** °neglect, °disregard, °fail, °forget, °overlook, let °slide, °ignore: *I omitted to tell you that your sister telephoned yesterday.*

once *adv.* **1** once upon a °time, °formerly, (at) one °time, on a °former °occasion, °previously, °before, in days gone by, in olden days, in the (good) °old days, long ago, some °time ago, years *or* ages *or* aeons ago, in days of yore: *Your hair is as long as mine once was. He was once a famous film star. That once revered leader has fallen.* **2** °one °time, on °one °occasion, a °single °time: *He has visited his family only once in all these years.* **3** ***once and for all***: °finally, °positively, °definitely, decidedly, conclusively, for good: *We must settle the itinerary once and for all before we can make the bookings.* **4** ***once in a while***: °occasionally, (every) °now and then, °now and again, at °times, °sometimes, periodically, from °time to time, at intervals, sporadically: *We go to the theatre once in a while.*
—*conj.* **5** (if) ever, as soon as, at any °time: *Once the bus comes, you'd best get on it straight away.*
—*n.* **6** ***at once***: **a** °immediately, °straight away, °right away, °directly, without °delay, °promptly, instantly, °post-haste; in a wink, in the twinkling of an eye, in a °minute *or* °moment *or* °second *or* split °second, in no time (at all), before you can turn around, before you can say 'Jack Robinson', in a trice, *Colloq* in a jiffy, in two shakes of a lamb's tail: *Watson, come here at once. I'll be there at once.* **b** together, at the same time, simultaneously, at a °stroke, in the same °instant, in the same breath, *Colloq* at °one go, at a go, in °one go: *You cannot be in two places at once.*

oncoming *adj.* **1** advancing, arriving, coming, nearing, approaching, onrushing, °imminent: *He swerved and just managed to avoid the oncoming lorry.*
—*n.* **2** °onset, °beginning, nearing, °arrival, °advance, °approach: *With the oncoming of spring, the birds returned.*

one *adj.* **1** °single, lone, °solitary, °individual, °sole, °only: *The one time I kissed Margie it was heaven.* **2** unified, °united, inseparable, joined, °undivided, one and the °same, °identical, °equal, at one, °harmonious, in °unison, °whole, °entire, °complete: *When he went into a trance, he felt one with his God.* **3** a °particular, a °certain, a given, a °specific: *I recall one occasion when she brought all her dogs into work.*
—*pron.* **4** a °person, an °individual, a °man *or* a °woman, everybody, °everyone, anybody, anyone; °people; *Possibly offensive* °man: *One ought to treat others as one would like to be treated. One cannot be too careful these days.*
—*n.* **5** °joke, °story, anecdote, chestnut, one-liner; limerick, °rhyme, ditty, °song; bromide: *Have you heard the one that begins, 'There was a young man from Loch Ness'?*

one-sided *adj.* **1** °partial, °biased, °partisan, °prejudiced, °bigoted, unfair, unjust, inequitable, close-minded, °narrow-minded, °intolerant: *His is a one-sided view of the problem.* **2** °lopsided, °unbalanced, unequal, unequalized, uneven, °disproportionate, *Slang* cock-eyed: *The swelling on his left cheek made Tom's face look very one-sided.* **3** unilateral, °independent, exclusionary, °exclusive: *They made a one-sided decision to halt production of nuclear weapons.*

ongoing *adj.* **1** continuing, continued, °continuous, °continual, ceaseless, unbroken, uninterrupted, °constant, °perpetual, °non-stop, °relentless, °persistent, unending, °endless, interminable, °running: *There has been an ongoing dispute with the museum over the authenticity of the sculpture.* **2** developing, evolving, growing, °successive, unfolding, progressing, °progressive: *Rather than come to a hasty decision, we decided to monitor ongoing developments.*

onlooker *n.* °spectator, °observer, looker-on, °eyewitness, °witness, watcher, viewer; °bystander, passer-by: *She was merely an onlooker, not a participant. Onlookers reported that the driver had run away from the accident.*

only *adj.* **1** °sole, °single, °solitary, lone, °one and only, °exclusive: *He is the only one who can identify the murderer.*
—*adv.* **2** solely, °just, exclusively, °alone: *He has a face that only a mother could love. They have been here only twice. She gets her own way only because she has a tantrum if anyone crosses her. Harry was correct in one respect only.* **3** °merely, °simply, °barely, at °best, at worst, at most, °just, purely, not *or* no more than, not *or* no greater than: *She is only seventeen. I received your note only today. Don't get excited, it's only a small present.*
—*conj.* **4** but, °however, on the other hand, on the °contrary, contrariwise: *The flowers are lovely, only they have no scent.*

onset *n.* **1** °attack, °assault, onrush, onslaught, °charge, °strike, °hit, °raid, storming, sally, sortie: *These troops had to bear the brunt of the onset.* **2** °beginning, °start, °outset, °initiation, inauguration, commencement, inception, °dawn, °birth, °origin, genesis, °appearance, début: *We must leave before the onset of the monsoon season. The sudden onset of a new policy will throw the ministers into a panic.*

onward *adj.* °forward, advancing, °progressive, progressing, °moving onward *or* forward: *They resumed their onward march, laying waste to the countryside as they went.*

onwards *adv.* °onward, forwards *or* forward, °ahead, in °front, on, forth: *They marched onwards through the dismal valley. From this day onwards afternoon visiting hours will be from two to four o'clock.*

ooze *n.* **1** slime, °muck, °mud, °mire, °silt, °sludge, °sediment, slush, *Colloq* goo, gunk, guck, *Slang US* glop, goop: *I stepped into the bog and the ooze rose over the tops of my shoes.*
—*v.* **2** exude, °weep, seep, °secrete, bleed, °leak, °drain, °trickle; °emit, °discharge: *Sap continues to ooze from the gash in the tree.*

opacity *n.* **1** opaqueness, darkness, murkiness, dimness, °obscurity, impermeability, impenetrability: *The opacity of the lens increases automatically in the presence of sunlight.* **2** °obscurity, density, impenetrability, unintelligibility, indefiniteness, vagueness, reconditeness, abstruseness, °ambiguity, equivocation, mystification: *For centuries scientists were unable to penetrate the opacity of the question of what occurred when substances burned.* **3** °stupidity, dullness, denseness, thickness, obtuseness: *A light finally dawned through the thick opacity of his brain.*

opalescent *adj.* opaline, iridescent, nacreous, °pearly, °lustrous: *The sea was opalescent in the moonlight.*

opaque *adj.* **1** °dark, °murky, °dim, turbid, °muddy, cloudy, °obscure, obscured, obfuscated, °black, °impermeable, impenetrable, clouded, non-transparent, untransparent, non-translucent, °hazy, blurred, blurry, smoky: *Solar eclipses should be viewed directly only through special opaque glass.* **2** unclear, °vague, °indefinite, °obscure, unfathomable, unplumbable, baffling, mystifying, °ambiguous, °equivocal, impenetrable, °cryptic, enigmatic, °puzzling, °perplexing, °mysterious, °elusive, abstruse, arcane, °recondite: *Despite years of study, the inscriptions on the tomb have remained opaque to scholars.* **3** unintelligent, °dense, °thick, °dull, °obtuse, °stupid, dull-witted, °stolid, thickheaded, dunderheaded, dunderpated, °slow, doltish, °backward, cloddish: *He was too opaque to notice the jeers of his colleagues.*

open *adj.* **1** ajar, gaping, agape, unfastened, unlocked, unbarred, unbolted, unlatched, unclosed: *Come on in—the door is open.* **2** yawning, agape, uncovered, revealed, unsealed, exposed, °bare: *Her uncle escaped by hiding for three nights in an open grave.* **3** unwrapped, unsealed, unfastened: *The package was open and the contents gone.* **4** °free, °accessible, °public, °available; obtainable; unrestricted, unobstructed, unencumbered *or* unincumbered, °unimpeded, unhindered, unhampered, unregulated, unconditional, °unqualified: *The parks are open to all. We were allowed open access to the library stacks.* **5** unprotected, unenclosed, unsheltered, °bare; uncovered, exposed: *They spent a week in an open boat before being rescued. The roof can be retracted, leaving the interior completely open to the sky.* **6** °unsettled, unagreed, unsigned, unsealed, unclinched, unestablished, unconcluded, undecided, °pending: *As far as I am concerned, the deal is open till the contract is signed.* **7** undecided, °unsettled, °unresolved, °debatable, arguable, °problematic, °moot, *US* up in the air: *Whether they should get married is a question that will remain open until he returns from abroad.* **8** unscheduled, unbooked, unspoken for, unreserved, uncommitted, °free, unpromised: *The doctor has an hour open at noon on Friday.* **9** °clear, unobstructed, wide open, uncluttered, °roomy, °spacious, °extensive, °expansive; treeless, uncrowded, unfenced, unenclosed; ice-free, °navigable, unblocked, °passable: *We travelled through open country for days. In the spring the shipping lanes will again be open.* **10** °available, unfilled, °vacant, untaken: *There are not many jobs open in this part of the country.* **11** °receptive, open-minded, °flexible, amenable, persuasible *or* persuadable, pliant, °willing, °responsive: *The management is open to suggestions for improving its products and services.* **12** exposed, °public, °well-known, °widely known, unconcealed: *That they are living together is an open secret.* **13** °evident, °obvious, °conspicuous, °manifest, °clear, unconcealed, unequivocal, °plain, palpable, °apparent, °patent, °downright, °out-and-out, °blatant, °flagrant, °glaring, °brazen: *He operates with open disregard for the law.* **14** °generous, °liberal, °charitable, unreserved, open-handed, munificent, magnanimous, big-hearted, beneficent, bounteous, °unselfish, unstinting, °humanitarian, altruistic: *They are quite open when it comes to giving to charity.* **15** unreserved, °candid, °frank, °outspoken, straightforward, °forthright, °direct, °honest, °sincere, guileless, °artless, °fair: *He found it difficult to be open with his wife.* **16** °free, unrestrained, unconstrained, °uninhibited, unreserved, unrestricted: *They have an open marriage, each aware of the other's affairs.* **17** unfolded, extended, °spread (out), outstretched, outspread: *She ran into my open arms.* **18** °liable, °subject, °susceptible, exposed, °inclined, predisposed, °disposed: *These fraudulent shipping documents may well leave the captain open to prosecution for barratry.* **19** unprotected, undefended, unfortified, exposed: *With the invaders at the gates, Paris was declared an open city.*

—*v.* **20** °begin, °start, °initiate, °commence, get under way, °inaugurate, °launch, °put in *or* into °operation, °activate, get going, °set in °motion; °establish, °set up; *Colloq* get *or* °start the ball rolling, get *or* put the show on the road, kick off: *The minister opened the proceedings with an interminable speech. Jeremy is planning to open a restaurant in Pebble Lane. The show opens in Manchester next week.* **21** unlock, unbar, unlatch, unbolt, unfasten; uncover; uncork, unseal; °undo, untie, unwrap; °pull out: *Open the door. Open the box. Open the bottle. Open your present. He opened the drawer.* **22** unblock, °clear, unobstruct, unclog, unstop: *They had to dig up the yard to open the drain. The new law has opened the way for increased exports.* **23** °disclose, °unveil, uncover, °expose, °display, °show, °exhibit, °reveal, divulge, bring to °light, °communicate, °bring out, unbosom, °explain, °present, °announce, °release, °publish, °air, °make known, advertise: *The wonders of the language were opened to me by my first dictionary.* **24** °expand, °spread (out), °stretch out, °open up *or* out, unfurl, °extend: *The flag opened to the breeze.* **25** °present, °offer, °furnish, °provide, °afford, °yield, °reveal, uncover, °raise, °contribute, °introduce: *Expansion of technology opens new business opportunities every day.*

opening *n.* **1** °break, °breach, °rent, °rift, cleft, °crack, °crevice, fissure, °cranny, °chink, °pit, °gap, °split, °slit, °slot, °aperture, °hole, orifice, °separation: *Flowers grew from openings in the wall.* **2** °opportunity, °chance, °occasion, toe-hold, foothold, *Colloq* °break, toe *or* foot in the door, *Brit* look-in: *I was waiting for an appropriate opening to make my presentation.* **3** °job, °position, °opportunity, °vacancy: *Is there likely to be an opening in the art department of your company?* **4** °beginning, commencement, °start, °birth, °origin, °outset, °onset, inauguration, °launch, send-off, °initiation, °presentation, début; vernissage, *US* start-off, start-up: *The opening of the autumn social season was marked by Malcolm's birthday party. Aren't you going to the opening at the museum tonight?*

openly *adv.* **1** brazenly, brashly, flagrantly, unabashedly, unashamedly, unreservedly, boldly, audaciously, flauntingly: *She has openly defied the direct orders of her employer.* **2** frankly, unreservedly, plainly, forthrightly, candidly, °directly, °outright, °freely, outspokenly: *The man admitted openly that he had stolen the plans for the missile.*

operable *adj.* workable, °practicable, °serviceable, usable, °functional, °fit, operational, in working order *or* condition: *Aircraft engines that rely on oxygen for burning fuel are not operable where the air is too thin.*

operate *v.* **1** °go, °run, °perform; °work, °function, °serve, °act: *This watch operates even under water. The drug operates to reduce blood pressure.* **2** °manage, °run, °direct, °conduct, °control, °carry on, °ply, °manipulate, °handle; *US* °drive: *Katherine has been operating as an antiques dealer for years. It is unsafe to operate this machinery without goggles.*

operation *n.* **1** °function, functioning, working, °running, °performance, °action, °motion, °movement: *The operation of the internal combustion engine is very simple.* **2** manipulation, handling, °direction, °running, °control, °management, managing; manoeuvring: *The operation of the aircraft is under the control of the captain.* **3** °undertaking, °enterprise,

°venture, °project, °affair, °deal, °procedure, °proceeding, (day-to-day) °business, °transaction: *Who will be in charge of the operation while the president is abroad?* **4** Often, ***operations***: °action, °manoeuvre, °mission, °task, °campaign, °exercise: *The generals directed military operations from positions close to enemy lines.* **5** ***in*** or ***into operation***: functioning, °operative, in °effect, in °force, operating, operational, °functional, °effective, °efficacious: *Is the factory in operation yet? The new regulations went into operation last week.*

operative *adj.* **1** See **operation, 5,** above. —*n.* **2** °worker, °hand, °employee; craftsman, craftswoman, artisan, mechanic, machinist: *We hired two more lathe operatives today.* **3** private °detective, (private) investigator, *Colloq* private eye, °sleuth, *Brit* sleuth-hound, *US* P.I., gumshoe, *Slang* (private) dick, *US* shamus, eye: *Our operatives reported that Jones had been seen in the company of a known enemy agent.* **4** espionage *or* °intelligence °agent, counter-espionage *or* counter-intelligence °agent, °spy, counter-spy, °undercover °agent *or* man, (FBI *or* CIA) °agent, *US* G-man, *Colloq US* company man, member of the firm: *We had an operative at the top level of the NKVD.*

operator *n.* **1** (bus *or* °taxi *or* °train) driver; °worker, °operative, manipulator, practitioner: *These operators are required to take safety courses.* **2** °director, administrator, °manager, °supervisor, °superintendent: *Shaughnessey is the operator of a roofing business in Tring.* **3** machinator, faker, °fraud, manipulator, manoeuvrer, *Colloq* finagler, °wise guy, *Slang* smooth *or* slick operator, smoothie, wheeler-dealer, bigshot, big-time operator, *Chiefly US and Canadian* big wheel: *Claude is a cunning operator who always gets what he goes after.*

opinion *n.* **1** °belief, °judgement, °thought, °sentiment, (°point of) °view, °viewpoint, °conviction, way of °thinking, °perception, °idea, °impression, °notion, °conception, theory, *idée reçu;* °mind: *It is my opinion that sickness benefits ought to be increased. In her opinion all men are chauvinists.* **2** °evaluation, °estimation, °estimate, appraisal, °appreciation, °impression: *Myra has a very low opinion of Ray's taste in architecture.*

opinionated *adj.* **1** °stubborn, pigheaded, °obstinate, doctrinaire, °inflexible, °dogmatic, °single-minded, cocksure, obdurate, °dictatorial, dogged, mulish, bullheaded, °overbearing: *Felix is too opinionated to change his mind even if he knows he is wrong.* **2** °prejudiced, °biased, °bigoted, °one-sided, °jaundiced, coloured, °partial, °partisan: *You can count on Joan for an opinionated view of social values.*

opponent *n.* °antagonist, °adversary, disputant, °contestant, °competitor, contender, °rival, foe, °enemy; the °opposition: *He may be my opponent in the chess competition, but we are the best of friends.*

opportune *adj.* **1** °favourable, °advantageous, auspicious, °good, felicitous, °happy, °propitious, °beneficial, °helpful, °fortunate, °lucky, °profitable: *As I need money, and you have it to invest, our meeting is most opportune.* **2** °timely, °well-timed, °seasonable, apt, °appropriate, germane, °pertinent, °convenient, °fitting, °suitable, °becoming: *If this is not an opportune time to bring up the matter of the money you owe me, just say so.*

opportunistic *adj.* °expedient, °selfish, taking °advantage, exploitive *or* exploitative, unprincipled, Machiavellian, opportunist: *Don't you agree that it was opportunistic of him to inform on his own brother for a reward?*

opportunity *n.* °chance, °occasion, °opening, °possibility, °moment, °time, *Slang* °break: *She has taken advantage of every opportunity to vilify her ex-employers.*

oppose *v.* **1** °resist, °counter, °object (to), °defy, take a °stand against, °withstand, °resist, °combat, °contest, °attack, counter-attack, °fight, °grapple with, contend with *or* against: *If it comes to that, we must oppose force with force.* **2** °check, °bar, °obstruct, °block, °hinder, °impede, °stop, °slow, °curb, °restrain, °inhibit, °interfere with, °restrict, °prevent, obviate, °preclude, °thwart, °foil, °frustrate: *Labour seeks to oppose the privatization of industry.* **3** °match, °offset, counterbalance, °contrast, °pit *or* °set against, °play off (against), °set off: *What can they call upon to oppose the power of the Devil?*

opposed *adj.* Often, ***opposed to***: against, in °opposition (to), °opposing, in °conflict (with), antipathetic, conflicting, °contrary (to), at °variance (with), antithetical (to), °hostile (to), inimical (to), °opposite (to), contrasting: *Harvey is among those opposed to abortion. All those who are opposed to the motion raise your hands.*

opposing *adj.* °opposite, conflicting, °contrary, antithetical, antagonistic, antipathetic, °hostile, inimical, contrasting, °rival, °contradictory, °incompatible, irreconcilable, °dissident, discrepant: *Those with opposing views will be heard from later.*

opposite *adj.* **1** °facing, vis-à-vis, *en face*: *The sniper was on the roof of the building opposite.* **2** °opposing, conflicting, °contrary, contrasting, °contradictory, antithetical, differing, °different, °divergent, °diverse, antagonistic, °inconsistent, irreconcilable: *William and his wife hold diametrically opposite political views.* —*n.* **3** °reverse, °converse, °contrary, antithesis: *Whatever you tell teenagers to do, their first reaction is to do the opposite.*

opposition *n.* **1** °hostility, °antagonism, unfriendliness, °resistance, counteraction, °disapproval, °objection, °conflict, defiance, °contrast, antipathy, adversity, *Colloq* °flak: *There is strong opposition to plans for an amusement arcade.* **2** °competition, °opponent, °adversary, °competitor, °antagonist, °enemy, foe, °rival, other °side: *We must overcome the opposition in order to win.* **3** ***in opposition***: competing, competitive, antagonistic, °hostile, conflicting, in °conflict, antithetic(al), °opposed, at daggers drawn, in deadly embrace: *Although they agree on some points, the parties are in opposition on others.*

oppress *v.* **1** °burden, °afflict, °trouble, °weigh down, °overload, °encumber, °wear (down), °press, °weary, overburden, °overwhelm, *Brit* pressurize, *US* °pressure: *He was oppressed by the heavy burden of responsibility.* **2** °crush, °repress, °put down, °suppress, °subjugate, °tyrannize (over), °subdue, °overpower, °enslave, °persecute, maltreat, °abuse, harry, °harass, °trample underfoot, ride roughshod over: *The Russian serfs had been oppressed for centuries before they finally rose up against tyranny.*

oppression *n.* °repression, °suppression, subjugation, °subjection, °tyranny, °despotism, enslavement, °persecution, maltreatment, °abuse, °torment, torture, °hardship, °injury, °pain, °anguish, °injustice: *People who have not known oppression cannot imagine the agonies suffered by the oppressed who once were free.*

oppressive *adj.* **1** °burdensome, °overpowering, °overwhelming, onerous, °heavy, cumbersome, °exhausting, racking, °unbearable, intolerable, °agonizing, unendurable, °harsh, °brutal, °severe, °tyrannical, °repressive; dispiriting, depressing, disheartening, discouraging, °grievous, distressing, dolorous, °miserable, °harrowing, °wretched: *The conquerors resorted to oppressive measures to keep the people subjugated.* **2** suffocating, stifling, °stuffy, °close, airless, unventilated, uncomfortable: *The atmosphere in the tiny cell quickly became oppressive, and a couple of people fainted.*

oppressor *n.* °bully, °tyrant, taskmaster, taskmistress, °despot, autocrat, persecutor, slave-driver, °dictator, overlord, iron hand, °scourge, tormentor *or* tormenter, torturer, intimidator: *The citizens finally banded together and overthrew their oppressors.*

optimistic *adj.* °sanguine, °positive, °cheerful, °buoyant, °bright, °hopeful, °expectant, °confident, bullish, °idealistic, Pollyannaish: *We have every reason to be optimistic that the venture will succeed.*

optimum *n.* **1** °best, finest, most °favourable, °ideal, °perfection, °model, °paragon, exemplar: *In all work, the optimum is difficult to achieve.* —*adj.* **2** °best, finest, most °favourable, °ideal, °perfect, choicest, optimal, °first-rate, first-class, °sterling, °prime, °capital, °excellent, °exceptional, °superlative, °extraordinary, °unique, °peerless, unequalled, unexcelled, unsurpassed: *These instruments keep the chamber at the optimum temperature. After months of training, Guy is in optimum condition to win the marathon.*

option *n.* **1** °choice, °selection, °alternative, °recourse, °opportunity, °way out: *There are fewer employment options open to the uneducated.* **2** °choice, °privilege, °election, °opportunity, °chance: *Investors pay for the option to buy at a fixed figure if the price of the shares goes up.*

optional *adj.* °voluntary, discretionary *or* discretional, elective, facultative, °free, °spontaneous, uncoerced, unforced, non-compulsory, uncompulsory, non-mandatory, unmandatory, non-requisite, unrequisite: *Life insurance is optional for those who have our hospitalization policy.*

opulent *adj.* **1** °wealthy, affluent, °rich, °prosperous, well-to-do, °well off, °comfortable, *Colloq* °flush, well-heeled, °loaded, rolling in it, made of °money, in clover, on Easy Street, *Brit* on velvet, *US* in velvet, in the chips: *Timothy was fortunate in having met and wed an opulent widow.* **2** °luxurious, °lavish, °sumptuous: *That poor little rich girl was raised in the most opulent of surroundings.* **3** °abundant, copious, °bountiful, °plentiful, °prolific, °profuse, plenteous: *We enjoyed a most opulent harvest this year.*

opus *n.* °work, °composition, °production, *œuvre*, °creation; *magnum opus*: *Her most important opus will be performed at the Albert Hall next week.*

oracle *n.* **1** °prophet, sibyl, °seer, soothsayer, augur, °fortune-teller, diviner, prognosticator, *US* reader (and °adviser *or* advisor), Cassandra, Nostradamus; °authority, guru, °mastermind, mentor, wizard: *He insists on consulting his oracle before making any final decision.* **2** °prophecy, augury, °prediction, divination, °advice, prognostication, °answer, °message, °divine utterance: *According to the oracle, the travellers would survive the perils of the journey.*

oral *adj.* °spoken, said, °verbal, uttered, voiced, vocal, vocalized, enunciated, °pronounced, articulated, word-of-mouth, viva voce: *Tomorrow James must make an oral presentation of his plan to the entire staff.*

oration *n.* °speech, °declaration, °address, °lecture, °recitation, discourse, monologue, declamation; valedictory, °eulogy, homily, panegyric; *Colloq* spiel: *Bentley delivered a long oration on the future of the economy.*

oratory *n.* °public speaking, speech-making, eloquence, °rhetoric, way with words, °command of the °language, °fluency, glibness, grandiloquence, magniloquence, declamation; elocution, °diction, enunciation, articulation, °address; *Colloq* gift of the gab: *The crowds who thronged to hear Churchill's oratory were seldom disappointed.*

orb *n.* °sphere, ball, °globe: *The golden orb of the sun sank into the sea.*

orbit *n.* **1** °circuit, °course, °path, °track, °revolution, °circle, °round, °cycle: *The earth's orbit round the sun is elliptical.* —*v.* **2** °revolve, °go °round, °circle, °encircle, °turn: *The earth orbits the sun in a year. Electrons orbit the nucleus of an atom.*

ordeal *n.* °trial, °test, tribulation(s), °hardship, °affliction, °trouble(s), °suffering, °distress, °anguish, nightmare, °misery, °grief, °misfortune, adversity, °tragedy, °disaster: *She never fully recovered from her ordeal at the hands of the kidnappers.*

order *n.* **1** °organization, °arrangement, grouping, °disposition, °form, °structure, categorization, systematization *or* systemization, classification, codification, disposal, layout, array, °sequence, *Colloq* °set-up: *The order of the library is of crucial importance if we are to find anything.* **2** °organization, °uniformity, °regularity, °system, °pattern, °symmetry, °harmony, tidiness, orderliness, neatness: *Some believe that there is an order of things in the universe, others that the universe tends to chaos.* **3** °category, °class, °caste, °level, °kind, °sort, °rank, °group, °scale, °importance, hierarchy, °position, °status, °degree, *Colloq* pecking °order: *Gregory's musical talents are of a very high order.* **4** °command, °direction, directive, °instruction, commandment, °dictate, mandate, edict, behest, °request, °demand, ukase, °decree, fiat, °proclamation, °pronouncement, pronunciamento; °rule, °regulation, °law, ordinance, statute, °requirement: *The police have issued an order to surrender all hand guns.* **5** °procedure, °proceeding(s), °discipline, °conduct: *The order of the meeting was breached by some rowdies.* **6** °condition, °state (of affairs): *Please leave everything in the order in which you found it.* **7** °purchase °order, °request, °requisition, commitment, commission, °instruction: *We received a large order for office furniture.* **8** °calm, °peace, peacefulness, tranquillity, °quiet, °serenity, °law and °order, °discipline, lawfulness: *After a brief commotion, order was restored.* **9** °brotherhood, °fraternity, sisterhood, sorority, °fellowship, sodality, °association, °organization, °society, guild, °sect, °company, community, °lodge, °body, knighthood: *One of her ancestors was a Knight of the Teutonic Order.* **10** ***in order***: **a** °neat, °clean, °tidy, °shipshape, °orderly, (°well-)organized, °ready, °prepared, arranged: *Is everything in order for the wedding tomorrow?* **b** °fitting, °suitable, °appropriate, °correct, °right, apt, called-for; required, demanded, needed: *I think that an apology is in order for the way you behaved.* **11** ***in order that***: so (that), with the °aim *or* °purpose that, to the °end that: *We invited him in order that you might meet him.* **12** ***in order to***: to, for the °purpose of: *In order to get there, you have to drive up the hill.* **13** ***out of order***: **a** disordered, non-sequential, out of °sequence, non-alphabetical, disorganized, unorganized, in °disorder: *The cards in this catalogue are out of order and I cannot find anything.* **b** °unseemly, out of °place, °improper, uncalled-for, unsuitable, indecorous, *Colloq chiefly Brit* not cricket: *Your remark about her religion was completely out of order.* **c** out of commission, °broken, in °disrepair, non-functioning, non-functional, not working, broken-down, inoperative, out of kilter *or Brit also* kelter, *Colloq* (gone) haywire, kaput, bust(ed), *US* out of whack, on the fritz, shot; *Slang* on the °blink, *Brit* wonky, gone phut: *The telly is out of order again.* —*v.* **14** °direct, °command, °instruct, °charge, °tell, °bid, °require, enjoin; °demand, ordain; °force, °make: *The sergeant ordered the men to run around the drill field with full packs. The council ordered that garden rubbish should be packed in special bags.* **15** °requisition, °ask for, °send (away) for, °call for, °apply for, °reserve, °engage, commission, °contract for; °purchase, °buy: *Have you ordered breakfast for tomorrow? Let's order a take-away from the Chinese restaurant.* **16** °organize, systematize, °arrange, classify, °categorize, codify, °lay out, °sort (out), °straighten (out *or* up): *The bottles were ordered in neat rows along the wall.*

orderly *adj.* **1** in (°good) °order, (°well-)organized, °neat, °shipshape, °tidy, arranged, °methodical, °systematic, systematized *or* systemized, °harmonious, °symmetrical, °regular, °uniform: *Before you leave, make sure that your room is orderly.* **2** well-behaved, disciplined, °decorous, law-abiding, well-mannered, °peaceable, °tranquil, mannerly, °polite, °courteous, °civil, civilized, non-violent: *Everyone left the burning theatre in an orderly fashion.* —*n.* **3** °assistant, adjutant, °attendant, °messenger; °menial, °servant; nurse's °aide; *Military Brit* batman; *US* candystriper; *Slang US and Canadian* gofer: *An orderly arrived with dispatches from the general. She has a job as a hospital orderly.*

ordinarily *adv.* °usually, normally, as a °rule, commonly, °generally, in °general, customarily, routinely, typically, habitually, by and large, for the most °part: *Ellie is ordinarily at her desk by nine o'clock.*

ordinary *adj.* **1** °usual, °normal, expected, °common, °general, °customary, °routine, °typical, °habitual, °accustomed, °traditional, °regular, °everyday, °familiar, °set, °humdrum: *This wine is quite good for ordinary drinking. Just display ordinary good manners when you meet the Queen.* **2** °common, °conventional, °modest, °plain, °simple, °prosaic, °homespun, commonplace, run-of-the-mill, °everyday, °average, unpretentious, workaday, °mediocre, °fair, °passable, °so so, °undistinguished, unexceptional, unremarkable, uninspired, °pedestrian, °bourgeois, °peasant, °provincial, °unrefined, *Colloq Brit* °common or garden, *US* common-or-garden variety, garden-variety: *They bought a rather ordinary house in an inferior neighbourhood.*
—*n.* **3** °standard, °norm, °average, °status quo, °convention, expected: *Saint-Gaudens' architectural designs are far from the ordinary.* **4 *out of the ordinary***: °extraordinary, °unusual, uncommon, °strange, °unfamiliar, °different, unexpected, unconventional, °curious, °eccentric, °peculiar, °rare, °exceptional, °original, °singular, °unique, °odd, °bizarre, °weird, °offbeat, °outlandish, °striking, °quaint, °picturesque: *She was looking for a gift that was a little out of the ordinary, so I suggested a pet tarantula.*

organ *n.* **1** °device, °instrument, °implement, °tool; °member, °part, °element, °unit, component, °structure, *Technical* process: *The eye, come to think of it, is a truly miraculous organ.* **2** °medium, °vehicle, °voice, °mouthpiece, forum, °publication, °paper, °magazine, newsletter, house organ, newspaper, annual, semiannual, °quarterly, monthly, fortnightly, weekly, hebdomadal, daily, °journal, °periodical: *The official organ of the Society is published in Abergavenny.*

organic *adj.* **1** living, °natural, biological, biotic, °animate, breathing: *Though coal may seem to be a mineral, it is organic, for it was formed from plants.* **2** °basic, °elementary, °essential, innate, °inborn, °natural, °native, °ingrained, °primary, °fundamental, visceral, constitutional, °inherent, structural, °integral: *The organic differences between the styles of writing are obvious.* **3** organized, °systematic, °coherent, coordinated, integrated, structured, °methodical, °orderly, °consistent: *The various elements of the painting blend into an organic whole.*

organism *n.* living thing, °structure, body; being, °creature: *It is the work of natural scientists to classify all kinds of organisms.*

organization *n.* **1** organizing, structuring, assembling, °assembly, putting together, coordination, systematizing, systematization, classifying, classification, categorizing, categorization, codifying, codification: *The organization of the school timetable took hours to complete.* **2** °structure, °pattern, configuration, °design, °plan, °scheme, °order, °system, °organism, °composition, °arrangement, constitution, °make-up, grouping, framework, °format, °form, °shape: *One must consider the organization as a whole, not merely its constituent elements.* **3** °body, °system, °institution, °federation, confederacy, confederation, °society, °group, °league, coalition, conglomerate, °combine, consortium, °syndicate, °organism: *The organization is a coherent structure made up of an enormous number of disparate elements.*

organize *v.* **1** °structure, °coordinate, systematize, systemize, °order, °arrange, °sort (out), classify, °categorize, codify, catalogue, °group, °tabulate, pigeonhole, °standardize: *These files ought to be organized so that you can find something when you need it.* **2** °form, °found, °set up, °establish, °institute, °start, °begin, °create, °originate, °initiate, °put together, °build, °develop, *US* pull together: *In 1969, we organized a company to publish reference books.*

orgy *n.* **1** bacchanalia, bacchanal, saturnalia, Dionysia, debauch, carousal, °carouse, °spree, °revel, °party, *Colloq* binge, °bender, °drunk, bust, *Slang* °jag, *US and Canadian* toot, tear: *The journalist represented the earl's party as a wild orgy.* **2** overindulgence, °splurge, °spree, °fling, *Slang US* °bender: *Trying to lift himself out of depression, Roger went on a spending orgy.*

orient *n.* **1** east: *Harriet is in the orient on business.*
—*adj.* **2** *Literary* oriental, eastern: *The grass was sown with orient pearls.*
—*v.* **3** °adjust, °adapt, acclimatize *or* acclimate, habituate, °accommodate, °condition, °accustom, °familiarize, feel one's °way, assess, get one's °bearings, *Colloq* orientate: *It is a new job and she needs a few days to orient herself.*

orientation *n.* **1** °placement, bearings, °attitude, alignment, °lie, placing, °situation, layout, °location, °position, positioning, °arrangement, °set-up: *The orientation of the buildings is such that the windows face south.* **2** introduction, training, °initiation, briefing, familiarization, assimilation, acclimatization, °preparation, °instruction: *The orientation of the new employees is scheduled for next week. We were given orientation lectures.*

origin *n.* **1** °source, °derivation, °rise, fountain-head, °foundation, °basis, °base, well-spring, fount, provenance, *Chiefly US* provenience: *The origins of many English words are unknown.* **2** °creation, genesis, °birth, birthplace, cradle, dawning, °dawn, origination, °start, °beginning, commencement, °outset, °launch, launching, inception, inauguration: *The origin of the notion of democracy can be traced to ancient Greece.* **3** Often, ***origins***: °parentage, ancestry, °extraction, descent, °lineage, °pedigree, genealogy, °stock, °heritage: *We have traced our family's origins back to the Middle Ages.*

original *adj.* **1** °initial, °first, earliest, °primary, °beginning, starting, °basic: *The original report made no mention of any missing jewellery.* **2** °native, °indigenous, autochthonous, °aboriginal, primordial, primeval *or Brit. also* primaeval, °primitive: *At first, we could find only slight traces of the original inhabitants.* **3** °master, °actual, °primary, °authentic, °true, °genuine, °real, °basic; prototypic(al), archetypal, °source: *I have the original document and my lawyer has a copy.* **4** °creative, °novel, innovative, °unique, °imaginative, °unusual, inventive, °ingenious; first-hand, °fresh, underived, unprecedented: *The film is based on a highly original story by Daphne du Maurier. The author has some original insights into Hamlet's relationship with Ophelia.*
—*n.* **5** °prototype, archetype, °source, °model, °pattern; °master: *The original hangs in the National Gallery.* **6** °eccentric, °nonconformist, °individualist, *Colloq* case, °card, °character, *Brit* °queer fish: *True to his reputation as an original, Wilde sauntered down the Strand with a lily in his hand.*

originality *n.* creativeness, creativity, inventiveness, °ingenuity, innovativeness, °innovation, °novelty, newness, unorthodoxy, unconventionality, cleverness, °daring, resourcefulness, °independence, individuality, uniqueness, nonconformity: *One must admire Dali for his originality.*

originally *adv.* in *or* at *or* from the °beginning, (at) first, from the °first, initially, to °begin with, at *or* from the °outset, at *or* from the °start, in the °first place *or* instance, *Colloq* from the word go, from day one: *Originally, we were to have gone in Patrick's car.*

originate *v.* **1** °create, °bring about, engender, give °birth to, beget, °conceive, °initiate, °inaugurate, °start, °begin, °introduce, °launch, °found, °set up, °institute, °establish, °invent, °coin, °devise, °pioneer, °design, contrive, concoct, °mastermind, °compose, °organize, °formulate, °form, °generate, °produce, °develop, evolve: *Wasn't it the Chinese who originated free public health schemes?* **2** °arise, °rise, °begin, °start, °come, °spring, °stem, °flow, °issue, °emerge, °emanate, °proceed, °grow, °develop, evolve, °derive, °result: *Where did the idea of the democratic form of government originate?*

ornament *n.* **1** enhancement, °embellishment, adornment, °decoration, ornamentation, gingerbread, trimming, garnish, garnishment, °frill, embroidery, beautification, °accessory; frippery; knick-knack, furbelow, °bauble, °gewgaw, *Slang US* tchotchke: *We spent a pleasant afternoon putting ornaments on the Christmas tree. The ornaments on the mantelpiece needed dusting.*
—*v.* **2** °decorate, °embellish, °enhance, adorn, °trim, garnish, embroider, °elaborate, °beautify, accessorize, deck (out), °dress up: *The cabinet is ornamented with ormolu fittings in the Empire style.*

ornamental *adj.* decorative, beautifying, adorning, garnishing, embellishing: *Nothing in the house is ornamental, everything is functional.*

ornate *adj.* °elaborate, florid, overdone, °laboured, rococo, baroque, gingerbread, arabesque, °fancy, °lavish, °rich, °flowery, °busy, °fussy, frilly, °intricate; high-flown, euphuistic, Ossianic, °bombastic, °pompous, °pretentious, °affected, °grandiose, fulsome, highfalutin *or* hifalutin, grandiloquent, °flamboyant: *Louis Quinze style is far too ornate for my tastes. We find his writing, with its contorted artificialities, far too ornate to appeal to the modern reader.*

orthodox *adj.* conformist, accepted, °authoritative, authorized, recognized, received, °official, standard, °prevailing, °prevalent, °common, °regular, °popular, °ordinary, doctrinal, established, °traditional, traditionalist, °accustomed, °conventional, °customary, °conservative: *The orthodox view is that he was killed by an assassin acting on his own.*

oscillate *v.* °fluctuate, °vibrate, waver, °see-saw, °swing, °sway; vacillate, °equivocate, °shilly-shally, hem and haw, tergiversate: *The needle is oscillating between the 'Safe' and 'Danger' marks. I wish he'd stop oscillating and make up his mind.*

ostensibly *adv.* °outwardly, externally, superficially, patently, ostensively, demonstrably, °apparently, °evidently, °seemingly; °clearly, plainly, °manifestly, conspicuously, °obviously, patently, noticeably, prominently: *Ostensibly, he was visiting his aunt, but we all know he went to see Stella.*

ostentation *n.* °show, °display, °exhibition, exhibitionism, showing off, °pretension, pretentiousness, flaunting, flashiness, °flourish, flamboyance, °parade, window-dressing: *His clothes are elegant without ostentation.*

ostentatious *adj.* °showy, °boastful, °braggart, vaunting, °vain, vainglorious, flaunting, °pretentious, °flamboyant, °theatrical, *Colloq* °flash: *It's terribly ostentatious of Lady Penny to wear her diamond tiara to the disco.*

ostracize *v.* blackball, blacklist, °banish, °exile, °boycott, °isolate, °segregate, °exclude, excommunicate, snub, °shun, °avoid, *Chiefly Brit* send to Coventry, *Colloq* °cut, cold-shoulder, give (someone) the cold °shoulder: *Marcus has been ostracized at the club ever since the court case.*

otherwise *adv.* **1** if not, or else, under other circumstances, in another °situation, on the other hand: *I learned something about you tonight that otherwise I should never have guessed.* **2** differently, in another °manner *or* °way: *You may travel unless the doctor advises otherwise.*

out *adv.* **1** °outside, outdoors, in *or* into the open °air: *If you go out take an umbrella.* **2** away (from), °abroad, °elsewhere, not (at) °home, gone (from), gone away (from), °absent (from): *She was out of the house when I phoned.* **3** in *or* into the open, to *or* into °public °notice, for all to see, out of the closet: *Everything will be brought out at the trial.* **4** revealed, exposed, °visible, °discernible, °manifest, in °sight, in °view: *Are the stars out tonight?* **5** °short, minus, missing, in °default, out of pocket: *He is out the £2,000 he invested in a Welsh diamond mine.* **6** °free, at °liberty, at °large, °loose, unconfined: *They let Matilda out after she served her sentence.* **7** °completely, °thoroughly, effectively, °entirely: *I was tired out after that long swim.*
—*adj.* **8** °unconscious, °senseless, °insensible, *Colloq* out °cold, out like a light: *He has been out for almost an hour.* **9** dated, out-dated, out-moded, °*passé*, °old-fashioned, °antiquated, °old hat, *démodé*, °obsolete, unfashionable: *Longer skirts were out in the mid-1960s.* **10** °often, ***outer***: outlying, °distant, far-off, °peripheral: *He was planning to travel to the outer reaches of his empire. Let's sail to some of the out islands.* **11** °exhausted, gone, finished, ended; over, completed: *Our food was out. Rescue came before the day was out.* **12** °inaccurate, °incorrect, °wrong, at °fault, °faulty, °off, °wide of the mark: *Your figures are out by a factor of four.* **13** °unacceptable, forbidden, prohibited, not allowed, *Colloq* not on: *Smoking is out in the dining room.* **14** extinguished, unlit; °off, doused; inoperative, nonfunctioning, out of °order *or* commission, unserviceable, °broken: *Make certain that all camp-fires are completely out. The light is out in the corridor.*
—*n.* **15** °alibi, °excuse, °escape, °loophole, °evasion: *She used your visit as an out to avoid calling on her mother.*

out-and-out *adj.* °complete, °unmitigated, unalloyed, °undiluted, °pure, utter, °perfect, consummate, °outright, °total, °downright, °unqualified, °thorough, thoroughgoing, through-and-through, dyed in the wool: *She was an out-and-out fool to turn down his marriage proposal.*

outburst *n.* outbreak, °eruption, °explosion, blow-up, flare-up, fulmination; upsurge, °surge, °outpouring, welling (forth), upwelling, outflow(ing), °rush, °flood, effusion, effluence *or* efflux; °fit, access, °attack, °spasm, °paroxysm, °seizure, °tantrum: *Another outburst like that, young man, and you'll be sent home.*

outcast *n.* pariah, °exile, °reject, *persona non grata*, leper, untouchable, expatriate, °refugee, displaced person, DP, evacuee: *In 1946, Europe swarmed with outcasts, the detritus of the war.*

outcome *n.* °result, consequence, °end (°result *or* °product), after-effect, °effect, °upshot, °sequel, °development, outgrowth, aftermath, °wake, °follow-up, *Medicine* sequela (usually *pl.* sequelae), *Colloq* °pay-off, bottom line: *One outcome of the new safety regulations will be higher fares. We eagerly awaited the outcome of the race.*

outcry *n.* °protest, protestation, decrial, °complaint, °indignation, °uproar, vociferation, clamour, clamouring, commotion, °outburst, °noise, hullabaloo, °howl, howling, hoot, hooting, boo, booing, °hiss, hissing: *The public outcry against terrorism was heard round the world.*

outdo *v.* °exceed, °surpass, °excel, °transcend, °beat, °outstrip, outshine, °top, °cap, trump, °overcome, °defeat, °outweigh: *Their prices are lower because they outdo us in cheapness of labour.*

outdoor *adj.* °outside, out of doors, alfresco, open-air: *Both of them enjoy outdoor activities like hiking and bicycling.*

outfit *n.* **1** °gear, °rig, °equipment, equipage, °apparatus, accoutrements *or US also* accouterments, °paraphernalia, °trappings, °tackle, °tack, utensils: *His mountain-climbing outfit turned out to be extremely expensive.* **2** °clothes, °costume, °ensemble; attire, garb, clothing, °dress; *Colloq* °get-up, togs: *She was wearing a very weird outfit that attracted a lot of stares.* **3** °firm, °concern, °business, °organization, °company, (military) °unit, corporation; °party, °set, °group; *Colloq* °set-up: *I joined the outfit when it consisted of only a hundred people.*
—*v.* **4** °fit (out *or* up), °equip, °kit out, °provision, °stock, accoutre *or US also* accouter, °rig (out *or* up), °supply, °furnish: *The shop is prepared to outfit anyone for anything from a walk in the country to an African safari or an Arctic expedition.*

outgoing *adj.* **1** departing, °retiring, ex-, °former, °past, emeritus, leaving, withdrawing: *It is our custom to honour the outgoing president with a banquet.* **2** °genial, °friendly, °amiable, °cordial, °warm,

°expansive, approachable, affable, °accessible, amenable, °easygoing, °amicable, °sociable, congenial, extrovert, °familiar, °informal, communicative: *Because of his outgoing attitude, Keith gets along well with most people.*

outing *n.* jaunt, junket, °excursion, °trip, °expedition, °tour, °ride, *Colloq* °spin: *This year, the annual church outing will again be to Torquay.*

outlandish *adj.* °unfamiliar, °strange, °odd, °queer, °offbeat, °peculiar, °curious, °exotic, °foreign, °alien, °unknown, °unheard-of, °different, °exceptional, °extraordinary, °quaint, °eccentric, °bizarre, °*outré*, °weird, °fantastic, °unusual, °singular, °unique; freakish, °grotesque, barbarous; *Colloq* far-out, °camp(y), °kinky: *Those youngsters wear the most outlandish hair-dos you have ever seen.*

outlast *v.* °survive, outlive; outwear; °weather: *Considering her condition, it seems doubtful that she will outlast her husband.*

outlaw *n.* **1** °criminal, °gangster, °robber, desperado, bandit, highwayman, brigand, footpad, picaroon *or* pickaroon, °pirate, °fugitive (from justice *or* the law), °renegade, *US* road-agent: *In Westerns, the sheriff always wins out over the outlaws.*
—*v.* **2** °forbid, disallow, °ban, interdict, °bar, °exclude, °prohibit, proscribe: *Some countries have outlawed prostitution, but with little effect.*

outlay *n.* °expense, °cost, °expenditure, spending, disbursement, °payment: *The city council refused to approve the outlay for a new swimming-pool.*

outlet *n.* **1** °way out, °exit, egress, °loophole, °relief, °escape, °escape hatch, °vent, °opening, °release, safety-valve, °discharge: *There seemed to be no outlet for his anger but to throw the cushion at her. The main outlet of the Great Lakes is the St Lawrence river.*
2 retailer, °shop, °store, °market: *The company is having difficulty finding outlets that will stock its products.*

outline *n.* **1** °profile, °silhouette, contour, °periphery, °boundary, footprint: *This outline is of the desk area occupied by the keyboard and monitor.* **2** °précis, °synopsis, résumé, °summary, °digest, °abstract, conspectus, °survey, overview, °run-down, recapitulation, °review, (°thumbnail) sketch, skeleton, (°overall) °plan, layout, framework, °draft, °scenario: *O'Brien presented an outline of what his company planned to do after the take-over.*
—*v.* **3** °trace, °draft, sketch, °rough out, °profile, °block (out), °plan (out), °lay out, °define, delineate: *None of the divers was particularly enthusiastic about the procedure outlined for bringing up the wreckage.*

outlook *n.* **1** °view, °position, °point of °view, °viewpoint, °prospect, °perspective, °slant, °angle, °standpoint, °attitude, °opinion: *His outlook on the situation in the Middle East is bound to be somewhat biased.*
2 °prospect, °forecast, °expectation(s): *What is the outlook for the value of the pound sterling over the next year?*

outlying *adj.* °distant, far-off, far-flung, outer, outermost, °out-of-the-way, °remote, °far-away, °peripheral, furthest *or* farthest: *In those days it took weeks for the news to reach the outlying parts of the empire.*

out-of-the-way *adj.* **1** untravelled, unfrequented, °isolated, °lonely, °outlying, °obscure, hidden, °secluded, °inaccessible: *She now lives in some out-of-the-way village in the Himalayas.* **2** °unusual, °odd, °peculiar, °extraordinary, °far-fetched, °remarkable, °*outré*, °exceptional, °outlandish, °strange, °rare, uncommon, °exotic, °unheard-of, unconventional, °queer, °weird, °bizarre: *His latest book is a treatise on some out-of-the-way subject.*

outpouring *n.* effusion, outflow, °flow, °outburst, °flood, deluge, °torrent, °spate, emanation, spouting, °spurt, gushing, efflux, effluence, outrush, tide, cascade, cataract, Niagara, *Technical* debouchment: *We scarcely expected such an outpouring of grief at her death. This writing appears to reflect the outpourings of his soul.*

output *n.* **1** °production, °result, °yield, crop, °harvest: *Nobody was quite ready for such a massive output.*
2 productivity, °achievement, °efficiency: *Job insecurity has diminished her output.*
—*v.* **3** °put out, °produce, °generate, °create, °manufacture, °yield, °achieve: *Our new laser printer outputs about ten pages a minute.*

outrage *n.* **1** °violence, °atrocity, inhumanity, barbarism, °enormity, °evil, °barbarity, savagery, brutality, malignity, malefaction, wrongdoing, evil-doing, maltreatment, °abuse, cruelty, °injury, °harm, °damage: *Wherever there is war there is misery and outrage.*
2 °resentment, affront, °bitterness, °indignation, °hurt, °shock, °anger, wrath, ire: *The minister felt outrage at being given a parking ticket.* **3** °insult, °indignity, °slight: *Contributors to the charity considered it an outrage that the fund-raisers should keep so much of the money.*
—*v.* **4** °offend, °insult, affront, vex, °displease, °distress, nettle, °chafe, °infuriate, °anger, °enrage, °madden, make one's blood °boil, raise (someone's) hackles, rile: *He was outraged to discover that the wretch had proposed to his daughter.* **5** °violate, °desecrate, defile, do °violence to, °injure, °harm, °abuse, °damage: *Such deeds outrage human feelings.* **6** °rape, °violate, °ravage, °ravish, deflower, °attack: *He seized the unhappy girl and outraged her.*

outrageous *adj.* **1** °excessive, °extravagant, °immoderate, °exorbitant, °enormous, °unreasonable, °preposterous, °shocking, °extreme, °unwarranted, exaggerated, °unconscionable, °inordinate, intolerable, °disgraceful, °shameful, °scandalous: *The prices at that restaurant are absolutely outrageous.*
2 °vicious, °cruel, heinous, °atrocious, barbaric, °inhuman, °abusive, °beastly, °horrible, horrid, horrendous, iniquitous, °villainous, °wicked, °evil, egregious, °flagrant, °grievous, °infamous, execrable, °abominable, °grisly, °hideous, °monstrous, °vile, °unthinkable, °foul, °awful, unspeakable, appalling, °offensive, °indecent: *The captives suffered the most outrageous treatment at the hands of their conquerors.*
3 °indecent, °offensive, °immoral, °rude, indelicate, °obnoxious, °profane, °obscene, °dirty, °filthy, °lewd, salacious, °foul, smutty, scatological, °pornographic, objectionable, °repellent, °repulsive, nauseating, °nauseous, °nasty, °gross, °revolting, °shocking, °repugnant, °disgusting, fulsome, °perverted, depraved, °dissolute, °degenerate, dissipated, debauched, °profligate; °explicit, unrestrained; foul-mouthed, thersitical, insulting; °unseemly, °inappropriate, indecorous, °improper, °naughty, appalling, °embarrassing; *Literary* Fescennine, *US* shy-making: *The sermon denounced the outrageous films, books, magazines, and television programmes to which children are exposed. Warren sometimes says the most outrageous things.*

outré *adj.* unconventional, °unusual, °extravagant, °bizarre, °weird, °strange, °odd, °peculiar, °grotesque, °outlandish, freakish, °out-of-the-way: *The attention of the media was turned upon the singer's outré behaviour on stage.*

outright *adj.* **1** °unqualified, °total, unreserved, unrestricted, full, °complete, unconditional, unequivocal, °clear, °direct, °definite, unmistakable: *The duke is the outright owner of the property.* **2** °undisguised, °unmitigated, utter, consummate, °pure, °out-and-out, all-out, °sheer, °absolute, °stark, bald, °thorough, arrant, thoroughgoing, through-and-through, °downright, °direct, °definite, unmistakable: *Her outright refusal to provide further help was met with dismay.*
—*adv.* **3** °directly, at °once, °immediately, °instantaneously, instantly, then and there *or* there and then, °straight *or* °right away, on the °spot, °right off: *One passenger was killed outright, the other died later in hospital.* **4** °completely, °entirely, °exactly, °precisely, °totally, *in toto*, °utterly, baldly, starkly, consummately, purely, °thoroughly, °directly, unhesitatingly,

°quite, °absolutely, explicitly, categorically, straightforwardly, plainly, °openly, forthrightly, unequivocally, unambiguously, candidly: *I wish that Henry wasn't so reticent and would say outright what he means.* **5** unrestrictedly, unqualifiedly, unreservedly, unconditionally: *The duke owns the property outright.*

outset *n.* °beginning, °start, inauguration, inception, °first, *Colloq* kick-off: *Had you let them know who you were at the outset, this wouldn't have happened.*

outside *n.* **1** °exterior, °face, °facing, °shell, °skin, °case, casing, °surface, °front; façade: *What is that on the outside of the box? The outside of the house is painted white.* **2** °aspect, °appearance, °look, demeanour, °face, °front, façade, mien, °mask, °disguise, °false °front, °pretence: *One cannot tell what people are really like from the outside they present to the world.* **3** °extreme, °limit, most, °maximum, utmost, best, worst, longest: *At the outside, you shouldn't pay more than half your income for housing. I'll wait for her for an hour at the outside.* **4** the world at °large: *We had to bring in someone from the outside to complete the work.* —*adj.* **5** °exterior, °external, out of doors, °outdoor: *They have added an outside swimming-pool to the house.* **6** °maximum, maximal, highest, best, worst, greatest, most, largest, longest, furthest *or* farthest: *What was their outside estimate for replacing the roof? The outside time for driving here from London is about an hour.* **7** °private, °home, cottage, °secondary, °peripheral, °independent, freelance: *Her outside job pays more than her regular work.* **8** °unlikely, °remote, °faint, *Colloq* °slim: *He has an outside chance of beating the world record.* **9** °foreign, °alien, °outward; unconnected, excluded, uninvolved, disinvolved, °independent, °separate, °different: *I'm worried that Phil might be subject to outside influences. An outside contractor is doing the work.* —*adv.* **10** outdoors, out of doors: *Perhaps you'd like to step outside to discuss the matter further?*

outsider *n.* non-member, non-initiate, °foreigner, °alien, outlander, °stranger, °newcomer, °guest, °visitor, trespasser, interloper, °intruder, squatter, invader, *Colloq* gatecrasher: *The others always treated Peter as an outsider. Why do I feel an outsider in my own home?*

outskirts *n.pl.* °periphery, °edge, environs, outer reaches, °vicinity, °border(s), suburb(s), exurb(s), general °area *or* °neighbourhood, purlieus, °fringes, vicinage, faubourg(s): *The university is on the outskirts of the city.*

outsmart *v.* °outwit, outfox, out-think, outmanoeuvre, outmanipulate, outplay, steal a march on, get the better *or* best of, °trick, °dupe, °hoodwink, °fool, °deceive, °hoax, gull, make a °fool of; °swindle, °cheat, °defraud, cozen, *Colloq* °put one over on, pull a fast one on, °take in, make a °monkey (out) of, bamboozle, con, *Brit* nobble, *Slang* °slip *or* °put one *or* something over on (someone): *'I have been outsmarted by bigger fools than you!', Mr White shouted.*

outspoken *adj.* °candid, °frank, °open, °free, °direct, unreserved, unreticent, straightforward, °forthright, °explicit, °specific, plain-spoken, plain-speaking, unequivocal, unceremonious, unambiguous, unsubtle, °uninhibited, unshrinking, °blunt, °bold, °brusque, °brash, undiplomatic, °tactless, °crude: *Linda was always quite outspoken in her opinions of her neighbours. Her outspoken observations are a fruitful source of gossip.*

outstanding *adj.* **1** °prominent, °eminent, °renowned, °famous, famed, unforgettable, °memorable, °celebrated, °distinguished, °special, °choice, °noteworthy, °notable, °noted, °important, °conspicuous, °exceptional, °excellent, °superior, first-class, °first-rate, °superb, °remarkable, °extraordinary, °marvellous, °sensational, *Colloq* smashing, °super: *Liszt was the outstanding pianist-composer of his time.* **2** °unsettled, on-going, °unresolved, °unpaid, °due, owed *or* owing, receivable *or* °payable; °remaining, °leftover: *The company has a few outstanding debts.*

outstrip *v.* °overcome, °surpass, °outdo, outperform, outshine, outclass, °better, °beat, °transcend, °best, worst, °exceed, °excel, outdistance, °overtake, °top, °cap, put in the °shade, °eclipse: *Bannister again outstripped everyone in the race.*

outward *adj.* °external, °exterior, outer, °outside, °outlying, °manifest, °obvious, °evident, °apparent, °visible, °observable; °superficial, °surface, °extrinsic, °skin-deep, °shallow, °pretended, °false, ostensible, °formal, °physical, bodily, fleshly, °carnal, mundane, °worldly, °secular, °temporal, °terrestrial, °material, non-spiritual: *She gave every outward sign of being the bereaved widow. Whatever outward trappings money may buy, A man's true wealth lies deep inside.*

outwardly *adv.* externally, °apparently, visibly, superficially, °ostensibly, °evidently, °seemingly, on the °surface, to all appearances, to all intents and purposes: *Though the town was outwardly quiet, we had a feeling of ominous foreboding.*

outwards *adv.* °outward, °outside, away, °out, without: *The towns of the early twentieth century centred on the railway station and radiated outwards.*

outweigh *v.* °overcome, outbalance, overbalance, overweigh, tip the scales, preponderate (over), °surpass, °prevail (over), override, take °precedence (over), °compensate (for), °make up for: *His feeling for his wife outweighed all else in his life.*

outwit *v.* See **outsmart,** above.

oval *adj.* egg-shaped, ovoid, ovate, oviform, obovoid, obovate; elliptical, ellipsoid(al): *His mother's picture hung in an oval frame over the mantel.*

ovation *n.* °applause, acclamation, acclaim, plaudits, °cheers, cheering, clapping, laudation, °praise, °kudos, *Colloq* (big) °hand: *At the conclusion of the concerto, the pianist was given a standing ovation.*

over *prep.* **1** above, on, upon, on °top of, atop (of): *She spread a tarpaulin over the boat to protect it.* **2** more than, greater than, upwards *or* upward of, in °excess of, (over and) above, (over and) beyond; °exceeding: *Of the 2,000 people questioned in our survey, over half said they think prunes are funny. The thieves took over £50,000-worth of paintings.* **3** across, to *or* from *or* on the other °side of; beyond: *The children crossed over the river to play in the woods on the other side.* **4** °for, during, in *or* over *or* during the °course of, °through, °throughout: *Over the next week she will be working in the Paris office.* **5** (all) through, °throughout, (all) about, all over: *We travelled over the entire country in the course of our holiday.* —*adj.* **6** done (with), finished, terminated, concluded, ended, °past, settled, closed, at an °end, over with: *I'm afraid it's all over between us, Carrie.* —*adv.* **7** to, onto, past, beyond, across: *This room looks out over the sea.* **8** °remaining, as a °remainder, as °surplus, °outstanding: *When we finished eating, there wasn't much left over.* **9** (once) again, once more, one more time: *This pot will have to be cleaned over again.* **10** down, to the ground *or* floor: *You almost knocked over the lamp.*

overall *adj.* °total, °complete, °comprehensive, all-inclusive, °inclusive, °whole, °entire, all-embracing, blanket: *The overall cost, including materials and labour, came to more than I had expected.*

overawe *v.* °overwhelm, °intimidate, cow, °daunt, awe, °bully, hector, °browbeat, °dominate, domineer, °frighten, °scare, °terrify, disconcert, °discomfit, °upset, abash: *The children were overawed by their father's slightest sign of displeasure.*

overbearing *adj.* °repressive, °domineering, bullying, imperious, °officious, °high and °mighty, high-handed, overweening, magisterial, lordly, °authoritarian, °wilful, °despotic, °dogmatic, autocratic, °tyrannical, °dictatorial, °peremptory, °arbitrary, °assertive, °arrogant, cavalier, °haughty, °superior, °supercilious, °pretentious, *Colloq* °bossy, °pushy, °hoity-toity, high-falutin *or* hifalutin, snooty, *Slang* snotty: *His temper was harsh and severe, his manner haughty and overbearing.*

overcast *adj.* cloudy, clouded, °sunless, moonless, starless, °murky, °grey, louring *or* lowering, °dull, °dark, darkened, °dreary, °sombre, °gloomy, °dismal, °threatening, °menacing: *The sky was overcast this morning, but the sun is now beginning to shine through.*

overcome *v.* **1** °beat, °defeat, °conquer, °overpower, °subdue, worst, °best, °triumph over, °win (out) (over), °prevail (over), °overthrow, °overwhelm, vanquish, get the better *or* best of, °whip, drub, °rout, °break, °subjugate, °suppress, °crush, °master, *Colloq* lick: *If we do not overcome these temptations, they will overcome us. The superior force easily overcame the tiny group of defenders.*
—*adj.* **2** beaten, defeated, overwhelmed, °subdued, worsted, bested; °affected, °speechless, swept off one's feet, rendered °helpless, overpowered, moved, influenced, at a loss (for words), *Colloq* bowled over: *The victim's parents were overcome with grief when the casualty list was published. Colin was too overcome to speak at the award presentation.*

overconfident *adj.* **1** °brash, °arrogant, cocksure, °cocky, °brazen, hubristic, swaggering, °audacious, °overbearing, vainglorious, *Colloq* °pushy: *It is harmful for a sportsman's morale to be overconfident of winning.* **2** °heedless, °foolhardy, °thoughtless, °shortsighted, °hasty: *Rock-climbers should not be overconfident and rely entirely on their ropes.*

overcritical *adj.* supercritical, hypercritical, captious, carping, °niggling, cavilling, °querulous, °fault-finding, °finicky, °fussy, °hair-splitting, °difficult, °fastidious, °harsh, °severe, °demanding, °exacting, small, °small-minded, *US and Canadian* picayune, *Colloq* picky, nit-picking, pernickety *or US also* persnickety: *You should not be overcritical of Maddy—she's only a child.*

overcrowded *adj.* jammed, °packed, °congested, °populous, over-populous, jam-packed, overpopulated; swarming, crawling, choked, °packed to the gunwales: *The planet is becoming overcrowded. We squeezed into an already overcrowded train.*

overdo *v.* **1** carry to °excess, overindulge, be intemperate, go *or* carry to °extremes, overact, °exaggerate, carry *or* go too far, overreach, not know when to stop, paint the lily, gild refined gold, out-Herod Herod, *Colloq* go overboard, do to death, lay it on thick, °lay it on with a trowel; go off the deep end: *Exercise a little judgement and try not to overdo it.* **2** °overwork, do too much, overtax, °exhaust, °fatigue, °overload, overburden, *Colloq* bite off more than one can chew, burn the candle at both ends: *Don't overdo it or you'll feel the results tomorrow.*

overdue *adj.* °late, °tardy, behindhand, behind, unpunctual, °belated, *US* past °due: *As it is now December, payment is long overdue. I've got an overdue library book to return.*

overeat *v.* °gorge, binge, gormandize, °stuff oneself, overindulge, guzzle, °feast, wolf down, overfeed, do the gavage, *Colloq* pack away, *Brit* pig, *US* pig out: *People not only overeat but they tend to eat the wrong foods.*

overgrown *adj.* covered, °overrun, overspread, °luxuriant, weedy, °abundant: *The walls are all overgrown with ivy.*

overhang *v.* **1** °jut (out), beetle, °bulge (out), °project (out), °protrude, °stick out, °loom (out), °extend (out), °hang (out) over: *The balcony overhangs the sea.* **2** impend, °threaten, °menace, imperil, °loom: *His life was overhung by the threat of blackmail.*
—*n.* **3** °ledge, °projection, °bulge, °protrusion, °extension: *A swallow nested under the overhang of the roof.*

overhaul *v.* **1** °overtake, °pass, °gain on *or* upon, °draw °ahead of, catch up with, get ahead of, °outstrip, outdistance, °leave behind, °lap: *We overhauled the ketch and were beginning to close on the yawl when the squall hit us.* **2** °renovate, °refurbish, recondition, rebuild, °restore, °repair, °service, °adjust, °patch (up), °mend, °fix (up): *The car engine needs to be thoroughly overhauled.*
—*n.* **3** reconditioning, overhauling, refurbishing, rebuilding, renovation, servicing, °adjustment, mending, fixing (up): *The overhaul of the die-stamping machine will require two months to complete.*

overhead *adv.* **1** (up) above, (up) in the °air *or* °sky, °high up, on °high, °aloft, skyward: *The aeroplanes passed overhead at dawn.*
—*adj.* **2** °elevated, raised, °upper: *The crane travels on an overhead track.*
—*n.* **3** *Brit* overheads, *US* overhead (basic *or* fixed) costs, operating °cost(s), °expense(s), °outlay, disbursement(s), °running °cost(s), °expenditure(s), °maintenance, °cost(s) of doing °business: *One way to increase profits is by reducing overheads.*

overjoyed *adj.* °delighted, °ecstatic, °elated, °happy, °rapturous, euphoric, jubilant, thrilled, cock-a-hoop, transported, *Colloq* tickled pink, in seventh °heaven, on cloud nine, *Brit* over the moon: *We were overjoyed to hear your news and to receive the invitation to your wedding.*

overlap *v.* **1** °lap (over), overlie, overlay, shingle, *Technical* imbricate, strobilate: *Note how the upper tiles overlap the lower to keep the rain out.* **2** °coincide, °correspond, intersect: *Our work shifts overlap by four hours.*
—*n.* **3** °lap, °flap, overlay, °fly (front) *or Brit* flies, imbrication: *The overlap conceals the buttons that close the skirt on the side.*

overload *v.* **1** °weigh down, °burden, overburden, °load (up), overtax, saddle with, °tax, °strain, °impede, °handicap, °oppress, °encumber, cumber, overcharge: *They overloaded me with so much work that I'll never finish.*
—*n.* **2** surcharge, overcharge, overburden, dead °weight, °oppression, °handicap, °tax, °load, °encumbrance, °impediment, °hindrance: *We had to hire extra people at Christmas to help deal with the overload.*

overlook *v.* **1** °miss, °slip up on, °omit, °neglect, °slight, °disregard, °fail to notice, °ignore, °pass over, °leave out, °forget, *Colloq* °pass up: *You overlooked an error on the first page.* **2** °blink at, wink at, °let go (by), °let pass, °let ride, turn a blind eye to, °shut (one's) eyes to, pretend not to °notice, take no °notice of, °ignore, °disregard, °forgive, °pardon, °excuse, °permit, °allow, °forget about, °write off, condone, make allowances (for), °let bygones be bygones, °gloss over: *I shall overlook your slowness if you will work late to compensate for it.* **3** °front on (to), °face, °give upon, °command *or* °afford a °view of, °look out on *or* over, have as a vista *or* °view: *My room overlooks the lake.*

overly *adv.* excessively, too, °exceedingly, immoderately, disproportionately, °unduly, inordinately, extraordinarily, °very, *Colloq* damned: *She seemed overly anxious for us to leave.*

overpower *v.* **1** °overcome, °overwhelm, °beat, vanquish, °conquer, °defeat, °crush, °put down, worst, °best, °prevail, °master, °quell, °subdue, °subjugate: *The thugs easily overpowered the elderly couple and took their money.* **2** °overcome, °overwhelm, °dumbfound *or* dumfound, °daze, °stagger, °amaze, °stun, stupefy, °nonplus, °strike, *Colloq* °floor: *I was quite overpowered by the grandeur of the house.*

overpowering *adj.* °overwhelming, °irresistible, °powerful, °telling, compelling, unendurable, °unbearable, °oppressive: *They presented an overpowering argument against the use of asbestos as an insulator.*

overrate *v.* overvalue, °make too much of, °exaggerate the °worth *or* value of, °attach too much °importance to, overprize, assess too °highly: *They insist that his value to the company is overrated and that he should be dismissed.*

overreact *v.* °exaggerate, make much ado about nothing, °make too much of (something), make a mountain out of a molehill, lose all *or* one's sense of proportion, °blow (up) out of (all) proportion: *I'd say that she overreacted by leaving him because he forgot her birthday.*

overriding *adj.* °dominant, dominating, °predominant, predominating, compelling, °prevailing, °primary, °prime, most °important, overruling, °overwhelming, °paramount, preponderant, °principal, °cardinal, °main, °chief: *His overriding reason for buying the larger dictionary was that it made a better doorstop.*

overrun *v.* invade, °defeat, °attack, °ravage, °destroy, °overwhelm, °conquer, harry, vandalize, °plunder, maraud, °scourge, despoil, °sack, °strip, °pillage, °storm, *Colloq* blitz: *Within a week the armies had overrun the country and captured the capital city.*

overseas *adv.* °abroad: *Did you serve overseas during the war?*

oversee *v.* °direct, °manage, °watch (over), °keep an °eye on, °administer, superintend, °run, °supervise, °operate, °manipulate, °handle, °control: *We employed Gertrude to oversee our offices in Frankfurt.*

overseer *n.* °superintendent, °supervisor, °manager, °foreman, forewoman, °superior, *Colloq* °boss, °chief, °super, *Brit* gaffer, *US* straw °boss, (°head *or* °chief) honcho: *Simon is too hard a taskmaster to be overseer of that sensitive operation.*

overshadow *v.* **1** °dominate, outshine, °eclipse, °dwarf, °diminish, °minimize, put in *or* throw into *or* leave the °shade, steal the limelight from, °tower over *or* above, °excel: *The Crown, overshadowed by the great barons, turned for aid to the Church.* **2** °spoil, °blight, °ruin, °mar, take (all) the pleasure from, put a damper on, take the edge off, °impair, take the enjoyment out of: *The news from the east overshadowed everyone's spirits at the party.*

oversight *n.* **1** °omission, inadvertence, °neglect, laxity, laxness, °fault, °failure, dereliction, °error, °mistake, °blunder, carelessness, heedlessness: *It was owing to an oversight by a clerk that the flight booking was not made.* **2** supervision, superintendence, °surveillance, °management, °direction, °guidance, °administration; °charge, °care, °custody, keeping, °hands, °protection, °auspices: *The matter of expenses must be left to the oversight of the committee established to deal with such things.*

overstate *v.* °exaggerate, °magnify, hyperbolize, embroider, overstress, °colour, °make (too) much of, overdraw, overemphasize, °stretch, °enlarge, °inflate, °blow up: *They might have overstated the problem by asking for a 24-hour police guard.*

overstep *v.* °exceed, °transcend, °surpass, °go beyond: *Again Hortense has overstepped the bounds of propriety by inviting herself to the reception.*

overt *adj.* °apparent, °evident, °plain, °clear, °obvious, °manifest, clear-cut, unconcealed, °patent, °open, °visible, °observable, °public: *Moving the troops to the border may be considered an act of overt hostility.*

overtake *v.* **1** catch (up with *or* to), °reach, draw °level *or* °even with, °overhaul, °gain on *or* upon, °move by *or* °past, °pass, °leave behind, °outstrip, outdistance: *The express train overtakes the local one at Amersham.* **2** °come upon, °seize, catch (unprepared), befall, °strike, °hit, °overwhelm: *The weaknesses of old age overtook the actress before she could finish writing her memoirs.*

overthrow *v.* **1** °defeat, °beat, °rout, °conquer, °overpower, °master, °bring down, depose, oust, °overwhelm, unseat, unhorse, °topple, °overturn, dethrone, thrash, worst, °best: *The new leader was overthrown by the partisans in two weeks. Cotswold Rangers overthrew Kent United in last night's match at Hurley.*
—*n.* **2** °defeat, °rout, °conquest, deposing, ousting, unseating, toppling, °overturn, overturning, °downfall, °end, °ruin, °fall, °collapse, °destruction, °suppression, quashing, crushing, subjugation, *US* ouster: *The overthrow of the military regime was followed by weeks of rioting and looting.*

overtone *n.* undertone, connotation, °hint, °suggestion, °innuendo, insinuation, intimation, °indication, °implication: *Do I detect overtones of regret now that you are finally leaving?*

overture *n.* Often, ***overtures***: °approach, °advance, °offer, °proposal, °proposition, °tender: *While they were winning, they rejected all peace overtures.*

overturn *v.* **1** °turn over, °knock down *or* over, °tip over, °capsize, up-end, °upset, °turn turtle, °turn upside down, °turn °topsy-turvy, invert: *The tanks overturned when they tried to drive past the huge concrete barriers. On his first day as a waiter, he overturned the soup in a guest's lap.* **2** °bring down, °overthrow, °throw over, °upset, depose, unthrone, unseat, oust, °eject: *The dictatorship was overturned and the country returned to being a democratic republic.*
—*n.* **3** overturning, °overthrow, unseating, ousting, toppling, °fall, °destruction, °ruin, °defeat, *US* ouster: *Could the overturn of the present regime be effected without force of arms?*

overwhelm *v.* **1** °overpower, °overcome, overtax, °devastate, °stagger, °crush, °defeat, °destroy, °subdue, °suppress, °quash, °quell, °conquer, °beat, °bring down, °prostrate, °weigh down, °oppress: *Overwhelmed by grief, she dissolved into tears.* **2** inundate, °overcome, engulf, °submerge, °flood (over); deluge, °swamp, °bury, °immerse: *A feeling of terror suddenly overwhelmed me as I watched my safety rope fray and break. In only a few hours the rising waters had completely overwhelmed the house.* **3** °overcome, °stagger, °astound, °astonish, °dumbfound *or* dumfound, °shock, °stun, °bewilder, °confuse, confound, °nonplus, °surprise, °take aback, *Colloq* °bowl over, °knock off one's feet *or* pins, blow one's °mind, discombobulate, *Brit* °knock for six: *We were overwhelmed by the friendly reception that awaited our return.*

overwhelming *adj.* **1** °overpowering, uncontrollable, °irresistible, °devastating, unendurable, °unbearable, crushing, °burdensome, °formidable: *He had an overwhelming sense of shame for what he had said.* **2** °awesome, awe-inspiring, stupefying, astounding, astonishing, staggering, bewildering, mind-shattering, °prodigious, mind-boggling, *Colloq* mind-blowing: *When I first went to live in London, I found its sheer size totally overwhelming.*

overwork *v.* **1** overexert, overstrain, overburden, °oppress, overtax, °overload, overuse: *We were so overworked that the quality had to suffer.* **2** °slave (away), burn the midnight oil, lucubrate: *She insisted on overworking in order to get the project finished on time.*
—*n.* **3** overexertion, overstrain, °strain: *I was ready to drop from overwork.*

overwrought *adj.* **1** °tense, °nervous, jittery, °jumpy, fidgety, °touchy, in a dither *or* °twitter, all a-twitter, overexcited, on °edge, over-stimulated, °frantic, frenetic, distracted, *Brit* strung up, *US* strung out, *Colloq* (all) worked up, edgy, in a tizzy, wound up, uptight: *They were quite overwrought worrying about the children's safety.* **2** overworked, °ornate, °elaborate, baroque, rococo, florid, °flowery, °fussy, °ostentatious, °busy, °gaudy, °garish: *Some of the Victorian houses were characterized by overwrought gingerbread decoration. A few of his poems are overwrought and difficult to digest.*

owe *v.* **1** be in °debt to, be °indebted to, be °beholden to: *It must be a good feeling not to owe anyone any money at all.* **2** ***owing to***: because of, on °account of, thanks to; °through, as a °result of, resulting from, *Colloq* °due to: *Owing to my schedule, I cannot stay the night. The higher tides are owing to the positions of the sun and moon.*

owner *n.* possessor, holder; °proprietor, proprietress: *The papers have been returned to their rightful owner. Who is the owner of the property?*

P

pace *n.* **1** °step, stride: *Please walk forward two paces.* **2** °rate (of °speed), °tempo, °speed, °velocity, *Colloq* °clip: *We were proceeding at a pace of five miles per hour.*
—*v.* **3** °walk, stride, tread; °traverse: *Alistair paced up and down nervously, waiting for word from the surgeon.* **4** °measure, °gauge *or* gage, °judge, °rate, °estimate, °determine, °reckon, °figure, °compute: *I was trying to pace myself to conserve some energy for a sprint finish.*

pack *n.* **1** °parcel, °package, °packet, °bundle, bale, backpack, knapsack, rucksack, haversack, kitbag, °kit, duffle *or* duffel °bag: *The stranger hoisted his pack onto his shoulder and loped off.* **2** °load, °lot, °bunch, multitude, °heap, °pile, °accumulation, °mass, amassment, °mess, barrel, peck: *She told the jury a pack of lies.* **3** °group, °collection, °assembly, assemblage, congregation, °gathering, °crowd, °number, °throng, horde, °mass, °crew, °gang, °body, °lots, loads, °band, °company, °party, °set, °flock, °herd, drove, °mob, °swarm, bevy, covey, °circle, coterie, °clique: *A huge pack of people were waiting at the stage door for the star to emerge.* **4** deck: *We ought to have two packs of cards for bridge.*
—*v.* **5** Often, ***pack in*** *or* ***into***: °package, bale, °bundle, °compact, °crowd, °cram, °jam, °fill, °stuff, °squeeze, °ram, °press, °wedge, tamp: *They packed us into the train like sardines. I packed as much as I could into the short time I had left.* **6** ***pack it in***: °stop, °cease, °end, °finish, °quit, °wind up, °terminate, °give up, call it a day, *Colloq* chuck: *Edward finally packed it in because they were giving him too much trouble.* **7** ***pack off***: °dismiss, °send off *or* away, °bundle off *or* out, °hustle off *or* out *or* away, get °rid of, °drive off *or* away, °order off *or* away *or* out, °send (someone) about his *or* her business: *At the beginning of the war, Sally's mother packed her off to America to stay with her aunt.* **8** ***pack up***: **a** °get *or* °gather together, °put away, °store: *Pack up your troubles in your old kit bag and smile, smile, smile.* **b** °quit, °stop, °break down, °fail, °give out, °stall, °die, give up the ghost, *Colloq* conk out, have had it: *After three days crossing the desert, the engine finally packed up.*

package *n.* **1** °packet, °parcel, °box, container, °case, carton, °bundle: *I am donating a package of clothing to the relief fund.* **2** °combination, °unit, package °deal: *Included in the package from the car dealer are several luxury features.*
—*v.* **3** °wrap, °pack, containerize, carton, °case, encase, °enclose, °include; °combine, °unite, coupled, °incorporate: *More and more merchandise comes packaged in plastic these days. A special sponge is packaged with the cleaning liquid.*

packed *adj.* filled, full, °loaded, crowded, stuffed, jammed, crammed, brim-full, chock-a-block, chock-full, jam-packed, overloaded, overflowing, °loaded *or* filled to the gunwales, up to there, bursting, groaning, °swollen, °replete, *Colloq* wall-to-wall: *The gallery was packed with the soprano's relatives, who cheered every note. The publicity for the show promised a packed programme of mirth and merriment.*

packet *n.* **1** °package, °parcel, °pack, °batch: *We found a packet of your old love-letters in a trunk in the lumber room.* **2** loads, °lot(s), °great °deal, °fortune, °mint, *Colloq* °bundle, pretty penny, °pile(s), °tidy °sum, king's ransom, *Brit* bomb: *He lost a packet on that property when they built a sewage plant alongside it.*

pact *n.* °agreement, °treaty, °bargain, °alliance, °contract, °compact, concord, covenant, concordat, entente, °understanding, °arrangement, °deal: *The companies entered into an illegal pact not to compete in the same markets.*

pad *n.* **1** °cushion, pillow, °wad, wadding, stuffing, padding, °filling, filler: *Wrap a soft cotton pad over the wound to protect it.* **2** writing-pad, note-pad, memo pad, °block (of paper), jotter, *US* filler: *You'd best take a pad with you to make notes at the lecture.* **3** °flat, apartment, °room(s), °home, °place, °quarters, *Colloq* hang-out, *Brit* digs *or* diggings, *Slang US* flop: *A few friends are crashing at my pad while they're in town.*
—*v.* **4** °cushion, °wad, °stuff, °fill; upholster: *The chair seats are padded with foam rubber, but the arms are bare.* **5** Sometimes, ***pad out***: °expand, °inflate, °stretch, dilate, °lengthen, protract, °extend, °blow up, °flesh out, °puff up, augment, °spin out, °amplify: *He pads his weekly newspaper column with trivia in order to fill the space.*

paddle *n.* **1** °oar, °sweep, scull: *A 'crab' occurs when you catch the water with the paddle blade on the return stroke.*
—*v.* **2** °row, scull, °oar: *Deftly she paddled the canoe over to the pier.* **3** °wade: *The children were paddling at the water's edge.* **4** °spank, thrash, °beat, °whip, °flog, *Colloq* paddywhack: *Dad threatened to paddle me if he caught me playing hookey again.*

paddy *n.* °rage, (fit of) °temper, °fit, °tantrum, *Colloq Brit* paddywhack *or* paddywack, wax: *She was in a proper paddy when she found out what you'd done.*

pagan *n.* **1** °heathen, unbeliever, idolater, polytheist, °infidel, Gentile: *He joined the religion of the pagans and worshipped the golden calf.*
—*adj.* **2** °heathen, °infidel, idolatrous, polytheistic, heathenish, Gentile: *Many churchmen condemned Renaissance scholars for their interest in pagan and pre-Christian writers.*

page[1] *n.* **1** leaf, folio, °side, °sheet, verso *or* recto: *On which page does the index begin?* **2** °episode, °phase, °period, °time, °stage, °point, °era, epoch, °age, chapter: *The early 1940s were among the darkest pages in Britain's history.*
—*v.* **3** paginate, folio, °number: *Roman numerals were used in paging the preface to the book.*

page[2] *n.* **1** °attendant, page-boy, °servant, errand-boy, °messenger, *Brit* foot-boy, *US* bellman, bellhop, *Offensive used of an adult* bellboy: *Please have a page deliver this message to Mr Simmonds.*
—*v.* **2** °announce, °summon (forth), °send for *or* after, °call, °call for, °call out: *They are paging your wife now to give her your message.*

pageant *n.* °spectacle, °display, °grandeur, °tableau, °show, °parade, °procession, °ceremony, °formality, °ritual, °event, °affair, °extravaganza, °presentation, °gala: *The children stage a medieval mystery play as a part of the annual Christmas pageant.*

pageantry *n.* °pomp, °ceremony, °display, magnificence, °extravagance, panorama, showiness, °show: *The pageantry of the Oberammergau passion play should be experienced at least once.*

pain *n.* **1** °hurt, °suffering, °discomfort, soreness, °ache, aching, °pang, °spasm, smarting, cramp: *I feel the pain in my back from lifting that box.* **2** °anguish, °agony, °affliction, °distress, °grief, °woe, °suffering, °misery, travail, wretchedness, °despair, °torment, tribulation, °trial, torture, dolour, discomposure, °ordeal, disquiet: *No one who has not experienced it can imagine the pain of losing a child.* **3** irritation, vexation, °annoyance, °bother, °nuisance, °pest, *Colloq* °pain in the neck, °headache, °drag, °bore, *Taboo slang* °pain in the *Brit* arse *or US* ass: *What a pain it is that you have forgotten your keys again! David can really be a pain when he goes on about the book he's writing.* **4** ***pains***: °effort, °trouble, °exertion, toil, °labour: *She went to great pains to make our stay comfortable.*
—*v.* **5** °hurt, °distress, °grieve, °wound, °injure; °trouble, °depress, °sadden, °sorrow, °cut to the quick: *It pained us to learn of Mrs McArthur's illness.*

painful *adj.* **1** hurting, °grievous, °hurtful, °sore, distressing, distressful, °excruciating, torturous, °agonizing, smarting, stinging, aching, achy, throbbing,

°burning, °piercing, stabbing, °sharp, °tender, °sensitive, °raw, °bitter, *Formal* nociceptive: *The bullet caused a painful wound in the knee. Mother's arthritis can be quite painful at times.* **2** vexing, vexatious, annoying, harassing, irritating, °irksome, aggravating, galling, exasperating, unpleasant, afflictive, °harrowing, worrisome, worrying, troubling, disquieting, °disturbing, distressing: *Fighting in the front lines was a painful experience for Rupert.* **3** °painstaking, °laborious, °careful, rigorous, °arduous, assiduous, sedulous, °diligent, °earnest, °conscientious, °meticulous, °scrupulous, °detailed, °thorough, thoroughgoing, °exacting, °demanding: *A great deal of painful research went into discovering the cause of yellow fever.*

painfully *adv.* agonizingly, distressingly, disagreeably, unpleasantly, unfortunately, °sadly, woefully, lamentably, ruefully, unhappily: *I became painfully aware that much of the relief destined for the poor never reached them.*

painkiller *n.* anodyne, analgesic, anaesthetic, °sedative, palliative: *When he wrenched his back, the doctor gave him a painkiller so that he could walk.*

painless *adj.* trouble-free, °easy, °simple, °comfortable, °effortless, *Colloq* °easy as 1, 2, 3 *or* as ABC, °easy as pie, a °piece of cake, °pushover, child's play, *Slang* cinch, no °sweat: *The procedure for assembling the bicycle is relatively painless.*

painstaking *adj.* See **painful, 3,** above.

paint *n.* **1** °colour, °tint, dye, colouring, pigment, °stain: *I bought the paint and brushes, and started work on the kitchen walls.* **2** coating, °coat, °surface; enamel: *The rust has come through the paint here and there.* **3** °make-up, cosmetics, *maquillage*, greasepaint, *Colloq* warpaint, face: *Sheila is in her room putting on some paint before we go out.*
—*v.* **4** depict, °portray, °picture, °show, °represent, delineate, °render, °draw, limn, °characterize, °describe: *Whistler painted a portrait of my grandmother. Correspondents painted a very grim picture of the plight of the hostages.* **5** °coat, °brush, °apply, °cover, daub: *The doctor painted the area with some medication that soothed the pain.* **6** °colour, °tint, dye, °stain, °decorate: *We are planning to paint the nursery pale blue.* **7** ***paint the town red***: make merry, °carouse, °revel, go on a °spree, go out on the town, *Colloq* whoop it up, live it up, (go on a) pub-crawl, °step out, *Slang* make whoopee, go on a °bender *or* °drunk *or* binge, °booze it up: *Saturday nights a few of the boys would go out and paint the town red till the wee hours.*

pair *n.* **1** °couple, twosome, two of a kind, °set of two, matched °set, duo, dyad, twins, °double, doublet; °brace, °span, yoke, °team, tandem: *A pair of silver candelabra disappeared during the party.*
—*v.* **2** °match (up), °mate, °pair off *or* up, °team (up), °put together, °partner, °twin, °double, °join, °unite, yoke; °wed, °marry, °join in wedlock *or* in holy matrimony: *Pair these gloves for me, would you? Husbands may not pair off with wives for the next dance.*

pal *n.* **1** °friend, consort, °comrade, *alter ego*, crony, °companion, amigo, °playmate, classmate, *Colloq* °chum, sidekick, °mate, *Chiefly US and Canadian* buddy: *Jim left a little while ago with a few of his pals.*
—*v.* **2** ***pal (up) with*** *or* ***about*** *or US* ***around (with)***: °associate (with), be *or* become °friendly *or* °friends (with), be *or* get *or* become on °friendly *or* °intimate terms (with), °go (around *or* about) with, °fraternize (with), consort (with), spend time together *or* with, keep °company (with), *Colloq* °hang out *or* about *or* around (with), °knock about *or* around (with): *Fiona and Isabel palled up last year. Do you still pal about with Timothy?*

palace *n.* mansion, °castle, °stately *or* °palatial °home *or* °residence, manor (house), (°country) °estate, château, *palazzo*, villa: *After the wedding, they went to the prince's palace and lived happily ever after.*

palatial *adj.* °luxurious, de luxe, °magnificent, °splendid, °stately, °sumptuous, °opulent, °majestic, °grand, °elegant, palatine, *Slang* °posh, ritzy, °swanky, classy: *After winning the pools, they moved into a palatial house in Belgravia.*

palaver *n.* **1** °nuisance, °procedure, red tape, to-do, °rigmarole *or* rigamarole, *Colloq* °song and dance, °bother, °nonsense, °business, carry-on, °performance: *He lost the certificates, so she now has to go through all the palaver of getting new ones.* **2** °chatter, °babble, °jabber, (°empty *or* °small) °talk, blather *or* blether, °gossip, prating, °prattle, prattling, palavering, *Brit* natter, nattering, *Scots* clishmaclaver, *Colloq* jawing, °hot air, *Colloq Brit* witter, wittering: *There is so much palaver at the annual meeting that nothing important ever gets said.* **3** °parley, °talk, °conference, °discussion, colloquy, °conversation, confabulation, °meeting, °get-together, round table, powwow, *Colloq* confab, °huddle, chin-wag: *The annual palaver of the regional general managers is scheduled for next week.*
—*v.* **4** °chatter, °babble, °jabber, blather *or* blether, °gossip, °prattle, prate, chit-chat, gabble, *Brit* natter, witter, *Colloq* jaw, chin-wag, *US and Canadian* shoot the breeze, *Slang* ya(c)k, ya(c)kety-ya(c)k: *Peter and I were palavering outside the supermarket when Sophie came along.* **5** °confer, °consult, °discuss, °parley, °talk, °converse, powwow, °meet, °get together, °sit down (together), confabulate, °negotiate, *Colloq* confab, °huddle, chew the fat *or* the °rag: *Management and union representatives will palaver tomorrow.*

pale[1] *adj.* **1** °colourless, °white, °wan, sallow, waxen, livid, ashen, ashy, pallid, bloodless, whitish, °pasty, whey-faced, washed out, anaemic, blanched, drained, °ghostly, °ghastly, °peaky *or* peakish, peaked, cadaverous: *If you had been through an ordeal like that, you'd look pale, too.* **2** °faint, °light, °dim, washed out, pastel: *She was wearing a pale green evening gown tonight.* **3** °feeble, °weak, °flimsy, °meagre, enfeebled, °ineffective, °ineffectual, °puny, °insignificant, °paltry, °lame, °poor, °inadequate, °half-hearted, °tame, spiritless, whey-faced, °empty, °sterile, °lifeless, uninspired, anaemic, *Colloq* half-baked: *The sequel was a pale imitation of the original film.*
—*v.* **4** blanch, blench, °dim, whiten: *He paled when they told him of the car crash.* **5** °diminish, lessen, °fade (away), °decrease, abate: *The works of most modern writers pale in comparison with those of the Elizabethans.*

pale[2] *n.* **1** paling, palisade, °picket, °upright, °post, °stake: *The pales are attached to horizontal rails to form a fence.* **2** °boundary, °limit(s), °restriction, °bounds, °border(s), confines: *Nothing is outside the pale of the imagination of a great novelist.* **3** ***beyond the pale***: °improper, °irregular, °unseemly, unsuitable, °indecent, °unacceptable, °inadmissible, forbidden, anathema, disallowed, prohibited, *verboten*, interdicted; *US* °unusual, °bizarre, °peculiar, °*outré*, °weird, °abnormal, °strange: *The committee have found your behaviour to be beyond the pale, Frances, and we demand your resignation.*

pall[1] *n.* **1** °shroud, covering, °mantle, °cloth, °veil: *A black velvet pall covered the coffin.* **2** °gloomy *or* °melancholy *or* °sombre *or* °grave *or* depressing °air *or* °mood *or* °atmosphere; damper, cold water, *Colloq* wet blanket: *The recently uncovered scandals have cast a pall over his successes in office.*

pall[2] *v.* **1** Often, ***pall on*** *or* ***upon***: °bore, °tire, °weary, °jade, °irk, °irritate, °sicken: *His position lost all its charm when the work began to pall on him.* **2** sate, °satiate, cloy, °glut, °surfeit, °gorge: *I had reached the point where even the finest foods began to pall me.*

paltry *adj.* °trifling, trivial, °petty, °small, °insignificant, °worthless, °pitiful, °pathetic, °pitiable, °puny, °sorry, °wretched, °miserable, °inconsequential, inconsiderable, unimportant, °meagre, °mean, beggarly, °base, °low, °contemptible, *Colloq* piddling, *Brit* twopenny, twopenny-halfpenny, mingy, *US* penny-ante, *Slang* Mickey Mouse: *Despite his wealth, his* *charitable contributions are paltry. We all recognize Denison for the paltry pedant he is.*

pamper *v.* °baby, °coddle, cosset, (over)indulge, °spoil, mollycoddle, °cater to, °pet, *Rare* cocker, *Irish* cosher: *The Simpsons pamper their children far too much.*

pamphlet *n.* booklet, °brochure, °tract, °essay, folder, °leaflet, °circular; handbill, °bill, °notice, °bulletin, °advertisement, hand-out, ad, *Brit* advert, *US* flyer, throw-away: *He was arrested for printing a pamphlet that denounced the government's repression of free speech. Yesterday we received our sixteenth pamphlet promoting replacement windows.*

pan *n.* **1** saucepan, frying-pan, skillet, °pot, casserole, *US* spider: *Melt a teaspoonful of butter in the pan, add the mixture, and stir briskly over a medium heat.* **2** °face, visage, mien, façade, *Slang* kisser, °mug, puss: *The worst part of Alf's not working is that I have to look at his ugly pan all day.* **3** °depression, °indentation, concavity, °cavity, °hollow, °pit, °hole, crater: *In a rain-shower, the pans fill with water and the desert blooms.*
—*v.* **4** °wash, °separate, °sift: *For years prospectors have panned for gold in these hills.* **5** °criticize, censure, find °fault, °put down, °reject, flay, excoriate, *Brit* hammer, *Colloq* °knock, roast, slate, *Slang Brit* °rubbish, *US* trash: *The critics panned the play and it closed after a week.* **6** ***pan out***: °succeed, °thrive, °prosper, °flourish, fare well, °make it; °work out, °turn out, °result, °come out, °end (up), conclude, culminate, eventuate: *Your grandiose plans for irrigating the Sahara didn't pan out, either! How did the election pan out?*

panache *n.* °flourish, °dash, *élan*, éclat, °chic, °sophistication, *savoir faire*, *savoir vivre*, flamboyance, °verve, °style, cultivation, (good) °taste, °flair, smartness, boldness, self-assurance, °swagger, °vigour, liveliness, °spirit, brio, °gusto, °zest, °animation, °enthusiasm, °energy: *Whatever needs to be done, you can count on Irena to carry it off with panache.*

pandemonium *n.* °bedlam, °chaos, turmoil, °disorder, °tumult, °frenzy, °uproar, *Brit* °furore *or US* furor, °confusion: *Pandemonium reigned after the first bomb struck.*

pander *v.* **1** Usually, ***pander to***: °satisfy, °gratify, °humour, °indulge, °fulfil, °bow to, °yield to, °truckle to, °cater to: *She is tired of pandering to his every wish.* **2** °procure, °pimp, °solicit: *I didn't believe he would sink so low as to pander for his business clients.*
—*n.* **3** panderer, °pimp, °procurer, °solicitor, whoremonger, White °slaver, *Slang* flesh-pedlar *or US also* flesh-peddler *or* flesh-pedler, *Brit* ponce, mack: *The word* pander *is an eponym for* Pandarus, *who acted as a sycophantic go-between for Troilus in Chaucer's* Troilus and Criseyde.

pane *n.* panel, °sheet, °glass, window-pane, °light, quarrel, bull's-eye: *Ring up the glazier and have that pane replaced in the door.*

pang *n.* **1** °pain, °stab, °ache, °pinch, °twinge, stitch, °spasm: *I felt a sharp pang of hunger.* **2** °qualm, hesitation, °scruple, °misgiving, °remorse, °regret, contrition, contriteness, self-reproach, mortification, °guilt, °anguish, °discomfort, malaise: *Does Claire feel the slightest pangs for treating him badly?*

panic *n.* **1** °terror, °alarm, °fear, °fright, °dread, °horror, °dismay, consternation, hysteria; °anxiety, apprehension, apprehensiveness, nervousness: *As the speeding car veered towards us, a feeling of panic gripped me.*
—*v.* **2** be terrified *or* alarmed *or* °fearful *or* frightened *or* terror-stricken *or* terror-struck, °dread, °fear, lose one's °nerve; °frighten, °scare; *Colloq* go to °pieces, °fall apart, *Brit* lose one's °bottle: *I panicked, turned the wheel the wrong way, and crashed the car into a tree. Gregory panics at the slightest sign of danger.* **3** °frighten, °scare, °alarm, °terrify, °unnerve: *Something panicked the horses and one kicked out his stall door.*

panic-stricken *adj.* panic-struck, terrified, alarmed, horrified, aghast, terror-stricken *or* terror-struck, panicky, frenzied, in a °frenzy, °hysterical, °beside oneself with °fear *or* °terror, °fearful, °afraid, °scared (stiff), °petrified, horror-struck *or* horror-stricken, frightened *or* °scared out of one's wits, appalled, stunned, stupefied, perturbed, unnerved, °nervous, distressed, °upset, jittery, °jumpy, (all) worked up, *Colloq* in a cold sweat, in a °flap, in a tizzy, *Taboo slang* °scared shitless, shitting green: *At the news of the leak at the nuclear plant, hundreds of panic-stricken people fled from the area.*

panoramic *adj.* °sweeping, commanding, °extensive, °comprehensive, °wide, °overall, °scenic, far-reaching, all-embracing, far-ranging, all-encompassing, °inclusive, bird's-eye, °general: *This room affords a panoramic view of the sea-coast.*

pant *v.* **1** °gasp, °huff (and °puff), °blow, °heave, °breathe hard, wheeze: *He was panting when he came into the room, having run up the stairs.* **2** Usually, ***pant for*** or ***after***: crave, °hanker after, °hunger *or* °thirst for *or* after, °yearn for, °ache for, °want, °desire, covet, °wish for, °long *or* pine *or* °sigh for, have one's heart set on, °die for, be dying for, *Colloq* have a yen for, give one's eye-teeth *or* right arm for: *Margery was the girl that all the boys panted after when we were ten.*

pants *n.pl.* **1** *In Britain*: (men's) drawers, smallclothes, underpants, boxer shorts, trunks, undershorts, Y-fronts, briefs, *Colloq* smalls; (women's) knickers, camiknickers, panties, bloomers, pantalettes, °tights, pantihose, undies: *The baby was dressed in a frilly dress and matching pants.* **2** *In US*: trousers, slacks, breeches, (Oxford) bags, knickerbockers, flannels, shorts, Bermuda shorts *or* Bermudas, pedal pushers, bell-bottoms, peg-tops, hip-huggers, (blue) jeans, dungarees, denims, *Trade Mark* Levis, *Scots* trews; *Scots and No. Eng.* breeks, *US* knickers, *Colloq* cut-offs: *Americans who go into British shops asking for a pair of pants are embarrassed to be offered only underwear.*

paper *n.* **1** newspaper, tabloid, daily, weekly, °journal, gazette, °publication, °periodical, newsletter, °organ, *Colloq* °rag, °sheet: *She is feature editor of a paper in Manchester.* **2** Often, ***papers***: **a** °document(s), °instrument, °legal papers, °form, certificate, °deed, ownership papers; credential(s), °identification: *Bring the papers to my office for signing. His papers are not in order. Many people lost their papers during the war.* **b** docket, files, dossier, °record(s), archive(s): *Your papers seem to have disappeared from our office.* **3** °stationery, letterhead, writing-paper, letter-paper, notepaper; foolscap; °scrap *or US also* scratch paper; wrapping paper, gift-wrapping, gift-wrap; wallpaper: *She wrote to me on the most beautiful engraved paper. We buy our Christmas paper from a museum shop.* **4** article, °composition, °essay, °assignment, °report, °thesis, °study, °tract, °analysis, critique, exegesis, treatise, dissertation, disquisition, manuscript, MS *or* ms, autograph, holograph, typescript, °script, °speech: *Adelaide will present her paper at the meeting of the Royal Academy this year.*
—*v.* **5** (hang) wallpaper, line; °post, °distribute: *The entire area was papered with posters announcing the meeting.*

par *adj.* **1** °standard, °normal, °average, expected: *A success rate of two per cent is par for these candidates.*
—*n.* **2** °level, °rank, °standing, °scale, °standard: *How can you place yourself on a par with her as a tennis player?* **3** ***above par***: above °average, °superior, °outstanding, °excellent, °exceptional; °choice, °select, °prime: *Since I stopped taking that medication, I've been feeling above par. I am pleased to announce that the test results were above par for the school as a whole.* **4** ***at par***: °average, °level, °even, °equal, °equivalent, °standard; °par value: *The shares are selling at par, or below their true market value.* **5** ***below*** or ***under par***: **a** below °average, substandard, °inferior, second-rate,

°mediocre, middling, not up to par, °poor, °inadequate, °unsatisfactory, °wanting, °bad, °wretched, °miserable, °awful, °terrible, *Colloq* °lousy, not up to snuff *or* °scratch: *Ian's goal-keeping has been below par all season.* **b** °ill, °sickly, °unhealthy, unwell, not (very) well, not oneself, not in good *or* the best °shape, in bad °shape, *Brit* °off form, °off colour; *Colloq* under the weather, °poorly, not up to snuff: *I was feeling below par.* **6** ***up to par***: all °right, °adequate, °average, °satisfactory, °good enough, °passable, °acceptable, *Colloq* °OK *or* okay, up to °scratch *or* snuff, °fair to middling: *If your game had been up to par, Davis would not have won.*

parable *n.* allegory, fable, °lesson, °morality °tale: *When we first read Aesop's* Fables *we didn't know they were parables.*

parade *n.* **1** °procession, °march, °train, °file, °promenade, cortège, column; entourage: *They held a parade to celebrate the soldiers' safe return from the war.* **2** °exhibition, (ostentatious) °display, °show, °spectacle, array, °pomp, °splash: *She often makes a parade of her knowledge of architecture.* **3** °promenade, °walk, (pedestrian) °way, mall, esplanade: *Let's meet in the Parade when you have finished shopping.*
—*v.* **4** °march, pass in °review, °promenade, °walk, °file: *The generals saluted smartly as the troops paraded past.* **5** °strut, °flaunt, °show (off), brandish, °wave, vaunt, °display, °air: *Why does he feel it necessary to parade every new girlfriend in front of all the neighbours?*

paradise *n.* **1** °heaven, City of God, Zion, Elysium, Elysian Fields, °happy hunting-grounds, Abraham's bosom, °heavenly kingdom, Promised Land, Celestial City, New Jerusalem, Avalon, Valhalla, Hesperides, Isles *or* Islands of the Blessed, seventh °heaven: *People all have their own ideas of paradise, but everyone agrees it's a nice place to be.* **2** °heaven on earth, (Garden of) Eden, (land of) Goshen, °Utopia, Shangri-La, Land of Beulah: *Early settlers of California thought it a paradise.* **3** °bliss, °happiness, °rapture, °heaven, °delight, blessedness, °ecstasy, seventh °heaven, °joy, dreamland, nirvana: *Being with you has been sheer paradise.*

paradox *n.* contradiction, self-contradiction, incongruity, inconsistency, °absurdity, °ambiguity, °enigma, °puzzle, °mystery, °quandary, °problem, °dilemma: *Can you explain away Zeno's paradox of Achilles and the tortoise? The paradox was that although it was Edward's fifth birthday, he was 20 years old.*

paradoxical *adj.* °contradictory, self-contradictory, conflicting, oxymoronic, °impossible, °improbable, °incongruous, illogical, °inconsistent, °absurd, °ambiguous, confusing, °equivocal, enigmatic, °puzzling, baffling, °incomprehensible, bewildering, °perplexing, °mysterious, °problematic: *It would be true, though it might sound paradoxical, to say that the Norman Conquest made England Saxon.*

paragon *n.* °epitome, archetype, °model, °prototype, °quintessence, °pattern, °standard, exemplar, °ideal, *beau idéal*, criterion: *He had previously regarded Michael as a paragon of virtue and was deeply shocked by the revelations.*

parallel *adj.* **1** °similar, corresponding, congruent, analogous, analogic(al), °correspondent, °like, °matching, homologous, °coordinate, °equivalent, coequal, °proportional, proportionate, *pari passu, mutatis mutandis*, in °proportion, °uniform; °contemporary *or* cotemporary, contemporaneous *or* cotemporaneous: *The situation in Northern Ireland could be compared with a parallel situation in Lebanon.*
—*n.* **2** analogue, °match, homologue, °equivalent, °complement, counterpart, °equal, coequal: *Campbell found many parallels among the legendary heroes of other cultures.* **3** analogy, parallelism, equivalence, complementarity, °relationship, °kinship, correspondence, °resemblance, °likeness, similarity, °symmetry, °equality, coequality, °parity, correlation; °proportion, °balance, equiponderance, equipoise, counterbalance, °offset: *One can draw parallels between the human arm, the fish's fin, and the bird's wing. By way of parallel, consider the flood in the Bible and that in the Gilgamesh epic.*
—*v.* **4** °correspond to *or* with, °match, equate to *or* with, be likened to, correlate to *or* with, °compare with *or* to, °imitate, °repeat, °echo, iterate, °reiterate, °duplicate, °follow, °agree with; keep °pace with, °conform (to), °balance, °set off, °offset, °even off *or* up, be accompanied by, °coincide with, *Colloq* jibe with: *In many respects, your attitudes towards life parallel mine when I was your age. A decrease in the rate of inflation supposedly parallels a rise in interest rates.*

paralyse *v.* **1** immobilize, inactivate, deactivate, °transfix; °halt, °stop: *The stroke paralysed his entire left side. As the thing approached, the children became paralysed by fear.* **2** °deaden, °numb, °freeze, anaesthetize, benumb, °render °insensible: *This injection will paralyse your thumb so that we can operate on it.* **3** disable, °cripple, °incapacitate, disenable: *His left leg was paralysed in the accident.*

paramount *adj.* °pre-eminent, °chief, °supreme, °dominant, °main, °predominant, °cardinal, °first, °prime, °primary, °principal, °essential, °vital, requisite, °basic: *The company feel that the independence of researchers is paramount. It is of paramount importance that you study trigonometry before calculus.*

paramour *n.* °lover, °love, inamorato *or* inamorata, amorist, °mistress, gigolo, concubine, *cicisbeo*, kept °woman, *Colloq* °flame, sugar-daddy, *US* POSSLQ (= 'Person of the Opposite Sex Sharing Living Quarters'), *Slang* fancy man *or* woman: *At eighty, she liked to reminisce about her many paramours.*

paraphernalia *n.* Usually *pl.* equipment, apparatus, °accessories, outfit, appliances, utensils, gear, rig, °material(s), *matériel*, °things, tackle, equipage, accoutrements, °effects, chattels, °possessions, °belongings, appurtenances, °trappings, property, baggage, impedimenta, °supplies, stuff, *Colloq* junk, *Brit* rubbish, clobber, *Slang* crap, *Taboo slang US* shit: *Bring along your scuba paraphernalia. It took us a month just to pack up all the paraphernalia we had in the flat.*

paraphrase *n.* **1** rephrasing, rephrase, rewording, restatement, rewriting, rewrite, °rehash, °rendition, °rendering, °version, *Technical* paraphrasis: *The editor wanted a revision, not merely a paraphrase of the original.*
—*v.* **2** rephrase, °reword, restate, rewrite, explicate, °explain: *Please paraphrase the specialized jargon to make it understandable to non-professionals.*

parasite *n.* leech, °hanger-on, *Colloq* freeloader, sponger *or* sponge, °bloodsucker, cadger, scrounger *or* °scrounge, barnacle, jackal, hyena *or* hyaena: *That parasite lives off Gemma's money and has never worked a day in his life.*

parcel *n.* **1** °package, °packet, carton, °box, container, °case: *We are sending food parcels to the needy.* **2** °portion, °plot, plat, °lot, piece, °section, °tract: *We have bought a small parcel of land and plan to build on it next year.* **3** °lot, °group, °batch, °collection, °pack, °bundle, °set: *She gathered a parcel of drawings and published them as a travel sketchbook.*
—*v.* **4** Often, ***parcel out***: apportion, °allot, °deal (out), °dole (out), °mete (out), °hand out, °distribute, °share (out), °divide, *Colloq* divvy (up): *Before he died he parcelled out his fortune amongst his grandchildren.*

parch *v.* °dry (out *or* up), desiccate, dehydrate, exsiccate; °scorch, sear, °burn, bake; °shrivel (up), wither: *The earth was parched by the unrelenting sun.*

pardon *n.* **1** °forgiveness, °forgiving, amnesty, °remission, °release, reprieval, absolution, °indulgence, °excuse, excusal, °allowance, overlooking, condonation, exoneration, exculpation: *Should there be any pardon for crimes against humanity?*
—*v.* **2** °forgive, °remit, °release, °reprieve, absolve, °indulge, °allow, °overlook, °let off, °excuse, condone,

exonerate, exculpate: *There are some crimes that ought not be pardoned.*

pare *v.* **1** °trim, °peel, °skin, °shave (off), shuck; decorticate, excoriate: *Pare the apples and then grate them coarsely.* **2** Often, ***pare down***: °reduce, °diminish, °decrease, °cut (back *or* down), °curtail, °slash (back), °lower, lessen: *Since his illness, Bob has pared down his time at the office. We'll have to pare our prices to stay competitive in the present climate.*

parent *n.* **1** °father *or* °mother, °progenitor, progenitrix, procreator, begetter, materfamilias *or* paterfamilias; foster-parent, stepmother *or* stepfather, °guardian, *Colloq* old lady *or* old man, *Brit old-fashioned or facetious* mater *or* pater: *Most teenagers clash with their parents sooner or later.* **2** °source, °origin, originator, well-spring, fountain-head, °root: *The liturgy of St James is undoubtedly the parent of the Armenian Rite.*

parentage *n.* °lineage, ancestry, °line, °family, °extraction, descent, °origin, °pedigree, °stock, °birth, °strain, bloodline, °heritage, roots: *As he was separated from his mother at birth, he knows nothing of his royal parentage.*

parenting *n.* (of children) rearing, °upbringing, raising, nurturing: *Brian and Betty take their parenting very seriously.*

parity *n.* **1** °equality, equivalence, consistency, °uniformity, °par, °likeness, similarity, analogy, congruity, similitude, conformity, congruence: *The ministers agreed that they would observe parity of power amongst themselves at the conference.* **2** °proportion, parallelism, analogy, °balance, correspondence: *We are trying to maintain parity between the Deutschmark and the pound sterling.*

park *n.* **1** garden, °green(s), °common(s), °preserve, °reserve, greensward, parkland, woodland, °estate, *Chiefly Brit* °reservation: *Twice a day he strolls through the nearby park.* **2** *Brit* car park, *US and Canadian and New Zealand* parking-lot: *I shall meet you in the car park at the railway station.*
—*v.* **3** °leave, °put, °deposit, °store: *It is illegal to park in this street.*

parlance *n.* way *or* manner of speaking, *façon de parler*, phrasing, phraseology, °speech, °wording, °language, °idiom, °dialect, °jargon, *Colloq* °lingo: *In the parlance of the yuppies, that's a ballpark figure.*

parley *n.* **1** °conference, °discussion, °dialogue, °palaver, deliberation, °meeting, colloquy, colloquium, confabulation, powwow, °talk(s), *Colloq* °huddle, confab: *The issue will be decided at the executive council's parley.*
—*v.* **2** °confer, °discuss, °palaver, °deliberate, °talk (over), °negotiate, °deal, *Colloq* °huddle: *Would Sitting Bull parley with General Custer?*

parliament *n.* **1** ***Parliament***: Houses of Parliament, House of Lords and House of Commons, Westminster, the House, Mother of Parliaments: *The new health bill got its second reading in Parliament today.* **2** legislature, °council, congress, °diet, °assembly, Upper and Lower House *or* °chamber: *The United States parliament consists of the Senate and the House of Representatives.*

parliamentary *adj.* °formal, ordered, °orderly, procedural, conforming, conformist, *US* according to *Roberts Rules of Order*: *The debate must follow parliamentary procedure.*

parlour *n.* living-room, *Old-fashioned or Brit* drawing-room, *Chiefly Brit* sitting-room, °reception (room), °lounge: *She invited us into the parlour where tea was laid out.*

parlous *adj.* °perilous, °risky, °precarious, °uncertain, °dangerous, °hazardous, °difficult, °ticklish, °awkward, *Colloq* chancy, iffy, *Slang* °hairy: *These are parlous times in the Middle East.*

parochial *adj.* regional, °provincial, °narrow, °local, insular, °isolated, °limited, restricted, °narrow-minded, °petty, °short-sighted, °hidebound, °conservative, °conventional, illiberal, °bigoted, °prejudiced, °intolerant, °one-sided, °partial, °biased, °stubborn, °opinionated, °dogmatic, °rigid, °stiff, stiff-necked, °immovable, intractable, unchangeable, unchanging, close-minded, °unsophisticated, unworldly, uncultivated, uncultured: *Uneducated and untravelled, Mr Shriver maintained a very parochial view of the world.*

parody *n.* **1** °burlesque, °lampoon, °satire, °caricature, °mockery, mimicry, *Colloq* °take-off, spoof, *Brit* send-up: *The more serious the intent of the original author's work, the easier it is to write a parody of it.* **2** travesty, °mockery, feeble *or* poor °imitation, distortion, °perversion, corruption, debasement: *The Inquisition was a parody of justice and of religion.*
—*v.* **3** °burlesque, °lampoon, °satirize, °caricature, °mock, °mimic, ape, °ridicule, °deride, °laugh at, °poke °fun at, °guy, °scoff at, °sneer at, rib, °tease, °twit, roast, pillory, make a laughing-stock (of), make °sport of, make °fun of, make a °monkey (out) of, *Archaic* fleer, *Colloq* °take off, spoof, kid, *Brit* °send up: *Swift parodied English political figures and policies of the day in* Gulliver's Travels.

paroxysm *n.* °fit, convulsion, °spasm, °throe, °seizure, °spell, °outburst, °eruption, °explosion, *Colloq* flare-up: *At the sight of George dressed as Madame Pompadour Melissa rolled on the floor in a paroxysm of hysterical laughter.*

parrot *n.* **1** imitator, °mimic, *Colloq* copycat: *She never has an original idea of her own: she's a mere parrot of others' fashions and fancies.*
—*v.* **2** °imitate, °mimic, ape, °copy, °echo, °repeat, °reiterate: *Mick doesn't understand the issues and just parrots what he hears on TV.*

part *n.* **1** piece, °portion, °division, °allotment, °share, °percentage, participation, °interest; °parcel, °fragment, °scrap, shard; some: *I bought a part of the company when it was available. I want no part of the deal now.* **2** °portion, component, °factor, constituent, °element, °ingredient: *A part of her problem is that she doesn't speak Japanese.* **3** °role, °function, °duty, °responsibility, °share; °say, °voice, °influence, participation, involvement, °business: *Every man must do his part. Don't thank me! I had no part in your getting the contract.* **4** °role, °character: *He plays the part of Tweedledum in the school play.* **5** °side, °interest, °cause, °behalf, °faction, °party: *Which part did you support in the argument? No explanation has been offered on either part.* **6** °neighbourhood, °quarter, °section, °district, °region, °area, corner, °vicinity, vicinage, *Colloq* neck of the woods: *I come from the same part of the country as you.* **7** °piece, °portion, °segment, °section; °department, °division, component, °unit: *Which part of the turkey do you prefer? In which part of the company do you work?* **8** ***for the most part***: mostly, °generally, °usually, °mainly, in the °main, by and large, on the °whole, °chiefly, °principally, essentially, for all practical purposes, to all intents and purposes, in most cases *or* instances: *The shops are for the most part closed on Sunday.* **9** ***in part***: °partly, °partially, to some °extent *or* °degree, in some °measure, °relatively, comparatively, °somewhat: *He is himself in part responsible for the present state of affairs.* **10** ***on the part of (someone)*** *or* ***on (someone's*** *or* ***one's) part***: °by, on *or US also* in °behalf of, (as) for, as regards, as far as (someone) is concerned, in the °name of, for the °sake of, in °support of: *Tyrannical acts on the part of the king were not condoned. For my part, I want nothing to do with it.* **11** ***take (a) part (in)***: °participate (in), °join (in), be (a) °party to, °play a part *or* °role (in), be °involved (in *or* with), °associate oneself (with), have *or* take a °hand in, °partake (of), °contribute (to): *Why insist that she take part in your nefarious plot? People began to sing, but she didn't feel like taking part.*
—*v.* **12** °separate, part company, °split up, °go his *or* her (*or* their) °separate °way(s), °break up, say *or* bid °goodbye (*or* adieu, etc.); °leave, °depart, °go (away *or* off): *We parted on the best of terms.* **13** °separate, °divide, °put *or* °pull °apart, °put asunder: *I saw a pale hand part the curtains for a brief moment. A fool and*

his money are soon parted. **14** ***part with***: °give up, °yield, °relinquish, °release, °sacrifice, °forgo, °renounce, °forsake, °let go, °surrender: *I doubt that you'll persuade Rover to part with his bone.*
—*adj.* **15** °partial, fractional, °limited: *Ronald is a part owner of the company.*

partake *v.* **1** Usually, ***partake in***: °share (in), °participate (in), take (a) °part (in), °enter (in *or* into): *We share each other's burdens and partake in each other's joys.* **2** Usually, ***partake of***: **a** °receive, °get, have a °share *or* °portion *or* °part (of), °share: *We were invited to partake of a meagre repast.* **b** °evoke, °suggest, °hint at, °intimate, °imply, °possess *or* have the °quality of: *Greater knowledge often partakes of insolence.*

partial *adj.* **1** °incomplete, °fragmentary, not °total *or* °whole, °imperfect: *They were able to afford only a partial restoration of the house. There will be a partial solar eclipse at noon.* **2** °prejudiced, °biased, °partisan, °inclined, influenced, °one-sided, °jaundiced, unfair, discriminatory: *It will be difficult to find a judge who is not partial.* **3** ***partial to***: in °favour of, predisposed to, °fond of, having a soft spot *or* °weakness for, having a °liking *or* °taste *or* predilection for, having a fondness for, feeling an °attraction *or* °affinity to *or* toward(s), °finding °enjoyment in: *She used to be partial to punk rockers. I am partial to Scotch beef.*

partiality *n.* **1** °prejudice, °bias, °inclination, °favouritism, predilection, predisposition, °leaning, °preference: *The losers of the contest accused the judges of partiality.* **2** °preference, °taste, °relish, °liking, fondness, °appreciation, °fancy, °love, °eye, °weakness, soft spot, °penchant; °fetish *or* fetich: *Alas, my wife has acquired a partiality for emeralds.*

partially *adv.* °partly, in °part, to some °extent *or* °degree, to a °limited *or* a °certain °extent *or* °degree, not °totally *or* °wholly *or* °entirely, restrictedly, incompletely, in some °measure, °relatively, comparatively, °moderately, (up) to a (given *or* certain) point, °somewhat: *Jon found the meal only partially satisfying and ordered another bread pudding.*

participant *n.* **1** participator, partaker, sharer, °party, contributor, prime mover: *The chief participants in the recent terrorist attack are in custody.*
—*adj.* **2** Usually, ***participant in*** *or* ***of***: participating, partaking, sharing: *As a shareholder, he will be participant in the profits.*

participate *v.* Often, ***participate in***: take °part (in), °share (in), °partake (in *or* of), °join (in), °engage (in), get *or* become °involved (in), be *or* become associated (with), °enter (in *or* into), °contribute (to): *We invited her to join the group, but she refuses to participate. I would like to participate in the venture.*

particle *n.* atom, molecule, scintilla, °spark, mote, °suggestion, °hint, °suspicion, °gleam, °bit, °crumb, °jot, tittle, whit, mite, °speck, °dot, °spot, iota, °grain, °morsel, °shred, °sliver, °scrap, *Colloq* smidgen *or* smidgin: *There isn't the slightest particle of evidence linking them with the murder.*

particular *adj.* **1** °certain, °specific, °special, °peculiar, °singular, °single, °isolated, °individual, °distinct, °discrete, °separate, °definite, °precise, °express: *These are not his particular sentiments but those of thousands of his followers. In this particular instance your theory does not apply.* **2** °marked, °special, especial, °exceptional, °remarkable, °noteworthy, °notable, °outstanding, °unusual: *The commendation is for her particular contribution to the treatment of nervous disorders. Vintage port is a particular favourite of mine.*
3 °detailed, itemized, item-by-item, °thorough, °minute, °precise, °exact, °exacting, °painstaking, °nice, rigorous, °close, blow-by-blow: *The inscriptions reveal the particular care taken in keeping daily records.* **4** °fussy, °meticulous, °finicky, finical, °fastidious, °discriminating, °selective, °demanding, hypercritical, °critical, *Colloq* pernickety *or US also* persnickety, °choosy, picky: *Daphne is very particular about whom she invites to dinner.*
—*n.* **5** Usually, ***particulars***: °detail, minutia, fine °point, °item, °specific, °element, °fact, °circumstance, °information: *The particulars may never be revealed, but we know in general what took place that fateful night.* **6** ***in particular***: °particularly, specifically, °precisely, °exactly, °especially, °specially; °particular, °specific, °special, °definite: *I told mother that I was just going out, not anywhere in particular.*

particularly *adv.* **1** °especially, °specially, exceptionally, peculiarly, singularly, distinctively, uniquely, unusually, uncommonly, °notably, outstandingly, markedly, extraordinarily, °very, °extremely, strikingly, surprisingly, amazingly: *Susannah went through a particularly bad patch but she's better now. Holroyd is a good writer, particularly of biography.* **2** in °particular, specifically, °especially, °principally, °mainly, exceptionally, °expressly, explicitly, °notably, markedly; °only, solely: *Maeterlinck was particularly interested in bees.*

parting *n.* **1** separating, splitting, dividing, breaking (up *or* °apart), sundering, cleaving; °separation, °split, °division, break-up, °rift, °rupture: *The high point of the film was the parting of the Red Sea. The parting between Harriet and Sam after twenty turbulent years was to be expected.* **2** leave-taking, °farewell, saying °goodbye, departure, leaving, going (away), making one's adieus *or* adieux; valediction: *Parting is such sweet sorrow.*
—*adj.* **3** closing, °final, concluding, °last, departing, valedictory; deathbed, °dying: *Her parting comment was, 'If you're leaving, take the rubbish'.*

partisan *n.* **1** partizan, °devotee, °follower, °supporter, adherent, °backer, °champion, °enthusiast, °fan, °zealot, °fanatic, *Chiefly US and Canadian* booster, *Colloq US* rooter: *He has long been a partisan of surrealism.* **2** °guerrilla *or* guerilla, °freedom fighter, °underground *or* °resistance fighter, irregular: *During the war the Yugoslav partisans were led by Marshal Tito.*
—*adj.* **3** °one-sided, factional, °biased, tendentious, °sectarian, °opinionated, °partial, °bigoted, °prejudiced, °parochial, myopic, °short-sighted, °near-sighted, °narrow, °narrow-minded, °limited: *She refuses to become involved in partisan politics.* **4** °guerrilla *or* guerilla, °freedom, °underground, °resistance, irregular: *They were both members of the Maquis, the French partisan group who fought against the Nazis.*

partition *n.* **1** °separation, °division, splitting (up), split-up, partitionment, break-up, breaking up, segmenting, segmentation: *One of the results of World War II was the partition of Germany.* **2** °allotment, allotting, apportionment, apportioning, °distribution, distributing, meting out, doling out, rationing (out), sharing (out), dividing (up), giving *or* handing *or* passing out, parcelling out, *Colloq* divvying up: *The partition of the estate is in the hands of our solicitors.* **3** (°room) divider, (dividing) °wall, °barrier, °screen, separator: *Let's put up a partition to divide this office into two.* **4** °compartment, °room, °chamber, °section, °part, °area, °division, subdivision, °cell, °stall, °booth: *In open floor planning, furniture, plantings, and other movables are used to create the partitions where people work.*
—*v.* **5** °divide (up), °separate, °cut up, subdivide, °split (up): *It is always a mistake to partition a country into smaller, potentially quarrelsome units.* **6** Often, ***partition off***: °divide, °separate, subdivide, °wall off, °screen (off), °fence off: *We must partition off the machine room so that the office staff are not disturbed by the noise.*

partly *adv.* See **partially,** above.

partner *n.* **1** sharer, partaker, °associate, °colleague, °participant, °accomplice, °accessory, confederate, °comrade, °ally, collaborator, °companion, team-mate, °fellow, *alter ego*, °friend, *Colloq* °pal, sidekick, °mate, *US and Canadian* buddy, °cohort: *His partner in the bank robbery was arrested this morning.* **2** wife *or* °husband, spouse, °mate, helpmate, helpmeet, consort: *She became my life partner more than 50 years ago.*

3 °companion, fellow-dancer: *Won't you change partners and dance with me?*

party *n.* **1** (social) °gathering, cocktail *or* dinner party, °celebration, °fête *or* fete, °function, °reception, soirée, levee, °festivity, festivities, °festival, °frolic, °spree, romp, carousal *or* °carouse, saturnalia, bacchanalia, debauch, °orgy, *Colloq* °get-together, bash, bust, shindig *or* shindy, ball, at-home, do, *Brit* beanfeast, beano, knees-up, *US* blow-out, *Slang Brit* °rave *or* rave-up, *Chiefly US and Canadian* wingding, bust-up, *US* °hop: *Campbell said he had a marvellous time at your birthday party.* **2** °group, °company, °band, °body, °corps, °gang, °crew, °team, °squad, troop, °platoon, °detachment, °detail, cadre, °unit, *Colloq* °bunch, °outfit: *A small party of men is trapped on the other side of the river.* **3** °side, °interest, °faction, °league, °club, coalition, bloc, °division, °sect, °denomination, °clique, coterie, °set, °cabal, °junta *or* junto, partisans, adherents, confederacy, confederation, °federation, *Chiefly US and Canadian* caucus: *The proliferation of political parties confuses the electorate.* **4** °participant, participator, confederate, °associate, °ally, °accomplice, °accessory, approver, ratifier, upholder, contributor, °supporter, °advocate, °backer, °aid, helper, seconder, promoter, °partisan, defender, exponent, °proponent, °champion: *I refuse to be a party to any illegal act.* **5** °individual, °person, °litigant, plaintiff, defendant, °side, °interest, signer, signatory, co-signatory, °participant, *US* co-signer: *The party of the first part accuses the party of the second part of infidelity. How many parties are there to this contract?*

parvenu *n.* **1** parvenue, °upstart, *arriviste, nouveau riche*, °intruder, °adventurer, social climber: *Usually one generation has to pass before a parvenu is accepted by the class with which his money associates him.* —*adj.* **2** *nouveau riche*, °upstart, °intrusive: *This parvenu industrialist tried to use his wealth to make up for his lack of refinement.*

pass *v.* **1** Often, ***pass by***: °proceed *or* °move °past, °go by *or* °past: *She passed me in the street. I didn't recognize her till she had passed. We met like ships that pass in the night.* **2** °proceed, °move (°onwards), °go (°ahead), °progress, °extend, °lie, °run, °flow, °fly, °roll, °course, °stream, °drift, °sweep: *A flock of geese passed overhead.* **3** °let pass, °let °go (by), °overlook, °disregard, °ignore, pay no °heed, °omit, °skip: *I think I'll pass on making a decision till the proper time comes.* **4** °qualify (in), pass °muster (in), °get *or* °come through, °succeed: *Deirdre didn't believe she would pass chemistry, but pass she did.* **5** °spend, °devote, °use (up), °expend, °employ, °occupy, °fill, while away, °take (up); °dissipate, °waste, °fritter away, °kill: *He passed his time on Devil's Island planning ways to escape.* **6** °surpass, °exceed, °outdo, °transcend, °go beyond, overshoot, °outstrip, outrun, surmount, outdistance: *She passed her own expectations in winning the scholarship. How Alan ever got a degree passes all comprehension.* **7** °allow, °tolerate, °permit, °approve, °sanction, °accept, °authorize, °endorse, °carry, °agree to, °confirm: *The customs inspectors passed my luggage without question. The bill passed the committee and came up for voting.* **8** °give, °hand °round *or* along *or* over, °transfer, pass on *or* over, °deliver, convey, *Sports US* hand off, *Colloq* °toss, °throw, °reach: *Please pass the salt. The sweeper passed the ball back to the goalkeeper.* **9** utter, °express, °issue, °declare, °pronounce, °deliver, °set forth, °offer: *Who is she to pass judgement on abstract paintings?* **10** °go away, °disappear, vanish, °evaporate, °fade away, °melt away, evanesce, °cease (to exist), (come to an) °end, °die out, go by the board, °terminate, *Literary* evanish, *Colloq* °blow over: *For an instant I was gripped by a horrible fear, but the feeling passed.* **11** °go (by), °expire, °elapse; °slip by *or* away, °fly; °crawl, °creep, °drag: *Weeks have passed since we last met. Time passes quickly when you're having fun.* **12** °evacuate, °void, °eliminate, excrete, °defecate, °urinate: *The tests showed that he had passed some gravel in his urine.* **13** ***come to pass***: befall, °happen, °occur, °take °place, °come about, °arise, *Colloq* °come off: *And it came to pass that a great pestilence was abroad in the land.* **14** ***pass away***: **a** °die, °expire, °perish, °succumb, breathe one's last, pass on, go to one's reward, go to one's final *or* last resting-place, (go to) meet one's Maker, *Colloq* go west, give up the ghost, *Slang* croak, kick the bucket, *Chiefly US* bite the dust, turn up one's toes: *He was the sole beneficiary when she passed away.* **b** vanish, °disappear, °go away, °stop, °cease, °end: *The feeling of vertigo simply passed away when the plane landed.* **15** ***pass by***: See **1**, above: *The strikers were urging people to pass by the shop.* **16** ***pass for*** *or* ***as***: **a** be °taken for, be °mistaken for, be regarded as, be accepted as: *He wrote a book about being a man who passed for a woman.* **b** impersonate, °imitate, °mimic, °pass (oneself) off as, °come *or* °go as, be disguised as, °disguise oneself as, °assume the °guise of, °masquerade as, °pose as, °assume the °role of, °act the part of, °act like, °pretend to be, °play: *Using her best cockney accent, she tried to pass as a Londoner.* **17** ***pass off***: °evaporate, °disappear, evanesce, be emitted: *The water passes off as steam, leaving the distillate in the flask.* **18** ***pass on***: **a** °proceed, °continue, °progress: *Let us now pass on to the next lesson.* **b** °bequeath, °hand down *or* on, °transfer, °make over, °will, °cede, °give: *The old gambler passed on to me the secret of never losing—Don't gamble.* **c** See **14 a** above. **19** ***pass (oneself) off as***: See **16 b**, above. **20** ***pass out***: **a** °faint, °collapse, swoon, black out, °drop, *Colloq* conk out, keel over: *When they told her of the accident, she passed out on the spot.* **b** °distribute, °dole out, °mete out, °deal (out), °hand out: *After we took our seats, the cabin staff passed out glasses of champagne.* **21** ***pass over***: See **3**, above: *I shall pass over his latest misdeeds without comment.* **22** ***pass up***: °reject, °decline, °refuse, °waive, °turn down, °dismiss, °spurn, °renounce; °deny (oneself), °skip, °give up, °forgo, °let °go (by), °abandon, forswear, °forsake, °let pass, °ignore, pay no °heed, °disregard, °omit: *If you don't buy this car, you are passing up an opportunity of a lifetime.* —*n.* **23** defile, °gorge, col, cwm, cut, °canyon, notch, °gap, °gully *or* gulley, couloir; °passage, °opening, °way, °route, °road: *We had mined the pass to prevent the enemy's advance.* **24** authorization, °permit, °licence, °approval, safe conduct, green light, °go-ahead; °permission, °freedom, °liberty, °authority, °clearance; *Colloq* °OK *or* okay: *He bribed an official for a pass to leave the country.* **25** °free pass, °complimentary ticket, *Slang US* twofer, Annie Oakley: *I have two passes to the opera tonight—Want to go?* **26** °state (of affairs), °condition, °situation, °stage, °juncture, °status, crux; °predicament, °crisis: *At that critical pass, it was too late to change policy. Things had come to a pretty pass.* **27** °attempt, °trial, °try, °effort, °endeavour: *Anita's first pass at a perfect score resulted in disaster. We made a pass at docking while under sail.* **28** (°sexual *or* °indecent) °overture *or* °advance(s), °proposition, °indecent °proposal: *That lecher has made a pass at every secretary he's ever had.* **29** °manoeuvre, °approach; °passage, °flight, fly-by, °transit: *The pilot's first pass over the airfield was at 500 feet.* **30** °transfer, °toss, °throw, *US* hand-off: *A forward pass is illegal in rugby.*

passable *adj.* **1** °satisfactory, °acceptable, °tolerable, all right, °adequate, admissible, allowable, °presentable, °average, °fair (enough), °fair to middling, °fairly °good, middling, not bad, unexceptional, °sufficient, °indifferent, *Colloq* °OK *or* okay, °so so: *I thought the play passable, but not up to his usual standard.* **2** traversable, °navigable, °open, unobstructed, unblocked: *The channel is passable till October, when the river freezes over.*

passage *n.* **1** °movement, moving, going, °transition, °transit, traversal, °traverse, °progress, crossing, °passing: *The Queen's passage through the town was attended by much jubilation. We observed the passage of Mercury across the sun's disc.* **2** °extract, °excerpt, °selection, °section, °part, °portion, °text, paragraph, canto, stanza, verse, °line, °sentence, °phrase, citation, °quotation: *I recognize this passage from* The Faerie Queene. **3** °way, °route, avenue, °course, °channel; °road, thoroughfare: *Amundsen found a navigable passage between the Atlantic and Pacific across North America.* **4** °corridor, °hall, passageway, hallway, vestibule, °lobby, foyer: *As I stepped into the passage outside my room I heard a door slam.* **5** °change, °mutation, °shift, conversion, °progression, passing: *In sublimation, the passage is directly between the solid and gaseous or vaporous states, without an intermediate liquid stage.* **6** °passing, °elapse, °progress, °progression, °flow, °march, °advance: *She may become more tractable with the passage of time.* **7** voyage, °trip, °journey, °cruise, crossing, °sail, °run, °travel, travelling; *Brit* °accommodation *or US* °accommodations, °arrangement(s), facilities: *In 1942 the trans-Atlantic passage was fraught with danger. The refugees were guaranteed safe passage to the border. We have been unable to book a passage to Majorca for tomorrow.* **8** safe conduct, °permission, °privilege, °liberty, °freedom, visa, authorization, °allowance: *Our troops were denied passage through Nepal.* **9** enactment, ratification, °sanction, °approval, acceptance, passing, adoption, °endorsement, endorsing, legitimatization *or* legitimization, legalization, legislation, constitutionalization, ordainment: *It appears that there is enough support to ensure passage of the bill.* **10** °traffic, trafficking, dealing, shipment, shipping, °commerce, °trade, °exchange, °transaction: *Representatives of several governments discussed putting a halt to the passage of narcotics from Colombia.* **11** °aperture, °hole, orifice, °opening; °entry, access, inlet; °exit, °outlet: *We found a tiny passage through which the termites were entering and leaving.*

passé *adj.* °old-fashioned, unfashionable, dated, out of °date, behind the °times, outmoded, °obsolete, °obsolescent, °antiquated, archaic, *démodé*, °quaint, °antique, superseded, *Colloq* out, not *or* no longer in, °old hat, back number: *She persisted in dressing in a style that had been passé at the turn of the century.*

passenger *n.* rider, °fare, °traveller, voyager, commuter: *The cruise ships have very comfortable accommodation for their passengers.*

passing *adj.* **1** disappearing, vanishing, ephemeral, °brief, going, fading (away), slipping away, °short-lived, expiring, °transient, transitory, °temporary, °momentary, °fleeting, transitional, impermanent: *I hope that Anne's obsession with acid rock is a passing fancy.* **2** °hasty, °superficial, °cursory, °casual, quick, °fleeting, °brief, °summary, °abrupt, dismissive; glancing: *The speaker paid only passing attention to those he disagreed with.* **3** ***in passing***: by the °way, °incidentally, by the by, parenthetically, *en passant*: *I might mention, in passing, that my train was late owing to the strike.*
—*n.* **4** °death, °dying, demise, °end, °loss, expiry, °expiration, °dying out, extinction, disappearance, vanishment: *Her passing is a great sorrow to all of us. Who thought we would live to see the passing of the steam engine?*

passion *n.* **1** Often, ***passions***: °ardour, ardency, °eagerness, °intensity, °fervour, fervency, fervidness, zeal, zealousness, avidity, avidness, °zest, zestfulness, vivacity, vivaciousness, °gusto, °verve, °emotion, °feeling, °animation, °spirit, spiritedness, °vigour, °enthusiasm; °zealotry, °fanaticism, feverishness: *The passions of the mob are uncontrollable. Passion and prejudice govern the world. Passions ran high at the political convention.* **2** °fit, °outburst, °frenzy, °paroxysm, °seizure, °spasm, convulsion, °eruption, °whirlwind, °tempest, °storm, °ferment, °fury, °furore *or US* furor: *Henry fell on his knees in a passion of grief.* **3** infatuation, °mania, °obsession, °craze, craving, °lust, (unquenchable) °thirst, (insatiable) °hunger, °itch, yearning, °longing, °desire, concupiscence, °love, °affection, °enthusiasm, compulsion, fondness, predilection, keenness, °fancy, °fascination, °partiality, °liking, °interest, °weakness, *Colloq* yen: *Would the world be a better place if the passion for spiritual values were as great as for material things? She has a passion for chocolates.* **4** °love, heart's °desire, °beloved, °idol, °hero *or* °heroine, °obsession, *Colloq* heartthrob, dream-girl *or* dream-boy: *He may not look much to you but he is the passion of every teenage girl.* **5** Usually, ***Passion***: °pain, °suffering, °agony, martyrdom: *Christ underwent his Passion at Calvary.*

passionate *adj.* **1** °ardent, °eager, °intense, fervid, zealous, avid, °earnest, zestful, °feverish, °fanatic(al), vehement, °impassioned, °emotional, °animated, °spirited, °enthusiastic, °vigorous, invigorated, °energetic: *Passionate environmentalists campaign for better governmental control of carbon dioxide emissions.* **2** aroused, °lustful, °lecherous, °erotic, °sexual, amorous, °sensual, *Colloq* °hot: *She tried to resist his passionate advances.* **3** °quick-tempered, irascible, °hotheaded, °fiery, °testy, huffy *or* huffish, °peevish, °cranky, peppery, choleric, °touchy, °bilious, °snappish, °volatile, °cross, °temperamental, °irritable, °quarrelsome, °pugnacious, °argumentative, contentious, °belligerent, *Rare* atrabilious *or* atrabiliar: *Valerie gets into a passionate mood whenever she thinks she is being treated unjustly.*

passive *adj.* **1** °inactive, non-aggressive, °inert, motionless, unresponsive, °quiet, °calm, °tranquil, °serene, placid, °still, °idle, unmoving, °unmoved, °impassive, untouched, °cool, °indifferent, °phlegmatic, uninterested, uninvolved, °dispassionate, apathetic, °lifeless, °listless, quiescent, unperturbed, °unaffected, imperturbable, unshaken, *Colloq* laid-back, out of it: *The comic was unable to get a reaction from the passive audience.* **2** °submissive, repressed, deferential, °yielding, compliant, complaisant, °receptive, °flexible, malleable, °pliable, °tractable, docile, °subdued, °sheepish, ovine, lamblike, cow-like, bovine, °tame, °gentle, °meek, °patient, unresisting, unassertive, forbearing, °tolerant, resigned, long-suffering, *Colloq US* excuse-me-for-living: *People tend to bully those of a more passive nature.* **3** unexpressed, °tacit, unrevealed, undisclosed, °implicit, unasserted: *We can no longer take a passive position regarding crime. Your passive support, while welcome, is not as effective as active campaigning.*

password *n.* watchword, °shibboleth, open sesame, countersign: *If you don't know the password, the guard won't let you in.*

past *adj.* **1** over, done, finished, (over and) done with, gone (and forgotten), °dead (and buried *or* gone), °defunct: *The day of the horse and carriage is past.* **2** °late, °former, one-time, °sometime, °previous, °prior, erstwhile, quondam, whilom; °last, °recent: *Past owners of the house had no idea that this treasure was buried in the basement.*
—*adv.* **3** on, (°close) by, °nearby: *I was standing here when he ran past.* **4** ago, °before, heretofore, since: *The previous owners moved out two years past.*
—*n.* **5** °history, °background, °life, lifetime, °existence, °career, lifestyle, biography: *She reveals all about her past in her new book.* **6** days *or* years *or* times gone by, days of yore, °old times, olden times *or* days, °former times, (good) °old days, days of °old, days beyond recall: *In the past, life proceeded at a more leisurely pace.*

pastiche *n.* °mixture, °medley, °blend, °compound, composite, °patchwork, olla podrida, °pot-pourri, motley, °miscellany, omnium gatherum, *mélange*, gallimaufry, farrago, °mishmash, °hotchpotch *or US and Canadian* hodgepodge, °tangle, *Colloq* °mess: *The room was furnished in a pastiche of styles from every imaginable period.*

pastime *n.* °hobby, avocation, °recreation, °diversion, °distraction, °amusement, °entertainment, °fun, °play, leisure-time °activity, °relaxation, °leisure, °sport, divertissement: *As a pastime, she collects books.*

pastor *n.* vicar, °clergyman, clergywoman, parson, °minister, churchman, churchwoman, rector, canon, reverend, °father, °divine, ecclesiastic, °priest, bishop: *The pastor led the congregation in prayer.*

pastoral *adj.* **1** bucolic, °idyllic, Edenic, °innocent, °simple, °tranquil, °serene, °quiet, °restful, °peaceful, °peaceable, placid, pacific, °harmonious, un-complicated, *Literary* Arcadian, georgic: *After a week in those pastoral surroundings, she felt inspired. Theocritus is noted for his pastoral poetry.* **2** °country, °rural, °rustic, °provincial, °farming, agricultural, agrarian; °humble: *He has chosen a pastoral setting for the play, which contrasts sharply with the emotional intensity of the characters.* **3** °clerical, ministerial, ecclesiastic(al), church(ly): *Our vicar discharges his pastoral duties with energy and sincerity.*
—*n.* **4** idyll, eclogue, georgic: *Flambeau did these marvellous engravings for a book of pastorals.*

pasture *n.* °meadow, meadow-land, pasture °land, grassland, °grass, lea, °range; pasturage: *How much pasture is needed for 200 head of cattle?*

pasty *adj.* °wan, pallid, pasty-faced, sallow, °pale, pale-faced, whey-faced, °sickly, anaemic: *He had the pasty complexion of a child raised in an industrial city.*

pat[1] *v.* **1** °tap, °touch, °dab, °pet, °stroke, °caress: *Being short, he hated it when people affectionately patted him on the head. Pat down the coverlet to smooth out the wrinkles.* **2** ***pat on the back***: °congratulate, commend, °praise, °compliment, °encourage, °reassure: *The sales manager patted me on the back for clinching the contract.*
—*n.* **3** °tap, °touch, °dab, °stroke, °caress: *Give the dog a pat and he'll leave you alone.* **4** (°small) piece, patty, °lump, °cake, °portion; patty: *The waiter put a pat of butter on my plate.* **5** ***pat on the back***: commendation, °praise, °compliment, °flattery, °encouragement, °credit, reassurance, °approval, °endorsement, °recognition; honeyed words: *I was expecting a big bonus, but all I got was a pat on the back.*

pat[2] *adv.* **1** °perfectly, °exactly, °precisely, faultlessly, flawlessly, °just so *or* °right, *Brit* off pat: *She has the new technique pat.* **2** aptly, suitably, appositely, °readily, °appropriately, fittingly, relevantly: *His reply came out a little too pat.*
—*adj.* **3** apt, °suitable, apposite, °ready, °appropriate, °fitting, °relevant: *The poet made a very pat comparison.*

patch *n.* **1** °piece, °scrap, °reinforcement; °shred, °snip, snippet, °tatter; pad: *Mother sewed colourful patches over the holes in my jeans.* **2** °area, °section, °segment, plat, °plot, °lot, °tract, °ground, °parcel, °field: *All he ever wanted was a little house on a little patch of land.* **3** °responsibility, °area, bailiwick, °territory: *The handling of customer complaints is in your patch, Gordon.* **4** °period, °interval, °spell, °stage, °episode, °time; °experience: *She went through a bad patch shortly after Starkey died.*
—*v.* **5** °patch up *or* over, °mend, °repair, vamp, °revamp, darn, °sew (up), °reinforce, °cover: *I had my trousers patched where the dog bit me. Her father always wore the same patched jacket to the club.* **6** Often, ***patch up***: °fix (up), °doctor, jury-rig, °improvise, °knock together *or* up: *Can you patch it up so I can drive it home?* **7** ***patch up***: °settle, set °right *or* °straight, °straighten out, °reconcile, °resolve, °heal; come *or* bring to °terms, bury the hatchet, kiss and °make up, °call a °truce: *Will the two girls ever patch up their differences?*

patchwork *n.* °pastiche *or* pasticcio, °mixture, °confusion, °hotchpotch *or US also* hodgepodge, gallimaufry, olio, olla podrida, °mishmash, °jumble, *mélange*, °medley, °hash, *US* crazy quilt, *Colloq* mixed bag: *The landscape is a patchwork of ploughland and pasture, with little copses and rivers. The concerto by Lindslade is 'derivative'—that is, it is a patchwork.*

patent *n.* **1** certificate of °invention, letters patent, °trade °name, °trade °mark, copyright, *US* service °mark; °licence, °permit, °charter, franchise, °grant; °control: *My brother holds the patent on a new piece of laboratory equipment. You think you have a patent on misery, but I have news for you.*
—*adj.* **2** °obvious, °clear, °transparent, °manifest, °apparent, °plain, °evident, °self-evident, unmistakable, °explicit, palpable, °tangible, °physical, °conspicuous, °flagrant, °blatant, °prominent: *The results are as patent as the fact that two and two make four.*

paternal *adj.* **1** °fatherly, °kindly, °indulgent, °solicitous, °fond, °concerned, °devoted, loving; patriarchal: *Uncle Charles takes a paternal interest in the welfare of his nieces and nephews.* **2** patrilineal *or* patrilinear, patriclinous *or* patroclinous *or* patriclinal *or* patroclinal *or* patriclinic *or* patroclinic, patrilateral, patrimonial: *She resembles her paternal grandmother. His fortune is partly paternal, partly acquired.*

paternity *n.* fatherhood, fathership; °parentage, descent, °heritage, °line, °lineage, °extraction, °family, °stock, °strain, blood, patrilineage: *The child's paternity was established through DNA tests.*

path *n.* **1** footpath, pathway, tow-path, °track, °trail, °walk, walkway, *Brit* footway: *A little kitten was sitting on the garden path.* **2** °way, °course, °track, °route, °road; °orbit, °trajectory, °circuit: *She had to overcome many obstacles in her path to the directorship. The path of the missile will take it outside the atmosphere.* **3** °course, °approach, °channel, °direction, °procedure, °process, °way, avenue, °means, °method, °technique, °strategy, °scheme, °plan, *Colloq US* game °plan, °scenario: *What path would you follow to accomplish your ends?*

pathetic *adj.* **1** °moving, °stirring, affecting, affective, °touching, °emotional, emotive, °poignant, °tragic, °heart-rending, heartbreaking, °pitiful, °pitiable, °piteous, plaintive, °wretched, °miserable, °sorrowful, °grievous, °sad, °doleful, dolorous, °mournful, woeful, °lamentable: *The boat people told a pathetic tale of the hardship of weeks in the open sea.* **2** °meagre, °paltry, °feeble, °inadequate, °poor, °petty, °puny, °sorry, piddling, *Colloq* °measly, *Slang* crummy: *He made a pathetic effort to pull himself together. A return of three per cent a year is pathetic.*

patience *n.* **1** °tolerance, forbearance, °restraint, toleration, sufferance, leniency, °submission, °resignation, °self-control, imperturbability, even °temper, unflappability, composure, calmness, °serenity, equanimity: *Many parents lose their patience when dealing with children.* **2** diligence, °tenacity, doggedness, indefatigability, °endurance, assiduity, °perseverance, constancy, °persistence, steadfastness, pertinacity, °determination, °resolve, °resolution, firmness, °stoicism, °fortitude, *Colloq US* stick-to-it-iveness: *Where do you get the patience to wait in those long queues?*

patient *adj.* **1** resigned, °submissive, °stoical, long-suffering, compliant, acquiescent, °passive, °self-possessed, °philosophical, °serene, unaggressive: *The staff who handle complaints must be extremely patient.* **2** °diligent, dogged, °tenacious, °persistent, assiduous, sedulous, °steadfast, °staunch, perseverant, unwavering, unswerving, °constant, unfaltering, unfailing, °untiring, °tireless, indefatigable, pertinacious, °determined, resolved, °resolute, °firm, unyielding: *Be patient, and don't do anything rash.* **3** forbearing, °tolerant, °forgiving, °lenient, °accommodating: *We have been patient long enough and must now put a stop to the vandalism.*
—*n.* **4** °invalid, sufferer, °case, valetudinarian: *Doctors were called in to treat patients who developed the symptoms.*

patriot *n.* nationalist, loyalist; flag-waver, jingo, jingoist, chauvinist: *She was among the patriots ready to do battle for their country.*

patriotic *adj.* nationalist(ic), loyalist; flag-waving, jingoist(ic), chauvinist(ic): *The fact that they criticize the government may show that they are more rather than less patriotic.*

patrol *n.* **1** °guard, sentry, °watch, °watchman, °sentinel, patrolman: *The patrol passes here once every hour.* **2** °rounds, policing, patrolling, °beat; protecting,

°protection, guarding, safeguarding, defending, watchfulness, °vigilance: *The patrol must be maintained night and day.*
—*v.* **3** °police, °guard, °protect, °defend, °watch over, walk a °beat, make (the) °rounds, stand *or* keep °guard *or* °watch (over), keep vigil: *Some of the local residents have taken to patrolling the neighbourhood at night.*

patron *n.* **1** patroness, °benefactor, benefactress, °philanthropist, Maecenas, °protector, °supporter, defender, °advocate, °champion, °guardian (angel), °sponsor, °backer, promoter, °sympathizer, °friend, *US* booster; °friend at court; *Colloq* angel: *Lady Agnes is a well-known patron of the arts.* **2** °customer, °client, purchaser, °buyer, patronizer, °*habitué*, °regular, frequenter: *The patrons habituate her shop because of the bargains to be found there.*

patronage *n.* **1** sponsorship, °support, °backing, °promotion, °encouragement, boosting, °aid, °help, °sympathy, financing, °auspices, °protection, guardianship, aegis: *The exhibition was organized with the duke's patronage.* **2** °trade, °business, °custom, trading, °traffic: *The shop could never succeed with our patronage.* **3** condescension, disdain, °scorn, °contempt, contumely, °superiority, patronizing, stooping, deigning, °humiliation: *There is an air of patronage about him when he finally does allow me a visit.* **4** °favouritism, °partiality, °preference, °bias, nepotism, political patronage, granting of indulgences, *US* °spoils (system): *Politicians have always used patronage to reward support.*

patronize *v.* **1** °look down on, °scorn, °look down one's nose at, °treat condescendingly, °talk down to, °treat as (an) °inferior, disdain, demean, °put down, °humiliate, *Formal* contemn: *He patronizes people by patting them on the head.* **2** bring °trade to, °deal *or* °trade with, do *or* °transact °business with, °buy *or* °purchase from, °frequent, °shop at, be a °customer *or* °client of: *You should patronize the local merchants in your town.* **3** °sponsor, °support, °back, °promote, °encourage, °boost, °aid, °assist, °help, °fund, °contribute *or* °subscribe to, °underwrite, °foster: *The fund has patronized the arts in this town for many years.*

patter[1] *v.* **1** tiptoe; °scurry, scuttle, °skip, °trip: *I could hear the squirrels pattering across the metal roof.* **2** °spatter, pitter-patter, °tap, pit-a-pat; °beat, °pelt: *The rain pattered on the tent with increasing intensity.*
—*n.* **3** °spatter, spattering, pit-a-pat, pitter-patter, tattoo, drum, thrum, °beat, beating, °tap, ratatat, tap-tap: *The rhythmical patter of the rain lulled me to sleep.*

patter[2] *n.* **1** °pitch, sales °talk, spiel, °line: *Anyone listening to his patter might be inclined to buy a time-share holiday.* **2** °chatter, °prattle, prate, babbling, °babble, gabble, gabbling, cackle, cackling, °palaver, °jabber, jabbering, chit-chat, °small °talk, °gossip, blather *or* blether, °gibberish *or* gibber, *Chiefly Brit* natter, nattering, *Scots* clishmaclaver, *Colloq* °gab, gabbing, *Slang* gas, °hot air, ya(c)kety-ya(c)k, ya(c)k: *The chap tapping our phone had to listen to the teenagers' patter for hours on end.*
—*v.* **3** °chatter, °prattle, prate, °babble, gabble, cackle, °palaver, °jabber, °rattle (on), chit-chat, chaffer, °gossip, blather *or* blether, gibber, *Chiefly Brit* natter, witter (on), *Colloq* °gab, *Slang* gas, ya(c)kety-ya(c)k, ya(c)k, jibber-jabber: *They just patter on about nothing in particular.*

pattern *n.* **1** °model, °original, archetype, °prototype, exemplar, °paragon, °ideal, °standard, °yardstick, criterion, °gauge, °measure: *Their life together could serve as a pattern for any couple.* **2** °figure, °motif, °design, °device, °decoration, °ornament: *The pattern of the wallpaper clashes with that of the curtains.* **3** °system, °order, °arrangement, °plan, °theme; °repetition, consistency, orderliness, °regularity, °sequence, °cycle: *By carefully noting the movements of the heavenly bodies, ancient observers were able to detect a pattern.* **4** blueprint, diagram, °plan, layout, °design, °draft, °guide, °template *or* templet, stencil, °mould, matrix: *These new lighting fixtures are made to a 19th-century pattern.* **5** °sample, °example, °instance, °specimen, °representation: *Were you able to match up your fabric pattern with one of those in the tailor's book?* **6** layout, configuration, °figure, °formation, °composition: *The geese often flew in a V-shaped pattern.*
—*v.* **7** Often, ***pattern on***: °model on, °imitate, °copy, °mimic, °duplicate, °follow, emulate, simulate: *She tried to pattern her behaviour on that of her older sister.* **8** °decorate, °figure, °ornament: *Cynthia's gifts were wrapped in a beautifully patterned paper.*

paunch *n.* belly, pot-belly, *Colloq* corporation, *US* bay window, *Slang* beer-belly: *Capitalism is often conventionalized as a top-hatted older man, in tails, with a huge paunch and a cigar.*

pauper *n.* have-not, °indigent, °down-and-out(er), bankrupt, °insolvent; °beggar, mendicant; °tramp, hobo, vagrant, *US* °bum: *The mortgage payments on such a lavish house soon made him a pauper.*

pause *v.* **1** °hesitate, °interrupt, °delay, °hold up, °discontinue, °break, °wait, mark time, °suspend, intermit, falter, °rest: *He paused for a moment to allow latecomers to take their seats.*
—*n.* **2** hesitation, °interruption, °delay, °lull, °lapse, °moratorium, °hold-up, °wait, °break, breather, breathing-space, discontinuity, lacuna, hiatus, °abeyance, discontinuation, discontinuance, *Prosody* caesura, *Music* fermata, *Colloq* °let-up: *There was a brief pause, then the altercation in the neighbouring flat resumed.*

pave *v.* **1** macadamize, tarmac, asphalt, tile, flag, °concrete, °cover, °surface: *Europeans thought that the streets of America were paved with gold.* **2** ***pave the way for*** or ***to***: °prepare *or* °smooth the °way for, °open the door for, make °easy *or* easier for; °facilitate, °ease: *If I talk to him first, perhaps I can pave the way for you to make your proposal.*

pawn[1] *v.* **1** °pledge, mortgage, hypothecate, °plight, °deposit, *Formal* pignorate, *Archaic* gage, *Colloq Brit* pop, *Chiefly US and Canadian* hock: *I had to pawn my watch to get enough money to eat.* **2** °venture, °stake, °risk, °gamble, °hazard, °chance, °jeopardize: *By agreeing to donate one of his kidneys, he pawned his life to save hers.*
—*n.* **3** collateral, guaranty *or* °guarantee, °pledge, surety, °security, °assurance, °bond, bail, °deposit: *She gave her jewels as pawn for the safe return of the children.*

pawn[2] *n.* °tool, cat's-paw, °puppet, instrument, °dummy, °dupe, *Colloq* stooge: *He's not important: he's just being used as a pawn by the powerful interests involved.*

pay *v.* **1** recompense, °compensate, remunerate, °reward, indemnify; °repay, refund, °reimburse; pay off, pay out, pay up, °satisfy, °clear, °remit, °discharge, liquidate, °settle, °honour, °meet: *Do you think that nurses are poorly paid? You have 30 days to pay this invoice.* **2** °reward, °benefit, recompense, °requite, °compensate: *Thurlew has been amply paid by having his name engraved on the roll of honour.* **3** °extend, °bestow, °transmit, °pass on, °give, °deliver: *Please pay my respects to your wife.* **4** °benefit, °profit, avail, (turn out to) be *or* prove °profitable *or* °worthwhile, °yield a °return, be °advantageous, produce results, pay off: *It no longer pays to complain about the service in the shops. Honesty pays.* **5** pay back, °repay, °retaliate, °settle (accounts) (with), °reciprocate, °requite, take *or* get °revenge on, avenge oneself for *or* on, °treat in kind, °hit *or* °strike *or* °get back (at), °settle *or* pay off *or* °even a °score *or* the °score (with), °exact one's pound of flesh (from), make (someone) pay (for), °punish, °chastise, °castigate, *Brit* pay out, *Colloq* get °even (with): *If I catch him, I'll pay him for turning informer.* **6** °suffer (the consequences), °answer (for), make °amends (for), °atone (for), get one's (just) deserts, °undergo °punishment (for), be punished (for): *If I catch him, I'll make him pay. Society requires that he pay for his crime.* **7** °produce *or* °make *or* °generate *or* °earn °money, °yield a °return, pay off: *His vending-machine business certainly pays well.* **8** ***pay back***:

a °recompense, °compensate, remunerate, °reward, indemnify; °repay, pay off, refund, °reimburse: *I paid back every penny I borrowed from the bank. I'll pay her back if it's the last thing I do.* **b** See **5,** above. **9** ***pay for***: See **6,** above. **10** ***pay off***: **a** See **4** and **7,** and **8a,** above. **b** °bribe, suborn, °buy off, grease (someone's) palm, give (someone) a °bribe *or* a °rebate, *Colloq* give (someone) a °kickback, slip (someone) something: *Did he really pay off the judges to select his daughter as Miss Tyneside?* **11** ***pay out***: **a** °distribute, °deal out, °give out, °disperse, disburse: *The managing director paid out bonuses to the entire staff.* **b** disburse, °expend, °spend, °contribute, *Colloq* °shell out, °lay out, *US and Canadian and Australian and New Zealand* kick in with, *Slang* cough up, fork out *or* over *or* up: *In the office, we are forever paying out for leaving presents.* **c** °release, °loosen, °let out, °slack *or* slacken off (on): *Pay out more rope so that he can reach it.* **d** See **5,** above: *We'll pay him out for everything he's done to you, never fear!*
—*n.* **12** °payment, compensation, recompense, °settlement, °return; °remuneration, °consideration, °reward, °money, wages, °salary, °fee, °honorarium, °remittance, °stipend, °income, takings, take-home (pay), °gain, °profit, *Colloq US* °take: *His sole pay for painting the kitchen was a big hug and a kiss. The work is tedious, but the pay isn't bad.*

payable *adj.* °due, owed, owing, °outstanding, °unpaid, receivable, °mature: *This bill is payable at the end of the month.*

payment *n.* **1** See **pay, 12,** above. **2** °expenditure, disbursement, °distribution, °outlay, °fee, contribution, °charge, °expense, payout: *You are not authorized to make payment of any amount over £100.*

pay-off *n.* **1** See **pay, 12,** above. **2** °result, °outcome, °upshot, conclusion, wind-up, °settlement, final °reckoning, *Colloq* punch-line, °crunch, grand finale, *Slang US and Canadian* kicker: *The pay-off was that permission to march on Sunday was denied.* **3** °bribe, °graft, °rebate; °ransom, blood-money, *Colloq* °kickback, °hush °money, *Chiefly US* payola, *US* plugola: *The pay-off was always made in cash, in used notes.*

peace *n.* **1** °serenity, tranquillity, °calm, calmness, placidity *or* placidness, peace of mind, °quiet, peacefulness, peaceableness, stillness: *For a summer holiday, we enjoy the peace of the Lakes.* **2** °harmony, °accord, harmoniousness, concord, amity, peacefulness, peacetime; cease-fire, armistice, °truce: *Since the Second World War, Europe has enjoyed more than 45 years of relative peace.*

peaceable *adj.* **1** See **peaceful, 1,** below. **2** pacific, °inoffensive, dovish, peace-loving, °mild, non-violent, non-belligerent, unbelligerent, unwarlike, non-warring, non-combative, °temperate, °agreeable, compatible, congenial, °genial, °friendly, °amiable, °amicable, °cordial, °civil: *Despite cultural differences, the two countries maintained peaceable relations.*

peaceful *adj.* **1** °peaceable, °serene, placid, °calm, °quiet, quiescent, °gentle, °restful, °tranquil, untroubled, undisturbed, unruffled: *After our week-end guests left, the house was again peaceful.* **2** See **peaceable, 2,** above.

peacemaker *n.* conciliator, pacifier, reconciler, propitiator, placater, pacificator, °mediator, arbitrator, intermediator, °intermediary, diplomat, appeaser, interceder, °go-between, referee, °umpire, adjudicator; peacemonger: *The ambassador was called upon to act as peacemaker between the warring nations.*

peak *n.* **1** °top, °pinnacle, °crest, °ridge, tor, °mountain °top, °summit, °mountain, eminence, °elevation, °hill: *We were just able to make out the snow-capped peaks in the distance.* **2** °top, °tip, tiptop, apex, °acme, culmination, apogee, °zenith, °high °point, °crown, °extreme, utmost, uttermost, °perfection, *ne plus ultra*, °consummation, °climax: *Irene has brought the office to a peak of efficiency.* **3** visor, °brim, *US* bill, nib: *The peak of the fisherman's cap serves as an eyeshade.*
—*v.* **4** °rise, °crest, culminate, (°reach a) °climax, °top (out): *Prices peaked during the Christmas shopping season.*

peaky *adj.* peakish, pinched, °unhealthy, °sickly, ailing, °ill, unwell, °infirm, °unwholesome, °pale, pallid, °wan, waxen, anaemic, °pasty, sallow, whey-faced, ashen, washed out, drained, °emaciated, wasted, °gaunt, hollow-eyed, °haggard, °drawn, °weak, °feeble, *US* peaked: *Paul has been looking a bit peaky of late.*

peal *n.* **1** ringing, °ring, carillon, °chime, chiming, °toll, tolling, clang, clangour, tintinnabulation, clamour, reverberation; knell; °clap, °crash, °roar, rumble, °thunder: *The constant peal of the bells nearly drove him mad. The doleful peal rang out for yet another fisherman lost at sea. A resounding peal of thunder shook the house.*
—*v.* **2** °ring, °toll, °chime, clang, tintinnabulate, reverberate, resonate, °resound; knell; °boom, °crash, °roar, °roll, rumble, °thunder: *The cowbells pealed plaintively, reminding me of my youth in the Alps. Lightning flashed, and the echoing thunder pealed through the valley.*

pearl *n.* °gem, °treasure, °prize, cream, °flower, °wonder, °nonpareil: *Wasn't Cuba once called the Pearl of the Antilles?*

pearly *adj.* nacreous, pearl-like, perlaceous, °lustrous, mother-of-pearl: *The dress was trimmed with pink lace and little pearly buttons.*

peasant *n.* °rustic, countryman, countrywoman, °farmer, °provincial, (°farm) °worker, (°country) bumpkin, bucolic; peon, fellah, muzhik *or* mouzhik *or* mujik; *Historical* esne, serf, *Archaic* swain, hind, churl, *Derogatory* yokel, hill-billy, bog-trotter, oaf, °lump, lout, °boor, churl, °clod, clodhopper; *Colloq US and Canadian* hick, galoot *or* galloot, *Derogatory* hayseed, rube, *Derogatory and offensive US* poor white (trash): *Regimes came and went, but the life of the medieval peasant endured.*

peccadillo *n.* °slip, °error, °lapse, °mistake, infraction, °violation, °misdeed, °shortcoming, °misstep, °blunder, *faux pas*, °indiscretion, gaffe, °botch, °stumble, °fault, °petty °sin, (°minor) °transgression, trespass, *Colloq* slip-up, goof: *We have to forgive the occasional peccadillo.*

peculiar *adj.* **1** °odd, °curious, °strange, °queer, °bizarre, °weird, °unusual, °abnormal, anomalous, aberrant, °deviant *or* °deviate, °eccentric, uncommon, °outlandish, °exceptional, °extraordinary, out of the °ordinary, °offbeat, °unorthodox, atypical, idiosyncratic, unconventional, °out-of-the-way, °quaint, °unique, °singular, °one of a kind, *sui generis*, °distinct, °distinguished, °special, °particular, quirky, °funny, freakish, *Slang* far-out, freaky, *Brit* rum: *Don't you agree that anyone who by choice goes barefoot in winter is a bit peculiar? She enjoys a peculiar immunity to colds.* **2** Usually, ***peculiar to***: °typical of, °characteristic of, characterized by, °natural to, °symptomatic of, °appropriate to *or* for, °distinctive of, restricted to, °specific to, indicative of, denotative of, °limited to, °individual to, °personal to, °special to, °unique to; seen *or* observed (°only) in, °local to, °native to, °indigenous to: *Such behaviour is peculiar to those who have served long prison sentences.*
—*n.* **3** *Typography* arbitrary, sort: *Characters with diacritical marks are called 'peculiars' in the printing trades.*

peculiarity *n.* **1** idiosyncrasy, °oddity, °eccentricity, °abnormality, irregularity, °quirk, °kink, crotchet, caprice: *Keeping alligators was only one of Jess's peculiarities.* **2** °feature, °characteristic, °property, °quality, °trait, °attribute, earmark, °hallmark, °mark, particularity, °singularity, *Brit* °speciality, *US* specialty: *One of the peculiarities of the books is their wide margins.*

pedantic *adj.* **1** didactic, doctrinaire, donnish, pedagogic, pedantical, preachy, professorial, bookish, °ostentatious, °pretentious, sententious, °pompous, °vain, °stuffy, °stilted, °stiff, °dry: *A pedantic approach* *to marketing may be all right in the classroom, but it doesn't sell products.* **2** °perfectionist, °scrupulous, overscrupulous, °finicky *or* finical, °fussy, punctilious, °fastidious, °meticulous, °exact, chop-logic, °hair-splitting, quibbling, *Colloq* nit-picking: *His secretary left because of his pedantic criticisms of her work.*

peddle *v.* °sell, hawk, °market, vend, huckster, *Colloq* °push, °flog: *He is a publishing tycoon today, but he started by peddling books door-to-door.*

pedestal *n.* **1** °foundation, °base, °platform, °stand, substructure, mounting, °pier, foot, °support, *Technical* plinth, socle, dado: *The statue crumbled away and only its pedestal remained.* **2** ***put*** *or* ***place*** *or* ***set on a pedestal***: °glorify, °exalt, °worship, deify, °revere, °idolize, °dignify, apotheosize, ennoble, elevate, °raise: *No woman is worth putting on a pedestal.*

pedestrian *n.* **1** walker, stroller, ambler, rambler, footslogger; itinerant, peripatetic: *A special crossing has been installed for pedestrians.*
—*adj.* **2** °boring, °dull, °banal, °tiresome, commonplace, mundane, °tedious, unimaginative, uninteresting, °monotonous, run-of-the-mill, °humdrum, °stock, °prosaic, insipid, °dry, °flat, jejune, °colourless, °dreary, °pale, °ordinary, hackneyed, trite, (as) °dull as ditch-water *or US also* dishwater, °vapid, °stale, uninspired, uninspiring, spiritless, °lifeless, °dead: *The dean delivered his customary pedestrian lecture to the new students.* **3** walking, strolling, ambulatory, on foot, rambling, peripatetic: *We were exhausted after taking a pedestrian tour of London.*

pedigree *n.* (°line of) descent, ancestry, genealogy, blood, bloodline, °line, °extraction, °lineage, °stock, °heritage, °family, °derivation, °birth, °parentage, °strain, °roots: *His pedigree is all right, but does he have brains as well as money?*

pedlar *n.* hawker, (door-to-door) salesman *or* saleswoman *or* °salesperson, vendor, huckster, °seller, colporteur, *US* peddler, drummer, *Archaic* chapman, *Colloq* cheapjack: *How can you expect the watch to work if you bought it from a street pedlar?*

peek *v.* **1** °peer, °peep, glimpse, °look, squint (at), squinny (at), *Scots* keek, *Colloq* take *or* have a gander (at), *Brit* take a dekko (at): *A small boy peeked out from under the blanket.*
—*n.* **2** °look, glimpse, °peep, °glance, *Scots* keek, *Colloq* gander, look-see: *I've had a peek at what Father hid in the cupboard.*

peel *v.* **1** Sometimes, ***peel off***: °skin, °strip (off), °pare, flay, °flake off, descale, decorticate; shuck, °hull, bark, °scale; desquamate: *Beulah, peel me a grape.* **2** °strip, undress, °disrobe; do a striptease: *In the last act, everyone peels to the bare skin.* **3** ***peel off***: °take off *or* doff, °strip off: *I peeled off my coat and dived into the canal to save her.*
—*n.* **4** °skin, °rind, coating, peeling: *Don't you like candied orange peel?*

peep *v.* **1** °chirp, tweet, cheep, squeak, °twitter, °pipe, chirrup: *The birds peeped excitedly when they saw the cat.*
—*n.* **2** °chirp, tweet, cheep, squeak, °twitter, °pipe, chirrup, chirr *or* chirre *or* churr: *The night was filled with the peep of the frogs at the pond.* **3** °sound, °complaint, °outcry, °protest, protestation, grumble, °murmur: *The students didn't let out a peep when ordered to remain after class.*

peer[1] *n.* **1** °noble, nobleman *or* noblewoman, °lord *or* lady, aristocrat; duke *or* duchess, marquess *or* marchioness, earl *or* countess, viscount *or* viscountess, baron *or* baroness: *As a peer of the realm, she had certain rights.* **2** °equal, coequal, compeer, °like, °match, confrère, °associate, °colleague: *Under law, he is entitled to trial by a jury of his peers.*

peer[2] *v.* **1** °peep, °peek, squint (at), squinny (at), °look, °examine; °spy: *Scrooge peered closely at the accounts ledger.* **2** °appear, °peep through *or* out, °break through, °show, become °visible, °emerge: *Now and then, the moon peered through the clouds.*

peerless *adj.* without °equal, unequalled, °matchless, unmatched, unrivalled, °unique, °incomparable, beyond °compare, °unparalleled, °nonpareil, inimitable, unexcelled, unsurpassed, °superior, °superb, °excellent, °supreme, °superlative, finest, °best, *ne plus ultra*, °sovereign, consummate, °pre-eminent, °paramount: *James's mother was a peerless beauty and the toast of her generation.*

peevish *adj.* °irritable, °testy, °touchy, °fretful, ill-humoured, °waspish, °petulant, crabbed, churlish, °querulous, °short-tempered, ill-natured, tetchy, °cross, bad-tempered, ill-tempered, °fault-finding, captious, carping, cavilling, crusty, curmudgeonly, crotchety, °cantankerous, grumpy *or* grumpish, pettish, acrimonious, splenetic, *Colloq* °bilious, *US and Canadian and Irish* °cranky: *He's very peevish today, so don't get on his wrong side.*

peg *v.* **1** °pin, dowel, °rod, °stick, °bolt; thole *or* thole-pin; clothes-peg, °hook: *Pegs and glue are often used for fastening good furniture together. Hang your coat on the peg.* **2** ***off the peg***: °ready-made, ready-to-wear, °stock: *As bespoke clothing is so dear, I buy mine off the peg.* **3** ***take down a peg (or two)***: °humble, °diminish, °lower, °subdue, °suppress, °downgrade, °dishonour, °mortify, °humiliate, °put down, abase, °debase, devalue *or* devaluate: *He was acting a bit high and mighty, so she took him down a peg or two.*
—*v.* **4** °fasten, °secure, make °fast, °fix, °attach, °pin: *They pegged the tent firmly to the ground.* **5** °fix, °attach, °pin, °set (by), °control by, °limit by, °restrict, confine, °freeze, °bind, °regulate, °govern: *In indexing, the rate of inflation is often used for pegging wages.* **6** °toss, °throw, °shy, °flip, °sling, °cast: *I'll bet a fiver you can't peg that stone across the river.* **7** ***peg away*** *or US also* ***along***: °work (away) (at), °persevere (at), °apply oneself (to), °persist (in *or* at), °go to *or* at (it), °keep at (it), °stick to *or* with *or* at (it), °stay with *or* at (it), °carry on (with *or* at), *Colloq* °plug away (at), beaver away (at), hammer *or* bang *or* peck away (at): *Trevor pegs away at his homework every evening.*

pell-mell *adv.* **1** °helter-skelter, slapdash, rashly, feverishly, incautiously, confusedly, chaotically, wildly, impulsively, recklessly, slap-bang, impetuously, °hastily, hurriedly, precipitately, spontaneously: *The ice-cream vendor pedalled down the street with the children running pell-mell after him.*
—*adj.* **2** °helter-skelter, slapdash, °rash, °feverish, incautious, °confused, disordered, °disorderly, disorganized, °wild, °mad, °chaotic, °tumultuous, panicky, °impulsive, °reckless, °precipitate, °impetuous, °hasty, °hurried: *Quick action by the soldiers was responsible for the pell-mell rout of the attackers.*
—*n.* **3** °confusion, °disorder, °chaos, °tumult, °pandemonium, turmoil, mêlée *or* melee, °furore *or US* furor, commotion, °bedlam, brouhaha, hubbub, °excitement: *In the pell-mell that followed, several bystanders were injured.*

pelt[1] *v.* **1** °bombard, °shower, °bomb, °pepper, strafe, °batter, °shell, assail, °assault, °attack, *US* pummel *or* pommel, °belabour, °pound, *Old-fashioned* °lay about, *Slang US* clobber, wallop, paste, work over: *The hooligans pelted the crowd with sticks and stones.* **2** Often, ***pelt down***: °beat, °dash, °pound, °hit; °come down, °teem, °pour, *Colloq* °rain cats and dogs, bucket down, *US* °rain pitchforks: *The rain came pelting down just as we were ready to go out.* **3** ***pelt along*** *or* ***over***: °hurry, °rush, °run, °dash, °shoot, scoot, °scurry: *The constables pelted along after the escaping thief.*
—*n.* **4** °stroke, °blow, whack, °hit, smack, °slap, thwack, bang, thump, *Colloq* wallop, °belt: *Chris received a pelt on the head from a rock.*

pelt[2] *n.* °skin, °hide, °coat, fur, °fleece: *The trappers traded the fox pelts for supplies.*

pen[1] *n.* **1** °writing °instrument, fountain-pen, ball-point (pen), *Brit trade mark* Biro, *Old-fashioned* quill: *Dearest, I have finally found time to put pen to paper. I prefer a pen with a fine point.*
—*v.* **2** °write (down *or* up *or* out), °jot down, (make a) °note (of), °draft, °draw up, °compose, put on °paper,

commit to °paper, commit to °writing, put in °writing, scribble, °scrawl, °scratch, *Formal* indite: *While he was in prison, he penned letters to many men of influence.*

pen[2] *n.* **1** coop, °enclosure, hutch, (pig)sty, pound, fold, °stall, confine, *US and Canadian* corral: *We kept the geese in a pen by the barn.*
—*v.* **2** Often, ***pen up***: °enclose, confine, coop up, °shut up, impound, °round up, *US and Canadian* corral: *It took three of us to pen the sheep. During the blockade, the ships remained penned up at Gibraltar.*

penal *adj.* correctional, °punitive, disciplinary: *Crime and its punishment are covered in the penal code. He was sent to a penal colony for life.*

penalize *v.* °punish, °discipline, mulct, °fine, °handicap, impose *or* invoke a °penalty against, impose a °penalty on, *Formal* amerce; °sentence: *This judge penalizes speeders mercilessly.*

penalty *n.* °punishment, °discipline, °penance, °sentence; °forfeit, °fine, °handicap, °price, mulct, *Formal* amercement; °imprisonment, incarceration: *The prosecution demanded the maximum penalty allowable under law for the crimes.*

penance *n.* **1** °punishment, °penalty, reparation, °amends, °atonement, self-punishment, self-mortification, °regret, repentance, contrition, °suffering, °penitence: *A year of public service was fair penance for the offence.* **2** ***do penance***: °pay, °suffer, make °amends *or* reparation(s), °atone, wear sackcloth and ashes *or* a hair-shirt: *She has done penance enough for her crime.*

penchant *n.* °inclination, °bent, proclivity, °leaning, °bias, predisposition, predilection, °partiality, proneness, propensity, °tendency, °affinity, °liking, °preference, fondness, °taste: *Agnes has a penchant for tennis and for men who play tennis.*

pendant *n.* °ornament, tassel, lavaliere *or* lavalière, medallion, locket, necklace, rivière, ear-drop, teardrop, drop, *Old-fashioned* carcanet: *I recognized the pendant she wore at her neck as my mother's.*

pending *prep.* **1** awaiting, waiting (for), depending on, °till, until, 'til, °till such time as; while, during: *Pending the outcome of the trial, he was remanded in custody.*
—*adj.* **2** °unsettled, undetermined, undecided, unconfirmed, unfinished, °inconclusive, up in the air, hanging °fire, in the °balance, in °abeyance; °forthcoming, °imminent, °impending, in the offing, *Colloq US* in a holding pattern, on hold: *The pending negotiations on the rent will determine whether we stay or move house. While the matter is pending, we can do nothing.*

pendulous *adj.* **1** pendent, hanging, drooping, sagging, dangling, suspended, pensile: *The weaver-bird's pendulous nest is a marvel of engineering.* **2** °swinging, swaying, waving, undulating, undulatory, oscillating, oscillatory: *I was hypnotized by the pendulous motion of the bell.*

penetrate *v.* **1** °enter, °go *or* °pass through *or* into, °pierce, °bore (into), °lance, spear, °probe, °stab, °puncture, °perforate, °drill: *The shell penetrated the tank's heavy armour.* **2** °permeate, °diffuse, °suffuse, pervade, °filter *or* seep through, °percolate through: *The soothing balm penetrated my aching body and I relaxed into a deep sleep.* **3** °reach, °get to, °get at, °touch, °affect, °hit, °strike: *Her cruel words penetrated the darkest recesses of my soul.* **4** °sink in, be °absorbed, be °understood, °register, °come *or* °get through, become °clear, °come across, be realized, *Colloq* °soak in, seep in: *It took a while for it to penetrate that she did not wish to see him again.* **5** °understand, °sense, become °aware *or* °conscious of, °see (through), gain °insight (in)to, discern, uncover, °discover, °find (out), °comprehend, °grasp, °work out, unravel, °fathom, °perceive, *Colloq* °get, °figure out, °dig, *Brit* suss out: *Will we ever penetrate all of nature's secrets?*

penetrating *adj.* **1** °incisive, °trenchant, °keen, searching, °deep, °acute, °sharp, °perceptive, perspicuous, percipient, quick, °discriminating, °intelligent, °sensitive, °clever, °smart, discerning: *This is a penetrating analysis of the situation which clarifies many of the issues.* **2** °piercing, °shrill, °strident, ear-splitting, ear-shattering, °pervasive; °pungent, °harsh, °biting, mordant, °strong, stinging: *I was awakened by a penetrating scream. The penetrating odour of ammonia assailed my nostrils.*

penetration *n.* **1** °piercing, perforation, puncturing, °incision, °puncture, °penetrating; °inroad, °entry, °entrance: *Penetration of the skull required great effort on the part of the surgeon. Tentatively we attempted the penetration of the jungle.* **2** °insight, keenness, °perception, percipience, °intelligence, perspicacity, perspicuity, perspicaciousness, perceptiveness, incisiveness, °sensitivity, sentience, °understanding, acuteness, discernment, °discrimination, cleverness, shrewdness, °wit, quick-wittedness: *We all admired the penetration that was shown by the examiner in the questions she asked.*

penitence *n.* °penance, contrition, °regret, repentance, regretfulness, °compunction, °remorse, °sorrow, sorrowfulness, ruefulness, °grief, °sadness, °shame, self-reproach: *Brendan's penitence for his former misdeeds was shown by his selfless devotion to good causes.*

penitent *adj.* contrite, °regretful, °repentant, °remorseful, °sorrowful, °sorry, rueful, grief-stricken, °sad, shamefaced, self-reproachful, °apologetic, conscience-stricken: *He said that he was truly penitent for all the heinous crimes of his youth.*

penmanship *n.* calligraphy, °hand, fine Italian *or* Italic °hand, handwriting, °script, °writing, longhand, chirography: *One must admire the penmanship of the medieval scribes.*

pennant *n.* °flag, °banner, pennon, °streamer, banderole, gonfalon, ensign, °colours, °standard, labarum, *Chiefly nautical* jack, *Nautical and yachting* burgee, *Technical* vexillum: *We saw from her pennant that she was a Spanish frigate.*

pension *n.* **1** °benefit, °allowance, annuity, subsistence, superannuation, °allotment, old-age pension, *US* social security, *Colloq* golden handshake: *She finds that her pension is not enough to live on.*
—*v.* **2** Usually, ***pension off***: (cause to) °retire, superannuate; °dismiss; *Colloq* °shelve, °put out to pasture: *The company cut back on staff by pensioning off everyone over 60.*

pensioner *n.* retiree, °veteran, °senior citizen, *Brit* OAP (= 'old-age pensioner'), *US* golden-ager, *Colloq Brit* wrinkly: *The housing units were specially designed for pensioners' needs.*

pensive *adj.* °thoughtful, °meditative, musing, in a brown °study, cogitative, contemplative, °reflective, °preoccupied, ruminative, °wistful, day-dreaming, in a °trance, in a °reverie, brooding, °sober, °serious, °grave: *I found the professor in a pensive mood, staring out the window.*

pent-up *adj.* restrained, constrained, repressed, stifled, bottled-up, corked-up, held in, checked, held back, curbed, °inhibited, restricted: *After weeks of frustration, he wanted to release his pent-up emotions in a scream. They went jogging to try to work off their pent-up energy.*

penurious *adj.* **1** stingy, °mean, penny-pinching, °miserly, °tight, tight-fisted, close-fisted, cheese-paring, niggardly, °cheap, ungenerous, parsimonious, skinflinty, °thrifty, begrudging, grudging, Scrooge-like, *Colloq* near, *Brit* mingy, *US* chintzy: *Even today, he is so penurious that he gives his children an allowance of only 50 pence a week.* **2** °poor, poverty-stricken, °destitute, °impoverished, penniless, °indigent, °needy, impecunious, necessitous, beggarly, bankrupt, *Colloq* (°dead *or* °flat) °broke, stony-broke, °hard up: *They lived in penurious circumstances.*

people *n.pl.* **1** °persons, °individuals, °men and °women, ladies and gentlemen, males and females, living souls; °mortals; bodies: *How many people can this aeroplane carry?* **2** °relations, relatives, °kin, kinsmen, kinsfolk *or US and Canadian* kinfolk, °family, kith and °kin; °ancestors, forebears: *His*

people left Russia in 1917. **3** masses, (general) °public, hoi polloi, consumers, multitude, °populace, °common people, °common °man *or* °woman, commoners, °subjects, citizenry, °plebeians, grass roots, proletariat, rank and file, the °crowd, commonalty *or* commonality, *mobile vulgus*, bourgeoisie; °man *or* °woman in the street, Everyman, Everywoman, Mr *or* Mrs Average, *Brit* A. N. Other, Joe Bloggs, °man *or* °woman on the Clapham omnibus, *US* John *or* Jane Doe *or* Roe, Mary Doe, Richard Roe, John Q. Public; *Colloq and often derogatory* proles, the °rabble, ragtag and bobtail, silent °majority, °common °herd, *Brit* plebs, admass: *Politicians unable to communicate with the people are seldom elected.*
—*n.sing.* **4** °race, community, °clan, °tribe, °folk, °nation, °population, °society: *On the subject of religion, they were a people divided. The anthropologists were studying the peoples south of the Sahara.*
—*v.* **5** °populate, colonize, °settle, °occupy: *The area was once peopled with Berber tribesmen.*

pep *n.* **1** °vigour, vim (and °vigour), °spirit, °animation, vivacity, °energy, °verve, °zest, °fire, sprightliness, °life, effervescence, °sparkle, ebullience, °dash, °enthusiasm, brio, *élan*, *Colloq* zip, zing: *He certainly has a lot of pep for an octogenarian.*
—*v.* **2** ***pep up***: °stimulate, invigorate, °animate, °enliven, °vitalize, vivify, °energize, exhilarate, °quicken, °arouse, breathe (some) °life into, °inspire, °activate, actuate, °fire, °cheer up, *Colloq* buck up, °spark, °work *or* °fire up, *US* °wind up: *After those defeats, the team needed to be pepped up.*

pepper *v.* sprinkle, °scatter, °dot, speckle, fleck, °spot, °spray, bespeckle, °spatter, stipple, mottle: *The letter was peppered with ink-spots. Their speech was peppered with swear-words.*

perceive *v.* **1** °see, °make out, discern, catch °sight of, glimpse, °spot, espy, apprehend, °take in, °notice, °note, °discover, descry, °observe, °mark, °remark, °identify, °distinguish, °detect: *I perceived his hesitation when a solo flight was suggested. She perceived a strange odour emanating from the cupboard.* **2** °appreciate, °grasp, °feel, °sense, apprehend, °understand, °gather, °comprehend, °deduce, °infer, °figure out, ascertain, °determine, conclude, °decipher, *Colloq* °dig, catch on: *She perceived that he was going to renege on his promise to take her to the Riviera.* **3** Often, ***perceive of***: °regard, °view, °look on, °consider, °contemplate, °judge, deem, °believe, °think: *Calthorpe perceives of himself as a great actor, but he is dreadful. This gesture is often perceived as threatening.*

percentage *n.* °share, °part, °portion, °proportion, °interest, °piece, *Colloq* °cut: *We are to get a percentage of the profits in return for our investment.*

perceptible *adj.* °discernible, detectable, °observable, perceivable, °noticeable, distinguishable, recognizable, °apparent, °evident, °notable, °obvious, °patent, °manifest, palpable, °plain, °clear, °prominent, unmistakable: *There are perceptible differences between your playing and Heifetz's.*

perception *n.* **1** °appreciation, °grasp, apprehension, °understanding, comprehension, °knowledge, °perspective, °view: *Mrs Hart's perception of the situation is quite different from mine.* **2** °intuition, °insight, °instinct, °feel, °feeling, °sense, °impression, awareness, °idea, °notion, consciousness, °realization: *Norton hasn't the slightest perception of what is going on behind his back at the office.*

perceptive *adj.* °astute, °alert, °attentive, quick, °alive, °quick-witted, °intelligent, °acute, °sharp, °sensitive, °sensible, percipient, discerning, °observant, perspicacious; on the qui vive; *Colloq* on the ball: *No one was sufficiently perceptive to predict the full extent of the recession. She is perhaps the most perceptive journalist writing on French politics today.*

perch *n.* **1** roost, °rest, °seat; °spot, °location, °position, °place, °site, vantage °point, °perspective: *From his perch at the top of the cliff, Martin had a clear view of the cave entrance.*
—*v.* **2** roost, °rest, °sit, °nest; °place, °put, °set, °situate, °locate, °position, °site: *The owl was perched in the tree, waiting for the vole to appear from its burrow.*

percolate *v.* seep, °steep, °transfuse, leach, °drip, °drain, °strain, °filter, pervade, infuse, °ooze, transude, filtrate, °trickle, °permeate, °suffuse, °penetrate: *The earth is too hard for the rainwater to percolate to the roots below. It slowly percolated through to me that Clare had told the police where I was hiding.*

perdition *n.* damnation, °hell, hell-fire, °doom, °ruin, condemnation, °destruction, ruination, °downfall: *If what divines call lust be punished with perdition, who is pure?*

peremptory *adj.* **1** commanding, °imperative, compelling, °obligatory, °mandatory, irrefutable, °incontrovertible, decretal: *After the sound of marching came a peremptory knock at the door.* **2** decisive, °final, preclusive, °arbitrary, °categorical, unequivocal, °dogmatic, unconditional, unreserved, °flat, °out-and-out, °outright, °unqualified, °unmitigated: *The juror was subject to peremptory dismissal because he was the defendant's cousin.* **3** imperious, °authoritative, °tyrannical, °despotic, °dictatorial, autocratic, °emphatic, °positive, °firm, °insistent, *Colloq* °bossy: *How dare you take such a peremptory tone when speaking to your father!*

perennial *adj.* **1** °durable, °lasting, continuing, °enduring, °constant, °stable, lifelong, °persistent, incessant, uninterrupted, °continual, °continuous, °chronic: *Once we expected our rivers to yield a perennial supply of fresh water. Bing Crosby has been a perennial favourite since the 1930s.* **2** °permanent, unfailing, never-failing, °endless, unending, ceaseless, unceasing, imperishable, undying, °perpetual, °everlasting, °timeless, °eternal, °immortal, *Literary* sempiternal: *The artificial flowers at her grave symbolize Ingrid's perennial youth.*

perfect *adj.* **1** °complete, °absolute, finished, (fully) realized, fulfilled, consummate, °pure, °entire, °whole, perfected, °best, °ideal: *Many have called the building a perfect example of the Palladian style.* **2** °sublime, °ideal, °superb, °supreme, °superlative, °best, °flawless, °faultless, °pre-eminent, °excellent, °exquisite, unexcelled, unrivalled, unequalled, unmatched, °matchless, °incomparable, °nonpareil, °peerless, inimitable: *At her throat she wore the most perfect emerald I had ever seen.* **3** °blameless, °righteous, °holy, °faultless, °flawless, °spotless, °immaculate: *Nobody's perfect.* **4** °fitting, °appropriate, (°just) °right, apt, °suitable, °correct, °proper, made to order, °best, *Brit* spot on: *Arthur would be perfect for the role of Quasimodo.* **5** °precise, °exact, °accurate, °correct, unerring, °true, °authentic, °lifelike, °right on, °excellent, °superlative, °superb, °reliable, *Brit* spot on: *These copies are perfect replicas of the original.* **6** utter, °absolute, °complete, °mere, °thorough, °out-and-out, through-and-through; 24-carat *or esp. US* 24-karat, °categorical, °unqualified, unalloyed, °unmitigated: *We were perfect strangers at the time. Once again, he's shown himself to be a perfect idiot.* **7** °expert, °proficient, °accomplished, °experienced, °practised, °skilful, skilled, °gifted, °talented, °adept, deft, adroit, °polished, °professional, masterly, °masterful: *The admirable Crichton was the perfect butler.*
—*v.* **8** °complete, °finish, °realize, °fulfil, consummate, °accomplish, °achieve, °effect, °execute, °carry out *or* through, bring (to °perfection): *The design of the bicycle was not to be perfected for several years.*
9 °rectify, °correct, emend, (put *or* set) °right, °improve, °refine, °polish, °cultivate, °better, ameliorate: *Viniculture has been perfected in the Bordeaux region of France.*

perfection *n.* **1** °purity, flawlessness, faultlessness, sublimity, °superiority, °excellence, °pre-eminence, transcendence: *Though we strive for perfection, we never can achieve it.* **2** °completion, completeness, °achievement, °fulfilment, °realization, °consummation, °accomplishment, attainment: *The building doesn't reach perfection till the last roof-tile is in place.*

3 °ideal, °paragon, °model, archetype, °pattern, °mould, °standard, idealization, °essence, °quintessence, °acme, °pinnacle, °summit: *Machiavelli probably achieved the perfection of political cunning.*

perfectionist *n.* **1** °purist, pedant, precisian, precisionist, stickler, *Colloq* fusspot, *US* fuss-budget: *The foreman is such a perfectionist that there's no satisfying him.*
—*adj.* **2** °meticulous, °precise, punctilious, °scrupulous, °exacting, °particular, °demanding, °fastidious, °fussy; °obsessive; *Colloq* picky, nit-picking: *She takes a perfectionist attitude towards everything she does.*

perfectly *adv.* **1** °completely, purely, °entirely, °absolutely, °utterly, °totally, °wholly, consummately, °thoroughly, °quite, °definitely, °positively, unambiguously, unequivocally, unmistakably, explicitly, °truly, °very, °extremely, extraordinarily, remarkably: *Your instructions for finding the house were perfectly clear.* **2** superbly, superlatively, flawlessly, faultlessly, impeccably, inimitably, incomparably, sublimely, exquisitely, marvellously, admirably, wonderfully: *Sally plays that Chopin étude perfectly.* **3** °exactly, °precisely, flawlessly, faultlessly, accurately, °literally, line for line, word for word, °verbatim, letter for letter, to the letter, *literatim*: *He knows the entire Koran perfectly.* **4** °very, full, °quite, *Dialect* °right, *Brit* jolly, *Slang* damned, bloody: *You know perfectly well that I hate cauliflower.*

perfidious *adj.* treacherous, °deceitful, °traitorous, treasonous, treasonable, °disloyal, °faithless, °false, unfaithful, °untrue, insidious, °hypocritical, °two-faced, Janus-faced, °corrupt, °dishonest: *His perfidious brother betrayed him to his enemies.*

perfidy *n.* perfidiousness, treachery, °deceit, traitorousness, treason, disloyalty, faithlessness, falseness, °falsity, unfaithfulness, °infidelity, insidiousness, °hypocrisy, °betrayal: *The name of Judas is a byword for perfidy.*

perforate *v.* °riddle, °puncture, °pierce, honeycomb, °drill, °bore, °punch; °enter, °penetrate, °pass into: *A perforated metal screen let through a pattern of light. The bullet perforated his lung but he survived.*

perform *v.* **1** °execute, °complete, °bring off *or* about, °accomplish, °effect, °carry out, °discharge, °dispatch, °conduct, °carry on, do, °fulfil, *Colloq* °pull off, °knock off, °polish off; put up or shut up: *Postmen perform their duties despite hazards such as vicious dogs.* **2** do, °act, °behave, °operate, °function, °run, °work, °go, °respond: *How does your new car perform?* **3** °present, °stage, °produce, °put on, °mount, do; °act, depict, °take, °play, °appear as: *The repertory group performs six shows weekly. He is performing the role of Scrooge.*

performance *n.* **1** °execution, °completion, bringing off *or* about, °accomplishment, effectuation, carrying out, °discharge, °dispatch, °conduct, carrying-on, doing, °fulfilment: *The soldiers acquitted themselves nobly in the performance of their duties.* **2** °show, °exhibition, °exhibit, °play, playing, °engagement, °act, °appearance, *Colloq* gig: *She does three performances nightly at the Blue Angel.* **3** playing, acting, °interpretation, °presentation, portrayal: *His performance in the courtroom scene was outstanding.* **4** °behaviour, °conduct, deportment, demeanour: *Her performance in the pub last night was outrageous.* **5** °scene, °show, °exhibition, °display: *The lad put on quite a performance till threatened with punishment by the headmaster.*

performer *n.* actor *or* actress, artiste, °Thespian, trouper, °player: *They received their training as performers in a repertory company.*

perfume *n.* **1** °essence, °extract, *parfum*, eau-de-Cologne, toilet water, °scent, °fragrance; °aroma, °odour, °smell, °bouquet, nose: *What is that wonderful perfume you're wearing? The perfume of the wine wafted over to me.*
—*v.* **2** °scent: *Orange blossoms perfumed the air.*

perfunctory *adj.* **1** °routine, °mechanical, °automatic, robot-like, °unthinking, businesslike, unspontaneous, °formal, dismissive, °inattentive, uninvolved, apathetic, °indifferent, unconcerned, removed, °distant, *dégagé*, °offhand, °heedless, uninterested, °hasty, °hurried, °superficial, °cursory, °fleeting, rushed: *I don't care for the perfunctory service in those fast-food restaurants.* **2** °careless, °slipshod, slovenly, negligent, °sketchy, °spotty: *The bill, made out in a perfunctory fashion, was incorrect.*

perhaps *adv.* °maybe, °possibly, it is °possible that, conceivably, as the case may be, it may be, *Archaic or literary* perchance, peradventure, *Archaic or dialect* mayhap: *Perhaps she'll be on the next train.*

peril *n.* °danger, °threat, °risk, °jeopardy, °exposure, vulnerability, susceptibility, uncertainty, insecurity: *You enter there at your peril. It was a time of peril for us all. The child's life was in peril.*

perilous *adj.* °dangerous, °risky, °hazardous, °vulnerable, °susceptible, °uncertain, °insecure, unsafe, unsure: *Why undertake such a perilous journey alone?*

perimeter *n.* °boundary, °border, borderline, °margin, °periphery, °limit(s), °bounds, ambit, circumference, °edge, °verge, °fringe(s), *Archaic or literary* bourn *or* bourne: *The perimeter of the military base is patrolled by sentry dogs.*

period *n.* **1** °interval, °time, °term, °span, duration, °spell, °space, °stretch; while; *Colloq chiefly Brit* °patch: *During the period of his absence, his children had grown up. I waited a short period, then phoned again. We went through a bad period last year.* **2** °era, °days, epoch, aeon, °age, years: *During the Old English period, very little was written down.* **3** full stop: *Place periods at the ends of sentences.*

periodic *adj.* °periodical, °intermittent, °regular, °recurrent, °repetitive, iterative, cyclic(al), repeated; episodic, °sporadic, °occasional: *We called in the plumber because of the periodic hammering in the pipes. The next periodic return of Halley's comet is expected in 2061-62.*

periodical *n.* °magazine, °journal, °paper, °publication, newsletter, °organ, serial, weekly, fortnightly, semi-monthly, monthly, bimonthly, °quarterly, semi-annual, annual, yearbook, almanac, *Rare* hebdomadal *or* hebdomadary: *Nicole's story will soon be published in an important literary periodical.*

peripheral *adj.* **1** °incidental, unimportant, °minor, °secondary, inessential *or* unessential, °non-essential, °unnecessary, °superficial, °tangential, °irrelevant, beside the point: *Let's ignore the peripheral issues for the time being and concentrate on the important ones.* **2** circumferential, °external, perimetric, °outside, outer: *The peripheral measurement of the figure is seven inches.*

periphery *n.* **1** °perimeter, circumference, °border, °edge, °rim, °brim, ambit, °boundary, °bound, °margin: *Trees will be planted along the periphery of the car park.* **2** °surface, °edge, °superficies: *Your analysis deals with the periphery, not the core, of the problem.*

perish *v.* °die, °expire, lose (one's) °life, be killed, be °lost, meet (one's) °death, be destroyed: *Three gnus perished in the fire at the zoo.*

perjury *n.* °lying, mendacity, mendaciousness, forswearing, prevarication, bearing °false °witness: *The defendant was acquitted and the prosecution witnesses charged with perjury.*

perk *n.* See **perquisite**, below.

perk up *v.* °cheer up, become °jaunty, °brighten, °liven up, invigorate, smarten up, °quicken, (re)vitalize, °pep up, °revive, inspirit, *Colloq* buck up: *The old lady perks up when her grandchildren come to visit. To perk up the party, Peter suggested we should all play a game.*

perky *adj.* °lively, cheery, °cheerful, °jaunty, bouncy, °bright, invigorated, °vigorous, vitalized, peppy, °spirited, °sprightly, °frisky, °animated, °vivacious, °effervescent, °bubbly, °buoyant, °gay, *Colloq* bright-eyed and bushy-tailed, full of °pep: *Sue's been quite perky since she started going with Trevor.*

permanence *n.* permanency, °stability, durability, fixedness, changelessness, °lasting quality, longevity, °endurance, °persistence, dependability, reliability, survival: *The new roofing material is being tested for permanence.*

permanent *adj.* **1** °everlasting, °eternal, unending, °endless, °perpetual, unceasing, °constant, undying, imperishable, °indestructible, °stable, °abiding, long-lasting, °lasting, °enduring, °perennial, long-lived, °durable: *The satellite is in permanent orbit around the earth.* **2** unchanging, °invariable, °changeless, °fixed, unchangeable, immutable, unalterable, °stable, °persistent: *This stain is permanent and will not come out in the wash. Bonham is a permanent member of the executive committee.*

permanently *adv.* for ever, for good, °once and for all, forevermore, °always, eternally, everlastingly; perpetually, constantly, incessantly, °non-stop, continuously, endlessly, ceaselessly, unendingly, interminably: *Is the boy permanently disabled? According to one theory the universe will not continue to expand permanently.*

permeate *v.* imbue, °diffuse, °penetrate, pervade, infiltrate, °enter, °spread through(out), °saturate, seep through(out), °percolate through, °soak through: *He felt the warmth permeate every limb. Greed seemed to permeate every level of society.*

permissible *adj.* allowable, admissible, °acceptable, allowed, permitted, °tolerable, °legal, licit, °lawful, °legitimate, authorized, °proper, (all) °right; pardonable, excusable, °venial, *Colloq* °OK *or* okay, kosher, legit: *Some things that are permissible are not necessarily honourable.*

permission *n.* °consent, assent, °leave, acquiescence, sufferance, °tolerance, laxity, leniency *or* lenience, °leave, °licence, °sanction, acceptance, authorization, °approval, approbation, countenance, °allowance, °liberty, °indulgence; franchise, enfranchisement: *Have you permission to watch television? She eats anything she likes with the doctor's permission.*

permissive *adj.* assenting, consenting, °indulgent, °lenient, latitudinarian, acquiescent, °lax, °easygoing, °liberal, °tolerant, non-constraining, non-restrictive, libertarian: *Allison grew up in the permissive society of the 1960s.*

permit *v.* **1** Often, ***permit to***: °allow, °agree (to), °consent (to), give °permission *or* °leave (to), °authorize, °sanction, °license, °tolerate, countenance, °suffer, °brook, °admit, °grant, °enable, empower, franchise, enfranchise; °let: *He permitted me to use his name as a reference. Do they permit smoking here?*
—*n.* **2** °licence, °authority, authorization, franchise, °warrant; °pass, passport, visa: *Your parking permit expired last week. Shirley has a permit to visit Tibet.*

perpendicular *adj.* **1** °erect, °upright, vertical, °plumb, °straight (up and down): *The plumb-line shows that the wall isn't perpendicular.* **2** Often, ***perpendicular to***: at right angles (to), at 90 degrees (to): *The two paths are perpendicular to one another.*

perpetrate *v.* °commit, °execute, °perform, °carry out *or* through, °effect, °effectuate, °accomplish, do, be °responsible for, °practise, *Colloq* °pull (off): *Atrocities were perpetrated on both sides in the war.*

perpetual *adj.* **1** °eternal, °infinite, °everlasting, never-ending, unending, °perennial, ageless, °timeless, long-lived, °permanent, unceasing, °lasting, °enduring, unvarying, unchanging, immutable, °invariable, undeviating, *Literary* sempiternal: *They declared their perpetual love for each other.* **2** °constant, uninterrupted, °continuous, unfailing, incessant, °persistent, unremitting, unending, °non-stop, °endless, °recurrent, °continual, °repetitive: *Why should we have to listen to the neighbours' perpetual bickering?*

perpetuate *v.* °continue, °maintain, °extend, °keep (on *or* up), °keep going, °preserve, °memorialize, °immortalize, eternalize: *Thoughtless jokes can perpetuate damaging stereotypes.*

perpetuity *n.* °permanence, constancy, timelessness; °eternity: *The estate was bequeathed to the townspeople in perpetuity.*

perplex *v.* °confuse, °bewilder, °puzzle, °mystify, °distract, baffle, befuddle, confound, °muddle, disconcert, °stump, °nonplus, °stymie, stupefy, °stun, °daze, °dumbfound *or* dumfound, flabbergast, *Colloq* bamboozle, hornswoggle, *Chiefly US and Canadian* discombobulate, °throw for a loop: *The more I tried to understand bathymetric semiotics, the more perplexed I became. Anne-Marie's reticence perplexed us all.*

perplexing *adj.* confusing, bewildering, °puzzling, mystifying, baffling, confounding, °disconcerting, stupefying, flabbergasting, enigmatic, °paradoxical, °incomprehensible, unfathomable, impenetrable, °recondite, arcane, °labyrinthine, complex, °complicated, Byzantine, °intricate, °involved, convoluted, twisted, knotty, Gordian: *The writing is filled with perplexing references to the author's personal experiences, of which the reader is told nothing.*

perplexity *n.* **1** °confusion, bewilderment, bafflement, °distress, °doubt, °difficulty: *My perplexity grew as he related his version of the event.* **2** intricacy, °complexity, complicatedness, arcaneness, reconditeness, impenetrability, impenetrableness, involvement, unfathomability, °obscurity, °difficulty: *The more deeply the enigma was probed, the greater its perplexity.* **3** °puzzle, °enigma, °mystery, °dilemma, °problem, °paradox, catch-22, °quandary, °predicament, °bind: *Because of the interlocking directorships of the companies, we faced many perplexities in trying to sort out what had happened to the funds.*

perquisite *n.* °consideration, emolument, °bonus, (fringe) °benefit, °extra, dividend, gratuity, °tip, douceur, baksheesh, token (of appreciation), *US* lagniappe *or* lagnappe, *Colloq* °perk: *It was traditional to provide each director with a company car as a perquisite.*

persecute *v.* **1** °oppress, °suppress, °subjugate, maltreat, °ill-treat, °abuse, °outrage, °molest, °victimize, °tyrannize, °afflict, °punish, martyr, °torment, torture: *For years black people had been persecuted.* **2** °bother, °annoy, °pester, °plague, hector, °bully, badger, harry, °harass, °irritate, °worry, vex, °trouble, importune, °hound: *Her lawyers continually persecuted him for non-payment of alimony.*

persecution *n.* **1** °oppression, °suppression, subjugation, maltreatment, ill-treatment, °abuse, °outrage, molestation, victimization, °tyranny, °affliction, °punishment, °torment, torture: *They suffered persecution because of their difference of religion.* **2** °bother, °annoyance, hectoring, bullying, badgering, harrying, harassing, irritation, °worry, vexation, °trouble: *The press is often guilty of the persecution of famous people.*

perseverance *n.* °persistence, steadfastness, °determination, °resolution, °resolve, decisiveness, °decision, firmness, purposefulness, pertinacity, staying power, °stamina, sedulousness, assiduity, °grit, °pluck, tirelessness, indefatigableness, indefatigability, °patience, °endurance, diligence, °devotion, °tenacity, doggedness, stubbornness, inflexibility, °obstinacy, obstinateness, obdurateness, *Colloq* guts, *US* stick-to-it-iveness: *Perseverance is essential for success in the theatre.*

persevere *v.* Often, ***persevere in*** *or* ***with*** *or* ***at***: °persist, °resolve, °decide, °endure, °continue, °carry on *or* through, °keep at *or* on *or* up, be °steadfast *or* °staunch *or* °constant, °keep going, stand °fast *or* °firm, °see through, be *or* °remain °determined *or* resolved *or* °resolute *or* °stalwart *or* °purposeful *or* uncompromising, be °tenacious *or* °persistent *or* °constant *or* pertinacious *or* assiduous *or* sedulous, be °tireless *or* °untiring *or* indefatigable, show °determination *or* °pluck *or* °grit, be plucky, be °patient *or* °diligent *or* °stubborn *or* °inflexible *or* adamant *or* °obstinate *or* obdurate, show *or* exhibit *or* demonstrate °patience *or* diligence *or* stubbornness *or* inflexibility *or* °obstinacy *or* obduracy, °remain dogged, °pursue doggedly, be intransigent *or* intractable, °cling to, °stick to, °support, stop at nothing, °sustain, *Colloq* °stick with, °stick (it) out: *We must persevere if we are to win. I shall persevere in my loyalty.*

persist *v.* **1** Often, ***persist in*** *or* ***at***: °persevere, be °persistent, °insist (on), stand °firm *or* °fast, be °steadfast *or* °staunch, °strive, toil, °labour, °work (°hard) (at): *She persists in arguing her innocence. Only those who persist will succeed.* **2** °remain, °continue, °endure, °carry on, °keep up *or* on, °last, °linger, °stay: *The bad weather persisted through the weekend.*

persistence *n.* °perseverance, °resolve, °determination, °resolution, steadfastness, °tenacity, constancy, assiduity, °stamina, tirelessness, indefatigability, indefatigableness, °pluck, °grit, °patience, diligence, pertinacity, doggedness, stubbornness, °obstinacy, obduracy: *By sheer persistence he got his own way.*

persistent *adj.* **1** persisting, persevering, °tenacious, °steadfast, °firm, °fast, °fixed, °staunch, °resolute, resolved, °determined, unfaltering, unswerving, undeviating, unflagging, °tireless, °untiring, indefatigable, dogged, unwavering, °stubborn, °obstinate, obdurate, °inflexible, °rigid: *He was persistent in his demands for justice. The inspector never gave up his persistent pursuit of criminals.* **2** continuing, °constant, °continuous, °continual, unending, interminable, unremitting, unrelenting, °perpetual, incessant, unceasing, °non-stop: *The persistent rainy weather began to depress us. At last he gave in to her persistent complaints and bought a washing machine.*

person *n.* **1** °individual, °human (being), being, °man *or* °woman *or* °child, (living) °soul; °mortal: *Not a single person knew the answer to my question.* **2** ***in person***: physically, °personally, bodily, °actually, myself *or* yourself *or* himself *or* herself *or* ourselves *or* yourselves, *or* themselves, *Colloq* in the °flesh: *The correspondent visited the battlefield in person to see for himself the extent of the carnage. I know their records, but I have never seen them in person.*

persona *n.* °face, °front, façade, °mask, °guise, °exterior, °role, °part, °character, °identity, self: *Her office persona is quite different from the one she displays at home.*

personage *n.* °celebrity, luminary, VIP, °name, °notable, °somebody, °personality, °star, superstar, magnate, °mogul, *Colloq* °big shot, °big wheel, hotshot, °hot stuff, *Brit* °big noise, *Theatre US* headliner: *My cousin is fast becoming a personage in the financial world.*

personal *adj.* **1** °individual, °physical, bodily, °actual, °live; in °person, in the °flesh: *The star is scheduled to make a personal appearance on tonight's chat show.* **2** °intimate, °exclusive, °private, °special, °particular: *Would you do me a personal favour? I hear they are having personal problems.* **3** °intimate, °close, °dear, °bosom, °familiar, °special: *Wendy happens to be a personal friend of ours.* **4** °intimate, °individual; disparaging, slighting, °offensive, °derogatory, °critical, deprecating, belittling, adverse, unfriendly, insulting: *He should confine his criticism to her acting and avoid personal remarks.*

personality *n.* **1** °character, °nature, temperament, °disposition, °make-up, °persona; °identity, °psyche: *Miles has an extremely abrasive personality that has upset many people.* **2** °celebrity, luminary, °star, superstar, °name, headliner, °somebody: *Whom shall we get as a personality to attract the crowds?*

personalized *adj.* monogrammed, initialled, individualized; signed: *They ordered personalized stationery with their new address on it.*

personally *adv.* **1** in °person, °alone, by oneself, on one's own, myself *or* yourself *or* himself *or* herself *or* ourselves *or* yourselves *or* themselves, *Colloq* in the °flesh: *She has not met them personally, but we have. They will see to the matter personally.* **2** in one's own °view *or* °opinion, for one's °part, for oneself, as far as one is concerned, from one's own °viewpoint, from where one stands, as one sees it *or* things, as for oneself: *Personally, I wasn't sure I would make it.* **3** as an °individual, as a °person, privately, in °private: *I like him personally but would never have him as my dentist.*

personify *v.* **1** °embody, °typify, °exemplify, epitomize, be the °embodiment of, °manifest, °represent, °stand for, °symbolize, *Archaic* impersonate, personate: *In my view, he personifies everything that is evil.* **2** humanize, personalize: *In literature, personifying inanimate things in nature with human attributes is called the pathetic fallacy.*

perspective *n.* **1** (°point of) °view, °viewpoint, °standpoint, °prospect, vantage °point, °position, °angle, *Colloq* where one is coming from: *I can see that my view would be illogical from his perspective.* **2** °attitude, °position, °angle, °approach, °sentiment, °outlook, °lookout: *Management has a different perspective on what is good for the company.*

perspiration *n.* °sweat, dampness, wetness; sweating; *Technical* sudor; diaphoresis: *I could feel the perspiration stand out on my forehead. They say that perspiration makes one cooler on a hot day.*

persuade *v.* **1** °urge, °induce, °prevail (up)on, °influence, exhort, importune, °dispose, °incline, °prompt, °sway, °press: *The officer persuaded him to surrender.* **2** °bring round, °convince, °win over, °talk *or* °argue into, °convert: *We persuaded her to open the door. He was persuaded to vote Labour.*

persuasion *n.* **1** °inducement, inducing, °influence, influencing, exhortation, exhorting, persuading: *At the bank's persuasion, the company tightened up its cash-flow management. She has extraordinary powers of persuasion at her command.* **2** °opinion, °belief, °creed, °faith, °set of °beliefs, °religion, (°religious) °conviction; °sect, °denomination, °faction, °school (of thought), affiliation: *Till he met Maggie, he had always been of the Baptist persuasion.*

persuasive *adj.* convincing, °telling, °influential, °effective, °productive, °impressive, °efficacious, cogent, °weighty, compelling, °forceful, valid, °winning, °authoritative, °dynamic: *His most persuasive argument for our leaving was that if we stayed we'd be shot.*

pert *adj.* **1** °forward, °brash, °brazen, °cheeky, °insolent, °impertinent, °flippant, saucy, °bold, °presumptuous, °impudent, °disrespectful, °audacious, °rude, °impolite, uncivil, °ill-mannered, unmannerly, *Archaic* malapert, *Colloq* °fresh, °flip, out of line, °brassy, big-mouthed, wise-guy, *Slang Brit* smart-arsed, *US* smart-ass(ed), wise-ass(ed): *He's a clever child, but I don't like his pert manner.* **2** °lively, °jaunty, °ebullient, °vivacious, °enthusiastic, bouncy, °sprightly, °brisk, °cheerful, °jolly, °bright, °perky, °animated, °nimble: *She is usually quite pert in the morning, becoming depressed as the day wears on.*

pertain *v.* Often, ***pertain to***: °concern, °refer to, °regard, have °reference *or* °relation (to), °apply (to), °relate (to), °include, °cover, °affect, appertain (to), be °appropriate (to), be °fitting (for), befit, °bear on, have °bearing (on): *The sign, 'Keep Off the Grass', does not pertain to the people who mow the lawn, Morris.*

pertinent *adj.* pertaining, °appropriate, °fitting, °suitable, apt, °relevant, germane, apropos, apposite: *Try to keep your comments pertinent to the subject under discussion.*

perturb *v.* °upset, °disturb, °fluster, °ruffle, unsettle, disconcert, make uneasy, °discomfit, vex, °worry, °agitate, °shake up, °alarm, disquiet, °confuse, discompose, °unnerve, addle, disorganize: *He became quite perturbed when the police asked him to help with their inquiries.*

perusal *n.* reading, °scrutiny, °check, °examination, °study, inspection, scanning, °review: *I saw nothing blasphemous in my perusal of the text.*

peruse *v.* °read, °study, °scan, °scrutinize, °examine, °inspect, °review, °browse, run one's °eye over: *As Gregory was perusing the ancient manuscript, a sudden draught blew out the candle.*

pervasive *adj.* °penetrating, pervading, omnipresent, °general, inescapable, °prevalent, °universal, widespread, ubiquitous, permeating, permeative: *A pervasive sense of doom in the castle made everyone feel uneasy.*

perverse *adj.* **1** °wrong, wrong-headed, awry, °contrary, wayward, °incorrect, °irregular, unfair, °improper, °contradictory: *It was most perverse of you to change your mind after all the arrangements had been made.* **2** °cantankerous, °testy, curmudgeonly, churlish, crusty, bad-tempered, °petulant, captious, °cross, cross-grained, °peevish, °waspish, °snappish, °bilious, splenetic, fractious, ill-tempered, °quarrelsome, irascible, °sullen, contentious, °touchy, °obstreperous, crabby, crabbed, °irritable, °surly, *Colloq* grouchy, *Brit* stroppy, *US and Canadian* °cranky: *With everything going wrong, Catherine feels particularly perverse today.* **3** °stubborn, °self-willed, wrong-headed, intractable, °wilful, obdurate, °obstinate, pigheaded, adamant, °inflexible, unbending, refractory, unyielding: *I refuse to give in to a perverse child just because he has a tantrum.*

perversion *n.* **1** deviation, irregularity, misdirection, corruption, °subversion, distortion, twisting, falsification, misrepresentation, °diversion, sidetracking: *The conduct of this trial has been a perversion of the course of true justice.* **2** °unnatural act, deviation, deviance *or* deviancy, °abnormality, depravity, °vice, aberration, debauchery, *Colloq* kinkiness, *Brit* °kink: *Every kind of perversion flourished in ancient Rome.*

pervert *v.* **1** °deflect, °divert, °sidetrack, °turn aside *or* away, °subvert, °misdirect, °distort, °twist, °abuse, °falsify, misapply, misconstrue, °misrepresent, °corrupt: *By withholding evidence, you have perverted the course of justice.* **2** °seduce, °lead astray, debauch, °degrade, °corrupt, °demoralize, °subvert: *He was accused of perverting young girls.*
—*n.* **3** °deviant, °degenerate, debauchee, *US* °deviate, *Colloq* °weirdo: *I worry about your being out late, when there are so many perverts about.*

perverted *adj.* °deviant, °deviate, °abnormal, amoral, unmoral, °immoral, °bad, depraved, °unnatural, warped, twisted, °profligate, °dissolute, °delinquent, °degenerate, °evil, °wicked, malign, malicious, malefic, malevolent, °evil-minded, °sinful, iniquitous, °base, °foul, °corrupt, unprincipled: *Members of the Hell-Fire Club yielded themselves up to the most perverted, abandoned behaviour.*

pessimistic *n.* °gloomy, °negative, despairing, °hopeless, °inauspicious, depressed, °despondent, °dejected, °melancholy, °downhearted, heavy-hearted, defeatist, °glum, °sad, °blue, °unhappy, cheerless, °joyless, cynical, °bleak, °forlorn: *The bears in the Stock Exchange take a pessimistic view of share prices.*

pest *n.* °nuisance, °annoyance, °nag, irritant, °bother, gadfly, bane, °trial, heckler, vexation, °curse, °thorn in one's flesh, *Colloq* °pain (in the neck), *Slang US* nudge *or* noodge *or* nudzh, nudnik, *Taboo slang* °pain in the *Brit* arse *or US* ass: *That man is such a pest, I wish he'd leave me alone.*

pester *v.* °annoy, °nag, °irritate, °irk, °bother, °get at *or* to, badger, °plague, vex, °fret, hector, °harass, harry, °heckle, nettle, °chafe, peeve, pique, °provoke, °exasperate, bedevil, °get *or* °grate on (someone's) °nerves, °get under (someone's) skin, °get in (someone's) hair, °try (someone's °patience), °torment, °persecute, *Brit* chivvy, *Colloq* drive (someone) up the °wall, needle, give (someone) the needle, hassle, °ride, give (someone) a °hard *or* °bad time, °bug: *Please stop pestering me about going to the football game.*

pestilence *n.* **1** °plague, °epidemic, pandemic, Black Death, *Rare* pest: *The pestilence raged throughout all Europe, killing 50 million people.* **2** °scourge, °blight, °curse, cancer, canker, bane, °affliction: *How are we to overcome the pestilence of greed?*

pet[1] *n.* **1** °darling, °favourite, °idol, apple of (one's) eye, *Colloq Brit* blue-eyed boy, *US* fair-haired boy: *You know that you were always Father's pet.*
—*adj.* **2** °tame, trained, domesticated: *Doesn't the landlord take a dim view of your keeping a pet alligator in the bath?* **3** °favourite, °favoured, preferred, cherished, °special, °particular; indulged, prized, treasured, °precious, dearest, adored, °darling: *Building the summer-house was Desmond's pet project. Elizabeth's pet pupil is Anne.*
—*v.* **4** °caress, °fondle, °stroke, °pat; °cuddle, nuzzle, °nestle, °snuggle, *Colloq* neck, smooch *or Australian and New Zealand also* smoodge *or* smooge, *Chiefly US and Canadian* make out: *Small children need to be petted a lot. Two teenagers were petting in the back seat of the car.* **5** °humour, °pamper, °favour, °baby, °coddle, cosset, mollycoddle, cocker, °spoil, °indulge, °dote on: *His mother pets him far too much.*

pet[2] *n.* (°bad *or* ill) °temper, pique, °sulk, (bad) °mood, °fume, *Colloq Brit* °paddy *or* paddywhack *or* paddywack: *He's in a terrible pet because they forgot to cancel the milk when they went on holiday.*

peter out *v.* °diminish, °evaporate, °wane, come to nothing *or* naught *or US also* nought, °die out, °disappear, °fail, °fade (out *or* away), °dwindle (into nothing), °run out, °give out, °flag, °melt away: *The path petered out after a mile or so and they realized that they had lost their bearings.*

petite *adj.* °delicate, °dainty, *mignon(ne)*, °diminutive, °small, °little, °slight, °tiny, small-boned, *Colloq Brit* dinky: *It was incongruous to see the basketball player with a petite blonde.*

petition *n.* **1** °request, °application, solicitation, °suit, entreaty, °supplication, °plea, °appeal: *An anti-pollution petition, signed by thousands of people, was delivered to the Department of the Environment.*
—*v.* **2** °request, °ask, °apply to, °apply for, °solicit, °sue, °call upon, entreat, supplicate, °plead, °appeal (to), °appeal (for), °beseech, implore, importune, *Rare* obsecrate: *The shopkeepers petitioned the council for better police protection.*

petrified *adj.* **1** horrified, horror-stricken *or* -struck, terrified, terror-stricken, °panic-stricken, frightened, °afraid, paralysed, numbed, benumbed, frozen: *The maiden stood petrified as the dragon, breathing fire, approached.* **2** shocked, °speechless, °dumbfounded *or* dumfounded, dumbstruck, stunned, °thunderstruck, astonished, astounded, confounded, stupefied, appalled, aghast, *Colloq* flabbergasted: *The firemen rescued three petrified children who were huddled in a corner.* **3** ossified, fossilized: *These were not stones but the petrified remains of ancient trees.*

petrify *v.* **1** °frighten, °scare, °horrify, °terrify, °paralyse, °numb, benumb: *I was petrified by the noise of the explosion.* **2** °shock, °dumbfound *or* dumfound, °stun, °astonish, °astound, °amaze, confound, disconcert, stupefy, °appal, *Colloq* flabbergast: *The sight of so much destruction petrified even hardened reporters.* **3** ossify, fossilize, turn to stone: *Over thousands of years the desert conditions petrify the wood.*

petty *adj.* **1** °insignificant, trivial, °paltry, °minor, °inferior, °niggling, °trifling, °negligible, °puny, inessential, °non-essential, °inconsequential, unimportant, °slight, nugatory, of no °account, *US* dinky, *Colloq* piddling, °measly, no great shakes, no big deal, °small-time, *Brit* twopenny-halfpenny *or* tuppenny-halfpenny, *US and Canadian* picayune: *He has been convicted only of petty crimes.* **2** °miserly, °mean, mingy, stingy, cheese-paring, grudging, °small-minded, °cheap, niggardly, parsimonious, °tight, tight-fisted, °close, close-fisted: *It was very petty of you to refuse the beggar a few pence.*

petulant *adj.* °peevish, pettish, °impatient, ill-humoured, °testy, °waspish, irascible, choleric, °cross, captious, ill-tempered, bad-tempered, splenetic, °moody, °sour, °bilious, crabby, crabbed, °irritable, huffish, huffy, °perverse, °snappish, crotchety, °cantankerous, curmudgeonly, grouchy, grumpy: *With a petulant gesture she hurled the rose away.*

phantom *n.* **1** apparition, °spectre, °ghost, °spirit, phantasm, °shade, wraith, revenant, °vision, *Formal* eidolon, phantasma, *Colloq* spook: *The so-called phantom of the opera turned out to be a real person.* **2** figment (of the °imagination), °illusion, °delusion, chimera *or* chimaera, °hallucination, °fancy, mirage: *She was a phantom of delight When first she gleamed upon my sight.*

Pharisaic *adj.* Pharisaical, °hypocritical, °insincere, °self-righteous, °pretentious, holier-than-thou, °sanctimonious, pietistic(al), formalistic, canting, unctuous, °oily, °slimy, *Literary* Tartuffian, Pecksniffian, *Colloq* goody-goody, *Chiefly Brit* smarmy: *I cannot tolerate his Pharisaic preaching.*

Pharisee *n.* °hypocrite, °pretender, dissembler, humbug, °fraud, whited sepulchre, pietist, formalist, canter, *Literary* Tartuffe, Pecksniff, *Colloq* °phoney *or US also* phony: *She is such a Pharisee with her pious little anecdotes.*

pharmacist *n.* pharmacologist, *Rather old-fashioned or formal* apothecary, *Brit* (pharmaceutical) chemist, *US and Canadian* °druggist, *Formal* posologist, *Colloq* °pill pusher, *US* °pill roller: *The pharmacist said that those pills have bad side-effects.*

pharmacy *n.* **1** dispensary, *Rather formal or old-fashioned* apothecary, *Brit* chemist's (°shop), *US and Canadian* drugstore, druggist's: *Stop off at the pharmacy and get me something for this headache, please.* **2** pharmaceutics, pharmacopoeia: *Research has vastly expanded modern pharmacy.*

phase *n.* **1** °stage, °period, °development, °step: *The boy is just going through a phase.* **2** °time, °moment, °juncture, °occasion: *At this phase of the discussion, I should like to introduce a new subject.* **3** °state, °form, °shape, configuration, °aspect, °appearance, °look, °condition, °status: *Here is a diagram of the phases of the moon at various points in its orbit.* **4** facet, °side, °angle, °viewpoint, °point of °view, *Colloq* °slant: *Only one phase of the argument has so far been presented.* —*v.* **5** ***phase in***: (°gradually) °introduce, usher in, °work in, °inject, °insert, °insinuate, °include, °incorporate: *The new work schedules will be phased in over the next month.* **6** ***phase out***: °ease out *or* off, °taper off, °wind up, put a °stop to, (°gradually) °eliminate, °remove, °withdraw, °discontinue, °end: *The use of non-biodegradable and non-recyclable packaging is being phased out.*

phenomenal *adj.* °outstanding, °remarkable, °exceptional, °extraordinary, °unusual, freakish, °rare, uncommon, °singular, °unorthodox, unprecedented, °unheard-of, °unparalleled, °unbelievable, °incredible, °marvellous, wonderful, °amazing, astonishing, astounding, staggering, °stunning, °prodigious, °miraculous, °fantastic, *Colloq* mind-boggling, mind-blowing: *She made a phenomenal recovery and can walk again.*

phenomenon *n.* **1** °event, °happening, °occurrence, °incident, °occasion, °experience, °fact: *Everyone knows the phenomenon of the souring of milk.* **2** °wonder, °curiosity, °spectacle, °sight, °sensation, °marvel, °rarity, °exception, miracle, *Slang* stunner: *An eight-year-old chess champion is truly a phenomenon, even in Russia.*

philanderer *n.* °flirt, °gallant, °roué, °rake, Casanova, Lothario, Don Juan, Romeo, °lover, °playboy, °gay dog, *Colloq* lady-killer, womanizer, *Old-fashioned* wolf, *Slang* stud: *In his memoirs it emerged what a philanderer he had been, often dallying with six women at once.*

philanthropic *adj.* °charitable, eleemosynary, °generous, magnanimous, munificent, °benevolent, open-handed, ungrudging, unstinting, beneficent, °humanitarian, altruistic, humane: *Finlay was always philanthropic, and spent much of his fortune on worthy causes.*

philanthropist *n.* contributor, °donor, °benefactor *or* benefactress, °patron *or* patroness, °sponsor, Maecenas, Good Samaritan, °humanitarian, altruist: *Some anonymous philanthropist provided the funds for the new school swimming-pool.*

philanthropy *n.* **1** generosity, °benevolence, °charity, °patronage, magnanimity, charitableness, public-spiritedness, big-heartedness, thoughtfulness, alms-giving, kind-heartedness, beneficence, benignity, liberality, open-handedness: *Carnegie's philanthropy was focused on libraries and education.* **2** °donation, contribution, °largesse, °aid, °grant, °assistance, °help: *Mrs Ander's recent philanthropy allows us to offer six new scholarships.*

philistine *n.* **1** °boor, °barbarian, yahoo, lowbrow, Boeotian, vulgarian, ignoramus, °bourgeois, *US* Babbitt: *Charlotte never could abide the philistines who put love of money above love of culture.* —*adj.* **2** uncultured, uncultivated, °tasteless, commonplace, unenlightened, °unrefined, unread, unlettered, °uneducated, untutored, unlearned, °narrow-minded, anti-intellectual, °boorish, lowbrow, °dull, °prosaic, °boring, °bourgeois, crass, commercial, °materialistic: *The television companies were accused of pandering to the basest appetites of the philistine viewer.*

philosophical *adj.* **1** philosophic, °abstract, esoteric, °learned, °scholarly, erudite, °theoretical, °rational, °logical, °impractical: *The person who is out of a job cares nothing about philosophical reasons for unemployment.* **2** °detached, unconcerned, unemotional, unimpassioned, composed, °thoughtful, °reflective, °meditative, cogitative, contemplative, °judicious, °sober, °level-headed, °realistic, °practical, pragmatic(al), down-to-earth, °cool, °calm, °serene, placid, °stoical, °patient, unruffled, cool-headed, °tranquil, unperturbed, even-tempered, °temperate, °moderate, °equable, equanimous, imperturbable: *Over the years, Evelyn had learned to take a philosophical attitude towards her husband's shortcomings.*

philosophy *n.* **1** metaphysics, epistemology, °logic, °natural *or* °moral *or* metaphysical philosophy, rationalism, °thinking, aesthetics: *He views philosophy as the attempt to describe and codify universal truths.* **2** °viewpoint, (°point of) °view, °outlook, °opinion, °attitude, °feeling, °sentiment, °idea, °notion, °ideology, (set of) °beliefs *or* values, °tenets, *Weltanschauung*, world-view: *Harold's philosophy of life is 'Live and let live'.* **3** °stoicism, °sang-froid, °control, °self-control, °restraint, coolness, composure, calmness, °serenity, placidity, cool-headedness, equanimity, thoughtfulness, imperturbability, self-possession, aplomb, dispassion, °patience, °resignation: *You may be sure that Paul allows nothing to disturb his philosophy.*

phlegmatic *adj.* **1** phlegmatical, stoic(al), unemotional, °unenthusiastic, unanimated, sluggish, apathetic, uninvolved, °lethargic, unfeeling, uncaring, °cold, unresponsive, °stolid, °unmoved, insensitive, °unaffected, °insensible, °indifferent, unconcerned, uninterested, °listless, °torpid, °indolent, °inactive, °passive, *Rare* hebetudinous: *Hutton is far too phlegmatic to be stirred by the fervour of the revolutionaries.* **2** phlegmatical, °self-possessed, self-controlled, controlled, restrained, composed, °calm, °serene, °tranquil, placid, cool-headed, equanimous, °cool, undisturbed, unperturbed, unruffled, imperturbable, even-tempered, °philosophical, °temperate, °moderate: *One has to learn to be phlegmatic about things going wrong at the office.*

phobia *n.* °fear, °horror, °terror, °dread, hatred, detestation, abhorrence, °loathing, execration, °aversion, °revulsion, repugnance, °dislike, °distaste, antipathy; disquiet, nervousness, °qualm, °distrust, °suspicion, apprehension, °worry: *He suffers from claustrophobia, which means that he has a phobia of enclosed places, and he avoids lifts and telephone booths.*

phoney *adj.* **1** °unreal, °fake, °synthetic, °artificial, °factitious, °false, °fraudulent, °imitation, °bogus, °spurious, °counterfeit, °mock, ersatz, paste, trumped up; °sham, °pretended, °insincere, °hypocritical, dissimulating, °deceitful, °dishonest; *US also* phony, *Colloq* pseudo *or Brit* pseud: *They were caught trying to collect insurance on the theft of a string of phoney pearls. Every time she wanted something, she'd turn on the phoney charm.*
—*n.* **2** °fake, °fraud, °imitation, °counterfeit, °forgery, °hoax, °sham, *US also* phony: *The diamond she's wearing is a phoney.* **3** trickster, faker, humbug, °impostor, °pretender, charlatan, mountebank, double-dealer, °counterfeiter, °quack, deceiver, *US also* phony, *Colloq Brit* pseud, *Slang US* paper-hanger: *Madame Tatiana claims to be able to communicate with the dead, but I think she's a phoney.*

photograph *n.* **1** snapshot, °print, °picture, slide, transparency; negative, positive, *Colloq* photo, snap, °shot, pic (*pl.* pix): *Heinrich has taken some marvellous photographs of the children.*
—*v.* **2** take a °picture (of), shoot, °film, take, *Colloq* °snap: *He photographed Jennifer holding her kitten.*

photographer *n.* lensman, lenswoman, cameraman, camerawoman, cinematographer, *paparazzo* (*pl. paparazzi*), *Old-fashioned* photographist: *The photographers clustered round the prime minister.*

photographic *adj.* **1** °vivid, °natural, °realistic, °graphic, °accurate, °exact, °precise, °faithful, °detailed, °lifelike, °true to life: *Many such neo-realist paintings are virtually photographic.* **2** cinematic, filmic, °pictorial: *Uncannily, a photographic image appeared on the Shroud under certain light.*

phrase *n.* **1** clause, noun phrase, verb phrase, prepositional phrase, adverbial phrase, adjectival phrase: *When asked for an example of a verb phrase, the student responded, 'Shut up'.* **2** °expression, word-group, collocation, locution, °idiom, idiomatic °expression, collocution, °proverb, °motto, °slogan, saying, catch-phrase, adage, °maxim, axiom, °saw, colloquialism, °cliché, platitude, commonplace, *Colloq* chestnut: *Do you know the source of Churchill's famous phrase, 'Blood, sweat, and tears'?* **3** phraseology, phrasing, °wording, °language, °usage, way *or* manner of speaking, °diction, °parlance, *façon de parler, modus loquendi, modus scribendi*, °speech habit, °style, choice of words, °word choice, syntax, vocabulary: *He was to 'let slip', to use Shakespeare's phrase, 'the dogs of war'.*
—*v.* **4** °express, °term, °word, °put, °frame, °formulate, °couch, °put into words, °put *or* °set forth, verbalize, articulate, °voice, utter, °say, °write; °describe, delineate: *I am pondering over the best way to phrase this example.*

physical *adj.* bodily, corporeal, corporal, fleshly, incarnate, °carnal, °mortal, °earthly, °natural, somatic; °material, °tangible, palpable, °real, °actual, °true, °concrete, °manifest, °solid: *Curtis doesn't have the physical strength to lift that weight. As a chemist, James deals with the physical, not the spiritual universe.*

physician *n.* °doctor, medical °doctor, M.D., °doctor of °medicine, medical practitioner, general practitioner, G.P., medical man *or* woman, °specialist, diplomate, *Brit navy* surgeon, *Colloq* doc, medico, medic, *US* man, *Slang* sawbones, bones: *You ought to see a physician if the pain persists.*

physique *n.* °build, °figure, °body, °frame, °shape, bodily °structure, °form, *Slang* chassis, *US* bod, built: *She has the physique of an Amazon but the disposition of a lamb.*

pick *v.* **1** Often, ***pick out***: °select, °choose, cull, °sort out, hand-pick, °single out, opt for, °fix *or* °decide upon *or* on, °elect, °settle upon *or* on, °screen (out), °sift (out): *Melanie was picked to succeed Hubert as president.* **2** °pluck, °gather, °collect, °harvest, °bring *or* °take in, °garner: *Scores of extra workers were brought in to pick apples.* **3** °provoke, °foment, °incite, °start, °initiate, °work *or* °stir up: *He tried to pick an argument with me about who is taller.* **4** ***pick at***: **a** °criticize, °carp at, find °fault with, °cavil (at *or* about), °quibble (at *or* about), °pick on, °nag (at), °niggle (at), °harass, °pester, °annoy, °irritate, °bother: *Stop picking at your brother!* **b** nibble (at), peck at: *We can't get him to eat a thing, he just picks at his food.* **5** ***pick off***: °shoot (down), °kill: *We picked them off one by one as they emerged from the trench.* **6** ***pick on***: °bully, °ride, °intimidate, °abuse, °browbeat, badger, harry, hector, °harass, °tease, °taunt, needle, °torment: *Robert must learn not to pick on the smaller boys.* **7** ***pick out***: **a** See **1**, above. **b** discern, °distinguish, °tell apart, °make out, °recognize, °separate, °discriminate: *I was able to pick out a distant rider, approaching swiftly. From amongst the forest sounds she picked out the song of the nightingale.* **8** ***pick up***: **a** °raise (up), °lift (up), heft, °hoist, °take up: *The stone is too heavy to pick up. Please pick up that piece of paper.* **b** °gather, °collect, glean, °take up: *I wish you would pick up your clothes.* **c** °tidy (up), °neaten, °straighten up *or* out, °clean (up): *She refuses to continue to pick up after him.* **d** °acquire, °learn, become °acquainted with; °master; *Colloq* get the hang of: *We picked up a little Spanish on our holiday.* **e** °acquire, °find, °come by, °get hold of, °obtain; °buy, °purchase, °get: *Basil picked up a few bad habits in the army. Let's pick up a bottle of wine on the way.* **f** °improve, get °better, °gain, °make °headway, °recover, °perk up, °rally, °recoup, (make) °progress, move °ahead, °increase, *Colloq* make a comeback: *Business usually picks up before Christmas.* **g** accelerate, °speed up: *The pace picked up as they approached the finish line.* **h** °arrest, apprehend, take into °custody, *Colloq* °pinch, collar, °nab, bust, °run in, °pull in, *Brit* °nick: *Two men were picked up trying to break into the bank.* **i** °call for, give a °lift *or* ride to, °collect, °go for *or US also* after, °go to get: *I'll pick you up at the railway station at noon.* **j** °meet, °introduce oneself to, °strike up an °acquaintance with, accost, make advances to: *I think she picked him up in a wine bar.* **k** catch, °come down with, °contract, °get: *He picked up a mystery virus in the Tropics.*
—*n.* **9** °selection, °choice, °option, °preference: *She could have had the pick of any man in the place. Take your pick.* **10** choicest, °best, *crème de la crème*, cream: *The early shoppers had already taken the pick of the crop.*

picket *n.* **1** °stake, °pale, °post, °peg, stanchion, °upright, vertical, palisade, paling: *The walls of the fort were of strong pickets tapered to a point at the top.* **2** demonstrator, protester *or* protestor, striker: *The police prevented the pickets from attacking workers who entered the factory.* **3** picquet, °sentinel, °watchman, °guard, °observer, °patrol, vedette *or* vidette *or* vedette boat: *The picket reported no unusual activity.*
—*v.* **4** °enclose, °shut in, °wall in, °fence (in), hem in, °box in: *We picketed the camp for the night.* **5** °protest, °demonstrate, blockade: *Strikers picketed the factory 24 hours a day.*

picnic *n.* **1** garden °party, *fête champêtre*, °meal alfresco, barbecue, *US* clam-bake, *US and Canadian* cookout: *The clouds had gone, and it was a great day for a picnic.* **2** child's play, *Colloq* °pushover, °snap, cinch, °piece of cake, walk-over, *US and Canadian* °breeze, lead-pipe cinch: *Sailing home with a quartering wind—it was a picnic all the way.* **3** ***no picnic***: °difficult, °arduous, torture, torturous, °agony, °agonizing, °painful, °disagreeable, discomfiting, °misfortune, *Colloq* °tough, °tough luck, °tough going, °rough, a °pain in the neck, *US* °tough sledding, *Taboo slang* °pain in the *Brit* arse *or US* ass: *Being marooned on a desert island for a month was no picnic, I assure you.*

pictorial *adj.* **1** °graphic, °picturesque, °vivid, °telling, °striking, °expressive, °plain, °explicit, °clear, lucid: *Many of the poet's images are amazingly pictorial.* **2** illustrated: *They published a pictorial history of biblical lands just for children.*

picture *n.* **1** °drawing, painting, °representation, °portrait, depiction, artwork, °illustration, sketch, °photograph: *Here is a picture of our cottage in the Cotswolds.*

2 °image, (perfect *or* exact) °likeness, (carbon) °copy, °double, °duplicate, °twin, (exact) °replica, °look-alike, °facsimile, *Colloq* spitting °image *or* °spit and °image, *Slang* (dead) ringer: *Isn't she just the picture of her mother?* 3 °impression, °idea, °notion, °understanding, °image: *I think I have a pretty good picture of the situation.* 4 °model, °prototype, °epitome, °essence, °embodiment, incarnation, personification, perfect °example: *From her autobiography, you might believe her to be the picture of sweet innocence.* 5 ***put (someone) in*** *or* ***into the picture***: °inform *or* °advise fully, *Colloq* °fill (someone) in: *Put me into the picture about what went on here last night.*
—*v.* 6 °envision, °envisage, visualize, °imagine, °fancy, °conceive of, °see in the mind's eye: *Picture yourself lying on a beach in the Bahamas.* 7 depict, °draw, °portray, °paint, °represent, °show, °illustrate, °display: *In this fresco, Salome is pictured dancing before Herod Antipas.*

picturesque *adj.* 1 colourful, °interesting, intriguing, °unusual, °unique, °original, charming, °idyllic, °fetching, °attractive, °pretty, °lovely, °quaint, °delightful, °pleasing, °scenic: *We came upon a picturesque village in which all the houses were half-timbered Tudor style with thatched roofs.* 2 colourful, °graphic, °realistic, °vivid, °striking: *Bernard has written a picturesque account of a walking trip through Bavaria.*

piece *n.* 1 °bit, °morsel, °scrap, chunk, hunk, °sliver, °lump, °portion, °particle, °fragment, °shred, shard *or* sherd, °remnant, °quantity: *All the beggar wanted was a piece of bread. A piece of shrapnel is still embedded in my arm.* 2 °wedge, °slice, serving, °helping, °portion: *You may not have a piece of pie till you've eaten your vegetables.* 3 °share, °portion, fraction, °part, °division, °segment, °section, °interest, holding, °percentage, °proportion: *It turned out that a piece of the company had been sold without shareholders' approval.* 4 (short) °story, article, °essay, °report, °theme, °draft; °poem; music, °opus, (°musical) number, °composition, °arrangement, °tune, °melody, °song, °air, °jingle, ditty; °production, °play, °drama, sketch, °show: *I read that piece about cholesterol in yesterday's paper. He wrote a piece for the flute. Which piece by Strindberg will you put on next?* 5 man, °token, chessman, chesspiece, chequer, *Brit* draughtsman: *Once you have touched a piece you must move it.* 6 ***go to pieces***: °fall °apart, °disintegrate, °crumble, °shatter; be shattered, be °upset, be °disturbed, have a nervous °breakdown, go out of *or* lose °control, °break down, *Colloq* °crack up: *Another earthquake and this wall will go to pieces. At the news of his son's death, Joe simply went to pieces.* 7 ***in pieces***: smashed, destroyed, ruined, shattered, °broken, in smithereens: *The vase lay in pieces at my feet. Though I had won the case, my life was in pieces.* 8 ***of a piece (with)***: °similar, similarly constituted, °alike, of the °same °sort *or* °kind *or* °type, °uniform, the °same, °part and parcel (of the °same thing), °identical; in °harmony, in °agreement, °harmonious, in keeping: *This book is of a piece with the others in the same series. All his paintings are of a piece.* 9 ***piece of cake***: *Colloq* snap, cinch, *US and Canadian* lead-pipe cinch, °breeze: *The French exam was a piece of cake.* 10 ***piece of (one's) mind***: scolding, °rebuke, °lecture, °reprimand, °tongue-lashing, chiding, °rap over *or* on the knuckles, *Colloq* °hell, what for, dressing-down, *US* bawling-out, chewing-out: *She gave him a piece of her mind about the amount of time he spent in the pub.* 11 ***piece of the action***: °share, °portion, °interest, °stake, °percentage, holding, °quota: *For £1,000 you can have a piece of the action.* 12 ***speak (one's) piece***: °have (one's) °say, °express (one's) °opinion, °say what is on (one's) mind; °vent (one's) spleen, *Colloq* get a load off (one's) mind *or* chest: *All were given a chance to speak their piece.*
—*v.* 13 ***piece together***: °assemble, °put together, °connect, °gather, °compose; °fix, °unite, °restore, °mend: *We pieced together what happened from the witnesses' accounts. You'll never be able to piece together the bits of that lamp.*

pièce de résistance *n.* highlight, (°special *or* °main) °feature *or* °attraction, *spécialité (de la maison)*, °masterpiece, *chef-d'œuvre*, *Brit* °speciality, *US* specialty: *The* pièce de résistance *of the meal was a magnificent gateau.*

piecemeal *adv.* 1 °piece by piece, °little by little, inch by inch, °bit by bit, inchmeal, °gradually, by °degrees, slowly, in °bits and °pieces, by °fits and starts, fitfully, intermittently, sporadically, disjointedly: *The ministry insisted that the plans should remain as one package and not be introduced piecemeal over the next two years.* 2 into fragments *or* shreds *or* °pieces: *He angrily took the cheque and tore it up piecemeal.*
—*adj.* 3 °fragmentary, °bit by bit, inchmeal, °gradual, °disjointed, °sporadic: *The South-east could become one huge traffic jam unless the Government drops its piecemeal approach to planning.*

pier *n.* 1 wharf, °landing (-stage *or* -place), jetty, quay, floating °dock, *Technically inaccurate* °dock: *The ship is tied up at the pier.* 2 °pile, piling, °post, °upright, column, °support, °buttress: *Owing to lack of maintenance, the piers supporting the building have crumbled.*

pierce *v.* 1 °stab, °puncture, °penetrate, °thrust *or* °poke into, °lance, spear, °spit, °run through *or* into, skewer, °impale, °fix, °transfix: *The arrow pierced his heart and he dropped down dead.* 2 °bore into *or* through, °penetrate, °drill, °perforate, °riddle, °punch through, °hole, °tunnel into: *The wall is pierced to provide ventilation.* 3 °penetrate, °fathom, °see, °understand, °comprehend, °grasp, °discover, °realize: *His keen analytical mind allowed him to pierce the mysteries of nature.* 4 °affect (keenly), °touch, °move, °melt, °stir, °rouse, °pain, °cut to the quick, °wound, °strike: *It pierced my heart to hear the child weep.*

piercing *adj.* 1 °strident, °shrill, °harsh, ear-splitting, ear-shattering, high-pitched, screaming, shrieking, screeching, °loud, blaring: *The piercing sound of the police siren made me sit bolt upright in bed.* 2 probing, searching, °penetrating, °sharp, °keen; °arresting, gripping, °spellbinding, °enthralling, fascinating, entrancing: *I was completely transfixed by her piercing green eyes.* 3 °penetrating, °icy, frosty, °frigid, chilling, °freezing, °cold, numbing, °keen, °wintry, arctic, °raw, °bitter, °fierce, °biting, nipping, nippy: *Shivering in that piercing wind I thought I'd never be warm again.* 4 stabbing, shooting, °excruciating, °exquisite, °acute, °sharp, °severe, °agonizing, °fierce, °intense, °painful, racking: *I suddenly felt a piercing pain in my left ear.*

piety *n.* 1 °devotion, devotedness, °respect, °deference, °dedication, dutifulness, °loyalty, °affection: *In filial piety he hung the painting of his parents prominently over the mantelpiece.* 2 piousness, °reverence, °veneration, devoutness, holiness, godliness, pietism, devotedness, °devotion, °observance, religiousness, °grace, °sanctity: *His life of piety had marked him out as a likely candidate for sainthood.*

pile[1] *n.* 1 °heap, °mound, °stack, °accumulation, stockpile, °mass, °supply, °deposit, °collection, assemblage, °batch, °hoard, aggregation, congeries, conglomeration, °assortment, agglomeration, concentration, amassment: *A huge pile of gravel was delivered today for the builders.* 2 °money, °fortune, °wealth, holdings, *Colloq* bundle, °loot, °mint, *Slang* °packet, °tidy °sum, *US* bankroll, °roll, °wad: *She made her pile selling arms to terrorists.* 3 Usually, ***piles***: °abundance, overabundance, superabundance, °plenty, °great °deal, °quantity, °ocean(s), °lot(s), °stack(s), plethora, *Colloq* oodles, ton(s), °bag(s), °heap(s), °bundle(s): *He made piles of money in the black market.* 4 See **pier, 2,** above.
—*v.* 5 Often, ***pile up***: °stack (up), °heap (up), °mound, °accumulate, stockpile, °amass, °collect, °assemble, °hoard, aggregate, cumulate: *Please pile the cartons in the corner.* 6 ***pile in*** *or* ***into***: °enter, °get in *or* into, °crowd in *or* into, °pack in *or* into, °flood in *or* into, °jam in *or* into, °crush in *or* into, *Colloq* °jump in *or* into: *All of us piled into my car to go to the cinema.* 7 ***pile it on***: °exaggerate: *Ronnie was really piling it on about how much his new job pays.* 8 ***pile on*** *or* ***onto***:

a °get in *or* into *or* on *or* onto, °crowd on *or* onto, °jump on *or* onto: *We piled on the train after the game. They piled onto the hay wagon for a ride home.* **b** °attack, °assault, °jump on, °overwhelm: *They all piled on me and I had to give up.* **9** ***pile out***: °leave, °get out (of) *or* down (from), °exit: *When we arrived, we all piled out of the bus. Hordes of people piled out of the theatre.* **10** ***pile up***: °accumulate, °amass, °collect: *The rubbish kept piling up during the strike.*

pile[2] *n.* °nap, shag, °plush; fuzz, bristles, °fleece: *The feet of the chairs have left marks in the carpet pile.*

piles *n.pl.* haemorrhoids.

pile-up *n.* **1** (road) °accident, smash, °crash, (multiple) (rear-end) °collision, *Colloq* smash-up: *Thirty cars were involved in that pile-up on the motorway.* **2** °accumulation, °heap, °stack, °mass, *Colloq* °mountain: *How will you ever get through that pile-up of work on your desk?*

pilfer *v.* °steal, °rob, °plunder, thieve, filch, °embezzle, °misappropriate, purloin, °take, walk off with, palm, *Colloq* °appropriate, °pinch, °snatch, °grab, °lift, borrow, *Brit* °nick, snaffle, *US* boost, *Slang* °hook, snitch, °swipe, °rip off: *The auditors found that he had pilfered small sums from the company for years.*

pilgrim *n.* hajji *or* hadji *or* haji, *Medieval history* palmer; crusader: *The pilgrims visited holy places in and near Jerusalem.*

pilgrimage *n.* hajj *or* hadj, holy °expedition, °crusade; °expedition, °journey, trek, voyage, °tour, °trip, °excursion: *Every year the entire family made a pilgrimage to grandfather's grave.*

pill *n.* **1** °tablet, capsule, bolus, pellet, pilule; °medicine, medication, medicament, °drug, pharmaceutical, °remedy, °cure; cough drop, pastille, lozenge, troche: *Doctor, can't you give me some kind of pill for this headache?* **2** °nuisance, °bore, °pest, *Colloq* °pain (in the neck), °crank, °drag: *I don't understand what she sees in Leonard—he's such a pill.*

pillage *v.* **1** °plunder, °raid, °ravage, °sack, despoil, °rob, °loot, °ransack, °rifle, maraud, depredate, °devastate, vandalize, °ruin, °demolish, °raze, °level, °strip: *The Goths pillaged every community they conquered and carried off the booty.*

—*n.* **2** °plunder, rapine, despoliation, looting, °robbery, °sack, sacking, ransacking, marauding, brigandage, piracy, freebooting, buccaneering, banditry, °depredation, devastation, vandalization, defilement, laying °waste, °destruction, razing, demolition, levelling, °ruin, stripping: *Pirates from Tripoli were responsible for the pillage of one coastal town after another.* **3** °plunder, °loot, °booty, spoils: *In the cave Ali Baba found the pillage from a thousand robberies.*

pillar *n.* **1** column, pilaster, °pile, piling, °pier, °upright, °post, °shaft, °prop; atlas, caryatid: *The roof is supported by a single pillar. Lot's wife was turned into a pillar of salt.* **2** °mainstay, °supporter, °worthy, upholder, °backbone, (°tower of) °strength, °leader: *Cummings has been a pillar of strength in our community.*

pilot *n.* **1** aviator, aviatrix, flier, airman, airwoman, aeronaut, captain: *The pilot announced that we would land in five minutes.* **2** steersman, helmsman, °navigator, *US* wheelman *or* wheelsman; °guide, °leader, cicerone, conductor: *The pilot knows his way through the shoals. A student acted as our pilot in our tour of Oxford.*

—*v.* **3** °guide, °steer, °run, °direct, °shepherd, °control, °lead, °navigate, °drive; °fly: *Only someone with local knowledge can pilot the ship into that harbour. The chairman piloted the company through turbulent times.*

pimp *n.* **1** °procurer, panderer *or* °pander, White °slaver, whoremonger, *Slang US* hustler: *The police rounded up the pimps and prostitutes for questioning.*

—*v.* **2** °procure, °pander, °solicit, *Slang US* °hustle: *He was well known as having pimped for three generations of the nobility.*

pimple *n.* pustule, papula, °boil, °swelling, °eruption, blackhead *or Technical* comedo, excrescence, *Brit* °spot, *Scots* plouk *or* plook, *US* whitehead, *Old-fashioned US* hickey: *The old witch had a pimple at the end of her nose.*

pin *n.* **1** °peg, dowel, °bolt, thole, thole-pin, °spike, rivet; *Brit* drawing-pin, *US* push-pin: *The table is held together by wooden pins. We need some more pins for the notice-board.* **2** °brooch, °clip; stickpin, tie-pin, scarf-pin, *US* tie tack: *She is wearing the cameo pin that her mother gave her. I had George's pin made into a brooch.*

—*v.* **3** °attach, °fix, affix, °fasten, °secure, °tack; °hold, °staple, °clip: *Let's play 'Pin the tail on the donkey'. Pin these papers together.* **4** ***pin down***: **a** °force, °make, compel, coerce, constrain, °press, *Brit* pressurize, *US* °pressure: *We must pin him down to give his decision by tomorrow.* **b** °define, °specify, pinpoint, °name, °identify, °determine, put *or* lay one's °finger on, home *or* °zero in on, °focus on: *The doctor was unable to pin down what is wrong with her.* **c** confine, °hold (down), °fix, immobilize, °tie down, constrain: *We were pinned down by enemy fire.* **5** ***pin on***: °blame, °hold °responsible *or* °accountable, point the °finger at, °accuse; °lay at (someone's) door: *They'll never be able to pin the murder on Drayton.*

pincers *n.pl.* pliers, nippers, tweezers: *Can you get the nail out with these pincers?*

pinch *v.* **1** °squeeze, °nip, °tweak, °press, compress, °grip, °grasp: *I pinched my finger in the drawer.* **2** °squeeze, cramp, confine, °crush, °hurt: *These shoes really pinch badly.* **3** °steal, thieve, °rob, °take, shoplift, filch, °pilfer, purloin, *Colloq* °lift, *Brit* °nick, *US* boost, *Slang* °swipe, °knock off: *I think it was Andrew who pinched my book.* **4** °arrest, apprehend, take into °custody, *Colloq* °nab, °run in, collar, bust, *Brit* °nick: *She was pinched for driving while under the influence.* **5** ***pinch pennies***: scrimp, °save, skimp, °economize: *We're pinching pennies now so that we can afford a nice holiday later.*

—*n.* **6** °squeeze, °nip, °tweak, °twinge: *Montrose gave the girl's cheek an affectionate pinch.* **7** °touch, (°tiny *or* °wee) °bit, soupçon, °jot, mite, °taste, *Colloq US* tad, smidgen *or* smidgin: *Add a pinch of salt to the boiling water.* **8** °predicament, °emergency, °crisis, °difficulty, °dilemma, (°ticklish *or* °delicate) °situation, °complication, *Colloq* pickle, °jam, °scrape, *Chiefly Brit* °crunch: *Sue will help me out in a pinch.*

pink[1] *n.* **1** ***in the pink***: at one's °best, °healthy, °hearty, in the °best of °health, in °top °form, in °good °shape, *Colloq US* up: *I saw Rob the other day, and he's in the pink.*

—*adj.* **2** °rosy, rose, rose-coloured, pinkish, flesh-colour(ed), salmon(-colour(ed)): *The designer suggests pink curtains for the bedroom.*

pink[2] *v.* serrate, °notch, scallop; °perforate, °puncture, °prick: *Pink the edge of the fabric to prevent fraying.*

pinnacle *n.* °top, °peak, apex, °acme, °summit, °zenith, °maximum, °climax, crowning °point, °consummation, utmost, °extreme, °perfection; °tip, °cap, °crest, °crown: *Being elected chairman was the pinnacle of Mark's career. The climbers reached the pinnacle, where they will rest overnight.*

pioneer *n.* **1** pathfinder, frontiersman, frontierswoman, trail-blazer, explorer, colonist, (early) °settler; ground-breaker, °forerunner, °precursor, °predecessor, innovator, °leader, trend-setter, pacemaker, pacesetter: *The pioneers who explored and settled the American west were daring men and women. Marconi was a pioneer in the development of radio.*

—*v.* **2** °create, °originate, °invent, °initiate, take the first °step, °introduce, °institute, actuate, trigger, °set off, °inaugurate, °start, °begin, °launch, °establish, °found, °set up, °develop, lay the °groundwork *or* °foundation, set *or* put in motion, take the °lead, °lead *or* show the way, blaze the trail, be a °prime mover, °open up, *Colloq* kick off, get the ball rolling: *Our company has pioneered systems for automatic typesetting.*

pious *adj.* **1** °devout, °religious, reverent, reverential, worshipful, °dutiful, God-fearing, °godly, °faithful, °holy, dedicated, °devoted, °spiritual, °moral, °good, °virtuous, right-minded, °saintly, angelic, °seraphic, Christ-like, °godlike: *Francis is a pious boy who attends church regularly.* **2** °hypocritical, °sanctimonious, pietistic, °self-righteous, °Pharisaic, °mealy-mouthed, °pretended, °fraudulent, °goody-goody, unctuous, °oily, *Colloq Brit* smarmy: *You are rationalizing your bad behaviour with a lot of pious cant.*

pipe *n.* **1** °pipeline, tube, duct, hose, °line, °main, conduit, °passage, conveyor, °channel: *The pipes are inspected regularly for corrosion.* **2** briar, meerschaum, corn-cob, calabash, clay pipe, water-pipe, hookah, narghile, chibouk *or* chibouque, peace-pipe *or* pipe of peace *or* calumet, brier, *Brit* hubble-bubble, *US* bong: *He slowly tamped down the tobacco in his pipe, then lit it.* **3** pan-pipe, whistle, boatswain's pipe, tooter, horn, wind, wind °instrument, woodwind, brass: *They play the pipes in the London Symphony.*
—*v.* **4** tootle, tweet, skirl, warble, whistle, °peep, cheep: *One was piping away on a flute, the other was dancing a jig.* **5** °transmit, °deliver, °channel, °conduct, convey, °supply: *The gas is piped directly into our homes.* **6** *US* °look at, °notice, °spot, °note, *Colloq* get a load of: *Pipe the guy trying to climb up the outside of that building.* **7** ***pipe down***: become quieter, °quiet(en) down, make less °noise, °hush (up), shush (up), °whisper, *Colloq* °belt up, °shut up: *I wish they'd pipe down, I can't sleep.* **8** ***pipe up***: °speak (up), °say, raise one's voice, make oneself heard, °offer, volunteer: *Sally piped up with the correct answer from the back of the classroom.*

pipeline *n.* **1** °pipe, tube, duct, hose, °line, °main, conduit, °passage, conveyor, °channel: *Pipelines carry gas from the North Sea throughout Britain. Very little information was flowing through the pipeline from Beirut.* **2** ***in the pipeline***: on the °way, under °way, in the offing, °ready, °imminent, coming, *Colloq* in the °works, cooking, *US* in °work: *They said that the contract was in the pipeline and should arrive soon.*

pirate *n.* **1** buccaneer, sea °rover, corsair, privateer, freebooter, sea-robber, filibuster, *Archaic* pic(k)aroon: *Captain Kidd and Blackbeard were actual pirates who looted shipping in the Americas in the 17th century.* **2** plagiarist, plagiarizer, infringer: *Some of these pirates offer unauthorized cheap reprints of expensive textbooks.*
—*v.* **3** plagiarize, °infringe, °copy, °reproduce, °steal, °appropriate, poach, *Colloq* °lift, °pinch, crib: *Our government has no jurisdiction over those who pirate books in countries with which we have no treaty.*

pirouette *n.* **1** °spin, whirl, °twirl, °turn, °revolution, pivoting: *Antoinette did a beautiful pirouette followed by a* pas de chat.
—*v.* **2** °spin, whirl, °turn (°round), °revolve, °pivot: *He was so happy that he fairly pirouetted round the room.*

pistol *n.* gun, handgun, °revolver, automatic, *Slang* rod, piece, shooting-iron, *Chiefly US* gat, *US* Saturday-night special, heater, roscoe: *In the United States, law enforcement officers are required to carry a pistol.*

piston *n.* plunger: *The piston in a bicycle pump is worked by hand.*

pit[1] *n.* **1** °hole, °excavation, °shaft, °cavity, °mine, mineshaft, °quarry, working, ditch, trench, trough: *Pits had been dug for the extraction of gravel.* **2** pothole, °hollow, °depression, dent, °indentation, dimple, pockmark: *His face was disfigured by the pits left by teenage acne.* **3** °abyss, chasm, °well, °crevasse, crater: *We found a bottomless pit that led to the centre of the earth.* **4** ***the pits***: °awful, °terrible, the worst, *Slang* °lousy: *That TV show last night was the pits. He thought that going to school was the pits.*
—*v.* **5** dent, pock-mark, °dig, °scar, °hollow out, °gouge: *The salt air has pitted the metal parts of my car.* **6** Often, ***pit against***: °match, °oppose, °set against; °contrast: *Shirley doesn't stand a chance if they pit her against Maria.*

pit[2] *n.* stone, °seed, pip: *I prefer seedless grapes, the ones without pits.*

pitch[1] *v.* **1** °toss, °throw, °cast, °fling, °hurl, °heave, °sling, °fire, °launch, °shoot, °send, let °fly, *Cricket* °bowl, *Colloq* chuck, °peg, °lob, *Brit* bung: *He rolled the paper into a ball and pitched it into the basket.* **2** °erect, °raise, °set *or* °put up, °position, °fix, °place: *We ought to pitch the tent in a level area.* **3** °plunge, °fall (headlong), °dive, °drop, °plummet, (take a) nosedive: *I caught my toe on the kerb and pitched forward onto the pavement.* **4** *Chiefly nautical* °toss about, °lurch, °plunge, °flounder, go °head over heels, go keel over truck, *US* pitchpole *or* pitchpoll: *The wind reached force ten as we pitched and rolled and yawed in the heavy seas.* **5** ***pitch in***: °contribute, °cooperate, °help, °assist, *Colloq* °chip in: *Everyone pitched in to make the church fair a success.* **6** ***pitch into***: **a** °attack, °lay into, assail, °lash out at, °abuse, °rail against, *Colloq* °lace into, °tear into, jump down (someone's) throat, °jump on: *Reggie's wife really pitched into him about going out with other women.* **b** °attack, °assault, °set upon, °belabour, *Colloq* °light into, sail into, °tear into: *They pitched into each other and fought like Kilkenny cats.* **7** ***pitch on*** *or* ***upon***: °determine, °decide on, °select, °pick, °choose, opt for, °elect, °nominate, °name, *Colloq* °light on: *They pitched on Carrie to be the best candidate for treasurer.*

pitch[2] *n.* tar, bitumen, asphalt: *Peter patched potholes with pitch.*

pitch-black *adj.* °black, °dark, ebon(y), Stygian, inky(-black), unlit, unlighted, pitch-dark, coal-black, jet-black; raven, sable: *The cellar was pitch-black. Her pale complexion was in stark contrast to her pitch-black hair.*

pitched *adj.* organized, planned, °deliberate, coordinated, arranged, systematized: *The two armies fought a pitched battle on the plain.*

piteous *adj.* °pitiable, °pathetic, °pitiful, plaintive, °miserable, °heart-rending, °poignant, distressing, °grievous, heartbreaking, °mournful, °sad, °doleful, dolorous, °tearful, °lamentable, °deplorable, °regrettable, rueful, woeful, °moving, °emotional: *We heard the piteous wailing of the mothers who had lost children in the disaster.*

pitfall *n.* **1** °trap, °pit: *Pitfalls were often used in Burma for trapping tigers.* **2** °danger, °peril, °hazard, catch, °difficulty, °snag: *You might well encounter pitfalls, but don't be discouraged.*

pith *n.* **1** °core, °heart, °kernel, °nucleus, crux, °gist, °focus, °focal °point, °essence, °meat, marrow, °nub, °point, °spirit, °substance, °quintessence: *As usual, Randolph came immediately to the pith of the argument.* **2** °weight, °burden, gravamen, °gravity, °force, °moment, °import, °importance, °significance, °substance, °depth, °matter: *I have something of great pith to tell you about.*

pitiable *adj.* See **piteous**, above.

pitiful *adj.* **1** See **piteous**, above. **2** °small, °little, °insignificant, °trifling, unimportant, beggarly, °sorry, °mean, °contemptible: *Does Hodges seriously expect us to praise him for that pitiful contribution of his?*

pittance *n.* mite, shoestring, *Slang* peanuts, chicken-feed, small potatoes: *The miserable pittance that she receives does not even cover the necessities of life. He's trying to run that business on a pittance.*

pitted *adj.* eaten away, corroded, eroded, pock-marked, defaced, marred, pierced, perforated: *The chrome plating is all pitted where the acid splashed.*

pity *n.* **1** °sympathy, commiseration, °sorrow, condolence, compassion, tenderness, *Archaic* ruth: *I really feel pity for Betty, being married to such a brute.* **2** (crying *or* damned) °shame, °sad thing, °disgrace, °misfortune, °sin, °sacrilege, *Colloq* crime: *It's a pity that no one can do anything.*
—*v.* **3** °sympathize, °feel for, commiserate with, °feel °sorry for, °feel *or* have compassion *or* tenderness for, bleed for, °weep for: *I pity any mother whose son goes off to war.*

pivot *n.* **1** pintle, gudgeon, hinge, °swivel, °pin, kingpin, spindle, fulcrum: *Use this stone as a pivot for the lever to lift the rock.* **2** °centre, °heart, °focal °point, °hub, nave, crux: *The finance minister regards the interest rate as the pivot on which the economy turns.* —*v.* **3** °rotate, °revolve, °turn, °spin, °twirl, whirl, °swivel: *The flywheel pivots on a bearing that requires constant lubrication.* **4** hinge, °depend, °hang, be contingent, °revolve around, °rely: *The whole deal pivots on the cooperation of the banks.*

pivotal *adj.* °critical, °central, °focal, °crucial, °significant, °important, °essential, °vital, °pressing, °urgent, °radical: *The attitude of the judge is pivotal in the jury's decision.*

place *n.* **1** °location, °site, °position, °point, °spot, locus, °area, °locale, °scene, °setting: *This looks like a nice place for a picnic. She likes to see a place for everything and everything in its place.* **2** °locale, °area, °neighbourhood, °vicinity, °district, °section, °part of the country, °quarter, °region; °city, °town, village, hamlet: *She comes from some place near Glasgow.* **3** °status, °station, °standing, °grade, °rank, °position, °niche, °slot, °situation, °estate, °state, °circumstance(s): *Angela was just saying how difficult it is today to find a servant who knows his place.* **4** °function, °role, °part, °purpose, °duty, °obligation, °task, °responsibility, °charge, chore, °burden, °concern, °mission: *It is scarcely my place to remind you of your appointments with the dentist.* **5** °position, °job, °post, berth, °appointment, livelihood; °employment, °occupation, *Colloq* billet: *Is there a chance of my earning a place in your new company?* **6** °home, °house, °flat, apartment, °room(s), °quarters, °lodgings, *Rather formal* °residence, °domicile, °dwelling, °abode, *Colloq* digs *or* diggings, °pad: *Why not stop by my place for tea on Sunday?* **7** stead; lieu: *As I cannot go, would you go in place of me?* **8** °position, °situation, circumstances, °condition: *Put yourself in my place and I think you would have done exactly the same.* **9** °seat, °chair, °position: *Kevin, please take your place at the head of the table.* **10** ***go places***: °succeed, become °successful, °get ahead, °advance, °prosper, °thrive, °flourish, go up in the world, °make good, strike it rich, *Colloq* °arrive, make a °splash, *US and Canadian* hit pay dirt, luck out: *That boy will go places one day.* **11** ***in place***: **a** °fitting, °suitable, °appropriate, °right, °proper, °correct, good °form: *I don't think it in place for you to tell me what to do.* **b** *in situ*, in (the right *or* proper *or* correct) °position, °ready, all °set, °set up, in °order, all °right, *Colloq* °OK *or* okay: *Is everything in place for tonight's party?* **12** ***out of place***: °awkward, uncomfortable, unsuitable, °inappropriate, °wrong, °improper, misplaced: *Compassion is out of place when dealing with war criminals.* **13** ***put (someone) in his*** *or* ***her*** *or* ***their place***: °humble, °mortify, °bring down, °embarrass, °squelch, *Colloq* °cut down to size, take down a °peg (or two): *Aunt Agatha used to put Uncle Wilfred in his place by reminding him who held the purse-strings.* **14** ***take place***: °happen, °occur, °go on, °come about; °arise, *Colloq* °transpire: *We shall never know what took place behind those locked doors.* —*v.* **15** °put (out), °position, °situate, °locate, °dispose, °arrange, °order, °set (out), °lay, °deposit; °station, °post, °spot, pinpoint, *Colloq* °stick, *Brit* bung: *Place the forks on the left and the knives on the right. They placed guards at the door of my room.* **16** °class, classify, °sort, °order, °arrange, °rank, °group, °categorize, °bracket, °grade; °regard, °view, °see, °consider: *She places love of family above love of country. Critics place him among the best writers of the century.* **17** °identify, put one's °finger on, °recall, °remember, °recognize; °associate: *I just can't place her for the moment. He finally placed me with those who had ragged him at school.* **18** °put, °set, °assign, °give: *People place too much importance on material things.*

placement *n.* **1** °arrangement, placing, °position, °distribution, array, °disposition, deployment, positioning, stationing, °organization, °order, ordering, °location, locating, arraying, emplacement, emplacing: *The placement of the chairs is all wrong for tonight's meeting.* **2** °employment, °appointment, °engagement, hiring: *Placement of qualified engineers has not been a problem.*

plagiarism *n.* plagiarizing, plagiary, piracy, pirating, °theft, purloining, °stealing, copying, appropriating, appropriation, thievery, usurpation, infringing, °infringement, °imitation, *Euphemistic* borrowing, *Colloq* lifting, cribbing: *The similarities between the two books could only be explained by plagiarism.*

plague *n.* **1** °scourge, °epidemic, °pestilence, °affliction, pandemic, °calamity, °curse, °evil, bane, °blight, °visitation: *The inhabitants turned a plague of locusts to advantage by eating them.* **2** irritation, °annoyance, °nuisance, °pest, vexation, °bother, °thorn in one's side *or* flesh, °torment, torture, *Colloq* °pain (in the neck), °headache, aggravation, *Slang* °drag, °bitch, hassle, *Taboo slang* °pain in the *Brit* arse *or US* ass: *It's a plague trying to find a place to park the car.* —*v.* **3** badger, harry, °hound, °pester, °annoy, vex, °irritate, °bother, °harass, °nag, nettle, °exasperate, °gall, °irk, °torment, torture, °anguish, °distress, *Brit* chivvy *or* chivy *or* chevy: *I wish the police would stop plaguing me with questions about Jonathan's whereabouts.*

plain *adj.* **1** °flat, °smooth, °even, featureless, °level, °plane: *I'd rather have a paper with a plain surface, not an embossed one, for the bedroom walls.* **2** °clear, °evident, °simple, °distinct, crystal °clear, lucid, °vivid, °transparent, °apparent, °obvious, °patent, °self-evident, °manifest, unmistakable, unequivocal, unambiguous, understandable, °intelligible, °graphic, °direct, in black and white: *His intentions regarding my daughter are plain enough. The plain fact is that she despises him.* **3** °open, °honest, straightforward, °forthright, °direct, °frank, °candid, °blunt, °outspoken, °ingenuous, °sincere, guileless, °artless, unreserved: *I want to see some plain talk between the two of us.* **4** °simple, °unadorned, undecorated, unembellished, °basic, austere, °stark, unostentatious, °colourless, °drab, °bare, °unvarnished, °Spartan: *Don't you find the average business suit a very plain affair?* **5** °homely, unattractive, ordinary-looking, unlovely, °ugly: *Who would believe that such a plain child could become such a beautiful woman?* —*n.* **6** prairie, grassland, °pasture, meadow-land, veld *or* veldt, pampas, campo, llano, savannah *or* savanna, steppe, tundra, champaign *or* campagna; heath; °moor, moorland; °plateau, flatland; down, downland, *Literary* wold, *Archaic or literary* mead: *The plain stretched out before us as far as the eye could see.*

plan *n.* **1** °design, layout, blueprint, °scheme, °method, °procedure, °system, °arrangement, °programme, °project, °formula, °pattern, *Colloq* °script, °scenario: *The plan called for monthly progress meetings. The best laid plans of mice and men gang aft agley.* **2** °drawing, sketch, °design, layout, blueprint, °chart, map, diagram, °representation: *This plan shows where the furniture will be placed.* —*v.* **3** °lay out *or* down, °design, °arrange, °devise, °outline, °organize, °plot, map out, delineate, °develop: *She has been invited to plan the new shopping mall.* **4** °intend, °expect, °envisage, °envision, °foresee, °aim, °contemplate, °propose: *Were you planning to go to the cinema tonight?*

plane *n.* **1** °flat *or* °level (°surface): *The lines meet in the same plane.* **2** aeroplane, aircraft, airliner, jet (plane): *I caught the next plane for Marrakesh.* —*adj.* **3** °flat, °even, °level, °smooth, °plain, °regular, unbroken, uninterrupted, °uniform, °horizontal: *We landed on the plane surface of the glacier.* —*v.* **4** °glide, °skim, skate, skid, °slip, °slide: *I swiftly planed along on my sailboard.*

plank *n.* °board, °timber, °slab: *The flooring was made up of wide planks laid side by side.*

plant *n.* **1** °flower, vegetable, herb, bush, shrub, tree, vine, weed: *Because of all the rain, the plants are flourishing this summer.* **2** °factory, °mill, °shop,

°works, workshop, foundry: *The new plant in Crawley is hiring lathe operators.* **3** °equipment, machinery, °apparatus; °gear, °fixtures: *The plant includes heavy cranes, JCBs, earth movers, and bulldozers.* **4** °spy, (°undercover *or* °secret) °agent, °informer, informant: *The new assistant is a plant, sent in by management to report on union activities.*
—*v.* **5** bed (out), °sow, °seed, °set (out), °transplant: *We planted a herbaceous border along the south wall of the garden.* **6** °implant, °establish, °root, °fix, ingrain, °lodge, °instil, °insinuate, °inject, °introduce, °impress, imprint: *Who planted the idea in your mind that you were a gifted writer?* **7** °place, °put, °position, °station, °assign, °situate: *Watch-towers are planted at 50-foot intervals around the prison.* **8** °hide, °secrete, °conceal: *The company has planted detectives in the store to watch out for shoplifters.*

planter *n.* flowerpot, cache-pot: *He poured the drugged wine into a nearby planter.*

plaque *n.* **1** °tablet, medallion, °plate, panel, marker, °slab, plaquette: *The plaque on the house marks it as the birthplace of Thomas Carlyle.* **2** badge, °brooch, °pin, °patch, medallion, medal, insignia *or* insigne: *The plaque shows him to be a member of the Royal Yacht Squadron.* **3** °prize, °honour, °award, °trophy: *At the annual dinner, she was presented with a plaque to mark her many years of service.*

plaster *v.* °smear, daub, bedaub, °spread, °coat, °cover, overlay, superimpose: *The mud was plastered all over my boots. They plastered the walls with posters.*

plastic *adj.* **1** mouldable, shapable *or* shapeable, fictile, °soft, malleable, workable, ductile, °flexible, pliant, °supple, °pliable, clayey, waxy: *The clay must be worked into the desired form while it is still plastic.* **2** °impressionable, °receptive, °open, persuadable *or* persuasible, °susceptible, °tractable, compliant, °responsive, °manageable, unformed, °inexperienced: *One encounters the children at an age when their minds and personalities are still plastic enough to be influenced.* **3** °artificial, °synthetic, °imitation, °fake, °counterfeit, ersatz, paste, °bogus, meretricious, °sham; °cheap, pinchbeck, °shoddy; *Colloq* °phoney *or US also* phony, crummy, *US* chintzy: *She was wearing a tawdry plastic brooch.*

plate *n.* **1** °platter, dish, *Archaic* trencher, charger: *I left the cold mashed potato on my plate.* **2** °course, serving, °portion, dish, °platter: *I ordered their speciality, a plate of spaghetti.* **3** layer, leaf, °sheet, °pane, panel, lamina, °slab: *In the condenser, insulation separates the thin metal plates.* **4** coating, °coat, plating, layer, lamination: *The plate on our cutlery is wearing thin.* **5** °illustration, °picture, °print, *US* °cut: *The book contains many beautiful colour plates of flowers.*
—*v.* **6** °cover, °coat, overlay, °face, laminate: *All the serving dishes were plated with gold.*

plateau *n.* **1** tableland, upland, highland, mesa: *We climbed till we reached a grassy plateau.* **2** °level, °lull, °pause, levelling off: *At 39, Julia seemed to have reached a plateau in her career.*

platform *n.* **1** °stand, dais, °stage, podium, °rostrum: *After the introduction, the speaker mounted the platform.* **2** °policy, party °line, °principle(s), °tenet(s), °programme, plank: *The main elements of our platform will be revealed at the party conference.*

platonic *adj.* non-physical, asexual, non-sexual, °celibate, °chaste, °dispassionate, °detached, °spiritual, °ideal, °intellectual: *Some say that their relationship has not always been purely platonic.*

platoon *n.* °company, °squad, squadron, °group, °patrol, °team, cadre, °body, °formation, °unit, *Colloq* °outfit: *A platoon of soldiers was marched to the barracks in close-order drill.*

platter *n.* serving dish, server, salver, tray, °plate, dish: *Waiters walked among the guests with platters of hot hors-d'œuvres.*

plausible *adj.* **1** °likely, believable, °reasonable, credible, °tenable, conceivable, °thinkable, °probable, imaginable, admissible, °sound, °sensible, °rational, °logical, °acceptable, °trustworthy, °presentable: *The police regarded our alibi as plausible.* **2** °specious, °deceptive, meretricious, misleading, °deceitful, casuistic, sophistical, Jesuitical, °smooth, °empty: *He was a cunning, plausible sort of fellow.*

play *v.* **1** °amuse oneself, °frolic, °frisk, °cavort, gambol, °caper, °sport, have °fun, have a good time, °enjoy oneself, disport (oneself), °carouse: *Ken's mother won't let him go out and play.* **2** °participate (in), take °part (in), °join (in), be occupied (in *or* with); °engage in, contend in, °take up, °occupy oneself in *or* with, °undertake: *He was invited for a game of poker, but he refused to play. I understand that you play bridge.* **3** °engage, contend with, °compete with *or* against, °challenge, °vie with, °pit oneself against, °take on, °rival: *The stranger played me at snooker, and I lost three games out of three.* **4** °portray, depict, °perform, act *or* take the °role *or* °part of, °act: *In the new production of* Othello *she plays Desdemona.* **5** perform (upon *or* on); put on: *Play 'Misty' for me. She plays the piccolo very well. Could you play that Caruso record?* **6** °operate: *I wish they wouldn't play their hi-fi so loud.* **7** °gamble, °bet, wager, °stake, °place, °put: *He played his last chip on number 14.* **8** ***play along***: **a** Often, ***play along with***: °cooperate, °participate, °go along (with), do *or* play one's °part, be a °party to: *I agreed to play along with her charade.* **b** °manipulate, °jolly along: *She played him along till he bought her a car.* **9** ***play around***: **a** °fool around, °tease, *Colloq* °monkey about *or* around, horse around *or* about: *Stop playing around and get to work.* **b** dally, °flirt, be unfaithful; philander, womanize; *Colloq* °fool around, °run around, °sleep around, play the field: *She found out about his playing around and filed for divorce.* **10** ***play at***: °pretend, make °believe, °fake, feign, simulate, °affect: *She's merely playing at enjoying skiing to please you.* **11** ***play ball***: °cooperate, °agree, °work together, work °hand in glove, play along: *They want him to smuggle diamonds, but he won't play ball.* **12** ***play by ear***: °improvise, extemporize, ad lib, *Colloq* wing it: *She can't read music and just plays by ear. With no definite plan of action, I'll just play it by ear.* **13** ***play down***: °belittle, °minimize, °diminish, °disparage, make °light of, deprecate, decry, de-emphasize: *He has always played down his role in the affair.* **14** ***play for time***: °delay, °procrastinate, °stall (for time), temporize, °hesitate, *Colloq* °drag one's feet: *They don't yet have the money to pay, so they are playing for time.* **15** ***play on*** *or* ***upon***: °use, °misuse, °abuse, °trade on, °exploit, take °advantage of, °impose on: *He plays on women's affections then persuades them to give him money.* **16** ***play the game***: °behave, °conduct oneself, deport oneself, °act: *It makes no difference whether you win or lose, it's how you play the game.* **17** ***play up***: **a** °stress, °emphasize, underscore, underline, accentuate, call °attention to, highlight, °spotlight, °dramatize, °build up: *Always try to play up your assets and play down your liabilities.* **b** °act up, °misbehave, give *or* cause °trouble, malfunction, *Colloq* go on the °blink *or US* fritz, *Brit* be wonky: *The bloody engine started playing up again, right in the middle of a rainstorm.* **18** ***play up to***: curry °favour with, °flatter, toady to, ingratiate oneself with, butter up, °truckle to, court, *Colloq* soft-soap, suck up to, boot-lick, *US* apple-polish, *Taboo slang* brown-nose: *Ray is always playing up to the teacher, trying to get a better mark.* **19** ***play with***: **a** °toy with, °trifle with, treat cavalierly *or* lightly, make °light of, think nothing of, dally with, °amuse oneself with: *He's just playing with her till he gets what he's after.* **b** °consider, °think about, °toy with, not treat seriously: *We were playing with the idea of a winter holiday this year.* **c** °mess with, °fiddle with, °toy with, °fidget with: *Stop playing with your food!*
—*n.* **20** °drama, °stage play, °show, °piece, °production, °entertainment: *We have tickets to a different play*

for every night this week. **21** °behaviour, °actions, deportment, °conduct, demeanour: *In the game of life, many have no regard for the rules of fair play. The police suspect foul play.* **22** °amusement, frivolity, °entertainment, °recreation, °fun, °pleasure, °sport, merrymaking, °revelry, tomfoolery, *Colloq* horseplay, skylarking, °monkey business, *Brit* °monkey tricks *or US* monkeyshines: *The time for play is past, and we must get down to serious business.* **23** °move, °manoeuvre, °action: *That last play might have won you the game.* **24** °flexibility, looseness, °freedom, °leeway, °margin, °room, °space, °movement, °motion, *Colloq* °give: *There's too much play in this gear lever.* **25** °treatment, coverage, °attention: *The newspapers gave Connie's new book a big play.*

playboy *n.* man about town, °roué, °rake, debauchee, °gay dog, womanizer, Don Juan, Casanova, Lothario, Romeo, *Colloq* wolf, lady-killer: *He fancies himself as a playboy, but no women seem to agree.*

player *n.* **1** °contestant, °participant, °competitor, contender; athlete, sportswoman, sportsman, *Colloq US* jock: *Chess players from all over the world came together for the championship. The referee sent three players off.* **2** actor *or* actress, °performer, entertainer, trouper, °Thespian: *The local drama group is the Allen Arts Players.* **3** gambler, °better *or especially US* bettor, gamester, speculator, *Brit* °punter: *J.B. is a big player in the commodities market.* **4** musician, instrumentalist, °performer, °virtuoso: *Gladys is one of the best tuba players in the band.*

playful *adj.* **1** (°high-)°spirited, °cheerful, °frisky, °frolicsome, °kittenish, °sprightly, fun-loving, °sportive, coltish, °mischievous, puckish, impish, elfish, °devilish: *The cat didn't mean to scratch you, she was just being playful.* **2** joking, facetious, teasing, roguish, waggish, jesting, °humorous, tongue-in-cheek: *Cleo's in a playful mood today, isn't she?*

playmate *n.* playfellow, °friend, °comrade, *Colloq* °pal, °chum, *US and Canadian* buddy: *Some of Molly's playmates are asking if she can come out to play.*

plaything *n.* **1** °toy, °game, knick-knack, °pastime: *Please pick up your playthings before supper.* **2** °tool, cat's-paw, °dupe, pigeon, °pawn, *Colloq US and Canadian* fall guy: *She had no use for Gerry except as a plaything.*

playwright *n.* °dramatist, dramaturge *or* dramaturgist, scriptwriter, screenwriter, scenarist: *The playwright has deftly caught the way people talk to each other.*

plea *n.* **1** °request, entreaty, °appeal, °petition, °supplication, °suit, °cry, solicitation: *Teenagers' mischievous behaviour is an earnest plea for attention.* **2** °answer, °defence, °argument: *She entered a plea of 'not guilty' to the charge.* **3** °excuse, °reason, °explanation, justification; °pretext: *His plea was that he had not received the bill and therefore couldn't pay it.*

plead *v.* **1** Often, ***plead for***: °request, °appeal (for), °cry (for), °ask (for), °seek, °beg (for), °pray (for), supplicate (for): *It was a hot day and the children were pleading for ice-creams every half hour.* **2** Usually, ***plead with***: °request (of), entreat, °appeal to, °petition, °ask, °apply to, implore, °beseech, °beg, importune, °solicit; °demand: *Bryan pleaded with us to let him go to the rock concert.* **3** assert, °say, aver, °allege, °argue, °maintain, °offer, °put forward, °declare, affirm, avow, °swear: *She pleaded that she was unaware that the goods she was selling had been stolen.*

pleasant *adj.* **1** °pleasing, °pleasurable, °nice, enjoyable, °satisfying, °good, °lovely, °attractive, °inviting, gratifying, °delightful, charming, °agreeable, °suitable, °fitting, °appropriate; °harmonious, euphonious, melodic, mellifluous; °delicious, delectable, palatable, °savoury, toothsome: *Travelling on the Orient Express was a most pleasant experience. The bedroom is decorated in a combination of pleasant colours. He simply doesn't find sunbathing particularly pleasant. That sauce has a very pleasant taste.* **2** °friendly, affable, °amiable, °amicable, gregarious, companionable, °sociable, °engaging, °attractive, °winning, °open, approachable, °outgoing, welcoming, °hospitable, °agreeable, °gracious, charming, congenial, °genial, °nice, °likeable, urbane, °cultivated, °genteel, °polite, °courteous, well-mannered, °suave, °debonair, °polished, °well-bred, cultured: *Murray always has a pleasant expression on his face. He is quite a pleasant fellow, once you get to know him.* **3** °fair, °sunny, °clear, °bright, cloudless, balmy, °nice, °fine: *What a pleasant day for an outing in the country!*

please *v.* **1** °delight, °gratify, °satisfy, °suit, °humour, °content, °cheer, °gladden, °amuse, °divert, °interest, °entertain: *I cannot tell you how much it pleases me to see you again.* **2** °like, °prefer, °choose, °desire, °want, see fit, °wish, °will, °elect, opt: *She may have her birthday party wherever she pleases.*

pleased *adj.* °happy, °delighted, °glad, gratified, satisfied, contented, thrilled; *Colloq* tickled pink, °pleased as Punch, on cloud nine, in seventh °heaven, on top of the °world, walking on air, *Brit* over the moon, chuffed: *His pleased look comes from his having won first prize.*

pleasing *adj.* **1** See **pleasant, 1,** above. **2** See **pleasant, 2,** above.

pleasurable *adj.* See **pleasant, 1,** above.

pleasure *n.* **1** °enjoyment, °happiness, °delight, °joy, °satisfaction, °fulfilment, contentment, °gratification; °comfort, °recreation, °amusement, °entertainment, °diversion: *It is a pleasure to meet you at last. Fred derives so much pleasure from tinkering with his model railways.* **2** °choice, °option, °desire, °wish, °preference, °fancy, °inclination, °discretion: *Feel free to come and go at your pleasure.*

plebeian *adj.* **1** proletarian, working-class, blue-collar, low-class, lower-class, °lowly, low-born, °common, °mean, °humble, °inferior, peasant-like, *Colloq* non-U: *What would you expect from someone with such a plebeian background?* **2** °unrefined, °coarse, °vulgar, ignoble, lowbrow, unpolished, uncouth, crass, brutish, gauche, °provincial, °rustic, °popular, commonplace, °undistinguished: *The entertainment caters to the most plebeian tastes.*
—*n.* **3** proletarian, °common °man *or* °woman, commoner, °man *or* °woman in the street, (any *or* every) Tom, Dick, or Harry, *Brit* °man *or* °woman on the Clapham omnibus, *Colloq* pleb, prole: *This art exhibition is not going to mean very much to the plebeians.*

plebiscite *n.* popular °vote *or* ballot, referendum, °poll: *The plebiscite revealed that the people were in favour of joining the Common Market.*

pledge *n.* **1** °promise, °oath, °vow, °word (of honour), covenant, °assurance, guaranty, °guarantee, °warrant, °warranty: *They have our solemn pledge that we will return within the hour.* **2** bail, surety, collateral, °security, °deposit, °earnest (money), °pawn, gage, °bond, guaranty, °guarantee: *They wanted something besides my signature as a pledge for the money.* **3** °toast, °tribute, °cheer, health: *They drank a pledge to the success of the voyage.*
—*v.* **4** °swear, °vow, °promise, give one's °word (of honour), °contract, °undertake, °agree, °vouch, °vouchsafe: *I pledge allegiance to the nation.* **5** °deposit, °pawn, mortgage, *Archaic* gage, *Colloq US and Canadian* hock: *He pledged his gold watch to pay for her birthday present.* **6** °toast, °drink (to), °drink (someone's) health: *Drink to me only with thine eyes And I will pledge with mine.*

plentiful *adj.* **1** °ample, °abundant, °profuse, copious, °lavish, plenteous, °bountiful, °generous, bounteous: *We found a plentiful supply of food in the markets.* **2** °fertile, °fruitful, °productive, bumper, °luxuriant, thriving, °prolific: *We thanked the Lord for a plentiful harvest.*

plenty *n.* **1** °abundance, more than °enough, °great °deal, °mass(es), °quantity *or* quantities, multitude(s), °number(s), °load(s), °mess, °scores, *Colloq* °lot(s), °mountain(s), °heap(s), °stack(s), °pile(s), °load(s), ton(s), °ocean(s), oodles, *US and Canadian* slew(s):

There is plenty of food, so it is just as well that plenty of people are coming. There's plenty of time before your bus arrives. **2** plentifulness, fertility, copiousness, °abundance, plenteousness, °wealth, °profusion, lavishness, °prodigality, plenitude, bountifulness: *It was a land of plenty, a land of milk and honey.*

pliable *adj.* **1** °flexible, pliant, °elastic, °plastic, fictile, malleable, workable, bendable, bendy, ductile, flexuous, °supple; lithe, limber: *This substance remains pliable only while it is warm.* **2** °tractable, °adaptable, °flexible, pliant, compliant, persuadable *or* persuasible, °impressionable, °susceptible, °responsive, °receptive, docile, °manageable, °yielding: *The other directors may not be as pliable when it comes to improving employee benefits.*

plight *n.* °condition, °state, circumstances, °situation, °case; °difficulty, °predicament, °quandary, °dilemma, catch-22, °straits, °trouble, °extremity, *Colloq* °hole, °jam, pickle, °spot, °scrape, °fix, °bind, hot water, °mess, fine kettle of fish, fine °state of affairs: *As soon as Elliott's sorry plight became known, we all rallied round to help.*

plod *v.* **1** Often, ***plod along***: trudge (along), °tramp, slog, °drag, tread, lumber, °labour, *Colloq* stomp, galumph: *We plodded wearily up the road carrying our heavy packs.* **2** Often, ***plod along or away***: °labour, °work, drudge, toil, moil, °slave (away), °grind (away *or* along), grub (on *or* along), °plug (along *or* away), *Brit* °peg away (at) *or* along: *Plodding through the compilation of the* Oxford Thesaurus, *he was only halfway through the letter P.*

plot[1] *n.* **1** °scheme, °plan, °intrigue, °machination, °cabal, °conspiracy: *The plot to blow up the Houses of Parliament was uncovered at a late stage.* **2** °story (-line), °chain of events, °theme, °outline, °scenario, °thread, skeleton: *Most operas have weak plots, but the music can be sublime.*
—*v.* **3** °scheme, °plan, °intrigue, machinate, °cabal, collude, conspire, °hatch, °devise, °design, °arrange, °organize, concoct, °dream up, °conceive, *Colloq* cook up: *Martin's wife had been plotting to murder him since their wedding night.* **4** °draw, °plan, diagram, °lay down, °outline, °calculate, °compute, °figure, °chart, map (out), °find, °determine, depict, °show: *The navigator plotted our position as being in the Strait of Malacca.*

plot[2] *n.* °lot, plat, °patch *or* °parcel (of °land), °tract, acreage, °area, *Brit* °allotment: *I have a small plot by the canal which is ideal for growing potatoes.*

plough *v.* **1** °till, °cultivate, °furrow, harrow, *Literary* delve: *They ought to finish ploughing the south field by tomorrow.* **2** °drive, °plunge, °push, bulldoze, °lunge, °dive, shove, °hurtle, °crash: *Out of control, a bus ploughed through the fence and into my garden.*

pluck *n.* **1** °courage, °spirit, °bravery, °grit, boldness, intrepidity, °backbone, mettle, °determination, gameness, °resolve, °resolution, steadfastness, hardiness, sturdiness, stout-heartedness, stoutness, °fortitude, °nerve, *Colloq* guts, °spunk, *US* sand, *Slang Brit* °bottle, *US* moxie: *She certainly showed pluck standing up to the boss like that.*
—*v.* **2** °pick, °remove, °withdraw, °draw out, °extract: *The children plucked flowers in the garden and made posies.* **3** °snatch, °grab, °yank, °jerk, °tear (away): *She was plucked from the jaws of death by Tarzan, who happened to be swinging by on a vine.* **4** °tug (at), °pull (at), catch (at), °clutch (at); vellicate: *An ancient crone plucked at his sleeve as he passed.*

plug *n.* **1** °stopper, stopple, bung, cork: *If you pull the plug out, the water will run out.* **2** chew, twist, quid, °wad, pigtail, cavendish: *As they forbade smoking, he would take snuff or chew a plug of tobacco.* **3** publicity, °mention, °promotion, °recommendation, °puff, blurb, PR; °advertisement, *Colloq* advert, hype: *His book was given a plug on yesterday's evening news.*
—*v.* **4** Often, ***plug up***: °stop (up), °close (up *or* off), °seal (off *or* up), cork, °stopper, bung, °block, °jam, °stuff, °clog, °obstruct, dam (up): *A piece of soap has plugged the drain.* **5** °publicize, °mention, °promote, °push, advertise, °puff, commend, *Colloq* °boost, beat the drum for: *It wasn't right to plug her brother's company in her article on double glazing.* **6** See **plod, 2,** above.

plum *n.* °find, catch, coup, °prize, °treasure; °bonus, cream: *Harvey's landed a plum job as overseas buyer.*

plumb *n.* **1** weight, (plumb-)bob, plummet, lead, sinker: *The plumb holds the string taut and exactly vertical.*
—*adj.* **2** vertical, °perpendicular, °straight up and down: *Make sure the jamb is plumb before hanging the door.*
—*adv.* **3** vertically, perpendicularly, °straight up and down: *The cord doesn't hang plumb because the shelf is in the way.* **4** °exactly, °precisely, °dead, °right, accurately, *Colloq* °slap, *Brit* bang, spot: *The navigator checked our position and we were plumb on course.*
—*v.* **5** °sound, °fathom, °measure, °probe, °explore, °measure, °gauge, delve, °penetrate: *The bathyscaphe has plumbed the deeps of the Indian Ocean. I plumb the depths of depression thinking of starving people everywhere.*

plummet *v.* See **plunge, 1,** below.

plump[1] *adj.* **1** °chubby, °stout, fleshy, °ample, full-bodied, portly, tubby, °rotund, squat, chunky, °buxom, corpulent, roly-poly, °fat, °obese, overweight, steatopygous, *Brit* podgy *or US* pudgy, *Colloq* busty, °beamy, hippy, beefy, well-upholstered: *They went on a diet because they were getting a bit plump.*
—*v.* **2** °puff up *or* out: *When you get up, please plump up the pillows on the sofa.*

plump[2] *v.* **1** °drop, °plummet, °fall, °plunge, °dive, °sink, °collapse, °flop: *I was so tired that all I could do was plump down in an armchair and watch TV.* **2** °deposit, °set *or* °put (down), plunk, plop: *She plumped down the defective mixer on the counter and asked for a refund.* **3** ***plump for***: °support, °choose, °select, °back, °side with, °campaign for: *Given the choice, they plumped for a film rather than the circus.*
—*n.* **4** °drop, plunk, °flop, thump, clunk, °clump, °thud, °bump: *He dropped the book on the floor with a plump.*
—*adv.* **5** abruptly, °suddenly, °directly, unhesitatingly, at °once, unexpectedly, surprisingly, without °warning, (all) of a °sudden, plunk, bang: *As I came out of the bank, I ran plump into a policeman.*
—*adj.* **6** °direct, unequivocal, unmistakable, unambiguous, °definite, °definitive, °blunt, °simple, °plain, °forthright, °downright, °straight, °matter-of-fact: *He asked her to marry him and she gave him a plump 'no'.*

plunder *v.* **1** °pillage, °loot, °rob, °ravage, °ransack, °rifle, despoil, °spoil, vandalize, °sack, °strip, maraud, °devastate, °desolate, lay °waste: *The attacking army plundered the villages.* **2** °prey on *or* upon, °pirate, °capture, °seize: *The buccaneers plundered the Spanish treasure ships on the high seas.*
—*n.* **3** °pillage, looting, °robbery, °depredation, rapine, despoliation, spoliation, vandalization, °sack, vandalism, vandalizing, sacking: *It is said that the plunder of Rome took no more than a fortnight.* **4** °booty, °loot, °spoils, °prizes, *Slang* boodle: *The police displayed an Aladdin's cave of plunder recovered from the thieves.*

plunge *v.* **1** °descend, °drop, °plummet, °dive, °pitch, nosedive, °fall (headlong): *They lost their footing, and both Holmes and Moriarty plunged into the abyss.* **2** °submerge, °sink, °immerse; engulf, °overwhelm: *I plunged my hand in the icy water to retrieve the keys. She plunged herself into her work to try to forget him.*
—*n.* **3** °dive, nosedive, °fall, °pitch, °plummet, °drop, descent; submersion, immersion: *After the scandal his career took a plunge from which it never recovered. Every winter they take a plunge into the icy waters of the Serpentine.* **4** °gamble, wager, °bet, °risk: *Are you taking the plunge with an investment in South America?*

plus *prep.* **1** and, added to, increased by, with the °addition of, with an °increment of, (coupled) with,

together with: *Two plus three equals five. Your initial deposit plus accumulated interest will make a substantial sum.*
—*adj.* **2** added, additional, °supplementary, °extra: *One must take into account the plus value of the good publicity.*
—*n.* **3** °addition, °bonus, °extra, °gain, °benefit, °asset, °advantage, °profit, °return: *Improvements constitute a big plus in evaluating the building.*

plush *adj.* °luxurious, °posh, costly, (de) luxe, °palatial, °lavish, °rich, °opulent, °sumptuous, °regal, °elegant, *Colloq* ritzy, classy, *Old-fashioned* swank(y): *I had no idea that you lived in such plush surroundings.*

ply *n.* layer, leaf, thickness, °fold: *These seams are sewn through two plies of fabric.*

pocket *n.* **1** °pouch, °sack, °bag, °receptacle, reticule, satchel: *You should always have a clean handkerchief in your pocket.* **2** °cavity, °pit, °hollow, crater: *We found water that had collected in pockets in the surface of the rock.* **3** °area, °island, °camp, °centre, °cluster, concentration: *Leaders encountered pockets of resistance to the new policies among the farmers.*
—*v.* **4** °take, °appropriate, °keep; filch, °embezzle, °steal, purloin, thieve, °pilfer, °help oneself to, palm, *Colloq* °walk off *or* away with, °pinch, °swipe, °rip off, °hook, °lift, snitch, *Brit* °nick, snaffle: *While collecting for charity, Johnson was known to have pocketed occasional contributions.*

poem *n.* verse, °lyric, °rhyme *or Archaic* rime, °song, ode, rhapsody, °jingle, ditty: *The anthology contains poems by politicians.*

poet *n.* poetess, versifier, metrist, lyricist *or* lyrist, versemaker, sonneteer, elegist, bard, °minstrel; rhymester *or* rimester *or* rhymer *or* rimer, poetaster: *A widely published poet, Constance is often invited to give readings.*

poetic *adj.* **1** poetical, °lyric(al), metrical, °musical, melodic; °idyllic, elegiac, georgic, °rhapsodic, epic, dithyrambic: *She bought a volume of the poetic works of John Keats.* **2** artistic, °aesthetic, Parnassian, Hippocrenian, °melodious: *The novel contains some poetic passages of surpassing quality.*

poetry *n.* verse, versification, metrical composition, metrics, °rhyme, *Archaic* poesy: *Modern poetry is often rather obscure.*

po-faced *adj.* stern-visaged, austere, °dour, disapproving, frowning, °grave, saturnine, °solemn, °sombre, humourless, °grim, °forbidding, °severe, °strait-laced, uncompromising, puritanical, prim, °prudish, °gruff, °bluff, curmudgeonly: *Despite having a po-faced approach to his work, William has a keen sense of humour when off duty.*

poignant *adj.* **1** distressing, upsetting, °agonizing, °grievous, °painful, woeful, °melancholy, °blue, °sad, °sorrowful, °tragic, °disastrous, °heart-rending, heartbreaking, °excruciating, °bitter, °pathetic, °pitiable, °piteous, °pitiful, °miserable, °moving, °touching: *The biography also covers the poignant early years, spent largely in orphanages and foster homes.* **2** °keen, °acute, °intense, °incisive, °sharp, stinging, °pointed, °piercing, °penetrating, barbed, °cutting, °caustic, acid, acerbic, °bitter, °biting, mordant, °sarcastic, °sardonic, °severe: *The headmaster's poignant remarks about honesty and loyalty really hurt.* **3** °sincere, °earnest, °heartfelt, °deep, °profound, °dramatic, deeply felt, °stirring, °moving, °touching, °emotional: *The reunion of the little boy and his dog was the most poignant moment in the film.*

point *n.* **1** °dot, °mark, °speck; (full) stop, °period; decimal point: *The writing is smudged, but that looks like a point at the end of the line.* **2** °tip, °peak, apex, °spike, °spur, prong, °sharp end: *Be careful of the point of that knife.* **3** °spot, °place, °stage, °position; °site, °station, °location, °locale: *We have reached the point of no return on that subject. I stopped at a few points along the way to admire the view.* **4** °time, °moment, °instant, °juncture: *At that point, we were summoned by the dinner bell.* **5** °focus, °essence, °meat, °pith, quiddity, °substance, °heart, °nucleus, crux, °nub, °core, °bottom, °details, *Colloq* guts, nitty-gritty: *I wish he would stop all the palaver and get to the point.* **6** °purpose, °intent, °intention, °aim, °goal, °object, °objective, °sense: *What was the point of bringing that piece of gossip into the discussion?* **7** °thrust, °drift, °theme, purport, °burden, °import, °implication, °significance, signification, °sense, °meaning; °application, applicability, relevancy, appropriateness: *We found it difficult to see the point of the argument.* **8** promontory, °projection, headland, °cape, peninsula: *It may take us a day to sail round the point.* **9** °brink, °verge: *We were on the point of leaving when the guest of honour finally arrived.* **10** °detail, °particular, °item, °element, nicety, °aspect, facet, °matter, °issue, °subject, °question; specifics: *Some of the points in her speech need clarification.* **11** °pointer, °hint, °suggestion, piece of °advice, °tip: *The golf pro at the club gave me some good points on improving my swing.* **12** °thought, °idea, °consideration; °notion, °view, °plan, °tactic; something: *That's a point to keep in mind if you buy another sailing-boat.* **13** °unit, °tally, °score: *She made her point and went on to win the match.* **14** °attribute, °characteristic, °feature, °aspect, °trait, °quality, °side, °property: *I suppose he has his good points, too.* **15** ***beside the point***: °irrelevant, inapt, °inappropriate, malapropos, °incidental, °immaterial, unimportant, °pointless, °inconsequential: *The fact that she's my sister is beside the point.* **16** ***in point of***: in °reference to, °regarding, as regards, in the °matter of, °concerning, with °respect to: *In point of date, the two events coincide perfectly.* **17** ***make a point of*** or *US also* ***make (it) a point to***: make an °effort (to), put *or* place °emphasis on, go out of one's way (to); °emphasize, °single out, °stress: *He made a point of apologizing to the hostess for his behaviour. She made a special point of forgiving him.* **18** ***to the point***: °relevant, °pertinent, °appropriate, °fitting, apropos, germane, apt, °applicable, apposite: *The speech was short and to the point.*
—*v.* **19** Often, ***point to***: °indicate, call *or* °direct attention to: *Desirée pointed to the building and asked what it was.* **20** °direct, °level, °aim, °train: *I awoke to find her pointing a gun at my head.* **21** ***point out***: **a** °designate, call *or* °direct attention to, °show, °exhibit, °indicate, °identify: *The taxi driver pointed out all the sights as we drove along.* **b** °say, °bring up, °mention, allude to, °emphasize, °stress, point up, °single out; call attention to, °remind: *I'd like to point out that you have rarely won at bridge. She pointed out the fallacy in his argument.* **22** ***point up***: °emphasize, °stress, accentuate, underline, underscore, °accent, °spotlight: *Such errors point up the need to double-check everything.*

point-blank *adj.* **1** °direct, °straight, °blunt, °flat, straightforward, °abrupt, °categorical, °explicit, uncompromising, °unmitigated, unalloyed, °downright, °outright, to the °point, °straight from the shoulder, (open and) °above-board, unreserved: *I asked her out to dinner and got a point-blank refusal.* **2** °close, °short, °nearby: *He was shot at point-blank range.*
—*adv.* **3** °directly, °straight (away), °right away, bluntly, °flat, flatly, abruptly, categorically, unqualifiedly, explicitly, uncompromisingly, unmitigatedly, °outright, unreservedly, plainly, frankly, °openly, candidly: *He turned her down point-blank when she offered him the job.* **4** °directly, °straight: *He fired point-blank at the target.*

pointed *adj.* **1** needle-shaped, °sharp, °acute, barbed, peaked, spiked, spiky, *Technical* acuminate, cuspidate, aciform, acicular, aciculiform, aculeous, apiculate, spiculate, serrate(d), mucroniform, mucronulate, mucronate(d), muricate, hebetate: *The child was poking holes in the sand with a pointed stick.* **2** °incisive, °piercing, °cutting, °sharp, °pungent, °keen, °penetrating, °telling, °trenchant, °biting, unmistakable: *The critic made a few pointed remarks about the actors' reading of the lines.*

pointer *n.* **1** °indicator, °rod, °stick; °index, °sign, arrow, *Typography* fist: *The pointer is used to call attention to something important.* **2** °tip, °advice, °hint, °suggestion, °recommendation, piece of °advice: *McLeod gave me a few pointers on how to improve the restaurant service.*

pointless *adj.* °purposeless, °aimless, °worthless, °ineffective, °meaningless, °ineffectual, °futile, unproductive, °fruitless, °bootless, °useless, °vain, °senseless, °absurd, °silly, °stupid, °inane, asinine, fatuous, °preposterous, °nonsensical, °ridiculous, °empty, °hollow: *After her paper, someone rose and wasted half an hour making pointless remarks.*

point of view *n.* **1** °viewpoint, °perspective, °approach, °position, °angle, °slant, °orientation, °outlook, °stance, °standpoint, vantage °point: *From his point of view, I can see why Fred thinks the research is a waste of time.* **2** °opinion, °view, °belief, (way of) °thinking, °principle, °doctrine: *Shouldn't everyone be entitled to express a point of view?*

poise *n.* **1** °balance, equilibrium, equipoise, equiponderance, °parity, °par: *The chariots of the gods in even poise, obeying the rein, glide rapidly.* **2** composure, °control, self-possession, aplomb, °assurance, °dignity, equanimity, °sang-froid, cool-headedness, imperturbability, °presence of mind, coolness, staidness, °reserve, sedateness, calmness, °serenity, tranquillity, *Colloq* °cool: *Jane's poise is remarkable, despite the heckling by the audience.*
—*v.* **3** °balance, be balanced, °hover, °hang, °float; make *or* be *or* get °ready, °prepare: *The boulder was poised on the edge of the cliff.*

poised *adj.* **1** composed, controlled, °self-possessed, unflappable, (self-)°confident, (self-)assured, °dignified, cool-headed, imperturbable, unruffled, °cool, °staid, °reserved, °sedate, °calm, °serene, °tranquil, *Colloq* together: *For a lad of eleven, Richard is quite poised.* **2** °ready, standing by, waiting, °prepared: *Our commando unit is poised to attack at your signal.* **3** teetering, hovering, tottering, wavering, suspended, trembling, wobbling, balanced: *In the present business climate, the company is poised on the brink of bankruptcy.*

poison *n.* **1** toxin, °venom, bane; miasma, mephitis: *The chemical plant was found to be releasing poisons into the atmosphere. He kills rats using poison.* **2** virus, bane, cancer, canker, °corrupt *or* °evil influence, °pestilence, °plague, °blight: *The drug barons continue to spread their poison throughout the world.*
—*v.* **3** defile, °adulterate, infect, °taint, °pollute; °contaminate, °debase, °pervert, °vitiate, °subvert, °warp, envenom: *Chemicals from the nearby plant have poisoned the drinking-water. Why have you poisoned the child's mind against eating spinach?* **4** °murder, °kill, do away with, °destroy, °dispatch *or* despatch: *Lucrezia Borgia poisoned her enemies in ingenious ways.*

poisonous *adj.* **1** °lethal, °deadly, °fatal, °mortal, toxic, septic, °virulent, noxious *or Rare* nocuous, °venomous, °malignant, pernicious, miasmic, mephitic: *Poisonous effluents were leaked into the rivers by the chemical plant.* **2** malicious, malevolent, °malignant, corruptive, °vicious, baleful, °evil, °foul, °diabolic(al), defamatory, libellous, °slanderous, °dangerous, deleterious: *They have been spreading poisonous gossip about him again.*

poke *v.* **1** °jab, °stick, °prod, °dig, goad, °stab, °thrust, °push, elbow, °nudge, °jog, jostle, °butt, shove: *Be careful not to poke someone in the eye with your umbrella. He tells a joke, then pokes me in the ribs to make sure I've got it.* **2** °punch, °hit, °strike, °box, cuff, smite, smack: *I made a suggestive remark and she poked me in the jaw.* **3** °pry, nose (about *or* around), stick one's nose into, °intrude, °dig, °probe, °investigate; °meddle, °interfere, °butt in, °tamper; *Colloq* °snoop: *I wish they would stop poking into my affairs.* **4** ***poke fun (at)***: °tease, °ridicule, °mock, make °fun of, °jeer (at), °chaff, °taunt, °twit, make °sport of, needle, *Colloq* kid, rib, *Brit* °send up, take the mickey out of: *People who don't understand something often poke fun at it. Stop poking fun at my hat.*
—*n.* **5** °jab, °prod, °dig, °stab, °thrust, °push, elbow, °finger, °nudge, °jog, jostle, °butt, shove: *Every time Rodney wants to emphasize a point, he gives you a poke.* **6** °punch, °hit, °box, °jab, cuff, smack, °blow: *If anyone says anything bad about you, I'll give him a poke in the nose.*

polar *adj.* **1** arctic, Antarctic, °frigid, °icy, glacial, °freezing, frozen, numbing, Siberian, hibernal, hyperborean, brumal, °wintry: *It is positively polar in the house without the heat turned on.* **2** °opposite, °opposed, antithetical, °contrary, °contradictory, diametric, antipodal, antagonistic, °hostile: *Dante felt Good and Evil to be the two polar elements of the Creation, on which it all turns.*

pole[1] *n.* °rod, °stick, °staff, °spar, °shaft, mast, °standard, °upright; flag-pole, flagstaff, jackstaff; beanpole, hop-pole: *We had to use a long pole to get the kite down from the tree.*

pole[2] *n.* **1** °extremity, °end, °limit, °extreme: *Their views are at opposite poles and they cannot agree.* **2** ***from pole to pole***: °everywhere, all over, °far and °wide, high and low, leaving no stone unturned, °throughout the world *or* the length and breadth of the land, *Colloq US* everyplace: *He searched for her from pole to pole.* **3** ***poles apart***: (very *or* completely) °different, worlds apart, at °opposite extremes, at °opposite ends of the earth, at °odds, irreconcilable: *I'm afraid that the union and management remain poles apart on the issue of working hours.*

police *n.* **1** constabulary, policemen, policewomen, police officers, *Colloq* boys in blue, the (long arm of the) °law, the cops, the gendarmes, *Slang* the coppers, the fuzz, *Brit* the (Old) Bill, *US* the heat: *There was a bit of an argument, so we called the police.*
—*v.* **2** °patrol, °guard, °watch, °protect: *Additional officers were assigned to police the neighbourhood.* **3** °enforce, °regulate, °administer, °oversee, °control, °observe, °supervise, °monitor: *A unit was established to police the terms of the agreement.*

police officer *n.* °officer, policeman, policewoman, °constable, *Brit* °police °constable, PC, WPC, *Chiefly US* peace °officer, patrolman, patrolwoman, *Colloq* cop, gendarme, *Brit* bobby; *Slang* copper, fuzz, flatfoot, *Brit* rozzer, Old Bill, *Offensive and derogatory* pig, *Historical* peeler, *US* bull, fuzz ball: *The police officers then asked if I wouldn't mind helping with their inquiries.*

policy *n.* °approach, °procedure, (game) °plan, °design, °scheme, °programme, °method, °system, °management, °conduct, °behaviour, °strategy, °tactic(s), °principle(s), °protocol, °regulation, °rule, °custom, °way, °practice, ways and °means, °action: *What policy should we follow regarding interest rates?*

polish *v.* **1** °shine, °brighten, burnish, buff, furbish, wax, °clean, °smooth, °rub, °gloss: *He polished up the handles so carefully That now he is the ruler of the Queen's navy.* **2** Often, ***polish up***: °refine, °improve, °perfect, °finish, °cultivate, ameliorate, °enhance; °correct, emend: *If you polish up the article we might consider it for publication.* **3** ***polish off***: **a** conclude, °end, °terminate, °finish: *Ned polished off his homework in less than an hour.* **b** °kill, slay, °murder, °dispatch *or* despatch, °destroy, °dispose of, do away with, liquidate, °eliminate, *Slang* °bump off, °rub out, do in, take for a °ride: *Three platoons were polished off quickly.* **c** °dispose of, °put away, °eat, °consume, wolf (down): *In a few minutes, MacGregor had polished off the entire meal.* **4** ***polish up***: °study, °review, °learn, *Archaic* con, *Colloq* bone up (on), *Slang Brit* swot up (on): *If you're going to Málaga, you'd better polish up your Spanish.*
—*n.* **5** °gloss, °shine, °lustre, °sheen, °glaze, smoothness, °brilliance, °sparkle, °gleam, °glow, brightness, °radiance: *You cannot imagine what a fine polish she put on that old table.* **6** wax, °oil: *The new polish really put a shine on the desk.*

polished *adj.* **1** °accomplished, °adept, °proficient, °expert, °fine, °outstanding, °skilful, °gifted, °masterful, masterly, °virtuoso, °excellent, °superior, °superb, °superlative; °flawless, °faultless, °perfect, °impeccable: *Edna is quite a polished cellist. She gave a polished performance.* **2** °refined, °elegant, °cultivated, °graceful, °debonair, °sophisticated, urbane, *soigné(e)*, courtly, °genteel, cultured, civilized, °well-bred, well-mannered, °polite: *Under her guidance, James has become a polished gentleman.*

polite *adj.* **1** °civil, °respectful, well-mannered, mannerly, °courteous, deferential, °diplomatic, °tactful, °formal, °proper, °cordial: *We asked our new neighbours to tea but were met with a polite refusal.* **2** See **polished, 2,** above.

politic *adj.* **1** °ingenious, °shrewd, °crafty, canny, cunning, °designing, °scheming, °clever, °wily, °foxy, °tricky, °artful, °Machiavellian, °evasive, °shifty, *Colloq* cagey: *Daniel is politic enough to know how to manoeuvre situations to his benefit.* **2** °tactful, °diplomatic, °discreet, °prudent, °judicious, °wise, °sage, sagacious, °sensible, °intelligent, percipient, °discriminating, °far-sighted, °expedient, °perceptive: *It was politic of the winner to share the prize with those who had helped him most.*

political *adj.* **1** governmental, civic, °civil, °public, °state, °national, federal; administrative, bureaucratic: *The movement began as an attempt to gain political freedom.* **2** °partisan, °factious, factional: *A coalition government was formed by the major political parties.*

politician *n.* legislator, lawmaker, statesman, stateswoman; °minister, *Brit* Member of Parliament, MP, *US* public *or* civil °servant, administrator, °official, bureaucrat, office-bearer, senator, congressman, congresswoman, °representative, assembly-man, assembly-woman, selectman; *Colloq US derogatory* politico, (°political) boss *or* hack, °machine politician, ward-heeler, wirepuller: *Some politicians have given a bad name to the art of politics.*

politics *n.* **1** °public affairs, °political science, civics, °civil affairs, °government, statecraft, °diplomacy, statesmanship: *Hume viewed politics as people united in society and dependent on each other.* **2** manoeuvring, manipulation, wirepulling, °machination: *Office politics are such that they wouldn't dare dismiss that department head.*

poll *n.* **1** voting, °vote, returns, °tally, figures: *The poll shows that the incumbents are not as secure as they thought.* **2** opinion poll, °survey, °canvass, census, ballot, °count: *A poll of home-owners shows that most would like to own washing machines.*
—*v.* **3** °sample, °survey, °question, °canvass, ballot, °ask, °interview; °count, °enumerate, °tally, °register, °record: *We polled teenagers to determine their reaction to a youth centre; those in favour polled 73 per cent.* **4** °receive, °get, °win, °register, °tally: *Cavendish polled more than 60 per cent of the votes cast.*

pollute *v.* **1** °contaminate, °adulterate, befoul, °foul, °soil, °spoil, °taint, °stain, °dirty, °sully, °blight, °poison: *These factories must be prevented from continuing to pollute the atmosphere.* **2** °corrupt, °desecrate, °profane, defile, °violate: *The altar was polluted because it had been touched by a non-believer.*

pollution *n.* contamination, adulteration, corruption, polluting, fouling, befouling, soiling, spoiling, tainting, staining, dirtying, sullying, blighting, poisoning, vitiation: *Laws were passed to prosecute those responsible for the pollution of the environment.*

pomp *n.* °glory, °grandeur, magnificence, °splendour, °show, °extravaganza, °pageantry, °ceremony, °spectacle, °brilliance, ceremoniousness: *The Chinese court's pomp and display of wealth had never before been seen by a westerner.*

pompous *adj.* **1** °vain, vainglorious, °proud, °arrogant, °pretentious, °ostentatious, °showy, °grandiose, °haughty, °overbearing, °conceited, °egotistical, °self-important, °boastful, °braggart, °inflated, °snobbish, magisterial, imperious, pontifical, °affected, exhibitionist, *Colloq* uppity, highfalutin *or* hifalutin, °hoity-toity, high-hat, *Slang* snooty, snotty: *Don't you despise the pompous way Marshall struts about in that ridiculous uniform?* **2** °bombastic, °flowery, grandiloquent, °pedantic, °stuffy, fustian, orotund, °ornate, embroidered, flatulent, °windy, turgid, °inflated, high-flown, euphuistic: *He's always making long-winded, pompous speeches because he loves the sound of his own voice.*

ponder *v.* °consider, °muse (over *or* on), °brood (over *or* upon *or* on), °mull over, °deliberate (over), °meditate (upon *or* on), °think (over *or* on *or* about), °weigh, ruminate (over), °chew over, cogitate, excogitate, °reflect (on *or* over), °contemplate: *I shall need a while to ponder the answer to that question. Give me a little more time to ponder.*

ponderous *adj.* **1** °weighty, °unwieldy, °heavy, °massive, °huge, °big, °large, °awkward, °clumsy, cumbersome *or* cumbrous: *A ponderous juggernaut bore down on us, completely out of control.* **2** °dull, °tedious, °laboured, °laborious, °tiresome, turgid, °boring, °dreary, °pedestrian, °stilted, °windy, °inflated, long-winded, °wordy, verbose, prolix, elephantine, °pompous, grandiloquent, overdone: *Many students faced with textbooks written in ponderous prose become disenchanted with learning.*

pool *n.* **1** pond, lake, tarn, mere, lagoon; swimming-pool, °leisure pool, *Brit* paddling pool, *US* wading pool, *Formal* natatorium: *We found an icy mountain pool where we went for a swim.* **2** °collection, °fund(s), °purse, stakes, °reserve(s), bank, *Colloq* °pot, jackpot, °kitty: *So far we have too little money in the pool for an office party at Christmas.* **3** °syndicate, °trust, °group, consortium, cartel, °combine: *The object of the pool was the private regulation of market prices, which is illegal.*
—*v.* **4** °accumulate, °collect, °gather, °combine, °merge, consolidate, °amalgamate, °league, bring *or* come *or* °band *or* °get together, °team (up) with: *We would do better if we pooled our resources.*

poor *adj.* **1** °needy, °destitute, °indigent, in °want, in °need, penniless, poverty-stricken, °impoverished, °badly off, necessitous, poor as a church-mouse, °straitened, pinched, in reduced °circumstances, impecunious, financially °embarrassed, down and out, out of pocket, ruined, °insolvent, bankrupt, *Colloq* °broke, °hard up, on one's uppers, °short, *US* wiped out, *Brit* in Queer Street, *Slang Brit* skint: *They were poor and didn't know where their next meal was coming from.* **2** °low, °bad, skimpy, °meagre, scant, °scanty, °inadequate, °deficient, °insufficient, °sparse: *How can a family of five survive on such a poor salary? These days, 3 per cent would be considered a poor return on investment.* **3** °barren, unproductive, unfruitful, °fruitless, °infertile, °sterile; depleted, °exhausted, °impoverished: *This is poor soil, and no amount of cultivation is likely to make it productive.* **4** °bad, °awful, °inadequate, °unsatisfactory, °unacceptable, bumbling, °inefficient, amateurish, °unprofessional, °inferior, second-rate, third-rate, low-grade, °shabby, °shoddy, °mediocre, °defective, °faulty, °flawed, substandard, °sorry, not up to °par *or* snuff, °slipshod, below *or* under °par, *Colloq* °rotten, °lousy: *They did a poor job repairing my car. Her latest recital was pretty poor.* **5** °insignificant, °slight, °paltry, °inconsequential, °mean, °modest, trivial, °trifling: *They made only a poor attempt to correct the problem.* **6** °unfortunate, unlucky, °pathetic, luckless, °pitiful, °pitiable, ill-fated, °miserable, °wretched, ill-starred, star-crossed, jinxed, hapless: *The poor chap lost his entire family in the disaster.* **7** °bad, °ill: *Aunt Theresa has been in poor health lately.*

poorly *adv.* **1** °badly, inadequately, unsatisfactorily, incompetently, inexpertly, improperly, crudely, unprofessionally, amateurishly: *The decorators you recommended have done their work very poorly indeed.*

—*adj.* **2** unwell, °indisposed, ailing, °sick, below °par, *Colloq* °rotten, under the °weather: *Charles is rather poorly, I'm afraid.*

pop *v.* **1** °burst, °explode, bang, °go off: *The balloon popped, making me jump.* **2** Often, ***pop in** or **out** or **by***: °visit, °stop, °call, °appear, *Colloq* °drop in, *Brit* °nip in: *Guess who popped in to see me on his way to the airport.* **3** °bulge, °protrude, °stick out, *US* bug out: *The little boy's eyes popped when they brought in the birthday cake.*
—*n.* **4** °explosion, bang, °report, °crack: *The Christmas cracker went off with a loud pop.* **5** soft °drink, soda (water); cola, *Brit* fizzy °drink, lemonade, *US* soda pop: *A bottle of pop for my daughter and a pint of bitter for me, please.*

populace *n.* °people, masses, commonalty *or* commonality, (general) °public, commoners, multitude, hoi polloi, °crowd, °throng, °rabble, peasantry, proletariat, °common °folk, rank and file, working °class, bourgeoisie, °mob, *Derogatory* great °unwashed, °riffraff, °rabble, *canaille*, ragtag and bobtail: *Some MPs act on behalf of their own constituencies rather than the populace at large.*

popular *adj.* **1** °favourite, °favoured, in °favour, accepted, well-received, approved, (°well-)liked, °fashionable, in °fashion, °stylish, in °vogue, °celebrated, °renowned, acclaimed, °famous, in °demand, sought-after, all the °rage, *Colloq* °trendy, in, °hot: *You would become a millionaire overnight if you could accurately predict the popular music of the coming year.* **2** °conventional, °stock, commonplace, °public, °normal, °standard, °general, °universal, °average, °everyday, °ordinary, °routine, °common, °habitual, °prevalent, °current, °prevailing, °dominant, °predominant, predominating, °customary: *His films cater to popular tastes in science fiction.* **3** °lay, non-professional, °amateur, understandable, °accessible, popularized, simplified: *He presents a popular astronomy programme on TV.*

popularity *n.* °favour, acceptance, °approval, °esteem, °regard, repute, °reputation, °vogue, °trend, stylishness, °renown, acclaim, °fame, °celebrity, lionization, (hero-)°worship, *Colloq* trendiness: *The immense popularity of her novels in America has made her very rich.*

popularly *adv.* commonly, °generally, °ordinarily, °usually, °universally, °widely, regularly, customarily, prevalently, habitually: *It is a popularly held belief among the French that their wine is the best in the world.*

populate *v.* colonize, °settle, °people, °occupy; °inhabit, °dwell in, reside in, °live in: *Shiploads of families braved the voyage to populate the New World.*

population *n.* °people, °populace, °inhabitants, °residents, °natives, °denizens, citizenry, °citizens, °folk: *In those days there was no one to look after the legal rights of the population.*

populous *adj.* crowded, (heavily) populated, peopled, teeming, thronged, crawling, swarming, jammed, jampacked, °packed: *The populous cities contrast with the sparsely inhabited rural areas.*

pore[1] *v.* ***pore over***: °study, °examine, °scrutinize, °peruse, °read, °go over, *Colloq* con: *Hamilton sits in the library, day after day, poring over books of forgotten lore.*

pore[2] *n.* °opening, orifice, °hole, °aperture, °vent, perforation, *Technical* spiracle, stoma: *A hot bath opens the pores in the skin.*

pornographic *adj.* °obscene, °lewd, °offensive, °indecent, °prurient, smutty, °taboo, °blue, °dirty, salacious, licentious, °nasty, X-rated, *Colloq* porno, *US* raunchy: *Some prudes consider anything concerning sex to be pornographic.*

pornography *n.* obscenity, smut, °filth, °dirt, erotica, *Colloq* porn: *The council voted to forbid the sale of pornography within the town precincts.*

porous *adj.* spongy, spongelike, permeable, pervious, penetrable: *The rainwater runs through the porous rock and collects in the pools below.*

port *n.* °harbour, haven, seaport; mooring, anchorage; °refuge: *We were bound east for the port of Cardiff.*

portable *adj.* transportable, °manageable, carriable, °handy, °light, lightweight, °compact, °pocket, pocket-sized, °little, °small, *US* carry-on, vest-pocket, shirt-pocket: *He needs a van just to transport his portable television, portable radio, portable hi-fi, portable typewriter, portable computer, and portable calculator.*

portentous *adj.* **1** °ominous, °threatening, °momentous, °sinister, °fateful, alarming, °menacing, °foreboding, ill-omened, °inauspicious, unfavourable, ill-starred, ill-fated, star-crossed, lowering *or* louring, °gloomy, °unpromising, unpropitious: *Precisely at midnight they appeared with the most portentous news.* **2** °extraordinary, °amazing, astonishing, astounding, °prodigious, °awesome, awe-inspiring, °remarkable, °marvellous, °phenomenal, °fabulous, °fantastic, mind-boggling, wondrous, °miraculous: *The coronation of a British monarch is truly a portentous event.*

porter[1] *n.* bearer, (baggage) °carrier *or* °attendant, *US airports* skycap, *US railways* redcap: *I tipped the porter to carry our bags to a taxi.*

porter[2] *n.* **1** concierge, cleaner, caretaker, *Chiefly US and Canadian* janitor, °superintendent, *Colloq US* super: *When we are away, the porter keeps our mail for us.* **2** door-keeper, °watchman, doorman, gatekeeper, concierge, *US* tiler: *He went to my club, but the porter would not let him in.*

portico *n.* porch, veranda *or* verandah, gallery, colonnade, galilee: *At the front of the mansion, six Corinthian pillars support a wide portico.*

portion *n.* **1** °segment, °part, °section, °division, subdivision, °parcel, °piece, hunk, chunk, °lump, °wedge, °slice, °sliver, fraction, °fragment, °bit, °morsel, °scrap: *A portion of the masonry fell into the street in the earthquake.* **2** °share, °part, °allotment, °quota, °ration, apportionment, °allowance, allocation, °assignment, °percentage, °measure, °division, °quantity: *The size of an investor's portion depends on the amount invested.* **3** °helping, serving; °ration, °plate, °platter: *He complained that the portions in* nouvelle cuisine *are too small.*
—*v.* **4** Often, ***portion out***: apportion, °share out, allocate, °ration, °allot, °partition, °assign, consign, °dole out, °deal (out), °parcel out, °distribute, °administer, °dispense, °disperse, °divide, °split up, °carve up, °cut up, °break up, °section, *Colloq* divvy up: *The conquered territories were then portioned out among the victors.*

portrait *n.* °picture, °likeness, °image, sketch, °rendering, vignette; °representation, °description, °profile, °thumbnail sketch, portrayal, picturization, depiction; °account, °story, characterization, °study, °record, °file, dossier: *We have the culprit's portrait in our rogues' gallery. We need a more accurate portrait of the kidnapper.*

portray *v.* **1** °represent, °picture, °show, depict, °paint, °render, °characterize, °describe, delineate: *She is portrayed wearing the Castelli tiara. Why must I always be portrayed as the villain?* **2** °act *or* °play (the part *or* role of), take the part *or* role of, °represent, °pose as, impersonate: *She portrays an aged crone who regains her youth in the last act.*

pose *v.* **1** °sit, °model; °position, °place, °arrange, °set (up), °put: *Would you let your husband or wife pose in the nude? She posed the model standing, looking out of the window.* **2** Usually, ***pose as***: °portray, °act *or* °play (the part *or* role of), take the part *or* role of, °represent, impersonate, be disguised as, °masquerade as, °pretend *or* °profess to be, °pass (oneself off) as, °pass for, °imitate, °mimic; attitudinize, °posture, put on °airs, *Colloq* °show off: *She posed as an art expert from Switzerland. She thinks him a roué, but he's only posing.* **3** °set, °put, °ask, °submit, °broach, °posit,

°advance, °present, predicate, postulate: *The interviewer posed some questions that were quite embarrassing.*
—*n.* **4** °position, °attitude, °posture, °stance: *Her profile is not shown to best advantage in that pose.* **5** °affectation, °act, °pretence, attitudinizing, affectedness, °display, façade, °show, °ostentation: *His interest in art is just a pose to impress her.*

poseur *n.* posturer, exhibitionist, °pretender, °impostor, masquerader, attitudinizer; °fake, faker, dissembler, °fraud, *Colloq* °show-off, °phoney *or US also* phony: *He talks about literature, but he's a poseur who just spouts the opinions of others.*

posh *adj.* (de) luxe, °luxurious, °elegant, °sumptuous, °lavish, °opulent, °rich, °royal, °regal, °luxury, °grand, °fashionable, *Colloq* swank(y), classy, ritzy, *Slang* snazzy: *You ought to see what a posh office my son has!*

posit *v.* postulate, hypothesize, °propound, °put *or* °set forth, °put forward, °advance, °propose, °pose, °offer, °submit, predicate: *If we posit a downturn in prices next year, how does that affect our profit forecasts?*

position *n.* **1** °posture, °attitude, °stance, °pose; °disposition, °arrangement, disposal: *Once in a while, he would change his position so that he faced the sun. With the pieces in this position the chess game is a draw.* **2** °site, °placement, °situation, °whereabouts, placing, emplacement, °location: *Those bearings put his present position about 20 miles west of Cádiz.* **3** °viewpoint, °point of view, °outlook, °attitude, °angle, °slant, °stance, °stand, °opinion, °inclination, °leaning, °bent, °sentiment, °feeling, way of °thinking: *My solicitor is pessimistic about my position in this case.* **4** °status, °condition, °state, °circumstances, °situation: *Our financial position* vis-à-vis *investment in gilt bonds has changed.* **5** °class, °caste, °place, °rank, °standing, °station, °status, °importance: *They insist on knowing the social position of the girl's family.* **6** °job, °occupation, °situation, °post, °office, °function, °appointment, °capacity, °place, °role, *Colloq* billet, berth, *Australian* possie *or* possy: *My mother's position as managing director had nothing to do with my getting a promotion.* **7** °hypothesis, °thesis, °principle, contention, °assertion, predication, °belief, °proposition, postulate: *His position is based on the implications of the third law of thermodynamics.*
—*v.* **8** °put, °place, °situate, °site, °set, °fix, °settle, °dispose, °arrange: *The pointer is again positioned at zero. Position your forces along this ridge and stay on full alert.* **9** °place, °locate, °establish, °determine, °fix, localize: *The scientists positioned the seismic activity as being along the San Andreas fault.*

positive *adj.* **1** °sure, °certain, °definite, unequivocal, °categorical, °absolute, °unqualified, unambiguous, unmistakable, clear-cut, °clear, °explicit, °express, decisive, °indisputable, indubitable, °unquestionable, unquestioned, incontestable, uncontested, undeniable, °reliable, °persuasive, convincing, irrefutable: *The police have positive evidence that the men are innocent of any crime. Spending this evening with you has been a positive delight.* **2** °definitive, °emphatic, °decided, °forceful, °firm, °peremptory, °definite: *He gave a positive denial when asked if he had agreed to let the hostages go. She made a positive commitment to meet me here at noon.* **3** °sure, °certain, °confident, convinced, satisfied: *Are you positive that the last train is at midnight?* **4** °beneficial, °favourable, °complimentary, °productive, °useful: *I heard many positive things about the way she handled herself at the interview.* **5** °overconfident, °dogmatic, doctrinaire, pontifical, °opinionated, pigheaded, °stubborn, °obstinate, obdurate, °arbitrary, overweening, °arrogant, °assertive, °dictatorial, °despotic, imperious, *Rare* thetic(al): *His problem is that he is quite positive about things that simply are not so.* **6** °practical, °realistic, utilitarian, °productive, °functional, pragmatic(al), °matter-of-fact, *Colloq* hard-nosed: *They have taken a positive approach to studying the economics of small businesses.* **7** encouraging, °supportive, °constructive, reassuring, °enthusiastic, °favourable, affirmative, yes, confirming: *Our plan to buy out the company has received a positive reaction from our bankers. Asked if they would buy our product, businessmen gave a positive response.* **8** auspicious, °promising, °propitious, encouraging; °optimistic, °favourable, °cheerful, °confident; *Colloq* bullish, °upbeat: *In the long run, the picture for home-owners looks positive. It pays to maintain a positive outlook and not get depressed.* **9** °complete, utter, °total, °perfect, °out-and-out, consummate, °unmitigated, °thorough, thoroughgoing; egregious, °glaring, °stark, °sheer, °outright, °unqualified, unequivocal: *You were a positive idiot not to let me know you needed help. All attempts at reconciliation ended in positive disaster.*

positively *adv.* °definitely, °absolutely, unquestionably, certainly, (most) assuredly, undeniably, °undoubtedly, °surely, to be °sure, emphatically, unmistakably, unqualifiedly, categorically, indisputably, beyond *or* without (a °shadow of) a °doubt, indubitably, beyond °question: *The wine list at Le Maître's is positively the best in the area.*

possess *v.* **1** be °possessed *or* in °possession of, °have, own, °enjoy, be blessed *or* endowed with: *In the 19th century, the family possessed great wealth.* **2** °have, be born *or* °gifted *or* endowed with, °contain, °embody, °embrace, °include: *He possesses a talent to amuse people. Man does not possess as keen a sense of smell as many animals.* **3** °dominate, °control, °govern, °consume, take °control of, preoccupy, °obsess; °charm, °captivate, °enchant, cast a °spell on *or* over, °bewitch, enthral: *What possessed her to think that I could help? He behaves as if he is possessed by the devil.* **4** ***be possessed with*** *or* ***of***: °have, be held *or* influenced *or* dominated by, be imbued *or* inspired *or* permeated *or* °affected with: *She became possessed with the notion that she could sing. Fiona believes herself the only person possessed of reason.* **5** ***possess oneself of***: °acquire, °achieve, °get, °come by, °gain, °come into, °win, °obtain, °procure, °secure, °take, °seize, °take *or* °gain °possession of: *Kevin has possessed himself of the only comfortable bed in the place.*

possessed *adj.* obsessed, driven, controlled, dominated, ridden, bedevilled, consumed, haunted, pressed, maddened, crazed, demented, frenzied, *Colloq* eaten up: *He behaved like a man possessed.*

possession *n.* **1** ownership, °title, proprietorship, °control, °hold, °tenure, keeping, °care, °custody, guardianship, °protection: *The paintings are now in my possession.* **2** holding, °territory, °province, °dominion, colony, protectorate: *How long will the Falkland Islands remain a possession of the Crown?* **3** ***possessions***: °belongings, °property, °effects, chattels, °assets, worldly °goods, °things: *The prison clerk placed all my possessions in an envelope, explaining that they would be returned when I was released.* **4** ***take*** *or* ***gain possession of***: °seize, °capture, °take, °conquer, °occupy, °acquire, °win, °possess oneself of, °secure, °obtain; repossess: *The raiding party gained possession of the port and surrounding area. The finance company has taken possession of my car.*

possessive *adj.* **1** °greedy, unyielding, °selfish, ungiving, ungenerous, stingy, niggardly, °materialistic, covetous, acquisitive: *He refuses to see anyone, as he is very possessive of his time.* **2** overprotective, controlling, °grasping, dominating, °domineering, °overbearing: *Anyone with a possessive parent finds it difficult to leave home.*

possibility *n.* **1** °chance, °odds, °prospect, conceivability, °feasibility, plausibility, °likelihood, admissibility: *There is a possibility of my leaving work early to meet you. What is the possibility that he might be honest? They deny even the possibility of God's existence.* **2** Often, ***possibilities***: °opportunity, potentiality, °potential, °capacity, °promise: *The old house has many large rooms and offers great possibilities.*

possible *adj.* **1** °feasible, °plausible, imaginable, conceivable, °thinkable, credible, °tenable, °reasonable, admissible: *It is remotely possible, though improbable,* *that she committed the crime.* **2** realizable, °practicable, workable, °practical, doable, achievable, attainable, reachable, accomplishable, °viable, *Colloq* on: *In the present state of the art, a fully interactive computer, operating in real time, is still not possible.*

possibly *adv.* **1** °maybe, °perhaps, God willing, *Deo volente*, if °possible, *Archaic or literary* perchance, mayhap, peradventure: *She is possibly the best person for the job.* **2** in any °way, under any circumstances, by any °chance, by any °means, at all: *Could you possibly help me find my contact lens? The weather forecast couldn't possibly be correct.*

post[1] *n.* **1** °pole, °stake, °upright, column, °pillar, °pale, °picket, °shaft, standard, newel, °pier, pylon, °pile, piling, °strut, shore, stanchion, °leg, °prop, °stay, °support, °brace: *A huge central post held up the roof.* —*v.* **2** advertise, °announce, °proclaim, °publish, °circulate, °propagate, promulgate; °put *or* °pin *or* °tack *or* °stick *or* °hang up, affix: *The notice of the meeting has been posted for all to see.*

post[2] *n.* **1** °assignment, °appointment, °position, °situation, °job, °place, °duty, °role, °function, °employment, °work, °task, chore: *Clarke was given a post as consul in some forgotten country.* —*v.* **2** °place, °put, °station, °assign, °appoint, °position, °situate, °set, °locate: *Guards have been posted around the enclosure.*

post[3] *n.* **1** postal service, °mail; °delivery; collection: *I am expecting an important letter in the post. It hasn't come in the first post.* —*v.* **2** °send, °dispatch *or* despatch, °transmit, *Chiefly US and Canadian* °mail: *I posted your cheque this morning.* **3** °record, °enter, °register, °list: *We post the daily receipts in this ledger.* **4** ***keep (someone) posted***: °inform, °advise, °brief, °notify, *Colloq* °fill (someone) in on: *Our observers have kept me posted as to your whereabouts every step of the way.*

poster *n.* placard, °notice, bill, °advertisement, °announcement, broadside, broadsheet; circular, flier: *Who designed that striking poster for the new play?*

posterior *adj.* **1** hind, °rear, °back, after, °hinder, rearward, *Nautical* aft: *The posterior legs are somewhat longer.* **2** later, after, latter, ensuing, following, succeeding, °subsequent: *Analysis has yielded evidence of the posterior origin of the lava.* —*n.* **3** °buttocks, °bottom, rump, °seat, *derrière*, behind, °rear, backside, *Colloq Brit* °bum, *US* hinie, tush *or* tushy *or* tushie, tokus *or* tochis *or* tuchis, °tail; *Taboo slang Brit* arse, *US* ass: *The term describing a person with a fat posterior is 'steatopygous'.*

posterity *n.* descendants, successors, heirs, children, °offspring, °issue, °progeny: *It is good that these buildings will be preserved for posterity. Posterity will be the judge of our success.*

post-haste *adv.* °quickly, at °once, without delay, °immediately, °directly, straight away, °right away, °promptly, speedily, °swiftly, instantly, before you can say 'Jack Robinson', before you can say 'knife', °rapidly, at full tilt, in a wink, in a trice, in the °twinkling of an eye, *Colloq* pronto, chop-chop, p.d.q. (= 'pretty damned quick'), *US and Canadian* lickety-split, like greased lightning: *He got me the report post-haste.*

post-mortem *n.* **1** autopsy, necropsy: *We'll know the cause of death after the post-mortem.* **2** °review, °analysis, *Slang US* Monday-morning quarterbacking: *We can do without the post-mortem on every bridge hand.*

postpone *v.* °delay, adjourn, °defer, keep in °abeyance, °put off *or* aside, °lay aside, °suspend, °shelve, put *or* keep on ice, temporize, dally, *Colloq* put on the back burner, *US* °table: *We ought to postpone further discussion till we have the facts.*

postponement *n.* °delay, adjournment, °abeyance, °suspension, °stay, deferment, deferral, °moratorium: *There has been a postponement of the meeting till Monday.*

posture *n.* **1** °pose, °position, °attitude, °stance, °appearance, °carriage: *She stood there in a defiant posture, with arms akimbo.* **2** °position, °condition, °situation, °state, °disposition; °arrangement, °organization, layout, array, °format: *The government adopted a conciliatory posture in the matter.* **3** °attitude, °stance, °position, °feeling, °sentiment, °outlook, (°point of) °view, °viewpoint, °orientation, °disposition, °frame of mind, °mood: *The interviewer tried to determine the general's posture on disarmament.* —*v.* **4** °pose, attitudinize, °affect, put on a °show, do for °effect, *Colloq* °show off: *Despite all her posturing, we believe her to be sincere.*

pot *n.* **1** °pan, saucepan, cauldron, cook-pot, stewpot; kettle: *How many politicians have promised the people 'a chicken in every pot'?* **2** jackpot, bank, °kitty: *You will have to add £5 to the pot to see my hand.* **3** pot-belly, °paunch, °gut, *Colloq* corporation, beer-belly, °spare tyre, *US* bay window: *If he exercised more, Patrick wouldn't have such a pot.*

potent *adj.* **1** °powerful, °strong; °mighty, °vigorous, °forceful, °formidable, °authoritative, °influential, *Literary* puissant: *A potent poison will kill those weeds. We have to reckon with an enemy that is quite potent.* **2** °effective, convincing, cogent, °persuasive, compelling, °efficacious, °telling, °sound, valid, °impressive: *Their argument is potent enough to convince the biggest sceptics.*

potential *adj.* **1** °possible, °likely, °implicit, implied, °imminent, developing, budding, embryonic, °dormant, hidden, concealed, covert, latent, quiescent, °passive, °future, unrealized, °undeveloped: *We are dealing with a potential threat to our liberty.* —*n.* **2** °capacity, °capability, °possibility, °aptitude, potency, *Colloq* the (right) stuff, what it takes: *All teenagers have potential; the problem is to teach them to exploit it to the best advantage.*

potion *n.* °draught, °brew, beverage, °drink, philtre, potation, °elixir, °tonic, cup, °dose, concoction, decoction: *The old crone gave him a tiny bottle containing the love potion.*

pot-pourri *n.* °mixture, °medley, °miscellany, °assortment, olla podrida, smorgasbord *or* smörgåsbord, gallimaufry, salmagundi, °patchwork, °collection, °hotchpotch *or US and Canadian* hodgepodge, *mélange*, motley, °pastiche *or* pasticcio, °mishmash, °jumble, °mess: *What a pot-pourri of styles is represented in that art gallery!*

potter *v.* °dabble (in *or* with), °toy with, °trifle with, fribble, °fool (with *or* about *or* around), °fritter (away), °mess (about *or* around *or* with), °tinker (with), meddle (with), °monkey (about *or* around *or* with), fidget (with), *US* putter (around *or* with), *Colloq* °fiddle (about *or* around *or* with), footle (around *or* about): *On Sundays I like to potter about in the garden.*

pottery *n.* earthenware, ceramics, terracotta, crockery, stoneware, porcelain, china, delftware: *Ornamented pottery has been found in pre-Columbian digs.*

pouch *n.* °pocket, °sack, °bag, °purse, reticule, *Dialect* poke: *A Highlander's pouch is called a sporran. As I was going out, I filled my tobacco pouch.*

pounce *v.* **1** Often, ***pounce on or upon***: °spring (on *or* upon), °leap (at *or* on), °swoop down (on *or* upon), °fall upon, °jump (at *or* on), °strike, take by °surprise *or* °unawares, °attack, °ambush, *Colloq* °mug: *As I rounded the corner, three youths pounced on me, stole my bag, and ran off.* —*n.* **2** °spring, °leap, °swoop, °jump: *The cat was on the mantel shelf in a single pounce.*

pound[1] *v.* **1** °beat, °batter, °pelt, hammer, pummel; thump, °belabour, thrash, bludgeon, cudgel, maul, °strike, *Colloq* °lambaste, *Slang* paste, clobber, work over, give (someone) the °works *or* a pasting: *She pounded on the door till someone came. It was satisfying to see him pound the class bully into submission.* **2** °crush, °powder, °pulverize, bray, comminute, triturate, mash, °pulp: *The corn must be pounded into a fine meal before use.* **3** °beat, throb, hammer, °pulse, °pulsate, palpitate: *My heart was pounding, waiting to*

see if the tiger would attack. **4** ***pound into***: °instil, °din into, °drill into, drub into, hammer into, °beat into: *Her parents have pounded into her that she must show respect to her elders.* **5** ***pound out***: °rid, °expel, °clear, °cleanse, °empty, °purge, °beat out, hammer out: *The last bit of stubbornness was pounded out of me at school.* **6** °beat out; hammer out, °produce: *The jungle drums pounded out the message that Tarzan was coming.*
—*n.* **7** pounding, °beat, beating, thump, °thumping: *The pound of horses' hooves heralded the arrival of the cavalry.*

pound[2] *n.* °enclosure, °pen, °compound, confine, yard: *My car was towed to the pound, and it cost a fortune to retrieve it.*

pour *v.* **1** °flow, °run, °gush, °rush, °flood, °stream, °course, °spout, °discharge, °spurt, °spew out, cascade: *Water was pouring from a crack in the dam.* **2** °empty, °discharge, °let out: *Pour the boiling water over the tea leaves and let them steep for a few minutes.* **3** °rain, °teem, *Colloq* come down in buckets *or* by the bucketful, bucket down, °rain cats and dogs, *US* °rain pitchforks: *It poured all night.* **4** °stream, °swarm, °crowd, °throng, °teem, °emerge, sally forth, °issue (forth), °go (forth): *The show over, people poured into the streets.*

pout *v.* **1** mope, °brood, °sulk, make a moue, pull a long °face, °frown, °lour *or* lower, °knit one's brows: *Don't pout—I'll buy you an ice-cream.*
—*n.* **2** °frown, moue, long °face: *Her pout was occasioned by her father's scolding.*

poverty *n.* **1** °want, penury, indigence, insolvency, destitution, pauperism, impecuniousness, neediness, beggary: *Her childhood was spent in poverty.* **2** °scarcity, scarceness, °want, °need, °lack, meagreness, insufficiency, °shortage, °dearth, paucity, inadequacy: *They criticized the poverty of talent among the current crop of actors.*

powder *n.* **1** dust; talc: *I couldn't remember whether the jar contained cornflour or baking powder. She dabbed her body all over with scented powder.* **2** ***take a (run-out) powder***: °run away, abscond, °escape, vanish, °disappear, *Slang Brit* scarper, do a moonlight flit, *US* take it on the lam: *The cops are coming, so I'm taking a powder.*
—*v.* **3** °pulverize, bray, °grind, °crush, °pound, granulate, triturate, comminute, levigate: *The rocks must first be crushed, then powdered.* **4** sprinkle, besprinkle, dust, dredge, °cover, °coat: *Lightly powder the top of the cake with icing sugar, and it is ready to serve.*

power *n.* **1** Sometimes, ***powers***: °capacity, °capability, °ability, °potential, °faculty, competency *or* competence, potentiality, *Colloq* what it takes, *US* the (right) °stuff, the goods: *Fishes have the power to change their buoyancy. He has remarkable powers of observation.* **2** °control, dominance, °authority, mastery, °rule, °influence, °sway, °command, ascendancy, °sovereignty, °dominion, °weight, clout, *Colloq* °pull, *US* drag: *He maintains a Svengali-like power over her. The prime minister has the power to appoint and dismiss cabinet ministers.* **3** °control, °command, °authority: *The party might not be in power for very long.* **4** °strength, °might, °vigour, °energy, °force, mightiness, potency, forcefulness, °brawn, muscle, *Literary* puissance: *His speech was delivered with great power and a certain wit. Has she the power it takes to toss the caber?* **5** °talent, °skill, °ability, °faculty, °gift, °aptitude, °genius, °knack: *They say that she has the power to see into the future.* **6** °authority, °licence, °right, authorization, °privilege, °warrant, °prerogative: *By the power vested in me, I now declare you man and wife. It is within her power to grant a stay of execution.* **7** Often, ***powers***: °activity, effectiveness, °effect, °ability, °capacity, °active °ingredient(s): *This mushroom has hallucinogenic powers.* **8** °energy, °momentum, °impetus, °drive, °force, °inertia: *The car rolled halfway up the next hill under its own power.* **9** (mechanical *or* electrical *or* atomic) energy, °electricity, °fuel: *Yesterday there was another demonstration against the use of nuclear power.* **10** ***powers that be***: °government, °administration, authorities, °incumbents: *It is up to the powers that be to investigate corruption.*

powerful *adj.* **1** °potent, °strong, °mighty, °vigorous, °robust, °energetic, °sturdy, °stalwart, °tough, resilient, °dynamic: *Leslie has a powerful physique. The cities of the Hanseatic League had powerful economies.* **2** °influential, °strong, compelling, °forceful, °potent, °substantial, °weighty, °authoritative, °effective; °important, °impressive, °telling, °effectual, °formidable, °persuasive: *Powerful arguments have been brought to bear against taking such action. She has many powerful friends.* **3** °strong, °potent; °intense, °substantial, °great, °high: *The drug is too powerful to be taken regularly. A powerful electrical charge was sent through the wire to test the connection.*

powerless *adj.* **1** °helpless, °incapable, °unable, unfit, °incompetent, °ineffectual, °ineffective: *Without his wand, the magician was powerless.* **2** incapacitated, °helpless, °weak, °feeble, debilitated, °crippled, paralysed, °disabled: *He is completely powerless without the use of his right hand.*

practicable *adj.* doable, °feasible, workable, performable, achievable, attainable, accomplishable, °possible, °viable: *We climbed up the glacier as far as was practicable. At last we had a practicable flying machine.*

practical *adj.* **1** pragmatic, °useful, usable *or* useable, °functional, °realistic, °reasonable, °sound, utilitarian, °applicable, °serviceable, °empirical, °efficient: *Whether the device is practical will depend on its cost effectiveness.* **2** °sensible, °reasonable, common-sense *or* commonsensical, °everyday, °ordinary, down-to-earth, °expedient, °matter-of-fact, mundane, businesslike, hard-headed, °judicious, *Colloq* hard-nosed: *Put theory aside and focus on a practical solution to the problem.* **3** applied, °field, hands-on, °personal, °everyday: *She has had practical experience in nursing the elderly.*

practically *adv.* **1** °almost, (very) °nearly, wellnigh, °virtually, in °effect, °just about, essentially, fundamentally, at °bottom, basically, when all is said and done, at the end of the day, to all intents and purposes: *We are practically there. I have practically finished the ironing.* **2** realistically, matter-of-factly, °clearly, °simply, reasonably, rationally, sensibly: *Practically, there was nothing to be done except let the fire burn itself out.*

practice *n.* **1** °custom, wont, °habit, °routine, °convention, °tradition, °rule, °procedure, °usage, °mode, °style, °way, modus operandi, °technique *or* technic, *Formal* praxis, *Colloq* MO (= 'modus operandi'): *She makes a practice of swimming for an hour every day. It is our practice to get patients out of bed as soon as possible after surgery.* **2** °exercise, °discipline, °drill, practising, °repetition, °rehearsal, training, °preparation, workout, warm-up; °application, °study: *She needs more practice on the beginner's slope before going down the main piste.* **3** °pursuit, °exercise, °work, °profession, °career, °vocation, °conduct; °business, °office: *He genuinely enjoys the practice of law. I heard of a veterinary practice for sale in Yorkshire.* **4** ***in practice***: °practically, °actually, day-to-day, realistically, in real life: *In practice no one would ever treat an injury the way this book recommends.* **5** ***out of practice***: °inexperienced, unpractised, °unaccustomed, rusty: *I once played a good game of chess, but I'm out of practice now.*

practise *v.* **1** °drill, °exercise, °work out, °train, °prepare, °rehearse, °run through, °repeat, °study, *US* practice: *I am practising for Sunday's tennis tournament. She practises the piano every day. You should practise your routine for the show.* **2** °carry on, make a °practice of, °perform, do, °act, °carry out, put into °practice, *US* practice: *She practises law. You should practise what you preach.*

practised *adj.* **1** °accomplished, °proficient, °expert, skilled, °experienced, °capable, °adept, °seasoned,

°able, °qualified, °gifted, °talented, °skilful, °masterful, consummate, °superb, °superior, *US* practiced: *She is a practised liar.* **2** trained, rehearsed, °versed, °cultivated, schooled, finished, perfected, *US* practiced: *He greeted them with the practised air of a veteran diplomat.*

praise *n.* **1** acclaim, °approval, approbation, °applause, plaudits, °kudos, °endorsement, acclamation, °tribute, accolade, compliments, commendation, encomium, °eulogy, panegyric, °ovation: *Sheila has received well-deserved praise for her work with paraplegic children. Would you expect me to sing the praises of my rival?* **2** °honour, glorification, adoration, exaltation, °devotion, °homage, °worship, °veneration, adulation, °reverence, °glory, hymn *or* song of praise, paean, hosanna: *The king rejoiced and said, 'Praise be to God'.*
—*v.* **3** acclaim, °approve, °laud, °applaud, °endorse, pay °tribute to, °compliment, commend, °eulogize, °extol, °honour, sing the praises (of): *The speaker praised Read for his many contributions to linguistics.* **4** °worship, °revere, °reverence, °exalt, °glorify, °adore, pay °homage to, °venerate, give °thanks to, °hallow: *Praise the Lord and pass the ammunition.*

praiseworthy *adj.* commendable, °laudable, °admirable, creditable, °worthy, °meritorious, °deserving, °exemplary: *However praiseworthy your motives were, you did not stop to consider the consequences.*

prance *v.* °caper, °dance, gambol, °skip, °cavort, romp, °leap, °frisk, °jump, °spring, °bound, *Dressage* curvet, capriole: *Ahead of the royal coach came a dozen riders on prancing horses.*

prank *n.* °trick, (practical) °joke, °frolic, escapade, antic, °caper, °stunt, °lark, jest, jape, °monkey tricks *or esp. US* monkeyshines, °mischief: *Those schoolboy pranks we once thought hilarious now seem quite silly.*

prattle *v.* **1** prate, °babble, blather *or* blether, blither, gibber, °jabber, jibber-jabber, °palaver, °tattle, twaddle, gabble, °chatter, °patter, °drivel, °twitter, °rattle on, °go on (and on), maunder, *Brit* natter, *Colloq* witter (on), gas, °gab, °spout, °gush, °run (on), *US* run off at the mouth, *Slang* jaw, ya(c)k, ya(c)kety-ya(c)k, shoot off one's mouth: *Do I have to listen to him prattle on and on about his grandchildren?*
—*n.* **2** prate, prating, °babble, babbling, blather *or* blether, blathering *or* blethering, gibber, gibbering, °jabber, jabbering, °palaver, palavering, °tattle, tattling, twaddle, °chatter, chattering, gabble, gabbling, °patter, °drivel, °twitter, twittering, rattling on, going on, maundering, cackle, *US* jibber-jabbering, twattle, clack, *Colloq* gas, °gab, running off at the mouth, *Slang* jawing, ya(c)kety-ya(c)k: *We were treated to constant prattle about eating healthy foods.* **3** jabberwocky, °gobbledegook *or* gobbledygook, °mumbo-jumbo, °rubbish, balderdash, (°stuff and) °nonsense, humbug, bunkum, tommy-rot, °trash, °rot, foolishness, *Colloq* pish and tush, °hot air, flapdoodle, °rigmarole *or* rigamarole, bunk, piffle, °moonshine, poppycock, claptrap, bull, hogwash, °swill, *Brit* tosh, fiddle-faddle, boloney, *Chiefly US* °garbage, horse feathers, *Slang* crap, hooey, guff, *Taboo slang* bullshit, *US* crock (of shit): *What they told you about guaranteeing your job is just a lot of prattle.*

pray *v.* **1** °beseech, °ask, °call upon *or* on, entreat, implore, °request, °appeal to, °plead (with), °beg (for), importune, °solicit, °petition, supplicate, *Rare* obsecrate: *I pray you to find it in your heart to approve my work.* **2** say one's °prayers, offer a °prayer: *We prayed for her safe return.*

prayer *n.* **1** °petition, °supplication, °request, entreaty, °plea, °suit, °appeal, *Rare* obsecration: *Our prayers were answered, and she returned safely.* **2** °devotion, praying, invocation, (°divine) °service, *Literary* orison: *Man ascends to God through prayer.*

preach *v.* **1** °deliver a °sermon, evangelize, °spread the Word *or* the Gospel; catechize: *The Most Reverend John Attwood will preach next week at Winchester.* **2** moralize, sermonize, °advise, °counsel, admonish, °reprimand, °lecture, °harangue, pontificate; °urge, inculcate, °advocate: *Mother used to preach to us about being charitable. Father preached restraint in all things.*

preacher *n.* °minister, evangelist, °clergyman, clergywoman, cleric, ecclesiastic, reverend, °divine, *Colloq* tub-thumper: *He studied for many years to become a preacher.*

preamble *n.* introduction, °foreword, prologue, °preface, *Formal* proem, prolegomenon, exordium: *As a preamble to today's proceedings, I should like to welcome our honoured guests.*

precarious *adj.* °uncertain, °unreliable, unsure, °risky, °hazardous, unpredictable, °insecure, °unstable, unsteady, °unsettled, °shaky, °doubtful, dubious, °questionable, °tricky, °delicate, °ticklish, °sensitive, °slippery, touch-and-go, (hanging) in the °balance, hanging by a thread, Damoclean, °perilous, treacherous, °dangerous, °difficult, °problematic, *Colloq* chancy, *Brit* °dodgy, °dicey, *US* iffy, *Slang* °hairy: *If sales continue to drop, the company will be in a precarious condition. We followed a precarious trail down the mountainside.*

precaution *n.* **1** °provision, °preventive °measure, °safety °measure, °safeguard, °insurance, °protection, °cover, °escape: *Unfortunately, he had failed to take any precautions against storm damage.* **2** °foresight, °prudence, °providence, °forethought, °caution, cautiousness, circumspection, °care, °attention, watchfulness, °vigilance, alertness, wariness, chariness, apprehension, far-sightedness, °anticipation: *Precaution is wiser than hindsight.*

precede *v.* °come *or* °go *or* °proceed before *or* °first, °go °ahead *or* in °advance (of), °lead (the way), °pave the °way (for), herald, usher in, °introduce, antecede; °foreshadow, antedate, predate: *His wife preceded him into the room. The* Decameron *preceded* The Canterbury Tales *by about fifty years.*

precedence *n.* precedency, °priority, °pre-eminence, °superiority, °supremacy, °preference, °privilege, °prerogative, °importance, °rank, °position, primacy: *Your school work must take precedence over football practice.*

precedent *n.* °prototype, °model, °example, exemplar, °pattern, paradigm, °yardstick, criterion, standard, °lead: *The French considered the War of American Independence a precedent for their revolution.*

preceding *adj.* °foregoing, °former, °previous, above, °prior, earlier, above-mentioned, aforementioned, above-stated, above-named: *The defendant in the preceding action was remanded in custody for a week.*

precept *n.* **1** °rule, °guide, °principle, unwritten °law, canon, guideline, °dictate, °code, °injunction, °law, commandment, °instruction, directive, °prescription, mandate, °charge; statute, °regulation, edict, ukase, °decree, °order, fiat, ordinance: *The Ten Commandments provide basic precepts of moral behaviour.* **2** °maxim, °proverb, axiom, °motto, °slogan, saying, °byword, aphorism, apophthegm *or* apothegm: *Does anyone follow the precepts set forth in Scripture?*

precinct *n.* **1** Usually, ***precincts***: °area, °territory, °region, °province, environs, purlieus, °borders, °bounds, confines: *Does he have any authority outside the precincts of the city?* **2** °sphere, °neighbourhood, °zone, sector, °section, °quarter, °district, °locale: *In some US cities, the area covered by a police station is called a precinct.*

precious *adj.* **1** °dear, dearest, costly, °expensive, high-priced, valuable, °invaluable, prized, °priceless, irreplaceable, *Colloq* °pricey *or* pricy: *The entire cabinet was filled with precious jewels.* **2** esteemed, °choice, cherished, °beloved, idolized, adored, loved, valued, prized, revered, venerated, °venerable, hallowed: *The church keeps its most precious relics in a special vault.* **3** °precise, °exquisite, overrefined, chichi, over-nice, °studied, °artificial, effete, °affected, overdone, °pretentious, euphuistic, alembicated, *Colloq Brit* °twee, *Slang US* cutesy: *His style is characterized by somewhat precious language.*

precipice *n.* °cliff, escarpment, °bluff, °crag: *We looked nervously over the edge of the precipice at the raging sea below.*

precipitate *v.* **1** accelerate, °hasten, °speed (up), °advance, °hurry, °quicken, °expedite, °bring on *or* about, trigger, °provoke, instigate, °incite, °facilitate, °further, °press, °push forward(s): *The rise in interest rates precipitated many bankruptcies.* **2** °hurl, °fling, °cast, °launch, °project: *The force of the impact precipitated him through the windscreen.* —*adj.* **3** headlong, °violent, °rapid, °swift, quick, °speedy, °meteoric, °fast: *A powerful counter-attack brought about the enemy's precipitate rout.* **4** °sudden, °abrupt, unannounced, unexpected, unanticipated: *Today's fall in share prices was as precipitate as yesterday's rise.* **5** °rash, °impetuous, °hasty, °volatile, °hotheaded, °careless, °reckless, incautious, injudicious, °foolhardy, °impulsive, unrestrained: *The selection of a career should not be a precipitate decision.*

precipitation *n.* showers, drizzle, °downpour, °rain, rainfall, snow, snowfall, hail, sleet: *Precipitation can be expected in advance of the low-pressure area pushing down from the north.*

precipitous *adj.* **1** °abrupt, °steep, °perpendicular, °sheer, bluff, acclivitous, declivitous: *I cannot see how anyone can climb up the precipitous face of that crag.* **2** See **precipitate, 5,** above.

précis *n.* °outline, °summary, °synopsis, *aperçu*, résumé, conspectus, °survey, overview, °abstract, °abridgement, °digest, compendium, recapitulation; °table of contents: *As I haven't the time to read the entire study document, let me have a précis of it.*

precise *adj.* **1** °correct, °exact, °definite, well-defined, °explicit, word-for-word, °verbatim, °literal, letter-for-letter, *literatim*, °faithful, °specific, unambiguous, unequivocal, °strict, °authentic, °perfect, °true, veracious, °truthful, unerring, error-free, °accurate: *Errors show that medieval scribes did not always succeed in making precise copies.* **2** °strict, °meticulous, °scrupulous, °careful, °conscientious, °exact, unconditional, rigorous, °rigid, puritanical, unbending, °inflexible, unyielding, °demanding, °severe, prim, °absolute: *He has been very precise about dates and facts. Margaret is precise in insisting on obedience to her orders.* **3** °fastidious, °particular, °finicky, finical, °fussy, °meticulous, °scrupulous, °careful, °conscientious, °nice, °exacting, °critical, °demanding: *Painting miniatures is very precise work.* **4** °exact, °very: *This is the precise spot where I found the body.*

precisely *adv.* **1** °exactly, °just, strictly, *Colloq* on the °nail, smack, °slap, on the nose, *Brit* bang on, spot on: *His view is precisely the opposite of hers. We left precisely at five o'clock. You phoned, and that is precisely why I came. The two paintings are not precisely the same.* **2** °exactly, exactingly, correctly, rigorously, °absolutely, punctiliously, minutely, carefully, meticulously, scrupulously, conscientiously, strictly, rigidly, inflexibly; in all respects, in every °way: *This judge follows the letter of the law precisely.*

precision *n.* **1** correctness, exactness, fidelity, faithfulness, exactitude, preciseness, °accuracy, °rigour, °perfection, flawlessness, faultlessness, literalism, unerringness: *This copy follows the original with precision.* **2** definiteness, °care, nicety, meticulousness, rigorousness, °rigour, fastidiousness, punctiliousness, scrupulousness, unambiguousness, strictness, explicitness: *The precision of the wording leaves no doubt about what the writer intended.*

preclude *v.* obviate, °bar, °prevent, °stop, °exclude, °prohibit, °shut out, °forestall, °rule out, debar, °check, °block, °obstruct, avert, °avoid, °thwart, °frustrate, °impede, °inhibit, °hinder, °interfere with: *To preclude misunderstanding, please repeat what you said. They may not engage in activities that preclude them from performing their regular duties.*

precocious *adj.* advanced, °mature, °bright, °gifted, °intelligent, °smart, quick: *It is hard to believe that Oliver was a precocious child.*

preconceived *adj.* beforehand, predisposed, prejudged, °predetermined, °prejudiced, °biased, anticipatory: *He has many false preconceived notions about people.*

preconception *n.* predisposition, prejudgement, predetermination, °prejudice, °bias, °presumption, °presupposition, assumption, *idée fixe*, prepossession, °preconceived notion *or* idea: *This production of* King Lear *will challenge your preconceptions of the play.*

precondition *n.* °prerequisite, °stipulation, °condition, °essential, °must, *sine qua non*, °imperative, °requirement, °proviso, °provision, °qualification, °necessity: *The release of the prisoners is a precondition for talks. Is great humanity a precondition of great music, or is it just a matter of the notes?*

precursor *n.* **1** °harbinger, herald, vanguard: *The glow on the eastern horizon is the precursor of another day.* **2** See **predecessor, 1,** below

predatory *adj.* **1** predacious *or* predaceous, carnivorous, preying, raptorial: *Despite domestication, dogs and cats are predatory animals.* **2** °rapacious, °ravenous, plundering, robbing, pillaging, marauding, despoiling, looting, piratical, vulturine, °avaricious, °greedy, °voracious, larcenous, thieving, extortionate, usurious: *Predatory pirates once ravaged the Mediterranean. Keep out of the hands of predatory moneylenders, my son.*

predecessor *n.* **1** °forerunner, antecedent: *I could not match the accomplishments of my predecessor in this post.* **2** forebear, forefather, °ancestor, antecedent: *Can you name the Tudor predecessors of Elizabeth I?*

predestination *n.* °destiny, °future, °lot, °fortune, kismet, karma; °doom, °fate; foreordainment, foreordination: *Meeting like this must have been predestination.*

predetermined *adj.* **1** °fixed, prearranged, pre-established, °set (up), °foregone, preplanned, pre-set: *A predetermined amount of milk is automatically poured into each cup of coffee.* **2** °fated, °doomed, °destined, ordained, foreordained, *Colloq* °cut and dried, *Brit* on the cards, *US* in the cards: *One gets the feeling that the outcome was predetermined.*

predicament *n.* °dilemma, °quandary, °difficulty, °trial, °situation, °state, °condition, imbroglio, °emergency, °crisis, °impasse, *Colloq* pickle, °jam, °fix, °pinch, °scrape, °spot, °bind, corner, °hole, °mess, *US* box: *I was hoping that you might help me out of a very awkward predicament.*

predict *v.* foretell, °prophesy, °forecast, °foresee, augur, °prognosticate, forewarn, presage, vaticinate; portend, °foreshadow, foretoken, forebode; °intimate, °hint, °suggest: *My mother predicted that there would be moments like this. If only I could predict the winner of the 2.30!*

predictable *adj.* foreseeable, foreseen, °probable, °likely, °liable, expected, anticipated, (reasonably) °sure *or* °certain, *Colloq Brit* on the cards, *US* in the cards: *Her angry reaction at being dismissed was quite predictable.*

prediction *n.* °forecast, °prophecy, augury, °prognosis; intimation, °hint, °suggestion: *The weatherman's predictions are more accurate than one might think. The prediction that he might be released the next day did not come true.*

predominance *n.* predominancy, °superiority, °influence, dominance, °pre-eminence, °preponderance, ascendancy, °precedence, °power, °supremacy, °hold, °sway, hegemony, °leadership, mastery, °control, °dominion, °sovereignty, transcendence *or* transcendency, °authority, the °upper hand, the whip hand, °advantage, the °edge: *We must re-establish the predominance of intellectual vigour over crass commercialism.*

predominant *adj.* °dominant, predominating, controlling, °sovereign, ruling, °pre-eminent, preponderant, ascendant, °superior, °supreme, °leading, °paramount, °main, °chief, transcendent, °important, °telling, °influential, °primary, °prevailing, °prevalent:

England was the predominant power in the world during the 19th century. The phlogiston theory was once predominant among scientists.

predominate *v.* Often, ***predominate over***: °dominate, °control, °rule, °reign, preponderate, °outweigh, °obtain, °prevail, °overshadow, get *or* have the °upper hand, °lord it over, hold °sway, overrule: *Though the American president is a Republican, the Democrats predominate in Congress.*

pre-eminence *n.* **1** See **predominance,** above. **2** peerlessness, magnificence, °excellence, °distinction, eminence, inimitability, °superiority: *There is no gainsaying the pre-eminence of Shakespeare as a poet and playwright.*

pre-eminent *adj.* **1** See **predominant,** above. **2** °peerless, °excellent, °distinguished, °eminent, inimitable, °superb, unequalled, °matchless, °incomparable, °outstanding, °unique, unrivalled, unsurpassed, °supreme, °superior: *In her opinion, Craig is the pre-eminent authority on the subject.*

pre-eminently *adv.* °primarily, °principally, by °far, °far and away, °manifestly, °eminently, °notably, conspicuously, prominently, signally, uniquely, extraordinarily, °supremely, superbly, matchlessly, incomparably, outstandingly: *There is no doubt that Nathalie is pre-eminently qualified to direct the play.*

pre-empt *v.* °appropriate, usurp, arrogate, °take over, °assume, °take °possession of, °seize, °acquire, °take, °possess, expropriate: *All the seats on the committee had been pre-empted by the ruling faction.*

preen *v.* **1** °trim, °clean, plume, °groom: *The gliding swans stopped now and then to preen their feathers.* **2** °primp, °dress up, titivate *or* tittivate, prettify, °beautify, prink, °spruce up, deck (out), *Colloq* doll up, *Brit* °tart up: *He made Sonia wait while he preened himself before the mirror.*

preface *n.* **1** introduction, °foreword, prologue, °preamble, *Formal* proem, prolegomenon, exordium: *By way of preface, I should like to say how happy I am to be here. The preface to the book is far too long.*
—*v.* **2** °precede, °introduce, prefix, °begin, °open: *The speaker prefaced his acceptance speech with a tribute to his predecessor.*

prefatory *adj.* °opening, °introductory, °preliminary, °preparatory: *Would you like to make a few prefatory remarks introducing this evening's speaker?*

prefer *v.* **1** °favour, °like better, °fancy, °lean *or* °incline towards *or* on the side of, be °inclined, be °partial to, °pick, °select, opt for, °choose, °single out, take a °fancy to, °embrace, espouse, °approve, °esteem: *Which flavour do you prefer, chocolate or coffee? I should prefer to take my own car.* **2** °present, °offer, °propose, proffer, °advance, °submit, °tender, °put forward, °file, °lodge, °enter: *They preferred charges against the hooligans for criminal damage.*

preference *n.* **1** °favourite, °choice, °selection, °desire, °option, °pick: *My preference is the Dover sole meunière.* **2** °partiality, proclivity, °prejudice, °favouritism, predilection, °liking, °fancy, predisposition, °bent, °inclination, °leaning: *She shows a marked preference for short men.*

preferential *adj.* °advantageous, °biased, °prejudiced, °favourable, °privileged, °partial, °better, °favoured, °superior: *What entitles her to preferential treatment?*

pregnant *adj.* **1** gravid, parturient, °expectant, (heavy) with child, enceinte, *Colloq* °expecting, in a family way, *Brit* preggers, *Slang* having a bun in the oven, *Brit* in the (pudding) club, up the spout: *Her twins are only seven months old and now she's pregnant again.* **2** charged, °fraught, °loaded, °weighty, °significant, °meaningful, °suggestive, °eloquent, °expressive, °pointed: *Although she said nothing, her smile was pregnant with meaning.* **3** °fruitful, teeming, °fertile, fecund, °rich, abounding, °replete, °productive: *My mind was so pregnant with ideas that I couldn't wait to get down to work.*

prehistoric *adj.* **1** primordial, primal, primeval *or Brit also* primaeval, °primitive, earliest, °early, antediluvian, Noachian *or* Noachic, fossil, °ancient: *The prehistoric remains of yet another skeleton have been found in the peat bogs.* **2** °antiquated, out-dated, °old-fashioned, °*passé*: *My mother makes me wear these absolutely prehistoric clothes to school.*

prejudice *n.* **1** °partiality, °preconception, prejudgement, °bias, °leaning, °warp, °twist, °preconceived notion, predisposition, predilection, °jaundiced eye, jaundice: *The judge showed an unfortunate prejudice against my client.* **2** °bigotry, unfairness, °bias, partisanship, °favouritism, cronyism, °discrimination, °intolerance, °inequality; racism, racialism, apartheid, Jim Crowism, sexism, (male) chauvinism: *There is still prejudice against many minority groups in society.*
—*v.* **3** °bias, °influence, °warp, °twist, °distort, °slant; °colour, jaundice, °poison: *Stop trying to prejudice me against the book, and let me form my own opinion. Are you prejudiced in favour of Anita's getting the job?*

prejudiced *adj.* **1** unfair, °one-sided, °biased, °jaundiced, °opinionated, predisposed, °partial, °partisan, non-objective, unobjective: *The prosecution objected to him as a prejudiced witness.* **2** °bigoted, °intolerant, °narrow-minded, closed-minded, °parochial, sexist, racist, chauvinistic: *We have no room in our organization for people who are prejudiced.*

prejudicial *adj.* °injurious, damaging, °detrimental, °harmful, unfavourable, inimical, deleterious, disadvantageous, counter-productive, pernicious: *Such an investment decision might prove prejudicial to her financial security.*

preliminary *adj.* **1** °advance, °prior, °introductory, °beginning, °initial, °opening, °preparatory, °prefatory, °preceding, antecedent, forerunning; premonitory; *Formal or technical* prodromal *or* prodromic: *The preliminary design for the swimming-pool is ready. After some preliminary remarks, the ceremonies got under way.*
—*n.* **2** introduction, °beginning, °opening, °preparation, °groundwork, prelude, °precedence; °overture: *We insist on rigorous training as a preliminary to working in the field.* **3** ***prelims***: *rarely*, ***preliminaries***: introduction, °preface, °foreword, °preamble, prologue, front matter, *Formal* proem, exordium, prolegomenon, prodromus, prodrome: *The manuscript is finished and we are waiting for the prelims.*

premature *adj.* **1** °immature, °undeveloped, underdeveloped, °unfledged, untimely, unready, °early, unripe, °green: *Much premature fruit has been blown down in the winds.* **2** °hasty, untimely, ill-timed, too °early, too °soon, beforehand, °unseasonable, overhasty, °impulsive, °inopportune: *The post may be slow, but still I think September a bit premature to send Christmas cards. The discovery that money was missing accounts for his premature departure.*

prematurely *adv.* **1** untimely, too °soon, too °early: *He died prematurely at the age of 46.* **2** rashly, (over-) °hastily, at half-cock, half-cocked: *She dismissed him prematurely, before he had the time to prove himself. The gun went off prematurely, with no chance to aim it.*

premeditated *adj.* planned, °conscious, °intentional, intended, °wilful, °deliberate, °studied, purposive; contrived, preplanned, °calculated, °preconceived: *The murder was coldly premeditated. I admit to being wrong, and I have no premeditated excuses.*

premier *n.* **1** °prime °minister, PM, °head of °state, °chief °executive, president, chancellor: *The premiers of the Commonwealth met at Kuala Lumpur in 1989.*
—*adj.* **2** °first, °prime, °primary, °chief, °principal, °head, °main, °foremost, top-ranking, highest-ranking, ranking, °leading, °top, °pre-eminent: *He is the premier expert in his field.*

première *n.* **1** premiere, °first night, °opening (night), début: *The première of* Aïda *was at the opening of the Suez Canal.*
—*v.* **2** °open, début: *The film will première at the Festival Cinema tomorrow.*

—*adj.* **3** °opening, début, °first, °original, °initial: *The première West-End performance is scheduled for May after a provincial tour.*

premise *n.* **1** premiss, assumption, °proposition, postulate, °hypothesis, conjecture, °assertion, °supposition, °thesis, °presupposition, °proposal, °theorem, °surmise, °basis, °ground: *He started out with the premise that time had a beginning and will have an end.*
—*v.* **2** °assume, °propose, postulate, hypothesize, hypothecate, conjecture, °posit, assert, °suppose, °presuppose, °theorize, °surmise, °put *or* °set forth, predicate, °argue: *If you accept what Einstein premised in the Special Theory of Relativity, then you accept that space is curved.*

premium *n.* **1** °bonus, °extra, dividend, °prize, °award, °reward, °perquisite: *In our slimming competition, a premium will be paid for each pound that you lose beyond five.* **2** °incentive, °inducement, stimulus, °incitement, °lure, bait, °spur, goad, °reward, *Colloq* °come-on, *Slang US and Canadian* freebie: *Many Building Societies offer premiums to first-time buyers.* **3** value, °importance, °regard, °stock, °store, °appreciation: *We place a premium on the way our staff treat customers.* **4** ***at a premium***: **a** °scarce, °rare, scant, °scanty, °sparse, hard to °come by, in °short supply, *Colloq* °scarce as hen's teeth, *Chiefly Brit* °thin on the ground: *Proficient, literate, experienced editors are at a premium these days.* **b** costly, °expensive, °dear, high-priced, *Colloq* °steep, °stiff: *The convertible model of this car is at a premium.*

premonition *n.* °intuition, °foreboding, presentiment, forewarning, °suspicion, °feeling, °hunch, *Colloq* funny °feeling, °sneaking °suspicion: *I had a premonition that something terribly evil was lurking in store for me.*

preoccupied *adj.* **1** engrossed, °lost in °thought, °rapt, °thoughtful, °pensive, °absorbed, cogitating, cogitative, meditating, musing, reflecting, °reflective, contemplative, contemplating, pondering, brooding, ruminating, in a brown study: *John is preoccupied, thinking about the speech he has to deliver tonight.* **2** °vague, °offhand, °far-away, °absent-minded, abstracted, °oblivious, °unaware, wrapped up, immersed, °inattentive, distracted, *distrait(e)*, *Colloq* turned off, *US* out of it: *From her preoccupied air it was obvious that something was wrong.*

preparation *n.* **1** Often, ***preparations***: **a** °groundwork, spadework, °provision(s), °foundation, preparing, measures, °proceedings: *Nothing will interfere with our preparation for the royal visit.* **b** °plans, °arrangements: *We are making preparations to leave tomorrow.* **2** °fitness, °readiness, readying, preparing, training, °education, teaching, °instruction, instructing, °tuition, briefing, grooming, *Colloq* gearing up, prep, *US* prepping: *The preparation of the students was your responsibility.* **3** °drawing up, draughting, planning, °setting up, putting together, organizing, °organization, composing, making: *How is your preparation of the new proposal coming along?* **4** °work, preparing, getting °ready, °study, studying, practising, °practice, *Colloq* cramming, *Brit* swotting: *All my preparation for the exam was to no avail.* **5** °substance, °compound, concoction, °mixture, °product, °material, °stuff, °composition: *This preparation is a furniture wax, not a suntan lotion.*

preparatory *adj.* **1** preparative, °preliminary, °introductory, °prefatory, °opening: *After some preparatory warnings about safety, the scuba-diving lessons began.* **2** °elementary, °basic, °essential, °fundamental, °primary, °rudimentary: *His preparatory training left him ill-equipped to deal with such a major problem.* **3** ***preparatory to***: °before, in °preparation for, °preceding: *Preparatory to the mission, we were briefed by MI5.*

prepare *v.* **1** (get *or* make) °ready, °prime, °arrange, (put in) °order, °organize, °provide for, make °provision(s) for, lay the °groundwork (for), make °fit, °fit (out), °equip, °outfit, °adapt: *Have you prepared adequately for the meeting? We prepared the house to receive guests.* **2** °train, (get *or* make) °ready, °study, °practise, *Colloq* °cram, *Brit* swot, °get up: *He is preparing to take an exam.* **3** °train, °educate, °teach, (get *or* make) °ready, °groom, °brief, °develop: *Her mother is preparing her for the next Olympics.* **4** cook (up), °make, do, *Colloq* °whip up, *US and Canadian* °fix: *I shall prepare dinner for eight o'clock.* **5** °manufacture, °fabricate, °produce, °make, °put out, °build, °construct, °assemble, °put together, °turn out, °fashion, °forge, °mould: *Our company prepares components for the printing industry.* **6** °brace, °strengthen, °steel, °fortify, °ready: *When I saw the doctor's face, I prepared myself for bad news.* **7** °process, °produce, °make, °treat, °change, °modify, °transform: *This fabric has been specially prepared to repel stains.*

prepared *adj.* **1** °ready, °set, °advance, prearranged, planned: *We have six prepared questions for the interview.* **2** treated, processed, modified, changed: *Using an etching needle, incise the lines on the prepared surface of the steel plate.* **3** °willing, °disposed, predisposed, °able, °inclined, of a °mind; °ready, (all) °set: *Are you prepared to apologize?* **4** oven-ready, microwave-ready, microwavable, °instant, convenience, ready-to-eat, ready-to-serve, precooked, °ready-made: *He lives alone and usually buys prepared dinners that just need reheating.*

preparedness *n.* °vigilance, alertness, °readiness, °fitness: *The armed forces were kept in a continuous state of preparedness.*

preponderance *n.* **1** °majority, greater °part, °bulk, °mass, lion's °share: *The preponderance of voters want a change of government.* **2** °weight, °influence, weightiness, °superiority, °supremacy, °predominance, primacy, ascendancy, °sway, °strength, °force, °power, °advantage, °control, °authority, hegemony, °leadership, °rule: *Good has always appeared to have an incontestable preponderance over evil.*

prepossessing *adj.* °attractive, appealing, °pleasing, °favourable, °engaging, charming, captivating, fascinating, winsome, °winning, °magnetic, alluring, bewitching, °taking, °fetching, °inviting, good-looking, °handsome, °lovely, °beautiful: *She is a woman of prepossessing appearance and a delightful nature.*

preposterous *adj.* °absurd, °ridiculous, °ludicrous, laughable, risible, asinine, °foolish, °senseless, irrational, °nonsensical, fatuous, fatuitous, °mindless, °insane, °crazy, crack-brained, °mad, idiotic, moronic, imbecilic, °incredible, °unbelievable, °outrageous, °extravagant, °extraordinary, °extreme, °exorbitant, °outlandish, *outré*, °weird, °bizarre, *Slang* barmy, nutty, screwy, batty, dotty, wacky, loony, cuckoo, *US* balmy: *To claim that it is all my fault is simply preposterous!*

prerequisite *adj.* **1** °essential, °necessary, requisite, °imperative, °indispensable, °obligatory, required, called-for, demanded: *Naval service is a prerequisite condition for joining the club.*
—*n.* **2** °precondition, °requirement, °qualification, requisite, °condition, *sine qua non*, °proviso, °provision, °necessity: *A thorough grounding in mathematics is a prerequisite for the study of advanced physics.*

prerogative *n.* °privilege, °right, °liberty, °power, °due, °advantage, °licence, franchise, °claim, °sanction, °authority, authorization: *As managing director, she exercises her prerogative to park her car closest to the door.*

prescribe *v.* ordain, °order, °direct, °dictate, °demand, °decree, °require, enjoin, °rule, °set (down), °stipulate, °command, °instruct, °define, °specify, °impose, °lay down, °exact, constrain: *The doctor prescribed rest. An independent journalist, Healey would not let anyone prescribe what he could or could not write.*

prescription *n.* **1** °formula, °recipe, °instruction, °direction: *The prescription is for three tablets a day, and this dose must not be exceeded.* **2** °remedy, medication,

°medicine, °drug, °preparation, medicament: *That prescription had no effect at all on my headache.*

prescriptive *adj.* °dictatorial, constrictive, didactic, restrictive, °dogmatic, °authoritarian, °overbearing, autocratic, imperious: *As grammar is a description of how language works, it cannot be prescriptive.*

presence *n.* **1** °proximity, nearness, closeness, adjacency, °vicinity, *Formal* propinquity: *The presence of a hospital near her home made Aunt Mary feel more secure.* **2** °attendance, °company, °companionship, °society, °association, °existence, °manifestation, manifestness, being: *The Queen honoured us by her presence at the unveiling of the plaque.* **3** °poise, self-assurance, °bearing, self-possession, °confidence, mien, °carriage, comportment, deportment, °air, °personality, °aspect, °aura, °appearance: *When Geoffrey entered, his presence created quite a stir.* **4** °spirit, wraith, °spectre, °shade: *I had the vague but pervading sense that an unidentifiable presence was with me in the empty room.* **5** ***presence of mind***: aplomb, °sophistication, coolness, cool-headedness, composure, imperturbability, phlegm, °sang-froid, self-possession, self-assurance, °calm, equanimity, level-headedness, quick-wittedness, alertness, *Colloq* °cool: *With great presence of mind, Grainger walked up to the man and took the gun from him.*

present[1] *adj.* **1** °current, °contemporary, present-day, existing, existent, up to °date, *Colloq* °now: *Do you understand the present generation?* **2** °nearby, nearest, °immediate, closest, adjacent, proximate, propinquitous; °close, °remaining; accounted for: *Everybody has been awful to me—present company excepted. All those present heard what she said to me.*

—*n.* **3** ***at present***: (right *or* just) °now, for the °time being, for the present, today, these days, *Non-Standard* °presently, *Colloq* at this °point in °time: *I am not ready to invest at present.* **4** ***the present***: the °time being, the °moment, the hour, the nonce, this °juncture, these days, our times; today, (right) °now, °nowadays; *Colloq* this °point in °time: *She lives for the present, and never thinks of the consequences.*

present[2] *n.* **1** °gift: *May I open my birthday presents now?* **2** °donation, °offering, °bounty, °grant, °largesse, contribution, °endowment: *I'll make you a present of the painting if you like it.* **3** °tip, gratuity, *pourboire*, baksheesh *or* backsheesh, °bonus; alms, hand-out, °dole, °aid, °allowance: *She gave the* maître d'hôtel *a present for looking after us so well.*

—*v.* **4** °introduce, °acquaint with, °make known: *I'd like to present my wife, Cordelia, who has been looking forward to meeting you.* **5** °offer, °give, °stage, °show, °exhibit, °put on (°show), °mount, °produce: *The local players will present a new production of* Blithe Spirit *tonight.* **6** °give (out), °award, °confer (on), °bestow (on), °turn *or* °hand over, °grant, °provide, °furnish; °dispense, °distribute, °dole out, °pass out, °deal out, °mete out: *They presented her with a prize for the best poem. Is it tonight that they present the awards?* **7** °offer, °bring (in *or* up), proffer, °tender, °introduce, °produce, °submit, °set *or* °put forth, °put forward, adduce; °register, °file, °record: *The lawyer for the defence presented evidence of his client's alibi.* **8** °introduce, °announce, *Brit* compère, *Colloq* emcee: *And here, to present our show, is the inimitable Reginald Norton!*

presentable *adj.* **1** °fit, °fitting, °suitable, °acceptable, °satisfactory, °adequate, °passable, °tolerable, admissible, all °right, allowable, up to °par *or* °standard *or* the °mark, °good °enough, *Colloq* up to °scratch, °OK *or* okay, up to snuff: *Whether that argument is presentable in a court of law is disputable.* **2** °decent, °proper, °polite, °decorous, °respectable, °well-bred, well-mannered, °fit to be seen: *After a bath, shave, and change of clothing he looked quite presentable.*

presentation *n.* **1** giving, bestowal, °offering, proffering, presenting, °award, awarding, conferral, conferring, °delivery; °donation: *The presentation of the prizes will be at the annual dinner.* **2** °appearance, °image, °display, visual(s), °spectacle, °show, °performance, °demonstration, °production: *The text of the proposal was fine, but the presentation could be improved.* **3** début, °launch, introduction, unveiling, disclosure: *We attended the presentation of the latest electric car.*

presently *adv.* °soon, by and by, in a little while, °shortly, after a short time, in due course, after a while *or* a time, before long, in a °moment *or* a °minute *or* a while, *Archaic or literary* anon, *Colloq* in a jiffy, in two shakes (of a lamb's tail), *Non-Standard* °now, at °present: *The show opens presently in the West End. I shall be with you presently.*

preservation *n.* **1** °upkeep, °maintenance, °care, °conservation: *The preservation of old paintings has become an art in itself.* **2** keeping, retention, retaining, perpetuation, perpetuating, continuation, °safe keeping, °security, safeguarding, °protection, protecting, °conservation: *Several charities are dedicated to the preservation of our heritage.*

preserve *v.* **1** °keep °safe, °protect, °guard, take °care of, °care for, °safeguard, °watch over, °shield, °shelter, °defend, °spare: *What can we do to preserve ourselves from this terrible pestilence? May God preserve me, I never expected to see you again!* **2** °keep (up), °maintain, °conserve, °spare, °perpetuate; °continue, °support, °sustain, °save: *We developed a technique to preserve antique furniture. The sea preserves much of the heat it absorbs in the summer. It is difficult to preserve one's sanity in this madhouse.* **3** °conserve, °put up, pickle, °cure, smoke, kipper, °salt, corn, marinate, can, °freeze, freeze-dry, °refrigerate, °dry, dehydrate, vacuum-pack; embalm, mummify: *The berries were preserved by bottling and freezing. Some of the remains were preserved for hundreds of years.*

—*n.* **4** Often, ***preserves***: °conserve(s), °jam, jelly, confiture, marmalade: *Susan likes thick toast with butter and preserves for tea.* **5** (°game) °reserve, °reservation, °sanctuary, *Brit* °park: *No hunting is allowed in this preserve.*

preside *v.* °supervise, °run, °oversee, °direct, °operate, °lead, °head (up), °govern, °rule, °manage, °handle, °control, °direct, °chair, °administer, administrate, °regulate, °officiate: *Melissa presides over the meetings of the board.*

press *v.* **1** °subject to *or* °exert °pressure *or* °force, °force, °push, impel, °thrust, °bear (on), °weigh on *or* upon, °jam, °cram, °crush; °pressure *or Brit also* pressurize: *The crowd was pressing against the door. Although hard pressed at first, we eventually won.* **2** °squeeze, compress, °depress, °push: *When the picture is in focus, press this button to release the shutter.* **3** °squeeze, °crush, compress, mash: *After harvesting, the grapes are pressed to extract the juice.* **4** iron, °smooth, °flatten, put through a mangle; steam: *I shall have to press my jacket before going out to dinner.* **5** °clasp, °embrace, °hug, °hold (°close *or* °tight(ly)), take in one's arms, throw one's arms about *or* around, °cleave to, *Archaic* clip: *She pressed the child to her with great affection.* **6** constrain, °urge, °force, °pressure, compel, °demand, °persuade, °induce, °prod, °provoke, importune, °beseech, °ask, °request, °beg, entreat: *They pressed me to tell where the money was hidden.* **7** °crowd, °flock, °gather, °mill, °swarm, °throng, °seethe, °cluster, congregate, °meet, °converge, °huddle: *The reporters pressed round the chancellor to catch every word.*

—*n.* **8** crowding, °gathering, thronging, converging, convergence, °crowd, °throng, °swarm, °cluster, °huddle, °pack, °herd, °host, multitude, horde, °mob, °crush: *When the doors opened, the huge press of people pushed onto the train.* **9** °urgency, °haste, °hurry, °hustle, bustle, °pressure, °stress: *The press of business required me to postpone my trip to Paris.* **10** ***the press***: **a** newspapers, the °papers, Fleet Street, the fourth estate, the media, the wire *or* °news services, broadcasting, °television, °radio: *The press will have a field-day when this news gets out.* **b** newspaper people, newspapermen *or* newspaperwomen, newsmen *or* newswomen, °reporters, °correspondents, ladies *or* gentlemen of the press, °journalists, commentators, *paparazzi*, *Brit* leader-writers, *US* °editorial °writers, *Colloq* news-hounds, *Brit* journos: *The doors were opened and the press were invited in.*

pressing *adj.* °urgent, compelling, °crucial, °pivotal, °burning, °grave, °serious, °major, °important, °vital, high-priority, °critical, °portentous, °momentous, °profound, °significant: *Some pressing matters kept me late at the office.*

pressure *n.* **1** °force, compression; °weight, °power, °strength: *The air pressure in your tyres is low. The pressure of the water burst the pipe.* **2** compression, °pressing, squeezing, compressing, °tension, °stress, crushing: *The pressure of a tourniquet has to be loosened now and then.* **3** °affliction, °oppression, °press, °weight, °burden, °load, albatross, °strain, °stress, °urgency, demands, exigency *or* exigencies, vexation, °distress, °trouble(s), adversity, °difficulty *or* difficulties, °straits, constraint(s), °problem(s): *Pressure of work prevents me from taking any time away from the office. When interest rates increase, we all feel financial pressure.* **4** °influence, °power, °sway, constraint, insistence, coercion, intimidation, arm-twisting; °inducement, °persuasion, urging, °pressing: *Without more pressure from local residents, the roadworks will not be completed in time.*
—*v.* **5** °persuade, °influence; °prevail upon *or* on, °press, °urge, °sway, °intimidate, bring pressure to bear (on), apply pressure (on *or* to), coerce, °force, compel, constrain, °require, °demand, °make, °insist upon *or* on, *Brit* pressurize, *Colloq* twist (someone's) arm, °lean on, turn the heat on, *Slang* put the screws on *or* to: *They pressured him to take the assignment in New Zealand.*

prestige *n.* °status, °reputation, °standing, °rank, stature, °importance, °significance, eminence, °esteem, °pre-eminence, °prominence, °predominance, primacy, °superiority, °supremacy, ascendancy, °distinction, °renown, °regard, °fame, °cachet, repute, °celebrity, °glamour, stardom: *To raise money, someone with prestige must be found to serve as director of the charity.*

prestigious *adj.* °important, °significant, °eminent, °estimable, °imposing, °impressive, °pre-eminent, °prominent, °distinguished, august, °dignified, °renowned, °famous, famed, °well-known, °illustrious, acclaimed, respected, °celebrated, °noted, °notable, °noteworthy, °outstanding, °glorious, honoured, °glamorous: *She may be a prestigious author, but she does not live at a very prestigious address.*

presumably *adv.* °probably, in all °likelihood, (very *or* most) °likely, in all °probability, °seemingly, °doubtless(ly), indubitably, no doubt, °undoubtedly, unquestionably, without a doubt, °surely, certainly, on the °face of it, all things considered, all things being equal: *Presumably, you have heard the one about the colonel's poodle.*

presume *v.* **1** °assume, take for granted, °suppose, °surmise, °infer, °presuppose, °take it, °gather, °understand, °think, °believe, °imagine, °suspect, °fancy, conjecture, postulate, °posit, °theorize, °speculate, hypothesize, hypothecate, *US and Canadian* °guess: *For some unaccountable reason, we presumed that your train would arrive on time. Dr Livingstone, I presume?* **2** °dare, take the °liberty, be so °presumptuous as, make (so) °bold (as), have the audacity *or* °effrontery, go so °far as, °venture: *Who is he to presume to judge others?* **3** Often, ***presume on*** *or* ***upon***: °encroach (on *or* upon), °impose (on *or* upon), take liberties (with), °intrude (on *or* upon *or* into): *I hate to presume on our friendship, but could you lend me some money?*

presumption *n.* **1** °arrogance, °pride, °effrontery, audacity, boldness, brazenness, °impudence, °impertinence, insolence, temerity, overconfidence, presumptuousness, forwardness, immodesty, *Colloq* pushiness, cheek, cheekiness, °nerve, °gall, chutzpah, °brass, *Brit* °brass neck: *He had the presumption to ask my age.* **2** assumption, °supposition, °presupposition, °preconception, °premise *or* premiss, °surmise, °proposition, postulation; °probability, °likelihood, plausibility, °feasibility: *The presumption of the innocence of a person accused of a crime is established in law.* **3** assumption, °stand, °position, °inference, °feeling, °deduction, conclusion, °conviction, °bias, °guess, theory, °hypothesis, conjecture, °belief, °thought; °suspicion: *Having examined the evidence, the pathologist's presumption was that the victim had died of natural causes.* **4** °ground(s), °reason, °basis, °evidence: *What is your presumption for thinking that you might win the lottery?*

presumptive *adj.* **1** °likely, °reasonable, °plausible, °tenable, believable, credible, conceivable, °acceptable, justifiable, °sensible, °rational, °sound: *There is strong presumptive evidence, but we need proof.* **2** inferred, presumed, °assumed, °supposed, °understood, predicted, predicated: *As King Richard was childless, his brother was heir presumptive to the Crown.*

presumptuous *adj.* °arrogant, °proud, prideful, °audacious, °bold, °brazen, saucy, °impudent, °impertinent, °insolent, temerarious, °brash, °overconfident, overweening, °forward, presuming, °immodest, °egotistical, *Colloq* °pushy, °cheeky, too big for one's boots, *Brit* °uppish: *He is presumptuous enough to think he can do no wrong.*

presuppose *v.* See **presume, 1,** above.

presupposition *n.* See **presumption, 1, 2,** above.

pretence *n.* **1** °show, °display, °pretension, °ostentation, °airs, °front, façade, °appearance, make-believe, fiction, °hypocrisy, fakery, faking, feigning, humbuggery, humbug, °deception, °artifice, °pretext, posturing, pretentiousness, pretending, °camouflage, cover-up: *Her charming manner was all pretence, for in reality she despised him.* **2** °hoax, humbug, °artifice, °pretext, °sham, °show, °pose, façade, °front, cover-up, °cover, °cloak, °veil, °mask, °masquerade, °disguise, °guise, °deception, °ruse, °dodge, °blind, °fabrication, °invention, fiction, °story, fable, make-believe, fairy °tale, figment, falsification, °impression: *His loyalty was a pretence under which he carried on many liaisons.* **3** °excuse, °pretext, °pretension: *They would ring for the butler on the slightest pretence, just to impress us.*

pretend *v.* **1** feign, °profess, °represent, °allege, °make °believe, °make out: *Let's pretend that we are royalty. Often, he pretends to be me.* **2** °try, °attempt, °endeavour, °venture, °presume, °undertake: *I could not pretend to guess the number of people attending last night's meeting.* **3** °make °believe, °act *or* °play, play-act, °fake, feign, put on an °act, dissemble, °sham, sail under false °colours: *Is she serious about wanting you to leave or was she just pretending?*

pretended *adj.* °so-called, °alleged, asserted, °reputed, °professed, ostensible, purported, °imaginary, make-believe, °fictitious, °fictional, °sham, °false, °fake, feigned, °bogus, °counterfeit, °spurious, *Colloq* °phoney *or US also* phony, pseudo, °pretend: *So this is the pretended hero of yesterday's battle!*

pretender *n.* claimant, aspirant, °candidate, °suitor, °rival, seeker: *He was the pretender to the Scottish throne.*

pretension *n.* **1** Often, ***pretensions***: °claim(s), °pretence(s), °aspiration(s), ambitiousness, °ambition(s): *He is known to have pretensions to the chancellorship.* **2** °pretext, °pretence, pretentiousness, °ostentation, pretending, °affectation, °hypocrisy: *Gladys has behaved without pretension and with great sincerity.*

pretentious *adj.* **1** °ostentatious, °showy, °superficial, °pompous, °arrogant, °bombastic, °inflated, high-flown, exaggerated, vainglorious, fastuous, °grandiose, grandiloquent, °extravagant, magniloquent: *The minister's pretentious language is a bit too much to take.* **2** °snobbish, °lofty, °haughty, flaunting, *Colloq* high and °mighty, highfalutin *or* hifalutin, °hoity-toity, high-hat, *Slang* snotty, *Brit* toffee-nosed: *That* *new couple next door are so pretentious—they think that nobody is good enough to associate with them!*

pretext *n.* **1** °pretence, °excuse, °camouflage, °guise, °disguise, °cover, °veil, °cloak, °colour: *They carried on the surveillance under pretext of working on the sewer.* **2** °ruse, red herring, °cover (°story), °rationale, °pretence, rationalization, °explanation: *What pretext did the thief use that made you let him in?*

pretty *adj.* **1** °comely, °attractive, good-looking, nice-looking, appealing, °lovely, °cute, mignon(ne), °graceful, °fair, °bonny, °fetching, charming, winsome, °beautiful, pulchritudinous, *Colloq* easy on the eye(s): *A pretty girl is like a melody. That's a very pretty cottage.* **2** °tuneful, melodic, °melodious, dulcet, °musical, °lyrical, °harmonious, catchy, mellifluous, euphonious: *He played a pretty tune on the piano.* —*adv.* **3** °rather, °quite, °fairly, °moderately, reasonably, tolerably; °somewhat; °very, °extremely, unbelievably, incredibly: *The children put on a pretty good performance, I thought. He had become pretty fat since we last saw him.*

prevail *v.* **1** hold °sway, °win (out), °predominate, °succeed, °triumph, gain *or* achieve a °victory, prove °superior, gain mastery *or* °control: *It is sometimes disappointing to learn that right does not always prevail.* **2** °predominate, be °prevalent *or* widespread *or* °current, preponderate, °dominate, be the order of the day: *As usual during Oktoberfest in Bavaria, revelry prevailed.* **3** ***prevail on*** *or* ***upon***: °persuade, °induce, °influence, °sway, °dispose; °incline, °win over, °bring round, °convince: *We prevailed on the guard to let us through the gate.*

prevailing *adj.* **1** °dominant, °predominant, °prevalent, °main, °chief, °principal, °common(est), °usual, °customary, °universal: *The prevailing winds are westerlies.* **2** °influential, °effective, °effectual, dominating, affecting, °powerful, °potent, °forceful, ruling, °telling, °main, °principal: *The prevailing religion there is Buddhism.*

prevalence *n.* **1** prevalency, frequency, commonness, currency, universality, ubiquitousness, ubiquity, pervasiveness, omnipresence, extensiveness; °predominance, °practice, acceptance, °popularity: *The prevalence of disease among the population is distressing.* **2** °sway, °control, °rule, primacy, ascendancy, mastery, °predominance: *The prevalence of bushido in Japan has diminished little since 1945.*

prevalent *adj.* °universal, °catholic, °common, °frequent, °prevailing, °current, ubiquitous, °pervasive, omnipresent, °general, °usual, °customary, commonplace, °extensive, widespread, established, ascendant, °dominant, °predominant, governing, ruling: *A desire for change is prevalent throughout the country.*

prevent *v.* °anticipate, °preclude, obviate, °forestall, avert, °avoid, °prohibit, °ban, °bar, °forbid, interdict, °taboo, enjoin, proscribe, °foil, °frustrate, °obstruct, debar, °intercept, °nip in the bud, abort, °thwart, °check, °block, °ward *or* °fend *or* stave off, baffle, balk *or* baulk, (put a) °stop (to), °arrest, (bring to a) °halt, °hinder, °impede, °curb, °restrain, °hamper, °inhibit, °delay, °retard, °slow, °mitigate, °control: *Some diseases can be prevented by inoculation or vaccination. There is nothing to prevent us from leaving. The barrier was built to prevent flooding.*

prevention *n.* preventing, °anticipation, preclusion, obviation, forestalling, avoidance, avoiding, °prohibition, prohibiting, °ban, banning, °bar, °barring, forbiddance, °forbidding, interdiction, interdicting, °taboo, tabooing, enjoining, °injunction, proscription, proscribing, foiling, frustration, frustrating, °obstruction, obstructing, debarment, debarring, interception, intercepting, abortion, aborting, thwarting, checking, °check, blocking, °block, warding *or* fending *or* staving off, balk *or* baulk, balking *or* baulking, stopping, °arrest, °arresting, °halt, °halting, °hindrance, hindering, impedance, impeding, °curb, curbing, °restraint, restraining, hampering, °inhibition, inhibiting, °delay, delaying, retardation, retarding, slowing, mitigation, °mitigating, °control, controlling: *The first item on the agenda is the prevention of cruelty to children. As the total prevention of crime is impossible, we must at least try to curb it.*

preventive *adj.* **1** preventative, preventing, hindering, impeding, restraining, hampering, inhibitive *or* inhibitory, inhibiting, restrictive: *We must take preventive steps to ensure the stability of the rate of exchange.* **2** preventative, prophylactic, precautionary, anticipatory *or* anticipative, °protective, counteractive: *Preventive means are available to limit heart disease.* —*n.* **3** preventative, °hindrance, °curb, °inhibition, °impediment, °block, °barrier, °obstacle, °obstruction: *Caffeine is one of the most powerful preventives of sleep that exists.* **4** preventative, prophylactic, °protection, °shield, °safeguard, °prevention, countermeasure, counteractant, counter-agent, inoculum *or* inoculant, vaccine, serum, °antidote, °remedy: *Heart specialists have recommended an aspirin every other day as a preventive to arterial blood clotting.*

preview *n.* °advance showing, °private showing; °opening, *vernissage*: *We saw the Picasso exhibition at a preview held for friends of the gallery.*

previous *adj.* **1** °former, °prior, °past, earlier, one-time, °foregoing, °sometime, erstwhile, °preceding, *Literary* quondam, *Archaic* whilom: *A previous owner of the house filled in the fish-pond.* **2** °prior, °former, °foregoing, above, °preceding, *Formal* antecedent, anterior, aforementioned, above-mentioned, before-mentioned, aforesaid, above-named: *Please see the previous examples in the Foreword.* **3** °premature, untimely, too °soon *or* °early: *Isn't putting up Christmas decorations in October being a bit previous?* **4** ***previous to***: °previously to, °before, °prior to, °preceding, anterior to, antecedent to: *Previous to the advent of motor cars, we had traffic jams of horse-drawn vehicles.*

previously *adv.* °before, °once, °formerly, earlier, at one °time, then, beforehand, heretofore, theretofore, hitherto, thitherto, in the °past, in days gone by, in days of old, in days *or* time °past, in the °old days, some time ago, a while ago, °once upon a time, yesterday, *Literary* in days of yore, in olden days *or* times: *The same thing had happened previously when I was in London. Previously, people lived more relaxed lives—or so we like to think.*

prey *n.* **1** °quarry, °kill, °game, °objective, °target: *The lioness singled out her prey from the herd of zebra.* **2** °victim, °target, °objective; °dupe, *Colloq* mark, *Slang* fall guy, °pushover, *Brit* °mug: *A public company with huge cash reserves, United Vector seemed easy prey for a take-over bid.* —*v.* **3** ***prey on*** *or* ***upon***: **a** °live off, °feed on *or* upon, °eat, °consume, °devour, °kill, °destroy, °stalk, °pursue, °hunt, °seize: *These snakes prey mostly upon other snakes.* **b** °victimize, °go after, °exploit, °use, take °advantage of, °intimidate, °bully, °cheat, °dupe, °swindle, gull, °trick, snooker, °defraud, °outwit, °outsmart, outfox, °hoodwink, *Literary* cozen, *Colloq* rook, bamboozle, flimflam: *An unscrupulous gang is preying on the elderly, persuading them to invest in non-existent properties.* **c** °oppress, °weigh on *or* upon, °burden, °depress, °distress, °strain, vex, °worry: *His wretched condition preyed very much on her mind.*

price *n.* **1** charge, °cost, °expense, °expenditure, °outlay, °payment, °amount, °figure, °fee; °quotation, appraisal, value, valuation, °evaluation, °worth: *The price of this lamp is too high. What is the price of that box? Can he afford the price of a ticket? The current price of a London flat is out of my reach.* **2** °sacrifice, °toll, °penalty, °cost, consequence: *Loss of his freedom was too high a price for standing by his principles.* **3** °reward, °bounty, °premium, °prize, °payment, °bonus, °honorarium, *Literary* guerdon: *The gunfighter had a price of $1,000 on his head.* **4** ***without price***: See **priceless, 1,** below. —*v.* **5** value, °evaluate, °rate, assay, assess, °cost (out): *How would you price a piece of furniture like this chair?*

priceless *adj.* **1** costly, °dear, °expensive, high-priced, valuable, °invaluable, °precious, °inestimable, incalculable; irreplaceable, °unique: *The vaults in the Vatican contain a king's ransom in priceless jewels.* **2** °hilarious, °riotous, (screamingly) °funny, side-splitting, °hysterical, droll, comical, amusing: *The expression on his face when he realized it was a joke was priceless.*

pricey *adj.* pricy, °expensive, °dear, costly, °exorbitant, °outrageous, °excessive, extortionate, *Colloq* °steep, *Brit* over the odds: *The restaurant where she took him was certainly pricey, but the food was excellent.*

prick *n.* **1** °puncture, pinhole, pinprick; °hole, perforation: *For the blood test, the doctor made a tiny prick in my finger with a needle.* **2** °sting, °pinch, °twinge, °prickle, tingle, °pain: *The teacher leapt from her chair the instant she felt the prick of the tack.*
—*v.* **3** °puncture, °pierce, °stab, °jab, °punch, °perforate, °riddle; °lance: *Using a pin, prick tiny holes in the paper to let the steam escape. The doctor pricked a boil on my neck.* **4** °stab, °sting, °hurt, °prickle, °pinch, °bite, °smart: *The hypodermic needle really pricked me when it went in.*

prickle *n.* **1** °spine, °bristle, barb, °thorn, bur *or* burr, needle, tine, °spike, °spur, prong: *The prickles make the brambles cling to your clothes.* **2** pricking, prickliness, °itch, itchiness, °sting, tingling, tingle: *I felt the prickle of the rough wool against my skin.*
—*v.* **3** tingle, °sting, °itch, °smart: *Sloane complained that the beard he had to grow for the pirate role made his face prickle.* **4** °stick, °jab, °prick: *The child's hands had been prickled by the chestnuts.*

prickly *adj.* **1** bristly, °thorny, brambly, spiny, barbed, briery *or* briary, spinous, spiky, *Technical* setaceous, setose, acanthoid, aciculate, aculeate, muricate, spiculate: *Dad's face is all prickly when he hasn't shaved.* **2** tingling, stinging, pricking, prickling, itchy, crawly, crawling: *The squeak of the chalk on the blackboard gives me a prickly feeling.* **3** °touchy, °irritable, °petulant, °cantankerous, °testy, °waspish, bad-tempered, °peevish, fractious, °short-tempered, curmudgeonly, *Colloq* °cranky: *Moira gets a bit prickly if you ask her why she married Noel.* **4** nettlesome, °thorny, °ticklish, °touchy, °troublesome, °intricate, °complicated, complex, knotty, °hard, °difficult, contentious: *The prickly problem of how to pay for the university must still be faced.*

pride *n.* **1** °honour, proudness, °self-esteem, °self-respect, *amour propre*, °dignity: *It is gratifying to be able to look with pride on one's children's achievements.* **2** °conceit, egotism, self-importance, °vanity, hubris, °arrogance, overconfidence, overweeningness, self-admiration, self-love, smugness, haughtiness, hauteur, °snobbery, snobbishness, *Colloq* uppitiness: *Pride goeth before a fall. Her pride stems from an exaggerated notion of her own worth.* **3** °boast, °flower, °best, °prize, °pride and °joy, °treasure, °jewel, °gem: *Those model railway trains are Eustace's pride and joy.*
—*v.* **4** Usually, ***pride oneself on***: be °proud of, take °pride in, °delight in, °revel in, °celebrate, °glory in: *Irena prides herself on having made her own way in life, without anyone's help.*

priest *n.* priestess, °clergyman *or* clergywoman, ecclesiastic, cleric, churchman *or* churchwoman, reverend, vicar, °divine, man *or* woman of the °cloth, man *or* woman of God, curate, confessor, °minister (of the Gospel), servant of God, °father, mother, °holy man *or* woman, °preacher, °missionary, evangelist, abbé, abbot *or* abbess, *Colloq* padre: *The oak tree was sacred to Druid priests.*

priestly *adj.* °clerical, ecclesiastical, °pastoral, hieratic, sacerdotal; ministerial, canonical, °missionary: *She has taken her priestly vows.*

prig *n.* (ultra-)°conservative, °prude, °purist, pedant, school-ma'm, °puritan, (Mrs) Grundy, Grundyite, Grundyist, precisionist, precisian, conformist, formalist, *Colloq* stuffed shirt, °stick-in-the-mud, °goody-goody: *A terrible prig, the headmaster forbade even the slightest hint of slang usage.*

priggish *adj.* (ultra-)°conservative, prim, demure, °prudish, °purist, puristic, °pedantic, school-marmish, °strait-laced, °hidebound, stiff-necked, puritanical, conformist, (Mrs) Grundyish, punctilious, °formal, formalistic, °strict, °severe, °fastidious, °fussy, °particular; °precious, *précieux* or *précieuse*, niminy-piminy, over-nice, *Colloq* °stick-in-the-mud, °goody-goody, °prissy, old-maidish, stuffed-shirt, °stuffy, uptight, nit-picking, *Brit* °twee: *Victorians were less priggish in their private behaviour than in their public image.*

primarily *adv.* **1** °principally, °mainly, °chiefly, °especially, at °bottom, °particularly, °first of all, °pre-eminently, basically, essentially, fundamentally, on the °whole, for the most °part, mostly, predominantly *or* predominately, °generally: *The rain in Spain falls primarily in the plain.* **2** initially, °originally, from *or* at the °start, °first (and °foremost), in the °first instance, *ab initio*: *The colonists, primarily refugees from England, began to settle the New World in the 17th century.*

primary *adj.* **1** °first, °prime, °principal, °chief, °main, °leading, °pre-eminent, °cardinal, °fundamental, °basic, °essential, °predominant, °elementary, °elemental, underlying: *The primary reason I want to see you is to discuss your future with the company. The primary meaning of a word is given first.* **2** earliest, °first, °original, °initial, °primitive, primeval *or Brit also* primaeval, primordial, embryonic, germinal, °beginning, °ultimate: *The primary source of life was possibly a sort of soup containing proteins and other molecules.* **3** firsthand, °direct, °immediate: *Bauxite is the primary source of aluminium ore.* **4** °elementary, °basic, °rudimentary, °fundamental: *One of the primary lessons we are taught is consideration for others.* **5** unmixed, unadulterated, °pure, °simple, °rudimentary, °fundamental, °principal: *The primary colours in art are red, yellow, and blue.*

prime *adj.* **1** See **primary, 1,** above. **2** °best, °foremost, °chief; °first-rate, first-class, °choice, °select, °superior, °pre-eminent, °leading, ranking, °predominant, °unparalleled, °matchless, °peerless, °noteworthy, °outstanding, °admirable, °worthy, °exceptional, °excellent, °extraordinary: *She is a prime example of the results of a modern education. Arthur is certainly a prime candidate for the position.* **3** °original, °fundamental, °basic, °elemental, °elementary: *The prime cause of scurvy is lack of fresh fruit and vegetables.*
—*n.* **4** °youth, springtime; °best years, heyday, °pinnacle, °acme, °peak, °zenith: *Some people reach the prime of life at 60.*
—*v.* **5** (make *or* get) °ready, °prepare, °educate, °teach, °instruct, °coach, °train, °tutor, °drill: *Has Sonia been fully primed to take over the chairmanship when Sir William steps down?* **6** °inform, °advise, °notify, apprise, °brief: *Having read your book, I am fully primed on American history.*

primitive *adj.* **1** °first, °original, °aboriginal, earliest, primordial, primal, primeval *or Brit also* primaeval, °pristine, °prehistoric; antediluvian, Noachian *or* Noachic, °old, °ancient: *In its most primitive state, life probably originated from some random strings of molecules. The most primitive farming tools date from some 10,000 years ago.* **2** °crude, °rude, °unrefined, °raw, barbaric, uncultured, °barbarian, °coarse, °rough, °uncivilized, °savage, uncultivated, °unsophisticated, uncouth: *I cannot tolerate Nigel's primitive table manners.* **3** °simple, °basic, simplistic, °naïve, °childlike, °unsophisticated, uncultivated, °unrefined, unpolished, °rough, untutored, untaught, untrained, unschooled, °undeveloped: *Gary collects paintings of the primitive school and has one by Grandma Moses.*

primp *v.* °preen, prink, prettify, titivate *or* tittivate, plume, °dress up, °groom, *Colloq* doll up, get (all) dolled up, °spruce up, put on one's °best bib and tucker, *Chiefly Brit* °tart up, get (all) tarted up, *Slang* deck out, trick out *or* up, put on one's glad °rags, *Brit* fig out, *US* gussy up, get (all) gussied up, °dude up: *She* *was primping before the mirror, awaiting the arrival of her beau.*

princely *adj.* **1** °lavish, °bountiful, °generous, °liberal, °ample, °substantial, °huge, °enormous: *They paid a princely sum for their stately home in Surrey.* **2** °lavish, °magnificent, °splendid, °luxurious, °majestic, °royal, °regal, °sumptuous, °superb, *Colloq* ritzy, swank(y), °posh, °plush: *The hotel laid on princely accommodation for us with rooms overlooking the sea.* **3** °royal, °noble, °regal, °sovereign, of °royal *or* °noble blood *or* rank: *Who would have thought that our humble home would ever shelter a princely guest?*

principal *adj.* **1** °chief, °primary, °prime, °paramount, °main, °first, °foremost, ranking, °pre-eminent, °predominant, °dominant, °prevailing; °leading, starring: *The principal reason I'm here is to see you. The principal food of the people is corn. The principal role was sung by Pavarotti.* **2** °important, °prominent, °leading, °key, °cardinal: *Cuba is a principal source of sugar.* —*n.* **3** °owner, °proprietor, chairman, chairwoman, chairperson, (managing) °director, °head, president, °chief, chief °executive officer, CEO, °manager *or Brit* manageress, °superintendent, °supervisor, *Colloq* °boss, *US* (°head *or* °chief) honcho: *We should talk to the principals about buying that company.* **4** dean, °director, *Chiefly Brit* headmaster, headmistress, °master, rector, (vice-)chancellor: *His appointment as principal is for a two-year period.* **5** (working) °capital, °capital funds, resources, investment, °backing, (cash) °reserve(s), °assets; °money: *She is fortunate to be able to live on the income from her investments, without touching the principal.* **6** °star, °lead, °heroine, °hero, °leading lady *or* man, °leading role, °main °part; diva, *première danseuse, premier danseur*, prima donna, prima ballerina: *The principal in the ballet company was a Russian.*

principally *adv.* °chiefly, °mainly, °first (and °foremost), °primarily, above all, in the °main, mostly, for the most °part, °largely, predominantly, on the °whole, at °bottom, in °essence, essentially, basically, fundamentally; °especially, °particularly: *He seems to be interested principally in money, with little regard for anything else.*

principle *n.* **1** °truth, °given, °precept, °tenet, °fundamental, °grounds, °law, °rule, dictum, canon, °doctrine, teaching, dogma, °proposition, (°basic) assumption, postulate, axiom, °maxim, °truism, °guide, °standard, criterion, °model: *The perpetual-motion machine violates a basic principle of physics.* **2** Often, ***principles***: °philosophy, °code, °attitude, (°point of) °view, °viewpoint, °sentiment, °belief, credo, °creed, °idea, °notion, ethic, sense of right and wrong: *He cynically conducts his life on the principle, 'Do unto others before they do unto you'. I am not sure I can condone his principles.* **3** (sense of) °honour, uprightness, °honesty, °morality, morals, °probity, °integrity, °conscience: *If you don't think him a man of principle, don't do business with him.* **4** ***in principle***: on principle, in theory, theoretically, basically, fundamentally, at °bottom, in °essence, essentially, °ideally: *I like your plan in principle, but in practice it cannot be accomplished that way.*

principled *adj.* °moral, °righteous, right-minded, °virtuous, °noble, high-minded, °ethical, °honourable, °proper, °correct, °right, °just, °upright, °honest, °scrupulous: *Michael is too highly principled to take bribes.*

print *v.* **1** °impress, imprint, °stamp, °publish, °issue, °run off, °put out; °copy; (pull a) proof: *We decided to print 500 copies of the book. You may have your name printed on the cover for an additional amount.* —*n.* **2** °reproduction, °copy, °replica, °facsimile; positive, °photograph, etching, (steel *or* wood-)°engraving, lithograph, woodcut, linocut, silk screen, rotogravure, *Trade Mark* Xerox; °picture, °illustration; *Colloq* photo, °cut, pic (*pl.* pix): *Today, a good print of a Picasso costs more than an original did fifty years ago.* **3** °text, printed matter, °type, °writing; °language, °wording, (choice of) °words, phrasing: *You'd be well advised to read the small print before signing the agreement.*

prior *adj.* **1** °former, °previous, earlier, one-time, ex-, erstwhile; °old, °last, °late, °latest, *Literary* quondam, whilom: *If you overdraw your account without prior arrangement, you will automatically be charged a higher rate of interest.* **2** ***prior to***: °before, °previous to, °previously to, °till, until, °preceding: *Prior to the earthquake, Valdivia was a river port.*

priority *n.* °precedence, precedency, primacy, °urgency, immediacy, °predominance, °pre-eminence, °preference, °rank, °superiority, °prerogative, °right, seniority, °importance, °weight: *The applications for aid will be processed in order of priority.*

prison *n.* °jail *or Brit also* gaol, °dungeon, oubliette, lock-up, °penal °institution, house of °correction, correctional °institution, reformatory, house of °detention; confinement, °detention; *Old-fashioned* °reform school, *Military* guardhouse; *Brit* remand centre, °detention centre, remand home, community home, *Military* glasshouse, *Formal* CHE (= 'community home with education on the premises'), *Old-fashioned* approved school; *US* penitentiary, *Military* brig; *Archaic Brit* bridewell; *Slang* clink, can, cooler, jug, °stir, *Brit* quod, chokey *or* choky, *US and Canadian* pokey *or* poky; *US* pen, calaboose, slammer, hoosegow, *Old-fashioned* big house: *He was released from prison last Friday after serving six months for burglary.*

prisoner *n.* °convict, trusty; internee, detainee; *Colloq* jailbird *or Brit also* gaolbird, lifer, *Slang* con, *Brit* (old) °lag, *Old-fashioned* ticket-of-leave man, *US* two-time *or* three-time loser: *Prisoners' letters were censored.*

prissy *adj.* °fussy, °precious, over-nice, °finicky *or* finical, °strait-laced, school-marmish, prim (and °proper), °prudish, °squeamish, °fastidious, *Colloq* old-maidish: *He is awfully prissy about changing on the beach.*

pristine *adj.* **1** °original, primal, °basic, primeval *or Brit also* primaeval, °primitive, primordial, earliest, °first, °initial: *It is impractical to try to return the world to what some regard as its pristine purity.* **2** uncorrupted, °pure, unsullied, undefiled, virginal, virgin, °chaste, untouched, °unspoiled *or* unspoilt, unpolluted, °untarnished, °spotless, °immaculate, °natural: *One must travel far today to experience the pristine beauty of nature. The car was in pristine condition.*

privacy *n.* **1** °seclusion, retirement, °solitude, isolation, °retreat, sequestration, reclusiveness, reclusion, solitariness; monasticism: *Coleman very much enjoys the privacy of living alone.* **2** °secrecy, secretiveness, clandestineness, confidentiality, surreptitiousness, covertness, concealment: *Many feel that the questions on census forms invade their privacy.*

private *adj.* **1** (top) °secret, °confidential, undisclosed, hidden, clandestine, concealed, covert, °surreptitious, off the °record, not for publication, °unofficial, *Colloq* hush-hush: *I think our relationship should be kept private for the time being. What I am about to tell you is strictly private.* **2** °privileged, restrictive, restricted, °exclusive, °special, °reserved, °personal, °inaccessible, non-public; °hidden, °secluded, concealed, °secret, °sneaking: *The house is situated on a private road. I had a private suspicion that they would cancel their trip.* **3** °personal, °individual, own, °intimate, °particular: *My private affairs are none of your business.* **4** °solitary, seclusive, °reclusive, °withdrawn, °retiring, °reticent, ungregarious, non-gregarious, °unsocial, unsociable, antisocial, °reserved, uncommunicative, hermitic(al), hermit-like, eremitic(al); sequestered, °secluded, retired: *You have to bear in mind that Edmund is a very private person.* —*n.* **5** private °soldier, infantryman, foot-soldier, *US* enlisted man, *Colloq Brit* Tommy, Tommy Atkins, squaddie, *US* GI (Joe), *Slang US* grunt: *Before cashiering him, they reduced him from colonel to private.* **6** ***in***

private: in °secret, °secretly, privately, *sub rosa*, °personally, confidentially, behind closed doors, in camera, off the °record, *US* on the q.t. *or* Q.T.; clandestinely, secretively, sneakily, sneakingly, surreptitiously, furtively, covertly, on the °sly: *Family matters should be discussed only in private. They met in private with agents of the rebel forces.* **7 *private parts*** *or* ***privates***: °genitals, °sexual *or* °sex organs, genitalia. *The natives wore loincloths to cover their private parts.*

privation *n.* °need, neediness, °want, deprivation, °hardship, indigence, °necessity, °poverty, penury, destitution, °strait(s), pauperism, beggary; °distress, °misery: *The lower classes in Victorian England suffered terrible privation.*

privilege *n.* °benefit, °advantage, °right, °prerogative, concession, °allowance, °indulgence, °immunity, °exemption, dispensation, °freedom, °liberty, franchise, °permission, °consent, °leave, authorization, °sanction, °authority, °licence, *carte blanche*: *The children were given the privilege of choosing where the family should go on holiday.*

privileged *adj.* **1** °favoured, advantaged, indulged, entitled, °élite, °special, honoured: *John was one of the privileged few to be told her private telephone number.* **2** protected, °exempt(ed), °immune; licensed, empowered, admitted, permitted, sanctioned, authorized, enfranchised, chartered: *This is a privileged institution as far as the dispensation of grants is concerned.* **3** °powerful, ruling; °wealthy, °rich: *He despised the privileged class till he became wealthy enough to be a member of it.* **4** °confidential, °secret, °private, °privy, °inside, off the °record, not for publication, restricted, *Colloq* hush-hush: *What I am about to tell you is privileged information.*

privy *adj.* **1** See **privileged, 4,** above. **2 *privy to***: °aware of, in on, on to *or* onto, sharing (in), cognizant of, apprised of, °informed *or* advised about *or* of, °informed on, °knowledgeable about, *Colloq* in the know about, *Slang* °hip to, °wise to, *Old-fashioned* hep to: *Was the minister's wife privy to what was discussed at cabinet meetings?*
—*n.* **3** °lavatory, (outside *or* outdoor) °toilet, latrine, water-closet, WC, *US* outhouse, *Colloq chiefly Brit* loo, *Slang Brit* bog, *US* crapper, *Taboo slang US* shithouse: *In those days, almost every home had an outside privy, as there was no interior plumbing.*

prize[1] *n.* **1** °reward, °award, °trophy, °premium; °honour, accolade, *Literary* guerdon: *The first prize was a week's holiday in the Bahamas.* **2** winnings, jackpot, °purse, receipts, °gain, °windfall, stakes, *Colloq* °haul, *Chiefly US* °take: *He used his prize from winning the lottery to buy a new car.* **3** °aim, °goal: *The prize they all strove for was a grant to carry on lexicographic research.* **4** °loot, °booty, °spoil(s), °trophy, °plunder, pickings: *The pirates took the galleon as their prize.*
—*adj.* **5** °choice, °excellent, (prize)winning, °best, °champion, °outstanding, °select, °superior, °superlative, °first-rate: *This dairy owns a prize herd of Guernseys.*

prize[2] *v.* value, °treasure, °esteem, °cherish, °appreciate, °rate highly, hold °dear: *I prize your friendship above all things.*

probability *n.* °likelihood, likeliness, °odds, °expectation, °chance(s), (distinct) °possibility, °presumption: *There is a high probability that it will rain.*

probable *adj.* (most) °likely, apt, (quite) °possible, presumed, °plausible, undoubted, indubitable, °apparent, °unquestionable, °evident, ostensible, odds-on, °feasible, believable, credible: *The probable cause of the flooding was a blockage in the drains. It is probable that most medieval churches had paintings round the walls.*

probably *adv.* (very) °likely, in all °likelihood, in all °probability, °undoubtedly, doubtlessly, indubitably, unquestionably, °presumably, all things considered, to all intents and purposes, °possibly, °perhaps, *Colloq* as °likely as not, °quite: *She is probably the best tennis player in the world at the moment.*

probe *v.* **1** °explore, °examine, °scrutinize, °investigate, °search (into), °look into, °go into, °study, °dig into, delve into, °poke about *or* around, *Colloq* °poke into: *They probed his background thoroughly but found nothing unusual.* **2** °poke, °prod, °explore, °examine; °plumb, °dig: *Snipe use their long bills to probe for worms in soft mud.*
—*n.* **3** °investigation, °examination, °exploration, °scrutiny, °search, °study, °inquiry *or* enquiry, inquest: *There will be a governmental probe into the mismanagement of the department.*

probity *n.* °integrity, uprightness, °honesty, °morality, °rectitude, °virtue, goodness, decency, righteousness, right-mindedness, °sincerity, trustworthiness, °honour, °equity, justness, °justice, fairness: *Lord Chancellors have consistently been men of unquestioned probity.*

problem *n.* **1** °difficulty, °trouble, °question, °dilemma, °quandary, °predicament, °complication, hornet's nest, imbroglio, °mess, °muddle, °stew, *Colloq* can of worms, fine kettle of fish, (pretty) pickle, *Brit* facer: *The Chancellor must constantly deal with the problems of the country's economy.* **2** °puzzle, conundrum, poser, °riddle, °question, °enigma, puzzler, *Colloq* mind-boggler, hard *or* tough nut to crack: *The problem is how to get the yolk out without breaking the shell.*
—*adj.* **3** °unruly, unmanageable, intractable, uncontrollable, °difficult, °ungovernable, refractory, °incorrigible, °obstreperous, °delinquent, maladjusted, °disturbed, emotionally °upset: *He teaches at a school where most of the students are problem children.*

problematic *adj.* problematical, °difficult, °uncertain, °questionable, questioned, °doubtful, doubted, °debatable, °disputable, disputed, °unsettled, °moot, undecided, °controversial, °tricky, °touchy, °sensitive, *Colloq* °hairy, iffy: *The value of treating colds with massive doses of vitamin C is problematic.*

procedure *n.* °way, °conduct, °course, °action, °course of °action, °method, methodology, °mode, °form, °system, °approach, °strategy, °plan (of °action), °scheme, modus operandi, °operation, °policy, ways and °means; °routine, °tradition, °practice, °custom, wont, standard operating procedure, *Colloq* MO (= 'modus operandi'), SOP (= 'standard operating procedure'), *Chiefly Brit* drill: *What procedure will you follow to regain the stolen property? The procedure in ballroom dancing has always been for the man to lead.*

proceed *v.* **1** Sometimes, ***proceed with***: °go *or* °move (on *or* ahead *or* forward), °advance, °continue, °progress, °carry on, °get *or* °move along, get going *or* moving *or* under °way, °start, °pass on, make °progress *or* °headway, °push *or* °press on *or* °onward(s), forge ahead; resume, °renew, °go on with, pick up (where one left off): *Proceed to the T-junction, then turn left. If the membership committee has finished, let us proceed to the report of the finance committee. After the break, the performance will proceed.* **2** Often, ***proceed from*** *or* ***out of***: °result from, °arise (from), °come (from), °stem from, °spring from, °develop (from), °issue (from *or* forth), °derive from, be derived (from), °descend from, °emerge (from), °grow (from *or* out of), °originate (in *or* from *or* with), °begin (with), °start (with *or* from): *The outcropping proceeds from glaciation and erosion. They say that more than half of a person's happiness proceeds from hope.*
—*n.* **3 *proceeds***: °profit(s), °gain, °yield; °income, °receipts, °return(s), °gate, box office, *US* °take: *The proceeds from the charity auction were better than ever this year.*

proceeding *n.* **1** °measure, °act, (°course of) °action, °move, °step, °undertaking, °deed, °procedure, °process, °operation, °transaction, °manoeuvre, °feat, °accomplishment: *Grace Darling's rescue of the shipwrecked men was truly a heroic proceeding.* **2 *proceedings***: **a** °transactions, °report(s), °minutes, °record(s), annals, °affairs, °dealings, °business, °account(s), archives, *Formal* acta: *The proceedings of the Society are published annually.* **b** °events, goings-on, doings; °celebration(s); °performance(s): *The proceedings were briefly interrupted while the hecklers were ejected from the hall.*

process *n.* **1** °procedure, °proceeding, °operation, °system, °method, °approach, °technique; °course of °action: *I am sure you understand how the process works. What process do they use to make paper out of wood?* **2** °activity, °function, °development: *The process of photosynthesis is the means by which plants synthesize carbohydrates.*
—*v.* **3** °treat, °prepare, (make *or* get) °ready, °change, °modify, °transform, °convert, °alter: *This is the room where the ingredients are processed before mixing.* **4** °handle, take °care of, °organize, °deal with, °manage; °dispose of, °answer, °manipulate: *After the earthquake the insurance companies processed thousands of claims.*

procession *n.* **1** °parade, °march, cavalcade, motorcade, cortege *or* cortège, column, °line, °file, °train, °march past: *A strange procession of thousands of beggars silently wound its way through the city.* **2** °succession, °cycle, °sequence, °string, °train, °chain, series, °course, °run, °progression, cavalcade: *He began to recount the procession of events that led up to the murder.*

proclaim *v.* **1** °announce, advertise, °circulate, °declare, °broadcast, °pronounce, °make known, bruit (about), trumpet, °publish, promulgate, herald; °profess, °protest, °enunciate, articulate: *Edgar was proclaimed king. She proclaimed her innocence.* **2** °brand, °accuse of being, °stigmatize as, °pronounce, °rule, °decree, °characterize, °report: *She found herself proclaimed a traitor.*

proclamation *n.* **1** °announcement, °advertisement, °declaration, °publication, promulgation, °statement, manifesto, pronunciamento, notification, °notice: *A proclamation was issued granting amnesty to all political prisoners.* **2** proclaiming, announcing, advertising, declaring, broadcasting, publishing, promulgating, heralding, making known, bruiting about: *The proclamation of his appointment as Chancellor came at a bad time.*

procrastinate *v.* **1** temporize, act evasively, °play for time, dally, °delay, °stall; °postpone, °defer, °put off *or* aside, °shelve, *US* °table: *I wish he would stop procrastinating and say what he plans to do.* **2** °hesitate, °pause, waver, vacillate, be undecided, °equivocate, tergiversate, °shilly-shally: *Helen procrastinates every time she is faced with making a decision.*

procure *v.* **1** °obtain, °acquire, °get, °come by, °secure, get *or* lay one's hands on, get (a) hold of, °gain, °win, °come into, °pick up, °find, °appropriate, °requisition; °buy, °purchase: *I have been trying to procure early editions of Defoe's works.* **2** °accomplish, °bring about, °effect, °cause, °produce: *Using every resource available to her, she finally procured his release.*

procurer *n.* °pander *or* panderer, °pimp, White °slaver, flesh-pedlar *or US also* flesh-peddler *or* flesh-pedler, *Archaic* whoremaster, bawd; madam, procuress: *He became a procurer for the wealthy men in the village.*

prod *v.* **1** °jab, °dig, °poke, °nudge, elbow: *Every time the comedian said something risqué, Aunt Flora would giggle and prod me in the ribs.* **2** °spur, °urge, impel, egg on, °push, °thrust, °prompt, °rouse, °stir, °incite, °move, °motivate, actuate, °activate, °provoke, °encourage, °stimulate: *My uncle keeps prodding me to continue with my studies.* **3** °incite, goad, needle, °irritate, °irk, °annoy, °pester, °harass, hector, badger, °plague, °nag, °hound, °carp at, °cavil; °henpeck: *My parents are constantly prodding me to go out and get a job.*
—*n.* **4** °jab, °dig, °poke, °nudge, elbow, °push: *I was quite black and blue from those prods I was getting from Aunt Flora.* **5** goad, °spur; needle, rowel: *These days electrified cattle prods are available.* **6** stimulus, °push, °prompt, °reminder, °signal, °cue: *Calvin needed that prod to make him finally go home after the party.*

prodigal *adj.* **1** °wasteful, °extravagant, °spendthrift, °lavish, °excessive, °profligate, squandering, °immoderate, intemperate, °wanton, °improvident, °reckless: *If the government were less prodigal, it would be possible to have a balanced budget.* **2** °generous, °bountiful, copious, °profuse, bounteous, °lavish, °liberal, °luxuriant, °sumptuous, °abundant, abounding, °rich, °plentiful, plenteous, superabundant, thriving, swarming, teeming: *He was prodigal of both compliments and criticism.*
—*n.* **3** °wastrel, °spendthrift, °profligate, squanderer, waster, big spender: *That prodigal went through his inheritance in less than a year.*

prodigality *n.* **1** wastefulness, °waste, °extravagance, °excess, excessiveness, immoderation, intemperateness, wantonness, recklessness, °profligacy, improvidence, °dissipation, squandering: *Surely his contemporaries must have condemned Shah Jehan's prodigality in building the Taj Mahal.* **2** lavishness, profuseness, °luxury, luxuriousness, luxuriance, °abundance, °plenty, °bounty, bountifulness, bounteousness, copiousness, °profusion, profuseness, sumptuousness, richness, plentifulness, plenteousness, superabundance, °exuberance: *The prodigality of Nature is unbounded.*

prodigious *adj.* **1** °vast, °immeasurable, °colossal, °enormous, °huge, °giant, °gigantic, °immense, mammoth, °monumental, tremendous, stupendous, titanic, Brobdingnagian, gargantuan, Herculean, Cyclopean, leviathan, °monstrous, °extensive, *Colloq US* ginormous, humongous: *There is a prodigious amount of water vapour contained in a cloudy sky. You may accuse her of being a workaholic, but consider the prodigious amount she gets done in a day.* **2** °amazing, astonishing, astounding, °startling, °extraordinary, °exceptional, °marvellous, wonderful, wondrous, °fabulous, °miraculous, °phenomenal, spectacular, °fantastic, °sensational, °unusual, staggering, °striking, dumbfounding *or* dumfounding, °remarkable, °noteworthy, °notable, *Colloq* flabbergasting, mind-boggling, mind-blowing: *In those days, running a mile in four minutes was considered a prodigious feat.*

prodigy *n.* **1** (child *or* girl *or* boy) °genius, wonder child, *Wunderkind*, °mastermind, °talent, °intellect, °intellectual *or* °mental giant, wizard, °virtuoso, *Colloq* °brain, Einstein, whiz-kid *or* whizz-kid, whiz *or* whizz, walking dictionary *or* encyclopedia *or* encyclopaedia: *She was a prodigy at the age of six and went on to become a great concert performer.* **2** °wonder, °marvel, °phenomenon, °sensation, miracle: *Some regarded the painting* Nude Descending a Staircase *a prodigy of cubist art.*

produce *v.* **1** °make, °develop, °turn out, °put *or* °bring out, °manufacture, °fabricate, °generate, °create; °construct, °assemble, °put together, °compose; °mould, °cast; extrude: *This machine is capable of producing 10,000 units an hour.* **2** °yield, give °rise to, °cause, °bring up, °bring forth, °spark, °initiate, °occasion, °bring about, °prompt, °evoke, °start, °create, °generate, beget, °originate: *He was unprepared for the laughter produced by his slip of the tongue.* **3** °generate, beget, °create, °put out *or* forth, °breed, °propagate, °bear, give birth to, °hatch, °grow: *See how the plant is producing buds at these nodes?* **4** °bring forward *or* in *or* out, °introduce, °present, °offer, °show, °exhibit, °display, °stage, °put on, °mount: *She was the first to produce Japanese Noh drama in the west.* **5** °disclose, °reveal, bring to °light, °show, °display, °draw: *When I refused to give him the money, he produced a gun.* **6** °supply, °furnish, °provide, °deliver, °distribute: *They are accused of continuing to produce fluorocarbons despite the government ban.*
—*n.* **7** vegetables, fruit, *Chiefly Brit* greengrocery: *The produce is delivered to the markets from the farms at the crack of dawn.*

producer *n.* **1** maker, °manufacturer, fabricator, processor, °creator; grower, farmer: *That company is the largest producer of microchips in the world.* **2** *In Britain*: °director, auteur, impresario, regisseur; *In US and Canada*: entrepreneur, (business *or* financial) °manager, organizer: *He was a producer of TV soap operas.*

product *n.* **1** °result, consequence, °output, °outcome, °issue, °effect, fallout, °yield, °upshot; spin-off, °offshoot, by-product: *It is evident that this work is the product of much thought. One product of her interest in literature is a new publishing company.* **2** artefact *or US* artifact, °good(s), °produce, commodity, °output, °merchandise, °offering, °work: *It doesn't matter how good the product is if nobody knows about it.*

production *n.* **1** producing, °manufacture, manufacturing, making, °fabrication, °preparation, origination, °creation, °output, putting out, °development; °formation, forming, forging, shaping, moulding, casting, °assembly, °building, construction: *Our business is the production of insulating materials.* **2** °product, (°end) °result, °work, °effort, handiwork, °output, °opus, *œuvre*: *These paintings are clearly productions of a fertile imagination.* **3** *In Britain*: artistry, °direction, staging; *In US and Canada*: °display, °presentation, *mise en scène*, °setting: *Both the acting and the production were superb.* **4** °drama, °play, (°stage *or* °television *or* °radio) °show, °performance; °film, motion *or* moving picture, °movie: *Our repertory company is putting on a production of* Othello *next week.*

productive *adj.* **1** °fruitful, °fertile, °rich, fecund, °plentiful, plenteous, °abundant, °bountiful, bounteous, °prolific, °dynamic: *Owing to a perfect balance of rain and sunshine, the earth has proved productive this year.* **2** °imaginative, °creative, inventive, °resourceful, generative, °ingenious, °fertile, °vigorous: *Her latest science-fiction trilogy is certainly evidence of a highly productive mind.* **3** °profitable, remunerative, °rewarding, valuable, °worthwhile: *Years ago he made an investment in computer shares that has turned out to be very productive. Discussing sales strategy is not as productive as getting out there and selling.*

profane *adj.* **1** °irreverent, °sacrilegious, °blasphemous, idolatrous, irreligious, °infidel, °heathen, °unbelieving, disbelieving, °pagan, atheist(ic), °impious, °godless, °ungodly, °sinful, °wicked, iniquitous, °contemptuous, °disrespectful: *The faithful attacked anyone who was seen to perform a profane act.* **2** unsanctified, unholy, unconsecrated, defiled, °impure, unclean, unhallowed, non-religious, non-sacred, unsacred; °lay, non-clerical, °secular, °temporal; *Judaism* tref *or* treif *or* treifa, non-kosher: *The missionaries persuaded them to abandon their profane rites and practices.* **3** °bad, °dirty, °filthy, smutty, °foul, foul-mouthed, °obscene, °vulgar, °coarse, uncouth, °low, °taboo, °blasphemous, °bawdy, ribald, °scurrilous, °off colour, °immodest, °improper, °naughty, °indecent, unprintable, °unmentionable, indecorous, indelicate, °common; °abusive, °vituperative, °venomous, thersitical, *Literary* Fescennine, *Colloq* °blue: *The boy was sent home from school for using profane language.*
—*v.* **4** °debase, °contaminate, °pollute, °taint, °vitiate, °degrade, defile, °desecrate, °violate, °pervert, °corrupt: *They swore undying retribution against those who had profaned their temple.*

profanity *n.* blasphemy, obscenity, cursing, curse-word(s), swearing, swear-word(s), °foul *or* °bad *or* °dirty *or* °vulgar *or* °coarse *or* °filthy *or* smutty *or* °taboo °language, four-letter word(s), billingsgate: *The film was held to be unfit for broadcasting as it contained so much obscenity and profanity.*

profess *v.* **1** assert, °claim, aver, asseverate, °state, affirm, °confirm, °confess, °declare, °say, °hold, °maintain, °present, °offer, proffer, °tender, °set forth, °put forward, °pronounce, enounce, °enunciate, °announce, utter, °vow, avow: *He professed himself satisfied with the judge's decision.* **2** °pretend, lay °claim, make a °pretence, purport, °act as if, simulate: *They professed to be legitimate businessmen, but I was always suspicious.*

professed *adj.* **1** °pretended, ostensible, °apparent, °alleged, purported, °so-called, would-be, °self-styled, *soi-disant*: *He was a professed wine 'expert' but the bottle he recommended turned out to be awful.* **2** confessed, avowed, sworn, admitted, acknowledged, confirmed, certified, declared: *What do you do when a professed friend betrays you?*

profession *n.* **1** °occupation, °calling, °work, °field, °vocation, °employment, *métier*, °trade, °business, °craft, °line, °sphere, °speciality *or US* specialty, °job, °position, °post, °situation, *Slang* °racket: *I know that she's a doctor, but what is her husband's profession?* **2** confession, affirmation, °statement, avowal, °assertion, asseveration, °declaration, °acknowledgement, °testimony, averment, °admission, °announcement: *I was uncertain whether to believe his professions of love.*

professional *adj.* **1** trained, °educated, °practised, °veteran, °experienced, °seasoned, °able, skilled, °skilful, °gifted, °talented, °qualified, °knowledgeable, licensed, °official, °expert, °masterful, masterly, °master, °efficient, °adept, °proficient, °competent, °polished, finished: *He is a professional ambulance driver who has to work as a plumber to make ends meet.* **2** °excellent, °proficient, °efficient, °skilful, masterly, °thorough, °prompt, °conscientious, °authoritative, businesslike: *She did a very professional job of repairing my car.*
—*n.* **3** °master, °expert, maestro, °virtuoso, past °master *or* mistress, °specialist, °authority, *Colloq* wizard, pro, whiz *or* whizz, *US* maven *or* mavin, *Brit* °dab hand: *You can always tell when the work has been done by a professional.*

proficiency *n.* °facility, °skill, °talent, adeptness, °expertise, expertness, skilfulness, °aptitude, °capability, °ability, °dexterity, competence *or* competency, °ingenuity, °knack, *savoir faire*, *Colloq* know-how: *The proficiency he displayed as a racing-car driver was second to none.*

proficient *adj.* °skilful, skilled, °talented, °adept, °gifted, °expert, °experienced, °practised, *au fait*, °veteran, well-versed, (highly) trained, °professional, °qualified, °capable, °able, °accomplished, °dexterous, °competent, °knowledgeable, top-notch, °first-rate, *Colloq* ace, crack, whiz-bang *or* whizz-bang, *Brit* wizard: *She is an extremely proficient surgeon.*

profile *n.* **1** °outline, °silhouette, contour, side-view: *His aquiline nose shows up prominently in this profile.* **2** biography, (biographical *or* °thumbnail *or* °character) sketch, °life, °portrait, vignette: *That profile of Allen in a well-known magazine did not do him justice.* **3** °analysis, °study, °survey, °examination; graph, diagram, °chart, °list, statistics: *The profile of the average newspaper reader revealed some interesting anomalies.*
—*v.* **4** °describe, °draw, sketch, limn: *The editor phoned to say that they want to profile you in the Gazette's Sunday colour supplement.*

profit *n.* **1** Often, ***profits***: °gross *or* °net profit, °net *or Brit also* nett, °return(s), °gain, °yield, °revenue, proceeds, bottom line, °surplus, °excess, *US* °take, *Slang* gravy, *US* vigorish: *The profits are down in the third quarter owing to the higher interest rate.* **2** °advantage, avail, °good, °benefit, °welfare, °gain, value, °interest, °use, °usefulness, *Archaic or literary* behoof: *Let me recommend a book that you will find of some profit.*
—*v.* **3** °advance, °further, be of profit to, °benefit, °promote, °aid, °help, be °advantageous *or* of °advantage, °serve, avail, °improve: *A few lessons from the club professional could profit your golf game.* **4** Often, ***profit from***: take °advantage of, °use, turn to °advantage *or* °account, °exploit, utilize, make (good) use of, make °capital (out) of, capitalize on, °maximize, make the most of, *Slang* cash in on: *I hope you profit from the experience.* **5** clear, °realize, °earn, °gain, *Colloq* make a °killing, clean up, °rake it in, make a °bundle *or* a

°packet: *Ernestine profited to the tune of £100,000 on the sale of her house.*

profitable *adj.* **1** °beneficial, °productive, lucrative, °fruitful, (well-)paying, well-paid, °worthwhile, °effective, cost-effective, °gainful, remunerative, money-making, °rewarding: *I had never thought of being a pavement artist as a profitable enterprise. Playing professional golf can be very profitable—if you win tournaments.* **2** °beneficial, °helpful, °useful, utilitarian, valuable, °worthwhile, °advantageous, °productive, °rewarding: *She gave me a lot of good advice that I found profitable in my professional life.*

profiteer *n.* **1** °racketeer, exploiter, extortionist, extortioner, blackmarketeer: *The profiteers turned to selling sugar at exorbitant prices.*
—*v.* **2** overcharge, °fleece, °exploit, °milk, make the most of; °extort; *US* °gouge: *The arms dealers are profiteering by selling banned* matériel *to the guerrillas.*

profligacy *n.* **1** debauchery, °vice, immorality, °sin, sinfulness, wickedness, °evil, °dissipation, dissoluteness, degeneracy, licentiousness, depravity, corruption, promiscuity, lechery, lasciviousness, lewdness, indecency, °perversion, carnality, libertinism, wantonness, unrestraint, eroticism, sybaritism, voluptuousness, sensuality: *Soho's reputation for profligacy is now much less deserved.* **2** °prodigality, °extravagance, °excess, °waste, wastefulness, recklessness, exorbitance, lavishness, improvidence, squandering: *The profligacy of the French court at the end of the 17th century was remarkable.*

profligate *adj.* **1** debauched, vice-ridden, °immoral, unprincipled, °sinful, °shameless, °evil, iniquitous, °wicked, dissipative, °dissolute, °degenerate, °loose, licentious, depraved, °corrupt, °promiscuous, °lecherous, °lascivious, °lewd, °indecent, °perverted, °carnal, °libertine, °wanton, unrestrained, °erotic, sybaritic, °voluptuous, °sensual, °wild, °abandoned: *The duke suddenly gave up his profligate life and became a monk.* **2** °extravagant, °prodigal, °wasteful, °reckless, squandering, °improvident, °spendthrift, °immoderate, °excessive: *As the family fortunes waned, my aunt had to curb her profligate ways.*
—*n.* **3** debauchee, °sinner, °degenerate, °pervert, sodomite, °reprobate, °rake, rakehell, °libertine, lecher, whoremonger, °roué, °wanton, °sybarite, voluptuary, °sensualist: *With the restraints removed, the profligate abandoned himself to every excess imaginable.* **4** °prodigal, °spendthrift, °wastrel, waster, squanderer: *Such are the extravagances indulged in by the profligates who never learnt the value of money.*

profound *adj.* **1** °deep, unfathomable, abstruse, °recondite, arcane, esoteric, °intricate, knotty, °involved, °tricky, inscrutable, indecipherable, cabbalistic, °incomprehensible, °obscure, °subtle, °occult, °secret, °cryptic, °puzzling, enigmatic, mystifying, °mysterious: *Some aspects of the theory of thought are even too profound for many specialists.* **2** °learned, °scholarly, °intellectual, erudite, discerning, °astute, sagacious, °sage, °wise, °penetrating, °sharp, °keen, insightful, analytical, °knowledgeable, °informed, °well-informed, well-read: *Russell was one of the most profound thinkers of his day.* **3** °deep, °great, °intense, °sincere; °heartfelt, °keen, °acute, utter, °extreme, °overpowering, °overwhelming: *He gave a profound sigh and fell asleep at once. It is with profound regret that I must tender my resignation.* **4** utter, °complete, °total, °perfect, °absolute, °thorough, thoroughgoing, °out-and-out, °downright, consummate; °awful, °terrible: *Her casual attitude stems from her profound lack of awareness of how important the work is. I was immediately struck by the profound silence in the house. Profound changes are under way.*

profoundly *adv.* °very, °extremely, °deeply, greatly, keenly, acutely, intensely, °sincerely; °terribly, °awfully: *We are profoundly sorry to have been so much trouble to you.*

profundity *n.* **1** °depth, profoundness, abstruseness, reconditeness, arcaneness, intricacy, °subtlety, °complexity, complicatedness, °difficulty, inscrutability, involvement, involvedness; indecipherability, incomprehensibility, incomprehensibleness, °obscurity: *I wouldn't claim to have fully grasped the profundity of his ideas.* **2** erudition, discernment, °scholarship, scholarliness, sagacity, °wisdom, sharpness, keenness, astuteness, acumen, insightfulness, knowledgeableness, knowledgeability: *I was amazed by the profundity of the argument of one so young.*

profuse *adj.* **1** °abundant, °ample, °plentiful, copious, unstinting, unsparing, ungrudging: *My profuse apologies if I have offended you in any way.* **2** °extravagant, °lavish, °bountiful, bounteous, °prolific, °luxuriant, °abundant, °exuberant, superabundant, °lush, °thick, teeming, overflowing, bursting, thriving, °productive, °fruitful, °rich: *From the seventh year onwards, the trees yielded profuse crops of pears and plums.* **3** °excessive, copious, °considerable, °prolific, °liberal, °lavish, °free, °abundant, °ample: *This stage of the fever is accompanied by profuse sweating.* **4** °generous, °abundant, °plentiful, copious, unsparing, °unselfish, unstinting, °exuberant, magnanimous, °liberal: *The audience was profuse in its applause and cries of 'Bravo!' and 'Encore!'*

profusion *n.* profuseness, °quantity, °abundance, °plenty, plentifulness, plenteousness, °bounty, copiousness, superabundance; °mass, °host, °hoard, °number, multitude, °lot, °mountain, °load, °mess, °stack, °pile, °heap, agglomeration, conglomeration, °accumulation, °wealth, °glut, °surplus, oversupply, °surfeit, plethora, °superfluity, *Formal* nimiety: *Ivy grew in profusion over the front of the house. We had never seen such a profusion of bric-à-brac as they had collected.*

progenitor *n.* **1** progenitrix, °ancestor, forefather, forebear: *They regarded the snake god as the progenitor of the human race.* **2** °predecessor, °forerunner, °precursor, antecedent, foregoer, °source, originator; °origin, °original, °prototype, archetype, °pattern, °guide: *The ancient philosophers were progenitors of many modern ideas. Some regard da Vinci's designs as the progenitors of some of today's machines.*

progeny *n.* °offspring, °children, °descendants, °issue, °young, °posterity, °heirs, scions, successors, sons and daughters, *Colloq* kids, °spawn, fry, *US* sprouts: *He dreamed that his progeny might have a freer, healthier life than his.*

prognosis *n.* °forecast, forecasting, °prediction, °prophecy, prognostication, °projection: *The doctor has recorded his prognosis for the course of the disease.*

prognosticate *v.* **1** °predict, foretell, °prophesy, °forecast, presage, °divine, forebode: *Those prophets of doom are always prognosticating disaster.* **2** betoken, augur, herald, °foreshadow, foretoken, °announce, °harbinger, °signal, portend: *The freshening breeze from the east prognosticates some rainy periods ahead.*

programme *n.* **1** °schedule, °plan, °scheme, agenda, °order of the day, °routine, °protocol, slate, °list, listing, °description, °outline, °abstract, °précis, °calendar, menu, bill of fare, curriculum, syllabus, °synopsis, °summary, °prospectus: *The programme shows the sequence of events. You cannot tell what is being offered without a programme.* **2** °performance, °production, °show, °presentation, (°radio *or* °television) °play, telecast, °broadcast, °recital, concert: *Television programmes seem to cater to lower levels of taste and intelligence every year.* **3** °proceedings, °events, °affairs, °activities: *The programme includes an hour of exercise before breakfast every day.*
—*v.* **4** °organize, °arrange, prearrange, °plan, °lay out, map (out), °design, °formulate, °set (up), °schedule, °book, *US* slate: *The solo pianist is programmed to follow the chamber orchestra.*

progress *n.* **1** (forward) °movement, going forward, °progression, °advance, °headway, advancement: *Progress through the dense underbrush was very slow.*

2 advancement, °advance, °promotion, °improvement, betterment, °elevation, °rise, °development, °furtherance: *Her progress in the company might have been impeded by the fact that she was a woman.* 3 advancement, °course, °development, °growth, °expansion, °increase, °evolution, maturation, ripening, burgeoning *or* bourgeoning, amplification, enlargement, °spread, °extension, broadening, °promotion, °furtherance, °advance, °encouragement: *Our publishing credo is that every book must contribute to the progress of culture or knowledge.* 4 ***in progress***: under °way, ongoing, going on, °happening, occurring, taking °place, at °work, in °operation, being done, °proceeding, *Colloq* in the °works: *Some of the plans for reorganization are already in progress.*
—*v.* 5 °advance, °move *or* °go (forwards *or* °onwards), °proceed, °continue, °go *or* forge °ahead, °go *or* °move along, make (one's) °way, make °headway, °travel, °go *or* °push *or* °press on: *Throughout the 19th century wagon trains of pioneers progressed across the prairies to settle the American West. I haven't progressed far enough in my reading to say whether I like the book or not.* 6 °advance, °improve, get °well, get °better, °develop, °grow, °expand, °increase, evolve, °mature, °ripen, burgeon *or* bourgeon, °amplify, °enlarge, °spread, °extend, broaden, °rise, °move up, upgrade: *Sarah's condition progressed to the point where she could get out of bed. Christmas sales of the new toy are progressing nicely. In only ten years, Michael progressed to a directorship in the company.*

progression *n.* 1 °movement forward *or* forward °movement, °advance, advancement, (making *or* gaining) °headway, °progress, ascension, °rise, °elevation: *This mode of progression requires enormous effort. It was interesting to watch her progression through the corridors of power.* 2 °progress, °development, °advance, advancement, °spread, spreading, °extension, extending, broadening, enlargement, °headway, intensification, °rise: *It seemed impossible to halt the progression of the disease.* 3 °order, °sequence, °succession, °train, °chain, concatenation, °course, °flow: *The report traces the progression of events leading up to the war.*

progressive *adj.* 1 advancing, continuing, developing, increasing, growing, ongoing, °continuous, °step by step, °gradual: *The doctors noted the progressive deterioration in his condition. With the onset of spring, we shall see progressive improvement in the weather.* 2 reformist, revisionist, °liberal, °radical, °revolutionary, °avant-garde, advanced, °dynamic: *Carrie was soon regarded as one of the more progressive thinkers of her day.*
—*n.* 3 reformist, reformer, revisionist, °liberal, leftist, left-winger: *Once a conservative, he did a complete volte-face after the war and became a progressive.*

prohibit *v.* 1 °bar, °ban, °forbid, disallow, interdict, °outlaw, °taboo, debar, proscribe: *Fishing without a permit is prohibited.* 2 °prevent, °stop, °preclude, °rule out, °obstruct, °block, °impede, °hinder, °hamper, °inhibit, °frustrate, °foil, °thwart, °restrain, °check: *A turnstile prohibits entry through the exit doors.*

prohibition *n.* 1 forbiddance, °barring, °bar, banning, °ban, disallowance, disallowing, interdiction, interdicting, outlawing, outlawry, °taboo, debarment, debarring, proscription, proscribing: *Did the members vote for the prohibition of smoking on club premises?* 2 °bar, interdict, °injunction, debarment, °embargo, proscription, °ban: *Imposition of an excessively high tariff on imported computer components has amounted to the prohibition of their use in this country.*

prohibitive *adj.* 1 discouraging, suppressive, °repressive, restrictive, prohibitory, inhibitory, restraining: *Prohibitive legislation has forced capital out of some profitable areas and into others less productive.* 2 °excessive, °exorbitant, °outrageous, °dear, °high, °outlandish, °abusive, extortionate, insupportable, criminal: *The prices of new designer dresses are prohibitive.*

project *n.* 1 °proposal, °plan, °scheme, °design, layout: *The project for housing low-income families had to be modified to allow for car parking.* 2 °activity, °enterprise, °programme, °undertaking, °venture, °assignment, commitment, °obligation, °contract, °engagement; °occupation, °job, °work: *What project will you move on to when you complete this one?*
—*v.* 3 °plan, °scheme, °prepare, °devise, conjure up, concoct, °think up, °contemplate, contrive, °invent, °work up *or* out, °propose, °present, °outline, °design, °draft, °draw up, delineate, °describe, °put forth *or* forward, *Colloq* cook up: *In his theory, he projects a quite different causal relationship.* 4 °cast, °hurl, °fling, °throw, °toss, °launch, °propel, °discharge; °shoot, °transmit; *Colloq* chuck, °lob: *A body projected into space will keep on travelling unless it strikes something. This device projects stereoscopic pictures on a screen.* 5 °jut out, °stick out, °protrude, °stand out, °bulge (out), °extend (out), °poke out, beetle (out), °overhang: *The cornice projects a full six feet over the street.* 6 °estimate, °reckon, °calculate, °predict, °forecast: *The economists projected a decline in inflation over the coming months.*

projectile *n.* °missile, °shell, bullet, °rocket: *Projectiles rained down on the enemy gun emplacement.*

projection *n.* 1 °protrusion, protuberance, °bulge, °extension, °overhang, °ledge, flange; °ridge, eminence, °prominence, °spur, °crag, outcropping: *The safety line caught on a projection of the building, and the man was saved. That projection off to the north is covered with ice all year long.* 2 °proposal, outlining, mapping, mapping out, presenting, °presentation: *The projection of the plan for the new development must be effective for the council to accept it.* 3 °plan, °scheme, blueprint, °programme, °design, °proposal, °outline, diagram, map, °representation, planning: *The council has approved the projection for the development of the waterfront.* 4 °estimate, prognostication, °forecast, °prediction, °calculation, °reckoning: *These sales projections for next year are quite optimistic.*

proliferate *v.* °grow, °increase, burgeon *or* bourgeon, multiply, mushroom, snowball; °breed, °reproduce: *Fast-food restaurants are proliferating everywhere. Failure to disinfect the wound allows germs to proliferate.*

proliferation *n.* °growth, °increase, burgeoning *or* bourgeoning, °expansion, °spread, escalation, build-up, °rise: *Some attribute the increase in violent crime to the proliferation of hand-guns.*

prolific *adj.* 1 °fertile, fecund, °productive, °fruitful, °abundant, copious, °bountiful, bounteous, °profuse, °plentiful, plenteous, °lush, °rich, rife: *The more perilous its natural survival, the more prolific a species is likely to be.* 2 °productive, °creative, °fertile: *He is a prolific author, and has more than 200 novels to his credit.*

prolong *v.* °extend, °lengthen, elongate, °stretch (out), °draw *or* °drag out, °drag (on), keep up, °string out, protract: *Not wishing to prolong the agony, we left after the first act. Aunt Caroline prolonged her visit by yet another week.*

promenade *n.* 1 °walk, °parade, esplanade, boulevard: *We strolled along the promenade as far as the pier.* 2 °walk, °stroll, °saunter, °ramble, °turn, constitutional, airing, turn: *After a brief promenade round the garden, she returned to the house.*
—*v.* 3 °walk, °stroll, °saunter, amble, °ramble, °parade, perambulate, take a °walk *or* °stroll: *Every Sunday, regardless of the weather, he promenades for an hour in the park.* 4 °flaunt, °show (off), °display, °parade, °strut: *Why he promenaded that awful person before all his friends is beyond me!*

prominence *n.* 1 °celebrity, eminence, °fame, °distinction, notability, °reputation, °pre-eminence, °standing, °position, °rank, °prestige, °renown, repute, °importance, °weight, °influence, °account, °name, consequence: *They are a family of considerable prominence in the county. She rose to prominence as an* *actress just last year.* **2** °hill, hillock, °rise, hummock, outcrop, outcropping, °spur, tor, °crag, arête, °spine, °ridge, °peak, °mount, °pinnacle; headland, °point, promontory: *We planted our flag on the prominence and constructed a small cairn.* **3** protuberance, °projection, °protrusion, °growth, excrescence, °swelling, tumefaction, tumescence, extrusion, outshoot, outgrowth, °spur, °bulge: *If that prominence on your elbow doesn't disappear in a day or so, I should see a doctor.*

prominent *adj.* **1** °conspicuous, °obvious, °evident, recognizable, °pronounced, °discernible, distinguishable, identifiable, °noticeable, °remarkable, °noteworthy, eye-catching, °striking, °outstanding, °chief, °main, °principal, °significant, °important; °apparent, unmistakable, °patent, °glaring, °salient, °flagrant, egregious: *The most prominent peak in the region is Annapurna. Some of the prominent shortcomings of the plan can be rectified easily.* **2** °eminent, °pre-eminent, °distinguished, °notable, °noteworthy, °noted, °leading, °foremost, °first, °outstanding, °well-known, famed, °illustrious, °famous, °celebrated, °renowned, acclaimed, honoured, °honourable, respected, °well-thought-of, °prestigious, °reputable, creditable: *A prominent politician is to be invited to cut the ribbon opening the new bridge.* **3** °protuberant, protruding, protrusive, projecting, jutting (out); excrescent, bulging, raised, °elevated: *She has a rather prominent chin. There is one prominent spot on the tabletop that needs more sanding.*

promiscuous *adj.* **1** °indiscriminate, undiscriminating, unselective, non-selective, non-discriminatory, unconscientious, °heedless, °haphazard, °indifferent, uncaring, uncritical, unfussy, unfastidious, disregardful, neglectful, negligent, °slipshod, slovenly, °irresponsible, °careless, °cursory, °perfunctory, °unthinking, °thoughtless, unconsidered: *The promiscuous massacre of civilians caused an international outcry.* **2** °lax, °loose, °unchaste, °wanton, °wild, °uninhibited, unrestrained, ungoverned, °uncontrolled, unbridled, uncurbed, °immoderate, °abandoned, amoral, °immoral, °indecent, °libertine, licentious, dissipated, °dissolute, depraved, °profligate, debauched, °fast; unfaithful, °faithless, °dishonourable: *Nothing you say could persuade me to condone your promiscuous behaviour.* **3** °mixed, °miscellaneous, heterogeneous, °random, intermixed, jumbled, °disorderly, disordered, °confused, °chaotic, motley, intermingled, scrambled, unorganized, disorganized, unsystematic, unsystematized, °helter-skelter, higgledy-piggledy, °hotchpotch *or US also* hodgepodge: *There is a somewhat promiscuous collection of books in his library that well reflects the eclecticism of his tastes.*

promise *n.* **1** °assurance, (solemn) °word (of °honour), °pledge, °vow, °oath, °undertaking, °engagement, °bond, commitment, guaranty, °guarantee, °warranty; °agreement, °contract, covenant, °compact: *You have my promise that the book will be completed by the deadline. She broke her promise to marry him. Unlike a contract, a promise does not imply a mutual commitment.* **2** °expectation, °potential, °capability; °likelihood, °probability: *This first novel shows a lot of promise. There is little promise that compensation will be paid to the victims by the government.*
—*v.* **3** °assure, give one's °word (of °honour), °pledge, °swear, °vow, take an °oath, °undertake, °engage, °commit oneself, °guarantee *or* guaranty, °warrant, cross one's heart (and hope to die): *Harold promised to do what cannot be done. We were promised a free ride on the roundabout. She promises she will repay the loan promptly. Make him pay for the damage as he promised.* **4** give °indication of, °hint at, °suggest, foretell, augur, °indicate, °show signs of, be in store for, look like, °seem *or* °appear °likely *or* °probable, *Brit* be on the cards, *US* be in the cards, *Literary* bid fair, betoken, bespeak: *Though the economic situation promised to improve, many were disappointed that it took so long.*

promising *adj.* °hopeful, encouraging, °favourable, auspicious, °positive, °rosy, °optimistic, °propitious, cheering, full of °promise, reassuring, heartening: *I see a promising future for you as a dancer.*

promote *v.* **1** °help, °further, °encourage, °assist, °advance, °support, °forward, °back, °sanction, °abet, °aid, °boost, °foster, °patronize, nurture, °develop, inspirit, °strengthen, °stimulate, °inspire: *Their continual bickering did little to promote domestic harmony. The sale of portable appliances has done much to promote the battery business.* **2** °advance, °move up, °raise, upgrade, elevate, °exalt, *Colloq* °kick upstairs: *He is to be promoted to floor manager next month.* **3** °recommend, °endorse, °sponsor, °support, espouse, commend, °advocate, °advance, °champion, °talk up, °speak for, °side with, °present, call °attention to: *She is promoting the cause of ecology in her campaign.* **4** advertise, °publicize, °push, °sell, *Colloq* beat the drum for, °plug, *Slang* hype, *Chiefly US* ballyhoo: *They are promoting the new chewing-gum by giving out free samples in Trafalgar Square.*

promotion *n.* **1** °furtherance, advancement, °advance, °encouragement, °support, °backing, °sanction, sanctioning, abetting, aiding, °helping, assisting, boosting, fostering, nurturing, cultivation, °development, developing, °improvement, improving, °inspiration, inspiriting, strengthening, stimulation, °stimulating: *The Society exists for the promotion of learning in a number of subjects.* **2** advancement, °advance, upgrading, upgrade, °rise, °elevation, preferment, exaltation: *He was envied for his promotion to the highest ranking post in the department.* **3** promoting, °recommendation, °presentation, espousal, commendation, advocacy, championing: *I am grateful for your promotion of my name for the job.* **4** advertising, publicity, public relations, °propaganda, selling, hard *or* soft °sell, °fanfare, plugging, *Colloq* puffery, *Slang* (media) hype, *Chiefly US* ballyhoo, hoop-la: *The manufacturer spent millions on the promotion of the new cola.* **5** °advertisement, advertising, °circular, °brochure, handbill, °bill, hand-out, °leaflet, °poster, *affiche*, placard, publicity, °space, (publicity) °release, hoarding, *US and Canadian* flier *or* flyer, billboard, broadside, *Colloq US* °puff piece, poop sheet: *The promotions for the new detergent use the celebrity endorsement technique.*

prompt *adj.* **1** quick, °ready, °immediate, instantaneous, °unhesitating, °rapid, °fast, °swift, °speedy, °punctual, °timely, on °time, °instant, °summary, °brisk, alacritous: *No matter what the question, Gemma gave a prompt response.* **2** °alert, °eager, °ready, quick, °expeditious, °ready and °willing, °disposed, predisposed, °unhesitating, °keen, avid: *Slow to praise, Alan was always prompt to criticize.*
—*v.* **3** °urge, egg (on), °prod, °nudge, °spur, exhort, °incite, °induce, impel, °provoke, °rouse, °arouse, °encourage, °work *or* °stir *or* °fire up, °move, °motivate, °cause, °influence, °put (someone) up to (something), °coax, °persuade, °cajole, °prevail upon *or* on, °talk (someone) into (something): *If he hadn't prompted her, she never would have apologized.* **4** °cue, °remind, feed lines (to), °help: *She never could remember her lines and needed to be prompted.* **5** °bring about, °inspire, °occasion, give °rise to, °elicit, °evoke, °provoke, °call forth, °stimulate, °awaken: *The mention of hostages prompted a question about what was being done to gain their release.*
—*n.* **6** °reminder, °cue, °hint, stimulus: *He always needs a prompt to remind him to send his mother flowers on her birthday.*

promptly *adv.* °quickly, at °once, *or* °straight away, °directly, °right away, °immediately, without °delay *or* hesitation, unhesitatingly, °swiftly, speedily, °readily, instantly, °instantaneously, punctually, expeditiously, with celerity, with alacrity, *Colloq US and Canadian* momentarily: *If this bill is not paid promptly, we shall have to discontinue your credit arrangements.*

prone *adj.* **1** face down *or* °downwards *or chiefly US* °downward, °prostrate, °lying down, reclining,

°recumbent, °horizontal, procumbent, *Formal or technical* decumbent, accumbent: *She was lying prone, resting between push-ups.* **2** °inclined, apt, °likely, °liable, °disposed, predisposed, of a °mind, °subject, °given, tending, °leaning: *They are prone to petty squabbles.*

pronounce *v.* **1** °declare, utter, °say, °voice, °express, articulate, °enunciate, vocalize, put into words: *He pronounced a curse on the family. Try to pronounce it one syllable at a time.* **2** °declare, affirm, °proclaim, °announce, °decree, °judge, aver, °state, asseverate, assert, °say to be: *I now pronounce you man and wife. The doctor pronounced mother to be out of danger.* **3** °announce, °proclaim, promulgate, °publicize, °publish, °deliver, °broadcast, °make known, °let (something) be known, °put out *or* forth, °set forth; °pass: *The judge will pronounce sentence tomorrow.*

pronounced *adj.* **1** °definite, °clear, °plain, well-defined, °decided, °conspicuous, °noticeable, recognizable, identifiable, °obvious, °striking, °prominent, °notable, °distinct, unmistakable, °marked, °strong: *There was a pronounced odour of bitter almonds in the room. Sophie spoke with a pronounced lisp.* **2** °definite, °distinct, unequivocal, unambiguous, °specific, °unqualified, °undisguised, °downright, °outright, °out-and-out, °decided, °complete, °total, °unmitigated, °strong, utter, unalloyed, unmixed, °clear, clear-cut, unmistakable: *A pronounced prejudice against fuzzy thinking emerges from his writings.*

pronouncement *n.* **1** °statement, °assertion, °observation, °comment, °opinion, °announcement, °proclamation, pronunciamento, manifesto, °declaration, avowal, affirmation, asseveration, averment, promulgation: *Occasionally he would issue a pronouncement on the sad state of English usage.* **2** °judgement, °decree, edict, °proclamation, dictum, °command, ukase, (papal) bull, °imperative, °order, ordinance: *The authorities made several official pronouncements regarding travel restrictions.*

pronunciation *n.* enunciation, articulation, elocution, °diction, °speech, °speech pattern, °manner of speaking, °delivery, °accent, accentuation, °intonation, inflection, modulation: *Standard pronunciations of English are so diverse that it is sometimes difficult for one native speaker to understand another. Rock singers seem always to imitate a Texan pronunciation.*

proof *n.* **1** °evidence, verification, corroboration, confirmation, validation, authentication, ratification, substantiation; documentation, °document, °facts, °data, certification, °testimony, *Colloq* ammunition: *Is there any proof that she was with you? The prosecution claims to have enough proof of his guilt to convict him of embezzlement.* **2** °test, °trial, °measure, °standard, °touchstone, criterion: *Do you intend to put his loyalty to the proof? The proof of the pudding is in the eating.* —*adj.* **3** impervious, impenetrable, able to °withstand *or* °resist, °protective, °strong, °tough, °impregnable, °resistant, tempered: *They maintain that this armour is proof against a nine-inch shell.*

prop *v.* **1** Often, ***prop up***: °support, °brace, °hold (up), °buttress, °stay, °bolster, °uphold, °bear, °sustain, shore up, °keep up: *A longer post is needed to prop up this end of the roof.* **2** °lean, °stand, °rest: *Do you mind if I prop my crutches against the desk while I sit down?* —*n.* **3** °support, °brace, truss, °stay, °buttress, °mainstay, °upright, vertical, shore: *Can you use this broomstick as a prop to support the shelf temporarily?*

propaganda *n.* **1** agitprop, disinformation, Newspeak, rumours, lies: *The state-controlled media spread propaganda about minorities to foster nationalism.* **2** advertising, °promotion, publicity, °public relations, °puff, °fanfare, *Colloq* puffery, ballyhoo, *Slang* hype, *US* hoop-la, whoop-de-do *or* whoop-de-doo: *All that propaganda was merely to launch a new washing-powder!*

propagate *v.* **1** °breed, °generate, °reproduce, multiply, °proliferate, °deliver, °bring forth, °bear, procreate: *Biologists are studying ways of making the species propagate at a faster rate.* **2** multiply, °increase, °spread, °grow, °develop: *These plants propagate very rapidly.* **3** °publicize, °promote, disseminate, °dispense, °distribute, °spread, °publish, °broadcast, °circulate, °make known, °transmit, °disperse, propagandize, °proclaim, promulgate, bruit about, noise abroad, herald: *The purpose of the organization is to propagate information about the state of the environment.*

propel *v.* °drive, impel, °move, actuate, set in °motion, get moving, °push, °thrust, °force, °send, °launch, °start: *Each galley was propelled by huge oars. The capsule is propelled by a rocket. Job opportunities propelled her to move to Bristol.*

proper *adj.* **1** °right, °appropriate, apropos, apt, °suitable, °fit, °fitting, °befitting, °becoming, suited, apposite, *de rigueur*, *comme il faut*, adapted, *Literary* °meet: *Is this the proper time to ask for a salary increase?* **2** °correct, °accurate, °exact, °right, °precise, °orthodox, °formal, expected, °normal, °usual, accepted, established, *Old-fashioned Brit* tickety-boo: *Some insist that the only proper way to pronounce 'controversy' is with the stress on the first syllable.* **3** °decorous, °dignified, °genteel, °fitting, °right, *de rigueur*, °appropriate, °becoming, °suitable, °decent, °seemly, °due, °correct, apt, *comme il faut*, conformist; gentlemanly, °ladylike, °polite, °refined, punctilious, °respectable: *Jeans are not proper attire for dinner at La Hacienda. Do you call that proper behaviour for the president of a learned society?* **4** °fitting, °suitable, °correct, °right, °satisfactory, °good, °sensible: *The kitchen is a proper place for the dishwasher, not the garage. Proper nutrition is very important.* **5** °complete, °perfect, utter, °thorough, thoroughgoing, °out-and-out, °unmitigated: *He felt a proper fool for having locked his keys inside his car.* **6** own, °individual, °separate, °distinct, °correct, °specific, °special, °particular, °respective; °characteristic, °distinctive, °peculiar, °singular, °unique: *When you have finished, return each book to its proper place.* —*quasi-adv.* **7** strictly speaking *or* °so-called, in the °strict(est) *or* °narrow(est) °sense, °only, solely, °alone, on (its *or* someone's) own: *Does the deed refer only to the house proper or are the outbuildings also included?*

properly *adv.* **1** °appropriately, fittingly, correctly, °well, becomingly, suitably, politely, decently, decorously, nicely: *If you cannot behave properly I shall have to ask you to leave.* **2** °duly, °appropriately, °well, suitably, rightly, correctly, aptly: *Are they properly equipped for the rescue mission?*

property *n.* **1** °possessions, °belongings, °effects, °gear, °paraphernalia, chattels: *All his worldly property fitted into the small Gladstone bag he carried everywhere.* **2** °assets, °means, °resources, holdings, °capital (°goods), °fortune, °riches, °estate, °worth: *We look on all our shares, personal belongings, and real estate as part of our property.* **3** °land, acreage, realty, real °estate *or* °property: *That property on the high street was recently sold to developers.* **4** °characteristic, °attribute, °quality, °feature, °trait, °mark, °hallmark, idiosyncrasy, °peculiarity, °oddity, °quirk, *Formal* haecceity, quiddity: *A property of iodine is that it changes directly from a solid to a vapour—and vice versa—without first liquefying.*

prophecy *n.* **1** forecasting, foretelling, °prediction, fortune-telling, divination, soothsaying, augury, prognostication, crystal-gazing, *Formal* vaticination: *The prophecy of future events lies outside the realm of science.* **2** °prediction, °forecast, °prognosis, °revelation: *Her prophecy warned of ice storms that would ravage the earth.*

prophesy *v.* **1** °predict, foretell, °forecast, forewarn, °prognosticate, vaticinate: *His father prophesied that he would come to no good if he quit college.* **2** augur, foretell (of), presage, °foreshadow, portend, °bode, °harbinger, herald, °promise, vaticinate: *The early disappearance of the swallows prophesies a long, cold winter.*

prophet *n.* prophetess, °oracle, forecaster, °seer, soothsayer, clairvoyant, prognosticator, °fortune-teller, augur, diviner, °witch, warlock, sibyl, haruspex, vaticinator; (*of doom*) Cassandra: *Statistically, the weather prophets have a fair record of accuracy.*

prophetic *adj.* predictive, prognostic, divinatory, oracular, inspired, prescient, sibylline, *Literary* fatidic, vatic: *His warnings of a drought proved to be prophetic.*

propitiatory *adj.* **1** conciliatory, pacifying, appeasing, expiatory, placative, propitiative, pacificatory, placatory: *He said that he was truly sorry and held out a propitiatory hand.* **2** deferential, °ingratiating, °obliging, obeisant, acquiescent, compliant, °tractable: *He was most propitiatory in his treatment of his stepchildren.*

propitious *adj.* °advantageous, °timely, °well-timed, °opportune, °lucky, °fortunate, °happy, °providential, °favourable, °bright, encouraging, auspicious, °promising, °rosy: *It was not a propitious moment to ask her to marry him.*

proponent *n.* proposer, promoter, °supporter, upholder, °backer, subscriber, °patron, espouser, adherent, °enthusiast, °champion, °friend, °partisan, defender, °advocate, exponent, pleader, apologist, spokesman, spokeswoman, spokesperson: *Ashley is a staunch proponent of the literacy movement.*

proportion *n.* **1** °ratio, (comparative) °relation, °relationship, °comparison: *The proportion of men to women on the course is three to one. The demand is out of all proportion to the supply.* **2** °balance, °agreement, concord, °harmony, suitableness, °symmetry, congruity, correspondence, correlation, °arrangement, °distribution: *The beauty of the building is at once apparent in the elegant proportion of its parts.* **3** °portion, °division, °share, °part, °percentage, °quota, °allotment, °ration, *Colloq* °cut: *Water covers a large proportion of the surface.* **4** ***proportions***: °size, °magnitude, dimensions, °measurements, °extent; °volume, °capacity, °mass, °bulk, °area, °expanse, °scope, °range, °degree: *The dragon suddenly assumed gigantic proportions.*
—*v.* **5** °adjust, °modify, °change, °modulate, °poise, °balance, °shape, °fit, °match, °conform, equate: *The punishment should be proportioned to the crime.*

proportional *adj.* proportionate, proportioned, comparable, analogous, analogic(al), °relative, °related, correlated, balanced, °symmetrical, corresponding, compatible, °harmonious, °consistent, commensurate, in accordance with: *The zeal with which their ideals are defended is directly proportional to the fierceness with which they are attacked.*

proposal *n.* **1** °offer, °presentation, °bid, °tender, °proposition, °recommendation, °suggestion, *Literary* proffer: *Her proposal was to provide the funding if we would do the work.* **2** °plan, °scheme, °outline, °draft, °design, layout; °programme, °proposition, °project: *The proposal for the new civic centre was rejected as too expensive.*

propose *v.* **1** °offer, °tender, proffer; °present, °introduce, °submit, °advance, °set forth, °put forward, °propound, °bid, °recommend, °suggest, °come up with, call °attention to, °broach, *Brit* °table: *Management proposed a wage increase of five per cent. The architect proposed that we consider an addition to the north wing.* **2** °offer, °mean, °intend, °plan, °expect, °aim: *We propose to make a start on the decorating once we have had our lunch.* **3** °nominate, °name, °put forward *or* forth, °suggest, °introduce, °submit, °put up: *His boss proposed him for membership of the golf club.*

proposition *n.* **1** See **proposal, 1,** above. **2** See **proposal, 2,** above.
—*v.* **3** accost, °solicit, make an °indecent *or* °sexual °advance *or* °proposal *or* °overture, *Colloq* make a °pass at: *She said she had been propositioned by him, but we never learnt if she accepted or not.*

propound *v.* °put *or* °set forth *or* forward, °propose, °offer, proffer, °suggest, postulate: *It was she who first propounded the idea of a unified country.*

proprietor *n.* **1** proprietress, °owner, landowner, °landlady, °landlord, landholder, title-holder, deed-holder, property °owner: *He is the proprietor of a large house in Chiswick.* **2** °owner, °partner, °landlord, restaurateur, innkeeper, hotel-keeper, hotelier, licensee, °manager, *Brit* publican: *The proprietor greeted us warmly and showed us to our rooms.*

propriety *n.* **1** correctness, properness, conformity, suitableness, appropriateness, suitability, aptness, °fitness, seemliness, °decorum; advisability, °wisdom: *I questioned the propriety of concealing this information from shareholders.* **2** °protocol, °good *or* °proper °form, punctilio, °etiquette, politeness, °courtesy, politesse, °refinement, sedateness, °dignity, modesty, °decorum, decency, °breeding, respectability, gentility, °grace, mannerliness: *He always behaved with the utmost propriety in the presence of his aunt.* **3** ***the proprieties***: the social graces, the amenities, the civilities, °formality *or* the formalities, social °convention *or* social conventions, social °procedure *or* °codes, accepted °practice, °tradition, °ceremony, °ritual: *He only observes the proprieties when he wants to make a good impression.*

propulsion *n.* °drive, impulse, °impetus, °thrust, °power, driving *or* propelling *or* propulsive °force, °pressure, °momentum, °push: *Enormous propulsion is required to lift the space shuttle into orbit.*

prosaic *adj.* °dull, °banal, overdone, °tedious, clichéd, commonplace, stereotyped, °pedestrian, °flat, stereotypical, hackneyed, °stock, °routine, °everyday, °ordinary, °common, workaday, °mediocre, °undistinguished, °bland, characterless, °homely, °plain, trite, °stale, °threadbare, °tired, °lifeless, °dead, °dry, jejune, °boring, °tiresome, unimaginative, unpoetic, unromantic, uninspiring, uninspired, insipid, uninteresting, °humdrum, °monotonous, Literary *ennuyant*, *Colloq* ho-hum, run-of-the-mill, °mouldy: *She found the law too prosaic and trained to become a jockey.*

prose *n.* (expository) °writing, °text, °language: *It came as a great revelation to learn that he had been speaking prose all his life.*

prosecute *v.* **1** arraign, °indict, °charge, put on *or* bring to °trial, °try, take to court, °sue, bring °suit *or* °action against, °accuse, *Brit* put in the °dock: *She threatened to prosecute him for slander.* **2** °pursue, °follow up *or* through, °see *or* °carry through, °persist, °go on with: *Will the same policy will be prosecuted in other countries?* **3** °carry on *or* out, °perform, do, °exercise, °conduct, °follow, °engage in, °practise, °continue: *The government needs popular support if it is to continue to prosecute the war successfully.*

prospect *n.* **1** °view, °scene, panorama, °landscape, seascape, °outlook, vista, °sight, °spectacle, °perspective, °aspect: *The sitting-room window offered a splendid prospect of the sea and cliffs below.* **2** °anticipation, contemplation, °outlook, °promise, °plan, °design, °intention, expectancy, °expectation, °thought, °likelihood: *The prospect of spending the Christmas holidays with your family is quite daunting.* **3** Often, ***prospects***: °future, °outlook, °chance(s), °hope(s), °possibility *or* possibilities, °likelihood, °opportunity *or* opportunities: *The prospects for her advancement are excellent.* **4** ***in prospect***: in °sight *or* °view, in the offing, on the °horizon, in °store, in the °wind, projected, °likely, °probable, °possible, *Brit* on the cards, on the table, *US* in the cards: *As a doctor, he has a number of opportunities in prospect.*
—*v.* **5** Often, ***prospect for***: °explore, °search (for), °look (for): *In 1896, his grandfather went to the Klondike to prospect for gold.*

prospective *adj.* anticipated, expected, awaited, looked-for, °future, °forthcoming, coming, approaching, °imminent, nearing, °pending, °impending, °destined, °potential, incipient: *Jane's prospective wedding had excited the entire family.*

prospectus *n.* °announcement, °plan, °scheme, °programme, °outline, conspectus, °description: *According to the prospectus for the fund, the minimum investment is £1000.*

prosper *v.* °flourish, °thrive, °succeed, °fare °well, °progress, get ahead, °grow, °develop; °profit, °gain, become °wealthy, grow °rich, make one's °fortune, °make good, *Colloq* °make it, make one's °pile: *With hard work, thrift, and perseverance, MacIntosh prospered and was soon able to buy the house he wanted.*

prosperity *n.* °success, (°good) °fortune, °wealth, °riches, affluence, °money, °luxury, °plenty, prosperousness, opulence, °bounty, *Colloq* life of Riley: *The basis of the family's prosperity was huge land holdings in Australia.*

prosperous *adj.* **1** °rich, °wealthy, moneyed *or* monied, affluent, well-to-do, °well off, *Colloq* well-heeled, °loaded, °flush, in the money, rolling in it *or* °wealth *or* °money, in clover, on Easy Street, *Slang* stinking °rich: *Anyone who owns six houses and four yachts must be prosperous.* **2** °successful, thriving, °flourishing, booming, prospering: *Frank owns a prosperous chain of video shops.*

prostitute *n.* **1** whore, call-girl, streetwalker, strumpet, trollop, harlot, lady of the night *or US also* evening, fallen *or* loose woman, *demi-mondaine*, *Archaic* cocotte, *fille de joie*, painted woman, woman of °ill repute, camp-follower, *Archaic* catamite, *Literary* hetaera *or* hetaira, courtesan *or* courtezan, *Brit* rent-boy, toy boy, *US* boy toy, *Archaic* bawd, quean, trull, cotquean, *Colloq* °tart, hustler, *Slang* pro, moll, *Brit* brass, hooker, *US* bimbo, working girl, chippy *or* chippie, roundheels: *There was a terrible scandal when the MP was found to have consorted with prostitutes.*
—*v.* **2** Often, ***prostitute oneself***: °degrade, demean, °lower, cheapen, °debase, °profane, defile, °desecrate, °pervert, °abuse, °misuse, devalue, *Colloq* °sell out: *To ward off starvation, he prostituted his talent by drawing comic strips.*

prostitution *n.* **1** whoredom, harlotry, the oldest profession, Mrs Warren's profession, streetwalking, °vice: *They argued strongly against the legalization of prostitution, saying that it would lead to a decline in public morals.* **2** °degradation, debasement, profanation, defilement, desecration, °misuse, °abuse, devaluation, lowering, °perversion, corruption: *Don't you regard pornography as a prostitution of the principle of freedom of expression?*

prostrate *v.* **1** Usually, ***prostrate oneself***: °lie down, °kowtow, °bow (down), °bow and °scrape, grovel, kneel, °fall to *or* on one's knees, °truckle, °crawl, °cringe, °submit, abase oneself: *The captives were forced to prostrate themselves before the emperor.* **2** °overwhelm, °overcome, °overpower, °crush, °lay *or* bring low, °paralyse, °fell, °bowl over, °floor, °bring down, °humble, make °helpless, °ruin; °exhaust, °fatigue, °weary, °wear down *or* out, °tire (out): *They were prostrated by grief at the loss of their son. Having been prostrated for months by glandular fever, she finally recovered and returned to work.*
—*adj.* **3** °prone, °horizontal, °lying down, laid low, stretched out, procumbent, °recumbent, *Formal or technical* accumbent, decumbent: *The prostrate bodies of the worshippers in their multicoloured garb resembled a huge patchwork quilt.* **4** overwhelmed, °overcome, overpowered, crushed, brought *or* laid °low, paralysed, felled, bowled over, brought down, humbled, °helpless, ruined, brought to one's knees, °powerless, °impotent, °defenceless, disarmed, *Colloq* floored: *She was prostrate at the news of the car crash. After the long war, the countries were struggling to revitalize their prostrate economies.* **5** °exhausted, drained, °fatigued, °spent, °worn out, wearied, °weary, °tired (out), °dead °tired, dog-tired, played out, *Colloq* fagged out, knocked out, all in, °beat, bushed, *US* wiped out, *Slang* shagged out, *US and Canadian* pooped (out): *We were prostrate after the long climb.*

prostration *n.* **1** genuflection *or Brit also* genuflexion, kowtowing, °kowtow, kneeling, bowing, °bow, salaaming, salaam, °submission: *Prostration before a superior was a mark of honour.* **2** °servility, °veneration, °worship, °humiliation, °respect, adulation, °deference, °obeisance, °homage: *Their silence betokened the profound prostration they felt before her superior intellect.* **3** °despair, °misery, °desolation, °desperation, dejection, °depression, despondency, wretchedness, unhappiness, °grief, °woe, woefulness: *Years of poverty created in him a spiritual prostration from which he never recovered.* **4** weariness, °exhaustion, °weakness, debility, feebleness, enervation, lassitude, paralysis, °collapse, °breakdown: *The diagnosis was nervous prostration and the treatment was bed rest for a week or more.*

protagonist *n.* **1** °hero, °heroine, anti-hero, anti-heroine, °principal, °leading °character; °lead, °leading role, °title role: *Mother was always the protagonist in our little domestic dramas.* **2** °leader, °supporter, °advocate, °backer, °prime mover, moving °spirit, °champion, °mainstay, standard-bearer, exponent: *He is considered the chief protagonist of reformist policies in the party.*

protean *adj.* °variable, ever-changing, multiform, mutable, °changeable, labile, polymorphous *or* polymorphic, kaleidoscopic: *The magic ring gave him protean powers to appear now as an eagle, now as a serpent.*

protect *v.* **1** °defend, °guard, °safeguard, keep °safe, °shield, °cover, °screen: *Company rules require the wearing of safety goggles to protect the eyes when operating any machine.* **2** °care for, °preserve, °keep, °shelter, °watch over, °safeguard, take °care of, °conserve, take under one's wing, °foster, nurture, °tend, °mind: *The best way of protecting wildlife is to conserve natural habitats.*

protection *n.* **1** °defence, °screen, °shield, °barrier, °guard, °safeguard, °immunity, °bulwark, buffer, °shelter, °refuge, haven, °sanctuary, °security, °safe keeping, °safety, °preservation: *They have not yet developed any protection from the common cold. How can we offer these fledglings protection against predators?* **2** °care, guardianship, aegis, °custody, °charge, °safe keeping, °patronage, sponsorship, keeping: *Even under the protection of the government, elephants continue to be slaughtered.* **3** extortion, °blackmail, °protection °money: *If we refuse to pay protection, they say that they will bomb the restaurant.*

protective *adj.* defensive, °jealous, °vigilant, watchful, heedful, °careful, °possessive; preservative, shielding, sheltering, safeguarding: *She is fiercely protective of her independence and will not accept help. Many animals rely on protective colouring as a defence against predators.*

protector *n.* protectress, defender, °benefactor, benefactress, °patron, patroness, °guardian (angel), °champion, knight in shining armour, paladin, bodyguard, *Slang Brit* °minder: *She came to regard him as her friend and protector.*

protégé *n.* protégée, °ward, °charge, dependant; °discovery, °student, °pupil: *He became her protégé and she has taught him everything he knows.*

protest *n.* **1** °objection, °opposition, °complaint, grumble, °grievance, dissent, °disapproval, protestation, °exception, °disagreement, demur *or* demurral, demurrer, disclaimer, °denial, °scruple, °compunction, °qualm, *Colloq* °gripe, grouse, °squawk, *US* kick, *Slang* beef, °bitch: *The Home Office has received many protests about the treatment of prisoners.* **2** ***under protest***: unwillingly, reluctantly, involuntarily: *I paid the fine under protest.*
—*v.* **3** °object, °oppose, °complain, grumble, dissent, °disapprove, take °exception, take °issue with, °disagree, demur, disclaim, °deny, °scruple, *Colloq* °gripe, grouse, °squawk, *Brit* °kick (against), *US* °kick, *Slang* beef, °bitch: *Bank employees protested at being expected to work on Saturday mornings.* **4** assert, °confirm,

°declare, aver, asseverate, affirm, °announce, °profess, °insist on, avow, avouch: *The convicted man went to the gallows protesting his innocence.*

protocol *n.* **1** °rule(s) *or* °code(s) *or* °standard(s) of °behaviour *or* °conduct, °convention(s), °custom(s), °diplomacy, °formality, formalities, °form, °etiquette, politesse, manners, °practice, °usage, °authority: *According to protocol, the lady stands at the right of the gentleman. Which protocol are you following, the British or the French?* **2** °treaty, °pact, °compact, covenant, °agreement, concordat; °memorandum, °minute, °note, °draft, °outline: *The original protocol must be checked before the ministers attach their signatures.*

prototype *n.* **1** °model, archetype, °first, °original, °pattern, exemplar, °precedent, °mould: *Many improvements were made as a result of tests on the original prototype.* **2** °example, °instance, °illustration, °sample, °norm, °paragon, °epitome, °model, °standard, analogue, referent, °metaphor: *Mrs Grundy is a common prototype for narrow-mindedness and prudishness.*

protracted *adj.* °long, long-drawn-out, interminable, prolonged, over-long, never-ending, extended, stretched out, marathon, °endless, °everlasting, long-winded: *The protracted union negotiations delayed the start of the work by six months.*

protrude *v.* °stick out, °jut (out), °project, °extend, °poke out, °stand out, °thrust out *or* forward, °start (from), exsert, *Rare* extrude; °bulge, balloon, °bag (out), belly (out); (of the eyes) °pop, goggle, *Colloq US* °bug (out): *Only the very tops of the plants protruded from the snow.*

protrusion *n.* °projection, protuberance, °prominence, °swelling, excrescence, tumescence, °bump, °lump, °knob, °bulge; *(condition of the eyes) Technical* exophthalmic goitre: *I can feel the slight protrusion of the nail-heads above the smooth surface.*

protuberant *adj.* protrusive, protruding, bulging, gibbous, jutting, bulbous, °swelling, °swollen, turgid, tumescent, distended, tumid, extrusive, excrescent, extruding, projecting, beetling, overhanging, °prominent: *She has large brown eyes that are a little protuberant.*

proud *adj.* **1** Often, ***proud of***: °pleased (with), satisfied (with), contented (with), °glad (about), °happy (with *or* about), °delighted (with *or* about), °elated (with *or* about); honoured, gratified: *He is very proud of his children and what they have achieved. I am proud to be your friend.* **2** °conceited, °boastful, self-satisfied, narcissistic, °self-important, °egotistical, °vain, vainglorious, prideful, self-centred, complacent, °snobbish, °haughty, °supercilious, °smug, °arrogant, °cocky, cocksure, °boastful, °braggart, *Colloq* high and mighty, snooty, stuck-up, *Slang* snotty, *Brit* toffee-nosed: *She's far too proud to have anything to do with the likes of us.* **3** °lofty, °dignified, lordly, °noble, °great, respected, honoured, °honourable, °important, °glorious, august, °illustrious, °estimable, creditable, °eminent, °prominent, °distinguished, °reputable, °worthy, °notable, °noted, °noteworthy: *His will always be a proud name in British military history.* **4** °stately, °majestic, °magnificent, °splendid, °grand: *Proud Edinburgh earned the sobriquet, 'Athens of the north'.*

prove *v.* **1** °verify, °authenticate, °confirm, °make good, corroborate, °demonstrate, °show, validate, °establish, °substantiate, °certify, affirm; °support, °sustain, back (up), °uphold: *Prove that he lied under oath, and we shall have him for perjury. If you cannot prove her guilt, she must be presumed innocent.* **2** °try, °test, °examine, °check, °analyse, assay: *Division can easily be proved by multiplication, and vice versa. The proving ground for military vehicles is off limits to the public. Come live with me and be my love, And we shall all the pleasures prove.* **3** °turn out, be °found, be °shown, be °established, °end up; °develop, °result: *The child proved to be his long-lost grandson.* **4** °show, evince, °demonstrate: *He proved his love many times over during their fifty years of marriage.*

provender *n.* **1** °provisions, °food, °supplies, victuals, rations, foodstuffs, groceries, eatables, edibles, comestibles, aliment, °nourishment, °sustenance, *Colloq* grub, eats: *The armies relied for their provender on farms they passed on the march.* **2** fodder, forage, °feed, hay, silage, corn, °grain: *Provender for the livestock was running low because of the long winter.*

proverb *n.* saying, °maxim, aphorism, °saw, adage, apophthegm *or* apothegm, axiom, °moral, moralism, homily, dictum, gnome, °epigram, commonplace, platitude, °truism, °cliché, bromide: *According to the old proverb, 'A fool and his money are soon parted'.*

proverbial *adj.* **1** axiomatic, aphoristic, °epigrammatic, apophthegmatic *or* apothegmatic, homiletic, moralistic; acknowledged, °well-known, accepted, °time-honoured, °traditional: *The language is full of proverbial sayings reflecting popular wisdom.* **2** °typical, archetypal, °exemplary: *The humanitarianism of Albert Schweitzer is proverbial.*

provide *v.* **1** °supply, °furnish, °equip, °outfit, fix up (with) °provision, °contribute, °accommodate, purvey, °cater, °stock (up), victual, °provender: *After providing us with a map and a compass, they sent us off across the moor.* **2** °produce, °yield, °afford, °lend, °give, °present, °offer, °accord: *The fertile land provided food in plentiful abundance. During those bleak years, the radio provided us not only with news but also entertainment.* **3** °stipulate, °lay down, °require, °demand, °specify, °state: *The lease provided that the rent be reviewed every five years.* **4** ***provide for***: °look after, °care for, °support, take °care of, take under one's wing, °minister to, °attend (to): *The bequest ensured that his widow would be amply provided for.* **5** ***provide for** or **against***: °arrange for, °prepare for, °anticipate, forearm, make *or* get °ready for, °plan for, take °precautions, take °measures: *It would seem that you have provided for any eventuality.*

providence *n.* **1** °foresight, °forethought, °preparation, °anticipation, °readiness, far-sightedness, °caution, °precaution, °discretion, °prudence, °care; °thrift, frugality, husbandry, thriftiness, °conservation, °economy: *Because of the providence of our founders, we were able to weather severe financial set-backs.* **2** Usually, ***(divine) Providence***: °protection, °care, °concern, beneficence, °direction, °control, °divine intervention, °guidance; °destiny, °fate, °lot, °fortune, karma, kismet: *Providence is always on the side of those who help themselves.*

provident *adj.* **1** °cautious, °wary, °discreet, canny, °prudent, °careful, °vigilant, °prepared, °far-sighted, °thoughtful, °wise, °shrewd, sagacious, °sage, °judicious: *In the fable, the grasshopper learns from the ant what it means to be provident.* **2** °frugal, °economic(al), °thrifty, °prudent: *Because he is not a provident man, he will always be poor.*

providential *adj.* °fortunate, °lucky, blessed, felicitous, °happy, °opportune, °timely: *It is providential that we left the house just before the earthquake.*

providing *conj.* Sometimes, ***providing that***: provided (that), on (the) °condition (that), if (only), only if, as long as, in the event (that), with the °proviso (that), in °case, with the °understanding (that): *Simon is always ready to go out to dinner, providing someone else pays for it.*

province *n.* **1** °territory, °state, °zone, °region, °quarter, °area, °district, °domain, dependency *or US also* dependancy, °division, °section: *Quebec is one of the administrative provinces of Canada.* **2** °country, °territory, °region, °dominion, °realm, strand, °tract: *During the war, those who escaped fled to distant provinces.* **3** °sphere *or* °area (of °responsibility), °responsibility, bailiwick, °concern, °function, °charge, °business, °field; *Colloq* °thing, °headache, °worry: *The payroll falls within the province of my department.* **4** ***provinces***: °outlying districts, countryside, hinterland(s), *Chiefly US* exurbia, *Slang US and Canadian* boondocks, boonies, hicksville: *Once a year, people flock into London from the provinces to do their Christmas shopping.*

provincial *adj.* **1** °local, regional: *Provincial administration is the responsibility of the sheriff.* **2** uncultured, uncultivated, °unsophisticated, °limited, °uninformed, °naïve, °innocent, °ingenuous, unpolished, °unrefined, °homespun, °rustic, °rude, °country, °parochial, insular, °narrow-minded, °boorish, loutish, cloddish, °awkward, °ungraceful, oafish, backwood(s), *Brit* parish pump, *US* small-town, *Colloq US and Canadian* hick, hick-town: *These paintings are unlikely to appeal to provincial tastes.*
—*n.* **3** °rustic, °country cousin, (°country) bumpkin, yokel, *US and Canadian* out-of-towner, hick, hayseed: *One could tell they were provincials by the cut of their clothes.*

provincialism *n.* **1** dialectalism, localism, regionalism; °idiom, patois, °dialect: *His northern speech is peppered with provincialisms unfamiliar to those who live in the south.* **2** narrow-mindedness, insularity, parochialism, narrowness, benightedness; unsophisticatedness, °simplicity, lack of awareness, °naïvety, ingenuousness, innocence, °inexperience: *Their provincialism made them suspicious of city people. There was something charming about the provincialism of this rough man from the outback.*

provision *n.* **1** °providing, supplying, furnishing; catering, victualling, provisioning, purveyance, purveying, equipping, °fitting out, outfitting, accoutrement *or US also* accouterment, °equipment: *The school is responsible for the provision of textbooks. The provision of a cruise ship of that size requires days.* **2** °stipulation, °proviso, °condition, °restriction, °qualification, clause, °term, °exception, °demand, °requirement, °prerequisite, *Colloq* °catch, °string, *US* hooker: *This provision of the contract calls for a penalty for each day's delay beyond the guaranteed completion date.* **3** °preparation, prearrangement, °arrangement, °measures, °steps: *They had failed to make provision for so many customers and soon ran out of food.* **4** Usually, ***provisions***: °supplies, °stores, stockpile, °stock(s), °quantity; °food, foodstuffs, eatables, edibles, drinkables, potables, victuals, viands, comestibles, °rations, groceries, °provender, °staples: *We had enough provisions to last a year.*
—*v.* **5** stockpile, °stock, °supply, victual, °cater, purvey: *They provisioned the expedition for a three-month period.*

provisional *adj.* **1** °temporary, interim, provisionary, transitional, °stopgap, *pro tempore*, *Colloq* pro tem: *The provisional government was expected to be in place for less than a month.* **2** conditional, contingent, provisory, °qualified, stipulatory, provisionary, probationary: *The appointment is provisional and will be reviewed in six months.*

proviso *n.* See **provision, 2,** above.

provocation *n.* **1** grounds, °reason, °cause, justification, instigation, °initiation, °incitement, stimulus, °incentive, motivation, °motive, °inducement: *What was the provocation for that unpleasant outburst?* **2** °insult, °offence, °taunt, irritation: *After a series of provocations, the final straw was his remark about my mother.*

provocative *adj.* **1** °inviting, alluring, °tempting, charming, tantalizing, teasing, intriguing, fascinating, °seductive, °stimulating, °voluptuous, °sensual, °sensuous, °suggestive, °erotic, arousing, °exciting, entrancing, °irresistible, bewitching, *Colloq* °sexy: *The council found the film too provocative to be shown to schoolchildren.* **2** irritating, annoying, galling, °irksome, nettlesome, harassing, plaguing, exasperating, infuriating, angering, incensing, maddening, enraging, vexing, vexatious, disquieting, challenging, upsetting, distressing, °disturbing, °outrageous, wounding, stinging, °offensive, humiliating, mortifying: *She is given to making provocative remarks that drive him to distraction.*

provoke *v.* **1** °stir (up), °stimulate, °move, °motivate, °push, impel, °drive, °get, °spur (on), egg on, goad, °force, compel, °prompt, °rouse, °arouse, waken, °awaken, °enliven, °animate, °activate, °induce, °encourage: *She did her best to provoke him to start his new novel.* **2** °start, °incite, instigate, °produce, °promote, °foment, °kindle, °work up: *Are you trying to provoke an argument?* **3** °irritate, °annoy, °irk, °pester, vex, pique, °anger, °enrage, °madden, incense, °infuriate, °gall, rile, nettle, °harass, hector, °plague, badger, °exasperate, get on one's °nerves, °try one's °patience, °frustrate, °upset, °disturb, °perturb, °distress, °outrage, °offend, °insult, affront: *If he continues to provoke me I shall punch him.*

prowess *n.* **1** °ability, °skill, skilfulness, °aptitude, adroitness, °dexterity, dexterousness, adeptness, °facility, °finesse, °expertise, mastery, °genius, °talent, know-how, °ingenuity, °capability, °proficiency: *Her prowess as a sculptor is unquestioned.* **2** °bravery, valour, °courage, boldness, °daring, intrepidity, dauntlessness, mettle, stout-heartedness, valiance, lion-heartedness, fearlessness, gallantry, doughtiness, °fortitude: *He was famed for his prowess in single combat.*

prowl *v.* **1** °lurk, °sneak, skulk, °steal, °slink: *I thought I saw someone prowling about in your back garden.* **2** °scour, scavenge, °range over, rove, °roam, °patrol, °cruise, °cover: *The police continued to prowl the waterfront looking for smugglers.*
—*n.* **3** ***on the prowl***: lurking *or* sneaking *or* skulking *or* stealing *or* slinking about *or* around, searching, seeking, hunting, tracking, stalking: *The lioness was on the prowl for wildebeest. After a few drinks, the boys went on the prowl for some female companionship.*

proximity *n.* nearness, closeness, adjacency, °neighbourhood, °vicinity, vicinage, contiguity, contiguousness, propinquity: *The proximity of the airport kept housing prices relatively low.*

proxy *n.* °substitute, °agent, °delegate, surrogate, °representative, °factor: *As I was unable to attend the owners' meeting, I sent Jane as my proxy.*

prude *n.* °prig, °puritan, Mrs Grundy, *Colloq* °goody-goody, *US* bluenose: *He was a bit of a prude and disapproved of anything even slightly suggestive.*

prudence *n.* **1** °discretion, °wisdom, sagacity, °judgement, °discrimination, common °sense, canniness, °presence of mind, awareness, wariness, °care, °tact, carefulness, °caution, cautiousness, circumspection, watchfulness, °vigilance, heedfulness: *You should proceed with prudence in this hazardous business.* **2** planning, °preparation, °preparedness, foresightedness, °forethought, °foresight, °providence, °precaution, far-sightedness; °economy, husbandry, °thrift, (good *or* careful) °management: *Owing to the prudence of her investments, Clara had accumulated a substantial nest egg.*

prudent *adj.* **1** °careful, °cautious, °discreet, discerning, °wise, °sage, sagacious, °politic, °judicious, °discriminating, °sensible, °reasonable, canny, °shrewd, °cautious, circumspect, watchful, °vigilant, heedful, °wary, °attentive, °alert, °guarded: *James had always found it prudent to listen to others before speaking his mind.* **2** °provident, °thrifty, °economic(al), °frugal, prudential: *Father favours prudent, conservative management of the family business.*

prudery *n.* prudishness, priggishness, puritanicalness, puritanism, squeamishness, Grundyism, primness, stuffiness, old-maidishness, precisianism: *She said that censorship was the result of prudery rather than concern for moral welfare.*

prudish *adj.* °priggish, puritanical, old-maidish, °prissy, prim, °fussy, °squeamish, °strait-laced, °stiff, °rigid, over-nice, over-modest, over-coy, °proper, demure, °decorous, °formal: *Victorian society was both prudish and prurient.*

prune *v.* °clip, °cut back, °lop, °dock, °pare (down), °trim: *If you prune fruit trees, they bear more abundantly. We have to prune the entertainment budget.*

prurient *adj.* **1** libidinous, °lecherous, °lascivious, °lewd, lubricious *or* lubricous, salacious, °lustful, concupiscent, licentious, °carnal, debauched, rakehell, °sensual, °randy, °voluptuous, °loose, goatish, ruttish, *Literary* Cyprian, Paphian, *Archaic* lickerish *or* liquorish, *Slang* horny, °hot: *The press takes a prurient interest in the private lives of famous people.* **2** °dirty, °lewd, °filthy, °pornographic, smutty, °obscene, °foul, °scurrilous, °vile, °indecent, °gross, °lurid, °blue, °bawdy, ribald, titillating, °suggestive, °coarse, °vulgar, °low, °crude, *Literary* Fescennine: *The police raid uncovered a store of prurient literature, films, and videos.*

pry *v.* **1** °investigate, ferret about, °examine, °peer, °peek, be °inquisitive, °inquire *or* °enquire: *They pried into her past but found nothing revealing.* **2** °intrude, °meddle, °interfere, *Colloq* °poke *or* °stick one's nose in *or* into, °snoop, be °nosy, nose about *or* around, °poke about *or* around: *They have no right to pry into my private affairs.*

pseudonym *n. nom de plume, nom de guerre,* alias, pen-name, stage °name, °incognito: *'George Eliot' was the pseudonym of Mary Ann Evans.*

psyche *n.* °soul, °spirit, °mind, *élan vital,* divine °spark, life-force, anima, self, °subconscious, °unconscious, °personality, (°essential) °nature, inner man *or* woman *or* °person, *Philosophy* pneuma: *To Homer, the psyche was more like an alter ego, or conscience.*

psychic *adj.* **1** psychical, °mental, °spiritual, psychologic(al), °subjective, psychogenic, cognitive, metaphysic(al), °intellectual, cerebral; philosophic(al): *The psychic effect of losing a loved one can have physical repercussions.* **2** psychical, extrasensory, °supernatural, °occult, magical, telepathic, telekinetic, preternatural, spiritualistic, °unearthly, extramundane, supermundane: *Many psychic phenomena have never been satisfactorily explained.*
—*n.* **3** °medium, spiritualist, clairvoyant, mind-reader, telepathist, °seer, seeress, crystal-gazer, soothsayer, astrologer, °fortune-teller, °prophet, prophetess, sibyl: *We were disturbed to learn that our political leaders consulted psychics.*

psychological *adj.* °mental, °intellectual, cerebral, cognitive, °psychic(al), °spiritual, °subjective, °subconscious, °unconscious, °subliminal, psychogenic; philosophic(al): *He has plenty of money, so there must be psychological reasons for his stealing.*

psychology *n.* (°mental) °make-up, constitution, °attitude, °behaviour, °thought processes, °thinking, °psyche, °nature, °feeling(s), °emotion(s), °rationale, °reasoning: *I cannot understand the psychology of fascism.*

psychotic *adj.* **1** °mad, °insane, psychopathic, °deranged, demented, lunatic, paranoiac *or* paranoid, °abnormal, °unbalanced, (mentally) °ill *or esp. US* °sick, °disturbed, *non compos mentis,* of °unsound mind, °exceptional, certifiable, °daft, unhinged, °raving, *Slang* °crazy, nuts, nutty, loony, off one's rocker *or* trolley *or* chump *or* head, cracked, crack-brained, °mental, out to lunch, batty, bats, having bats in one's belfry, having a screw loose, not all there, touched (in the head), bonkers: *The doctors diagnosed him as psychotic and insisted he be hospitalized.*
—*n.* **2** °madman, madwoman, °maniac, psychopath, lunatic, paranoid *or* paranoiac, schizophrenic, bedlamite, *Slang* nut, nutter, screwball, crackpot, °crazy, loony *or* looney *or* luny, schizo, *US* kook: *How many psychotics do you think are wandering about loose?*

pub *n.* public house, alehouse, tavern, inn, °bar, cocktail °lounge, saloon, taproom, hostelry, *Brit* saloon *or* °lounge °bar, *US* bar-room, *Colloq Brit* °local, *Slang* boozer, watering-hole, °joint, °dive, *Chiefly Brit* gin-palace, *US* barrelhouse, gin-mill, honky-tonk: *We went down to the pub for a pint and a game of darts.*

puberty *n.* pubescence, °sexual °maturity, adolescence, juvenescence, teens; nubility: *The anxiety of parents for the health of an infant is as nothing compared with their concerns when their child reaches puberty.*

public *adj.* **1** communal, community, °common, °general, collective, °universal, °catholic, °popular, worldwide: *One need only compare early and new films to see how public taste has changed.* **2** °civil, civic, °social, societal, community, communal: *Although they may seem restrictive, these laws are for the public good.* **3** °accessible, °open, °free, unrestricted, non-exclusive, communal, community, °available: *He does much of his research in the public library.* **4** °open, °manifest, exposed, °overt, projected, °plain, °obvious, °apparent, °patent, °clear, clear-cut, acknowledged, known, admitted, °visible, viewable, °conspicuous: *Her public image is quite different from her private persona.* **5** °visible, viewable, °conspicuous, unconcealed, unshrouded, °flagrant, °blatant: *Has Alfie made a public spectacle of himself again?* **6** °well-known, °prominent, °eminent, °celebrated, °famous, °renowned, °noted, °notable, °influential, °illustrious; °notorious, °disreputable, °infamous: *Invite a well-known public figure to open the exhibition if you can.* **7** ***make public***: See **publish**, below.
—*n.* **8** community, °people (at °large *or* in general), citizenry, °citizens, °nation, °populace, °population, °society, °masses, multitude, hoi polloi, bourgeoisie, °plebeians, proletariat, °rank and file, middle class, third °estate, commonalty *or* commonality, voters, °man *or* °woman in the street, *Brit* admass, *US* John Q. Public, Mr *or* Mrs Average, *Colloq* (any *or* every) Tom, Dick, and Harry: *The public has responded generously to the charity appeal.* **9** °clientele *or Brit also* clientage, °customers, °custom, °patrons, °followers, °supporters, °buyers, consumers, purchasers, following, °business, °trade: *How can you expect to attract the public without advertising?* **10** sector, °segment, special-interest °group, °portion: *The commuting public will no longer tolerate these excessive train delays.* **11** ***in public***: publicly, °openly, in the °open, *Colloq* out of the closet: *Jarvis has finally confessed in public what we long suspected privately.*

publication *n.* **1** dissemination, promulgation, publicizing, publishing, °proclamation, issuance, reporting, °announcement, °advertisement, advertising, °pronouncement, airing, putting out, °revelation, °declaration, °appearance: *The publication of the news about the sale of the company was no surprise to us.* **2** °book, booklet, °pamphlet, °brochure, °leaflet, broadside *or* broadsheet, flier *or* flyer, handbill, hand-out; °periodical, °magazine, °journal, newsletter, newspaper, °paper, tabloid; annual, semi-annual, °quarterly, bimonthly, monthly, semi-monthly, fortnightly, biweekly, weekly, hebdomadal *or* hebdomedary, semi-weekly, °daily: *He buys every publication he can find dealing with model railways.*

publicize *v.* °promote, advertise, give publicity to, *Colloq* beat the drum for, °plug, °puff, *US* °push, *Slang* hype: *They once hired an elephant to publicize a huge department-store sale.*

publish *v.* make °public, °put out, °broadcast, °spread (about *or* around), advertise, °make known, let (something) be known, °announce, °publicize, °report, °proclaim, promulgate, bruit about, °reveal, divulge, °disclose, °break the °news (about), *Colloq* °leak: *The minister resigned the day the news of the scandal was published.*

pucker *v.* **1** °gather, °draw together, compress, °purse, crinkle, ruck, shirr, °ruffle, corrugate, °furrow, °wrinkle, crease, °screw up, °tighten, °contract, °squeeze: *Pucker up your mouth and give me a kiss. The shirring is done by puckering up the fabric and stitching it through with decorative thread.*
—*n.* **2** °gather, tuck, pleat, pleating, shirr, shirring, °ruffle, ruck, ruche, ruckle, °wrinkle, wrinkling, °fold, crinkle, crinkling: *The curtains have some puckers that need ironing.*

puerile *adj.* °childish, °immature, babyish, °infantile, °juvenile, °silly, asinine, °foolish, trivial, °ridiculous,

°irresponsible, °shallow, °inconsequential, °insignificant, *US* sophomoric: *Stop that puerile horseplay and settle down.*

puff *n.* **1** °blow, °breath, °wind, whiff, °draught, °gust, °blast, °huff: *A slight puff through the open window stirred the curtains.* **2** °draught, °draw, °pull, *Colloq* drag: *She took a puff from her cigarette and blew the smoke in his face.* **3** °advertisement, °praise, °mention, °word, °item, °review, °notice, publicity, puffery, *Colloq* °plug, blurb, *Slang* hype: *The late editions of the papers carry puffs for your new restaurant.*
—*v.* **4** °blow, °breathe, °huff, °pant, °gasp, wheeze: *Victor came huffing and puffing up to the finishing line.* **5** °draw, °pull (at *or* on), °inhale, suck, smoke, *Colloq* drag: *Holmes was puffing silently on his pipe.* **6** Usually, ***puff up*** *or* ***out***: °inflate, distend, bloat, °swell (up *or* out), °stretch, balloon, °expand, °pump up, °enlarge: *Calvin swaggered in, all puffed up with pride about his new job.* **7** °publicize, advertise, °promote, °push, trumpet, ballyhoo, °extol, commend, °praise, *Colloq* °plug, beat the drum (for): *He has been shamelessly puffing his book on every radio and TV show.*

pugilism *n.* boxing, prizefighting; the manly art of self-defence, fisticuffs; *Colloq* the boxing *or* °fight game: *His career in pugilism came to an abrupt end in the second minute of the third round.*

pugilist *n.* boxer, prizefighter, fighter, contender, °contestant, battler, combatant, *Colloq* °bruiser, scrapper, champ, *Slang* slugger, pug: *The pugilists came out of their corners and at once started jabbing away at each other.*

pugnacious *adj.* °aggressive, °belligerent, combative, °quarrelsome, bellicose, antagonistic, °argumentative, °hostile, litigious, contentious, disputatious, °disagreeable, fractious, °petulant, °testy, irascible, hot-tempered, choleric, unfriendly, curmudgeonly, °irritable, °short-tempered: *The Gothic tribes were very pugnacious, always ready to fight with little or no provocation.*

pukka *adj.* **1** pukkah *or* pucka, °well done *or* made, °properly *or* °perfectly done, °first-class: *That was a pukka meal.* **2** pukkah *or* pucka, °genuine, °good, °authentic, °reliable, °honourable, °fair, °right, °proper, °thorough, °out-and-out: *They always referred to him as 'pukka sahib'.*

puling *adj.* whining, wailing, °querulous, whimpering, snivelling, weeping, caterwauling: *The third-class carriage was filled with chickens, pigs, and puling infants.*

pull *v.* **1** °draw, °haul, °drag, °lug, °tow, °trail: *Do you think the car is strong enough to pull that load?* **2** °tug, °jerk, °yank, °wrench, °pluck: *He suddenly pulled on the door and it opened.* **3** Sometimes, ***pull out*** *or* ***up***: °pluck (out), °withdraw, °extract, °uproot, °pick (up *or* out), °snatch out *or* up, °tear *or* °rip out *or* up, cull, °select, °draw out, °take out, °remove: *We pulled out all the weeds and threw them on the compost heap. He has a collection of jokes pulled from his speeches.* **4** Often, ***pull apart***: °tear *or* °rip (up *or* °apart), °rend, pull asunder, °wrench (°apart), °stretch, °strain: *This fabric is so weak it pulled apart as soon as I touched it. I think I pulled a muscle in my calf.* **5** Often, ***pull in***: °attract, °draw, °lure, °entice, allure, °catch, °captivate, °fascinate, °capture: *We need something besides the 'Sale' sign to pull the customers into the shop.* **6** ***pull apart***: pull to pieces *or* shreds, °criticize, °attack, °pick *or* take °apart *or* to pieces, flay, °run down, *Colloq* °put down, °pan, °knock, °devastate, °destroy, slate, *Slang* °slam: *The critics really pulled apart her new play.* **7** ***pull away***: °withdraw, °draw *or* °drive *or* °go *or* °move away; outrun, outpace, °draw °ahead of: *She pulled away abruptly when he touched her hand. The green car is pulling away from the others.* **8** ***pull back***: **a** °withdraw, °draw back, back off *or* away, °recoil, °shrink (away *or* back) from, °shy, °flinch (from), °jump, °start: *The burglar pulled back when he saw the ferocious dog.* **b** °withdraw, (beat a) °retreat, take °flight, °flee, °turn tail, °drop *or* °fall back, back out: *We cheered when we saw the enemy troops pulling back.* **9** ***pull down***: **a** °demolish, °raze, °level, °destroy, °wreck: *It takes only hours to pull down a house that it has taken generations to build.* **b** °draw, °receive, °get, be paid, °earn: *He pulls down much more at his new job.* **c** °lower, °debase, °diminish, °reduce, °degrade, °dishonour, °disgrace, °discredit, °humiliate: *When his fortunes declined, he pulled down all his friends with him.* **10** ***pull for***: °hope *or* °pray for, be °enthusiastic for, be °supportive of, °support, °campaign for, °cheer for, °encourage, °boost, *US* °root for: *We are all pulling for you to win.* **11** ***pull in***: **a** °drive up, °arrive, °come, °draw up *or* in, °reach: *The train finally pulled in at midnight. We need petrol, so pull in at the next filling station.* **b** °arrest, apprehend, take into °custody, *Colloq* °pinch, °nab, collar, °nail, *Brit* °nick, *Slang* bust: *The cops pulled him in for possession of narcotics.* **12** ***pull off***: **a** °detach, °rip *or* °tear off, °separate, °wrench off *or* away: *When he was cashiered from the army, they pulled off all his insignia and medals.* **b** °accomplish, do, °complete, °succeed, °carry out, °bring off, °manage, °perform: *Three men pulled off the robbery in broad daylight.* **13** ***pull oneself together***: °recover, get a °grip on oneself, °get over it, °recuperate, *Colloq* °snap out of it, buck up: *Try to pull yourself together and stop crying.* **14** ***pull out***: **a** °uproot, °extract, °withdraw: *In the ensuing scrap, someone tried to pull out his hair. Two survivors were pulled out of the rubble.* **b** °withdraw, °retreat, beat a °retreat, °recede, °draw back, °leave, °depart, °go *or* °run away *or* off, °evacuate, *Colloq* beat it, do a bunk, *Brit* do a moonlight flit: *The artillery unit pulled out yesterday.* **c** °leave, °go, °depart, °take off: *When that train pulls out, I want you on it!* **d** °withdraw, °quit, °abandon, °resign (from), °give up, °relinquish: *You can still pull out of the deal if you want to.* **15** ***pull someone's leg***: °tease, °chaff, rib, °have on, °rag, °twit, poke °fun at, make °fun of, °hoodwink, °ridicule: *He said that I'd just eaten a fly, but he was pulling my leg.* **16** ***pull strings***: use °influence *or* connections, *US* use pull, pull wires: *His uncle pulled strings to get him the job.* **17** ***pull through***: °survive, °recover, °improve, get °better, °get over (it), °rally; °live: *Murphy was at death's door, but luckily he pulled through.* **18** ***pull up***: **a** °stop, °halt, come to a °standstill: *We pulled up in a lay-by for a few minutes' rest.* **b** °uproot, °root out, °dig out, deracinate, eradicate: *Your dog has pulled up all the flowers in my garden.* **c** draw °even *or* °level with, °come up to, °reach: *On the fifth lap, Manson pulled up to, then passed Sabbatini.*
—*n.* **19** °draw, °tug; °yank, °jerk: *Give the bell-rope a strong, steady pull, and try not to yank it suddenly.* **20** °attraction, °draw, °magnetism, °appeal, drawing *or* pulling °power, seductiveness, seduction, °lure: *The pull that golf has on certain people is hard to explain.* **21** °influence, °authority, °connections, °prestige, °weight, leverage, *Colloq* clout, muscle: *You'd better treat her nicely, for she has a lot of pull with the boss.* **22** °puff, °draw, inhalation, *Colloq* drag: *He took a long, meditative pull on his cigarette and blew some smoke rings.*

pulley *n.* sheave, °block: *The rope is run through a system of pulleys, called a tackle, for lifting weights.*

pulp *n.* **1** marrow, °pith, °heart, °soft part, °flesh: *After removing the seeds, add two tablespoonfuls of sugar and mix into the pulp.* **2** mush, paste, mash, pap, pomace, °mass, *Technical* triturate: *Water is added to the waste paper, which the machines then reduce to a pulp.*
—*v.* **3** mash, squash, °pulverize, *Technical* levigate, triturate: *The entire print run of the book was pulped after she threatened to sue the publishers.*
—*adj.* **4** °lurid, °sensational, trashy, °cheap: *What he considers great literature you would call pulp fiction.*

pulsate *v.* °beat, °pulse, throb, °pound, thrum, drum, thump, °thud, reverberate, hammer, palpitate, °vibrate; °oscillate, °quiver: *Throughout the voyage, I could feel the ship's engines pulsating.*

pulse *n.* **1** °beat, beating, throb, throbbing, pulsing, pulsating, pulsation, pounding, thrumming, drumming, °thumping, thudding, reverberation, reverberating, hammering, palpitation, palpitating, vibration, vibrating: *The pulse of the jungle drums became louder and faster.*
—*v.* **2** See **pulsate,** above.

pulverize *v.* **1** °powder, comminute, °grind, °crush, °mill, granulate, °crumble, °break up, bray, °pound, *Technical* triturate, levigate: *This machine pulverizes the rock, after which the binding agents are added.* **2** °devastate, °destroy, °demolish, °crush, smash, °shatter, °ruin, °wreck, annihilate: *The four battalions were pulverized in the attack.*

pump *v.* **1** °send, °force, °deliver, °push: *The heart pumps blood around the body.* **2** interrogate, °question, °examine, cross-examine, °quiz, °probe, *Colloq* grill, give (someone) the third degree: *They pumped her for hours, but she told them nothing about my whereabouts.* **3** ***pump out***: pump °dry *or* °empty, °empty, °drain, bail out, °draw *or* °drive *or* °force out, siphon (out): *After the flood it took two days to pump out my basement.* **4** ***pump up***: **a** °inflate, °blow up; dilate, °swell, bloat, °expand, °puff out *or* up: *If you don't repair the tyre, pumping it up will accomplish nothing.* **b** °excite, °inspire, °stimulate, °animate, inspirit, °electrify, galvanize, °energize, °motivate, *Colloq* enthuse: *The coach is talking to the team, trying to pump them up before the big game.* **c** °intensify, °concentrate, °emphasize, °stress, °increase: *We ought to pump up our promotion campaign just before Christmas.*

pun *n.* play on words, °quip, *(bon) mot,* °witticism, °*double entendre, Literary* equivoque, *Technical* paronomasia: *Dennis made some awful pun on 'nose' and 'knows' that nobody got.*

punch[1] *v.* **1** °hit, °clip, °jab, whack, thwack, °knock, smack, °box, pummel, °strike, cuff, *Colloq* clout, bop, slug, wallop, thump, °lambaste, °slam, *Slang* sock, biff, °plug, °belt, °lace (into), *US* paste: *Anyone says anything about my girl, I'll punch him in the jaw!*
—*n.* **2** °clip, °jab, whack, thwack, °knock, smack, °box, cuff, upper-cut, °left *or* °right, *Colloq* clout, bop, slug, wallop, thump, °slam, *Slang* sock, °belt, biff, haymaker, °plug, paste: *The punch knocked him down.* **3** °effect, °impact, effectiveness, °force, forcefulness, °power, °vitality, °gusto, °vigour, °life, vim, °zest, ginger, *Colloq* it, oomph, what it takes, *Slang* zing, zip: *These advertisements are pretty, but they are lacking in punch.*

punch[2] *n.* **1** awl, auger, bodkin, perforator; °drill, °brace and bit: *Use the punch to make another hole in your belt.*
—*v.* **2** °pierce, °stab, °puncture, °perforate; °bore, °drill: *She uses a needle to punch a tiny hole in each end of the egg.*

punctual *adj.* on °time, °timely, °prompt, *Colloq* on the °dot: *Please be punctual, as I don't fancy waiting about in the street.*

punctuate *v.* **1** °interrupt, °break, intersperse; °pepper, sprinkle: *The speeches were punctuated by frequent shouts from the audience.* **2** °accent, accentuate, underline, underscore, °emphasize, °stress, °mark: *He punctuated each element of his argument with a sharp rap of his pencil on the lectern.*

puncture *n.* **1** °hole, perforation, °opening, °leak; °flat (tyre): *I haven't the tools needed to patch the puncture in the tyre.* **2** perforation, perforating, holing, puncturing, °piercing, stabbing, punching: *The puncture of the balloon means that we shall have to postpone our trip.*
—*v.* **3** °perforate, °hole, °pierce, °stab, °penetrate, °go through, °prick, °nick, °rupture: *An arrow punctured the side of the tent.* **4** deflate, °disillusion, bring up °short, °discourage, °humble, °dash, °destroy, °ruin: *Any hopes I had of winning the marathon were punctured when I tripped and fell, spraining my ankle.*

pungent *adj.* **1** °spicy, °hot, °sharp, °strong, °penetrating, °aromatic, °seasoned, peppery, piquant, tangy, flavourful, °tasty, sapid: *The pungent odours of devilled kidneys dominated the dining-room.* **2** °sharp, °biting, stinging, °caustic, °severe, astringent, °stern, acrid, °harsh, °sour, acid, °tart, acrimonious, °bitter, °cutting, °keen, barbed, °trenchant, °scathing, °incisive, mordant, °sarcastic: *This week's* Review *carries a pungent criticism of his new novel.* **3** distressing, upsetting, °poignant, °painful, °hurtful, °penetrating, °piercing, stabbing, °intense, °severe, °acute, °agonizing, °oppressive, °excruciating, racking, consuming: *Only when surgery eased the pressure was he relieved of the pungent pain.*

punish *v.* **1** °penalize, °chastise, °castigate, °discipline, °chasten, °scold, °rebuke, take to °task, °reprove, °dress down, admonish, °correct, teach someone a °lesson, °give a °lesson to, throw the book at, °rap (someone's) knuckles, °slap (someone's) wrist, have *or US* call on the carpet, *Colloq* take it out on (someone): *A child's first taste of injustice is being punished for something she did not do.* **2** °imprison, °jail *or Brit also* gaol, incarcerate, °lock up; °fine, mulct, amerce; °lash, °flog, °beat, °scourge, °spank, °whip, cane, birch, put across *or US also* turn over (one's) knee, *US* °paddle; pillory, crucify; tar and feather, °exile, °banish, excommunicate, cashier, drum out of the corps; °hang, °execute, electrocute, draw and quarter, send to the gas chamber, *Colloq* °put away, *Slang Brit* °send down, *US* °send up: *They were punished for their crimes.* **3** °hurt, °harm, °injure, °damage, °abuse, maltreat, °rough up, °knock about *or* around, maul, thrash, °beat, trounce, °manhandle, °batter, *Slang* °beat up: *The challenger punished the champion so badly that he could not come out for the tenth round.*

punishing *adj.* gruelling, °hard, °arduous, °strenuous, °laborious, °exhausting, tiring, wearying, fatiguing, wearing, taxing, °demanding, °burdensome, back-breaking, torturous: *Laying railway track was the most punishing job I ever had. This punishing schedule is beginning to tell on me.*

punishment *n.* **1** chastisement, chastising, castigation, castigating, °discipline, disciplining, chastening, scolding, °rebuke, °reproof, dressing-down, admonishment, admonition, °correction, °punitive measures: *Every society must continually revise its approach to the punishment of criminals.* **2** °penance, °penalty, °sentence, sentencing, °just °deserts; °imprisonment, incarceration, jailing *or Brit also* gaoling; lashing, flogging, beating, °whipping, scourging, °spanking, caning, birching, *US* paddling; °exile, banishment, excommunication, cashiering; hanging, °execution, electrocution, drawing and quartering: *Her punishment is to perform 20 hours a week of public service for a year. Stop whimpering and take your punishment like a man.* **3** °injury, °harm, °damage, °abuse, maltreatment, mauling, beating, °thrashing, trouncing, manhandling, battering, torture: *How are professional wrestlers able to withstand so much punishment?*

punitive *adj.* chastening, castigatory, disciplinary, retributive, punitory, retaliatory, correctional: *A punitive expedition was sent there to quell the colonists' uprising.*

punk *n.* **1** ruffian, °hoodlum, hooligan, °delinquent, °tough, °thug, vandal, yahoo, °barbarian, *Colloq* goon, °mug: *A couple of young punks were standing at the bar, trying to look important.*
—*adj.* **2** °inferior, °rotten, unimportant, °worthless, °bad, °poor, °awful, *Colloq* °lousy: *I thought that the lead in the play was a punk actor.*

punt *v.* **1** °bet, wager, °stake, °gamble, °speculate, °lay a °bet *or* °stake *or* wager: *Herbert spends all the grocery money punting at the races.*
—*n.* **2** °bet, wager, °stake, °gamble: *In roulette, Janet always placed her punt on number 14.*

punter *n.* **1** *Brit* better *or US also* bettor, gambler, gamester, °player, speculator, °backer, wagerer, *Brit* °punt, *Colloq* crap-shooter: *The punters are putting all their money on United to win the cup.* **2** °fellow, °chap, °person, °individual, °man *or* °woman in the street;

°customer, °client, °buyer, *Colloq* °guy, *Brit* bloke, geezer: *The average punter likes a beer now and then.*

puny *adj.* **1** °small, °little, °insignificant, °petty, unimportant, °inconsequential, °paltry, trivial, °trifling, °minor, °negligible, nugatory, of °little *or* no account, °inferior, °worthless, °useless, *Colloq* piddling, *Slang Brit* not much cop: *Farr's contribution to the success of the business was really quite puny.* **2** °small, °little, °diminutive, °tiny, °minute: *Mattson looks so puny alongside that sumo wrestler.* **3** °weak, °feeble, °frail, °sickly, weakly, underfed, undernourished, °undersized, underdeveloped, °stunted, °dwarf, midget, pygmy: *You cannot expect such a puny chap to lift such a great weight.*

pup *n.* puppy, whelp, °upstart, whippersnapper, popinjay, cub, jackanapes, °show-off, °braggart: *That young pup had the gall to tell me I was too old to be running the company.*

pupil *n.* °student, °learner, °scholar, schoolchild, schoolgirl, schoolboy, °disciple, °apprentice; beginner, °novice, neophyte, tiro *or* tyro, *Chiefly ecclesiastical* catechumen: *A number of Geoffrey's former pupils have organized a dinner to honour him.*

puppet *n.* **1** hand-puppet, finger-puppet, glove puppet, doll; marionette, string puppet: *The children built a little theatre and put on a puppet show.* **2** °figurehead, cat's-paw, °pawn, °dupe, °tool, hireling, °yes-man *Colloq* °front (man), *Slang* stooge, °sucker, patsy: *He is without authority and is merely a puppet of the drug dealers. The army of occupation set up a puppet government to rule the country.*

purchase *v.* **1** °buy, °acquire, °procure, °obtain, °get, °secure, °pay for: *He recently purchased a new personal computer and cannot get it to work. Not long ago, a shilling purchased a loaf of bread.* **2** °win, °gain, °achieve, °realize, attain, °obtain: *His liberty was purchased by the betrayal of his colleagues.*
—*n.* **3** °acquisition, acquiring, buying, purchasing, obtaining, securing, procurement: *The purchase of books for the university library is the responsibility of Ms Turnbull.* **4** °buy, °acquisition: *Tom returned from the shop carrying his purchases.* **5** °grip, °hold, °support, toe-hold, foothold, °grasp; leverage, °position, °advantage, °edge: *The climber was having trouble getting a good purchase on the icy ledge.*

pure *adj.* **1** unmixed, unadulterated, unalloyed, simon-pure; 24-carat *or US also* 24-karat, °sterling, °solid; °real, °genuine, °authentic, °flawless, °faultless, °perfect, °natural, °true, °simple: *We have made every effort to keep the blood-line of these horses completely pure. Pure gold is not used for coins or jewellery because it is too soft. She wore a dress of the purest white.* **2** uncontaminated, °clear, °clean, °wholesome, °sanitary, uninfected, disinfected, pasteurized, sterilized, °sterile, antiseptic, unpolluted, °spotless, °immaculate, unsullied, unbesmirched, unblemished, unmarred, unstained, untainted: *It was refreshing to breathe pure air again. Stringent tests ensure that the substances are pure before they go on the market.* **3** °chaste, virginal, virgin, °intact, maidenly, vestal, undefiled, °innocent, guileless, °virtuous, °modest, °moral, °correct, °proper, °decent, °decorous, uncorrupted, °blameless, sinless, °impeccable: *As far as we can tell, she led a totally pure life.* **4** °theoretical, °hypothetical, conjectural, °speculative, °abstract, conceptual, notional, °philosophical, °academic(al): *His field is pure science, and he cares little how the results of his work might be applied to everyday life.* **5** unalloyed, °simple, °unmitigated, °sheer, utter, °absolute, °unqualified, °complete, °total, °perfect, °thorough, °outright, °downright, °out-and-out, °mere: *Many regarded the notion that man could ever fly as pure nonsense. Any resemblance to a living person is pure coincidence.* **6** °honourable, (highly) °principled, °righteous, °upright, °honest, straightforward, high-minded, °pious, °worthy, °good, °ethical, °virtuous, °sincere, above °suspicion, above reproach, like Caesar's wife: *Can anyone doubt that their motives in striving for international peace are pure?*

pure-bred *adj.* full-blooded, thoroughbred, pedigreed: *We raise only pure-bred Angus cattle.*

purgative *n.* **1** laxative, cathartic, aperient, °purge, physic, depurative: *The doctor prescribed a mild purgative, and she felt much better next day.*
—*adj.* **2** laxative, cathartic, aperient, evacuant, diuretic, depurative; abstergent: *We were totally unprepared for the purgative effects of the spicy food.*

purge *v.* **1** °cleanse, °purify, °clean (out), °clear, °scour (out), depurate, deterge, °wash (out): *The tanks must be purged before filling them with the new fuel.* **2** °eject, eradicate, °expel, °eliminate, get °rid of, °dismiss, °clear out *or* away, °sweep away *or* out, oust, °remove, °rout out, weed out, °root out; do away with, °exterminate, liquidate, °kill, °destroy: *After the coup, the old guard was purged from all the governmental agencies. The rebels purged the entire council of elders.* **3** °clear, exonerate, absolve, °forgive, °purify, °pardon, exculpate: *He was given every opportunity to purge himself of the charge of contempt of court.*
—*n.* **4** °ejection, eradication, °expulsion, elimination, °dismissal, clearing out *or* away, ousting, ouster, °removal, routing out, weeding out, rooting out, unseating; defenestration; extermination, liquidation, °killing, °murder, °slaughter: *The bloody purge of dissidents was carried out by the secret police.* **5** See **purgative, 1,** above.

purify *v.* **1** °cleanse, °clean, °clarify, °wash, sanitize, depurate, decontaminate, °freshen, °disinfect; °fumigate: *The water is then purified by passing it through sand.* **2** exonerate, exculpate, absolve, °clear, °redeem, shrive, lustrate, acquit, °pardon, °forgive, °excuse: *Before the aspirants can be admitted to the church they must be purified.*

purist *n.* pedant, precisian, formalist, stickler, bluestocking, dogmatist, °Pharisee, °fanatic, *Colloq* diehard, stuffed shirt: *Language purists are often unaware of their own grammatical and semantic blunders.*

puritan *n.* **1** moralist, pietist, religionist, °fanatic, °zealot, °purist: *It seems to me that all religions have their puritans.*
—*adj.* **2** °prudish, puritanical, prim, °proper, °strait-laced, ascetic, austere, moralistic, pietistic, °intolerant, disapproving, °bigoted, °narrow-minded, °stuffy, stiff-necked, °rigid, uncompromising, hard-line, °stern, °severe, °strict, *Colloq* uptight, hard-nosed: *Puritan notions about women's clothing have often put propriety before practicality.*

purity *n.* **1** pureness, faultlessness, correctness, flawlessness, °perfection, spotlessness, cleanness, cleanliness, °clarity; healthfulness, wholesomeness, salubrity; innocuousness, harmlessness: *The purity of the drinking-water has been affected by the nearby chemical plant.* **2** °chastity, chasteness, virginity, virtuousness, °virtue, °morality, °propriety, °honesty, °integrity, °rectitude, properness, innocence, guilelessness, decency, decorousness, modesty, blamelessness, sinlessness: *We never had any reason to doubt the purity of their character.*

purpose *n.* **1** °object, °intention, °intent, °end, °goal, °ambition, °objective, °target, °aim, °principle, °point, °rationale, °reason; °scheme, °plan, °design, °motive, motivation, °view: *What purpose was served by her confession? If your purpose in inviting me was to insult me, I shall leave now. I fail to understand Laura's purpose in warning me against David.* **2** °resolution, firmness, °determination, °persistence, °drive, single-mindedness, deliberation, deliberateness, purposefulness, steadfastness, °tenacity, doggedness, °will, °resolve, resoluteness, °perseverance, stubbornness: *She admired the strong purpose behind his refusal to compromise with quality.* **3** °use, practicality, avail, °effect, utility, °usefulness, °outcome, °result; °advantage, °profit, °gain, °good, °benefit: *To what purpose are you planning to put this knowledge? I cannot see the purpose in pursuing this line of questioning.* **4 on purpose**: **a** purposely, intentionally, °deliberately,

wilfully, by °design, consciously, knowingly, designedly, wittingly: *That was no accident: you kicked me on purpose!* **b** °especially, °specially, °expressly, °exactly, °precisely, specifically, in °particular: *He kicked me on purpose, Mum, just to make me cry!*
—*v.* **5** °plan, °intend, °design, °resolve, °mean, °aim, have in °mind *or* °view, have a °mind, °propose, °consider, °contemplate, °aspire, long, °yearn: *They purpose to open an office of their own.*

purposeful *adj.* °intentional, intended, planned, °deliberate, resolved, settled, °determined, °resolute, °decided, confirmed, affirmed, °sure, °certain, °positive, °definite, °staunch, °steadfast, °persistent, strong-willed, dogged, °tenacious, pertinacious, unfailing, unfaltering, °firm, °fixed: *Her purposeful manner inclines other people to defer to her.*

purposeless *adj.* °pointless, °bootless, °meaningless, °empty, vacuous, °senseless, °aimless, °rambling, °discursive, wandering, disorganized, unorganized: *He made what we thought was a purposeless trip to the branch office, but it ultimately proved invaluable.*

purse *n.* **1** °pouch, (money-)°bag, °wallet, °pocket, *Dialect* poke, *Highland dress* sporran, *US and Canadian* (woman's) handbag, pocketbook: *The money goes out so fast I think there is a hole in my purse.* **2** °money, °wealth, °resources, °funds, °finances, exchequer, °treasury, °capital, °revenue, °income, °means, °cash, °riches; pounds, shillings, and pence, l.s.d., dollars, shekels, *Derogatory* Mammon, pelf, (filthy) lucre, *US* almighty dollar, *Slang Brit* °ready *or* readies, lolly, dosh, °loot, dough, *US and Canadian* bucks, °scratch: *The spread of capitalism shows that the power of a man's purse can transcend his political idealism.* **3** °prize, °reward, °award, °present, °gift: *The purse for the next race will be 5,000 guineas.*
—*v.* **4** °pucker (up), °contract, °wrinkle, compress, °press together: *Robert pursed his lips thoughtfully.*

pursue *v.* **1** °follow, °chase, °go *or* °run after, °hunt (after *or* down *or* for *or* up), °trace, °trail, °track, °run down, °take off after, dog, °stalk, °shadow, *Brit* chivvy *or* chivy *or* chevy, *Colloq* °tail: *The police pursued the escaped convicts across the moor.* **2** °follow (up *or* on with), °trace, °carry on with, °continue, °conduct, °devote *or* °dedicate oneself to, °cultivate, °undertake, °practise, °persist *or* °persevere in, °maintain, °exercise, °proceed with, adhere to, °stay with, °apply oneself to, *Colloq* °stick with: *If you pursue such a course, you are certain to land in jail.* **3** °aspire to, °aim for, °work for *or* toward(s), °try *or* °strive for, °purpose, °seek, °search for, °go in °search of, °quest after *or* for, be °intent on, be °bent upon *or* on: *Jonathan is pursuing a doctorate in history at Oxford.* **4** woo, (pay) court (to), °seek the hand of, *Formal* °press (one's) °suit with, pay °suit *or* court *or* (one's) addresses to, *Colloq* set one's cap for, *Slang* °chase (after): *Jack is pursuing Jacquelyn with matrimony in mind.*

pursuit *n.* **1** pursuing, chasing, following, hunting, °hunt, going *or* °running after, tracing, trailing, tracking, °running down, dogging, stalking, shadowing, *Brit* chivvy *or* chivy *or* chevy, *Colloq* tailing: *We all joined in the pursuit of the animal. The police set off in hot pursuit of the thieves.* **2** pursuance, striving after, seeking, searching, °search, looking for: *Many think that the pursuit of wealth is the only worthwhile thing in life.* **3** °work, °line (of °work), °employment, °field, °area, °speciality *or US and Canadian only* specialty, specialization, °business, °profession, °trade, °vocation, °calling, °career, life-work, °activity; °hobby, °pastime, avocation, °interest; *Slang* °racket: *What pursuits are open to Jack Ketch now that hanging has been abolished?*

push *v.* **1** °thrust, shove, °drive, °move, set in °motion, get °moving, °propel; °press: *Push the boat away from the pier. He pushed the door shut.* **2** °press, °depress: *Push the button if you want anything.* **3** shove, °thrust, elbow, °shoulder, °force, jostle, °nudge: *We pushed our way through the crowd.* **4** °urge, °encourage, °press, °induce, °ask, °persuade, °get, egg on, °prod, °spur, goad, °rouse, °prompt, °incite, °move, °motivate, °stimulate, °influence, impel, °make, compel, °force, dragoon, coerce, constrain; badger, °hound, °pester, °harass, °plague, °nag, °browbeat; °beg, importune, entreat: *His family is pushing him to find work. I'll soon have the work done, but stop pushing me.* **5** °force, °strain, overstrain, °tax, overtax, °burden, overburden: *You might have got away with it this time, but don't push your luck.* **6** °promote, °publicize, advertise, °boost, propagandize, °puff, *Colloq* °plug, *Slang* ballyhoo, hype: *Because we have too much stock, we are pushing suntan oil this week.* **7** ***push about*** *or* ***around***: °intimidate, °bully, cow, domineer, °tyrannize, bullyrag, °torment, °force, coerce: *Don't push people about if you want them to do what you want.* **8** ***push away***: °reject, °deny, °brush off *or* aside, give (someone) the cold °shoulder, °rebuff, °distance oneself from: *She pushes everyone away and then wonders why she has no friends.* **9** ***push off***: **a** shove off, °sail away *or* off: *We stepped into the dinghy and pushed off.* **b** °leave, °depart, °go away, *Colloq* light out, °take off, hit the road, skedaddle, scram, make oneself scarce, *Slang* °beat it: *I have to push off now if I'm to make that train.* **10** ***push on*** *or* ***forward(s)*** *or* ***along***: °move °onwards *or* °onward *or* °ahead *or* forward, °continue, °proceed, °advance, press on *or* °onwards *or* °onward: *If we stay the night here, we shall have to push on first thing in the morning.* **11** ***push through***: °force, °press, *Colloq* °railroad: *The bill was pushed through committee without delay.* **12** ***push (up) daisies***: be °dead (and buried), be six feet under: *Her husband's pushing up daisies.*
—*n.* **13** shove, °thrust, °nudge: *My car needs a push to get it started.* **14** °effort, °energy, °dynamism, °drive, °force, °enterprise, °ambition, °vigour, °determination, °initiative, °eagerness, °spirit, °enthusiasm, zeal, °verve, *Colloq* get-up-and-go, zing, zip, °gumption, °go: *If he had a bit more push, he might succeed.* **15** °campaign, °attack, °assault, °advance, °offensive, °charge, onslaught, foray, sortie, °invasion, incursion, °raid, sally, blitzkrieg, blitz, °strike: *The troops were massed along the coast, ready for the big push inland.* **16** ***the push***: °dismissal, °notice, *Colloq* marching orders, *Chiefly Brit* the °sack, the °boot, *Chiefly US and Canadian* walking papers, a pink slip: *He'd been with the company for twenty years, but they still gave him the push when sales fell.*

pushover *n.* **1** °sure thing, *Colloq* °piece of cake, child's play, °snap, °picnic, walk-over, *US* °breeze, *Slang* cinch, *Brit* doddle, *US* lead-pipe cinch: *The Latin exam was a pushover.* **2** *Colloq* walk-over, chump, °soft touch, °soft *or* °easy mark, °easy °prey *or* °game, *Slang* patsy, °sucker, stooge, °sap, *Brit* °mug, *US and Canadian* milquetoast: *I spotted him at once as a pushover for the find-the-lady con.*

pushy *adj.* °forward, (self-)°assertive, °forceful, °aggressive, °obnoxious, °arrogant, bumptious, °brassy, °brazen, °impertinent, °insolent, pushing, °presumptuous, °officious, °loud, °showy, °cocky, °brash, °offensive, °bold, *Colloq* °cheeky: *I hate pushy salesmen who won't take 'No' for an answer.*

pussyfoot *v.* **1** °sneak, °creep, °slink, °prowl, °steal, tiptoe: *I wish she'd stop pussyfooting about the house.* **2** beat about the bush, hem *or* hum and haw, °equivocate, °hesitate, be °evasive, °evade the °issue, prevaricate, tergiversate, be °noncommittal, be *or* sit on the °fence, °blow hot and cold: *Don't pussyfoot with me—just come out and say what you really think.*

put *v.* **1** °place, °position, °situate, °set, °lay, °station, °stand, °deposit, °rest, °settle; °locate: *Please put all books where they belong.* **2** °assign, °commit, °cause, °set, consign, °subject: *I joined the army to fight for my country, and they put me to work peeling potatoes.* **3** °subject, cause to °experience *or* °undergo *or* °suffer, consign, °send: *He was put to death for his beliefs, not his actions.* **4** °express, °word, °phrase; °say, utter, °write: *How did they put it?—'We hold these truths to be self-evident, that all men are created equal...' To put it to you straight, shape up or ship out! Can you put that* into French? **5** °offer, °advance, °bring forward, °present, °propose, °submit, °tender, °set before: *I put it to you that you have been lying to the court and that you did leave your house that night.* **6** °bet, °gamble, wager, °stake, play, °chance, °risk, °hazard: *I put two pounds on the horse to win.* **7** °throw, °heave, °toss, °fling, °cast, °pitch, °bowl, °lob, °send, °shy, °shoot, °snap, catapult: *How far did you say you can put a 10-pound shot?* **8** °place, °assign, °attribute, °lay, °pin, °attach, °fix: *They try to put the blame on me for everything that goes wrong around here.* **9** ***put about***: °broadcast, °publish, °make known, °publicize, °announce, °spread about *or* around: *They have been putting about some story linking the two of us romantically.* **10** ***put across*** *or* ***over***: make °clear, °get across, make (something *or* oneself) °understood *or* understandable, °explain, °spell out, convey, °communicate: *She is quite adept at putting across her ideas.* **11** ***put aside***: °set *or* °lay aside, °ignore, °disregard, pay no °heed to, °push aside, shrug off: *They put aside their differences and discovered they had much in common. Isn't it time you put aside childish things?* **12** ***put aside*** *or* ***by*** *or* ***away***: °lay aside *or* by, °set aside; °save, °store, °stow *or* °store *or* °salt *or* squirrel away, °lay away, °cache, bank: *You ought to put a little money aside for a rainy day.* **13** ***put away***: **a** See **12,** above. **b** °jail *or Brit also* gaol, °imprison, incarcerate, *Colloq* °send, °jug, confine, °commit, institutionalize, remand, *Brit* °send down, *US* °send up: *She wants rapists and child molesters put away for a long, long time.* **c** See **16 d,** below. **d** °consume, °gorge, gormandize *or US also* gourmandize: *It is unbelievable how much that man can put away at one sitting.* **14** ***put back***: °return, °replace, °restore: *He insists that he put back all the money he took. Put the pictures back where they belong.* **15** ***put by***: See **12,** above. **16** ***put down***: **a** °record, °register, °write down, °set down, °enter, °list; log, °note (down), °jot down, make a °note *or* °notation of: *You may put me down for a contribution of £5. Please put down your name and address in the box provided.* **b** depose, put an °end to, °topple, °crush, °overthrow, °subdue, °suppress, °check, °quash, °quell: *The loyalists put down the rebellion in short order.* **c** ascribe, °assign, °attribute: *The doctor put my feelings of fatigue and listlessness down to anaemia.* **d** °kill, °exterminate, °destroy, put to death, put to sleep, put away, do away with: *We had to have our cat put down, which was very upsetting for us all.* **e** abash, °humiliate, °crush, °silence, °mortify, °lower, take down (a °peg *or* a notch), °shame, snub, deflate, °slight, °reject, °dismiss: *Waiters have a way of putting people down if they behave presumptuously.* **f** °take for, °reckon, °account, °count, °categorize, °regard: *Don't put Martin down as a dunce just because he acts the fool now and then.* **g** °belittle, °diminish, °disparage, deprecate, °depreciate, °criticize, disdain, °look down on, °despise, contemn: *They deny being prejudiced, but they put down everyone who isn't exactly like them.* **17** ***put forth***: **a** °propose, °offer, °set forth, °advance: *Several theories have been put forth on the function of mitochondrial DNA.* **b** °grow, °produce, °send out *or* forth, bud, °flower: *When the plant puts forth suckers, they must be pinched back.* **c** °begin, °set out, °set forth, °start: *We put forth on our voyage with great enthusiasm.* **d** promulgate, °issue, °publish, °make known, °make °public: *The committee have not put forth any suggestions for improving traffic flow.* **18** ***put forward***: **a** °propose, °present, °tender, °nominate, °name; °recommend: *Your name has been put forward as chair for next year's committee.* **b** °suggest, °offer, °propose, °set forth, put forth, °present, °submit, °tender, proffer, °introduce, °advance, °propound, °air, °make known, °announce: *No new solutions to the problem were put forward.* **19** ***put in***: **a** °insert, °introduce: *Why did you put in a reference to your mother?* **b** °spend, °devote: *During the holiday season I plan to put in a lot of time reading.* **c** °make: *So, you finally decided to put in an appearance.* **20** ***put in for***: **a** °apply for, °request, °ask for, °petition for: *He has put in for a transfer twice and has been refused both times.* **b** °seek, °apply for, °pursue, °file: *Do you really think that Jamieson will put in for re-election?* **21** ***put off***: **a** °postpone, °delay, °defer, put back, °stay, °hold off, °shelve, put *or* °set aside, *Chiefly US* put over, °table: *Consideration of your request has been put off till tomorrow.* **b** °dismiss, get °rid of, °send away, °turn away; °discourage, *Colloq* give (someone) the °brush-off, *US* °brush off: *The manager put me off when I went in to ask about a salary increase.* **c** °dismay, disconcert, °upset, °confuse, °disturb, °perturb, abash, °distress, *Colloq* °throw, °rattle: *Curiously, Michael didn't seem a bit put off to learn about the murder.* **d** °repel, °disgust, °sicken, °revolt, °nauseate: *That television programme on open-heart surgery really put me off.* **e** °leave, °depart, °go (off), °set off: *We put off tomorrow morning for Rockall.* **22** ***put on***: **a** don, °clothe *or* attire *or* °dress (oneself) in, get dressed in, change *or* slip into: *We put on our best clothes to come to your party.* **b** °assume, °take on, °pretend, °affect, feign, °bluff, make a °show of: *She puts on an air of indifference, but she really does care.* **c** °add, °gain: *Bill put on quite a bit of weight when he stopped smoking.* **d** °stage, °mount, °produce, °present, °perform: *Our local repertory group is putting on* Hedda Gabler *this weekend.* **e** °tease, °mock, *Colloq* kid, pull (someone's) °leg, rib, °rag, *Brit* °have on: *When he told you that all holidays had been cancelled he was only putting you on.* **23** ***put out***: **a** °inconvenience, discommode, °disturb, °embarrass, °trouble, °bother, °impose upon *or* on, *Colloq* put on the °spot: *Her arriving an hour early didn't put me out one bit.* **b** °annoy, vex, °irritate, °anger, °exasperate, °irk, °perturb, °provoke, *Slang* °bug: *Donald was very much put out to discover that the appointment had gone to someone else.* **c** snuff out, °extinguish, °blow out, douse, °quench, °smother: *We put out the fire on the stove before it could spread.* **d** °exert, °put forth, °expend, °use, °exercise: *We put out considerable effort moving the furniture before she decided she liked it the way it had been.* **e** °publish, °issue, °broadcast, make °public, °circulate, °spread, °make known, °release: *The information office put out the news that the summit meeting had been a great success.* **24** ***put out of (one's) misery***: °release, °relieve, °free, °deliver, °rescue, °save, °spare: *Just tell him what they said and put him out of his misery.* **25** ***put over***: **a** put *or* °get across, convey, °communicate, °set *or* put forth, °relate: *I am trying to put the point over to you that I cannot leave now.* **b** See **21a,** above. **26** ***put (one*** *or* ***something) over on (someone)***: °fool (someone), °pull (someone's) leg, °deceive (someone), °mislead (someone), pull the wool over (someone's) eyes, °trick (someone), °hoodwink (someone): *She really put one over on me when she said she loved me. I think that Manfred is trying to put something over on you.* **27** ***put through***: **a** °carry out *or* through, °execute, (put into) °effect, °bring off, °accomplish, °complete, °finish, conclude, *Colloq* °pull off: *If they succeed in putting through their plan, the company will be bankrupt.* **b** °process, °handle, °organize, °see to, °follow up on: *I will personally see that your application is put through the proper channels.* **c** °connect, °hook up: *I asked the operator to put me through to the chairman himself.* **28** ***put up***: **a** °erect, °build, °construct, °raise, °set up, °put together, °fabricate: *They demolished a row of Georgian houses and put up some ugly County offices in their place.* **b** °accommodate, °lodge, °board, °house, °take in, °quarter, *Chiefly military* billet: *As our house is small, we were able to put up only three people.* **c** °preserve, can; °cure, pickle: *There are many foods that can be put up for later consumption.* **d** °contribute, °pledge, °offer (as collateral), °stake, mortgage, °post: *We put up the house as security for the loan.* **e** °contribute, °give, °supply, °donate, ante (up), °advance, °pay, °invest: *We put up all our savings to secure our retirement pension.* **f** °increase, °raise, °boost, elevate: *As soon as there is a hint of an oil shortage, they put up the price of petrol.* **g** See **18 a,** above. **h** °offer, °tender, put *or* place on the °market: *They put their house up for sale and are planning to move to the Riviera.* **29** ***put up to***: °incite, °urge, goad, °spur, egg on, °encourage, °prompt, instigate: *Was it* *you who put Reggie up to playing that prank on the teacher?* **30** ***put up with***: °tolerate, °abide, °take, °brook, °stand (for), °stomach, °accept, °resign oneself to, °bear, °endure, °swallow: *Why do you put up with his outrageous behaviour?*

put-down *n.* °dig, °sneer, snub, disparaging *or* denigrating °remark, °slight, °offence, °insult: *The worst put-down was to tell her she looks like her sister, whom she hates.*

put-on *n.* **1** °deception, °hoax, °trick, leg-pull, jest, (practical) °joke, °prank, °pretence, *Colloq* spoof: *He was completely taken in by my put-on about being from the Nobel prize committee.* **2** °take-off, °parody, °satire, °burlesque, °caricature, °act, *Brit* send-up, *Colloq* spoof: *You shouldn't be offended, it was only a put-on.*

putrefy *v.* °rot, °decompose, °decay, moulder, °go °bad, °spoil, °deteriorate, °go off: *We traced the smell in the larder to a putrefying leg of lamb.*

putrid *adj.* °rotten, rotting, decomposed, decomposing, decayed, decaying, °mouldy, mouldering, spoilt *or* spoiled, putrefied, putrescent, putrefying, °foul, fetid, °rank, tainted, °corrupt: *Only the vultures continued to hover about the putrid carcass.*

put-up *adj.* (secretly) °preconceived, prearranged, plotted, preconcerted: *If the butler had a hand in it, you know it was a put-up job.*

put-upon *adj.* imposed upon, inconvenienced, put out, taken °advantage of, exploited, °abused: *I shall be happy to help, and I don't feel put-upon at all.*

puzzle *v.* **1** baffle, °bewilder, °confuse, confound, °mystify, °flummox, °perplex, °nonplus, °stymie, °stump: *I am completely puzzled by what you wrote in your last letter.* **2** Usually, ***puzzle over***: °study, °ponder (over), °mull over, °contemplate, °meditate on *or* upon *or* over, °consider, °muse over *or* on, °reflect on *or* over, °think about *or* over *or* on: *If you puzzle over it long enough, the problem may vanish of its own accord.* **3** ***puzzle out***: °solve, °decipher, °crack (the °code), unravel, °work out, °figure out, °think through, °sort out, unlock: *I finally puzzled out the inscription on this old coin. It might take a while, but I can puzzle out the solution to this crossword.*
—*n.* **4** °enigma, °problem, °question, °paradox, poser, °mystery, °riddle, conundrum, *Colloq* brain-teaser: *The puzzle is how the murder was committed when the door was locked from the inside.*

puzzling *adj.* mystifying, enigmatic(al), bewildering, baffling, confounding, °perplexing, confusing, °ambiguous, °contradictory, abstruse: *It is a bit puzzling to see Catherine so often in the company of the husband she recently divorced.*

Q

quack *n.* **1** charlatan, °impostor, °pretender, °fake(r), °fraud, *Colloq* °phoney *or US also* phony: *The quack diagnosed Franny as having appendicitis, but it turned out that she was pregnant.*
—*adj.* **2** °fake, °fraudulent, °sham, °counterfeit, *Colloq* °phoney *or US also* phony: *Are you still going to see that quack doctor—the one who told you to take aspirin to relieve the pain from your ulcer?*

quaint *adj.* **1** °curious, °odd, °strange, °bizarre, °peculiar, °unusual, °queer, uncommon, °singular, °unorthodox, °eccentric, °whimsical, °offbeat, °fanciful, °outlandish, unconventional, °fantastic: *Her sitting-room was furnished in a quaint mixture of Gothic and Victorian styles.* **2** °old-fashioned, archaic, °antiquated, out-dated, °picturesque, °antique: *A rotund little figure appeared, dressed in the quaint clothing of another era.*

quake *v.* **1** °tremble, °shake, °quiver, °shudder; °vibrate, °stagger: *The children were quaking with fear as they crept past the abandoned house.* **2** earthquake, tremor, temblor *or* trembler *or* tremblor, seismic(al) activity, *Rare* seism: *In a few moments the quake levelled three cities that had stood for thousands of years.*

qualification *n.* **1** Often, ***qualifications***: °fitness, °ability, °aptitude, °capability, competence *or* competency, °capacity, suitableness, suitability, eligibility, °proficiency, °skill, °knowledge, *Colloq* know-how: *You cannot persuade me that Powell has the qualifications needed to do the job.* **2** limitation, °restriction, modification, °reservation, caveat, °condition, °stipulation, °proviso, °prerequisite, °requirement: *The only qualification for use of the club's facilities is that one must be a member. My support for the proposal is without qualification.*

qualified *adj.* **1** °able, °suitable, °capable, °competent, °fit, °fitted, equipped, °prepared, °ready, trained, °proficient, °accomplished, °expert, °talented, °adept, °skilful, skilled, °experienced, °practised, °knowledgeable, °well-informed: *Is Kimble qualified to become foreman?* **2** contingent, conditional, restricted, modified, °limited, °provisional: *The chairman has given his qualified approval to the scheme.*

qualify *v.* **1** °equip, °fit (out), °ready, °prepare, °condition, make °eligible; °certify: *His training in the air force qualified him to be a pilot.* **2** be °eligible, meet the °requirements, be °fit *or* °suitable *or* equipped *or* °ready *or* °prepared, make the °grade: *Sue will qualify as a doctor if she passes just one more exam.* **3** °temper, °mitigate, °modify, °moderate, °modulate, °restrict, °limit: *In the light of their later behaviour, I shall have to qualify my recommendation that you accept them as students.*

quality *n.* **1** °property, °attribute, °characteristic, °mark, °distinction, *je ne sais quoi*, °trait: *Can you describe the qualities needed to be a good musician?* **2** °grade, °calibre, °rank, °status, °importance, value, °worth: *In the curiosity shop items of high and low quality are mixed together haphazardly.* **3** *Old-fashioned* eminence, °prominence, °importance, °excellence, °superiority, °distinction, °standing, °supremacy, °dignity, °grandeur, °nobility, blue blood: *Despite her shabby appearance, one could see from her bearing and speech she was a person of quality.*

qualm *n.* second thought, °doubt, uncertainty, °misgiving, hesitation, °scruple, uneasiness, °compunction, °reluctance, disinclination, queasiness, apprehension, apprehensiveness, °twinge, °pang, °worry, °concern, *Colloq* °funny °feeling, °sinking °feeling: *He had some qualms about leaving the town where he had lived for over thirty years.*

quandary *n.* °dilemma, °predicament, °difficulty, °plight, cleft stick, uncertainty: *The management is in a quandary: should it risk overstretching the company by making further capital investment, or should it risk being left behind by its competitors by playing safe?*

quantity *n.* °amount, °extent, °volume; °sum, °number, °total; °weight, °measure: *There seemed to be no limit to the quantity of gold in the mine. The person who most accurately guesses the quantity of beans in the jar wins a prize. What quantity of flour should I buy to make enough cakes for fifty people?*

quarrel *n.* **1** °dispute, °argument, °disagreement, °debate, °controversy, °discord, °difference (of opinion), contention, °misunderstanding; wrangle, °tiff, °row, squabble, altercation, set-to, scuffle, °feud, °fight, °fray, °fracas, °brawl, Donnybrook, mêlée *or* melee, °riot, °battle (royal), *Colloq* dust-up, barney, °scrap, *US* spat: *I have no quarrel with my accountant—it's the tax man that's the problem. A quarrel broke out over whose turn it was to wash the dishes.*
—*v.* **2** °argue, °disagree, °dispute, altercate, have an altercation, °differ, wrangle, be at °odds *or* loggerheads, °clash, squabble, °feud, °fight, °brawl, °battle, *Colloq* °fall out, °scrap: *When we were children, my sister and I quarrelled all the time, but we still loved each other.*

quarrelsome *adj.* °testy, °petulant, irascible, °irritable, °disagreeable, fractious, °querulous, °peevish, °cross, choleric, curmudgeonly, °contrary, dyspeptic,

°cranky, grouchy, °argumentative, combative, squabbling, disputatious, °hostile, antagonistic, dissentious, dissentient, °dissident, °pugnacious, bellicose, °belligerent, contentious: *I have to listen to the continual bickering of my quarrelsome neighbours.*

quarry[1] *n.* °prey, °game, °prize, °object: *The hunter's dogs had run their quarry to ground. Wealthy widows were regarded as fair quarry by the swindlers.*

quarry[2] *n.* **1** °mine, °pit, °excavation: *Only one quarry yielded the statuary marble needed by those sculptors.*
—*v.* **2** °mine, °extract, °obtain, °get: *Gault's ideas were all quarried from the jottings of obscure writers.*

quarter *n.* **1** fourth: *Statistics showed that a quarter of the population attended church regularly.* **2** three-month period, three months, ninety days, thirteen weeks; fifteen minutes; °phase (of the moon), quadrature: *The first quarter's rent is now due. We waited a quarter of an hour. The moon is in its third quarter.* **3** °area, °region, °part, °section, °district, °zone, °division, °territory, °place, °neighbourhood, locality, °locale, °location, °point, °spot; °direction: *The army was called in to patrol the quarter of the city where looting had occurred. It was difficult to tell from which quarter the wind was blowing.* **4** °mercy, compassion, mercifulness, clemency, leniency, °forgiveness, °favour, °humanity, °pity: *The hostages expected no quarter from their captors.* **5** ***quarters***: living quarters, °lodging(s), dwelling-place, °dwelling, °accommodation(s), rooms, chambers, °residence, °shelter, habitation, °domicile, °home, °house, °abode; *Military* billet, barracks, cantonment, casern *or* caserne: *We found comfortable quarters in which we remained during our stay in the area.*
—*v.* **6** °lodge, °accommodate, °house, °board, °shelter, °put up; *Military* billet, °post, °station: *The tour guide stayed at the best hotel, while we were quartered in a youth hostel.*

quarterly *adj.* **1** trimonthly, three-monthly: *She is editor of a quarterly medical journal.*
—*adv.* **2** every three months, every ninety days, every thirteen weeks, four times a year: *The landlady insisted on being paid quarterly, in advance.*

quash *v.* **1** annul, nullify, °void, declare *or* render null and °void, invalidate, °revoke, °vacate, °set aside, rescind, °cancel, °reject, °throw out, °reverse, °overthrow, °discharge, overrule: *When the real culprit confessed, my conviction was quashed and I was set free.* **2** °suppress, °subdue, °quell, °put down, °squelch, °repress, °overthrow, °crush, °overwhelm: *The rebellion was quashed by the secret police.*

quasi- *adv.* **1** Sometimes, ***quasi***: as if, as it were, °seemingly, °apparently, °partly, to some °extent, to all intents and purposes, more or less, °virtually, °almost: *Her apology seemed only quasi-sincere to me. His function in the proceedings was quasi-judicial.*
—*adj.* **2** Often, ***quasi***: so to °speak, °kind of, °sort of; °pretended, °fake, pseudo, °so-called, °supposed, °artificial, °mock, °sham, *Colloq* °phoney *or US also* phony: *His quasi excuse does not diminish the horror of what he did.*

quaver *v.* **1** °tremble, °quiver, °shake, °shiver, °vibrate, waver, °shudder, °fluctuate, °oscillate, °flutter: *His voice quavered with emotion as he described his rescue.*
—*n.* **2** trembling, °tremble, °quiver, quivering, tremor, shaking, vibration, wavering, °break, °fluctuation, oscillation: *Only a slight quaver in her voice betrayed her feeling of panic.*

queasy *adj.* **1** uncomfortable, uneasy, °nervous, apprehensive, °ill at ease, troubled, °worried, discomfited; °doubtful, °hesitant: *I had a queasy feeling that I was being watched. The manager was a bit queasy about giving Denis so much responsibility.* **2** °sick, °nauseous, °nauseated, °ill, °bilious, °queer, *Colloq* green around *or* about the gills, °groggy, woozy: *Catherine felt very queasy after the ride on the roller coaster.*

queen *n.* **1** °sovereign, °monarch, ruler; empress; queen consort; queen mother; queen dowager: *She was absolutely thrilled when she was invited to a garden party at Buckingham Palace and met the Queen.* **2** beauty queen, movie queen, °star, prima donna, diva; °epitome, °model, °idol, °leading light, cynosure, °leader: *At the height of her career, she was known as 'the Queen of the Silver Screen'. 'Queen of the Antilles' was once a nickname of Cuba.*

queer *adj.* **1** °odd, °strange, °different, °peculiar, °funny, °curious, uncommon, unconventional, °unorthodox, atypical, °singular, °exceptional, anomalous, °extraordinary, °unusual, °weird, °bizarre, uncanny, °unnatural, freakish, °remarkable, °offbeat, °irregular, °unparalleled, °incongruous, °outlandish, °*outré*, °exotic, °eccentric, fey, °quaint, °absurd, °ridiculous, °ludicrous, unexampled: *How do you explain Basil's queer behaviour at the office party? Her attire could only be described as queer, given her age and status.* **2** °questionable, dubious, °suspicious, °suspect, °doubtful, °puzzling, °mysterious, *Colloq* °fishy, °shady: *We had a feeling that something queer was going on when the clocks started running backwards.* **3** (slightly) °ill, °queasy, °sick, unwell, °poorly, °faint, uneasy, °dizzy, °giddy, vertiginous, light-headed: *It's not surprising that you feel queer after drinking all that wine.* **4** °mad, °unbalanced, unhinged, demented, °deranged, °insane, °daft, touched, *Colloq* dotty, potty, nutty, nuts, loony, batty, cracked: *Francis seems to have gone a bit queer—fancies himself a reincarnation of Cicero.*
—*v.* **5** °ruin, °spoil, °bungle, °botch, °muddle, muff, °mar, °wreck, °destroy, *Colloq* make a °hash *or* °mess of, gum up (the works), *Slang* °muck up, °screw up, louse up, *US* ball up, *Taboo slang Brit* balls up: *Grimstone queered the deal by telling the buyer the company was worth half what we were asking.*

quell *v.* **1** °suppress, °put down, °repress, °subdue, °quash, °overcome, °crush, °squelch: *The army arrived to quell the uprising at the prison.* **2** °moderate, mollify, soothe, assuage, alleviate, °mitigate, allay, °quiet(en), °calm; pacify, °tranquillize, °compose: *Any feelings of bitterness were quelled by her comforting words.*

quench *v.* **1** °satisfy, °slake, sate, °surfeit, °satiate, allay, appease: *My thirst isn't quenched by those sweet fizzy drinks.* **2** °put out, °extinguish, douse, °smother, snuff out, °stifle, °kill, °destroy, °suppress, °squelch, °repress, °overcome, °subdue: *Even the most totalitarian regime cannot entirely quench the fire of freedom in the hearts of the oppressed.*

querulous *adj.* complaining, carping, °critical, criticizing, hypercritical, °fault-finding, °finicky, finical, °fussy, over-particular, censorious, °petulant, whining, murmuring, grumbling, °peevish, °testy, °touchy, °irritable, irritated, annoyed, piqued, in a pique, irascible, fractious, °perverse, °quarrelsome, ill-natured, ill-humoured, °cantankerous, curmudgeonly, crusty, crotchety, °fretful, bad-tempered, ill-tempered, °waspish, crabby, °cross, splenetic, choleric, °sour, dyspeptic, grumpy, *Colloq* grousing, pernickety *or US also* persnickety, *Slang* bitching: *He objected to almost all the television programmes and sent querulous letters to the broadcasters telling them so.*

query *n.* **1** °question, °inquiry *or* enquiry: *The information office will answer any query you may have about social security benefits.* **2** °doubt, uncertainty, °scepticism, °reservation, °problem: *She wants to see the manager about some query concerning her bank balance.*
—*v.* **3** °ask (about), °inquire *or* °enquire (about), °question; °challenge, °doubt, °dispute: *I am writing to query the third item on your latest bill.*

quest *n.* **1** °search, °pursuit, °exploration, °expedition, voyage (of °discovery), °pilgrimage, °mission, °crusade; °chase, °hunt: *When a child, he was inspired by the legend of Sir Launcelot's quest for the Holy Grail.*
—*v.* **2** Usually, ***quest after*** *or* ***for***: °seek (after *or* for), °search after *or* for, °hunt (for), °track down, °pursue, °stalk: *In 1928, joined by his father, he quested for gold along the Orinoco river.*

question *n.* **1** °query, °inquiry *or* enquiry: *I asked you a simple question, 'Where were you last night?', and I expect a civil answer.* **2** °problem, °difficulty, °confusion, °doubt, dubiousness, uncertainty, °query, °mystery, °puzzle: *Is there some question about the qualifications of the new employee?* **3** °matter, °issue, °point, °subject, °topic, °theme, °proposition: *Whether you stay is not the question. The question remains, How are you going to earn a living?* **4** ***beyond (all** or **any) question***: beyond (the °shadow of) a °doubt, without °question, without a °doubt, indubitably, °undoubtedly, doubtlessly, °definitely, certainly, assuredly: *He is guilty beyond all question.* **5** ***call in** or **into question***: °question, °doubt, °query, °challenge, °dispute, harbour *or* entertain *or* have doubts *or* suspicions about, °suspect, cast °doubt *or* °suspicion on: *I cannot see why he has called her loyalty into question.* **6** ***in question***: **a** under °discussion *or* °consideration: *The person in question never worked for this company.* **b** °questionable, °debatable, at °issue, in °doubt, °doubtful, open to °debate: *Her honesty was never in question.* **7** ***out of the question***: °unthinkable, °impossible, °absurd, °ridiculous, °preposterous, °inconceivable, beyond °consideration, insupportable: *An increase in salary at this time is out of the question.* **8** ***without question***: See **4,** above.
—*v.* **9** °ask, °examine, interrogate, °query, °interview, °sound out, °quiz, *Colloq* °pump, grill, *Slang* give (someone) the third degree: *He was questioned for six hours as to his whereabouts.* **10** call in *or* into question, °doubt, °query, °mistrust, °distrust, cast °doubt upon, °dispute, °suspect: *Investigators have long questioned the relationship between the banks and the drug barons.*

questionable *adj.* °doubtful, dubious, °debatable, °moot, °disputable, borderline, °suspect, °suspicious, °shady; open to °question, in °question, in °dispute, °problematic(al), °uncertain, arguable, unsure, °unreliable, °ambiguous: *The evidence shows that the defendant engaged in questionable banking practices while a director of Offshore Ltd. The advantages of quick divorce are questionable.*

queue *n.* **1** °line, °row, °file, column, °string, °train, cortege *or* cortège, °retinue, °procession, °succession, °chain, concatenation, series, °order, cordon, *Brit* tailback, *Colloq Brit* crocodile, *Military* °picket: *There were dozens of people in the queue in front of me.* **2** pigtail, °braid, plait; °tail, pony-tail: *Not long ago, Chinese men wore their hair in a queue.*
—*v.* **3** Often, ***queue up***: °line up, get in *or* into *or* form a °line *or* queue *or* °file, get into *or* in °line, *Military* fall in: *All he remembers about the war is that everyone had to queue up for everything and wait.*

quibble *v.* **1** °equivocate, split hairs, °evade, be °evasive, palter, chop logic, bandy words, °cavil, pettifog, *Colloq* nit-pick: *While people continued to be kept in slavery, the politicians quibbled over the difference between 'liberty' and 'freedom'.*
—*n.* **2** quibbling, equivocation, °hair-splitting, splitting hairs, °evasion, paltering, sophistry, *Colloq* nit-picking: *Lawyers often become involved in a quibble over the* mot juste *and forget their clients.* **3** °cavil, sophism, °subtlety, nicety: *It's a quibble whether you say 'either' and 'neither' to rhyme with 'peek' or 'pike'.*

quick *adj.* **1** °rapid, °fast, °speedy, °swift, °fleet; °expeditious, °express: *We made a quick descent to reach the camp before dark. The hand is quicker than the eye. Can you arrange the quick delivery of this parcel to Aylesbury?* **2** °sudden, °precipitate, °hasty, °brisk, °short, °abrupt, °hurried, °perfunctory, °summary; °immediate, °prompt, °timely, instantaneous: *There is no quick answer to your question about the causes of World War II. Don't be so quick to criticize others. I had a quick response to my letter complaining about service.* **3** °agile, °lively, °nimble, °energetic, °vigorous, °alert, °animated, °keen, °sharp, °acute, spry, °spirited, °vivacious, °rapid, °swift: *In three quick steps she was at my side. Antonia is known for her quick mind.* **4** °intelligent, °bright, °brilliant, facile, °adept, adroit, °dexterous, apt, °able, °expert, °skilful, deft, °astute, °clever, °shrewd, °smart, °ingenious, °perceptive, perspicacious, discerning, °far-sighted, °responsive; nimble-witted, °quick-witted: *You can rely on Rob's quick thinking to come up with a solution to the problem.* **5** °excitable, °touchy, °testy, °petulant, irascible, °irritable, °impatient: *She said that I have a quick temper because of my red hair.*

quicken *v.* **1** accelerate, °hasten, °speed up: *As we neared the house, our pace quickened.* **2** °expedite, °hurry, accelerate, °hasten, °speed (up): *We did everything we could to quicken her departure.* **3** °stimulate, °arouse, °kindle, °spark, invigorate, °excite, °animate, °vitalize, vivify, galvanize, °enliven, °awaken, °energize, °revive, resuscitate, reinvigorate: *Olivia's inspiring lectures quickened the imagination of everyone who heard them.*

quickly *adv.* **1** °rapidly, °swiftly, speedily, °fast: *Although share prices dropped in the morning, they recovered quickly during afternoon trading.* **2** °rapidly, °swiftly, speedily, °fast, with °dispatch *or* despatch, apace, °post-haste, at *or* on the °double, with all °speed, °quick, *Colloq US and Canadian* lickety-split: *Run quickly, and you'll get there before the shop closes.* **3** instantly, °promptly, °hastily, at °once, °immediately, °straight away, °right away, °shortly, without °delay, (very) °soon, hurriedly, °quick, *Colloq* pronto: *You'll have to leave quickly to catch your train.*

quick-tempered *adj.* °excitable, °impulsive, °temperamental, hot-tempered, °waspish, choleric, splenetic, °impatient, °short-tempered, °touchy, irascible, °irritable, °snappish, °abrupt, °short, short-spoken, °quarrelsome, °testy, °volatile, hot-blooded, bad-tempered, ill-tempered, churlish, highly-strung, *US* high-keyed: *Len is very quick-tempered these days and flies into a rage at the slightest provocation.*

quick-witted *adj.* °acute, °sharp, °clever, °smart, nimble-witted, °alert, °keen, °astute, °perceptive, perspicacious: *Hallam is known for his quick-witted responses to hecklers in the audience.*

quiet *adj.* **1** °silent, soundless, °noiseless, hushed, °still: *We have to be very quiet so as not to wake the children.* **2** °still, °serene, °silent, °peaceful, unperturbed, °calm, °tranquil, placid, pacific, °smooth, °mild, °restful, unagitated: *The sea was very quiet as we rowed towards the beach.* **3** °dormant, quiescent, °inactive, retired, °withdrawn, °unobtrusive: *His last days were spent living a quiet life in the Outer Hebrides.* **4** °still, motionless, unmoving, °fixed, stationary, at °rest, °inactive, composed, °temperate, unexcited, °calm: *There was a knock at the door and everyone suddenly became quiet.*
—*n.* **5** °silence, stillness, soundlessness, noiselessness, °hush, quietness, quietude, °ease, °rest, calmness, °serenity, tranquillity, °peace, °peace of mind, °repose: *In the quiet of the cave I could hear my heart beating.*
—*v.* **6** See **quieten,** below.

quieten *v.* Often, ***quieten down***: °quiet (down), °still, °silence, °hush, °calm, °tranquillize, °lull: *He gradually quietened down the audience, and the curtain rose.*

quietly *adv.* **1** °silently, soundlessly, noiselessly, inaudibly, in °silence, softly: *She tiptoed quietly out of the room.* **2** in hushed tones, in whispers: *In a corner of the room a young couple were quietly conversing.* **3** peacefully, calmly, serenely, peaceably, meekly, mildly: *When the police explained they only wanted him to help in their inquiries, he went with them quietly.* **4** modestly, humbly, demurely, unpretentiously, unostentatiously, unobtrusively, unassumingly, sedately: *The applicants sat quietly, waiting to be called in for the interview.*

quintessence *n.* °essence, °heart, °core, quiddity, essentialness, essentiality, °pith, marrow, °sum and °substance, °epitome, °nonpareil, °embodiment, personification, °model, °prototype, exemplar, °ideal, *beau idéal*, °paragon: *Hernandez considered the ancient Greek temple the quintessence of classic design.*

quip *n.* **1** (*bon*) *mot*, °witticism, sally, jest, ad lib, °joke, °gibe, barb, aphorism, °epigram, apophthegm *or* apothegm, °pun, °*double entendre*, equivoque *or* equivoke, *Colloq* °gag, one-liner, crack, °wisecrack, wheeze, chestnut: *In his worst quip he attributed the breakdown of his computer to a slipped diskette.*
—*v.* **2** °joke, jest, °gibe, *Colloq* °wisecrack, *US* crack wise: *As Mae West quipped, 'It's not the men in my life that count; it's the life in my men'.*

quirk *n.* °peculiarity, caprice, vagary, °eccentricity, °fancy, °twist, °warp, aberration, idiosyncrasy, °oddity, °kink, °characteristic, crotchet, whim, °trick: *By some strange quirk of fate, after weeks in an open boat I was cast ashore at Cap d'Antibes.*

quit *v.* **1** °leave, °depart from, °go (away) from, °get away from, decamp, °exit, °desert, °flee, °forsake, °abandon, *Colloq* °take off, °beat it, °skip: *They think that he will try to quit the country if he is released on bail.* **2** °resign, °give up, °relinquish, °leave, °renounce, °retire from, °withdraw from: *Would you really quit your job to sail around the world?* **3** °cease, °stop, °discontinue, °leave off, desist from: *They would always quit laughing when I walked into the room.*
—*adj.* **4** °free, °clear, discharged, °rid of, released (from), °exempt (from): *When my ex-wife remarried I was quit of the burden of paying alimony.*

quite *adv.* **1** °completely, °very, °totally, °utterly, °entirely, from head to toe, from A to Z, fully, °wholly, °thoroughly, unequivocally, °absolutely, °perfectly, °altogether, unreservedly: *Her trouble is that she is quite certain of many things that are simply not the case. The last time I saw him, he was quite drunk.* **2** °rather, °fairly, °moderately, °somewhat, °relatively, to some *or* a certain °extent *or* °degree, noticeably: *I thought that the paintings were quite well done.* **3** °rather: *We had quite a good dinner last night.* **4** °very much, °totally, °entirely, °wholly, °altogether; °really, °actually, °truly, °definitely, °positively, °undoubtedly, indubitably, °absolutely, unequivocally, certainly, °surely, unreservedly, °honestly: *What you are talking about is quite another matter. Your home-made chutney is quite the best I have ever tasted.*

quiver *v.* **1** °shake, °tremble, °vibrate, °shiver, °quaver; °shudder, tremor, °oscillate, °fluctuate, wobble: *He felt his lips quivering as he told her that he was dying. The outcome of the contest quivered in the balance.*
—*n.* **2** °tremble, °quaver, °shudder, °spasm, °shake, tremor, °shiver: *Pierced by the dart, the tiny bird fell to the earth, gave a little quiver, and lay still.*

quixotic *adj.* °idealistic, °impractical, °impracticable, °unrealistic, unrealizable, °visionary, °romantic, °fantastic, chimerical, °fanciful, °dreamlike, °dreamy, nephelococcygeal, starry-eyed, °optimistic, °rash, °absurd, °mad, °foolhardy, °reckless, °wild, °preposterous, °ridiculous: *When he was young, he had a quixotic notion that he could improve the world.*

quiz *n.* **1** °examination, °test, *Colloq* exam: *We have a ten-minute quiz every week on our reading assignment.*
—*v.* **2** °question, interrogate, °ask, °examine, *Colloq* grill, °pump: *The police have quizzed everyone in the neighbourhood about what they might have seen.*

quizzical *adj.* °curious, °queer, °odd, inquiring *or* enquiring, questioning, puzzled: *The interviewer had a quizzical expression, as if he didn't quite understand his own questions.*

quota *n.* apportionment, °portion, °allotment, allocation, °allowance, °ration, °share, °part, °proportion, °percentage, °equity, °interest, *Colloq* °cut: *Each shareholder is allowed a quota of the new shares based on the number now held.*

quotation *n.* **1** °quote, °passage, citation, °reference, allusion, °extract, °excerpt, °selection: *For many years Frances collected quotations from the speeches of politicians.* **2** °quote, (bid *or* asking *or* offer *or* market) °price, °charge, °fixed °price, °rate, °cost; value: *The quotation for Universal General International stood at 486 pence at the close of the market on Friday.*

quote *v.* **1** cite, °mention, °recite, °repeat, retell, °reproduce, °duplicate, °call up, °bring up, °bring in, °instance, °exemplify, °refer to, °reference, °extract, °excerpt: *Let me quote to you the relevant passage from* Paradise Lost.
—*n.* **2** See **quotation,** above.

R

rabble *n.* **1** °mob, °crowd, horde, °throng, °swarm, °gang: *We narrowly escaped the wrath of the rabble fighting the police in the square.* **2** ***the rabble***: *Derogatory* °masses, proletariat, hoi polloi, commoners, peasantry, ragtag and bobtail, vermin, °outcasts, °riff-raff, scum, °dregs (of society), lower °classes, *canaille*, commonalty *or* commonality, *Colloq* °trash, the great °unwashed: *He always refers to blue-collar workers as 'the rabble'.*

rabble-rouser *n.* °agitator, demagogue, instigator, inciter, firebrand, incendiary, °radical, °troublemaker, *agent provocateur*, °revolutionary, insurrectionist, *Colloq* hell-raiser: *The crowd was whipped into a frenzy by a rabble-rouser who was not identified.*

rabid *adj.* **1** °unreasonable, unreasoning, °extreme, °fanatical; raging, °furious, °violent, crazed, frenzied, °maniacal, °wild, °mad, infuriated, frenetic, °berserk: *Please don't mention politics to Nigel—he gets rabid on the subject.* **2** hydrophobic, °mad: *Animals from abroad are kept in quarantine to make sure they are not rabid.*

race[1] *n.* **1** foot-race, horse-race, marathon, °rally *or* rallye; °competition, °contest, °rivalry, contention: *How many will be running in Saturday's race? Several countries had joined the race to complete a workable anti-gravity device.* **2** sluice, flume, °chute, watercourse, °course, °channel, bed, mill-race, raceway, spillway; °track: *The water in the race enabled us to wash the sand in order to extract the gold. The ball-bearings don't fall out because they are retained in the race.* **3** ***the races***: horse-races, dog-races, the dogs, the °track, the °turf, *Brit* racecourse, race °meeting, *US* racetrack: *We're off to the races at Newmarket.*
—*v.* **4** °speed, °hurry, °hasten, °dash, sprint, °fly, °rush, °scramble, °step lively, *Colloq* °tear, °rip, zip, °step on the gas, °step on it, °hop to it, get a °move on, *Brit* hare, *US* get a wiggle on: *You're going to have to race to catch the last bus.* **5** °compete (with): *I'll race you to the gate and back.*

race[2] *n.* **1** °stock, °line, °lineage, °type, °tribe, °nation, °people, °folk, °clan, °family: *The citizens constitute a mix of all imaginable races.* **2** blood, descent, °breed, °kin, °family, °stock, °line, °lineage: *You say you are liberal, but how would you feel about your daughter's marrying someone of a different race?*

racial *adj.* ethnic, genetic, genealogical, ethnological, °folk; tribal; °national: *Bigots emphasize racial differences rather than racial similarities.*

rack *n.* **1** framework, °frame, trestle, holder, °support; °stand, scaffold, scaffolding, °structure, hat-rack, hatstand, coat-rack, *Technical* stretcher, tenter, *US* hattree: *The fish are hung out on long racks in the sun to dry. Please take your luggage off the seat and put it on the overhead rack.* **2** °suffering, °torment, torture, °agony, °anguish, °pain, °misery, °distress, °affliction, °scourge, adversity: *Only those who have experienced it can know the severe rack of gout.*
—*v.* **3** °distress, °torment, torture, agonize, °oppress, °pain, °persecute, °anguish, beleaguer, °plague, °harass, harrow, °hurt: *Gruber was racked by the feeling that he had been responsible for the road accident. Quentin has been racked by the pain of arthritis for ten years.* **4** °beat, °strain, °wrench, °tear at, °lash

(at), °batter, °shake, °damage: *Winds of hurricane force racked villages along the coast last night.*

racket *n.* **1** °noise, °din, °uproar, °disturbance, clamour, hubbub, °row, °rumpus, hullabaloo, °fuss, ado, commotion, to-do, hue and °cry, °outcry, brouhaha, °tumult, babel, °pandemonium, *Elizabethan theatre* alarums and excursions, *Colloq* ballyhoo: *How can you sleep through the racket from your neighbour's all-night parties?* **2** (organized) °crime, °criminal *or* °illegal activity *or* enterprise, °trickery, °trick, °dodge, °scheme, °swindle, °stratagem, °artifice, °game, °ruse, *Slang* °caper, scam, gyp: *Their racket is selling 'protection' to shop-owners.* **3** °business, °line, °profession, °occupation, °trade, °vocation, °calling, °job, °employment, livelihood: *I'm in commodities; what's your racket?*

racketeer *n.* mobster, °gangster, Mafioso: *The Chicago racketeers of the 1930s seem tame compared with today's terrorists.*

raconteur *n.* storyteller, anecdotalist *or* anecdotist, °narrator, relater *or* relator, *Colloq* spinner of yarns: *The after-dinner speaker was a marvellous raconteur with a wealth of stories about the theatre.*

racy *adj.* **1** °fresh, °lively, °animated, °spirited, °sprightly, °buoyant, °vivacious, °energetic, °vigorous, °dynamic, zestful, °stimulating, mettlesome *or* mettled, *Colloq* full of vim and °vigour, peppy, full of °pep, full of beans: *Tabloid journalists are told that their writing must be racy—straightforward reporting is out of fashion.* **2** °risqué, ribald, °bawdy, °naughty, °lusty, °earthy, °gross, °off colour, salty, °suggestive, °sexual, °immodest, indelicate, °indecent, °blue, smutty, °lewd, salacious, °vulgar, °dirty, °filthy, °pornographic, °obscene, sex-oriented, °adult, °rude, °crude, °coarse, *Colloq* raunchy, °sexy, °spicy, °hot: *By mistake my name got on the mailing list of some company selling racy videos.* **3** °spicy, piquant, °tasty, flavourful, °pungent, °strong, °savoury, °sharp, zesty, tangy, °tart, °hot: *That curry you served last night had quite a racy flavour.*

radiance *n.* **1** radiancy, °splendour, brightness, °brilliance, resplendence, luminosity, luminousness, °dazzle, °sparkle, coruscation, scintillation, °twinkle, effulgence, refulgence, incandescence, °glow, phosphorescence, °gleam, °lustre, °shimmer, °shine: *As Aladdin rubbed the ring, it began to glow with an inner radiance and then—suddenly—a genie appeared.* **2** °warmth, gladness, °joy, °pleasure, °happiness, cheeriness, °delight: *It was good to see again the radiance of the family at Christmas dinner.*

radiant *adj.* **1** shining, °bright, beaming, °burning, °ablaze, blazing, °brilliant, °luminous, resplendent, °splendid, splendorous, °lustrous, gleaming, °glowing, phosphorescent, shimmering, °shiny, °glossy, glistening, °incandescent, alight, effulgent, refulgent, sparkling, °dazzling, glittering, coruscating, °scintillating, °twinkling; aglow: *In her hair she wore a diamond tiara, a radiant crown whose glory was diminished only by her beauty. The room was radiant with sunshine.* **2** °happy, °overjoyed, °ecstatic, °rapturous, °delighted, °joyful, °blithe, blithesome, blissful, beatific, °glad, °gleeful, joyous, °gay, bubbling, °bubbly, jubilant, °elated, °rhapsodic, °exultant, exhilarated, in seventh °heaven, in °heaven, *Colloq* on cloud nine, *Brit* over the moon: *Carrie was absolutely radiant when she learned she was pregnant.*

radiate *v.* **1** °shine, °beam, °burn, °blaze, °gleam, °glow, °shimmer, °glisten, °sparkle, °dazzle, °glitter, coruscate, scintillate, °twinkle: *The jewel seemed to radiate with an inner light.* **2** °emanate, disseminate, °disperse, °spread, °diffuse, °shed, °send out, °emit, °give off *or* out, *Rare* irradiate: *He radiated goodwill the way a fire radiates heat and light.*

radiation *n.* emission, emanation, diffusion, dispersal, shedding: *Because the night was cloudless, unhindered radiation of the earth's heat rapidly cooled the air.*

radical *adj.* **1** °basic, °fundamental, °elementary, °inherent, constitutional, °elemental, °essential, °cardinal, °principal, °primary, °deep, deep-seated, deep-rooted, °profound, underlying, °organic, °natural, °rudimentary: *There is a radical error in your approach to the problem. There are radical differences in the ways we regard the English language.* **2** °thorough, thoroughgoing, °complete, °entire, °total, °exhaustive, °sweeping, (all-)°inclusive, °comprehensive, all-embracing, °out-and-out, °drastic, °severe, °extreme, extremist, °revolutionary: *We have made radical changes in the way we live. Every political party that is not in power promises radical reform.* **3** extremist, °revolutionary, °fanatic(al), °militant, anarchist(ic), °immoderate: *A staunch conservative, Vincent regarded as radical anyone who disagreed with him.*
—*n.* **4** extremist, °revolutionary, °fanatic, °zealot, °immoderate, anarchist, °militant: *The radicals favour reform, the conservatives the status quo—but there is nothing new in that.* **5** communist, leftist, left-winger, red, Bolshevik, Bolshevist, pink, *Slang US* pinko: *Carlo, recently arrested as a spy, had been a radical since his days at university.*

radio *n.* **1** receiver, °portable (radio), *Old-fashioned* crystal °set, *Brit and US old-fashioned* wireless, *Colloq* transistor, *Slang* ghetto-blaster, *Brit* tranny *or* trannie, *US* boom box: *He listens to BBC World Service on his short-wave radio.*
—*v.* **2** °transmit, °broadcast, °air, disseminate, °announce, °present: *Weather reports are radioed continuously to ships at sea and aircraft.*

raffle *n.* °lottery, °draw, sweepstake *or US* sweepstakes, sweep *or US* sweeps: *The church is holding a raffle for a new car next week.*

rag[1] *n.* **1** °tatter, °piece, °shred, °scrap, °fragment, °bit, *Dialect* clout: *Take a clean rag and dust the bookshelves when you get the chance.* **2** newspaper, °periodical, °magazine, °publication, °journal: *You can't believe anything you read in that rag.* **3** ***rags***: *Facetious* clothes, clothing, attire, °dress, °garments, *Old-fashioned* duds: *I bought some new rags at the post-Christmas sales.* **4** ***rag trade***: garment-industry, clothing °business, °fashion °industry: *Peggy has been a model in the rag trade for years.* **5** ***chew the rag***: **a** °converse, °talk, °gossip, °chat: *We bought a bottle of wine and just sat about chewing the rag all evening.* **b** *Brit* argue, wrangle: *They are constantly chewing the rag over trivial nonsense.*

rag[2] *v.* °tease, °taunt, °belittle, °twit, °ridicule, °mock, make °fun of, °pull (someone's) °leg, *Brit* °rally, *Colloq* kid: *The boys at school were always ragging him about his lisp.*

ragamuffin *n.* (street) urchin, (street) Arab, waif, mudlark, gamin, little lost lamb, babe in the wood, °stray, °guttersnipe, scarecrow: *We took in a poor little ragamuffin who was shaking from the cold.*

rage *n.* **1** °anger, °fury, wrath, ire, high dudgeon, exasperation, vehemence, °passion: *Imagine her rage when Simon phoned to say that he couldn't make it home for dinner!* **2** °fury, °passion, °frenzy, hysterics, °tantrum, °fit, °temper, *Colloq Brit* °paddy *or* paddywhack *or* paddywack, wax: *He flies into a rage if Grace is as little as five minutes late for an appointment.* **3** °fashion, °craze, °vogue, the (°latest *or* newest) °thing, last word, *dernier cri*, °mode, *Colloq* °fad: *Miniskirts were all the rage in the 1960s.*
—*v.* **4** °rant, °rave, °storm, go °mad *or* °crazy *or* bonkers *or* °wild *or* out of one's °mind, go °berserk, run amok *or* amuck, behave *or* act *or* be like one °possessed, °fret, be beside oneself (with °anger *or* °fury), lose one's °temper, have a °tantrum, fulminate, °explode; °fume, foam at the mouth, °stew, °smoulder, °boil, °seethe, °simmer, *Colloq* have kittens, lose one's cool, °fly off the handle, go off the deep end, *Slang* get into *or* work oneself up into a °lather *or* °stew *or* °sweat, get all worked up, °blow one's top, °blow a gasket, °blow up, °flip one's top *or* lid, hit the ceiling *or* roof, °freak out, be fit to be tied, be ready for a strait-

jacket, *Brit* throw a wobbly, *US and Canadian* °blow one's °stack, °flip one's wig, °blow a fuse, have a haemorrhage, go ape, do a slow burn, have a conniption °fit: *Father raged for hours when he found that Donald had borrowed the car without permission.*

ragged *adj.* **1** °rough, °shaggy, °shabby, °seedy, °tattered, °unkempt, scraggy, torn, rent, ripped, frayed, °worn (out), °threadbare, patched, patchy, ravelled, *Chiefly Brit* tatty, *Brit* down at °heel, *US* down at the °heel(s), *Colloq US* frazzled, beat-up: *On weekends, Charles put on his most ragged clothes to work in the garden.* **2** °rough, uneven, °irregular, nicked, °jagged; °serrated, sawtooth(ed), zigzag, °notched, toothed, denticulate(d), ridged: *Every morning on his way to work, his first sight of the factory was the ragged edge of its roof.* **3** °worn out, °tired, °exhausted, on one's last legs, the worse for °wear, °dead °tired, overtired, °fatigued, °weary, fagged out, °spent, *Colloq* all in, dog-tired, *Slang* °dead (on one's feet), (°dead) °beat, *Brit* knackered, *US and Canadian* pooped (out): *The emergency crew was run ragged by thirty hours on duty without rest.* **4** °bad, °rough, patchy, °imperfect, °shabby, messy, disordered, °disorderly, °run-down, battered, broken-down, neglected, deteriorated, °dilapidated, *Colloq* beat-up: *From its ragged condition, it's clear that the building isn't properly maintained.* **5** °rough, °harsh, °discordant, °grating, rasping, hoarse, °scratchy, croaking: *His voice, once a beautiful lyric tenor, was ragged after years of alcoholism.* **6** uneven, °bad, °poor, °shabby, patchy: *The guests gave a ragged rendition of 'Happy Birthday' as their host entered the room.*

ragman *n.* rag-dealer, rag-picker, °scrap °dealer, *Brit* rag-and-bone man, knacker, *US* °junk °dealer, junkman: *When the ragman comes round, give him those old curtains.*

raid *n.* **1** (°surprise) °attack, incursion, °invasion, °onset, onslaught, blitz, sortie, sally, °expedition, *Slang* (police) bust: *The partisans made a raid on the arsenal last night and got away with guns and ammunition.*
—*v.* **2** °attack, invade, °assault, °storm, °set upon, °descend upon, °swoop down on *or* upon, °pounce upon, *Military* forage; °sack, °plunder, °pillage, °loot, °ransack, °rifle, °strip, maraud, depredate, *Slang* bust: *The commandos raided the enemy stronghold and destroyed it.*

rail[1] *n.* **1** °bar, °rod, handrail, foot-rail, towel-rail; railing, banisters, balustrade, baluster, °fence: *Don't lean on the rail or it will break.* **2** ***by*** *or* ***via rail***: by °train, by °railway *or US also* °railroad: *We travelled by rail from Paris to Geneva.*

rail[2] *v.* Usually, ***rail at*** *or* ***against***: °vituperate, vociferate, fulminate, be *or* become °abusive, revile, °attack, °berate, °scold, °upbraid, °criticize, censure, decry, °condemn, °denounce: *She continues to rage and rail against those who would deny equal rights to women.*

raillery *n.* °banter, badinage, persiflage, °repartee, frivolity, joking, jesting, chaffing, teasing, °ridicule, *Colloq* kidding: *You shouldn't get upset over what was nothing more than some good-natured raillery.*

railroad *n.* **1** See **railway,** below.
—*v.* **2** °force, compel, °expedite, coerce, °intimidate, °push (through), *Brit* pressurize, *US* °pressure, °bully, hector, °tyrannize, dragoon, °browbeat, bullyrag, *Colloq* bulldoze, °squeeze, °lean on: *Clayton was railroaded into appointing Pinbury to head the committee to investigate corruption.*

railway *n.* °train, °rail, rolling-stock, *Archaic* iron horse, *US* °railroad: *Railway service could be improved on some suburban lines. Diamond Jim Brady, the American millionaire, made his money from the railway.*

rain *n.* **1** °precipitation, drizzle, sprinkle, °downpour, °shower, thunder-shower, cloudburst, rainstorm, squall, deluge, *US* sunshower: *After the rain the sun came out.* **2** rainfall, °precipitation: *The rain in Spain falls mainly in the plain.* **3** °flood, °torrent, °shower, °volley, °stream, °outpouring: *Arriving home, she could barely shield herself from the rain of children's kisses.*
—*v.* **4** come down, °pour, °teem, sprinkle, drizzle, °spit, *Brit dialect* mizzle, *Colloq* come down in buckets *or* by the bucketful, rain cats and dogs: *The weatherman said it would rain today, so take an umbrella.* **5** °trickle, °pour, °run, °fall: *Tears rained down her sallow cheeks.* **6** °descend, °shower: *Blows rained on him from the tiny fists of the furious child.* **7** °bestow, °lavish, °shower: *He rained kisses on her upturned face.*

raise *v.* **1** °lift (up), elevate; °hoist, °pull up, °haul up, run up, *Literary* upraise: *She raised the glass to her lips. We raised the mainsail and sailed out of the harbour.* **2** °erect, °put up, °construct, °build, °produce, °create, put together, °assemble, °frame: *With the help of some neighbours, the barn was raised in less than a day.* **3** °farm, °grow, °cultivate, °plant, °bring up, nurture, °harvest, °propagate: *During that year's mild winter, we were able to raise three crops.* **4** °bring up, nurture, °rear; °mother, °father, °parent: *His grandmother raised ten children, six girls and four boys.* **5** °assemble, °gather, bring *or* °gather *or* °get together, °muster, °mobilize, °round up, °rally, °collect, convene, °recruit, *Colloq* pull together: *Do you think you could raise an army quickly enough to defend us against attack?* **6** °increase, °boost, °advance, °put up, jack up, run up, °inflate, escalate: *Why are consumer petrol prices always raised at the vaguest hint of an increase in oil prices?* **7** °cultivate, °foster, nurture, °heighten, °stimulate, °buoy, °lift, uplift, °boost, °arouse, °quicken, °encourage, °develop: *The news about the new company raised our hopes of finding jobs.* **8** °open, °introduce, °initiate, °broach, °bring up, °bring *or* °put forward, °present, °suggest, °mention, °moot: *It is regrettable that you saw fit to raise such a delicate issue.* **9** °remove, °relieve, °lift, °abandon, °eliminate, °discontinue, (bring to an) °end, °terminate: *Restrictions on travel to south-east Asia were about to be raised.* **10** °cause, °provoke, °evoke, °occasion, put *or* set in °motion, °institute, °prompt, engender, °stir up, instigate, °inspire, give °rise to, °bring about, °arouse, °originate: *Objections to the relaxation of safety regulations were raised by relatives of the victims of the earlier disaster.* **11** utter, °express, °bring up, °put forward, °shout, °call: *Was it you who raised the alarm at the first sign of smoke?* **12** °assemble, °obtain, °get, °collect, °amass, °solicit: *We raised twice as much for charity as last year.* **13** invigorate, °animate, °vitalize, vivify, °buoy, °lift, uplift, °cheer (up), exhilarate, elate: *Our spirits were raised considerably by the news from head office.*

rake[1] *v.* **1** Often, ***rake up***: °scrape together, °gather (together *or* up), °collect, °draw together: *You really must rake up the leaves from the lawn and burn them.* **2** °scrape, comb, °scratch, °grate, graze: *Don't you just hate the sound of a fingernail being raked across a blackboard?* **3** ***rake in***: °collect, °gather (up *or* in), pull in, °make: *Pamela is raking in the royalties from her latest thriller.* **4** ***rake it in***: °coin °money, °make °money (hand-over-fist), *Brit* °coin it in: *The new record shop in the mall is really raking it in.* **5** ***rake out***: °sift (out), °screen, °remove, °clear, °eliminate: *Please rake out the cinders from the grate.* **6** ***rake over*** *or* ***through***: °search, °probe, °ransack, °scour, comb, °rummage through, °pick through *or* over, °go through *or* over (with a fine-tooth(ed) comb), °rifle (through): *The police raked through her entire flat but found nothing incriminating.* **7** ***rake up***: **a** See **1,** above. **b** °revive, resuscitate, °resurrect, °raise, °bring up, °recall: *Must you persist in raking up those bad memories?* **8** ***rake up*** *or* ***together***: °gather, °scrape up *or* together, °collect, °drag together, °pick up, °dig up, dredge up, °find, °unearth: *Were you able to rake up the others for a game of poker tonight?*

rake[2] *n.* °libertine, womanizer, lecher, °roué, °playboy, ladies' man, Don Juan, Casanova, Lothario, debauchee, voluptuary, °profligate, °prodigal; °scoundrel, °rascal, cad, *Archaic* rakehell, masher; *Colloq* lady-killer, *Colloq old-fashioned* wolf, *Brit* bounder: *Lady Anne was led stray by some young rake, a friend of the Prince Regent's.*

rake-off *n.* °kickback, commission; °discount, markdown, °rebate, *Colloq* °cut, °piece: *Does Mac get a rake-off for every buyer he sends to the shop?*

rakish *adj.* °dashing, °jaunty, °dapper, °spruce, °debonair, raffish, °smart, °breezy, °flashy, °chic, °fashionable, °elegant; °dandy, foppish: *Adjusting his trilby to a rakish angle, Peter strode along the boulevard.*

rally *n.* **1** °gathering, (mass) °meeting, °meet, convocation, °convention, assemblage, °assembly, °muster: *There is to be a political rally tonight in the town square. Are you taking your Daimler to the vintage car rally?* **2** °recovery, °improvement, °revival, °turn for the °better, recuperation, renewal: *His doctors said that the rally might be only temporary.*
—*v.* **3** Often, ***rally round***: bring *or* call *or* °get together, °round up, °assemble, convene, °group, congregate, °organize, come together, troop; marshal, °mobilize, °summon, °gather, °muster: *All Sally's friends rallied round her when her father died. He rallied every last ounce of strength in the dash for the finishing line.* **4** °revive, °rouse, °recover, °improve, get better, take a °turn for the °better, °recuperate, °perk up, °pick up, *Colloq* °snap out of it, make a comeback: *According to the nurse, he rallied during the night and asked for something to eat.*

ram *v.* **1** °jam, °force, °drive, °cram, °crowd, °pack, compress, °stuff, °squeeze, °thrust, tamp, °pound, hammer: *We rammed as much filler as we could into the crevices.* **2** °butt, °bump, °strike, °hit, °collide with, °dash, °crash, °slam: *Their car rammed into mine in the garage.*

ramble *v.* **1** amble, °wander (off), °stroll, °saunter, °walk, perambulate, °go (off *or* away), °travel, °drift, °range, rove, °go *or* °move about, hike, trek, *Colloq* mosey: *Don't ramble too far as dinner will be ready soon. We used to ramble over those hills, but the area is now an industrial site.* **2** °meander, °wander, digress, maunder: *Fiona tends to ramble off the main topic of conversation.* **3** Sometimes, ***ramble on***: °babble, °chatter, gibber, °rave, °go on (and on), °rattle on, *Colloq Brit* witter on, rabbit on *or* away: *If you didn't stop him, Hugh would ramble on for ever about his grandchildren.*
—*n.* **4** °stroll, amble, °saunter, °walk, °promenade, constitutional, walkabout, °tour, °tramp, hike, trek: *We went on a short ramble through the park.*

rambling *adj.* **1** °discursive, °roundabout, circuitous, °tortuous, °incoherent, °diffuse, °unsettled, °disconnected, °disjointed, disorganized, unorganized, illogical, maundering, °aimless, °confused, muddled, jumbled, scrambled, unintelligible, °inarticulate, periphrastic, circumlocutory, circumlocutional, circumlocutionary, ambagious, °wordy, verbose, prolix, °endless, interminable: *We couldn't make heads or tails of the professor's rambling lecture.* **2** unplanned, straggling, °irregular, sprawling, °spread out, spreading, straggly: *The Wilsons live in that big old rambling Victorian house down the road.* **3** roving, wandering, °travelling, peripatetic, itinerant, wayfaring, migratory, nomadic: *For five years he led a rambling life as a folk-singing banjo player.*

ramification *n.* **1** consequence, °result, °effect, °upshot, °implication, °subtlety; °complication, °difficulty: *Have you considered the ramifications of your decision to retire?* **2** °branch, °extension, outgrowth, subdivision, °offshoot: *Courier services may be considered a ramification of services that were once performed by the post office.*

ramp *n.* °slope, °grade, gradient, °incline; °rise, ascent, acclivity; descent, °dip, declivity: *There is a special ramp in the theatre for wheelchair access.*

rampage *n.* **1** °excitement, °agitation, recklessness, °riot, °tumult, °uproar, °frenzy, °fury, °rage, °furore *or* *US* furor, turmoil: *His latest rampage was prompted by their serving him a cup of cold coffee.* **2** *Brit* **on the *rampage***, *US* ***on a rampage***: berserk, °mad, °crazy, amok *or* amuck, °wild, out of control: *Pete regularly drank too much whisky and then went on the rampage.*
—*v.* **3** °storm, °rage, °rant, °rave, go °berserk, run amok *or* amuck: *He rampaged like a man possessed when he got his second parking ticket of the day.*

rampant *adj.* **1** unchecked, °uninhibited, unrestrained, °wild, °uncontrolled, out of control, out of hand, frenzied, unbridled, uncontrollable, °violent: *He was a victim of rampant jealousy. Jennie could hardly be described as a rampant feminist.* **2** °profuse, unbounded, abounding, °flourishing, rife, widespread, °everywhere, °epidemic, pandemic, °prevalent, unrestrained, unchecked, running °wild, °uninhibited, °indiscriminate, °wild, °uncontrolled; in °control, holding °sway, in full °sway, °dominant, °predominant; °exuberant, °rank, °luxuriant: *Before Masterson became sheriff, vice and crime were rampant in the town.*

rampart *n.* °defence, bastion, °guard, fortification, °security, °stronghold, °bulwark, barricade, °wall; earthwork, breastwork, parados, gabion: *The old town is surrounded by seven rows of ramparts leading up to the cathedral at the summit. They regard religion as an impenetrable rampart against immorality.*

ramshackle *adj.* °dilapidated, °tumbledown, crumbling, broken-down, °rickety, unsteady, jerry-built, °decrepit, °flimsy, °shaky, °unstable, tottering, unsubstantial *or* °insubstantial, ruined, in °disrepair, beyond repair, °run-down, neglected, °derelict: *He lives in a ramshackle hut on the outskirts of town.*

rancid *adj.* °stinking *or* reeking (to high heaven), foul-smelling, ill-smelling, evil-smelling, noisome, mephitic, miasmic *or* miasmal *or* miasmatic(al), °smelly, °rank, malodorous, fusty; °nasty, °disagreeable, odious, fetid *or* foetid, °rotten, decayed, spoilt *or* spoiled, turned, °bad, °awful, °sour, tainted, °high, gamy, °ripe, °putrid, °corrupt, °stale: *To rid your fridge of that rancid smell, wash it out with a solution of baking soda.*

rancorous *adj.* °hateful, °spiteful, °resentful, °hostile, malign, °malignant, °bitter, malevolent, malicious, °venomous, °vindictive, vengeful, splenetic, acrimonious: *Olivia felt rancorous towards her brother-in-law when he refused to lend her money.*

rancour *n.* hatred, °hate, antipathy, °spite, °resentment, resentfulness, °antagonism, °hostility, malignity, °bitterness, malevolence, malice, venomousness, °venom, vindictiveness, vengefulness, spleen, acrimony, animus, °animosity, enmity, bad feeling, bad blood: *Owing to the rancour between them, the brothers had not exchanged a word in forty years.*

random *adj.* **1** °haphazard, °chance, fortuitous, serendipitous, aleatory, °arbitrary, °casual, °stray, °occasional, °indefinite, °indiscriminate, non-specific, unspecific, unspecified, unordered, unorganized, undirected, °unpremeditated, unplanned, °accidental, uncalculated, unsystematic, adventitious, °incidental, hit-or-miss: *He used a computer program to generate random numbers. A random selection of slips was drawn from the drum and Madelaine's name was on one of them.* **2** ***at random***: randomly, haphazardly, fortuitously, by °chance, serendipitously, arbitrarily, casually, °occasionally, (every) °now and then, (every) °once in a while, irregularly, indefinitely, erratically, indiscriminately, unsystematically, adventitiously, °incidentally, unpremeditatedly: *They picked names from a hat at random. They drove up and down the road, firing at random.*

randy *adj.* aroused, °lustful, °lecherous, *Brit* on °heat *or US* in °heat, *Brit* in oestrus *or US* in estrus, *Slang* °hot, horny, in rut, rutting, at stud: *Seeing Betty always made Len feel terribly randy.*

range *n.* **1** °scope, °sweep, °reach, °limit, °extent, °span, °area, radius, °distance, compass, latitude, °stretch, °sphere, °orbit: *The gun has a range of about*

200 yards. This radio transmitter is effective only within a thirty-mile range. The minister is trying to broaden the range of his influence. **2** °assortment, series, °collection, °lot, °spread, °selection, °choice, °number, °variety, °kind, °sort, °scale, °gamut, °register: *The courses offered cater to a wide range of interests.* **3** °rank, °row, °tier, °line, °file, series, °string, °chain: *From my window I could see the range of hills stretching away into the distance.* **4** kitchen range, (cooking-) stove, *Chiefly Brit* cooker, *Brit trade mark* Aga, *US* cook-stove: *In every French farmhouse there was always a pot of soup on the range.*
—*v.* **5** °line up, °rank, °order, align, °order, array: *The teacher ranged the children according to their height.* **6** °vary, °fluctuate, °spread, °run the °gamut, °extend, °stretch, °run, °go: *The students range in age from eight to eighty.* **7** °organize, °categorize, catalogue, °arrange, classify, °sort, °class, °group, °rank, °bracket, pigeon-hole, °file, °index, °break down, °grade, °distribute: *The books are ranged according to their subject-matter.* **8** °cover, °traverse, °roam, rove, °travel over *or* across, °go *or* °pass over, °drift, °migrate, °wander, °move, °extend: *The wildebeest ranges far and wide over vast tracts of grazing land in Africa.*

rank[1] *n.* **1** °status, °standing, °position, °place, °level, °stratum, °class, °caste, circumstances, echelon, °grade: *It is virtually impossible to determine rank simply by looking at a person.* **2** °weight, °authority, °power, °superiority, seniority, ascendancy, °priority, °influence, eminence: *Caldwell uses the privilege of rank to cover up some of his more questionable transactions.* **3** °nobility, °title, high °birth, aristocracy, °dignity, °prestige, (blue) blood; peerage: *Gentlemen of rank should behave with honour, my boy.* **4** °line, °row, column, °queue, series, °formation; °sequence: *We gazed on the serried ranks of warriors, golden shields glistening in the sun.* **5** ***ranks***: °soldiers, °workers, °staff, °employees: *Smithers rose from the ranks to become chief executive officer.*
—*v.* **6** °grade, °rate, classify, °class, °categorize; °dispose, °organize, °order, °sort, assort, °arrange, array, align, °range, °graduate: *He was ranked among the best in the school. The applicants are ranked according to their test scores.* **7** °rate, °count, °stand, have °standing *or* value *or* °prestige, be °important *or* °distinguished: *To Janet, character ranks far above wealth. Phil is so mean that Scrooge would rank high on a list of charitable men in comparison with him.*

rank[2] *adj.* **1** °lush, °luxuriant, °abundant, °flourishing, °profuse, °prolific, °dense, superabundant, °exuberant, °fertile, °productive, fructuous: *The expedition could hardly make its way through the rank undergrowth of th jungle.* **2** °corrupt, °foul, °low, °base, °gross; °downright, utter, °sheer, °absolute, °complete, °out-and-out, °blatant, °flagrant, unalloyed, °unmitigated, °undiluted: *I cannot understand the rank treachery of the man after all that we have done for him. I ventured my opinion, even though a rank outsider.* **3** °offensive, °loathsome, °disgusting, °gross, °foul, °corrupt, °indecent, °shocking, °immodest, indecorous, °shameless, °risqué, °lurid, °off colour, °outrageous, °blue, °nasty, °vulgar, °vile, °dirty, °filthy, smutty, scatological, °pornographic, °obscene: *Those bigots always resort to the rank vocabulary of malice and hate. In a secret cupboard was a collection of the rankest literature.* **4** °offensive, °loathsome, °disgusting, °gross, °foul, foul-smelling, °smelly, °rancid, noisome, °stinking, reeky, reeking, mephitic, miasmic *or* miasmal *or* miasmatic(al), fetid *or* foetid, noxious, °rotten, °putrid, °musty, °stale, °disagreeable, °strong, °pungent: *The rank stench from the open sewers pervades the air in those pockets of poverty.*

rank and file *n.* (general) membership, °members, °majority: *The union's rank and file must now vote on whether to accept management's pay offer.*

rankle *v.* °gall, °fester, °irk, vex, °plague, °chafe, °grate, nettle, °torment, °pain, °hurt, °provoke, °anger, °exasperate, °get (to), °upset: *Although she had forgiven him, the insult still rankled.*

ransack *v.* **1** °search, °examine, °go through *or* over (with a fine-tooth(ed) comb), comb, °rake *or* °rummage through, °scour, °explore, °scrutinize, turn inside out: *I ransacked the second-hand bookshops for a copy but had no success.* **2** °rob, °plunder, °pillage, °sack, despoil, °loot, °strip; burgle, *US and Canadian* burglarize: *The thieves who ransacked the shop apparently missed the most valuable jewel.*

ransom *n.* **1** redemption, °rescue, deliverance; °release, °liberation: *The envoy was held to ransom by a fanatical band of zealots.* **2** °payment, payout, °payoff, °price: *The police refuse to reveal the amount of the ransom given to the kidnappers.*
—*v.* **3** °redeem, °rescue, °release, °deliver: *The boy was ransomed for £10,000.*

rant *v.* **1** declaim, °hold forth, expound, expatiate, orate, perorate, pontificate, trumpet, °preach, °harangue, °lecture, deliver (oneself of) a °tirade *or* diatribe *or* °speech, °speak: *The minister ranted pompously about his accomplishments.* **2** vociferate, °bluster, °rave, rant and °rave, °bellow, °rage: *The master kept ranting on about his newspaper having been creased.*
—*n.* **3** °tirade, philippic, °bluster, flatulence, °rhetoric, °bombast, pomposity, turgidity, gasconade, rodomontade, theatrics, histrionics, °act: *As he carried on his rant, the theatre gradually emptied till he was alone.*

rap *v.* **1** °knock, °strike, °tap, °hit: *The policeman rapped smartly at the door with his truncheon.* **2** °criticize, °rebuke, °scold, °reprimand, rap over the knuckles, *Colloq* °knock, *Brit* tick off: *We were severely rapped for dropping litter on the pavement.* **3** °converse, °talk, °chat, °gossip, *Colloq* °gab, *Slang* °chew the fat *or* the °rag: *That guy was so fascinating—we could rap with him for hours.*
—*n.* **4** °knock, °tap, °hit, °blow, °crack, °stroke, cuff, whack, thwack, °punch, *Colloq* °belt, clout, *Slang* sock, slug, biff: *The punishment for failing to complete the assignment was a severe rap on the knuckles.* **5** °conversation, °discussion, °chat, confabulation, °talk, °dialogue, discourse, colloquy, *Colloq* confab, *Slang chiefly US and Canadian* bull session, rap session: *We used to get together for a nice long rap now and then.* **6** °responsibility, °blame; °punishment, °sentence; °charge, °accusation, indictment: *Why should he have to take the rap for something you did? The witness failed to show up, so Baxter beat the rap.*

rapacious *adj.* °greedy, covetous, °grasping, °avaricious, °mercenary, usurious, acquisitive, °predatory, predacious, °ravenous, ravening, °voracious, insatiable, insatiate, wolfish, wolflike, lupine, vulturine, raptorial: *That rapacious swindler took everything they had in the world.*

rapacity *n.* °greed, greediness, cupidity, covetousness, °avarice, acquisitiveness, predaciousness, ravenousness, voracity, voraciousness, insatiability, insatiableness, rapaciousness: *The rapacity of the invading hordes of Mongols knew no bounds.*

rape *n.* **1** ravishment, defloration, deflowering, °violation, sexual °assault, defilement: *The police are investigating reports of rape by a masked man.* **2** rapine, despoliation, spoliation, despoilment, °pillage, °depredation, ravagement, ravaging, °plunder, plundering, °sack, sacking, looting, ransacking: *He travelled in disguise to document the rape of the war-torn areas.* **3** abduction, carrying-off, kidnapping, °seizure, °capture, snatching: *History debates whether the ancient Romans were truly responsible for the rape of the Sabine women.*
—*v.* **4** °violate, °ravish, °assault sexually, deflower, defile, force to submit to sexual intercourse, have one's way with, take advantage of: *The defendant raped three women before he was caught.* **5** despoil, spoliate, °pillage, depredate, °ravage, °plunder, °sack, °loot: *Throughout history the city has been raped by marauding tribes.*

rapid *adj.* °quick, °fast, °swift, °speedy, high-speed, °brisk, °expeditious, °prompt, °express, °fleet, lightning(-fast), alacritous; °hurried, °hasty, °precipitate, °impetuous, °immediate, instantaneous, °instant, °sudden: *The company we use offers rapid delivery service. What do you suppose occasioned Flannery's rapid departure?*

rapidity *n.* quickness, swiftness, °speed, speediness, briskness, expeditiousness, promptness, promptitude, alacrity, celerity, immediateness, °dispatch *or* despatch, instantaneousness: *The rapidity with which they responded to our request is truly commendable.*

rapidly *adv.* **1** °quickly, °fast, °swiftly, speedily, briskly, expeditiously, like a °shot, at the speed of light, double-quick, at full °speed, like one °possessed, at a gallop, tantivy, *Colloq* like blazes, like (greased) lightning, *US* lickety-split, *Slang* like a bat out of hell, like °mad: *He cycled down the High Street as rapidly as he could go.* **2** °promptly, instantly, °instantaneously, instanter, without °delay, at °once, °straight away, °right away, in a °moment, in a trice, like a shot, in a wink, in (less than) no °time, double-quick, in a °flash, at the °speed of light, before you (can) turn around, *Colloq* in a jiffy, in two shakes (of a lamb's tail), like (greased) lightning, before you can say 'Jack Robinson', *US and Canadian* (right) off the bat, lickety-split, *Slang* like a bat out of hell: *When I mentioned that you were coming, she left rapidly.*

rapport *n.* empathy, °relationship, °sympathy, °harmony, °affinity, °accord, °bond, °relationship, (mutual) °understanding, camaraderie: *The minute we met we established a rapport.*

rapprochement *n.* °reconciliation, °understanding, °settlement: *The party needs to bring about a* rapprochement *between the radicals and the reactionaries.*

rapt *adj.* **1** entranced, fascinated, spellbound, mesmerized, hypnotized, engrossed, enthralled, bewitched, °absorbed, transported, captivated, °delighted: *She gave her last performance of* 'Giselle' *before a rapt audience.* **2** enraptured, °rapturous, °delighted, °elated, °happy, °ecstatic, blissful, °overjoyed, joyous, °joyful, beatific: *You should have seen the rapt expression on the child's face when Santa Claus appeared.*

rapture *n.* °ecstasy, °delight, °joy, joyfulness, joyousness, °pleasure, exaltation, elation, °thrill, °enchantment, euphoria, beatitude, °transport: *Nothing could compare with the rapture he felt at seeing his daughter win the Nobel prize.*

rapturous *adj.* °ecstatic, °delighted, °joyful, joyous, °elated, thrilled, °enchanted, euphoric, in seventh °heaven, °overjoyed, °rhapsodic, *Colloq* on cloud nine, *Brit* over the moon: *He was rapturous over qualifying for the Olympics.*

rare[1] *adj.* **1** uncommon, °unfamiliar, °unusual, °exceptional, out of the °ordinary, °extraordinary, atypical; °scarce, °unparalleled, °choice, recherché, °phenomenal, infrequent, °few and far between, °sparse, °scanty, °limited, °seldom encountered *or* met with *or* seen; °unique, °singular, one of a kind; *Chiefly Brit* °thin on the ground: *It was rare to see Liz in such good humour. Specimens in such perfect condition are rare. A copy of the first edition in this condition is rare.* **2** °fine, °good, °admirable, °excellent, °choice, °select, °special, °first-rate, first-class, °exquisite, °superior, °superlative, °peerless, unequalled, °matchless, °incomparable, in a °class by itself *or* herself *or* himself *or* themselves, *sui generis*, °outstanding; collectible *or* collectable: *O, rare Ben Jonson! On exhibit was a black pearl of rare beauty and remarkable size. Consideration for others seems a rare quality these days.*

rare[2] *adj.* underdone, undercooked, *bleu(e), saignant(e)*: *Do you want your steak rare, medium, or well-done?*

rarefied *adj.* **1** °thin, °lean, attenuated, diluted, °sparse, scant, °scanty: *As we climbed higher, the rarefied atmosphere made breathing more difficult.* **2** °exalted, °lofty, °elevated, high, °sublime, °noble: *I feel out of place in the rarefied atmosphere of academia.* **3** cliquish, clannish, °exclusive, °private, °select, esoteric: *Clarence copes well in the rarefied atmosphere of Whitehall's corridors of power.*

rarely *adv.* °seldom, °infrequently, on °rare occasions, °hardly (°ever), °scarcely (°ever), °almost °never, *Colloq* °once in a blue moon: *He rarely attends formal dinners at his club.*

rarity *n.* **1** °curiosity, °oddity, curio, collector's item, °find, °treasure, conversation piece, *Brit* one-off, *Colloq Brit* oner: *Among the rarities in his collection is a stuffed dodo.* **2** unusualness, uncommonness, rareness, uniqueness, °scarcity: *The rarity of the first edition makes this book all the more valuable.*

rascal *n.* °imp, °devil, scamp, mischief-maker; rapscallion, °rogue, °scoundrel, cad, °villain, blackguard, knave, °good-for-nothing, ne'er-do-well, °wastrel, scapegrace, dastard, °wretch, *Colloq* scallywag *or* scalawag, *Brit* rotter, blighter, bounder: *That little rascal has eaten all the cherry tarts. They've caught the rascals who were vandalizing parked cars.*

rash[1] *adj.* °impetuous, °impulsive, °unthinking, °thoughtless, °foolhardy, unconsidered, ill-considered, °ill-advised, injudicious, °imprudent, °indiscreet, °precipitate, °hasty, °careless, °heedless, °reckless, headlong, °wild, madcap, °hare-brained, °hotheaded, °adventurous, °quixotic, °venturesome, °audacious, °bold, °dashing, °brash, devil-may-care: *It was rash of him to try to sail round the world single-handed, but he did it.*

rash[2] *n.* **1** °eruption, eczema, redness, efflorescence, dermatitis: *One of the symptoms of measles is a skin rash.* **2** °number(s), °quantity, °lot(s), multitude, °profusion, outbreak, series, °succession, °spate, °wave, °flood, deluge, °plague, °epidemic: *There's been a rash of burglaries in the neighbourhood.*

rasp *n.* **1** °grating, °scrape, scraping, °scratch, scratching, grinding, stridulation: *One could hear the rasp of the file as they tried to cut through the door.* **2** °file, grater: *The coarser rasp is for use on wood.*
—*v.* **3** °scrape, abrade, °grate, °file: *First, rasp the horseradish, then combine the gratings with a little vinegar.* **4** °irritate, °jar (upon), °grate upon *or* against, °rub (someone) (up) the wrong way, nettle, °irk, °annoy, vex, °wear on, °get, *Literary* gride: *She has a rasping metallic voice that gets on my nerves.* **5** croak, °squawk, screech: *The sergeant rasped out another command and the company marched forward.*

rate[1] *n.* **1** °measure, °pace, gait, °speed, °velocity, *Colloq* °clip: *We moved along at a pretty fast rate. Rates of production must increase.* **2** °charge, °price, °fee, °tariff, °figure, °amount; °toll: *The rate for a hotel room has increased enormously in the past few years.* **3** °percentage, °scale, °proportion: *What is the current rate of interest on government savings bonds?* **4** Usually, ***-rate***: °rank, °grade, °place, °standing, °status, °position, °class, classification, °kind, °sort, °type, rating, worth, value, valuation, °evaluation: *After a few years, he had improved from a second-rate typist to a first-rate secretary.* **5** ***at any rate***: in any °case, in any °event, anyway, at all events, anyhow, under any circumstances, °regardless, °notwithstanding: *At any rate, with their last child out of university, they have no more worries about paying education costs.*
—*v.* **6** °rank, °grade, °class, classify, °evaluate, °estimate, °calculate, °compute, °count, °reckon, °judge, °gauge, assess, appraise, °measure: *How do you rate your chances of beating the champion?* **7** °merit, be entitled to, °deserve, be °worthy of, have a °claim to: *The play doesn't rate all the attention it's been getting in the press.* **8** °count, °place, °measure: *She rates very high among her friends.*

rate[2] *v.* °scold, °berate, °reprimand, °rebuke, reproach, °reprove, take to °task, °upbraid, censure, *Colloq* °bawl out, °dress down, *US and Canadian* °chew out: *I was rated severely for staying out after midnight.*

rather *adv.* **1** °quite, °very, °somewhat, °fairly, °moderately, to a certain °extent *or* °degree *or* °measure, to some °extent *or* °degree *or* °measure, more or less, pretty, °slightly, *Colloq* °sort of, kind of: *I suppose she was rather good-looking, but at that age I didn't pay much attention to girls. This coffee tastes rather strange.* **2** preferably, sooner, °instead, more °readily *or* °willingly: *Given an option, I choose to live alone rather than marry.* **3** ***would*** or *Colloq US* ***had rather***: °prefer, °choose: *Given a choice, I would rather live alone.*

ratify *v.* °approve, °sanction, °endorse, °support, corroborate, °uphold, °back (up), °sustain, °establish, validate, °substantiate, °verify, °authenticate, °guarantee, °warrant, °certify, affirm, °ensure, °clinch, °settle: *The pact was ratified by all members.*

ratio *n.* °proportion, °relationship, correlation, correspondence: *What is the ratio of male to female students at Oxford University? In that area, the ratio of tenants to home-owners is about two to one.*

ration *n.* **1** °share, °quota, °allotment, °portion, °helping, °part, °provision, °measure, °dole, °percentage, °amount: *Each person is permitted a weekly fixed ration of butter, sugar, coffee, meat, etc. We shall have to go on short rations till we are rescued.* **2** ***rations***: °supplies, provisions, °food, °provender, victuals, viands, eatables, edibles, comestibles, *Brit* commons: *It was not till the third week with our rations running low that we really began to worry.*
—*v.* **3** Often, ***ration out***: °allot, apportion, °dole (out), °give out, °distribute, °deal out, °mete out, °parcel out, °measure out, °hand out: *As water was in short supply, we had to ration it. One cup was rationed out to each of us every morning.* **4** budget, °schedule, °restrict, °control, °limit: *Water had to be rationed to one cup a day for each of us.*

rational *adj.* **1** °well-balanced, °sane, °sound, °normal, °reasonable, °reasoning, °logical, ratiocinative, clear-headed, clear-eyed, °sober; of °sound mind, *Colloq* all there: *Desmond is a rational human being who would be able to advise you about your problem.* **2** °discriminating, °intelligent, °thinking, °enlightened, °prudent, °wise, °knowledgeable, °informed: *We could not have elected a more rational representative for our cause than Robert Brown.* **3** °sensible, common-sense, commonsensical, °practical, pragmatic, down-to-earth, °everyday, °acceptable, °reasonable, °logical: *Philippa thinks she has a rational explanation for the strange light we saw in the sky last night.*

rationale *n.* °reason, °explanation, °logical °basis, grounds, °logic, °reasoning, °philosophy, °principle, theory: *Do you understand the rationale of a policy for curbing inflation that sets interest rates at a level where business, initiative, and productivity are stifled?*

rationalize *v.* **1** make °plausible *or* believable *or* understandable *or* °acceptable *or* °reasonable, make °allowance(s) *or* excuses for, °vindicate, °account for, °justify, °excuse, °reason away, °explain away: *How can you rationalize taking my car without my permission?* **2** °think through, °reason out; apply °logic to, ratiocinate: *He warps the statistics to rationalize his argument. The fundamentalists make no attempt to rationalize their literal interpretation of the Scripture.*

rattle *v.* **1** clatter: *An acorn dropped from an overhanging tree and rattled down the tin roof.* **2** °shake, °vibrate, °jar, joggle, °jiggle: *The wind was strong enough to rattle the windows in their frames.*
3 °unnerve, disconcert, °discomfit, °disturb, °perturb, °shake, discountenance, °upset, °agitate, °put off, *Chiefly US and Canadian* faze: *They are only trying to rattle us by saying that we might lose our jobs if we strike.* **4** jounce, °bounce, °bump, °jolt, °speed, °hurtle: *The stagecoach came rattling down the road, swaying wildly.* **5** ***rattle off***: °recite, °list, utter, °reel off, run through, °enumerate, call off: *The announcer rattled off a long list of trains cancelled because of the storm.*
6 ***rattle on***: °chatter, °babble, °jabber, gibber, prate, °prattle, blabber, cackle, blather, °ramble, *Chiefly Brit* witter, natter, *Slang US* run off at the mouth: *The speaker kept rattling on and on about the delights of collecting beer cans.*
—*n.* **7** clatter, °racket, °noise; rale *or* râle, crackle, crackling; death-rattle: *I heard the rattle of the beans and knew you were about to grind the coffee. The doctor said he didn't like the rattle in my chest.* **8** °clapper, sistrum, *US* noise-maker: *Rattles have been used as musical instruments for thousands of years.*

rattletrap *n.* flivver, rattler, *Colloq* jalopy, tin Lizzie, *US* Model T: *This old rattletrap won't get us all the way to Hawkhurst.*

ratty *adj.* **1** °irritable, °cross, °testy, °touchy, annoyed, crabbed, irritated, °angry, °short-tempered, °impatient, °disagreeable: *He's always ratty in the mornings when he has a hangover.* **2** °dirty, °greasy, straggly, °unkempt, matted: *His hair was all ratty and he hadn't bathed in a month.*

raucous *adj.* °harsh, rasping, °rough, °husky, hoarse, °grating, scratching, °scratchy, °discordant, dissonant, jarring; °strident, °shrill, °noisy, °loud, ear-splitting, °piercing: *You could hear Ramsay's raucous voice above the others. A raucous scream came from the parrot's cage.*

ravage *v.* **1** lay °waste, °devastate, °ruin, °destroy, °demolish, °raze, °wreck, °wreak °havoc (up)on, °damage: *The hurricane ravaged outlying areas but did little damage in the city.* **2** °pillage, °plunder, despoil, °ransack, °sack, °loot: *The police tried to prevent hooligans from ravaging the shops in the town centre.*
—*n.* **3** Usually, ***ravages***: °destruction, °damage, °depredation(s), devastation, wrecking, °ruin, demolition: *All about us we saw the ravages of war.*

rave *v.* **1** °rant, °rage, °storm, fulminate, °roar, °thunder, °howl, °yell, caterwaul, yowl, °bellow, °shout, °scream, °fly off the handle, *Colloq* °flip one's °top *or* lid, *Slang* raise hell: *He kept raving on about his coffee mug having been pinched.* **2** ***rave about***: °praise, °laud, rhapsodize over, °applaud, °gush over: *Bernard can't stop raving about that new Thai restaurant.*
—*n.* **3** °praise, acclaim, °favour, °enthusiastic °reception, °tribute, °testimonial, encomium, °bouquet, plaudits, accolade, °admiration, *US* hosanna: *The play got raves in all the newspapers when it opened.* **4** °rage, °fashion, °vogue, °trend, °thing, last word, *dernier cri*, °craze, °mania, *Colloq* °fad: *The rave that year was for stiletto heels.* **5** °party, °fête *or* fete, soirée, *Colloq* do, *Slang* bash, blow-out, *Brit* rave-up, *US* wingding, °blast: *Monica threw quite a rave to celebrate her new job.*

ravenous *adj.* **1** °hungry, °famished, starving, °starved: *We were ravenous after the long hike.* **2** °voracious, °gluttonous, °greedy, insatiable, ravening, swinish, piggish, °hoggish, edacious, wolfish: *With my family's ravenous appetites, there are rarely any leftovers.*

ravine *n.* °gorge, °canyon, °pass, cleft, defile, °gully *or* gulley, °valley, *Brit dialect* clough, *Scots* linn, *US* °gap, gulch, arroyo: *At the spring thaw, torrents filled the ravines.*

raving *adj.* **1** °mad, °insane, °berserk, raging, °crazy, crazed, irrational, manic, °maniacal, °frantic, frenzied, °delirious, °hysterical; out of one's °mind *or* head: *He stood there shouting and screaming, like a raving lunatic.* **2** °extraordinary, °outstanding, °unusual, °rare, uncommon, °phenomenal, °great, °striking, °ravishing, *Colloq* °stunning: *Diana had been a raving beauty in her time.*
—*n.* **3** Often, ***ravings***: °rant, ranting, °bombast, pomposity, grandiloquence, magniloquence, rodomontade, °rhetoric, °bluster, blustering, claptrap, balderdash, puffery, bunkum, flatulence, hyperbole, vapouring, fustian, *Colloq* °hot air, bunk: *Why must we be subjected to the ravings of this politician?* **4** gabble, °babble, babbling, °gibberish, *Colloq* °gab: *This is nothing more than the raving of a maniac.*

ravish *v.* **1** °enrapture, °delight, °captivate, enthral, °fascinate, °charm, °entrance, spellbind, °bewitch, °transport: *I was ravished at the prospect of seeing you again.* **2** °rape, °violate, have one's way with, deflower, defile: *The soldiers attacked the village and ravished the women.*

ravishing *adj.* °dazzling, °beautiful, °gorgeous, °striking, °radiant, charming, alluring, °attractive, entrancing, captivating, °enthralling, bewitching, °spellbinding, *Colloq* °stunning: *Daphne was even more ravishing than her sister Diana.*

raw *adj.* **1** uncooked, °unprepared, °fresh: *Many vegetables can be eaten raw.* **2** unprocessed, untreated, °unrefined, unfinished, °natural, °crude: *The raw sugar is shipped to the plant where it is refined. The raw statistics revealed that many women had refused to respond to the questionnaire.* **3** °new, °inexperienced, unseasoned, °immature, °green, °untried, °fresh, untrained, unskilled, untested: *They sent us raw recruits who had never seen battle.* **4** exposed, unprotected, uncovered, °open; °sore, °tender, °inflamed, °painful, °sensitive: *When he mentioned her name, it was as if he had touched a raw nerve.* **5** °chill, °chilly, chilling, °cold, °damp, °frigid, °freezing, °biting, stinging, nippy, nipping, °sharp, °keen, °piercing, °penetrating: *You should wrap up warmly if you're going out in that raw wind.* **6** °brutal, °frank, °candid, °blunt, °direct, °unvarnished, unmollified, unembellished, °realistic, °honest, °plain, unreserved, unrestrained, °uninhibited, °bluff, straightforward: *The producer felt that no domestic audience could stomach a raw depiction of the horrors of war.*
—*n.* **7** ***in the raw***: °naked, °stark °naked, undressed, unclothed, °nude, in the °nude, *Brit* starkers, *Colloq* in the buff, in the altogether, in one's birthday suit: *For punishment, they made us stand outside, in the freezing cold, in the raw.*

raw-boned *adj.* °gaunt, °lean, gangling, °thin, °skinny, °spare, °meagre, °scrawny, underfed, bony, °emaciated, half-starved, wasted, hollow-cheeked, cadaverous: *They'll take that raw-boned youngster into the army and put some meat on him.*

ray *n.* **1** °beam, °shaft, °bar, °streak, pencil, °gleam, °flash: *A single ray from the setting sun illuminated the head of the statue.* **2** glimmer, °trace, °spark, scintilla, °flicker: *As he had not been rejected outright, there was still a ray of hope that he might be accepted.*

raze *v.* °tear *or* °pull *or* bring *or* °knock *or* throw down, °demolish, °destroy, °level, °flatten, bulldoze: *As usual, beautiful old buildings were razed to make way for a new shopping centre.*

reach *v.* **1** Often, ***reach out***: °hold out, °extend, °stretch (out), °stick out, °thrust out, outstretch, outreach: *He reached out his hand and grasped mine warmly.* **2** °arrive at, °get to, come to, go to, end up at *or* in; °land at *or* in, *Colloq* °make (it to): *I won't reach the office till noon today. Have we reached the point of no return?* **3** °get, °get in touch with, °communicate with, establish *or* make °contact with, °get through to, °get (a) hold of: *I tried to reach her at home, but she was out.* **4** attain, °achieve, °accomplish, °make, °get *or* go to, °get *or* go as far as: *Do you think that McClintock will reach the semi-finals?* **5** come *or* go *or* get up to, °amount to, attain, °climb to, °rise to, °run to, °equal, °match: *It looks as though the trade deficit might reach last year's figure.* **6** °get through *or* across to, °register with, °communicate with, reach into the mind of, °impress, °influence, °sway, °move, °stir, °carry °weight with: *It is very difficult for teachers to reach teenagers, who have a natural suspicion of adults.*
—*n.* **7** °range, ambit, °scope, °orbit, compass, °sphere, °territory: *Those outlying areas are beyond our reach. Padua is within easy reach of Venice.* **8** °capability, °capacity: *Tragedy often occurs when one's ambition exceeds one's reach.*

react *v.* **1** °act, °behave, °conduct oneself, °proceed; °retaliate, °reciprocate, °get °even: *I wonder how you would have reacted if someone had insulted you!* **2** °respond, °answer, °reply, °retort: *The crowd reacted to the police presence by becoming very nasty. She reacted with surprise on learning of his arrest.*

reaction *n.* **1** °response, °reply, °answer, °effect, feedback: *Did you get any reaction when you told her I had been arrested? Her reaction was to turn over and go back to sleep.* **2** repulsion, °resistance, counteraction, counterbalance, compensation: *A rocket derives forward thrust by reaction against its own exhaust, hence can operate in a vacuum.* **3** retaliation, reciprocation, °reprisal, °revenge: *He shot her in reaction to her announcement that she was leaving him.*

reactionary *adj.* **1** (ultra-)°conservative, °right, rightist, right-wing, blimpish; traditionalist; *South African* verkrampte: *Reactionary governments tend to reduce social services.*
—*n.* **2** (ultra-)°conservative, rightist, right-winger, Colonel Blimp; traditionalist; *South African* verkrampte: *As a reactionary, he feels that the status quo is fine and change unnecessary.*

read *v.* **1** °peruse, °scan, °skim, °review, °study, °look over, °pore over: *I have read the article twice but still cannot understand it.* **2** °understand, °know, be °familiar with, °comprehend, °interpret, °decipher: *Can you read Greek? Madame Sonja reads tea leaves.* **3** °announce, °present, °deliver: *Anna reads the news on TV at six o'clock every evening.* **4** ***read into***: °assign to, °impute (to), °infer (from), °assume (from), °presume (from), conclude (from): *You might be reading too much into that letter of commendation.*

readable *adj.* **1** °intelligible, comprehensible, understandable, °easy to °understand, °easily °understood, °plain: *Surprisingly, the instructions for operating the computer are fairly readable.* **2** °entertaining, °easy to °read, enjoyable, °pleasurable, °absorbing, °interesting, °engaging, °stimulating, °worthwhile: *Her latest thriller is so readable that I stayed up all night to finish it.* **3** °legible, decipherable, °distinct: *The print on that microfiche is too small to be readable.*

readily *adv.* **1** cheerfully, °willingly, eagerly, ungrudgingly, unhesitatingly, °freely, °gladly, °happily, agreeably, graciously, charitably: *He always gave readily of his time to anyone who sought his help, and we shall miss him sorely.* **2** effortlessly, °easily, smoothly, without °difficulty: *I was able to get the wheel off readily enough, getting it back on was the problem.* **3** °promptly, °quickly, speedily, °swiftly, apace, at °once, without °delay, in no °time, °immediately, instantly, °instantaneously, instanter, °straight away, °right away, at *or* on short notice, *Colloq* pronto: *The police came readily but were unable to catch the thieves, who had already escaped.*

readiness *n.* **1** willingness, cheerfulness, good °will, °eagerness, agreeableness, graciousness: *Her readiness to help marked her as truly charitable.* **2** promptness, quickness; °facility, °ease, °skill, adroitness, expertness, °proficiency: *The readiness with which he gave expert advice on gardening made him very popular with his neighbours.* **3** ***in readiness***: See **ready, 1,** below.

ready *adj.* **1** °prepared, (all) °set, in °readiness, in (°proper) °shape; up, primed, °ripe, °fit, in °condition; *Colloq* psyched (up): *The charge is ready for detonation. I'm ready for a good run in the park. Are these apples ready for eating? Are you ready to meet the girl of your dreams?* **2** °agreeable, consenting, acquiescent, °willing, °content, °eager, °keen, °happy, °cheerful, °genial, °gracious, °cordial, °friendly, well-disposed, °enthusiastic, *Colloq* °game: *Tim was always a ready accomplice to any mischief devised by his brother.* **3** apt, °likely, °inclined, °disposed, °given, °prone: *She was all too ready to believe anything she was told.* **4** about, °liable, °likely, apt; on the °verge of, °subject to, in °danger of, on the °brink of, on the °point of, °close to: *The volcano seemed ready to erupt at any moment.* **5** °prompt, °rapid, quick, °immediate, °speedy, °swift, °punctual, °timely: *Alistair seems to have a ready answer for everything.* **6** °clever, °keen, °sharp, °agile, deft, °skilful, adroit, °alert, °bright, °intelligent, °perceptive, °quick: *It was Carlotta's ready wit that first*

attracted me. **7** on *or* at *or* to °hand, °handy, °available, °accessible, at (one's) fingertips, at the ready, °close at °hand, °convenient: *I don't have the ready cash for a new car at the moment.*
—*n.* **8** ***readies***: °money, °cash, wherewithal: *If you have the readies, please pay me what you owe me.* **9** ***at the ready***: **a** waiting, on °tap, °expectant, in °position, °poised: *Keep your pistol at the ready in case there's trouble.* **b** See **7,** above.
—*v.* **10** °prepare, make *or* get ready, °set, °fit out, °equip, °organize, psych up: *He readied himself as best he could for the ordeal.*

ready-made *adj.* **1** ready-to-wear, finished, prefabricated, *Brit* off the °peg: *Ready-made clothes fit me better than custom-made.* **2** °convenient, °expedient, °serviceable, usable, °handy, °useful, °suitable, °adaptable; °plausible, credible, believable: *The storm provided a ready-made excuse for cancelling the appointment.* **3** stereotyped, stereotypic(al), hackneyed, °time-worn, trite, °stale, °conventional, unoriginal, °stock, °pedestrian, °routine, run-of-the-mill: *His speeches are always full of ready-made clichés.*

real *adj.* **1** °genuine, °true, °actual, °authentic, verified, verifiable, °legitimate, °right, bona fide, °official; °legal, licit, °natural, valid, °veritable: *He says that his name is Smith, but what is his real name? Her diamonds are not real. It has been proved beyond the shadow of a doubt that he is the real father.* **2** °genuine, °actual, °true, existent, °authentic, °natural; °material, °physical, °tangible, palpable, corporeal: *How can one distinguish between the real object and what one sees, which is merely its image?* **3** °genuine, °sincere, °heartfelt, °true, °actual, unfeigned, °unaffected, °earnest, °honest, °truthful, °legitimate, valid: *Deirdre's face is so impassive that it is impossible to tell what her real feelings are. What's the real reason that you're here?* **4** °genuine, °actual, °true, °loyal, °trustworthy, trusted, °honest: *You are a real friend, and I know I can count on you.* **5** °intrinsic, °actual, °true, °genuine, °proper, °essential: *The £150 million sale of the company fell significantly below its real value.*
—*adv.* **6** See **really,** below.

realistic *adj.* **1** °practical, °matter-of-fact, down-to-earth, pragmatic, common-sense, °sensible, °reasonable, °level-headed, °rational, °sane, hard-headed, businesslike, °no-nonsense, unromantic, unsentimental, °tough, tough-minded, *Colloq* hard-nosed, hard-boiled: *Kevin's realistic grasp of the problems may make the company profitable at last.* **2** °natural, °lifelike, °true to °life, naturalistic, °vivid, °genuine, °real, °graphic: *This painting is so realistic that it looks like a photograph. Harriet's description was so realistic that I felt I had actually been to Benidorm.*

reality *n.* **1** actuality, °fact, °truth, genuineness, authenticity, *Aristotelianism* entelechy: *It is important to deal with the reality not the potentiality of the situation.* **2** ***in reality***: See **really,** below.

realization *n.* **1** °conception, °understanding, comprehension, apprehension, awareness, °appreciation, °perception, °recognition, °cognizance: *Full realization of what he had done finally dawned on him.* **2** actualization, °consummation, °accomplishment, °achievement, °establishment, °fulfilment, materialization, effectuation: *The realization of the dream of a united Europe seems possible in the last decade of the 20th century.*

realize *v.* **1** make °real, °effect, °bring about, make happen, make a °reality, actualize, °accomplish, °produce, °achieve, °fulfil, °materialize, °effectuate: *Many of Leonardo da Vinci's inventions were not realized in his lifetime.* **2** °understand, °appreciate, °comprehend, be °aware of, °conceive of, °grasp, °perceive, discern, be *or* become °conscious *or* °aware *or* appreciative of, °recognize, °see, *Colloq* °catch on (to), cotton (on) to, *Brit* °twig: *Did Clare fully realize the consequences of her actions?* **3** °return, °gain, °clear, °profit, °make, °earn, °bring *or* take in, °net, °produce, °get: *We have realized a substantial profit on the sale of the shares bought when the company was privatized.*

really *adv.* **1** genuinely, °actually, °truly, °honestly, in °reality, in actuality, in (point of) °fact, as a matter of °fact, °surely, °indeed, °absolutely, °definitely: *Is he really going to do the high-wire act without a net?* **2** °indeed, °actually, °absolutely, unqualifiedly, °positively, categorically, unquestionably, °definitely, undeniably: *She is really the musical one in the family.* **3** in °effect, in °reality, °actually, in °fact, de facto, in the end, at °bottom, in the final analysis, at the end of the day, *Colloq* deep down: *Despite the sergeant's protests to the contrary, it was really Andrews who saved the platoon.* **4** °very, °extremely, °quite, exceptionally, remarkably, unusually, uncommonly, extraordinarily, °exceedingly, *Non-Standard* °real: *I saw a really good film last night.*

realm *n.* **1** °domain, °kingdom, empire, °monarchy, principality, palatinate, duchy *or* dukedom: *They searched the realm for a girl whose foot would fit into the glass slipper.* **2** °territory, °area, bailiwick, °department, °responsibility, °jurisdiction: *Collecting taxes is not within the realm of our office.* **3** °area, confines, °sphere, °limits: *Cooperation with foreign companies is certainly well within the realms of possibility.*

ream *v.* °drill (out), °bore (out), °open up, °tap: *The carpenter reamed three holes in the beam.*

reap *v.* **1** °harvest, °garner, glean, °gather (in), °mow, °take in *or* up: *The land was fertile, and a bountiful crop was reaped. As ye sow, so shall ye reap.* **2** °profit, °bring in, °gain, °procure, °acquire, °get, °obtain, take in: *It is impossible to reap much when there is so small a margin between cost and selling price.*

rear[1] *n.* **1** °back (part), °end, hind part, *Nautical* °stern, *Colloq* °tail (end), fag-end, *US and Canadian* tag end: *The rear of the column was attacked as it marched through the defile. We took seats at the rear of the auditorium.* **2** hindquarters, °posterior, rump, °buttocks, bottom, behind, backside, rear end, *Colloq Brit* °bum, *US* hinie, tush *or* tushy *or* tushie, tokus *or* tochis *or* tuchis, *Taboo Slang Brit* arse, *US* ass: *As he left, he felt someone give him a pat on the rear.*
—*adj.* **3** °back, °last, end, rearmost, *Nautical* aft, after, °stern: *The rear window is all misted over.*

rear[2] *v.* **1** °raise, °bring up, °care for, nurture, °nurse; °cultivate, °educate, °train; °breed, °produce: *They reared six children in that tiny house. Is this where they rear Aberdeen Angus cattle?* **2** °erect, °raise, °build, °put up, °construct, °fabricate, °create: *The family reared an elaborate mausoleum in memory of Lord Percy.* **3** °raise, °lift, °put up, upraise, uplift, °hold up: *He said that élitism was rearing its ugly head again, and that equality of opportunity was proving a myth.*

reason *n.* **1** justification, °argument, °case, °explanation, °rationale, °ground(s), °pretext, vindication, °defence, why (and wherefore), *Literary* apologia, apology: *What reason did they give for confiscating our luggage?* **2** °judgement, common °sense, °intelligence, °sanity, °sense(s), saneness, °insight, perspicacity, percipience, °understanding, rationality, °reasoning, °mind, °intellect: *He must have lost his reason to accuse you of embezzlement.* **3** °purpose, °aim, °intention, °object, °objective, °goal, °motive, °end, °point: *His reason for leaving now is to be on time for the curtain.* **4** °excuse, rationalization: *Ignorance of the law is not an accepted reason for breaking it.* **5** ***by reason of***: because of, on account of, owing to, by °virtue of, as a °result of; °due to: *He was declared unfit to stand trial by reason of insanity.* **6** ***within*** *or* ***in reason***: °reasonable, °sensible, justifiable, °rational, °fitting, °proper, °acceptable: *We will consider any offer for the house that is within reason.*
—*v.* **7** °think, conclude, °calculate, °reckon, °estimate, °figure (out), °work out, °deduce, act *or* °think rationally *or* logically, ratiocinate, use (one's) °judgement *or* common °sense, use (one's) °head, put two and two together: *I reasoned that she would be arriving at the station at that very moment. Roy certainly hasn't lost his powers of reasoning.* **8** ***reason with***: °argue with, remonstrate with, °debate with, °discuss with, °talk over with, °plead with, °convince; °persuade, dissuade,

°urge, °prevail (up)on: *George is very stubborn and can't be reasoned with.*

reasonable *adj.* **1** °sensible, °rational, °sane, °logical, °sober, °sound, °judicious, °wise, °intelligent, °thinking: *I had always thought Philip a reasonable man.* **2** credible, believable, °plausible, °tenable, reasoned, arguable, well-thought-out, well-grounded: *Her story about having found the child wandering in the street doesn't sound very reasonable to me.* **3** °moderate, °tolerable, °acceptable, within °reason, °equitable, °fair; °inexpensive, unexcessive, unextravagant, °economical, °conservative: *Considering inflation, we thought the price increases were reasonable.* **4** °appropriate, °suitable, °proper, °sensible, °right: *The car was travelling at a reasonable speed, considering conditions.*

reasoning *n.* **1** °thinking, °logic, °analysis, rationalization: *The entire argument falls to pieces because of faulty reasoning.* **2** reasons, arguments, premises, °rationale, postulate, °hypothesis, theory, °explanation, explication: *His reasoning had no effect on her—she simply refused to listen.*

reassure *v.* °comfort, °encourage, hearten, °buoy (up), °bolster, °cheer, uplift, inspirit, °brace, °support, restore °confidence to, set *or* put (someone's) mind at rest, set *or* put (someone) at ease, °settle (someone's) doubts: *The minister reassured the public regarding the safety of public transport.*

rebate *n.* **1** °discount, reduction, °deduction, °allowance, mark-down, cut-back, refund, repayment, *Colloq US* °rake-off: *This coupon entitles you to a rebate of ten per cent on the purchase of four new tyres.* **2** °kickback, °percentage, °rake-off, commission, °cut, °bribe, °graft, *Colloq chiefly US* payola, *US* plugola: *He gets a rebate of five per cent on every client he refers to the solicitor.*
—*v.* **3** °discount, °reduce, °deduct, °mark down, refund, °repay; kick back: *Periodicals rebate fifteen per cent of their gross advertising revenue to the agencies that place ads.*

rebel *v.* **1** °revolt, °mutiny, °rise up: *The people will rebel if subjected to more oppression.* **2** Often, ***rebel against***: °defy, °flout, °dare, °challenge; °disobey, dissent: *It is in the nature of young people to rebel against authority and the status quo.*
—*n.* **3** °revolutionary, revolutionist, insurgent, insurrrectionist, mutineer, resister, °resistance fighter, freedom fighter: *We call ourselves fighters for justice, but the unjust call us rebels and traitors.* **4** heretic, °nonconformist, apostate, dissenter, recusant, °schismatic: *James's problem was that he was a rebel without a cause.*

rebellion *n.* **1** °uprising, °revolution, °mutiny, insurrection, °revolt, insurgence *or* insurgency: *Rebellion is the last recourse against tyranny.* **2** insubordination, disobedience, defiance, °resistance, rebelliousness, contumacy: *Her rebellion against parental authority led her to leave home at sixteen.*

rebellious *adj.* **1** °insubordinate, °defiant, °mutinous, °revolutionary, contumacious, insurgent, insurrectionary, °seditious: *The more rebellious students organized mass meetings against the university authorities.* **2** unmanageable, °disobedient, °incorrigible, °ungovernable, °unruly, °difficult, refractory, °stubborn, °obstinate, °recalcitrant: *They resented being treated as rebellious children.*

rebirth *n.* °renaissance *or* renascence, °revival, renewal, reawakening, °resurgence, revitalization, resurrection, regeneration, rejuvenation, °restoration, new °beginning, reincarnation; metempsychosis, palingenesis: *The 15th century marked the rebirth of learning in Europe after the so-called Dark Ages.*

rebound *v.* **1** °spring back, °bounce, °recoil, ricochet, resile: *The ball rebounded from the goalpost.*
—*n.* **2** °bounce, °recoil, ricochet, °return, comeback, °repercussion, °backlash, reflex: *Carter caught the ball on the rebound.*

rebuff *n.* **1** °rejection, snub, °check, °denial, °repulse, °refusal, °dismissal, °defeat, repudiation, °slight, discouragement, *Colloq* cold °shoulder, °cut, °put-down, °brush-off, *Slang US* °brush: *Ellie's friendly approach was met with an abrupt rebuff.*
—*v.* **2** °reject, snub, °check, °deny, °repel, °drive away, °spurn, °repulse, °refuse, °dismiss, °defeat, °repudiate, °slight, °ignore, send (someone) to Coventry, *Colloq* give (someone) the cold °shoulder, °cut, °put (someone) down, °brush (someone) off, give (someone) the °brush-off, tell (someone) where to go *or* get off, tell (someone) where to get lost, *Slang* give (someone) his *or* her walking papers, °freeze (someone) out, *US* give (someone) the °brush, show (someone) the door: *She rebuffed everyone who proposed marriage to her, preferring to remain a spinster.*

rebuke *v.* **1** °scold, reproach, admonish, °reprove, °reprimand, °lecture, censure, chide, reprehend, °berate, °castigate, °criticize, take to °task, °upbraid, revile, *Colloq* °dress down, °bawl out, give (someone) a piece of one's °mind, haul (someone) over the coals, let (someone) have it, give (someone) hell *or* what for, °tell (someone) off, tell (someone) where to get off, *Brit* carpet, tear (someone) off a strip, tick (someone) off, wig, °blow (someone) up, give (someone) a wigging, *US and Canadian* rake (someone) over the coals, give (someone) the business, °chew out: *The headmaster severely rebuked those boys who had violated the school curfew.*
—*n.* **2** scolding, reproach, admonition, °reproof, °reprimand, °lecture, censure, chiding, reprehension, berating, castigation, °criticism, upbraiding, revilement, °tongue-lashing, *Colloq* dressing-down, what for, *Brit* wigging, blow-up *or* blowing up, *Slang* °hell: *Rawlings was let off with nothing more than a rebuke.*

rebut *v.* refute, °deny, °disprove, confute, invalidate, negate, °discredit, belie, °contradict, controvert, °puncture, expose, °destroy, °ruin, °devastate, *Colloq* shoot full of holes, knock the bottom out of, shoot down, blow sky-high: *We have all the evidence needed to rebut the contention that our client was anywhere near the scene of the crime.*

rebuttal *n.* °answer, °reply, °retort, °response, rejoinder, counter-argument, riposte, retaliation, °denial, refutation, contradiction, confutation, *Colloq* comeback: *In rebuttal, the defence tried to prove that the witness for the prosecution had been bribed.*

recalcitrant *adj.* °stubborn, °obstinate, °wilful, °defiant, refractory, headstrong, °perverse, °contrary, contumacious, °mutinous, °rebellious, fractious, °unruly, unmanageable, °ungovernable, uncontrollable, wayward, °insubordinate, intractable, unsubmissive, unyielding, unbending, adamant, °immovable, °inflexible, °stiff, °firm: *Recalcitrant students who refuse to obey the rules risk expulsion.*

recall *v.* **1** °remember, °recollect, °think back to, °reminisce over *or* about, call to °mind: *I like to recall the happy days we had at Biarritz.* **2** °withdraw, °retract, °call back, °summon: *The legions guarding the frontier provinces were recalled to Rome.* **3** rescind, °cancel, annul, nullify, °retract, °withdraw, °revoke, °recant, °take back, call back; disavow, disown, °deny: *Despite the fact that you might have been hasty, you cannot recall your promise.*
—*n.* **4** °memory, °recollection, remembering, °remembrance: *He had a loving and near-photographic recall of their holiday in the Alps.* **5** withdrawal, recantation, °cancellation, revocation, annulment, nullification, recision, rescission, retraction, °repeal, disavowal, °denial: *The decision was made without any possibility of recall.* **6** withdrawal, retraction, °return: *The manufacturer's recall of the shipment of defective toasters was voluntary.*

recant *v.* °recall, forswear, °deny, rescind, °repudiate, disavow, disclaim, °withdraw, °revoke, °retract, °forsake, °abandon, apostasize, °renounce, abjure, °take back: *He was given three days to recant: otherwise, he would be executed for heresy.*

recapitulate *v.* summarize, °sum up; °repeat, °go over (again), °reiterate, restate, °review; °recount, °enumerate, °recite, °relate, °list, *Colloq* recap: *I shall* *begin by recapitulating some of the issues which I covered in my last lecture.*

recede *v.* **1** °ebb, °subside, °fall *or* °go *or* move back, abate, °return, °withdraw, °retreat, back up: *As the flood waters receded, people began to go back to their homes.* **2** °diminish, lessen, °decline, °dwindle, °shrink, °wane, °fade, °become more °distant *or* less likely: *The likelihood of our being rescued receded with each passing day.*

receipt *n.* **1** sales receipt, register receipt, sales °slip, ticket, °stub, counterfoil, °proof of °purchase, voucher: *Any request for a return or exchange must be accompanied by a receipt.* **2** °delivery, acceptance, °reception, °arrival: *He has acknowledged receipt of the merchandise.* **3** ***receipts***: °income, °proceeds, °gate, takings, °gains, °return, *Colloq* °take: *The receipts from ticket sales were below expectations.*

receive *v.* **1** °get, °obtain, °come by, °collect, °take (into one's °possession), °accept, be given, °acquire, °come into, °inherit, °gain, °profit, °make: *She received a large sum of money from the sale of the house. What will he receive when his aunt dies?* **2** °earn, be paid, °make, °draw, °gross, °net, °clear, °pocket, *Colloq* °take, walk off *or* away with, *US* °pull down: *He receives a bigger weekly salary than I make in a year.* **3** °greet, °meet, °welcome; °show in, give entrée, °let in, °admit: *We received our guests in the foyer.* **4** °experience, °undergo, °endure, °suffer, °bear, °sustain, be subjected to, °meet with: *In return for helping him all I received was a punch in the nose.* **5** °gather, °hear, °learn, ascertain, be told, be informed *or* notified of, °find out, °pick up: *We only received the information yesterday that you were coming to stay for a month.*

recent *adj.* °late, °latest, °new, °just out, °brand-new, °fresh; °current, °modern, up to °date, late-model: *This feature is now supplied as standard on all our more recent models. Recent arrivals will be interviewed by the committee.*

receptacle *n.* container, holder, repository; °box, tin, can, °case, °casket, °chest, reliquary, °vessel, °bag, basket: *Please put the rubbish into the receptacle. She kept the diamond in a velvet-lined receptacle which she always carried with her.*

reception *n.* **1** °welcome, °greeting, °treatment, °reaction, °response: *My suggestion that we open a bottle of champagne met with a warm reception.* **2** °party, levee, °social, soirée, °function; °opening, °preview, vernissage, *Colloq* do: *Would you like to go to a reception at the new art gallery next week?*

receptive *adj.* **1** °open, °hospitable, amenable, pervious, persuasible, °tractable, °flexible, pliant, °interested, °willing, °responsive: *I have always found Peggy receptive to suggestions on improving productivity and efficiency.* **2** °quick, °alert, °perceptive, °astute, °intelligent, °keen, °sharp, °bright, °sensitive: *Julia has a receptive mind.*

recess *n.* **1** alcove, °niche, °nook, °cranny, bay, °hollow: *The statuette fits perfectly in that recess outside the library.* **2** °respite, rest, °interlude, time off, °break, °intermission, breather, breathing-space, °pause; °holiday, vacation: *A brief recess has been scheduled to allow us to relax before continuing.* **3** ***recesses***: innermost reaches, corners, °secret places, °depths, penetralia: *I searched for her name in the recesses of my mind.*

recession *n.* °set-back, (economic) downturn, °slump, °decline, °dip, °depression: *The slowing of the economy led to a recession which soon deepened into a depression.*

recipe *n.* **1** °formula, °prescription: *Elizabeth gave me a marvellous recipe for chocolate cake.* **2** °plan, °procedure, °method, °approach, °technique, °way, °means, °system, °programme, modus operandi, *Colloq US* MO: *The minister insists that his recipe for conquering inflation will work.*

recipient *n.* receiver, beneficiary, °heir *or* heiress, legatee: *Who is the current recipient of her favours?*

reciprocal *adj.* °mutual, exchanged, returned, complementary, correlative, °common, shared, °joint, requited: *The reciprocal courtesies enjoyed among our neighbours benefit us all.*

reciprocate *v.* °repay, recompense, °requite, °exchange, °return, °trade, °match, °equal, °correspond: *You have always been very kind to me and I want to reciprocate in any way I can.*

recital *n.* **1** (°solo) concert, °performance, musicale, °presentation, °show, °entertainment: *We have tickets to a recital for that night.* **2** °report, °narration, °account, °recitation, °description, °relation, °telling, recounting, °narrative, °rendition, °interpretation, °version, recapitulation, °rehearsal, °repetition, *Colloq* recap: *A reporter who was on the flight provided us with a recital of the events leading up to the crash.*

recitation *n.* **1** reciting, °performance, reading, monologue: *At the age of four Simon delighted his parents with his recitation of 'The Charge of the Light Brigade'.* **2** See **recital, 2,** above.

recite *v.* **1** °quote, °repeat, °present: *In the old days, children were often called upon to recite poems they had learned by heart.* **2** °report, °narrate, °recount, °relate, °tell, °describe, °detail, °chronicle, °list, °share, °recapitulate, °repeat, *Colloq* recap: *Again I recited every particular of the hold-up that I could recall.*

reckless *adj.* °careless, °rash, °thoughtless, incautious, °heedless, °foolhardy, °imprudent, unwise, injudicious, °impulsive, °irresponsible, negligent, unmindful, °foolish, devil-may-care, °daredevil, °wild, °breakneck, °dangerous, madcap, °mad, °hare-brained: *I won't go with Oliver because he's a reckless driver.*

reckon *v.* **1** Often, ***reckon up***: °calculate, °compute, °add (up), °figure (up), °tally (up), °sum up, °total (up), °work out *or* up: *If you reckon up the bill, I'll pay it at once.* **2** °include, °count, °number, °enumerate, °list, °name, °consider, °account, °judge, deem, look upon, °regard, °view, °think of, °hold, °gauge, °estimate, appraise, value, °rank, °rate, °class: *I have always reckoned Arthur as being among my closest friends.* **3** °suppose, °think, °assume, °presume, °dare say, °venture, °imagine, °fancy, °consider, conclude, be of the °opinion, *US or colloq* °guess: *She reckoned that no one could accuse her of idle chatter.* **4** ***reckon on*** *or* ***upon***: °count on, °rely on, °depend on, °lean on, °trust in, take for granted, *Colloq* bank on: *I was reckoning on your help, and I hope you won't disappoint me.* **5** ***reckon with***: **a** °settle (accounts) with, take °care of, °look after, °see *or* °attend to, °deal with, °handle, pay °attention to, °think about: *I have to go now, but I'll reckon with you later.* **b** take into °account *or* °consideration, °consider, °contemplate, °account for, °remember, bear in °mind: *He thought he had got away with it, but he failed to reckon with Inspector Harris of the CID.*

reckoning *n.* **1** counting, calculating, °calculation, computation, enumeration, °addition: *The reckoning of Old Style dates used the Julian calendar.* **2** °bill, °account, invoice, *US* °check, *Colloq chiefly US and Canadian* °tab: *If you let me have the reckoning, I'll pay it with my credit card.* **3** (last) °judgement, °retribution, final °account(ing) *or* °settlement, °doom: *On the day of reckoning we must all face the music.*

reclaim *v.* °restore, °recover, °rescue, °redeem, °salvage, °save, regain, °retrieve, regenerate, °rejuvenate: *Much of the farmland was reclaimed from the sea.*

recline *v.* °lie (down), °lie back, °lean back, °lounge, °rest, °repose, °sprawl, loll, °stretch out: *Just recline on the sofa and make yourself comfortable.*

recluse *n.* °hermit, anchorite *or* anchoress, °monk *or* nun, eremite: *For the past ten years, he has been living the life of a recluse.*

reclusive *adj.* °solitary, lone, °secluded, °isolated, eremitic(al), hermitic(al), anchoritic, monastic, cloistered, sequestered, °retiring, °shut off: *She insists that she enjoys her reclusive existence.*

recognition *n.* **1** °identification, detection: *Her recognition of the man on TV led to his arrest.*

2 °acknowledgement, °notice, °attention, °cognizance, acceptance, awareness, °perception, °admission; °honour, °appreciation: *The award was a recognition of his contributions to scientific knowledge.*

recognize *v.* 1 °identify, °detect, °place, °recall, °remember, °recollect, °know (again): *I recognized him from seeing his picture in the newspaper.* 2 °acknowledge, °perceive, °understand, °realize, °see, °admit, °accept, own, °concede, °allow, °grant, °appreciate, °respect, be °aware of: *He refuses to recognize that he is responsible for his own actions.* 3 °approve, °sanction, °endorse, °accept, validate, °ratify: *A totalitarian government refuses to recognize the rights of the individual.* 4 °honour, give °recognition to, °salute, show °gratitude *or* °appreciation, °reward, °distinguish, pay °respect, do °homage: *The society recognizes Dr Jackson for his many contributions to science.*

recoil *v.* 1 °jerk *or* °jump *or* °spring back, °start, °flinch, wince, °shrink, blench, balk *or* baulk, shy (away) (from): *He recoiled when confronted with the evidence of the gruesome experiments with live animals.* 2 °rebound, °bounce back, resile, °kick back: *When fired, the gun recoiled, bruising his shoulder.*
—*n.* 3 °kick, °rebound, °repercussion, °backlash: *He was unprepared for the violent recoil of the old gun.*

recollect *v.* °recall, °remember, call to °mind: *Now that you mention it, I do recollect your asking me to buy some milk when I went out.*

recollection *n.* °memory, °recall, °remembrance, °impression, °reminiscence: *My brother's recollection of our grandparents is quite different from mine.*

recommend *v.* 1 °counsel, °advise, °guide, °urge, exhort, °suggest, °advocate, °propose, (°put) °forward, °propound, °persuade: *He recommended that the entire system should be changed.* 2 °endorse, °praise, commend, °mention °favourably, °vouch for, °second, °subscribe to, °back, °push, °favour, °approve, °underwrite, °stand up for, °support, °promote, *Colloq* °tout, °plug: *I wish Charles would stop recommending his brother-in-law for a job with us.* 3 make °attractive *or* °advisable *or* °interesting *or* °acceptable: *Wendover has little to recommend it as a tourist spot.*

recommendation *n.* 1 °counsel, °advice, °guidance, urging, exhortation, °direction, °encouragement, °suggestion, prompting, advocacy, °proposal: *It was on your recommendation that we tried that restaurant.* 2 °endorsement, °praise, commendation, °favourable °mention, °backing, °blessing, °approval, approbation, °support, °promotion, good word, °testimonial, °say-so: *The chairman of the board gave Caswell's brother-in-law his personal recommendation.*

reconcile *v.* 1 °get *or* bring (back) together, °unite, reunite, °settle *or* °resolve differences between, °restore °harmony between, make °peace between, placate, make compatible: *Do you think that a marriage counsellor could help reconcile John and Martha?* 2 °resign, °submit, °accommodate, °adjust: *Lady Mary Wortley Montague wrote that she was reconciled to being a woman when she reflected that she was thus in no danger of ever marrying one.*

reconciliation *n.* 1 conciliation, appeasement, propitiation, pacification, placation, *rapprochement*, reconcilement, °understanding, détente, reunion, °harmony, concord, °accord, amity, °rapport: *It was with great effort that the reconciliation between the two families was finally arranged.* 2 compromise, °settlement, °agreement, arbitration, conformity, compatibility, °adjustment: *Reconciliation of their differences seems difficult but not impossible.*

recondite *adj.* abstruse, arcane, °obscure, esoteric, °deep, °profound, °incomprehensible, unfathomable, impenetrable, undecipherable, °opaque, °dark, °occult, cabbalistic *or* kabbalistic, °inexplicable, enigmatic: *I have difficulty following the more recondite aspects of information theory.*

reconnaissance *n.* °survey, °examination, scouting, °exploration, reconnoitring, °investigation, inspection, °scrutiny, *Slang Brit* recce: *Their reconnaissance showed that the enemy forces had withdrawn.*

reconnoitre *v.* °survey, °examine, °scout (out), °scan, °explore, °investigate, °inspect, °scrutinize, °check out, °check up (on), *Slang Brit* recce: *We reconnoitred the territory and reported the enemy troop movements.*

record *v.* 1 °write (down), °transcribe, °document, °register, °note, make a °notation (of), °take down, °put *or* °set down, log, °chronicle, °report, °itemize, °list, °enumerate: *I recorded the events of the day in my diary.* 2 °tell of, °relate, °recount, °narrate, °recite: *The chronicle records an eyewitness account of the battle.*
—*n.* 3 recording, °report, °document, log, °journal, °memorandum, °note, °notation, °minute(s), transactions, archive(s), annal(s), °chronicle, °diary, °account, dossier, °register, °list, catalogue: *Patricia has kept a careful record of all the men whose books she has ever read.* 4 documentation, °data, °information, °evidence; °memorial, °memento, souvenir: *There is no record of your birth in the church archive. I took away a piece of the Berlin Wall as a record of my visit.* 5 (°best) °performance, track record, °accomplishment; time; distance; °height: *Her records for the 110-metre hurdles and the high jump still stand.* 6 °accomplishment(s), °deed(s), °history, °reputation, curriculum vitae, CV, *Colloq* track record: *He has a record of being late everywhere. His criminal record is none too savoury.* 7 disc, recording, album, release, LP (= 'long playing'), 78, 33⅓, 45, EP (= 'extended play'), compact disc, CD, *Brit* gramophone record, *US* phonograph record, *Colloq* single, *Slang US* platter: *We put a jazz combo together and cut a few records last year.* 8 ***off the record***: °confidential(ly), °private(ly), not for publication, °secret(ly), in °confidence, °unofficial(ly), sub rosa: *We cannot publish his statement, which was off the record. Off the record, I'll tell you where Hazel is staying.*
—*adj.* 9 record-breaking, °extreme: *Last week we had a record snowfall.*

recount *v.* 1 °relate, °narrate, °tell, °recite, °report, °communicate, °impart, °unfold: *The old man recounted for us the legend of the two-headed lamb.* 2 particularize, °review, °detail, °describe, °enumerate, °specify: *Must I recount every particular all over again?*

recoup *v.* regain, °make good, °make up, recompense, °repay, °recover; refund, °redeem, °reimburse, remunerate: *From his profits on the Culpepper deal, he recouped all the losses he had sustained when Cranston Ltd failed.*

recourse *n.* 1 °resort, access, entrée, °admittance, availability: *They are completely isolated and without recourse to help from the outside world.* 2 °resource, backup, °reserve, °refuge, place to turn, °alternative, °remedy: *The company has no recourse against the authorities.*

recover *v.* 1 regain, °get *or* °take *or* °win *or* make back (again), °recoup, repossess, retake, recapture, °restore, °retrieve, °reclaim, °redeem: *It was impossible to recover the time lost. After a fierce battle, the territory was recovered.* 2 get °well *or* °better, °recuperate, °convalesce, °mend, °return to °health, regain one's °strength *or* °health, be on the °mend, °heal, °improve, °revive, °rally, take a °turn for the °better, get back on one's feet, °pull through: *It took me a week to recover from the operation. Lucy had a virus, but she's recovering now.* 3 °save, °salvage, °deliver, °rescue, °return, °bring back, °reclaim, °retrieve: *They never did recover the gold from the sunken ship.*

recovery *n.* 1 recuperation, convalescence, °restoration, °improvement, healing, °rally, °turn for the °better; °rise, °revival, °increase, amelioration, bettering, betterment, °advance, °gain, advancement, *Colloq* pick-up, comeback: *After so serious an illness, Bentley has made a remarkable recovery. Share prices staged a recovery after the reduction in interest rates.* 2 retrieval, recouping, repossession, retaking, °restoration, reclamation; recapture, redemption: *The recovery of the stolen gems was credited to excellent* *detective work. Hard fighting resulted in the recovery of the land west of the river.* **3** °salvage, °delivery, deliverance, °rescue, °return, °saving, reclamation, retrieval: *Recovery of the climbers' bodies from the ravine was very hazardous.*

recreation *n.* °entertainment, °amusement, °enjoyment, °diversion, °distraction, °fun and games, °leisure (°activity), °pastime, °relaxation, °sport, °play: *What do you like to do for recreation? His favourite recreation is building model aeroplanes.*

recrimination *n.* counter-accusation, countercharge, retaliation, counter-attack, blaming, °aspersion, °reprisal: *Recriminations for real and imagined ills were continually exchanged throughout their marriage.*

recruit *v.* **1** °draft, °induct, °enlist, °enrol, °muster, °raise, °call up, conscript, °mobilize, impress, levy: *Owing to the nefarious enemy attack, there was little time to recruit men for a strong fighting force.* —*n.* **2** conscript, trainee, beginner, °apprentice, °initiate, °novice, neophyte, tiro *or* tyro, *US* draftee, enlistee, *Colloq* °greenhorn, rookie: *The new recruits have to be issued with their uniforms and other gear.*

rectify *v.* °correct, °revise, redress, put *or* set °right, °cure, °repair, °remedy, °improve, emend, °fix, °adjust, °square, ameliorate: *What do you intend to do to rectify the damage you have done?*

rectitude *n.* °propriety, correctness, °morality, uprightness, °probity, °virtue, decency, goodness, °honesty, °integrity, incorruptibility, righteousness, °principle, °good °character, respectability, unimpeachability: *Fred's unquestioned moral rectitude makes him an outstanding candidate for membership.*

recumbent *adj.* reclining, °lying down, °flat on one's back, °horizontal, °lying, reposing, accumbent, decumbent, °supine, stretched out; °leaning (back): *Oscar resumed his recumbent posture, sprawled out on the cushions.*

recuperate *v.* °improve, °recover, °convalesce, get °better, °rally, °revive, °mend, °heal, get back on one's feet, regain one's °health *or* strength, °pull through, °survive, take a °turn for the °better: *Paul went to Ibiza to recuperate from his illness.*

recur *v.* °return, °happen *or* °occur again, reoccur, °repeat, come (back) again, reappear: *The condition recurred after a year, and he was obliged to have another operation.*

recurrent *adj.* repeated, recurring, returning, reoccurring, reappearing, °frequent, °periodic, cyclical, °regular, °repetitive, °repetitious, °persistent, incessant, °continual, °intermittent, °habitual, iterative: *She told the psychiatrist about her recurrent dream of flying.*

redeem *v.* **1** °reclaim, °recover, regain, repossess, °retrieve, °get back, °buy back, repurchase; °pay off, *Brit* °clear: *He went into the pawn shop to redeem the gold watch.* **2** °rescue, °ransom, °deliver, °free, °save, °liberate, set °free, °emancipate, °release: *He was able to redeem the boy only after paying the kidnappers.* **3** °exchange, °cash (in), collect on, °trade in: *These coupons must be redeemed before the end of the month.* **4** °rehabilitate, °save, °reform, °convert, absolve, °restore to °favour, reinstate: *She can be redeemed only by atoning for her sins.* **5** make °amends for, °make up for, °atone for, redress, °compensate for, °offset, make °restitution for: *Do you think that 200 hours of community service was enough to redeem his crime of snatching handbags in the shopping centre?* **6** °perform, °fulfil, °keep, °make good (on), °discharge, °satisfy, °abide by, keep °faith with, be °faithful to, hold to, °carry out, °see through: *Helen is here to redeem her promise to help at the charity bazaar.*

red-handed *adj.* in the (very) °act, (in) flagrante delicto, *Colloq* with one's hand in the till, *US* with one's hand in the cookie-jar: *There's no doubt that Rick did it—he was caught red-handed.*

redolent *adj.* **1** °fragrant, sweet-smelling, °aromatic, perfumed, odorous, scented, °savoury: *The entire house was redolent with the odour of pine needles.* **2** ***redolent with*** *or* ***of***: °reminiscent of, °suggestive of, evocative of, remindful of, °characteristic of, having the earmarks *or* °hallmark of: *The style of the film is redolent of 1930s Hollywood.*

reduce *v.* **1** °cut (back), °cut down (on), °decrease, °diminish, °moderate, abate, lessen, °shorten, truncate, °abbreviate, °abridge, °curtail, crop, °trim, compress, °restrict, °limit, °stunt: *We must reduce expenses this year.* **2** °ease (up on), °let up (on), °decrease, °mitigate, °tone down, slacken up (on): *It will reduce the burden of your costs if you share with me.* **3** lose weight, °slim (down), °diet, °trim down, *Chiefly US* slenderize: *You'll have to reduce to fit into that dress, Betty.* **4** °change, °modify, °adjust, °turn, °convert; °break down *or* up, °grind, °rub, triturate, °pulp, °powder: *Payment of the debt reduced me to poverty. The first step is to reduce the liquid to a thick extract.* **5** °cut, °decrease, °trim, °bring down, °lower, °drop, °mark down, °slash, *Colloq* °knock down: *The prices on these shoes have been reduced for a quick sale.* **6** demote, °degrade, °lower, °downgrade, °break; °humble; *Military US and Canadian* bust: *He was reduced in rank from sergeant to private.* **7** °diminish, lessen, °bring down, °depreciate, °subdue, °belittle, °minimize: *He was reduced in her estimation when she saw the deprecating way his friends treated him.* **8** *Medicine* set, °adjust, reset: *The doctor caused little pain when he reduced her dislocated finger.*

redundant *adj.* **1** °superfluous, °unnecessary, °surplus, inessential *or* unessential, °non-essential, unneeded, unwanted, *de trop*, in °excess, °excessive: *He was made redundant at the age of forty-five and was unable to find another job.* **2** °wordy, verbose, prolix, over-long, long-winded, °repetitious, tautological *or* tautologous, circumlocutory, °roundabout: *The book would be improved if certain redundant passages were improved.*

reek *v.* **1** stink *or* °smell (to high heaven), *Slang Brit* pong, hum: *Allie reeks from cleaning out the stable.* **2** smoke, steam: *It is because it used to reek so badly that Edinburgh acquired its nickname, 'Auld Reekie'.* —*n.* **3** stink, °stench, fetor *or* foetor, miasma, mephitis, °odour, °smell, *Slang Brit* hum, pong: *The reek of rotting vegetation permeated the atmosphere.* **4** °fumes, smoke, steam, °vapour, °exhalation, cloud, °mist: *He delighted in the redolent reek that arose from the haggis.*

reel *v.* **1** °stagger, °totter, waver, °stumble, °lurch, falter, °roll, °rock, °sway, °flounder, °pitch: *Chris came reeling down the lane, dead drunk.* **2** ***reel off***: °list, °recite, °rattle off, °enumerate, °review, °itemize, °name, °read off, °call off, °run through, °run over: *Under questioning, the suspect began to reel off the names of his accomplices.*

refer *v.* **1** Often, ***refer to***: allude to, make °reference to, °mention, make mention of, °touch on, °bring up, advert to, °speak of, turn *or* call *or* direct °attention to, °direct to, °point to, °indicate, °specify, °name, °concern, °quote, cite, make a °note of, take °note of, °note: *A footnote refers to the author's article on netsukes.* **2** °assign, °hand over, °pass on *or* over, °send, °direct, °commit: *I was referred to your office for information about rates. The question will be referred to committee.* **3** Usually, ***refer to***: °look at, °use, °study, °check, °consult, °resort to, have °recourse to, °turn to, °appeal to, °confer with; °talk to, °ask, °inquire *or* °enquire of, °apply to: *For information about words, you should refer to a dictionary. Refer to the departmental office for Professor Clarke's address.* **4** Usually, ***refer to***: °mean, °signify, °denote, °say: *What are you referring to?*

reference *n.* **1** allusion, °mention, °remark, referral, °direction, °indication, °specification, naming, °quotation, citation, °note, °notation, notification, °hint, intimation, °innuendo, insinuation: *I can't find a reference in any footnote. Few readers make use of the bibliographical references in scholarly articles. Her persistent references to my baldness embarrass me.*

2 °regard, °concern, °connection, °respect, °relation, °relevance, pertinence: *People are selected without reference to race, creed, colour, sex, or age.* 3 °endorsement, °recommendation, °testimonial, certification; credentials: *I relied on my former employer to give me a good reference. We shall not be needing to take up your references.*

refine *v.* 1 °purify, °cleanse, °clear, °clarify, decontaminate: *They continued to refine the liquid till all the impurities were gone.* 2 °cultivate, °civilize, °polish, °improve, elevate, °perfect: *He is trying to refine his speech by getting rid of his country accent.* 3 hone, °sharpen, °concentrate, °focus, subtilize: *We ought to refine our argument for higher wages before approaching the management.*

refined *adj.* 1 °cultivated, cultured, civilized, °polished, °sophisticated, urbane, °elegant, °well-bred, °genteel, courtly, °ladylike, gentlemanly, °polite, °courteous, mannerly, well-mannered, °gracious, °gentle, °noble, aristocratic, °dignified, °elevated, *Colloq* °posh: *It is seldom that I find myself in such refined company.* 2 °subtle, °discriminating, discerning, °sensitive, °fastidious, °nice, °precise, °exacting, cultured, °educated, °cultivated, °knowledgeable, advanced, °sophisticated: *Her taste in the visual arts is fairly refined, but she knows little about music.* 3 °exact, °precise, °fine, °subtle, °sensitive, °nice, °sophisticated: *In his poetry one encounters an extremely refined use of metaphor. These new devices are far more refined than any previously available.* 4 purified, clarified, cleansed, °pure, °clean; distilled: *Only refined chemicals may be used in pharmaceuticals.*

refinement *n.* 1 °culture, °polish, °elegance, °sophistication, urbanity, urbaneness, °breeding, cultivation, gentility, °propriety, courtliness, °civility, politeness, politesse, °delicacy, °tact, °diplomacy, °finesse, suavity, suaveness, °taste, tastefulness, °discrimination, discernment, °sensitivity: *He drank thirstily, with no pretence at refinement.* 2 °subtlety, nicety, nuance, °distinction, °detail, °fine °point, °delicacy, minutia; fastidiousness, finickiness: *The latest version contains refinements that are beyond the appreciation of all but a few.* 3 refining, purification, purifying, clarification, clarifying, cleaning, cleansing; filtration, distillation: *The sugar must undergo refinement before being sold commercially.* 4 °improvement, betterment, bettering, enhancement, °development, °perfection: *She is working on the refinement of her technique before performing in public.*

reflect *v.* 1 °mirror, send *or* throw back, °reproduce, °return; °echo: *The smooth surface of the lake reflected the sunlight. The radio waves are reflected and focused by this parabolic dish.* 2 °show, °demonstrate, °exhibit, °illustrate, °exemplify, °reveal, °lay °bare, expose, °display, °disclose, bring to °light, uncover, °point to, °indicate, °suggest, °evidence: *They say that your true emotions are reflected in your dreams. His crime reflects the depths of depravity to which a person can sink.* 3 Often, ***reflect about*** *or* ***on***: °think (about *or* over *or* on), °contemplate, °muse (about *or* on), °consider, °ponder (about *or* over *or* on), °deliberate (on *or* over), ruminate *or* °meditate (about *or* on *or* over), cogitate (about *or* on *or* over); °mull over, °weigh, °evaluate, °examine: *I was just sitting here reflecting. I was reflecting on what you said about wanting to quit your job.* 4 ***reflect on*** *or* ***upon***: °result in, °end in, °bring, °attract, °cast, °throw: *The success of the team reflects credit on the coach.*

reflection *n.* 1 °image, °echo, *Brit* reflexion: *Sonar works by detecting the reflection of generated sound waves.* 2 °thought, °thinking, meditation, meditating, °consideration, cogitation, rumination, deliberation, deliberating, pondering, °study, cerebration: *After a moment's reflection, I arrived at the same conclusion as you had.* 3 °aspersion, °imputation; °effect: *Any reflection on his reputation might harm his career.* 4 °result, °sign, °token, °symbol, °mark; °evidence, °testimony, testament, °proof, substantiation, corroboration: *Her tears are a reflection of how she feels about having betrayed me.*

reflective *adj.* reflecting, °thoughtful, °pensive, contemplative, meditating, musing, °meditative, cogitating, cogitative, ruminating, deliberative, deliberating, pondering: *I found Alan in a reflective mood, staring out of the window.*

reform *v.* 1 °improve, °better, ameliorate, meliorate, emend, °rectify, °correct, °mend, °repair, °fix, °remedy, redo, °revise, revolutionize, °rehabilitate, remodel, refashion, °renovate, reorganize, rebuild, °recover: *The first thing to be done was to reform the political system.* 2 °mend one's ways, turn over a new leaf, *Colloq* go °straight: *After three convictions in as many years, there seemed little chance that he would reform.* —*n.* 3 °improvement, betterment, amelioration, melioration, emendation, rectification, °correction, rehabilitation, °change, modification, perestroika, reorganization, renovation, °recovery: *Many believe that prison reform would reduce crime by second offenders. The many reforms introduced by the president were condemned by hard-line party members.*

reform school *n. Brit* youth custody centre, CHE (= 'community home (with education on the premises)'), *Formerly* Borstal, approved school, *US* reformatory: *He was sent to a reform school because of his persistent misbehaviour.*

refrain[1] *v.* 1 Usually, ***refrain from***: °keep (from), forbear, abstain (from), eschew, °avoid: *Whatever you do, refrain from whistling on board his boat.* 2 °stop, °cease, °give up, °discontinue, desist, °quit, °leave off, °renounce: *You must refrain from calling the headmaster 'Pops', even if he is your father.*

refrain[2] *n.* °melody, °song, °tune, chorus, °burden, reprise: *It was one of those long boring folk songs with a refrain that we were all supposed to join in.*

refresh *v.* 1 °enliven, °renew, °revive, °freshen (up), resuscitate, bring back to °life, breathe °new °life into, invigorate, °vitalize, °energize, °brace, °fortify, exhilarate, revitalize, reinvigorate, reanimate: *I felt fully refreshed after a short nap.* 2 °arouse, °rouse, °awaken, waken, reawaken, °stimulate, °jog, °prod, °activate: *Would you mind refreshing my memory as to when and where we last met?* 3 °fix up, °repair, redo, °revamp, °overhaul, °spruce up, recondition, °renovate, °refurbish, refurnish; °renew, restock, °restore: *We took the opportunity of the ship's arrival to refresh our supplies.*

refreshing *adj.* °invigorating, °stimulating, °bracing, °exhilarating, °fresh, inspiriting, fortifying, °tonic, like a breath of °fresh air, rejuvenating, enlivening, vitalizing, revitalizing; cooling, thirst-quenching, slaking: *It's refreshing to be around young people. I would love a cool refreshing glass of beer right now.*

refreshment *n.* 1 Usually, ***refreshments***: °nourishment, nutriment, °sustenance, restorative, °food, °drink(s), edibles, eatables, °bite, °snack(s), °titbit(s), *Slang* grub, eats, chow, nosh: *Will they be serving refreshments after the meeting?* 2 stimulation, invigoration, exhilaration, °tonic, rejuvenation, enlivenment, °revival, °restoration, renewal, resuscitation, fortification, °reinforcement: *The library provides an oasis of mental refreshment.*

refrigerate *v.* °cool, °chill, keep °cool *or* °cold *or* chilled, ice, °freeze: *The soufflé must be refrigerated for three hours to allow it to set.*

refuge *n.* 1 °sanctuary, °shelter, haven, asylum, °protection, °cover, °retreat, °harbour, °security, °safe °house, °stronghold, citadel, bolt-hole, °hideaway, hide-out, *Colloq* hidy-hole *or* hidey-hole: *The abandoned mine served as a refuge from the storm.* 2 °excuse, °pretext, °resort, °recourse, °ruse, °trick, °stratagem, °subterfuge, °dodge, °evasion, °expedient: *Patriotism is often the last refuge of a scoundrel.*

refugee *n.* °fugitive, °runaway, escapee, displaced °person, DP, °exile, émigré: *The problem of the refugees was most acute after the war.*

refurbish *v.* °restore, refurnish, redecorate, °clean (up), °polish, °renew, °renovate, °spruce up, remodel, refit, °overhaul, °repair, recondition, °revamp, rebuild, *Colloq* do up, *US* °fix up: *The person who bought the house refurbished it completely, at enormous expense.*

refusal *n.* **1** °denial, °rejection, °disapproval, turn-down: *She pleaded against the grand vizier's refusal to grant amnesty to her brother.* **2** °option, °choice, °privilege, disposal: *We were promised first refusal on the house should it come on the market.*

refuse[1] *v.* **1** °decline, °reject, °spurn, °repudiate, °turn down, °rebuff, give (something) the °thumbs down, *US* °turn °thumbs down on, *Colloq* °pass by *or* up: *They refused our application to build a hotel here. Did he actually refuse a knighthood?* **2** °deny, °deprive (of), °withhold, disallow, not °allow *or* °permit: *They refused me my right to vote.*

refuse[2] *n.* °rubbish, sweepings, °waste, °litter, dust, °dirt, °dregs, dross, °garbage, debris, detritus, cast-offs, °junk, *Chiefly US* °trash: *Refuse collection is scheduled for once a week.*

regal *adj.* **1** °royal, kingly, queenly, °princely, °fit for *or* °befitting a °king *or* °queen, °noble, lordly, °sovereign, °majestic, °imperial, °stately, °splendid, °magnificent, °grand, resplendent, °palatial, °exalted: *The regal throne was decorated with gold and precious stones.* **2** °disdainful, °haughty, °proud, °scornful, contumelious, °contemptuous, °derisory, derisive, °pompous, lordly: *She was dismissed with a regal wave of the hand.*

regale *v.* °entertain, °amuse, °delight, °divert, °indulge, °please, °gratify, °captivate, °fascinate, °entrance, °enchant, spellbind, °bewitch, °charm, °enrapture: *She regaled them with entertaining tales of her travels.*

regalia *n.* °finery, °decorations, insignia, °emblems, accoutrements *or US also* accouterments, furnishings, °apparatus, °gear, °paraphernalia, °trappings, °tackle, appurtenances, °equipment, equipage: *The Bishop was dressed in full regalia with mitre and crook.*

regard *v.* **1** °view, °look at *or* upon *or* on, °observe, °note, °notice, °watch, °eye, keep an °eye on, °gaze at *or* upon, °stare at: *The children regarded the magician's performance with great interest.* **2** °contemplate, °consider, °perceive, °view, °look upon *or* on, °treat: *The lion looked at me as if he regarded me as his dinner. Smith appears to regard his appointment as treasurer as a licence to steal.* **3** °respect, °esteem, value: *Gwen's friends regard her very highly indeed.* **4** °consider, °view, °look upon *or* on, °think (of), °judge, deem, °rate, °believe (to be), °gauge, °see, pay °heed *or* °attention to, °esteem, °account, take into °account, °imagine, °reckon, °evaluate: *I don't regard her as a likely suspect. He regards his professor as his mentor.* **5** °concern, °relate to, be °relevant to, °pertain to, °apply to, °refer to, °affect, have (a) °bearing on, °bear on *or* upon, °involve, °have to do with, °go for: *Our discussion regarded the disappearance of £10 from petty cash.*

—*n.* **6** °reference, °relation, °relevance, relevancy, °association, pertinence, °application, °bearing, °connection, °link, °tie-in: *We would like to talk to you with regard to your application for the post of assistant editor.* **7** °respect, °consideration, °attention, °reverence, °veneration, awe, °deference, °honour, °favour, °esteem, high °opinion, °approval, approbation, °appreciation, °admiration, °affection, fondness: *They have no regard for the law.* **8** °point, °particular, °respect, °aspect, °detail, °matter: *In this regard, I must take your past record into consideration.* **9** °care, °concern, °thought, °consideration, °respect, °sympathy, °feeling, °sentiment; °heed, °attention, °notice, °mind: *The police behave as if they have no regard for the safety of the hostages. This work reflects the artisan's regard for detail.* **10** ***regards***: °best wishes, °good wishes, °compliments, °greetings, °respects, salutations, *Archaic* devoirs: *Please give my regards to your father.*

regarding *adj.* °concerning, °about, respecting, with °regard to, with °respect to, in *or* with °reference to, in the °matter of, pertaining to, on the °subject of, apropos, re, *Law* in re, *Archaic or Scots* anent, *Dialect* anenst: *We have received your letter regarding poor service. Regarding your claim, the processing of it has been delayed because you failed to sign the form.*

regardless *adj.* **1** Sometimes, ***regardless of***: °despite, °notwithstanding; in °spite of, °heedless of, *Non-Standard* irregardless: *Regardless of her father's protestations, she continued to go out with William.*

—*adv.* **2** °notwithstanding, °nevertheless, no matter what, in any °event, in any °case, at all events, anyway, anyhow, *Non-Standard* irregardless: *She heard his threats but is going out with William regardless.*

regime *n.* régime, regimen, °reign, °government, °rule, °regulation, °administration, °direction, °order, °leadership, °management, °system, °discipline: *Persistent offenders were given harsh penalties under the new regime.*

regiment *v.* °discipline, °order, °organize, systematize, whip into °shape, °standardize, °regulate, °control: *I dislike the way management regiments people in this establishment, as if they were schoolchildren.*

region *n.* **1** °district, °area, °zone, °territory, °division, locality, sector, °section, °tract, °part, °dominion, °precinct, °province, °quarter, °department: *Each region is under the suzerainty of a powerful dictator.* **2** °sphere, °territory, °domain, °province, °field, ambit, °pale, °jurisdiction, bailiwick: *She is an expert in the region of climatology.*

register *n.* **1** °record, °roll, roster, rota, catalogue, annal(s), archive(s), °journal, daybook, °diary, appointment °book, °calendar, °chronicle, °schedule, °programme, directory, ledger, °file, °index, inventory, °list, listing, °poll, °tally: *The council holds a register of all houses sold since 1900 with the names of both sellers and buyers.* **2** cash register, cash-drawer, °till, °money °box, cash-box: *The money in the register does not agree with the figures for receipts.*

—*v.* **3** °record, °write *or* °jot *or* °take *or* °put *or* °set down, °list, °enrol, °sign in *or* on *or* up, °enter, catalogue, log, °index, °chronicle, °note, make *or* take °note (of): *All transactions must be registered.* **4** °show, °display, °express, °indicate, °manifest, °reveal, °betray, divulge, °record, °reflect: *James pretended to like my book, but his contempt for it was registered on his face.* **5** °make known, °inform of, °advise, °transmit, °communicate, °record, °note, make °note of, °report, °write down, °minute: *I wish to register my disapproval of the way prisoners are treated here.* **6** °check in, °sign in *or* on, log in: *In the US, all aliens are required to register each year in January. We registered in the hotel as man and wife.* **7** Sometimes, ***register with*** *or* ***on***: °sink in, °impress, become °apparent (to), make an °impression (on), come °home (to), °get through (to); °dawn on *or* upon, °occur to: *I heard what you said, but it just didn't register. The name didn't register with me at first, but I now know who you are.* **8** °indicate, °read, °mark, °represent, °measure, °point to, °specify, °exhibit, °show, °manifest: *The earthquake registered 7 on the Richter scale.*

regret *v.* **1** rue, °mourn, °lament, °bemoan, °bewail, °repent, be *or* feel °sorry for, feel °remorse for, feel *or* be °remorseful over, be *or* feel °upset, never forgive oneself, deplore, deprecate, °weep *or* °cry over: *You will regret speaking to me that way! The management regrets any inconvenience caused by the redecoration of the restaurant.*

—*n.* **2** Sometimes, ***regrets***: repentance, °guilt, °sorrow, °disappointment, contrition, °remorse, regretfulness, (°pang *or* pangs of) °conscience, self-reproach, self-condemnation, °qualm, second thoughts, rue, ruefulness, °grief, °woe, °sadness, mournfulness, *Literary* dolour: *He felt no regret for his evil deeds. Do you ever have any regrets over the way you treated him?* **3** ***regrets***: °refusal, non-acceptance, non-consent, *US* turn-down: *Thank you for the invitation, but I must tender my regrets.*

regretful *adj.* rueful, °mournful, °sad, °repentant, °guilty, °sorry, °sorrowful, °disappointed, contrite,

°remorseful, °apologetic, °penitent: *He was most regretful for the way he had behaved.*

regrettable *adj.* °lamentable, °deplorable, woeful, °sad, distressing, upsetting, °unhappy, °unfortunate, unlucky, too °bad, °awful, °terrible, execrable, reprehensible, °wrong, °shameful, shaming, *Colloq* °tough, °rough: *It is regrettable that he had the car crash, but he had been warned about drinking and driving.*

regular *adj.* **1** °routine, °ordinary, °common, °everyday, °customary, °accustomed, wonted, commonplace, °normal, °usual, °traditional, °time-honoured, °conventional, °typical, °habitual, °natural, °familiar, °standard, °predictable, scheduled, °fixed, unvarying, °invariable, °methodical: *The attack occurred while Eric was taking his regular evening stroll.* **2** scheduled, °routine, °systematic, ordered, °steady, °consistent, °rhythmic(al), °automatic, °uniform, °periodic, cyclic(al); hourly, °daily, weekly, hebdomadal, semiweekly, biweekly, fortnightly, semi-monthly, monthly, bimonthly, seasonal, °quarterly, semiannual, annual: *The patrol made their regular rounds, as usual. The printers' strike might delay regular publication of the magazine.* **3** °symmetrical, °uniform, °even, even-sided, equal-sided, equilateral, equal-angled, equiangular; °harmonious: *Any six-sided plane figure is a hexagon, but if it has six equal angles and six sides equal in length, it is a regular hexagon.* **4** undistorted, °even, well-proportioned, °proportional, °symmetrical, °classic: *He was classically good-looking, with regular features.* **5** °even, °smooth, °level, °straight, °uniform, uninterrupted, unvarying, °continuous, °flat, °plane, °plumb: *The surface of the wing is regular except for the spoilers.* **6** dependable, °methodical, (well-)regulated, (well-)ordered, °orderly; °proper, °correct, °legal, °official, bona fide, °legitimate, established, recognized, °orthodox, approved, *Colloq* kosher, °OK *or* okay: *Everything about the council election was entirely regular.* **7** °usual, expected, °normal, °habitual, °accustomed, °familiar: *Our regular doctor was on holiday, and we had to see a locum.* **8** °acceptable, accepted, °estimable, °fine, °good, °likeable, °popular, °pleasant: *We all consider Bob to be a regular fellow and a friend.* **9** °complete, utter, thoroughgoing, °unmitigated, unalloyed, °unqualified, consummate, °perfect, °thorough, °absolute, °well-known, acknowledged: *The man is a regular dunce when it comes to repairing cars.* **10** °permanent, °career: *She's in the regular navy.* **11** °conventional, °usual, °common, conformable, °ordinary, °systematic, *Colloq US* ruly: *Regular English verbs form their past by the addition of -d or -ed to the infinitive.*

—*n.* **12** °fixture, °habitué, (°steady) °customer, °patron, °client, frequenter: *Jan has been a regular at the Star and Garter pub for years.*

regularity *n.* **1** consistency, constancy, °uniformity, evenness, sameness, °symmetry, °balance, °harmony, harmoniousness, orderliness, °order, °stability, predictability: *To the casual observer, nothing interferes with the regularity of planetary movement.* **2** °routine, reliability, dependability, steadiness, invariability; °pace, °rhythm, °cadence: *Mr Warbridge listens to the six o'clock evening news with unfailing regularity. Our business depends on the regularity of the postal service. The regularity of the ticking of the clock is driving me mad.*

regulate *v.* **1** °adjust, °modify, °modulate, °control, °balance, °set, °fix, °order, °govern, °organize, °maintain, °manage: *The mixture of air and fuel in modern cars is regulated by an injection system. The responsibility of this department is to regulate prices.* **2** °control, °monitor, °govern, °run, °operate, °administer, °handle, °guide, °steer, °conduct, °direct, °supervise, superintend, °oversee, °manage: *The foreman's job is to regulate the work on the assembly line.*

regulation *n.* **1** °adjustment, modification, modulation, °control, °balance, balancing, °setting, fixing, °organization, °maintenance: *The regulation of the temperature is accomplished by the thermostat.* **2** °rule, ruling, °law, °code, by-law *or* bye-law, edict, °order, ordinance, statute, °decree, directive, °dictate: *There are strict regulations governing the sale, disposal, and movement of radioactive materials.* **3** edict, ukase, °pronouncement, fiat, (papal) bull, °proclamation: *A regulation was issued against meetings of more than five people.*

—*adj.* **4** °standard, accepted, °official, required, prescribed, °mandatory: *The soldier was not wearing a regulation uniform.* **5** °usual, °normal, °ordinary, °customary, °typical: *If you use anything but regulation accessories, the guarantee will be null and void.*

regurgitate *v.* °vomit, disgorge, return one's dinner, °spew up, (*of birds of prey*) cast; retch, °gag; *Colloq* °throw up, upchuck, *Slang* puke, *US* spiff one's biscuits, barf: *The child regurgitated its dinner all over the inside of the car.*

rehabilitate *v.* **1** °restore, °save, °reclaim, °rescue, °redeem, re-establish, reinstate, re-educate, reorient, °reform, *US* °straighten out, *Colloq US* rehab: *They have had marked success at rehabilitating criminals.* **2** °renew, redecorate, °renovate, °refurbish, °restore, °fix (up), °repair, reconstruct, rebuild, °change, °transform: *Sam has plans to rehabilitate vintage cars for a living.*

rehash *v.* **1** rework, °go over again, restate, redo, rearrange, reshuffle, reuse: *Heverton has nothing new to offer—he just keeps on rehashing the same old material.*

—*n.* **2** reworking, restatement, redoing, rearrangement, reshuffle, reshuffling, reuse, rewording: *Her speech was a mere rehash of what she's said scores of times already.*

rehearsal *n.* **1** °practice, °exercise, dry run, °drill, °run-through, read-through, dress rehearsal, *Technical* undress rehearsal: *Is there a rehearsal of the school play scheduled for tonight?* **2** °narration, recounting, °relation, °recital, °telling, °description, enumeration, °account, °repetition, °repeat: *Do we have to listen to yet another rehearsal of your great-uncle's exploits in the war?*

rehearse *v.* **1** °practise, °exercise, °run through, °read through, °study, °repeat: *Sorry, Annie, but we are going to have to rehearse the scene till you get it right.* **2** °repeat, °relate, °recite, °tell, °describe, °recount, °review, °go through *or* over, °report, °recapitulate, *Colloq* recap: *I shall go mad if I hear him again rehearse the events leading up to the final acceptance of his novel.*

reign *n.* **1** °rule, °sovereignty, ascendancy, °power, hegemony, °influence, °command, suzerainty, °administration, °jurisdiction, °leadership, °government, °direction, °control, °domination, mastery; °kingdom, °monarchy, empire: *During her reign, the kingdom saw its greatest prosperity.*

—*v.* **2** °rule, °control, °command, °govern, °lead, °direct, °dominate, °supervise, °manage, hold °sway, wear the °crown, °wield the sceptre, occupy the throne, *Colloq* °run the show, °rule the roost, *Slang* call the shots: *During the sixth Egyptian dynasty, Pepi II Nefektare reigned for 94 years, the longest in recorded history.* **3** °prevail, be *or* become °prevalent, °predominate, hold °sway, °obtain, be *or* become °rampant, be *or* become °universal: *An argument broke out, which developed into a fist fight, and soon pandemonium reigned.*

reimburse *v.* °repay, recompense, refund, °pay back, °compensate, remunerate, indemnify: *Don't worry—we'll reimburse you for any money you spent.*

rein *n.* **1** °check, °curb, °control, °restraint, constraint, limitation, harness, °bridle, °brake: *You are going to have to put a rein on your expenses.* **2 reins**: °control, °command, °administration, °running, °leadership, °power, °rule, tiller, °helm: *He should hand over the reins to a younger person.*

—*v.* **3 rein in**: °check, °curb, °control, °restrain, °limit, harness, °bridle, °restrict, pull back on: *You will have to rein in your passions: it is not becoming to behave in this way at your age.*

reinforce *v.* °strengthen, °buttress, °bolster, °support, °fortify, °prop (up), shore up, augment, °brace, °stay, °steel: *The bookshelf needs to be reinforced with another bracket, or it'll fall down.*

reinforcement *n.* **1** °buttress, °support, °prop, °brace, °stay, °bolster: *This iron reinforcement ought to be strong enough to secure the wall.* **2** strengthening, buttressing, bolstering, shoring (up), augmentation, °bracing: *This shelf is wobbly and in need of reinforcement.* **3** ***reinforcements***: °reserves, auxiliaries, men, soldiers, °forces, personnel: *We cannot hold out till reinforcements arrive.*

reiterate *v.* °repeat, restate, iterate, °labour, harp on, °dwell on, °rehash, °recapitulate, *Colloq* recap: *I must reiterate my warning to you to be careful.*

reject *v.* **1** °decline, °refuse, disallow, °spurn, °veto, °turn down, give (something) the °thumbs down, °set aside, *US* turn °thumbs down (on); °deny, °repudiate, °renounce, °rebuff, °shun, °brush aside, turn a °deaf ear to, will not °hear of: *Jim has rejected my plan for a holiday in Torremolinos. She rejects any suggestion that she might be wrong.* **2** °refuse, °repel, °repulse, °spurn, °rebuff, say no to, °turn down, °decline, °brush aside; °jilt, °drop, °dismiss, °throw over, give (someone) the cold °shoulder, show (someone) the door, send (someone) away *or* on his *or* her *or* their way, turn one's back on, *Slang* give (someone) the °brush-off *or US also* the °brush, give (someone) his *or* her walking papers, *Brit* give (someone) the boot: *Ted proposed, but Alice rejected him.* **3** °throw away *or* out, °discard, disown, jettison, °eliminate, °scrap, *Colloq* °junk, °scratch: *The inspector rejects all defective merchandise.*
—*n.* **4** °second, °irregular, °discard, cast-off: *The rejects are sold at reduced prices in the factory shop.*

rejection *n.* °refusal, °denial, repudiation, °rebuff, °dismissal, spurning, renunciation, turn-down; cold °shoulder, *Slang* °brush-off *or US also* °brush, the (old) heave-ho: *The union voted for the rejection of management's offer of a 9.2 per cent increase. Her advances were met with rejection.*

rejoice *v.* °delight, °exult, °glory, °celebrate, °revel, be °happy *or* °delighted *or* °pleased *or* °overjoyed *or* °elated *or* °glad, *Colloq* be tickled (pink): *We all rejoiced to be home once again after the ordeal.*

rejuvenate *v.* °restore, °refresh, reinvigorate, revitalize, revivify, °renew, reanimate, regenerate, recharge, breathe new °life into: *I think a week in Barbados would rejuvenate me.*

relapse *v.* **1** get back, backslide, °fall back, °lapse, °slip back, regress, retrogress, recidivate; °go back, °return, °retreat, °revert: *Lottie has relapsed into her bad habits.* **2** °decline, °deteriorate, °weaken, °degenerate, °fail, °fade, °sink, °sicken, °worsen, get *or* become worse: *Just when we thought he was improving, he relapsed into a coma and died.*
—*n.* **3** backsliding, falling *or* going back, °lapse, lapsing, °return, returning, reversion, reverting, regression, regressing, retrogression, retrogressing, recidivism, apostasy: *The church's main concern was a relapse into idolatry.* **4** °decline, deterioration, weakening, degeneration, °failing, °failure, fading, °sinking, worsening: *Barry was getting better but has now suffered a relapse.*

relate *v.* **1** °associate, °connect, °couple, °link, °tie, °ally, correlate, °coordinate: *Volta first enabled us to relate the forces of chemistry and electricity.* **2** °recount, °narrate, °tell, °report, °present, °describe, °recite, °detail, °set forth, °communicate, divulge, °impart, °reveal, delineate, make known, give an °account of, °rehearse: *It was not till years later that Olivia related to me the strange events of that night.* **3** °apply to, °coordinate with, °respect, °regard, °bear upon *or* on, have a °bearing on, have °reference to, have to do with, °pertain to, °refer to, appertain to, °belong with *or* to: *Does your comment really relate to the matter in hand?* **4** Often, ***relate to***: be in *or* en °rapport with, °understand, empathize, °sympathize, °communicate with, °identify with, °grasp, °comprehend, be in °tune with, °deal with, °handle, °cope with, *Colloq* °dig, °tune in to, be °hip to, be turned on to, be *or* get into: *I have been having trouble relating to my new psychiatrist. Your favourite music is reggae?—Man, I can relate to that.*

related *adj.* **1** °associate(d), affiliate(d), connected, coupled, linked, tied up, allied, correlated, °coordinate(d), interconnected, interrelated, interdependent, °mutual, °reciprocal, °common, °joint, cognate: *She and her husband work for related companies.* **2** °kin, °kindred, consanguineous, cognate, agnate; °akin: *Just how are you two related? Are you cousins?*

relation *n.* **1** °relationship, °connection, affiliation, °association, °bearing, °link, °tie, °tie-in, °reference, pertinence, interconnection, interdependence, correspondence, °kinship: *The relation between time and money is rarely disputed these days.* **2** °kinship, °relationship: *Just what is your relation to this lady?* **3** °relative, kinsman *or* kinswoman, blood °relative, in-law, °family member: *Is she a relation of yours?* **4** °narration, °narrative, °telling, recounting, °description, °report, °recital, °recitation, delineation, portrayal, °story, recapitulation: *She amused them all with her relation of what had happened to her that night.* **5** ***in relation to***: °concerning, °about, °regarding, respecting, pertaining to, with °regard to, with °respect to, referring to, in *or* with °reference to, in the °matter *or* °subject of, apropos, re, *Archaic or Scots* anent, *Dialect* anenst: *I should like to talk to you in relation to the matter of company expenses.* **6** ***relations***: **a** sexual °intercourse, coitus, °sex, criminal conversation; carnal °knowledge: *It is well known that he had relations with his secretary.* **b** °dealings, °intercourse, °link(s), °association(s), °liaison, °relationship, *Colloq* doings, °truck: *We have no relations with that company.*

relationship *n.* See **relation, 1, 2,** above.

relative *adj.* **1** °related, connected, associated, allied, °affiliated, interconnected, interrelated, °pertinent, °relevant, germane, °applicable; apropos: *Your comments are not relative to the matter at hand.* **2** Sometimes, ***relative to***: comparative, comparable, proportionate, °proportional, commensurate; analogous to, contingent on, dependent on, reliant on, conditioned by, °subject to, °attendant on, °correspondent *or* corresponding to, °provisional on, appurtenant to; °subordinate to, ancillary to: *Well, as they say, everything is relative. Relative humidity depends on the temperature of the air. The yield is relative to the effort.*
—*n.* **3** See **relation, 3,** above.

relatively *adv.* more or less, °somewhat, comparatively, °rather, to some °degree *or* °extent: *Business has been relatively quiet lately.*

relax *v.* **1** °loosen, let go, °release, °let up (on), °relieve, °ease, °reduce, °moderate, slacken, °remit, *Colloq* °ease up on, slacken up on: *He relaxed his grip on the rope and fell to his death on the rocks below.* **2** °diminish, °decrease, lessen, °reduce, abate, °weaken, °mitigate, °modify, °tone down, °moderate, °modulate, °lighten (up on), °check, °temper, °curb: *We must not relax our vigilance. I hope that they don't relax the regulations concerning smoking in the office.* **3** °ease up, °slow down, °loosen up, put one's feet up, °rest, unbend, *Colloq* take it °easy, unwind: *Why not come for a weekend and relax a bit?* **4** °calm down, °cool down, °quiet(en) down, stay °calm, °cool and °collected, *Colloq* take it °easy, *Slang* °cool it: *You ought to relax and not get so excited.*

relaxation *n.* **1** °ease, °repose, °rest, °leisure, °recreation, °amusement, °entertainment, °fun, °pleasure, °diversion, *Colloq* R and R ('rest and relaxation'): *For relaxation we usually charter a boat and go sailing.* **2** easing (up *or* off), relief, alleviation, abatement, diminution, lessening, mitigation, moderation, slackening, °remission, weakening, letting up, *Colloq* °letup: *What do you think about the proposed relaxation of the laws against pornography?*

relaxed *adj.* °nonchalant, °easygoing, °calm, °peaceful, °tranquil, °serene, pacific, °carefree, insouciant, °blasé, languorous, languid, devil-may-care, °free and °easy, happy-go-lucky, °mellow, at °ease, composed, °cool: *Richard takes a relaxed view of life.*

release *v.* **1** °let °go, (set) °free, °liberate, (set *or* °let *or* turn) °loose, unloose, untie, unchain, unfetter, unshackle, °deliver, °let out, disenthral, °discharge, °let off, °emancipate, manumit, °rescue, °save: *They kept up a strenuous campaign until all the political prisoners were released.* **2** °issue, °publish, make °available, °put out, °pass out, °hand out, °come out with, °circulate, °distribute, disseminate; °launch, °unveil, °present: *The government refuses to release information that is considered harmful to its interests. The band's new album will be released tomorrow.*
—*n.* **3** freeing, releasing, liberating, loosing, unloosing, delivering, emancipating, manumitting, rescuing, °saving, °freedom, °liberation, deliverance, °discharge, emancipation, manumission, °rescue, °remission, salvation: *The release of the prisoner is scheduled for noon. It would be a great release to be rid of housework.* **4** °press *or* publicity release, °announcement, publicity, °notice, °story, °report: *The press office sent out a release to the media about Randolph's appointment.*

relegate *v.* **1** consign, °banish, °exile, °transfer, °dispatch *or* despatch: *Owing to his disagreement with the Foreign Office, Kendall was relegated to some outpost in the Indian Ocean.* **2** °downgrade, demote: *I fear that Corporal Jones has been relegated to private.* **3** °assign, °commit, °hand over, °refer, °transfer, °pass on: *She relegates most of her everyday correspondence to her secretary for reply.*

relent *v.* °relax, °soften, °yield, °give, °give °way *or* ground, °bend, °comply, acquiesce, compromise, °capitulate, come round, be °merciful, show °pity *or* compassion, °melt, show °mercy, °succumb: *They finally relented and allowed me to have visitors.*

relentless *adj.* **1** unyielding, inexorable, unstoppable, unrelenting, dogged, °implacable, °inflexible, unbending, unmoving, °unmoved, unrelieved, °stiff, °hard, stiff-necked, °rigid, °obstinate, adamant, obdurate, intransigent, °determined, unswerving, undeviating, intractable, persevering, °steely, °tough, unsparing, uncompromising, pitiless, unforgiving, °ruthless, °merciless, °cruel, °unmerciful, °remorseless: *The novel is about the relentless horde of Mongols that swept across Europe in the 13th century.* **2** °non-stop, °persistent, incessant, unrelenting, unremitting, unstoppable, °perpetual, unfaltering, unfailing, unflagging, unrelieved, unabated, unbroken, °continual, °continuous, ceaseless, °constant, unceasing, °steady, °habitual, °regular: *Won't you ever stop your relentless nagging?*

relevance *n.* relevancy, appropriateness, aptness, pertinence, °bearing, °connection, °affinity, °tie-in, °relation, °significance, suitability, suitableness, applicability, °application, applicableness: *What you just said has no relevance whatsoever to the issue under discussion.*

relevant *adj.* °pertinent, °appropriate, apt, °related, °relative, °significant, suited, °applicable, °fitting, °proper, germane, °akin, allied, associated, apposite, to the °point: *Alan's suggestion is not strictly relevant to our plans.*

reliable *adj.* dependable, °trustworthy, °honest, trusty, trusted, °principled, °conscientious, punctilious, °honourable, credible, believable, °safe, °sure, °certain, °secure, °sound, °responsible, °predictable, °stable, unfailing, °infallible, °reputable: *Would a reliable employee like Susan abscond with the money?*

reliance *n.* °confidence, °trust, °faith, dependence: *You may be placing too much reliance on the smoke alarm.*

relic *n.* **1** °memento, °keepsake, °memorial, °remembrance, souvenir, heirloom, °token, artefact *or* artifact: *It has been argued again and again that the Turin shroud, though old, is not a genuine relic of Christ.* **2** °remains; °fragment, °trace, °scrap, shard *or* sherd, °remnant: *Deep in the jungle, archaeologists unearthed relics of a previously unknown civilization.*

relief *n.* **1** °ease, easing, abatement, easement, deliverance, °remedy, redress, alleviation, °release, °remission, assuagement, °liberation, °recess: *We would all welcome relief from this blistering heat. Contributions for the relief of famine in Africa would be most welcome.* **2** °aid, °help, °support, °assistance, succour; °comfort: *How many troops can we send for the relief of the besieged garrison?* **3** °elevation, °projection, °contrast, °prominence; bas-relief *or* basso-rilievo ('low relief'), mezzo-rilievo ('medium relief'), alto-rilievo ('high relief'): *The Greek reliefs brought to England by Lord Elgin are on display at the British Museum.* **4** °substitute, surrogate, replacement, °alternate, locum (tenens), °stand-in; °understudy, °double: *I wish that my relief would arrive so I could go home.*

relieve *v.* **1** °ease, lessen, °reduce, °diminish, abate, °lift, °raise, alleviate, °mitigate, palliate, °soften, soothe: *Business will suffer if nothing is done to relieve the burden of high interest rates. The doctor gave me something to relieve the pain.* **2** disburden, °free, °rid, °liberate, disencumber, unburden, °rescue, °save, °release: *Winning the lottery relieved me of any immediate worries of poverty.* **3** °help, °aid, °assist, °support, succour, °rescue, °save, °deliver: *Will the cavalry arrive in time to relieve the fort, which is under attack?* **4** °stand in (for), °replace, °substitute for, take over for *or* from, *US* °spell, *Colloq* sub for: *I thought you were coming to relieve me at noon.*

religion *n.* °creed, °belief, °faith; °doctrine, dogma: *People must be treated equally, regardless of their religion.*

religious *adj.* **1** °devout, churchgoing, °pious, God-fearing, °holy, spiritual-minded: *You never struck me as a particularly religious person.* **2** °scrupulous, °exact, °precise, °conscientious, rigorous, °strict, °fastidious, °meticulous, °faithful, punctilious, unerring, unswerving, undeviating: *Edmund's work is characterized by religious devotion to detail.*

relinquish *v.* **1** °yield, °give up, °cede, °waive, °leave, °quit, °abandon, °drop, °forsake, forswear, °desert, °abdicate, °resign, °renounce, let go, °surrender, °vacate, °retire from: *Richard was forced to relinquish the throne.* **2** let go, °give up, °release, unloose, °loose, °free: *He refused to relinquish his grasp on her arm.*

relish *n.* **1** °enjoyment, °pleasure, °delight, °gusto, °eagerness, avidity, °anticipation, °taste, °appetite, °zest, °liking, °appreciation, fondness, °fancy, °partiality, °preference: *The children attacked the birthday cake with great relish.*
—*v.* **2** °enjoy, °delight in, take °pleasure in, °fancy, be °partial to, °appreciate, °savour, °look forward to, °anticipate: *After all that dining out, I'd really relish a home-cooked meal. I don't relish having to tell her she is being made redundant.*

reluctance *n.* unwillingness, disinclination, °aversion, °dislike, disrelish, hesitancy: *Cooper's reluctance to leave before the end of the play was understandable.*

reluctant *adj.* unwilling, °disinclined, °averse, °hesitant, °loath, °unenthusiastic, °indisposed, °opposed, antagonistic; °cautious, chary, °wary, °leery, circumspect, °careful: *I remember how reluctant you were to try raw oysters, and then you couldn't get enough of them.*

rely *v.* ***rely on or upon***: °depend on *or* upon, °lean on *or* upon, °count on *or* upon, bank on *or* upon, have °confidence in, °bet on, °trust in, °swear by, be °sure *or* °certain of: *You can rely on Philippa to come through when you need a friend. I am relying on the fact that interest rates are likely to stay at their present levels.*

remain *v.* **1** °stay (behind), be °left, °tarry, °linger, °wait, *Colloq* °stay put: *I remained to help with the washing-up.* **2** be °left, be there: *How many days remain before your trip?* **3** °stay, °continue, °carry on, °abide; °endure, °persist, °last, °persevere: *She refuses*

to remain with him another minute. His last book will remain a monument to his scholarship.
—*n.* **4** ***remains***: **a** leavings, °remnants, °crumbs, debris, detritus, °remainder, °balance, °residue, leftovers, °scraps, °vestiges, °traces, °fragments, oddments, °odds and ends: *The remains of a half-eaten meal were on the table.* **b** °body, °cadaver, °corpse; carcass: *The remains of the impala were being picked over by vultures.*

remainder *n.* **1** °rest, °balance, °remains, °residue: *He spent the remainder of his life in penury.* **2** °excess, overage, °surplus, °residue, residuum, leftovers: *I have used all I needed and don't know what to do with the remainder.*

remaining *adj.* **1** °left (over), extant, °outstanding: *I did as much as I could in the time remaining.* **2** °leftover, surviving, °residual; °unused, uneaten, unconsumed: *The remaining books will be sold at auction.*

remark *v.* **1** °note, °notice, °observe, °perceive, °regard, °look at, take °notice *or* °note of: *His friends remarked his tired and overworked appearance and suggested that he should take a holiday.* **2** °comment (on *or* upon), °say, °observe, °reflect, °mention, °declare, °state, assert: *Carrie remarked that she had seen Ted the night before.*

remarkable *adj.* **1** °extraordinary, °unusual, °singular, °exceptional, °noteworthy, °notable, uncommon, °incredible, °unbelievable, °impressive, °phenomenal, astonishing, astounding, surprising: *With remarkable swiftness the falcon dropped on its prey.* **2** °striking, °distinguished, °signal, °special, wonderful, °marvellous, out of the °ordinary, °unique, °significant, °outstanding, °rare, °memorable, unforgettable, never-to-be-forgotten: *This novel is truly a remarkable achievement.* **3** °strange, °different, °odd, °peculiar, °curious: *Contortionists can do truly remarkable things with their bodies.*

remedy *n.* **1** °cure, °treatment, °therapy, °antidote, counteractant, countermeasure, medication, medicament, °medicine, °prescription, °drug, pharmaceutical, cure-all, panacea, nostrum, restorative, °specific: *What remedy did the doctor recommend?* **2** °cure, °antidote, cure-all, panacea, nostrum, countermeasure, relief, redress, °answer, °solution: *Knowledge is the only remedy for superstition.*
—*v.* **3** °cure, °treat, °heal, °mend, °restore, °relieve, soothe, °control, °ease, °mitigate, alleviate: *The ointment will remedy the itching but not the infection causing it.* **4** °correct, °rectify, °reform, °improve, ameliorate, redress, °repair, put *or* set °right, °straighten out: *How can I remedy a situation that has already gone too far?*

remember *v.* **1** call to °mind, bear in °mind; °recall, °recollect: *Can you remember her funny little laugh? Yes, I remember.* **2** °muse (on *or* about), °reminisce over *or* about, °think back on *or* about, °memorialize, °commemorate, °recognize: *He will be remembered for his many achievements.* **3** °retain, keep in °mind, °recall: *He was unable to remember his own name or where he lived.* **4** °tip, °reward: *The Elliotts always remembered the servants at Christmas.*

remembrance *n.* **1** °memory, °recollection; °reminiscence: *My remembrance of her is quite different from yours.* **2** °memento, °reminder, souvenir, °keepsake, °memorial: *I keep this piece of shrapnel as a remembrance of being wounded in the war.*

remind *v.* °prompt, °cue, cause to °remember, °jog the °memory, put in °mind of: *Remind me to set the clock back an hour tonight.*

reminder *n.* mnemonic, refresher; °cue, °prompt: *I tied this string round my finger as a reminder, but I don't know of what.*

reminisce *v.* Sometimes, ***reminisce about***: °remember, °recollect, °think back, °look back, turn one's °mind *or* thoughts back; call to °mind, hark back, °return: *Most of the time we just sit about and reminisce. The other day we were reminiscing about the time Alex was arrested for shoplifting.*

reminiscence *n.* Usually, ***reminiscences***: anecdote(s), °memory *or* memories, °reflection(s), °memoir(s): *The Sunday Clarion has paid a six-figure sum to Charlotte for her reminiscences as a cleaner at Whitehall.*

reminiscent *adj.* Usually, ***reminiscent of***: recalling, °redolent of, evocative of, indicative of, °suggestive of, °similar to, comparable with *or* to: *The odour of burning cabbage is reminiscent of my husband's cooking.*

remiss *adj.* °slack, °careless, negligent, neglectful, °heedless, unheeding, °inattentive, unmindful, °thoughtless, °forgetful, °unthinking, °slow, °indolent, °lazy, dilatory, °delinquent: *You were remiss in failing to turn off the bath water.*

remission *n.* **1** °forgiveness, °pardon, deliverance, amnesty, °reprieve, exoneration, °release, absolution, exculpation, °indulgence, °excuse, °exemption, acquittal: *As we were granted remission of our crimes, we were freed.* **2** diminution, abatement, °decrease, lessening, subsidence, alleviation, mitigation, assuagement, ebbing, °relaxation, easing: *Remission of the disease may occur, but most sufferers deteriorate rapidly.*

remit *v.* **1** °send, °transmit, °forward, °dispatch *or* despatch; °pay, °compensate, °settle, liquidate: *We have remitted in full the amount requested.* **2** abate, °diminish, slacken, °decrease, lessen, °subside, alleviate, °mitigate, assuage, °ebb, °dwindle, °reduce, °relax, °ease (up *or* off), °fall off: *The fever ought to remit on the sixth day.*

remittance *n.* °payment, °settlement: allowance, consideration: *Remittance was made regularly on the tenth of the month. He lives on remittances he receives from home.*

remnant *n.* **1** °scrap, °shred, °fragment, °end, °bit, °piece, °trace, °vestige, °relic: *A silver button was the only remnant of the splendid uniform.* **2** °leftover, °remainder, °residue, °rest, remains, °part: *The surviving remnant of the battalion made its way across the desert to Djibouti.*

remorse *n.* °regret, repentance, ruefulness, °sorrow, °woe, °anxiety, °guilty *or* °bad °conscience, °pangs of °conscience, °humiliation, °embarrassment, °guilt, self-reproach, mortification, °shame, contrition, contriteness, °penitence, °compunction, °bitterness: *It is impossible to describe the remorse he felt at having run over the little girl's puppy.*

remorseful *adj.* °regretful, °repentant, rueful, °sorry, °apologetic, °sorrowful, woeful, °anxious, °guilty, °bad, conscience-stricken, guilt-ridden, humiliated, humbled, °embarrassed, mortified, °shamefaced, °shameful, °ashamed, shamed, contrite, °penitent, °bitter: *Harold made a remorseful confession of all his sins.*

remorseless *adj.* **1** °cruel, °heartless, °callous, °harsh, hard-hearted, stony-hearted, °savage, °merciless, °unmerciful, pitiless, °ruthless: *The heavyweight champion administered a remorseless beating to the challenger.* **2** °relentless, unrelenting, unremitting, unstoppable, inexorable, °implacable: *The remorseless storm thrashed at our tiny vessel, tearing away every last shred of rigging.*

remote *adj.* **1** °distant, °far-away, far-off, removed, °outlying, °inaccessible: *The more remote the transmitter, the weaker the signal.* **2** °lonely, °isolated, God-forsaken, °secluded, °out-of-the-way, sequestered, tramontane, ultramontane: *They spent their holiday on a remote island in the Indian Ocean.* **3** °unfamiliar, °obscure, arcane, °recondite, °subtle, °alien, °far-fetched, °unusual, °unlikely: *Her writing is scattered with references remote to the average reader's experience.* **4** °unrelated, °irrelevant, °inappropriate, unconnected, °outside: *Her conclusions were not remote from what we now know to be the truth.* **5** °slight, °faint, foggy: *I haven't the remotest idea what you're talking about.* **6** °slight, °faint, °slender, °insignificant, °slim,

°small, °meagre, °outside, °poor, inconsiderable, °negligible, °improbable, °unlikely, °implausible: *There is only a remote chance that the experiment will succeed.* **7** °aloof, °detached, °withdrawn, °reserved, °indifferent, °standoffish, abstracted: *He keeps himself quite remote from the hurly-burly of everyday life.* **8** °early, °ancient, far-removed, °distant: *The archaeopteryx is a remote ancestor of modern birds.*

removal *n.* **1** elimination, removing, eradication, taking away: *The removal of the wallpaper revealed that the plaster underneath was in very poor condition.* **2** extermination, °murder, elimination, °killing, slaying, assassination, °execution, liquidation, eradication, °massacre, °slaughter, °purge, doing away with, *Slang* bumping off, rubbing out, doing in, *US* rub-out, wasting: *The removal of the finance minister was accomplished by the secret police.* **3** °dismissal, °transfer, transference, transferral, shifting, °discharge, throwing over, throwing out, deposition, unseating, dethroning, dethronement, displacement, °expulsion, ouster, ousting, riddance, °purge, *Colloq* firing, sacking: *The company functions better since the removal of the former chairman.* **4** °move, °transfer, departure, °moving: *Her removal to a branch office was requested by top management.* **5** moving, house-moving: *We hired a removal van when we moved to Shropshire.*

remove *v.* **1** °take off, doff, °shed, °cast off: *Gentlemen are requested to remove their hats in her presence.* **2** °take away, get °rid of, °carry away *or* off, °shift; °transfer: *When I arrived this morning, my desk had been removed. The threat of war has been removed. Kindly remove your elbows from the table.* **3** °obliterate, °delete, °erase, expunge, eradicate, efface, °eliminate, °take off, °wipe *or* °rub out, °wipe *or* °rub off, get °rid of: *Use chemicals to remove the graffiti from the wall.* **4** °murder, assassinate, °kill, slay, °execute, °exterminate, °eliminate, liquidate, eradicate, °massacre, °slaughter, do away with, °dispose of, get °rid of, °purge, *Slang* °rub *or* °wipe out, do in, °bump off, *US* °waste: *We brought in some of the boys to remove the competition.* **5** °discharge, °dismiss, depose, unseat, °displace, °expel, oust, °turn out, get °rid of, °purge, *Colloq* °fire, °sack, °kick out: *Andrews must be removed from his job before he does any more harm.* **6** relocate, °move, °transfer, °shift: *I removed to a quieter place where I could write in peace.* **7** °take out, unfasten, °detach, °disconnect, °separate, °undo: *They have to remove the transmission to overhaul it.*
—*n.* **8** °distance, °space, °interval, °separation: *They tried to keep the girls and the boys at some remove from one another.*

remuneration *n.* **1** °payment, compensation, °salary, wages, °earnings, emolument, °income, °pay, °stipend, °consideration, °reward: *What remuneration will she expect to receive if appointed?* **2** recompense, repayment, reimbursement, °restitution, reparation(s), damages, °indemnity, indemnification, redress: *Have they received any remuneration for their loss of property during the earthquake?*

renaissance *n.* renascence, °rebirth, °revival, reawakening, °restoration, resumption, renewal, °resurgence, °return, regeneration, rejuvenation, °new °dawn, °new °birth: *The Renaissance is so called because of the return to classical tradition. Hugh seems to have undergone a renaissance since taking that rest cure.*

rend *v.* **1** °rip *or* °tear *or* °pull (to pieces *or* apart *or* asunder), °wrench, °mangle, °shred: *The bully threatened to rend me limb from limb.* **2** °split, °tear, °rip, °rupture, °cleave, rive, °separate, °slice, °lacerate: *When the balloon was rent from top to bottom, the basket fell to the ground.* **3** °pain, °distress, °pierce, °stab, smite, °wound, °afflict, °torment, wring, °hurt: *My heart was rent by conflicting emotions.*

render *v.* **1** depict, °picture, °represent, °reproduce, °portray, °create, °produce, do, °execute, °make, °accomplish, °achieve: *The artist rendered this portrait of the family from a photograph.* **2** °make, °cause to be or °become: *The news of winning the lottery rendered me speechless.* **3** °give (up), °yield (up), °surrender, °relinquish, °resign, °cede, °deliver, °hand over, °tender, °offer, proffer, °present, °furnish, °provide: *The inscription on the tomb has still not rendered up its secret. To Caesar will I render my legions and my horse.* **4** °play, °perform: *She rendered a fugue most beautifully on a harpsichord.* **5** °deliver, °return: *The jury rendered a verdict of Guilty.* **6** °translate, decode, °decipher, °transcribe, °convert, °explain, °interpret, °put, restate, °reword, rephrase: *She rendered the passage into idiomatic English.* **7** °deliver, °hand in, °present, °offer, proffer, °furnish, °provide, °tender: *They rendered their invoice for the work already done.* **8** Usually, *Brit* ***render down***: °melt, °clarify, °extract: *The fat must be rendered down before it can be used for making soap.*

rendering *n.* depiction, showing, °presentation, °interpretation, °conception, °version, °rendition, °representation, delineation, portrayal, °picture: *This is the architect's rendering of what the building will look like when completed.*

rendition *n.* **1** °performance, °interpretation, °execution, °conception, concept, °understanding, construction, reading, °rendering: *I have never before heard such an exquisite rendition of a Bach cantata.* **2** See **rendering,** above.

renegade *n.* **1** °deserter, °turncoat, heretic, °defector, °traitor, apostate, *Archaic* renegado: *The renegade has organized a conspiracy against us.*
—*adj.* **2** °traitorous, treacherous, °perfidious, treasonous, apostate, °heretical, °disloyal: *A renegade band of deserters has turned against the army leaders.*

renege *v.* **1** *Cards* revoke: *When you renege you fail to follow suit.* **2** °go back on, back out, °default, °repudiate, °go back on *or* °break (one's) °promise *or* °word, °recant, abrogate, abjure, *Slang* welsh (on): *You swore you would keep your word, and now you're reneging.*

renew *v.* **1** °restore, °refresh, °rejuvenate, revitalize, reinvigorate, resuscitate, °revamp, redo, °rehabilitate, °transform, regenerate, °refurbish, refurnish, °renovate, refit, °overhaul, recondition, °modernize, redecorate, do over: *The entire interior of the hotel has been renewed at considerable expense.* **2** resume, °resurrect, restart, °pick *or* °take up again, recommence, °return to, reopen: *They renewed their argument in favour of the teaching of Latin.* **3** °restore, °replace, restock, °replenish: *We must renew our supply of claret.* **4** °repeat, °reiterate, reaffirm, °confirm, reconfirm, restate, reassert: *Each autumn she renews her promise to return in the spring.*

renounce *v.* °give up, forswear, °surrender, °abandon, °desert, abjure, °reject, °repudiate, °spurn, °swear off, abstain from, °deny, °forgo, °forsake, eschew, disown, °throw off *or* out, °shun, °avoid: *He renounced his claim to the throne and retired to a monastery.*

renovate *v.* redecorate, °modernize, do over, °refurbish, refurnish, refit, remodel; recondition, °rehabilitate, °restore, °repair, °revamp, °overhaul, °patch up, *Colloq* do up, *US* °fix up: *We are having the entire house renovated by an interior decorator. It was quite costly to have those paintings renovated.*

renown *n.* °fame, °celebrity, °glory, °distinction, °esteem, acclaim, °reputation, °prominence, eminence, °note, °mark, °honour, °prestige, repute, éclat, °lustre, illustriousness, stardom: *She enjoys great renown as a rock star.*

renowned *adj.* °famous, famed, °celebrated, °distinguished, acclaimed, °prominent, °eminent, °well-known, °noted, °notable, honoured, °illustrious: *He was one of the most renowned authors of the 19th century.*

rent[1] *v.* **1** °let (out), °lease, °hire (out), °charter (out), °farm out: *Eric owns a three-bedroom house that he rents out. I should like to rent a yacht for a cruise this summer.*
—*n.* **2** rental, °hire, °lease, °fee: *The rent comes to about a quarter of my salary.*

rent[2] *n.* °tear, °rip, °split, °gash, °slash, °hole, °slit: *The skirt has a six-inch rent in it.*

repair *v.* **1** °mend, °patch (up); °renew, put *or* set °right, °restore, °fix (up), °service, put (back) in *or* into working order, vamp, °revamp, °adjust: *Can you repair the tear in my trousers? I must remember to ask the garage to repair the brakes on my car.* —*n.* **2** °mend, °patch; °restoration, fixing (up), servicing, °improvement, °adjustment, renovation, revamping, renewal: *The cost of the repairs to our roof after the storm was covered by our insurance.* **3** °form, °condition, fettle, °state, working °order, *Colloq* °shape, *Brit* °nick: *The engine, I'm afraid, has not been kept in good repair.*

repartee *n.* °banter, badinage, persiflage, °patter, (°witty) °conversation, wordplay, °raillery, °give and take, *Literary* deipnosophism: *Simon's witty repartee makes him a most welcome dinner guest.*

repay *v.* °pay back, recompense, °compensate, °requite, °reciprocate, °return the °favour *or* °compliment, °reward, °square with, °settle (up) with; refund, °give back, °return, °reimburse, °restore: *How can I ever repay you for what you have done? Alan repaid the money he borrowed from me.*

repeal *v.* **1** °revoke, °recall, rescind, °reverse, °cancel, annul, nullify, invalidate, °void, °set aside, °abolish, abrogate, *Law* °vacate: *They have repealed the rule forbidding guests to wear shorts in the restaurant.* —*n.* **2** revocation, °recall, rescission, rescindment, °reversal, °cancellation, annulment, nullification, invalidation, voiding, °abolition, abrogation: *Alcoholic beverages were forbidden in the US until the repeal of Prohibition.*

repeat *v.* **1** °reiterate, restate, °echo, retell, °recite, °quote, °rehearse, °recount, °recapitulate, *Colloq* recap: *Would you please repeat to Anne what you told me?* **2** °duplicate, °reproduce, replicate: *History repeated itself on the playing field here today, when Queens Park Rangers defeated Manchester United, 2-0.* —*n.* **3** °repetition, °duplicate, °copy, duplication, replication, °reproduction, °replica, rerun, rebroadcast, replay, encore, reprise: *This is a repeat of a show we saw last year.*

repeatedly *adv.* again and again, over again, over and over, °frequently, °often, °time and (time) again, °time after time, recurrently, repetitively, repetitiously: *The needle stuck, and the record player kept playing the same thing repeatedly.*

repel *v.* **1** °repulse, °drive back *or* away *or* off, °reject, °fend off, parry, °ward off, °hold off, °rebuff, °resist, °withstand, keep at bay *or* arm's length: *They were completely defenceless and unable to repel attackers.* **2** °revolt, °offend, °disgust, °sicken, °nauseate, turn one's stomach, make one's skin crawl, *Colloq* give one the creeps, turn one off: *The idea of eating sheep's eyes repels me.*

repellent *adj.* °repulsive, repelling, °revolting, °disgusting, nauseating, °nauseous, stomach-turning, sickening, °offensive, °loathsome, °repugnant, °distasteful, vomit-provoking, sick-making, °disagreeable, °obnoxious, off-putting: *He described some of the more repellent examples of vivisection he had encountered.*

repent *v.* °regret, feel contrition, °lament, °bemoan, °bewail, be °sorry, rue, feel °remorse, feel °remorseful *or* °penitent, show °penitence: *She repented having reported him to the police. Now that the evil deed is done he can but repent.*

repentant *adj.* °regretful, contrite, rueful, °remorseful, °apologetic, °sorry, °ashamed, °embarrassed, °penitent: *It was terrible that she wasn't the least bit repentant for what she had done.*

repercussion *n.* Often, ***repercussions***: °reaction, °response, °effect, °outcome, consequence, reverberation, °result, aftermath, after-effect, °upshot, fallout, °backlash, °echo: *We were dealing with the repercussions of that decision long afterwards.*

repertory *n.* repertoire, °store, reservoir, °collection, °hoard, °cache, repository, °stock, °supply, inventory, stockpile: *Cosgrove felt compelled to run through his entire repertory of jokes at dinner.*

repetition *n.* **1** Often, ***repetitions***: reiteration(s), duplication(s), redundancy *or* redundancies, °repeats, °tautology *or* tautologies: *The book is full of boring repetitions.* **2** reiteration, °repeat, °echo, echoing, repeating, duplication, duplicating, °rehearsal, recapitulation, restatement, replication, rereading, retelling, relisting, °recital, reprise, rerun, rerunning: *We sat through a repetition of every name for the benefit of any who might have missed it the first time.*

repetitious *adj.* °tiresome, °tedious, °boring, °redundant, prolix, °windy, long-winded, °wordy, tautological, pleonastic: *Streatham's lectures are very repetitious—he makes the same point over and over again.*

repetitive *adj.* iterative, °repetitious, incessant, °monotonous, repeated, °redundant, °humdrum, unceasing, ceaseless, °relentless, unremitting, °persistent, °recurrent, °non-stop, uninterrupted, °continual, °constant, °continuous: *The repetitive beat of that rock music is driving me mad.*

replace *v.* **1** °change, put in °place of, °substitute, °supplant, °renew: *If the toy won't work, try replacing the batteries.* **2** °succeed, °supersede, °substitute for, °take over from, °supplant: *Tim will be replacing David as department head.* **3** °restore, °return, °put back, make good (on), °repay, refund, make °restitution for: *Are you going to replace the money you took?*

replenish *v.* refill, restock, °restore, °renew, °replace, °fill, °top up; °furnish, °provide: *They stopped off in Bordeaux to replenish their supplies.*

replete *adj.* **1** Often, ***replete with***: °full (of), filled up (with), overflowing (with), well supplied *or* well provided *or* well stocked (with), chock-full (of), crammed *or* jammed *or* jam-packed (with), brim-full (with), chock-a-block, bursting, teeming, °loaded, overloaded (with), gorged (with), stuffed (with), *Colloq* up to the eyes *or* ears (in), up to here *or* there (in), *US* up to the old wazoo (in), *Slang* °lousy (with), *Taboo slang* up to the *Brit* arse (in) *or US* ass (in): *His speech was replete with names, dates, and precise quotations, all delivered without a note of any kind.* **2** satisfied, sated, satiated: *After a meal like that, anybody would feel replete.*

replica *n.* °copy, °duplicate, °facsimile, °reproduction, °likeness, °imitation, carbon °copy, photocopy, duplication, *Colloq* °dupe, *US* °knock-off: *The hall was dominated by a replica of Michelangelo's David.*

reply *v.* **1** °answer, °respond, rejoin, °retort, °return, come back, °acknowledge: *When I asked where he had been, he refused to reply and walked out of the room.* —*n.* **2** °answer, °response, rejoinder, °retort, comeback, riposte, °reaction, *US* rise: *I have written to the prime minister but as yet have had no reply.*

report *n.* **1** °account, °description, °story, article, write-up, °piece, °statement, °dispatch *or* despatch, communication, communiqué, °announcement, °narrative, °record; °news, °information: *Stanley hasn't yet sent in the full report of his meeting with John. Is there any report from the front?* **2** °explosion, bang, °boom, °shot, gunshot, gunfire, backfire, °discharge, °crack, °blast, detonation: *In the distance we heard the report of a gun, and later a muffled explosion.* —*v.* **3** °relate, °recount, °describe, °narrate, °tell of, °detail, give an °account of, °write up, °document: *Our man in Kuala Lumpur reported a disturbance in a remote village.* **4** °publish, promulgate, °publicize, °put out, °announce, °set forth, °reveal, °disclose, divulge, °circulate, make °public, °broadcast: *Two newspapers and a television station reported the arrest of the suspect.* **5** °arrive, °appear, °surface, °check in, °sign in, clock in *or* on, °turn up, °come in, *US* report in: *We were asked to report for duty at 0800 on Friday.* **6** ***report on***: °investigate, °cover, °examine, °explore, °look into, °inquire into, °check into *or* on, °check (up) on, °research, °study, °probe, °scrutinize, *Slang* °check out, *Brit* suss out: *The new journalist was assigned to report on allegations of bribery in the council.*

reporter *n.* °journalist, newspaperman, newspaperwoman, newsman, newswoman, °correspondent, columnist, newswriter, gentleman *or* lady of the °press, gentleman *or* lady of the fourth estate, *Brit* pressman, presswoman; newscaster, news-presenter, commentator, broadcaster, anchorman, anchorwoman; photojournalist, cameraman, camerawoman, *Colloq* newshound, news-hawk, news-hen, stringer: *Reporters swarmed around the footballers who had returned home with the World Cup.*

repose *n.* **1** °rest, °inactivity, °calm, °respite, tranquillity, °quiet, restfulness, °peace, °relaxation: *A half hour's repose would be welcome after a long day coping with lively toddlers.* **2** °sleep, °nap, °doze, catnap, siesta, slumber, *Colloq* forty winks, snooze, *Slang* zizz, shut-eye: *The short repose refreshed, and she felt ready to tackle anything.* **3** composure, calmness, °calm, °serenity, equanimity, °poise, self-possession: *He became angry in a flash, his face changing from quiet repose to livid distortion.*
—*v.* **4** °lie, °abide, be, °lodge, rest: *The power to make the modifications reposes with you.*

represent *v.* **1** °substitute for, °stand (in) for, °replace, °act for: *I have appointed her to represent me in all legal matters.* **2** Often, ***represent oneself as***: °present (oneself), depict (oneself), °put *or* °set (oneself) forth, °masquerade as, take (on) *or* assume the °guise *or* role *or* °part of, °characterize as, impersonate, °pretend to be, °pose as, °imitate, °mimic: *He represents himself as a plumber in order to get into houses to rob them. His wife was represented to me as a social worker.* **3** °describe, delineate, °reproduce, °report, assert, °state, °put *or* °set forth, °show, °reflect, °mirror, °characterize, °define, °note, °outline, sketch, depict, °picture, °portray, °draw, °paint; °pretend: *What took place that fateful day is not as represented in Inspector Taylor's testimony.* **4** °symbolize, °stand for, °typify, °exemplify, °embody, epitomize; °illustrate: *He represents all that is good in the world today.*

representation *n.* **1** °reproduction, °image, °likeness, °portrait, °picture, depiction, portrayal, °semblance, °model, °manifestation: *This is an accurate representation of the town's appearance in the 18th century.* **2** °agency: *The sales representation for this area is under Wright's direction.* **3** °statement, °account, °exposition, °declaration, deposition, °assertion, °presentation, °undertaking: *Certain representations have been made concerning harassment by the police.* **4** °replica, °reproduction, °figure, figurine, °statue, statuette, bust, °head, °model, effigy: *This representation of the goddess Athena was found in Kios.*

representative *adj.* **1** °symbolic, °typical, °characteristic, °emblematic, archetypal, evocative, illustrative: *Is this a representative sample? These poems are not representative of your best work.* **2** elected, chosen, °democratic: *They are struggling to establish a representative form of government.*
—*n.* **3** °agent, °deputy, legate, °ambassador, (papal) nuncio, spokesman, spokeswoman, °proxy, °delegate, °envoy, emissary, °missionary, commissioner; Member of Parliament, MP, Councillor, Congressman, Congresswoman, Assemblyman, Assemblywoman: *We like to think that our representatives are acting on our behalf.* **4** °agent, (travelling) salesman *or* saleswoman, *Colloq* rep: *We have hired a new representative to sell refrigerators in the north of the country.*

repress *v.* °suppress, °put down, (keep in) °check, °curb, °quash, °stifle, °overcome, °squelch, (keep under) °control, °contain, °restrain, constrain, °limit, °keep back, °quell, °hold back *or* in, °subdue, °inhibit, °hamper, °hinder, °deter, °frustrate, °discourage, disallow: *The government tried to repress freedom of expression.*

repression *n.* **1** °restraint, °suppression, subjugation: *Increasing repression of their liberties finally led the people to revolt.* **2** °check, squelching, °control, °inhibition, hampering, hindering, °hindrance, stifling, deterring, frustration, frustrating: *The repression of the revolt was unsuccessful.*

repressive *adj.* °tyrannical, °oppressive, °dictatorial, °despotic, °brutal, suppressive, °authoritarian, °totalitarian; Fascist(ic): *In some countries, the people were unable to rebel against the repressive regime.*

reprieve *v.* **1** °respite, °rescue, °save; °let off, °spare: *The Home Secretary reprieved the prisoner from execution pending further investigation.*
—*n.* **2** °delay, °postponement, °suspension, °remission, °respite, °stay, amnesty: *The governor granted the condemned man a reprieve at the eleventh hour.*

reprimand *n.* **1** scolding, °reproof, °rebuke, admonition, upbraiding, castigation, reproach, °lecture, censure, °criticism, °disapproval, remonstrance, remonstration, reprehension, °tongue-lashing, *Colloq* dressing-down, talking-to, telling-off, ticking-off, rap over *or* on the knuckles, slap on the wrist, *Brit* slating, *US and Canadian* chewing-out, *Slang Brit* wigging: *Brown received a severe reprimand for violating the curfew.*
—*v.* **2** °scold, chide, °reprove, °rebuke, admonish, °upbraid, °castigate, reproach, °berate, °lecture, censure, °criticize, find °fault with, °attack, flay (alive), reprehend, read (someone) the riot act, slap on the wrist, rap over the knuckles, take to °task, *Colloq* °bawl out, °dress down, give a dressing-down, °tell off, tick off, haul over the coals, give (someone) a °piece of (one's) °mind, *Brit* slate, give (someone) a row, send (someone) away *or* off with a flea in his *or* her ear, tell (someone) a thing or two, carpet, wig, skin (alive), *US and Canadian* °chew out, rake over the coals, call on the carpet, pin (someone's) ears back: *Nigel deserves to be reprimanded for what he did.*

reprisal *n.* retaliation, °revenge, °retribution, redress, °requital, °vengeance, repayment, recompense, vindication, getting °even, °indemnity: *She refused to be named because she feared reprisals. How many hostages did they shoot in reprisal?*

reproachful *adj.* °fault-finding, °critical, censorious, disapproving, disparaging, upbraiding, reproving, scolding, admonitory, condemnatory, hypercritical: *She was quite reproachful after seeing what I had written about her in my book.*

reprobate *adj.* **1** unprincipled, °immoral, amoral, °abandoned, depraved, °despicable, °dissolute, °low, low-life, °base, °mean, debased, damned, accursed, cursed, °degenerate, °profligate, °shameful, °shameless, °vile, °evil, °wicked, °villainous, °sinful, irredeemable, °foul, iniquitous, reprehensible: *Such reprobate behaviour soon brought him to the attention of the church fathers.*
—*n.* **2** °scoundrel, blackguard, °miscreant, °rake, °profligate, °roué, °villain, °wastrel, °wretch, °degenerate, unprincipled person, °villain, evil-doer, debauchee, °libertine, °good-for-nothing, ne'er-do-well, cur, rapscallion, scamp, knave, °rascal, *US* low-life, *Colloq* scallywag *or* scalawag: *I can't understand what she sees in that old reprobate.*

reproduce *v.* **1** °duplicate, °copy, replicate, °match, recreate, °repeat, °imitate, simulate: *The printer thinks he can reproduce successfully the colours of the original picture in a print.* **2** °breed, multiply, °propagate, procreate, °spawn, °produce *or* °bring forth *or* beget °young; regenerate: *These animals normally reproduce twice a year.*

reproduction *n.* **1** duplication, copying, printing: *Unlicensed reproduction of this film is against the law.* **2** °duplicate, °copy, °print, clone, carbon (°copy), °facsimile, °replica, °look-alike, °double, °twin, °imitation: *The reproductions look better than the original.* **3** propagation, °breeding, spawning, °proliferation, °production: *Today's lecture concerns the reproduction and breeding habits of large sea-mammals.*

reproof *n.* See **reprimand, 1,** above.

reprove *v.* See **reprimand, 2,** above.

repudiate *v.* °reject, °scorn, °turn down, °renounce, °retract, rescind, °reverse, °abandon, abrogate, forswear, °forgo, °deny, disown, °discard: *The government* *has repudiated its earlier policy of refusing to negotiate with the strikers.*

repugnant *adj.* °repulsive, °abhorrent, °disgusting, off-putting, °offensive, °repellent, °revolting, °vile, °abominable, °loathsome, °foul, °distasteful, °unpalatable, °unsavoury, execrable, intolerable, °obnoxious, noisome, nauseating, °nauseous, sickening, unpleasant, objectionable: *I find the very thought of seeing them again repugnant.*

repulse *v.* **1** °repel, °rebuff, °drive back, °ward off, °fight *or* °beat off, °check: *With a mighty effort, they were able to repulse the attacking forces.* **2** °refuse, °spurn, snub, °reject, °rebuff, °fend off, °resist, °turn down, give the cold °shoulder to: *She repulsed his offer of marriage, and he left, never to see her again.* —*n.* **3** °rejection, °rebuff, °refusal, °denial, snub, cold °shoulder, spurning: *Alistair told himself he could not accept another repulse.*

repulsive *adj.* °disgusting, °revolting, °abhorrent, °loathsome, °repugnant, °repellent, °offensive, °obnoxious, objectionable, °gross, °unsavoury, °distasteful, °nasty, unpleasant, displeasing, °disagreeable, °ugly, off-putting, sickening, nauseating, °nauseous, °beastly, °vile, °dreadful, °awful, °rotten, feculent, °foul, odious, °horrible, horrid, °abominable, execrable, fulsome: *I have seldom had so repulsive an experience as the tour of that abattoir. The repulsive sights and smells were more than I could bear.*

reputable *adj.* °respectable, °honourable, °well-thought-of, °estimable, respected, °trustworthy, trusted, °honest, °reliable, dependable, °principled, °virtuous, °good, °worthy: *Alan is one of Aylesbury's most reputable businessmen.*

reputation *n.* **1** repute, °name, °standing, stature, °position, °status: *Jean is a woman of excellent reputation in the community.* **2** ***have a reputation for***: be known *or* °noted *or* °notorious *or* °famous for: *The company has a reputation for dismissing employees without notice.*

reputed *adj.* °alleged, purported, °supposed, °assumed, presumed; rumoured, said, deemed, held, regarded, viewed, looked on *or* upon, judged, considered, thought, believed: *The police arrested three reputed gang members. They are reputed to be international drug dealers.*

request *v.* **1** °ask for, °seek, °plead for, °apply for, °put in for, °requisition, °call for, °demand, °insist on, °solicit, °beg, entreat, °beseech, importune: *They request my cooperation. I requested to be excused. He requested her to open the door for him.* —*n.* **2** °plea, °petition, °application, °requisition, °call, °demand, solicitation, entreaty: *We receive many requests for information.*

require *v.* **1** °order, °command, °ask (for), °call (for), °press (for), °instruct, coerce, °force; °insist, °demand; °make: *I am required to appear in court on Monday. The teacher required that I bring my mother to school.* **2** °need, °want, °lack, be lacking, be missing, be °short (of); °desire: *We require one more trainee in order to fill our quota.*

requirement *n.* **1** requisite, °prerequisite, °demand, °precondition, °condition, °qualification, °stipulation, *sine qua non*, °provision, °proviso, °necessity, °essential, desideratum, °must: *It is a requirement of the loan agreement that you maintain an account with this bank.* **2** °need, °want, °demand: *We hope the new design will meet all your requirements.*

requisition *n.* **1** °request, °order, °demand, °call, authorization, mandate, voucher: *A requisition was issued by headquarters for the delivery of 200 desks and chairs.* —*v.* **2** °request, °order, °demand, °call, °authorize, mandate: *Have you requisitioned the office furniture we need?* **3** °seize, °appropriate, commandeer, °confiscate, °take °possession of, °take (over), °occupy; expropriate: *The army of occupation has requisitioned all available sleeping accommodation in the town.*

requital *n.* **1** repayment, °return, recompense, redress, °restitution, reparation, °remuneration, quittance, °amends, °satisfaction, compensation, °payment: *I look forward to an opportunity to make requital for all the favours you have done for me.* **2** °revenge, retaliation, °retribution, °reprisal, °vengeance; quid pro quo, Roland for an Oliver: *In requital for his shameful treachery, MacFallon was sent into exile.*

requite *v.* **1** °repay, °reward, °reciprocate, recompense, °compensate for, °respond to: *Her years of tender care were requited with abuse and scorn.* **2** °retaliate for, °revenge, avenge, make °restitution for, redress, °pay back for, give tit for tat for, make °amends for: *Who can requite the wrongs inflicted on these poor people?*

rescue *v.* **1** °save, °deliver, (°set) °free, °liberate, °let °go (°free), °release, (°let) °loose: *We rescued all the men who were being held prisoner. Jane was rescued by a very handsome lifeguard.* —*n.* **2** deliverance, °saving; freeing, liberating, °release: *The seaman's rescue was conducted by a navy helicopter team. Because of the heavy guard, the prisoners' rescue is out of the question.*

research *n.* **1** °investigation, investigating, °exploration, delving, digging, enquiry *or* °inquiry, fact-finding, scrutinization, °scrutiny, °examination, inspection, probing, °analysis, experimentation: *Her research into the causes of the disease have yielded good results. The government no longer supports much research.* —*v.* **2** °investigate, °explore, delve into, °dig into, °enquire *or* °inquire into, °scrutinize, °examine, °study, °analyse, °inspect, °check in *or* into *or* (up) on, °probe, °experiment with, *Colloq* °check out: *We are researching ways in which the virus attacks the blood cells.*

resemblance *n.* °likeness, similarity; correspondence, congruity, °coincidence, conformity, °accord, °agreement, equivalence, comparableness, comparability, °comparison: *There is a striking resemblance between your wife and mine. Any resemblance is purely a matter of chance.*

resemble *v.* °look *or* °sound *or* °taste *or* °seem *or* be °like *or* °similar to, °bear (a) °resemblance to, °approximate, smack of, °correspond to, have (all) the °hallmarks *or* earmarks of, °take after, *Colloq* °favour: *You are right, the taste does resemble that of liquorice. Does she resemble her mother?*

resent *v.* feel °embittered *or* °bitter about, feel °envious *or* °jealous of, °begrudge, have hard feelings about, be displeased *or* °disgruntled at, be °angry about: *I resent having to go to work while you sit about the house all day.*

resentful *adj.* °embittered, °bitter, acrimonious, °spiteful, °envious, °jealous, begrudging, °vindictive, °indignant, displeased, °disgruntled, °dissatisfied, unsatisfied, °unhappy, peeved, irritated, irked, annoyed, provoked, riled, °angry, piqued, irate, °furious, incensed, °agitated, °upset, worked up, antagonistic, °hostile: *Ronald is resentful because you got the promotion that he considered rightfully his.*

resentment *n.* °bitterness, acrimony, °rancour, °envy, jealousy, °grudge, °indignation, °displeasure, °dissatisfaction, unhappiness, irritation, °annoyance, °provocation, pique, °anger, ire, °fury, °agitation, °upset, °anxiety, °ill will, malice, °antagonism, °hostility, °animosity, enmity, antipathy, °hate: *Some believe that inequality among people provokes resentment.*

reservation *n.* **1** keeping *or* holding back, withholding, reticence, °reluctance, hesitation, hesitancy, hedging: *It was not without some reservation that I gave the book my endorsement.* **2** °qualm, °scruple, °qualification, hesitancy, limitation, °exception, °objection, demur *or* demurral *or* demurrer, °condition, °proviso, °provision: *He has no reservations about revealing the most intimate details in his autobiography.* **3** booking, °appointment, °arrangement: *I'll* *make a reservation for dinner for the two of us.* **4** °preserve, °sanctuary, °reserve, °area, °tract, °territory, °region, °section, °plot: *In North America, many Indians still live on reservations.*

reserve *v.* **1** °keep *or* °hold (back), °withhold, °save, °set *or* °put aside, °conserve, °preserve, °retain, °keep (to *or* for oneself), °hold over, °postpone, °delay, °put off, °defer: *Reserve judgement till you have heard all the facts. I shall reserve my answer to that question for another day.* **2** °hold, °keep, °book, °register, °save, °put *or* °set aside, °charter, °engage, °secure, °contract for: *I have reserved two seats for the matinee.*
—*n.* **3** Often, ***reserves***: °store, °stock, stockpile, inventory, °supply, nest egg, reservoir, °fund, °hoard, °cache: *We prayed for rain, as our water reserves were getting low.* **4** reticence, (self-)°restraint, (self-) °control, taciturnity, aplomb, °formality, coolness, aloofness, guardedness, standoffishness, remoteness, °detachment: *I had to admire Paul's reserve in the face of such insults.* **5** Often, ***reserves***: °auxiliary, °alternate, °substitute, reinforcements, backup, °spare: *If the battle goes badly, we shall have to call out the reserves.* **6** See **reservation, 4,** above. **7** °reservation, °restriction, °restraint, hesitancy, hesitation, °limit, limitation, hedging, avoidance, °evasion, dodging, fudging: *The lawyer acknowledged without reserve that the case was weak.* **8** ***in reserve***: °ready, in °readiness, on °hand, °available, on °call, °accessible, as backup, in °store, on °tap, at (one's) fingertips: *We have huge resources in reserve should we require them.*

reserved *adj.* °reticent, restrained, controlled, °silent, °taciturn, uncommunicative, unforthcoming, close-mouthed, unresponsive, undemonstrative, unemotional, poker-faced, °cool, °formal, °aloof, °guarded, °standoffish, °unsocial, antisocial, °distant, °remote, °detached, °retiring, °withdrawn, °sedate, demure, °dignified, prim, °rigid, °strait-laced, °icy, °frigid, ice-cold: *She was always very reserved, not showing any emotion.*

residence *n.* **1** °abode, °home, °domicile, °dwelling, dwelling-place, °place, °house, habitation, (living) quarters: *A crowd was waiting to greet them outside their residence.* **2** residency, °stay, °sojourn, °visit, °tenancy: *During his residence in Cape Province, he became bilingual in Xhosa.* **3** mansion, villa, manor (°house), stately °home, °estate, château, °castle, °palace, *Brit* °hall: *The ambassadorial residence was a very imposing structure.*

resident *adj.* **1** in °residence, residing, living, staying, °abiding, °dwelling, °remaining: *Is he resident in this country?* **2** °local, °neighbourhood, °district, regional, °neighbouring: *Our resident astronomer mentioned there would be an eclipse of the moon tonight.*
—*n.* **3** °denizen, dweller, °inhabitant, °citizen, householder, home-owner, °tenant, °local: *Parking permits are available only to residents.*

residual *adj.* °remaining, °leftover, °surplus, °spare, °extra, residuary: *Residual units of the army are still bivouacked in the field. How would we survive nuclear fall-out and the subsequent residual contamination?*

residue *n.* °remainder, °leftover, °surplus, remains, rest, °excess, °dregs, residuum: *The residue of the tatterdemalion force escaped into the forest.*

resign *v.* **1** °quit, °leave, °go, °abdicate, give °notice; °retire (from), °abandon, °give up, °forsake, °hand over, °yield up, °renounce, °relinquish, let go, °release, °vacate, °surrender, °deliver up, °turn over: *Amanda resigned because she was offered a better job elsewhere. Anthony refused to resign the last of his responsibilities till he was ninety.* **2** ***resign (oneself) (to)***: °reconcile (oneself) (to), be *or* become resigned *or* reconciled (to), °accommodate (oneself) (to), °adjust (oneself) (to), °adapt (oneself) (to), acclimatize *or* acclimate (oneself) (to), °submit (oneself) (to): *Knowing that no one had ever escaped from the prison, he resigned himself to his fate.*

resignation *n.* **1** °notice; abandonment, abdication, resigning, renunciation, forgoing, relinquishment: *After the incident in the boardroom, Kim was asked for her resignation. Stuart's resignation of his responsibilities led to a severe reprimand.* **2** °reconciliation, reconcilement, °adjustment, °adaptation, acclimatization *or* acclimation, °submission, acceptance, compliance, capitulation, abandonment, acquiescence, passivity: *His resignation to his fate won admiration from those around him.*

resilience *n.* °rebound, °recoil, °bounce, °elasticity, springiness, °spring, buoyancy, °flexibility, suppleness, °ability to °recover: *The resilience of youth is astonishing, and William was soon on his feet again.*

resist *v.* **1** °stop, °hinder, °prevent, °hold out (against), be °proof (against), °keep *or* °hold at bay, °hold the line (against), °thwart, °impede, °block, °obstruct, °inhibit, °restrain, °preclude, °check, °control, °curb, °stem, °bridle, °hold back, °withstand, °weather, °last (against), °endure, °outlast, °stand up (to *or* against); °combat, °fight (against), °battle, countervail (against), °counteract, °oppose, °rebuff, °defy: *He was jailed for attempting to resist arrest. It is pointless to resist.* **2** °refuse, °deny, °turn down, °forgo: *I cannot resist a rich sweet for dessert.*

resistance *n.* **1** °opposition, defiance, °refusal, °denial, °obstruction, intransigence, rebelliousness, recalcitrance, stubbornness: *The child puts up considerable resistance to any form of discipline.* **2** °defences: *My resistance is low, I can deny you nothing.* **3** ***Resistance***: °underground, partisans, °freedom fighters, °guerrilla *or* guerilla °movement, guerrillas *or* guerillas, irregulars, Maquis, *US* resisters: *During the war, he was a member of the Resistance and engaged in sabotage against the invaders.*

resistant *adj.* **1** °opposed, against, °defiant, °averse, unsubmissive; impervious, °unaffected: *The organisms are resistant to any change.* **2** °recalcitrant, °stubborn, °obstinate, intransigent, °rebellious, °immovable, intractable, refractory, °wilful, °ungovernable, unmanageable, °unruly, uncompliant, uncooperative: *We have run up against a highly resistant group of activists.* **3** Often, ***resistant to***: impervious (to), impenetrable (to), °repellent (to); °proof (against); shedding: *You need a more resistant material. This fabric is resistant to rain and snow.*

resolute *adj.* resolved, °determined, °purposeful, °steadfast, °firm, °stubborn, adamant, °set, °decided, °staunch, °bold, dogged, undaunted, °dauntless, persevering, persisting, °persistent, perseverant, pertinacious, °tenacious, °single-minded, dedicated, °devoted, bulldog, purposive, °deliberate, °inflexible, unwavering, unshakeable *or* unshakable, unshaken, unflagging, °untiring, indefatigable, °tireless, unfaltering, °unhesitating, unhesitant, unswerving, °irreversible, undeviating, unchanging, °changeless, unchangeable, immutable, unalterable: *We remain resolute in our determination to end injustice.*

resolution *n.* **1** °resolve, resoluteness, °determination, °purpose, purposefulness, steadfastness, firmness, decidedness, °decision, staunchness, boldness, doggedness, dauntlessness, stubbornness, °obstinacy, °perseverance, °persistence, relentlessness, pertinacity, °tenacity, single-mindedness, °dedication, °devotion, constancy, devotedness, deliberation, deliberateness, inflexibility, inflexibleness, unshakeability *or* unshakability, fixedness, indefatigability, indefatigableness, irreversibility, changelessness, unchangeability, immutability, immutableness, unalterability, *Colloq US* stick-to-it-iveness: *The boys showed extraordinary resolution in deciding to continue despite the hardships.* **2** °promise, commitment, °pledge, °word (of honour), °oath, °vow, °undertaking, °obligation; °intention: *I find that my New Year's resolutions last till about January 5th.* **3** °motion, °resolve, °proposal, °proposition, °plan, °suggestion, °idea, °notion; °determination, verdict, °decision, °judgement: *The committee votes today on the resolution to increase membership fees.* **4** °answer, answering, °solution, solving, unravelling, disentanglement, sorting out, explication; °outcome, °issue, °result, °end

(°result): *The resolution of a family problem is seldom easy. Can there be a final resolution of the question of a free market economy?* **5** acutance, sharpness, °precision, °accuracy, exactness, exactitude, fineness, °discrimination, detailing, distinguishability: *The new optical system provides for a much better resolution.*

resolve *v.* **1** °determine, °decide, make up one's °mind, °agree, °undertake, °settle, °fix, conclude: *When did you resolve to move to Australia? Let us resolve never to let this happen again.* **2** °work out, °figure out, °solve, °clear up, °answer: *How have you resolved the problem of looking after the cats while you are away?* **3** °adopt, °pass, °approve, °decide: *It was resolved that membership fees should be raised.* **4** ***resolve into***: °change into, °convert into, °alter into, °transform into, transmute into, metamorphose into, be °convert(ed) into, °become, °dissolve into, °break down into, liquefy into, °disintegrate into, °reduce to *or* into: *O, that this too too solid flesh would melt, Thaw, and resolve itself into a dew!*
—*n.* **5** See **resolution, 1,** above. **6** See **resolution, 2,** above: *She kept her resolve never to marry again.*

resonant *adj.* vibrating, vibrant, resounding, (re-)echoing, reverberating, reverberant, pulsating, ringing, booming, thundering, °thunderous, °loud: *The resonant pealing of the bells almost drove me mad.*

resort *n.* **1** spa, °retreat, *Chiefly Brit* watering-place: *We go to a lovely resort in the Alps every summer.* **2** °resource, backup, °reserve, °refuge, place to turn, °alternative, °remedy: *He will see a doctor only as a last resort.*
—*v.* **3** ***resort to***: have °recourse to, °turn to, °look to, °fall back on, °repair to, °take to, °frequent, °patronize, °attend; °visit, °haunt, °hang out in: *I have to resort to father for a small loan. She was said to be resorting to the lowest dens in the Casbah.*

resound *v.* °boom, resonate, °ring (out), °boom (out), (re-)°echo, reverberate, °pulsate, °thunder: *The laughter resounded around the entire office.*

resource *n.* **1** Often, ***resources***: °initiative, °ingenuity, °talent, inventiveness, °imagination, imaginativeness, cleverness, quick-wittedness, °capability, resourcefulness, °aptitude, °qualifications, °strength, °quality, °forte, *Colloq Brit* °gumption, *Slang* °guts: *Has he the inner resources for the job that lies ahead?* **2** Often, ***resources***: °capital, °assets, °money, °possessions, °wealth, °property, °cash, °funds: *She has sufficient resources to retire at fifty if she wants to.*

resourceful *adj.* °ingenious, inventive, °imaginative, °clever, Daedalian, °creative, °skilful, °smart, °slick: *Sylvia is resourceful enough to get out of any situation.*

respect *n.* **1** °regard, °consideration, °admiration, °esteem, (high) °opinion, °appreciation: *We have great respect for Samuel Simpson, our president.* **2** °regard, °consideration, °courtesy, politeness, °civility, attentiveness, thoughtfulness, °etiquette, °deference, °reverence, °veneration: *Few treat Alastair with the respect he deserves.* **3** °reference, °relation, °connection, °comparison, °regard, °bearing: *What are they planning to do with respect to the flooding?* **4** °detail, °point, °element, °aspect, °characteristic, °feature, °quality, °trait, °particular, °matter, °attribute, °property: *Describe the respects in which the War of American Independence and the French Revolution were similar.* **5** ***respects***: °regards, °good *or* °best wishes, °greetings, compliments, *Formal* salutations, *Formal or archaic* devoirs: *I went to pay my respects to my aunt on her 90th birthday.*
—*v.* **6** °consider, °admire, °esteem, °honour, °appreciate, value, °defer to, pay °homage to, °think °highly *or* °well of, °look up to, °revere, °reverence, °venerate: *I am not sure that I like Mrs Horne, but I certainly respect her for what she has done for the poor.* **7** °heed, °obey, show °consideration *or* °regard for, °pay °attention to, °attend to, be °considerate *or* °polite *or* °courteous to, °defer to: *Children are no longer taught to respect their elders.*

respectable *adj.* **1** °proper, demure, °decorous, °seemly, °estimable, °worthy, °dignified, °decent, °upright, °honest, respected, °genteel, °refined, °reputable, °above-board, unimpeachable, law-abiding: *Patricia Smythe is a very respectable member of the community. I'll have you know that I run a respectable boarding house!* **2** °moderate, appreciable, °goodly, °reasonable, °fair, not inconsiderable, °considerable, °tolerable, °satisfactory, sizeable, good-sized, °substantial, not °insignificant, °significant, *Colloq* °tidy: *She earns a respectable living. A respectable number of people showed up. Climbing Annapurna, though it is not Everest, is a respectable feat.* **3** °presentable, °moral, °decent, °proper, °modest, °chaste, °innocent, °pure, °clean: *The board decided that the film is not respectable enough to be shown to schoolchildren.*

respectful *adj.* °courteous, °polite, well-mannered, well-behaved, mannerly, °civil, °cordial, gentlemanly, °ladylike, °gracious, °obliging, °accommodating, °considerate, °thoughtful: *On entering, Captain Gregory made a respectful bow to the ladies.*

respective *adj.* °separate, °individual, °particular, °pertinent, °specific, °special, °personal, own, °relevant, corresponding, °several: *Each retired to his respective room for the night. All of you know your respective duties.*

respectively *adv.* °separately, °individually, °singly, severally, *mutatis mutandis*, each to each: *Ron and Daniel are, respectively, president and secretary of the association.*

respite *n.* **1** °interval, °intermission, °break, °interruption, °recess, breather, °rest; °holiday, *Chiefly US and Canadian* vacation: *I haven't had a moment's respite since six o'clock this morning. We are planning a brief respite from work in August.* **2** °pause, °delay, hiatus, °stay, °extension, °reprieve, °postponement: *After a ten-minute respite, the infernal noise began again.*

respond *v.* **1** °answer, °reply, °come back, °return, °react, °reciprocate, °counter; rejoin, °retort: *When Sean insulted her, Una responded with a slap to his face. I said, 'Good morning!' and Adrian responded, 'What's good about it?'* **2** Often, ***respond to***: be °responsive (to), °react (to), empathize (with), °sympathize (with), commiserate (with), °feel for, °pity, be °affected *or* moved *or* touched (by): *Many respond to those charity appeals for the crippled and disabled.*

response *n.* °answer, °reply, °retort, rejoinder; °reaction, °effect, feedback, °return, *Colloq* comeback: *Whatever you say to Ronnie Farrago, he always has a snappy response. The response to our advertising has been quite good.*

responsibility *n.* **1** °accountability, °liability, chargeability, answerability, °obligation: *Responsibility is one of the burdens a parent must undertake.* **2** °charge, °duty, onus, °burden, °trust, °job, role, °task: *Has Ted taken on more responsibilities than he can handle? It is your responsibility to see that the children are awakened in time for school.* **3** °blame, °guilt, °fault, culpability: *Professor Davies assumed full responsibility for the failure of the experiment.* **4** dependability, reliability, trustworthiness, °stability, °accountability, creditability: *Before accommodating you with a loan, Mr Stokes, we must confirm your financial responsibility.*

responsible *adj.* **1** °accountable, answerable, °liable, chargeable: *The court determined that she was not responsible for her actions.* **2** °reliable, °trustworthy, dependable, °stable, creditable, °accountable, °ethical, °honest: *If teenagers can show that they are sufficiently responsible, the bank will lend them money for their enterprise.* **3** °executive, °leading, °authoritative, administrative, °important, decision-making, managerial, directorial, °principal, °chief, °top, *US* front-office: *Oliver played a responsible role in the running of the company.* **4** °guilty, to °blame, at °fault, culpable: *We never found out who was responsible for putting the frog in the teacher's desk.*

responsive *adj.* °alert, °alive, (wide-)°awake, reactive, communicative, °sharp, °keen, °receptive, °sensitive, °open, °sympathetic: *I was delighted to find students who were so responsive to the ideas put forth in my lectures.*

rest[1] *n.* **1** °repose, °sleep, °nap, °doze, siesta, slumber, *Chiefly Brit* lie-down, *Colloq* forty winks, zizz, snooze; shut-eye: *I think I'll have a bit of a rest before dinner.* **2** °relaxation, °intermission, °interval, °interlude, entr'acte, rest °period, cessation, (tea *or* coffee) °break, °recess, breather, breathing-space, °respite, °time off, °holiday, *Chiefly US and Canadian* vacation: *Why don't you take a rest for a while?* **3** °ease, °relaxation, °leisure, °indolence, °idleness, °inactivity, loafing, dozing: *His well-deserved rest was disturbed by an urgent request from Interpol to investigate a smuggling operation.* **4** °prop, °support, holder, °brace, trestle, shelf, °bracket: *Those old guns were too heavy to hold and fire without using a rest.* **5** ***come to rest***: °stop, °end up, °turn up, °arrive: *The ball rolled down the slope and came to rest in a puddle.*
—*v.* **6** (go to) °sleep, °doze, °relax, take a rest, (take one's) °repose, °lie down, °recline, go *or* take to one's bed, take one's °ease, unwind, loll, languish, laze about, be °idle, °idle about, °lounge, (take a) °nap, put one's feet up, *Colloq* take it °easy, snooze, count sheep, have a zizz, catch *or* grab some shut-eye, get *or* take forty winks, *US* catch *or* log a few zees (Z's), *Slang Brit* kip, doss down, hit the °sack, hit the hay, *US* °sack out: *Rest now—you'll feel better tomorrow.* **7** reside, be situated, be lodged, °lie, be placed, hinge, be found, °remain, °stay: *The responsibility for passenger safety rests with the captain and the crew. The blame for this fiasco rests on you.* **8** °place, °position, °put, °lay, °set, °lean, °prop: *Rest your head on my shoulder.* **9** °lie, °remain, °stay: *Can't you let the matter rest?* **10** allay, °calm, °quiet, °still, °stay: *Rest your fears—I shall let nothing happen to you.*

rest[2] *n.* **1** °remainder, °balance; °remains, °remnants, leftovers, °residue, residuum, °excess, °surplus, overage: *If you carry these bags, I'll take the rest. Martin bought up all the best books and left the rest for us.*
—*v.* **2** (°continue to) be, °remain, °keep on being: *Rest assured, the situation is bound to get easier as we go along.*

restful *adj.* **1** relaxing, °soothing, comforting, tranquillizing, °sedative, calming, sleep-inducing, hypnotic, soporific, somnolent: *Don't you find the sound of the waves restful?* **2** °tranquil, °calm, °peaceful, °quiet, °still, °serene, pacific, °comfortable, °relaxed, reposeful: *After a hectic day in the city, I was happy to return to the restful atmosphere of the country.*

restitution *n.* **1** °amends, compensation, redress, recompense, °remuneration, reparation, °requital, indemnification, °indemnity: *It was agreed that victims of the raids were entitled to restitution for what had been taken from them.* **2** °restoration, °return, re-establishment, reinstatement, °recovery: *A commission is to investigate the restitution of plundered property.*

restive *adj.* See **restless,** below.

restless *adj.* °restive, uneasy, edgy, on °edge, on tenterhooks, fidgety, °nervous, skittish, °excitable, highly-strung, high-strung, worked up, °agitated, °fretful, °jumpy, apprehensive, itchy, *Colloq* jittery, *Slang* uptight, *US* antsy, hyper: *The crowd in the square were becoming restless as they waited for the speeches to start.*

restoration *n.* **1** See **restitution, 2,** above. **2** renovation, refurbishment, rehabilitation, renewal, °repair, rejuvenation, reconstruction, resurrection, reconversion, °revival: *The programme for the restoration of ancient buildings suffers from lack of funding.*

restore *v.* **1** °give *or* °hand back, °return, make °restitution, bring back: *We must restore to the people the land that is rightfully theirs.* **2** °revive, °rejuvenate, re-establish, °renew, bring back, °give (someone) back, resuscitate, °resurrect, rekindle, reinvigorate, °refresh, °stimulate, revitalize, °strengthen: *Your kindness has restored my faith in mankind.* **3** °renovate, °refurbish, °renew, °repair, °rejuvenate, °resurrect, °revive, reconstruct, °rehabilitate, rebuild; °mend, °fix, °retouch, °touch up; *Colloq US* °fix up: *They live in a 17th-century cottage that has been lovingly restored. Antiques often lose their value entirely if they are restored.* **4** °replace, reinstate, °put back; °return, bring back: *They said that they would not rest until they had restored the rightful king on the throne. The doctor said she would soon be restored to good health.* **5** °replace, °reimburse, °repay, °return, °pay *or* °put *or* °give back: *Even though he has restored all the money he took, she refuses to forgive him.*

restrain *v.* **1** (keep under *or* in) °control, (keep *or* hold in) °check, °hold (back *or* in), °curb, °govern: *A poor rider, he was unable to restrain his horse. Something must be done to restrain the general's power.* **2** °limit, °restrict, °inhibit, °regulate, °suppress, °repress, °bar, debar, °curtail, °stifle, °hinder, °interfere with, °hamper, °handicap: *Trade between the two countries was restrained because of tariff disputes.* **3** (place under) °arrest, confine, °imprison, incarcerate, detain, °hold, °lock up, °jail *or Brit also* gaol, °shut in *or* up: *For his most recent offence, he was restrained for two months.*

restraint *n.* **1** °control, °check, °curb, °rein, °bridle, °restriction, constraint, °limit, limitation, curtailment, °taboo, °ban, interdict *or* interdiction, proscription, delimitation, °bound(s), °embargo: *The law places restraints on executives' buying and selling shares in their own companies. In 1863, a bill for the restraint of the press was brought before the House of Commons.* **2** °control, °restriction, constraint, confinement; °bondage, °bonds, fetters, °shackles, °handcuffs, gyves, bilboes, pinions, manacles, ball and °chain, strait-jacket, *Colloq* cuffs, bracelets: *Despite the restraints to his liberty, he felt a free man. He became violent and had to be put under restraint.* **3** °control, °reserve, °self-control, self-possession, °poise, equanimity, self-discipline, self-restraint: *Heather Gorse exhibited admirable restraint in remaining silent when teased about her name.*

restrict *v.* °limit, confine, °bound, circumscribe, delimit, °mark off, demarcate, °regulate; °qualify, °restrain, °impede: *Smoking is allowed only in restricted areas. The opposition party said that they would restrict the movement of heavy goods by road.*

restriction *n.* **1** °condition, °provision, °proviso, °qualification, °stipulation: *One restriction is that purchasers of shares in the utility must be resident in the UK.* **2** See **restraint, 1,** above.

result *n.* **1** °outcome, consequence, °effect, °end (result), °fruit; conclusion, °upshot, °issue, °development, °sequel, °follow-up, denouement *or* dénouement: *It will take years to evaluate the results of the new educational curriculum. As a result of his speeding ticket, his driving licence was suspended.*
—*v.* **2** Often, ***result from***: °develop, °emerge, °follow, °happen, °occur, °come (about), °come to °pass, °arise, evolve, be produced: *Severe burns can result from allowing children to play with matches. The mixture that results may be highly volatile.* **3** ***result in***: °end, conclude, culminate, °terminate: *The explosion resulted in a heavy loss of life. The experience gained often results in better safety devices.*

resume *v.* °continue, °carry on, take up again, °pick up (where one left off): *After prison, it is not easy to resume one's life where it left off. When the audience quieted, the speaker resumed.*

résumé *n.* **1** °summary, °digest, °abstract, °synopsis, °précis, °outline, °review, recapitulation, °epitome, *Colloq* °run-down, recap: *Give me a résumé of what went on at the board meeting.* **2** curriculum vitae, CV, °summary, biography, °work *or* °job °history, °career °description, *Formal* prosopography, *Colloq* bio, *US* vita: *Suitably qualified candidates are invited to send their résumés to the address below.*

resurgence *n.* °renaissance, renascence, °rebirth, °revival, reawakening, °restoration, renewal, resumption, °return, resurrection, regeneration, rejuvenation, new °dawn, new °birth: *Simone is banking her entire future on a resurgence of interest in seventies' fashion.*

resurrect *v.* °revive, bring back, °return, reawaken, °restore (to °life), reintroduce, °renew, regenerate, °rejuvenate, °raise (from the dead), resuscitate, breathe new °life into, reanimate, reincarnate: *Some antiquated law was resurrected in order to prevent their using the land for grazing.*

retain *v.* **1** °keep (°possession of), °hold (on to), °save, °preserve, *Colloq* °hang on to: *Retain the receipt in case you wish to exchange the merchandise.* **2** °engage, °hire, °employ, commission, °take on: *We have retained a caretaker to look after the estate.* **3** °hold, absorb, °contain, °soak up, °preserve: *This type of soil retains little water.* **4** °remember, °keep *or* bear *or* have in °mind, °recall, remain aware of, °memorize, impress on the °memory, °recollect: *As he aged, he found it increasingly difficult to retain even the simplest information such as names and dates.*

retaliate *v.* °repay, °pay back (in kind), °counter, °strike back (at), take °revenge (on), °wreak °vengeance (on), °revenge oneself (on), avenge, °reciprocate, °settle a °score (with); give a Roland for an Oliver, give tit for tat, take an eye for an eye (and a tooth for a tooth), give as good as one gets, give (someone) a taste of his *or* her *or* their own medicine, °pay (someone) back in his *or* her own coin; *Colloq* get °even (with), °get back (at): *After government forces bombed their mountain headquarters, the guerrillas retaliated by destroying bridges and railway lines.*

retard *v.* **1** °slow (down *or* up), °hold up *or* back, °set back, °hinder, °impede, °delay, °keep back, °stall, °thwart, balk, °block, °restrict, °hold in °check, °frustrate, °interfere with: *Growth of the economy was severely retarded by the war.*
—*n.* **2** *Offensive and derogatory*: idiot, moron, °fool, imbecile, dunce, *Slang chiefly US and Canadian* °jerk: *Why she invites that retard to her parties I can't imagine.*

reticent *adj.* °quiet, °shy, °timid, °retiring, °reserved; °taciturn, °silent, unresponsive, °tight-lipped, unforthcoming: *If you are proud of your accomplishments, why be reticent about saying so? Colin is reticent about how he acquired his gold earring.*

retinue *n.* entourage, °escort, convoy, cortège, °company, °train, °suite, followers, attendants, following, hangers-on, *Colloq* groupies: *The rock band arrived at the airport accompanied by a retinue of flunkeys.*

retire *v.* **1** °withdraw, rusticate, °go off *or* away, °take off, °retreat; hibernate, aestivate *or US* estivate, seclude *or* sequester *or* cloister oneself: *I think I'll retire to some mountain-top to finish my book.* **2** °stop *or* °give up work(ing), be pensioned off, (be) put out to grass *or* pasture, take the golden handshake, be given the gold watch, go on social security, go on a pension, be superannuated, go out of circulation: *Gemma Frobisher has retired from her job in the bakery, and is now living with her daughter in Norfolk.* **3** go *or* take to (one's) bed *or* bedroom, (go to) °sleep, °lie down, (take one's) °repose, (take a) °nap, put one's feet up, *Colloq* take it °easy, snooze, count sheep, have a zizz, catch *or* grab some shut-eye, get *or* take forty winks, *US* catch *or* log a few zees (Z's), *Slang* hit the °sack, °sack out, hit the hay, *Brit* kip, doss down: *I usually retire around midnight.*

retiring *adj.* °shy, °bashful, °coy, demure, °modest, diffident, °timid, unpretentious, unassuming, °humble, self-effacing, timorous, °meek, °reticent, °reserved, °unsocial, unsociable, °aloof, removed, °standoffish, °distant, °reclusive, eremitic(al): *Howard is of a retiring disposition, preferring to keep to himself.*

retort *n.* **1** °response, °reply, rejoinder, °answer, riposte, °rebuttal, *Colloq* comeback: *Faced with criticism of the novel, the author's retort was a four-letter word.*
—*v.* **2** °fling *or* °hurl back, rejoin, °answer back, riposte, °rebut, °counter, come back with, °return, °respond, °answer, °reply, °retaliate: *'And don't expect a Christmas present from me, either!', she retorted vehemently.*

retouch *v.* °touch up, °correct, °restore, °repair, recondition, °refresh, °brush up, °adjust, °improve, °finish, put the finishing touches on: *Only an expert restorer could have retouched the damaged painting so skilfully.*

retract *v.* **1** °withdraw, °pull *or* °draw back: *The instant he felt the heat, he retracted his hand.* **2** °take back, °withdraw, rescind, °revoke, °repeal, °deny, disavow, °recant, °renounce, abjure, °cancel, forswear, °repudiate, disclaim, disown, °reverse: *If they refuse to retract their statement, I shall sue them for libel.*

retreat *n.* **1** retirement, withdrawal, pulling *or* falling *or* drawing back, giving ground, evacuation, °flight: *The regiment's retreat in the face of overwhelming odds is complete.* **2** retirement, °seclusion, withdrawal, isolation, °solitude, rustication: *Since her retreat from public life, she has devoted herself to painting.* **3** °sanctuary, °sanctum (sanctorum), °refuge, °shelter, den, haven, asylum, °resort, °hideaway, hide-out: *Antonia insisted on having her own retreat where she could occasionally escape from the children.*
—*v.* **4** °withdraw, decamp, °run (away), °turn tail, °depart, give *or* lose ground, °pull *or* °fall *or* °draw back, °retire, °evacuate, °flee, take °flight: *We must retreat to the shelter of the hills, where we can regroup.* **5** °ebb, °draw *or* move back, °recede: *The waves, constantly advancing and retreating across the pebbly strand, lulled me to sleep.*

retribution *n.* °vengeance, °revenge, °reprisal, retaliation, °requital, redress, quid pro quo, °satisfaction, °punishment, °justice, just °deserts, recompense, compensation: *It is a moral question whether society's treatment of malefactors should be an act of retribution or the setting of an example to others.*

retrieve *v.* **1** bring *or* °get (back), °fetch, come back with: *Simon trained his dog to retrieve his slippers.* **2** °recover, °save, °rescue, °take back, °recoup, regain, °reclaim: *I tried using a fishing line to retrieve my hat from the lake.* **3** °make up, make °amends for, °recover, °cover, °redeem, °repay, °pay for, °return, °get back, regain, be repaid *or* reimbursed for: *Will we be able to retrieve our losses when we sell the business?*

retrospect *n.* hindsight, reconsideration, °review, remembering, afterthought, °recollection, looking back: *In retrospect, I am not sure we did the right thing.*

return *v.* **1** come *or* °go back, °revert, °turn back: *She is returning to her old habits. I shall return to this subject later if I have time.* **2** come back, reappear, resurface, crop up again, °turn *or* °show up again, put in an °appearance again; °recur, reoccur, *Colloq* pop up again: *Will he return before March? The symptoms returned.* **3** °replace, °put back, °restore, give back, bring *or* carry back: *The missing books have mysteriously been returned.* **4** °exchange, bring back *or* carry back: *You may return any merchandise, for any reason, for refund or exchange, within ten days of its purchase.* **5** °yield, °earn, °gain, °profit, °benefit: *Where else can you find a secure investment that returns more than 15 per cent?* **6** °deliver, °render, °give, °offer, °turn in, proffer, °report: *The jury returned a verdict of Not Guilty.*
—*n.* **7** recurrence, reappearance, °repetition, renewal, recrudescence, resurfacing, re-emergence: *There was a return of the symptoms when I stopped taking the medicine.* **8** replacement, replacing, °restoration, restoring, °restitution: *We shall see to the return of the stolen items to their rightful places.* **9** Sometimes, ***returns***: °yield, °earnings, °profit, °gain, °benefit, °income, °revenue, °proceeds, °interest, takings, °results: *The return on my investment was almost 100 per cent!* **10** °arrival, advent, coming, home-coming: *A*

small crowd had gathered to await his return. **11** reciprocity, reciprocation, repayment, recompense, reimbursement, compensation, °payment, reparation, °indemnity, indemnification, °consideration, °amends, redress, °requital: *If I give you my bike, what will I get in return?*

revamp *v.* °overhaul, redo, recondition, °renovate, °repair, °fix, do up, refit, °refurbish, °restore, °rehabilitate, *US* °fix up: *To bring it into line with the 21st century, the constitution may need to be revamped completely.*

reveal *v.* expose, °display, divulge, °disclose, °show; make known, °let on, °let out, let it be known, let °slip, °communicate, give °vent to, °air, ventilate, °leak (out): *The increasing light of dawn revealed a no-man's-land of utter devastation. The book is said to reveal everything you would prefer not to know about factory-farming.*

revel *v.* **1** Usually, ***revel in***: (take) °delight (in), take °pleasure (in), °rejoice (in), °luxuriate (in), bask (in), °wallow(in), °lap up, crow (about *or* over), °glory (in), °savour, °relish: *Gavin revelled in the news that his ex-wife was remarrying and he would no longer have to pay her alimony.* **2** make °merry, °carouse, °celebrate, cut loose, go on a °spree, *Colloq* live it up, °whoop it up, make whoopee, paint the town red, °party, *Brit* push the boat out, *Slang Brit* have a °rave *or* rave-up: *The night after exams finish, the students traditionally revel till dawn.*
—*n.* **3** °spree, °party, merrymaking, debauch, °carouse, °festival, °fête *or* fete, carousal, °celebration, °gala, ball, romp, °fling, carnival, °jamboree, bacchanal, saturnalia: *Everyone joined in the revels on New Year's Eve, and had a good time.*

revelation *n.* °news, °information, °proclamation, °publication, °bulletin, communiqué, °announcement, °pronouncement, °declaration, °statement, °leak; °admission, confession; °discovery, unveiling, uncovering, °exposure, disclosure, exposé: *We were shocked at the revelation that they had been married all these years. Scientists' revelations about the depletion of the ozone layer are causing widespread concern.*

revelry *n.* merrymaking, °fun, revelling, carousal, carousing, °gaiety, °festivity, jollity, °mirth, °celebration, ball, high jinks *or* hijinks, °spree, *Colloq* partying, *Slang Brit* rave *or* rave-up: *The revelry went on into the wee hours of the morning.*

revenge *n.* **1** °vengeance, retaliation, °reprisal, °retribution, vindictiveness, spitefulness, repayment, °satisfaction: *They think he set fire to the place in revenge for having been dismissed.*
—*v.* **2** avenge, get °even for, take revenge for, make °reprisal for, exact °retribution *or* °payment *or* repayment for: *She was seeking ways to revenge the murder of her brother.* **3** ***revenge oneself* (on)**: settle a °score *or* an old °score (with), °pay (someone) back in his *or* her own coin, give a Roland for an Oliver, give tit for tat, take an eye for an eye (and a tooth for a tooth), °punish, *Colloq* °get, °get °even (with), give (someone) his *or* her *or* their comeuppance, give (someone) a taste of his *or* her *or* their own medicine: *He found ways to revenge himself on them for all that they had done to him.*

revenue *n.* (gross) °income, °proceeds, °receipts, °return(s), °yield, °interest, takings, net (°income), °gate; °profits, °gain, *Colloq chiefly US* °take: *The revenue from the drugs operation must run into billions.*

revere *v.* °adore, adulate, °reverence, °venerate, °worship, °idolize, enshrine, °sanctify, beatify, °glorify, °esteem, °admire, °respect, °honour: *He was revered as the founding father of British psychology.*

reverence *n.* **1** °honour, °respect, °esteem, °admiration, glorification, beatification, sanctification, idolization, °worship, °veneration, adulation, adoration, °homage, fealty, °obeisance, °deference, awe: *Their totalitarian discipline was able to succeed because of the people's reverence for authority.*
—*v.* **2** See **revere,** above.

reverie *n.* °day-dream, °fantasy, brown study, wool-gathering, absent-mindedness; meditation, °thought: *I shouldn't disturb Kevin—he's deep in a reverie.*

reversal *n.* **1** °reverse, °turn-about, turn-round, U-turn, °change, volte-face, (complete) °switch, *Brit* °about-turn, *US* about-face: *This represents a reversal of former policy, doesn't it?* **2** See **reverse, 8,** below. **3** annulment, nullification, nulling, °cancellation, revocation, °repeal, rescission: *The present case is an appeal against the reversal of an earlier judgement.*

reverse *adj.* **1** °opposite, °contrary, inverse, °converse; inverted, upside down, °mirror, reversed, °backward: *Now try turning the wheel in the reverse direction. What appears on the retina is a reverse image, which the brain inverts.*
—*v.* **2** invert, °overturn, °turn upside down, °turn °topsy-turvy, °turn over, up-end; °exchange, °change, interchange, °transpose: *Using your finger to keep the mercury from running out, reverse the tube in the dish of mercury. Perhaps the car will start if you reverse the leads to the battery.* **3** °overturn, °overthrow, °upset, °set aside, °quash, override, annul, nullify, °vacate, °abandon, °revoke, negate, °veto, declare null and °void, disaffirm, invalidate, °cancel, °repeal, rescind, overrule, countermand, °undo: *The superior tribunal reversed the decision of the lower-court judge.* **4** °alter, °change, °modify; °renounce, °recant, °take back: *Reverse the polarity of the wiring. I reversed my opinion after hearing her sing.* **5** °back up, move *or* go °backwards *or US also* °backward, backtrack, *Nautical* make sternway: *You will be in the right spot if you reverse a yard or two.*
—*n.* **6** °opposite, °contrary, °converse, antithesis: *Whatever she tells you, I suggest you do the reverse.* **7** °back, °rear, wrong side, verso, underside; flip side, B-side; tail side: *Read what it says on the reverse.* **8** °setback, °disappointment, °misfortune, °reversal, °mishap, misadventure, °trouble, °problem, °difficulty, °vicissitude, adversity, °defeat; °disaster, °catastrophe, débâcle, °rout, *Colloq* °washout: *We suffered a temporary reverse or two in business, but we're all right now. United suffered a humiliating reverse against Wanderers in the cup last week.*

revert *v.* °return, come *or* °go back, take *or* pick up again, °lapse, backslide, regress, °relapse, °retreat: *He reverted to his old beliefs about male superiority.*

review *v.* **1** °survey, °examine, °regard, °look at, °study, con, °consider, °weigh, °inspect, °look over, °scrutinize: *Would you be good enough to review the work of the new employees? She is coming to review the troops this weekend.* **2** re-examine, reconsider, °go over again, °look at *or* over again, reassess: *Billings reviewed once more all the bad things he had done in his lifetime.* **3** °criticize, critique, assess, °judge, °evaluate, give one's °opinion of, °comment on *or* upon, °discuss: *Who reviewed your latest book?*
—*n.* **4** °criticism, critique, review article, assessment, °judgement, °evaluation, commentary, °study, °comment, °notice: *The play received rave reviews from almost all the critics.* **5** °survey, °examination, °study, °consideration, inspection, °scrutiny, °analysis; reviewing, reading: *After a detailed review of the circumstances, we have decided to let you off easy this time, Finnegan.* **6** re-examination, reconsideration, rehashing *or* °rehash, °post-mortem, reassessment, rethinking, rethink: *Why do you always insist on a review of all the bidding on every hand, whenever we play bridge?* **7** °periodical, °journal, °magazine: *Have you read Stonehouse's article in the latest Birmingham Review?* **8** °parade, °procession, array, cavalcade, °march past, fly-past *or chiefly US* flyover: *A great naval review was held at Spithead.*

revise *v.* **1** °edit, emend, °improve, °correct, °rectify, °modify, °revamp, redact, rework, °overhaul, update; rewrite: *A revised edition of the dictionary has been published every ten years.* **2** °alter, °change, °amend: *Since hearing him sing, I have been forced to revise my taste in music.*

revision *n.* editing, revising, emendation, °improvement, °correction, rectification, modification, revamping, reappraisal, re-examination, reinterpretation, reassessment, redaction, reworking, °overhaul, overhauling, updating, update; rewrite, °edition, °version, °rendition: *Her revision of the text is based on a newly discovered manuscript. The fourth revision will be available next April.*

revival *n.* **1** resurrection, resuscitation, renewal, °restoration, revitalization, resurfacing, °return, returning: *How much more often we see the revival of out-moded fashions than the introduction of new ideas!* **2** °rebirth, °renaissance *or* renascence, °resurgence, awakening, quickening, reanimation: *Do you regard the current trend towards fundamentalism as a genuine revival of religion?* **3** °recovery, °improvement, °increase, upsurge, upturn, °boost, upswing, °advance, advancement, °progress, °rise, escalation, *Colloq* pick-up, comeback: *This week saw a revival in the metals market.*

revive *v.* **1** (re)awaken, °wake (up), come *or* °bring (a)round, waken, resuscitate; °recover, (re)gain consciousness: *Dashing cold water in his face revived him at once. I revived to find her leaning over me.* **2** reawaken, °stir up again, °renew, resume, reopen, °refresh: *You can blame Andy for reviving the feud between our families.* **3** bring back, reactivate, °renew, °resurrect, re-establish, resume, reopen, revitalize, breathe life into, reinvigorate, °rejuvenate: *Perhaps we ought to revive the practice of putting hooligans, vandals, and delinquents into stocks in the market square.*

revoke *v.* °cancel, °deny, invalidate, annul, declare null and °void, °void, nullify, negate, °repudiate, °renounce, rescind, °repeal, °recall, °recant, °quash, °veto, °set aside, abrogate, °abolish, °withdraw, °take back, °retract: *He warned that if they refused to comply with local authority rulings he had the power to revoke their licence.*

revolt *n.* **1** °rebellion, °revolution, °uprising, °mutiny, insurrection, *coup d'état*, putsch, take-over: *The council ordered the secret police to suppress the revolt.* —*v.* **2** °rebel, °rise up, °mutiny; °protest, dissent: *After years of oppression, the people revolted and deposed their leaders.* **3** °repel, °offend, °disgust, °shock, °horrify, °repulse, °nauseate, °sicken: *I was revolted by the poverty and sickness I saw in that country.*

revolting *adj.* °disgusting, sickening, nauseating, °nauseous, stomach-turning, stomach-churning, vomit-provoking, sick-making, °foul, °loathsome, °abhorrent, horrid, °horrible, °nasty, °vile, °obnoxious, °repulsive, appalling, °abominable, °repellent, °offensive, objectionable, off-putting, °beastly, °gross, °rotten, °rancid, inedible, °disagreeable, unpleasant, *Slang* icky, °yucky: *Rick served up some revolting mess for dinner and then took offence when we didn't eat it.*

revolution *n.* **1** °mutiny, °revolt, °rebellion, coup, *coup d'état*, °uprising, insurgency, insurrection, putsch, take-over, °overthrow: *If the government fails to ensure that the people have food, there will be a revolution.* **2** °upheaval, cataclysm, °transformation, (°drastic *or* radical *or* major) °change, sea °change, metamorphosis: *Recent successes of capitalism have sparked a revolution in the political philosophies of communist nations.* **3** rotation, °turn, °orbit, °circuit, °spin, °lap, °round, °cycle, °circle, gyration; °wheel, whirl, °pirouette: *At each revolution of the gear (A), the ratchet (B) moves one notch. The rapid revolutions of the ice-skater dissolved her into a blur of colour.*

revolutionary *adj.* **1** °mutinous, °rebellious, insurgent, insurrectionist, insurrectionary, °radical, °rebel, °seditious, °subversive: *They had dreamed for years of the revolutionary overthrow of the government.* **2** °novel, innovative, °creative, °new, °different, °original, °avant-garde: *The firm hopes that its revolutionary new product will make a clean sweep in the marketplace.* —*n.* **3** °rebel, mutineer, insurgent, insurrectionist, insurrectionary, revolutionist, sansculotte *or* sansculottist, anarchist, °radical, extremist, °terrorist: *In his younger days at university, Charles fancied himself a revolutionary, without quite knowing what he might rebel against.*

revolve *v.* **1** °spin, °turn, °pivot, °rotate, °gyrate, whirl, °twirl, °reel, °wheel, °go (a)round, °circle, °cycle, °orbit; °swivel: *As the earth revolves on its axis, the moon revolves round the earth.* **2** °turn, °depend, °pivot, °rely: *His decision to buy a new car revolves on his finances.* **3** °turn over (in one's mind), °ponder, °weigh, °consider, °meditate upon *or* on, °think about, °reflect upon *or* on, ruminate over *or* on, °chew over, °contemplate: *I have been revolving in my mind your most attractive proposal, but I regret I must turn it down.*

revolver *n.* °pistol, gun, side-arm, firearm, *Chiefly US and Canadian* handgun, *Colloq US* six-gun, six-shooter, *Slang US* rod, gat, roscoe, piece, Saturday-night special, shooting-iron: *How do you explain the fact that your fingerprints were found on the revolver with which she was shot?*

revulsion *n.* °loathing, detestation, °disgust, repugnance, abomination, abhorrence, °aversion, hatred, antipathy, odium, execration: *I cannot describe the revulsion I felt at seeing those elephants slaughtered for their ivory.*

reward *n.* **1** °award, °favour, recompense, compensation, °return, °payment, °pay, °requital: *For your good deeds you will have to seek your reward in heaven; dishonesty is recompensed here on earth.* **2** °prize, °award, °tribute, °honour, *Literary* guerdon: *The Victoria Cross was instituted as a reward for military valour in 1856.* **3** °retribution, °punishment, just °deserts, *Colloq* comeuppance: *Hanging was the reward of treason.* —*v.* **4** recompense, °compensate, °pay, °repay, remunerate, redress, °requite, make (something *or* it) worth someone's while: *Only if they reward him will Fuller give information leading to the capture of the thief.*

rewarding *adj.* °satisfying, gratifying, °worthwhile, enriching, enriched, °fruitful; °profitable, °advantageous, °productive, °gainful: *Laurence says that his most rewarding experience has been seeing his children again.*

reword *v.* °paraphrase, rephrase, put into different words, put another way, express differently, °revise, recast, rewrite: *Perhaps if you reworded your request in politer terms it might get more sympathetic consideration.*

rhapsodic *adj.* rhapsodical, °ecstatic, °enthusiastic, °elated, °overjoyed, °effusive, °rapturous, thrilled, blissful, transported, orgasmic, intoxicated, euphoric, walking on air, °delighted, °happy as a sandboy, °happy as a pig in clover, (sitting) on top of the °world, *Brit* in the seventh °heaven, *US* in seventh °heaven, °happy as a cow in clover, *Taboo slang US* °happy as a pig in shit: *What kind of society have we that is scornful of intellect and rhapsodic about celebrities?*

rhetoric *n.* **1** eloquence, expressiveness, elocution, way with words, *Colloq* gift of the gab: *His rhetoric, though it defied analysis, exactly reflected the emotions of the Labour movement.* **2** °bombast, °bluster, fustian, rodomontade, grandiloquence, magniloquence, °oratory, windiness, high-flown poppycock, wordiness, sesquipedality, verbosity, prolixity, long-windedness, turgidity, flatulence, gasconade, *Colloq* °hot air, puffery: *Her threats are mere rhetoric and I refuse to take notice of them.*

rhetorical *adj.* **1** stylistic, linguistic, °poetic, °expressive, oratorical: *Zeugma, hysteron proteron, and anacoluthon are all terms for rhetorical devices.* **2** °artificial, contrived, for °effect, unanswerable, not °literal: *The question, 'Why don't you drop dead', was purely rhetorical.* **3** °pretentious, °bombastic, °flamboyant, °extravagant, florid, fustian, high-flown, °inflated, °grandiose, euphuistic, turgid, grandiloquent, magniloquent, long-winded, °windy, orotund, °wordy, prolix, sesquipedalian, *Colloq* highfalutin *or* hifalutin: *The rhetorical style of Crampton's parliamentary speeches appear to be doing the party more harm than good.*

rhyme *n.* **1** rime, °poem, °poetry, verse, versification, metrical composition, °song: *The art of rhyme may well be coincident with the earliest stages of language.* **2** ***rhyme or reason***: (common) °sense, °logic, °intelligence, °meaning, °wisdom, rationality, °rationale, soundness, °organization, °structure: *There appears to be no rhyme or reason behind the bombing of the library.*

rhythm *n.* °tempo, °beat, °cadence *or* cadency, throb, throbbing, °accent, accentuation, °time, timing, °stress *or* rhythmic(al) pattern, °measure, metre, °pulse, lilt, *Music* downbeat, thesis, upbeat, arsis: *The song is in samba rhythm.*

rhythmic *adj.* rhythmical, °measured, cadenced, throbbing, pulsing, pulsating, °regular, °steady, beating: *The rhythmic sound of the waves soon sent me to sleep.*

ribaldry *n.* °vulgarity, immodesty, °indelicacy, indecency, coarseness, bawdiness, earthiness, wantonness, raciness, naughtiness, shamelessness, lustfulness, rakishness, rascality, dissoluteness, lubricity, lasciviousness, looseness, scurrility *or* scurrilousness, lewdness, salaciousness, licentiousness, grossness, offensiveness, rankness, rudeness, smuttiness, smut, °dirt, °filth, foulness, obscenity: *The ribaldry of some of Chaucer's tales makes them not altogether suitable for schoolchildren.*

rich *adj.* **1** °wealthy, affluent, °prosperous, well-to-do, °well off, well provided for, °opulent, moneyed, in clover, on velvet, *Colloq* °flush, °loaded, on Easy Street, rolling in it *or* °money *or* °wealth, in the chips *or* the dough *or* the °money, well-heeled, *US* well-fixed: *A year ago Montmorency was a rich man, but that was before Blue Thursday on the Stock Exchange.* **2** Sometimes, ***rich in***: °abundant (in), overflowing (with), °fertile (in), fecund (in), °productive (of), copious (in), abounding in, well supplied (with), well stocked (with), rife (with), °replete (with), °profuse (in *or* with): *The rich prairie land was soon yielding abundant harvests. The surrounding mountains were rich in minerals of all kinds.* **3** valuable, °precious, °invaluable, °priceless: *For centuries the islanders have enjoyed the rich bounty of the seas. The thieves who broke into the vaults got a rich haul.* **4** costly, °expensive, °dear, valuable, °invaluable, °precious, °priceless, °lavish, °sumptuous, °lush, °luxurious, °palatial, °elaborate, °splendid, °exquisite, °superb, °elegant: *The caravans returned laden with rich treasures of the Orient—silks, jewels, spices, rare woods, and other luxuries.* **5** °intense, °dark, °deep, °warm, vibrant, °strong, °lustrous: *At the rajah's court the rich colours of the carpets and hangings dazzle the eye.* **6** °fat, fattening, °heavy, creamy, °succulent, °savoury, mouth-watering, °luscious, sapid, °delicious: *When Vicky complained that her sweet was too rich, Arthur ate hers, too.* **7** °mellow, mellifluous, °resonant, sonorous, °full: *Edgar's rich basso filled the cavernous amphitheatre.* **8** °aromatic, ambrosial, °savoury, °fragrant, °redolent, °pungent, °strong: *The house was filled with the rich odour of freshly made coffee.* **9** °productive, °plentiful, °abundant, °ample, °bountiful, °prolific, °fruitful, °fertile, fecund, copious, °profitable, °potent: *The letters proved a rich source of intimate details about their private life.* **10** laughable, °funny, °hilarious, °comic(al), °humorous, amusing, *Colloq* side-splitting: *He had many rich anecdotes to relate about the practical jokes they used to play on one another.* **11** °ridiculous, °preposterous, °outlandish, °ludicrous, °absurd, °nonsensical: *One particularly rich episode involved a chimpanzee.*

riches *n.pl.* °wealth, affluence, opulence, °plenty, °prosperity, °abundance, °fortune, °means, °resources; lucre, pelf: *It was rumoured that the family had acquired its apparently endless riches in the slave trade, in the 18th century.*

richly *adv.* **1** sumptuously, lavishly, luxuriously, splendidly, elaborately, exquisitely, elegantly, superbly: *The flat was richly appointed with Chinese antiques, thick oriental carpets, and silk hangings.* **2** °well, °thoroughly, °amply, fully, °appropriately, fittingly, condignly: *Shirley's work was at last given the recognition it so richly deserved.*

rickety *adj.* wobbly, unsteady, broken-down, °decrepit, °shaky, tottering, teetering, °ramshackle, °flimsy, °frail, °precarious, °dilapidated, in °disrepair, °tumbledown, unsecure: *Don't put such a heavy lamp on that rickety table!*

rid *v.* **1** ***rid of***: °deliver from, °relieve of, °free from *or* of, °rescue, °save: *What can we do to rid ourselves of that appalling smell?* **2** ***be*** *or* ***get rid of***: °banish, °exile, °eject, °expel, °dispose of, °throw out *or* away, °eliminate, °dispense with; °refuse, °reject, °dismiss, shrug off: *If she had wanted to be rid of him, she would have divorced him long ago. I am having a spot of bother trying to get rid of my old car: nobody wants to buy it.*

-ridden *adj.* afflicted *or* harassed *or* °affected *or* dominated by, infected *or* infested with: *They were shocked when they first came to this drought-ridden province of Northern Ethiopia. Only foreign aid can salvage the debt-ridden economy of this state.*

riddle[1] *n.* conundrum, °puzzle, °enigma, poser, °question, °mystery, °problem, brain-teaser *or Brit* brain-twister: *The cracker contained a whistle, paper hat, and the inevitable riddle.*

riddle[2] *v.* **1** °perforate, °pepper, °puncture, °pierce, honeycomb: *The back of the bookcase was riddled with tiny worm-holes.* **2** °penetrate, °infest, infect, pervade, °permeate, °fill, °spread: *An investigation revealed that the entire department was riddled with corruption.*
—*n.* **3** sieve, colander *or* cullender, strainer, °grating, °screen, sifter, °filter: *He shovelled the dirt through the riddle to sift out the larger stones.*

ride *v.* **1** °sit on *or* in, °travel *or* °journey *or* °go *or* °proceed on *or* in, be borne *or* carried *or* conveyed (on *or* in), °take; °propel *or* °control *or* °drive (a horse *or* a bicycle *or* a motor cycle): *They ride the bus to work each day. The film began with a witch riding a broomstick. Do you know how to ride a motor bike?* **2** °float, °lie: *The yacht is riding at anchor off Portsmouth.* **3** °tyrannize, terrorize, °intimidate, °dominate, °oppress; °bully, °rag, harry, °harass, hector, °nag, °provoke, °heckle, badger, °plague, °pester, °annoy, °irritate, *Colloq* hassle: *He has been ridden by obsessive ambition all his life.*
—*n.* **4** °drive, °journey, °trip, °excursion, °tour, jaunt, °outing, °expedition, *Colloq* °spin: *Let's go for a ride in the country!* **5** ***take for a ride***: **a** delude, °swindle, °trick, °deceive, °defraud, humbug, gull, °take in, °cheat, bamboozle: *Those tricksters with the loaded dice certainly took Charlie for a ride last night!* **b** (°kidnap and) °murder *or* °kill *or* °execute *or* do in, *Slang* °bump off, *US* (°snatch and) °rub out *or* °waste: *They said that if he identified them, they would take him for a ride.*

ridge *n.* °crest, °line, °strip, °top °edge, arête: *The mountain ridge was partly obscured by clouds.*

ridicule *n.* **1** °derision, deriding, °jeer, jeering, °taunt, taunting, °mockery, mocking, °gibe *or* jibe, gibing *or* jibing, °raillery, *Colloq* ribbing, *US and Canadian* razzing, joshing: *Nick was often subjected to ridicule because of his outlandish clothes.*
—*v.* **2** °deride, °jeer at, °taunt, °tease, °mock, °gibe *or* jibe, °guy, °chaff, °laugh at, °caricature, °poke °fun at, make °fun *or* °sport of, °lampoon, °burlesque, travesty, °parody, make a laughing-stock (of), *Colloq* rib, roast, *Brit* °send up, take the mickey out of, *US and Canadian* razz, josh: *In a democracy, it is an inalienable right of the people to ridicule their leaders and government.*

ridiculous *adj.* °absurd, laughable, °preposterous, °weird, comical, °funny, °humorous, °ludicrous, °farcical, droll, amusing, mirthful, °hilarious, side-splitting, risible; °silly, °inane, °nonsensical, °foolish, °stupid, °outlandish, °bizarre, °grotesque, °queer,

°crazy, °insane, °zany, °wild, *Slang* far-out: *You look absolutely ridiculous in that outfit! Where did she ever get the ridiculous notion that she would marry a prince?*

riff-raff *n.* °rabble, hoi polloi, ragtag and bobtail, scum, *canaille*, masses, °dregs (of society), *Colloq* great °unwashed: *I am shocked that you continue your membership in a club to which riff-raff like Barnes belong.*

rifle *v.* **1** °rob, °loot, °ransack, °plunder, despoil, burgle, °pillage, *US* burglarize: *We caught the man who had rifled the till.* **2** °search, °ransack, °go through, °rummage through: *She rifled through the files till the will was found.*

rift *n.* **1** °separation, °break, °split, °schism, cleft, °gulf, °gap; °disagreement, °conflict, disruption, °difference, °breach, break-up, °division, °distance, alienation: *The continued bitterness served only to intensify the rift between them.* **2** °tear, °rent, °opening, °hole, °crack, °chink, °crevice, cleavage, °fracture, °flaw, °fault: *Water was pouring through an ever-widening rift in the dam.*

rig *v.* **1** Often, ***rig out** or **up***: °fit (out *or* up), °equip, °set up, °outfit, °supply, °provision, accoutre *or US also* accouter, caparison, *Chiefly Brit* °kit out: *Good Sports was the shop that rigged us out completely for our Himalayan climbing expedition.* **2** °falsify, °manipulate, °doctor, °juggle, °fix, °tamper with, °fake, *Colloq* °fiddle (with), cook: *The accountants rigged the books to make the company appear profitable enough to merit a bank loan.*
—*n.* **3** °equipment, equipage, °gear, °tackle, °apparatus, °outfit, °kit, accoutrements *or US also* accouterments, °paraphernalia, appurtenances, *Colloq* °things, °stuff: *It cost a fortune to transport his diving rig by plane.*

right *adj.* **1** °just, °moral, °good, °proper, °correct, °legal, °lawful, licit, °honest, °upright, °righteous, °virtuous, °ethical, °fair, °true, °honourable, right-minded, °principled, °open, °above-board: *There is no doubt in my mind that Simon can be relied on to do the right thing.* **2** °correct, °fitting, °suitable, °proper, °accurate, °exact, °precise, °perfect; °factual, °truthful, veracious, valid, °sound, *Colloq Brit* bang on, spot on: *Have you bought the right kind of nail to go into plaster? Jennie had nine right answers out of ten. How many of yours are right?* **3** °propitious, °convenient, °strategic, °advantageous, °beneficial, °favourable, auspicious, preferred, preferable, °promising: *I waited for the right moment to ask his advice.* **4** °sound, °sane, °normal, °rational, lucid, °healthy: *Is she right in the head, letting him drive in his condition?* **5** right-hand, dextral, dexter, *Nautical* starboard: *In the United Kingdom, drivers sit on the right side.* **6** rightist, right-wing, °conservative, °reactionary, Tory: *The right wing of the liberal party is not so very different from the left wing of the conservatives.* **7** °face, °upper, °principal, °front: *Have you laid the tablecloth right side up?* **8** utter, °complete, °perfect, °unmitigated, unalloyed, °out-and-out, °thorough, thoroughgoing, 24-carat *or esp. US* 24-karat, dyed in the wool, °pure, °absolute, °real, *Brit* °proper: *I've been a right idiot not to realize that he loved only her.*
—*n.* **9** °privilege, °prerogative, °licence, °power, °claim, °title, °freedom, °liberty: *We must allow nothing to interfere with our democratic rights, such as our right to vote.* **10** °justice, °reason, °fact, °truth, fairness, °equity, °good, goodness, °integrity, °virtue, virtuousness, °honesty, honourableness, °morality, °propriety, °rectitude, right-mindedness, high-mindedness, °nobility, uprightness: *He believes that he has right on his side.* **11** right side *or* hand *or* fist, *Nautical* starboard: *She stood on his right. She gave him a quick right to the jaw.* **12** ***by rights***: °properly, °fairly, justly, to be °just, to be °fair, in fairness, °honestly, in all °honesty, to be °honest: *By rights, because I paid for it, the house is mine.*
—*adv.* **13** °directly, °straight, straight away, right away *or* off, in a beeline, as the crow flies, forthwith; unhesitatingly, °immediately, °promptly, at °once, instantly, without hesitating *or* hesitation, without °delay, °quickly, °swiftly, speedily, *Colloq* pronto, °straight off: *The minute he walked into the room, he went right to the wall-safe. Please come over right now.* **14** °exactly, °precisely, unerringly, accurately; °just: *She hung the paintings right where they belonged.* **15** °just, °only: *I stopped right now—when you walked in.* **16** °well, satisfactorily, advantageously, profitably, °favourably, opportunely: *I hope that everything turns out right for you.* **17** correctly, accurately, °properly, °precisely, °well, sensibly, fittingly, suitably, aptly: *If you can't do it right, why bother doing it at all!*
—*v.* **18** °straighten (up *or* out), set °upright *or* aright: *I righted all the chairs the children had knocked over.* **19** put *or* set *or* make right, put *or* set to rights, °correct, °straighten out, redress, °amend, °make up for, °rectify, °sort out, °repair, °fix: *She has always felt that her mission in life was to right wrongs.* **20** avenge, °retaliate for, °vindicate, °repay, °revenge, °settle, *Colloq* get °even for: *Langdon swore that he would right the injury done to his father's name.*

righteous *adj.* **1** °moral, °just, °virtuous, upstanding, °upright, °good, °honest, °ethical, °honourable, °fair, °reputable, °trustworthy: *He insists that his father was a righteous man who had been unjustly accused.* **2** °right, °correct, justifiable, justified, °appropriate, condign, °fitting, apt, °self-righteous: *Her righteous indignation at being criticized stems from her overweening pride.*

rightful *adj.* **1** °legal, °lawful, °legitimate, licit, de jure, °correct, °proper, bona fide, valid, °true, authorized, °right: *If the deed is in his name, then he is the rightful owner.* **2** °just, °fair, °equitable, °right: *Emily has supported rightful causes all her life.*

rigid *adj.* **1** °stiff, unbending, unbendable, °firm, °hard, °strong: *Are those brackets rigid enough to support such a heavy shelf?* **2** °inflexible, inelastic, unyielding, undeviating, unalterable, °set, °firm, °hard, adamant, hard-line, unbending, adamantine, °steely, iron, °strong, uncompromising, unrelenting, intransigent, stringent, °severe, °strict, rigorous, °stern, °harsh, austere: *Frank is known to favour rigid discipline in the classroom.* **3** rigorous, °exact, °precise, unwavering, °unqualified, unswerving, undeviating, °demanding, °strict, °hard and °fast, °literal, °nice, °close, °thorough, °scrupulous, °careful, °conscientious, °painstaking, °meticulous, punctilious, °exacting, °strait-laced: *Rigid observance of the regulations produced the desired results. Pinwell's rigid parsimony met with little favour from his family.* **4** °obstinate, °stubborn, pigheaded, °inflexible, °immovable, adamant, adamantine, °fixed, °set, obdurate, °wilful, headstrong, dogged, persevering, °determined, °resolute, °steadfast, resolved, °tenacious, °relentless, unrelenting, uncompromising, unadaptable, mulish, close-minded: *Candida remained rigid in her opposition to birth control.*

rigmarole *n.* rigamarole, motions, °complication(s), formalities, red tape, °bureaucracy, punctilio, ceremoniousness, °ceremony, °ritual, °procedure, °mess, °mumbo-jumbo, °gobbledegook *or* gobbledygook, bunkum *or* buncombe, °bother, balderdash, °rubbish, °nonsense, foolishness, *Colloq* hassle, bunk, *Slang* crap, *US* meshugaas *or* mishegaas: *Why must one go through such a rigmarole just to get a driving licence?*

rigour *n.* **1** Usually, ***rigours***: °severity, harshness, °hardship, inhospitableness, bleakness, inclemency *or* inclementness, °bitterness, °cold: *I am not sure that my grandmother can endure the rigours of another Scottish winter.* **2** strictness, rigidity, °precision, preciseness, punctilio, literalness, exactness, meticulousness, stringency, inflexibility, rigorism, harshness, °severity, °hardship, asperity, austerity, sternness: *If you work with radioactive materials, safety regulations must be observed with rigour. The rigour of monastic life has toughened him over the years.*

rim *n.* °edge, °brim, lip, °border, °periphery, °perimeter: *To make a margarita, you first coat the rim of a cocktail glass with coarse salt.*

rind *n.* °peel, °skin, husk: *Cut the thin outer part of the rind of a lemon into thin strips and soak them in brandy.*

ring[1] *n.* **1** °loop, hoop, °band, °circle, ringlet, circlet, annulus, grommet, eyelet, quoit, noose, cincture, °belt, girdle, cestus, °border, °halo, aureole, nimbus, corona, cuff, collar, necklace, neckband, bandeau, fillet, bracelet, armlet, torque *or* torc, °crown, coronet, tiara, diadem, (laurel-)wreath, °garland, *Mechanics* gland, bearing, *US and Canadian* bushing *or Brit also* bush, washer, O-ring, *Nautical* thimble, *Architecture and heraldry* annulet, *Literary* roundlet, *Anatomy* cingulum: *The rings brought up from the wreck of the ancient Greek trading vessel are worth a great deal.* **2** rink, °enclosure, arena, circus, bullring, Spanish *plaza de toros*, boxing ring: *I would no sooner get into the ring with him than with a bull!* **3** °circle, °organization, °gang, °band, °pack, °cell, °team, °crew, confederacy, confederation, °combination, cartel, °mob, bloc, coterie, °set, °clan, °clique, °fraternity, °brotherhood, sorority, sisterhood, guild, (secret) °society, °junta *or* junto, °cabal, °faction, °group, °league, °alliance, °federation, coalition, °union, affiliation, camorra, camarilla, Bund: *She was running an international ring of jewel thieves who worked only in the most exclusive resorts.*
—*v.* **4** °encircle, °surround, °bind, gird, girt, °circle; °loop, compass, °envelop, encompass, °embrace: *The swimming-pool is ringed with dense shrubbery. After the vase is fired, I intend to ring the base with a gold band.*

ring[2] *v.* **1** °peal, °chime, °toll, knell, tintinnabulate, ding-dong, gong, °sound, resonate, °resound, °echo, re-echo, reverberate; clang, °jangle; tinkle, clink, °jingle, ding-a-ling, ring-a-ding-ding, *Archaic or dialect* knoll: *The bells rang out their joyous announcement of peace on earth.* **2** °telephone, ring up, phone, °call, give (someone) a ring, *Colloq* (give (someone) a) °buzz, give (someone) a tinkle, °get (someone) on the blower *or* horn, *US* (give (someone) a) jingle: *I'll ring you when I am next in town.*
—*n.* **3** ringing, °peal, pealing, °chime, chiming, °toll, tolling, tintinnabulation, knell, sounding, resonating, °echo, echoing, re-echo, re-echoing, reverberation, reverberating; clang, clanging, °jangle, jangling; tinkle, tinkling, clink, clinking, °jingle, jingling, ding-a-ling, ring-a-ding-ding, *Archaic or dialect* knoll: *I couldn't hear the ring at the door because the water was running.* **4** (telephone *or* phone) °call, *Colloq* °buzz, tinkle, *US* jingle: *Don't forget to give your mother a ring on Sunday.*

rinse *v.* **1** °wash (out *or* off), °wash up, °clean, °cleanse, bathe, °drench, °flood, °flush, irrigate, *Chiefly Brit* °swill (out), *Literary* lave: *Use plenty of fresh water to rinse all the soap out of the clothes.* **2** °tint, dye, °touch up, highlight: *The hairdresser rinsed a little blue into Martine's greying hair.*
—*n.* **3** rinsing, °wash, washing, bath, bathing, cleaning, cleansing, ablution, drenching, °flood, flushing, irrigation, *Medicine* lavage, *Literary* laving: *The softening agent should be added in the final rinse.* **4** °tint, dye: *I had no idea that she used a rinse—I thought her hair was naturally reddish.*

riot *n.* **1** rioting, °riotous behaviour, °disturbance, °uproar, °tumult, turmoil, (civil) °disorder, lawlessness, hubbub, °rumpus, turbulence, °fracas, °fray, affray, mêlée *or* melee, °pandemonium, Donnybrook, °brawl, °row, °unrest, commotion, °bother, imbroglio, °outburst, anarchy, disruption, °violence, °strife, *Colloq* ruckus, ruction, to-do, do, *Brit* bovver, punch-up: *The government is unable to quell the food riots, which have become more frequent and more violent.* **2** °funny man *or* woman, °comedian *or* comedienne, °hilarious event *or* bit *or* shtick *or* thing *or* piece of business, *Colloq* gas, *US* °panic, laugh-riot: *Benny's closing routine with the model is an absolute riot.*
—*v.* **3** mount the barricades, take to the streets, °rebel, °revolt, create *or* cause a °disturbance, °brawl, °fight, (go on the *or US also* a) °rampage, run riot, °storm: *The prisoners rioted to protest against the crowded conditions.*

riotous *adj.* **1** °tumultuous, unrestrained, °wild, °noisy, °uncontrolled, uncontrollable, unmanageable, °chaotic, °disorderly, disordered, °lawless, turbulent, °violent, brawling, °obstreperous: *The headmaster warned that he would not tolerate such riotous behaviour.* **2** °rowdy, °boisterous, °unruly, °uproarious, rollicking, roisterous, °wild, rumbustious, unrestrained, °uninhibited, *Archaic* robustious, *Colloq* rambunctious, no-holds-barred: *Bernard's retirement party was certainly a riotous affair.*

rip *v.* **1** °tear (apart *or* asunder), °rend, be torn *or* rent, °split, °cut (apart): *I ripped my trousers on that nail. The paper ripped because you yanked it out of my hand.* **2** ***rip off***: **a** °steal, purloin, °rob, °snatch, °pilfer, filch, °take, shoplift, *Colloq* °pinch, *Brit* °nick, *Slang* °lift, °swipe, *US* boost, promote: *They broke into my car and ripped off my tape deck.* **b** °cheat, °swindle, °trick, °fleece, bilk, °dupe, °deceive; °defraud, °embezzle, *Colloq* con, bamboozle, *Slang* skin, gyp, rook: *A smooth couple got £100 by using the old 'stuffed wallet' trick to rip me off.*
—*n.* **3** °tear, °rent, °split, °gash, °slash; °rift, cleft, °rupture: *The vandals tore a foot-long rip in the top of my new convertible.*

ripe *adj.* **1** °mature, matured, °seasoned, (fully) grown, (well-)ripened, developed, °mellow, °ready, °fit, *US* (fully) °aged, well-aged: *The grapes are ripe for picking.* **2** °prepared, °ready, °fit, °appropriate, °experienced, °veteran, °seasoned, °sage, °wise, °sophisticated, °mature, °informed, °qualified, dependable, °reliable: *Henry is ripe in judgement and understanding.* **3** ***ripe for***: **a** °timely, °opportune, °propitious, °favourable, auspicious, °ideal, °right, °suitable, apt, °proper, suitably advanced: *Is the time yet ripe for another revival of* Heartbreak House*?* **b** °ready, °eager, °enthusiastic, °prepared, °fit, in °readiness: *The mob is ripe for revolt.*

ripen *v.* °develop, °mature, °age, °season, maturate, bring *or* come to °maturity; °perfect: *The peaches need another day to ripen.*

rip-off *n.* **1** °stealing, purloining, robbing, pilfering, °taking, filching, pilferage, °theft, °robbery, larceny; shoplifting, *Colloq* pinching, *Brit* nicking, *Slang* lifting, swiping, *US* boosting: *The rip-off of books from the library is a disgrace.* **2** °swindle, confidence °trick, swindling, cheating, °cheat, °fraud, °deception, defrauding, defalcation; °embezzlement, *Colloq* con (°job *or* °trick): *A husband-and-wife team are being sought for executing a rip-off of thousands from the Outland Bank using a forged letter of credit.* **3** overcharging, exploitation, *Colloq* highway *or chiefly Brit* daylight °robbery: *It's a rip-off to charge two pounds for something that costs only three pence to make.*

ripping *adj.* fine, splendid, marvellous, excellent, exciting, thrilling, stirring, spine-tingling: *Buchan and Henty and Haggard all wrote ripping adventure novels.*

ripple *n.* **1** wavelet, °wave, °ruffle, ruffling, cat's-paw, purl, purling, undulation, *US* riffle, riffling: *There wasn't even the slightest breath of air to cause a ripple on the mirror-like surface of the lake.* **2** (slight) °disturbance, °upset, perturbation, °agitation, °flurry, °flutter, °suggestion, °hint, soupçon: *The divorce occasioned only a ripple of dissent in the royal family.*
—*v.* **3** °ruffle, purl, undulate, °wave; °splash, °wash, *US* riffle: *I sat musing, watching the water ripple over the stones in the brook.*

rise *v.* **1** °get up, °arise, °stand (up), °get to one's feet, *Brit* be upstanding: *All rise when the judge enters the court.* **2** °get up, °arise, °awaken, waken, °wake up, start *or* begin the day, *Nautical or colloq* hit the deck, *Colloq* turn out: *We usually rise at about six o'clock.* **3** ascend, be °elevated, °arise, °climb, °lift, °go up, °mount: *The smoke slowly, almost furtively, rose from*

the camp-fire into the still night air. The morning star can be seen tomorrow rising in the sky just before dawn. Some of those skyscrapers rise to a height of 110 storeys. **4** Often, ***rise (up) (against)***: °rebel, °revolt, °mutiny, kick over the traces, take up arms, mount the barricades, take to the streets: *If the food shortages persist, the people are sure to rise up and overthrow the present regime.* **5** °swell, °flood, °increase, °grow; wax: *Owing to the heavy rains, the river is rising rapidly.* **6** °slant *or* °incline *or* °slope (upwards), ascend, °climb, go uphill: *The path rises steeply just beyond the cwm.* **7** °fly, take °flight, take wing, take to the air, °take off, °arise, °lift, °climb, °soar, °mount: *At the roar of the gun, tens of thousands of flamingoes rose from the lakes.* **8** °advance, °improve one's lot *or* position, °progress, °get °ahead, go *or* get somewhere, °succeed, make something of oneself, be promoted, °prosper, °thrive, °make good, *Colloq* °make it, °make the °grade, go places: *Fielding could well have risen in the company had his attitude been different.* **9** °start, °begin, °originate, °arise, °occur, °happen, take °place: *I cannot explain how so much bad feeling rose between us.* **10** °increase, be °elevated *or* lifted *or* boosted, °grow, °go up, move upwards, °climb, escalate, ascend, snowball: *When interest rates rise, they contribute to the inflation that raising them was supposed to reduce.* **11** °arise, be nurtured, be produced, be generated, be created, °spring up, be engendered: *The feelings that rose within him were spurred on by sheer hatred of the man.* **12** ***rise to***: **a** °arise, come up, °meet, be °equal to, prove °adequate to: *If you need a good man, you can count on Michael to rise to the occasion.* **b** come to get, °take, °swallow, °react to, °respond to, °succumb to, be tempted by: *Sue rose to the bait of a company car and accepted our offer.*
—*n.* **13** ascent, °hill, hillock, °knoll, eminence, °prominence, °elevation, upland, highland, (upward) °slope *or* °incline, acclivity, *US* upgrade: *As we climbed a slight rise, we saw the mountains gleaming in the distance.* **14** °increase, °increment, °gain, °addition: *In return for only a slight rise in wages, they are being asked to take on much more responsibility.* **15** ascent, ascension, °elevation, °flight, °climb, °take-off: *The balloon's rise was suddenly halted when the basket caught in a tree.* **16** ***get*** *or Brit also* ***take a rise out of (someone)***: °provoke, °stimulate, °incite, instigate, °foment, goad, °encourage, °press, °push, °shake up, waken, °awaken, °move, °motivate, °activate, °agitate, °stir (up), °inflame, impassion: *We finally got a rise out of Sidney by threatening to charge him for cleaning his room.* **17** ***give rise to***: °start, engender, °generate, °begin, °commence, °produce, °bring out, °cause, °bring about, bring into being: *We never discovered what gave rise to Tom's dislike of dogs.*

risk *n.* **1** °danger, °peril, °jeopardy, °hazard, °chance, °gamble: *I would take up skydiving, but my mother won't let me because of the risk.*
—*v.* **2** °endanger, imperil, °jeopardize, °hazard, °chance, °gamble: *Would you really risk all your money on one roll of the dice?*

risky *adj.* °dangerous, °perilous, °hazardous, chancy, touch-and-go, °precarious, *Colloq* iffy, °dicey, °dodgy, °touchy: *Futures trading is a very risky business, as many have discovered to their dismay.*

risqué *adj.* indelicate, °unrefined, indecorous, °indecent, °improper, °broad, °naughty, °spicy, salty, °off colour, °racy, °bawdy, °erotic, °suggestive, °wicked, °blue, ribald, °daring, salacious, °gross, *Colloq Brit* near the knuckle: *Some of those photographs of beauty contest queens are pretty risqué.*

rite *n.* °ceremony, °ritual, °ceremonial, °observance, °formality, °custom, °practice, °routine, °procedure, °solemnity, solemnization, liturgy: *This weekend I have to perform the annual rite of having tea with great-aunt Elizabeth at the Ritz.*

ritual *adj.* **1** °ceremonial, °ceremonious, sacramental: *The celebrants undergo ritual washing before preparing the sacrifice.* **2** procedural, °formal, °conventional, °customary, °habitual, °routine, prescribed, °usual, °automatic, °perfunctory: *Each time they meet, Harold and Bill have to go through a ritual handshaking routine—a hangover from their school-days, I think.*
—*n.* **3** °formality, °routine, °custom, °practice, °convention, °protocol: *If everyone goes through this tea-drinking ritual twice a day, how do you get any work done?* **4** See **rite,** above.

rival *n.* **1** °competitor, °opponent, contender, challenger, °antagonist, °adversary; °opposition: *This year there are many formidable rivals for the championship.*
—*v.* **2** °compete with *or* against, contend with *or* against, °oppose, °challenge, °contest, °struggle with *or* against, °vie with, °combat, °compare with, °equal, °measure up to, (be a) °match (for): *Jan's prowess at tossing the caber rivalled that of anyone else in Craigie.*

rivalry *n.* °competition, competitiveness, contention, vying; °dispute, °feud, feuding, °conflict, °struggle, °strife, °controversy, °dissension, °discord, °difference(s): *Once again the two local teams meet in a rivalry that has been traditional for over a century. It appeared unlikely that the rivalry between the brothers would be settled amicably.*

river *n.* **1** watercourse, °branch, °tributary, °stream, waterway, estuary, rivulet, °creek, °brook, streamlet, runnel, rill, *Scots and No. Eng.* burn, *Brit* beck, *US* kill: *We used to sail our toy boats on the river here when I was a lad.* **2** °stream, °flood, °torrent, °quantity, cataract, °flow, cascade: *Rivers of sweat poured down me as I toiled in the humid heat of the jungle.*

riveting *adj.* °spellbinding, engrossing, hypnotic, hypnotizing, transfixing, fascinating, °enthralling, gripping, captivating, °absorbing: *The programme was absolutely riveting—one of the best I have ever seen.*

road *n.* **1** °way, °means, °approach, °route, °procedure, °technique, °method, °passage, °street, avenue, °course, °track, entrée, access, °direction: *Our researchers arrived at the identical results via a completely different road.* **2** thoroughfare, °way, byway, highway, roadway, high road, low road, avenue, boulevard, °street, lane, alley(way), *Brit* motorway, carriageway, *US* turnpike, expressway, freeway, parkway, throughway *or* thruway, German *Autobahn*, Italian *autostrada*, French *autoroute*, *Colloq US* pike: *The roads are jammed with traffic on Sunday evenings during the summer.*

roam *v.* °wander, rove, °ramble, °range, °walk, °drift, dally, °dawdle, °cruise, °stroll, amble, °meander, °saunter, °stray, °prowl, perambulate, °travel, voyage, peregrinate, circumambulate, traipse, gallivant, jaunt, *Colloq* mosey, swan: *They spent a year roaming about the continent, staying wherever they pleased.*

roar *v.* **1** °bellow, °thunder; °howl, °bawl, squall, °cry, °yell, yowl; bay, °snarl, growl: *A train roared by. The crowd roared appreciation. A lion roared once in the night.* **2** °laugh, guffaw, °howl (with °laughter), hoot: *They fell about roaring when he told the joke about the egg and the taxi.*
—*n.* **3** roaring, °bellow, °thunder, rumble, °boom; °howl, °bawl, squall, °cry, °yell, yowl, clamour, °outcry; °snarl, snarling, growl, growling: *The roar of the falls could be heard miles away. There was a roar of indignation at the proposal. The beast's roar was enough to strike terror into our hearts.* **4** guffaw, °outburst, °howl, hoot: *Everything she said was met by a roar of laughter from the gallery.*

rob *v.* **1** burgle, °loot, °rifle, °ransack, °plunder, depredate, °raid; hijack; °pillage, °sack; *US* burglarize, *Colloq* °hold up, *Slang* °stick up, °rip off: *They robbed a jeweller's shop last week.* **2** °prey upon *or* on, *Colloq* °hold up, °mug, *Slang chiefly US* °stick up, °rip off, *Chiefly US and New Zealand* °roll: *These hooligans rob old ladies in the street.* **3** ***rob (someone) (of)***: °deprive (of), °cheat *or* °swindle (out of), °defraud (of), °strip (of), °fleece (of), bilk (of), °victimize, mulct (of), *US* euchre ((out) of), *Colloq* rook ((out) of), do *or* diddle (out of), gyp (out of), *Slang Brit* nobble (of): *I was robbed of my last penny by those confidence men. We* *were robbed by a taxi driver who offered to change our money. She robbed me of my self-respect.*

robber *n.* °thief, pickpocket, shoplifter, °burglar, bandit, housebreaker, sneak-thief, cat °burglar, safe-breaker, highwayman, gentleman of the road, brigand, °pirate, freebooter, buccaneer, privateer, corsair, *Colloq* mugger, °hold-up man, *Slang* cracks-man, °rip-off artist, safe-cracker, safe-blower, *Chiefly US* stick-up man, *US* second-story *or* second-storey man: *The police were making every effort to catch the robbers.*

robbery *n.* robbing, °theft, thievery, thieving, burglary, burgling, pilfering, pilferage, °stealing, plundering, °plunder, looting, °sack, sacking, ransacking, °depredation, °pillage, pillaging, hijacking, hijack, larceny, breaking and entering, *Colloq* pinching, °hold-up, holding up, mugging, *Slang* °rip-off, ripping-off, *Chiefly US* stick-up, sticking-up, *Brit* nicking, *US* heist: *The robbery of the paintings took place in broad daylight. The robbery of the shop was aided by a former employee. The robbery of elderly persons is on the increase.*

robe *n.* **1** °cloak, °dress, garment, vestment, °habit, frock, cassock, caftan, muu-muu, surplice, bathrobe, dressing-gown, lounging °robe, housecoat, kimono, house-dress, peignoir, °wrapper, French *robe de chambre*, °costume: *A woman wearing a green robe came to the door and asked what I wanted.* **2** ***robes***: °costume, °habit, °uniform, garb, attire, vestments, °apparel, raiment, livery, clothing, °garments, °outfit, accoutrements *or US also* accouterments, °regalia, °finery, °trappings, panoply, °gear, °paraphernalia, appurtenances, equipage, °rig, *Archaic* vesture: *She looked absolutely splendid decked out in the full robes of state.*
—*v.* **3** °cloak, garb, °dress, °cover, enrobe, °clothe: *The dish consists of ladyfingers topped with fresh strawberries robed in chocolate, with whipped cream spread over the top.*

robot *n.* **1** automaton, °mechanical man *or* monster, android: *In the future, much of the drudgery will be taken over by electronic robots.* **2** drudge, °clod, °tool, °puppet, cat's-paw, myrmidon, °mechanical man, automaton: *The company has a number of robots on its payroll who carry out orders without question.*

robust *adj.* **1** °healthy, °fit, °sound, °hale (and °hearty), °sturdy, °hardy, °hearty, °strong, °stout, °tough, able-bodied, strapping, °brawny, °sinewy, °rugged, °muscular, °powerful, well-knit, athletic, °staunch, °vigorous; in fine *or* good fettle, *Colloq* °husky: *Kelly was such a robust chap one might have thought he'd live forever.* **2** °pungent, °strong, flavourful, sapid, °rich, full-bodied, nutty, fruity: *He gave me a glass of an excellent robust tawny port.*

rock[1] *n.* **1** stone; boulder: *In the avalanche, the rocks thoroughly destroyed the ski lodge.* **2** °crag, tor, escarpment, scarp, *Brit* outcrop, *US* outcropping: *We used to go rock climbing when I had the strength.* **3** ***on the rocks***: **a** on ice: *I'd like a whisky on the rocks, thanks.* **b** in (a) °shambles, destroyed, in ruins, ruined, finished, broken-down, beyond repair: *He lost his job and his marriage went on the rocks.* **c** °destitute, poverty-stricken, °indigent, penniless, bankrupt: *Unable to find another job, he's been on the rocks for a year, now.*

rock[2] *v.* **1** °sway, °swing, °lull: *Her father used to rock her to sleep in his arms.* **2** °roll, °reel, °lurch, °toss, °swing, °sway, wobble: *The building rocked so during the earthquake that I thought it was going to fall down.* **3** °astound, °astonish, °shock, °surprise, °jar, °stagger, °amaze, °stun, °dumbfound *or* dumfound, °daze, stupefy, °overwhelm, disconcert, °unnerve, *Colloq* set (someone) back on his *or* her *or* their heels, °throw, °rattle, °shake up: *I was really rocked by the news that Sue was marrying Craig.*

rocket *v.* zoom, °take off, sky-rocket, °shoot up, °climb, °rise rapidly, °soar, °spiral upwards, *Colloq* go through the roof: *The day controls were lifted, prices rocketed, almost doubling overnight.*

rocky[1] *adj.* **1** °stony, pebbly, shingly, boulder-strewn, craggy; °bumpy, °difficult, °hard, uncomfortable, °arduous: *The beach at Nice might be romantic, but it's very rocky to lie on. The road to love can be very rocky indeed.* **2** °stony, adamant, adamantine, °firm, unyielding, rocklike, °tough, unbending, flinty, °solid, °steadfast, °steady, unfaltering, °staunch, unflinching, °determined, °resolute, unwavering, unchanging, unvarying, invariant, °invariable, °reliable, dependable, °sure, °certain: *I knew we could depend on Charles's rocky determination to see the project through.* **3** °stony, flinty, unfeeling, °unsympathetic, unemotional, emotionless, °impassive, °cold, °cool, apathetic, °indifferent, uncaring, °detached, *dégagé*, callous, °thick-skinned, °tough, °hard: *Beneath that rocky exterior beats a tender heart.*

rocky[2] *adj.* °unstable, tottering, teetering, unsteady, °shaky, °rickety, unsure, °uncertain, °unreliable, °weak, °flimsy, wobbly, wobbling, vacillating, dubious, °doubtful, °questionable, *Colloq* iffy: *The project will be very rocky till we are assured proper funding.*

rod *n.* **1** °bar, °pole, baton, °wand, °staff, °stick, dowel, cane, °shaft: *Steel rods are used to reinforce the concrete in modern buildings.* **2** cane, birch, °switch, °scourge, °lash; °punishment, chastisement, castigation, °discipline, chastening, °correction: *As they say, spare the rod and spoil the child.*

rogue *n.* **1** trickster, °swindler, °cheat, cad, ne'er-do-well, °wastrel, °good-for-nothing, °miscreant, *Rather old-fashioned* scamp, °scoundrel, blackguard, knave, °rascal, rapscallion, scapegrace, dastard, cur, churl, °wretch, °villain, charlatan, mountebank, *Brit* bounder; *Colloq* louse, °stinker, rat, °creep, *Brit* rotter, blighter, *Chiefly US and Canadian* son of a gun, *Slang* bastard, *Chiefly US and Canadian* son of a bitch, SOB *or* s.o.b., °bum: *She met some clever rogue in Capri who conned her out of fifteen thousand lire.*
—*adj.* **2** °independent, °undisciplined, uncontrollable, °ungovernable, unmanageable, unpredictable, °disobedient, °incorrigible, fractious, °self-willed, °unruly, intractable, unrestrained, °wild, °lawless, strong-willed, headstrong, refractory, contumacious, °recalcitrant, cross-grained, rampageous: *Part of the village was destroyed when a rogue elephant ran amok. Perkins quit the company to start up his own rogue concern.*

role *n.* **1** rôle, °part, °character, impersonation; lines: *She had the role of Maria in a recent production of* Twelfth Night. **2** °function, °position, °situation, °place, °post, °capacity, °job, °duty, °task, °responsibility: *Hermione's role in the company is that of managing director.*

roll *v.* **1** °rotate, °cycle, °turn (over (and over)), °wheel, trundle; °revolve, °go (a)round, °orbit, °tumble, somersault *or* somerset *or* summersault *or* summerset: *The landlord rolled another barrel beer into the pub. The children loved rolling about in the ride at the fun fair.* **2** °pass, °go, °flow, °slip, °flit, °glide, °slide, °move (on); °expire, °elapse, °disappear, vanish, °evaporate: *The time certainly rolls by quickly when you're having fun.* **3** °move, °drive, °bowl, be carried *or* conveyed, °cruise, °sail, °coast, °ride, °float, °fly: *We rolled down the road, singing and laughing.* **4** undulate, billow, °rise and °fall: *The countryside rolled away before us as far as the eye could see.* **5** °roar, °echo, re-echo, rumble, reverberate, °resound, °sound, °boom, °peal, resonate, °thunder: *The roar of the explosion rolled over us as we ran for cover.* **6** °rob, °steal from: *They got their money by rolling drunks.* **7** Often, ***roll out***: °flatten, °level (off *or* out), °smooth (out), °even (out), °grade: *After cutting, the lawn ought to be rolled.* **8** Usually, ***roll over***: °turn (over), °rotate, °spin: *Roll onto your stomach so I can examine your back.* **9** Usually, ***roll up***: furl, °coil, curl, °wind (up), °wrap (up); enwrap, °swathe, enfold, °envelop, °shroud, enshroud: *Every night he takes down the banner and carefully rolls it. Cleopatra was rolled up in a rug to be smuggled past the guards.* **10** ***roll in***: **a** °arrive, °come in, °pour in,

°flow in, °turn up, °show up: *The contributions really started to roll in after the appeal.* **b** °luxuriate in, °revel in, °wallow in, °savour, bask in, °delight in, take °pleasure in, °indulge in, °rejoice in, °relish: *Basil has been rolling in unaccustomed wealth since his aunt died.* **11** ***roll out***: unroll, unfurl, °spread (out), °unfold, uncoil, uncurl, unwind, °open (out): *Roll out the bolt of cloth so that we can measure it.*

—*n.* **12** °reel, spool, cylinder, scroll; tube: *The message was written on a long roll of paper.* **13** °list, rota, °register, °record, directory, listing, roster, slate, docket, catalogue, inventory, °muster, °index, census, annal(s), °schedule, °chronicle(s), *Sports* line-up: *With great ceremony, the clerk read the roll.* **14** rolling, billowing, waving, °wave action, °wave, billow, °swell, undulation, pitching, rocking, tossing: *With each roll of the boat, I felt more seasick.* **15** °peal, rumble, reverberation, °boom, °echo, °thunder, °roar: *A roll of thunder drowned out her shouts.* **16** rotation, °spin, °toss, whirl, °twirl: *I decided to bet everything on one last roll of the dice.* **17** bun; scone, croissant; *Brit* bread-roll, bap, split: *Waiter, would you please bring some more rolls?* **18** bankroll, °money, °wad, °bundle: *He took out a roll of notes and peeled off five twenties.*

roller *n.* **1** drum, cylinder, barrel, calender; tube; windlass; rolling-pin; mangle, wringer: *Make certain that the roller is clean.* **2** billow, °wave, comber, breaker, °swell: *After the storm, the heavy rollers continued to pound the sea wall.*

romance *n.* **1** (°love) °affair, amour, °affair of the heart, *affaire (de cœur* or *d'amour)*, °liaison, °relationship, dalliance, °intrigue: *Wasn't Rick the one from Canada with whom Diana had a romance?* **2** (true) °love: *You are lucky if you find romance even once in your lifetime.* **3** °novel, °narrative, fiction, °story, °mystery, thriller, horror °story, ghost °story, science fiction, °fantasy, Western, melodrama, gothic *or* Gothic *or* Gothick °novel *or* °tale, (fairy) °tale, love °story, idyll, epic, °legend: *It is probably accurate to say that the romance is the most popular form of fiction.* **4** °sentiment, nostalgia, °mystery, °intrigue, °fantasy, °imagination, imaginativeness, °adventure, °excitement, °fascination, exoticism, °glamour, °colour, colourfulness: *It was the romance of Morocco that entranced me.* **5** °tall °tale *or* °story, °fantasy, °fabrication, fairy °tale, °exaggeration, prevarication, concoction, flight of °fancy, °fib, (white) °lie, balderdash, fiction, °nonsense, °imagination: *That episode with the girl on the train that David told you about was all romance.*

—*v.* **6** make °love to; woo, court: *Steve has been romancing Maria ever since they met.* **7** °pander to, °flatter, curry °favour with, toady (up) to, *Colloq* butter up, soft-soap, *Taboo slang* brown-nose: *The new restaurant is romancing neighbourhood office executives, and luring them in for business lunches.*

romantic *adj.* **1** °imaginary, imagined, °fictitious, °fictional, °ideal, idealized, °fancied, °fabulous, made-up, dreamed-up, dreamt-up, fantasized, °fanciful, fairy-tale, °mythical, °idyllic, Utopian, °illusory: *Vivian isn't a real person—she's just Howard's romantic notion of the girl he wants to marry.* **2** °impractical, °visionary, °fictitious, unpractical, °unrealistic, °ideal, °abstract, °quixotic, chimerical, °absurd, °extravagant, °wild, crackpot, °mad: *She had romantic notions of how she would be running her own international business by the time she was thirty.* **3** nostalgic, °sentimental, °emotional, °sweet, °tender, °picturesque, °exotic, °glamorous; mawkish, °maudlin, saccharine, *Colloq* soppy, sugary, °mushy, °sloppy: *I can think of a lot more romantic places than a hamburger bar to eat on our anniversary. Fred hates it when I get too romantic.* **4** amorous, °affectionate, aroused, °impassioned, °passionate, libidinous, °lustful, over-friendly, *Colloq* lovey-dovey; °fresh: *After a drink or two Mike starts getting romantic—if you know what I mean.*

—*n.* **5** romanticist, °dreamer, Don Quixote, °visionary, idealist, sentimentalist: *I've never lost my taste for soft lights and sweet music—I suppose I'm just a romantic at heart.*

room *n.* **1** °space, °area, °scope, °extent, °allowance, latitude, elbow-room, °range, °leeway, °margin: *There is room for one more inside.* **2** °chamber, apartment, °compartment, °office, °cell, cubicle: *For years Pablo occupied a small room on the top floor.* **3** ***rooms***: °quarters, °lodgings, °accommodation, °flat, °dwelling: *We had rooms in an old house downtown.*

—*v.* **4** °live, °lodge, °dwell, °abide, reside, °stay: *Did you really room with the daughter of a prime minister?*

roomy *adj.* °spacious, capacious, commodious, °large, sizeable, °big, °ample: *For what appears to be a small car, it has a surprisingly roomy interior.*

root[1] *n.* **1** °base, °basis, °foundation, °source, °seat, °cause, fountain-head, °origin, fount, well-spring: *Love of money is the root of all evil.* **2** rootstock, rootstalk, °tap root, rootlet; tuber; *Technical* radix, radicle, radicel, rhizome, rhizomorph: *When transplanting seedlings, special care should be taken not to damage the roots.* **3** ***root and branch***: radically, °completely, °utterly, °entirely, °wholly, °totally: *The Romans sought to destroy Carthage root and branch.* **4** ***roots***: °origins, °heritage, °family, °lineage, °house, antecedents, forefathers, foremothers, descent, genealogy, °family tree, forebears, ancestors, predecessors, °stock, °pedigree; birthplace, motherland, °fatherland, °native °land *or* °country *or* °soil, cradle: *Carlotta spent years tracing her roots to ancient Rome. The roots of civilization first appeared in Mesopotamia.* **5** ***take root***: become °set *or* established *or* settled, germinate, °sprout, °grow, °develop, °thrive, burgeon, °flourish, °spread: *Good work habits should take root at an early age; then they will last a lifetime.*

—*v.* **6** °plant, °set, °establish, °found, °fix, °settle, embed *or* imbed; entrench, °anchor: *The cuttings failed to grow because they were not properly rooted. Hilary's fear of heights is rooted in a childhood fall from a tree.* **7** ***root out***: **a** °Sometimes, ***root up***: °uproot, eradicate, °eliminate, °destroy, extirpate, °exterminate: *Any subversives in the organization must be rooted out.* **b** °find, uncover, °discover, °dig up *or* out, °unearth, °turn up, bring to °light: *The survey of accounts is aimed at rooting out customers who are slow in paying.*

root[2] *v.* rootle, forage, °dig, °pry, nose, °poke, ferret, °burrow, °rummage, delve, °search, °ransack: *Harvey has been rooting about in the garage looking for his tennis racket.*

root[3] *v.* Usually, ***root for***: °cheer (for), °applaud (for); °boost, °support, °encourage, °urge on: *I'm rooting for our side to win.*

rooted *adj.* °firm, established, °set, °fixed, °fast, settled, deep-rooted, deep-seated, °entrenched, °ingrained *or* engrained, (°firmly) embedded *or* imbedded, implanted, instilled; °chronic, inbred, °inherent, °intrinsic, °essential, °fundamental, °basic, °radical: *Have you any rooted objections to the principle of living with someone of the opposite sex without being married?*

rope *n.* **1** °line, °cord, °cable, hawser; strand, °string: *This rope is too light for mooring the boat. She wore a rope of baroque pearls.* **2** ***the ropes***: the °routine, the °procedure, one's way around, the ins and outs; the °truth, the (real) °situation; *Colloq* what's what, the °score, *Brit* the gen: *It didn't take her long to learn the ropes.*

—*v.* **3** °tie, °bind, °lash, °hitch, °fasten, °secure; °tether, °attach: *Rope these two crates together. The horses were roped to the post.* **4** ***rope in***: °attract, °draw (in), °tempt, °entice, °lure, °persuade: *They are going to use a lottery to rope the customers in to supporting our cause.*

ropy *adj.* **1** ropey, viscous, °stringy, viscid, glutinous, mucilaginous, gluey, gummy, thready, fibrous, filamentous: *The plastic resin emerging from the vat looks somewhat ropy, like mozzarella cheese.* **2** °questionable, °inadequate, °inferior, °deficient, °indifferent, °mediocre, substandard, °unsatisfactory, °poor, °sketchy: *Greenwood's plan for increasing profit* *margins looks pretty ropy to me.* **3** °sickly, °ill, unwell, hung-over, below °par, out of sorts, *Colloq* under the °weather, °poorly, °rough, not up to snuff, off one's feed: *I was feeling pretty ropy on Saturday morning after that do at your place on Friday.*

rostrum *n.* °platform, °stage, dais, podium, °stand; pulpit; lectern, reading-stand: *As the crowd hooted and booed, the speaker descended from the rostrum.*

rosy *adj.* **1** °pink, rose-coloured, red, roseate, reddish, pinkish, cherry, cerise, ruddy, flushed, °glowing, blushing, ruby, rubicund, florid; rose-red: *During the skiing holiday, they all developed healthy rosy complexions.* **2** °optimistic, °promising, °favourable, auspicious, °hopeful, encouraging, °sunny, °bright: *Caldwell has a rosy future ahead of him.*

rot *v.* **1** °decay, °decompose, °fester, °spoil, °go °bad *or* °off, be tainted, be ruined, °mould, moulder, °putrefy; corrode, rust, °disintegrate, °deteriorate, °crumble *or* go *or* °fall to °pieces: *When the power went off, all the food in the freezer rotted. The piers holding up the far end of the bridge have all rotted away.* **2** °waste away, wither away, languish, °die, moulder, °decline, °deteriorate, °degenerate, °decay, atrophy: *Despite repeated appeals for clemency, he's been rotting away in jail all these years.*
—*n.* **3** °decay, decomposition, °mould, putrefaction, putrescence, °blight, corrosion, corruption, disintegration, deterioration: *Once the rot has set in, the job of revitalization can be overwhelming.* **4** (°stuff and) °nonsense, balderdash, °rubbish, bunkum, tommy-rot, twaddle, °drivel, hogwash, eyewash, °trash, *Colloq* claptrap, bunk, boloney *or* boloney, bosh, malarkey, °moonshine, poppycock, tosh, *Slang* crap, bull, codswallop, *Brit* (a load of (old)) cobblers, *Taboo* balls, bullshit: *He knows nothing whatsoever about linguistics and is just talking a lot of rot.*

rotate *v.* **1** °turn, °revolve, °go °round, °spin, °gyrate, °pirouette, whirl, °twirl, °wheel, °pivot, °reel: *As the gear rotates, its teeth mesh with those of the other gear, causing it to turn in the opposite direction.* **2** °change, °exchange, °alternate, interchange, °switch, °trade places; take °turns, *Colloq* swap *or* swop: *Rotate the positions of the tyres for more even wear. We rotate the chores in our family.*

rote *n.* **1** °routine, °ritual: *He acquired a rote knowledge of the words, without knowing what they mean.* **2** ***by rote***: **a** by heart, from °memory: *He can recite the entire Prologue of* Canterbury Tales *by rote.*
b unthinkingly, automatically, mechanically: *She learned the French dialogue by rote but doesn't understand a word of it.*

rotten *adj.* **1** rotted, decayed, decomposed, decomposing, °putrid, putrescent, putrescing, °mouldy, mouldering, spoilt *or* spoiled, mildewed, °rancid, fetid *or* foetid, °stale, °rank, °foul, feculent, tainted, contaminated, festered, festering, °corrupt, °bad, °off, turned, overripe, soured, °sour: *One rotten apple in the barrel can spoil the rest. The stench of rotten meat filled the room.* **2** rotted, rusted, corroded, deteriorating, disintegrating, crumbling, crumbly, falling to pieces, friable: *He stepped on a spot where the wood was rotten and his foot went right through the stair.* **3** °immoral, °corrupt, °dishonest, °deceitful, °venal, °shameless, °degenerate, °villainous, iniquitous, °evil, °wicked, °vile, debased, °base, °perverted, depraved, °unscrupulous, unprincipled, amoral, warped, *Slang* °bent: *These drug dealers are rotten at the core.*
4 heinous, °evil, °vile, °base, °miserable, °despicable, °wretched, °awful, °terrible, °horrible, horrific, °nasty, °contemptible, °filthy, °mean, low, *Colloq* °lousy, °stinking, °low-down, dirty-rotten: *Pairing me off with Vera at the dance was a rotten trick.* **5** °ill, unwell, °sick, °nauseated, °awful; hung-over, *Colloq* °lousy, °ropy *or* ropey, rough: *I feel really rotten—maybe it was those mushrooms I ate last night.*

rotund *adj.* **1** °round(ed), °circular, orbicular, globular, °spherical: *His rotund, cherubic little face simply invited a pinch of the cheek.* **2** °full, full-toned, °deep, °resonant, reverberant, reverberating, sonorous, °rich, °round, °mellow; pear-shaped: *They thrilled to hear the rotund notes issuing from Caruso's lips as he sang 'Vesti la Giubba'.* **3** °chubby, podgy *or chiefly US* pudgy, (pleasingly) °plump, portly, tubby, °heavy, fleshy, corpulent, °stout, °fat, °obese, overweight, *Colloq* roly-poly: *Jack's rotund figure was easily recognizable waddling up the street.*

roué *n.* °playboy, womanizer, ladies' man, °rake, lecher, Lothario, Don Juan, Romeo, Casanova, °charmer, °flirt, °libertine, debauchee, *Old-fashioned* masher, gay dog, *Colloq* wolf, lady-killer, dirty old man, *Taboo slang* gash-hound: *Alistair was quite a roué in his youth but has settled down since turning 50.*

rough *adj.* **1** uneven, °irregular, °coarse, °jagged, °rugged, °bumpy, °lumpy, °broken: *The next mile or so we slogged over some very rough terrain.* **2** °agitated, turbulent, choppy, °stormy, storm-tossed, °tempestuous, roiled: *We negotiated a very rough patch of water before sailing into the calm, sheltered bay.* **3** °brusque, °bluff, °curt, °short, °abrupt, unpleasant, churlish, °discourteous, °impolite, rough-spoken, °ungracious, °surly, °disrespectful, °rude, uncouth, loutish, °unrefined, uncivil, °uncivilized, uncultured, °vulgar, unladylike, ungentlemanly, °coarse, °ill-mannered, ill-bred, °inconsiderate: *Ian can be a bit rough, I know, but underneath he is a true and loyal friend.* **4** °tough, rough-and-tumble, roughneck, °rowdy: *There are some very rough characters frequenting that pub.* **5** °harsh, °violent, unfeeling, unjust, °severe, °cruel, °tough, °hard, °brutal, °extreme; ungentle: *They were subjected to very rough treatment when being questioned by the police.* **6** °dirty, °obscene, smutty, °pornographic, °vulgar, °crude, °raw, °rude: *After midnight they watch the rough shows beamed by satellite from Italy.* **7** °hard, °tough, °Spartan, °difficult, °arduous, °laborious, °rugged, unpleasant: *It was pretty rough going with almost no money and all those expenses.* **8** °harsh, °grating, cacophonous, °discordant, jarring, °strident, °raucous, rasping, unmusical, inharmonious, °gruff, °husky: *In acknowledgement he made a rough, growling noise.* **9** unfinished, °incomplete, uncompleted, °imperfect, °rudimentary, °crude, °rude, formless, unformed, °raw, rough-and-ready, rough-hewn, roughcast, °undeveloped, unshaped, unworked, unwrought, unprocessed, °unrefined; uncut, unpolished; °shapeless, undressed: *I only saw the sculpture in its rough state and cannot say how it looked when finished. The stones are rough, as they were when taken from the ground.* **10** °general, °approximate, °inexact, °cursory, °quick, °hasty, °sketchy, °vague, °hazy; foggy, *Colloq* ballpark: *Can't you give me even a rough idea of how much you want for the house?* **11** unfair, unjust, °bad, °tough; unlucky, °unfortunate: *We went through a spell of rough luck last year. This is a rough time for everyone.* **12** See **rotten, 5,** above.
—*n.* **13** °rowdy, °tough, hooligan, ruffian, °thug, brawler, yahoo, *Slang* roughneck, *Australian* larrikin, *US* mug: *Phil will get into trouble if he continues to associate with those roughs at the Lantern.* **14** sketch, (rough) °draft, mock-up, °outline: *Let me see roughs of the presentation before the meeting with the client.*
—*v.* **15** ***rough out*** *or* ***in***: sketch, °draft, mock-up, °outline, °mark out, °trace, °block out: *Our escape plan was roughed out by Captain Gallagher.* **16** ***rough up***: °beat (up), thrash, °attack, °batter, °assault, pummel *or* pommel, lay on, °knock about, °belabour, °lambaste, *Colloq* wallop: *Some of the boys roughed him up a bit when they learned that he was an informer.*
—*adv.* **17** violently, savagely, brutally, brutishly: *You'd best not mention Cassie or Henry might cut up rough.*

rough-house *n.* **1** boisterousness, rowdiness, °rowdyism, °violence, brawling, disorderliness, °disorderly conduct, ruffianism: *The police were called in to quell the rough-house that broke out at the dance.*
—*v.* **2** °brawl: *If you want to rough-house, do it outside!*

roughly *adv.* **1** °approximately, °around; °about, °nearly: *The British Museum is roughly in the same direction as Euston. It cost roughly two weeks' wages.*

Roughly two years later I saw her again. **2** harshly, unkindly, °severely, sternly, unsympathetically, brutally, violently, savagely, inhumanly, mercilessly, unmercifully, ruthlessly, pitilessly, cruelly, heartlessly: *The police were accused of dealing too roughly with those suspected of harming a fellow officer.* **3** clumsily, rudely, crudely, awkwardly, primitively, inexpertly, amateurishly, maladroitly, heavy-handedly, ineptly, inefficiently, unskilfully, inartistically: *This roughly hewn block of local granite is what the council paid a fortune for as 'sculpture'.*

round *adj.* **1** °circular; disc-shaped, discoid, disc-like: *I prefer a round table to a square one. She made a round motion to demonstrate the shape.* **2** ring-shaped, annular, hoop-shaped, hoop-like: *The track is oval, not round.* **3** °spherical, ball-shaped, ball-like, globular, spheroid, spheroidal, globe-shaped, globelike, globate, orb-shaped, orb-like, orbicular: *You will never convince me that the earth is round—I know what I see.* **4** curved, curvilinear, rounded, arched: *The round chisel is used to cut these grooves.* **5** °exact, °precise, °complete, °entire, °full: *That makes a round hundred times you have asked me the same question.* **6** °approximate, °rough, rounded (off *or* up *or* down), °whole: *In round numbers, that makes 40 per cent For and 60 per cent Against.* **7** rounded, °mellow, °full, vibrant, reverberant, reverberating, sonorous, °rich, mellifluous, orotund, pear-shaped: *Couldn't you listen forever to those beautiful round tones sung by Fischer-Dieskau?* **8** °plain, °honest, straightforward, °direct, °unvarnished, unembellished, unelaborated, °outspoken, °candid, °truthful, °frank, °open, °blunt, *Colloq* upfront: *They delivered what they had to say in round, assertive statements.* **9** *Chiefly Brit* return: *We made the round trip to Bristol in less than three hours.*
—*n.* **10** °circle, disc; °ring, hoop, annulus; ball, °sphere, °globe, °orb, bead: *The moulding has a repeated pattern of a round alternating with three vertical grooves.* **11** °cycle, series, °sequence, °succession, °bout, °spell: *The current round of talks on the economy is expected to last for three days. There was the usual round of parties on New Year's Eve.* **12** Often, ***rounds***: °beat, °route, °routine, °circuit, °course, °tour, °turn, ambit: *The milkman still makes his daily rounds in England.* **13** °heat, °stage, °level, °turn: *After each round in the tournament, the losers are eliminated, reducing the competitors by half.* **14** °spell, °period, °run, °spate, °bout, °outburst, °burst, °volley: *Each new acrobat who added to the human pyramid got a round of applause.* **15** bullet, cartridge, charge, °shell, (single) °shot: *Each man was given only ten rounds of ammunition.*
—*v.* **16** °turn, °go (a)round: *The car rounded the corner on two wheels.* **17** °orbit, circumnavigate, °go (a)round, °circle, °encircle: *He rounded the earth in the fastest recorded time.* **18** ***round off*** *or* ***out***: °complete, °close, °end, bring to an °end *or* °completion *or* a °close, °finish: *Tim suggested we round off the evening with a rubber of bridge.* **19** ***round up***: °gather, °assemble, °muster, draw *or* pull *or* °get together, °collect, °herd, marshal, *US and Canadian* (of cattle *or* horses) corral, wrangle: *The police are rounding up witnesses who might have seen the shooting. More than 10,000 head of cattle have been rounded up for the drive.*
—*prep.* **20** °about, °around, encircling, enclosing; orbiting: *The fence round the site ought to keep out the curious. The new bypass round town ought to reduce local traffic.* **21** here and there in, °about, °around, °throughout, all over, °everywhere in: *Dad used to smoke and kept dozens of ash trays round the house.* **22** °about, around, °nearby, in the °neighbourhood *or* °vicinity *or* (general) °area of: *Whenever I want to see you alone, there are always people round you. Just look round you if you don't believe me.*
—*adv.* **23** around, °about, in a °circle *or* °ring, on all sides: *Gather round and I'll tell you a story. Pass the hat round for Harry's farewell party.* **24** from beginning to end, from start to finish, °through: *He now lives in France the year round.* **25** in °perimeter *or* °periphery, °around: *The indoor track is exactly one fifth of a mile round.* **26** °about, °around, in the °neighbourhood *or* °vicinity *or* (general) °area: *There isn't a soul for miles round.* **27** around, in a °circle *or* °circuit, in *or* by a °circular *or* circuitous route *or* path, circuitously: *This road goes round to the other side of the lake.*

roundabout *adj.* **1** circuitous, °circular, °indirect, °long: *We had plenty of time so we came the more scenic, roundabout way.* **2** °devious, circuitous, °evasive, °indirect, °oblique: *If you wanted to borrow some money, asking me for tax advice was quite a roundabout way of asking.*
—*n.* **3** merry-go-round, carousel *or* carrousel, *Old-fashioned or dialect* whirligig: *The children weren't the only ones who enjoyed themselves on the roundabout.* **4** *Brit* mini-roundabout, *US and Canadian* rotary, traffic circle: *When you come to the roundabout, turn right and keep going till you come to a traffic light.*

round-up *n.* **1** °gathering, °assembly, °rally, °collection, herding, *US and Canadian* (of cattle *or* horses) corralling, wrangling: *The round-up of suspects by the police was focused on the Bournemouth area.* **2** °summary, °synopsis, °digest, °outline, recapitulation, °review, °survey, *Colloq* recap: *And now, with a round-up of the news, here is Moira Lawley.*

rouse *v.* **1** °arouse, °call, waken, °awaken, °wake (up), °get up, °arise: *I was roused from a deep slumber by a dog's barking.* **2** °stir (up), °arouse, bestir, °stimulate, inspirit, °animate, invigorate, °electrify, °excite, °provoke, °prompt, goad, °prod, galvanize, °incite, °whet, °move, °work up, °fire up: *Bruce's unquenchable enthusiasm roused many to become involved in the campaign.*

rousing *adj.* °stimulating, inspiriting, animating, enlivening, energizing, inspiring, °invigorating, vitalizing, electrifying; °fervent, °vigorous, °energetic, °enthusiastic, °spirited, °brisk, °lively, °animated, *Colloq* peppy: *The huge crowd gave the team a rousing cheer as they jogged out onto the field.*

rout *n.* **1** °defeat, trouncing, °ruin, °overthrow, subjugation, vanquishment, débâcle, °conquest, °thrashing, drubbing, beating; dispersal, °retreat, °collapse; *Colloq* licking, hiding, *US and Canadian* shellacking: *Owing to the government's overwhelming forces, there was a complete rout of the rebels.*
—*v.* **2** °defeat, °win (out) over, trounce, °ruin, °overthrow, °bring down, °subjugate, °subdue, °suppress, vanquish, °conquer, °overwhelm, °overpower, put to rout *or* °flight, worst, °best, °trample, °overrun, thrash, °trim, °whip, drub, °beat, °crush, °batter, smash, °shatter, °cut to pieces *or* ribbons *or* shreds, °destroy, °devastate, °wipe out, °eliminate, °put down, seal the °doom *or* the °fate of, eradicate, °obliterate, *Colloq* lick, wipe the floor with, °polish off, °knock off, *Hyperbolic sports jargon* °pulverize, make mincemeat of, ride roughshod over, °demolish, °mangle, °ravage, °mutilate, °flatten, squash, °topple, lay °waste, wreak °havoc (up)on, °massacre, °murder, °exterminate, annihilate, liquidate, °smother, °stifle, do away with, *Slang* clobber, do in, *US* skunk, *Chiefly US and Canadian* cream: *Queens Park Rangers routed Manchester United 6-0.*

route *n.* **1** °way, itinerary, °course, °direction, °path, °road, avenue: *If you have the time, take the scenic route. John's route to the chairmanship is strewn with his colleagues' corpses.*
—*v.* **2** °direct, convey, °carry: *Goods destined for Cleveland will be routed through Northampton.*

routine *n.* **1** °custom, °habit, °procedure, °practice, °method, °schedule, °plan, °programme, °formula, °pattern, °way, °usage, wont, *Colloq chiefly Brit* °drill: *Chalmers has always been a stickler for routine. What's the routine here when you want to order a new chair?* **2** °act, °piece, °bit, °performance, °number, °part, *Colloq* °thing, shtick: *The fat lady doesn't sing till after Joe Miller finishes his routine.*
—*adj.* **3** °customary, °habitual, °usual, °rote, °accustomed, °familiar, °conventional, °regular, °ordinary,

°everyday; programmed, assigned, designated, scheduled: *Her routine responsibilities include proofreading.* **4** °boring, °tedious, °tiresome, unimaginative, uninteresting; hackneyed, trite, stereotypic(al), clichéd, run-of-the-mill, °ordinary; unvaried, unvarying, unchanging, °monotonous, uneventful, °rote, °automatic, °mechanical, °perfunctory: *He has a routine job on the assembly line.*

rover *n.* wanderer, bird of passage, itinerant, °traveller, rolling stone, nomad, gypsy, wayfarer, gadabout, sojourner, °tourist; °drifter, °tramp, °vagabond, vagrant, *US* hobo, °bum: *He's a born rover and will never settle down.*

row[1] *n.* °line, °rank, °tier, bank, °string, series, °file: *A row of trees serves as a wind-break along one side of the farm.*

row[2] *n.* **1** altercation, °argument, °dispute, °quarrel, °disagreement, squabble, spat, °tiff, °conflict, °fracas, *Colloq* shouting match, °scrap, falling-out, *Brit* slanging-match: *We had a silly row about where we should spend the Christmas holidays.* **2** commotion, °disturbance, clamour, hubbub, °racket, °din, °rumpus, °tumult, °uproar, brouhaha, °fuss, °stir, turmoil, hullabaloo; °bedlam, °pandemonium, °chaos; *US* foofaraw, *Colloq* ruckus: *There was a tremendous row over the increase in membership fees.*
—*v.* **3** °dispute, °quarrel, °argue, °disagree, wrangle, cross swords, have words, °bicker, °tiff, *Colloq* °scrap, °fall out: *They are constantly rowing over something, usually some insignificant detail.*

rowdy *adj.* **1** °boisterous, °uproarious, °disorderly, °noisy, °loud, °obstreperous, °unruly: *It only takes a couple of rowdy youths to start trouble at a match.*
—*n.* **2** ruffian, °tough, hooligan, yahoo, brawler, lout, *Brit* lager lout, skinhead, *Chiefly US and Canadian* °hoodlum, hood, *Slang Brit* bovver boy: *The police arrested three of the rowdies involved in last night's fight.*

rowdyism *n.* rowdiness, ruffianism, hooliganism, °rough-house, barbarism, troublemaking, brawling, unruliness, boisterousness, *Slang Brit* bovver: *Have you any suggestions about what to do to curb rowdyism at football matches?*

royal *adj.* **1** queenly, kingly, queenlike, kinglike, °regal, °imperial, °sovereign, °princely, °majestic: *The Royal Family usually spend their summer holidays at Balmoral. The establishment proudly boasts royal patronage.* **2** °grand, °splendid, °stately, °impressive, august, °imposing, °superior, °superb, °magnificent, °majestic: *She arrived at the ball in a royal coach drawn by six white horses.*
—*n.* **3** °king, °queen, prince, princess, duke, earl, duchess, viscount, viscountess, baron, baroness, °noble, nobleman, noblewoman, °peer: *Her greatest ambition is to meet a royal in the flesh.* **4** ***royals***: °royalty, °nobility, °nobles, peerage: *He writes the daily column reporting on the activities of the royals.*

royalty *n.* **1** queenship, kingship, °royal °house *or* °line *or* °family, °sovereignty: *Royalty does have its privileges, doesn't it?* **2** °percentage, commission, °share, °payment, compensation: *He receives a royalty every time his song is played or sung commercially, anywhere in the world.* **3** °nobility, °nobles, peerage, *Colloq Brit* °royals: *It is ironic that Americans are more impressed than the British with royalty.*

rub *v.* **1** °massage, knead, °stroke; °scour, °scrub, °scrape, abrade, °chafe, °clean; °wipe, °smooth, °polish, °shine, buff, burnish: *Rub my back, would you?—Not there, a little lower down. You are not supposed to rub those plastic baths with abrasive cleansers. Before the guests arrived, we rubbed the silver till you could see yourself in it.* **2** ***rub in*** or ***on***: °apply, °smooth, °smear, °spread, °put: *The ache may be relieved a bit if you rub on some liniment.* **3** ***rub (it*** or ***something) in***: °emphasize, °stress, make an °issue of, harp on, °reiterate, °dwell on, hammer away, °dramatize: *It's bad enough that Caroline did better than I did—you don't have to keep rubbing it in.* **4** ***rub off*** or ***out***: expunge, °erase, °remove, °delete, °cancel, °eliminate, eradicate: *It's a pity, Peter, that you rubbed out the right reply and wrote in the wrong one. The boys were released on the condition that they would rub the graffiti off the wall.* **5** ***rub off (on)***: °affect, be transferred (to), be communicated *or* transmitted (to), be passed on *or* along (to), be imparted to: *Your mother and I had hoped that some of our love of music might have rubbed off on you.* **6** ***rub out***: °murder, °kill, °execute, slay: *The Godfather ordered all witnesses to be rubbed out.* **7** ***rub shoulders with***: °rub elbows with, °associate with, °socialize with, °mix with, °fraternize with, keep °company with, consort with, *Colloq US* °run *or* °pal *or* °chum around with: *Since getting his knighthood Charles no longer rubs shoulders with the likes of us.* **8** ***rub (someone) (up) the wrong way***: °annoy, °irritate, °irk, °anger, °provoke, go against the grain, *Colloq* °bug, get under one's *or* someone's skin, peeve: *I don't know what it is about Underbridge, but every time we meet he manages to rub me up the wrong way.*
—*n.* **9** °wipe, °stroke, rubbing: *You will have to give that stain a good rub to make it come out.* **10** °massage, rub-down: *After exercising, Jane always has an alcohol rub.* **11** ***the rub***: the *or* a °catch *or* °hitch *or* °snag *or* °hindrance *or* °set-back, the *or* an °obstacle *or* °impediment, the *or* a °difficulty *or* °problem *or* °trouble: *The only rub I can see is that Warren may not agree to resign.*

rubberneck *v.* **1** °gape, °stare, goggle, °gawk: *They spent a weekend in New York, rubbernecking at the skyscrapers.*
—*n.* **2** °tourist, °sightseer, rubbernecker, *US* out-of-towner: *Buses for the rubbernecks leave Trafalgar Square every hour or so.*

rubbish *n.* **1** °refuse, °waste, debris, rubble, detritus, °litter, °garbage, sweepings, dross, °dregs, °residue, °leftovers, °remnants, lees, °scraps, °fragments, leavings, residuum, °junk, °rejects, *Chiefly US* °trash *Slang chiefly US* dreck: *Private companies are now contracted to remove household rubbish weekly.* **2** (°stuff and) °nonsense, balderdash, °moonshine, °gibberish, °gobbledegook *or* gobbledygook, tommy-rot, bunkum, °trash, °garbage, twaddle, *Colloq* °rot, flapdoodle, crap, hokum, codswallop, bosh, piffle, hooey, bunk, malarkey, poppycock, boloney *or* baloney, eyewash, hogwash, bilge-water, bull, *Scots* havers, *Brit* tosh, gammon, *US* a crock, horse feathers, gurry, *Brit* (a load of (old)) cobblers, *Taboo slang* bullshit, horseshit, *US* a crock of shit: *What she told you about how I treated her is absolute rubbish.*
—*v.* **3** °criticize, °attack, °destroy, *Colloq* clobber, °pan, *Chiefly US* °trash, *Slang* °jump on, *Chiefly US and Canadian* bad-mouth, °jump all over: *In his latest book he rubbishes the newspaper that had given his previous book a bad review.*

rude *adj.* **1** °impolite, °discourteous, °disrespectful, °ungracious, ungallant, unmannerly, °ill-mannered, uncivil, bad-mannered, ungentlemanly, unladylike, ill-bred, °unrefined, unpolished, uncouth, °boorish, churlish, oafish, loutish, °coarse, °uncivilized, uncultured, unceremonious: *It was rude of him not to get up when she came in, but he doesn't know any better.* **2** °impertinent, °impudent, °discourteous, insulting, °insolent, °offensive, saucy, °bold, °disrespectful, uncivil, °flippant, °brusque, °curt, °gruff, °tactless, °outrageous, *Colloq* °fresh: *I simply asked the chambermaid to make up my room early and she responded with a rude remark.* **3** °naughty, °unrefined, ribald, °bawdy, °indecent, indelicate, °vulgar, °obscene, °dirty, °filthy, lubricious *or* lubricous, °lewd, °gross, smutty, °taboo, °pornographic: *Chris has an extensive collection of rude photographs.* **4** °crude, °rough, °clumsy, °awkward, unskilful, unskilled, °artless, inartistic, °imperfect, unpolished, °inaccurate, gauche, bumbling, °raw, inelegant, °makeshift, °homespun, °primitive, °misshapen, ill-formed, unfinished, rough-hewn, °simple, °basic, °bare: *The replica on view in the local museum is only a rude approximation of the original.*

rudimentary *adj.* **1** °basic, °essential, °elementary, °fundamental, rudimental, °primary, °introductory, abecedarian, formative, °first, °initial, °elemental, primal, °seminal: *The purpose of the course is provide students with a rudimentary knowledge of computer programming.* **2** °crude, °coarse, unshaped, unfinished, °imperfect, °primitive, °undeveloped, °vestigial, embryonic, primordial, °immature: *These fish, which spend their lives in darkness, have only a rudimentary organ for an eye.*

rudiments *n.pl.* basics, °elements, essentials, °fundamentals, °first °principles: *She learnt the rudiments of musical composition from the maestro himself.*

ruffle *n.* **1** trimming, °flounce, °frill, ruff, peplum, °flare, smocking, ruche, ruching, gather, gathering: *Doesn't that ruffle at the back of the skirt make it look a bit old-fashioned?* **2** °ripple, wavelet, °disturbance, °flurry, bustle, °stir, perturbation, wrinkle: *The news of the divorce caused a slight ruffle at court.*
—*v.* **3** °agitate, disconcert, °confuse, discompose, °discomfit, °upset, °disturb, °stir up, °perturb, unsettle, disorient, °unnerve, °fluster, °affect, °bother, °intimidate, unstring, °put out, vex, °trouble, °worry, *Colloq* °rattle, °throw, °shake up, *Chiefly US and Canadian* discombobulate, voodoo, hex, psych out, *Slang chiefly US and Canadian* get (someone) all shook up, spook: *She was ruffled by questions concerning her relationship with the deceased.* **4** disarrange, dishevel, °disorder, °rumple, °mix up, °tousle, °tangle, *Colloq* °mess *or* muss (up): *His unpleasant attitude ruffled quite a few feathers in the department.*

rugged *adj.* **1** °rough, uneven, °broken, °stony, °rocky, °irregular, °bumpy, °pitted, °jagged, °ragged: *The horses picked their way slowly across the rugged terrain.* **2** °tough, °rough, °severe, °hard, °harsh, °difficult, °arduous, °Spartan, rigorous, onerous, °stern, °demanding, °burdensome: *It is amazing how that small band of pioneers withstood the rugged life in the untamed West.* **3** °hardy, °durable, °strong, °sturdy, °hale, °robust, °tough, °vigorous, °hard, rough-and-ready, °stalwart; °independent, individualistic, self-reliant, °self-confident, °self-sufficient, °bold: *WANTED: Five rugged pioneering types to join an expedition to the source of the Amazon river.* **4** °rude, uncouth, uncultured, °uncivilized, °unrefined, unpolished, °crude, °ungraceful, churlish: *I admit that Charlie's manners are a bit rugged, but he's one of the best men we have.*

ruin *n.* **1** °downfall, °destruction, devastation, °havoc, °breakdown, breakup, débâcle, °collapse, °fall, disintegration, ruination, °dissolution, wiping out, °failure, °decay, °undoing, °end; °conquest, °defeat, °overthrow; bankruptcy, liquidation: *Alexander was responsible for the ruin of the Persian empire. Overwhelming debts spelt Theo's financial ruin.* **2** °degradation, °dishonour, debasement, defilement, corruption, vitiation, seduction, °degrading, dishonouring, debasing, defiling, corrupting, vitiating, seducing; deflowering, defloration: *Who was the libertine who brought about the ruin of Lord Harecombe's daughter?* **3** nemesis, °curse, °end, bane: *That boy will be my ruin!* **4** gin, mother's ruin, blue ruin, *Slang* rot-gut: *After eating, we sat down and polished off a bottle of mother's ruin.* **5** °hag, °witch, crone, beldam; dotard, (old) °fogy *or* fogey, fossil, fuddy-duddy, °antique, *Brit* OAP (= 'old-age pensioner'), *Chiefly US* retiree, *Colloq* (old) geezer, °wreck, *Slang* dodo: *It's hard to understand what those two old ruins see in each other.* **6** ***ruins***: debris, °wreckage, °fragments, rubble, °remains: *He stood among the ruins of the burnt-out house wondering what to do next. She was trying to piece together the ruins of her disastrous marriage.*
—*v.* **7** °destroy, °devastate, °demolish, annihilate, °dissolve, °wipe out, °undo, °overthrow, lay °waste, °raze, °shatter, °wreck, °crush, °flatten, wreak °havoc (up)on, °reduce to °nothing *or* °naught, °pulverize, smash, bring to °ruin: *The bomb ruined the entire centre of the city.* **8** °spoil, disfigure, °damage, °botch, °mess up, make a °mess of, °mar, uglify: *The county office building completely ruins the Aylesbury skyline.* **9** °spoil, °destroy, °wreck, nullify, °damage, °harm, °hurt, °impair, °poison, *Slang* louse up, °screw up, put the kibosh on, *US* bollix up, *Taboo slang chiefly Brit* make a balls-up of: *I think that your behaviour at the office party may just have ruined your prospects for promotion.* **10** bankrupt, pauperize, impoverish, reduce to penury *or* °poverty *or* destitution *or* indigence: *Paying off the loan virtually ruined me.* **11** °violate, deflower, °ravish, °seduce, °lead astray, °dishonour, defile, °corrupt, °debase: *She claimed that it was the local squire who ruined her, despite evidence to the contrary.*

ruinous *adj.* °disastrous, °destructive, catastrophic, °calamitous, deleterious, pernicious, crippling, cataclysmic, baleful, °fatal, toxic, °poisonous, noxious, °harmful, °injurious, °nasty, *Archaic* baneful: *Smoking can be ruinous to your health. Who was behind the ruinous decision to move the factory to the north-east?*

rule *n.* **1** °regulation, °order, °law, ordinance, ruling, °decree, ukase, statute, °principle, °direction, °guide, guideline, °precept: *We go by the Golden Rule here, Jim, 'Do unto others before they do unto you'.* **2** °dominion, °authority, °control, °sovereignty, °sway, °command, ascendancy, °direction, °oversight, supervision, mastery: *How could such a despised monarch maintain rule over a people for so long?* **3** °fact, °standard, customs, °practice, °form, °routine, °convention, °policy, way things are: *Honesty and integrity among our students are the rule rather than the exception.* **4** ***as a rule***: °generally, °usually, normally, customarily, for the most °part, mostly, °ordinarily, °mainly, in the °main, °chiefly, on the °whole, commonly, more often than not: *As a rule, we require payment in advance.*
—*v.* **5** Sometimes, ***rule over***: °reign (over), °govern, be in °control *or* °charge *or* °command (of *or* over), be in °power (over), hold °sway (over), °wield the sceptre, wear the °crown, °run; °prevail, °dominate, °predominate, °control: *The hand that rocks the cradle rules the world. Supposedly, the majority rules in a democracy.* **6** °direct, °guide, °manage, °control, °lead, °head (up), °preside (over), superintend, °oversee, °supervise, °regulate, °govern, °run: *The company is ruled by a committee made up of employees and directors.* **7** °decide, °judge, hand down a °judgement *or* °decision, °decree, deem, °resolve, °settle, °determine, °find, °declare, °pronounce: *The referee ruled that Jones had committed a foul.* **8** ***rule out***: °ban, °bar, °prohibit, °exclude, °eliminate, °forbid, °preclude, proscribe, negate, °dismiss, °disregard, °bypass, °ignore, °overlook: *The programme committee ruled out Birmingham as the site of next year's conference.*

rummage *v.* **1** °search, °hunt, comb, °scour, scrabble, °look through, °sift through, °turn inside out *or* upside down, °examine, *Colloq* °scrounge: *We rummaged about in four dustbins before finding the discarded receipt.*
—*n.* **2** °jumble, miscellanea, knick-knacks, °odds and ends, °hotchpotch *or US also* hodgepodge: *May we borrow your car to collect items for the church rummage sale?*

rumour *n.* **1** °news, °gossip, hearsay, °information, °scoop, tidings, °chat, chit-chat, tittle-tattle, *on dit;* °grapevine, jungle telegraph, *Colloq* °low-down, info, *US and Canadian* poop, *Slang chiefly US nautical* scuttlebutt: *The rumour is that they are moving from Reading to Exeter. Rumour has it that you are not going with them.*
—*v.* **2** bruit about, °noise abroad, °circulate, °pass around, °intimate, °breathe, °suggest, °whisper, °leak, °reveal, °make known, °put about, °say, °report, °tell: *It has been rumoured that she is going to have his baby.*

rumple *v.* Sometimes, ***rumple up***: °wrinkle, °crumple, °crush, crease, °fold, crinkle, dishevel, °ruffle, °tousle, scrunch (up), °pucker, muss (up), °mess (up): *When she stood up, the back of her dress was all rumpled.*

rumpus *n.* commotion, °disturbance, °fuss, °confusion, °uproar, °tumult, to-do, ado, °mayhem, °bedlam, brouhaha, °stir, pother, affray, °fracas, °row, mêlée *or* melee, °rough-house, °brawl: *You have no idea what a rumpus he created just because my dog went in his garden.*

run *v.* **1** sprint, °race, scamper, °scurry, °scud, dart, °bolt, °dash, °flit, °tear (along), scoot, scuttle, zip, whiz *or* whizz, gallop, °jog, °trot, lope; °rush, °hurry (up), °hasten, °scramble, °hustle, °step °lively, hop (to) it, °step on it, put on some °speed, *Archaic* hie, *Colloq* get a °move on, hoof it, °leg it, hotfoot (it), °stir one's stumps, *Brit* hare, *US* °step on the gas, hump (it), *Slang* get cracking, *US* get the lead out (of one's pants *or taboo* ass), *Chiefly US* get a wiggle on: *If you run, you might catch her before she gets on the train.* **2** run away *or* off, °flee, °escape, take °flight, take to one's °heels, °bolt, decamp, °make off, °clear out, show a clean pair of °heels, abscond, cut and run, (beat a (hasty)) °retreat, °retire, make a °getaway, (make a) run for it, *Colloq* °beat it, scram, skedaddle, °take off, °skip (out), take French °leave, °fly the coop, *Slang* head for the hills, *Brit* scarper, do a bunk, *US and Canadian* take a (run-out) °powder, lam out of (somewhere), take it *or* go on the lam, *US* vamoose: *The minute the enemy appeared, the entire troop ran. Cavendish ran, hoping the police wouldn't catch him.* **3** °go, °cover, °pass over, sprint, °race: *He ran the mile in just under four minutes.* **4** °wander, rove, °roam, °meander, °drift: *Some farmers allow their animals to run free, rather than penning them up.* **5** Often, ***run for***: °compete (for), be a °candidate (for), °vie, °struggle, contend, °fight (for), °stand (for): *As she has already said she would not stand again, I doubt that she will run for re-election in the council elections.* **6** °pass, °flow, °pour, °stream, °flood, °gush, °spill, dribble, °spurt, °issue, °move, °trickle, seep, °discharge, cascade, °spout: *You can see where the rain-water has run down this crack in the roof and into the room below.* **7** °flow, °diffuse: *The colour ran when he washed his red underwear with some white shirts in very hot water.* **8** °melt, liquefy, °dissolve, °fuse: *It was so hot that the icing on top of the cake began to melt and run down the sides.* **9** °keep, °maintain, °support, °sustain, °manage: *It is very expensive to run a large house.* **10** °operate, °manage, °direct, °supervise, °oversee, °conduct, superintend, °control, °handle, °manipulate, °head, °carry on, °lead, °regulate, take °care of, °look after, °administer, be in °charge of, °coordinate: *She must be a terrifically high achiever to run a huge international conglomerate like that!* **11** °operate, °perform, °function, °work, tick, °go: *Even after all that abuse, the watch kept running and kept good time.* **12** °extend, °stretch, °reach; °amount, °add up, °total up, °come (up): *The balance of payments deficit is running to twice last year's figure. His bill at the restaurant last night ran to more than £200.* **13** convey, °transport, give (someone) a °lift, °drive, °take, °bring: *Tom said he would run me home in his new car.* **14** bootleg, smuggle, °deal *or* °traffic in, *Chiefly US and Canadian* rustle: *During Prohibition, his father ran whisky from Canada to the US.* **15** be in °effect *or* °force, be °effective, have °force *or* °effect: *This lease has another year to run.* **16** °incur, invite, °encourage, °attract, be subjected to: *Aren't you running a risk asking Sheila to handle your money?* **17** °propel, °drive; °steer, °guide, °navigate: *If you are inept enough to run a boat aground, at least have the sense to do it at low tide.* **18** unravel, come °undone, *Chiefly Brit* ladder: *My stocking ran just before I had to leave for the dance!* **19** Sometimes, ***run off***: °print, °offset, lithograph, °reproduce, °publish, °display; imprint, °position, °place, °locate, °lay out: *They are going to run his story in the next issue of* The Londoner! *We'll run the photographs of the fire alongside the article on page one.* **20** ***run across***: °meet (up with), run into, °come across, °find, °stumble on *or* upon, °hit *or* °chance *or* °happen upon, *Colloq* °bump into: *Guess whom I ran across at Harrods yesterday.* **21** ***run after***: °chase, °pursue, °go after, court, woo, *Colloq* set one's cap for: *The City is filled with young men and women running after big money. Mick is running after this girl half his age, and he hasn't a clue that she's leading him on.* **22** ***run along***: °go away, °leave, *Slang* get °lost: *Sue wanted to get rid of Wayne and told him to run along.* **23** ***run around***: philander, be unfaithful, gallivant, *Colloq* sleep around, play the field: *How does she cope with his constant running around?* **24** ***run around with***: °associate with, spend time with, dally with, consort with: *Cynthia is running around with a bad crowd these days.* **25** ***run away***: See **2,** above. **26** ***run down***: **a** °trace, °track, °hunt, °stalk, °follow, °pursue, dog, °shadow; °find, °locate, °track down, °discover: *We ran down the suspect in an abandoned barn in Little Fakenham.* **b** °criticize, decry, defame, °vilify, °disparage, deprecate, °depreciate, denigrate, *Colloq* °knock, °pan: *If you keep running him down like that he'll develop an inferiority complex before he's seven.* **c** °weaken, °tire, °expire, play (itself) out, °burn out, run out, °fail, *Colloq* peter out: *Once the batteries have run down, we will no longer be able to transmit a distress-signal.* **d** °strike, °hit, smash *or* °crash *or* °slam into, run over, °knock over *or* down, °collide with: *On the way home, he almost ran down a boy on a bicycle.* **27** ***run in***: °arrest, take into °custody, °jail, apprehend, take *or* bring in, *Colloq* °pinch, °nab, °pull in, bust, collar, *Brit* °nick: *This is the third time this week that Minette has been run in for soliciting.* **28** ***run into***: See **20,** above. **29** ***run off***: **a** See **2,** above. **b** °duplicate, °print, °copy, °turn out, °produce, °make, °manufacture, °generate, *Colloq* do, churn out: *How quickly can you run off 1,000 copies of this brochure?* **30** ***run out***: **a** be °exhausted, °expire, °terminate, (come *or* draw to a) °close, °end, °cease: *The time for renewing your subscription has run out.* **b** °finish, °go, be °exhausted, be used up, *Colloq* peter out: *The food had run out and we had no water when we were rescued.* **31** ***run out of***: °use up, °consume, °eat up, °exhaust, be out of: *We've run out of milk—can you nip down to the shop and get some?* **32** ***run out on***: °desert, °abandon, °leave high and dry, °forsake, °leave in the lurch, °leave holding the baby: *Despite all his promises, Edgar ran out on her when she became pregnant.* **33** ***run over***: **a** See **26 d,** above. **b** °scan, run through, °go over, °look over, °flip *or* leaf *or* °thumb through, °look at, °skim (through), °browse through, °dip into, °review: *I promised Casey I would run over his article if I had the time.* **c** overflow, °spill (over), °brim over, slosh over, °pour over; °extend, °reach, °spread over, °stretch over; °exceed, go beyond, overreach, overshoot, °surpass, °transcend: *She accidentally let the bath run over, ruining the ceiling below. This article will run over onto the next page. McClelland always runs over the time allotted to his part of the proceedings.* **d** °rehearse, run through, °repeat, °practise, °review, °go over, °study, °learn, °memorize: *You'd best run over your speech again before the banquet.* **34** ***run through***: **a** °pierce, °stab, °transfix, °stick, °spit: *In the last scene, the hero runs the villain through with his sword before succumbing to his own wounds.* **b** squander, °consume, °use up, °waste, °fritter away, °exhaust, deplete, °spend, °dissipate, °throw away, *Slang* °blow: *It didn't take Hugh more than a year to run through his inheritance.* **c** See **33 b,** above.

—*n.* **35** sprint, °dash, °race, °jog, °trot: *They go for a two-mile run every morning before breakfast.* **36** °trip, °journey, °visit, °drive, °expedition, trek, °outing, °excursion, jaunt, junket, °sojourn, *Colloq* °spin, joyride: *He has to make a run over to Paris for the weekend, supposedly on business.* **37** °route, °routine, °circuit, °passage, °trip, °cycle, °round; °beat: *I was on the Murmansk run during the war.* **38** °period, °spate, °interval, °time, °spell, °stretch, °course; °engagement, booking, *Colloq* °patch: *Roger has had a run of bad luck and could use some help. The show had a long run on Broadway.* **39** access, °freedom, °liberty: *The children had the run of the house for a week while their parents were away.* **40** °return, °satisfaction, °reward, recompense, compensation, °requital, expiation, °atonement, repayment, °remuneration: *Although the odds are never in your favour, you get a good run for* *your money at Diamond Lil's Gambling Emporium.* **41** series, °sequence, °stream, °spate, °string, °succession, °progression: *Will attributed his poor showing at the tournament to a bad run of cards.* **42** °stream, °brook, runnel, °creek, rill, rivulet, *Brit* beck, *Scots* burn, *US* branch, kill: *There is a small run at the bottom of the hill.* **43** °demand, °call, °request: *Bouillon cubes seem to have enjoyed quite a run lately.* **44** °type, °category, °class, °kind, °sort: *Mark seems to be a bit more refined than the usual run of guest at Lisa's parties.* **45** °trail, °track, piste, °path, °slope; °way, runway: *She skied down the north run in record time.* **46** °enclosure, yard, °pen, °compound, runway; paddock; °pound: *There is a good-sized run at the kennel where we board the dogs when we go on holiday.* **47** *Music* roulade, cadenza, arpeggio, riff: *The soprano treated us to a marvellous run in which each note was distinct and pure.* **48** ***in the long run***: °eventually, °finally, after all, °ultimately, in (due) °time, in due course, in fine, in the °end, at the °end of the day, in the °final °analysis, all things considered, when all is said and done: *Regardless of early troubles, things always seem to turn out all right in the long run in his plays.* **49** ***on the run***: **a** °hastily, in °haste, hurriedly, while under °way, in a °hurry, at °speed, in a °rush: *It isn't supposed to be good for you to eat breakfast on the run every day.* **b** on the °loose, fleeing, escaping, in °flight, °running (away), *Slang US* on the lam: *He was on the run from the police and desperate to find Duncan.* **c** °running, retreating, on the °move *or* the °go: *They kept the enemy on the run for a week.* **50** ***the runs***: diarrhoea, dysentery, °upset °stomach, *Jocular* tummy rot, Delhi belly, Aztec hop, turista *or* tourista, Mexican foxtrot *or* two-step *or* toothache, Montezuma's revenge, curse of Montezuma, Rangoon runs, Tokyo trots, Lambeth run(s): *I came down with the runs when we got to Ankara.*

run-around *n.* °evasive treatment; °slip: *Every time he applied for help he was given the run-around.*

runaway *n.* **1** °fugitive, escapee, °refugee, °deserter, °truant, absconder: *The lad is a notorious runaway who has escaped four times before.*
—*adj.* **2** °wild, °uncontrolled, unchecked, °rampant, °renegade, unsuppressed; driverless, riderless, °loose; escaped: *Runaway inflation is ruining the economy of the country. The runaway horses were finally brought back.* **3** °easy, °effortless, °overwhelming, uncontested: *The incumbent enjoyed a runaway victory in yesterday's election.*

run-down *adj.* **1** wearied, °exhausted, debilitated, weakened, °worn out, peaked, °fatigued, enervated, °tired, drained, °spent, out of °shape *or* °condition, below °par, in °bad °shape; °unhealthy, °sickly, °ill: *He was found in a badly run-down condition, but was soon back on his feet.* **2** °ramshackle, °dilapidated, °tumble-down, °decrepit, °rickety, broken-down: *The family lives in a run-down cottage on the edge of the moor.*
—*n.* **3** °run-through, °synopsis, °summary, °survey, °précis, résumé, (°thumbnail) sketch, °outline, °rough °idea, °review, recapitulation, briefing; highlights, high points: *Give me a quick run-down of what happened while I was gone.*

run-in *n.* °disagreement, °argument, °dispute, altercation, °quarrel, confrontation, contretemps: *We had a run-in with our neighbour about playing his hi-fi too loud.*

runner *n.* **1** sprinter, racer, jogger, hurdler, miler: *Gordon is one of our best runners and ought to make the Olympic team.* **2** °messenger, courier, errand-boy, errand-girl, messenger-boy, messenger-girl, °page, dispatch-bearer *or* despatch-bearer, dispatch-rider *or* despatch-rider, *Colloq US* gofer: *The runner said that the package fell off his motor cycle and he lost it.* **3** sucker, tendril, creeper, °shoot, °branch, °stem: *Tie these runners to the frame in order to train the vine.* **4** °blade: *The runners on your skates need sharpening.*

running *n.* **1** °operation, °management, °direction: *Who attends to the everyday running of the business while you are away?* **2** °competition, °contest, °meet, °tournament, °race, °match; °event, °game: *If he is found to take steroids, he'll be out of the running.*
—*adj.* **3** °continuous, on-going, °continual, °perpetual, °sustained, °constant, uninterrupted, ceaseless, unceasing: *Where do they get the energy to keep up a running argument on the same silly subject?*

runt *n.* °dwarf, pygmy, midget: *Save the runt of the litter for me.*

run-through *n.* **1** °rehearsal, °practice, °trial, °test: *Let's have one more run-through before tomorrow's dress rehearsal.* **2** See **run-down,** above.

rupture *n.* **1** °break, °rift, °split, fissure, °fracture, cleavage, bursting; breaking, splitting, break-up, °breach, °schism, disunity, breaking up, severance, °division, °separation: *The rupture was caused by the expansion of the water on freezing. There was no rupture in friendly relations between the families.* **2** hernia: *He is to undergo surgery for a rupture.*
—*v.* **3** °break (up *or* apart), °split, °fracture, °cleave, °divide, °breach, °separate; °disrupt, °part, sunder: *The fabric of the balloon ruptured, the gas escaped, and the basket plummeted earthward.*

rural *adj.* **1** °country, °pastoral, sylvan, bucolic, °rustic, Arcadian, exurban; agricultural, agrarian, *Literary* georgic: *They always preferred rural life to life in the city. Constable painted mainly rural scenes. He sells farm equipment, strictly a rural business.* **2** See **rustic, 2,** below.

ruse *n.* °trick, °device, °deception, °manoeuvre *or chiefly US* maneuver, °dodge, °pretence, °pretext, °subterfuge, °stratagem, ploy, °hoax, °wile, °artifice, imposture: *His feigned friendship was only a ruse to get them to reveal their next move.*

rush *v.* **1** °hurry (up), °hasten, °run, °race, °hustle, bustle, make °haste, °dash, °speed, °scurry, °scramble, scoot, °jump, sprint, scamper, scuttle, *Colloq* °move (it), hotfoot (it), skedaddle, °step on it, make it °snappy, *US* hightail (it), °step on the gas, *Slang* get °moving, get cracking, get a wiggle on, go like a bat out of hell, shake a °leg: *If you want the job, you'll have to rush to send in your application. Don't rush—there's plenty for everyone.* **2** °attack, °assault, °charge, °storm, blitz: *If we rush them, we might take them by surprise.*
—*n.* **3** °hurry, °haste, °hustle, bustle, °dash, °speed, turmoil, turbulence, °flurry, commotion, °ferment, pother, ado, to-do, °excitement, °pell-mell, harum-scarum: *What's the rush?* **4** °surge, °sensation, °thrill, °charge: *I felt a rush of pleasure when I saw her coming down the street.*
—*adj.* **5** °urgent, hurry-up, exigent, high-priority, top-priority, °emergency: *This is a rush job that must be completed today.*

rustic *adj.* **1** See **rural, 1,** above. **2** °peasant, °plain, °simple, uncomplicated, °unsophisticated, °naïve, °ingenuous, guileless, °artless, °unrefined, unpolished, countrified, uncultivated, uncultured, °boorish, °crude, °rough, unmannerly, hill-billy, backwoods, °awkward, ungainly, cloddish, plodding, oafish, gawky, lumpen, loutish: *Who could dream that such a rustic homebody would some day be famous for the most fashionable literary salon in London?*
—*n.* **3** °peasant, bumpkin, °boor, yokel, hill-billy, countryman, countrywoman, °country boy *or* girl, oaf, °country cousin, *Colloq* clodhopper, *Derogatory and offensive* bog-trotter, *US and Canadian* hayseed, hick: *In those days, few rustics ever even visited a city.*

rustle *v.* **1** °whisper, °swish, sibilate, susurrate: *Outside my window, the leaves rustled in the evening breeze.*
—*n.* **2** °whisper, whispering, rustling, °swish, swishing, sibilation, sibilance, susurration, susurrus: *I heard the faint rustle of satin and knew she was listening at the door.*

rut *n.* **1** °groove, °furrow, wheel-mark, °track, trough: *In the winter the ruts in the lane fill with water and freeze, making driving difficult.* **2** °pattern, °habit, °routine, °groove, °grind, treadmill, dead end, *Colloq* rat race: *After 27 years as a horse groom, I'm beginning to feel I'm stuck in a rut.*

ruthless *adj.* pitiless, unpitying, °cruel, °unsympathetic, °merciless, °unmerciful, °harsh, °fierce, °remorseless, uncompassionate, °vicious, °savage, °ferocious, hard-hearted, °callous, unfeeling, °tough, °severe, °heartless, °inhuman, °brutal, brutish, unrelenting, °relentless, *Chiefly US and Canadian* °mean: *The jail houses some of the country's most ruthless criminals. In all of history there was no more ruthless a tyrant.*

S

sabotage *n.* **1** °destruction, °damage, wrecking, °impairment: *Enemy infiltrators were responsible for the sabotage of our radar.* **2** °subversion, treachery, treason: *When the radar was found damaged, sabotage was suspected.*
—*v.* **3** °undermine, °subvert, °disrupt, °spoil, °ruin, °cripple; °damage, °incapacitate, disable, °destroy, °wreck, *Colloq Brit* throw a spanner in(to) the works, *US* throw a monkey wrench into the machinery, *Slang Brit* °queer (someone's pitch): *Only someone who had something to lose would have sabotaged our plan for reorganization. The engine had been sabotaged by pouring sand into the fuel tank.*

sack *n.* **1** °pouch, °bag, *Scots and US dialect* poke; *Technical* sac: *She bought a 10-pound sack of potatoes.* **2** ***hit the sack***: °retire, °turn in, go to bed *or* to °sleep, *Slang* hit the hay, *Brit* kip (down), *US* sack out: *I need my beauty sleep so I'm going to hit the sack.* **3** ***the sack***: °dismissal, °discharge, firing, *Colloq* heave-ho, the axe, marching orders, *US* pink slip, bounce, *Chiefly US and Canadian* walking papers, *Slang Brit* the boot, the chop, the °push: *Ten of us got the sack when the new management took over.*
—*v.* **4** °dismiss, °discharge, °fire, let go, °lay off, *Brit* make *or* declare °redundant, *Colloq* give (someone) the axe *or* the (old) heave-ho, give (someone) his *or* her marching orders, *Brit* give (someone) the sack, *US* bounce, *Slang Brit* give (someone) the boot *or* the chop *or* the °push: *Now that he's been sacked, Norman will be able to spend more time with the children.*

sacred *adj.* **1** consecrated, dedicated, hallowed, °holy, blessed, blest, sanctified, revered, °divine, awe-inspiring, °venerable, venerated, sainted, heaven-sent: *This is a most sacred Islamic site.* **2** inviolable, inviolate, untouchable, protected, sacrosanct: *They held nothing sacred as they ransacked the temple.* **3** °religious, °spiritual, °ceremonial, church(ly), ecclesiastical, °priestly, hieratic, °ritual, °solemn, sacramental, liturgical: *He continued to carry out his sacred duties despite the war.*

sacrifice *n.* **1** immolation, °surrender, forfeiture, forgoing, giving up, yielding up, °offering (up), °offer, *Christian religion* oblation: *The Aztec religion demanded the sacrifice of human beings.* **2** forfeiture, forgoing, giving up, relinquishment, °loss: *Mrs Clinton continues her charitable work at the sacrifice of much of her time.*
—*v.* **3** immolate, °offer (up), °yield (up), °give up: *In their religion, they were required to sacrifice small animals to propitiate the gods.* **4** °give up, °forgo, °forfeit, °relinquish, °surrender, °let °go, °lose, °yield, °renounce, forswear; forbear, desist, °cease, °stop, °refrain from: *She was quite ready to sacrifice her inheritance to see justice done. If you sacrificed smoking you could give the money you save to charity.*

sacrificial *adj.* **1** sacrificed, immolated, surrendered, given up, yielded: *They led the sacrificial lamb to the slaughter.* **2** atoning, expiatory, °propitiatory, conciliatory: *The solemn sacrificial ceremonies were carried out by the high priestess.*

sacrilege *n.* **1** desecration, profanation, debasement, °violation, °prostitution, dishonouring, vitiation, defilement, befouling, fouling, contamination, befoulment, °misuse, °abuse, °perversion, maltreatment: *The horrendous Buckinghamshire county office building is an example of architectural sacrilege.* **2** impiety, heresy, profanation, °outrage, °violation, °profanity, blasphemy, impiousness, irreverence, °disrespect, secularization: *It was an unscrupulous sacrilege to appropriate to his own use the offerings to the gods.*

sacrilegious *adj.* °profane, °impious, °heretical, °blasphemous, °irreverent, °disrespectful: *The inscription contains a curse on any who perpetrate any sacrilegious act against the remains of the pharaoh.*

sad *adj.* **1** °unhappy, °melancholy, downcast, °dejected, depressed, °low, °sorrowful, °gloomy, morose, °glum, lugubrious, °mournful, heartsick, crestfallen, chapfallen, disheartened, °downhearted, °blue, °despondent, °broken-hearted, °heartbroken, °woebegone, °miserable, °wretched: *Danny was so sad when his dog died that he wept for a week.* **2** depressing, °gloomy, disheartening, °dreary, °dismal, °funereal, °sombre, lugubrious, saddening, heartbreaking, °bleak, distressing, dispiriting, °calamitous: *It was a sad day for all of us here when the England team lost the semifinal.* **3** °unfortunate, °unsatisfactory, °awful, °bad, °shabby, °dirty, °lamentable, °miserable, °sorry, °wretched, °pathetic, °pitiful, °pitiable, °deplorable, °terrible, *Colloq* °lousy, °rotten: *After two weeks under water, the sofa was in pretty sad shape.*

sadden *v.* °depress, deject, °sorrow, dishearten, °distress, dispirit, °discourage, °grieve, aggrieve: *It saddens me to think of all the starving people.*

sadistic *adj.* °cruel, °monstrous, °brutal, brutish, °beastly, °ruthless, °perverse, *Technical* algolagnic: *She derives sadistic pleasure from reminding me of all my failures. The scars and bruises confirmed the sadistic treatment he had undergone.*

sadly *adv.* **1** unfortunately, alas, unhappily, unluckily, lamentably, regrettably, deplorably, °sad to relate: *Sadly, all our oldest oaks were uprooted in the hurricane.* **2** unhappily, gloomily, morosely, mournfully, despondently, miserably, wretchedly, dejectedly, dismally, sombrely, lugubriously: *He told me sadly that he did not expect to return to England again.*

sadness *n.* unhappiness, dolour, °misery, °sorrow, dispiritedness, °grief, °depression, dejection, dejectedness, sorrowfulness, despondency, °melancholy, °gloom, gloominess: *It is hard to describe the sadness we all felt when she left.*

safe *adj.* **1** unharmed, °whole, uninjured, unhurt, (safe and) °sound, °secure, protected, shielded, sheltered, out of harm's way, all right, *Colloq* °OK *or* okay: *You'll be safe here with me.* **2** °harmless, non-toxic, non-poisonous, innocuous; unpolluted: *This medication is safe if you do not exceed the recommended dosage. Is the water safe to drink?* **3** °sure, °secure, °sound, protected, risk-free, riskless, safe as the Bank of England, °reliable, dependable, °solid, bona fide, °conservative, tried and °true, *Brit* safe as houses: *It was previously thought that an investment in Alfordyce Ltd was safe.* **4** all right, allowable, °permissible, °acceptable, °satisfactory, °appropriate, °suitable, °timely, °right, °correct, °proper, justifiable, justified, *Colloq* °OK *or* okay: *Is it safe to come out now?* **5** secured, protected: *The children are safe in bed. Your secret is safe with me.*
—*adv.* **6** safely, securely: *I won't breathe easy till he's safe behind bars.*
—*n.* **7** vault, °crypt, strongbox, safe-deposit *or* safety-deposit °box, coffer, °chest, repository: *The necklace is kept in the safe and I never get a chance to wear it.*

safeguard *n.* **1** °protection, °defence, °security: *Such a flimsy fence is hardly a sufficient safeguard.*
—*v.* **2** °protect, °defend, °shield, °shelter, keep °safe, °guard; °conserve, °save, °keep, °care for, °look after: *What is being done to safeguard the passengers from attacks by bandits?*

safe keeping *n.* °charge, °protection, keeping, °custody, °care, guardianship: *The deed to the house is in the safe keeping of Mr Williams, my solicitor.*

safety *n.* safeness, °protection, aegis, °cover, °shelter, °security, °refuge; °sanctuary, °safe keeping: *There's safety in numbers, so the more the merrier. We retreated to the safety of the castle dungeon.*

sag *v.* **1** °droop, °sink, °slump, °bend, °dip; swag, °bag: *The board sagged precariously under his weight. Without a breath stirring, the banners sagged in the humid air.* **2** °drop, °decrease, °decline, °go *or* come down, °fall, °slide, °slip, °weaken, °slump, °descend, °diminish, lessen, °droop, °subside, °flag, falter, °wilt: *The value of the dollar sagged in world markets today.* —*n.* **3** sagging, °drop, °droop, °sinking, sinkage, subsidence, °dip; reduction, °decrease, °decline, °fall, °slide, weakening, °slump, lessening, flagging, faltering: *If you stand over here you can see a definite sag in the roof. The sag in profits was attributed to a poor response to the new model.*

saga *n.* (heroic) °legend, °narrative, epic, Edda, °chronicle, °romance, *roman-fleuve*, °story, °tale, °adventure: *Are you really interested in the continuing saga of the inhabitants of Coronation Street?*

sage *adj.* **1** °wise, sagacious, °prudent, °sensible, perspicacious, °profound, °intelligent, discerning, °reasonable, °logical, °judicious, common-sense, commonsensical: *The old woman gave her some sage advice about men, which she promptly forgot.* —*n.* **2** °wise man, savant, °expert, °elder, doyen *or* doyenne, guru, Nestor, pundit, Solomon, philosopher, °oracle, °authority: *The sage whose counsel you seek lives deep in the forest.*

sail *v.* **1** °navigate, °pilot, °steer: *Sail as close to the shore as possible to avoid the whirlpool.* **2** go sailing *or* boating *or* yachting, °cruise, set sail, put (out) to sea: *Would you like to sail to the Isle of Wight for the weekend?* **3** °drift, °move lightly, breeze, °flow, °waft, °sweep, °coast, °float, °scud, °glide, °slide, °slip, °plane, °skim, °fly, °flit: *It was delightful to watch the tiny boats sailing, tacking, beating, and running in the brisk wind.* —*n.* **4** canvas: *The schooner was carrying all the sail she could.*

sailor *n.* seaman, seafarer, °seafaring man *or* woman, seagoing man *or* woman, mariner, (old) °salt, sea dog, bluejacket, shellback, yachtsman, yachtswoman, boatman, boatwoman, deck-hand, captain, °skipper, *Literary* Jack Tar, *Colloq* tar, *Naval US* swab, swabbie, gob: *When she said she had married a sailor I didn't know she meant that he had a 100-foot yacht.*

saintly *adj.* °holy, blessed, blest, beatific, °godly, sainted, angelic, °seraphic, °pure, °righteous, °virtuous, °blameless: *Donald was such a saintly man, it was impossible to think ill of him.*

sake *n.* **1** °benefit, °welfare, well-being, °good, °advantage, °behalf, °profit, °gain, °account: *Joe and I stayed together for the sake of the children. She felt pleased, for his sake, that he had managed to get away.* **2** °purpose(s), °reason(s), °objective(s): *Just for the sake of comparison, let us now look at the situation in Taiwan.*

salary *n.* °income, °pay, °earnings, compensation, °remuneration, emolument; °wage(s): *I can't afford a new car on my present salary.*

sale *n.* **1** selling, °traffic, vending, marketing, trafficking, trading; °trade, °exchange, °transaction: *The sale of alcoholic beverages on Sundays is prohibited. Provide a receipt for each sale.* **2** °trade, °purchase; trading, buying, purchasing: *We must do something to boost sales. The house is very reasonably priced for a quick sale.* **3** sales event, mark-down, white sale, jumble sale, *Brit* car-boot sale, *US* rummage sale, garage sale, tag sale, yard sale, *Colloq* sellathon, sales marathon: *We are having a sale to clear out things we no longer want or need.* **4** °transaction: *She hasn't made a sale in a week.* **5** ***on sale***: *US* marked down, cut-price, bargain-priced; reduced (in price): *Bacon is on sale this week at half price.* **6** ***(up) for sale***: on the market, °available, in stock, *Chiefly Brit* on sale, on offer, *US* on the block: *Their house is for sale to the highest bidder.*

salesperson *n.* salesman, saleswoman, saleslady, salesgirl, sales-clerk, clerk, *Chiefly Brit* shop-girl, *Brit* shop °assistant, *Old-fashioned* counter-jumper: *The shop is noted for its wide range of merchandise and the efficiency and courtesy of its salespeople.*

salient *adj.* °conspicuous, °outstanding, °pronounced, °noticeable, °prominent, °significant, °important, °marked, °impressive, °striking, °remarkable, distinguishing, °distinctive, °unique, °eminent, °noteworthy, °notable, °principal, °chief, °primary: *A salient feature of this policy is that it can be converted at any time from a straight life to an endowment policy.*

salt *n.* **1** common *or* table salt, sodium chloride, sea salt, rock-salt: *A little salt will bring out the flavour.* **2** °spice, spiciness, °zest, zestiness, pungency, °vigour, °vitality, liveliness, °pep, °pepper, poignancy, piquancy, °relish, °bite, °savour, °seasoning, °taste, *Colloq* zip, zing, °punch: *Yes, do invite Randolph, for he can be relied on to add a little salt to the dinner conversation.* **3** (Attic) °wit, Attic salt, °dry °humour, °sarcasm: *Her conversation is sprinkled with the salt of clever aphorisms.* **4** See **sailor,** above. **5** ***with a grain*** *or* ***pinch of salt***: *cum grano salis*, warily, cautiously, qualifiedly, qualifyingly, doubtfully, sceptically, suspiciously, reservedly, with °reservation(s) *or* °qualification(s): *You have to take what he says with a grain of salt.* —*v.* **6** °season, °spice, °flavour, °pepper: *The pirate's speech was salted with expressions like 'Shiver me timbers!', 'Avast there!', and 'Blow me down!'* **7** pickle, °cure, °preserve, corn, marinate, souse: *The book gives several recipes for curing ham and salting beef.* **8** ***salt away***: °save (up), °hoard, °put *or* °lay *or* °set by *or* aside, squirrel away, °store up, stockpile, °amass, °accumulate, °pile up, *Colloq* stash away, *US and Canadian* sock away: *They were always terribly stingy, claiming they were salting something away for their old age.* —*adj.* **9** salty, saline, brackish, briny: *The water had a salt taste.* **10** pickled, kippered, marinated, soused; corned; cured: *Do you like salt herring?*

salute *v.* **1** °greet, °hail, °address, accost: *The moment I stepped in at the door I was saluted with the peremptory question, 'Where have you been?'* **2** pay °respects *or* °homage *or* °tribute to, °honour, °recognize, °acknowledge: *Wherever she went she was saluted as a heroine.* —*n.* **3** °greeting, °address, salutation: *He returned my salute with a nod.*

salvage *v.* **1** °save, °recover, °rescue, °redeem, °deliver, °retrieve, °reclaim: *Were you able to salvage anything of value after the fire?* —*n.* **2** °recovery, °rescue, retrieval, redemption, deliverance, reclamation, salvation: *The salvage of a vessel or cargo at sea invests the salvager with legal rights under certain conditions.*

salve *n.* **1** balm, °ointment, unguent, dressing, cream, °lotion, demulcent, embrocation, liniment: *The doctor applied a salve to the wound and bandaged it.* **2** emollient, balm, palliative, °tranquillizer, opiate, anodyne, °narcotic, relief, assuagement: *The money was more a salve to his conscience than a token of his charity.* —*v.* **3** °mitigate, °relieve, °ease, alleviate, assuage, palliate, soothe, mollify, °comfort, appease: *There must be something you can do to allow them to save face and to salve their wounded pride.*

same *adj.* **1** °identical, °exact (same), selfsame; °very: *When I said they were wearing the same dress I meant that they were wearing identical dresses. That's the same tie you wore when we first met.* **2** unchanged, unchanging, °changeless, unmodified, unaltered, °constant, °uniform, unvaried, unvarying; word-for-word, °verbatim: *As you can see, it's the same old Charley you used to know and love. Professor Spicer is still giving the same lecture that he has given all these years.* **3** ***all the same***: at the same time, °nevertheless, °nonetheless, °even so, °yet, but, anyway, anyhow, in any °case, in any °event, at any °rate, °regardless, °still (and all), in °spite of *or* °despite the fact, °notwithstanding, for all that, that (having been) said, having said that, after all is said and done, just the same: *Of course you have a right to go; all the same, I wish you had let me know.*

sample *n.* **1** °specimen, °example, °representative, °representation, °illustration, sampling, sampler, cross-section; swatch; °bite, nibble, °taste: *I should like to see a sample before deciding whether to place an order with you.*
—*v.* **2** °test, °try, °taste, °experience: *Anyone is welcome to sample the merchandise on request.*
—*adj.* **3** °representative, °specimen, illustrative, representational, °trial, °test: *A sample copy of the book is available for examination.*

sanatorium *n.* rest-home, convalescent °home, nursing °home, clinic, health farm, *US also* sanitarium: *After spending a month recuperating in a Swiss sanatorium, Gladys was as good as new.*

sanctify *v.* **1** consecrate, °hallow, make °sacred *or* °holy, °glorify, °exalt, canonize, enshrine; *Rom Cath Ch* beatify: *The site was sanctified and is visited by pilgrims throughout the year.* **2** °purify, °cleanse: *According to Scripture, some are sanctified before birth.* **3** °confirm, °sanction, °ratify, °justify, °legitimate, legitimatize *or* legitimize, legalize, °license: *Her family insisted that the marriage be sanctified at the church in Suffolk, where they live.*

sanctimonious *adj.* °hypocritical, °self-righteous, canting, °mealy-mouthed, holier-than-thou, Pharisaical, pietistic, unctuous, Tartuffian, *Colloq* °goody-goody, *Chiefly Brit* smarmy, *Slang Brit* pi: *I wondered what happened to all that sanctimonious talk about putting his family first?*

sanction *n.* **1** confirmation, ratification, secondment, authorization, legalization, legitimatization *or* legitimization, validation, °licence, certification, °approval, °permission, imprimatur, °seal *or* °stamp (of °approval), signet: *If you get the sanction of the rest of the members, then I shall agree.* **2** °help, °aid, °encouragement, °support, advocacy, °backing, sponsorship, °favour, countenance: *You will need the sanction of the entire committee in order to win a vote of confidence.* **3** °agreement, concurrence, acceptance, affirmation, assent, acquiescence, compliance, °approval, °OK *or* okay: *He would never have proceeded with the invasion without the sanction of his generals.* **4** °ban, °penalty, °punishment, °retribution, °discipline, retaliation, redress: *The government decided to introduce sanctions against the regime on account of their atrocious record on human rights.*
—*v.* **5** °confirm, °ratify, °second, °authorize, legalize, legitimatize *or* legitimize, validate, °license, °certify, °approve, °permit, °allow, notarize, °vouchsafe, °subscribe to, commission, °consent to: *If the board sanctions the purchase of the company, it is then up to the shareholders to vote.* **6** °support, °encourage, °advocate, °back, °sponsor, °favour, countenance, °help: *You know I cannot be seen to sanction your plan in preference to others.*

sanctity *n.* °piety, holiness, saintliness, divinity, °grace, sacredness, godliness, °devotion, °dedication: *The arguments of the anti-abortionists were based on a belief in the sanctity of all human life.*

sanctuary *n.* **1** °sanctum, shrine, chapel, °temple, church, house of °worship, house of God; synagogue, mosque, pagoda: *All of us retire at this time to the sanctuary for evening prayer.* **2** asylum, °refuge, °retreat, °protection, °shelter, °safety: *Formerly, criminals could seek sanctuary in churches.* **3** (nature *or* wildlife) reserve *or* °preserve, °reservation, conservation area, national °park: *If housing is built here, it will destroy the bird sanctuary.*

sanctum *n.* **1** °sanctuary, holy of holies, shrine: *No one is allowed into the sanctum except the high priestess.* **2** sanctum sanctorum, den, °study, °retreat; hiding-place, hide-out, °hideaway, cubby-hole: *After dinner Roger goes to his sanctum to write.*

sane *adj.* °normal, of °sound mind, °rational, *compos mentis*, °well-balanced, right-minded, °level-headed, °reasonable, °sensible, °judicious, *Colloq* °right in the head, all there: *They decided that the killer was sane and fit to stand trial.*

sang-froid *n.* cold-bloodedness, coolness, cool-headedness, °indifference, composure, phlegm, self-possession, °self-control, °poise, imperturbability, equanimity, *Colloq* unflappability, °cool, coolth: *What amazed us was the remarkable sang-froid displayed by even the smallest children in the face of bullying.*

sanguinary *adj.* **1** °bloodthirsty, °cruel, °brutal, brutish, °gory, °merciless, °remorseless, °ruthless, pitiless, °heartless, °savage, barbarous, slaughterous, °grim, fell, °murderous, °homicidal: *The axe murder was the most sanguinary crime that the division had ever been required to investigate.* **2** bloody, sanguineous, sanguinolent: *I am unsure how I survived such a sanguinary battle.*

sanguine *adj.* °optimistic, °rosy, °confident, °hopeful, forward-looking, anticipatory, °expectant, °enthusiastic, fervid, zealous: *Some experts took a more sanguine view, saying that they expected to see the start of an economic upturn in the next few months.*

sanitary *adj.* °clean, °sterile, °hygienic, antiseptic, disinfected, aseptic, germ-free, bacteria-free; °healthy, unpolluted, salubrious, healthful, salutary, °wholesome: *With such shortages of personnel and equipment, it was impossible to maintain a sanitary hospital environment.*

sanity *n.* saneness, °reason, mental °health *or* soundness, normality, rationality, reasonableness, °stability, °balance: *Have you any reason for suspecting her sanity?*

sap[1] *n.* **1** (vital) °juice *or* °fluid, bodily *or US also* body °fluid, lifeblood, °essence, *Literary* ichor: *He apostrophized about how the sap of youth had shrunk from his veins.* **2** °fool, idiot, nincompoop, ninny, ninnyhammer, simpleton, ignoramus, nitwit, dim-wit, dunce, ass; °dupe, gull, *US* thimble-wit; *Colloq* chump, °drip, *Brit* (right) charlie, noddy, noodle, °wet, *Chiefly Brit* °twit, *Slang* patsy, °sucker, (easy) mark, °pushover, sap-head, *Brit* muggins, *US* schnook, schlemiel *or* schlemihl *or* shlemiel, fall guy: *You certainly were a sap to fall for that old line!*
—*v.* **3** bleed, °drain, °draw, °tap, °rob, °milk: *I could feel the strength being sapped from my body.*

sap[2] *v.* °undermine, °sabotage, °weaken, °cripple, °wreck, devitalize, deplete, °drain, °erode, °enervate, debilitate: *They did everything they could to sap my self-confidence.*

sarcasm *n.* °scorn, contumely, °derision, °ridicule, °bitterness, acrimony, acrimoniousness, acerbity, harshness, acridity, acridness, asperity, °venom, °poison, venomousness, poisonousness, °virulence, °spite, spitefulness, malice, maliciousness, malevolence, °satire, irony, cynicism, disdain: *Kathy was too thick-skinned to appreciate the sarcasm of Tom's cutting commentary on her acting.*

sarcastic *adj.* °scornful, contumelious, derisive, °derisory, ridiculing, °bitter, °biting, °cutting, °trenchant, °incisive, acrimonious, acerbic, acid, acidic, acidulous, °harsh, acrid, aspersive, °venomous, °poisonous, °virulent, °spiteful, malicious, malefic, malevolent, satiric(al), ironic(al), cynical, °disdainful, mocking, °contemptuous, °critical, censorious, captious, carping, cavilling, °sardonic, °scathing, °caustic, °nasty: *I don't think he knows how hurtful his sarcastic remarks can be.*

sardonic *adj.* ironic(al), derisive, °derisory, mocking, cynical, °sarcastic: *She said that she was leaving him, but his only response was a sardonic smile.*

satanic *adj.* **1** °diabolic(al), °fiendish, °devilish, Mephistophelian, demonic, demoniac(al), cacodemonic, °ghoulish, hellish, °infernal, °evil, °wicked, iniquitous, °corrupt, depraved, °perverted, °perverse, °godless, °ungodly, °impious, unholy, °sinister, °dark, °black, °immoral, amoral: *They practise witchcraft and other satanic inventions.* **2** dire, °monstrous, heinous, °atrocious, °hideous, °horrible, horrendous, horrid, horrifying, °loathsome, °vile, °abhorrent, unspeakable, unutterable, °damnable, °despicable, °abominable: *The miners worked under positively satanic conditions.*

satellite *n.* **1** moon, spacecraft, *Old-fashioned* sputnik: *The sky is crowded with artificial satellites orbiting the earth.* **2** °follower, °attendant, retainer, °disciple, acolyte, °aide, aide-de-camp, minion, lieutenant, °assistant, helper, °hanger-on, dependant, °shadow, right-hand man, vassal, °parasite, sycophant, *Colloq* sidekick: *Boswell became the obsequious satellite of Samuel Johnson.*

satiate *v.* **1** °stuff, °glut, °gorge, cloy, °surfeit, overfill, overstuff, °pall, overindulge, °saturate, °choke, deluge, °flood, suffocate, °weary, °exhaust, °bore, °tire, °jade: *The travellers were so satiated with food and drink that nothing could wake them.* **2** °slake, °satisfy, °quench, °content, °gratify, sate: *I felt it would take at least a gallon of water to satiate my thirst.*

satiety *n.* °surfeit, °glut, superabundance, overindulgence, saturation, nimiety, °excess, °superfluity: *The painting exudes a mood of sexual languor and satiety.*

satire *n.* **1** °ridicule, irony, °sarcasm, °mockery, spoofing, °exaggeration, °caricature: *Often, the best way to comment on a distasteful political situation is through satire.* **2** °burlesque, °lampoon, °parody, travesty, pasquinade, spoof, cartoon, °caricature, *Colloq* °take-off, *Chiefly Brit* send-up: *For several years he wrote mainly satires of life among the wealthy.*

satirical *adj.* satiric, ironic, °sarcastic, mocking, spoofing, °irreverent, exaggerating, Hudibrastic, derisive, disparaging, °abusive, °scornful, °flippant, ridiculing, chaffing: *After a number of satirical plays, he returned to writing novels, which, he felt, reached a wider audience.*

satirize *v.* °lampoon, °burlesque, °parody, °caricature, travesty, °poke °fun at, (hold up to) °ridicule, make °fun *or* °sport of, pillory, °deride, °mock; °mimic, °imitate; *Colloq* °take off, °put down, *Brit* °send up: *Since ancient times writers have satirized the follies of their age.*

satisfaction *n.* **1** °gratification, °comfort, °fulfilment, contentment, °delight, °joy, °enjoyment, °pleasure, °happiness: *They get a great deal of satisfaction out of seeing their children happily married.* **2** °payment, °requital, repayment, compensation, recompense, °remuneration, reparation, °indemnity, indemnification, °restitution, vindication, °damages, °amends, redress, °atonement, expiation: *The purpose of the lawsuit is to demand satisfaction for the wrongs done to our family.*

satisfactory *adj.* °adequate, °sufficient, °acceptable, °passable, all right, not bad, °good enough, °fair, *Colloq* °OK *or* okay: *I'd say that the food at Michelle's is satisfactory but not outstanding.*

satisfy *v.* **1** °gratify, °fulfil, °comfort, °please, °content, placate, appease, pacify: *It takes a lot to satisfy him: he is one of the fussiest men I have ever worked with.* **2** °fill, °meet, °fulfil, °provide for, °look after *or* to, °serve, °answer, °comply with, °resolve, °solve, °gratify, °indulge; °slake, °quench, sate, °satiate: *Your desire for better working conditions can probably only be satisfied by a change of job. What will it take to satisfy your thirst for adventure?* **3** °convince, °persuade, °reassure, °assure, put (someone's) mind at rest, °content: *He was satisfied that emigration to Australia was the only option open to him.* **4** °pay, °repay, redress, °make good, indemnify, °write off, liquidate: *I shall see to it that the debt is satisfied at once.*

satisfying *adj.* gratifying, °satisfactory, fulfilling, °filling, satiating; comforting, °pleasing, pacifying, °pleasurable: *That was a very satisfying meal. It is a satisfying feeling to know that you are happy.*

saturate *v.* °soak, °wet, °drench, °steep, °fill, imbue, souse, °suffuse, °impregnate, °permeate; waterlog; *Technical* ret: *I got caught in the rain and came home saturated. Make sure that you saturate the earth round the tree once you have finished planting.*

sauce *n.* **1** gravy, condiment: *That sauce on the meat was truly delicious.* **2** °impertinence, sauciness, °impudence, audacity, insolence, brazenness, pertness, °disrespect, disrespectfulness, *Colloq* cheek, cheekiness, lip, back °talk, backchat, °brass, °nerve, °gall, *Slang* crust, *US and Canadian* sass, sassiness: *She had the sauce to tell me to pay at once or get out.*

saunter *v.* °walk, °stroll, amble, °meander, °ramble, °wander, *Colloq* mosey, traipse: *An oddly dressed man sauntered over and asked if I had ever bet on a horse before.*

savage *adj.* **1** °wild, °untamed, undomesticated, feral, unbroken: *These savage beasts had never seen a man before.* **2** °vicious, °ferocious, °fierce, °beastly, bestial, brutish, °bloodthirsty, °brutal, °cruel, °ruthless, pitiless, °merciless, °harsh, bloody, °unmerciful, fell, barbarous, barbaric, °murderous, demonic, demoniac, °sadistic: *The boy was subjected to a savage attack by the defendant's dog. The king's guards were selected for their savage nature.* **3** °wild, °uncivilized, uncultivated, °primitive, °inhuman, bestial, barbaric, barbarous, °untamed, °rude: *The savage behaviour of some New Guinea tribes included cannibalism.*
—*n.* **4** °wild man *or* woman, °brute, °barbarian; Caliban: *When the explorers landed on the island, they were welcomed by the savages who lived there.*

save *v.* **1** (come to someone's) °rescue, °deliver; (set) °free, °liberate, °release, °redeem, bail (someone) out; °recover, °salvage, °retrieve: *What can be done to save me from the drudgery of doing the laundry? She saved only one thing of value from the fire.* **2** °keep, °preserve, °guard, °safeguard, °protect, °conserve, °secure, °shelter, °shield: *One way to save dried flowers is to press them between the leaves of a book.* **3** lay *or* °put aside, lay *or* °put by, lay *or* °put away, °keep, °retain, °set °apart, °hold, °reserve, °preserve, °conserve; °economize, scrimp, °scrape: *Soon he had saved enough money to buy a new car. If you keep on saving, you may soon have enough for a new suit.* **4** obviate, °preclude, °spare, °prevent: *A little extra care taken now will save a lot of trouble later on.*

saving *adj.* **1** redeeming, redemptory *or* redemptive *or* redemptional, compensating, °compensatory, qualifying, °extenuating, extenuatory: *His one saving grace is that he has a lot of money.* **2** parsimonious, °economical, °thrifty, °provident, °frugal, °sparing, °prudent: *It was only because of Alison's saving nature that we had enough to live on during the strike.*
—*n.* **3** economizing, economization, °economy, °thrift, °providence, frugality, °prudence, scrimping, scraping, sparingness: *It was only by her saving that we survived.* **4** ***savings***: °resources, °reserve, °cache, °hoard, nest egg: *Our savings are to pay for your education, not for having a good time.*

saviour *n.* **1** rescuer, salvation, °friend in need, Good Samaritan, liberator, redeemer, deliverer, emancipator, °champion, knight errant, knight in shining armour: *Because he gave her a job when she most needed it, she regarded him as her saviour.* **2** ***the*** *or* ***our Saviour***: *Christian religion* Christ (the Redeemer), Jesus, the °Messiah, Lamb of God, Our Lord, Son of God, King of Kings, Prince of Peace, *Islam* Mahdi.

savoir faire *n.* °tact, tactfulness, °sophistication, °finesse, urbanity, °discretion, knowledgeability, °diplomacy, smoothness, °polish, suavity *or* suaveness, °poise, °grace, °style, °skill, adroitness, °knowledge, comprehension, *Slang* savvy: *She felt a vague sense of social inferiority, an uneasy lack of savoir faire.*

savoir vivre *n.* °breeding, °upbringing, comity, °knowledge, °sophistication, °polish: *He has at least enough savoir vivre to know that one doesn't drink red wine with oysters.*

savour *n.* **1** °taste, °flavour, °zest, °tang, smack, piquancy: *These poached peaches have a savour of brandy about them.* **2** °hint, °suggestion, °odour, °scent, °fragrance, °smell, °perfume, redolence, °bouquet, °breath, °trace, °quality, soupçon, °dash: *He*

preferred talking about the savour rather than the odour of sanctity, for alliteration's sake.
—*v.* **3** °taste, °sample, °perceive, °detect, °sense, discern, °mark, descry, °observe, °notice, °note, °identify; °enjoy, °luxuriate in, °relish, °indulge in, bask in, °appreciate, °revel in, °delight in, value, °cherish, *Colloq* lick *or* smack one's lips *or* chops over: *One could savour a trace of honey in the wine. For a week we savoured the delights of the Costa Brava.*

savoury *adj.* **1** palatable, °delicious, delectable, °tasty, toothsome, appetizing, flavourful, flavorous, flavoursome, ambrosial, °luscious: *Pettigrew bit greedily into the savoury flesh of the ripe melon.* **2** °tasteful, °honest, °proper, °decent, °reputable, °respectable, °honourable, creditable, °upright, °decorous, °seemly, °wholesome, °innocent: *I am not sure that Victoria is travelling in particularly savoury society.*
—*n.* **3** appetizer, °hors-d'œuvre; °dessert, °sweet; °morsel, °dainty, °titbit *or US* tidbit, *Chiefly Brit* starter, *Archaic* warner: *I think I'd like the Welsh rabbit as a savoury.*

saw *n.* °proverb, °maxim, (old) saying, aphorism, apophthegm *or* apothegm, axiom, adage, °epigram, gnome; °slogan, °motto, catchword, catch-phrase, °byword; dictum, platitude, °truism, °cliché, commonplace: *She always quoted to him the old saw, 'A fool and his mother are soon parted'.*

say *v.* **1** °state, affirm, °declare, °maintain, °hold, aver, °remark, assert, °claim, asseverate, °announce: *She said that I had to go at once, and I said, 'I shall never leave you!'* **2** assert, °allege, °report, °mention, °rumour, °reveal, bruit about, °disclose, divulge, bring to °light, °put about, °noise abroad, °suggest, °hint, °whisper: *It was said that spies had already infiltrated the party.* **3** °pronounce, articulate, utter; °phrase, rephrase, °translate: *How do you say* gemütlich? *How do you say it in English?* **4** °tell, °put, °express, verbalize, °communicate, °explain, °reveal, °bring up, °break, °impart: *I don't quite know how to say this, Harry, but you have bad breath.* **5** °reply, °respond, °answer: *What have you to say to her allegation that it is all your fault?* **6** °guess, °estimate, conjecture, °venture, °judge, °imagine, °believe, °think: *I'd say you look about 60 years old.* **7** mean *or* intend *or* try to say, °think, °contemplate, °imply, °suggest: *Are you saying that you would steal if you had the opportunity?* **8** °predict, °prognosticate, foretell: *The newspaper says that shares will go down.* **9** °signify, °denote, °symbolize, °communicate, °indicate, convey, °suggest, °imply, °mean: *What does a red light say to you?* **10** °order, °require, °demand, °bid, °stipulate, °command, give the word: *If I say that you are to go, then you go—and quickly.* **11** °deliver, utter, °speak: *Say your lines and exit stage left without waiting for a reply.*
—*n.* **12** °voice, °authority, °influence, °power, °weight, °sway, clout: *Does she have that much say about how the money should be spent?* **13** °turn, °chance, °opportunity, °vote: *You've had your say, now let's hear from Ackroyd.*
—*adv.* **14** °approximately, °about, °roughly, *circa*, °nearly: *The snake was, say, twenty feet long.* **15** for °example, for °instance, as *or* for an °illustration, eg *or US* e.g.: *Take any novel, say,* Wuthering Heights, *and analyse the characters.*

say-so *n.* °authority, °word, °say, °order, dictum; authorization: *I shouldn't do it just on his say-so if I were you.*

scale[1] *n.* Often, ***scales***: °balance: *We need new bathroom scales: the old one gives too high a reading.*

scale[2] *n.* **1** °flake, imbrication; scurf, dandruff; *Technical* squama, °plate, scute *or* scutum, lamina, lamella: *Scrape the scales off the fish with a sharp knife before gutting it.* **2** coating, encrustation *or* incrustation, crust, overlay, layer, cake, caking, tartar, °plaque: *The hardness of the water causes the scale inside the kettle.*

scale[3] *n.* **1** °range, compass, °rank, ranking, gradation, graduation, °register, spectrum, calibration, °progression, hierarchy, °scope, °gamut: *As we ascend in the scale of life we rise in the scale of longevity.* **2** °proportion, °ratio: *The scale of these drawings is One Foot = One Centimetre.*
—*v.* **3** °climb, ascend, °mount, clamber up, surmount, °go up, escalade: *Using grappling hooks and ropes, we scaled the wall in minutes.* **4** °regulate, °adjust, °proportion, *Chiefly US and Canadian* prorate: *The size of the cable is scaled to the weight it must carry.* **5** ***scale up*** *or* ***down***: °increase, °enlarge, °raise; °decrease, °reduce, °diminish, °lower: *Depending on the expanse of the façade, the windows ought to be scaled up or down accordingly.*

scaly *adj.* **1** °rough, imbricated, shingly, *Technical* lamellar, laminar, lamellate, scutate: *The scaly covering of reptiles and fishes is related to the feathers of birds.* **2** scabby, scabrous, squamous, squamulose, squamosal, squamose, scurfy, furfuraceous, scruffy: *The medication causes the skin to dry and become temporarily scaly.*

scan *v.* **1** °glance at *or* through, °look over, °skim, °read over, °flip *or* °thumb *or* leaf through: *I didn't have time to read it thoroughly, but I did scan it.* **2** °study, °pore over, °examine, °investigate, °scrutinize, °inspect, delve into, °research, °explore (in depth), °sweep, *Archaic* con: *Scan the horizon for hostile planes.*
—*n.* **3** °look, °survey, inspection, °examination, overview: *A microscopic scan revealed no trace of blood.*

scandal *n.* **1** °shame, °disgrace, °embarrassment, °sin, °outrage: *It is a scandal how much of the money raised for charity goes into the pockets of the fund-raisers.* **2** °discredit, °damage, calumny, ignominy, obloquy, °dishonour, °degradation, disrepute, °infamy: *The scandal resulting from their being found together could never be lived down. The breath of scandal never touched her.* **3** °slander, °libel, °aspersion, °innuendo, insinuation, °abuse, °dirt, defilement, defamation, °slur, °smear, °taint, °blemish, °spot, °stigma, smirch, black °mark *or* °spot, °blot (on the escutcheon), (badge of) °infamy, skeleton in the cupboard, *Brit* °blot on one's copybook: *His cowardice brought scandal to the name that could never be lived down.*

scandalize *v.* °appal, °shock, °outrage, affront, °offend, °horrify, °upset, °disturb; °rankle, stick in (someone's) craw *or* throat, °gall: *They were scandalized to learn the truth about Cooksley's father.*

scandalous *adj.* **1** °shocking, °disgraceful, ignominious, °improper, indecorous, °unseemly, °infamous, °outrageous, °shameful, °immodest, °dishonourable, °disreputable, °sordid, °despicable, flagitious, °wicked, °sinful, °evil, iniquitous, °profligate, °immoral, °indecent, °lewd, °lascivious, °lustful, licentious, °lecherous, °atrocious, heinous, °disgusting, fulsome, °taboo, °unmentionable, unspeakable: *The scandalous goings-on at the Hellfire Club are well documented.* **2** defamatory, libellous, °slanderous, calumnious, calumniatory, aspersive, °abusive, °scurrilous, °injurious: *The newspaper published a scandalous article about him which they refused to retract.*

scanty *adj.* **1** scant, °sparse, °scarce, °little, °meagre, °minimal; °barely adequate *or* sufficient, °limited, restricted, *Colloq* °measly: *The news from the front was scanty. We received only scanty support from the Arts Council.* **2** skimpy, °short, °small, °sparse, °minimal, °meagre, in °short supply, *Colloq chiefly Brit* °thin on the ground: *Investor interest in the new share offering seemed to be scanty.*

scapegoat *n.* °victim, °front, °dupe, gull, cat's-paw, whipping-boy, *Brit* man of straw, Aunt Sally, *US* straw man, *Colloq* fall guy, *Slang* °sucker: *We have to find a scapegoat to take the punishment for us.*

scar *n.* **1** °blemish, °mark, °damage, disfigurement, °wound, °injury, °scratch, °mar, °cut, °burn, °brand, cicatrix: *Fortunately, the cut is shallow and shouldn't leave a scar.*
—*v.* **2** °blemish, °mark, °damage, disfigure, °wound, °injure, °scratch, °mar, °cut, °burn, °brand; dent: *The blow scarred him for life.*

scarce *adj.* °scanty, scant, °insufficient, °inadequate, °deficient, °wanting, lacking, °rare, °unusual, at a °premium, in °short supply, °meagre, °few and far between, °seldom met with, hard to come by, *Chiefly Brit* °thin on the ground: *Good editors are very scarce.*

scarcely *adv.* **1** °hardly, °barely, (only) °just, not quite: *He had scarcely uttered the magic words when the rock split open.* **2** (probably *or* certainly *or* surely *or* definitely) not, in no way, not at all, not in the least, by no °means, on no °account, under no circumstances, nowise, *Colloq US* noway: *I scarcely need remind you that you are getting married tomorrow.*

scarcity *n.* °lack, °want, °need, paucity, °dearth, insufficiency, °shortage, inadequacy, inadequateness: *The teaching of foreign languages is not improved by the scarcity of qualified teachers.*

scare *v.* **1** °frighten, °alarm, °startle, °shock, °dismay, °daunt, °appal, give (someone) a °shock *or* a °fright, °terrify, terrorize, °threaten, °menace, cow, °intimidate, °horrify, *US and Canadian* spook, *Colloq* scare the pants off, scare the life *or* the living daylights *or* the hell out of, scare out of one's wits, make one's hair stand on end, make one's flesh creep *or* crawl, give one goose bumps *or* goose-pimples, *US* scare the bejesus out of, *Taboo slang* scare *or* °frighten the shit out of, scare shitless, *US* scare shitty: *A sudden noise scared me, and I ran out of the cave as fast as I could.* **2** ***scare up***: °scrape together *or* up, °find, °gather, °collect, °raise, °dig up, °get, °come by, °scrounge (up): *I can't scare up that much money in one day!*
—*n.* **3** °fright, °shock, °surprise, °start: *I had a terrible scare when I saw what I thought was blood.*

scared *adj.* frightened, alarmed, °afraid, appalled, shocked, terrified, horrified, startled: *Don't be scared, I won't hurt you.*

scary *adj.* °frightening, °eerie, °terrifying, °frightful, hair-raising, unnerving, blood-curdling, horrifying, spine-chilling, intimidating, daunting; horrendous, horrid, °horrible, creepy, crawly, *Colloq* spooky: *Aren't you afraid to watch scary movies on TV when you're home alone?*

scathing *adj.* searing, °withering, damaging, °harmful, °severe, °harsh, °stern, °nasty, °biting, acrid, acrimonious, mordant, °incisive, °cutting, °sharp, °keen, °virulent, vitriolic, acid, °scorching, °burning, °fierce, °savage, °ferocious: *She was totally unprepared for the critics' scathing attack on her book.*

scatter *v.* **1** °spread, °diffuse, °shower, °litter, sprinkle, °strew, °circulate, °distribute, disseminate, °sow, °broadcast: *As the seeds of dissent were scattered far and wide, we became aware of a ground swell of hatred for the regime.* **2** °disperse, °separate, °dissipate, dispel, °disband, °break up, °go off: *My notes were scattered all over the floor. Immediately after dividing up the loot, the gang scattered to the four winds.*

scatterbrained *n.* °hare-brained, rattle-headed, rattle-brained, °frivolous, flibbertigibbet, °giddy, dazed, °flighty, wool-gathering, *Colloq* dippy, °dizzy, dopey *or* dopy, slap-happy: *It irritates me to think that our lives might depend on such a scatterbrained fool.*

scattering *n.* smattering, sprinkling, °trifle, °bit, °suggestion, soupçon, °hint: *It is true, there was a scattering of rebellious sentiment in the town.*

scenario *n.* **1** (master *or* ground *or* floor) °plan, (grand) °scheme, °plot, schema, °design, °outline, layout, framework, °structure; °sequence of events, °routine: *According to this scenario, the bank will provide the financing and we shall organize the takeover.* **2** (plot) °summary, °précis, résumé, °synopsis; (working *or* shooting) °script, screenplay: *The scenario for the film was a joint venture between the director and the author of the book on which it was based.*

scene *n.* **1** °location, °site, °place, °area, °locale, °spot, locality, °whereabouts, °sphere, °milieu, backdrop, °background: *The scenes of my youth are always in my mind.* **2** °action, °episode, °part, chapter, °section, °segment; (stage) °setting, *mise en scène;* scenery: *The next scene takes place in Venice. Is the Venice scene ready?* **3** commotion, °upset, °exhibition, °display, °row, brouhaha, °disturbance, °furore *or US* furor, °tantrum, °argument, altercation, uncomfortable *or* disagreeable situation, °episode, °incident: *She made an unpleasant scene in the restaurant when he refused to sit next to her.* **4** °view, scenery, °sight, °landscape, seascape, panorama, vista, °picture, °prospect: *The scene from the terrace was completely tranquil.* **5** ***behind the scenes***: °secretly, privately, clandestinely, confidentially, surreptitiously, on the q.t. *or* Q.T.: *Sigrid operated behind the scenes and her identity was never revealed to MI5.* **6** ***make*** *or* ***do the scene***: °socialize, °appear, °get around *or* about, °go out, °participate: *We used to make the scene in the Village back in the forties, but no more.*

scenic *adj.* °picturesque, °panoramic, pretty, °beautiful, °grand, °awesome, awe-inspiring, °impressive, °striking, spectacular, breathtaking: *The train passes through some incredibly scenic routes in Switzerland.*

scent *n.* **1** °fragrance, °aroma, °perfume, redolence, °smell, °odour, °bouquet, whiff, °trace: *The room was filled with the scent of wild flowers.* **2** °trail, spoor, °track: *In drag hunting, the scent is laid down by a sack dragged along the ground.*
—*v.* **3** °perceive, °detect, °find out, °determine, discern, °distinguish, °recognize, °sense, °smell, °sniff (out), get °wind of, °learn *or* °hear about: *Scenting possible trouble, he decided he had better take along my revolver.* **4** °perfume: *She had left behind her handkerchief, scented with Chanel No. 19.*

sceptic *n.* doubter, questioner, doubting Thomas, disbeliever, nullifidian, agnostic, scoffer, cynic: *You'll always find some sceptics who don't believe that a woman could be a good prime minister.*

sceptical *adj.* doubting, dubious, °doubtful, questioning, disbelieving, °incredulous, agnostic, scoffing, cynical, mistrustful, °distrustful: *We were sceptical at first whether anything would come of it, but then things began to happen.*

scepticism *n.* °doubt, dubiety, dubiousness, doubtfulness, disbelief, incredulity, incredulousness, agnosticism, cynicism, °mistrust, °distrust, mistrustfulness, distrustfulness: *At first, the entire matter was greeted with some scepticism; but then the Berlin Wall came tumbling down.*

schedule *n.* **1** °programme, °timetable, °plan, °calendar, agenda, °outline, °list, listing, °record, °register: *I'd like a complete schedule of your work for the next month on my desk tomorrow.*
—*v.* **2** °programme, °organize, °plan, °outline, °list, °record, °register, °arrange, °book, °time, slate, °appoint, °assign, °allot, °dedicate, earmark: *Schedule the next meeting for the 15th of the month. Alistair is scheduled to speak tomorrow.*

schematic *adj.* **1** diagrammatic(al), representational, °graphic, charted: *We have the schematic drawings showing the placement of the equipment.*
—*n.* **2** diagram, blueprint, layout, (floor *or* °game) °plan, °scheme, °design, °representation, graph, (flow *or* PERT) °chart: *Give copies of the schematics to the electricians so that they can plan where to put the wiring.*

scheme *n.* **1** °plan, °plot, °design, °programme, °system, °course (of action), schema, °outline, °exposition, °projection, °draft, °method, °technique, °approach, °game °plan, °scenario: *In my scheme, compensation would be dependent on productivity, merit, and length of service.* **2** °pattern, °arrangement, layout, °design, diagram, blueprint, °chart, map, °drawing, °schematic, °disposition, °order, °organization, schema: *This alternative scheme shows the executive offices on the second floor.* **3** °plot, °plan, ploy, °manoeuvre, °strategy, °stratagem, °tactic, °machination, °subterfuge, °trick, °device, °dodge, °wile, °ruse, °intrigue, *Colloq* °racket, °game, °move: *Ashton's scheme was to lure the security guards into the outer room, then lock them in.*

—*v.* **4** °plan, °plot, °devise, contrive, °intrigue, °organize, °formulate, °hatch, conspire, machinate, °manoeuvre, connive, concoct, *Colloq* cook up: *Clifton had been scheming to get his revenge on them ever since the Manchester episode.*

scheming *adj.* conniving, plotting, nefarious, treacherous, °crafty, cunning, °artful, °sly, °wily, °devious, Machiavellian, intriguing, °slick, °calculating, °tricky, °foxy, °slippery, underhanded, duplicitous, °deceitful: *Wait till I lay my hands on the scheming little thief!*

schism *n.* °split, °rift, °break, °breach, °division, °rupture, °separation, disunion: *The schism was caused by a group of left-wing idealists.*

schismatic *adj.* schismatical, separatist, breakaway, divisive, °dissident, °heretical: *The schismatic movement in art was marked by one faction's abandonment of realism.*

scholar *n.* **1** °academic, professor, °teacher, pedagogue, °authority, °expert, pundit, savant, bookman, book-woman, man *or* woman of letters, °intellectual, °highbrow, °bookworm, *Colloq* egghead, °brain, *US* longhair: *Professor Read is one of the most respected linguistics scholars in the world.* **2** °student, °pupil, schoolboy, schoolgirl, undergraduate: *Cosgrove was a failure as a scholar, preferring football to physics.*

scholarly *adj.* °learned, erudite, °lettered, scholastic, °profound, °deep, °intellectual, °academic, °highbrow(ed), ivory-tower(ed), *Colloq* egghead, brainy, *US* longhair, long-haired: *Her scholarly achievements are not limited to scholarly articles for learned journals.*

scholarship *n.* **1** °learning, erudition, °knowledge, °lore, °education, °schooling, training, °preparation, *Colloq* know-how: *Elsa Cairn brings to her appointment as headmistress considerable scholarship and experience.* **2** °grant, °endowment, °award, °fellowship, *Brit* °exhibition, *Chiefly Scots and New Zealand* bursarship, bursary: *Without the scholarship, I should never have been able to continue my education.*

school *n.* **1** (°educational) °institution, kindergarten, nursery school, primary *or* grammar *or* secondary *or* high school, °institute, college, university, °seminary; Alma Mater; boarding-school, day-school; public school, private school, *Brit* State school; *lycée;* Lyceum, *Brit* first *or* middle school, *US* junior high school: *His mother was very upset when he hinted that he might quit school.* **2** °set, coterie, °circle, °clique, °group, °denomination, °faction, °sect, °followers, °devotees, adherents, votaries, °disciples; °style, °kind, °form, °manner, °fashion: *Burne-Jones belonged to the Pre-Raphaelite School of painters.* **3** °philosophy, principles, °creed, set of beliefs, way of life, °persuasion, credo, dogma, teaching, °view, °opinion, °faction, °approach: *Regarding the creation of the universe, do you support the big-bang school or the steady-state school?*

—*v.* **4** °teach, °educate, °drill, inculcate, °instil, °indoctrinate, °instruct, °tutor, °train, °discipline, °coach, °prepare, °prime, °equip, °ready; °mould, °shape, °form; imbue with, infuse with: *Young ladies were schooled in all the social graces.*

school-book *n.* °text(book), primer, grammar (-°book), reader, °manual, handbook, exercise °book, notebook, copybook, *Rare* enchiridion, *Old-fashioned* hornbook, abecedarium: *All I did was ask if I could carry her school-books!*

schooling *n.* °education, teaching, °instruction, tutelage, °tuition, °guidance, training, °preparation, indoctrination, °edification, enlightenment; °learning, °study, °research: *How many years of schooling are needed to become a doctor?*

schoolteacher *n.* °teacher, professor, °instructor, °tutor, pedagogue, schoolmaster, schoolmistress, *Scots* dominie, *Colloq* school-ma'm: *It is not often realized what a profound influence schoolteachers have on one's entire life.*

science *n.* **1** (body of) °knowledge *or* °information, (body of) °laws *or* °principles, °discipline, °study, °branch, °field, °area, °subject, °realm, °sphere: *Many new sciences have sprung up even in the past fifty years. DNA research falls properly into the science of microbiologic genetics.* **2** °skill, °art, °technique, °expertise, °proficiency, °method, °system: *He made a science of brewing tea.*

scientific *adj.* (well-)organized, (well-)regulated, (well-)controlled, (well-)ordered, °orderly, °systematic, °methodical, °precise, °meticulous, °thorough, °painstaking, °detailed: *A scientific approach to the problem would start with a complete analysis of present conditions.*

scintillating *adj.* **1** sparkling, coruscating, flashing, °dazzling, gleaming, glittering, °twinkling, shimmering, glistening, shining, °lustrous, °radiant, effulgent, °brilliant, *Literary* nitid: *Madame Irena appeared wearing a scintillating silver lamé gown.* **2** °exciting, °engaging, °lively, °effervescent, fascinating, entrancing, °stimulating, °invigorating, °dynamic, °vivacious: *I cannot remember when I last found myself in such scintillating company.*

scoff[1] *v.* Often, ***scoff at***: °deride, °belittle, °dismiss, °disparage, °mock, make °light of, °sneer (at), °poke °fun (at), °ridicule, spoof, °lampoon, °jeer (at), °chaff, °tease, °twit, rib, kid, *Brit* °rag: *It's easy for you to scoff at Clare's tantrums—you don't have to live with her. Don't scoff: your turn might come next.*

scoff[2] *v.* **1** °devour, °put away, °gorge oneself on, wolf (down), °bolt, °stuff (oneself with), gobble (up *or* down), guzzle, °gulp (down), *Brit* gollop: *The two of them scoffed every crumb they could find.*

—*n.* **2** °food, victuals, °rations, edibles, °provisions, *Colloq* grub, eats, chow, *Slang Brit* prog: *In no time at all, they had cleared out every last bit of scoff in the larder.*

scold *v.* **1** °reprimand, chide, °reprove, °upbraid, °criticize, censure, find °fault (with), °rebuke, reproach, °lecture, °berate, °rate, °castigate, take (someone) to °task, °rap (someone's) knuckles, °slap (someone's) wrist, *Colloq* °bawl out, °dress down, give (someone) hell, give (someone) what for, °jump on (someone), °jump down (someone's) throat, call (someone) to account, bring (someone) to book, let (someone) have it with both barrels, give (someone) a °piece of (one's) °mind, give (someone) a °tongue-lashing *or* a talking-to, give (someone) a hard time, rake *or* haul (someone) over the coals, °tell (someone) off, tick (someone) off, skin (someone) alive, call *or* have (someone) on the carpet, °light *or* °rip *or* tear *or* °lace *or* sail into (someone), *US* °chew out, °jump all over (someone), *Brit* carpet: *When their mother scolded them, they began to cry.*

—*n.* **2** °nag, °shrew, termagant, virago, fishwife, beldam, harridan, hell-cat, °fury, amazon, tigress, Xanthippe, *Colloq* battleaxe: *In the old days, they used to take scolds, tie them in a chair at the end of a pole, and dunk them in a pond till they cooled off.*

scoop *n.* **1** ladle, dipper, bailer, spoon: *Use the scoop to skim the fat off the soup.* **2** °exclusive: *Fergus's story on the minister's illegal business dealings was a real scoop for the paper.* **3** (°latest) °news, (°inside) °story, °revelation, °truth, *Colloq* °latest, °low-down, info, °dope, *Brit* gen, *US* poop: *What's the scoop on that man who moved in next door?*

—*v.* **4** Often, ***scoop up***: bail, °dip, ladle, spoon: *They scooped up some sand and spread it on the ice for traction.* **5** ***scoop out***: °gouge out, °excavate, spoon out, °hollow out, °dig, °cut: *Scoop out some melon balls for the fruit salad.* **6** ***scoop up***: °pick up, °gather (up), °sweep up *or* together, °take up *or* in: *He scooped up the money and ran out of the bank.*

scope *n.* **1** °range, °reach, °field, °area, °extent, compass, °expanse, °breadth, °sphere, °orbit, °span: *The scope of her interests includes both the sciences and the arts.* **2** °leeway, °space, °room, elbow-room, °freedom, °opportunity, °capacity, °stretch, latitude, °spread: *Have you allowed enough scope for growth?*

scorch *v.* sear, °blacken, °burn, roast, °singe, char: *Though scorched in the fire, the papers were saved intact.*

scorching *adj.* **1** °hot, °torrid, searing, parching, shrivelling, tropical, hellish, sizzling, broiling, boiling, °sweltering: *Scorching heat waves are dangerous for the very young and the elderly.* **2** °critical, °caustic, °scathing, mordant, °vituperative, excoriating, °harsh, acrimonious, °bitter: *The shadow minister for finance issued a scorching condemnation of the government's tax policies.*

score *n.* **1** °record, °account, °reckoning, °register, °tally, °amount, °number, °count, °sum, °total; °mark, °grade: *What was your best golf score? Chester got a score of 80 in the French test.* **2** °nick, °groove, °scratch, °line, °mark, °stroke, °notch, °cut, *Archery* nock: *Every time he won, he made a score on his walking-stick.* **3** twenty: *And the days of our lives shall be three score years and ten.* **4** Often, ***scores***: dozens, hundreds, (tens *or* hundreds of) thousands, millions, °number(s), drove(s), horde(s), °host(s), multitude(s), °herd(s), legion(s), °lot(s), °mass(es), myriad(s), shoal(s), °pack(s), covey(s), bevy *or* bevies, °swarm(s), °flock(s), army *or* armies, °crowd(s), °throng(s): *Passengers by the score angrily protested against the airline's policy of overbooking flights. Scores of animals were fleeing before the forest fire.* **5** music, accompaniment, *Technical* full *or* short *or* vocal score: *Boito might have written the libretto, but the score was by Verdi.* **6** °situation, °story, °news, °status (quo), °condition, °word, *Colloq* °latest, °scoop, *US* poop: *What's the score on your applications to medical school?* **7** °dupe, gull, °victim, °greenhorn, *Colloq* fall guy, chump, goat, sitting duck, *Slang* °sucker, patsy, mark, *Brit* °mug: *That fellow in the Hawaiian shirt looks a likely score for our little scam.* **8** °ground(s), °basis, °account, °reason, °rationale, °provocation, °cause: *On what score can you justify eliminating him from the competition?* **9** ***settle*** *or* ***pay off*** *or* ***even a score*** *or* ***the score*** *or* ***old scores***: get °revenge, °retaliate, get °even, avenge, °repay, get an eye for an eye, give tit for tat, give measure for measure, °pay (someone) back in his *or* her own coin, give (someone) a taste *or* a dose of his *or* her *or* their own medicine, *Colloq* get one's own back: *He tried to find out where MacTavish had moved to as he had an old score to settle with him.*
—*v.* **10** °mark, °line, incise, °scratch, °nick, °notch, °cut, °groove, °graduate; °scrape, °deface, °mar, °gouge, °slash: *The dipstick is scored at intervals to indicate how much oil is in the crankcase.* **11** gain *or* make a °point *or* points, °record, °tally, °account for: *George scored a hat trick in the game against Hotspurs.* **12** °count (for), °reckon for *or* as: *The ace scores either 1 or 11 in vingt-et-un.* **13** °succeed, be °successful, °triumph, °win, make an °impression, have an °impact, *Colloq* make a °hit: *Your plan really scored with the boss.* **14** succeed in seducing, *Slang* make out, get laid: *Did you score with Ava last night?*

scorn *n.* **1** contumely, °contempt, contemptuousness, disdain, deprecation; °rejection, °dismissal: *He treated their demands with the utmost scorn.* **2** °mockery, °derision, derisiveness, sneering, °ridicule, scoffing, jeering, taunting: *The crowd's scorn was directed at the politicians who failed to deliver what they had promised.*
—*v.* **3** °reject, °rebuff, disown, disavow, °disregard, °ignore, °shun, snub, °flout, contemn, treat with *or* hold in °contempt, have no use for, disdain, °spurn, °despise, turn up one's nose at, curl one's lip at, °look down on *or* upon, °look down one's nose at, °thumb one's nose at, *Colloq* pooh-pooh, °put down, *Brit* cock a snook at: *His parents offered to finance his education, but he scorned their help.* **4** °mock (at), °deride, °sneer at, °ridicule, °scoff at, °jeer at, °taunt, °poke °fun at, make °fun of, °laugh at: *People scorned him because he said the earth was round.*

scornful *adj.* contumelious, °contemptuous, °disdainful, deprecative, disparaging, °derisory, derisive, snide, °supercilious, mocking, sneering, scoffing, °haughty, overweening, high-handed, °superior, *Colloq* snooty, *Slang* snotty: *The people were scornful of his attempt to reassure them, and continued to demand action.*

scoundrel *n.* °villain, °rogue, °wretch, °good-for-nothing, scapegrace, blackguard, °rascal, scamp, cur, *Old-fashioned* bounder, cad, knave, *Colloq* °heel, *Slang* louse, *Brit* rotter: *Politicians tend to treat their opponents as liars and scoundrels.*

scour *v.* **1** °scrub, °clean, °cleanse, °wash, °rub, abrade, °polish, burnish, buff, °shine: *The pots were scoured until they shone.* **2** °scrape (about *or* around), °rake, comb, turn upside down, °search, °ransack: *I scoured the shops looking in vain for the coffee filters you wanted.*

scourge *n.* **1** °curse, °misfortune, bane, °evil, °affliction, °plague, adversity, °torment, °misery, °woe: *He questions whether AIDS should be considered the scourge of the 20th century. Was it Attila who proved himself the scourge of Rome?* **2** °whip, °lash, cat-o'-nine-tails, knout, quirt, horsewhip, bull-whip: *They saw fit to punish themselves with scourges.*
—*v.* **3** °whip, °flog, °beat, °lash, horsewhip, whale, °belt, flagellate: *Some medieval sects scourged themselves as they went in procession through the cities.* **4** °punish, °castigate, °chastise, °discipline, °afflict, °torment: *In the old days, students were scourged if they made a mistake.*

scout *v.* **1** Often, ***scout about*** *or* ***around***: °reconnoitre, °investigate, °study, °research, °examine, °explore, °spy, °search *or* °look (about *or* around) (for), °hunt (about *or* around) (for), °cast around *or* about (for), *Colloq* °check (about *or* around): *I am going to scout about to find a key that fits.* **2** ***scout up*** *or* ***out***: °discover, °find, °locate, uncover, *Colloq* °dig up: *I was finally able to scout up a key that fits.*

scowl *v.* **1** glower, °frown, grimace, °glare, look daggers, °lower *or* °lour: *It's hard to tell if he's ever pleased because he's always scowling.*
—*n.* **2** °frown, grimace, °glare, dirty °look: *I do wish she would wipe that scowl off her face and try to look more pleasant.*

scramble *v.* **1** °climb, clamber, °crawl, scrabble, °struggle: *We scrambled up the rocky hillside with the big cat in pursuit.* **2** °rush, °hurry, scamper, °run, °hasten, °race, °scurry, scoot, scuttle, °dash, hotfoot (it), °hustle, *Chiefly US and Canadian*, hightail (it), *Colloq* skedaddle: *When the siren sounded, we scrambled down to the air raid shelter.* **3** Often, ***scramble up***: °mix up, °confuse, °jumble, intermingle, °mingle, commingle: *Contestants, spectators, and officials were all scrambled together.*
—*n.* **4** °scrimmage, °struggle, tussle, contention, °clash, °competition, °contest, °race, °rush, °conflict, °disorder, commotion, °riot, mêlée *or* melee, °pandemonium, *Colloq* free-for-all, hassle, *Brit* scrum *or* scrummage: *Thousands were involved in the scramble for tickets to the rock concert. In the scramble for a directorship Jeremy lost.* **5** °struggle, °climb: *She twisted her ankle in the scramble over the rocks.*

scrap[1] *n.* **1** mite, °bit, °shred, °bite, °morsel, °piece, °fragment, shard *or* sherd, °particle, °sliver, snippet, °snip, °crumb, whit, iota, °jot *or* tittle, °snatch, °drop, °drip, °grain, °speck, molecule, atom, °dab, °trace, scintilla, °hint, °suggestion: *There wasn't a scrap of evidence to link him with the crime.* **2** ***scraps***: °remnants, °remains, °leftovers, leavings, °residue, °vestiges, °traces, scrapings, °discards, rejections, °rejects: *In the alley, two cats were fighting over some scraps of garbage.* **3** °waste, debris, °rubbish, *Colloq* °junk: *Any computer more than five years old isn't even worth its weight as scrap.*
—*v.* **4** °discard, °throw away, °reject, °abandon, °give up, consign to the scrap heap, °forsake, °forget, get °rid of, °dispose of, °dispense with, *Colloq* °junk, *US* °trash: *If I were you, I would buy a new car and scrap this one.*

scrap[2] *n.* **1** °fight, °brawl, °fracas, °fray, affray, °rumpus, scuffle, Donnybrook, °battle (royal); °row,

°dispute, °argument, °quarrel, °disagreement, wrangle, squabble, °tiff, spat, *Colloq* ruckus, set-to, dust-up: *A terrible scrap broke out in the pub last night and the police were called in. Our neighbours were having a scrap about who should take the dog for a walk.*
—*v.* **2** °fight, °brawl, °spar, scuffle, °battle, °row, wrangle, °argue, °disagree, squabble, °bicker: *Let's not scrap over trifles—only important things.*

scrapbook *n.* album, portfolio, °collection: *She keeps a scrapbook of reviews of her stage triumphs.*

scrape *v.* **1** abrade, graze, °scratch, bark, scuff, °skin, °bruise, °damage, °injure: *I scraped my knee on the pavement when I fell.* **2** Often, ***scrape off*** *or* ***away*** *or* ***out***: °remove, °rub off *or* away, °scour *or* °scrub *or* °clean (off *or* away), °scratch off *or* away, °claw (at *or* away *or* out), °gouge out, scrabble (at), °dig out *or* away at: *As I scraped away the grime, a beautiful mosaic was revealed. Each sled dog scraped out a hole in the snow and snuggled into it.* **3** skimp, scrimp (and °scrape), °save, °stint, be °frugal *or* stingy *or* parsimonious *or* °thrifty, °pinch and °save *or* scrape, °economize; °struggle, *US* scrabble: *Only by scraping were we able to pay the increased taxes.* **4** ***bow and scrape***: make °obeisance, °kowtow, salaam, genuflect, kiss the feet *or* hem *or* ring, grovel, demean *or* °lower oneself, °prostrate oneself, toady, *Colloq* boot-lick: *He can bow and scrape all he likes, but Jones will get nowhere with the foreman.* **5** ***scrape by*** *or* ***through***: °get by, °cope, (barely) °manage, °survive, scrape *or* °get along, *Colloq* squeak by, barely make it: *We are just about able to scrape by on the little that Nigel is making.* **6** ***scrape together*** *or* ***up***: glean, °garner, scratch *or* °get *or* °rake together *or* up, dredge up, scrabble for, °gather, °save (up), get hold of, marshal, °amass, °muster, °accumulate, aggregate, °compile, °pile up, °stack up, °assemble, *Colloq* °scrounge (up): *By the time we finally managed to scrape up enough for a down payment on a house, the prices had gone up.*
—*n.* **7** abrasion, °bruise, °scratch, graze, scuff, °damage, °injury: *He was very annoyed when he found a scrape on his brand-new car.* **8** °predicament, °difficulty, °quandary, °dilemma, °plight, (fine) kettle of fish, °muddle, °stew, °situation, °position, °pinch, *Colloq* pickle, °fix, °mess, the °crunch, (tight *or* tough) °spot: *I got into a terrible scrape by forgetting our wedding anniversary. Can you lend me some money to help me out of a scrape?*

scratch *v.* **1** °mar, °mark, °gouge (out), °gash, abrade, graze, scuff, °grate against, °bruise, °damage, °injure; °claw: *If you glue some felt to the bottom, the lamp won't scratch the table.* **2** °chafe, °rub: *If you scratch those mosquito bites you might get an infection.* **3** Often, ***scratch out*** *or* ***off***: °erase, °obliterate, °rub out *or* off, °cross out, °delete, °strike out *or* off, expunge; °exclude, °eliminate, *US* x out: *You can scratch my name from the list of candidates. She scratched out what she had written and started again.*
—*n.* **4** °mark, °gouge, °gash, abrasion, °scrape, graze, scuff, °bruise, °damage, °injury; °line: *Where did you get that scratch on your face? 'It's only a scratch', Sandy protested as they tried to remove the spear from his shoulder.* **5** ***up to scratch***: up to °standard *or* °par, °adequate, °sufficient, good enough, °competent, °satisfactory, competitive, *Colloq* up to snuff: *Cynthia's performance is not yet up to scratch, so she might not make the team.*
—*adj.* **6** °hasty, °hurried, impromptu, unplanned, °haphazard, °rough, °casual, °informal, °unprepared, °unpremeditated, °makeshift, extempore, *Colloq* off the cuff, *US* pick-up: *We didn't have time to practise, so we are racing with a scratch crew.*

scratchy *adj.* **1** itchy, irritating, °prickly: *The pullover was as scratchy as a hair shirt.* **2** °rough, hoarse, °raw, °grating, °sore, raspy, °dry: *My throat feels a bit scratchy and I need something to drink.*

scrawl *n.* **1** scribble, *Colloq* squiggle, *US* hen-scratch, chicken-scratch: *I can't read that scrawl of his.*
—*v.* **2** scribble, °scratch, doodle: *How do pharmacists read the prescriptions that doctors scrawl?*

scrawny *adj.* bony, °skinny, °spare, °drawn, reedy, °haggard, °lean, lank(y), scraggy, °gaunt, °raw-boned, angular, °emaciated, cadaverous; anorectic *or* anorexic: *She certainly has changed from that scrawny kid I used to know.*

scream *v.* **1** °shriek, screech, squeal, yowl, wail, caterwaul, °howl, °cry: *She screamed when I applied iodine to the cut.* **2** °laugh, °roar, hoot, °howl, guffaw: *The women screamed hysterically as the male stripper got down to the bare essentials.*
—*n.* **3** °shriek, screech, squeal, yowl, wail, caterwaul, °howl, °cry: *When she saw what had happened, she let out a blood-curdling scream.* **4** *Colloq* card, °panic, °riot, thigh-slapper: *Phyllis is such a scream when she talks about the silly things that happen to her.*

screen *n.* **1** °partition, (room) divider, paravent, °wall: *In their one-room flat a bookcase serves as a screen to separate the living area from the sleeping area.* **2** °shelter, °protection, °shield, °cover: *A row of poplars acts as a screen against the wind.* **3** curtain, °blind, °shroud, °cloak, °cover; concealment, °camouflage: *The gauze fabric was too transparent to act as a screen.* **4** sieve, °mesh, strainer, °filter, colander, °riddle: *The sand has to be shovelled through a screen to get rid of the stones.* **5** motion pictures, movies, silver screen; °television, small screen, home screen, *Colloq* box, telly, *US* boob tube: *She is a star of both the big and small screens.*
—*v.* **6** °partition (off), °separate, °divide, °wall off: *Why not use a beaded curtain to screen the kitchen area from the dining-room?* **7** °shelter, °protect, °shield, °cover, °guard, °conceal, °camouflage, °mask, °veil, °hide: *A decorative pierced wall screens the ladies of the harem from the prying eyes of visitors.* **8** °sift, °separate (out), °sort (out), °filter, °select, cull, °process, °interview, °evaluate, °grade, °gauge, °qualify, °examine, °scan, *Chiefly Brit* °vet: *The agency screens all candidates before sending them to see a client.*

screw *n.* **1** °bolt, screw-bolt, machine screw, lag-bolt, lag-screw: *This screw is too small to hold that door hinge.* **2** helix, °spiral, corkscrew: *The screw of a spiral staircase should not be too small for safety.* **3** sexual °intercourse; sexual °partner, *Slang* °lay, *Taboo slang* fuck: *When arrested for kerb-crawling, he said that he was just looking for a screw.* **4** ***put the screws on (someone)***: °pressure, °influence, °force, constrain, °press, °oblige, °require, °demand, coerce, compel, apply °pressure, bring °pressure to bear (on); °insist; *Chiefly Brit* pressurize, *Colloq* °twist (someone's) arm, put the °squeeze on (someone): *I believe that someone put the screws on him to leave town.*
—*v.* **5** °twist, °turn, °rotate: *Screw the bolt in clockwise.* **6** Often, ***screw out of***: °defraud, °cheat, °swindle, gull, bilk, do out of, *Slang* °take, °clip, °fleece: *They screwed him by convincing him that the bonds were real. He was screwed out of all his savings.* **7** ***screw up***: **a** °raise, °increase, °stretch, °strain; °summon, °call up, °call upon, °tap, °draw on *or* upon: *I screwed up my courage to ask for a salary increase.* **b** °ruin, °destroy, make a °mess of, °botch, °bungle, °muddle, mismanage, °mishandle, *Colloq* make a °hash of, *Slang* louse up, *Brit* make a muck-up of, *US* bollix up, *Taboo slang* fuck up, *Brit* °bugger up, ballocks *or* bollocks up, make a balls-up of: *It is hard to see how they could have screwed up such a simple operation.* **c** contort, °twist, deform, °warp: *At the suggestion of cauliflower, Ambrose screwed up his face in displeasure.*

scribe *n.* **1** copyist, copier, transcriber, *Archaic* scrivener; amanuensis, clerk, secretary: *Before the invention of movable type printing, copies of books and documents were prepared by scribes.* **2** °writer, °author, penman, scrivener, wordsmith, scribbler, °hack, penny-a-liner; °dramatist, dramaturge, °playwright, °poet, novelist, essayist, columnist, technical °writer; °journalist, gentleman *or* lady of the °press, newspaperman, newspaperwoman, °reporter, rewrite man *or* woman *or* person, °editor, reviewer, commentator,

newswriter, sob sister, agony aunt *or* uncle, Miss Lonelyhearts, gossip columnist, member of the fourth estate, *Brit* paragraphist, leader-writer, *US* Grub Streeter, *Colloq Brit* journo: *In a general way, he refers to all writers as 'scribes', but particularly those he considers a bit old-fashioned.*
—*v.* **3** inscribe, incise, °etch, °engrave, °mark, °scratch, °score, grave, scrimshaw, °carve, chase *or* enchase: *The shotgun was scribed with the most beautiful designs, some inlaid in gold.*

scrimmage *n.* °skirmish, scuffle, °fray, affray, °disturbance, brouhaha, mêlée *or* melee, °riot, °row, °brawl, °struggle, °scramble, tussle, °fracas, °rumpus, Donnybrook, °battle, °fight, *Colloq* ruckus, set-to, dust-up, free-for-all, °scrap, *Brit* scrum *or* scrummage, *Slang Brit* (bit of) bovver: *The police were called when what started as a minor scrimmage began to develop into a riot.*

script *n.* **1** handwriting, °hand, (cursive) °writing, °penmanship; calligraphy: *These love-letters are written in an unusually beautiful script.* **2** manuscript, °scenario, °book, °play, screenplay, teleplay, libretto, continuity: *Stick to the script—I don't want you ad libbing!*
—*v.* **3** °write, °pen, °prepare, °create: *The new series was scripted by the same writer who wrote 'Out in the Outback'.* **4** °plan, °organize, °design, °arrange, °lay out, °order, configure, °pattern: *The take-over of the company had not been scripted in their business forecasts.*

Scripture *n.* Scriptures, °sacred writings, Bible, Good Book, Holy Writ *or* Scripture(s), Word of God, Gospel(s); Book of Mormon; Koran; Upanishad(s), Bhagavad-Gita: *Throughout his life, he did only those things approved in Scripture.*

scrounge *v.* **1** ferret out, °seek out, nose *or* °smell out, come up with, °scrape together *or* up, °scratch up; importune, cadge, °beg (, °borrow, or °steal), *Colloq US* freeload, °bum: *Did Hedley try to scrounge some money from you, too?*
—*n.* **2** scrounger, cadger, °parasite, *Colloq* sponger, *US* freeloader: *Hedley, that scrounge, has just asked me for a cigarette.*

scrub *v.* **1** See **scour, 1,** above. **2** °cancel, °call off, abort, °scratch, °drop, °terminate, °give up, °end, °abandon, °stop, °cease, °discontinue, do away with: *Something went wrong with the fuel computer, so they scrubbed today's satellite launch.*

scruple *n.* **1** °compunction, °qualm, °reluctance, °misgiving, second thoughts, °doubt, (twinge of) °conscience, hesitation, uneasiness, °discomfort, squeamishness: *Peter hadn't the slightest scruple about taking the money from his aunt.*
—*v.* **2** °pause, falter, °hesitate, vacillate, have °doubts *or* °compunction (about), demur, waver, °shrink from *or* at, have °misgivings *or* °qualms (about *or* over), be °loath *or* loth (to), think twice (about), °stick at, be °reluctant, balk (at), have scruples (about): *Susan didn't scruple for a moment about keeping the money she found in the street.*

scrupulous *adj.* **1** °careful, °cautious, °meticulous, °exacting, °precise, over-nice, °strict, °rigid, rigorous, °severe, °critical, °fastidious, °neat, °conscientious, °finicky *or* finical, °fussy, °painstaking, punctilious: *Andrew has always been scrupulous about his toys, his books, his clothes, etc.* **2** °ethical, °honourable, upstanding, °moral, °righteous, °principled, high-minded, °just: *Meg was always scrupulous in her business dealings.*

scrutinize *v.* °examine, °analyse, dissect, °investigate, °probe, °study, °inspect, °sift, °go over *or* through, °check: *I have scrutinized the results of the blood tests and can find nothing abnormal.*

scrutiny *n.* °examination, °analysis, °investigation, °probe, probing, °study, inspection, sifting, °inquiry *or* enquiry, °exploration, °check: *The tax inspectors have subjected the company books to close scrutiny but have found nothing amiss.*

scud *v.* °fly, °skim, °race, scoot, °speed, °shoot: *We scudded along in the catamaran at a good 30 knots.*

sculpture *n.* **1** °figure, figurine, °statue, statuette, group, head, bust, °relief; bronze, marble: *His favourite sculpture is Rodin's* Burghers of Calais.
—*v.* **2** sculpt *or* sculp, °model, °chisel, °carve, °cast, °form, °fashion: *The students are learning how to sculpture in clay.*

scurrilous *adj.* foul-mouthed, thersitical, °gross, °indecent, °profane, Fescennine, °vulgar, °obscene, licentious, Sotadean *or* Sotadic, °foul, °vituperative, °low, °coarse, scabrous, °vile, °nasty, defamatory, °derogatory, disparaging, vilifying, calumnious *or* calumniatory, malign, aspersive, opprobrious, °offensive, °abusive, insulting: *Clifford was an inveterate collector of scurrilous limericks.*

scurry *v.* °dash, °scramble, scamper, scoot, dart, °fly, °race, sprint, scuttle, °hurry, °hasten, °speed, °hustle, °rush, °tear, zoom, zip, °bolt, °rip, °scud: *A rat scurried across the floor. We went scurrying round the shops on Christmas Eve.*

scurvy *adj.* °low, °miserable, °contemptible, °vile, °base, °despicable, °rotten, °sorry, °bad, ignoble, °dishonourable, °mean, °worthless, °shabby: *Robbing poor old ladies is a pretty scurvy activity.*

sea *n.* **1** °ocean, °deep blue sea, high seas, *Literary* (briny) °deep, (bounding) main, Neptune's *or* Poseidon's kingdom *or* domain, *Nautical* blue °water, Davy Jones's locker, *Colloq* briny, °drink, pond (= 'Atlantic Ocean'): *For years he sailed the seas in search of adventure.* **2** °swell, breaker, °wave: *As the wind increased, huge seas began to wash over the boat.* **3** plethora, °quantity, °abundance, °surfeit, °profusion, °flood, multitude, °spate, legion, °mass, *Colloq* °lot(s), °heap(s), °pile(s), ton(s), °mountain(s), °load(s), oodles, gobs, scads: *Hamlet's sea of troubles was nothing compared to mine if this book isn't completed soon!* **4 *(all) at sea*:** °confused, disoriented, at sixes and sevens, bewildered, perplexed, baffled, mystified, °lost, adrift: *They were clearly not expecting her and were completely at sea as to what to do.*

sea-coast *n.* seashore, shore, °coast, seaside, seaboard, shoreline, coastline, littoral, sand(s), °beach, strand: *The people in the villages along the sea-coast depend mainly on fishing for their livelihood.*

seafaring *adj.* maritime, °nautical, naval, °marine: *Britain was at one time the largest seafaring nation in the world.*

seal *n.* **1** °symbol, °token, °mark, insigne (*pl.* insignia), °sign, signet, °crest, °bearing, coat of arms, escutcheon, °emblem, badge, monogram, °identification, cartouche, °design, imprint, °stamp: *The seal on his ring showed a crouching lion.* **2** authentication, confirmation, verification, validation, affirmation, attestation, ratification, corroboration, °assurance, °guarantee *or* guaranty, °endorsement, substantiation, °evidence, °notice, notification: *Management set their seal of approval on the plans.*
—*v.* **3** Sometimes, ***seal off*** *or* ***up***: °close (off *or* up), °shut (off), zip up, °plug (up), °stop (up), °lock, °bolt, °secure, batten down, make airtight *or* waterproof; cork: *All exits had been sealed off. They sealed up the windows so that no air could get in.* **4** °authenticate, °confirm, °verify, validate, affirm, °attest, °ratify, °clinch, corroborate, °assure, °ensure, °guarantee, °endorse: *The peace treaty was sealed by the marriage of the king to the emperor's daughter.*

seam *n.* **1** °junction, °juncture, °joint, suture, *Technical* commissure; °scar, °ridge, °line, cicatrix: *It is easy enough to see the seam where the parts meet.* **2** lode, °vein, °stratum, bed, layer, thickness: *The miners have been working on a new seam discovered at the end of Tunnel 4.*

seamy *adj.* °sordid, °nasty, °dark, °disreputable, °shameful, °unwholesome, °unpalatable, °unsavoury, °distasteful, °unseemly, squalid, °low, depraved, °degenerate, degraded, °foul, °vile, odious, °abhorrent, °contemptible, °scurvy, °rotten, unattractive, °ugly,

°repulsive, °repellent: *In his later work, he painted the seamy side of life in the slums.*

search *v.* **1** Often, ***search through***: °examine, °scrutinize, °check, comb (through), °explore, °go through, °investigate, °scout out, °inspect, °look at *or* into, °probe, °scour, °sift through, °pry into, °hunt *or* °rummage through; °inquire *or* °enquire of, *Colloq* plough through: *She searched through several encyclopedias but could not find the information she was looking for. Search your conscience to determine the best course.* **2** Often, ***search for***: °look (about *or* around), °cast about, °seek, leave no stone unturned: *I searched high and low but couldn't find my key.*
—*n.* **3** °hunt, °pursuit, °quest: *The search for the killer went on for years.* **4** researching, °analysis; °exploration, °examination, °scrutiny, °probe, °study, °perusal, sifting, inspection, scouring, °inquiry *or* enquiry: *A thorough search of the documents failed to turn up anything useful. The police made a house-to-house search of the neighbourhood.*

searchingly *adv.* penetratingly, piercingly, °intently, °deeply, fixedly, concentratedly, eagerly: *She looked searchingly into my eyes for some glimmer of hope.*

season *n.* **1** °time, °period, °occasion, °opportunity: *This is the season when the birds migrate north. Is the silly season upon us again so soon?* **2** ***in season***: °ripe, °ready, °edible, °seasoned, °seasonable, °available: *Fresh strawberries will be in season soon.*
—*v.* **3** °spice, °salt, °flavour, °pep up, °enliven: *One of the great things about chicken is that you can season it in many different ways.* **4** °ripen, °mature, °age, °condition, °mellow: *The wood should be well seasoned before being made into furniture.*

seasonable *adj.* °appropriate, °opportune, °suitable, apt, °timely, °fitting, °providential, °well-timed, °proper, °fit, °propitious, °welcome, well-suited, °happy, °lucky, °fortunate, °convenient, auspicious, °favourable, °advantageous, °expedient: *The success of the book was owing largely to its seasonable publication, just at the end of the cold war.*

seasoned *adj.* °experienced, trained, long-standing, long-serving, °practised, well-versed, habituated, acclimatized *or* acclimated, °accustomed, familiarized, °prepared, established, °veteran, tempered, hardened, toughened, inured: *It was a pleasure to be working with so seasoned a performer as Margie.*

seasoning *n.* °spice, °zest, °flavour, °relish, °sauce: *The fact that a former film star was running for office lent just the right seasoning to the campaign.*

seat *n.* **1** °place, °chair, bench, sofa, settee, °settle, stool, throne: *He found a seat and waited to be called.* **2** °focus, °base, °centre, °heart, °hub, °site, °capital, cradle, headquarters, fountain-head: *In those days, Paris was the main seat of learning in western Europe. Istanbul was established as the seat of the Turkish empire.* **3** membership, °position, incumbency: *His grandfather held a seat in the House of Commons.* **4** °bottom, °buttocks, °posterior(s), rump, hindquarters, fundament, *derrière*, behind, backside, °rear (end), *Colloq Brit* °bum, *US* hinie, tush *or* tushy *or* tushie, tokus *or* tochis *or* tuchis, butt, °tail, *Taboo slang Brit* arse, *US* ass: *He needs a swift kick in the seat to get him to move.* **5** °abode, °residence, °home, °domicile, °estate, mansion: *The duchess used to spend the summer at her country seat in Norfolk.*
—*v.* **6** °hold, °accommodate, have room *or* °space *or* capacity for, °contain, °sit: *The new auditorium will seat more than four thousand.* **7** °install *or* instal, enthrone, ensconce, instate, °invest, °establish, °place, swear in: *Once the new judge has been seated, it will be difficult to get rid of him.*

seating *n.* °accommodation, °capacity, °space, °room: *At present, the auditorium has seating for only 500.*

secede *v.* °withdraw *or* °resign *or* °retire (from), °abandon, °forsake, apostasize, °break with *or* away (from), °drop *or* °pull out (of), turn one's °back to *or* on, °quit, °separate from, °leave, °wash one's hands of, have nothing further to do with: *The City of New York occasionally threatens to secede from the United States.*

secession *n.* withdrawal, seceding, defection, °break, breaking, disaffiliation, retirement, °separation, splitting off *or* away, apostasy: *The secession of the splinter group was welcomed by virtually all the other members.*

secluded *adj.* **1** °private, °separate, °isolated, °lonely, cloistered, sequestered, °detached, °solitary, retired, eremitic, monastic: *He lives a very secluded life on an island in the Outer Hebrides.* **2** off the beaten track, °out-of-the-way, °remote, °far-away, far-off, °separate, segregated, °private: *He chose a secluded island in the Outer Hebrides for his vacation.*

seclusion *n.* °privacy, °private, °separation, isolation, loneliness: *He prefers to live in complete seclusion.*

second[1] *adj.* **1** °subsequent, following, next: *He let the first target go by and aimed for the second one.* **2** °subordinate, next: *If the colonel isn't here, who is the second officer?* **3** °alternative, second-best: *She refuses to settle for second choice.* **4** °alternate, other: *The laundry is picked up and delivered every second Tuesday. His second language is Italian.* **5** other, later, younger, newer, more recent: *After his first wife died, he took her nurse as his second wife.* **6** another, °duplicate: *The boy is a second Einstein.*
—*n.* **7** °defective *or* °imperfect *or* damaged *or* °faulty *or* °deficient *or* °flawed *or* impaired *or* marred *or* blemished *or* bruised *or* °inferior °merchandise: *The prices of these shirts have been reduced because they are seconds.* **8** °subordinate, °assistant, number two, lieutenant, aide-de-camp, man Friday, girl Friday, right hand; °understudy, °stand-in, °substitute, surrogate, °double, °alternate, °backer, °supporter; *Colloq US* gal Friday: *Not being ambitious, Helen would prefer to be a second to the person who runs the business.*
—*v.* **9** °support, °back, °aid, °help, °assist, °approve (of), °advance, °promote, °subscribe to, espouse, °sponsor, °patronize, °favour, °encourage, °go along with: *Madam Chairwoman, I would like to second this proposal.* **10** °transfer, °move, °assign, °shift, relocate: *After the Falklands War, he was seconded to fleet headquarters for a year.*
—*adv.* **11** secondly, in the second place, secondarily, (number) two, b *or* B: *I want to go: first, because it'll be interesting, and second, because Jake'll be there.*

second[2] *n.* °moment, °instant, °flash, °minute, °twinkling *or* wink *or* bat (of an eye), split second, *Colloq* sec, jiffy, two shakes (of a lamb's tail), *Brit* tick, half a mo: *I'll be with you in a second, as soon as I finish writing this letter.*

secondary *adj.* **1** less important, unimportant, inessential *or* unessential, °non-essential, non-critical, °subsidiary, ancillary, °minor, °inferior, °subordinate: *These secondary matters can be dealt with after the important ones.* **2** °derivative, derived, °indirect, °second-hand, unoriginal, not °original; copied, imitated: *His biography of Queen Victoria was based entirely on secondary sources.* **3** °auxiliary, second-line, backup, °extra, °reserve, °spare, °provisional, supporting, °supportive, °alternate, °alternative: *We were forced to rely on our secondary defences after the enemy cavalry broke through.*

second-hand *adj.* °used, old, °worn, *Colloq* hand-me-down: *When we were children our parents could only afford to dress us in second-hand clothes. His much-vaunted novels are for the most part based on second-hand ideas.*

secrecy *n.* **1** °mystery, concealment, confidentiality, °stealth, secretiveness, surreptitiousness, °privacy, furtiveness, covertness, clandestineness: *Why was there so much secrecy surrounding the publication date of Jennie's book?* **2** ***in secrecy***: °secretly, mysteriously, confidentially, stealthily, secretively, surreptitiously, privately, furtively, covertly, clandestinely, sneakily: *They carry on much of their business in secrecy.*

secret *adj.* **1** concealed, °hidden, °private, covert, shrouded, clandestine; °confidential, °quiet, under

cover, °secretive, unpublishable, unpublished, *Colloq* hush-hush: *There is a secret passageway leading from the cave to the cove. Keep secret what I shall tell you. She revealed to me her most secret desires.* **2** °cryptic, °private, arcane, °mysterious, °incomprehensible, esoteric, °recondite, abstruse; cryptographic, encrypted, encoded: *We used to communicate by secret code. Did you receive my secret message?*
—*n.* **3** °private *or* °confidential matter *or* affair, °mystery: *If I tell you my secret will you tell me yours?* **4** ***in secret***: privately, confidentially, °secretly, on the q.t. *or* Q.T.; surreptitiously, under cover, by °stealth, stealthily, furtively, °quietly, on the °sly, clandestinely: *The office manager told me in secret that John was going to resign. They see one another in secret.*

secrete[1] *v.* °hide, °conceal, °cache, °bury, °cloak, °shroud, enshroud, °camouflage, °mask, °disguise, *Slang* stash away: *They secreted the haul from the robbery in the cellar of a house in Balham.*

secrete[2] *v.* °yield, excrete, °pass, °generate, °release, °ooze, seep, exude, °discharge, °leak, °drip, °drop, dribble, °trickle, °run, °drain, °emit, °give off, °emanate, transude, *Technical* extravasate: *The ants herd aphids for the substance they secrete. The wound will secrete pus for a while.*

secretion *n.* secreting, °release, °escape, oozing, seeping, seepage, °discharge, discharging, °leak, leaking, leakage, °drip, dripping, °drop, dropping, dribbling, trickling, °trickle, °running, °drain, draining, emission, emitting, giving off, exudation, transudation, excretion, excreting, emanation, emanating, °generation, *Technical* extravasation; transudate, excreta, *Technical* extravasate: *The secretion of perspiration may be profuse under such circumstances. The secretion is highly acid in content.*

secretive *adj.* °reticent, °silent, close-mouthed, °taciturn, uncommunicative, °reserved, °tight-lipped, °close, *Colloq* °mum: *Robert is very secretive about where he goes every day at lunch-time.*

secretly *adv.* surreptitiously, °quietly, privately, covertly, on the q.t. *or* Q.T., furtively, stealthily, mysteriously, clandestinely, in °secret, confidentially, on the °sly, slyly, sub rosa, sub sigillo: *I can tell you secretly that she is wanted by the police. Henry secretly rents videotape cartoons to watch at weekends.*

sect *n.* **1** °religious °order *or* °group *or* °denomination *or* °body *or* cult *or* °persuasion *or* subdivision: *At times it seems as if there are as many sects as worshippers.* **2** °school (of thought), °faction, ism, °set, °clique, °cabal: *He belonged to a small sect that promulgated the Ptolemaic cosmogony.*

sectarian *adj.* **1** cultist, cultish, clannish, cliquish, °partisan, °partial, °dogmatic, doctrinaire, factional: *They seldom mingle with others, maintaining their sectarian existence.* **2** °parochial, °narrow, °narrow-minded, °limited, insular, °provincial, °rigid, °fanatic(al), °prejudicial, °prejudiced, °bigoted: *Because they refused to consider ideas other than their own, they gradually became more and more sectarian in their views.*
—*n.* **3** adherent, °member, sectary, votary, cultist, °partisan: *They tried to banish Anabaptists, Lutherans, Calvinists, and other sectarians.* **4** (true) believer, dogmatist, °fanatic, bigot, °zealot, extremist, *Slang* nut, °bug, °fiend: *Some of the sectarians engage in the ritualistic handling of live rattlesnakes.*

section *n.* **1** °part, °division, °department, °branch, sector, °group, °detachment, °segment, °portion, subdivision, component, °element: *Sadler has been assigned to work in the research section. I never read the sports section in the Sunday papers. Which sections of the country will vote for you? The string section needs practice before tonight's concert.* **2** °sample, °slice, cross-section, fraction: *It can be faulty to assume that the characteristics of the whole are necessarily represented in a small section of it. I examined a section of tissue under the microscope.* **3** °part, °stage, °segment, °portion, °leg: *The first section of the journey was more comfortable than the last.*
—*v.* **4** °cut (up), °divide (up), °segment, °split, °cleave, °measure out, apportion, °allot, allocate: *The land was sectioned into four-acre parcels.*

secular *adj.* °worldly, °terrestrial, mundane, °temporal, °material, °lay, laic *or* laical, non-clerical, non-ecclesiastic(al), non-spiritual, non-religious, °civil, °state: *Once he had taken his vows, he put aside secular matters.*

secure *adj.* **1** °safe, shielded, sheltered, protected, °immune, unthreatened, unexposed, unimperilled, °snug, °cosy: *Fiona feels quite secure in her new house. Considering the success of the company, Bill's job looks secure.* **2** °firm, °steady, °stable, °fixed, °fast, moored, anchored, °immovable, closed, °shut, fastened, locked (up), °tight, °sound, °solid, °sturdy, °strong: *That button on your jacket doesn't look very secure. Make sure that the house is secure before you go to sleep.* **3** °reliable, °safe, °good, °profitable, °healthy, °solid: *Telephone shares looked like a secure investment at the time.* **4** °sure, °certain, assured, ensured, °definite, °inevitable, °assumed, °evident, °obvious, °unquestionable, established, °probable, °easy: *With only two minutes left to play, victory seemed secure for Rangers.*
—*v.* **5** °obtain, °get (hold of), °come by, °acquire, °procure, °win; °gain, °get *or* °take °possession of, arrogate: *Tim has secured a responsible position at the bank. She always manages to secure the sympathy of older men.* **6** °guarantee, °underwrite, hypothecate, collateralize: *We used our house to secure the loan.* **7** °protect, °shelter, °shield, °defend, °guard, °safeguard, °preserve: *It seems impossible to secure young children from bullying at school.* **8** °fasten, make °fast, °fix, affix, °attach, °anchor: *Secure the cases to the roof-rack with strong rope.*

security *n.* **1** °safety, °shelter, °protection, fastness, °refuge, °safe keeping, °sanctuary, asylum: *During the air raids, we retired to the security of the basement.* **2** °confidence, °certainty, surety, °assurance, °conviction: *He has the security of knowing that he is right in this instance.* **3** °guarantee *or* guaranty, collateral, °deposit, gage, °pledge, °insurance: *What are you going to offer as security for the loan?* **4** °surveillance, safeguarding, guarding, °safe keeping, °protection, °custody, custodianship, °care: *What plans does the company have for the security of the office building?*

sedate *adj.* **1** composed, °serene, °peaceful, °calm, °tranquil, °cool, °collected, even-tempered, °detached, imperturbable, unruffled, undisturbed, unperturbed, controlled, placid, °grave, °serious, °sober, °solemn, *Colloq* unflappable: *Despite all the turmoil round her, Sarah remained quite sedate.* **2** °dignified, °decorous, °refined, °formal, °stiff, °staid, °proper, °strait-laced, °prudish, °fussy, prim, °conventional, °old-fashioned: *Donald prefers a sedate waltz to boogying and jiving.*

sedative *n.* **1** °narcotic, °tranquillizer, opiate, sleeping-pill, soporific, calmative, anodyne, depressant, hypnotic, barbiturate, lenitive, *Colloq* downer, knockout drop, *Slang* Mickey (Finn): *The doctor has given him a sedative and he should sleep now.*
—*adj.* **2** °narcotic, tranquillizing, relaxing, °soothing, calming, allaying, opiate, soporific, sleep-inducing, calmative, anodyne, lenitive, depressing, hypnotic: *I found that listening to a recording of surf splashing on a beach has a sedative effect.*

sedentary *adj.* seated, sitting, stationary, °fixed, immobile, unmoving, housebound, desk-bound: *You should find a more sedentary occupation to follow while you recover. As a writer, I lead a sedentary existence and get little exercise.*

sediment *n.* lees, °dregs, °deposit, °grounds, °precipitate, °remains, °residue, settlings, residuum, detritus: *Periodically, the sediment must be cleaned out of the filters.*

sedition *n.* °agitation, °incitement (to °riot), rabble-rousing, fomentation, instigation, firing-up, stirring up, °whipping up; °mutiny, insurrection, insurgency *or* insurgence, °rebellion; treason, treachery: *Because he had organized the strike in the munitions plant during wartime, he was accused of sedition.*

seditious *adj.* °rebellious, °mutinous, °revolutionary, insurgent, °inflammatory, rabble-rousing, insurrectionist, insurrectionary, refractory, °subversive, treacherous, °dissident, °disloyal, °turncoat, unfaithful: *One seditious action on the part of the colonists was to dump tea into the harbour at Boston, Massachusetts.*

seduce *v.* **1** °lure, °entice, °attract, allure, °tempt, °mislead, °beguile, °deceive, °decoy, draw on, °charm, °captivate, vamp, entrap, ensnare, °trap, *Colloq* sweet-talk: *He was seduced into giving her his life's savings.* **2** °dishonour, °ruin, °corrupt, °lead astray, defile, debauch, deflower, °violate, °ravish: *How many girls have been seduced in the name of undying love?*

seducer *n.* See also **seductress,** below; °rake, °libertine, °roué, °playboy, lady-killer, lecher, debauchee, debaucher, °lover, *cicisbeo*, Don Juan, Lothario, Casanova, *Colloq* wolf: *She can't really be going out with that wretched seducer!*

seductive *adj.* alluring, °attractive, °tempting, tantalizing, enticing, °inviting, seducing, °enchanting, entrancing, bewitching, fascinating, °flirtatious, coquettish, captivating, beguiling, °provocative, °siren, °irresistible, °winning, appealing, °prepossessing, *Colloq* °sexy: *He was lured into the whirl of the financial world by the seductive five-letter word—money. Never had Helena looked more seductive than on that night in Rio.*

seductress *n.* See also **seducer,** above; °temptress, °siren, *femme fatale*, enchantress, Circe, Lorelei, Jezebel, vamp: *That clever seductress will soon have him eating out of her hand.*

see *v.* **1** °perceive, °note, °notice, °mark, °spot, °watch, °witness, °recognize, °behold, discern, °distinguish, °observe, °look at, °regard, °sight, catch °sight of, descry, espy, °spy, °make out, °look upon, °view, glimpse, catch a glimpse of, *Slang* get a load of, *US* glom: *I saw him buy a bottle of whisky. We saw two yellow-bellied sapsuckers in one day! Can you see the sea from your suite? Did you see the Houses of Parliament when you were in London?* **2** °understand, °comprehend, apprehend, °perceive, °appreciate, °fathom, °grasp, °take in, °realize, °know, be °aware *or* °conscious of, °get the °idea *or* °meaning of, *Colloq* °dig, °get, °get the °drift *or* the °hang of: *I see what you are saying, but I don't agree. After her speech, I saw Gladys in a new light.* **3** °foresee, foretell, °imagine, °envisage, °envision, visualize, °picture, °divine, °conceive (of), °dream of, conjure up, °accept: *I can see a day when warming from the greenhouse effect will make the sea level rise. Ted said he can't see you as a married man.* **4** °determine, ascertain, °find out, °investigate, °discover, °learn: *See if the bakery has any macaroons. I'll see what she thinks.* **5** Often, ***see to it***: °ensure, °assure, make °sure *or* °certain, °mind, be °vigilant: *It's cold outside, so see that you dress warmly.* **6** °accompany, °escort, °show, °lead, °conduct, usher, °take, convoy, °bring, °walk, °drive: *I was seeing Nellie home from a soirée at Aunt Dinah's.* **7** °go out with, °socialize with, keep °company with, consort with, °associate with; court, woo; *Colloq* go °steady with, *Chiefly US* °date: *Are you still seeing that boy you met at the school dance?* **8** make up one's °mind, °think over, °mull over, °consider, °ponder (on *or* over), °contemplate, °decide, °reflect (on), °meditate (on *or* over *or* about), ruminate (on *or* over), °brood over: *Mother said she'd see whether I could go. Then I asked father, and he said he'd see.* **9** °receive, °meet (with), °talk *or* °speak with, °confer with, °consult (with), have a word with, sit down with, °visit with, °interview; °welcome, °greet: *The ambassador will see you now.* **10** °undergo, °experience, °go through, °endure, °survive: *He saw service overseas during the war.* **11** °help, °aid, °assist, °support, °finance, °pay the way for; °guide, °shepherd: *She saw three children through university without anyone's help.* **12** ***see about***: **a** see to, °attend to, °look after, take °care *or* °charge of, °look to, °organize, °manage, do, °undertake, °sort out; °think about, °consider, give some °thought to, pay °attention *or* °heed to: *Could you please see about feeding the horses while I am away? I asked Martin and he said he'd see about it.* **b** °investigate, °study, °probe, °look into, make enquiries *or* °inquiries, °enquire *or* °inquire about: *The teacher said she would see about letting us out early before the holiday.* **13** ***see off***: bid adieu *or* bon voyage: *We went to the airport to see them off.* **14** ***see through***: **a** °penetrate, °detect, °perceive, *Slang* be °wise to: *She saw through your subterfuge at once.* **b** ***see (something) through***: °persevere, °persist, °manage, °survive, °last, °ride out, *Colloq* °stick out: *Once you start on something, I wish you'd see it through.* **c** ***see (someone) through***: provide with °help *or* °aid *or* °assistance, °help, °aid, °assist, °last: *We'll give you enough money to see you through.* **15** ***see to***: See **12 a,** above.

seed *n.* **1** °grain, spore, °kernel, °pit, tuber, bulb, corm, *Technical* ovum, ovule, embryo, egg, °germ: *Add water and the seeds will soon germinate.* **2** °origin, °source, °cause, °root, °provocation, °reason, °basis, °grounds; °motive, motivation, motivating factor: *The seeds of suspicion were sown by the continuous police presence in the neighbourhood.* **3** °offspring, °children, °progeny, °young, °issue, °descendants, °heirs, successors: *Yea, and verily I say unto you that his seed shall populate the earth.* **4** ***go*** *or* ***run to seed***: °run down, become °dilapidated *or* °worn out *or* °shabby, °decay, go downhill, °decline, °degenerate, °deteriorate, go to rack and °ruin, *Colloq* go to pot: *If he doesn't start to look after it, the entire place will go to seed.* —*v.* **5** °scatter, °sow, °distribute: *Don't walk on the freshly seeded lawn.*

seedy *adj.* **1** °shabby, °dilapidated, °worn (out), decayed, deteriorated, °run-down, broken-down, °mangy, grubby, decaying, tatty, scruffy, squalid, °sleazy, *Colloq* °ratty: *They live in a seedy little shack on the other side of town.* **2** °tired, °weary, wearied, °run-down, °worn out, unwell, out of °sorts, ailing, °ill, °sickly, *Colloq* °poorly, under the °weather, off one's feed: *I begged off at dinner time because I was feeling a bit seedy.*

seeing *conjunction.* in °view of (the fact that), whereas, in (the) °light of, inasmuch as, since, °considering: *Seeing that you are here, you might as well tell her yourself.*

seek *v.* **1** °look (for), °search (for), °hunt (for), go *or* be after, °quest after, °pursue: *They are seeking a really good site for a grand luxury hotel. Seek and ye shall find.* **2** °hope, °aim, °aspire, °try, °essay, °endeavour, °undertake: *They are seeking to recruit members for the new party.* **3** °ask for, °request, °beg, °solicit, invite; °demand: *He sought her help and she refused him.*

seem *v.* °appear, °look (as if *or* like), °sound, °feel, have (all) the hallmarks *or* earmarks of, give every °indication *or* °appearance of: *He seems all right to me. She seems to have forgotten her key again. It seems as if I've never been away at all. He seemed frightened.*

seeming *adj.* °apparent, °evident, ostensible, °outward, °superficial, °surface, °assumed, feigned, °pretended, °false, °so-called, °alleged, °specious, purported, °professed: *She was shocked by his seeming indifference to her problems.*

seemingly *adv.* °apparently, °evidently, °ostensibly, °outwardly, superficially, falsely, allegedly, speciously, purportedly, professedly, on the °face of it, °possibly, feasibly, conceivably, plausibly, believably: *The purpose of this seemingly honest confession was to throw the detectives off the scent.*

seemly *adj.* **1** °proper, °fitting, °appropriate, °becoming, suited, °suitable, °fit, °befitting, apt, *comme il faut*, °right, apropos, apposite, °characteristic, °meet, °reasonable, °sensible: *You can count on Felix to do the seemly thing in such cases.* **2** °decent, °decorous, °proper, °dignified, °genteel, gentlemanly, °ladylike, °diplomatic, °discreet, °prudent, °politic: *She behaved* *in a seemly manner, in keeping with what was expected of a princess.*

seer *n.* soothsayer, °fortune-teller, sibyl, °oracle, °prophet, prophetess, augur, vaticinator, prophesier, clairvoyant, °psychic, crystal-gazer, star-gazer: *The seer foretold a grave famine and much suffering in the land.*

see-saw *n.* **1** teeter: *The children were playing on the see-saw.*
—*v.* **2** °teeter, °totter, waver, °vary, vacillate, °oscillate, °alternate, °fluctuate, °swing, °switch: *He couldn't make up his mind and kept see-sawing between staying and going.*

seethe *v.* **1** °boil, °stew, °simmer, °foam: *In the kitchen, a large pot of stew seethed on the stove.* **2** °stew, °simmer, °foam (at the mouth), °fume, °smoulder, °burn, °rage, °rant, °rave, become livid *or* °feverish, be in °ferment, be °furious *or* incensed, *Colloq* °blow one's °stack *or* top, carry on, take on, get °hot under the collar, get red in the face, get all steamed up: *The ball sailed through Mr Griffiths' new greenhouse and he came out seething with rage.*

see-through *adj.* °sheer, diaphanous, gauzy, °transparent, translucent, gossamer, °filmy, peekaboo: *She was wearing a see-through negligée when she appeared at the door.*

segment *n.* **1** °section, °part, °division, °portion, component, °element; °piece, fraction, °fragment, °length, °joint, °slice, °wedge: *Only a narrow segment of the population supports the new measures. She divided the orange into three equal segments.*
—*v.* **2** °divide, °partition, °section, °separate, °part, °cleave, °split, subdivide, °fragment: *The department was then further segmented into smaller units, each with its own manager.*

segregate *v.* °separate, °segment, °partition, °isolate, seclude, sequester, °set apart, compartmentalize, °exclude, °ostracize, °discriminate against: *In the sorting process, each size must be segregated into its own compartment. Their policy was to segregate the Blacks from the rest of the population.*

segregation *n.* °separation, segmentation, °partition, isolation, °seclusion, sequestration, setting apart, compartmentalization, °exclusion, ostracism, °discrimination, apartheid, *US* Jim Crowism: *No modern culture can long survive a segregation of the races.*

seize *v.* **1** Sometimes, ***seize on***: °grab, °grasp, °clutch, °take (hold of), °grip, °snatch: *Robin felt that he had to seize every opportunity that presented itself. The dog seized the robber by the seat of the pants.* **2** °capture, °catch, °arrest, take into °custody, take °prisoner, apprehend, °round up, *Colloq* °pinch, °nab, collar, °pick up, *Brit* °nick, *Slang* bust: *The police seized him as he was trying to leave the country.* **3** °catch, °transfix, °stop, °hold, °possess, take °possession of, °afflict, °beset, °visit, °subject: *I was seized by a sudden desire to kiss those quivering, pouting lips.* **4** take °advantage of, make good use of: *When their attention was diverted, I seized the opportunity to escape.* **5** °confiscate, °take (away), commandeer, °appropriate, °capture, °take °possession of, impound: *Ten tons of cannabis was seized in the raid.* **6** °Sometimes, ***seize up***: °bind, °jam, °stop, °lock (up), °stick, °freeze (up): *Because of the excessive heat, the gears seized and the engine stalled.*

seizure *n.* **1** seizing, confiscating, confiscation, appropriation, impounding, commandeering, °capture, taking, °possession, annexation, sequestration, usurpation: *Police today announced the seizure of a shipment of 2,000 pounds of cocaine.* **2** °spasm, °attack, °fit, °paroxysm, convulsion, *Technical* ictus: *He has had another seizure and is not expected to live.*

seldom *adv.* °rarely, °infrequently, not °often, °hardly ever, very °occasionally: *Since they moved away, we seldom see the Pattersons.*

select *v.* **1** °choose, °pick, °show (a) °preference for, °prefer, opt for, °single out, hand-pick, °distinguish: *Select any two books from this pile. Anne was delighted to be selected from hundreds of candidates.*
—*adj.* **2** selected, chosen, hand-picked, °choice, °special, preferred, preferable, °favoured, °favourite, °exceptional, °excellent, °first-rate, first-class, °superior, °supreme, °prime, °better, °best, finest, tiptop: *We have set aside some of our select jewels for you to consider, Your Ladyship.* **3** °limited, restricted, restrictive, °exclusive, °privileged, °élite, closed: *He belongs to one of those select clubs that accept you only if your family can be traced back five hundred years.*

selection *n.* **1** °choice, °pick, °preference, °option: *Please make your selection from the merchandise in this display.* **2** °assortment, °variety, °collection, °range, °batch, °number, °set, series, °group: *Tonight I shall play for you a selection of jazz recordings made at the Savoy.* **3** selecting, choosing, picking, singling out, electing, settling on, voting for, opting for, °choice, °pick, °election: *Selection has been delayed till tomorrow.* **4** °extract, °quotation, °excerpt, °abstract, °passage, °piece, °quote: *I shall read you a selection from Blake's* Songs of Innocence and Experience.

selective *adj.* °particular, discerning, discriminative, °discriminating, discriminatory, eclectic, °exacting, °demanding, °choosy, *Colloq* picky: *Thea has been very selective in her choice of partners.*

self-abuse *n.* masturbation, onanism, self-gratification, auto-eroticism *or* autoerotism, self-stimulation, self-manipulation, self-pollution, self-defilement, self-contamination, *Technical* manustupration: *Victorian schoolboys were punished if suspected of self-abuse.*

self-confidence *n.* °confidence, self-assurance, °self-respect, °self-esteem, °assurance, °poise, aplomb, self-reliance, self-sufficiency: *Harrigan has demonstrated that he has the self-confidence to run the department.*

self-confident *adj.* °confident, self-assured, assured, °poised, self-reliant, °secure, °sure of oneself, °positive, °definite, °assertive, °independent: *She seems much more self-confident, relaxed, and contented these days.*

self-conscious *adj.* °embarrassed, °coy, diffident, °shy, °modest, self-effacing, °sheepish, shrinking, °retiring, unsure, apprehensive, °reserved, °insecure, °affected, °awkward, °nervous, uncomfortable, °hesitant, °timid, timorous: *Phil felt a bit self-conscious about asking Maria to the dance.*

self-contained *adj.* **1** °self-possessed, unemotional, self-controlled, in °control, composed, °serene, °peaceful, °calm, °tranquil, °cool, °collected, even-tempered, °detached, imperturbable, unruffled, undisturbed, unperturbed, controlled, placid, °grave, °serious, °sober, °solemn, *Colloq* unflappable: *Sometimes I think Frank is a little too self-contained.* **2** °reserved, controlled, °distant, °aloof, °formal, °withdrawn, °reticent, °standoffish: *Gregory is so self-contained that he did not tell anyone that he was ill, not even his wife.* **3** °whole, °entire, °complete, stand-alone, unitary: *The house has been divided into five self-contained apartments.*

self-control *n.* **1** self-discipline, self-restraint, °restraint, °self-denial, °control, will-power, °strength (of character *or* of mind *or* of °will), mettle, °fortitude, moral °fibre, °determination, self-possession, resoluteness, °resolve, °will, constancy, steadfastness, °perseverance, doggedness, obduracy, °persistence, *Facetious US* won't-power: *Can I exercise the self-control needed to stop smoking?* **2** calmness, tranquillity, °serenity, placidity, imperturbability, cool-headedness, coolness, °poise, level-headedness, °patience, aplomb, °dignity, equanimity, forbearance, °control, °restraint, self-restraint, °even °temper: *You exhibited marvellous self-control by not losing your temper when you were insulted.*

self-denial *n.* **1** self-sacrifice, self-abnegation, renunciation, selflessness, °altruism, unselfishness, magnanimity: *His contributions must have been made at the cost of some self-denial.* **2** °hardship, °suffering, self-mortification, asceticism, °privation, renunciation, renouncing, abstemiousness, abstinence, abstention, self-deprivation, keeping away from, °refusal, refusing, giving up, desisting, *Colloq* swearing off: *As far as certain foods are concerned, a little self-denial is good for one's health.* **3** See **self-control, 1,** above.

self-esteem *n.* **1** °conceit, °vanity, egoism, narcissism, self-centredness, egotism, *amour propre*, self-approbation, self-satisfaction, self-admiration, self-love, self-adulation, self-idolatry, smugness, self-importance, self-regard: *The arrogant, overweening self-esteem of some of the club members is unbearable.* **2** See **self-confidence,** above.

self-evident *adj.* °evident, °obvious, °patent, °clear, °incontrovertible, °definite, °express, °distinct, clear-cut, °apparent, unmistakable, undeniable, inescapable, incontestable, °plain, axiomatic, °proverbial, °manifest, °true, palpable, °tangible: *Her guilt seemed self-evident at first. The gradual destruction of the beaches is self-evident.*

self-government *n.* **1** self-rule, °independence, self-determination, home rule, autonomy, °freedom: *The satellite countries, one by one, voted for self-government.* **2** See **self-control, 1,** above.

self-important *adj.* °conceited, self-centred, self-seeking, self-absorbed, °vain, egotistic(al), self-satisfied, °smug, °pompous, swollen-headed, swell-headed *or* swelled-headed, °arrogant, overweening, °overbearing, vainglorious, self-glorifying, self-engrossed, °presumptuous, °snobbish, °haughty, *Colloq* snooty, *Slang* snotty, stuck-up: *That self-important little cockalorum ought to be taken down a few pegs.*

self-indulgent *adj.* self-gratifying, °selfish, °extravagant, °sensual, intemperate, overindulgent, °greedy, °immoderate, hedonistic, sybaritic, °epicurean, °gluttonous, gormandizing, pleasure-bound, pleasure-seeking, °dissolute, dissipating, licentious, °profligate, debauching: *David's self-indulgent habits take no account of his wife and children.*

selfish *adj.* **1** °greedy, covetous, °grasping, °avaricious, °self-indulgent, self-aggrandizing, acquisitive, self-seeking, self-loving, self-centred, self-absorbed, self-interested, self-serving, egotistic(al), °egoistic(al): *They pursue success for their own selfish ends.* **2** stingy, °mean, °mercenary, °tight, tight-fisted, °narrow, °penurious, parsimonious, °miserly, niggardly, penny-pinching, cheese-paring, ungenerous, illiberal, grudging, uncharitable, °possessive, °inconsiderate, °thoughtless: *He is so selfish that he won't even give you the right time.*

selfless *adj.* °open, °charitable, °unselfish, self-denying, °generous, altruistic, ungrudging, magnanimous, °considerate, °thoughtful; self-sacrificing: *Always ready to help anyone with a need, Archer is the most selfless man I know.*

self-made *adj.* °independent, self-reliant, entrepreneurial, °self-sufficient: *She is a self-made woman and has accomplished it all without anyone else's help.*

self-possessed *adj.* composed, °cool, °serene, placid, °collected, self-assured, °peaceful, °calm, °tranquil, even-tempered, °detached, imperturbable, unruffled, undisturbed, unperturbed, controlled, °dignified, °refined, *Colloq* unflappable: *Considering what she has been through, Tanya is quite self-possessed for a teenager.*

self-respect *n.* °honour, °dignity, °integrity, self-regard, °self-esteem, °pride, *amour propre*, °morale: *He managed to maintain a semblance of his self-respect despite the accusations hurled at him.*

self-righteous *adj.* °Pharisaic(al), °sanctimonious, holier-than-thou, pietistic, °mealy-mouthed, °hypocritical, complacent, °smug, self-satisfied, °priggish, °superior, Tartuffian, canting, *Colloq* °goody-goody, *Slang Brit* pi: *Butter would not melt in the mouth of that self-righteous hypocrite!*

self-styled *adj.* would-be, self-called, *soi-disant*, °professed, self-appointed, self-christened, °so-called, °quasi-: *The building has been designed by a firm of self-styled 'neo-traditionalist' architects.*

self-sufficient *adj.* °independent, self-reliant, self-supporting, self-sustaining: *Agriculture will soon reach the point where the country is self-sufficient for food.*

self-willed *adj.* headstrong, °determined, °forceful, refractory, °stubborn, °obstinate, pigheaded, °wilful, °ungovernable, uncontrollable, °unruly, unmanageable, intractable, °contrary, °perverse, uncooperative, contumacious, °recalcitrant, stiff-necked, vexatious, °difficult, °incorrigible, °disobedient: *That self-willed, overindulged little brat needs a good spanking.*

sell *v.* **1** vend, °transfer, convey (title), °trade, barter, °exchange, °dispose of: *Sorry, but I sold that car last week.* **2** °market, °deal in, °merchandise, °trade in, °traffic in, °peddle, vend, hawk, °handle, retail, °carry, °stock, °furnish, °supply, °offer, *Colloq* °push, *Slang Brit* °flog: *We no longer sell that model. She has a shop selling second-hand clothes.* **3** Often, ***sell out***: °betray, °inform against, °deliver up, °give away, *Slang* rat on, °grass on, °tell on, °tattle on, sell down the river, blow the whistle on, °double-cross, *Brit* °shop: *He swore he'd get the man who sold him.* **4** °promote, °push, °put across *or* over: *He couldn't sell sand to a beach flea.* **5** ***be sold on***: persuaded, convinced, won over: *After seeing that film, I was sold on a holiday in Mexico.*

seller *n.* °dealer, vendor, °merchant, retailer, shopkeeper, °salesperson, salesman, saleswoman, saleslady, sales °agent, °representative, °traveller, travelling salesman, peddler, hawker, colporteur, sutler, chandler, *Old-fashioned* counter-jumper, *Brit* shop °assistant, -monger (*as in* costermonger, ironmonger, fishmonger, etc.), *US and Canadian* salesclerk, clerk, shop-girl, *Colloq* rep, *US* drummer: *Time ran out on his job as a seller of water-clocks and hourglasses.*

semblance *n.* **1** °appearance, °image, °likeness, °resemblance, °form, °figure, °bearing, °aspect, °air, °look, mien, °exterior, °mask, façade, °front, °face, °show, °veneer: *Beneath that semblance of tranquillity lies a turbulent, tortured mind.* **2** °guise, °face, °front, façade, °air, °show, °veneer, °look, °pretence, °cloak, simulation, °impression, °affectation, *Rare* °superficies: *You might try to give the sculpture at least a semblance of reality.*

seminal *adj.* **1** °original, °basic, °creative, °primary, °prime, formative, innovative, °imaginative, °new, unprecedented, precedent-setting, °landmark, benchmark, °important, °influential, °telling: *Michaelson's paper is considered the seminal work on the subject. It sets forth many seminal ideas.* **2** embryonic, germinal, °potential, °undeveloped, incipient: *Each seed contains a seminal plant.*

seminary *n.* academy, °school, °institute, °institution, college, university, training ground: *His three daughters had all attended an exclusive seminary on the East Coast.*

send *v.* **1** Sometimes, ***send off***: °dispatch *or* despatch, commission, °charge, depute, °delegate, °assign: *The Pope sent an emissary to London.* **2** °communicate, °transmit, convey, °deliver, consign, °address to, °mail, °post, fax, °remit, °ship, °forward; °broadcast, telecast, televise, °radio, telegraph: *The message is being sent to all concerned.* **3** °release, °discharge, °shoot, °propel, °fire, °fling, °project, °hurl; °cast, °throw, °toss, let °fly: *With a great burst of flame the satellite was sent into orbit.* **4** °delight, °please, °charm, °enrapture, °stir, °thrill, °move, °electrify, *Slang* °turn (someone) on: *That saxophone solo really sends me.* **5** ***send down***: °imprison, incarcerate, send away, °jail *or Brit also* gaol *Slang US* send up (the river): *If she doesn't mend her ways, she'll be sent down.* **6** ***send for***: °call for, °summon, °order, °request, °ask for: *I have sent for a taxi which should be here shortly.* **7** ***send forth*** *or* ***out***: °emit, °radiate, °discharge, °give off, exude, °grow: *The object sent forth a strange phosphorescent glow. In the spring, the vine sends forth tendrils.* **8** ***send off***: send (someone) away, send (someone) away *or* off with a flea in his *or* her ear, °dismiss, °discharge, send (someone) packing, send (someone) about his *or* her business, *Colloq* give (someone) his *or* her walking papers, *Slang* give (someone) the °brush-off, *US* give (someone) the °brush: *I went to the office as you instructed, but they just sent me off with no explanation.* **9** ***send up***: **a** °lampoon, °satirize, °burlesque, °parody, make °fun of, *Colloq* °take off, spoof, *Brit* take the mickey out of: *In Britain one of the enduring forms of humour is in sending up the government.* **b** °imprison, incarcerate, send away, °jail *or Brit also* gaol, *Slang US* send up the river: *He was sent up for insider trading.*

senile *adj.* (*of a woman*) anile; senescent, °decrepit, declining, °failing, in one's dotage, doting, °doddering, in one's second childhood, dotty, °simple, °feeble-minded; °forgetful, *Colloq* past it: *He's senile and needs constant care.*

senility *n.* (*of a woman*) anility; °senile dementia, Alzheimer's disease, senescence, °decrepitude, °decline, dotage, second childhood, loss of one's faculties: *Senility has robbed my grandmother of her memory.*

senior *adj.* °elder, older, *Brit* (*postpositive*) °major; (higher-) ranking, °superior, °chief: *The senior members of the club are impossibly stuffy. You must not address your senior officer in such a manner.*

senior citizen *n.* °elderly person, retired person, °pensioner, *Brit* OAP (= 'old-age pensioner'), °grey panther, *Chiefly US* retiree, golden-ager: *Special tax provisions have been made for senior citizens.*

sensation *n.* **1** °feeling, °sense, °impression, °perception, °foreboding, presentiment, prescience, awareness, °suspicion, *Colloq* sneaking °suspicion, funny °feeling, °hunch: *I had the distinct sensation of having been there before.* **2** commotion, °stir, °thrill, °furore *or US* furor; °excitement: *The news of the wedding caused a sensation.* **3** °hit, *coup de théâtre*, °success, *Colloq* show-stopper, crowd-puller, crowd-pleaser: *Edith Piaf was a sensation at Le Théâtre de la Verdure in Nice.*

sensational *adj.* **1** °exciting, °stimulating, electrifying, galvanizing, °shocking, hair-raising, spine-tingling, °thrilling, °stirring, breathtaking, °amazing, astonishing, astounding, staggering, mind-boggling, °unbelievable, °incredible, spectacular, *Slang* mind-blowing: *They certainly put on a sensational show—the best I have ever seen.* **2** °lurid, °vivid, overdone, overdrawn, °extreme, °melodramatic, exaggerated, °dramatic, °extravagant: *The weekly I worked for insisted that each issue's first page carry a sensational story—whether it was true or not.* **3** (very) °good, °great, °marvellous, wonderful, °superior, °superb, °matchless, °peerless, unequalled, °nonpareil, °extraordinary, °terrific, °phenomenal, °splendid, °fabulous, °fantastic, stupendous, *Colloq* °super, smashing, *Slang* far-out: *Suzanne Peters's performance in* Carmen *was sensational.*

sense *n.* **1** °faculty: *It's not always easy to tell if Brown's senses are all functioning.* **2** common sense, °intelligence, °perception, quick-wittedness, quickness, (mother) °wit, °judgement, °reason, °wisdom, sagacity, °discrimination, discernment; °sanity, *Colloq* °brains, *Slang Brit* nous: *Fancy doing something like that!—she hasn't the sense she was born with!* **3** See **sensation, 1,** above. **4** °meaning, intelligibility, coherence, head or tail, °drift, °gist, °import, purport, nuance, °significance, °message, °substance: *I was unable to get any sense out of what she was saying. Yes, I wasn't able to make sense out of it either.* **5** °sentiment, °atmosphere, °impression, °intuition, °sensation: *I had a sense of being* de trop *— that I was not wanted.*
—*v.* **6** °feel, °perceive, °detect, °divine, intuit, have a °hunch *or* °feeling, have *or* get *or* be under the °impression that, °suspect, *Colloq* have a funny °feeling that, °feel (something) in one's bones, pick up: *I sensed a certain antagonism in that last remark. I sensed that he was getting bored with me.*

senseless *adj.* **1** °insensible, °unconscious, (knocked) °out (cold), stunned, insensate, comatose: *Agatha's head hit the fire-grate and she was borne senseless to her room.* **2** °numb(ed), insensate, unfeeling, benumbed, °insensible, anaesthetized, °dead, deadened, insentient: *My feet are senseless from the cold.* **3** °pointless, °purposeless, °ridiculous, °ludicrous, unintelligent, illogical, irrational, °incongruous, °meaningless, °absurd, °wild, °mad, °crazy, demented, °insane, asinine, °nonsensical, imbecilic *or* imbecile, idiotic, moronic, simple-minded, fatuous, °stupid, °foolish, °silly, °dizzy, °halfwitted, °mindless, brainless, witless, empty-headed, thimble-witted, pea-brained, bird-brained, °hare-brained, feather-headed, rattle-brained, addle-pated, muddle-headed, *Colloq* °daft, *US* daffy, nutty, batty, *Slang* wacky, dippy: *Many of the government's objections to the plan are just senseless posturing. He is promoting some senseless plan for double-decker motorways.*

sensibility *n.* **1** See **sensitivity, 3,** below. **2** Often, ***sensibilities***: °feelings, responsiveness, responsivity, °emotions, °sentiments: *Personal events are more likely to affect our sensibilities than major disasters in which we are not involved.*

sensible *adj.* **1** °reasonable, °realistic, °logical, common-sense, commonsensical, °rational, reasoned, °sound, °practical, °prudent, °judicious, °discreet, °intelligent, °sage, °wise, °sane; down-to-earth, °matter-of-fact, well-thought-out: *Do you really think it sensible to go out in this storm? Andrew has a very sensible way of dealing with junk mail—he returns it to sender.* **2** perceivable, °perceptible, detectable, °evident, °discernible, recognizable, ascertainable, apprehensible, cognizable, °manifest, palpable, °physical, °tangible, corporeal, substantive, °material, °visible, °observable, seeable: *Some maintain that in addition to the sensible world there is another world, an anti-world, that we do not normally encounter.* **3** sentient, °feeling, °sensitive, °live, °conscious, °aware: *Who among us ever regards microbes as sensible creatures?* **4** Usually, ***sensible of*** *or* ***to***: °conscious (of), °aware (of), °acquainted (with), cognizant (of), °sensitive (to), °alive to, °mindful (of), understanding (of), in °touch (with), °observant (of), °awake (to), °alert (to), *Slang* °wise (to), °hip *or old-fashioned* hep (to): *The people of the village are ever sensible to the needs of their neighbours. There are some things to which we are not at all sensible.* **5** appreciable, °significant, °considerable, °substantial, substantive, °noticeable: *The theory is that an increased interest rate will have a sensible effect on the rate of inflation.*

sensitive *adj.* **1** °delicate, °tender, °sore, °susceptible: *My arm is still sensitive where I got the injection.* **2** °touchy, °susceptible, susceptive, reactive, °responsive, attuned, °impressionable, °emotional, thin-skinned, °vulnerable, supersensitive, hypersensitive, °testy, irascible, °quarrelsome, °irritable, °volatile, °excitable, °temperamental, °petulant, hot-tempered, °quick-tempered: *Liz is very sensitive on the subject of being unmarried, and I shouldn't bring it up.* **3** finely tuned, °delicate, °responsive, °subtle, °acute, reactive, °receptive: *We need a more sensitive test to detect neutrinos. This radio is not sensitive enough to receive distant stations.*

sensitivity *n.* **1** sensitiveness, °delicacy, touchiness, over-sensitivity, hypersensitivity, supersensitivity; soreness, irritability: *The sensitivity of teenagers to criticism is well known to teachers and parents. She complained of sensitivity and pain in the pelvic region.* **2** compassion, °concern, °sympathy, tenderness, tender-heartedness, kind-heartedness, kindliness, °warmth, °feeling: *The nurses exhibit a genuine sensitivity for the problems of the handicapped.* **3** awareness, consciousness, acuteness, °perception, °understanding, °intuition, °feeling, °sense, sensitiveness, receptivity *or* receptiveness, receptibility, °appreciation, appreciativeness, susceptibility, susceptivity *or* susceptiveness: *Harvey has a keen sensitivity for the feelings of others. Sometimes I think the duke lacks the sensitivity needed to sympathize with the needy.*

sensual *adj.* °physical, appetitive, °voluptuous, °carnal, bodily, fleshly, °erotic, °sexual, °lustful, °unchaste, °abandoned, °dissolute, °profligate, dissipated, licentious, °lewd, °lascivious, lubricious *or* lubricous, goatish, hircine, °lecherous, libidinous, salacious, °prurient, °rakish, °wanton, debauched, Cyprian, °loose, °dirty, *Slang* °randy: *Cranston pursued his sensual pleasures with no regard for morality.*

sensualist *n.* lecher, °profligate, °wanton, debauchee, °roué, °rake, Romeo, Don Juan, Casanova, Lothario, °libertine; voluptuary, hedonist, °sybarite, bon viveur, *bon vivant*, °epicure, °epicurean, °gourmet, gourmand, gastronome, pleasure-seeker: *The main character in the film is a self-seeking sensualist who betrays every woman in his life.*

sensuous *adj.* sensory, sybaritic, °epicurean, hedonist(ic), °sumptuous, °luxurious, °rich: *She felt sensuous delight in the scents and sounds of the island.*

sentence *n.* °judgement, °decision, ruling, verdict, °decree, °determination; °punishment, *Slang* °rap: *It is up to the judge to announce the sentence of the court. Asked by his teacher for an example of a short sentence, Johnny replied, 'Thirty days'.*

sentiment *n.* **1** °attitude, °feeling, °sensibility, °emotion, susceptibility, tenderness, tender-heartedness, °sentimentality, sentimentalism: *He wanted to preserve the old village square more out of sentiment than because it was historically important.* **2** Often, ***sentiments***: °view, °outlook, °opinion, °position, °attitude, °judgement, °thought, °belief, °feeling, °emotion: *His sentiments regarding apartheid are better left unexpressed.*

sentimental *adj.* **1** °emotional, °sympathetic, compassionate, °tender, warm-hearted, tender-hearted: *Has he returned for sentimental reasons or for practical and mercenary ones?* **2** °romantic, nostalgic, °emotional, °maudlin, mawkish, over-emotional, °tender, °tearful, weepy, sickening, nauseating, simpering, °sweet, saccharine, *Colloq* °sloppy, °gooey, °sticky, °tacky, °mushy, slushy, °gushy, soppy, drippy, tear-jerking, ill-making, sick-making, *Slang* corny, schmaltzy, icky, °yucky *or* yukky: *His last tune is always some sentimental ballad like 'Good Night, Sweetheart'.*

sentimentality *n.* romanticism, nostalgia, pathos, emotionalism, maudlinism, bathos, mawkishness, over-emotionalism, tenderness, tearfulness, weepiness, sweetness, *Colloq* sloppiness, gooeyness, mushiness, slushiness, gushiness, soppiness, drippiness, *US* stickiness, tackiness, *Slang* corn, corniness, schmaltz, schmaltziness, ickiness, yuckiness *or* yukkiness: *The role of the bereaved mother was overplayed with enough gushing sentimentality to make one sick.*

sentinel *n.* sentry, °guard, °watchman, °watch, °picket, °lookout, °patrol: *The sentinels measured out the ramparts of the fortress with their regular paces.*

separable *adj.* distinguishable, segregable, detachable, divisible, severable, removable, fissile, scissile: *Unfortunately, as history demonstrates, morality and religion are separable.*

separate *v.* **1** disjoin, °pull *or* take *or* °break °apart, °come *or* °fall °apart, °fall *or* °take *or* °break to pieces, °split *or* °divide *or* °break (up), °split *or* °break (off *or* away), °disconnect, °disengage, °part, °partition, °sort (out), uncouple, disarticulate, disassemble, unhook, °detach, disunite, unyoke, disentangle, unravel: *In order to clean it, I first have to separate all the individual elements of the motor. The glue didn't hold, and the vase separated into a dozen fragments. Separate this yarn into different piles.* **2** °distinguish, °discriminate, °analyse, °sort, °break down, classify, °segregate, °single out, sequester, °type, codify, °organize, °split up; °group, collate: *What criteria are used to separate the men from the boys, the sheep from the goats, or the wheat from the chaff?* **3** °split *or* °break up, °part (company), °divide (up), °disband, °divorce: *After ten years we separated, and each went our own way.* **4** fork, °split (up *or* off), bifurcate, °diverge, °branch: *Beyond the river, the road to Norton separates from the main road.*
—*adj.* **5** divided, separated, disjoined, °disconnected, °detached, °isolated, °discrete, °distinct, °individual, °independent, °solitary, °different: *Sort these books by subject into separate piles.* **6** °different, °independent, °unrelated, other: *How you behave when you are not at home is a separate matter.* **7** °withdrawn, °solitary, °alone, °shut *or* closed off *or* away, °apart, °detached, removed, cloistered, °secluded, sequestered, °isolated, separated: *He prefers a separate existence, far away from the rest of the world.*

separately *adv.* °individually, independently, °singly, one by one, one at a time, °personally, °alone, severally: *Each child approached separately to wish her Bon Voyage.*

separation *n.* **1** °rift, °break, °split, split-up, °divorce, break-up, disunion, estrangement: *Their separation, after forty years, was a surprise.* **2** °partition, °division, °split, °schism, dividing line, dissociation, disassociation, severance: *The United States constitution provides for the separation of church and state.* **3** disintegration, shattering, break-up, fragmentation, dismemberment, taking *or* keeping °apart, °segregation, °division, disjoining, disjunction, fission, scission, °rupture, °schism, splitting, °split, fracturing, °fracture, °break: *After a crash, investigators supervise the separation of the aeroplane into its tens of thousands of component parts.*

sepulchre *n.* °tomb, mausoleum, burial-vault, °grave, °crypt, pyramid, burial-place: *Beneath the floor of the church are the sepulchres of important people.*

sequel *n.* °follow-up, °upshot, °issue, °result, consequence, °development, °supplement: *The ruling went against him, but there was a curious sequel when he was suddenly offered an out-of-court settlement. They are showing the film* Jean de Florette, *together with its sequel* Manon des Sources.

sequence *n.* °succession, °progression, °order, series, °chain, °string, °course, °cycle, °arrangement, °organization, °train, °line, °set, °run, concatenation, °system: *His description conflicts with the sequence of events as recorded by the video camera. Some of these dates are out of sequence.*

sequential *adj.* °successive, ordered, °orderly, serial, °progressive, organized, °systematic, cyclic, °continuous: *Would you please put these periodicals into sequential order?*

seraphic *adj.* angelic, °celestial, °divine, °heavenly, blissful, °sublime, empyrean, Elysian, ethereal, °holy, °saintly, °godly: *In her later years, Anna's beauty took on a detached, seraphic quality.*

serene *adj.* **1** °peaceful, °tranquil, °calm, pacific, °peaceable, °restful, halcyon, °idyllic, bucolic, °pastoral, undisturbed, unruffled, imperturbable, unperturbed, untroubled, °quiet, °still: *With the turmoil of the love affair behind her, Sharon looked ahead to a more serene life.* **2** °calm, °cool, °collected, placid, composed, °self-possessed, °poised, unexcitable, even-tempered, °temperate, °nonchalant, °easygoing, cool-headed, °easy, *Colloq* unflappable: *William's serene exterior disguised his violent nature.*

serenity *n.* **1** peacefulness, °peace, tranquillity, °calm, calmness, restfulness, °quiet, stillness: *The serenity of the warm summer's evening was shattered by an enormous explosion.* **2** tranquillity, peacefulness, peaceableness, unexcitability, calmness, °calm, composure, self-possession, °poise, aplomb, even-temperedness, °temperance, nonchalance, cool-headedness, placidity, *Colloq* unflappability: *The serenity of her nature was like a safe harbour to the friends who sought comfort from the turbulence of their lives.*

serious *adj.* **1** °grave, °solemn, °earnest, unsmiling, poker-faced, straight-faced, °sedate, °sober, °pensive, °thoughtful; humourless, °sombre, °grim, °dour, °severe: *One should be wary of the person who is always serious, who cannot see the ludicrous side of life.*

2 °grave, °important, °vital, °dangerous, °weighty, °significant, °momentous, °crucial, consequential, life-and-death *or* life-or-death, °urgent, °pressing; no laughing matter, of consequence *or* °moment *or* °importance: *Things like the greenhouse effect and the hole in the ozone layer are serious concerns for all mankind.* **3** °sincere, straightforward, not joking *or* fooling, °genuine, °honest: *Is he serious about wanting me to fetch him a left-handed wrench?* **4** °acute, °critical, life-threatening, °bad, °dangerous, °nasty, °perilous, alarming, °grave, °severe, °precarious: *His condition is serious and we might have to operate tonight. She had no idea that measles could be such a serious illness.*

seriously *adv.* **1** gravely, °badly, °severely, critically: *Two men were seriously injured in the explosion.* **2** °really, °honestly, Scout's honour, °sincerely, °truly, candidly, °openly, *Colloq* joking *or* kidding aside, no joking *or* kidding *or* fooling, cross one's heart (and hope to die): *Seriously, kids, I meant what I said about going to bed on time, or no treats tomorrow at the beach.* **3** soberly, earnestly, unquestioningly, without a doubt, at face value: *What teacher takes seriously that old story about a grandmother's illness as an excuse for absence?*

sermon *n.* **1** °lecture, °lesson, preaching, °reprimand, reproach, °reproof, remonstration, remonstrance, scolding, °harangue, *Colloq* talking-to, dressing-down: *Mother gave me a long sermon last night about getting home late.* **2** homily, °address, exhortation, °lesson, °lecture, °speech, °talk, discourse: *We thought that Father Keiller's sermon on vanity was especially appropriate.*

serpentine *adj.* **1** °evil, °bad, diabolic(al), °satanic, Mephistophelian, reptilian, °devilish, °wily, cunning, conniving, °sneaky, °shrewd, °artful, °crafty, °slick, °sly, insidious, °shifty, °tricky, °scheming, plotting, Machiavellian: *With serpentine deceit she swore that she had returned the ring.* **2** twisting, winding, °tortuous, snaking, snakelike, sinuous, anfractuous, °roundabout, °meandering, ambagious, °indirect, °devious, °crooked, °labyrinthine, vermicular, vermiculate, complex, °complicated, Byzantine: *The amulet was traced through a serpentine trail of ownership back to Xerxes.*

serrated *adj.* sawlike, saw-shaped, sawtooth(ed), toothed, °notched, zigzag, °jagged, serrate, serriform, serratiform, serrulate(d), crenellated, crenulate, crenate, denticulate: *A knife with a serrated edge would cut the meat more easily.*

serried *adj.* ranked, tiered, row on row, ranged, assembled, °packed, °close, compacted, °compact: *The serried army of brightly clad warriors stretched as far as the eye could see.*

servant *n.* **1** °domestic (servant), °help, retainer; °maid, maidservant, parlour-maid, upstairs °maid, lady's °maid, cleaner, cleaning °man, cleaning °woman, amah; housekeeper, chatelaine, major-domo, factotum, steward, seneschal, butler, houseman, houseboy, °boy, °page; valet, °man, gentleman's gentleman, manservant, serving-man, footman, foot-boy, chauffeur, driver, °attendant, °groom; governess, au pair (°girl), °nurse, nursemaid, ayah; cook, chef, °waiter, waitress, stewardess, wine steward, *sommelier (des vins)*; °menial, lackey, dogsbody, *Archaic* servitor, *Historical* coachman, postilion, serving-woman, serving-girl, servant-girl, serving-wench, scullery-maid, scullion, *Literary* cup-boy, Ganymede, *Chiefly Brit* nanny, *Brit* boots, charwoman, charlady, daily, tweeny, *US* scrubwoman: *Who can afford to keep domestic servants these days?* **2** ***civil servant***: civil-service employee *or* worker, public servant, (°government *or* State) °official, office-holder, °government worker: *In his capacity as a civil servant, Richard has worked for several different governments.*

serve *v.* **1** °attend (to), °wait on *or* upon, °minister to, °look after (the needs of), be at (someone's) beck and call, °assist, °help, be of °assistance *or* °help, be in the °service of, °oblige, °accommodate, °gratify: *After a patron is seated and settled, approach him and ask, 'May I serve you, Sir (or Madam, as the case may be)?' We serve all customers with equal consideration.* **2** °fulfil *or* °carry out *or* °perform *or* °discharge (a °function *or* a °duty *or* one's °duty), °work (for), do (°duty) (as *or* for), do one's °part, °suffice, be °used *or* of °use *or* °useful (to *or* for), °function (as *or* to), °act (as *or* to), fill the bill, be °serviceable (as *or* for), be °available (for), °answer (for), be °sufficient *or* °adequate *or* °suitable, °suit, be °advantageous *or* of °advantage (to); fight (for), be °obedient (to), take one's part: *This catch will serve to keep the door closed. I had no screw driver, but a coin served just as well. They also serve who only stand and wait.* **3** °distribute, °deal out, °dole out, °give out, °present, °set out, °provide, °supply, °offer, °pass out *or* about *or* around, make °available, come (a)round with, dish up *or* out: *They will serve hors-d'œuvres at seven-thirty. Dinner is served, Madam.* **4** be °convenient *or* °opportune *or* °favourable (to): *If the opportunity serves me, I shall repay you many times over.* **5** not fail, not play tricks (on), °work *or* °function (for), be °accurate *or* °correct: *If memory serves, he was last here about ten years ago.* **6** °go through, °complete, °spend, °last, °endure, °survive: *Henryson served ten years in Dartmoor for that crime.*

service *n.* **1** °help, °assistance, °aid, °use, °usefulness, utility, °benefit, °advantage: *May I be of service to you? You could do me a great service by not saying anything of this to my mother.* **2** °maintenance, °overhaul, servicing, checking, °repair, mending: *Must we send the copier out for service or can they do it in the office?* **3** serving, °accommodation, amenities, waiting, °care: *The food is good but the service leaves much to be desired.* **4** °employment, °employ: *How long have you been in my service, Jones?* **5** °use, utilization, °usage, handling: *This old teapot has seen much service.* **6** °assignment, °post, °appointment, *Military Brit* secondment: *Oscar was on service in the Far East during the war.* **7** °rite, °ceremony, °ritual, °worship: *I shall be attending a memorial service for Grimes on Saturday.* **8** Often, ***services***: army, °navy, air force, marines; armed forces *or* services, °military: *He was a pianist before joining the service.* **9** Often, ***services***: °talents, °help, professional °care, °work, °advice: *You will need the services of a good accountant.* **10** °serve, serving; putting into play: *Clarke's tennis service is faster and more accurate than before.*

serviceable *adj.* **1** workable, working, °functional, functioning, usable, °useful, °operative, operating: *It seems unlikely that the old tractor will still be serviceable.* **2** hard-wearing, long-wearing, °durable, utilitarian, long-lasting, °tough, wear-resistant: *I need to buy a serviceable pair of hiking boots.*

servile *adj.* °submissive, subservient, °menial, craven, acquiescent, abject, cringing, slavish, °mean, fawning, deferential, mean-spirited, °vile, °low, °base, °ingratiating, °grovelling, °obsequious, toadying, toadyish, sycophantish, sycophantic, truckling, wheedling, unctuous, °slimy, °flattering, °time-serving, boot-licking, *Colloq chiefly Brit* smarmy, *US and Canadian* apple-polishing, *Slang Brit* arse-kissing, *US* ass-kissing, *Taboo slang* brown-nosing, *Brit* arse-licking, *US* ass-licking: *Victor is constantly trying to gain favour with the directors in the most servile way.*

servility *n.* submissiveness, °submission, subservience, servileness, acquiescence, abjectness, abjection, cringing, slavishness, meanness, fawning, mean-spiritedness, vileness, baseness, °grovelling, obsequiousness, obsequence, toadying, toadyism, sycophancy, sycophantism, truckling, wheedling, unctuousness, sliminess, °flattery, boot-licking, *Colloq chiefly Brit* smarminess, *US and Canadian* apple-polishing, *Slang Brit* arse-kissing, *US* ass-kissing, *Taboo slang* brown-nosing, *Brit* arse-licking, *US* ass-licking: *We are sick of the servility with which Victor treats the directors.*

servitude *n.* °bondage, °slavery, thraldom, serfdom, subjugation, enslavement, °subjection, vassalage: *They were sentenced to ten years' penal servitude.*

session *n.* **1** sitting, °seating, °assembly, °conference, °meeting, hearing: *Parliament is in session at this very moment.* **2** °term, °period: *The bill will be introduced again at the next session of Parliament.*

set *v.* **1** set down, °place, °put, °situate, °locate, °site, °plant, °position, °station, °stand, °lay, °install *or* instal, °lodge, °mount, °park, °deposit, °plump, °drop, plunk *or* plonk (down): *Please set that blue box over here.* **2** °go down, °sink, °decline, °subside: *The sun is setting.* **3** °jell *or* gel, congeal, °freeze, °solidify, °stiffen, °harden, clot, °coagulate, °thicken, °cake: *The concrete takes a long time to set in this weather.* **4** °establish, °fix, °fasten on, °appoint: *The date of the wedding has been set for May 23rd.* **5** °focus on, home *or* °zero in on, pinpoint, °pin down: *When Ivor sets his mind on doing something, it usually gets done.* **6** °adjust, °regulate, °turn, synchronize, °fix, °calibrate, °coordinate: *Set your watches to Greenwich Mean Time. Set the counter back to zero.* **7** °present, °introduce, °establish, °determine, °stipulate, °lay down, °define, °indicate, °designate, °specify; set *or* °mark off, delineate: *Who set the pattern for such behaviour? You'll have to set the rules.* **8** °prepare, set up, concoct, °lay, °arrange, °fix: *I think we ought to set a trap for the burglar.* **9** set forth, °propound, °present, °devise, °work out *or* up, °make up, °select, °choose, °decide, °settle, °establish: *Who is going to set the questions for the examination?* **10** °arrange, °lay, °spread: *If you set the table, I'll serve dinner.* **11** °adjust, °move, °tilt, °fix, °place, °position, °lodge: *He set his hat at a jaunty angle and strode out of the restaurant.* **12** ***set about***: **a** get *or* make ready, °start, °begin, get to work, set in motion, get under °way, °start the ball rolling, break the ice, °undertake, °launch, °tackle, °address oneself to, °enter upon, *Colloq* get cracking: *It's time you set about deciding what you want to do for a living.* **b** °attack, assail, °assault, °beat up: *The gang set about him with clubs.* **13** ***set against***: **a** °compare, °evaluate, °rate, °balance, °weigh, juxtapose, °contrast: *If you set his assets against his liabilities, he comes off pretty well.* **b** antagonize, set at °odds, °alienate, °divide, disunite: *They succeeded in setting brother against brother.* **14** ***set apart***: **a** °distinguish, °separate, °differentiate: *His talent for language sets him apart from the others.* **b** °reserve, °put *or* set aside, °store, earmark, °put away, °lay away, set by, °save, °keep back: *I set apart this piece of chocolate just for you.* **15** ***set aside***: **a** See **14 b,** above. **b** annul, °cancel, nullify, declare *or* render null and °void, °reverse, °repudiate, abrogate, °quash, °overturn, overrule, °discard: *The judge set aside the ruling of the lower court.* **16** ***set back***: put back, °hinder, °slow, °hold up, °retard, °delay, °impede, °obstruct, °stay, °thwart, °frustrate, °inhibit: *Completion has been set back because the materials failed to arrive.* **17** ***set down***: **a** °write (down), put in °writing, °put down, °record, °register, °mark *or* °jot down, °list: *The secretary laboriously set down every word the official said.* **b** ascribe, °assign, °attribute, °impute, °charge: *She set down her failure to win promotion to prejudice on the part of management.* **c** °put down, °land: *See if you can set the plane down in that field over there.* **18** ***set forth***: **a** °express, °voice, °propose, °propound, °state, °offer, °submit, °suggest, °broach, make a °motion, °move: *Hugo set forth various proposals for the expansion of the company.* **b** set out *or* off, °put forth *or* out, °begin, °start (out), get under °way, °go, °embark, sally forth, °push off, °depart, °leave: *After much hemming and hawing, Clive finally set forth on his big adventure.* **c** set out, °present, °declare, °describe, °propose, °state, articulate, °enunciate: *Hermione's theory is set forth in a lengthy report.* **19** ***set in***: °begin, become established, °arrive, °come: *Winter has set in quite early this year.* **20** ***set off***: **a** ignite, °kindle, detonate, °light, °touch off, trigger, °trip: *That little spark set off an explosion that destroyed the entire plant.* **b** °dramatize, °enhance, highlight, throw into °relief, °show (off), °display: *The engraving is beautifully set off by the new mat and frame.* **c** See **18 b**, above. **21** ***set on***: set upon, °attack, °assault, °pounce on *or* upon, °fall on *or* upon, °fly at: *You were set on by a pack of dogs in the park?* **22** ***set out***: **a** See **17 b** and **c,** above. **b** put out, °lay out, °arrange, °dispose, °display: *The stallholders are all setting out their wares for the jewellery fair this morning.* **23** ***set up***: **a** °build, °put up, °erect, °assemble, °construct, °raise, elevate, °put together, °arrange, °prepare: *They are setting up the Christmas displays over the weekend.* **b** °start, °begin, °initiate, °organize, °establish, °found; °finance, °fund, °invest in, °back, °subsidize: *The Crockers are setting up their third shop in Halsted. His father set him up in business.* **24** ***set upon***: °attack, °assault, °ambush, °beat up, °fall upon, set about, *Colloq* °mug: *The gang set upon him as he was getting home from work.*

—*n.* **25** °collection, °group, °combination, °number, grouping, °assortment, °selection, °arrangement, series: *Brackenhall bought a set of Hogarth etchings from the gallery.* **26** °clique, coterie, °group, °company, °circle, °ring, °crowd, °faction, °sect, °gang: *The set she associates with think nothing of flying to Rio for the weekend.* **27** °kit, °outfit, °rig; °equipment, °apparatus: *When I was ten, my father bought me a chemistry set.* **28** °setting, stage set *or* °setting, °scene, *mise en scène*, mounting, scenery: *Hunter's set for* Waiting for Godot *won a prize.*

—*adj.* **29** °fixed, established, °determined, °predetermined, arranged, prearranged, °decided, °customary, °usual, °normal, °regular, agreed, °conventional, °habitual, °definite, defined, °firm, unvarying, unvaried, unchanging, wonted, °rigid, °strict, settled, scheduled: *There is a set order in which these things are done.* **30** stereotyped, trite, hackneyed, °routine, °standard, °traditional, unchanged, unvaried, °invariable: *He made his set welcoming speech, as usual dripping with condescension, to the incoming classes.* **31** °prepared, °ready, °fit, primed: *Are you all set to go?*

set-back *n.* °hindrance, °hitch, °check, °reverse, °reversal, °impediment, °block, °obstruction, °defeat, °hold-up, °delay, °check, °rebuff, °upset; °relapse; *Colloq* hiccup: *The reduction in arts funding has resulted in some severe set-backs in certain programmes. Derek has suffered a set-back and will remain in hospital for a while.*

setting *n.* mounting, scenery, °background, backdrop, °locale, °location, surroundings, °habitat, °home, environs, °environment, °milieu, °frame, °context, °site, °placement; stage °set *or* setting, *mise en scène*, °scene: *It is quite interesting to see how the animals live in their natural setting. The setting of Hardy's novels is in the West Country.*

settle *v.* **1** °arrange, °order, °dispose, °organize, °straighten out, put in *or* into °order, °compose, °sort out, classify, °coordinate, °resolve, set to rights, °reconcile: *Ben settled his affairs before undergoing surgery.* **2** Often, ***settle on*** *or* ***upon***: °fix (on), °decide (on), °establish, °appoint, °set, °confirm, affirm, conclude, make °sure *or* °certain (of), °determine, °agree (upon *or* on), °pick, °choose, °select: *Have you been able to settle on a suitable time to visit Max and Maddy?* **3** °decide, °reconcile, °resolve, put an °end to, conclude, °clear up, °patch up, °adjust, °negotiate, mediate: *We have settled our differences.* **4** Often, ***settle down***: take up °residence, go *or* come *or* °move to, °dwell, reside, make one's °home, °abide, °remain, °stay, °live, set up °home *or* °house, put down roots, °locate, °inhabit, *US* °set up housekeeping, °locate: *They have decided to settle in Australia after George retires.* **5** Sometimes, ***settle down***: °light, alight, °land, °come down, put down, °set down, (come to) °rest *or* roost, °descend, °perch: *The butterfly settled on the tip of Alice's nose.* **6** °populate, °people, colonize, °pioneer: *That part of the country wasn't settled till late in the 19th century.* **7** Usually, ***settle down***: °calm down, °subside, °quiet down, be *or* become °tranquil, *Chiefly Brit* °quieten (down): *The class settled down and we began the lesson. I must settle down and get back to work.* **8** °calm, °quiet, soothe, °tranquillize, °relax, *Chiefly Brit* °quieten: *He drank some camomile tea to settle his nerves.* **9** °subside, °sink, °decline, °fall: *A great crack appeared in the wall when the house settled a bit.* **10** Often, ***settle up***: °pay, °square, °dispose of, °clear, °balance, liquidate, °discharge: *If you settle the bill, we can leave.* **11** Often, ***settle out***: gravitate, °sink, °fall, precipitate (out): *Stop shaking the container and let the sand settle to the bottom.* **12** °clarify, °clear: *After a few days the pond will settle.*

settlement *n.* **1** colony, outpost, °post, °camp, community, encampment, village, hamlet: *The first colonists established a small settlement on the bank of the river.* **2** colonization, settling, populating: *The settlement of the valley was mainly by Scandinavians.* **3** °agreement, °*rapprochement*, °resolution, °adjustment, elimination, °reconciliation, working-out, °accommodation, arbitration, °arrangement: *Settlement of the dispute was supervised by a union representative.* **4** °payment, defrayal, °discharge, liquidation, °satisfaction, settling, quittance, clearing, °clearance: *The settlement of our debts is of paramount importance.* **5** deciding, settling, °setting, °decision, conclusion, confirmation, affirmation, °establishment, stabilization, °determination, °agreement, °choice, °selection: *The only thing on his mind was the settlement of their holiday destination—should it be France or Thailand?*

settler *n.* colonist, frontiersman, frontierswoman, °pioneer, °immigrant: *The early settlers cleared the land for farming.*

set-up *n.* **1** °arrangement, °system, °organization, layout, regime, °structure, °make-up, °composition, framework, °frame, construction; °conditions, °circumstances: *This set-up of interlocking directorships makes it difficult to see who answers to whom and who owns what. What, exactly, is the set-up between you and Eustace?* **2** prearrangement, °trap, *Slang* °put-up job: *As soon as I saw the police car, I knew we had walked into a set-up.*

sever *v.* **1** °cut off *or* °apart *or* in two, °lop *or* °chop *or* hew *or* °hack off, °slice *or* shear off, °cleave, dock, bob, dissever, °split, °separate, °divide, disjoin, °detach, °disconnect: *The animal's foot was severed by the trap.* **2** °separate, disunite, °dissolve, °break off *or* up, °terminate, °end, °cease, °stop, °discontinue, °suspend, °abandon, put an °end to: *The final divorce decree severed us from one another once and for all.*

several *adj.* **1** some, a °few, not too *or* very °many, a °handful *or* a sprinkling *or* a °number of: *Several people asked for you at the party last night.* **2** °various, °sundry, a °variety of, °diverse, °divers, °different, °respective, °individual, °distinct, disparate, °particular, °certain, °specific, °discrete, °dissimilar: *There are several stages one must go through before reaching the end.*

severe *adj.* **1** °strict, °harsh, rigorous, austere, °hard, °stony, stony-hearted, hard-hearted, flinty, inexorable, iron-handed, °oppressive, unbending, °rigid, uncompromising, °relentless, unyielding, obdurate, pitiless, °punitive, °merciless, °unsympathetic, unfeeling, °cruel, °brutal, °mean, °savage, °inhuman, °beastly, °ruthless, °despotic, °dictatorial, °tyrannical, autocratic, °demanding, °exacting, °painstaking, °fastidious, exigent, taxing: *Nicholas Nickleby was subjected to extremely severe treatment at Dotheboys Hall. Mr Bradshaw was a severe taskmaster.* **2** °stern, °forbidding, °dour, glowering, °grave, °grim, °stiff, °strait-laced, °serious, unsmiling, °sober, °cold, °frigid, °aloof, austere: *If he so much as dropped a spoon the master would give Nicholas a severe look.* **3** °dangerous, °critical, °dreadful, °awful, life-threatening, °acute, dire; °mortal, °fatal, °terminal: *She has had a severe attack of the flu.* **4** stringent, °punitive, °harsh, °punishing, °burdensome, °tough, onerous, °grievous, °painful, Draconian *or* Draconic: *There are severe penalties for breaking the parking laws in this city.* **5** °harsh, °bitter, °cold, °inclement, °keen, °violent, °stormy, °intense, turbulent, °fierce, °wicked: *Granny couldn't live through another severe winter at Fort William.* **6** °stark, °bare, °plain, austere, °Spartan, ascetic, °primitive, °simple, °sparse, °spare, monastic, °modest, °unadorned, unembellished, °crude, undecorated, unembroidered: *The severe décor in the servants' quarters gave the appearance of a prison.*

severely *adv.* **1** acutely, °seriously, °badly, °dangerously, dreadfully; °permanently, fully, °entirely: *The accident left him severely handicapped.* **2** strictly, harshly, rigorously, austerely, oppressively, relentlessly, mercilessly, cruelly, brutally, savagely, inhumanly, tyrannically: *The boys were severely maltreated at the school.* **3** sternly, forbiddingly, dourly, gloweringly, gravely, °seriously, grimly, unsmilingly, soberly, coldly, coolly, austerely: *Mrs Gladwin regarded me severely over the top of her pince-nez.* **4** stringently, punitively, harshly, onerously, grievously, °painfully: *One is punished severely for the slightest infraction of the law.* **5** °dangerously, acutely, critically, dreadfully, °awfully; mortally, fatally, terminally: *I am afraid to say that your mother is severely ill.* **6** starkly, plainly, °barely, modestly, austerely, ascetically, monastically, primitively, °simply, crudely, sparsely, sparely: *The room is furnished a bit severely for my taste.*

severity *n.* **1** strictness, harshness, °rigour, rigorousness, austerity, hardness, flintiness, inexorability, inexorableness, stringency, °oppression, oppressiveness, rigidity, inflexibility, relentlessness, obduracy, obdurateness, pitilessness, mercilessness, cold-bloodedness, abusiveness, cruelty, brutality, meanness, savagery, inhumanity, beastliness, ruthlessness, °despotism, °tyranny, fastidiousness, exigency: *The severity of the discipline was almost unbearable.* **2** coldness, aloofness, sternness, °gravity, grimness, frigidity, austerity, °solemnity: *The severity of his look froze me to the spot.* **3** dangerousness, acuteness, seriousness, °gravity, ferocity, fierceness, °virulence, °violence, °intensity: *The severity of the fits has diminished since we put the patient on new medication.* **4** stringency, punitiveness, °punishment, harshness, onerousness, grievousness, painfulness, burdensomeness, oppressiveness: *The severity of the sentence is not inappropriate to the heinousness of the crime.* **5** harshness, inclemency, °violence, storminess, °intensity, ferocity, fierceness, °fury, furiousness, tempestuousness: *The severity of the weather has interfered with our maintenance of the electrical power lines.* **6** plainness, starkness, austerity, asceticism, bareness, modesty, °simplicity, primitiveness, spareness, sparseness, monasticism, crudeness: *The severity of the cells at the monastery was equalled by the austerity of the regimen.*

sew *v.* sew up, stitch, darn, °mend, °repair; sew on, °attach, °fasten; °tack, baste, hem: *Would you sew up a hole in my sweater for me and, while you're at it, would you mind sewing a button on my shirt?*

sex *n.* **1** gender: *It is difficult to determine the sex of some of the lower animals.* **2** sexual °intercourse *or* relations, coitus, coition, mating, copulation, (sexual) congress *or* °union, intimacy, lovemaking, making °love, coupling, *Colloq* making out, going to bed, shacking up, *Slang* having it away, *Taboo slang* screwing, shafting, shagging, fucking, *Chiefly Brit* bonking: *They feel that there is too much sex and violence on television these days.*

sexual *adj.* **1** sex, reproductive, genital, procreative *or* procreant, progenitive, propagative: *Their current project is an investigation of sexual behaviour in young adults.* **2** °sensual, °sensuous, °erotic, °carnal, fleshly, °voluptuous, libidinous, °earthy, bodily, °physical, °lustful, °animal, *Colloq* °sexy: *They have a deep sexual attraction to one another.*

sexy *adj.* **1** °erotic, arousing, °exciting, °sensual, °sensuous, °seductive, °suggestive, °provocative, °inviting, alluring, bedroom, °flirtatious, appealing, fascinating, °striking, °tempting, captivating, °enchanting, °stunning, *Colloq* come-hither: *She thought he had a sexy smile.* **2** sex, °dirty, °pornographic, °obscene, °filthy, smutty, °lewd, °foul, °lascivious, °indecent, °explicit, °gross, X-rated, °vulgar, °rude, °coarse, °off colour, °risqué, titillating, °bawdy, ribald, °lusty, °immodest, °rough, indelicate, °suggestive, °unseemly, °improper, indecorous, °naughty, °shameless, *Slang* raunchy: *They sat there leering over a sexy magazine.*

shabby *adj.* **1** °worn, °dingy, faded, °worn out, °threadbare, tatty, °tattered, frayed, raggedy, °ragged, scruffy, °dilapidated, °ratty, °dirty, °bedraggled, °mangy, °run-down, °seedy, (much) the worse for wear, *Brit* down at °heel, *US* down at the °heel(s), *Colloq* grubby, scrubby, gungy, °tacky, *US* grungy: *He was wearing a shabby suit and down-at-heel shoes.* **2** °poor, °peremptory, unpleasant, °nasty, °disagreeable, °mean, °contemptuous, demeaning, grudging, ungenerous, °impolite, °rude, unfriendly, unhelpful, °shoddy, ungentlemanly, unladylike, °dishonourable, °unworthy, °scurvy, *Colloq* °rotten: *We were subjected to very shabby treatment at the office where we applied for work.* **3** °dilapidated, °tumbledown, broken-down, shattered, battered, °run-down, °ramshackle, °seedy, neglected, °dirty, squalid, slum-like, slummy, *Colloq* beat-up, crummy: *Sam lives in a shabby little house near the canal.* **4** °mean, stingy, ungenerous, niggardly, °contemptible, °low, °lowly, °base, mean-spirited, °despicable, °vile, uncouth, discreditable, °inferior, °disreputable, °infamous, °abominable, °dishonourable, ignoble, °atrocious, ignominious, odious, detestable, opprobrious: *The shabby apology for their behaviour fell on deaf ears.*

shack *n.* °hut, °hovel, shanty, °cabin, lean-to, *Colloq* °dump: *The shack was built out of scrap lumber and cardboard boxes.*

shackle *n.* **1** Often, ***shackles***: fetter(s), leg-iron(s), °chains, iron(s), bilboes, gyve(s), ball and °chain, °manacle(s), handcuff(s), °restraint(s), °bond(s), °trammel(s), *Colloq* cuff(s), *Slang* bracelet(s), *Brit* darbies: *When those shackles went round his ankles, he thought he'd never see them taken off.* **2** Usually, ***shackles***: °restriction, °restraint, °deterrent, °impediment, °check, °obstacle, °obstruction, °barrier, °hindrance, °bar, °encumbrance: *When shall we throw off the shackles of ignorant prejudice and see a truly free world?*
—*v.* **3** °chain, fetter, °manacle, handcuff, °bind, °restrain, °tie, °secure, truss, pinion, °tether: *He was shackled to the mast and whipped for disobedience. In this glorious spring weather I resent being shackled to a desk.* **4** °restrain, °hold back, °check, °deter, °hinder, °discourage, °hobble, °handicap, °restrict, °curb, °rein, °bridle, °control, fetter, °inhibit, °limit: *Freedom of expression has been shackled during all those years of oppression.*

shade *n.* **1** °shadow, shadiness, dimness, duskiness, semi-darkness, gloominess, murkiness, °dusk, °gloom, murk, darkness, °obscurity, *Literary* shades: *We rested in the shade of an old oak to get out of the hot sun.* **2** °tint, tinge, °tone, °colour, °hue, °intensity: *The curtains should be of a lighter shade to match the wallpaper.* **3** °hint, intimation, tinge, °suggestion, °modicum, sprinkling, soupçon, °trace, °suspicion, undertone, °overtone, °touch, °speck, °dash, nuance, atom, °grain, scintilla, iota, °jot *or* tittle: *Did I detect a shade of sarcasm in your voice, Aloysius?* **4** °ghost, °spectre, apparition, °phantom, phantasm, °spirit, wraith, °vision, banshee, *Colloq* spook: *As night came on, horrifying shades took shape amongst the leafless trees.* **5** °blind, window-blind, curtain, venetian °blind; lampshade; °screen, °cover, covering, °protection, °veil, awning, canopy, °shield, °shelter, °umbrella, parasol: *We need shades to reduce the glare of the light. We had only a light tent as a shade against the broiling sun.* **6** fraction, hair's breadth, °bit, °hair, *Colloq* smidgen *or* smidgin: *Try moving the picture a shade to the left.* **7** °variation, °variety, nuance, °degree: *Do you really think his approval would make a shade of difference to me?* **8** ***put (someone) in*** *or* ***into the shade***: °overshadow, °exceed, °surpass, °outstrip, outclass, °eclipse, outshine, °best, °better, °beat, put to °shame, outplay, outperform, °outdo, *Colloq* run rings *or* circles around, °show up: *Your record time in the 1000-metre put other contenders in the shade.* **9** ***shades***: sun-glasses: *Take off those shades so I can see what you are thinking.*
—*v.* **10** °screen, °protect, °shield, °shelter, °cover: *You should shade your eyes from the direct sunlight.* **11** darken, °opaque, black out, °blacken: *She shaded in parts of the diagram to give a better effect.* **12** °dim, °shadow, °veil, °blot out, cloud, °conceal, °hide, °obscure, °shroud, °screen, °mask, °camouflage, °disguise: *The house is shaded from view by trees on the south side.*

shadow *n.* **1** darkness, °gloom, dimness, °dusk, °obscurity: *In the shadow I could make out the dim outline of a figure.* **2** °cover, °screen, covering, °shield, °veil, curtain, °protection, concealment: *He stole past the sentry under the shadow of darkness.* **3** °hint, intimation, °suggestion, °suspicion, °trace, °vestige; °remnant: *I do not have the slightest shadow of doubt that she is telling the truth. Martin is merely a shadow of his former robust self.* **4** cloud, °blight, °curse: *A terrible shadow has fallen upon the family name.* **5** See **shade, 4,** above. **6** °companion, alter ego, °comrade, *Colloq* sidekick, crony, °chum, (°bosom) °pal, *US* (°bosom) buddy: *Boswell was Johnson's shadow for almost twenty years.*
—*v.* **7** °follow, °trail, °track, dog, °stalk, °pursue, °trace, *Colloq* °tail, *US and Canadian* bird-dog: *For a month detectives shadowed the suspect.*

shadowy *adj.* **1** °dark, °shady, bowery, °leafy, shaded, °gloomy, °dusky, °dim, *Literary* bosky: *The hotel bar was a shadowy place with pink lights on the tables.* **2** °vague, °dim, °dark, °obscure, °faint, °indistinct, °indefinite, °hazy, ill-defined, unclear, indeterminate: *The photograph was too shadowy for us to identify anyone in it. The years before he came to London are part of his shadowy past.* **3** °spectral, °ghostly, °phantom, phantasmal, wraithlike, phantasmagoric(al), °illusory, °dreamlike, °imaginary, °visionary, chimerical, hallucinatory, °unreal, unsubstantial, °fleeting, impalpable, transitory, ethereal, °immaterial: *He saw shadowy figures lurking near the tomb. The plaintiff's case is shadowy, to say the least.* **4** See **shady, 2,** below.

shady *adj.* **1** See **shadowy, 1,** above. **2** °indistinct, °indefinite, °questionable, °doubtful, °uncertain, °unreliable, °suspicious, °suspect, dubious, °shifty, °disreputable; °devious, °tricky, °slippery, underhand(ed), unethical, °unscrupulous, °dishonourable, °dishonest, *Colloq* °fishy, °crooked, °bent, not (strictly) kosher: *The minister's shady past will be revealed in the next issue of* Tribune. *She got involved with some shady character who had just come out of prison.*

shaft *n.* **1** °pole, °rod, °staff, °stick, °stem, shank, °handle, helve; °pillar, column, °post, stanchion, °upright: *The shaft of the harpoon splintered as the whale suddenly plunged downwards. These shafts help support the upper storey.* **2** °beam, °ray, °gleam, °streak, pencil: *At exactly noon on the winter solstice a shaft of light struck the altar at the centre of the stone circle.* **3** °thrust, barb, °sting, dart, °gibe *or* jibe, *Colloq* °slap (in the face), °knock, °put-down: *After the episode in the restaurant, Barbara had to suffer the shafts of her colleagues and their teasing.* **4** mine-shaft, °tunnel, adit, °well, °pit; air-shaft, duct, flue: *How many men went down the shaft in the first shift? The screen over the ventilating shaft must be kept clean.*

shaggy *adj.* °hairy, °woolly, °unkempt, unshorn, uncut, hirsute, dishevelled, matted, °untidy: *They had a large black dog with shaggy hair and a great bushy tail.*

shake *v.* **1** °quiver, °quake, °shudder, waver, wobble, °tremble, °shiver: *The poor child is shaking from the cold.* **2** wiggle, °wriggle, °squirm, shimmy, twitch, joggle, °jiggle, waggle, °sway, °swing, °roll, °bump, °grind, °vibrate, °oscillate, °pulsate, °gyrate: *When Lola shakes her hips the strongest men have been known to weaken.* **3** °weaken, undermine, °impair, °harm, °damage, °discourage; disenchant, °disappoint,

disaffect: *The incident shook my faith in the political party I had supported all my voting life.* **4** °wave, brandish, °flourish, °display, °show off, °parade, °exhibit, vaunt, waggle, °flap, °flutter: *It was thrilling to see the once-banned flag being shaken under the noses of the deposed leaders.* **5** Often, ***shake up***: °agitate, °stir (up), °mix (up); °upset, °distress, °frighten, °scare, °shock, °disturb, °unnerve, unsettle, disconcert, °discomfit, °worry, °fluster, disquiet, confound, °confuse, °perplex, °puzzle, *Colloq* °rattle, get to, *US* °throw (for a loop): *Shake the medicine before taking it. I was really shaken by the news that Sheila had quit.* **6** ***shake down***: **a** °break in, °condition, °test, °prove, *Colloq* debug: *We shook down the submarine on a 30-day cruise.* **b** °blackmail, °extort *or* °extract *or* °squeeze *or* wrest money from, °hold up, °squeeze, °threaten: *The shopkeepers were so frightened that the gang easily shook them down.* **7** ***shake off***: get °rid of, °discard, dislodge, °drop, °brush off, °elude, °evade, °lose, °throw off, °rid oneself of, give the °slip to: *We finally shook off our pursuers: at last we felt safe.*
—*n.* **8** shaking, quivering, quaking, shuddering, wavering, wobbling, trembling, shivering, °quiver, °quake, °shudder, waver, wobble, °tremble, °shiver, wiggle, °wriggle, twitch, joggle, °jiggle, °sway, °swing, °roll, gyration: *The dog gave a shake of its tail and bounded towards them.* **9** agitating, °agitation, shaking, stirring (up), °jolt, °jar, jarring, jounce, jolting, jouncing: *Give him a good shake and he'll wake up.* **10** ***the shakes***: trembling, tremors, delirium tremens, *Colloq* D.T.'s: *She's had so much to drink that she's got the shakes.*

shake-up *n.* reorganization, rearrangement, °overhaul, °revamp, restructuring, rehabilitation, makeover, realignment: *With new owners you can expect a complete shake-up of top management.*

shaky *adj.* **1** °uncertain, wobbly, °unstable, °precarious, °unsound, °flimsy, °weak, unsteady, unsupported, unsubstantiated, undependable, °unreliable, °tenuous, untrustworthy, dubious, °questionable, °doubtful, *Colloq* iffy: *The evidence against him is very shaky indeed.* **2** wobbly, wobbling, °unstable, °precarious, °dilapidated, °ramshackle, on its last °legs, °decrepit, falling down *or* °apart, °rickety, °flimsy, unsteady, °insecure, °unsound, unsubstantial, °insubstantial, °feeble: *Surely, you can't expect that shaky old chair to support your weight!*

shallow *adj.* **1** °surface, °skin-deep, °superficial, °thin, °empty, °flimsy, trivial, unimportant, °slight, °frivolous, °idle, °foolish: *If you read only comic books, your thoughts are bound to be shallow.*
—*n.* **2** Often, ***shallows***: shoal(s), sand °bar, sandbank, bank, shelf: *This boat draws too much water to go fishing in the shallows.*

sham *n.* **1** °fake, °fraud, °counterfeit, °imitation, °hoax, humbug, °pretence, °forgery, °copy, imposture, *Colloq* °phoney *or US also* phony: *Their call for reform is a sham, as they have no intention of disturbing the status quo.*
—*adj.* **2** °fake, °fraudulent, °counterfeit, °imitation, paste, simulated, °false, make-believe, °fictitious, made-up, °bogus, °spurious, °mock, ersatz, °artificial, °synthetic, *Colloq* °phoney *or US also* phony, pseudo: *He sat there feigning interest, a sham smile on his face.*

shambles *n.* °chaos, devastation, °mess, °disaster, Augean stables, pigsty, °muddle, pigpen: *I can't find anything in this shambles. The campaign degenerated into a complete shambles.*

shambling *adj.* shuffling, lumbering, dragging, scuttling, °awkward, °clumsy, lurching, unsteady, faltering: *The old beggar hobbled off with a shambling gait.*

shame *n.* **1** °embarrassment, °humiliation, mortification, chagrin, ignominy, shamefacedness, loss of °face, abashment: *Watts felt abysmal shame at being discovered stealing from petty cash.* **2** °disgrace, ignominy, °dishonour, disrepute, °degradation, opprobrium, vilification, calumniation, °infamy, obloquy, odium, °contempt, °scandal, denigration, loss of °face, defamation, °discredit, disesteem, °disfavour, derogation, disparagement: *To think that one knight's single act of cowardice in 1249 could have brought such shame to all his descendants.* **3** °pity, °calamity, °disaster, °catastrophe; °outrage: *What a shame that Gerry failed the exam!* **4** °humility, modesty, (sense of) decency *or* °decorum *or* °propriety, respectability, decorousness, diffidence, shyness, coyness, prudishness, timidity, shamefacedness: *The people who wear bathing suits like that obviously have no shame at all.* **5** ***put to shame***: **a** °surpass, °eclipse, outclass, °overshadow, cast into the °shade, °outdo, °outstrip, outshine, °show up: *Cochrane put his opponents to shame when they failed to score a single point against him.* **b** See **8**, below.
—*v.* **6** °embarrass, °humiliate, °mortify, °humble, chagrin, disconcert, discountenance, °put down, bring down, abash, °chasten, *Colloq* bring (someone) down a °peg, °suppress, °subdue: *He hated the teacher because she had shamed him in front of his friends.* **7** coerce, °force, °drive, °bully, °push; °embarrass, °humiliate, °mortify, °humble: *The other boys shamed him into admitting that he had done it.* **8** °disgrace, °embarrass, °dishonour, °scandalize, calumniate, °degrade, °debase, defame, °discredit, °stigmatize; °smear, °blacken, °stain, °taint, besmirch, °tarnish: *I am sure, son, that nothing you ever do would shame the family or me.*

shamefaced *adj.* **1** °bashful, °shy, °modest, self-effacing, diffident, °timid, °meek, °coy, °sheepish, timorous: *He felt shamefaced as a schoolboy when they awarded him a medal for bravery.* **2** °ashamed, shamed, abashed, °embarrassed, humiliated, dishonoured, mortified, humbled, chastened, chagrined, uncomfortable, discomfited, °remorseful, red-faced: *Shamefaced, she finally admitted the truth about where she had been.*

shameful *adj.* °disgraceful, °dishonourable, °base, low, °mean, °vile, °degrading, °indecent, inglorious, °deplorable, discreditable, °corrupt, °disreputable, °infamous, ignominious, humiliating, °embarrassing, mortifying, humbling, chastening, discomfiting, shaming, blameworthy, °scandalous, °outrageous, unprincipled: *Quentin was known for his shameful behaviour both at school and in the army.*

shameless *adj.* °wild, °flagrant, unreserved, °uncontrolled, °immodest, °wanton, indecorous, °indecent, °rude, °improper, °forward, °bold, unembarrassed, unblushing, °audacious, °brazen, °brash, °unabashed, unashamed, °impudent, °shocking, °outrageous: *He was roundly condemned for his shameless neglect of his responsibilities. Her behaviour was shameless, even wanton.*

shape *n.* **1** °form, °figure, °build, °body, °physique; lines, °profile, °silhouette, contours: *I've never heard anyone complain about Marilyn Monroe's shape.* **2** °form, °pattern, configuration, °structure, °aspect: *The discussion is on the shape of things to come in the double-glazing trade. The new swimming-pool will be in the shape of a figure of eight.* **3** °form: *Gradually, the shopping mall began to take shape.* **4** °state, °condition, fettle, °status, (°state of) °health, °order, °trim: *When I saw Wayne yesterday, he seemed in very good shape indeed.* **5** °guise, °disguise, °form, °appearance, °likeness, °image: *Zeus visited Danäe in the shape of a golden shower, and fathered Perseus on her.*
—*v.* **6** °form, °fashion, °mould, °cast, °make, °model, °sculpture, sculpt; °cut, °carve, hew, °hack, °trim: *Using primitive tools, they were able to shape the clay into bowls. The topiary shrubs were shaped into the forms of birds.* **7** °determine, give °form to, °control, °govern, °regulate, °affect, °condition, °influence, °decree, °frame, °define,: *There are many factors that shape our future.* **8** °word, °express, °embody in words, °put, °formulate, °form: *Perhaps you could shape your question differently.* **9** °change, °modify, remodel, °accommodate, °fit, °adapt, °adjust: *The box was shaped especially for this bottle.* **10** ***shape up***: **a** take °form, take shape, °develop, evolve, °proceed: *The plan is shaping up very nicely.* **b** °conform, °improve,

°progress, go *or* move *or* °come along, show °improvement, °come up to snuff; behave better: *Those who cannot shape up will have to ship out.*

shapeless *adj.* **1** amorphous, formless, °nebulous, unformed, °indefinite, unstructured, °vague: *Sculptors start with a shapeless mass of clay.* **2** unshapely, °deformed, °misshapen, distorted, twisted, °bent, battered: *The wreckage was a shapeless tangle of steel and mortar.*

shapely *adj.* curvaceous, °comely, well-proportioned, °graceful, °neat, well turned out, good-looking, °pleasing; °voluptuous, *Colloq* °sexy: *That slinky black dress certainly sets off her shapely figure to advantage.*

share *n.* **1** °portion, °allotment, °division, apportionment, allocation, °ration, appropriation, dispensation, °allowance, °part, due, °percentage, °interest, dividend, °quota, °helping, serving, *Colloq* °cut: *Each of us is entitled to a share in the profits. We made sure that all participants got their shares.* **2** °interest, °piece, °part, °stake, °equity, °slice: *Do you own any shares in the stock market? My share in United Telephone is worth twice what I paid for it.*
—*v.* **3** share out, °divide up, °allot, apportion, allocate, °ration, °appropriate, °share in, °split, °partition, °parcel *or* °deal *or* °dole out, °pay out: *Ownership in the company is shared equally among the employees. Let's just take one car, and share the expenses.*

sharp *adj.* **1** °acute, °keen; razor-sharp, knife-like, knife-edged, sharpened; °pointed, needle-sharp: *How do you keep the telescope in sharp focus? You need an extremely sharp knife for boning fish. This pencil isn't sharp enough.* **2** °abrupt, °sudden, °precipitous, °sheer, vertical, °marked: *Just round the corner is a sharp dip in the road. There was a sharp rise in prices on the London Stock Exchange today.* **3** °keen, keen-witted, keen-minded, sharp-witted, °shrewd, °intelligent, °smart, °alert, °bright, quick, °agile, °astute, °clever, on the qui vive, °penetrating, °observant: *Penny has a very sharp mind and a good eye for detail.* **4** °caustic, °bitter, °biting, acrid, °hot, °spicy, °pungent, piquant, tangy, °harsh, °sour, acid, acidulous, °tart: *That lemon sorbet is a little too sharp for my taste.* **5** acid, acidulous, acerbic, vitriolic, acrimonious, °cutting, piquant, °biting, °bitter, °unkind, °strict, °hurtful, °spiteful, °virulent, °sarcastic, °sardonic, °trenchant, °severe, °scathing, malicious, °nasty, °malignant, °venomous, °poisonous: *How does one escape the sharp comments of the critics? She was unprepared for the sharp exchange between the guests on her chat show.* **6** °clever, °shrewd, °artful, °crafty, °sly, cunning, °foxy, °calculating, °unscrupulous, °dishonest, *Colloq* °sneaky, fly: *There is evidence that the stock manipulators were engaged in very sharp practice.* **7** high-pitched, °shrill, °penetrating, °piercing, °strident, °harsh, ear-splitting, °loud: *Jane gave a sharp cry when she felt the ice break under her feet.* **8** °poignant, °severe, °cutting, °intense, °sudden, °piercing, °extreme, °acute, °fierce: *Complaining of a sharp pain in his chest, he fell down.* **9** °chic, °dapper, °spruce, °stylish, °smart, °fashionable, °dressy, *Colloq* °snappy, natty, classy, °nifty, °swell, °swanky: *If you want to see the latest collection of sharp clothes, go to the disco.*
—*adv.* **10** °sharply, °precisely, °exactly, punctually, on the °dot, *Colloq* on the button, *US* on the nose: *Our appointment was for seven o'clock sharp.* **11** °sharply, °suddenly, abruptly: *I was pulled up sharp by her mention of the Black Rose.* **12** °sharply, alertly, attentively, vigilantly, watchfully, carefully: *Listen sharp to what I tell you.*

sharpen *v.* hone, °grind, strop, °whet: *Of what use is a knife if you don't sharpen it periodically?*

sharp-eyed *adj.* sharp-sighted, °eagle-eyed, hawk-eyed, lynx-eyed, gimlet-eyed, keen-sighted, wide °awake, °wakeful, watchful, °observant, (on the) °alert, on the qui vive, °wary, circumspect, Argus-eyed, °cautious, °careful: *It takes quite a sharp-eyed person to check the accuracy of these circuits.*

sharply *adv.* **1** °severely, sternly, harshly, cuttingly, acerbically, peremptorily, angrily, strictly, °firmly: *Her teacher sharply rebuked Hilary for smiling.* **2** °suddenly, °quickly, abruptly, precipitously, precipitately: *Prices increased sharply for the third day in succession.* **3** acutely, distinctly, °definitely, definitively: *These new cameras automatically remain sharply focused on the object.*

shatter *v.* **1** °disintegrate, °burst, °pulverize, °shiver, smash, °demolish, °break (to smithereens), °splinter, °fragment, °fracture, °dash to pieces: *If you hadn't caught the vase, it would have shattered into a million pieces.* **2** °destroy, °ruin, °devastate, °wreck, °dash, °crush, °demolish, torpedo, °undermine, °blast: *Any dreams he might have had of being published were shattered by the rejection letter.* **3** °upset, °disturb, °perturb, °trouble, °unnerve, °overcome, °overwhelm, °crush, °devastate, °depress, deject, °rattle, °shake (up), unsettle, °agitate, confound, °confuse, stupefy, °daze, °stun, °paralyse, *Colloq* °throw: *He was shattered by the news of Mill's death.*

shave *v.* **1** shear (off), °cut (off), °trim, °clip, crop, °snip off, °remove: *He made a mistake in shaving off his beard, as it hid his weak chin.* **2** °pare, °scrape, °plane, °whittle: *If you shave just a hair off this side, it will fit into the hole.*
—*n.* **3** ***close shave***: °narrow °escape, *Colloq* °narrow *or* °near squeak, *US* squeaker: *That was a close shave!—You almost fell out the window!*

shed[1] *n.* lean-to, °shelter, °structure, °addition, penthouse, °hut, °shack, °stall, °booth, °pen, cote, hutch: *The tools are in the shed alongside the barn.*

shed[2] *v.* **1** °spill: *Much blood has been shed in the name of freedom.* **2** °shine, °spread, °scatter, °throw, °cast, let fall, °impart, °release, °focus, °pour forth, °radiate: *Can you shed a little light on a matter that has puzzled me for years?* **3** °pour *or* °stream *or* °flow *or* °surge *or* °spill (out *or* forth), °discharge, °emanate, °emit, °drop; exude, °ooze, °weep: *The clouds shed their snow and the world below turned white. Don't shed any tears over me.* **4** °cast off, doff, °drop, °abandon; moult, defoliate, desquamate, °peel (off), °flake (off): *The trees shed their leaves. She rushed into the bathroom, shedding her clothes as she went.*

sheen *n.* °shine, °gleam, °polish, °lustre, shininess, burnish, brightness, °gloss, °glow, glimmer, °shimmer, °radiance, glint, °dazzle: *The sheen of the horse's coat glistened in the sunlight.*

sheepish *adj.* **1** °timid, °withdrawn, °passive, docile, °obedient, compliant, sheeplike, manipulable, °tractable, °pliable, °meek, amenable: *Dashworth might seem sheepish but he doesn't like to be bullied.* **2** See **shamefaced,** above.

sheer *adj.* **1** °steep, °precipitous, °abrupt, °perpendicular, °bluff, vertical: *There is a sheer drop of 2000 feet to the valley below.* **2** °absolute, °unmitigated, °unqualified, °downright, °out-and-out, unalloyed, unadulterated, °pure, unmixed, °plain, °simple, °rank, °total, °complete, arrant, °thorough, thoroughgoing, utter: *Johnson said that he had got his definition of 'pastern' wrong out of 'sheer ignorance'.* **3** °transparent, °see-through, °thin, diaphanous, °filmy, gauzy, gossamer, translucent, peekaboo: *Kathryn was wearing the sheer nightgown he had given her for her birthday.*

sheet *n.* **1** bed-sheet, crib-sheet, fitted sheet, flat sheet, *US* contour sheet: *How often do you change the sheets on your bed?* **2** leaf, folio, °page: *He tore a sheet of paper from the notebook.* **3** °pane, panel, °plate, °slab: *The desk has a sheet of glass on top for protection.* **4** lamina, lamination, layer, °stratum, °veneer, membrane: *Plywood is made up of a number of thin sheets of pressed wood bonded together for strength.* **5** °area, °expanse, °stretch, layer, °film, °coat, coating, covering, blanket, °cover, °surface, °skin, °veneer: *The sheet of ice on the road made driving hazardous.* **6** newspaper, °journal, °paper, tabloid, gazette, daily, weekly, monthly, *Colloq* °rag: *Have you got a copy of the sheet that published the article about you?*

shell *n.* **1** cartridge, °projectile, °shot: *We huddled in the foxhole as the shells whistled overhead.* **2** °exterior, °outside, façade, framework, °frame, chassis, externals, skeleton, °hull: *After the earthquake, only the shell of the building was left standing.*
—*v.* **3** shuck, husk, °peel, °hull, excorticate, decorticate: *Would you mind shelling the peas while I peel the potatoes?* **4** °fire on *or* upon, °bombard, barrage, °attack, °bomb, blitz, cannonade, *Slang Brit* prang: *The enemy shelled our position relentlessly.* **5** ***shell out***: °pay out, °give out, disburse, °spend, °expend, °hand over, °hand out, *Colloq* °lay out, fork out, dish out, *Chiefly US* ante up: *I had to shell out a month's salary for that suit.*

shelter *n.* **1** °protection, °cover, °refuge, asylum, °sanctuary, haven, °safety, °security: *During the hailstorm, we sought shelter in a cave.* **2** °cover, covering, concealment, °screen, °umbrella: *Under the shelter of a moonless night, they stole quietly past the guards.* **3** dwelling-place, habitation, °home, °dwelling, °housing, °accommodation: *He feels that everyone is entitled to food, clothing, and shelter.*
—*v.* **4** °protect, °screen, °shield, °safeguard, °guard, °keep, °secure, °harbour: *The parapet sheltered the guards from the icy wind.* **5** seek *or* take °refuge *or* shelter, °hole up, *Colloq* °lie *or* °lay low: *Mike sheltered in a mountain hut until the hue and cry died down.*

shelve *v.* °postpone, °defer, °put off *or* aside *or* on ice *or* on the shelf, pigeon-hole, °lay aside, hold in °abeyance, *US* °table: *We will have to shelve this matter until we have more information.*

shepherd *v.* °lead, convoy, °escort, °conduct, °guide, usher, °take, °pursue: *I want you, personally, to shepherd Miss Jones through the plant. As this project requires special care, I shall shepherd it through personally.*

shibboleth *n.* °password, catchword, catch-phrase, buzz-word, °byword, watchword, °jargon: *As Simon knew none of the shibboleths of teenagers' slang, he remained an outsider to his classmates.*

shield *n.* **1** °protection, °guard, °safeguard, °defence, °screen, °bulwark, °shelter: *Education is a poor shield against poverty.*
—*v.* **2** °protect, °guard, °safeguard, °keep, °defend, °screen, °shelter: *The mother bear will shield the cubs from harm or die in the attempt.*

shift *v.* **1** °move, °change position; °edge, budge, relocate, rearrange, °transpose, °switch: *Shift the picture slightly to the left. Marla shifted over closer to me on the bench. I almost broke my leg because you shifted the chair as I was about to sit on it.* **2** Usually, ***shift for (oneself)***: °manage, °succeed, °make do, °look after, take °care of, °get *or* °scrape by *or* along, °fend for (oneself), °make it, paddle one's own canoe: *Cyril prefers to live alone and shift for himself.* **3** °sell, °market, move: *The object of advertising is to shift merchandise.*
—*n.* **4** hours, °stint, °schedule; workforce, relay, °crew, cadre, °staff, workers, °squad, °team, °corps, °group, °party, °gang: *I prefer to work the morning shift. The night shift comes on at 1600.* **5** °change, °movement, °switch, °transfer, °swerve, deflection, veer: *Owing to a wind shift, it became impossible to manoeuvre among the rocks.* **6** smock, chemise, muumuu; caftan *or* kaftan: *A light cotton shift is the most comfortable thing to wear in such scorching weather.*

shiftless *adj.* unambitious, °lazy, °indolent, uninspired, unmotivated, °idle, °lackadaisical, °irresponsible, uncaring, unenterprising, °aimless, °slothful, otiose, °ineffective, ne'er-do-well, °good-for-nothing, fainéant, pococurante: *He calls Geoff a shiftless vagabond, virtually a tautology.*

shifty *adj.* °tricky, °artful, °shrewd, canny, cunning, °foxy, °wily, °sharp, °devious, °slick, °evasive, °smooth, °slippery, °scheming, °designing, conniving, °calculating, underhand(ed), conspiratorial, treacherous, °traitorous, °deceitful, deceiving, duplicitous, °two-faced, Janus-faced, °dishonest, °crooked, untrustworthy, *Colloq* °bent: *The shifty scoundrel gave me a bad cheque and did a moonlight flit.*

shilly-shally *v.* hem and haw, dilly-dally, teeter-totter, °see-saw, yo-yo, vacillate, waver, °alternate, °fluctuate, dither, falter, tergiversate, *Brit* haver, hum and haw, *Scots* swither; °delay, °hesitate, °dawdle: *Stop shilly-shallying and decide whether you want chocolate or strawberry!*

shimmer *v.* **1** °shine, °gleam, °glow, glimmer, glint, °glisten, °ripple, °flicker: *The desert shimmered like a lake under the relentless sun.*
—*n.* **2** shimmering, °shine, °gleam, °glow, glimmer, glint, °gloss, °flicker, °light: *As Julia slunk up to the microphone, the spotlight picked up the shimmer from her black satin gown.*

shin *v.* Usually, ***shin up***: °climb, clamber up, °scramble up, °scale, *US* shinny up: *The lad shinned up the flag-pole carrying the banner.*

shine *v.* **1** °gleam, °glow, °shimmer, °radiate, °beam, °glare, °flare, °glisten, °glitter, coruscate, °twinkle, °sparkle, scintillate, glint, °flash, °flicker: *The light of a candle shone from her window. The stars are shining brightly. I want that brass polished till it shines.* **2** °polish, burnish, °rub (up *or* down), buff, °brush, °brighten: *You'd best shine your shoes before going for the job interview.* **3** °excel, °surpass, °stand out, outshine, be °outstanding *or* °pre-eminent *or* °excellent *or* °prominent *or* °conspicuous: *She had shone at tennis from a very early age, and first entered Wimbledon when she was twelve.*
—*n.* **4** °gleam, °glow, °shimmer, °sparkle, brightness, °radiance, °gloss, °lustre, °sheen, °glaze, patina: *That shine was achieved with a little wax and elbow-grease.* **5** ***take a shine to***: °like, be attracted to, take a °fancy to, °fancy: *Her Great Dane has taken a shine to me and likes to sit on my lap.*

shiny *adj.* gleaming, °glowing, shimmering, °glossy, shimmery, °lustrous, °glassy, °radiant, °bright, beaming, glistening, °polished, burnished, glittering, °dazzling, coruscating, °twinkling, sparkling, °scintillating, glinting, flashing, °flashy, flickering, lambent, fulgent: *She loves riding about in her shiny new car.*

ship *n.* **1** °vessel, (ocean *or* passenger) liner, steamer, wind-jammer, cutter: *The statue is dedicated to the men who go down to the sea in ships.*
—*v.* **2** °send, °move, ferry, °transport, °deliver, °carry, °dispatch *or* despatch, °freight, °haul, °truck, °cart: *You need a specialized company that ships computers and other delicate equipment.* **3** ***ship out***: °leave, °depart, °embark, set °sail, °take off, °get out, °quit, *Slang* scram: *You'll ship out if you know what's good for you.*

shipshape *adj.* °neat, °trim, °spotless, °orderly, Bristol fashion, spick and °span, °tidy: *Pick up your clothes and make this room shipshape at once!*

shirk *v.* °avoid, °evade, °shun, °dodge, °get out of, °shrink from, *Colloq* °duck (out of), *Brit* skive, *Military Brit* scrimshank, *US* gold brick: *Stop shirking your responsibilities and get to work! Is Callum shirking again?*

shiver[1] *v.* **1** °shake, °quake, °tremble, °shudder, °quiver: *We sat in our wet clothes, shivering in the cold. The old shack shivered in the wind.* **2** °vibrate, luff, °flap, °flutter, °chatter, °rattle, °shake, wallop: *The sails shivered violently in the stiff breeze.*
—*n.* **3** °shake, °quake, °tremble, °shudder, °quiver, °thrill, *frisson*, trembling, tremor, °flutter: *She gave a little shiver and then snuggled into my arms.* **4** ***the shivers***: trembling, shivering, goose-pimples *or* goose bumps, *Colloq* the shakes, *US* the chills: *He's had malaria and occasionally gets the shivers. Those horror films give me the shivers.*

shiver[2] *v.* °shatter, °fragment, °splinter, °disintegrate, °rupture, °explode, implode, smash (to smithereens), °crash: *The light-bulb fell and shivered into a million fragments.*

shock *v.* **1** °startle, °surprise, °stagger, °jar, °jolt, °shake (up), °stun, °numb, °paralyse, °daze, stupefy, °dumbfound *or* dumfound, °bowl over, °appal, °astonish, °astound, °frighten, °scare, °petrify, traumatize, °horrify, °outrage, °disgust, °nauseate, °repel, °revolt, °sicken, °upset, disquiet, °disturb, °perturb, discompose, unsettle, *Colloq* °throw, *US* °throw for a loop, flabbergast, give (someone) a °turn: *He shocked us when he announced his resignation. We were shocked to learn of the train wreck.*
—*n.* **2** trauma, °stupor, paralysis, °prostration, °breakdown, °collapse, nervous °exhaustion: *He is in a state of shock after the accident.* **3** °surprise, thunderbolt, °bolt from the blue, °bombshell, °revelation, shocker, eye-opener, °jolt: *It came as a shock to learn whom I had been talking to so casually. The death of her husband was a terrible shock.* **4** tingle, °jolt, °impact: *You'll get a nasty shock if you touch those wires.*

shocking *adj.* **1** surprising, astounding, astonishing, °amazing, °striking, stupefying, numbing, °sudden, unexpected, electrifying, °startling, *Colloq* mind-boggling, mind-blowing: *It was shocking to see the way the neighbourhood had deteriorated.* **2** °disgusting, °revolting, nauseating, °nauseous, sickening, °repulsive, °abominable, °hideous, °horrible, horrifying, horrific, horrid, °foul, °loathsome, °abhorrent, °ghastly, unspeakable, °dreadful, distressing, °outrageous, appalling, °monstrous, °scandalous: *The conditions in the concentration camps were shocking.*

shoddy *adj.* °shabby, tatty, °inferior, °poor, rubbishy, °cheap, pinchbeck, meretricious, °tawdry, °gaudy, Brummagem, °plastic, °artificial, tinsel, tinselly, second-rate, trashy, junky, *Colloq* crappy, cheapjack, °tacky, *US* chintzy: *They can't get away for long with selling such shoddy merchandise.*

shoo *interjection.* **1** Scat!, Go away!, Away with you!, Be off!, Get out!, Begone!, *Colloq* Get lost!, Beat it!, Scram!: *I shouted 'Shoo!' and the chickens scattered.*
—*v.* **2** Often, ***shoo away*** *or* ***off***: °scare off, °frighten away, °drive away, force to leave: *She shoos away anyone who disturbs her while she is painting.*

shoot *v.* **1** scoot, dart, °whisk, °speed, °bolt, °run, °race, °rush, °flash, °fly, °dash, °hurtle, °streak, scuttle, °bound, °leap, °spring, *Colloq* zip, whiz: *The instant the baby cried out, its mother shot over to protect it.* **2** °discharge, °fire, open °fire; let °fly, °launch, °propel, °project, °fling, °hurl, °throw, °toss: *Don't shoot till you see the whites of their eyes! With all his strength he shot the arrow into the beast's neck.* **3** °wound, °hurt, °harm, °injure; °kill, slay, assassinate, °execute, *Slang* fill *or* pump full of lead, °plug, °blast, °zap, °knock off, snuff (out): *He insulted her, so she shot him. He's to be shot at sunrise.* **4** °sprout, germinate, burgeon, °flourish, °grow, °spring up, mushroom, °develop: *Owing to the perfect weather, the corn shot up very quickly.*
—*n.* **5** °sprout, °stem, bud, °branch, °offshoot, °slip, scion, °sucker: *If you want fruit, the new shoots have to be pinched back.*

shop *n.* **1** °store, boutique, department °store: *Would you stop at the shop and buy some lettuce?* **2** workshop, machine shop: *Henry gained experience in operating a lathe at my father's shop.*
—*v.* **3** °betray, °inform on *or* against, *Slang* peach on, rat on, snitch on, blow the whistle on: *The police persuaded Luke to shop his accomplices in exchange for a lighter sentence.* **4** ***shop for***: °buy, °purchase, °seek, °look for, °research: *I've been shopping for a new dishwasher.*

short *adj.* **1** °small, °little, °slight, °petite, °diminutive, °wee, °tiny, °elfin, minuscule; midget, dwarfish, squat, °dumpy, runty, stubby, °stunted, *Colloq* pint-sized, knee-high to a grasshopper, sawn-off: *Did you know that Queen Victoria was quite short?* **2** shortened, °brief, °concise, compressed, compendious, °compact, °pocket, *US* vest-pocket; °abbreviated, abridged, °cut: *A short version of the book was published in paperback.* **3** laconic, °terse, °succinct, pithy, sententious, °epigrammatic: *He made a few short remarks that were very much to the point.* **4** °abrupt, °curt, °terse, °sharp, °blunt, °bluff, °brusque, °offhand, °gruff, °testy, °snappish, °discourteous, uncivil, °impolite: *It is unnecessary to be so short with the staff.* **5** °direct, °straight, straightforward, short and sweet: *In reply to your request for permission to leave early, the short answer is 'No'.* **6** Usually, ***short of***: °deficient (in), lacking (in), needful (of), °wanting, °inadequate, °shy (of), °low (on): *The hotel is short of clean linen because the laundry failed to deliver.* **7** °brief, °limited; transitory, °temporary, °short-lived, °momentary, °quick, °transient: *HQ had a short life but a happy one. I'll just make a short stop in here and will join you in a moment.* **8** impecunious, °straitened, pinched, underfunded, °poor, penniless, °deficient: *I'm a bit short today and wonder if you could lend me some money?* **9** ***in short supply***: °rare, °scarce, °scanty, unplentiful, °meagre, °sparse, *Colloq chiefly Brit* °thin on the ground: *Good editors are in short supply these days.* **10** ***short of***: °before, °failing, excluding, °exclusive of, °barring, eliminating, precluding, excepting, °except for, leaving out, °apart from, setting aside: *Short of killing him, I am not sure what she could have done in the circumstances.*
—*adv.* **11** abruptly, °suddenly, peremptorily, without warning, instantly, unexpectedly, hurriedly, °hastily, out of the blue: *She stopped short in the middle of the road and made me get out.* **12** ***cut short***: **a** °trim, °curtail, °shorten, °abbreviate, °cut: *I must cut my visit short because I have a train to catch.* **b** °stop, °cut off, °terminate, °cut in on, °break in on, °interrupt; °butt in: *I am sorry to cut you short, but it is getting on for midnight.* **13** ***fall*** *or* ***come short***: °fail, be *or* prove °inadequate *or* °insufficient: *These grades fall short of our expectations, Bobby.*
—*n.* **14** ***in short***: °briefly, in a °word, all in all, to make a long story short, in a nutshell: *He told me, in short, that there was no job and there never had been one.* **15** ***shorts***: Bermuda shorts, knee-breeches, knee-pants, hot °pants: *I usually wear shorts to play tennis.*

shortage *n.* °deficit, deficiency, shortfall, °dearth, °scarcity, °lack, °want, paucity: *They are predicting a shortage of water again this summer.*

shortcoming *n.* °failure, °defect, deficiency, °weakness, °frailty, °drawback, °liability, °imperfection, °weak point, °flaw: *One might justifiably regard colour-blindness as a shortcoming in an interior decorator.*

shorten *v.* **1** °cut, °curtail, °cut off *or* down *or* °short, °reduce, °diminish, °trim; °lop off, °dock, °prune; hem: *Please shorten the time you spend in the bathroom in the mornings. This skirt has already been shortened.* **2** condense, °abridge, °abbreviate, °digest, compress: *Can one shorten the book without losing too much of the characterization?*

short-lived *adj.* ephemeral, evanescent, °temporary, °fleeting, transitory, °transient, °passing, fugacious, °volatile: *He enjoyed a short-lived reputation that died with him.*

shortly *adv.* **1** °soon, °presently, anon, before long, in a (little) while, by and by, *Archaic* ere long: *I'll see you shortly.* **2** °just, °immediately, °soon, °right: *We had dinner with him shortly before he went abroad.* **3** abruptly, °briefly, peremptorily, curtly, brusquely, °sharply, tersely, testily, gruffly, rudely, tartly: *'Leave me alone', said Bill shortly.*

short-sighted *adj.* **1** °near-sighted, myopic, dim-sighted: *He wears thick spectacles because he's so short-sighted.* **2** unimaginative, unprogressive, °improvident, °imprudent, injudicious, °rash, °brash, °impulsive, °reckless, impolitic, °limited, °unwary, incautious, °careless, °thoughtless, unmindful: *Lewis's short-sighted view makes no provision for the future.*

short-staffed *adj.* undermanned, short-handed, understaffed: *We are usually short-staffed during the summer because of the holiday schedules.*

short-tempered *adj.* °testy, irascible, °short, °curt, °abrupt, °gruff, °peremptory, °bluff, °rude, °tart, acid, acidulous, °terse, °brusque, crabbed, crabby, °irritable, °touchy, °petulant, °peevish, bearish, °snappish,

P S

°waspish, shrewish, curmudgeonly, crusty, °surly, °discourteous, grouchy, °disagreeable, °caustic, acrimonious, acerbic: *Henry is often short-tempered if he has slept badly.*

short-winded *adj.* short of *or* out of breath, winded, °breathless, panting, huffing (and puffing), gasping (for air *or* for breath), *Technical* dyspnœal: *He is very short-winded because he smokes too much.*

shot *n.* **1** °discharge, shooting: *The town was captured without a shot being fired.* **2** bullet, ball, slug, cannonball, buckshot, pellet, °projectile, °missile: *A dumdum bullet is a piece of soft shot with a hollowed-out nose.* **3** °attempt, °try, °opportunity, °chance, °go, °essay, °endeavour, °guess, conjecture, *Colloq* °stab, °crack, whack: *You are allowed three shots at the answer.* **4** marksman, markswoman, sharpshooter, sniper, rifleman: *Geraghty is an excellent shot and favourite for an Olympic gold.* **5** °photograph, snapshot, °picture, *Colloq* °snap, photo: *Miller took some excellent action shots using stroboscopic lighting.* **6** injection, inoculation, vaccination: *The doctor gave me a flu shot this morning.* **7** °drink, jigger, °tot, dram, °nip, spot, °swallow, *Colloq* finger, swig, slug, snort: *Will you have a shot of whisky with me, Muldoon?* **8** (space) °launch *or* launching: *The moon shot scheduled for today has been postponed owing to technical difficulties.* **9** ***call the shots***: °run *or* °direct *or* °manage *or* °administer *or* °control things *or* affairs *or* matters, °run the show, °rule the roost, be in °command *or* the driver's seat: *Ravelli calls the shots around here, and don't you forget it.* **10** ***like a shot***: °quickly, °swiftly, °rapidly, speedily, hurriedly, °hastily, at °once, like a °flash, °immediately, instantly, °instantaneously, *Colloq* in two shakes of a lamb's tail, like greased lightning, before you can say 'Jack Robinson': *All I had to do was mention ice-cream, and the children were in here like a shot.* **11** ***(not) by a long shot***: no way, under no circumstances, by no °means, on no account, by no chance, °never: *You ask if he can get elected and my response is, 'Not by a long shot'.* **12** ***shot in the arm***: °boost, stimulus, °encouragement, °incentive, °inducement, °provocation, motivation: *The team needs a shot in the arm to improve morale.*

shoulder *n.* **1** °side, °edge, °verge, °margin; breakdown lane: *If you have a flat tyre, drive onto the hard shoulder and phone for help.* **2** ***give (someone) the cold shoulder***: °rebuff, snub, °ostracize, send (someone) to Coventry, cold-shoulder, °put (someone) down, °reject, °exclude, °freeze (someone) out, °shun, °avoid, *Colloq* °cut (dead): *After his court case, they gave Nicholas the cold shoulder at his club.* **3** ***put (one's or the) shoulder to the wheel***: make every °effort, make an °effort, °strive, °work hard, °pitch in, °apply oneself, roll up one's sleeves, set *or* get to °work, *Colloq* knuckle down, °buckle down: *If we put our shoulders to the wheel, we ought to be able to get our candidate elected.* **4** ***rub shoulders (with)***: °associate (with), °hobnob (with), °socialize (with), consort (with), °mix (with), °fraternize (with), keep °company (with): *Once in a while, she condescends to come down and rub shoulders with the common people.* **5** ***shoulder to shoulder***: °side by °side, °united, as one, cooperatively, jointly, arm in arm, °hand in °hand, in partnership: *If we fight shoulder to shoulder, we can defeat this menace and regain our freedom.* **6** ***straight from the shoulder***: °directly, straightforwardly, candidly, frankly, °honestly, °openly, unabashedly, unashamedly, unambiguously, unequivocally, plainly, bluntly, man to man, (with) no holds barred, °outright, *Colloq* without beating about the bush, without pulling (any) punches: *I want to tell you, straight from the shoulder, Willie, you're the best pal in the world.*
—*v.* **7** °push, shove, jostle, °hustle, °thrust aside, elbow, °force: *She shouldered everyone aside roughly to fight her way to the bargain counter.* **8** °support, °carry, °bear, °take upon oneself, °take on, °accept, °assume: *Are you ready to shoulder the responsibilities of caring for a family?*

shout *v.* **1** °yell, °scream, °bellow, °bawl, °howl, °roar, °cry (out), °call (out), °whoop, *Colloq* holler: *We lined up when the sergeant shouted out our names.*
—*n.* **2** °yell, °scream, °bellow, °howl, yelp, °roar, °cry, °call, °whoop, *Colloq* holler: *Nobody on shore could hear the boys' shouts when their boat capsized.*

show *v.* **1** °display, °present, expose, °demonstrate, °indicate, °exhibit, °manifest, (°lay) °bare, °disclose, °reveal, °betray, °make known, divulge, °register, °express, °make °clear *or* °plain *or* °manifest, elucidate, °clarify, °explain: *Show your identification as you enter. Your persistent refusal to associate with Dominic shows how you feel very clearly. They showed me how the new machine works.* **2** °escort, °accompany, °conduct, usher, °lead, °guide, °direct; °steer: *Please show Mr Sorenson to his table.* **3** °prove, °demonstrate, °confirm, corroborate, °verify, °substantiate, °bear out, °certify, °authenticate: *This signature shows that the will was signed personally by your father.* **4** °teach, °instruct, °tell, °inform, let (someone) in on, give (someone) an idea of: *Would you please show me how to use this washing-machine?* **5** °appear, become *or* be °visible, °peek through, can *or* may be seen: *The floor was showing through a hole in the carpet.* **6** °exhibit, °reveal, °indicate, °display, °register: *A thermometer shows the temperature, a barometer the atmospheric pressure.* **7** make an °appearance, °appear, show up, °arrive, °come: *Do you really think that the Jack Nicholson will show at the club tonight?* **8** °represent, °symbolize, depict, °portray, °picture, °illustrate: *This drawing shows what happens to children who bite their fingernails.* **9** °present, °play, °put on, °stage, °screen; be (being) presented *or* played *or* playing *or* °put on *or* staged *or* screened: *They are showing* The Maltese Falcon *at the local cinema. What is showing there tomorrow?* **10** °grant, °accord, °bestow: *They finally showed mercy and let the hostages go.* **11** ***show off***: make an °exhibit *or* a °spectacle of, °flaunt, advertise, °display, °parade; °pose, °swagger, °posture, °boast, °brag, *US and Canadian* grandstand: *They invited us to show off their new house. Quilty shows off too much for my taste.* **12** ***show up***: **a** expose, °give away, °reveal: *His collection of animal trophies shows him up for what he really is.* **b** °stand out, be °conspicuous, be °noticeable, °contrast: *The white dress shows up nicely against your suntan.* **c** °embarrass, (put to) °shame, °mortify, upstage, °overshadow, outshine, °eclipse: *John only runs in the marathon to show me up.*
—*n.* **13** °display, °demonstration, °exhibition, °exposition, °fair, °presentation, *Colloq* expo: *There will be a computer show at the convention centre next week.* **14** °production, °presentation, °drama, °musical, °entertainment: *We flew to New York for a week to see a few Broadway shows.* **15** °ostentation, °display, °appearance, pretentiousness, °pretension, °affectation: *Those paintings are there just for show, not because they enjoy art.*

showdown *n.* confrontation, °climax, moment of truth, final °settlement, moment of decision, *US* face-off: *It's come to the point where we must have a showdown about who's boss.*

shower *n.* **1** sprinkle, sprinkling, drizzle: *Scattered showers are predicted for this afternoon.* **2** deluge, °torrent, °flood, °stream, barrage, overflow, °abundance, °profusion: *Showers of confetti rained on the parade from the offices.*
—*v.* **3** sprinkle, °rain, °pour, °spray, °bombard, °fall, °descend, °drop: *Debris and ash from the volcano showered down on the village.* **4** °lavish, inundate, °overwhelm, °heap, °load (down): *On return from her triumphant tour, Sylvia was showered with gifts and praise.*

showman *n.* °producer, impresario, °director: *P. T. Barnum was possibly the greatest showman in modern history.*

show-off *n.* °braggart, exhibitionist, swaggerer, egotist, boaster, *Colloq* blowhard, windbag: *Sit down and stop being such a show-off, Tetsworth.*

showy *adj.* °flashy, °garish, °flamboyant, °conspicuous, °ostentatious, °pretentious, bravura, °gaudy, *US* °show-off; °elaborate, °fancy, florid, °ornate, °fussy, °intricate, baroque, rococo, Byzantine, arabesque: *Their house is very showy, with gargoyles and lions and unicorns everywhere you look.*

shred *n.* **1** °scrap, °fragment, °bit, °tatter, °sliver, snippet, °rag, °remnant, °chip, °piece; atom, °trace, whit, °grain, °jot *or* tittle, scintilla, °hint, °suggestion, iota, °speck: *We found shreds from his shirt caught on the thorn-bushes. There isn't a shred of evidence to suggest that she killed him.*
—*v.* **2** °fragment, °tear (up), °tatter, °rip (up); °destroy, °demolish; °throw away, °dispose of, °scrap, *US* °trash: *At the news of the break-in, he dashed to his office and shredded the incriminating evidence.*

shrew *n.* harridan, virago, termagant, vixen, °scold, fishwife, °nag, °fury, spitfire, maenad, harpy, °witch, °hag, crone, hell-cat, beldam, °bitch, banshee, Xanthippe, Thyiad *or* Thyad, *Colloq* battleaxe, dragon: *His mother is an old shrew who does nothing but complain all the time.*

shrewd *adj.* °clever, °smart, °astute, cunning, canny, °acute, °sharp, keen-minded, °keen, °quick-witted, °crafty, °artful, manipulative, °calculating, °calculated, °foxy, °sly, °wily, °perceptive, percipient, perspicacious, discerning, °wise, °sage, sagacious, long-headed, °intelligent, °ingenious, Daedalian, inventive, °resourceful: *He is a shrewd politician, very good at knowing exactly what people want to hear him say.*

shriek *n.* **1** °scream, °cry, screech, squeal, °squawk, squall: *The girls collapsed in shrieks of laughter.*
—*v.* **2** °scream, °cry, screech, squeal, °squawk, squall: *It is very boring to listen to one's neighbours shrieking at each other day and night.*

shrill *adj.* high-pitched, ear-splitting, °piercing, ear-piercing, °sharp, piping, screeching, screechy, °penetrating: *She let out a shrill cry when she saw what had happened.*

shrink *v.* **1** wither, °shrivel (up), °contract: *My woollen pullover shrank because you washed it in hot water.* **2** Often, ***shrink from***: °withdraw (from), °draw back, °recoil (from), back away (from), °retreat (from), cower, °cringe, °flinch, °shy away (from), wince, balk (at): *Once committed to a responsibility, nothing could persuade Ella to shrink from it.*

shrivel *v.* Often, ***shrivel up***: °shrink, °wrinkle, °pucker (up), curl (up), wizen, °contract; wither, °wilt, °dry up, desiccate, dehydrate: *The soil had dried up and all the plants had shrivelled.*

shroud *v.* **1** °screen, °veil, °mask, °disguise, °camouflage, °cover, °shield, blanket, °shade, °hide, °conceal, °protect, °cloak, °swathe, °wrap, °envelop: *The tanks were shrouded from view in the forest. His activities are shrouded in mystery.*
—*n.* **2** winding-sheet, cerement, cerecloth, graveclothes: *They wrapped his body in a shroud and buried him in the churchyard.* **3** °veil, °cover, °shield, °cloak, blanket, °mask, °mantle, °pall, °screen, covering, cloud: *A shroud of secrecy descended over the Morocco affair.*

shrubbery *n.* shrubs, planting(s), hedge(s), hedging, hedgerow, °thicket, underbrush, brake, bracken, undergrowth, coppice *or* copse: *The fox lay low in the shrubbery till the dogs flushed him out.*

shudder *v.* **1** °quiver, °shake, °tremble, °shiver, °jerk, convulse, °quaver, °quake; °vibrate, °rattle: *I shudder to think what he might do next. Olive slammed on the brakes and the ancient car shuddered to a stop.*
—*n.* **2** °quiver, °shake, °tremble, twitch, °shiver, convulsion, °paroxysm, °spasm, °quaver, °quake; vibration, °rattle: *He gave a shudder at the prospect of having to clean out the stable.*

shuffle *v.* **1** °mix (up), intermix, disarrange, rearrange, interfile, intersperse, °jumble, °confuse; °shift (about), °mess up, °turn °topsy-turvy, °scatter, disorganize: *I shall cut the cards after you have shuffled them. Osbert shuffled the papers on his desk.* **2** scuff *or* °drag (one's feet), °scrape along, shamble: *The boy shuffled into the headmaster's office, guilt written all over his face.* **3** °equivocate, hem and haw, bumble, shift, °cavil, °fence, be °evasive *or* °shifty, °dodge, °niggle, split hairs, °quibble, prevaricate, *Brit* hum and haw, *Colloq* °waffle: *The suspect shuffled when asked the names of his accomplices.*
—*n.* **4** shamble, °shambling, scuffling, scraping: *Whenever he was lying, he did a funny little shuffle with his feet.* **5** °sidestep, °evasion, °subterfuge, °trick, °dodge, °shift, prevarication, °quibble, shuffling: *Tell me what you've done with the money—and no shuffle!*

shun *v.* °avoid, keep *or* °shy away from, °steer °clear of, eschew, °shrink from, °fight °shy of, °run *or* °turn (away) from, °flee *or* °escape from; °forgo, °give up; disdain, °spurn, °rebuff, °reject, cold-shoulder, give the cold °shoulder to: *After her experience, Penelope shunned the company of men for several years.*

shut *v.* **1** °close, °fasten, °secure, shut up; °lock, °bolt, °seal: *Come in and shut the door.* **2** ***shut down***: °close down, °discontinue, °cease, °suspend, °halt, °leave off, shut up; °switch *or* °turn *or* shut off, °stop: *We shut down operations at the Enfield factory last week. Make sure you shut down the machinery before leaving.* **3** ***shut in***: **a** confine, seclude, °keep in, °pen, °fence in, °secure: *We shut the dog in before we went out.* **b** See **6 a,** below. **4** ***shut off***: **a** °switch *or* °turn off, shut down, *Colloq* °kill, douse, °cut (off): *They shut off the lights while I was shaving.* **b** °separate, °isolate, seclude, °segregate, sequester, °bar, shut out, °cut off, send to Coventry: *The more violent cases are shut off in another wing.* **c** °close (off), °shut (down): *To save on heating, we shut off part of the house in the winter.* **5** ***shut out***: **a** °exclude, °eliminate, °bar, debar, °lock out, °ban, °keep out *or* away, disallow, °prohibit: *Aliens without work permits are shut out from employment. We shut out all hooligans and rowdies.* **b** °keep out, °screen, °exclude, °block out, °cut out: *This window shade shuts out the direct sunlight.* **c** °screen, °mask, °hide, °conceal, °veil, °cover: *The house is shut out from view by the hedge.* **6** ***shut up***: **a** confine, shut in, coop (up), °cage (in), °bottle up, °box in; °imprison, °jail, incarcerate, intern, immure: *People suspected of being subversives were shut up during the war.* **b** °silence, keep °quiet, °stifle, °mute, °gag, shush, *Chiefly Brit* °quieten: *As soon as Colin wants to say something, Sidonie shuts him up.* **c** See **1,** above. **d** See **2,** above.
—*adj.* **7** closed (up), sealed (up), locked (up), bolted, fastened: *There is not much hope of penetrating their shut minds on this issue.*

shuttle *v.* commute, °alternate: *He shuttles daily between London and Paris.*

shy *adj.* **1** diffident, °coy, °bashful, °retiring, °withdrawn, withdrawing, °reserved, °timid, °meek, °modest, °sheepish, unconfident, °self-conscious, introverted, °nervous, apprehensive, timorous, *Rare* verecund: *Casey is quite shy and you have to draw him out gently.* **2** timorous, °cautious, °wary, chary, °leery, °guarded, °afraid, °fearful, frightened, °anxious, °worried, °suspicious, °distrustful, °cowardly, craven, uncourageous: *The local people are shy of anyone or anything unfamiliar.* **3** missing, lacking, °deficient in, °short of: *The shipment is shy a few dozen shoelaces we ordered.*
—*adv.* **4** ***fight shy of***: °avoid, be unwilling *or* °reluctant *or* °averse *or* °loath *or* loth *or* °disinclined *or* not disposed; be °wary *or* °cautious *or* watchful: *The children fight shy of talking to strangers.*

sick *adj.* **1** *Chiefly Brit* nauseated, °queasy, sick to one's stomach, °squeamish, qualmish; seasick, carsick, airsick, *Colloq* green around the gills: *Patrick felt a bit sick after the rough ferry crossing.* **2** °ill, unwell, °unhealthy, °sickly, °indisposed, °infirm, ailing, °diseased, afflicted, *Colloq* under the °weather, on the sick-list, °poorly, laid up, not (feeling) up to snuff: *If you feel sick, you'd best see a doctor. I've been sick for a week.* **3** °affected, troubled, °stricken, heartsick, °wretched, °miserable, burdened, weighed down:

I was sick with worry to learn of the problems you have been having with your business. **4** °mad, °crazy, °insane, °deranged, °disturbed, °neurotic, °unbalanced, psychoneurotic, °psychotic, *Colloq* °mental, *US* off ((one's) rocker *or* trolley): *Anyone who could have committed such a crime must be sick.* **5** °peculiar, unconventional, °strange, °weird, °odd, °bizarre, °grotesque, °macabre, °shocking, °ghoulish, °morbid, °gruesome, stomach-turning, °sadistic, masochistic, sado-masochistic, *Colloq* °kinky, °bent, far-out, *US* °off: *In 30 years as a policeman, I've seen some sick things, but this is the end.* **6** sickened, shocked, put out, °upset, appalled, °disgusted, revolted, repulsed, offended, repelled, °nauseated; annoyed, chagrined, irritated: *She was sick at what she saw in the army field hospital. The way you do things sometimes makes me sick.* **7** Sometimes, ***sick of***: (sick and) °tired, bored, °weary, *Colloq* fed up with: *Don't you get sick of telling them the same thing so many times?*

sicken *v.* **1** fall °ill, take °sick, °contract, be °stricken by, °come down with *or* °catch something *or* a °bug, °fail, °weaken: *After he seemed to be recovering so well, he suddenly sickened and died.* **2** make °ill *or* °sick, °afflict, °affect, °disgust, °nauseate, turn one's stomach, °upset, °appal, °shock, °repel, °revolt, °repulse, °offend, make one's gorge rise; °put out: *The scene in the abattoir sickened me.*

sickly *adj.* **1** See **sick, 2,** above. **2** ailing, °feeble, °delicate, °wan, °weak, pallid, °pale, °drawn, peaked, °peaky, peakish: *Jennie looks sickly and must build up her resistance.* **3** °mushy, mawkish, °maudlin, cloying, insipid, °weak, °watery: *The sickly sentimentality of the episode about the boy and his lost puppy was unbearable.*

side *n.* **1** Sometimes, ***sides***: °flank(s), °edge(s), °verge, °margin(s), °rim, °brim, °brink, °border(s); bank; °boundary *or* boundaries, °perimeter, °periphery, °limit(s): *This side of the road is in West Sussex, the other in East Sussex. The sides of the swimming-pool are tiled.* **2** °surface, °face, °plane; facet: *The smallest possible number of sides of a pyramid is four.* **3** °faction, °interest, °party, °part, °sect, °camp, (point of) °view, °viewpoint, °aspect, °opinion, °standpoint, °stand, °cause, °angle, °position, °attitude, °school, °philosophy: *Which side do you support in the controversy?* **4** °team; string, °squad; *American football* and *Association Football* or *Soccer* and *Cricket* eleven, *Australian Rules football* eighteen, *Baseball* nine, *Basketball* five, *Gaelic football* and *Rugby Union* fifteen, *Rugby League* thirteen: *Whichever side Craig is on seems likely to win. The local side is now coming out onto the field.* **5** °affectation, °pretension, haughtiness, °arrogance, insolence, pretentiousness, °airs: *Chauncy puts on a bit too much side for my taste.* **6** ***side by side***: together, jointly, cheek by jowl: *These paintings should not have been hung side by side.* **7** ***take sides***: show °preference, be °partial, show °favouritism: *A judge must avoid taking sides.*
—*adj.* **8** °secondary, °incidental, °subordinate, °tangential, °subsidiary, °indirect, ancillary, °marginal, lesser, °minor, unimportant, °inconsequential, inconsiderable, °insignificant: *The main point is that he refuses to cooperate, and his reasons are entirely a side issue.* **9** °auxiliary, °secondary: *We live in a quiet side-road just off the High Street.*
—*v.* **10** ***side with***: take sides with, show °preference for, be °partial to, °show °favouritism to *or* for, °support, °favour, °prefer, °go in *or* along with, °join ((up) with), °ally with, be *or* become allied with, *Colloq US* throw in with, °team up with: *You can be sure that Kenneth will always side with the favourite candidate.*

sidelong *adj.* °oblique, °indirect, °sideways, covert, °surreptitious: *He marched straight ahead, without so much as a sidelong glance in her direction.*

sidestep *v.* °avoid, °dodge, circumvent, skirt, °evade, °shun, °steer °clear of, *Colloq* °duck: *The minister neatly sidestepped all questions about her retirement.*

sidetrack *v.* °divert, °deflect, °draw off *or* away, °distract, °turn aside; shunt: *Where was I? I got sidetracked by your comment about being overweight.*

sidewalk *n.* °walk, *Chiefly Brit* pavement, footpath, footway: *You may play on the sidewalk, but don't you dare step into the street.*

sideways *adv.* obliquely, laterally, edgeways, edge on, °sidelong, crabwise, indirectly, *US and Canadian* edgewise: *The dresser will go through the door if you turn it sideways.*

sidle *v.* °edge: *She sidled towards the door, opened it, and was gone.*

siege *n.* **1** blockade, encirclement, beleaguerment, besiegement: *The siege of Troy lasted ten years.*
—*v.* **2** lay siege to, °besiege, blockade, beleaguer, cordon off, °encircle, °box *or* °pen *or* °shut in, °bottle up: *They sieged the city and the inhabitants surrendered when they ran out of food and water.*

sift *v.* **1** °strain, sieve, °riddle, °filter, °screen, bolt; winnow, °separate, weed out, °sort out, °select, °choose, °pick: *It is not easy to sift out the promising manuscripts.* **2** °examine, °analyse, °study, °probe, °screen, °scrutinize, °investigate: *The police are sifting the evidence of the witnesses.*

sigh *v.* **1** °breathe, sough; suspire: *Troilus sighed forth his soul to the tent where sleeping Cressid lay.* **2** ***sigh for***: °bemoan, °lament *or* °mourn *or* °grieve *or* °weep for, °bewail; °yearn *or* pine for: *Now and then, all of us sigh for the good old days.*
—*n.* **3** °murmur, °exhalation, °sound; suspiration: *I gave a sigh of relief as the train left the station.*

sight *n.* **1** eyesight, °vision, °eyes: *His sight was completely restored by the operation.* **2** field of °view *or* of °vision, °range of °vision, ken, °perception, °view, eyeshot, °gaze: *We turned a corner, and at last the welcoming lights of the pub came into sight.* **3** °spectacle, °scene, °show; °rarity, °marvel, °wonder, °phenomenon; °pageant: *I shall never forget the sight of Joe wearing a strapless ballgown in the pantomime. We went to Rome to see the sights.* **4** °mess, °disaster, eyesore, °monstrosity, *Colloq* °fright, °atrocity: *The flat looked a sight after the boys finally moved out.* **5** ***catch sight of***: °spot, °notice, descry, °spy, espy, °glance at, (catch a) glimpse (of), (get a) °look *or* °peep *or* °peek at, *Colloq* take a gander at, get a look-see at, *Slang* get a load of, *US* glom, pipe: *We caught sight of a sinister-looking person slipping behind a pillar.* **6** ***out of sight***: **a** °remote, °distant, °far-away, unseeable, °imperceptible, °invisible: *She soon walked out of sight down the road. The mortar emplacement is out of sight, over the hill.* **b** °unusual, °rare, °extraordinary, °outrageous, °imaginative, awe-inspiring, °incredible, °shocking, °unreal, °moving, jolting, *Colloq* °neat, °cool, *Brit* °brilliant, brill: *The gig last night was out of sight, man.*
—*v.* **7** °look, °view, (take) °aim, °peer, °peek, °peep, draw a bead: *Sight along this stick and you'll see a cluster of stars called the Pleiades.* **8** °spot, °see, catch sight of, °mark, °observe, °behold, °view, °distinguish, discern, °identify, °note, °notice, °remark, glimpse, descry, espy, °spy: *A group of bird-watchers have sighted a golden eagle recently in the Grampians.*

sightseer *n.* °tourist, °traveller, globe-trotter, *Colloq* °rubberneck(er), *Brit* tripper, day-tripper: *As usual, the streets of Oxford were crowded with sightseers and tourists.*

sign *n.* **1** °token, °symbol, °indication, °mark, °signal, °indicator; °notice: *I interpreted the shouts of the crowd as a sign that I had won the race.* **2** °movement, °gesture, °motion, °signal, °cue, gesticulation: *She made a sign motioning me to come over.* **3** °trace, °indication, °evidence, °mark, °clue, °hint, °suggestion, °vestige: *She waited for an hour but there was no sign of him.* **4** °device, °mark, °symbol, °representation, °emblem, trade °mark, badge, °brand, °stamp, °seal, ideogram, ideograph, lexigram, phonogram, grapheme, hieroglyph, cartouche, rebus, logo(type), colophon, ensign, °standard, °banner, °flag; monogram,

°initials, cipher *or* cypher: *Sir Roger fought under the sign of a rampant lion.* **5** signboard, °advertisement, placard, °poster, *US* broadside; shingle, °notice, °announcement: *You can't miss the huge supermarket sign at the corner.* **6** °omen, augury, °warning, fore-warning, °foreboding, portent, °indication, writing on the wall, °prophecy, prognostication, foreshadowing: *We took the rumbling as a sign of an imminent earthquake.*

—*v.* **7** autograph, put one's signature on *or* to, inscribe, countersign, °endorse, °witness, put *or* set one's hand to, °mark; sign on the dotted line; *Colloq US* put one's John Hancock on *or* to: *I have already signed the petition, have you? The painting is valueless unless signed by the artist.* **8** ***sign away***: °forgo, °relinquish, °give up, °abandon, °abandon *or* °quit claim to, °waive, °release, °surrender, °dispose of, °sacrifice, get °rid of: *With one stroke of the pen, he signed away most of his fortune.* **9** ***sign off***: °close down, °discontinue (broadcasting, writing a letter, *etc.*): *It is midnight, time for us to sign off till tomorrow.* **10** ***sign on*** *or* ***up***: **a** °enrol, °enlist, °register, volunteer, °join (up), °contract: *I signed on to be a bodyguard, not a nursemaid.* **b** °enrol, °enlist, °hire, °employ, put under °contract, °retain, °engage, °take on, *Colloq* °take on board, °bring aboard: *We signed up three new engineers this week.* **11** ***sign over***: °assign, consign, °transfer, °make over, °deliver, °give, °donate, °present, °dispose of, turn over: *Aunt June was persuaded to sign over the ownership of the business to her nephews.*

signal *n.* **1** See **sign, 1,** above. **2** °incitement, stimulus, °spur, °impetus, goad, °prick: *The waving of the flag will be the signal to advance.*

—*adj.* **3** °remarkable, °conspicuous, °striking, °extraordinary, °unusual, °unique, °singular, °special, °noteworthy, °notable, °exceptional, °significant, °important, °outstanding, °momentous, consequential, °weighty: *The British forces won a signal victory at Khartoum that day. Winning the competition is a signal accomplishment.*

—*v.* **4** °motion, °indicate, °gesture, gesticulate, °communicate, °announce, °notify; whistle, wink, °blink, °nod, °beckon, °wave, °sign: *When your turn comes, a clerk will signal you to approach the counter. Peter raised his hand as a request to leave the room and the teacher signalled his assent.*

significance *n.* **1** °meaning, °sense, signification, denotation, °message, °idea, °point, °import, purport, °implication, portent, °content, °pith, °essence; °gist, °drift, °vein, °impression, connotation: *The significance of words like* God *and* love *is different for almost everyone who uses them.* **2** °importance, °weight, weightiness, consequence, °moment, °relevance, value: *The significance of the agreement lay not in its wording but in the fact that it was drawn up at all.*

significant *adj.* **1** °important, °weighty, °momentous, consequential, °critical, °substantial, substantive, °noteworthy, °notable, valuable, valued, °meritorious, °outstanding, °impressive, °historic, °relevant, °signal: *Appleton made significant contributions to knowledge about the ionosphere.* **2** °meaningful, °eloquent, pithy, °expressive, °pregnant, °suggestive, °informative: *It is significant that they prefer the term* Britain *to* England, Scotland, and Wales.

signify *v.* **1** °sign, °signal, °indicate, °communicate, °make known, convey, °symbolize, betoken, °represent, °express, °announce, °declare, °denote, °say, °mean, °specify; connote, °intimate, °suggest, °reveal, °disclose, °impart: *She signified her agreement by a nod. What does the phrase 'pursuit of happiness' signify to you?* **2** °matter, °count, be °significant *or* °important *or* consequential, be of °significance *or* of °importance *or* of consequence, carry °weight, °impress, °stand out, deserve *or* merit consideration: *It signifies little that they were found innocent of a crime we all believe they committed.*

silence *n.* **1** °quiet, quietness, stillness, soundlessness, noiselessness, °calm, calmness, °hush, quietude, tranquillity, °peace, peacefulness, °serenity: *The silence was so complete that I could hear my heart beating.* **2** speechlessness, muteness, dumbness, reticence, taciturnity, uncommunicativeness: *Do not construe his silence as agreement.*

—*v.* **3** °quiet, °mute, °hush, °still, shush, °calm, °tranquillize, soothe, *Chiefly Brit* °quieten: *The audience was silenced by the start of the overture.* **4** °mitigate, °temper, mollify, take the sting out of, propitiate, pacify, °blunt, °suppress, °repress, °restrain, °subdue, draw the fangs *or* teeth of, °inhibit, °put down, °damp, °mute, °squelch, °quash, emasculate, muzzle, °muffle, °shut off, °gag, °stifle, °smother, °deaden (the effect of): *Only a full account of what lay behind these events will silence criticism in the media.*

silent *adj.* **1** °quiet, °still, soundless, °noiseless, °tranquil, hushed, shushed, °mute; °calm, °serene, placid, °peaceful, pacific, unagitated, unruffled, untroubled, undisturbed, *Literary* stilly: *After the children left the house fell silent. Not a mouse stirred in the silent city.* **2** uncommunicative, °mute, close-mouthed, °taciturn, °reticent, °reserved, °mum, °tight-lipped, °secretive: *Millie told me a great deal about her children but was silent on the subject of her own activities.* **3** unspeaking, unspoken, °mute, unexpressed, °tacit, °understood, °implicit, implied, unstated, unsaid: *There is a silent agreement among the islanders not to reveal where the whisky is hidden.* **4** °inactive, non-participating, °passive, quiescent, *Brit* sleeping: *Although John runs the company, he has several silent partners.* **5** unpronounced, unuttered, not sounded, *Technical* aphonic: *The* g *in* sign *is silent, like the* k *in* know *and the* l *in* could.

silently *adv.* °quietly, soundlessly, noiselessly, with catlike tread, as °quietly as a mouse, stealthily; wordlessly, speechlessly, mutely: *They fold their tents like the Arabs, And silently steal away. He stood by silently, allowing his brother to do all the talking.*

silhouette *n.* °outline, °profile, contour, °form, °figure, °shape, °shadow, configuration, °periphery, °perimeter: *I could see the silhouette of a person on the window-blind.*

silky *adj.* silken, silklike, °delicate, °sleek, °soft, °smooth, satiny, °shiny, °glossy, °lustrous, *Technical* sericeous: *Her long, silky black hair hung below her shoulders.*

silly *adj.* **1** °senseless, °nonsensical, °absurd, °ridiculous, °ludicrous, laughable, risible, asinine, °inane, °preposterous, idiotic, °childish, °puerile, °foolish, °foolhardy, °irresponsible, °unreasonable, illogical, irrational, °pointless, fatuous, °stupid, unwise, imbecilic, °crazy, °mad, °insane: *It would be silly to pay for it if you can get it for nothing.* **2** stunned, stupefied, dazed, °giddy, °dizzy, muzzy, benumbed: *Culley said something rude and the girl knocked him silly with a karate chop.*

—*n.* **3** °fool, nincompoop, idiot, dunce, ninny, °halfwit, simpleton, numskull *or* numbskull, dim-wit, booby, °dolt, jackass, °twit, blockhead, bonehead, nitwit, ignoramus, °clod, *US* thimble-wit, *Colloq* °dope, °dummy, knuckle-head, goose, °drip, silly billy, *Brit* clot, *Slang US and Canadian* °jerk, nerd: *Warren is such a silly to spend so much money on a girl who cares nothing for him.*

silt *n.* **1** °deposit, °sediment, alluvium, °ooze, °sludge: *The irrigation pumps get clogged up with silt.*

—*v.* **2** Usually, ***silt up*** *or* ***over***: become clogged *or* choked *or* obstructed *or* dammed *or* °congested: *The channel silts up and has to be dredged yearly so that the boats can pass through.*

silver *n.* **1** silverware, °sterling, (silver) °plate; cutlery, *US* flatware; hollowware: *Guests are coming so I'll have to polish the silver.* **2** °white, greyish, whitish-grey, greyish-white, °grey: *When your hair has turned to silver, I will love you just the same.*

—*adj.* **3** silvery, °shiny, shining, °polished, burnished, °lustrous, °pearly, nacreous, °bright, gleaming, *Literary or heraldry* argent; °white: *The moon's silver crescent hung low in the sky. Her hair is more silver than grey.* **4** silvery, silver-toned, silver-tongued, °sweet, pretty, euphonious, °melodious, mellifluous, mellifluent, dulcet, °musical: *The silver tones of the muezzin echoed in the streets, calling the faithful to prayer.*

similar *adj.* **1** °like, almost °identical, comparable, °equivalent, nearly the °same; °alike: *That brooch is similar to the one I bought for my mother. The two may be similar, but they are not the same.* **2** ***be similar to***: °resemble, be °like, °correspond to, °compare favourably with: *This letter is very similar to the one I received yesterday.*

simmer *v.* **1** °seethe, °stew, cook, °boil, °bubble: *A huge cauldron of soup simmered on the fire.* **2** °chafe, °seethe, °stew, steam, °smoulder, °fume, °rage, °burn, *Colloq US* do a slow burn: *Father is still simmering because you scratched his car.* **3** ***simmer down***: °calm *or* °cool down, °cool off, °calm oneself, become °quiet, °control oneself, get °control of *or* over oneself, *Chiefly Brit* °quiet(en) down, *Slang* °cool it: *Yesterday he was in a towering rage, but he has simmered down a bit today.*

simple *adj.* **1** uncomplicated, °plain, uninvolved, °unsophisticated, understandable, °intelligible, (easily) °understood, comprehensible, °clear, lucid, straightforward, °easy, °elementary, °basic: *At the age of four, Jan was able to do simple mathematical calculations.* **2** °plain, °unadorned, undecorated, unembellished, °basic, °fundamental, °elementary, °elemental, °mere, unostentatious, unassuming, unpretentious, °modest, °classic, uncluttered, °stark, °clean, °severe, austere, °Spartan, °homely; °unvarnished, °naked, °honest: *Thea was stunning in a simple black dress with a colourful scarf and gold jewellery. The simple truth is that he came home from work to find the house broken into and his wife gone.* **3** °sincere, °frank, °candid, °open, °unaffected, uncomplicated, unpretentious, straightforward, °above-board, simple-hearted, uncontrived, °direct, °upright, °square, °forthright, four-square, °righteous, °honest, °naïve, guileless, °artless, undesigning, °childlike, °ingenuous, °unsophisticated, °innocent, °green: *The colonel was a simple man who was respected because he always said just what he meant. A simple heart may be its own best guide.* **4** °unsophisticated, °naïve, °slow, slow-witted, °stupid, °thick, thickheaded, simple-minded, °feeble-minded, oafish, bovine, °dense, °obtuse, °dull, dull-witted, witless, °halfwitted, brainless, °backward, imbecilic *or chiefly Brit* imbecile, cretinous, *Colloq* °dumb, moronic: *That chap Dawson is far too simple to understand what you are asking him.* **5** °lowly, °humble, °inferior, °mean, °base, subservient, °common, °subordinate: *The lord of the manor regarded his tenants as simple folk, a breed apart from himself and his family.*

simplicity *n.* **1** uncomplicatedness; understandability, comprehensibility, lucidity, straightforwardness, °clarity, intelligibility, decipherability: *Consider the simplicity of some life forms in contrast to the complexity of others. The simplicity of the Bible can be deceptive.* **2** plainness, cleanness, °clarity, °severity, starkness, austereness, asceticism, °restraint, bareness, °purity: *She prefers the simplicity of classical or very modern design to baroque and rococo clutter.* **3** °sincerity, openness, artlessness, °candour, guilelessness, frankness, unsophisticatedness, ingenuousness, straightforwardness, forthrightness, unaffectedness, unpretentiousness, modesty, °naïvety; plainness, directness, inelegance, rusticity, pastoralism: *Many have been charmed by the simplicity of the local folk art.* **4** °stupidity, slow-wittedness, thickheadedness, simple-mindedness, feeble-mindedness, oafishness, cloddishness, obtuseness, dullness, dull-wittedness, witlessness, halfwittedness, imbecility, brainlessness: *The simplicity of some of those yokels is incredible.*

simplify *v.* °clarify, °clear up, make °easy, °paraphrase, °explain, explicate, disentangle, untangle, unravel, streamline: *Simplify your request and we shall be able to do what you ask.*

simply *adv.* **1** °merely, °barely, purely, °only, solely, °just, °entirely, fully, °totally, °wholly, °altogether, °absolutely, °really: *Is it true that they met regularly simply to discuss politics?* **2** °totally, °completely, °altogether, °entirely, °just, plainly, °obviously, °really, unreservedly, unqualifiedly: *If you believe that, you're simply too stupid for words!* **3** naïvely, artlessly, guilelessly, °openly, innocently, ingenuously, unaffectedly, unpretentiously, plainly, °naturally: *He asked her very simply what she did as a 'working girl'.* **4** plainly, modestly, starkly, °severely, sparely, sparsely, austerely, ascetically: *His home is simply furnished, without paintings or any other decoration.* **5** distinctly, unambiguously, plainly, °obviously, unmistakably: *The instructions must be written simply so that they are understandable to anyone.*

simultaneous *adj.* coincident, coinciding, concurrent, contemporaneous, synchronous; °contemporary: *The simultaneous appearance of two books on such an obscure subject was very unusual.*

sin *n.* **1** trespass, °transgression, °offence, °wrong, impiety, °misdeed, profanation, desecration, iniquity, °evil, °devilry, °sacrilege, °crime, infraction, °misdeed, dereliction, °infringement, °violation, misdemeanour, °fault, °foible, °peccadillo: *How many sins have been committed in the name of righteousness! It's a sin to tell a lie. The seven deadly sins are anger, covetousness, envy, gluttony, lust, pride, and sloth.* **2** wickedness, sinfulness, °vice, corruption, ungodliness, badness, °evil, wrongfulness, iniquity, iniquitousness, immorality, depravity, impiety, irreverence, impiousness, °sacrilege: *His brother Edmund was conceived in sin, and sin ruled his entire life.*
—*v.* **3** °transgress, °offend, °fall (from grace), °lapse, go °wrong, °stray, go astray, °err, *Biblical or archaic* trespass: *Strictly speaking, we can sin only against God.*

sincere *adj.* °honest, °truthful, °true, veracious, °genuine, °heartfelt, true-hearted, undissembling, unfeigned, °open, (°open and) °above-board, straightforward, °direct, °frank, °candid, guileless, °artless, *Colloq* upfront, on the °level, on the up and up: *I took her criticism as a sincere desire to see improvement in my work. You have always been sincere in your emotional involvements.*

sincerely *adv.* °truly, °honestly, °really, wholeheartedly, candidly, frankly, unequivocally, °seriously, earnestly, genuinely, °deeply, fervently: *When they say they love each other, they mean it sincerely.*

sincerity *n.* °honesty, truthfulness, straightforwardness, openness, forthrightness, frankness, °candour, candidness, seriousness, genuineness, uprightness: *Everyone appreciates sincerity in dealings with others.*

sinew *n.* **1** ligament, tendon; muscle, thew: *After the climb, I ached in every sinew.* **2** Usually, ***sinews***: °strength, °force, °power, °energy, °brawn, °vigour, °might, °stamina, °vitality: *The sinews of his argument were considerably weakened by her disarming candour.*

sinewy *adj.* °strong, °powerful, °muscular, °mighty, °stout, °wiry, °robust, °tough; strapping, °brawny, °burly: *She looked so tiny and fragile cradled in his huge sinewy arms.*

sinful *adj.* °corrupt, °evil, °wicked, °bad, °wrong, wrongful, iniquitous, °vile, °base, °profane, °immoral, °profligate, depraved, °criminal, °sacrilegious, °ungodly, unholy, demonic, irreligious, °impious, °irreverent: *Anything that you like as much as you like chocolate must be sinful. They would never condone such sinful behaviour in our church.*

sing *v.* **1** °chant, intone, carol, vocalize, trill, croon, °pipe, °chirp, warble; chorus; yodel: *It was a wonderful spring day and Barbara felt like singing. Can you sing* On the Road to Mandalay? **2** whistle, °pipe, °peep: *I have just bought a singing kettle.* **3** °tell, °tattle, °name names, *Slang* rat, snitch, squeal, blow the whistle, peach, °spill the beans: *They found out that Johnny had been singing to the cops about the bank job.*

singe *v.* char, °blacken, sear, °scorch, °burn: *Unfortunately, I singed the tail of my shirt while ironing it.*

singer *n.* °vocalist, soloist, songster, crooner, *chanteuse*, nightingale, °minstrel, troubadour, balladeer, caroller, chorister, choirboy, choir girl, choir member, chorus-boy, chorus girl, chorus-member, *Colloq* songbird, canary, thrush: *She used to be a professional singer.*

single *adj.* **1** °unmarried, unwed, °unattached, °free; °celibate: *She remained single till she was twenty-two.* **2** °singular, °individual, °distinct, °solitary; °one, °only, °sole, lone, °unique, °isolated: *There wasn't a single person there who could think for himself. A single shot rang out.* **3** °separate, °distinct, °individual, °solitary: *Every single hair is rooted in its follicle.*
—*v.* **4** ***single out***: °select, °choose, °pick, °separate, take *or* °put *or* °set aside *or* °apart, °distinguish, cull, °segregate, °fix *or* °fasten on: *Why was she singled out for special treatment?*

single-handed *adj.* **1** °solo, lone, °solitary, °independent, unaided, unassisted: *Chichester was the first winner of the single-handed transatlantic sailing race.*
—*adv.* **2** single-handedly, by oneself, °alone, °solo, on one's own, independently: *He sailed round the world single-handed.*

single-minded *adj.* dedicated, °devoted, °resolute, °steadfast, persevering, °firm, °determined, dogged, unswerving, unwavering, °tireless, °purposeful: *Single-minded perseverance saw him through the completion of the work in eight years.*

singly *adv.* one at a time, °separately, °individually, one by one, successively, one after the other, seriatim: *Taken singly, the facts are not hard to assimilate.*

singular *adj.* **1** °unusual, °different, atypical, °eccentric, °extraordinary, °remarkable, °special, uncommon, °strange, °odd, °peculiar, °bizarre, °outlandish, °curious, °queer, outré, °offbeat, *Slang* far-out: *Ideas that yesterday were considered singular have today become quite commonplace.* **2** °outstanding, °prominent, °eminent, °pre-eminent, °noteworthy, °significant, °important, °conspicuous, °particular, °notable, °signal, °exceptional, °superior: *Stempel made a singular contribution to the development of microscopy.* **3** lone, °isolated, °single, °separate, uncommon, °rare, °unique, °distinct, one of a kind: *Some medieval philosophers denied the existence of general realities, and claimed that all things that exist were particular and singular.*

singularity *n.* **1** individuality, distinctiveness, uniqueness, idiosyncrasy: *Personality demonstrates its singularity even in handwriting.* **2** °eccentricity, °peculiarity, strangeness, oddness, queerness, outlandishness, uncommonness: *The singularity of the marriage ceremony among these tribes was often remarked on by anthropologists.* **3** *Technical* black hole: *The ultimate collapse of the star results, theoretically, in a singularity.*

sinister *adj.* **1** °fateful, °inauspicious, unfavourable, °foreboding, °threatening, °menacing, minacious, minatory *or* minatorial, °portentous, °ominous, unpropitious, °disastrous, °dark, °gloomy: *There was a sinister meaning in the look he gave her.* **2** °evil, °bad, °corrupt, °base, malevolent, °malignant, malign, °harmful, pernicious, treacherous, nefarious, °wicked, °diabolic(al), baleful, °villainous, insidious, °sneaky, °furtive, underhand(ed): *The poor girl fell under the sinister influence of a real-life Svengali.*

sink *v.* **1** °founder, °submerge, °go down, °go under, °plunge, °descend, be engulfed: *The ship was struck below the water-line and sank in minutes.* **2** °subside, °cave in, °collapse, °settle, °drop, °fall in, °go down, °slip away: *The earth suddenly sank beneath our feet.* **3** °descend, °go down, °drop, °fall, move down *or* °downward(s), °go down to *or* on: *The parachute slowly sank to the ground. When he saw the statue move, he sank to his knees, terrified.* **4** °decline, °weaken, °worsen, °degenerate, °subside, °deteriorate, °flag, °fail, °diminish, °die, °expire; languish; *Colloq* go downhill: *Grandfather, sinking fast, summoned the family to his bedside.* **5** °disappear, vanish, °fade away, °evaporate; °set, °go down, °descend, °drop: *After a meteoric rise, many rock stars sink into oblivion. As the sun sank slowly in the west, we returned to our hotel to reminisce about our day at the pyramids.* **6** °settle, °precipitate, °descend, °drop: *After a few minutes, the sand sinks to the bottom.* **7** °bore, put down, °drill, °dig, °excavate, °drive: *A special shaft will be sunk just for ventilating the mine.* **8** °submerge, °immerse, °plunge: *He sank his hand deep into the mud and came up with a small box.* **9** °stoop, °bend, °get, °go, °lower *or* °humble oneself: *I never dreamt that he would sink so low as to beg in the streets.* **10** °invest, °venture, °risk, °put: *He sank his life's savings into his son's business, only to see it go bankrupt.* **11** ***sink in***: be °understood, °penetrate, °register, make an °impression on, °get through to: *How many times do I have to tell you in order for it to sink in?*
—*n.* **12** basin, wash-basin, wash-bowl, lavabo; *Church* font, stoup, piscina: *The kitchen has a large double sink.* **13** cesspool, cesspit, °pit, hell-hole, den of iniquity, sink-hole, *Colloq* °dive: *We found him playing piano in some sink frequented by the worst element of society.*

sinking *adj.* **1** °queasy, °nervous, uneasy, °tense, apprehensive, unquiet, °fretful, °shaky, jittery, °jumpy, °anxious: *Just thinking about the way they treat hostages gave me a sinking feeling in the pit of my stomach.* **2** depressed, °dejected, °miserable, dolorous, °doleful, °mournful, °forlorn, woeful, °desolate, despairing, °stricken, heavy-laden: *I had a sudden sinking feeling when she announced that she had something important to tell me.*

sinner *n.* °transgressor, wrongdoer, °miscreant, °offender, evil-doer, malefactor, °reprobate, *Biblical or archaic* trespasser: *Few people nowadays believe that sinners are punished in hell for all eternity.*

sip *v.* **1** °taste, °sample, sup: *She was sitting on a bar stool, sipping a cocktail.*
—*n.* **2** °taste, °sample, soupçon, °drop, °bit, °swallow, °mouthful, spoonful, thimbleful, °nip, dram, *Colloq* swig: *She took a sip, savoured it, then turned to me with a smile.*

siren *n.* **1** whistle, warble, wailer, horn, foghorn; °signal, °alarm, °warning, °alert, tocsin: *The air raid siren sounded and everyone ran for shelter.* **2** °temptress, °seductress, enchantress, °charmer, sorceress, *femme fatale*, Circe, Lorelei, *Colloq* vamp, *US* mantrap: *Have you seen the latest siren to whom John has fallen prey?*

sissy *n.* °milksop, mama's boy, mummy's boy, namby-pamby, °weakling, °baby, cry-baby, mollycoddle, *US* milquetoast, *Colloq* softie *or* softy, *Brit* °wet: *The boy you remember from school as a sissy is now a football star.*

sit *v.* **1** be seated, °settle, sit down, take a °seat, rest, *Colloq* take the weight *or* a load off one's feet: *Come in and sit with me for a while. If you sit on that chair it will break.* **2** hold a °session, be in °session, °assemble, °meet, convene; °gather, °get together: *The Supreme Court of the United States will be sitting next week.* **3** Often, ***sit on***: have *or* hold *or* occupy a °seat (on), °participate (in), be a °member (of): *Kathy sits on the board of directors.* **4** °remain, °stay, °lie, rest; °relax, mark time, °abide, °dwell: *Let the dough sit a while to rise. Anita sat in Vienna awaiting her instructions.* **5** °seat, °contain, °hold, °accommodate, have seats *or* °seating for, have °room *or* °space *or* °capacity for seating: *The auditorium sits only 600.* **6** ***sit in***: **a** Often, ***sit in on***: °play, °join (in), °participate (in), take °part (in); °observe, °watch: *Mind if I sit in on your poker game? We invited Mary Lou to sit in during our discussion.* **b** °substitute, °fill in, °stand in, °double, *Colloq* °cover, sub, *US* pinch-hit: *Mary Lou often sat in for our pianist if he had another gig.* **7** ***sit out***: °wait out, outwait, outstay, °outlast, outlive, °last through, °live through: *Will sat out endless dances. He sat out the whole evening merely waiting to walk home with*

Lily. **8 *sit tight*:** °wait, °hang back, °hold back, be °patient, bide (one's) time, play a waiting game, take no action, °delay, temporize, *Colloq* hold (one's) horses: *Just sit tight till you hear from them—don't jump the gun.* **9 *sit up*:** °awaken, pay °attention, °notice, become °alert *or* °interested *or* °concerned: *Jennie's performance in the hurdles made many track coaches sit up.* **10 *sit (with)*:** Often, ***sit well** or **right (with)***: °agree with, be °agreeable to; °seem, °appear, °look: *The way Ashton handled the matter did not sit well with the directors.*

site *n.* **1** °location, °place, °plot, plat, °spot, °locale, °area, °milieu, °neighbourhood, locality, purlieus, °placement, °position; °situation, °orientation: *A site near that of ancient Pergamum has been acquired for the building. The site alongside the river has much to recommend it.*
—*v.* **2** °locate, °position, °place, °put, °situate, °install *or* instal: *The building has been sited to take maximum advantage of the sun.*

situate *v.* °place in a °position *or* °situation *or* °location, °place, °position, °locate, °set, °spot, °put, °install *or* instal: *Harwood is very well situated to learn what the high command is planning. The greenhouse should be situated on the south side of the house.*

situation *n.* **1** °place, °position, °location, °spot, °site, °locale, °setting: *The situation of the monastery, high on the mountain, makes it almost inaccessible.* **2** °state (of affairs), °condition, °circumstances, °case, °status (quo), lay of the land, °picture; °plight, °predicament; *Colloq* ball game; kettle of fish: *The present situation calls for careful planning. The chancellor's policies have done little to improve the economic situation.* **3** °position, °place, °job, °employment, °post, *Colloq* berth: *Jenkins likes his new situation as Lord Fortescue's valet.*

size *n.* **1** °magnitude, largeness, bigness, °bulk, °extent, °scope, °range, dimensions, °proportions, °measurement(s), °expanse, °area, square footage, °volume, °mass, °weight; hugeness, immensity, greatness, vastness, °enormousness: *How do astronomers determine the distance and size of stellar objects? A shape of extraordinary size suddenly loomed up in the darkness.*
—*v.* **2** dimension, °measure: *The furnishings are sized in proportion to these miniature room displays.* **3 *size up*:** assess, °judge, °evaluate, °measure, take the °measure of, appraise, assay, make an °estimate of, °estimate, value, °gauge, °rate: *She looked him up and down, sizing him up as a prospective husband.*

sketchily *adv.* cursorily, superficially, incompletely, patchily, °roughly, perfunctorily, skimpily, °vaguely, imperfectly, crudely, °hastily, hurriedly: *His account of the event was sketchily written.*

sketchy *adj.* °cursory, °superficial, °incomplete, patchy, °rough, °perfunctory, skimpy, °imperfect, °crude, °hasty, °hurried, °vague, ill-defined, °fuzzy, °indistinct, °inexact, °imprecise, °unrefined, unpolished, rough-hewn, unfinished: *We received only sketchy reports of what was going on in the capital. This will do as a sketchy outline, but eventually the details will need to be filled in.*

skilful *adj.* skilled, °accomplished, °adept, adroit, °dexterous, °expert, °proficient, masterly, °masterful, °gifted, apt, °able, °clever, °talented, °capable, °professional, trained, °qualified, °experienced, °practised: *Julio is a skilful enough driver to race tomorrow. I have to admire the skilful way he handles people.*

skill *n.* **1** °talent, °ability, °aptitude, expertness, °expertise, °facility, skilfulness, °art, artistry, cleverness, adeptness, adroitness, mastery, °dexterity, handiness, °ingenuity, °experience, °proficiency, °finesse, °knack, quickness, deftness, °technique: *It requires great skill to operate this machine.* **2** °accomplishment, °forte, °strength, °gift, °capability, know-how, °faculty: *Her skill is in teaching others how to be skilful sales people.*

skim *v.* **1** Often, ***skim off***: °separate, cream, °scoop *or* ladle off, °take off, °remove: *After the water has come to a boil, skim off the scum that has collected on top.* **2** Often, ***skim through** or **over***: °scan, °flip *or* °thumb *or* leaf through, °skip through, °glance at *or* through, °dip into: *I only had time to skim through your report, but at a glance it looks good.* **3** °soar, °glide, skate, °slide, °sail, °fly: *Along came Calabro on his sailboard, skimming along the tops of the waves.*

skin *n.* **1** epidermis, derma, integument, °hide, °pelt, °fleece, fell: *Her skin reddens in the sun. How many skins are needed to make a coat?* **2** °coat, °film, coating, crust, incrustation, husk, °peel, °rind, °outside, °shell, pellicle, °veneer, outer layer, lamina, overlay: *The frame is first covered with a tough plastic skin to make it waterproof.*
—*v.* **3** flay, °strip, decorticate, excoriate: *I shall skin that boy alive if I catch him!* **4** °peel, °hull, husk, °shell: *This machine skins the fruit automatically.* **5** abrade, °scrape, graze, bark: *She skinned her knee on the edge of the coffee table.*

skin-deep *adj.* °superficial, °shallow, °surface, °slight, °external, unimportant, trivial, unprofound, °insubstantial: *The impression he makes on people is only skin-deep.*

skinny *adj.* °thin, underweight, °gaunt, bony, scraggy, lank, °lanky, gangly, gangling, °raw-boned, °meagre, °spare, °emaciated, half-starved, undernourished, pinched, hollow-cheeked, wasted, shrunken: *Two skinny children were clinging to their mother's skirts.*

skip *v.* **1** °leap, °cavort, °caper, gambol, °frisk, °prance, °jump, °hop, romp, °bound, °dance: *Eleanor came skipping down the walk to the house.* **2** °omit, °leave out, °pass by, °overlook, °pass over, °avoid, °ignore, °disregard, °steer clear of, °cut: *In my haste, I skipped over your name. Please skip the reading of the roll today.*
—*n.* **3** °leap, °cavort, °caper, gambol, °frisk, °prance, °jump, °bound, °dance, °hop, romp: *He had a curious way of walking, giving a little skip before each step.* **4** lacuna, °gap, °omission, avoidance, °disregard; °miss, *Colloq* go-by: *There was a skip of 32 pages after page 64. If you take my advice, you will give that restaurant a skip.*

skipper *n.* captain, °master, commander; °boss, °leader, °chief: *The skipper gave orders to put him in irons.*

skirmish *n.* **1** °fight, °encounter, °fray, °brush, °clash, °engagement, confrontation, °showdown, °combat, °battle, °conflict, °struggle, set-to, °contest, °scrimmage, °fracas, tussle, mêlée *or* melee, *Law* affray, *Colloq* °scrap, dust-up, *Brit* scrum: *There was a brief skirmish when the troops met a band of partisans.*
—*v.* **2** °fight, °clash, °struggle, °battle, tussle: *At the edge of the convoy a destroyer skirmished with a submarine.*

sky *n.* **1** °heaven(s), skies, arch *or* vault of °heaven, °firmament, (wild) blue (yonder), ether, *Archaic or literary* welkin, empyrean, azure: *The dour, overcast sky gave the bleak moor a chilling sense of foreboding.* **2 *to the skies*:** °overly, excessively, extravagantly, fulsomely, profusely, inordinately, °highly: *If I praise him to the skies people will get the idea that I benefit from his success.*

slab *n.* °slice, °wedge, °piece, hunk, chunk, tranche, *Colloq Brit* wodge: *The keeper threw a large slab of meat into the lion's cage.*

slack *adj.* **1** °remiss, °careless, °indolent, negligent, °lax, °lazy, °idle, neglectful, °delinquent, °inattentive, otiose, dilatory, cunctatory, °laggard, °easygoing, °slothful, sluggish, °lethargic, °shiftless, do-nothing, fainéant, *Colloq* asleep at the switch *or* the wheel, asleep on the job: *Production has fallen off because the workers are getting slack.* **2** °loose, °flabby, flaccid, °soft, °limp, baggy, drooping, droopy, bagging, sagging, floppy: *The flag hung down, slack in the still air.*
—*v.* **3** Often, ***slack** or **slacken off** or **up***: **a** let go, let run, let °loose, °release, slacken, °loose, °loosen, °relax, °ease (out *or* off), °let up (on): *Slack off the stern line a bit.* **b** °slow (down *or* up), °delay, reduce speed, °tire,

°decline, °decrease, °diminish, °moderate, abate, °weaken: *Barnes could not keep up his terrific pace and is beginning to slack off. Business has slackened off since Christmas.* **4** °neglect, °shirk, *Colloq Brit* skive (off), *US* goof around *or* off, *Chiefly military* gold-brick, *Taboo slang US* fuck the dog: *Don't let the foreman find you slacking.*
—*n.* **5** °lull, °pause, °inactivity, cut-back, lessening, reduction, abatement, drop-off, downturn, diminution, °decline, fall-off, °decrease, dwindling: *How do you compensate for the slack in sales of ski equipment during the summer?* **6** °room, looseness, slackness, play, °give: *There's too much slack in that mooring line.*

slacker *n.* shirker, °loafer, °idler, *Slang Brit* skiver, *Military* scrimshanker, *US* gold brick, goof-off: *We have tight deadlines to meet, so there is no room for slackers on the team.*

slake *v.* °satisfy, °quench, °gratify, allay, assuage, °ease, °relieve: *Nothing would slake my thirst better right now than a pint of ice-cold lager.*

slam *v.* **1** °shut, fling closed, bang: *Gillian said that she hated encyclopedias, and slammed the door in the salesman's face.* **2** °crash, smash, smack, °dash, °ram, bang, °slap: *Not looking where he was going, Newland slammed his car into a street lamp.* **3** °criticize, °attack, °vilify, pillory, °run down, °disparage, denigrate, °denounce, °put down, flay, °pounce on *or* upon, *Colloq* °shoot down, °pan, *Chiefly Brit* slate: *The critics slammed his play because of the way it portrayed women.*

slander *n.* **1** defamation (of character), calumny, obloquy, misrepresentation, °slur, vilification; °libel: *He spread lies about me and I am suing him for slander.*
—*v.* **2** defame, calumniate, °disparage, °slur, traduce, malign, °smear, °vilify, decry; °libel: *He must be stopped from slandering people and ruining their reputations.*

slanderous *adj.* defamatory, calumnious, calumniatory, disparaging, smear, deprecatory, depreciative, discrediting, decrying; libellous: *I understand that she made some slanderous remarks about your relationship with your ex-wife.*

slant *n.* **1** °angle, °viewpoint, (point of) °view, °standpoint, °approach, °twist, °idea, °aspect, °attitude: *The article reflects a new slant on why governments are sometimes out of touch with the electorate.* **2** °bias, °prejudice, °partiality, one-sidedness, °turn, °bent: *Carla's reporting has a feminist slant which occasionally distorts the facts.* **3** °slope, °incline, °tilt, °ramp, gradient, °pitch, °lean, °leaning, deflection, °angle, °rake, °cant, camber: *A window sill normally has an outward slant. The road has a slant downwards to the right on right-hand curves.*
—*v.* **4** °tilt, °angle, °incline, °pitch, °cant, °slope, °bend, °lean, °list, °tip, bevel, °shelve: *The land slants downwards near the lake. Notice how his writing slants upwards at the ends of the lines. Cut the edges to slant outwards.* **5** °bend, °distort, °deviate, °twist, °warp, °colour, °weight, °bias: *The editor slanted the story to put the minister in a favourable light.*

slap *v.* **1** smack, cuff, whack, °rap; °spank; *Colloq* clout, wallop: *He said something extremely rude so she slapped him.* **2** °flap, slat, °whip, °beat, bat: *Can't you stop that blind from slapping in the wind?* **3** °fling, °toss, °splash, °hurl, °throw, °sling: *If you slap some paint on it, no one will know the difference.*
—*n.* **4** smack, °blow, cuff, whack, °rap, *Colloq* clout, wallop: *He got a hard slap on the cheek for using foul language.* **5** Often, ***slap in the face***: °reprimand, °reproof, °rebuff, °criticism, censure, °rebuke, shot, °thrust, °attack, °put-down, °insult, °offence, smack in the eye: *The speaker's reference to Anne's paper as 'trivial' was a severe slap in the face.*
—*adv.* **6** ***slap on***: °exactly, °directly, °precisely, °straight, °point-blank, °right, squarely, °plumb, smack, bang: *As usual, Barry's comments were slap on the mark.*

slash *v.* **1** °cut, °gash, °hack, °score, °slit, °knife, °lacerate; °wound; °scar: *The guide slashed away at the undergrowth with his machete.* **2** °lash, °whip, °scourge, °flog, °beat, horsewhip, flail, flagellate, flay, °lambaste, thrash: *In those days, a convicted felon was beaten and slashed in front of a crowd in the marketplace.* **3** °cut, °reduce, °decrease, °drop, °mark down, °trim, °lower: *Prices were slashed to clear out last season's styles.*
—*n.* **4** °cut, °gash, °incision, °slit, °slice, °gouge, °rent, °rip, °score, laceration: *There is a slash in each sleeve that reveals the colourful fabric underneath.* **5** °cut, reduction, °decrease, mark-down: *The department stores continued their price slashes to the end of January.*

slattern *n.* slut, °tramp, sloven, trollop, hussy, °wanton, whore, °prostitute, harlot, streetwalker, lady of the evening, woman of ill repute, °loose *or* fallen woman, *trottoise*, *Colloq* call-girl, pro, *Slang* °tart, hooker, hustler, *US* roundheels, bimbo: *His reputation will not be enhanced if he associates with slatterns.*

slaughter *n.* **1** butchery, butchering, *Rare* abattage: *Most of the cattle were sent for slaughter.* **2** °massacre, °killing, °bloodshed, blood bath, °murder, homicide, manslaughter, °carnage, extermination, °execution, liquidation, slaying, blood-letting, butchery, pogrom, genocide, mass °murder *or* °execution *or* extermination, °sacrifice, hecatomb: *1940 to 1945 saw the slaughter of millions in Europe and the Far East.*
—*v.* **3** °butcher, °kill, °murder, slay, °execute, °exterminate, °massacre, put to the sword, put to death, liquidate, °destroy: *How many more must be slaughtered before war is made obsolete?* **4** °defeat, °beat, °win (out) over, vanquish, °overcome, °overwhelm, smash, °crush, thrash, °destroy, °rout, °upset, trounce, *Colloq* clobber: *Our school soccer team slaughtered the visitors 10--0.*

slave *n.* **1** lackey *or* lacquey, scullion, serf, slave-girl, slaveling, odalisque, bondservant, bondslave, bondsman *or* bondman, bondswoman *or* bondwoman, bondmaid, vassal, *Derogatory chiefly Brit* skivvy, *Archaic* esne, helot, hierodule, *Colloq Brit* slavey: *In ancient times, captured peoples and those of lower social status were kept as slaves.* **2** drudge, workhorse, °hack, °grind, toiler, °labourer, *Chiefly Brit* °fag, dogsbody, *Colloq US* gofer: *Susan was a slave to her job for years, only to be sacked without a pension by the new owners.*
—*v.* **3** °labour, toil, moil, °grind, grub, drudge, °sweat, burn the midnight oil, lucubrate, °work one's fingers to the bone, °work like a Trojan *or* a horse, *Brit* skivvy: *He was slaving over an essay that was due the following morning.*

slaver[1] *v.* **1** drool, salivate, slobber, °drivel, dribble, °spit, *Dialect* slabber: *The wolf opened its slavering jaws.*
—*n.* **2** drool, saliva, °drivel, dribble, °spit, spittle, *Dialect* slabber: *The slaver formed on his lips as he raged on.* **3** °nonsense, °drivel, °rubbish, twaddle, piffle: *The slaver spewed forth by the critics set her teeth on edge.*

slaver[2] *n.* **1** slave ship, slave-trader: *Conditions were so bad aboard the slavers that many of the poor souls died before reaching their destination.* **2** blackbirder, slave-trader; White slaver, °pimp, panderer: *He was ashamed that his grandfather had been a South Sea slaver.*

slavery *n.* **1** enslavement, °bondage, thraldom, thrall, enthralment, °servitude, serfdom, vassalage, yoke; subjugation, °captivity, *Historical US* peculiar institution: *All of those ancient cultures that we venerate practised slavery.* **2** slave-trade, blackbirding: *No one ever mentions that the family fortune had been made from slavery.* **3** toil, moil, °drudgery, travail, °grind, °strain, (hard) °labour: *She remembered the years of slavery she had spent at the kitchen sink.*

sleazy *adj.* **1** unsubstantial *or* °insubstantial, °flimsy, °slight, °shabby, °poor, gimcrack, jerry-built, °tawdry, °cheap, tatty, °ramshackle, °rickety, °slipshod, *Colloq* *US* chintzy: *Her garish dress was made from some* *sleazy synthetic material.* **2** °disreputable, low-class, low-grade, squalid, °dirty, °base, °seedy, °sordid, °contemptible, trashy, °run-down, °mean, °cheap, *Colloq* crummy, slummy, *Slang* crappy, cheesy: *He was lying low in a sleazy hotel while the police searched for him.*

sleek *adj.* **1** °smooth, °slick, velvety, °lustrous, °shiny, shining, °glossy, °silky, silken: *The seals' sleek fur glistened in the sunlight.* **2** °graceful, °trim, °streamlined: *For her birthday Edmund gave her a sleek convertible.* **3** °suave, unctuous, °slimy, fawning, °oily, °specious, °hypocritical, *Chiefly Brit* smarmy: *His explanations sounded plausible enough, but we soon found out what a sleek rogue he really was.*

sleep *v.* **1** °doze, (take a) °nap, catnap, °rest, °repose, slumber, drowse, °drop *or* °nod off, be in the land of Nod, be in the arms of Morpheus, snore, *Colloq* snooze, saw wood, catch *or* log a few zees (Z's), take *or* have a zizz, catch forty winks: *I was so tired, I slept for a full ten hours.*
—*n.* **2** °nap, °doze, slumber, rest, siesta, *Colloq* forty winks, snooze, zizz, beauty sleep: *As she grew older, she found she needed less sleep.*

sleepless *adj.* **1** °restless, °wakeful, insomniac, °disturbed: *Your mother and I spent a sleepless night worrying about you.* **2** °alert, watchful, °vigilant, unsleeping: *Mark's wife kept a sleepless vigil at his bedside.*

sleepwalking *n.* **1** noctambulism, somnambulism, noctambulation, somnambulation: *Because of his sleepwalking, he had to be strapped in at night.*
—*adj.* **2** noctambulant, somnambulant: *Proper drugs will control her sleepwalking activities.*

sleepy *adj.* **1** °drowsy, somnolent, °tired, °nodding, dozy, °lethargic, °torpid, slumberous, sluggish, oscitant; °weary, °fatigued, °exhausted, *Colloq* °dead on one's feet, (knocked) out, °beat, *US and Canadian* pooped: *All that exercise has made me sleepy.* **2** °boring, °inactive, °dull, °quiet, soporific, °slow, sluggish: *He grew up in a sleepy little village in the Outer Hebrides.*

slender *adj.* **1** °slim, °lean, °willowy, sylphlike, svelte, lissom *or* lissome, lithe, °graceful, snake-hipped, °thin, °spare, °slight, °lanky: *By exercising regularly, she has retained her slender figure.* **2** °slim, °narrow, °slight, °poor, °unlikely, °small, °little, °scanty, °remote, °meagre, °weak, °feeble: *Prospects for a quick recovery of the stock market are slender.* **3** °slim, °slight, °little, °scanty, °inadequate, °insufficient, °insignificant, °trifling: *The evidence against the defendant was too slender for a conviction.*

sleuth *n.* (private) °detective, (private) investigator, *US* P.I., *Colloq* private eye, Sherlock, °snoop, *Brit* tec *or* 'tec, *US* hawkshaw, *Slang US* dick, shamus, *US and Canadian* gumshoe: *Dissatisfied with the progress of the police, we hired a private sleuth to investigate the theft.*

slice *n.* **1** °slab, °piece, rasher, collop, shaving, layer, *Cookery* scallop, escalope, scaloppine (*pl. of* scaloppina) *or* scaloppini (*pl.*): *May I have another slice of ham?* **2** °portion, °piece, °part, °wedge, °share, °sliver, °helping: *He wants to make certain he gets his slice of the pie.* **3** spatula; slicer: *The Cabots gave us a silver fish slice for a wedding present.*
—*v.* **4** °cut, °carve, °divide: *They watched their mother slicing bread for sandwiches.*

slick *adj.* **1** °smooth, °sleek, °glossy, °silky, silken, °shiny, shining, °glassy, °slippery: *His slick hair looked as if it had been greased.* **2** °smooth, urbane, °suave, smooth-spoken, °glib, °smug, °plausible; sycophantic, unctuous, *Colloq* smarmy: *Thomas was a slick operator and managed to worm his way into a position of power.* **3** °smooth, °clever, °skilful, adroit, °dexterous, °professional, °ingenious, °imaginative, inventive, °creative, *Colloq* °neat: *The performance was slick and well-rehearsed.* **4** °superficial, °shallow, meretricious, °specious, °glib: *They have made a lot of money publishing slick magazines for the yuppy market.*
—*v.* **5** Often, ***slick down***: °smooth, °plaster down, grease, °oil: *He likes his hair slicked down to look like Valentino's.*

slicker *n.* **1** confidence man *or* woman, °cheat, °swindler, mountebank, *Colloq* con man, city slicker: *That slicker she met in Paris tricked Harriet out of a lot of money before he disappeared.* **2** oilskin (raincoat): *Best wear your slicker if you're going out in this storm, James.*

slide *v.* **1** °glide, °slip; °coast, °skim, glissade, skate, °plane, skid, toboggan, °slither: *The drawer slid smoothly out on its runners. Terry came sliding down the icy hill, arms and legs flailing.* **2** °creep, °steal, °slip, °slink, °move: *My contact slid into the seat beside me and slipped me a note.* **3** °decline, °decrease, °drop, °fall: *Shares slid to an all-time low on this morning's market.* **4** ***let slide***: °forget, °ignore, °neglect, °gloss *or* °pass over, pay no °heed *or* °mind (to): *When Mr Bartlett borrowed my lawnmower, I let the matter slide till he began to think of it as his own, and offered to lend it to me!*
—*n.* **5** landslide, earth-slip, avalanche, mud-slide: *A dozen houses were destroyed in the slides caused by the recent torrential rains.*

slight *adj.* **1** °small, °little, °minor, °negligible, °unlikely, °insignificant, °inconsequential: *There is always a slight chance that you might be wrong, you know.* **2** °trifling, °tiny, °slender, °minute, infinitesimal; trace, °perceptible: *He didn't attach the slightest importance to the rumours that were going round. You'd best wash it again, as there is still a slight odour of garlic.* **3** °small, °short, °petite, °thin, °slim, °slender, °delicate, °diminutive, °tiny, °miniature, bantam, °wee, °pocket, pocket-sized, *US* vest-pocket, *Colloq* pint-sized: *Charlotte's slight build seems totally unaffected by the amount she eats.* **4** °insubstantial *or* unsubstantial, °weak, °feeble, °delicate, °dainty, °frail, °unstable, °fragile, °flimsy, lightly made *or* built, °precarious, °inadequate, °rickety, °insecure: *This table is too slight to support the computer and the printer. His arguments were far too slight to carry conviction.*
—*v.* **5** °disregard, °ignore, disdain, °scorn, snub, °rebuff, °cut, °disrespect, cold-shoulder: *He thought she had slighted him deliberately at the dance.* **6** °insult, °offend, affront, °mortify, °diminish, °minimize, °depreciate, °disparage: *Siobhan felt slighted by Harry's inattention.*
—*n.* **7** °insult, affront, °slur, °indignity, °outrage, °offence, °disrespect: *It is hard to understand why she tolerates his persistent slights.* **8** inattention, °neglect, °disregard, °indifference, snub, cold °shoulder, coldness, ill-treatment: *Perhaps she misinterprets his obsessive occupation in his work as a slight to her.*

slightly *adv.* a °little, °somewhat, to a certain *or* slight *or* minor extent *or* °degree *or* measure, marginally: *Yes, I do feel slightly better, thank you.*

slim *adj.* **1** See **slender, 1,** above. **2** See **slender, 2, 3,** above.
—*v.* **3** reduce, lose *or* shed weight, °diet, *Chiefly US* slenderize: *I really must slim if I am to fit into my summer clothes.*

slimy *adj.* **1** oozy, °slippery, mucky, squashy, squishy, viscous, °sticky, gluey, mucilaginous, uliginous, glutinous, mucous, °clammy, °mushy, *US* squushy *or* squooshy, *Colloq* °gooey, gunky, *US* gloppy: *He had cleverly buried the bag of diamonds in a mass of slimy waste where no one would want to look.* **2** °slippery, unctuous, °obsequious, sycophantic, toadying, °servile, creeping, °grovelling, abject, *Colloq* smarmy: *I don't mind his trying to sell me insurance, but why does he have to be so slimy about it?*

sling *v.* **1** °toss, °throw, °cast, °propel, °hurl, °shy, °fling, °fire, °shoot, °pitch, let °fly, °launch, °heave, °lob, *Colloq* chuck: *He slung his briefcase onto the desk and flopped into a chair.*
—*n.* **2** slingshot, catapult, trebuchet *or* trebucket: *It is said that David slew Goliath with a stone from his sling.* **3** °support, strap, °band; °belt: *The doctor ordered him to keep his sprained arm in a sling for a*

few days. The military rifles are supplied with leather slings.

slink *v.* °sneak, °creep, °steal, °prowl, skulk: *The dog slunk out of the room with its tail between its legs.*

slip[1] *v.* **1** °slide, skid, °glide, °slither: *Waxing the runners helps the sleigh slip along more easily.* **2** °stumble, lose one's °footing *or* °balance, miss one's °footing, °trip; °fall, °tumble: *Mother slipped on the ice but luckily didn't fall down.* **3** Often, ***slip up***: °err, °blunder, make a °mistake, °miscalculate, go °wrong, °botch (up), *Slang* °screw up: *He slipped up again by failing to give you your telephone messages.* **4** ***let slip***: °reveal, divulge, °blurt out, °leak, °let out, °disclose, °expose, *Colloq* come out with, °blab: *He accidentally let slip the news that you were back in town.* **5** ***slip away*** *or* ***by***: °pass, °elapse, vanish, °go by: *The hours just slipped away when I was with Irena.* **6** ***slip away*** *or* ***off*** *or* ***out***: °escape, °disappear, °leave, vanish, °steal, °go *or* °run away *or* off *or* out, °break away, °get away, give (someone) the slip; °sneak away *or* off *or* out: *After the speech, he slipped away before we could interview him.* **7** ***slip in***: °enter, °get in, °sneak in; °put in: *A field mouse slipped in past the wire netting. I managed to slip in my suggestion before the meeting was adjourned.*
—*n.* **8** °blunder, °error, °mistake, °fault, °oversight, slip of the tongue *or* pen, inadvertence, °indiscretion, °impropriety, °transgression, °peccadillo, faux pas, *Colloq* slip-up, *Chiefly US* blooper, *Slang Brit* boob, bloomer: *She made so many slips in the letter that she had to retype it.*

slip[2] *n.* **1** °piece, °scrap, °strip, °sliver; °paper, °note, chit, °permit, °permission, °pass, °document: *I'll put my phone number on this slip of paper. To go on the outing, each child will have to bring in a slip signed by a parent.* **2** °shoot, scion, °cutting, sprig, °twig, °sprout, °runner, °offshoot: *After the slip is inserted, the branch must be bandaged up firmly.*

slippery *adj.* **1** °slick, °sleek, °slimy, °icy, °glassy, °smooth, °greasy, °oily, lubricated, *Colloq* skiddy: *Be careful! Those stairs can be slippery when they're wet.* **2** °evasive, °devious, °shifty, °unreliable, undependable, °questionable, untrustworthy, °dishonest, treacherous, °disloyal, °perfidious, °slick, °crafty, °sly, °foxy, cunning, °tricky, °sneaky, °false, reptilian, °faithless, *Colloq* °shady: *I have dealt with some very slippery characters over the years, but this one is downright evil.*

slipshod *adj.* °careless, slovenly, slapdash, °haphazard, messy, °untidy, disorganized, °lax, unorganized, *Colloq* °sloppy: *We refused to pay the bill because of the slipshod way they did the repairs.*

slit *v.* **1** °split, °cut, °slash, °gash, °knife, °slice: *The bark of the log is first slit open, then carefully peeled back.*
—*n.* **2** °split, °cut, °gash, °incision, fissure, °groove, °slash, cleft, °aperture, °opening: *Off-stage, the rest of the actors were watching the audience through a slit in the curtain.*

slither *v.* °slide, worm, °snake, °slip, °slink, °glide, skitter, °creep, °crawl: *After regarding me for a moment, the cobra turned and slithered away.*

sliver *n.* °fragment, °piece, shard, °shred, °splinter, °slip, shaving, paring, °flake, °chip, °bit, °scrap, snippet, °snip: *Two weeks later, we were still finding tiny slivers of glass from the broken vase.*

slob *n.* oaf, °boor, pig, lout, churl, yahoo, *Slang Brit* yob, yobbo, *Chiefly US* galoot *or* galloot, Slobbovian: *He was a complete slob—he never tidied his room, and hardly ever washed.*

slogan *n.* war °cry, battle-cry, rallying °cry, catchword, watchword; °motto: *The magazine's slogan was 'If you love words, you'll love* Word'.

slope *v.* **1** °incline, °decline, ascend, °descend, °rise, °fall, °dip, °sink, °drop (off), °angle, °slant, °pitch, °tilt, °tip: *The lawn slopes downwards from the house, then upwards towards that grove of trees.*
—*n.* **2** °incline, °decline, ascent, descent, acclivity, declivity, °rise, °fall, °ramp, °dip, °sink, °drop, °angle, °slant, °pitch, °tilt, °rake, °tip, camber, °cant, bevel, °hill, bank, °mount, gradient, *US* °grade, upgrade, °downgrade: *Sheep can be seen grazing on the grassy slopes.*

sloppy *adj.* **1** messy, °dirty, slovenly, °careless, °slipshod, °untidy, disordered, °disorderly; draggle-tailed, °bedraggled, dishevelled, °unkempt, °dowdy, frumpy, frumpish, °shabby, scruffy, *Colloq US* grungy: *She is certainly a sloppy housekeeper. John's teacher complained about his sloppy work.* **2** °wet, slushy, °watery, soggy, soppy, sopping, sodden, sloshy, °muddy, rainy: *The roads were sloppy after all the rain. You're lucky you don't have to go out in this sloppy weather.* **3** °sentimental, °gushy, gushing, mawkish, °maudlin, °mushy, over-emotional, *Colloq* slushy, *Brit* °wet, soppy: *She starts to cry whenever she watches a sloppy film on TV.*

slot *n.* **1** °groove, fissure, °notch, °slit, °opening, °hollow, °depression, °channel, sulcus: *Each of these pieces fits into its own slot. Drop a coin in the slot and watch what happens.* **2** °opening, °position, °vacancy, °job, °place, °assignment, °niche, °space, °spot, pigeonhole: *We filled that slot in the sales department. They scheduled the new programme into the half-hour slot after the six o'clock news.*
—*v.* **3** °groove, fissure, °notch, °slit, °hollow out: *We slotted the stanchions to accommodate the shelf brackets.* **4** °assign, °schedule, °place, °position, pigeon-hole, °fit: *Can we slot this interview into the documentary on China?*

sloth *n.* °idleness, laziness, °indolence, slothfulness, °inertia, apathy, °indifference, accidie, °torpor, fainéance, pococurantism *or* pococuranteism, torpidity, °sluggishness, languor, languidness, °lethargy, phlegm, *Rare* hebetude: *The maharajahs lived a life of sloth and luxury at the expense of their poverty-stricken subjects.*

slothful *adj.* °idle, °lazy, °indolent, apathetic, °indifferent, °torpid, °inert, pococurante, °slack, °lax, °shiftless, fainéant, °inactive, do-nothing, sluggish, sluggard(ly), °slow, °laggard, languorous, languid, °lethargic, °lackadaisical, °phlegmatic, hebetudinous: *One cannot pursue a slothful attitude and expect to get anywhere in life.*

slouch *v.* **1** °droop, °sag, °stoop, loll, °slump, °hunch: *Sit up straight and stop slouching.*
—*n.* **2** °stoop, °sag, °droop, °slump, °hunch: *He seems to have developed a slouch from the burden of his responsibilities.* **3** Usually, ***no slouch***: sloven, °loafer, sluggard, °laggard, °loafer, °idler, malingerer, lazybones: *Nellie is certainly no slouch when it comes to exercising to keep fit.*

slow *adj.* **1** lagging, °laggard, dawdling, sluggish, sluggard(ly), slow-moving, °leaden, °ponderous, °unhurried, plodding, snail-like, tortoise-like, °torpid, leaden-footed, creeping, crawling; °deliberate, slow-paced, leisurely, °gradual, °easy, °relaxed, °lax, °lackadaisical, °lazy, *US* lallygagging *or* lollygagging: *They walked at a slow pace back to the house. Philip has become a little slower in his old age.* **2** °gradual, °progressive, °moderate, perceptible, almost imperceptible, measurable: *The church elders have noted a slow decline in moral standards.* **3** °unhurried, slow-moving, slow-paced: *The slow funeral cortege crept through the streets.* **4** behindhand, unpunctual: *I missed the train because my watch is five minutes slow.* **5** °late, °tardy, behindhand, dilatory, delayed, unpunctual: *You were so slow in getting here that everyone has gone.* **6** °slack, °inactive, °quiet, sluggish, unproductive: *Business is always a bit slow after the holidays.* **7** °dense, °dull, slow-witted, dull-witted, °obtuse, °backward, bovine, °dim, dim-witted, °stupid, unresponsive, blockish, cloddish, unintelligent, doltish, °simple, °stolid, unimaginative, Boeotian, *Colloq* slow on the uptake, °thick, °dumb: *I'm afraid I'm a bit slow when it comes to particle physics.* **8** °conservative, unprogressive, °old-fashioned, out of °date, °backward, old-fogyish *or* old-fogeyish, behind

the times, *Colloq* °square, not with it, past it, *US* out of it: *The council has been rather slow in realizing the needs of the community.* **9** °boring, °dull, °tiresome, ennuyant, °tedious, °sleepy, somnolent, °torpid, soporific, wearisome, dry-as-dust, uninteresting, °monotonous, °tame, uneventful, °humdrum, *Colloq* ho-hum, °dead, *Brit* dead-and-alive: *This town becomes really slow in the autumn, till the tourists reappear in the spring.* **10** °reluctant, not quick, unwilling, °hesitant, °disinclined, °averse, °loath *or* loth, °indisposed: *Even when provoked, Cassie tends to be slow to anger.*
—*adv.* **11** slowly, unhurriedly, cautiously, carefully, circumspectly: *He failed his test because he drove too slow.* **12** behindhand, tardily, °late, unpunctually: *All the trains seem to be running a bit slow tonight.* **13** slowly, °easy, leisurely, °easily: *They told him to take things slower or he'd have another heart attack.*
—*v.* **14** Often, ***slow down*** *or* ***up***: °slack *or* slacken off, °reduce speed, hold back, put on the brakes, take it easy: *You'd better slow down before you come to Deadman's Hill.* **15** °relax, take it easy, *Colloq* °ease up: *The doctor suggested that at my age I ought to slow down a little.*

sludge *n.* °muck, °mire, °ooze, °mud, slime, °dregs, °silt, °residue, °precipitate, *Colloq* goo: *The mechanic said that there was a lot of sludge in the engine.*

sluggishness *n.* °sloth, laziness, slothfulness, languor, lassitude, °lethargy, languidness, laggardness, °torpor, phlegm, lifelessness, stagnation, shiftlessness, pococurantism *or* pococuranteism, fainéance, accidie, *Rare* hebetude: *A few days' golfing in Scotland will help to shake off the sluggishness of your Caribbean holiday.*

slum *n.* Often, ***slums***: ghetto, warren, shanty town, *US* skid row *or* Skid Road: *Many very famous men emerged from the slums of the Lower East Side in New York.*

slump *n.* **1** °dip, trough, depreciation, °decline, downturn, downslide, °recession, °depression, falling-off, fall-off, °fall, °drop, °plunge, descent, °crash, °collapse, °failure; nosedive, tailspin: *A slump in the housing market was one of the early signs of the impending recession. The market went into a slump this morning from which it barely recovered before closing.*
—*v.* **2** °decline, °slip, °recede, °fall (off), °drop, °plunge, °descend, °sink, °crash, °collapse, °dive, °plummet, take *or* go into a nosedive *or* tailspin: *Prices on the stock market slumped following announcement of a rise in interest rates.* **3** See **slouch, 1,** above.

slur *n.* **1** °smear, °insult, calumny, °aspersion, affront, °stigma, °stain, °blot, °spot, (black) °mark, °discredit, insinuation, °innuendo, °imputation, °slander, °libel, °slight, *Colloq* °put-down: *She resents any slur on her husband's character.*
—*v.* **2** °mumble, misarticulate, °garble, stutter, lisp: *Some people nowadays slur their speech so badly that one can hardly understand them.* **3** ***slur over***: °gloss over, °pass over, °disregard, give short shrift to, °ignore: *The eulogies at the memorial service slurred over his faults and focused on his accomplishments.*

sly *adj.* **1** cunning, °artful, °crafty, °clever, °wily, guileful, underhand(ed), °deceitful, treacherous, °foxy, °scheming, plotting, °designing, conniving, °furtive, °shrewd, °sneaky, °stealthy, insidious, °devious, °disingenuous, °tricky, °shifty, °sharp, canny, *Colloq* °shady: *It was devilishly sly of him to manoeuvre you into paying for his party.* **2** impish, elfish, roguish, °mischievous, puckish, °devilish, scampish, °naughty, °arch, waggish: *Even as he was flirting with Allison he was giving Antonia sly, conspiratorial winks.*
—*n.* **3** ***on the sly***: slyly *or* slily, °quietly, surreptitiously, covertly, stealthily, furtively, sneakily, underhandedly, clandestinely, *Colloq* on the q.t. *or* Q.T., on the side: *Although her parents had forbidden her to see him again, Antonia continued to meet Kevin on the sly.*

small *adj.* **1** °little, °tiny, °short, °diminutive, °petite, mignon(ne), °wee, teeny, °elfin, Lilliputian, midget, °miniature, °minute, minuscule, °baby, bantam, °pocket(-sized), mini; °undersized, °immature, °young, under age; *Colloq* pint-sized, *US* peewee: *She was once small enough to fit into a size 7. When I was very small, my father took me to my first cricket match.* **2** °slight, °secondary, °insignificant, trivial, °inconsequential, lesser, °puny, °negligible, °minor, °trifling, unimportant, °paltry, nugatory: *The opinions of other people were not of the smallest importance to him.* **3** unimaginative, °shallow, unoriginal, mundane, °everyday, °limited, unprofound, uninspired, commonplace, °matter-of-fact, °flat, two-dimensional: *With their small minds they were incapable of fully appreciating the scope of the project.* **4** skimpy, niggardly, stingy, uncharitable, ungenerous, °scanty, °meagre, °cheap, °petty, parsimonious, grudging, stinting, °selfish, °miserly, °tight, tight-fisted, close-fisted, °close; °poor, °insignificant, °inadequate, °insufficient, °unsatisfactory, °negligible, °trifling, °humble, small-scale, °modest, unpretentious, *Colloq* piddling, °measly: *With all your money, it was very small of you not to contribute more to the scholarship fund. We all thought their cheque was too small.* **5** °insignificant, °limited, °negligible, °trifling, °tiny; °little, °minor, diminished, reduced, °slight: *Only a small number of people came to the opening night. It was small consolation to be told that he had come a good second.* **6** ***feel small***: feel °embarrassed *or* °ashamed *or* shamed *or* humiliated *or* °foolish, feel discomfited *or* °disconcerted *or* uncomfortable, feel mortified *or* chagrined, *Colloq* feel °put down: *Doreen always managed to make some remark that made Andrew feel small.*

small-minded *adj.* °small, °petty, °selfish, stingy, grudging, niggardly, ungenerous, °mean, °narrow-minded, °narrow, close-minded, uncharitable, °hidebound, °rigid, °intolerant, unimaginative, °short-sighted, °near-sighted, myopic: *Charging members of staff for local telephone calls seems rather small-minded.*

small-time *adj.* °small, small-scale, unimportant, °petty, piddling, °minor, °insignificant, °trifling, trivial: *In less than ten years he succeeded in building a small-time used-car business into a national chain.*

smart *adj.* **1** °intelligent, °clever, °bright, °brilliant, °quick-witted, °sharp, °acute, °astute, °capable, °adept, apt, °quick, °ingenious: *Emily is one of the smartest children in the class.* **2** canny, perspicacious, °perceptive, percipient, discerning, °knowledgeable, *au fait*, well-educated, well-read, erudite, °learned, well-versed, °aware, °shrewd, streetwise, *Slang* °hip, tuned in, *US* savvy: *Brendan is smart enough to avoid trouble.* **3** °elegant, °chic, °fashionable, °stylish, modish, à la °mode, °well-groomed, °trim, °neat, °dapper, °spruce, soigné(e), *Colloq* °snappy, natty: *You must admit that both Della and Paul are smart dressers.* **4** °pert, °pointed, saucy, °witty, nimble-witted, °poignant, °trenchant, °effective: *I wish he would stop making smart remarks when I am trying to explain something.* **5** °brisk, °vigorous, °animated, °active, °energetic, °spirited, °lively; °quick, °alert, °jaunty, °perky, °breezy: *The enemy launched a smart counterattack at dawn. He set off down the road at a smart pace.* **6** °quick, °swift, °stiff, smarting, stinging, °sharp, °severe: *The mugger gave him a smart blow on the back of the neck.*
—*v.* **7** °sting, °hurt, °pinch, °pain, °ache, tingle, °prickle, °burn, throb, °stab, °pierce: *The antiseptic may smart a bit when it is put on the cut. The smoky atmosphere made her eyes smart.*
—*n.* **8** °injury, °harm, °pain, °pang, °twinge, °affliction, °suffering, smarting: *For years he silently endured the smart of his colleagues' ridicule.*

smear *v.* **1** daub, °rub, anoint, °spread, °cover, °coat, °wipe, °plaster, bedaub; besmirch, °dirty, smudge, °stain, °soil, begrime: *The baby smeared ice-cream all over his face. The car windows were smeared with dirt from the road.* **2** °blacken, besmirch, °soil, °sully, calumniate, °slander, °discredit, °tarnish, defile, °vilify, °scandalize, °stigmatize, *Colloq* drag through the mud: *Politicians regularly smear their opponents with all sorts of accusations.*

—*n.* **3** smudge, daub, °stain, splodge *or chiefly US* splotch, °blot, °taint, °spot: *These outrageous lies constitute a smear on my good reputation. There was a smear of blood on his collar.* **4** °slander, °scandal, °libel, vilification, mud-slinging, defamation, calumny, °aspersion, °reflection: *The article contains several smears on the character of an MP.*

smell *n.* **1** °odour, °scent, °aroma, °perfume, °fragrance, °bouquet, °breath, whiff: *Don't you love the smell of freshly brewed coffee in the morning?* **2** stink, °stench, fetor *or* foetor, fetidness, mephitis, effluvium, *Colloq Brit* pong: *The smell from the rubbish tip was overpowering.*
—*v.* **3** °scent, °sniff, *Colloq* get a whiff of: *The moment I smelt that perfume I knew that Nicole had been there.* **4** stink, °reek, *Colloq Brit* pong, hum: *The milk had gone off and smelled to high heaven.*

smelly *adj.* malodorous, evil-smelling, foul-smelling, °foul, mephitic, fetid, °putrid, reeky, °stinking, noisome, °rank, °offensive, miasmic *or* miasmatic *or* miasmatical *or* miasmal, odoriferous, °rancid, high, gamy, *Slang Brit* whiffy: *She hid the diamond in a washing basket full of smelly clothes.*

smile *v.* **1** grin, °beam: *He smiled and said he was pleased to meet me.*
—*n.* **2** grin: *Georgina bestowed on me a sweet, wistful smile.*

smirk *n.* **1** °leer, °sneer, grin, grimace, simpering °smile: *Wipe that conceited smirk off your face.*
—*v.* **2** °sneer, grimace, °leer: *Instead of saying, 'I told you so', he just stood there smirking.*

smitten *adj.* **1** °affected, afflicted, °beset, °stricken, troubled, distressed, burdened, crushed, plagued, haunted, °worried, bothered, vexed: *Offers of help for the smitten town came pouring in.* **2** captivated, enthralled, struck, bewitched, °enchanted, beguiled, °charmed, enraptured, °infatuated, enamoured, ensorcelled, swept off one's feet, *Colloq* bowled over, gaga: *Anthea met some rock star and was totally smitten. They were so smitten by the beauty of the island that they returned every year.*

smooth *adj.* **1** °regular, °even, °flush, °flat, °level, °plane, unruffled, unbroken, unwrinkled, undisturbed, °tranquil, °peaceful, °calm, °serene, °glassy: *A light breeze rose to ripple the smooth surface of Alan's martini.* **2** °slick, °sleek, °shiny, °glossy, °glassy, mirror-like, °uniform, °polished, burnished; °silky, silken, velvety, satiny: *Optical mirrors for telescopes must be as smooth as modern technology can made them. He ran his fingers over the smooth fabric.* **3** unobstructed, °easy, °effortless, °free, uncluttered, °even, °orderly, well-ordered, uneventful, flowing, °fluent, unconstrained, uninterrupted: *There were no obstacles in the way of a smooth return to normal operations. The road to ruin is short and smooth.* **4** °hairless, bald, °bare, °naked, clean-shaven, smooth-shaven, depilated, glabrous: *His smooth pate shone in the moonlight.* **5** °soothing, °mellow, °pleasant, °bland, °mild, °soft: *That is a very smooth whisky indeed.* **6** °suave, °slick, °slippery, unctuous, silken, °silky, °glib, urbane, soigné(e), °agreeable, °winning, °plausible, facile, °nonchalant, courtly, °eloquent, honey-tongued, smooth-spoken, °persuasive, °oily, °slimy, syrupy, *Colloq chiefly Brit* smarmy: *With his quick understanding and smooth manner, Edward was a very successful salesman.* **7** °sweet, dulcet, pear-shaped, °mellow, well-modulated, silver-tongued: *The smooth tones of his serenade wafted through the evening air.* **8** °slick, °scheming, conniving, °crafty, °shrewd, cunning, °tricky, °shifty, °sly, °foxy, Machiavellian, °sophistic(al), °plausible, credible, believable, *Colloq* cagey: *Robinson came up with a very smooth plan to bilk wealthy widows out of their money.*
—*v.* **9** Often, ***smooth out*** *or* ***away***: °flatten, °even, °level, iron, °press, °mangle, calender: *Please smooth the wrinkles out of this shirt so that I can wear it tonight.* **10** °prepare, °lay, °pave, °ease, °ready, °clear, °open, °prime, lubricate, °facilitate: *What is your policy for smoothing the way for employees joining the firm?* **11** sand, °plane, °polish, buff, burnish: *The wood is smoothed to a glassy finish before being used for the cabinets.* **12** Often, ***smooth over***: ameliorate, assuage, allay, °calm, °gloss over, °minimize, °mitigate, lessen, soothe, °reduce, °temper, mollify, smoothen, °soften, palliate, appease: *An otherwise uncomfortable situation was smoothed over by her quiet words.*

smother *v.* **1** suffocate, °stifle, °choke, asphyxiate; throttle, strangle, snuff (out), °kill: *He was accused of trying to smother his wife with a pillow.* **2** be suffocated *or* stifled *or* asphyxiated, be choked *or* strangled, be killed: *The infant apparently smothered in the blanket.* **3** °overwhelm, °overcome, blanket, inundate, °cover, °shower; °envelop, °wrap, enshroud, °surround: *The children crowded round and smothered her with kisses. The banquet table was smothered in white roses.* **4** °repress, °subdue, °suppress, °conceal, °hide, keep *or* °hold back, °cover up, °mask, °choke back *or* down, °check; °stifle, °muffle, blanket, °blank out: *He managed to smother his grief and put on a brave face. Our whispers were smothered by the noise of the hi-fi.* **5** °extinguish, °put out, snuff out: *The foam from the fire extinguisher smothered the blaze in a few moments.*

smoulder *v.* °burn; °seethe, °simmer, °chafe, °rage, °fume, °foam, °boil, °stew, °fester, *Colloq* get hot under the collar, get (all) steamed up, see red, *US* do a slow burn, get (all) burnt up: *The fire continued to smoulder, then flared up again a week later. He has been smouldering ever since his wife confessed she was going out with another man.*

smug *adj.* self-satisfied, complacent, holier-than-thou, °self-important, °overconfident, °conceited: *She is a bit too smug about the security of her job and might get a nasty shock some day soon.*

snack *n.* **1** °bite, nibble, °morsel, °titbit *or chiefly US* tidbit, °refreshment(s), *Brit* elevenses, *Colloq* nosh: *Have a little snack or you'll be hungry later.*
—*v.* **2** °bite, nibble, *Colloq* nosh: *He gained all that weight just from snacking between meals.*

snag *n.* **1** °hitch, °catch, °problem, (stumbling) °block, °stricture, bottleneck, °complication, °obstacle, °impediment, °obstruction, °hindrance, °difficulty, *US* hang-up: *A snag developed that prevented my keeping my promise to you.*
—*v.* **2** °catch, °tear, °rip: *He snagged his new jacket on a nail.*

snake *n.* **1** reptile, serpent, ophidian, viper: *A specialist in snakes is called a herpetologist.* **2** snake in the grass, °traitor, °turncoat, Judas, quisling, betrayer, double-crosser, °informer, rat, *US* Benedict Arnold, *Slang chiefly US and Canadian* fink, ratfink: *Eventually they caught the snake who was giving away their plans to the enemy.*
—*v.* **3** °slither, °glide, °creep, °crawl, worm: *To avoid being seen, he snaked along on his stomach for a few yards.* **4** °twist, °wind, curve, °bend, °turn, zigzag, worm, °wander, °loop, crook, °meander: *The road snakes through the jungle for 50 miles or more.*

snap *v.* **1** °break (off), °separate, °crack; °cleave, °split, °fracture, °give °way, °part: *The wind snapped off tree branches like matchsticks. The back legs of the chair snapped in two as she sat on it.* **2** click; °pop; °crack: *The door snapped shut.* **3** Often, ***snap at***: **a** °bite (at), °nip, gnash *or* °snatch at: *The postman ran down the street, the dog snapping at his heels.* **b** °attack, °lunge at, °lash out (at), °snarl at, growl (at), bark (at), be °brusque *or* °short *or* °curt (with), *Colloq* jump down (someone's) throat, °fly off the handle (at): *Robin is in a bad mood today, snapping at everyone.* **4** Usually, ***snap up*** *or US also* ***off***: °grab (up), °snatch (up), °seize, °pluck, °pounce on *or* upon, °make off with, °take (away), °capture, °catch, °get, °secure: *The people who arrived early at the sale had snapped up all the bargains.* **5** °shoot, snapshot, °photograph, click, °catch: *He always has his camera with him so that he can snap anything interesting.* **6** ***snap one's fingers at***: disdain, °scorn, °flout, °dismiss, contemn, °disregard, °ignore, °defy, °mock, °deride, °thumb one's nose at, *Brit* cock a snook at: *He merely snapped his fingers*

at the dangers when I mentioned them. **7** ***snap out of it***: °recover, °come °round *or* around, °revive, °awaken, °wake up, °perk up, °liven up, °cheer up; get a grip *or* (a) hold on *or* of oneself, °pull oneself together, (re)gain control of oneself: *I was feeling very blue yesterday but managed to snap out of it.*
—*n.* **8** °crack, crackle, °pop, click: *The lid shut with a snap.* **9** °spell, °period, °interval, °wave: *During that cold snap we thought we were in for a terrible winter.* **10** °catch, spring °catch, (snap-)fastener, °fastening, °clasp: *Do you want snaps or buttons sewn on this shirt?* **11** °energy, °vigour, °animation, liveliness, °vitality, °bounce, alertness, sprightliness, élan, °dash, °sparkle, °verve, *Colloq* zip, zing, get-up-and-go, °pep, pizazz *or* pizzazz: *Granny certainly has a lot of snap left in her.* **12** easy job, *Slang* °picnic, *US and Canadian* °breeze: *There had been no need for her to worry, for the exam turned out to be a snap.*
—*adj.* **13** °abrupt, °sudden, °precipitate, °hurried, hasty, incautious, °rash, °unpremeditated, unplanned, not well-thought-out, °quick, instantaneous, °instant: *This is too important a matter for a snap decision.*

snappish *adj.* **1** °short-tempered, °testy, °petulant, °peevish, °irritable, °prickly, °touchy, irascible, quick to anger, °quick-tempered, hot-tempered, °waspish, *Brit* °snappy, *US* on a short string *or* tether: *He fancies that being snappish goes with his 'artistic' temperament.* **2** °curt, °short, °abrupt, °brusque, curmudgeonly, °cantankerous, °sharp, °cross, grouchy, °gruff, °cranky, crusty, crabby, crabbed, acid, °tart, acerbic, churlish, dyspeptic, choleric, splenetic, ill-humoured, ill-tempered, °temperamental, °moody, *Brit* snappy: *Grandad tended to be snappish when he became impatient with our lack of experience.*

snappy *adj.* **1** °quick, °sharp, °brisk, °smart, °crisp, °lively, °rapid, °speedy: *If you want to come with us, you'd better make it snappy.* **2** °fashionable, °chic, °sharp, °smart, °stylish, °dapper, modish, *Colloq* natty, *Brit* °trendy: *Your new friend is a very snappy dresser, isn't he?*

snare *n.* **1** °trap, °net, springe, noose, gin: *They had caught only a pigeon in the snare.*
—*v.* **2** °trap, °catch, entrap, °seize, °capture, ensnare: *Using a different bait, William snared some partridges.*

snarl[1] *v.* **1** growl; °snap: *I admit I found three snarling Dobermans a bit off-putting. The clerk snarled at me when I asked for a form.*
—*n.* **2** growl: *With a snarl the dog leapt at his throat.*

snarl[2] *v.* **1** Often, ***snarl up***: °tangle, °entangle, °complicate, °confuse, °scramble, °muddle, °twist, °mix *or* °mess up, *Colloq* ball up, °screw up: *This situation is so snarled up that we'll never straighten it out.* **2** °tangle, °entangle, °knot, °twist, ravel, °jam, °kink: *The rope won't feed through the pulley because it's all snarled.*
—*n.* **3** °tangle, entanglement, °complexity, °snag, °problem, °difficulty, °complication, °muddle, °mess, °predicament, °fix, °quandary, °dilemma, *Colloq* snarl-up, °tight °spot, pickle: *The situation was full of snarls and problems.* **4** jungle, °maze, labyrinth, °knot: *The drain was clogged by a snarl of hair.*

snatch *v.* **1** °grab, °grasp, °seize, °clasp, °clutch, °pluck, °take (hold of), °catch, lay hold of, wrest, latch on to, °capture, °snap up, °win, °get, lay *or* get one's hands on: *The thief snatched her purse and ran away. One must snatch every available opportunity for happiness.* **2** *Chiefly US* kidnap, °abduct: *They snatched the kid and are holding him for ransom.* **3** °save, °rescue, °deliver, °remove: *At the very last moment, we were snatched from the jaws of death.*
—*n.* **4** °grab, °clutch, °grasp: *He made a snatch for her necklace, but she managed to duck out of the way.* **5** °scrap, °bit, °fragment, snippet, °segment, °morsel, °specimen, °sample: *We were able to hear only brief snatches of their conversation through the closed door.*

sneak *v.* **1** °lurk, °slink, °steal, °creep, skulk, cower, °lurk, °pad, °prowl, °sidle, *Colloq* °pussyfoot: *We caught Francis sneaking about the house last night.*
—*n.* **2** °informer, *Colloq* tattle-tale, *Brit* °grass, *Slang* stool-pigeon, snitch, *Brit and Australian* nark, *US* stoolie, shoo-fly. *Chiefly US and Canadian* fink, ratfink: *Frank picked up a little money acting as a sneak for the police.*

sneaking *adj.* **1** °persistent, °lingering, lurking, °nagging, worrying, worrisome, °niggling, intuitive, deep-rooted, deep-seated, *Slang* °gut: *She had a sneaking suspicion that Stephen was a police informer.* **2** innate, intuitive, °inherent, °private, °secret, suppressed, °hidden, unexpressed, undeclared, unvoiced, unavowed, unconfessed, unrevealed, unadmitted, undivulged, undisclosed, covert: *I have a sneaking sympathy with the underdog.*

sneaky *adj.* underhand(ed), °devious, °furtive, °sly, °slippery, °disingenuous, °deceitful, °dishonest, °unscrupulous, °shifty: *He took a sneaky look at his friend's homework before starting his own.*

sneer *v.* **1** °smirk, curl one's lip, °sniff: *Don't sneer—you might be the next to lose your job.* **2** °scorn, disdain, °despise, contemn, turn up one's nose (at), °sniff (at), °jeer (at), °laugh (at), °deride, °mock, °ridicule; underrate; *Colloq* °sneeze at, *Slang* °knock: *They sneered at her ambition to become a serious athlete.*
—*n.* **3** °scorn, °jeer, disdain, °contempt, °derision, °mockery, °ridicule; sneering, jeering: *Barry endured his classmates' sneers without a word.*

sneeze *v.* **1** sternutate: *I was about to sneeze, so I grabbed a tissue.* **2** ***sneeze at***: See **sneer, 2,** above.
—*n.* **3** sternutation; sneezing: *The sneeze is an involuntary convulsive action.*

snicker *v.* **1** snigger, °chuckle, °giggle, °titter, °laugh up one's sleeve, °mock, °scorn, °laugh (at), °jeer (at): *It was embarrassing when the audience began to snicker at the ineptitude of the juggler.*
—*n.* **2** snigger, °chuckle, °giggle, °titter: *The villain gave a little snicker when he thought he had her in his clutches.*

sniff *n.* **1** whiff, °breath, °odour, °scent: *I got a sniff of her perfume as she walked by.* **2** °hint, °spirit, °feeling, °suggestion: *There is the sniff of spring in the air.*
—*v.* **3** °smell, snuffle, snuff: *Why is your dog always sniffing at my shoes?* **4** ***sniff (at)***: See **sneer, 2,** above.

snip *v.* **1** °nip, °clip, crop, °cut, °lop, °prune, °dock: *When the blossoms begin to fade, snip them off.*
—*n.* **2** °cut, °slit, °gash, °slash, °incision, °nick: *We could watch the audience through a small snip in the curtain.* **3** °bit, °scrap, °shred, snippet, °fragment, °cutting, clipping, °remnant, °morsel: *You are welcome to the leftover snips of fabric.* **4** ***snips***: scissors, shears, tinsnips: *This duct can be cut with the snips.*

snipe *v.* Usually, ***snipe at***: °shoot at, °fire at; °attack, °criticize, °deride, find °fault with, °carp at, °pick apart: *Newby has been sniping at the organization for years and we simply ignore him.*

snivel *v.* sniffle, snuffle, blubber, whimper, whine, mewl, pule; °cry, *Colloq Brit* whinge: *I'll buy some of your matches, little girl, but only if you stop snivelling.*

snobbery *n.* snobbism, snobbishness, pretentiousness, °pretension, hauteur, haughtiness, superciliousness, condescension, loftiness, contemptuousness, presumptuousness, lordliness, disdainfulness, disdain, pompousness, pomposity, °affectation, inflatedness, self-importance, °conceit, vainness, °vanity, narcissism, self-admiration, self-centredness, egotism, smugness, *Colloq* uppishness, uppitiness, snootiness, snottiness: *It is commonplace to criticize the nouveau riche for their snobbery.*

snobbish *adj.* °condescending, °superior, patronizing, °arrogant, °haughty, lordly, °lofty, putting on airs, °disdainful, °supercilious, °contemptuous, °pretentious, °smug, °scornful, °self-important, °affected, °conceited, egotistic(al), °vain, self-satisfied, complacent, °pompous, *Colloq* snooty, snotty, highfalutin *or* hifalutin, on one's high horse, uppity, °hoity-toity, high and mighty, stuck-up, *Brit* °uppish, *Chiefly US* high-hat, *Slang Brit* toffee-nosed: *Since he got his knighthood, Cathcart has become so snobbish he'll have nothing to do with us.*

snoop *v.* **1** °pry, °spy, °interfere, °meddle, °intrude, °butt in(to), *Colloq* stick *or* °poke one's nose; be °nosy, nose around *or* about: *He couldn't stop snooping into other people's affairs.*
—*n.* **2** °busybody, Paul Pry, meddler, °spy, °intruder, snooper, peeper; private °detective *or* investigator; *Colloq* Nosy Parker, *US* buttinsky *or* buttinski; private eye, *US* shamus: *There was a snoop here today, asking a lot of personal questions.*

snug *adj.* °cosy, °comfortable, °intimate, relaxing, °restful, °warm, sheltered, °friendly, °easy, °homely, °casual, *Colloq* comfy: *Curled up on the sofa, Chris looks as snug as a bug in a rug.*

snuggle *v.* °cuddle, °snug down, °nestle, nuzzle: *The puppies snuggled up close to their mother for warmth and protection.*

soak *v.* **1** °drench, °saturate, °wet, °immerse, souse, douse *or* dowse, bathe, °steep, inundate, ret: *You'd better let the tablecloth soak for a while to get out those wine stains.* **2** ***soak up***: absorb, °take in, sponge up; assimilate, °learn: *The parched earth soaked up the water like a sponge. Let me just lie here and soak up some sunshine. She spent years soaking up the culture of the Cameroons.*
—*n.* **3** °alcoholic, drunkard, °drunk, dipsomaniac, drinker, tippler, toper, sot, *Slang* sponge, souse, boozer, *US* dip, lush, juicer: *You'll never get a straight answer out of that old soak.*

soaking *n.* **1** drenching, wetting, dousing *or* dowsing, immersing, saturating: *We got a thorough soaking when we were caught in the storm.*
—*adj.* **2** °wet, sopping, drenched, dripping, saturated, soaked, wringing °wet, streaming, sodden, waterlogged: *Take off your soaking clothes and sit by the fire in this robe.*

soar *v.* **1** °rise, °fly, °hover, °float, °hang: *The glider soared over the hills, catching every updraught.* **2** °rise, °increase, escalate, °climb, °spiral upwards, °shoot up *or* upwards, °rocket, sky-rocket: *To counteract inflation, interest rates began to soar.*

sob *v.* °cry, °weep, blubber, °shed tears, °snivel, whimper, °sniff, snuffle, pule, wail, °moan, boohoo, mewl, °bawl, °howl, yowl: *The poor, lonely child sobbed quietly.*

sober *adj.* **1** teetotal, °temperate, *US* °dry, *Colloq* on the (water-) wagon: *Because he was driving, he stayed sober at the party while everyone else got drunk.* **2** °serious, °solemn, °earnest, °dispassionate, unruffled, unflustered, unexcited, unperturbed, °steady, °sedate, °staid, composed, °dignified, °cool, °calm, °serene, °tranquil, °collected, cool-headed, °level-headed, °sane, balanced, °practical, °realistic, °rational, clear-headed, *Slang* together: *We invited you because we respect your sober judgement.* **3** °sedate, °sombre, °plain, °simple, °subdued, °quiet, repressed, °dreary, °dark, °drab, °colourless, °neutral: *At the funeral the widow wore a sober black costume.*
—*v.* **4** ***sober up***: detoxify, °recover, *Colloq* dry out: *When she finally sobered up she awoke to find herself in custody.*

sobriety *n.* **1** teetotalism, abstemiousness, abstention, abstinence, non-indulgence, °temperance: *Since taking the pledge, Oscar has been a model of sobriety.* **2** seriousness, soberness, °solemnity, staidness, °gravity, temperateness, sedateness, °formality, °dignity: *They made him promise to do nothing to upset the sobriety of the memorial service.*

so-called *adj.* **1** styled, °self-styled, designated, *soi-disant*, called, °professed: *They found themselves fighting for Kolchak, the so-called supreme ruler of all the Russias.* **2** °alleged, °pretended, °supposed, ostensible; misnamed, misdesignated; °suspect: *She bought it through the so-called Honest Used Car Dealers Association.*

sociable *adj.* °friendly, affable, approachable, °social, gregarious, °outgoing, extrovert(ed) *or* extravert(ed), companionable, °accessible, °amiable, °amicable, °genial, congenial, convivial, °warm, °cordial, °neighbourly, hail-fellow-well-met, *Colloq* °chummy, °cosy: *The people in this area are quite sociable, and we get together often.*

social *adj.* **1** communal, community, °common, collective, °group, °public, °popular, societal: *In many New England towns, the business of government is a social activity. Crime is a social, not an individual problem.* **2** °sexual, sexually transmitted, °venereal: *The clinic was established specifically to deal with social diseases.* **3** See **sociable,** above.

socialize *v.* °mix, °get together, °fraternize, keep °company, °go out, °get out; °associate: *They haven't had much time for socializing since the birth of their baby.*

society *n.* **1** °fellowship, °brotherhood, °association, °intercourse, °companionship, °company, camaraderie, °friendship: *Few people can be happy for long without the society of others.* **2** mankind, °people, the °public: *I fear that Bob is not yet ready to mingle with society again. Do you believe that society demands too much?* **3** °culture, °civilization, community, way of life, °world; °organization, °system: *The hunting society was replaced largely by the agricultural some 10,000 years ago.* **4** high society, *haut monde, beau monde*, °upper classes, polite society, °élite, °gentry, *Colloq* °upper crust: *The purpose of the debutante ball is to introduce young ladies of about 18 to society.* **5** °organization, °club, °association, °circle, °league, °institute, academy, °alliance, guild, °group, °fraternity, sorority, °brotherhood, sisterhood, °fellowship, °union, consociation, sodality, *Verein*, bund *or* Bund: *The society, founded to advance and support linguistic scholarship, is now 100 years old.*

soft *adj.* **1** °yielding, cushiony, plushy, spongy, squeezable, compressible, squashy, squashable, °flexible, °plastic, °pliable, pliant, °supple, flexile, flexuous, unstarched: *This mattress is much too soft for my back.* **2** °easy, °comfortable, undemanding, *Colloq* cushy: *His uncle got him a soft job at the Labour Ministry.* **3** °gentle, °mild, balmy, °pleasant, °moderate, °warm, halcyon, springlike, summery, °restful, °tranquil, relaxing, °lazy: *Alexandra was looking forward to a week in the soft Caribbean climate.* **4** °subdued, toned *or* turned down, muted, °low, °quiet, °melodious, mellifluous *or* mellifluent, °mellow, °gentle, °faint, softened, °soothing, °smooth: *Riley thought she might succumb to the influences of the wine and the soft music and lights.* **5** °easygoing, °tolerant, °kind, compassionate, °gentle, °merciful, °lenient, °indulgent, °permissive, °liberal, °lax, °easy, docile, °tame, °submissive, deferential, °benign, tender-hearted, °sympathetic, kind-hearted, °kind: *Some believe that the jailers were too soft with the criminals. His parents were far too soft.* **6** Usually, ***soft in the head***: °foolish, °silly, °simple, *Colloq chiefly Brit* °daft, *US* °off: *Kevin must have gone a bit soft in the head if he thinks that Clara still loves him.* **7** depressed, declining, in °decline, in °recession, °slow, °unprofitable, borderline, °questionable, °weak: *Owing to the stormy, cold summer, the resort business has been soft this year.* **8** downy, °silky, silken, satiny, furry, °fluffy, feathery, fleecy, °fuzzy, velvety, °smooth (as a baby's bottom): *The wool from the lambs is much softer.* **9** pastel, °pale, °delicate, °fine, °subdued, °light, mat *or* matt, °quiet, °diffuse(d), °soothing: *He wanted the bedroom painted in soft shades of greenish blue.* **10** °harmless, non-addictive: *Some consider cannabis a soft drug.* **11** °fuzzy, °woolly, blurred, blurry, foggy, °diffuse(d): *The soft focus photos of the wedding looked very romantic.* **12** °weak, °feeble, °frail, effete, °delicate, non-physical, non-muscular, °puny, °flabby, out of training *or* °condition *or* °shape, pampered; namby-pamby, °effeminate, unmanly, unmanful, *Colloq* sissified, °sissy: *He had been out of the marines for so long they thought he had gone soft.* **13** °easy, °luxurious, pampered, °rich, °opulent, °plush, °posh, *Colloq* ritzy, swank(y): *Since selling his business, Aubrey has been living the soft life on the Costa del Sol.*

soften *v.* **1** Often, ***soften up***: °melt, °affect, mollify, °mellow, palliate, soothe, °relax, appease: *Nothing would soften the heart of that cruel tyrant.* **2** °mitigate, assuage, °diminish, °moderate, °reduce, °cushion, lessen, °weaken, allay, °ease, °lighten, abate, °temper, °relieve: *Can't you think of some way to soften the blow of such bad news?* **3** °muffle, °deaden, damp, soft-pedal, °lower, °still, °quiet, °tone down, lessen, °diminish, °lighten, °turn down, °quell, *Chiefly Brit* °quieten: *Try to soften the high notes and bring up the bass.* **4** °give in, °succumb, °surrender, °yield, °agree, °consent, concur, assent, give °way, °relax, °ease (up), °let up: *The committee finally softened and allowed the park to be used for games.*

soft-hearted *adj.* tender-hearted, compassionate, °tender, warm-hearted, °sentimental, °charitable, °generous, giving, °sympathetic, °indulgent, °kind, kind-hearted, °responsive: *Alison is quite soft-hearted when it comes to animal causes and contributed willingly.*

soil[1] *v.* **1** °dirty, °stain, begrime, °muddy, °smear, °spot: *His shirts were returned by the laundry still soiled.* **2** °pollute, °contaminate, °sully, defile, °foul, befoul, °tarnish, besmirch, °disgrace, °muddy, °smear, °blacken; °blot: *The scandal soiled his previously spotless reputation.*
—*n.* **3** °dirt, °filth, °muck, °mire, °mud, °sludge, °dregs, °refuse; excrement, °waste (matter): *The soil is carried away by these pipes into the main sewer.*

soil[2] *n.* °earth, loam, °dirt, °ground, °turf, humus; clay: *The men who dug the swimming-pool took away the soil from the pit.*

sojourn *n.* **1** °stay, °stop, stopover, °visit, °rest, °holiday, vacation: *We had a very pleasant sojourn in Toronto on our way home.*
—*v.* **2** °stay, °stop (over), °visit, rest, °holiday, vacation, °tarry: *Next year we plan to sojourn in Bermuda for a while.*

solace *n.* **1** °comfort, consolation, condolence, relief, balm, °support, °help, succour; reassurance, °cheer: *The children brought her solace in her bereavement.*
—*v.* **2** °comfort, °console, condole, °support, °help, succour, soothe, allay, alleviate, ameliorate, °mitigate, assuage, °relieve; °cheer (up), °reassure, hearten: *There was little to solace James's misery.*

soldier *n.* **1** serviceman, servicewoman, °recruit, fighter, infantryman, foot-soldier, trooper, warrior, military man, man-at-arms, *Brit* Tommy (Atkins), *US* enlisted man *or* woman, *Colloq Brit* squaddie, *US* GI *or* G.I. (Joe), *Old-fashioned* (*WWI*) doughboy: *Enemy soldiers had been reconnoitring our position during the night.* **2** fighter, °stalwart, °supporter, °militant: *He has been a soldier in the fight against poverty all his life.*
—*v.* **3** °serve (in the army): *In his family the men have been soldiering for generations.* **4** ***soldier on***: °continue, °persist, °persevere, °endure, °drive, °keep going, °keep on *or* at, °grind, drudge: *Despite the setbacks, they soldiered on to complete the project in time.*

sole *adj.* lone, °only, °singular, °unique, °solitary; °particular, °exclusive, °individual, °personal: *As Susan is the sole surviving heir, she has the right to sell the house if she wishes.*

solecism *n.* °error, °slip, °impropriety, °fault, °breach, °violation, °lapse, °mistake, misusage, incongruity, inconsistency, barbarism, °blunder, gaffe, °bungle, °fumble, gaucherie, faux pas, °botch *or* botch-up, *Colloq* boo-boo, *US* flub, *Slang* boner, *Brit* boob, bloomer, *Chiefly US and Canadian* blooper: *Solecisms in his writing include failure of subject and verb to agree.*

solemn *adj.* **1** °serious, °sober, °reserved, °grave, °earnest, °sedate, °staid, °taciturn; morose, °morbid, mirthless, unsmiling, °gloomy, °sombre, °grim; °glum, long-faced, saturnine: *We observed a moment of solemn silence in memory of our fallen comrades. They knew from their father's solemn expression that something was wrong.* **2** °ceremonial, ritualistic, liturgical, °religious, ecclesiastical, °holy, °divine, °sacred, hallowed, sacramental, reverential, devotional: *We attended a solemn service to celebrate the return of the hostages.* **3** °ceremonious, °ritual, °formal, °dignified, °stately, °grand, august, °imposing, °impressive, awe-inspiring, °awesome, °important, °momentous: *The Trobriand islanders regarded the rites of passage as most solemn.*

solemnity *n.* solemnness, °gravity, seriousness, soberness, °reserve, sedateness, taciturnity, staidness, earnestness, impressiveness, °grandeur, °importance, momentousness, consequence: *All who attended the service were affected by the solemnity of the lighting of the eternal flame.*

solicit *v.* **1** entreat, °beseech, °ask (for), implore, °petition, importune, °appeal for *or* to, °call on *or* upon, °beg, supplicate, °pray, crave: *He has solicited my help on more than one occasion.* **2** accost, °approach, °entice, °lure, °pander to, *Slang* °hustle: *You can't go out in that neighbourhood without being solicited.*

solicitor *n.* °lawyer, attorney, *US* counselor-at-law: *I have turned the matter over to my solicitor.*

solicitous *adj.* **1** °concerned, caring, °considerate, uneasy, troubled, °anxious, apprehensive, °worried: *She seemed genuinely solicitous over the state of my health.* **2** °eager, °earnest, zealous, °keen, °anxious, °desirous, °ardent, avid: *She seems sincerely solicitous to please the firm's customers.*

solicitude *n.* °concern, °consideration, °regard, disquiet, disquietude, uneasiness, °anxiety, apprehension, °worry, nervousness, °fear, fearfulness, °alarm: *As she had not yet made him her sole heir, his solicitude over her health was understandable.*

solid *adj.* **1** three-dimensional, cubic: *The perspective drawing is a representation of a solid object.* **2** filled (in *or* up), °packed, jammed, crowded, teeming, °congested, crammed, swarming, compressed, concentrated, *Colloq* chock-a-block, jam-packed, chock-full: *By the time I arrived, the gallery was solid with people.* **3** °compact, °firm, °hard, °stable; unshakeable *or* unshakable, unshaky, °substantial, °concrete, °sturdy, °sound, °stout, °strong: *The vessel floated through the air before coming to rest on solid ground. His theories rest on a solid foundation.* **4** °consistent, °homogeneous, °uniform, unalloyed, unmixed, °pure, °continuous, unbroken, °real, °authentic, °true, °genuine, 24-carat *or esp. US* 24-karat, unadulterated, *Slang* honest-to-God: *This mountain seems to be solid iron all the way through. John gave me a solid gold necklace for my birthday.* **5** law-abiding, upstanding, °upright, °decent, °stout, °substantial, °powerful, °reliable, °regular, °steady, °steadfast, °stalwart, °straight, °estimable, °sure, trusty, °trustworthy, true-blue, °worthy, dependable, °sober: *Mr Hart is one of the solid citizens of this town. He has always been a solid defender of the underdog.* **6** °steady, °stable, °stalwart, dependable, °sturdy, °strong, °substantial, °sound, °firm, well-built, well-constructed, well-made, °tough, °durable, °rugged, °stout: *That chair is not solid enough for you to stand on.* **7** cogent, °sound, °concrete, °weighty, proved, provable, valid, °reasonable, °sensible, °rational, °sober, well-founded, °authoritative, °indisputable, °incontrovertible, irrefutable, incontestable, °good, °powerful, °potent, °forceful, convincing, °persuasive: *He presents a solid argument for a sales tax.* **8** °firm, °downright, °vigorous, °telling, °effective, °forceful, °potent, °powerful, °mighty, °dynamic, °thorough, through-and-through, °intensive: *Jan struck a solid blow against the supporters of abortion.* **9** See **solvent, 1,** below. **10** °entire, °complete, °whole, °continuous; uninterrupted, °undivided, unbroken, unrelieved, °blank, windowless: *I had to wait at the dentist's for a solid hour. Around the park they erected a solid wall.*

solidarity *n.* °unity, unanimity, unification, °accord, concord, concordance, °harmony, concurrence, like-mindedness, °agreement, mutuality, single-mindedness, singleness (of purpose), community of interest, esprit de corps, camaraderie, comradeship, sodality, *Solidarność*: *It was through solidarity, not the pursuit of individual interest, that freedom was achieved.*

solidify *v.* **1** °harden, °freeze, °set, °cake, °compact, compress, crystallize; °jell *or* gel, clot, congeal, °coagulate, °thicken, *Technical* inspissate; sublime: *The lava flowed round the bodies of those who died and solidified, preserving them in their final attitudes.* **2** consolidate, °unite, °unify, pull *or* draw together: *Studying the speeches of politicians enables me to solidify my own views.*

solitary *adj.* **1** lone, °single, °sole, °individual; unattended, °solo, companionless, friendless, °lonesome, °lonely, °unsocial, cloistered, °secluded, °reclusive, °separate, eremitic(al), hermitic(al), °remote, °withdrawn, °distant, °out-of-the-way, unfrequented, °desolate: *There is not a solitary exception to the rule. Flora's solitary style of living allows her to concentrate on her writing. There is a solitary little inn where we go for weekends.*
—*n.* **2** solitary confinement: *The prisoner has been in solitary for striking a guard.*

solitude *n.* **1** solitariness, aloneness, isolation, °seclusion, °privacy: *Peter enjoys the solitude of living on an island.* **2** loneliness, remoteness; °emptiness, wilderness: *How long could one person survive in the solitude of interstellar space?*

solo *adv.* **1** °alone, °unaccompanied, on one's own: *Jack flew solo for the first time yesterday.*
—*adj.* **2** °individual, °unaccompanied, °solitary: *Let Eugene play the solo trombone part.*

solution *n.* **1** solving, working *or* figuring out, °discovery, °finding out, unravelling, explication, deciphering, decipherment, elucidation, °revelation, clarification, °explanation; °answer, °key: *The solution of the problem should be left up to the experts. Several solutions have been found through computer analysis.* **2** °settlement, settling, °resolution, °result, denouement *or* dénouement, °outcome, conclusion: *It seems unlikely that we shall be able to bring this matter to a solution in a one-day meeting.* **3** °mixture, °blend, °compound, infusion; °liquid, °fluid; *Technical* emulsion, °suspension, colloid *or* colloidal solution *or* colloidal °suspension: *After mixing the powder with water, use the solution to bathe the wound.* **4** dissolving, °dissolution, mixing, °mixture: *The solution of these ingredients in alcohol was first accomplished in ancient times.*

solve *v.* °work *or* °figure out, unravel, disentangle, untangle, °clarify, °clear up, make °plain *or* °clear, °interpret, explicate, °decipher, °crack, °explain, elucidate, °reveal, °answer, °resolve: *Oedipus' problems began in earnest when he solved the Riddle of the Sphinx.*

solvent *adj.* creditworthy, (financially) °sound, °solid, °reliable; debt-free; °profitable: *The auditors rate the business as solvent.*

sombre *adj.* **1** °gloomy, morose, lugubrious, °funereal, °morbid, louring *or* lowering, °melancholy, °sad, °dismal, °unhappy, cheerless, °joyless, °serious, °sober, °doleful, dolorous, °mournful, depressed, depressing, °grave, °grim, grim-faced, grim-visaged, *Literary* melancholic, darksome: *Despite his sombre appearance, Sid was one of the funniest men I've ever met.* **2** °dark, °gloomy, °foreboding, °bleak, depressing, °shadowy, °murky, °leaden, °grey, °black, °dismal, °dreary, °overcast, °dusky, °dim, °dingy, darkling, °dull, subfusc *or* subfuscous: *The sombre sky set the mood for the proceedings that were to follow.* **3** °staid, °sedate, °sober, °solemn, °dark, °dull, subfusc: *A young person like you ought to dress in less sombre colours.*

somebody *pron.* **1** °one, someone, some person: *There must be somebody who will take you to the dance.*
—*n.* **2** °personage, °celebrity, °dignitary, VIP, luminary, °notable, °star, superstar, *Colloq* hotshot, °bigwig, °big wheel, °big gun, °big noise, °big White Chief, °big Daddy, °big Chief, big-timer; hot stuff; *Old-fashioned* °big cheese; *US* Mr Big: *He must be a somebody to merit such treatment.*

somehow *adv.* someway, in one °way or another, in some °way, somehow or other, by °hook or by crook, by fair means or foul, *Colloq* come hell or high water: *Somehow, we have to get into the vault for those papers.*

sometime *adj.* **1** °former, erstwhile, °past, °recent, one-time, quondam: *Crawford was a sometime student of the occult.*
—*adv.* **2** at some °time or other, someday, one day, any °time, on a future occasion, when *or* if the opportunity arises, °soon, by and by, one of these days: *Come up and see me sometime.* **3** sooner or later, in (due) °time, in the fullness of °time, in the long °run, one fine day, *Un bel di*, °eventually, when all is said and done, before long, before you know it: *You can be sure that the tax man will find out about it sometime.*

sometimes *adv.* °occasionally, on occasion, (every) °now and then, °now and again, off and on, at times, from °time to °time, every so often, (every) °once in a while: *Sometimes Ambrose used to visit his grandchildren twice a week.*

somewhat *adv.* °rather, °quite, °relatively, more or less, °moderately, pretty, °fairly, to some *or* a certain °extent *or* °degree *or* °measure, °slightly, a bit, a °little, *Colloq* °sort of, kind of: *Ingrid was somewhat put out by my refusal.*

song *n.* **1** °tune, °air, °melody, ditty, °number: *Together, they wrote some of the most popular songs of this century.* **2** ***for a song***: cheaply, inexpensively, at a °bargain price: *That old book you wanted went for a song at the auction.* **3** ***(old) song and dance***: **a** °fuss, to-do, commotion, °bother, ado, *Colloq* °flap, °performance, *Brit* kerfuffle: *I cannot see why they made such a song and dance of telling us they couldn't come.* **b** °evasion, °tale, prevarication, (long) °story, (long) °explanation: *To excuse his absence he gave me the old song and dance about his grandmother being ill.*

soon *adv.* **1** before long, °presently, ere long; in the near future, any minute (now), before you know it, in good time, in a little while, in a °minute *or* a °moment, momentarily, °shortly, anon, in a °second, *Colloq* in a jiffy: *Soon another year will have passed. The doctor will be with you soon.* **2** °quickly, speedily, at °once, °promptly, °immediately, °directly, without delay, °straight away, °right away, forthwith, in short order, at the °double, in two shakes (of a lamb's tail), in a wink, *tout de suite*, *Colloq* pronto, *US and Canadian* lickety-split: *If he doesn't come soon, dinner will be spoilt.* **3** °quickly, speedily, °promptly, °swiftly: *I'll be there as soon as I can.* **4** °willingly, lief, °gladly, °happily, °readily: *I'd just as soon be left alone, if you don't mind.* **5** ***sooner or later***: at some °time or other, some °time, one day, in °time, in due course, °eventually, °ultimately, in the end, when all is said and done, at the end of the day, in the last *or* final analysis, at °bottom: *Don't worry, she'll come home sooner or later. Sooner or later they will have to yield.*

soothing *adj.* **1** relaxing, °restful, °serene, °peaceful, pacifying, °calm, calming, °quiet, °soft, quieting: *I put on some soothing music and offered her a cocktail.* **2** mollifying, comforting, palliative, lenitive, demulcent, balsamic, emollient: *The doctor prescribed a soothing ointment to relieve the pain.*

sophistic *adj.* sophistical, °specious, fallacious, °deceptive, °hypocritical, °false, °unsound, baseless, °groundless, casuistic(al), Jesuitic(al), captious, misleading, °bogus, °sham, °untenable: *The politicians advanced their usual sophistic arguments for continuing a war that no one wanted to support.*

sophisticated *adj.* **1** °cultivated, cultured, °refined, °experienced, °worldly, cosmopolitan, °polished, °elegant, urbane, worldly-wise, °knowledgeable, °knowing, °suave, soigné(e), °blasé, chichi, °slick, *Slang* °hip *or* hep, °cool, with it: *The Gordons mix with a pretty sophisticated crowd.* **2** advanced, complex, °complicated, °intricate, °elaborate, °subtle, °refined, multifaceted: *The desk-top computers of today are* *much more sophisticated than most older main-frame systems.*

sophistication *n.* **1** worldliness, urbanity, °culture, °refinement, °knowledge, knowledgeability, cosmopolitanism, °polish, °elegance, °poise, suavity *or suavité*, savoir faire, savoir vivre, °finesse, °discrimination, discernment, awareness, °taste, tastefulness, °style: *They want him on the board of directors of the museum because he lends it sophistication.* **2** °complexity, intricacy, °subtlety, °refinement: *There is a staggering amount of sophistication built into modern integrated circuits.*

sorcerer *n.* sorceress, magus, necromancer, wizard, °witch, warlock, enchanter, enchantress, °magician, thaumaturgist, shaman, witch-doctor, medicine man: *The law demanded death for the sorcerers and for those who dealt with them.*

sorcery *n.* witchcraft, °enchantment, sortilege, necromancy, wizardry, (black *or* white) °magic, shamanism, black art, diabolism: *Once Vera works her sorcery on you, you obey her every whim.*

sordid *adj.* **1** °base, °vile, °corrupt, °low, ignoble, debased, degraded, abased, °mean, ignominious, °dishonourable, °despicable, °disreputable, °shabby, °shameful, °scurvy, °rotten, execrable: *He forced his family to do the most sordid things to raise money.* **2** °avaricious, °greedy, °grasping, °mercenary, piggish, °hoggish, °selfish, °rapacious, money-grubbing, stingy, parsimonious: *His most sordid plan was to pretend he was collecting money for the handicapped.* **3** °dirty, °foul, °filthy, squalid, unclean, °untidy, °mean, slummy, °seamy, °seedy, °wretched, unsanitary, insanitary, °offensive, defiled, polluted, fetid, feculent, mucky, maggoty, °putrid, fly-blown, °slimy: *The conditions of some of the homes the social workers visit are indescribably sordid.* **4** °wretched, °miserable, °poor, poverty-stricken, down-and-out, °impoverished, °ramshackle, hovel-like, °tumbledown, °dingy, °seamy, °seedy, slummy, deteriorated, °sleazy, back-alley: *When he first came to town, he lived in a sordid shack lent him by a farmer.*

sore *adj.* **1** °painful, °sensitive, °tender, °raw, °angry, °burning, stinging, smarting, hurting; irritated, °inflamed, chafed: *My finger is still sore round the cut.* **2** °sensitive, °delicate, °tender, °embarrassing, °awkward, °ticklish, °touchy, °thorny, °prickly: *Failing to complete medical school is a sore point with her.* **3** dire, °serious, °acute, °extreme, °critical, °urgent, °pressing, °desperate: *He is in sore need of some good advice.* **4** °angry, angered, annoyed, irritated, vexed, irked, °upset, *Colloq* peeved: *Don't get sore at me because you got low marks in your exams.* **5** °painful, °troublesome, °grievous, aggrieved, distressing, distressful, °harrowing, °severe, °agonizing, °bitter, °fierce, °burdensome, onerous, °heavy, °oppressive: *Melanie's marital troubles proved a sore trial for her friends.* **6** ***sore straits***: °difficulty, °trouble, °distress, °danger, °dangerous *or* °precarious condition: *The business is in sore straits, I fear.*
—*n.* **7** °injury, °damage, °swelling, rawness, infection, °inflammation, °bruise, abrasion, °cut, laceration, °scrape, °burn, canker, °ulcer: *If that sore on your arm doesn't heal, you'd better see a doctor.*

sorrow *n.* **1** °sadness, heartbreak, °grief, unhappiness, dolour, °misery, °woe, °anguish, °distress, °suffering, °torment, °agony, wretchedness, heartache, °desolation, desolateness: *How can one deal with the sorrow of the loss of a child?* **2** °affliction, °trouble, °trial, tribulation, °misfortune, °hardship, adversity, bad *or* hard luck, °cares, °pressure, °strain, travail: *It is unbelievable that anyone could survive a life filled with such sorrow.*
—*v.* **3** °grieve, °lament, °mourn, °regret, °keen, °bemoan, agonize, °moan, °bewail: *She is sorrowing over the loss of her nephew.*

sorrowful *adj.* **1** °sad, °unhappy, °regretful, °sorry, depressed, °dejected, crestfallen, chap-fallen, °gloomy, downcast, °blue, dispirited, °melancholy, in the doldrums, °wretched, °woebegone, °miserable, heartsick, disheartened, °piteous, heavy-hearted, °broken-hearted, rueful, woeful, °tearful, disconsolate, °inconsolable, grief-stricken, *Colloq* down in the °mouth, down in the dumps: *The entire family was sorrowful to learn of Carriston's death.* **2** distressing, °lamentable, °doleful, °unfortunate, °bitter, distressful, troublous, °grievous, unlucky, hapless, afflictive: *What a sorrowful life some of those miners' families have led!*

sorry *adj.* **1** °regretful, °penitent, °remorseful, contrite, conscience-stricken, guilt-ridden, °repentant, °apologetic, penitential: *I am sorry if I offended you.* **2** abject, °miserable, depressing, °wretched, °pitiful, °pitiable, °pathetic, °deplorable, °stark, °grim, °sordid, °dismal, °base, star-crossed, ill-starred: *Crackham has led a rather sorry life, most of it as a vagrant. Agnes again made a sorry spectacle of herself at the Christmas party.* **3** See **sorrowful, 1,** above: *I was indeed sorry to learn that you are moving away, Peggy.*

sort *n.* **1** °kind, °variety, °type, °class, classification, °group, °category, °brand, °make, °mark, °stamp, °description, °mould, °stripe, ilk, feather, kidney, °character, °nature; °manner, species: *A 1928 Alfa-Romeo coupé is not exactly the right sort of car for a family. Lewis is a person of a different sort. What sort of person is he?* **2** °kind, °type, °manner: *This sort of behaviour must stop.* **3** species, genus, °family, phylum, subgenus, subspecies, °race, °breed, °strain, °stock, °kind, °variety, °type: *Aberdeen Angus is a better sort of beef for steaks.* **4** °person, °individual, °lot; °thing: *He is not really such a bad sort.* **5** ***of sorts***: of a sort, of a °mediocre *or* °passable *or* admissible *or* not (too) bad *or* °fair *or* sufficiently good *or* °adequate *or* °undistinguished *or* °indifferent kind *or* quality *or* proficiency: *Yes, one might say that he is a violinist of sorts.* **6** ***out of sorts***: not oneself, not up to snuff, unwell, ailing, °indisposed, (slightly) °ill, °low, *Colloq* off one's feed, under the °weather: *He is out of sorts after last night's revelries.* **7** ***sort of***: See **somewhat,** above.
—*v.* **8** assort, classify, °file, °order, °rank, °grade, °class, °categorize, °separate, °divide, °combine, °merge, °arrange, °organize, systemize, systematize, catalogue, °group, sort out: *Sort these names into alphabetical order.* **9** °describe, °characterize, °categorize, °cast, °throw, °combine, °mould, type: *I did not enjoy being sorted together with thieves and murderers.* **10** ***sort out***: **a** °organize, set *or* put °straight, °straighten out, °resolve, °tidy (up), °clarify, °clear up, °solve; °decide: *Someone will have to sort out how we are to proceed.* **b** °choose, °select, °separate, °divide: *Sort out all the books that you want to keep from those to be donated to the library.*

so so *adj.* °mediocre, all right, °average, °undistinguished, °passable, not (too) bad *or* good, °adequate, °fair (to middling), middling, °indifferent, °ordinary, °tolerable, *comme ci, comme ça*, °modest: *Sabrina, whose singing is just so so, will never be a star.*

soul *n.* **1** (vital) °spirit *or* °force, being, (inner *or* true) self, °essence, °psyche, °heart, °mind, °intellect, °reason, anima: *He finally surrendered, body and soul.* **2** °person, °individual, °man, °woman, °mortal, (°human) being: *I won't tell a soul about our conversation. What a sweet old soul she is!* **3** incarnation, °embodiment, personification, typification, °essence, °quintessence: *You can count on me as the soul of discretion.* **4** °emotion, °feeling, °sentiment, °sincerity, °fervour, °ardour, °warmth, °dynamism, vivacity, °energy, °spirit, °vitality, °force: *Alice puts a lot of soul into her singing, and that comes across to the audience.*

soulful *adj.* °sincere, °deep, °profound, °moving, °emotional, °warm, °ardent, °intense, °fervent, °expressive: *The lovers exchanged soulful looks.*

sound[1] *n.* **1** °tone; °noise; °din; cacophony; °report: *This piano has a tinny sound. We could hear the sound of laughter from below. I heard nothing over the sound of the crowd. Sounds of gunfire echoed in the valley.* **2** °ring, °tone, °impression, °characteristic, °quality, °effect, °aspect, °look: *I didn't like the sound of that*

remark. **3** hearing, °range, earshot: *Anyone within the sound of his voice could tell that he was angry.*
—*v.* **4** °resound, reverberate, °echo, resonate: *The noises sound very close.* **5** °seem, °appear, °look; °strike °one, give one the °impression *or* °feeling *or* °sense (that); °resemble, °seem *or* °look °like: *It sounds as if you don't want to come to my party. That sounds like Russian to me.* **6** °ring, (be) °activate(d), (be) °set *or* °touch(ed) off, °signal: *Anyone walking into the room sounds the alarm. The alarm sounds when the beam is broken.* **7** Sometimes, ***sound out***: articulate, °pronounce, °enunciate, utter; °voice, vocalize: *I was taught to speak clearly, to sound each consonant and vowel.* **8** Sometimes, ***sound out*** *or* ***off***: °shout (out), °cry out, °yell (out): *Sound out those numbers loud and clear!* **9** ***sound off***: °vituperate, °complain, °bluster, grumble, *Slang* °bitch: *Today Mr Morrison was again sounding off about the service in the café.*

sound[2] *adj.* **1** undamaged, uninjured, °whole, unmarred, in °good °condition *or* °shape, °intact, unimpaired, °unscathed: *When the vase was sold to you it was sound.* **2** °healthy, °hale (and °hearty), °fit (as a fiddle), °robust, °vigorous, blooming, °rosy, ruddy: *Old Tom is as sound as ever.* **3** °firm, °solid, °substantial, °strong, °sturdy, °tough, °rugged, °durable, well-built, well-constructed, dependable: *A business, like a building, must be built on sound foundations if it is to last.* **4** °sane, balanced, °normal, °rational, °wholesome, °reasoning, °reasonable, clear-headed, lucid, right-minded, °responsible, °practical, °prudent, °politic, °wise, °sensible, °logical, common-sense, commonsensical, °astute, °far-sighted, °perceptive, perspicacious, percipient; valid, °good, °judicious, °reliable, °useful: *As Juvenal said, 'Mens sana in corpore sano,' or 'A sound mind in a sound body'. My old teacher gave me a lot of sound advice.* **5** °safe, °secure, °good, °conservative, non-speculative, °solid, riskless; °profitable: *Are you sure that utilities are a sound investment now?* **6** unbroken, uninterrupted, undisturbed, untroubled, °peaceful, °deep: *I drank the potion and at once fell into a sound sleep.*

sound[3] *v.* **1** Often, ***sound out***: °plumb, °probe, °test, °check (out *or* into), °fathom, °inquire *or* °enquire of, °question, °poll, °canvass, °investigate, °examine, °survey: *Sound out the membership on their feelings about increasing the dues.* **2** °dive, °plunge, °submerge: *The great whale sounded, almost taking the tiny boat down with it.*

sound[4] *n.* inlet, °strait(s), fiord *or* fjord, bight, (sea) loch, bay, arm of the sea, cove, *Scots* firth: *The breeze freshened as we sailed across the Sound of Mull.*

sour *adj.* **1** acid, acidic, °tart, vinegary, lemony, acidulous *or* acidulent, acidulated, acescent, acerbic: *This apple has a pleasant, slightly sour taste. Do you like sour dill pickles?* **2** turned, °bad, (gone) °off, fermented, curdled, °rancid, spoilt *or* spoiled: *If the food is sour, throw it away.* **3** °disagreeable, unpleasant, °distasteful, °bad, °nasty, °bitter, °terrible: *The poor service and facilities made the entire holiday a very sour experience.* **4** acrimonious, °bitter, °embittered, unpleasant, churlish, ill-natured, ill-tempered, bad-tempered, crusty, curmudgeonly, crabbed, crabby, grouchy, °cross, °cranky, °testy, °petulant, °impatient, °abrupt, °nasty, °curt, °caustic, °brusque, °peevish, °snappish, edgy, °sullen, morose, °gloomy, °discontented: *The waitress's sour expression matched her sour disposition.*
—*v.* **5** °turn, °spoil, curdle, go °bad *or* °off, °ferment: *Milk sours quickly in this climate if you don't refrigerate it.* **6** embitter, acerbate, disenchant, °exasperate, vex, *Colloq* peeve: *Being forced to practise for hours when a child was what soured my enjoyment of playing the piano.*

source *n.* **1** fountain-head, well-spring, °origin, provenance, provenience, inception, °start, °outset, °beginning, °root(s), commencement, °rise: *We set out to find the source of the Blue Nile. The mineral bauxite is the source of aluminium.* **2** originator, °author, °creator, begetter: *Who is credited as the source of this quotation?* **3** °authority, documentation; informant, *Colloq* horse's mouth: *To verify the information, go to the source.*

sovereign *n.* **1** °monarch, ruler, emperor, empress, °king, °queen, prince, princess, potentate, °chief, °master, °mistress, shah, sultan; Akund (of Swat), Gaekwar (of Baroda), Nizam (of Hyderabad), Mehtar (of Chitral), Nucifrage of Nuremberg, Sheikh of Araby, *Colloq* supremo: *She is the sovereign and must be obeyed.*
—*adj.* **2** °supreme, °paramount, highest, °principal, °foremost, greatest, °predominant, °dominant, ranking, °leading, °chief, °superior, °pre-eminent, ruling, regnant, reigning, governing, all-powerful, °absolute, °unlimited: *The first-born of the monarch is vested with sovereign authority upon the monarch's death.* **3** °royal, °regal, °majestic, °noble, lordly, aristocratic, kingly, queenly: *He was hailed as the sovereign ruler of all the islands.*

sovereignty *n.* suzerainty, hegemony, °dominion, °rule, °pre-eminence, °power, °jurisdiction, °authority, °leadership, °command, °sway, °supremacy, ascendancy, primacy: *Anyone who doubted his sovereignty was seized and thrown into a dungeon.*

sow *v.* °seed, disseminate, °broadcast, °plant: *The grand vizier sowed the seeds of dissension amongst the subjects of the caliph.*

space *n.* **1** spaciousness, °room, °place, °expanse, elbow-room, °leeway, °margin, latitude, °play: *There was no space for another desk.* **2** °blank: *When the spaces are filled in, the puzzle is done.* **3** °interval, °lapse, °period, °time, hiatus, lacuna, °span, while, duration, °extent, °spell, °stretch, °pause, °wait, °intermission, °gap, °break, °interruption: *After a short space we were home again.* **4** °accommodation, °seat, berth, °room, °place: *Luckily, I got the last available space on the plane.*
—*v.* **5** °arrange, °organize, array, °set out, align, °range, °order, °rank, °lay out, °measure (out): *Space the trees about eight feet apart.*

spacious *adj.* °vast, °large, °extensive, °enormous, °wide, °broad, commodious, °ample, °expansive, °roomy, °huge, sizeable, capacious, °great, °immense, outsized, °voluminous, oversize(d): *The house was more spacious than it looked from the outside. Siberia offers spacious territory, ripe for habitation over the next century.*

span *n.* **1** °bridge, °link, °stretch, overpass, *Chiefly Brit* flyover: *We drove across the entire span in less than five minutes.* **2** °course, °extent, °interval, °stretch, °period, °time, °term, °spell: *In the short span of six hours we had crossed the Atlantic.*
—*v.* **3** °cross, °stretch over, °reach over, °extend over, °go over, °bridge: *A rude bridge spans the river at Lexington. Their lives spanned more than a century.*

spank *v.* °slap, smack, put *or* take over one's knee, thrash, °paddle; °chastise, °punish, °castigate; *Colloq* wallop, tan (someone's) °hide, paddywhack, whack, give (someone) a (good) licking *or* hiding: *In those days when you misbehaved you were spanked.*

spanking *adj.* **1** spick and span, °smart, °bright, °snappy, gleaming, °brand-new, °fine, °remarkable, °outstanding, °big, °large, °great: *You ought to see Jim Trowbridge's spanking new yacht.* **2** °brisk, °lively, °crisp, °bracing, °fresh, freshening, rattling, °strong, °invigorating, blustery: *A spanking breeze blew up from the west.* **3** °quick, °rapid, °swift, °lively, °snappy, °fast, °smart, °energetic, °vigorous, °brisk: *The pony drew the dogcart at a spanking pace.*

spar[1] *n.* mast, yard, yard-arm, boom, boomkin, gaff, jigger, mizen, *Colloq* °stick, °pole: *The first gusts of the storm tore the remaining canvas from the spars.*

spar[2] *v.* **1** °fight, °box, exchange blows; shadow-box: *He was once the champion's sparring partner.* **2** °dispute, °argue, °bicker, squabble, wrangle, bandy words, have words; °fight, *Colloq* °scrap: *I have better things to do than spar with you over breakfast every day.*

spare *adj.* **1** °extra, °surplus, supernumerary, °auxiliary, °supplementary, additional; °odd, °leftover; in °reserve, in °addition: *We got a puncture, so Dad stopped and put on the spare wheel. Give them the spare room. Have you a spare cigarette?* **2** unoccupied, °leftover, °leisure, °free, °surplus, °extra; not spoken for: *Her demanding job left her very little spare time.* **3** °thin, °skinny, °scrawny, cadaverous, °gaunt, °rawboned, °meagre, gangling, lank(y), °wiry, °slim, °slender; all skin and bones: *The spare, ragged figure crouched in the shadows, his hand outstretched in supplication.* **4** See **sparing,** below. **5** °meagre, °frugal, °small, skimpy, °modest, °scanty: *Their meals were spare but wholesome.*
—*v.* **6** °save, °rescue, °deliver, °redeem: *Bill spared me from a fate worse than death. Spare me the embarrassment of having to ask for my money back.* **7** °pardon, let go, °release, have °mercy on, °let off, °free, °liberate: *At the last moment, the judge spared him.* **8** °allow, °relinquish, let go (of), °give, °award, °bestow, let have, °donate, °part with, °yield: *She decided she could spare a couple of pounds for the disaster appeal. Buddy, can you spare a dime?* **9** °avoid, °dispense with, manage *or* do without, °give up, °forgo, °forsake, °surrender, °sacrifice: *We spared a great deal of trouble by settling the dispute. Spare the rod and spoil the child.*

sparing *adj.* **1** °thrifty, °saving, °frugal, °spare, °careful, °prudent, parsimonious, °economical, °penurious, °mean; penny-pinching, stingy, niggardly, °miserly, °close, close-fisted, °cheap, *Colloq* °tight, tight-fisted, *Brit* mingy: *As sparing in his praise as he was in his purse, General Waller rarely complimented his troops.* **2** See **sparse, 2,** below.

spark *n.* **1** scintilla, °flicker, glimmer, glint, °sparkle, °speck, °hint, °suggestion, °vestige, atom, whit, °jot (or tittle), iota: *As long as a spark of life remained in his body he fought for freedom and justice.*
—*v.* **2** Often, ***spark off***: °set *or* °touch off, ignite, °kindle, enkindle, °electrify, °animate, trigger, °energize, galvanize, °activate, °excite, °stimulate, set in °motion, °bring about, °start (up), °begin, °initiate, °inspire, inspirit, °provoke, °precipitate: *Was there any single factor that sparked the Renaissance?*

sparkle *v.* **1** °glitter, scintillate, glint, °flicker, °shine, °twinkle, wink, °blink, glimmer, °flash, coruscate, °blaze, °burn, °flame: *The setting sun sparkled on the sea. Brian's eyes sparkled with an inner fire.* **2** effervesce, °fizz, °bubble: *We ordered a jeroboam of sparkling Burgundy.*
—*n.* **3** °glitter, scintillation, °twinkle, coruscation, °dazzle, °spark, °gleam, brightness, °brilliance, °radiance: *I fear that the sparkle has gone out of her smile.* **4** vivacity, liveliness, °fire, brightness, wittiness, effervescence, ebullience, °excitement, °animation, °vigour, °energy, °spirit, °cheer, °joy, light-heartedness, élan, zeal, °gusto, °dash, °life, °gaiety, °cheer, cheerfulness; certain something; *Colloq* vim, zip, zing, pizazz *or* pizzazz, oomph: *It is easy to see that she gets her sparkle from her mother.*

sparse *adj.* **1** °thin (on the °ground), °few (and far between), °meagre, °scanty, (widely) dispersed *or* scattered, °spread out, °spotty, in °short supply, °scarce: *Tourists are sparse in Scotland in January. Sparse blooms appeared on the rose-bushes this year.* **2** °little, °limited, °meagre, scant, °sparing, inappreciable, not much, °insignificant: *Sparse use was made of the new tennis court because of the rain.*

Spartan *adj.* austere, °strict, °severe, °harsh, °hard, °stern, rigorous, °rigid, ascetic, stringent, controlled, disciplined, self-denying, abstinent, abstemious: *He gave up all luxuries and today lives a Spartan life in the forest.*

spasm *n.* **1** convulsion, °throe, °fit, twitch, °paroxysm: *Deprived of his medication, Brian might go into spasms.* **2** °fit, °seizure, convulsion, °paroxysm, °spell, °outburst, °burst, °eruption: *After that, every time he said 'furniture', the crowd went into spasms of laughter.*

spasmodic *adj.* **1** spasmodical, paroxysmal, convulsive, jerky, jerking, °sudden, *Technical* spastic: *John was quite uneasy, unaware that Cynthia's spasmodic winking was due to a tic.* **2** °fitful, °irregular, °intermittent, arrhythmic, °random, interrupted, °sporadic, °erratic, °occasional, °periodic, unsustained, discontinuous, pulsating, cyclic(al), °broken: *Spasmodic peals of thunder shook the house.*

spate *n.* °flood, inundation, onrush, °onset, °rush, deluge, °outpouring, outflow, outflowing, °flow: *What did I say to provoke that spate of foul language?*

spatter *v.* °splash, splatter, speckle, bespatter, °spray, °dabble, daub, bedaub, sprinkle, besprinkle, *Brit* splodge, *US* splotch: *When she dropped the pan the grease spattered all over my new white flannels.*

spawn *v.* give birth to, °yield, °bear, °bring forth, °breed, beget, °create, °father, sire, °produce, °generate, engender, give °rise to, °bring about, °cause: *Donald's arrogance over his wealth spawned a great deal of resentment.*

speak *v.* **1** °talk, °converse, discourse: *We were not allowed to speak during lessons.* **2** °talk to, °converse *or* discourse with, °address, °say (something *or* anything) to: *She was speaking quietly to the children. That is no way to speak to your elders.* **3** °talk, °communicate in, discourse *or* °converse in, utter in, articulate in, °use: *Can you really speak Chinese?* **4** °express, utter, °say, °state, °tell, °pronounce, °enunciate, °voice; articulate, °make known, °communicate, °reveal, °indicate: *He is speaking the truth.* **5** °symbolize, betoken, °signify, °communicate, convey, °indicate: *Her refusal to return your love-letters speaks volumes.* **6** ***so to speak***: as it were, in a manner of speaking, figuratively *or* metaphorically (speaking): *When it comes to employee benefits, the boss is Scrooge himself, so to speak.* **7** ***speak for***: **a** °support, °uphold, °defend, °stand up for, °plead for, make a plea for, °recommend, *Colloq* °stick up for: *Be quiet and let Simon speak for himself.* **b** act on *or* in behalf of, act for, °represent, act as agent for: *He is speaking for the whole staff when he expresses worries about the cuts.* **c** °demand, °require, °beg, °request, °ask for: *The situation speaks urgently for an effective drug rehabilitation programme.* **8** ***speak for itself***: be °self-evident, be °obvious, be °significant: *The fact that both your son and the ring are missing speaks for itself.* **9** ***speak of***: °mention, advert to, allude to, °refer to, make °reference to, °comment on, speak *or* °talk about: *I begged you not to speak of her again in my presence.* **10** ***speak on***: °discuss, °address, discourse upon *or* on, speak to, °treat (of), °deal with, °examine, °touch upon *or* on: *In his presentation Dr Andrews spoke on the role of natural predators in pest control.* **11** ***speak out*** *or* ***up***: **a** °talk (more) loudly *or* °clearly, make oneself heard: *I cannot hear you unless you speak up a bit.* **b** °talk °freely *or* unreservedly, °express one's opinion, speak one's mind, °declare, come out, °state one's position, take a stand: *I heard a mother of ten speak out against birth control.* **12** ***speak to***: **a** °reprove, °scold, °reprimand, °rebuke, admonish, °warn, °lecture: *After his father spoke to him, Nicholas stopped staying out so late.* **b** be °meaningful to, °appeal to, °influence, °affect, °touch: *Constance's poetry effectively speaks to the heart.* **c** accost, °address, °talk to, *Formal* apostrophize: *I have to speak to the teacher after class.* **d** See **10,** above. **13** ***spoken for***: °reserved, °engaged, bespoke, °set aside, accounted for, chosen, selected: *I'm afraid that the purple dress has already been spoken for, madam.*

speaker *n.* orator, lecturer; keynoter; °rabble-rouser, demagogue, *Colloq* tub-thumper, spieler: *It was my function to introduce the speaker.*

spearhead *v.* **1** °launch, °initiate, °lead (the way), take the °initiative, °pioneer, blaze the trail, break the ice, take the °lead, be in the van *or* vanguard: *He spearheaded medical research into arthritis.*
—*n.* **2** vanguard, advance guard, van, forefront, cutting edge: *They claim to be the spearhead of space technology.*

special *adj.* **1** °particular, °specific, °exceptional, uncommon, especial, °rare, °unusual, out of the °ordinary, °extraordinary, °different, °unorthodox, unconventional, °unique, °precise, °individual, °singular, °distinctive, specialized, °certain, °remarkable, inimitable, idiosyncratic, °curious, °peculiar, °odd, °strange, °bizarre, °weird, one of a kind; °distinguished, °notable, °noteworthy: *They have a special way of communicating with each other. I bought something very special for your birthday. A special relationship sprang up between us.* **2** °significant, °important, °momentous, earth-shaking, °memorable, red-letter; °gala, festive, celebratory: *The fifth of September is a special day in our family.* **3** °pointed, concerted, °deliberate, °particular, °extra, °determined: *After I had made a special effort to get there, nobody was home.* **4** °exclusive, °express, °individual, °extra: *Send the packet by special messenger.* **5** °dear, °intimate, °particular, °good, °close, °bosom, °staunch, °loyal, °faithful, °devoted, °steadfast; dearest, °best, closest; esteemed, valued: *I wasn't aware that John Spencer was a special friend of yours.* **6** °prime, °primary, °major, °prominent, °paramount: *I shouldn't attach any special importance to her demands.*
—*n.* **7** See **speciality, 2,** below.

specialist *n.* °expert, °authority, °professional, °master, connoisseur, maestro, artiste, artist, °adept: *Pierre Legrand is a specialist in matching antique furniture finishes. Such work requires specialist knowledge.*

speciality *n.* **1** °expertise, °talent, °genius, °gift, °skill, °aptitude, °trade, °craft, °accomplishment, °ability, °strength, °forte, strong point, °capability, adeptness, °art, °sphere, °field, °area, °subject, concentration, specialization, métier, *Chiefly US and Canadian* specialty, *Colloq* °bag, °thing, cup of tea, baby, claim to fame: *Dr Mann's speciality is tropical diseases.* **2** *pièce de résistance, spécialité de la maison,* °special, *Chiefly US and Canadian* specialty, *US* blueplate °special: *Today's speciality is calves' brains au beurre noir.*

specially *adv.* °especially, °particularly, °custom, °expressly, exclusively: *I had this suit specially made for me.*

specific *adj.* **1** °definite, °precise, °exact, °particular, °explicit, °express, unambiguous, °definitive, clear-cut, unequivocal, (well-)defined, °determined, specified, °individual, °peculiar, °certain, °limited, indicated, °predetermined, established, spelt *or* spelled out, delineated, °set, °distinct, °fixed, circumscribed, restricted: *Each part has its specific function.* **2** Often, ***specific to***: °characteristic (of), °unique to, °individual (to), *sui generis,* °proper (to), °typical (of), °peculiar to, identified with, °personal (to), °discrete (to), °special (to), associated with: *The disease is specific to one area only. Are these problems group-specific?*

specification *n.* **1** °identification, identifying, °description, describing, particularization, particularizing, specifying, naming: *The police were relying on a specification of the ringleaders by an informer.* **2** itemization, itemizing, °list, listing, check-list, inventory, °list of °particulars, °detail, enumeration: *When can you let me have the specifications for the new building?* **3** °requirement, °qualification, °condition, °restriction, °stipulation, °consideration: *The specification called for green marble and no substitute.*

specify *v.* particularize, °enumerate, °itemize, °name, denominate, °list, °indicate, °mention, °identify, cite, °define, °detail, °stipulate, °spell out, °set out *or* forth, individualize, be °specific about, delineate, °determine, disambiguate, °establish: *You must specify the source of each quotation.*

specimen *n.* °sample, °example, °instance, exemplar, °representative, °representation; °illustration, °case (in point), °type, °model, °pattern: *This is a specimen taken from the Pre-Cambrian strata. Using this as a specimen, can you reproduce the entire fabric?*

specious *adj.* °deceptive, °superficial, casuistic, ostensible, misleading, °apparent, °seeming, fallacious, °sophistic(al), °plausible, °likely, conceivable, °possible, °supposed, purported, presumed, presumable, °alleged, °so-called: *The candidate affected a specious show of liberality merely to attract votes. Do not be misled by specious reasoning.*

speck *n.* °spot, °dot, fleck, mote, speckle, °mark, °bit, °particle; °crumb, iota, °jot (or tittle), whit, atom, molecule, °touch, °hint, °suggestion, °suspicion, tinge, °modicum, °amount, °grain, smidgen *or* smidgin: *There's a speck of soot on your collar. Is there a speck of truth in what she says about you?*

speckled *adj.* spotted, °mottled, dotted, sprinkled, °flecked, stippled, °dapple(d), freckled, brindle(d); discoloured, spattered, bespattered: *I can see by looking at it that it's a speckled trout.*

spectacle *n.* **1** °show, °display, °sight, °performance, °event, °presentation, °exhibition, °exhibit, °exposition, °demonstration, °extravaganza, °marvel, °wonder, °sensation: *Instead of criticizing everything in life, why not just sit back and enjoy the spectacle?* **2** °fool, laughing-stock, °curiosity: *Joan makes a spectacle of herself by her solo dancing when she gets a little tipsy.* **3** ***spectacles***: eyeglasses, °glasses, *Colloq* specs: *He wears spectacles only for reading.*

spectator *n.* °witness, °eyewitness, °observer, viewer, °onlooker, looker-on, watcher, beholder: *There were more spectators than participants at the spring dance.*

spectral *adj.* °ghostly, ghostlike, °phantom, °eerie, wraithlike, incorporeal, °unearthly, °supernatural, °weird, *Colloq* spooky: *I could have sworn there was a spectral figure, dressed in white, standing near the window.*

spectre *n.* **1** °ghost, °phantom, wraith, apparition, °vision, °spirit, °shade, revenant, *doppelgänger,* chimera, *Colloq* spook, bogeyman *or* bogyman: *Each year the spectre appeared to her on Christmas Eve.* **2** °image, °vision, (mental) °picture: *Again the horrible spectre of war and pestilence arose.*

speculate *v.* **1** Often, ***speculate on*** *or* ***upon*** *or* ***about*** *or* ***over***: °reflect (on *or* about *or* over), °consider, °muse (on *or* about *or* over), °meditate (on *or* over *or* about), °contemplate (on *or* about), cogitate (on *or* about), °think (about *or* over *or* on), °ponder (over *or* about), °mull over, °chew on *or* over, ruminate (on *or* over *or* about), °wonder (about), °deliberate (over *or* on *or* about), °weigh, °judge, °evaluate, °theorize (on *or* about), conjecture (on *or* about), postulate, hypothesize: *I have been speculating about whether I should take a holiday in the Algarve. Why not go and enjoy yourself instead of speculating on the world's injustices?* **2** °gamble, wager, take a °chance, *Colloq* have a flutter, play the market, take a °plunge: *She is too conservative to speculate in the stock market.*

speculation *n.* **1** conjecture, °guess, °hypothesis, theory, guesswork, postulation, °surmise, °supposition, °opinion: *My speculations have often proved true. Both the steady-state and the big-bang theories of the origins of the universe are pure speculation.* **2** °thinking, rumination, cogitation, °reflection, meditation, contemplation, °consideration, cerebration, pondering, wondering, deliberation, °evaluation: *All serious philosophers engage in idle speculation.* **3** gambling, °gamble, wagering, wager, taking (a) °chance(s) *or* °risk(s), chance-taking: *Her speculation on the market paid off handsomely.*

speculative *adj.* **1** °intellectual, ideational, °abstract, cogitative, notional, °theoretical, °hypothetical, conjectural, suppositional, supposititious *or* suppositious, suppositive, °rational, ratiocinative, °ideal, idealized, °idealistic, °unrealistic, unpractical, °impractical, analytical: *Frank's theories about climate change were entirely speculative and substantially wrong.* **2** °risky, °hazardous, °uncertain, °unreliable, untrustworthy, °doubtful, dubious, untested, unproven, unproved, *Colloq* iffy, chancy, *Slang* °dicey: *You ought to invest your money in less speculative enterprises.*

speech *n.* **1** speaking, talking, articulation, °diction, °language, °expression, enunciation, elocution, speech pattern; communication: *His speech is marred by a lisp. Martha studied speech at a well-known drama school.* **2** °oration, °address, °lecture, °talk, discourse, disquisition, °sermon, homily; °tirade, °harangue, philippic; (sales) pitch, °line, °song and dance; *Colloq* spiel, blast: *Her speech left her audience awed with her knowledge of the subject. When the householder opens the door, you launch into your speech about the encyclopedia.* **3** °dialect, idiolect, °jargon, °parlance, °idiom, *façon de parler*, °language, °tongue, *Colloq* °lingo: *English speech varieties range from Scots to Cockney to Texan to Jamaican.*

speechless *adj.* **1** °mute, °dumb, voiceless: *He was speechless and in shock for two days following the accident. They claim to speak for animals who are, of course, speechless themselves.* **2** °dumbfounded *or* dumfounded, dumbstruck *or* dumbstricken, wordless, struck °dumb, °tongue-tied, °thunderstruck, shocked, dazed, °inarticulate, paralysed, nonplussed, *Slang Brit* gobsmacked: *He was speechless with fury to find his car missing.*

speed *n.* **1** °rapidity, fleetness, quickness, speediness, swiftness, °velocity, °dispatch *or* despatch, °hurry, hurriedness, °haste, hastiness, celerity, alacrity, expeditiousness, °expedition, briskness, promptness, timeliness; suddenness, precipitateness, precipitousness, abruptness: *We reached a speed of Mach 2. What is the speed of your new computer? The speed of her reactions will be recorded during the experiment.* —*v.* **2** Often, ***speed up***: accelerate, °move, °expedite, °forward, °advance, °facilitate, °boost, °further, °promote, °help, °assist, °aid, *Colloq* give a °leg up: *He vowed to do anything he could to speed the troops' return from the battlefield.* **3** °hasten, make °haste, °hurry, °rush, °charge, dart, °bolt, °shoot, °run, °race, sprint, °fly, °streak, °scurry, °tear, °hustle, °scramble, scamper, °career, °bowl along, °go *or* °fly like the wind, *Colloq* °go °hell for leather, °go like a bat out of hell, belt along, °step on it, put one's foot down, zip, zoom, skedaddle, °go like a °shot, *US* hightail it, step on the gas, °go like greased lightning, make tracks, *Slang US* burn rubber: *Where the road is straight, cars speed along at up to 120 miles per hour.*

speedy *adj.* **1** °quick, °rapid, °swift, °brisk, °expeditious, °fast, °immediate, °prompt: *What happened to the form of justice under which the accused were guaranteed a speedy trial?* **2** °hasty, °precipitate, °precipitous, °hurried, °summary: *Some of the townspeople favoured the wrong kind of speedy justice—by lynching.* **3** °fleet, °nimble, wing-footed, winged, °fast, °quick, °rapid, °swift: *Carol is one of the speediest sprinters on our team.*

spell[1] *n.* **1** °period, °interval, °time, °term, °season; °stint, °turn, °run, °course, °shift, °tour (of duty), °watch, °round: *We had a spell of bad weather. Each of us had a spell at the tiller during the crossing.* —*v.* **2** °relieve, °replace, °substitute for, °take over for *or* from: *After 36 hours of uninterrupted duty, I needed someone to spell me for a while.*

spell[2] *n.* **1** °enchantment, allure, °charm, °magic, witchcraft, witchery, °fascination, captivation, enthralment: *She had them all under her spell.* **2** incantation, °formula, °charm: *The priest uttered some spell and I found myself unable to move.* **3** °attraction, °lure, allure, °appeal, °draw, °pull, °magnetism, °fascination, °influence, mesmerism, hypnotic effect: *We were drawn ever onward by the spell of the jungle.*

spell[3] *v.* **1** augur, portend, presage, °promise, hold °promise of, °signify, °point to, °indicate, °omen, °bode, look like, °amount to, °mean: *Harry's conviction will spell the end of his career as a bank robber.* **2** ***spell out***: °specify, delineate, make °clear *or* °plain *or* °explicit, °clarify, elucidate: *She despises you—I can't spell it out for you more plainly than that.*

spellbinding *adj.* fascinating, °enchanting, °enthralling, captivating, enrapturing, bewitching, mesmerizing, charming, °overpowering: *The preacher put on one of his most spellbinding performances.*

spend *v.* **1** °pay out, disburse, °expend, °lay out, *Colloq* fork out, dish out, °shell out, *Brit* splash out: *That man spends more for a suit than you earn in a year.* **2** squander, °throw away, °fritter away, °waste, °go through, °splurge, °lavish, °dissipate: *He spends money as if it's going out of style.* **3** °devote, °allot, °assign, °invest, °put in, °pass: *If you don't spend more time with the children they'll forget they have a father.*

spendthrift *n.* **1** °profligate, °wastrel, (big) spender, squanderer, °prodigal: *Because her nephew is such a spendthrift, she put his inheritance in a trust fund.* —*adj.* **2** °wasteful, free-spending, °prodigal, °profligate, squandering, °extravagant, °improvident: *The chancellor's spendthrift budget will increase inflation.*

spent *adj.* **1** drained, °exhausted, °prostrate, °tired, °fatigued, fagged out, °weary, wearied, °worn out, *Colloq* (°dead) °beat, done in, done for, all in, dog-tired, played out, burnt- *or* burned-out, °used up, *Brit* knackered, done up, *US* pooped: *He was totally spent after sitting in the airport all night during the storm.* **2** °exhausted, °used up, emptied, gone, expended, finished, *fini*, consumed, depleted: *At 70, he was wrong to feel that his life was spent.*

spew *v.* Often, ***spew forth*** *or* ***out*** *or* ***up***: belch (up *or* out *or* forth), °vomit (up *or* forth), °regurgitate, °spit up *or* out, °spout, °discharge, °emit, °eject, °send forth, °spurt, °gush, °throw up *or* out, disgorge, *Slang* puke: *The volcano spewed forth lava for six days and nights.*

sphere *n.* **1** °globe, °orb, globule, spherule; °drop, droplet, °bubble: *Flotation is provided by thousands of hollow plastic spheres.* **2** °society, °class, °level, °caste, °rank, °domain, walk of life, °station, °stratum, °position: *They did not belong to the same social sphere.* **3** °area, °field, °province, °subject, °discipline, °range, °speciality *or US* specialty, °forte, *Colloq* bailiwick, °territory, °department, °thing, °bag: *Are Gregorian chants within Stanley's sphere of interest?*

spherical *adj.* spheric, globular, °round, ball-shaped, ball-like, globelike, globe-shaped, globose *or* globous, globoid, globate(d), spheroid(al): *They chose simple, spherical lampshades for the sitting-room.*

spice *n.* **1** condiment, °relish, °seasoning, °flavour(ing); herb: *Much of the purpose of early explorers was to search for spices.* **2** °zest, spiciness, piquancy, °tang, pungency, °bite, sharpness, poignancy, °gusto, °excitement, °seasoning, °dash, élan, °colour, °life, °vigour, °interest, stimulation, °stimulant, °spirit, *Colloq* vim, zip, °pep, °kick, pizazz *or* pizzazz, °punch, ginger, °pepper: *A holiday in the Bahamas will add a little spice to our lives.* —*v.* **3** °season, °flavour: *Highly spiced food does not agree with many people.* **4** Often, ***spice up***: °enliven, inspirit, °stimulate, invigorate: *The proprietor felt that the new editor should try to spice up the magazine.*

spicy *adj.* **1** zesty, zestful, piquant, tangy, (well-) spiced, (well-)°seasoned, °hot, peppery, °sharp, °pungent, °snappy, °biting, full-bodied, °aromatic, °savoury, flavoursome, flavourful: *This curry is a little too spicy for my taste.* **2** °off colour, indelicate, °suggestive, °risqué, °improper, °indecent, indecorous, ribald, °racy, °bawdy, °unseemly, °offensive, titillating, °sexy, *Colloq* °hot: *This magazine often publishes spicy nude photos.* **3** °scandalous, °sensational, °outrageous, °notorious, revealing, revelatory, °intimate: *She likes to read about the spicy goings-on in Hollywood.*

spike *n.* **1** skewer, °stake, prong, treenail, °nail, °peg, °picket, °pin, pike, °spine: *To subdue a vampire, drive a wooden spike through its heart.* —*v.* **2** °impale, °stab, °stick, spear, °pierce, °spit, °lance: *He was spiked through the thigh by a bayonet.* **3** disable, °thwart, nullify, °disarm, °block, °frustrate, °foil, °void, balk, °check, °cancel, annul: *Our plans for the picnic were spiked by the weather.* **4** °strengthen;

°drug, °poison, *Slang* slip in a Mickey (Finn): *I passed out because my drink was spiked.*

spill *v.* **1** °pour (out *or* over), overflow, slop *or* °run *or* °brim over: *The milk spilt all over the floor.* **2** °waste, °throw out, °lose: *Don't cry over spilt milk.* **3** ***spill the beans***: °reveal *or* °tell *or* °disclose *or* divulge all *or* everything, °blab, °tattle, let the cat out of the bag, °confess, *Slang* squeal, be a stool-pigeon *or* stoolie, spill one's guts, °sing (like a canary), *Brit* blow the gaff: *Finnegan spilled the beans to the cops.*
—*n.* **4** °outpouring, °flood, °leak, leakage: *Don't tell me there's been another oil spill!* **5** °fall, °tumble, °accident, *Colloq* cropper, header: *Crutchley had a nasty spill at the third fence in the Grand National.*

spin *v.* **1** °revolve, °turn, °rotate, °gyrate, °twirl, whirl, °twist, °reel, °pirouette, °pivot: *The car spun out of control on the ice. Fred spun Ginger around the dance floor.* **2** °invent, concoct, °make up, °devise, °produce, °fabricate; °weave, °relate, retail, °recount, °narrate, °tell, °unfold: *Each night, father would spin a new chapter in the yarn of the vagabond princess.* **3** be °dizzy, suffer °vertigo, swim, whirl, be °giddy: *My head was spinning from so much attention by the media.* **4** ***spin off***: °separate, °derive: *The manufacturer spun off two new companies specializing in parts and service.* **5** ***spin out***: °prolong, protract, °drag *or* °draw out, °stretch out, °perpetuate, °continue, °extend, keep alive, keep going: *The case was spun out for years in the courts.*
—*n.* **6** whirl, whirling, °twirl, twirling, °turn, turning, gyration, °reel, °pirouette, °revolution, revolving, rotation, rotating: *He puts a spin on the ball when he throws it. Is the spin of all planets in the same direction?* **7** °drive, whirl, joyride, °ride, °tour, °excursion, °outing, jaunt: *On Sunday afternoons we sometimes went for a spin in the car.*

spine *n.* **1** °backbone, spinal column, vertebrae: *He can't stand up straight—he has curvature of the spine.* **2** °thorn, needle, barb, °spike, °spur, prong, quill, °ray, barbel, °bristle, °prickle, *Technical* barbule, spicule *or* spiculum *or* spicula: *The surface of the sea urchin is covered with needle-like spines.*

spineless *adj.* **1** *Technical* invertebrate: *There are more species of spineless creatures than those with internal backbones.* **2** °weak, °feeble, °flabby, °irresolute, weak-willed, °indecisive, °ineffectual, °ineffective, °impotent, °powerless: *After her reign, any king would appear spineless.* **3** °cowardly, dastardly, pusillanimous, timorous, lily-livered, white-livered, craven, °fearful, °timid, spiritless, °squeamish, *Colloq* yellow, chicken-hearted, chicken, yellow-bellied, wimpish: *She said you were spineless because you refused to go into the lions' cage.*

spiral *n.* **1** helix, °coil, corkscrew, °screw, scroll; whorl, volute, °turn, curl: *In earlier Greek motifs, the spiral is commoner than the rectangular fret.*
—*adj.* **2** helical, coiled, screw, corkscrew, cochlear *or* cochleate; scrolled, volute(d), whorled: *A spiral staircase is attractive and space-saving, but hard to use.*

spire *n.* **1** column, °tower, belfry; steeple, *flèche*: *The spire of the church was repeatedly struck by lightning that night.* **2** °top, °pinnacle, apex, °peak, °summit, °acme, °tip, °crest, °crown, °vertex: *We climbed till we stood on the highest spire above the valley.*

spirit *n.* **1** anima, °breath, °life, °vitality, vital spirit, pneuma, °soul, consciousness, °psyche, self, °heart, °essence: *Though past eighty, Mr Wilkins has a great deal of spirit. Even though she is gone, Annabel's spirit is still with us.* **2** °character, temperament, °temper, °persona, °disposition, °mind, °will, will-power, °attitude, °bent, °inclination, °energy, °ardour, °desire, °impetus, °drive, °urge, °eagerness, °zest, zeal, zealousness, °fire, °passion(s), °enthusiasm, motivation, mettle, °resolution, °resolve, °intention, °enterprise: *We have always admired the spirit of the early pioneers. Bill has shown a lot of the right spirit.* **3** °zest, pungency, piquancy, °warmth, °fire, °animation, °life, liveliness, vivacity, vivaciousness, °panache, élan, °dash, °spice, *Colloq* °sauce, °pepper: *He needs to put more spirit into his sales presentation.* **4** See **spectre, 1,** above. **5** °bravery, °courage, °grit, °backbone, valour, °pluck, °daring, stout-heartedness, manfulness, manliness, gameness, resoluteness, °will, will-power, *Colloq* vim, °spunk, get-up-and-go, (right) °stuff, °guts, *US* sand: *Johnston has the spirit to be a marine.* **6** °meaning, °sense, °tenor, signification, purport, °intent, °intention, °purpose, °aim, °implication, °message, °essence, °quintessence, °core, °heart, °meat, °pith, °substance, marrow: *The spirit of the agreement is different from the way the lawyers worded the contract. Is it in keeping with the spirit of the law?* **7** °attitude, °principle, °thought, °idea, °inspiration, °notion, °feeling, °inclination, impulse: *Christmas is associated with the spirit of giving.* **8** Often, ***spirits***: °temper, °mood, °sentiments, °feelings, °cheer, °humour, °frame of °mind; °morale: *I hope he took my criticism in good spirit. You seem to be in pretty good spirits today. My spirits are quite low.* **9** ***spirits***: **a** °feelings, °mood, °temper, °sentiments; °morale, esprit de corps, team spirit: *Spirits were high at the annual boat races.* **b** °alcohol, °liquor, °whisky, strong °drink, *Colloq* °booze, fire-water, *Slang chiefly US and Canadian* hooch *or* hootch: *It is illegal to sell spirits to minors.*
—*v.* **10** ***spirit away*** *or* ***off***: °abduct, °make off *or* away with, °carry off, °transport, °take away, °kidnap, °steal (off *or* away with), °whisk away, abscond with; make °disappear: *A thief spirited away a painting from the exhibition. She was spirited away by a band of elves.*

spirited *adj.* °lively, °sprightly, °energetic, °vigorous, °animated, sparkling, °dynamic, °buoyant, °effervescent, °vivacious, °ardent, mettlesome: *The horse I chose was a bit too spirited. The barrister presented a spirited defence for his client. The 1970s saw spirited revivals of art nouveau and art deco styles.*

spiritual *adj.* **1** °sacred, ecclesiastic(al), churchly, °clerical, °priestly, devotional, °holy, °divine, sacerdotal, °religious, non-secular: *Father Craig was in charge of the spiritual aspects of our lives.* **2** non-material, incorporeal, °psychic(al), °mental, °psychological, inner: *Spiritual needs are less easily satisfied than physical needs.*

spit *v.* **1** expectorate; dribble, salivate, drool, °slaver, sputter, splutter; °discharge, °spew (forth), °eject: *Spitting is forbidden. Don't you hate people who spit when they talk? The volcano spat huge boulders into the sky.* **2** ***spitting image*** or ***spit and image***: °twin, °duplicate, clone, °image, counterpart, °likeness, °copy: *She is the spitting image of her mother.*
—*n.* **3** spittle, saliva, drool, *Technical* sputum: *A large gobbet of spit clung to his beard.*

spite *n.* **1** spitefulness, maliciousness, malice, malevolence, malignity, °ill will, °venom, spleen, °rancour, °animosity, °gall (and wormwood), °resentment, °bitterness, °hostility, °antagonism, hatred, °hate, *Colloq* bitchiness: *Just out of spite, Marian saw to it that he didn't get the job.* **2** ***in spite of***: °despite, °notwithstanding, °regardless of, ignoring, in defiance of: *In spite of his efforts to be helpful, she despises him.*
—*v.* **3** °annoy, °irritate, vex, °upset, disconcert, °offend, °provoke, °discomfit, pique, °put out, °hurt, °injure, °wound, *Colloq* peeve, get under (someone's) skin, needle, *US* do a number on: *He would cut off his nose to spite his face. He told her he was happy only to spite her for having divorced him.*

spiteful *adj.* °rancorous, °bitter, acrimonious, malevolent, malicious, °venomous, °hateful, invidious, °hostile, antagonistic, unfriendly, unforgiving, retaliative *or* retaliatory, °punitive, retributive *or* retributory: *Cutting off Colin's allowance because he forgot your birthday was a spiteful thing to do.*

splash *v.* **1** °spatter, bespatter, splatter, °shower, °spray, sprinkle, besprinkle, *Brit* splodge *or US also* splotch; mottle, °spot: *The painters splashed paint all over the floor. My freshly washed car was soon splashed with mud again.* **2** blazon, °spread, °plaster: *Was that your picture splashed across the front page of yesterday's paper?*

—*n.* **3** °spatter, °spray, splatter, sprinkle, °spot, °stain, °smear, smudge, *Brit* splodge *or US also* splotch: *There's a splash of tomato sauce on the tablecloth.* **4** °impression, °show, °uproar, ado, brouhaha, °sensation, commotion, °excitement, *US* foofaraw, *Colloq* to-do: *After all the advance publicity, he was sure to make a big splash in the theatre.*

splendid *adj.* **1** splendorous, °magnificent, resplendent, °dazzling, °gorgeous, °showy, °dashing, °marvellous, spectacular, °grand, °glorious, °lavish, °ornate, °sumptuous, °majestic, °brilliant, °extraordinary, °exceptional, °superb, °supreme, °imposing, °impressive, awe-inspiring, °awesome, °lush, °plush, °rich, °luxurious, *Colloq* splendiferous, °posh, swank(y), ritzy: *The mausoleum built by Shah Jehan for his wife was far more splendid than his own palace.* **2** °impressive, °marvellous, °brilliant, °eminent, °prominent, °superior, °noteworthy, °notable, °celebrated, °illustrious, °famous, °distinguished, °exemplary, °remarkable, °admirable, °conspicuous, °outstanding, °sublime, °striking, °extraordinary, °successful, °meritorious, creditable: *His splendid victory at Waterloo was the climax of his military career.* **3** °excellent, °superior, °pre-eminent, °fine, °marvellous, °extraordinary, °exceptional, °unbelievable, °incredible, first-class, unequalled, unsurpassed, °fabulous, °peerless, °matchless, °nonpareil, °superlative, °praiseworthy, °laudable, *Brit* °brilliant, *Colloq* °great, °colossal, supercolossal, stupendous, fab, °fantastic, °super, smashing, A-1 *or* A-one, tiptop, °capital, *Brit* brill, *Slang* far-out, °way-out, °dandy, °cool, keen, *US* solid, out of °sight, fantabulous, boss, °neat, major: *Bill is a splendid dancer.*

splendour *n.* **1** magnificence, °grandeur, °brilliance, °display, °radiance, resplendence, sumptuousness, stateliness, majesty, panoply, °spectacle, °show, °glory, °pomp, gorgeousness, °dazzle, refulgence, °beauty, splendidness, exquisiteness, luxuriousness, richness, lavishness, °luxury, *Colloq* swankiness, poshness, swank, ritziness: *There was nothing to match the splendour of the court of Louis XIV.* **2** °brilliance, °shine, °lustre, °light, effulgence, brightness, °glitter, °dazzle, refulgence, luminosity, luminousness, °gloss: *The splendour of the city's golden domes was reflected in the setting sun.*

splice *v.* **1** °join, °unite, °marry, °bind, conjoin; °knit, °entwine, intertwine, °braid, plait, °twist, interlace: *After the two rope ends are spliced together, they should be seized with marline.*
—*n.* **2** joining, °union, splicing, °joint, °connection *or Brit* connexion, °tie, °bond, binding, °fastening, linking, linkage: *A proper splice will probably be stronger than the single cable.*

splinter *n.* **1** °sliver, °fragment, °piece; °scrap, shard, °shred, °chip: *A splinter of glass is stuck in my finger.*
—*v.* **2** °shatter, °break, °fragment, °split, °disintegrate, smash to smithereens: *The lamp hit the floor and splintered into a million pieces.*

split *v.* **1** Often, ***split up*** *or* ***apart***: °divide, °separate, °cleave, °cut *or* °chop apart, °cut *or* °chop in two, °pull *or* °tear °apart, °rend, °break *or* °snap apart *or* in two, °break up, °come apart, °rupture, °partition, °detach, become °detached; bisect, dichotomize: *He split the log with one blow of his axe. The ship split apart on the reef. The party may split on the tax issue.* **2** Often, ***split up***: °divorce, °separate, go °separate ways, °break up, °part company: *After 30 years, the Hitchcocks have decided to split up.* **3** Often, ***split up***: °branch, fork, °diverge, °separate: *The road splits to pass round the pond.* **4** Often, ***split up***: °divide (up), apportion, °deal out, °dole out, °distribute, °allot, °share *or* °parcel out, °carve up: *Why don't we split the dinner bill five ways?* **5** °burst, °crack *or* °break up, °fall apart *or* about, *Slang* bust: *I laughed so much I thought I'd split!* **6** °leave, °depart, °go, *Slang* take a (run-out) °powder, take it on the lam, °beat it, scram, skedaddle: *When they heard the sirens of the police cars, they split.*
—*n.* **7** °crack, cleft, fissure, °chink, °cranny, °slit, °slot, °crevice, °groove, °furrow, °channel, sulcus; °gap, hiatus, lacuna, °opening, °separation, °division, chasm; °rift, °break, °rupture, °fracture; °slash, °gash, °tear, °rip, °rent: *The edges of the tectonic plates mark splits in the earth's crust. Pressure caused the splits in these plaster columns. I had to borrow a tablecloth to cover up the split in my trousers.* **8** °division, dichotomy, °schism, °breach, °rupture, °partition, disunion, °discord; °break, °separation: *Don't you think that the issue will cause a split within the party?*
—*adj.* **9** divided, separated; halved, bisected, cleft; °cut, °broken, fractured: *The result was a split vote along party lines. Their first containers were of split bamboo.*

splurge *n.* **1** °display, °show, ostentatiousness, °extravagance, °indulgence, access, °splash, °burst, °outburst, °spree: *In his final splurge he bet everything on the number 14.*
—*v.* **2** Often, ***splurge on***: squander *or* °dissipate *or* °waste *or* °burn (up) *or* °throw away money (on), °show off *or* °flaunt one's money, *Slang* °blow everything (on): *Victor splurged on toys for the children.*

spoil *v.* **1** °ruin, °destroy, °wreck, °queer, °mess up, °upset, °demolish, °harm, °damage, *Colloq* °kill: *You really spoiled everything by telling Mum about my pet frog. Spare the rod and spoil the child.* **2** °damage, °mar, °injure, °harm, °deface, disfigure, °scar, °blemish: *The painting was spoiled by some fanatic who slashed it.* **3** °baby, mollycoddle, °coddle, °indulge, °pamper, °dote on, spoonfeed, *Rare* cocker: *Barbara really spoils her family terribly by indulging their every whim.* **4** °turn, °go °off *or* °bad, curdle, moulder, °decay, °decompose, become addle(d), °rot, °putrefy, mildew: *The milk will spoil if not refrigerated.* **5** ***be spoiling for***: °itch (for *or* after), °yearn (for), be °eager (for), be °keen (for), °look for, be °bent on, be °desirous of, crave, be after: *If you give Tom a drink he'll be spoiling for a fight.*
—*n.* **6** ***spoils***: °loot, °booty, °plunder, °pillage, °prizes, pickings, *Slang* swag, °take, °goods, boodle: *The Nazis took the paintings as spoils of war.*

spoilsport *n.* °killjoy, damper, dog in the manger, *Colloq* wet blanket, *US* party pooper: *Some spoilsport tipped off Jane about her surprise birthday party.*

spoken *adj.* **1** °oral, vocal, °verbal, viva voce: *My spoken commentary was recorded for later broadcast. He has an excellent command of spoken French.* **2** ***spoken for***: See **speak, 13,** above.

sponsor *n.* **1** °backer, °supporter, promoter, angel, °patron, Maecenas, subsidizer: *Make a contribution and we will list you as a sponsor of the games.* **2** (radio *or* television) advertiser: *The American broadcasting catch-phrase 'A word from our sponsor' is not to be taken literally.*
—*v.* **3** °back, °support, °promote, °fund, °patronize, °subsidize, °finance, °underwrite: *Hughes agreed to sponsor a campaign to clean up the environment.*

spontaneous *adj.* **1** unannounced, °unpremeditated, unplanned, impromptu, °extemporaneous, extempore, °unprepared, unrehearsed, °offhand, ad lib, spur-of-the-moment, *Colloq* off the cuff: *Miss Malkin's spontaneous speech could not have been better had it been written out.* **2** °natural, unforced, unbidden, °instinctive, instinctual, °unconscious, reflex, °automatic, °mechanical, °immediate, °offhand, °unguarded, °unthinking, unwitting, °involuntary, °impetuous, °impulsive, *Slang* knee-jerk: *How could you doubt the sincerity of such an outburst of spontaneous affection? My spontaneous reaction is to beg you not to take up sky-diving.*

sporadic *adj.* °occasional, °intermittent, °random, °irregular, uneven, °erratic, °chance, unexpected; °spasmodic(al), °fitful, °periodic(al): *There has been sporadic unrest in that area of the city.*

sport *n.* **1** °recreation, °diversion, °pastime, °amusement, °entertainment, °play, °distraction, °relaxation, divertissement, °pleasure, °enjoyment, °fun: *I fish for sport, not to earn a living.* **2** jest, °humour, °fun, °mockery: *They often call him rude names, but only in*

sport. **3** ***make sport of***: °tease, °deride, make a laughing-stock (of), (hold up to) °ridicule, make a °fool of: *She doesn't like it when you make sport of her husband.*
—*v.* **4** °frolic, gambol, °cavort, romp, °caper, °play, °frisk, °lark, rollick, °skip about: *These octogenarians are sporting about like young foals.* **5** °show off, °exhibit, °flaunt, °display, °wear: *Keith arrived, sporting the latest in Italian footwear.*

sportive *adj.* °frisky, gambolling, cavorting, frolicking, romping, capering, rollicking, °sprightly, coltish, °spirited, °frolicsome, °buoyant, gamesome, °gay, °kittenish, °merry, °playful, °gleeful, light-hearted, °blithe, prankish, waggish: *He watched a sportive group of children playing hide-and-seek.*

sportsmanship *n.* °fair °play, sportsmanliness, fairness, honourableness, °honesty, °honour, °probity, scrupulousness, °integrity, uprightness, °justice, justness: *Good sportsmanship requires that the loser congratulate the winner.*

sporty *adj.* °informal, °casual; °stylish, °chic, °smart, °trendy, °fashionable, modish, à la °mode, up to °date, °showy, °rakish, *Colloq* swank(y), °loud, *Slang* classy, °swell, °flashy, snazzy, °sharp, *US and Canadian* spiffy: *He came to dinner wearing sporty clothes. Yes, I suppose you might call Fred a sporty dresser.*

spot *n.* **1** °mark, °patch, °speck, °blot, blotch, °blemish, speckle, fleck, °particle, mote, macula, smudge, °stain, °stigma, discoloration, *Brit* splodge *or US also* splotch: *There's a spot of ink on your shirt.* **2** °site, °place, °locale, °location, locality, °scene, °setting, °section, °area, °neighbourhood, °quarter: *The Coopers picked out a lovely spot to build their new house.* **3** °morsel, °bit, °bite, *Colloq* smidgen *or* smidgin: *Let's stop in here for a spot of tea.* **4** °predicament, °situation, °quandary, °mess: *John said he was in a bit of a spot, and needed to borrow £20 until the end of the week.* **5** ***spots***: eruptions, °pimples, acne, pustules, blackheads, comedos *or* comedones, whiteheads; °boils, blains, wens; pockmarks; *Old-fashioned US and Canadian* hickeys: *Teenagers often get spots.*
—*v.* **6** °see, catch °sight of, glimpse, discern, °identify, °pick out, °distinguish, °single out, °detect, °sight, °recognize, °make out, descry: *I think I spotted Molly in the crowd.* **7** °mark, °stain, fleck, speckle, °spray, °splash, °spatter, bespatter, °sully, °soil, °dirty, °taint, besmirch, smudge: *The car's shiny new paintwork was spotted with mud.*

spotless *adj.* **1** °immaculate, °clean, gleaming, °shiny, °polished, unspotted, spick and span: *The floor is so spotless you could eat off it.* **2** °pure, unsullied, unassailable, °flawless, °faultless, °untarnished, °blameless, °irreproachable: *Samantha has a spotless reputation.*

spotlight *n.* **1** arc °light, searchlight, *US* pin spotlight, *Colloq US* (pin) spot: *I couldn't see the audience with the spotlight shining in my eyes.* **2** °focus (of attention), limelight, public eye: *How does it feel to have been in the spotlight most of your life, Miss Hallward?*
—*v.* **3** °light (up), °illuminate, °focus (light) upon *or* on, °shine *or* °shed *or* °throw *or* °cast light upon *or* on, °emphasize, highlight, draw attention to, °feature, give °prominence to, °stress, accentuate, °accent, °point up, underscore, underline: *The students held a sit-in to spotlight the cuts in their grants.*

spotty *adj.* **1** spotted, dotted, °speckled, freckled, °flecked, blotched, blotchy, stained, °marked, pied, piebald, brindle(d), skewbald, °mottled, motley, °dapple(d), macular, foxed; soiled, °dirty; *Brit* splodgy, splodged *or US also* splotchy, splotched: *Pages of some old books are spotty with brown stains.* **2** pimply, pimpled, blotched, blotchy, acned, pock-marked, pocky, bad, *Scots* plouky *or* plooky: *Ian used to have a spotty complexion, but it's clear now.* **3** patchy, °irregular, uneven, °erratic, °sporadic, °capricious, °fitful: *Radio reception in our area is spotty during electrical storms.*

spout *v.* **1** °discharge, °emit, squirt, °spurt, jet, °shoot, °gush, °erupt, °spew (up *or* out *or* forth), °spit, °eject, disgorge, °vomit (up *or* forth), °pour (out *or* forth), °flow, °stream: *Steam spouts from many vents in Iceland. The water came spouting out of the hose and drenched me.* **2** °ramble on, °rant, °rave, carry on, pontificate, orate, declaim, °hold forth, maunder (on), witter on, expatiate, speechify, °talk, *Colloq* °go on, *Brit* rabbit on: *Harry, as usual, was spouting about his golf handicap.*
—*n.* **3** waterspout, gargoyle, downspout, duct, °drain, °outlet, conduit: *The rainwater drains into the gutters, then into the spouts.* **4** ***up the spout***: gone, °lost, destroyed, beyond hope *or* °recovery, to be written off *or* °abandoned: *Our dream of finding the treasure was now up the spout.*

sprawl *v.* **1** °spread (out), °stretch (out), straddle, °ramble, °meander, °wander, °straggle, °branch out: *Greater Los Angeles sprawls over a huge area of some 450 square miles.* **2** °spread out, °stretch out, loll, °lounge, °slouch, °slump, °recline, °lie about *or* around: *A dozen guests were sprawled on blankets at the beach party.*
—*n.* **3** °spread, °stretch, °expansion, °extension: *Some suburbs of large cities have been swallowed up in urban sprawl.*

spray[1] *v.* **1** sprinkle, °spatter, °scatter, °shower, °disperse, °diffuse, atomize, °spread: *Try to spray the insecticide evenly over the plants.*
—*n.* **2** °shower, sprinkling, drizzle, °mist, sprinkle, spindrift *or* spoondrift: *The strong wind carried the spray from the whitecaps right up into the streets of the town.* **3** atomizer, sprayer, sprinkler, vaporizer, aerosol: *Richard bought me a cologne spray for Mother's Day.*

spray[2] *n.* flower *or* floral arrangement, nosegay, posy, °bouquet, sprig, °branch, bough: *The scores of tiny roses were interspersed with sprays of baby's-breath.*

spread *v.* **1** Often, ***spread out***: °diffuse, °distribute, °disperse, disseminate, °broadcast, °sow, °scatter, °strew, °shed, dispel, °dissipate: *Spread the mulch as evenly as possible to a depth of several inches.* **2** Often, ***spread about*** *or* ***around***: °broadcast, °publicize, °make known, bruit about, °air, televise, °circulate, °publish, °distribute, disseminate, trumpet, °announce, °pronounce, promulgate, advertise, enounce, make °public, °tell the world, herald, °repeat, °recite: *Start spreading the news: I'm leaving today.* **3** Often, ***spread out***: °unfold, °draw out, °display, °stretch out, °open out, °extend, °lay out, °fan out, unroll, unfurl: *Please spread the cloth on the table.* **4** Often, ***spread out***: °stretch (out), °extend, protract, °prolong, °drag out, °distribute, °disperse: *The bank said I could spread the payments over twenty years.* **5** Often, ***spread out***: °stretch, °extend, °separate, put apart *or* out, °part: *He spread his arms and Lorna rushed into them.* **6** °grow, °develop, °increase, broaden, °expand, °extend, °widen, °enlarge, mushroom, °proliferate, °sprawl, °branch out; metastasize: *To meet the demand for the pies, bakeries began to spread throughout the country. The cancer, unchecked, was bound to spread.* **7** °smear, °apply, °smooth, °put, °rub, °cover, layer, °plaster, °plate, °coat, °wash, °glaze, °paint, varnish, overlay, overspread; °cloak, °mantle, swaddle, °wrap, blanket: *I was careful to spread the paint evenly, avoiding streaks. When the cake has cooled, spread the chocolate icing over it.*
—*n.* **8** spreading, °extension, extending, °expansion, expanding, enlargement, enlarging, °development, developing, °increase, increasing, °proliferation, proliferating, broadening, °growth, widening, mushrooming, dispersion, dispersal, dispersing, dissemination, disseminating, °distribution, distributing, dispensation, dispensing: *The spread of the disease is uncontrolled. One of the functions of a university is to encourage the spread of knowledge.* **9** °extent, °expanse, °area, °span, °sweep, vastness, °stretch, °reach, °breadth, °depth, °size, dimensions, compass, °limits, °bounds, °boundary *or* boundaries: *As our craft accelerated past the moon, we were awed by the spread of empty space that lay before us.* **10** °range, °extent,

°scope, °span, °difference: *There was too much of a spread between the cost and the selling price.* **11** °feast, °banquet, °meal, dinner, repast, barbecue; °table; *Colloq* °feed: *I have never seen a spread like the one laid on for the returning champions.* **12** butter, margarine, °jam, jelly, °preserve, °conserve, confiture, paste, *US old-fashioned* oleo: *What kind of spread do you like on your toast?* **13** ranch, landholding, holding, °property, °place, plantation, °farm, homestead: *His spread in Texas eventually amounted to 10,000 acres.* **14** bed-spread, counterpane, coverlet, bed-cover, °cover, quilt, eiderdown, duvet, afghan, *US* comforter, *US and Canadian* throw: *Leave the spread off the bed, Carlotta, as I want to take a nap.*

spree *n.* °frolic, romp, °lark, °outing, escapade, °revel, wild °party, °fling, debauch, °orgy, bacchanalia; drinking-bout, carousal, *Colloq* °bender, binge, °jag: *Bruce has gone off on another of his sprees.*

sprightly *adj.* °lively, chipper, spry, °vivacious, °cheerful, °gay, °brisk, °animated, °sportive, °active, °alert, °nimble, °agile, °energetic, °jaunty, °perky, °playful, °spirited: *She is quite sprightly for a grandmother of 78.*

spring *v.* **1** °leap, °bound, °jump, °hop, vault, dart, °fly, °bounce: *He sprang to his feet when she came into the room. When Tom came to the stream, he sprang over it. The leprechaun sprang out from behind a tree.* **2** °arise, °appear, °grow, °come up, °rise, °come into being *or* °existence, be born, °emerge, °sprout, °shoot up, °burst forth: *Where the dragon's teeth were sown, an entire army sprang up.* **3** Often, ***spring up*** *or* ***from***: °originate, °begin, °start, evolve; °proceed from, °stem from, °descend from, °derive from, °come from, °develop from: *He learned how the practice of scratching the head in perplexity had sprung up. I wondered where the term* horse latitudes *sprang from.* **4** start *or* begin *or* experience *or* cause to occur *or* appear *or* happen °suddenly *or* unexpectedly, °broach, °pop, introduce *or* divulge *or* reveal *or* disclose °suddenly *or* unexpectedly: *The canoe sprang a leak and started to sink. He likes to spring trick questions at candidates in an interview.* **5** ***spring for***: °pay for, °treat (someone) to, assume the °expense(s) of: *If you go to a place I choose, I'll spring for dinner.*

—*n.* **6** °leap, °bound, °jump, °hop, vault, °bounce, °skip: *In one spring the cat cleared the garden wall and was off.* **7** bounciness, °bounce, resiliency, °resilience, springiness, buoyancy, °elasticity, sprightliness, airiness, °flexibility: *Despite her age, there's still a lot of spring in her step.* **8** °source, fount, fountain-head, well-spring, °well, °origin, °beginning, °root: *From what secret spring does his understanding arise?* **9** springtime, Eastertide, Maytime: *At 35, James is still in the spring of life.*

—*adj.* **10** vernal: *We exulted in the spring sunshine.*

sprout *v.* bud, germinate, °come up, °arise, °begin, bloom, blossom, °flower: *With this warm weather, everything in my garden is beginning to sprout.*

spruce *adj.* **1** °neat, °dapper, °smart, °trim, well turned out, °well-groomed, °elegant, *Colloq* natty: *Peter Thornton turned up for dinner looking as spruce as can be.*

—*v.* **2** ***spruce up***: °tidy (up), °neaten (up), °primp, °clean (up), °straighten out *or* up, smarten (up), titivate *or* tittivate: *Some people are coming to dinner, so first spruce up your room and then spruce yourself up.*

spunk *n.* °nerve, °courage, °pluck, °spirit, gameness, °resolve, °resolution, mettle, °heart, °grit, spunkiness, °backbone, marrow, *Colloq* °guts, °gumption, *Brit* °bottle, *US* sand: *Frances has shown she has tremendous spunk to have got this far despite her handicap.*

spur *n.* **1** goad, °prod, urging, impulse, °incitement, instigation, prompting, °pressure, stimulus, stimulation, °incentive, °provocation, °inducement, °encouragement, °motive, motivation: *The company paid the workers a bonus for each piece they completed as a spur to productivity.* **2** °projection, prong, °spike, °spine, gaff, barb, quill, tine, barbel, barbule, process: *The hook has a spur that prevents the fish from disengaging.* **3** ***on the spur of the moment***: impetuously, impulsively, unthinkingly, unpremeditatedly, impromptu, on the spot; rashly, thoughtlessly, recklessly, °hastily, brashly, incautiously, unexpectedly, °suddenly: *On the spur of the moment, we decided to fly to Cap d'Antibes for the weekend.*

—*v.* **4** goad, °prod, °urge, egg on, impel, °incite, °prompt, °press, °push, °pressure *or Brit* pressurize, °stimulate, °drive, °provoke, °induce, °encourage, °motivate, °excite, °animate: *The sales force are spurred on by the huge bonuses the company offers.*

spurious *adj.* °false, °counterfeit, °sham, °fake, °fraudulent, °bogus, °mock, °imitation, simulated, unauthentic, ungenuine, forged, feigned, °pretended, °deceitful, meretricious, contrived, °factitious, °artificial, ersatz, °synthetic, *Colloq* pseudo, °phoney *or US also* phony: *His brother was jailed for peddling spurious Egyptian burial artefacts to archaeologists.*

spurn *v.* °reject, disdain, °scorn, contemn, °despise, °rebuff, °repudiate, °refuse, °sneer at, snub, °brush off, °turn down, turn one's °back on *or* upon, °look down on *or* upon, *Colloq* cold-shoulder, turn one's nose up at, °sneeze at: *Judith spurned her father's offer of a loan.*

spurt *n.* **1** °burst, access, °effort, outbreak, °spell, °interval, °spate, °moment, °instant: *With a sudden spurt of speed he caught up with me.* **2** °increase, °advance, acceleration, °rise, °improvement: *After a brief spurt in business in January, everything stopped.*

—*v.* **3** °gush, °spew, squirt, jet, °shoot, °erupt, °burst, °surge: *The minute the plumber left, water began spurting out of the drain again.*

spy *n.* **1** double °agent, foreign °agent, secret(-service) °agent, intelligence °agent, °undercover °agent, mole, fifth-columnist, CIA man *or* woman *or* °agent, MI5 *or* MI6 man *or* woman *or* °agent; °informer, informant, *Colloq* mole, *Slang* stool-pigeon, stoolie, fink, ratfink: *In those days, everyone was a spy and you could trust no one.*

—*v.* **2** Usually, ***spy on*** *or* ***upon***: °follow, °shadow, °trail, °watch, °observe, °reconnoitre, keep under °surveillance, *US* surveil, *Colloq* °tail, °check out, case: *Why should anyone from a foreign government be spying on my mother?* **3** espy, glimpse, °spot, catch °sight *or* a glimpse of, descry, °note, °notice, °see, discern: *I spied him getting into a yellow convertible.*

spying *n.* espionage, °undercover work, secret service; detection, °intelligence, °surveillance: *Virtually every government engages in spying.*

squad *n.* °unit, °team, °band, °company, °crew, °force, troop, cadre, °gang, °section, °group, squadron, °platoon, °party: *They decided to call in the drugs squad. Has the work squad returned to base yet?*

square *adj.* **1** equilateral, quadrangular, rectangular, right-angled, quadrilateral, four-sided, cubic, cubed, six-sided, boxy: *She bought a work of art consisting of three square pieces of red plastic on a mauve ground. He keeps trying to put square pegs into round holes.* **2** °equal, on a °par, °even, on °equal terms, settled, balanced: *With this payment, our accounts are now all square.* **3** °even, °true, °exact, °straight, °accurate, °precise, °correct: *Make sure that the corners are perfectly square.* **4** °honourable, °upright, °honest, straightforward, °fair (and square), °decent, °ethical, °open, (°open and) °above-board, °right, (°right and) °proper, °clean, °just, °equitable, *Colloq* on the °level, on the up and up: *I have never had anything but square dealings with Fred Latham.* **5** healthful, °healthy, °nutritious, °substantial, °solid, °full, °generous, °satisfying, °filling, unstinting: *You could always count on three square meals a day when staying at Auntie Maisie's.* **6** °naïve, °innocent; °bourgeois, °conservative, °conventional, °unsophisticated, °provincial, °old-fashioned, conformist, °strait-laced, unimaginative, °predictable, *Colloq* antediluvian, uptight, out of it, not with it, not in the know, not °hip *or* hep, unhip, °stuffy, behind the times, °straight, *US* L-7: *We were at the age when anyone over 25 was considered square.*

—*n.* **7** rectilinear figure, rectangle; cube, °block: *He took a square of wood and quickly carved it into the shape of a duck.* **8** plaza, piazza, place, °park, (village) °green, market-place, °market (square), agora, quadrangle: *We like to sit on the benches in the square outside my house and chat with the neighbours.* **9** °bourgeois, °conservative, conformist, traditionalist, (old) °fogy *or* fogey, die-hard; °outsider; *Colloq* stuffed shirt, fuddy-duddy, *US* longhair, L-7, *Slang US* nerd, dweeb: *My parents did not understand me—they were real old squares.*
—*v.* **10** °stiffen, throw back, °straighten (up), °tense: *I squared my shoulders and prepared for the worst.* **11** Usually, ***square with***: °meet, °match (with), °conform to *or* with, °obey, °correspond to *or* with, °tally with, °accord with, °agree with, °reconcile with *or* to: *These activities do not square with the plans set out by the directors.* **12** °adapt, °adjust, °change, °modify, harmonize, °accommodate, °arrange, °comply with, °fit: *Ronald was unable to square his beliefs with what they were teaching him at the seminary.* **13** °settle, °arrange, come to °terms, °patch up, °clear up, °satisfy, °fix: *Don't worry about the customs officials—I'll square it with them later on.*

squawk *v.* **1** cackle, screech, °shriek, °yell, yowl, °whoop, hoot, °scream, °call, °cry: *The parrot kept squawking 'Where is the treasure? Where is the treasure?'* **2** °complain, grumble, whine, grouse, °protest, °object, (make a) °fuss, °yap, yowl, *Slang* bellyache, °bitch, kick, beef, °gripe, kick up a °fuss: *Oh, stop squawking and get on with your work!*
—*n.* **3** °complaint, grouse, grumble, °protest, *Colloq* kick, beef, °gripe: *If you have a squawk, take it up with the sergeant.*

squeamish *adj.* **1** °dainty, °delicate, °prudish, punctilious, °demanding, °critical, °exacting, °difficult, °fussy, °scrupulous, °fastidious, °meticulous, °painstaking, °finicky *or* finical, *Colloq* persnickety *or* pernickety, fuddy-duddy: *The museum directors were too squeamish to put on an exhibition of nudes.* **2** °nauseous, qualmish, easily °disgusted *or* revolted *or* °nauseated: *Sam was too squeamish to watch open-heart surgery on the TV.*

squeeze *v.* **1** °press, compress, °compact, °crush, squash, wring, °pinch, °nip, °grip, °tweak: *Each morning Anne squeezes an orange to make fresh juice for Edgar. Everyone knows that squeezing the nose between the thumb and forefinger means that something smells.* **2** °extract, wrest, °exact, °extort, °milk, °wrench, °pry (out), °tear, *Colloq* bleed: *It is doubtful that they will be able to squeeze a contribution out of old Scrooge.* **3** °milk, *Colloq* °shake down, bleed, °lean on, put the °screws to, put the squeeze on, °twist (someone's) arm, *US* put the arm on: *You'll have to squeeze Fletcher if you want to get paid.* **4** °ram, °jam, °pack, °stuff, °cram, °crowd, °force, °press, °wedge: *We were squeezed into the train so tightly that I could hardly breathe.* **5** °clasp, clench, °embrace, °hug, °hold, enfold, °fold, °clutch, *Archaic* clip: *She squeezed him close as they bade goodbye.* **6** ***squeeze through*** *or* ***by***: °get through *or* by, °pass, (barely) °succeed, *Colloq* squeak through *or* by, (barely) °make it: *He managed to squeeze through the exam with a pass mark, but it was touch-and-go.*
—*n.* **7** °clasp, °embrace, °hug, °clutch, *Colloq* °clinch: *She gave me a little squeeze to signal her affection.* **8** °pressure: *I was beginning to feel the squeeze between inflation and high interest rates.* **9** °crush, °jam, °crowd, squash, °press: *There was such a squeeze of people at the sale that I couldn't get in.* **10** girlfriend, °mistress, °sweetheart, *Colloq* sweetie, *Slang* moll, °broad, *Archaic* doxy: *Willie showed up with his current squeeze.* **11** ***put the squeeze on***: °press, bring °pressure to bear on, °urge, °influence, *Brit* pressurize, *US* °pressure: *The bank was beginning to put the squeeze on me to repay my overdraft.*

squelch *v.* **1** °suppress, °subdue, °put down, °quell, °quash, °defeat, °overcome, °outdo, °humiliate, *Colloq* shoot *or* slap down, take down a °peg (or two), take the °wind out of (someone's) sails, settle (someone's) °hash: *The slightest sign of disapproval from Noël was enough to squelch the most arrogant toady.*
—*n.* **2** riposte, °retort, comeback, °quip, sally, °gibe *or* jibe, barb, *Colloq* °wisecrack, °put-down: *One of the best squelches was when Oscar Wilde said, referring to a bon mot, 'I wish I'd said that', to which Whistler said, 'You will, Oscar. You will.'*

squire *v.* **1** °escort, °accompany, °conduct, °go with, °take; convoy: *Who will squire my sisters to the prince's ball?*
—*n.* **2** esquire, gentleman, landowner, landholder, landed °proprietor: *The old squire held his head high among the county aristocracy.*

squirm *v.* °wriggle, writhe, °twist, °flounder, °shift, °fidget, be (very) uncomfortable, agonize, *Colloq* °sweat: *The boy squirmed under the stern gaze of the headmaster.*

stab *v.* **1** °stick, °puncture, °prick, °lance, °jab, °pierce, °run through, °impale, °gore, °transfix, °knife, bayonet, skewer, °spike, °spit, spear, °pin; °plunge, °poke, °thrust: *In the melee, George was stabbed in the arm. It is said that she stabbed a fork into his hand.* **2** ***stab in the back***: °harm, °betray, °sell out, °double-cross, give the Judas kiss, play false with: *As soon as he had left, they stabbed him in the back by phoning the authorities.*
—*n.* **3** °puncture, °jab, °thrust, (stab-)°wound: *The coroner's office reported that the body had six stabs in the abdomen.* **4** °attempt, °try, °essay; °guess, conjecture: *Even if you are wrong, you lose nothing by making a stab at the right answer.* **5** °pang, °twinge, °pain, °ache, °hurt, stitch: *Doctor, I get a terrible stab of pain in my side when I turn that way.* **6** ***stab in the back***: treachery, °betrayal, °double-cross, Judas kiss, kiss of death, duplicity: *Informing on someone to the tax inspector is a really nasty stab in the back.*

stability *n.* **1** steadiness, solidity, firmness, soundness, sturdiness, °strength: *These flimsy structures are not known for their stability.* **2** steadfastness, constancy, dependability, reliability, °tenacity, °resolve, resoluteness, °perseverance, °determination, °persistence, durability, °lasting quality, solidity, °permanence: *The stability of the government was in doubt as the crisis continued.*

stable *adj.* **1** °steady, °solid, °firm, °sound, °sturdy, °strong, °durable, well-founded, °fast, °sure, established, deep-rooted, °stout: *The building is designed to remain stable even in a severe earthquake.* **2** °lasting, °enduring, long-lasting, long-standing, °secure, °steadfast, °steady, °strong, unchanging, unchanged, unchangeable, unalterable, °fixed, °invariable, unwavering, immutable, °permanent: *A stable relationship has existed between our countries for generations. The relationship you and I enjoy has remained stable all our lives.* **3** °sane, (°well-)balanced, °responsible, °reasonable, °sensible, °competent, °accountable: *He seemed a nice, stable young man, and nobody would have guessed that he had a drugs habit.*

stack *n.* **1** °pile, °heap, °mound, °mass, °accumulation, °hill, °mountain, °store, °stock, bank, °deposit, °supply, stockpile, °hoard, °load, °bundle, bale, *Colloq US and Canadian* stash: *This stack of paper ought to be enough to last through the next printing.* **2** haystack, cock, haycock, rick, rickle, hayrick, *Brit* clamp: *The stacks were covered with a tarpaulin before it started to rain.* **3** °collection, aggregation, °accumulation, agglomeration, amassment, °mass, °load, °pack, °amount, °abundance, °plenty, °profusion, °volume, array, °sea, °throng, multitude, °swarm, °host, °number, °quantity, °pile-up: *We have a huge stack of orders to process this morning.* **4** smokestack, chimney, chimney-stack, funnel; *Building* soil stack: *They built the stack very tall to carry the fumes away from the town below.* **5** ***blow one's stack***: °anger, become °angry, become °furious *or* infuriated, °rage, °rant, lose one's °temper, *Slang* °blow *or* lose one's cool, get hot under the collar, °blow one's top: *The boss will blow his stack if we miss the deadline.*

—*v.* **6** Often, ***stack up***: °pile (up), °heap, °accumulate, °amass, °store, °stock, stockpile, °hoard, °collect, aggregate, agglomerate, *Colloq* stash (away), squirrel away: *Stack those boxes neatly in the corner. Has he stacked up enough points to qualify?* **7** ***stack up***: **a** make sense, add up, °agree, jibe, be verifiable, *Colloq* °check out: *The ledgers don't stack up with the cheque-book. The two sets of figures simply don't stack up.* **b** °compare, °measure up, hold a candle to, be on a °par (with), be as good as: *He could never stack up to Olivier.*

stadium *n.* arena, °ground, amphitheatre, hippodrome, coliseum *or* colosseum, circus: *The new football stadium can accommodate 60,000 spectators.*

staff *n.* **1** °stick, °pole, °standard, baton, °rod, pikestaff, pike, °stake, cane, stave, °shaft, alpenstock, shillelagh, °club, truncheon, mace, crook, crozier, sceptre, °wand, caduceus: *Carrying the ceremonial staff and dressed in full regalia, the officer impressively opened the royal court proceedings.* **2** personnel, °employees, °help, workforce, °crew, °team, °organization: *Before we introduced computers, we had a staff of fifty doing nothing but filing.*

stage *n.* **1** °position, °situation, °grade, °level, °stratum, °tier, echelon, °step, °station, °place, °point, °spot, °juncture, °division, °phase, °lap; °status, °condition: *We have to reach the third stage before going on to the fourth.* **2** °platform, dais, podium; °rostrum: *After the performance, the audience threw flowers onto the stage.* **3** ***the stage***: show business, the °theatre, the boards, the footlights, Broadway, *Chiefly Brit* the West End; acting, Thespianism; *Colloq* showbiz: *That first burst of applause decided her to make the stage her career.*
—*v.* **4** °put on, °produce, °present, °mount, °exhibit: *If we can't get the theatre, why don't we stage the show in Mr Kimble's barn?* **5** °put on, contrive, °organize, °originate, °devise, °make up, concoct, °fake, trump up, stage-manage, °manipulate, °manoeuvre: *It seems that the enthusiastic reception given his wife had been staged solely for his benefit.*

stagger *v.* **1** °totter, °reel, °lurch, °teeter, °sway, walk unsteadily *or* shakily, °pitch, °rock, wobble: *When he staggered in, they thought he was drunk till they saw the knife in his back. I was already staggering under the burden of a heavy mortgage and three children and two elderly parents to care for.* **2** °surprise, °amaze, °astound, °astonish, °overwhelm, °overcome, °dumbfound *or* dumfound, °shock, stupefy, °stun, °nonplus, °floor, confound, °bewilder, °startle, °jolt, °shake (up), take one's °breath away, make one's head swim, °take (someone) aback, throw (someone) off balance, °tax, °burden, *Colloq* flabbergast, °flummox, °bowl over, *Slang* blow (someone's) mind: *The cost of cleaning up the oil spill will be staggering. He was staggered by her announcement.* **3** °alternate, °space (out), °vary, rearrange, zigzag, *US* change off: *Working hours will be staggered during the holiday period. We could strengthen the structure by staggering the positions of the columns.*

stagnant *adj.* motionless, °standing, °still, °quiet, sluggish, unmoving, immobile, °flat; °stale, °foul, °putrid, putrescent, putrefied, polluted, °dirty, contaminated, °filthy: *The malarial mosquitoes thrive in pools of stagnant water in the tropical swamps.*

stagnate *v.* languish, °idle, vegetate, °deteriorate, °degenerate, °decline, go to °seed *or* pot, °decay, rust, moulder, °decompose, °spoil, °rot: *He felt he had stagnated in a backwater of civilization for far too long.*

staid *adj.* °sedate, °rigid, °stiff, prim, °dignified, °sober, °calm, composed, °quiet, restrained, °solemn, °serious, serious-minded, °grave, sober-sided: *One expects a judge to be rather staid in his behaviour.*

stain *n.* **1** °blot, °mark, °spot, discoloration, blotch, smutch, smirch, °speck, *Brit* splodge *or US also* splotch: *There's a stain on your tie.* **2** °mark, °blot (on the escutcheon), °stigma, °blemish, *Brit* °blot on one's copybook, *Colloq US* black eye: *His cowardice in battle was a permanent stain on his reputation.* **3** dye, °colour, colouring, °tint, tinge, pigment: *An indigo stain was used to bring up certain features in microscopy.*
—*v.* **4** °blot, °mark, °spot, discolour, blotch, speckle, dye, °spatter, splatter, tinge, smudge, smutch, °splash: *The tablecloth was stained red from the spilt wine.* **5** °spoil, defile, °ruin, smirch, besmirch, °taint, °tarnish, °stigmatize, °shame, °disgrace, °sully, °contaminate, °soil, °corrupt: *Her reign was stained with the blood of the thousands she had tortured and executed.*

stake[1] *n.* **1** °stick, °post, °spike, °picket, paling, °pale, °pole, pike, stave; palisade, °upright, °pillar, column: *They tied the goat to a stake and hid, waiting for the tiger to catch the scent.* **2** ***pull up stakes***: °move (house), resettle, °move on, °migrate, °emigrate, °leave, °depart: *It was time to pull up stakes and find a new camp-site.*
—*v.* **3** °tether, °tie (up), °secure, °fasten, °picket, °lash, leash, °hitch, °chain: *The ponies were staked out in the pasture.* **4** Usually, ***stake out***: **a** °fence (in *or* off), confine, °pen, °enclose, °close in *or* off, hem in, °shut in, impound, °cage, °wall in: *We hired a man to stake out a large enough area to keep the horses.* **b** °mark off *or* out, °define, delimit, °outline, demarcate, delineate, circumscribe: *The pioneers had already staked out the land they planned to cultivate.*

stake[2] *n.* **1** °bet, wager, ante, °risk, °hazard: *If you want to make the game interesting, you'll have to raise the stakes.* **2** investment, °interest, °share, involvement, concern: *Myra has a considerable stake in the outcome of the shareholders' meeting.* **3** ***at stake***: at °hazard, hazarded, at °risk, risked, on the table, in °jeopardy, jeopardized, °concerned, °involved: *Don't take the matter lightly, as Tom's reputation is at stake.*
—*v.* **4** °risk, °jeopardize, °venture, put (money) on, °chance, °hazard, °gamble, wager, °bet: *I had staked my last penny on that gold-mine.*

stale *adj.* **1** old, past its prime, unfresh, °dry, dried-out, hardened, °limp, wilted, withered, °flat, °sour, turned, (gone) off, °mouldy, °musty, spoiled, °rotten: *All the food is stale because you failed to wrap it carefully.* **2** °old, °banal, overused, °antiquated, °old-fashioned, °threadbare, trite, clichéd, unoriginal, hackneyed, stereotyped, °tired, °weary, °boring, °tiresome, warmed-over, shop-worn, °familiar, °stock, °well-known, *Colloq* hand-me-down, *Brit* reach-me-down: *These comedians come up with the same old stale jokes year after year.*

stalemate *n.* °impasse, °deadlock, stand-off, °standstill, (dead *or* full) °stop, °tie; °check, checkmate, mate; *US* Mexican stand-off: *As both parties refused to back down, the situation was a stalemate.*

stalk[1] *v.* °follow, dog, °haunt, °shadow, °trail, °track (down), °hunt (down), °pursue, °hound, °chase, *Colloq* °tail: *The leopard stalked its prey in complete silence.*

stalk[2] *n.* °stem, °trunk, cane, main axis, leaf-stalk, °shaft, °spike: *The leaves cluster at the very top, leaving the entire stalk of the plant bare.*

stall[1] *v.* **1** °stop, °halt, °die, °quit, °shut down, °fail, cease operating, come to a °standstill, *Colloq* conk out: *My car stalled in the middle of rush-hour traffic—isn't that typical?*
—*n.* **2** °compartment, °stand, °booth, cubicle, alcove, °section, °space, °area, °slot, °enclosure, °quarters; °counter, table: *Several antiques dealers had hired stalls in the market.* **3** °shed, pen, cote, fold, coop, sty, corral, °enclosure, cowshed, barn, stable: *The animals belong in their stalls at night.*

stall[2] *v.* **1** °delay, °dawdle, dilly-dally, dally, loiter, °linger, temporize, °equivocate, °hesitate, prevaricate, play for time, waste time, stonewall, be obstructive, °put (someone *or* something) off; vacillate, dither, hedge, °procrastinate; *Brit* haver, *Colloq* beat about the bush, °drag one's feet, give (someone) the °run-around: *He managed to stall for a while before handing over the money.*
—*n.* **2** stalling, °delay, hedge, hedging, °pretext, °subterfuge, °wile, °trick, °ruse, °artifice, °stratagem, °manoeuvre, °move, stonewalling, obstructionism, playing

for time, procrastination, procrastinating, *Colloq* beating about the bush, °run-around, foot-dragging: *Her claim that she was dressing was nothing but a stall to give her time to hide the pistol.*

stalwart *adj.* **1** °robust, °stout, °strong, °mighty, °powerful, °rugged, °staunch, °hardy, °sturdy, °vigorous, °lusty, °indomitable, °solid, able-bodied, °brawny, °sinewy, °muscular, °fit, °healthy, °hale, (°hale and) °hearty, *Colloq* °husky, °hefty, beefy: *We shall need a dozen stalwart men to carry out the raid.* **2** redoubtable, °intrepid, undaunted, °resolute, °firm, °determined, unbending, °steadfast, °tenacious, unswerving, unwavering, unfaltering, unflinching, uncompromising, unyielding, persevering, °persistent, unflagging, °relentless, °tireless, °untiring, indefatigable: *Although they lost, their lawyers put up a stalwart defence.* **3** °brave, °courageous, °daring, °intrepid, valiant, °heroic, °manly, manful, °fearless, °indomitable, stout-hearted, °bold, °audacious, °game, red-blooded, plucky, mettlesome, lion-hearted, °spirited: *These stalwart knights met at dawn on the battlefield.*
—*n.* **4** °supporter, upholder, sustainer, °partisan, loyalist, (party) °faithful, trouper, °hero, °heroine: *And most of all I want to thank those stalwarts who have supported me throughout this victorious campaign.*

stamina *n.* ruggedness, °vigour, vigorousness, (intestinal) °fortitude, robustness, indefatigability, staying °power, °endurance, °energy, °power, °might, mettle, (inner) °strength, staunchness, stalwartness, °courage, indomitability, *Colloq* °grit, °guts, starch, *US* stick-to-it-iveness, sand, *Taboo slang* balls: *Even at the age of 70, she still had the stamina to run in the marathon.*

stammer *v.* **1** stutter, °hesitate, hem and haw, °stumble, falter, °pause, *Brit* hum and haw: *Is he stammering from embarrassment or because he has a speech defect?*
—*n.* **2** stutter: *Many young people who have a stammer lose it when they get out of their teens.*

stamp *v.* **1** °trample, bring down one's foot; tread, °step, °tramp; *Colloq* stomp (on): *He flew into a rage and stamped on the floor, like a petulant child.* **2** °impress, °mark, imprint, °print, °record, °document, °register, log; °engrave, emboss, inscribe; °sign, °initial: *That last night in Rio is stamped forever in my memory. Their passports were stamped at the frontier.* **3** °brand, °label, °mark, °tag, °term, °name, °style, °identify, °categorize, classify, °characterize, °designate, denominate, °show to be: *The episode on Friday stamped him as someone not to be trifled with.* **4** ***stamp out***: °eliminate, eradicate, °abolish, get °rid of, annihilate, °exterminate, °kill, snuff out, °terminate, °end, put an °end to, °destroy, °put down, °put out, °extinguish, extirpate; °quell, °subdue, °suppress, °squelch, °repress: *Something must be done to stamp out the drug traffic.*
—*n.* **5** °mark, °sign, °hallmark, earmarks, °traits, °features, °characteristics: *Her work bears the stamp of genius.* **6** die, block, punch, °seal, matrix, °plate, die-stamp, stereotype, °mould; signet(-ring): *The stamps for the binding are not quite ready.* **7** °seal, (trade *or* service) °mark, °brand, logo, logotype, °symbol, °representation, colophon, imprint, °emblem, insigne (*singular of* insignia), °label, monogram, °sign, °crest, coat of arms, escutcheon, cartouche, signature, initials: *As it bears his stamp, it must belong to him.* **8** °character, °kind, °sort, °make, °fashion, °type, °cast, °mould, °grade, °style, °cut, °genre, °class, °level, kidney, feather, °stripe, classification, species, genus, °variety, °description: *Men of Randolph's stamp are hard to find amongst gentlemen and scholars alike.*

stampede *n.* **1** °rout, °flight, °scattering, °panic, °rush, °dash: *When the store opened its doors for its annual sale, we were nearly trampled in the stampede.*
—*v.* **2** °panic, °frighten, °rush, °scatter, °rout: *Millions of buffalo were killed by stampeding them off cliffs.* **3** °rush, °run, °race, °charge, take to one's °heels, °flee, take °flight: *At the cry of 'Fire!', the audience stampeded for the exits.*

stance *n.* °carriage, °bearing, deportment; °position, °posture, °attitude, °standpoint, °stand, °viewpoint, °point of °view: *Legs apart and arms akimbo, she assumed a defiant stance at the door. Her stance was that she must protect the children at all costs.*

stanch *v.* °staunch, °stop, °stem, °halt, °check, °arrest, °stay, °end, °cease; °prevent: *Apply pressure with a pad to stanch the flow of blood from the wound.*

stand *v.* **1** °rise, °arise, °get up, *Brit* be upstanding: *We all stood when the master of ceremonies proposed a toast to McArthur.* **2** Sometimes, ***stand up***: **a** °set, °place (°upright), °position, °put, °move; up-end: *Please stand the cabinet in the corner.* **b** °stay, °remain (°standing): *Just for that you can go and stand in the corner!* **3** °endure, °survive, °tolerate, °brook, countenance, °face, confront, °last through, °abide, °allow, °accept, °take, °suffer, °bear, °withstand, °undergo, °experience, °cope with, °brave, stand *or* °bear up under, stand for, °withstand, °stomach, °weather, °handle, *Colloq* °put up with: *I could not stand another year in the tropics. She can stand neither hypocrites nor vanilla ice-cream.* **4** °continue, °remain, °persist, be *or* °remain in °effect *or* in °force, °prevail, °obtain, °apply, °exist: *The law will stand as it is till it is rescinded or modified by the court.* **5** ***stand by***: **a** °support, °defend, °back, stand *or* °stick up for, stand behind, be *or* °remain °loyal *or* °faithful to, °uphold, take the °side of, °side with, °sympathize with, *US* go to bat for: *No matter what he did, she always stood by him.* **b** °wait (in the wings), stand *or* °wait *or* stay *or* remain on the sidelines, be *or* stand °ready *or* °available *or* °accessible, be *or* stand in °readiness: *Would you mind standing by in case we need your help?* **c** °stick to, adhere to, °support, °maintain, °persist in, affirm, reaffirm, °confirm, °abide by: *We shall stand by every word of the agreement.* **6** ***stand down***: °resign, °quit, °step aside, °withdraw: *When it was revealed that she was taking steroids, she agreed to stand down from the team.* **7** ***stand for***: **a** °symbolize, betoken, °represent, °signify, °mean, be °emblematic of, °exemplify, epitomize, °illustrate, °typify, °refer to, allude to: *The initials in P. G. Wodehouse's name stand for 'Pelham Grenville'.* **b** °support, °advocate, °favour, °sponsor, °promote, espouse (the cause of), °subscribe to, °back, °champion, lend support *or* one's name to, °second: *Norma has always stood for the principles of democratic freedom.* **c** °campaign for, be *or* °present (oneself) as a °candidate for, *US* °stump for, °run for: *Who will stand for chairman this year?* **d** See **3**, above. **8** ***stand in***: °substitute (for), °understudy (for), °replace, °relieve, °double for, take the place of, *US and Canadian* pinch-hit (for), *Colloq* °cover for: *If you can't get to the rehearsal, I'll stand in for you.* **9** ***stand out***: **a** be °prominent *or* °conspicuous *or* °noticeable, be °notable *or* °noteworthy: *With her green spike hairdo and a safety pin through her cheek, Kylie really stands out in a crowd. His farewell speech stands out in my mind as one of his best.* **b** °protrude, °project, °stick out, °jut out, °bulge, °obtrude, beetle, °overhang, °extend: *The balcony stands out over the village square.* **10** ***stand up***: **a** stand, °rise, °arise, get to one's feet, °get up: *The boys had been taught to stand up when a woman entered the room.* **b** °endure, °last, °wear (well), °survive: *Today's products, with their built-in obsolescence, don't stand up to long use.* **c** °jilt, °break *or* fail to keep an °appointment with: *After waiting for two hours, he realized that he had been stood up.* **11** ***stand up for***: °support, °defend, take the °side of, °side with, °champion, °uphold, *Colloq* °stick up for: *I shall never forget how you stood up for me when they accused me of cheating.* **12** ***stand up to***: **a** confront, °brave, °challenge, °encounter, °dispute, °question, °resist, °defy, °withstand: *He's a coward when it comes to standing up to authority.* **b** °resist, °defy, °withstand, °endure, °outlast, °last through, °suffer: *This material will stand up to years of abuse.*
—*n.* **13** °position, °attitude, °stance, °posture, °policy, °philosophy, °point of °view, °viewpoint, °standpoint, °belief, °opinion, °sentiment, °feeling, °line: *I disagree*

completely with the Chancellor's stand on the economy. **14** °defence, °resistance, °effort: *This campaign will be our last stand in trying to retrieve some of the market we lost.* **15** °stop, stopover, °halt, °stay; °performance, °show: *We do some one-night stands in the country before returning to Manchester.* **16** °counter, °booth, °stall, table; wagon *or Brit* waggon, barrow, °cart: *He sells fruit from a stand in the street.* **17** °rack, °frame, °bracket; hatstand, coat-rack: *This stand is for displaying a china plate. I left my hat on the stand in your office.* **18** staging, °platform, dais, °stage, bandstand, summer-house: *We like to go to the stand in the park to hear the band play.* **19** copse, grove, wood, °thicket, brake, *Brit* spinney, coppice: *Near the house was a small stand of beeches.*

standard *n.* **1** criterion, °measure, benchmark, °model, °pattern, archetype, °touchstone, °yardstick, °gauge, °guide, guideline, paradigm, °paragon, exemplar, °example, °sample, °type, °ideal, *beau idéal*, °rule, canon, °law, °requirement, °precept, °principle: *The metric system has become the standard in many countries. People resent having imposed on them the standards of another culture.* **2** °mean, °average, °norm, °par, °level, rating: *With many luxuries now necessities, the standard of living has improved enormously. The course was for students of intermediate standard.* **3** °flag, °banner, ensign, °emblem, °pennant, burgee, insigne (*singular of* insignia), guidon, gonfalon *or* gonfanon, labarum: *The black knight bore a curiously coloured standard into battle.* **4** °pole, °post, stanchion, lamppost, column, °pillar, °support, °pedestal, °pier, °footing, (upright) °bar *or* °rod *or* timber: *The car went out of control and knocked down two lighting standards.*
—*adj.* **5** accepted, approved, °definitive, defined, °authoritative, °official, required, regulative, regulatory, textbook: *Must we follow standard procedure? The tests were conducted according to the standard methods.* **6** recognized, °prevailing, °prevalent, °usual, °customary, °habitual, °orthodox, °set, established, °regular, °familiar, °ordinary, °traditional, °classic, °stock, °typical, °normal, °staple, °conventional, °universal: *People in the south usually regard themselves as speakers of standard English.*

standardize *v.* °regiment, systematize, codify, °normalize, homogenize: *We could save money if we standardized the dimensions of the books we publish.*

stand-by *n.* **1** °supporter, defender, °backer, upholder, °partisan, °sympathizer, adherent, °stalwart: *His mother had always been his stand-by against the severity of his father.* **2** °substitute, surrogate, replacement, backup, °understudy, °second, *US and Canadian* °alternate: *They had a second ambulance as a stand-by in case the first broke down or needed servicing.* **3** °resource, °support, replacement: *I knew I could always count on you as a stand-by in case I had trouble.*

stand-in *n.* °double, °substitute, stunt man *or* woman; surrogate, replacement, °stand-by, backup, °understudy, °second, *US and Canadian* °alternate: *Any time they had to shoot a dangerous scene, my stand-in went through the motions.*

standing *adj.* **1** established, °set, °standard, °conventional, °customary, °usual, °normal, °regular, °fixed, °permanent, continued, continuing: *The club has standing rules concerning use of the card-room.* **2** °stagnant, motionless, unmoving, stationary, °still, °static: *Insects bred in the standing pools of rainwater.* **3** °continuous, °fixed, °ongoing, °perpetual, unbroken: *Michael placed a standing order for six cases of Beaujolais Nouveau every November.* **4** °erect, °upright, on one's feet, vertical, unseated: *Please remain standing till the signal is given to be seated.*
—*n.* **5** °status, °rank, °station, °position, °place, °grade, °order, °level, °stratum: *Considering her standing in the party, Mrs Miller ought to win the nomination easily.* **6** eminence, °prominence, repute, °reputation: *Foster is a surgeon of considerable standing.* **7** Usually, ***long standing***: (considerable) °age *or* longevity *or* °experience *or* seniority *or* duration: *Ivan is an art expert of long standing.*

standoffish *adj.* °aloof, °haughty, °unsocial, °reserved, °cool, frosty, °withdrawn, °remote, removed, °distant, °detached, °unapproachable, °inaccessible, uncongenial, unfriendly, unsociable; Olympian, lordly, °pompous, *Colloq* highfalutin *or* hifalutin, snooty: *Oliver is much too standoffish to deign to come to my party.*

standpoint *n.* °viewpoint, °point of °view, vantage point, °perspective, °position, °angle, °view: *From the standpoint of mice, cats do not make good pets.*

standstill *n.* (dead *or* full) °stop, °halt: *The car came to a standstill with the front wheels overhanging a cliff.*

staple *adj.* **1** °basic, °elementary, °essential, °necessary, requisite, required, °vital, °indispensable, °critical, °fundamental, °primary, °principal, °main, °chief: *These people cannot afford even staple commodities like flour and salt.* **2** °standard, °usual, °habitual, °ordinary, °customary, °prevailing, °normal, °conventional, °universal: *The staple fare on television seems to consist of old and new sitcoms.*
—*n.* **3** Often, ***staples***: °necessities, essentials, basics, °fundamentals: *Supermarkets disperse low-cost staples such as bread, tea, and milk to force shoppers to pass luxury items. Marital and financial problems are the staples of soap operas.*

star *n.* **1** °celestial *or* °heavenly body; evening star, morning star, falling star, shooting star, comet; nova, supernova: *It was a beautiful clear night and the sky was full of stars.* **2** °celebrity, °personage, °dignitary, VIP, °name, °somebody, luminary, °leading light, °leading man *or* woman *or* lady, °lead, °principal, diva, prima donna, °hero, °heroine, °idol, superstar, *Colloq* big shot, (big) draw, celeb, big °name, *Slang* top banana, headliner: *Clancy knows many of the big stars personally.*
—*adj.* **3** °principal, °major, °leading, °important, °celebrated, °famous, famed, °prominent, °eminent, °preeminent, °distinguished, °brilliant, °illustrious, unequalled, °peerless, °matchless, °incomparable, unrivalled, inimitable, unmatched, °unparalleled, °top, °foremost: *A new local rock band was the star attraction at the Hippodrome.*
—*v.* **4** °feature *or* be featured; play *or* act *or* take the °lead *or* the °leading part *or* role: *He began his career starring in spaghetti westerns.*

stare *v.* **1** °gaze, °gape, goggle, °gawk, °watch, *Colloq* °rubberneck, *Slang Brit* gawp: *The people were powerless to do anything but stare as the molten lava engulfed the city.*
—*n.* **2** °fixed *or* °blank °look; goggle, °gaze: *The teacher fixed her with a stare and she blushed with guilt.*

stark *adv.* **1** °completely, °utterly, unqualifiedly, °wholly, °absolutely, °entirely, °totally, fully, °altogether, plainly, °obviously, °clearly, certifiably: *Is that an elephant on the beach, or am I going stark staring mad? The children were running around stark naked.*
—*adj.* **2** °plain, °simple, °Spartan, °severe, unembellished, °unadorned, °cold, °bare, °harsh, °hard, °grim, bald, °blunt: *The room looks less stark with curtains. Just give me the stark facts without all the elaboration.* **3** °harsh, °severe, °bleak, austere, °barren, °desolate, °dreary, °grey, depressing, ravaged, °empty, °vacant, *Literary* drear, *Colloq US* spooky: *As day dawned, I looked out over the stark landscape of the nuclear winter.* **4** °sheer, °complete, utter, °absolute, °perfect, °pure, °thorough, thoroughgoing, arrant, °unmitigated, °out-and-out, °downright, °outright, °total, unconditional, °unqualified, °clear, °plain, °evident, °obvious, °patent, °flagrant, °gross, °rank: *They were shocked by the stark poverty they saw in the rural areas.*

start *v.* **1** Often, ***start off*** *or* ***up***: °begin, °commence, get (something) going, get off the ground, °originate, °initiate, °open, set in motion, °activate, °embark on; °turn *or* °switch on, °crank up, *Colloq* kick off: *They started operations at once. I can't start my car.* **2** Often,

start off** or **up** or **in: °arise, °come up, come to be *or* into being, °emerge, crop up, °develop, °begin, °commence, get under °way, °originate: *How did this situation start?* **3** Often, ***start off** or **up** or **in***: °go, °leave, °depart, get going, °move (off *or* out *or* on), get under °way, °set off *or* out *or* forth, *Colloq* hit the road, get the show on the road: *You start and I'll follow shortly.* **4** Often, ***start in***: °begin, °commence, get *or* start the ball rolling, get things under °way, be on one's °way, get going: *When I went in I found that she had started without me.* **5** °jump, °flinch, blench, quail, °shy, °recoil, wince, °shrink, °draw back: *He started when he saw her suddenly behind him in the mirror.* **6** cause to °spring *or* °leap *or* dart *or* °jump *or* °bound: *Any abrupt movement will start the plovers from cover.* **7** °establish, °found, °begin, °set up, °initiate, °institute, °create, °father, give birth to, beget: *It was her ideas that started the current trend in mystery novels.* **8** °bulge, °protrude, °stick out; *Colloq US* bug out: *Warping caused these boards to start from the floor. When he saw what was in his swimming-pool, his eyes started from their sockets.*
—*n.* **9** °beginning, °opening, °move: *This is not very good, but it's a start.* **10** °beginning, commencement, °opening, °outset, °onset, inception, start-up: *The start of the race is set for ten o'clock.* **11** °beginning(s), inception, °birth, °initiation, °onset, °rise, genesis, °creation, °emergence, °origin: *The start of the blues can be traced to New Orleans.* **12** °opportunity, °chance, °beginning; °help, °assistance, °aid, °backing, financing, sponsorship, °encouragement, *Colloq* °break: *Her father-in-law gave her the start she needed in business.* **13** head start, °advantage, °edge, °lead, *Colloq* (the) jump, *US and New Zealand* drop (on someone): *Having the inside track gave her a start on the competition. If he has a ten-minute start, we'll never catch him.* **14** inauguration, °opening, °beginning, °initiation, *Colloq* kick-off: *When is the start of the salmon fishing season this year?* **15** °beginning(s), founding, °foundation, °establishment, inception, °birth, °origin: *This company had its start in 1781.*

startle *v.* °frighten, °surprise, °scare, °disturb, unsettle, °upset, discompose, make (someone) °jump, °jolt, °jar, °dismay, °perturb, °stun, °take (someone) aback, °shock, °astound, °astonish, *Colloq* °shake up, give (someone) a turn, *US* discombobulate: *He jumped out from behind the door and startled me. She was startled when she was told that she had to leave at once.*

startling *adj.* °shocking, °terrifying, °frightening, astounding, astonishing, °awesome, staggering, jarring, °disturbing, °unsettling, upsetting, °amazing, surprising: *Monica fainted when told the startling news.*

starved *adj.* **1** starving, (extremely) °hungry, °famished, °ravenous: *Harry came in from the fields, declaring he was starved and ready to eat a horse.* **2** ***starved** or **starving for***: yearning for, dying for, hankering for, °hungry *or* hungering for, pining for, °longing for, °burning for, craving, thirsting for *or* after, °desirous of, aching for, *Colloq* hurting for: *I was starved for a pint of cold lager.* **3** ***starved of***: °deprived of, in °need *or* °want of, lacking, bereft of: *The children seemed starved of affection.*

state *n.* **1** °condition(s), °circumstance(s), °situation, state of affairs, °status, °shape, °position: *He was concerned about the state of the company's finances.* **2** °structure, °form, constitution, °shape, °phase, °stage: *One does not see iodine in its gaseous state outside the laboratory.* **3** °grandeur, °pomp, °style, °splendour, magnificence, °glory, °brilliance: *The prince was met at the airport and escorted in state to the palace.* **4** °nation, °country, °land, body politic: *No longer a colony, it became an independent state in 1952.*
—*adj.* **5** governmental, °government, °national, federal: *The State schools in the town had a good reputation.* **6** °ceremonial, °formal, °dignified, °stately, °solemn, °official; °royal, °regal, °imperial, °majestic: *We attended a state dinner at the White House. The Queen travelled in the state coach from Buckingham Palace to Westminster.*
—*v.* **7** aver, assert, asseverate, °declare, affirm, °express, °report, articulate, °voice, °specify, delineate, °claim, °maintain, °allege, °submit, °confirm; °say, °testify, °hold, have: *He has often stated his firm belief in democracy. He stated firmly that he was not in the house on the night of the murder.*

stately *adj.* °dignified, august, °solemn, °distinguished, °impressive, °striking, °imposing, °awesome, °grand, °lofty, °elevated, °noble, °majestic, °regal, °royal, °imperial: *The stately procession wound through the streets of the capital.*

statement *n.* °assertion, °allegation, °declaration, °expression, °report, °account, affirmation, asseveration, averral, °announcement, annunciation, °proclamation, utterance, communication, communiqué, disclosure: *Your statement is subject to interpretation. He made a long and detailed statement about the future of the project.*

static *adj.* **1** °immovable, immobile, unmoving, motionless, stationary, °fixed, °stagnant, °inert, °still, unchanging, unchanged, °changeless, unvarying, °invariable, °constant: *The situation remained static for years. A living language is not static but dynamic.*
—*n.* **2** °interference, °noise, atmospherics; °difficulty *or* difficulties, °trouble, °problem(s), *Colloq* °flak: *With all the static, I couldn't understand what she was saying. You can expect some static about being late for your wedding.*

station *n.* **1** °place, °position, °spot, °post, °site, °location: *The sentry is not to leave his station till relieved.* **2** °position, °place, °status, °rank, °caste, °standing, °class, °level: *As a doctor, he attained a station in life far above that of his father.* **3** railway station, train station, passenger station, bus station, *US and Canadian* depot: *Let's meet in the waiting-room in the station.*
—*v.* **4** °position, °place, °spot, °post, °site, °locate, °assign, °appoint, garrison, °install *or* instal, *Colloq* billet: *He was stationed in three different places in four years.*

stationery *n.* writing-paper, letterhead(s), °paper and envelopes, writing implements *or* supplies; °office supplies *or* equipment: *We consider stationery costs as part of overheads.*

statue *n.* °sculpture, °figure, figurine, statuette, carving, casting, °model, bronze, °image, icon *or* ikon, effigy, °representation; bust, atlas, caryatid, colossus, °figurehead, *Biblical* graven °image: *A statue of Disraeli stands in the market square of Aylesbury.*

statuesque *adj.* °imposing, °impressive, °majestic, °regal, °stately, °magnificent, °noble, °dignified, august, °grand, well-proportioned, °comely, °handsome, queenly, Junoesque: *Julie's statuesque figure was well set off by the draped silk gown.*

status *n.* **1** eminence, °prominence, °pre-eminence, °standing, stature, °importance, °significance, repute, °reputation, °rank, °station: *Few could approach Keith's status as a pathologist.* **2** See **standing, 5,** above.

staunch *adj.* **1** °steadfast, °loyal, °firm, unflinching, °steady, unshrinking, unswerving, dependable, °reliable, (tried and) °true, °devoted, true-blue, trusty, trusted, °faithful, unfaltering, undeviating, unwavering: *Charles has always been a staunch supporter of the party.* **2** °strong, °solid, °sturdy, °sound, well-built, °stout, °substantial, well-constructed, well-made, °tough, °rugged, long-lasting; °watertight, seaworthy: *The ship's staunch oaken hull has withstood much abuse over the years.*

stay[1] *v.* **1** °remain, °stop, °continue, °tarry, °wait, °stand, *Colloq* °freeze: *Stay where you are or I'll shoot!* **2** °remain, °stop, °lodge, °sojourn, °abide, reside, °dwell, °live, °visit: *I heard that Sheila was back in town, staying at her aunt's.* **3** °keep, °remain, °continue to be: *I was having trouble staying awake.* **4** °stop,

°arrest, °thwart, °prevent, put an °end to, °halt, °interrupt, °block, °check; °curb, °retard, °slow, °impede, °foil, °obstruct, °hamper, °hinder, °discourage, °deter; °delay, °postpone, °put off, °discontinue, °defer, *Technical* prorogue: *Only one man has the authority to stay the execution. What can be done to stay the advance of the killer bees?* **5** °linger, loiter, °wait, °tarry, °stop, °remain, *Archaic* bide: *I like this part of the world and plan to stay here a while.*
—*n.* **6** °stop, stoppage, °arrest, °set-back, °check, °halt, °prevention, discontinuance, discontinuation, °interruption, blockage, °delay, °postponement, deferment, deferral, °reprieve: *Have you been able to arrange a stay in carrying out the sentence?* **7** stopover, °sojourn, °visit, °stop: *We really enjoyed our stay at Fred's house in Fort Lauderdale.*

stay[2] *n.* **1** guy, °line, °rope, °cable, °chain, °support, °brace, °reinforcement; *Technical* head-stay, (running) backstay, forestay, °mainstay, mizen-stay: *If one of those stays gives way, the entire structure may fall.*
—*v.* **2** °support, °strengthen, °secure, °reinforce, °brace, °buttress, gird, shore (up): *The mast is stayed by two steel cables, fore and aft.*

steadfast *adj.* °resolute, °determined, persevering, resolved, °single-minded, °steady, unflinching, unfaltering, unwavering, unswerving, indefatigable, dependable, °immovable, °stable, °firm, °fixed, °constant, °persistent, unflagging, °tireless, °enduring, dedicated, deep-rooted, °faithful, °true, °loyal, °staunch: *For years Janet has been steadfast in supporting the cause. Stephen was a steadfast friend and will never be forgotten.*

steady *adj.* **1** °stable, °firm, °solid, °substantial, °sound, °stout, °strong: *Is this chair steady enough to stand on?* **2** °even, °regular, °uniform, °habitual, °invariable, unvarying, unfluctuating, unwavering, undeviating, °changeless, unchanging, °continuous, °constant; °perpetual, °non-stop, round-the-clock, °persistent, uninterrupted, unbroken, unrelieved, unceasing, ceaseless, incessant, °relentless, unremitting, never-ending, unending, °endless: *Steady trade winds could be relied on to carry vessels to the Caribbean. Inflation has remained steady for a year. How do the children manage to survive on a steady diet of junk food? The economists fear a steady rise in inflation.* **3** unflinching, unblinking, °fixed, °constant, unfaltering, °continuous, °direct: *The boy began to quail under the headmaster's steady gaze.* **4** °calm, °cool, balanced, °equable, controlled: *Steady nerves are needed to handle this new breed of fighter plane.* **5** °devoted, °firm, °staunch, °faithful, °loyal, long-standing, inveterate, °consistent, confirmed, °persistent: *The Pendergasts have always been steady supporters of the museum.* **6** °staid, °sedate, °sober, °dignified, °poised, °sophisticated, civilized, °sensible, down-to-earth, settled, °serious, °level-headed, °reliable, *Colloq* unflappable: *WANTED: Steady person as housekeeper to eccentric editor.*
—*adv.* **7** °firmly, solidly: *His wife was holding the ladder steady while he mended the gutter.* **8** ***go steady***: keep company, °date, °socialize: *Is Jane still going steady with Hubert?*
—*n.* **9** boyfriend, girlfriend, (regular) °fellow *or* °girl, °sweetheart, *Colloq* guy, gal, woman, man: *Yes, Hubert is still Jane's steady.* **10** °regular, °habitué, °customer, frequenter, familiar face: *Gil has been a steady here ever since we opened.*
—*v.* **11** stabilize, hold fast; °brace, °secure, °support, °strengthen: *Prices steadied after the first hour of trading. To steady the table, merely tighten the screws holding the legs.*

steal *v.* **1** °take (away), °appropriate, filch, shoplift, °pilfer, purloin, °make *or* walk off *or* away with, get away with; °embezzle, °misappropriate, peculate; *Colloq* °lift, °pinch, °hook, snitch, borrow, *US* boost, °liberate, heist, hijack, *Slang* °swipe, *Brit* °nick, prig, *US* hoist: *The thieves stole only the emeralds, leaving the diamonds. The bookkeeper stole the money by diverting it into his own account.* **2** plagiarize, °pirate, °copy, °imitate, °appropriate, usurp, °take: *He claims that the story of the film was stolen from his short story.* **3** °sneak, °creep, °slip, tiptoe, °prowl, °lurk, skulk, *Colloq* °pussyfoot: *Silently, we stole into the garden at the rear of the house.*
—*n.* **4** °bargain, (good) °buy, *Colloq* give-away: *At that price, the rug was a steal!*

stealing *n.* °theft, °robbery, robbing, larceny, pilferage, shoplifting, poaching, °embezzlement, peculation, thievery, thieving, filching, burglary, °plagiarism, plagiarizing, piracy, pirating: *Stealing from the church poor-box must be one of the lowest things a person can do.*

stealth *n.* furtiveness, °secrecy, clandestineness, surreptitiousness, sneakiness, slyness, underhandedness: *What the thieves lacked in stealth they compensated for in knowledge of art.*

stealthy *adj.* stealthful, °furtive, °secretive, °secret, °sly, clandestine, °surreptitious, °sneaky, °sneaking, skulking, covert, °undercover, underhand(ed), backstairs, hugger-mugger, closet: *He was as stealthy as a cat in his movements. They were stealthy collectors of pornography.*

steamy *adj.* **1** °humid, steaming, °damp, °moist, °muggy, °sticky, dank, sweaty, °sweltering, sodden, °sultry, boiling, °wet: *We were not prepared for the steamy jungle of equatorial Africa.* **2** steamed (up), fogged (up), befogged, °misty, misted, °hazy, clouded, cloudy, beclouded, °dim, blurred: *Every time I take a hot shower, the bathroom mirror gets all steamy.* **3** °erotic, °passionate, (sexually) °exciting, arousing, °hot, *Colloq* °sexy, *Slang* horny: *The film was notorious for its steamy scenes.*

steel *n.* **1** sword, °dagger, °blade, °knife, dirk, stiletto: *He saw the flash of the cold steel in the moonlight.*
—*v.* **2** °brace, °nerve, °stiffen, °fortify, grit one's teeth, °bear up, bite the bullet, screw up one's courage (to the sticking point); inure, °insulate, °protect: *People must learn to steel themselves against criticism in this business.*

steely *adj.* **1** greyish, °grey: *His steely blue eyes pierced deep into her soul.* **2** iron, °tough, indurate, adamant, adamantine, °hard, °strong, °rugged, unyielding, flinty, °sturdy: *She was a woman of steely determination.*

steep[1] *adj.* **1** °sheer, °abrupt, °precipitous, °bluff, °sharp, nearly vertical *or* °perpendicular *or* °upright: *In those days, a car had to be in first gear to climb such a steep hill.* **2** °expensive, °dear, high, overpriced, °exorbitant, °excessive, °extravagant, extortionate, *Colloq* °stiff: *The house prices in the city centre were much too steep for all but the highest-paid executives.*

steep[2] *v.* **1** °soak, °submerge, souse, °drench, °immerse, °saturate, douse, °wet, ret; pickle, marinate: *Before cooking, the meat has to be steeped in brine for at least six hours to tenderize it.* **2** imbue, °fill, °saturate, °immerse, inundate; °bury: *He learnt Japanese by steeping himself in the language for six months.*

steer *v.* **1** °guide, °pilot, °conduct, °direct; °manage, °control, °channel: *Steer the boat closer to the pier. David has steered the company to greater profits than ever before.* **2** ***steer clear of***: °avoid, °dodge, keep away from, °shun, circumvent, give (something *or* someone) a wide berth: *You'd best steer clear of Melissa when she's angry.*
—*n.* **3** Usually, ***bum steer***: (bad *or* poor) °tip *or* °suggestion *or* °hint; (bad *or* poor) °guidance *or* °advice *or* °information: *He avoids me because I once gave him a bum steer on a horse.*

stellar *adj.* **1** astral, star, sidereal: *The sidereal year is based on stellar calculations.* **2** °chief, starring, °principal, °leading, °main, headlining: *For years Lee has been a stellar performer on the golf circuit.*

stem[1] *n.* **1** °trunk, °stalk, °stock; *Technical* peduncle, pedicel, petiole, °shoot: *Three white blossoms are borne on each stem of the plant.* **2** bows, prow, stem-post: *The ship shook from stem to stern.*

—*v.* **3** °come, °arise, °develop, °derive, °issue, °flow, °generate, °originate, °spring, °emanate, °sprout, °grow, °descend, °result, °proceed: *The dispute stems from basic differences in the ways the parties regard property.*

stem[2] *v.* **1** °check, °stop, °halt, °stanch *or* °staunch, °arrest, °stay, °curb, °control, °quell, °suppress; °retard, °slow, lessen, °diminish, °reduce, °cut (back (on)): *The government introduced legislation to stem immigration. I was able to stem the bleeding by applying the tourniquet.* **2** ***stem the tide (of)***: °resist, °withstand, go *or* make °headway *or* °advance *or* make °progress against, °prevail over *or* against: *They were unable to stem the tide of public opinion.*

stench *n.* stink, °reek, noisomeness, mephitis, fetor *or* foetor, foul °odour, effluvium, *Colloq Brit* pong: *A terrible stench emanated from the cupboard. For decades their government has wallowed in the stench of corruption.*

stenographer *n.* secretary, amanuensis, stenotypist, tachygrapher, phonographer: *The court stenographer read back part of the testimony.*

stenography *n.* shorthand, stenotypy, tachygraphy, speedwriting: *Her qualification in stenography proved most useful.*

step *n.* **1** °movement, °move: *The steps of the dance were very intricate.* **2** footfall, °footstep, tread: *I think I hear father's step on the stair.* **3** °footstep, footprint, °trace, spoor, °track, mark, °impression; imprint, °vestige: *In his master's steps he trod, where the snow lay dinted.* **4** °action, °initiative, °measure, °activity, °procedure, °move, °motion: *What steps are needed to improve the situation?* **5** °stage, °move, gradation, °degree, °progression: *Can we not proceed from one to the other in easy steps?* **6** °pace, °footstep, stride: *My mother's cottage is just a few steps away, at the bottom of the garden.* **7** ***in step (with)***: in keeping (with), in °harmony *or* °agreement (with), °harmonious (with), °agreeable (with), according (with *or* to), concordant (with), attuned (to), in °tune (with), consonant (with), °consistent (with), °appropriate (to), °fitting (for); °conventional, °traditional, °routine: *Do you think that her ideas of discipline are in step with the times? I am not sure they are in step at all.* **8** ***out of step (with)***: out of keeping (with), out of *or* not in °harmony *or* °agreement (with), not °harmonious (with), not °agreeable (with), not according (with *or* to), °discordant (with), not concordant (with), not attuned (to), out of °tune (with), not consonant (with), °inconsistent (with), °inappropriate (to), not °fitting (for); °offbeat, unconventional, °eccentric, *Slang* °kinky: *You must admit that her views are out of step with the committee's.* **9** ***step by step***: °gradually, a step at a time, slowly, steadily: *The way to unravel the problem is to analyse it step by step.* **10** ***steps***: **a** °course, °way, °route, °direction, °path, °movement, °passage; °journey, journeying, °travels, °travelling: *After leaving the village, I directed my steps southward, towards the coast.* **b** stairway, stairs, stair, staircase, stepladder, *US and Canadian* stoop: *Claire walked down the steps to greet me.* **11** ***take steps***: °proceed, °move, °begin *or* °start *or* °commence to act *or* to take action, do something: *We must take steps to prevent this from happening again.* **12** ***watch one's step***: tread carefully *or* cautiously, be °cautious *or* °careful, exercise °care *or* °caution, be °wary *or* °discreet, be on the qui vive, be *or* remain °alert, be on one's °guard, have *or* keep one's wits about one, take care *or* heed, *Colloq* °pussyfoot about: *You must really watch your step with Marnie to avoid upsetting her.*

—*v.* **13** °move, °walk, look; °pace, stride: *Step lively or you'll miss your last chance to see the elephants.* **14** ***step down***: **a** °resign, °abdicate, °quit, bow out, °retire: *Don't you think it time you stepped down from the chairmanship?* **b** °decrease, °diminish, °reduce: *Using this transformer, we can step down the voltage gradually.* **15** ***step in***: °intervene, °interfere, intercede, become °involved: *It seemed the right time for us to step in and take over the company.* **16** ***step on it***: °hurry (up), make °haste, °hasten, °speed up: *He'd better step on it if he is going to catch his plane.* **17** ***step out***: **a** °go °outside *or* out of doors, °leave: *Would you mind stepping out for a few minutes while we settle this in private?* **b** °go out, °socialize: *Notice how quickly Genevieve has started stepping out again after her bereavement.* **c** become disinvolved, °withdraw, °secede: *Our firm stepped out of the negotiations when we saw who was bidding.* **18** ***step up***: **a** °improve, °progress: *George has certainly stepped up in the world since I knew him at university.* **b** °increase, accelerate, °raise, °intensify, °boost, escalate, up, °speed up: *They stepped up the pace until she could no longer keep up with them.*

sterile *adj.* **1** °barren, °fruitless, unfruitful, childless, unproductive, °infertile, infecund: *The first great disappointment of Napoleon's life was that Josephine was sterile.* **2** °pure, aseptic, uninfected, unpolluted, uncontaminated, disinfected, °sanitary, sterilized, germ-free, antiseptic: *Make sure that you always use a sterile bandage for a wound.* **3** °barren, unproductive, °stale, effete: *Vanessa's greatest fear was that her mind would become sterile and she would run out of ideas.*

sterilize *v.* **1** °purify, °disinfect, °cleanse, °clean, °fumigate, depurate, *Technical* autoclave: *Sterilize the instruments before using them.* **2** castrate (males), emasculate (males), geld (horses), spay (female animals), alter (animals), °neuter (animals), caponize (male fowl), eunuchize (males), *Technical* ovariectomize (females), vasectomize (males), *Colloq* fix (animals), cut (male animals), *Slang* tie (someone's) tubes: *Steers—that is, sterilized bulls—yield tenderer meat.*

sterling *adj.* **1** °genuine, °authentic, °real, °true, °pure: *Is this candle-snuffer sterling silver?* **2** °excellent, °superior, °superb, °superlative, first-class, °exceptional, °matchless, °peerless, unequalled, °nonpareil, °incomparable, °fine, very °good, °worthy, °estimable, °admirable: *Commander Johnston has acquitted himself as an officer of sterling character.*

stern *adj.* **1** austere, °severe, °strict, stringent, °demanding, °critical, °rigid, rigorous, flinty, °steely, °authoritarian, uncompromising, °hard, °tough, °inflexible, °firm, °immovable, °unmoved, unrelenting, unremitting, °steadfast, °resolute, °determined, unyielding, adamant, adamantine, obdurate, hard-hearted, °stony, stony-hearted, unsparing, unforgiving, °unsympathetic, °harsh: *Discipline in the French Foreign Legion is said to be quite stern.* **2** °serious, frowning, °grim, °forbidding, °grave, °gloomy, °dour, °sombre, saturnine, lugubrious, °gruff, °taciturn, crabby, crabbed, crusty, churlish, °sour: *Beneath that terribly stern exterior he really is a pussy-cat.*

stew *n.* **1** gallimaufry, goulash, salmagundi, °hash, °mess, olla podrida, olio, °mixture, °mishmash, *Brit* °hotchpotch, *US also* hodgepodge: *His book is a stew of many different opinions, none of them his own.* **2** state of °excitement *or* °alarm *or* °anxiety, dither, pother, °bother, °lather, °sweat, *Colloq* tizzy, state: *She really worked herself up into a stew over the boy Paula is engaged to.*

—*v.* **3** °simmer, °seethe, agonize, °fret, dither, °chafe, °burn, °smoulder, *Colloq* get steamed (up) (over *or* about), °work (oneself) (up) into a °sweat *or* °lather *or* state (over): *Paula's father is all stewed up over her leaving school to get married.*

stick[1] *v.* **1** °pierce, °thrust, °stab, °transfix, °pin, °spike, °impale, spear, °spit, °run through, °poke, °gore, °jab, °prick, °puncture, °punch, °penetrate, °drill, °bore, °riddle, °perforate: *He stuck the wild boar with his spear.* **2** °put, °drop, °place, °deposit, *Colloq* shove, plonk, plunk, plop: *Stick another ice cube in my drink, would you?* **3** °put, °poke, °push, °thrust, °prod, °dig; °insert: *She stuck her head out of the window to get a better look. Stop sticking your finger in my ribs!* **4** °attach, °fasten, affix, °fix, °nail, °pin, °tack; °glue, °cement, paste, gum, °weld, solder, °bind, °tie, °tape, wire; °bond, °melt, °fuse, °unite, °join: *What shall we used to stick the poster to the wall? How can I stick the* *pieces of the vase together again?* **5** Often, ***stick together***: cohere, adhere, °stay *or* °remain *or* °cleave *or* °cling together: *I cannot make these parts stick together.* **6** °hold, °last, °endure, °go through, be upheld, be *or* remain effective, remain attached: *The prosecutor was unable to make a charge of murder stick.* **7** °linger, °dwell, °remain (fixed), °continue, °stay; be *or* become lodged *or* stopped *or* °fixed *or* °fast *or* °immovable *or* stationary, be *or* become entangled *or* enmired *or* bogged down: *Something sticks in my mind about your leaving next week. We were stuck in the Sunday traffic for hours. The wheel is stuck in the sand.* **8** °burden, °weigh down, °encumber, saddle with, °charge, °impose on, °force on: *We stuck Tony with the nasty job of changing the tyre.* **9** baffle, °puzzle, °bewilder, °perplex, °confuse, °stump, stop, °nonplus: *I was totally stuck for a solution.* **10** °stand, °abide, °tolerate, °endure, °bear: *I can't stick people watching me while I am painting.* **11** ***stick around*** or ***about***: °wait, °tarry, °linger, °stay, °stand by, °remain, *Colloq* °hang around *or* about *or* on: *Can you stick around for a few minutes after the meeting?* **12** ***stick at***: °stop at, °hesitate at, °pause at, °scruple at, be deterred *or* °put off by, take °exception to, °shrink from *or* at, balk at: *Barnes sticks at nothing to get his way.* **13** ***stick by***: °support, be °loyal *or* °faithful to, °stand by: *Arnold will stick by you, come what may.* **14** ***stick it (out)***: °persevere, °persist, stand fast, °bear it, be °resolute, °soldier on, hold (one's) ground, grin and °bear it, °see it through, °weather it, *Colloq US* tough it out: *It was a very hard job, but I stuck it out to the very end.* **15** ***stick out*** or ***up***: °protrude, °jut (out), °extend, °project, poke (out); °bulge, °obtrude, °stand out, °overhang, beetle: *Stick out your tongue. What is sticking out of your ear? Balconies stick out from all sides of the building.* **16** ***stick together***: **a** °unite, °unify, °join (forces), consolidate, °merge, confederate, °amalgamate, °cooperate, work together: *The family always sticks together at times of crisis.* **b** See **5**, above. **17** ***stick up***: **a** °rob, °mug, *Colloq* °hold up, *US* heist: *They stuck up a bank courier this morning, in broad daylight!* **b** °put up, °post, affix, °display: *We went round town sticking up posters for our candidate.* **18** ***stick up for***: rally to the °support of, °support, °stand by *or* up for, °defend, °speak for *or* on *or* in behalf of, take up the cudgels for; put one's money where one's mouth is, have the courage of one's convictions: *A person must stick up for what he thinks is right.* **19** ***stick with***: °persevere, °persist, °stay *or* °remain *or* °continue with, not change one's mind about: *Stick with me, kid, and you'll wear diamonds. I'll stick with the smoked eel as a starter.*

stick[2] *n.* **1** °stake, °twig, °branch, baton, °wand, °staff, °rod, cane, °pole, pike, walking-stick: *We put a stick in the ground to mark the place.* **2** °person, °man, °fellow, °chap, *Colloq* °guy, *Brit* geezer, bloke: *Desmond isn't such a bad old stick after all.* **3** ***the sticks***: the °country, the °provinces, the countryside, the backwoods, the bush, *Brit* the hinterland *or US* the hinterlands, *Australian* the outback, *US* the boondocks, the boonies: *He hates the city and now lives somewhere in the sticks.* **4** ***wrong end of the stick***: °misunderstanding, misreading, misconstruction, misinterpretation: *When it comes to understanding a regulation, Ed always seems to get hold of the wrong end of the stick.*

stick-in-the-mud *n.* (old) °fogy *or* fogey, °conservative, °anachronism, *Colloq* fuddy-duddy, fossil, °square, back number: *Her husband was a terrible stick-in-the-mud and would never try anything new.*

sticky *adj.* **1** gluey, gummy, viscous, °tacky, glutinous, viscid, *Colloq* °gooey: *Children, please keep your sticky fingers off the car windows.* **2** °awkward, °ticklish, °tricky, °sensitive, °delicate, uncomfortable, discomfiting, discomforting, °embarrassing, *Slang* °hairy: *Inviting Steve with his ex-wife might be a bit sticky, don't you think?* **3** °humid, °clammy, dank, °damp, °muggy, °close, °sultry, °oppressive, °sweltering: *The weather was oppressive and sticky, and they kept the fan on constantly.*

stiff *adj.* **1** °firm, °rigid, inelastic, unbending, °inflexible, °hard, unbendable, °tough, °solid, solidified, stiffened, unyielding, °brittle: *The table napkins were so stiff with starch that I almost cracked one.* **2** °severe, °harsh, °punitive, °hurtful, °punishing, °abusive, torturous, distressing, afflictive, °painful, °overwhelming, °unbearable, tormenting, °merciless, excruciating, °cruel, °drastic, *US* °cruel and unusual: *The government here has stiff penalties for drug traffickers.* **3** °strong, °potent, °powerful, °overpowering, °alcoholic: *After that kind of an ordeal, you could use a stiff drink, I'm sure.* **4** °vigorous, °energetic, °staunch, dogged, °tenacious, °resolute, resolved, °determined, °stubborn, °obstinate, unyielding, °indomitable, °relentless: *They met with stiff opposition in trying to capture the fort.* **5** °strong, °steady, °powerful, °fresh, °brisk, °spanking, gusty, °forceful, howling: *We had to reduce sail because of a stiff westerly wind.* **6** °excessive, °exorbitant, °high, °steep, °expensive, °dear: *They are asking a pretty stiff price these days for a bottle of good vintage port.* **7** °cool, °haughty, °rigid, °wooden, °stuffy, °aloof, °tense, °intense, unrelaxed, °forced, °pompous, °stilted, °mannered, °ceremonious, austere, °formal, °chilly, °cold, unfriendly, °standoffish, °reserved, °snobbish, *Colloq* snooty, *Slang* uptight: *Vince is warm and friendly, but his wife is as stiff as a poker.* **8** °stilted, unrelaxed, °wooden, °forced, °artificial, °laboured, °pedantic, turgid, °formal, prim, *Colloq* °stuffy: *I have always found her writing to be rather stiff.* **9** °difficult, °hard, °steep, uphill, °laborious, °arduous, tiring, fatiguing, °exhausting, °harrowing, °toilsome, rigorous, challenging, *Colloq* °rough, °tough: *It is quite a stiff climb to the top of the pyramid of Cheops. That was a stiff homework assignment.* **10** °solid, semi-solid, °firm, °hard, °thick, °dense, °compact: *If you add a bit more water the next time, the jelly won't get quite so stiff.*
—*n.* **11** °corpse, °body, °cadaver: *Barry had to go down to the morgue to identify some stiff they hauled out of the river.* **12** skinflint, °miser, *Colloq* cheapskate, *Slang* piker, *US and Canadian* tightwad: *A stiff is a customer who fails to leave a tip.*

stiffen *v.* **1** °thicken, °coagulate, clot, °harden, °jell, °set, °solidify, congeal, crystallize: *Beat the egg-whites with a whisk until they stiffen.* **2** °brace, °reinforce, tauten, rigidify, toughen, °strengthen: *The weak support was stiffened by means of a steel bar.*

stifle *v.* **1** suffocate, °smother, °choke, strangle, throttle, asphyxiate: *The firemen were almost stifled by the smoke from the chemical fire.* **2** °choke back, keep *or* °hold back, °withhold, °repress, °suppress, °hold in, °restrain, °prevent, °curb, °cover up, °control: *I stifled a yawn as John went on about his grandchildren.* **3** °destroy, °crush, °demolish, °extinguish, °stamp out, °kill, °quash, °silence, °stop, °check: *Under his tyrannical rule all artistic creativity was stifled for fifty years.*

stigma *n.* °brand, (bad) °mark, °blot, smirch, °stain, °spot, °taint, °blemish, demerit, °blot on the escutcheon, *Brit* °blot in one's copybook: *Bankruptcy is no longer the social stigma that it used to be.*

stigmatize *v.* °brand, °mark, °scar, °blemish, besmirch, °sully, °disparage, °depreciate, °denounce, °condemn, calumniate, defame, pillory, °slander: *His foul treachery stigmatized his entire family.*

still *adj.* **1** °quiet, °serene, placid, °calm, °tranquil, motionless, unmoving, °peaceful, pacific, at rest, quiescent, °even, °flat, °smooth, °inert, stationary, undisturbed, unruffled: *In the moonlight, the lake lay still and dark.* **2** °silent, °quiet, °noiseless, soundless; hushed, °restful, *Literary* stilly: *Be still or they'll hear you! In the still night I heard the distant sound of an owl.*
—*n.* **3** stillness, °hush, °quiet, °silence, tranquillity, noiselessness, peacefulness, °calm: *In the still of the evening came the call of the nightingale.*
—*adv.* **4** even now, to *or* till *or* until this *or* that time, (up) till *or* until now, °yet: *Henry came for dinner five years ago, and he's here still. Do you still smoke?*

5 °even, in °addition: *Hugh weighed twenty stone when you last saw him, but he's heavier still today.* **6** °notwithstanding, °yet, °even then: *Are you still going to Sue's party, despite what she said?.* **7** motionless(ly), °quiet(ly), °silent(ly), stock-still: *Lie still while I put on this bandage.*
—*conj.* **8** °however, but, °notwithstanding, °nevertheless, °even so, in any °event, in any °case: *She said she'd be here; still, you never know, she may come later.*
—*v.* **9** °calm, allay, assuage, alleviate, °relieve, °silence, °lull, °quiet(en), pacify, soothe, mollify, appease, °subdue, °suppress: *A few kind words and she had stilled my fears.*

stilted *adj.* °awkward, °ungraceful, graceless, °clumsy, °wooden, °stiff, turgid, °affected, °artificial, °unnatural, °mannered, °laboured; °pretentious, °formal, °pompous, °lofty, °bombastic, grandiloquent, high-flown, °inflated: *Francis has a stilted way of expressing himself.*

stimulant *n.* **1** stimulus, °incentive, °provocation, °spur, °prompt, goad, °urge, °prod, fillip, °impetus, °incitement, °drive, impulse, °push, °pull, °draw: *She yielded readily to the stimulants of literature, science, and the fine arts.* **2** energizer, antidepressant, °tonic, restorative, *Colloq* bracer, pick-me-up, shot in the arm, *Slang* °pep pill, upper, bennie, speed: *He found he couldn't get through the day without a stimulant.*

stimulate *v.* **1** °rouse, °arouse, waken, °awaken, °wake up, °excite, °incite, °inspire, °encourage, °spur, °quicken, °fire, °fuel, °nourish, °activate, °whip *or* °stir up, goad, galvanize, °jolt, inspirit: *What can be done to stimulate students to study history? Their teacher eventually found a way to stimulate their interest.*
2 °increase, °encourage, °prompt, °provoke, °quicken: *This drug stimulates the circulation of the blood.*

stimulating *adj.* °exciting, inspirational, inspiring, arousing, °stirring, animating, °exhilarating, °provocative, thought-provoking: *I cannot recall having spent a more stimulating evening in the theatre.*

sting *v.* **1** °prick, °stab, °pierce, °stick; °bite: *Bees, wasps, and scorpions sting you, but mosquitoes, spiders, and snakes bite.* **2** °hurt, °wound, °pain, °injure, °distress, nettle, °cut to the quick: *He was really stung by Maria's callous remarks.* **3** See **stimulate, 1,** above: *We were stung into action by the minister's inspiring speech.* **4** °cheat, overcharge, °swindle, °fleece, °defraud, *Slang* °rob, °soak, °rip off, take for a °ride: *You really were stung if you paid that much for such an old piano.*

stinker *n.* °wretch, °villain, °scoundrel, cad, °heel, °beast, cur, viper, °snake in the grass, skunk, swine, polecat, *Rather old-fashioned* blackguard, °rogue, *Archaic* knave, varlet, dastard, (base) caitiff, *Colloq* stinkpot, louse, °creep, rat, *Brit* °nasty °piece of °work, sod, *Old-fashioned* rotter, bounder, blighter, *Slang* (rotten) bastard, son of a bitch, *Brit* toerag, °bugger, *US* SOB *or* s.o.b., °bum, stinkeroo *or* stinkaroo, *Taboo slang* shit, *Brit* arse-hole, *US* ass-hole: *They were a lovely couple, but their son was a real stinker.*

stinking *adj.* **1** foul-smelling, °smelly, fetid *or* foetid, mephitic, °rank, noisome, malodorous, reeking, °putrid, miasmal *or* miasmatic(al) *or* miasmic, °rancid, gamy, *Colloq Brit* pongy, whiffy: *They were kept in a stinking dungeon with little food for a month.*
2 °wretched, °villainous, °beastly, °vile, °contemptible, °low, °despicable, °mean, °nasty, °disgusting, °rotten, °terrible, °awful, *Old-fashioned* dastardly, *Colloq* °lousy, *Taboo slang* shitty: *Taking my clothes while I was swimming was a stinking thing to do.* **3** drunken, °drunk (as a lord *or US also* a skunk), intoxicated, inebriated, (be)sotted, under the °influence, over the limit, °high, °maudlin, tipsy, woozy, *Colloq* pie-eyed, °loaded, in one's cups, under the °weather, three sheets to the wind, *Slang* sozzled, soused (to the gills), potted, plastered, smashed, bombed, pissed, boozed, boozy, tanked, stoned, canned, *US* in the bag: *The last time I saw Bob, he was so stinking I had to pour him onto his train.*

stint *n.* **1** °share, °quota, °allotment, °bit, °assignment, °stretch, °shift, °term, °time, °job, chore, °task, °routine, °turn, °tour, °duty, °responsibility, °obligation, °charge: *She had done her stint of washing-up and refused to do any more.* **2** °control, °curb, °limit, limitation, °restriction, °check, °restraint, constraint, °condition, °qualification, °reservation: *The committee is free to exercise without stint its power to raise membership fees.*
—*v.* **3** °control, °curb, °limit, °restrict: *Don't stint yourself, lunch is on the firm.* **4** skimp, scrimp, be stingy *or* °cheap *or* °penurious *or* parsimonious *or* °sparing *or* °frugal, °hold back (on), °withhold, °economize, °pinch (pennies), cut corners, *Colloq Brit* be mingy: *They certainly didn't stint on the food and drink at Andrea's party.*

stipend *n.* °pay, °salary, °payment, °remuneration, °remittance, recompense, compensation, °reward, emolument, °earnings, °income; °grant, subvention, °scholarship, °subsidy, °allowance, °allotment, (financial) °support: *His stipend barely covers his basic expenses.*

stipulate *v.* °specify, °demand, °require, covenant, °set forth, °agree (to), °provide (for), °guarantee, °warrant, °promise, °insist (upon *or* on); °call for: *The agreement stipulates that the goods be received prior to payment. The compensation stipulated in the contract has been paid.*

stipulation *n.* °condition, °demand, °essential, °given, °requirement, requisite, °prerequisite, °specification, °undertaking, °obligation, covenant, clause, °proviso, °term, °agreement, °provision, °guarantee, °warranty, °promise: *This stipulation calls for payment on delivery in full and in sterling.*

stir *v.* **1** Often, ***stir up***: °agitate, °shake (up), °mix (up), °scramble, °amalgamate, °mingle, commingle, intermingle, °merge, °blend, °fold (in), churn (up), °beat, °whip (up): *Stir all the ingredients together.* **2** °move, °rise, °arise, °get up, bestir (oneself), be up and about, *Colloq* get a °move on, get moving, get a wiggle on, shake a °leg, look *or* step lively, look alive, stir one's stumps: *It is about time you were up and stirring.*
3 °disturb, °trouble, °affect, °upset, °stimulate, °activate: *The play stirred the conscience of the king. Mention 'diet' to Roberta and you'll stir up a wasp's nest.*
4 Often, ***stir up***: °motivate, °encourage, °stimulate, °energize, galvanize, °electrify, °animate, °excite, °inspire, °provoke, °move, °rouse, °arouse, °get, °prompt, °urge, °incite, °spur, °prod, °induce, °persuade, °convince: *What will it take to stir the council to take action? The usual rabble-rousers were there, stirring up the crowd.* **5** Often, ***stir up***: °awaken, °rouse, (cause to) °recall *or* call to mind, °revive, resuscitate: *Those photographs stir up so many old memories!*
—*n.* **6** bustle, °activity, °movement, °stirring, °action, commotion, °flurry, °confusion, °tumult, ado, to-do, °fuss, °disturbance, °excitement, hubbub, *Colloq Brit* kerfuffle: *There was a stir at the door, which was flung wide to allow Kitty to sweep in. The news of her marriage caused quite a stir.* **7** °prison, °jail *or Brit also* gaol, jail-house, clink, penitentiary, lock-up, *Military Brit* glasshouse, *US* brig, *Slang chiefly Brit* quod, *US* big house, °pen, slammer, can, calaboose: *He claims he's in stir for something he didn't do.*

stirring *adj.* °moving, °telling, °emotional, emotive, emotion-charged, °rousing, °stimulating, inspiring, gripping, evocative, °exciting, °thrilling, °melodramatic, °dramatic, heady, °intoxicating, °spirited, inspiriting, °exhilarating, awe-inspiring: *He was treated to the stirring experience of hearing fifty thousand people shouting his name in unison, again and again.*

stock *n.* **1** °supply, °store, inventory, stockpile, °reserve, reservoir, °cache, °hoard; °wares, °merchandise, °goods, °selection, °assortment, °range, °variety, array: *One can select something suitable from the stock at the local wine shop.* **2** °pedigree, bloodline, °house, °dynasty, (°line of) descent, genealogy,

°extraction, °roots, °lineage, °family, ancestry, °parentage, °breeding, °heritage: *Her mother was concerned that she should marry someone of good stock.* **3** °source, °progenitor, °creator, °father, begetter, forefather, °ancestor, °precursor, °forerunner, forebear; °founder: *He might well provide the stock for a new line of kings.* **4** livestock, (domestic *or* farm) animals, °cattle, beasts; horses, cows, oxen, sheep, goats: *Don't forget to water the stock before driving to the village.* **5** °share, ownership, investment, °capital, °funds; °property, °assets: *He owned ten shares of stock in the corporation. The company's stock is worth next to nothing today.* **6** ***take stock***: °weigh (up), °estimate, °review, appraise, °look at, *Colloq* °size up: *We must take stock of the situation and decide what to do.*
—*adj.* **7** °routine, stereotyped, °banal, clichéd, commonplace, °usual, hackneyed, °ordinary, °stale, °staple, run-of-the-mill, °tired, old, °everyday, °customary, °set, °standard, °traditional, trite, °worn out, *Colloq* corny: *Ask him how he is and you always get his stock reply, 'Fair to meddling'.* **8** °standard, °ordinary, °regular, °routine, °staple: *The shop does not carry 'extra tall' or 'extra short', only stock sizes.*
—*v.* **9** °carry, °have, °have *or* make °available, °handle, °deal in, °market, °sell, °supply, °furnish, °provide, °offer, °trade in, °keep: *The shop stocked a wide range of hardware.* **10** Often, ***stock up (on)***: °accumulate, °amass, °pile up, stockpile, °hoard, °store (up), °cache, °lay in, inventory: *Everyone stocked up on food in case the village was blocked by snow.*

stocky *adj.* thickset, °sturdy, chunky, °dumpy, °solid, stumpy, °burly, beefy, heavy-set, squat, pyknic, mesomorphic: *He is stocky and powerfully built.*

stodgy *adj.* °stuffy, °dull, °heavy, °ponderous, elephantine, °boring, °tedious, °humdrum, °tiresome, turgid, uninteresting, unimaginative, dry-as-dust, jejune, °vapid, °dreary, °flat, °colourless, °bland, *Colloq* ho-hum, blah, °deadly: *The speaker was boring and gave the stodgiest talk I have ever heard.*

stoical *adj.* stoic, °impassive, resigned, apathetic, °cool, unemotional, emotionless, °frigid, imperturbable, °calm, °dispassionate, °indifferent, °phlegmatic, long-suffering, °stolid, disciplined, °self-possessed, (self-)controlled, *Colloq* unflappable: *Bertram remained stoical as the judge read out the sentence of death.*

stoicism *n.* °indifference, self-possession, austerity, °self-control, °fortitude, calmness, °calm, coolness, imperturbability, longanimity, forbearance, °patience, fatalism, °resignation, *Colloq* unflappability: *The people accepted the news of one defeat after another with increasing stoicism.*

stole *n.* tippet, scarf, boa, shawl: *Mandy was too embarrassed to wear her mink stole to the charity ball.*

stolid *adj.* °impassive, °dull, doltish, °obtuse, °thick, °dense, bovine, °wooden, °slow, lumpish, unemotional, clod-like, °phlegmatic, °lethargic, apathetic, °indifferent, uninterested: *He was a stolid character, very different from his dynamic younger brother.*

stomach *n.* **1** abdomen, belly, °gut, pot-belly, °pot, °paunch, *Colloq* corporation, bay window, tummy, bread basket, spare tyre: *His huge stomach hung over and concealed his belt.* **2** °tolerance; °taste, °appetite, °desire, °hunger, °thirst, craving, °need, °inclination, °relish, °longing, yearning, hankering: *I have no stomach for those TV sitcoms featuring precocious four-year-olds.*
—*v.* **3** °abide, °tolerate, °endure, °stand, °bear, °suffer, °take, °accept, °swallow, °resign *or* °reconcile oneself to, °put up with, countenance, °brook, *Brit* °stick: *He walked out when he could no longer stomach her continual criticism.*

stony *adj.* **1** °rocky, pebbly, shingly, shingled: *Some of the beaches along the Riviera are too stony to lie on directly.* **2** °hard, obdurate, adamant, adamantine, °heartless, stony-hearted, hard-hearted, °indifferent, °unsympathetic, °implacable, intractable, insensitive, °insensible, unfeeling, unsentimental, °merciless, pitiless, °cold, °cold-hearted, °chilly, °frigid, °icy, °tough, °callous, °steely, °inflexible, unresponsive, *Colloq* hard-boiled: *He listened to her pleadings in stony silence.* **3** bankrupt, penniless, °indigent, poverty-stricken, °poor, *Colloq* °broke, *Chiefly Brit* stony-broke, skint: *At the time, I was so stony I didn't have two pennies to rub together.*

stoop *v.* **1** Sometimes, ***stoop down***: °bend (down), °bow, °duck (down), °lean (down), °hunch (down), hunker (down), °crouch (down), scrunch down: *She had to stoop down to talk to the child.* **2** Often, ***stoop low***: °condescend, °deign, °lower *or* abase *or* °degrade oneself, °sink, °humble oneself; be demeaned *or* diminished: *She had to stoop pretty low to accept a job paying only half of what she had demanded.*
—*n.* **3** °hunch, °slouch, scrunch, °crouch, stooping, slouching, *Technical* lordosis, curvature of the spine, torticollis, wryneck: *The orthopaedist thought his stoop could be corrected by a back brace.*

stop *v.* **1** °discontinue, °halt, °terminate, °cease, °break off, °end, put an °end *or* a stop to, bring to a stop *or* a °halt *or* an °end *or* a °close, °give up, °quit, °leave off, °finish, conclude, desist (from), °refrain (from), °abandon; draw to a °close, be over, come to a stop *or* a °halt *or* an °end *or* a °close; *Colloq* °cut (out), °lay off, *Brit* °pack in: *Stop shouting, I'm not deaf. The car stopped suddenly. Will the fighting ever stop?* **2** bring to a stop *or* a °halt *or* a °standstill, °check, °cut off; °arrest, °suppress, °restrain, °thwart; °block, °bar, °obstruct, dam, keep *or* °hold back, °prevent, °hinder; °slow, °impede, °stem, °stanch *or* °staunch: *The main problem was how to stop drug trafficking. Can we stop the river from flooding? This tourniquet will stop the bleeding.* **3** Often, ***stop up***: °obstruct, °block (up), °jam (up), °plug (up), °clog (up), °choke (up), °stuff (up), °fill (up), °close (up *or* off): *The drain was all stopped up with paper.* **4** peter out, be over, °end: *He gave me an injection and the pain finally stopped.* **5** °pause, °break, take a °break, °interrupt, °tarry; °sojourn, rest, °stay, °put up, °lodge, °visit, stop off *or* in *or* over; pull over, °pull up: *I'd like to stop for a cup of coffee. I stopped at The Bell Inn on my way here. We stopped short at the sign.*
—*n.* **6** °halt, °end, cessation, °termination, °ban, °prohibition; °close, °standstill, conclusion: *The new law put a stop to door-to-door selling. We must bring that practice to a stop.* **7** °stay, °sojourn, °visit, °break, °rest, stopover, *US* layover: *We thoroughly enjoyed our stop in Brighton.* **8** stopping-place, °station, °terminal, °stage, terminus, *US and Canadian* depot: *There is a bus stop in the next street.* **9** blockage, blocking, stopping (up), stoppage, closing up, °obstruction, °block: *A stop in the water supply was soon cleared up.*

stopgap *n.* **1** °makeshift, improvisation, °substitute: *The wire served as a stopgap until they could get the proper part.*
—*adj.* **2** °makeshift, °temporary, improvised, impromptu, °substitute, °emergency, °provisional, °stand-by; jury-rigged: *A broomstick served as a stopgap mast for the dinghy's sail.*

stopper *n.* stopple, cork, °plug, bung: *I had problems getting the stopper out of the barrel.*

store *v.* **1** °stock, °collect, °accumulate, °put by, lay away, °set aside, °pile (up), aggregate, °amass, cumulate; °hoard; °assemble: *The corn is stored in huge silos.* **2** °keep, °hold, °stow (away), °preserve, °warehouse, stockpile: *Apples should be stored in a cool, dry place.*
—*n.* **3** °supply, inventory, °collection, °accumulation, °stock, stockpile, reservoir, °cache, °fund: *We keep a large store of dry foods for an emergency. Grandfather has an endless store of tales about the sea.* **4** °shop, department store, °market, retailer, °outlet, cooperative (store), *Colloq* co-op: *You might get a good fridge at a department store.* **5** ***set*** or ***lay store by***: give credence to, °believe (in), °have °faith *or* °trust in, °trust (in), bank *or* °rely on, °depend on *or* upon, °count on, value: *I shouldn't set much store by what that old gossip tells you.*

storehouse *n.* °warehouse, depository *or* depositary, repository, storeroom, bank, °store, (*In Asia*) godown; arsenal, °magazine, armoury: *The company maintains storehouses in a dozen countries to better supply their customers.*

storey *n.* °floor, °level, °tier, *Chiefly US* story: *The new building is five storeys high.*

storm *n.* **1** °tempest, °disturbance, turbulence; windstorm, mistral, °gale, °whirlwind, °hurricane, tornado, typhoon, cyclone, *US and Canadian* williwaw; °shower, cloudburst, °downpour, rainstorm, deluge, monsoon, thunder-shower, thunderstorm, electrical °storm; dust-storm, sandstorm, simoom *or* simoon *or* samiel, harmattan, khamsin, sirocco; snowstorm, blizzard; hailstorm, ice-storm: *People were evacuated from the area where it was thought the storm would strike.* **2** °outburst, °outcry, °explosion, °eruption, °outpouring, °furore *or US* furor: *The proposed taxes were met by a storm of protest.* **3** °disturbance, °rumpus, °stir, commotion, °agitation, °furore *or US* furor; turbulence, °strife, turmoil, °disorder: *I am not sure the company could weather another serious financial storm.*
—*v.* **4** °rage, °rant, °rave, °bluster, °fume, °explode, °thunder, °roar, raise the roof, raise hell, raise Cain, *Colloq* °fly off the handle, °blow one's top, *US* °blow one's °stack: *When she found out where Laura had gone, mother stormed round the house.* **5** °blow, °rain, °hail, snow, sleet, °rage, °bluster, squall, °howl: *It stormed for a week, and much property was destroyed.* **6** °attack, °assault, assail, °raid, blitz, blitzkrieg, °bombard, barrage, °fire upon *or* on, °shell; °besiege, lay °siege to, °siege: *The enemy stormed the castle again and again without effect.*

stormy *adj.* **1** °violent, °tempestuous, blustery, turbulent, °wild, howling, raging, roaring, °foul, °nasty, °bad, not fit for man or beast, °inclement: *It was always stormy along the eastern coast of the island.* **2** °violent, °tempestuous, turbulent, °fierce, °fiery, °frantic, frenetic, °nerve-racking *or* nerve-wracking, frenzied, °feverish, °raving, °wild: *He and Kate enjoyed—if that is the right word—a stormy relationship for thirty years.*

story *n.* **1** °narrative, °tale, recounting, anecdote, °yarn; °account, °recital, °chronicle, °record, °history; °legend, °myth, fairy °tale *or* story, °romance, gest *or* geste, fable, fabliau; epic, °saga, Edda; °joke, *Colloq* °gag; °mystery, detective story, whodunit, thriller; horror story; allegory, °parable; °piece, article: *In olden days, the historians were the story tellers. George really knows how to tell a story. Have any of your stories been published?* **2** contention, °testimony, °assertion, °version, °statement, °representation, °allegation: *That's his story and he's sticking to it.* **3** °fib, confabulation, (white *or* black) °lie, °alibi, °excuse, untruth, °falsehood; °tall °tale, fishing *or* fish story: *He told us some story about having sailed round the world single-handed in a dinghy. Did you believe her story about being of royal blood?* **4** article, °item, °report, °dispatch, °news, tidings, °release, °information, °copy, °feature; °scoop, °exclusive: *A story about China appears on page two.* **5** story-line, °plot, °scenario, (°plot) °outline, °summary, °book: *The story needs some revision before the dialogue can be rewritten.* **6** biography, curriculum vitae, °life (story); °facts, °experiences, °adventures, °fortunes: *His story is going to be made into a film.*

stout *adj.* **1** °fat, °obese, tubby, overweight, thickset, heavy-set, °big, °burly, corpulent, fleshy, °heavy, °plump, portly: *She squeezed onto the seat between the door and a rather stout man.* **2** valiant, °brave, undaunted, °dauntless, °hardy, °courageous, °gallant, plucky, valorous, °staunch, °resolute, doughty, °bold: *'Stout fellow!' exclaimed the colonel, the ultimate compliment he was ever heard to utter.* **3** °strong, °tough, °substantial, °durable: *Tie stout cord round the box before posting it.* **4** °brawny, °sturdy, °healthy, °robust, strapping, °stalwart, °lusty, °hulking, athletic, *Colloq* beefy, °husky: *Two stout bouncers flanked the entrance to the club.*

stow *v.* °pack, °store, °load, °deposit, °put (away), °place; °cram, °stuff, °wedge, °bundle, °jam; °hide, °secrete, °conceal, °cache, *Colloq* stash (away): *We stowed our gear the moment we went aboard. They couldn't stow another thing in the basement. Where did he stow the pistol when the police searched the place?*

straggle *v.* °stray, °ramble, loiter, rove, °prowl, °range, °drift, °wander, °meander, (be) °spread, *Colloq* mosey: *Thousands of refugees straggled along the road away from the bombed village.*

straight *adj.* **1** °direct, unbending, undeviating, uncurved, °regular, linear: *The tracks are straight for as far as the eye can see.* **2** °erect, vertical, °upright, upstanding, °perpendicular; °plumb: *Stop slouching and stand up straight. He stood straight as a ramrod.* **3** °even, °square, °true, °right, °flat, °smooth, °horizontal, °level: *Are you sure that the billiard table is straight?* **4** °honest, °frank, straightforward, °direct, °forthright, °legitimate, (°fair and) °square, °fair, °equitable, °just, °above-board, °upright, °respectable, °decent, °trustworthy, °honourable, dependable, °reliable, *Colloq* upfront: *Sternway seems to be perfectly straight in his business dealings.* **5** unequivocal, unambiguous, straightforward, °candid, °plain, °simple, °explicit, °blunt, unembellished, unelaborated, °unqualified, °outright, °accurate: *The straight facts are given in this article. The police cannot get a straight story out of him as to his whereabouts last night.* **6** °direct, °point-blank, straightforward, straight from the shoulder, °candid, °outright, °plain, °frank, °no-nonsense: *Do you mind answering a straight question?* **7** °shipshape, °orderly, °neat, °tidy, in °order, arranged, organized, sorted out, °spruce, straightened out: *I wish Leonard would put his room straight before the guests arrive.* **8** °sober, °staid, °sedate, °serious, unsmiling, unemotional, °impassive, emotionless, °taciturn, composed, mask-like: *It was impossible to keep a straight face during the school play.* **9** °undiluted, °neat, unmixed, °pure, unadulterated, uncut, unmodified, unaltered, unalloyed: *He likes his whisky straight.* **10** °even, °square, settled, straightened out, agreed: *The account will be straight when Dick makes the last payment.* **11** heterosexual, °normal, *Slang* hetero: *Till Evelyn came out of the closet, I thought he was straight.*
—*adv.* **12** °directly, °right, undeviatingly, unswervingly; as the crow flies, in a beeline: *I should have known she would go straight to the police.* **13** (straight) °ahead: *Go straight for a mile and you'll see it on the right.* **14** Sometimes, ***straight out***: °directly, unequivocally, unambiguously, forthrightly, straightforwardly, °point-blank, candidly, plainly, °simply, in °plain *or* °simple English, explicitly, °outright, °honestly, accurately: *Just give me the story straight, without beating about the bush.* **15** Often, ***straight away*** *or* ***off***: °immediately, at °once, without °delay, instantly, °summarily, °directly, °right (away *or* off), °right off the bat, °promptly, *Colloq* p.d.q. (= 'pretty damned quick'): *She went back to work straight after having the baby. I told him straight off to leave town.* **16** ***straight up***: without ice: *I like my gin straight up.*

straighten *v.* **1** Often, ***straighten out***: uncurl, untangle, disentangle, unsnarl, unravel, unkink; °clear (up), °settle, °resolve, °sort out, set *or* put °straight *or* °right *or* to rights, °correct, °adjust, °rectify: *She decided to have her hair straightened. They are busy straightening out the matter of father's will.* **2** Often, ***straighten out***: °reform, °rehabilitate, °organize, reorganize: *Perhaps psychotherapy will straighten him out.* **3** Often, ***straighten out*** *or* ***up***: °tidy (up), °arrange, rearrange, °neaten, °spruce up, put in °order, °clean (up): *Would you help me straighten up the place before you leave?*

strain[1] *v.* **1** °stretch, °force, °tax, overtax, °burden, overburden, °overwork, °push; °exceed, °surpass: *His story that a bushy-haired intruder had shot her strained the jury's credulity.* **2** °push, °pull, °tug,

°heave, °stretch, °twist, °wrench, °struggle: *As he strained at his bonds the rope cut more deeply into his wrists.* **3** °injure, °hurt, °harm, °impair, °damage, °overwork, °tax, °pull, °tear, °twist, °wrench: *I strained my back lifting that box of books.* **4** °stretch, crane, °twist; °try (hard), °struggle, °strive, °labour, toil, °push, make an °effort, °exert oneself: *She strained to catch a glimpse of the prince. They strained to hear every word.* **5** °filter, °sift, °drain, °screen, sieve; winnow, °draw off, °separate; °purify, seep, °percolate: *Strain the soup to remove the bones. Strain the dregs from the wine. The water is then strained through sand.*
—*n.* **6** sprain, °injury, °damage, °harm, °wrench: *Strains often hurt more than broken bones.* **7** °anxiety, °worry; °effort, °exertion, °stress, °tension, °pressure, °burden; °tax, °demand, °obligation: *The strain began to tell on all of us. Another rope was needed to relieve the strain on the first. This advertising budget will put a great strain on our resources.* **8** Often, ***strains***: °air, °melody, °tune, °song, °sound, music: *In the distance I made out the faint strains of skirling bagpipes.* **9** °tenor, °tone, °drift, °inclination, °tendency, °quality, °spirit, °mood, °humour, °character, complexion, °cast, °impression, °thread, °vein, °theme: *I detected a mellowing strain in her letters.*

strain[2] *n.* **1** °family, °stock, ancestry, °roots, °extraction, °derivation, (°family) °background, °heritage, descent, °parentage, °lineage, °pedigree, bloodline, °race, °line, descendants: *This sample of sweet pea came from an entirely different strain.* **2** °trace, °hint, °suggestion, °suspicion, soupçon, °streak, °trait, °mark, °indication, °vestige, °evidence, °sign: *There was a definite strain of ruthlessness in her character.*

strained *adj.* °laboured, °forced, °artificial, °stiff, °tense, °awkward, uneasy, uncomfortable, °difficult, tension-ridden, °self-conscious, °unnatural, °insincere, °put-on: *His already strained relations with his wife scarcely improved when he met Lisa.*

strait *adj.* **1** °narrow, °tight, constricted, constricting, confining, confined, restricting, restricted, °limited, limiting, rigorous, °demanding, °exacting; °difficult, °straitened: *Strait is the gate and narrow is the way which leadeth unto life, and few there be that find it.*
—*n.* **2** Usually (except in gazetteers), ***straits***: narrows, °channel: *We coasted through the Straits of Magellan with all sails flying.* **3** ***dire*** or ***desperate*** or ***sore straits***: bad *or* poor °state *or* °condition, °trouble, °predicament, °plight, °mess, °dilemma, °tight °spot, hot water, *US* °bind, *Colloq* pickle, °jam, °scrape, pretty *or* fine kettle of fish, *US* box: *We shall be in dire straits if father's cheque doesn't come soon.*

straitened *adj.* °inadequate, °insufficient, reduced, oppressed, distressed, °needy, necessitous, °poor, poverty-stricken, °indigent, °impoverished, °destitute, penniless, °insolvent, *Colloq* °hard up, *US* strapped: *As a writer, he was accustomed to living in straitened circumstances between sales of his stories.*

strait-laced *adj.* °priggish, prim, °conservative, °old-fashioned, Victorian, old-maidish, °proper, °prudish, puritanical, moralistic, °strict, °narrow-minded, (over-)°scrupulous, °fussy, *Colloq* pernickety *or US also* persnickety, °stuffy, °goody-goody: *Her aunt has the strait-laced notion that girls ought to be home by ten o'clock.*

strange *adj.* **1** °odd, °peculiar, °bizarre, °weird, °curious, uncommon, °unusual, °rare, °singular, °exceptional, °eccentric, °funny, °quaint, °fantastic, out of the °ordinary, °extraordinary, °out-of-the-way, °queer, °outlandish, °unheard-of, °grotesque, °abnormal, °remarkable, surprising, °inexplicable, °unaccountable, uncanny, *Colloq* °offbeat, far-out, *Slang* °kinky, *Brit* rum, *US* kooky: *I had a strange dream last night.* **2** °unfamiliar, °unknown, °unaccustomed: *The children were warned not to get into strange cars. She was overwhelmed by the strange culture of her husband's country.*

stranger *n.* °foreigner, outlander, °alien, °newcomer, °visitor: *The people in these parts don't take kindly to strangers.*

stratagem *n.* °trick, °artifice, °device, °dodge, °subterfuge, °lure, °wile, °ruse, °plan, °scheme, °plot, °intrigue, °manoeuvre, ploy, °tactic: *What stratagem did they use to tempt you to attend this boring affair?*

strategic *adj.* °tactical, °key, °crucial, °principal, °cardinal, °critical, °vital, °key: *That line of supply is of strategic importance. Sending in the landing force was a strategic manoeuvre.*

strategy *n.* °plan, °tactic(s), °design, °policy, °procedure, °scheme, blueprint, *Colloq* game *or* master °plan, °scenario: *The enemy's strategy calls for quick air strikes by low-flying bombers.*

stratum *n.* **1** layer, °level, stratification, °table, °vein, °seam, °plane: *These coal strata have been mined for hundreds of years.* **2** °level, °caste, °class, °rank, °station, °standing, °status, °bracket, °group, °estate: *She married someone from a higher stratum of society.*

stray *v.* **1** °wander, °roam, rove, °range, °straggle, °drift, °meander: *They found the ponies straying up the valley and across the moor.* **2** °deviate, °diverge, °wander, digress, °ramble, divagate, get *or* go off the track *or* subject, go off on *or* at a tangent, get sidetracked: *She let her mind stray from the matter in hand.*
—*n.* **3** straggler, vagrant, waif, *US* dogie: *They have always taken in and cared for strays.*
—*adj.* **4** vagrant, °lost, roving, roaming, wandering, °homeless, °derelict, °abandoned: *The problem with stray pets increases when people abandon them on returning home after the summer.* **5** °random, °casual, °chance, °accidental, °haphazard, °singular, °freak, unexpected: *A stray bullet caught him in the leg.* **6** °isolated, °separate(d), lone, °odd, °single: *She brushed a stray hair from her face.*

streak *n.* **1** °stripe, striation, °strip, °stroke, °bar, °band, °line, °mark, °smear, °slash, °dash, °touch, daub, fleck, °trace; °vein, layer, °seam, °stratum: *The male bird is marked with a streak of bright reddish-orange on its throat. A red streak marks the iron deposit.* **2** °flash, °bolt: *I saw the dark figure in the light from a streak of lightning.* **3** °spell, °spate, °period, °stretch, °run: *They were celebrating their streak of good luck at the roulette table.*
—*v.* **4** °stripe, striate, °line, °bar, °mark, °smear, daub, °slash: *Dawn was beginning to streak the sky when she left the party.* **5** °race, °run, °rush, °dash, sprint, dart, °hurtle, °fly, scoot, °speed, °hasten, °hurry, °tear, whistle, zip, zoom, *Colloq* whiz *or* whizz: *The gang streaked through the village on their motor cycles and were gone.*

stream *n.* **1** °brook, brooklet, streamlet, rivulet, °tributary, °river, freshet, °run, watercourse, waterway, °channel, *Chiefly literary* rill, runnel, *Literary or No. Brit dialect* beck, burn, *Archaic NE US except in place-names* kill, *US* °creek, °branch: *If the streams continue to swell, flooding can be expected in low-lying areas.* **2** °flow, °current, °outpouring, effluence *or* efflux, effusion, °rush, °spurt, °surge, °fountain, geyser, °torrent, °flood, deluge, cataract, cascade: *A stream of bubbles showed where the diver was swimming. A stream of obscenities poured from his lips.* **3** °flow, °rush, °swarm, tide, °flood, deluge, °succession, series, °row, °line, °string, °chain, barrage, *Brit* °queue: *Simon has had a constant stream of visitors all morning.*
—*v.* **4** °run, °flow, °course, °glide, °rush, °slide, °slip, °surge; °pour, °issue, °emanate, °gush, °flood, °spout, °well up *or* out *or* forth, squirt, °spurt, °shoot, jet; cascade: *The rain streamed down the windows.* **5** °issue, °emanate; °rush, °surge, °pour, °flood, °file, °proceed, °march, °walk, °move: *People streamed in and out of the building all day long.*

streamer *n.* °pennant, °banner, pennon, °flag, bannerette *or* banneret, banderole *or* banderol *or* bannerol, gonfalon *or* gonfanon, jack, burgee: *A long streamer fluttered from the mast.*

streamlined *adj.* **1** aerodynamic, hydrodynamic, curved, curvilinear; °smooth, flowing: *Streamlined* *design began to appear in cars and boats in the 1930s.* **2** °modern, ultra-modern, modernistic, modernized, up to °date, time-saving, labour-saving, °compact, (°well-)organized, °efficient, automated: *Mother always dreamt about having a streamlined kitchen.* **3** well-run, °smooth, °efficient, automated, labour-saving, time-saving, °profitable, °productive, simplified: *He designed a fully streamlined manufacturing process for us.*

street *n.* **1** thoroughfare, °way, °road, roadway, high °road, avenue, concourse, boulevard, lane, °drive, terrace, °circle, °row, °passage, alley, byway: *I don't know the name of the street where she lives.* **2** ***up (someone's)*** *Brit* ***street*** *or US* ***alley***: (someone's) cup of tea, in (someone's) bailiwick, suiting (someone) to a T: *Crossword puzzles are very much up Eugene's street.*

strength *n.* **1** °power, °might, °force, mightiness, robustness, toughness, stoutness, sturdiness, °brawn, browniness, muscle, °sinew: *Do you have the strength to lift that by yourself?* **2** °fortitude, °backbone, °stamina, °tenacity, tenaciousness, will-power, °perseverance, °persistence, resoluteness, °resolution, pertinacity, °nerve, °grit, °pluck, °determination, gameness, intrepidity, firmness, °stability, *Colloq* °guts, gutsiness, °spunk, *US* intestinal °fortitude, stick-to-it-iveness: *Sally was a tower of strength when I needed her the most.* **3** °talent, °ability, °aptitude, °gift, °strong point, °asset: *One of his strengths is being able to sight-read music.* **4** concentration, concentratedness, °intensity, potency: *Coffee of that strength would keep me awake all night.* **5** °vigour, °force, °energy, °power, potency, °intensity: *The strength of the wind was great enough to pick up cars and toss them about.* **6** durability, °power, toughness, °stability, reliability, °resistance, solidity, °stamina, ruggedness, °endurance, soundness: *The manufacturer claims that his product has the strength to resist wear for a hundred years.* **7** persuasiveness, cogency, °weight, °force, convincingness, incisiveness, soundness: *There is no disputing the strength of the argument against smoking.*

strengthen *v.* **1** °reinforce, °renew, °bolster, °fortify, °support, °confirm, corroborate, °substantiate, °buttress, °step up, °boost: *A thousand troops were sent to strengthen the garrison at Fort Old.* **2** °encourage, hearten, invigorate, °fortify, °rejuvenate, °nourish, °energize, °vitalize, toughen, °brace (up), °steel, innervate, °stiffen: *Whatever she said seems to have strengthened his determination to succeed.*

strenuous *adj.* **1** °demanding, taxing, °tough, °arduous, °laborious, °toilsome, °burdensome, tiring, °exhausting, °difficult, °hard, uphill: *Hauling in the fishing nets was strenuous work.* **2** °energetic, °active, °vigorous, °enthusiastic, zealous, °earnest, °dynamic, °intense, indefatigable, °tireless, °persistent, dogged, °determined, °tenacious, pertinacious, °resolute, °sincere, °eager: *He has made a strenuous effort to be more accommodating.*

stress *n.* **1** °emphasis, °force, °pressure, forcefulness, °accent, accentuation, °prominence, *Technical* ictus: *Many people place the stress on the first syllable of 'controversy'.* **2** °emphasis, °significance, °importance, °weight, °force, insistence, °urgency: *She lays too much stress on looks.* **3** (stress and) °strain, °burden, °anxiety, °worry, °distress, °pain, °grief, °suffering, °anguish, °pressure, tenseness, °tension: *She has four elderly people to care for, and the stress is beginning to show.*
—*v.* **4** °emphasize, °accent, accentuate, lay stress *or* °emphasis on, underscore, underline, °mark, °note, make a °point of, bring °home, °focus on, bring into °prominence, °spotlight, °feature, highlight: *The conference succeeded in stressing the importance of a good home life.* **5** °strain, put under °strain *or* stress, °upset, °disturb, °burden, °worry, °distress, *Brit* pressurize *or US* °pressure: *Duncan was terribly stressed after a few months in the new job.*

stretch *v.* **1** °extend, °reach; °span, °spread: *Her memory stretches back to the first World War. His Texas ranch stretches as far as the eye can see.* **2** distend, °lengthen, elongate, °widen, broaden, °swell, °draw *or* °pull out, balloon, °inflate, °enlarge, °expand, °increase, dilate, °blow up: *Stretch the netting to cover the frame.* **3** overtax, overextend; °warp, °strain, °distort, °bend, °break: *We like to stretch our employees in this company. He is stretching the rules by allowing undergraduates to take his course.*
—*n.* **4** °elasticity, °give, °resilience, resiliency, stretchability, stretchiness: *There isn't much stretch left in this old rubber band.* **5** °extent, °reach, °span, °spread, °expanse, °sweep, °area, °tract, *US* °section: *There is a stretch of desert just south of the coast.* **6** °time, °stint, °period, °spell, °term, °tour (of duty), *Colloq US and Canadian* °hitch: *He signed up for a two-year stretch in the navy. He once did a six-month stretch in prison for assault.*

strew *v.* °scatter, bestrew, sprinkle, °disperse, °spread, °toss, °distribute; °litter: *Rubbish was strewn all over the floor.*

stricken *adj.* **1** Usually, ***stricken by***: struck (down) (by), °hit (by), laid °low (by *or* with), °affected (by *or* with), afflicted (with), racked (by *or* with): *He was stricken by pneumonia but is recovering.* **2** °affected (by), °smitten (by), overwhelmed (by *or* with), °overcome (by *or* with), plagued (by *or* with), tormented (by); °broken, crushed, demoralized, °broken-hearted, grief-stricken: *He was stricken by her beauty. During the plague year, commerce virtually ceased with the stricken city of London.*

strict *adj.* **1** rigorous, °narrow, °close, undeviating, confining, constricting, constrictive, °rigid, defined, °precise, °exact, °exacting, stringent, °meticulous, °compulsive, punctilious, °finicky *or* finical, °scrupulous, °attentive, °conscientious, °faithful, °thorough, °complete: *The judge's strict interpretation of the law left no room for leniency or sympathy.* **2** °severe, austere, °authoritarian, autocratic, °stern, °firm, °hard, °tough, uncompromising, °inflexible, °cold-blooded, iron-fisted, °tyrannical, °harsh, °ruthless, pitiless, °unsympathetic: *Miss Wells is remembered by all her students as a strict disciplinarian.*

stricture *n.* **1** interdiction, blockage, °restriction, °restraint, constraint, °deterrent, °impediment: *The strictures imposed on credit have throttled trade.* **2** °criticism, censure: *He deplored conservative strictures against anything new in the arts.*

strident *adj.* °shrill, °raucous, °harsh, °loud, °grating, stridulous, stridulant, scraping, scratching, °scratchy, grinding, hoarse, °rough, guttural, °husky, gravelly, rasping, jarring, °discordant, unharmonious, unmelodious, unmusical, cacophonous, croaking, creaking: *Her strident voice could be heard all over the building.*

strife *n.* **1** °discord, disharmony, °disagreement, °difference, °conflict, °rivalry, °competition, contention, °dispute, °dissension, °struggle, squabbling, bickering, arguing, quarrelling: *The nation is torn by the strife of perpetual labour disputes.* **2** °animosity, °friction, hard feelings, bad feeling(s), bad blood, °antagonism, °ill will, hatred, enmity, °hostility, unfriendliness: *The strife between us will continue because our philosophies differ so radically.*

strike *v.* **1** °hit, deal a °blow to, °knock, smack, thump, thwack, °crown, cuff, °punch, smite; °beat, hammer, °belabour, °batter, pummel *or* pommel, °pelt, buffet, thrash; cudgel, bludgeon, °club, °whip, horsewhip, °scourge, °lash, cane, °flog, birch, °slap, *Colloq* wallop, slug, whack, clout, sock, conk, °belt, bash, °lambaste, bop: *Small wonder he struck you after what you called his wife.* **2** °deliver, °deal, °aim, °direct: *He struck a blow for freedom.* **3** °hit, °collide with, °land on *or* in *or* against, smash *or* °bump *or* bang *or* °crash *or* °dash into, °go *or* °run into, °impact: *Mrs Humphrey's car went out of control and struck a tree.* **4** °remove, °take away, °take apart, dismantle, °knock down; °take *or* °pull *or* °haul down: *Stage-hands struck the set. As the wind piped up we struck the mainsail.* **5** Usually, ***strike off*** *or* ***from*** *or* ***out***: °obliterate, expunge, °erase, eradicate, °blot out, °delete, °scratch, °eliminate, °rub out, °cross (out), °cancel, °wipe out, *US* x out: *After the*

scandal, his name was struck off the register. Strike out any references that might be thought libellous. **6** °light, ignite: *He struck a match to see where he was going.* **7** °affect, °impress, °influence, °afflict, *Colloq* °hit: *The death of her kitten struck Mandy to the heart.* **8** °make, °reach, attain, conclude; °agree *or* °settle (on), °ratify, °confirm: *We struck a bargain on the sale of the car.* **9** °occur *or* °come to, °dawn on *or* upon, *Colloq* °hit, °register (with): *It suddenly struck me that you are leaving tomorrow.* **10** °impress, °print, °stamp, °punch, °mint, °make: *They have struck a new gold coin for collectors.* **11** °instil, °implant, °induce: *Horror films struck fear into our hearts when we were children.* **12** °assume, °adopt, °put on, °display, °affect, °take on, feign: *He struck a supercilious pose of insouciant hauteur that annoyed her intensely.* **13** Often, ***strike down***: °afflict, °affect, °attack, indispose, °incapacitate, disable, °cripple, °invalid: *Polio struck her down in the prime of life.* **14** °encounter, come *or* °happen *or* °hit upon, °come across, °chance upon, °discover, °stumble on, °find: *The news is that they've struck oil in the North Sea.* **15** °revolt, °rebel, °mutiny, °walk out (of the job), walk off the job: *The machinists struck at midnight, bringing the industry to a halt.* **16** ***strike on*** *or* ***upon***: °dream up, °devise, conjure up, °improvise, °work out, °invent, contrive, come up with, °hit on *or* upon, °arrive at: *The alchemist never did strike upon a way to turn lead into gold.* **17** ***strike out***: **a** °fail, get nowhere, *Colloq US* miss the boat, °flop, come a cropper, *Slang US* °blow it, blow the gaff, come to nothing *or* naught *or* nought: *Tim always strikes out when it comes to girls.* **b** See **5,** above. **18** ***strike up***: (cause to) °begin *or* °start *or* °commence: *The band struck up. We struck up an acquaintance aboard ship.*
—*n.* **19** °attack, °assault: *A dawn air strike is planned.* **20** walk-out, sit-down (strike), job action, slow-down, go-slow, work-to-rule: *They will call a strike if negotiations break down.*

striking *adj.* °remarkable, astounding, astonishing, °amazing, wondrous, awe-inspiring, °awesome, °stunning, °impressive, °imposing, °fabulous, out of the ordinary, °unusual, °rare, °exceptional, °marvellous, °extraordinary, °magnificent, °superb, °splendid, stupendous, *Colloq* °great, smashing, *Slang old-fashioned Brit* °ripping, ripsnorting, top-hole, topping: *I met the most striking girl at the golf club.*

string *n.* **1** °line, °cord, °thread, °twine, °fibre, °rope, °cable, ligament, strand, filament: *To fly a kite one needs the right weight of string.* **2** leash, °lead, °leader: *Why does he let her drag him around on the end of a string?* **3** °line, °row, series, °sequence, °succession, °chain, °procession, °stream, °train, °file, *Chiefly Brit* °queue: *A string of coincidences led to their meeting again after twenty years.* **4** necklace, °chain, °loop, strand, dog-collar, choker, chaplet, wreath, rivière, *Archaic* carcanet: *In her hair was a string of pearls.* **5** ***pull strings*** *or* ***wires***: use *or* exert °influence, *Colloq* throw one's weight around: *He had to pull strings to get his son a job on the paper.* **6** ***pull the strings***: be in °control, °control, °run, °operate, °dominate, be in °command, be in the driver's seat, hold the reins, °manipulate: *She is the one who pulls the strings when it comes to new investments.* **7** ***strings***: °conditions, °stipulations, provisos, °qualifications, °requirements, °prerequisites, °terms, °obligations, limitations, °provisions, °musts, *Colloq* °catches: *I might have known that there would be strings attached to their offer of a free holiday in Corfu.*
—*v.* **8** °thread, °join: *The children were busy stringing beads to make necklaces.* **9** Often, ***string together*** *or* ***up***: °loop, festoon, °link, °drape, °suspend, °sling, °hang, array, concatenate, °chain together: *At holiday time, coloured lights are strung round the town square.* **10** ***string along***: **a** °follow, °go along (with), °agree, concur, °collaborate: *I said I would string along with the plan for the time being.* **b** keep waiting *or* dangling, keep on a string, keep on tenterhooks, *Colloq* play fast and loose with (someone): *She's just stringing you along till her boyfriend comes back.* **c** °fool, °deceive, °bluff, °dupe, °cheat, °trick, °hoax, *Colloq* take someone for a ride, put one *or* something over on (someone): *They strung Harold along for months before they made off with his life savings.* **11** ***string out***: **a** °stretch, °reach, °extend: *The line of refugees strung out as far as one could see.* **b** °delay, °postpone, °drag out, protract, °spin out: *He strung out the repayment for as long as possible.* **12** ***string up***: °hang, lynch: *He knew that if the jury didn't convict him the townspeople would string him up.*

stringy *adj.* fibrous, chewy, °sinewy, gristly, °ropy, leathery, °tough: *The beef was somewhat stringy and the potatoes were overcooked.*

strip[1] *n.* °band, ribbon, fillet, °belt, °swath *or* °swathe, °stripe: *She wore a strip of embroidered silk tied round her head. They began farming the strip of land near the lake.*

strip[2] *v.* **1** °peel, °skin, °bare, uncover, denude, °lay °bare, decorticate, excoriate, flay: *The woodwork will need stripping before you repaint it.* **2** °disrobe, undress, get undressed, unclothe, strip down to nothing *or* to the skin *or* to the buff *or* to (one's) birthday suit, °take off *or* °peel off *or* °divest (oneself) of *or* °shed (one's) clothes *or* clothing, get °naked: *The doctor told me to go behind the screen and strip.* **3** (do a) striptease, *US* work the runway: *Sugar Caine says she enjoys stripping for an appreciative audience.* **4** °remove, °take away, °confiscate, °seize, expropriate, *Slang* °rip off: *He was accused of stripping the assets from the companies he purchased.* **5** °rob, °pillage, despoil, °plunder, °ransack, °loot, °sack: *Armies could be raised only by letting them strip the cities they conquered.*

stripe *n.* **1** °band, °bar, striation, °strip, °streak, °line, °stroke, °slash, °length: *Each railway car has a bright orange stripe along each side.* **2** °style, °kind, °sort, °class, °type, complexion, °character, °nature, °description, °persuasion, kidney, feather: *These new students are of a completely different stripe.*

striped *adj.* streaked, lined, striated: *Why not wear your striped dress to the party?*

stripling *n.* °lad, °boy, °adolescent, °juvenile, °minor, schoolboy, youngster, °teenager, °youth, °young °fellow *or* °man, fledgling *or Brit also* fledgeling, *Dialect* gossoon, °young 'un, *Archaic* hobbledehoy: *The police cadet was a callow youth, a mere stripling.*

strive *v.* **1** °endeavour, °strain, °struggle, make every °effort, °attempt, °try (hard), do one's °best *or* utmost, °exert oneself, °work at, *Colloq* give (it) one's all, go all out: *Jim strove to keep his self-control. Jennie strives for perfection in all she does.* **2** °compete, contend, °fight: *One must often strive against unbelievable odds to achieve a goal.*

stroke *n.* **1** °blow, °rap, °tap, thump, °knock, smack, whack, °swipe, °slam, °strike, *Colloq* wallop: *One stroke of the hammer and the nail went in.* **2** °action, °motion, °go, °move, °movement, °feat, °achievement: *She won the leading role and defeated her shyness at one stroke.* **3** °flourish, °movement, °gesture; °mark, °dash, *Colloq* °splash: *With a stroke of the pen the man's fate was sealed.* **4** °beat, throb, °pulse, pulsation, thump: *His heart was beating at exactly 72 strokes a minute.* **5** °attack, °seizure, °fit, apoplexy, apoplectic °fit, °spasm, paralytic attack *or* °fit; *Technical* embolism, thrombosis, cerebrovascular accident, aneurysm: *Gerry has been incapacitated since he had a stroke.* **6** °pat, °touch, °caress: *A few strokes of her fingers on my brow and the headache was gone.* **7** °achievement, °accomplishment, °feat, °act, °action, °work; °example; °touch: *Your idea of having a jazz concert to raise money is a stroke of genius.* **8** °bit, °jot or tittle, °scrap, iota, °touch, stitch, °hint, °suggestion: *You haven't done a stroke of work all morning.* **9** °occurrence, °happening, °matter: *It was just a stroke of luck that I came along when I did.*
—*v.* **10** °caress, °pet, °pat, °fondle; °massage, °rub, soothe: *His heart beat faster when she stroked his hand lightly with her fingertips.*

stroll *v.* **1** amble, °saunter, °ramble, °walk, °wander, °promenade, °meander, °stray, *Colloq* mosey: *I think I'll stroll over and buy a newspaper.*
—*n.* **2** amble, °ramble, °saunter, °walk, °wander, °promenade, °meander, constitutional: *Father rarely missed his Sunday stroll in the park.*

strong *adj.* **1** °powerful, °muscular, °mighty, °brawny, strapping, °robust, °sturdy, °stalwart, °burly, °stout, °sinewy, athletic, °wiry, *Colloq* beefy, °hefty, °husky: *He was so strong he carried both wounded men 500 yards to safety.* **2** °powerful, concentrated, °intense, °pungent, °potent, °sharp, piquant, acrid, heady, °penetrating, °aromatic, °fragrant, °hot, °spicy: *There was a strong odour of ammonia. The flavour is a little too strong for my taste.* **3** °smelly, odoriferous, noisome, °stinking, °foul, mephitic, miasmic, °putrid, putrescent, °rotten: *There is a strong smell of rotting flesh.* **4** concentrated, °undiluted, °potent, intensified: *How can you drink such strong coffee and still sleep?* **5** °vigorous, °active, °dynamic, °energetic, °eager, unflagging, °tireless, unfailing, °diligent, indefatigable, °staunch, true-blue, °steadfast, dedicated, °enthusiastic, °ardent, °fervent, fervid, vehement, °rabid, zealous, °resolute, °determined, unwavering, unswerving, °firm, uncompromising, °regular, °persistent, °tenacious, sedulous, assiduous, hard-working: *We could use other strong party supporters like Sandy.* **6** °competent, °talented, skilled, °qualified, °knowledgeable, °able, °experienced, well-versed, trained, °efficient, °capable: *We are looking for someone who is particularly strong in writing advertising copy.* **7** °influential, °persuasive, convincing, compelling, °trenchant, unmistakable, °telling, °great, °profound; °effective, °efficacious, °effectual, °powerful, °formidable: *His evidence had a strong effect on the jury. She was taking very strong medicine for her migraine.* **8** well-supported, irrefutable, well-substantiated, cogent, °forceful, °substantial, convincing, conclusive: *The police made out a very strong case against her for premeditated murder.* **9** °well-established, well-founded, redoubtable, °substantial, °powerful, °formidable: *The position inside the fortress was quite strong.* **10** °likely, °definite, °substantial, °good, better than average, °reasonable, sizeable: *There is a strong possibility that she will be elected. Sales of cars were strong during the first quarter.* **11** °stable, °sound, °solvent, °prosperous, °flourishing, thriving, affluent: *The economists think that the economy will remain strong.* **12** °solid, °sturdy, °substantial, °tough, well-built, reinforced, heavy-duty, °durable; hard-wearing: *Is the cage strong enough to hold the beast?* **13** °drastic, °extreme, Draconian, high-handed, °severe, °forceful, rigorous, °harsh, stringent, °aggressive, °strenuous, °stiff, °tough, *Colloq* hard-nosed: *We had to resort to strong measures.* **14** numerous, °large, °considerable, °great; numerically, in number, in °strength: *They arrived on the battlefield with a strong force of ten thousand men. Their army was ten thousand strong.* **15** °vivid, °graphic, etched, engraved, imprinted, impressed; °definite, clear-cut, °clear, °pronounced, °distinct, °striking, °marked: *The memory of her embrace was still strong in my mind. He bears a strong resemblance to his brother.* **16** °wilful, °aggressive, combative, defensive, °difficult, °assertive, °incisive, °dogmatic, doctrinaire, °opinionated, °self-willed, hard-headed, °strong-minded, °recalcitrant, °stubborn, °obstinate, °emphatic, *Colloq* °pushy: *One cannot deny that Caroline has a strong personality.* **17** °vigorous, °forceful, °powerful, °heavy: *Strong winds lashed the west coast last night.* **18** °rugged, craggy, °rough, weather-beaten: *She was attracted by Martin's strong, suntanned good looks.* **19** °dazzling, °glaring, °bright, °garish, °brilliant, °vivid, °bold, blinding: *The strong sunlight made her blink. Shocking pink is too strong a colour for a small room.* **20** °urgent, strongly-worded, °emphatic, °assertive: *A proposal to repeal the tax was met by strong protests.* **21** unvarying, the °same, °steady, °stable, °firm, balanced: *The market has remained strong all day.* **22** °emotional, deep-felt, deep-rooted, °basic, °intense, °fervent, °passionate, °deep, °earnest: *Doris has very strong feelings on the subject of feminism.*
—*adv.* **23** overbearingly, overenthusiastically, offensively, aggressively, antagonistically, truculently: *He always comes on a bit strong when he's enthusiastic about something.*

strong-arm *adj.* °threatening, °menacing, bullying, high-pressure, thuggish, °violent, °brutal, brutish, °aggressive, terrorizing, °terrorist, intimidating, minacious: *The gang use strong-arm tactics to force shopkeepers to buy protection.*

stronghold *n.* fortress, °bulwark, bastion, fastness, fortification, citadel: *The eastern district was one of the last strongholds of the Labour Party.*

strong-minded *adj.* strong-willed, °obstinate, °firm, °determined, uncompromising, °resolute, resolved, °independent: *He found he was dealing with a very strong-minded young woman.*

structure *n.* **1** °form, °shape, configuration, °organization, °arrangement, °make-up, framework, °order, °design, °formation, °system, °nature, °character: *The career structure of the company has served as a model for similar firms.* **2** °building, edifice, °house, construction: *Planning regulations allow only a certain kind of structure in the residential areas.*
—*v.* **3** °construct, °build, °organize, °design, °form, °shape, °arrange, systematize: *Their language seems to be structured in an unusual way.*

struggle *v.* **1** °strive, °strain, °expend °energy, °exert oneself, °labour, °endeavour, °try, °attempt: *He struggled to keep his head above water.* **2** contend, °fight, °wrestle, °battle: *They struggled against the twin odds of poverty and sickness.* **3** °wriggle, wiggle, °squirm, writhe, °twist, worm: *She finally struggled free of the ropes.*
—*n.* **4** °effort, °exertion, °strain; toil, °work, travail, °labour, °drudgery, striving, struggling: *Earning even a humble living was a struggle in those days. Was the outcome worth the struggle?* **5** contention, °competition, °contest, °battle, °fight, tussle, °match, °clash, °encounter, °strife: *The struggle between good and evil continues.*

strut *v.* °swagger, °parade, °promenade, peacock, °prance: *She goes strutting about the office as if she were the boss.*

stub *n.* **1** °butt, °end, °stump, °tail (°end), °remnant, *Colloq Brit* fag-end: *He produced a stub of pencil from his pocket and began to make notes.* **2** counterfoil; °receipt: *You will need your ticket stub for any claim.*

stubborn *adj.* °obstinate, unyielding, °inflexible, intransigent, intractable, uncompromising, mulish, pigheaded, refractory, wayward, adamant, °recalcitrant, bull-headed, °persistent, °tenacious, pertinacious, unrelenting, dogged, °determined: *He remains stubborn in his refusal to join the group.*

student *n.* **1** °pupil, °learner, °scholar, undergraduate, schoolboy, schoolgirl, schoolchild, trainee, °apprentice, °disciple; *Colloq Brit* swot *or* swotter, *US* °grind: *Only students of advanced standing are admitted to this class.* **2** °devotee, °follower, °admirer, °observer, evaluator, commentator, critic: *Nicole is a perceptive student of human nature.*

studied *adj.* °premeditated, °deliberate, °calculated, planned, °intentional, °wilful, well-thought-out, °conscious, contrived, feigned, °forced, °laboured: *He treated even the greatest crisis with a studied air of insouciance.*

studious *adj.* **1** assiduous, sedulous, °diligent, °industrious, °attentive, °careful, °painstaking, °thorough, °tireless: *Miniaturists must pay studious attention to detail.* **2** °scholarly, bookish, °academic: *She refused to allow her athletic achievements to interfere with her studious pursuits.*

study *v.* **1** °learn (about), °read, con, °memorize, burn the midnight oil, lucubrate, *Colloq* bone up (on), °cram, *Brit* swot, °mug up: *I want to study music. She has to study for an exam.* **2** °contemplate, °consider,

°reflect on, °think over *or* about, ruminate on, °chew over, °turn over, °weigh, °ponder, °deliberate over *or* on *or* about, °muse about *or* on, °mull over, °meditate on *or* about *or* over: *I want to study the problem before deciding what to do.* **3** °look *or* °go into *or* over, °look at, °scan, °examine, °analyse, °inspect, °investigate, °scrutinize, °survey, °observe: *The crime squad studied every square inch of the murder scene. Avoiding the issue as usual, Joyce silently studied her fingernails.* —*n.* **4** °analysis, °review, °examination, °survey, °inquiry *or* enquiry, °investigation, °scrutiny, °research, °exploration: *Government funds are paying for a study of the ecosystem of the Norfolk Broads.* **5** °learning, lessons, bookwork, °work, reading, contemplation, °investigation, *Colloq* boning up, cramming, *Brit* swotting: *The study of anthropology is what led him to his theory of linguistic universals.* **6** library, reading *or* writing-room, °sanctum (sanctorum), °haunt, studio, °retreat, den, workroom, °office: *Let's go into the study and talk business.*

stuff *n.* **1** °substance, °material, °matter, °fabric, ingredients, °essence, essentials, fundamentals, building blocks, makings: *This is the stuff that dreams are made on. Is hydrogen the basic stuff of the universe?* **2** °equipment, °goods, °gear, °trappings, °kit, °tackle, °accessories, °paraphernalia, accoutrements *or US also* accouterments, °effects, °belongings, °possessions, °things, °bits and °pieces, impedimenta, baggage, °property, chattels, °furniture, *Brit* °lumber, *Colloq* °junk, °rubbish, crap, *Brit* clobber, *Taboo slang* shit: *Graham left all his stuff with his mother when he went west.* **3** °spirit, °attitude, °grit, °substance, makings, °talent(s), °abilities, °capabilities, °qualities, °attributes: *Is Simon the stuff of which commandos are made?* **4** °nonsense, °trash, °rubbish, stuff and nonsense, twaddle, humbug, bunkum, tommy-rot, balderdash, *Colloq* °rot, °garbage, bunk, tripe, poppycock, crap, malarkey, boloney *or* baloney, bosh, hogwash, °swill, claptrap, piffle, °hot air, flapdoodle, fiddle-faddle, codswallop, bull, *US* horse feathers, *Taboo slang* bullshit, horseshit: *You don't believe all that stuff you've been reading about me, do you?* **5** °creations, °accomplishments, °things, °works, °materials, °matter: *Without the attributions, I'd have trouble telling their stuff apart.* —*v.* **6** °jam, °ram, °cram, °crowd, compress, °pack, °press, °squeeze, squash, shove, °thrust, °force: *You couldn't stuff another handkerchief into that suitcase.* **7** °line, °fill, °pack: *Stuff the chicken with the following mixture.* **8** °overeat, °gorge, overindulge, gormandize, gluttonize, *Colloq* make a pig *or* a hog of oneself: *They really stuffed themselves at the wedding reception.* **9** ***stuff up***: °clog, °plug, °obstruct, °choke, °block (up), °stop *or US also* °pack up: *Phone the plumber: the drain is stuffed up again. The cold had given her a headache and a stuffed-up nose.*

stuffy *adj.* **1** °close, airless, unventilated, °oppressive, stifling, suffocating, °stale, °musty, fusty, °mouldy, mildewy, °muggy, fetid *or* foetid, frowzy *or* frouzy *or* frowsy, *Brit* frowsty: *It was stuffy in the ancient tomb.* **2** °pompous, °pedantic, °self-important, self-centred, °stodgy, old-fogyish *or* old-fogeyish, °old-fashioned, °strait-laced, °staid, °conventional, prim (and °proper), °priggish, niminy-piminy, °stilted, °stiff, °rigid, *Colloq* fuddy-duddy, uptight: *What a bore to be trapped for an entire evening with those stuffy old codgers!*

stumble *v.* **1** falter, °blunder, °slip, °trip, °miss one's footing, °stagger, °lurch, °flounder: *Minnie caught her heel in the grating and stumbled.* **2** falter, °pause, °hesitate, °trip, °slip, °blunder: *He was very nervous and stumbled his way through his speech.* **3** ***stumble on*** *or* ***upon***: °chance *or* come *or* °happen on *or* upon, °hit upon, °come *or* °run across, °find, °discover, °encounter, *Colloq* °bump into: *I stumbled on a great new pub when I was out on Saturday.*

stumbling-block *n.* °impediment, °obstacle, °bar, °block, °obstruction, °hurdle, °hindrance, °barrier, °difficulty, °snag: *It was often labour unions that proved the stumbling-blocks to technological progress.*

stump *n.* **1** °stub, °butt, °end: *The branches were lopped off, leaving only the stumps.* —*v.* **2** °mystify, °confuse, °perplex, °bewilder, °flummox, °foil, °puzzle, baffle, confound, °dumbfound *or* dumfound, °stop, °stymie, °nonplus, bring up short: *I am completely stumped as to how the trick was done.* **3** °campaign, °electioneer, °canvass, *US and Canadian* barnstorm: *The candidates are out stumping in the farm areas in Iowa.* **4** ***stump up***: °pay up *or* out, °contribute, °donate, *Colloq* cough up, °chip in, °shell *or* fork out: *Everyone at the office stumped up for Peter's leaving present.*

stun *n.* **1** °daze, °numb, benumb, °knock out: *I was stunned by an unexpected blow to the solar plexus.* **2** °astonish, °daze, °paralyse, °stagger, stupefy, °overcome, °overwhelm, °astound, °jar, °shock, °jolt, strike °dumb, °amaze, confound, °bewilder, take (someone's) breath away, *Colloq* °shake up, °bowl over, discombobulate, flabbergast: *The children were stunned to hear that their mother had been arrested.*

stunning *adj.* **1** stupefying, paralysing, staggering, benumbing, numbing; °knockout: *Another stunning punch to the head and McGinty went down.* **2** °beautiful, °dazzling, °brilliant, °gorgeous, spectacular, °ravishing, °sensational, °extraordinary, °remarkable, °marvellous, stupendous, °fabulous, wonderful, °superb, °grand, °divine, °heavenly, °sublime, °lovely, °exquisite, °glorious, astonishing, astounding, °amazing, °striking, °splendid, staggering, °overpowering, mind-boggling, earth-shaking, °magnificent: *There stood the most stunning creature I had ever laid eyes on. The team won a stunning victory in the county tournament.*

stunt[1] *n.* °caper, °act, °deed, °feat, *tour de force*, °exploit, °trick, *US* dido: *The dangerous stunts are done by a stand-in for the star.*

stunt[2] *v.* °stop, °limit, delimit, °restrict, °check, °arrest, put an °end to, °end; °impede, °hamper, °hinder, °slow, °retard: *My parents always told me that smoking would stunt my growth.*

stunted *adj.* dwarfed, shrunken, °undersized, °small, °tiny, °diminutive, °little, °wee: *We saw a bonsai—a stunted Japanese potted tree—that was hundreds of years old.*

stupid *adj.* **1** unintelligent, fatuous, °obtuse, bovine, °dull, °dense, lumpish, doltish, °simple, simple-minded, moronic, imbecilic, cretinous, Boeotian, subnormal, °feeble-minded, weak-minded, °stolid, dull-witted, °dim, dim-witted, °halfwitted, °thick, thick-witted, thickheaded, slow-witted, witless, brainless, °mindless, empty-headed, bird-brained, feather-brained, feather-headed, rattle-brained, rattle-headed, ox-like, boneheaded, addle-pated, addle-headed, addled, *Chiefly Brit* imbecile, *Chiefly US* °dumb, jerky, thimble-witted, *Colloq* dopey, *Brit* dozy: *He seemed really stupid in comparison with his precocious younger sister.* **2** °foolish, °silly, °frivolous, asinine, °hare-brained, °crazy, °insane, °mad, crack-brained, °scatterbrained, °absurd, °inane, idiotic, °ridiculous, risible, laughable, °ludicrous, °nonsensical, °senseless, °bootless, °irresponsible, irrational, °ill-advised, °foolhardy, half-baked, *Colloq* cuckoo, cock-eyed, damn-fool, *Chiefly Brit* °daft, barmy *or* balmy, *US* cockamamie *or* cockamamy: *He came up with one stupid plan after another.* **3** insipid, °dull, °tedious, °boring, °tiresome, °humdrum, °prosaic, °monotonous, unimaginative, uninspired, uninteresting, °vapid, vacuous, *Colloq* ho-hum: *Most sitcoms feature stupid characters doing stupid things.*

stupidity *n.* **1** fatuity, obtuseness, dullness, denseness, lumpishness, doltishness, °simplicity, simple-mindedness, imbecility, cretinism, feeble-mindedness, weak-mindedness, stolidity, dull-wittedness, dimness, dim-wittedness, halfwittedness, thick-wittedness, slow-wittedness, thimble-wittedness, witlessness, brainlessness, mindlessness, empty-headedness, feather-headedness, rattle-headedness, boneheadedness: *In public affairs stupidity is more dangerous* *than knavery.* **2** foolishness, °folly, asininity, craziness, °insanity, °madness, °absurdity, absurdness, inanity, idiocy, ridiculousness, risibility, ludicrousness, °nonsense, senselessness, bootlessness, irresponsibility, irrationality, foolhardiness: *The stupidity of such a venture is obvious when you consider the enormous risk and the minuscule return.*

stupor *n.* insensibility, stupefaction, °torpor, °lethargy, listlessness, languor, laziness, lassitude, lifelessness, supineness, °inertia; inertness, coma, °trance, unconsciousness, numbness: *His stupor might be caused by the medication he is taking for his cold.*

sturdy *adj.* **1** °strong, °solid, °stout, °rugged, °tough, well-built, °substantial; strapping, °muscular, °powerful, °brawny, °burly, °robust, well-muscled, athletic, °hardy, *Colloq* °husky, °hefty: *This ladder should be sturdy enough to hold you. James got that sturdy build from exercise.* **2** °stalwart, °staunch, °steadfast, °resolute, °firm, °vigorous, °determined, uncompromising, unyielding, unwavering, unswerving, unfaltering, °enduring, °indomitable: *One must admire her sturdy independence in the face of all that criticism.*

style *n.* **1** °type, °kind, °variety, °category, °genre, °sort, °manner, °mode, °make, °design, °fashion, °look, °period, °pattern, configuration, °line, °cut, °shape, °form: *That style of jacket looks really good on you. They are planning to build the house in the pointed Gothic style.* **2** °fashion, °trend, °vogue, °mode, °look, °rage, °craze, *Colloq* °fad, (latest) °thing: *The current style is for shorter skirts.* **3** °luxury, high style, °comfort, opulence, °splendour, °elegance: *Now that he's won all that money, they live in style on the Costa Smeralda.* **4** °chic, stylishness, °taste, smartness, °flair, °dash, élan, °panache, °cachet, tastefulness, fashionableness, °elegance, °refinement, °polish, °sophistication, sophisticatedness, cosmopolitanism, *Colloq* pizazz *or* pizzazz; ritziness: *Irena has more style in her little finger than you have in your whole body.* **5** °quality, °character, °mode of °expression, °approach, °treatment, °vein, colouring, °spirit, °mood, °form, °technique; °tenor, °tone, °wording, phraseology, phrasing, °language, vocabulary, word choice, °diction, sentence °structure: *The pointillist style of painting appeals to many. His style of writing is reminiscent of Stevenson's.* **6** ***in style***: See **stylish,** below.
—*v.* **7** °characterize, °designate, denominate, °call, °name, °term, °label, °tag, °brand: *The use of the indicative for the subjunctive is no longer styled a solecism in British English.* **8** °fashion, °design, °arrange, °set, do, °cut, °tailor, °shape, °form: *Antoine styled my hair in a page-boy for the reception.*

stylish *adj.* °chic, °fashionable, °smart, à la °mode, modish, in °style *or* °fashion *or* °vogue, °elegant; chichi; *Colloq* in, with it, °swanky, *Chiefly Brit* °trendy, *Slang* °swell, °neat, classy, snazzy, *US* spiffy: *Nicole always looks so stylish.*

stymie *v.* °thwart, °obstruct, °block, °frustrate, snooker, °defeat, °spike, °ruin, °foil, confound, °stump, °nonplus, °hinder, °impede, *Colloq* °flummox: *The government has stymied all efforts to have him extradited.*

styptic *adj.* astringent: *The styptic effect of alum stops bleeding.*

suave *adj.* °debonair, °sophisticated, urbane, cosmopolitan, °worldly, °smooth, °gracious, °nonchalant, civilized, °cultivated, °courteous, °diplomatic, °polite, charming, °agreeable, affable, °bland: *Fictional detectives range from the suave Simon Templar to the earthy Philip Marlowe.*

subconscious *adj.* **1** °subliminal, °unconscious, suppressed, °hidden, latent, repressed, inner, innermost, underlying, deep-rooted, *Colloq* Freudian: *Despite his belligerence, he has a subconscious desire to be loved.*
—*n.* **2** (collective) °unconscious, inner self; °heart: *Her subconscious tells her that all confined areas are dangerous.*

subdue *v.* **1** °put *or* °beat down, °quell, °repress, °suppress, °quash, °crush, °control, °master, °overpower, gain mastery *or* °control *or* the °upper hand over, get the °better of, °dominate, °triumph over, hold *or* keep in °check, °bridle, °tame: *Having subdued the uprising, government forces are again in control.* **2** °conquer, vanquish, °defeat, °overcome: *The Mongol horde subdued all the people in their path.* **3** °quiet(en) *or* °tone down, °moderate, °mellow, °temper, °soften, soft-pedal, °check, °curb, °control: *His anger was subdued by her calm words.*

subdued *adj.* **1** °quiet, °mellow(ed), toned down, °moderate(d), tempered, hushed, muted, low-key, °unenthusiastic, repressed, restrained, °peaceful, °tranquil, placid, °calm(ed), °temperate, °reserved: *There was a little subdued criticism at first, but the bill was passed.* **2** chastened, °sober, sobered, °solemn, saddened, °dejected, °sad, down in the °mouth, crestfallen, downcast, °grave, °serious: *He looked subdued when he emerged from the headmaster's office.*

subject *n.* **1** (subject-)°matter, °topic; °issue, °theme, °angle, °thesis, °gist, °substance, °business, °affair, °point: *What is the subject of conversation today? The subject under discussion was of crucial importance.* **2** °course (of °study), °field, °area, °discipline, °branch of °knowledge: *In which subject did Frank take his doctorate?* **3** °cause, °ground(s), °motive, °reason, °basis, °source, °rationale; °excuse: *Increased taxes are always a subject of complaint.* **4** °participant, °case, guinea-pig, testee: *The subjects of the experiment were all in their thirties.* **5** °citizen, °national; taxpayer, voter; liegeman, vassal: *She became a British subject after her marriage to Frank.*
—*adj.* **6** Usually, ***subject to***: exposed (to), °open (to), °vulnerable (to), °susceptible (to), °prone (to), °disposed (to), at the °mercy (of), °liable (to suffer *or* undergo): *She is subject to asthma attacks. This kind of wood is subject to worm infestation.* **7** discussed, under °discussion, referred to, above: *The subject book was not returned before the due date.* **8** ***subject to***: **a** answerable to, °responsible for, °bound by, °obedient to, subservient to, °submissive to, controlled by, under the °control of: *You are subject to the same laws as everyone else.* **b** dependent on, conditional on, contingent on: *All leave is subject to the approval of the departmental head.*
—*v.* **9** ***subject to***: expose, lay °open, °submit, °put through, °impose on, cause to °undergo: *How could anyone subject another human being to such cruelty?* **10** °conquer, °subjugate, °dominate, °subdue, °enslave, enthral, °crush, °humble: *The peoples subjected by the Romans sometimes fared better than when independent.*

subjection *n.* subordination, °domination, °conquest, subjugation, enslavement, enthralment, humbling, °humiliation: *Their goal was the subjection of all peoples in the Mediterranean area.*

subjective *adj.* **1** personal, °individual, idiosyncratic; °prejudiced, °biased: *His review of the play was entirely subjective.* **2** self-centred, °egoistic, egocentric, °selfish, self-serving: *Your approach is much too subjective to be of interest to others.*
—*n.* **3** *Technical* nominative: *The subjective of 'me' is 'I'.*

subjugate *v.* °dominate, °enslave, enthral, °crush, °humble, °subject, °oppress, °suppress, °put down, °tyrannize, °subdue, °reduce, °quell, °overcome, °overpower, make subservient *or* °submissive, °humiliate: *Few peoples have been subjugated so ignominiously as the American Indians.*

sublimate *v.* transmute, °alter, °transform; °channel, °divert: *He sublimates his aggressions by jogging and marathon running.*

sublime *adj.* **1** °lofty, °high, °supreme, °exalted, °elevated, empyrean *or* empyreal, °heavenly, °noble, °glorious, °grand, high-minded; °honourable, ennobled, °eminent, °glorified, beatified, canonized, sanctified, °great, °good: *Her poetry evokes sublime emotions.* **2** °awesome, °overwhelming, inspiring, mind-boggling, °overpowering, humbling, awe-inspiring, °majestic, °splendid, empyrean: *The architecture of the cathedral was truly sublime.*

subliminal *adj.* °subconscious, °unconscious, °suggestive: *Advertisers know that subliminal techniques can be very effective in TV commercials.*

submerge *v.* **1** °plunge, submerse, °immerse, inundate, °dip, °wash, °soak, °drench, °saturate, °wet, douse, *Colloq* dunk: *To cleanse, submerge the garment in a basin of warm water for ten minutes.* **2** °dive, °plunge, °go down, °descend, °sink, °sound, °plummet: *The order to submerge was given as soon as the planes were spotted.* **3** °flood, °immerse, inundate, °swamp, °bury, engulf, °overwhelm, deluge, °drown; °conceal, °hide, °camouflage, °obscure, °cloak, °veil, °shroud: *He was quickly submerged under an enormous pile of correspondence.*

submission *n.* **1** concession, acquiescence, capitulation, °surrender, °yielding, °deference, giving in, °obedience, compliance, °resignation, submissiveness, tractability; meekness, docility, passivity, timidity, unassertiveness: *After years of oppression their abject submission to a new tyrant was not altogether surprising.* **2** submittal, °offering, °tender, contribution, °entry: *Submissions for the essay competition should be sent to the address given below.*

submissive *adj.* **1** °yielding, acquiescent, deferential, compliant, °obedient, °tractable, amenable, °agreeable, °accommodating, °passive, unresisting, pliant, °flexible, °manageable, unassertive, docile, °meek, °timid, resigned, uncomplaining: *As a child she was very submissive but she rebelled in adolescence.* **2** °obsequious, abject, subservient, °servile, °humble, deferential, slavish, °ingratiating, truckling, biddable, sycophantic, toadying, *Colloq* boot-licking, *Taboo slang* brown-nosing, *Brit* arse-kissing, arse-licking, *US* ass-kissing, ass-licking: *She keeps a few submissive lackeys about to do her bidding.*

submit *v.* **1** Often, ***submit to***: °surrender (to), °yield (to), °capitulate (to), °give in *or* up (to), °comply (with), °agree (to), °concede (to), °consent (to), accede (to), °defer (to), °bow *or* °bend (to), °succumb (to), °truckle (to), knuckle under (to), °resign (oneself) (to), be *or* become resigned (to); °respect, °accept, *Colloq* °put up with: *Despite the threats, he refused to submit. The government eventually submitted to the union's demands.* **2** °offer, proffer, °tender, °enter, °propose, °present: *Many of the suggestions that Alan submitted have been accepted.*

subordinate *adj.* **1** Often, ***subordinate to***: °minor; °inferior (to), °lower (than), lesser (than), °secondary (to), °second (to), °junior (to), °subsidiary (to); next to, °below, °beneath, °under: *He had to accept a subordinate position in the new company. His new job is subordinate to that of purchasing director.*
—*n.* **2** °assistant, °aide, °junior, subaltern, °staff °member; underling, hireling, °inferior, lackey, °servant, °slave, vassal; *Colloq US* staffer: *She is a subordinate to the editor-in-chief.*
—*v.* **3** make (something) °secondary: *Too many subordinate community interest to personal greed.*

subscribe *v.* **1** Often, ***subscribe to***: °endorse, °support, °underwrite, °advocate, back (up), °approve (of), °agree (with *or* to), °accept, °consent (to), assent (to), countenance, °tolerate, condone, °allow, °permit, °brook: *I sympathize with many of their arguments but I cannot subscribe to terrorism.* **2** Often, ***subscribe to***: °contribute (to), °support, °give (to), °donate (to), °pledge, °promise, °sign (up) (for), *Colloq* °chip in (to *or* for): *Mrs Donaldson has subscribed thousands to Amnesty International.*

subscription *n.* **1** °payment, °remittance, investment; commitment, °dues, °fee, °price, °cost: *The subscription is now £100 a year.* **2** °obligation, °pledge, °promise, underwriting: *If we get enough subscriptions, we shall be able to print the book.*

subsequent *adj.* **1** succeeding, following, ensuing, next, °future, later, °successive; resultant, resulting, consequent: *Subsequent governments have failed to solve the problem.*
—*prep.* **2** ***subsequent to***: after, following, succeeding, in the °wake *or* aftermath of: *Further problems arose subsequent to their second term of office.*

subsequently *adv.* later (on), afterwards *or US also* afterward: *Subsequently, the law was changed to protect witnesses.*

subside *v.* **1** °sink (down), °drop (down), °go down, °recede, °descend, °decline; °lower, °settle: *The waters of the swollen river subsided. The volcano's centre subsided, leaving a caldera.* **2** abate, °quiet(en) (down), °calm (down), °moderate, °let up, °decrease, °diminish, lessen, °die (down *or* off *or* out), °pass (away), °wear off: *His enthusiasm for sky-diving subsided a bit after he broke both legs. When the clamour had subsided, the president rose to speak.*

subsidiary *adj.* Often, ***subsidiary to***: ancillary (to), °secondary (to), °auxiliary (to), lesser (than), additional (to), °supplementary *or* supplemental (to), complementary (to), °accessory (to), °subordinate (to), adjuvant (to): *The company offers removal of hazardous waste as a subsidiary service.*

subsidize *v.* °fund, °finance, °support, °aid, °sponsor, subvene, °maintain, °underwrite; capitalize, *Slang US and Canadian* bankroll: *Bill and Sue can only afford to live in that big house because her parents subsidize them.*

subsidy *n.* funding, financing, subsidizing, sponsoring, sponsorship, °assistance, °aid, contribution, °support, °grant, subvention, °maintenance, underwriting, capitalization: *Farmers are hoping for increased subsidies.*

subsistence *n.* **1** °existence, living, survival, subsisting, being: *You are worried about buying beer when I feel my very subsistence threatened!* **2** °food, rations, victuals, °provision, °sustenance, °board, °nourishment, nutriment, aliment; °maintenance, °keep, °upkeep: *We depend on your salary for our subsistence, so forget about quitting your job.*

substance *n.* **1** °material, °matter, °stuff; °fabric, °composition, °make-up: *She couldn't recognize the substance in the bottle. The comet's substance is mainly ice and dirt.* **2** °essence, °pith, °heart, °core, °gist, °burden, °theme, °meat, °kernel, °nub, crux, °sum total, °sum and substance, °point, gravamen, haecceity, °quintessence, quiddity: *Explain, in 500 or fewer words, the substance of Hegel's dispute with Kant.* **3** °meaning, °import, °significance, purport, signification, °point: *Our visit to San Francisco gave substance to all we had read about it.* **4** °reality, corporeality, solidity, actuality, concreteness: *You must learn to deal with the substance, not the shadows.* **5** °means, °wealth, °property, °possessions, °riches, °resources, affluence, assets: *John Culver was a citizen of some substance in this town.*

substantial *adj.* **1** °material, °considerable, °significant, °great, °worthwhile, consequential, °ample, °goodly, °respectable, °abundant, °generous, °big, °large, sizeable, °major, *Colloq* °tidy, °healthy: *We understand that he made a substantial payment to keep his name out of the papers.* **2** °strong, °solid, well-built, °durable, °sound, °stout, °sturdy; °big, °large, °massive, °huge, sizeable, °impressive, °vast; numerous, °numberless: *A substantial mausoleum was constructed for his family. A substantial crowd had gathered.* **3** well-founded, °sound, °weighty, °solid, °well-established, °telling, °good, valid, °actual: *Many economists produced substantial arguments in favour of another cut in interest rates.* **4** °wealthy, well-to-do, °rich, affluent, °prosperous, °profitable, °successful; landed, propertied: *The Trevelyan Ironworks is a substantial business, and Mr Trevelyan is one of our more substantial businessmen.*

substantially *adv.* in °substance, essentially, at °bottom, fundamentally, basically, in °essence, intrinsically, in °reality, at °heart, °sincerely, °truly, °actually, in °truth, veritably, °indeed, in °fact, as a matter of °fact; °largely, to a °large extent, in °large measure, °materially, °practically, in the °main, for the most °part, mostly, °virtually, to all intents and purposes; *Archaic* verily: *The article was substantially sound. Do you agree substantially with the ruling of the court?*

substantiate *v.* °confirm, affirm, corroborate, °support, °sustain, back up, °bear out, °authenticate, °show (clearly), °prove, °document, °verify, °certify, validate: *Do not make accusations that cannot be substantiated by evidence.*

substitute *v.* **1** Sometimes, ***substitute for***: °replace, °exchange, °displace, °relieve, °supplant; °switch; take the °place of, °stand in for, °double for, *Colloq* sub for, °cover for, swap *or* swop, *US and Canadian* pinch-hit for: *She substituted the real diamond with a paste replica. I will substitute for you while you are away.* —*n.* **2** °substitution, replacement, °alternative, °relief, °representative, °deputy, °delegate, °stand-in, °stand-by, °understudy, surrogate, succedaneum, *Brit* locum (tenens), *US and Canadian* °alternate: *In those days a man could hire a substitute to serve in his place in the militia.*

substitution *n.* **1** °exchange, exchanging, °change, changing, replacement, replacing, supplanting, °switch, switching, interchange, interchanging, *Colloq* swap *or* swop, swapping *or* swopping: *The substitution of certain words distorted the sense.* **2** See **substitute, 2,** above.

substratum *n.* substrate, °foundation, underlayer, °basis, fundament, °base, substructure, °groundwork: *The agreement rests on a substratum of mutual trust and respect.*

subterfuge *n.* °artifice, °trick, °device, °stratagem, °manoeuvre, ploy, °evasion, °deception, °dodge, °feint, °shift, °excuse, °expedient, contrivance, °intrigue: *Although he told no lies, he used every subterfuge to avoid telling the truth.*

subtle *adj.* **1** °delicate, °fine, °refined, °exquisite, °nice, *Archaic* subtile: *I became aware, almost subconsciously, of the subtle odour of jasmine. These subtle shades of green are so peaceful.* **2** abstruse, arcane, °recondite, °remote, °deep, °profound, concealed, °hidden, °shadowy, °nebulous, °vague, °obscure, °veiled, °thin, airy, °insubstantial, °elusive, °faint; °sophistic(al): *The symbolism is so subtle as to be meaningful to the poet alone. A subtle hint gave me to understand that I ought to go.* **3** °tricky, °shrewd, cunning, °wily, °sly, °devious, °crafty, °smart, °clever, °foxy, °artful, °scheming, °designing, underhand(ed), °deceptive, Jesuitical, Machiavellian, °ingenious, °skilful, °strategic, insidious, casuistic, °shifty, °slick, °slimy, *Chiefly Brit* smarmy: *You were a fool to allow that subtle serpent to insinuate himself into your confidence.*

subtlety *n.* **1** °refinement, nicety, °delicacy, exquisiteness, intricacy, fineness, acuteness, °elegance, °sophistication: *The subtlety of the detail in this work is quite unique. One must admire the subtlety of expression in her writing.* **2** treachery, guile, insidiousness, casuistry, cunning, artfulness, craftiness, deviousness, slyness, deceptiveness: *The subtlety of her deception was revealed only after the war.*

subtract *v.* **1** °deduct, °take away, °take off, °take (something) from: *First calculate the discount, then subtract it from the price.* **2** Sometimes, ***subtract from***: °detract (from), °diminish, °take away (from): *Nothing could subtract from the exhilaration of that moment.*

subversion *n.* °overthrow, °ruin, °destruction, undermining, °upheaval, displacement: *The dictator used extreme tactics to avoid the subversion of his leadership.*

subversive *adj.* **1** subversionary, °seditious, seditionary, treasonous, treacherous, °traitorous, °revolutionary, insurrectionary: *The government regarded as subversive anything and anyone disagreeing with their policies.* —*n.* **2** °traitor, insurgent, saboteur, fifth-columnist, collaborator, collaborationist, quisling, °radical, °revolutionary, insurrectionist, insurrectionary; °dissident, °defector: *The security agencies were removing subversives from sensitive jobs.*

subvert *v.* °overthrow, °ruin, °destroy, °undermine, °topple, °demolish, °wreck, °sabotage: *The regime was subverted from within, not by outside forces.*

subway *n.* **1** *In US*: underground (°railway), tube: *She takes the subway to work.* **2** *In Britain*: tunnel, underpass: *Use the subway to cross the road in safety.*

succeed *v.* **1** °follow, °come after, supervene: *The end of the war in the Pacific succeeded the surrender in Europe.* **2** be successor (to), °follow, be °heir (to), °replace, take the °place of, °inherit *or* °take over from: *Elizabeth I succeeded Mary in 1558.* **3** Often, ***succeed in*** *or* ***at***: °make good, °thrive, °prosper, °flourish, be a °success, be °successful, °progress, °advance, °get ahead *or* on, attain *or* °gain *or* °achieve °success, °win, °triumph, *Colloq* °make it, °arrive, °get to the °top: *Has she succeeded in persuading you to sing? He always wanted to make a lot of money and now he has succeeded. They have succeeded at whatever they have tried.*

success *n.* **1** °good *or* °happy °result *or* °outcome, good °fortune, °achievement, °triumph, attainment, ascendancy, °prosperity: *The success of the fast food business is evident everywhere.* **2** °star, °celebrity, (big) °name, °sensation: *She was a great success as a singer, dancer, and actress.*

successful *adj.* **1** °wealthy, °rich, °prosperous, °fortunate, °lucky, °flourishing, thriving, prospering, well-to-do, affluent, *Colloq* °loaded, well-heeled, °flush, in the °money, *US* well-fixed: *He is a very successful investor.* **2** lucrative, booming, °profitable, °fruitful, moneymaking, remunerative: *The shares they bought proved to be a successful investment. How successful was last year for the company?* **3** °famous, °well-known, famed, °celebrated, °renowned, °eminent; °prominent, °pre-eminent, °popular, °leading, °top, best-selling: *Constance is one of our most successful poets. That book of mine was also successful.* **4** °victorious, °triumphant; °first; °winning: *Henry was successful in his bid for the chairmanship. I want to see a successful conclusion to the tour.*

succession *n.* **1** °passing (on), handing down *or* on, transmittal, °transmission, °transfer, transferral, °shift, conveyance, conveyancing: *According to her will, the succession of the property is via her first-born.* **2** °sequence, °progression, °order, series, °turn, °course, °flow, °chain, °train, °procession: *The succession of events was as he described.* **3** accession, assumption, attainment, °elevation, °promotion; °inheritance: *What was the year of Charles II's succession to the Spanish throne?* **4** °lineage, descent, birthright, °dynasty, ancestry, descendants, bloodline: *The 18th century began with the War of the Spanish Succession.* **5** ***in succession***: one after *or* behind the other, at intervals, successively, consecutively, in a °row, °running, without °interruption, uninterruptedly, in °order, in °line: *They published several historical novels in quick succession.*

successive *adj.* uninterrupted, °continuous, unbroken, °continual, consecutive, succeeding: *Last season he scored in sixteen successive matches.*

succinct *adj.* °compact, °brief, °concise, pithy, °terse, °short, compressed, condensed, °epigrammatic: *He prefers a succinct style of writing, one that gets to the point.*

succulent *adj.* °juicy, °rich, °luscious, mouth-watering, toothsome: *He was eating a succulent peach with evident enjoyment.*

succumb *v.* °yield, °give up, °give °way, °surrender, accede, °submit, °capitulate: *I finally succumbed and agreed to their request for help.*

sucker *n.* °dupe, goat, gull, °victim, °butt, cat's-paw, °fool, *Colloq* (easy) °mark, °easy *or* fair °game, chump, °pushover, soft touch, *Chiefly US and Canadian* fall guy, *Slang* °sap, pigeon, *Brit* °mug, *Chiefly US and*

Canadian patsy: *He's asking far too much for his car, but some sucker will buy it.*

sudden *adj.* unexpected, unannounced, unanticipated, °unforeseen; °unwonted, surprising, °startling; °precipitate, °abrupt, quick, °immediate, °rapid, °swift, °brisk; °impetuous, °hasty, °rash, °impulsive: *His sudden turn caught us off balance. Your change of heart was quite sudden.*

suddenly *adv.* **1** in a °flash *or* a °moment *or* a split °second, all at °once, instantly, °instantaneously, momentarily, fleetingly, in the °twinkling of an eye, in a trice; °quickly, abruptly, °swiftly, speedily, °rapidly: *Suddenly, my whole life flashed before me. He suddenly realized why the head of MI6 had summoned him.* **2** all of a °sudden, out of the blue, unexpectedly, without °warning, on the °spur of the moment, °hastily, hurriedly, feverishly: *Suddenly, she turned on her heel and stormed out.*

sue *v.* **1** proceed *or* move *or* act (against), take (°legal) °action *or* bring °suit *or* °prefer charges (against); °summon(s), °charge, °accuse: *He threatened to sue. They are suing him for the injuries they sustained.* **2** °petition, °beg, °plead, entreat, °pray, °request, °solicit, °apply, °beseech, implore, supplicate: *After five years of constant warfare, the country is suing for peace.*

suffer *v.* **1** Sometimes, ***suffer from*** *or* ***with***: agonize, °smart, °hurt, writhe, °sweat, °ache: *He is suffering with a stomach virus. How terribly they suffered when their child was kidnapped!* **2** °endure, °undergo, °experience, °bear, °live *or* °go through, °tolerate, °withstand, °sustain, °take, °submit to, °abide, *Colloq* °put up with: *He suffered years of ill health before he finally died.* **3** °allow, °tolerate, °permit, °let, °admit, °humour, °indulge: *They suffer the storks to build their nests on their chimneys.* **4** °deteriorate, °diminish, °decline, °go down, °fall off, be reduced *or* diminished: *If you discontinue advertising, sales will suffer.*

suffering *n.* °pain, °agony, °distress, °misery, °affliction, °hardship, °torment, torture, tribulation, °trial: *The man's suffering is written in his face.*

suffice *v.* °satisfy, °serve, do, be °sufficient *or* °enough *or* °adequate, °answer, sate, °satiate, °quench: *If you are merely thirsty, water should suffice.*

sufficient *adj.* °adequate, °enough: *Have we sufficient food to last through the winter?*

suffix *n.* **1** ending, desinence, °addition; affix: *The suffix* -ness *is added to many English adjectives to form nouns.*
—*v.* **2** °add (on), °join, °fasten to, subjoin, °amend, *Colloq* °tack on: *One can suffix* -ness *to a huge number of adjectives to form nouns.*

suffrage *n.* (°right to) °vote, voting °right(s), franchise, °voice, °say, ballot, °option, °choice: *They campaigned for universal adult suffrage.*

suffuse *v.* overspread, imbue, °pour *or* °spread over, bathe, °cover, °permeate, pervade, °flood, °flush, °penetrate, °saturate, °mantle, infuse, °transfuse, imbrue *or* embrue: *A rosy glow suffused her face.*

suggest *v.* **1** °propose, °advance, °recommend, °urge, °advocate, °support, °offer, proffer, °put *or* °set forward, °present, °mention, °introduce: *He suggested going out to a pub for dinner. Can you suggest an alternative?* **2** call to °mind, °bring up, °hint (at), °imply, °insinuate, °intimate, make one think, °lead one to believe, °indicate: *His silence suggested that this was not the right time to pursue the matter.*

suggestible *adj.* °impressionable, °susceptible, °receptive, impressible, susceptive, °open, mouldable, fictile: *Patricia was very suggestible at that age and readily believed everything that she was told.*

suggestion *n.* **1** °proposal, °proposition, °recommendation, °plan, °advice, °counsel, °idea, °notion, °opinion; prompting, urging: *The committee rejected your suggestion that membership fees should be increased.* **2** °indication, °trace, °whisper, insinuation, °innuendo, °implication, intimation, °hint, soupçon, °touch, tinge, °suspicion, °breath, iota, °jot or tittle: *There wasn't the slightest suggestion of animosity in her criticism.*

suggestive *adj.* **1** Often, ***suggestive of***: °reminiscent (of), evocative (of), indicative (of): *To me, the smell of orange blossom is always suggestive of southern California.* **2** °provocative, °naughty, °risqué, ribald, °off colour, °racy, °bawdy, °earthy, °lusty, °rude, indelicate, °unseemly, °immodest, °improper, °indecent, °prurient, °blue, °offensive, °vulgar, smutty, °dirty, °pornographic, °lewd, salacious, *Colloq* °sexy, °spicy, *Slang* raunchy: *He used to sing his suggestive songs in night clubs.*

suit *v.* **1** °adapt, °accommodate, °fit, °adjust, °tailor, make °appropriate *or* °suitable: *It will require some reorganization to suit the office space to our needs.* **2** °please, °satisfy, °fill (someone's) needs, °gratify, be °acceptable *or* °suitable *or* °convenient to *or* for, befit; °conform to: *Choose whichever room suits you. The schedule does not suit my personal plans at all.*
—*n.* **3** jacket and trousers *or* skirt, °outfit, °uniform, °ensemble, °costume, °habit; garb, clothing, °clothes, livery: *He showed up wearing a new silk suit.* **4** lawsuit, °action, °case, °proceeding, °process, °cause, °trial; °litigation: *I do not want to enter into a suit over the damage to my car.* **5** °petition, °plea, °request, entreaty, °prayer, solicitation, °application, °appeal, °supplication; courtship: *The king rejected all suits for his daughter's hand in marriage.*

suitable *adj.* °appropriate, apt, °fit, °fitting, °befitting, °becoming, °right, °proper, °correct, °acceptable, °satisfactory, °applicable, °meet, °seemly; °timely, °opportune: *John has at last found suitable employment. A chandelier is not suitable at all for such a low room. Is this a suitable time for me to ask you a favour?*

suitcase *n.* °bag, valise, overnight °bag, holdall, °grip *or Brit* handgrip, *Brit formerly* portmanteau: *She packed enough for a week's holiday into one small suitcase.*

suite *n.* **1** °set, series, °collection, °number: *They gave us a beautiful suite of rooms at the hotel.* **2** °set: *She bought a new suite of dining-room furniture.* **3** following, °retinue, entourage, °train, cortège, convoy, °escort; followers, attendants, retainers: *Her suite includes advisors, secretaries, hairdressers, and bodyguards.*

suitor *n.* °admirer, beau, wooer; boyfriend, °paramour, °lover, inamorato, *cicisbeo*, °escort, *Archaic* swain: *Madelaine has more suitors than I can count.*

sulk *v.* mope, °brood, °pout, be °sullen *or* °moody *or* ill-humoured: *I wish you'd get a job instead of sulking about the house all day.*

sullen *adj.* sulky, sulking, morose, brooding, pouting, °gloomy, °moody, °temperamental, °dour, lugubrious, °funereal, °dismal, °dreary, °grim, depressing, depressed, churlish, ill-humoured, °glum, grumpy, °sombre, out of humour, antisocial, unsociable, °cross, °petulant, °perverse, crusty, crotchety, choleric, crabby, ill-natured, ill-tempered, bad-tempered, splenetic, °peevish, dyspeptic, out of sorts, *US* °cranky: *He remained quite sullen and refused to associate with anyone.*

sully *v.* besmirch, °stain, smirch, °blemish, °mar, defile, °soil, °disgrace, °dirty, °tarnish, °pollute, °spoil, °ruin, °destroy, °wreck: *Sadly, his reputation was sullied when his company was found to be involved in insider trading.*

sultry *adj.* **1** °hot, °humid, °sticky, °stuffy, stifling, °oppressive, °close, °muggy, °steamy, steaming, °moist, °damp, °sweltering, suffocating: *I was happy to be languishing again in the sultry warmth of St Lucia.* **2** °lusty, °lustful, °passionate, °erotic, °seductive, °voluptuous, °provocative, °sensual, *Colloq* °sexy, °hot: *She continued her sultry, slow, sinuous dance.*

sum *n.* **1** °total, aggregate, grand °total, sum °total, °whole, °totality; °amount, °quantity: *The sum of money found in the satchel was not revealed by the police. He would give the neighbourhood children small sums to spend on sweets.*

—*v.* **2** ***sum up***: **a** °recapitulate, summarize, encapsulate, synopsize, °digest, °abridge, condense, consolidate, epitomize, °review: *He summed up by reminding the children not to accept gifts from strangers.* **b** °reckon, °add up, °calculate, °total, °tot up, °measure (up), take the °measure of: *They summed up their chances of escaping.* **c** °estimate, °evaluate, °size up, assess: *She had summed him up the minute she saw him.*

summarily *adv.* **1** °immediately, at °once, straight away, °directly, °quickly, without °delay, unhesitatingly, without hesitation, forthwith, °promptly, °swiftly, speedily, expeditiously, instantly, *Colloq* p.d.q. (= 'pretty damned quick'): *Any dog caught without a muzzle will be impounded summarily.* **2** °suddenly, without °warning, abruptly, peremptorily, precipitately: *He was summarily dismissed, with no advance notice.*

summary *n.* **1** summarization, recapitulation, encapsulation, compendium, °synopsis, °digest, °abridgement, condensation, shortening, consolidation, °epitome, epitomization, °review, distillate, conspectus, °brief, °outline, °précis, résumé: *I want a summary of the meeting on my desk in the morning.* —*adj.* **2** °abrupt, °peremptory, °short, quick, °brief, laconic, °perfunctory, °curt, °terse: *My simple request for some time off was denied with a summary, 'No!'*

summit *n.* °peak, °top, apex, °acme, °pinnacle, °zenith, °crown; culmination, °climax: *The winds at the summit of Annapurna reached hurricane force. There was no doubt that I had reached the summit of my achievements.*

summon *v.* **1** °call, °assemble, convoke, convene, °send for, invite, °muster, °get together, °arouse, °rouse: *Why would he summon us to the office at midnight?* **2** Often, ***summon up***: °call *or* °draw on *or* upon, °draw up, °mobilize, °muster (up), °work up, °gather, invoke: *I had to summon up all my courage to ask Eve to go out.*

sumptuous *adj.* °expensive, costly, °extravagant, °exorbitant, °dear, °rich; °lavish, °luxurious, de luxe, °opulent, °palatial, °royal, °majestic, °regal, °magnificent, °dazzling, °splendid, °showy, *Colloq* °posh, °plush, ritzy: *The family treated us to a sumptuous repast to celebrate our 50th wedding anniversary.*

sun *n.* **1** (old) Sol, Helios, Phoebus (Apollo), Ra, Sunna, day-star: *Many early cultures worshipped the sun.* —*v.* **2** tan, suntan, sunbathe, bask, bake, brown, bronze: *They spent their holidays sunning themselves on the beach.*

sundries *n.pl.* knick-knacks, trinkets, °small items, notions, miscellanea, °miscellany, kickshaws, Brummagem, frippery, °bric-à-brac *or* bric-a-brac, °odds and ends: *We might find a button for your shirt in a shop that sells sundries.*

sundry *adj.* °various, °varied, °miscellaneous, assorted, °different, °mixed, diversified, °diverse, divers: *In addition to food, supermarkets stock sundry other items.*

sunken *adj.* **1** °hollow, hollowed-out, °haggard, °drawn: *From her sunken cheeks the child looked as if she hadn't eaten for weeks.* **2** submerged, undersea, underwater, submersed: *The boat hit a sunken wreck and foundered.* **3** buried, °underground, in-ground, below-ground, settled, lowered: *The old term for a sunken fence is 'ha-ha'.*

sunless *adj.* °dark, °grim, cheerless, °unhappy, °joyless, °funereal, depressing, °dreary, drear, °sombre, °gloomy, °grey, Stygian, °black, pitchy, inky, °shadowy, tenebrous, unlit, unlighted, °dusky, subfusc *or* subfuscous, darkling: *It was an overcast sunless day, with rain in the offing.*

sunny *adj.* **1** sunlit, sunshiny, °brilliant, °bright, °radiant, °fair, °fine, cloudless, °clear, unclouded: *The enchanting scenery and warm sunny climate makes it a perfect place for holidays.* **2** °cheerful, cheery, °happy, joyous, °joyful, light-hearted, smiling, beaming, °buoyant, °blithe, °gay, mirthful, °jolly, °bubbly, °ebullient, °genial, °warm, °friendly, °outgoing: *Being with someone who has a sunny disposition was a pleasant change.*

super *adj.* wonderful: See **superb,** below.

superb *adj.* wonderful, °marvellous, °excellent, °superior, °gorgeous, °glorious, °magnificent, °outstanding, °exquisite, °fine, °splendid, unequalled, °sensational, °noteworthy, °admirable, °peerless, °matchless, unrivalled, °first-rate, °superlative, °perfect, °classic, °exceptional, °extraordinary, °striking, °brilliant, °dazzling, °miraculous, °incredible, °unbelievable, °fantastic, °fabulous, stupendous, staggering, mind-boggling, breathtaking, °divine, *Colloq* °great, °super, smashing, °magic, °terrific, fantabulous, °unreal, out of this °world, mind-blowing, *Slang* out of °sight, far-out, boss, solid, cool, hot, bad: *The curator said he had never seen such a superb collection. She does a superb* Hedda Gabler. *We were treated to a superb dinner.*

supercilious *adj.* °haughty, °contemptuous, °superior, °snobbish, °disdainful, °arrogant, °condescending, patronizing, °overbearing, °scornful, lordly, high and mighty, °pompous, °lofty, °stuffy, °pretentious, *Colloq* °hoity-toity, highfalutin *or* hifalutin, uppity, snooty, stuck-up, *Brit* toffee-nosed, °uppish, la-di-da *or* lah-di-dah *or* la-de-da: *She was very supercilious towards her customers.*

superficial *adj.* **1** °surface, °external, °exterior, °shallow, °skin-deep, °slight, °outside: *I suffered a superficial wound to the forehead.* **2** °surface, °slight, °external, °apparent, °skin-deep, °outward, °cursory, °insignificant, °passing, unimportant, trivial, °empty, °insubstantial; paying lip-service, for appearances' sake, cosmetic: *She bears a superficial resemblance to your sister. His interest in your welfare is entirely superficial.* **3** °cursory, slapdash, quick, °hurried, °hasty, °perfunctory, °nominal, °meaningless, °passing: *The machinery is subjected to a superficial inspection before shipping.*

superficies *n.* (outer) °surface, façade, °face, externals, °outside: *The superficies may appeal to children, but adults appreciate the book's profundities.*

superfluity *n.* °excess, superabundance, over-abundance, °surplus, oversupply, °surfeit, °glut, superfluousness, °profusion, plethora, oversupply, supersaturation: *The middle and upper classes wallow in a superfluity of goods.*

superfluous *adj.* °excessive, °excess, superabundant, over-abundant, supererogatory, °surplus, unneeded, uncalled-for, °unnecessary, °redundant, °extra; °needless, °dispensable, °gratuitous: *The superfluous grain that remains unsold should be donated to third-world countries. They knew each other so well that words were superfluous between them.*

superhuman *adj.* **1** °heroic, Herculean, °godlike, °legendary, valiant, °courageous, °brave, °daring, °dangerous, death-defying, °extraordinary, °miraculous, °phenomenal, °incredible, °fabulous, °fantastic, °unbelievable, °amazing: *His superhuman feats would never be duplicated.* —*n.* **2** superman, °hero, superhero, *übermensch*, Hercules: *They still believe that one day a superhuman will come along to lead them.*

superintendent *n.* °supervisor, °foreman, °overseer, °manager, administrator, °chief, °head, °boss; governor, controller, °director, conductor: *Alan has been appointed superintendent of the new project.*

superior *adj.* **1** higher, higher-ranking, higher-level, higher-class, higher-calibre, °upper, upper-level, °upper-class, loftier, nobler, °better; of a higher °order *or* °status *or* °standing, *Colloq* classier, tonier: *He was reported to his superior officer.* **2** °high-class, °elevated, °first-rate, °distinguished, °exceptional, °excellent, preferred, °choice, °select, élitist, °outstanding, °superlative, °matchless, unequalled, °peerless, °nonpareil, °sterling, °supreme, °fine, °noteworthy, °notable,

°worthy, °estimable: *Kenneth has had the benefit of a superior education.* **3** See **supercilious,** above.
—*n.* **4** See **supervisor,** below.

superiority *n.* **1** ascendancy, °pre-eminence, °supremacy, °leadership, °lead, dominance, °predominance, primacy, hegemony: *Her superiority in the field is unchallenged.* **2** °excellence, greatness, peerlessness, matchlessness, inimitability, superlativeness, °prominence, eminence, °importance, °distinction, °prestige, °renown: *All commented on the superiority of Mark's contribution.*

superlative *adj.* unsurpassed, °paramount, °supreme, consummate, °superior, °best, choicest, finest, °matchless, °peerless, unequalled, unrivalled, °singular, °unique, °incomparable, °excellent, °superb, °sterling, °dazzling, °first-rate, °exceptional, °extraordinary, °marvellous, spectacular, °capital, *Colloq* tiptop, °super, smashing, °great, ace, °terrific, °fantastic, *Slang* crack: *Max turned in a superlative performance in the tournament.*

supernatural *adj.* preternatural, °unusual, °extraordinary, °exceptional, °unnatural, °miraculous, °remarkable, °fabulous, preterhuman, °ghostly, °spectral, °abnormal, °inexplicable, unexplainable; metaphysical, other-worldly, °unearthly, ultramundane, supramundane, extramundane, °occult, mystic, paranormal, °psychic, uncanny, °weird, °mysterious, arcane, °unreal, magical, °dark: *Some claim to hear supernatural voices speaking to them. Many characters in children's stories have supernatural powers.*

supersede *v.* °replace, °succeed, °displace, °supplant, oust, take the °place of, °substitute for: *The 286 computers have been superseded by 386 models.*

supervise *v.* °oversee, °overlook, °watch (over), °manage, °run, °control, superintend, °govern, °direct, be in *or* have °charge (of), °handle, keep an °eye on, °administer: *They are moving you up to supervise the production department.*

supervisor *n.* °overseer, °foreman, °manager, controller, °superintendent, °superior, governor, °director, °boss, °chief, °head, administrator: *As supervisor, you are responsible for the work done in your department.*

supervisory *adj.* managerial, administrative, °executive: *Do you think that Len is ready for supervisory responsibilities?*

supine *adj.* **1** °flat (on one's back), °lying (down), °prostrate, °recumbent, *Formal or technical* procumbent, accumbent, decumbent: *When I found him, he was supine, staring up at the stars.* **2** °indolent, °lazy, °lethargic, °idle, °listless, °indifferent, apathetic, unconcerned, uninterested, °torpid, languid, languorous, sluggish, °slothful, °phlegmatic, lymphatic, °lackadaisical, °inert, °inactive, °passive, motionless, °inanimate, spiritless, abject: *During the entire crisis, the town council was completely supine and uncaring.*

supplant *v.* °replace, °displace, oust, °turn out, °eject, °remove, °expel, °dismiss, unseat, °supersede, °substitute, °exchange: *The council should be supplanted by a new group more sympathetic to the needs of the people.*

supple *adj.* **1** °flexible, flexile, pliant, bendable, °elastic, resilient, °pliable, tractile, fictile: *He made a rug-beater out of some supple lengths of bamboo.* **2** °willowy, lithe, limber, °nimble, pliant, lissom *or* lissome, °graceful, athletic: *She has the supple body of a dancer.* **3** °tractable, compliant, °yielding, °accommodating, °obliging, complaisant, acquiescent, °submissive, unresistant, unresisting, °servile, °obsequious, °ingratiating, fawning, toadying: *With supple words the miserable sycophant wormed his way into father's confidence.*

supplement *n.* **1** addendum, °addition, appendix, epilogue, end-piece, postscript, appendage, °extension, continuation, adjunct, annexe, appurtenance, °accessory, codicil, °insert, °sequel; supplementation; *Technical* suppletion: *The later version includes the 1909 supplement.*
—*v.* **2** °add (on *or* to), °extend, augment; °complement: *Various scholars supplemented the earlier work with their own notes and comments. He supplements his income by working at a restaurant.*

supplementary *adj.* **1** additional, added, annexed, adjunct, °new: *The supplementary buildings increased the size of the hospital greatly.* **2** supplemental, °supportive, contributory, ancillary, °secondary, °subordinate, annexed, additional, °attached, added, appended, °subsidiary, adscititious; °extraneous, adventitious, supervenient, °extra, °excess; *Technical* suppletive: *The supplementary material expanded the original work fivefold.*

supplicant *adj.* **1** suppliant, supplicating, entreating, petitioning, supplicatory, beseeching, praying, imploring, °solicitous, importunate, begging, mendicant: *In 1897, he carved a supplicant group in white marble, now in the Fraser Museum.*
—*n.* **2** suppliant, applicant, petitioner, beseecher, °suitor, pleader, aspirant, appellant, plaintiff, °beggar, mendicant: *He came to me as a supplicant, begging forgiveness for what he had done.*

supplication *n.* **1** entreaty, °petition, °prayer, °appeal, pleading, °plea, °suit, solicitation, obsecration, obtestation, impetration: *Heeding the pitiful supplications of the beggars, they gave them some money.* **2** supplicating, begging, pleading, soliciting, petitioning, entreating, beseeching: *All his supplication could not wring a farthing from the old skinflint.*

supply *v.* **1** °furnish, °provide, °give, endow, °present, purvey, °deliver, come up with, °contribute, °distribute, °sell; stock, °accommodate, °afford, °equip, °outfit, °gear (up), °rig (out), °fit (out), °provision, °cater to, *Chiefly Brit* °kit out *or* up; victual: *Her company supplies radios to the army. Her husband's firm supplies the navy with anti-fouling paint.* **2** °yield, °give, °contribute, come up with, °deliver, °provide, °furnish: *The farm supplies our basic foods.* **3** °satisfy, °fulfil, °replenish, °fill: *Can you supply the demand for clothing?*
—*n.* **4** °stock, stockpile, °store, inventory, °quantity, reservoir, °reserve, °cache, °hoard, °accumulation, °fund: *Our supply is big enough to serve the entire area.* **5** furnishing, °provision, °providing, purveying, supplying, °distribution, equipping, outfitting, provisioning, °delivery, stocking, stockpiling: *The supply of microchips on a large scale is beyond our capacity.*

support *v.* **1** back (up), °stand by, °help, °bolster, °uphold, °brace, °strengthen, °fortify, °buttress, °prop (up), shore up, °reinforce, °boost, °champion, °assist, take up the cudgels for, °aid, °promote, °forward, °second, °advance, °advocate, °stand up for, be °supportive (of *or* in), *Colloq* °stick up for: *Peterson agreed to support him in his bid for the presidency.* **2** °brace, °hold up, °carry, °prop (up); °strengthen, shore up, °reinforce, °fortify, °buttress: *You need a column to support this beam.* **3** °tolerate, °bear, °stand (for), °suffer, °submit to, °undergo, °brook, °stomach, °endure, °abide, countenance, °face, *Brit* °stick, *Colloq* °put up with: *He cannot support the notion that she might be guilty.* **4** °pay for, °fund, °maintain, °keep, °finance, °subsidize, °underwrite, °sponsor, *Colloq US* bankroll: *I can no longer support myself or my family.* **5** °sustain, °withstand, °stand, °take, °bear, °tolerate, °hold up under, °weather: *His legs were too weak to support his own weight.* **6** °verify, corroborate, °authenticate, °vouch for, °endorse, °confirm, affirm, °bear out, °attest to, °certify, °substantiate, validate, °ratify: *Can anyone support his alibi?*
—*n.* **7** °help, °backing, backup, °reinforcement, bolstering, °encouragement, reinforcing, fortifying, °assistance, °aid, succour, °sustenance: *Thank you for your support over the years.* **8** °brace, °prop, °stay, °frame, °foundation, underpinning, substructure, truss, °beam, column, °pillar, °strut, guy, guy wire, °mainstay, °buttress, °bolster, °reinforcement, °supporter: *The supports failed under the grandstand and it fell, injuring a few. Alan was a tremendous support during my illness.* **9** °sustenance, (living) expenses, °keep, °maintenance, °subsistence, °upkeep; finances,

funding: *Mona is suing David for the support of their child. He lives mainly on government support.*

supportable *adj.* **1** °tolerable, °bearable, endurable, °acceptable, sufferable: *Thoughts of death are more supportable when it seems remote.* **2** defensible, confirmable, verifiable, °demonstrable, °tenable, believable: *The argument that we should keep the old tax structure is simply not supportable.*

supporter *n.* **1** °enthusiast, °champion, promoter, °fan, aficionado, °devotee, °admirer, °backer, °follower, °support, °advocate, exponent, adherent, °aid, °assistant, helper: *I wish to thank my many supporters, who were there when I needed them.* **2** See **support, 8,** above.

supportive *adj.* °helpful, sustaining, supporting, encouraging, °sympathetic, °understanding, reassuring: *Among our many friends, Cleo was the most supportive during the recent trouble.*

suppose *v.* **1** °assume, °presume, °presuppose, °surmise, °take, °take as °given *or* as read, °take for granted; °believe, °think, °fancy, °imagine; *Colloq* °take it: *Don't people usually suppose that civil servants are honest? I supposed her to be his wife. Do you suppose you could return my key today?* **2** hypothesize, °theorize, postulate, °posit, °assume: *Supposing a reduced rate of inflation, will they reduce interest rates? Suppose that you have lost the election—what will you do?*

supposed *adj.* **1** °alleged, °assumed, putative, °reputed, presumed, °hypothetical, °theoretical, theorized, imagined, suppositious, supposititious: *Her supposed drug addiction turned out to be a myth.* **2** °obliged, expected, required; meant, intended: *You were supposed to return my key. What is that supposed to mean?*

supposedly *adv.* allegedly, reputedly, theoretically, hypothetically, °presumably; °rumour has it: *The bridge was blown up, supposedly by terrorists.*

supposing *conj.* if, °even if, in the °event that, °despite the °fact that, although, °though: *Supposing he says no, what will you do?*

supposition *n.* assumption, °presumption, °surmise, °belief, °thought, °fancy, theory, °hypothesis, postulate, °proposal, °proposition: *On the supposition that your calculations are correct, we will have made a profit this year.*

suppress *v.* **1** °end, °discontinue, °cut off, °cease, °stop, °terminate, put an °end to, °halt, °prohibit, °preclude, °prevent, °repress, censor, °forbid, interdict, °block, °obstruct, °withhold, °stifle, °inhibit, °hinder, °arrest: *They have been unable to suppress the publication of the book.* **2** °put down, °quell, °crush, °squelch, °quash, °subdue, °check, °stamp out, snuff out, °smother, °extinguish, °quench, °crack down on: *The uprising was suppressed with the shooting of the students.* **3** °keep down, °control, °keep under °control, °keep *or* °hold in °check, °restrain, °hold in *or* back, °repress, °cover up, °conceal, °hide, °keep °quiet *or* °secret, °mute, °muffle, °quiet(en), °silence: *Objections to the guest speaker were suppressed at the request of the university's chancellor.*

suppression *n.* suppressing, ending, °end, discontinuation, discontinuing, °cutting off, cut-off, cessation, ceasing, surcease, stopping, °stop, terminating, °termination, °halting, °halt, prohibiting, °prohibition, preclusion, precluding, preventing, °prevention, repressing, °repression, censoring, censorship, °forbidding, forbiddance, interdicting, interdiction, blocking, obstructing, °obstruction, withholding, stifling, hindering; putting down, °put-down, quelling, crushing, squelching, quashing, subduing, checking, °check, stamping out, smothering, snuffing out, extinguishing, extinction, elimination, quenching, cracking down on, crack-down; °control, controlling, restraining, °restraint, concealing, concealment, hiding, muting, muffling, quieting, silencing: *That constitutes suppression of the freedom of speech. The suppression of heresy is a perennial church problem. Dictators confuse the suppression of ideas with the oppression of people.*

supremacist *n.* supremist, bigot, racist, racialist, dogmatist, °zealot, °fanatic: *Supremacists' philosophies are based on hatred, not love.*

supremacy *n.* **1** transcendency, °pre-eminence, °superiority, ascendancy, °excellence, primacy, peerlessness, matchlessness, incomparability, inimitability: *Colonialism depends on military supremacy.* **2** °sovereignty, °dominion, °sway, mastery, °control, dominance, (°supreme *or* °absolute) °rule *or* °authority, autarchy, omnipotence, hegemony: *They maintained their supremacy over the Iberian peninsula for centuries.*

supreme *adj.* **1** highest, loftiest, topmost, greatest, °first, °foremost, °principal, unsurpassed, °top, °uppermost, °chief, °paramount, °sovereign: *There is no appeal to a decision of the supreme tribunal.* **2** greatest, °maximum, °extreme, uttermost, utmost, °ultimate: *I fear that your son has made the supreme sacrifice, Mrs Atkins.* **3** °best, greatest, °first, °outstanding, °pre-eminent, °first-rate, °prime, °primary, unexcelled, °leading, crowning, consummate: *Many regard her as the supreme artist of her day.* **4** °superb, °marvellous, °excellent, °outstanding, °superlative, °matchless, °peerless, °incomparable, °unparalleled, °masterful, masterly, °sublime, °brilliant, °transcendent, inimitable, °choice: *There is no doubt that she is a supreme artist.*

supremely *adv.* °very, °extremely, °completely, °perfectly, superlatively, sublimely, transcendently: *I have never been so supremely happy as I was in Capri in '38.*

sure *adj.* **1** °certain, assured, convinced, persuaded, °positive, °definite, unwavering, unswerving, unflinching, °steadfast, °steady, unshakeable *or* unshakable, °confident, satisfied, undeviating, unfaltering: *How can you be so sure in your opinion that Jack did it? I'm sure I've met you before.* **2** established, °firm, °solid, trusty, °stable, °steadfast, °secure, °safe, °trustworthy, °reliable: *I never travel without my sure companions, courage and caution.* **3** °accurate, °reliable, dependable, tried and °true, unfailing, °infallible, °foolproof, °effective, *Colloq* sure-fire: *A high temperature is a sure sign of illness.* **4** °certain, °inevitable, indubitable, °unavoidable, ineluctable, inescapable, guaranteed: *He who enters the Devil's Cave meets sure death.*

surely *adv.* **1** certainly, to be °sure, °positively, °absolutely, °definitely, °undoubtedly, indubitably, unquestionably, beyond the shadow of a °doubt, beyond °question, °doubtless, doubtlessly, assuredly, *Colloq* °sure, *US* absotively-posolutely: *He is surely one of the finest riders I've ever seen.* **2** °firmly, solidly, confidently, unfalteringly, steadily, unswervingly, unhesitatingly, determinedly, doggedly, securely: *Slowly but surely, the Great Bamboni stepped out onto the tightrope stretched across the Reichenbach Falls.*

surface *n.* **1** °exterior, covering, °outside, °top, °skin, integument, façade, °face, °boundary, interface, °superficies; °side, °plane: *Most of the earth's surface is covered by water. How many surfaces on an icosahedron?* **2** ***on the surface***: superficially, to all appearances, at first glance, °outwardly, to the casual observer, extrinsically, °ostensibly: *It looks pretty enough on the surface, but it is rotten underneath.* —*v.* **3** °appear, °show up, °emerge, °materialize, °arise, °rise, °come up, *Colloq* °pop up, crop up: *Guess who surfaced after ten years in Tierra del Fuego! An enormous turtle surfaced near our boat.* **4** °pave, °concrete, tarmac: *They are surfacing the road in front of my house.*

surfeit *n.* over-abundance, superabundance, plethora, °glut, °excess, °surplus, oversupply, overdose, °satiety, overflow, °flood, deluge, °superfluity, nimiety: *There has been a surfeit of those dolls on the market. She is suffering from a surfeit of rich food and alcohol.*

surfeited *adj.* gorged, overfed, satiated, sated, stuffed, glutted, °jaded: *He passed the sleeping surfeited diners and stole into the library unseen.*

surge *v.* **1** °swell, °wave, billow, °bulge, °heave, °roll, undulate, °well forth *or* up, °rise and °fall, °ebb and °flow, °pulsate; °rush, °gush, °pour, °flood, °stream, °flow: *The sea surged through the narrow gorge with a roar. The crowd surged round their hero.*
—*n.* **2** °swell, °wave, billow, °roller, whitecap, white horse, breaker, comber, upsurge, °eddy, °rush, °gush, °flood, °stream, °flow: *The raft was caught by a surge and tossed high up on the beach.*

surly *adj.* unpleasant, °rude, crusty, °cantankerous, curmudgeonly, churlish, crabby, crabbed, choleric, splenetic, dyspeptic, °bilious, °temperamental, °cross, crotchety, grouchy, grumpy, bearish, °testy, °touchy, °short-tempered, ill-tempered, bad-tempered, ill-natured, bad-natured, ill-humoured, °peevish, °quarrelsome, °argumentative, °obnoxious, uncivil, °rough, °obstreperous: *I see no reason to shop where the sales staff are surly.*

surmise *v.* **1** °imagine, °guess, conjecture, °speculate, °suppose, hypothesize, °theorize, °assume, °presume, conclude, °gather, °infer, °understand, °fancy, °suspect, °feel, °sense: *I surmised that the treaty terms were arranged by deputies long before the summit.*
—*n.* **2** °guess, conjecture, °speculation, °notion, °hypothesis, theory, °supposition, assumption, °presumption, conclusion, °understanding, °fancy, °suspicion, °feeling, °sense: *It was an early surmise of the experts that man could not survive passing through the Van Allen belts.*

surpass *v.* °exceed, °excel, °go *or* °pass beyond, °outdo, °beat, worst, °better, °best, °outstrip, outdistance, outperform, outclass, outshine, °eclipse, °overshadow, °top, °cap, °transcend, °prevail over, leave behind: *He easily surpassed the statesmen of his time.*

surpassing *adj.* °excessive, °extraordinary, °great, °enormous, unrivalled, °matchless, °peerless, unmatched, unequalled, unsurpassed: *I could not believe the surpassing gall of the man.*

surpassingly *adv.* °exceedingly, extraordinarily, incomparably, *Literary* °surpassing: *The girls on the beach were surpassingly beautiful.*

surplus *n.* **1** surplusage, overage, °excess, °leftover(s), °surfeit, over-abundance, oversupply, overdose, °glut: *The price of oil dropped owing to the surplus in the market.*
—*adj.* **2** °excess, °leftover, °extra, °spare, over-abundant, °superfluous, °unused, °redundant: *The surplus grain is sold abroad.*

surprise *v.* **1** °shock, °astound, °astonish, °amaze, disconcert, °nonplus, °dumbfound *or* dumfound, °stagger, °take aback, °strike, °hit, *Colloq* °floor, °bowl over, flabbergast, °rock *or* set (someone) back on his *or* her *or chiefly Brit* their heels, *Brit* knock (someone) for six, *US* knock (someone) for a loop: *What surprised me was her coolness in the face of danger.* **2** take *or* °catch °unawares, °catch °red-handed *or* in the act *or* in flagrante delicto, °catch napping *or* off guard, °discover: *When Samuel Johnson's wife found him with a maid, she said, 'Dr Johnson! I am surprised!', to which he replied, 'No, madam: you are amazed. I am surprised.'*
—*n.* **3** °shock, °astonishment, °amazement, stupefaction, °wonder, incredulity: *Imagine my surprise to learn that I was being arrested.* **4** °blow, °jolt, shocker, °bolt from *or US also* out of the blue, °bombshell, eye-opener: *It came as a surprise to me that my sister was pregnant.*

surrender *v.* **1** °give up, °yield, °let go (of), °relinquish, °deliver (up), °hand over, °forgo, °forsake, °turn over, °turn in, °part with, °cede, °concede: *We were forced at gunpoint to surrender our valuables.* **2** °give up, °yield, °quit, cry quits, °capitulate, throw in the sponge *or* the towel, raise the white flag, throw up one's hands, °succumb, °submit, °give °way, acquiesce, °comply, °give in, °concede, °crumble: *The argument is so overwhelming that I must surrender.*
—*n.* **3** °submission, capitulation, °yielding, renunciation, relinquishment, transferral, °transfer, transference, handing *or* turning over, conveyancing, ceding, cession, concession: *The official surrender of the disputed territory took place in the following year.*

surreptitious *adj.* °furtive, °secret, clandestine, °stealthy, underhand(ed), covert, (on the) °sly, °secretive, °private, concealed, °hidden, °veiled, *Colloq* °sneaky: *She stole surreptitious glances at him.*

surround *v.* **1** encompass, °encircle, °envelop, °enclose, hem in, °ring: *She likes being surrounded by flowers. Troops surrounded the building.*
—*n.* **2** environs, °environment, surroundings, °atmosphere, ambience *or* ambiance, °setting: *The formal gardens make a charming surround for the art gallery.*

surrounding *adj.* °nearby, °neighbouring, °local, °adjoining, °neighbourhood, adjacent, bordering, abutting, circumambient, circumjacent: *The surrounding countryside was bursting into bloom.*

surveillance *n.* °observation, °watch, °scrutiny, °reconnaissance: *The police kept him under constant surveillance.*

survey *v.* **1** °examine, appraise, °evaluate, take the °measure of, °inspect, °study, °scan, °scrutinize, °measure, °size up, assess, °investigate, °look into *or* over, °review: *He surveyed the situation and found nothing wrong.* **2** °view, °look at, get a bird's eye view of, °contemplate: *From the top of the tower I surveyed the surrounding countryside.*
—*n.* **3** surveying, °examination, appraisal, °evaluation, °measure, °study, °scan, scanning, °scrutiny, °inquiry *or* enquiry, °measurement, °investigation, inspection: *Our survey of the company finances yielded some very interesting information.*

survive *v.* **1** °continue, °last, °live (on), °persist, subsist, °pull through, °endure: *The village was destroyed, but its people survived.* **2** °outlast, outlive: *At the age of 114, MacMurtagh has survived all his children and many of his grandchildren.*

susceptible *adj.* **1** Often, ***susceptible of*** *or* ***to***: °open (to), °prone (to), °subject (to), °disposed (to), predisposed (to), °receptive (to), °affected by, °responsive (to): *Brass is susceptible of a high shine. Are you still susceptible to her blandishments?* **2** °impressionable, influenceable, °vulnerable, reachable, °accessible, credulous, °suggestible, °gullible, °naïve: *Susceptible youngsters need protection from commercial exploitation.*

suspect *v.* **1** disbelieve, °doubt, °mistrust, °distrust, harbour *or* have suspicions about *or* of, be °suspicious of: *Do you suspect the butler?* **2** °feel, °think, °believe, °sense, have a °feeling, °fancy, °imagine, °theorize, °guess, °surmise, have a sneaking °suspicion, think it likely *or* probable, *Colloq* °expect: *I suspect that the butler might have done it.*
—*adj.* **3** °suspicious, °questionable, °doubtful, dubious, °shady, °shadowy; suspected: *If you ask me, his behaviour since boarding the Orient Express has been highly suspect.*

suspend *v.* **1** °hold up *or* off (on), °withhold, °put off, put *or* °hold *or* keep in *or* into °abeyance, °shelve, °postpone, °delay, °defer, °interrupt, °stop *or* °check *or* °cease *or* °discontinue temporarily, *US* °table: *We suspended payment pending inspection of the work already done. Train services on this route will be suspended till further notice. Suspend your disbelief for a moment to consider the possible motive for stealing a prune.* **2** °hang, °attach, °fasten, °dangle, °swing: *She suspended the cameo from a gold chain which she wore as a necklace.* **3** debar, °exclude, °eliminate, °reject, °expel, °eject, °evict; °deprive of the rights of, °deny the privileges of; blackball: *A member may be suspended if his dues are six months or more in arrears.*

suspense *n.* **1** uncertainty, indefiniteness, insecurity, °doubt, irresolution, expectancy, °indecision, not knowing: *May I have the envelope please?—I cannot stand the suspense!* **2** °anxiety, °tension, apprehension, nervousness, °agitation, anxiousness, °anticipation, °expectation, °excitement: *A story that creates suspense for the reader is often suitable for film treatment.*

suspension *n.* **1** debarring, disbarment, °exclusion, elimination, °rejection, °expulsion, °ejection, °eviction, deprivation, °denial: *The suspension of privileges cannot last for more than a fortnight.* **2** °intermission, °moratorium, deferment, °hold-up, °delay, delaying, °interruption, °postponement, postponing, discontinuing, discontinuation, °stay: *Luckily, the suspension of hostilities lasted till the summer.*

suspicion *n.* **1** °doubt, dubiousness, dubiety, °misgiving, °mistrust, °distrust, °scepticism, °qualm, wariness, apprehension, apprehensiveness, cautiousness, hesitation, second thought(s), uncertainty, leeriness, *Colloq* funny °feeling, bad °vibes: *We all had our suspicions about Edward's genuine intentions. My worst suspicions have now been confirmed.* **2** °notion, °inkling, °suggestion, °hint, °trace, °flavour, soupçon, °taste, °dash, glimmer, tinge, °touch, °shadow, °shade, scintilla, *Colloq chiefly US and Canadian* tad: *If you have even a suspicion of doubt, do not find the defendant guilty. Did I detect a suspicion of a sneer?*

suspicious *adj.* **1** °doubtful, in °doubt, dubious, °questionable, °debatable, °suspect(ed), under °suspicion, °open to °doubt *or* °question *or* misconstruction, *Colloq* °shady, °fishy: *There is something very suspicious about his behaviour.* **2** mistrustful, °distrustful, °doubtful, in °doubt, °sceptical, suspecting, disbelieving, °unbelieving, °leery, apprehensive, °wary, °uncertain, uneasy: *I was suspicious of Douglas from the very beginning.*

sustain *v.* **1** °uphold, °support, °keep up, °maintain, °continue, °keep (someone *or* something) going, °keep °alive, °preserve; °prolong, °persist in: *He has been sustained on a life-support system for weeks. If Georgette can sustain the pretence of loving him, he won't change his will.* **2** °support, °carry, °bear, °bolster, °buoy (up), °reinforce, °keep (someone) going, °strengthen, shore up, underpin, °prop up, °buttress: *During those long months as a hostage, only prayer sustained him.* **3** °endure, °stand, °withstand, °bear up under, °put up with, °suffer, °undergo, °experience, °tolerate, °weather, °brave: *It is amazing how much punishment the human body can sustain.* **4** °bear, °carry, °support: *This column is supposed to sustain the weight of half the building.* **5** °uphold, °recognize, °allow, °admit, °approve, °ratify, °sanction, °authorize, °endorse, validate: *The judge sustained the objection by the defence.*

sustained *adj.* continued, °continuous, °continual, prolonged, unremitting, °steady, ceaseless, unceasing, incessant, interminable; °uniform, °even, °level, unchanged, unchanging: *The neighbours keep up that sustained caterwauling every night. The audience was thrilled by her sustained top C.*

sustenance *n.* **1** nutriment, °nourishment, °food (and °drink), daily bread, °rations, victuals, provisions, °provender, groceries, aliment, °edibles, eatables, foodstuff(s), viands, °meat, *Colloq* grub, eats, chow, nosh, *Slang Brit* prog, °scoff: *My first concern is sustenance for my family.* **2** livelihood, °support, °maintenance, °upkeep, °keep, °subsistence, living: *The fur trade provided the sustenance of early Canadian settlers.*

swagger *v.* **1** °strut, °prance, °parade, *Archaic* swash, *Colloq US* sashay, cut a swath: *Look at that Charlie swaggering down the street in his new suit!* **2** °boast, °brag, °show off, vaunt, crow, *Colloq Brit* swank: *He is always swaggering on about his war experiences.*
—*n.* **3** °strut, °prance, strutting, swaggering, °show, °display, showing off, °ostentation, braggadocio, °arrogance, boastfulness: *Paul's outrageous swagger developed only after he was promoted.*

swallow *v.* **1** °eat, °consume, °devour, ingest, °dispatch *or* despatch; °drink, °gulp, guzzle, down, *Colloq* °put *or* pack away, swig, °swill: *Snakes swallow their prey whole. The amount that man can swallow at one meal is incredible.* **2** °accept, °allow, °credit, °believe, °take, *Colloq* °buy, °fall for: *She swallowed that tale about an aeroplane hook, line, and sinker.* **3** Often, ***swallow up***: absorb, make disappear, engulf, °consume, assimilate: *The fugitive was swallowed up by the crowd.* **4** Sometimes, ***swallow back***: keep *or* °choke back *or* down, °repress, °suppress, °control, °stifle, °smother, °overcome, °conquer: *Harriet swallowed back the tears. Try swallowing your pride just this once.*
—*n.* **5** °bite, nibble, °morsel, °mouthful; °drink, °gulp, guzzle, *Colloq* swig: *Have a swallow of this to warm you up a little.*

swamp *n.* **1** °bog, fen, °marsh, quagmire, °morass, °moor, *Chiefly literary* slough, *Scots and No. Eng. dialect* moss, *So. US* everglade: *The draining of swamps destroys the breeding places of mosquitoes.*
—*v.* **2** °overwhelm, °overcome, °flood, inundate, °submerge, °immerse, deluge, °overload, overtax, overburden, *Colloq* snow under: *I'm so swamped with work I'm sleeping at the office.* **3** scuttle, °sink, °founder: *A huge wave swamped the boat and she sank quickly.*

swanky *adj.* °smart, °stylish, °fashionable, °chic, chichi, °fancy, °luxurious, °grand, °elegant, *Colloq* swank, snazzy, °neat, °nifty, °plush, °posh, ritzy, *Brit* °swish: *Living in a swanky house and wearing swanky clothes—what else would anyone want?*

swarm *n.* **1** °throng, horde, army, °host, multitude, hive, °herd, °mob, °mass, drove, °flood, °stream, cloud, °flock, °pack, shoal, °bunch: *Swarms of people showed up for our garden party.*
—*v.* **2** °throng, °mass, °crowd, congregate, °flock, °gather, °flood, °stream, °flow: *The fans swarmed round the rock group.* **3** ***swarm with***: Often, ***be swarming with***: °crawl with, °abound in *or* with, °throng with, °teem with, °burst with, °bristle with, be °overrun with: *In two minutes the place was swarming with police.*

swarthy *adj.* swart, °black, ebon, ebony, sable, °pitch-black, jet-black, coal-black, raven, °dark: *His swarthy complexion contrasted with her china-like pallor.*

swashbuckling *adj.* °adventurous, °daring, °daredevil, swaggering, roisterous, °bold, °dashing, °flamboyant: *Those old swashbuckling films with Errol Flynn, Richard Green, and Douglas Fairbanks, formed a genre all their own.*

swath *n.* °swathe, °path, °belt, °strip: *A flock of birds was feeding along the swath cut by the harvester.*

swathe *v.* °tie, °bind, bandage, °wrap, enwrap, swaddle, °bundle (up), °envelop, °shroud, °muffle (up): *I can't tell who he is as his head is swathed in bandages.*

sway *v.* **1** °wave, waver, °swing, °sweep, °oscillate, undulate, °reel, °totter, °swing *or* °move to and fro *or* back and forth *or* from side to side *or* backwards and forwards, °rock, °fluctuate; °bend, °lean: *The reeds swayed in the breeze.* **2** °move, °incline, °divert, °tend, veer, °tilt, °lean, °slant, °bias; °influence, °persuade, °impress, °win over, °bring round, °convince, °talk into: *The wind is causing the trees to sway towards the east. We tried to sway him to our way of thinking.*
—*n.* **3** °sweep, °wave, °swing, (period of) oscillation, libration: *There must be a sway of twenty feet in the top of that skyscraper.* **4** °influence, °control, °power, °command, °authority, °dominion, °rule, °sovereignty, °leadership, mastery; °grip, clutches, °grasp: *His ambition was to get the mountain people under his sway.*

swear *v.* **1** depose, aver, asseverate, °declare, °insist, assert, solemnly affirm *or* °state, °testify, °promise, take an °oath, °undertake, °vow, avow, °vouchsafe, °warrant, °pledge, give one's °word, °agree: *He swore he had not done any such thing.* **2** °curse, °blaspheme, imprecate, use °profanity, utter profanities, execrate, *Colloq* cuss: *Priscilla stopped her ears at the men's swearing.* **3** ***swear by***: °trust (in), °believe in, °rely on, have °confidence in, °count on: *The colonel swears by the same old fountain-pen he has used for years and will use no other.* **4** ***swear off***: forswear, °renounce, abjure, go off, °forgo, °shun, °avoid, °give up, eschew, °forsake, °throw over: *Brian tells me he's sworn off alcohol for a while.*

sweat *v.* **1** perspire, °glow: *That workout made me sweat.* **2** Often, ***sweat out***: °worry, be °anxious, agonize, °anguish, bite (one's) nails, be on pins and

needles, °fret, °fuss, °stew, torture *or* °torment oneself, lose sleep (over), *Colloq* sweat blood, be in a tizzy, *US* sweat bullets: *The professors really like to make students sweat, don't they? Fiona is sweating it out till the results are posted.* **3** °slave (away), °labour, drudge, °grind, toil and moil, slog, °work like a Trojan *or* a horse, *Slang Brit* swot: *I sweat over a hot stove all day while you're out and about town.* **4** °ooze, exude, °squeeze out, transude: *When a boy, he believed that dew came from flowers sweating water.*
—*n.* **5** °perspiration, *Technical* diaphoresis, sudor: *In addition to body moisture, salt and other minerals are lost in sweat.* **6** (hard) °work, °labour, laboriousness, °grind, toil, °drudgery, slogging, sweating, *Slang Brit* swotting: *Nothing worthwhile is gained without some sweat.* **7** state of °confusion *or* °upset *or* °excitement *or* °distraction *or* °agitation *or* °anxiety *or* °distress *or* °worry; pother, *Colloq* dither, tizzy, °lather: *Henry has really worked himself up into a sweat over this problem.* **8** ***No sweat!***: No problem!, Don't worry!, Everything is taken care of!, All is well!, That presents no difficulty!: *When asked to change a flat tyre, the stranger's response was, 'No sweat!'*

sweep *v.* **1** °brush, °whisk, °clean, °clear, °tidy up: *This weekend I have to sweep out the basement.* **2** Often, ***sweep away***: °carry *or* °take (away *or* off), °destroy, °wipe out, °demolish, °remove, °wash (away); °blow (away): *The raging torrent swept away the bridge. The wind swept the debris before it.* **3** °swoop, °flounce, °glide, °sail, °march, °parade, °skim, °tear, °dash, zoom: *Hattie swept into the room majestically.* **4** curve, arc, °arch, °bend, °bow, °circle, °turn: *The long drive to the house sweeps round the pond and gardens.*
—*n.* **5** °pass, °clearance, °stroke; °purge: *In one clean sweep the police rounded up all the suspects.* **6** curve, arc, °arch, °bow, °bend, curvature, flexure: *Note the sweep of those main arches holding up the dome.* **7** °range, °extent, compass, °reach, °stretch, °scope, °swing, °span: *The Hubbell space telescope has a farther sweep than any on earth.*

sweeping *adj.* **1** °comprehensive, (all-)°inclusive, °general, °extensive, °universal, all-embracing, °broad, widespread, °wide(-ranging), far-ranging, blanket, °umbrella, °catholic, °exhaustive, °radical, °thorough(-going), °out-and-out, across the °board, wholesale, *Colloq* wall-to-wall: *We must institute sweeping reforms of the party before the election.* **2** °complete, °total, °overwhelming, decisive: *The first team enjoyed a sweeping victory in track and field events.*

sweet *adj.* **1** sugary, honey-like, honeyed, sweetened: *Sweet breakfast cereals are bad for your teeth.* **2** °fragrant, perfumed, scented, °aromatic, ambrosial, sweet-smelling, sweet-scented, balmy, °redolent: *The night air was sweet with jasmine.* **3** °harmonious, °melodious, sweet-sounding, euphonious, dulcet, °musical, °tuneful, euphonic, mellifluous, °mellow, °lyric, silvery, bell-like, °golden: *I could hear McCormick's sweet voice singing 'Danny Boy'.* **4** °gentle, °amiable, °agreeable, °genial, °warm, °friendly, °kind, °nice, unassuming, °easygoing; °attractive, appealing, charming, °winning, °pleasant, °pleasing, °lovely; °cute, pretty: *Jane normally has such a sweet disposition. Old Mrs Hughes was always sweet to me when I was little. Amy looks so sweet in her new dress. What a sweet little kitten!* **5** °dear, °beloved, °precious, prized, treasured, wonderful, °marvellous, °splendid, *Colloq* °great: *How sweet life can be!* **6** °considerate, °attentive, °solicitous, °thoughtful, °sympathetic, compassionate, °kind, kind-hearted, °generous, °gracious, °accommodating: *How sweet it was of you to bring flowers!* **7** cloying, °sentimental, syrupy, saccharine, treacly, °precious, honeyed, sickening, *Colloq* gushing, °gushy, °sloppy, soppy, °maudlin, °sticky, *Brit* °twee, *Colloq* icky: *Claire is so sweet that she really overdoes it sometimes.* **8** ***sweet on***: °fond of, °taken with, °keen on, °devoted to, enamoured of, °infatuated with, (°head over heels) in °love with, *Colloq* °wild *or* °mad *or* °crazy about, nuts about *or* over, *Slang* gone on, stuck on, batty about: *We were teasing Rick about being sweet on Anne.*
—*n.* **9** Often, ***sweets***: bon-bon, chocolate, confection, sweetmeat, *Old-fashioned* comfit, *US* °candy: *Harry always brings a box of sweets for my mother when he comes to see me.* **10** °dessert, *Brit* pudding, *Colloq Brit* pud, afters: *For a sweet we can offer you a choice between chocolate gateau and gooseberry pie.*

sweeten *v.* **1** sugar, sugar-coat: *Can you think of nothing that would sweeten the bad news?* **2** °dress up, make more °attractive *or* °agreeable, sugar-coat, °embellish, embroider; make less painful, °mitigate, alleviate, assuage, °lighten, °soften, palliate, mollify, °ease, allay, °moderate, °temper: *Perhaps the shareholders would be more amenable to the take-over were the buyers to sweeten the offer.*

sweetheart *n.* girlfriend, boyfriend, °friend, °admirer, beau, °darling, °dear, °love, °beloved, °lover, °paramour, inamorato, inamorata, lady-love, betrothed, intended, fiancé(e), *Archaic* swain, *Colloq* heartthrob, °flame, sweetie, °steady: *She married her childhood sweetheart and lived happily ever after.*

swell *v.* **1** Often, ***swell out*** *or* ***up***: °grow, °increase, °enlarge, °expand, °blow *or* °puff up *or* out, distend, °inflate, dilate, wax; mushroom, belly, balloon, bloat, °bulge, billow, fatten, °rise, tumefy: *After cooking, the mixture swells to twice its original volume.* **2** °grow, °increase, mushroom, snowball, °accumulate, °mount: *Forgotten for years, her savings had swelled to become a small fortune.* **3** °increase, °raise, augment, °enlarge, °boost, °step up: *Something must be done to swell the number of recruits.*
—*n.* **4** enlargement, broadening, °increase, °extension, °spread, °swelling, inflation, °expansion, °rise, °surge: *Have you noted the swell in popularity of health foods?* **5** °wave, °surge, billow: *As we rose to the top of each swell, we could see the shore.* **6** fop, °dandy, gay °blade, fashion plate, Beau Brummell, *Archaic* coxcomb, *Historical* macaroni, *Colloq* clothes-horse, *US* fancy Dan, *Slang* nob, *Archaic* lounge lizard, *Brit* toff: *He frequented the clubs populated by the other London swells.*
—*adj.* **7** °smart, °chic, °stylish, °fashionable, modish, °grand, °luxurious, de luxe, °elegant, °first-rate, first-class, top-grade, *Colloq* °posh, swank, °swanky, ritzy: *Charlie always took Diane to the swellest places.* **8** °marvellous, °thrilling, °splendid, spectacular, °first-rate, °fine, *Colloq* °great, °super, °terrific: *I really had a swell time at your party.*

swelling *n.* enlargement, distension, tumescence, protuberance, °bump, °prominence, °bulge, °lump, excrescence, °protrusion, °tumour, node, nodule: *It is a good idea to have any unexplained swelling examined by the doctor.*

sweltering *adj.* °hot, °torrid, steaming, °sultry, °steamy, °muggy, °sticky, °oppressive, stifling, °stuffy, suffocating, °clammy, °humid, °wet, broiling, boiling, °scorching, roasting, baking, wilting, melting, tropical, *Colloq* °close: *I cannot live through another sweltering summer in the Amazon jungle.*

swerve *v.* veer, °career, °swing, °diverge, °deviate, °sheer off, skew, °stray, °turn (aside): *The car swerved wildly off the road and into a ditch.*

swift *adj.* °fleet, °fast, °rapid, °speedy, °hasty, °lively, °nimble, °expeditious; quick, °brisk, °sudden, °abrupt: *The postman was bent on the swift completion of his rounds. What Bill needs is a swift kick to jolt him out of his lethargy.*

swiftly *adv.* °fast, °quickly, speedily, °rapidly, expeditiously; briskly, hurriedly, °hastily, °suddenly, abruptly, in a °flash, in a trice, in the wink of an eye, before you can say 'Jack Robinson', before you can say 'knife', like a shot, in an °instant, in (less than) no time, precipitately, unexpectedly, *Colloq* like greased lightning, *US* lickety-split, in a jiffy, *Slang* pronto, like a bat out of hell: *The assembly is done much more swiftly by machine. Swiftly, I ducked into a doorway to avoid being seen.*

swill *n.* **1** hogwash, pigswill, °refuse, pigwash, slop(s), °garbage, °waste: *If you saw the swill that pigs eat, you might not eat pork.* **2** °nonsense, °rot, °rubbish, *Slang* crap: *That novel of hers was the worst swill I've read in a long time.*
—*v.* **3** °drink, guzzle, quaff, °swallow, *Colloq* swig, toss off *or* down, throw down, °polish off, °knock back *or* off, *US* chug-a-lug: *They waste every evening swilling beer.*

swimmingly *adv.* smoothly, °easily, effortlessly, °well, successfully, without a °hitch *or* a °problem, like a dream, cosily, like clockwork, without °difficulty, °handily, °readily: *The plan has gone swimmingly thus far.*

swindle *v.* **1** °cheat, cozen, bilk, °defraud, °deceive, °hoodwink, °take in, °fleece, °dupe, °fool, mulct, gull, make a °fool *or* °sucker (out) of, °victimize, °exploit, °trick, *Old-fashioned or literary* euchre, *Archaic* chouse, *Colloq* bamboozle, °chisel, diddle, pull a fast one on, flimflam, pluck, burn, take (someone) for a °ride, *Brit* °fiddle, *US* buffalo, *Slang* con, °sting, °screw, rook, gyp, °rip (someone) off: *The gang has swindled several elderly people out of their life savings.*
—*n.* **2** °fraud, confidence game *or* trick, cheating, swindling, defrauding, °deception, °racket, °trickery, °sharp practice, thimblerigging, °chicanery, knavery, *Colloq Brit* °fiddle, swizzle *or* swizz, *Slang* °rip-off, scam, con (game), gyp, *US* bunco: *Those old-time swindles are nothing compared with the activities of unscrupulous stock brokers.*

swindler *n.* °cheat, confidence man *or* woman, hoaxer, mountebank, charlatan, knave, °scoundrel, sharper, °fraud, trickster, thimblerigger, °villain, *Technical* defalcator, *Colloq* flimflam man *or* artist, *Slang* con man *or* woman, *US* bunco-artist, four-flusher: *Swindlers tricked them out of all their cash and traveller's cheques.*

swing *v.* **1** °sway, °move *or* °go to and fro *or* back and forth *or* °backwards and forwards, °come and °go, °wave, °fluctuate, °flap, °oscillate, °vibrate, librate, waver, wobble, waggle, zigzag, wigwag, °flourish: *The branches swung in the wind. They swung their arms in time to the music.* **2** °hang, °dangle; be hanged, be suspended: *They watched the monkeys swinging from tree to tree. He will swing for his crime.*
—*n.* **3** swinging, °sway, swaying, toing and froing, coming and going, waving, °fluctuation, fluctuating, flapping, °flap, oscillation, oscillating, vibration, vibrating, libration, waver, wavering, wobble, wobbling, waggle, waggling, zigzag, zigzagging, wigwag, wigwagging, °flourish, flourishing, °stroke: *Catch the rope on its next swing. He was caught on the shoulder by a wild swing of the bat.* **4** °sweep, °scope, °range, °trend, °limit(s); °change, °switch, °shift: *The swing of public opinion is unpredictable in these matters. There has been a small percentage swing to the Conservatives.* **5** °pace, °routine, °groove, °pattern: *Don't you find it hard to get into the normal swing of things after a long holiday?* **6** ***in full swing***: in (full) °operation, under °way, in °business, °animated, °lively, on the °move, °moving, going, *Colloq* on the hop, cooking: *The party was in full swing when we arrived.*

swingeing *adj.* °huge, °immense, °enormous, °considerable, °drastic, °severe, °harsh, stringent, °punishing, °devastating, °painful, °excruciating, °major, daunting, Draconian, °oppressive, °exorbitant, °excessive, °violent, *Colloq* °thumping: *They have instituted a truly swingeing increase in commuter fares. She gives me a swingeing headache.*

swinging *adj.* °fashionable, °chic, up to °date, °modern, *Colloq* à gogo, in the swim, with it, *Chiefly Brit* °trendy, *Slang* °hip, groovy, in the groove: *That's what the swinging '60s were like in London.*

swipe *v.* **1** Usually, ***swipe at***: °swing at, °strike at, °hit at, °lash out at: *He swiped away at the golf ball but kept missing it.* **2** °steal, filch, °pilfer, purloin, *Colloq* °pinch, °lift, snitch, *Chiefly Brit* °nick, °whip, snaffle: *They caught Freddie swiping a bag of mints at Woolworth's.*
—*n.* **3** °swing, °strike, °clip: *Ronald took a swipe at the ball with his racket.*

swirl *v.* **1** whirl, °spin, °eddy, churn, °circulate, °gyrate, °surge, °boil, °seethe: *Faster and faster the water swirled round in the maelstrom.* **2** °twist, whirl, whorl, curl, °roll, furl, °spin, curve, °spiral, °twirl, °wind (round): *She swirled her hair round her head and fastened it with a large clip.*
—*n.* **3** °twist, whirl, curl, °roll, °twirl, °spiral: *At the fabric exhibition swirls of textiles were decoratively displayed.*

swish *v.* **1** °hiss, °whisk, °rustle, °whisper, susurrate: *I heard Elena swish up behind me in her taffeta dress.*
—*n.* **2** °hiss, hissing sound, whoosh, swoosh, °rustle, whistle: *With a quick swish the machete knifed through the underbrush.*
—*adj.* **3** °elegant, °fashionable, °stylish, *de rigueur*, °smart, *Colloq* °posh, °plush, ritzy, °swell, swank(y): *Liza bought a swish new outfit for the wedding.* **4** °homosexual, °gay, °effeminate; *All the following are offensive and derogatory*: *Colloq chiefly Brit* °bent, *Slang* °queer, °camp, campy, °kinky, *Chiefly US* fruity, limp-wristed, faggy, swishy: *He used to bring his swish friends here, but not lately.*

switch *n.* **1** twitch, °lash, °rod, °whip, birch (°rod), °scourge: *He picked up the switch as if to hit me with it.* **2** °change, °alteration, °exchange, °shift, change-over, °reversal, deflection, °trade, swap *or* swop: *A switch of costume was done swiftly backstage, yielding the expression 'quick-change artist'.*
—*v.* **3** twitch, °lash, °whip, birch, °beat, °strike, thrash, °scourge, °flog: *The headmaster switched the boys for the slightest misdemeanour.* **4** °change, °shift, °exchange, °divert, °deviate: *The colonel switched to another subject. They switched the two stones, leaving the fake emerald.* **5** °divert, °turn, rechannel, redirect, °direct: *They switched the funds to another project.*

swivel *v.* **1** °pivot, °turn, °rotate, °spin, °revolve, °pirouette, °move freely: *This joint allows the arm to swivel in all directions.*
—*n.* **2** °pivot, elbow-joint, gimbal, ball-and-socket °joint: *The stern-chaser is fitted with a swivel, allowing it to be fired at any angle.*

swollen *adj.* enlarged, distended, °inflated, °bloated, bulging, puffed up *or* out, tumid, tumescent, expanded, turgid, puffy, oversized, outsized, *Technical* dropsical, hypertrophied, proud: *My knee was swollen for three days after that knock.*

swoop *v.* **1** °descend, °dive, °sweep down, °pounce, °stoop: *The eagle swooped down across the stream, catching a salmon in its talons.*
—*n.* **2** descent, °dive, °sweep, °pounce, °stoop, °stroke, °blow, °rush: *The police raid caught several drug dealers in one fell swoop.*

sybarite *n.* °epicure, °epicurean, hedonist, voluptuary, °sensualist, °aesthete, gastronome, °gourmet, *bon vivant*, *bon viveur*, pleasure-seeker, °playboy, jet-setter: *These sybarites spend all their time and their parents' money in the fleshpots of the world.*

symbol *n.* °representation, °figure, °metaphor, allegory, insigne (*singular; plural is* insignia), °token, °sign, °emblem, badge, °image, logotype, °mark, °trade °mark, colophon, °brand, °code, °abbreviation, phonogram, initialism, cryptogram, acronym, monogram, °password, °shibboleth, watchword, °code word; arms, °bearing, armorial °bearing, °crest, escutcheon, °coat of arms, °banner, °flag, °pennant, °standard, *Colloq* logo: *This jewel is a mere symbol of my devotion and love for you.*

symbolic *adj.* Often, ***symbolic of***: symbolical (of), tokening, betokening, °emblematic (of), figurative, allegoric(al), °typical (of), °representative (of), °symptomatic (of), °characteristic (of), °metaphoric(al), allusive (of), denotative (of), connotative (of), mnemonic (of): *From ancient times the laurel, or bay, has been regarded as symbolic of praiseworthiness.*

symbolize *v.* °represent, °stand for, °denote, connote, °suggest, °express, °imply, °signify, °mean, °typify,

°exemplify, betoken, °illustrate, °embody, epitomize: *Green symbolizes envy and jealousy, red anger, blue sadness, white purity, and so on.*

symmetrical *adj.* symmetric, (°well-)balanced, proportionate, °proportional, well-proportioned, °orderly, (well-)ordered, in °proportion, °even, °regular, congruous, congruent, °uniform, °harmonious; °equal, mirror-image, mirror-like: *The temple was exactly symmetrical, with a wing on each side. The two wings are symmetrical.*

symmetry *n.* °balance, °proportion, evenness, °order, orderliness, °regularity, °uniformity, congruity, congruousness, correspondence, °agreement, °harmony, consistency, °equality: *With the crudest of tools, the pyramid builders achieved incredible symmetry.*

sympathetic *adj.* **1** Often, ***sympathetic to*** *or* ***toward(s)***: compassionate (to *or* toward(s)), commiserating (with), commiserative (with), °understanding (of), °supportive (of), caring (to *or* toward(s)), °concerned (about *or* with), °solicitous (of *or* to *or* (toward(s)), warm-hearted (to *or* toward(s)), kind-hearted (to *or* toward(s)), °responsive (to *or* toward(s)), well-meaning, well-intentioned, °good-natured (to *or* toward(s)), °considerate (of *or* to *or* toward(s)), empathetic *or* empathic (with *or* to *or* toward(s)); sympathizing, °kindly, comforting, consoling: *The social workers are sympathetic to the people's problems. One should be more sympathetic. Julie takes a sympathetic outlook.* **2** Often, ***sympathetic to*** or ***toward(s)***: °agreeable, °pleasant, °friendly, well-disposed, °favourably °disposed, encouraging, like-minded, °responsive, congenial, *en rapport, simpatico*: *You will find a sympathetic ear at the council. The people are not sympathetic to a tax increase.*

sympathize *v.* **1** Often, ***sympathize with***: °suffer *or* °grieve *or* °mourn (with), °feel (°sorry) (for), have °pity (for), empathize (with), condole (with), commiserate (with): *I sympathized with you over the loss of your grandfather. Now that mine is gone, it is your turn to sympathize.* **2** Often, ***sympathize with***: harmonize (with), °get along (with), °relate (to), °identify (with), °go along (with), see eye to eye (with), °agree (with), °side (with), °understand, be *en rapport* (with), be in °sympathy (with), be *simpatico* (with), have (a) °rapport (with), *Colloq* be *or* vibrate on the same frequency *or* wavelength (with), *Slang* °dig: *I can sympathize with anyone who despises terrorism.*

sympathizer *n.* condoner, approver, conspirator, co-conspirator, collaborator, °accomplice, °accessory, °supporter, fellow-traveller, °ally: *At one time, they tried to incarcerate all suspected of being Fascist sympathizers.*

sympathy *n.* **1** compassion, commiseration, °pity, °concern, tenderness, empathy, °understanding, solicitousness, °warmth, tender-heartedness, warm-heartedness, *Archaic* ruth: *We feel great sympathy for any child who loses a pet.* **2** °agreement, °harmony, compatibility, °rapport, concord, °accord, fellow-feeling, congeniality, °affinity, closeness, °unity, communion, °fellowship, camaraderie: *It is amazing that there can be so much sympathy between two such different people.*

symptom *n.* °manifestation, °evidence, syndrome, °mark, °token, °indication, °cue, °clue, (°warning) °sign, °characteristic, °trait, °feature, earmark, marker: *Esmeralda is extremely jealous—I recognize the symptoms.*

symptomatic *adj.* Often, ***symptomatic of***: indicative (of), °representative (of), °suggestive (of), °characteristic (of), °emblematic (of), °symbolic (of), °peculiar (to), °specific (to), idiosyncratic (of); indicating, suggesting: *A high fever is symptomatic of many illnesses.*

syndicate *n.* **1** °trust, monopoly, bloc, cartel, syndication: *They were part of a syndicate that controlled the worldwide sale of nickel.* **2** (crime) family, Cosa Nostra, mafia: *Guido used to be an enforcer for the syndicate.*
—*v.* **3** affiliate, °ally, °associate, °amalgamate, consolidate, °league, confederate, synthesize: *Mrs Cartwright was successful in syndicating the milk producers in the entire county.* **4** serialize, °distribute: *His business is syndicating old movies to television stations.*

synonymous *adj.* Often, ***synonymous with*** *or* ***to***: °equal (to), °equivalent (to), tantamount (to), identified (with), corresponding (to *or* with); transposable (with), exchangeable (with), °identical (to *or* with), interchangeable (with), the °same (as): *A word is almost never truly synonymous with another in all respects. Even terms like 'salt' and 'sodium chloride' are not synonymous.*

synopsis *n.* °summary, condensation, °abridgement, epitomization, °outline, °abstract, °digest, °précis, °epitome, compendium, conspectus, *aperçu*, résumé: *He was assigned to write a ten-page synopsis of a 600-page book.*

synthesis *n.* °blend, °compound, °merge, °union, °amalgamation, coalescence, integration, unification, composite, °composition, °mixture, °combination; compounding, combining, blending, merging, integrating, mixing, fusing, fusion, unifying: *This mixture is a synthesis of many different ingredients. How do they effect the synthesis of coal, water, and air to make nylon?*

synthetic *adj.* °artificial, man-made, manufactured, ersatz; °fake, °false, °counterfeit, °sham, °bogus, °spurious, °mock, °imitation, pseudo, °plastic, *Colloq* °phoney *or US also* phony: *Because of the animal rights activists, many women today wear synthetic fur.*

system *n.* **1** organized °whole, °organization, °set, °group, °combination; °structure, °arrangement, °pattern, °set-up: *Some believe that the universe is a vast ordered system, others that it is chaos in which only man sees order. It took years to establish the banking system in this country.* **2** °scheme, °method, °approach, modus operandi, °way, procedure, methodology, °technique, °plan, °process, °practice, °routine: *There is a proper system for doing the job and you should keep to it.*

systematic *adj.* organized, systematized, planned, °methodical, businesslike, °orderly, well-organized, well-ordered, °regular, °routine, standardized, °standard: *There are several systematic ways for cataloguing books.*

T

tab *n.* **1** °flap, °tag, °loop, ticket, sticker, °label, °flag, lappet, strap, °handle: *Pull on the red tab and the life jacket inflates automatically.* **2** °charge, °bill, °account, °reckoning, *Chiefly US* °check: *They left me to pick up the tab at the restaurant for everyone.*

table *n.* **1** °food, victuals, °provender, comestible(s), °edibles, eatables, °fare, °board, °provisions: *One can rely on a fine table at Mrs McGuire's.* **2** °plain, flatland, mesa, tableland, °plateau, steppe: *The area is barren lava table from horizon to horizon.* **3** (tabular *or* columnar) °list *or* listing, °register, °record, tabulation, °chart, catalogue, °index, inventory, itemization, °précis, table of contents: *The figures are easier to understand when arranged in a table.*
—*v.* **4** °submit, °present, °offer, proffer, °bring forward, °bring up, °propose: *The bill will be tabled for action today.* **5** °shelve, °postpone, °defer, °suspend, °put off, °stay, pigeon-hole, mothball, *Colloq* put on ice: *When the bill came up we tabled it for six months.*

tableau *n.* °scene, °sight, °spectacle, °picture, °image; °composition, °arrangement, grouping, °effect: *The children raptly listening to their father telling a story—what a charming tableau!*

tablet *n.* **1** (scribbling *or* writing- *or* note- *or* memo) °pad, (spiral(-bound)) notebook, *US* scratch °pad:

I write all my dreams in a little tablet in case I forget to relate them to my psychiatrist. **2** °slab, °plaque, °plate, panel, plaquette: *The tablet on the base of the statue says it is of Disraeli.* **3** stone, gravestone, headstone, °tombstone, °memorial: *We each contributed to the tablet that marks Croombender's grave.* **4** °pill, capsule, troche, pellet, pastille, drop, lozenge, bolus: *Take three tablets twice a day.*

taboo *adj.* **1** tabu, anathema, forbidden, interdicted, off limits, out of bounds, *verboten*, proscribed, banned, prohibited, restricted, °unmentionable, unspeakable; censored, censorable, °unacceptable, °rude, °impolite, indecorous, °dirty, °explicit; outlawed, °illegal, °illicit, °unlawful: *Our holiday in Benidorm is a taboo subject in my house. Many people dislike hearing taboo language used on radio or television.*
—*n.* **2** tabu, anathema, interdict, interdiction, proscription, °ban, °prohibition, °restriction: *There is still a strict taboo against mentioning bodily functions in public.*
—*v.* **3** tabu, °forbid, interdict, proscribe, °ban, °prohibit: *The hotel taboos the sharing of a room by unmarried couples.*

tabulate *v.* systematize, °organize, °order, °group, °list, °arrange, classify, °categorize, °rate, °grade, catalogue, codify, pigeon-hole, °sort, assort, °index, °itemize; °record, note: *We shall report the results of the poll as soon as they have been tabulated.*

tacit *adj.* unspoken, undeclared, unsaid, unstated, unvoiced, unuttered, °silent, °understood, unexpressed, implied, °implicit: *The sisters have a tacit agreement not to poach each other's boyfriends. He gave me a look of tacit gratitude.*

taciturn *adj.* °silent, uncommunicative, °mum, °mute, °reticent, °reserved, unforthcoming, °tight-lipped, close-lipped, untalkative, °quiet: *Even when he was small, Chris was quite taciturn, saying little but evidently thinking much.*

tack *n.* **1** °pin, push-pin, °nail, *Brit* drawing-pin, tintack, *US* thumbtack: *Someone keeps stealing the tacks from the bulletin board.* **2** °fastening, stitch, baste: *Could you put some tacks in the hem so I can try on the skirt?* **3** °direction, °bearing, heading, °course, °approach; °way, °path, °procedure, °method, °technique, °attack, °line: *Our new tack was due east. They may have to take a different tack to win the contract.* **4** °tackle, °gear, °equipment, equipage, harness, saddlery, °fittings, fitments, °kit, °outfit, °rig, rigging, accoutrements *or US also* accouterments: *He has ordered all new tack for his horse.*
—*v.* **5** °pin, °attach, °fasten, °secure, °join, °couple, °unite, °combine, °stick, °fix, affix, °staple, °nail, skewer, °peg, °screw, °bolt, rivet; baste, stitch, °sew, °bind, °tie; paste, °glue, °cement, solder, braze, °weld: *You were only supposed to tack these together lightly, but now I can't pull them apart.* **6** °change direction *or* heading *or* course, *Nautical* °go *or* °come about; zigzag, veer off *or* away, *Nautical* °beat: *We tacked quickly to avoid striking the buoy.* **7** ***tack on***: °add (on), append, annex, °attach, tag on: *When they tacked on a rider to the contract, we refused to sign it.*

tackle *n.* **1** °gear, °rig, °fittings, °equipment, equipage, rigging, °paraphernalia, °outfit, °tools, °apparatus, °trappings, accoutrements *or US also* accouterments, *Colloq Brit* clobber: *The steeplejack brought along all his tackle and made ready for his climb.* **2** block (and tackle), fall, hoisting °gear, °pulley, sheave: *You'll need heavier tackle to lift this cargo.*
—*v.* **3** come to grips with, °grapple with, °approach, °take on, °try to solve, (°try to) °deal *or* °cope with, °stand *or* °face up to, °face, confront, °address oneself to, °attend to, °set about, °pursue, *Colloq* take a crack at, have a °go at: *Perhaps you'd better tackle the parking problem yourself. I'll tackle the boss on the matter as soon as I see him.* **4** °attack, °fall upon, °devour, °consume, °demolish, °destroy: *You've seen nothing till you've seen Graham tackle a roast turkey.*

tacky[1] *adj.* °sticky, gluey, gummy, adhesive, °ropy, viscous, viscid, *Colloq* °gooey: *The varnish is still tacky and must dry before sanding.*

tacky[2] *adj.* °tawdry, °cheap, brummagem, °gaudy, °tasteless, °vulgar, °shabby, tatty, °sleazy, chintzy, °shoddy, °seedy: *Richard consistently buys the tackiest suits on the market.*

tact *n.* °discretion, °diplomacy, °sensitivity, savoir faire, °judgement, politesse, °delicacy, °finesse, cleverness, °prudence, °care, carefulness, °dexterity, dexterousness, discernment, judiciousness, adroitness, °skill, acumen, acuteness, °perception, °understanding, °consideration, thoughtfulness, politeness: *You can count on Robert to handle such matters with consummate tact.*

tactful *adj.* °discreet, °diplomatic, °sensitive, °politic, °judicious, °delicate, °clever, °prudent, °careful, °dexterous, discerning, adroit, °skilful, °acute, °perceptive, °considerate, °understanding, °thoughtful, °polite: *Even the people working in the complaints department are tactful.*

tactic *n.* **1** °move, °manoeuvre, ploy, °caper, °plan, °strategy, °stratagem, °device, °ruse, °plot, °scheme, °design: *Inviting her husband along was a tactic merely to avert suspicion.* **2** ***tactics***: manoeuvres, °strategy, plans, °campaign, generalship, military science, military °operation(s), orchestration, engineering, masterminding: *Entirely different tactics must be employed in jungle fighting.*

tactical *adj.* °artful, °clever, cunning, °shrewd, adroit, °strategic, °skilful, °adept, °politic, °smart, °tactful: *The general was noted for his dazzling strategies and tactical genius.*

tactician *n.* strategist, campaigner, °mastermind, intriguer, plotter, planner, schemer, manipulator, manoeuvrer, orchestrator, *Colloq* °operator: *Montgomery was regarded by some as a master tactician.*

tactless *adj.* °coarse, °boorish, °uncivilized, °unsophisticated, °rough, °rude, uncouth, °discourteous, ungentlemanly, unladylike, °crude, °gruff, °bluff, °abrupt, °blunt, °brusque, °impertinent, °disrespectful, uncivil, °impolite, insensitive, °awkward, bungling, °clumsy, maladroit, °inept, undiplomatic, °thoughtless, gauche, unskilful, impolitic, °imprudent, °inconsiderate, injudicious, °indiscreet, unwise: *It was pretty tactless of him to ask her out in front of his ex-girlfriend.*

tag *n.* **1** °label, name *or* price tag, °mark, marker, °tab, ticket, sticker, °stub, docket: *The tag was clearly marked with a bar-code.* **2** °name, epithet, °label, designation, °title, appellation, °nickname, *Slang* handle, moniker *or* monicker: *Called 'Eddie the dip', he got his tag 'the dip' because he's a pickpocket.*
—*v.* **3** °label, °mark, ticket, °identify, earmark: *Please tag all these cartons so we'll know what's in them without opening them.* **4** °label, °name, °call, dub, °nickname, °style, °entitle, °christen, baptize: *I have already said that Eddie was tagged 'the dip' because he was a pickpocket.* **5** ***tag along***: °follow, °trail (along) after, °tail, °shadow, °attend, °accompany, °drag along with *or* after: *Does your little brother have to tag along wherever we go?*

tail *n.* **1** appendage, brush (*of a fox*), scut (*of a hare, rabbit, or deer*), dock, caudal fin (*of a fish*), uropygium (of a bird), pope's *or* parson's nose, tailpiece, flag: *I just caught a glimpse of the fox's tail as it leapt the fence.* **2** °rear °end, tail-end, backside, °buttocks, croup, rump, °posterior(s), °bottom, behind, *Colloq Brit* °bum, *US* hinie, *Taboo slang Brit* arse, *US* ass: *When I catch you, I'll kick your tail!* **3** °reverse: *The obverse of a coin is the head, the reverse is the tail.*
—*v.* **4** dog, °follow, °trail, °stalk, °shadow, °track: *We tailed the suspect from Newcastle to New Mexico.*

tailor *n.* **1** couturier, couturière, costumier, °dressmaker, modiste, clothier, garment-maker, outfitter, seamstress: *She has all her clothing made by her tailor.*
—*v.* **2** °fit, °adapt, °suit, °adjust, °alter, °accommodate, °modify, °change, °convert, °cut, °fashion, °mould,

°stretch, °accustom: *Your telephone system can be tailored to your most exacting demands.*

tailor-made *adj.* **1** °fitted, custom-made, made to order, bespoke; made to measure: *He would not wear anything but tailor-made clothes.* **2** °ideal, °perfect, customized, made to order, custom-made, suited, °suitable, (just) °right, *Colloq* right up one's *Brit* °street *or US* alley: *The job of lighthouse-keeper was tailor-made for a misanthrope.*

taint *n.* **1** °stain, °blot, °blemish, °slur, tinge, tincture, (°black *or* °bad) °mark, °stigma, °imperfection, °flaw, °scar, °defect; °discredit, °dishonour: *His writing suffers from the taint of pedantry.*
—*v.* **2** °sully, °tarnish, °stain, °stigmatize, °smear, °harm, °hurt, °damage, °debase, °vitiate, °blacken, °foul, °contaminate, °pollute, °dirty, °muddy, smirch, besmirch, °blemish, °soil, °corrupt, °spoil, defile, °ruin, °destroy: *It takes very little to taint one's reputation in a small village.*

take *v.* **1** °grip, °seize, °grasp, °clasp, °get, °get *or* take °hold of, °grab, °snatch, °clutch, °catch, °capture, °obtain, °lay °hold of, °lay (one's) hands on, °procure, °acquire, °gain (°possession of), take °possession of, °secure, °win, °carry off, °abduct, *Colloq* °nab: *The police took him into custody. He takes what he can get. When it comes to ineptitude, Sue certainly takes the prize.* **2** °pick, °select, °choose, opt for, °settle *or* °decide *or* °fasten on *or* upon: *When you get to the fork, take the road to the left.* **3** °appropriate, arrogate, °extract, °carry off *or* away, °steal, purloin, °pilfer, filch, palm, °rob, shoplift, °pocket, °remove, °walk off *or* away with, °run *or* °make off *or* away with; °embezzle, °misappropriate, peculate; plagiarize, °pirate; *Colloq* °lift, °swipe, snitch, *Chiefly Brit* °pinch, °nick, *Slang* °knock off, °hook, °rip off, °liberate, *US* boost, crook: *They took what didn't belong to them.* **4** °reserve, °book, °engage; °hire, °rent, °lease: *He took a room in a small hotel, where he began to write detective fiction.* **5** °acquire, °get, °adopt; °assume, °derive, °obtain, °draw, °receive, °inherit: *He has taken his bad manners from you. The film takes its title from the book.* **6** °accept, °receive, °bear, °withstand, °stand, °endure, °weather, °tolerate, °abide, °brave, °go through, °undergo, °suffer, °submit to, °swallow, *Colloq* °put up with, °brook, °stomach, *Brit* °stick: *She took the news about Leon's relapse quite well. I have taken quite enough from you already.* **7** °assume, °bear, °undertake, °adopt, arrogate; °acknowledge, °accept: *Kevin took full responsibility for the mistake.* **8** °believe, °think, °judge, deem, °hold, °feel; take for, assess (as), °consider (as), °regard (as), °view (as), °accept (for): *I take people to be honest till proven otherwise. She took him for a fool when they first met.* **9** °carry, convey, °bear, °transport, °bring, °deliver, ferry; °haul, °cart: *Will this train take me to Aylesbury? They took the bicycle to Old Lyme in a van.* **10** take up, °study, be °involved *or* occupied in *or* with, °apply oneself to, °learn; °read, *Colloq* °tackle: *I cannot believe that Doreen is taking home economics. He took a course in car maintenance.* **11** prove *or* be °effective *or* °efficacious *or* °operative *or* °functional, take °effect, take °hold, °operate, °function, °work, °perform, *Colloq* do the °trick: *If the transplant fails to take, the doctors will have to operate again.* **12** °exact, °extract, °get: *She took revenge by denying him certain privileges.* **13** °swallow, °eat, °consume, ingest, °devour, °gulp down, gobble up *or* down, wolf, °bolt; °drink, imbibe, quaff; °inhale: *Rudolf takes pills of every conceivable colour. The doctor said I could take a wee nip now and then. Sonya stepped out to take a breath of fresh air.* **14** °subtract, °deduct, °remove, take away, take from, take off: *Take three from five. Five, take away two, leaves three. It's cheaper when you've taken off the discount.* **15** °end, °terminate, annihilate, °wipe out; °kill: *The assault on Leningrad took tens of thousands of lives. The Lord giveth and the Lord taketh away.* **16** °require, °demand, °need, necessitate, °call for: *Remember, it takes two to tango. It took him two years to complete the fresco. It takes six to sail his yawl.* **17** °hold, °contain, °accommodate, °accept, °fit in: *This storage bin cannot take anything else, it's completely full.* **18** convey, °lead, °conduct; °escort, convoy, °guide, °accompany: *This road takes you directly to the yacht club. He asked to be taken to the manager's office.* **19** °understand, °gather, °interpret, °perceive, apprehend, °deduce, conclude, °infer, °judge, deem, °assume, °suppose, °imagine, °see: *I take him to be a fool. I take it from your expression that you've had bad news.* **20** °charm, °captivate, °capture, °attract, °lure, allure: *There was something about him that took her fancy.* **21** °use, °employ, make °use of, °establish, put in(to) °place, °adopt, put into effect, °effect, °apply; °resort to, have °recourse to, °turn to: *The police have taken measures to ensure that it doesn't happen again.* **22** °clear, °get *or* °go over *or* past *or* round *or* through: *Browning's Delight took the last jump easily. He must have taken that corner at 90!* **23** °experience, °entertain, °feel: *She seemed to take an instant dislike to me.* **24** °express, °voice, °raise, °put forth: *I hope you will not take objection or exception to what I am about to tell you.* **25** °cause *or* °make *or* °induce *or* °drive *or* °persuade (someone) to go *or* be: *What takes you to Málaga in August?* **26** °act, °assume, °play, °perform: *I'm taking the part of the wicked witch in the local pantomime.* **27** bilk, °cheat, °swindle, °defraud, *Colloq* con, *Brit* °fiddle: *When he examined his wallet he realized he'd been taken.* **28** ***take aback***: °astound, °astonish, °surprise, °startle, °shock: *She was really taken aback at the news.* **29** ***take after***: **a** °resemble, °look °like, be the spitting °image *or* the °spit and °image of, °favour, °remind one of, *Colloq* be a chip off the old block: *He takes after his grandfather.* **b** Sometimes, ***take off after***: °chase, °follow, °run after, °pursue: *When the man stole the newspaper and ran, the shopkeeper took after him at a gallop.* **30** ***take back***: °retract, °withdraw, °recant, disavow, °repudiate: *He now wants to take back what he said about you.* **31** ***take down***: **a** °note, make a °note *or* memo *or* °memorandum of, °write down, °record, °put *or* °set down, °put in °writing, °document, °transcribe, °chronicle: *Please take down what I am about to tell you.* **b** °debase, deflate, °lower, °diminish, °belittle, °depreciate, deprecate, °humble, °humiliate, °shame, °disparage, °degrade, °disgrace: *She certainly took that pompous ass down a peg or two.* **32** ***take in***: **a** °accommodate, °receive, °let in, °quarter, °board, °lodge: *When her children grew up and left home, she decided to take in lodgers.* **b** °deceive, °fool, °trick, °impose upon, overcharge, °cheat, mulct, °defraud, cozen, bilk, °dupe, gull, °hoodwink, °swindle, *Colloq* bamboozle, con, pull the wool over (someone's) eyes, *Slang Brit* do: *He was really taken in by that time-share deal.* **c** °include, subsume, °embrace, comprise, °cover, encompass, °contain: *Our sales figures take in all of North America, not just Canada.* **33** ***take it***: **a** °withstand *or* °tolerate *or* °survive punishment *or* abuse, °survive: *The Marines are extremely tough and can take it.* **b** See **19,** above. **34** ***take off***: **a** °remove, doff, °strip *or* °peel off, °discard, °divest (oneself) of: *Take off your hat in the house.* **b** °satirize, °lampoon, °caricature, °mock, °parody, travesty, °burlesque, °mimic, °imitate, *Colloq* spoof, *Brit* °send up: *It is not always easy to take off members of the Cabinet.* **c** °depart, °leave, °go (away), decamp; °fly off, °become airborne, °lift off, °blast off; *Colloq* skedaddle, make (oneself) scarce, *Slang* hit the road, scram, °beat it, °split: *You'd better take off before they find you here. The plane is due to take off at 18.35.* **35** ***take on***: **a** °hire, °engage, °employ, °enrol, °enlist, °retain: *We are so busy that we have taken on ten new people.* **b** °challenge, °rival, °face, contend against, °oppose, °match *or* °pit (oneself) against, °vie with, °fight: *Are you in any condition to take on the champion?* **c** °assume, °accept, °undertake, °tackle: *You might be taking on more than you bargained for.* **36** ***take out***: °entertain, °escort, invite out; court, woo: *He took her out to dinner at a Chinese restaurant.* **37** ***take over***: °assume *or* take *or* usurp *or* °gain °control *or* °possession *or* °command of: *A huge conglomerate is trying to take over our*

company. **38** ***take to***: **a** °like, find °pleasant *or* °pleasing, feel °affection *or* °liking *or* °affinity for, find °suitable: *We took to each other the very first time we met. He took to computers as a duck takes to water.* **b** °leave *or* °depart *or* take off for, °run for, °head for, °flee to, °make for: *When the attack came, the villagers took to the hills.* **39** ***take up***: **a** °pick up, °accept, °agree to, acquiesce to, accede to: *She took up his offer, and they've been married for forty years.* **b** °assume, °resume, °carry on, °continue, °go on with, °follow on with, °pick up: *After a pause, he took up the thread of the story once more.* **c** espouse, °embrace, become °interested *or* °involved in, °support, °sponsor, °advocate: *She took up the cause of women's rights at her age?* **d** °occupy, °cover, °use (up), °fill (up): *Bernard's exercise equipment now takes up half the living-room.* **e** °deal with, °treat, °consider, °bring up, °raise: *Next week our panellists will take up the question, 'Who benefits from education?'*
—*n.* **40** °revenue, takings, °yield, °return, receipts, proceeds, °gain, °profit(s); °gate, °box °office: *How much was the take from the first day?*

taken *adj.* captivated, entranced, °enchanted, °charmed, bewitched, °infatuated: *I was so taken with Lucinda that I started blushing like a teenager.*

take-off *n.* **1** °flight, flying, taking off, departure, leaving, going; °launch, lift-off: *The take-off was delayed by bad weather.* **2** °satire, °lampoon, °caricature, °mockery, °parody, travesty, °burlesque, °imitation, *Colloq* spoof, *Brit* send-up: *The annual students' entertainment was as usual a take-off of the teachers.*

taking *adj.* °attractive, alluring, °engaging, captivating, °winning, winsome, charming, entrancing, °enchanting, bewitching, °fetching, fascinating, °delightful, °irresistible, compelling, intriguing, °prepossessing: *Cassie's taking ways won her many friends.*

tale *n.* **1** °story, °narrative, °report, °account, °record, °chronicle, °history, °narration, °recital, anecdote: *We were brought up on tales of the supernatural. Her tale of what happened does not agree with the facts.* **2** °falsehood, °lie, fiction, °fib, °fabrication, untruth, falsification, °exaggeration, *Colloq* °tall tale *or* °story, (cock-and-bull) °story, *US* fish °story: *He told some tale about having been captured by urban guerrillas.* **3** °rumour, °gossip, °slander, °allegation, tittle-tattle, °libel, °story, *US chiefly naval* scuttlebutt: *I have been hearing tales about wild parties at the neighbours' again.*

talebearer *n.* °gossip, rumour-monger, gossipmonger, taleteller, talemonger, scandalmonger, telltale, °troublemaker, quidnunc, tattler, °informer, sieve, *Chiefly US and Canadian* tattle-tale, *Slang* bigmouth, °blabbermouth, squealer, stool-pigeon, stoolie, rat, *Brit* °sneak, nark, *US* fink, ratfink: *The words, spoken in private, were repeated to him by some talebearer.*

talent *n.* **1** °ability, °power, °gift, °faculty, °flair, °genius, °facility, °aptitude, °capacity, °knack, °ingenuity, °forte, °strength; °endowment: *Bill's extraordinary talent for playing the trombone was widely acclaimed.* **2** °tendency, proclivity, propensity, °penchant, predilection, predisposition, °bent, °inclination: *Annabel certainly has a talent for saying the wrong thing.*

talented *adj.* °gifted, °accomplished, °brilliant, skilled, °skilful, °masterful, °expert, °adept, adroit, °dexterous, deft, °clever, °good, °polished, °proficient, °first-rate, top-drawer, °excellent, *Colloq* ace, crack, top-notch, *Brit* wizard, whizzo, *US* crackerjack: *Leslie is the most talented player in the school hockey team.*

talisman *n.* °amulet, °charm, tiki, °fetish *or* fetich, juju, periapt, abraxas; wishbone, rabbit's foot, *Brit* merry thought: *He was given a talisman that was supposed to protect its wearer from bad luck.*

talk *v.* **1** Sometimes, ***talk in***: °speak (in), °use, °communicate in, °converse in, °express (oneself) in, discourse in: *If you talk English I might understand.* **2** °confer, °consult, °parley, have a (little) talk, (have a) °chat, confabulate, *Colloq* confab, *Slang US* °rap: *I think we ought to talk before you decide which offer to accept.* **3** °chatter, prate, °prattle, °jabber, blather *or* blether, gibber, jibber-jabber, cackle, °babble, °patter, °rattle on, °go on, *Brit* natter, witter, rabbit on, *Colloq* °gab, *Slang* gas, jaw, *US* run off at the mouth: *They talk continuously, mostly about nothing.* **4** °chat, °gossip, °palaver, *Slang* °chew the fat *or* the °rag, shoot the breeze, *US* chin, schmooze, °rap, have a bull session, bat the breeze, shoot the bull: *We were just sitting around talking when Tom suggested we go for a swim.* **5** °inform, °confess, °give the game away, °blab, *Colloq* come °clean, *Slang* rat, squeal, °sing, °spill the beans, *Brit* °grass: *If they give him the third degree, you can be sure he'll talk.* **6** °speak, give *or* deliver a °speech *or* a talk *or* an °address, °lecture: *I believe that Professor Hale is talking at the County Library tonight.* **7** ***talk about*** *or* ***over*** *or* ***of***: °discuss, °confer about *or* on, °parley about: *I don't want to talk about football all the time. Can't we talk it over? She talks only of you.* **8** ***talk big***: °boast, °brag, vaunt, crow, °bluster, °exaggerate, blow *or* toot (one's) own horn: *He was never in the war—he just talks big.* **9** ***talk down***: **a** °depreciate, deprecate, denigrate, °disparage, °belittle, °minimize, °diminish, °criticize, *Colloq* °knock, °pan, °put down: *It's the only thing he's ever done, and you shouldn't talk it down.* **b** Usually, ***talk down to***: °condescend to, °patronize: *I resent your talking down to me in that way.* **10** ***talk into***: °convince, °bring round, °sway, °persuade: *We have been trying to talk him into running in the marathon.* **11** ***talk over***: °discuss: *We talked over the best way to prepare the advertising proposal.* **12** ***talk to*** *or* ***with***: °speak to *or* with, °communicate with, °converse with: *Since the episode with the monkey, she refuses to talk to me. I talked with him yesterday.* **13** ***talk up***: °promote, °support, °sponsor, advertise, °publicize, °push, *Colloq* °plug, hype, ballyhoo: *She has been talking up the book on her radio show.*
—*n.* **14** °oration, °lecture, °address, °presentation, °speech, discourse, °report, disquisition, dissertation; °sermon; °harangue, °tirade, *Colloq* spiel: *Claire delivered a talk on computational linguistics. Every week we have to listen to the same talk about sin.* **15** °conversation, °conference, °discussion, °meeting, consultation, °dialogue, colloquy, °parley, °palaver, °chat, °tête-à-tête, confabulation, *Colloq* confab, powwow, *Slang* chin-wag, head-to-head, *US* one-on-one, °rap session: *We must have a little talk about your school report.* **16** subject *or* topic of °conversation *or* °gossip *or* °rumour: *Her behaviour at the wedding was the talk of the town for weeks.* **17** °gossip, °rumour, hearsay, °information, °news, °report, *Colloq* info, *Slang* °dope: *There is some talk that you might be leaving.* **18** °palaver, °gossip, claptrap, °prattle, prattling, °chatter, verbiage, cackle, bunk, °nonsense, °rubbish, balderdash, poppycock, °hot air, °stuff and °nonsense, twaddle, *Colloq* malarkey, piffle, hooey, hokum, bunkum, bosh, hogwash, horse feathers, *Slang* bilge(-water), crap, bull, tripe, *Brit* tosh, balls, *US* apple-sauce, *Taboo slang* horseshit, bullshit: *That's just a lot of talk.* **19** °dialect, °speech, way *or* manner of speaking, *façon de parler*, °language, °jargon, argot, °cant, patois, °accent, *Colloq* °lingo: *Can you understand musicians' talk? My parents' talk is peppered with words long obsolete in standard English.*

talkative *adj.* garrulous, loquacious, verbose, long-winded, °voluble, prolix, °wordy, chatty, gossipy, °effusive, talky, logorrhoeic *or* logorrhoeal, *Colloq* gabby, blabby, *Slang* big-mouthed; *US* running off at the mouth: *The children are so talkative I can't get a word in edgeways.*

talker *n.* **1** °speaker, lecturer, orator, speech-maker, keynoter, spellbinder, tub-thumper, °rabble-rouser, demagogue, haranguer, ranter: *You might disagree with what he says, but you must admit he's a great talker.* **2** blusterer, blatherskite, swaggerer, °show-off, *Slang* windbag, gasbag, lot of °hot air, blowhard: *He is a big talker, but he never gets anything done.*

tall *adj.* **1** °high, °towering, °big, soaring, °lofty, °giant, °gigantic; multi-storey: *The giant sequoias of California are the tallest trees in the world. There are many tall buildings in most major cities.* **2** °lanky, gangling, rangy, leggy, long-legged, °big, °giant, °huge, °gigantic, °large: *Some of those basketball players are unbelievably tall.* **3** exaggerated, overblown, °far-fetched, °improbable, °unbelievable, °incredible, °preposterous, °outrageous, overdone, °absurd, *Colloq Brit* °steep: *He told us some amusing tall tales about his fishing adventures.*

tally *v.* **1** °agree, °coincide, °accord, °correspond, °fit, °compare, °match (up), °square, °conform, concur, harmonize, *Colloq US* jibe: *Nothing I could do would make my figures tally with those of the bank.* **2** Sometimes, ***tally up***: °count (up *or* out), °enumerate, °record, °register, °reckon, °add (up), °total (up), °tabulate, °itemize, °list, °calculate, °compute: *Please tally up what I owe you.*
—*n.* **3** °count, enumeration, °record, °register, °reckoning, °addition, °total, tabulation, itemization, listing, °calculation, computation: *According to my tally, you owe £156.72.* **4** ticket, °label, °mark, marker, °tag, °tab: *Each plant can be identified by its own tally.* **5** counterfoil, °stub, counterpart, °duplicate, °mate: *If you lose your tally you cannot get your luggage back.*

tame *adj.* **1** tamed, docile, disciplined, °obedient, domesticated, house-broken, trained, °broken: *He used to keep a tame fox in his back garden.* **2** °mild, °gentle, °fearless, unafraid: *It is amazing how tame animals can be when they do not perceive man as a threat.* **3** °tractable, pliant, compliant, °meek, °submissive, °mild, under (someone's) °control *or* °thumb, °subdued, suppressed; unassertive, °feeble, °ineffectual, °timid, timorous, °cowardly, pusillanimous, chicken-hearted, °faint-hearted, white-livered, lily-livered, yellow, *Colloq* wimpish: *Charles is far too tame to defy Kate.* **4** °boring, °tedious, °tiresome, °dull, insipid, °bland, °lifeless, °flat, °vapid, °prosaic, °humdrum, °bland, unexciting, uninspired, uninspiring, run-of-the-mill, °ordinary, uninteresting, °dead, *Colloq* °wishy-washy: *As a nightclub, the place is much too tame for my tastes.*
—*v.* **5** °break, domesticate, °train, house-train, °gentle, °master, °subdue, °subjugate: *The brown bear is a most difficult animal to tame.* **6** °calm, °subdue, °control, mollify, pacify, °mute, °temper, °soften, °curb, °tone down, °moderate, °mitigate, °tranquillize: *After a week the Lord tamed the violent sea and our tiny craft was allowed to continue.*

tamper *v.* °interfere, °meddle, intermeddle, °intrude, °tinker, °mess (about *or* around), *Colloq* °fiddle *or* °fool (about *or* around), °monkey (about *or* around), °muck (about *or* around): *Anyone caught tampering with the machinery will be prosecuted.*

tang *n.* **1** pungency, piquancy, °bite, °zest, zestiness, sharpness, poignancy, spiciness, °nip, °edge, °spice, °taste, °flavour, °savour, °aroma, °smell, °odour, *Colloq* zip, °kick: *Ginger root gives the dish just the right tang.* **2** tinge, °flavour, °hint, °suggestion, soupçon, °trace, °dab, smack, °touch, smattering: *The new version has the tang of the original without its obsolete words.* **3** prong, °tab, °projection, °tongue, °strip, tine, shank, °pin, °spike: *The tang of a good knife goes right through to the end of the handle.*

tangential *adj.* °divergent, digressive, off *or* beside the °point, °peripheral, °irrelevant, °extraneous, °unrelated: *The matter of cost is tangential to the main issue.*

tangible *adj.* °material, °real, °physical, corporeal, bodily, somatic, °solid, °concrete, touchable, tactile, °manifest, palpable, °evident, °actual, °substantial, °visible, seeable, °discernible, °perceptible, ponderable, °objective, ostensive: *Leaving aside intangibles like taste, smell, and colour, the important tangible characteristic of food is texture.*

tangle *n.* **1** °confusion, °knot, gnarl, °mesh, °snarl, °twist, °kink, entanglement, °jam, °snag, °jumble, °mess, skein, °web, °coil: *It took hours to straighten out the tangle of ribbons.* **2** °muddle, °complication, °jumble, °puzzle, °medley, °complexity, °complication, °scramble, °mishmash, °mix-up, °hotchpotch *or US and Canadian also* hodgepodge, jungle, °maze, labyrinth: *She was rather bewildered by the vast tangle of information on the subject.*
—*v.* **3** Often, ***tangle up***: °confuse, °knot, °mesh, °snarl, gnarl, °twist, °kink, ravel, °entangle, °jam, °snag, intertwist, intertwine, interlace, interweave, °jumble, °mess up, °scramble, °shuffle, °muddle: *Now you've tangled all the ribbons I carefully straightened out earlier.* **4** Often, ***tangle with***: wrangle (with), contend (with), °fight (with *or* against), (come into) °conflict (with), come *or* go up against, lock horns (with), °dispute (with), cross swords (with), °disagree (with): *The sheriff is the last person I want to tangle with.*

tantalize *v.* °tease, °taunt, °provoke, °torment, torture, bait, °tempt, °plague, °frustrate: *They tantalized him by hanging the keys to his cell just outside his reach.*

tantamount to *adj.* amounting to, as good as, °virtually the °same as, (pretty) much the °same as, °equal to, °equivalent to, °like, of a °piece with, comparable to, commensurate with: *His response, for all its politeness, was tantamount to a rejection.*

tantrum *n.* °fit (of °anger *or* of °passion), °outburst, °eruption, blow-up, °explosion, flare-up, °storm, °rage, °fury, *Colloq Brit* °paddy, wax: *He has a tantrum every time he fails to get his own way.*

tap[1] *v.* **1** °rap, °knock, °dab, °strike, peck; drum, °beat: *Must you continually tap on the table with that blasted pencil?*
—*n.* **2** °rap, °knock, °dab, °strike, peck, °pat; tapping, tap-tap, rapping, knocking, pecking, °beat, beating, °patter, pattering: *I felt a tap on my shoulder. The tap, tap, tap of the dripping water was driving me mad.*

tap[2] *n.* **1** cock, stopcock, pet-cock, sillcock, seacock, spigot, °spout, valve, *US* faucet: *Replace the washer in the tap to stop the leak.* **2** bung, °stopper, cork, spile, °plug, stopple, °peg: *Move the tap from the empty barrel to the new one.* **3** wire-tap, °bug, listening °device, electronic eavesdropper: *I think there's a tap on my phone.* **4** ***on tap***: **a** on draught, out of the barrel *or* keg: *They have real ale on tap.* **b** °ready, °available, on *or* at °hand, waiting, in °reserve, on °call: *He promised to be on tap if I needed him for anything.*
—*v.* **5** °drain, °draw (off), siphon off *or* out, °extract, °withdraw: *We tapped the wine directly from the casks.* **6** °open, °drain, unplug, °sap, bleed, °milk, °broach, °mine, °use, utilize, make °use of, put to °use, °draw on *or* upon, turn to account: *Whenever she needed money, she tapped her savings.* **7** °bug, °eavesdrop on, wire-tap: *M.I.5 still taps her phone.*

tape *n.* **1** °strip, °band, fillet, °stripe, strap, °belt, ribbon: *She wore a colourful woven tape round her head to hold her hair.* **2** (tape) recording, °reel, spool, cassette, video: *He played us the tape of the whole interview.*
—*v.* **3** strap, °band, °bind; °seal, °stick: *If you tape the packet, customs cannot open it for inspection.* **4** °record; tape-record, video: *Programmes can be taped automatically when we are out.*

taper *v.* **1** °narrow (down), °thin, °diminish, come *or* go down: *Note how the trousers taper towards the ankles.* **2** Often, ***taper off***: °diminish, °reduce, °thin out, °wind down, °decrease, °fade, lessen, peter out, °wane, °subside, °let up, slacken, °die away *or* down *or* off *or* out, °decline, °slow (down *or* up), °weaken, abate, °ebb, °slump, °drop (off), °fall (off), °plummet: *Sales of ice skates can be expected to taper off during the summer.*

tardy *adj.* **1** °late, unpunctual, behind schedule, °overdue, behindhand: *Yet again you have been somewhat tardy in completing your assignments.* **2** °slow, dilatory, °belated, °slack, retarded, sluggish, °reluctant, °indolent, °lackadaisical, °listless, °phlegmatic, °slothful, °lethargic, languid: *They have been tardy in acknowledging the importance of Allen's work.*

target *n.* °goal, °object, °objective, °aim, °end; °butt, °quarry: *The target of the charity drive is to raise £30,000. Why make Peter the target of your ridicule?*

tariff *n.* **1** °tax, assessment, °duty, excise, levy, impost, °toll, *Brit* °rate: *The tariff on imported clothing may be increased.* **2** °schedule (of charges), price-list; bill of fare, menu: *I stopped by the hotel to ask about their tariff.*

tarnish *v.* °sully, °disgrace, °taint, °blacken, °blemish, °stain, °blot, °soil, °spot, °dirty, °contaminate, defame, °injure, °spoil, °ruin, °damage, °harm, °hurt, °stigmatize, °debase, °degrade, denigrate, °dishonour, asperse, calumniate: *By his behaviour, he has tarnished the reputation of his entire family.*

tarry *v.* **1** °delay, °pause, °wait, °linger, loiter, °stall, °procrastinate, °dawdle, bide (one's) time, temporize, °hang back, *Colloq* °hang on *or* about *or* (a)round: *They tarried in the pub, and missed their train.* **2** °remain, °sojourn, °stay, °stop, °rest, °dwell, bide (one's) time, °settle: *She plans to tarry at Eastbourne for a while.*

tart[1] *adj.* **1** °sour, acidic, acidulous, acidulated, lemony, citrusy, vinegary, acetous, acescent; °sharp, tangy, astringent, acerb, acerbic, acrid, °bitter, °pungent, piquant, °harsh: *Those grapes are a bit tart for my taste.* **2** °biting, °bitter, °caustic, acid, corrosive, mordant, astringent, acrimonious, °trenchant, °harsh, °scathing, stinging, acerbic, °incisive, °cutting, °keen, barbed, °nasty, curmudgeonly, °testy, crusty, °abusive, °virulent, °sarcastic, °sardonic, satiric(al), °vicious, cynical: *You can rely on Henry for a tart rebuff every time.*

tart[2] *n.* **1** pie, tartlet, pastry, °turnover, flan, quiche, patty, *Brit* pasty: *Three guesses who stole the tarts from the Queen of Hearts.* **2** strumpet, streetwalker, °prostitute, whore, harlot, fallen woman, trollop, °wanton, working girl, *fille de joie*, call-girl, °loose woman, slut, drab, °jade, demi-mondaine, courtesan, woman of ill repute, hussy, doxy, lady of the evening *or* the night, woman of easy virtue, *Slang* floozie *or* floozy *or* floosie, hooker, *US* chippy, roundheels, bimbo: *The paper claimed that the minister was involved with a woman that it described as 'a tart'.*

task *n.* **1** °duty, °assignment, °business, °job, °charge, °stint, °mission, °work, chore, °undertaking: *It will be your task to keep the others working.* **2** (major) °effort, °test (of strength), piece of °work, °struggle, °strain: *Getting him to do anything at all was quite a task.* **3** ***take to task***: °scold, °reprimand, call to °account, °blame, censure, recriminate, reproach, °reprove, °rebuke, °criticize, °lecture, °upbraid, chide, reprehend: *I was taken to task for failing to notify the police of the break-in.*

taste *n.* **1** °drop, soupçon, °dash, °pinch, °touch, °hint, °suggestion, °grain, °trace, °bit; °flavour, °savour, °relish, °tang: *I added just the tiniest taste of coriander to the sauce.* **2** °sample, °morsel, °bite, °mouthful, °bite, °sip, °nip, °swallow: *I had a taste of the sauce and it's superb.* **3** palate, °desire, °inclination, °leaning, °partiality, °disposition, °penchant, °liking, °fancy, °preference, fondness, °appetite, °relish, stomach, °tolerance: *She developed a taste for caviare and champagne while working in television.* **4** discernment, °discrimination, °perception, °judgement, cultivation, °refinement, stylishness, °grace, °polish, °elegance: *Her unerring taste leads her to select only the best.* **5** °style, °mode, °fashion, °manner, °form, °design, °motif: *The room was decorated in Moorish taste.* **6** °decorum, °discretion, tactfulness, °delicacy, °refinement, politesse, politeness, correctness, °propriety, tastefulness: *Evan's taste would never allow him to say anything rude.*
—*v.* **7** °savour, °sample, °examine, °try, °test: *Taste this and see if it's too salty.* **8** °experience, °sample, °know, have knowledge of, °undergo, °encounter, °meet (with), come up against: *As a young man he had tasted the pleasures of Paris.*

tasteful *adj.* in good °taste, °decorous, °refined, finished, °tactful, °polite, °polished, restrained, °correct, °harmonious, °fitting, °fit, °proper, °discriminating, °aesthetic, discriminative, °fastidious, °cultivated, *comme il faut*, °elegant, °graceful, charming: *Though a bit shabby, her clothes were demure and tasteful.*

tasteless *adj.* **1** in bad *or* poor °taste, °garish, °gaudy, °loud, °tawdry, meretricious, °cheap, °flashy, °unrefined, inelegant, unaesthetic; °improper, °wrong, indecorous, indelicate, uncultivated, uncouth, uncultured, gauche, °boorish, maladroit, °distasteful, °unsavoury, °coarse, °crude, °gross, °vulgar, °base, °low: *That is the most tasteless dress I have ever seen. He made a tasteless remark about her table manners.* **2** insipid, °bland, °dull, °flat, °watery, °vapid, flavourless, °unsavoury, *Colloq* °wishy-washy: *The tea served there is completely tasteless.*

tasty *adj.* °delicious, delectable, °luscious, flavorous, flavoursome, flavourful, °savoury, toothsome, palatable, appetizing, sapid, mouth-watering, ambrosial, *Colloq* °yummy, scrumptious: *They serve a very tasty curry at that Indian restaurant.*

tatter *n.* **1** Often, ***tatters***: °scrap(s), °rag(s), °shred(s), °bit(s), °piece(s): *Tatters from the culprit's clothing were found on a thorn-bush.* **2** ***in tatters***: in °ruins, in °shreds, destroyed, ruined, shattered, in disarray, demolished: *My life has been in tatters ever since she left me.*

tattered *adj.* °ragged, torn, shredded, °rent, °threadbare: *Above the altar in the chapel hang the tattered standards of the regiment, dating from the Crimean War.*

tattle *v.* **1** °blab, °tell, °reveal *or* divulge, °give away secrets, *Slang* squeal: *Though sworn to silence, Davis tattled.* **2** °gossip, °prattle, prate, °babble, °chatter, °jabber, blather *or* blether, *Brit* natter, witter, *Slang* ya(c)k: *The old crones were tattling away in the kitchen.*

taunt *v.* **1** °tease, °jeer (at), °flout, °twit, °mock, °torment, °annoy, make °fun *or* °sport of, °poke °fun at, °deride, °sneer (at), °scoff (at), °insult, °ridicule, °burlesque, °lampoon, *US* °ride, *Colloq* kid, rib, roast, °put down, *Brit* °guy, *Slang* °bug, °rag, hassle, *US* get on (someone's) case: *The boys used to taunt him, calling him 'Shrimpo' because he was so short.*
—*n.* **2** °jeer, °gibe, brickbat, °insult, °scoff, °derision, °sneer, °slap (in the face), raspberry, *Colloq* °dig, *US* Bronx cheer: *At 17, he was six feet tall and no longer had to tolerate his classmates' taunts.*

taut *adj.* **1** °tight, °tense, °strained, stretched, °rigid, °stiff: *When his jaw goes taut like that I know he's angry.* **2** *Nautical* neat, °tidy, Bristol fashion, °shipshape, °spruce, (in) °trim, °smart, °orderly, well-organized; well-disciplined: *Captain Scriven runs a taut ship, no doubt about it.*

tautology *n.* °repetition, redundancy, battology, pleonasm, iteration, tautologism; repetitiousness, repetitiveness, wordiness, prolixity, verbiage, verbosity, long-windedness: *Clichés like 'null and void' and 'cease and desist' are tautologies. Tautology, when called 'repetition', is often used for rhetorical effect.*

tawdry *adj.* °gaudy, °cheap, °flashy, brummagem, °showy, meretricious, °garish, °loud, tatty, tinsel, tinselly, °plastic, °tinny, °shabby, *US* °tacky, *Colloq* cheapjack: *She was wearing a tawdry outfit picked up at a church jumble sale.*

tax *n.* **1** levy, impost, °duty, °tariff, assessment, °tribute, °toll, excise, customs, °charge, contribution, *Archaic* scot, tithe, *Brit* octroi, cess, °rate(s), °dues: *Most people try to pay the lowest taxes they can get away with.* **2** onus, °burden, °weight, °load, °encumbrance, °strain, °pressure: *The admission of fifty new children put a heavy tax on the school's resources.*
—*v.* **3** assess, °exact, °demand, °charge, °impose *or* levy a tax (on), *Archaic* tithe: *If the government doesn't tax citizens, where will the money come from?* **4** °burden, °strain, put a °strain on, °try; °load, °overload, °stretch, °exhaust; °encumber, °weigh down,

saddle, *Brit* pressurize, *US* °pressure: *This misbehaviour is really taxing my patience. Our meagre resources were taxed to the limit. Mother was taxed with the responsibility of caring for us.*

taxi *n.* **1** taxi-cab, °cab, hackney, *Colloq* hack: *Please hurry, as I have a taxi waiting.*
—*v.* **2** °drive, °ride (on the ground): *After landing, the plane taxied to the gate.*

teach *v.* °instruct (in), °inform (about), °communicate (to), °educate, °guide, °train, °tutor, °coach, °enlighten, edify, °indoctrinate, inculcate, °instil, °school in, °demonstrate, °show, °familiarize *or* °acquaint with, give lessons (in) (to); °drill, °discipline: *She is qualified to teach chemistry. Captain Ross taught many youngsters to sail. She wants to teach when she completes her training.*

teacher *n.* °schoolteacher, educator, °instructor, professor, °doctor, °tutor, °fellow, lecturer, °master, °mistress, schoolmaster, schoolmistress, °coach, trainer, °guide, mentor, guru, cicerone, °counsellor, advisor; educationist; *Brit* don, *Scots* dominie, *US* docent, *Colloq* schoolma'm: *One can be counted extremely lucky to have inspiring teachers.*

team *n.* **1** °side, line-up, °group, °band, °gang, °body, °crew, °party, troupe: *Which team does Lineker play for?* **2** °pair, yoke, °span, duo, °set, °rig, tandem: *They hitched a fresh team of horses to the coach and we were soon back on the road.*
—*v.* **3** Often, ***team up***: °join (up *or* together), °band *or* °get *or* work together, °unite, °combine, °link (up), °cooperate, °collaborate; conspire: *If we team up, we'll get the job done better and in half the time.*

tear *v.* **1** °rip, °rend, rive, °rupture, °pull °apart, °shred, °mutilate, °mangle, °claw, °split, °divide, °separate, °sever: *The tiger is tearing its quarry to shreds. He tore the contract in half and stormed out.* **2** °pull, °snatch, °wrench: *The force of the blast tore the attaché case from my grasp. The child was torn from her mother's arms by the soldier.* **3** °dash, °fly, °run, gallop, °race, sprint, °rush, scoot, °shoot, °speed, °bolt, dart, °flit, °scurry, scuttle, °career, zoom, °hurry, °hasten, *Colloq* zip: *He is tearing around trying to find the money to cover his loan.*
—*n.* **4** °rip, °rent, °rupture, °hole, °split, °slash, °gore, °cut, °score, °slit, °gash, fissure, °rift, laceration: *Nobody will see the tear in your trousers if you remain seated.*

tearful *adj.* weeping, crying, in tears, sobbing, whimpering, dewy-eyed, blubbering, snivelling, lachrymose, *Colloq* weepy: *She was tearful as she told him they could not meet again.*

tease *v.* **1** bait, °taunt, °torment, °harass, bedevil, °bother, nettle, °plague, °chaff, °pester, °annoy, °irritate, needle, goad, badger, °provoke, vex, °twit, °tantalize, °frustrate, *Non-Standard* °aggravate, *Colloq* °guy, °pick on, rib, drive mad *or* crazy, drive up the °wall, *Brit* take the mickey out of, *Slang* °rag: *Stop teasing the animals! Frances would tease me by agreeing to go out and then begging off with a headache.* **2** °coax, °worry, winkle, °work, °manipulate: *He was finally able to tease the broken piece of key out of the lock.*

technical *adj.* **1** complex, °complicated, °detailed, °intricate, specialized: *This is a technical matter, not easily understood by the layman.* **2** °mechanical, applied, industrial, polytechnic, technologic(al): *We thought he would be happier attending a technical school.*

technique *n.* **1** technic, °method, °approach, °manner, °mode, °fashion, °style, °procedure, °system, °tack, °line, modus operandi, standard operating °procedure, *Colloq* MO (= 'modus operandi'), SOP (= 'standard operating procedure'): *After many years, he has developed his own technique for building hot-air balloons.* **2** technic, °art, craftsmanship, artistry, °craft, °knack, °touch, °skill, skilfulness, adroitness, adeptness, dexterousness, °facility, competence, °faculty, °ability, °aptitude, °performance, °proficiency, °talent, °gift, °genius, know-how, °knowledge, °expertise: *Jason's technique remains unsurpassed.*

tedious *adj.* over-long, long-drawn-out, prolonged, °endless, unending, °monotonous, unchanging, °changeless, unvarying, °laborious, long-winded, wearing, wearying, wearisome, tiring, °exhausting, fatiguing, °tiresome, °boring, °dreary, °dull, dry-as-dust, °drab, °colourless, °vapid, insipid, °flat, uninteresting, °banal, unexciting, °prosaic, prosy, soporific, °humdrum, °routine, °repetitious, °repetitive, °mechanical, automaton-like, °automatic, *Colloq* ho-hum, *Slang* °dead, *US* blah: *For almost fifty years my father had a tedious job on an assembly line.*

tedium *n.* tediousness, monotony, changelessness, invariability, long-windedness, wearisomeness, tiresomeness, °boredom, ennui, dreariness, dullness, drabness, colourlessness, vapidity, insipidity, insipidness, two-dimensionality, banality, °routine, repetitiousness: *How do you survive the tedium of getting up and going to an office every day?*

teem[1] *v.* Usually ***teem with***: °proliferate (with), be °prolific (with), °abound, be °abundant, °swarm (with), be °alive (with), °crawl (with), °bristle (with), overflow (with), °overrun (with), be °full (of), °brim (with): *When the panel was removed, the entire foundation was seen to be teeming with termites.*

teem[2] *v.* °pour, °rain, °stream (down), *Colloq* come down (in buckets *or* by the bucketful), °bucket down, °rain *or* °pour cats and dogs: *It teemed with rain continuously when we were on holiday.*

teenager *n.* °adolescent, °youth, °boy, °girl, °young °man, °young lady, °juvenile, °minor, *Colloq* kid: *The town ought to provide a place where teenagers can get together.*

teeter *v.* °balance, wobble, °rock, °sway, °totter, waver, °tremble, °stagger: *She screamed when she saw Bruce teetering on the edge of the precipice.*

telegram *n.* °cable, cablegram, radiogram, radio-telegram, wire, telex, (*In France*) *bleu, pneu, Brit trade mark* Telemessage, *US trade mark* Mailgram: *She received a telegram from him, saying that he would be arriving on Monday.*

telephone *n.* **1** handset, phone, *Colloq* blower, *Chiefly US* horn: *Mr Fraser, the Managing Director is on the telephone for you.*
—*v.* **2** phone, °ring (up), °call (up), give (someone) a °ring *or* a °call, *Colloq* get (someone) on the blower *or chiefly US* the horn, give (someone) a tinkle *or* a °buzz, °buzz: *Telephone when you have a chance.*

telescope *n.* **1** spyglass, *Old-fashioned* °glass; refracting telescope, reflecting telescope, radio telescope: *Through the telescope, he could just discern the American coastline.*
—*v.* **2** °shorten, compress, °abbreviate, °curtail, condense, summarize, °précis, °digest, °tighten (up), °boil down, °abridge, truncate, °abstract: *Telescope the report into two columns for page 2.* **3** concertina, squash, °crush: *The first three carriages of the train were telescoped in the crash.*

television *n.* TV, video (receiver), small °screen, *Colloq* box, idiot box, *Brit* telly, *US* boob tube, *Slang* tube, *Brit* goggle-box: *My television was not working over the weekend.*

tell[1] *v.* **1** °relate, °narrate, °recount, °recite: *Tell me a story.* **2** Sometimes, ***tell of***: °say, °mention, °hint at, °refer to, °touch on, utter, °state, °declare, °proclaim, °announce, °publish, °broadcast, °communicate, °make known, °report, °impart, °indicate, °release, °break, let (something) be known, advertise, trumpet, herald, bring to °light, °disclose, divulge, °intimate, °leak, °admit, °betray, °acknowledge, °confess, disbosom oneself, get (something) off (one's) chest, unburden *or* disburden (oneself), °blab, °tattle, *Colloq* °talk, °let the cat out of the bag, °spill the beans, °let out, °let °slip, blow the whistle on, °give away the (whole) show, *US* pull the plug on, *Slang* squeal, squeak, rat, peach, *US* spill (one's) guts: *She told of her fears. He refuses to tell where the money is hidden. She* *talked a lot but told very little.* **3** apprise, °advise, °inform, let (someone) know, °notify, °acquaint (someone) with (something): *He has told me everything. Tell them that I shall be late. He told them nothing of his illness.* **4** °recount, °describe, delineate, °outline, °portray, depict, °express, °put, °word, °explain: *I am not sure how to tell you this.* **5** °order, °command, °require, °demand (that), °charge, °direct, °dictate (that), °instruct, °bid: *Tell them I want no visitors today. She told him to go.* **6** carry °weight, be °influential, be °effective, have (an) °effect: *What we accomplished here today is bound to tell in our favour.* **7** °determine, °say, °confirm, aver, assert, asseverate, °swear, take an °oath, be °sure *or* °certain *or* °positive, °know (for °sure *or* for °certain): *It just shows you never can tell.* **8** ascertain, °determine, °perceive, °understand, °make out, discern, °identify, °recognize, °distinguish, °discriminate, °differentiate: *I cannot tell if that is George or not. I can't tell George from John in this photograph.* **9** °predict, °prophesy, °forecast, foretell, °foresee, °determine, ascertain, °know: *Who can tell what tomorrow will bring?* **10** ***tell off***: °scold, °reprimand, °berate, chide, °castigate, censure, take to °task, °rebuke, °lecture, reproach, °reprove, *Colloq* give (someone) a °tongue-lashing, rake *or* haul (someone) over the coals, give (someone) a °piece of (one's) mind, tick off, *Slang* tear a strip off, *US* °chew out: *He was told off for being late for dinner again.* **11** ***tell on***: °tattle on, °blab about, *Brit* °grass on: *Charlotte never forgave Tim for telling on her to Aunt Jane.*

tell[2] *n.* tumulus, °mound, barrow, hillock: *Excavation of the tell exposed ancient skeletons.*

telling *adj.* **1** °effective, °effectual, °influential, °weighty, °important, °powerful, °forceful, °potent, °significant, °considerable, °striking: *The new colour scheme in the office has had a telling effect on morale.* —*n.* **2** tattling, (too) revealing, *Colloq* letting the cat out of the bag, giving away the whole show: *I cannot say why her key was found in his pocket—that would be telling.*

temper *n.* **1** °mood, °disposition, temperament, °humour, °state *or* °frame of mind, °character, °personality, °nature, °make-up, constitution: *Practising law did not suit his temper, so he became a social worker.* **2** composure, °self-control, self-possession, calmness, equanimity, °balance, °sang-froid, coolness, *Colloq* °cool: *He would lose his temper if she ever mentioned another man.* **3** °ill °humour, °ill temper, °foul temper, irascibility, irritability, petulance, volatility, peevishness, huffishness, surliness, churlishness, hotheadedness, hot-bloodedness: *At the first sign of temper, just ignore him.* **4** (temper) °tantrum, °fury, °fit (of pique), °rage, °passion, *Colloq Brit* wax, °paddy: *She went off into a temper at the mere mention of his name.* —*v.* **5** °modify, °moderate, assuage, mollify, °soften, °cushion, °tone down, allay, soothe, °mitigate, palliate, °reduce, °relax, slacken, °lighten, appease: *The cold currents from the poles are tempered by the equatorial waters. She used all her wiles to temper his fury.* **6** anneal, toughen, °strengthen, °harden: *Plunge the heated blade into water to temper it.*

temperamental *adj.* **1** °moody, °sensitive, °touchy, hypersensitive, °volatile, irascible, °irritable, °petulant, °testy, °short-tempered, hot-tempered, °hotheaded, hot-blooded, °excitable, °explosive, on a short fuse, °capricious, °impatient, bad-humoured, °curt, °brusque, °short, °gruff, °bluff, curmudgeonly, °waspish, °snappish, °peevish, crabby, crabbed, grumpy, huffish, huffy, crotchety, *US* °cranky, *Colloq* grouchy: *He's not usually temperamental—must be something he ate.* **2** °erratic, uneven, °unreliable, °inconsistent, undependable, unpredictable: *That car of mine is getting temperamental in its old age.*

temperance *n.* **1** (self-)°restraint, moderation, (self-) °control, forbearance, (self-)°discipline, continence: *Temperance is one of the four cardinal virtues, alongside justice, prudence, and fortitude.* **2** abstemiousness, teetotalism, abstinence, °sobriety, Rechabitism; °prohibition: *We have always preached temperance to our children.*

temperate *adj.* **1** °moderate, °reasonable, (self-) restrained, disciplined, controlled, forbearing, °sensible, °sane, °rational, not excessive, composed, °steady, °stable, even-tempered, °equable, °sober, sober-sided, sober-minded, °mild, °dispassionate, unimpassioned, °cool, cool-headed, unexcited, °calm, unruffled, °tranquil, imperturbable, unperturbed, °self-possessed, °quiet, °serene: *Even the most temperate of women would lose her cool when dealing with a man like that.* **2** abstemious, teetotal, abstinent, continent, °moderate, °sober; °chaste, °celibate, austere, ascetic, self-denying, puritanical: *Those who lead temperate lives seem to live no longer than those who yield to dissipation.*

tempest *n.* **1** °storm, wind-storm, hailstorm, rainstorm, °hurricane, typhoon, tornado, cyclone, squall, thunderstorm: *The Red Spot on Jupiter is the centre of a perpetual, violent tempest.* **2** °storm, commotion, °disturbance, °upheaval, disruption, °furore *or US* furor, turbulence, °ferment, °tumult, °agitation, perturbation, hurly-burly, °disorder, outbreak, °unrest, °riot, °chaos, °uproar, brouhaha, *Colloq* hoo-ha: *After the tempest of protest died down, a vote was taken and saner heads prevailed.*

tempestuous *adj.* °stormy, °wild, °uncontrolled, uncontrollable, disrupting, disruptive, turbulent, °tumultuous, °riotous, °chaotic, °uproarious, °boisterous, °frantic, frenzied, frenetic, °furious, wrathful, vehement, °fiery, °impassioned, °fierce: *They had a tempestuous relationship, and did not live together for very long.*

template *n.* templet, °pattern, °mould, °guide, °model, °die: *The work on the lathe is matched to the template.*

temple *n.* place *or* house of °worship, °holy place, house of God, church, synagogue, mosque, pagoda, cathedral, °sanctuary, chapel, shrine, *Yiddish* shul *or* schul: *Temples to gods are found throughout the world.*

tempo *n.* °cadence, °rhythm, °beat, °time, °pulse, metre, °measure; °pace, °speed, °rate: *The melody should be played in waltz tempo. Living in the country, Tom is unaccustomed to the tempo of big-city life.*

temporal *adj.* **1** °earthly, °terrestrial, terrene, mundane, °worldly, non-spiritual, non-clerical, °lay, laic(al), °secular, non-religious, non-ecclesiastic(al), °material, °civil, °profane, fleshly, °mortal: *He believed that his temporal miseries would be compensated for by an eternity in the seventh heaven.* **2** See **temporary,** below.

temporarily *adv.* **1** for the °time being, in the interim, *pro tempore*, pro tem, in *or* for the °meantime *or* the °meanwhile, for °now: *Mr Peters is temporarily out of the office, and will contact you on his return.* **2** °briefly, fleetingly, for a (°short *or* °little) while *or* °time, for the °moment: *Your size is temporarily out of stock, madam.*

temporary *adj.* impermanent, °makeshift, °stopgap, °stand-by, °provisional; *pro tempore*, pro tem, transitory, °transient, °fleeting, °fugitive, °passing, ephemeral, °temporal, evanescent, °short-lived, °momentary: *I suppose it will have to do as a temporary substitute.*

tempt *v.* **1** °attract, °entice, °lure, allure, °draw (in), invite, °lead on, °whet (one's) appetite, °seduce, °captivate, °persuade, °coax, °cajole: *They had a special offer to tempt new customers.* **2** °lead, °induce, °persuade, °prompt, °move, °incline, °dispose: *I would be tempted to resign if they treated me that way.* **3** °provoke, °dare, (put to the) °test: *I shouldn't tempt Providence if I were you.*

temptation *n.* **1** °tempting, enticing, leading on, seducing, captivating, persuading, coaxing, cajoling: *The temptation by advertisers never stops, does it?* **2** °enticement, seduction, captivation, °persuasion, allurement, °invitation, °attraction, °draw, °lure, °inducement, °snare, *Colloq* °pull, °come-on: *I could never resist a temptation like that.*

tempting *adj.* **1** °seductive, enticing, °inviting, alluring, captivating, °attractive, tantalizing, appealing, °irresistible, titillating; °fetching, winsome, °prepossessing, °ravishing, °voluptuous, °sensuous, *Colloq* °sexy, *US* °foxy: *They made her a very tempting offer which she found hard to refuse. He was continually distracted by thoughts of tempting young girls.* **2** appetizing, mouth-watering, °delicious, °savoury, delectable, °succulent, °luscious, toothsome: *Why does food always look most tempting when I am on a diet?*

temptress *n.* °seductress, vamp, °siren, *femme fatale*, coquette, °flirt, enchantress, sorceress, Circe, *Slang* sexpot, man-eater, *US* °foxy lady, fox, mantrap: *You warned me against that temptress because you wanted her for yourself.*

tenable *adj.* defensible, °supportable, justifiable, maintainable, workable, °viable, defendable, °plausible, °reasonable, °rational, arguable, believable, credible, creditable, imaginable, conceivable, °possible: *Copernicus showed that Ptolemaic cosmology was no longer tenable.*

tenacious *adj.* **1** °persistent, dogged, unfaltering, pertinacious, unswerving, °determined, °diligent, °resolute, °staunch, °stalwart, °steadfast, °strong, °sturdy, unwavering, strong-willed, °strong-minded, unshaken, unshakeable *or* unshakable, °obstinate, intransigent, °stubborn, adamant, obdurate, refractory, °immovable, °inflexible, °rigid, °firm, unyielding, uncompromising: *Despite his age, Christopher maintains a tenacious grip on reality.* **2** cohesive, °strong, °tough; adhesive, °sticky, clinging; gummy, gluey, mucilaginous, glutinous, viscous, viscid: *The bricks are then smeared over with a tenacious mud, which dries hard.* **3** Often, ***tenacious of***: clinging (to), °grasping, maintaining, keeping (up), staying with, retentive (of), persisting *or* °persistent (in), retaining: *She is tenacious of the old ways of doing things.* **4** retentive, °good: *Aunt Agatha has a very tenacious memory.*

tenacity *n.* **1** tenaciousness, °persistence, doggedness, °perseverance, pertinacity, °determination, °grit, diligence, resoluteness, °resolution, purposefulness, °resolve, staunchness, steadfastness, °stamina, assiduity, sedulousness, °strength, strong-mindedness, unshakeability *or* unshakability, °obstinacy, intransigence, stubbornness, obduracy, inflexibility, rigidity, firmness, uncompromisingness, *Colloq US* sand, stick-to-it-iveness: *He persisted with the tenacity of the English bulldog.* **2** tenaciousness, cohesiveness, °strength, °power, toughness, °resilience; adhesiveness, stickiness, gumminess, glueyness, mucilaginousness, glutinousness, viscousness, viscidity, *US* °cling: *The texture of the surfaces affects the tenacity of the bonding cement.*

tenancy *n.* occupancy, °occupation, °possession, °tenure: *Our tenancy of the house expires next month. The tenancy of this position is a year.*

tenant *n.* °occupant, lessee, renter, leaseholder, occupier, °resident, °inhabitant: *We could not redecorate the premises while the tenants were there.*

tend[1] *v.* be °inclined *or* °disposed, be °liable *or* apt *or* °likely, °incline, °lean, have *or* show *or* exhibit *or* demonstrate a °tendency, °favour, °verge, gravitate, be °biased; be °prone: *The judge might tend towards leniency in your case. I tend to agree. Tree growth here tends towards the horizontal.*

tend[2] *v.* °care for, take °care of, °look after, °look out for, °watch over, °see to, keep an °eye on, °attend (to), °wait on, °cater to, °minister to, °serve, °nurse, nurture: *Marie tended her father lovingly throughout his long illness.*

tendency *n.* °inclination, °bent, °leaning, °disposition, propensity, predisposition, proclivity, predilection, susceptibility, proneness, °readiness, °partiality, °affinity, °bias, °drift, °direction, °trend, °movement: *Brian has always had a tendency to be overweight. The particles exhibit a tendency to align themselves north and south.*

tender[1] *adj.* **1** °sensitive, °delicate, °fragile, °frail, °infirm, °unstable, °shaky, °weak, °feeble, unwell, °sickly, ailing, °unsound: *His condition is still a bit too tender for him to go outside.* **2** chewable, °edible, eatable, °soft: *The steak will become more tender if it is marinated.* **3** °young, youthful, °immature, °juvenile, °inexperienced, °impressionable, °vulnerable, °green, °new, °raw, °undeveloped, untrained, uninitiated, °callow: *At his tender age he could not have known about such things.* **4** °sensitive, °touchy, °ticklish, °dangerous, °troublesome, °provocative, °difficult, °tricky: *Please avoid mentioning the wedding, it's a tender subject around here.* **5** °gentle, °soft, °delicate, °light, °sensitive, °soothing: *Oh, how he yearned for her tender touch at his fevered brow.* **6** °kind, kind-hearted, loving, °affectionate, °fond, °gentle, °mild, compassionate, °considerate, humane, °benevolent, °sympathetic, °feeling, °thoughtful, °soft-hearted, °warm, caring, °merciful, °solicitous, tender-hearted, warm-hearted, °good-natured: *Wounded and helpless, he succumbed to the tender care of the nurses.* **7** °touching, °emotional, °moving, °stirring, soul-stirring, °heart-rending, °heartfelt, °passionate, °impassioned, impassionate, °poignant, °sentimental, mawkish, °maudlin: *Who could forget the tender scene as Cedric bade farewell to his mother and went off to war?* **8** °sore, °raw, °painful, °sensitive, °inflamed; smarting, °burning, hurting, aching, °agonizing: *This spot, right here, is so tender that it hurts just to think about it.* **9** loving, °affectionate, amatory, amorous, adoring, °romantic: *They exchanged tender, knowing looks.*

tender[2] *v.* **1** °offer, proffer, °present, °propose, °put forward, °extend, °hold out, °submit, °advance, °put up, °set before: *Donald tendered his resignation yesterday. She has tendered the committee an excellent proposal.*

—*n.* **2** °offer, °bid, °presentation, °proposal, °proposition: *The city is accepting tenders for the construction of a new bridge.* **3** currency, °money, specie, (bank) °notes, °cash, °bills; °payment, compensation: *Pound notes are no longer legal tender in England and Wales.*

tender[3] *n.* **1** dinghy, gig, skiff, °launch, °boat, row-boat *or* rowing-boat, jolly-boat: *The yacht moved easily through the water towing a tender.* **2** wagon *or Brit* waggon, °truck, °vehicle: *The tender of Felix's toy train was filled with sweets for his birthday.*

tenet *n.* °belief, credo, °creed, article of °faith, °ideology, °precept, °conviction, °principle, dogma, °idea, °opinion, °position, °view, °viewpoint, °maxim, axiom, canon, teaching, °doctrine: *They accept the Golden Rule as a fundamental tenet of their organization.*

tenor *n.* °drift, °tone, °spirit, °essence, °character, °gist, °bias, °import, °substance, °effect, °significance, °meaning, °sense, connotation, °theme, °thread, °implication, °inference, °intent, °purpose, °tendency, purport, °direction: *The general tenor of Mark's letters was unfriendly.*

tense *adj.* **1** °taut, °strained, °stiff, under °tension, °rigid: *One could see how tense the muscles were under the skin.* **2** °intense, °nervous, °anxious, under (a) °strain, highly-strung, high-strung, °strained, on °edge, wrought up, keyed up, worked up, °taut, on tenterhooks, apprehensive, distressed, °upset, °disturbed, °worried, edgy, on pins and needles, °jumpy, fidgety, °overwrought, *Colloq* wound up, jittery, having a case of the °jitters, *Brit* strung up, *US* strung out, *Slang* uptight, *US* antsy: *Try to relax and not be so tense.* **3** °nervous, °anxious, worrying, worrisome, distressing, °disturbing, stressful, °nerve-racking *or* nerve-wracking, °fraught, disquieting: *Those were tense moments while we waited for the winner's name to be posted.*

—*v.* **4** °tighten, °stretch, °strain, tauten, °tension: *The mast will be secure once the stays have been tensed.*

tension *n.* **1** °stress, tightness, tautness, °strain, °pull, °traction, °pressure, tenseness, °force: *Can this cable withstand so much tension?* **2** nervousness, °anxiety, anxiousness, °strain, edginess, apprehension, °suspense, tautness, °distress, °upset, °worry, jumpiness, fidgetiness, *Colloq* jitteriness, (a case of) the °jitters: *I could feel the tension building among the audience.*

tentative *adj.* **1** °experimental, °speculative, exploratory, probative, °trial, °provisional: *We have tentative plans for introducing a new work methodology.* **2** unsure, °hesitant, °uncertain, °indecisive, °cautious, °timid, °shy, diffident, uneasy, apprehensive: *The child gave him a tentative smile, not knowing what to expect.*

tenuous *adj.* **1** °thin, °slender, °fine, attenuated, °delicate, gossamer, diaphanous, °fragile: *The spider descended slowly on its tenuous thread.* **2** °flimsy, °insubstantial *or* unsubstantial, °paltry, °weak, °feeble, °frail, °meagre, °vague, °negligible, °insignificant, °trifling, °sketchy, °hazy, °nebulous, dubious, °doubtful, °shaky: *Your case rests on very tenuous evidence.*

tenure *n.* **1** °possession, holding, occupancy, incumbency, tenantry, °tenancy, °occupation, residency, °residence: *The laws on tenure are extremely complicated.* **2** (job) °security, °permanence, permanency: *After five years he was automatically guaranteed tenure.*

tepid *adj.* **1** °lukewarm, warmish: *The gelatine should be tepid before refrigerating it.* **2** °lukewarm, °unenthusiastic, °cool, °indifferent, apathetic, uninterested, unconcerned, °nonchalant, uncaring, °neutral, °blasé: *How can he remain tepid on an issue like apartheid?*

term *n.* **1** °name, °title, designation, appellation; °word, °expression, locution, °phrase: *The term for that is* venturi tube. Habeas corpus *is a term of art in law.* **2** semester; °time, °period (of °time), °interval, °length of °time, °span (of °time), duration, °spell, °stretch, while: *During the summer term we played cricket every Saturday. He was sentenced to a long term of imprisonment.* **3** sitting, °stint, °session, °course; incumbency, °administration: *During their latest term of office, interest rates were raised twice.* **4** Often, ***terms***: °condition(s), °provision(s), article(s), clause(s), °proviso(s); °stipulation(s), °qualification(s), assumption(s): *According to the terms of the will, proceeds from the patent go into a trust fund.* **5** ***come to terms***: °agree, come to *or* reach an °agreement *or* an °arrangement *or* an °understanding, °reconcile, °arrange, °settle, compromise: *Can we come to terms on the price? He will simply have to come to terms with his conscience.* **6** ***in terms of***: °concerning, °regarding, as regards, with °regard to, in °relation to, °relative to, relating to, in the °matter of: *The psychiatrist offered little in terms of direct solutions to my problems.* **7** ***terms***: **a** °payment, °schedule, rates: *What terms have they offered to settle the debt?* **b** °standing, °position, °basis, °relationship, relations, °footing: *I always thought you two were on good terms.*
—*v.* **8** °call, °name, °label, °designate, denominate, °entitle, °title, °style, dub; °nickname: *Abraham Lincoln was termed, among other things, 'The Great Emancipator'.*

terminal *adj.* **1** closing, concluding, terminating, ending, °final, °ultimate, °extreme; °maximum, greatest: *Spencer wrote that the human being is at once the terminal problem of biology and the initial factor of sociology.* **2** °deadly, °mortal, °fatal, °lethal, °incurable: *The cancer was diagnosed as terminal.*
—*n.* **3** terminus, (terminal) °station, °end of the line, depot: *We arrived at the air terminal with five minutes to catch our plane.* **4** keyboard, °monitor, °position, °station, VDU (= 'visual display unit'), PC (= 'personal computer'), module, CRT (= 'cathode ray tube'), °screen, (control) panel: *The computer system supported a terminal for each member of the team.* **5** °connection, wire, connector, coupler, coupling, conductor: *Do I attach the red cable to the positive or the negative terminal?*

terminate *v.* °stop, °end, come to an °end, °finish; put an °end to, °cease, conclude, °discontinue, °drop, abort, bring to an °end *or* a °close, °wind up *or* down, °sign off, °cut off: *The railway line once terminated at the port. They said they wanted to terminate the contract.*

termination *n.* **1** °end, ending, °stop, stopping, stoppage, ceasing, cessation, discontinuation, abortion, *Colloq* wind-up, winding up, °close, °finish, finishing, conclusion: *The rights revert to us at the termination of the agreement. Because of her condition, termination of the pregnancy was recommended.* **2** °suffix, desinence, ending: *The English termination* -ly *usually denotes an adverb but is occasionally adjectival, as in* sickly.

terminology *n.* nomenclature, vocabulary, °language, words, locutions, °wording, terms, phraseology, phrasing, °jargon, shop-talk, argot, °cant, *Colloq* °lingo: *Medical terminology requires specialized dictionaries.*

terrain *n.* topography, °landscape, °ground, °territory: *These vehicles are specially designed for rough terrain.*

terrestrial *adj.* **1** °earthly, earthbound, °worldly, terrene, tellurian *or* telluric, °global, sublunary, subastral; mundane: *He insists that we tackle our terrestrial problems before spending a fortune on space travel.*
—*n.* **2** earth-man, earth-woman, earth-person, earthling, °mortal, °human: *My experiences are beyond the imaginations of you mere terrestrials.*

terrible *adj.* **1** °bad, °serious, °grave, °severe, °acute, distressing, °disagreeable, °nasty, °foul, °unbearable, °dreadful, °loathsome, °hideous, °vile, intolerable, °awful, *Colloq* °rotten, °lousy, °beastly: *I've had a terrible virus.* **2** °bad, °remorseful, °regretful, rueful, °sorry, contrite, °ashamed, conscience-stricken, °guilty, distressed, °dreadful, °awful, *Colloq* °rotten, °lousy, °beastly: *I felt terrible having to tell the neighbours about their cat.* **3** °unhappy, unpleasant, °disagreeable, °awful, °miserable, °joyless, °wretched, °unfortunate, *Colloq* °rotten, °lousy, °beastly: *We spent an absolutely terrible evening at the theatre.* **4** °gruesome, °grisly, °macabre, °gory, °grotesque, °brutal, °savage, °horrible, horrendous, °terrifying, °terrific, °harrowing, horrid, horrifying, °ghastly, °frightening, °frightful, unspeakable, °monstrous, °dread, appalling, °shocking, alarming, °awful, °foul: *The casualties that were arriving had the most terrible wounds.* **5** °disgusting, °revolting, nauseating, °nauseous, °offensive, vomit-provoking, °obnoxious, stomach-turning, stomach-churning, °abominable, mephitic, noisome, noxious, °loathsome, °horrible, °hideous, °terrific, °awful, °evil, °vile, °rotten: *The compost heap was giving off the most terrible stench.* **6** °terrifying, °frightening, °frightful, °fearsome, °formidable, redoubtable, °awesome, awe-inspiring, °terrific: *The animal gave a terrible roar and charged into the clearing.*

terribly *adv.* °very, °extremely, °exceedingly, °thoroughly, decidedly, unbelievably, incredibly, monumentally, outrageously, °awfully, fabulously, *Colloq* °frightfully: *They were terribly apologetic about being late. I missed him terribly when he left.*

terrific *adj.* **1** See **terrible, 4, 5, 6,** above. **2** wonderful, °marvellous, °splendid, breathtaking, °extraordinary, °outstanding, °magnificent, °exceptional, °unbelievable, °incredible, mind-boggling, stupendous, °superb, °excellent, first-class, °superior, *Colloq* °great, ace, °fantastic, °fabulous, °sensational, smashing, °super: *They really put on a terrific show.*

terrify *v.* °alarm, °frighten, °scare, terrorize, °shock, make one's flesh crawl *or* creep, °horrify, make one's blood run cold, make one's hair stand on end, °stun, °paralyse, °petrify: *Are you trying to terrify the child with those horror stories?*

terrifying *adj.* alarming, °frightening, °scary, °shocking, horrifying, paralysing, petrifying: *Being chased by a bull is a terrifying experience.*

territory *n.* **1** °area, °region, °district, °neighbourhood, °zone, sector, °tract, °land, °precinct, °quarter, vicinage, °vicinity, purlieu: *Each one of these animals stakes out its own territory and protects it.* **2** °area, bailiwick, °domain, °province, haunts, °patch, *Colloq* stamping-ground, *US* °turf: *Richard would be best advised to stick to his own territory.*

terror *n.* **1** °fright, °dread, °fear, °horror, °panic, °shock, °alarm, °anxiety, °dismay, consternation, intimidation, awe: *They felt a sense of terror when they caught sight of the enemy forces.* **2** °scourge, °demon, °brute, °monster, °fiend, °devil, *US* mad dog: *The gang of teenagers was the terror of the neighbourhood. Her daughter is a little terror.*

terrorist *n.* °subversive, °radical, insurgent, °revolutionary, anarchist, nihilist; bomber, arsonist, incendiary; desperado, gunman, °thug, °felon, °criminal: *The shooting was carried out by a previously unknown gang of terrorists.*

terse *adj.* **1** °concise, °brief, °short, °compact, pithy, °succinct, °summary, laconic, °short and sweet, to the °point, sententious, °crisp, °epigrammatic, aphoristic; distilled, condensed, compendious, °abbreviated, abridged, shortened, concentrated: *He gave a terse account of what had happened.* **2** °abrupt, °curt, °short, °brusque, °blunt, °gruff, °bluff, °ungracious, °petulant, °tart, °rude: *His answer was terse and unhelpful.*

test *n.* **1** °trial, °examination, exam, °proof, °evaluation, assay, °check, check-up, °investigation, °study, °analysis: *My physics test is tomorrow. Have you had a blood test lately?*
—*v.* **2** °try (out), °check (up) (on), °examine, °evaluate, assess, assay, °prove, °probe: *Someone ought to test the water for purity.*

testify *v.* °state, aver, assert, °attest, °swear, °say, affirm, °declare, give °evidence *or* °testimony, bear °witness, avow, °vouchsafe, °proclaim, °announce: *He testified that he saw you there. Is your mother going to testify at the trial? The fingerprints testify to the fact that she was here.*

testimonial *n.* °endorsement, certification, commendation, (letter of) °recommendation, °reference, *Colloq* blurb: *I am happy to write a testimonial for you.*

testimony *n.* °evidence, attestation, affirmation, confirmation, verification, authentication, corroboration, avowal, deposition, °statement, affidavit, °declaration, °assertion, °claim, averral, asseveration, °information: *We have only his testimony that the woman caused the accident.*

testy *adj.* °irritable, bad-tempered, irascible, °short-tempered, °petulant, °touchy, tetchy, °querulous, °peevish, hot-tempered, crusty, °cross, grumpy, grouchy, bearish, crabby, crabbed, °fretful, captious, °waspish, °snappish, °quarrelsome, fractious, contentious, choleric, splenetic, ill-humoured, °disagreeable, ill-tempered, edgy, on °edge, °quick-tempered, crotchety, °cantankerous, *US* °cranky, *Colloq and US and Canadian dialect* ornery: *The old colonel made a few testy remarks about the boys' haircuts. Why make excuses for his being so testy?*

tête-à-tête *n.* **1** (cosy *or* personal) °chat, °dialogue, causerie, pillow °talk, private °talk *or* °word, °parley, °interview, *Colloq* confab, *US* one-on-one: *Will we have time for a brief tête-à-tête after dinner?*
—*adv.* **2** intimately, privately, in °private, °face to face, confidentially, °secretly, *à deux*, in °secret, *Colloq US* one-on-one: *Could we meet tête-à-tête some time?*
—*adj.* **3** °intimate, °private, *intime*, °cosy: *I arranged a little tête-à-tête dinner at my flat.*

tether *n.* **1** °lead, leash, °rope, °cord, fetter, °restraint, halter, °tie, °chain: *The dog had broken loose from its tether and was running around in the yard.*
—*v.* **2** °tie (up *or* down), °restraint, fetter, °chain (up *or* down), leash, °manacle, °secure, °shackle, °fasten, °picket, °stake: *Why don't you tether the goat where the grass is more plentiful?*

text *n.* **1** °wording, words, °content, (°subject-)°matter; printed °matter, (main) °body (text), °contents: *The editor had no right to make changes in the text without consulting the author. The text is in 10-point roman type, the footnotes in 8-point.* **2** °extract, °abstract, °section, °quotation, °part, paragraph, °passage, verse, °line: *What text from the Scripture are we discussing next week?* **3** °subject(-matter), °topic, °theme, °motif, °issue, °focus: *For today's talk I have chosen for my text the problem of alcoholism.* **4** textbook, °school-book, reader, °manual, primer, workbook, exercise °book, *Archaic* hornbook: *Today's science texts are much more advanced than those of twenty years ago.*

texture *n.* °feel, °surface, °character, °grain, features, consistency, °weave; configuration, °nature, °structure, °fabric, constitution, °substance: *The material has a rough texture. The texture of the plot is reinforced by the dialogue.*

thank *v.* **1** express *or* show (one's) °gratitude *or* thanks *or* °appreciation, say thank you *or* thanks, give *or* offer *or* tender thanks: *Don't forget to thank your uncle for the gift, William.* **2** °blame, hold °responsible, °credit, °acknowledge: *You have your mother to thank for the present state of affairs.*
—*n.* **3** ***thanks***: °gratitude, °appreciation, gratefulness, °acknowledgement, °recognition, thanksgiving: *I gave thanks that I was again on dry land.* **4** ***thanks to***: owing to, because of, as a °result of, thanks be given to, in consequence of, as a consequence of, by °reason of, °through, *Sometimes non-standard* °due to: *Thanks to you, I have to commute to work by train.*

thankful *adj.* °grateful, appreciative, °indebted, °pleased, °glad, °obliged, obligated, under °obligation, °beholden to: *I am most thankful that you came, doctor.*

thankless *adj.* unappreciated, unacknowledged, °useless, unrewarding, °fruitless, °unprofitable, profitless, unrequited, °vain, °futile, °bootless: *She always regarded housekeeping as a thankless task.*

thaw *v.* **1** Sometimes, ***thaw out***: °melt, de-ice, liquefy, defrost, °warm (up), °heat (up), unfreeze: *We cannot leave till the river thaws. Why not thaw out the shepherd's pie for dinner?* **2** °soften, °warm, become (more) °cordial *or* °friendly, °relax, °yield, °relent, °bend, unbend, let (oneself) go: *After he got to know some of us better he began to thaw.*

theatre *n.* **1** playhouse, (opera) °house, (music-) °hall, auditorium, amphitheatre, theatre-in-the-round, coliseum, hippodrome, arena (theatre): *A long run in a West End or Broadway theatre is every playwright's dream.* **2** °drama, stagecraft, dramaturgy, melodrama, theatrics, histrionics, staginess, acting, performing, °performance: *Even the way Mary serves dinner is pure theatre.* **3** ***the theatre***: °drama, the °stage, dramaturgy, °dramatic *or* °Thespian *or* histrionic art(s), the boards, show business, *Colloq* showbiz: *The theatre is a risky profession.* **4** °area, arena, °scene, °sphere *or* °place *or* °field of action, °setting: *In which theatre of war did you serve?*

theatrical *adj.* **1** theatric, °dramatic, °stage, histrionic, °Thespian; °repertory: *He joined a theatrical company and his family disowned him.* **2** stagy, overdone, °camp, campy, °melodramatic, °overwrought, exaggerated, °forced, overacted, overacting, °sensational, sensationalistic, °fake, °false, °mannered, °affected, °unnatural, °artificial, °showy, °ostentatious, spectacular, °extravagant, *Colloq* °phoney *or US also* phony, ham *or* hammy, grandstand: *Does Fergus's theatrical behaviour ever embarrass you?*

theft *n.* °robbery, °stealing, pilferage, pilfering, filching, shoplifting, thievery, purloining, °embezzlement, hijacking, larceny, *Colloq* lifting, appropriation, pocketing, pinching, swiping, snitching, *Chiefly Brit* nicking, *US* boosting, *Slang* heist, knocking off, °rip-off: *The theft of the jewellery was reported to the police immediately.*

theme *n.* **1** °subject(-matter), °topic, °idea, °notion, concept, °thesis, °text, °thread, keynote, °gist, °core, °substance, °point, °essence: *What is the central theme of your article?* **2** °essay, °paper, °composition, °review, article, °story, °piece, °exposition, °study, °exercise, °monograph, °tract, °thesis, dissertation, disquisition, treatise: *I have to hand in two themes next week.*

theorem *n.* **1** °hypothesis, °proposition, assumption, conjecture, °thesis, postulate: *He has set forth a clever proof of the binomial theorem.* **2** °statement, dictum, °rule, °deduction, °formula, axiom, °principle: *After a* *lifetime of experience, his theorem is that honesty is the best policy.*

theoretical *adj.* **1** °hypothetical, conjectural, °speculative, untested, unproved, unproven, °moot, putative, °debatable, supposititious, suppositional: *The theoretical trajectory will take it beyond Uranus.* **2** °impractical, °unrealistic, °pure, °ideal, °abstract, °academic: *The suggestion was purely theoretical, since we have no means of carrying it out.*

theorist *n.* theoretician, speculator, hypothecator, hypothesizer, theorizer, philosopher, °dreamer: *Leave guesswork to the theorists: we need hard facts.*

theorize *v.* °guess, hypothesize, conjecture, °speculate: *It is logically illogical to theorize about articles of faith.*

therapeutic *adj.* therapeutical, healing, curative, remedial, restorative, salutary, health-giving, °healthy, °beneficial, corrective, salubrious, medical, °medicinal: *Primitive medicine men knew of the therapeutic powers of these herbs.*

therapist *n.* psychotherapist, psychologist, analyst, therapeutist, psychiatrist, psychoanalyst, °counsellor, advisor, *Colloq* shrink: *For some problems it is best to seek the advice of a trained counsellor or therapist.*

therapy *n.* **1** °remedy, °treatment, remedial programme; °cure: *As therapy, he suggested I swim a mile every day.* **2** psychotherapy, psychoanalysis, °analysis, group therapy: *If it weren't for my weekly therapy sessions, I'd never see anyone.*

therefore *adv.* °consequently, so, °thus, as a °result *or* consequence, °hence, ergo, for this *or* that °reason, wherefore, °accordingly, that being so *or* the °case: *Demand for our products has fallen dramatically, and we cannot therefore expect to make a profit this year.*

thesaurus *n.* **1** °treasury, °treasure trove, °storehouse, armoury, arsenal, repository, °cache: *It is hoped that this book will be regarded as a thesaurus of linguistic treasures.* **2** synonym °dictionary, synonymy, °dictionary, lexicon: *He checked in his thesaurus for a synonym of 'idea'.*

thesis *n.* **1** °argument, theory, °proposition, °point, contention, °belief, °idea, °premise *or* premiss, assumption, °view, °assertion, °precept, °opinion, °notion, °theorem, axiom, postulate: *Think how many centuries it took man to come to grips with the thesis that all men are created equal.* **2** See **theme, 2,** above.

Thespian *adj.* **1** °dramatic, °theatrical *or* theatric, histrionic, acting, performing; *Colloq* ham, hammy: *His Thespian talents went unnoticed until he appeared as an extra in a James Bond movie.*
—*n.* **2** actor, actress, °performer, trouper, °player; supernumerary; matinée °idol, °star; *Colloq* ham: *For many years she was one of the most beloved Thespians who ever trod the boards.*

thick *adj.* **1** °broad, °wide, °solid, thickset, °burly, °ample, °bulky, °substantial, °beamy: *He sank his teeth into the thickest sandwich I have ever seen. She is a bit thicker in the mid-section than I had remembered, but a good ketch nonetheless.* **2** Usually, ***thick with***: °dense, °solid, °compact, concentrated, condensed, °packed, close-packed, compressed, crowded, choked, filled, °full, °deep, clotted, chock-full *or* choke-full *or* chuck-full, chock-a-block, teeming, swarming, °alive, bristling, crawling, bursting, crammed, jammed, brimming, *Colloq* °lousy with: *The gallery was thick with visitors.* **3** °compact, condensed, compressed, choking, °packed, impenetrable, impassable, °dense; pea-soup, soupy, °murky, °misty, foggy, smoggy, smoky, °opaque, °obscure, obscuring, °hazy: *We plunged deeper into the thick jungle. A thick fog blanketed the valley.* **4** °abundant, °plentiful, bushy, °luxuriant: *Her thick red hair tumbled down over her shoulders.* **5** °dense, viscid, viscous, gelatinous, mucilaginous, gluey, glutinous, °ropy, coagulated, clotted, congealed, jelled, jellied, inspissated, stiffish; °stiff, °firm, °rigid, °solid: *For a thicker sauce, use cornflour.* **6** thick-headed, thick-witted, thick-skulled, °dense, °stupid, °slow, slow-witted, °dull, dull-witted, °stolid, °obtuse, gormless, boneheaded, fat-headed, pin-headed, wooden-headed, addle-pated, °halfwitted, block-headed, doltish, Boeotian, cretinous, imbecilic, moronic, *US* thimble-witted; insensitive, °thick-skinned; *Colloq* dim-witted, *Slang* dopey: *How could anyone so thick have become an executive?* **7** guttural, hoarse, throaty, raspy, rasping, °rough, °husky, °grating, gravelly, °indistinct, distorted, °inarticulate; °gruff, °raucous: *'I need you,' he moaned, his voice thick with emotion.* **8** °close, °friendly, like that, inseparable, °devoted, °hand in glove, on good terms, on the best (of) terms, °intimate, *Colloq* °chummy, pally, (as) thick as thieves, *Brit* matey, well in, *US* palsy-walsy: *We were thick in the old days, going everywhere together.* **9** °marked, °pronounced, °strong, °decided, °obvious, °typical: *She speaks English with a thick Polish accent.*
—*n.* **10** °core, °heart, °centre, °middle, °focus, °midst: *If it's a fight, you can be sure that Timothy will be in the thick of it.*

thicken *v.* °coagulate, clot, congeal, °jell, gel, °set, °solidify, °stiffen, °harden, °firm up, °cake, incrassate, inspissate: *Cornflour can be used to thicken sauces.*

thicket *n.* copse, °brake, grove, covert, wood, *Brit* spinney: *We concealed our horses in the thicket and stole ahead on foot.*

thick-skinned *n.* insensitive, insensate, °dull, °obtuse, °stolid, °callous, °numb(ed), steeled, hardened, toughened, °tough, unsusceptible, inured, unfeeling, case-hardened, impervious, pachydermatous, *Colloq* hard-boiled: *You must be very thick-skinned not to realize that they were getting at you.*

thief *n.* **1** °robber, °burglar, cat °burglar, housebreaker, picklock, sneak-thief, safe-cracker, pilferer, shoplifter, purloiner; embezzler, peculator; pickpocket, cutpurse, purse-snatcher, mugger, highwayman, footpad, brigand, bandit, °thug, dacoit, ruffian, °outlaw, desperado, hijacker, gunman, plunderer; poacher; *Technical* kleptomaniac, *Australian* bush-ranger, *US* road-agent, *Colloq* °hold-up man, crook, *US* second-story *or* second-storey man, bandito *or* bandido, *Slang* cracksman, box man, dip, stick-up man: *They caught the thief who took the paintings.* **2** °cheat, °swindler, confidence man, mountebank, charlatan, sharper, trickster, flimflam artist *or* man, thimblerigger, *Colloq* con man, con artist, shell-game artist, *US* highbinder: *That thief cheated them out of their savings.* **3** °pirate, (sea) rover, picaroon *or* pickaroon, corsair, freebooter, buccaneer, marauder, filibuster, privateer: *They might seem romantic in retrospect, but at the time, pirates were no more than common thieves.*

thin *adj.* **1** °slim, °slender, °lean, °spare, °slight, °lanky, spindly, °skinny, thin as a rail *or* reed *or* rake, wispy, twiggy, skeletal, °gaunt, gangling, bony, °emaciated, cadaverous, °meagre, °scrawny, all skin and bones, scraggy, undernourished, underfed, underweight, °undersized, °puny, °sparse, hollow-cheeked, (half-) °starved, pinched, withered, shrunken, shrivelled (up): *Douglas is quite thin as a result of his illness.* **2** °sparse, unsubstantial, °poor, scant, °insufficient, °inadequate, °slight, °worthless, unimportant, °deficient, skimpy, unplentiful, °paltry, piddling: *This year's harvest has been very thin.* **3** attenuated, threadlike, stringlike, pencil-thin, °fine; °narrow: *Draw a thin line between the columns. Please slice the bread thin.* **4** °flimsy, °weak, °feeble, °slight, unsubstantial, °insubstantial, °fragile, °frail, °poor, °lame; °unbelievable, unconvincing: *Harry gave some thin excuse for being late.* **5** airy, °filmy, diaphanous, gossamer, °sheer, °light, °delicate, chiffon, °silky, silken, gauzy, translucent, °see-through, °transparent: *She had nothing but a thin negligee to protect her from the cold.* **6** °watery, watered down, °dilute(d), °weak, unsatisfying: *My dinner, as usual, consisted of thin gruel and a dry crust.* **7** ***thin on the ground***: °rare, uncommon, °scarce, °few (and far between), °unusual, °hard to come by *or* find, scant, °scanty: *Good managers are thin on the ground.*
—*v.* **8** Often, ***thin down***: °draw out, attenuate, °reduce, °trim, °cut down, °prune; °sharpen: *At one*

end, thin the dowel to a point. **9** Often, ***thin down*** or ***out***: °dilute, °water (down), °decrease, °reduce, °diminish: *They always thin the wine with some water. The crowd thinned out after a while.*

thing *n.* **1** °item, (inanimate) °object, article, °possession: *They went without leaving a thing behind.* **2** °item, °subject, °matter, °detail, °feature, °aspect, °affair, constituent, °element, °factor, °point: *There's one thing that I forgot to mention. It's a small thing, but I like coffee with my breakfast.* **3** °fad, °trend, °fashion: *Let me show you the latest thing in sports cars.* **4** °feeling, °reaction, °attitude, °sentiment, emotional °attachment; °quirk, °fixation, preoccupation, °obsession; °fetish *or* fetich, *idée fixe*, °affection, °liking, °partiality, predilection, °fancy, °love, °passion, °mania; °phobia, °fear, °terror, °aversion, °loathing, °horror, detestation, °dislike, *Colloq* hang-up: *A chocoholic has a thing about chocolate. Pet snakes are not Patricia's thing. Roger has a thing about going out in public.* **5** °device, °item, °gadget, °object, °entity, °mechanism, contrivance, °apparatus, °instrument, utensil, *Colloq* dingus, doodah, doodad, whatchamacallit, thingumajig, whosis, whatsis, thingummy, thingumabob, *Chiefly US and Canadian* gismo *or* gizmo: *Where's the thing that is supposed to hold the flywheel in place?* **6** chore, °task, °responsibility, °matter; °act, °action, °deed, °activity, °proceeding: *The first thing I must do is to phone home.* **7** °opportunity, °chance, °possibility: *See me first thing tomorrow.* **8** ***things***: **a** °affairs, °matters, °business, °concerns: *I have to take care of some things at the office today.* **b** °circumstances, °events, °happenings: *Things are rarely what they seem.* **c** °belongings, °luggage, baggage, impedimenta, °possessions, °paraphernalia, °effects, °clothes, clothing, °goods; °equipment, °tools, utensils, °implements, °apparatus, *Colloq* °gear, °stuff, *Slang Brit* clobber, *US* crap, °junk, *Taboo slang US* shit: *Take your things and leave at once! The plumber left his things at the shop.*

think *v.* **1** °believe, °imagine, °expect, °dream, °fantasize, °suppose: *When do you think that you will retire?* **2** °judge, °reckon, °consider, deem, °regard (as), °characterize (as), °believe, °assume, °mark: *They thought him a fool for making such a fuss.* **3** °contemplate, cogitate (on *or* over *or* about), ruminate (over *or* about), °reflect (on), °meditate (on *or* over *or* about), °muse (on *or* over *or* about), °deliberate (on *or* over *or* about), °think about *or* of *or* over: *He likes to sit in the bath and think. I need time to think over your proposal.* **4** Often, ***think of***: °recall, °remember, °recollect, °call to °mind: *I simply cannot think of the name of that film we saw last week.* **5** ***think of*** or ***about***: **a** °consider, °ponder, °weigh, °contemplate, °muse over, have in °mind, °mull over, °entertain the °idea *or* °notion of, °intend, °propose: *Do you ever think of retiring?* **b** assess, °evaluate, value, °judge: *What do you think about their latest suggestion?* **6** ***think up*** or ***of***: °devise, concoct, contrive, come up with, °invent, °conceive (of), °dream up, °create, °make up, °improvise: *Who thinks up the plots for these dreadful TV series?*

thinkable *adj.* conceivable, °possible, imaginable, °feasible, °reasonable, °tenable, not °unlikely, °plausible, believable, credible: *It is hardly thinkable that they can be serious.*

thinker *n.* °sage, °wise man, savant, Nestor, Solomon, pundit, °mastermind, philosopher, °scholar, °learned person, mentor, °expert: *She has been looked on as one of the great thinkers of her time.*

thinking *adj.* **1** °rational, °sensible, ratiocinative, °intelligent, °reasoning, °reasonable; °meditative, contemplative, °reflective, °philosophical, cogitative, °pensive, °thoughtful, °intellectual: *Any thinking person would have done the same as you.*
—*n.* **2** °opinion, °judgement, °belief, °thought, °point of °view, °viewpoint, assessment, °evaluation, theory, °reasoning, conclusion, °idea, °philosophy, °outlook: *There is nothing either good or bad, but thinking makes it so. Do you concur with the current thinking on education?*

thirst *n.* **1** craving, °desire, °appetite, °hunger, °eagerness, avidity, ravenousness, voracity, voraciousness, °lust, °passion, °enthusiasm, °fancy, hankering, °longing, yearning, *Colloq* °itch, yen: *It was the thirst for gold that drove them mad. She has an insatiable thirst for knowledge.*
—*v.* **2** Often, ***thirst for*** or ***after***: crave, °desire, °hunger for *or* after, °lust for *or* after, °fancy, °hanker for *or* after, °long for, °yearn for, °wish for: *These men are thirsting for power.*

thirsty *adj.* **1** parched, °dry, dehydrated; arid: *I need another drink—I'm really thirsty. The thirsty land welcomes the rain.* **2** °desirous, °hungry, avid, °eager, °ravenous, °voracious, °burning, °greedy, °avaricious, hankering, yearning, craving, *Colloq* itching: *The students are thirsty for knowledge and very hard-working.*

thorn *n.* **1** barb, °spine, °spike, °prickle, °bristle, brier *or* briar, bur *or* burr, °point, bramble, cocklebur: *My sleeve caught on the thorn and tore.* **2** Often, ***thorn in (one's) side***: °bother, irritation, °annoyance, °nuisance, vexation, °torment, torture, °scourge, °plague, °affliction, irritant, bane, *Colloq* °pain in the neck, *Taboo slang* °pain in the *Brit* arse *or US* ass: *His nagging brother has been a thorn in his side for years.*

thorny *adj.* **1** °prickly, barbed, spiny, spiked, brambly, spinous, *Technical* spinose, acanthoid, spiculose, spiculate, spinulose, aciculate, muricate, barbellate, setigerous, setaceous, setiferous, setose: *The insect's feet have tiny thorny projections.* **2** °difficult, °hard, °tough, °prickly, nettlesome, °painful, °ticklish, °delicate, °intricate, °critical, complex, °complicated, °problematic, vexatious, knotty, tangled, °involved, °troublesome, °controversial, °nasty, worrying, *Colloq* °sticky, *Slang* °hairy: *Many thorny questions have vexed us throughout the ages.*

thorough *adj.* **1** thoroughgoing, °complete, °downright, °perfect, through-and-through, °total, °unmitigated, °undiluted, unmixed, unalloyed, °out-and-out, °unqualified, °sheer, utter, arrant, °absolute, °proper: *I have rarely encountered such thorough stupidity.* **2** °exhaustive, °extensive, °painstaking, °meticulous, assiduous, °careful, °scrupulous, °particular, °conscientious, °methodical: *Police conducted a thorough search but found nothing.* **3** °extensive, °exhaustive, °detailed, in-depth, °comprehensive, °full, °complete, all-inclusive, °total, all-embracing, °encyclopedic *or* encyclopaedic, °universal, A-to-Z, *Colloq* all-out: *We need someone who has a thorough knowledge of the terrain.*

thoroughly *adv.* **1** °completely, °downright, °perfectly, °totally, unqualifiedly, °utterly, °absolutely, °entirely, °extremely, unreservedly, °wholly, fully, °positively, °definitely, °quite: *He is thoroughly stupid, as we all know.* **2** carefully, painstakingly, exhaustively, extensively, assiduously, sedulously, methodically, conscientiously, scrupulously, meticulously, intensively, comprehensively, °completely, °throughout, from top to bottom, from stem to stern, backwards and forwards, in every nook and cranny: *Police searched thoroughly again, but could still find no murder weapon.*

though *conj.* **1** although, °even though, while, in °spite of *or* °despite the fact that, °notwithstanding that, albeit, granted, granting *or* conceding that, allowing *or* admitting that, °even if, °supposing: *Though it is the right size, I hate the colour.*
—*adv.* **2** °however, °nonetheless, °nevertheless, °yet, but, °still, °even so, be that as it may, all the same, °notwithstanding, for all that: *She lost the original; I kept a copy though.*

thought *n.* **1** °thinking, °reflection, reflecting, meditation, meditating, contemplation, contemplating, cogitation, cogitating, musing, pondering, rumination, ruminating, brooding, °mental activity, mentation, brown study; brainwork, cerebration, deliberation, deliberating, °consideration, °considering: *She was deep in thought. The solution may require considerable thought.* **2** °idea, °notion, brainstorm,

°observation: *I have a thought that I'd like to share with you.* **3** °consideration, contemplation, planning, °plan, °scheme, °design, °intention, °expectation, °hope, °prospect, °anticipation, °dream, °vision: *Any thought of taking a few days off had to be abandoned.* **4** thoughtfulness, °consideration, kindliness, kind-heartedness, °concern, compassion, tenderness, °kindness, °sympathy, attentiveness, °regard, °solicitude: *I don't need any help, but I appreciate the thought.* **5** Often, ***thoughts***: °recollection(s), °memory *or* memories, °remembrance(s), °reminiscence(s): *Now and then he comforted himself with thoughts of his happy childhood.* **6** °intellect, °intelligence, °reasoning, rationality, ratiocination, °reason: *Some believe that only humans are capable of thought.* **7** °bit, °trifle, °touch, small amount, °trace, soupçon, °little, tinge: *This champagne is a thought too sweet.*

thoughtful *adj.* **1** °considerate, °kind, °kindly, kind-hearted, compassionate, °tender, °sympathetic, °attentive, °solicitous, °helpful, °charitable: *Wasn't it thoughtful of Simon to offer his help?* **2** contemplative, °pensive, °reflective, musing, in a brown study, pondering, °meditative, engrossed, introspective, °rapt, °wistful, brooding, wool-gathering, day-dreaming: *Every time I mentioned Clarissa, he would become thoughtful.* **3** °prudent, °wary, °cautious, °mindful, heedful, °thinking, °attentive, circumspect, °careful, caring: *The crew are ever thoughtful of the passengers' safety.*

thoughtless *adj.* **1** °inconsiderate, °rude, °impolite, insensitive, °tactless, undiplomatic, untactful, °unthinking: *It was thoughtless of you to mention her son, who is serving time for possession of drugs.* **2** °rash, °imprudent, negligent, °foolish, °stupid, °careless, neglectful, °reckless, °silly, °unthinking, unreflective, °absent-minded, °forgetful, °remiss, ill-considered, °heedless, °inadvertent, °inattentive: *How thoughtless of me to forget your birthday!*

thrashing *n.* **1** beating, drubbing, °whipping, flogging, °assault, caning, belting, mauling, lashing, trouncing, basting, battering, pounding, *Colloq* hiding, tanning, lambasting, hammering, pasting: *Every time he stepped into the ring he got a thrashing.* **2** °punishment, chastisement, disciplining, °discipline, castigation: *He dreaded the thrashing his father administered at any sign of disobedience.*

thread *n.* **1** °fibre, filament, strand, (piece of) °yarn; °string, °line, °cord, °twine: *Threads from his jacket were found clutched in the victim's hand. The glass is spun out into fine threads.* **2** °theme, °plot, story-line, °subject, °motif, °thesis, °course, °drift, °direction, °tenor, °train (of thought), °sequence *or* °train *or* °chain of events: *It is difficult to follow the thread of the story when it has so many digressions.*
—*v.* **3** °string: *Carefully thread the beads onto the wire.* **4** °file, °wind, °pass, °squeeze (through), pick *or* make (one's) way (through), inch, °ease: *He threaded his way through the crowd to reach the dais.*

threadbare *adj.* **1** frayed, °worn (out), °worn to a frazzle, °ragged, moth-eaten, °tattered, tatty, scruffy, °shabby, °seedy, torn, °wretched, °sorry, slovenly: *My old winter coat is looking a bit threadbare.* **2** trite, hackneyed, overused, overworked, reworked, °stale, °tired, stereotyped, commonplace, clichéd, cliché-ridden, °banal, °prosaic, °dull, °monotonous, °tedious, °tiresome, °boring, played out, *Colloq* °old hat: *You'll never make it as a comedian by relying on that threadbare material of yours.*

threat *n.* **1** intimidation, °menace, commination, °warning, °peril, °risk, °danger, Damoclean sword: *It is not honesty but the threat of punishment that deters many from crime.* **2** °omen, presage, portent, °foreboding, forewarning, intimation: *The villagers lived under a constant threat from the smoking volcano.*

threaten *v.* **1** °intimidate, °menace, terrorize, °daunt, cow, °bully, °browbeat, °warn, °caution: *The headmaster threatened those who misbehaved with the most dire punishment.* **2** imperil, put at °risk, °endanger, °jeopardize, put in °jeopardy: *All life is threatened if the environment is not better looked after.* **3** impend, °loom; augur, portend, presage, forebode: *The creatures crawl into their burrows if danger threatens. The gathering clouds threatened rain.*

threatening *adj.* °ominous, °menacing, °portentous, °sinister, looming, °inauspicious, minatory, minacious, comminatory, intimidating, °foreboding, °imminent, °impending: *Threatening storm clouds began to build in the western sky.*

threshold *n.* **1** sill, door-sill, doorstep; doorway, °entrance: *He stood at the threshold and peered into the room.* **2** °brink, °verge, °edge, °beginning, commencement, °outset, °start, °dawn: *The emigrants were at the threshold of a new life.*

thrift *n.* °economy, husbandry, °care, carefulness, °prudence, parsimony, frugality, thriftiness, sparingness, scrimping, skimping; penuriousness, close-fistedness, tight-fistedness, niggardliness, stinginess, miserliness: *Only through our thrift were we able to save enough for a new car.*

thrifty *adj.* °economical, °careful, °prudent, parsimonious, °frugal, °sparing, scrimping, skimping; °penurious, close-fisted, tight-fisted, niggardly, stingy, °miserly, penny-pinching, °cheap: *He talked about the need to save money and be thrifty in every way.*

thrill *n.* **1** °excitement, titillation, frisson, tingle, tingling (°sensation), stimulation, *Colloq* °kick, bang, °charge, °buzz: *Victor feels a tremendous thrill when his daughter wins a tennis match.* **2** tremor, °quiver, quivering, °shudder, shuddering, °tremble, trembling, °flutter, throb, throbbing, pulsation, vibration: *The only warning was a slight thrill in the earth just before the main quake.*
—*v.* **3** °excite, °stimulate, °animate, °electrify, galvanize, °enliven, °stir, titillate, °touch, °strike, °move, impassion, °arouse, *Slang* °send, give (someone) a kick: *They were thrilled to discover that they had won an award.*

thrilling *adj.* °exciting, °stimulating, animating, electrifying, galvanizing, enlivening, °stirring, titillating, °striking, °moving, arousing, °rousing, gripping, °sensational, °riveting, spine-tingling, soul-stirring: *Last year's Cup Final was a thrilling match, with most sides playing their hearts out. I have never had such thrilling rides at the fun fair.*

thrive *v.* °succeed, °prosper, °boom, °advance, °flourish, °grow, bloom, burgeon, °develop, wax, °increase, fructify, °ripen: *They thrived in the invigorating mountain air.*

throe *n.* Usually, ***throes***: °pang, °anguish, °struggle, °chaos, turmoil, °tumult, °paroxysm, °spasm, °fit, °seizure, convulsion, *Technical* ictus: *She was in the throes of despair at the dreadful news from home.*

throng *n.* **1** horde, °crowd, °host, assemblage, °assembly, °gathering, °mass, °crush, °jam, multitude, congregation, °press, °swarm, °herd, °flock, bevy, drove: *Throngs of people packed the shopping mall on Saturday.*
—*v.* **2** °crowd (into), °fill, °pack (into), °cram (into), °crush (into), °jam (into), °press (into), °swarm (into), °herd (into), °flock (into *or* to); °assemble (in *or* at), °gather (in *or* at), °mass (in *or* at), congregate (in *or* at): *Thousands thronged the stadium to watch the tennis matches.*

through *prep.* **1** because of, on °account of, owing to, as a consequence *or* °result of, by °virtue of, via, by °means of, by °way of, with the °aid *or* °help of, under the aegis *or* °auspices of, *Sometimes non-standard* °due to: *It was through his good graces that I got the appointment.* **2** during, °throughout, in the °course *or* °middle of: *The dog barked all through the night.* **3** °inclusive of, including: *When I say 'the third through the sixth' I mean 'including the sixth'.* **4** to; into: *I went through a lot of trouble to find this book.*
—*adj.* **5** Often, ***through with***: done (with), finished (with); at the end of one's tether (with), washing (one's) hands (of): *Let me know when you are through.*

How many times has she sworn she was through with him forever?
—*adv.* **6** °by, °past: *I am just passing through.* **7** °entirely, through and through, °completely, °thoroughly, °totally, °wholly, °utterly, fully, to the core, from head to foot *or* toe, from top to bottom, from stem to stern, from one end to the other, in every way, in all respects: *By the time I got home, I was soaked through.*

throughout *prep.* **1** during, all (the way) °through, from the beginning to the end of: *We worked throughout the day and night. Throughout his life he felt the need for constant support.* **2** °everywhere in, all over, in every part of, in every nook and cranny of, from one end to the other of: *I searched throughout the house for my keys.*
—*adv.* **3** all (the way) °through, °everywhere, from one end to the other, °wholly, °entirely, °completely, fully: *They were busy tidying the house throughout before his mother came to stay.*

throw *v.* **1** °toss, °cast, °hurl, °fling, °sling, °pitch, °dash, °propel, °project, °shy, °bowl, °send, °launch, *Colloq* chuck: *He threw the ball to the batter with all his might.* **2** °cast, °shed, °project: *I was hoping you might throw some light on the subject. Coming events throw their shadow before them.* **3** °throw *or* °bring down, °floor, °fell, °knock down *or* over, °overthrow, °upset, °overturn: *He threw the vase on the floor.* **4** °dismay, confound, °confuse, °dumbfound *or* dumfound, baffle, disconcert, °unnerve, throw off *or* out, unsettle, °put off, °put (someone) off his *or* her *or* their stride *or* pace *or* stroke, *Colloq* discombobulate: *Her frank questions about my private life really threw me.* **5 *throw away*:** **a** °discard, °cast off, °dispose of, jettison, get °rid of, °scrap, throw out, °dispense with, *Colloq* °dump, °trash, chuck out, *Slang* ditch: *He is a hoarder, refusing to throw anything away.* **b** °waste, squander, °lose, °forgo, °fritter away, fail to exploit *or* take advantage of, *Slang* °blow: *He threw away his last chance for a decent life when he left her.* **6 *throw off*:** **a** °eject, °expel, °emit, throw up *or* out: *The volcano throws off rocks every so often.* **b** °shake off, °rid *or* °free (oneself) of, get °rid of, °reject, °renounce, °repudiate: *He finally managed to throw off his mother's pernicious influence.* **c** °deceive, °mislead, °decoy, misguide, °misdirect, °distract, °divert, °bewilder, confound, °confuse, *Colloq* °flummox, bamboozle: *He doubled back to throw the dogs off.* **d** See **4,** above. **7 *throw out*:** **a** °radiate, °emit, °send forth, °give out *or* off, °diffuse, °put out *or* forth, disseminate: *The substance throws out a greenish light.* **b** °expel, °eject, °force out, °evict, *Colloq Brit* °turf out, *Slang* bounce: *Henry was thrown out of the pub for rowdy behaviour.* **c** See **5 a,** above. **d** See **6 a,** above. **8 *throw over*:** °jilt, °leave, °abandon, °desert, °forsake, °break *or* °split up with, *Colloq* °walk out on, chuck, °drop: *She was heartbroken when he threw her over and married her sister.* **9 *throw up*:** **a** °vomit, °spit up, puke, °spew up, be °sick; °regurgitate, disgorge, *Colloq* °heave (up): *He felt as if he was going to throw up.* **b** °abandon, °quit, °leave, throw over, °give up, °relinquish, °resign, °renounce, *Colloq* chuck: *He threw up a perfectly good job to go and live on a boat.* **c** °reveal, °bring out *or* up, °bring to the surface *or* the top, °bring forward *or* forth, bring to °light *or* to notice: *Their treachery was thrown up in high relief by the events that followed.* **d** throw *or* °slap *or* °knock together, jerry-build: *The house was thrown up overnight—and it looks like it.* **e** See **6 a,** above.

thrust *v.* **1** °push, shove, °drive, °force, impel, °ram, °jam, °butt, °propel, °prod, °urge, °press; °shoulder, jostle, elbow: *A stranger thrust this note into my hand. She thrust her way through the crowd.* **2** °stab, °plunge, °stick, °jab, °poke; °lunge: *He thrust the dagger into the man's back. She thrust at me with an ice pick.* **3** Usually, ***thrust upon*:** °press (upon *or* on), °impose (upon *or* on), °force (upon *or* on), °urge (upon *or* on): *They were willing to help, but rather thought the problem had been thrust upon them.*
—*n.* **4** shove, °push, °drive, °lunge, °poke, °prod, °stab: *He depended on his agility to avoid the thrusts of the rapier.* **5** °propulsion, °force, °power, °energy: *The thrust of the photon engines drives the spaceship at nearly the speed of light.*

thud *n.* clunk, thump, whomp, wham, clonk, °bump: *His head hit the wall with a thud.*

thug *n.* hooligan, °gangster, desperado, gunman, °terrorist, °hoodlum, °robber, assassin, °murderer, °killer, °cutthroat, ruffian, Mafioso, *In Paris* apache, mugger, *Technical* p'hansigar, *Brit* °rough, *Slang* °tough, hood, crook, °hit man, heavy, *US* goon, *Australian* larrikin: *Some thugs roughed him up and took his wallet.*

thumb *n.* **1** *Technical* pollex. **2 *all thumbs*:** °awkward, °clumsy, maladroit, *Colloq* butter-fingered, ham-fisted, cack-handed: *I am all thumbs when it comes to threading needles.* **3 *give (something) the thumbs down* or *turn thumbs down (on)*:** °disapprove (of), °reject, °rebuff, °turn down: *We turned thumbs down to the idea of a picnic.* **4 *turn* or *give thumbs up (to)*:** °approve (of), °accept, °welcome, *Colloq* °OK *or* okay: *The boss gave thumbs up to our request for a Christmas party.* **5 *under (one's) thumb*:** under (one's) °control, wrapped (a)round (one's) little °finger, in the palm of (one's) hand, eating out of (one's hand), at (one's) beck and call: *She has the directors under her thumb.*
—*v.* **6** hitchhike, *Colloq* °hitch, *US* hook a ride: *They thumbed their way across the country.* **7** Often, ***thumb through*:** leaf (through), flick *or* °flip (through), riffle (through), °skim (through), °browse (through): *I was thumbing through* City Life *and came across your picture, Bernard!* **8 *thumb (one's) nose at*:** °scoff at, °deride, °jeer at, °mock, °dismiss, °scorn, °flout, be °contemptuous of, show °contempt for, exhibit defiance for, be °defiant of, contemn, *Brit* cock a snook at: *He has thumbed his nose at authority all his life.*

thumbnail *adj.* °rough, undetailed, °cursory, °sketchy, °superficial; °brief, °short, quick; °compact, °concise, pithy, °succinct: *His poetry is a chilling, thumbnail sketch of the way we live now.*

thumping *adj.* **1** °great, °huge, °colossal, stupendous, °gigantic, °enormous, °immense, °monumental, °massive, titanic, elephantine, behemoth, gargantuan, mammoth, °jumbo, *Colloq* °whopping, thundering, walloping: *That is the biggest thumping beach ball I have ever seen! That was a thumping lie.* **2** °complete, utter, °unmitigated, 24-carat *or esp. US* 24-karat, °perfect: *Anyone who would turn down a salary increase must be a thumping idiot.*

thunder *n.* **1** °roll, reverberation, °boom, booming, °roar, roaring, pealing, rumble, rumbling; °crash, crashing, °crack, cracking, °explosion, °blast: *We were deafened by the thunder of the tanks crossing the bridge above us.*
—*v.* **2** °roll, reverberate, °boom, °roar, rumble, °resound; °explode, °crash, °crack, °blast: *The noise of the jets thundered through the valley.* **3** °shout, °yell, °scream, °bellow, bark, °roar; °denounce, fulminate against, °swear (at), °rail (at), °curse (at), execrate; °threaten, °intimidate, °menace: *'Fee, fie, foe, fum!' thundered the giant. No secretary will tolerate his thundering at her.*

thunderous *adj.* roaring, booming, thundering, °tumultuous, °noisy, °loud, ear-splitting, deafening: *They took curtain calls to thunderous applause.*

thunderstruck *adj.* °dumbfounded *or* dumfounded, astonished, astounded, awestruck, awed, °speechless, struck °dumb, amazed, °taken aback, staggered, stunned, shocked, dazed, °numb, paralysed, aghast, open-mouthed, nonplussed, *Colloq* flabbergasted, floored, bowled over, *Brit* knocked for six: *We were thunderstruck to learn that our team had been disqualified.*

thus *adv.* **1** so, in this °manner *or* °way *or* °fashion *or* wise, as follows, *Non-Standard* thusly: *On receipt of the payment, I wrote thus to him.* **2** °therefore, ergo,

°consequently, as a consequence, as a °result, °accordingly, (and) so, then, for this *or* that °reason, °hence, in which °case *or* °event, that being the °case, that being so: *He has already decided; thus, your efforts to persuade him are useless.*

thwart *v.* **1** °frustrate, °impede, °check, °stymie, baffle, °stop, °foil, °stump, °hinder, °obstruct, balk, °block, °oppose, negate, nullify, *Colloq* short-circuit: *They have thwarted all our efforts to become friendly.* —*n.* **2** °brace, cross-brace; (rowing-)seat, bench: *These canoes are fitted with two thwarts.*

tickle *v.* titillate, °delight, °please, °gratify, °amuse, °entertain, °divert, °captivate, °thrill, tickle pink *or* to death: *The show we saw last night really tickled my fancy. She was tickled to receive the flowers.*

ticklish *adj.* **1** °uncertain, unsteady, unsure, °unstable, °unsettled, °fickle, touch-and-go, °touchy: *Power that relies on the sword has a ticklish basis.* **2** °delicate, °precarious, °risky, °hazardous, °dangerous, °critical, °thorny, °fragile, °awkward: *As the canoe drifted towards the waterfall, we found ourselves in a very ticklish predicament.* **3** °delicate, °sensitive, hypersensitive, °difficult, °touchy, °prickly: *Cornelia is a bit ticklish on the subject of her holiday plans.*

tidy *adj.* **1** °neat, °orderly, °trim, °shipshape, °spruce, spick and span, °clean, well-kept, °well-groomed: *Change your clothes and come back when you're tidy.* **2** well-organized, organized, well-ordered, °methodical, °systematic, °trim: *They refused to clean his office till he had made it tidy.* **3** °respectable, sizeable, °significant, °considerable, °substantial, °good, °goodly, good-sized, °ample, °large, °big, °fair, °generous, not °insignificant; *Colloq* not to be sneezed at: *They settled a tidy sum on their daughter when she was married.* —*v.* **4** Often, ***tidy up***: °neaten (up), °straighten (out *or* up), °clean (up), put in °order, *Colloq* °fix (up), °spruce up, °organize, reorganize, °arrange, rearrange: *You can't watch television until you've tidied up your room. Please tidy up the files by the end of the week.*

tie *v.* **1** °bind, °fasten, make °fast, tie up, °lash, °secure, truss, °attach, °tether, °rope, °chain, °moor; °connect, °join, °knot, °link, °couple, °splice, °unite: *He keeps a vicious dog tied to a stake in his garden. Tie the ends of the rope together.* **2** °bind, truss (up), tie up, °lash, pinion, °restrict, confine, °restrain; °limit, tie down, °curtail, °curb, cramp, °hamper, °hinder: *His hands are tied behind his back. According to the terms of the agreement, my hands are tied and I can do nothing.* **3** °connect, °associate, °unite, °join, °link, °bind (up), affiliate, °ally, °league, °team (up): *Our business interests are tied to those of the major banks.* **4** °equal, °even, be °equal *or* °even (with), °match, be neck and neck (with): *We tied them for first place. Yesterday, we were tied for second.* **5** ***tie down***: **a** °clinch, °secure, °confirm, *Colloq* °nail down: *I tied down the PBT contract this morning.* **b** °restrict, °restrain, constrain, confine, °curtail: *He won't marry because he doesn't want to feel tied down.* **6** ***tie in***: **a** be °consistent, make °sense, °correspond, °coincide, °fit (in), be °logical, °coordinate: *His alibi ties in with the witness's testimony.* **b** °relate, °connect, °link, °associate, °coordinate: *They cleverly tie in concern for the environment with their product.* **7** ***tie up***: **a** °occupy, °engage, (keep) °busy: *This affair will tie me up till Tuesday.* **b** °use, °take up, °encroach on, °impose on: *I won't tie up your time any longer.* **c** °stop, °halt, bring to a °standstill: *The traffic was tied up for hours.* **d** °commit, °oblige, °obligate, °bind: *We have tied up all their output for a year.* **e** See **1**, above. **f** See **2**, above. —*n.* **8** °link, °fastening, °bond, °band, °connection, °tie-up, °relationship, affiliation, °liaison, involvement, entanglement: *Isn't there some tie between those two companies?* **9** °string, °cord, °lace, °rope, thong, ribbon, °band, ligature, shoelace, °line, leash, stop: *The tie of her dressing-gown came loose.* **10** °equality, dead heat, °deadlock, °draw, °stalemate: *When there is a tie, the game ought to go into 'sudden death' overtime.* **11** cravat, *US* necktie: *Please put on a tie for dinner.* **12** railway tie, sleeper: *Ties in Europe are now made of concrete.*

tie-in *n.* °tie-up, °relationship, °relation, °association, °connection, °link, linkage: *They say that there is a tie-in between smoking and lung cancer.*

tier *n.* °row, °line, °level, °order, °range, °course, series, °stratum, layer, echelon, °file, °rank, °storey: *The trireme is said to have had three tiers of oarsmen.*

tie-up *n.* **1** *In US and Canada*: slow-down, slow-up, entanglement, stoppage, °jam, log-jam, traffic °jam, °delay, congestion: *The tie-up was caused by fog on the highway.* **2** See **tie-in,** above.

tiff *n.* (petty) °quarrel, °disagreement, °misunderstanding, °dispute, °argument, °difference (of opinion), squabble, °bicker, °row, wrangle, *US* spat: *Clare and Geoff have had their first tiff.*

tiffin *n.* luncheon, lunch, light repast, °snack: *The new arrivals were to join us for tiffin.*

tight *adj.* **1** °secure, °firm, °fast, °fixed, secured, close-fitting, °snug, sealed, hermetically sealed, leak-proof, °hermetic, impervious, impenetrable, °impermeable, airtight, °watertight, waterproof: *Make sure that the lid is tight.* **2** °taut, stretched, °tense, constricting, (too) °small, ill-fitting: *She was wearing a very tight dress.* **3** °strict, binding, restrictive, stringent, °severe, °tough, uncompromising, unyielding, rigorous, °stern, austere, autocratic, °harsh, °hard and °fast, °inflexible: *You can't get away with anything under such tight regulations. I have a tight schedule next week.* **4** *Chiefly nautical* taut, (well-)disciplined, °orderly, °neat, well-organized, °trim, °tidy, °smart: *He runs a tight ship.* **5** stingy, niggardly, °mean, °penurious, °miserly, parsimonious, penny-pinching, tight-fisted, close-fisted, *Colloq Brit* mingy: *Glenn is much too tight to buy anyone a drink.* **6** °close, (°almost) °even, (highly) competitive, neck and neck, evenly matched: *It is going to be a tight race.* **7** °difficult, °trying, °dangerous, °perilous, °risky, °hazardous, °touchy, °problematic, °sticky, °tricky, °ticklish, °precarious, touch-and-go: *The strike has created a tight situation at the office.* **8** tipsy, °drunk, intoxicated, *Colloq* °high, woozy, under the °influence, *Brit* tiddly: *When I saw her, she was too tight to drive.* **9** °scarce, °scanty, hard to find *or* come by, °rare; °dear, °expensive: *Entrepreneurs have found investment money to be pretty tight this year.* —*adv.* **10** °tightly, securely, °firmly; closely: *Keep this door closed tight. Hold me tight. Her hands were clasped tight in prayer.* **11** compactly, densely, solidly, °firmly, closely: *We were packed so tight in the bus that no one could move.*

tighten *v.* **1** Sometimes, ***tighten down*** *or* ***up***: °anchor, °fasten, °fix, °tense, °secure: *Tighten those last two screws and you're finished.* **2** make tighter *or* tenser *or* stronger, °strengthen: *He tightened his grip on my hand.* **3** Sometimes, ***tighten up***: make more rigorous *or* °strict *or* stringent *or* °severe *or* restrictive, close gaps in: *We ought to tighten security at the warehouse.* **4** Sometimes, ***tighten up***: tauten, °stiffen, °tense, °close: *I felt the noose begin to tighten round my neck.*

tight-lipped *adj.* close-mouthed, °silent, °quiet, °mum, °mute, close-lipped, °noncommittal, °reticent, °secretive, °taciturn, unforthcoming, uncommunicative, °reserved: *He remained tight-lipped about his activities during the war.*

tightly *adv.* closely, tensely, °vigorously, rigorously: *It was a tightly fought race.*

tights *n.pl. US and Canadian and New Zealand* panty hose, *Australian and US also* pantihose: *It was much too hot to wear tights.*

till[1] *v.* °plough *or US also* plow, °cultivate, °farm, °work, °dig, hoe, harrow, manure, *Literary* delve: *My family has tilled this land for seven generations.*

till[2] *n.* money *or* cash-drawer, cash-box *or* °register: *He insists that the money was in the till when he left last night.*

tilt *v.* **1** °lean, °slant, °incline, °slope, °angle, °tip, °heel over, °pitch, °list, °cant: *She caught the lamp just as the table tilted.* **2** ***tilt at***: joust with, °compete with, °battle

against, contend with, °spar with, cross swords with, °attack: *In tilting at the media, he has chosen some formidable opponents.*
—*n.* **3** °lean, °slant, °incline, °slope, °angle, °tip, °heel, °list, °pitch, °cant, °inclination: *The wall is at a perilous tilt and could easily fall.* **4** joust, tourney, °tournament, °meeting, tilting, °engagement, °encounter, °match, °contest, °test, °trial, °fight, °combat; °dispute, °argument, °difference, °quarrel, altercation, squabble, °tiff, *US* spat, *Colloq* set-to: *I have enjoyed the various tilts I have had with the editor over the years.*

timber *n.* **1** trees, forest, woodland: *The standing timber has been seriously depleted in Brazil.* **2** wood, °beams, °boards, °planks, *US and Canadian* °lumber: *The timber for our new house arrived today.* **3** °material, °potential, °stuff, °character, °quality, °talent, °prospect: *Agatha seems to be good management timber.*

timbre *n.* °tone (°colour *or* °quality), tonality, °colour, resonance: *Kurt's voice has a rich, full timbre.*

time *n.* **1** °period, °interval, °stretch, °spell, °patch: *I was going through a bad time when we last met.* **2** °period, °interval, °stretch, while, °span, °space, °term, duration: *It is a long time since I have seen you. In the time I took to write this, she had vanished.* **3** hour; °point, °moment: *What time is it? At what time is our appointment?* **4** °age, °period, epoch, °era, lifetime, heyday, °day(s): *The novel is set in the time of the Caesars.* **5** °opportunity, °chance, °occasion: *You must make time to visit your mother.* **6** °experience: *I had a wonderful time at your party.* **7** °tempo, °beat, °rhythm, metre, °measure: *They are playing 'Teddy Bears' Picnic' in march time.* **8** °ease, °leisure; convenience: *He'll be there in his own time.* **9** Often, ***times***: °life, °things, °circumstance, °conditions, °everything, °culture, mores, °habits, values: *How times have changed since we were young!* **10** ***ahead of time***: (bright and) °early, °prematurely, beforehand, in good time: *He arrived ahead of time and had to wait.* **11** ***all the time***: °always, °ever, constantly, continuously, continually, perpetually, at all times, without surcease, unceasingly: *Mother is after me all the time to do my homework.* **12** ***at one time***: **a** °once, °once upon a time, on one °occasion, °previously, in days of yore, °formerly, heretofore, in the (good) °old days: *At one time you thought me beautiful.* **b** simultaneously, (all) at °once, at the same time, together, all together, in °unison: *The car can only carry five people at one time.* **13** ***at the same time***: **a** all the °same, °nonetheless, °yet, °even so, but, °however, be that as it may, °nevertheless, °notwithstanding, just the °same: *I love her; at the same time, I cannot live with her.* **b** See **12 b,** above. **14** ***at times***: from time to time, °occasionally, (every) °now and then, °once in a while, on °occasion, at intervals, °sometimes, *Colloq* every so °often: *At times, Ingrid would come over and cook dinner for me.* **15** ***behind the times***: °old-fashioned, out-dated, dated, outmoded, °antiquated, °passé, °obsolescent, °obsolete, *Colloq* °old hat, °dead: *Isn't 'The Lambeth Walk' a bit behind the times?* **16** ***for the time being***: for °now, for the °present, for the °moment, °meanwhile, °temporarily, *pro tempore*, *Colloq* pro tem, *Archaic* for the nonce: *He has been appointed chairman for the time being.* **17** ***in no time***: at °once, forthwith, straight away, °immediately, °quickly, speedily, without °delay, °swiftly: *The pizza we ordered was delivered in no time.* **18** ***in time***: **a** in °timely fashion, °early, in good time, in the nick of time: *The doctor arrived in time to save the baby.* **b** °soon, one of these days, °sometime, someday, one day, °eventually, sooner or later, anon: *In time, people might be living on the moon.* **19** ***on time***: **a** punctually, on the °dot, in good time: *He is never on time for his appointments.* **b** in instalments, on terms, on account, on credit, *Colloq Brit* on the never-never, on hire purchase *or* h.p.: *We bought the car on time.* **20** ***take (one's) time***: °dawdle, dilly-dally, °shilly-shally, °delay, °linger, loiter: *He's certainly taking his time with his report.* **21** ***time and again***: again (and again), °repeatedly, (over and) over again, time and time again, time after time, °frequently, °often, °many times, on °many °occasions: *Time and again I warned him he'd get a ticket if he parked there.*
—*v.* **22** °schedule, °set, °regulate, °control: *The trains are timed to arrive five minutes apart.* **23** °schedule, °set, °organize, °adjust, °fix: *She timed her entrance to coincide exactly with the crash of the cymbals.*

time-honoured *adj.* established, °traditional, °habitual, °customary, °rooted, °conventional, age-old, °set, °fixed; °venerable, venerated, respected, revered, honoured: *We observed the time-honoured custom of kissing the Blarney Stone.*

timeless *adj.* °eternal, °everlasting, °immortal, undying, °endless, unending, ceaseless, °abiding, °deathless, ageless, °changeless, unchanged, immutable, unchanging, °permanent, °indestructible: *He was enraptured by the timeless beauty of the heavens.*

timely *adj.* °punctual, °prompt, °well-timed, °propitious, °opportune, °convenient, °favourable, auspicious: *We welcomed the timely arrival of our rescuers.*

time-serving *adj.* self-seeking, self-serving, °selfish, °self-indulgent, °ambitious, °mercenary, °venal, °greedy, profit-oriented, fortune-hunting, gold-digging, °opportunistic, °hypocritical, °obsequious, sycophantic, toadying, toad-eating, boot-licking, subservient, *Colloq* on the °make, on the take, *Slang US* out for numero uno, *Taboo slang* brown-nosing: *Members of the party were known to be time-serving and untrustworthy.*

timetable *n.* °schedule, °calendar, curriculum, °programme, agenda, *Chiefly Brit* °diary: *My timetable doesn't allow for long lunches.*

time-worn *adj.* ageing, °old, °tired, °worn, time-scarred, °decrepit, °dilapidated, °tumbledown, °ramshackle, °run-down, dog-eared, °ragged, moth-eaten, °threadbare, °seedy, °shabby, archaic, °antique, well-worn, °worn out, °passé, broken-down, °old-fashioned, out-dated, dated, °antiquated, °ancient, °obsolescent, °obsolete, stereotyped, stereotypic(al), hackneyed, °stale, trite, overused, *Colloq* °old hat: *She went into her time-worn routine about two living as cheaply as one.*

timid *adj.* °shy, °retiring, °modest, °coy, °bashful, diffident, timorous, °fearful, apprehensive, °mousy, °scared, frightened, °nervous, °cowardly, pusillanimous, craven, *Colloq* chicken-hearted, yellow, yellow-bellied, chicken, chicken-livered, lily-livered, gutless: *I knew this strapping marine when he was a timid little boy.*

tinker *v.* °trifle, °dabble, °meddle, °mess (around *or* about), °toy, °fool *or* °play (around *or* about), *Brit* °potter *or US* putter (about *or* around), *Colloq* °fiddle *or* °monkey *or* °muck (about *or* around): *Graham has always enjoyed tinkering with engines.*

tinny *adj.* **1** °shabby, °flimsy, flimsily *or* °poorly made, °shoddy, °inferior, °cheap, °tawdry: *He bought himself a tinny old rattletrap of a car.* **2** metallic, °harsh, twangy: *She plays that tinny old trumpet day and night.*

tint *n.* **1** tincture, °wash, °hue, °colour, °cast; tinge, °touch, °hint, °trace, °dash, colouring, °shade, °tone, °suggestion: *In the west a tint of pink lingered in the sky. I thought I detected a tint of anger in his voice.* **2** dye, °rinse, wash, °stain, tincture, colourant, colouring, touch-up: *What's the harm in granny's using blue hair tint?*
—*v.* **3** dye, °stain, °colour, °rinse, tinge, °touch up: *Sandra tints her hair to give it a coppery sheen.* **4** tinge, °colour, °influence, °affect, °taint, °stain: *A deep pessimism tints all his writing.*

tiny *adj.* microscopic, infinitesimal, °minute, minuscule, °diminutive, °wee, °small, °little, °miniature, micro, mini, pocket, pocket-sized, bantam, pygmy, midget, Lilliputian, °petite, °delicate, °dainty, °elfin, °slight, °insignificant, °negligible, °trifling, °paltry, °inconsequential, °puny, *Colloq* pint-sized, teeny, teeny-weeny, teensy-weensy, itty-bitty, itsy-bitsy: *She wore the tiniest bikini I had ever seen. When I saw them together I realized how tiny she is. Forgetting my birthday was only a tiny thing.*

tip[1] *n.* **1** °end, °extremity, °peak, apex, °summit, °vertex, °cap, °top, °pinnacle, tiptop, °crown, °head, °terminal, ferrule *or* ferule, finial, nib *or* neb, °point: *The tip of the mountain showed above the clouds. He broke off the tip of the billiard cue.*
—*v.* **2** °top, °cap, °crown, surmount: *The foil is tipped with a rubber button to prevent injury.*

tip[2] *v.* **1** Often, ***tip over***: °upset, °overthrow, °knock *or* °cast *or* °throw down, up-end, °knock over, °overturn, °topple (over), °capsize: *His elbow tipped the lamp, which fell with a crash.* **2** °slant, °lean, °incline, °tilt, cant: *The statue is tipped a bit off the vertical.* **3** °empty, °unload, °dump, °deposit, *Slang Brit* ditch: *They tipped their load of gravel all over my driveway.*
—*n.* **4** (°rubbish *or US* °garbage) °dump, °rubbish *or* °refuse *or* °trash °heap, dumping-ground: *This old chair belongs in the tip.*

tip[3] *n.* **1** gratuity, baksheesh, *pourboire*, douceur, lagniappe *or* lagnappe, °present, °gift, *Colloq* little something: *That waiter didn't deserve a tip.* **2** tip-off, (inside) °information, °warning, °advice, °suggestion, °clue, °hint, °pointer, °forecast, °prediction, *Colloq Brit* gen: *Louie had a tip that the police were coming. Her tip was 'Flapdoodle' to win the fifth race.*
—*v.* **3** °reward: *Why did you tip the barmaid?*
4 Usually, ***tip off***: °advise, °warn, °caution, °alert, forewarn, °notify, let (someone) °know, *Colloq* let (someone) in on: *The thieves were tipped off and never arrived.*

tirade *n.* declamation, °harangue, diatribe, philippic, °outburst, onslaught, screed, jeremiad, denunciation, °stream of °abuse, invective: *He let loose with such a vituperative tirade that I walked out.*

tire *v.* **1** °weary, tire out, °fatigue, °exhaust, °wear out, °drain, °sap, °enervate, debilitate, °weaken, *Colloq* take it out of, °fag (out), *The long climb tired me.*
2 °bore, °exasperate, °weary, °irk, °irritate, °annoy, °bother: *I wish you wouldn't tire me with your accounts of your shopping expeditions.*

tired *adj.* **1** °exhausted, tired out, °worn out, °weary, °fatigued, °spent, drained, *Colloq* all in, (°dead) °beat, knocked out, fagged (out), dog-tired, ready to drop, °dead tired, done in, *Brit* knackered, whacked, *US* bushed, pooped, wiped out: *I was really tired after that ten-hour flight.* **2** Usually, ***tired of***: bored with, exasperated by, °weary of, irked *or* irritated *or* annoyed *or* bothered by, °sick (and tired) of, *Colloq* fed up (to here) with: *Perhaps she's tired of your constant nagging.*
3 overworked, overused, clichéd, stereotyped, stereotypic(al), hackneyed, unimaginative, trite, °stale, °worn out, unoriginal, commonplace, *Colloq* bromidic: *The gossip columns are filled with the same old tired rubbish day after day.*

tireless *adj.* °energetic, °vital, °vigorous, °dynamic, °spirited, °lively, indefatigable, hard-working, °industrious, °untiring, unflagging, unfaltering, unfailing, °persistent, dogged, °tenacious, pertinacious, persevering, °staunch, sedulous, unwavering, unswerving, undeviating, °steady, °steadfast, °resolute, °determined: *We all appreciate the honorary secretary's tireless efforts on behalf of our fund-raising this year.*

tiresome *adj.* **1** °boring, °dull, fatiguing, °humdrum, °monotonous, °flat, °tedious, wearisome, tiring, uninteresting, insipid, °bland, dry-as-dust, soporific, hypnotic: *Ibsen wrote plays that actors love and audiences find tiresome.* **2** irritating, °irksome, vexing, vexatious, annoying, bothersome, exasperating, °trying, °disagreeable, °troublesome, unpleasant: *I wish she would take her tiresome problems elsewhere.*

tissue *n.* °fabric, °network, °web, interweaving, °combination, °chain, series, °accumulation, conglomeration, concatenation, °pile, °mass, °pack: *Their entire testimony was a tissue of lies.*

titbit *n.* °delicacy, (°dainty) °morsel, °treat, °choice °item, *bonne bouche*, *US* tidbit, *Colloq* goody: *Sally likes to steal little titbits off my plate. I heard a juicy titbit of gossip this morning.*

title *n.* **1** °name: *You cannot tell much from a book's title.* **2** designation, appellation, epithet: *Aubrey is now an earl, but he rarely uses his title.* **3** caption, inscription, headline, °head, subtitle, °legend, subhead, rubric: *The title on this picture has nothing to do with its subject.* **4** championship, °crown: *He holds the world heavyweight boxing title.* **5** °right, °interest, °privilege, entitlement, ownership, °possession, °tenure; (°title-)°deed, documentation of ownership: *My aunt has sole title to these lands.*
—*v.* **6** °name, °call, °designate, °style, °label, °term, °entitle, °christen, baptize, °nickname, denominate, °tag, dub: *Harold was titled King of the Revels.*

titter *v.* **1** °chuckle, °snicker, chortle, °giggle; snigger: *He told the most awful jokes at which his staff would titter politely.*
—*n.* **2** °chuckle, °snicker, °giggle, (suppressed) °laughter, chortle, snigger: *A titter ran through the audience.*

titular *adj.* °nominal, °so-called, so-designated, so-styled, °self-styled, *soi-disant*, °token, putative, °theoretical: *He may be the titular head of the company, but his brother is really the boss.*

toast *n.* **1** °tribute, °pledge, salutation(s), °greeting(s), felicitations, °honour, good wishes, °appreciation, °remembrance(s), °cheers: *The speaker proposed a toast to the editor-in-chief.* **2** °heroine, °hero, °favourite, °darling, °idol: *Jenny was the toast of the town.*
—*v.* **3** °pay °tribute to, °salute, °drink to, °honour, °greet, °congratulate, felicitate: *We toasted our fallen comrades.*

toilet *n.* **1** (water) closet, WC, men's (room), ladies' (room), (public) convenience, °facility *or* facilities, washroom, bathroom, °lavatory, °privy, outhouse, urinal, In France *pissoir, vespasienne; Nautical* head, *Chiefly military* latrine, *Chiefly US* rest room, *New England* °necessary, *Colloq* the Gents, the Ladies('), powder-room, little girls' room, little boys' room, *Brit* loo, smallest room (in the house), *Military* ablutions, *Slang Brit* bog, karzy, *US and Canadian* john, can, crapper: *They excused themselves to go to the toilet.*
2 *Formal or literary* grooming, dressing, making up, *Brit* toilette: *She was still at her toilet when we arrived.*

toilsome *adj.* °arduous, °laborious, °tough, °hard, °difficult, °strenuous, °burdensome, onerous, backbreaking, °exhausting, fatiguing, tiring, enervating, wearying, draining: *After a toilsome ascent we finally reached the first camp.*

token *n.* **1** °coin, disc: *You need to buy a token to get through the turnstile.* **2** °symbol, °sign, °mark, marker, badge, °emblem, °indication, °proof, °evidence: *The purple trim on a Roman toga was a token of its wearer's elevated status.* **3** souvenir, °memento, °keepsake, °reminder, °remembrance, *Archaic* remembrancer: *The miniature Statue of Liberty and Eiffel Tower are tokens of our trips abroad.*
—*adj.* **4** °symbolic, °emblematic, °representative: *The panel was made up of three men and a token woman.*
5 °superficial, cosmetic, °surface, °perfunctory, °minimal, °slight, °nominal: *We encountered only token resistance when taking over the communications centre.*

tolerable *adj.* **1** °bearable, °supportable, allowable, endurable, °acceptable, sufferable: *The heat and humidity are barely tolerable.* **2** °acceptable, unexceptional, °common, °fair, common-or-garden variety, middling, °ordinary, °average, °so so, °mediocre, °adequate, run-of-the-mill, °passable, °indifferent, *Colloq* °OK *or* okay, not (too) °bad, pretty *or* fairly °good: *They serve a tolerable lunch in the hotel bar.*

tolerance *n.* **1** open-mindedness, toleration, forbearance, broad-mindedness, permissiveness, magnanimity, °indulgence, sufferance, °patience, freedom from °bigotry *or* °prejudice: *You must exercise more tolerance in dealing with people who are poorer than you.*
2 °play, °clearance, °allowance, °variation: *The tolerance between these parts is less than a ten-thousandth of a millimetre.* **3** toleration, °resistance, °endurance,

imperviousness; °immunity, insensitivity: *His tolerance of the outrages of stupidity seems limitless. She has a low tolerance for sugar.*

tolerant *adj.* open-minded, °objective, forbearing, °unprejudiced, unbigoted, °dispassionate, broad-minded, °indulgent, magnanimous, °patient, °generous, °charitable, °catholic, latitudinarian, °permissive, °liberal, big-hearted, °fair, even-handed, °considerate: *I am more tolerant of people than of their ideas.*

tolerate *v.* **1** °stand (for), °allow, °permit, °bear, °suffer, °brook, countenance, °abide, °admit, °indulge, °concede, °sanction, °swallow, °stomach, turn a blind eye to, *Colloq* °put up with, *Brit* °stick: *The teacher refused to tolerate any more misbehaviour.* **2** °bear, °stand, °submit to, °endure, °weather, °take, °accept, °undergo: *Tests show that the product can tolerate considerable wear and tear.*

toll[1] *v.* **1** °ring, °peal, °chime, °strike, °sound: *The clock tower bell tolled three.*
—*n.* **2** °ring, ringing, °peal, pealing, °chime, chiming, °striking, °sound, sounding, tolling, knell: *Each toll of the bell marked the death of another victim.*

toll[2] *n.* **1** °charge, °fee, °dues, assessment, °tariff; excise, °duty, impost, levy, °tribute: *New motorways will be funded by means of a toll on traffic using them.* **2** °loss, °penalty, °cost, °damage(s); exaction: *The death toll from the earthquake reached 50,000.*

tomb *n.* °sepulchre, °crypt, vault, mausoleum, °grave, catacomb, burial-chamber, final *or* last resting-place: *Every year his tomb is visited by a mysterious woman in black.*

tombstone *n.* gravestone, headstone, marker, °monument, cenotaph: *The tombstones in the military cemetery stood in serried ranks.*

tone *n.* **1** °sound, note: *Odd tones emanated from the electronic music-maker.* **2** °stress, °emphasis, °force, °accent, °intonation, modulation, phrasing, inflection, °pitch, tonality, °timbre, °sound (°colour), tone °colour *or* °quality, colour *or* colouring, resonance, sonorousness, sonority, fullness, richness: *The tone of his voice is extraordinarily melodic.* **3** °manner, °style, °attitude, °air, °aspect, °approach, note, °tenor, tone of °voice, °mode of °expression, °temper, °vein, °spirit, °air: *Do not take that imperious tone with me!* **4** °tint, tinge, °shade, °hue, °colour, colouring, °cast: *The fabric has a silvery tone that makes it shimmer.*
—*v.* **5** ***tone down***: °temper, °modify, °reduce, °moderate, °modulate, °soften, °quiet(en), °dampen, °dull, °subdue, °mute, soft-pedal: *Please tone down your voice or the neighbours will hear you.* **6** ***tone up***: (re)invigorate, °tune (up), °brighten (up), (re)vitalize, °freshen (up), limber up, get into °condition *or* °shape: *I really have to tone up my body before I put on a swimsuit this summer.*

tongue *n.* **1** °language, °speech; °dialect, patois,Creole, °idiom, °parlance, argot, °talk, °vernacular, *façon de parler*: *The people in that area speak a strange tongue.* **2** (°verbal) °expression, utterance, °voice, articulation: *Michael is reluctant to give tongue to his real feelings.* **3** ***hold (one's) tongue***: be *or* °remain *or* °keep °silent, °keep °mum, °say °nothing *or* nought, not breathe a word, °keep (one's) °counsel, not °say a word, *Slang* °shut up: *Hold your tongue till you are spoken to!* **4** ***slip of the tongue***: °slip, °mistake, gaffe, °blunder, faux pas, Freudian °slip, *Colloq Brit* boob: *Saying 'bald' when I meant 'bold' was a slip of the tongue.* **5** ***(with (one's)) tongue in (one's) cheek***: facetiously, whimsically, ironically, jocularly, jokingly, not °seriously, in jest, jestingly, in °fun, to be °funny, *Colloq* kiddingly: *As he is my older brother, I call him 'Dad' with tongue in cheek, of course.*

tongue-lashing *n.* scolding, berating, °reproof, °rebuke, °reprimand; (°verbal) °abuse, castigation, chastisement, vituperation, revilement, *Colloq* dressing-down, telling-off, talking-to, *Brit* slating, ticking-off, wigging: *For all his efforts to please, he only got a tongue-lashing for interfering.*

tongue-tied *adj.* °speechless, at a °loss for words, struck °dumb, °dumbfounded *or* dumfounded, °mute, °inarticulate: *I was so nervous when the Prince of Wales spoke to me that I got tongue-tied.*

tonic *n.* **1** °stimulant, restorative, invigorant, °boost, refresher; *Obsolete or literary* ptisan *or* tisane, *Technical* roborant, analeptic, *Colloq* bracer, pick-me-up, pick-up, °shot in the arm, *US* picker-upper: *His father made his money selling snake-oil tonic.*
—*adj.* **2** °stimulant, °stimulating, restorative, °invigorating, fortifying, °bracing, strengthening, reviving, enlivening, °refreshing, *Technical* analeptic, roborant: *Seeing Maddie and Max again had a tonic effect.*

tool *n.* **1** utensil, °implement, °instrument, °device, °apparatus, appliance, contrivance, °aid, °machine, °mechanism, °gadget, *Colloq* °contraption, °gimmick, *Chiefly US and Canadian* gismo *or* gizmo: *The work would go faster if you had the proper tools.* **2** °means, °way, °agency, weapon, °medium, °vehicle, instrumentality, avenue, °road: *Education is the tool you need to get anywhere in life.* **3** °puppet, cat's-paw, °pawn, °dupe, *Slang* stooge, °sucker: *I had been used merely as a tool in her ambitious rise to the top.*
—*v.* **4** °work, °carve, °cut, °embellish, °decorate, °ornament, °dress, °shape: *This is the shop where the leather is tooled and gold-stamped.*

top *n.* **1** °summit, apex, °peak, °acme, °crest, °head, °pinnacle, °vertex, °zenith, meridian, °crown, culmination, °high °point, °height, apogee: *They reached the top of the mountain at dawn. For a change, I should like to be at the top looking down. Samantha remains at the top of her profession.* **2** lid, °cover, °cap, covering, °stopper, cork: *Put the top back on the bottle when you're through.*
—*v.* **3** °surpass, °better, °best, °outstrip, °exceed, °outdo, °excel, °beat, °transcend: *It would be impossible to top some of his achievements.* **4** surmount, °cover, °cap, °crown, °tip; °finish, °complete, garnish: *The entire concoction was topped by a maraschino cherry.* **5** °trim, crop, °lop *or* °cut off, °clip, °prune, °nip, °pinch (back): *All the trees in this area have been topped to let in more sunlight.* **6** °scale, °climb, ascend, surmount: *The party topped Annapurna the next day.* **7** ***top up***: °fill (up), °refresh, refill, °replenish, *US* °freshen (up): *He asked the barman to top up our drinks.*
—*adj.* **8** °best, greatest, °foremost, °leading, °pre-eminent, °eminent, °first, °first-rate, °principal, °prime, finest, choicest, topmost; °excellent, °superior, °superb, top-drawer, top-grade, top-notch, °supreme, °peerless, unequalled, °incomparable, *Colloq* crack, ace, A-1 *or* A-one: *Is he the top man in his field? She is a top economics adviser to the government.* **9** °uppermost, topmost, highest: *The top fruit is the best.*

topic *n.* °subject(-matter), °matter, °issue, °question, °point, °thesis, °theme, °text, keynote, °field *or* °area of °study *or* of °inquiry: *We need to decide on a topic for tonight's discussion.*

topical *adj.* **1** °contemporary, °current, up to °date, °timely: *Drug addiction is certainly a topical subject.* **2** °local, °superficial: *For a minor injury we give a topical, not a general anaesthetic.*

topple *v.* **1** °upset, up-end, °knock down *or* over, °bring down, °fell, °capsize, °collapse: *Scores of buildings were toppled by the tornado.* **2** °bring *or* °throw down, °overthrow, °defeat, vanquish, °overcome, °overturn, unseat, oust: *The leaders of the coup succeeded in toppling the government in a week.* **3** °fall (over *or* down), °drop, °collapse, keel over, °tumble down: *Seven guardsmen toppled over because of the heat on the parade ground.*

topsy-turvy *adj.* **1** upside down, °wrong side up, °head over heels, inverted, reversed, °backwards, °vice versa: *The children were wearing their pyjamas topsy-turvy.* **2** °chaotic, muddled, jumbled, °disorderly, disordered, disorganized, °confused, mixed-up, messy, °untidy, in a °muddle, higgledy-piggledy, *Colloq* arsy-versy, every which way: *The room was completely topsy-turvy and it was impossible to find anything.*

torment *v.* **1** torture, °abuse, maltreat, °mistreat, °distress, agonize, excruciate, crucify, harrow, °rack, °pain: *Hunger tormented his weary body.* **2** °worry, °trouble, °plague, °annoy, bedevil, vex, harry, badger, hector, °harass, °pester, °nag, °persecute, needle, nettle, °irk, °irritate, °bother, torture, °afflict, *Brit* chivvy *or* chivy *or* chevy: *I was tormented by the suspicion that something was wrong.*
—*n.* **3** °agony, wretchedness, °anguish, °distress, °misery, °pain, °woe, painfulness, torture, °suffering, °curse, °hell: *How can parents endure the torment of losing a child?* **4** °worry, vexation, °annoyance, harassment, °ordeal, °persecution, needling, °nuisance, bane, irritation, °bother, °affliction, °scourge, torture: *For yet another day I had to suffer the torment of their company.*

torpid *adj.* sluggish, °slow, slow-moving, slow-paced, tortoise-like, °lethargic, apathetic, °indolent, °passive, °slothful, °dull, stupefied, °sleepy, somnolent, °inactive, °inert, languid, languorous, °phlegmatic, spiritless, °lifeless, °listless, fainéant, °lackadaisical, pococurante, °indifferent, uncaring, unconcerned, insouciant: *Johnson said that it is a man's own fault if his mind grows torpid in old age.*

torpor *n.* °sluggishness, °sloth, °lethargy, apathy, °indolence, passivity, slothfulness, dullness, stupefaction, drowsiness, sleepiness, somnolence, °inactivity, °inertia, inertness, languor, laziness, phlegm, lifelessness, listlessness, °idleness, fainéance, pococurant(e)ism, °indifference, unconcern, insouciance: *The heat produced a certain torpor in all of us.*

torrent *n.* °stream, °rush, °flood, deluge, effusion, gushing, °outburst, °outpouring, °spate, inundation, °flow, overflow, tide, cascade: *In minutes the brook became a rushing torrent. They assailed us with a torrent of abuse.*

torrential *adj.* rushing, streaming, copious, °profuse, teeming, °relentless, °violent; °fierce, vehement, vociferous, °ferocious: *The torrential monsoons inundated the land. I had never heard such a torrential outpouring of oaths.*

torrid *adj.* **1** °hot, °fiery, °sultry, stifling, °sweltering, broiling, sizzling, roasting, blazing, °burning, baking, cooking, boiling, blistering, blistery, °scorching, scorched, parched, parching, arid; °humid, °steamy, steaming, °muggy; tropical: *It seemed impossible that any creature could survive in such a torrid climate.* **2** °fervent, fervid, °passionate, °intense, °ardent, °inflamed, °impassioned, °lustful, amorous, °erotic, *Colloq* °sexy, °hot: *The film was noted for its torrid love scenes.*

tortuous *adj.* **1** twisted, twisting, winding, wandering, °serpentine, turning, °crooked, sinuous, °bent, curled, curling, curved, curvy, curvilinear, flexuous, anfractuous, convoluted, involuted, zigzag, maze-like, mazy, °labyrinthine: *They followed a tortuous trail through the jungle.* **2** °roundabout, °indirect, °devious, °intricate, °involved, unstraightforward, °complicated, °ambiguous, ambagious, circuitous, warped, °crooked, °tricky, misleading, °deceptive: *We could not help being intrigued by the tortuous Machiavellianism of the scheme.*

toss *v.* **1** °throw, °cast, °lob, °pitch, °fling, °hurl, °heave, °shy, °launch, °send, °let °fly, °propel, catapult, °sling, °bowl, *Colloq* chuck: *The goalkeeper tossed the ball into the middle of the field.* **2** °shake, °jerk, °stir up, °agitate, °fling: *Lucy disdainfully tossed her head.* **3** °shake (up), °stir (up), °agitate, °jiggle, °tumble, joggle; °wave, °lash, thrash: *Don't you put the dressing on before you toss the salad? The branches of the huge oak were being tossed about in the storm.* **4** writhe, °wriggle, °squirm, toss and °turn, thrash: *I tossed all night, unable to get a moment's sleep.* **5** °pitch, yaw, °wallow, °roll, °lurch, undulate, °plunge: *Our little boat was tossed this way and that in the heavy seas.*
—*n.* **6** °throw, °lob, °pitch, °heave, °shy: *His toss went wild and the ball rolled over the cliff.*

tot *n.* °child, toddler, infant, °baby: *Can you recall when you were a tiny tot?*

total *n.* **1** °sum (total), °totality, aggregate, °whole, °amount, total °number: *The total of wounded came to only fifteen.*
—*adj.* **2** °whole, °entire, °complete, °full, °gross, °overall, °comprehensive: *Total rainfall in that area is only three inches per annum.* **3** °complete, unalloyed, °unmitigated, °unqualified, unconditional, utter, °out-and-out, °thorough, thoroughgoing, °perfect, °outright, °downright, all-out, °absolute: *My son is a total failure in everything he attempts.*
—*v.* **4** °add (up), °tot up, °sum up, °reckon, °compute: *Please total my bill.* **5** °amount to, °add up to, °come to, °mount up to: *The bill totals twice the amount I paid yesterday.*

totalitarian *adj.* °absolute, absolutist, °arbitrary, °authoritarian, autocratic, °dictatorial, Fascist(ic), undemocratic, illiberal, °monolithic, Nazi, °oppressive, °despotic, °tyrannical: *Sooner or later, totalitarian governments get overthrown.*

totality *n.* °total, aggregate, °sum (°total), °whole, °entirety, beginning and end, alpha and omega, be-all and end-all: *The totality of his interests lies in watching soap operas on TV.*

totally *adv.* °completely, °utterly, °entirely, fully, unqualifiedly, unconditionally, °perfectly, °absolutely, °thoroughly, °wholly, consummately: *We then decided on a totally different approach. The weather was totally awful.*

totter *v.* waver, °topple, falter, °tremble, °teeter, °sway, °rock, °stagger, °stumble, wobble, °quiver, °shake, °quake, °shiver, dodder: *He seemed to totter a bit as he left the pub.*

touch *v.* **1** put (one's) hand on, °feel, °handle: *She leant forward and touched my hand.* **2** bring into °contact with, °apply, °put, °set: *He touched a match to the fuse and ran.* **3** Sometimes, ***touch (up) against***: be in °contact (with), °border, adjoin, °meet, come up *or* be (up) against, °push *or* °press *or* °lean (up) against, °brush *or* °rub (up) against, come *or* be together, abut: *The ladder is touching the freshly painted wall.* **4** °lay a hand *or* finger on; °meddle with, have to do with, °interfere with, come °near, °approach: *If you touch me, I'll scream.* **5** °drink, °eat, °consume, °partake of, °take, °use, °taste, have to do with: *He swore that he would never touch alcohol again.* **6** °affect, °impress, °influence, °disturb, °move, °stir, °arouse, °excite, impassion, °stimulate, °strike, *Colloq* °get to: *We were touched by your sympathetic note.* **7** °rival, °match, °equal, °compare with, come up to, be on a °par with, be a °match for, be in the °same league *or* class as *or* with, be on an °equal footing with, °reach, come *or* get °near *or* °close to, hold a candle to, °measure up to *or* against, *Colloq US* °stack up to *or* with *or* against: *No other car can touch our new model for speed and safety.* **8** Usually, ***touch on*** *or* ***upon***: °refer to, °have °reference to, °pertain to, °relate to, have a °bearing on, °regard, °mention, allude to, °speak *or* °write of, °tell of, °bring up *or* in, °raise, °deal with, °cover: *I must now touch upon a delicate matter.* **9** have access to, access, °use, °employ, make °use of, °put to °use, avail (oneself) of, °take, °get, °take °advantage of: *I do not touch the principal, but try to live off the interest.*
10 ***touch down***: °land, alight, come to °earth: *We touched down for fuel at Gander, Newfoundland.*
11 ***touch off***: **a** detonate, °spark (off), °set alight, °set off, ignite, °light, °fire, put a match to: *We touched off the gunpowder and blew up the arsenal.* **b** instigate, °initiate, °begin, °start, set in °motion, ignite, °set off, trigger, °provoke, °foment, °cause, give °rise to: *Her offhand remark touched off a family row that lasted for years.* **12** ***touch up***: °retouch, °patch up; °beautify, °enhance, titivate, °renovate, °spruce up: *She said that the painting had recently been touched up. Mandy is upstairs touching up her make-up.*
—*n.* **13** °feeling, °feel, °texture: *She wants nothing but the touch of silk next to her body.* **14** °pat, °tap, °blow, °hit, °stroke, °brush, °caress: *She hated him so much*

that she cringed at the touch of his hand. **15** °dash, °hint, intimation, °suggestion, soupçon, °bit, °pinch, °jot, °spot, °trace, tinge, °taste, °suspicion, smattering, colouring, smack, °speck, °drop, whiff, °odour, °scent, °smell: *Cynthia has a touch of hypocrisy about her. The salad dressing could use a touch more garlic.* **16** °ability, deftness, °expertise, °dexterity, adroitness, °facility, °skill, skilfulness, °knack, °capability, °genius, °talent, °gift, °flair: *Richard has a master's touch in everything he does.* **17** °response, °feel, responsiveness, °feeling, °movement, °operation, performance level: *This piano action has an excellent touch.* **18** signature, °trade °mark, °characteristic, °influence, °approach, °style, °manner, °technique, °execution, °method: *I thought I recognized your touch in the furniture selection. A woman's touch might have helped.*

touching *adj.* °moving, °stirring, °emotional, °tender, °poignant, °pathetic, soul-stirring, °heart-rending, heartbreaking, °sad, °pitiful, distressing, distressful: *The most touching scene is the one where the boy meets his father for the first time.*

touchstone *n.* °standard, °yardstick, criterion, °reference, benchmark, °test, °norm, °measure: *His craftsmanship is the touchstone by which the others are judged.*

touchy *adj.* **1** (over-)°sensitive, supersensitive, hypersensitive, highly-strung, °tense, thin-skinned, crabby, crabbed, °testy, irascible, °irritable, tetchy, °temperamental, grouchy, °peevish, °querulous, °petulant, pettish, splenetic, captious, bad-tempered, °short-tempered, hot-tempered, °quick-tempered, crusty, °cross, curmudgeonly, °cantankerous, choleric, dyspeptic, °waspish, bearish, snarling, °snappish, °argumentative, disputatious, contentious, *US* high-strung, °cranky: *She is very touchy on the subject of her family. He's always touchy in the morning.* **2** °critical, touch-and-go, °sensitive, °ticklish, °risky, °precarious, °hazardous, chancy, unsure, °uncertain, °close, hair-breadth, °dangerous, hair-raising, °frightening, °terrifying, °nerve-racking *or* nerve-wracking, *Jocular* °parlous, *Colloq* °hairy: *There was a touchy moment when the fuel leaked into the astronauts' cabin.*

tough *adj.* **1** °hard, °firm, °durable, long-lasting, wear-resistant, °substantial, °strong, °stout, °rugged, °sturdy, °sound, well-built: *Only one kind of material is tough enough to endure such conditions for so long.* **2** °stiff, °hard, leathery, °inflexible, chewy, fibrous, cartilaginous, °sinewy, °ropy, °wiry, °stringy: *That steak was as tough as shoe-leather.* **3** °strong, °stalwart, °brawny, °burly, °muscular, °powerful, virile, °manly, °sturdy, doughty, °intrepid, °stout, °rough, °vigorous, strapping, athletic: *Two tough-looking characters moved towards us, so we left.* **4** °difficult, °demanding, °exacting, °hard, °troublesome; °laborious, taxing, °strenuous: *We deal with tough complaints every day. It's a tough job.* **5** baffling, °thorny, °puzzling, °perplexing, mystifying, knotty, °irksome, °difficult: *The examiners asked us some very tough questions.* **6** °stubborn, hardened, inured, °obstinate, obdurate, °hard, °harsh, °severe, °stern, °inflexible, refractory, intractable, adamant, unyielding, ungiving, °rigid, unbending, unsentimental, unfeeling, °unsympathetic, °callous, hard-boiled, uncaring, °cold, °cool, °icy, °stony, *Colloq* hard-nosed: *He's a tough man to work for, but he's fair.*
—*interj.* **7** *Colloq* Too bad!, Tough luck!, Hard luck!, *Brit* Hard cheese!, *Slang* Tough titty!, *Taboo slang* Tough shit!: *When I told him that my money had been stolen, he said 'Tough!'*
—*n.* **8** °bruiser, hooligan, °bully (boy), °rowdy, °thug, ruffian, *Colloq* roughneck, °bruiser, tough guy, gorilla: *A couple of toughs who had been threatening the cashier disappeared when they saw our uniforms.*

tour *n.* **1** °journey, °trip, °excursion, °outing, °expedition, voyage, trek, peregrination, jaunt, junket: *We went on a guided tour because we were short of time and wanted to see everything.* **2** °stroll, perambulation, walkabout, °ramble, °walk, °drive; °round, °circuit, ambit: *The government representatives are on a tour of all nuclear facilities.* **3** °spell, °shift, °assignment, °turn, *Military* °period of °service *or* enlistment: *His tour of duty is not finished till midnight.*
—*v.* **4** °journey, °travel, voyage, °visit, °trip, trek, sightsee, °cruise; *Colloq* globe-trot: *On retirement we spent a year just touring around Europe.*

tourist *n.* °traveller, voyager, °visitor, °sightseer, *Colloq* °rubberneck(er), out-of-towner, *Brit* tripper, day-tripper, holiday-maker: *During the summer, this place is inundated with tourists.*

tournament *n.* tourney, °competition, °contest, °match, °meeting, °event, °meet: *The tennis tournament was delayed by rain.*

tousle *v.* dishevel, °disorder, °ruffle, disarrange, °tangle (up), °mess (up), °rumple, disarray, *US* muss (up): *Her hair was all tousled by the wind.*

tout *v.* **1** hawk, °peddle, °sell, °promote, °talk up, *Colloq* °push, °plug: *They tout these new headache tablets as miraculous.*
—*n.* **2** tipster: *He is often seen with racetrack touts.*

tow *v.* °pull, °drag, °draw, °haul, °lug, °trail, °tug, trawl: *The boat was towing a long purse seine. I arrived just as the police were towing away my car.*

towards *prep.* **1** toward, in the °direction of, to; °for, so as to °approach *or* °near, on the way *or* road to: *She turned towards me. I'd appreciate a lift if you're going towards Aston Clinton.* **2** toward, to, °for, as a help to, supporting, promoting, assisting: *We welcome any contribution towards the charitable works of our order.* **3** toward, °near, nearing, °close to, approaching, °shortly before: *Towards the close of day, the cattle wander back to the barns.*

tower *n.* **1** bell-tower, campanile, minaret, pagoda, obelisk; belfry, °spire, turret, steeple, flèche: *There was a time when the church tower was the tallest building in the town.* **2** fortress, citadel, °stronghold, °castle, fastness; °keep, °dungeon, °prison: *The princess was imprisoned in the tower for a year and a day.*
—*v.* **3** Often, ***tower over*** *or* ***above***: °loom, °soar, °rise, ascend, °rear: *These ugly high-rise buildings tower over everything, blocking out the sun.*

towering *adj.* **1** °lofty, °tall, °high, soaring, °outstanding, °elevated, sky-scraping, sky-high, °great, °impressive, °imposing, °huge, °gigantic, °supreme, °superior, °paramount, °extraordinary, unmatched, unequal, unrivalled, °unparalleled, unsurpassed: *The towering American economy dominated the world for decades after World War II.* **2** °violent, °fiery, °burning, °passionate, °excessive, vehement, °intense, consuming, °mighty, °overwhelming, unrestrained, °immoderate, °inordinate, intemperate, °extreme, °colossal, °enormous: *Every time she mentioned Valentino, he went into a towering rage.*

town *n.* township, village, hamlet, community; °municipality, °city, °metropolis, borough, burgh: *She was born in Stornoway, a small town in the Outer Hebrides. We have to drive into the town to do our shopping.*

toy *n.* **1** °plaything: *Whenever he visited, Uncle Jed brought toys for the children.* **2** °trifle, trinket, °bauble, °gewgaw, gimcrack, knick-knack, bagatelle, kickshaw, bit of frippery: *After marrying her, he treated her as a rich man's toy.*
—*v.* **3** Usually, ***toy with***: °trifle (with), dally (with), °play (with), °sport (with), °fool (with), °fiddle (with), °tinker (with): *He kept toying with his watch chain.* **4** Usually, ***toy with***: °flirt (with), dally (with), dilly-dally (with), °play (with), deal with carelessly, °amuse oneself with: *The cad was only toying with her affections.*
—*adj.* **5** °miniature, °tiny, °diminutive, °small, °dwarf: *She breeds toy poodles.* **6** °imitation, °fake, °phoney *or US also* phony, simulated, °artificial: *This is only a toy watch and doesn't work.*

trace *n.* **1** °hint, intimation, °sign, °token, °suggestion, °touch, °vestige, °indication, °mark, °record, °evidence, °clue: *There wasn't any trace of the intruders.* **2** °bit, °spot, °speck, °jot, °drop, °dash, °suspicion, °remnant,

tinge, soupçon, iota, whiff, °suggestion, °trifle: *The traces of mud on the suspect's shoes proved he had been there.* **3** Often, ***traces***: °track(s), °trail, spoor, footprint(s), °print(s), footmark(s): *They were following the traces of a buffalo.*
—*v.* **4** dog, °pursue, °follow (in the footsteps of), °stalk, °track (down), °shadow, °trail, *Colloq* °tail: *We traced him to a seedy hotel in Caracas.* **5** °investigate, °discover, ascertain, °detect, °determine, °find, °seek, °search for, °hunt down *or* up, °unearth, °track: *Have you traced her whereabouts? I am able to trace my ancestry back to the time of the First Crusade.* **6** delineate, °outline, °copy, °draw, map, °chart, °mark (out), °record, °reproduce, sketch: *We traced Marco Polo's route to China and back.*

track *n.* **1** °line, °rail(s), °way, °railway, *US* °railroad: *New track was laid between London and Manchester.* **2** °path, °trail, °route, footpath, °course, °road, °street, alley: *A rough track leads over Sty Head Pass. Are you sure you're on the right track?* **3** spoor, °trail, footprint(s), °print(s), °trace(s), footmark(s), °scent, °slot, °wake: *The last time I saw him he was following the track of a yeti.* **4** ***keep track of***: °trace, track, °keep an °eye on, °follow, °pursue, °monitor, °supervise, °oversee, °keep up with *or* on, °watch, °keep a °record of *or* on, °record: *Using an electronic tag, we were able to keep track of the animal's movements.* **5** ***lose track of***: °lose, misplace, °mislay, °lose sight of, °forget: *She lost track of some important papers. I lost track of what I was saying.*
—*v.* **6** °follow, dog, °pursue, °trace, °stalk, °shadow, °trail, °hunt down, °chase, *Colloq* °tail: *She was tracked to Istanbul, where they lost her.* **7** See **4,** above. **8** ***track down***: °find, °seek out, ferret out, °hunt down, °trace, °catch, apprehend, °capture, smell *or* sniff out, °run to earth *or* ground, *Colloq* °run down: *We finally tracked him down at his mother's house in Putney.*

trackless *adj.* °empty, pathless, untrodden, unexplored, °uncharted, virgin, untrod: *We found ourselves in the trackless wilderness of central Australia.*

tract[1] *n.* °region, °area, °stretch, °territory, °expanse, °zone, °portion, °section, sector, °quarter, °district, °patch, °plot, °parcel, *US* °lot: *The developers own a tract of land where they plan to build a shopping mall.*

tract[2] *n.* treatise, °monograph, °essay, article, °paper, dissertation, disquisition, homily, °sermon, critique; °pamphlet, booklet, °brochure, °leaflet: *Daphne was distributing tracts to passers-by in front of the church.*

tractable *adj.* **1** docile, amenable, °tame, °manageable, biddable, persuadable *or* persuasible, compliant, °easygoing, °willing, °submissive, °obedient, governable, °yielding: *It was a pleasure to teach a student who was so tractable.* **2** °manageable, handleable, workable, °adaptable, malleable, °pliable, °plastic, ductile, fictile: *The new materials are quite tractable and can be drawn or moulded with ease.*

traction *n.* °grip, gripping power, °drag, °purchase, °friction, adhesion: *Unable to get any traction on the ice, the car skidded off the road.*

trade *n.* **1** °commerce, °business, °traffic, °exchange, barter, dealing(s), buying and selling, merchandising, marketing, mercantilism, °truck: *Have we any trade in shoes with South Korea? We are establishing trade with Eastern Europe?* **2** °calling, °occupation, °pursuit, °work, °business, °employment, °line (of °work), métier, °job, °vocation, °craft, °career, °profession: *Just what trade are you engaged in?* **3** swap *or* swop, °exchange, interchange, barter: *Was exchanging your microwave cooker for a hi-fi set a good trade?* **4** customers, °clientele, °custom, °patrons, following, °patronage, shoppers: *Her shop caters chiefly to the holiday trade.*
—*v.* **5** °transact *or* do °business, °buy, °sell, °deal, °traffic, °merchandise, have °dealings: *There are laws against Sunday trading in some areas.* **6** °exchange, swap *or* swop, interchange, °switch, barter; °return: *Having traded his car for the boat, Sam has no way of reaching the marina.*

trader *n.* °dealer, °merchant, businessman, businesswoman, °broker, merchandiser, distributor, °seller, salesman, saleswoman, °salesperson, vendor, °buyer, purchaser, retailer, wholesaler: *All sorts of traders can be found in the covered market.*

tradesman *n.* **1** °merchant, °dealer, shopkeeper, retailer, vendor, °seller: *A tradesman had been ringing at the door for several minutes.* **2** artisan, craftsman, journeyman, handicraftsman: *He is a tradesman, a skilled cabinet-maker by profession.*

tradition *n.* °custom, °practice, °habit, °usage, °convention, °ritual, °rite, unwritten °law, °institution, °form, praxis, °lore: *Exchanging gifts on Christmas Eve has long been a tradition in our family.*

traditional *adj.* °customary, °usual, °routine, °habitual, °standard, household, stock, °time-honoured, established, °well-known, °conventional, °ritual, unwritten, °accustomed, °historic, °old, ancestral: *Mazetta mocha tarts were the traditional birthday cakes at home when I was a child.*

traffic *n.* **1** °movement, conveyance, shipping, °transport, °freight, *Chiefly US* transportation: *Traffic across the border has resumed.* **2** See **trade, 1,** above: *Drug traffic has increased greatly in recent years.*
—*v.* **3** See **trade, 5,** above: *The police think that Baines is trafficking in stolen goods.*

tragedy *n.* °catastrophe, °calamity, °disaster, °misfortune, adversity, °blow: *The death of their dog was a terrible tragedy, especially for the children.*

tragic *adj.* °sad, depressing, °lamentable, °unhappy, °funereal, °forlorn, °melancholy, cheerless, °mournful, lachrymose, dolorous, °grievous, morose, lugubrious, °dismal, °piteous, °pitiable, °pitiful, °pathetic(al), appalling, °wretched, °dreadful, °awful, °terrible, °horrible, °deplorable, °miserable, distressing, °disturbing, upsetting, °shocking, unlucky, °unfortunate, hapless, ill-fated, °inauspicious, star-crossed, ill-omened, ill-starred, °calamitous, catastrophic, crushing, °disastrous; tragical: *It was really tragic that we couldn't get there in time to say goodbye.*

trail *n.* **1** (beaten) °path, °way, footpath, °route, °track, °course: *There is a well-worn trail through the wood.* **2** °track, spoor, °scent, °smell, °trace, footsteps, footprints, °path, °wake: *The trail of the elephant herd was quite easy to follow.* **3** See **train, 2,** below: *She was always followed by a trail of admirers.*
—*v.* **4** °tow, °draw, °drag (along), °haul, °pull, °tag along, trawl, °bring along (behind), °carry along (behind): *We were moving slowly because we were trailing a dinghy.* **5** °drag, °pull, °move, be °drawn, °stream, °sweep, °dangle: *I heard the whisper of silken gowns trailing across Persian carpets.* **6** °lag (behind), °dawdle, loiter, °linger, °follow, °straggle, bring up the °rear, °hang back, °fall *or* °drop behind: *Our team was trailing three-five in the final.* **7** °follow, °pursue, dog, °trace, °shadow, °stalk, °track, °chase, °hunt, *Colloq* °tail: *We trailed the suspect to Victoria Station, where we lost him.* **8** ***trail off*** *or* ***away***: °diminish, °decrease, °fade away *or* out, °disappear, °dwindle, lessen, °die out *or* away, peter out, °subside, °taper off, °weaken, grow °faint *or* °dim: *As they drove away, the noise of their blasting radio trailed off.*

train *n.* **1** °carriage, °coach, *Baby-talk* choo-choo: *Will this train take me to Newcastle?* **2** °retinue, entourage, cortège, °suite, following, °escort, °guard, attendants, retainers, followers, °trail; °staff, court, household: *After the duke's coffin came a train of several hundred hangers-on.* **3** °line, °queue, °procession, °succession, °string, °set, °sequence, °chain, °progression, caravan, cavalcade, °parade, column, °file: *The baggage train of the advancing army stretched for miles.*
—*v.* **4** °discipline, °exercise, °tutor, °teach, °coach, °drill, °school, °instruct, °prepare, °educate, edify, °guide, °bring up, °indoctrinate, °rear, °raise: *We had been trained to put things away and avoid clutter.* **5** °work out, °exercise, °practise: *Hannah is training for the next Olympics.*

trait *n.* °feature, °characteristic, °attribute, °quality, °peculiarity, idiosyncrasy, °quirk, lineament, °mark, °property: *He has some unpleasant traits, like spitting when he talks.*

traitor *n.* °turncoat, Judas, quisling, betrayer, °renegade, fifth-columnist, *US* Benedict Arnold, *Colloq* double-crosser, °snake in the grass, double-dealer, two-timer: *Some traitor in their midst had revealed their plans to the enemy.*

traitorous *adj.* treacherous, °perfidious, °seditious, °subversive, insurrectionist, °renegade, insurgent, °disloyal, °deceitful, °untrue, unfaithful, °faithless; treasonable, *Colloq* double-crossing, double-dealing, two-timing: *They identified the traitorous wretch and hanged him. Consorting with the enemy is a traitorous act.*

trajectory *n.* flight °path, °course, °track: *The missile has a high trajectory.*

tram *n.* tramcar, trolley bus, *US and Canadian* streetcar, trolley(-car): *Most cities with a traffic problem have replaced trams with buses.*

trammel *n.* **1** Usually, ***trammels***: °impediment(s), °hindrance(s), °shackle(s), °handicap(s), °check(s), °restriction(s), °restraint(s), °curb(s), °deterrent(s), constraint(s), °hitch(es), °snag(s), (stumbling) °block(s), °obstacle(s), °bar: *He managed to avoid the trammels of domesticity.*
—*v.* **2** °impede, °hinder, °handicap, °check, °restrain, °curb, °deter, constrain, °block, °obstruct, fetter, confine: *Do not let the limitations of what's practical and possible trammel your imagination.*

tramp *v.* **1** °march, hike, trudge, °plod, slog, °plough, tread, trek, °walk, *US* mush: *I must have tramped across half of England looking for work.* **2** Usually, ***tramp on*** or ***upon***: See **trample, 1,** below.
—*n.* **3** °march, trudge, °plod, slog, trek, hike, °walk: *Every day we had to make the five-mile tramp into the village for water.* **4** °derelict, °vagabond, vagrant, °drifter, °rover, gypsy, beachcomber, *Brit* dosser, down-and-out, *Australian* swagman, *US* hobo, °bum, down-and-outer: *The police do not allow tramps to sleep in public parks.* **5** °step, tread, footfall, °footstep: *She couldn't get to sleep until she heard her husband's tramp on the stair.*

trample *v.* **1** trample on *or* upon, °tramp (on *or* upon), °stamp (on), tread (on), °step on, °crush, °press, squash, °flatten, *Colloq* stomp (on *or* upon), squish, squush *or* squoosh: *After the harvest, we would take turns trampling the grapes.* **2** Often, ***trample on*** or ***upon***: °violate, °damage, °harm, °hurt, °infringe *or* °encroach on, ride roughshod over, set at naught, °scorn, contemn, disdain, °defy, °disregard, °ignore, °fly in the face of, fling *or* cast *or* throw to the winds: *The military regime trampled on the people's civil rights.* **3** Usually, ***trample out***: trample down, trample underfoot, °stamp out, °extinguish, °put out, °destroy, °crush, °break down: *The left-wing parties were trampled in a military coup.*

trance *n.* °daze, °stupor, semi-conscious *or* half-conscious *or* hypnotic *or* cataleptic *or* °dream state, state of semi-consciousness *or* half-consciousness *or* catalepsy *or* suspended animation *or* stupefaction *or* abstraction *or* (complete) absorption *or* exaltation *or* °rapture *or* °ecstasy; brown study: *He walked about all day in a trance, oblivious to what was going on around him.*

tranquil *adj.* °calm, °serene, placid, °quiet, °peaceful, °still, °smooth, unagitated, halcyon, °relaxed; unruffled, °sedate, °steady, °regular, °even, °dispassionate, °self-possessed, °cool, self-controlled, cool-headed, unexcited, undisturbed, untroubled, unperturbed: *He often thought back to the tranquil, sultry summer days of his youth. How can Eleanor be so tranquil when everything about her is so chaotic?*

tranquillize *v.* °calm, soothe, pacify, °still, °quiet(en), °relax, °lull, °compose, °sedate: *He soon fell asleep, tranquillized by the medication that had been administered to him.*

tranquillizer *n.* bromide, barbiturate, opiate, °sedative, anti-psychotic, anti-anxiety °drug, *Slang* downer, red: *She had been prescribed tranquillizers, and developed severe side-effects.*

transact *v.* do, °carry on *or* out, °conduct, °manage, °handle, °negotiate, °administer, °discharge, °perform, °enact, °settle, conclude, °complete, °finish: *We are flying to Frankfurt today to transact some business.*

transaction *n.* **1** °deal, dealing, °negotiation, °matter, °affair, °business, °action, °proceeding, °agreement, °arrangement, °bargain: *This transaction must not be revealed to the stock market.* **2** ***transactions***: °proceedings, °record(s), °acts, °minutes, annals, *Colloq* goings-on, doings: *The Society's transactions are published annually.*

transcend *v.* °surpass, °outstrip, °exceed, go beyond, outdistance, °overstep, °outdo, °excel, °overshadow, °top, outvie, °rise above, outshine, °beat: *Her performance at La Scala transcended that of every other Mimi I have heard.*

transcendent *adj.* °peerless, °incomparable, unequalled, °matchless, unrivalled, °unparalleled, °unique, consummate, °paramount, °superior, °surpassing, °supreme, °pre-eminent, °sublime, °excellent, °superb, °magnificent, °marvellous; transcendental: *Can there be any doubt of Einstein's transcendent genius?*

transcribe *v.* **1** °copy, °reproduce, replicate, °duplicate: *I am busy transcribing my lecture notes.* **2** °translate, transliterate, °write out, °render, °represent, °show, °interpret: *The Rosetta Stone has the same text transcribed in Egyptian hieroglyphics and in demotic as well as in Greek.*

transcript *n.* **1** transcription, °translation, transliteration, °rendering, °interpretation, °representation: *Most linguists regarded writing as a mere transcript of language.* **2** (carbon *or* machine *or* Xerox *or* photostatic *or* xerographic) °copy, carbon, °duplicate, duplication, photocopy, °reproduction, Photostat, *Colloq* dupe; *I have requested a transcript of the court proceedings.*

transfer *v.* **1** °move, °transport, convey, °remove, °carry, °take, °deliver, °bring, °transmit, °cart, °haul, °shift, °hand (on *or* over), °turn over, °give, °pass (on *or* along *or* over): *The documents will be transferred to you today.*
—*n.* **2** °move, conveyance, transmittal, °transmission, °delivery, °change: *The papers documenting the transfer of the property are here.*

transfix *v.* **1** °pin, °fix, °impale, skewer, °nail, °pierce, spear, °spike, °spit, °stick: *The shrike, or butcher-bird, transfixes its prey on a thorn, then picks its bones clean.* **2** °enrapture, galvanize, °electrify, °hypnotize, mesmerize, rivet, °fascinate, °bewitch, °enchant, ensorcell, engross, °root to the spot, °stun, °paralyse, *Colloq* °stop °dead (in one's tracks): *The felon stood transfixed with terror as the judge pronounced sentence.*

transform *v.* °change, °modify, transfigure, °alter, transmute, metamorphose, °turn into, °convert, transmogrify, mutate, permute: *What will it take to transform these students into civilized human beings?*

transformation *n.* °change, modification, transfiguration, transfigurement, °alteration, transmutation, metamorphosis, conversion, transmogrification, °mutation, permutation: *The transformation in her appearance over a few short months was miraculous.*

transfuse *v.* **1** °instil, °transmit, °transfer, °inject: *Her greatest success was to transfuse a sense of history into her students.* **2** infuse, °permeate: *An embarrassed blush transfused his face.*

transgress *v.* **1** °sin, trespass, °offend, °err, °lapse, °fall from grace, °disobey, °misbehave, go °wrong *or* astray, do °wrong: *She knew she had transgressed and was ready to atone.* **2** °break *or* °violate *or* contravene *or* go beyond *or* °exceed *or* °overstep *or* °infringe *or* °defy *or* °disobey (the law): *He had blatantly transgressed the laws of decency.*

transgression *n.* °sin, trespass, °offence, °error, °lapse, °fall from grace, disobedience, °misbehaviour, °wrong, °violation, °fault, °misdeed, misdemeanour, °crime, wrongdoing, infraction: *How should he be punished for his transgressions?*

transgressor *n.* °sinner, °offender, °criminal, °felon, °culprit, lawbreaker, trespasser, wrongdoer, evil-doer, °villain, °miscreant, malefactor, °delinquent: *The majority of transgressors are apprehended within 24 hours of the crime.*

transient *adj.* transitory, °temporary, °brief, °fleeting, °momentary, °passing, ephemeral, fugacious, °fugitive, evanescent, °short-lived, short-term, impermanent, °fly-by-night, °volatile: *The peace was transient, as the outbreak of civil war soon followed. A souvenir shop obviously sells more to the transient trade than to residents.*

transit *n.* **1** °moving, °movement, °travel, °travelling, °motion, °passing, °progress, °progression, °transition; °passage, °traverse, traversal, traversing: *We were unable to mail any letters while we were in transit. The overland transit of the island took three days.* **2** °transport, transportation, °carriage, haulage, cartage, conveyance, °transfer, transference, transferral, transmittal: *The transit of the merchandise will be handled by our regular shipping company.*
—*v.* **3** °cross, °traverse, °go *or* °move *or* °pass *or* °travel across *or* over *or* through: *They were advised to check with authorities of every country visited or transited during their journey.*

transition *n.* **1** °change, °alteration, metamorphosis, change-over, °transformation, transmutation, °mutation, °development, °evolution, conversion, modification, metastasis: *Tracing the transition from tadpole to frog is exciting for young pupils.* **2** See **transit, 1,** above.

translate *v.* **1** °convert, °paraphrase, °change, rewrite, °interpret, °transcribe, °render, decode, °decipher, metaphrase: *Can you translate this German document?* **2** °transform, °convert, °change, mutate, °turn, transmute, metamorphose, transubstantiate, °alter, transmogrify: *Why are people always trying to translate the dross of reality into the gold of dreams?* **3** °interpret, rewrite, °explain, °reword, elucidate, °spell out: *Can you translate this technical legal jargon into plain English?* **4** °transfer, convey, °carry, °move, °transport, °forward, °ship, °send, °dispatch *or* despatch: *Soon after being made bishop of Worcester, he was translated to Winchester.*

translation *n.* **1** conversion, °paraphrase, °interpretation, transcription, transliteration, °rendering, °rendition, metaphrase, °gloss, decipherment, decoding: *It was Michael Ventris who was responsible for the translation of Linear B.* **2** metamorphosis, °change, °alteration, transmutation, transfiguration, °transformation, transmogrification, transubstantiation, conversion: *The translation from the caterpillar to the butterfly is miraculous.* **3** °interpretation, rewriting, rewrite, °explanation, rewording, elucidation: *He is well known for his translation of abstract ideas into terms that an intelligent layman could cope with.* **4** °transfer, transference, transferral, conveyance, carrying, °moving, °movement, transportation, °transport, forwarding, shipping, shipment, sending, °transmission, °dispatch *or* despatch: *His translation to a minor consular post in the south Pacific was expected.*

transmission *n.* **1** °transfer, transference, transferral, transferring, conveyance, carrying, °moving, °movement, transportation, °transport, transporting, forwarding, shipping, shipment, sending, transmittal, transmitting, °dispatch *or* despatch, dispatching *or* despatching: *We were unable to arrange for the transmission of the papers in time for the meeting.* **2** °broadcast, broadcasting, sending, telecasting, dissemination, communication: *Transmission of the new programmes begins next year.*

transmit *v.* **1** °send, °transfer, convey, °communicate, °pass on, °deliver, °forward, °dispatch *or* despatch; °post, °ship, °cable, °radio, telegraph, fax, telex, °telephone, phone, *Chiefly US and Canadian* °mail, *Colloq* wire: *Your message was transmitted last night.* **2** °pass *or* °go through, °pass on, °send, °put, °direct, °conduct, °channel: *The mirror transmits the light through this filter.*

transparent *adj.* **1** (crystal) °clear, pellucid, diaphanous, °see-through, limpid, crystalline, °sheer, transpicuous: *I want completely transparent glass in this window, instead of that frosted glass.* **2** °plain, °apparent, °obvious, °evident, unambiguous, °patent, °manifest, unmistakable, (crystal) °clear, as °plain as day, as °plain as the nose on (one's) face, °undisguised, recognizable, understandable, transpicuous: *The origin of many English words is transparent because of their spelling.* **3** °candid, °open, °frank, plain-spoken, °direct, unambiguous, unequivocal, straightforward, °ingenuous, °forthright, °above-board, °artless, guileless, °simple, °naïve, undissembling, *Colloq* on the °level, upfront: *His transparent honesty makes Clive unsuited to a career in diplomacy.*

transpire *v.* **1** become known, be rumoured, be revealed, come to °light: *It transpired that she had been seeing him while she was still married.* **2** (*Disputed*): happen, °occur, take °place, °come about, °come to °pass, °materialize, °arise, °turn out: *No improvement has yet transpired in their living conditions.*

transplant *v.* °displace, °move, °remove, relocate, °shift, °uproot, resettle, °transfer: *This is the third time the company has transplanted Harry in a year!*

transport *v.* **1** °carry, °bear, convey, °move, °remove, °transfer, °deliver, °fetch, °bring, °get, °take, °ship, °haul, °transmit, °send, °forward: *The goods were transported by ship.* **2** °exile, °banish, deport, °send away: *Australia was settled mainly by people who had been transported from England.* **3** °carry away, °enrapture, °captivate, °delight, °charm, spellbind, °bewitch, °fascinate, °enchant, °entrance, °hypnotize, mesmerize, °electrify, °ravish: *Flavia's parents were totally transported by her winning the decathlon.*
—*n.* **4** transportation, °carrier, conveyance, shipping, °transfer, transferral, shipment, haulage, cartage, °carriage, °moving: *Can't you give me any idea of what the transport costs might come to?* **5** Usually, ***transports***: °rapture, °ecstasy, exaltation, exultation, euphoria, °delight, (seventh) °heaven, °happiness, °bliss, elation, exhilaration, °thrill, Elysium, °paradise; Elysian Fields, *Colloq* cloud nine: *Helen succumbed to transports of delight at seeing her son receive such an important award.*

transpose *v.* °exchange, interchange, metathesize, °switch, swap *or* swop, °trade, commute, °transfer: *The bank transposed two figures on my statement, reducing my balance by £450.*

trap *n.* **1** °snare, °pitfall, gin, springe, deadfall, booby-trap: *After the Pied Piper left, Hamelin had no further need for rat traps.* **2** °trick, °subterfuge, °wile, °ruse, °stratagem, °ambush, °deception, °device, °artifice, ploy: *Oscar was the man for whom Esther set a neat trap.* **3** °mouth, *Slang* °yap, °gob, mush, °face: *Shut your trap or get out.*
—*v.* **4** °snare, ensnare, entrap, °catch, °net: *We dug a pit to trap the marauding lion.* **5** °imprison, confine, °lock, °hold, °keep: *The boy was trapped in the cave without a means of escape.* **6** °trick, °deceive, °fool, °dupe, °beguile, inveigle: *Esther finally trapped Oscar into marrying her.*

trappings *n.pl.* accoutrements *or US also* accouterments, panoply, caparison, equipage, °apparatus, °equipment, °paraphernalia, appointments, furnishings, °furniture, °gear, °rig, habiliments, °decoration(s), °embellishment(s), °accessories, frippery *or* fripperies, adornment(s), trimmings, raiment, °fittings, °finery: *Many respect the trappings of office more than the office-holder.*

trash *n.* **1** °rubbish, (°stuff and) °nonsense, balderdash, °moonshine, °gibberish, °gobbledegook *or* gobbledygook, tommy-rot, bunkum, °garbage, twaddle, *Colloq* °rot, flapdoodle, crap, codswallop, bosh, piffle, hooey, bunk, malarkey, poppycock, boloney *or* baloney, eyewash, hogwash, bilge-water, bull, *Scots* havers, *Brit* tosh, gammon, *US* a crock, hokum, gurry, horse feathers, *Slang Brit* (a load of (old)) cobblers, *Taboo slang* bullshit, horseshit, *Brit* balls, *US* a crock of shit: *Don't believe him—he is talking trash.* **2** *Chiefly in US and Canada*: °junk, brummagem, knick-knacks, gewgaws, °trifles, °bric-à-brac *or* bric-a-brac, frippery *or* fripperies, bits and pieces, °odds and ends, trinkets, tinsel, 'Not Wanted on Voyage': *There was mostly trash in the flea market, but there were one or two more valuable items.* **3** *In US and Canada*: °rubbish, °litter, °garbage, °waste, °refuse, °junk, debris, rubble, °dregs, dross, scoria, slag, off-scourings, °dirt, sweepings, *Slang* crap: *The service comes to remove the trash once a week.*
—*v.* **4** *Slang chiefly in US*: destroy, °ruin, °wreck, vandalize, °deface: *The lodgers trashed the flat before doing a moonlight flit.*

traumatic *adj.* °shocking, upsetting, °disturbing, °painful, °agonizing, distressing, °harmful, °hurtful, °injurious, damaging, wounding, traumatizing: *Few experiences are more traumatic than losing a child.*

travel *n.* **1** °travelling, tourism, touring, globe-trotting: *Travel is an enriching experience. Travel by air is the commonest means of long-distance transport.* **2** ***travels***: °trips, °expeditions, °journeys, °excursions, °tours, voyages, touring, treks, trekking, °travelling, wanderings, peregrinations, junkets, °pilgrimages: *In all your travels, have you ever encountered an honest man?*
—*v.* **3** °journey, °go, °move, °proceed, °roam, rove, °traverse, °tour, take *or* make a °trip *or* °tour *or* °excursion *or* junket *or* °journey, trek, voyage: *As one who has travelled far and wide, what is your favourite country?* **4** °go, °move, °socialize, °fraternize, °associate, *Colloq* °hang around *or* about: *Cordelia and I do not travel in the same circles.*

traveller *n.* °tourist, voyager, °sightseer, globe-trotter, gypsy, wanderer, hiker, °rover, wayfarer, *Jocular* bird of passage, *Colloq* °rubberneck(er), jet-setter, *Chiefly Brit* tripper, day-tripper, holiday-maker: *Travellers have been greatly inconvenienced by the strike of customs officials.*

travelling *adj.* itinerant, wandering, peripatetic, roving, °mobile, nomadic, touring, wayfaring, migratory, °restless: *At fourteen, he joined a travelling circus.*

traverse *v.* **1** °cross, criss-cross, °pass *or* °move over *or* through, °walk, °cover, °travel (over *or* through), °roam, °wander, °range, °tramp, °tour: *He has traversed the country from end to end innumerable times.* **2** °cross, criss-cross, °go across; °lie *or* °extend across *or* athwart, °bridge, intersect: *The road traverses the river several times at Newtown.* **3** °oppose, °cross, °thwart, go *or* act against, go *or* act in °opposition *or* °counter to, °conflict (with), controvert, contravene, °counter, °obstruct, °contradict, gainsay, °deny: *The policies of today seem to traverse those set forth only last year.* **4** °examine, °look into, °scrutinize, °inspect, °investigate, °review, °study, °look at, °consider, °contemplate, °scan, °look over, °check, °survey, °reconnoitre, °observe: *Certain areas of knowledge are seldom traversed by scholars.*

treasure *n.* **1** °wealth, °riches, °money, °fortune, valuables, °cash, °cache, °hoard: *The existence of the treasure came to light only last week.* **2** °pride (and °joy), °delight, °joy, °darling, °ideal, apple of (one's) eye, *Colloq* °jewel, °gem, °prize, °find, °catch: *Kathy is a treasure and I don't know what we did before we hired her.*
—*v.* **3** °hold °dear, °cherish, value, °prize, °esteem, rate *or* value highly: *We treasure the signed letter that Churchill wrote to my father. I treasure every moment we can spend together.*

treasury *n.* exchequer, bank, °cache, resources, funds, °money(s): *There was not enough money in the treasury to pay for the scheme. The Treasury indicated their concern at the current state of the economy.*

treat *v.* **1** °handle, °manage, °behave *or* °act toward(s), °deal with; °use: *Why should we treat female employees any differently?* **2** °handle, °manage, °deal with, °discuss, °touch on *or* upon, °consider, °take up, °study, °examine, °explore, °investigate, °scrutinize, °analyse, °go into, °probe, °survey, expound (on), °criticize, °review, critique: *That subject is treated in Chapter VI.* **3** °nurse, °doctor, °attend, °care for, °look after, °prescribe for, medicate: *He is being treated for gallstones.* **4** °entertain, °take out, °pay for, °regale, play °host to; wine and dine: *Our visitors treated us when we went out to dinner yesterday.* **5** ***treat (someone) to (something)***: °pay (the bill) for, °buy (something) for: *Edward treated us all to ice-cream.*
—*n.* **6** °favour, °gift, °present, °boon, °bonus, °premium, *Colloq US and Canadian* freebie: *Put your money away—this is my treat.*

treatment *n.* **1** Often, ***treatment of***: °behaviour (towards), °conduct (towards), °action (towards), handling (of), °care (of), °management (of), dealing(s) (with), manipulation (of), °reception (of); °usage (of): *I am not accustomed to such rude treatment. Your treatment of our customers must be more courteous, Miss Davidson.* **2** °therapy, °care, curing, remedying, healing: *They received extensive medical treatment for the injuries they had sustained.*

treaty *n.* °pact, °agreement, °alliance, concordat, entente, covenant, °deal, °contract, °compact, °accord: *They entered into a treaty not to violate each other's borders.*

tremble *v.* **1** °quiver, °shake, °quake, °shiver, °shudder, °quaver, quail; °vibrate, °rock: *Her first big role and she was trembling like a leaf! The earth trembled as the tanks rolled past.*
—*n.* **2** °quiver, °shake, °quake, °shiver, °shudder, °quaver, tremor; vibration: *There was a little tremble, and then the building collapsed.*

tremulous *adj.* **1** trembling, a-tremble, quivering, shaking, quaking, shivering, shuddering, quavering, °hesitant, wavering, unsure, unsteady, faltering, °doubtful, °nervous, °shaky, palpitating, °jumpy, *Colloq* jittery: *His tremulous hands revealed just how apprehensive he was.* **2** °timid, °shy, °bashful, °anxious, °worried, timorous, °fearful, °afraid, frightened, °scared: *I cannot remember when I felt so tremulous before meeting someone.*

trenchant *adj.* °cutting, °keen, °acute, °sharp, °pointed, °poignant, °penetrating, °incisive, °biting, mordant, mordacious, °sarcastic, °bitter, acerbic, acid, vitriolic, °tart, acrid, acrimonious, acidulous, corrosive, °caustic: *The critics dismissed the play with a few trenchant remarks.*

trend *n.* **1** °tendency, °leaning, °bias, °bent, °drift, °course, °inclination, °direction: *The trend seems to be towards shorter skirts.* **2** °fashion, °style, °vogue, °mode, °look, °rage, *Colloq* °fad, °craze, °thing: *Why is she so compulsive about keeping up with the latest trends?*
—*v.* **3** °tend, °lean, be °biased, °bend, °drift, °incline, veer, °turn, °swing, °shift, °head: *At the convention, the party leaders trended more to the left of centre.*

trendy *adj.* **1** °fashionable, °stylish, à la °mode, °modern, up to °date, up to the °minute, in °vogue, voguish, all the °rage, *Slang* °hot, °now, with it, groovy, in the °groove, in, °flash: *Sibyl travels with that trendy set from Belgravia.*
—*n.* **2** °show-off, clothes-horse, coxcomb, exhibitionist, *Slang Brit* pseud, grandstander: *Don't you just hate those trendies down at Cole's wine bar?*

trial *n.* **1** °test, testing, °experiment, °proof, try-out, °trying out, trial run, °examination, °check, checking, *Colloq* dry run: *The trials of the new life-jackets are to be conducted soon.* **2** hearing, enquiry *or* °inquiry,

°examination, inquisition, °litigation, °judicial °proceeding, lawsuit, °contest: *Throughout the trial, the accused protested his innocence.* **3** °try, °attempt, °endeavour, °effort, °venture, °essay, *Colloq* °go, °shot, °stab, °fling, whirl, crack, whack: *This was their first trial at climbing the north face.* **4** °trouble, °affliction, tribulation, °hardship, adversity, °suffering, °grief, °woe, °misery, °distress, bad *or* hard °luck, °misfortune, hard times: *Mona acknowledged the trial of having ten children and no husband.* **5** °nuisance, irritation, °bother, bane, °annoyance, °pest, irritant, °thorn in the flesh *or* side, *US* bur *or* burr under the saddle, *Colloq* °plague, hassle, °pain (in the neck), °headache, *Taboo slang* °pain in the *Brit* arse *or US* ass: *William, who is full of mischief, is a constant trial to his mother.*
—*adj.* **6** °sample, °experimental, exploratory, °provisional, probationary, °tentative, conditional, °pilot: *Will you consider a trial subscription to* Verbatim, *The Language Quarterly?*

tribe *n.* °race, °stock, °strain, °nation, °breed, °people, °seed, (ethnic) °group, gens, °clan, blood, °pedigree, °family, sept, °dynasty, °house; °caste, °class: *It was important in that society to marry someone from the same tribe.*

tribunal *n.* court (of °justice), °bar, bench, judiciary, Inquisition, Star Chamber: *Should he be tried before a judicial tribunal or pilloried by the tribunal of public opinion?*

tributary *n.* °branch, °offshoot, streamlet, feeder, °brook, rivulet, °run, rill, runnel, runlet, *Scots and No. Eng.* burn, *No. Eng.* beck, *US* °creek, *NE US* kill: *The Teviot is one of the tributaries of the Tweed.*

tribute *n.* **1** °honour, °homage, °recognition, °celebration, °respect, °esteem, °testimonial, °compliment, encomium, °acknowledgement, acclaim, acclamation, commendation, °praise, °kudos, laudation, panegyric, °eulogy, glorification, exaltation: *No greater tribute could be bestowed than recognition by one's fellows.* **2** °tax, exaction, impost, °duty, excise, levy, °dues, assessment, °tariff, °charge, surcharge, °payment, contribution, °offering, °gift; °ransom; tithe, Peter's *or* Peter pence: *In exchange for their freedom, the king demanded an annual tribute of a thousand oxen.*

trick *n.* **1** °ruse, °artifice, °device, °stratagem, °wile, °deception, °manoeuvre, °deceit, °fraud, °hoax, imposture, °intrigue, °machination, °conspiracy, °subterfuge, °dodge, confidence trick, °sham, *Slang* con: *The government's 'dirty tricks squad' perpetrated crimes against their political adversaries.* **2** °prank, °frolic, antic, (practical) °joke, °hoax, tomfoolery, °caper, jape; °sport, horseplay, °mischief; *Scots* cantrip, *Colloq* leg-pull, °gag, shenanigans, *US* dido: *The boys meant no harm, they're just up to their tricks.* **3** °art, °knack, °technique, °skill, °secret, °gift, °ability, *Colloq* hang: *He has developed the trick of persuading people to buy life insurance.* **4** Usually, ***no mean trick***: °feat, °accomplishment, °deed: *It was no mean trick to train a cat to fetch his slippers.* **5** sleight of hand, legerdemain, °magic, °stunt: *I have taught him all the tricks I know.* **6** °trait, °characteristic, °peculiarity, idiosyncrasy, °eccentricity, °quirk, °practice, °habit, °mannerism, crotchet, °weakness, °foible: *He has an odd trick of winking while giving a sly smile.* **7** ***do the trick***: °work, °answer, °fulfil the need, °suffice, be °effective, °solve *or* take °care of the problem, do *or* °accomplish the necessary, *US* turn the trick, *Colloq* fill the bill: *Replacing the battery cable did the trick.*
—*v.* **8** °fool, °hoodwink, °dupe, °mislead, °outwit, outmanoeuvre, °deceive, misguide, °misinform, gull, bilk, °cheat, °defraud, cozen, °take in, °swindle, humbug, *Colloq* bamboozle, °take, °put something over on (someone), pull the wool over (someone's) eyes, *Brit* gammon, *Slang* rook: *I knew I had been tricked when I missed my wallet. For years the couple made a living tricking tourists out of their money. She tricked me into taking her to dinner.*
—*adj.* **9** See **tricky, 3,** below.

trickery *n.* °chicanery, °deception, °deceit, guile, shrewdness, craftiness, slyness, shiftiness, evasiveness, artfulness, °artifice, °craft, imposture, swindling, knavery, duplicity, double-dealing, °fraud, cheating, *Colloq* °hanky-panky, skulduggery, funny *or* monkey business, jiggery-pokery: *He separated her from her money by trickery.*

trickle *v.* **1** °drip, °drop, dribble, drizzle, °run, °flow, °spill; °ooze, seep, °leak, exude: *The water trickled onto the floor. Blood is trickling from the wound.*
—*n.* **2** °drip, seepage, °spill, dribble, runnel, runlet, rivulet: *A tiny trickle of saliva appeared at the corner of his mouth.*

tricky *adj.* **1** °deceitful, °shady, °deceptive, °shifty, °dodgy, °artful, guileful, °crafty, duplicitous, °shrewd, cunning, °dishonest, °devious, °sly, °wily, °slippery, °foxy, double-dealing, cheating: *Arthur is a tricky chap and I shouldn't trust him.* **2** °ticklish, °risky, °hazardous, °sensitive, °delicate, touch-and-go, °thorny, °difficult, °awkward, complex, °complicated, knotty, °uncertain, °debatable, *Colloq* iffy, °sticky: *It is a tricky decision whether you tell a patient how ill he really is.* **3** unfair, unjust, unsportsmanlike, °deceptive, *Colloq* °trick: *There were some tricky questions in today's exam.*

trifle *n.* **1** knick-knack, trinket, °bauble, bagatelle, °toy, °gewgaw, °nothing, °plaything, bêtise, *Colloq* doodah: *Oh, it's nothing, just a trifle I picked up in the Seychelles.* **2** °little, °bit, °drop, iota, scintilla, °suggestion, °dash, °dab, °pinch, whiff, mite, whit, °jot, tittle, *Colloq* smidgen *or* smidgin, *US* tad: *I'd like a trifle more sugar in my coffee, if you don't mind.*
—*v.* **3** Usually, ***trifle with***: dally (with), °flirt (with), °wanton (with), °mess about *or* around (with), °toy (with); °play (with), °fiddle (with), dandle, °tinker (with), °fidget (with): *I hated to see the way he trifled with my sister's affections. While trifling with this knob, I was able to get Radio Moscow.*

trifling *adj.* trivial, °insignificant, unimportant, °puny, °minor, °paltry, °slight, °petty, °inconsequential, °frivolous, °superficial, °incidental, °negligible, commonplace, inconsiderable, °shallow, valueless, °worthless, *US and Canadian* picayune, *Colloq* piddling: *Their contribution to musical scholarship has been trifling.*

trim *adj.* **1** °neat, °tidy, °orderly, well-ordered, °well-groomed, well turned out, well-kempt, °smart, °crisp, °dapper, spick and span, °spruce, °shipshape (and Bristol fashion), *Archaic or dialectal* trig, *Colloq* natty, *US* spiffy: *Nancy arrived wearing her trim new flight-attendant's uniform.* **2** in good *or* fine fettle, °fit (as a fiddle), athletic, °slim, °slender, clean-cut, °shapely, °streamlined, °compact: *Larry looks so trim that I asked him if he had lost weight. The new convertible model is a very trim little motor car.*
—*v.* **3** °curtail, °shorten, °prune, °pare, °lop (off), crop, bob, °clip, °cut, °shave, shear, °snip, °dock; barber: *They trimmed the article by cutting two paragraphs from the end. He had shaved off his beard and trimmed his moustache.* **4** °decorate, °embellish, °dress up, embroider, adorn, °ornament, deck out, caparison, °beautify: *When should we trim the Christmas tree?*
—*n.* **5** trimming, edging, piping, purfling, ricrac *or* rickrack, embroidery, °border, hem, °frill, °fringe, °ornament, ornamentation, °decoration, °embellishment, adornment: *The skirt was spoilt by a rather cheap trim round the hem.* **6** °condition, °state, fettle, °health, °form, °order, °fitness, °repair, *Colloq* °shape: *Sid's car seemed to be in good trim when I saw it yesterday.*

trio *n.* threesome, trilogy, triad, triplex, triple, troika, triptych, triumvirate, triplet, trine, triune, trinity, three: *An interesting trio showed up for dinner.*

trip *n.* **1** °stumble, °slip, °blunder, °false °step, °misstep, °fall: *He sprained his ankle in that trip on the stair.* **2** °stumble, °slip, °blunder, °false °step, °misstep, faux pas, °error, °mistake, °indiscretion, °lapse, °slip of the tongue, *lapsus linguae*, erratum, °oversight; Freudian °slip; *Slang Brit* boob: *If it hadn't been for*

that one trip, we would have had a perfect score. **3** °tour, °journey, °excursion, °outing, °expedition, voyage, trek, peregrination, jaunt, junket, °drive: *We took a short side-trip to visit Khios.*
—*v.* **4** °dance, °caper, °skip, °cavort, gambol, °frisk, °hop, °spring: *Joanne came tripping gaily down the Champs Élysées.* **5** °stumble, °slip, °blunder, °misstep, °fall (down), °tumble, °topple, °dive, °plunge, °sprawl, °lurch, °flounder, °stagger, falter: *I tripped on the doorstep and went head over heels.* **6** Often, ***trip up***: °trap, °trick, °catch out, unsettle, °throw off, disconcert: *She has been trying to trip me up and confess to something I didn't do.* **7** °journey, °travel, voyage, °visit, °tour, trek, sightsee, °cruise; *Colloq* globe-trot: *They have been tripping all over Europe this summer.* **8** detonate, °set off, trigger, °operate, °release, °explode, °spark off: *When he touched the wire, he tripped the charge.* **9** Often, ***trip out***: hallucinate, *Slang* °freak out, °turn on: *There's no talking to him when he's tripping out on coke.*

triumph *n.* **1** °victory, °conquest, °success, °achievement, °accomplishment, attainment, coup, ascendancy: *The discovery of the drug was perhaps the greatest of his many triumphs.* **2** exultation, rejoicing, exulting, elation, °delight, °rapture, exhilaration, jubilation, °happiness, °joy, °celebration, °glory: *There was great triumph on winning the World Cup.*
—*v.* **3** Often, ***triumph over***: °win, °succeed, carry the day, be °victorious, °gain a °victory, take the honours, °thrive, °dominate, °prevail; °defeat, °beat, °rout, vanquish, °best, °conquer, °overcome, °overwhelm, °subdue: *Does justice always triumph? The book is about how man triumphed over pain.*

triumphal *adj.* celebratory, °rapturous, jubilant, °joyful, °glorious, °exultant; commemorative: *A holiday was declared to celebrate her triumphal entry into the city. This triumphal arch commemorates Trajan's victory over the Dacians.*

triumphant *adj.* °victorious, °successful, conquering, °winning; undefeated: *The triumphant hero returns tonight!*

triviality *n.* **1** smallness, unimportance, insignificance, meaninglessness, inconsequentiality *or* inconsequentialness *or* inconsequence *or* inconsequentness, trivialness, pettiness, paltriness: *I have difficulty coping with the triviality of some of my boss's requests.* **2** °trifle, technicality, °non-essential, °small matter, unimportant *or* °insignificant *or* °inconsequential *or* trivial *or* °petty °detail, bêtise: *He tends to get bogged down in trivialities, unable to see what is important.*

trivialize *v.* °belittle, denigrate, lessen, °minimize, undervalue, °depreciate, °underestimate, underrate, make °light of, °laugh off, underplay, °dismiss, °disparage, misprize, °beggar, deprecate, °slight, °scoff at, °scorn, °run down, decry, *Colloq* °put down, °play down, pooh-pooh: *Edward tends to trivialize the work of others.*

trophy *n.* **1** °prize, laurel(s), wreath, cup, °award, °reward, °honour(s), medal, citation, palm, bays; °booty, °spoils, *Colloq* gold, °silver, silverware: *He has won trophies for more boat races than I have participated in.* **2** °memento, souvenir, °token, °record, °reminder, °remembrance, °keepsake: *That scar is a trophy of a hand-to-hand fight near El Alamein.*

trot *v.* **1** °jog, °run; bustle, °hustle, °hurry, °hasten, scamper, scoot, *Colloq* skedaddle: *I trot round the park every morning for exercise. As I need some butter, I'd better trot down to the shop before it closes.* **2** ***trot out***: °bring out, °show, °display, °exhibit, °flaunt, °come out with; dredge up, °drag out; °recite, °repeat: *Our neighbour trotted out his new lawnmower for us to admire.*
—*n.* **3** °jog, lope, single-foot, °pace; °run: *It was a delight to watch the young horses in a fast trot round the track.* **4** °translation, °gloss, °interpretation, crib, *Colloq US* pony, horse: *He couldn't read Homer without a trot.*

trouble *v.* **1** °bother, °upset, °anguish, °alarm, °worry, °afflict, °agitate, disquiet, °discomfit, make uncomfortable, °grieve, °perturb, discommode, °inconvenience, discompose, discountenance, °put out, °burden, °encumber, °weigh down: *I don't mean to trouble you with my problems, but I have no one else to turn to.* **2** °annoy, °irritate, °irk, vex, °bother, °plague, °pester, °torment, °harass, hector, harry, °provoke, nettle, °exasperate, °ruffle, *Colloq* get *or* grate on (someone's) °nerves, give (someone) a hard time, get under (someone's) skin: *Vincent keeps troubling me for advice on starting a new business.* **3** discommode, incommode, °impose on, °inconvenience, °put out, thank: *I'll trouble you to turn off the light when you leave the room.* **4** °care, be °concerned, take the trouble *or* the time, go to the trouble, °bother, °exert (oneself), °concern (oneself), take °pains: *He never troubled to find out if his family was safe.*
—*n.* **5** °distress, °worry, °concern, °difficulty, °discomfort, unpleasantness, °inconvenience, vexation, °grief, °woe, °affliction, disquiet, °suffering, tribulation, °anxiety, °torment, °anguish, °strife: *Her trouble began when her ex-husband stopped paying for child support. How can someone so insignificant cause so much trouble?* **6** °annoyance, °bother, tormentor *or* tormenter, irritation, °nuisance, °nag, heckler, °pest, *Slang US* nudnik: *Ever since she lost her job, she's been a trouble to her family.* **7** °disorder, °agitation, °row, °disturbance, turbulence, °tumult, °upset, °dissatisfaction, °unrest, °discord, °dispute, turmoil, °rebellion, °revolt, °uprising, outbreak, fighting, °fight, skirmishing, °skirmish: *The trouble began when workers refused to allow management to hire replacements.* **8** °affliction, °defect, °disability, °disease, °ailment, °illness, sickness, °disorder, °complaint: *With her trouble she ought to see a doctor.* **9** ***in trouble***: **a** in deep trouble, in a °mess, in a °predicament, in dire °straits, *Colloq* in a pickle, in hot water, on the °spot, in a °scrape, *Slang Brit* in shtook *or* shtuk *or* shtuck *or* schtuck, *Taboo slang* in deep shit, up shit creek (without (the vestige of) a paddle): *They will be in terrible trouble if the bank forecloses on the mortgage.* **b** unmarried *or* unwed and impregnated *or* °pregnant *or* with child *or* °expecting *or* in a delicate condition *or colloq* in a family way: *Most of the girls who are in trouble are teenagers.*

troublemaker *n.* mischief-maker, °rabble-rouser, gadfly, firebrand, *agent provocateur*, stormy petrel, incendiary, gossip-monger, scandalmonger, malcontent, instigator, meddler, °agitator: *As far as the police were concerned, any protester was, by definition, a troublemaker.*

troublesome *adj.* worrisome, worrying, annoying, °irksome, irritating, vexatious, bothersome, distressing, °difficult, °burdensome, *Colloq* pestiferous, *US and Canadian* pesky: *We sometimes have to put up with troublesome motor-cycle gangs.*

truant *n.* **1** malingerer, °runaway, absentee, °delinquent, dodger, shirker, °idler, °loafer, layabout, *Slang Brit* skiver, *Brit military* scrimshanker: *Truants were warned that their parents would be required to visit the school.*
—*adj.* **2** malingering, °runaway, °absent, absentee, °delinquent, shirking, loafing, *Slang Brit* skiving: *The officer brought in three truant boys found fishing at the lake.*

truce *n.* **1** armistice, cease-fire, °suspension of hostilities, °lull, °moratorium, °respite, °let-up, °intermission, °interval, °interlude: *It looked as if the truce might last.* **2** °pact, °treaty, °compact, °agreement, cease-fire, armistice: *If both sides abide by the truce the war might be over.*

truck *n.* **1** °merchandise, commodities, goods, stock, °wares, °stuff, °odds and ends, °sundries, °junk, °rubbish, *US* °trash: *There was no one in the shop and all the truck was stacked in the corner.* **2** dealing(s), °traffic, °business, °transaction, °trade, °commerce, communication, °contact, °connection, (business *or* social) °relations: *She refuses to have any truck with the likes of you.*

truckle *v.* °kowtow, be °obsequious, toady, °defer, °bow, °scrape, genuflect, salaam, °drop to the ground *or* to (one's) knees *or* down on (one's) knees, °submit, °yield, cower, °cringe, grovel, °crawl, quail, fawn (on *or* upon), *Colloq* butter up, fall all over, lick (someone's) boots, boot-lick, *US* apple-polish, *Slang* suck up to, *Taboo slang* brown-nose, kiss (someone's) *Brit* arse *or US* ass: *Just look how Caroline is always truckling to the boss, hoping for favours.*

truculent *adj.* °surly, °sullen, bad-tempered, ill-tempered, unpleasant, °nasty, °obstreperous, °rude, °ferocious, °fierce, °savage, feral, barbarous, °harsh, °scathing, °virulent, combative, °belligerent, antagonistic, bellicose, °hostile, contentious, °warlike, °violent, °pugnacious, *Colloq* scrappy: *I don't care enough for this job to endure the boss's truculent attitude a moment longer.*

true *adj.* **1** °accurate, °correct, °truthful, °faithful, °literal, °authentic, veracious, °actual, °factual, °realistic, °genuine, °right, valid, unelaborated, °unvarnished, unadulterated, verified, verifiable: *Do you swear that this is a true account of what actually took place?* **2** °staunch, °faithful, °devoted, dedicated, °loyal, °fast, °firm, unswerving, °steady, °steadfast, °trustworthy, trusty, °dutiful, °upright, °honourable, °constant, unwavering, °stable, dependable, °sincere, °reliable, true-blue: *D'Artagnan proved himself to be a true friend.* **3** °proper, °exact, °accurate, unerring, °correct, °precise, °right, *Slang Brit* spot on: *It is important that these matters be seen in their true perspective. If this is a true copy of the original, please sign it.*
—*adv.* **4** °truly, truthfully, °honestly, accurately, candidly, frankly, °sincerely, straightforwardly: *Tell me true, do you love me? If the report speaks true, then we must find the culprit.* **5** °exactly, correctly; geographically: *We sail true north to Iceland.* **6** ***come true***: come to °pass, °occur, take °place, °happen, be realized, become a °reality, be fulfilled: *Her dreams finally came true when she bought a little house in Kent.*

truism *n.* commonplace, platitude, bromide, axiom, °cliché, °maxim: *You can rely on Vera to utter a truism like, 'It's a nice day', on a warm, sunny day.*

truly *adv.* **1** truthfully, °actually, °really, °honestly, in °fact, in °truth, in actuality, in °reality, in all °honesty, °sincerely, genuinely: *Are you truly giving up your job to get married? I truly believed her to be guilty.* **2** °properly, rightly, rightfully, justly, legitimately, justifiably, °duly, °well and truly, accurately: *In the circumstances, can we truly condemn him for behaving as he did?* **3** °definitely, °really, °actually, °undoubtedly, indubitably, beyond (the shadow of) a doubt, beyond question, without a doubt, °indeed, unquestionably, °absolutely, °positively, decidedly, certainly, °surely: *I believed her to be truly guilty.* **4** in °truth, °indeed, °really, °honestly, °sincerely, genuinely, *Archaic* (yea,) verily, *Usually ironic* forsooth: *I love you, darling, truly I do.*

trunk *n.* **1** main °stem, °stalk, °stock, *Technical* bole: *After the tornado, only the trunks of the trees remained upright.* **2** torso, °body: *All that was found of the corpse was the trunk.* **3** °chest, locker, foot-locker, °box, °case, bin, coffer, °casket: *We found a trunk full of old books in the attic.* **4** snout, proboscis: *The elephant reached for the food with its trunk.* **5** *US and Canada*: luggage compartment, *Brit* boot: *We cannot get all the luggage into the trunk of the car.*

trust *n.* **1** °confidence, °reliance, °faith, °conviction, certitude, °certainty, sureness, positiveness, °assurance, °belief: *Place your trust in me.* **2** °credit, reliability, dependability, credibility, trustworthiness: *The company will sell you the piano on trust.* **3** °custody, °care, keeping, °charge, guardianship, °protection, °safe keeping, trusteeship: *The money is in trust for Gillian's grandchildren.* **4** monopoly, cartel; °group, corporation, conglomerate: *An international trust controls the world market in diamonds.*
—*v.* **5** °rely (on *or* upon), have °faith *or* °confidence (in), confide (in), °depend *or* bank *or* °count (on *or* upon), pin (one's) °faith *or* °hopes on *or* upon: *I trust that you will attend the meeting. In God we trust—others must pay cash. Can I trust you to keep a secret? Don't trust to luck.* **6** °entrust, °commit, °give, °delegate, °make *or* turn *or* °sign *or* °hand over, depute, °assign, empower, consign: *I shouldn't trust my money to her.*

trusting *adj.* trustful, unsuspicious, confiding, °confident, °unsuspecting; °naïve, °innocent, °gullible, incautious, credulous: *It is a good thing that her husband has a trusting nature. Samantha might be a little too trusting and could easily be deceived.*

trustworthy *adj.* °reliable, trusty, dependable, °accurate; °responsible, °steady, °steadfast, °loyal, °faithful, (tried and) °true, °honourable, °honest, °ethical, °principled, °moral, incorruptible: *Is this thermometer trustworthy? Isaac's former employer said that he is completely trustworthy.*

truth *n.* **1** genuineness, °reality, actuality, correctness, °accuracy, °fact: *The truth of the matter is that he's in love with you.* **2** °fact(s): *To tell the truth, I came here to kill you.* **3** ***in truth***: in °fact, °truly, °actually, °really: *In truth, his name is not Jack Armstrong at all but Ebenezer Braithwaite.*

truthful *adj.* °true, °accurate, °factual, veracious, true to life, °honest, °realistic, °reliable, °faithful, °trustworthy, straightforward, °candid, °frank, °sincere, °earnest, °forthright, °unvarnished, unembellished: *He gave a truthful account of his experiences in the jungle.*

try *v.* **1** °attempt, °endeavour, °essay, °seek, °undertake, °venture, °strive, °struggle, make an °effort, try (one's) hand at, *Colloq* have a °stab *or* °go *or* whack (at), take a °shot *or* crack (at): *He tried to help me with my homework.* **2** °test, °try out, °prove, °evaluate, °examine, °inspect, °check out, °sample, appraise, assay, °look over, °analyse, °scrutinize, assess, °judge: *I'll try your way of solving the problem. You won't know if it works till you try it.* **3** °test, °prove, °strain, °tax: *You are trying my patience with your silly questions.* **4** °hear, sit on, adjudicate, °judge, adjudge: *There are three more cases to try this month.*
—*n.* **5** °attempt, °endeavour, °essay, °undertaking, °venture, °struggle, °effort, °turn, *Colloq* °go, °stab, whack, °fling, °shot, crack: *You have three tries to pin the tail on the donkey.*

trying *adj.* irritating, exasperating, frustrating, annoying, °irksome, infuriating, maddening, bothersome, °tiresome, vexing, °troublesome, worrying, worrisome, distressing, disquieting, upsetting, dispiriting, taxing, °demanding, °tough, stressful, °difficult, tiring, fatiguing: *This must be a trying time for you, caring for eight small children.*

tug *v.* **1** °pull, °tow, °yank, °jerk, °draw, °drag, °haul, °wrench: *The boy was tugging a little puppy along on a lead.*
—*n.* **2** °pull, °tow, °yank, °jerk, °drag, °haul, °wrench: *I gave a tug and the doorknob came away in my hand.*

tuition *n.* °education, teaching, tutelage, training, °schooling, °instruction, °guidance, °preparation: *The course fees cover tuition and accommodation.*

tumble *v.* **1** °fall (down), °pitch, °turn end over end *or* °head over heels, °roll, °drop: *Giggling hysterically, we tumbled in a heap on the lawn.* **2** °drop, °toss, °dump, °jumble: *The waiter tumbled several spoonfuls of berries on to my plate.* **3** ***tumble to***: °understand, apprehend, °perceive, °comprehend, °see the °light, *Colloq* °get the °signal *or* °message, °catch on, *Brit* °twig to, *Slang* °get °wise, °wise up, dig: *I finally tumbled to what she was trying to tell me.*
—*n.* **4** °fall, °slip, °stumble, *Colloq* header, °spill: *Joshua took a bad tumble on the stairs yesterday.*

tumbledown *adj.* °ramshackle, °dilapidated, ruined, in ruins, °decrepit, °rickety, °shaky, falling °apart *or* to °pieces, disintegrating, tottering, broken-down, crumbling, gone to rack and °ruin: *He lived for years in a tumbledown shanty near the railway.*

tumour *n.* neoplasm, cancer, melanoma, sarcoma, malignancy, carcinoma, °growth, °lump, °swelling, protuberance, excrescence: *The doctor found a tumour that he said ought to be removed.*

tumult *n.* commotion, °disturbance, °upset, °uproar, °riot, °disorder, disquiet, insurrection, °agitation, °bedlam, °chaos, brouhaha, °fracas, hubbub, °stir, °pandemonium, hullabaloo, °furore *or US* furor, °brawl, Donnybrook, affray, °row, mêlée *or* melee, turbulence, °ferment, ado, turmoil, °confusion, °rampage, °frenzy, °rage, °excitement, °rumpus, *Colloq US* ruckus: *The tumult caused by the football hooligans spread through the city.*

tumultuous *adj.* clamorous, °noisy, °boisterous, °disorderly, turbulent, °violent, °uproarious, °chaotic, frenzied, °furious, °excited, °agitated, °hectic, °riotous, °rowdy, °unruly, unrestrained, °fierce, °savage, °wild, °hysterical, °frantic, rumbustious, °obstreperous, °tempestuous, °stormy: *The heroes received a tumultuous welcome on their return.*

tune *n.* **1** °melody, °air, °song, °strain, °motif, °theme: *David presents a marvellous half-hour radio programme of show tunes every week.* **2** euphony, °pitch, °harmony, °accord, accordance, consonance, °unison, correspondence, conformity: *She cannot sing in tune. The guitar is out of tune with the piano. Her husband is out of tune with today's fashion.*
—*v.* **3** °tune up, °calibrate, °adjust, °regulate, °coordinate, °adapt, attune, align, °set: *That garage charges too much for tuning an engine.* **4** ***tune in (on)***: °attend (to), pay °attention (to), °listen (to), °understand, be °aware (of), be on the qui vive, be °alert (to), *Slang* be on the same wavelength *or* frequency (with): *I am not sure that Bernard is tuned in to what his sister does for a living.* **5** ***tune out***: °ignore, °disregard, turn a blind eye to, be °blind to, turn one's back on, turn a deaf ear to: *Sally is able to tune out anything she doesn't like to hear.*

tuneful *adj.* melodic, °musical, sweet-sounding, °melodious, euphonious, dulcet, mellifluent, mellifluous, harmonic, catchy, °mellow, °smooth, °rich, °rhythmic, *Colloq* easy on the ear(s): *Irving Berlin wrote some of the most tuneful music that we have.*

tunnel *n.* **1** °shaft, °subway, (°underground) °passage(way), underpass; °burrow, °hole; Channel Tunnel, *Colloq* Chunnel: *The cat got out through this tunnel.*
—*v.* **2** °burrow, °dig, °hole, °excavate, °penetrate, °mine: *The prisoners tunnelled under the wall and escaped.*

turf *n.* **1** sod, sward, °green, °grass, greensward, °lawn: *We bought some turf for the new lawn.* **2** °territory, bailiwick, °area, °neighbourhood, backyard, *Colloq* stamping-ground, °home ground, (personal) °space: *You're on my turf now, so you'll do as I say.* **3** ***the turf***: horse-racing, racing, the racing world, racecourse, racetrack: *The attractions of the turf keep them from other pursuits.*
—*v.* **4** ***turf out***: °eject, °dismiss, °expel, °throw out, oust, °banish, °exile, *Colloq* °sack, °bounce, give (someone) the boot *or* the °sack *or* the (old) heave-ho, chuck *or* toss *or* kick *or* °boot out, °fire: *The committee said he had brought the sport into disrepute and turfed him out of the team.*

turn *v.* **1** °rotate, °revolve, °spin, °roll, °reel, °circle, °gyrate, whirl, °wheel, °go (a)round *or* about, °pivot, °swivel: *The earth turns on its axis. Turn the crank to raise the bucket.* **2** °move, °shift, °wheel, veer, °swing, °face: *As she turned I noticed a horrible scar.* **3** °reverse, turn (a)round, °alter, °change, °adapt, reorganize, remodel, °modify, refashion, reshape, °reform, °transform, °make over, °convert, bring over: *He has been trying to turn the business into a profit-making enterprise. He has turned defeat into advance. She managed to turn one of the most loyal members of the government.* **4** °go *or* °pass *or* °move (a)round, veer, °drive, °walk: *Turn left at the corner.* **5** go °bad, become °rancid, °spoil, curdle, addle, °sour, °decay, moulder, °rot, °putrefy, *Colloq* °go off: *All the milk in the fridge had turned because of the power cut.* **6** °apply, °put, °use, °employ: *Is there any way we can turn this situation to our advantage?* **7** Sometimes, ***turn aside*** *or* ***away***: °block, avert, °thwart, °prevent, balk *or* baulk, parry, °deflect, °fend off, °check: *He deftly turned aside the thrust of the dagger.* **8** °form, °make up, °fashion, °formulate, °construct, °cast, °create, °coin, concoct, °express: *Donald certainly knows how to turn a felicitous phrase.* **9** °direct, °aim, °point: *He turned the gun on himself and pulled the trigger.* **10** °twist, sprain, °wrench: *I have turned my ankle and cannot walk.* **11** °twist, °wind, °snake, curve, °bend, arc, °coil, °loop, °meander, zigzag: *The road turned this way and that, following the river bank.* **12** ***turn against***: °defy, °mutiny, °rebel, °revolt, °rise (up) against: *The captain had not expected the first mate to turn against him, too.* **13** ***turn back***: **a** °reverse, °repulse, °repel, °rebuff, °drive back, °beat back: *At last we turned back the enemy's advance.* **b** °go back, retrace (one's) steps, °return: *We must turn back before it is too late.* **14** ***turn down***: **a** °refuse, °reject, °rebuff, °decline, °deny: *My request for help was turned down.* **b** °decrease *or* °diminish *or* lessen *or* °lower *or* °soften the sound of: *Turn down the radio, I'm on the phone.* **15** ***turn in***: **a** go to bed *or* °sleep, °retire, °withdraw, call it a day, *Slang* hit the °sack *or* the hay: *I usually turn in by eleven o'clock.* **b** °hand in *or* over, turn over, °deliver, °give in, °submit, °offer, proffer, °tender, °give back, °return, °surrender, °yield: *Please turn in your visitors' badges before you leave.* **c** turn over, °deliver (up), °inform on, °betray, *Colloq* squeal on, rat on, °finger, °tell on: *For enough money, he'd turn in his own mother.* **16** ***turn into***: **a** turn to, °become, °change into *or* to, metamorphose into *or* to: *Right before her, the prince turned into a frog again.* **b** °go *or* °come into, °drive into, °pull into, °walk into: *They lost sight of the suspect when he turned into a side-street.* **17** ***turn off***: **a** °stop, °switch off, deactivate, °discontinue; °extinguish: *First turn off the water, then the light.* **b** °disillusion, °depress, °cool (off), disenchant, disaffect, °alienate, °repel, °repulse, °bore, °offend, °put off, °displease, °sicken, °nauseate, °disgust: *People who don't brush their teeth turn me off.* **c** °deviate, °diverge: *When you come to the fork, turn off to the right.* **18** ***turn on***: **a** °start (up), °switch on, °energize, °activate, set in °motion, cause to °function *or* °operate: *Turn on the light.* **b** °depend on *or* upon, be contingent on, hinge on *or* upon, be °subject to: *The success of the venture turns on our ability to capitalize it.* **c** °excite, °thrill, °arouse, °stimulate, titillate, °work up, impassion: *He was really turned on by the girl in the bar.* **19** ***turn on*** *or* ***upon***: **a** °concern, °revolve about, °relate to: *The discussion turned on his ability to write music.* **b** be °hostile to, °attack, assail, °set upon, *Colloq* °tear into: *Oliver is so unpopular that his own dog turned on him and bit him.* **20** ***turn out***: **a** °make, °form, °shape, °construct, °build, °fabricate, put together, °assemble, °manufacture, °produce, °put out, °bring out: *The plant turns out a thousand cars a week.* **b** °develop, evolve, eventuate, °happen, °result, °prove, °occur, °end up, °arise: *As it turned out, he lost anyway. It turns out that he knows my sister.* **c** °eject, °evict, °throw out, °expel, oust, °dismiss, °terminate, cashier, *Colloq* °fire, °sack, kick out, axe, *Brit* °turf out: *When they found I wasn't a member, they turned me out.* **d** °dress, °fit out, °equip, °rig out, accoutre *or US also* accouter: *She was well turned out in a beautiful ball gown.* **e** °come, °arrive, °appear, °attend, °assemble, °meet, *Colloq* °show (up), °surface: *55,000 turned out for the rock concert.* **21** ***turn over***: **a** °consider, °muse *or* ruminate over *or* about, °revolve, °ponder (over): *I needed a while to turn over the job offer in my mind.* **b** °reverse, invert, turn upside down: *Turn over the clock and read the inscription on the bottom.* **c** °overturn, °upset, °knock over: *In my haste, I turned over the punch bowl.* **d** °sell, °merchandise: *A shop in that location ought to turn over a million a year.* **e** °rotate, °revolve, °spin, °kick over: *The engine turns over, but it won't start.* **22** ***turn tail***: °run away, °flee, °bolt, scoot,

show a clean pair of heels, cut and °run, take to (one's) heels, beat a hasty °retreat, *Colloq* °take off, °beat it, scram, skedaddle: *He turned tail when I shouted for help.* **23** ***turn to:*** **a** °appeal to, °apply to, °resort to: *She turned to me for help.* **b** advert to, °refer to, °pick *or* °take up, have °recourse to: *Please turn to your exercise books now.* **c** get to °work, °pitch in, buckle *or* knuckle down: *The neighbours turned to in helping clean up the mess after the storm.* **d** turn into, °change to, °convert into, °become: *Lot's wife was turned to salt.* **24** ***turn turtle***: °capsize, °overturn, keel over, °upset, up-end, *Colloq* go bottoms up: *The overloaded barge turned turtle and sank in the river.* **25** ***turn up***: **a** °surface, °appear, °arrive, *Colloq* °show (up), show one's face: *Guess who turned up at our wedding?* **b** °come up, °arise, *Colloq* crop up, °pop up: *Something will turn up soon for you.* **c** uncover, °discover, °find, °unearth, °come across, °hit upon, °dig up, °expose, °disclose, °reveal, bring to °light: *We turned up a formerly unknown fact about the shipwreck.* **d** °increase *or* °raise *or* °amplify *or* °intensify the sound of: *Turn up the TV—I can't hear what they're saying.*
—*n.* **26** °revolution, rotation, °cycle, °spin, whirl, °circuit, °round, °roll, °twirl; °pirouette: *He gave the top another turn, just to make sure it was on securely.* **27** curve, °bend, turning, corner, sinuosity, dog-leg, hairpin °bend *or* curve, irregularity, °meander, °twist, zigzag, *Colloq* toing and froing: *There are many dangerous turns on that road.* **28** °loop, °coil, °spiral, °twist: *Take two turns of this rope round your waist, then knot it.* **29** deviation, turning, °detour, °shift, °change of direction *or* course: *A turn to the right is not permitted at this corner.* **30** °opportunity, °chance, °say, °round, °spell, °time, °watch, °shift, °stint, °tour (of duty), °move, °trick, *Colloq* whack, crack, °shot, °go: *You have had your turn, now let someone else go.* **31** °drive, °spin, °ride; airing, constitutional, °ramble, °saunter, °stroll, °walk, °promenade, amble: *Let's take a short turn round the park.* **32** °trend, °direction, °drift: *The conversation took a new turn.* **33** °change, °alteration, °switch: *The doctor says that Valerie has taken a turn for the better.* **34** Usually, ***bad turn***: °disservice, °harm, °injury, °wrong: *If you do someone a bad turn, what can you expect?* **35** Usually, ***good turn***: °favour, (°good) °deed, °act (of °kindness), °courtesy, °boon, °mercy: *One good turn deserves another.* **36** °shock, °fright, °surprise, °start, °scare: *You really gave me a turn, jumping out like that!* **37** °form, °style, °manner, °mode: *Each turn of phrase in her writing seems original and refreshing.* **38** °disposition, °inclination, °bent, °bias, °leaning, °tendency: *Alistair is of a rather dour turn of mind tonight.* **39** ***at every turn***: °everywhere, constantly, °always, all the °time: *In Scotland, we met with kindness and hospitality at every turn.* **40** ***by turns***: alternately, reciprocally, in rotation, successively, in °succession: *The book is fascinating and frustrating by turns.* **41** ***in turn***: sequentially, one after the other, in °succession, successively, in (proper) °order: *Each patient will be treated in turn.* **42** ***out of turn***: **a** out of °sequence, out of °order: *I don't want you answering questions out of proper turn, Jonathan.* **b** imprudently, indiscreetly, improperly, disobediently, inappropriately: *I apologize if I am speaking out of turn on this issue.* **43** ***take turns***: °alternate, °vary, °rotate, °exchange: *Let's take turns looking through the telescope.*

turn-about *n.* reciprocity, °exchange: *Turn-about is fair play.*

turncoat *n.* °renegade, °traitor, betrayer, °deserter, fifth-columnist, °double agent, apostate, tergiversator, °defector, backslider, Vicar of Bray, *US* Benedict Arnold, *Colloq* °snake in the grass: *Labour members who voted with the Tories on the issue were branded turncoats.*

turn-off *n.* **1** °exit, side-road, feeder (°road), °auxiliary (°road), °ramp, *Brit* slip-road, *US* (°exit *or* °entrance) °ramp: *Our shop is at the first turn-off after the traffic light.* **2** damper, °killjoy, *Colloq* wet blanket, *Slang US* freeze-out: *It was a real turn-off to discover that his hobby was model railways.*

turnout *n.* **1** assemblage, °muster, °attendance, audience, °crowd, °gate, °throng, °gathering: *The turnout for the first day of the sale was enormous.* **2** °output, °production, out-turn, °volume; gross national °product, GNP, gross domestic °product, GDP: *Turnout has improved since the settlement of the labour dispute.* **3** °gear, °outfit, clothing, °apparel, °apparatus, °equipment, °trappings, °fittings, equipage: *Have you seen Charlie in his mountain-climbing turnout?*

turnover *n.* gross (°revenue), (total) °business, °volume: *Although turnover increased by ten per cent, profits were down by two per cent.*

tutor *n.* **1** °teacher, °instructor, educator, °coach, mentor, guru: *Bernard engaged a tutor to coach him through the examinations.*
—*v.* **2** °teach, °instruct, °coach, °educate, °school, °train, °indoctrinate, °drill, °enlighten, °advise, °direct, °guide, °prepare, °ground: *Twitchell needs someone to tutor him in the fine art of going out with girls.*

tweak *v.* **1** °pinch, °nip, twitch, °squeeze, °jerk, °grip: *I do wish that adults would refrain from tweaking my nose, though it is pretty cute.*
—*n.* **2** °pinch, °nip, twitch, °squeeze, °jerk, °grip: *He gave her nose an affectionate little tweak.*

twee *adj.* °precious, °sweet, °sentimental, °quaint, °dainty, °cute, mignon(ne), bijou: *The tearoom atmosphere is a bit too twee for my taste.*

twiddle *v.* **1** °play with, °twirl, °fiddle (with), wiggle, °juggle, °toy with, °fidget with, *Colloq* °fool with, °mess with, °monkey with: *Stop twiddling with the dial on that radio!* **2** ***twiddle (one's) thumbs***: do °nothing, be °idle, °idle *or* while away (the) time, °waste time, bide (one's) time: *I sat there, twiddling my thumbs, while you were being entertained royally.*

twig[1] *n.* sprig, °stem, °shoot, °offshoot, branchlet, °stick, °sucker, °sprout, withe *or* withy, tendril: *Gather up some dry twigs for kindling.*

twig[2] *v.* °understand, °grasp, °fathom, °get, °comprehend, °see, °know, °sense, °divine, *Colloq* °catch on, be *or* get *or* become °wise to, °tumble to, *Slang* rumble, dig: *She twigged the situation at once but didn't let on she knew.*

twilight *n.* **1** °dusk, sunset, gloaming, sundown, half-light, crepuscule *or* crepuscle: *We enjoyed dinner at twilight on the terrace overlooking the sea.* **2** °decline, °wane, waning, °ebb, downturn, down-swing, °slump, °decay, weakening, declination, diminution: *Even at the twilight of his career, Jonas enjoyed the respect of his colleagues.* **3** ***Twilight of the Gods***: Götter-dämmerung, Ragnarök *or* Ragnarok: *The world ends at the Twilight of the Gods, only to be born anew.*
—*adj.* **4** °evening, crepuscular, dimming, darkening, darkish, darksome, °shadowy, °shady, °dim, °dark, °obscure, °sombre, °gloomy, *Literary* darkling: *The Nymphs in twilight shade of tangled thickets mourn.* **5** ***twilight zone***: °limbo: *He lives in the twilight zone, unable to distinguish reality from fantasy.*

twin *n.* **1** °double, clone, °duplicate, °look-alike, counterpart, *Slang* ringer: *I cannot distinguish these twins.*
—*adj.* **2** °identical, °matching, matched, °duplicate, corresponding, °look-alike: *The bedroom had twin beds with pink covers.*
—*v.* **3** °pair, °match, yoke, °join, °link, °couple, °combine, °connect, °associate: *Many towns in Britain are twinned with similar towns on the Continent.*

twine *n.* **1** °cord, °string; °rope, °cable, °yarn: *Have you some twine for tying up this package?*
—*v.* **2** °entwine, °braid, °twist, intertwine, curl, wreathe, °spiral, °wind, °weave, interweave, °encircle, °wrap: *Annette's front door has roses twined all round it.*

twinge *n.* **1** °stab, °pang, cramp, °spasm, °pinch, stitch, (sharp) °pain, °prick, °bite, °gripe: *I get a terrible twinge in my back when I lift anything heavy.* **2** °pang, °pain: *I felt a twinge of remorse at leaving.*

twinkle *v.* **1** scintillate, °sparkle, coruscate, °glitter, °shimmer, wink, °flicker, °glisten, glint, °flash, fulgurate, °spark, °dance, °blink, °shine, °gleam: *The stars were twinkling in the icy black sky. Nicole's eyes twinkled as she told me about Max's latest success.* —*n.* **2** °twinkling, scintillation, °scintillating, °sparkle, sparkling, coruscation, coruscating, °glitter, glittering, °shimmer, shimmering, winking, °flicker, flickering, glistening, glint, °flash, flashing, fulguration, °spark, sparking, dancing, blinking, °shine, shining, °gleam, gleaming, °dazzle, °dazzling: *From far off, I caught the twinkle of the sun on car windscreens.*

twinkling *n.* **1** (split) °second, °flash, twinkling *or* wink of an eye, °instant, trice, *Colloq* jiffy, two shakes (of a lamb's tail), tick: *Liza called out, and in a twinkling, Joseph was at her side.* **2** See **twinkle, 2,** above.

twirl *v.* **1** °spin, whirl, °rotate, °revolve, °wheel, °turn, °gyrate, °twist, °wind (about *or* around): *The windmills twirled in the breeze. Katherine absently twirled a lock of hair round her finger.* —*n.* **2** twirling, °spin, spinning, whirl, whirling, °turn, turning, °revolution: *He was hypnotized by each twirl of the roulette wheel.* **3** whorl, winding, convolution, °spiral, helix, °coil, volute: *The pattern consists of interlocking twirls of green and brown.*

twist *v.* **1** plait, °braid, °weave, °entwine, intertwine, °twine, interweave, pleach, °splice, wreathe, interlace: *She twisted together some daisies to make a garland for her hair.* **2** °distort, °warp, contort, °pervert, °alter, °change, °slant, °bias, °colour, °falsify, misquote, misstate, °garble, miscite, °misrepresent, °violate; °misinterpret, mistranslate, °misunderstand, misconstrue: *He twisted her words so that she seemed to be saying the opposite of what she intended.* **3** °wriggle, worm, °squirm, writhe, wiggle: *The little beggar twisted out of my grasp and ran for his life.* **4** °wind, °snake, °meander, °turn, zigzag, worm, °bend, curve: *I lost sight of the stream where it twisted through the undergrowth.* **5** °wrench, °turn, sprain, rick *or* wrick: *I twisted my ankle on a faulty step.* **6** ***twist (one's*** *or* ***someone's) arm***: °force, coerce, °make, °persuade, °bully, *Brit* pressurize, *US* °pressure: *I didn't want to go, but she twisted my arm.* —*n.* **7** °coil, °spiral, skew, zigzag, dog-leg, °turn, curve, °angle, °bend, °bow, °meander: *The road is full of twists and turns.* **8** °interpretation, °analysis, °understanding, °slant, °angle, construction, construal; °treatment, °approach, °version, °variation: *This book puts a new twist on the fall of the Roman Empire.* **9** distortion, misinterpretation, contortion, °perversion, warping, °alteration, °change, departure, °bias, colouring, falsification, misquotation, °misstatement, garbling, misrepresentation; mistranslation, °misunderstanding, misconstrual, misconstruction: *It was a twist of fate that brought us together again. She gave everything he said such a twist that he scarcely recognized his own ideas.* **10** °quirk, idiosyncrasy, crotchet, °peculiarity, °oddity, °trick, °eccentricity, incongruity, inconsistency, irregularity; °weakness, °flaw, °fault, °foible, °failing: *Owing to a twist in his character, he has developed a hatred of women.* **11** ***round the twist***: °mad, °crazy, °insane, °eccentric, *Colloq* °daft, *Brit* round the bend, *Slang* nuts, nutty, bonkers, cuckoo, batty, off (one's) rocker, *Brit* barmy *or* balmy: *Kevin's gone round the twist if he thinks I am going out with his sister.*

twister *n.* **1** °cheat, °swindler, confidence man *or* woman, °rogue, °scoundrel, trickster, mountebank, deceiver, °fraud, °impostor *or* imposter, *Colloq* con man *or* woman, crook: *This particular twister preys on the elderly.* **2** tornado, cyclone, typhoon, °hurricane, °whirlwind; waterspout: *The twister picked up my bicycle and dropped it in my neighbour's garden.*

twit[1] *v.* °tease, °cajole, °taunt, °jeer (at), make °fun of, °banter, °tweak, °gibe *or* jibe, °chaff, °ridicule, °mock; °blame, °berate, °deride, °scorn, contemn, censure, revile, reproach, °upbraid; *Colloq* kid, pull (someone's) °leg: *She never seemed to mind being twitted about her height.*

twit[2] *n.* nitwit, nincompoop, ass, ninny, ninnyhammer, °fool, imbecile, blockhead, °halfwit, idiot, simpleton, *Colloq* chump, moron, *Brit* °silly billy, *Slang* °dope, *US and Canadian* °jerk: *That silly twit told the teacher what we were planning.*

twitter *v.* **1** °peep, cheep, tweet, °chirp, warble, trill, chirrup, °chatter: *The birds twitter so loudly that they wake me every morning.* **2** °chatter, °prattle, °gossip, °giggle, prate, °titter, °snicker, snigger, simper: *I was embarrassed because my classmates always twittered when I did a recitation.* —*n.* **3** °peep, peeping, cheep, cheeping, twittering, tweet, tweeting, chirrup, chirruping, °chirp, chirping, warble, warbling, trill, trilling: *The twitter of the birds was driving me mad.* **4** ado, bustle, °excitement, °flutter, dither, whirl, °agitation, *Colloq* °stew, tizzy: *The girls were in a twitter of apprehension.*

two-faced *adj.* double-dealing, °hypocritical, duplicitous, dissembling, °deceitful, Janus-faced, treacherous, °dishonest, untrustworthy, °insincere, °scheming, °designing, °crafty, Machiavellian, °sly, °perfidious, °lying, mendacious: *That two-faced liar told you one story and me another!*

tycoon *n.* °mogul, magnate, baron, °financier, (multi)-millionaire, billionaire, °merchant prince, potentate, *Colloq* °big shot, (big-time) °operator, wheeler-dealer, big-timer, *US* °big wheel, °big cheese: *What makes you think that Castenado is an oil tycoon?*

type *n.* **1** °class, °category, classification, °kind, °sort, °genre, °order, °variety, °breed, species, °strain, °group, genus, ilk, kidney: *Just what type of person would you say the president is?* **2** typeface, *Brit* fount, *US* font: *The body text ought to be set in Bodoni Book type, the headings in Times bold.* **3** °prototype, paradigm, archetype, °epitome, exemplar, °model, °specimen, °pattern, personification, °standard, °quintessence: *She doesn't consider him to be the usual type of businessman.* —*v.* **4** typewrite; keyboard; °transcribe: *She types at a speed of about sixty words a minute.*

typical *adj.* **1** °representative, °characteristic, °conventional, °normal, °standard, °ordinary, °regular: *On a typical day I get up at 6.30.* **2** °orthodox, °classic, °conventional, in °character, in keeping, °usual, commonplace, run-of-the-mill, °natural, °customary, °common, to be expected, °ordinary: *His way of looking at life is typical for someone of his educational and social background.*

typify *v.* °exemplify, °instance, epitomize, °personify, °represent, °characterize, °embody, evince, °symbolize, °suggest: *John's views typify the conservative approach.*

tyrannical *adj.* tyrannous, °oppressive, °dictatorial, Fascistic, °despotic, autocratic, °authoritarian, °arbitrary, imperious, °overbearing, unjust, high-handed, °severe, °harsh, iron-handed, °heavy-handed: *The people suffered under one tyrannical form of government after another for generations.*

tyrannize *v.* Often, ***tyrannize over***: domineer over, °bully, °subjugate, enthral, °enslave, °dominate, °intimidate, °dictate to, °order about *or* around, ride roughshod over, °browbeat, keep under (one's) °thumb, °oppress, °subdue, °suppress, keep down: *The people have been tyrannized long enough.*

tyranny *n.* autocracy, Fascism, authoritarianism, absolutism, °despotism, dictatorship, Stalinism, Nazism; arbitrariness, °oppression, °suppression, subjugation, enslavement, enthralment, °domination: *Tyranny would not survive long were it not expedient for its supporters.*

tyrant *n.* °dictator, °despot, autocrat, martinet, Hitler, °bully, °oppressor, °authoritarian, hard taskmaster, slave-driver, Simon Legree, overlord: *It seems that no people or part of the world is immune from tyrants.*

U

ugly *adj.* **1** unattractive, unlovely, unprepossessing, °unsightly, °hideous, °grotesque, °gruesome, °ghastly, °offensive, repulsive-looking, °plain, plain-looking, plain-featured, bad-featured, ill-favoured, dreadful-looking, awful-looking, terrible-looking, horrible-looking, frightful-looking, monstrous-looking, *US and Canadian* °homely: *The Georgian houses were demolished and replaced by ugly tower-blocks.* **2** objectionable, °disagreeable, unpleasant, °offensive, °nasty, °loathsome, °repellent, °repugnant, °repulsive, noisome, nauseating, °nauseous, °revolting, sickening, °disgusting, °obnoxious, mephitic, °rotten, °corrupt, °filthy, °vile, heinous, °bad, °sordid, °evil, °foul, °perverted, °immoral, depraved, °degenerate, °base, debased, detestable, °hateful, °abominable, execrable, °despicable, odious: *The East End murders were among the ugliest crimes of the century. He sprang from his seat with an ugly curse on his lips.* **3** disquieting, uncomfortable, discomforting, °troublesome, °awkward, disadvantageous, °ominous, °dangerous, °perilous, °hazardous: *He found himself in a very ugly position, with no apparent means of escape.* **4** unpleasant, °disagreeable, °surly, °hostile, °nasty, °spiteful, bad-tempered, ill-tempered, currish, irascible, curmudgeonly, °cantankerous, crabby, crabbed, crotchety, °cross, °cranky, °mean: *He's in an ugly mood till he's had his coffee.*

ulcer *n.* **1** °sore, lesion, abscess, ulceration, canker, chancre, °boil, gumboil, °eruption, carbuncle, °inflammation: *That ulcer should be treated before it gets any worse.* **2** cancer, canker, festering spot, °blight, °scourge, °poison, °disease, °pestilence, °curse, bane, °plague: *We must purge this ulcer before it corrupts the entire organization.*

ulcerous *adj.* ulcerative, cancerous, cankerous, festering, ulcerated, suppurating, suppurative, gangrenous, septic, *Technical* furuncular, furunculous, necrotic, necrosed, sphacelated: *The wound is in an ulcerous condition and requires immediate surgery.*

ulterior *adj.* **1** °hidden, concealed, covert, °secret, unrevealed, undisclosed, unexpressed, °private, °personal, underlying, °surreptitious, underhand(ed): *She had an ulterior motive for arriving early.* **2** °outside, beyond, °further, °remote, remoter: *What you propose is ulterior to our immediate plan.*

ultimate *adj.* **1** °final, °last, terminating, °terminal, °end, °eventual, conclusive, concluding, decisive, deciding: *The ultimate outcome will not be known till next week. Who is the ultimate authority in such matters?* **2** °final, °maximum, highest, greatest, °supreme, utmost, °paramount: *Her ultimate goal is to win the gold medal.* **3** °elemental, °basic, °fundamental, underlying, °primary, °essential, °final: *He believes that the ultimate truths were set down in Scripture.* **4** remotest, furthest, farthest, °extreme, uttermost, °last, °final: *The ultimate stage of the experiment will be at a distance of five light-years.*

ultimately *adv.* °finally, at long °last, in the °final *or* °last analysis, in the °end, at the °end of the day, after all is said and done, at (the) °last, in the long run; fundamentally, essentially, basically, at °bottom: *I thought it might ultimately come to this. He came to understand that ultimately people must depend on each other.*

ultimatum *n.* °demand(s), °term(s), °condition(s), °stipulation(s), °requirement(s): *If we refuse to comply with his ultimatum, he'll kill the hostage.*

ultra- *adj.* °extreme, °immoderate, °excessive, °drastic, °radical, °fanatic(al), °unmitigated, °outrageous, °unqualified, °sheer, °blatant, °out-and-out, °complete, °thorough, thoroughgoing, dyed in the wool, die-hard, °rabid, °opinionated, unregenerate, °unrepentant, unreformed, fundamentalist, °prejudiced, °bigoted, *Colloq* hard-nosed: *Ultra-conservativism marked his views till the day he died.*

umbrage *n.* Usually, ***take umbrage***: feel *or* be °offended, take °offence, feel °displeasure *or* °annoyance *or* exasperation *or* °indignation *or* vexation *or* °bitterness *or* °resentment, be piqued *or* displeased *or* annoyed *or* exasperated *or* °indignant *or* vexed *or* °resentful, harbour a °grudge: *She took umbrage at the way he seemed to ignore her.*

umbrella *n.* **1** parasol; *Colloq chiefly Brit* gamp, *Brit* brolly, *US* bumbershoot: *You will need an umbrella today.* **2** °protection, °cover, coverage, aegis, °shield, °screen, °patronage, °agency: *What benefits are included under the umbrella of this policy?*

umpire *n.* **1** referee, arbiter, °judge, °moderator, adjudicator, arbitrator; °official; *Colloq* ref, *Australian* umpy, *US* ump: *The sides agree to abide by the decision of the umpire.*
—*v.* **2** referee, arbitrate, °judge, °moderate, adjudicate; °officiate: *When Peter Jones umpires a game, the players know they will get a fair decision.*

umpteen *adj.* a °lot of, °many, innumerable, unnumbered, countless, a °huge °number of, very °many, numerous, hundreds of, thousands of, millions of, billions of, trillions of: *You've been told umpteen times, 'Don't go near the water'.*

unabashed *adj.* unashamed, unblushing, unembarrassed, °brazen, °blatant, °bold, undaunted, unawed, undismayed, unconcerned: *I couldn't put up with his unabashed conceit for another moment.*

unable *adj.* not °able, °powerless, unfit, °unqualified, °impotent: *The company was unable to give guarantees about continuity of employment.*

unabridged *adj.* **1** uncut, °whole, full-length, °entire, °complete, °intact, uncondensed, unshortened; unbowdlerized, unexpurgated: *This is the original, unabridged edition, with nothing removed.* **2** °extensive, °thorough, °comprehensive, °exhaustive, all-encompassing, (all-)°inclusive: *That word is too rare to be listed in anything but an unabridged dictionary.*

unaccented *adj.* unstressed, unemphasized, unaccentuated, °weak, *Technical* lenis: *The first syllable of 'before' is unaccented.*

unacceptable *adj.* °unsatisfactory, objectionable, °wrong, °bad, °improper, unallowable, °undesirable, not *de rigueur*, °distasteful, °disagreeable, unsuitable, °inappropriate, unpleasant, °tasteless: *Murder is generally regarded as an unacceptable way to relieve oneself of unwanted company.*

unaccompanied *adj.* °alone, °solo, on (one's) own, unescorted, unchaperoned, unattended, *Music* a cappella, *Colloq* stag: *We went to the dance unaccompanied.*

unaccountable *adj.* **1** unexplained, °inexplicable, unexplainable, °mysterious, inscrutable, °incomprehensible, unintelligible, °strange, °puzzling, baffling, °peculiar, °odd, °bizarre, unfathomable: *I found it unaccountable that anyone would arrive for an appointment four hours early.* **2** not answerable, not °responsible: *How can you have a governmental committee that is unaccountable to anyone?* **3** °weird, °unheard-of, °extraordinary, °unusual, °unorthodox, uncanny: *Sophie has unaccountable powers of perception.*

unaccustomed *adj.* **1** °unfamiliar, °unusual, °rare, unexpected, uncommon, unprecedented, unanticipated, °curious, °peculiar: *They encountered unaccustomed hostility from local people.* **2** ***unaccustomed to***: °unused to, °inexperienced in *or* at, amateurish at, unpractised in *or* at, °unfamiliar with, uninitiated in: *Unaccustomed as I am to public speaking, I had better be brief.*

unadorned *adj.* °plain, °simple, unembellished, undecorated, unornamented, °stark, °bare, austere: *She prefers an unadorned style, without frills.*

unaffected[1] *adj.* °genuine, °real, °sincere, °natural, °simple, °plain, unpretentious, unassuming, °ingenuous, °unsophisticated, unstudied, °honest, guileless, °artless, unartificial, straightforward, unfeigned: *He conveyed in simple unaffected language a clear impression of the nightmarish quality of that day.*

unaffected[2] *adj.* Usually, ***unaffected by***: impervious (to), °immune (to), untouched (by), °unmoved (by), unresponsive (to), °aloof (to *or* from), uninfluenced (by), unimpressed (by), °remote (to *or* from), °cool *or* °cold (to), unconcerned (by), unstirred (by): *The duchess remained totally unaffected by the children's appeals for help.*

unapproachable *adj.* **1** °distant, °remote, °aloof, °reserved, °standoffish, austere, °withdrawn, unfriendly, °forbidding, °chilly, °cool, °cold, °frigid: *James seems unapproachable, but in fact he's a very warm person.* **2** °inaccessible, °remote, unreachable, °out-of-the-way, out of °reach, beyond °reach: *Her house is unapproachable except from the sea.*

unarmed *adj.* unprotected, °defenceless, weaponless: *The army began shooting unarmed civilians.*

unasked *adj.* uninvited, unrequested, undemanded, °unsolicited, unsought, unwanted, unprompted, °gratuitous, unbidden, °spontaneous, °unwelcome, °unasked for: *I wish he would keep his unasked opinions to himself.*

unattached *adj.* **1** °separate, unconnected, °detached, °independent, unaffiliated, self-governing, self-regulating, self-regulated, autonomous, self-reliant, self-sustaining, self-sustained: *The committee was established as an unattached body, not associated with any organization.* **2** °single, °unmarried, uncommitted, unengaged, on (one's) own, unspoken for: *I joined the club hoping to meet some unattached people.*

unauthorized *adj.* unsanctioned, unapproved, °unofficial, °unlawful, °illegal, °illicit, °illegitimate: *Unauthorized use of the company's parking spaces is prohibited.*

unavoidable *adj.* inescapable, ineluctable, °inevitable, °irresistible, inexorable, °sure, °certain, °fated, °destined, predestined, °determined, °predetermined, unchangeable, unalterable, settled, °fixed, °definite: *Punishment is an unavoidable consequence of getting caught for something you shouldn't have done.*

unaware *adj.* °ignorant, °oblivious, unknowing, °unsuspecting, °unconscious, °uninformed, unenlightened, incognizant, inobservant, °insensible, °heedless, unmindful: *She was totally unaware of the huge spider dangling directly over her.*

unawares *adv.* **1** unexpectedly, abruptly, by °surprise, °suddenly, off (one's) guard: *We caught the sentry unawares.* **2** inadvertently, unconsciously, unintentionally, unknowingly, unwittingly, by °mistake, mistakenly, by °accident, accidentally, in an °unguarded moment: *She had betrayed her closest friend unawares.*

unbalanced *adj.* **1** uneven, asymmetric(al), unsymmetric(al), °lopsided, unequal, overbalanced, °unstable, wobbly, °shaky, unsteady: *That stack of chairs is unbalanced and could fall any minute.* **2** °mad, demented, certifiable, °crazy, °insane, °eccentric, *non compos mentis*, touched (in the head), °unstable, unhinged, °deranged, °disturbed, of °unsound mind, out of (one's) head, *Colloq* daffy, °dizzy, *Chiefly Brit* °daft, *Slang* nuts, batty, off (one's) rocker, *Chiefly Brit* bonkers, *US* out of one's gourd, loco: *The boy is clearly unbalanced, but that doesn't excuse his appalling behaviour.*

unbearable *adj.* intolerable, unsupportable, unendurable, °insufferable, °unacceptable, too much: *The pain in her side was almost unbearable.*

unbeatable *adj.* unsurpassable, undefeatable, °excellent, unexcelled, °incomparable, °matchless, unrivalled, °peerless, °unparalleled, °superlative, °supreme: *She'll go far with such an unbeatable combination of looks and brains.*

unbecoming *adj.* **1** unsuited, unsuitable, °inappropriate, ill-suited, unfitting, unfit, inapt, unapt, out of °character, out of °place: *It is unbecoming to wear your mink coat to the Save the Animals fund-raising dinner.* **2** indecorous, °unseemly, indelicate, °improper, ungentlemanly, unladylike, °offensive, °tasteless: *Father said it was unbecoming for her to use such foul language.*

unbelievable *adj.* °incredible, °preposterous, °inconceivable, unimaginable, mind-boggling, °implausible, °unthinkable: *The amount of money they spend on clothes is unbelievable. He told an unbelievable tale about having been picked up by a flying saucer.*

unbelieving *adj.* °incredulous, disbelieving, nonbelieving, doubting, mistrusting, distrusting, mistrustful, °distrustful, °suspicious, °sceptical, unpersuaded, unconvinced: *The unbelieving world thinks that the age of miracles is past.*

uncertain *adj.* **1** unsure, indeterminate, unpredictable, undeterminable, unforeseeable, unascertainable, °haphazard, °chance, °arbitrary, °random, aleatory, serendipitous, hit-or-miss, °casual: *It is uncertain whether interest rates will rise again next month.* **2** unsure, in *or* of two minds, vacillating, undecided, unclear, ambivalent, °irresolute, °indecisive, °hesitant, hesitating, undetermined, shilly-shallying, *Brit* at a loose °end, *US* at loose °ends: *Julia is uncertain about what to do next.* **3** unsure, indeterminate, up in the air, °indefinite, unpredictable, °unresolved, °unsettled, in the balance, conjectural, °speculative, °debatable, touch-and-go, °unreliable, °doubtful, dubious, °questionable, °vague, °hazy: *The future of the company is now uncertain. The results of the election are still uncertain.* **4** °variable, °changeable, °inconstant, unfixed, °unsettled, °irregular, °fickle, °erratic, °fitful, unsteady, wavering, °unreliable, °sporadic, °occasional; unmethodical, unsystematic: *The pictures in the cave danced in the uncertain light of the torch. How can we make an appointment if your plans are so uncertain?*

uncharted *adj.* unmapped, °unknown, unexplored, undiscovered, °unfamiliar, °strange, virgin, °trackless: *For weeks he wandered lost in the uncharted jungle.*

unchaste *adj.* °impure, °wanton, °immoral, unvirtuous, °promiscuous, °immodest, Cyprian, debased, °lecherous, °lewd, °lascivious: *Her unchaste conduct was a topic of conversation throughout the school.*

uncivilized *adj.* **1** barbarous, °savage, °wild, uncultivated, °barbarian, barbaric, °crude, °primitive, brutish: *He was an uncivilized man living in uncivilized surroundings.* **2** °unrefined, uncultured, uncouth, loutish, °coarse, °uneducated, untutored, unpolished, churlish, °boorish, °philistine, °provincial, °rough, °rude, unlearned, °ill-mannered, incondite, unmannerly, °unsophisticated, inelegant, °gross, gauche: *Anna's father forbade her to go out with the uncivilized boors in the nearby town.*

unconscionable *adj.* **1** conscienceless, °unscrupulous, amoral, unprincipled, °immoral, unethical, °evil, °criminal, unjust, °wicked, arrant: *This unconscionable thief stole from his own mother.* **2** °excessive, extortionate, egregious, °extreme, °unwarranted, °unreasonable, °outrageous, °inordinate, °immoderate, °exorbitant, indefensible, unpardonable, °inexcusable, unforgivable: *When I questioned the unconscionable size of his bill, the plumber explained that he charges extra for house calls.*

unconscious *adj.* **1** °insensible, out (cold), knocked out, °senseless, °numb, stunned, comatose, °dead to the world, *Colloq* blacked-out: *The patient was unconscious for hours.* **2** Often, ***unconscious of***: °heedless (of *or* to), unheeding, unheedful (of), insensitive (to), °mindless, unmindful (of), reflex, °automatic, °involuntary, unintentional, °instinctive, °subliminal, °unthinking, °unpremeditated, °subconscious, unwitting; °blind (to), °unaware (of), °oblivious (to *or* of),

°deaf (to): *For Tim, scratching his head is an unconscious act. Tim is totally unconscious of how irritating his mannerisms are.*

uncontrolled *adj.* unrestrained, ungoverned, unchecked, untrammelled, °undisciplined, °wild, °unruly, °boisterous, °riotous, out of hand *or* of °control, °rampant, frenzied, °frantic; going °berserk, running amok *or* amuck: *He hit his brother in a moment of uncontrolled anger.*

under *prep.* **1** °beneath, °below, underneath, covered by: *What is under that blanket? The wreck lies a mile under the surface.* **2** °subordinate to, answerable to, °inferior to, °second to, °secondary to, subservient to, °below, °beneath, underneath, °junior to, directed *or* supervised *or* controlled by, under (the) °control of, at the °mercy of, at the beck and call of: *The bashi-bazouks were under the sultan's top officers.* **3** included *or* comprised in *or* under, subsumed under: *This should be under the heading, 'What is the Stupidest Thing you have done Today?' Under which category is 'Software'?* **4** under the aegis *or* °protection *or* °eye *or* guardianship *or* °care of: *The prince was trained under the grand vizier.* **5** less than, °lower than: *I paid under £200 for my VCR.* **6** ***under the influence***: °drunk, tipsy, °high, impaired: *The police charged him with driving while under the influence.*
—*adv.* **7** °below, underneath, °beneath: *You looked on top of the bed, but have you looked under?* **8** underwater, beneath the waves, down, out of °sight: *We watched helpless as he went under for the third time.*

underclothes *n.* underclothing, underwear, undergarments, lingerie, *Old-fashioned* °unmentionables, *Colloq* underthings, undies, *Brit* smalls, *Old-fashioned Brit* small-clothes, *US* skivvies: *When a salesman she met on the train said he was in ladies' underclothes, she moved to another carriage.*

undercover *adj.* °secret, °private, clandestine, °confidential: *He doesn't look much like an undercover agent.*

undercurrent *n.* **1** undertow, cross-current, rip tide, rip (°current), underflow: *Caught in the undercurrent, he was carried out to sea.* **2** undertone, subcurrent, °trend, °tendency, °overtone, °tenor, °suggestion, °murmur, °implication, connotation, °sense, °feeling, °aura, tinge, °flavour, °atmosphere, ambience *or* ambiance; vibrations, *Colloq* °vibes: *There is a sinister undercurrent of gloom about this place.*

undercut *v.* **1** °undermine, °excavate, °hollow out, °cut out *or* away, °gouge out: *If you undercut the roadway it will collapse.* **2** underprice, undercharge, °sacrifice, °sell cheaply *or* at a loss, undersell: *The supermarkets undercut prices and put the independent grocers out of business.*

underdog *n.* °loser, °scapegoat, °victim; vanquished, °defenceless; *Colloq* fall guy, little fellow *or* guy: *It has always been our policy to fight for the underdog.*

underestimate *v.* undervalue, underrate, °discount, misjudge, °miscalculate, misprize, °minimize, °depreciate, °belittle, not do justice to, fail to appreciate, set (too) little °store by, think (too) little of: *No one should underestimate the physical and mental effort involved.*

undergo *v.* °suffer, °bear, °endure, °experience, °live *or* °go through, be subjected to, °subject oneself to, °sustain, °submit to, °weather, °stand, °withstand: *The hotel has recently undergone extensive refurbishing.*

underground *adj.* **1** subterranean, buried, belowground, °sunken, covered: *They crept through the underground passage into the treasure room.* **2** °secret, clandestine, concealed, °hidden, covert, °undercover, °surreptitious, °stealthy, °private: *The secret service has a worldwide underground network of agents.* **3** °alternative, °radical, °experimental, °avant-garde, °nonconformist, °revolutionary: *Some underground newspapers that sprang up in the 1960s are still being published.*
—*n.* **4** tube, metro, underground °railway, *US* °subway: *Two more stops on the underground and we'll be there.* **5** °resistance, partisans *or* partizans, freedom fighters, *in France* Maquis, insurgents, seditionaries *or* seditionists, insurrectionists, guerrillas *or* guerillas, extremists, revolutionaries; fifth-columnists, fifth column, saboteurs, subversives: *The underground helped the family to escape to England. The government blames the underground for the bombings.*

undermine *v.* **1** °sap, °drain, disable, °weaken, debilitate, °threaten, °sabotage, °subvert, °damage, °hurt, °harm, °impair, °ruin, °dash, °wreck, °spoil, *Slang* °queer, °bugger (up): *He said that the entire campaign would be undermined if the events of January 17th were ever revealed.* **2** See **undercut, 1,** above.

undersized *adj.* under-size, °little, °short, °small, °petite, °tiny, °elfin, bantam, °slight, mignon(ne); °stunted, underdeveloped, runty, runtish, dwarfish, dwarfed, pygmy, squat; underweight, °undeveloped: *These cattle are a bit undersized for market.*

understand *v.* **1** °grasp, °comprehend, °see, °perceive, discern, °make out, °get the °drift *or* the hang of, °appreciate, °interpret, take °cognizance of, °recognize, be °aware *or* °conscious of, be conversant with, °know, °realize, °conceive of, apprehend, °penetrate, *Colloq* °get (it), °dig, °catch on (to), °tumble to, cotton on (to), *Brit* °twig: *I can understand what you are saying. I didn't think you understood.* **2** °accept, °agree, °arrange, covenant, °take: *I understand the terms of the agreement.* **3** °interpret, °take, °read, °gather from, construe, °surmise from, °assume from, °infer from, °view, °see: *As I understand the regulation, only residents may use the facilities.* **4** °hear (of), °gather, get °wind (of), °take it, be told *or* °informed *or* advised, have found out *or* learnt, *Colloq* °hear tell: *I understand that you've applied for another job.* **5** °sympathize *or* empathize (with), be in °sympathy (with), show compassion (for), commiserate (with); °accept, °tolerate, °allow, °forgive: *Surely your employer will understand your being late because of the funeral.*

understanding *n.* **1** °agreement, °contract, °arrangement, °bargain, covenant, concession, °pact, °compact, °accord, °treaty, concordat, entente, °alliance, °truce, armistice, °reconciliation, °settlement: *They reached an understanding with respect to nuclear weapons.* **2** discernment, °sensitivity, sensitiveness, °sympathy, empathy, °perception, °insight, good °sense, °intuition, enlightenment, percipience, sagacity, sageness, sapience, °wisdom, *Colloq* savvy: *Georgianna brings so much understanding to her treatment of the aged.* **3** Usually, ***understanding of***: comprehension *or* awareness *or* °grasp *or* °control *or* °idea *or* °conception *or* °knowledge *or* mastery (of), °acquaintance *or* °familiarity *or* intimacy *or* °dexterity *or* skilfulness *or* deftness *or* adroitness *or* adeptness (with), competence *or* °skill *or* expertness *or* know-how *or* °proficiency *or* °expertise (in), *Colloq US* fix (on), handle (on): *I know no one with a better understanding of medieval Welsh.* **4** reading, °interpretation, °opinion, °judgement, °estimation, °notion, °view, °perception, apperception, apprehension: *My understanding of what took place is at odds with yours.* **5** °intellect, °intelligence, °mind, °brain, brainpower, °sense, °reason, °reasoning power, °wisdom, *Colloq* brains: *I'm afraid that he lacks the understanding needed to cope with the subtleties of the situation.*

understated *adj.* °subtle, restrained, low-key, °simple, °basic, unembellished, °unadorned: *Alexandra was wearing an understated black dress with a string of pearls.*

understood *adj.* accepted, agreed, arranged, °given, covenanted, settled, conceded: *It was understood that we would be dining together that night. The terms of the agreement are now fully understood.*

understudy *n.* **1** °second, °substitute, °stand-in, °alternate, backup, °double, sub, °reserve, *US* pinch-hitter: *The understudy got her break one night when the star fell ill.*
—*v.* **2** °substitute for, °stand in for, back up, °double for, °second, °replace, *US* pinch-hit for: *He is understudying Hamlet as well as playing the part of Laertes.*

undertake *v.* **1** °assume, °take on *or* upon (oneself), °accept, °take *or* °assume *or* °bear the responsibility for, °enter upon, °begin, °start, °set about, °embark on, °tackle, °try, °attempt: *Gates might be undertaking a bit too much, considering his condition.* **2** °promise, covenant, °agree, °contract, °pledge, °vow, °swear, °warrant, °guarantee, °bargain, °commit (oneself), °stipulate, °engage: *Is it not true that you undertook to complete the work in six months?*

undertaker *n.* mortician, °funeral °director: *The body is available for viewing at the undertaker's tonight.*

undertaking *n.* **1** °enterprise, °affair, °business, °project, °task, °effort, °venture, °work, °feat: *The scope of the undertaking was far beyond her capacity.* **2** doing, performing, °performance, °realization, °achievement: *Giles's undertaking of the work makes me feel more confident.* **3** °promise, °pledge, commitment, °assurance, °contract, °agreement, °vow, °guarantee *or* guaranty, °warranty: *You gave an undertaking to complete the work by Friday.*

underworld *n.* **1** Usually, ***the underworld***: organized crime, the °syndicate, the Mafia, the °mob, Cosa Nostra, °criminals, the °criminal element, *Colloq* gangland: *Lorenzo was fast becoming a well-known figure in the underworld.* **2** nether regions, abode of the dead, Hades, Hell, Avernus, Dis, Orcus, *Facetious* Egyptian °underground: *I think I prefer contemplating the Happy Hunting Ground of the American Indian to the underworlds of Christianity and classical Mediterranean culture.*

underwrite *v.* **1** back (up), °finance, °support, °invest in, °subsidize, °sponsor, °uphold, °approve, insure, °guarantee, *US* subvene: *The company has agreed to underwrite the development of your invention.* **2** °subscribe to, °endorse *or* indorse, °sign, countersign, °consent to, °agree to, °confirm, accede to, °sanction, °ratify, °approve, validate, *Colloq* °OK *or* okay: *The government underwrote the action one day, then denied knowledge of it the next.*

undesirable *n.* **1** *persona non grata*, pariah, °outcast, °exile, °reject, leper: *The police had many requests to run the undesirables out of town.*
—*adj.* **2** unwanted, objectionable, °offensive, °unacceptable, °obnoxious, °unsavoury, °unwelcome, disliked, °distasteful, °repugnant, unfit, °unbecoming, unsuitable: *The parks are filled with tramps, drug addicts, and other undesirable elements.*

undeveloped *adj.* embryonic, °premature, °immature, incipient, inchoate, °potential, latent: *His sense of beauty remained undeveloped till he visited Rome.*

undiluted *adj.* °pure, °neat, °straight, unmixed, uncut, unblended, unadulterated, unwatered, unalloyed: *No ice, please—I like my whisky undiluted. How do you like the undiluted gall of the fellow walking in here uninvited!*

undisciplined *adj.* untrained, unschooled, °unprepared, untutored, °uneducated, untaught, unpractised, °uncontrolled, °disobedient, °naughty, °bad, °wilful, wayward, unrestrained, °erratic, unpredictable, °unruly, °wild: *The sergeant has taken quite a few undisciplined recruits and knocked them into shape.*

undisguised *adj.* °open, °out-and-out, unmistakable, °overt, unconcealed, unreserved, unrestrained, unfeigned, unpretended, °obvious, °evident, °patent, °clear, °explicit, °transparent, °sincere, °heartfelt, unalloyed, °unmitigated: *They regarded the traitor with undisguised contempt.*

undisputed *adj.* unquestioned, °unquestionable, beyond °question, accepted, acknowledged, admitted, °indisputable, indubitable, undoubted, °certain, °sure, unmistakable, °definite, °explicit, °clear, (self-)°evident, °obvious, uncontested, unchallenged, incontestable, irrefutable, °incontrovertible, undeniable, conclusive: *He proved once again that he is the undisputed heavyweight champion of the world.*

undistinguished *adj.* °ordinary, commonplace, °common, °everyday, run-of-the-mill, °pedestrian, unexceptional, °plain, °homespun, °simple, °prosaic, unremarkable; °mediocre, middling, °indifferent, unexciting, unimpressive, unpretentious, *Brit* °homely, *Colloq* °so so, no °great shakes, no big deal, °nothing to write home about, °nothing °special *or* °unusual *or* °extraordinary: *It was an undistinguished modern building near the roundabout.*

undivided *adj.* **1** °whole, °entire, unbroken, uncut, °intact, unseparated, °complete, unsplit: *The family lands remained undivided for generations.* **2** undiverted, °whole, °entire, °devoted, concentrated, °full, °complete, °exclusive, undistracted: *You have my undivided attention.*

undo *v.* **1** °loosen, °loose, °open, unfasten, unhook, unlace, unzip, unsnap, unbutton, untie, unpin; unlock, unbolt: *Help me undo my blouse. Don't undo the gate—you'll let the dogs out.* **2** unwrap, uncover, °open, untie, unbind: *Why have you allowed the children to undo their Christmas presents a week early?* **3** °cancel, annul, rescind, nullify, °void, declare null and °void, °reverse, invalidate: *If one could undo things there would be no such thing as regret.*

undoing *n.* **1** °ruin, ruination, °destruction, devastation, °defeat, °downfall, °overthrow, °fall, °collapse, descent, debasement, °degradation, abasement, mortification, °humiliation, °shame, °disgrace: *It is not easy to identify the factors that brought about the demagogue's undoing.* **2** °curse, °misfortune, bane, °affliction, °trouble, °blight: *As the novelists would have it, a beautiful woman was his undoing.*

undone[1] *adj.* **1** ruined, °lost, wrecked, crushed, destroyed, devastated, shattered, brought to °ruin, defeated, prostrated, °overcome: *Brian was completely undone by that gold-digging heart-breaker he met in Caracas. If the headmaster finds out about the glue, we are undone!* **2** °open, °loose, loosened, untied, unfastened, °detached, unhooked, unlaced, unzipped, unsnapped, unbuttoned, unpinned, unstuck: *Your shoelaces are undone. The knot came undone.*

undone[2] *adj.* unaccomplished, uncompleted, °incomplete, unfinished, omitted, neglected, left (out), skipped, missed, passed over, forgotten, unattended to: *From this list of chores, how many are still undone?*

undoubtedly *adv.* indubitably, without (a) °doubt, indisputably, unquestionably, beyond (a *or* the shadow of a) °doubt, certainly, °definitely, °surely, assuredly, unmistakably, explicitly, °clearly, °obviously, incontestably, irrefutably, incontrovertibly, undeniably: *If they win, they will undoubtedly go to the pub to celebrate.*

unduly *adv.* **1** disproportionately, excessively, °overly, unnecessarily, inordinately, unreasonably, irrationally, unjustifiably, improperly, inappropriately: *He claimed that he was being unduly harassed by the police.* **2** immoderately, lavishly, profusely, extravagantly: *Don't be unduly generous in tipping our waiter—he did spill the soup in your lap.*

unearth *v.* °dig up, disinter, exhume; °excavate, dredge up, °mine, °quarry, °find, °pull *or* °root out, °come across, °discover, °turn up, expose, uncover: *The artefacts were unearthed at Boghazköy, ancient Hattusas. They had unearthed some evidence that would put him away for years.*

unearthly *adj.* **1** °supernatural, °unnatural, preternatural, unworldly, other-worldly, °psychic(al), extramundane, extraterrestrial, extrasensory, supersensory, out-of-(the-)body, asomatous, incorporeal, °sublime, °celestial, astral: *They speculated about what unearthly experiences space travel might lead to.* **2** °weird, °bizarre, °macabre, °nightmarish, uncanny, °eerie, °strange, °ghostly, °spectral, °unreal, *Literary* eldritch, *Colloq* spooky, creepy: *An unearthly creature appeared in a mist before her.* **3** °strange, °odd, °peculiar, °unusual, °abnormal, °absurd, out of the °ordinary, °extraordinary, °outrageous; °unheard-of, °unreasonable, *Colloq* °ungodly: *The baby wakes up at the unearthly hour of three o'clock every morning.*

uneducated *adj.* unschooled, untaught, uncultivated, unread, uncultured, °illiterate, unlettered, °ignorant, unenlightened: *It is debatable whether the fault for being uneducated lies with the student, the teacher, or the system.*

unemployed *adj.* out of °work, jobless, °idle, laid off, out of a °job, unoccupied, °inactive, *Brit* °redundant, *Colloq Brit* on the °dole, *Facetious* resting, at °liberty, at °leisure: *He has been unemployed ever since he was made redundant.*

unenthusiastic *adj.* °lukewarm, °cool, °cold, uninterested, °indifferent, °blasé, unresponsive, apathetic, unexcited, unimpressed: *Bentley presented the new design, but the directors were unenthusiastic and turned it down.*

unenviable *adj.* uncoveted, °undesirable, unwished for, unattractive: *He was given the unenviable task of informing the victim's family.*

unfamiliar *adj.* **1** °new, °novel, °unknown, unconventional, °unusual, °different, uncommon, °strange, °odd, °peculiar, °bizarre: *The man spoke in a tongue that was totally unfamiliar to me.* **2** Usually, ***unfamiliar with***: unacquainted with, °unaccustomed to, °inexperienced in *or* with, °unused to, unconversant with, °uninformed about, °ignorant of, unpractised in, unskilled in *or* at, uninitiated in, unversed in: *The Americans were as unfamiliar with cricket as the Englishmen were with baseball.*

unflattering *adj.* **1** °harsh, °unsympathetic; °realistic, °stark, °candid: *Her hairstyle was unflattering and made her face look rather heavy.* **2** uncomplimentary, insulting, unfavourable: *Saying that I look just like my grandmother is quite unflattering.*

unfledged *adj.* °undeveloped, °immature, unmatured, °inexperienced, °green, °callow, °young, °raw, ungrown: *Take these unfledged recruits and turn them into men.*

unfold *v.* **1** °open (out *or* up), °spread (out), unfurl, °stretch out, °expand, uncoil, unwind, °straighten out: *Emerging from the pupa, it unfolds its wings and becomes a beautiful butterfly.* **2** °develop, evolve, °happen, take °place, °occur, be divulged, be disclosed *or* revealed: *What will unfold next in our little drama?*

unforeseen *adj.* unexpected, surprising, unanticipated, unpredicted, unlooked-for, unsought, unhoped for, undreamed of *or* undreamt of, unthought of, °startling, °surprise, °chance, fortuitous: *The sales manager's resignation was an unforeseen event.*

unfortunate *adj.* **1** unlucky, luckless; cursed, out of °luck, unblessed, *Colloq* down on (one's) °luck: *She was unfortunate enough to have married early and divorced late.* **2** °poor, °miserable, °wretched, °woebegone, °pathetic, °dismal, °unhappy, °forlorn, °pitiable, °doomed, ill-starred, star-crossed, ill-fated: *These unfortunate refugees have nowhere to go if we refuse them asylum.* **3** °deplorable, °terrible, °awful, catastrophic, °disastrous, °calamitous, °tragic, °lamentable, °regrettable, distressing, upsetting, °disturbing, °inauspicious, °grievous, °ruinous: *It was an unfortunate decision, and led to many problems. The flood was a most unfortunate sequel to the earthquake.*

unfounded *adj.* baseless, °groundless, °unwarranted, unjustified, unsupported, unsupportable, °unsound, unjustifiable, unattested, unproven: *Reports of a typhoid outbreak are completely unfounded.*

ungodly *adj.* **1** °wicked, °sinful, °impious, °blasphemous, °heretical, irreligious, iconoclastic, atheist(ic), anti-religious, °sacrilegious, demonic, demoniac(al), °diabolic(al), °satanic, °fiendish, hellish, °infernal; depraved, °godless, °corrupt, °immoral, °evil, iniquitous, °bad, °villainous, heinous, flagitious, °profane, °vile: *The crusaders believed that they had a duty to deliver Jerusalem from the ungodly heathens.* **2** °awful, °outrageous, °indecent, °monstrous, °nasty, °dreadful, °terrible, appalling, °frightful, °shocking, *Colloq* God-awful, °unearthly, *Brit* °beastly: *Margot and I were subjected to another ungodly evening at the Dawsons'.*

ungovernable *adj.* °unruly, refractory, intractable, unmanageable, uncontrollable, °rebellious, °wild, °disobedient, unrestrainable, °incorrigible: *The nursemaid was saddled with two ungovernable children whom she had to cosset.*

ungraceful *adj.* **1** °awkward, °clumsy, ungainly, lubberly, *Colloq* all °thumbs, butter-fingered, *Slang US and Canadian* klutzy: *People in the aerobics class are always ungraceful to start off with.* **2** inelegant, graceless, °coarse, °crude, inartistic, °vulgar, °tasteless, unaesthetic, °unrefined, barbarous, unlovely, °ugly, unharmonious, unattractive, ill-proportioned, unsymmetric(al), asymmetric(al): *Some regard the Albert Memorial as a paragon of ungraceful Victorian design.*

ungracious *adj.* °discourteous, °overbearing, churlish, gauche, °rude, uncivil, °impolite, ill-bred, bad-mannered, unmannerly, ungentlemanly, unladylike, °gruff, °bluff, °brusque, °abrupt, °surly, curmudgeonly: *It was ungracious of him not to acknowledge the help of his staff.*

ungrateful *adj.* unthankful, unappreciative, °rude; °selfish, °heedless: *That ungrateful wretch never thanked me for all my help.*

unguarded *adj.* **1** incautious, °unwary, °careless, °inattentive, °heedless, inobservant, °inadvertent, °unthinking, unwatchful, unvigilant: *He let the intruder past him in an unguarded moment.* **2** °defenceless, unprotected, undefended, unfortified, °open, uncovered, exposed, °vulnerable: *The sentry insisted that he had left his post unguarded for only a few minutes.* **3** °indiscreet, °careless, °imprudent, unwise, °hasty, °unthinking, °thoughtless; guileless, incautious: *He was anxious to restore good relations after his unguarded remarks about their associates.*

unhappy *adj.* **1** °sad, depressed, °blue, °dejected, °melancholy, °despondent, downcast, °gloomy, °downhearted, dispirited, heavy-hearted, long-faced, disconsolate, °sorrowful, °miserable, crestfallen, cheerless, °forlorn, low-spirited, °glum, distressed, °tearful, *Formal* lachrymose, *Colloq* down, *Slang US* bummed out: *Mary is very unhappy that John is to be away a whole month.* **2** unlucky, °unfortunate, unpropitious, °inauspicious, unfavourable, luckless, hapless, cursed, °wretched, ill-omened, ill-fated, ill-starred, star-crossed, jinxed, °disastrous: *Let me tell you how this unhappy state of affairs came about.* **3** infelicitous, unfitting, °inappropriate, unsuitable, unsuited, °wrong, inexpedient, °ill-advised, °poor, °unfortunate: *Vivian was an unhappy choice as his successor.*

unhealthy *adj.* **1** ailing, unwell, °ill, °sickly, °infirm, °feeble, °frail, debilitated, °unsound, °sick, in °poor *or* °delicate health *or* condition, °indisposed, °invalid, valetudinary: *The boys had pasty, unhealthy faces.* **2** °unwholesome, °harmful, noxious, °detrimental, insalubrious, damaging, °injurious, °destructive, malign: *The doctor said that this climate is unhealthy for people with respiratory disorders.* **3** °risky, °dangerous, °perilous, life-threatening, touch-and-go: *You might find it unhealthy to criticize the government here.*

unheard-of *adj.* **1** °unknown, °unfamiliar, °obscure, °unidentified, °nameless, °unsung: *She is busy trying to promote some unheard-of sculptor.* **2** unimaginable, undreamed of *or* undreamt of, unprecedented, unimagined, °unbelievable, °inconceivable, °unusual: *They took the unheard-of step of requiring that refunds be paid. Her starting salary is an unheard-of £100,000.* **3** °shocking, °offensive, °outrageous, °disgraceful, °extreme, °unthinkable, °outlandish: *The victims were subjected to unheard-of tortures.*

unheralded *adj.* unannounced, unpublicized, unadvertised; unexpected, °surprise, unanticipated, °unforeseen, unpredicted: *Published by some obscure company, the book turned out to be an unheralded success.*

unhesitating *adj.* **1** °swift, °rapid, quick, °immediate, instantaneous, °prompt, °ready, unhesitant: *The response was an unhesitating 'No!'* **2** unfaltering, unwavering, °wholehearted, °unqualified, unswerving, undeviating, °staunch, °steadfast, °implicit, °resolute: *We appreciate your unhesitating devotion to duty.*

unhurried *adj.* leisurely, unrushed, °easy, °easygoing, °casual, °gradual, °deliberate, °steady, °sedate, °calm: *We proceeded at an unhurried pace, eventually arriving at dusk at the castle gates.*

unidentified *adj.* °nameless, anonymous, °unknown, unmarked, unnamed, °unfamiliar, unrecognized, °mysterious: *The police found the body of an unidentified woman in the park.*

uniform *adj.* **1** °homogeneous, °consistent, unvaried, unchanged, unaltered; unvarying, unchanging; °invariable, unchangeable, unalterable, regimented, °standard; ordered, °orderly, °equal, °even, °like, °identical; °alike: *The mixture is uniform throughout. The rules are uniform for everyone. Line up in ten uniform rows of ten each.* **2** °even, unbroken, °smooth, °regular, °flat: *Not one irregularity marred the uniform surface of the plain.*
—*n.* **3** livery, °habit, °regalia, °costume, °outfit; regimentals: *When I next saw him, he was in the uniform of a Gestapo officer.*

uniformity *n.* **1** °regularity, similarity, sameness, homogeneity, consistency, °symmetry, evenness, invariability, unchangeability, similitude, conformity, °agreement, concord, °accord, harmoniousness; °harmony, concordance, accordance, conformance, correspondence: *One can easily see the lack of uniformity even in what is supposed to be a classless society.* **2** dullness, monotony, drabness, sameness, °tedium, featurelessness, flatness, invariability, lack of °variety, changelessness: *After a few days, the uniformity of the routine began to get on my nerves.*

unify *v.* consolidate, °unite, °combine, °amalgamate, coalesce, bring together, °fuse, °join, °weld, °merge, confederate, °integrate: *The separate elements were unified into a coherent whole. Successive Reform Bills unified the nation.*

unimpeded *adj.* unblocked, unchecked, °free, unconstrained, unrestrained, unhindered, unhampered, unencumbered, °open, untrammelled, unrestricted: *They insist on having unimpeded access to the files.*

unimposing *adj.* unimpressive, nugatory, trivial, °trifling, °minor, unimportant, °puny, inconsiderable, °negligible: *It was an unimposing building sandwiched between two office blocks. A more unimposing little cockalorum has seldom assailed my sensibilities.*

uninformed *adj.* °ignorant, nescient, unknowledgeable, unenlightened, °uneducated, unschooled, untutored, untaught, uninstructed, °unaware, incognizant: *The problem is not that they are stupid, merely uninformed and misinformed.*

uninhabited *adj.* °desolate, °empty, °abandoned, °deserted, unoccupied, °vacant, vacated, tenantless, untenanted; °desert, unpopulated, unpeopled, °trackless, depopulated, °waste, °barren: *Tristan da Cunha, in the south Atlantic, is an uninhabited island.*

uninhibited *adj.* °wild, unchecked, unbridled, uncurbed, intemperate, °boisterous, unrepressed, unconstrained, unrestrained, °uncontrolled, unselfconscious, unreserved, °relaxed, °casual, °easygoing, °free (and °easy), °open, °frank, °candid, °outspoken, *Colloq* upfront: *Their behaviour at the party was totally uninhibited. I will tell you what I think only if I can be totally uninhibited about it.*

uninviting *adj.* °repulsive, °repellent, °offensive, unappealing, unattractive, unpleasant, °disagreeable, °distasteful, unappetizing, °unsavoury, sickening, °revolting, °obnoxious, °nasty, °disgusting, *Brit* off-putting: *The food he put on the table was cold and uninviting.*

union *n.* **1** uniting, °unity, combining, °combination, joining, °junction, conjoining, conjunction, allying, °alliance, associating, °association, coalition, amalgamating, °amalgamation, fusing, fusion, marrying, °marriage, confederating, confederation, confederacy, synthesizing, °synthesis, mixing, °mixture, °federation, togetherness: *Monarchies favour the union of Church and State.* **2** °alliance, °association, °organization, °society, °circle, °fraternity, °club, °fellowship, °team, °ring, °gang, °syndicate, coalition, °party, confederation, confederacy, °federation, Bund, °league, consortium, bloc, cartel, °trust: *The countries formed a union to control their joint economies.* **3** °joint, °seam, °splice, °junction, conjunction, °graft, °weld; coupling: *The union between the two pieces may be stronger than the material itself.* **4** °agreement, °accord, °harmony, harmoniousness, congruity, coherence, compatibility, unanimity, °unity: *The union of the various elements in the painting was skilfully effected.*

unique *adj.* **1** °single, lone, (°one and) °only, °solitary, °one of a kind, *sui generis*: *Natural forces conspired to create this unique situation.* **2** unequalled, °unparalleled, unrivalled, °incomparable, inimitable, °peerless, unmatched, unsurpassed, unexcelled, second to none: *Stimble's genius is unique in the annals of cardiology.*

unison *n.* ***in unison (with)***: in °harmony, together, corresponding °exactly, in (perfect) °accord, consonant, °harmonious: *Why is his singing never in unison with ours? We all responded in unison with a rousing 'No!'*

unit *n.* °element, component, °entity, °part, °item, constituent, °piece, °portion, °segment, °section, module: *The units fit together almost seamlessly.*

unite *v.* **1** °combine, °unify, °merge, coalesce, °amalgamate, °mix, °mingle, commingle, intermix, °blend, consolidate, °fuse: *The splinter parties have united to form a coalition.* **2** °join (forces), °unify, °wed, °marry, °link, °connect, °merge: *The two families are united by marriage.* **3** °bond, °fuse *or* °weld *or* solder *or* °glue *or* °stick *or* °tie *or* °bind *or* °fasten *or* °fix *or* °fit (together): *Unite these pieces and the job is done.*

united *adj.* **1** unified, °common, °mutual, combined, merged, coalesced, pooled, shared, collective, °joint, amalgamated, connected: *The new law will serve our united interests.* **2** °joint, cooperative, °common, communal, collaborative, synergetic *or* synergistic, collective, concerted, coordinated, allied; partnership: *We must make a united effort if we are to survive.* **3** agreed, unanimous, in °agreement, of °one °mind, of °like °mind *or* opinion, like-minded, in °accord, in °harmony, °harmonious: *We are united in our assessment of last night's performance.*

unity *n.* **1** consistency, unanimity, constancy, °uniformity, sameness, consensus, °agreement, concord, concordance, °accord, °solidarity, compatibility, concurrence, continuity, consentaneousness, °rapport, °sympathy, like-mindedness: *All members of the association enjoy a unity of purpose.* **2** oneness, °singularity, °integrity, singleness, congruity, °uniformity, congruousness, homogeneity, °identity, sameness, °resemblance, °likeness, similarity, similitude: *If there is little unity between your ideas and those of the organization, perhaps you should resign.* **3** unification, uniting, °combination: *In unity is strength.*

universal *adj.* **1** °prevalent, °prevailing, °general, worldwide, widespread, ubiquitous, omnipresent, °limitless, °unlimited, °common, pandemic, °epidemic: *The end of the 20th century is marked by a universal preoccupation with greed.* **2** cosmic, °infinite, °boundless, °limitless, °unlimited, measureless, °endless, uncircumscribed, all-inclusive, all-embracing, all-encompassing, wide-ranging, °comprehensive: *Renaissance man was regarded as possessing universal knowledge.*

universally *adv.* in every case *or* instance, in all cases *or* instances, unexceptionally, without exception, uniformly, °always, invariably: *In those days, it was universally accepted that the earth was flat.*

universe *n.* **1** cosmos, °creation, macrocosm: *What arrogance makes man believe that in all the vast universe God pays him any heed?* **2** °world, bailiwick,

°sphere, °province, °domain, °circle, °milieu, °territory, corner, °quarter, microcosm: *Such behaviour may be acceptable in her tiny universe.*

unkempt *adj.* dishevelled, uncombed, tousled, disarranged, ungroomed, wind-blown, °untidy, disordered, mussed (-up), messy, messed-up, °bedraggled, °shaggy, scruffy, rumpled, slovenly, frowzy *or* frouzy *or* frowsy, blowzy, *Archaic* draggle-tailed, *Colloq* °sloppy: *Mother would refuse to allow us to the table if we were unkempt.*

unkind *adj.* °inconsiderate, unthoughtful, °thoughtless, unfeeling, unconcerned, insensitive, unkindly, °unsympathetic, uncharitable, unchristian, uncaring, hard-hearted, °heartless, flinty, °hard, °rigid, °callous, °tough, °inflexible, unyielding, unbending, °severe, °harsh, °stern, °cruel, °mean, °inhuman: *It was very unkind of you to refuse the beggar.*

unknown *adj.* **1** unrecognized, °unfamiliar, °strange, unnamed, anonymous, °nameless, °unidentified; °obscure, °unheard-of, little-known, °humble, °undistinguished, °unsung: *Some unknown person left this package for you. Bill is in some unknown place for the weekend. An unknown poet won the competition.* **2** °unfamiliar, unexplored, uninvestigated, unresearched, unrevealed, °mysterious, °uncharted, °unidentified, °dark: *We were now going into unknown territory.* **3** unbeknownst, °untold, unrevealed: *Unknown to me, the thieves were at that moment breaking in through the kitchen window.*

unlamented *adj.* unmissed, unmourned, unbemoaned, unbewailed, unloved: *They destroyed a statue of the late, unlamented Joseph Stalin.*

unlawful *adj.* °illegal, °illicit, against the °law, °illegitimate, under the table, under the counter, °criminal, felonious; outlawed, banned, prohibited, forbidden, interdicted, disallowed, proscribed, *verboten*; °unauthorized, unlicensed, unsanctioned: *Unlawful payments had been made to councillors. Gambling has been declared unlawful in that county.*

unlike *adj.* **1** °different (from), °dissimilar (to), unalike, °distinct (from), °opposite (from *or* to), contrasting *or* contrastive (with *or* to), °separate (from), °divergent (from), °incompatible (with), distinguishable (from), far apart (from), °far (from), °distant (from), ill-matched (with), unequal (to), unequivalent (to): *His notions of right and wrong are unlike those of other people. Although they're brothers, they look quite unlike each other.* **2** atypical, uncharacteristic, untypical: *It is unlike you to complain.*
—*prep.* **3** °different from, differing from, in contradistinction to, in °contrast with *or* to, °dissimilar to, °distinct from, °opposite from *or* to, contrasting with *or* to, °divergent from, °incompatible with, distinguishable from, ill-matched with, unequal to, unequivalent to: *Unlike you, I've been there and know what it's like.*

unlikely *adj.* **1** °improbable, °doubtful, dubious, °remote, °unthinkable, unimaginable, °inconceivable, °implausible: *His story was unlikely, but she decided to believe him. It is not unlikely that he will come even if we ask him to stay away.* **2** °unseemly, °inappropriate, unfit, unfitting, unsuitable, uncongenial, objectionable, °unbecoming, °unacceptable, unattractive, °distasteful: *Claire had seldom seen a more unlikely prospect for a husband.* **3** unpropitious, °unpromising, °inauspicious: *The tiny shop seemed an unlikely place to find a great treasure.*

unlimited *adj.* **1** unrestricted, unrestrained, °limitless, unconstrained, °unqualified, °full, °absolute, unconditional, far-reaching, unchecked, °uncontrolled: *He has unlimited authority to issue all the paper money he wishes.* **2** °limitless, °boundless, °endless, °vast, unbounded, °immense, °immeasurable, measureless, °numberless, innumerable, °inexhaustible, interminable, never-ending, °infinite, myriad, °extensive: *As the wealthiest woman in the world, she has unlimited resources to do as she pleases.*

unload *v.* °empty, °dump, unpack, offload, °discharge; disburden, unburden: *We unloaded the cargo at Sulawesi. The camels must be unloaded every night.*

unmarried *adj.* °single, unwed(ded), bachelor, spinster, old-maid, °maiden, °unattached, unengaged, unbetrothed, unplighted, unpromised, °free, uncommitted: *He was thirty-five, unmarried, and lived alone in a tiny flat.*

unmentionable *adj.* **1** unspeakable, unutterable, °ineffable, °taboo, °scandalous, forbidden, interdicted; °inexpressible: *I will not have Karen or her unmentionable boyfriend in this house again!* **2** °disgraceful, °indecent, °immodest, °shameful, °shocking, appalling, °dishonourable, indescribable, °obscene, °filthy: *In carnivals, geeks do unmentionable things with live chickens.*
—*n.* **3** ***unmentionables***: °underclothes, underclothing, underwear, undergarments, lingerie, *Archaic* small-clothes, *Colloq* underthings, undies, *Brit* smalls, *US* skivvies: *The woman next door insists on hanging out her unmentionables in full view of the whole street.*

unmerciful *adj.* °merciless, pitiless, unsparing, °unkind, °relentless, unpitying, °heartless, stony-hearted, hard-hearted, flinty, unfeeling, °unsympathetic, unforgiving, °mean, °cruel, °savage, °brutal, brutish, °vicious, barbarous: *The boys gave him an unmerciful beating for cheating.*

unmitigated *adj.* °undiluted, unalloyed, unmixed, untempered, unmoderated, unmodified, unabated, unlessened, undiminished, unreduced, unrelieved, °oppressive, unalleviated, unmollified, unsoftened, °relentless, °unqualified, °out-and-out, °thorough, thoroughgoing, °outright, °downright, °categorical, °absolute, °immoderate, °sheer, °complete, consummate, °total, °perfect, °true, °pure, arrant, utter, °plain: *That man is an unmitigated bore. The project was an unmitigated disaster.*

unmoved *adj.* °cool, °aloof, °calm, °collected, °unaffected, untouched, °unsympathetic, unstirred, undisturbed, apathetic, stoical, °impassive, °dispassionate, unemotional, unfeeling, unconcerned, °indifferent, unreactive, unresponsive, °stolid, °stony, adamant, stony-hearted, hard-hearted: *Despite her child's tears, she remained totally unmoved.*

unnatural *adj.* **1** *Derogatory* abnormal, °perverse, °perverted, °monstrous, °unusual, °peculiar, °strange, aberrant, °improper, °unseemly; *Slang* kinky, *Chiefly Brit* °bent: *There was a scandal when the senator was found to have engaged in some unnatural act.* **2** sodomitic(al), bestial, tribadic, tribadistic: *They still coyly referred to homosexual activities as 'unnatural acts'.* **3** uncharacteristic, out of °character, °odd, °peculiar, °strange, unexpected, °abnormal, °unusual: *Isn't it unnatural for someone who has won the sweepstakes to look so unhappy?* **4** °laboured, °forced, °stilted, °stiff, restrained, °artificial, °false, °insincere, feigned, contrived, °affected, °mannered, °self-conscious, °theatrical, stagy: *She has an irritating, unnatural laugh.* **5** °outlandish, °weird, uncanny, °strange, °odd, °unaccountable, °supernatural, preternatural, °queer, °grotesque, °bizarre, °extraordinary, °eccentric, freakish: *Let me tell you about the unnatural events that took place in that house.*

unnecessary *adj.* unneeded, °needless, unrequired, °dispensable, °disposable, °expendable, unwanted, °surplus, °superfluous, supererogatory, inessential, unessential, °non-essential: *The children were asleep, so we asked the workmen to avoid making any unnecessary noise.*

unnerve *v.* °upset, °agitate, °perturb, °ruffle, °fluster, °rattle, °discomfit, unsettle, disconcert, °dismay, °intimidate, °stun, stupefy, *Colloq* °shake (up), faze: *Peter drove home slowly: the accident he had seen had unnerved him.*

unnoticed *adj.* unnoted, overlooked, unobserved, undiscovered, unremarked, unmarked, unperceived; unseen, unheard: *Fortunately, Martha's nasty aside went unnoticed.*

unobtrusive *adj.* °inconspicuous, unostentatious, low-key, °retiring, °modest, self-effacing, unpresuming, unpretentious, unassuming, °quiet, °humble, unaggressive, unassertive, non-assertive, °subdued, °reserved, °reticent, suppressed: *Agatha may seem unobtrusive, but she's a tigress when aroused.*

unofficial *adj.* °informal, °unauthorized, undocumented, off the °record, °private, °secret, unpublicized, unannounced: *The builder acknowledged having had unofficial meetings with the council.*

unopened *adj.* closed, °shut: *The book lay, unopened, on the bedside table.*

unorthodox *adj.* °irregular, unconventional, °nonconformist, unconforming, nonconforming, aberrant, aberrational, °deviant, heteroclite, °unusual, °abnormal, uncustomary, uncommon: *Roebuck's unorthodox methods almost lost him his job.*

unpaid *adj.* **1** °payable, °outstanding, owed, owing, °due, unsettled: *In the end he absconded, leaving a pile of unpaid bills.* **2** unsalaried, °voluntary, volunteer, °honorary, *US* dollar-a-year: *On retirement, she took an unpaid job with Oxfam.*

unpalatable *adj.* °distasteful, °disagreeable, unpleasant, °unsavoury, unappetizing, unattractive, °repugnant, °nasty, °offensive; °rancid, °sour, °off, turned, °bitter, inedible, uneatable: *Without an education, they are often offered the unpalatable jobs. We found heavy claret totally unpalatable with the sole.*

unparalleled *adj.* unequalled, °incomparable, °matchless, °peerless, unrivalled, unmatched, inimitable, unexcelled, °superior, °supreme, °superlative, unsurpassed, °unusual, °special, °singular, °rare, °unique, °exceptional, consummate: *In our experience, the food and service aboard the* Normandie *were unparalleled.*

unperfumed *adj.* unscented, °plain, °natural: *This deodorant is available in sandalwood, forest pine, mint, or unperfumed.*

unpopular *adj.* out of °favour, in bad odour, unliked, disliked, shunned, avoided, snubbed, ignored, unsought after, unaccepted, unwanted, rejected, °unwelcome, °undesirable; unloved, friendless: *New taxes are always unpopular. James had always been an unpopular boy at school.*

unprejudiced *adj.* unbigoted, unbiased, °impartial, unjaundiced, °just, °fair, °objective, °disinterested, fair-minded, °non-partisan, °liberal, open-minded, undogmatic: *An unprejudiced opinion would be difficult to find, since everyone has an axe to grind.*

unpremeditated *adj.* °unprepared, unplanned, unarranged, uncontrived, unstudied, °coincidental, °spontaneous, spur-of-the-moment, last-minute, impromptu, °extemporaneous *or* extemporary, extempore, ad lib, °offhand, °casual, °impulsive, °natural, °involuntary, °automatic, °unconscious, *Colloq* off the cuff: *I had no inkling of her plans, so my running into her was entirely unpremeditated. Her immediate, unpremeditated reaction was to run away.*

unprepared *adj.* **1** unready, surprised, °taken aback, (caught) napping *or* off guard, °dumbfounded *or* dumfounded, at sixes and sevens, *Colloq* (caught) with (one's) °pants down, *Brit* caught on the hop, *US* asleep at the switch: *The sudden squall found us unprepared and we lost a sail.* **2** unfinished, °incomplete, uncompleted: *Dinner was still unprepared at eight o'clock.* **3** unwarned, unreadied, not set up, not forewarned: *I was unprepared for the strange events that followed.* **4** See **unpremeditated,** above.

unprofessional *adj.* **1** °unbecoming, °improper, unethical, unprincipled, °unseemly, undignified, unfitting, unbefitting, °unworthy, unscholarly, negligent, °lax: *The Medical Association is quick to act against doctors whose conduct might be judged unprofessional.* **2** amateurish, °amateur, inexpert, °inexperienced, untrained, untutored, unschooled, °incompetent, unskilled, unskilful, °inferior, second-rate, °inefficient, °poor, °shoddy, low-quality, °sloppy: *It was an astonishingly unprofessional way to audit accounts.* **3** non-technical, unspecialized, non-specialist, °lay, °everyday, °ordinary, °plain (English), understandable: *What does all that gobbledegook mean when translated into unprofessional language?*

unprofitable *adj.* **1** profitless, ungainful, unremunerative, unfruitful, non-profit-making; breaking even; losing, loss-making: *The last quarter was unprofitable for car manufacturers.* **2** °bootless, °pointless, °purposeless, unavailing, °futile, °useless, unproductive, °worthless, °ineffective, °inefficient: *Having employees sitting about waiting for the telephone to ring is unprofitable.*

unpromising *adj.* °inauspicious, unpropitious, unfavourable, °gloomy, °ominous, adverse, °portentous, baleful, °hopeless: *The forecast for the economy looked unpromising yesterday but has suddenly brightened.*

unqualified *adj.* **1** °ineligible, unfit, untrained, ill-equipped, unsuited, unequipped, °unprepared: *He was rejected as unqualified for the job of repairing computers.* **2** unrestricted, unreserved, unconditional, °categorical, °outright, °unmitigated, °downright, °out-and-out, °pure (and °simple), °true, °perfect, utter, °absolute, consummate: *If he told you that he flew jets in the RAF, he is an unqualified liar. Cato's unqualified 'Delenda est Cartago' was echoed in every speech he made in the Roman senate.*

unquenchable *adj.* insatiable, unslakeable *or* unslakable, unsatisfiable; °inextinguishable, unsuppressible, °irrepressible, °indestructible: *She had an unquenchable thirst for knowledge. Those principles have kindled an unquenchable fire in the hearts of the oppressed.*

unquestionable *adj.* unexceptionable, indubitable, undoubted, °indisputable, incontestable, unimpeachable, undeniable, °certain, °sure, °positive, irrefutable, °manifest, °obvious, °patent, °clear, °definite, °incontrovertible, unequivocal, unmistakable, conclusive: *Their integrity is unquestionable, and I have complete confidence in them.*

unreal *adj.* **1** °imaginary, °fantastic, chimerical, °fanciful, °fancied, °illusory, make-believe, phantasmagoric(al), phantasmal, °spectral, figmental, °unrealistic, °non-existent: *Fear made the whole scene unreal to Martha.* **2** °theoretical, °hypothetical, °mythical, °imaginary, made-up, °fictitious, make-believe, °fanciful: *Although the example is unreal, it will serve its purpose in my argument.* **3** °artificial, °synthetic, synthesized, °mock, °false, °fake(d), °counterfeit, °fraudulent, °dummy, °spurious, falsified, °pretend(ed), °sham, pseudo, make-believe: *The countryside looked a little unreal, too luxuriant and too sculptured.*

unrealistic *adj.* **1** °impractical, illogical, °unreasonable, unworkable, unrealizable, °quixotic, °romantic, °fanciful, °visionary, delusional, delusive, delusory: *However exciting it is to think of travelling faster than light, the notion is unrealistic.* **2** °unreal, unlifelike, °unnatural, unauthentic, non-representational, unrepresentative, °inaccurate: *The background paintings are poorly done and unrealistic.*

unreasonable *adj.* **1** irrational, illogical, °unthinking, °absurd, °foolish, °senseless, °nonsensical, °mindless, brainless, °thoughtless, °silly, °mad, °crazy, °insane, idiotic, moronic, imbecilic, °stupid, fatuous, °ridiculous, °ludicrous, laughable, °preposterous, °far-fetched, °short-sighted, unperceptive, unperceiving, undiscerning, myopic, °blind: *Some people have an unreasonable aversion to anything scientific. Is it unreasonable to expect you to spend a little time with your mother?* **2** °excessive, °outrageous, °exorbitant, °extravagant, °immoderate, extortionate, °inordinate, °unconscionable, unjust, °unwarranted, inequitable, unfair, unequal, °improper, unjustified, unjustifiable, uncalled-for: *The new tax puts an unreasonable demand on those with lower incomes.* **3** °inappropriate, unapt *or* inapt, unsuitable, unbefitting, °impractical, °unrealistic: *His conduct was quite unreasonable for a man of the cloth.*

unrefined *adj.* **1** °coarse, °rude, °rough, °unsophisticated, uncultured, °uncivilized, uncultivated, unpolished, inelegant, ill-bred, °impolite, °discourteous, unmannerly, °ill-mannered, bad-mannered, ignoble, °plebeian, undignified, unladylike, ungentlemanlike, ungentlemanly, uncourtly, °ungracious, °boorish, loutish, °gross, °vulgar, uncouth, cloddish, bumbling, °awkward, gauche: *Consider their background before criticizing them for being unrefined.* **2** °impure, unpurified, unclarified, °raw, °crude, °coarse, untreated, unfinished, °natural, unprocessed: *The unrefined ore is first washed thoroughly.*

unrelated *adj.* °independent, °separate, °distinct, °different, °dissimilar, °incompatible, °inappropriate, °foreign, °alien, unassociated, unaffiliated, unconnected, uncoupled, unlinked, unallied, uncoordinated: *Why raise a totally unrelated issue?*

unreliable *adj.* °irresponsible, °disreputable; untrustworthy, undependable, °uncertain, °unstable, treacherous, °flimsy, °weak: *He is unreliable and unlikely to be there when you need him. The equipment was expensive, slow, and unreliable.*

unrepentant *adj.* unrepenting, unremorseful, impenitent, unapologetic, unregretful, unashamed, unembarrassed, unselfconscious, °remorseless, unreformed, unrehabilitated, unregenerate, recidivist *or* recidivistic *or* recidivous: *They were quite unrepentant, though they had seen for themselves the harm they had done.*

unresolved *adj.* °unsettled, °open, up in the air, °moot, °pending, °debatable, arguable, °problematic(al), °indefinite, °vague, open to °question, °questionable, unanswered, unsolved; undetermined, undecided, °uncertain, unsure, ambivalent, wavering, vacillating, °irresolute: *The matter of joining the monetary union remained unresolved. I am still unresolved on the issue.*

unrest *n.* disquiet, uneasiness, °distress, °anxiety, anxiousness, nervousness, °anguish, unease, °worry, °concern, °agitation, turmoil, °disturbance, °trouble, °strife, °agony: *The proximity of the huge army on our borders caused considerable unrest among the populace.*

unruly *adj.* unmanageable, °ungovernable, uncontrollable, °undisciplined, unregulated, °lawless, °disobedient, °insubordinate, °rebellious, °mutinous, fractious, refractory, contumacious, °obstreperous, °wilful, headstrong, °stubborn, °recalcitrant, intractable, °defiant, uncooperative, wayward, °disorderly, turbulent, °riotous, °tumultuous, °violent, °stormy, °tempestuous: *She had no idea of how to handle a capricious and unruly teenager. The first reading of the bill led to an unruly session of Parliament.*

unsatisfactory *adj.* °insufficient, °inadequate, °inferior, °poor, °unacceptable, displeasing, °disappointing, °unworthy, °inappropriate, °deficient, °weak, °wanting, lacking, unsuitable, °imperfect, °flawed, °defective, °faulty: *The report was unsatisfactory in that it failed to meet the committee's demands. Why put up with unsatisfactory workmanship?*

unsavoury *adj.* °distasteful, objectionable, unpleasant, °disagreeable, unappetizing, °unpalatable, °offensive, °repugnant, °obnoxious, °repellent, °nasty, °repulsive, °revolting, °disgusting, nauseating, sickening: *Her ex-husband is a totally unsavoury character. Even the most unsavoury swill tasted like ambrosia to the starving inmates.*

unscathed *adj.* unharmed, unhurt, uninjured, unmarked, untouched, undamaged, unscarred, unscratched, °safe and °sound, in one piece, as °new, *Archaic* scatheless, *Colloq* like °new: *Miraculously, he came out of the battle unscathed.*

unscrupulous *adj.* °unconscionable, conscienceless, unprincipled, amoral, unethical, °immoral, °dishonourable, °corrupt, °dishonest, °deceitful, °sly, cunning, °artful, insidious, °shifty, °sneaky, °slippery, roguish, knavish, °disingenuous, treacherous, °perfidious, °faithless, °false, untrustworthy, °wicked, °evil, *Colloq* °crooked: *Some people are totally unscrupulous in the pursuit of their ambitions.*

unseasonable *adj.* unsuitable, °inopportune, °inappropriate, untimely, ill-timed, inexpedient: *Unseasonable frosts in April caused severe damage to the flower buds.*

unseemly *adj.* **1** °improper, °unrefined, °unbecoming, indecorous, indelicate, unladylike, ungentlemanly, undignified, in poor *or* bad °taste, °disreputable, discreditable, °risqué, °naughty, °indecent, °shameful, °offensive, °lewd, °lascivious, °obscene, °rude, °coarse: *Out of desperation, they engaged in some unseemly activities.* **2** impolitic, unwise, °imprudent, inapt, °inappropriate, °inopportune, °inconvenient, uncalled-for, unsuitable, °improper, inadvisable, °ill-advised, unbefitting, unfitting, out of °place *or* keeping, °awkward, °inauspicious, inexpedient, °unfortunate, ill-timed, untimely: *It would be unseemly for you to become involved with such a notorious individual.*

unselfish *adj.* °generous, °charitable, open-handed, ungrudging, unstinting, unsparing, giving, magnanimous, °philanthropic, °humanitarian, °free, °liberal, altruistic, °selfless, self-sacrificing: *We were all greatly impressed by her unselfish concern for the well-being of her colleagues.*

unsettled *adj.* **1** unfixed, °unstable, changing, varying, °variable, °changeable, °inconstant, ever-changing, °protean, unpredictable, °uncertain: *The weather remained unsettled all week. They told me of their unsettled life as gypsies.* **2** °disturbed, turbulent, riled, °agitated, disquieted, °upset, perturbed, ruffled, rattled, flustered, °restive, °restless, unnerved, *US* roiled: *It was being kept in the dark about Father that made us feel unsettled.* **3** disoriented, °confused, °mixed up, unorganized, disorganized, °disorderly, disordered, °tumultuous: *The unsettled situation in the east worried us.* **4** See **unresolved,** above: *Some questions about Ian remain unsettled.*

unsettling *adj.* unnerving, upsetting, °disturbing, perturbing, discomfiting, °disconcerting: *Sorry for being a wet blanket, but I have had some unsettling news from home.*

unsightly *adj.* °ugly, °hideous, awful-looking, °horrible, frightful-looking, unattractive, unprepossessing, unlovely, unpretty, °plain, *US and Canadian* °homely: *The property borders an unsightly junk-yard.*

unsocial *adj.* unsociable, unfriendly, °cool, °cold, °chilly, °aloof, uncongenial, unamiable, unforthcoming, °standoffish, °inhospitable, °withdrawn, °reserved, °solitary, °retiring, °distant, °detached, °reclusive, hermitic(al), eremitic(al), anchoritic *or* anchoretic(al); antisocial, °misanthropic, °hostile: *Erwin, who prefers to be alone, is definitely unsocial. Donna, who despises other people, is unsocial for different reasons.*

unsolicited *adj.* unlooked-for, unsought, unsought after, unrequested, °unasked for, uncalled-for, °gratuitous, uninvited; *Colloq US* over-the-transom: *Tanya is always offering unsolicited advice on every conceivable subject. The publishers receive scores of unsolicited book manuscripts each week.*

unsophisticated *adj.* **1** °naïve, °inexperienced, °simple, °childlike, unworldly, °innocent, °ingenuous, °artless, guileless: *Is the unsophisticated consumer sufficiently protected against unscrupulous traders?* **2** °simple, °plain, uncomplicated, undetailed, uninvolved, °unrefined: *The computers of twenty years ago were unsophisticated compared with those of today.*

unsound *adj.* **1** °weak, °feeble, °frail, °rickety, °shaky, °ramshackle, °infirm, °unstable, wobbly, tottering, unsteady, broken-down, crumbling, disintegrating, °dilapidated, °defective, °imperfect, °faulty, decayed, °rotten: *The building inspector condemned the structure as unsound and unsafe.* **2** °unhealthy, °diseased, °ill, afflicted, in °poor °health, ailing, °sickly, °sick, unwell, °delicate, injured, wounded: *The attack of flu left him unsound in wind and limb.* **3** °insane, °mad, °psychotic, °unbalanced, °unstable, demented, °deranged: *The doctors said that she was still of* *unsound mind and ought not be released.* **4** illogical, °faulty, °flawed, fallacious, °untenable, °invalid, °groundless, °unfounded, °erroneous, °defective, °specious: *We thought that his arguments were unsound, so we rejected his recommendations.*

unspoiled *adj.* unspoilt, unsullied, °pristine, virgin, °whole, untainted, unstained, °immaculate, uncorrupted, unpolluted, °spotless, stainless: *The house has been preserved in its original condition, unspoiled by modern additions.*

unstable *adj.* **1** °changeable, °variable, unsteady, °inconstant, °inconsistent, °insecure, °capricious, °fickle, °irregular, unpredictable, °unreliable, °erratic, °volatile, fluctuating, °flighty, mercurial, vacillating, tergiversating, °indecisive, undecided, °irresolute, °indefinite, °unsettled: *He seems too unstable to maintain a long-standing relationship.* **2** See **unsound, 1,** above.

unsuccessful *adj.* **1** °unfortunate, unavailing, °vain, abortive, °useless, °bootless, °fruitless, unfruitful, unproductive, °ineffective, °ineffectual, °inefficacious, °worthless, °unprofitable, °sterile: *We made an unsuccessful attempt to regain control of the company.* **2** unlucky, hapless, °unfortunate, luckless, defeated, beaten, jinxed, cursed, foiled, frustrated, balked: *Trevor complained that he had been unsuccessful in business all his life.*

unsung *adj.* uncelebrated, unrecognized, unglorified, unexalted, unpraised, unhonoured, °unnoticed, disregarded, °unknown, anonymous, °unidentified, °nameless, °obscure, °insignificant, °inconspicuous: *I have no wish to add to the long list of unsung authors of the twentieth century.*

unsuspecting *adj.* unsuspicious, °unwary, unknowing, °ignorant, °unconscious, °gullible, credulous, °naïve, °ingenuous, °innocent, °trusting; °unaware, off guard: *Martin became an unsuspecting dupe in Lambert's plot to embezzle money from the bank.*

unsympathetic *adj.* uncaring, unconcerned, °callous, unfeeling, °unaffected, untouched, °unmoved, °indifferent, unemotional, °dispassionate, uncompassionate, unreactive, unresponsive, °impassive, °stolid, °cold, °cool, °aloof, unstirred, apathetic, insensitive, stoical, °stony, adamant, stony-hearted, hard-hearted, unpitying, pitiless, °ruthless: *We were unable to understand Taylor's unsympathetic attitude to the suffering around him.*

untamed *adj.* undomesticated, °wild, unbroken, unsubdued, uncontrollable, °savage, °fierce, feral, °ferocious: *In the story, the wolf boy behaves like an untamed beast.*

untarnished *adj.* unsoiled, unsullied, °immaculate, °spotless, unspotted, untainted, °faultless, uncorrupted, unfouled, °chaste, lily-white, undefiled, virginal: *Despite the obloquy heaped on his colleagues, his own reputation remained untarnished.*

untenable *adj.* insupportable *or* unsupportable, indefensible, unsustainable, unmaintainable, unjustified, unjustifiable, baseless, °groundless, °unfounded, °flawed, °faulty, °weak, illogical, °specious, °implausible, °unreasonable, °unsound: *It is beyond me why he holds so tenaciously to such untenable views.*

unthinkable *adj.* **1** °inconceivable, °unbelievable, unimaginable, °incredible, °incomprehensible, beyond °belief, °extraordinary, *Colloq* mind-boggling, *Slang* mind-blowing: *It seemed unthinkable that such a mild-mannered man could have been a mass murderer.* **2** °unacceptable, °absurd, illogical, °impossible, °improbable, °unlikely, out of the °question, °preposterous, °ridiculous, laughable, °ludicrous, *Colloq* not on: *It is simply unthinkable for her to go to the ball unattended.*

unthinking *adj.* **1** °thoughtless, °mindless, undiscriminating, unconsidered, unwitting, unreflecting, unthoughtful, irrational, °unreasonable, illogical, unperceptive, unperceiving, undiscerning, witless, brainless, °foolish, °senseless, °nonsensical, °rash, °stupid, °silly, °mad, °crazy, °insane, idiotic, moronic, imbecilic, °hasty, °short-sighted: *It was unthinking of me to ask her mother to go out to dinner with us.* **2** °inconsiderate, °impolite, °tactless, °rude, °thoughtless, undiplomatic, °discourteous, uncivil, °imprudent, unwise, °indiscreet, neglectful: *On the other hand, it would have been unthinking of me not to ask her mother.*

untidy *adj.* °disorderly, messy, dishevelled, °unkempt, slovenly, slatternly, °bedraggled, rumpled, frowzy *or* frouzy *or* frowsy, °sloppy, °dirty; littered, cluttered, °chaotic, °helter-skelter, jumbled, *Archaic* draggle-tailed, *Colloq US* mussy, mussed-up: *You should never go to the door looking so untidy. Ken's papers are always so untidy.*

untiring *adj.* unflagging, °determined, indefatigable, dogged, persevering, perseverant, °tireless, unwearying, unwearied, dedicated, unfailing, unfaltering, °steady: *Kim has always been an untiring perfectionist.*

untold *adj.* **1** countless, uncounted, uncountable, unnumbered, °numberless, innumerable, myriad, incalculable; °immeasurable, measureless, °unlimited: *Untold millions are lost through tax fraud each year.* **2** unrecounted, unnarrated, undescribed, unpublished, unrevealed, undisclosed, undivulged, unreported, °private, °hidden, °secret: *How many untold stories are there in the naked city?* **3** °inexpressible, unutterable, indescribable, unimaginable, °inconceivable, °unthinkable, unspeakable: *The untold agony that man went through because of his family's illnesses!*

untoward *adj.* **1** adverse, unfavourable, unpropitious, discouraging, °inopportune, °unpromising, °bleak, °inauspicious, °bad, °unfortunate: *The rainstorm created untoward conditions, causing the river to rise dangerously.* **2** °unbecoming, unfitting, °awkward, °inappropriate, unapt, unsuitable, °improper, °impolite, °rude, °boorish, ungentlemanly, unladylike, indecorous, indelicate, °unwarranted, uncalled-for, °unrefined, °unseemly, unwise, °imprudent, undiplomatic, °tactless, untactful, ill-conceived, °silly, °foolish, °stupid, ill-timed, vexatious, vexing, irritating, annoying: *Charles made some untoward remark about the size of Sandra's feet.*

untried *adj.* untested, unproved *or* unproven, °new: *He may be good at homes, but he is as yet untried as the designer of a library.*

untrue *adj.* **1** unfaithful, °faithless, °disloyal, °fickle, °capricious, undependable, °unreliable, °dishonourable, untrustworthy, °false, °hypocritical, °dishonest, °insincere, °two-faced, duplicitous, °devious, °deceitful, treacherous, °perfidious: *Only when I saw her with Henry did I realize that Pauline had been untrue to me.* **2** °wrong, °false, °inaccurate, °incorrect, °erroneous, misleading, °mistaken, distorted: *What you said about Pauline was simply untrue.* **3** °inexact, non-standard, substandard, °imprecise, °imperfect: *How unfortunate for legend had William Tell's aim been untrue!*

unused *adj.* **1** (°brand-)°new, untouched, °pristine, °original, °intact, °fresh, firsthand: *He sold me his unused computer for half what it cost.* **2** °disused, °abandoned, °derelict, neglected, given up: *We hid in an old unused factory building.* **3** unconsumed, °leftover, °remaining, °left: *If dissatisfied with this product, return the unused portion for a full refund.* **4** ***unused to***: °unaccustomed to, °unfamiliar with, °inexperienced in *or* at, amateurish at, unpractised in *or* at, uninitiated in: *I am quite unused to doing that sort of thing.*

unusual *adj.* uncommon, °exceptional, atypical, untypical, °different, unexpected, °singular, out of the °ordinary, °extraordinary, °odd, °peculiar, °curious, °bizarre, °strange, °queer, °remarkable, °unique, freakish, unprecedented, unconventional, °unorthodox, *Slang* off-the-wall: *It takes an unusual person to be as charitable as Jean. Don't you agree that an egg-laying mammal is a bit unusual?*

unvarnished *adj.* °plain, °simple, °pure, unembellished, straightforward, °straight, °direct, °honest, unelaborated, °naked, °stark, °sincere, °frank, °candid,

°outspoken: *My dear, let me tell you the unvarnished truth about Marnie and Jim.*

unveil *v.* °reveal, °expose, uncover, °lay °bare *or* °open, °bare, bring to °light: *They will unveil a rival bid at tomorrow's meeting. Only after William died did Cynthia unveil the truth about his double life.*

unwarranted *adj.* uncalled-for, °unasked (for), unjustified, indefensible, unjust, unfair, °unconscionable, °unworthy, °improper, °inexcusable, °gratuitous, unmerited, undeserved, unprovoked, °outrageous, °excessive, °unreasonable, unrestrained, intemperate, untempered, °immoderate, undue, °unnecessary: *The police were accused of unwarranted use of force in ejecting the rowdies from the pub.*

unwary *adj.* °heedless, °careless, °hasty, incautious, °unguarded, °imprudent, °rash, °foolhardy, °reckless, °thoughtless, °indiscreet, °unthinking, °mindless, unwise: *Many perils await the unwary traveller. It was unwary of you not to lock the doors and windows.*

unwashed *adj.* **1** °dirty, uncleaned, unclean, uncleansed: *Separate your personal things from the unwashed laundry in the hamper.*
—*n.* **2** ***the (great) unwashed***: *Derogatory* the rabble, the masses, the °mob, the plebs, °people (at large *or* in general), the °population, the °populace, the man *or* woman in the street, Mr (& Mrs) Average, the working class(es), most °people, the (silent) majority, *US* John Q. Public: *The effort to sell expensive brandy to the great unwashed failed miserably.*

unwelcome *adj.* **1** uninvited, unsought for, unwished for, undesired, °undesirable, displeasing, unpleasing, °distasteful, unpleasant: *My day was further ruined by the unwelcome arrival of all those bills.* **2** unwanted, rejected, unaccepted, excluded; *persona non grata*, anathema: *Following that episode, Curshaw was made to feel unwelcome at the club.*

unwholesome *adj.* **1** °unhealthy, unhealthful, °detrimental, deleterious, pernicious, insalubrious, unhygienic, insalutary, °harmful, noxious, toxic, °injurious, °destructive: *Fernthwaite finally succumbed to the unwholesome climate and had to be sent home.* **2** °corrupt, °immoral, °bad, °wicked, °evil, °sinful, °perverted; demoralizing, depraved, °degrading, corrupting, perverting: *The social worker said it was wrong for a child to be raised in such an unwholesome atmosphere.* **3** °ill, ailing, °sickly, °sick, °pale, °wan, anaemic, pallid, °pasty: *Their unwholesome complexion comes from malnutrition.*

unwieldy *adj.* °awkward, °clumsy, °bulky, oversized, cumbersome, ungainly, unmanageable, unhandy, unmanoeuvrable: *The huge oil tankers, though economical, often proved unwieldy in the ports they visited.*

unwonted *adj.* infrequent, °unusual, uncustomary, uncommon, °unfamiliar, unprecedented, °rare, °singular, atypical, °abnormal, °peculiar, °odd, °strange, °irregular, unconventional, °unorthodox: *All this unwonted physical exercise made them exhausted by evening.*

unworthy *adj.* **1** unequal, meritless, unmerited, substandard, °inferior, second-rate, °menial, °puny, °petty, °paltry, °unprofessional, °mediocre, °despicable, °contemptible, °dishonourable, ignoble, °disreputable, discreditable, °unqualified, °ineligible, unfit, undeserving: *I consider Patrick an unworthy opponent.* **2** ***unworthy of***: °unbecoming to, °inappropriate to, unsuitable for, unfit for, out of °character for, °inconsistent with *or* for, out of °place with *or* for, °incongruous with *or* for: *That sort of petty haggling is unworthy of your position and of you.*

upbeat *adj.* °positive, °optimistic, °sanguine, °favourable, °cheerful, encouraging, heartening, °buoyant, light-hearted: *Christopher has a very upbeat attitude towards life despite his age.*

upbraid *v.* °scold, °rebuke, °reprimand, reproach, °berate, °castigate, °chastise, °reprove, chide, censure, take to °task, *Colloq* °tell off, tick off, °dress down, give a dressing-down, give (someone) a piece of (one's) °mind, °tell (someone) a thing or two, rake (someone) over the coals, °jump on *or* all over, °bawl out, *US* °chew out: *The boys were soundly upbraided for going near the railway tracks.*

upbringing *n.* rearing, raising, training, °education, cultivation, nurture, °breeding: *The way one behaves through life is really a matter of upbringing.*

upheaval *n.* °upset, °unrest, commotion, °change, cataclysm, disruption, °disturbance, °disorder, °confusion, °chaos, °furore *or US* furor: *Those were times of drastic political upheaval in Asia.*

uphold *v.* °support, °maintain, °sustain, °preserve, °hold up, °defend, °protect, °advocate, °promote, espouse, °embrace, °endorse, °back, °champion, °stand by: *All demagogues claim to uphold democratic principles.*

upkeep *n.* **1** °maintenance, °repair, °support, °sustenance, °preservation, °conservation, °subsistence, °running, °operation: *The upkeep of the infrastructure came to ten per cent of the annual budget last year.* **2** (operating) °costs, (°running) °expenses, °outlay, °expenditure, *Brit* °overheads, oncosts, *US* °overhead: *Have you included upkeep in the annual expenses?*

upper *adj.* **1** higher (up), loftier, topmost, more °elevated, °uppermost: *Air is less dense in the upper parts of the atmosphere. Our flat is on an upper floor. Her best notes are sung in the upper register.* **2** higher, upland, more °elevated; (more) northerly, northern: *We visited the cataracts on the upper reaches of the Nile. We spent the holiday in upper Canada.* **3** later, more °recent: *These strata were laid down in the Upper Cretaceous period.* **4** ***upper case***: °capital letter(s), °capital(s), majuscule (letters *or* characters): *The heading ought to be in upper case.* **5** ***upper crust***: upper °class, °élite, aristocrats, °nobles, blue bloods, °wealthy, *US* Four Hundred: *Gregory thinks of himself as a member of the upper crust and won't associate with us.* **6** ***upper hand***: °advantage, °control, °authority, °power, °sway, °superiority, °supremacy, °command, dominance, ascendancy, *Colloq* °edge: *Purvis kowtows to whoever has the upper hand.*
—*n.* **7** ***on (one's) uppers***: °poor, °indigent, °destitute, poverty-stricken, *Colloq* °broke: *Stanley has been on his uppers since losing his job.*

upper-class *adj.* **1** °élite, aristocratic, blue-blooded, well-born, °noble, high-born, patrician, *Colloq* °upper crust: *Eunice comes from an upper-class Irish family.* **2** °high-class, °elegant, °fancy, °luxurious, °first-rate, de luxe, °royal, °regal, °sumptuous, *Colloq* swank(y), ritzy, °posh: *I'll have you know that we stayed only in upper-class hotels on our tour.*

uppermost *adj.* **1** highest, topmost, loftiest, °top: *These curious animals live in the uppermost branches of the trees.* **2** °foremost, °first, most °important *or* °prominent *or* °influential *or* °telling, °principal, °paramount, °pre-eminent, °predominant: *Uppermost in my mind is the safety of the children.*

uppish *adj.* °affected, putting on airs, °snobbish, °conceited, overweening, °self-important, *Colloq* uppity, snooty, °high and mighty, °hoity-toity, highfalutin *or* hifalutin, stuck-up, on (one's) high horse, *Slang* snotty, *Brit* toffee-nosed: *Even if she is in charge she doesn't have to be so uppish.*

upright *adj.* **1** °erect, °perpendicular, vertical, on °end, °straight up and down, °plumb, stand-up, °standing up, *Brit* upstanding: *Few upright columns of the Greek temple remained.* **2** °moral, °principled, high-minded, °ethical, °virtuous, upstanding, °straight, °righteous, straightforward, °honourable, °honest, °just, °trustworthy, unimpeachable, uncorrupt(ed), incorruptible, °decent, °good: *David had long been an upright member of the church council.*
—*n.* **3** °post, °pole, column, vertical, °perpendicular: *We need another upright to support the floor over here.*
—*adv.* **4** perpendicularly, vertically, upward(s), °straight up (and down): *The javelin was sticking upright out of the ground.* **5** °right side up: *Miraculously, the platter with the roast on it landed upright on the floor.*

uprising *n.* °rebellion, °revolt, °mutiny, °revolution, insurrection, rising, putsch, coup, *coup d'état*: *The government quelled the uprising with water cannons and tear gas.*

uproar *n.* clamour, hubbub, °disturbance, commotion, hullabaloo, brouhaha, °din, °racket, °pandemonium, °tumult, turmoil, pother, °outcry, °outburst, °bedlam, °agitation, °frenzy, °broil, °rumpus, °fuss; affray, °fracas, °brawl; *Colloq* hoo-ha, to-do, *US* hoopla, *Brit* kerfuffle *or* carfuffle *or* kurfuffle: *The announcement of the new taxes caused a nationwide uproar.*

uproarious *adj.* **1** clamorous, °noisy, deafening, °tumultuous, turbulent, °tempestuous, °excited, frenzied, °rowdy, °riotous, °disorderly, °wild: *We had an uproarious party on New Year's Eve.* **2** °hilarious, °hysterical, (screamingly) °funny, side-splitting, *Colloq* too °funny for words, killing: *Leslie told his uproarious story about Colonel Cholmondley and the tiger.*

uproot *v.* **1** °transfer, °transplant, °move, °displace; °exile, °banish: *Finney has been uprooted five times in his career with the firm.* **2** deracinate, extirpate, °root out, °dig out, °pluck out, °tear out; °destroy, °demolish, °ruin, eradicate, annihilate, °kill, °devastate, °ravage: *Thousands of trees were uprooted by the hurricane.*

upset *v.* **1** °disturb, °agitate, °distress, unsettle, °put off, °put out, °perturb, disquiet, °fluster, °ruffle, °frighten, °scare, disconcert, °dismay, °trouble, °worry, °bother, discompose, make (someone) °nervous: *We once had a nanny who told the children horror stories just to upset them.* **2** °overturn, °capsize, °topple, up-end, °tip over, °knock over *or* down, invert, °turn °topsy-turvy *or* upside down, °spill: *That is the third time this week you have upset the cream jug.* **3** °disturb, derange, °disrupt, disarrange, °mess up, disorganize, °snarl up, °jumble, °muddle, *Colloq Brit* kerfuffle *or* carfuffle *or* kurfuffle: *The boys upset the entire house with their horseplay.* **4** °overthrow, °defeat, °beat, worst, thrash, °rout, °conquer, °overcome, °win out over, get the °better of, get *or* gain the °advantage over, °triumph over, be °victorious over, vanquish: *The question is whether the challenger will upset the champion in the Wimbledon finals.* **5** °defeat, °ruin, °spoil, °thwart, °interfere with, °destroy, °demolish, °mess up, °disturb, *Colloq* throw a *Brit* spanner in(to) *or US* monkey wrench into (the °works), *US* discombobulate, *Slang* °screw up, gum up, put the kibosh on, *Taboo slang* fuck up, *Brit* °bugger up: *Your coming early upset my plan to shampoo my hair.*
—*adj.* **6** capsized, overturned, upside down, bottom side up, inverted, reversed, toppled, tipped over, °topsy-turvy: *We clung to the bottom of the upset boat till help arrived.* **7** °sick, °queasy: *Eve has an upset stomach and cannot go.* **8** perturbed, °disturbed, disquieted, °disconcerted, °agitated, distressed, °worried, troubled, unnerved, distracted, apprehensive, °nervous, frightened, °scared, °afraid: *We found Vladimir in a terribly upset state at Natasha's disappearance.* **9** disordered, °confused, disorganized, messed-up, jumbled, muddled, °disturbed, disarranged: *The house is never so upset as after a party.* **10** °angry, irate, °furious, beside oneself, °mad, *Colloq* fit to be tied, *Slang* freaked out: *Father was upset because I took the car without his permission.*
—*n.* **11** °defeat, upsetting, °conquest, °overthrow, °rout, °thrashing, °triumph, °victory: *We celebrated the upset of Queen's Park Rangers by Manchester United.* **12** °surprise, unexpected event *or* occurrence: *The upset of the season was when Carridoff won the Derby.*

upshot *n.* °result, °end (°result), °outcome, ending, conclusion, °termination, °effect, after-effect, fallout, °wake, backwash, °repercussion, after-clap, feedback, °resolution, culmination, denouement *or* dénouement, °issue, *Colloq* °pay-off, *US* wrap-up: *The upshot of the nasty business was that Bowles was sent to prison for life.*

upstart *n.* °parvenu(e), arriviste, nouveau riche, (social) climber, status-seeker, °pretender, °nobody: *That upstart husband of Dora's tried to get me to invest in some scheme of his.*

uptake *n.* comprehension, °understanding, apprehension, °grasp, °perception, °insight, perspicaciousness, perspicacity, perceptiveness, °sensitivity: *Billie was very quick on the uptake, and knew immediately what the man was after.*

urge *v.* **1** °press, °push, °drive, °force, impel, °speed, accelerate, °hurry, °rush, °hustle, °move, goad, °prod, egg on, °spur: *He urged his steed onward.* **2** °press, goad, °prod, egg on, °spur, °prompt, °induce, °incite, constrain, exhort, °encourage, °demand, °request, °ask, °plead (with), °beseech, °beg, entreat, importune: *We've been urging the police for months to investigate the goings-on at that house.* **3** °coax, °persuade, °induce, °prevail (up)on, °campaign (with), °sway, °influence, °talk into, °advise, °suggest, °counsel: *The agents urged them to sell their house while the market was good.* **4** °argue, °set forth, affirm, °state, °allege, assert, °hold, °advise, °advocate, °demand: *The residents urged that the planning board should deny permission for a supermarket.*
—*n.* **5** °pressure, °impetus, °desire, compulsion, impulse, °itch, °longing, yearning, °drive, °fancy, °hunger, °thirst, craving, *Colloq* yen: *We stopped because Corey felt the urge to have some ice-cream.*

urgency *n.* imperativeness, °pressure, °stress, °extremity, °importance, seriousness, importunity, °necessity, °need, insistence, exigency, °emergency: *She was told to ring back as a matter of some urgency.*

urgent *adj.* **1** °immediate, °instant, °imperative, °pressing, compelling, °vital, life-and-death *or* life-or-death, °important, °serious, °necessary, exigent, °rush, °emergency, °pressing, high-priority: *There was an urgent need to do something at once, so she screamed.* **2** supplicative, begging, °solicitous, °earnest, importunate, °insistent, °loud, clamorous, °active, °energetic, pertinacious, °tenacious, °forceful, °firm: *Both parties were urgent in pressing for tax reform.*

urinate *v.* pass *or* make °water, *Technical* micturate; *Babytalk* (make a) wee, (go) wee-wee, (have a *or US also* take a) pee, (make) pee-pee, do number one, tinkle, piddle; *Euphemistic* go to the men's *or* ladies' (room), go to the °lavatory, excuse (oneself), wash (one's) hands, go to the bathroom, go to the powder-room; *Mincing* go to the little boys' *or* girls' room; *Colloq Brit* spend a penny, go to the loo, *Slang* (take *or* have a) piss, *Brit* have a *or* go for a slash: *One symptom of cystitis is pain when urinating.*

usage *n.* **1** °use, °custom, °habit, °practice, °routine, °convention, °form, °tradition: *British usage reflects decreasing use of the subjunctive mood.* **2** °treatment, °use, °management, handling, °operation, manipulation: *It would appear that the car has been subjected to some rough usage.*

use *v.* **1** °employ, make use of, put into °practice *or* °operation, °practise, utilize, °exercise, bring into play, have °recourse to, °resort to, put *or* press into °service, put to use, avail (oneself) of; °say, utter, °speak: *If you use a hammer you might damage the surface. Why do you have to use bad language?* **2** capitalize on, turn to °account, °profit by *or* from, °exploit, utilize, make use of, take °advantage of, °manipulate, °manoeuvre, °handle, °abuse, °misuse, °play, °work: *She used her smile to lure men on. Dorothy never forgave Conrad for the way he used her and her contacts to get his job.* **3** °consume, °eat, °drink, smoke, °take, °partake of, ingest, °inject, *Slang* °shoot (up): *He has never used a habit-forming substance.* **4** °consume, °buy, °purchase, °employ, utilize: *Which kind of detergent do you use?* **5** ***use up***: °consume, °exhaust, °expend, °run through, °run out of, deplete; °waste, squander, °fritter away, pour down the °drain, °throw away: *He used up all the toothpaste. She used up her entire inheritance gambling.*
—*n.* **6** °usage, °application, °employment, utilization; using: *The use of unleaded fuel is recommended.* **7** °function, utility, °application; °advantage, °benefit, °good, °service, °interest, °profit, avail: *What's the use*

of a radio that doesn't work? **8** °wear (and tear), utilization, °treatment, °usage, handling: *Long use has worn the workbench smooth.* **9** usability, °usefulness, utility, utilization, °usage, °function, functioning, °service(s), serviceability, °power: *He lost the use of his right arm in an accident at work.* **10** °licence, °permission, °permit, °privilege: *We paid a high fee for the use of this parking space.* **11** consumption, °purchase, buying, °acquisition: *The use of cigarettes has diminished in the last decade.* **12** °advantage, °purpose, °point, °end, °object, °reason, °basis, °ground: *I have tried to help him overcome his habit, but what's the use? Many are the uses of adversity.* **13** °demand, °need, °necessity, °urgency, exigency: *The world has as much use for art as for engineering.* **14** See **usage, 1,** above. **15** ***have no use for***: execrate, °detest, °abhor, °hate, °despise, °scorn, contemn, °spurn, °reject, °dislike: *We have no use for cowards in this regiment.*

used *adj.* **1** °second-hand, cast-off, °old, °worn, *Euphemistic* pre-owned, *Colloq* hand-me-down, *Brit* reach-me-down: *You're better off buying a good used car, since new ones depreciate so quickly.* **2** utilized, employed, occupied; in °use: *We slept in a rarely used room.* **3** ***used to***: °accustomed to, habituated to, acclimatized *or* acclimated to, adapted to, hardened *or* toughened *or* inured to *or* against, tempered to, °tolerant of; °familiar *or* °acquainted with: *After all those years, Amanda was used to Bill's shouting.*

useful *adj.* utilitarian, °functional, °serviceable, °practical, usable, of °use, °beneficial, salutary, °advantageous, °expedient, °profitable, valuable, °gainful, °helpful, °fruitful, °productive, °effective, °worthwhile: *Does this knob serve any useful purpose? We had some very useful conversations with the bank manager.*

usefulness *n.* utility, applicability, practicability, °purpose, purposefulness, °point, practicality, °benefit, °advantage, expediency, °profit, profitability, value, °gain, °help, fruitfulness, effectiveness, °worth: *I never could see the usefulness of all the forms one has to fill in.*

useless *adj.* **1** °ineffective, °ineffectual, unserviceable, °impractical, °impracticable, unpractical, unavailing, °vain, °pointless, °purposeless, °idle, °futile, unproductive, °unsuccessful, °impotent, effete, °sterile, °barren, abortive, unusable, °bootless, °worthless, *Rare* inutile: *The treatment that she tried was quite useless.* **2** °inefficient, °incompetent, unproductive, °ineffectual, °ineffective, °hopeless, °inept: *My dachshund has proved totally useless as a watchdog.*

user *n.* **1** consumer, °buyer, purchaser, °owner; °operator: *Users of the equipment report excellent results.* **2** (alcohol *or* drug *or* narcotic) °addict: *The police have been interviewing users in order to obtain more information about the dealers.*

user-friendly *adj.* °simple, °practicable, usable, °explicit, °accommodating, understandable: *The system is designed to be particularly user-friendly.*

usual *adj.* °same, °customary, °habitual, °accustomed, °familiar, °well-known, °common, °everyday, established, °traditional, °set, °time-honoured, °old, °conventional, workaday, stock, wonted, °regular, °ordinary, °normal, expected, °routine, °typical, run-of-the-mill, stereotypic(al), hackneyed, trite, °prosaic, °worn out, shop-worn, °predictable, unexceptional, unoriginal, unremarkable, unimaginative: *The usual answer I get is 'Why?' I missed my usual train this morning. They still sing the usual drinking songs.*

usually *adv.* customarily, as a °rule, °generally (speaking), most of the time, for the most °part, most °often, mostly, almost °always, inveterately, on the °whole, normally, commonly, regularly, predominantly, °chiefly, all things considered, in the °main, °mainly, by and large, as °usual, *Colloq* as per °usual: *I usually walk home from the office. Johnson usually interviews applicants in the morning.*

Utopia *n.* °paradise, °heaven, seventh °heaven, (Garden of) Eden, °bliss, cloud-cuckoo-land, Nephelococcygia, never-never land, Shangri-La, Cockaigne *or* Cockayne, °heaven on earth, °perfection: *He dreams about a Utopia where everyone is rich and there are no taxes.*

utterly *adv.* °completely, °perfectly, °absolutely, °thoroughly, fully, °entirely, °wholly, unreservedly, °totally, unqualifiedly, °out-and-out, °altogether, overwhelmingly, unequivocally, categorically, °definitely, °properly; °extremely, *Brit dialect* proper; (with) no holds barred, body and soul, °head over heels: *The proposal was utterly defeated in the Commons. That was an utterly foolish act. She gave herself to him utterly.*

V

vacancy *n.* **1** °emptiness, °void, °gap, lacuna, hiatus, °blank, deficiency, °opening, °breach, vacuum: *Only after she left did Hubert sense the vacancy in his life.* **2** (°job) °opening, °slot, °position, °post, °situation: *Her promotion created a vacancy in the personnel department.* **3** blankness, °emptiness, vacuity, absent-mindedness, inanity, vacuousness, incomprehension, fatuity, unawareness: *I knew by the vacancy of his look that he hadn't any idea of what I was talking about.*

vacant *adj.* **1** °empty, °void, °hollow, unoccupied, untenanted, °uninhabited, °abandoned, °deserted: *The house remained vacant all summer.* **2** °blank, expressionless, deadpan, °empty, vacuous, °dull, °absent-minded, °inane, uncomprehending, fatuous, °unaware: *After the accident, she would just sit, for hours on end, with a vacant look on her face.* **3** unoccupied, °free, °unused, unutilized, °spare, °extra, °idle, unfilled, unengaged, unspoken for: *The doctor has a vacant hour tomorrow at ten and could see you then.*

vacate *v.* **1** °leave, °depart (from), °withdraw from, °quit, °evacuate, °get *or* °go out of; °desert, °abandon: *In a fire drill, employees must vacate the building in five minutes.* **2** °give up, °relinquish, °sacrifice, °renounce, let go, °resign, °abdicate, °cede, °give up right *or* claim to, °abandon: *We vacated all claims to my aunt's property.* **3** annul, declare null and °void, nullify, °void, °repudiate, override, overrule, rescind, °revoke, °recall, °quash, °set aside, invalidate: *The judge vacated the defendant's plea of diminished capacity.*

vade-mecum *n.* handbook, °manual, ready °reference, °book, °guide: *She always had with her a vade-mecum on rare poisons.*

vagabond *n.* **1** gypsy, °tramp, vagrant, wayfarer, °rover, wanderer, itinerant, °migrant, bird of passage, rolling stone, beachcomber, °derelict, *Chiefly US and Canadian* hobo, *Australian* swagman, *Colloq US* °bum, *Slang US* bindle-stiff: *The police interviewed every vagabond they could find for a clue to the murder.* —*adj.* **2** vagrant, wayfaring, roving, wandering, itinerant, °migrant, derelict, nomadic, gypsy, °rambling, roaming, drifting, peripatetic, °transient, peregrinating: *When will he give up his vagabond ways and settle down?*

vague *adj.* **1** °indefinite, °indistinct, °imprecise, °inexact, unclear, °confused, unspecified *or* non-specified, °general, generalized, unspecific *or* non-specific, inexplicit *or* unexplicit, ill-defined, °hazy, °fuzzy, °ambiguous, °obscure, amorphous; °shapeless, blurred, blurry, °filmy, °dim, °shadowy, °veiled, bleary, foggy, °misty, cloudy, clouded, hardly *or* barely distinguishable *or* discernible: *I have only a vague recollection of our having met. She must have had a vague idea of your intentions. Leon could almost make out the vague shape of an approaching figure.* **2** undetermined, indeterminate, unfixed, °indefinite, °inexact, unspecified *or* non-specified, unspecific *or* non-specific, °ambiguous, °doubtful, in °doubt, °uncertain, °equivocal: *For security reasons, her time of* *arrival was left vague.* **3** °veiled, concealed, °hidden, shrouded, °obscure, ill-defined, unspecific *or* non-specific, inexplicit *or* unexplicit, °ambiguous: *There had been a vague threat of kidnapping, which should not have been ignored.* **4** °subliminal, °subconscious, indefinable, unexplained: *I had a vague sensation of being followed.* **5** °indefinite, °ambiguous, °wishy-washy, undecided, °indecisive, °irresolute, vacillating, wavering, °inconstant, °unsettled, °uncertain, °nebulous, up in the air: *Leonore is vague about her plans to run for re-election.* **6** °vacant, °empty, °blank, expressionless, vacuous, °dull; puzzled: *By their vague expressions I could see they hadn't understood a word.*

vaguely *adv.* **1** distantly, remotely, indefinitely, dimly, subliminally, subconsciously, inexplicably: *I became vaguely aware of another presence in the room.* **2** ambiguously, imprecisely, inexactly, unclearly, confusedly, confusingly, hazily, fuzzily, nebulously, obscurely: *Kenston claims that he expresses his theories vaguely to allow for broad interpretation.* **3** °idly, vacantly, detachedly, absent-mindedly, dreamily, absently, distractedly: *Manton listened only vaguely to the judge's words.*

vain *adj.* **1** °proud, °conceited, °haughty, °arrogant, °boastful, °egotistical, °cocky, °self-important, vainglorious, narcissistic, *Colloq* big-headed, swell-headed *or* swelled-headed, stuck-up, swollen-headed: *They are so vain that they have mirrors in every room.* **2** °worthless, profitless, °bootless, °pointless, °unsuccessful, °empty, °futile, °useless, unavailing, unproductive, °fruitless, °ineffective, abortive: *Peter sent Carol flowers every day in a vain attempt to win her back.* **3** ***in vain***: **a** vainly, futilely, unsuccessfully, fruitlessly, bootlessly: *In vain, we sought the help of the police.* **b** irreverently, blasphemously, disrespectfully, improperly: *Despite his mother's admonitions, he continues to take the Lord's name in vain.*

valley *n.* glen, dale, dell, vale, dingle, °hollow, coomb *or* coombe *or* combe *or* comb, *No. Brit and Welsh* cirque *or* corrie *or* cwm, *Scots* strath: *Oh, to stroll once again the cool valleys and the heathered hills of home!*

vanity *n.* **1** °conceit, conceitedness, egotism, narcissism, °arrogance, cockiness, self-importance, vainglory, haughtiness, °pride, self-admiration, self-worship, *Colloq* swell-headedness, big-headedness: *It is disgraceful what some people do to satisfy their vanity.* **2** vainness, °emptiness, hollowness, worthlessness, futility, unreality, bootlessness, pointlessness, uselessness, °folly, vapidity, silliness, vacuousness, vacuity, foolishness, fatuity, frivolousness: *The vanity of trying to complete the book in a year must be obvious by now.*

vapid *adj.* insipid, flavourless, °tasteless, °bland, °watery, watered down, °wishy-washy, jejune, °colourless, °unpalatable, °flat, °tame, °lifeless, °boring, °tedious, °tiresome, uninteresting, trite, wearisome, wearying, °humdrum, *Colloq* blah, ho-hum: *The minister attacked green politics as vapid romanticism.*

vapour *n.* **1** °mist, °fog, steam, cloud, smoke, smog, °exhalation: *There arose from the bog a suffocating, miasmic vapour.* **2** ***the vapours***: morbidity, hypochondria, hysteria, nervousness, °depression, rheuminess, *Archaic* distemper, *Colloq* the pip: *Charlotte suffered an attack of the vapours and retired to her room.*

variable *adj.* °changeable, °protean, changing, °inconstant, varying, wavering, mercurial, °fickle, °capricious, unsteady, unfixed, °unstable, °uncertain, undependable, unpredictable, fluctuating, vacillating, mutable, chameleonic, chameleon-like: *The weather can be quite variable depending on the season.*

variance *n.* **1** °variation, °difference, °disparity, °discrepancy, °disagreement, deviation, inconsistency, divergence, incongruity: *The monitor takes account of minute variance in blood pressure.* **2** °disagreement, °misunderstanding, °discord, °difference (of opinion), °dissension, contention, °dispute, dissent, °controversy, °quarrel, °conflict, °argument, °debate, lack of harmony, falling out, °schism, °rift: *There has never been any variance between us about the disciplining of the children.* **3** ***at variance***: in °dispute, in °disagreement, quarrelling, in contention, in °conflict: *The workforce was at variance with management in the matter of day care.*

variant *n.* **1** °alternative, modification, °variation: *'Labor' is an American spelling variant of 'labour'.* —*adj.* **2** varying, °variable, changing, altering, °unstable, °deviant, deviating, °different, differing; °separate, °distinct: *It is claimed that the law is given variant interpretations depending on the social standing of the suspect.*

variation *n.* **1** °change, changing, °alteration, altering, °variety, varying, modification, modifying, °difference, differing, diversification, °diversity, diversifying, modulation, modulating, conversion, converting, permutation, permuting: *We have to allow for variation in the intensity of the light.* **2** °variety, °choice, °novelty, °diversity, departure (from the norm *or* usual), °change of pace, divergence, variegation, deviation (from the norm): *This restaurant offers considerable variation in its menu.*

varied *adj.* **1** °diverse, diversified, °mixed, °miscellaneous, assorted, heterogeneous: *An insufficiently varied diet may lead to malnutrition.* **2** See **various,** below. **3** See **variegated,** below.

variegated *adj.* multicolour(ed), particolour(ed), varicoloured, many-coloured, motley, pied, piebald, brindled, °mottled, polychrome, polychromatic; nacreous, changeant, °opalescent, opaline: *Plants with variegated foliage always add interest to a garden.*

variety *n.* **1** °diversity, diversification, multifariousness, multiplicity, °number, °range, °assortment, °medley, °mixture, °mix, °miscellany, heterogeneity, °choice, °selection, °collection: *Don't you find that the variety of foods in supermarkets today is astonishing? There was certainly a wide variety of people at their party.* **2** °difference, heterogeneity, °discrepancy, °diversity, °disparity, °variation, °contrast: *The flora and fauna of Australia display great variety.* **3** °sort, °brand, °make, °mark, °kind, °class, °category, °breed, °type, °order, °genre, species, genus, classification, °strain: *Which variety of washing powder do you prefer? Rex cultivated only the rarest varieties of orchid.*

various *adj.* **1** °different, a °number of, a °variety of, diversified, °diverse, °several, °many, numerous, °sundry, heterogeneous, °miscellaneous, *Literary* °divers: *We are considering various offers for the painting. Catherine held various executive positions in the company.* **2** °different, °distinct, °individual: *There are various ways of looking at the problem.*

vary *v.* **1** °change, °alter, °diversify, °transform, reshape, remodel, restyle, °modify, reorganize: *We vary the programme each month to make it more interesting.* **2** °change, °switch, °alternate, °fluctuate, vacillate: *The manager's attitude varies from helpful to downright rude.* **3** °depart, °deviate, °differ, °diverge, °shift, veer: *These results do not vary from the average by more than five per cent.*

vast *adj.* °infinite, °unlimited, °boundless, °limitless, unbounded, interminable, °endless, never-ending, °inexhaustible, indeterminate, °immeasurable, incalculable, measureless; °immense, °enormous, °huge, tremendous, °great, °prodigious, stupendous, °gigantic, °massive, °voluminous, capacious, °colossal, °monumental, mammoth, °jumbo, elephantine, behemoth, Cyclopean, Brobdingnagian, titanic, *Literary* vasty, *Colloq* ginormous, humongous: *It is difficult to comprehend the vast distances of space. There is a vast difference between the climates of California and the Midwest.*

vastly *adv.* immensely, greatly, hugely, enormously, considerably, °substantially, (almost) entirely, infinitely, °exceedingly, °extremely, °very much, *Colloq* worlds: *Their new house was vastly different from the* *way I had pictured it. Katy looks vastly better since she lost two stone.*

vehicle *n.* **1** conveyance: *The police report that two vehicles were damaged in the crash.* **2** °means, °channel, °mechanism, °carrier, conduit, °agency, °instrument: *Water is the vehicle used in many sprays.*

veil *n.* **1** covering, °cover, °screen, °camouflage, °cloak, curtain, °mask, °shroud: *A veil of silence has been drawn over the meetings. He stole away under the veil of darkness.*
—*v.* **2** °cover, °conceal, °hide, °camouflage, °cloak, °mask, °disguise, °shroud, °shield, °obscure: *The writer's identity was veiled from us till recently.*

veiled *adj.* concealed, °hidden, masked, °obscure, unrevealed, covert, disguised, °secret, sub rosa, °subtle: *There seemed to be a veiled threat in the way he said goodbye.*

vein *n.* **1** blood-vessel; nervure: *He killed himself by opening a vein in his wrist.* **2** °streak, °seam, °stripe, striation, stria, °thread, °line: *The reddish vein gives this marble a warm feeling.* **3** °seam, lode, °stratum, °course, °deposit, bed: *The prospector discovered a vein of almost pure gold in the old mine.* **4** °thread, °hint, °suggestion, °touch, °trace, °streak, °line, °strain, °mood, °spirit, °tone, note, °tenor, °feeling, °attitude, °disposition, °humour, °temper; °tendency *or* °inclination *or* proclivity toward(s): *Underlying her apparent kindness is a vein of bitter hatred.* **5** °way, °manner, °course, °fashion, °style, °mode, °pattern: *He would have continued in that same vein if the chairman hadn't stopped him.*

velocity *n.* °speed, swiftness, °rapidity, fleetness, quickness, briskness, alacrity, celerity, °pace, °rate of °speed, miles per hour, m.p.h., kilometres per hour, km/hr: *Our velocity slowed as we neared the outer atmosphere.*

venal *adj.* °corrupt, corruptible, bribable, buyable, purchasable, °mercenary, unprincipled, °dishonourable, °rapacious, °avaricious, °greedy, simoniacal, *Colloq* °crooked, *Slang* °bent: *All we had to do was to find a venal official, cross his palm with silver, and they would release our son.*

vendetta *n.* (blood) °feud, °quarrel, °dispute, °conflict, °rivalry, enmity, °bitterness, hatred, °ill will, bad blood: *Fifty years after leaving Palermo, the vendetta between their families still persisted.*

veneer *n.* °gloss, façade, °finish, °pretence, (false) °front, (°outward) °show *or* °display, °appearance, °mask, °guise, °aspect, °superficies: *Beneath that veneer of elegance and refinement lie the heart and soul of a monstrous criminal.*

venerable *adj.* °respectable, °honourable, °estimable, respected, honoured, esteemed, august, °sedate, °impressive, revered, reverenced, worshipped: *Venerable old military men were called on for advice.*

venerate *v.* °respect, °honour, °esteem, °revere, °reverence, °worship, °hallow, °adore, °admire, °look up to: *Schweitzer was widely venerated for his charitable works.*

veneration *n.* °respect, °honour, °esteem, °reverence, °deference, °homage, °devotion, °worship, °admiration, adoration, idolization, awe: *Their veneration for their hero turned to contempt when his past was revealed.*

venereal *adj.* °sexual; genital; °social, sexually transmitted, gonorrhoeal *or* gonorrhoeic, syphilitic: *Syphilis was once the most feared venereal disease.*

vengeance *n.* **1** °revenge, retaliation, °retribution, °requital, °reprisal: *Her vengeance for what he had done was to disinherit him.* **2** ***with a vengeance***: **a** violently, °fiercely, ferociously, wildly, vehemently, furiously, forcefully: *The wind blew with a vengeance all night.* **b** energetically, to the fullest extent, to the utmost *or* the fullest *or* the limit, (with) no holds barred, enthusiastically, wholeheartedly: *Give Richard a job to do and he goes at it with a vengeance.*

venial *adj.* forgivable, excusable, pardonable, °tolerable, tolerated, °minor, °petty, °insignificant, unimportant, remittable *or* remissible: *That hypocrite considers even his most heinous crimes to be venial.*

venom *n.* **1** °poison, toxin: *The snakes are 'milked' of their venom, which is collected for research in antitoxins and pharmaceuticals.* **2** malice, maliciousness, malevolence, °ill will, malignity, °animosity, °hate, hatred, °hostility, °antagonism, °spite, spitefulness, spleen, °rancour, °bitterness, embitteredness, °gall, °poison, poisonousness, °virulence: *Vinnie was totally unprepared for the venom of the attack.*

venomous *adj.* **1** °poisonous, °deadly, toxic, °dangerous, life-threatening, °lethal: *There are few venomous snakes in the British Isles.* **2** °poisonous, °virulent, malicious, malevolent, malign, °malignant, °savage, baleful, envenomed, °hostile, antagonistic, °spiteful, splenetic, acerbic, °rancorous, °bitter, °embittered, °mean, °vicious: *That venomous little man caused me to lose my job.*

vent *n.* **1** °opening, °slit, °slot, °hole, °aperture, air-hole, blow-hole, spiracle, orifice, °outlet, inlet, funnel, flue, duct, °passage; fumarole, fissure, °pipe, mofette: *The tepee has a vent at the peak to let the smoke of the fire escape.* **2** ***give vent to***: See **3,** below.
—*v.* **3** give vent to, °express, verbalize, °air, articulate, °enunciate, °declare, °voice, °announce, °communicate, °pronounce, °proclaim, °reveal, °release, let go, let °loose, allow to become known, °make known, °blurt out, make °public, °broadcast: *Has Margie ever vented her true feelings about your work as a bomb disposal expert? Arnold vents his spleen on any unfortunate who will stand for it.* **4** °discharge, °release, °emit, °eject, °issue, °empty, °dump, °expel, °send *or* °pour out *or* forth, °throw out: *It is illegal to vent poisonous fumes into the atmosphere.*

venture *n.* **1** °risk, °chance, °hazardous °undertaking, °experiment, °speculation, °gamble, °plunge, °fling: *Their new publishing venture turned out to be quite a success.*
—*v.* **2** °dare(say), make °bold, °hazard, volunteer, °tender, °offer, °broach, °advance, proffer, °put forward: *Ambrose ventured some nasty remark and was asked to leave.* **3** °jeopardize, °risk, °endanger, °hazard, imperil; °gamble, °bet, wager, °plunge, °put down: *Thomas ventured his last chip on the number four.*

venturesome *adj.* **1** °daring, °bold, °intrepid, °adventurous, °courageous, plucky, adventuresome, °audacious, °fearless, doughty, °brave, °spirited: *Henderson felt that he was being truly venturesome by sailing single-handed round the Isle of Wight.* **2** °risky, °rash, °reckless, sporting, °game, °daredevil: *Taking one's family into the American West was truly a venturesome undertaking—even in the 20th century.*

verbal *adj.* **1** °spoken, °oral, vocal, said, uttered, expressed, enunciated, articulated, colloquial, conversational, viva voce, word-of-mouth, unwritten: *We had a verbal agreement that you would behave yourself.* **2** word-for-word, °verbatim, °literal: *We have an accurate verbal transcript of the proceedings.* **3** °word, lexical, vocabulary: *She did very well on the verbal parts of the examination but poorly on the mathematics.*

verbatim *adj.* **1** word-for-word, verbatim et literatim (= 'word-for-word and letter for letter'), °literal, °exact, °precise, °accurate, °faithful, °strict: *This verbatim translation may be accurate but all the poetic expressiveness is lost.*
—*adv.* **2** word for word, verbatim et literatim, °literally, °exactly, °precisely, accurately, faithfully, to the letter, strictly: *To make certain there would be no misunderstanding, the speech was copied verbatim.*

verge[1] *n.* **1** °edge, °border, °boundary, °margin, °brink, °threshold, °brim: *Frances is jealous of John to the verge of insanity.* **2** ***on the verge of***: about to, °ready to, on the (very) °point of, preparing to, °soon to: *Many smaller companies are on the verge of bankruptcy.*

—*v.* **3** Often, ***verge on***: °border (on), °approach, come °close *or* °near (to), *Technical* be asymptotic to: *Cathy's idea of comfort verges on what is more commonly thought of as luxury. Her charitable contributions last year verged on zero.*

verge[2] *v.* °incline, °lean, °tend, °extend, °stretch, °turn; °approach, °draw, °move: *The road verges southwards after the bridge.*

verify *v.* affirm, °confirm, °testify to, °attest (to), bear °witness to, °vouch for, corroborate, °support, °substantiate, °clinch *or* clench, °prove, °demonstrate, °show, °bear out, °authenticate, validate, °certify, °guarantee, back up, °warrant: *Can you verify the accuracy of his testimony?*

veritable *adj.* °real, °true, °virtual, °genuine, °actual, °legitimate, °authentic: *Frank becomes a veritable monster if denied his daily doughnut.*

vernacular *adj.* **1** °native, °local, regional, °indigenous, autochthonous: *Old Hebrew fell out of use, to be replaced by vernacular Aramaic.* **2** °popular, °informal, colloquial, conversational, °ordinary, °familiar, °everyday, °spoken, °vulgar, vulgate; °plain, °simple, straightforward, °easy: *We have both the vernacular and the formal, literary, or clerical levels of language. Can you translate this scientific gobbledegook into vernacular English that we can understand?*
—*n.* **3** °jargon, patois, argot, °cant, °idiom, phraseology, °language, °talk, °speech: *Alf occasionally slips into the vernacular of a Billingsgate fishmonger (his former calling).*

versatile *adj.* **1** °adaptable, °resourceful, all-round, all-purpose, many-sided, multi-purpose, multifaceted, °flexible, adjustable, °protean, °dexterous, °handy, facile: *Everett is a versatile painter who works in many media and styles.* **2** °variable, °changeable, °protean, changing, °flexible, fluctuating: *Any versatile organization should be able to accommodate staff losses.*

versed *adj.* Usually, ***well-versed in***: well-read *or* (°well-)°informed in *or* (well-)trained *or* (well-)grounded *or* (well-)schooled *or* (well-)°educated *or* (well-)tutored *or* °learned *or* cultured *or* °lettered *or* °cultivated *or* literate *or* °competent *or* °accomplished *or* skilled in, (well) posted on, °knowledgeable in *or* about, °proficient *or* °experienced *or* °practised *or* °expert *or* °good in *or* at, conversant *or* °familiar *or* (well-)°acquainted with: *The applicant appears to be sufficiently well-versed in several subjects to be qualified to teach them.*

version *n.* **1** °form, °variant, °variation, °type, °model, °style, °kind, °variety, °manifestation, portrayal, °adaptation, °rendition, °interpretation, °construct, construction, °conception, °idea: *This is yet another modern designer's version of 1920s' and 1930s' art deco.* **2** °story, °account, °rendering, °rendition, °translation, °interpretation, reading, °understanding, °view, °side: *Simon's version of what happened is completely distorted.*

vertex *n.* °top, °tip, °extremity, °zenith, meridian, apogee, °peak, apex, °acme, °summit, °pinnacle, °crest, °crown, °cap, °height(s): *The building is surmounted by a pyramidal dome at the vertex of which is a statue of Osiris.*

vertigo *n.* dizziness, light-headedness, giddiness, instability, *Colloq* wooziness: *Vertigo suddenly overcame me, and I grabbed a rail to steady myself.*

verve *n.* °spirit, vivacity, vivaciousness, °vitality, °life, liveliness, °animation, °sparkle, °energy, °vigour, °exuberance, briskness, brio, esprit, élan, °dash, °flair, °panache, °flourish, °enthusiasm, zeal, °zest, °gusto, *Colloq* pizazz *or* pizzazz, zip, vim, get-up-and-go, zing, oomph: *Helen's verve adds much to this production of* Carmen.

very *adv.* **1** °extremely, °truly, °really, to a °great extent, °exceedingly, greatly, (very) much, °profoundly, °deeply, acutely, unusually, extraordinarily, uncommonly, exceptionally, remarkably, °absolutely, °completely, °entirely, °altogether, °totally, °quite, °rather, hugely, °vastly, *Dialect* right, *Brit* jolly, *Colloq* °damn(ed), °terribly, °awfully, darned, *US dialect* danged, plumb, *Slang Brit* bleeding, *Chiefly Brit* bloody: *The Bell Inn has a very fine wine list. Vicky was very attached to her pony. I shall be there very soon.* **2** most, °extremely, certainly, °surely, °definitely, decidedly, unequivocally, unquestionably, °quite, °entirely, °altogether: *If you ask her out, she is very likely to say no.*
—*adj.* **3** °exact, °precise, °perfect; °same, selfsame, °identical, °particular: *Her hopes were the very opposite of his. I arrived the very day she left. He is the very model of a hard-working student.* **4** least, °mere, merest, °bare, barest, °sheer, sheerest; utter, °pure, °simple: *The very thought of war makes me ill. The very mention of her name strikes terror into the hearts of the local residents.*

vessel *n.* **1** container, °receptacle, utensil, holder: *Food was stored in vessels neatly arrayed around the sarcophagus.* **2** °craft, °boat, °ship, ark, *Literary* barque *or US also* bark: *The vessel docked gently at the airlock of the space station.*

vestige *n.* °trace, °suggestion, soupçon, °hint, glimmer, °inkling, °suspicion, °sign, °evidence, °mark, °token, °scent, whiff, tinge, °taste; °remnant, °scrap, °fragment, °memorial, °residue, °relic, remains: *Vestiges of an ancient city have been found in the sea off Cyprus.*

vestigial *adj.* °imperfect, °undeveloped, underdeveloped, °rudimentary, °incomplete: *Anatomists regard the coccyx in man and apes as a vestigial tail.*

vet *v.* °examine, °review, °investigate, °scrutinize, °inspect, °check (out), °look over, °scan; validate, °authenticate; *Colloq* give (something *or* someone) the once-over, °size up: *We engaged an expert to vet the definitions of culinary terms for the new dictionary.*

veteran *n.* **1** °old hand, past °master, old-timer, trouper, *Colloq* warhorse: *Barlow was a veteran of twenty years' experience in the service.*
—*adj.* **2** °experienced, °practised, °seasoned, °mature, long-serving, battle-scarred: *Did it never occur to this veteran politician that there are degrees of misconduct?*

veto *v.* **1** °stop, °block, °deny, °ban, °turn down, °reject, disallow, °rule out, °quash, °prevent, °prohibit, interdict, °taboo, °outlaw, proscribe, °preclude, *Colloq* put the kibosh on, °kill, nix: *Father vetoed the idea that we go to Brighton for the holiday. Any measure he proposed was summarily vetoed.*
—*n.* **2** °denial, °ban, stoppage, °block, °embargo, turndown, °rejection, disallowance, quashing, °prevention, °prohibition, interdiction, °taboo, proscription, preclusion, vetoing, *Colloq* °killing, nixing: *The home secretary's veto of the abortion measure greatly angered the women's groups.*

viable *adj.* sustainable, °supportable, °sensible, °reasonable, °practical, °practicable, °applicable, workable, °feasible, °possible: *We have three days to come up with a viable plan for continuing the research project.*

vibes *n.pl.* vibrations, °feelings, °sensations, resonance(s), °rapport, empathy, °sympathy: *I felt the place had really good vibes the minute I walked in.*

vibrate *v.* °quiver, °shiver, °shudder, °fluctuate, °quake, °shake, °tremble, throb, °pulsate, °oscillate, °pulse, reverberate, resonate, *Brit* judder: *The house began to vibrate, the windows rattled, and the dishes danced off their shelves.*

vicarious *adj.* surrogate, delegated, deputed, commissioned, assigned, °indirect, substituted: *He derived vicarious pleasure from seeing his children do the things that he no longer could.*

vice *n.* **1** immorality, corruption, °evil, badness, depravity, °degradation, degeneracy, iniquity, villainy, venality, evil-doing, wickedness, °profligacy, °sin, sinfulness, °transgression: *She described the town as a den of indecency, exhibitionism, and vice.* **2** °flaw, °defect, °fault, °imperfection, °blemish, °shortcoming,

°failing, °weakness, °frailty, °foible, °infirmity, deficiency: *Rejection without due consideration is a prejudicial vice of editors.*

vice versa *adv.* conversely, contrariwise, to *or* on the °contrary, reversed, the other °way around: *She made the facts fit her conclusions, instead of vice versa.*

vicinity *n.* °area, °neighbourhood, °locale, vicinage, environs, locality, precincts, purlieus, °territory: *All people living in the vicinity of the nuclear plant were tested for radiation poisoning.*

vicious *adj.* **1** °immoral, unprincipled, amoral, barbarous, °corrupt, °evil, °bad, °base, depraved, °vile, °atrocious, execrable, degraded, °degrading, °degenerate, °venal, iniquitous, heinous, odious, °perverted, nefarious, °wicked, flagitious, °devilish, °diabolic(al), °fiendish, °monstrous, °profligate, °shameful, °shameless, °abominable, °sinful: *The vicious, bloody dictatorship on the island lasted only a dozen years.* **2** malicious, °spiteful, °mean, °nasty, °hateful, malevolent, °malignant, °bitter, acrimonious, °rancorous, °venomous, °vindictive, defamatory, °slanderous, °scandalous, *Slang* °rotten, bitchy: *When they argued, they said terribly vicious things to one another.* **3** °savage, °wild, °untamed, °ferocious, °fearful, °brutal, °fierce, °fiendish, bestial, feral, brutish, ravening, *Literary* fell: *The local children were terrified of his vicious Rottweiler.*

vicissitude *n.* **1** °change, °mutation, °alteration, changeability, changeableness, mutability, °variation, variability, °variety, °alternation, °flux, °fluctuation, unpredictability: *Who seeks stability in life often encounters its vicissitude.* **2** ***vicissitudes***: °fluctuations, °changes, °variations, °contrasts, °inconstancy, unpredictability, uncertainties, *Colloq* ups and downs, flukiness: *His success is amazing in the light of the vicissitudes he survived.*

victim *n.* **1** sufferer, martyr, °casualty, °scapegoat, °sacrificial lamb, injured °party: *It is a pity that you had to be the victim of her greed.* **2** °dupe, gull, °fool, °butt, fair °game, *Colloq* chump, fall guy, *Slang* °sucker, °sap, *Chiefly US and Canadian* patsy, *US* schnook, schlemiel *or* schlemihl *or* shlemiel: *She was an easy victim for any confidence man.*

victimize *v.* **1** °prey on, °pursue, go after, °pick on, °bully, take °advantage of, °persecute, °exploit, °use: *Increasingly, older people are being victimized by unscrupulous relatives.* **2** °cheat, °swindle, bilk, °defraud, °dupe, °hoodwink, °deceive, gull, °fool, °trick, °outwit, °outsmart, outfox, *Colloq* snooker, flimflam, *Slang* suck *or* °sucker in, °screw, shaft, °take (in), rook: *The confidence team used the old Spanish handkerchief trick to victimize unsuspecting tourists.*

victor *n.* °winner, °champion, conqueror, prizewinner: *They came home unchallenged victors by an overwhelming 11 point margin.*

victorious *adj.* °triumphant, °successful: *Caesar was victorious over the Gauls.*

victory *n.* °triumph, °conquest, °supremacy, °superiority, °success, overcoming, mastery, °winning, quelling, crushing: *Alexander's victory over Darius at Arbela was one of the decisive battles of history.*

vie *v.* °compete, contend, °struggle, °strive: *The brothers constantly vied for their father's affection.*

view *n.* **1** °outlook, °aspect, °prospect, °scene, °perspective, vista, panorama, °spectacle, °picture, °tableau; °landscape, seascape, cityscape: *From the tower we had a view of the devastation below.* **2** °opinion, °point of view, °approach, °position, °judgement, °belief, way of °thinking, °conception, °understanding, °impression, °feeling, °sentiment, °notion: *Denham's view is that the country's defences are inadequate.* **3** °aspect, °angle, °position, °prospect, °perspective, °vision, °representation, °projection: *Here is a termite's-eye view of the timbers in your house.* **4** inspection, °survey, °vision, °sight, °observation, °scrutiny, °examination, contemplation, °study: *The shroud was pulled away, exposing the revolting object to our view.* **5** °aim, °direction, °intent, °intention, °purpose, °objective, °object, °expectation, °prospect, °vision, °hope, °dream: *We cultivated their friendship with a view to being invited aboard their yacht.* **6** ***in view of***: in (the) °light of, °considering, in °consideration of, because of, on °account of: *In view of your failure to respond to our letters, we must refer the matter to our lawyers.*
—*v.* **7** °look at *or* upon *or* over, °see, °take in, °watch, °observe, °scrutinize, °examine, °regard, °behold: *From this vantage point one can view the entire valley.* **8** °witness, °see, °watch, °observe, °take in: *We viewed the entire robbery as it took place.* **9** °regard, °consider, °think of, °look on *or* upon, °judge, deem, °believe, °hold, °estimate, °rate, °gauge, assess: *Control views Craven as a threat.*

viewpoint *n.* °standpoint, (°point of) °view, °attitude, °angle, °slant, °position, °stance, vantage °point, °perspective, °frame of reference, °way of °thinking, °context: *From our viewpoint, widening the road only encourages speeding.*

vigilance *n.* watchfulness, alertness, °observance, guardedness, circumspection, attentiveness, °caution: *While the dog remains loose, we must exercise vigilance.*

vigilant *adj.* watchful, °alert, °sharp, °observant, °guarded, circumspect, °attentive, °wakeful, °cautious, °careful, °wary, chary, on one's °guard, on the °alert, on the °lookout, °eagle-eyed, hawk-eyed, Argus-eyed, on the qui vive, on one's toes, with one's eyes open, *Colloq* with one's eyes skinned *or* peeled: *As long as we remain vigilant, they will never be able to take us by surprise.*

vigorous *adj.* °energetic, °active, °vivacious, °dynamic, °brisk, °lively, °spirited, °robust, °strong, °hardy, °hale, °hearty, °vital, °fit, °lusty, °stalwart, in good *or* fine fettle, spry, °sprightly, resilient, *Colloq* peppy, full of °pep, full of get-up-and-go, full of beans: *At 63, he is just as vigorous as he was at 40.*

vigorously *adv.* energetically, actively, vivaciously, dynamically, briskly, spiritedly, robustly, strongly, hardily, heartily, lustily, stalwartly, eagerly, with °might and °main, with a °vengeance, strenuously, *Colloq* like °mad, like crazy, hammer and tongs: *It may not be good for you to exercise vigorously every day.*

vigour *n.* °vitality, °resilience, °strength, °power, °energy, forcefulness, °force, °stamina, °endurance, mettle, mettlesomeness, °pith, °dynamism, °spirit, liveliness, °animation, °verve, vivacity, °exuberance, brio, briskness, °zest, zealousness, °enthusiasm, °gusto, °eagerness, *Colloq* °spunk, °pep, pizazz *or* pizzazz, vim, oomph, zing, get-up-and-go: *When attacked, they defended themselves with extraordinary vigour.*

vile *adj.* **1** °base, abject, °contemptible, debased, °degenerate, depraved, °bad, iniquitous, execrable, °atrocious, °sordid, °immoral, amoral, °wicked, °evil, °sinful, hellish, °fiendish, ignoble, °revolting, °despicable, horrid, °horrible, °dreadful, °terrible, °corrupt, °mean, °wretched, °miserable, °degrading, ignominious, °disgraceful, °shameful, °shameless: *In every age, the vilest specimens of human nature are to be found among demagogues.* **2** °disgusting, °nasty, sickening, °nauseous, nauseating, °foul, °loathsome, °offensive, noxious, °repulsive, °repellent, °repugnant: *It is, indeed, a vile disease, but at least it is not contagious. She had prepared some vile cocktail that I refused to drink.*

vilify *v.* °depreciate, devalue, deprecate, °debase, °disparage, denigrate, °diminish, traduce, defame, speak °ill of, revile, °slander, °libel, °abuse, defile, °sully, °smear, °tarnish, malign, calumniate, asperse, °run down, decry, *Rare* vilipend, *Colloq US* bad-mouth: *His political and religious views became notorious and were often vilified.*

villain *n.* °wretch, evil-doer, °criminal, °miscreant, blackguard, °rogue, °rascal, cad, scallywag *or* scalawag, malefactor, °scoundrel, dog, cur, viper, reptile, °snake in the grass, rat, *Archaic* rapscallion, *Literary* knave, caitiff, *Colloq Brit* bounder, blighter, *Slang* bastard, son of a bitch, *Brit* rotter, *US* SOB *or* s.o.b. (= 'son of a bitch'): *The villain of the film is a smooth-talking charmer who swindles old ladies out of their savings.*

villainous *adj.* **1** treacherous, °perfidious, °dishonest, °unscrupulous, °traitorous, °corrupt, °faithless, °criminal, felonious, °murderous, *Colloq* °crooked, °bent: *Few activities are more villainous than being a double agent.* **2** See **vile, 1,** above.

vindicate *v.* **1** °clear, exonerate, absolve, acquit, exculpate, °excuse: *She was vindicated of any complicity in the affair.* **2** °justify, °support, °uphold, °prove: *Subsequent events vindicated his actions.*

vindictive *adj.* avenging, vengeful, vindicatory, revengeful, retaliatory, °spiteful, unforgiving, splenetic, °resentful, °rancorous, °implacable: *She later turned vindictive, attacking everyone for real or imagined slights.*

vintage *n.* **1** year, crop, °harvest, °origin, °generation: *Which vintage is the better for Bordeaux, 1949 or 1954?* —*adj.* **2** °quality, °choice, °superior, °better, °good, °select, °best, °classic; °aged, °seasoned, °mature(d), °mellow(ed): *Mark has become an expert in vintage wines.* **3** °antiquated, °old-fashioned, old-fogyish *or* old-fogeyish, °antique, °bygone, old-time, °collector *or* collector's, *Colloq* over the hill: *Claud used to drive his vintage car to work every day.*

violate *v.* **1** °break, °breach, °disobey, °disregard, contravene, °infringe, °ignore: *He habitually violated the law by carrying a pistol.* **2** °dishonour, °desecrate, °profane, defile, °degrade, °debase, treat irreverently: *Vandals were found to have violated the sacred shrine.* **3** °rape, debauch, °ravish, °ravage, °molest, °attack, °assault, °outrage: *The victim identified the man who had violated her.*

violation *n.* **1** °infringement, °breach, °disregard, disobedience, contravention, °abuse; ignoring, infringing, breaching, disregarding, disobeying, contravening, abusing, violating: *Parking here is a violation of the law. Violation of the rules will be dealt with summarily.* **2** profanation, profaning, °sacrilege, desecration, desecrating, defilement, defiling, °degradation, °degrading, °dishonour, dishonouring, debasement, debasing, violating: *The authorities take a serious view of the violation of a place of worship or a cemetery.* **3** °rape, ravishment, molestation, °attack, °outrage, °assault, violating: *The defendant is charged with the violation of three women.*

violence *n.* **1** (brute *or* physical) °force, °might, mightiness, °power, °strength, °severity, °intensity, °energy, vehemence, ferocity, ferociousness, fierceness, °fury, °vigour; destructiveness, °virulence: *The violence of the storm continued unabated throughout the night. The violence of the seizures diminished after she was given the medication.* **2** bestiality, brutality, °barbarity, savagery, cruelty, bloodthirstiness, wildness, ferocity, °frenzy, °fury, °passion, fierceness, vehemence, murderousness: *The marauders attacked with a violence that terrified the villagers.* **3 *do violence to***: **a** °harm, °damage, °injure: *The scandal did violence to her reputation. Humphrey's singing could do violence to any melody.* **b** °warp, °twist, °distort: *In reporting that her views are antifeminist, the newspaper did violence to the import of her speech.*

violent *adj.* **1** °wild, °physical, °destructive, vehement, °brutal, brutish, °beastly, °nasty, °cruel, °mean, barbarous, °inhuman, °savage, °fierce, °ferocious, °furious, frenzied, uncontrollable, °untamed, °ungovernable, raging, °raving, irrational, °insane, crazed, *Colloq* fit to be tied: *Tony turned into a violent maniac when he suspected her of seeing another man.* **2** °harmful, °injurious, damaging, °detrimental, °destructive, deleterious, catastrophic, cataclysmic, °ruinous, °devastating: *This was the most violent earthquake to hit Mexico in recorded history.* **3** °acute, °serious, °severe, °extreme, °harsh, °trenchant, °virulent, °intense, °energetic, °forceful, vehement, °passionate, °impetuous,°tempestuous: *The proceedings were interrupted by an outburst of violent abuse from the public gallery.*

virtual *adj.* °effective, °essential; °practical, °understood, accepted: *In rush hours, the motorway traffic comes to a virtual standstill.*

virtually *adv.* essentially, effectively, °practically, °almost, to all intents and purposes, for all practical purposes, more or less, °nearly, as good as, °substantially, in °effect, in °essence: *He had virtually won the Brisbane-London sailing race when he passed the Lizard, but then he hit a rock.*

virtue *n.* **1** °morality, high-mindedness, °honour, goodness, justness, righteousness, fairness, °integrity, right-mindedness, °honesty, °probity, uprightness, °rectitude, decency, °worth, worthiness, °nobility, °character, respectability: *You will find the Billingses to be people of unassailable virtue.* **2** virginity, °chastity, chasteness, °honour, innocence, °purity: *As Healey had six daughters, he was kept quite busy protecting their virtue.* **3** °quality, °credit, °strength, °good °point, °asset: *Opposing the seven deadly sins are the three theological virtues, faith, hope, and charity, and the four cardinal virtues, fortitude, justice, prudence, and temperance.* **4 *by virtue of***: by dint of, owing to, thanks to, by °reason of, because of, on °account of: *Gerry was a part owner by virtue of his investment in the company.*

virtuosity *n.* (technical) °skill, °technique, °ability, °expertise, mastery, °excellence, °brilliance, craftsmanship, °craft, °flair, °dash, élan, éclat, °panache, pyrotechnics, showmanship, °show, staginess, *Colloq* razzle-dazzle: *The concerto was performed with signal virtuosity but little imagination or understanding.*

virtuoso *n.* **1** °master, maestro, °expert, °genius, °talent, °prodigy, °old hand, *Colloq* wizard, whiz *or* whizz *or* wiz, whiz-kid *or* whizz-kid, *Chiefly Brit* °dab hand, *US* maven *or* mavin: *Walter is a veritable virtuoso on the harmonica.* —*adj.* **2** °masterful, masterly, °expert, °talented, °brilliant, °dazzling, bravura, °prodigious, °excellent, °superb, °extraordinary, °exceptional, °superior, °first-rate, °superlative, °matchless, °peerless, °sterling, °marvellous, °remarkable: *His virtuoso performance of the B minor sonata won him a standing ovation.*

virtuous *adj.* **1** °moral, °honourable, °ethical, °honest, °good, upstanding, high-principled, °upright, °righteous, °pure, uncorrupted, incorruptible, °just, °fair, right-minded, fair-minded, high-minded, °scrupulous, °trustworthy: *Thomas has proved himself a virtuous young man.* **2** °chaste, °innocent, virginal, virgin; °decent, °proper, unsullied, °faithful, °true, uncorrupted: *A virtuous woman makes a virtuous wife.*

virulence *n.* **1** virulency, poisonousness, venomousness, toxicity, noxiousness, deadliness, perniciousness, injuriousness, destructiveness, malignity, malignancy, °violence, balefulness: *The virulence of his affliction was not recognized till it was too late.* **2** virulency, acrimony, acrimoniousness, °bitterness, acerbity, °rancour, spleen, °poison, poisonousness, °venom, venomousness, malignity, malevolence, maliciousness, malice, °spite, °hostility, °resentment, °antagonism, hatred: *We were taken aback by the virulence of the priest's attack on Miss Thompson's morals.*

virulent *adj.* **1** °lethal, life-threatening, °deadly, °fatal, pernicious, septic, °poisonous, toxic, baleful, noxious, °dangerous, °harmful, °injurious, °detrimental, deleterious, °destructive, °unhealthy, °unwholesome: *He died from a virulent form of dysentery that he caught in the tropics.* **2** °vicious, °venomous, °bitter, °spiteful, °malignant, malign, malicious, malevolent, °poisonous, splenetic, acrimonious, acerbic, acid, mordant, °sarcastic, °nasty, °trenchant, °caustic, antagonistic, °hateful, °hostile: *What did I do to the reviewer of* The Herald *to merit such a virulent review?*

visible *adj.* **1** seeable, perceivable, °perceptible, °discernible, detectable, discoverable, °noticeable, unmistakable, °clear, °obvious, °observable; visual: *The visible part of the energy spectrum is relatively small. The entrance holes to their burrows were clearly visible.* **2** °obvious, °conspicuous, °evident, °apparent, °prominent, °manifest, °distinct, °patent, well-defined, identifiable: *The consequences of the Act of Union of 1707 are still visible in Scotland today.*

vision *n.* **1** eyesight, °perception, °sight: *The optician said there is nothing wrong with MacKenzie's vision.* **2** far-sightedness, °understanding, °imagination, °foresight, foresightedness, °insight: *MacKenzie has brought great vision to this scheme for developing the Australian outback.* **3** °view, °perspective, °perception, envisioning, envisaging, °dream, °idea, °plan, °scheme: *MacKenzie's vision of making the desert bloom seemed impossibly remote.* **4** °phantom, apparition, chimera, °delusion, °hallucination, mirage, °spectre, °shade, eidolon, revenant, phantasm, materialization, °illusion, °ghost, wraith: *A vision appeared to MacKenzie as he slept, telling him that her name was Alice Springs.* **5** °sight for sore eyes, (welcome) °sight, °dream, °epitome: *To MacKenzie Alice was a vision of great beauty, and he proposed marriage.*

visionary *adj.* **1** °dreamy, °speculative, unpractical, °impractical, °fanciful, °imaginary, °unrealistic, °unreal, °romantic, °idealistic, unworkable, Utopian: *It is a pity that none of MacKenzie's visionary plans ever came to pass.*
—*n.* **2** °dreamer, idealist, °romantic, fantast, wishful °thinker, Don Quixote: *The world needs more visionaries like MacKenzie.*

visit *v.* **1** (go *or* come to) °see, °call (in *or* on *or* upon), °look in on, °stop in *or* by, *Colloq* °pop in *or* by, °drop in (on), °take in: *I plan to visit Leslie. Did you visit the Smithsonian Institution?* **2** °afflict, °attack, befall, °fall upon, assail, °seize, smite, °scourge, °descend upon, °inflict, °affect: *Horrible diseases and tortures were said to visit those who denied God.*
—*n.* **3** °stay, °call, °sojourn, °stop, stopover: *The minister will be here for only a brief visit.*

visitation *n.* **1** staying, °calling, visiting, sojourning, stopping (over): *The father has visitation rights to his children on weekends.* **2** °affliction, °ordeal, °trial, °punishment, °disaster, °catastrophe, cataclysm, °calamity, °tragedy, °curse, °scourge, °blight, °plague, °pestilence: *In the story, the tyrant succumbed finally to a visitation from the Almighty.*

visitor *n.* caller, °guest, °company; visitant: *May I phone you back after my visitors have gone?*

vital *adj.* **1** °imperative, °essential, °necessary, needed, requisite, required, °indispensable, °mandatory, compulsory, °cardinal, °fundamental, °basic, °critical, °crucial, °central, °pivotal: *Air and water are vital for the existence of most known organisms.* **2** °important, °key, °central, °critical, °crucial, life-and-death *or* life-or-death, °pivotal, °paramount, °main: *In an emergency, the captain must make the vital decision whether to abandon ship. This is a matter of vital concern for us all.* **3** °lively, full of °life, °vivacious, °spirited, °vigorous, °dynamic, °alive, °animated, °brisk, °energetic: *We have lost a vital member of the community. She took a vital interest in community affairs.* **4** °invigorating, quickening, life-giving, animating, vitalizing, reviving, vivifying, enlivening, rejuvenating: *I could feel the vital energies returning to my limbs.*

vitality *n.* **1** °energy, °life, life-force, °vigour, °power, °intensity, °force, liveliness, vivacity, vivaciousness, °animation, °sparkle, spiritedness, °exuberance, *Colloq* zing, °pep, pizazz *or* pizzazz, oomph, get-up-and-go, zip, vim: *My great-grandfather has the vitality of a forty-year-old.* **2** °stamina, hardiness, °endurance, °energy, °strength, robustness: *Does this society have the vitality needed to take it into the next decade?*

vitalize *v.* °stimulate, °activate, °arouse, vivify, °animate, °awaken, inspirit, invigorate, °enliven, °inspire, °revive, °rejuvenate, innervate, °energize, °fortify, reinvigorate, °renew, °refresh, °charge (up): *The tonic vitalized him to the point where he felt young again.*

vitiate *v.* **1** °spoil, °ruin, °harm, °impair, °mar, °sully, °corrupt, °pervert, °contaminate, °adulterate, °weaken, °degrade, °downgrade, °depreciate, °diminish, °depress, vulgarize, °lower, °reduce, °undermine: *Words appropriated from other languages tend to enrich rather than vitiate modern English.* **2** °debase, deprave, °pervert, °corrupt, °demoralize, defile: *Despite other strengths his entire character was vitiated by overriding avarice.* **3** invalidate, °destroy, °delete, °cancel, nullify, annul, °revoke, °void, abrogate, °abolish, °withdraw, °quash, °suppress: *The invoice was effectively vitiated by the plaintiff's failure to deliver the goods.*

vituperate *v.* °berate, °rate, reproach, revile, °vilify, execrate, °abuse, °denounce, decry, deprecate, °disparage, devalue, °diminish, °put down, °run down, devaluate, °depreciate, °blame, inculpate, censure, find °fault with, °attack, assail, °castigate, °scold, °reprimand, °upbraid, °rebuke, chide, °chasten: *From the pulpit he continued to vituperate the vices of the court.*

vituperative *adj.* °abusive, calumniatory, calumnious, °scurrilous, °derogatory, belittling, depreciatory, depreciative, detractory, °contemptuous, damning, denunciatory, denigrating, deprecatory, censorious, aspersive, defamatory, °slanderous, libellous, castigatory, condemnatory, malign, °scornful, °withering, °harsh, °sardonic, °sarcastic, °biting, acid, contumelious, opprobrious, insulting, *Formal* vilipenditory, *Colloq* down-putting: *Why should he have directed this vituperative speech at the very person whom he loves?*

vivacious *adj.* °lively, °spirited, °sprightly, °energetic, °animated, °brisk, °ebullient, °effervescent, °bubbly, °gay, °cheerful, °happy, °blithe, °jaunty, light-hearted, °sunny, °merry, high-spirited, °buoyant, chipper, *Colloq* up, peppy, full of °pep, full of beans, zippy: *Had he not gone on the cruise, Michael would never have met the vivacious redhead who became his bride.*

vivid *adj.* **1** °intense, °strong, °brilliant, °fresh, °bright, °dazzling, lucid, °rich, °clear, colourful, °glowing: *Michelle looked splendid in a silk dress of vivid yellow.* **2** °clear, °detailed, °sharp, °realistic, °graphic, true to life, °lifelike, °distinct, °powerful, °strong, °memorable, °dramatic, °striking: *It brought back to me vivid memories of our first meeting in 1985.* **3** °prolific, °fruitful, °fertile, fecund, inventive, °creative: *That kiss, which never took place, is a figment of Bagley's vivid imagination.*

vocalist *n.* °singer, soloist, choirboy, choir girl, choir member, chorus-boy, chorus °girl, chorus-member, chorister, caroller; diva, prima donna, *chanteuse*; cantor, crooner; *Colloq* songbird, canary, thrush, nightingale: *It was sung by a female vocalist with a high-pitched girlish voice.*

vocation *n.* °calling, °trade, métier, °business, °profession, °occupation, °career, °employment, °job, °pursuit, life's-work, life-work, °line (of °work), *Slang* °bag, °thing: *I left university with no particular vocation in mind.*

vogue *n.* **1** °fashion, °mode, °style, °look, °taste, °trend, °rage, °craze, °last °word, *dernier cri*, (°latest) °thing, *Colloq* °fad, the °latest: *Black leather boots were in vogue once again.* **2** °popularity, °favour, °preference, acceptance, currency, °prevalence, fashionableness: *They are capitalizing on the vogue for torn jeans.*

voice *n.* **1** °speech, utterance, articulation, words, °expression: *Keith found it difficult to give voice to his innermost thoughts.* **2** °share, °part, °vote, participation, °say, °decision, °option, °turn, °chance: *As a junior member of the board, Nicholas had no voice in major decisions.* **3** spokesman, spokeswoman, spokesperson, °representative, °agent, °agency, °instrument; °organ, °medium, °vehicle, forum, °publication: *Throughout his time in government, Logan had served as the voice of the miners.* The Clarion *views itself as*

the voice of all the people, though it actually represents only a few.
—*v.* **4** °express, utter, articulate, °enunciate, °present, verbalize, put into °words, give utterance *or* voice *or* °expression *or* °vent to, °communicate, convey, °declare, assert, °make known, °reveal, °disclose, °raise, °bring up, °air: *I must voice my misgivings about the step you are planning to take.*

void *adj.* **1** null and void, °invalid, not (legally) binding, inoperative, unenforceable, °ineffectual, °futile, °ineffective, °vain, unavailing, °idle, °useless, °pointless, °bootless: *Owing to irregularities, the election was declared void. If a card is turned face-up, the deal is void.* **2** °empty, °vacant, unoccupied, °unused, unutilized, unfilled, °blank, °clear; °deserted: *It is up to the council to appoint new members as places become void.* **3** ***void of***: devoid of, without, lacking, °destitute of: *The man was utterly void of imagination. In a minute, the room was void of people.*
—*n.* **4** °emptiness, vacantness, vacuum, blankness, nothingness: *Without a word, he leaped off the edge and plunged into the void.* **5** °space, °niche, °slot, °opening, °place, °vacancy, °gap, °emptiness: *Who will fill the void left by Edgar's departure?*
—*v.* **6** nullify, annul, °cancel, °delete, disannul, declare *or* render null and void, invalidate, °quash, °vacate, °discharge, °abandon, disestablish, °neutralize, disenact, °set *or* °put aside, rescind, °reverse, abnegate, abrogate: *They had to void the accusation for lack of evidence.* **7** °evacuate, °discharge, °expel, °emit, °purge, °clear, °empty, °drain, °eject; °pass, excrete, °urinate, °defecate: *The tanker went far out to sea before voiding its tanks. This medication will help in voiding the patient's bowels.*

volatile *adj.* **1** vaporizing, evaporable, evaporative: *A volatile solvent, which evaporates quickly, is the vehicle for thermosetting plastics.* **2** °changeable, °fickle, °flighty, °inconstant, °erratic, °restless, °unstable, °variable, mercurial, °capricious: *She was so volatile that one could never predict what she would do next.* **3** °explosive, hair-trigger, °sensitive, charged, eruptive, °tense, tension-ridden: *Be careful of Christine's volatile temper.*

volition *n.* (free) °will, °choice, °option, choosing, °choice, °discretion, °preference: *She pursued a course of her own volition.*

volley *n.* **1** salvo, bombardment, barrage, cannonade, fusillade, °discharge, °hail, °shower: *A volley of shot struck the tower, which collapsed.* **2** °outpouring, °torrent, °flood, deluge, inundation, °burst, °storm, outbreak: *The cracks of the muleteer's whip were accompanied by a volley of abuse.* **3** °give and take, to-and-fro, interaction, reciprocity, °exchange, volleying, crossfire, badinage, bantering: *Samuel enjoyed the volley of haggling that accompanied every sale.*

voluble *adj.* °talkative, °glib, °fluent, loquacious, garrulous, chatty, °profuse, gossipy, °exuberant, long-winded, °bombastic, °windy, °wordy, *Colloq* blessed with the gift of the °gab: *He is the House of Commons' most voluble advocate of capital punishment.*

volume *n.* **1** °amount, °quantity, °supply, °mass, °bulk, °abundance, °sum °total, aggregate: *The volume of ore from the mine created a pile hundreds of feet high. Her volume of output is greater than yours and mine together.* **2** °capacity, °size, °measure: *The volume of this bottle is not more than a litre.* **3** loudness: *Turn down the volume on that ghetto-blaster.* **4** °book, tome: *I bought a twenty-volume set of Dickens.*

voluminous *adj.* **1** °large, °extensive, °great, °spacious, capacious, °expansive, °roomy, °loose, °ample, °big, °bulky, cavernous, copious, °massive, °huge, °substantial, tremendous, °enormous, °gigantic, mammoth, °vast: *Rose's voluminous skirt was supported by a farthingale.* **2** oversized, outsized, °ample, billowing: *The voluminous spinnaker filled and we wafted down the estuary at hull speed.*

voluntarily *adv.* °freely, °willingly, spontaneously, of (one's) own °free °will, on (one's) own (°initiative *or* recognizance *or* °responsibility), without prompting, without being prompted *or* asked, gratis, gratuitously; by °choice, intentionally, purposely, on °purpose, °deliberately: *Some of the students spent their summer vacation voluntarily helping the needy.*

voluntary *adj.* **1** °free, elective, °willing, °spontaneous, °unsolicited, unbidden, °unasked, °gratuitous, contributed: *All work done on behalf of the cause is voluntary.* **2** discretionary *or* discretional, unconstrained, °intentional, °wilful, °deliberate, intended, °premeditated, planned, volitional, °optional: *His confession was entirely voluntary, and he was not coerced in any way.*

voluptuous *adj.* **1** °sensual, sensualistic, °sensuous, °luxurious, voluptuary, sybaritic, hedonist(ic), pleasure-seeking, pleasure-loving, luxury-loving, (self-)°indulgent: *He longed to taste once again the voluptuous delights of the Corinthian court.* **2** °seductive, °attractive, °desirable, °beautiful, °tempting, °inviting, appealing, enticing, alluring, °ravishing, °luscious, °delicious, °gorgeous, °shapely, °buxom, well-proportioned, well-endowed, well-built, *Colloq* curvaceous, °sexy, eye-filling, *Slang* (well-)stacked, busty, *US* built: *As he lolled on silken cushions, voluptuous houris danced round him in tightening circles.*

vomit *v.* °spew out *or* up, °spit up, belch forth; °regurgitate, °throw up, °gag, retch, °heave, *US* keck, *Colloq* puke, °return (food), *Brit* °sick up, *Slang chiefly Australian* chunder, *US* barf, upchuck, toss (one's) cookies, spiff (one's) biscuits: *The ancient steam engine vomited smoke and cinders from its huge stack. The very thought of going on a sea voyage almost made me vomit.*

voracious *adj.* **1** insatiable, °gluttonous, °ravenous, ravening, °rapacious, piggish, °hoggish, predacious, edacious, devouring, °greedy, °avaricious, esurient, uncontrollable, °uncontrolled, °unquenchable, °enormous, °prodigious, *US* cormorant: *Is there no satisfying the man's voracious appetite?* **2** °thirsty, °hungry, °desirous, avid, °eager, zealous, °enthusiastic, °fervent, fervid, °ardent, °earnest, °passionate, °devoted: *It was becoming difficult to satisfy the public's voracious demand for gossip.*

vote *n.* **1** ballot, ticket, show of hands; referendum, °plebiscite: *We must have a vote on the issue.* **2** °suffrage, franchise: *Women did not have the vote in those days.* **3** °opinion; voter, elector: *Do you think your platform can win over the liberal vote?*
—*v.* **4** opt, °choose, come out (for *or* against), express *or* signify (one's) °opinion *or* °preference *or* °desire: *Many people vote for a party rather than an individual.*

vouch *v.* Usually, ***vouch for***: °support, °guarantee, °back (up), °endorse, °certify; °uphold, °sponsor, bear °witness, °attest to: *My neighbour will vouch for me. Can she vouch for your not leaving the house all evening?*

vouchsafe *v.* **1** °offer, °give (up), °yield, °accord, °supply, °grant, °impart, °bestow, °deign *or* °condescend to give: *The minister vouchsafed no information regarding interest rates.* **2** °permit, °allow, °suffer: *The government vouchsafed the hostages safe passage out of the country.*

vow *v.* **1** °swear, °pledge, °promise, °assure, °state, °declare, give (one's) (solemn) °word (of honour): *I vowed to return after the war to care for those who had helped me escape.*
—*n.* **2** °oath, °pledge, °promise, °agreement; (solemn) °word (of honour): *She will keep her vow, you may be certain.*

vulgar *adj.* **1** indelicate, °boorish, uncultured, uncultivated, °low, °unrefined, °common, °plebeian, inelegant, unladylike, ungentlemanly, gauche, uncouth, °coarse, °tasteless, °ostentatious, ignoble, low-class, *Colloq* °flash: *The boss's wife was known for her vulgar behaviour at the dinner table.* **2** °tasteless, indelicate, °indecent, °rude, °crude, °naughty, °dirty, °improper, °off colour, °risqué, ribald, °blue, indecorous, °nasty, °offensive, °gross, °lustful, °obscene, °lewd, °lascivious, licentious, smutty, salacious, scatological, °filthy,

°pornographic, *Slang US* raunchy: *He made a lot of money through publishing vulgar magazines and videos.* **3** °popular, °vernacular, °ordinary, °everyday, °general, °homespun, commonplace, household, °average: *Dictionaries should record the vulgar language as well as the literary.*

vulgarity *n.* **1** coarseness, lack of refinement *or* sophistication, crudeness, rudeness, °indelicacy, tawdriness, baseness, humbleness, unsophistication, gaucherie, gaucheness, ignobility: *When you consider his upbringing you can scarcely blame him for his vulgarity.* **2** °impropriety, lewdness, grossness, foulness, vileness, filthiness, obscenity, *Slang US* raunchiness: *The magazine was refused an import licence because of its vulgarity.*

vulnerable *adj.* exposed, °defenceless, °weak, °sensitive, unprotected, °unguarded, unshielded, °helpless, °powerless: *She felt vulnerable to those who prey on the elderly.*

W

wad *n.* **1** °pad, °mass, °lump, °clod, ball, °plug, chunk, hunk, °block, °pack: *He had a wad of cotton wool in each ear.* **2** °roll, pocketful, °heap, °quantity, °load, *Colloq US* bankroll: *Over coffee James handed him a wad of notes.*

waddle *v.* toddle, °shuffle, wobble *or* wabble, °totter, °paddle, °pad, waggle, duck-walk, *Brit dialect* wamble: *He waddled down the road, a shopping-bag on each arm.*

wade *v.* **1** ford, °cross, °traverse, °walk, make one's way: *The water is only knee-deep, and you can wade across.* **2** °paddle, °play, °splash: *There is a shallow pool where the little children can wade.* **3** ***wade in*** *or* ***into***: **a** °enter, °get in (*or* into), °join (in): *When the fight began, Patrick waded in with arms flailing.* **b** °attack, °approach, get *or* °set to work, °plunge *or* °dive into: *I have to wade into an enormous pile of mail that accumulated while I was away.* **4** ***wade through***: °plough through, °work (one's) way through, hammer *or* °pound away at, °plod through, °peg away at: *You really have to wade through that entire book to write your report.*

waffle *v.* **1** Often, ***waffle on***: °carry on, °jabber (on), °prattle (on), prate, blather (on *or* away), *Colloq* run on, *Brit* witter (on), natter (on), rabbit on, *Slang* run off at the mouth: *He kept waffling on about his new computer and, frankly, I wasn't listening.* **2** °equivocate, hedge, °quibble, °shuffle, tergiversate, hem and haw, prevaricate, *Brit* beat about the bush, *US* beat around the bush, *Colloq* fudge: *I wish he would stop waffling and say what he means.*
—*n.* **3** °talk, °palaver, verbiage, °prattle, twaddle, blather, prolixity, wordiness, °jabber, jibber-jabber, *Colloq* °hot air: *All I got was a lot of waffle when I asked for the best interest rate on a loan.*

waft *v.* **1** °drift, °float, °blow, whiff, be borne *or* carried *or* transported: *The scent of jasmine wafted towards me on the warm breeze.*
—*n.* **2** °breath, °suggestion, °puff, whiff, °hint: *A waft of cool, fresh air momentarily eased the stench of the dungeon.*

wag[1] *v.* **1** °wave, waggle, °oscillate, °fluctuate, °sway, undulate, °flutter, °flap, °flip, °flicker, °shake, °vibrate, °quiver, °nod, °rock, °dance, wobble, bob, bobble, waver, *Rare* vellicate: *Misty's tail wagged as I approached the house.*
—*n.* **2** °wave, waggle, oscillation, °fluctuation, °sway, undulation, °flutter, vellication, °flap, °flip, °flicker, °shake, vibration, °quiver, °nod, wobble, bobble, waver: *The dying animal recognized me and gave a feeble wag of her tail.*

wag[2] *n.* °comedian, comedienne, °wit, punster, pundit, °joker, jester, °comic, jokester, droll, °merry andrew, °clown, *Colloq* °card: *A wag said that tailors were like storks—known for their big bills.*

wage *n.* **1** Often, ***wages***: °pay, compensation, emolument, °remuneration, °payment, °fee, °salary, °stipend, recompense, °reward, °earnings; °honorarium: *The strikers wanted a ten per cent increase in their hourly wage.*
—*v.* **2** °carry on, °pursue, °conduct, °engage in, °undertake, °practise, °prosecute, °proceed with: *History shows that wars are often waged over trifling differences.*

wait *v.* **1** °tarry, °linger, °hold on, °stay, bide (one's) time, mark time, °stand by, *Colloq* cool (one's) heels, °stick around, °sit tight, °hang on, *Brit* °hang about, *US* °hang around: *If you wait till I've finished this, I'll join you for dinner.* **2** be delayed *or* postponed *or* deferred *or* shelved *or* °put off, *US* be tabled, *Colloq* be put on ice *or* on the back burner: *The quarterly sales figures can wait—we haven't yet completed those for this month.* **3** ***wait on*** *or* ***upon***: °serve, °attend (to), °minister (to): *Rose made such a fuss that the restaurant staff refused to wait on her.*
—*n.* **4** °delay, °pause, °stay, °hold-up, °interval, °halt, °stop, stoppage, °break, hiatus, lacuna, °gap, °respite, °rest (°period), °intermission, discontinuation, °recess: *There was an extra long wait between trains because of track repairs further up the line.*

waiter *n.* waitress, head waiter, maître d'hôtel, °host, hostess, *sommelier* (*des vins*), wine steward, stewardess; cup-bearer, Ganymede, Hebe: *Marie asked the waiter to bring her a clean plate.*

waive *v.* **1** °give up, °relinquish, °renounce, °resign, °forsake, °forgo, °cede, °sign away, °surrender, °abandon, °yield, °dispense with: *I waived my right to the inheritance in favour of my daughters.* **2** °set *or* °put aside, °except, °ignore, °disregard, °overlook, °abandon, °defer, °postpone: *We are happy to waive the rules in your case, madam.*

waiver *n.* renunciation, relinquishment, forgoing, ceding, cession, °resignation, °surrender, abandonment, setting *or* putting aside, deferral, °remission, °postponement: *Her waiver of all rights to the inheritance was duly recorded.*

wake[1] *v.* **1** Often, ***wake up***: °awaken, °awake, °rouse, waken, °bring around; °stir, bestir (oneself), °get up, °come to, get going: *Wake me when it is over. She didn't wake up till noon.* **2** °awake, waken, °awaken, °animate, °stimulate, °enliven, galvanize, °fire, °quicken, inspirit, °inspire, °activate, °liven up, vivify, °kindle, °vitalize, °stir, °arouse, get (someone) going, bring to °life: *When I feel this tired, it takes a lot to wake me up. Seeing Margo woke a spark in me I thought had long since died.*
—*n.* **3** vigil, °watch, death-watch, °funeral: *If you have ever been to an Irish wake, you will know what I mean.*

wake[2] *n.* **1** °track, °trail, aftermath, °path, backwash, °wash, bow °wave; °trace, spoor, °scent: *The wake from the passing boats damages the docks. No matter where he went, they followed in his wake.* **2** ***in the wake of***: following (on *or* upon), after, °subsequent to; as a °result *or* consequence of, on °account of, because of, owing to, by °virtue of: *In the wake of the law's enactment, scores of abortions were performed.*

wakeful *adj.* **1** °awake, °sleepless, waking, unsleeping, °restless, °restive, insomniac: *The children were wakeful the entire night in anticipation of a visit from Santa Claus.* **2** watchful, (on the) °alert, on the qui vive, °sharp, °attentive, °vigilant, °wary, °cautious, °observant, heedful, on the °lookout: *We remained wakeful, alert to any footstep.*

walk *v.* **1** °advance, °proceed, °move, °go, wend, °go *or* make (one's) way by foot, tread, °step, perambulate, °stalk, stride, °tramp, °stroll, amble, °ramble, ambulate, shamble, °pad, °shuffle, °saunter, trudge, trek, °plod, slog, hike, °parade, °promenade, °strut, °swagger, °prance, °march, goose-step, °pace, °trip, °sidle, tiptoe, sashay, °flounce, °stagger, °lurch, °limp, °waddle, °stamp, mince, °slink, °steal, °prowl, skulk,

°sneak, °creep, *Colloq* go by *or* ride by shanks's *or* shanks' mare *or* pony, hoof it, foot it, traipse, °pussyfoot, *Slang US* boogie: *Guthrie certainly has a peculiar way of walking.* **2** °take, convoy, °accompany, °escort, °go with; °conduct, °lead; °empty: *Let me walk you to the station. I have to walk the dog twice a day.* **3** °patrol, °trace out, °stalk, °cover, °haunt, °prowl, °wander, °roam, rove *or* °range about in *or* on, °frequent: *Her mother could not understand why Maizie walked the streets nightly.* **4** ***walk out***: **a** °leave, °depart, °desert: *She just walked out and no one has seen her since.* **b** °strike, go (out) on °strike, °protest, take industrial action, *Brit* down tools: *Negotiations reached an impasse, so the employees walked out.*

—*n.* **5** °path, lane, pathway, pavement, footpath, °promenade, esplanade, boardwalk, *Brit* footway, *US* °sidewalk: *We strolled along the pleasant walks that lead through the park.* **6** gait, °step, °carriage, °bearing, stride: *He had great fun imitating Groucho Marx's slinky walk.* **7** constitutional, °stroll, amble; slog, °tramp, hike: *Lettie likes to take a walk in the park after dinner. We had a five-day walk through the jungle before reaching civilization.*

wall *n.* **1** °screen, °partition, divider, °enclosure, separator, bulkhead, °barrier, °obstruction, °obstacle, °impediment, °block, °fence: *Marcie built round herself a wall of resentment which no one could penetrate.* **2** barricade, fortification, °protection, °bulwark, breastwork, embankment, °rampart, palisade, stockade: *It was questionable whether the walls would withstand the cannon-balls.* **3** ***drive up the wall***: drive crazy *or* insane *or* mad, °madden, °exasperate, derange, °try, °irritate, °infuriate, °enrage: *The constant caterwauling from the next flat is driving me up the wall.* **4** ***go to the wall***: °fail, °collapse, be ruined, face °ruin, go bankrupt, lose everything, *Colloq* go °broke, °go under, °fold (up), *Slang* go bust: *Unicold went to the wall because of increased costs and decreased sales.*

—*v.* **5** Often, ***wall up*** *or* ***off***: °enclose, °partition (off), °close (off), °brick up, immure: *A bricklayer was hired to wall up the openings where the windows had been.*

wallet *n.* °purse, pocketbook, *Brit* notecase, *US* billfold: *An anonymous good Samaritan found my wallet and sent it to me intact, with all the money in it.*

wallow *v.* **1** °roll *or* loll about *or* around, °welter, writhe, °tumble, °splash *or* plash: *He enjoys watching the pigs wallowing in the mud.* **2** Usually, ***wallow in***: °luxuriate in, bask in, °revel in, °glory in, °indulge (oneself) in, °give (oneself) up to, °succumb to, °take to, °appreciate, °fancy, °enjoy, °like, °love, °savour, *Slang* get a kick *or* a bang *or* a boot from *or* out of: *Now that Gabriel is a big rock star, he simply wallows in all the attention he is getting.* **3** °stumble, °stagger, °lurch, °flounder, °teeter, °totter, falter, °pitch: *Without its engines, the ship was lifted skyward by a wave one moment only to wallow in a trough the next.*

wan *adj.* **1** °white, °sickly, °pale, pallid, livid, °pasty, ashen, bloodless, waxen, whey-faced, sallow, °colourless, deathly, °ghostly, °ghastly, cadaverous: *I almost wept at seeing the child's wan face against the pillow.* **2** °weary, °weak, °hollow, °feeble, °frail, °ineffectual, °sorry, °pitiful: *She offered no more than a wan smile in response to questions about her family.*

wand *n.* baton, °stick, °staff: *The magician pointed with his wand and a bottle of gin appeared.*

wander *v.* **1** °walk, °go, °roam, rove, °range, °stray, °ramble, °stroll, °saunter, °meander, °drift, °cruise, °prowl, *Colloq* mosey: *We wandered about the village square, chatting and window-shopping.* **2** °wind, °meander, zigzag, °turn this way and that: *A trout stream wanders past our house.* **3** digress, go off, become °absent-minded, go wool-gathering, lose concentration *or* focus: *My mind wandered as the speaker droned on.* **4** °deviate, digress, °turn, divagate, °stray, °drift, °depart, go off at a tangent, lose (one's) train of thought, °lapse: *The speaker tended to wander occasionally.*

wane *v.* **1** °decrease, °diminish, grow less, lessen, °decline, °die out, abate, °ebb, °subside, °fade (away), °dim, °taper off, peter out, °wind down, °weaken: *The waning moon cast its pale light on the dying knight. As his strength waned he could no longer lift his sword.* **2** draw to a °close, °end, °terminate: *The day waned into a gloomy evening.*

—*n.* **3** °decrease, diminution, lessening, °decline, abatement, °ebb, subsidence, fading, tapering off, petering out, winding down, weakening, deterioration, degeneration: *The 1970s saw the wane in popularity of large, gas-guzzling cars.* **4** ***on the wane***: on the °decrease *or* °decline *or* °ebb, diminishing, decreasing, declining, abating, subsiding, fading, tapering off, petering out, winding down, weakening, deteriorating, degenerating: *The economy is recovering, and inflation is on the wane. Since that latest illness, my energy has been on the wane.*

wangle *v.* °scheme, °plot, °work out, contrive, °manoeuvre, °engineer, °manage, °manipulate, machinate, *Colloq* °fix, °fiddle, °work, °pull off, finagle, °swing: *I hear that you were able to wangle an audience with the pope.*

want *v.* **1** °desire, crave, °wish (for), °long for, pine for, °hope (for), °fancy, covet, °hanker after, °lust after, °hunger for *or* after, °thirst for *or* after, °yearn for, *Colloq* have a yen for: *I want you near me. Ignore his crying—he just wants some ice-cream. Maybe he's crying because he wants to go.* **2** °need, °lack, °miss, °require, °call for, °demand, be °deficient in, be *or* stand in want *or* in °need of, necessitate; be *or* °fall °short of: *This engine wants proper maintenance. The bottle wants only a few more drops to fill it.*

—*n.* **3** °need, °lack, °shortage, deficiency, °dearth, °scarcity, scarceness, insufficiency, scantiness, inadequacy, paucity: *For want of good writers, the literary quarterly diminished in size and finally disappeared.* **4** °appetite, °hunger, °thirst, craving, °desire, °fancy, °wish, °longing, yearning, hankering, °demand, °necessity, °requirement, requisite, °prerequisite, *Colloq* yen: *She gave up trying to satisfy his wants.* **5** °poverty, °need, indigence, homelessness, destitution, °privation, pauperism, penury, neediness, impecuniousness: *The civilized nations are trying to solve the problems of want, which seem to increase daily.*

wanting *adj.* **1** °deficient, °inadequate, not up to °par *or* expectations, °insufficient, leaving much to be desired, °unsatisfactory, unsatisfying, °disappointing, second-rate, °inferior, °poor, °shabby, °shoddy, °flawed, °faulty, °imperfect, °incomplete, unfinished, °defective, patchy, impaired, damaged, °broken, °unsound: *These robots were tested at the factory and were found wanting.* **2** °absent, missing, lacking, °short (of), *US and Canadian* °shy (of): *What good is a banjo wanting its strings?*

wanton *adj.* **1** °immoral, °dissolute, °profligate, dissipated, depraved, °loose, °promiscuous, °lustful, licentious, °lecherous, °wild, libidinous, °lewd, °lascivious, °unchaste: *She is a wanton hussy who is no better than she ought to be.* **2** °abandoned, unrestrained, °undisciplined, ungoverned, °ungovernable, unmanageable, °outrageous, °immoderate, intemperate, untempered: *It is not the boy's fault, it is the wanton company he keeps.* **3** °reckless, °rash, uncaring, °lavish, °extravagant, °wilful, °heedless, °irresponsible, °careless: *This situation arises from the parents' wanton disregard for their children's moral training.* **4** °wicked, °evil, malevolent, malicious, °merciless, inhumane, °vicious, °cruel, °violent, unjustified, unprovoked, uncalled-for, °purposeless, motiveless, unjustifiable, °arbitrary, °gratuitous: *We were subject to wanton attacks by the hill people.*

—*n.* **5** vamp, strumpet, whore, harlot, °loose woman, °prostitute, voluptuary, slut, trollop, Jezebel, *Colloq* °tart, *Slang* hooker, working girl, call-girl: *Who invited that wanton, with her tight-fitting, shamelessly low-cut dress?*

war *n.* **1** warfare, °combat, °conflict, fighting, °clash, hostilities, °battle, °struggle, °engagement, °encounter,

°strife, contention: *The war, in which several millions died, lasted six years.* **2** ***at war***: fighting, battling, in °combat, in °conflict; in °disagreement, in °dispute, in contention, struggling, antagonistic, at daggers drawn: *They are at war because an ambassador refused to retract some silly insult.*
—*v.* **3** do °battle *or* °fight *or* °struggle *or* (°engage in) °combat with *or* against, make *or* °wage war with *or* against, take up arms *or* °strive *or* °campaign *or* °tilt against, cross swords *or* contend *or* joust with: *We must continue to war against the forces of evil.*

ward *n.* **1** °district, °division, °precinct, °section, °zone, °quarter: *Perkin was running for re-election as councillor of the Eastgate ward.* **2** °minor, dependant: *The child was made a ward of the court.*
—*v.* **3** ***ward off***: °fend off, °repel, avert, °avoid, °block, °thwart, keep away *or* off *or* at bay *or* at arm's length, °check, °repulse, °chase away *or* off, °forestall: *This brandy should help ward off the night chill.*

wardrobe *n.* **1** (collection *or* stock of) clothing *or* °clothes *or* attire *or* °apparel: *At the time, my entire wardrobe consisted of a pair of jeans, a shirt, and a dinner suit.* **2** clothes-press, closet, clothes-cupboard: *In her wardrobe they found more than three thousand pairs of shoes.*

warehouse *n.* °storehouse, °store, storeroom, depository, stockroom, depot, go-down: *The books are kept in a warehouse and shipped to customers as needed.*

wares *n.pl.* °merchandise, °goods, commodities, manufactures, °produce, stock-(in-trade), °supplies, °lines: *A blind man peddled his wares on this corner for twenty years.*

warlike *adj.* combative, °belligerent, bellicose, °aggressive, °pugnacious, °hostile, °bloodthirsty; hawkish, militaristic, jingoistic, warmongering: *Violation of the border was a warlike act that must be punished. There are warlike factions in every government.*

warm *adj.* **1** °heated, °tepid, °lukewarm, °cosy, °comfortable, not uncomfortable, balmy: *We chose a beautiful warm day for our picnic.* **2** °passionate, °impassioned, °excited, °animated, °fervent, fervid, °spirited, °lively, °ardent, zealous, °keen, °eager, °emotional, °heated, °intense, irritated, annoyed, vexed, °angry, irate, °furious, °testy, °short-tempered, °touchy, °quick-tempered, irascible, °irritable, °stormy, turbulent, °vigorous, °violent, *Colloq* worked up, °hot under the collar, steamed up: *Charles occasionally became a bit warm on the subject of architecture. The debate grew warm as we joined in.*
3 °amiable, °friendly, °cordial, affable, °pleasant, °genial, °cheerful, °kindly, °hospitable, °hearty; °affectionate, °tender, °mellow, loving, amorous: *After a warm greeting from our host, we went in to meet the other guests. Her generous gifts to charity revealed that she really has a warm heart.* **4** °ardent, °enthusiastic, °earnest, °eager, °sincere: *Our ideas for the new campaign met with warm approval from the client.*
5 uncomfortable, °awkward, unpleasant, °strained, °tense: *The people in this town tend to make things a bit warm for strangers.* **6** Often, ***getting warm***: °close *or* °near to making a discovery, about to make a discovery: *From her look as I approached the cabinet, I knew I was getting warm.*
—*v.* **7** °heat (up), warm up *or* over: *I warmed myself by the fire.* **8** Often, ***warm to***: become less antagonistic *or* hostile to *or* toward(s), become °enthusiastic *or* °supportive of, become °excited *or* °animated about *or* over, be attracted to *or* toward(s), °like, feel °affection for: *Martin never did warm to my idea of using the village notice-board for his message.* **9** °stir, °move, °please, °delight, make (one *or* someone) feel good: *It warmed me to know that she had at last found someone to love.*

warm-blooded *adj.* **1** *Technical* homoeothermic *or* homoeothermal *or* homoiothermic *or* homoiothermal *or* homeothermic *or* homeothermal: *Birds and mammals are warm-blooded, reptiles and fish are cold-blooded.* **2** °passionate, °ardent, fervid, hot-blooded, °impetuous, *Colloq* °randy: *He tried to excuse his behaviour towards her by saying that he was just a normal, warm-blooded man.*

warmly *adv.* **1** affectionately, tenderly, °fondly, lovingly: *Linda kissed him warmly to thank him for the gift.* **2** cordially, amiably, amicably, solicitously, warm-heartedly: *We were greeted warmly by the manager on our arrival and shown to our rooms.*
3 earnestly, eagerly, fervently, enthusiastically, °well, °kindly: *The directors are warmly disposed to your plan for reorganization.* **4** °vigorously, intensely, °fiercely, intensively, °intently, energetically, doggedly, persistently, zealously, fervently, fervidly, °hotly, ardently, enthusiastically: *We learned that she was being warmly pursued by Interpol.* **5** heatedly, vehemently, vociferously, forcefully, energetically, °vigorously, feverishly, frantically, furiously, angrily, violently: *The sending of a peace-keeping force was being warmly debated in the UN.*

warmth *n.* **1** °heat: *We basked in the welcome warmth of the sun.* **2** cordiality, heartiness, friendliness, geniality, amiableness, kindliness, tenderness, affability, °love: *Mother thrives on the warmth of a family environment and should not be put in a nursing home.*
3 °ardour, effusiveness, °enthusiasm, zeal, excitedness, °fervour, vehemence, °vigour, ebullience, °passion: *I was taken aback by the warmth of the stranger's greeting. The resolution was debated with considerable warmth.* **4** irritation, °annoyance, pique: *The warmth of his reaction to the accusation is understandable.*

warn *v.* **1** °caution, admonish, °advise, °notify, apprise, °inform, give (fair) °warning, °alert, give (prior) °notice, put (someone) on °notice *or* on guard *or* on the °alert, make (someone) °aware (of), forewarn, °tip off, *Rare* premonish: *The entire population has been warned about the imminent hurricane.* **2** °advise, °counsel, °caution: *You did warn me against investing in llama farms.*

warning *n.* **1** °caution, admonition, °advice, °counsel, caveat, word (to the wise), °tip, notification, °notice, °threat; °lesson, °example: *Cyril never took seriously his doctor's warning about his cholesterol level. Let that be a warning to you not to drink and drive.* **2** °omen, °sign, °signal, °indication, augury, foretoken, portent, foreshadowing, forewarning, °prophecy: *Sailors take that kind of sky and a falling barometer as warning of a hurricane.*

warp *v.* **1** °twist, contort, °distort, deform, °bend out of shape, °wrench, °pervert, misshape: *Using steam, the timber was warped to fit the hull. You certainly have a warped idea of what Yvette does for a living.*
—*n.* **2** °twist, contortion, distortion, °bias, deformity, deformation, °bend, °wrench, °perversion, °kink, idiosyncrasy, °quirk, deviation: *There is too much of a warp in this veneer to repair it. Harry has to overcome a serious warp in his attitude towards food.*

warrant *n.* **1** authorization, °sanction, °reason, justification, °approval, validation, °licence, °right, certification, entitlement, grounds, °cause, °rationale, °basis, °assurance, *carte blanche*, °guarantee, °pledge, °security, °charter, °warranty: *We demand to know what warrant may exist for such an action.* **2** writ, °order, affidavit, °paper, °document, credential, °permit, entitlement, °licence, summons, subpoena, mandate, °decree, fiat, edict, ukase: *Do not let them search the premises without a warrant. A warrant has been issued for her arrest.*
—*v.* **3** °guarantee, °promise, °assure, °ensure *or* insure, °answer for, be answerable for, °certify, °vouch for, °underwrite, °back up, °uphold, °stand by *or* behind: *All these products are warranted by the manufacturer for one year.* **4** °authorize, °sanction, °justify, °explain, °approve, °verify, validate, °permit, °allow, provide *or* offer grounds *or* justification *or* cause *or* reason for, °call for, necessitate, °entitle, empower, °excuse, °license: *What is it that warrants such accusations of malfeasance?*

warranty *n.* °guarantee, °assurance, °promise, commitment, covenant, °undertaking, °agreement, °pledge, °bond: *There is a maker's warranty that repairs of any defects will be made at no cost to the buyer.*

wary *adj.* °cautious, °careful, on (one's) guard, circumspect, °prudent, apprehensive, chary, watchful, °vigilant, on the qui vive, heedful, °observant, on (one's) toes, *Colloq* cagey, *Slang* °leery (of): *Phoebe is wary of going out with someone she doesn't know.*

wash *v.* **1** °wash up, °clean (up), °cleanse, bathe, °shower, douche, douse, °scrub (up), shampoo, soap up, °lather, °launder, °scour, °soak, °rinse, °flush, °wet, °drench, deterge, sponge (off), *Facetious* perform (one's) ablutions, *Archaic* absterge, *Formal or literary* lave, *Brit* bath: *Please wash the dishes when you have finished eating. I must wash before I do anything else.* **2** Sometimes, ***wash away*** *or* ***out*** *or* ***off***: °remove, °move, °transport, °carry, °bear, convey, °deliver, °deposit, °drive, °sweep: *The silt, with the gold dust, is washed downstream. In this process, the impurities are washed away.* **3** °splash, °spatter, splatter, plash, °dash, °beat, °pound, thrash, °break, °toss, °surge, undulate, °rush, °run, °lap, °ripple, °roll, °flow: *We stood watching the sea washing against the breakwater.* **4** Usually, ***wash away*** *or* ***off***: °erode, °wear off *or* away, °remove, °delete, °erase, expunge, °destroy, eradicate, °obliterate, °extinguish, °blot out, °wipe out: *After 5,000 years, the action of the waves had washed away all traces of the Vengorian civilization.* **5** Often, ***wash away*** *or* ***out***: °erode, °cut *or* °dig *or* °wear *or* °eat *or* dredge (away *or* out), °excavate, °channel: *The river eventually washed out a new course, fifteen miles to the west.* **6** decontaminate, °purify, °sift, °filter, depurate: *The wastes are thoroughly washed in these tanks before being discharged into the ocean.* **7** overlay, °film, °coat, °paint, °glaze; °plate: *What do you think of the colour they washed the wall?* **8** °hold up, °stand up, stand the test of time, carry weight, bear scrutiny, °prove °true, make sense, be believable *or* credible, *Colloq* hold °water: *I'm afraid that Helen's explanation of her whereabouts at the time of the murder simply won't wash.* **9** ***wash down***: °swallow: *Here, wash the pill down with this.* **10** ***wash (one's) hands of***: stay *or* keep away from, disown, °repudiate, turn (one's) °back on, have nothing more *or* further to do with, get °rid of, °rid (oneself) of, °desert, °abandon, °leave: *After Neil took the money, Violet washed her hands of him and his problems.*
—*n.* **11** washing, cleaning, cleansing, scrubbing, °scrub, scouring, shampoo, shampooing, bath, bathing, °shower, sponge bath, tub-bath; laundering; *Facetious* ablutions; *Colloq Brit* tub, tubbing: *He always likes a good wash and shave before breakfast.* **12** °wave, °wake, °surge, backwash: *The wash from passing ships almost swamped our skiff.* **13** °lotion, °rinse, liniment, °salve, embrocation, emulsion, °preparation; mouthwash, gargle; eyewash, collyrium: *Use this wash twice a day till the condition disappears.* **14** °flow, °wave, °swell, welling, °sweep, °sweeping, ebb and flow, °surge, surging, undulation, rise and fall: *Shellfish in the gap cleanse themselves of impurities in the constant tidal wash running through there.* **15** °coat, coating, °film, overlay, °glaze; plating: *There is a microscopic wash of gold over the tin to lend the bracelet a little cachet.*

washed out *adj.* **1** °wan, °pale, pallid, °colourless, faded, °lacklustre, °flat; blanched, bleached, etiolated: *Gene looks washed out because he never gets out in the sun. She was wearing washed-out jeans and a torn t-shirt.* **2** °exhausted, °spent, °tired, °tired out, °weary, °worn out, °fatigued, drained, *Colloq* dog-tired, bone-tired, done in, all in, fagged out, bushed, *Brit* knocked up, *US* knocked out, *Slang* °beat, *US and Canadian* tuckered out, pooped: *After a hard day in the office, I feel completely washed out.*

washed up *adj.* finished, °through, failed, done for, played out, over (and done with), *Slang* kaput, fini: *After that last fiasco, he's no more than a washed-up has-been.*

washout *n.* °failure, °disaster, débâcle, (total) °loss, °fiasco, °disappointment, *Colloq* °flop, °dud, *Brit* damp squib, *US* lead balloon: *His attempts to revive the hula-hoop craze were a washout.*

waspish *adj.* irascible, bad-tempered, foul-tempered, °temperamental, °testy, grouchy, °sensitive, °volatile, °querulous, edgy, °petulant, °spiteful, °peevish, °cantankerous, curmudgeonly, °cross, crabby, crabbed, crotchety, splenetic, grumpy, captious, °cranky, crusty: *Elaine is feeling very waspish today—no one can do anything right.*

waste *v.* **1** squander, °misuse, °throw away, °fritter away, misspend, °splurge, °dissipate, *Slang* °blow: *Why I wasted so much time on him I'll never know. Don't waste your money on such frivolities.* **2** Often, ***waste away***: °diminish, °deteriorate, °dwindle, °decline, °decay, atrophy, wither, °shrink, °weaken, °become debilitated, °fade, °become enervated *or* enfeebled, regress, °ebb, °sink: *She is just wasting away, and I am seriously worried that she may not recover.* **3** °enervate, enfeeble, emaciate, °gnaw, °destroy, °consume, debilitate, °exhaust, disable: *Arkwright contracted a terrible wasting disease while in the tropics.* **4** assassinate, °murder, °kill, *Slang* °put away, °rub out, *US* ice: *Don't worry, Boss, we'll waste Andy and you won't have no more trouble.*
—*n.* **5** °misuse, misapplication, squandering, °dissipation, misemployment, °abuse, °neglect: *What a terrible waste of talent to have such a person doing such lowly work! Do not let that genius go to waste.* **6** wasting, °extravagance, °prodigality, wastefulness, squandering, °indulgence, lavishness, °profligacy, dissoluteness, improvidence, overindulgence: *Government waste is one of our biggest problems.* **7** °refuse, °rubbish, °garbage, °dregs, debris, leavings, °scrap, offscourings, sweepings, °litter, *Archaic* orts, *US and Canadian* °trash: *Techniques are being developed to process the waste in order to avoid using landfills, incineration, or dumping at sea.* **8** wasteland, °desert, wilderness, barrens, °wilds, °emptiness, vastness: *Beyond that system were vast wastes of uninhabited space.*
—*adj.* **9** °extra, °leftover, °unused, °superfluous, °worthless, °useless: *The waste food was usually fed to the animals.* **10** °barren, unproductive, unusable, unsalvageable, °useless, unrecyclable, °unprofitable, °worthless: *The waste products of manufacture are a big problem.* **11** ***lay waste***: °devastate, °destroy, °demolish, despoil, °ruin, °wreck, °ravage, °pillage, °sack, °plunder, °loot, °rob, °strip, °spoil, °gut, °ransack, °wreak °havoc (up)on, °crush, °raze, annihilate, eradicate, extirpate, °wipe out: *These lands and cities, laid waste by the invaders, have never recovered.*

wasteful *adj.* °extravagant, °spendthrift, °profligate, °prodigal, °lavish, °improvident, unthrifty, uneconomical, overindulgent, open-handed, free-handed, penny wise and pound foolish: *It was very wasteful of you to buy me that expensive jewellery.*

wastrel *n.* **1** °spendthrift, °profligate, waster, °prodigal, big spender, squanderer: *That wastrel went through his inheritance in a year.* **2** °idler, layabout, malingerer, °loafer, shirker, °good-for-nothing, ne'er-do-well, *Chiefly Brit* drone, *Slang Brit* skiver: *The workhouse is the place for wastrels like you!*

watch *v.* **1** °observe, °regard, °look at, °gaze at *or* on, °take in, °contemplate: *Daniel loves to watch the bears at the zoo.* **2** °look after, °tend, °mind, keep an °eye on, watch over, °guard, °care for, take °care of, °safeguard, °protect, °shield, keep safe, °supervise, superintend; chaperon, °accompany, °attend; *Colloq* babysit (for), sit (with): *Could you please watch Suzie while I go shopping?* **3** °observe, note, °notice, make *or* take note of, °see, pay °attention (to), °attend (to), °follow, (take) °heed (of), °examine, °inspect, °scrutinize, °pore over; °eye, °peer at; °ogle, make °eyes at: *Watch the way I bone this fish. Ted enjoys watching the* *girls going by.* **4** Often, ***watch (out) for***: °look for, be on the watch *or* °lookout *or* °alert *or* qui vive (for), °guard (against), keep an °eye open (for), be watchful (for), note, take note *or* °notice of, be °vigilant (for *or* of), keep (one's) °eyes open (for), keep a (sharp) °lookout (for), be prepared *or* °ready for, be °careful of, °anticipate, await, °wait (for), *Colloq* keep (one's) °eyes peeled *or* skinned (for), keep a weather °eye open (for): *We were watching for irregularities in the test results. Watch where you're going! Watch out for that last step!* —*n.* **5** vigil, °surveillance, °observation, °lookout: *Our six-hour watch was rewarded by the appearance of a yellow-bellied sapsucker.* **6** clock, timepiece, pocket watch, wrist-watch; chronometer: *I always set my watch by the GMT time signal on the radio.* **7** sentry, °sentinel, °guard, °watchman: *The midnight watch just returned from his rounds.* **8** ***on the watch (for)***: on the °alert (for), on the °lookout (for), on (one's) °guard (for), on the qui vive (for), °alert (for *or* to), °awake (to), °observant (of), watchful (of), °cautious (of), °wary (of), °vigilant, circumspect: *We remained on the watch for the slightest movement in the bushes.*

watchman *n.* (°security) °guard, °sentinel, sentry, °watch, night-watchman, custodian, caretaker; watch-dog: *After retiring from the police, he worked as a watchman.*

water *n.* **1** H_2O; distilled water, °tap water, drinking-water, bottled water, spa water, still water, soda (water), effervescent water, mineral water; sea water, salt water; ditch-water, dishwater, bath-water, *US* branch water, *Facetious* Adam's ale, *Technical or Latin* aqua; *Technical* heavy water *or* deuterium oxide *or* D_2O; *Brit* fizzy water: *Pure water is odourless, tasteless, and colourless.* **2** ***not hold water***: be illogical *or* °unsound *or* °invalid, not be sensible, be °inconsistent, not make sense, be °unbelievable *or* °incredible, be indefensible, be unfeasible *or* unworkable, not work, not function, not hold up under *or* bear scrutiny *or* examination, not ring true, ring false, *Colloq* not °wash: *Her account of her whereabouts that day just doesn't hold water.* **3** ***like water***: lavishly, extravagantly, °freely, wastefully, profligately, open-handedly, liberally, excessively, copiously, unstintingly, unreservedly: *They've been spending money like water since they won the football pools.* **4** ***make water***: °urinate, pass water, *Colloq* pee, piss: *When a dog makes water, it marks off a territory bounded by its scent.* **5** ***of the first water***: of °superior *or* °excellent *or* °first *or* top *or* A-one *or* the finest *or* the highest *or* the °best °quality *or* °grade; first-grade, top-grade: *These were not industrial stones but diamonds of the first water.* —*v.* **6** inundate, °flood, °drench, °saturate, °soak, douse, irrigate, hose, °wet, °shower, °splash, °spray, sprinkle, moisten, °damp, °dampen, bedew: *If you don't water the garden, the vegetables will die.* **7** Often, ***water down***: °dilute, °weaken, °thin out, °adulterate; °cut; mollify, °modify, °soften, °tone down, °qualify: *We no longer go there because they water the drinks. They told the children a watered-down version of what had happened.*

water-colour *n.* aquarelle: *John's water-colours sell as fast as he paints them.*

waterfall *n.* cascade, cataract, °fall(s), °chute, Niagara, *No. Brit* force, *Scots* linn: *In front of them, a waterfall tumbled down a rock-face into a deep pool.*

watertight *adj.* **1** sealed, waterproof: *The escape hatch has been made watertight.* **2** unassailable, °impregnable, °solid, airtight, °flawless, °faultless, °incontrovertible; without °loopholes: *Landry has a watertight alibi for the night of the crime.*

watery *adj.* **1** °weak, °dilute(d), watered down, °tasteless, insipid, flavourless, °bland, °flat, °dull, °thin, runny, pallid, anaemic, *Colloq* °wishy-washy: *He asked me in, then gave me some watery tea to drink.* **2** weeping, teary, °tearful, °running, weepy, lachrymose, rheumy: *The child looked up at him with watery eyes and then collapsed, sobbing.* **3** °wet, swampy, boggy, marshy, aqueous, squelchy; soggy, °moist, °damp, °humid; *Colloq* squushy *or* squooshy: *It took days to make our way across that watery plain to the high ground.*

wave *n.* **1** °swell, undulation, billow, °sea, °heave, °roller, whitecap, white horse; °ripple, wavelet, breaker, comber: *A huge wave tossed me up on the beach.* **2** °surge, °swell, welling up, ground °swell, °movement, °flood, upsurge, °uprising, °current, tide: *The period is marked by a wave of materialism and greed that swamped all morality and integrity.* **3** °signal, °sign, gesticulation, °gesture: *Was his wave intended for you or for me?* —*v.* **4** undulate, billow, °move to and fro, °flap, °flutter, °quiver, flip-flop, °swing, °sway, °ripple, °oscillate, zigzag, °fluctuate, °shake; °wag, whiffle, wigwag, wiggle, waggle, brandish: *The streamer waved slowly in the quickening breeze. Stop waving that knife at me!* **5** °signal, °sign, °indicate, °signify; °gesture, gesticulate: *Hazel waved goodbye from the train.*

way *n.* **1** °manner, °method, °mode, °fashion, °means, °system, °course (of action), procedure, °approach, °scheme, °technique, °practice, modus operandi, *Colloq* MO (= 'modus operandi'): *That's no way to talk to your mother! We have ways of making you talk. Is that any way to treat a lady?! It's the wrong way to deal with the problem.* **2** °manner, °spirit, °feeling, °sense, °character, °approach, °personality, temperament, °disposition, modus vivendi (= 'lifestyle'), °nature, °technique, °style, °conduct, °habit, °behaviour °pattern, °custom: *He has such a pleasant way about him. Lucinda certainly has a way with children and dogs. You city people may not approve of our down-to-earth country ways.* **3** °path, °road, °street, avenue, °course, °route, °trail, °direction: *Show me the way to go home. The way to the village lies through dark woods.* **4** °distance; °route, °trail, °course, °road: *You've come a long way since we last met.* **5** °progress, °passage, °advance, °headway; °speed, °velocity, °motion, (forward) °movement: *We made our way to the front of the crowd. Who has the right of way at the crossing? The tide was too strong for us to get any way on.* **6** °aspect, °respect, °particular, °detail, °point, °sense, °feature: *In certain ways, you remind me of Attila the Hun.* **7** °clearance, pathway, avenue, °scope, °freedom, °opportunity: *When you hear a siren, drive to the side and give way. Make way for the Lord High Executioner!* **8** °condition, °situation: *She prefers the prissy 'in a family way' to the straightforward 'pregnant' and the vulgar 'have a bun in the oven'. I saw Luke yesterday and he was really in a bad way.* **9** ***by the way***: °incidentally, °moreover, by the by, parenthetically: *By the way, have I told you how beautiful you look tonight?* **10** ***by way of***: **a** via, °through, by °means of: *We drove from London to Oxford by way of Reading.* **b** (functioning) as, in (the) way of, in the capacity of, °equivalent to, more or less, something °like: *Richard is by way of being an expert on eccentric behaviour.* **11** ***give way***: **a** °collapse, °break (down), °fail, °cave in, °fall (down), °crumble, °crumple, °disintegrate, go to °pieces: *The cable gave way, causing the bridge to collapse.* **b** °yield, °surrender, °retreat, °concede, °withdraw, accede, make concessions, acquiesce, °acknowledge: *The trouble is that they both think they are in the right and neither will give way.* **12** ***under way***: proceeding, progressing, on the °move, moving, advancing, going, begun, started, in °progress, operating, functioning, at work, *US* in °work, *Colloq* in the works, *US* in the °pipeline: *Once under way, it takes the ship three days to make the crossing. Plans are under way to reclaim the slum area for a park.*

waylay *v.* **1** °ambush, lie in wait for, await, °intercept, °pounce upon *or* on, °swoop down on *or* upon, accost: *You'll have to waylay him on his way to lunch if you want to speak to him.* **2** °attack, °mug, °seize, °assault, accost, °set upon: *He was waylaid by a band of thieves and stripped of his belongings.*

way-out *adj.* **1** °bizarre, °mad, °weird, °crazy, °strange, °odd, °peculiar, freakish, freaky, °eccentric, °queer, °abnormal, °offbeat, °outrageous, °wild, °exotic, esoteric, *Colloq* °kinky, *Slang* kooky, off-the-wall, far-out, screwy, nutty, *US* flaky, screwball: *The police did not take kindly to the boys' way-out behaviour after the party.* **2** °avant-garde, advanced, °original, innovative, °unorthodox, unconventional, °experimental, precedent-setting, °progressive, exploratory, ground-breaking, *Slang* far-out: *Spencer thinks that the way-out art of the 1960s will have great value one day.*

weak *adj.* **1** °feeble, °frail, °fragile, unsubstantial, °flimsy, breakable, frangible, °delicate, °rickety, unsteady, °unsound, °decrepit, °shaky, °infirm: *That chair is too weak for you to stand on.* **2** °frail, °infirm, debilitated, enervated, °delicate, °sickly, anaemic, wasted, °decrepit, °puny, effete, °worn out, °tired, °exhausted: *When I last saw Tindell he was so weak he could hardly lift his brandy glass.* **3** unassertive, °retiring, namby-pamby, °spineless, °irresolute, °impotent, °ineffectual, °ineffective, °incompetent, feckless, °inept, °wishy-washy, °timid, °meek, craven, timorous, °cowardly, pusillanimous, lily-livered, chicken-hearted, *Colloq* chicken, yellow: *We know which is the weaker partner in that marriage, don't we?* **4** °feeble, °lame, half-baked, °poor, °miserable, unconvincing, unpersuasive, °empty, °shallow, °flimsy, °hollow, °pathetic, °pitiful, °unbelievable, °untenable: *Edward made some weak excuse for being late. I found Mona's argument against birth control very weak indeed.* **5** weak-minded, dim-witted, dull-witted, slow-witted, °foolish, °feeble-minded, °simple, simple-minded, soft-headed, °stupid, °dull, moronic, imbecilic, *Colloq* °dumb: *They seek out people of weaker intelligence and make fools of them.* **6** °faint, °dim, °poor, °dull, °pale, faded, °indistinct, °vague, °hazy, °imperceptible, indiscernible, unclear, blurred, blurry, muzzy, wavering, faltering, ill-defined, °feeble, flickering, °subdued: *I could hardly see her face in the weak light of the candle.* **7** °feeble, °subdued, °low, °soft, hushed, muffled, muted, almost °inaudible, stifled, °indistinct: *When the victim finally spoke, his voice was very weak.* **8** See **watery, 1,** above. **9** ***weak point***: See **weakness, 3,** below.

weaken *v.* **1** debilitate, enfeeble, °enervate, emasculate, °mitigate, °moderate, °dilute, deplete, °diminish, lessen, °depress, °lower, °reduce, °sap, °undermine, °exhaust, impoverish: *The continuous torture helped to weaken Errol's resolve.* **2** °fade, °dwindle, °tire, °droop, °sag, fail, give °way, °crumble, °flag: *My determination weakened when I saw what had happened to the children.* **3** °give in, °relent, acquiesce, give °way, °yield, accede, °consent, °agree, assent, °soften, °bend, °ease up, °let up, °ease off, °relax: *If you ask very politely, she might weaken and allow you to go out and play.* **4** °water (down), °dilute, °thin (out): *Adding the water so weakened the soup that it tasted like dishwater.*

weakling *n.* °milksop, °baby, mollycoddle, lightweight, namby-pamby, *US and Canadian* milquetoast, *Colloq* °sissy *or Brit also* cissy, °loser, cream puff, jellyfish, °pushover, softie *or* softy, *Slang* wimp, twerp *or* twirp, *US* weak sister, schnook, schlemiel *or* schlemihl *or* shlemiel: *If you count on a weakling like Geoffrey, nothing will ever get done.*

weakness *n.* **1** feebleness, °frailty, fragility, °delicacy, delicateness, vulnerability, °infirmity, °decrepitude: *They discovered a weakness in the structure of the bridge, so it had to be closed.* **2** incapacity, irresolution, irresoluteness, °impotence, powerlessness, puniness: *He is ashamed of his weakness in being unable to stop smoking.* **3** °weak point, °foible, °failing, °fault, °shortcoming, °flaw, Achilles' heel, °defect, °imperfection, °liability: *Her one great weakness is her inability to deny her children anything.* **4** soft spot, fondness, °affection, °liking, °preference, °bent, °leaning, °inclination, °fancy, °penchant, predilection, proneness, proclivity, predisposition, °partiality, °appreciation, °appetite, sweet tooth, °taste, °eye: *The two of them share a weakness for good food and wine.*

wealth *n.* **1** affluence, °riches, °money, opulence, °prosperity, °property, holdings, °capital, assets, wherewithal, °cash: *Most of their wealth comes from illicit trade in diamonds.* **2** °profusion, °abundance, °bounty, plenteousness, bounteousness, copiousness, °mine, plenitude, fullness, °store, cornucopia, richness: *Janet has a wealth of ideas for situation-comedy plots.*

wealthy *adj.* °rich, affluent, °well off, °prosperous, well-to-do, °opulent, °comfortable, moneyed, *Colloq* in the °money, on Easy Street, °flush, well-heeled, in clover, *Slang* °loaded, stinking (°rich), filthy °rich, quids in, rolling in it: *Bill has a wealthy aunt who sends him a little something now and then.*

wear *v.* **1** be dressed *or* clothed in, °dress in, °put on, don, be in, step *or* °get into *or* in, °have on, °sport: *I shall wear my new suit tonight.* **2** °display, °show, °exhibit, °have, °adopt, °assume: *I wondered why she wore such a curious expression.* **3** Often, ***wear down*** *or* ***away*** *or* ***off***: °damage, °impair, °harm, °fray, °erode, abrade, corrode, °rub (off): *The water has worn down the rocks till they are round and shiny. The inscription on the stone is worn away. After years of use, the paint has worn off.* **4** Often, ***wear well***: °last, °endure, °survive, °hold up, °bear up, °stand up: *I wrote to the makers telling them the shoes have worn well.* **5** °drag, °pass slowly, °creep by *or* along, °go by gradually *or* tediously: *The hours wore on as I waited for the test results.* **6** Often, ***wear out***: °tire, °fatigue, °exhaust, debilitate, °weary, °enervate, °drain, °burden: *You must be worn out from carrying those heavy books.* **7** °bore, °exasperate, °harass, vex, °annoy, °irritate, °tax, °strain: *I find it wearing to listen to that music all day long.*

—*n.* **8** wearing, °use, utilization; attire, garb, clothing, °clothes, °apparel, °dress, °gear: *Did you get much wear out of your new hat? Suzanne is modelling a silver lamé dress for evening wear.* **9** wear and tear, attrition, deterioration, °damage, fraying, chafing, abrasion, °erosion, corrosion, °friction: *As the engine ages, heavier oil is needed to offset the normal wear.*

weary *adj.* **1** °tired, °fatigued, °exhausted, °worn out, drained, °spent, *Colloq* all in, ready to drop, fagged (out), done in, °dead (on (one's) feet), frazzled, °dead °beat, dog-tired, *Brit* knocked up, *US* knocked out, *Slang Brit* whacked, knackered, *US* pooped, zonked (out), shot: *He is so weary after work that he can scarcely eat his dinner.* **2** °boring, °irksome, irritating, °tedious, vexing, annoying, exasperating, °burdensome, wearying, tiring, fatiguing, draining, taxing, wearisome: *We walked many a weary mile before reaching the oasis.* **3** bored, °impatient, °jaded, °blasé, *Colloq* fed up, °sick and °tired, *Taboo slang* browned off: *I wish he would wipe that weary expression off his smug face.*

—*v.* **4** Often, ***weary of***: °tire (of), be *or* become bored (with *or* by) *or* °impatient (with) *or* °jaded (with *or* by), *Colloq* be *or* become fed up (with) *or* °sick and °tired (of): *I soon wearied of her nagging.* **5** °exhaust, °enervate, °fatigue, °tire, debilitate, °drain, °tax, °wear *or* °tire out: *The long trek across country had wearied us all.*

weather *n.* **1** (meteorological) condition(s), °climate: *The weather suddenly changed, and we arrived home cold and wet.* **2** ***under the weather***: ailing, °ill, °sickly, unwell, °indisposed, out of sorts, °sick, *Colloq* °poorly, °seedy: *I didn't go sailing because I was feeling a bit under the weather.*

—*v.* **3** °stand, °survive, °suffer, °bear up against, °endure, °withstand, rise above, ride out, °live through, °brave: *Gemma didn't think she could weather much more sarcasm from the critics.*

weave *v.* **1** °loom; °braid, plait, °entwine, intertwine, interlace, interweave, °knit (together): *These fabrics were woven by hand. Weave these leather strands together to make a belt.* **2** °blend, °combine, °fuse, °merge, °unite, intermingle, °mesh, °splice, dovetail, °join: *The threads of their lives are inextricably woven together.* **3** °construct, °make, contrive, °build, °create, °fabricate, °compose, °spin, °design: *Oh, what a tangled web we weave When first we practise to deceive!* **4** zigzag, criss-cross, wend *or* make (one's) way,

°dodge, bob and weave, °shift: *Look at that motor cyclist weaving in and out of the traffic!* **5** ***get weaving***: get started, get a °move on, °hurry (up), °start, *Colloq* shake a °leg, *Brit* get *or* pull (one's) °finger out, *Chiefly US* get a wiggle on: *If you're going to get to work on time, you'd best get weaving.*

web *n.* spider's web, cobweb; °net, °network, entanglement, °snare, °trap: *Don't you just hate getting those webs in your hair? She became entangled in a web of deception.*

wed *v.* **1** °marry, espouse, get married, become husband and wife, say *or* take (one's) (°marriage) vows, °join *or* °unite in holy wedlock *or* matrimony; lead down the aisle, lead to the altar, *Archaic* wive; *Colloq* tie the knot, get hitched, get spliced: *They were wed on the fourth of July, 1921. That was when Harry wed Annabel.* **2** °combine, °unite, °ally, °marry, °blend, °merge, °join, °mingle, intermingle, commingle, coalesce, °mix, intermix, °amalgamate, °compound, °alloy, °fuse, homogenize: *As a chef, he is extremely fortunate to be able to wed business to pleasure.*

wedded *adj.* Usually, ***wedded to***: intimately *or* obstinately °attached *or* connected (to), enamoured (of): *He has always been wedded to the notion of living alone on an island.*

wedding *n.* **1** °marriage (ceremony), wedding ceremony, nuptials; confarreation: *Our son's wedding was attended by members of the royal family.* **2** combining, °combination, uniting, °union, joining, °juncture, blending, °blend, allying, °alliance, associating, °association, marrying, °marriage, merging, °merger, mingling, intermingling, commingling, coalescing, coalescence, mixing, °mixture, intermixing, amalgamating, °amalgamation, compounding, °compound, alloying, °alloy, fusing, fusion, homogenizing, homogenization: *Through her wedding of vision to observation she has produced some truly remarkable paintings.*

wedge *n.* **1** °block, chock: *A shoe with a wedge heel is called a 'wedgie'. We forced wedges into the cracks in the stone to split it.* **2** °separation, separator, °division, °partition, °split, fissure, cleavage: *That woman tried to drive a wedge between me and my husband.*
—*v.* **3** °ram, °jam, °stuff, °cram, °crowd, °force, °squeeze, °pack, °thrust: *You couldn't have wedged another person into the back seat of that Mini with a shoehorn.*

wee *adj.* **1** °tiny, °small, °diminutive, °little, minuscule, midget, °minute, °miniature, Lilliputian, microscopic, *Colloq* itty-bitty, itsy-bitsy, teeny(-weeny), teensy-weensy: *Johnny caught his wee little finger in the door.* **2** unimportant, °insignificant, trivial, °little, °puny: *It was only a wee thing, of no interest to anyone but me.*

weep *v.* **1** °cry, °shed tears, °bawl, blubber, °keen, sob, °lament, °mourn, °bemoan, °bewail, °moan, °grieve, whine, whimper, mewl, pule, °snivel, *Colloq* blub, boohoo, *Brit and Australian* whinge: *A small child, sitting by herself, was weeping bitterly.* **2** °ooze, seep, exude, °drip: *The wound had started weeping and needed bandaging.*

weigh *v.* **1** Sometimes, ***weigh in at*** *or* ***out at***: *Colloq* tip the scales at: *The sailboard weighed in at 250 pounds. I weigh more than I should.* **2** °consider, °ponder, °contemplate, °think on *or* over *or* about, °mull over, °turn over in the *or* (one's) mind, ruminate over, °chew over, °reflect on *or* upon, °brood over, °pore over, °study, °examine: *After weighing the qualifications of the candidates, we voted for you. Weigh your words carefully before responding.* **3** °judge, °estimate, assess, °evaluate, value, °determine: *It is not easy to weigh each person's contribution to the effort.*
4 Usually, ***weigh on*** *or* ***upon***: °lie heavy on, °burden, °depress, °prey on, °oppress, °disturb, °perturb, °upset: *Loneliness weighs heavily on Dave's widow.* **5** °matter, °count, have (an) °effect *or* °influence, carry °weight, be of value *or* °account, *Colloq* cut any ice: *Certain factors—like the sizes of the bribes—are likely to weigh heavily with the judges of this particular beauty contest.* **6** ***weigh down***: °burden, overburden, °load, °overload, °encumber, °tax, overtax, °strain, °trouble, °worry, °depress, °oppress: *He's been weighed down by financial worries since losing his job.*

weight *n.* **1** heaviness, avoirdupois, °mass, tonnage, *Dialect* heft: *They sell peaches by weight but melons are individually priced. The weight of these books must be enormous.* **2** °burden, °load, millstone, onus, °pressure, °strain, albatross, °cross: *He has to support the weight of the entire family's expenses.* **3** °influence, °authority, °power, °substance, °force, °moment, °importance, consequence, °impact, persuasiveness, value, °worth, *Colloq* clout: *Clyde brought down his full weight in favour of the liberal candidate. Clyde's opinion carries little weight with me. He must stop throwing his weight around.* **4** °mass, °majority, °preponderance *or* preponderancy, °bulk, °superiority: *The weight of the voters is in favour of reducing taxes. The weight of the evidence is against us.*
—*v.* **5** °load, °charge, ballast: *The policemen's truncheons are weighted with lead.* **6** °arrange, °manipulate, °bias, °incline, °slant, *Colloq* °rig: *The statistics are weighted so as to make the advertiser's product look superior.*

weighty *adj.* **1** °heavy, °ponderous, °massive, °huge, °bulky, °substantial, °ample, °large, mammoth, °colossal, °immense, °enormous, °gigantic, °prodigious; corpulent, °fat, °obese, adipose, *Colloq* °hefty: *I found myself face to face with a rather weighty gentleman who was blocking the doorway.* **2** °important, consequential, °significant, °momentous, °grave, °crucial, °portentous, thought-provoking, °provocative: *These are weighty matters and should be handled with circumspection.* **3** °influential, convincing, °persuasive, °impressive, °telling, °powerful, °potent, °leading; °forceful: *Weighty arguments have been put forward in support of these proposals.*

weird *adj.* °strange, °odd, °peculiar, °bizarre, °unnatural, °eerie, °queer, °grotesque, freakish, °outlandish, uncanny, °unearthly, other-worldly, °supernatural, preternatural, *Literary* eldritch, *Colloq* spooky, freaky, °kinky, *Slang* far-out, °way-out: *There was something decidedly weird about the creature at the door.*

weirdo *n.* °eccentric, °madman, madwoman, lunatic, °psychotic, *Colloq* °crazy, weirdie, nutcase, oddball, queer fish, °crank, *Slang* °freak, loony, psycho, *Brit* nutter, *US* screwball, nut, kook: *Why belong to a club whose members are weirdos who refuse to talk to one another?*

welcome *v.* **1** °greet, °hail, °meet, °receive, °accept, offer °hospitality (to): *Everywhere she went she was welcomed with open arms.*
—*adj.* **2** accepted, °acceptable, well-received, °desirable, °agreeable, gratifying, appreciated: *Norma is always a welcome guest at my house. Ice-cream was a welcome relief from the perennial plum duff.* **3** freely permitted *or* allowed, invited, entitled, suffered: *At that hotel, guests are welcome to dine when they please.*
—*n.* **4** °reception, °greeting, salutation: *We gave the ambassador a warm welcome.*

weld *v.* **1** °unite, °combine, °merge, °fuse, °connect, °link, °join; solder, braze, °cement, °bond: *We felt welded together in a brotherhood that would last forever. The brace must be welded all the way along the edge.*
—*n.* **2** °seam, °joint, °juncture, commissure: *The weld must be filed down smooth.*

welfare *n.* °benefit, °good, °advantage, well-being, °prosperity, (good) °fortune, °profit, °interest, (good) °health, °happiness, felicity: *It is up to the parents to look after their children's welfare.*

well[1] *adv.* **1** satisfactorily, sufficiently, adequately, agreeably, nicely, (well) enough, *Colloq* °OK *or* okay: *Alan is doing well these days.* **2** successfully, °famously, marvellously, wonderfully, fabulously, incredibly, splendidly, admirably, spectacularly, excellently, superbly: *Barbara and David really get along well together.* **3** articulately, understandably, expressively, correctly, accurately, °properly, proficiently, effectively, artistically, poetically; grammatically: *Henry will make a good announcer because he speaks well.* **4** comfortably, luxuriously, prosperously, extravagantly, showily, pretentiously, ostentatiously, sumptuously, grandly, opulently: *How can Rita live so well with no visible income? Living well is the best revenge.* **5** graciously, °kindly, °highly, °favourably, glowingly, approvingly, °warmly, genially, cordially, amiably, kind-heartedly, warm-heartedly, affectionately, lovingly: *Rudolph has always spoken well of you, Aileen.* **6** skilfully, expertly, adeptly, proficiently, ably: *Does Anne play well enough to compete professionally? Paul sings well.* **7** °far, by a long way, immeasurably, (°very) much; °far and away, °definitely, °positively, °obviously, °clearly, plainly, °manifestly, °evidently, unquestionably, decidedly, beyond (the shadow of a) doubt, *Colloq* by a long chalk: *Keep well away from the fuel tank before lighting that cigarette. She is well beyond the beginner stage. This painting is well worth what you paid.* **8** good-naturedly, equably, coolly, serenely, calmly, soberly, unexcitedly, sedately: *Burt took the bad news about his car very well.* **9** °likely, °probably, in all probability, doubtlessly, without doubt, not unexpectedly, °indeed: *He might well say he needs no help.* **10** °easily, without difficulty: *Though he gave her the money, he could not well spare it.* **11** °completely, °entirely, °wholly: *Before she could well finish her sentence, he was out of the house.* **12** °thoroughly (cooked), (cooked) through and through, °completely (cooked): *He likes his roast beef well done.* **13** intimately, closely, familiarly, °personally; °thoroughly, °profoundly, soundly, fully: *Do you know Boris well? I learnt my lesson well.* **14** °fairly, justly, suitably, °properly, adequately, reasonably, fully, generously, °amply: *James is well paid for his work.* **15** °happily, mercifully, fortunately, luckily: *After the divorce, both said they were well rid of each other.*

—*adj.* **16** °healthy, °fit, °hale, °robust, °vigorous, °hearty, in fine *or* good fettle, *Colloq* in good shape: *Wendy felt really well after her holiday.* **17** °satisfactory, °pleasing, °agreeable, °good, °right, all °right, °fine, °proper, °OK *or* okay: *When he phoned the office, they told him all was well.*

well[2] *n.* **1** well-spring, °spring, °fountain, well-head, fountain-head, fount, °source, reservoir: *The well provided a constant supply of cool clear water.*

—*v.* **2** Often, ***well up*** *or* ***out*** *or* ***forth***: °flow, °spring, °surge, °rise, °stream, °trickle, °brim over, °swell, °start; °gush, °spurt, jet, °spout; °ooze, seep, °leak: *Tears welled up in the child's eyes when she saw the broken doll.*

well-advised *adj.* °prudent, °wise, °sensible, °intelligent, °smart: *You would be well-advised to avoid Chichicastenango at this time of year.*

well-balanced *adj.* **1** °rational, °sane, °sensible, °reasonable, °level-headed, °sober, °sound, well-adjusted, °cool(-headed), *Slang* together: *Ray is as well-balanced as people seem to be these days.* **2** °even, symmetrical, °harmonious, well-proportioned, °orderly, well-ordered, well-disposed: *Note the well-balanced arrangement of the windows in this Palladian façade.*

well-bred *adj.* °well brought up, well-mannered, °polite, °decorous, mannerly, °refined, °courteous, °cultivated, °polished, cultured, gentlemanly, °ladylike, °elegant, °suave, urbane, °sophisticated, °gracious, courtly, °genteel, °gallant, °chivalrous: *Jane prefers bikers to the well-bred gentlemen her mother selects for her.*

well-established *adj.* long-standing, °traditional, °set, °venerable, °well-known, accepted, well-founded: *He works for a well-established firm of solicitors. It's a well-established fact that the English discuss the weather a lot.*

well-fed *adj.* °plump, chunky, thickset, °chubby, rounded, °rotund, portly, °stout, fleshy, overweight, adipose, °fat, °obese, °gross, *Brit* podgy *or US* pudgy: *On the westward crossing we were seated with a well-fed Austrian couple.*

well-groomed *adj.* °neat, °dapper, °fastidious, °tidy, °trim, °smart, clean-cut, °spruce, natty, well-dressed, *Colloq* °nifty, *Slang US and Canadian* spiffy: *Well-groomed gentleman sought as escort to attractive widow.*

well-informed *adj.* °knowledgeable, °learned, well-read, well-versed, well-educated, literate, °educated, *Colloq* in the °know, °wise, *US* vibrating on the right frequency, *Slang* °hip *or* hep: *With access to all the media, what excuse have you for not being well-informed?*

well-known *adj.* **1** known, °familiar, (°well-)established, acknowledged, °customary, °everyday: *Plain salt is a well-known remover of wine stains.* **2** °famous, °noted, °notable, °celebrated, °renowned, °illustrious, famed, °prominent, °eminent, °pre-eminent: *The scandal linked a former Cabinet Minister with several well-known City names.*

well off *adj.* °comfortable, °wealthy, °rich, affluent, °prosperous, well-to-do, *Colloq* well-heeled, *US* well-fixed: *They are well off and live in a charming house on the edge of the Cotswolds.*

well-thought-of *adj.* admired, °highly regarded, respected, °reputable, venerated, esteemed, revered, looked-up-to, valued: *Timothy is a well-thought-of member of the community.*

well-timed *adj.* °timely, °seasonable, °opportune, auspicious, °favourable, °advantageous, °beneficial: *Tax incentives gave a well-timed boost to the economy.*

welsher *n.* non-payer, °cheat, cheater, °swindler, *Slang* dead-beat, *US* welcher: *That welsher never paid the money he lost to me at poker.*

welt *n.* **1** bead, °ridge, °seam, °edge, wale, °stripe: *The cushion has a welt of contrasting colour binding it.* **2** °bruise, contusion, °bump, °lump, °scar, weal *or* wale *or* wheal: *The boy's back was covered with red welts where he had been birched.*

welter *n.* **1** °mass, °mess, °jumble, °tangle, °confusion, °mishmash, °muddle, °clutter, *Brit* °hotchpotch *or US also* hodgepodge: *Her assignment was to sort out a welter of discarded clothing for the poor. My mind was assailed by a welter of disorganized images.*

—*v.* **2** be sunk *or* °involved in, °flounder, be bogged down in, be entangled *or* ensnarled in: *Till I found a new secretary, I would have to continue weltering in a sea of correspondence and unfiled papers.*

wet *adj.* **1** °moist, moistened, °damp, dampened, soaked, °soaking, sopping, wringing, dripping, sodden, soppy, saturated, drenched: *During the rainy season, the ground is far too wet for planting.* **2** rainy, raining, teeming, pouring, drizzling, showery: *We have had a very wet spring this year.* **3** °feeble, °weak, °irresolute, effete, namby-pamby, °foolish, °ineffectual, °ineffective, °spineless, timorous, °cowardly: *She considered some of her colleagues too wet to take the tough action needed.*

—*n.* **4** moisture, °water, wetness, dampness, °damp, humidity, °liquid: *The wet stood out on his forehead.* **5** °rain, wetness, °mist, dew, °fog, °damp, humidity: *Come in out of the wet, and warm yourself by the fire.* **6** °milksop, softie *or* softy, lightweight, *Colloq* °drip, °loser, *Brit* weed, *Slang* wimp, *US* weak sister: *Why is he such a wet about standing up for his rights?*

wheedle *v.* °coax, °cajole, inveigle, °charm, °beguile, °persuade, °talk; butter up; *Colloq* con, sweet-talk: *Irena always managed to wheedle someone into taking her dancing.*

wheel *n.* **1** disc, °ring, annulus, °circle, hoop: *It seems odd that no culture in the western hemisphere ever invented the wheel.*

—*v.* **2** °spin, °turn, veer, °swivel, °pivot, °swing, whirl: *Medusa wheeled to face him and he promptly turned to stone.*

whereabouts *n.pl.* or *sg.* **1.** location, position, place, site, situation, locale, neighbourhood, vicinity: *Her*

present whereabouts are unknown to me. The culprit concealed his whereabouts from the police.
—*adv.* **2** where, in *or* at *or* to what °place, whither: *Whereabouts are you going to spend your holiday? Whereabouts are you going?*

whet *v.* **1** °sharpen, hone, °grind, °file, put an °edge on, strop: *He whetted the knife on an oiled stone till it was razor-sharp.* **2** pique, °sharpen, °awaken, °arouse, °stimulate, °kindle, °fire, °increase, °excite, °enhance: *The cruise on Bill's yacht whetted my appetite to own a small sailing-boat.*

whimsical *adj.* **1** °quaint, fey, °fanciful, °odd, °curious, °unusual, chimerical, °queer, °singular, °peculiar, °funny, °fantastic(al), pixyish, °playful, puckish, °absurd, °preposterous, *Colloq* °offbeat: *When Andrew's whimsical drawings caught on they were bought by greetings card makers.* **2** °capricious, °erratic, °eccentric, wavering, °flighty, °unsettled, °fickle, mercurial, fluctuating, unpredictable, °inconsistent, °volatile, unsteady: *The buses in our village run on what could best be termed a whimsical timetable.*

whip *v.* **1** °beat, thrash, °lash, °flog, horsewhip, °scourge, °switch, cane, birch, flagellate, leather, °spank, strap; °castigate, °chastise, °punish, °discipline; *Slang* tan, *US* wale: *They learnt right from wrong because father whipped them when they were wrong.* **2** trounce, °defeat, °beat, °conquer, °overwhelm, °rout, °overcome, °overpower, °thwart, °check, °best, worst, drub, °stop, °outdo, *Colloq* lick, wipe the floor with, °batter, *Slang* °pulverize, clobber, °destroy, °ruin, °murder, °slaughter, °kill, squash, smash, *US* cream: *Karpilova whipped O'Meara 6-0, 6-2 at today's match.* **3** °run, scamper, scoot, °race, °scurry, °scramble, °hurry, °flit, °rush, °dash, dart, *Colloq* zip, zoom, skedaddle: *I whipped round the corner and dived behind a tree to hide.* **4** °beat, °whisk, °fluff up: *Whip the egg-whites till they are stiff.* **5** *Nautical* seize, °bind, °wind, °fasten, °tie: *The end of the line is whipped to prevent its unravelling.* **6** ***whip out***: °yank out, °jerk out, °pull (out), °whisk out, °present, °exhibit, °flash, °produce: *He suddenly whipped out a gun and started shooting.* **7** ***whip up***: **a** °stir up, °agitate, °arouse, °rouse, °work up, °excite, °incite: *The rabble-rousers whipped the crowd into a frenzy.* **b** °improvise, put together *or* °assemble *or* °prepare °quickly *or* hurriedly, *Colloq* knock together, °knock up, *US* slap together: *Tina whipped up a snack while we were waiting for Ken to arrive.*
—*n.* **8** °scourge, knout, °lash, cat-o'-nine-tails, rawhide, quirt, horsewhip, bull-whip, cane, birch, °switch, thong, (riding-)crop, *Colloq* cat: *We dreaded it when Dr Hazen eyed the whip hung behind the classroom door.*

whipping *n.* **1** beating, °thrashing, lashing, flogging, horsewhipping, scourging, switching, caning, birching, flagellation, °spanking: *Once he had had a whipping, the boy would not misbehave again.* **2** *Nautical* seizing, binding, tying, winding, fastening: *The whipping will prevent the end of the line from unravelling.*

whirlpool *n.* maelstrom, vortex, °eddy, whirl, °swirl, *Heraldry* gurges: *As we watched in horror, the canoe was drawn down into the whirlpool and disappeared.*

whirlwind *n.* **1** waterspout, dust devil, cyclone, typhoon, anticyclone, °hurricane, extra-tropical cyclone, tropical cyclone, *Nontechnical* tornado, *Nautical* white squall, *Australian* willy-willy, *Colloq US* whirly: *A whole row of houses was destroyed in the whirlwind.*
—*adj.* **2** °speedy, °quick, °swift, °sudden, °precipitous, lightning, headlong, °hasty, °rash, °impetuous: *It was one of those whirlwind romances that last till the wind dies down.*

whisk *v.* **1** °rush, dart, °sweep, °brush: *Agatha whisked about the room, aimlessly moving small objects about on tables and shelves.* **2** °speed, °rush, °carry, °whip, °hasten, °hustle, °hurry: *The taxi came and whisked Fran off to the airport.* **3** See **whip, 4,** above.
—*n.* **4** °sweep, °wave, °brush, flick: *With a whisk of his hand he dismissed the servants.* **5** °brush, fly-whisk: *The chief flicked his whisk to signal that the audience was ended.* **6** beater, °whip: *It is quicker to whip cream with a whisk.*

whisky *n.* whiskey, °alcohol, spirits, John Barleycorn, usquebaugh, Scotch, home-brew, mother's ruin (= 'gin'), *Scots* barley-bree, *US* rye, bourbon, white lightning, white mule, °moonshine, *Colloq* °booze, hooch, rot-gut, *US* corn, fire-water, *Slang US* Sneaky Pete, smoke: *Peter is a welcome guest who always remembers to bring a bottle of whisky.*

whisper *v.* **1** °breathe, °murmur, °mutter, °mumble, °hiss, °speak *or* °say softly *or* under (one's) breath, °sigh, susurrate: *He whispered sweet nothings in her ear.* **2** °gossip, bruit about, °noise abroad, °murmur, °insinuate, °hint, °rumour, °disclose, divulge, °reveal, °breathe a word: *We have all heard Corin whispering of your wife's infidelities.*
—*n.* **3** °murmur, undertone, hushed tone(s): *Why do you always speak in whispers when talking about Nesta?* **4** °hint, °suggestion, soupçon, °suspicion: *There was never the slightest whisper of gossip about Eleanor.*

white *adj.* **1** snow-white, snowy, chalk-white, chalky, ivory, creamy, milky, milk-white, oyster-white, off-white; °silver, hoary: *Many buildings in the tropics are painted white. Do you believe that a person's hair can turn white overnight?* **2** °pale, pallid, °pasty, °wan, whey-faced, ashen, bloodless, drained, whitish, waxen, °ghastly, °ghostly, anaemic, °dead white, deathly white, cadaverous, corpse-like: *Her black dress contrasted starkly with her white complexion.* **3** °innocent, °pure, unsullied, stainless, unblemished, °spotless, °immaculate, virginal, °virtuous, undefiled, °chaste: *She came to you with white hands, which you have sought to dirty with your vicious accusations.* **4** Caucasian, Caucasoid, light-skinned, fair-skinned, pale-complexioned: *The American Indian was—and still is—treated very unfairly by the White man.*

whitewash *v.* °gloss over, °cover up, sugar-coat, °hide, °camouflage, °conceal, °qualify, °minimize, extenuate, °diminish, °play down, downplay, make °light of, °rationalize, °excuse: *We are being accused of whitewashing the dishonest actions of the previous administration.*

whittle *v.* **1** °pare (down *or* away), °shave, °trim, °cut, °carve, hew, °shape: *Remember when Grandpapa used to whittle those tiny figures of elves when we were children?* **2** Usually, ***whittle away at*** *or* ***down***: °pare, °shave, °cut, °trim, °reduce, °diminish, °erode, °eat away at: *If he keeps whittling away at his trust fund, he might have to get a job.*

whole *adj.* **1** °entire, °complete, uncut, °full, °intact, unbroken, °total: *I can't believe she ate the whole chicken. Were you here the whole time?* **2** in °one piece, °intact, unharmed, undamaged, °unscathed, unimpaired, unhurt, uninjured: *How could anyone emerge whole from that smash-up?* **3** °well, °healthy, °sound, °fit, °strong: *The surgeons have made him whole again.*
—*n.* **4** °everything, aggregate, (°sum) °total, °totality, °lot, °entirety; °ensemble; *Colloq* whole kit and caboodle: *I look at the whole and don't bother about petty details.* **5** ***on the whole***: °largely, mostly, °usually, more often than not, for the most part, in °general, °generally, by and large, with few exceptions, all things considered, all in all, as a rule, °chiefly, °mainly, in the °main, predominantly: *On the whole, our clients collect only originals, not copies or prints.*

wholehearted *adj.* °devoted, dedicated, committed, °earnest, °sincere, °unqualified, °unmitigated, unreserved, °complete, °entire, unstinting, °real, °true, °genuine, °hearty, °heartfelt, °serious, °enthusiastic, zealous, °warm, °fervent, °ardent, °spirited, °eager, °energetic: *Once I agree to help, you can rely on my wholehearted support.*

wholesome *adj.* **1** healthful, °healthy, health-giving, °nutritious, nourishing, °beneficial, °tonic, salutary, salubrious, strengthening, °bracing, °stimulating: *Everyone should regularly engage in wholesome exercise.* **2** °moral, °ethical, °righteous, °upright, °honourable, °decent, °principled, °proper, °fit, °meet: *I am not sure that the child is being brought up in a wholesome atmosphere.*

wholly *adv.* **1** °altogether, °entirely, °absolutely, °quite, °totally, °thoroughly, °completely, *in toto*, fully, in all respects, in every way, all in all, °utterly, unqualifiedly, every inch, 100%; lock, stock, and barrel; root and branch; backwards and forwards; from the ground up; *Colloq* bag and baggage; °hook, line, and sinker; to the nth degree; (the) °whole hog, *US* up one side and down the other: *We are wholly on your side in this matter. The company has been wholly reorganized.* **2** °only, exclusively, solely, unexceptionally, categorically, unequivocally, unambiguously, explicitly: *The success or failure of the plan depends wholly on you.*

whoop *n.* **1** °shout, °shriek, °yell, °roar, °bellow, hoot, (battle *or* war) °cry, war-whoop, °outcry, °scream, screech, squeal, yelp, yowl, °howl, bark; °cheer, hurrah, huzzah; *Colloq* holler: *At his whoop of joy we knew he had passed the exam.*
—*v.* **2** °shout, °shriek, °yell, °roar, °bellow, hoot, °cry (out), °scream, screech, squeal, yelp, yowl, °howl, bark; °cheer, hurrah, huzzah; *Colloq* holler: *He heard the tribesmen whooping as they descended on the fort.*

whopping *adj.* **1** °huge, °great, °enormous, °colossal, °gigantic, °immense, tremendous, °prodigious, °monstrous, °thumping, mammoth, °massive, Brobdingnagian: *With that whopping Great Dane of yours in the kitchen there's no room to move about.* **2** °flagrant, °outrageous, °extravagant, °terrible, °awful: *Jones tells such whopping lies I don't know when to believe him.*

wicked *adj.* **1** °evil, °bad, °immoral, amoral, unprincipled, °sinful, °impious, irreligious, °blasphemous, °profane, °sacrilegious, °ungodly, °godless, °diabolic(al), °satanic, Mephistophelian, demonic, demoniac(al), hellish, °infernal, accursed, °damnable, °fiendish, °ghoulish: *How wicked must one be to murder one's own child? She has done many wicked things, but this was the worst.* **2** depraved, °dissolute, °villainous, black-hearted, iniquitous, °horrible, horrid, °hideous, heinous, °beastly, °base, °low, °vile, debased, °degenerate, °perverse, °perverted, °corrupt, °foul, °offensive, °abominable, °disgraceful, °shameful, °dreadful, °awful, °gross, °gruesome, °grim, appalling, °grisly, °loathsome, °lawless, °unrepentant, unregenerate, °incorrigible, °criminal, felonious, rascally, knavish, °terrible, egregious, execrable: *The Deluge was regarded as divine vengeance on a wicked world. He was a wicked man, in league with the devil himself.* **3** °dirty, °pornographic, °filthy, °erotic, °obscene, °lewd, °offensive, °indecent, °prurient, smutty, °rude, °taboo, °blue, °coarse, °bawdy, °vulgar, salacious, licentious, °nasty, X-rated, *Colloq US* raunchy: *The townspeople took the wicked books and burnt them all.* **4** °vicious, °beastly, °savage, °nasty, °bad, °violent, °mean, °cruel: *Graham has a wicked temper. The boys were subjected to the most wicked treatment.* **5** °naughty, °mischievous, impish, °sly, °devilish, rascally, roguish, scampish, puckish; vexatious, exasperating, annoying, irritating, °irksome, °trying, galling, bothersome: *What trouble have those wicked children got themselves into now? It is wicked of you to make pig noises every time I mention Bertha.* **6** °foul, °offensive, pernicious, baleful, mephitic, °disgusting, °revolting, sickening, °repulsive, °repellent, °nauseous, °repugnant, °rotten, pestilential, noxious: *That liniment the doctor prescribed has a wicked odour.* **7** °expert, °ingenious, °superior, °superb, °superlative, °outstanding, °masterful, masterly, °skilful, deft, °adept: *That chap Gough plays a wicked game of tennis.*

wide *adj.* **1** °spacious, °roomy, °ample, °extensive, °broad: *The road is wide enough for two cars to pass. If the book is set in wider type, it will have more pages.* **2** °broad, °extensive, °comprehensive, °encyclopedic *or* encyclopaedic, °inclusive, far-reaching, wide-ranging, widespread: *He has wide interests, from music to archaeology to sport.* **3** °extreme, °considerable, °substantial, sizeable, °major, °big, °large; widespread: *There have been wide fluctuations in market prices.* **4** ***wide of the mark***: off the °mark, astray, °deviant, deviating, off (the) °target, not on °target, °inappropriate: *Forecasts from analysts were based on erroneous assumptions and proved to be very wide of the mark.*
—*adv.* **5** astray, afield, wide of the °mark, off the °mark, off (the) °target, to one side: *He took careless aim and the shot went wide.* **6** all the way, as much as °possible, fully, °completely, to the utmost: *The dentist said, 'Open wide'. When I heard the drill, I was suddenly wide awake.*

widely *adv.* **1** extensively, °thoroughly, °universally, °everywhere, °generally, by °many: *In the days when it was widely believed that the earth was flat, perhaps it was.* **2** to a °large *or* a °great extent, greatly, °largely, °very much, °extremely, considerably, °substantially: *Opinions differ widely regarding the origin of the universe.*

widen *v.* distend, dilate, °spread, °stretch, °enlarge, °increase, °expand; °extend, broaden, °supplement, °add to, augment: *It will be necessary to widen the opening to allow insertion of the device. We are planning to widen the news coverage we provide our readers.*

width *n.* **1** °breadth, wideness, compass, broadness, °span; diameter, °calibre, °bore; °measure; *Nautical* °beam: *What is the standard width of railway track in this country? The width of the cannon-ball is three inches.* **2** °reach, °scope, °range, °breadth, °extent, extensiveness: *There is an impressive width of choice at the restaurant.*

wield *v.* **1** °flourish, °swing, brandish, °wave, °handle, °use, °employ: *He wields that machete as if he means business.* **2** °exercise, °have, °employ, °exert, °use, utilize: *Since Juan is the one who wields the power, he is the one to deal with.*

wife *n.* °mate, helpmeet, helpmate, spouse, bride, °partner, *Colloq* better half, little woman, the missis *or* missus, old lady *or* woman, ball and chain, *Slang* trouble and strife: *Doesn't your wife mind your going out every night?*

wild *adj.* **1** undomesticated, °untamed, unbroken, °savage, feral: *The only four-legged animals inhabiting the island were wild pigs.* **2** uncultivated, °uninhabited, °waste, °desert, °desolate, virgin, unpopulated, °empty, °trackless, °barren, °lifeless; °deserted: *The cottage overlooks an expanse of wild moorland.* **3** °savage, °uncivilized, barbarous, °primitive, °rude, uncultured, uncultivated, brutish, barbaric, °fierce, °ferocious: *Some early explorers studied the wild people they encountered in far-off lands.* **4** °uncontrolled, unrestricted, unrestrained, untrammelled, unbridled, unfettered, unshackled, °free, unchecked, °lively, °impetuous, unconventional, °undisciplined, °disobedient, °insubordinate, °self-willed, wayward, °mutinous, °rowdy(ish), °boisterous, °unruly, °tumultuous, turbulent, °tempestuous, °uproarious; uncontrollable, unmanageable, °ungovernable, intractable, unrestrainable: *Peter led quite a wild youth. We cannot cope with their wild behaviour after they have had too much to drink.* **5** °mad, °maniac(al), crazed, °crazy, irrational, distracted, frenzied, °frantic, °distraught, °hysterical, °raving, raging, unhinged, demented, °delirious; °berserk; run amok *or* amuck: *William had a wild look about him. Nellie has been driven wild by the pressures of business.* **6** °exciting, °excited, vehement, °passionate, °romantic, turbulent, °chaotic, °tempestuous, °reckless, madcap: *At the time, Ernest was having a wild love affair with Charles's widow.* **7** °absurd, irrational, °unreasonable, °extravagant, °fantastic, °imprudent, °foolish, °foolhardy, °impractical, °impracticable, unpractical, unworkable, °ridiculous, °reckless, °silly, °giddy, °flighty, madcap, °outrageous, °preposterous, °bizarre, °strange, °odd, °peculiar, *Colloq* °offbeat: *He lost thousands on some* *wild scheme for reducing shipping costs by filling bubble packing with helium.* **8** tousled, wind-blown, °unkempt, dishevelled, °untidy, disordered, °disorderly, messed-up, *Colloq* mussed-up: *Her hair was in wild disarray.* **9** °enthusiastic, avid, °eager, °agog, *Colloq* °crazy, °mad, °daft, dotty, *Brit* potty, *Slang* nutty, nuts: *I'm just wild about Harry, And Harry's wild about me.*

—*n.* **10** Usually, ***wilds***: wasteland, wilderness, °desert, vastness, °emptiness, *Colloq* °sticks, middle of nowhere, back of beyond: *His idea of adventure was to trek through the wilds of Hyde Park.*

wile *n.* Often, ***wiles***: °trick, °stratagem, °ruse, °artifice, °subterfuge, °dodge, °trap, °snare, °manoeuvre, ploy, contrivance, °move, gambit, °plot, °scheme, °machination, *Colloq* (little) °game: *You won't get far trying to work your wiles on me, young lady.*

wilful *adj.* **1** °intentional, °deliberate, °voluntary, °conscious, intended, °purposeful, °premeditated, *US* willful: *The jury decided that such a wilful act of vandalism must be punished. She is accused of wilful neglect of her children.* **2** °stubborn, headstrong, pigheaded, °obstinate, mulish, °inflexible, adamant, obdurate, intransigent, unyielding, °self-willed, °ungovernable, °recalcitrant, °unruly, °immovable, intractable, dogged, °determined, refractory, uncompromising, wayward, °perverse, °contrary: *Jim is far too wilful, and tends to have a tantrum if he fails to get his own way.*

will *n.* **1** °desire, °wish, °longing, °liking, °inclination, °disposition, °drive, purposefulness, °purpose, °intent, °intention, °resolve, commitment, °resolution, °determination; will-power: *Where there's a will there's a way. Some believe that taking medication is against God's will. Marguerite seems to have lost the will to live.* **2** °choice, °wishes, °desire, °inclination: *He was forced to submit against his will.* **3** (last will and) testament, last °wishes: *In accordance with his will, Josiah was buried at sea.* **4** ***at will***: as *or* when (one) pleases *or* wishes *or* thinks °fit(ting), at (one's) °desire *or* whim *or* °pleasure *or* °discretion: *If he brings his own car, then he can leave at will.*

—*v.* **5** °want, °desire, °wish, °choose, see °fit, °make, compel, °force, °command, °order, ordain, °require: *When she willed him to appear, there was a flash of lightning and he was there.* **6** °leave, °bequeath, °devise, °hand down *or* on, °pass on, °transfer; settle upon *or* on: *My great-uncle Philip willed me his collection of 19th-century theatre memorabilia.*

willing *adj.* °agreeable, acquiescent, compliant, amenable, consenting, assenting, °passive, complaisant, docile, °ready, well-disposed, °happy, °content, °pleased, °delighted, °enthusiastic, avid, °eager, zealous, *Colloq* °game: *Albert might not have thought up the pranks, but he was a willing accomplice.*

willingly *adv.* °readily, °happily, contentedly, °gladly, cheerfully, amenably, agreeably, °freely, passively, docilely, of (one's) own °accord *or* °free °will, on (one's) own, ungrudgingly, by °choice, °voluntarily, unhesitatingly, nothing loath, eagerly, enthusiastically, zealously, avidly, *Colloq* at the drop of a hat: *We did not coerce him in any way—he went along quite willingly. You can rely on Hubert to give willingly and generously to support any good cause.*

willowy *adj.* **1** lissom *or* lissome, pliant, lithe, °flexible, °supple, limber, loose-limbed: *Everyone enjoys watching the willowy athletes training for the Olympics.* **2** °slim, °slender, °graceful, sylphlike, svelte, °thin, long-limbed, clean-limbed: *How does Jeanne keep her willowy figure without dieting?*

willy-nilly *adv.* **1** whether one likes it or not, inevitably, °necessarily, of °necessity, perforce, whether or no, like it or not, *nolens volens, bon gré, mal gré*: *Having borrowed the money, you must, willy-nilly, repay it.*

—*adj.* **2** °necessary, °unavoidable, °inevitable, °involuntary: *He joked about a willy-nilly choice, meaning one offering no alternatives.*

wilt *v.* **1** °sag, °droop, wither, °shrink, °shrivel (up *or* away), °diminish: *My house-plants wilted because they weren't watered.* **2** °sag, °droop, °bow, °weaken, °sink, °wane, wither, lose courage *or* nerve, °flag, °dwindle, languish: *The lad wilted under the stern glare of the headmaster.*

wily *adj.* °shrewd, cunning, °crafty, °sly, °artful, guileful, °clever, °foxy, vulpine, °disingenuous, °shifty, °scheming, plotting, °calculating, °designing, °sharp, canny, °deceitful, deceiving, °deceptive, treacherous, °perfidious, °false, double-dealing, °dishonest, underhand(ed), °tricky, °smooth, °slick, °slippery, °oily, unctuous, *Scots and No. Eng.* pawky, *Colloq* cagey, °crooked, two-timing, *Slang chiefly Brit* fly: *Rats are wily and cunning, and have to be taken seriously.*

win *v.* **1** come (in *or* out) °first, carry the day, °conquer, °overcome; carry off (the palm), finish °first (in), °achieve °first place (in), °triumph (in), be °victorious (in), be the °victor (in), °gain a °victory (in), °prevail (in), °succeed (in), take °first °prize (in), *Colloq* bring home the bacon: *Which team is more likely to win today? We seem to have won the battle but not the war.* **2** °gain, °carry off *or* away, attain, °acquire, °get, °obtain, °secure, °procure, °receive, °collect, °net, °bag, °earn, °realize, °pick up, glean: *Look at all those trophies Gillian has won playing golf!* **3** ***win over***: °influence, °sway, °incline, °persuade, °charm, °prevail (up)on, °convert, °induce, °bring °round *or* around, °convince: *Don't think that Gilbert can be won over without a strong argument.*

—*n.* **4** °victory, °conquest, °triumph, °success: *So far this season we have recorded six wins and one loss for the Surrey Scouts.*

wind[1] *n.* **1** °breeze, zephyr, °puff, °gust, °breath, °draught, light °air, °current (of °air): *A gentle wind wafted our little boat across the bay.* **2** puffery, °bombast, rodomontade, °bluster, boasting, braggadocio, vain speech, blather, (idle *or* empty) °talk, fustian, °nonsense, twaddle, humbug, °babble, °gibberish, *Colloq* °gab, °hot air, claptrap, hogwash, °rot, hooey, boloney, *Slang Brit* (load of (old)) cobblers: *I went there for advice and all I got was a lot of wind.* **3** gas, flatulence, windiness, flatus, borborygmus (= 'stomach rumbling (as from gas)'), heartburn, *Taboo slang* fart (= 'anal °release of gas'): *I have to take a pill to relieve this wind.* **4** ***before the wind***: *Nautical* downwind, off the wind: *We were racing before the wind with every scrap of sail flying.* **5** ***break wind***: *Taboo slang* fart: *It is considered rude to break wind.* **6** ***get*** or ***have wind of***: °hear of, °learn of, come to °know, °pick up, be made *or* become °aware of, °gather, °understand, °hear on the °grapevine, *Colloq* °hear tell of: *We got wind of the company's plans to close this plant.* **7** ***get*** or ***have the wind up***: take °fright, become frightened *or* °afraid *or* apprehensive: *When I heard a window being raised I got the wind up.* **8** ***in the wind***: around, °about, rumoured, in the air, detectable, °discernible, discoverable, °imminent, °impending, approaching, °close (at °hand), about to °happen *or* take °place *or* °occur, afoot, in the offing, °near, on the way, *Colloq Brit* on the cards, *US* in the cards: *We knew that a change was in the wind, but never expected the chairman to resign.* **9** ***off the wind***: See **5**, above. **10** ***on the*** or ***a wind***: *Nautical* upwind, windward, to the wind, into (the teeth *or* the eye of) the wind; °near the wind: *Because 'Syrena' was a sloop, she could sail closer on the wind than the schooner.* **11** ***put the wind up***: °scare, °frighten, °alarm: *The leakage at the nuclear plant really put the wind up everyone living in the area.* **12** ***sail close*** or ***near to the wind***: take °risks, throw caution to the winds, play with °fire, skate on thin ice, take (one's) life in (one's) hands, *Colloq* stick (one's) neck out, *Slang* go for broke: *One nude scene is highly salacious, and we think the director is sailing very close to the wind by including it.* **13** ***take the wind out of (someone's) sails***: deflate (someone), disconcert (someone), destroy (someone's) advantage, ruin (someone's) superiority *or* supremacy *or* ascendancy: *It rather took the wind* *out of her sails when he announced that he was leaving anyway.*

wind[2] *v.* **1** °turn, °bend, °twist, °snake, worm, °twine, zigzag, slew, °swerve, °loop, °coil, curve, °meander, °ramble, veer: *The river winds along the valley floor.* **2** °reel, °roll, °spiral, °turn, °twist, curl, °coil, °wrap, °twine, wreathe; °crank (up), wind up: *The streamers are wound around the columns for decoration.* **3** ***wind down***: **a** °taper off, °slow down, °diminish, °reduce, °close out, slacken *or* °slack off (on), °ease (up on), °decrease, °cut back *or* down (on); wind up: *They were going to wind down their sportswear department, but then business suddenly perked up.* **b** °relax, become °calm *or* °tranquil, °calm down, °cool off *or* down, regain (one's) equilibrium, °ease up *or* off, *Colloq* unwind, let (one's) hair down, take it °easy: *It takes me a couple of days to wind down from the hectic activity in the office.* **4** ***wind up***: **a** °terminate, conclude, come *or* bring to an °end *or* a °close *or* a conclusion, °end (up), °close down *or* up, °finish (up), °wrap up; liquidate, °settle: *After calmly winding up his affairs, Evan sailed off in his boat and was never seen again.* **b** °end up, °finish (up), °become °ultimately: *I understand that Sally wound up as a bar girl in Tampico.* **c** °excite, innervate, °energize, °stimulate, invigorate, °stir up: *After getting us all wound up about that weekend party in Paris, she called the whole thing off.* **d** °agitate, °fluster, disconcert, °ruffle: *Don't let such trifles get you so wound up.* **e** See **3 a,** above.

windfall *n.* bonanza, °godsend, stroke of (good) °fortune, serendipitous °find, °boon, piece of (good) °luck, jackpot, (°lucky) strike: *The sale of the house provided a windfall that saved them from imminent bankruptcy.*

windy *adj.* **1** blustery, blowing, blowy, °breezy, gusting, gusty, °wild, squally, °tempestuous; windswept: *It is quite windy today. I waited at that windy corner for you and you never showed up!* **2** °talkative, long-winded, garrulous, °wordy, verbose, prolix, loquacious, °rambling, °voluble, °fluent, °effusive, °glib, turgid, °bombastic, °pompous, longiloquent: *Potter does tend to be windy at times.*

winner *n.* °victor, °champion, prizewinner, titleholder, conqueror, conquering °hero, *Colloq* champ: *The winner will receive a new car.*

winning *adj.* **1** °engaging, °attractive, alluring, captivating, °endearing, °prepossessing, winsome, bewitching, °fetching, °taking, °enchanting, °pleasing, °delightful, charming, °amiable, °friendly, °pleasant, °sweet: *Maggie's winning ways are a tremendous asset in making friends.* **2** °triumphant, conquering, °victorious, °successful: *The winning team is invited to dine at the Red Lion.*

wintry *adj.* **1** hiemal, brumal, hibernal; °icy, snowy, °freezing, frozen, frosty, °cold, °frigid, °bitter (°cold), °chilly, chilling, °piercing, °cutting, glacial, Siberian, arctic, hyperborean: *It was cold and the sky was clear and wintry with premonitions of frost.* **2** °cold, °frigid, °chilly, °cool, chilling, glacial: *She got a very wintry reception from Dan's parents, who disliked the idea of their living together.* **3** °forbidding, °bleak, °dismal, cheerless, °dreary, °harsh, unfriendly, °ugly, °menacing, °ominous, °threatening, °dark: *His comment about her age evoked only a wintry look from Margot.*

wipe *v.* **1** Sometimes, ***wipe off*** or ***out*** or ***up***: °rub, °clean (off *or* out *or* up), °cleanse; °dry (off *or* out *or* up), dust (off), mop (up), swab, sponge (off *or* up): *For God's sake, wipe your nose! Please wipe the crumbs off the table when you've finished eating. Stop crying and wipe up the spilt milk.* **2** Often, ***wipe off***: °remove, °erase, °take off *or* away, get °rid of: *Wipe that grin off your face, stranger.* **3** ***wipe out***: °kill (off), annihilate, °massacre, °destroy, °finish (off), °dispose of, eradicate, °obliterate, °exterminate, do away with, °stamp out, get °rid of, °remove, wipe off the face of the earth: *Scientists have succeeded in wiping out smallpox.*

wiry *adj.* °muscular, °sinewy, °lean, lank, °thin and °strong, °tough and °flexible: *He was a stocky and wiry little man, rather like a short-legged terrier.*

wisdom *n.* **1** sagacity, sageness, °judgement, discernment, °reason, °prudence, judiciousness, (common) °sense, °insight, °penetration, sapience, °understanding, rationality, clear-sightedness, clear-headedness, perspicacity, perspicuity, percipience, °perception, perceptiveness, °intelligence, acuteness, acumen, astuteness, sharpness, shrewdness, long-headedness: *At least she had the wisdom not to shoot the intruder. Allen's wisdom stems from long experience in such matters.* **2** °knowledge, °learning, erudition, °lore, °scholarship, enlightenment: *The wisdom of the ages is locked away in these books.*

wise *adj.* **1** °sage, sagacious, °judicious, °reasonable, commonsensical, °prudent, °sensible, insightful, sapient, °understanding, °rational, °sound, clear-sighted, clear-headed, discerning, perspicacious, perspicuous, percipient, °perceptive, °intelligent, °acute, °astute, °sharp, °shrewd, °crafty, °clever, °bright, °quick-witted, °smart, °brilliant, long-headed, *Colloq* brainy: *Among the wisest of men were Solomon, Confucius, Buddha, and, perhaps, Aristotle.* **2** °knowledgeable, °learned, °enlightened, °informed, erudite; (well-)°educated, °knowing, well-read, well-versed, °lettered, °scholarly: *We saw to it that they escaped, and the police were none the wiser. Wise heads prevailed at the college on what constituted worthwhile research.* **3** °well-advised, °advisable, °judicious, °sensible, °expedient, °reasonable, °strategic, °tactful, °tactical, °prudent, °politic, °discreet, °diplomatic, well-thought-out, well-considered, °proper, °fitting, °appropriate, °meet: *Do you think it wise to punish the child so severely?* **4** ***put wise (to)***: °inform *or* °advise *or* °warn (of *or* about): *If you must know how he found out, it was Myrna who put him wise. Did she also put him wise to where the money is hidden?* **5** ***wise to***: °aware *or* °knowledgeable *or* °informed of *or* about, °sensitive to, on to *or* onto, *Colloq* in the know about: *You are wrong if you think she isn't wise to your little tricks. Get wise to what's going on, man.*

—*v.* **6** ***wise up (to)***: become °informed *or* °aware (of *or* about), °wake up (to), *Colloq* get °wise (to) *or* in the know (about): *If Cooley doesn't wise up, he'll be in deep trouble. Was it you who wised Meg up to the fact that Tom no longer cares?*

wisecrack *n.* **1** °joke, °quip, rejoinder, °witticism, °pun, barb, jest, °gibe *or* jibe, *Colloq* °gag; °dig: *Everything is a potential subject for a wisecrack.*

—*v.* **2** °joke, °quip, °pun, °gibe *or* jibe: *Get serious and stop wisecracking for a change.*

wise guy *n.* wiseacre, °smart alec *or* aleck, *Archaic* witling, *Colloq* know-all *or* know-it-all, *Brit* Clever Dick *or* cleverdick, *Slang* smarty-pants, smarty, *Brit* smart-arse, *US* smart-ass, wisenheimer: *There's always some wise guy waiting to make a clever remark.*

wish *v.* **1** °desire, °want; °yearn, crave, °long, °hope, °hanker, have a °mind, (have a) °fancy, °choose, °care: *I wish you'd go now. If you had Aladdin's lamp, what would you wish for?* **2** °require, °request, °demand, °order, °specify: *Did you wish lemon or milk in your tea?* **3** °foist *or* °force *or* °thrust *or* °impose upon, *Colloq* fob off on *or* upon, palm off on: *The job of treasurer was wished on me when Jock left.*

—*n.* **4** °desire, °request, whim, °want, craving, °longing, hankering: *Your every wish is my command.* **5** °desire, °longing, craving, °need, yearning, hankering, °passion, keenness, °thirst, °appetite, °hunger, whim, °urge, °liking, fondness, °fancy, °preference, predisposition, °disposition, °inclination, *Colloq* yen, *Slang* °itch: *She expressed a wish for nightingale tongues, truffles, and champagne.*

wishy-washy *adj.* **1** neither here nor there, undecided, °indecisive, °irresolute, °half-hearted, shilly-shallying, tergiversating, vacillating, °uncertain, of *or* having °mixed feelings, of two minds: *Make up your mind and stop being so wishy-washy about everything!* **2** °feeble, °weak, °watery, watered down, °thin, °vapid,

°flat, °bland, runny, diluted, °tasteless, insipid, flavourless, °stale: *Isabel served me some wishy-washy tea and sent me on my way.*

wisp *n.* °shred, °scrap, strand, °thread, snippet, tuft, °lock: *The laboratory matched the wisp of hair found in the victim's hand with the hair of the suspect.*

wistful *adj.* **1** °melancholy, °mournful, °sad, morose, °sorrowful, disconsolate, heartsick, °forlorn, woeful, °woebegone, °desirous, °longing, yearning: *She gave a last, wistful look at the aeroplane as it rose into the clouds.* **2** °thoughtful, contemplative, °pensive, absent-minded, °detached, °absorbed, in a brown study, °preoccupied, meditating, °meditative, °reflective, ruminating, ruminative, °dreamy, dreaming, day-dreaming, musing: *Some might have misinterpreted his wistful gaze at her photograph.*

wit *n.* **1** °intelligence, brains, °mind, (common) °sense, °judgement, °understanding, discernment, °wisdom, sagacity, °insight, astuteness, cleverness, *Slang* savvy: *He hasn't the wit to know when he's being insulted.* **2** °humour, drollery, °levity, joking, °repartee, °raillery, facetiousness, waggishness, badinage, jocularity, wordplay, paronomasia; °amusement, °entertainment: *Some say that sarcasm is the lowest form of wit.* **3** °comedian, comedienne, humorist, °comic, °wag, °joker, *farceur*, *farceuse*, punster, madcap, °zany; parodist, satirist, caricaturist; *Colloq* pundit, °card, °character: *In the face of such a devastating remark, even the club wit was struck dumb.*

witch *n.* **1** sorceress, enchantress, °magician, sibyl, pythoness; warlock: *The witches prophesied that Macbeth would be king.* **2** °hag, °fury, battleaxe, crone, gorgon, Medusa, ogress, Xanthippe, °shrew, virago, harridan, fishwife, termagant, *Archaic* beldam, *Offensive* old °bag, bitch: *How could you stand living with the old witch for so many years?*

withdraw *v.* **1** °draw back, °retract, °pull back, °recoil, °shrink back: *He would suddenly withdraw into his cocoon whenever she said the name, 'Elsie'.* **2** °retract, °recall, °take back, °cancel, rescind, °recant, disavow, disclaim, abjure, °void, annul, °go back on, °back down (on): *If she doesn't withdraw that remark, I shall sue her for slander.* **3** °pull out, °extract, °remove, *Technical* retrude: *Afterwards, she withdrew the knife, washed it, and replaced it in the rack.* **4** °retire, °retreat, °go, °repair: *After dinner, we withdrew to the drawing-room for brandy and cigars.* **5** °leave, °depart, °go, make (oneself) scarce, °absent (oneself), °retire: *We waited till the servants withdrew before exchanging news about Cora.*

withdrawn *adj.* **1** °reserved, °detached, °distant, °standoffish, °aloof, °shy, diffident, °bashful, °timid, timorous, introverted, °taciturn, °reticent, °silent, °quiet, °retiring, shrinking: *Why is Henry acting so withdrawn tonight?* **2** °remote, °distant, °isolated, °solitary, °hidden, °secluded, °private, °out-of-the-way, °reclusive: *Sarah and Ben have led a withdrawn existence since the children married and moved away.*

withering *adj.* °destructive, °devastating, death-dealing, °murderous, °deadly: *The enemy laid down a withering barrage of machine-gun fire.*

withhold *v.* **1** °hold *or* °keep back, °retain, °reserve, °restrain, °control, °repress, °check, °hide, °conceal: *He could withhold his anger no longer.* **2** °hold *or* °keep back, °deduct, °retain, °reserve: *The company is required to withhold a percentage of wages and salaries for taxes.*

withstand *v.* °resist, °oppose, °stand (up to), °face, °defy, confront, °combat, °grapple with, °fight (against), °cope with, °hold out against, °weather, °suffer, °survive, °tolerate, °take, °bear, °last through, °endure, °brave, *Colloq Brit* °stick: *Can Brian withstand the pressure of his new job? Our small force withstood the attack for days.*

witness *n.* **1** °observer, °onlooker, °spectator, viewer, °eyewitness, °bystander, watcher, *Rare* earwitness: *Were you a witness to what took place here?* **2** deponent, testifier, corroborating °witness, corroborator: *The defence will call its witnesses today.* **3** ***bear witness (to or of)***: °testify (to), °attest (to), be *or* give *or* provide *or* furnish *or* constitute °evidence *or* °proof *or* °testimony (of *or* to), °verify, °confirm, corroborate, °show, °prove: *The bent poker bears witness to the violence of the attack.*
—*v.* **4** °see, °observe, °watch, °look on *or* at, °view, °behold, °mark, note, °notice, °take in, *Colloq* °spot, °catch: *I did witness the way they looked at each other.* **5** countersign, °sign, °certify, °endorse, °substantiate, °document, certificate: *Would you mind witnessing our signatures, Miss Cabot?* **6** See **3**, above.

witticism *n.* °pun, °quip, play on words, bon mot, jest, °joke, °epigram, °clever °remark, sally, *Archaic or literary* °conceit, *Colloq* °gag, one-liner: *Clive is just as likely to utter a witticism as say something excruciatingly banal.*

witty *adj.* °ingenious, °subtle, °clever, °humorous, °sarcastic, °sardonic, piquant, °comic(al), °farcical, °ludicrous, facetious, amusing, jocular, waggish, droll, °funny: *Corbett, not ready with his usual witty riposte, shouted an obscenity at the bus driver.*

wizened *adj.* wrinkled, shrunken, shrivelled (up), withered, °gnarled, dried up, wilted, faded, wasted: *The wizened old crone is his grandmother.*

woe *n.* °trouble, °hardship, adversity, °misery, °anguish, tribulation, °calamity, °trial, wretchedness, °grief, unhappiness, °desolation, dolour, °melancholy, °gloom, °depression, °sadness, disconsolateness, °misfortune, °affliction, °sorrow, °distress: *How much more woe could beset one small family?*

woebegone *adj.* troubled, °miserable, anguished, °wretched, grief-stricken, °unhappy, °desolate, °doleful, dolorous, °melancholy, melancholic, °gloomy, °mournful, °sorrowful, depressed, °dejected, °sad, °glum, crestfallen, chap-fallen, lugubrious, downcast, disconsolate, °unfortunate, star-crossed, afflicted, distressed, woeful, °forlorn, °downhearted, °broken-hearted, °heartbroken, disheartened, *Slang US* bummed out: *Timmy has been so woebegone since his puppy was stolen!*

woman *n.* **1** female, lady; °girl: *Elvira was the first woman to be elected to the board.* **2** °wife, spouse, bride, lady-love, °sweetheart, lady, °girl, girlfriend, °mistress, concubine, °mate, helpmeet, helpmate, °partner, *Colloq* sweetie, better half, little woman, the missis *or* missus, old lady *or* woman, ball and chain, *Slang* trouble and strife: *In this scene, Porgy tells Bess that she is his woman, now and forever.* **3** °lass, °maid, °maiden, °miss, lassie, *Slang* gal, dame, bird, skirt, chick, bit of fluff, °broad, piece (of work), number, baggage, moll, popsy: *The soldiers went into town to try to find some women for an evening's entertainment.* **4** °domestic, housekeeper, °maid, cleaning woman *or* lady, maidservant, chambermaid, handmaiden, abigail, lady-in-waiting, *Brit* charwoman, *Colloq Brit* char, °daily: *They have a woman who comes in every other day.*

wonder *n.* **1** °marvel, °prodigy, °phenomenon, °spectacle, °rarity, °sight, °curiosity, miracle, *Slang* °knockout, stunner, mind-blower, mind-boggler, °trip: *Surely, the wheel must rank high among the wonders of technology. And still he gazed, and still the wonder grew, That one small head could carry all he knew.* **2** awe, °astonishment, °admiration, °amazement, wonderment, °surprise, stupefaction, °fascination: *Facsimile transmission, which used to excite so much wonder, is now used in offices all over the world.*
—*v.* **3** °ponder, °muse, °meditate, °think, °theorize, conjecture, °puzzle, °query, °question, °inquire, be °inquisitive, be °curious, °ask oneself, °speculate, cudgel (one's) brains: *I wondered if I would be invited to the dance. Have you ever wondered what makes the world go round?* **4** °marvel (at), goggle, °gawk, °gape, °stare, be awed, be °thunderstruck, be amazed, be astonished: *We wondered at the death-defying skills of the trapeze artistes.* **5** ***wonder about***: °question *or*

°doubt the sanity *or* reason *or* reasonableness of: *I wondered about Tammy after that streaking episode.*

wooded *adj.* sylvan, forested, bosky, tree-covered, woody, timbered: *We rested and had our lunch in the coolness of a wooded glen.*

wooden *adj.* **1** wood, woody, ligneous, xyloid: *The wooden cabinet for the kitchen is almost finished.* **2** °stiff, °rigid, °artificial, °clumsy, °stilted, °unnatural, °awkward, ungainly, spiritless, unanimated, °dead, °lifeless, °dry, passionless, unimpassioned, °impassive, °vacant, °empty, °colourless, expressionless, deadpan: *The understudy gave a wooden performance as Uncle Vanya.* **3** unintelligent, blockheaded, °stupid, °dull, insensitive, slow-witted, dull-witted, °obtuse, oafish, doltish, tiny-minded, dim-witted, dunderpated, *Colloq* °thick, wooden-headed, knuckle-headed: *Clancy has some pretty wooden ideas about how to run a business.*

woolly *adj.* **1** fleecy, woollen, wool-bearing, laniferous, lanate *or* lanose, lanuginose *or* lanuginous, downy, °fuzzy, °shaggy, flocculent *or* floccose, flocky: *He was wearing a woolly hat. After two days one test tube contained a woolly precipitate.* **2** °hazy, °fuzzy, unclear, °obscure(d), foggy, °indistinct, °confused, °vague, cloudy, clouded, °nebulous, ill-defined: *My recollection of the event is a bit woolly after all these years.*

word *n.* **1** (little) °talk, (brief) °conversation, °chat, °discussion, consultation, °dialogue, °huddle, °parley, °tête-à-tête, chit-chat, confabulation, °conference, °interview, *Colloq* powwow, confab: *Could I have a word with you before you leave for the day?* **2** °news, °intelligence, °information, °facts, °data, °report, °story, tidings, °account, communiqué, °bulletin, °dispatch *or* despatch, °advice, °message, *Colloq* °low-down, *Slang* info, °dope, *Brit* gen, *US* poop: *Have you had any word about the situation in the Middle East?* **3** °name, °term, designation, locution, appellation, °expression, °phrase: *What is the word for 'write' in Greek?* **4** °promise, °pledge, °vow, °oath, (solemn) word of honour, °undertaking, °assurance, °warrant, °guarantee *or* guaranty, °warranty: *You have my word that I won't mention this to anyone.* **5** utterance, °expression, °declaration, °statement: *Let me give you a word of warning, my friend.* **6** °suggestion, °hint, scintilla, °bit: *I promise that I won't breathe a word of this to anyone.* **7** °command, °order, °signal, °direction, °instruction, *Colloq US* high °sign: *I shall not press the red button till you give the word.* **8** ***in a word***: succinctly, °briefly, in °brief, in a °few words, concisely, in °short, in °summary, in °sum, not to mince words, to make a long story short, when all is said and done, in the final analysis, not to beat about the bush, *Colloq* in a nutshell: *His bedside manner was, in a word, menacing.* **9** ***words***: **a** °quarrel, °dispute, °argument, unpleasantness: *Paul and Kitty had words and are not on speaking terms.* **b** lyrics, °book, libretto, °text: *Did Irving Berlin write the words as well as the music to his songs?*

—*v.* **10** °put (forth), °say, °couch, °express, °phrase, utter, °state, °term, °style, °set forth: *Had you worded your complaint in politer language, you might have spared yourself a punch in the eye.*

wording *n.* phraseology, °language, phrasing, °choice of words, °word °choice: *From the confused wording of this note I cannot tell whether you are coming to my party or not.*

wordy *adj.* verbose, prolix, °rambling, long-winded; pleonastic, °redundant, garrulous, °windy, °talkative, loquacious: *This contract is too wordy and could be cut to two pages. Try to make your replies less wordy.*

work *n.* **1** °labour, toil, °effort, °drudgery, travail, °exertion, °industry: *Few people make it to the top and stay there without hard work.* **2** °employment, °business, °occupation, °vocation, °calling, °profession, °trade, °line, métier, °career, livelihood, °job, °post, °position, °situation: *Does your work as a test pilot interfere much with your home life?* **3** °task, °function, °duty, °assignment, °charge, °responsibility, chore, commission, °undertaking, °stint: *When you are finished with that work, clean out the cellar.* **4** °feat, °achievement, °creation, °accomplishment, °opus, handiwork, *oeuvre*, °production, °composition, °piece, master-work, °masterpiece, *chef-d'œuvre, magnum opus*, °output: *Some of Edwin's recent works have won prizes.* **5** ***in work***: in °production, under °way, being done, in the works, being planned, in the planning stage(s): *The budget has been approved and the project is already in work.* **6** ***out of work***: °unemployed, °idle, jobless, at °liberty, between engagements, °available, °free, *Brit* °redundant, *Colloq Brit* on the °dole, *US* on *or* collecting unemployment: *How long have you been out of work?*

—*v.* **7** °labour, toil, °exert oneself, °sweat, moil, °slave (away), °peg away, slog (away): *His father worked in the mines from the age of nine till he died of black-lung disease at forty.* **8** °till, °plough, °farm, °cultivate: *Would he have been healthier and longer-lived had he worked the land?* **9** have a °job, °hold (down) a °post *or* °position, °earn a living, be °employed: *His wife works as a designer in a Parisian fashion house.* **10** °control, °manage, °manipulate, °manoeuvre, °wield, °handle, °operate, °use, make °use of, utilize, °exploit, °deal with, bring into play: *Are you sure you know how to work all those dials and buttons?* **11** °function, °operate, °run, °go, °develop, °turn out, *Colloq* °pan out: *Are you sure that the plan is working to your advantage?* **12** °function, °operate, °run, °go: *The drill works better if you turn on the power.* **13** knead, °mould, °form, °fashion, °shape; °mix, °stir, °incorporate: *Work the clay into long, narrow strips. Try to work the colour in with your fingers.* **14** °manoeuvre, °manipulate, °guide: *See if you can work him over into a corner where you can grab him.* **15** °operate, °use, °employ, put to (good *or* effective) °use, °wield, °manipulate, °ply, °apply, °exploit: *Tanya must have worked her magic on Eustace to make him that docile.* **16** °bring about, °effect, °accomplish, °carry out *or* off, °make, °produce, °achieve, engender, beget, °create, do, °put through, °execute, °fulfil, °effectuate, °implement, °realize: *I doubt that the new sports centre will work many changes in the area.* **17** ***work in***: find °time *or* °space for, °include, °insert, °introduce, °fit in, °squeeze in, °accommodate: *I'll try and work in your comments when I write up my report.* **18** ***work on***: °wheedle, °coax, importune, °press, *Brit* pressurize, *US* °pressure; °influence, °persuade, °act on, °prevail (up)on, °induce, °dispose, °urge: *Keep working on him to try to change his mind.* **19** ***work out***: **a** °exercise, do callisthenics, do aerobics, °warm up, do setting-up exercises, do (one's) daily dozen, °jog, lift weights, °train, °drill: *I try to work out for an hour every day.* **b** Often, ***work out at*** *or* ***to***: °equal, °total (up to), °result in, °amount to, °come to: *Let's see—that works out at one car for every 4.7 people.* **c** °clear up, °resolve, °solve, *Slang Brit and New Zealand* suss out: *Thaddeus is old enough to work out his own problems. Can they work out their differences?* **d** evolve, °develop, °succeed, °prosper, °come out all °right, prove satisfactory, °go °well, be °effective, *Colloq* °pan out: *How can you be so sure that everything will work out?* **e** °formulate, work up, contrive, °draw up, °detail, °plan, °develop, °devise, put together, °elaborate, °expand, °enlarge (on): *The captain worked out a way for them to escape.* **20** ***work up***: **a** °excite, make °excited, °agitate, °inflame, enkindle, °arouse, °rouse, °stir, °move, °animate, °incite, °spur, *Colloq* °fire (up), get (someone) (all) steamed *or* hopped *or* het up: *Those fire-and-brimstone preachers used to get the people all worked up.* **b** °prepare, (make *or* get) °ready, whip into shape, °develop, come up with, °write up, put together, °produce, °turn out: *Can you work up that proposal in time for Monday's meeting?* **c** °advance, ascend, °rise, °move up *or* ahead *or* on: *In no time at all, Greg worked his way up from assembler to foreman.* **d** See **19 e,** above.

worker *n.* °labourer, working man *or* woman, workman, °hand, °employee, artisan, craftsman, °tradesman, white-collar worker, blue-collar worker, proletarian, breadwinner, wage-earner: *It seems unlikely that the workers would strike for longer hours and less pay.*

workmanship *n.* handicraft, °craft, craftsmanship, artistry, °art, °technique, handiwork, °skill, skilfulness, mastery, *US* artisanship: *One cannot help but admire the workmanship in those marquetry tabletops.*

works *n.pl.* **1** °plant, °factory, workshop, °shop, °mill: *We were taken on a tour of the works to see how the marble is carved.* **2** °mechanism, machinery, workings, (moving *or* working) parts; clockwork, *Colloq* innards, insides, *Slang* guts: *We once had a clock with all the works exposed.* **3** ***the works***: **a** °everything, the °lot, *Colloq* the whole kit and caboodle, the whole shooting match, °everything but the kitchen sink, *Chiefly US and Canadian* the whole shebang: *We ordered two hamburgers with the works.* **b** a °thrashing, a beating, a drubbing, a battering, a flogging, a lambasting: *When he refused to tell them where the money was hidden, they gave him the works.*

world *n.* **1** °earth, planet, °sphere, °globe, Terra; °universe, cosmos, °existence, °creation, °life: *Do you believe the world is round? Buckland lives in his own, private world.* **2** °humanity, mankind, °people, the human °race, °society, the °public, men, humankind, everybody, °everyone, the world at °large: *We know what he thinks of the world, but what does the world think of him?* **3** °area, °sphere, °domain, community, °clique, °crowd, °circle, °fraternity, °faction, °set, coterie: *What value does the art world place on Longchamps' paintings?* **4** °period, °time(s), °age, °era, epoch: *They have produced an excellent series of programmes on the ancient world.* **5** ***bring into the world***: **a** °deliver, °have, give birth to, beget, *Rare or dialect* birth: *Grandmother brought sixteen children into the world.* **b** °deliver, midwife: *The town family doctor brought hundreds of children into the world in his long career.* **6** ***for all the world***: °precisely, °exactly, in all °respects, in every °respect, in every °way, °just: *He behaved for all the world like a man possessed by the devil.* **7** ***on top of the world***: °ecstatic, °delighted, °elated, °happy, °exultant, °overjoyed, °rapturous, *Brit* in the seventh °heaven, *US* in seventh °heaven, *Colloq* on cloud nine, *Brit* over the moon: *George has been on top of the world ever since Prudence agreed to marry him.* **8** ***out of this world***: °marvellous, wonderful, °exceptional, °unbelievable, °incredible, °excellent, °superb, *Colloq* °great, smashing, °fantastic, °fabulous, *Slang* out of °sight, far-out, *Brit* °magic, *US* to the max: *The place we stayed at Ibiza was out of this world!*

worldly *adv.* **1** mundane, °earthly, °terrestrial, °temporal, °physical, °carnal, fleshly, corporeal, °human; °lay, non-spiritual, non-religious, civic, °secular, °profane: *Theo indulged in worldly pleasures in the fleshpots of the continent. Veronica put aside worldly things and took the veil.* **2** urbane, °suave, °sophisticated, cosmopolitan, worldly-wise, *Slang* with it, °hip, °cool: *Behind that worldly manner is the heart of a peasant.*

worn *adj.* **1** °shabby, °threadbare, tatty, °tattered, °ragged, frayed: *Burt wears an old, worn tweed jacket when he's around the house.* **2** °haggard, °drawn: *He looked anxiously at his mother's thin, worn face.* **3** ***worn out***: °tired, °fatigued, °exhausted, frazzled, °spent, °jaded, played out, °haggard, °drawn, the worse for wear, *Colloq* dog-tired, all in, done in, *Slang* °dead (on one's feet), °beat, *US* pooped: *I was completely worn out from climbing those stairs.*

worried *adj.* °fearful, apprehensive, °anxious, distressed, °nervous, uneasy, anguished, disquieted, agonized, °agonizing, °distraught, on °edge, on tenterhooks, °ill at ease, troubled, °fretful, °agitated, perturbed, °upset, °suffering: *The two worried mothers waited at the police station for news of their children.*

worry *v.* **1** be °anxious, be °fearful, be °concerned, °fret, agonize, be distressed, be vexed, *Colloq* °stew, bite *or* chew (one's) nails, go *or* get grey, get grey hair, *Slang* °sweat blood, *US* °sweat bullets: *I worry about you when you stay out so late.* **2** °annoy, °irk, °pester, nettle, harry, °harass, °tease, °bother, °tantalize, °torment, °plague, hector, badger, nettle, °gall, peeve, *Colloq* hassle: *The police have been worrying me the way a dog worries a bone.*
—*n.* **3** °concern, °care, °responsibility; °problem, °bother, °trouble, °affliction, irritation, °annoyance, vexation: *I cannot see why that is your worry. I am sorry to hear about your financial worries.* **4** °anguish, °anxiety, uneasiness, unease, nervousness, °distress, apprehension, disquiet, perturbation, °agitation, °upset, °misgiving: *Your association with that crowd has caused your mother and me a great deal of worry.*

worsen *v.* **1** °increase, exacerbate, °heighten, °intensify, °aggravate: *The recent rains have worsened the drainage problem.* **2** °weaken, °deteriorate, °decline, °degenerate, °decay, °slip, °sink, °slide, °fail, °disintegrate, take a turn for the worse, get worse, go from bad to worse, *Colloq* go downhill: *Her condition continues to worsen.*

worship *v.* **1** °venerate, °revere, °reverence, °extol, °honour, °exalt, °praise, °admire, °adore, adulate, °glorify, deify, °idolize, be °devoted to, pay °homage to, °bow down before, kneel before, put on a °pedestal: *When he arrived, he found the people worshipping huge stone idols.*
—*n.* **2** °veneration, °reverence, adoration, °devotion, °homage, °honour, °respect, °esteem, exaltation, °praise, °admiration, adulation, glorification, deification, idolatry: *A healthy respect for security should not be confused with the worship of money.*

worth *n.* °quality, °merit, value, °advantage, °benefit, °good, °importance, °significance, °usefulness: *You have underestimated Roberta's worth to the community.*

worthless *adj.* **1** valueless, unimportant, °insignificant, inessential *or* unessential, °dispensable, °disposable, °paltry: *His contribution to the work of the committee proved utterly worthless.* **2** °pointless, °bootless, °silly, °inane, °vain, unavailing, °useless, °futile, °fruitless, unproductive, °unprofitable: *It is worthless to try to salvage that wreck.* **3** °cheap, valueless, °tawdry, °poor, trashy, rubbishy, °shabby, °wretched, *Colloq* °tinny, crappy, cheesy, *Slang* chintzy: *The deceased's handbag contained only a few items of worthless jewellery.*

worthwhile *adj.* **1** °profitable, justifiable, °productive, °gainful, °rewarding, °fruitful, cost-effective, remunerative: *Would it be worthwhile to buy up that land as a long-term investment?* **2** °useful, valuable, °good, °helpful, °beneficial, °worthy, beneficent, °desirable, °exemplary, °matchless, °honourable, °upright, °sterling, °irreproachable: *Brian Smith is one of the most worthwhile people I met at university.*

worthy *adj.* **1** °worthwhile, °deserving, meriting, °meritorious, °praiseworthy, °good, °estimable, °qualified, creditable: *He is a worthy recipient of the honour.* **2** See **worthwhile, 2,** above.
—*n.* **3** °dignitary, °personage, °notable, eminence, luminary: *The dinner was attended by all the local worthies.*

wound *n.* **1** °damage, °hurt, °injury, trauma, traumatism; laceration, °puncture, °cut, °gash, °slash, lesion, °bruise, contusion: *We dressed and bandaged the wounds of the victims.* **2** °slight, °damage, °injury, °harm, °blow, °distress, mortification, °torment, torture, °anguish, °pain, °insult: *Hugh takes the slightest criticism as a deep wound to his self-esteem.*
—*v.* **3** °damage, °harm, °injure, °hurt, traumatize; °cut, °slash, °gash, °lacerate, °slit, °stab, °shoot, *Colloq* wing: *He was wounded in the leg in the war.* **4** °slight, °distress, °damage, °mortify, °insult, °hurt, °pain, °grieve, °offend, aggrieve, °wrong: *I was terribly wounded by the things she said about me.*

wrap *v.* **1** Sometimes, ***wrap up***: °swathe, swaddle, °bind, °cover, enwrap, °envelop, °wind, enshroud, °shroud, enfold, °fold, °muffle, °enclose, sheathe, encase; °pack, °package, do up, gift-wrap: *Wrap up*

well—it's cold outside. I've just finished wrapping some Christmas presents. **2** ***wrapped up in***: immersed in, submerged in, buried in, °absorbed in, engrossed in, °bound up in, °involved in, occupied with *or* by *or* in, °engaged in, dedicated to, °devoted to: *While Irma is completely wrapped up in her grandchildren, Henry is wrapped up in his books.* **3** ***wrap up***: **a** °complete, conclude, °finish, °end, bring to a °close, °terminate, °wind up, °settle, °tidy up: *We'll be able to wrap things up in an hour and go home.* **b** ***Wrap up!***: Be °silent!, Be °quiet!, Stop talking!, Hold your °tongue!, *Slang* °Shut up!, Shut your face!, Shut your °trap!, Shut your °mouth!, *Brit* Put a sock in it!: *He would have kept on wittering away if she hadn't told him to wrap up.*
—*n.* **4** °stole, shawl, °mantle, poncho, serape, °cloak, °cape: *Sonia adjusted her evening wrap before going out to dinner.*

wrapper *n.* **1** housecoat, °robe, dressing-gown, bathrobe, kimono, negligee, lounging °robe, peignoir, *US* house-dress: *Peggy threw on a wrapper and went to answer the door.* **2** envelope, °package, packing, wrapping, covering, jacket, °case, casing, container: *Throw the wrapper in the dustbin.*

wreak *v.* °inflict, °exercise, °exert, °carry out, °bring (to bear), °visit, °effect, °work, unleash, °execute, °impose, °force, °vent, let go: *The tribesmen wreaked vengeance on the hill people for destroying their farms.*

wreck *v.* **1** °destroy, °ruin, °devastate, °demolish, smash, °shatter, °spoil, °dash (to °pieces), reduce to nothing, turn into °scrap, annihilate: *He drove my motor-bike into a tree and wrecked it.* **2** °sink, scuttle, run aground, °founder, °capsize: *The ship was wrecked on a reef near Rarotonga.*
—*n.* **3** °hulk, shipwreck, °ruins: *The wreck finally rusted away to nothing.* **4** °mess, °disaster, °ruin; °havoc: *That man made a wreck of her life.* **5** °destruction, °loss, °sinking, devastation, foundering, grounding, °capsize, capsizing, disabling, disablement, wrecking; demolition, demolishing, levelling, tearing down, razing, pulling down, obliteration: *The wreck of the* Titanic *was a major news event in 1912. The wreck of the old tower block is scheduled for next month.*

wreckage *n.* debris, fragments, remains, rubble, °ruin(s): *The wreckage of the building is being searched for survivors.*

wrench *v.* **1** °yank, °twist, °jerk, °force, °pull, °tug, °tear, wring, °rip, wrest: *The gun was wrenched from my grasp, breaking my finger.* **2** °strain, sprain, °twist, overstrain: *After she wrenched her ankle on the ladder, Mary couldn't walk for a week.* **3** °extract, wrest, wring, °force, °pry, °draw: *The only way they could wrench the information from Michael was by torturing him.*
—*n.* **4** °yank, °twist, °jerk, °pull, °tug, °rip: *One wrench at the doorknob and it came off in my hand.* **5** °pang, °pain, °agony, torture, °blow, °ache, °throe, °anguish, °sadness, °grief, heartbreak: *The severest wrench at my heartstrings came when we had to part.* **6** *Brit* spanner, shifting spanner, adjustable spanner, *US* monkey wrench: *We need metric wrenches to work on your car.*

wrestle *v.* °battle, °fight, °struggle, tussle, °strive: *After thirty years Garth wrestled his way to the top in the company.*

wretch *n.* **1** °scoundrel, blackguard, worm, °villain, cur, °beast, dog, swine, °rogue, °good-for-nothing, knave, varlet, scallywag *or* scalawag, °rascal, rapscallion, *Archaic* caitiff, whoreson, *Colloq* rat, °stinker, louse, creep, *Slang* bastard, *Brit* rotter, bounder, blighter, *US* °bum: *That wretch not only stole my wife but asked me for money to support her!* **2** °unfortunate, °poor °fellow *or* °chap, °miserable °creature, °poor °devil, pilgarlic, *Slang* °poor bastard *or* son of a bitch, *Brit* °poor °bugger *or* sod, *US* °sad sack: *The poor wretch cannot keep a job and lives off others' charity.*

wretched *adj.* **1** °miserable, °awful, °terrible, °atrocious, °deplorable, *Colloq* °lousy, °rotten: *We had the most wretched weather throughout our holiday.* **2** °unhappy, °sad, °miserable, °woebegone, woeful, °dismal, °downhearted, °heartbroken, °brokenhearted, heartsick, °dejected, depressed, melancholic, °melancholy, °mournful, disconsolate, °inconsolable, °doleful, cheerless, crestfallen, °joyless, °desolate: *If you want to see a wretched human being, look at a boy whose dog is lost.* **3** °pitiable, °pathetic, °sorry, °pitiful, hapless, °hopeless, °unfortunate, °miserable: *The poor in these tropical paradises are some of the most wretched people on earth.* **4** °vile, °shameful, °scurvy, underhand(ed), treacherous, °contemptible, °despicable, °base, °low, °mean, °paltry, mean-spirited, detestable: *It was hard to see how the people could support such a wretched little demagogue.*

wriggle *v.* **1** wiggle, wobble, °shake, °tremble, °quiver, °jiggle, waggle, writhe, °twist, °fidget: *She managed to wriggle free of the ropes and run away. The dog was wriggling with excitement at seeing its master.* **2** °twist, °squirm, °snake, worm, writhe, °slither, °crawl: *He wriggled through the narrow opening into the strongroom.*
—*n.* **3** wiggle, zigzag, wavy °line, *Colloq* squiggle, squiggly °line: *The page had no writing on it, only a lot of wriggles.* **4** wriggling, writhing, °squirm, squirming, wiggle, wiggling, shaking, trembling, °quiver, quivering, shimmying, waggle, waggling, twisting, °twist: *Don't confuse that rhythmic wriggle of the hips with dancing.*

wrinkle[1] *n.* **1** crease, °fold, °line, °furrow, crinkle, crow's-foot, corrugation, °pucker, °ridge: *She hasn't a wrinkle on her face—but then she's only nine.*
—*v.* **2** crease, °fold, °line, °furrow, crinkle, corrugate, °pucker, °gather, ruck, crimp, °screw up, °rumple, °crumple: *I love the way you wrinkle your nose when you're perplexed.*

wrinkle[2] *n.* °dodge, °gimmick, °device, ploy, °ruse, °scheme, °trick, °idea, °plan, °plot, °stunt, °way, °approach, °technique, °method, *Slang chiefly Brit* wheeze: *Leave it to Edmund to come up with a new wrinkle for fleecing pensioners.*

write *v.* **1** °pen, scribble, get off, °dash off; indite, inscribe, °make out: *I was writing you a note when you phoned. She wrote out a cheque for £1,000.* **2** °correspond (with), °send a letter *or* a note *or* a postcard *or US also* a postal °card, °communicate (with): *You don't write home often enough. Write and let me know when you get a job.* **3** °compose, °create, °make up, °author: *We saw the house in which Elgar wrote the 'Enigma' Variations.* **4** ***write down***: **a** °register, °list, catalogue, note, make a note *or* °notation, °record, °transcribe, °set *or* °jot *or* °take down, note, put in writing, put in black and white: *The teacher was known for Irish bulls like, 'All absent students must write down their names'.* **b** derogate, decry, °disparage, °put down, °minimize, make little of, °play down, °detract, °belittle: *Cumberland's contributions have been written down by his critics.* **5** ***write off***: °delete, °cancel, °disregard, °ignore, °forgive, °forget (about), annul, eradicate, °erase: *The bad debts have been written off.*

writer *n.* °author, novelist, littérateur, essayist, man of letters, °scribe, scribbler, wordsmith, freelancer, penny-a-liner, °hack, Grub Streeter, °journalist, newsman, °reporter, °correspondent, member of the fourth estate, (gossip) columnist, stringer, *Brit* paragraphist, *US* paragrapher, *Colloq* pen-pusher, pencil-pusher, sob sister, *Brit* journo: *These days all those who know how to write call themselves writers.*

writing *n.* **1** handwriting, longhand, °penmanship, °script, calligraphy *or* chirography, scribble: *I sometimes have trouble reading your writing.* **2** Sometimes, ***writings***: (°literary) °work(s), °composition, °theme, °book, article, critique, °criticism, °review, °editorial, column, exposé, °essay, °poetry, °poem, °novel, non-fiction, fiction, °document, letter, correspondence, °publication, *Chiefly Brit journalism* leading article *or* leader, *Chiefly US journalism* op-ed article: *Her writing has been widely published. Poe's writings are collected in this book.* **3** °literature, belles-lettres, letters: *I don't agree that British writing has declined since 1900.*

wrong *adj.* **1** °improper, unjust, unfair, injudicious, unethical, °terrible, °foul, °awful, °bad, °immoral, °sinful, °evil, iniquitous, °villainous, °wicked, °vile, °diabolic(al), °infernal, °fiendish, °corrupt, °dishonest, reprehensible, °abominable, °dreadful, °dishonourable, blameworthy, °naughty, °shameful, °disgraceful, opprobrious, °criminal, felonious, °illegal, °illicit, °unlawful, °illegitimate, *Colloq* °crooked: *They believe that all war is wrong. It was wrong of you to come here while my husband was away.* **2** °mistaken, in °error, °erroneous, °incorrect, °inaccurate, °imprecise, °inexact, fallacious, askew, °false, °wide of the mark; °strange, °odd, °peculiar, °curious; *Colloq* off target *or US also* off the target, *Brit* off beam, *US* off the beam: *The answers to these four questions were all wrong. You certainly have some wrong ideas about me.* **3** °incorrect, °improper, unsuitable: *They must have given us the wrong baby at the hospital.* **4** °inappropriate, inapt, °improper, indecorous, °unseemly, unfitting, °unacceptable, °undesirable, °incongruous, °unbecoming, out of °place, ill-considered, wrong-headed, °imprudent, °misguided, inexpedient, impolitic, infelicitous, *Colloq* out of line: *You saw nothing wrong in inviting girls to stay with you in your rooms? Your mother thinks she's the wrong girl for you.* **5** out of °order, not working, °faulty, awry, °amiss, the °matter, °defective, °imperfect, °unsound, °flawed, °deficient: *Considering the noise my car makes, there must be something wrong.* **6** °opposite, °reverse, °incorrect, °improper: *That is the wrong direction to the post office.*
—*adv.* **7** awry, imperfectly, incorrectly, improperly, inappropriately, °amiss, °badly, wrongly, *Scots and No. Eng. and literary* agley, *Colloq* out of sync: *You've wired up the video all wrong.* **8** ***go wrong***: **a** go astray, falter, °fail, °lapse, °err, °fall from grace, go to the °bad, °deteriorate, go downhill, backslide, regress, retrogress, recidivate: *Her father was convinced that she would go wrong if she went into the theatre.* **b** °fail, malfunction, °break down, °miscarry, backfire, °fall through, *Colloq* °flop, come to °grief, go kaput, *Brit* go phut: *The entire plan went wrong when Clara started screaming.*
—*v.* **9** °abuse, °mistreat, °injure, °misuse, maltreat, ill-use, °ill-treat, °discredit, asperse, calumniate, malign, °dishonour, °impose upon, take °advantage of, °harm, °damage, °oppress: *He believes he was wronged by his commanding officer.*

wry *adj.* **1** distorted, contorted, twisted, °lopsided, °deformed, °crooked, aslant, °one-sided, askew, °bent, tilted, off-centre: *He is afflicted by a rheumatic disorder, which gives his neck a wry appearance.* **2** °dry, droll, °witty, °sardonic, °sarcastic, ironic(al), amusing; °perverse, fey; *Scots* pawky: *Bill has a wry sense of humour that does not appeal to everyone.*

Y

yank *v.* **1** °jerk, °jolt, °tug, °wrench, °snatch, °hitch: *He yanked the chair from beneath me just as I sat down.*
—*n.* **2** °jerk, °jolt, °tug, °wrench, °snatch, °hitch: *Give two yanks on the rope when you want me to pull you up.*

yap *v.* **1** bark, yelp: *Their dog was yapping away all night.* **2** gabble, °babble, blither *or* blather, °chatter, °jabber, °tattle, °prattle, prate, *Colloq chiefly Brit* witter, natter, *Slang* jaw, run on, *US* run off at the mouth: *I wish she'd stop her yapping and give me some peace.*
—*n.* **3** °mouth, *Slang* °trap, °gob, *US* bazoo: *If only Sam would shut his big yap once in a while!*

yardstick *n.* °measure, benchmark, criterion, °standard, °gauge, °basis, °touchstone, °scale, exemplar: *We thought she sang beautifully, but then we had no yardstick against which to judge.*

yarn *n.* **1** °thread, °fibre, strand: *I haven't enough yarn to finish knitting these socks.* **2** °tale, °story, °account, °narrative, anecdote; °tall °tale, fable, °fabrication, fiction, cock-and-bull °story, *Colloq* whopper, *Brit* fishing °story, *US* fish °story, fish °tale: *The old salt had many yarns to spin during the long evenings by the fire.*

yearly *adv.* **1** annually, perennially, every year, °once a year, year after year, year in (and) year out, regularly: *We watch the Canada geese migrate north yearly.* **2** per year, per annum, by the year, each year: *What is the interest rate yearly?*
—*adj.* **3** annual, °perennial, once-a-year, °regular: *Those yearly migrations told us when to plant the first crop.*

yearn *v.* °long, pine, °ache, °hanker, °itch, °hunger, °thirst, crave, have a craving, °desire, °wish, °want, °fancy, °prefer: *I yearn to see the green-clad hills of home once more, Before my vessel bears me from this mortal shore.*

yell *v.* **1** °shout, °scream, °bellow, °howl, screech, yowl, °roar, °bawl, caterwaul, squall, yelp, *Colloq* holler: *'Stop yelling at your sister!' shouted my father.*
—*n.* **2** °shout, °scream, °cry, °bellow, °howl, screech, yowl, °roar, caterwaul, squall, yelp, *Colloq* holler: *I think I heard a yell for help.*

yeomanly *adj.* yeoman, workmanlike, °useful, °staunch, °courageous, °loyal, dedicated, °faithful, °steadfast, unswerving, unwavering, °firm, °sturdy, °reliable, °solid: *Carruthers certainly did a yeomanly job on reorganizing the system.*

yes-man *n.* toady, sycophant, toad-eater, time-server, °hanger-on, lickspittle, bootlicker, truckler, °flunkey, courtier, jackal, spaniel, lap-dog, *Taboo slang Brit* arse-kisser, arse-licker, *US* ass-kisser, ass-licker, brown-noser: *He surrounds himself with yes-men, then says he refuses to take no for an answer.*

yet *adv.* **1** as yet, (up) till *or* until now, so °far, thus far, hitherto, to the °present (time): *She hasn't arrived yet.* **2** °still, up to this °time, up to °now, even now, till *or* until now, to this day: *She was there earlier and I think she's there yet.* **3** °moreover, furthermore, °besides, °further, °still: *He made yet another excuse.* **4** in the °future, in °time to come, later, °eventually: *Despite the life I've led, I might yet get to heaven.* **5** °still, °notwithstanding, anyway, anyhow, °nonetheless, °nevertheless, °regardless, in °spite of *or* °despite everything, just *or* all the °same, °even so, after all, *US* still and all: *Despite the life I've led, I might get to heaven yet.*
—*conj.* **6** °notwithstanding, in °spite of *or* °despite it *or* that *or* the fact, °still, °nevertheless, but: *He goes out every night, yet never oversleeps in the mornings.*

yield *v.* **1** °surrender, °give up (the fight *or* struggle), °give in, knuckle under, °submit, °cede, cry quits, throw in the towel *or* the sponge, °capitulate, °succumb, raise the white flag: *The captain of the enemy company asked if we would yield.* **2** °give up, °surrender, °give over, °hand in *or* over, °abandon, °relinquish, °renounce, °cede: *We agreed to yield our arms to the enemy.* **3** °agree, °consent, °comply, °concede, °relent, assent, give °way, accede, concur: *He did his best to persuade me, and I finally yielded.* **4** °earn, °return, °pay, °bring in, °supply, °generate, °produce, °net: *She has investments that yield more than 15% a year.*
—*n.* **5** °return, °production, °output, °revenue, takings, °gate, °earnings, °income, °proceeds, °profit, °gain: *The yield from that operation is not even enough to pay the rent.*

yielding *adj.* **1** pliant, flexile, °flexible, °pliable, °soft, °plastic, fictile, °elastic, resilient, °supple, springy, bouncy, spongy, rubbery: *The frame is of a yielding material that gives way under pressure.* **2** °accommodating, docile, °submissive, amenable, °tractable, compliant, °obedient, °flexible, acquiescent, °agreeable, °obliging, °manageable, manipulable: *He wanted a wife with a yielding temperament who would tolerate his foibles.*

young *adj.* **1** youthful, teenage(d), °adolescent, prepubescent, pubescent, °juvenile, °minor, °junior, under °age: *Would you believe that she has young children?* **2** °boyish, girlish; °immature, °callow, °green, °inexperienced, °unfledged, uninitiated, °unsophisticated, °childlike, °innocent, °naïve: *This programme may contain material unsuitable for young ears.* **3** °childish, °puerile, °infantile, babyish, *US* sophomoric: *He's too young to invite to the party.*
—*n.* **4** °offspring, babies, °issue, little ones, °progeny, °litter, °brood; children: *The cat's young should stay with her for a few weeks.*

youth *n.* **1** °childhood, boyhood, girlhood, °young manhood, °young womanhood, prepubescence, pubescence, adolescence, salad days; immaturity, minority: *In our youth we do many foolish things we might later regret.* **2** °child, youngster, schoolchild, °teenager, teen, °minor, °juvenile, °adolescent; °boy, schoolboy, °stripling, °young °boy *or* °man, °lad, laddie, whippersnapper; °girl, °lass, lassie, schoolgirl, °maid, °maiden, *Literary* damsel, demoiselle, mademoiselle, *Colloq* kid, (little) shaver, *US and Canadian* tad, *Slang* teeny-bopper, *Brit* sprog: *As youths, they used to spend time at rock concerts.* **3** children, youngsters, juveniles, adolescents, °young °people, °young, *Colloq* kids: *The youth of today have little respect for their elders.*

yucky *adj.* yukky *or US also* yuchy, °disgusting, °repugnant, °repellent, unappetizing, vomit-provoking, sick-making, ill-making, °nauseous, nauseating, °revolting, °foul, mucky, °beastly, °awful, *Slang Brit* grotty: *We get this yucky mess at school that we call 'mystery meat'.*

yummy *adj.* °delicious, mouth-watering, °luscious, appetizing, °tasty, toothsome, °savoury, delectable, ambrosial, *Colloq* scrumptious: *At our school tuck shop we get the most yummy ice-cream.*

Z

zany *adj.* **1** clownish, °mad, °wild, °frolicsome, °sportive, °playful, °gay, °merry, slapstick, °crazy, °funny, °comic(al), amusing, °hilarious, °absurd, °nonsensical, °ludicrous, °silly, °foolish, °inane, *Colloq* wacky, loony, madcap, crackpot, nutty, goofy, *US* kooky: *The buskers put on the zaniest show I have seen for some time.*
—*n.* **2** °clown, °comic, jester, °fool, °joker, buffoon, °wag, °comedian, comedienne, °merry andrew, laughing-stock, *Slang* nut, *US* screwball: *The two zanies kept the crowd in stitches while the pickpockets stole their wallets.*

zap *v.* °destroy, °kill, °slaughter, annihilate, °murder, slay, assassinate, liquidate, °erase; °shoot, electrocute, *Slang* °rub out, °polish off, °knock off, °bump off, snuff (out), °waste, °hit, *US* ice: *The baddies got zapped by the ray gun, one after the other.*

zealot *n.* °fanatic, extremist, °radical, bigot, °maniac, °militant: *We have to deal with ruthless zealots who are willing to die for their cause.*

zealotry *n.* °fanaticism, extremism, radicalism, °bigotry, militantism, terrorism, single-mindedness, monomania, °fervour, °frenzy, hysteria, °obsession, obsessiveness: *Their attacks on innocent civilians show how far their zealotry can take them.*

zenith *n.* meridian, °summit, °acme, apex, °vertex, apogee, °high °point, °top, °peak, °pinnacle: *The dictator reached the zenith of his power very quickly.*

zero *n.* **1** °nil, null, °nothing, nought *or* °naught, aught, cipher, *Cricket* duck, *Colloq* nix, *US* goose-egg, nada, niente, *Slang Brit* (sweet) Fanny Adams *or* F.A., bugger-all, *US* zilch: *Temperatures have remained below zero all day. The visiting team won three games, we won zero.* **2** (rock) °bottom, nadir: *On a scale of one to ten, she is a zero.* **3** °nobody, °nothing, nonentity, *Slang US* nebbish, bupkis: *That fellow she married is a real zero.*
—*v.* **4** ***zero in on***: °focus on, pinpoint, °fix on, home in on, °concentrate on, bring to bear on: *We zeroed in on the problem and then rapidly found the answer.*

zest *n.* **1** °spice, °relish, °gusto, °tang, °pepper, ginger, piquancy, pungency, °edge, °bite, °flavour, *Colloq* zing, zip, pizazz *or* pizzazz: *Put in a little of my home-made sauce to add some zest.* **2** °eagerness, zestfulness, °exuberance, °appetite, °interest, °enthusiasm, °hunger, °thirst: *Where does Sidney get his zest for life?*

zone *n.* °area, °quarter, °district, °region, sector, °section, °sphere, °belt, °territory, °province, °realm, °domain, °precinct, bailiwick, °department, °terrain, °circle, locality, °locale, *Slang US* °turf: *A duty-free zone will allow for quicker transshipment of goods. The northern and southern hemispheres each have a frigid, temperate, and torrid zone.*

zoo *n.* **1** zoological garden, menagerie, *Tiergarten*, (safari) °park: *When I was a child, I enjoyed going to the zoo almost as much as I do now.* **2** madhouse, °mess; °chaos, °pandemonium, °bedlam, *Colloq US* three-ring circus, Chinese fire-drill: *When my husband and the three children get ready in the morning the kitchen is like a zoo.*

INDEX

How to Use the Index

THE Index lists in alphabetical order the words and phrases that occur, either as main headwords in their own right or as synonyms of some other headword, in the text of the *Thesaurus*.

When you want to find synonyms for a word, you can either start by looking for that word as a main entry in the text or you can come straight to the Index to find out how many times your chosen word is mentioned and where. If you look first in the text and fail to find the word that interests you entered there as a main entry, you may still find it entered in the Index because it is listed in the text as a synonym of one or more other headwords.

The degree sign (°) is used in the Index to indicate that a word or phrase has its own list of synonyms in the text. If, for example, you were interested in finding synonyms for *advisory* and looked first for it in the Index, you would find an entry reading

advisory°

meaning that the word *advisory* has its own entry and list of synonyms but does not occur anywhere else in the *Thesaurus* as a synonym of any other word. If you looked for the word *adult* in the Index, you would find an entry reading

adult°
mature 1
racy 2

This means that *adult* has its own entry and list of synonyms, and in addition to this it occurs as a synonym of *mature* and *racy*, and can be found in the list of synonyms at sense 1 of *mature* and sense 2 of *racy*. So, if you had failed to find the group of synonyms that you were seeking in the main entry, you could then move on to the words listed near *adult* in the entries for *mature* and/or *racy*.

The degree sign, when used in the Index, does not always point to a main entry. In the text, separate lists of synonyms are sometimes given for a phrase, for the plural form of a noun, etc. These too are given a degree sign in the Index to show that a list of synonyms is available. If the word or phrase is not a main entry in its own right, the degree sign is followed by the word *at* and the entry and sense number at which the list of synonyms can be found, printed in **small bold type**. For example, the entry

argue out of°
at **argue 6**

means that the phrase *argue out of* has its own list of synonyms at sense 6 of *argue*, but is not entered as a synonym of any other word or phrase in the text, while

bear in mind°
at **mind 9**
consider 2
heed 1
reckon 5b
remember 1
retain 4

means that a list of synonyms for the phrase *bear in mind* can be found at sense 9 of the entry for *mind*, but the phrase itself also occurs as a synonym of *consider* (sense 2), *heed* (sense 1), *reckon* (sense 5b), etc.

All the words and phrases in the Index are listed in letter-by-letter alphabetical order, that is in alphabetical order of the actual letters that occur in them, without taking account of hyphens and spaces within them. For example, the order of entries at *cry-* is as follows:

cry
cry-baby
crying
cry out

cry out for
cry over
crypt
cryptic
etc.

As can be seen from this example, phrases mostly occur as main headings in the index in their alphabetical places; this applies not just to phrasal verbs of the type *cry out* and *cry out for*, but also to verbal idioms like *corner the market* (between *cornerstone* and *corniness*) and *count sheep* (between *country-wide* and *count upon*), to noun phrases like *crack of dawn* (between *crackle* and *crackpot*) and *everything but the kitchen sink* (between *everything* and *everything considered*), and to compound words like *cream puff* (between *cream* and *creamy*). Only phrases which begin with a preposition or the verb *be* are entered as subheadings under a keyword. For example, the phrase *at one's convenience* will be found as a subheading under *convenience* and *to the core* as a subheading under *core*. Subheadings are introduced by a rule (—). For example, the Index entry

cup
mug 1
potion
trophy 1
—in one's cups
drunk 1
stinking 3

means that *cup* occurs as a synonym of *mug*, *potion*, and *trophy*, and in addition the phrase *in one's cups* is listed as a synonym of *drunk* (sense 1) and *stinking* (sense 3).

Subheadings are also used for the plural form of a headword. For example, the index entry

curio
antique 2
curiosity 3
rarity 1
—curios
bric-à-brac

means that, while *curio* occurs in its singular form as a synonym of *antique*, *curiosity*, and *rarity*, it is also used in the plural as a collective term, and this is listed as a synonym at *bric-à-brac*.

When an Index entry contains more than one subheading, even if they include both of these types, the subheadings are listed in a strict letter-by-letter alphabetical sequence like the one used for main headings. Thus at *day*, the subheadings come in the order

—days
—in days gone by *etc.*
—in this day and age
—to this day

but at *contrast*, the plural comes in the middle of the alphabetical sequence:

—as contrasted with
—contrasts
—in contrast to

abnormal (*cont.*)
unwonted
way-out 1
abnormality°
freak 2
impropriety 1
peculiarity 1
perversion 2
Abo
aboriginal
aboard
board 5
abode°
domicile 1
dwelling
habitat
home 1
house 1
place 6
quarter 5
residence 1
seat 5
abode of the damned
hell 1
abode of the dead
underworld 2
abolish°
cancel 1
dispense 3b
erase 2
extinguish 2
forgive 3
repeal 1
revoke
stamp 4
vitiate 3
abolition°
cancellation 1, 2, 3
repeal 2
abominable°
abhorrent
atrocious 1
awful 1
beastly 2
black 6
damnable
deplorable 2
diabolic 2
disagreeable 2
evil 1
foul 4
frightful 2
ghoulish 2
grisly
gruesome
hateful 1
hideous 2
horrible 1
infamous 2
loathsome
nameless 3
obnoxious
obscene 1
offensive 3
outrageous 2
repugnant
repulsive
revolting
satanic 2
shabby 4
shocking 2
terrible 5
ugly 2
vicious 1
wicked 2
wrong 1
abominate
abhor
detest
dislike 1
hate 1
loathe
abomination
infamy 2
revulsion
aboriginal°
indigenous 1
native 2, 5
original 2
primitive 1
aborigine
aboriginal
native 7
abort
fail 1
fizzle 2
founder[2] 2
miscarry
misfire 1, 2
prevent
scrub 2
terminate
abortion
fiasco
miscarriage
monster 2
prevention
termination 1
abortive
fruitless
futile
idle 4
unsuccessful 1
useless 1
vain 2
abound°
crawl 4
teem[1]
abound in°
at **abound 2**
fill 6
swarm 3
abounding
abundant 2
fraught 1
luxuriant 2
pregnant 3
prodigal 2
rampant 2
rich 2
abound with°
at **abound 3**
swarm 3
about°
almost
approximately
around 1, 2, 3, 4, 5, 6
by 6
close 21
concern 1
concerning
nearby 1
nearly 1
neighbourhood 2
over 5
ready 4
regarding
relation 5
roughly 1
round 20, 21, 22, 23, 26
say 14
wind[1] 8
about-face
about-turn
reversal 1
about to
fit[1] 4
verge[1] 2
warm 6
wind[1] 8
about-turn°
reversal 1
above°
aloft
deception 1, 2
foregoing
free 11
further 3
over 1, 2
overhead 1
preceding
previous 2
subject 7
above all°
at **above 6**
chiefly
especially 2
mainly
principally
above and beyond
besides 2
above-board°
artless 1
candid 1
fair[1] 2
forthright
frank 2
free 9
honest 2, 3
honestly 2
honourable 3
ingenuous 1
level 15
point-blank 1
respectable 1
right 1
simple 3
sincere
square 4
straight 4
transparent 3
above-mentioned
preceding
previous 2
above-named
preceding
previous 2
above-stated
preceding
abracadabra
hocus-pocus 2
mumbo-jumbo 2
abrade
chafe 2
erode
fray[2]
gall[2] 3
grind 1
rasp 3
rub 1
scour 1
scrape 1
scratch 1
skin 5
wear 3
abrading
erosion
friction 1
Abraham's bosom
heaven 1
paradise 1
abrasion
bruise 1
chafe 4
erosion
friction 1
gall[2] 1
scrape 7
scratch 4
sore 7
wear 9
abrasive
gritty 1
abraxas
talisman
abridge°
abbreviate 2
abstract 4
curtail
cut 5
digest 4
diminish 1
minimize 1
reduce 1
shorten 2
sum 2a
telescope 2
abridged
brief 2
concise
cut 27
short 2
terse 1
abridgement°
brief 4
digest 5
epitome 2
précis
summary 1
synopsis
abroad°
elsewhere
out 2
abroad (*cont.*)
overseas
abrogate
cancel 1
contradict 2
renege 2
repeal 1
repudiate
revoke
set 15b
vitiate 3
void 6
abrogation
cancellation 1
repeal 2
abrupt°
bluff[2] 1
blunt 2
brief 3
brusque
curt
dead 16
disagreeable 3
discourteous
fretful
gruff 1
harsh 3
immediate 1
impetuous
moody 2
offhand 2
passing 2
point-blank 1
precipitate 4
precipitous 1
quick 2
quick-tempered
rough 3
sharp 2
sheer 1
short 4
short-tempered
snap 13
snappish 2
sour 4
steep[1] 1
sudden
summary 2
swift
tactless
terse 2
ungracious
abruptly
cold 11
dead 19
plump[2] 5
point-blank 3
sharp 11
sharply 2
short 11
shortly 3
suddenly 1
summarily 2
swiftly
unawares 1
abruptness
speed 1
abscess
boil[2]
ulcer 1
abscond
beat 8
bolt 8
carry 10b
depart 1
desert[1] 4
escape 1
flee 1
flight[2] 3
fly 2
make 26
powder 2
run 2
spirit 10
absconder
deserter
runaway 1
absence°
dearth
lack 1
–in the absence of
failing 2
absent°
absent-minded
dreamy 2
elsewhere
far-away 2
miss[1] 1
out 2
truant 2
wanting 2
withdraw 5
absentee
truant 1, 2
absently
vaguely 3
absent-minded°
careless 2
dreamy 2
far-away 2
forgetful
inattentive
oblivious
preoccupied 2
thoughtless 2
vacant 2
wander
wistful 2
absent-mindedly
vaguely 3
absent-mindedness
reverie
vacancy 3
absent oneself
miss[1] 1
absolute°
arbitrary 2
authoritarian
bare 5
blank 6
categorical
certain 4
clear 14
complete 3
dead 14
decided 1
definitive 3
despot
despotic
dictator
dictatorial 1
entire 1
exclusive 1
explicit 1
final 2
flat 4
implicit 2
inalienable
incontrovertible
indisputable
inevitable
main 4
mere
outright 2
perfect 1, 6
positive 1
precise 2
profound 4
pure 5
rank[2] 2
regular 9
right 8
sheer 2
sovereign 2
stark 4
thorough 1
total 3
totalitarian
unlimited 1
unmitigated
unqualified 2
absolutely°
actually
altogether
certainty 3
clean 7
clearly 2
cold 11
completely 2
dead 18, 19
definitely
doubtless 1
downright 2
exactly 2
absolutely (*cont.*)
expressly 1
fairly 3
finally 2
flat 16
indeed 1
mean[3] 2a
outright 4
perfectly 1
positively
precisely 2
quite 1, 4
really 1, 2
simply 1
stark 1
surely 1
thoroughly 1
totally
truly 3
utterly
very 1
wholly 1
absolutely not
mean[3] 5
absolution
excuse 5
forgiveness 1
immunity 1
pardon 1
remission 1
absolutism
despotism
monarchy 2
tyranny
absolutist
totalitarian
absolve
clear 21
discharge 1
excuse 1, 2
exempt 1
forgive 2
justify
let[1] 6b
pardon 2
purge 3
purify 2
redeem 4
vindicate 1
absolved
clear 32
absorb
busy 4
catch 14a
comprehend
consume 3
cushion 2
devour 3
distract 2
divert 3
engage 2
fascinate
get 21
grip 7
hold 4
immerse 2
interest 7
intrigue 1
kill 3
occupy 3
penetrate 4
retain 3
soak 2
swallow 3
absorbed°
absent-minded
bury 3
deep 4
devour 3
engaged 2
full 6
intent 4
interested 1
muse
preoccupied 1
rapt 1
wistful 2
wrap 2
absorbing°
enthralling
interesting
readable 2
riveting

accessary
accessory 2
accident 3
accomplice
accessible°
accommodating 2
available
convenient 2
forthcoming 3
free 3
friendly 2
hand 9
handy 1
home 4b
nearby 2
open 4
outgoing 2
popular 3
public 3
ready 7
reserve 8
sociable
stand 5b
susceptible 2
accession
succession 3
accessorize
ornament 2
accessory°
accident 3
accomplice
ally 1
associate 3, 6
attachment 4
attendant 1
auxiliary 1, 2, 3
extra 1, 3
fellow 3
fixture 2
further 1
indirect 2
instrumental
non-essential 1
occasional 2
ornament 1
partner 1
party 4
subsidiary
supplement 1
sympathizer
-accessories
fitting 2
furniture 2
gear 2
paraphernalia
stuff 2
trappings
accident°
casualty 1
catastrophe 2
coincidence 3
disaster
fluke
luck 1
misfortune 2
pile-up 1
spill 5
-by accident
unawares 2
accidental°
casual 1
chance 6
circumstantial 2
coincidental
haphazard 1
inadvertent 1
incidental 1
indirect 2
random 1
stray 5
accidentally
chance 5a
incidentally 2
unawares 2
accidie
sloth
sluggishness
acclaim
applause
attention 2
clap 1
credit 4
eulogize
eulogy

acclaim *(cont.)*
extol
fame
glorify 2
hail[1] 2
honour 6
kudos
laud
laurels
ovation
popularity
praise 1, 3
rave 3
renown
tribute 1
acclaimed
celebrated
famous
honourable 4
illustrious
legendary 3
noble 3
notable 1
noted
popular 1
prestigious
prominent 2
renowned
acclamation
applause
eulogy
kudos
laurels
ovation
praise 1
tribute 1
acclimate
accustom
adapt 2
adjust 3
condition 7
orient 3
resign 2
acclimated
seasoned
used 3
acclimation
resignation 2
acclimatization
orientation 2
resignation 2
acclimatize
accustom
adapt 2
adjust 3
condition 7
orient 3
resign 2
acclimatized
seasoned
used 3
acclivitous
precipitous 1
acclivity
grade 4
hill 3
incline 4
ramp
rise 13
slope 2
accolade
eulogy
honour 2
kudos
praise 1
prize[1] 1
rave 3
accommodate°
adapt 2
adjust 3
board 7
contain 2
entertain 2
favour 8
fit[1] 7
fix 16a
gear 5
hold 8
house 8, 9
lodge 4
minister 3
oblige 1
orient 3
provide 1

accommodate *(cont.)*
put 28b
quarter 6
reconcile 2
resign 2
seat 6
serve 1
shape 9
sit 5
square 12
suit 1
supply 1
tailor 2
take 17, 32a
work 17
accommodating°
agreeable 2
attentive 2
considerate
decent 4
dutiful
easy 4
elastic 2
favourable 1
gracious
helpful
human 3
kind[1]
obliging
patient 3
respectful
submissive 1
supple 3
sweet 6
user-friendly
yielding 2
accommodation°
abode
adaptation 2
domicile 1
flat 18
home 1
housing 1
loan 1
lodging
passage 7
quarter 5
room 3
seating
service 3
settlement 3
shelter 3
space 4
-accommoda-tions
accommodation 4
home 1
lodging
passage 7
quarter 5
accommodative
adaptable
agreeable 2
favourable 1
accompanied
fraught 1
parallel 4
accompaniment
score 5
accompany°
attend 4, 5
bring 2
call 8b
escort 4
follow 3
go 20a, 40b
join 3
see 6
show 2
squire 1
tag 5
take 18
walk 2
watch 2
accompanying
attendant 1
accomplice°
accessory 2
ally 1
associate 3
cohort 3
partner 1
party 4

accomplice *(cont.)*
sympathizer
accomplish°
achieve 1, 2
bring 7, 11
carry 10c, 12
complete 5
discharge 5
dispatch 4
effect 7
effectuate
execute 1
finish 2
fulfil 1
implement 2
make 14
negotiate 2
notch 4
perfect 8
perform 1
perpetrate
procure 2
pull 12b
put 27a
reach 4
realize 1
render 1
work 16
accomplishable
possible 2
practicable
accomplished°
able 2
adept 1
brilliant 3, 4
capable 1
complete 2
experienced 1
expert 2
fine[1] 4
good 12
great 6
learned
masterful 1
old 7
perfect 7
polished 1
practised 1
proficient
qualified 1
skilful
talented
versed
accomplishing
consummation 1
accomplish-ment°
achievement 1, 2, 3
act 1
completion 1
consummation 1
deed 2
discharge 12
effort 3
execution 1
exploit 1
fact 2
feat
fulfilment
perfection 2
performance 1
proceeding 1
realization 2
record 5, 6
skill 2
speciality 1
stroke 7
trick 4
triumph 1
work 4
-accomplish-ments
laurels
record 6
stuff 5
accord°
agree 1
agreement 1
award 1
coincide
coincidence 2
comply
conform 2
correspond 1

accord *(cont.)*
extend 4
give 1
go 37a
harmony 1
identity 1
impart 1
match 7
peace 2
provide 2
rapport
reconciliation 1
resemblance
show 10
solidarity
sympathy 2
tally 1
treaty
tune 2
understanding 1
uniformity 1
union 4
unity 1
vouchsafe 1
-in accord
agreeable 2
conform 2
consistent 1
harmonious
line[1] 19b
unison
united 3
-of one's own accord
freely 2
willingly
accordance
accord 2
coincidence 2
observance 1
tune 2
uniformity 1
-in accordance
conform 2
consistent 1
line[1] 19b
proportional
accordant
consistent 1
according
step 7
accordingly°
consequently
duly 1
hence 1
therefore
thus 2
according to°
step 7
accord with
conform 2
go 40a
square 11
step 7
accost
address 4
buttonhole 1
greet 2
hail[1] 1
molest 2
pick 8j
proposition 3
salute 1
solicit 2
speak 12c
waylay 1, 2
accoucheur, -euse
midwife
account°
bill[1] 1
bulletin
chronicle 1
chronology
description 2
distinction 2
entry 4
esteem 2
explanation 1
favour 4
history 1, 5
importance 1
mark 8
memoir 1, 2

account *(cont.)*
narrative 1
news 2
portrait
proceeding 2a
prominence 1
put 16f
recital 2
reckon 2
reckoning 2
record 3
regard 4
rehearsal 2
report 1
representation 3
sake 1
score 1, 8
statement
story 1
tab 2
tale 1
version 2
word 2
yarn 2
-accounts
memoir 2
proceeding 2a
-of account
weigh 5
-on account
time 19b
-on account of
for 7
owe 2
reason 5
through 1
view 6
virtue 4
wake[2] 2
accountability°
debt 1
fault 3
liability 1
obligation 1
responsibility 1, 4
accountable°
answer 7a
debt 2
fault 5
liable 2
responsible 1, 2
stable 3
accountableness
accountability
accountant
bookkeeper
accounted for
present[1] 2
speak 13
account for°
at **account 1**
cover 7
explain 2
rationalize 1
reckon 5b
score 11
accounting
account 2
clerical 2
finance 1
accoutre
clothe 1
dress 1
equip
outfit 4
rig 1
turn 20d
accoutrement
attachment 4
provision 1
-accoutrements
equipment
fitting 2
furniture 2
gear 2, 4
kit
outfit 1
paraphernalia
regalia
rig 3
robe 2
stuff 2
tack 4
tackle 1

accoutrement *(cont.)*
trappings

accredit
assign 4
confirm 1
delegate 2
license 2

accredited
official 1

accrual
increment

accrument
increment

acculturate
civilize 1, 2

accumbent
prone 1
prostrate 3
recumbent
supine 1

accumulate°
amass
assemble 2
cluster 3
collect 1
compile
form 11
garner
gather 1
get 50a
heap 3
hoard 2
keep 3
lay[1] 19a
mass 8
mount 7
pile[1] 5, 10
pool 4
salt 8
scrape 6
stack 6
stock 10
store 1
swell 2

accumulation°
collection 1, 2
deposit 4
drift 5
formation 1
group 2
heap 1
hoard 1
mass 1
mountain 2
pack 2
pile[1] 1
pile-up 2
profusion
stack 1, 3
store 3
supply 4
tissue

accumulator
collector

accuracy°
precision 1
resolution 5
truth 1

accurate°
authentic
authoritative 2
correct 8
dead 17
deadly 6
definitive 3
exact 1, 2
express 5
factual 2
faithful 2
faultless
graphic 1
meticulous
nail 5
nice 3
perfect 5
photographic 1
precise 1
proper 2
right 2
serve 5
square 3
straight 5
sure 3

accurate *(cont.)*
true 1, 3
trustworthy
truthful
verbatim 1

accurately
exactly 1, 2
letter 4
perfectly 3
plumb 4
right 14, 17
straight 14
true 4
truly 2
verbatim 2
well[1] 3

accursed
damnable
diabolic 2
doomed 2
evil 1
lost 7
reprobate 1
wicked 1

accusation°
allegation
charge 6
imputation
rap 6

accuse°
blame 1
charge 11
denounce 1
fault 8
finger 8
impeach 1
incriminate
indict
pin 5
proclaim 2
prosecute 1
sue 1

accused
culprit 1
litigant

accustom°
adapt 2
adjust 3
break 18b
condition 7
familiarize
orient 3
tailor 2

accustomed°
conventional
customary 2
everyday 2
general 2
given 3
habitual 1
ordinary 1
orthodox
regular 1, 7
routine 3
seasoned
traditional
usual
used 3

AC/DC
bisexual 2

ace
dab hand
divine 3
expert 1
fabulous 3
first-rate
gifted
good 2
master 2
proficient
superlative
talented
terrific 2
top 8

acerb
cutting 2
gruff 1
tart[1] 1

acerbate
sour 6

acerbic
bitter 1
cutting 2
harsh 3

acerbic *(cont.)*
incisive 2
keen[1] 2
poignant 2
sarcastic
sharp 5
short-tempered
snappish 2
sour 1
tart[1] 1, 2
trenchant
venomous 2
virulent 2

acerbically
sharply 1

acerbity
bitterness 1
gall[1] 1
ill will
sarcasm
virulence 2

acescent
sour 1
tart[1] 1

acetous
tart[1] 1

Achates
friend 1
intimate[1] 5

ache°
anxiety 2
die 5
discomfort 2
distress 1
gripe 3
hurt 2, 6
lust 3
pain 1
pang 1
pant 2
smart 7
stab 5
suffer 1
wrench 5
yearn

Acheron
hell 1

achievable
feasible
possible 2
practicable

achieve°
accomplish
bring 7, 11
complete 5
effect 7
effectuate
execute 2
finish 2
fulfil 1
gain 1
hit 6
implement 2
make 14
notch 4
output 3
perfect 8
possess 5
prevail 1
purchase 2
reach 4
realize 1
render 1
succeed 3
win 1
work 16

achievement°
accomplishment 1
act 1
consummation 1
deed 2
discharge 12
effort 3
execution 2
exploit 1
feat
fruition
fulfilment
gain 10
output 2
perfection 2
realization 2
stroke 2, 7
success 1

achievement *(cont.)*
triumph 1
undertaking 2
work 4

achieving
consummation 1

Achilles' heel
weakness 3

aching
anxious 2
desperate 3
pain 1
painful 1
starved 2
tender[1] 8

achromatic
neutral 2

achy
painful 1

acicular
pointed 1

aciculate
prickly 1
thorny 1

aciculiform
pointed 1

acid
caustic 2
cutting 2
devastating 1
embittered
gruff 1
incisive 2
keen[1] 2
poignant 2
pungent 2
sarcastic
scathing
sharp 4, 5
short-tempered
snappish 2
sour 1
tart[1] 2
trenchant
virulent 2
vituperative

acid-head
addict 1

acidic
sarcastic
sour 1
tart[1] 1

acidulous
sarcastic
sharp 4, 5
short-tempered
sour 1
tart[1] 1
trenchant

aciform
pointed 1

acknowledge°
abide 4
accept 2
admit 4
allow 1
clean 8
concede 1
confess
credit 6
face 18a
figure 9
hail[1] 2
keep 6
mention 1
nod 1
recognize 2
reply 1
salute 2
take 7
tell[1] 2
thank 2
way 11b

acknowledged
given 2
professed 2
proverbial 1
public 4
regular 9
undisputed
well-known 1

acknowledgement°
admission 3, 4
appreciation 1
credit 2
mention 4
profession 2
recognition 2
thank 3
tribute 1

acknowledging
acknowledgement 1
admission 3

acme°
climax 1
consummation 2
extreme 8
height 2
high 15
ideal 2
maximum 2
peak 2
perfection 3
pinnacle
prime 4
spire 2
summit
top 1
vertex
zenith

acne
spot 5

acned
spotty 2

acolyte
satellite 2

acquaint°
accustom
inform 1
introduce 1
pick 8d

acquaintance°
connection 3
contact 2
experience 1
exposure 3
familiarity 1
friend 1
knowledge 3
understanding 3

acquaintanceship
acquaintance 1
familiarity 1
knowledge 3

acquainted°
knowledgeable 1
sensible 4

acquainted with°
at **acquainted 2**
familiar 4
know 1
sensible 4
used 3
versed

acquaint with°
at **acquaint**
expose 3
present[2] 4
teach
tell[1] 3

acquiesce
acknowledge 1
admit 3
agree 2, 3
capitulate 2
comply
consent 1
defer[2]
go 20b
nod 2
obey 1
relent
surrender 2
take 39a
way 11b
weaken 3

acquiescence
consent 4
deference 2
nod 6
obedience

acquiescence *(cont.)*
permission
resignation 2
sanction 3
servility
submission 1

acquiescent
agreeable 2
dutiful
easy 4
meek 2
obedient
patient 1
permissive
propitiatory 2
ready 2
servile
submissive 1
supple 3
willing
yielding 2

acquire°
achieve 2
assume 2
buy 1
come 9a, 12
conquer 2
contract 3
derive 1
draw 8
find 5
finger 5b
form 10
gain 1
get 1, 5
have 2
inherit
land 7
learn 2
line[1] 23b
make 7
obtain 1
pick 8d, 8e
possess 5
possession 4
pre-empt
procure 1
purchase 1
reap 2
receive 1
secure 5
take 1, 5
win 2

acquired
derivative 1

acquirement
achievement 1
acquisition 1

acquiring
acquisition 1
purchase 3

acquisition°
achievement 1
buy 4
catch 16
gain 10
purchase 3, 4
use 11

acquisitive
avaricious
grasping
greedy 2
hoggish
hungry 3
mercenary 1
possessive 1
rapacious
selfish 1

acquisitiveness
avarice
greed 1
rapacity

acquit
clear 21
conduct 6
discharge 1
excuse 1
forgive 2
get 40d
justify
let[1] 6b
purify 2
vindicate 1

adamantine
hard 1
immovable 2
rigid 2,4
rocky[1] 2
steely 2
stern 1
stony 2
Adam's ale
water 1
adapt°
accommodate 1,2
adjust 3
alter
arrange 3
condition 5,7
conform 1
differentiate 2
edit 1
fit[1] 7
gear 5
groom 4
measure 12
modify 1
orient 3
prepare 1
resign 2
shape 9
square 12
suit 1
tailor 2
tune 3
turn 3
adaptability
elasticity 2
flexibility 2
obedience
adaptable°
elastic 2
flexible 2
lend 3
obedient
pliable 2
ready-made 2
tractable 2
versatile 1
adaptation°
accommodation 1
alteration
arrangement 4
resignation 2
version 1
adapted
calculated 1
fit[1] 1
proper 1
used 3
add°
allow 6
attach 2
enumerate 2
introduce 5
lend 2
mix 3
number 4
put 22c
reckon 1
suffix 2
supplement 2
tack 7
tally 2
total 4
added
extra 1
extraneous 1
plus 2
supplementary 1, 2
added attraction
icing 2
addendum
addition 3
amendment 2
extension 3
extra 3
insert 2
supplement 1
addict°
demon 2
devotee
enthusiast
fan
fiend 2
addict (*cont.*)
freak 4
addicted
fond 3
given 3
addiction
abuse 5
habit 2
addictive
hard 11
adding
addition 1
adding machine
calculator
adding up
addition 2
addition°
accessory 1
accident 3
amendment 2
attachment 4
extension 3
extra 3
frill 2
gain 9
increase 4
increment
insert 2
plus 3
reckoning 1
rise 14
shed[1]
suffix 1
supplement 1
tally 3
-in addition°
at **addition 6**
besides 1
boot 1
extra 7
further 3
likewise 2
measure 10
moreover
spare 1
still 5
-in addition to°
at **addition 5**
besides 2
-with the addition of
plus 1
additional
accessory 3
alternative 1
auxiliary 2
extra 1
extraneous 1
fresh 4
further 1
indirect 2
new 3
non-essential 1
occasional 2
plus 2
spare 1
subsidiary
supplementary 1, 2
additionally
addition 6
besides 1,2
boot 1
extra 7
further 3
measure 10
moreover
addle
bemuse 1
intoxicate 1
mix 4b
perturb
spoil 4
turn 5
addle-brained
daft 1
insane 2
mindless 1
addled
groggy
muddy 2
stupid 1
addle-headed
stupid 1
addle-pated
daft 1
feeble-minded
foolish 2
insane 2
mindless 1
senseless 3
stupid 1
thick 6
add on
suffix 2
supplement 2
tack 7
address°
apply 5
call 10a
dedicate 3
dedication 2
direct 5
greet 2
hail[1] 1
harangue 1
lecture 1
message 2
oration
oratory
salute 1,3
send 2
sermon 2
speak 2,10,12c
speech 2
talk 14
addressee
occupant
address oneself to°
at **address 5**
set 12a
tackle 3
add to°
at **add 4**
amplify 1
complement 4
compound 3
contribute 2
enhance
enlarge 1
enrich 1
extend 2
heighten 2
maximize 1
supplement 2
widen
adduce
mention 1
present[2] 7
add up
calculate
count 1
number 4
reckon 1
run 12
stack 7a
sum 2b
tally 2
total 4
add up to
amount 1a
come 18a
make 8
total 5
adept°
able 2
accomplished
capable 1
clever 1
dab hand
experienced 1
expert 2
genius 1
good 12
great 8
handy 3
home 5
ingenious
master 2,4
masterful 1
old 7
perfect 7
polished 1
practised 1
professional 1
adept (*cont.*)
proficient
qualified 1
quick 4
skilful
smart 1
specialist
tactical
talented
wicked 7
adeptly
well[1] 6
adeptness
ability 1
capability
ease 2
efficiency 1
finesse 1
ingenuity
knowledge 3
proficiency
prowess 1
skill 1
speciality 1
technique 2
understanding 3
adequacy
enough 2
fitness 1
adequate°
acceptable 1
ample 4
comfortable 4
competent 1
decent 3
due 3
effectual 1
enough 1
equal
fair[1] 4
fit[1] 2
good 1,16
OK 3
par 6
passable 1
presentable 1
satisfactory
scratch 5
sort 5
so so
sufficient
tolerable 2
-be adequate
go 35b
measure 15b
rise 12a
serve 2
suffice
adequately
enough 3
fairly 1
OK 7
well[1] 1,14
à deux
face 8
intimate[1] 4
tête-à-tête 2
adhere
attach 5
cement 2
cling 1
stick[1] 5
adherence
dedication 1
devotion 3
observance 1
adherent
addict 2
admirer 1
devotee
disciple 2
enthusiast
fan
follower 1
friend 4
observant 2
partisan 1
proponent
sectarian 3
stand-by 1
supporter 1
-adherents
party 3
school 2
adhere to
abide 4
follow 2,10
keep 6
obey 1
observe 1
pursue 2
stand 5c
adhering
observance 1
adhesion
traction
adhesive
cement 1
glue 1
tacky[1]
tenacious 2
adhesiveness
tenacity 2
adieu
farewell 1,3
goodbye
leave[1] 1
part 12
parting 2
ad infinitum
cease 2
adios
farewell 3
goodbye
adipose
fat 2
large 1
oily 1
weighty 1
well-fed
adit
shaft 4
adjacency
presence 1
proximity
adjacent
about 9
adjoining
border 9
close 9,20
flush[2] 1
immediate 2
join 4
near 5,9
nearby 2
neighbouring
present[1] 2
surrounding
adjectival phrase
phrase 1
adjoin
border 9
join 4
meet[1] 4
touch 3
adjoining°
local 1
near 5
neighbouring
surrounding
adjourn
defer[1]
dissolve 3
postpone
adjournment
dismissal 2
dissolution 2
postponement
adjudge
decree 2
determine 1
judge 4
try 4
adjudicate
decide 1
judge 4
officiate
try 4
umpire 2
adjudication
judgement 2
adjudicator
judge 2
peacemaker
umpire 1
adjunct
accessory 1
attachment 4
extension 3
supplement 1
supplementary 1
adjust°
accommodate 1
adapt 2
alter
calibrate
conform 1
correct 4
differentiate 2
dispose 1
fit[1] 7
fix 3
gear 5
measure 12
modify 1
modulate
orient 3
overhaul 2
proportion 5
reconcile 2
rectify
reduce 4,8
regulate 1
repair 1
resign 2
retouch
scale[3] 4
set 6,11
settle 3
shape 9
square 12
straighten 1
suit 1
tailor 2
time 23
tune 3
adjustability
elasticity 2
flexibility 2
adjustable
elastic 2
fluid 3
versatile 1
adjustableness
flexibility 2
adjustable spanner
wrench 6
adjusted
calculated 1
adjusting
adaptation 1
adjustment 1
adjustment°
accommodation 1
adaptation 2
alteration
difference 3
overhaul 3
reconciliation 2
regulation 1
repair 2
resignation 2
settlement 3
adjutant
orderly 3
adjuvant
subsidiary
ad lib
extemporaneous
improvise 1
offhand 3,4
play 12
quip 1
spontaneous 1
unpremeditated
admass
hoi polloi
people 3
public 8
administer°
apply 2
conduct 3
deal 1,4
deliver 5
direct 1
dispense 2
dose 2
enforce 1

administer (*cont.*)
handle 3
head 11
inflict
manage 1
oversee
police 3
portion 4
preside
regulate 2
run 10
shot 9
supervise
transact
administering
administration 3
direction 1
administer the *coup de grâce*
finish 4
kill 1
administrate
administer 1
preside
administration°
bureaucracy
conduct 2
direction 1
establishment 3
execution 2
executive 2
government 1, 2
leadership
management 1, 2
oversight 2
power 10
regime
reign 1
rein 2
term 3
administrative
executive 3
political 1
responsible 3
supervisory
administrator
boss 1
director 1
executive 1
head 2
manager
officer 1
operator 2
politician
superintendent
supervisor
admirable°
beautiful 2
bully 3
desirable 4
divine 3
estimable
excellent
exemplary 2
fine[1] 1, 11
first-rate
glorious 4
good 2
grand 5
laudable
meritorious
noble 5
praiseworthy
prime 2
rare[1] 2
splendid 2
sterling 2
superb
admirably
beautifully 2
perfectly 2
well[1] 2
admiration°
appreciation 3
attachment 3
esteem 3
estimation 2
homage
honour 2
love 1
rave 3
regard 7
respect 1

admiration (*cont.*)
reverence 1
veneration
wonder 2
worship 2
admire°
adore 1
appreciate 1
esteem 1
follow 9
go 28c
honour 5
idolize
look 12
love 7
respect 6
revere
venerate
worship 1
admired
beloved 1
dear 1
estimable
well-thought-of
admirer°
addict 2
disciple 2
enthusiast
fan
gallant 5
student 2
suitor
supporter 1
sweetheart
admissibility
possibility 1
admissible
acceptable 1
good 1, 3
legal 1
passable 1
permissible
plausible 1
possible 1
presentable 1
sort 5
admission°
acknowledge-
ment 1
allowance 1
entrance[1] 1
entry 1
initiation 2
profession 2
recognition 2
revelation
-admissions
gate 2
admit°
accept 2
acknowledge 1
agree 3
allow 1, 2
bear 4
clean 8
concede 1
confess
contain 2
face 18a
grant 2
initiate 2
let[1] 5, 7a
permit 1
receive 3
recognize 2
suffer 3
sustain 5
tell[1] 2
tolerate 1
admit defeat
give 13
lose 3
admittance°
admission 1, 3
entrance[1] 1
entry 1
initiation 2
recourse 1
admitted
privileged 2
professed 2
public 4
undisputed

admitting
acknowledge-
ment 1
admission 3
though 1
admixture
alloy 1
amalgam
amalgamation
admonish
advise 1
caution 3
correct 2
lambaste 2
lecture 4
notice 7
preach 2
punish 1
rebuke 1
reprimand 2
speak 12a
warn 1
admonishment
caution 1
punishment 1
admonition
advice 1
advisory 2
caution 1
example 3
injunction 2
lesson 3
punishment 1
rebuke 2
reprimand 1
warning 1
admonitory
advisory 1
exemplary 3
ominous 2
reproachful
ado
bother 8
excitement 2
fanfare 2
flap 4
flurry 1
furore 1
fuss 1
hurry 3
racket 1
rumpus
rush 3
song 3a
splash 4
stir 6
tumult
twitter 4
adolescence
childhood
puberty
youth 1
adolescent°
boyish 1
child 2
juvenile 1, 2
minor 3
stripling
teenager
young 1
youth 2
-adolescents
youth 3
adopt°
affect[2] 1, 2
assume 1, 2
borrow
embrace 2
favour 6
follow 2
go 29a
resolve 3
strike 12
take 5, 7, 21
wear 2
adoption
passage 9
adorable°
cute 1
darling 4
lovable
adoration
glory 2
love 1

adoration (*cont.*)
praise 2
reverence 1
veneration
worship 2
adore°
bless 1
delight 2
dote
esteem 1
glorify 2
honour 5
idolize
like[2] 1
love 7
praise 4
revere
venerate
worship 1
adored
beloved 1
darling 3
dear 1
pet[1] 3
precious 2
adoring
fond 1
tender[1] 9
adoringly
fondly
adorn
beautify
become 4
decorate 1
drape 1
dress 2
elaborate 3
embellish 1
enrich 2
grace 6
illuminate 3
illustrate 2
ornament 2
trim 4
adorning
ornamental
adornment
decoration 1
elaboration 1
embellishment 1
flourish 3
ornament 1
trappings
trim 5
-adornments
trappings
adrift
disorientated
end 6
lost 3
sea 4
adroit
adept 1
astute 1
clever 1, 4
cute 2
expert 2
good 12
great 8
handy 3
home 5
ingenious
masterful 1
neat 4
nimble 1
perfect 7
quick 4
ready 6
skilful
slick 3
tactful
tactical
talented
adroitly
handily 2
adroitness
art 1, 4
dexterity 1
diplomacy 1
efficiency 1
expertise
facility 1
faculty 1
finesse 1

adroitness (*cont.*)
ingenuity
knack
prowess 1
readiness 2
savoir faire
skill 1
tact
technique 2
touch 16
understanding 3
adscititious
accessory 3
indirect 2
non-essential 1
supplementary 2
adulate
adore 3
honour 5
idolize
like[2] 1
love 7
revere
worship 1
adulation
flattery
love 1
praise 2
prostration 2
reverence 1
worship 2
adulatory
flattering 2
adult°
mature 1
racy 2
adulterate°
alloy 2
contaminate
corrupt 4
cut 6
debase 2
degrade 3
dilute
doctor 4
foul 12
garble 1
poison 3
pollute 1
vitiate 1
water 7
adulterated
foul 2
impure 2
mixed 1
adulteration
filth 2
impurity 1
pollution
adulterer
libertine 1
adultery
infidelity 2
intrigue 4
adulthood
age 2
majority 2
maturity 1
adumbrate
extinguish 3
obscure 7
advance°
abet 2
appreciation 2
approach 1, 6
benefit 3
better[1] 10
bolster
bring 6, 9b
broach
climb 3
come 1
contribute 2
course 2
cultivate 3
develop 1
development 2
draw 13b
ease 8
elevation 3
encourage 2
evolution
exalt 1

advance (*cont.*)
expedite 2
extend 4
facilitate
far 6a
favour 8
foment
forward 1, 6, 8
foster 1
front 10
further 5
gain 3, 7, 9
get 28d, 28e
glorify 1
go 1, 19
growth 3
headway 2
hold 16b
improve 2
improvement 2, 3
increase 2
inroad 2
introduce 2
jump 5, 9
laud
lay[1] 6, 18b
lead 12
leg 4
lend 1
lift 2
loan 1, 2
moot 2
move 1, 7
movement 6
nourish 3
offer 3
oncoming 2
overture
pass 28
passage 6
place 10
pose 3
posit
precipitate 1
prefer 2
preliminary 1
prepared 1
proceed 1
profit 3
progress 1, 2, 3, 5, 6
progression 1, 2
promote 1, 2, 3
promotion 1, 2
propose 1
push 10, 15
put 5, 17a, 18b, 28e
raise 6
recovery 1
revival 3
rise 8
second[1] 9
speed 2
spurt 2
succeed 3
suggest 1
support 1
tender[2] 1
thrive
venture 2
walk 1
way 5
work 20c
-advances
approach 4
inroad 2
pass 28
-in advance°
at **advance 10**
ahead 1
before 2, 4
front 8
advanced
avant-garde
early 5
far 5a
forward 3
lead 11
new 2
precocious
progressive 2
refined 2
sophisticated 2
way-out 2

-of advanced age
elderly 1
old 1
advance guard
spearhead 2
advancement
advantage 2
development 2
elevation 3
furtherance
growth 3
progress 1, 2, 3
progression 1, 2
promotion 1, 2
recovery 1
revival 3
advance payment
deposit 3
advance showing
preview
advance word
foreboding 2
advancing
move 13c
oncoming 1
onward
progressive 1
way 12
advantage°
account 3
asset 2
beauty 3
benefit 1
better[1] 8
blessing 2
boon
edge 4
enjoyment 2
fruit
gain 8
good 19
interest 3
lead 12
merit 2
occasion 1
odds 2
plus 3
predominance
preponderance 2
prerogative
privilege
profit 2
purchase 5
purpose 3
sake 1
service 1
start 13
upper 6
use 7, 12
usefulness
welfare
worth
-for the advantage of
behalf
-of advantage
profit 3
serve 2
-to advantage°
at **advantage 3**
advantaged
favoured 2
inside 4
privileged 1
advantageous°
behove
beneficial 1
constructive 1
convenient 1
desirable 4
expedient 2
favourable 1
fortunate 2
fruitful 2
gainful
golden 7
good 13
happy 2
helpful
inside 4
instrumental
lucky 2
advantageous *(cont.)*
opportune 1
pay 4
preferential
profit 3
profitable 2
propitious
rewarding
right 3
seasonable
serve 2
useful
well-timed
advantageously
advantage 3
favourably 2
right 16
advent
appearance 1
arrival 1
dawn 2
return 10
adventitious
accessory 3
accidental
circumstantial 2
extra 1
extraneous 1
haphazard 1
incidental 1
indirect 2
non-essential 1
random 1
supplementary 2
adventitiously
random 2
adventure°
enterprise 1
episode 1
experience 2
lark 1
romance 4
saga
-adventures
fortune 3
history 3
story 6
adventurer°
daredevil 1
parvenu 1
adventuresome
adventurous
venturesome 1
adventuress
adventurer 1, 2
adventurous°
audacious 1
bold 1
daring 2
enterprising
foolhardy
game 7, 8
intrepid
rash[1]
swashbuckling
venturesome 1
adventurousness
daring 1
enterprise 2
adverbial phrase
phrase 1
adversarial
negative 1
adversary°
antagonist
competitor
contestant
enemy
entry 5
negative 1
opponent
opposition 2
rival 1
adversative
negative 1
adverse
bad 4
contrary 3
destructive 2
detrimental
adverse *(cont.)*
discordant 1
foul 8
hostile 1
ill 4
injurious 1
low[1] 14
miserable 2
negative 1
personal 4
unpromising
untoward 1
adversely
ill 10, 11
adverse weather
element 3a
adversity
affliction 1
calamity 2
disaster
distress 2
grief 2
hardship
ill 8
misery 3
misfortune 1
opposition 1
ordeal
pressure 3
rack 2
reverse 8
scourge 1
sorrow 2
tragedy
trial 4
woe
advert
advertisement 1
announcement 3
hint 3
imply 2
insert 2
leaflet
pamphlet
plug 3
refer 1
speak 9
turn 23b
advertise
announce 1
broadcast 2
celebrate 4
circulate 2
display 1
feature 4
merchandise 2
open 23
plug 5
post[1] 2
proclaim 1
promote 4
publicize
publish
puff 7
push 6
show 11
spread 2
talk 13
tell[1] 2
advertisement°
announcement 3
circulation 2
insert 2
leaflet
pamphlet
plug 3
poster
proclamation 1
promotion 5
publication 1
puff 3
sign 5
advertiser
sponsor 2
advertising
advertisement 2
proclamation 2
promotion 4, 5
propaganda 2
publication 1
advice°
caution 1
clue 1
advice *(cont.)*
counsel 1
guidance 2
hint 1
information
instruction 1
intelligence 2
news 1
notice 5
oracle 2
pointer 2
recommendation 1
service 9
steer 3
suggestion 1
tip[3] 2
warning 1
word 2
advisability
propriety 1
advisable°
behove
expedient 2
wise 3
advise°
acquaint
alert 5
brief 6
caution 3
clue 2
counsel 4
direct 2
enlighten
fill 9c
guide 3
help 4
inform 1
notice 7
notify 1
post[3] 4
preach 2
prime 6
recommend 1
register 5
tell[1] 3
tip[3] 4
tutor 2
urge 3, 4
warn 1, 2
wise 4
-be advised
hear 2
know 5
understand 4
advise against
discourage 2
advised
current 4
informed 2
privy 2
advise fully
picture 5
advisement
guidance 2
adviser°
consultant 2
counsel 3
counsellor
guide 5
instructor
teacher
therapist
-advisers
board 4
cabinet 2
advisory°
advocacy
cooperation 2
defence 3
furtherance
office 5
promotion 3
recommendation 1
sanction 2
advocate°
agent 1
backer 1
champion 2, 4
endorse 1
favour 6
follower 3
friend 4
lawyer
maintain 4
advocate *(cont.)*
move 7
party 4
patron 1
preach 2
promote 3
proponent
protagonist 2
recommend 1
sanction 6
stand 7b
subscribe 1
suggest 1
support 1
supporter 1
take 39c
uphold
urge 4
advocating
furtherance
aegis
auspices
office 5
patronage 1
protection 2
safety
umbrella 2
-under the aegis of
through 1
under 4
aeon
age 4
once 1
period 2
aerate
air 6
fluff 5
froth 3
aerie
nest 1
aerobics
exercise 4
work 19a
aerodynamic
streamlined 1
aeronaut
pilot 1
aeroplane
craft 4
flight[1] 3
plane 2
aerosol
spray[1] 3
aerosphere
atmosphere 1
aesthete°
dilettante
epicure
highbrow 1
sybarite
aesthetic°
highbrow 2
poetic 2
tasteful
aesthetician
aesthete
aestheticism
discrimination 2
aesthetics
philosophy 1
aestivate
retire 1
aestivation
inactivity 2
afar
far 1
off 2
affability
familiarity 2
fellowship 3
warmth 2
affable
amiable
bluff[2] 2
cordial
debonair 1
easy 6
expansive 2
familiar 3
forthcoming 3
friendly 2
affable *(cont.)*
genial
gracious
hearty 1
homely 1
kind[1]
mild 1
neighbourly
outgoing 2
pleasant 2
sociable
suave
warm 3
affair°
adventure 1
arrangement 2
bag 5
business 1, 2
circumstance 2
concern 4, 8
episode 1
event 1
experience 2
function 2
incident 2
infidelity 2
interest 5
intrigue 4
issue 3
job 3
liaison 3
love 5a
matter 2
occasion 3
occurrence 1
operation 3
pageant
romance 1
subject 1
thing 2
transaction 1
undertaking 1
-affairs
dealings
finance 1
proceeding 2a
programme 3
thing 8a
affaire°
at **affair 4**
affaire d'amour
affair 4
liaison 3
romance 1
affaire de coeur
affair 4
liaison 3
love 5a
romance 1
affair of the heart
romance 1
affect°
afflict
ail 1
assume 4
attack 4
bear 8
colour 4
come 16b
concern 2
determine 4
disturb 3, 5
fake 2
get 16
hit 4
hurt 3
impact 4
impress 1
influence 3
interest 7
involve 3
let[1] 7b
make 25
mould[1] 6
move 3, 4
penetrate 3
pertain
pierce 4
play 10
posture 4
put 22b
regard 5
rub 5
ruffle 3

ageless
classic 2
perpetual 1
timeless
agency°
agent 2
bureau 2
cause 2
hand 3
instrument 2
mean[3] 4a
mechanism 3
medium 5
ministry 3
representation 2
tool 2
umbrella 2
vehicle 2
voice 3
agenda
programme 1
schedule 1
timetable
agent°
ambassador
broker
cause 1, 2
dealer
delegate 1
deputy
envoy
factor 2
go-between
instrument 2
intermediary
liaison 2
merchant 3
minister 2
mouthpiece 2
negotiator
officer 1
operative 4
plant 4
proxy
representative 3, 4
speak 7b
voice 3
agent provocateur
agitator
rabble-rouser
troublemaker
age-old
aged
old 4
time-honoured
agglomerate
stack 6
agglomeration
assortment 2
ensemble 3
group 2
heap 1
hotchpotch
mass 1
medley
pile[1] 1
profusion
stack 3
aggrandizement
appreciation 2
magnification
aggravate°
compound 3
exasperate 2
get 17
inflame 2
irk
magnify 1
tease 1
worsen 1
aggravating
irksome
painful 2
aggravation
annoyance 1
gall[2] 2
plague 2
aggregate
accumulate
alloy 1
amass
amount 1a, 3
cluster 3
aggregate (*cont.*)
combination 3
come 18a
composition 3
ensemble 3
everything
gross 2
heap 3
lump[1] 3
mass 8
muster 2
pile[1] 5
scrape 6
stack 6
store 1
sum 1
total 1
totality
volume 1
whole 4
aggregation
accumulation 1, 3
collection 1
combination 3
gathering
group 2
heap 1
knot 2
mass 1
muster 2
pile[1] 1
stack 3
aggression°
assault 1
invasion 2
aggressive°
assertive
belligerent 2
defiant
enterprising
fierce 2
forceful 1
forcible 2
hostile 3
industrious
liberty 5
make 43
militant 1
offensive 1
officious
pugnacious
pushy
strong 13, 16
strong-arm
warlike
aggressively
strong 23
aggressiveness
aggression 1
drive 8
enterprise 2
initiative 2
aggressor°
militant 3
aggrieve
cut 3
hurt 3
sadden
wound 4
aggrieved
hurt 7
sore 5
aggro
aggression 1
aghast
abhor
panic-stricken
petrified 2
thunderstruck
agile°
active 3
alert 2
clever 1
dexterous 1
fleet[2]
graceful 1
light[2] 7
lively 1
mobile 4
nifty 2
nimble 1, 2
quick 3
ready 6
sharp 3
agile (*cont.*)
sprightly
agitate°
affect[1] 2
disrupt 1
distract 3
disturb 2, 4
excite 1, 2
exercise 3
ferment 2
flurry 2
fluster 1
incite
inflame 1
infuriate
jar[2] 1
jiggle 1
kindle
move 3, 4
mutiny 2
perturb
rattle 3
rise 16
ruffle 3
shake 5
shatter 3
stir 1
toss 2, 3
trouble 1
unnerve
upset 1
whip 7a
wind[2] 4d
work 20a
agitated°
beside 3
disconcerted
distraught
disturbed 1
emotional 4
excited 1
frantic
hectic
impatient 1
jumpy
nervous 1
resentful
restless
rough 2
tumultuous
unsettled 2
upset 8
worried
agitating
incitement 1
shake 9
agitation°
dismay 3
distraction 1
excitement 1
flap 4
flurry 1
fluster 2
frenzy 1
fuss 1
heat 2
hurry 3
incitement 2
motion 1
rampage 1
resentment
ripple 2
sedition
shake 9
storm 3
suspense 2
sweat 7
tempest 2
trouble 7
tumult
twitter 4
unrest
uproar
worry 4
agitator°
rabble-rouser
troublemaker
agitprop
propaganda 1
agley
wrong 7
aglow
ablaze 2
bright 1
fiery 2
aglow (*cont.*)
glowing 1
luminous 2
lurid 4
radiant 1
agnate
kin 2
kindred 2
related 2
agnomen
nickname 1
agnostic
faithless 1
godless 2
heathen 1, 2
heretical
infidel
non-believer
sceptic
sceptical
agnosticism
scepticism
ago
back 16
past 4
agog°
anxious 2
breathless 3
fanatical
goggle-eyed
impatient 1
keen[1] 1
marvel 1
wild 9
à gogo
swinging
agonize
brood 4
fret 1
nail 3
rack 3
sorrow 3
squirm
stew 3
suffer 1
sweat 2
torment 1
worry 1
agonized
worried
agonizing°
excruciating
exquisite 4
hard 5
harrowing
heart-rending
nerve-racking
nightmarish
oppressive 1
painful 1
picnic 3
piercing 4
poignant 1
pungent 3
sore 5
tender[1] 8
traumatic
worried
agonizingly
hard 14
painfully
agony°
anguish 1
distress 1
evil 7
grief 1
hell 2, 3
hurt 6
pain 2
passion 5
picnic 3
rack 2
sorrow 1
suffering
torment 3
unrest
wrench 5
agony aunt
scribe 2
agony uncle
scribe 2
agora
square 8
agrarian
pastoral 2
rural 1
agree°
accept 2, 3
accord 1
approve 1
check 5
close 4
coincide
commit 4
comply
conform 2
consent 1
contract 2
correspond 1
cut 9
defer[2]
deign
engage 3
fix 15
get 28a
go 6, 20b, 37a
grant 2
keep 6
like[2] 1
make 16
match 7
nod 2
obey 1
permit 1
play 11
pledge 4
resolve 1
settle 2
soften 4
stack 7a
stipulate
strike 8
string 10a
submit 1
subscribe 1
swear 1
sympathize 2
tally 1
term 5
understand 2
undertake 2
weaken 3
yield 3
agreeability
obedience
agreeable°
acceptable 2
amiable
comfortable 3
delicious 2
delightful 1
desirable 2
easy 6
engaging
fair[1] 8
friendly 2
genial
get 28a
good 1
good-natured
gracious
harmonious
hospitable 1
indulgent
likeable
lovely 2
mellow 4
neighbourly
nice 1
obedient
obliging
peaceable 2
pleasant 1, 2
ready 2
sit 10
smooth 6
step 7
suave
submissive 1
sweet 4
sympathetic 2
welcome 2
well[1] 17
willing
yielding 2
agreeableness
flexibility 2
obedience
agreeableness (*cont.*)
readiness 1
agreeably
favourably 1
happily 3
kindly 2
nice 6
readily 1
well[1] 1
willingly
agreed
conventional
fixed 3
given 1
OK 1
set 29
straight 10
understood
united 3
agreed-upon
given 1
agreeing
consistent 1
agreement°
accord 2, 3, 4
approval
arrangement 3
bargain 1
bond 2
charter 1
coincidence 2
consent 4
contract 1
deal 5
deed 3
engagement 3
harmony 1
identity 1
instrument 3
kinship 2
likeness 1
negotiation 2
nod 6
obedience
obligation 2
OK 6
pact
promise 1
proportion 2
protocol 2
reconciliation 2
resemblance
sanction 3
settlement 3, 5
solidarity
stipulation
symmetry
sympathy 2
transaction 1
treaty
truce 2
understanding 1
undertaking 3
uniformity 1
union 4
unity 1
vow 2
warranty
–in agreement
according to 1
agreeable 2
consistent 1
line[1] 19b
piece 8
step 7
united 3
agree to°
at **agree 2**
abide 4
accept 2
allow 2
approve 1
consent 2
defer[2]
enable 3
fix 2
go 20b
grant 2
hear 3
hold 23
keep 6
make 16
obey 1
OK 5

agree to (*cont.*)
pass 7
permit 1
stipulate
submit 1
subscribe 1
take 39a
underwrite 2
agree with°
at **agree 4**
conform 2
get 28a
go 6, 40a
hold 23
parallel 4
sit 10
square 11
subscribe 1
sympathize 2
agribusiness
farming
agricultural
pastoral 2
rural 1
agriculture
farming
agriculturist
farmer
agronomist
farmer
agronomy
farming
ague
chill 2
cold 10
ahead°
advance 10a, 10b
before 2, 3, 4
early 1
first 4
forward 4
front 8
lead 4
onwards
straight 13
ahead of time°
at **time 10**
advance 10a
early 1
aid°
abet 1
accommodation 5
advance 2
assist 1
assistance
assistant 1
auxiliary 3
back 2a
backing 1
benefit 1, 3
bolster
boost 2, 5
contribute 2
cooperation 2
ease 8
enable 2
encourage 2
encouragement 2
endowment 1
facilitate
far 6b
favour 8
forward 6
foster 1
further 5
furtherance
hand 2
help 1, 6
kindness 2
largesse
militate 2
minister 3
nourish 3
office 5
party 4
patronage 1
patronize 3
philanthropy 2
present[2] 3
profit 3
promote 1
relief 2
relieve 3
sanction 2
aid (*cont.*)
second[1] 9
see 11, 14c
service 1
speed 2
start 12
subsidize
subsidy
support 1, 7
supporter 1
tool 1
-in aid of
boot 4
-with the aid of
mean[3] 3
through 1
aide°
accessory 2
assistant 1
attendant 2
auxiliary 4
help 8
satellite 2
subordinate 2
aide-de-camp
aide
assistant 1
satellite 2
second[1] 8
aiding
auxiliary 1
promotion 1
ail°
ailing
diseased
feeble 1
frail 2
ghastly 3
ill 1
indisposed 1
infirm 1
invalid[1] 1
peaky
poorly 2
seedy 2
sick 2
sickly 2
sort 6
tender[1] 1
unhealthy 1
unsound 2
unwholesome 3
weather 2
ailment°
bug 2
disease 1
disorder 3
illness
infirmity 2
trouble 8
aim°
ambition 3
aspiration
aspire
design 7
direct 4
drift 4
end 3
endeavour 1
eye 6
fasten 2
function 1
goal
head 10
idea 4
intend
intent 1
intention
lay[1] 7
level 10
mark 6
mean[1] 1
mission 1
motive 2
object 2
objective 2
order 11
plan 4
point 6, 20
prize[1] 3
propose 2
purpose 1, 5
reason 3
seek 2
aim (*cont.*)
sight 7
spirit 6
strike 2
target
turn 9
view 5
aim at°
at **aim 2**
aim for
go 28e
make 30a
pursue 3
aiming
direction 1
aimless°
disjointed 2
end 6
erratic 3
pointless
purposeless
rambling 1
shiftless
aimlessly
helter-skelter 2
aimlessness
emptiness 2
air°
appearance 2
atmosphere 1, 2
aura
bearing 1
broadcast 1
carriage 2
circulate 2
climate 2
display 1
exhalation 2
expose 1
expression 3
feel 11
feeling 6
flavour 2
freshen 3
front 4
guise 1
lay[3]
look 14
manner 2
melody 1
odour 2
open 23
parade 5
piece 4
presence 3
put 18b
radio 2
reveal
semblance 1, 2
song 1
spread 2
strain[1] 8
tone 3
tune 1
vent 3
voice 4
-airs°
at **air 5**
affectation 2
genteel 1
pose 2
pretence 1
side 5
snobbish
uppish
-in the air
about 5
aloft
current 2
impending
overhead 1
wind[1] 8
airborne
take 34c
aircraft
craft 4
flight[1] 3
plane 2
airfield
field 2
air force
military 2
service 8
air-hole
vent 1
airily
gaily 2
airiness
spring 7
airing
excursion 1
exposure 1
expression 1
promenade 2
publication 1
turn 31
airless
close 12
oppressive 2
stuffy 1
airliner
flight[1] 3
plane 2
airman
pilot 1
air pocket
bubble 1
air-shaft
shaft 4
airsick
nauseated
sick 1
airtight
hermetic
seal 3
tight 1
watertight 2
airwoman
pilot 1
airy
breezy 1, 2
carefree
fluffy 1, 2
frivolous 2
hare-brained 1
immaterial 2
insubstantial 2
intangible
subtle 2
thin 5
airy-fairy
fluffy 2
frivolous 2
ait
island
ajar
open 1
akin°
alike 1
homogeneous
kin 2
kindred 1
like[1] 1
related 2
relevant
Akund (of Swat)
sovereign 1
alacritous
prompt 1
rapid
alacrity
dispatch 5
expedition 2
facility 1
haste 1
rapidity
speed 1
velocity
-with alacrity
promptly
à la mode
chic 1
contemporary 2
current 3
dashing 2
date 5
elegant 2
fashionable
minute[1] 3
modern
smart 3
sporty
stylish
trendy 1
alarm°
alert 4, 5
appal
daunt
dismay 1, 3
disturb 4
dread 1, 2
fear 1
fright 1
frighten
horrify 1
horror 2
intimidate
menace 1
panic 1, 3
perturb
scare 1
siren 1
solicitude
stew 2
terrify
terror 1
trouble 1
wind[1] 11
alarmed
fearful 1
panic 2
panic-stricken
scared
alarming
awesome
disturbing
dreadful 2
formidable 1
frightening
grim 3
harrowing
nightmarish
portentous 1
serious 4
terrible 4
terrifying
alarmingly
dangerously 2
alar(u)ms and excursions
noise 1
racket 1
alas
sadly 1
albatross
burden 1
encumbrance
load 1
pressure 3
weight 2
albeit
though 1
album
journal 2
record 7
scrapbook
alchemic(al)
occult 2
alchy
alcoholic 2
drunk 3
alcohol°
booze 1
bottle 3
drink 5
liquor 1
spirit 9b
whisky
alcohol addict
user 2
alcoholic°
drunk 3
hard 10
intoxicating 1
soak 3
stiff 3
alcoholic drink
bottle 3
alcoholism
drunkenness
alcove
compartment
niche 1
nook 1
recess 1
stall[1] 2
ale
brew 4
aleatory
haphazard 1
incidental 1
random 1
uncertain 1
alehouse
pub
alembicated
precious 3
alert°
acute 5
agile 2
alarm 1
alive 2, 3
astute 2
attentive 1
awake 2, 4
bright 6
careful 1
cautious
close 14
conscious 1
eagle-eyed
fresh 5
hip
informed 2
intelligent
look 9
lookout 2
mindful
mobile 4
nimble 2
notify 1
observant 1
perceptive
prompt 2
prudent 1
quick 3
quick-witted
ready 6
receptive 2
responsive
sensible 4
sharp 3
sharp-eyed
siren 1
sit 9
sleepless 2
smart 5
sprightly
step 12
tip[3] 4
tune 4
vigilant
wakeful 2
warn 1
watch 8
-on the alert
awake 4
vigilant
watch 4, 8
alertly
sharp 12
alertness
caution 2
intelligence 1
precaution 2
preparedness
presence 5
snap 11
vigilance
alexipharmic
antidote
medicinal
alfresco
outdoor
algolagnic
sadistic
alias
pseudonym
alibi°
excuse 6
out 15
story 3
alien°
exile 2
exotic 1
exterior 2
external 2
extraneous 2
fantastic 1
foreign 1

alien (*cont.*)
foreigner
immigrant
irrelevant
newcomer 1
outlandish
outside 9
outsider
remote 3
stranger
unrelated

alienate°
divide 3
exile 3
set 13b
turn 17b

alienated
estranged

alienation
breach 2
rift 1

alight
ablaze 1,2
bright 1
disembark
fire 5
get 36a, 40a
incandescent
land 5
light[1] 13
light[2] 13
live 3
luminous 1
radiant 1
settle 5
touch 10

alighting
landing 1

align
arrange 1
even 13
line[1] 23d
range 5
rank[1] 6
space 5
tune 3

aligned
line[1] 19a

alignment
adjustment 2
arrangement 1
orientation 1

-in alignment
line[1] 19a

alike°
akin
equal 1
equivalent 1
homogeneous
identical 2
indistinguish-able 1
piece 8
similar 1
uniform 1

aliment
diet[1] 1
food
provender 1
subsistence 2
sustenance 1

alimentary
nutritious

alimony
maintenance 3

alive°
animate 4
awake 4
bristle 4
flesh 4
lively 3
lousy 4
mindful
perceptive
responsive
teem[1]
thick 2
vital 3

alive to°
at alive 2
sensible 4

alkie
alcoholic 2
drunk 3

alky
alcoholic 2
drunk 3

all
entirety 2
everyone
everything
lot 6
mass 4

-above all
above 6
chiefly
especially 2
mainly
principally

-after all
eventually
however 1
run 48
yet 5

-after all is said and done
same 3
ultimately

-at all
ever 1
possibly 2

-before all
first 5

-for all
around 3

-for all that
nevertheless
same 3
though 2

-for all to see
above-board 1
out 3

-in all
altogether

-to all
among 2
face 11

all about
around 4

all and sundry
everyone

all at once
suddenly 1

allay
alloy 3
charm 6
dampen 2
dull 9
ease 6
hush 5
mitigate
quell 2
quench 1
rest[1] 10
slake
smooth 12
soften 2
solace 2
still 9
sweeten 2
temper 5

allaying
sedative 2

all being well
hopefully 2

all but
almost
nearly 1

allegation°
accusation
aspersion
charge 6
grievance 2
imputation
statement
story 2
tale 3

allege°
charge 11
claim 4
maintain 3
plead 3
pretend 1

allege (*cont.*)
say 2
state 7
urge 4

alleged°
pretended
professed 1
reputed
seeming
so-called 2
specious
supposed 1

allegedly
seemingly
supposedly

allegiance
dedication 1
devotion 3
duty 2
faith 3
homage
loyalty

allegorical
mystical 1
mythical 1
symbolic

allegory
myth 1
parable
story 1
symbol

all-embracing
catholic
expansive 3
extensive 1
overall
panoramic
radical 2
sweeping 1
thorough 3
universal 2

all-encompassing
exhaustive
full 2
inclusive 1
obsessive
panoramic
unabridged 2
universal 2

alleviate
deaden 2
ease 6
help 2
lighten[2]
mitigate
moderate 5
quell 2
relieve 1
remedy 3
remit 2
salve 3
solace 2
still 9
sweeten 2

alleviation
relaxation 2
relief 1
remission 2

alley
road 2
street 1
track 2

-up someone's alley
street 2

alliance°
affinity 1
association 1
belonging
brotherhood 1
club 2
combination 2
federation
fellowship 2
friendship 1
group 1
institute 1
kinship 2
league 1
marriage 3
match 3
pact
ring[1] 3

alliance (*cont.*)
society 5
treaty
understanding 1
union 1,2
wedding 2

allied
akin
associate 6
fall 15
fellow 5
kindred 1
league 2
like[1] 1
related 1
relative 1
relevant
side 10
united 2

alligator
crack 6

all in
exhausted 1
fatigued
prostrate 5
ragged 3
spent 1
tired 1
washed out 2
weary 1
worn 3

all in all
altogether
considering
mainly
short 14
whole 5
wholly 1

all-inclusive
catholic
exhaustive
full 2
general 1,3
overall
thorough 3
universal 2

all-in-one
inclusive 1

allocate
allot
allow 5
assign 1
commit 1
devote 1
dispense 1
divide 2
dole 3
fix 9
give 15b
grant 1
measure 14
mete
portion 4
section 4
share 3

allocation
allowance 3
assignment 1
distribution 1
dole 2
portion 2
quota
share 1

all of a sudden
suddenly 2

allot°
apply 3
appoint 1
appropriate 3
assign 1
carve 2
commit 1
deal 1
devote 1
dispense 1
dispose 3c
distribute 1
divide 2
dole 3
find 8
give 15b
invest 2
job 6
measure 14

allot (*cont.*)
mete
parcel 4
portion 4
ration 3
schedule 2
section 4
share 3
spend 3
split 4

allotment°
assignment 1
distribution 1
division 1
dole 1
donation 2
endowment 1
farm 1
lot 4
measure 5
part 1
partition 2
pension 1
plot[2]
portion 2
proportion 3
quota
ration 1
share 1
stint 1
stipend

allotting
partition 2

all out
entirely 1

all-out
dead 14
exhaustive
intensive
outright 2
thorough 3
total 3

all over
about 8
around 2
over 5
pole[2] 2
round 21
throughout 2

allow°
accept 1,2,4
acknowledge 1
admit 2,3
agree 3
approve 1
authorize
believe 1
brook[2]
buy 2
concede 1
consent 2
enable 1,3
entertain 3
entitle 1
excuse 3
face 18a
forgive 1
give 1,11
grant 2
let[1] 1
license 1
loan 2
lump[2]
OK 5
overlook 2
pardon 2
pass 7
permit 1
recognize 2
sanction 5
spare 8
stand 3
subscribe 1
suffer 3
sustain 5
swallow 2
tolerate 1
understand 5
vouchsafe 2
warrant 4

allowable
good 3
lawful 2
passable 1
permissible

allowable (*cont.*)
presentable 1
safe 4
tolerable 1

allowance°
acknowledge-ment 2
admission 3
allotment 1
benefit 2
clearance 1
complement 2
discount 4
dole 1
endowment 1
forgiveness 1
grant 3
indulgence 1
loan 1
lot 4
maintenance 3
margin 3
measure 5
pardon 1
passage 8
pension 1
permission
portion 2
present[2] 3
privilege
quota
rebate 1
room 1
share 1
stipend
tolerance 2

allowed
free 10
given 2
lawful 2
permissible
welcome 3

allow for
account 7
bargain 4
include 3

allow in
admit 1
let[1] 5

allowing
admission 3
allowance 1

allowing for
for 11

allowing that
though 1

alloy°
adulterate
amalgam
combination 3
composition 3
compound 5
degrade 3
mix 1,7
mixture 2
wed 2
wedding 2

alloyed
impure 2

alloying
mixture 2
wedding 2

all-powerful
dictatorial 1
sovereign 2

all-purpose
versatile 1

all right
acceptable 1
adequate 2
competent 1
decent 3
fair[1] 4
fine[1] 12
good 1
OK 1,2,4,7
par 6
passable 1
place 11b
presentable 1
safe 1,4
satisfactory
so so
well[1] 17

amass (*cont.*)
heap 3
hoard 2
keep 3
lay[1] 19a
mass 7
pile[1] 5, 10
raise 12
salt 8
scrape 6
stack 6
stock 10
store 1
amassing
accumulation 1
amassment
collection 1
pack 2
pile[1] 1
stack 3
amateur°
dilettante
green 2
homespun
lay[2] 2
newcomer 2
novice
popular 3
unprofessional 2
amateurish
amateur 2
green 2
homespun
poor 4
unaccustomed 2
unprofessional 2
unused 4
amateurishly
badly 3
poorly 1
roughly 3
amatory
erotic 2
tender[1] 9
amaze°
astonish
breath 3
daze 1
dumbfound
electrify 1
floor 5
jolt 3
overpower 2
petrify 2
rock[2] 3
stagger 2
stun 2
surprise 1
amazed
breathless 2
daze 4
dumbfounded
goggle-eyed
marvel 1
thunderstruck
wonder 4
amazement°
astonishment
surprise 3
wonder 2
amazing°
awesome
exciting 1
extraordinary 2
fabulous 2
good 2
incredible 2
marvellous
miraculous
phenomenal
portentous 2
prodigious 2
sensational 1
shocking 1
startling
striking
stunning 2
superhuman 1
amazingly
extra 6
frightfully
particularly 1
amazon
giant 1
scold 2
ambagious
diffuse 2
equivocal 1
indirect 1
rambling 1
serpentine 2
tortuous 2
ambagiousness
gobbledegook 2
ambassador°
delegate 1
deputy
envoy
minister 2
negotiator
representative 3
ambience
air 1
atmosphere 2
aura
climate 2
context
feel 11
feeling 6
flavour 2
medium 4
milieu
surround 2
undercurrent 2
ambiguity°
confusion 3
mystery 2
opacity 2
paradox
ambiguous°
confused 1
contradictory
double 3
equivocal 2
evasive
imprecise
indefinite 2
indistinct 2
left-handed 2
mealy-mouthed
obscure 2
opaque 2
paradoxical
puzzling
questionable
tortuous 2
vague 1, 2, 3, 5
ambiguously
vaguely 2
ambiguousness
confusion 3
mystery 2
obscurity 2
ambisextrous
bisexual 2
ambit
circuit 1, 2
course 1
girth 1
lap[2] 1
perimeter
periphery 1
reach 7
region 2
round 12
tour 2
ambition°
aim 5
aspiration
drive 8
enterprise 2
goal
hope 1
initiative 2
intention
lust 2
motive 2
objective 2
pretension 1
purpose 1
push 14
ambitious°
enterprising
go-ahead 2
grandiose 2
time-serving
ambitiousness
drive 8
initiative 2
pretension 1
ambivalence
indecision
ambivalent
contradictory
end 6
equivocal 1
hesitant 1
indecisive 1
mind 11
uncertain 2
unresolved
amble
meander 1
mill 6
promenade 3
ramble 1, 4
roam
saunter
stroll 1, 2
turn 31
walk 1, 7
ambler
pedestrian 1
ambrosial
delicious 1
fragrant
luscious
rich 8
savoury 1
sweet 2
tasty
yummy
ambulant
mobile 5
ambulate
walk 1
ambulatory
mobile 5
pedestrian 3
ambuscade, ambuscado
ambush 1, 2
ambush°
pounce 1
set 24
trap 2
waylay 1
ameliorate
amend 1
better[1] 10
break 3
elaborate 4
enrich 1
improve 1
lift 2
mend 2
perfect 9
polish 2
rectify
reform 1
remedy 4
smooth 12
solace 2
amelioration
amendment 1
elaboration 1
euphemism
improvement 1
recovery 1
reform 3
amenable
agreeable 2
easy 4
feminine 1
flexible 2
hospitable 2
manageable
obedient
obliging
open 11
outgoing 2
receptive 1
sheepish 1
submissive 1
tractable 1
willing
yielding 2
amenably
willingly
amend°
correct 1
improve 1
modify 1
revise 2
right 19
suffix 2
amendment°
correction 1
amends°
atonement
indemnity 1
penance 1
requital 1
restitution 1
return 11
satisfaction 2
amenity
-amenities
manner 3
propriety 3
service 3
amerce
fine[2] 2
penalize
punish 2
amercement
fine[2] 1
forfeit 1
penalty
amiability
civility
friendship 2
amiable°
amicable
brotherly
comfortable 3
cordial
easy 6
expansive 2
fatherly
forthcoming 3
friendly 2
genial
good-natured
gracious
hearty 1
homely 1
kind[1]
likeable
mellow 4
mild 1
neighbourly
nice 1
obliging
outgoing 2
peaceable 2
pleasant 2
sociable
sweet 4
warm 3
winning 1
amiableness
warmth 2
amiably
kindly 2
warmly 2
well[1] 5
amicability
fellowship 3
friendship 2
hospitality
amicable°
amiable
brotherly
easy 6
friendly 1
good-natured
hearty 1
hospitable 1
kind[1]
nice 1
outgoing 2
peaceable 2
pleasant 2
sociable
amicably
kindly 2
warmly 2
amid°
among 1
amidst
amid
among 1
amigo
pal 1
amiss°
erroneous
false 1
improper 1
inaccurate
mistaken 1
wrong 5, 7
amity
companionship
fellowship 1
friendship 1
love 1
peace 2
reconciliation 1
ammunition
fuel 2
proof 1
ammunition dump
magazine 2
amnesiac
forgetful
amnesty
forgiveness 1
immunity 1
pardon 1
remission 1
reprieve 2
amok
berserk
homicidal
rampage 2
among°
amid
among 2
amongst
amid
among 1
amoral
abandoned 2
bad 3
criminal 2
dissolute
foul 4
libertine 2
obscene 1
perverted
promiscuous 2
reprobate 1
rotten 3
satanic 1
unconscionable 1
unscrupulous
vicious 1
vile 1
wicked 1
amorist
paramour
amorous
erotic 2
flirtatious
passionate 2
romantic 4
tender[1] 9
torrid 2
warm 3
amorphous
lax 2
nebulous
shapeless 1
vague 1
amount°
batch 1
breadth 2
calculation 2
deal 6
dose 1
gauge 4
incidence
matter 5
measure 1, 5
measurement 2
price 1
quantity
rate[1] 2
ration 1
run 12
score 1
speck
stack 3
sum 1
total 1
amount (*cont.*)
volume 1
amounting to
tantamount to
amount to°
at **amount 1**
come 18a
make 8
reach 5
spell[3] 1
total 5
work 19b
amour
affair 4
infidelity 2
intrigue 4
liaison 3
love 5a
romance 1
amour propre
conceit 1
dignity 3
pride 1
self-esteem 1
self-respect
amphibolic
ambiguous 1
equivocal 1
amphibological
ambiguous 1
amphibologism
ambiguity 2
amphibology
ambiguity 1
amphibolous
ambiguous 1
equivocal 1
amphiboly
ambiguity 1
amphitheatre
hall 2
stadium
theatre 1
amphora
jar[1]
ample°
abundant 1
adequate 1
big 2
bountiful 2
broad 1
chubby
due 3
enough 1, 2
full 5
generous 3
good 16
goodly
handsome 2
hearty 4
heavy 2
large 2, 3
liberal 1
plentiful 1
plump[1] 1
princely 1
profuse 1, 3
rich 9
roomy
spacious
substantial 1
thick 1
tidy 3
voluminous 1, 2
weighty 1
wide 1
amplification
elaboration 2
extension 1
magnification
progress 3
amplified
inflated 1
amplify°
add 4
blow[1] 8d
develop 1
enhance
enlarge 1, 2
expand 3, 4
heighten 2
inflate 3
magnify 1

amplify (*cont.*)
pad 5
progress 6
turn 25d
amplitude
extent 1
measure 1
measurement 2
amply°
freely 4
richly 2
well[1] 14
amputate
lop
mutilate 1
amputee
cripple 1
amuck
homicidal
rampage 2
amulet°
charm 1
fetish 1
talisman
amuse°
beguile 3
delight 1
distract 2
divert 3
entertain 1
occupy 3
please 1
regale
tickle
amusement°
cabaret 2
delectation
dissipation 3
distraction 2
diversion 3
enjoyment 1
entertainment 1, 2
enthusiasm 2
festivity 2
fête 1
fun 1
game 1
interest 5
mirth
pastime
play 22
pleasure 1
recreation
relaxation 1
sport 1
wit 2
amuse oneself
play 1, 19a
toy 4
amusing
comic 1
delicious 2
delightful 1
entertaining
farcical
fine[1] 3
funny 1
hilarious
humorous
light[2] 11
priceless 2
rich 10
ridiculous
witty
wry 2
zany 1
anachronism°
stick-in-the-mud
anacreontic
erotic 2
anaemic
pale[1] 1, 3
pasty
peaky
unwholesome 3
watery 1
weak 2
white 2
anaesthetic
narcotic 1, 2
painkiller
anaesthetize
deaden 1
drug 4

anaesthetize
(*cont.*)
numb 2
paralyse 2
anaesthetized
insensible 1
senseless 2
anaglyph
engraving 1
analeptic
medicinal
tonic 1, 2
analgesic
drug 2
painkiller
analogic(al)
metaphoric
parallel 1
proportional
analogize
compare 1
analogous
kindred 1
like[1] 1
matching 2
metaphoric
parallel 1
proportional
relative 2
analogue
metaphor
parallel 2
prototype 2
analogy
equality 2
likeness 1
metaphor
parallel 3
parity 1, 2
analphabetic
illiterate
analyse°
break 16b
canvass 2
criticize 1
decompose 1
diagnose
examine 1
explore 2
gloss[2] 2
go 30b
investigate
prove 2
research 2
scrutinize
separate 2
sift 2
study 3
treat 2
try 2
analysis°
breakdown 3
criticism 1
discussion
examination 1
explanation 1
exploration
gloss[2] 1
interpretation 2
investigation
paper 4
post-mortem 2
profile 3
reasoning 1
research 1
review 5
scrutiny
search 4
study 4
test 1
therapy 2
twist 8
analyst
therapist
analytical
inquisitive 1
judicial 2
profound 2
speculative 1
Ananias
liar
anarchic(al)
disobedient 2
lawless 1

anarchist
radical 4
revolutionary 3
terrorist
anarchist(ic)
lawless 1
radical 3
anarchy
riot 1
anathema
pale[2] 3
taboo 1, 2
unwelcome 2
anathematize
curse 4
anatomize
analyse 1
decompose 1
anatomy
form 2
ancestor°
father 2
forerunner 1
predecessor 2
progenitor 1
stock 3
–ancestors
family 3
people 2
root[1] 4
ancestral
hereditary 2
traditional
ancestry
birth 3
derivation
extraction 3
family 3
house 2
line[1] 15
lineage 1
origin 3
parentage
pedigree
stock 2
strain[2] 1
succession 4
anchor°
announcer
base[1] 5
connect 3
dock 2
fasten 1
mainstay
moor[2]
root[1] 6
secure 8
tighten 1
anchorage
harbour 1
port
anchored
firm 2
fixed 1
immovable 1
secure 2
anchoress
hermit
recluse
anchoret
hermit
misanthrope
anchoretic(al)
isolated 2
unsocial
anchorite
hermit
misanthrope
recluse
anchoritic
reclusive
unsocial
anchorman
announcer
journalist
moderator
reporter
anchor to wind-ward
mainstay
anchorwoman
announcer
journalist

anchorwoman
(*cont.*)
moderator
reporter
ancient°
aged
antiquated
date 4
decrepit 1
early 6
elderly 1
extinct 2
former 2
grey 3
history 6
mouldy
musty 2
obsolete
old 2
prehistoric 1
primitive 1
remote 8
time-worn
anciently
early 2
ancillary
accessory 3
auxiliary 2
extra 1
incidental 2
indirect 2
instrumental
relative 2
secondary 1
side 8
subsidiary
supplementary 2
and
plus 1
androgyne
bisexual 3
androgynous
bisexual 1
android
human 1
robot 1
anecdotal
narrative 2
anecdotalist
narrator
raconteur
anecdote
joke 1
one 5
reminiscence
story 1
tale 1
yarn 2
anecdotist
narrator
raconteur
anechoic
dead 13
anenst
regarding
relation 5
anent
about 11
concerning
regarding
relation 5
aneurysm
stroke 5
anfractuosity
–anfractuosities
meander 2
anfractuous
circular 2
devious 2
intricate 1
meandering
serpentine 2
tortuous 1
angel
backer 2
benefactor
financier
friend 4
love 3
nurse 1
patron 1
sponsor 1

angelic
divine 1
godlike 1
good 5
heavenly 1
pious 1
saintly
seraphic
anger°
aggravate 2
displease
displeasure 2
enrage
exasperate 1
flare 3
flip 2
fury 1
gall[2] 4
get 17
indignation
inflame 1
infuriate
irritate
madden 1
offend 1
outrage 2, 4
provoke 3
put 23b
rage 1
rankle
resentment
rub 8
stack 5
angered
huff 1
indignant
offence 3
sore 4
angering
provocative 2
angle°
aspect 2, 4
bend 1
bias 2
inclination 2
incline 1
motive 2
outlook 1
perspective 1, 2
phase 4
point of view 1
position 3
side 3
slant 1, 3, 4
slope 1, 2
standpoint
subject 1
tilt 1, 3
twist 7, 8
view 3
viewpoint
angled
oblique 1
angling
oblique 1
angrily
sharply 1
warmly 5
angry°
bilious
black 7
blow[1] 8a
bristle 3
cross 7
dirty 5
embittered
fierce 2
fit[1] 4
flare 3
flip 2
furious 1
hard 9
heated
indignant
inflamed
mad 4
ratty 1
resent
resentful
sore 1, 4
stack 5
upset 10
warm 2

angst
anxiety 1
distress 1
fear 4
horror 2
misery 1
anguish°
agony
care 1
desolation 2
despair 1
desperation 2
distress 1
evil 7
grief 1
hell 3
hurt 6
melancholy 2
misery 1
mourning 2
oppression
ordeal
pain 2
pang 2
plague 3
rack 2, 3
sorrow 1
stress 3
sweat 2
throe
torment 3
trouble 1, 5
unrest
woe
worry 4
wound 2
wrench 5
anguished
woebegone
worried
angular
gaunt 1
lean[1] 1
scrawny
anile
doddering
elderly 1
senile
anility
senility
anima
psyche
soul 1
spirit 1
animadversion
comment 1
innuendo
animadvert
mention 2
observe 4
animal°
beast 1, 2
brute 2
carnal
inhuman 2
sexual 2
–animals
stock 4
animalistic
animal 3
animate°
activate
awake 2
electrify 2
encourage 1
energize
enliven 1
exalt 3
excite 1
fire 8b
flush[1] 3
gladden
heat 4
inflame 1
inspire 1
interest 7
intoxicate 2
kindle
live 1
liven 2
organic 1
pep 2
provoke 1
pump 4b

appropriateness (*cont.*)
- relevance

appropriating
- plagiarism

appropriation
- occupation 3
- plagiarism
- seizure 1
- share 1
- theft

approval°
- acknowledgement 2
- applaud 1
- applause
- auspices
- backing 1
- clearance 2
- consent 3,4
- endorsement 1
- esteem 3
- favour 1
- go 27e
- go-ahead 1
- nod 6
- OK 6
- pass 24
- passage 9
- pat[1] 5
- permission
- popularity
- praise 1
- recommendation 2
- regard 7
- sanction 1,3
- warrant 1

approve°
- abet 2
- agree 3
- allow 5
- applaud 1
- authorize
- charter 4
- confirm 1
- consent 2
- enable 1,3
- endorse 1
- favour 6
- go 36b
- hail[1] 2
- hear 3
- hold 23
- honour 5
- initial 2
- license 1
- make 23
- OK 5
- pass 7
- praise 3
- prefer 1
- ratify
- recognize 3
- recommend 2
- resolve 3
- sanction 5
- second[1] 9
- subscribe 1
- sustain 5
- thumb 4
- underwrite 1,2
- warrant 4

approved
- correct 7
- popular 1
- regular 6
- standard 5

approved school
- Borstal
- prison
- reform school

approve of°
- *at* approve 1
- abet 2
- agree 2
- hear 3
- hold 23
- like[2] 1
- second[1] 9
- subscribe 1
- thumb 4

approver
- party 4
- sympathizer

approving
- agreeable 2
- good 17

approvingly
- highly 3
- well[1] 5

approximate°
- approach 2
- broad 4
- compare 2
- estimate 1
- evaluate 2
- general 4
- near 10
- resemble
- rough 10
- round 6

approximately°
- about 2,6
- almost
- around 1,6
- close 21
- generally 2
- nearly 1
- neighbourhood 2
- roughly 1
- say 14

approximation
- estimate 3
- estimation 3
- evaluation 2
- idea 2

appurtenance
- extra 3
- supplement 1

–appurtenances
- equipment
- gear 2
- kit
- paraphernalia
- regalia
- rig 3
- robe 2

appurtenant
- relative 2

apropos
- about 11
- applicable
- appropriate 1
- befitting
- concerning
- due 2
- expedient 1
- fit[1] 1
- fitting 1
- incidentally 1
- pertinent
- point 18
- proper 1
- regarding
- relation 5
- relative 1
- seemly 1

apt
- applicable
- appropriate 1
- capable 1
- correct 6,8
- disposed
- due 2
- elegant 4
- fit[1] 1
- fitting 1
- happy 2
- inclined 2
- ingenious
- intelligent
- liable 1
- likely 4
- nifty 3
- opportune 2
- order 10b
- pat[2] 3
- perfect 4
- pertinent
- point 18
- probable
- prone 2
- proper 1,3
- quick 4
- ready 3,4
- relevant
- righteous 2
- ripe 3a

apt (*cont.*)
- seasonable
- seemly 1
- skilful
- smart 1
- suitable
- tend[1]

aptitude°
- ability 1
- art 1,4
- bent 5
- capability
- capacity 2
- facility 1
- faculty 1
- flair 1
- forte
- genius 2,3
- gift 2
- head 4
- instinct
- intelligence 1
- knack
- mind 3
- potential 2
- power 5
- proficiency
- prowess 1
- qualification 1
- resource 1
- skill 1
- speciality 1
- strength 3
- talent 1
- technique 2

–aptitudes
- endowment 3

aptly
- appropriately
- pat[2] 2
- properly 2
- right 17

aptness
- aptitude 1,3
- fitness 1
- ingenuity
- propriety 1
- relevance

aqua
- water 1

aquarelle
- water-colour

aquatic
- marine 2
- oceanic

aqueduct
- channel 1

aqueous
- fluid 2
- watery 3

Arab
- guttersnipe
- lad
- ragamuffin

arabesque
- flowery
- ornate
- showy

arable
- farm 1
- field 1

arbiter
- authority 3
- intermediary
- judge 2,3
- mediator
- moderator
- negotiator
- umpire 1

arbitrarily
- random 2

arbitrariness
- tyranny

arbitrary°
- absolute 3
- authoritarian
- character 1
- despotic
- dictatorial 1
- dogmatic
- domineering
- haphazard 1
- imperative 2

arbitrary (*cont.*)
- masterful 2
- overbearing
- peculiar 3
- peremptory 2
- positive 5
- random 1
- totalitarian
- tyrannical
- uncertain 1
- wanton 4

arbitrate
- adjust 1
- decide 1
- determine 1
- judge 4,6
- moderate 6
- umpire 2

arbitration
- decision 1
- negotiation 1
- reconciliation 2
- settlement 3

arbitrator
- intermediary
- judge 2
- mediator
- moderator
- negotiator
- peacemaker
- umpire 1

arborescent
- leafy

arc
- sweep 4,6
- turn 11

Arcadian
- idyllic
- pastoral 1
- rural 1

arcana
- occult 3

arcane
- cryptic 2
- dark 6
- deep 2
- heavy 12
- hidden
- incomprehensible
- mysterious 2
- mystical 1
- obscure 5
- occult 1
- opaque 2
- perplexing
- profound 1
- recondite
- remote 3
- secret 2
- subtle 2
- supernatural

arcaneness
- perplexity 2
- profundity 1

arcanum
- obscurity 2

arch°
- astute 1
- bend 2
- elfin 1
- hump 2
- sly 2
- sweep 4,6

archaic
- ancient 3
- antiquated
- date 4
- disused
- extinct 2
- musty 2
- obsolete
- old 2
- passé
- quaint 2
- time-worn

arched
- round 4

archetypal
- classic 1
- exemplary 1
- model 11
- original 3
- proverbial 2
- representative 1

archetype
- epitome 1
- example 2
- image 4
- model 2
- original 5
- paragon
- pattern 1
- perfection 3
- progenitor 2
- prototype 1
- standard 1
- type 3

archfiend
- devil 1

archipelago
- island

architect
- author
- creator 1
- designer 1
- engineer 1
- father 3
- founder[1]
- mastermind 2

architecture
- fabrication 1

archive
- chronicle 1,2
- paper 2b
- record 3
- register 1

–archives
- paper 2b
- proceeding 2a
- record 3
- register 1

archness
- devilry 1

arch of heaven
- sky 1

arc light
- spotlight 1

arctic
- chill 4
- cold 1
- freezing
- frigid 1
- icy 1
- piercing 3
- polar 1
- wintry 1

ardency
- animation 1
- devotion 3
- feeling 4
- fire 2
- passion 1

ardent°
- animated 1
- anxious 2
- bookworm
- burning 2
- deep 6
- devoted
- devout 3
- eager
- earnest 2
- emotional 1
- enthusiastic
- excited 2
- favourable 2
- fervent 1
- feverish
- fiery 3
- fire 5
- great 9
- hard 7
- heartfelt
- heated
- hot 3,4
- impassioned
- intense 2
- keen[1] 1
- mad 6
- passionate 1
- solicitous 2
- soulful
- spirited
- strong 5
- torrid 2
- voracious 2
- warm 2,4
- warm-blooded 2

ardent (*cont.*)
- wholehearted

ardently
- hard 13
- hotly
- mad 5
- madly 4
- warmly 4

ardour°
- animation 1
- dash 6
- devotion 3
- electricity
- enthusiasm 1
- expression 4
- feeling 4
- fervour
- fire 2
- flame 2
- heat 2
- inclination 4
- inspiration 1
- intensity
- love 1
- passion 1
- soul 4
- spirit 2
- warmth 3

arduous°
- difficult 1
- exhausting 2
- formidable 3
- hard 2
- killing 3
- laborious 1
- murderous 2
- painful 3
- picnic 3
- punishing
- rocky[1] 1
- rough 7
- rugged 2
- stiff 9
- strenuous 1
- toilsome

arduously
- hard 13

arduousness
- difficulty 1

area°
- beat 12
- belt 2
- breadth 2
- business 1
- calling
- category
- discipline 5
- district
- domain 2
- dominion 2
- expanse
- extent 3
- field 1,4
- ground 2
- job 1
- jurisdiction
- kingdom 2
- limit 3
- line[1] 7
- measurement 2
- neighbourhood 1
- office 3
- part 6
- partition 4
- patch 2,3
- place 1,2
- plot[2]
- pocket 3
- precinct 1
- proportion 4
- province 1,3
- pursuit 3
- quarter 3
- range 1
- realm 2,3
- region 1
- reservation 4
- room 1
- scene 1
- science 1
- scope 1
- sheet 5
- site 1
- size 1
- speciality 1

area (*cont.*)
sphere 3
spot 2
spread 9
stall[1] 2
stretch 5
subject 2
territory 1,2
theatre 4
tract[1]
turf 2
vicinity
world 3
zone
arena
area 5
ring[1] 2
stadium
theatre 1,4
arenose
gritty 1
arête
prominence 2
ridge
argent
silver 3
argie-bargie
dispute 3
argle-bargle
dispute 3
argosy
navy
argot
cant 2
dialect
idiom 1
jargon 1
language 1
lingo
talk 19
terminology
tongue 1
vernacular 3
arguable
debatable
disputable
moot 1
open 7
questionable
reasonable 2
tenable
unresolved
argue°
advocate 1
bicker
clash 3
contest 3
contradict 1
debate 3
defend 3
differ 2
disagree 2
discuss
dispute 1,2
fight 4
insist 1
issue 9
object 4
plead 3
premise 2
quarrel 2
reason 8
row[2] 3
scrap[2] 2
spar[2] 2
urge 4
argue into°
at **argue 6**
persuade 2
argue out of°
at **argue 6**
arguing
strife 1
argument°
battle 2
clash 2
conflict 2
contest 2
controversy 1,2
debate 1
defence 3
difference 2
disagreement 3
discussion

argument (*cont.*)
dispute 3
exchange 3
feud 1
fight 8
flap 5
fracas 2
friction 2
ground 3
matter 4
misunder-standing 2
objection
plea 2
quarrel 1
reason 1
row[2] 1
run-in
scene 3
scrap[2] 1
thesis 1
tiff
tilt 4
variance 2
word 9a
-arguments
reasoning 2
argumentation
controversy 1
debate 1
argumentative°
contrary 2
controversial 3
factious
negative 1
passionate 3
pugnacious
quarrelsome
surly
touchy 1
Argus-eyed
sharp-eyed
vigilant
argy-bargy
dispute 3
arid
boring
desert[1] 2
dreary 2
dry 1
lean[1] 2
thirsty 1
torrid 1
aright
adjustment 1
arise°
appear 1
begin 3
breed 4
climb 3
come 19a, 19c
dawn 4
derive 2
develop 4
emerge 1
follow 7
form 11
get 51a
grow 2
issue 11
loom 1
mount 3
occur 1
originate 2
pass 13
place 14
proceed 2
result 2
rise 1,2,3,7,9,11, 12a
rouse 1
spring 2
sprout
stand 1,10a
start 2
stem[1] 3
stir 2
surface 3
transpire 2
turn 20b, 25b
aristocracy
élite 1
gentry
nobility 3

aristocracy (*cont.*)
rank[1] 3
aristocrat
lord 2
noble 1
peer[1] 1
-aristocrats
élite 1
upper 5
aristocratic
cultivated
distinguished 2
élite 2
exclusive 2
genteel 2
high-class 2
ladylike
lofty 2
noble 2
refined 1
sovereign 3
upper-class 1
arithmetical
mathematical
ark
vessel 2
arm
branch 1
defend 2
division 3
extort
squeeze 3
-arms
extremity 2
hardware 2
symbol
-at arm's length
aloof 1
-be in the arms of Morpheus
sleep 1
armada
fleet[1]
navy
armament(s)
hardware 2
armchair
chair 1
armed forces
service 8
armed services
service 8
arm in arm
shoulder 5
armistice
peace 2
truce 1,2
understanding 1
armlet
ring[1] 1
arm of the sea
sound[4]
armorial bear-ing
symbol
armour
defence 2
armoury
magazine 2
storehouse
thesaurus 1
arm-twisting
force 2
pressure 4
army
force 3
host[2]
military 1,2
number 2
score 4
service 8
swarm 1
-armies
score 4
aroma°
aura
bouquet 2
flavour 1,2
fragrance
fume 3
odour 1

aroma (*cont.*)
perfume 1
scent 1
smell 1
tang 1
aromatic°
fragrant
pungent 1
redolent 1
rich 8
spicy 1
strong 2
sweet 2
around°
about 1,2,5,6,7,8
approximately
by 6
nearby 1
nearly 1
neighbourhood 2
neighbouring
roughly 1
round 20,21,22,23, 25,26,27
wind[1] 8
arousal
agitation 2
flush[1] 6
heat 2
incitement 2
inspiration 1
arouse°
activate
agitate 1
animate 2
awake 2
electrify 2
energize
enliven 1
excite 3
find 7
fire 8b
flush[1] 3
gall[2] 4
get 16
incite
incur
inflame 1
infuriate
inspire 1
interest 7
intrigue 1
jog 2
kindle
knock 7b
motivate
move 5,6
pep 2
prompt 3
provoke 1
quicken 3
raise 7,10
refresh 2
rouse 1,2
stimulate 1
stir 4
summon 1
thrill 3
touch 6
turn 18c
vitalize
wake[1] 2
whet 2
whip 7a
work 20a
aroused
agitated
awake 4
fire 5
heated
impassioned
passionate 2
randy
romantic 4
arousing
erotic 3
impressive
incitement 1
provocative 1
sexy 1
steamy 3
stimulating
thrilling
arpeggio
run 47

arraign
accuse 2
impeach 1
indict
prosecute 1
arraignment
accusation
arrange°
adjust 1,4
appoint 1
categorize
class 5
close 4
compose 2
coordinate 1
devise 1
dispose 1
distribute 3
divide 5
draw 15c
dress 2
edit 4
engineer 5
file 3
fix 2,12
float 3
get 9, 51d
group 4
have 6
juggle
lay[1] 2, 18a
let[1] 2
line[1] 23a, 23b
make 15,16
mount 5
negotiate 2
order 16
organize 1
place 15,16
plan 3
plot[1] 3
pose 1
position 8
prepare 1
programme 4
provide 5
range 7
rank[1] 6
schedule 2
script 4
set 8,10,22b,23a
settle 1
sort 8
space 5
square 12,13
straighten 3
structure 3
style 8
tabulate
term 5
tidy 4
understand 2
weight 6
arranged
calculated 1
cut 29a
fixed 3,4
given 1
inside 5
order 10a
orderly 1
pitched
set 29
straight 7
understood
arrangement°
adjustment 2
bargain 1
bouquet 1
cast 3
composition 2
contract 1
deal 5
design 6
disposition 2
distribution 3
engagement 1
fix 18
form 1
format 2
formation 3
frame 3
get-up 2
make-up 3
mechanism 2

arrangement (*cont.*)
method 2
mould[1] 2
mount 8
negotiation 2
network 2
order 1
organization 2
orientation 1
pact
passage 7
pattern 3
piece 4
placement 1
plan 1
position 1
posture 2
proportion 2
provision 3
reservation 3
scheme 2
sequence
set 25
set-up 1
settlement 3
structure 1
system 1
tableau
transaction 1
understanding 1
-arrangements°
at **arrangement 5**
passage 7
preparation 1b
arrant
barefaced 2
blatant 1
flagrant
great 11
outright 2
sheer 2
stark 4
thorough 1
unconscionable 1
unmitigated
arras
drapery
array
arrange 1
arrangement 1
assortment 2
combination 1
display 4,5
dispose 1
drape 1
dress 1,2
equip
formation 3
line[1] 23d
order 1
parade 2
placement 1
posture 2
range 5
rank[1] 6
review 8
space 5
stack 3
stock 1
string 9
arraying
placement 1
arrear(s)
liability 2
-in arrears
back 13,17
debt 2
delinquent 3
due 1
fall 10
arrest°
capture 1,2
catch 1
check 1
delay 2
get 8
grab 3
hinder 2
intercept
nab
nick 4
nip[1] 2
obstruct 1

arrest (*cont.*)
pick 8h
pinch 4
prevent
prevention
pull 11b
restrain 3
run 27
seize 2
stanch
stay[1] 4, 6
stem[2] 1
stop 2
stunt[2]
suppress 2
-under arrest°
at **arrest 6**
arrested
arrest 6
arresting°
magnetic
piercing 2
prevention
arrhythmic
spasmodic 2
arrière pensée
motive 2
arrival°
appearance 1
dawn 2
entrance[1] 3
entry 3
immigrant
landing 2
oncoming 2
receipt 2
return 10
arrive°
appear 1, 3
check 6
come 2, 13c, 17b
dawn 4
derive 2
draw 11
face 12
get 10, 38b, 38d
land 5
make 32b
place 10
pull 11a
report 5
rest[1] 5
roll 10a
set 19
show 7
succeed 3
turn 20e, 25a
arrive at°
at **arrive 3**
fix 2
gain 6
get 10, 47, 49a, 50c
hit 6, 9a
make 14
reach 2
strike 16
arrivederci
goodbye
arriving
incoming 1
oncoming 1
arrivisme
ambition 1
arriviste
parvenu 1
upstart
arrogance°
air 5
bravado
conceit 1
effrontery
freedom 7
liberty 5
presumption 1
pride 2
side 5
swagger 3
vanity 1
arrogant°
cocky
conceited
disdainful
dogmatic
domineering

arrogant (*cont.*)
haughty
hoity-toity
immodest 2
impudent
lofty 4
macho
majestic 2
masterful 2
overbearing
overconfident 1
pompous 1
positive 5
presumptuous
pretentious 1
proud 2
pushy
self-important
snobbish
supercilious
vain 1
arrogantly
big 9
arrogate
adopt 2
appropriate 2
assume 1
grab 2
help 5
pre-empt
secure 5
take 3, 7
arrondissement
area 3
arrow
bolt 1
pointer 1
arroyo
canyon
gully
ravine
arse
bottom 1
bum 1
buttocks
posterior 3
rear[1] 2
seat 4
tail 2
-up to the arse (in)
replete 1
arse-hole
stinker
arse-kisser
flatterer
yes-man
arse-kissing
flattery
grovelling
obsequious
servile
servility
submissive 2
arse-licker
flatterer
yes-man
arse-licking
flattery
grovelling
obsequious
servile
servility
submissive 2
arsenal
magazine 2
storehouse
thesaurus 1
arsis
rhythm
arsonist
terrorist
arsy-versy
topsy-turvy 2
art°
craft 1
execution 4
ingenuity
science 2
skill 1
speciality 1
technique 2
trick 3

art (*cont.*)
workmanship
-arts°
at **art 6**
artefact
product 2
relic 1
artery
channel 4
artful°
arch 2
astute 1
clever 2
crafty
deceitful
deep 5
designing
dexterous 2
disingenuous
foxy 1
fraudulent 2
insincere
knowing 1
mealy-mouthed
politic 1
scheming
serpentine 1
sharp 6
shifty
shrewd
sly 1
subtle 3
tactical
tricky 1
unscrupulous
wily
artfulness
art 5
artifice 1
craft 2
dexterity 2
finesse 1
subtlety 2
trickery
arthritic
gnarled
article
composition 1
editorial
entity 1
essay 1
exposition 3
feature 2
item 1
paper 4
piece 4
report 1
story 1, 4
term 4
theme 2
thing 1
tract[2]
writing 2
-articles
term 4
article of faith
doctrine
tenet
article of virtu
antique 2
articulate
coherent 2
eloquent 1
enunciate 1
express 1
fluent
formulate 1
go 14
mouth 7
phrase 4
proclaim 1
pronounce 1
say 3
set 18c
sound[1] 7
speak 3, 4
state 7
vent 3
voice 4
articulated
jointed
oral
verbal 1

articulately
well[1] 3
articulateness
fluency
articulation
accent 3
delivery 4
diction 2
intonation
oratory
pronunciation
speech 1
tongue 2
voice 1
artifact
product 2
relic 1
artifice°
chicanery
deceit 2
deception 2
delusion 1
device 2
evasion 2
feint
finesse 2
fraud 1
game 3
gimmick 1
hocus-pocus 1
intrigue 3
machination
manoeuvre 1
move 9
pretence 1, 2
racket 2
ruse
stall[a] 2
stratagem
subterfuge
trap 2
trick 1
trickery
wile
-artifices
art 6
artificer
designer 1
artificial°
affected 1
camp[2] 1
counterfeit 2
factitious
false 3
fictitious 2
flowery
forced
glossy 2
hollow 4
imitation 5
insincere
laboured 2
mannered
mock 3
phoney 1
plastic 3
precious 3
quasi- 2
rhetorical 2
sham 2
shoddy
spurious
stiff 8
stilted
strained
synthetic
theatrical 2
toy 6
unnatural 4
unreal 3
wooden 2
artificiality
affectation 1
artisan
operative 2
tradesman 2
worker
artisanship
craft 1
workmanship
artist
designer 1
natural 11
specialist

artiste
performer
specialist
artistic
aesthetic 1, 2
creative
elegant 1, 2
great 6
poetic 2
artistically
well[1] 3
artisticness
art 2
artistry
art 1, 2
production 3
skill 1
technique 2
workmanship
artless°
above-board 2
camp[2] 1
candid 1
careless 4
childlike
frank 2
honourable 3
ingenuous 1
innocent 4
naïve
natural 4
open 15
plain 3
rude 4
rustic 2
simple 3
sincere
transparent 3
unaffected[1]
unsophisticated 1
artlessly
simply 3
artlessness
ease 4
naïvety
simplicity 3
art-lover
aesthete
collector
artwork
cut 25
picture 1
as
for 13
way 10b
ascend
arise 2
climb 1, 3
get 51c
incline 1
mount 2
rise 3, 6, 10
scale[3] 3
slope 1
top 6
tower 3
work 20c
ascendancy
domination 1
dominion 1
hold 26
influence 1
jurisdiction
might 2
power 2
predominance
preponderance 2
prestige
prevalence 2
rank[1] 2
reign 1
rule 2
sovereignty
success 1
superiority 1
supremacy 1
triumph 1
upper 6
ascendant
dominant 1
mighty 1
predominant
prevalent

ascension
progression 1
rise 15
ascent
climb 6
grade 4
incline 4
ramp
rise 13, 15
slope 2
ascertain
calculate
compute
detect 1
determine 2
discover 1
evaluate 2
fathom
find 2
get 30e
hear 2
learn 1
measure 11
perceive 2
receive 5
see 4
tell[1] 8, 9
trace 5
ascertainable
sensible 2
ascertained
determined 2
ascertaining
determination 3
discovery 1
ascertainment
determination 3
measurement 1
ascetic
celibate 2
puritan 2
severe 6
Spartan
temperate 2
ascetically
severely 6
simply 4
asceticism
self-denial 2
severity 6
simplicity 2
ascribe
assign 4
attach 4
attribute 2
credit 6
fix 9
impute
lay[1] 7
put 16c
set 17b
ascription
assignment 4
attribution
credit 2
imputation
aseptic
hygienic
sanitary
sterile 2
asexual
neuter 1
platonic
ash
-ashes
embers
ashamed°
blush
embarrassed 1
guilty 2
hang 8
remorseful
repentant
shamefaced 2
small 6
terrible 2
ashen
colourless 1
deadly 4
ghastly 2
grey 1
lurid 3
pale[1] 1

ashen (*cont.*)
peaky
wan 1
white 2
ashore
disembark
ashram
monastery
ashy
pale[1] 1
aside
abeyance
apart 1
by 8
digression 1
single 4
aside from
apart 4
bar 10
barring
besides 2
independent 8
asinine
absurd 2
crazy 2
daft 1
foolish 2
halfwitted
hare-brained 2
inane
insane 2
ludicrous
meaningless 1
mindless 1
nonsensical
pointless
preposterous
puerile
senseless 3
silly 1
stupid 2
asininity
folly 1
stupidity 2
as it were
quasi- 1
speak 6
ask°
bid 2
call 10a
charge 13
claim 3
consult 1
demand 2,4
enquire 1
like[2] 2
petition 2
plead 1,2
poll 3
pose 3
pray 1
press 6
push 4
query 3
question 9
quiz 2
refer 3
require 1
solicit 1
urge 2
wonder 3
-without being asked
voluntarily
ask about°
at **ask 5**
query 3
ask after°
at **ask 5**
askew
crooked 2
lopsided 1
nonsensical
oblique 1
wrong 2
wry 1
ask for°
at **ask 6**
beg 1
call 8a
claim 3
demand 2,4
desire 2
fire 11
ask for (*cont.*)
hit 8
order 15
plead 1
put 20a
request 1
require 1
seek 3
send 6
solicit 1
speak 7c
aslant
oblique 1
wry 1
asleep
dormant 1
numb 1
slack 1
unprepared 1
Asmodeus
devil 1
asomatous
unearthly 1
aspect°
angle[1] 2
appearance 2
attitude 1
bearing 1,3
detail 1
exposure 4
expression 3
face 2
factor 1
feature 1
form 2
format 1
front 4
guise 1
image 6
landscape
look 14
manner 2
outside 2
phase 3
point 10,14
presence 3
prospect 1
regard 8
respect 4
semblance 1
shape 2
side 3
slant 1
sound[1] 2
thing 2
tone 3
veneer
view 1,3
way 6
asperity
gall[1] 1
rigour 2
sarcasm
asperse
blacken 2
discredit 1
disgrace 4
foul 14
impeach 2
insult 1
libel 4
tarnish
vilify
wrong 9
aspersion°
discredit 5
disgrace 2
dishonour 5
flak
imputation
indignity
insult 2
jeer 2
libel 2
recrimination
reflection 3
scandal 3
slur 1
smear 4
aspersive
foul 6
sarcastic
scandalous 2
scurrilous
aspersive (*cont.*)
vituperative
asphalt
pave 1
pitch[2]
asphyxiate
choke 1
smother 1,2
stifle 1
aspirant
candidate
pretender
supplicant 2
aspiration°
aim 5
ambition 3
end 3
goal
objective 2
pretension 1
aspire°
endeavour 1
hope 3
purpose 5
seek 2
aspire to°
at **aspire**
aim 2
pursue 3
aspiring
ambitious 1
ass
bottom 1
bum 1
buttocks
clod 2
dolt
dummy 3
fool 1
gawk 1
halfwit
monkey 2
posterior 3
rear[1] 2
sap[1] 2
seat 4
tail 2
twit[2]
assail
abuse 3
assault 3
attack 1
beset
besiege 3
bombard 2
charge 14
denounce 3
encounter 3
fall 17
go 22,28d
lace 5a
lay[1] 13
light[2] 14
make 30b
pelt[1] 1
pitch[1] 6a
set 12b
storm 6
turn 19b
visit 2
vituperate
assailant°
aggressor
assassin
cutthroat 1
killer 1
murderer
thug
assassinate
bump 5
cut 13b
dispatch 3
eliminate 4
execute 3
kill 1
murder 3
remove 4
shoot 3
waste 4
zap
assassination
destruction 2
dispatch 7
execution 3
assassination (*cont.*)
murder 1
removal 2
assault°
aggression 2
attack 1,6
attempt 3
batter 2
bombard 2
charge 7,14
come 8
descend 4
fall 17
go 22,28d
invasion 2
lace 5a
lay[1] 13
light[2] 14
make 30b
mistreatment
mug 5
offensive 5
onset 1
pelt[1] 1
pile[1] 8b
pitch[1] 6b
push 15
raid 2
rape 4
rough 16
rush 2
set 12b,21,24
storm 6
strike 19
thrashing 1
violate 3
violation 3
waylay 2
assaulter
assailant
assay
analyse 2
analysis 1
price 5
prove 2
size 3
test 1,2
try 2
assay-mark
hallmark 1
assegai
lance 1
assemblage
accumulation 3
assembly 1
attendance 2
body 6
cluster 2
collection 2
company 2
ensemble 3
fabrication 1
gate 2
gathering
group 1,2
herd 1
host[2]
knot 2
mass 1
mob 1
muster 2
pack 3
pile[1] 1
rally 1
throng 1
turnout 1
assemble°
accumulate
amass
build 1
call 4
cluster 3
collect 1
compile
construct 1
crowd 3
edit 4
fabricate 1
flock 2
form 7
frame 6
garner
gather 1,2
get 50a,50b
assemble (*cont.*)
group 4
herd 3
hoard 2
hold 10
integrate
line[1] 23a
make 1
manufacture 1
mass 8
meet[1] 2
mobilize
muster 1
piece 13
pile[1] 5
prepare 5
produce 1
raise 2,5,12
rally 3
round 19
scrape 6
set 23a
sit 2
store 1
summon 1
throng 2
turn 20a,20e
whip 7b
assembled
serried
assembling
organization 1
assembly°
attendance 2
body 6
chamber 1
cluster 2
company 2
composition 2
convention 1
council 1
diet[2]
fabrication 1
flock 1
gathering
group 1
host[2]
house 3
manufacture 3
meeting 2
muster 2
organization 1
pack 3
parliament 2
production 1
rally 1
round-up 1
session 1
throng 1
assembly hall
hall 2
assembly-man
politician
representative 3
assembly room
chamber 2
assembly-woman
politician
representative 3
assent
accept 2
agree 2,3
approve 1
belief 2
consent 3
enable 3
go 20b
hear 3
nod 2,6
permission
sanction 3
soften 4
subscribe 1
weaken 3
yield 3
assenting
permissive
willing
assert
allege
announce 3
argue 5
assure 4
assert (*cont.*)
attest
charge 11
claim 4
declare 1
insist 2
maintain 3
plead 3
premise 2
profess 1
pronounce 2
protest 4
remark 2
represent 3
say 1,2
state 7
swear 1
tell[1] 7
testify
urge 4
voice 4
asserted
pretended
assertion°
allegation
argument 2
claim 1
declaration 1
evidence 2
expression 1
position 7
premise 1
profession 2
pronouncement 1
representation 3
statement
story 2
testimony
thesis 1
assertive°
aggressive 2
decided 2
dogmatic
dominant 1
emphatic
insistent
make 43
overbearing
positive 5
pushy
self-confident
strong 16,20
assess
analyse 2
balance 1
calculate
charge 12
criticize 1
estimate 1
evaluate 1
examine 1
gauge 2
judge 5
lay[1] 17b
mark 14
measure 11
orient 3
price 5
rate[1] 6
review 3
size 3
sum 2c
survey 1
take 8
tax 3
test 2
think 5b
try 2
view 9
weigh 3
assessment
charge 3
criticism 1
estimate 3
evaluation 1
examination 1
interview 2
judgement 5
measure 4
measurement 1
review 4
tariff 1
tax 1
thinking 2
toll[2] 1

assessment (*cont.*)
tribute 2
asset°
advantage 2
beauty 3
blessing 2
plus 3
strength 3
virtue 3
-assets°
at asset 1
capital 3
estate 2
finance 2
fortune 1
fund 2
good 21b
merit 2
money 2
possession 3
principal 5
property 2
resource 2
stock 5
substance 5
wealth 1
asseverate
allege
announce 3
assure 4
attest
certify 1
declare 1
insist 2
profess 1
pronounce 2
protest 4
say 1
state 7
swear 1
tell[1] 7
asseveration
allegation
assertion 1
declaration 1
expression 1
profession 2
pronouncement 1
statement
testimony
asseverative
assertive
decided 2
ass-hole
stinker
assiduity
application 3
exertion
industry 2
patience 2
perseverance
persistence
tenacity 1
assiduous
attentive 1
close 14
diligent
earnest 1,2
enterprising
hard 7
industrious
laborious 2
painful 3
patient 2
persevere
strong 5
studious 1
thorough 2
assiduously
hard 13
intently
thoroughly 2
assiduousness
exertion
assign°
allot
allow 5
apply 3
appoint 1,2
appropriate 3
attach 2,4
attribute 2
award 1
assign (*cont.*)
cast 8
charge 9
commit 1
credit 6
dedicate 1,3
delegate 2,3
designate 2
destine 2
detail 6
devise 2
devote 1
dispense 1
distribute 1
enable 1
entrust
find 8
fix 9
give 15b,16
grant 1
impute
job 6
leave[1] 7
make 23,38b
measure 14
mete
place 18
plant 7
portion 4
post[2] 2
put 2,8,16c
read 4
refer 2
relegate 3
schedule 2
second[1] 10
send 1
set 17b
sign 11
slot 4
spend 3
station 4
trust 6
assignation
appointment 1
date 2
meeting 1
assigned
routine 3
vicarious
assignee
nominee
assignment°
appointment 2,3
attribution
dedication 1
disposition 3
distribution 1
duty 1
errand 2
function 1
job 2
lesson 1
lot 4
mission 1
office 4
paper 4
portion 2
post[2] 1
project 2
service 6
slot 2
stint 1
task 1
tour 3
work 3
-between assignments
idle 2
assimilate
comprehend
digest 1,2,3
incorporate
soak 2
swallow 3
assimilation
orientation 2
assist°
abet 1
advance 2
aid 1
back 2a
bolster
boost 5
cooperate 2
assist (*cont.*)
ease 8
enable 2
encourage 2
facilitate
favour 8
forward 6
foster 1
further 5
help 1,4
leg 4
minister 3
patronize 3
pitch[1] 5
promote 1
relieve 3
second[1] 9
see 11,14c
serve 1
speed 2
support 1
assistance°
accommodation 5
aid 2
auxiliary 3
backing 1
boost 2
cooperation 2
furtherance
hand 2
help 6,7
kindness 2
leg 4
philanthropy 2
relief 2
see 14c
service 1
start 12
subsidy
support 7
-be of assistance
serve 1
assistant°
accessory 2
accomplice
aide
attendant 2
auxiliary 4
help 7,8
orderly 3
satellite 2
second[1] 8
subordinate 2
supporter 1
assisting
auxiliary 1
promotion 1
towards 2
ass-kisser
flatterer
yes-man
ass-kissing
flattery
grovelling
obsequious
servile
servility
submissive 2
ass-licker
flatterer
yes-man
ass-licking
flattery
grovelling
obsequious
servile
servility
submissive 2
associate°
accessory 2
accomplice
acquaintance 2
ally 1,2
attach 2
brother
chum 2
club 6
cohort 3
colleague
combine 1
communicate 2
companion 1
compare 1
comrade
associate (*cont.*)
connect 2
fellow 2,5
fraternize
friend 2
get 28a
go 33c
henchman
hobnob
identify 2
implicate 1,2
intimate[1] 5
league 3
link 4
mate 1
member
mingle 2
mix 2
pal 2
partner 1
party 4
peer[1] 2
place 17
relate 1
related 1
shoulder 4
socialize
syndicate 3
tie 3,6b
travel 4
twin 3
-associates
company 1
associated
accompany 2
affiliated
akin
associate 6
attend 5
belong
fall 15
fellow 5
involved 3
kindred 1
league 2
mixed 3
participate
related 1
relative 1
relevant
specific 2
associate with°
at **associate 1**
chum 3
communicate 2
fall 15
fraternize
get 28a
go 21b,40b
hang 4b
involve 3
join 2,3
knock 3b
mix 2
pal 2
part 11
rub 7
run 24
see 7
shoulder 4
associating
mixture 2
union 1
wedding 2
association°
alliance 1
amalgamation
assembly 2
belonging
body 6
brotherhood 2
club 2
combination 2
connection 2
contact 3
federation
fellowship 1,2
fraternity 2,3
group 1
identification 4
implication 1
institute 1
kinship 2
league 1
link 2
association (*cont.*)
marriage 3
mixture 2
order 9
presence 2
regard 6
relation 1,6b
society 1,5
tie-in
union 1,2
wedding 2
-associations
relation 6b
assort
bunch 3
categorize
class 5
distribute 3
divide 5
group 3
rank[1] 6
sort 8
tabulate
assorted
different 3
divers
diverse
general 3
manifold
many 2
miscellaneous
sundry
varied 1
assortment°
batch 2
bunch 2
confusion 5
group 2
line[1] 16
lot 1
mass 1
medley
miscellany
mix 7
mixture 1
pile[1] 1
pot-pourri
range 2
selection 2
set 25
stock 1
variety 1
assuage
charm 6
comfort 1
console
deaden 2
dull 9
ease 6
melt 2
mitigate
quell 2
remit 2
salve 3
slake
smooth 12
soften 2
solace 2
still 9
sweeten 2
temper 5
assuagement
relief 1
remission 2
salve 2
assume°
accept 3
affect[2] 1
believe 1,3
deduce
divine 4
embark 2
expect 2
fancy 10
figure 9
gather 4
guess 2
hold 7
imagine 2
imply 2
infer
pass 16b
pre-empt
premise 2
assume (*cont.*)
presume 1
put 22b
read 4
reckon 3
represent 2
shoulder 8
spring 5
strike 12
suppose 1,2
surmise 1
take 5,7,19,26,35c, 37,39b
think 2
understand 3
undertake 1
wear 2
assumed°
affected 2
alleged
artificial 3
fictitious 2
foregone
given 2
hypothetical, presumptive 2
reputed
secure 4
seeming
supposed 1
assuming
arrogant 1
assumption
expectation 2
given 4
guess 3
hope 2
hypothesis
inference
preconception
premise 1
presumption 2,3
principle 1
succession 3
supposition
surmise 2
term 4
theorem 1
thesis 1
assurance°
belief 1
certainty 2
confidence 2
conviction 3
faith 1
guarantee 1
indemnity 2
insurance
pawn[1] 3
pledge 1
poise 2
promise 1
seal 2
security 2
self-confidence
trust 1
undertaking 3
warrant 1
warranty
word 4
assure°
commit 4
ensure 1
guarantee 2
promise 3
satisfy 3
seal 4
see 5
vow 1
warrant 3
assured
certain 2,5
clear 10
confident 1
definite 2
hopeful 1
inevitable
mind 12
poised 1
secure 4
self-confident
sure 1
assuredly
absolutely 3
certainty 3

attendance°
company 1
gate 2
presence 2
turnout 1
-in attendance°
at **attendance 3**
attendant°
boy 2
companion 3
escort 2
follower 2
henchman
keeper
minister 3
orderly 3
page[2] 1
porter[1]
relative 2
satellite 2
servant 1
-attendants
retinue
suite 3
train 2
attended
fraught 1
attending
attendance 3
attend to°
at **attend 3**
care 4, 6a
deal 4
get 37
hear 1
keep 6
mark 12
mind 16
minister 3
note 11
notice 1
observe 1
provide 4
reckon 5a
respect 7
see 12a
serve 1
tackle 3
tend[2]
tune 4
wait 3
watch 3
attention°
application 3
care 2
concern 5
ear 1
emphasis
eye 7
heed 2
interest 1
mind 8
note 7
notice 3, 4
observance 1
observation 1
occur 2
play 25
precaution 2
recognition 2
regard 7, 9
attentive°
alert 1
awake 4
careful 2
close 14
conscientious 3
considerate
diligent
dutiful
gallant 2
intent 4
mindful
nice 3
observant 1, 2
perceptive
prudent 1
strict 1
studious 1
sweet 6
thoughtful 1, 3
vigilant
wakeful 2
attentively
intently
jealously
sharp 12
attentiveness
application 3
consideration 1
interest 1
respect 2
thought 4
vigilance
attenuate
thin 8
attenuated
narrow 1
rarefied 1
tenuous 1
thin 3
attest°
certify 1
evidence 4
guarantee 2
manifest 3
seal 4
support 6
testify
verify
vouch
witness 3
attestable
demonstrable
attestation
declaration 1
evidence 1
seal 2
testimony
attested
bona fide
Atticism
epigram 1
Attic salt
salt 3
attire
apparel
clothe 1
clothes
costume
cover 5
dress 1
ensemble 1
equip
garments
gear 3
get 51e
habit 3
have 12a
outfit 2
put 22a
rag[1] 3
robe 2
wardrobe 1
wear 8
attitude°
approach 7
bearing 1
carriage 2
conduct 1
disposition 1
fashion 3
form 2
frame 5
habit 2
inclination 3
manner 2
mentality 2
mind 6
mood 1
morale
orientation 1
outlook 1
perspective 2
philosophy 2
pose 4
position 1, 3
posture 1, 3
principle 2
psychology
sentiment 1, 2
side 3
slant 1
spirit 2, 7
stance
stand 13
stuff 3
attitude (*cont.*)
thing 4
tone 3
vein 4
viewpoint
attitudinize
pose 2
posture 4
attitudinizer
poseur
attitudinizing
pose 5
attocerebral
daft 1
feeble-minded
halfwitted
insane 2
attorney
advocate 3
counsel 3
counsellor
lawyer
mouthpiece 3
solicitor
attract°
appeal 2
ask 6a
attach 3
bring 3
captivate
catch 11, 12
command 4
decoy 2
draw 4
enchant 2
engage 4
entice
fascinate
incur
interest 7
intrigue 1
lure 1
pull 5
reflect 4
rope 4
run 16
seduce 1
take 20
tempt 1
attractant
attraction 2
attracted
care 6b
fancy 11
go 28c
incline 3
interested 1
like[2] 1
love 8
shine 5
warm 8
attracting
attractive
magnetic
attraction°
affinity 2
appeal 4
beauty 3
come-on
decoy 1
draw 16
enticement 2
fancy 7
fascination
feature 2
glamour
gravity 1
grow 5
haul 3
inducement
invitation 2
love 1, 2
lure 2
magnetism
motive 1
partial 3
pièce de
résistance
pull 20
spell[2] 3
temptation 2
attractive°
adorable
appeal 2
attractive (*cont.*)
beautiful 1
becoming
bonny
buxom 1
catching 2
comely
cute 1
darling 4
delightful 2
desirable 2
enchanting
endearing
engaging
exquisite 3
fair[1] 7
fetching
fine[1] 10
foxy 2
glamorous 1
good 10
handsome 1
interesting
inviting
likeable
lovable
lovely 1
magnetic
nice 1
picturesque 1
pleasant 1, 2
prepossessing
pretty 1
ravishing
seductive
sweet 4
taking
tempting 1
voluptuous 2
winning 1
attractively
beautifully 1
attractiveness
affinity 2
beauty 1
charm 2, 3
fascination
glamour
magnetism
attribute°
accuse 2
aspect 4
assign 4
attach 4
character 2
characteristic 2
credit 6
feature 1
fix 9
impute
lay[1] 7
mark 2
peculiarity 2
point 14
property 4
put 8, 16c
quality 1
respect 4
set 17b
trait
-attributes
endowment 3
nature 1
stuff 3
attribution°
credit 2
imputation
attrition
erosion
friction 1
wear 9
attune
tune 3
attuned
sensitive 2
step 7
a-twitter
overwrought 1
atypical
character 9
eccentric 1
freak 5
odd 1
peculiar 1
atypical (*cont.*)
queer 1
rare[1] 1
singular 1
unlike 2
unusual
unwonted
au courant
aware 1
current 4
familiar 4
knowledgeable 1
level 5
audacious°
adventurous
barefaced 2
bold 1, 2
brash 2
brazen
cheeky
cool 6
daredevil 2
daring 2
dauntless
defiant
enterprising
fearless
flagrant
foolhardy
forward 2
heroic 1
impertinent
impudent
indiscreet
intrepid
liberty 5
overconfident 1
pert 1
presumptuous
rash[1]
shameless
stalwart 3
venturesome 1
audaciously
openly 1
audaciousness
freedom 7
audacity
assurance 4
effrontery
enterprise 2
face 5
freedom 7
gall[1] 2
gumption 2
gut 3a
impertinence
impudence
indiscretion 1
mouth 4
nerve 2
presumption 1
sauce 2
audibly
clearly 3
audience
attendance 2
gate 2
interview 1
turnout 1
audit
attend 1
monitor 3
audition
apply 6
auditorium
hall 2
house 5
theatre 1
au fait
aware 1
current 4
experienced 1
expert 2
familiar 4
informed 2
intelligent
knowledgeable 1
learned
level 5
proficient
smart 2
au fond
essence 3
auf Wiedersehen
farewell 3
goodbye
Augean stables
shambles
auger
drill 3
punch[2] 1
aught
naught
nil
zero 1
augment
add 4
amplify 1
compound 3
enhance
enlarge 1
expand 3
extend 2
follow 11b
fortify 3
heighten 2
increase 1
inflame 2
intensify
magnify 1
maximize 1
pad 5
reinforce
supplement 2
swell 3
widen
augmentation
addition 3
expansion 1
extension 1
gain 9
increase 3
increment
reinforcement 2
augur
announce 4
bode
forecast 1
foresee
foreshadow
fortune-teller
mean[1] 3
oracle 1
predict
prognosticate 2
promise 4
prophesy 2
prophet
seer
spell[3] 1
threaten 3
augural
ominous 3
augury
foreboding 2
forecast 2
forerunner 2
harbinger
indication 3
omen
oracle 2
prediction
prophecy 1
sign 6
warning 2
august
ceremonial 2
dignified
grand 2
heroic 6
imperial 2
imposing
lofty 2
magnificent
noble 3
prestigious
proud 3
royal 2
solemn 3
stately
statuesque
venerable
augustness
grandeur 2

au naturel
naked 1
nude
auntie
homosexual 1
Aunt Sally
butt[1]
scapegoat
au pair
servant 1
aura°
air 1, 3
aroma 2
climate 2
halo
mystique
odour 2
presence 3
undercurrent 2
aureate
golden 1, 2
aureola
halo
aureole
glory 4
halo
ring[1] 1
au revoir
goodbye
auric
golden 2
auriferous
golden 2
aurora
dawn 1
aurous
golden 2
auspices°
cooperation 2
guidance 1
office 5
oversight 2
patronage 1
-under the auspices of
through 1
auspicious
bright 4
favourable 1
fortunate 2
golden 7
happy 2
hopeful 2
lucky 2
opportune 1
positive 8
promising
propitious
right 3
ripe 3a
rosy 2
seasonable
timely
well-timed
austere
chaste 2
dour 2
frigid 2
hard 5
harsh 2
joyless 2
plain 4
po-faced
puritan 2
rigid 2
severe 1, 2, 6
simple 2
Spartan
stark 3
stern 1
stiff 7
strict 2
temperate 2
tight 3
unadorned
unapproachable 1
austerely
severely 2, 3, 6
simply 4
austereness
simplicity 2
austerity
hardship
rigour 2
severity 1, 2, 6
stoicism
autarchy
despotism
independence 1
supremacy 2
auteur
producer 2
authentic°
actual 1
authoritative 1, 2
bona fide
concrete
factual 1
genuine 1
good 8
hearty 2
historical
honest 2
legitimate 1
lifelike
natural 6
official 1
original 3
perfect 5
precise 1
pukka 2
pure 1
real 1, 2
solid 4
sterling 1
true 1
veritable
authenticate°
check 3, 11
confirm 1
document 2
establish 3
prove 1
ratify
seal 4
show 3
substantiate
support 6
verify
vet
authentication
check 15
hallmark 1
identification 1
proof 1
seal 2
testimony
authenticity
hallmark 1
reality 1
author°
compose 2
creator 1
designer 1
father 3, 6
founder[1]
narrator
scribe 2
source 2
write 3
writer
authoritarian°
arbitrary 2
despotic
dictatorial 1, 2
dogmatic
domineering
imperative 2
masterful 2
mighty 1
overbearing
prescriptive
repressive
stern 1
strict 2
totalitarian
tyrannical
tyrant
authoritarianism
monarchy 2
tyranny
authoritative°
absolute 4
authentic
authoritative *(cont.)*
categorical
classical 1
definitive 2
dominant 1
inevitable
influential
orthodox
peremptory 3
persuasive
potent 1
powerful 2
professional 2
responsible 3
solid 7
standard 5
authoritatively
highly 4
authoritativeness
certainty 2
authority°
adept 2
administration 2
auspices
balance 5
carte blanche
chair 2
charter 2
command 7
control 4
crown 2
dab hand
domination 1
dominion 1
expert 1
freedom 4
government 1
grip 2
hand 8
hold 26
intellectual 4
judge 3
jurisdiction
licence 1
lock[1] 2
master 2
might 2
nobility 1
oracle 1
pass 24
permit 2
power 2, 3, 6
predominance
preponderance 2
prerogative
privilege
professional 3
protocol 1
pull 21
rank[1] 2
rule 2
sage 2
say 12
say-so
scholar 1
source 3
sovereignty
specialist
supremacy 2
sway 4
upper 6
weight 3
-authorities°
at **authority 4**
bureaucracy
establishment 3
power 10
-on the authority of
according to 1
authorization
approval
authority 1
clearance 2
consent 3
endorsement 1
faculty 4
freedom 4
go-ahead 1
leave[2] 1
liberty 2
licence 1
OK 6
authorization *(cont.)*
pass 24
passage 8
permission
permit 2
power 6
prerogative
privilege
requisition 1
sanction 1
say-so
warrant 1
authorize°
allow 2
appoint 1
approve 1
assign 2
charter 4
confirm 1
consent 2
delegate 2
enable 1
enact 1
endorse 1
entitle 1
legitimate 4
let[1] 1
license 1
make 23
OK 5
pass 7
permit 1
requisition 2
sanction 5
sustain 5
warrant 4
authorized
formal 2
lawful 2
legal 1, 2
legitimate 1
official 1
orthodox
permissible
privileged 2
rightful 1
auto
car 1
machine 2
autobiography
life 6
memoir 2
autochthon
aboriginal
native 7
autochthonous
domestic 3
indigenous 1
native 2
original 2
vernacular 1
autoclave
sterilize 1
autocracy
despotism
monarchy 2
tyranny
autocrat
despot
dictator
oppressor
tyrant
autocratic
absolute 3
arbitrary 2
authoritarian
despotic
dictatorial 1
domineering
heavy-handed 2
imperative 2
masterful 2
mighty 1
overbearing
peremptory 3
prescriptive
severe 1
strict 2
tight 3
totalitarian
tyrannical
auto-eroticism
self-abuse
autoerotism
self-abuse
autograph
paper 4
sign 7
automated
animated 2
automatic 1
mechanical 1
streamlined 2, 3
automatic°
cut 29c
immediate 1
instinctive 2
involuntary
mechanical 1, 2
perfunctory 1
pistol
regular 2
ritual 2
routine 4
spontaneous 2
tedious
unconscious 2
unpremeditated
automatically
necessarily
rote 2b
automaton
robot 1, 2
automaton-like
tedious
automobile
car 1
machine 2
autonomous
democratic
free 1
independent 1
unattached 1
autonomy
freedom 1
independence 1
liberty 1
self-government 1
autopsy
post-mortem 1
autumn
fall 23
auxiliary°
accessory 3
assistant 2
extra 1
fellow 5
further 1
occasional 2
reserve 5
secondary 3
side 9
spare 1
subsidiary
turn-off 1
-auxiliaries
reinforcement 3
avail
boot 4
embrace 2
good 19
interest 3
pay 4
profit 2, 3
purpose 3
touch 9
use 1, 7
availability
recourse 1
available°
accessible
appear 5
convenient 2
disposable 2
eligible 2
free 3
hand 9
handy 1
home 4b
leisure 3a
open 4, 10
public 3
ready 7
reserve 8
sale 6
season 2
available *(cont.)*
serve 2
stand 5b
tap[2] 4b
work 6
avalanche
slide 5
Avalon
heaven 1
paradise 1
avant-garde°
progressive 2
revolutionary 2
underground 3
way-out 2
avarice°
greed 1
rapacity
avaricious°
ambitious 3
grasping
greedy 2
hoggish
mercenary 1
miserly
predatory 2
rapacious
selfish 1
sordid 2
thirsty 2
venal
voracious 1
avariciousness
greed 1
avenge
fix 14
pay 5
requite 2
retaliate
revenge 2
right 20
score 9
avenging
vindictive
avenue
channel 4
direction 2
mean[3] 4a
measure 6
medium 5
method 1
passage 3
path 3
road 1, 2
route 1
street 1
tool 2
way 3, 7
aver
allege
announce 3
attest
certify 1
confess
declare 1
insist 2
maintain 3
plead 3
profess 1
pronounce 2
protest 4
say 1
state 7
swear 1
tell[1] 7
testify
average°
adequate 2
common 1
decent 3
fair[1] 4
indifferent 3
mean[3] 1, 6
mediocre
medium 1, 3
mill 4
moderate 3
norm 1
normal 1
ordinary 2, 3
par 1, 4, 6
passable 1
popular 2
so so

average (*cont.*)
standard 2
tolerable 2
vulgar 3
-above average
exceptional 2
par 3
-below average
exceptional 3
off 8
par 5a
-on average°
at **average 2**
generally 1
averment
assertion 1
evidence 2
profession 2
pronouncement 1
Avernus
hell 1
underworld 2
averral
statement
testimony
averse°
backward 1
disinclined
dislike 1
hate 1
hostile 1
indisposed 2
loath
reluctant
resistant 1
shy 4
slow 10
aversion°
disgust 2
dislike 2
distaste 2
dread 2
grudge 1
hate 3
horror 1
hostility 1
ill will
loathing
phobia
reluctance
revulsion
thing 4
avert
deflect
divert 2
fend 2
forestall
head 13b
preclude
prevent
turn 7
ward 3
aviate
fly 5
aviator
pilot 1
aviatrix
pilot 1
avid
agog
anxious 2
ardent
crazy 4
eager
enthusiastic
hard 7
hot 4
hungry 2
intent 5
keen[1] 1
mad 6
passionate 1
prompt 2
solicitous 2
thirsty 2
voracious 2
wild 9
willing
avidity
ambition 2
eagerness 1
enthusiasm 1
greed 1
gusto

avidity (*cont.*)
lust 2
passion 1
relish 1
thirst 1
avidly
willingly
avidness
lust 2
passion 1
avocation
bag 5
hobby
interest 5
pastime
pursuit 3
avoid°
boycott 1
bypass 1
cut 7
decline 1
dodge 2
duck 3
elude 1
equivocate
escape 2
evade 1
fence 4
fight 6
flee 1, 2
forgo 1
get 44e, 46a
help 3
hold 18a
isolate
jump 3
miss[1] 1
ostracize
preclude
prevent
refrain[1] 1
renounce
shirk
shoulder 2
shun
shy 4
sidestep
skip 2
spare 9
steer 2
swear 4
ward 3
avoidance
evasion 1
prevention
reserve 7
skip 4
avoided
unpopular
avoiding
prevention
avoirdupois
obesity
weight 1
avouch
declare 1
protest 4
avow
allege
confess
declare 1
insist 2
maintain 3
plead 3
profess 1
protest 4
swear 1
testify
avowal
acknowledge-
ment 1
allegation
assertion 1
declaration 1
manifestation
oath 1
profession 2
pronouncement 1
testimony
avowed
alleged
professed 2

await
expect 1
hope 3
look 7a
watch 4
waylay 1
awaited
forthcoming 2
prospective
awaiting
pending 1
awake°
alert 1
arise 1
attentive 1
call 6
come 18b
conscious 1
responsive
sensible 4
wake[1] 1, 2
wakeful 1
watch 8
awaken°
arouse 1, 2
awake 1, 2
call 6
come 18b
enliven 1
exalt 3
find 7
fire 8b
foment
get 51a
heat 4
incite
inspire 1
prompt 5
provoke 1
quicken 3
refresh 2
revive 1
rise 2, 16
rouse 1
sit 9
snap 7
stimulate 1
stir 5
vitalize
wake[1] 1, 2
whet 2
awakening
dawn 2
incitement 1
inspiration 1
revival 2
awake to°
at **awake 3**
sensible 4
watch 8
award°
bestow
boon
bounty 3
come 9b
confer 2
decoration 2
dole 1
donate
donation 1
endowment 1, 2
give 1
grant 1, 3
indemnity 1
plaque 3
premium 1
present[2] 6
presentation 1
prize[1] 1
purse 3
reward 1, 2
scholarship 2
spare 8
trophy 1
-awards
laurels
awarding
award 3
endowment 2
presentation 1
aware°
acquaint
acquainted 2
acute 5

aware (*cont.*)
alert 1
alive 2
appreciate 3
awake 3
careful 1
conscious 1
current 4
enlighten
enlightened
familiar 4
feel 3
find 2
get 43c
hip
informed 2
intelligent
judicious
know 5
knowing 2
knowledgeable 1
mind 9
mindful
observant 1
penetrate 5
privy 2
realize 2
recognize 2
see 2
sensible 3, 4
smart 2
tune 4
understand 1
warn 1
wind[1] 6
wise 5, 6
awareness
acquaintance 1
appreciation 3
cognizance
concern 5
familiarity 1
feeling 2
grasp 5
grip 3
idea 2
illumination 2
impression 1
knowledge 1
notice 3
observation 1
perception 2
prudence 1
realization 1
recognition 2
sensation 1
sensitivity 3
sophistication 1
understanding 3
away
abroad 3
absent 1
absent-minded
aloof 1
back 14
beside 2
by 8
distant 2
elsewhere
far 1
hence 2
off 1, 2
out 2
outwards
away with you
shoo 1
awe
admiration
amaze
amazement
bully 2
daunt
discourage 1
dismay 3
fear 2
horror 2
intimidate
overawe
regard 7
reverence 1
terror 1
veneration
wonder 2
-be in awe of
fear 6

awed
marvel 1
thunderstruck
wonder 4
awe-inspiring
admirable
awesome
colossal 2
conspicuous 3
fearsome
formidable 1
impressive
incredible 2
magnificent
monumental 1
overwhelming 2
portentous 2
sacred 1
scenic
sight 6b
solemn 3
splendid 1
stirring
striking
sublime 2
terrible 6
awesome°
amazing
conspicuous 3
divine 3
fearsome
formidable 1, 2
impressive
incredible 2
majestic 1
monumental 1
overwhelming 2
portentous 2
scenic
solemn 3
splendid 1
startling
stately
striking
sublime 2
terrible 6
awestruck
breathless 2
goggle-eyed
thunderstruck
awful°
abominable 2
abysmal 1
atrocious 1, 2
awesome
bad 1, 3, 4, 11
beastly 2
black 6
bum 4
calamitous
damnable
deplorable 1, 2
diabolic 2
disastrous 1, 2
dreadful 1
evil 1, 5
fearful 3
fierce 3
flagrant
frightful 2
ghastly 1, 3
great 11
grievous 2
grim 3
grisly
gruesome
heavy 4
horrible 1, 2
infamous 2
lamentable
lousy 1, 2
lurid 2
miserable 2, 4
monstrous 1
monumental 4
mortal 5
nightmarish
obnoxious
obscene 2
off colour 1
outrageous 2
par 5a
pit[1] 4
poor 4
profound 4

awful (*cont.*)
punk 2
rancid
regrettable
repulsive
rotten 4, 5
sad 3
severe 3
stinking 2
terrible 1, 2, 3, 4, 5
tragic
unfortunate 3
ungodly 2
whopping 2
wicked 2
wretched 1
wrong 1
yucky
awful-looking
ugly 1
unsightly
awfully°
badly 3
fearfully 2
frightfully
profoundly
severely 5
terribly
very 1
awfulness
monstrosity 2
awkward°
affected 1
artless 3
bashful 1
bulky
clumsy
difficult 5
disconcerting
embarrassing
halting
heavy-handed 1
hefty 1
hulking
ill 6
incompetent
inconvenient
inept 1
lame 2
left-handed 1
nasty 2
parlous
place 12
ponderous 1
provincial 2
rude 4
rustic 2
self-conscious
shambling
sore 2
sticky 2
stilted
strained
tactless
thumb 2
ticklish 2
tricky 2
ugly 3
ungraceful 1
unrefined 1
unseemly 2
untoward 2
unwieldy
warm 5
wooden 2
awkwardly
roughly 3
awkwardness
embarrassment 1
inconvenience 1, 2
ineptitude 1
awl
punch[2] 1
awning
blind 7
shade 5
awry
amiss 1, 2
bent 2
crooked 2
deformed 1
erroneous
inaccurate
lopsided 1

bad *(cont.)*
run-down 1
-in bad straits
impoverished 1
-in bad taste
abominable 2
indecent 1
tasteless 1
unseemly 1
-in someone's bad books
favour 4
-on bad terms
odds 4
-too bad
regrettable
tough 7
bad actor
hoodlum
miscreant 1
bad blood
animosity
feud 1
friction 2
rancour
strife 2
vendetta
bad breeding
incivility
bad condition
strait 3
bad conscience
guilt 2
remorse
baddy
criminal 3
hoodlum
miscreant 1
bad faith
betrayal 1
bad-featured
ugly 1
bad feeling
rancour
strife 2
bad fortune
grief 2
badge
character 1
colour 2b
crest 2
decoration 2
device 3
emblem
identification 3
mark 2
plaque 2
seal 1
sign 4
symbol
token 2
badger
annoy 2
browbeat
exasperate 2
gall[2] 4
gnaw 3
grind 5
harass
heckle
hound
madden 3
molest 1
nag[1] 1
persecute 2
pester
pick 6
plague 3
prod 3
provoke 3
push 4
ride 3
tease 1
torment 2
worry 2
badgering
persecution 2
bad guy
criminal 3
bad hat
criminal 3
bad-humoured
temperamental 1
badinage
banter
chaff 1
raillery
repartee
volley 3
wit 2
bad judgement
lunacy 2
bad language
curse 3
profanity
bad luck
catastrophe 2
grief 2
hardship
misfortune 1
sorrow 2
trial 4
badly°
amiss 2, 3
awfully
card 13
hard 14, 16
ill 10, 11, 12
poorly 1
seriously 1
severely 1
wrong 7
badly behaved
disobedient 1
badly off
deprived
destitute 1
impoverished 1
poor 1
bad-mannered
disagreeable 3
discourteous
disrespectful
rude 1
ungracious
unrefined 1
bad manners
incivility
bad match
misalliance
bad-mouth
disparage 2
libel 4
rubbish 3
vilify
bad move
misstep 1
mistake 1
bad-natured
surly
badness
evil 6
harm 2
misbehaviour
mischief 1
sin 2
vice 1
bad news
misfortune 2
bad off
impoverished 1
bad state
strait 3
bad taste
impropriety 3
indelicacy
bad-tempered
bilious
black 7
cantankerous
disagreeable 3
disgruntled
fretful
gruff 1
irritable
mean[2] 5
nasty 4
peevish
perverse 2
petulant
prickly 3
querulous
quick-tempered
sour 4
sullen
surly
bad-tempered *(cont.)*
testy
touchy 1
truculent
ugly 4
waspish
bad turn°
at **turn 34**
disservice
bad vibes
suspicion 1
Baedeker
guide 8
baffle
beggar 3
bewilder
confuse 1
daze 2
defy 2
discomfit 2
elude 2
escape 4
floor 5
flummox
fluster 1
foil[1]
frustrate 1
get 18
muddle 1
mystify
nonplus
perplex
prevent
puzzle 1
stick[1] 9
stump 2
throw 4
thwart 1
baffled
confused 2
daze 4
disconcerted
dumbfounded
groggy
helpless 2
lost 3
sea 4
bafflement
fluster 2
perplexity 1
baffling
confused 1
difficult 2
disconcerting
hard 3
incomprehensible
indefinite 2
inexplicable
labyrinthine
mysterious 1
obscure 2
occult 2
opaque 2
paradoxical
perplexing
puzzling
tough 5
unaccountable 1
bag°
catch 2, 15
concern 4
gain 1
get 8
grip 4
hag
haul 4
land 6
net[1] 2
pile[1] 3
pocket 1
pouch
protrude
purse 1
receptacle
sack 1
sag 1
speciality 1
sphere 3
suitcase
vocation
win 2
-bags
luggage
mass
pile[1] 3
-in the bag
stinking 3
bag and baggage
wholly 1
bagatelle
bauble
gewgaw
nothing 3
toy 2
trifle 1
baggage
bag 2
gear 4
jade 2
luggage
paraphernalia
stuff 2
thing 8c
woman 3
bagging
slack 2
baggy
flabby 1
loose 3
slack 2
bag lady
bum 2
bagnio
brothel
house 6
bail
pawn[1] 3
pledge 2
scoop 4
bailer
scoop 1
bailiwick
area 3
beat 12
department 2
domain 2
field 4
habitat
home 2
jurisdiction
kingdom 2
patch 3
province 3
realm 2
region 2
sphere 3
street 2
territory 2
turf 2
universe 2
zone
bail out
flee 1
pump 3
save 1
bait
come-on
decoy 1, 2
enticement 2
harass
heckle
inducement
invitation 2
lure 2
madden 3
premium 2
tantalize
tease 1
bake
parch
sun 2
baking
sweltering
torrid 1
baksheesh
consideration 2
gift 1
perquisite
present[2] 3
tip[3] 1
balance°
adjustment 2
comparison 1
compensate 2
balance *(cont.)*
composition 2
difference 5
equalize
even 14
footing 3
harmony 2
leftover 1
modulate
offset 1
parallel 3, 4
parity 2
poise 1, 3
proportion 2, 5
regularity 1
regulate 1
regulation 1
remain 4a
remainder 1
rest[2] 1
sanity
scale[1]
set 13a
settle 10
symmetry
teeter
temper 2
-in the balance
pending 2
precarious
uncertain 3
-off balance
stagger 2
-on balance
mainly
balanced
equal 2
even 5
level-headed
methodical
moderate 1
poise 3
poised 3
proportional
sober 2
sound[2] 4
square 2
stable 3
steady 4
strong 21
symmetrical
balancing
comparison 1
regulation 1
bald
bare 2
hairless
obvious
outright 2
smooth 4
stark 2
balderdash
drivel 3
fiddlesticks
gab 2
gibberish
gobbledegook 1
jargon 2
moonshine 2
nonsense 1
prattle 3
raving 3
rigmarole
romance 5
rot 4
rubbish 2
stuff 4
talk 18
trash 1
bald-faced
obvious
bald-headed
hairless
baldly
flat 17b
outright 4
bald-pated
hairless
bale
bundle 1
pack 1, 5
stack 1
baleful
black 5
deadly 1
destructive 1
fearful 3
harmful
ill 4
lurid 3
mischievous 2
poisonous 2
ruinous
sinister 2
unpromising
venomous 2
virulent 1
wicked 6
balefulness
virulence 1
balk
bar 9
block 3
check 13
defeat 2
disappoint 3
foil[1]
frustrate 1
hamper[1]
hesitate 1
hinder 1
prevent
prevention
recoil 1
retard 1
scruple 2
shrink 2
spike 3
stick[1] 12
thwart 1
turn 7
balked
disappointed 2
unsuccessful 2
balking
prevention
ball
dance 2
fête 1
gala 1
globe 2
orb
party 1
revel 3
revelry
round 10
shot 2
wad 1
-balls
drivel 3
face 5
fiddlesticks
gab 2
gall[1] 2
gibberish
gumption 2
gut 3a
machismo
nerve 1
rot 4
stamina
talk 18
trash 1
-on the ball
alert 1
bright 6
experienced 1
ingenious
perceptive
ballad(e)
lay[3]
balladeer
minstrel
singer
ball and chain
restraint 2
shackle 1
wife
woman 2
ball-and-socket joint
swivel 2
ballast
weight 5
balled up
confused 2

ball game
situation 2
ballistic missile
missile
ball-like
round 3
spherical
ballocks
botch
bugger 3
butcher 4
fiddlesticks
flannel 1
screw 7b
ballocksed
confused
ballo in maschera
masquerade 1
balloon
inflate 1
protrude
puff 6
stretch 2
swell 1
ballot
poll 2, 3
suffrage
vote 1
ballpark
approximate 1
neighbourhood 2
rough 10
ball-point
pen[1] 1
ball-shaped
round 3
spherical
balls up
bugger 3
confuse 2
fluff 4
queer 5
ruin 9
screw 7b
balls-up
hash 2
mess 3
mix-up
muddle 4
ball up
bugger 3
confuse 2
fluff 4
queer 5
snarl[2] 1
ballyhoo
advertisement 2
fanfare 2
noise 1
promote 4
promotion 4
propaganda 2
puff 7
push 6
racket 1
talk 13
ballyrag
carp
balm
fragrance
help 9
lotion
ointment
salve 1, 2
solace 1
bal masqué
masquerade 1
balmy
calm 3
crazy 1
deranged
fine[1] 2
foolish 2
fragrant
gentle 1
mad 1
mental 2
mild 2
pleasant 3
preposterous
soft 3
stupid 2

balmy *(cont.)*
sweet 2
twist 11
warm 1
baloney
drivel 3
nonsense 1
rubbish 2
stuff 4
trash 1
balsamic
soothing 2
baluster
rail[1] 1
balustrade
rail[1] 1
bamboozle
beguile 1
blind 5
bluff[1] 1
cheat 2
chisel 2
deceive
dupe 3
fool 4
hoax 2
hoodwink
lead 7
mislead
mystify
outsmart
perplex
prey 3b
ride 5a
rip 2b
swindle 1
take 32b
throw 6c
trick 8
ban°
bar 3, 9
black 8
boycott 2
embargo 1, 2
exclude 1
exclusion 1
exile 3
expel 2
forbid
freeze 4
outlaw 2
prevent
prevention
prohibit 1
prohibition 1, 2
restraint 1
rule 8
sanction 4
shut 5a
stop 6
taboo 2, 3
veto 1, 2
banal°
common 6
hack[2] 4
humdrum
monotonous
pedestrian 2
prosaic
stale 2
stock 7
tedious
threadbare 2
banality
cliché
tedium
bananas
crazy 1
deranged
mad 1
mental 2
banausic
monotonous
band°
bar 2
belt 2
body 6
braid 2
cabal 2
circle 1
clan 2
club 6
cluster 2, 3
cohort 2

band *(cont.)*
combine 1
company 2
complement 2
crew
ensemble 2
flock 1
gang 1, 3
group 1
junta
knot 2
league 1, 3
line[1] 2
pack 3
party 2
ring[1] 1, 3
sling 3
squad
streak 1
strip[1]
stripe 1
tape 1, 3
team 1
tie 8, 9
bandage
bind 3
dress 3
swathe
B & B
hotel
bandeau
band[1] 1
ring[1] 1
banderole
banner 1
pennant
streamer
bandido
thief 1
bandit
gangster
outlaw 1
robber
thief 1
banditry
pillage 2
bandleader
leader 2
bandmaster
leader 2
bandstand
stand 18
band together
ally 2
club 6
flock 2
pool 4
team 3
bandy words
quibble 1
spar[2] 2
bane
curse 2
headache 2
pest
pestilence 2
plague 1
poison 1, 2
ruin 3
scourge 1
thorn 2
torment 4
trial 5
ulcer 2
undoing 2
baneful
black 5
destructive 1
fatal 1
harmful
hurtful 1
mischievous 2
ruinous
bang
boom 1
clap 5
crack 2
crash 3, 4
explosion 1
full 14
hit 1, 3, 10, 12
knock 1
love 6

bang *(cont.)*
peg 7
pelt[1] 4
plumb 4
plump[2] 5
pop 1, 4
report 2
slam 1, 2
slap 6
strike 3
thrill 1
bang on
exactly 2
faultless
marvellous
precisely 1
right 2
bangtail
nag[2]
banish°
dismiss 2
displace 2
exile 3
expel 2
extinguish 2
isolate
ostracize
punish 2
relegate 1
rid 2
transport 2
turf 4
uproot 1
banishment
ejection 2
exile 1
punishment 2
banisters
rail[1] 1
bank
bar 4
beach 1
deposit 2
drift 5
heap 3
incline 1
mound 1
pool 2
pot 2
put 12
row[1]
shallow 2
side 1
slope 2
stack 1
storehouse
treasury
trust 5
bank card
card 9
banked
oblique 1
banker
factor 3
financier
banking
finance 1
oblique 1
banknote
bill[1] 2
note 4
-banknotes
cash 1
money 1
bank on
count 3
depend 2
go 26b
reckon 4
rely
store 5
trust 5
bankroll
back 2a
finance 3
pile[1] 2
roll 18
subsidize
support 4
wad 2
bankrupt
back 7b
break 5

bankrupt *(cont.)*
broke
destitute 1
hard 17
impoverished 1
insolvent
pauper
penurious 2
poor 1
rock[1] 3c
ruin 10
stony 3
bankruptcy
collapse 6
failure 4
ruin 1
banned
taboo 1
unlawful
banner°
colour 2a
flag[1] 1
pennant
sign 4
standard 3
streamer
symbol
banneret
flag[1] 1
streamer
bannerol
streamer
banning
prevention
prohibition 1
banquet°
dine
feast 1
function 2
spread 11
banshee
ghost 1
shade 4
shrew
bantam
little 1
miniature
minute[2] 1
slight 3
small 1
tiny
undersized
banter°
chaff 1, 2
fool 5
humour 1
joke 4
raillery
repartee
twit[1]
bantering
volley 3
bap
roll 17
baptize
call 2
christen 1
entitle 2
name 4
tag 4
title 6
bar°
ban 1
barrier 1, 2
barring
beam 1
block 2, 3
bolt 2
cake 2
counter 2
deterrent
disqualify
dive 3
embargo 1, 2
except 1
exclude 1
exclusion 1
exile 3
expel 2
hamper[1]
handicap 1, 2
hinder 1
hurdle 1
impede

bar *(cont.)*
impediment
inhibit
inhibition
isolate
leave[1] 10
lock[1] 1, 3, 8
lounge 4
measure 9
obstacle
obstruct 1
obstruction 1
oppose 2
outlaw 2
preclude
prevent
prevention
prohibit 1
prohibition 1, 2
pub
rail[1] 1
ray 1
restrain 2
rod 1
rule 8
shackle 2
shut 4b, 5a
standard 4
stop 2
streak 1, 4
stripe 1
stumbling-block
trammel 1
tribunal
-behind bars
hold 6
imprison
lock[1] 9
barb
bristle 1
insult 2
prickle 1
quip 1
shaft 3
spine 2
spur 2
squelch 2
thorn 1
wisecrack 1
barbarian°
boor 2
boorish
devil 2
heathen 3
merciless
philistine 1
primitive 2
punk 1
savage 4
uncivilized 1
barbaric
atrocious 1
barbarian 3
beastly 1
brutal 1
cold-blooded 3
cruel 2
cutthroat 3
deadly 3
ferocious
fierce 1
ghoulish 2
heathen 3
inhuman 1
merciless
monstrous 1
outrageous 2
primitive 2
savage 2, 3
uncivilized 1
wild 3
barbarism
misuse 2
outrage 1
rowdyism
solecism
barbarity°
atrocity 1
enormity
monstrosity 2
outrage 1
violence 2
barbarous
atrocious 1
barbarian 3

barbarous (*cont.*)
beastly 1
brutal 1
cold-blooded 3
cruel 2
cutthroat 3
deadly 3
ferocious
fierce 1
inhuman 1
merciless
monstrous 1
murderous 1
outlandish
sanguinary 1
savage 2, 3
truculent
uncivilized 1
ungraceful 2
unmerciful
vicious 1
violent 1
wild 3
barbarousness
barbarity
barbate
hairy 1
barbecue
broil
picnic 1
spread 11
barbed
poignant 2
pointed 1
prickly 1
pungent 2
tart[1] 2
thorny 1
barbel
spine 2
spur 2
barbellate
thorny 1
barber
trim 3
barbiturate
sedative 1
tranquillizer
barbule
spine 2
spur 2
bard
minstrel
poet
bare°
barren 2
blank 1
bleak 3
desert[1] 2
desolate 1
develop 1
disclose 2
disrobe
dry 1
empty 1, 3
exhausted 2
expose 1
gaunt 2
hard 8
lean[1] 2
lifeless 4
meagre 1, 3
mere
naked 1, 4
nude
open 2, 5
plain 4
rude 4
severe 6
show 1
smooth 4
stark 2
strip[2] 1
unadorned
unveil
very 4
bare-ass
bare 1
bare-boned
meagre 2, 3
bared
bare 4
naked 1
barefaced°
brazen
flagrant
naked 3
barely°
almost
hardly
just 5
little 3, 8
merely 2
narrowly 1
nearly 1
only 3
scarcely 1
scrape 5
severely 6
simply 1
bareness
emptiness 1
severity 6
simplicity 2
barest
very 4
barf
regurgitate
vomit
barfly
alcoholic 2
bargain°
agreement 1
buy 5
contract 1
deal 5
dicker 1, 2
engage 3
engagement 3
find 10
haggle
negotiate 1
negotiation 2
pact
steal 4
transaction 1
understanding 1
undertake 2
–at a bargain price
song 2
–into the bargain
addition 6
besides 1
boot 1
measure 10
moreover
bargain for°
at **bargain 4**
bargaining
negotiation 1
bargain-priced
cheap 1
sale 5
barge in
interrupt 1
intrude
baring
exposure 1
bark
hack[1] 2
peel 1
scrape 1
skin 5
snap 3b
thunder 3
vessel 2
whoop 1, 2
yap 1
barking up the wrong tree
misguided
mistaken 1
barley-bree
whisky
barmy
crazy 1
curious 3
deranged
foolish 2
halfwitted
insane 1
mad 1
mental 2
odd 1
preposterous
barmy (*cont.*)
stupid 2
twist 11
barn
stall[1] 3
barnacle
bloodsucker
parasite
barney
argument 1
fracas 2
quarrel 1
barnstorm
stump 3
barnyard
enclosure 1
barometer
glass 5
measure 3
baron
lord 2
merchant 3
mogul
peer[1] 1
royal 3
tycoon
baroness
peer[1] 1
royal 3
baroque
busy 3
elaborate 2
fancy 1
flamboyant 1
flowery
luxuriant 3
ornate
overwrought 2
showy
barque
vessel 2
barrack
cheer 7
heckle
jeer 1
–barracks
quarter 5
barracuda
fraud 3
barrage
fire 3
hail[2] 1, 2
shell 4
shower 2
storm 6
stream 3
volley 1
barrel
keg
lot 5b
pack 2
roller 1
–barrels
lot 5b
mass 2
–on the barrel-head
nail 6
–out of the barrel
tap[2] 4a
barrelhouse
pub
barren°
bare 4
bleak 3
dead 8
desert[1] 2
desolate 1
dry 1
empty 1, 3
exhausted 3
fruitless
futile
gaunt 2
impotent 3
impoverished 2
ineffectual 1
infertile
inhospitable 2
lean[1] 2
lifeless 4
lonely 2
meagre 4
barren (*cont.*)
non-productive 1
poor 3
stark 3
sterile 1, 3
uninhabited
useless 1
waste 10
wild 2
–barrens
waste 8
barrenness
desolation 1
emptiness 1
famine
barricade
bar 3, 9
block 3
defence 2
enclosure 2
fence 1
hamper[1]
jump 10
rampart
riot 3
rise
wall 2
barrier°
bar 3
block 2
bulwark 1
embargo 1
enclosure 2
fence 1
gate 1
handicap 1
hindrance 1
hurdle 1
impediment
inhibition
liability 3
obstacle
obstruction 1
partition 3
preventive 3
protection 1
shackle 2
stumbling-block
wall 1
barring°
bar 10
besides 2
except 1
exclusive 4
independent 8
prevention
prohibition 1
short 10
barrister
advocate 3
counsel 3
counsellor
lawyer
bar-room
bar 6
pub
barrow
cart 1
hump 1
knoll
mound 2
stand 16
tell[2]
barter
bargain 3
dicker 1
exchange 1, 2
give 2
haggle
sell 1
trade 1, 3, 6
base°
abominable 1
awful 1
bad 2
basis 1
bottom 2
build 2
cheap 3
common 4
contemptible
damnable
dark 4
degenerate 1
base (*cont.*)
despicable
diabolic 2
dirty 6
disgraceful 1
dishonourable 1, 2
disreputable 1
earthly 2
elixir 3
evil 1
floor 3
footing 1
foul 4
found 2
foundation 1, 2
germ 2
ground 3, 5
groundwork
grovelling
home 2
humble 3
immoral 1
infamous 2
installation 3
locate 1
lousy 1
low[1] 7, 12
mangy
mean[2] 2
menial 1
miscreant 2
monstrous 2
obnoxious
origin 1
paltry
pedestal 1
perverted
rank[2] 2
reprobate 1
root[1] 1
rotten 3, 4
scurvy
seat 2
servile
shabby 4
shameful
simple 5
sinful
sinister 2
sleazy 2
sordid 1
sorry 2
substratum
tasteless 1
ugly 2
vicious 1
vile 1
wicked 2
wretched 4
–off base
cock-eyed
inaccurate
inapplicable
base-born
humble 3
low[1] 7
baseless
gratuitous 2
groundless
ill-founded
sophistic
unfounded
untenable
basement
cellar
crypt
foundation 1
baseness
degradation 1
evil 6
filth 2
servility
vulgarity 1
bash
batter 1
beat 1
fête 1
fling 3
hit 1
party 1
rave 5
strike 1
bashful°
backward 1
coy
bashful (*cont.*)
modest 1
retiring
shamefaced 1
shy 1
timid
tremulous 2
withdrawn 1
bashfulness
embarrassment 1
humility
bashibazouk
guard 3
basic°
bare 2, 5
critical 2
effective 3
elemental
elementary 2
essential 2
first 3
fundamental 1
great 11
gut 6
ingrained
inherent
integral 1
intrinsic
introductory 2
literal 2
main 3
master 5
mere
mill 4
native 3
natural 3
necessity 1
need 3
organic 2
original 1, 3
paramount
plain 4
preparatory 2
primary 1, 4
prime 3
primitive 3
pristine 1
radical 1
rooted
rude 4
rudimentary 1
seminal 1
simple 1, 2
staple 1
strong 22
ultimate 3
understated
vital 1
–basics
element 3b
heart 3
meat 2
rudiments
staple 3
basically
bottom 5
effect 5
essence 3
inside 6
largely
materially
merely 1
practically 1
primarily 1
principally
principle 4
substantially
ultimately
basin
bowl[2]
hollow 7
sink 12
basis°
base[1] 2
bottom 3
cause 3
elixir 3
evidence 1
excuse 4
footing 1
foundation 1, 2
gauge 3
germ 2
ground 3
groundwork

bear witness°
at **witness 3**
attest
certify 1
finger 8
testify
verify
vouch
beast°
animal 2
bag 4
brute 2
devil 2
hag
monster 1
stinker
wretch 1
-beasts
stock 4
beastlike
animal 4
beastliness
severity 1
beastly
abominable 2
beastly°
brutal 1
cruel 1
foul 1
hideous 1, 2
horrible 2
monstrous 1
obnoxious
obscene 2
outrageous 2
repulsive
revolting
sadistic
savage 2
severe 1
stinking 2
terrible 1, 2, 3
ungodly 2
violent 1
wicked 2, 4
yucky
beat°
accent 1
assault 5
batter 1
belabour
belt 3
best 11
better[1] 11
cadence
cap 4
chastise
club 5
conquer 1, 3
crush 4
dead 9
defeat 1
downtrodden
exceed 1
excel
exhausted 1
fatigued
finish 4
flap 1, 2
flog 1
floor 4
go 27c
hail[2] 1
hide[2] 2
hippie
hit 1
jaded 1
knock 3d
lace 5a
lambaste 1
lash[1] 3
lather 4
light[2] 14
lose 3
manhandle
measure 9
mishandle 1
mystify
outdo
outstrip
overcome 1
overpower 1
overthrow 1
overwhelm 1
paddle 4
beat *(cont.)*
patrol 2
patter[1] 2, 3
pelt[1] 2
pound[1] 1, 3, 4, 7
prostrate 5
pulsate
pulse 1
punish 2, 3
rack 4
ragged 3
rhythm
rough 16
round 12
rout 2
run 37
scourge 3
shade 8
slap 2
slash 2
slaughter 4
sleepy 1
spent 1
stir 1
strike 1
stroke 4
surpass
switch 3
tack 6
tap[1] 1, 2
tempo
time 7
tired 1
top 3
transcend
triumph 3
upset 4
wash 3
washed out 2
whip 1, 2, 4
worn 3
beat about the bush
equivocate
fence 4
pussyfoot 2
stall[2] 1
waffle 2
-without beating about the bush
direct 9
shoulder 6
beat a retreat
flee 1
fly 2
make 26
nick 5
pull 14b
turn 22
beat back
turn 13a
beat down
subdue 1
beaten
broken 3
downtrodden
overcome 2
unsuccessful 2
-off the beaten track
isolated 3
secluded 2
beater
whisk 6
beatific
godlike 2
heavenly 1
radiant 2
rapt 2
saintly
beatification
reverence 1
beatified
heavenly 1
sublime 1
beatify
immortalize
revere
sanctify 1
beating
assault 2
defeat 3
patter[1] 3
pound[1] 7
beating *(cont.)*
pulse 1
punishment 2, 3
rhythmic
rout 1
tap[1] 2
thrashing 1
whipping 1
works 3b
beat it°
at **beat 8**
bugger 5
clear 30
depart 1
exit 3
flee 1
fly 2
leave[1] 1
make 26
nick 5
pull 14b
push 9b
quit 1
run 2
shoo 1
split 6
take 34c
turn 22
beatitude
rapture
beatnik
hippie
beat off°
at **beat 9**
repulse 1
beat one's brains out
exert 2
beat one's breast
bewail
beat out
beat 2
pound[1] 5, 6
beat the drum
plug 5
promote 4
publicize
puff 7
beat up
assault 5
knock 3d
manhandle
mishandle 1
punish 3
rough 16
set 12b, 24
beat-up
ragged 1, 4
shabby 3
beau
admirer 2
dandy 1
date 3
escort 3
fellow 4
flame 3
friend 3
gallant 5
love 3
suitor
sweetheart
Beau Brummell
dude 1
swell 6
beau geste
favour 2
beau idéal
model 3
paragon
quintessence
standard 1
beau monde
society 4
beauteous
fair[1] 7
lovely 1
beautification
ornament 1
beautiful°
aesthetic 1
bonny
brilliant 2
beautiful *(cont.)*
comely
cute 1
divine 3
elegant 1
exquisite 3
fair[1] 7
fine[1] 10
glorious 4
gorgeous 1
lovely 1
prepossessing
pretty 1
ravishing
scenic
stunning 2
voluptuous 2
beautifully°
beautiful people
élite 1
beautify°
decorate 1
embellish 1
enrich 2
grace 6
ornament 2
preen 2
touch 12
trim 4
beautifying
becoming
ornamental
beauty°
charm 3
delicacy 1
elegance 2
glory 3
splendour 1
beauty queen
queen 2
beauty sleep
sleep 2
beaver away
peg 7
because
for 7, 13
owe 2
reason 5
thank 4
through 1
view 6
virtue 4
wake[2] 2
beck
brook[1]
river 1
run 42
stream 1
tributary
-at one's beck and call
serve 1
thumb 5
under 2
beckon°
motion 6
signal 4
beckoning
inviting
becloud
dim 3
dull 10
fog 3
mist 2
obscure 7
beclouded
filmy 2
steamy 2
become°
amount 1b
change 8
fit[1] 5
get 6, 7
go 7
grow 4
make 10, 11
resolve 4
turn 16a, 23d
become of°
at **become 5**
happen 2
becoming°
appropriate 1
befitting
decent 1
decorous
fit[1] 1
fitting 1
flattering 1
opportune 2
proper 1, 3
seemly 1
suitable
becomingly
appropriately
properly 1
becomingness
grace 4
bed
border 6
bottom 4
cot
lay[1] 8
plant 5
race[1] 2
seam 2
vein 3
bedabble
dabble 1
bed and breakfast
hotel
bedaub
plaster
smear 1
spatter
bedazzle
daze 1
bedazzled
daze 4
bedazzling
dazzling
bedchamber
chamber 4
bedclothes
cover 13
linen
bed-cover
spread 14
bedding
cover 13
bedeck
beautify
decorate 1
drape 1
dress 1
embellish 1
bedevil
annoy 2
madden 3
obsess
pester
tease 1
torment 2
bedevilled
doomed 2
possessed
bedew
dampen 1
water 6
bedfellow
friend 3
bedim
blur 3
dim 4
dull 10
fog 3
obscure 7
bedlam°
chaos
confusion 2
disorder 2
noise 1
pandemonium
pell-mell 3
row[2] 2
rumpus
tumult
uproar
zoo 2
bedlamite
psychotic 2
bed linen(s)
linen
bed out
plant 5
bedraggled°
dirty 1
disreputable 2
filthy 2
shabby 1
sloppy 1
unkempt
untidy
bedroom
chamber 4
sexy 1
bed-sheet
sheet 1
bedsit
flat 18
bedsitter
flat 18
bedspread
spread 14
bedtime
nightly 2
bedwetting
incontinent 3
beef
cattle
complain
complaint
grievance 2
gripe 1, 2
groan 2, 4
moan 2
protest 1, 3
squawk 2, 3
beefy
big 2
brawny
burly
fat 1
hefty 2
husky 1
plump[1] 1
stalwart 1
stocky
stout 4
strong 1
beeline
directly 1
head 10
right 13
straight 12
Beelzebub
devil 1
beer
brew 4
beer-bellied
heavy 11
beer-belly
gut 2
paunch
pot 3
bee's knees
killer 2
beeswax
affair 2
beetle
bug 1
jut
leave[1] 1
overhang 1
project 5
stand 9b
stick[1] 15
beetling
protuberant
befall
chance 7
come 4a
happen 2
occur 1
overtake 2
pass 13
visit 2
befit
become 3
behove
fit[1] 5
pertain
suit 2
befitting°
applicable
appropriate 1

befitting (*cont.*)
becoming
correct 6
expedient 1
fit[1] 1
fitting 1
proper 1
seemly 1
suitable

befittingly
duly 1

befog°
fog 4
blur 3
mist 2
muddle 1
muddy 4

befogged
obscure 1
steamy 2

before°
advance 10a, 10b
ahead 1
by 4
first 4
formerly
front 8
once 1
past 4
preparatory 3
previous 4
previously
prior 2
short 10

beforehand
advance 10a
before 1
early 1
first 4
preconceived
premature 2
previously
time 10

before-mentioned
previous 2

befoul
contaminate
desecrate
dirty 7
foul 12
mire 4
pollute 1
soil[1] 2

befouled
dirty 1
muddy 1

befouling
pollution
sacrilege 1

befoulment
sacrilege 1

befriend
fall 15

befuddle
bemuse 1
bewilder
confuse 1
daze 2
disorder 4
distract 3
fluster 1
intoxicate 1
muddle 1
perplex

befuddled
daze 4
dizzy 2
groggy

befuddlement
distraction 1
fluster 2

beg°
appeal 1
ask 3
beseech
bid 2
bum 5
cry 3
hit 8
plead 1, 2
pray 1
press 6

beg (*cont.*)
push 4
request 1
scrounge 1
seek 3
solicit 1
speak 7c
sue 2
urge 2

beg, borrow, or steal
scrounge 1

beget
breed 2
conceive 1
create 2
father 5
generate 2
have 8
originate 1
produce 2, 3
reproduce 2
spawn
start 7
work 16
world 5a

begetter
parent 1
source 2
stock 3

begetting
generation 1

beggar°
bum 2
devil 3
down and out 2
pauper
supplicant 2
trivialize

beggared
impoverished 1

beggarly
measly
paltry
penurious 2
pitiful 2

beggary
need 4
poverty 1
privation

begging
supplicant 1
supplication 2
urgent 2

begin°
arise 4
attack 3
break 17
brew 3
commence 1, 2, 3
dawn 4
develop 4
embark 2
enter 4
establish 1
excite 1
fall 21
flow 3
go 18, 24b, 29a
inaugurate 1
initiate 1
institute 4
introduce 4
launch 1
lead 8
move 12a
open 20
organize 2
originate 1, 2
pioneer 2
preface 2
proceed 2
put 17c
rise 9, 17
set 12a, 18b, 19, 23b
spark 2
spring 3
sprout
start 1, 2, 4, 7
strike 18
touch 11b
undertake 1
way 12

-to begin with
first 5
originally

beginner
apprentice 1
greenhorn
initiate 4
innocent 5
learner
newcomer 2
novice
pupil
recruit 2

beginning°
birth 2
conception 1
creation 1
dawn 2
derivation
early 5
elementary 2
entrance[1] 4
first 2, 6
front 3
generation 3
germ 2
infancy 2
initial 1
initiation 1
introductory 1
oncoming 2
onset 2
opening 4
origin 2
original 1
outset
preliminary 1, 2
primary 2
source 1
spring 8
start 9, 10, 11, 12, 14, 15
threshold 2

-at the beginning
early 2
first 5
originally

-beginnings
infancy 2
start 11, 15

-from beginning to end
completely 1
round 24
throughout 1

-from the beginning
originally

-in the beginning
first 8
originally

beginning and end
totality

begin the day
rise 2

begone
depart 1
shoo 1

beg pardon
apologize 1

begrime
blacken 1
dirty 7
mire 4
muddy 5
smear 1
soil[1] 1

begrimed
dirty 1
filthy 2

begrudge°
envy 3
grudge 2
resent

begrudging
envious
penurious 1
resentful

beguile°
amuse 1
appeal 2

beguile (*cont.*)
bewitch
cajole
captivate
coax
dazzle 1
defraud
divert 3
enchant 2
enrapture
entice
fascinate
flatter 3
intrigue 1
lead 9b
occupy 3
seduce 1
trap 6
wheedle

beguiled
infatuated
smitten 2

beguilement
amusement 1
cajolery
enchantment 2
enticement 1
flattery

beguiling
enchanting
enthralling
glamorous 1
inviting
magnetic
seductive

behalf°
interest 3
part 5
sake 1

-in behalf of° *at* **behalf**
favour 5
for 1, 3, 5
part 10
speak 7b

-on behalf of° *at* **behalf**
favour 5
for 1, 3, 5
part 10

behave°
act 5
card 13
conduct 6
deal 3
function 3
perform 2
play 16
react 1
treat 1

behave badly
misbehave

behave better
shape 10b

behave improperly
misbehave

behave like one possessed
rage 4

behaviour°
action 8
bearing 1
breeding 2
carriage 2
conduct 1
decorum 1
discipline 3
form 6
guise 1
manner 2, 3
moral 4
morality 2
performance 4
play 21
policy
psychology
treatment 1

behaviour pattern
way 2

behead°

behemoth
giant 1
thumping 1
vast

behest
command 6
demand 5
dictate 2
order 4

behind
back 5, 17
backward 4
bottom 1
bum 1
buttocks
favour 5
last[1] 5
overdue
posterior 3
rear[1] 2
seat 4
tail 2

behindhand
back 13, 17
backward 3
belated
late 1
overdue
slow 4, 5, 12
tardy 1

behold°
contemplate 1
discover 2
eye 10
look 1
see 1
sight 8
view 7
witness 4

beholden°
debt 2
indebted
obliged 1
owe 1
thankful

beholder
observer
spectator

behoof
interest 3
profit 2

behoove
become 3

behove
become 3

beige
dead 10
neutral 2

being
animal 1
attendance 1
beast 1
creature 1
entity 1
essence 1
existence 1, 3
life 1
organism
person 1
presence 2
soul 1, 2
subsistence 1

belabour°
batter 1
beat 1
chastise
club 5
hit 1
labour 6
lace 5a
lambaste 1
lash[1] 4
lather 4
lay[1] 13
light[2] 14
manhandle
pelt[1] 1
pitch[1] 6b
pound[1] 1
rough 16
strike 1

belated°
late 1
overdue

belated (*cont.*)
tardy 2

belatedly
late 7

belch
erupt 1
spew
vomit

belching forth
eruption 1

beldam
bag 4
fury 3
hag
jade 2
ruin 5
scold 2
shrew
witch 2

beleaguer
besiege 1
molest 1
rack 3
siege 2

beleaguerment
siege 1

belfry
crazy 1
head 1
spire 1
tower 1

Belial
devil 1

belie
contradict 2
explode 2
garble 1
misrepresent
rebut

belief°
cause 4
confidence 1
conviction 2
credit 1
creed
doctrine
estimate 4
expectation 2
faith 1, 2
feeling 2
hope 2
idea 3
ideology
impression 1
judgement 4
mind 6
moral 4
opinion 1
persuasion 2
point of view 2
position 7
presumption 3
principle 2
religion
sentiment 2
stand 13
supposition
tenet
thesis 1
thinking 2
trust 1
view 2

-beliefs
ideology
lore 1
philosophy 2

-beyond belief
incredible 1
unthinkable 1

believable
good 8
plausible 1
presumptive 1
probable
ready-made 2
reasonable 2
reliable
smooth 8
supportable 2
tenable
thinkable
wash 8

believably
seemingly

bent°
shapeless 2
shifty
sick 5
slant 2
spirit 2
spoil 5
swish 4
talent 2
tendency
tortuous 1
trend 1
turn 38
unnatural 1
venal
villainous 1
weakness 4
wry 1
benumb
bemuse 2
daze 1
deaden 1
drug 4
dull 11
numb 2
paralyse 2
petrify 1
stun 1
benumbed
chill 5
dead 2
groggy
insensible 1
numb 1
petrified 1
senseless 2
silly 2
benumbing
stunning 1
be off
shoo 1
bequeath°
devise 2
donate
hand 15a
inherit
leave[1] 6
pass 18b
will 6
bequeathed
hereditary 2
bequest°
donation 1
endowment 1
grant 3
inheritance
berate°
abuse 3
attack 2
chastise
correct 2
damn 1
dress 4
lace 5b
lambaste 2
lash[1] 4
lecture 4
light[2] 14
mind 10
nag[1] 1
rail[2]
rate[2]
rebuke 1
reprimand 2
scold 1
tell[1] 10
twit[1]
upbraid
vituperate
berating
abuse 8
lecture 2
rebuke 2
tongue-lashing
bereave°
bereavement
loss 1
mourning 2
bereft
destitute 2
forlorn 2
starved 3
Bermuda shorts
short 15
berserk°
deranged
distraught
frantic
homicidal
hysterical 1
mad 4
maniacal 2
rabid 1
rampage 2
raving 1
wild 5
berth
appointment 3
cabin 2
dock 1, 2
job 1
land 5
moor[2]
office 4
place 5
position 6
situation 3
space 4
beseech°
appeal 1
ask 3
beg 1
hit 8
petition 2
plead 2
pray 1
press 6
request 1
solicit 1
sue 2
urge 2
beseecher
supplicant 2
beseeching
supplicant 1
supplication 2
beset°
assault 3
harass
haunt 2
infest
mob 3
seize 3
smitten 1
beside°
about 9
by 1
beside oneself°
at **beside 3**
ecstatic
excited 1
frantic
furious 1
hysterical 1
panic-stricken
rage 4
upset 10
besides°
addition 5, 6
apart 4
barring
boot 1
further 3
independent 8
likewise 2
measure 10
moreover
yet 3
besiege°
beset
bombard 2
siege 2
storm 6
besiegement
siege 1
besmeared
dirty 1
besmirch
blacken 2
blemish 2
dirty 7
discredit 1
disgrace 4
foul 14
libel 4
mire 4
muddy 5
shame 8
besmirch (*cont.*)
smear 1, 2
soil[1] 2
spot 7
stain 5
stigmatize
sully
taint 2
besmirched
dirty 1
besmirchment
filth 2
besom
brush[2] 1
besotted
daft 3
drunk 1
far 5b
infatuated
bespatter
dabble 1
muddy 5
spatter
splash 1
spot 7
bespattered
speckled
bespeak
engage 1
indicate 2
promise 4
bespeckle
dapple 2
dot 3
pepper
bespoke
fitted
speak 13
tailor-made 1
besprinkle
dabble 1
powder 4
spatter
splash 1
best°
beat 2
better[1] 5
choice 3, 4
defeat 1
dress 5a
élite 2
end 8b
excellent
finish 4
floor 4
flower 2
foremost 1
good 15
great 6
leading 2
native 3
optimum 1, 2
outside 3, 6
outstrip
overcome 1
overpower 1
overthrow 1
peerless
perfect 1, 2, 4
pick 10
pride 3
prime 2
prize[1] 5
rout 2
select 2
shade 8
special 5
superlative
supreme 3
surpass
top 3, 8
triumph 3
vintage 2
whip 2
-at best
ideally 1
just 4
only 3
-at one's best
pink[1] 1
-in the best of circumstances
ideally 1
-in the best of health
pink[1] 1
-of the best quality
water 5
-on the best terms
thick 8
best bib and tucker
best 7
finery
best clothes
best 7
dress 5a
bested
lose 3
overcome 2
bestial
animal 4
beastly 1
brutal 1
ferocious
fierce 1
inhuman 2
libertine 2
savage 2, 3
unnatural 2
vicious 3
bestiality
violence 2
bestir
incite
rouse 2
stir 2
wake[1] 1
bestir oneself
awake 1
move 12a
best-liked
favourite 2
bestow°
award 1
confer 2
contribute 1
devise 2
dispose 3c
donate
extend 4
give 1
grant 1
heap 4
impart 1
lavish 5
lend 2
pay 3
present[2] 6
rain 7
show 10
spare 8
vouchsafe 1
bestowal
award 3
disposition 3
donation 2
endowment 2
presentation 1
best part
feature 2
majority 1
mass 4
bestraddle
mount 4
bestrew
strew
bestride
mount 4
best-seller
novel 2
best-selling
successful 3
best wishes
compliment 2
congratulations
greeting 3
regard 10
respect 5
best years
prime 4
bet°
adventure 4
back 1
bet (*cont.*)
chance 8
gamble 1, 2, 4
lay[1] 4
play 7
plunge 4
punt 1, 2
put 6
rely
stake[2] 1, 4
venture 3
bête noire
fear 3
be that as it may
however 1
nevertheless
though 2
time 13a
betide
chance 7
happen 1
betimes
early 3
bêtise
trifle 1
triviality 2
betoken
announce 4
argue 4
bode
denote 2
express 2
foreshadow
imply 2
import 2
indicate 2
involve 2
mean[1] 2
prognosticate 2
promise 4
signify 1
speak 5
stand 7a
symbolize
betokening
symbolic
betray°
blab
deceive
denounce 2
disclose 1
display 1
double-cross
exhibit
expose 1
finger 8
give 12b
grass 1
inform 2
let[1] 7a
manifest 2
register 4
sell 3
shop 3
show 1
stab 2
tell[1] 2
turn 15c
betrayal°
perfidy
stab 6
betrayer
informer
snake 2
traitor
turncoat
betrothal
engagement 2
match 3
betrothed
attached 4
engaged 1
fiancé(e)
girl 2
love 3
sweetheart
better°
advantage 3
amend 1
benefit 3
cap 4
dignify
elaborate 4
enhance
better (*cont.*)
enrich 1
exceed 1
help 2
high-class 1
improve 1
increase 2
lift 2
mend 2
outstrip
perfect 9
preferential
reform 1
select 2
shade 8
superior 1
surpass
top 3
vintage 2
better half
mate 2
wife
woman 2
bettering
recovery 1
refinement 4
betterment
advance 7
advantage 2
amendment 1
elaboration 1
improvement 1
progress 2
recovery 1
refinement 4
reform 3
better part
majority 1
mass 4
better than average
strong 10
bettor
backer 3
better[2]
player 3
punter 1
betwixt and between
end 6
bevel
slant 4
slope 2
beverage
brew 4
drink 4
potion
bevy
flight[1] 4
flock 1
number 2
pack 3
score 4
throng 1
bewail°
grieve 1
keen[2] 1
lament 1
moan 2
mourn
regret 1
repent
sigh 2
sorrow 3
weep 1
beware°
look 9
mistrust 1
bewhiskered
hairy 1
bewilder°
astound
bemuse 1
bother 3
confuse 1
daze 2
demoralize 3
distract 3
dumbfound
elude 2
entangle 2
floor 5
flummox
flurry 2

bewilder (*cont.*)
fluster 1
fog 4
get 18
knock 6b
mix 4b
muddle 1
mystify
overwhelm 3
perplex
puzzle 1
stagger 2
stick[1] 9
stump 2
stun 2
throw 6c
bewildered
blank 5
confused 2
daze 4
disconcerted
disorientated
dumbfounded
groggy
helpless 2
lost 3
sea 4
bewildering
disconcerting
indefinite 2
inexplicable
mysterious 1
overwhelming 2
paradoxical
perplexing
puzzling
bewilderment
distraction 1
fluster 2
perplexity 1
bewitch°
captivate
catch 11
charm 5
dazzle 1
enchant 1
enrapture
entrance[2]
fascinate
hypnotize
intoxicate 2
jinx 3
possess 3
ravish 1
regale
transfix 2
transport 3
bewitched
charmed 1
doomed 2
infatuated
rapt 1
smitten 2
taken
bewitching
catching 2
darling 4
devastating 2
enchanting
enthralling
glamorous 1
inviting
lovely 1
magic 6
magnetic
prepossessing
provocative 1
ravishing
seductive
spellbinding
taking
winning 1
bewitchment
glamour
magic 3
beyond
above 4
addition 5
advance 10b
besides 2
escape 4
further 3
independent 8
over 2, 3, 7
ulterior 2
beyond (a) doubt
doubtless 1
easily 4
far 3
indisputable
positively
question 4
surely 1
truly 3
undoubtedly
well[1] 7
beyond belief
incredible 1
unthinkable 1
beyond compare
incomparable
matchless
peerless
beyond the pale
extreme 6
beyond words
ineffable 2
Bhagavad-Gita
Scripture
bias°
bent 5
bigotry
colour 4
discriminate 2
discrimination 1
drift 3
fanaticism 2
favour 3
favouritism
inclination 3
incline 2
inequality 2
influence 3
injustice 1
intolerance
leaning
liking 1
mind 5
partiality 1
patronage 4
penchant
preconception
prejudice 1, 2, 3
presumption 3
slant 2, 5
sway 2
tendency
tenor
trend 1
turn 38
twist 2, 9
warp 2
weight 6
biased°
biased
bigoted
incline 3
interested 2
intolerant 2
jaundiced 1
lean[2] 3
lopsided 2
narrow-minded
near-sighted 2
one-sided 1
opinionated 2
parochial
partial 2
partisan 3
preconceived
preferential
prejudiced 1
subjective 1
tend[1]
trend 3
bib and tucker
dress 5
primp
bibber
drunk 3
bibelot
antique 2
-bibelots
bric-à-brac
Bible
Scripture
bibliography
list[1] 1
bibliophage
bookworm
bibliophile
bookworm
bibulate
booze 2
bibulousness
drunkenness
bicker°
argue 1
disagree 2
feud 2
fight 4
haggle
jar[2] 2
row[2] 3
scrap[2] 2
spar[2] 2
tiff
bickering
feud 1
fight 8
friction 2
strife 1
biconcave
crescent 2
bid°
apply 6
ask 4
attempt 2
beckon
call 4
charge 10
command 1
demand 1, 5
direct 3
instruct 2
offer 1, 5
order 14
proposal 1
propose 1
say 10
tell[1] 5
tender[2] 2
bid adieu
exit 3
kiss 3
part 12
see 13
bid bon voyage
see 13
biddable
obedient
submissive 2
tractable 1
bidding°
call 14
command 6
dictate 2
invitation 1
bide
stay[1] 5
bide one's time
sit 8
tarry 1, 2
twiddle 2
wait 1
bid fair
promise 4
bid goodbye
leave[1] 1
part 12
biff
jab 2, 4
knock 9
punch[1] 1, 2
rap 4
bifocals
glass 7
bifurcate
separate 4
big°
beamy
burly
considerable 1
extensive 2
gigantic
great 1
gross 1
handsome 2
hefty 1
large 1, 2, 3, 4
liberal 1
big (*cont.*)
long[1] 1
major 2
massive
merciful
mighty 3
ponderous 1
roomy
spanking 1
stout 1
substantial 1, 2
tall 1, 2
tidy 3
voluminous 1
wide 3
big apple
city
Big Board
exchange 4
big boss
master 1
big break
fluke
big-busted
bosomy
buxom 2
big cheese
bigwig 1
boss 1
chief 1
dignitary
director 1
executive 1
head 2
leader 1
master 1
mogul
name 3
somebody 2
tycoon
big Chief
chief 1
dignitary
mogul
somebody 2
big Daddy
chief 1
dignitary
mogul
somebody 2
bigener
mongrel
big fish
master 1
bigger
better[1] 2
major 1
biggest
main 2
major 2
master 6
biggie
dignitary
biggish
considerable 1
big gun
bigwig 1
dignitary
mogul
somebody 2
big-headed
vain 1
big-headedness
vanity 1
big-hearted
generous 1
kind[1]
large 2
liberal 1
open 14
tolerant
big-heartedness
charity 2
philanthropy 1
big house
jail 1
prison
stir 7
bight
gulf 1
sound[4]
big-mouth
blabbermouth
braggart
gossip 3
talebearer
big-mouthed
pert 1
talkative
big name
dignitary
name 3
star 2
bigness
magnitude 1
mass 5
size 1
big noise
dignitary
mogul
personage
somebody 2
bigot
sectarian 4
supremacist
zealot
bigoted°
hidebound
intolerant 2
jaundiced 1
narrow-minded
near-sighted 2
one-sided 1
opinionated 2
parochial
partisan 3
prejudiced 2
puritan 2
sectarian 2
ultra-
bigotry°
discrimination 1
fanaticism 2
injustice 1
intolerance
prejudice 2
zealotry
big screen
movie 2
big shot
bigwig 1
dignitary
mogul
name 3
notable 3
operator 3
personage
star 2
tycoon
big spender
prodigal 3
wastrel 1
big-time operator
operator 3
big-timer
somebody 2
tycoon
big wheel
bigwig 1
dignitary
master 1
mogul
operator 3
personage
somebody 2
tycoon
big White Chief
chief 1
dignitary
somebody 2
bigwig°
dignitary
mogul
name 3
somebody 2
-bigwigs°
at **bigwig 2**
bijou
gewgaw
jewel 1
twee
bijouterie
jewellery
bilboes
restraint 2
shackle 1
bile
gall[1] 1
bilge
drivel 3
fiddlesticks
gobbledegook 1
moonshine 2
muck 2
mumbo-jumbo 1
nonsense 1
rubbish 2
talk 18
trash 1
bilious°
cantankerous
harsh 3
passionate 3
peevish
perverse 2
petulant
queasy 2
surly
bilk
cheat 2
chisel 2
clip[2] 4
defraud
dupe 3
fleece
fraud 2, 3
gouge 2
rip 2b
rob 3
screw 6
swindle 1
take 27, 32b
trick 8
victimize 2
bilker
fraud 3
bill°
act 4
advertisement 1
charge 12
check 19
damage 2
fee 1
leaflet
measure 7
note 4
pamphlet
peak 3
police 1
poster
promotion 5
reckoning 2
tab 2
-bills
cash 1
money 1
tender[2] 3
bill and coo
cuddle 2
billboard
promotion 5
billet
abode
accommodate 4
board 7
house 8
lodge 4
place 5
position 6
put 28b
quarter 5, 6
station 4
billet-doux
love letter
note 2
billfold
wallet
billingsgate
abuse 8
profanity
billion
number 2
-billions
mint 1
umpteen

black eye
stain 2
blackguard
criminal 3
heel[1] 2
miscreant 1
rascal
reprobate 2
rogue 1
scoundrel
stinker
villain
wretch 1
blackguardly
black 6
black hat
criminal 3
blackhead
pimple
-blackheads
spot 5
black-hearted
dark 4
evil 1
fiendish
wicked 2
black hole
dungeon
singularity 3
blackjack
club 1
blackleg°
blacklist
black 8
boycott 1,2
ostracize
blacklisting
boycott 2
black look
glare 2
black magic
magic 1
occult 3
blackmail°
extort
gouge 2
protection 3
shake 6b
blackmailer
bloodsucker
black mark
disgrace 2
dishonour 5
scandal 3
blackmarketeer
profiteer 1
blackness
dark 11
gloom 1
night 1
oblivion 1
obscurity 1
black out
faint 3
pass 20a
shade 11
blackout
faint 4
black sheep
good-for-nothing 2
black spot
scandal 3
blade°
dagger
dandy 1
knife 1
runner 4
steel 1
blah
bland 2
lacklustre
stodgy
tedious
vapid
blains
spot 5
blame°
accuse 1
charge 11
come 11
condemn 1
correct 2
blame (*cont.*)
damn 1
denounce 1
fault 3,8
flak
guilt 1
impeach 1
imputation
incriminate
indict
pin 5
rap 6
recrimination
responsibility 3
task 3
thank 2
twit[1]
vituperate
-to blame
answer 7a
fault 5
responsible 4
blameable
fault 5
liable 2
blameless°
clean 4
clear 12
impeccable
innocent 1
irreproachable
perfect 3
pure 3
saintly
spotless 2
blamelessness
purity 2
blameworthiness
guilt 1
blameworthy
fault 5
guilty 1
liable 2
shameful
wrong 1
blaming
recrimination
blanch
bleach 1
fade 1
pale[1] 4
blanched
colourless 1
pale[1] 1
washed out 1
bland°
benign 2
colourless 2
dead 10,12
flat 5
lacklustre
meek 1
mild 1,3
nondescript
prosaic
smooth 5
stodgy
suave
tame 4
tasteless 2
tiresome 1
vapid
watery 1
wishy-washy 2
blandiloquent
ingratiating
blandish
entice
blandishment
cajolery
caress 1
enticement 1
flattery
blank°
block 4b
empty 5,6
form 4
glassy 2
solid 10
space 2
vacancy 1
vacant 2
vague 6
blank (*cont.*)
void 2
blanket
cover 3,13
general 3
inclusive 1
mantle 2
overall
sheet 5
shroud 1,3
smother 3,4
spread 7
sweeping 1
blank look
stare 2
blankness
emptiness 1,3
oblivion 1
vacancy 3
void 4
blank out
block 4b
smother 4
blare°
bellow 1
blast 2
din 1
fanfare 1
noise 1
blaring
din 1
loud 1
noisy
piercing 1
blarney
flannel 1
gab 2
line[1] 18
blasé°
blithe 2
carefree
casual 3
disenchanted
lackadaisical 2
nonchalant
offhand 1
relaxed
sophisticated 1
tepid 2
unenthusiastic
weary 3
blaspheme°
curse 5
desecrate
flout
swear 2
blasphemous°
godless 1
impious
irreverent 1
oath 2
profane 1,3
sacrilegious
ungodly 1
wicked 1
blasphemously
vain 3b
blasphemy
curse 3
oath 2
profanity
sacrilege 2
blast°
blare 1,2
blaze 5
blight 3
blow[1] 2,8b
boom 1,3
crash 4
criticize 2
curse 4
damn 1
din 1
explode 1
explosion 1
fanfare 1
fête 1
gale 1
gust 1,2
noise 1
puff 1
rave 5
report 2
shatter 2
blast (*cont.*)
shoot 3
speech 2
thunder 1,2
blasted
flaming
blasting
noise 1
noisy
blast off
take 34c
blatant°
barefaced 1
conspicuous 2
flagrant
flaming
glaring 1
gross 4
manifest 1
naked 3
open 13
patent 2
public 5
rank[2] 2
ultra-
unabashed
blather
drivel 2
gab 1,2
gibberish
gossip 4
gush 2
hot air
jabber 1
jargon 2
moonshine 2
mumbo-jumbo 1
nonsense 1
palaver 2,4
patter[2] 2,3
prattle 1,2
rattle 6
talk 3
tattle 2
waffle 1,3
wind[1] 2
yap 2
blatherskite
gossip 3
talker 2
blaze°
burn 1
fire 1
flame 1,4
flare 1,4
flash 1,4
glare 1
radiate 1
sparkle 1
blaze away°
at **blaze 5**
blaze the trail
pioneer 2
spearhead 1
blazing
ablaze 1
burning 1,4
fiery 1
fire 5
full 10
glaring 2
radiant 1
torrid 1
blazon
splash 2
bleach°
fade 1
bleached
washed out 1
bleak°
cold 4
dark 3
desolate 1
dismal
dreary 1
gaunt 2
harsh 2
heavy 9
joyless 2
lifeless 4
murky
pessimistic
sad 2
sombre 2
bleak (*cont.*)
stark 3
untoward 1
wintry 3
bleakness
rigour 1
blear
film 4
bleary
filmy 2
indistinct 1
vague 1
bleat
gripe 1
bleed
drain 5
extort
feel 8
fleece
gouge 2
milk
ooze 2
pity 3
sap[1] 3
squeeze 2,3
tap[2] 6
bleeding
flaming
very 1
bleep
edit 2
blemish°
blot 1
bruise 1
deface
defect 2
discredit 5
disgrace 2
dishonour 5
failing 1
fault 1
flaw 1
foible
imperfection
mark 1,10
nick 1
scandal 3
scar 1,2
spoil 2
spot 1
stain 2
stigma
stigmatize
sully
taint 1,2
tarnish
vice 2
blemished
disfigured
second[1] 7
blench
bleach 1
blink 3
cringe 1
dread 1
fade 1
flinch
pale[1] 4
recoil 1
start 5
blend°
alloy 1
amalgam
amalgamate
amalgamation
beat 6
chime 5a
combination 3
combine 2,3
compound 1,2,5
converge
cross 2
fuse
go 6,40a
incorporate
integrate
lump[1] 3
match 7
medley
melt 3
merge
merger
mingle 1
mix 1,7
blend (*cont.*)
mixture 1,2
neologism
pastiche
solution 3
stir 1
synthesis
unite 1
weave 2
wed 2
wedding 2
blended
general 3
blending
amalgamation
merger
mixture 2
synthesis
wedding 2
bless°
dedicate 2
hallow 1
blessed
favoured 2
fortunate 1
godlike 1
golden 5
heaven 1
heavenly 1
holy 1
lucky 1
possess 1
providential
sacred 1
saintly
blessedness
bliss
paradise 3
blessing°
approval
boon
cooperation 2
glory 2
godsend
grace 5
honour 3
joy 3
recommendation 2
blest
godlike 1
golden 5
sacred 1
saintly
blether
drivel 2
gab 1,2
gibberish
gossip 4
gush 2
hot air
jabber 1
jargon 2
moonshine 2
mumbo-jumbo 1
nonsense 1
palaver 2,4
patter[2] 2,3
prattle 1,2
talk 3
tattle 2
blethering
prattle 2
bleu
rare 2
telegram
blight°
disease 2
mar 2
mould[2]
overshadow 2
pestilence 2
plague 1
poison 2
pollute 1
rot 3
shadow 4
ulcer 2
undoing 2
visitation 2
blighter
rascal
rogue 1
stinker

boat trip
cruise 2

boatwoman
sailor

bob
clip[2] 1
dodge 1
duck 1
float 1
plumb 1
sever 1
trim 3
wag[1] 1

bobble
fumble 2
wag[1] 1,2

bobby
constable
police officer

bobby-soxer
miss[2]

bod
build 5
figure 1
form 2
physique

bode°
foreshadow
prophesy 2
spell[3] 1

bodiless
disembodied

bodily
carnal
flesh 4
material 5
mortal 2
outward
person 2
personal 1
physical
sensual
sexual 2
tangible

bodily structure
physique

bodkin
punch[2] 1

body°
assembly 1
band[2] 1
build 5
cadaver
camp[1] 2
chamber 1
cluster 2
cohort 2
committee
company 2
corps
corpse
council 2
crew
figure 1
flesh 2
flock 1
form 2
frame 4
group 1
host[2]
hull 1
mass 4
mob 1
order 9
organism
organization 3
pack 3
party 2
physique
platoon
remain 4b
shape 1
stiff 11
team 1
text 1
trunk 2

-bodies
people 1

-in a body
large 5b

body and soul
utterly

body count
casualty 2b

body fluid
sap[1] 1

bodyguard
bruiser
escort 1
follower 2
guard 3
henchman
minder 2
protector

body of instruction
doctrine

body politic
state 4

body text
text 1

Boeotian
philistine 1
slow 7
stupid 1
thick 6

boffin
expert 1

bog°
facility 2b
flat 14b
lavatory
marsh
mire 1
morass 1
privy 3
swamp 1
toilet 1

bog down°
at **bog 2**
delay 2

-be bogged down
stick[1] 7
welter 2

bogey
fear 3
fly 10
ogre

bogeyman
monster 1
ogre
spectre 1

boggart
ghost 1

boggle at
hesitate 1

boggy
muddy 1
mushy 1
watery 3

bog-trotter
peasant
rustic 3

bogus°
affected 2
artificial 2
assumed 2
bum 3
counterfeit 1
deceptive 2
factitious
fake 5
false 3
fictitious 2
glossy 2
mock 3
phoney 1
plastic 3
pretended
sham 2
sophistic
spurious
synthetic

bogy
see **bogey**

bogyman
see **bogeyman**

Bohemian°
hippie
offbeat

boil°
brew 1
bristle 3
bubble 3

boil *(cont.)*
evaporate 1
ferment 1
fume 1
lump[1] 2
pimple
rage 4
seethe 1
simmer 1
smoulder
swirl 1
ulcer 1

-boils
spot 5

boil down
diminish 1
telescope 2

boiling
furious 1
hot 1
scorching 1
steamy 1
sweltering
torrid 1

boisterous°
blatant 2
disorderly 2
high 8
irrepressible
noisy
obstreperous
riotous 2
rowdy 1
tempestuous
tumultuous,
uncontrolled
uninhibited
wild 4

boisterousness
festivity 2
hilarity
rough-house 1
rowdyism

bold°
adventurous,
aggressive 2
assertive
audacious 1,2
barefaced 2
brash 2
brave 1
confident 2
cool 6
courageous
dare 2
daredevil 2
daring 2
dauntless
defiant
downright 1
enterprising
familiar 3
fearless
flagrant
foolhardy
forward 2
fresh 8
gallant 1
game 8
hardy 2
heroic 1
immodest 2
impertinent
impudent
independent 3
indiscreet
ingenuous 2
insolent
intrepid
liberty 5
manly
officious
outspoken
pert 1
presumptuous
pushy
rash[1]
resolute
rude 2
rugged 3
shameless
stalwart 3
stout 2
strong 19
swashbuckling

bold *(cont.)*
unabashed
venturesome 1

boldly
openly 1

boldness
assurance 4
bravado
confidence 2
courage
daring 1
effrontery
enterprise 2
face 5
familiarity 3
freedom 7
gumption 2
gut 3a
heart 2
impertinence
impudence
indiscretion 1
liberty 5
manhood 2
mouth 4
nerve 1
panache
pluck 1
presumption 1
prowess 2
resolution 1

bole
trunk 1

bollixed (up)
confused 2

bollix up
botch
bugger 3
butcher 4
ruin 9
screw 7b

bollocks
fiddlesticks
flannel 1

bollocksed (up)
confused 2

bollocks up
botch
bugger 3
butcher 4
screw 7b

boloney
drivel 3
fiddlesticks
flannel 1
nonsense 1
prattle 3
rot 4
rubbish 2
stuff 4
trash 1
wind[1] 2

Bolshevik
radical 5

Bolshevist
radical 5

bolster°
cushion 1
follow 11b
fortify 1
prop 1
reassure
reinforce
reinforcement 1
strengthen 1
support 1,8
sustain 2

bolstering
follow-up
reinforcement 2
support 7

bolt°
career 2
connect 3
dash 3,5
devour 1
escape 1,5
flash 5
flee 1
flight[2] 3
fly 2
gorge 3
gulp 1
hasten 1

bolt *(cont.)*
lock[1] 1,3
peg 1
pin 1
run 1,2
scoff[2] 1
screw 1
scurry
seal 3
shoot 1
shut 1
speed 3
streak 2
tack 5
take 13
tear 3
turn 22

bolted
shut 7

bolt from the blue°
at **bolt 6**
blow[2] 2
bombshell
jolt 5
shock 3
surprise 4

bolt-hole
refuge 1

bolt upright°
at **bolt 12**

bolus
pill 1
tablet 4

bomb°
bolt 6
bombard 1
bombshell
fall 12
flop 3,4
killing 2
mint 1
packet 2
pelt[1] 1
shell 4

bombard°
batter 2
blaze 5
bomb 2
hail[2] 1
pelt[1] 1
shell 4
shower 3
storm 6

bombardment
fire 3
hail[2] 2
volley 1

bombast°
bluff[1] 3
exaggeration
hot air
mouth 3
nonsense 1
rant 3
raving 3
rhetoric 2
wind[1] 2

bombastic°
flowery
grandiose 1
inflated 2
ornate
pompous 2
pretentious 1
rhetorical 3
stilted
voluble
windy 2

bombed (out of one's mind)
drunk 1
stinking 3

bomber
terrorist

bombilate
hum 1

bombinate
hum 1

bombshell°
blow[2] 2
bolt 6
bomb 1

bombshell *(cont.)*
jolt 5
shock 3
surprise 4

bona fide°
authentic
concrete
factual 1
genuine 1
honest 2
literal 2
natural 6
official 1
real 1
regular 6
rightful 1
safe 3

bonanza
godsend
killing 2
windfall

bon-bon
candy
sweet 9

bond°
alliance 1
association 2
assurance 1
attach 1
attachment 1
bridge 2
cement 1,2
chain 2
combine 3
connection 1
fasten 1
fastening
guarantee 1
insurance
knot 1
link 1
marry 2
obligation 2
pawn[1] 3
pledge 2
promise 1
rapport
shackle 1
splice 2
stick[1] 4
tie 8
unite 3
warranty
weld 1

-bonds
restraint 2
shackle 1

bondage°
captivity
occupation 2
restraint 2
servitude
slavery 1

bonding
association 2

bondmaid
slave 1

bondservant
captive 1
slave 1

bondslave
slave 1

bond(s)man
captive 1
slave 1

bond(s)woman
slave 1

bone
grievance 2
mug 6
polish 4
study 1

-bones
doctor 1
physician

bone-chilling
freezing
frigid 1

bonehead
dolt
fool 1
silly 3

boneheaded
daft 1
feeble-minded
foolish 2
obtuse 2
stupid 1
thick 6
boneheadedness
stupidity 1
boner
blunder 2
error 1
fault 2
howler
indiscretion 2
solecism
bone structure
frame 4
bone-tired
beat 13
jaded 1
washed out 2
bone to pick
grievance 2
bone up (on)
mug 6
polish 4
study 1
bone-weary
jaded 1
bone-yard
graveyard
bonfire
beacon
bong
pipe 2
bon gré
willy-nilly 1
Boniface
landlord 1
boning up
study 5
bonk
love 6
bonkers
crazy 1
deranged
disturbed 2
inane
insane 1
mad 1
mental 2
psychotic 1
twist 11
unbalanced 2
bonking
sex 2
bon mot
epigram 1
joke 1
witticism
bonne bouche
titbit
bonny°
beautiful 1
comely
fine[1] 10
pretty 1
bonus°
bounty 3
extra 3
gift 1
icing 2
perquisite
plum
plus 3
premium 1
present[2] 3
price 3
treat 6
-as a bonus
measure 10
-bonuses
largesse
bon vivant
epicure
gourmet
sensualist
sybarite
bon viveur
epicure
gourmet
bon viveur (*cont.*)
sensualist
sybarite
bony
emaciated
gaunt 1
lean[1] 1
meagre 2
raw-boned
scrawny
skinny
thin 1
bonzer
excellent
fine[1] 1
boo
hiss 2, 3
jeer 2
outcry
boob
breast 1
dupe 1
err 1
error 1
fault 2
mistake 1
slip[1] 8
solecism
tongue 4
trip 2
-boobs
bosom 1
boo-boo
blunder 2
error 1
fault 2
mistake 1
solecism
boob tube
screen 5
television
booby
fool 1
silly 3
booby-trap
trap 1
boodle
booty
loot 1
money 1
plunder 4
spoil 6
boofhead
fool 1
boogie
walk 1
boohoo
sob
weep 1
book°
engage 1
get 1
list[1] 2
lyric 4
programme 4
publication 2
reserve 2
schedule 2
script 2
story 5
take 4
vade-mecum
volume 4
word 9b
writing 2
-in someone's (good, bad) books
favour 4
booked
bound[3] 5
booking
engagement 4
reservation 3
run 38
bookish
highbrow 2
intellectual 2
literary 1
pedantic 1
studious 2
bookkeeper°
bookkeeping
clerical 2
booklet
brochure
leaflet
pamphlet
publication 2
tract[2]
book-lover
bookworm
bookman
scholar 1
Book of Mormon
Scripture
book-woman
scholar 1
bookwork
study 5
bookworm°
scholar 1
boom°
blare 1, 2
blast 2
crash 3, 4
explosion 1
flourish 1
peal 2
report 2
resound
roar 3
roll 5, 15
spar[1]
thrive
thunder 1, 2
boom box
radio 1
boomerang°
backlash
booming
deep 7
flourishing
going 1
loud 1
prosperous 2
resonant
successful 2
thunder 1
thunderous
boomkin
spar[1]
boon°
blessing 2
bosom 4
find 10
godsend
jewel 2
treat 6
turn 35
windfall
boondocks
country 3
province 4
stick[2] 3
boong
aboriginal
boonies
country 3
province 4
stick 3
boor°
barbarian 2
clod 2
clown 2
gawk 1
peasant
philistine 1
rustic 3
slob
boorish°
barbarian 3
beastly 1
brutal 2
coarse 2
discourteous
ignorant 4
impolite
philistine 2
provincial 2
rude 1
rustic 2
tactless
tasteless 1
boorish (*cont.*)
uncivilized 2
unrefined 1
untoward 2
vulgar 1
boorishness
incivility
indelicacy
boost°
appropriate 2
encourage 2
encouragement 2
enhance
exalt 1
fortify 3
furtherance
glorify 1
hand 2
help 5
increase 4
inflate 2
inspire 2
jump 9
leg 4
lift 2, 9
magnify 1
make 27
patronize 3
pilfer
pinch 3
plug 5
promote 1
pull 10
push 6
put 28f
raise 6, 7
revival 3
rip 2a
rise 10
root[3]b
shot 12
speed 2
steal 1
step 18b
strengthen 1
support 1
swell 3
take 3
tonic 1
booster
enthusiast
fan
follower 3
partisan 1
patron 1
boosting
furtherance
patronage 1
promotion 1
rip-off 1
theft
boot°
discharge 9
dismiss 1
dismissal 1
ejection 3
eviction
expulsion
kick 1
lay[1] 16a
push 16
sack 3
trunk 5
-boots
servant 1
-to boot°
at **boot 1**
addition 6
besides 1
further 3
likewise 2
measure 10
moreover
bootee
boot 2
booth°
partition 4
shed[1]
stall[1] 2
stand 16
Boot Hill
graveyard
bootlace
lace 2
bootleg
moonshine 3
run 14
bootless°
fond 2
fruitless
futile
hollow 5
hopeless 4
idle 4
ineffective 1
ineffectual 1
meaningless 2
non-productive 2
pointless
purposeless
stupid 2
thankless
unprofitable 2
unsuccessful 1
useless 1
vain 2
void 1
worthless 2
bootlessly
vain 3a
bootlessness
stupidity 2
vanity 2
boot-lick
cringe 2
flatter 1
play 18
scrape 4
truckle
bootlicker
flatterer
inferior 4
menial 4
yes-man
boot-licking
flattery
grovelling
ingratiating
menial 2
obsequious
servile
servility
submissive 2
time-serving
boot out
dismiss 1
dispossess
eject 1, 3
evict
fire 11
lay[1] 16a
turf 4
booty°
loot 1
pillage 3
plunder 4
prize[1] 4
spoil 6
trophy 1
booze°
alcohol
bottle 3
carouse 1, 2
drink 2, 5
liquor 1
paint 7
spirit 9b
whisky
boozed
drunk 1
stinking 3
booze-hound
alcoholic 2
boozer
alcoholic 2
bar 6
carouse 2
drunk 3
pub
soak 3
boozing
drunkenness
boozy
drunk 1
stinking 3
bop
dance 1, 2
hit 1, 10
bop (*cont.*)
knock 9
punch[1] 1, 2
strike 1
borborygmus
wind[1] 3
bordello
brothel
house 6
border°
band[1] 1, 2
bound[1] 1
boundary
brink 1
circuit 1
division 4
edge 1
extremity 1
flank 2
frame 2
fringe 1, 2, 3
frontier
girth 2
join 4
limit 2
line[1] 2, 4, 22
margin 1, 2
outskirts
pale[2] 2
perimeter
periphery 1
rim
ring[1] 1
side 1
touch 3
trim 5
verge[1] 1, 3
-borders
border 2
bound[1] 1
boundary
outskirts
pale[2] 2
precinct 1
side 1
bordering (on)
adjoining
almost
neighbouring
surrounding
borderline
border 5
division 4
line[1] 4
marginal 1, 2
perimeter
questionable
soft 7
bore°
annoyance 2
bind 6
burrow 2
calibre 1
drag 7
drill 1
drip 3
fag 2
nuisance 2
pain 3
pall[2] 1
penetrate 1
perforate
pierce 2
pill 2
punch[2] 2
ream
satiate 1
sink 7
stick[1] 1
tire 2
turn 17b
wear 7
width 1
boreal
freezing
frigid 1
bored
blasé 1
jaded 2
sick 7
tired 2
weary 3, 4
boredom°
tedium

borehole
bore[1] 1

boring°
bland 2
colourless 2
cut 29b
dead 12
deadly 5
dreary 2
dry 2
dull 4
flat 5
heavy 7
humdrum
irksome
lacklustre
lengthy
lifeless 3
literal 3
matter-of-fact
monotonous
pedestrian 2
philistine 2
ponderous 2
prosaic
repetitious
routine 4
sleepy 2
slow 9
stale 2
stodgy
stupid 3
tame 4
tedious
threadbare 2
tiresome 1
vapid
weary 2

born
native 6

-be born with
possess 2
spring 2

borne
ride 1
waft 1

born loser
loser

born on the wrong side of the blanket
illegitimate 2

born out of wedlock
illegitimate 2

born yesterday
gullible
inexperienced
naïve

borough
city
municipal
municipality
town

borrow°
bum 5
hook 7
make 27
pilfer
scrounge 1
steal 1

borrowed
derivative 1

borrowing
plagiarism

Borstal°
jail 1
reform school

boscage
brush[1] 2

bosh
drivel 3
fiddlesticks
gobbledegook 1
hot air
jargon 2
moonshine 2
mumbo-jumbo 1
nonsense 1
rot 4
rubbish 2
stuff 4
talk 18

bosh (*cont.*)
trash 1

bosky
leafy
shadowy 1
wooded

bosom°
breast 1
intimate[1] 1
personal 3
special 5

bosomy°
buxom 2

boss°
bigwig 1
chief 1
director 1
employer 1
executive 1
foreman
head 2
knob
leader 1
lord 3
manager
master 1
monarch 2
neat 5
nub 1
overseer
politician
principal 3
skipper
splendid 3
superb
superintendent
supervisor

-bosses
management 2

boss around
lord 3

bossman
chief 1
leader 1
master 1

bossy°
assertive
authoritarian
dictatorial 2
domineering
imperative 2
masterful 2
overbearing
peremptory 3

botch°
bitch 4
blow[1] 3
bugger 3
bungle
butcher 4
confuse 2
err 1
fiasco
fluff 4
foul 16b
fumble 2
hash 2,3
mess 5b
mishandle 2
mistake 1
mix-up
muck 4
peccadillo
queer 5
ruin 8
screw 7b
slip[1] 3
solecism

botched (up)
confused 1
erroneous

botch up
slip[1] 3

botch-up
solecism

bother°
afflict
aggravate 2
ail 1
annoy 1
annoyance 1
beset
bind 6
bug 7

bother (*cont.*)
concern 3
discomfort 2
distract 3
distress 3
disturb 1,4
exasperate 2
fluster 1,2
fuss 1
gall[2] 2,4
get 17
gnaw 3
handful 2
harass
headache 2
heckle
inconvenience 1,3
infuriate
irritate
jar[2] 3
job 4
molest 1,2
nag[1] 1
nuisance 1
pain 3
palaver 1
persecute 2
persecution 2
pest
pester
pick 4a
plague 2,3
put 23a
rigmarole
riot 1
ruffle 3
song 3a
stew 2
tease 1
thorn 2
tire 2
torment 2,4
trial 5
trouble 1,2,4,6
upset 1
worry 2,3

botheration
annoyance 1

bothered
concerned 2
disturbed 1
mind 15
smitten 1
tired 2

bothersome
burdensome
inconvenient
irksome
tiresome 2
troublesome
trying
wicked 5

bothy
cabin 1

bottle°
alcohol
courage
daring 1
drink 5
grit
gumption 2
gut 3a
jar[1]
jug
nerve 1
pluck 1
spunk

bottled-up
pent-up

bottled water
water 1

bottleneck
impediment
jam 4
obstruction 1
snag 1

bottle up°
at **bottle 4**
box[1] 3
keep 14a
shut 6a
siege 2

bottom°
base[1] 1
basis 1
bum 1
buttocks
floor 3
foundation 1
point 5
posterior 3
rear[1] 2
seat 4
tail 2
zero 2

-at bottom°
at **bottom 5**
above 6
effect 5
essence 3
inside 6
largely
mainly
materially
merely 1
practically 1
primarily 1
principally
principle 4
really 3
soon 5
substantially
ultimately

bottomless°
abysmal 2
deep 1
exotic 3
infinite 1

bottomless gulf
abyss

bottomless pit
hell 1

bottom line
essence 1
outcome
profit 1

bottom-line
grand 4
net[2] 2

bottom side up
upset 6

bottoms up
bottom 6

bough
branch 1
offshoot 1
spray[2]

bought
mercenary 2

bouillon
broth

boulder
rock[1] 1

boulder-strewn
rocky[1] 1

boulevard
promenade 1
road 2
street 1

boulevardier
dude 1

bounce°
bound[2] 1,3
discharge 9
dismissal 1
dispossess
ejection 3
exclude 3
expulsion
fire 11
flounce 2
glance 3
hustle 4
jar[2] 1
jog 3
jolt 1,4
life 9
rattle 4
rebound 1,2
recoil 2
resilience
sack 3,4
snap 11
spring 1,6,7
throw 7b

bounce (*cont.*)
turf 4

bouncer
bruiser

bounciness
spring 7

bouncy
bubbly 2
bumpy
buoyant 2
elastic 1
lively 1
perky
pert 2
yielding 1

bound°
border 2
bounce 1,3
boundary
cavort
circuit 1
dash 3,5
destined 2
edge 1
enclose 1
end 1
extremity 1
fast[1] 3
fence 3
finite
frontier
hop 1,3
indebted
jump 1,8
leap 1,5
limit 1,2
lunge 3
margin 2
measure 8
obliged 2
periphery 1
prance
restraint 1
restrict
shoot 1
skip 1,3
spring 1,6

-be bound by
subject 8a

-be bound for
make 30a

-be bound (to)
belong 1

-bounds
border 2
boundary
extent 2
extreme 6,7,8
extremity 3
fringe 2
frontier
limit 1,2
margin 2
pale[2] 2
perimeter
precinct 1
restraint 1
spread 9

-out of bounds
taboo 1

boundary°
barrier 3
border 3
bound[1] 1
circuit 1
division 4
edge 1
enclosure 2
end 1
extremity 1
fringe 2
frontier
limit 2
line[1] 4
margin 2
outline 1
pale[2] 2
perimeter
periphery 1
side 1
spread 9
surface 1
verge[1] 1

-boundaries
side 1
spread 9

boundary line
barrier 3
bound[1] 1
division 4
margin 2

bounded
finite

bounder
adventurer 2
heel[1] 2
rake[2]
rascal
rogue 1
scoundrel
stinker
villain
wretch 1

boundless°
endless 1
immeasurable
indefinite 4
inestimable 2
inexhaustible 1
infinite 1
limitless
universal 2
unlimited 2
vast

boundlessness
eternity

bound up in
wrap 2

bounteous
abundant 1
bountiful 1,2
fertile
fruitful 3
generous 1,3
liberal 1
luxuriant 1
open 14
plentiful 1
prodigal 2
productive 1
profuse 2
prolific 1

bounteousness
exuberance 2
prodigality 2
wealth 2

bountiful°
abundant 1
charitable 1
free 7
fruitful 3
generous 1
large 2
lavish 2
liberal 1
opulent 3
plentiful 1
princely 1
prodigal 2
productive 1
profuse 2
prolific 1
rich 9

bountifulness
exuberance 2
plenty 2
prodigality 2

bounty°
blessing 2
gift 1
largesse
present[2] 2
price 3
prodigality 2
profusion
prosperity
wealth 2

bouquet°
aroma 1
bunch 1
compliment 1
fragrance
odour 1
perfume 1
rave 3
savour 2
scent 1

brass hat
bigwig 1
-brass hats
bigwig 2
brassiness
impertinence
brass neck
face 5
presumption 1
brassy°
barefaced 2
brash 2
brazen
fresh 8
impertinent
impudent
insolent
pert 1
pushy
brat
boy 1
guttersnipe
imp
bravado°
bluff[1] 3
bluster 3
bombast
brave°
adventurous
audacious 1
bold 1
challenge 3
courageous
daredevil 2
daring 2
dauntless
defy 1
enterprising
face 14, 18b
fearless
gallant 1
game 8
go 36a
gritty 2
hardy 2
heroic 1
indomitable
intrepid
manly
martial 2
stalwart 3
stand 3, 12a
stout 2
superhuman 1
sustain 3
take 6
venturesome 1
weather 3
withstand
bravery°
chivalry
courage
daring 1
grit
gut 3a
heart 2
manhood 2
nerve 1
pluck 1
prowess 2
spirit 5
bravura
showy
virtuoso 2
brawl°
battle 1
conflict 1
disorder 2
dispute 4
disturbance 2
fight 1, 7
fracas 1, 2
fray[1]
quarrel 1, 2
riot 1, 3
rough-house 2
rumpus
scrap[2] 1, 2
scrimmage
tumult
uproar
brawler
rough 13
rowdy 2
brawling
riotous 1
rough-house 1
rowdyism
brawn°
power 4
sinew 2
strength 1
brawniness
brawn
strength 1
brawny°
big 2
burly
hefty 2
husky 1
large 1
mighty 2
muscular
robust 1
sinewy
stalwart 1
stout 4
strong 1
sturdy 1
tough 3
bray
blare 1
din 1
grind 1
mill 5
pound[1] 2
powder 3
pulverize 1
braying
din 1
braze
attach 1
cement 2
connect 3
tack 5
weld 1
brazen°
arrogant 1
audacious 2
barefaced 2
blatant 1
bold 2
brash 2
brassy 1
brave 3
cheeky
cool 6
defiant
flagrant
flippant 2
forward 2
fresh 8
ill-mannered
immodest 2
impertinent
impudent
insolent
open 13
overconfident 1
pert 1
presumptuous
pushy
shameless
unabashed
brazen-faced
brazen
brazenly
face 13
flat 17b
openly 1
brazenness
assurance 4
effrontery
flippancy 2
freedom 7
gall[1] 2
impertinence
impudence
nerve 2
presumption 1
sauce 2
brazen out
brave 3
defy 1
face 18b
breach°
break 25
crack 1
breach *(cont.)*
flaw 2
fracture 2, 3
gap 1
gulf 2
hole 2
infringement
jump 12
offence 1
opening 1
rift 1
rupture 1, 3
schism
solecism
split 8
vacancy 1
violate 1
violation 1
breaching
violation 1
breach of faith
betrayal 1
breach of the peace
disorder 2
disturbance 2
bread
cash 1
food
fund 2
money 1
bread-and-butter letter
note 2
bread basket
stomach 1
breadline
-on the breadline
needy
bread-roll
roll 17
breadth°
area 4
extension 2
measure 1
measurement 2
scope 1
spread 9
width 1, 2
breadwinner
worker
break°
back 7b, 18
breach 1, 2
break 19b
burst
check 13
come 7
crack 1, 5
cranny
crevice
crush 1
dash 1
dawn 3
degrade 1
disengage,
disobey
enervate
escape 5
flaw 2
force 8
fracture 1, 2, 3
fragment 3
gap 1
go 25
hold-up 2
hole 2
holiday 1
humble 4
infringe 1
interlude
interruption 1, 2
interval 1
jump 12
lapse 2
leak 2
let-up
loosen 2
luck 2
lull 1
opening 1, 2
opportunity
overcome 1
break *(cont.)*
pause 1, 2
punctuate 1
quaver 2
recess 2
reduce 6
respite 1
rest[1] 2
rift 1
rupture 1, 3
say 4
schism
secession
separate 1
separation 1, 3
shatter 1
snap 1
space 3
splinter 2
split 1, 7, 8
start 12
stop 5, 7
stretch 3
tame 5
tell[1] 2
transgress 2
violate 1
wait 4
wash 3
way 11a
-breaks
fate 1
breakable
brittle 1
crisp 1
delicate 1
flimsy 1
fragile
weak 1
breakage
fracture 1
break an appointment
stand 10c
break and enter
break 18c
break apart
break 1
come 7
crumble
disintegrate
fall 7
loosen 2
rupture 3
separate 1
split 1
break asunder
break 1
burst
break away°
at **break 15**
bolt 8
break 12
depart 2
get 31a
secede
separate 1
slip[1] 6
breakaway
schismatic
break bread
dine
eat
break down°
at **break 16**
analyse 1
cave 2a
collapse 1, 2, 4
come 7
decompose 1
destroy 1
founder[2] 2
give 9
miscarry
pack 8b
piece 6
range 7
reduce 4
resolve 4
separate 2
trample 3
way 11a
wrong 8b
breakdown°
analysis 1
collapse 5, 7
destruction 3
dissolution 1
downfall
failure 2
loss 5
miscarriage
prostration 4
ruin 1
shock 2
breakdown lane
shoulder 1
breaker
roller 2
sea 2
surge 2
wave 1
break faith with
betray 1
breakfast
dine
eat
meal 1
break forth
break 12, 13
break free
escape 1
get 31a
break from
disengage
break ground°
at **break 17**
break in°
at **break 18**
chime 5b
chip 4b
discipline 6
disrupt 2
interrupt 1
intervene 1
intrude
shake 6a
short 12b
breaking
fracture 1
infringement
parting 1
rupture 1
secession
breaking and entering
robbery
breaking apart
parting 1
breaking down
destruction 1
dissolution 1
breaking even
unprofitable 1
breaking up
destruction 1
dissolution 1
division 1
parting 1
partition 1
rupture 1
break into
disrupt 2
dissolve 2
go 31f
break in two
split 1
break loose°
at **loose 8**
break 12
breakneck°
hurried 1
reckless
-at breakneck speed
flat 17a
break of day
dawn 1
break off°
at **break 19**
break 10
cease 1
cut 15b
disconnect
discontinue
break off *(cont.)*
dissociate
end 9
interrupt 2
separate 1
sever 2
snap 1
stop 1
break out°
at **break 20**
erupt 1, 2
escape 1
flare 1
get 31a
go 31f
break-out
escape 5
break the back of°
at **back 7**
break the connection
hang 12
break the ice°
at **break 21**
break 17
move 12a
set 12a
spearhead 1
break the news
publish
break the spell
disillusion
break through°
at **break 22**
breach 4
peer[2] 2
breakthrough
inroad 2
break to pieces
separate 1
break to smithereens
shatter 1
break up°
at **break 23**
break 1, 11, 16b, 24a
collapse 2
come 7
crumble
decompose 1
destroy 1
disband
disintegrate
disperse 2
dissipate 1
dissociate
dissolve 3
diversify
divide 1
fall 7
fragment 3
laugh 1
let[1] 8d
part 12
portion 4
pulverize 1
reduce 4
rupture 3
scatter 2
separate 1, 3
sever 2
split 1, 2, 5
throw 8
breakup
breach 2
destruction 3
dissolution 1
divorce 1
parting 1
partition 1
rift 1
ruin 1
rupture 1
separation 1, 3
break with°
at **break 24**
disengage
jilt
secede
breast°
bosom 1
chest 2

breast-feed
nurse 3
breastwork
rampart
wall 2
breath°
air 2
breeze 1
draught 1
exhalation 1,2
expectant
hint 2
odour 2
puff 1
savour 2
smell 1
sniff 1
spirit 1
suggestion 2
waft 2
wind[1] 1
-out of breath
breathless 1
shortwinded
breathe°
blow[1] 1
draw 7
exhale
exist 1
heave 3
live 6
puff 4
rumour 2
sigh 1
tongue 3
whisper 1
breathe a word
whisper 2
breathe hard
pant 1
breathe in
draw 7
inhale
breathe (new) life into
animate 1
pep 2
refresh 1
rejuvenate
resurrect
revive 3
breathe one's last
die 1
expire 2
pass 14a
breathe out
exhale
expire 3
breather
break 28
pause 2
recess 2
respite 1
rest[1] 2
breathing
alive 1
animate 4
live 1
organic 1
breathing one's last
moribund 1
breathing-space
interlude
leisure 2
pause 2
recess 2
rest[1] 2
breathless°
agog
short-winded
breath of air
draught 1
breathtaking
awesome
dramatic 2
gorgeous 1
marvellous
scenic
sensational 1
superb
terrific 2
breech
bottom 1
breed°
bear 6
bring 15a
description 3
extraction 3
form 3
generate 2
grow 3
hatch 1
kind[2] 1
like[1] 8
mate 5
nationality 2
produce 3
proliferate
propagate 1
race[2] 2
rear[2] 1
reproduce 2
sort 3
spawn
tribe
type 1
variety 3
breeding°
background 1
class 3
culture 1
grace 2
propriety 2
refinement 1
reproduction 3
savoir vivre
stock 2
upbringing
breeding ground
hotbed
breeze°
air 2
breath 1
draught 1
gust 1
picnic 2
piece 9
pushover 1
sail 3
snap 12
wind[1] 1
breezy°
carefree
rakish
smart 5
windy 1
brevity°
economy 2
brew°
ferment 1
potion
brewing
impending
briar
see **brier**
briary
see **briery**
bribable
accommodating 2
mercenary 2
venal
bribe°
buy 3
corrupt 5
fix 11
get 30d
kickback
pay 10b
pay-off 3
rebate 2
bribery
fix 18
graft[2]
bric-à-brac
curiosity 3
gewgaw
sundries
trash 2
brick°
block 1
loaf[1] 1
brickbat
missile
taunt 2
-brickbats
flak
brick up
wall 5
bridal°
nuptial
bride
mate 2
wife
woman 2
bridegroom
groom 2
husband 1
bride-to-be
fiancée
bridewell
prison
bridge°
span 1,3
traverse 2
bridle°
bristle 3
contain 3
curb 2
discipline 7
govern 2
inhibit
limit 5
master 8
rein 1,3
resist 1
restraint 1
shackle 4
subdue 1
brief°
abbreviated
compact 3
concise
curt
fast[1] 1
fleeting
fly-by-night 1
fugitive 3
groom 4
hasty 3
hurried 1
inform 1
instruction 1
little 4
meteoric 1
momentary
passing 1,2
post[3] 4
prepare 3
prime 6
short 2,7
succinct
summary 1,2
terse 1
thumbnail
transient
-briefs
pants 1
-in brief°
at **brief 5**
word 8
briefcase
bag 2
briefed
informed 2
briefing
instruction 1
orientation 2
preparation 2
run-down 3
briefly°
brief 5
short 14
shortly 3
temporarily 2
word 8
briefness
brevity
economy 2
brier
pipe 2
thorn 1
briery
prickly 1
brig
hole 4
jail 1
prison
stir 7
brigade
cohort 1
corps
brigand
gangster
outlaw 1
robber
thief 1
brigandage
pillage 2
bright°
ablaze 2
brilliant 1,4
broad 2
buoyant 2
cheerful 2
clear 3,4
dazzling
fair[1] 5
fine[1] 2
fresh 5
full 10
gay 2,3
glowing 2
golden 3
hopeful 2
hot 8
ingenious
intelligent
keen[1] 6
light[1] 13
liquid 3
lively 4
luminous 1
optimistic
perky
pert 2
pleasant 3
precocious
propitious
quick 4
radiant 1
ready 6
receptive 2
rosy 2
sharp 3
shiny
silver 3
smart 1
spanking 1
strong 19
sunny 1
vivid 1
wise 1
brighten°
cheer 6
dawn 3
enliven 2
gladden
illuminate 1
light[1] 16,18
lighten[1] 1,2
liven 1
perk up
polish 1
shine 2
tone 6
bright-eyed and bushy-tailed
fresh 5
perky
brightly
clear 17
gaily 1
brightly-lit
ablaze 2
brightness
blaze 3
brilliance 1
depth 4
gaiety 3
glare 1
gloss[1] 1
glow 2
illumination 1
intelligence 1
light[1] 1
polish 5
radiance 1
brightness *(cont.)*
sheen
shine 4
sparkle 3,4
splendour 2
brill
capital 6
good 2
sight 6b
splendid 3
brilliance°
blaze 3
dazzle 3
depth 4
flare 4
gaiety 3
genius 2
glamour
glare 1
glitter 4
glory 3
glow 2
ingenuity
lustre 2
polish 5
pomp
radiance 1
sparkle 3
splendour 1,2
state 3
virtuosity
brilliant°
ablaze 2
bright 1,5,6
dazzling
fiery 2
fine[1] 4
flamboyant 2
full 10
gay 3
gifted
glaring 2
glorious 4
glowing 2
golden 3
good 2
gorgeous 1
great 6
hot 8
ingenious
jewel 1
light[1] 13
liquid 3
lively 4
luminous 1
magnificent
meteoric 2
nimble 2
quick 4
radiant 1
scintillating 1
sight 6b
smart 1
splendid 1,2,3
star 3
strong 19
stunning 2
sunny 1
superb
supreme 4
talented
virtuoso 2
vivid 1
wise 1
brilliantly
ablaze 2
gaily 1
brim°
brink 1
edge 1
flow 2
peak 3
periphery 1
rim
side 1
teem[1]
verge[1] 1
brim-full
full 1
loaded 1
packed
replete 1
brimming
full 1
loaded 1
thick 2
brim over
run 33c
spill 1
well[2] 2
brindle
speckled
spotty 1
brindled
dapple 1
mottled
speckled
spotty 1
variegated
bring°
cart 2
collect 1
deliver 1
fetch 1,3
get 4
lead 2
perfect 8
present[2] 7
reflect 4
retrieve 1
run 13
see 6
take 9
transfer 1
transport 1
wreak
bring aboard
sign 10b
bring about°
at **bring 7**
achieve 1
arrange 2
brew 2
bring 5,12b
cause 6
effect 7
effectuate
excite 1
execute 1
found 1
fulfil 1
implement 2
induce 2
lead 6
make 3
motivate
negotiate 2
occasion 5
originate 1
perform 1
precipitate 1
procure 2
produce 2
prompt 5
raise 10
realize 1
rise 17
spark 2
spawn
work 16
bring action against
prosecute 1
bring along (behind)
trail 4
bring an end to
destroy 2
bring around°
at **bring 14**
convince
revive 1
wake[1] 1
win 3
bring back
fetch 1
get 4
recover 3
refresh 1
restore 1,2,4
resurrect
retrieve 1
return 3,4
revive 3

bring credit to oneself
mark 9
bring down°
at **bring 8**
defeat 1
depress 2
downgrade 1
finish 4
floor 4
humble 4
lower[1] 2
mortify 1
overthrow 1
overturn 2
overwhelm 1
place 13
prostrate 2,4
raze
reduce 5,7
rout 2
shame 6
throw 3
topple 1,2
bring forth°
at **bring 9**
bear 6
breed 2
deliver 6
develop 1
draw 4
elicit
fetch 2
hatch 1
produce 2
propagate 1
reproduce 2
spawn
throw 9c
bring forward
lay[1] 6
lodge 6
moot 2
produce 4
put 5
raise 8
table 4
throw 9c
bring home°
at **home 11**
impress 3
stress 4
win 1
bring honour upon oneself
mark 9
bring in°
at **bring 10**
broach
cost 2
earn 2
fetch 3
gain 2
gross 6
import 1
inject 2
introduce 2,4
mention 1
nab
net[2] 4
pick 2
present[2] 7
produce 4
quote 1
realize 3
reap 2
run 27
touch 8
yield 4
bringing about
execution 2
performance 1
bringing off
performance 1
bringing-up
breeding 1
bring into being
create 1
generate 2
rise 17
bring into contact with
expose 3
touch 2
bring into disfavour
discredit 1
bring into disrepute
discredit 1
foul 14
bring into focus
focus 4
bring into play
exert 1
use 1
work 10
bring into prominence
stress 4
bring into the world°
at **world 5**
deliver 6
have 8
bring low
prostrate 2,4
bring off°
at **bring 11**
accomplish
achieve 1
carry 10c
execute 1
fulfil 1
manage 3
negotiate 2
perform 1
pull 12b
put 27a
bring on°
at **bring 12**
cause 6
incur
induce 2
lead 6
occasion 5
precipitate 1
bring out°
at **bring 13**
circulate 2
develop 1
draw 4
elicit
introduce 4
mean[1] 2
open 23
produce 1,4
rise 17
throw 9c
trot 2
turn 20a
bring over
turn 3
bring pressure to bear (on)
influence 3
lean[2] 4b
lobby 3
pressure 5
screw 4
squeeze 11
bring round°
at **bring 14**
convince
get 14
persuade 2
prevail 3
revive
sway 2
talk 10
win 3
bring someone to their knees
prostrate 4
bring suit against
prosecute 1
sue 1
bring to a close
halt 2
round 18
stop 1
terminate
wind[2] 4a
wrap 3a
bring to a conclusion
wind[2] 4a
bring to a halt
stop 1,2
bring to an end
accomplish
close 3
complete 5
demolish 2
destroy 2
end 9
get 45c
halt 2
round 18
stop 1
terminate
wind[2] 4a
bring to an impasse
deadlock 2
bring to a standstill
deadlock 2
obstruct 1
stop 2
tie 7c
bring to a stop
stop 1,2
bring to bear
enforce 1
exercise 1
exert 1
wreak
zero 4
bring to book
scold 1
bring to completion
fulfil 1
round 18
bring to fruition
mature 6
bring together
assemble 1,2
close 8b
concentrate 3
gather 1
group 4
integrate
pool 4
raise 5
rally 3
reconcile 1
unify
bring to life
wake[1] 2
bring to light
bare 7
dig 6
discover 1
elicit
expose 1
find 2
lay[1] 9
open 23
produce 5
reflect 2
root[1] 7b
say 2
tell[1] 2
throw 9c
turn 25c
unveil
bring to maturity
ripen
bring to mind
finger 5a
bring to notice
throw 9c
bring to perfection
perfect 8
bring to ruin
ruin 7
undone[1] 1
bring to terms
patch 7
bring to the surface
throw 9c
bring to the top
throw 9c
bring trade to
patronize 2
bring up°
at **bring 15**
arise 3
bring 9b
broach
come 19a
dig 6
educate
excavate 2
foster 2
introduce 2
lead 10b
mention 1
moot 2
point 21b
present[2] 7
produce 2
quote 1
raise 3,4,8,11
rake[1] 7b
rear[2] 1
refer 1
say 4
suggest 2
table 4
take 39e
throw 9c
touch 8
train 4
voice 4
bring upon
incur
bring up short
nonplus
puncture 4
stump 2
bring up the rear
follow 1
trail 6
bring up to date
fill 9c
brink°
border 5
brim 1
edge 1
eve 2
margin 1
point 9
side 1
threshold 2
verge[1] 1
-on the brink of
almost
ready 4
briny
deep 9
drink 7
ocean 1
salt 9
sea 1
brio
dash 6
life 7
panache
pep 1
verve
vigour
brisk°
active 1
agile 1
alive 3
breezy 1
energetic
excited 2
expeditious
fast[1] 1
fresh 5,7
hasty 1
jaunty 1
lively 1
nimble 1
pert 2
prompt 1
quick 2
rapid
rousing
smart 5
snappy 1
spanking 2,3
brisk *(cont.)*
speedy 1
sprightly
stiff 5
sudden
swift
vigorous
vital 3
vivacious
briskly
double 8
fast[1] 6
rapidly 1
swiftly
vigorously
briskness
haste 1
rapidity
speed 1
velocity
verve
vigour
bristle°
bridle 3
prickle 1
spine 2
swarm 3
teem[1]
thorn 1
-bristles
pile[2]
bristling
thick 2
bristly
coarse 1
hairy 1
harsh 1
prickly 1
Bristol fashion
shipshape
taut 2
Bristols
bosom 1
brittle°
crisp 1
fragile
stiff 1
broach°
bring 15b
come 19a
introduce 2
lead 10b
mention 1
moot 2
pose 3
propose 1
raise 8
set 18a
spring 4
tap[2] 6
venture 2
broad°
ample 1,2,6
bawdy
beamy
catholic
comprehensive
deep 1
encyclopedic
expansive 3
extensive 1
full 2,5,10
general 3,4
girl 1
global
heavy 8
inclusive 1
jade 2
large 1,3
lax 2
liberal 3
loose 5
meagre 3
obscene 1
off colour 2
risqué
spacious
squeeze 10
sweeping 1
thick 1
wide 1,2
woman 3
broadcast°
air 7
announce 1
blab
carry 8
celebrate 4
circulate 2
circulation 2
declare 2
deliver 4
diffuse 3
disperse 1
enunciate 2
give 15c
issue 10
proclaim 1
programme 2
pronounce 3
propagate 3
publish
put 9,23e
radio 2
report 4
scatter 1
send 2
sow
spread 1,2
tell[1] 2
transmission 2
vent 3
broadcaster
journalist
reporter
broadcasting
circulation 2
issue 6
press 10a
proclamation 2
transmission 2
broad daylight
day 1
daylight 2
broaden
amplify 1
civilize 2
develop 1
enlarge 1
expand 3
extend 2
flare 2
grow 1
increase 1
liberalize 1
maximize 1
progress 6
spread 6
stretch 2
widen
broadening
extension 1
flare 6
growth 1
progress 3
progression 2
spread 8
swell 4
broad in the beam
beamy
fat 1
broadly
abroad 2
amply 1
generally 2
broad-minded
enlightened
liberal 3
tolerant
broad-mindedness
tolerance 1
broadness
breadth 1
width 1
broadsheet
poster
publication 2
broad-shouldered
muscular
broadside
advertisement 1
fire 3
insert 2

broadside (*cont.*)
poster
promotion 5
publication 2
sign 5
Broadway
stage 3
Brobdingnagian
big 1
colossal 1
enormous
gigantic
great 1
huge
immense
large 3
massive
prodigious 1
vast
whopping 1
brochure°
advertisement 1
insert 2
leaflet
pamphlet
promotion 5
publication 2
tract[2]
-brochures
literature 2
brogue
dialect
broil°
fight 1, 7
uproar
broiling
scorching 1
sweltering
torrid 1
broke°
destitute 1
down and out 1
embarrassed 2
hard 17
heel[1] 3
impoverished 1
indigent
insolvent
penurious 2
poor 1
stony 3
upper 7
broken°
blink 6
defective 1
dud 2
duff
faulty
gentle 2
hurt 8
intermittent
meek 2
mouth 6
order 13c
out 14
piece 7
rough 1
rugged 1
spasmodic 2
split 9
stricken 2
tame 1
wanting 1
broken-down°
at **broken 7**
decrepit 2
dilapidated
leg 7
old 3
order 13c
ragged 4
ramshackle
rickety
rock[1] 3b
run-down 2
seedy 1
shabby 3
time-worn
tumbledown
unsound 1
broken-hearted°
desolate 3
heartbroken
inconsolable
broken-hearted (*cont.*)
low[1] 8
miserable 1
sad 1
sorrowful 1
stricken 2
woebegone
wretched 2
broken up
mouth 6
broker°
dealer
intermediary
merchant 3
negotiator
trader
brolly
umbrella 1
bromide
cliché
one 5
proverb
tranquillizer
truism
bromidic
tired 3
Bronx cheer
hiss 2
taunt 2
bronze
sculpture 1
statue
sun 2
brooch°
clasp 1
pin 2
plaque 2
brood°
family 2
fret 1
hatch 1
incubate
litter 2
muse
offspring
ponder
pout 1
sulk
young 4
brooding
meditative
moody 1
pensive
preoccupied 1
sullen
thought 1
thoughtful 2
brood on°
at **brood 3**
contemplate 2
ponder
brood over°
at **brood 3**
contemplate 2
muse
ponder
see 8
weigh 2
broody
moody 1
brook°
abide 1
accept 4
admit 2
allow 4
bear 4
creek 2
digest 2
feel 5
go 36a
lump[2]
permit 1
put 30
river 1
run 42
stand 3
stomach 3
stream 1
subscribe 1
support 3
take 6
tolerate 1
tributary
brooking
allowance 1
brooklet
stream 1
broom
brush[2] 1
broth°
liquor 2
brothel°
house 6
brother°
clergyman 2
equal 4
monk
brotherhood°
clan 2
club 2
fellowship 1, 2
fraternity 1
friendship 1
love 4
order 9
ring[1] 3
society 1, 5
brotherliness
brotherhood 1
fraternity 2
brotherly°
amicable
fraternal
friendly 1
brought to one's knees
prostrate 4
brouhaha
disorder 2
disturbance 2
excitement 2
fanfare 2
fracas 1
furore 1
fuss 1
pell-mell 3
racket 1
row[2] 2
rumpus
scene 3
scrimmage
splash 4
tempest 2
tumult
uproar
browbeat°
bully 2
enforce 2
face 17
hound
intimidate
overawe
pick 6
push 4
railroad 2
threaten 1
tyrannize
brown
dark 8
mousy 1
sun 2
-in a brown study
absent-minded
dreamy 2
inattentive
meditate 1
muse
pensive
preoccupied 1
thoughtful 2
wistful 2
browned off
angry 1
discontented
disgruntled
furious 1
weary 3
brownie
goblin
imp
brownish
mousy 1
brownish-grey
mousy 1
brown-nose
cringe 2
cultivate 4
flatter 1
kowtow
menial 4
play 18
romance 7
truckle
brown-noser
flatterer
flunkey 2
menial 4
yes-man
brown-nosing
flattery
grovelling
ingratiating
menial 2
obsequious
servile
servility
submissive 2
time-serving
brown off
infuriate
brown study
fog 2
reverie
thought 1
trance
-in a brown study
absent-minded
dreamy 2
inattentive
meditate 1
muse
pensive
preoccupied 1
thoughtful 2
wistful 2
browse°
peruse
run 33b
thumb 7
bruise°
assault 5
batter 3
blemish 2
chafe 4
mark 10
scrape 1, 7
scratch 1, 4
second[1] 7
sore 7
welt 2
wound 1
bruised
hurt 8
bruiser°
pugilist
tough 8
bruit
circulate 2, 3
get 25a
gossip 4
noise 3
proclaim 1
propagate 3
publish
rumour 2
say 2
spread 2
whisper 2
bruited about
current 2
bruiting about
proclamation 2
brumal
cold 1
polar 1
wintry 1
Brummagem
garish
gaudy
novelty 2
shoddy
sundries
tacky[2]
tawdry
trash 2
brunette
dark 8
brunt°
impact 2
brush°
brush[1] 1
encounter 5
fight 7
kiss 2
paint 5
rebuff 1, 2
rejection
shine 2
skirmish 1
sweep 1
tail 1
touch 3, 14
whisk 1, 4, 5
brush aside
disregard 1
ignore 1
laugh 2b
push 8
reject 1, 2
brush off
discount 3
disregard 2
ignore 1
jilt
push 8
put 21b
rebuff 2
shake 7
spurn
brush-off°
rebuff 1
rejection
brush up
retouch
brushwood
brush[1] 1
brusque°
abrupt 3
blunt 2
brief 3
crude 4
curt
disagreeable 3
discourteous
gruff 1
harsh 3
impatient 2
offhand 2
outspoken
rough 3
rude 2
short 4
short-tempered
snap 3b
snappish 2
sour 4
tactless
temperamental 1
terse 2
ungracious
brusquely
shortly 3
brutal°
abusive 2
atrocious 1
beastly 1
bloodthirsty
cold-blooded 3
cruel 2
cutthroat 2, 3
deadly 3
ferocious
fierce 1
ghoulish 2
grim 2
hard 4
harsh 2
heartless
inhuman 2
merciless
monstrous 1
murderous 1
oppressive 1
raw 6
repressive
rough 5
ruthless
sadistic
sanguinary 1
savage 2
severe 1
brutal (*cont.*)
strong-arm
terrible 4
unmerciful
vicious 3
violent 1
brutality
outrage 1
severity 1
violence 2
brutalization
mistreatment
brutalize
mishandle 1
mistreat
brutally
rough 17
roughly 2
severely 2
brute°
animal 2
barbarian 1
beast 2
devil 2
main 4
monster 1
ogre
savage 4
terror 2
brutish
brute 1
cutthroat 3
fierce 1
grim 2
hard 4
harsh 2
inhuman 2
monstrous 1
plebeian 2
ruthless
sadistic
sanguinary 1
savage 2
strong-arm
uncivilized 1
unmerciful
vicious 3
violent 1
wild 3
brutishly
rough 17
brutishness
barbarity
BS
moonshine 2
B-side
reverse 7
bubble°
boil[1] 1
ferment 1
fizz 1
flow 1
foam 2
froth 3
gurgle 1
simmer 1
sparkle 2
sphere 1
-bubbles°
bubble 2
foam 1
froth 1
bubble over
gush 2
bubbling
ebullient
effervescent 1, 2
fizz 2
gay 2
gurgle 2
irrepressible
radiant 2
bubbly°
effervescent 1, 2
gay 2
perky
radiant 2
sunny 2
vivacious
buccaneer
pirate 1
robber
thief 3

bumptious
arrogant 1
pushy
bumpy°
gnarled
irregular 1
lumpy
rocky[1] 1
rough 1
rugged 1
bum steer°
at **steer 3**
bum-sucker
flatterer
bum-sucking
flattery
bun
cake 1
roll 17
–with a bun in the oven
expecting
bunch°
band[2] 1
batch 2
bouquet 1
bundle 1
clump 2,3
cluster 1,2,3
crowd 2
flock 1
group 2
herd 1
huddle 1
knot 2
lump[1] 3
mass 1,2
number 2
pack 2
party 2
swarm 1
–bunches
mass 2
bunch up°
at **bunch 4**
bunco
swindle 2
bunco-artist
swindler
buncombe
rigmarole
bund
ring[1] 3
society 5
union 2
bundle°
bunch 1
cluster 1
group 2
mass 1
mint 1
money 2
pack 1,5
package 1
packet 2
parcel 3
pile[1] 2,3
profit 5
roll 18
stack 1
stow
swathe
–bundles
pile 3
bundle off°
at **bundle 3**
pack 7
bundle out°
at **bundle 3**
pack 7
bung
block 5
pitch[1] 1
place 15
plug 1,4
stopper
tap[2] 2
bungalow
cabin 1
cottage
bungle°
bitch 4
blow[1] 3
bungle (*cont.*)
botch
bugger 3
butcher 4
err 1
fluff 4
foul 16b
fumble 2
hash 3
mess 5b
mishandle 2
muck 4
muddle 2
queer 5
screw 7b
solecism
bungled
erroneous
bungler
amateur 1
butcher 2
duffer
gawk 1
bungling
amateur 2
artless 3
awkward 1
clumsy
heavy-handed 1
incompetent
inept 1
tactless
bung up
block 5
bunk
cot
gab 2
gibberish
gobbledegook 1
jargon 2
moonshine 2
mumbo-jumbo 1
nonsense 1
prattle 3
raving 3
rigmarole
rot 4
rubbish 2
stuff 4
talk 18
trash 1
bunk-mate
friend 3
bunkum
gab 2
hot air
mumbo-jumbo 1
nonsense 1
prattle 3
raving 3
rigmarole
rot 4
rubbish 2
stuff 4
talk 18
trash 1
bunting
flag[1] 1
buoy°
encourage 1
enliven 2
float 5
fortify 2
gladden
inspire 2
raise 7,13
reassure
sustain 2
buoyancy
cheer 2
exuberance 1
gaiety 1
joy 2
merriment
mirth
resilience
spring 7
buoyant°
breezy 2
cheerful 2
debonair 2
ebullient
effervescent 2
exuberant 1
buoyant (*cont.*)
gay 2
irrepressible
jaunty 1
joyful 1
lively 1
merry 1
optimistic
perky
racy 1
spirited
sportive
sunny 2
upbeat
vivacious
buoying up
encouragement 1
buoy up°
at **buoy 2**
cheer 6
encourage 1
enliven 2
gladden
inspire 2
reassure
sustain 2
bupkis
zero 3
bur
prickle 1
thorn 1
burble
babble 1
drivel 2
gurgle 1,2
burden°
bother 2
bow 4
brunt
charge 1,9
curse 6
depress 1
duty 1
encumber 1
encumbrance
exercise 3
fill 1
grief 2
heap 4
impact 2
implication 3
impose 4a
imposition 2
inconvenience 1
job 4
labour 7
liability 1,3
lie[2] 4
load 1,4
lumber 3
misery 3
nuisance 1
obligation 1
oppress 1
overload 1
pith 2
place 4
point 7
pressure 3
prey 3c
push 5
refrain[2]
responsibility 2
stagger 2
stick[1] 8
strain[1] 1,7
stress 3,5
substance 2
tax 2,4
trouble 1
wear 6
weigh 4,6
weight 2
burdened
downtrodden
heavy 13
labour 7
loaded 1
sick 3
smitten 1
burdening
back 8
burdensome°
arduous 1
difficult 1,4
exacting
exhausting 2
formidable 3
hard 2
heavy 4
inconvenient
irksome
laborious 1
leaden 1
oppressive 1
overwhelming 1
punishing
rugged 2
severe 4
sore 5
strenuous 1
toilsome
troublesome
weary 2
burdensomeness
inconvenience 2
severity 4
bureau°
cabinet 1
department 1
ministry 3
bureaucracy°
rigmarole
bureaucrat
functionary
officer 1
politician
bureaucratic
political 1
burg
city
burgee
banner 1
colour 2a
pennant
standard 3
streamer
burgeon
boom 2
flourish 1
flower 3
grow 1
increase 1
progress 6
proliferate
root[1] 5
shoot 4
thrive
burgeoning
boom 4
expansion 1
explosion 3
flourishing
progress 3
proliferation
burgess
citizen 2
burgh
city
town
burglar°
intruder 1
robber
thief 1
burglarize
break 18c
ransack 2
rifle 1
rob 1
burglary
caper 2
job 5
robbery
stealing
burgle
break 18c
ransack 2
rifle 1
rob 1
burgling
robbery
burial°
funeral
burial-chamber
tomb
burial-ground
graveyard
burial-place
sepulchre
burial-vault
sepulchre
buried
absorbed
lost 4
sunken 3
underground 1
wrap 2
burke
choke 1
burlesque°
caricature 1,2
derision
imitate 2
imitation 2
lampoon 1,2
mock 2
mockery 2
parody 1,3
put-on 2
ridicule 2
satire 2
satirize
send 9a
take 34b
take-off 2
taunt 1
burly°
big 2
brawny
hefty 2
husky 1
large 1
mighty 2
muscular
sinewy
stocky
stout 1
strong 1
sturdy 1
thick 1
tough 3
burn°
blaze 4
brook[1]
creek 2
fire 8
flame 4
flash 4
flush[1] 1
glow 5
hurt 2
light[1] 15
parch
radiate 1
river 1
run 42
scar 1,2
scorch
seethe 2
simmer 2
singe
smart 7
smoulder
sore 7
sparkle 1
splurge 2
stew 3
stream 1
swindle 1
tributary
burnable
flammable
inflammable
burning°
ablaze 1
caustic 1
fanatical
fervent 1
feverish
fiery 1
fire 5
glow 3
glowing 1
hot 1,4
incandescent
intense 2
live 3
burning (*cont.*)
lurid 4
painful 1
pressing
radiant 1
scathing
sore 1
starved 2
tender[1] 8
thirsty 2
torrid 1
towering 2
burning desire
ardour
burnish
brighten 2
glaze 1
gloss[1] 1,3
polish 1
rub 1
scour 1
sheen
shine 2
smooth 11
burnished
glossy 1
lustrous
shiny
silver 3
smooth 2
burn money (on)
splurge 2
burn out
blow[1] 5,7c
bolt 7
run 26c
burn rubber
speed 3
burn the candle at both ends
dissipate 4
overdo 2
burn the midnight oil
cram 2
grind 4
mug 6
overwork 2
slave 3
study 1
burnt-out
exhausted 1
extinct 3
spent 1
burn up
dissipate 3
enrage
infuriate
irritate
madden 1
splurge 2
burr
dialect
prickle 1
thorn 1
trial 5
burrow°
deepen 1
dig 1
excavate 1
excavation
hole 1
lair 1
root[2]
tunnel 1,2
bursarship
scholarship 2
bursary
scholarship 2
burst°
blast 3
blow[1] 7b, 8b
break 1
discharge 10
explode 1
explosion 1,2
flare 4
flash 1,4
flurry 1
gale 2
gush 1,3
pop 1

Byzantine (*cont.*)
intricate 1
involved 2
labyrinthine
perplexing
serpentine 2
showy

C

CA
bookkeeper
cab°
taxi 1
cabal°
combination 2
conspiracy
design 8
faction 1
junta
machine 3
party 3
plot^{1} 1,3
ring^{1} 3
sect 2
cabaret°
club 4
cabbage
money 1
cabbala
occult 3
cabbalism
occult 3
cabbalistic
cryptic 1
mystical 1
occult 1
profound 1
recondite
cabin°
cottage
hut
lodge 1
shack
cabinet°
board 4
committee
council 2
cabinet member
minister 2
cable°
flex 1
lead 17
line^{1} 11,13
main 5
rope 1
stay^{2} 1
string 1
telegram
transmit 1
twine 1
cablegram
cable 2
telegram
caboose
kitchen
cache°
fund 1
garner
hide^{1} 1
hoard 1
put 12
repertory
reserve 3
saving 4
secrete^{1}
stock 1,10
store 3
stow
supply 4
thesaurus 1
treasure 1
treasury
cache-pot
planter
cachet°
prestige
style 4
cack-handed
awkward 1
clumsy
cack-handed (*cont.*)
left-handed 1
thumb 2
cackle
chatter 1,3
gab 2
gibberish
giggle 1,2
jargon 2
nonsense 1
patter^{2} 2,3
prattle 2
rattle 6
squawk 1
talk 3,18
cackling
patter^{2} 2
cacodemon
demon 1
devil 1
cacodemonic
devilish
fiendish
ghoulish 1
satanic 1
cacoethes
hunger 2
mania 1
cacophonous
discordant 2
harsh 1
noisy
rough 8
strident
cacophony
jangle 3
noise 1
sound^{1} 1
cad
adventurer 2
heel^{1} 2
ogre
rake^{2}
rascal
rogue 1
scoundrel
stinker
villain
cadaver°
body 1
corpse
remain 4b
stiff 11
cadaverous
deadly 4
emaciated
gaunt 1
ghastly 2
haggard
macabre
pale^{1} 1
raw-boned
scrawny
spare 3
thin 1
wan 1
white 2
caddy
box^{1} 1
chest 1
cadence°
accent 1
measure 9
regularity 2
rhythm
tempo
cadenced
measured 3
rhythmic
cadency
rhythm
cadency mark
device 3
cadenza
run 47
cadge
beg 2
borrow
bum 5
scrounge 1
cadger
beggar 1
parasite
scrounge 2
cadre
cohort 1
corps
detail 3
faction 1
party 2
platoon
shift 4
squad
caduceus
staff 1
caducity
decrepitude 1
caesura
interruption 2
lapse 2
lull 1
pause 2
café°
bar 6
cafeteria
café
caff
café
caftan
robe 1
shift 6
cag
coat 1
cage°
hole 4
lock^{1} 9
shut 6a
stake^{1} 4
caged
captive 2
cage in°
at cage 2
shut 6a
cage up°
at cage 2
cagey
evasive
foxy 1
guarded
politic 1
smooth 8
wary
wily
cagoule
coat 1
cagy
foxy 1
cahoots
–in cahoots
hand 10
league 2
caird
bum 2
cairn
monument 1
caitiff
boy 2
milksop
miscreant 1
stinker
villain
wretch 1
cajole°
beg 1
coax
deceive
entice
flatter 3
get 14,46b
induce 1
make 34b
motivate
prompt 3
tempt 1
twit^{1}
wheedle
cajolery°
enticement 1
flattery
cajoling
ingratiating
temptation 1
cake°
loaf^{1} 1
lump^{1} 1
pat^{1} 4
scale^{2} 2
set 3
solidify 1
thicken
caking
scale^{2} 2
calabash
pipe 2
calaboose
jail 1
prison
stir 7
calamitous°
disastrous 1
evil 4
fatal 2
grievous 2
hard 5
monumental 4
mournful 2
ruinous
sad 2
tragic
unfortunate 3
calamity°
accident 1
affliction 2
blight 2
casualty 1
catastrophe 1
crisis 2
disappointment 1
disaster
distress 2
evil 7
fatality 1
grief 2
grievance 1
ill 8
misery 3
misfortune 2
plague 1
shame 3
tragedy
visitation 2
woe
calculate°
compute
count 1
enumerate 2
estimate 1
evaluate 2
expect 3
figure 8,9,12a
forecast 1
gauge 1
make 21
measure 11
number 4
plot^{1} 4
project 6
rate^{1} 6
reason 7
reckon 1
sum 2b
tally 2
calculated°
cool 3
deliberate 1
forced
measured 2
premeditated
shrewd
studied
calculatedly
deliberately
calculating°
astute 1
crafty
designing
disingenuous
foxy 1
hard 6
reckoning 1
scheming
sharp 6
shifty
shrewd
wily
calculatingly
deliberately
calculation°
account 2
estimate 3
evaluation 2
forecast 2
measurement 1
projection 4
reckoning 1
tally 3
calculator°
calendar°
chronology
diary
programme 1
register 1
schedule 1
timetable
calender
roller 1
smooth 9
Caliban
ogre
savage 4
calibrate°
graduate 2
measure 11
set 6
tune 3
calibrating
adjustment 1
calibration
adjustment 1
scale^{3} 1
calibre°
quality 2
width 1
call°
appeal 3
beckon
buzz 7
call 12b
cause 3
christen 2
claim 2,3
cry 6
demand 1
designate 4
drop 12
entitle 2
exclaim
exclamation
fetch 2
hail^{1} 1
hold 10
invitation 1
label 5
market 3
name 4
need 2
occasion 2
page^{2} 2
pop 2
raise 11
request 2
require 1
requisition 1,2
ring^{2} 2,4
rouse 1
run 43
shout 1,2
squawk 1
style 7
summon 1
tag 4
telephone 2
term 8
title 6
visit 1,3
–on call°
at call 16
demand 8
reserve 8
tap^{2} 4b
–within call°
at call 17
call a truce
patch 7
call attention to
distinguish 4
emphasize
feature 4
indicate 1
call attention to (*cont.*)
mention 1
note 13
play 17a
point 19,21a,21b
promote 3
propose 1
refer 1
call back
recall 2,3
call down°
at call 7
lambaste 2
called
so-called 1
called-for
indispensable 1
order 10b
prerequisite 1
caller
company 3
guest
visitor
–callers
company 3
call for°
at call 8
claim 3
cry 3
demand 1,3
entail
exact 3
indicate 4
insist 1
need 1
order 15
page^{2} 2
pick 8i
request 1
require 1
send 6
stipulate
take 16
want 2
warrant 4
call forth°
at call 9
arouse 3
elicit
evoke
excite 1
occasion 5
prompt 5
call-girl
bitch 2
prostitute 1
slattern
tart^{2} 2
wanton 5
calligraphic
neat 3
calligraphy
hand 7
penmanship
script 1
writing 1
call in
visit 1
calling°
business 1
career 1
craft 3
duty 1
employment 1
job 1
line^{1} 7
mission 2
occupation 1
profession 1
pursuit 3
racket 3
trade 2
visitation 1
vocation
work 2
calling-card
card 2
call into disrepute
foul 14
call into doubt
challenge 1

call into question°
at **question 5**
challenge 1
fault 8
question 10
callisthenics
exercise 4
work 19a
call it a day
pack 6
turn 15a
call off°
at **call 11**
rattle 5
reel 2
scrub 2
call on°
at **call 10**
call 5
castigate
drop 12
fall 9
look 11b
pray 1
solicit 1
summon 2
visit 1
call on (to) the carpet
castigate
punish 1
reprimand 2
scold 1
callous°
cold 3
cold-blooded 2
cold-hearted
cruel 1
dead 4
dull 2
frigid 2
hard 1,4
heartless
icy 2
impassive
indifferent 1
inhuman 1
insensible 2
merciless
remorseless 1
rocky[1] 3
ruthless
stony 2
thick-skinned
tough 6
unkind
unsympathetic
callousness
heart 2
indifference 1
call out
call 1
challenge 2
exclaim
page[2] 2
shout 1
callow°
fresh 3
green 2
immature 2
inexperienced
new 6
tender[1] 3
unfledged
young 2
callowness
inexperience
naïvety
call the shots°
at **shot 9**
direct 1
dominate 1
reign 2
call the tune
command 2
control 1
dominate 1
call to account
accuse 1
fault 8
scold 1
task 3
call together
assemble 1
muster 1
rally 3
call to mind
finger 5a
recall 1
recollect
remember 1
reminisce
stir 5
suggest 2
think 4
call up°
at **call 12**
buzz 7
call 3
enlist 1
evoke
find 7
induct 2
look 11b
mobilize
occasion 5
quote 1
recruit 1
screw 7a
telephone 2
call upon°
at **call 10**
fall 9
petition 2
pray 1
screw 7a
solicit 1
summon 2
visit 1
calm°
bland 1
charm 6
collected
compose 4
console
cool 2
dead 11
deliberate 3
dispassionate 1
ease 5
easy 2
equable 1
even 4
gentle 1
hush 5
impassive
level-headed
lull 2,3
mild 1
mitigate
moderate 1,5
nonchalant
order 8
passive 1
peace 1
peaceful 1
philosophical 2
phlegmatic 2
poised 1
presence 5
quell 2
quiet 2,4
quieten
relaxed
repose 1,3
rest[1] 10
restful 2
sedate 1
self-contained 1
self-possessed
serene 1,2
serenity 1,2
settle 8
silence 1,3
silent 1
smooth 1,12
sober 2
soothing 1
staid
steady 4
still 1,3,9
stoical
stoicism
subdued 1
subside 2
tame 6
temperate 1
calm (*cont.*)
tranquil
tranquillize
unhurried
unmoved
wind[2] 3b
calmative
sedative 1,2
calm down°
at **calm 5**
compose 4
relax 4
settle 7
simmer 3
subside 2
wind[2] 3b
calmed
subdued 1
calming
dreamy 3
mild 3
restful 1
sedative 2
soothing 1
calmly
easy 7
quietly 3
well[1] 8
calmness
calm 2
ease 1
lull 2
patience 1
peace 1
philosophy 3
poise 2
quiet 5
repose 3
self-control 2
serenity 1,2
silence 1
stoicism
temper 2
calm oneself
simmer 3
calumniate
abuse 3
blaspheme 2
discredit 1
libel 4
shame 8
slander 2
smear 2
stigmatize
tarnish
vilify
wrong 9
calumniation
abuse 8
shame 2
calumniatory
abusive 1
foul 6
injurious 2
scandalous 2
scurrilous
slanderous
vituperative
calumnious
abusive 1
foul 6
injurious 2
scandalous 2
scurrilous
slanderous
vituperative
calumny
abuse 8
aspersion
libel 2
scandal 2
slander 1
slur 1
smear 4
calvous
hairless
camaraderie
association 3
brotherhood 1
companionship
fellowship 1
fraternity 2
rapport
society 1
camaraderie (*cont.*)
solidarity
sympathy 2
camarilla
faction 1
junta
ring[1] 3
camber
slant 3
slope 2
cambered
oblique 1
cameo
engraving 1
camera
-in camera
private 6
cameraman, camerawoman
photographer
reporter
camiknickers
pants 1
camorra
ring[1] 3
camouflage°
conceal 1
cover 15
disguise 1,3
dissimulate
dress 5b
face 3
gloss[1] 2,4
hide[1] 2
keep 14a
mask 2,3
masquerade 2
pretence 1
pretext 1
screen 3,7
secrete[1]
shade 12
shroud 1
submerge 3
veil 1,2
whitewash
camouflaged
invisible 2
camp°
base[1] 4
faction 1
homosexual 2
installation 3
outlandish
pocket 3
settlement 1
side 3
swish 4
theatrical 2
campagna
plain 6
campaign°
agitate 2
battle 2
canvass 1,3
crusade 1,2
drive 10
electioneer
movement 5
operation 4
plump[2] 3
pull 10
push 15
stand 7c
stump 3
tactic 2
urge 3
war 3
campaigner
champion 3
tactician
campanile
tower 1
camp-follower
prostitute 1
camp(ing)-ground
camp[1] 1
camp(ing)-site
camp[1] 1
campo
plain 6
campy
camp[2] 1
effeminate
homosexual 2
outlandish
swish 4
theatrical 2
can
bottom 1
bum 1
buoy 1
buttocks
dismiss 1
fire 11
jail 1
lavatory
preserve 3
prison
put 28c
receptacle
stir 7
toilet 1
canaille
mob 2
populace
rabble 2
riff-raff
canal
channel 1
canary
informer
singer
vocalist
can-buoy
buoy 1
cancel°
abolish
call 11
correct 4
counteract
cross 3
delete
destroy 3
dispense 3b
disturb 5
eliminate 3
erase 1
forgive 3
kill 6
lift 4
militate 1
neutralize
offset 1
omit 1
quash 1
recall 3
repeal 1
retract 2
reverse 3
revoke
rub 4
scrub 2
set 15b
spike 3
strike 5
undo 3
vitiate 3
void 6
withdraw 2
write 5
cancellation°
abolition
dismissal 2
recall 5
repeal 2
reversal 3
cancelled
off 9
cancelling
cancellation 1
negative 3
cancel out°
at **cancel 3**
destroy 3
militate 1
neutralize
offset 1
cancer
disease 2
pestilence 2
poison 2
tumour
ulcer 2
cancerous
ulcerous
cancer stick
fag 5
candent
glowing 1
incandescent
candid°
above-board 2
artless 1
blunt 2
brazen
broad 5
direct 10
dispassionate 2
downright 1
explicit 2
forthright
frank 1,2
front 9b
genuine 2
honest 3
ingenuous 2
naïve
natural 4
open 15
outspoken
plain 3
raw 6
round 8
simple 3
sincere
straight 5,6
transparent 3
truthful
unflattering 1
uninhibited
unvarnished
candidate°
entry 5
match 4
nominee
pretender
-be a candidate for
line[1] 20
run 5
stand 7c
-candidates
field 3
candidly
above-board 1
face 13
freely 1
honestly 2
naturally 3
openly 2
outright 4
point-blank 3
seriously 2
shoulder 6
sincerely
straight 14
true 4
candidness
freedom 6
sincerity
candle
light[1] 2
candlelight
light[1] 1
candour°
freedom 6
honesty 2
naïvety
simplicity 3
sincerity
candy°
sweet 9
candystriper
orderly 3
cane
beat 1
chastise
hit 1
lambaste 1
punish 2
rod 1,2
staff 1
stalk[2]
stick[2] 1
strike 1
whip 1,8

caning
punishment 2
thrashing 1
whipping 1
canker
pestilence 2
poison 2
sore 7
ulcer 1, 2
cankerous
ulcerous
canned
stinking 3
cannibal°
cannily
gingerly 1
canniness
dexterity 2
ingenuity
prudence 1
cannonade
fire 3
shell 4
volley 1
cannon-ball
shot 2
canny
acute 5
astute 1
calculating
clever 2
crafty
deep 5
dexterous 2
gingerly 2
incisive 1
ingenious
intelligent
keen[1] 6
knowing 1
noncommittal
politic 1
provident 1
prudent 1
shifty
shrewd
sly 1
smart 2
wily
can of worms
mess 3
problem 1
canon
clergyman 1
doctrine
law 1
pastor
precept 1
principle 1
standard 1
tenet
canonical
clerical 1
priestly
canonize
glorify 2
immortalize
sanctify 1
canonized
sublime 1
canoodle
kiss 1
love 6
canopy
mantle 2
shade 5
cant°
dialect
idiom 1
jargon 1
language 1
lingo
list[2] 1, 2
slant 3, 4
slope 2
talk 19
terminology
tilt 1, 3
tip[2] 2
vernacular 3
cantankerous°
cranky 2
cross 6
cantankerous (*cont.*)
gruff 1
irritable
mean[2] 5
moody 2
nasty 4
peevish
perverse 2
petulant
prickly 3
querulous
snappish 2
surly
testy
touchy 1
ugly 4
waspish
cantankerousness
obstinacy
canted
oblique 1
canteen
bar 6
café
canter
Pharisee
canticle
chant 1
canting
oblique 1
Pharisaic
sanctimonious
self-righteous
canto
passage 2
cantonment
quarter 5
cantor
vocalist
cantrip
trick 2
canvas
sail 4
canvass°
electioneer
poll 2, 3
sound[3] 1
stump 3
canyon°
gorge 1
gully
pass 23
ravine
cap°
capital 1, 4
cover 11
crest 3
crown 5
outdo
outstrip
pinnacle
surpass
tip[1] 1, 2
top 2, 4
vertex
capability°
ability 2
aptitude 2
calibre 2
capacity 2
efficiency 1
faculty 1
genius 3
gift 2
ingenuity
might 2
potential 2
power 1
proficiency
promise 2
prowess 1
qualification 1
reach 8
resource 1
skill 2
speciality 1
touch 16
–capabilities
endowment 3
stuff 3
capable°
able 1
competent 2
effective 1
effectual 1
efficacious
experienced 1
fit[1] 2
gifted
good 12
practised 1
proficient
qualified 1
skilful
smart 1
strong 6
capable of°
at **capable 2**
equal 3
capably
handily 2
capacious
extensive 2
great 1
large 3
roomy
spacious
vast
voluminous 1
capaciousness
extent 1
capacitate
enable 2
capacity°
ability 1, 2
aptitude 3
brain 1
calibre 2
capability
character 7
content[1] 1
effect 2
extension 2
faculty 1
gauge 4
genius 3
gift 2
instinct
intelligence 1
knack
measure 1
measurement 2
mentality 1
might 2
mind 3
position 6
possibility 2
potential 2
power 1, 7
proportion 4
qualification 1
reach 8
role 2
scope 2
seating
talent 1
volume 2
–capacities
endowment 3
–in the capacity of
way 10b
caparison
clothe 2
decorate 1
embellish 1
equip
rig 1
trappings
trim 4
cape°
cloak 1
mantle 1
point 8
wrap 4
caper°
bound[2] 3
cavort
clown 3
dance 1
frisk 1
frolic 2, 3
hop 1, 3
job 5
caper (*cont.*)
jump 1
lark 1, 2
leap 2
move 9
play 1
prance
prank
racket 2
skip 1, 3
sport 4
stunt[1]
tactic 1
trick 2
trip 4
capering
nonsense 2
sportive
cap in hand°
at **cap 3**
capital°
asset 1
big 8
estate 2
excellent
finance 2
fund 2
good 2
high 6
mean[3] 4b
metropolis
monetary
money 2
neat 5
optimum 2
principal 5
property 2
purse 2
resource 2
seat 2
splendid 3
stock 5
superlative
upper 4
wealth 1
–capitals
upper 4
capital funds
principal 5
capital goods
property 2
capitalist
financier
capitalistic
bourgeois 1
capitalization
subsidy
capitalize
finance 3
fund 3
profit 4
subsidize
use 2
capital letter(s)
upper 4
capitally
famously
capital punishment
execution 3
capitulate°
bow 2
defer[2]
fall 5
give 13, 17b
lose 3
relent
submit 1
succumb
surrender 2
yield 1
capitulation
fall 28
resignation 2
submission 1
surrender 3
capon
neuter 2
caponize
fix 13
neuter 2
sterilize 2
cappella
unaccompanied
caprice
conceit 2
eccentricity 2
fancy 8
freak 3
kink 4
notion 2
peculiarity 1
quirk
capricious°
arbitrary 1
changeable 1
cranky 1
erratic 1
fanciful 1
fancy 2
fickle
fitful
flighty 1
giddy 2
inconsistent 2
inconstant
kinky 1
moody 3
spotty 3
temperamental 1
unstable 1
untrue 1
variable
volatile 2
whimsical 2
capriciousness
eccentricity 1
extravagance 2
inconstancy
capriole
prance
capsize°
overturn 1
tip[2] 1
topple 1
turn 24
upset 2
wreck 2, 5
capsized
upset 6
capsizing
wreck 5
capsule
pill 1
tablet 4
captain
chief 1
director 2
govern 1
lead 3
leader 1
navigate 2
pilot 1
sailor
skipper
captaincy
direction 1
caption
legend 4
title 3
captious
fault-finding 2
fretful
hair-splitting
overcritical
peevish
perverse 2
petulant
sarcastic
sophistic
testy
touchy 1
waspish
captiousness
fault-finding 1
captivate°
attract
bewitch
catch 11
charm 5
dazzle 1
delight 1
enchant 2
enrapture
entrance[2]
fascinate
captivate (*cont.*)
hypnotize
interest 7
intrigue 1
love 8
possess 3
pull 5
ravish 1
regale
seduce 1
take 20
tempt 1
tickle
transport 3
captivated
fervent 3
infatuated
love 8
rapt 1
smitten 2
taken
captivating
absorbing
adorable
attractive
catching 2
delightful 2
desirable 2
devastating 2
enchanting
endearing
enthralling
exciting 2
fetching
glamorous 1
interesting
inviting
lovely 1
magnetic
prepossessing
ravishing
riveting
seductive
sexy 1
spellbinding
taking
temptation 1
tempting 1
winning 1
captivation
fascination
glamour
spell[2] 1
temptation 2
captive°
convict 2
hostage
inmate
captivity°
detention
duress 2
slavery 1
capture°
arrest 2, 4
bag 6
carry 6, 10a
catch 1, 15
conquer 2
engage 4
fall 28
gain 1
get 8
grab 3
hook 6
interest 7
kidnap
land 6
nab
net[1] 2
obtain 1
occupy 1
plunder 2
possession 4
pull 5
rape 3
seize 2, 5
seizure 1
snap 4
snare 2
snatch 1
take 1, 20
track 8
–be captured
fall 5

car°
carriage 1
machine 2
carafe
jar[1]
jug
caravan
train 3
caravanserai
hotel
caravan site
camp[1] 1
carbon
copy 1
facsimile
reproduction 2
transcript 2
carbonated
effervescent 1
carbonation
bubble 2
fizz 2
foam 1
carbon copy
copy 1
facsimile
replica
reproduction 2
car-boot sale
sale 3
carbuncle
boil[2]
lump[1] 2
ulcer 1
carcanet
pendant
string 4
car-card
advertisement 1
card 8
carcass
body 1
corpse
remain 4b
carcinoma
tumour
card°
character 6
eccentric 2
greeting 2
joker 1
line[1] 8
missive
oddity 2
original 6
scream 4
wag[2]
wit 3
-cards°
at **card 14**
dismissal 1
fire 11
-in, on the cards°
at **card 12**
certain 3
destined 4
forthcoming 1
impending
predetermined 2
predictable
promise 4
prospect 4
wind[1] 8
cardinal°
capital 5
central 2
first 3
fundamental 1
great 11
head 9
leading 1
main 1
overriding
paramount
primary 1
principal 2
radical 1
strategic
vital 1
care°
caution 2
charge 1, 4
concern 5
care (*cont.*)
consideration 1
custody 1
damn 5
discomfort 1
discretion 1
foresight 1
hand 8
load 1
love 4
maintenance 1
mind 15
oversight 2
possession 1
precaution 2
precision 2
preservation 1
protection 2
providence 1, 2
prudence 1
regard 9
safe keeping
security 4
service 3
tact
thrift
treatment 1, 2
trouble 4
trust 3
wish 1
worry 3
-cares
sorrow 2
-under the care of
under 4
careen°
beach 2
list[2] 1
career°
calling
careen
job 1
journey 2
occupation 1
past 5
practice 3
pursuit 3
regular 10
speed 3
swerve
tear 3
trade 2
vocation
work 2
career description
résumé 2
care for°
at **care 6**
attend 3
bring 15a
foster 2
keep 2
look 4
maintain 2
mind 18
minister 3
mother 5
nourish 1
nurse 2
preserve 1
protect 2
provide 4
rear[2] 1
safeguard 2
tend[2]
treat 3
watch 2
carefree°
blasé 2
blithe 2
breezy 2
buoyant 2
comfortable 2
debonair 2
easy 2
easygoing
gay 2
merry 1
relaxed
careful°
accurate 2
anxious 1
beware
careful (*cont.*)
cautious
ceremonious 2
close 14
conscientious 2, 3
conservative 2
deliberate 2, 3
diligent
discreet
exact 2
faithful 3
frugal 1
gingerly 2
good 11
guarded
judicious
laborious 2
leery
look 9
measured 2
meticulous
mind 17
narrow 3
nice 3
noncommittal
painful 3
precise 2, 3
protective
provident 1
prudent 1
reluctant
rigid 3
scrupulous 1
sharp-eyed
sparing 1
step 12
studious 1
tactful
thorough 2
thoughtful 3
thrifty
vigilant
wary
watch 4
carefully
gingerly 1
hard 15
jealously
narrowly 2
precisely 2
sharp 12
slow 11
thoroughly 2
carefulness
care 2
prudence 1
tact
thrift
careless°
blithe 2
breakneck
derelict 2
desperate 2
foolhardy
forgetful
haphazard 2
hasty 2
helter-skelter 1
improvident 2
imprudent
inadvertent 2
inattentive
indiscreet
indiscriminate 1
irresponsible
lax 1, 2
loose 5, 6
nod 4
offhand 1
perfunctory 2
precipitate 5
promiscuous 1
rash[1]
reckless
remiss
short-sighted 2
slack 1
slipshod
sloppy 1
thoughtless 2
unguarded 1, 3
unwary
wanton 3
carelessly
badly 1
carelessness
indiscretion 1
neglect 3
negligence
oversight 1
caress°
cuddle 2
feel 2
fondle
handle 2
love 6
pat[1] 1, 3
pet[1] 4
stroke 6, 10
touch 14
caressingly
fondly
caretaker
keeper
porter[2] 1
watchman
careworn
haggard
carfuffle
disorder 2
uproar
upset 3
cargo°
freight 2
load 2
caricature°
burlesque 1, 3
derision
guy 2
imitate 2
imitation 2
joke 3
lampoon 1, 2
mimic 3
mock 2
mockery 2
parody 1, 3
put-on 2
ridicule 2
satire 1, 2
satirize
take 34b
take-off 2
caricaturist
mimic 4
wit 3
carillon
chime 1
peal 1
caring
affectionate
benevolent
concerned 1
consideration 1
devoted
fatherly
fond 1
helpful
maternal
solicitous 1
sympathetic 1
tender[1] 6
thoughtful 3
carious
mouldy
carload
cargo
carnage°
bloodshed
gore[1]
holocaust 2
killing 1
massacre 1
murder 2
slaughter 2
carnal°
animal 4
earthly 2
epicurean 1
erotic 3
immoral 2
intimate[1] 3
lecherous
lewd
libertine 2
lustful
obscene 1
outward
physical
carnal (*cont.*)
profligate 1
prurient 1
sensual
sexual 2
worldly 1
carnality
profligacy 1
carnal knowledge
intercourse 2
relation 6a
carnival
festival 2
fête 1
gala 1
jamboree
revel 3
carnivorous
predatory 1
carol
chant 1, 2
sing 1
caroller
singer
vocalist
carom
glance 3
carousal
bender
carouse 2
drunk 4
orgy 1
party 1
revel 3
revelry
spree
carouse°
banquet 2
bender
dissipate 4
drink 2
drunk 4
jag
jamboree
merry 2
orgy 1
paint 7
party 1
play 1
revel 2, 3
carousel
roundabout 3
carousing
dissipation 1
dissolute
revelry
carp°
cavil 2
complain
criticize 2
fault 6
get 30c
gripe 1
henpeck
knock 2
nag[1] 1
niggle
pick 4a
prod 3
snipe
car park
park 2
carpet
castigate
rebuke 1
reprimand 2
scold 1
carpet-bag
bag 2
carping
critical 1
fault-finding 1, 2
fretful
gripe 2
hair-splitting
overcritical
peevish
querulous
sarcastic
carriable
portable
carriage°
attitude 1
bearing 1
car 2
coach 1
form 2
freight 1
motion 3
posture 1
presence 3
stance
train 1
transit 2
transport 4
walk 6
carriageway
road 2
carrier°
porter[1]
transport 4
vehicle 2
carrier bag
bag 1
carrion
filth 1
carrot
incentive
inducement
carrousel
roundabout 3
carry°
bear 1, 2, 5
bring 1, 4
cart 2
conduct 5
contain 1, 2
deliver 1
fetch 1
haul 2
hold 1, 8
hump 3
lug
mean[1] 2
pass 7
ride[1] 1
roll 3
route 2
sell 2
ship 2
shoulder 8
stock 9
support 2
sustain 2, 4
sweep 2
take 9
transfer 1
translate 4
transport 1
waft 1
wash 2
whisk 2
carry-all
grip 4
carry along (behind)
trail 4
carry a torch for
adore 3
carry away°
at **carry 9**
remove 2
sweep 2
take 3
transport 3
win 2
carry back
fetch 1
return 3
carrying
translation 4
transmission 1
carrying-on
performance 1
carrying out
execution 1
fulfilment
performance 1
carrying through
fulfilment
carry off°
at **carry 10**
abduct

carry off (*cont.*)
accomplish
bring 11
execute 1
float 3
fulfil 1
kidnap
negotiate 2
remove 2
spirit 10
sweep 2
take 1, 3
win 1, 2
work 16

carry on°
at **carry 11**
act 5
administer 2
conduct 3
continue 1, 3, 4
extend 1, 3
follow 6
go 32a
hang 7c
hold 10, 20a
keep 5
last[2] 1
maintain 1
manage 3
misbehave
operate 2
peg 7
perform 1
persevere
persist 2
practise 2
proceed 1
prosecute 3
pursue 2
remain 3
resume
run 10
seethe 2
spout 2
take 39b
transact
waffle 1
wage 2

carry-on
palaver 1
portable

carry-on bag, luggage
bag 2

carry out°
at **carry 12**
accomplish
achieve 1
administer 2
bring 11
carry 10c
commit 3
discharge 5
dispense 2
effect 7
effectuate
enforce 1
execute 1
fill 8
finish 2
follow 10
fulfil 1
honour 7
implement 2
make 31c
manage 3
meet[1] 5
obey 2
perfect 8
perform 1
perpetrate
practise 2
prosecute 3
pull 12b
put 27a
redeem 6
serve 2
transact
work 16
wreak

carry the day
triumph 3
win 1

carry through°
at **carry 12**
accomplish
execute 1
fulfil 1
perfect 8
perpetrate
persevere
prosecute 2
put 27a

carry to excess
overdo 1

carry to extremes
meal 2
overdo 1

carry too far
meal 2
overdo 1

carry weight
mean[1] 4
reach 6
signify 2
tell[1] 6
wash 8
weigh 5

carsick
nauseated
sick 1

cart°
carry 1
deliver 1
haul 2
ship 2
stand 16
take 9
transfer 1

cartage
carriage 3
transit 2
transport 4

***carte blanche*°**
freedom 4
liberty 2
licence 1
privilege
warrant 1

carte de visite
card 2

cartel
combination 2
fellowship 2
firm 6
pool 3
ring[1] 3
syndicate 1
trust 4
union 2

carter
carrier 1

cartilaginous
tough 2

carton
box[1] 1
case[2] 1
package 1, 3
parcel 1

cartoon
caricature 1
satire 2

cartouche
seal 1
sign 4
stamp 7

cartridge
round 15
shell 1

carve°
chisel 1
cut 2, 17a
engrave 1
etch 1
model 7
scribe 3
sculpture 2
shape 6
slice 4
tool 4
whittle 1

carve out°
at **carve 2**
frame 7
model 7

carve up°
at **carve 2**
cut 17a
portion 4
split 4

carving
statue

caryatid
pillar 1
statue

Casanova
charmer
libertine 1
philanderer
playboy
rake[2]
roué
sensualist

cascade
fall 1, 25
flow 2
gush 1, 3
outpouring
pour 1
river 2
run 6
stream 2, 4
torrent
waterfall

case°
argument 2
box[1] 1
casket 1
cause 4
chest 1
eccentric 2
eventuality
examine 1
example 1, 4
file 1
grip 4
housing 2
hull 2
illustration 1
inmate
instance 1
litigation
observe 2
original 6
outside 1
package 1, 3
parcel 1
patient 4
plight
reason 1
receptacle
situation 2
specimen
spy 2
subject 4
suit 4
trunk 3
wrapper 2

–as the case may be
perhaps

–be the case
hold 11

–in all cases
ever 2
universally

–in any case
always 3
event 3
ever 1
however 1
means[3] 2b
nevertheless
rate[1] 5
regardless 2
same 3
still 8

–in case
providing

case-hardened
thick-skinned

case in point
example 4
illustration 1
instance 1
specimen

case-mounting
frame 2

casern(e)
quarter 5

cash°
capital 3
change 4
coin 1
finance 2
fund 2
honour 8
monetary
money 1
purse 2
ready 8
redeem 3
resource 2
tender[2] 3
treasure 1
wealth 1

cash-box, -drawer
register 2
till[2]

cashier
bookkeeper
degrade 1
discharge 2
dismiss 1
displace 2
eject 3
expel 2
fire 11
lay[1] 16a
punish 2
turn 20c

cashiering
ejection 3
punishment 2

cash in°
at **cash 2**
redeem 3

cash in on
profit 4

cash in one's checks, chips
die 1

cash register
register 2

casing
case[2] 2
frame 2
housing 2
outside 1
wrapper 2

cask
keg

casket°
box[1] 1
case[2] 1
chest 1
coffin
receptacle
trunk 3

Cassandra
killjoy
misery 4
oracle 1
prophet

casserole
pan 1

cassette
tape 2

cassock
robe 1

cast°
clap 3
colour 1
company 2
dash 2
deliver 5
fibre 3
figure 1, 4
fling 1
fly 8a
forge 1
form 1
go 9
heave 2
hue
hurl
image 6
inclination 3
like[1] 8
make-up 2

cast (*cont.*)
mould[1] 1, 5
nature 4
peg 6
pitch[1] 1
precipitate 2
produce 1
project 4
put 7
reflect 4
regurgitate
sculpture 2
send 3
shape 6
shed[2] 2
sling 1
sort 9
stamp 8
strain[1] 9
throw 1, 2
tint 1
tone 4
toss 1
turn 8

cast about°
at **cast 10**
scout 1
search 2

cast aside°
at **cast 11**
abandoned 1
cast 14
junk 2
old 3

cast a slur on
denounce 3

cast a spell on, over
bewitch
enchant 1
fascinate
hypnotize
intoxicate 2
possess 3

cast aspersions
blacken 2
impeach 2

cast away°
at **cast 12**
cast 11
maroon

castaway°

cast doubt
question 5, 10

cast down
depress 1
tip[2] 1

caste°
class 1
degree 1
estate 3
order 3
position 5
rank[1] 1
sphere 2
station 2
stratum 2
tribe

castigate°
berate
call 7b
chasten 1
correct 3
damn 1
discipline 8
dress 4
flog 1
lace 5b
lambaste 2
mind 10
mortify 2
pay 5
punish 1
rebuke 1
reprimand 2
scold 1
scourge 4
spank
tell[1] 10
upbraid
vituperate
whip 1

castigation
correction 2
discipline 2
hell 4
lesson 4
punishment 1
rebuke 2
reprimand 1
rod 2
thrashing 2
tongue-lashing

castigatory
punitive
vituperative

casting
cast 4
production 1
statue

casting out, up
ejection 1

cast into the shade
shame 5a

castle°
palace
residence 3
tower 2

castle in Spain, the air
day-dream 1

cast light on, upon
illuminate 1, 2
spotlight 3

cast off°
at **cast 13**
abandoned 1
back 9
drop 8
forsake 2
loose 12
old 3
remove 1
shed[2] 4
throw 5a

cast-off
castaway
discard 2
reject 4
used 1

–cast-offs
refuse[2]

cast out°
at **cast 14**
banish 2
cast 11
empty 8
exile 3
expel 1

castrate
fix 13
neuter 2
sterilize 2

cast suspicion on
question 5

cast to the winds
trample 2

casual°
accidental
blithe 2
Bohemian
breezy 2
careless 1, 4
chance 6
easy 2
easygoing
familiar 3
free 8
frivolous 2
haphazard 2
incidental 1
indiscriminate 2
informal 1, 2
irregular 2
lax 1
loose 5
nodding
nonchalant
occasional 1
odd 2
offhand 1

casual (*cont.*)
passing 2
random 1
scratch 6
snug
sporty
stray 5
uncertain 1
unhurried
uninhibited
unpremeditated
-to the casual observer
surface 2
casually
easy 7
incidentally 2
offhand 5
random 2
casualness
ease 4
casualty°
accident 1
fatality 2
victim 1
-casualties°
at **casualty 2b**
casuistic
evasive
plausible 2
sophistic
specious
subtle 3
casuistry
falsity
subtlety 2
cat
guy 1
lash[1] 1
whip 8
catachresis
abuse 4
misuse 2
cataclysm
calamity 1
catastrophe 1
disaster
evil 7
fatality 1
ill 8
revolution 2
upheaval
visitation 2
cataclysmic
calamitous
disastrous 1
fatal 2
fateful 2
ill 4
ruinous
violent 2
catacomb
crypt
tomb
cataleptic state
trance
catalogue
brochure
detail 5
enrol 2
enumerate 1
group 3
identify 1
include 2
index 1
journal 2
list[1] 1,2
litany 2
organize 1
range 7
record 3
register 1,3
roll 13
sort 8
table 3
tabulate
write 4a
catalogue raisonné
list[1] 1
cataloguing
distribution 3
identification 2
cataloguing (*cont.*)
litany 2
catalyst
instrument 2
catalytic
instrumental
catamite
prostitute 1
catapult
fire 9
launch 3
put 7
sling 2
toss 1
cataract
fall 25
flood 2
outpouring
river 2
stream 2
waterfall
catastrophe°
accident 1
affliction 2
calamity 1
casualty 1
crisis 2
disaster
distress 2
evil 7
fatality 1
grief 2
ill 8
misery 3
misfortune 2
reverse 8
shame 3
tragedy
visitation 2
catastrophic
calamitous
disastrous 1
evil 3
fatal 2
fateful 2
ill 4
monumental 4
mournful 2
ruinous
tragic
unfortunate 3
violent 2
cat burglar
burglar
robber
thief 1
catcall
hiss 2
jeer 2
catch°
arrest 2
bag 6
bolt 2
brace 3
buckle 1
capture 2
clasp 1
claw 3
come 12
contract 3
detect 2
deterrent
drawback
engage 4
entangle 1
fastening
field 5
find 10
follow 8
foul 13
get 5,11,20
grab 1,3
grapple 1
grasp 2
haul 4
hear 1
hitch 4
hook 1,6
intercept
interest 7
involve 3
jewel 2
joker 2
catch (*cont.*)
land 6
lock[1] 1
lodge 5
lure 1
mesh 3
nab
net[1] 2
obstacle
obstruction 1
occupy 3
overtake 1,2
pick 8k
pitfall 2
pluck 4
plum
provision 2
pull 5
rub 11
seize 2,3
snag 1,2
snap 4,5,10
snare 2
snatch 1
take 1
track 8
trap 4
treasure 2
witness 4
-catches
string 7
catch a few zees, Z's
doze 1
nap[1] 1
rest[1] 6
retire 3
sleep 1
catch a glimpse of
discover 2
see 1
spy 3
catch forty winks
nap[1] 1
sleep 1
catch hold of
grab 1
grasp 1
lay[1] 11
catch in flagrante delicto
surprise 2
catching°
capture 1
infectious
catch in the act
surprise 2
catch napping
surprise 2
catch off guard
surprise 2
catch on°
at **catch 13**
figure 12b
grasp 2
learn 3
perceive 2
realize 2
tumble 3
twig[2]
understand 1
catch one's breath
gasp 1
catch out
trip 6
catch-phrase
byword
phrase 2
saw
shibboleth
catchpole
officer 2
catch red-handed
spy 3
surprise 2
catch sight of°
at **sight 8**
discover 2
find 2
catch sight of (*cont.*)
perceive 1
see 1
sight 8
spot 6
spy 3
catch some shut-eye
rest[1] 6
retire 3
catch-22
catch 18
dilemma
fix 71
hole 5
joker 2
perplexity 3
plight
catch unawares
surprise 2
catch unprepared
overtake 2
catch up°
at **catch 14**
entangle 1
gain 4
overhaul 1
overtake 1
catchword
byword
motto
saw
shibboleth
slogan
catchy
memorable
pretty 2
tuneful
catechism
examination 3
catechize
examine 2
preach 1
catechumen
convert 3
initiate 4
pupil
categorical°
absolute 2
dead 14
definitive 3
direct 9
dogmatic
downright 1
emphatic
explicit 1
express 5
flat 4
peremptory 2
perfect 6
point-blank 1
positive 1
unmitigated
unqualified 2
categorically
absolutely 1
completely 3
dead 18
definitely
expressly 1
flat 16
outright 4
point-blank 3
positively
really 2
utterly
wholly 2
categorization
identification 2
order 1
organization 1
categorize°
bunch 3
class 5
coordinate 1
distinguish 2
distribute 3
divide 5
file 3
grade 6
group 3
identify 1
categorize (*cont.*)
include 2
label 5
order 16
organize 1
place 16
put 16f
range 7
rank[1] 6
sort 8,9
stamp 3
tabulate
categorizing
identification 2
organization 1
category°
assortment 1
bracket 3
class 2
description 3
division 3
genre
grade 1
nature 4
order 3
run 44
sort 1
style 1
type 1
variety 3
cater°
entertain 2
feed 1
lay[1] 17a
provide 1
provision 5
cater for°
at **cater 2**
entertain 2
feed 1
lay[1] 17a
catering
provision 1
caterpillar
bug 1
cater to°
at **cater 2**
entertain 2
indulge 1
oblige 1
pamper
pander 1
supply 1
tend[2]
caterwaul
rave 1
scream 1,3
yell 1,2
caterwauling
noise 1
puling
cathartic
purgative 1,2
cathedra
chair 2
cathedral
temple
cathode-ray
monitor 2
catholic°
broad 7
extensive 1
general 3
prevalent
public 1
sweeping 1
tolerant
catholicity
breadth 3
cat-house
brothel
house 6
catlike
-with catlike tread
silently
catnap
doze 1,2
nap[1] 1,3
repose 2
sleep 1
cat on a hot tin roof
fidget 2
cat on hot bricks
fidget 2
cat-o'-nine-tails
lash[1] 1
scourge 2
whip 8
cat's-paw
breeze 1
dupe 2
fool 3
inferior 4
pawn[2]
plaything 2
puppet 2
ripple 1
robot 2
scapegoat
sucker
tool 3
cattle°
stock 4
Caucasian
white 4
Caucasoid
white 4
caucus
cabal 2
council 1,2
meeting 2
party 3
caudal fin
tail 1
caught
foul 10
caught on the hop
unprepared 1
cauldron
pot 1
caulk
fill 7
cause°
agent 2
bottom 3
breed 2
brew 2
bring 5,7
call 15
case[1] 2
effect 7
effectuate
entail
excite 1
excuse 4
execute 1
explanation 3
factor 1
generate 3
get 14
give 4,10
ground 3
have 9
implement 2
induce 2
lead 2,6
let[1] 2
make 2,3,5
motivate
motive 1
occasion 2,5
part 5
procure 2
produce 2
prompt 3
provocation 1
put 2
raise 10
rise 17
root[1] 1
score 8
seed 2
side 3
spawn
subject 3
suit 4
touch 11b
warrant 1,4
cause a disturbance
riot 3

charge *(cont.)*
price 1
prosecute 1
protection 2
protégé
province 3
push 15
quotation 2
rap 6
rate[1] 2
responsibility 2
round 15
rush 2, 4
safe keeping
send 1
set 17b
speed 3
stampede 3
stick[1] 8
stint 1
sue 1
tab 2
task 1
tax 1, 3
tell[1] 5
thrill 1
toll[2] 1
tribute 2
trust 3
vitalize
weight 5
work 3
-be in charge
boss 2
govern 1
head 11
manage 1
rule 5
run 10
supervise
-charges
check 19
dues
-without charge
free 13
chargeability
responsibility 1
chargeable
responsible 1
charged
electric
explosive 1
fraught 1
hot 9
live 5
loaded 2, 3
momentous
pregnant 2
volatile 3
chargé d'affaires
minister 2
charger
mount 9
plate 1
charily
gingerly 1
chariness
mistrust 2
precaution 2
charisma
glamour
magnetism
mystique
charismatic
magnetic
charitable°
benevolent
big 6
bountiful 1
chivalrous
considerate
free 7
generous 1, 2
good 6
good-natured
human 3
kind[1]
large 2
lenient
liberal 1
merciful
open 14
philanthropic

charitable *(cont.)*
selfless
soft-hearted
thoughtful 1
tolerant
unselfish
charitableness
altruism
benevolence 1
bounty 1
humanity 3
kindness 1
philanthropy 1
charitably
readily 1
charity°
altruism
benevolence 1
bounty 1
gift 1
grace 3
kindness 1
largesse
love 4
mercy
philanthropy 1
charivari
jamboree
noise 1
charlady
servant 1
charlatan
adventurer 2
cheat 1
fake 4
fraud 3
hypocrite
impostor
phoney 3
quack 1
rogue 1
swindler
thief 2
charlatanism
hypocrisy
charlatanry
hypocrisy
charlie
sap[1] 2
charm°
amulet
appeal 4
attract
beguile 3
bewitch
captivate
catch 11
coax
dazzle 1
disarm 2
enchant 2
enchantment 1, 2
enrapture
entrance[2]
fascinate
fascination
fetish 1
glamour
hypnotize
intrigue 1
lure 1, 2
magic 3
magnetism
mumbo-jumbo 2
possess 3
ravish 1
regale
seduce 1
send 4
spell[2] 1, 2
take 20
talisman
transport 3
wheedle
win 3
-charms°
at **charm 3**
charmed°
delighted
infatuated
lucky 1
smitten 2
taken

charmer°
roué
siren 2
charming
adorable
attractive
beautiful 1
darling 4
debonair 2
delicious 2
delightful 2
enchanting
engaging
exciting 2
fetching
glamorous 1
idyllic
likeable
lovable
magic 6
nice 1
picturesque 1
pleasant 1, 2
prepossessing
pretty 1
provocative 1
ravishing
spellbinding
suave
sweet 4
taking
tasteful
winning 1
charmingly
beautifully 1
chart°
design 5
plan 2
plot[1] 4
profile 3
schematic 2
scheme 2
table 3
trace 6
charted
schematic 1
charter°
enable 1
hire 2, 3, 4
law 2
lease 2
let[1] 3
licence 1
patent 1
rent[1] 1
reserve 2
warrant 1
chartered
privileged 2
chartered accountant
bookkeeper
charterhouse
monastery
charwoman
servant 1
woman 4
chary
backward 1
careful 1
discreet
distrustful
gingerly 2
leery
reluctant
shy 2
vigilant
wary
Charybdis
eddy 1
chase°
flight[2] 2
follow 4
heel[1] 5
hunt 1, 3
pursue 1, 4
quest 1
run 21
scribe 3
stalk[1]
take 29b
track 6
trail 7

chase away°
at **chase 3**
flight[2] 3
ward 3
chase off
flight[2] 2
ward 3
chasing
pursuit 1
chasm
aperture
breach 3
crevasse
depth 5
gorge 1
gulf 2
pit[1] 3
split 7
chasmal
deep 1
chasmic
deep 1
chassis
figure 1
frame 1
physique
shell 2
chaste°
celibate 2
clean 4
decent 5
flawless 1
good 5
holy 2
immaculate 2
innocent 2
maiden 2
platonic
pristine 2
pure 3
respectable 3
temperate 2
untarnished
virtuous 2
white 3
chasten°
castigate
chastise
correct 3
humble 4
mortify 1
punish 1
shame 6
vituperate
chastened
shamefaced 2
subdued 2
chasteness
purity 2
virtue 2
chastening
lesson 4
punishment 1
punitive
rod 2
shameful
chastise°
call 7b
castigate
chasten 1
correct 3
discipline 8
flog 1
mind 10
pay 5
punish 1
scourge 4
spank
upbraid
whip 1
chastisement
correction 2
discipline 2
lesson 4
punishment 1
rod 2
thrashing 2
tongue-lashing
chastising
punishment 1
chastity°
celibacy 2
honour 4

chastity *(cont.)*
purity 2
virtue 2
chat°
chew 2
communicate 2
conversation
converse
dialogue 1
discuss
discussion
gossip 1
rag[1] 5a
rap 3, 5
rumour 1
talk 2, 4, 15
tête-à-tête 1
word 1
château
castle 2
palace
residence 3
chatelaine
servant 1
chattel
-chattels
belongings
effects
estate 2
furniture 1
gear 4
good 21a
paraphernalia
possession 3
property 1
stuff 2
chatter°
babble 1, 3
converse
drivel 2
gab 1, 2
gibberish,
go 32f
gush 2
jabber 1
jargon 2
palaver 2, 4
patter[2] 2, 3
prattle 1, 2
ramble 3
rattle 6
shiver[1] 2
talk 3, 18
tattle 2
twitter 1, 2
yap 2
chatterbox
gossip 3
chatterer
blabbermouth
chattering
babble 3
chatter 3
prattle 2
chatty
forthcoming 3
talkative
voluble
chat up
approach 3
chat 3
flirt 1
chauffeur
servant 1
chauvinism
jingoism
prejudice 2
chauvinist
nationalistic
patriot
patriotic
chauvinistic
national 2
nationalistic
patriotic
prejudiced 2
CHE
prison
reform school
cheap°
base[2] 3, 5
common 4
economical 1, 2

cheap *(cont.)*
empty 4
flashy 1
garish
gaudy
inexpensive
little 6
mean[2] 1
miserly
near 6
penurious 1
petty 2
plastic 3
pulp 4
shoddy
sleazy 1, 2
small 4
sparing 1
stint 4
tacky[2]
tasteless 1
tawdry
thrifty
tinny 1
worthless 3
-on the cheap°
at **cheap 7**
cheapen
degrade 2
depreciate 1
depress 2
diminish 2
disparage 1
prostitute 2
cheaper than
below 5
cheapjack
pedlar
shoddy
tawdry
cheaply
cheap 5, 6, 7
song 2
cheapskate
miser
stiff 12
cheat°
adventurer 2
beguile 1, 2
chisel 2
clip[2] 4
deceive
defraud
double-cross
dupe 3
fake 4
fiddle 1
fleece
fool 4
fraud 2, 3
gouge 2
hoax 1
hocus-pocus 1
impostor
outsmart
prey 3b
ride 5a
rip 2b
rip-off 2
rob 3
rogue 1
screw 6
slicker 1
sting 4
string 10c
swindle 1
swindler
take 27, 32b
thief 2
trick 8
twister 1
victimize 2
welsher
cheater
fraud 3
welsher
cheating
chicanery
deceit 1
deception 1
dishonest
fraud 1
infidelity 2
rip-off 2

cheating *(cont.)*
swindle 2
trickery
tricky 1

check°
arrest 1, 5
bill[1] 1
bog 2
bond 1
brake 1
bridle 1, 2
catch 8
chain 2
chip 2
contain 3
control 2, 5
crack 1
cranny
curb 1, 2
damage 2
dampen 2
defeat 2
delay 2
deter
deterrent
discipline 4, 7
discomfit 2
embargo 1, 2
examination 1
examine 1
flag[1] 3
foil[1]
follow 11a
frisk 2
frustrate 1
gag[1] 1, 3
govern 2
halt 2
handicap 1, 2
hinder 1, 2
hindrance 1
hold 14a, 15a, 17a
hurdle 1
impede
impediment
inhibit
inhibition
inspect
intercept
interview 4
keep 13
limit 1, 5
look 8, 10
manacle 3
master 8
monitor 3
nip[1] 2
nonplus
observe 2
obstacle
obstruct 1
obstruction 1
offset 2
oppose 2
perusal
preclude
prevent
prevention
prohibit 2
prove 2
put 16b
rebuff 1, 2
reckoning 2
refer 3
rein 1, 3
relax 2
report 6
repress
repression 2
repulse 1
resist 1
restrain 1
restraint 1
scout 1
scrutinize
scrutiny
search 1
set-back,
shackle 2, 4
smother 4
sound[3] 1
spike 3
stalemate
stanch
stay[1] 4, 6

check *(cont.)*
stem[2] 1
stifle 3
stint 2
stop 2
stunt[2]
subdue 3
suppress 2
suppression
tab 2
test 1, 2
thwart 1
trammel 1, 2
traverse 4
trial 1
turn 7
vet
ward 3
whip 2
withhold 1

-checks
bond 1
trammel 1

checked
chequered 1
pent-up

check in°
at **check 6**
come 2
register 6
report 5
research 2

checking
obstruction 2
prevention
service 2
suppression
trial 1

check into°
at **check 7**
look 8
report 6
research 2
sound[3] 1

check-list
specification 2

checkmate
foil[1]
stalemate

check off°
at **check 9**
enumerate 1
flag[1] 3

check out°
at **check 10**
check 3, 5, 8
depart 1
examination 1
examine 1
follow 11a
frisk 2
hunt 2
interview 4
leave[1] 1
look 8, 10
monitor 3
note 11
observe 2
reconnoitre
report 6
research 2
sound[3] 1
spy 2
stack 7a
try 2
vet

check over°
at **check 11**
check 10b
look 10
observe 2

check temporarily
suspend 1

check-up
examination 1
test 1

check up (on)°
at **check 12**
check 3, 8, 10b
examine 1
follow 11a
inspect
monitor 3

check up (on) *(cont.)*
observe 2
reconnoitre
research 2

cheek
assurance 4
brass
disrespect
effrontery
face 5
flippancy 2
gall[1] 2
impertinence
mouth 4
nerve 2
presumption 1
sauce 2

-cheeks
buttocks

cheek by jowl
side 6

cheekiness
flippancy 2
presumption 1
sauce 2

cheeky°
audacious 2
barefaced 2
brash 2
brassy 1
brazen
cocky
disrespectful
flippant 2
foolhardy
forward 2
fresh 8
immodest 2
impertinent
impudent
insolent
irreverent 2
pert 1
presumptuous
pushy

cheep
chirp 1, 2
peep 1, 2
pipe 4
twitter 1, 3

cheeping
twitter 3

cheer°
amuse 2
applaud 1
bear 10b
bliss
clap 1
comfort 1, 2
console
content[2] 4
delight 1
encourage 1
enliven 2
extol
feast 6
flush[1] 3
follow 9
fortify 2
fun 1
gladden
glee
gratify
hail[1] 2
happiness
joy 2
lighten[1] 2
liven 1
merriment
please 1
pledge 3
pull 10
raise 13
reassure
root[3]
solace 1, 2
sparkle 4
spirit 8
whoop 1, 2

-cheers
applause
bottom 6
goodbye

cheer *(cont.)*
ovation
toast 1

cheerful°
blithe 1
breezy 2
bright 8
bubbly 2
buoyant 2
content[2] 3
debonair 2
elevated 3
exuberant 1
gala 2
gay 2
genial
gleeful
happy 1
high 8
hilarious
jaunty 1
jolly 1
joyful 1
light[2] 9
lively 1, 4
mellow 4
merry 1
optimistic
perky
pert 2
playful 1
positive 8
ready 2
sprightly
sunny 2
upbeat
vivacious
warm 3

cheerfully
gaily 2
gladly
happily 2
readily 1
willingly

cheerfulness
cheer 2
exuberance 1
gaiety 1
glee
happiness
hilarity
joy 2
merriment
readiness 1
sparkle 4

cheerily
gaily 2
happily 2

cheeriness
gaiety 3
happiness
radiance 2

cheering
applause
cheerful 2
encouragement 1
exhilarating 2
heart-warming 1
ovation
promising

cheering up
lift 9

cheerio
goodbye

cheerless
bleak 1
broken-hearted
cold 4
dark 3
desolate 3
dingy
dismal
doleful
dour 1
drab
dreary 1
forlorn 1
gloomy 2, 3
grey 2
heavy 6
joyless 1, 2
melancholy 1
moody 1
mournful 1

cheerless *(cont.)*
pessimistic
sombre 1
sunless
tragic
unhappy 1
wintry 3
wretched 2

cheerlessness
melancholy 2

cheer up
brighten 1
cheer 6
console
encourage 1
enliven 2
light[1] 18
lighten[1] 2
pep 2
perk up
raise 13
snap 7
solace 2

cheery
breezy 2
bubbly 2
cheerful 1, 2
gala 2
genial
happy 1
hilarious
jolly 1
lively 1
merry 1
perky
sunny 2

cheesecloth
filter 1

cheesed off
angry 1
discontented
disgruntled
furious 1

cheese off
infuriate

cheese-parer
miser

cheese-paring
cheap 4
close 18
frugal 2
miserly
near 6
penurious 1
petty 2
selfish 2

cheesy
sleazy 2
worthless 3

chef
servant 1

chef-d'oeuvre
gem 2
masterpiece
pièce de résistance
work 4

chemise
shift 6

chemist
druggist
pharmacist

chemist's (shop)
pharmacy 1

cheque
draft 2

chequer
piece 5

chequer-board
chequered 1

chequered°

cherish°
adore 3
appreciate 1
cling 2
esteem 1
harbour 3
love 7
nourish 2
nurse 2
prize[2]
savour 3
treasure 3

cherished
beloved 1
bosom 4
darling 3
dear 1
golden 6
intimate[1] 1
lovable
pet[1] 3
precious 2

cherry
rosy 1

chessman
piece 5

chess-piece
piece 5

chest°
bosom 1
box[1] 1
breast 1
bureau 1
cabinet 1
case[2] 1
casket 1
receptacle
safe 7
trunk 3

chest cold
cold 10

Chesterfieldian
elegant 1

chestnut
cliché
one 5
phrase 2
quip 1

chest of drawers
bureau 1
cabinet 1

chest-on-chest
cabinet 1

chesty
buxom 2

chevy
harass
nag[1] 1
plague 3
pursue 1
pursuit 1
torment 2

chew°
bite 1
crunch 1
gnaw 1
morsel 1
munch
plug 2

chewable
tender[1] 2

chewing-out
lecture 2
piece 10
reprimand 1

chew nails
worry 1

chew on
contemplate 2
speculate 1

chew out°
at **chew 3**
castigate
dress 4
lambaste 2
lecture 4
mind 10
rate[2]
rebuke 1
reprimand 2
scold 1
tell[1] 10
upbraid

chew over°
at **chew 4**
consider 1
contemplate 2
meditate 2
mull
muse
ponder
revolve 3
speculate 1
study 2
weigh 2

chew the fat°
at **chew 2**
chat 2
palaver 5
rap 3
talk 4
chew the rag°
at **chew 2**
chat 2
palaver 5
rap 3
talk 4
chewy
stringy
tough 2
chibouk, chibouque
pipe 2
chic°
becoming
dapper
dashing 2
dressy 1
elegant 2
exclusive 2
exquisite 3
fashionable
flair 2
flash 6
glamorous 2
jaunty 2
modern
new 2
nifty 1
panache
rakish
sharp 9
smart 3
snappy 2
sporty
style 4
stylish
swanky
swell 7
swinging
chicane
deceit 1
deception 1
dodge 4
evasion 2
chicanery°
artifice 1
deceit 1
deception 1
evasion 2
foul play
fraud 1
hanky-panky
hocus-pocus 1
hypocrisy
intrigue 3
swindle 2
trickery
chichi
precious 3
sophisticated 1
stylish
swanky
chick
broad 9
girl 1
woman 3
chicken
coward
faint-hearted 1
spineless 3
timid
weak 3
chicken-feed
pittance
chicken-hearted
cowardly
faint-hearted 1
spineless 3
tame 3
timid
weak 3
chicken-heartedness
cowardice
chicken-livered
cowardly
faint-hearted 1
timid
chicken-scratch
scrawl 1
chicly
beautifully 1
chide
berate
correct 2
lambaste 2
lecture 4
rebuke 1
reprimand 2
scold 1
task 3
tell[1] 10
upbraid
vituperate
chiding
lecture 2
lesson 4
piece 10
rebuke 2
chief°
arch 1
bigwig 1
boss 1
capital 5
cardinal
central 2
director 1
dominant 2
employer 1
essential 2
executive 1
first 1
foremost 1
grand 6
head 2, 9
high 11
lead 18
leader 1
leading 1
main 1
major 1
manager
master 1, 5
monarch 2
overriding
overseer
paramount
predominant
premier 2
prevailing 1
primary 1
prime 2
principal 1, 3
prominent 1
responsible 3
salient
senior
skipper
sovereign 1, 2
staple 1
stellar 2
superintendent
supervisor
supreme 1
chief executive (officer)
executive 1
head 2
premier 1
principal 3
chief honcho
boss 1
director 1
master 1
chiefly°
above 6
especially 2
large 5b
largely
mainly
part 8
primarily 1
principally
rule 4
usually
whole 5
chieftain
chief 1
leader 1
master 1
chifferobe
bureau 1
cabinet 1
chiffon
thin 5
chiffonier
bureau 1
cabinet 1
child°
baby 1
bugger 2
descendant
human 4
innocent 5
issue 7
minor 3
offspring
person 1
tot
youth 2
-children
brood 1
family 2
issue 7
posterity
progeny
seed 3
young 4
youth 3
-with child
expecting
pregnant 1
trouble 9b
childbirth
birth 1
delivery 3
labour 4
childhood°
youth 1
childish°
absurd 1
boyish 2
frivolous 2
immature 2
infantile
juvenile 1
mad 2
puerile
silly 1
young 3
childless
barren 1
sterile 1
childlike°
childish
immature 2
ingenuous 1
innocent 4
naïve
primitive 3
simple 3
unsophisticated 1
young 2
child-minder
minder 1
child's play
painless
picnic 2
pushover 1
chill°
brisk 3
chilly 1, 2
cold 1
cool 1, 7, 9
cutting 1
dampen 2
freeze 1
freezing
frigid 1
icy 1, 2
lukewarm 2
nip[1] 4
raw 5
refrigerate
-chills
shiver[1] 4
chilled
chill 5
cold 2
cool 1
freezing
chilliness
cool 7
chilling
chill 4
cold 3, 4
cool 1
harrowing
icy 1
piercing 3
raw 5
wintry 1, 2
chilly°
aloof 3
bleak 2
brisk 3
chill 4, 6
cold 1, 2, 3
cool 1
frigid 1
icy 1, 2
lukewarm 2
raw 5
stiff 7
stony 2
unapproachable 1
unsocial
wintry 1, 2
chime°
jingle 1, 2
peal 1, 2
ring[2] 1, 3
toll[1] 1, 2
chime in°
at **chime 5**
chip 4b
interrupt 1
chimera
fantasy 2
hallucination
illusion 2
phantom 2
spectre 1
vision 4
chimeric(al)
dreamlike
fanciful 2
groundless
ideal 5
imaginary
insubstantial 2
mythical 2
non-existent
quixotic
romantic 2
shadowy 3
unreal 1
whimsical 1
chiming
chime 2
jingle 2
peal 1
ring[2] 3
toll[1] 2
chimney(-stack)
stack 4
chin
talk 4
china
friend 1
intimate[1] 5
mate 1
pottery
china plate
intimate[1] 5
Chinese fire-drill
zoo 2
chink°
aperture
crack 1
cranny
crevice
flaw 2
gap 1
jingle 1, 2
leak 2
opening 1
rift 2
split 7
chinking
jingle 2
chinless wonder
milksop
chintzy
cheap 3
gaudy
chintzy (*cont.*)
miserly
penurious 1
plastic 3
shoddy
sleazy 1
tacky[2]
worthless 3
chin-wag
chat 1
conversation
discussion
gossip 1
palaver 3, 4
talk 15
chip°
carve 1
check 18
counter 1
crisp 3
flake 1, 2
flaw 2
fragment 1
mark 10
nick 1
shred 1
sliver
splinter 1
-chips
check 10d
-in the chips
flush[2] 3
loaded 4
opulent 1
rich 1
chip in°
at **chip 4**
chime 5b
pitch[1] 5
stump 4
subscribe 2
chip off the old block
take 29a
chipped
jagged
chipper
gay 2
lively 1
sprightly
vivacious
chippie
prostitute 1
chippy
prostitute 1
tart[2] 2
chips and plaice
feature 3
chirography
penmanship
writing 1
chirp°
peep 1, 2
sing 1
twitter 1, 3
chirping
twitter 3
chirpy
lively 1
chirr
chirp 1, 2
peep 2
chirrup
chirp 1, 2
peep 1, 2
twitter 1, 3
chirruping
twitter 3
chisel°
carve 1
chip 3
engrave 1
fleece
gouge 1
sculpture 2
swindle 1
chit
check 17
memorandum
slip[2] 1
chit-chat
chat 1, 2
conversation
chit-chat (*cont.*)
gab 2
gossip 1
jargon 2
palaver 4
patter[2] 2, 3
rumour 1
word 1
chitter
chirp 1, 2
chitty
memorandum
chivalrous°
fearless
gallant 2
genteel 2
heroic 1
manly
noble 4
well-bred
chivalry°
chivvy, chivy
harass
nag[1] 1
pester
plague 3
pursue 1
pursuit 1
torment 2
chlorine
bleach 2
chock
wedge 1
chock-a-block
full 1
loaded 1
packed
replete 1
solid 2
thick 2
chock-full
full 1
loaded 1
packed
replete 1
solid 2
thick 2
chocolate
sweet 9
choice°
alternate 5
alternative 2
appointment 2
capital 6
dainty 3
delicious 1, 2
desirable 3
discretion 2
disposition 4
elect 3
election
elegant 1
élite 2
excellent
exclusive 2
exquisite 1, 5
fancy 3
favoured 1
favourite 1, 2
fine[1] 1
good 2
option 1, 2
outstanding 1
par 3
pick 9
pleasure 2
precious 2
preference 1
prime 2
prize[1] 5
range 2
rare[1] 1, 2
refusal 2
select 2
selection 1, 3
settlement 5
suffrage
superior 2
supreme 4
variation 2
variety 1
vintage 2
volition,
will 2

-by choice
voluntarily
willingly
choice item
titbit
choice of words
phrase 3
wording
choicest
best 3
flower 2
optimum 2
pick 10
superlative
top 8
choir
ensemble 2
choirboy
singer
vocalist
choir girl, member
singer
vocalist
choke°
clog
flood 5
foul 15
gag[1] 2
glut 4
gulp 2
satiate 1
silt 2
smother 1, 2
stifle 1
stop 3
stuff 9
choke back°
at **choke 4**
gulp 2
smother 4
stifle 2
swallow 4
choked
congested
foul 9
overcrowded
silt 2
thick 2
choke down°
at **choke 4**
smother 4
swallow 4
choke-full
full 1
thick 2
choke off°
at **choke 3**
choker
string 4
chokey
jail 1
prison
choking
thick 3
choky
jail 1
prison
choler
anger 1
fury 1
indignation
choleric
bilious
cantankerous
cranky 2
cross 6
embittered
fretful
harsh 3
hasty 4
passionate 3
petulant
pugnacious
quarrelsome
querulous
quick-tempered
snappish 2
sullen
surly
testy
touchy 1
chomp
munch
choo-choo
train 1
choose°
affect[2] 2
appoint 2
assign 3
cast 8
decide 2
designate 2
determine 3
draw 9
elect 1
extract 4
favour 6
fix 15
go 28c
make 23
mind 13
name 5
nominate
pick 1
pitch[1] 7
please 2
plump[2] 3
prefer 1
rather 3
select 1
set 9
settle 2
sift 1
single 4
sort 10b
take 2
vote 4
will 5
wish 1
choosing
choice 1
election
selection 3
volition
choosy°
finicky 1
fussy 1
particular 4
selective
chop°
cleave
cut 17a
hack[1] 1, 3
mangle
sack 3
split 1
-chops
mouth 1
chop away°
at **chop 1**
chop-chop
post-haste
chop down°
at **chop 1**
cut 13a
chop logic
quibble 1
chop-logic
pedantic 2
chop off°
at **chop 1**
cut 4, 15a
lop
sever 1
choppy
rough 2
chop up°
at **chop 2**
cut 17a
mangle
chore
assignment 2
drudgery
duty 1
fag 2
function 1
grind 7
job 2, 3
labour 3
office 4
place 4
post[2] 1
stint 1
task 1
chore (*cont.*)
thing 6
work 3
choreograph
arrange 2
manipulate 1
chorister
singer
vocalist
chortle
chuckle 1, 2
giggle 1, 2
laugh 1, 3
titter 1, 2
chortling
laughter
chorus
ensemble 2
refrain[2]
sing 1
chorus-boy, -girl, -member
singer
vocalist
chosen
elect 2
favoured 1
favourite 2
representative 2
select 2
speak 13
chouse
fool 4
swindle 1
chow
food
meat 1
refreshment 1
scoff[2] 2
sustenance 1
chowhound
glutton
chrestomathy
collection 2
Christ
lord 3
saviour 2
christen°
call 2
designate 4
entitle 2
name 4
tag 4
title 6
Christ-like
pious 1
Christmas card
card 3
chroma
hue
chronic°
habitual 2
nagging
perennial 1
rooted
chronicle°
account 4
calendar 2
describe 1
description 2
diary
document 1, 2
enrol 2
history 5
journal 2
list[1] 2
narrate
narration 1
narrative 1
note 12
recite 2
record 1, 3
register 1, 3
roll[1] 3
saga
story 1
take 31a
tale 1
-chronicles
roll 13
chronicler
narrator
chronicling
narration 1
narrative 2
chronologize
file 3
chronology°
calendar 2
chronicle 1
memoir 2
chronometer
watch 6
chubbiness
fat 5
fatness
obesity
chubby°
beamy
dumpy
fat 1
heavy 11
obese
plump[1] 1
rotund 3
well-fed
chuck
cast 1, 7
dash 2
drop 7
dump 2
fling 1
fly 8a
give 17a
heave 2
hurl
lob 1
pack 6
pitch[1] 1
project 4
sling 1
throw 1, 8, 9b
toss 1
chuck-full
full 1
thick 2
chuckle°
giggle 1, 2
laugh 1, 3
snicker 1, 2
titter 1, 2
chucklehead
dolt
fool 1
chuckling
chuckle 2
laughter
chuck out
dump 2
throw 5a
turf 4
chuffed
elated
glad 1
pleased
chug-a-lug
drink 2
gulp 1
swill 3
chum°
boy 3
brick 2
brother
comrade
friend 1
intimate[1] 5
mate 1
pal 1
playmate
shadow 6
chum around°
at **chum 2**
rub 7
chummy°
familiar 3
friendly 1
sociable
thick 8
chump
dolt
dupe 1
fool 1, 3
loaf[1] 2
mug 3
pushover 2
chump (*cont.*)
sap[1] 2
score 7
sucker
twit[2]
victim 2
-off one's chump
crazy 1
deranged
insane 1
mad 1
psychotic
chum up with°
at **chum 3**
chunder
vomit
chunk
block 1
brick 1
cake 2
clod 1
clump 1
gob
loaf[1] 1
lump[1] 1
mass 3
mouthful
piece 1
portion 1
slab
wad 1
chunky
beamy
bulky
burly
chubby
dumpy
large 1
lumpy
plump[1] 1
stocky
well-fed
Chunnel
tunnel 1
chunter
mutter 2
church
denomination 1
establishment 3
ministry 1
pastoral 3
sacred 3
sanctuary 1
temple
church elders
ministry 2
churchgoing
devout 1
religious 1
churchly
clerical 1
pastoral 3
sacred 3
spiritual 1
churchman, churchwoman
clergyman 1
divine 5
minister 1
pastor
priest
churchyard
graveyard
churl
barbarian 2
gawk 1
peasant
rogue 1
slob
churlish
barbarian 3
brusque
cranky 2
gruff 1
impolite
mean[2] 5
nasty 4
peevish
perverse 2
quick-tempered
rough 3
rude 1
rugged 4
churlish (*cont.*)
snappish 2
sour 4
stern 2
sullen
surly
uncivilized 2
ungracious
churlishness
indelicacy
temper 3
churn
agitate 3
disturb 2
stir 1
swirl 1
churning
agitation 1
churn out
grind 6
run 29b
churr
peep 2
chute°
race[1] 2
waterfall
chutzpah
assurance 4
gall[1] 2
grit
impertinence
impudence
nerve 2
presumption 1
CIA
firm 6
CIA agent
spy 1
ciao
farewell 3
goodbye
cicatrix
scar 1
seam 1
cicerone
adviser
director 2
escort 2
guide 5
pilot 2
teacher
cicisbeo
paramour
suitor
ci-devant
former 1
CID man
detective
cig
fag 5
cigarette
fag 5
ciggy
fag 5
Cimmerian
obscure 1
cinch
breeze 2
girth 2
painless
picnic 2
piece 9
pushover 1
cincture
belt 1
girth 2
ring[1] 1
cinders
embers
cinema
movie 2
cinematic
photographic 2
cinematographer
photographer
cingulum
ring[1] 1
cipher
code 2
cog 2
figure 7

cipher (*cont.*)
nobody 2
non-essential 2
nothing 2
sign 4
zero 1
circa
around 1, 6
say 14
circadian
daily 1
diurnal
everyday 1
Circe
charmer
magician 1
siren 2
temptress
circle°
assembly 1
brotherhood 2
circuit 2
circulate 1
clan 2
clique
coil 2
company 2
crowd 2
cycle 1, 2
encircle
faction 1
fellowship 2
flank 3
fraternity 1
gang 2
garland 2
group 1
halo
lap[2] 1
loop 1, 2
orbit 1, 2
pack 3
revolution 3
revolve 1
ring[1] 1, 3, 4
round 10, 17
school 2
set 26
society 5
street 1
sweep 4
turn 1
union 2
universe 2
wheel 1
world 3
zone
-in a circle
round 23, 27
circlet
crown 1
garland 1
glory 4
ring[1] 1
circuit°
beat 12
belt 2
circulation 1
course 1
girth 1
lap[2] 1
orbit 1
path 2
revolution 3
round 12
run 37
tour 2
turn 26
-in a circuit
round 27
circuitous
circular 2
detour 1
devious 2
diffuse 2
discursive
indirect 1
meandering
oblique 2
rambling 1
round 27
roundabout 1, 2
tortuous 2
-by a circuitous route
round 27
circuitously
round 27
circular°
advertisement 1
insert 2
leaflet
pamphlet
poster
promotion 5
rotund 1
round 1
roundabout 1
-by a circular route
round 27
-circulars
literature 2
circulate°
air 7
announce 1
diffuse 3
disperse 1
distribute 1
flow 1
get 25a
go 21a
issue 10
mingle 2
noise 3
post[1] 2
proclaim 1
propagate 3
put 23e
release 2
report 4
rumour 2
scatter 1
spread 2
swirl 1
circulation°
distribution 2
issue 6
-in circulation
current 2
circumambient
indirect 1
surrounding
circumambulate
circle 3
roam
circumference
circuit 1
girth 1
perimeter
periphery 1
circumferential
peripheral 2
circumjacent
surrounding
circumlocution
gobbledegook 2
circumlocutory
circular 2
diffuse 2
equivocal 1
indirect 1
mealy-mouthed
oblique 2
rambling 1
redundant 2
circumnavigate
circle 3
round 17
circumscribe
bound[1] 2
circle 4
define 1
fence 3
restrict
stake[1] 4b
circumscribed
limited 1
narrow 4
specific 1
circumspect
careful 1
cautious
conscientious 3
discreet
distrust 1
circumspect (*cont.*)
gingerly 2
guarded
judicious
mindful
noncommittal
prudent 1
reluctant
sharp-eyed
thoughtful 3
vigilant
wary
watch 8
circumspection
calculation 3
care 2
caution 2
discretion 1
foresight 1
precaution 2
prudence 1
vigilance
circumspectly
gingerly 1
slow 11
circumstance°
aspect 4
case[1] 1
condition 1
context
development 1
event 1
eventuality
experience 2
factor 1
fortune 3
happening
incident 1
occasion 1
particular 5
place 3
state 1
time 9
-circumstances°
at **circumstance 1**
condition 1, 4
context
environment
fortune 3
place 3, 8
plight
position 4
rank[1] 1
set-up 1
situation 2
state 1
thing 8b
-under any circumstances
possibly 2
rate[1] 5
-under no circumstances
never 1
scarcely 2
shot 11
-under other circumstances
otherwise 1
-under the best of circumstances
ideally 1
circumstantial°
detailed 1
circumvent
avoid
bypass 1
evade 1
foil[1]
get 46a
sidestep
steer 2
circus
ring[1] 2
stadium
cirque
valley
cissified
feminine 2
cissy
coward
feminine 2
milksop
weakling
citadel
castle 1
refuge 1
stronghold
tower 2
citation
accusation
excerpt 1
extract 6
mention 3
passage 2
quotation 1
reference 1
trophy 1
cite
accuse 1
charge 11
detail 5
enumerate 1
excerpt 2
extract 4
indict
mention 1, 3
name 6
quote 1
refer 1
specify
citizen°
brother
denizen
inhabitant
national 3
native 7
resident 3
subject 5
-citizens
population
public 8
citizenry
folk
people 3
population
public 8
citizenship
nationality 1
citrusy
tart[1] 1
city°
local 2
metropolis
municipal
municipality
place 2
town
city-dweller
citizen 2
City of God
paradise 1
cityscape
view 1
city slicker
slicker 1
civic
municipal
political 1
public 2
worldly 1
civics
politics 1
civil°
amicable
attentive 2
ceremonious 2
courteous
debonair 1
fair[1] 8
genteel 2
interior 2
municipal
national 1
neighbourly
obliging
orderly 2
peaceable 2
polite 1
political 1
public 2
respectful
civil (*cont.*)
secular
temporal 1
civil affairs
politics 1
civil disorder
disorder 2
civilian
civil 1
civility°
breeding 2
courtesy
deference 1
etiquette
manner 3
refinement 1
respect 2
-civilities
propriety 3
civilization°
culture 2
society 3
civilize°
educate
refine 2
civilized
civil 3
courteous
cultivated
educated 2
enlightened
orderly 2
polished 2
refined 1
steady 6
suave
civil servant°
at **servant 2**
politician
clack
prattle 2
clad
face 16
cladding
facing
claim°
allegation
application 4
argue 5
argument 2
call 8a
charge 13
declare 1
demand 2
exact 3
maintain 3
prerogative
pretension 1
profess 1
right 9
say 1
state 7
testimony
claimant
pretender
claimed
alleged
claim to fame
speciality 1
clairvoyant
fortune-teller
prophet
psychic 3
seer
clam-bake
picnic 1
clamber
climb 4
scramble 1
clamber up
climb 1
mount 2, 4
scale[3] 3
shin
clamminess
damp 2
clammy°
damp 1
humid
moist 1
muggy
slimy 1
clammy (*cont.*)
sticky 3
sweltering
clamorous
blatant 2
boisterous
chaotic 2
demanding 2
loud 1
noisy
obstreperous
tumultuous
uproarious 1
urgent 2
clamour
blare 2
din 1
disorder 2
jangle 3
mob 3
noise 1
outcry
peal 1
racket 1
roar 3
row[2] 2
uproar
clamouring
outcry
clamp°
brace 3
clasp 3
fasten 1
fix 1
stack 2
clamp down
enforce 1
clam up
hush 1
clan°
fellowship 2
folk
fraternity 3
house 2
kin 1
lineage 2
nationality 2
native 4
people 4
race[2] 1
ring[1] 3
tribe
clandestine
furtive 1
illicit 2
inside 4
mystical 1
oblique 2
private 1
secret 1
stealthy
surreptitious
undercover
underground 2
clandestinely
back 6
incognito 2
private 6
scene 5
secrecy 2
secret 4
secretly
sly 3
clandestineness
privacy 2
secrecy 1
stealth
clang
chime 3
clash 1
jangle 1, 3
peal 1, 2
ring[2] 1, 3
clanger
error 1
flop 4
howler
mistake 1
clanging
chime 2
jangle 3
ring[2] 3
clangorous
noisy

clangour
clash 1
din 1
jangle 3
noise 1
peal 1
clank
clash 1
jangle 1, 3
clanking
jangle 3
clannish
exclusive 2
rarefied 3
sectarian 1
clannishness
fraternity 2
clap°
applaud 1
cheer 7
crack 2
explosion 1
hand 6
noise 1
peal 1
clap in irons
manacle 2
clapper°
rattle 8
clapping
applause
ovation
claptrap
gibberish
hot air
jargon 2
moonshine 2
mouth 3
mumbo-jumbo 1
nonsense 1
prattle 3
raving 3
rot 4
stuff 4
talk 18
wind[1] 2
claque
combination 2
crowd 2
clarification
comment 1
definition 2
demonstration 2
explanation 1
exposition 2
illumination 2
interpretation 1
key 4
light[1] 5
refinement 3
solution 1
clarified
refined 4
clarify°
clear 20, 22, 31a
define 2
explain 1
filter 2
illuminate 2
interpret 1
light[1] 12
purify 1
refine 1
render 8
settle 12
show 1
simplify
solve
sort 10a
spell[3] 2
clarifying
definitive 3
refinement 3
clarion
clear 11
noisy
clarity°
daylight 2
definition 1
purity 1
simplicity 1, 2
clash°
action 6
battle 1
combat 5
compete
conflict 3, 4
disagreement 3
encounter 3, 5
engage 5
faction 2
fall 18
feud 2
fight 1, 7
jangle 1, 3
jar[2] 2
noise 1
quarrel 2
scramble 4
skirmish 1, 2
struggle 5
war 1
clashing
harsh 1
incompatible
mixed 2
odds 4
clasp°
brace 3
brooch
buckle 1
catch 17
clamp 1, 2
clinch 2
cling 3
clip[1] 1, 2
embrace 1
fastening
fix 1
fold 2
grapple 1
grasp 1, 3
grip 1, 6
hold 1, 2, 24
hook 1
hug 1, 3
lock[1] 1, 4
press 5
snap 10
snatch 1
squeeze 5, 7
take 1
class°
assortment 1
bracket 3
bunch 3
caste
categorize
category
circle 2
course 5
degree 1
denomination 2
description 3
distribute 3
division 3
estate 3
family 4
genre
grade 1, 3, 6
group 3
instruction 2
kind[2] 1
label 5
lesson 2
nature 4
nobility 2
order 3
place 16
position 5
range 7
rank[1] 1, 6
rate[1] 4, 6
reckon 2
run 44
sort 1, 8
sphere 2
stamp 8
station 2
stratum 2
stripe 2
tribe
type 1
variety 3
-be in a class with
compare 2
-in a class by itself
rare[1] 2
-in the same class
touch 7
classic°
immortal 3
monumental 1
regular 4
simple 2
standard 6
superb
typical 2
vintage 2
classical°
heroic 5
classics
letter 3
classier
superior 1
classification
assortment 1
bracket 3
breakdown 3
category
class 2
denomination 2
distribution 3
division 3
family 4
identification 2
inclusion
label 2
order 1
organization 1
rate[1] 4
sort 1
stamp 8
type 1
variety 3
classified
advertisement 1
confidential
classify
bracket 4
bunch 3
categorize
certify 2
class 5
coordinate 1
distinguish 2
distribute 3
divide 5
file 3
grade 6
group 3
identify 1
include 2
label 5
order 16
organize 1
place 16
range 7
rank[1] 6
rate[1] 6
separate 2
settle 1
sort 8
stamp 3
tabulate
classifying
denomination 3
identification 2
organization 1
classism
intolerance
classist
intolerant 2
classless
democratic
classmate
pal 1
classroom
hall 2
classy
dapper
dressy 2
exclusive 2
flash 6
classy (*cont.*)
genteel 2
high-class 2
palatial
plush
posh
sharp 9
sporty
stylish
clatter
chatter 2
din 1
jangle 1, 3
rattle 1, 7
claudication
hobble 3
limp[1] 2
clause
amendment 2
phrase 1
provision 2
stipulation
term 4
claw°
lacerate
nail 2
scrape 2
scratch 1
tear 1
clay
dirt 2
earth 2
ground 1
mud
soil[2]
clayey
plastic 1
clay pipe
pipe 2
clean°
brush[2] 4
chaste 1, 2
clarify 2
clean 11a
cleanse 1
clear 19, 20
decent 2
disinfect
empty 6
filter 2
flawless 1
fresh 7
go 34c
gut 4
holy 2
hygienic
immaculate 1
launder 1
neat 1
neaten
order 10a
pick 8c
polish 1
preen 1
pure 2
purge 1
purify 1
refined 4
refurbish
respectable 3
rinse 1
rub 1
sanitary
scour 1
scrape 2
simple 2
spotless 1
spruce 2
square 4
sterilize 1
straighten 3
sweep 1
tidy 1, 4
wash 1
wipe 1
clean-cut
clean 3
trim 2
well-groomed
cleaner
detergent 1
disinfectant
porter[2] 1
servant 1
cleaning
detergent 2
refinement 3
rinse 3
wash 11
cleaning man
servant 1
cleaning woman
servant 1
woman 4
clean-limbed
willowy 2
cleanliness
purity 1
cleanly
clean 2
clear 19
freely 5
cleanness
purity 1
simplicity 2
clean out°
at **clean 10**
exhaust 3
flush[1] 2
gut 5
purge 1
wipe 1
cleanse°
clean 9, 11a
clear 20
disinfect
flush[1] 2
fumigate
launder 1
pound[1] 5
purge 1
purify 1
refine 1
rinse 1
sanctify 2
scour 1
sterilize 1
wash 1
wipe 1
cleansed
clean 2
refined 4
cleanser
detergent 1
disinfectant
clean-shaven
smooth 4
cleansing
detergent 2
refinement 3
rinse 3
wash 11
clean up°
at **clean 11**
edit 2
neaten
pick 8c
profit 5
refurbish
spruce 2
straighten 3
tidy 4
wash 1
wipe 1
clear°
apparent 1
appear 4
bold 3
bright 2
broad 3
clarify 2
clean 11b
clear 31b
coherent 2
conspicuous 1
decided 1
definite 3
defray
direct 9
discernible 1
discharge 6
distinct 1
earn 2
ease 8
easy 1
elementary 1
empty 6, 8
evacuate 1
clear (*cont.*)
evident
excavate 2
excuse 1
explicit 1
express 5
fair[1] 3, 5, 6
fine[1] 2
focus 2
forgive 2
free 10
fresh 7
gain 2
get 3
glaring 1
graphic 1
hard 12
honour 8
hook 5
innocent 1
intelligible
lead 10a
leap 1
legible
let[1] 6b
liquid 3
luminous 3
make 7
manifest 1
navigable 1
negotiate 3
net[2] 2, 4
noticeable 1
observable
obvious
open 9, 13, 22
outright 1
overt
patent 2
pay 1
penetrate 4
perceptible
pictorial 1
plain 2
pleasant 3
positive 1
pound[1] 5
profit 5
pronounced 1, 2
public 4
pure 2
purge 1, 3
purify 2
quit 4
rake[1] 5
realize 3
receive 2
redeem 1
refine 1
self-evident
settle 10, 12
simple 1
smooth 10
stark 4
straighten 1
strong 15
sunny 1
sweep 1
take 22
transparent 1, 2
undisguised
undisputed
unquestionable
vindicate 1
visible 1
vivid 1, 2
void 2, 7
-in the clear°
at **clear 32**
clearance°
discharge 13
excuse 5
pass 24
settlement 4
sweep 5
tolerance 2
way 7
clear away°
at **clear 26**
purge 2
clear-cut
clear 7
concrete
conspicuous 1
cut 29a

clear-cut (*cont.*)
definite 3
distinct 1
evident
express 6
noticeable 1
obvious
overt
positive 1
pronounced 2
public 4
self-evident
specific 1
strong 15
cleared
hook 5
clear-eyed
luminous 3
rational 1
clear-headed
luminous 3
rational 1
sober 2
sound[2] 4
wise 1
clear-headedness
judgement 1
wisdom 1
clearing
excuse 5
field 1
purge 4
settlement 4
clearly°
apparently 1
clear 18
completely 3
definitely
easily 2
entirely 2
evidently 1
expressly 1
far 3
manifestly
naturally 1
notably 1
obviously
ostensibly
practically 2
stark 1
undoubtedly
well[1] 7
clearness
clarity 1
clear off°
at **clear 30**
bugger 5
fly 2
clear out°
at **clear 26**
bugger 5
clean 10b
escape 1
evacuate 1
exhaust 3
flee 1
fly 2
make 26
purge 2
run 2
clear-sighted
wise 1
clear-sightedness
wisdom 1
clear the way
lead 10a
make 41
clear up°
at **clear 22**
clarify 1
explain 1
fix 16c
illuminate 2
interpret 1
resolve 2
settle 3
simplify
solve
sort 10a
square 13
straighten 1
work 19c
cleavage
fracture 2
rift 2
rupture 1
wedge 2
cleave°
attach 5
chop 1
cling 3
cut 15a
disengage
divide 1
embrace 1
follow 2
fracture 3
gash 2
press 5
rend 2
rupture 3
section 4
segment 2
sever 1
snap 1
split 1
stick[1] 5
cleaving
parting 1
cleft
aperture
chink
crack 1
cranny
crevice
flaw 2
gap 1
gash 1
notch 1
opening 1
ravine
rift 1
rip 3
slit 2
split 7, 9
cleft stick
quandary
clemency
forgiveness 2
grace 3
quarter 4
clement
forgiving
merciful
mild 2
clench
hold 2
nail 7
squeeze 5
verify
Cleopatra
charmer
clergy
cloth 2
ministry 2
clergyman°, clergywoman
divine 5
father 4
minister 1
pastor
preacher
priest
-clergymen
ministry 2
cleric
clergyman 1
divine 5
minister 1
preacher
priest
clerical°
pastoral 3
priestly
spiritual 1
clericals
ministry 2
clerk
bookkeeper
salesperson
scribe 1
seller
clever°
able 2
acute 5
clever (*cont.*)
arch 2
artful 2
astute 1
bright 6
brilliant 4
capable 1
comic 1
crafty
cute 2
deep 5
dexterous 2
disingenuous
elegant 4
foxy 1
good 12
great 8
handy 2, 3
imaginative 1
ingenious
intelligent
keen[1] 6
knowing 2
neat 4
nifty 3
penetrating 1
politic 1
quick 4
quick-witted
ready 6
resourceful
sharp 3, 6
shrewd
skilful
slick 3
sly 1
smart 1
subtle 3
tactful
tactical
talented
wily
wise 1
witty
Clever Dick
wise guy
cleverly
handily 2
cleverness
ability 2
art 5
craft 1
dexterity 2
faculty 1
finesse 1
gumption 1
ingenuity
intellect 1
intelligence 1
originality
penetration 2
resource 1
skill 1
tact
wit 1
cliché°
idiom 2
maxim
phrase 2
proverb
saw
truism
clichéd
banal
common 6
musty 2
prosaic
routine 4
stale 2
stock 7
threadbare 2
tired 3
click
snap 2, 5, 8
client°
buyer
customer 1
patron 2
punter 2
regular 12
-be a client
patronize 2
-clients
clientele
clientele°
public 9
trade 4
cliff°
bluff[2] 3
crag
height 3
precipice
climactic
maximum 3
climate°
air 1
atmosphere 2
feel 11
feeling 6
milieu
weather 1
climatic conditions
element 3a
climax°
acme
close 3
consummation 2
crown 5
end 9
head 5
height 2
issue 2
maximum 2
peak 2, 4
pinnacle
showdown
summit
climb°
arise 2
get 45a, 51c
mount 2
reach 5
rise 3, 6, 7, 10, 15
rocket
scale[3] 3
scramble 1, 5
shin
soar 2
top 6
climb along°
at **climb 4**
climb down (from)°
at **climb 5**
descend 1
get 36a, 40a
climber
upstart
climb up°
at **climb 1**
get 51c
mount 2, 4
clime
climate 1
clinch°
clip[1] 1
close 4
confirm 2
determine 1
embrace 4
finalize
finish 2
hug 3
nail 7
ratify
seal 4
squeeze 7
tie 5a
verify
clincher°
cling°
cement 2
hang 7a
harbour 3
hold 19a, 19b
hug 2
persevere
tenacity 2
clinging
tenacious 2, 3
cling together°
at **cling 3**
stick[1] 5
clinic
hospital
infirmary
sanatorium
clink
jail 1
jingle 1, 2
prison
ring[2] 1, 3
stir 7
clinker
dud 1
howler
loser
clinking
jingle 2
ring[2] 3
clip°
brace 3
buckle 1
catch 17
clamp 1, 2
clasp 1, 3
cut 4
diminish 1
embrace 1
fleece
fold 2
hit 1
hook 1
hug 1
jab 2, 4
lop
nip[1] 1
pace 2
pin 2, 3
press 5
prune
punch[1] 1, 2
rate[1] 1
screw 6
shave 1
snip 1
squeeze 5
swipe 3
top 5
trim 3
clipping
cutting 3
extract 6
snip 3
clip someone's wings
foil[1]
clique°
brotherhood 2
cabal 2
camp[1] 2
circle 2
clan 2
combination 2
crowd 2
faction 1
fellowship 2
fraternity 1
gang 2
group 1
junta
machine 3
pack 3
party 3
ring[1] 3
school 2
sect 2
set 26
world 3
cliquish
rarefied 3
sectarian 1
clishmaclaver
gossip 1
palaver 2
patter[2] 2
cloaca
drain 1
cloak°
camouflage 1, 2
cape[2]
cover 15
envelop 2
mantle 1, 2, 3
mask 2
muffle 1
obscure 6
cloak (*cont.*)
pretence 2
pretext 1
robe 1, 3
screen 3
secrete[1]
semblance 2
shroud 1, 3
spread 7
submerge 3
veil 1, 2
wrap 4
clobber
batter 1
beat 1
clothes
effects
equipment
furniture 2
gear 3
hit 1
light[2] 14
manhandle
paraphernalia
pelt[1] 1
pound[1] 1
rout 2
rubbish 3
slaughter 4
stuff 2
tackle 1
thing 8c
whip 2
clock
face 1
mug 2
watch 6
clock off
knock 5
clock on
come 2
report 5
clock-watcher
idler
clockwise
forward 4
clockwork
measured 4
works 2
clod°
barbarian 2
boor 2
clown 2
clump 1
dolt
fool 1
gawk 1
hulk 2
lump[1] 1
peasant
robot 2
silly 3
wad 1
cloddish
clumsy
dull 1
obtuse 2
opaque 3
provincial 2
rustic 2
slow 7
unrefined 1
cloddishness
simplicity 4
clodhopper
boor 2
clod 2
clown 2
gawk 1
peasant
rustic 3
clod-like
dull 1
stolid
clodpate
fool 1
clodpole
fool 1
clog°
block 5
bog 2
choke 2
foul 15

clog (*cont.*)
glut 3
hamper[1]
jam 2
obstruct 1
plug 4
silt 2
stop 3
stuff 9
clogged
foul 9
silt 2
cloister
isolate
monastery
cloistered
isolated 2
reclusive
secluded 1
separate 7
solitary 1
cloister oneself
retire 1
clone
double 7
duplicate 2, 3
image 2
look-alike
reproduction 2
spit 2
twin 1
clonk
thud
Clootie
devil 1
close°
about 2
adjust 4
area 5
bosom 4
by 6
chummy
clammy 2
clasp 3
close 5, 8a, 8b
compact 3
completion 1
cramped
dense 1
enclosure 1
end 2, 9
equivalent 1
expiration
expire 1
faithful 2
familiar 3
fast[1] 5
fight 1
fill 7
fine[1] 13
finish 5, 9
fold 3
forthcoming 1
friendly 1
frugal 2
gain 4
great 10
greedy 3
halt 1
hand 9
handy 1
hard 1
imminent
impending
intimate[1] 1
kindred 1
let[1] 8d
like[1] 1
lock[1] 4
mean[2] 1
miserly
muggy
narrow 2, 3, 6, 7
near 1, 4, 5, 6, 7, 8
nearby 2
nice 3
old 8
oppressive 2
particular 3
personal 3
petty 2
plug 4
point-blank 2
present[1] 2
rigid 3

close (*cont.*)
round 18
run 30a
seal 3
secretive
serried
shut 1, 4c
small 4
sparing 1
special 5
sticky 3
stop 3, 6
strict 1
stuffy 1
sultry 1
sweltering
termination 1
thick 8
tight 6
tighten 4
touchy 2
wall 5
warm 6
wind[1] 8
close at hand
convenient 2
imminent
near 1
nearby 1
ready 7
wind[1] 8
close by°
at **by 6**
about 1, 9
available
close 20
forthcoming 1
hand 9
handy 1
imminent
local 1
near 1, 5
nearby 1
closed
close 10
exclusive 2
impermeable
over 6
secure 2
select 3
shut 7
unopened
-behind closed doors
private 6
closed-minded
prejudiced 2
closed off
separate 7
close down°
at **close 5**
close 8a
fail 4
fold 3
halt 2
knock 5
shut 2
sign 9
wind[2] 4a
close-fisted
avaricious
close 18
economical 2
frugal 2
grasping
greedy 3
mean[2] 1
miserly
near 6
penurious 1
petty 2
small 4
sparing 1
thrifty
tight 5
close-fistedness
avarice
greed 2
thrift
close-fitting
tight 1
close in
enclose 1
gain 4

close in (*cont.*)
stake[1] 4
close-knit
close 15
close-lipped
taciturn
tight-lipped
closely
exactly 1
fast[1] 8
hand 10
immediately 2
intently
literally 1
narrowly 2
nearly 2
tight 10, 11
tightly
well[1] 13
closely guarded
close 16
closely-knit
compact 1
close-matched
close 13
close-minded
hidebound
intolerant 2
narrow-minded
near-sighted 2
one-sided 1
parochial
rigid 4
small-minded
close-mindedness
fanaticism 2
close-mouthed
close 17
mum 1
reserved
secretive
silent 2
tight-lipped
closeness
affinity 1
familiarity 2
fraternity 2
friendship 1
harmony 2
presence 1
proximity
sympathy 2
close off°
at **close 6**
block 3
close 1
plug 4
seal 3
shut 4c
stake[1] 4
stop 3
wall 5
close on°
at **close 21**
close one's eyes to°
at **close 7**
close out
lock[1] 8
wind[2] 3a
close-packed
thick 2
close quarters
clinch 2
close shave°
at **shave 3**
closest
immediate 2
present[1] 2
special 5
closet
stealthy
toilet 1
wardrobe 2
-out of the closet
out 3
public 11
close to°
at **close 21**
about 2, 6
approximately
beside 1

close to (*cont.*)
by 1
fast[1] 8
like[1] 1
near 2, 3, 9
nearly 1
neighbourhood 2
ready 4
towards 3
close up°
at **close 8**
adjust 4
bar 8
close 1, 5
fail 4
fold 3
halt 2
plug 4
seal 3
stop 3
wind[2] 4a
closing
expiration
final 1
finish 9
last[1] 4
net[2] 3
parting 3
terminal 1
clot
coagulate
dolt
lump[1] 1
set 3
silly 3
solidify 1
stiffen 1
thicken
cloth°
fabric 1
filter 1
good 21d
material 2
ministry 1, 2
pall[1] 1
clothe°
cover 5
dress 1
equip
get 51e
mantle 3
put 22a
robe 3
-be clothed in
have 2a
wear
cloth-eared
insensible 2
clothes°
apparel
costume
dress 1, 5a
ensemble 1
garments
gear 3
habit 3
outfit 2
rag[1] 3
suit 3
thing 8c
wardrobe 1
wear 8
clothes-brush
brush[2] 1
clothes-cupboard
wardrobe 2
clothes-horse
dandy 1
swell 6
trendy 2
clothes-peg
peg 1
clothes-press
wardrobe 2
clothier
tailor 1
clothing
apparel
clothes
costume
ensemble 1
garments

clothing (*cont.*)
gear 3
habit 3
outfit 2
rag[1] 3
robe 2
suit 3
thing 8c
turnout 3
wardrobe 1
wear 8
clothing business
rag[1] 4
clotted
thick 2, 5
cloud
dull 10
fade 1
film 3, 4
flight[1] 4
fog 1, 3
mist 1, 2
muddy 4
obscure 7
reek 4
shade 12
shadow 4
shroud 3
swarm 1
vapour 1
-in the clouds
absent-minded
dreamy 2
forgetful
inattentive
cloudburst
downpour
rain 1
storm 1
cloud-cuckoo-land
fairyland
Utopia
-in cloud-cuckoo-land
forgetful
clouded
black 7
dim 1
dull 5
filmy 2
inauspicious
murky
nebulous
obscure 1
opaque 1
overcast
steamy 2
vague 1
woolly 2
cloudiness
blur 1
gloom 1
obscurity 1
cloud-land
fairyland
-in cloud-land
forgetful
cloudless
bright 2
clear 1, 23
fair[1] 5
fine[1] 2
pleasant 3
sunny 1
cloud nine
transport 5
-on cloud nine
ecstatic
elated
exalted 3
exuberant 2
exultant
happy 1
joyful 2
overjoyed
pleased
radiant 2
rapturous
world 7
cloud over
fade 1
fog 5

cloud over (*cont.*)
mist 2
cloud up
fog 5
mist 2
cloudy
dark 5
dim 1
dull 5
filmy 2
gloomy 1
grey 2
hazy 1
heavy 9
imprecise
inauspicious
misty
murky
obscure 1
opaque 1
overcast
steamy 2
vague 1
woolly 2
clough
ravine
clout
batter 1
beat 1
blow[2] 1
box[2] 2, 3
clip[2] 3, 6
effect 2
hit 1
hold 26
influence 1
knock 9
might 2
power 2
pull 21
punch[1] 1, 2
rag[1] 1
rap 4
say 12
slap 1, 4
strike 1
weight 3
clover
-in clover
money 4
opulent 1
prosperous 1
rich 1
wealthy
clown°
boor 2
clod 2
comedian
fool 2
joker 1
wag[2]
zany 2
clown about°
at **clown 3**
clowning
fun 2
nonsense 2
clownish
boorish
zany 1
cloy
glut 4
pall[2] 2
satiate 1
cloyed
jaded 2
cloying
excessive 2
gooey 2
gushy
sickly 3
sweet 7
club°
beat 1
brotherhood 2
cabal 2
cabaret 1
dive 3
fellowship 2
fraternity 1, 3
gang 3
group 1
hit 1

club (*cont.*)
league 1
party 3
society 5
staff 1
strike 1
union 2
-in the club
expecting
pregnant 1
clubbable
friendly 2
clubbiness
fellowship 3
friendship 1
clubby
friendly 1
clubhouse
club 3
club soda
fizz 4
club together°
at **club 6**
clue°
conception 2
evidence 3
hint 1,3
idea 2
index 2
indication 1
inkling
key 2
lead 14
line[1] 10
note 6
sign 3
symptom
tip[3] 2
trace 1
-clues
indication 4
clue someone in°
at **clue 2**
clump°
bunch 1
huddle 1
lump[1] 1
plump[2] 4
clumsily
roughly 3
clumsiness
embarrassment 1
ineptitude 1
clumsy°
amateur 2
artless 3
awkward 1
heavy 8
heavy-handed 1
hefty 1
hulking
incompetent
inept 1
lame 2
left-handed 1
ponderous 1
rude 4
shambling
stilted
tactless
thumb 2
ungraceful 1
unwieldy
wooden 2
clunk
bump 1
plump[2] 4
thud
cluster°
bunch 1,2,4
centre 2
clump 2
concentrate 3
crowd 3
gather 2
herd 1
huddle 1,3
knot 2
mass 8
pocket 3
press 7,8
clutch°
bunch 2
clasp 5
cling 3
cluster 1
embrace 4
grab 1,4
grapple 1
grasp 1
grip 1,6
hang 7a
hold 1,2,19a,24
lock[1] 4
pluck 4
seize 1
snatch 1,4
squeeze 5,7
take 1
-clutches°
at **clutch 2**
grasp 3
hand 8
jurisdiction
mesh 2
sway 4
clutter°
disorder 1
jumble 2
litter 4
lumber 1
mess 1
welter 1
cluttered
disorderly 1
untidy
clutter up°
at **clutter 3**
mess 5c
coach°
brief 6
carriage 1
discipline 6
drill 2
educate
enlighten
groom 4
ground 6
initiate 3
instruct 1
instructor
prime 5
school 4
teach
teacher
train 1,4
tutor 1,2
coaching
instruction 2
coachman
servant 1
coadjutor
aide
ally 1
coagulate°
cake 3
jell 1
set 3
solidify 1
stiffen 1
thicken
coagulated
thick 5
coal-black
black 1,3
pitch-black
swarthy
coalesce
blend 2
combine 3
compound 2
fuse
incorporate
integrate
merge
mix 1
unify
unite 1
wed 2
coalesced
united 1
coalescence
amalgamation
merger
synthesis
coalescence (*cont.*)
wedding 2
coalescing
amalgamation
wedding 2
coalfield
mine 1
coalition
alliance 1
association 1
combination 2
federation
fellowship 2
league 1
merger
organization 3
party 3
ring[1] 3
union 1,2
coarse°
animal 4
barbarian 3
base[2] 4
bawdy
beastly 1
blue 2
boorish
brassy 1
broad 8
brutal 2
crude 3
dirty 2
earthy
filthy 3
foul 5
gross 3
harsh 1
heavy 8
homespun
immodest 1
impolite
indecent 2
irregular 1
lascivious 2
low[1] 3
nasty 3
obscene 1
plebeian 2
primitive 2
profane 3
prurient 2
racy 2
rough 1,3
rude 1
rudimentary 2
scurrilous
sexy 2
tactless
tasteless 1
uncivilized 2
ungraceful 2
unrefined 1,2
unseemly 1
vulgar 1
wicked 3
coarse language
profanity
coarseness
incivility
indelicacy
ribaldry
vulgarity 1
coast°
beach 1
cruise 1
drift 1
glide
roll 3
sail 3
sea-coast
slide 1
coastline
coast 1
sea-coast
coat°
cloak 1
cover 3
face 16
film 1,4
glaze 1
paint 2,5
pelt[2]
plaster
coat (*cont.*)
plate 4,6
powder 4
sheet 5
skin 2
smear 1
spread 7
wash 7,15
coating
coat 2
exterior 3
facing
film 1
foil[2]
glaze 2
icing 1
paint 2
peel 4
plate 4
scale[2] 2
sheet 5
skin 2
wash 15
coat of arms
device 3
seal 1
stamp 7
symbol
coat-rack
rack 1
stand 17
coax°
cajole
drag 2
entice
flatter 3
get 14,46b
induce 1
lure 1
motivate
prompt 3
tease 2
tempt 1
urge 3
wheedle
work 18
coaxing
cajolery
enticement 1
temptation 1
cobber
comrade
friend 1
cobblers
drivel 3
gobbledegook 1
nonsense 1
rot 4
rubbish 2
trash 1
wind[1] 2
cobweb
web
cobwebby
filmy 1
cochlear
spiral 2
cochleate
spiral 2
cock
flannel 1
stack 2
tap[2] 1
cock-a-hoop
ecstatic
exultant
happy 1
overjoyed
Cockaigne
Utopia
cockamamie
daft 1
stupid 2
cock-and-bull story
fabrication 3
falsehood
fib 1
lie[1] 2
myth 2
yarn 2
cock a snook at
defy 1
disobey
fly 6
jeer 1
mock 1
scorn 3
snap 6
thumb 8
Cockayne
Utopia
cock crow
dawn 1
morning 1
-at cock crow
early 3
cocker
coddle
friend 1
pamper
pet[1] 5
spoil 3
cock-eyed
daft 1
lopsided 1
mistaken 2
nonsensical
one-sided 2
stupid 2
cockiness
vanity 1
cocklebur
thorn 1
cocksure
cocky
confident 2
impudent
opinionated 1
overconfident 1
proud 2
cocktail lounge
bar 6
lounge 4
pub
cock-teaser
flirt 3
cock up
bugger 3
fluff 4
cock-up
flop 4
cocky°
confident 2
impudent
inflated 1
overconfident 1
proud 2
pushy
vain 1
co-conspirator
accessory 2
accomplice
sympathizer
coconut
head 1
cocotte
prostitute 1
coddle°
baby 2
cater 2
dote
favour 7
humour 4
indulge 2
make 34b
mother 6
nurse 2
pamper
pet[1] 5
spoil 3
coddled
hothouse 2
code°
etiquette
institution 4
law 2
legend 3
notation 2
precept 1
principle 2
regulation 2
symbol
code of behaviour
etiquette
protocol 1
code of practice
institution 4
code word
symbol
codicil
supplement 1
codification
distribution 3
embodiment 2
order 1
organization 1
codify
coordinate 1
embody 3
form 7
formulate 1
order 16
organize 1
separate 2
standardize
tabulate
codifying
organization 1
codswallop
drivel 3
fiddlesticks
flannel 1
gab 2
gibberish
gobbledegook 1
jargon 2
rot 4
rubbish 2
stuff 4
trash 1
coed
miss[2]
coenobite
monk
coequal
equal 1
even 5
parallel 1,2
peer[1] 2
coequality
equality 1
parallel 3
coerce
blackmail 2
drive 1
enforce 2
extort
force 7
hustle 4
make 2
oblige 2
pin 4a
pressure 5
push 4,7
railroad 2
require 1
screw 4
shame 7
twist 6
coercion
duress 1
force 2
pressure 4
coercive
compulsive
forcible 2
coetaneous
contemporary 1
coeval
contemporary 1
current 1
coevality
coincidence 1
coexistent
contemporary 1
coextension
coincidence 1
coextensive
even 2
join 4
coffee-break
break 28
coffee-shop
café

coffer
box[1] 1
casket 1
chest 1
safe 7
trunk 3
coffin°
casket 2
coffin-nail
fag 5
cog°
gear 1
cogency
force 4
strength 7
cogent
concise
eloquent 1
forceful 2
good 8
persuasive
potent 2
solid 7
strong 8
cogitate
consider 1
contemplate 2
deliberate 4
meditate 1
mull
muse
ponder
reflect 3
speculate 1
think 3
cogitating
preoccupied 1
reflective
thought 1
cogitation
consideration 3
debate 2
reflection 2
speculation 2
thought 1
cogitative
meditative
pensive
philosophical 2
preoccupied 1
reflective
speculative 1
thinking 1
cognate
kin 2
kindred 2
like[1] 1
related 1, 2
cognition
brain 1
knowledge 1
cognitive
mental 1
psychic 1
psychological
cognizable
sensible 2
cognizance°
device 3
familiarity 1
notice 3
realization 1
recognition 2
cognizant
alive 2
appreciate 3
aware 1
familiar 4
know 5
knowledgeable 1
mind 9
privy 2
sensible 4
cog-wheel
gear 1
cohere
bond 4
cement 2
hang 11b
stick[1] 5
coherence
connection 2
integrity 2
coherence *(cont.)*
sense 4
union 4
coherent°
hang 11b
logical 3
organic 3
cohesive
tenacious 2
cohesiveness
tenacity 2
cohort°
accomplice
aide
attendant 2
corps
friend 2
henchman
mate 1
partner 1
coiffure
hairdo
coil°
coil 1
entwine
garland 2
kink 1
loop 1, 2
meander 2
roll 9
spiral 1
tangle 1
turn 11, 28
twirl 3
twist 7
wind[2] 1, 2
coiled
spiral 2
coin°
change 4
forge 2
form 8
generate 4
invent 1
make 39c
mint 2
money 1
originate 1
token 1
turn 8
-coins
change 4
money 1
coinage
neologism
coincide°
accord 1
agree 1
check 5
conform 2
converge
correspond 1
join 4
overlap 2
parallel 4
tally 1
tie 6a
coincidence°
equality 2
resemblance
coincident
simultaneous
coincidental°
contemporary 1
unpremeditated
coinciding
simultaneous
coin it in°
at coin 4
rake[1] 4
coin of the realm
cash 1
coinstantaneity
coincidence 1
coition
intercourse 2
sex 2
coitus
intercourse 2
relation 6a
sex 2
col
pass 23
cola
pop 5
colander
filter 1
riddle[2] 3
screen 4
cold°
bare 2
biting
bitter 6
bleak 2
brisk 3
callous
chill 1, 2, 4, 6
chilly 1, 2
cold-hearted
cool 1, 3, 4, 5
cutting 1
dead 4
distant 3
dour 1
freezing
frigid 1, 2, 3
glassy 2
hard 4, 8
heartless
hostile 2
icy 1
impassive
impersonal 2
inaccurate
inanimate
indifferent 1
inhospitable 1
lackadaisical 2
mechanical 3
merciless
nail 4b
negative 2
phlegmatic 1
piercing 3
raw 5
rigour 1
rocky[1] 3
severe 2, 5
stark 2
stiff 7
stony 2
tough 6
unaffected[2]
unapproachable 1
unenthusiastic
unsocial
unsympathetic
wintry 1, 2
-in a cold sweat
panic-stricken
cold-blooded°
brutal 1
chill 6
cold 3
cool 3, 4
cruel 1
cutthroat 2
deadly 3
deliberate 1
heartless
impassive
inhuman 1
strict 2
cold-bloodedness
barbarity
sang-froid
severity 1
cold cash
money 1
cold feet
dread 2
cold-hearted°
callous
cold 3
cold-blooded 2
cool 3, 4
cutthroat 2
frigid 2
stony 2
coldish
chilly 1
coldly
severely 3
coldness
chill 1
cold 9
indifference 1
nip[1] 4
severity 2
slight 8
cold shoulder
brush-off
cut 23
disregard 2
rebuff 1
rejection
repulse 3
slight 8
cold-shoulder
neglect 1
ostracize
shoulder 2
shun
slight 5
spurn
cold water
discourage 2
pall[1] 2
colic
gripe 3
coliseum
stadium
theatre 1
collaborate°
ally 2
cooperate 1
league 3
string 10a
team 3
collaborating
league 2
collaboration
cooperation 1
collaborative
joint 4
united 2
collaborator
accessory 2
accomplice
ally 1
associate 3
partner 1
subversive 2
sympathizer
collapse°
break 16c
breakdown 1, 2
buckle 2
cave 2a
crash 5
decay 3
destruction 3
disrepair
dissolution 1
dissolve 2
downfall
drop 6
failure 2
faint 3, 4
fall 2, 7, 11a, 12, 14, 24, 26
fate 2
fizzle 2
flake 3a
flop 1
fold 3
founder[2] 2, 3
give 9
go 12, 27c, 38b
loss 5
miscarriage
naught
overthrow 2
pass 20a
plump[2] 1
prostration 4
rout 1
ruin 1
shock 2
sink 2
slump 1, 2
topple 1, 3
undoing 1
wall 4
way 11a
collapsed
flat 3, 6
collapsing
dead 9
collar
arrest 2, 4
capture 1, 2
catch 1
get 8
grab 3
hook 6
nab
nick 4
pick 8h
pinch 4
pull 11b
ring[1] 1
run 27
seize 2
collate
compile
separate 2
collateral
extra 1
indirect 2
pawn[1] 3
pledge 2
security 3
collateralize
secure 6
collation
meal 1
colleague°
accessory 2
accomplice
acquaintance 2
aide
associate 2
brother
chum 1
companion 1
comrade
equal 4
fellow 2
friend 2
intimate[1] 5
mate 1
member
partner 1
peer[1] 2
collect°
accumulate
amass
assemble 1, 2
bunch 4
bundle 2
call 4, 8b
clump 3
cluster 3
compile
concentrate 3
crowd 5
derive 1
earn 2
embody 3
flock 2
gain 1
garner
gather 1, 2
get 1, 50a
group 4
harvest 2, 3
heap 3
herd 3
hoard 2
lump[1] 3
mass 8
meet[1] 2
muster 1
pick 2, 8b, 8i
pile[1] 5, 10
pool 4
raise 5, 12
rake[1] 1, 3, 8
receive 1
round 19
scare 2
stack 6
store 1
win 2
collectable
antique 2
rare[1] 2
-collectables
bric-à-brac
collected°
cool 2
deliberate 3
equable 1
level-headed
nonchalant
sedate 1
self-contained 1
self-possessed
serene 2
sober 2
unmoved
collectible
see **collectable**
collecting
accumulation 1
collection 1
collection°
accumulation 3
assortment 2
batch 2
bunch 2
bundle 1
cluster 1, 2
embodiment 2
ensemble 3
flock 1
group 2
heap 1
herd 1
hoard 1
kitty
knot 2
lot 1
mass 1
medley
mob 1
pack 3
parcel 3
pile[1] 1
pool 2
post[3] 1
pot-pourri
range 2
redeem 3
repertory
round-up 1
scrapbook
selection 2
set 25
stack 3
store 3
suite 1
variety 1
collective
common 5
joint 4
public 1
social 1
united 1, 2
collector°
editor
vintage 3
collector's item
antique 2
rarity 1
colleen
girl 1
lass
miss[2]
college
institution 2
school 1
seminary
collegiate
academic 1
collide°
bump 3
compete
collide with°
at **collide 2**
bump 3
hit 3
impact 3
ram 2
run 26d
strike 3
colliery
mine 1
collision°
bump 1
clash 2
hit 10
impact 1

collision (*cont.*)
pile-up 1
collocation
phrase 2
collocution
phrase 2
colloid(al) solution
combination 3
solution 3
collop
slice 1
colloquial
informal 3
verbal 1
vernacular 2
colloquialism
phrase 2
colloquium
conference
parley 1
colloquy
chat 1
conference
conversation
dialogue 1, 2
discussion
palaver 3
parley 1
rap 5
talk 15
collude
league 3
plot[1] 3
collusion
conspiracy
intrigue 3
-in collusion
hand 10
league 2
collusively
hand 10
collyrium
wash 13
collywobbles
dread 2
Colonel Blimp
reactionary 2
colonist
emigrant
newcomer 1
pioneer 1
settler
colonization
settlement 2
colonize
inhabit
people 5
populate
settle 6
colonnade
portico
colony
possession 2
settlement 1
colophon
device 3
sign 4
stamp 7
symbol
coloration
camouflage 1
colossal°
big 1
enormous
gigantic
great 1, 11
heroic 4
huge
immense
large 3
massive
monolithic
monstrous 3
monumental 2
prodigious 1
splendid 3
thumping 1
towering 2
vast
weighty 1
whopping 1
colosseum
stadium
colossus
giant 1
statue
colour°
bias 4
blush
distort 2
drift 4
flesh 6
flush[1] 1, 4
form 3
garble 1
glow 6, 7
hue
make 34a
maximize 2
misrepresent
nature 4
overstate
paint 1, 6
prejudice 3
pretext 1
romance 4
shade 2
slant 5
spice 2
stain 3
timbre
tint 1, 3, 4
tone 2, 4
twist 2
-colours°
colour 2
decoration 2
pennant
-off colour°
blue 2
broad 8
dirty 2
foul 5
improper 3
nasty 3
naughty 3
obscene 1
par 5b
profane 3
racy 2
rank[2] 3
risqué
sexy 2
spicy 2
suggestive 2
vulgar 2
colourant
tint 2
coloured
black 2
jaundiced 1
opinionated 2
colourful
brave 2
dramatic 3
gorgeous 1
jaunty 2
juicy 2
picturesque 1, 2
vivid 1
colourfully
gaily 1
colourfulness
gaiety 3
romance 4
colouring
camouflage 1
cast 6
paint 1
stain 3
style 5
tint 1, 2
tone 2, 4
touch 15
twist 9
colourless°
dead 10
drab
dreary 2
grey 1
lacklustre
lifeless 3
literal 3
matter-of-fact
mechanical 3
colourless (*cont.*)
monotonous
mousy 1
neutral 2
nondescript
pale[1] 1
pedestrian 2
plain 4
sober 3
stodgy
tedious
vapid
wan 1
washed out 1
wooden 2
colourlessness
tedium
colporteur
pedlar
seller
coltish
frisky
frolicsome
jolly 1
playful 1
sportive
column
corps
editorial
feature 2
file 2
leg 2
line[1] 6
parade 1
pier 2
pillar 1
post[1] 1
procession 1
queue 1
rank[1] 4
shaft 1
spire 1
stake[1] 1
standard 4
support 8
train 3
upright 3
writing 2
columnist
editor
journalist
reporter
scribe 2
writer
coma
fog 2
stupor
comate
hairy 1
comatose
dormant 1
lethargic 1
senseless 1
unconscious 1
comb
rake[1] 2, 6
ransack 1
rummage 1
scour 2
search 1
valley
combat°
action 5
battle 1, 3
conflict 1
contest 2
engage 5
engagement 5
fight 1, 7
hostility 2
oppose 1
resist 1
rival 2
skirmish 1
tilt 4
war 1
withstand
-in combat
war 2
combatant
champion 3
militant 2, 3
pugilist
combating
militant 2
combative
aggressive 1
argumentative
belligerent 2
hostile 3
militant 1
offensive 1
pugnacious
quarrelsome
strong 16
truculent
warlike
combativeness
aggression 1
combe
valley
comber
roller 2
surge 2
wave 1
combination°
alliance 1
alloy 1
amalgam
amalgamation
arrangement 2
band[2] 2
blend 3
chain 1
composition 2, 3
compound 5
cross 2
embodiment 2
ensemble 2
federation
hybrid
junction
league 1
match 3
medley
merger
mix 7
mixture 1, 2
package 2
ring[1] 3
set 25
synthesis
system 1
tissue
union 1
unity 3
wedding 2
combine°
add 1, 2
ally 2
amalgamate
associate 1a
association 1
blend 1
bracket 4
cement 2
club 6
combination 2
compound 1, 2
couple 3
embody 3
fuse
gang 3
incorporate
integrate
join 1
knit 1
league 3
lump[1] 3
marry 2
match 5
merge
mingle 1
mix 1, 3
organization 3
package 3
pool 3, 4
sort 8, 9
tack 5
team 3
twin 3
unify
unite 1
weave 2
wed 2
weld 1
combined
affiliated
general 3
joint 4
united 1
combining
addition 1
confusion 4
mixture 2
synthesis
union 1
wedding 2
combo
band[2] 2
ensemble 2
combustible
flammable
fuel 1
inflammable
live 4
come°
appear 1
arrive 1
collect 1
emanate 1
enter 1
fall 1
flow 3
get 9, 10
hop 2
intervene 2
originate 2
proceed 2
pull 11a
result 2
run 12
set 19
show 7
stem[1] 3
turn 20e
-to come
before 3
future 2
impending
come about°
at **come 4**
chance 7
come 19a
develop 4
go 32b
happen 1
occur 1
pass 13
place 14
result 2
tack 6
transpire 2
come a cropper
misfire 1
strike 17a
come across°
at **come 5**
bump 4
come 16a
find 1
light[2] 15
locate 2
meet[1] 1, 3
penetrate 4
run 20
strike 14
stumble 3
turn 25c
unearth
come after
follow 1
succeed 1
come again
recur
come along°
at **come 6**
shape 10b
come and go
swing 1
come apart°
at **come 7**
break 1
collapse 4
decompose 1
disintegrate
fragment 3
give 9
grief 3
separate 1
come apart (*cont.*)
split 1
come around
come 18b
revive 1
snap 7
come around with
serve 3
come at°
at **come 8**
come back
get 32a
reply 1
respond 1
retort 2
retrieve 1
return 1, 2
revert
comeback
answer 1
rebound 2
rebuttal
recovery 1
reply 2
response
retort 1
revival 3
squelch 2
come before
precede
come between
intervene 2
come by°
at **come 9**
acquire
buy 1
drop 12
finger 5b
gain 1
get 1, 2, 11
inherit
obtain 1
pick 8e
possess 5
procure 1
receive 1
scare 2
secure 5
come clean°
at **clean 8**
card 14
confess
talk 5
come close (to)
approach 1, 2
approximate 2
draw 13b
halt 2
near 10
touch 7
verge[1] 3
comedian°
card 11
clown 1
fool 2
joker 1
riot 2
wag[2]
wit 3
zany 2
comedo
pimple
spot 5
come down
descend 1
fall 1, 3
get 36a
land 5
light[2] 13
pelt[1] 2
rain 4
sag 2
settle 5
taper 1
teem[2]
come down in buckets
pour 3
rain 4
teem[2]

commandment *(cont.)*
precept 1
comme ci, comme ça
fair[1] 4
so so
comme il faut
correct 6, 7
fitting 1
proper 1, 3
seemly 1
tasteful
commemorate°
immortalize
keep 10
memorialize
observe 5
remember 2
commemorated
go 27d
commemoration
celebration 1
feast 2
festival 1
monument 1
occasion 3
commemorative
ceremonial 1
memorial 1
monumental 3
triumphal
commence°
begin 1, 3
break 17
dawn 4
develop 4
embark 2
enter 4
fall 21
inaugurate 1
initiate 1
institute 4
lead 8
move 12a
open 20
rise 17
start 1, 2, 4
strike 18
commencement
beginning 1, 2
conception 1
dawn 2
entrance[1] 4
first 6
infancy 2
initiation 1
onset 2
opening 4
origin 2
source 1
start 10
threshold 2
commencing
initial 1
commend
advise 1
applaud 2
approve 2
compliment 3
extol
glorify 2
laud
pat[1] 2
plug 5
praise 3
promote 3
puff 7
recommend 2
commendable
deserving
desirable 4
estimable
exemplary 2
fine[1] 11
good 1
laudable
meritorious
nice 2
praiseworthy
commendation
applause
bouquet 3
compliment 1
commendation *(cont.)*
credit 4
eulogy
pat[1] 5
praise 1
promotion 3
recommendation 2
testimonial
tribute 1
commendatory
complimentary 1
favourable 2
commensurability
comparison 2
commensurate
according to 2
equal 1, 2
equivalent 1
proportional
relative 2
tantamount to
commensuration
measurement 1
comment°
gloss[2] 1
note 3
notice 6
observation 2
observe 4
pronouncement 1
remark 2
review 4
comment about°
at **comment 4**
note 13
commentary
comment 2
criticism 3
description 2
explanation 1
exposition 3
gloss[2] 1
note 3
notice 6
observation 2
review 4
commentator
journalist
reporter
scribe 2
student 2
-commentators
press 10b
comment on°
at **comment 4**
gloss[2] 2
note 13
observe 4
remark 2
review 3
speak 9
commerce°
business 3
dealings
exchange 2
finance 1
industry 1
intercourse 1
passage 10
trade 1
truck 2
commercial
advertisement 1
announcement 3
economic 1
hot 6
mercantile
philistine 2
commercial traveller
merchant 2
commination
menace 3
threat 1
comminatory
threatening
commingle
blend 1
combine 3
commingle *(cont.)*
fuse
merge
mingle 1
mix 1
scramble 3
stir 1
unite 1
wed 2
commingling
amalgamation
blend 3
merger
wedding 2
comminute
break 23b
grind 1
mill 5
pound[1] 2
powder 3
pulverize 1
comminuted
fine[1] 7
granular
commiserate (with)
feel 8
pity 3
respond 2
sympathize 1
understand 5
commiserating
sympathetic 1
commiseration
pity 1
sympathy 1
commiserative
sympathetic 1
commission
appoint 2
assignment 2
authorize
charge 9
charter 4
committee
cut 20
delegate 2
employ 1
enable 1
engagement 4
errand 2
function 1
job 6
kickback
license 1
make 23
mission 1, 3
office 2, 4
order 7, 15
rake-off
rebate 2
retain 2
royalty 2
sanction 5
send 1
work 3
-out of commission
broken 7
ill 1
indisposed 1
order 13c
out 14
commissioned
vicarious
commissioner
delegate 1
functionary
officer 1
representative 3
commissure
seam 1
weld 2
commit°
apply 5
dedicate 1
deliver 2
devote 1, 2
leave[1] 7
lock[1] 6b
obligate
perpetrate
put 2, 13b
commit *(cont.)*
refer 2
relegate 3
tie 7d
trust 6
undertake 2
commitment
application 3
assurance 1
contract 1
dedication 1
engagement 1
order 7
project 2
promise 1
resolution 2
subscription 1
undertaking 3
warranty
will 1
commit oneself°
at **commit 4**
decide 2
promise 3
commit perjury
lie[1] 1
committed
devoted
earnest 1
heartfelt
intent 5
wholehearted
-be committed to
have 12b
committee°
board 4
body 6
cabinet 2
council 2
mission 3
commit to memory
learn 4
memorize
commit to paper
pen[1] 2
commode
cabinet 1
commodious
convenient 1
extensive 2
roomy
spacious
commodity
product 2
-commodities
good 21b
merchandise 1
truck 1
wares
common°
accustomed 1
average 3, 4
banal
base[2] 3
conventional
current 2
customary 1
daily 2
everyday 2
familiar 1
field 1
frequent 1
general 1, 2
going 2
green 4
habitual 1
humble 3
humdrum
joint 4
kindred 1
low[1] 3
mean[2] 2
mill 4
mutual 2
natural 1
nondescript
normal 1
ordinary 1, 2
orthodox
park 1
plebeian 1
popular 2
prevailing 1
common *(cont.)*
prevalent
profane 3
prosaic
public 1
reciprocal
regular 1, 11
related 1
simple 5
social 1
tolerable 2
typical 2
undistinguished
united 1, 2
universal 1
usual
vulgar 1
-commons
food
park 1
ration 2
commonalty
people 3
populace
public 8
rabble 2
common cold
cold 10
commoner
plebeian 3
-commoners
people 3
populace
rabble 2
commonest
prevailing 1
common folk
populace
common herd
herd 2
hoi polloi
people 3
common knowledge
come 15a
commonly
frequently 2
generally 1
often
ordinarily
popularly
rule 4
usually
common man, woman
people 3
plebeian 3
commonness
prevalence 1
common or garden
common 1
informal 1
mediocre
mill 4
nondescript
ordinary 2
tolerable 2
common people
hoi polloi
mass 6
people 3
commonplace
average 4
banal
cliché
common 1
conventional
customary 1
daily 2
dead 12
dry 2
everyday 2
familiar 1
hack[2] 4
homely 1
humdrum
indifferent 3
mediocre
monotonous
natural 1
nondescript
ordinary 2
commonplace *(cont.)*
pedestrian 2
philistine 2
phrase 2
plebeian 2
popular 2
prevalent
prosaic
proverb
regular 1
saw
small 3
stock 7
threadbare 2
tired 3
trifling
truism
typical 2
undistinguished
vulgar 3
common sense
discretion 1
experience 3
intuition
judgement 1
prudence 1
reason 2, 7
sense 2
common-sense
enlightened
practical 2
rational 3
realistic 1
sage 1
sensible 1
sound[2] 4
commonsensical
enlightened
judicious
legitimate 3
level-headed
moderate 1
practical 2
rational 3
sage 1
sensible 1
sound[2] 4
wise 1
commotion
agitation 2
bedlam
bother 8
confusion 2
din 1
disorder 2
disturbance 2
excitement 2
fanfare 2
flap 4
flurry 1
fluster 2
fracas 1
furore 1
fuss 1
hurry 3
incident 2
mayhem
motion 1
noise 1
outcry
pell-mell 3
racket 1
riot 1
row[2] 2
rumpus
rush 3
scene 3
scramble 4
sensation 2
song 3a
splash 4
stir 6
storm 3
tempest 2
tumult
upheaval
uproar
communal
common 5
general 1
joint 4
mutual 2
public 1, 2, 3
social 1

composure *(cont.)*
sang-froid
serenity 2
temper 2
compound°
alloy 1
amalgam
amalgamate
amalgamation
combination 3
combine 2, 3
complicated
composition 3
elixir 2
enclosure 1
fuse
hybrid
mingle 1
mix 7
mixture 2
pastiche
pound[2]
preparation 5
run 46
solution 3
synthesis
wed 2
wedding 2
compounding
amalgamation
combination 3
composition 3
mixture 2
synthesis
wedding 2
comprehend°
appreciate 3
catch 10, 13a
conceive 3
cover 7
digest 3
embrace 3
follow 8
get 19
grasp 2
include 1
involve 1
know 1
make 37d
penetrate 5
perceive 2
pierce 3
read 2
realize 2
relate 4
see 2
tumble 3
twig[2]
understand 1
comprehensibility
clarity 2
simplicity 1
comprehensible
clear 6
coherent 2
evident
intelligible
manifest 1
readable 1
simple 1
comprehension
appreciation 3
conception 2
eye 3
familiarity 1
grasp 5
grip 3
insight
perception 1
realization 1
savoir faire
understanding 3
uptake
-beyond comprehension
deep 2
-past comprehension
deep 2
comprehensive°
broad 6
catholic

comprehensive *(cont.)*
detailed 1
elaborate 1
encyclopedic
exhaustive
expansive 3
extensive 1
full 2, 12
general 1, 3
grand 4
inclusive 1
intensive
overall
panoramic
radical 2
sweeping 1
thorough 3
total 2
unabridged 2
universal 2
wide 2
comprehensively
depth 6
detail 4
thoroughly 2
compress
abbreviate 1
abridge
contract 4
crowd 5
crush 3
digest 4
diminish 1
edit 3
pinch 1
press 2, 3
pucker 1
purse 4
ram 1
reduce 1
shorten 2
solidify 1
squeeze 1
stuff 6
telescope 2
compressed
brief 2
close 11
compact 1
concise
dense 1
firm 1
hard 1
short 2
solid 2
succinct
thick 2, 3
compressible
elastic 1
soft 1
compressing
pressure 2
compression
pressure 1, 2
comprise
compose 3
cover 7
embody 3
embrace 3
form 9
have 4
hold 9
include 1
incorporate
involve 1
take 32c
-be comprised of
make 39b
comprised
under 3
comprising
inclusive 2
compromise
accommodation 2
give and take
medium 3
reconciliation 2
relent
term 5
compulsion
duress 1
fetish 2

compulsion *(cont.)*
fixation
force 2
habit 2
life 8
mania 1
obligation 1
passion 3
urge 5
compulsive°
fanatical
strict 1
compulsory
imperative 1
incumbent 1
indispensable 2
mandatory
necessary 1
obligatory
vital 1
compunction°
penitence
protest 1
qualm
remorse
scruple 1
computation
account 2
calculation 1
evaluation 2
measurement 1
reckoning 1
tally 3
compute°
calculate
count 1
enumerate 2
evaluate 2
figure 8, 12a
gauge 1
measure 11
number 4
pace 4
plot[1] 4
rate[1] 6
reckon 1
tally 2
total 4
computer
calculator
comrade°
aide
ally 1
associate 4
brick 2
chum 1
cohort 3
colleague
companion 1
fellow 2
friend 1
intimate[1] 5
mate 1
pal 1
partner 1
playmate
shadow 6
-comrades
company 1
comradely
fraternal
friendly 1
comradeship
association 3
brotherhood 1
companionship
fellowship 1
fraternity 2
friendship 1
solidarity
con
brush[2] 8
cheat 2
convict 2
deceit 2
deceive
defraud
dupe 3
finesse 4
fool 4
hoax 1, 2
hocus-pocus 1
hoodwink

con *(cont.)*
line[1] 18
misinform
mislead
moonshine 2
mull
navigate 2
outsmart
polish 4
pore[1]
prisoner
review 1
rip 2b
rip-off 2
scan 2
study 1
swindle 1, 2
take 27, 32b
trick 1
wheedle
con artist
charmer
devil 4
fraud 3
thief 2
concatenate
link 3
string 9
concatenation
chain 1
progression 3
queue 1
sequence
tissue
concave
hollow 2
concavity
depression 1
pan 3
concavo-concave
crescent 2
conceal°
blind 6
blot 4a
blur 4
bury 4
cache 3
camouflage 2
cloak 3
colour 6
cover 2
disguise 1
dissimulate
eclipse 1
envelop 2
gloss[1] 4
harbour 2
hide[1] 1, 2
hold 17b
hush 4
keep 14a
mantle 3
mask 3
muffle 1
obscure 6
plant 8
screen 7
secrete[1]
shade 12
shroud 1
shut 5c
smother 4
stow
submerge 3
suppress 3
veil 2
whitewash
withhold 1
concealed
close 19
dark 7
dormant 2
hidden
incognito 1
invisible 2
mysterious 2
mystical 1
obscure 3
occult 1
potential 1
private 1, 2
secret 1
subtle 2
surreptitious

concealed *(cont.)*
ulterior 1
underground 2
vague 3
veiled
concealment
camouflage 1
cloak 2
cover 14, 15
eclipse 3
mask 2
privacy 2
screen 3
secrecy 1
shadow 2
shelter 2
suppression
concede°
acknowledge 1
admit 3, 4
agree 3
allow 1, 2
capitulate 2
confess
consent 1
deign
figure 9
give 5, 11, 17b
grant 2
recognize 2
submit 1
surrender 1, 2
tolerate 1
way 11b
yield 3
conceded
given 2
understood
conceding
admission 3
conceding that
though 1
conceit°
arrogance
notion 2
pride 2
self-esteem 1
snobbery
vanity 1
witticism
conceited°
arrogant 1
boastful
cocky
egotistical
haughty
hoity-toity
inflated 1
pompous 1
proud 2
self-important
smug
snobbish
uppish
vain 1
conceitedly
big 9
conceitedness
vanity 1
conceivability
chance 3
possibility 1
conceivable
earthly 4
likely 2
plausible 1
possible 1
presumptive 1
specious
tenable
thinkable
conceivably
chance 5b
perhaps
seemingly
conceive°
coin 3
comprehend
create 1
design 1, 2
devise 1
discover 3
envisage 1
envision

conceive *(cont.)*
fancy 9
forge 2
form 8
formulate 2
frame 7
imagine 1
invent 1
mastermind 1
meditate 2
originate 1
picture 6
plot[1] 3
realize 2
see 3
think 6
understand 1
conceiver
mastermind 2
concentrate°
apply 5
centre 2
collect 2
deepen 2
embody 3
essence 2
extract 5
extraction 2
fasten 2
fix 4, 6
focus 4
get 37
intensify
liquor 2
narrow 9
pump 4c
refine 3
zero 4
concentrated
close 14
compact 1
diligent
firm 1
focal
heavy 10
intensive
intent 4
solid 2
strong 2, 4
terse 1
thick 2
undivided 2
concentratedly
depth 6
intently
searchingly
concentratedness
strength 4
concentrating
absorbed
attentive 1
concentration
attention 1
embodiment 2
extract 5
extraction 2
focus 1
intensity
mind 8
pile[1] 1
pocket 3
speciality 1
strength 4
concept
conception 2
doctrine
idea 1, 2
image 3
motif
notion 1
rendition 1
theme 1
conception°
design 5
discovery 1
fancy 5
idea 1, 2
image 3
invention 1
knowledge 1
notion 1
opinion 1
realization 1

conception (*cont.*)
rendering
rendition 1
understanding 3
version 1
view 2
conceptual
abstract 1
ideal 5
mental 1
pure 4
conceptualize
imagine 1
concern°
affair 1, 2
anxiety 1, 2
bag 5
bear 8
bother 2
business 1, 4
care 2
cause 4
charge 1
come 18c
company 4
consideration 1
department 2
domain 2
dread 2
enterprise 3
establishment 2
exercise 3
fear 4
feeling 3
firm 6
fret 2
function 1
go 28b
heart 5
house 4
implicate 2
importance 1
interest 1, 2, 5, 8
involve 3
job 2
lookout 3
love 4
matter 2
misgiving
moment 3
outfit 3
pertain
place 4
providence 2
province 3
qualm
refer 1
reference 2
regard 5, 9
sensitivity 2
solicitude
stake[2] 2
sympathy 1
thought 4
trouble 4, 5
turn 19a
unrest
worry 3
-concerns
thing 8a
-of concern
momentous
concerned°
anxious 1
disturbed 1
full 6
interested 1, 2
involved 1
nervous 1
paternal 1
sit 9
solicitous 1
stake[2] 3
sympathetic 1
-be concerned
care 5
damn 5
fret 1
trouble 4
worry 1
concerning°
about 11
for 12
point 16

concerning (*cont.*)
regarding
relation 5
term 6
concert
accord 2
programme 2
recital 1
-in concert
cooperate 1
hang 11a
concerted
special 3
united 2
concert-hall
house 5
concertina
telescope 3
concert-master
director 2
leader 2
concession
admission 3, 4
allowance 1, 5
charter 2
grant 3
privilege
submission 1
surrender 3
understanding 1
concierge
porter[2] 1, 2
conciliate
disarm 2
conciliation
reconciliation 1
conciliator
mediator
peacemaker
conciliatory
accommodating 1
forgiving
mild 1
propitiatory 1
sacrificial 2
concise°
brief 2
compact 3
curt
epigrammatic
short 2
succinct
terse 1
thumbnail
concise edition
abridgement 3
concisely
brief 5
briefly 1
word 8
concision
brevity
economy 2
conclave
assembly 2
convention 1
council 1
gathering
meeting 2
conclude
accomplish
carry 12
clinch 1
close 3, 4
come 15c, 17b
complete 5
cut 9
decide 1
deduce
determine 1, 2
dispatch 4
dispose 3a
dissolve 3
end 9
expire 1
finalize
finish 1, 5
fix 2
follow 10
gather 4
get 48c
guess 2

conclude (*cont.*)
halt 2
infer
judge 4, 7
live 7
mind 13
nail 10
negotiate 2
pan 6
perceive 2
polish 3a
put 27a
read 4
reason 7
reckon 3
resolve 1
result 3
settle 2, 3
stop 1
strike 8
surmise 1
take 19
terminate
transact
wind[2] 4a
wrap 3a
concluded
complete 2
over 6
concluding
eventual 1
expiration
final 1
last[1] 3
net[2] 3
parting 3
terminal 1
ultimate 1
conclusion
accomplishment 1
close 22
completion 1
consummation 2
decision 2
deduction 2
determination 2
dissolution 2
effect 1
end 2, 5
event 2
expiration
finding 2
finish 9
head 5
implication 3
inference
issue 2
judgement 2
kill 9
law 3
pay-off 2
presumption 3
result 1
settlement 5
solution 2
stop 6
surmise 2
termination 1
thinking 2
upshot
conclusive
authoritative 1
definitive 1
demonstrable
final 2
last[1] 4
net[2] 3
strong 8
ultimate 1
undisputed
unquestionable
conclusively
easily 2
finally 2
once 3
conclusiveness
decision 3
finality
concoct
brew 2
coin 3
compound 1
devise 1
fabricate 2
form 8

concoct (*cont.*)
formulate 2
hatch 2
imagine 1
improvise 2
invent 1, 2
make 39c
manufacture 2
originate 1
plot[1] 3
project 3
scheme 4
set 8
spin 2
stage 5
think 6
turn 8
concocted
artificial 2
false 2
concoction
brew 4
fabrication 2
fantasy 3
mess 2
potion
preparation 5
romance 5
concomitance
coincidence 2
concomitant
attendant 1
contemporary 1
fellow 3
concord
accord 2
agreement 2
coincidence 2
harmony 1
pact
peace 2
proportion 2
reconciliation 1
solidarity
sympathy 2
uniformity 1
unity 1
concordance
solidarity
uniformity 1
unity 1
-in concordance
consistent 1
concordant
harmonious
step 7
concordat
agreement 1
negotiation 2
pact
protocol 2
treaty
understanding 1
concourse
street 1
concrete°
hard 1
material 5
pave 1
physical
solid 3, 7
surface 4
tangible
concreteness
substance 4
concretion
mass 3
concretization
embodiment 1
concretize
embody 1
concubine
friend 3
mistress 1
paramour
woman 2
concupiscence
desire 3
lust 1
passion 3
concupiscent
carnal
erotic 3

concupiscent (*cont.*)
hot 7
immoral 2
lecherous
lewd
lustful
prurient 1
concur
accord 1
agree 1, 3
comply
conform 2
consent 1
fall 15
go 20b
hold 23
nod 2
soften 4
string 10a
tally 1
yield 3
concurrence
agreement 2
approval
coincidence 1
consent 4
nod 6
sanction 3
solidarity
unity 1
concurrent
contemporary 1
simultaneous
concurring
agreeable 2
condemn°
attack 2
blame 1
criticize 2
damn 1, 2
denounce 3
disapprove
jinx 3
rail[2]
stigmatize
condemnation
blame 3
criticism 2
disapproval
flak
judgement 3
knock 10
perdition
condemnatory
destructive 2
reproachful
vituperative
condemned°
condemn 3
doomed 1, 2
condensation
abridgement 1, 3
abstract 3
brief 4
digest 5
epitome 2
summary 1
synopsis
condense
abbreviate 2
abridge
abstract 4
concentrate 2
contract 4
cut 5
digest 4
diminish 1
dwindle
edit 3
shorten 2
sum 2a
telescope 2
condensed
brief 2
compact 1, 3
concise
dense 1
firm 1
hard 1
succinct
terse 1
thick 2, 3

condescend°
deign
descend 3
lower[1] 4
patronize 1
stoop 2
talk 9b
vouchsafe 1
condescending°
haughty
lofty 4
snobbish
supercilious
condescension
patronage 3
snobbery
condign
deserved
just 3
righteous 2
condignly
richly 2
condiment
sauce 1
spice 1
condition°
break 8, 18b
bug 2
capacity 3
circumstance 1
degree 1
depend 1
determine 4
development 1
discipline 6
disease 1
fitness 2
footing 2
form 5
frame 5
grade 1
hang 7e
health 1
lie[2] 6
matter 2
mode[1] 2
order 6
orient 3
pass 26
phase 3
place 8
plight
position 4
posture 2
precondition
predicament
prerequisite 2
provision 2
qualification 2
qualify 1
repair 3
requirement 1
reservation 2
restriction 1
score 6
season 4
shake 6a
shape 4, 7
situation 2
specification 3
stage 1
state 1
stint 2
stipulation
strait 3
term 4
trim 6
ultimatum
way 8
weather 1
-conditions°
at **condition 4**
circumstance 1
environment
set-up 1
state 1
string 7
term 4
time 9
ultimatum
weather 1
-on condition
providing

-in conflict
afoul
discordant 1
foul 18
opposed
opposition 3
variance 3
war 2
conflicting
contradictory
contrary 1
destructive 2
different 1
discordant 1
dissident 2
divergent
factious
incompatible
incongruous
mixed 2
odds 4
opposed
opposing
opposite 2
opposition 3
paradoxical
confluence
junction
meeting 3
conform°
accord 1
agree 1
check 5
comply
consent 1
correspond 1
fit[1] 6
go 6
normalize
obey 1
parallel 4
proportion 5
shape 10b
tally 1
conformability
flexibility 2
obedience
conformable
flexible 2
obedient
regular 11
conformable to
according to 2
conformably
accordingly 2
conformance
fulfilment
obedience
uniformity 1
-in conformance
consistent 1
conformation
accommodation 1
figure 1
form 1
conforming
consistent 1
observance 1
parliamentary
conformist
conservative 2
normal 1
observant 2
orthodox
parliamentary
prig
priggish
proper 3
square 6, 9
conformity
accommodation 1
accord 2
coincidence 2
decorum 2
equality 2
flexibility 2
formality 3
fulfilment
obedience
observance 1
parity 1
propriety 1
reconciliation 2
resemblance
conformity (*cont.*)
tune 2
uniformity 1
-in conformity
accordingly 2
according to 1, 2
line[1] 19b
conform to
abide 4
answer 5
follow 2
fulfil 2
obey 1
observe 1
parallel 4
square 11
suit 2
confound
amaze
bewilder
complicate 1
confuse 1, 2, 3
devastate 2
discomfit 1
disorder 4
distract 3
disturb 5
dumbfound
elude 2
entangle 2
fight 2
floor 5
flummox
fluster 1
get 18
impede
jumble 1
mix 4b, 6
muddle 1
mystify
nonplus
overwhelm 3
perplex
petrify 2
puzzle 1
shake 5
shatter 3
stagger 2
stump 2
stun 2
stymie
throw 4, 6c
confounded
dumbfounded
groggy
helpless 2
lost 3
petrified 2
confoundedly
devil 5
confounding
confusion 3
disconcerting
inexplicable
labyrinthine
mysterious 1
perplexing
puzzling
confrère
brother
cohort 3
colleague
companion 1
comrade
friend 2
intimate[1] 5
peer[1] 2
confront
brave 3
challenge 3
defy 1
encounter 3
face 14, 17, 18b
fight 2
grip 5
stand 3, 12a
tackle 3
withstand
confrontation
challenge 5
combat 3
controversy 1
encounter 5
confrontation (*cont.*)
run-in
showdown
skirmish 1
confronting
face 8, 9
confusable
ambiguous 2
confuse°
bemuse 1
bewilder
bother 3
complicate 1
daze 2
demoralize 3
discomfit 1
disorder 4
distract 3
disturb 5
dumbfound
elude 2
entangle 2
floor 5
flummox
flurry 2
fluster 1
fog 4
garble 2
get 18
jumble 1
mistake 4
mix 4b, 4d, 6
muddle 1, 2
muddy 4
mystify
nonplus
overwhelm 3
perplex
perturb
put 21c
puzzle 1
ruffle 3
scramble 3
shake 5
shatter 3
shuffle 1
snarl[2] 1
stick[1] 9
stump 2
tangle 3
throw 4, 6c
confused°
amiss 1
awkward 3
bashful 1
blank 5
chaotic 1
complicated
daze 4
disconcerted
disconnected 2
disjointed 2
disorderly 1
disorientated
dizzy 2
dumbfounded
fog 2
foolish 2
frantic
groggy
hairy 3
helpless 2
helter-skelter 1
inarticulate 1
incoherent
indefinite 2
indiscriminate 2
indistinct 1, 2
involved 2
lost 3
mixed 2
muddy 2
neurotic
obscure 2
pell-mell 2
promiscuous 3
rambling 1
sea 4
topsy-turvy 2
unsettled 3
upset 9
vague 1
woolly 2
confusedly
helter-skelter 2
pell-mell 1
vaguely 2
confusing
confused 1, 3
disconcerting
hairy 3
indefinite 2
involved 2
labyrinthine
mysterious 1
obscure 2
paradoxical
perplexing
puzzling
confusingly
vaguely 2
confusion°
bedlam
chaos
clutter 1, 2
daze 3
disorder 1
distraction 1
flummox
fluster 2
hash 1
havoc 2
jumble 2
mayhem
mess 1
mix-up
morass 2
muddle 4
pandemonium
patchwork
pell-mell 3
perplexity 1
question 2
rumpus
stir 6
sweat 7
tangle 1
tumult
upheaval
welter 1
confutable
moot 1
confutation
rebuttal
confute
contest 3
deny 1
destroy 4
disprove
dispute 1
fight 2
rebut
confuted
moot 1
con game
deceit 2
hoax 1
hocus-pocus 1
swindle 2
congé
dismissal 2
ejection 3
farewell 2
congeal
cake 3
coagulate
fix 7
freeze 2
jell 1
set 3
solidify 1
stiffen 1
thicken
congealed
thick 5
congenial
amiable
amicable
benign 1, 3
comfortable 3
delightful 2
friendly 1
genial
harmonious
homely 1
hospitable 1
kind[1]
congenial (*cont.*)
like[2] 1
likeable
outgoing 2
peaceable 2
pleasant 2
sociable
sympathetic 2
congeniality
fellowship 3
friendship 1
hospitality
sympathy 2
congenital
hereditary 1
inborn
inherent
instinctive 1
intrinsic
native 1
congenitally
naturally 2
congeries
heap 1
mass 1
pile[1] 1
congest
block 5
choke 2
clog
jam 2
silt 2
congested°
full 1
mobbed
overcrowded
silt 2
solid 2
congestion
jam 4
tie-up 1
conglomerate
combination 3
firm 6
organization 3
trust 4
conglomeration
assortment 2
combination 3
ensemble 3
group 2
heap 1
hotchpotch
mass 1
medley
pile[1] 1
profusion
tissue
congratulate°
compliment 3
extol
hail[1] 2
pat[1] 2
toast 3
congratulations°
congratulatory
complimentary 1
congregate
assemble 1
cluster 3
collect 1
concentrate 3
crowd 3
flock 2
gather 2
get 50b
herd 3
mass 8
meet[1] 2
press 7
rally 3
swarm 2
throng 2
congregation
assembly 1
cluster 2
convention 1
council 1
fellowship 2
flock 1
group 1
knot 2
meeting 2
congregation (*cont.*)
muster 2
pack 3
throng 1
congress
assembly 2
body 6
chamber 1
conference
convention 1
council 1
diet[2]
gathering
house 3
meeting 2
muster 2
parliament 2
sex 2
congressman, congresswoman
politician
representative 3
congruence
accord 4
coincidence 2
equality 2
identity 1
parity 1
congruent
equal 2
parallel 1
symmetrical
congruity
coincidence 2
harmony 2
parity 1
proportion 2
resemblance
symmetry
union 4
unity 2
congruous
correspond 1
equal 2
harmonious
meet[2]
symmetrical
conjectural
academic 2
alleged
doubtful 1
experimental 1
hypothetical
pure 4
speculative 1
theoretical 1
uncertain 3
conjecture
believe 3
divine 4
estimate 2, 3
expect 2
expectation 2
fancy 10
guess 1, 3
imagine 2
judge 7
premise 1, 2
presume 1
presumption 3
say 6
shot 3
speculate 1
speculation 1
stab 4
surmise 1, 2
theorem 1
theorize
wonder 3
conjectured
hypothetical
conjoin
associate 1a
combine 1
match 5
splice 1
conjoining
junction
union 1
conjugal
bridal
matrimonial

conjugal (*cont.*)
nuptial
conjunction
association 2
combination 1
contact 1
junction
meeting 3
union 1, 3
conjuration
enchantment 1
mumbo-jumbo 2
conjurer
magician 1
conjure up
conceive 3
dream 2
envisage 1
evoke
fancy 9
project 3
see 3
strike 16
conjuring
hocus-pocus 3
magic 2
conjuror
magician 1
conjury
enchantment 1
conk
head 1
hit 1, 10
knock 9
strike 1
conk out
pack 8b
pass 20a
stall[1] 1
con man
charmer
cheat 1
devil 4
fraud 3
hypocrite
impostor
slicker 1
swindler
thief 2
twister 1
connate
inborn
inherent
connect°
assemble 3
associate 1a
attach 1, 2
bind 4
bolt 11
bridge 4
close 8b
combine 1
couple 3
fasten 1
fix 1
go 4
hitch 1
identify 2
implicate 2
install 2
involve 3
join 1
link 4
mix 5
piece 13
put 27c
relate 1
tie 1, 3, 6b
twin 3
unite 2
weld 1
connected
about 11
affiliated
akin
attached 1
belong 1
concern 1
continuous 1
fast[1] 3
mixed 3
near 7
related 1
relative 1

connected (*cont.*)
united 1
connecting
connection 1
connection°
affinity 1
alliance 1
assembly 3
association 2
attachment 1, 2
bearing 3
belonging
bond 3
bridge 2
contact 1, 2
identification 1, 4
implication 1
installation 2
joint 1
junction
kinship 2
liaison 1
link 2
marriage 3
reference 2
regard 6
relation 1
relevance
respect 3
splice 2
terminal 5
tie 8
tie-in
truck 2
-connections°
at **connection 3**
influence 2
pull 16, 21
connector
link 1
terminal 5
connexion
affinity 1
bridge 2
splice 2
connivance
conspiracy
design 8
connive
cabal 3
engineer 5
intrigue 2
scheme 4
conniver
designer 2
conniving
calculating
design 8
designing
scheming
serpentine 1
shifty
sly 1
smooth 8
connivingly
hand 10
connoisseur
aesthete
collector
epicure
expert 1
gourmet
highbrow 1
judge 3
specialist
connoisseurship
discrimination 2
connotation
implication 3
import 3
meaning 2
overtone
significance 1
tenor
undercurrent 2
connotative
symbolic
connote
imply 2
mean[1] 2
signify 1
symbolize

connubial
bridal
matrimonial
nuptial
conquer°
beat 2
best 11
crush 4
defeat 1
finish 4
floor 4
occupy 1
overcome 1
overpower 1
overrun
overthrow 1
overwhelm 1
possession 4
rout 2
subdue 2
subject 10
swallow 4
triumph 3
upset 4
whip 2
win 1
-be conquered
fall 5
lose 3
conquering
triumphant
winning 2
conqueror
champion 1
victor
winner
conquest°
catch 16
defeat 3
fall 28
occupation 3
overthrow 2
rout 1
ruin 1
subjection
triumph 1
upset 11
victory
win 4
consanguineous
kin 2
kindred 2
related 2
consanguinity
kinship 1
conscience°
principle 3
regret 2
scruple 1
conscienceless
faithless 2
unconscionable 1
unscrupulous
conscience-stricken
apologetic
bad 8
guilty 2
penitent
remorseful
sorry 1
terrible 2
conscientious°
accurate 2
careful 2
diligent
dutiful
earnest 2
faithful 3
hard 7
industrious
mindful
painful 3
precise 2, 3
professional 2
reliable
religious 2
rigid 3
scrupulous 1
strict 1
thorough 2
conscientiously
hard 13
precisely 2

conscientiously (*cont.*)
thoroughly 2
conscious°
alive 2
appreciate 3
awake 3, 4
aware 2
deliberate 1
familiar 4
feel 3
know 5
mindful
penetrate 5
premeditated
realize 2
see 2
sensible 3, 4
studied
understand 1
wilful 1
consciously
deliberately
purpose 4a
consciousness
cognizance
feeling 2
impression 1
knowledge 1
notice 3
perception 2
sensitivity 3
spirit 1
conscript
call 12a
enlist 1
induct 2
mobilize
recruit 1, 2
consecrate
bless 1
celebrate 1
commemorate
dedicate 1, 2
devote 1
hallow 1
sanctify 1
consecrated
divine 1
holy 1
sacred 1
consecration
blessing 1
dedication 3
devotion 2
faith 3
installation 1
consecutive
successive
consecutively
end 7b
succession 5
consensus
unity 1
consent°
accept 2
agree 3
approval
clearance 2
comply
grant 2
leave[2] 1
nod 2, 6
obey 1
OK 6
permission
permit 1
privilege
soften 4
submit 1
subscribe 1
weaken 3
yield 3
consentaneousness
unity 1
consenting
agreeable 2
permissive
ready 2
willing
consent to°
at **consent 2**
abide 4

consent to (*cont.*)
accept 2
agree 2
allow 2
authorize
grant 2
hear 3
obey 1
OK 5
permit 1
sanction 5
submit 1
subscribe 1
underwrite 2
consequence
account 5
distinction 2
effect 1
end 4
event 2
fruit
impact 2
import 4
importance 1
interest 2
issue 2
magnitude 2
mark 8
matter 4
moment 3
note 8
outcome
price 2
product 1
prominence 1
ramification 1
repercussion
result 1
sequel
significance 2
solemnity
weight 3
-as a consequence
consequently
naturally 1
thank 4
therefore
through 1
thus 2
wake[2] 2
-consequences
fruit
impact 2
-in consequence (where of)
accordingly 1
-of consequence
considerable 2
matter 6
serious 2
signify 2
consequent
attendant 1
eventual 2
natural 9
subsequent 1
consequential
big 4
eventful
fateful 1
goodly
great 4
high 6
historic
important 1
material 6
meaningful 1
momentous
serious 2
signal 3
significant 1
signify 2
substantial 1
weighty 2
consequently°
accordingly 1
hence 1
naturally 1
therefore
thus 2

conservation°
economy 1
maintenance 1
preservation 1, 2
providence 1
upkeep 1
conservational
frugal 1
conservation area
sanctuary 3
conservationist
environmentalist
green 3, 5
conservatism
economy 1
conservative°
economical 2
extreme 4
fogy
frugal 1
hidebound
narrow-minded
orthodox
parochial
prig
priggish
reactionary 1, 2
reasonable 3
right 6
safe 3
slow 8
sound[2] 5
square 6, 9
stick-in-the-mud
strait-laced
-conservatives
establishment 3
conservatory
hothouse 1
conserve°
husband 2
keep 1
preserve 2, 3, 4
protect 2
reserve 1
safeguard 2
save 2, 3
spread 12
-conserves
preserve 4
consider°
account 7
allow 4
balance 1
chew 4
contemplate 2, 3
count 2
debate 4
deliberate 4
digest 3
entertain 3
esteem 2
estimate 2
feel 4
figure 9, 11b
find 4
flirt 2
hear 3
heed 1
hold 7
imagine 1
investigate
judge 5, 7
look 1
meditate 2
mind 9, 13
mull
muse
note 11
observe 2
perceive 3
place 16
play 19b
ponder
purpose 5
puzzle 2
reckon 2, 3, 5b
reflect 3
regard 2, 4
respect 6
review 1
revolve 3
see 8, 12a

consider (*cont.*)
speculate 1
study 2
take 8, 39e
think 2, 5a
traverse 4
treat 2
turn 21a
view 9
weigh 2

considerable°
dramatic 2
extensive 2
good 16, 18
goodly
great 3
handsome 2
hefty 3
high 4, 13
large 2
marked
nifty 4
noticeable 2
profuse 3
respectable 2
sensible 5
strong 14
substantial 1
swingeing
telling 1
tidy 3
wide 3

considerably
degree 4b
exceedingly
far 2, 3
materially
vastly
widely 2

considerate°
accommodating 1
attentive 1, 2
benevolent
charitable 2
chivalrous
courteous
decent 4
deliberate 3
discreet
dutiful
gallant 2
good 6
good-natured
gracious
helpful
human 3
kind[1]
merciful
neighbourly
obliging
respect 7
respectful
selfless
solicitous 1
sweet 6
sympathetic 1
tactful
tender[1] 6
thoughtful 1
tolerant

considerately
kindly 2

considerateness
charity 2
consideration 1
grace 4

consideration°
account 5
allowance 5
charity 2
civility
concern 5
counsel 2
debate 2
deference 1
ear 1
factor 1
favour 4
grace 2
heart 5
heed 2
humanity 3
indemnity 1
inducement
interest 3

consideration (*cont.*)
kindness 1
mercy
moment 3
notice 4
pay 12
perquisite
point 12
reflection 2
regard 7, 9
remuneration 1
respect 1, 2
return 11
review 5
solicitude
specification 3
speculation 2
tact
thought 1, 3, 4

-beyond consideration
question 7

-in consideration of
light[1] 11
view 6

-into consideration
forward 5

-under consideration
line[1] 20
question 6a

-without consideration
despite

-without considering
despite

considered
deliberate 1, 3
intentional
judicious
measured 2
reputed

considering°
light[1] 11
seeing
thought 1
view 6

consign
assign 1
commit 1
deposit 2
forward 7
give 5
job 6
leave[1] 7
portion 4
put 2, 3
relegate 1
send 2
sign 11
trust 6

consigned
condemn 3

consignment
cargo
freight 2
load 2
lot 1

consistency
body 7
coincidence 1
connection 2
harmony 2
parity 1
pattern 3
regularity 1
symmetry
texture
uniformity 1
unity 1

consistent°
accord 1
according to 1, 2
coherent 1
conform 2
equable 2
even 3
hang 11b
homogeneous
level 3, 4

consistent (*cont.*)
logical 3
natural 9
organic 3
proportional
regular 2
solid 4
steady 5
step 7
tie 6a
uniform 1

consistently°
for ever 2

consist in, of
compose 3

consistory
council 1

consociate
colleague
friend 2

consociation
society 5

consolation
cheer 3
comfort 2
solace 1

console°
bracket 1
cheer 5
comfort 1
solace 2

consolidate
amalgamate
cake 3
combine 2
concentrate 1
embody 3
firm 5
fix 7
follow 11b
fuse
incorporate
integrate
knit 1
lump[1] 3
merge
pool 4
solidify 2
stick[1] 16a
sum 2a
syndicate 3
unify
unite 1

consolidated
compact 1

consolidation
amalgamation
compound 5
embodiment 2
follow-up
merger
summary 1

consoling
sympathetic 1

consommé
broth

consonance
coincidence 2
harmony 2
tune 2

consonant
consistent 1
harmonious
natural 9
step 7
unison

consort
associate 1b
fraternize
hang 4b
hobnob
knock 3b
mate 2
mingle 2
mix 2
pal 1, 2
partner 2
rub 7
run 24
see 7
shoulder 4

consortium
association 1
chamber 1
club 2
combination 2
fellowship 2
organization 3
pool 3
union 2

conspectus
abstract 3
digest 5
epitome 2
outline 2
précis
prospectus
summary 1
synopsis

conspicuous°
apparent 1
bold 3
discernible 1
effective 2
eminent 1, 2
evident
famous
figure 10
flagrant
flaming
glaring 1
important 2
manifest 1
marked
naked 3
notable 2
noticeable 1
obvious
open 13
outstanding 1
patent 2
prominent 1
pronounced 1
public 4, 5
salient
shine 3
show 12b
showy
signal 3
singular 2
splendid 2
stand 9a
visible 2

conspicuously
especially 1
notably 1
ostensibly
pre-eminently

conspiracy°
cabal 1
combination 2
design 8
intrigue 3
plot[1] 1
trick 1

conspirator
accessory 2
accomplice
designer 2
sympathizer

conspiratorial
furtive 1
knowing 1
shifty

conspire
cabal 3
engineer 5
intrigue 2
league 3
plot[1] 3
scheme 4
team 3

conspiring
designing
league 2

conspiringly
hand 10

constable°
detective
officer 2
police officer

constabulary
police 1

constancy
determination 1
loyalty
patience 2
perpetuity
persistence
regularity 1
resolution 1
self-control 1
stability 2
unity 1

constant°
abiding
certain 1
changeless 2
consistent 2
continual
continuous 2
determined 1
devoted
diligent
endless 2
equable 2
eternal 2, 3
even 3
everlasting
faithful 1
fast[1] 5
firm 4
frequent 1
habitual 2
homogeneous
immortal 1
indestructible
invariable 1
level 3
loyal
non-stop 2
ongoing 1
patient 2
perennial 1
permanent 1
perpetual 2
persevere
persistent 2
relentless 2
repetitive
running 3
same 2
static 1
steadfast
steady 2, 3
true 2

constantly
cease 2
consistently 1
daily 3
ever 2
firmly 2
for ever 2
non-stop 3
permanently
time 11
turn 39

consternation
alarm 2
dismay 3
dread 2
fear 1
fright 1
panic 1
terror 1

constituent
element 1
factor 1
ingredient
link 1
part 2
thing 2
unit

-constituents
content[1] 2
material 3

constitute
compose 1, 3
establish 1
form 9
make 8, 39b

constitution
composition 5
fabric 2
fibre 3
format 2
health 1
law 2

constitution (*cont.*)
make-up 2, 3
nature 1
organization 2
psychology
state 2
temper 1
texture

constitutional
fundamental 1
inborn
instinctive 1
intrinsic
lawful 1
legal 2
native 1
organic 2
promenade 2
radical 1
ramble 4
stroll 2
turn 31
walk 7

constitutionalization
passage 9

constrain
bind 2
drive 1
force 7
lock[1] 6b
obligate
pin 4a, 4c
prescribe
press 6
pressure 5
push 4
repress
screw 4
tie 5b
trammel 2
urge 2

constrained
bound[3] 2
compulsive
modest 3
pent-up

constraint
bond 1
brake 1
check 14
duress 1
force 2
handicap 1
inhibition
measure 8
necessity 1
need 2
obligation 2
obstruction 1
pressure 3, 4
rein 1
restraint 1, 2
stint 2
stricture 1
trammel 1

-without constraint
freely 1

constrict
choke 2
contract 4
gather 3
narrow 8

constricted
narrow 1
strait 1

constricting
strait 1
strict 1
tight 2

constrictive
extreme 4
prescriptive
strict 1

construal
interpretation 2
twist 8

construct°
assemble 3
build 1
design 2
engineer 4

construct (*cont.*)
erect 2
fabricate 1
fashion 5
forge 1
form 1,7
frame 3,6
generate 4
idea 1
lay[1] 3
make 1,39c,39e
manufacture 1
mould[1] 4
prepare 5
produce 1
put 28a
raise 2
rear[2] 2
set 23a
structure 3
turn 8,20a
version 1
weave 3

construction
arrangement 2
assembly 3
building
composition 2
design 6
establishment 1
fabric 2
fabrication 1
form 1
frame 1,3
make-up 3
manufacture 3
mould[1] 2
production 1
rendition 1
set-up 1
structure 2
twist 8
version 1

constructive°
beneficial 1
helpful
positive 7

construe
interpret 2
understand 3

consul
minister 2

consult°
confer 1
discuss
huddle 4
negotiate 1
palaver 5
refer 3
see 9
talk 2

consultant°
adviser

consultation
counsel 2
huddle 2
talk 15
word 1

consultative
advisory 1

consumable
good 7

consume°
devour 2,3
dispose 3d
drain 5
eat
erode
exhaust 1
expend 2
finish 3
gnaw 2
go 16
kill 7
lap[1] 3a
lose 4
occupy 4
polish 3c
possess 3
prey 3a
put 13d
run 31,34b
swallow 1,3
tackle 4

consume (*cont.*)
take 13
touch 5
use 3,4,5
waste 3

consumed
exhausted 2
full 6
possessed
spent 2

consumer
buyer
customer 1
user 1

-consumers
people 3
public 9

consuming
intense 2
pungent 3
towering 2

consummate
absolute 1
accomplished
arch 1
complete 4
crown 5
definitive 2
exact 1
execute 2
exquisite 5
fine[1] 4
finish 2
float 3
follow 10
fulfil 1
great 11
ideal 4
masterful 1
model 11
out-and-out
outright 2
peerless
perfect 1,8
positive 9
practised 1
profound 4
regular 9
superlative
supreme 3
transcendent
unmitigated
unparalleled
unqualified 2

consummated
mature 3

consummately
outright 4
perfectly 1
totally

consummation°
accomplishment 1
complement 1
execution 2
fruition
fulfilment
issue 2
maturity 3
peak 2
perfection 2
pinnacle
realization 2

consumption
exhaustion 1
use 11

consumptive
emaciated
frail 2

contact°
connection 3
experience 1
exposure 3
get 12,48b
impact 1
intercourse 1
liaison 1,2
truck 2

-be in contact (with)
communicate 2
correspond 2
touch 3

contagion
disease 2

contagious
catching 1
infectious

contain°
bottle 4a
check 2
control 2
cover 7
curb 2
enclose 2
govern 2
have 4
hold 5,9,17a
house 9
include 1
involve 1
possess 2
repress
retain 3
seat 6
sit 5
take 17,32c

contained
impassive

container
bottle 1
box[1] 1
case[2] 1
casket 1
housing 2
jar[1]
package 1
parcel 1
receptacle
vessel 1
wrapper 2

containerize
case[2] 3
package 3

contaminant
impurity 2

contaminate°
adulterate
alloy 2
corrupt 4
debase 2
desecrate
foul 12
poison 3
pollute 1
profane 4
soil[1] 2
stain 5
taint 2
tarnish
vitiate 1

contaminated
bad 6
diseased
foul 2
impure 2
rotten 1
stagnant

contamination
impurity 1
pollution
sacrilege 1

contemn
despise
dislike 1
disregard 2
flout
fly 6
look 5
neglect 1
patronize 1
put 16g
scorn 3
snap 6
sneer 2
spurn
thumb 8
trample 2
twit[1]
use 15

contemplate°
brood 3
consider 1
design 1
entertain 3
envisage 1
expect 1
eye 10
flirt 2

contemplate (*cont.*)
gaze 1
get 30b
hope 3
imagine 1
intend
look 1
mean[1] 1
meditate 1,2
mull
muse
note 11
observe 2
perceive 3
plan 4
ponder
project 3
purpose 5
puzzle 2
reckon 5b
reflect 3
regard 2
revolve 3
say 7
see 8
speculate 1
study 2
survey 2
think 3,5a
traverse 4
watch 1
weigh 2

contemplating
preoccupied 1
thought 1

contemplation
consideration 3
debate 2
prospect 2
speculation 2
study 5
thought 1,3
view 4

contemplative
meditative
pensive
philosophical 2
preoccupied 1
reflective
thinking 1
thoughtful 2
wistful 2

contemporaneity
coincidence 1

contemporaneous
contemporary 1
current 1
parallel 1
simultaneous

contemporarily
now 2

contemporary°
current 1
date 5
going 2
live 2
modern
new 2
now 5
parallel 1
present[1] 1
simultaneous
topical 1

-contemporaries
generation 4

contempt°
animosity
derision
disgrace 1
disgust 3
dislike 2
disregard 3
mockery 1
patronage 3
scorn 1,3
shame 2
sneer 3

-beneath contempt
despicable

-beyond contempt
despicable

contemptible°
abhorrent
base[2] 1
despicable
dirty 6
disgraceful 1
dishonourable 3
flagrant
hateful 1
hideous 2
horrible 2
loathsome
lousy 1
low[1] 12
mangy
mean[2] 3
miserable 3,4
paltry
pitiful 2
rotten 4
scurvy
seamy
shabby 4
sleazy 2
stinking 2
unworthy 1
vile 1
wretched 4

contemptuous°
arrogant 2
condescending
cutting 2
derisory
despise
disdainful
disreputable 1
flagrant
hateful 2
haughty
injurious 2
insolent
lofty 4
profane 1
regal 2
sarcastic
scornful
shabby 2
snobbish
supercilious
thumb 8
vituperative

contemptuousness
scorn 1
snobbery

contend
argue 3,5
claim 4
combat 5
compete
contest 3
debate 3
disagree 2
fight 1
issue 9
maintain 3
play 2
run 5
strive 2
struggle 2
tangle 4
vie

contender
antagonist
competitor
contestant
enemy
opponent
player 1
pugilist
rival 1

contend with
battle 3
cope 2
encounter 2,3
fight 1
grapple 2
grip 5
oppose 1
play 3
rival 2
take 35b

contend with (*cont.*)
tangle 4
tilt 2

content°
capacity 1
format 2
matter 4
meaning 1
please 1
ready 2
satiate 2
satisfy 1,3
significance 1
text 1
willing

-contents
filling
format 2
index
inside 1
précis
table 3
text 1

contented
carefree
comfortable 1,2
content[2] 3
glad 1
happy 1
pleased
proud 1

contentedly
happily 3
willingly

contentedness
content[2] 1,2

contention
antagonism 2
argument 2
assertion 1
competition 1
conflict 2
contest 2
controversy 1
debate 1
disagreement 3
discord
dissension
encounter 5
faction 2
feud 1
friction 2
position 7
quarrel 1
race[1] 1
rivalry
scramble 4
story 2
strife 1
struggle 5
thesis 1
variance 2
war 1

-in contention
issue 8
variance 3
war 2

contentious
argumentative
belligerent 2
controversial 3
cranky 2
dissident 2
factious
fault-finding 2
hasty 4
legalistic
militant 1
offensive 1
passionate 3
perverse 2
prickly 4
pugnacious
quarrelsome
testy
touchy 1
truculent

contentment
content[2] 1
ease 1
heaven 3
joy 1
pleasure 1

contentment (*cont.*)
satisfaction 1
conterminous
join 4
contest°
battle 1, 2
bout 3
campaign 2
challenge 1, 3
combat 2, 6
competition 2
debate 3
disagree 2
dispute 1
encounter 5
fight 2, 7
game 2
match 2
meet[1] 7
oppose 1
race[1] 1
rival 2
running 2
scramble 4
skirmish 1
struggle 5
tilt 4
tournament
trial 2
contestable
moot 1
contestant°
belligerent 3
competitor
enemy
entry 5
opponent
player 1
pugilist
-contestants
field 3
contested
moot 1
context°
frame 3
matter 4
setting
viewpoint
contiguity
proximity
contiguous
adjoining
join 4
near 5
neighbouring
contiguousness
proximity
continence
celibacy 2
chastity
temperance 1
continent
celibate 2
chaste 1
temperate 2
contingency
condition 2
eventuality
contingent
cohort 1
depend 1
hang 7e
pivot 4
provisional 2
qualified 2
relative 2
subject 8b
continual°
constant 2
continuous 2
endless 2
eternal 2
everlasting
frequent 1
habitual 2
nagging
non-stop 2
ongoing 1
perennial 1
perpetual 2
persistent 2
recurrent
continual (*cont.*)
relentless 2
repetitive
running 3
successive
sustained
continually
always 2
cease 2
daily 3
ever 2
for ever 2
frequently 1
night 3
non-stop 3
often
time 11
continuation
endurance 2
existence 2
maintenance 2
preservation 2
supplement 1
continue°
abide 3
add 3
carry 11a, 12
endure 1
exist 1
extend 1, 2, 3
follow 10
go 15, 19, 32a
hold 20a, 21b
keep 5
last[2] 1
lengthen
live 7
maintain 1
pass 18a
perpetuate
persevere
persist 2
preserve 2
proceed 1
progress 5
prosecute 3
pursue 2
push 10
remain 3
resume
soldier 4
spin 5
stand 4
stay[1] 1, 3
stick[1] 7, 19
survive 1
sustain 1
take 39b
continued
ongoing 1
standing 1
sustained
continuing
chronic 1
enduring
frequent 1
non-stop 2
ongoing 1
perennial 1
persistent 2
progressive 1
standing 1
continuity
script 2
unity 1
continuous°
constant 2
continual
endless 2
entire 3
eternal 2
everlasting
flush[2] 1
nagging
non-stop 1, 2
ongoing 1
perennial 1
perpetual 2
persistent 2
progressive 1
regular 5
relentless 2
repetitive
running 3
sequential
continuous (*cont.*)
solid 4, 10
standing 3
steady 2, 3
successive
sustained
continuously
cease 2
daily 3
end 7b
ever 2
for ever 2
intently
night 3
non-stop 3
permanently
time 11
contort
distort 1
screw 7c
twist 2
warp 1
contorted
crooked 2
deformed 1
gnarled
misshapen
wry 1
contortion
twist 9
warp 2
contour
form 2
line[1] 5
outline 1
profile 1
silhouette
-contours
shape 1
contour sheet
sheet 1
contraband
booty
contract°
abbreviate 1
abridge
accord 3
agreement 1
apprentice 2
arrangement 3
bargain 1
bond 2
catch 5
charter 1, 3, 5
come 12
deal 5
decrease 1
deed 3
diminish 1
dwindle
engage 3
engagement 3
farm 4
flex 3
form 10
gather 3
get 5
instrument 3
job 6
knit 3
let[1] 3
match 3
negotiation 2
obligation 2
pact
pick 8k
pledge 4
project 2
promise 1
pucker 1
purse 4
shrink 1
shrivel
sicken 1
sign 10a
treaty
understanding 1
undertake 2
undertaking 3
-under contract
fascinate
contract for
engage 1
line[1] 23b
order 15
reserve 2
contractile
elastic 1
contraction
abbreviation
abridgement 1
decrease 2
epitome 2
-contractions
labour 4
contradict°
deny 1
destroy 4
differ 2
disprove
fight 2
fly 6
rebut
traverse 3
contradiction
confusion 3
denial 1
disagreement 2
paradox
rebuttal
contradictory°
confused 1
contrary 1
destructive 2
differ 2
discordant 1
incompatible
incongruous
mixed 2
negative 1
opposing
opposite 2
paradoxical
perverse 1
polar 2
puzzling
contradistinction
difference 1
-in contradistinction to
unlike 3
contradistinguish
differentiate 1
contraption°
apparatus
device 1
gadget
gimmick 2
implement 1
instrument 1
invention 2
machine 1
tool 1
contrariety
difference 1
discrepancy
diversity 1
contrarily
contrary 5
contrariness
obstinacy
contrarious
contrary 2
contrariwise
contrary 5
only 4
vice versa
contrary°
cantankerous
destructive 2
different 1
difficult 3
discordant 1
disobedient 2
hostile 1
incompatible
incongruous
insubordinate
negative 1
obstinate
opposed
opposing
contrary (*cont.*)
opposite 2, 3
perverse 1
polar 2
quarrelsome
recalcitrant
reverse 1, 6
self-willed
wilful 2
-on the contrary
only 4
vice versa
contrast°
compare 3
comparison 1
differ 1
difference 1
differentiate 1
disparity
distinction 1
diversity 1
oppose 3
opposition 1
pit[1] 6
relief 3
set 13a
show 12b
variety 2
-as contrasted with
instead 2
-contrasts
vicissitude 2
-in contrast to
unlike 3
contrasting
comparison 1
different 1
dissimilar
distinct 2
opposed
opposing
opposite 2
unlike 1, 3
contrastive
different 1
unlike 1
contravene
break 9
contradict 2
disobey
fight 2
fly 6
infringe 1
transgress 2
traverse 3
violate 1
contravened
broken 5
contravention
breach 1
infringement
violation 1
contretemps
misfortune 2
run-in
contribute°
afford 2
chip 4a
cooperate 2
donate
far 6b
finger 6
give 1
impart 1
invest 2
lay[1] 18b
lend 2
open 25
part 11
participate
pay 11b
pitch[1] 5
provide 1
put 28d, 28e
stump 4
subscribe 2
supply 1, 2
contributed
voluntary 1
contribute to°
at **contribute 2**
advance 2
bring 5
contribute to (*cont.*)
lead 6
make 30c
part 11
participate
patronize 3
subscribe 2
contribution
benevolence 2
charity 3
donation 1, 2
endowment 1
gift 1
grant 3
job 2
largesse
maintenance 3
offering
payment 2
philanthropy 2
present[2] 2
submission 2
subsidy
tax 1
tribute 2
contributor
donor
participant 1
party 4
philanthropist
contributory
instrumental
supplementary 2
con trick
deceit 2
rip-off 2
contrite
apologetic
bad 8
guilty 2
penitent
regretful
remorseful
repentant
sorry 1
terrible 2
contrition
compunction 1
guilt 2
pang 2
penance 1
penitence
regret 2
remorse
repent
contrivance
arrangement 2
artifice 2
contraption
deceit 2
device 1, 2
dodge 4
expedient 3
fabrication 2
fixture 2
gadget
gimmick 2
implement 1
instrument 1
invention 1, 2
machine 1
mechanism 1
medium 5
subterfuge
thing 5
tool 1
wile
contrive
arrange 2
brew 2
compose 2
conceive 2
create 2
design 2
devise 1
discover 3
draw 6
engineer 4
fix 12
form 8
frame 7
generate 4
get 9
hatch 2

contrive (*cont.*)
improvise 2
invent 1
make 1
manoeuvre 3
manufacture 2
muddle 3
originate 1
project 3
scheme 4
stage 5
strike 16
think 6
wangle
weave 3
work 19e
contrived
affected 1
artificial 3
forced
glossy 2
imaginative 2
intentional
laboured 2
mannered
premeditated
rhetorical 2
spurious
studied
unnatural 4
contriver
engineer 1
mastermind 2
contriving
calculating
disingenuous
invention 1
control°
administer 1
assurance 5
auspices
authority 1
balance 5
better[1] 8
bond 1
boss 2
bottle 4a
brake 1
bridle 1, 2
care 3
chain 2
charge 4
charm 5
check 2, 14, 15
clutch 2b
command 2, 3, 5, 7, 8
conduct 2, 3
contain 3
cool 8
curb 1, 2
department 2
direct 1
direction 1
discipline 4, 7
disposition 4
dominate 1
domination 1
dominion 1
drive 2
economy 1
finger 10
fluency
govern 1, 2
government 1
grasp 4
grip 2
guard 2
guidance 1
guide 3
hand 8
handle 3, 4, 6
head 11
helm 2
hold 14a, 15a, 17a, 26
influence 1
inhibit
jurisdiction
keep 1
leadership
lock[1] 2
manacle 3
manage 1, 2, 3
management 1

control (*cont.*)
manipulate 1, 2
master 8
measure 8, 12
monopolize
mortify 2
mould[1] 6
normalize
obsess
occupation 2
operate 2
operation 2
oversee
patent 1
peg 5
philosophy 3
pilot 3
poise 2
police 3
possess 3
possession 1
power 2, 3
predominance
predominate
preponderance 2
preside
prevalence 2
prevent
prevention
providence 2
ration 4
regiment
regulate 1, 2
regulation 1
reign 1, 2
rein 1, 2, 3
remedy 3
repress
repression 2
reserve 4
resist 1
restrain 1
restraint 1, 2, 3
ride 1
rule 2, 5, 6
run 10
self-control 1, 2
shackle 4
shape 7
shot 9
steer 1
stem[2] 1
stifle 2
stint 2, 3
string 6
subdue 1, 3
supervise
suppress 3
suppression
supremacy 2
swallow 4
sway 4
take 37
tame 6
temperance 1
time 22
understanding 3
upper 6
withhold 1
work 10
-in control
line[1] 19c
rampant 2
rule 5
self-contained 1
string 6
-out of control
obstreperous
rampage 2
rampant 1
uncontrolled
-under (someone's) control
cool 2
line[1] 19c
subject 8a
tame 3
thumb 5
under 2
controllable
gentle 2
manageable
navigable 2

controlled
collected
cool 2
impassive
moderate 1
phlegmatic 2
poised 1
possessed
reserved
scientific
sedate 1
self-contained 1, 2
self-possessed
Spartan
steady 4
stoical
subject 8a
temperate 1
under 2
controller
master 1
superintendent
supervisor
controlling
dominant 1
influential
master 5
obsessive
possessive 2
predominant
prevention
suppression
control oneself
compose 4
simmer 3
controversial°
debatable
disputable
doubtful 3
moot 1
problematic
thorny 2
controversy°
argument 1
combat 2
conflict 2
contest 2
debate 1
disagreement 3
dispute 3
faction 2
friction 2
issue 4
misunderstanding 2
quarrel 1
rivalry
variance 2
controvert
contradict 1
deny 1
disprove
rebut
traverse 3
contumacious
contrary 2
defiant
disobedient 2
insubordinate
mutinous 2
obstinate
rebellious 1
recalcitrant
rogue 2
self-willed
unruly
contumacy
obstinacy
rebellion 2
contumelious
contemptuous
derisory
disdainful
lofty 4
regal 2
sarcastic
scornful
vituperative
contumely
contempt
derision
indignity
mockery 1
patronage 3

contumely (*cont.*)
sarcasm
scorn 1
contuse
bruise 2
contusion
bruise 1
welt 2
wound 1
conundrum
enigma
mystery 1
problem 2
puzzle 4
riddle[1]
conurbation
city
convalesce°
improve 3
mend 3
recover 2
recuperate
convalescence
improvement 2
recovery 1
convalescent
mend 5
convalescent home
hospital
sanatorium
convalescing
mend 5
convene
assemble 1
call 4
collect 1
gather 2
get 50b
hold 10
mass 8
meet[1] 2
muster 1
raise 5
rally 3
sit 2
summon 1
convenience
accommodate 5
accommodation 3
facility 2b
lavatory
prepared 4
time 8
toilet 1
-at one's convenience
leisure 3b
convenient°
available
cosy 2
favourable 1
fit[1] 1
hand 9
handy 1
leisure 3b
lucky 2
opportune 2
ready 7
ready-made 2
right 3
seasonable
serve 4
suit 2
timely
convention°
assembly 2
ceremony 2
code 3
company 2
conference
council 1
custom 1
etiquette
form 6
formality 1
gathering
get-together
habit 1
meeting 2
motif
muster 2
observance 2

convention (*cont.*)
ordinary 3
practice 1
protocol 1
rally 1
ritual 3
rule 3
tradition
usage 1
-conventions
ceremony 2
code 3
protocol 1
conventional°
bourgeois 1
ceremonious 2
common 1
conservative 2
correct 7
customary 1
everyday 2
formal 1
habitual 1
hidebound
narrow-minded
normal 1
ordinary 2
orthodox
parochial
popular 2
ready-made 3
regular 1, 11
ritual 2
routine 3
sedate 2
set 29
square 6
standard 6
standing 1
staple 2
step 7
stuffy 2
time-honoured
traditional
typical 1, 2
usual
conventionalism
convention 2
conventionality
formality 1
conventionally
generally 1
convention hall
hall 2
converge°
centre 2
collect 1
concentrate 1
focus 4
press 7
convergence
focus 1
meeting 3
press 8
convergent
focal
conversance
familiarity 1
knowledge 3
conversancy
exposure 3
conversant
acquainted 2
familiar 4
home 5
informed 2
understand 1
versed
conversation°
chat 1
dialogue 1
discussion
gossip 1
interview 1
palaver 3
rap 5
repartee
talk 15
word 1
conversational
verbal 1
vernacular 2

conversationalist°
conversation piece
curiosity 3
rarity 1
converse°
chat 2
chew 2
communicate 2
confer 1
discuss
opposite 3
palaver 5
rag[1] 5a
rap 3
reverse 1, 6
speak 1, 2, 3
talk 1, 12
conversely
vice versa
conversion
adaptation 1
alteration
difference 3
passage 5
transformation
transition 1
translation 1, 2
variation 1
convert°
alter
change 8
differentiate 2
make 9
persuade 2
process 3
redeem 4
reduce 4
render 6
resolve 4
tailor 2
transform
translate 1, 2
turn 3, 23d
win 3
convertible
changeable 2
liquid 4
converting
variation 1
convey
bear 1
bring 2, 4
carry 1, 2, 3
cart 2
cede
channel 5
communicate 1
conduct 5
deliver 1
devise 2
dispatch 2
distribute 1
express 2
fetch 1
give 3
haul 2
impart 1
import 2
insinuate 1
make 38b
mean[1] 2
pass 8
pipe 5
put 10, 25a
route 2
run 13
say 9
sell 1
send 2
signify 1
speak 5
take 9, 18
transfer 1
translate 4
transmit 1
transport 1
voice 4
wash 2
-be conveyed
ride 1
roll 3

conveyance
delivery 1
freight 1
medium 5
succession 1
traffic 1
transfer 2
transit 2
translation 4
transmission 1
transport 4
vehicle 1
conveyancing
succession 1
surrender 3
conveyor
pipe 1
pipeline 1
convey title
sell 1
convict°
captive 1
condemn 2
criminal 3
inmate
prisoner
conviction°
belief 3
certainty 2
confidence 2
doctrine
faith 1
hope 2
idea 3
obsession
opinion 1
persuasion 2
presumption 3
security 2
tenet
trust 1
-convictions
ideology
convince°
argue 6
assure 3
bring 14b
induce 1
lead 2
persuade 2
prevail 3
reason 8
satisfy 3
stir 4
sway 2
talk 10
win 3
convinced
believe 2
clear 10
confident 1
positive 3
sell 5
sure 1
convincing
eloquent 1
forceful 1, 2
good 8
persuasive
positive 1
potent 2
solid 7
strong 7, 8
weighty 3
convincingness
strength 7
convivial
friendly 1
gala 2
genial
hearty 1
jolly 1
merry 1
sociable
conviviality
festivity 1
friendship 1
gaiety 2
hilarity
convocation
assembly 2
council 1
gathering
meeting 2

convocation *(cont.)*
muster 2
rally 1
convoke
assemble 1
call 4
hold 10
muster 1
summon 1
convoluted
elaborate 2
intricate 1
involved 2
labyrinthine
meandering
perplexing
tortuous 1
convolution
complexity 1
complication 1
twirl 3
-convolutions
maze
meander 2
convoy
accompany 1
attend 4
escort 1, 5
fleet[1]
flock 1
guard 1, 4
retinue
see 6
shepherd
squire 1
suite 3
take 18
walk 2
convulse
shudder 1
convulsion
fit[2] 1
paroxysm
passion 2
seizure 2
shudder 2
spasm 1, 2
throe
convulsive
spasmodic 1
co-occur
coincide
co-occurrence
coincidence 1
cook
brew 1, 3
fabricate 3
falsify
fiddle 1
happen 1
juggle
make 17
manipulate 3
prepare 4
rig 2
servant 1
simmer 1
cooker
range 4
cookhouse
kitchen
cookie
broad 9
fate 1
cookie-cutter
flat 7
cooking
pipeline 2
swing 6
torrid 1
cookout
picnic 1
cook-pot
pot 1
cook someone's goose
fix 14
cook-stove
range 4
cook up
brew 2
devise 1

cook up *(cont.)*
fabricate 3
formulate 2
hatch 2
imagine 1
invent 2
make 39c
manufacture 2
plot[1] 3
prepare 4
project 3
scheme 4
cooky
broad 9
cool°
aloof 3
bland 1
blasé 2
brisk 3
calm 4
casual 3
chill 4, 7
chilly 1, 2
cold 3
cold-blooded 2
cold-hearted
collected
confident 2
dampen 2
dead 4
deliberate 3
dispassionate 1
distant 3
equable 1
even 4
excellent
fabulous 3
fine[1] 1
fresh 7
frigid 2
half-hearted
hard 6
hip
icy 2
impassive
impersonal 2
indifferent 1
inhospitable 1
insensible 2
lackadaisical 2
level-headed
listless
lukewarm 2
minute[1] 3
moderate 1
neat 5
negative 2
nonchalant
noncommittal
offhand 1
passive 1
philosophical 2
phlegmatic 2
poise 2
poised 1
presence 5
refrigerate
relaxed
reserved
rocky[1] 3
sang-froid
sedate 1
self-contained 1
self-possessed
serene 2
sight 6b
sober 2
sophisticated 1
splendid 3
standoffish
steady 4
stiff 7
stoical
superb
temper 2
temperate 1
tepid 2
tough 6
tranquil
turn 17b
unaffected[2]
unapproachable 1
unenthusiastic
unmoved
unsocial

cool *(cont.)*
unsympathetic
well-balanced 1
wintry 2
worldly 2
cool down
calm 5
loose 9
relax 4
simmer 3
wind[2] 3b
cooler
jail 1
prison
cool-headed
calm 4
cool 2
philosophical 2
phlegmatic 2
poised 1
serene 2
sober 2
temperate 1
tranquil
well-balanced 1
cool-headedness
philosophy 3
poise 2
presence 5
sang-froid
self-control 2
serenity 2
cooling
cool 1
refreshing
cool it
relax 4
simmer 3
coolly
severely 3
well[1] 8
coolness
assurance 5
calm 2
chill 1, 3
confidence 2
cool 7
detachment 2
distance 2
indifference 1
nerve 1
philosophy 3
poise 2
presence 5
reserve 4
sang-froid
self-control 2
stoicism
temper 2
cool off
calm 5
loose 9
simmer 3
turn 17b
wind[2] 3b
cool one's heels
dangle 3
wait 1
coolth
cool 7
sang-froid
coomb
valley
co-op
store 4
coop
cage 1, 2
fence 3
hovel
jail 1
pen[2] 1
shut 6a
stall[1] 3
cooperate°
club 6
collaborate
fall 15
hang 11a
pitch[1] 5
play 8a, 11
stick[1] 16a
team 3

cooperation°
give and take
cooperative
accommodating 1
association 1
flexible 2
good-natured
helpful
joint 4
store 4
united 2
cooperatively
shoulder 5
cooperative store
store 4
coop up
cage 2
hold 5
keep 14b
lock[1] 6c, 9
pen[2] 2
shut 6a
coordinate°
line[1] 23a
match 7
moderate 6
mount 5
organize 1
parallel 1
relate 1, 3
related 1
run 10
set 6
settle 1
tie 6a, 6b
tune 3
-coordinates
ensemble 1
coordinated
organic 3
pitched
related 1
united 2
coordinating
coordinate 3
coordination
adjustment 2
organization 1
coordinative
coordinate 3
coordinator
moderator
cop
constable
detective
officer 2
police officer
-cops
police 1
copacetic
fabulous 3
cope°
get 28b
make 29
muddle 3
scrape 5
cope with°
at cope 2
face 14, 18b
field 6
grapple 2
grip 5
handle 4, 6
manage 2
relate 4
stand 3
tackle 3
withstand
copied
derivative 1
secondary 2
copier
scribe 1
copious
abundant 1
ample 4, 6
bountiful 2
fertile
fruitful 3
full 5
generous 3
heavy 2

copious *(cont.)*
lavish 1
liberal 1
luxuriant 1
opulent 3
plentiful 1
prodigal 2
profuse 1, 3, 4
prolific 1
rich 2, 9
torrential
voluminous 1
copiously
amply 3
water 3
copiousness
abundance
exuberance 2
plenty 2
prodigality 2
profusion
wealth 2
cop out
evade 2
cop-out
excuse 6
copper
constable
detective
officer 2
police officer
-coppers
change 4
police 1
copperplate
neat 3
coppice
shrubbery
stand 19
copse
brush[1] 2
clump 2
shrubbery
stand 19
thicket
copulate
lay[1] 8
mate 5
copulation
intercourse 2
sex 2
copy°
counterfeit 4
double 6, 7
dummy 2
duplicate 2, 3
echo 2, 4
edition
extract 4
facsimile
follow 2
forge 3
image 2
imitate 1, 2
imitation 3, 4
impression 4
issue 5
knock 5b
knock-off
lift 6
likeness 2
match 1
mimic 1, 2
model 1, 9, 10
monkey 4
news 4
number 3
parrot 2
pattern 7
picture 2
pirate 3
print 1, 2
repeat 3
replica
reproduce 1
reproduction 2
run 29b
sham 1
spit 2
steal 2
story 4
trace 6
transcribe 1
transcript 2

copybook
school-book
copycat
mimic 4
parrot 1
copy-edit
edit 1
copy editor
editor
copying
imitation 1
plagiarism
reproduction 1
copyist
scribe 1
copyright
patent 1
coquette
flirt 1, 3
temptress
coquettish
flirtatious
kittenish
seductive
cor
indeed 3
corbel
bracket 1
cord°
bond 1
flex 1
lace 2
lead 15
line[1] 11
rope 1
string 1
tether 1
thread 1
tie 9
twine 1
cordial°
amicable
benign 1
brotherly
civil 3
comfortable 3
familiar 3
friendly 2
genial
good-natured
gracious
hearty 1
hospitable 1
kind[1]
mellow 4
neighbourly
nice 1
outgoing 2
peaceable 2
polite 1
ready 2
respectful
sociable
thaw 2
warm 3
cordiality
civility
fellowship 3
hospitality
kindness 1
warmth 2
cordially
kindly 2
warmly 2
well[1] 5
cordon
circle 1
queue 1
cordon off
siege 2
core°
base[1] 3
body 4
bosom 2
bowels
breast 2
centre 1
elixir 3
essence 1
fabric 2
focus 1
gist
heart 3
core (*cont.*)
hub
inside 1
interior 6
kernel 2
meat 2
nub 2
nucleus
pith 1
point 5
quintessence
spirit 6
substance 2
theme 1
thick 10
-to the core
home 10
through 7
cork
plug 1, 4
seal 3
stopper
tap[2] 2
top 2
corked-up
pent-up
corkscrew
screw 2
spiral 1, 2
corm
seed 1
cormorant
greedy 1
voracious 1
corn
cure 3
grain 2
lump[1] 2
preserve 3
provender 2
salt 7
sentimentality
whisky
corn-cob
pipe 2
corned
salt 10
corner
angle[1] 1
bend 1
buttonhole 1
fix 17
hole 5
monopolize
nook 1
part 6
predicament
recess 3
turn 27
universe 2
-around the corner
hand 9
cornerstone
essence 1
fundamental 2
groundwork
keystone
corner the market
monopolize
corniness
sentimentality
cornucopia
wealth 2
corny
banal
mushy 2
sentimental 2
stock 7
corollary
law 3
corona
glory 4
halo
ring[1] 1
coronach
lament 2
coronate
crown 4
coronation
installation 1
coronet
crown 1
ring[1] 1
corporal
mortal 2
physical
corporation
business 4
company 4
employer 2
firm 6
gut 2
office 1
outfit 3
paunch
pot 3
stomach 1
trust 4
corporeal
earthly 2
flesh 3
material 5
mortal 2
physical
real 2
sensible 2
tangible
worldly 1
corporeality
flesh 2
substance 4
corporealization
image 4
corps°
band[2] 1
body 6
cohort 2
crew
group 1
party 2
shift 4
corpse°
body 1
cadaver
remain 4b
stiff 11
corpse-like
white 2
corpulence
fat 5
fatness
obesity
corpulent
burly
fat 1
gross 1
heavy 11
large 1
obese
plump[1] 1
rotund 3
stout 1
weighty 1
corpus juris
code 1
law 2
corral
catch 2
crowd 4
enclose 1
enclosure 1
herd 4
pen[2] 1, 2
round 19
stall[1] 3
corralling
round-up 1
correct°
accurate 1
adjust 1
amend 2
appropriate 1
castigate
ceremonious 2
chasten 1
chastise
counteract
cure 2
decorous
discipline 8
due 2
edit 1
ethical
correct (*cont.*)
exact 1
expedient 1
factual 2
faithful 2
faultless
fit[1] 1
fix 3
formal 1
good 3
grade 7
honourable 2
impeccable
improve 1
incorrupt 2
ladylike
legitimate 3
make 31a
mark 14
mend 1, 2
nail 5
OK 2
order 10b
perfect 4, 5, 9
place 11a
polish 2
precise 1
principled
proper 2, 3, 4, 6
punish 1
pure 3
rectify
reform 1
regular 6
remedy 4
retouch
revise 1
right 1, 2, 19
righteous 2
rightful 1
safe 4
serve 5
square 3
straighten 1
suitable
tasteful
true 1, 3
correction°
adjustment 1
amendment 1
discipline 2
punishment 1
reform 3
revision
rod 2
correctional
penal
punitive
correctional institution
prison
corrective
therapeutic
correctly
appropriately
duly 1
exactly 1
precisely 2
properly 1, 2
right 17
true 5
well[1] 3
correctness
accuracy
decorum 2
formality 2
precision 1
propriety 1
purity 1
rectitude
taste 6
truth 1
correlate
answer 5
compare 3
coordinate 2
parallel 4
relate 1
correlated
proportional
related 1
correlation
bearing 3
connection 2
correlation (*cont.*)
parallel 3
proportion 2
ratio
correlative
coordinate 3
reciprocal
correspond°
accord 1
agree 1
check 5
coincide
communicate 2
compare 2
conform 2
contact 4
equal 5
fit[1] 6
hang 11b
match 7
overlap 2
parallel 4
reciprocate
resemble
similar 2
square 11
tally 1
tie 6a
write 2
correspondence
accord 4
coincidence 1
equality 2
kinship 2
letter 2
likeness 1
mail 1
note 2
parallel 3
parity 2
proportion 2
ratio
relation 1
resemblance
symmetry
tune 2
uniformity 1
writing 2
correspondent°
coordinate 3
equal 2
journalist
like[1] 1
parallel 1
reporter
writer
-correspondents
press 10b
corresponding
equal 2
equivalent 1
identical 2
like[1] 1
matching 1, 2
parallel 1
proportional
relative 2
respective
synonymous
twin 2
unison
corridor°
gully
hall 1
lobby 1
passage 4
corrie
valley
corrigendum
correction 1
corroborate
authenticate
bear 9
certify 1
check 3
confirm 3
document 2
establish 3
manifest 3
prove 1
ratify
seal 4
show 3
corroborate (*cont.*)
strengthen 1
substantiate
support 6
verify
witness 3
corroboration
check 15
evidence 1
identification 1
proof 1
reflection 4
seal 2
testimony
corroborator
witness 2
corrode
attack 5
erode
etch 1
gnaw 2
rot 1
wear 3
corroded
pitted
rotten 2
corrosion
attack 9
erosion
rot 3
wear 9
corrosive
caustic 1
tart[1] 2
trenchant
corrugate
contract 5
furrow 3
pucker 1
wrinkle[1] 2
corrugation
furrow 1
wrinkle[1] 1
corrupt°
abandoned 2
abusive 3
adulterate
bad 2, 3
base[2] 6
bent 2
bribe 2
buy 3
contaminate
criminal 2
debase 2
decadent 2
degenerate 1
demoralize 2
desecrate
diabolic 2
dirty 3
disgraceful 1
dishonest
dishonourable 2
dissolute
evil 1, 2
filthy 3
fix 11
foul 7
garble 1
get 30d
ill 2
immoral 1
improper 3
jaundiced 1
lawless 2
loose 7
lost 7
mercenary 2
miscreant 2
perfidious
pervert 1, 2
perverted
pollute 2
profane 4
profligate 1
putrid
rancid
rank[2] 2, 3
rotten 1, 3
ruin 11
satanic 1
seduce 2

corrupt *(cont.)*
shameful
sinful
sinister 2
sordid 1
stain 5
taint 2
ugly 2
ungodly 1
unscrupulous
unwholesome 2
venal
vicious 1
vile 1
villainous 1
vitiate 1, 2
wicked 2
wrong 1
corrupted
bent 2
degenerate 1
impure 4
corruptible
accommodating 2
venal
corrupting
ruin 2
unwholesome 2
corruption
abuse 7
degradation 1
dirt 3
evil 6
filth 2, 3
graft[2]
impurity 3
misuse 2
parody 2
perversion 1
pollution
profligacy 1
prostitution 2
rot 3
ruin 2
sin 2
vice 1
corruptive
poisonous 2
corsage
buttonhole 2
corsair
pirate 1
robber
thief 3
cortège
escort 1
line[1] 6
march 2
parade 1
procession 1
queue 1
retinue
suite 3
train 2
coruscate
blink 2
flash 4
radiate 1
shine 1
sparkle 1
twinkle 1
coruscating
brilliant 1
nimble 2
radiant 1
scintillating 1
shiny
twinkle 2
coruscation
flash 1
radiance 1
sparkle 3
twinkle 2
coryza
chill 2
cold 10
Cosa Nostra
syndicate 2
underworld 1
cosh
club 1
cosher
pamper
co-sign
enter 8
co-signatory
party 5
cosily
swimmingly
cosmetic
flashy 2
superficial 2
token 5
-cosmetics
make-up 1
paint 3
cosmic
extensive 1
universal 2
cosmopolitan
cultivated
extensive 1
genteel 3
international
sophisticated 1
suave
worldly 2
cosmopolitan-ism
sophistication 1
style 4
cosmos
creation 2
nature 2
universe 1
world 1
cosset
baby 2
cater 2
cherish 2
coddle
humour 4
indulge 2
make 34b
pamper
pet[1] 5
cost°
charge 2
damage 2
expenditure
expense 1, 2
fare 2
fee 1
fetch 3
hire 5
outlay
overhead 3
price 1, 2, 5
quotation 2
subscription 1
toll[2] 2
upkeep 2
-at any cost
means[3] 2b
-at cost
cheap 7
-costs
expense 1
overhead 3
upkeep
-without cost
free 4
cost-effective
economic 2
economical 1
profitable 1
worthwhile 1
cost-free
free 4
costly
dear 2
expensive
extravagant 3
high 3
hollow 5
invaluable
plush
precious 1
premium 4b
priceless 1
pricey
rich 4
sumptuous
costume°
disguise 3
dress 5b, 6
costume *(cont.)*
ensemble 1
garments
get-up 1
habit 3
outfit 2
robe 1, 2
suit 3
uniform 3
costume party
masquerade 1
costumier
tailor 1
cosy°
cajole
easy 2
home 4a
homely 2
intimate[1] 4
secure 1
snug
sociable
tête-à-tête 3
warm 1
cot°
cabin 1
cottage
hut
cote
enclosure 1
hut
shed[1]
stall[1] 3
cotemporaneous
parallel 1
coterie
cabal 2
camp[1] 2
circle 2
clan 2
clique
company 2
crowd 2
faction 1
fellowship 2
fraternity 1
gang 2
group 1
junta
pack 3
party 3
ring[1] 3
school 2
set 26
world 3
cotquean
prostitute 1
cottage°
cabin 1
lodge 1
outside 7
cotton on (to)
get 43c
realize 2
understand 1
couch°
lounge 5
phrase 4
word 10
cough
hack[1] 2
cough drop
pill 1
cough up
pay 11b
stump 4
coulée
canyon
couloir
pass 23
council°
assembly 2
board 4
body 6
cabinet 2
committee
convention 1
diet[2]
house 3
municipal
parliament 2
Councillor
representative 3
counsel°
advice 1
advise 1
adviser
advocate 3
caution 1, 3
counsellor
direct 2
enlighten
guidance 2
guide 3, 5
lawyer
preach 2
recommend 1
recommenda-tion 1
suggestion 1
urge 3
warn 2
warning 1
counselling
advisory 1
guidance 2
counsellor°
adviser
consultant 2
counsel 3
guide 5
teacher
therapist
counselor-at-law
advocate 3
counsellor
lawyer
solicitor
count°
add 2
calculate
calculation 2
detail 1
enumerate 2
figure 8
include 3
itemize
lord 2
matter 6
number 4
poll 2, 3
put 16f
rank[1] 7
rate[1] 6, 8
reckon 2
score 1, 12
signify 2
tally 2, 3
trust 5
weigh 5
countable
finite
countenance
abet 2
allow 4
approve 1
authorize
endorse 1
expression 3
face 1
feature 3
front 4
hold 23
look 14
mug 2
permission
permit 1
sanction 2, 6
stand 3
stomach 3
subscribe 1
support 3
tolerate 1
countenancing
allowance 1
counter°
bar 7
check 18
chip 2
contest 3
contradict 2
cover 10
fly 6
foil[1]
frustrate 1
militate 1
counter *(cont.)*
oppose 1
respond 1
retaliate
retort 2
stall[1] 2
stand 16
traverse 3
-under the coun-ter
furtive 1
unlawful
counter-accusation
recrimination
counteract°
cancel 3
contradict 2
correct 4
destroy 3
fly 6
frustrate 1
neutralize
offset 1
resist 1
counteractant
antidote
preventive 4
remedy 1
counteraction
backlash
offset 2
opposition 1
reaction 2
counteractive
preventive 2
counter-agent
preventive 4
counter-argument
rebuttal
counter-attack
oppose 1
recrimination
counterbalance
balance 3
cancel 3
compensate 2
correct 4
counteract
cover 10
neutralize
offset 1, 2
oppose 3
parallel 3
reaction 2
countercharge
recrimination
counter-clockwise
backwards 1
counter-espionage agent
operative 4
counterfeit°
act 8
affect[2] 1
affected 2
artificial 2
assume 4
assumed 2
base[2] 5
bogus
deceitful
deceptive 2
disguise 2
dishonest
dissimulate
duff
erroneous
fabricate 3
factitious
fake 1, 3, 5
false 3, 4
fictitious 2
forge 3
forgery 2
fraudulent 1
glorified 2
glossy 2
hollow 4
imitation 3
mimic 5
counterfeit *(cont.)*
mock 3
phoney 1, 2
plastic 3
pretended
quack 2
sham 1, 2
spurious
synthetic
unreal 3
counterfeiter°
phoney 3
counterfeiting
forgery 1
counterfoil
check 17
receipt 1
stub 2
tally 5
counterglow
light[1] 1
counter-intelligence agent
operative 4
counterirritant
antidote
counter-jumper
salesperson
seller
countermand
cancel 1
reverse 3
countermeasure
preventive 4
remedy 1, 2
countermine
fly 6
counterpane
cover 13
spread 14
counterpart
double 7
equal 4
equivalent 2
fellow 3
image 2
like[1] 7
match 1
mate 3
parallel 2
spit 2
tally 5
twin 1
counterpoise
balance 3
compensate 2
offset 1
counter-productive
prejudicial
countersign
endorse 2
enter 8
execute 2
password
sign 7
underwrite 2
witness 5
counter-signature
endorsement 2
counter-spy
operative 4
counter-statement
answer 2
countervail
cancel 3
fly 6
foil[1]
militate 1
offset 1
resist 1
countess
peer[1] 1
count in
involve 1
counting
calculation 1
inclusion

counting (*cont.*)
reckoning 1
counting up
addition 2
countless
frequent 1
great 2
inestimable 2
limitless
lot 5c
numberless
umpteen
untold 1
count on°
at **count 3**
anticipate 3
bargain 4
depend 2
expect 3
fall 9
figure 11a
gamble 2
go 26b
hope 3
lean[2] 4a
look 6c, 7b
reckon 4
rely
store 5
swear 3
trust 5
count out
exclude 2
leave[1] 10
tally 2
countrified
rustic 2
country°
dominion 2
fatherland
land 4
monarchy 1
nation
pastoral 2
province 2
provincial 2
rural 1
state 4
stick[2] 3
country cousin
provincial 3
rustic 3
country-like
green 1
countryman, countrywoman
peasant
rustic 3
countryside
country 3
landscape
nature 3
province 4
stick[2] 3
country-wide
national 1
count sheep
rest[1] 6
retire 3
count upon°
at **count 3**
expect 3
fall 9
figure 11a
hope 3
look 7b
rely
trust 5
county
genteel 1
high-class 2
local 2
coup
accomplishment 2
hit 11
killing 2
plum
revolution 1
triumph 1
uprising
coup de grâce
clincher
finish 4
coup de grâce (*cont.*)
kill 1, 9
knockout 1
coup d'état
revolt 1
revolution 1
uprising
coup de théâtre
sensation 3
coup d'oeil
glance 4
minute[1] 1
couple°
brace 4
connect 3
fix 1
handful 1
hitch 1
join 1
lay[1] 8
link 3
marry 2
mate 4, 5
pair 1
relate 1
tack 5
tie 1
twin 3
coupled
double 1
package 3
related 1
coupler
brace 3
terminal 5
coupling
brace 3
connection 1
link 1
marriage 3
sex 2
terminal 5
union 3
courage°
backbone 3
bottle 2
bravery
character 3
chivalry
confidence 2
daring 1
enterprise 2
fortitude
grit
gumption 2
gut 3a
heart 2
nerve 1
pluck 1
prowess 2
spirit 5
spunk
stamina
courageous°
adventurous
audacious 1
bold 1
brave 1
confident 2
daredevil 2
daring 2
dauntless
enterprising
fearless
gallant 1
game 8
gritty 2
hardy 2
heroic 1
indomitable
intrepid
manly
martial 2
stalwart 3
stout 2
superhuman 1
venturesome 1
yeomanly
courier
messenger
runner 2
course°
approach 5
beat 12
chain 1
channel 4
circuit 2
circulate 1
circulation 1
current 6
cycle 1
direction 2
discipline 5
drift 3
education 3
flow 1, 5
form 4
hunt 1, 3
journey 2
line[1] 9
mean[3] 4a
measure 6
medium 5
method 1
mode[1] 1
movement 7
orbit 1
pass 2
passage 3
path 2, 3
plate 2
pour 1
procedure
procession 2
progress 3
progression 3
race[1] 2
road 1
round 12
route 1
run 38
scheme 1
sequence
span 2
spell[1] 1
step 10a
stream 4
subject 2
succession 2
tack 3
term 3
thread 2
tier
track 2
trail 1
trajectory
trend 1
vein 3, 5
way 1, 3, 4
-in the course of
for 10
over 4
through 2
-of course°
at **course 6**
absolutely 3
indeed 1
mean[3] 2a
naturally 1
necessarily
needless 2
obviously
-off course
erroneous
course of action
measure 6
procedure
process 1
scheme 1
way 1
course of study
education 3
subject 2
course of treatment
cure 1
court
area 5
bar 5
chase 2
cultivate 4
flatter 1
go 33c, 40b
play 18
pursue 4
romance 6
court (*cont.*)
run 21
see 7
take 36
train 2
tribunal
courteous°
amicable
attentive 2
ceremonious 2
chivalrous
civil 3
cordial
debonair 1
decent 4
diplomatic
fair[1] 8
gallant 2
genteel 2
good-natured
graceful 2
gracious
hospitable 1
kind[1]
ladylike
neighbourly
nice 1
obliging
orderly 2
pleasant 2
polite 1
refined 1
respect 7
respectful
suave
well-bred
courteously
kindly 2
courteousness
civility
courtesy
hospitality
courtesan
prostitute 1
tart[2] 2
courtesy°
chivalry
civility
deference 1
etiquette
favour 2
hospitality
propriety 2
respect 2
turn 35
courtier
flatterer
yes-man
courtliness
chivalry
courtesy
decorum 1
dignity 1
elegance 1
refinement 1
courtly
attentive 2
ceremonious 2
chivalrous
civil 3
courteous
dignified
elegant 1
gallant 2
genteel 2
graceful 2
ladylike
polished 2
refined 1
smooth 6
well-bred
courtroom
bar 5
courtship
suit 5
courtyard
area 5
enclosure 1
couturier, couturière
dressmaker
tailor 1
cove
chap
character 6
creek 1
gulf 1
sound[4]
covenant
agreement 1
arrangement 3
bargain 1
bond 2
charter 1
commit 4
contract 2
engage 3
engagement 3
negotiation 2
obligation 2
pact
pledge 1
promise 1
protocol 2
stipulate
stipulation
treaty
understand 2
understanding 1
undertake 2
warranty
covenanted
understood
cover°
bind 3
blind 7, 8
blot 4a
brood 2
camouflage 1, 2
cap 2, 5
case[2] 2
cloak 2
coat 3
conceal 1
defence 1
defray
eclipse 1
envelop 1, 2
face 6, 16
film 1, 4
flood 7
flow 4
front 5
glaze 1
hide[1] 2
housing 2
include 1
insulate 2
insurance
involve 1
line[2] 1
make 19
man 4
mantle 2, 3
mask 2, 3
muffle 1
obscure 6
occupy 4
paint 5
patch 5
pave 1
pertain
plaster
plate 6
powder 4
precaution 1
pretence 2
pretext 1, 2
protect 1
prowl 2
range 8
refuge 1
report 6
retrieve 3
robe 3
run 3
safety
screen 2, 3, 7
shade 5, 10
shadow 2
sheet 5
shelter 1, 2
shroud 1, 3
shut 5c
sit 6b
smear 1
smother 3
cover (*cont.*)
spread 7, 14
stand 8
substitute 1
suffuse
take 32c, 39d
top 2, 4
touch 8
traverse 1
umbrella 2
veil 1, 2
walk 3
wrap 1
-covers°
at **cover 3**
-under cover
incognito 2
secret 1, 4
coverage
play 25
umbrella 2
covered
invisible 2
overgrown
under 1
underground 1
covering
case[2] 2
coat 2
cover 11, 15
eclipse 3
exterior 3
film 1
glaze 2
housing 2
inclusive 2
mantle 2
pall[1] 1
shade 5
shadow 2
sheet 5
shelter 2
shroud 3
surface 1
top 2
veil 1
wrapper 2
coverlet
cover 13
spread 14
cover over°
at **cover 2**
cover story
pretext 2
covert
furtive 1
hidden
lair 1
mysterious 2
potential 1
private 1
secret 1
sidelong
sneaking 2
stealthy
surreptitious
thicket
ulterior 1
underground 2
veiled
covertly
private 6
secrecy 2
secretly
sly 3
covertness
privacy 2
secrecy 1
cover up°
at **cover 2**
blot 4a
bury 4
camouflage 2
cloak 3
disguise 1
dissimulate
gloss[1] 4
hide[1] 2
hush 4
mask 3
muffle 1
smother 4
stifle 2
suppress 3

cover up (*cont.*)
whitewash
cover-up
camouflage 1
cover 15
disguise 3
front 5
mask 2
masquerade 2
pretence 1,2
covet
desire 1
envy 3
grudge 2
hanker
long[2]
pant 2
want 1
covetable
enviable
coveted
demand 7
desirable 1
covetous
avaricious
desperate 3
envious
greedy 2
hungry 2
jealous 1
mercenary 1
miserly
possessive 1
rapacious
selfish 1
covetousness
avarice
envy 2
greed 1
rapacity
covey
flight[1] 4
number 2
pack 3
score 4
cow
break 7
browbeat
bully 2
daunt
discourage 1
dismay 1
face 17
frighten
intimidate
lean[2] 4b
menace 1
overawe
push 7
scare 1
threaten 1
-cows
cattle
stock 4
-till the cows come home
ever 2
for ever 1
coward°
milksop
cowardice°
fear 1
cowardliness
cowardice
cowardly°
afraid 1
base[2] 1
faint-hearted 1
fearful 2
shy 2
spineless 3
tame 3
timid
weak 3
wet 3
cowboy
fly-by-night 2
cowed
downtrodden
cower
crawl 3
cringe 1
flinch

cower (*cont.*)
shrink 2
sneak 1
truckle
cowering
grovelling
mousy 2
cow-like
passive 2
co-worker
colleague
friend 2
mate 1
cow-pat
dung
cowshed
stall[1] 3
coxcomb
dandy 1
dude 1
swell 6
trendy 2
coy°
backward 1
bashful 2
delicate 5
flirtatious
kittenish
modest 1
retiring
self-conscious
shamefaced 1
shy 1
timid
coyness
shame 4
cozen
bluff[1] 1
deceive
defraud
dupe 3
fool 4
hoax 2
mislead
outsmart
prey 3b
swindle 1
take 32b
trick 8
cozy
see **cosy**
CPA
bookkeeper
crabbed
edge 5
gruff 1
moody 2
nasty 4
peevish
perverse 2
petulant
ratty 1
short-tempered
snappish 2
sour 4
stern 2
surly
temperamental 1
testy
touchy 1
ugly 4
waspish
crabby
bad 7
cantankerous
cranky 2
fretful
irritable
moody 2
perverse 2
petulant
querulous
short-tempered
snappish 2
sour 4
stern 2
sullen
surly
temperamental 1
testy
touchy 1
ugly 4
waspish

crabwise
sideways
crack°
aperture
attempt 2
breach 3
break 1,26
chink
clap 5
collapse 4
cranny
crevasse
crevice
dead 17
dig 8
effort 2
endeavour 2
expert 2
explosion 1
first-rate
flaw 2
fling 3
force 8
fracture 2,3
gag[2] 1
gap 1
gibe 2
gifted
go 12,42
hole 2
joke 1
leak 2
masterful 1
nook 1
opening 1
pop 4
proficient
puzzle 3
quip 1
rap 4
report 2
rift 2
shot 3
snap 1,2,8
solve
split 7
superlative
talented
thunder 1,2
top 8
trial 3
try 5
turn 30
crack-brained
crazy 1
deranged
foolish 2
preposterous
psychotic 1
stupid 2
crack-down
suppression
crack down
enforce 1
suppress 2
cracked
broken 1
crazy 1
deranged
mad 1
psychotic 1
queer 4
crackerjack
expert 2
gifted
ingenious
master 2
talented
crackers
crazy 1
insane 1
mad 1
mental 2
cracking
good 2
thunder 1
crackle
crack 6
rattle 7
snap 8
crack of dawn
dawn 1

crackpot
character 6
crazy 1,2
hare-brained 1
madman
maniac 1
psychotic 2
romantic 2
zany 1
cracksman
robber
thief 1
crack up
collapse 4
laugh 1
piece 6
split 5
crack-up
breakdown 2
collapse 7
collision
crack wise
joke 4
quip 2
cradle
cot
hold 2
origin 2
root[1] 4
seat 2
craft°
art 1,3
artifice 1
boat
career 1
deceit 1
employment 1
fraud 1
ingenuity
job 1
occupation 1
profession 1
speciality 1
technique 2
trade 2
trickery
vessel 2
virtuosity
workmanship
craftiness
art 5
artifice 1
craft 2
deceit 1
finesse 1
subtlety 2
trickery
craftsman, craftswoman
master 2
operative 2
tradesman 2
worker
craftsmanship
art 1
technique 2
virtuosity
workmanship
crafty°
arch 2
artful 1
astute 1
calculating
clever 2
cute 2
deceitful
deep 5
designing
devious 1
dexterous 2
disingenuous
foxy 1
fraudulent 2
furtive 2
ingenious
insincere
keen[1] 6
knowing 1
Machiavellian
politic 1
scheming
serpentine 1
sharp 6
shrewd

crafty (*cont.*)
slippery 2
sly 1
smooth 8
subtle 3
tricky 1
two-faced
wily
wise 1
crag°
cliff
height 3
precipice
projection 1
prominence 2
rock[1] 2
craggy
irregular 1
mountainous 1
rocky[1] 1
strong 18
cram°
coach 3
crowd 4,5
devour 1
fill 1
glut 4
gorge 3
grind 4
huddle 3
jam 1
load 3
mug 6
pack 5
prepare 2
press 1
ram 1
squeeze 4
stow
study 1
stuff 6
throng 2
wedge 3
crammed
congested
full 1
loaded 1
packed
replete 1
solid 2
thick 2
crammer
coach 2
cramming
preparation 4
study 5
cramp
gripe 3
kink 2
pain 1
pinch 2
tie 2
twinge 1
cramped°
close 11
hidebound
narrow 2
crane
hoist 2
strain[1] 4
cranium
head 1
crank°
eccentric 2
oddity 2
pill 2
weirdo
wind[2] 2
crank out
grind 6
crank up
start 1
wind[2] 2
cranky°
bad 7
cantankerous
cross 6
disgruntled
eccentric 1
fretful
hasty 4
irritable
moody 2
nasty 4

cranky (*cont.*)
passionate 3
peevish
perverse 2
prickly 3
quarrelsome
snappish 2
sour 4
sullen
temperamental 1
testy
touchy 1
ugly 4
waspish
cranny°
chink
crevice
nook 1
opening 1
recess 1
split 7
crap
defecate
drivel 3
effects
fiddlesticks
flannel 1
gab 2
garbage
gibberish
gobbledegook 1
jargon 2
moonshine 2
mumbo-jumbo 1
nonsense 1
paraphernalia
prattle 3
rigmarole
rot 4
rubbish 2
stuff 2,4
swill 2
talk 18
thing 8c
trash 1,3
crapper
privy 3
toilet 1
crappy
inferior 3
shoddy
sleazy 2
worthless 3
crap-shoot
gamble 3
crap-shooter
better[2]
punter 1
crapulence
drunkenness
gluttony
crapulent
drunk 1
epicurean 1
crash°
break 1
bump 3
camp[1] 5
clap 5
clash 1
collide 1,2
collision
dash 1
explosion 1
failure 4
hit 3
impact 1
jangle 1,3
noise 1
peal 1,2
pile-up 1
plough 2
ram 2
run 26d
shiver[2]
slam 2
slump 1,2
strike 3
thunder 1,2
crashing
impact 1
thunder 1

crass
brutal 2
crude 3
dull 1
gross 3
philistine 2
plebeian 2
crate
box[1] 1,2
cage 1
car 1
case[2] 1,3
crater
cavity
excavation
hole 1
hollow 7
pan 3
pit[1] 3
pocket 2
cravat
tie 11
crave
ache 2
beg 1
desire 1
die 5
fancy 11
feel 9
hanker
hunger 3
itch 2
long[2]
lust 3
pant 2
solicit 1
spoil 5
thirst 2
want 1
wish 1
yearn
craven
afraid 1
coward
cowardly
servile
shy 2
spineless 3
timid
weak 3
cravenness
fear 1
craving
ambition 1
appetite 2
aspiration
avarice
desire 3
desperate 3
eager
famished
fancy 7
greed 1
greedy 2
hope 1
hunger 2
hungry 2
inclination 4
itch 4
longing
mania 1
passion 3
starved 2
stomach 2
thirst 1
thirsty 2
urge 5
want 4
wish 4,5
crawl°
bristle 4
climb 4
creep 1,2
cringe 2
drag 3
edge 6
pass 11
prostrate 1
scramble 1
slither
snake 3
swarm 3
teem[1]
truckle
crawl (*cont.*)
wriggle 2
crawling
alive 4
grovelling
lousy 4
obsequious
overcrowded
populous
prickly 2
slow 1
thick 2
crawly
prickly 2
scary
crayon
colour 3
craze°
bug 3
crack 6
enthusiasm 2
fad
fashion 2
furore 2
mania 1
mode[2]
passion 3
rage 3
rave 4
style 2
trend 2
vogue 1
crazed
berserk
crazy 1
delirious 2
deranged
hysterical 1
insane 1
mad 1
possessed
rabid 1
raving 1
violent 1
wild 5
craziness
absurdity 1
folly 1
lunacy 1
madness 2
stupidity 2
crazy°
absurd 1
beside 3
daft 3
delirious 1
deranged
devilish
distraught
disturbed 2
exotic 2
flighty 2
foolish 2
impossible 2
improbable
imprudent
inane
insane 1,2
love 7
ludicrous
mad 1,6
maniacal 2
marvellous
mental 2
mind 14
miraculous
nonsensical
off 4
preposterous
psychotic 1,2
rampage 2
raving 1
ridiculous
senseless 3
sick 4
silly 1
stupid 2
sweet 8
twist 11
unbalanced 2
unreasonable 1
unthinking 1
way-out 1
weirdo
wild 5,9
crazy (*cont.*)
zany 1
crazy quilt
patchwork
creaking
decrepit 2
grating 2
strident
creaky
decrepit 2
cream
choice 3
flower 2
gem 2
gentry
lotion
model 3
ointment
pearl
pick 10
plum
rout 2
salve 1
skim 1
whip 2
cream puff
weakling
creamy
rich 6
white 1
crease
contract 5
crumple
crush 2
fold 1,4
furrow 1,3
knit 3
line[1] 3
pucker 1
rumple
wrinkle[1] 1,2
create°
begin 2
breed 2
bring 5
cause 6
coin 3
compose 2
conceive 2
construct 2
design 2
devise 1
draw 6
effect 7
erect 3
establish 1
fabricate 2
fashion 5
father 6
forge 2
form 8
formulate 2
found 1
frame 7
generate 1,3,4
get 51d
imagine 1
induce 2
invent 1
lead 6
make 1,4,5,39c
manufacture 1,2
mastermind 1
occasion 5
organize 2
originate 1
output 3
pioneer 2
produce 1,2,3
raise 2
rear[2] 2
render 1
script 3
spawn
start 7
think 6
turn 8
weave 3
work 16
write 3
–be created
rise 11
create a disturbance
riot 3
create difficulties
bugger 4b
creation°
beginning 1
birth 2
composition 4
effort 3
establishment 1
fabrication 2
fancy 5
formation 1,2
foundation 3
gadget
generation 3
institution 1
invention 1,2
manufacture 3
nature 2
opus
origin 2
production 1
start 11
universe 1
work 4
world 1
–creations
stuff 5
creative°
brilliant 4
clever 3
imaginative 1
ingenious
new 1
novel 1
original 4
productive 2
prolific 2
resourceful
revolutionary 2
seminal 1
slick 3
vivid 3
creativeness
fancy 5
ingenuity
originality
creative power(s)
imagination 1
creative writing(s)
literature 1
creativity
fancy 5
fantasy 1
imagination 1
ingenuity
originality
creator°
author
cause 2
deity
designer 1
father 3
founder[1]
lord 3
mastermind 2
producer 1
source 2
stock 3
creature°
animal 1
beast 1
existence 3
mortal 6
organism
creature comforts°
at **creature** 2
credence
belief 2
believe 1
credit 1
faith 1
credential
licence 2
paper 2a
warrant 2
–credentials
background 1
identification 3
licence 2
paper 2a
reference 3
credibility
trust 2
credible
believe 1
good 8
likely 2
plausible 1
possible 1
presumptive 1
probable
ready-made 2
reasonable 2
reliable
smooth 8
tenable
thinkable
wash 8
credit°
allowance 4
apply 3
attribute 2
attribution
believe 2
distinction 2
honour 3
impute
lap[1] 3b
loan 1,2
pat[1] 5
swallow 2
thank 2
trust 2
virtue 3
–on credit
time 19b
creditability
responsibility 4
creditable
believe 1
deserving
estimable
good 8
honest 1
laudable
meritorious
praiseworthy
prominent 2
proud 3
responsible 2
savoury 2
splendid 2
tenable
worthy 1
creditably
honestly 1
creditation
credit 2
credit card
card 9
creditworthy
solvent
credo
creed
doctrine
ideology
principle 2
school 3
tenet
credulity
naïvety
credulous
childlike
easy 4
gullible
innocent 4
naïve
susceptible 2
trusting
unsuspecting
credulousness
naïvety
creed°
belief 3
doctrine
faith 2
ideology
persuasion 2
creed (*cont.*)
principle 2
religion
school 3
tenet
creek°
brook[1]
gulf 1
river 1
run 42
stream 1
tributary
creel
hamper[2]
creep°
climb 2,4
crawl 1,2
drag 3
edge 6
jerk 5
pass 11
pussyfoot 1
rogue 1
slide 2
slink
slither
snake 3
sneak 1
steal 3
stinker
walk 1
wear 5
wretch 1
creeper
runner 3
creeping
slimy 2
slow 1
creepy
eerie
ghostly 1
nightmarish
scary
unearthly 2
creepy-crawly
bug 1
cremation
funeral
crème de la crème
choice 3
élite 1
flower 2
gem 2
gentry
model 3
pick 10
crenate
notched
serrated
crenellated
notched
serrated
Creole
cant 2
dialect
jargon 1
lingo
tongue 1
crepuscular
dim 1
twilight 4
crepuscule
twilight 1
crescendo
head 5
crescent°
crescent-shaped
crescent 2
crest°
climax 4
device 3
emblem
head 5
height 2
maximum 2
peak 1,4
pinnacle
ridge
seal 1
spire 2
stamp 7
symbol

crest (*cont.*)
top 1
vertex
crestfallen
blue 1
dejected
gloomy 2
glum
heartbroken
heavy 6
joyless 1
low[1] 8
melancholy 1
moody 1
mouth 6
sad 1
sorrowful 1
subdued 2
unhappy 1
woebegone
wretched 2
cretinism
stupidity 1
cretinous
daft 1
halfwitted
simple 4
stupid 1
thick 6
crevasse°
gorge 1
pit[1] 3
crevice°
aperture
chink
crack 1
cranny
gap 1
leak 2
nook 1
opening 1
rift 2
split 7
crew°
complement 2
man 4
pack 3
party 2
ring[1] 3
shift 4
squad
staff 2
team 1
crib
cot
house 6
hovel
lift 6
pirate 3
trot 4
cribbing
plagiarism
crib-sheet
sheet 1
crick
kink 2
crikey
indeed 3
crime°
atrocity 2
caper 2
foul play
guilt 1
job 5
misdeed
offence 1
pity 2
racket 2
sin 1
transgression
criminal°
accessory 2
accomplice
bad 3
black 6
crooked 1
culprit 2
delinquent 1
evil 2
felon
fraudulent 2
gangster
illegal
lawless 2

criminal (*cont.*)
miscreant 1, 2
offender
outlaw 1
prohibitive 2
sinful
terrorist
transgressor
unconscionable 1
unlawful
villain
villainous 1
wicked 2
wrong 1
-criminals
underworld
criminal activity
racket 2
criminal conversation
relation 6a
criminal element
underworld 1
criminality
guilt 1
crimp
fold 1, 4
kink 1
wrinkle[1] 2
crimped
kinky 3
crimson
flush[1] 1
cringe°
crawl 3
dread 1
flinch
kowtow
prostrate 1
shrink 2
truckle
cringing
grovelling
menial 2
obsequious
servile
servility
crinite
hairy 1
crinkle
crumple
crush 2
fold 4
furrow 3
kink 1
line[1] 3
pucker 1, 2
rumple
wrinkle[1] 1, 2
crinkling
pucker 2
crinkly
crisp 2
cripple°
break 7
demoralize 1
destroy 4
drain 5
frustrate 1
hurt 4
impair
incapacitate
invalid[1] 2
maim
mangle
mutilate 1
paralyse 3
sabotage 3
sap[2]
strike 13
crippled°
decrepit 1
deformed 2
disabled
frail 2
helpless 1
infirm 1
lame 1
misshapen
powerless 2

crippling
exhausting 2
ruinous
crisis°
climax 2
crunch 2
emergency
head 5
necessity 4
pass 26
pinch 8
predicament
crisp°
brisk 3
chilly 1, 2
kinky 3
snappy 1
spanking 2
terse 1
trim 1
crispy
crisp 2
criss-cross
network 2
traverse 1, 2
weave 4
criterion
code 3
example 2
gauge 3
guide 6
ideal 1
mark 3
measure 3
norm 2
paragon
pattern 1
precedent
principle 1
proof 2
standard 1
touchstone
yardstick
critic
judge 3
student 2
critical°
acute 2
caustic 2
crucial
delicate 4
desperate 4
destructive 2
difficult 5
discriminating
educated 2
essence 4
explanatory
explosive 1
fastidious
fateful 1
fault-finding 2
fine[1] 9
finicky 1
fundamental 1
grave[2] 2
great 4
hard 6
heavy 3
important 1
incisive 2
instant 4
jaundiced 2
judicial 2
key 6
landmark 3
low[1] 14
main 3
major 2
meticulous
momentous
narrow 3
nasty 5
nervous 2
nice 4
particular 4
personal 4
pivotal
precise 3
pressing
querulous
reproachful
sarcastic
scorching 2
scrupulous 1

critical (*cont.*)
serious 4
severe 3
significant 1
sore 3
squeamish 1
staple 1
stern 1
strategic
thorny 2
ticklish 2
touchy 2
vital 1, 2
critically
badly 5, 7
ill 11
narrowly 2
seriously 1
severely 5
critical moment
crisis 1
crunch 2
criticism°
analysis 2
attack 7
blame 3
comment 1
disapproval
explanation 1
fault-finding 1
flak
gloss[2] 1
hell 4
judgement 3
knock 10
lecture 2
note 3
notice 6
observation 2
rebuke 2
reprimand 1
review 4
slap 5
stricture 2
writing 2
-beneath criticism
dishonourable 3
criticizable
exceptionable
criticize°
analyse 2
attack 2
belittle
blame 1
blast 6
carp
castigate
cavil 2
come 11
condemn 1
damn 1
denounce 3
disapprove
discipline 8
disparage 1
fault 6, 8
get 30c
gloss[2] 2
knock 2
lash[1] 4
nag[1] 1
niggle
pan 5
pick 4a
pull 6
put 16g
rail[2]
rap 2
rebuke 1
reprimand 2
review 3
rubbish 3
run 26b
scold 1
slam 3
snipe
talk 9a
task 3
treat 2
criticizing
querulous
critique
analyse 2
analysis 2

critique (*cont.*)
criticism 3
exposition 3
gloss[2] 1, 2
note 3
notice 6
paper 4
review 3, 4
tract[2]
treat 2
writing 2
croak
check 10d
die 1
pass 14a
rasp 5
croaking
grating 2
ragged 5
strident
crock
jar[1]
crocked
drunk 1
crockery
pottery
crock of shit
gibberish
prattle 3
rubbish 2
trash 1
crocodile
line[1] 6
queue 1
croft
farm 1
croissant
roll 17
crone
bag 4
devil 2
hag
jade 2
ruin 5
shrew
witch 2
crony
boy 3
comrade
friend 1
henchman
intimate[1] 5
mate 1
pal 1
shadow 6
cronyism
prejudice 2
crook
bend 1, 2
criminal 3
gangster
hoodlum
hump 2
miscreant 1
offender
snake 4
staff 1
take 3
thief 1
thug
twister 1
crooked°
abusive 3
bent 1, 3
corrupt 1
criminal 1
deceitful
deformed 1
designing
devious 1, 2
dishonest
evil 2
faithless 2
fixed 4
fly-by-night 2
foul 7
fraudulent 2
gnarled
indirect 1
insincere
lawless 2
lopsided 1
meandering
misshapen

crooked (*cont.*)
oblique 1
serpentine 2
shady 2
shifty
tortuous 1, 2
unscrupulous
venal
villainous 1
wily
wrong 1
wry 1
croon
sing 1
crooner
singer
vocalist
crop
chop 1
clip[2] 1
cut 4, 5
diminish 1
edit 3
generation 4
growth 2
harvest 1
lop
lower[1] 3
nip[1] 1
output 1
reduce 1
shave 1
snip 1
top 5
trim 3
vintage 1
whip 8
cropper
spill 5
crop up
appear 1
arise 3, 4
come 19a
emerge 1
occur 1
start 2
surface 3
turn 25b
cross°
bad 7
bilious
bridge 3
burden 1
cantankerous
cover 9
curse 2
disagreeable 3
disgruntled
encumbrance
fretful
get 45a
gruff 1
harsh 3
hybrid
irritable
load 1
navigate 1
negotiate 3
passionate 3
peevish
perverse 2
petulant
quarrelsome
querulous
ratty 1
snappish 2
sour 4
span 3
strike 5
sullen
surly
testy
touchy 1
transit 3
traverse 1, 2, 3
ugly 4
wade 1
waspish
weight 2
-at cross purposes
odds 4
cross-brace
thwart 2

cross-bred
mixed 1
cross-breed
cross 2
hybrid
mongrel
cross-current
undercurrent 1
cross-examination
examination 3
inquiry 1
interrogation
cross-examine
examine 2
pump 2
crossfire
volley 3
cross-grained
cantankerous
contrary 2
disobedient 2
perverse 2
rogue 2
crossing
passage 1, 7
cross one's heart
promise 3
seriously 2
cross out°
at cross 3
cancel 2
cut 16a
delete
eliminate 3
erase 1
omit 1
scratch 3
strike 5
crossroads
climax 2
junction
cross-section
sample 1
section 2
cross someone's mind
occur 2
cross swords
clash 3
encounter 3
fight 1
row[2] 3
tangle 4
tilt 2
war 3
cross to bear
curse 2
encumbrance
crotchet
eccentricity 2
fancy 8
foible
freak 3
kink 4
notion 2
oddity 3
peculiarity 1
quirk
trick 6
twist 10
crotchety
bad 7
cantankerous
capricious
cranky 2
cross 6
gruff 1
irritable
kinky 1
moody 2
nasty 4
peevish
petulant
querulous
sullen
surly
temperamental 1
testy
ugly 4
waspish
crouch°
duck 1
stoop 1, 3
croup
tail 2
crow
bluster 2
boast 2
brag
chuckle 1
gloat
glory 5
revel 1
swagger 2
talk 8
-as the crow flies
directly 1
right 13
straight 12
crowd°
abound 2
assembly 1
attendance 2
besiege 2
bunch 2, 4
circle 2
clan 2
clique
cluster 2, 3
company 2
concentrate 3
crush 6
faction 1
fill 1
flock 1, 2
flood 6
fraternity 1
gang 1
gate 2
gather 2
group 1
herd 1
hoi polloi
host[2]
huddle 1, 3
hustle 3
jam 1, 5
knot 2
many 3
mass 2
mill 6
mob 1, 3
number 2
pack 3, 5
people 3
pile 6, 8a
populace
pour 4
press 7, 8
rabble 1
ram 1
score 4
set 26
squeeze 4, 9
stuff 6
swarm 2
throng 1, 2
turnout 1
wedge 3
world 3
crowded
abound 2
alive 4
congested
cramped
dense 2
full 1
loaded 1
mobbed
packed
populous
solid 2
thick 2
crowding
press 8
crowd-puller
attraction 2
sensation 3
crowing
chuckle 2
egotistical
crown°
capital 1
complete 6
crown *(cont.)*
crest 3
garland 1, 2
glory 4
hit 1
peak 2
pinnacle
ring[1] 1
spire 2
strike 1
summit
tip[1] 1, 2
title 4
top 1, 4
vertex
crowned head
king
monarch 1
crowning
installation 1
maximum 3
supreme 3
crowning blow
clincher
crowning point
pinnacle
crow's-foot
furrow 1
line[1] 3
wrinkle[1] 1
crow to pluck
grievance 2
crozier
staff 1
CRT
monitor 2
terminal 4
crucial°
acute 2
critical 2
desperate 4
essence 4
fateful 1
fundamental 1
good 2
grave[2] 2
great 4
heavy 3
imperative 1
indispensable 1
key 6
landmark 3
main 3
major 2
momentous
pivotal
pressing
serious 2
strategic
vital 1, 2
weighty 2
crucifix
cross 1
crucify
punish 2
torment 1
crud
filth 1
cruddy
filthy 1
crude°
amateur 2
animal 4
artless 3
barbarian 3
bawdy
beastly 1
bluff[2] 1
boorish
brutal 2
coarse 1, 2
earthy
garish
gaudy
gross 3
harsh 1
homespun
impolite
incomplete
insolent
lewd
low[1] 3
merciless
nasty 3
crude *(cont.)*
outspoken
primitive 2
prurient 2
racy 2
raw 2
rough 6, 9
rude 4
rudimentary 2
rugged 4
rustic 2
severe 6
sketchy
tactless
tasteless 1
uncivilized 1
ungraceful 2
unrefined 2
vulgar 2
crudely
poorly 1
roughly 3
severely 6
sketchily
crudeness
indelicacy
severity 6
vulgarity 1
cruel°
abusive 2
atrocious 1
beastly 1
bitter 3, 5
bloodthirsty
brutal 1
cold-blooded 3
cold-hearted
cutthroat 3
devilish
diabolic 2
ferocious
fiendish
fierce 1
flagrant
ghoulish 2
grim 2
hard 4
harsh 2
heartless
hurtful 2
ill 3
implacable
inhuman 1
mean[2] 4
merciless
monstrous 2
murderous 1
nasty 4
outrageous 2
relentless 1
remorseless 1
rough 5
ruthless
sadistic
sanguinary 1
savage 2
severe 1
stiff 2
unkind
unmerciful
violent 1
wanton 4
wicked 4
cruelly
badly 6
roughly 2
severely 2
cruelty
atrocity 1
barbarity
devilry 2
outrage 1
severity 1
violence 2
cruise°
excursion 1
journey 1, 3
navigate 1
passage 7
prowl 2
roam
roll 3
sail 2
tour 4
trip 7
cruise *(cont.)*
wander 1
crumb°
bit 1
fragment 1
grain 3
little 10
modicum
morsel 2
particle
scrap[1] 1
speck
-crumbs
leftover 1
remain 4a
crumble°
collapse 1
come 7
decay 1b
deteriorate 2
disintegrate
fall 7
grind 1
piece 6
pulverize 1
rot 1
surrender 2
way 11a
weaken 2
crumbling
decrepit 2
dilapidated
leg 7
old 3
ramshackle
rotten 2
tumbledown
unsound 1
crumbly
crisp 1
rotten 2
crummy
bad 1
bum 4
inferior 3
pathetic 2
plastic 3
shabby 3
sleazy 2
crumpet
chap
fluff 2
girl 1
halfwitted
head 1
insane 1
crumple°
buckle 2
collapse 1
crush 2
fall 2
rumple
way 11a
wrinkle[1] 2
crunch°
crush 1
mill 5
munch
pay-off 2
pinch 8
scrape 8
crunchy
crisp 1
crusade°
battle 2
campaign 1
drive 10
movement 5
pilgrimage
quest 1
crusader
pilgrim
crush°
beat 2
best 11
bow 4
break 4, 7
conquer 1
crumple
crunch 1
defeat 1
demolish 2
demoralize 1
destroy 1
crush *(cont.)*
floor 4
grind 1, 5
herd 1
humble 4
jam 5
mangle
mill 5
mob 1
mortify 1
oppress 2
overcome 1
overpower 1
overwhelm 1
pile[1] 6
pinch 2
pound[1] 2
powder 3
press 1, 3, 8
prostrate 2
pulverize 1, 2
put 16b, 16e
quash 2
quell 1
rout 2
ruin 7
rumple
shatter 2, 3
slaughter 4
squeeze 1, 9
stifle 3
subdue 1
subject 10
subjugate
suppress 2
telescope 3
throng 1, 2
trample 1, 3
waste 11
-be crushed
break 16c
crushed
broken 3
broken-hearted
fine[1] 7
heartbroken
prostrate 4
smitten 1
stricken 2
undone[1] 1
crusher
mill 1
crushing
overthrow 2
overwhelming 1
pressure 2
suppression
tragic
victory
crust
gall[1] 2
heel[1] 1
nerve 2
sauce 2
scale[2] 2
skin 2
crusty
cantankerous
cross 6
curt
gruff 1
irritable
moody 2
peevish
perverse 2
querulous
short-tempered
snappish 2
sour 4
stern 2
sullen
surly
tart[1] 2
testy
touchy 1
waspish
crux
crunch 2
essence 1
heart 3
keystone
meat 2
nub 2
pass 26
pith 1

crux (*cont.*)
pivot 2
point 5
substance 2
cry°
bawl 2
call 1, 13
cheer 4
complain
exclaim
exclamation
grieve 2
howl 1, 2
interjection
moan 3
plea 1
plead 1
roar 1, 3
scream 1, 3
shout 1, 2
shriek 1, 2
snivel
sob
squawk 1
weep 1
whoop 1, 2
yell 2
cry-baby
milksop
sissy
crying
instant 4
lamentation
tearful
cry out
call 1
exclaim
shout 1
sound[1] 8
whoop 2
cry out for°
at **cry 3**
demand 3
cry over
bewail
regret 1
crypt°
grave[1]
safe 7
sepulchre
tomb
cryptic°
ambiguous 2
dark 7
hidden
incomprehensible
indefinite 2
mysterious 2
mystical 1
obscure 2
opaque 2
profound 1
secret 2
cryptogram
code 2
symbol
cryptographic
secret 2
cry quits
surrender 2
yield 1
crystal
glass 1
crystal clear
graphic 1
plain 2
crystal-gazer
fortune-teller
psychic 3
seer
crystal-gazing
prophecy 1
crystalline
clear 2
transparent 1
crystallization
formation 1
crystallize
jell 2
solidify 1
stiffen 1
crystal set
radio 1

cub
pup
cubby-hole
compartment
sanctum 2
cube
block 1
brick 1
cake 2
chop 2
cut 17a
loaf[1] 1
lump[1] 1
square 7
cubed
square 1
cubic
solid 1
square 1
cubicle
booth 2
cell
compartment
room 2
stall[1] 2
cuckoldry
infidelity 2
cuckoo
crazy 1
deranged
foolish 2
inane
insane 1
mad 1
preposterous
stupid 2
twist 11
cuddle°
caress 1, 2
clinch 2
embrace 1
fondle
hug 1
love 6
nestle
pet[1] 4
snuggle
cuddly
lovable
cudgel
beat 1
club 1, 5
hit 1
lambaste 1
pound[1] 1
strike 1
cudgel one's brains
exert 2
wonder 3
cue°
hint 3
key 2
lead 14
nod 5
note 6
prod 6
prompt 4, 6
remind
reminder
sign 2
symptom
cuesta
cliff
cuff
clip[2] 3, 6
hit 1
jab 2, 4
knock 9
manacle 2
poke 2, 6
punch[1] 1, 2
rap 4
ring[1] 1
shackle 1
slap 1, 4
strike 1
-cuffs
handcuffs
manacle 1
restraint 2
shackle 1

-off the cuff
extemporaneous
offhand 3, 4
scratch 6
spontaneous 1
unpremeditated
cull
derive 1
excerpt 2
extract 4
pick 1
pull 3
screen 8
single 4
cullender
riddle[2] 3
cully
mate 1
culminate
climax 4
complete 6
crest 4
crown 5
end 9
finish 5
pan 6
peak 4
result 3
culmination
accomplishment 1
acme
climax 1
close 22
completion 1
consummation 2
finish 9
head 5
height 2
issue 2
peak 2
summit
top 1
upshot
culpability
accountability
blame 4
fault 3
guilt 1
responsibility 3
culpable
fault 5
guilty 1
responsible 4
culprit°
criminal 3
delinquent 1
felon
offender
transgressor
cultish
sectarian 1
cultist
sectarian 1, 3
cultivate°
breed 3
cherish 2
develop 1
educate
elaborate 4
farm 3
follow 6
foment
form 10
foster 1
grow 3
nourish 3
nurse 2
perfect 9
plough 1
polish 2
pursue 2
raise 3, 7
rear[2] 1
refine 2
till[1]
work 8
cultivated°
aesthetic 2
discriminating
educated 1, 2
elegant 1
enlightened
genteel 3
highbrow 2

cultivated (*cont.*)
informed 1
lettered
literary 1
pleasant 2
polished 2
practised 2
refined 1, 2
sophisticated 1
suave
tasteful
versed
well-bred
cultivation
breeding 1
charm 2
civilization 1
culture 1
education 1
elevation 4
farming
grace 2
growth 1
panache
promotion 1
refinement 1
taste 4
upbringing
culture°
charm 2
civilization 1, 2
elegance 1
grace 2
learning
letter 3
lore 1
refinement 1
society 3
sophistication 1
time 9
cultured
cultivated
educated 1
genteel 3
highbrow 2
informed 1
knowledgeable 2
ladylike
learned
lettered
literary 1
pleasant 2
polished 2
refined 1, 2
sophisticated 1
versed
well-bred
culvert
drain 1
cumber
overload 1
cumbersome
bulky
burdensome
gross 1
hefty 1
hulking
inconvenient
oppressive 1
ponderous 1
unwieldy
cumbersomeness
inconvenience 2
cumbrous
ponderous 1
cum grano salis
salt 5
cummerbund
girth 2
cumshaw
gift 1
cumulate
accumulate
amass
heap 3
pile[1] 5
store 1
cunctatory
slack 1
cunning
arch 2
art 5
artful 1

cunning (*cont.*)
artifice 1
astute 1
clever 2
craft 2
crafty
cute 1, 2
deceit 1
deceitful
deep 5
designing
dexterity 2
dexterous 2
disingenuous
evasion 2
evasive
finesse 1
foxy 1
furtive 2
ingenious
ingenuity
insincere
keen[1] 6
Machiavellian
politic 1
scheming
serpentine 1
sharp 6
shifty
shrewd
slippery 2
sly 1
smooth 8
subtle 3
subtlety 2
tactical
tricky 1
unscrupulous
wily
cup
mug 1
potion
trophy 1
-in one's cups
drunk 1
stinking 3
cup-bearer
waiter
cupboard
cabinet 1
cup-boy
servant 1
cupidity
avarice
greed 1
hunger 2
rapacity
cup of tea
speciality 1
street 2
cup that cheers
alcohol
drink 5
cur
mongrel
reprobate 2
rogue 1
scoundrel
stinker
villain
wretch 1
curable
benign 4
curate
minister 1
priest
curative
medicinal
therapeutic
curb°
brake 1
bridle 1, 2
catch 8
chasten 2
check 1, 2, 14
contain 3
control 2, 3, 5
discipline 4, 7
gag[1] 1, 3
govern 2
halt 2
hamper[1]
handicap 1, 2
hindrance 2

curb (*cont.*)
hold 14a, 17a
impede
impediment
inhibit
inhibition
keep 13
limit 1, 5
manacle 3
oppose 2
prevent
prevention
preventive 3
rein 1, 3
relax 2
repress
resist 1
restrain 1
restraint 1
shackle 4
stay[1] 4
stem[2] 1
stifle 2
stint 2, 3
subdue 3
tame 6
tie 2
trammel 1, 2
curbed
pent-up
curbing
prevention
curdle
coagulate
sour 5
spoil 4
turn 5
curdled
sour 2
cure°
antidote
correct 1
doctor 2
drug 1
heal 1
help 2, 9
pill 1
preserve 3
put 28c
rectify
remedy 1, 2, 3
salt 7
therapy 1
curé
father 4
minister 1
cure-all
cure 1
drug 1
elixir 1
medicine
remedy 1, 2
cured
better[1] 4
salt 10
curing
treatment 2
curio
antique 2
curiosity 3
rarity 1
-curios
bric-à-brac
curiosity°
eccentricity 2
freak 2
interest 1
intrigue 1
oddity 2
phenomenon 2
rarity 1
spectacle 2
wonder 1
-curiosities
bric-à-brac
curious°
bizarre 1
deviant 1
eccentric 1
extraordinary 1
fanciful 3
foreign 2
funny 2
grotesque 2

curious (*cont.*)
inquisitive 1
interested 1
mysterious 1
nosy
odd 1
ordinary 4
outlandish
peculiar 1
quaint 1
queer 1
quizzical
remarkable 3
singular 1
special 1
strange 1
unaccustomed 1
unusual
whimsical 1
wonder 3
wrong 2
curiously
notably 1
curiousness
oddity 1
curl
kink 1
lock[2]
loop 2
roll 9
shrivel
spiral 1
swirl 2, 3
twine 2
wind[2] 2
-curls
hair 1
curled
tortuous 1
curlicue
flourish 3
kink 1
curling
tortuous 1
curl one's lip (at)
scorn 3
sneer 1
curl someone's hair
horrify 1
curl up
nestle
shrivel
curly
crisp 2
kinky 3
curmudgeonly
bad 7
cantankerous
cranky 2
cross 6
gruff 1
harsh 3
irritable
moody 2
nasty 4
peevish
perverse 2
petulant
po-faced
prickly 3
pugnacious
quarrelsome
querulous
short-tempered
snappish 2
sour 4
surly
tart[1] 2
temperamental 1
touchy 1
ugly 4
ungracious
waspish
currency
cash 1
coin 1
money 1
note 4
prevalence 1
tender[2] 3
vogue 2

current°
actual 2
air 2
contemporary 2
date 5
draught 1
drift 3
familiar 1
flow 5
force 6
going 2
home 5
immediate 3
late 2
latest 2
live 2
modern
popular 2
present[1] 1
prevail 2
prevalent
recent
stream 2
topical 1
wave 2
wind[1] 1
curriculum
programme 1
timetable
curriculum vitae
background 1
history 4
record 6
résumé 2
story 6
currish
base[2] 6
contemptible
nasty 4
ugly 4
curry
brush[2] 4
curry favour with
cultivate 4
flatter 1
play 18
romance 7
curse°
abuse 3
affliction 2
blaspheme 1
blast 7
blight 2
damn 3
expletive 2
grief 2
jinx 1, 3
misery 3
oath 2
pest
pestilence 2
plague 1
ruin 3
scourge 1
shadow 4
swear 2
thunder 3
torment 3
ulcer 2
undoing 2
visitation 2
cursed
damnable
doomed 1
fated 2
lost 7
reprobate 1
unfortunate 1
unhappy 2
unsuccessful 2
curse of Montezuma
run 50
curse-word
curse 3
profanity
cursing
profanity
cursorily
offhand 5
sketchily

cursory°
careless 1
hasty 3
hurried 2
offhand 1
passing 2
perfunctory 1
promiscuous 1
rough 10
sketchy
superficial 2, 3
thumbnail
curt°
abrupt 3
bluff[2] 1
blunt 2
brief 3
brusque
disagreeable 3
discourteous
fretful
gruff 1
harsh 3
impatient 2
moody 2
offhand 2
rough 3
rude 2
short 4
short-tempered
snap 3b
snappish 2
sour 4
summary 2
temperamental 1
terse 2
curtail°
abbreviate 1
abridge
cut 5, 8
decrease 1
diminish 1
hamper[1]
minimize 1
pare 2
reduce 1
restrain 2
short 12a
shorten 1
telescope 2
tie 2, 5b
trim 3
curtailed
brief 2
concise
cut 27
curtailment
abridgement 2
cut 21
decrease 2
restraint 1
curtain
blind 7
drape 2
drapery
mantle 2
screen 3
shade 5
shadow 2
veil 1
curtly
briefly 1
shortly 3
curtness
economy 2
curtsy
bend 3
bow 1, 5
curvaceous
full 7
shapely
voluptuous 2
curvature
bend 1
stoop 3
sweep 6
curve
bend 1, 2
flex 2
hump 2
meander 2
misinform
snake 4
sweep 4, 6

curve (*cont.*)
swirl 2
turn 11, 27
twist 4, 7
wind[2] 1
curved
bent 1
round 4
streamlined 1
tortuous 1
curvet
caper 1, 3
cavort
frisk 1
frolic 3
leap 2
prance
curvilinear
round 4
streamlined 1
tortuous 1
curving(s)
meander 2
curvy
meandering
tortuous 1
cushion°
deaden 2
insulate 2
moderate 5
pad 1, 4
soften 2
temper 5
cushioning
euphemism
cushiony
soft 1
cushy
fat 4
soft 2
cusp
angle[1] 1
cuspidate
pointed 1
cuss
swear 2
cuss-word
expletive 2
custodian
guard 3
guardian
keeper
monitor 1
watchman
custodianship
custody 1
security 4
custody°
captivity
care 3
charge 4
detention
grip 2
hand 8
imprisonment
oversight 2
possession 1
protection 2
safe keeping
security 4
trust 3
-in custody
arrest 6
hold 6
custody centre
Borstal
custom°
civilisation 2
clientele
code 3
convention 2
etiquette
form 6
formality 1
habit 1, 2
institution 4
moral 4
morality 2
observance 2
patronage 2
policy
practice 1
procedure

custom (*cont.*)
protocol 1
public 9
rite
ritual 3
routine 1
specially
trade 4
tradition
usage 1
way 2
-customs°
at **custom 2**
civilization 2
code 3
culture 2
duty 3
etiquette
moral 4
morality 2
protocol 1
rule 3
tax 1
customarily
average 2
frequently 2
generally 1
ordinarily
popularly
rule 4
usually
customary°
accustomed 1
average 3
common 1
conventional
correct 7
everyday 2
familiar 2
formal 1
frequent 1
general 2
going 2
habitual 1
natural 1
normal 1
obtain 3
ordinary 1
orthodox
popular 2
prevailing 1
prevalent
regular 1
regulation 5
ritual 2
routine 3
set 29
standard 6
standing 1
staple 2
stock 7
time-honoured
traditional
typical 2
usual
well-known 1
customer°
buyer
chap
client
fellow 1
guest
guy 1
patron 2
punter 2
regular 12
steady 10
-be a customer
patronize 2
-customers
clientele
public 9
trade 4
customer acceptance
demand 6
customer base
market 3
customization
adaptation 2
customize
accommodate 1
customized
tailor-made 2

custom-made
fitted
tailor-made 1, 2
cut°
abbreviate 2
abridge
abstract 4
accomplish
adulterate
brief 2
bring 8b
carve 1, 2
chisel 1
chop 1, 3
cleave
clip[2] 1, 2
curtail
decrease 1, 2
delete
digest 4
dilute
diminish 1
disregard 2
divide 1
doctor 4
edit 2, 3
eliminate 3
engrave 1
engraving 1
etch 1
excavate 1
excavation
execute 1
figure 1
fix 13
flaw 2
form 1
furrow 1, 2
gash 1, 2
groove
gully
hack[1] 1, 3
hairdo
hurt 3
ignore 2
incision
indentation
interest 4
isolate
knife 2
lacerate
lash[1] 2
leak 2
loosen 2
lower[1] 1
lunge 3
make 37c
mangle
mark 10, 15b
minimize 1
mould[1] 2
mow 1
neuter 2
nick 1
nip[1] 1
notch 1, 3
omit 1
ostracize
pain 5
pare 2
pass 23
percentage
pierce 4
plate 5
print 2
proportion 3
quota
rake-off
rebate 2
rebuff 1, 2
reduce 1, 5
rip 1
scar 1, 2
scoop 5
score 2, 10
section 4
sever 1
shape 6
share 1
shave 1
short 2, 12a
shorten 1
shoulder 2
shut 4a
skip 2

D

D
F

dastard (*cont.*)
rogue 1
stinker
dastardly
black 6
cowardly
low[1] 12
spineless 3
stinking 2
data°
dope 3
evidence 1
fact 3
file 1
good 21c
indication 4
information
intelligence 2
knowledge 2
line[1] 10
literature 2
low-down
material 4
proof 1
record 4
word 2
date°
appointment 1
day 2
engagement 1
era
escort 3
go 33c, 40b
see 7
steady 8
-out of date°
***at* date 4**
antiquated 1
antique 1
belated
extinct 2
musty 2
obsolete
old 2
old-fashioned
passé
slow 8
-to date
far 8a
-up to date°
***at* date 5**
contemporary 2
current 3, 4
fashionable
fresh 2
informed 2
knowledgeable 1
late 2
level 5
minute[1] 3
modern
new 2
now 5
present[1] 1
recent
sporty
streamlined 2
swinging
topical 1
trendy 1
date back (to)
go 24b
date-book
calendar 1
diary
dated
antiquated
date 4
extinct 2
obsolete
old 2
old-fashioned
out 9
passé
time 15
time-worn
daub
dab 1, 3
paint 5
plaster
smear 1, 3
spatter
streak 1, 4
daughter
child 1
descendant
issue 7
-daughters
issue
progeny
daunt°
alarm 3
appal
bully 2
demoralize 1
desolate 6
deter
discourage 1
foil[1]
frighten
intimidate
menace 1
overawe
scare 1
threaten 1
daunting
awesome
fearsome
formidable 1
frightening
harrowing
scary
swingeing
dauntless°
bold 1
brave 1
confident 2
courageous
fearless
gallant 1
gritty 2
heroic 1
indomitable
intrepid
manly
resolute
stout 2
dauntlessness
courage
grit
nerve 1
prowess 2
resolution 1
Davenport
couch 1
lounge 5
davit
hoist 2
Davy Jones's locker
bottom 4
deep 9
drink 7
ocean 1
sea 1
dawdle°
bugger 4a
delay 3
drag 4
fool 7b
lag 1
linger 2
roam
shilly-shally
stall[2] 1
tarry 1
time 20
trail 6
dawdler
idler
laggard
dawdling
delay 6
idleness 2
slow 1
dawn°
beginning 1
infancy 2
light[1] 4
morning 1
onset 2
origin 2
threshold 2
-at dawn
early 3
dawning
beginning 1
dawn 1, 2
origin 2
dawn on°
***at* dawn 5**
hit 5
occur 2
register 7
strike 9
day°
date 1
era
generation 2
time 4
-days
era
generation 2
period 2
time 4
-in days gone by
etc.
formerly
once 1
previously
time 12a
-in this day and age
now 2
-to this day
yet 2
day after day
daily 3
day-bed
couch 1
lounge 5
day before
eve 1
daybook
register 1
daybreak
dawn 1
light[1] 4
morning 1
-at daybreak
early 3
day by day
consistently 1
day-dream°
dream 1
fancy 6
fantasize
fantasy 2
hallucination
illusion 2
muse
reverie
day-dreamer
dreamer
day-dreaming
absent-minded
dreamy 2
inattentive
pensive
thoughtful 2
wistful 2
Day-Glo
bright 5
day in day out
non-stop 3
often
daylight°
day 1
light[1] 1
daylight robbery
rip-off 3
day one
beginning 1
-from day one
originally
day-school
school 1
days gone by *etc.*
history 6
past 6
-in days gone by
formerly
once 1
previously
time 12a
day-spring
dawn 1
morning 1
day-star
sun 1
days to come
future 1
daytime
day 1
diurnal
day-to-day
diurnal
everyday 1
practice 4
day-tripper
sightseer
tourist
traveller
daze°
astonish
distract 3
fluster 1
fog 2
jolt 3
knock 6b
overpower 2
perplex
rock[2] 3
shatter 3
shock 1
stun 1, 2
trance
-in a daze°
***at* daze 4**
dazed
blank 5
confused 2
dizzy 1
dumbfounded
glassy 2
goggle-eyed
groggy
scatterbrained
speechless 2
thunderstruck
dazzle°
amaze
blind 6
breath 3
brilliance 1
captivate
daze 1
flare 1, 4
flash 1, 4
fluster 1
glare 1
life 7
radiance 1
radiate 1
sheen
sparkle 3
splendour 1, 2
twinkle 2
dazzled
daze 4
dumbfounded
dazzling°
amazing
arresting
bright 1
brilliant 1
flamboyant 2
flash 6
full 10
glaring 2
glorious 2
golden 3
gorgeous 1
hot 8
luminous 1
meteoric 2
radiant 1
ravishing
scintillating 1
shiny
splendid 1
strong 19
stunning 2
sumptuous
superb
superlative
twinkle 2
virtuoso 2
vivid 1
deacon
clergyman 1
deactivate
disarm 1
disband
incapacitate
paralyse 1
turn 17a
dead°
boring
broke
casualty 2b
cold 5, 6
defunct 1, 2
dreary 2
exhausted 1
extinct 1
fatigued
flat 5, 8
inanimate
jaded 1
late 3
lifeless 1, 2
lost 5
mechanical 3
needy
numb 1
obsolete
old-fashioned
past 1
pedestrian 2
plumb 4
prosaic
push 12
ragged 3
senseless 2
slow 9
tame 4
tedious
time 15
weary 1
wooden 2
worn 3
dead-and-alive
slow 9
dead and buried
past 1
dead beat
beat 13
fatigued
weary 1
welsher
dead broke
needy
dead duck
failure 3
deaden°
dampen 2
drug 4
dull 11
kill 3
muffle 2
mute 3
numb 2
paralyse 2
silence 4
soften 3
dead end
impasse
rut 2
deadened
dead 13
dull 8
noiseless
numb 1
senseless 2
deadening
cold 4
deadfall
trap 1
dead heat
draw 17
tie 10
dead letter
history 7
deadliness
virulence 1
deadlock°
dilemma
draw 17
impasse
stalemate
tie 10
deadly°
black 5
calamitous
cutthroat 3
destructive 1
evil 3
fatal 1
fateful 2
homicidal
hopeless 1
lethal
macabre
malignant 1
mortal 3, 4
murderous 1
poisonous 1
stodgy
terminal 2
venomous 1
virulent 1
withering
-in deadly embrace
opposition 3
dead on one's feet
exhausted 1
ragged 3
sleepy 1
weary 1
worn 3
deadpan
empty 5
vacant 2
wooden 2
dead tired
fatigued
jaded 1
prostrate 5
ragged 3
tired 1
dead to the world
dead 3
unconscious 1
dead weight
overload 2
deaf°
heedless
insensible 2
unconscious 2
deafening
loud 1
noisy
thunderous
uproarious 1
deal°
administer 3
agreement 1
allot
bargain 1
contract 1
deliver 5
dicker 1, 2
dispense 1
divide 2
dole 3
find 10
give 15b
haggle
hand 17
mete
negotiate 1
negotiation 2
operation 3
pact
parcel 4
parley 2
pass 20b
portion 4
strike 2
trade 5
transaction 1
treaty
deal a blow to
strike 1
dealer°
broker
merchant 1
seller
trader
tradesman 1

deal in
handle 5
market 4
merchandise 2
run 14
sell 2
stock 9
dealing
business 3
exchange 2
passage 10
trade 1
transaction 1
treatment 1
truck 2
-dealings°
intercourse 1
proceeding 2a
relation 6b
trade 1
treatment 1
truck 2
deal out
allot
dispense 1
dispose 3c
distribute 1
divide 2
dole 3
give 15b
hand 17
measure 14
mete
parcel 4
pass 20b
pay 11a
portion 4
present[2] 6
ration 3
serve 3
share 3
split 4
deal with°
at **deal 4**
attend 2
cope 2
cover 7
dispose 3a
face 14, 18b
field 6
grapple 2
grip 5
handle 6, 7
manage 2
meet[1] 5
patronize 2
process 4
reckon 5a
relate 4
speak 10
tackle 3
take 39e
touch 8
treat 1, 2
work 10
dean
clergyman 1
elder 3
minister 1
principal 4
dear°
adorable
beloved 1
bosom 4
darling 1, 3
dearly 3
expensive
extravagant 3
high 3
intimate[1] 1
invaluable
lovable
old 8
personal 3
precious 1
premium 4b
priceless 1
pricey
prohibitive 2
rich 4
special 5
steep[1] 2
stiff 6
sumptuous
sweet 5
dear (*cont.*)
sweetheart
tight 9
dear boy
boy 3
dearest
beloved 1, 2
darling 1
love 3
pet[1] 3
precious 1
special 5
dearly°
dear 4
dear one
love 3
dearth°
absence 2
famine
lack 1
need 5
poverty 2
scarcity
shortage
want 3
deasil
forward 4
death°
doom
end 5
fatality 2
fate 2
finish 10
kill 9
killing 1
loss 7
passing 4
-at death's door
dying
moribund 1
-be the death of
carry 10d
deathbed
parting 3
-on one's death-bed
dying
deathblow
kill 9
death-dealing
homicidal
withering
death-defying
daredevil 2
superhuman 1
deathless°
classic 2
everlasting
immortal 1
timeless
deathlike
dead 3
deadly 4
macabre
deathly
black 5
dead 3
deadly 4
macabre
murderous 1
wan 1
death notice
obituary
death-rattle
rattle 7
death-watch
wake[1] 3
débâcle
disaster
downfall
flood 1
flop 4
reverse 8
rout 1
ruin 1
washout
debar
ban 1
disqualify
exclude 1
expel 2
forbid
debar (*cont.*)
freeze 4
isolate
lock[1] 8
obstruct 3
preclude
prevent
prohibit 1
restrain 2
shut 5a
suspend 3
debark
disembark
land 5
light[2] 13
debarment
exception 2
prevention
prohibition 1, 2
debarring
prevention
prohibition 1
suspension 1
debase°
adulterate
alloy 2
contaminate
corrupt 3
degrade 2
demoralize 2
desecrate
diminish 2
disgrace 4
dishonour 2
foul 14
humble 4
lower[1] 4
peg 3
poison 3
profane 4
prostitute 2
pull 9c
ruin 11
shame 8
taint 2
take 31b
tarnish
vilify
violate 2
vitiate 2
debased
bad 2
base[2] 5
corrupt 2
decadent 1
degenerate 1
disgraceful 1
dishonourable 1
impure 2, 4
monstrous 2
reprobate 1
rotten 3
sordid 1
ugly 2
unchaste
vile 1
wicked 2
debasement
degradation 2
disgrace 1
filth 2
parody 2
prostitution 2
ruin 2
sacrilege 1
undoing 1
violation 2
debasing
degrading
derogatory
disgraceful 1
ruin 2
violation 2
debatable°
controversial 1
disputable
doubtful 1
implausible
moot 1
open 7
problematic
question 6b
questionable
suspicious 1
theoretical 1
debatable (*cont.*)
tricky 2
uncertain 3
unresolved
debate°
argue 1, 2, 3
argument 1
contest 2, 3
controversy 1
deliberate 4
disagree 2
disagreement 3
discuss
discussion
dispute 1, 2, 3
fight 4
knock 3c
negotiate 1
quarrel 1
reason 8
variance 2
debauch
demoralize 2
dishonour 3
dissipate 4
fling 2
orgy 1
party 1
pervert 2
revel 3
seduce 2
spree
violate 3
debauched
abandoned 2
decadent 2
dissolute
immoral 2
incontinent 2
indecent 2
lascivious 1
lewd
libertine 2
loose 7
obscene 1
outrageous 3
profligate 1
promiscuous 2
prurient 1
sensual
debauchee
degenerate 3
libertine 1
pervert 3
playboy
profligate 3
rake[2]
reprobate 2
roué
sensualist
debauchery
dissipation 1
excess 2
perversion 2
profligacy 1
debauching
self-indulgent
debilitate
break 6
cripple 2
depress 2
drain 5
enervate
exhaust 2
sap[2]
tire 1
undermine 1
waste 3
weaken 1
wear 6
weary 5
debilitated
broken 3
crippled 1
decrepit 1
delicate 3
exhausted 1
feeble 1
helpless 3
impotent 1
infirm 1
limp[2] 2
low[1] 4
powerless 2
run-down 1
debilitated (*cont.*)
unhealthy 1
waste 2
weak 2
debilitating
exhausting 1
killing 3
debilitation
decrepitude 1
exhaustion 2
impairment
impotence 1
debility
decline 7
infirmity 1
prostration 4
debit
charge 3, 12
liability 2
loss 6
debonair°
elegant 1
gay 2
genteel 2, 3
jaunty 2
pleasant 2
polished 2
rakish
suave
debouchment
issue 1
mouth 2
outpouring
debris
fragment 2
garbage
junk 1
leftover 1
litter 1
odds 5
refuse[2]
remain 4a
rubbish 1
ruin 6
scrap[1] 3
trash 3
waste 7
wreckage
debt°
charge 3
liability 2
obligation 3
-in debt°
at **debt 2**
beholden
embarrassed 2
owe 1
debt-free
solvent
debug
shake 6a
debunk
explode 2
début°
initiation 1
onset 2
opening 4
première 1, 2, 3
presentation 3
decadence
decay 3
decadent°
degenerate 1
lecherous
libertine 2
decamp
bolt 8
bundle 3
clear 30
depart 1
drop 13
escape 1
evacuate 2
flee 1
flight[2] 3
fly 2
go 2, 23, 31d
leave[1] 1
make 26
move 2
quit 1
retreat 4
decamp (*cont.*)
run 2
take 34c
decampment
escape 5
decanter
bottle 1
jug
decapitate
behead
decarbonated
flat 8
decay°
decline 7
decompose 2
decrepitude 2
degenerate 2
deteriorate 2
disintegrate
disrepair
dissolution 2
ebb 2, 4
fade 2
fail 3
failure 2
fall 24
fester 1
filth 1
mortify 3
putrefy
rot 1, 2, 3
ruin 1
seed 4
spoil 4
stagnate
turn 5
twilight 2
waste 2
worsen 2
decayed
bad 6
decrepit 2
dilapidated
foul 2
mouldy
musty 1
old 3
putrid
rancid
rotten 1
seedy 1
unsound 1
decaying
decadent 1
decrepit 2
dilapidated
mouldy
putrid
seedy 1
decease
death 1
die 1
expire 2
deceased
dead 1
defunct 1
late 3
deceit°
art 5
craft 2
deception 1
dissimulation
evasion 2
falsity
finesse 2
fraud 1
hocus-pocus 1
hypocrisy
lying 1
perfidy
trick 1
trickery
deceitful°
artful 1
crafty
deceptive 2
designing
devious 1
dirty 3
dishonest
disingenuous
disloyal
double 5
evasive

deceitful (*cont.*)
false 2
fraudulent 2
furtive 1
game 6
hollow 4
hypocritical
insincere
lying 2
Machiavellian
mealy-mouthed
oblique 2
perfidious
phoney 1
plausible 2
rotten 3
scheming
shifty
sly 1
sneaky
spurious
traitorous
tricky 1
two-faced
unscrupulous
untrue 1
wily
deceitfully
back 6
deceitfulness
deceit 1
falsity
hypocrisy
deceive°
beguile 1
betray 3
blind 5
bluff[1] 1
cheat 2
defraud
disappoint 2
disguise 2
dissimulate
double-cross
dupe 3
equivocate
finesse 4
flummox
fool 4
have 12c
hoax 2
hoodwink
jolly 2
lead 7
leg 8
misinform
mislead
outsmart
put 26
ride 5a
rip 2b
seduce 1
string 10c
swindle 1
take 32b
throw 6c
trap 6
trick 8
victimize 2
-be deceived by
fall 13b
labour 7
deceiver
cheat 1
fraud 3
hypocrite
impostor
phoney 3
twister 1
deceiving
deceptive 1
dishonest
hypocritical
shifty
wily
decelerate
brake 2
decency
grace 2
honour 1
integrity 1
kindness 1
morality 1
nobility 1
probity

decency (*cont.*)
propriety 2
purity 2
rectitude
shame 4
virtue 1
decent°
chaste 1
clean 4
considerable 1
correct 6
decorous
ethical
fair[1] 4
honest 1
honourable 2
just 2
moral 1
noble 4
presentable 2
proper 3
pure 3
respectable 1, 3
savoury 2
seemly 2
solid 5
square 4
straight 4
upright 2
virtuous 2
wholesome 2
decently
honestly 1
properly 1
deception°
act 3
artifice 1
blind 8
bluff[1] 3
camouflage 1
chicanery
deceit 1
delusion 1
disguise 4
dissimulation
dodge 4
evasion 2
feint
finesse 2
foul play
fraud 1, 2
gimmick 1
gobbledegook 2
hanky-panky
hoax 1
hocus-pocus 1
hypocrisy
illusion 1
intrigue 3
masquerade 2
pretence 1, 2
put-on 1
rip-off 2
ruse
subterfuge
swindle 2
trap 2
trick 1
trickery
deceptive°
devious 1
dishonest
false 2
fraudulent 2
hollow 4
hypocritical
illusory
insincere
lying 2
oblique 2
plausible 2
sophistic
specious
subtle 3
tortuous 2
tricky 1, 3
wily
deceptiveness
falsity
gobbledegook 2
subtlety 2
decern
decree 2

decide°
arrange 2
choose
decree 2
determine 1, 3
dispose 3a
distinguish 1
finalize
fix 2, 15
judge 4
make 16
mind 13
persevere
resolve 1, 3
rule 7
see 8
set 9
settle 2, 3
sort 10a
-to be decided
issue 8
decided°
bent 4
certain 1
cut 29a
determined 1
emphatic
fated 1
firm 4
fixed 3
grim 1
intent 5
marked
mind 12
positive 2
pronounced 1, 2
purposeful
resolute
set 29
thick 9
decidedly
absolutely 1
definitely
degree 4b
far 2, 3
highly 2
once 3
terribly
truly 3
very 2
well[1] 7
decidedness
decision 3
resolution 1
decide on°
at **decide 2**
fix 15
make 16
pick 1
pitch[1] 7
settle 2
take 2
deciding
settlement 5
ultimate 1
decimal point
dot 1
point 1
decimate
kill 1
massacre 2
mow 2
decimation
killing 1
murder 2
decipher°
figure 12b
interpret 1
make 37d
perceive 2
puzzle 3
read 2
render 6
solve
translate 1
decipherability
simplicity 1
decipherable
intelligible
legible
readable 3
decipherment
interpretation 1
solution 1

decipherment (*cont.*)
translation 1
decision°
decide 1
decree 1
determination 2
disposition 4
finding 2
judgement 2
negotiation 2
perseverance
resolution 1, 3
sentence
settlement 5
voice 2
decision-making
responsible 3
decision time
crunch 2
decisive
critical 2
crucial
decided 2
definitive 1
fateful 1
final 2
firm 4
last[1] 4
momentous
peremptory 2
positive 1
sweeping 2
ultimate 1
decisively
finally 2
firmly 2
decisiveness
decision 3
finality
perseverance
deck
beautify
decorate 1
drape 1
embellish 1
equip
floor 1, 2
ornament 2
pack 4
preen 2
deck-hand
sailor
deck out
beautify
decorate 1
dress 1, 2
equip
get 51e
ornament 2
preen 2
primp
trim 4
declaim
denounce 3
harangue 2
hold 16a
impeach 2
lecture 3
mouth 7
rant 1
spout 2
declamation
harangue 1
lecture 1
oration
oratory
tirade
declaration°
admission 4
allegation
announcement 1
answer 2
assertion 1
exposition 2
expression 1
finding 2
manifestation
message 2
observation 2
oration
proclamation 1
profession 2

declaration (*cont.*)
pronouncement 1
publication 1
representation 3
revelation
statement
testimony
word 5
declaratory
assertive
declare°
admit 4
air 7
allege
announce 1, 3
attest
certify 2
claim 4
confess
deliver 4
enunciate 2
exclaim
find 9
insist 2
issue 10
maintain 3
make 33
manifest 2
notify 2
observe 4
pass 9
plead 3
proclaim 1
profess 1
pronounce 1, 2
protest 4
remark 2
rule 7
say 1
set 18c
signify 1
speak 11b
state 7
swear 1
tell[1] 2
testify
vent 3
voice 4
vow 1
declared
professed 2
declare null and void
quash 1
reverse 3
revoke
set 15b
undo 3
vacate 3
void 6
declare redundant
eject 3
fire 11
sack 4
declaring
proclamation 2
declension
downgrade 3
declination
twilight 2
decline°
collapse 2
decay 1b, 3
decrease 1, 2
degenerate 2
deny 2
depression 3
descend 2
deteriorate 1, 2
die 2
diminish 1
dip 2, 5
dissolve 1
downgrade 3
drop 4, 6, 11
dwindle
ebb 2, 4
eclipse 4
fade 2
fail 3
failure 2
fall 3, 4, 16, 24, 26, 27

decline (*cont.*)
flag[2] 2
go 12, 27b
grade 4
hill 3
lapse 3, 4
melt 4
movement 6
pass 22
recede 2
recession
refuse[1] 1
reject 1, 2
relapse 2, 4
rot 2
sag 2, 3
seed 4
senility
set 2
settle 9
sink 4
slack 3b, 5
slide 3
slope 1, 2
slump 1, 2
stagnate
subside 1
suffer 4
taper 2
turn 14a
twilight 2
wane 1, 3
waste 2
worsen 2
-in decline
soft 7
-on the decline
infirm 1
obsolescent
wane 4
declining
decadent 1
downgrade 4
downward
moribund 2
obsolescent
senile
soft 7
wane 4
declivitous
precipitous 1
declivity
decline 8
drop 4
fall 27
grade 4
hill 3
incline 4
ramp
slope 2
decoction
broth
extract 5
extraction 2
potion
decode
decipher 1
interpret 1
render 6
translate 1
decoding
interpretation 1
translation 1
decollate
behead
décolleté
low[1] 11
decompose°
attack 5
break 16b
decay 2
deteriorate 2
disintegrate
dissolve 1
fester 1
mortify 3
putrefy
rot 1
spoil 4
stagnate
decomposed
foul 2
mouldy
putrid

decomposed (*cont.*)
rotten 1
decomposition
breakdown 3
decay 4
dissolution 2
rot 3
decompound
decompose 1
decontaminant
disinfectant
decontaminate
clean 11b
disinfect
fumigate
purify 1
refine 1
wash 6
decontaminated
clean 1
decontaminator
disinfectant
decontrol
laissez-faire
decorate°
appoint 3
beautify
drape 1
dress 2
elaborate 3
embellish 1
enrich 2
fix 16b
furnish 2
garland 2
grace 6
illuminate 3
illustrate 2
ornament 2
paint 6
pattern 8
tool 4
trim 4
decorated
busy 3
elaborate 2
fancy 1
flamboyant 1
flowery
luxuriant 3
decoration°
attachment 4
elaboration 1
embellishment 1
finery
flourish 3
frill 1
fringe 1
motif
ornament 1
pattern 2
regalia
trappings
trim 5
-decorations
finery
regalia
trappings
trim 5
decorative
fancy 1
ornamental
decorator
designer 1
decorous°
correct 6
courteous
decent 2,5
genteel 2
good 3
ladylike
official 2
orderly 2
presentable 2
proper 3
prudish
pure 3
respectable 1
savoury 2
sedate 2
seemly 2
tasteful
well-bred
decorously
properly 1
decorousness
purity 2
shame 4
decorticate
pare 1
peel 1
shell 3
skin 3
strip[2] 1
decorum°
ceremony 2
discipline 3
etiquette
form 6
formality 3
grace 2
manner 3
propriety 1,2
shame 4
taste 6
decoy°
entice
enticement 2
lead 7
lure 1,2
seduce 1
throw 6c
decrease°
contract 4
cut 8,21
decay 1
decline 2,6
deduction 1
depreciate 1
die 2
dilute
diminish 1
drop 11
dwindle
ease 6
ebb 2,4
fall 3,16,26
flag[2] 2
go 27b
impairment
lag 2
let[1] 9
lower[1] 1
mark 15b
melt 4
minimize 1
mitigate
moderate 5
modify 2
movement 6
narrow 8
pale[1] 5
pare 2
reduce 1,2,5
relax 2
remission 2
remit 2
sag 2,3
scale[3] 5
slack 3b,5
slash 3,5
slide 3
step 14b
subside 2
taper 2
thin 9
trail 8
wane 1,3
wind[2] 3a
-on the decrease
wane 4
decreasing
wane 4
decree°
act 4
appoint 1
command 1
decision 2
declare 2
dictate 1,2
enact 1
establish 1
finding 2
judge 4
judgement 2
law 1
order 4
decree (*cont.*)
precept 1
prescribe
proclaim 2
pronounce 2
pronouncement 2
regulation 2
rule 1,7
sentence
shape 7
warrant 2
decreed
fatal 3
fated 1
inevitable
decrement
decrease 2
decrepit°
dilapidated
doddering
elderly 1
feeble 1
fragile
infirm 1
leg 7
low[1] 4
ramshackle
rickety
run-down 2
senile
shaky 2
time-worn
tumbledown
weak 1,2
decrepitude°
infirmity 1
senility
weakness 1
decretal
decree 1
peremptory 1
decrial
attack 7
mockery 1
outcry
decry
abuse 3
attack 2
belittle
blaspheme 2
denounce 3
depreciate 2
disapprove
disparage 1
downgrade 2
flout
hiss 3
jeer 1
minimize 2
mock 1
play 13
rail[2]
run 26b
slander 2
trivialize
vilify
vituperate
write 4b
decrying
slanderous
decrypt
decipher 1
decumbent
prone 1
prostrate 3
recumbent
supine 1
decussation
mesh 1
dedal
intricate 1
dedicate°
apply 5
celebrate 1
commemorate
devote 1,2
give 5
hallow 1
schedule 2
dedicated
devoted
devout 1
earnest 1
faithful 1
dedicated (*cont.*)
given 3
great 10
heartfelt
loyal
pious 1
resolute
sacred 1
single-minded
steadfast
strong 5
true 2
untiring
wholehearted
wrap 2
yeomanly
dedicate oneself to
follow 6
pursue 2
dedication°
application 3
devotion 2
faith 3
fanaticism 1
loyalty
morale
piety 1
resolution 1
sanctity
deduce°
derive 1
extract 2
gather 4
infer
perceive 2
reason 7
take 19
deduced
circumstantial 1
constructive 2
deduct°
allow 6
discount 1
rebate 3
subtract 1
take 14
withhold 2
deduction°
allowance 4
discount 4
inference
law 3
logic 1
presumption 3
rebate 1
theorem 2
-after deductions
net[2] 2
deductive
logical 1
deed°
achievement 2
act 1
action 3
adventure 1
effort 3
exploit 1
fact 2
feat
move 9
paper 2a
proceeding 1
record 6
stunt[1]
thing 6
title 5
trick 4
turn 35
deed-holder
proprietor 1
deem
consider 3
count 2
esteem 2
feel 4
guess 2
hold 7
imagine 2
judge 4
mind 13
perceive 3
reckon 2
deem (*cont.*)
regard 4
rule 7
take 8,19
think 2
view 9
deemed
reputed
de-emphasize
belittle
minimize 2
play 13
deemster
judge 1
deep°
abyss
dark 6
dead 15
deeply 1
depth 5
drink 7
exquisite 2
full 11
gruff 2
gulf 2
heartfelt
heavy 12
highbrow 2
incomprehensible
intense 1,2
intimate[1] 2
keen[1] 3
meaningful 1
ocean 1
penetrating 1
poignant 3
profound 1,3
radical 1
recondite
rich 5
rotund 2
scholarly
sea 1
soulful
sound[2] 6
strong 22
subtle 2
thick 2
-in deep trouble
trouble 9a
-off the deep end
disturbed 2
excited 1
insane 1
deep down
deeply 1
really 3
deepen°
gather 5
heighten 2
inflame 2
intensify
deeper down than
below 6
deep-felt
strong 22
deep-freeze
freeze 1,5
-in the deep-freeze
abeyance
delay 1
deep in thought
meditative
deeply°
deep 10
depth 6
hard 14
head 8
home 10
profoundly
searchingly
sincerely
very 1
deeply felt
poignant 3
deepness
depth 1
deep-rooted
deep 6
entrenched
gut 6
deep-rooted (*cont.*)
inborn
ingrained
radical 1
rooted
sneaking 1
stable 1
steadfast
strong 22
subconscious 1
deep-water
oceanic
de-escalate
decrease 1
de-escalation
decrease 2
deface°
blemish 1
damage 4
hack[1] 1
mar 1
mutilate 2
score 10
spoil 2
trash 4
defaced
disfigured
pitted
de facto
really 3
defalcate
embezzle
misappropriate 1
defalcation
embezzlement
rip-off 2
defalcator
swindler
defamation
aspersion
discredit 5
dishonour 5
insult 2
libel 1
scandal 3
shame 2
slander 1
smear 4
defamatory
abusive 1
foul 6
injurious 2
poisonous 2
scandalous 2
scurrilous
slanderous
vicious 2
vituperative
defame
abuse 3
blacken 2
blaspheme 2
blast 6
discredit 1
disgrace 4
disparage 2
foul 14
insult 1
libel 3
run 26b
shame 8
slander 2
stigmatize
tarnish
vilify
default°
deficit
failure 1
neglect 4
omission 2
renege 2
-in default
failing 2
out 5
defaulting
delinquent 2
defeat°
back 7b
beat 2
best 11
break 4
conquer 1

defeat (*cont.*)
conquest 1
crush 4
demolish 2
demoralize 1
disappoint 3
disappointment 1
discomfit 2
downfall
enervate
fall 28
finish 4,10
floor 4
foil[1]
frustrate 1
kill 6
loss 5
miscarriage
outdo
overcome 1
overpower 1
overrun
overthrow 1,2
overturn 3
overwhelm 1
rebuff 1,2
reverse 8
rout 1,2
ruin 1
set-back
slaughter 4
squelch 1
stymie
subdue 2
topple 2
triumph 3
undoing 1
upset 4,5,11
whip 2
-be defeated
fall 5
go 27c
lose 3
defeated
broken 3
disappointed 2
overcome 2
undone[1] 1
unsuccessful 2
defeatism
desperation 2
defeatist
naysayer
pessimistic
defecate°
go 17
pass 12
void 7
defect°
blemish 3
default 1
desert[1] 4
disability 1
disadvantage 1
drawback
failing 1
fault 1
flaw 1
foible
frailty 2
imperfection
infirmity 2
kink 3
nick 1
shortcoming
taint 1
trouble 8
vice 2
weakness 3
defection
secession
defective°
amiss 1
bad 1
deficient 1,2
fail 1
faulty
flawed
hurt 8
imperfect
inadequate 1
incomplete
inferior 3
poor 4
second[1] 7
defective (*cont.*)
unsatisfactory
unsound 1,4
wanting 1
wrong 5
defectively
badly 1,3
defector°
deserter
renegade 1
subversive 2
turncoat
defence°
answer 2
argument 2
bulwark 1
excuse 4
guard 5
inhibition
plea 2
protection 1
rampart
reason 1
safeguard 1
shield 1
stand 14
-defences
resistance 2
defenceless°
human 2
insecure 2
leg 6
prostrate 4
unarmed
underdog
unguarded 2
vulnerable
defence mechanism
inhibition
defend°
apologize 2
bulwark 2
champion 4
cover 1
excuse 3
guard 1
justify
maintain 4
patrol 3
preserve 1
protect 1
safeguard 2
secure 7
shield 2
speak 7a
stand 5a,11
stick[1] 18
uphold
defendable
tenable
defendant
litigant
party 5
defender
advocate 2
champion 2
guardian
party 4
patron 1
proponent
protector
stand-by 1
defending
patrol 2
defenestration
purge 4
defensible
supportable 2
tenable
defensive
protective
strong 16
defer°
bow 2
cringe 2
delay 1
hinder 1
hold 18a,21a
postpone
procrastinate 1
put 21a
reserve 1
defer (*cont.*)
shelve
stay[1] 4
submit 1
suspend 1
table 5
truckle
waive 2
-be deferred
wait 2
deference°
duty 2
homage
honour 2
obeisance
piety 1
prostration 2
regard 7
respect 2
reverence 1
submission 1
veneration
deferential
attentive 2
dutiful
feminine 1
humble 2
meek 1
obsequious
passive 2
polite 1
propitiatory 2
servile
soft 5
submissive 1,2
deferment
delay 4
postponement
stay[1] 6
suspension 2
deferral
delay 4
postponement
stay[1] 6
waiver
defer to
esteem 1
honour 5
keep 6
obey 1
respect 6,7
submit 1
defiance
challenge 5
opposition 1
rebellion 2
resistance 1
-in defiance of
despite
face 9
spite 2
defiant°
audacious 2
disobedient 1
flagrant
insubordinate
mutinous 2
naughty 2
rebellious 1
recalcitrant
resistant 1
thumb 8
unruly
deficiency
absence 2
dearth
defect 1
deficit
failure 1
famine
fault 1
imperfection
incompetence
inferiority 2
lack 1
non-completion
shortage
shortcoming
vacancy 1
vice 2
want 3
deficient°
absent 2
defective 1,2
deficient (*cont.*)
destitute 2
empty 7
exceptional 3
fail 1
fall 19
feeble-minded
hopeless 2
imperfect
inadequate 1
incomplete
inefficient 1
insufficient
lack 2
low[1] 2
meagre 3,4
poor 2
ropy 2
scarce
short 6,8
shy 3
thin 2
unsatisfactory
want 2
wanting 1
wrong 5
deficiently
badly 1
deficit°
lack 1
shortage
defied
broken 5
defile
canyon
contaminate
corrupt 4
debase 2
desecrate
dirty 7
dishonour 3
foul 12,14
gorge 1
gully
mire 4
outrage 5
pass 23
poison 3
pollute 2
profane 4
prostitute 2
rape 4
ravine
ravish 2
ruin 11
seduce 2
smear 2
soil[1] 2
stain 5
sully
taint 2
vilify
violate 2
vitiate 2
defiled
filthy 1
foul 2
impure 1,4
profane 2
sordid 3
defilement
abuse 7
filth 2
impurity 1
pillage 2
prostitution 2
rape 1
ruin 2
sacrilege 1
scandal 3
violation 2
define°
bound[1] 2
characterize
describe 2
distinguish 2
explain 1
fix 2
formulate 1
gloss[2] 2
interpret 1
limit 7
outline 3
pin 4b
prescribe
define (*cont.*)
represent 3
set 7
shape 7
specify
stake[1] 4b
defined
set 29
specific 1
standard 5
strict 1
definite°
assertive
certain 2,3,5,6
clean 3
clear 5,6,7,10
concrete
decided 1,2
determined 2
distinct 1
emphatic
explicit 1,2
express 5
firm 4
fixed 2,3
flat 4,10
formal 2
hard 12
incontrovertible
indisputable
manifest 1
outright 1,2
particular 1,6
plump[2] 6
positive 1,2
precise 1
pronounced 1,2
purposeful
secure 4
self-confident
self-evident
set 29
specific 1
strong 10,15
sure 1
unavoidable
undisputed
unquestionable
definitely°
absolutely 1,3
certainty 3
clearly 2
course 6
downright 2
easily 2
entirely 2
exactly 2
expressly 1
far 3
finally 2
flat 16
indeed 1
mean[3] 2a
OK 1
once 3
perfectly 1
positively
question 4
quite 4
really 1,2
sharply 3
surely 1
thoroughly 1
truly 3
undoubtedly
utterly
very 2
well[1] 7
definitely not
mean[3] 5
definiteness
certainty 2
clarity 2
precision 2
definition°
clarity 2
description 2
determination 3
explanation 1
gloss[2] 1
interpretation 1
-by definition
necessarily
definitive°
classic 1
concrete
emphatic
final 2
incontrovertible
indisputable
last[1] 4
plump[2] 6
positive 2
specific 1
standard 5
definitively
easily 2
finally 2
sharply 3
definitiveness
finality
deflate
collapse 1
mortify 1
puncture 4
put 16e
take 31b
wind[1] 13
deflated
flat 6
deflating
derogatory
deflect°
bend 6
distract 1
divert 1,2
fend 2
intercept
pervert 1
sidetrack
turn 7
deflected
bent 1
deflection
shift 5
slant 3
switch 2
defloration
rape 1
ruin 2
deflower
dishonour 3
outrage 6
rape 4
ravish 2
ruin 11
seduce 2
deflowering
rape 1
ruin 2
defoliate
bare 8
shed[2] 4
defoliated
bare 4
deform
deface
distort 1
mangle
screw 7c
warp 1
deformation
warp 2
deformed°
crooked 2
disfigured
grotesque 1
misshapen
shapeless 2
wry 1
deformity
abnormality 2
freak 1
kink 3
monster 2
warp 2
defraud°
beguile 2
cheat 2
chisel 2
double-cross
dupe 3
fleece
fool 4
gouge 2
hoax 2

defraud (*cont.*)
hoodwink
misinform
outsmart
prey 3b
ride 5a
rip 2b
rob 3
screw 6
sting 4
swindle 1
take 27, 32b
trick 8
victimize 2
defrauder
fraud 3
defrauding
rip-off 2
swindle 2
defray°
clear 29
cover 10
meet[1] 5
defrayal
settlement 4
defrost
thaw 1
deft
clever 4
dexterous 1
graceful 1
handy 3
ingenious
masterful 1
neat 4
nimble 1
perfect 7
quick 4
ready 6
talented
wicked 7
deftly
handily 2
deftness
dexterity 1
facility 1
ingenuity
skill 1
touch 16
understanding 3
defunct°
dead 1
extinct 1
inanimate
past 1
defuse
moderate 5
defy°
beggar 3
brave 3
break 9
challenge 1, 3
combat 6
dare 1
disobey
fight 2
fly 6
mock 1
oppose 1
rebel 2
resist 1
snap 6
stand 12a, 12b
trample 2
transgress 2
turn 12
withstand
dégagé
casual 5
detached 2
perfunctory 1
rocky[1] 3
degeneracy
degradation 1
evil 6
profligacy 1
vice 1
degenerate°
corrupt 2
decadent 2
decay 1b
decline 4
deteriorate 1
die 2
degenerate (*cont.*)
dissolute
flag[2] 2
go 12
immoral 1
impure 4
indecent 2
kinky 2
lecherous
libertine 2
mean[2] 2
obscene 1
outrageous 3
pervert 3
perverted
profligate 1, 3
relapse 2
reprobate 1, 2
rot 2
rotten 3
seamy
seed 4
sink 4
stagnate
ugly 2
vicious 1
vile 1
wicked 2
worsen 2
degenerating
decadent 1
wane 4
degeneration
decay 3
decline 7
degradation 1
ebb 4
impurity 3
relapse 4
wane 3
degradation°
discredit 4
disgrace 1
downfall
evil 6
filth 2
humiliation
prostitution 2
ruin 2
scandal 2
shame 2
undoing 1
vice 1
violation 2
degrade°
belittle
corrupt 3
cut 6
debase 1
desecrate
deteriorate 1
diminish 2
discredit 1
disgrace 4
dishonour 2
flout
foul 14
humble 4
lower[1] 4
mortify 1
pervert 2
profane 4
prostitute 2
pull 9c
reduce 6
shame 8
take 31b
tarnish
violate 2
vitiate 1
degraded
base[2] 2
corrupt 2
degenerate 1
disgraceful 1
low[1] 12
mean[2] 2
seamy
sordid 1
vicious 1
degrade oneself
stoop 2
degrading°
base[2] 2
disgraceful 1
dishonourable 1
menial 1
ruin 2
shameful
unwholesome 2
vicious 1
vile 1
violation 2
degree°
breadth 2
calibre 3
gauge 4
grade 1
incidence
indication 2
measure 5
notch 2
order 3
proportion 4
shade 7
step 5
-at 90 degrees
perpendicular 2
-by degrees°
at **degree 3**
piecemeal 1
-to a degree°
at **degree 4**
moderately
partially
quite 2
slightly
somewhat
dehydrate
dry 4
evaporate 1
parch
preserve 3
shrivel
dehydrated
dry 1
thirsty 1
dehydration
evaporation 1
de-ice
thaw 1
deific
divine 1
deification
worship 2
deiform
divine 1
deify
glorify 2
idealize
idolize
lift 2
pedestal 2
worship 1
deign°
condescend
lower[1] 4
stoop 2
vouchsafe 1
deigning
patronage 3
deipnosophism
repartee
deipnosophist
conversationalist
deity°
creator 2
god
deject
chill 8
depress 1
desolate 6
get 36c
sadden
shatter 3
dejected°
bad 9
blue 1
broken 3
broken-hearted
desolate 3
despondent
disappointed 1
doleful
downhearted
dejected (*cont.*)
forlorn 1
gloomy 2
heartbroken
heavy 6
hopeless 3
hurt 7
joyless 1
low[1] 8
melancholy 1
miserable 1
moody 1
morbid 3
mouth 6
pessimistic
sad 1
sinking 2
sorrowful 1
subdued 2
unhappy 1
woebegone
wretched 2
dejectedly
sadly 2
dejection
depression 2
despair 1
desperation 2
disappointment 2
gloom 2
grief 1
melancholy 2
prostration 3
sadness
de jure
lawful 1
legitimate 2
rightful 1
dekko
glance 4
delay°
arrest 1
dawdle
defer[1]
drag 6
fire 4
forestall
gap 1
hamper[1]
hang 6
hesitate 1
hinder 1
hold 18a, 21a, 22b
hold-up 2
impede
impediment
interval 1
lag 1
lull 1
moratorium
obstruct 2
pause 1, 2
play 14
postpone
postponement
prevent
prevention
procrastinate 1
put 21a
reprieve 2
reserve 1
respite 2
retard 1
set 16
set-back
shilly-shally
sit 8
slack 3b
stall[2] 1, 2
stay[1] 4, 6
string 11b
suspend 1
suspension 2
tarry 1
tie-up 1
time 20
wait 4
-be delayed
fire 4
hang 6, 10
wait 2
-without delay
demand 8
directly 2
double 8
delay (*cont.*)
flat 17b
hastily 1
immediately 1
instantaneously
nail 6
now 3
once 6a
post-haste
promptly
quickly 3
rapidly 2
readily 3
right 13
soon 2
straight 15
summarily 1
time 17
delayed
belated
late 1
slow 5
delaying
prevention
suspension 2
dele
cancel 2
cut 16a
delete
obliterate 1
omit 1
delectable
dainty 3
delicious 1
luscious
pleasant 1
savoury 1
tasty
tempting 2
yummy
delectation°
delight 3
enjoyment 1
delegate°
agent 1
ambassador
appoint 2
assign 3
cast 8
commit 1
deputy
designate 2
detail 6
enable 1
entrust
envoy
farm 4
make 23
minister 2
mouthpiece 2
name 5
proxy
representative 3
send 1
substitute 2
trust 6
delegated
vicarious
delegation
mission 3
delete°
abolish
blot 4b
cancel 2
cross 3
cut 16a
edit 2
eliminate 3
erase 1
forgive 3
neutralize
obliterate 1
omit 1
remove 3
rub 4
scratch 3
strike 5
vitiate 3
void 6
wash 4
write 5
deleterious
bad 2
destructive 1
detrimental
deleterious (*cont.*)
evil 3
harmful
hurtful 1
ill 4
injurious 1
mischievous 2
poisonous 2
prejudicial
ruinous
unwholesome 1
violent 2
virulent 1
deletion
cut 22
omission 1
delftware
pottery
Delhi belly
run 50
deliberate°
balance 1
calculated 2
confer 1
conscious 2
consider 1
consult 1
contemplate 2
cool 3
debate 4
discuss
intentional
measured 2
methodical
moderate 1
mull
muse
parley 2
pitched
ponder
premeditated
purposeful
reflect 3
resolute
slow 1
special 3
speculate 1
studied
study 2
think 3
unhurried
voluntary 2
wilful 1
deliberately°
purpose 4a
voluntarily
deliberateness
purpose 2
resolution 1
deliberating
reflection 2
reflective
thought 1
deliberation
calculation 3
consideration 3
counsel 2
debate 2
discussion
parley 1
purpose 2
reflection 2
resolution 1
speculation 2
thought 1
delicacy°
dainty 4
finesse 3
frailty 1
refinement 1, 2
sensitivity 1
subtlety 1
tact
taste 6
titbit
weakness 1
delicate°
awkward 5
brittle 2
dainty 1
dodgy
elegant 1
explosive 1

delicate (*cont.*)
exquisite 1
fastidious
feeble 1
feminine 1
filmy 1
fine[1] 5, 6, 9
finicky 1, 2
flimsy 1, 3
fragile
gingerly 2
hot 10
hothouse 2
light[2] 4, 5
mincing
nice 3, 4
petite
precarious
sensitive 1, 3
sickly 2
silky
slight 3, 4
soft 9, 12
sore 2
squeamish 1
sticky 2
subtle 1
tactful
tender[1] 1, 5
tenuous 1
thin 5
thorny 2
ticklish 2, 3
tiny
tricky 2
unsound 2
weak 1, 2
-in delicate health
unhealthy 1
delicately
gingerly 1
delicateness
weakness 1
delicious°
dainty 3
luscious
mellow 1
pleasant 1
rich 6
savoury 1
tasty
tempting 2
voluptuous 2
yummy
delight°
admiration
amuse 2
bliss
carry 9
charm 5
content[2] 1, 4
delectation
distract 2
ecstasy 1
enchant 2
enjoyment 1
enrapture
entertain 1
entrance[2]
exult
feast 3, 6
flush[1] 3, 6
fun 1
gaiety 1
gladden
glee
gloat
glory 5
gratification
gratify
gusto
happiness
honour 3
joy 1, 3
love 2
luxury 3
paradise 3
please 1
pleasure 1
radiance 2
rapture
ravish 1
regale
rejoice

delight (*cont.*)
relish 1
revel 1
satisfaction 1
send 4
tickle
transport 3, 5
treasure 2
triumph 2
warm 9
delighted°
blithe 1
charmed 3
content[2] 3
ecstatic
elated
enchanted
exuberant 2
exultant
glad 1
gleeful
happy 1
joyful 2
merry 1
overjoyed
pleased
proud 1
radiant 2
rapt 1, 2
rapturous
rejoice
rhapsodic
willing
world 7
delightedly
happily 2
delightful°
acceptable 2
adorable
agreeable 1
beautiful 2
delicious 2
enchanting
engaging
entertaining
exhilarating 2
glorious 3
golden 4
heavenly 2
lovely 2
nice 1
picturesque 1
pleasant 1
taking
winning 1
delightfully
beautifully 1
nice 6
delight in°
at **delight 2**
admire 1
enjoy 1
gloat
like[2] 1
love 8
luxuriate 1
pride 4
relish 2
revel 1
roll 10b
savour 3
delimit
bound[1] 2
define 1
limit 6
measure 13
restrict
stake[1] 4b
stunt[2]
delimitation
definition 1
determination 3
restraint 1
delimited
finite
delineate
characterize
define 1, 2
describe 2
design 2
designate 1
detail 5
draft 3
draw 5

delineate (*cont.*)
explain 1
get 39b
outline 3
paint 4
phrase 4
plan 3
portray 1
project 3
relate 2
represent 3
set 7
specify
spell[3] 2
stake[1] 4b
state 7
tell[1] 4
trace 6
delineated
given 1
graphic 2
specific 1
delineation
definition 1
design 6
explanation 1
relation 4
rendering
delinquency
default 2
misbehaviour
delinquent°
derelict 2
disgraceful 2
disobedient 1
guilty 1
perverted
problem 3
punk 1
remiss
slack 1
transgressor
truant 1, 2
deliquesce
dissolve 1
melt 1
delirious°
distraught
drunk 2
ecstatic
mad 1
raving 1
wild 5
delirium tremens
shake 10
deliver°
abandon 1
address 3
administer 3
bring 1
catch 6
commit 1
communicate 1
distribute 1
emancipate
enunciate 1
execute 2
extricate
fetch 1
forward 7
give 1
hand 14, 18a
have 8
issue 10
lecture 3
liberate 1
loose 11, 13
make 18, 31c
pass 8, 9
pay 3
pipe 5
preach 1
produce 6
pronounce 3
propagate 1
pump 1
put 24
ransom 3
rant 1
read 3
recover 3
redeem 2
release 1
relieve 3

deliver (*cont.*)
render 3, 5, 7
rescue 1
return 6
rid 1
salvage 1
save 1
say 11
send 2
ship 2
sign 11
snatch 3
spare 6
strike 2
supply 1, 2
surrender 1
talk 6
take 9
transfer 1
transmit 1
transport 1
turn 15b, 15c
wash 2
world 5a, 5b
deliverance
delivery 1, 2
freedom 2, 3
liberation
ransom 1
recovery 3
release 3
relief 1
remission 1
rescue 2
salvage 2
delivered
free 2
deliverer
Messiah
saviour 1
delivering
delivery 1
release 3
deliver the goods
make 31c
deliver up
abandon 1
cede
resign 1
sell 3
surrender 1
turn 15c
delivery°
administration 3
birth 1
diction 2
execution 4
expression 6
freight 1
intonation
issue 6
labour 4
liberation
post[3] 1
presentation 1
pronunciation
receipt 2
recovery 3
supply 5
transfer 2
dell
hollow 7
valley
Delphic
ambiguous 2
obscure 2
delude
beguile 1
bluff[1] 1
deceive
defraud
dupe 3
finesse 4
fool 4
hoodwink
misinform
ride 5a
-be deluded
labour 7
deludedly
blindly

deluge
downpour
drown 1, 2
flood 1, 3, 4
flow 6
flush[1] 5
glut 3
outpouring
overwhelm 2
rain 1
rash[2] 2
satiate 1
shower 2
spate
storm 1
stream 2, 3
submerge 3
surfeit
swamp 2
torrent
volley 2
delusion°
dream 1
fallacy
fancy 6
fantasy 2
hallucination
illusion 1
misconception
phantom 2
vision 4
delusional
blind 3
dreamlike
unrealistic 1
delusive
dreamlike
fancy 2
non-existent
unrealistic 1
de luxe
fancy 3
luxurious 1
palatial
sumptuous
swell 7
upper-class 2
delve
burrow 2
plough 1
plumb 5
root[2]
till[1]
delve into
dig 5
fathom
go 30b
look 8
probe 1
research 2
scan 2
delving
research 1
demagogic
inflammatory
demagogue
agitator
rabble-rouser
speaker
talker 1
demand°
appetite 2
ask 2
bid 3
bidding 2
call 8a, 14
challenge 6
charge 5, 13
claim 1, 3
command 1, 4
condition 2
cry 3
desire 2, 4
dictate 1, 2
drive 1
enforce 2
entail
exact 3
expect 3
expectation 3
have 9
indicate 4
insist 1
lay[1] 10, 17b

demand (*cont.*)
look 6a
market 3
need 1, 2
obligation 1
oblige 2
order 4, 14
plead 2
prescribe
press 6
pressure 5
provide 3
provision 2
request 1, 2
require 1
requirement 1, 2
requisition 1, 2
run 43
say 10
screw 4
seek 3
speak 7c
stipulate
stipulation
strain[1] 7
take 16
tax 3
tell[1] 5
urge 2, 4
use 13
want 2, 4
wish 2
-demands
pressure 3
ultimatum
-in demand°
at **demand 7**
enviable
indispensable 1
popular 1
-on demand°
at **demand 8**
demanded
imperative 1
indispensable 1
mandatory
necessary 1
obligatory
order 10b
prerequisite 1
demanding°
choosy
difficult 1, 4, 5
exacting
fussy 1
hard 4
impatient 2
incumbent 1
meticulous
narrow 3
officious
overcritical
painful 3
particular 4
perfectionist 2
precise 2, 3
punishing
rigid 3
rugged 2
selective
severe 1
squeamish 1
stern 1
strait 1
strenuous 1
tell[1] 5
tough 4
trying
ultimatum
demand note
note 4
demarcate
define 1
restrict
stake[1] 4b
demarcation
definition 1
line[1] 4
démarche
manoeuvre 1
dematerialization
evaporation 2

depart from (*cont.*)
quit 1
vacate 1
departing
outgoing 1
parting 3
department°
bag 5
branch 2
bureau 2
category
district
division 3
domain 2
faculty 2
field 4
ministry 3
office 1, 2
part 7
realm 2
region 1
section 1
sphere 3
zone
departmentalize
categorize
department store
shop 1
store 4
departure
digression 1
diversion 1
diversity 1
escape 5
exception 3
exit 2
farewell 2
flight[2] 1
leave[2] 3
licence 3
mutation 2
parting 2
removal 4
take-off 1
twist 9
variation 2
depend°
dangle 1
hang 1, 7e
pivot 4
revolve 2
trust 5
dependability
credit 3
loyalty
permanence
regularity 2
responsibility 4
stability 2
trust 2
dependable
authoritative 2
certain 2
consistent 2
constant 1
durable
faithful 4
foolproof
good 8
honest 1
infallible 2
loyal
regular 6
reliable
reputable
responsible 2
ripe 2
rocky[1] 2
safe 3
solid 5, 6
sound[2] 3
staunch 1
steadfast
straight 4
sure 3
true 2
trustworthy
dependably
consistently 2
honestly 1
dependant
hanger-on
protégé
satellite 2
ward 2
dependence
abuse 5
belief 1
faith 1
reliance
dependency
province 1
dependent (on)
depend 1
hang 7e
helpless 1
relative 2
subject 8b
depending (on)
attendant 1
pending 1
depend on°
at **depend 1**
count 3
credit 5
draw 13a
fall 9
feed 3
figure 11a
go 26b, 32g
hang 7e
lean[2] 4a
reckon 4
rely
store 5
trust 5
turn 18b
depict
characterize
describe 3
draw 5
enact 2
exemplify 2
express 1, 2
mirror 3
paint 4
perform 3
picture 7
play 4
plot[1] 4
portray 1
render 1
represent 2, 3
show 8
tell[1] 4
depiction
description 1
drawing
history 1
illustration 2
picture 1
portrait
rendering
representation 1
depilated
smooth 4
deplane
disembark
get 40a
land 5
light[2] 13
deplaning
landing 2
deplete
clean 10a
consume 2
drain 5
erode
evacuate 1
exhaust 1, 4
expend 2
run 34b
sap[2]
use 5
weaken 1
-be depleted
give 15d
depleted
exhausted 2, 3
impoverished 2
poor 3
spent 2
depletion
drain 2
exhaustion 1
loss 2
deplorable°
abominable 1
grievous 2
lamentable
miserable 3, 4
mournful 2
piteous
regrettable
sad 3
shameful
sorry 2
tragic
unfortunate 3
wretched 1
deplorably
sadly 1
deplore
disapprove
grieve 1
moan 2
mourn
regret 1
deploy
draw 15c
deployment
distribution 1, 2, 3
placement 1
depollute
clean 11b
depone
attest
deponent
witness 2
depopulate
desolate 4
depopulated
uninhabited
deport
banish 1
behave
conduct 6
exile 3
expel 2
isolate
transport 2
deportation
ejection 2
exile 1
deportee
exile 2
deportment
action 8
bearing 1
behaviour
carriage 2
conduct 1
decorum 1
form 6
guise 1
manner 2
performance 4
play 21
presence 3
stance
deport oneself
act 5
play 16
depose
allege
attest
bring 8a
degrade 1
displace 2
downgrade 1
overthrow 1
overturn 2
put 16b
remove 5
swear 1
deposing
overthrow 2
deposit°
advance 9
dregs 1
dump 1
earnest 3
ground 4
lay[1] 1
lodge 5
deposit (*cont.*)
mine 2
park 3
pawn[1] 1, 3
pile[1] 1
place 15
pledge 2, 5
plump[2] 2
put 1
security 3
sediment
set 1
silt 1
stack 1
stick[1] 2
stow
tip[2] 3
vein 3
wash 2
deposition
allegation
assertion 1
declaration 1
deposit 4
evidence 2
removal 3
representation 3
testimony
depository
mine 2
storehouse
warehouse
depot
installation 3
station 3
stop 8
terminal 3
warehouse
deprave
corrupt 3
demoralize 2
vitiate 2
depraved
abandoned 2
bad 3
corrupt 2
criminal 2
degenerate 1
diabolic 2
dissolute
evil 1
evil-minded 1
filthy 3
ill 2
immoral 1
impure 4
kinky 2
lecherous
libertine 2
low[1] 12
miscreant 2
monstrous 2
outrageous 3
perverted
profligate 1
promiscuous 2
reprobate 1
rotten 3
satanic 1
seamy
sinful
ugly 2
ungodly 1
unwholesome 2
vicious 1
vile 1
wanton 1
wicked 2
depravity
degradation 1
evil 6
impurity 3
perversion 2
profligacy 1
sin 2
vice 1
deprecate
abuse 3
attack 2
belittle
blaspheme 2
debase 1
degrade 2
depreciate 2
diminish 2
deprecate (*cont.*)
disapprove
discredit 1
disparage 1
flout
impeach 2
knock 2
libel 3
minimize 2
play 13
put 16g
regret 1
run 26b
take 31b
talk 9a
trivialize
vilify
vituperate
deprecation
attack 7
libel 1
scorn 1
deprecatory
abusive 1
critical 1
foul 6
injurious 2
personal 4
scornful 1
slanderous
vituperative
depreciate°
belittle
blaspheme 2
debase 1
degrade 2
depress 2
deteriorate 1
detract
diminish 2
discredit 1
disparage 1
flout
foul 14
libel 3
minimize 2
put 16g
reduce 7
run 26b
slight 6
stigmatize
take 31b
talk 9a
trivialize
underestimate
vilify
vitiate 1
vituperate
depreciation
dishonour 4
fall 26
humiliation
libel 1
slump 1
depreciative
abusive 1
critical 1
derogatory
foul 6
slanderous
vituperative
depredate
gut 5
loot 2
pillage 1
raid 2
rape 5
rob 1
depredation°
desolation 1
pillage 2
plunder 3
rape 2
ravage 3
robbery
depress°
chill 8
crush 5
debase 1
demoralize 1
depreciate 1
desolate 6
get 36c
hurt 3
pain 5
depress (*cont.*)
press 2
prey 3c
push 2
sadden
shatter 3
turn 17b
vitiate 1
weaken 1
weigh 4, 6
depressant
sedative 1
depressed
bad 9
blue 1
broken-hearted
dejected
desolate 3
despondent
disturbed 2
doleful
downhearted
dreary 1
flat 11
forlorn 1
gloomy 2
heartbroken
heavy 6
hollow 2
hopeless 3
hurt 7
joyless 1
low[1] 8
melancholy 1
miserable 1
moody 1
morbid 3
pessimistic
sad 1
sinking 2
soft 7
sombre 1
sorrowful 1
sullen
unhappy 1
woebegone
wretched 2
depressing
bleak 1
cold 4
dingy
dismal
doleful
dreary 1
dull 5
funereal
gloomy 3
grey 2
heart-rending
heavy 5
joyless 2
mournful 2
oppressive 1
sad 2
sedative 2
sombre 1, 2
sorry 2
stark 3
sullen
sunless
tragic
depression°
despair 1
desperation 2
dip 5
disappointment 2
distress 1
gloom 2
grief 1
hole 1
hollow 7
hurt 6
impression 3
indentation
melancholy 2
misery 1
pan 3
pit[1] 2
prostration 3
recession
sadness
slot 1
slump 1
vapour 2
woe

deprivation
disadvantage 1
hardship
loss 1
need 4
privation
suspension 1
deprive°
beguile 2
bereave
divest 1
evacuate 1
refuse[1] 2
rob 3
suspend 3
-be deprived of
forfeit 2
go 41
lose 1
deprived°
destitute 2
hungry 3
needy
starved 3
depth°
breadth 2
dead 21
expression 4
extreme 8
further 4
gulf 2
measurement 2
pith 2
profundity 1
spread 9
-depths°
at **depth 5**
bottom 4
bowels
dead 21
interior 6
ocean 1
recess 3
-in depth°
at **depth 6**
detail 4
length 4c
depurate
cleanse 2
purge 1
purify 1
sterilize 1
wash 6
depurative
purgative 1,2
deputation
mission 3
depute
delegate 2,3
designate 2
enable 1
make 23
send 1
trust 6
deputed
vicarious
deputize
appoint 2
make 23
deputy°
agent 1
alternate 5
ambassador
assistant 2
factor 2
representative 3
substitute 2
deracinate
abolish
cancel 2
pull 18b
uproot 2
deracination
extraction 1
derange
upset 3
wall 3
deranged°
crazy 1
delirious 1
insane 1
mad 1
maniacal 1
deranged (*cont.*)
mental 2
psychotic 1
queer 4
sick 4
unbalanced 2
unsound 3
derangement
disorder 4
insanity 1
lunacy 1
mania 2
deregulation
freedom 4
laissez-faire
derelict°
bum 2
decrepit 2
delinquent 2
dilapidated
disobedient 1
down and out 2
homeless 1
hulk 1
ramshackle
stray 4
tramp 4
unused 2
vagabond 1,2
dereliction
default 1
failure 1
neglect 4
negligence
offence 1
omission 2
oversight 1
sin 1
deride°
depreciate 2
flout
fun 5
gibe 1
hiss 3
jeer 1
laugh 2a
mock 1
parody 3
ridicule 2
satirize
scoff[1]
scorn 4
snap 6
sneer 2
snipe
sport 3
taunt 1
thumb 8
twit[1]
deriding
ridicule 1
de rigueur
correct 6,7
proper 1,3
swish 3
derision°
gibe 2
jeer 2
mockery 1
ridicule 1
sarcasm
scorn 2
sneer 3
taunt 2
derisive
abusive 1
burlesque 4
contemptuous
derisory
disdainful
foul 6
haughty
irreverent 2
left-handed 2
regal 2
sarcastic
sardonic
satirical
scornful
derivation°
derivative 2
extraction 2,3
family 3
origin 1
derivation (*cont.*)
pedigree
strain[2] 1
derivative°
offshoot 3
secondary 2
derive°
base[1] 5
deduce
extract 2
get 21
infer
mine 3
originate 2
spin 4
stem[1] 3
take 5
derived
constructive 2
derivative 1
secondary 2
derive from°
at **derive 2**
enjoy 1
proceed 2
spring 3
derive pleasure (from)
enjoy 1
like[2] 1
love 8
derma
skin 1
dermatitis
rash[2] 1
dernier cri
craze
fashion 2
rage 3
rave 4
vogue 1
derogate
belittle
depreciate 2
diminish 2
disparage 1
foul 14
libel 3
look 5
write 4b
derogation
dishonour 4
humiliation
libel 1
shame 2
derogatory°
abusive 1
destructive 2
foul 6
injurious 2
personal 4
scurrilous
vituperative
derrière
bottom 1
bum 1
buttocks
posterior 3
seat 4
derring-do
daring 1
descale
peel 1
descant
chant 1,2
descend°
climb 5a
decline 3
dip 2
dive 1
drop 6
fall 1
get 36a, 40a
incline 1
light[2] 13
plunge 1
rain 6
sag 2
settle 5
shower 3
sink 1,3,5,6
slope 1
descend (*cont.*)
slump 2
stem[1] 3
submerge 2
subside 1
swoop 1
descendant°
child 1
issue 7
offshoot 2
-descendants
house 2
issue 7
lineage 2
posterity
progeny
seed 3
strain[2] 1
succession 4
descend from
get 40a
proceed 2
spring 3
descending
downward
descend on°
at **descend 4**
come 8
raid 2
visit 2
descent
birth 3
class 1
climb 6
decline 6,8
derivation
downgrade 3
drop 3
extraction 3
fall 22,27
family 3
grade 4
incline 4
kinship 1
lapse 3
line[1] 15
lineage 1
origin 3
parentage
paternity
pedigree
plunge 3
race[2] 2
ramp
root[1] 4
slope 2
slump 1
stock 2
strain[2] 1
succession 4
swoop 2
undoing 1
describe°
characterize
chronicle 2
define 1,2
demonstrate 2
document 2
explain 1
get 39b
label 5
narrate
paint 4
phrase 4
portray 1
profile 4
project 3
recite 2
recount 2
rehearse 2
relate 2
report 3
represent 3
set 18c
sort 9
tell[1] 4
describer
narrator
description°
account 4,6
character 2
chronicle 1
definition 2
demonstration 2
description (*cont.*)
explanation 1
exposition 2
form 3
history 1
key 4
kind[2] 2
label 2
narration 1
narrative 1
nature 4
portrait
programme 1
prospectus
recital 2
rehearsal 2
relation 4
report 1
sort 1
specification 1
stamp 8
stripe 2
-beyond description
ineffable 2
descriptive
explanatory
graphic 1
descry
behold
discover 2
distinguish 3
find 2
make 37a
perceive 1
savour 3
see 1
sight 5,8
spot 6
spy 3
desecrate°
outrage 5
pollute 2
profane 4
prostitute 2
violate 2
desecration
prostitution 2
sacrilege 1
sin 1
violation 2
desegregate
integrate
deselect
dismiss 1
desensitize
deaden 1
dull 11
desert°
abandon 2,3
defect 3
desolate 1
drop 7
evacuate 2
fail 2
flight[2] 3
forsake 1,2
fruit
inhospitable 2
jilt
kiss 3
leave[1] 1,4
lifeless 4
lurch[1]
maroon
quit 1
relinquish 1
renounce
run 32
throw 8
uninhabited
vacate 1
walk 4a
wash 10
waste 8
wild 2,10
-deserts
fruit
deserted°
abandoned 1
alone 1
derelict 1
desert[1] 2
deserted (*cont.*)
desolate 1
empty 3
forlorn 2
gaunt 2
lonely 2
lonesome 1
uninhabited
vacant 1
void 2
wild 2
desertedness
emptiness 1
deserter°
defector
fugitive 1
renegade 1
runaway 1
turncoat
deserve°
earn 1
merit 3
rate[1] 7
deserved°
due 2
just 3
deservedly
duly 1
deserving°
praiseworthy
worthy 1
desex
fix 13
neuter 2
desiccate
dry 4
evaporate 1
parch
shrivel
desiccated
dry 1
desiccation
evaporation 1
desideratum
desire 4
necessity 1
need 3,5
requirement 1
design°
block 4a
chart 3
conceive 2
conception 3
create 2
crest 2
destine 2
device 3
devise 1
discover 3
draft 3
draw 5
drawing
eye 6
fabricate 2
fabrication 2
figure 7
format 1
formulate 3
frame 3
game 3
hatch 2
idea 1
intend
intent 1
intention
invent 1
lay[1] 18a
machination
mastermind 1
mean[1] 1
meditate 2
method 2
model 6
mould[1] 2
objective 2
organization 2
originate 1
pattern 2,4
plan 1,2,3
plot[1] 3
policy
programme 4
project 1,3
projection 3

design (*cont.*)
proposal 2
prospect 2
purpose 1, 5
scenario 1
schematic 2
scheme 1, 2
script 4
seal 1
strategy
structure 1, 3
style 1, 8
tactic 1
taste 5
thought 3
weave 3
-by design
purpose 4a
-designs°
at **design 8**
designate°
appoint 2
assign 2, 3
call 2
cast 8
delegate 2
denote 1
destine 2
distinguish 2
elect 1
entitle 2
express 2, 3
indicate 1
label 5
make 23
mark 11
mean[1] 2
name 5
nominate
point 21a
set 7
stamp 3
style 7
term 8
title 6
designated
alleged
routine 3
so-called 1
designated hitter
alternate 5
designation
appointment 2
assignment 3, 4
denomination 3
election
identification 1
label 2
name 1
tag 2
term 1
title 2
word 3
designed
calculated 1
destined 1
intentional
designedly
purpose 4a
designee
nominee
designer°
author
creator 1
engineer 1
founder[1]
designing°
arch 2
calculating
crafty
deep 5
devious 1
disingenuous
foxy 1
machination
politic 1
shifty
sly 1
subtle 3
two-faced
wily
desinence
suffix 1
termination 2
desirability
charm 2
glamour
desirable°
choice 4
demand 7
enviable
expedient 2
glamorous 1
voluptuous 2
welcome 2
worthwhile 2
desire°
aim 5
ambition 3
anxiety 2
appetite 1, 2
ardour
aspiration
aspire
avarice
burn 3
demand 6
device 4
die 5
eagerness 2
envy 2
expectation 3
fancy 7, 11
feel 9
hanker
hope 1, 4
hunger 2, 3
inclination 3, 4
intent 2
itch 2, 4
long[2]
longing
lust 2, 3
mania 1
mind 7
motive 2
pant 2
passion 3
please 2
pleasure 2
preference 1
require 2
spirit 2
stomach 2
taste 3
thirst 1, 2
urge 5
vote 4
want 1, 4
will 1, 2, 5
wish 1, 4, 5
yearn
-at desire
will 4
desired
demand 7
desirable 1
enviable
desirous°
anxious 2
desperate 3
eager
envious
hungry 2
solicitous 2
spoil 5
starved 2
thirsty 2
voracious 2
wistful 1
desist
abandon 4
cease 1
cut 16c
give 17a
halt 2
lay[1] 16b
leave[1] 9
quit 3
refrain[1] 2
sacrifice 4
stop 1
desisting
self-denial 2
desk
bureau 1, 2
desk-bound
sedentary
desolate°
alone 1
bleak 3
desert[1] 2
deserted
devastate 1
empty 3
forlorn 1
gaunt 2
gloomy 2
impoverished 2
inconsolable
joyless 2
lifeless 4
lonely 2
miserable 1
moody 1
mournful 1
plunder 1
sinking 2
solitary 1
stark 3
uninhabited
wild 2
woebegone
wretched 2
desolateness
sorrow 1
desolation°
calamity 2
distress 1
emptiness 1
gloom 2
grief 1
havoc 1
misery 1
mourning 2
prostration 3
sorrow 1
woe
despair°
brood 4
depression 2
desolation 2
desperation 2
give 17b
gloom 2
misery 1
mourning 2
pain 2
prostration 3
despairing
desperate 6
gloomy 2
hopeless 3
inconsolable
miserable 1
mournful 1
pessimistic
sinking 2
despatch
bulletin
bump 5
bundle 3
course 3
execute 1
execution 1
expedite 1
expedition 2
finish 3, 4
forward 7
haste 1
hasten 2
kill 1
launch 3
letter 2
mail 2
message 1
news 2
poison 4
polish 3b
post[3] 2
rapidity
relegate 1
remit 1
report 1
send 1
ship 2
speed 1
swallow 1
translate 4
despatch (*cont.*)
translation 4
transmission 1
transmit 1
word 2
-with despatch
quickly 2
despatch-bearer
runner 2
despatch-case
bag 2
despatching
transmission 1
despatch-rider
runner 2
desperado
criminal 3
gangster
hoodlum
outlaw 1
terrorist
thief 1
thug
desperate°
deplorable 1
drastic
heroic 3
hopeless 1
lost 8
miserable 1
sore 3
desperately
mad 5
madly 3, 4
desperate straits
strait 3
desperation°
despair 1
misery 1
prostration 3
despicable°
abominable 1
base[2] 1
contemptible
damnable
dirty 6
disgraceful 1
dishonourable 2
disreputable 1
hateful 1
horrible 2
infamous 2
lamentable
loathsome
lousy 1
low[1] 12
mangy
miserable 3
obnoxious
obscene 2
reprobate 1
rotten 4
satanic 2
scandalous 1
scurvy
shabby 4
sordid 1
stinking 2
ugly 2
unworthy 1
vile 1
wretched 4
despise°
detest
dislike 1
disregard 2
hate 1
loathe
look 5
put 16g
scorn 3
sneer 2
spurn
use 15
despite°
even 11
face 9
for 11
irrespective of
notwithstanding 2
regardless 1
same 3
spite 2
despite (*cont.*)
though 1
yet 5, 6
despite that
even 12
however 1
nevertheless
notwithstanding 1
despite the fact that
notwithstanding 3
supposing
despoil
desolate 5
divest 1
gut 5
loot 2
overrun
pillage 1
plunder 1
ransack 2
rape 5
ravage 2
rifle 1
strip[2] 5
waste 11
despoiling
depredation
predatory 2
despoliation
depredation
desolation 1
havoc 1
pillage 2
plunder 3
rape 2
despondency
depression 2
despair 1
desperation 2
gloom 2
grief 1
melancholy 2
misery 1
mourning 2
prostration 3
sadness
despondent°
blue 1
dejected
desolate 3
desperate 6
forlorn 1
gloomy 2
heartbroken
heavy 6
hopeless 3
joyless 1
low[1] 8
melancholy 1
miserable 1
moody 1
morbid 3
mournful 1
mouth 6
pessimistic
sad 1
unhappy 1
despondently
sadly 2
despot°
dictator
disciplinarian
oppressor
tyrant
despotic°
absolute 3
arbitrary 2
authoritarian
bossy
dictatorial 2
domineering
hard 4
heavy-handed 2
imperative 2
masterful 2
overbearing
peremptory 3
positive 5
repressive
severe 1
totalitarian
tyrannical
despotism°
domination 2
monarchy 2
oppression
severity 1
tyranny
desquamate
flake 2
peel 1
shed[2] 4
dessert°
savoury 3
sweet 10
destination°
end 3
fate 3
object 2
destine°
appoint 1
cut 16e
design 4
destined°
bound[3] 4, 5
card 12
certain 3
condemn 3
doomed 1
eventual 2
fatal 3
fated 1
for 8
inevitable
predetermined 2
prospective
unavoidable
destiny°
doom
fate 1
fortune 2
lot 2
luck 1
predestination
providence 2
destitute°
broke
deprived
down and out 1
heel[1] 3
impoverished 1
indigent
insolvent
lean[1] 3
low[1] 6
needy
penurious 2
poor 1
rock[1] 3c
straitened
upper 7
destitute of°
at **destitute 2**
empty 7
void 3
destitution
misery 2
necessity 3
need 4
poverty 1
privation
want 5
destroy°
abolish
attack 5
back 7b
blast 5, 6
blot 4b
blow[1] 8b
break 4, 16a
bugger 3
bump 5
consume 4, 5
dash 1
deface
defeat 1
demolish 1, 2
desolate 5
devastate 1
devour 2
dispose 3d
disprove
disturb 3, 5
eliminate 4
end 10
erase 2

devoted°
affectionate
attached 3
brotherly
cling 2
close 15
constant 1
devout 1,3
earnest 1,2
enthusiastic
faithful 1
fast[1] 5
godly
great 9,10
hard 7
heartfelt
keen[1] 1,7
loyal
maternal
paternal 1
pious 1
resolute
single-minded
special 5
staunch 1
steady 5
sweet 8
thick 8
true 2
undivided 2
voracious 2
wholehearted
worship 1
wrap 2
devotedly
consistently 2
hard 13
devotedness
dedication 1
devotion 1,2
enthusiasm 1
fanaticism 1
loyalty
piety 1,2
resolution 1
devotee°
addict 2
admirer 1
disciple 2
enthusiast
fan
fiend 2
follower 3
freak 4
partisan 1
student 2
supporter 1
-devotees
school 2
devote oneself to
address 5
attend 3
follow 6
pursue 2
devotion°
application 3
attachment 3
dedication 1
enthusiasm 1
faith 3
fanaticism 1
friendship 2
love 1
loyalty
perseverance
piety 1,2
praise 2
prayer 2
resolution 1
sanctity
veneration
worship 2
devotional
devout 2
solemn 2
spiritual 1
devour°
attack 5
consume 1,5
dispose 3d
eat
feed 2
finish 3
devour *(cont.)*
gnaw 2
gorge 3
gulp 1
prey 3a
scoff[2] 1
swallow 1
tackle 4
take 13
devouring
voracious 1
devout°
devoted
godly
hearty 2
holy 2
pious 1
religious 1
devoutness
devotion 1
piety 2
dew
wet 5
dewy
damp 1
moist 1
dewy-eyed
tearful
dexter
right 5
dexterity°
art 1,4
craft 1
efficiency 1
expertise
facility 1
faculty 1
ingenuity
knack
proficiency
prowess 1
skill 1
tact
touch 16
understanding 3
dexterous°
adept 1
agile 2
artful 2
clever 1,4
expert 2
handy 3
ingenious
masterful 1
neat 4
nimble 1
proficient
quick 4
skilful
slick 3
tactful
talented
versatile 1
dexterously
handily 2
dexterousness
ingenuity
prowess 1
tact
technique 2
dextral
right 5
diablerie
devilry 1,2
diabolic°
devilish
fiendish
ghoulish 1
infernal 2
poisonous 2
satanic 1
sinister 2
ungodly 1
vicious 1
wicked 1
wrong
diabolical
black 6
cruel 2
devilish
diabolic 1,2
dreadful 2
ferocious
diabolical *(cont.)*
fiendish
ghoulish 1
infernal 2
inhuman 2
poisonous 2
satanic 1
serpentine 1
sinister 2
ungodly 1
vicious 1
wicked 1
wrong 1
diabolism
magic 1
sorcery
diacritic
accent 2
diadem
crown 1
ring[1] 1
diagnose°
identify 3
diagnosis
interpretation 2
diagonal
bias 2
line[1] 1
oblique 1
diagram
chart 2
design 5
draft 1,3
figure 5
pattern 4
plan 2
plot[1] 4
profile 3
projection 3
schematic 2
scheme 2
diagrammatic
graphic 2
schematic 1
dial
call 3
control 6
face 1,7
mug 2
dialect°
cant 2
idiom 1
jargon 1
language 1
lingo
parlance
provincialism 1
speech 3
talk 19
tongue 1
dialectalism
provincialism 1
dialectic
controversial 2
dialectics
logic 1
dialogue°
conversation
discussion
parley 1
rap 5
talk 15
tête-à-tête 1
word 1
diameter
calibre 1
width 1
diametric
polar 2
diaphanous
filmy 1
fine[1] 6
flimsy 3
insubstantial 1
see-through
sheer 3
tenuous 1
thin 5
transparent 1
diaphoresis
perspiration
sweat 5
diarrhoea
run 50
diary°
calendar 1
chronicle 1
journal 2
memoir 2
record 3
register 1
timetable
diatribe
harangue 1
lecture 1
tirade
dice
chop 2
cut 17a
fate 1
dicey°
dodgy
explosive 1
hazardous
precarious
risky
speculative 2
dichotomize
split 1
dichotomy
split 8
dick
detective
officer 2
operative 3
sleuth
dickens
devil 6
dicker°
bargain 3
haggle
negotiate 1
dicky°
dodgy
hazardous
ill 1
dictate°
bid 3
bidding 2
charge 5
decree 1,2
determine 4
direct 3
injunction 2
lay[1] 10
order 4
precept 1
prescribe
regulation 2
tell[1] 5
tyrannize
dictator°
despot
disciplinarian
oppressor
tyrant
dictatorial°
absolute 3
arbitrary 2
authoritarian
bossy
despotic
dogmatic
domineering
hard 4
heavy-handed 2
imperative 2
masterful 2
officious
opinionated 1
overbearing
peremptory 3
positive 5
prescriptive
repressive
severe 1
totalitarian
tyrannical
dictatorship
despotism
domination 2
tyranny
diction°
expression 6
language 4
diction *(cont.)*
oratory
phrase 3
pronunciation
speech 1
style 5
dictionary°
glossary
literal 2
thesaurus 2
dictum
decree 1
principle 1
pronouncement 2
proverb
saw
say-so
theorem 2
didactic
pedantic 1
prescriptive
diddle
cheat 2
defraud
fleece
rob 3
swindle 1
dido
caper 2
stunt[1]
trick 2
die°
disappear 2
end 9
expire 2
fail 3
fall 6,20
farm 2
fizzle 2
flag[2] 2
founder[2] 2
go 13,33a
itch 2
miscarry
mould[1] 1
pack 8b
pass 14a
perish
rot 2
sink 4
stall[1] 1
stamp 6
subside 2
template
die away°
at **die 2**
diminish 3
dwindle
fade 2
fail 3
fizzle 2
taper 2
trail 8
die-cast
mould[1] 5
died out
extinct 1
die down°
at **die 2**
dwindle
subside 2
taper 2
die for
desire 1
pant 2
die-hard
purist
square 9
ultra-
die off°
at **die 4**
disappear 2
subside 2
taper 2
die out°
at **die 2**
diminish 3
disappear 2
dwindle
end 9
fade 2
fail 3
fizzle 2
go 33a
die out *(cont.)*
pass 10
peter out
subside 2
taper 2
trail 8
wane 1
die-stamp
stamp 6
diet°
assembly 2
chamber 1
convention 1
fare 3
fast[2] 1,2
house 3
parliament 2
reduce 3
slim 3
differ°
clash 3
conflict 4
contrast 2
depart 2
disagree 1
dispute 2
fall 18
quarrel 2
vary 3
difference°
balance 7
change 2
clash 2
combat 3
conflict 3
contrast 3
disagreement 1,2
discrepancy
disparity
dispute 3
dissimilarity
distinction 1
diversity 1
fight 8
gap 2
inequality 1
misunderstanding 2
odds 3
quarrel 1
rift 1
rivalry
spread 10
strife 1
tiff
tilt 4
variance 1,2
variation 1
variety 2
different°
alternative 1
contrary 1
cry 8
deviant 1
discordant 1
dissimilar
distinct 2
divergent
divers
diverse
exotic 2
extreme 1,5
fresh 2
incongruous
kinky 1
new 1,4
notable 2
noteworthy
novel 1
odd 1
opposite 2
ordinary 4
outlandish
outside 9
pole[2] 3
queer 1
remarkable 3
revolutionary 2
reword
separate 5,6
several 2
singular 1
special 1
sundry
unfamiliar 1

different (*cont.*)
unlike 1,3
unrelated
unusual
variant 2
various 1,2
differentiate°
contrast 1
discriminate 1
distinguish 1
know 4
set 14a
tell[1] 8
differentiating
judicial 2
differentiation
distinction 1
differently
otherwise 2
differing
discordant 1
divergent
divers
diverse
odds 4
opposite 2
unlike 3
variant 2
variation 1
difficile
difficult 5
difficult°
arduous 1
awkward 5
choosy
deep 2
demanding 1
deplorable 1
dicey
dodgy
exacting
exhausting 2
fastidious
finicky 1
formidable 3
fussy 1
hairy 3
hard 2,3,5
heavy 12
killing 3
laborious 1
laboured 1
lean[1] 3
murderous 2
nasty 2
nervous 2
overcritical
parlous
picnic 3
precarious
prickly 4
problem 3
problematic
rebellious 2
rocky[1] 1
rough 7
rugged 2
self-willed
squeamish 1
stiff 9
strained
strait 1
strenuous 1
strong 16
tender[1] 4
thorny 2
ticklish 3
tight 7
toilsome
tough 4,5
tricky 2
troublesome
trying
difficulty°
complication 2
delicacy 3
dilemma
discomfort 1
distress 2
drawback
embarrassment 2
emergency
fix 17
fly 10
grief 2
difficulty (*cont.*)
hardship
headache 2
hitch 4
hole 5
hurdle 1
inconvenience 1
interference 2
issue 4
jam 6
job 4
kink 3
lookout 3
matter 3
mess 3
mischief 2
necessity 3
need 4
nuisance 1
perplexity 1,2
pinch 8
pitfall 2
plight
predicament
pressure 3
problem 1
profundity 1
quandary
question 2
ramification 1
reverse 8
rub 11
scrape 8
snag 1
snarl[2] 3
sore 6
static 2
stumbling-block
sweat 8
trouble 5
-difficulties°
at **difficulty 3**
necessity 3
pressure 3
static 2
-in difficulty
debt 2
-without difficulty
easily 1
readily 2
swimmingly
well[1] 10
diffidence
fear 1
humility
shame 4
diffident
backward 1
bashful 1
coy
faint-hearted 1
fearful 2
modest 1
mousy 2
retiring
self-conscious
shamefaced 1
shy 1
tentative 2
timid
withdrawn 1
diffidently
fearfully 1
diffuse°
discursive
disperse 1
dissipate 1
dissolve 1
distribute 2
penetrate 2
permeate
radiate 2
rambling 1
run 7
scatter 1
soft 9,11
spray[1] 1
spread 1
throw 7a
diffusion
circulation 2
dissipation 2
radiation
diffusive
diffuse 2
dig°
bore[1] 2
burrow 2
cut 23
drive 4
enjoy 1
excavate 1
figure 12b
follow 8
gibe 2
go 28c
gouge 1
grasp 2
hollow 8
identify 4
insult 2
jab 1,3
like[2] 1
mine 3
nudge 1,2
penetrate 5
perceive 2
pit[1] 5
poke 1,3,5
probe 2
prod 1,4
put-down
relate 4
root[2]
scoop 5
scrape 2
see 2
sink 7
stick[1] 3
sympathize 2
taunt 2
till[1]
tumble 3
tunnel 2
twig[2]
understand 1
wash 5
wisecrack 1
digest°
abbreviate 2
abridge
abridgement 3
abstract 3,4
brief 4
consume 1
cut 5
epitome 2
outline 2
précis
résumé 1
round-up 2
shorten 2
sum 2a
summary 1
synopsis
telescope 2
digging
research 1
-diggings
abode
domicile 1
home 1
pad 3
place 6
dig into°
at **dig 5**
look 8
probe 1
research 2
digit
figure 7
finger 1
number 1
dignified°
ceremonial 2
ceremonious 1
decent 2
decorous
distinguished 2
elegant 1
elevated 2
eminent 1
exalted 1
formal 3
gallant 3
grand 2
ladylike
lofty 2
dignified (*cont.*)
majestic 1
measured 1
noble 3
poised 1
prestigious
proper 3
proud 3
refined 1
reserved
respectable 1
sedate 2
seemly 2
self-possessed
sober 2
solemn 3
staid
state 6
stately
statuesque
steady 6
dignify°
exalt 2
glorify 1
grace 7
honour 6
lift 2
pedestal 2
dignitary°
celebrity 2
name 3
notable 3
officer 1
somebody 2
star 2
worthy 3
dignity°
cachet 2
decorum 1
elegance 1
elevation 4
face 4
glory 1
gravity 3
mark 8
nobility 1
poise 2
pride 1
propriety 2
quality 3
rank[1] 3
self-control 2
self-respect
sobriety 2
dig out°
at **dig 6**
bore[1] 2
deepen 1
excavate 1
hollow 8
pull 18b
root[1] 7b
scrape 2
uproot 2
wash 5
digress
deviate 1
diverge 2
ramble 2
stray 2
wander 3,4
digressing
digression 2
discursive
digression°
diversion 1
excursion 2
digressive
diffuse 2
discursive
inarticulate 1
tangential
digs
abode
accommodation 4
domicile 1
flat 18
home 1
pad 3
place 6
dig up°
at **dig 6**
detect 1
discover 1
dig up (*cont.*)
excavate 1,2
hollow 8
line[1] 23b
rake[1] 8
root[1] 7b
scare 2
scout 2
turn 25c
unearth
dilapidated°
decrepit 2
derelict 1
far 5a
flimsy 1
hurt 8
leg 7
old 3
ragged 4
ramshackle
rickety
run-down 2
seed 4
seedy 1
shabby 1,3
shaky 2
time-worn
tumbledown
unsound 1
dilapidation
decay 3
decrepitude 2
disrepair
dilatable
expansive 1
dilate
enlarge 1
expand 2
increase 1
inflate 1
pad 5
pump 4a
stretch 2
swell 1
widen
dilation
expansion 2
dilatory
derelict 2
late 1
lazy 1
remiss
slack 1
slow 5
tardy 2
dilemma°
bind 5
complication 2
difficulty 2
embarrassment 2
fix 17
hole 5
jam 6
matter 3
mess 3
paradox
perplexity 3
pinch 8
plight
predicament
problem 1
quandary
scrape 8
snarl[2] 3
strait 3
dilettante°
amateur 1,2
diligence
application 3
exertion
follow-through
industry 2
patience 2
perseverance
persevere
persistence
tenacity 1
diligent°
busy 2
conscientious 2
dutiful
earnest 2
enterprising
expeditious
industrious
diligent (*cont.*)
laborious 2
painful 3
patient 2
strong 5
studious 1
tenacious 1
-be diligent
persevere
diligently
hard 13
dilly
killer 2
dilly-dally
dawdle
delay 3
drag 4
hesitate 1
shilly-shally
stall[2] 1
time 20
toy 4
dilly-dallying
delay 6
idleness 2
dilute°
adulterate
cut 6
degrade 3
doctor 4
thin 6,9
water 7
watery 1
weaken 1,4
diluted
rarefied 1
thin 6
watery 1
wishy-washy 2
dim°
backward 2
blot 4a
blunt 4
blur 3
dark 2
dense 3
dingy
dull 1,10
dusky 2
extinguish 3
fade 1
faint 1
feeble 3
film 4
filmy 2
fog 3
foolish 2
fuzzy 2
gloomy 1
hazy 2
indefinite 3
indistinct 1
intangible
light[2] 3
mist 2
misty
muddy 2,4
murky
nebulous
obscure 1,7
opaque 1
pale[1] 2,4
shade 12
shadowy 1,2
slow 7
sombre 2
steamy 2
stupid 1
twilight 4
vague 1
wane 1
weak 6
dimension
extension 2
format 1
gauge 4
length 1
mass 5
measure 1
measurement 2
size 2
-dimensions
capacity 1
extension 2

dimension (*cont.*)
extent 1
format 1
gauge 4
magnitude 1
proportion 4
size 1
spread 9
diminish°
alloy 2
belittle
bring 8b
clip[2] 2
collapse 2
consume 2
contract 4
cool 10
curtail
cut 8
dampen 2
deaden 2
debase 1
decay 1
decline 2
decrease 1
depreciate 1, 2
depress 2
deride
detract
die 2
dilute
discount 2
discredit 1
dismiss 2
disparage 1
dissipate 2
dissolve 1
drop 11
dwarf
dwindle
ease 6
ebb 2
erode
fade 2
fail 3
fall 3, 16
flag[2] 2
hamper[1]
hold 15a
lag 2
lapse 4
let[1] 9
lower[1] 1, 3
melt 4
minimize 1
moderate 5
modify 2
narrow 8
overshadow 1
pale[1] 5
pare 2
peg 3
peter out
play 13
pull 9c
put 16g
recede 2
reduce 1, 7
relax 2
relieve 1
remit 2
sag 2
scale[3] 5
shorten 1
sink 4
slack 3b
slight 6
soften 2, 3
stem[2] 1
step 14b
subside 2
subtract 2
suffer 4
take 31b
talk 9a
taper 1, 2
thin 9
trail 8
vilify
vitiate 1
vituperate
wane 1
waste 2
weaken 1

diminish (*cont.*)
whitewash
whittle 2
wilt 1
wind[2] 3a
-be diminished
stoop 2
suffer 4
diminished
cut 28
small 5
diminishing
derogatory
extenuating
wane 4
diminution
decline 6, 7
decrease 2
deduction 1
ebb 4
fall 26
impairment
lapse 3
let-up
loss 2
relaxation 2
remission 2
slack 5
twilight 2
wane 3
diminutive°
elfin 2
little 1
miniature
minute[2] 1
nickname 2
petite
puny 2
short 1
slight 3
small 1
stunted
tiny
toy 5
wee 1
dimly
vaguely 1
dimming
eclipse 3
twilight 4
dimness
blur 1
gloom 1
obscurity 1
opacity 1
shade 1
shadow 1
stupidity 1
dimple
depression 1
indentation
pit[1] 2
dim-sighted
short-sighted 1
dim-wit
dolt
dummy 3
fool 1
halfwit
sap[1] 2
silly 3
dim-witted
backward 2
blind 2
daft 1
dense 3
dim 2
dull 1
feeble-minded
foolish 2
halfwitted
obtuse 2
slow 7
stupid 1
thick 6
weak 5
wooden 3
dim-wittedness
stupidity 1
din°
blast 2
jangle 3
noise 1
pound[1] 4

din (*cont.*)
racket 1
row[2] 2
sound[1] 1
uproar
dine°
eat
feast 4
diner
café
ding-a-ling
dolt
ring[2] 1, 3
dingbat
dolt
ding-dong
chime 2
ring[2] 1
dinghy
launch 6
tender[3] 1
dingle
valley
dingus
gadget
gimmick 2
thing 5
dingy°
drab
lacklustre
leaden 3
mangy
muddy 3
shabby 1
sombre 2
sordid 4
din into
pound[1] 4
dinky
neat 1
petite
petty 1
dinner
feast 1
function 2
meal 1
spread 11
dint
-by dint of
mean[3] 3
virtue 4
diocese
city
Dionysia
orgy 1
dip°
dabble 1
decline 3, 5
depression 1
descend 2
dive 1
duck 1
hollow 7
immerse 1
incline 4
ramp
recession
sag 1, 3
scoop 4
slope 1, 2
slump 1
soak 3
submerge 1
thief 1
dip into°
at **dip 3**
run 33b
skim 2
diplomacy°
civility
discretion 1
finesse 3
politics 1
protocol 1
refinement 1
savoir faire
tact
diplomat
ambassador
envoy
minister 2
negotiator
peacemaker

diplomate
physician
diplomatic°
courteous
discreet
judicious
polite 1
politic 2
seemly 2
suave
tactful
wise 3
dipper
scoop 1
dippy
crazy 1
deranged
flighty 2
foolish 2
inane
off 4
scatterbrained
senseless 3
dipsomania
drunkenness
dipsomaniac
alcoholic 2
drunk 3
soak 3
dire
calamitous
disastrous 1
drastic
dreadful 2
evil 4
fearful 3
fierce 3
frightening
grim 3
infernal 2
macabre
mortal 5
satanic 2
severe 3
sore 3
-in dire straits
back 10
debt 2
needy
trouble 9a
direct°
above-board 2
administer 1
aim 1
artless 1
bare 2
bend 4
blunt 2
boss 2
broad 3, 5
candid 1
card 14
categorical
chair 4
channel 5
charge 10
clear 16
coach 3
command 1
concentrate 1
concise
conduct 3, 5
control 1
decree 2
deliver 5
dictate 1
discipline 7
dispense 2
dominate 1
downright 1
emphatic
explicit 2
express 5, 7
fasten 2
fix 4
flat 4
forthright
frank 1
free 9
front 9b
govern 1
guide 1, 2, 3
handle 3
head 11

direct (*cont.*)
honest 3
immediate 2
ingenuous 2
instant 4
instruct 2
lay[1] 7
lead 3
level 10, 15
manage 1
manipulate 2
matter-of-fact
moderate 6
mould[1] 6
navigate 2
non-stop 1
obvious
officiate
open 15
operate 2
order 14
outright 1, 2
outspoken
oversee
pilot 3
plain 2, 3
plump[2] 6
point 20
point-blank 1
prescribe
preside
primary 3
raw 6
refer 1, 2
regulate 2
reign 2
round 8
route 2
rule 6
run 10
short 5
shot 9
show 2
simple 3
sincere
steady 3
steer 1
straight 1, 4, 6
strike 2
supervise
switch 5
tell[1] 5
transmit 2
transparent 3
turn 9
tutor 2
unvarnished
direct attention to
indicate 1
mention 1
point 19, 21a
refer 1
directed (by)
bound[3] 5
under 2
directing
direction 1
management 1
direction°
administration 1
aim 4
bearing 4
bent 5
bidding 2
care 3
charge 5
command 6, 7
conduct 2
control 4
counsel 1
course 4
dictate 2
discipline 4
drift 3
exposure 4
gist
government 1
guidance 1
injunction 2
instruction 1
lead 13
leadership
line[1] 9
management 1

direction (*cont.*)
measure 6
operation 2
order 4
oversight 2
path 3
prescription 1
production 3
providence 2
quarter 3
recommendation 1
reference 1
regime
reign 1
road 1
route 1
rule 1, 2
running 1
step 10a
tack 3
tendency
tenor
thread 2
trend 1
turn 32
view 5
way 3
word 7
-directions°
at **direction 2**
formula
manual
-in all directions
about 8
around 5
helter-skelter 2
-in the direction of
for 6
towards 1
directionless
disjointed 2
erratic 3
directive
decree 1
injunction 2
instruction 1
law 1
order 4
precept 1
regulation 2
directly°
dead 20
due 5
expressly 1
face 13
flat 16, 17b
flush[2] 4
full 14
hastily 1
immediately 1, 2, 3
instantaneously
once 6a
openly 2
outright 3, 4
plump[2] 5
point-blank 3, 4
post-haste
promptly
right 13
shoulder 6
slap 6
soon 2
straight 12, 14, 15
summarily 1
directness
candour 1
honesty 2
simplicity 3
director°
boss 1
employer 1
executive 1
guide 5
head 2
leader 1, 2
manager
master 1
officer 1
operator 2
principal 3, 4
producer 2
showman

director (*cont.*)
superintendent
supervisor
-directors
board 4
council 2
management 2
directorate
board 4
council 2
direction 1
executive 2
management 2
directorial
responsible 3
directorship
board 4
chair 2
direction 1
executive 2
helm 2
leadership
management 1
directory
council 2
index 1
list[1] 1
register 1
roll 13
diremption
division 1
dire straits°
at **strait 3**
dirge
chant 1
keen[2] 2
lament 2
dirk
dagger
steel 1
dirt°
earth 2
filth 1
grime
ground 1
impurity 2
information
land 2
low-down
mire 2
mould[3]
muck 2
mud
news 1
pornography
refuse[2]
ribaldry
scandal 3
soil[1] 3
soil[2]
trash 3
dirtiness
impurity 1, 3
dirty°
abusive 1
base[2] 4
bawdy
beastly 2
bedraggled
blue 2
broad 8
coarse 3
dingy
dishonourable 3
disreputable 2
earthy
erotic 3
evil 2
evil-minded 1
filthy 1, 2, 3
foul 5, 7, 11, 12
gross 3
immodest 1
immoral 2
impure 1, 4
incontinent 2
indecent 2
lascivious 2
lewd
libertine 2
lousy 1
low[1] 3
mangy
mess 5c

dirty (*cont.*)
mire 4
muddy 1, 5
nasty 1, 3
naughty 3
obscene 1
outrageous 3
pollute 1
pornographic
profane 3
prurient 2
racy 2
rank[2] 3
ratty 2
rough 6
rude 3
sad 3
sensual
sexy 2
shabby 1, 3
sleazy 2
sloppy 1
smear 1
soil[1] 1
sordid 3
spot 7
spotty 1
stagnant
suggestive 2
sully
taboo 1
taint 2
tarnish
untidy
unwashed 1
vulgar 2
wicked 3
dirtying
pollution
dirty language
profanity
dirty look
frown 3
glare 2
scowl 2
dirty-minded
evil-minded 1
filthy 3
lecherous
dirty old man
libertine 1
roué
dirty-rotten
rotten 4
dirty trick(s)
foul play
machination
dirty word
curse 3
expletive 2
oath 2
dirty work
conspiracy
foul play
Dis
hell 1
underworld 2
disability°
ailment
disease 1
handicap 1
illness
trouble 8
disable
cripple 2
destroy 4
exhaust 2
handicap 2
hurt 4
incapacitate
lay[1] 19b
maim
mutilate 1
paralyse 3
sabotage 3
spike 3
strike 13
undermine 1
waste 3
disabled°
crippled 1
decrepit 1
helpless 1
invalid[1] 1

disabled (*cont.*)
lame 1
powerless 2
disablement
disability 1
wreck 5
disabuse
alienate
disillusion
disabused
disenchanted
disaccord
disagreement 1
disadvantage°
catch 18
detriment
drawback
encumbrance
handicap 1, 2
hurt 5
inconvenience 1
liability 3
loss 3, 5
-be disadvantaged by
labour 7
disadvantaged
deprived
needy
disadvantageous
detrimental
hurtful 1
inconvenient
prejudicial
ugly 3
disadvantageousness
inconvenience 2
disaffect
divide 3
shake 3
turn 17b
disaffected
estranged
disaffection
dislike 2
disaffiliation
secession
disaffirm
contradict 2
deny 1
reverse 3
disaffirmation
denial 1
disagree°
argue 1
clash 3
conflict 4
differ 2
dispute 1
exception 4
fall 18
feud 2
fight 4
issue 9
jar[2] 2
protest 3
quarrel 2
row[2] 3
scrap[2] 2
tangle 4
disagreeable°
abominable 2
argumentative
bad 4
beastly 2
bitter 2
cantankerous
distasteful
evil 5
foul 8
fretful
frightful 2
harsh 3
horrible 2
nasty 2, 4
picnic 3
pugnacious
quarrelsome
rancid
rank[2] 4
ratty 1

disagreeable (*cont.*)
repellent
repulsive
revolting
shabby 2
short-tempered
sour 3
terrible 1, 3
testy
tiresome 2
ugly 2, 4
unacceptable
uninviting
unpalatable
unsavoury
disagreeably
painfully
disagreeing
discordant 1
dissident 2
divergent
incongruous
odds 4
disagreement°
argument 1
clash 2
combat 2
conflict 2, 3
controversy 1, 2
difference 1, 2
discord
discrepancy
dispute 3, 4
dissension
division 5
encounter 5
exchange 3
faction 2
feud 1
fight 8
fracas 2
friction 2
gap 2
misunderstanding 2
protest 1
quarrel 1
rift 1
row[2] 1
run-in
scrap[2] 1
strife 1
tiff
variance 1, 2
-in disagreement
discordant 1
odds 4
variance 3
war 2
disallow
ban 1
contradict 2
deny 2
exclude 1
forbid
keep 13
outlaw 2
prohibit 1
refuse[1] 2
reject 1
repress
shut 5a
veto 1
disallowance
exclusion 1
prohibition 1
veto 2
disallowed
impure 3
inadmissible
pale[2] 3
unlawful
disambiguate
clear 22
specify
disannul
void 6
disappear°
collapse 2
depart 1
die 2
disperse 2
dissipate 2

disappear (*cont.*)
dissolve 1
drain 6
escape 1
evaporate 2
exit 3
fail 3
finger 9
flee 1
get 31a
go 10
leave[1] 1
lift 5
melt 3, 4
pass 10, 14b, 17
peter out
powder 2
roll 2
sink 5
slip[1] 6
trail 8
disappearance
collapse 6
dissipation 2
evaporation 2
loss 1
passing 4
disappearing
passing 1
disappoint°
defeat 2
disillusion
fail 2
fall 19
foil[1]
frustrate 1, 2
hurt 3
let[1] 4
shake 3
disappointed°
disenchanted
disgruntled
dissatisfied
heartbroken
regretful
disappointing°
bad 1
fall 11b, 19
inadequate 1
off 8
unsatisfactory
wanting 1
disappointment°
dissatisfaction 1
let-down
loss 5
mockery 3
regret 2
reverse 8
washout
disapprobation
blame 3
disapproval
disfavour 1
flak
disapproval°
blame 3
criticism 2
disfavour 1
displeasure 1
flak
judgement 3
objection
opposition 1
protest 1
refusal 1
reprimand 1
disapprove°
criticize 2
discourage 2
disfavour 3
frown 2
mind 15
object 4
protest 3
thumb 3
disapproving
destructive 2
jaundiced 2
po-faced
puritan 2
reproachful

disarm°
melt 2
spike 3
disarmed
prostrate 4
disarrange
disorder 4
displace 1
jumble 1
mess 5a
muddle 2
ruffle 4
shuffle 1
tousle
upset 3
disarranged
disorderly 1
indiscriminate 2
unkempt
upset 9
disarrangement
confusion 1
disturbance 1
mess 1
disarray
clutter 2
confuse 2
confusion 1
disorder 1
disturbance 1
jumble 2
mess 1, 5a
tousle
-in disarray
disorderly 1
loose 4
tatter 2
disarticulate
separate 1
disassemble
separate 1
disassociate
dissociate
distance 3
divorce 2
disassociated
estranged
disassociation
separation 2
disaster°
accident 1
affliction 2
calamity 1
casualty 1
catastrophe 1, 2
crash 5
crisis 2
disappointment 1
distress 2
evil 7
fatality 1
fate 2
fiasco
flop 4
grief 2
hash 2
ill 8
misery 3
misfortune 2
muddle 4
naught
ordeal
reverse 8
shambles
shame 3
sight 4
tragedy
visitation 2
washout
wreck 4
disastrous°
black 5
calamitous
deplorable 1
evil 3
fatal 2
fateful 2
hard 5
ill 4, 5
mortal 3
mournful 2
poignant 1
ruinous
sinister 1

disconcert (*cont.*)
floor 5
flurry 2
fluster 1
foil[1]
horrify 2
jar[2] 3
overawe
perplex
perturb
petrify 2
put 21c
rattle 3
rock[2] 3
ruffle 3
shake 5
shame 6
spite 3
surprise 1
throw 4
trip 6
unnerve
upset 1
wind[1] 13
wind[2] 4d
disconcerted°
agitated
blank 5
confused 2
dumbfounded
embarrassed 1
excited 1
frantic
insecure 1
small 6
upset 8
disconcerting°
disappointing
disturbing
embarrassing
harrowing
perplexing
unsettling
disconnect°
detach
disengage
dissociate
divide 1
hang 12
remove 7
separate 1
sever 1
disconnected°
broken 6
desultory
detached 1
discrete
disjointed 1
fragmentary
incoherent
independent 2
intermittent
loose 1, 5
odd 2
rambling 1
separate 5
disconnection
detachment 1
disconsolate
bad 9
broken-hearted
dejected
desolate 3
doleful
forlorn 1
heartbroken
heavy 6
hopeless 3
inconsolable
joyless 1
low[1] 8
melancholy 1
miserable 1
moody 1
mournful 1
sorrowful 1
unhappy 1
wistful 1
woebegone
wretched 2
disconsolateness
melancholy 2
woe
disconsonant
incongruous
discontent°
discontented
disgruntled
dissatisfaction 1
dissatisfied
discontented°
disappointed 1
disgruntled
dissatisfied
sour 4
discontentment
discontent
displeasure 1
dissatisfaction 1
distaste 1
discontinuation
break 27
cancellation 2
check 13
dissolution 2
expiration
failure 2
pause 2
stay[1] 6
suppression
suspension 2
termination 1
wait 4
discontinue°
abandon 4
break 10, 19a
call 11
cease 1
close 5
cut 15b
drop 7
end 9
expire 1
halt 2
interrupt 2
leave[1] 9
lift 3
pause 1
phase 6
quit 3
raise 9
refrain[1] 2
scrub 2
sever 2
shut 2
sign 9
stay[1] 4
stop 1
suppress 1
suspend 1
terminate
turn 17a
-be discontinued
lapse 1
discontinued
disused
discontinuing
suppression
suspension 2
discontinuity
break 27
check 13
gap 1
pause 2
discontinuous
broken 6
discrete
disjointed 2
intermittent
loose 5
odd 2
spasmodic 2
discord°
antagonism 2
conflict 3
disagreement 1
dispute 4
dissension
division 5
faction 2
feud 1
fight 8
fracas 2
friction 2
jar[2] 2
misunderstanding 2
discord (*cont.*)
quarrel 1
rivalry
split 8
strife 1
trouble 7
variance 2
discordance
disagreement 1
discord
discrepancy
dissension
noise 1
discordant°
dissident 2
factious
grating 1
harsh 1
incompatible
incongruous
mismatched
noisy
ragged 5
raucous
rough 8
step 8
strident
discount°
allowance 4
dismiss 2
lower[1] 1
mark 15b
rake-off
rebate 1, 3
underestimate
discounted
cut 28
discountenance
disfavour 3
displeasure 1
embarrass
frown 2
horrify 2
rattle 3
shame 6
trouble 1
discountenanced
embarrassed 1
discounting
irrespective of
discourage°
break 7
browbeat
choke 3
dampen 2
daunt
demoralize 1
depress 1
desolate 6
deter
dismay 2
fend 2
frustrate 1, 2
gag[1] 1
get 36c
hinder 2
inhibit
keep 13
militate 1
puncture 4
put 21b
repress
sadden
shackle 4
shake 3
stay[1] 4
discouraged
broken 3
dejected
desolate 3
despondent
disappointed 1
downhearted
hopeless 3
discouragement
depression 2
despair 1
desperation 2
deterrent
disappointment 2
lesson 3
rebuff 1
discouraging
bad 5
cold 4
disappointing
oppressive 1
prohibitive 1
untoward 1
discourse
address 1
conversation
converse
hold 16a
lecture 1, 3
oration
rap 5
sermon 2
speak 1, 2, 10
speech 2
talk 1, 14
discourteous°
abrupt 3
blunt 2
brusque
disagreeable 3
disrespectful
flippant 2
harsh 3
ignorant 4
ill-mannered
impertinent
impolite
irreverent 2
offensive 2
rough 3
rude 1, 2
short 4
short-tempered
tactless
ungracious
unrefined 1
unthinking 2
discourtesy
disrespect
flippancy 2
impertinence
incivility
indignity
insult 2
discover°
catch 4
check 12b
come 5a
detect 1
determine 2
dig 6
divine 4
expose 1
find 1, 2, 3, 4
finger 5b
get 43c
hear 2
hit 9a
learn 1
light[1] 9
locate 2
make 37a
penetrate 5
perceive 1
pierce 3
root[1] 7b
run 26a
scout 2
see 4
strike 14
stumble 3
surprise 2
trace 5
turn 25c
unearth
-be discovered
light[1] 10
discoverable
visible 1
wind[1] 8
discovery°
find 10
finding 1
location 2
observation 1
protégé
revelation
solution 1
discredit°
belittle
blacken 2
blast 6
brand 3
degradation 2
degrade 2
depreciate 2
diminish 2
disfavour 2
disgrace 1, 4
dishonour 4
disparage 1
disprove
distrust 1
doubt 1
explode 2
flaw 4
foul 14
humiliation
impeach 2
infamy 1
libel 4
lower[1] 4
notoriety
pull 9c
rebut
scandal 2
shame 2, 8
slur 1
smear 2
taint 1
wrong 9
discreditable
degrading
dishonourable 2
disreputable 1
infamous 1
notorious 1
shabby 4
shameful
unseemly 1
unworthy 1
discrediting
slanderous
discreet°
cautious
conscientious 3
deliberate 3
diplomatic
inconspicuous
judicious
politic 2
provident 1
prudent 1
seemly 2
sensible 1
step 12
tactful
wise 3
discrepancy°
difference 1
disagreement 1
disparity
dissimilarity
diversity 1
gap 2
hole 6
inequality 1
odds 3
variance 1
variety 2
discrepant
contradictory
divergent
incongruous
opposing
discrete°
different 1
distinct 2
diverse
individual 1
particular 1
separate 5
several 2
specific 2
discretion°
age 2
calculation 3
carte blanche
caution 2
diplomacy 1
disposition 4
finesse 3
freedom 4
discretion (*cont.*)
intelligence 1
judgement 1
pleasure 2
providence 1
prudence 1
savoir faire
tact
taste 6
volition
-at one's discretion
will 4
discretionary
optional
voluntary 2
discriminate°
contrast 1
differentiate 1
distinguish 1
pick 7b
segregate
separate 2
tell[1] 8
discriminating°
acute 5
aesthetic 2
choosy
delicate 5
fine[1] 9
fussy 1
judicial 2
judicious
keen[1] 5, 6
nice 3
particular 4
penetrating 1
politic 2
prudent 1
rational 2
refined 2
selective
tasteful
discrimination°
culture 1
discretion 1
distinction 1
ear 2
eye 3
grace 2
injustice 1
intolerance
judgement 1
penetration 2
prejudice 2
prudence 1
refinement 1
resolution 5
segregation
sense 2
sophistication 1
taste 4
discriminative
judicial 2
judicious
keen[1] 6
nice 3
selective
tasteful
discriminatory
intolerant 2
judicial 2
partial 2
selective
disc-shaped
circular 1
round 1
discursive°
diffuse 2
erratic 3
inarticulate 1
purposeless
rambling 1
discuss°
argue 2
bring 15b
comment 4
confer 1
consult 1
converse
criticize 1
debate 3
dispute 2
get 39b

disinclined *(cont.)*
incapable 2
indisposed 2
loath
reluctant
shy 4
slow 10
disinfect°
clean 11b
fumigate
purify 1
sterilize 1
disinfectant°
disinfected
clean 1
hygienic
pure 2
sanitary
sterile 2
disinformation
misinformation
propaganda 1
disingenuous°
artful 1
deceitful
foxy 1
insincere
sly 1
sneaky
unscrupulous
wily
disinherit
cut 15d
disintegrate°
break 16c, 23a
collapse 2
come 7
crumble
decay 1b
decompose 1, 2
deteriorate 2
die 2
dissolve 1
fall 7
fragment 3
go 12
piece 6
resolve 4
rot 1
shatter 1
shiver[2]
splinter 2
way 11a
worsen 2
disintegrated
broken 1
old 3
disintegrating
rotten 2
tumbledown
unsound 1
disintegration
collapse 6
decay 3
dissolution 1
rot 3
ruin 1
separation 3
disinter
dig 6
excavate 2
unearth
disinterest
equity
indifference 1
objectivity
disinterested°
detached 2
dispassionate 2
equitable
even 7
fair[1] 1
generous 2
honourable 3
impartial
impersonal 1
independent 4, 7
indifferent 1, 2
liberal 3
neutral 1
non-partisan 2
objective 1
unprejudiced

disinterestedly
honestly 1
disinterestedness
equity
honesty 3
indifference 3
disinvolve
disengage
disinvolved
outside 9
disjoin
detach
disconnect
disengage
dissociate
divide 1
separate 1
sever 1
disjoined
detached 1
disjointed 1
incoherent
separate 5
disjoining
separation 3
disjointed°
broken 6
disconnected 2
fragmentary
inarticulate 1
incoherent
piecemeal 3
rambling 1
disjointedly
piecemeal 1
disjunction
separation 3
disk
see **disc**
dislike°
aversion 1, 2
disfavour 1, 3
disgust 3
displeasure 1
distaste 1
grudge 1
hate 1, 2
horror 1
ill will
mind 15
objection
phobia
reluctance
thing 4
use 15
disliked
undesirable 2
unpopular
dislocate
displace 1
dislodge
clear 24
dispossess
evict
expel 1
shake 7
dislodgement
eviction
disloyal°
betray 1
dirty 3
dishonourable 2
faithless 2
fickle
perfidious
renegade 2
seditious
slippery 2
traitorous
untrue 1
disloyalty
betrayal 1
infidelity 1
perfidy
dismal°
black 5
bleak 1
blue 1
cold 4
dark 3
desolate 3
dingy

dismal *(cont.)*
dour 1
drab
dreary 1
dull 5
forlorn 1
funereal
gaunt 2
gloomy 2, 3
glum
grey 2
heavy 9
hurt 7
joyless 2
lacklustre
leaden 3
low[1] 6
mean[2] 3
melancholy 1
miserable 1
moody 1
mournful 1
murky
obscure 1
overcast
sad 2
sombre 1, 2
sorry 2
sullen
tragic
unfortunate 2
wintry 3
wretched 2
dismally
sadly 2
dismantle
demolish 1
strike 4
dismay°
alarm 2, 3
appal
confuse 1
desolate 6
discourage 1
dissatisfaction 2
dread 2
fear 1
fright 1
frighten
horrify 2
horror 2
intimidate
nonplus
panic 1
put 21c
scare 1
startle
terror 1
throw 4
unnerve
upset 1
dismaying
frightening
harrowing
nightmarish
dismember
butcher 3
mutilate 1
dismembered
disjointed 1
dismemberment
separation 3
dismiss°
banish 1, 2
brush[2] 6, 7
diminish 2
discharge 1, 2
discount 3
disperse 2
displace 2
disregard 1, 2
dissolve 3
drop 10
eject 3
excuse 2
expel 1, 2
fire 11
flight[2] 2
forget 3
jilt
kiss 3
laugh 2b
lay[1] 16a
light[2] 12
pack 7

dismiss *(cont.)*
pass 22
pension 2
purge 2
put 16e, 21b
rebuff 2
reject 2
remove 5
rid 2
rule 8
sack 4
scoff[1]
send 8
snap 6
supplant
thumb 8
trivialize
turf 4
turn 20c
-be dismissed
go 9
dismissal°
brush-off
discharge 8, 9
dissolution 2
ejection 3
expulsion
purge 4
push 16
rebuff 1
rejection
removal 3
sack 3
scorn 1
dismissive
flippant 1
passing 2
perfunctory 1
dismount
get 36a, 40a
land 5
light[2] 13
disobedience
breach 1
infringement
misbehaviour
non-compliance
rebellion 2
transgression
violation 1
disobedient°
bad 10
defiant
disorderly 2
insubordinate
mutinous 2
naughty 2
rebellious 2
rogue 2
self-willed
undisciplined
ungovernable
unruly
wild 4
disobediently
turn 42b
disobey°
break 9
defy 2
infringe 1
misbehave
mutiny 2
rebel 2
transgress 1, 2
violate 1
disobeyed
broken 5
disobeying
violation 1
disobliging
disagreeable 3
mean[2] 4
disorder°
ailment
bother 8
brawl 1
bug 2
chaos
confuse 2
confusion 1, 2
disease 1
displace 1
disrupt 1
distraction 1

disorder *(cont.)*
disturb 2
disturbance 1, 2
fracas 1
havoc 2
illness
infirmity 2
jumble 1, 2
mayhem
mess 1
muddle 2, 4
pandemonium
pell-mell 3
riot 1
ruffle 4
scramble 4
storm 3
tempest 2
tousle
trouble 7, 8
tumult
upheaval
-in disorder
loose 4
order 13a
disordered
chaotic 1
confused 1
desultory
disorderly 1
disreputable 2
incoherent
indiscriminate 2
inordinate 2
loose 4
morbid 1
neurotic
order 13a
pell-mell 2
promiscuous 3
ragged 4
riotous 1
sloppy 1
topsy-turvy 2
unkempt
unsettled 3
upset 9
wild 8
disorderliness
disorder 1
misbehaviour
rough-house 1
disorderly°
chaotic 1
confused 1, 3
desultory
disjointed 2
haphazard 2
helter-skelter 1
inordinate 2
irregular 2
obstreperous
pell-mell 2
promiscuous 3
ragged 4
riotous 1
rowdy 1
sloppy 1
topsy-turvy 2
tumultuous
unruly
unsettled 3
untidy
uproarious 1
wild 8
disorderly conduct
misbehaviour
rough-house 1
disorganization
disorder 1
dissolution 2
disturbance 1
mess 1
disorganize
confuse 2
disband
disorder 4
disrupt 1
jumble 1
muddle 2
perturb
shuffle 1
upset 3

disorganized
chaotic 1
confused 1, 3
desultory
disjointed 2
disorderly 1
haphazard 2
helter-skelter 1
indiscriminate 2
inefficient 2
loose 4
order 13a
pell-mell 2
promiscuous 3
purposeless
rambling 1
slipshod
topsy-turvy 2
unsettled 3
upset 9
disorient
confuse 1
muddle 1
ruffle 3
disorientated°
disoriented
confused 2
daze 4
disorientated
lost 3
sea 4
unsettled 3
disown
abdicate
back 9
cut 15d
deny 3
recall 3
reject 3
renounce
repudiate
retract 2
scorn 3
wash 10
disparage°
abuse 3
attack 2
belittle
blaspheme 2
condemn 1
debase 1
depreciate 2
deride
detract
diminish 2
discredit 1
disgrace 4
disregard 2
downgrade 2
flout
foul 14
hiss 3
impeach 2
knock 2
libel 3
look 5
minimize 2
mock 1
play 13
put 16g
run 26b
scoff[1]
slam 3
slander 2
slight 6
stigmatize
take 31b
talk 9a
trivialize
vilify
vituperate
write 4b
disparagement
aspersion
attack 7
criticism 2
dishonour 4
humiliation
libel 1
mockery 1
shame 2
disparaging
abusive 1
critical 1
derogatory

disparaging (*cont.*)
destructive 2
foul 6
injurious 2
jaundiced 2
left-handed 2
personal 4
reproachful
satirical
scornful
scurrilous
slanderous
disparaging remark
put-down
disparate
different 1
disproportionate
divergent
incongruous
mismatched
several 2
disparity°
contrast 3
disagreement 2
discrepancy
disproportion
dissimilarity
diversity 1
gap 2
inequality 1
odds 3
variance 1
variety 2
dispassion
indifference 3
objectivity
philosophy 3
dispassionate°
calm 4
casual 3
cold 3
cold-blooded 2
cool 3
deliberate 3
detached 2
disinterested
equitable
half-hearted
hard 4
impassive
impersonal 1
indifferent 1, 2
insensible 2
liberal 3
neutral 1
non-partisan 2
nonchalant
objective 1
passive 1
platonic
sober 2
stoical
temperate 1
tolerant
tranquil
unmoved
unsympathetic
dispatch°
bulletin
bump 5
bundle 3
course 3
execute 1
execution 1
expedite 1
expedition 2
finish 3, 4
forward 7
haste 1
hasten 2
kill 1
launch 3
letter 2
mail 2
message 1
missive
news 2
perform 1
performance 1
poison 4
polish 3b
post[3] 2
rapidity
dispatch (*cont.*)
relegate 1
remit 1
report 1
send 1
ship 2
speed 1
story 4
swallow 1
translate 4
translation 4
transmission 1
transmit 1
word 2
-with dispatch
quickly 2
dispatch-case
bag 2
dispatching
dispatch 7
transmission 1
dispatch-rider
messenger
runner 2
dispel
diffuse 3
disperse 2
evaporate 2
scatter 2
spread 1
-be dispelled
dissipate 1
dispelling
evaporation 2
dispensable°
expendable
needless 1
non-essential 1
superfluous
unnecessary
worthless 1
dispensary
hospital
infirmary
pharmacy 1
dispensation
administration 3
disposition 3
distribution 2
dole 2
exemption
faculty 4
leave[2] 1
licence 1
privilege
share 1
spread 8
dispense°
administer 3
allot
deal 1
diffuse 3
dispose 3c
distribute 1
divide 2
dole 3
dose 2
give 15b
hand 17
measure 14
mete
portion 4
present[2] 6
propagate 3
dispense with°
at **dispense 3**
discard 1
rid 2
scrap[1] 4
spare 9
throw 5a
waive 1
dispensing
spread 8
dispersal
dissipation 2
dissolution 2
distribution 2
radiation
rout 1
spread 8
disperse°
break 11, 23a
diffuse 3
disperse (*cont.*)
disband
dismiss 3
dissipate 1
dissolve 1, 3
distribute 2
evaporate 2
flight[2] 2
measure 14
pay 11a
portion 4
propagate 3
radiate 2
scatter 2
spray[1] 1
spread 1, 4
strew
dispersed
diffuse 1
loose 4
sparse 1
dispersion
dissipation 2
evaporation 2
spread 8
dispirit
chill 8
daunt
demoralize 1
depress 1
desolate 6
discourage 1
get 36c
sadden
dispirited
blue 1
broken 3
dejected
desolate 3
despondent
forlorn 1
gloomy 2
glum
heartbroken
joyless 1
melancholy 1
mournful 1
mouth 6
sorrowful 1
unhappy 1
dispiritedness
melancholy 2
sadness
dispiriting
bitter 3
cold 4
gloomy 3
joyless 2
oppressive 1
sad 2
trying
displace°
downgrade 1
exile 3
expel 1
lose 1
remove 5
substitute 1
supersede
supplant
transplant
uproot 1
displaced person
emigrant
exile 2
outcast
refugee
displacement
movement 1
removal 3
subversion
display°
affectation 2
air 7
appearance 3
arrangement 1
bear 5
bring 13a
carry 7
demonstrate 2
demonstration 1, 2
develop 3
display (*cont.*)
evidence 4
exemplify 2
exhibit
exhibition
expose 1
exposition 1
flash 2
flaunt
float 6
flourish 4
formation 3
hold 22d
indicate 3
indicator
liberty 5
manifest 2
manifestation
model 8
monitor 2
mount 5
open 23
ostentation
pageant
pageantry
parade 2, 5
performance 5
picture 7
pose 5
presentation 2
pretence 1
produce 4, 5
production 3
promenade 4
reflect 2
register 4
reveal
run 19
scene 3
set 20b, 22b
shake 4
show 1, 6, 11, 13, 15
spectacle 1
splendour 1
splurge 1
sport 5
spread 3
stick[1] 17b
strike 12
swagger 3
trot 2
veneer
wear 2
displease°
anger 2
offend 1
outrage 4
turn 17b
displeased
discontented
disgruntled
dissatisfied
resent
resentful
umbrage
displeasing
distasteful
off 8
offensive 2
repulsive
unsatisfactory
unwelcome 1
displeasure°
anger 1
disapproval
discontent
disfavour 1
dislike 2
dissatisfaction 1, 2
distaste 1
offence 3
resentment
umbrage
disport
flaunt
play 1
disposable°
dispensable
expendable
unnecessary
worthless 1
disposal
dispatch 7
disposition 2, 3, 4
disposal (*cont.*)
hand 8
order 1
position 1
refusal 2
-at one's disposal
available
dispose°
arrange 1
coordinate 1
give 10
group 4
incline 2
interest 8
lead 2
persuade 1
place 15
position 8
prevail 3
rank[1] 6
set 22b
settle 1
tempt 2
work 18
disposed°
capable 2
fit[1] 4
given 3
glad 2
incline 3
inclined 1
lean[2] 3
liable 1
like[1] 2
likely 4
mood 2
open 18
prepared 3
prompt 2
prone 2
ready 3
subject 6
susceptible 1
sympathetic 2
tend[1]
dispose of°
at **dispose 3**
clinch 1
cope 2
demolish 2
devise 2
discard 1
dispatch 3
dispense 3b
dump 2
eliminate 2, 4
finish 3, 4
meet[1] 5
polish 3b, 3c
process 4
remove 4
rid 2
scrap[1] 4
sell 1
settle 10
shred 2
sign 8, 11
throw 5a
wipe 3
-be disposed of
go 9
disposition°
appetite 1
aptitude 2
arrangement 1
attitude 1, 2
bent 5
bias 1
cheer 1
device 4
discretion 2
distribution 3
fate 3
favour 4
formation 3
frame 5
habit 2
humour 3
inclination 3
love 2
make-up 2
mentality 2
mind 5
mood 1
disposition (*cont.*)
morale
nature 1
order 1
personality 1
placement 1
position 1
posture 2, 3
scheme 2
spirit 2
taste 3
temper 1
tendency
turn 38
vein 4
way 2
will 1
wish 5
dispossess°
bereave
deprive
divest 1
downgrade 1
evict
expel 1
dispossessed
homeless 1
dispossession
ejection 2
eviction
disproportion°
disproportionate°
excessive 1
exorbitant
extreme 6
inordinate 1
lopsided 2
one-sided 2
disproportionately
fault 7
overly
unduly 1
disprove°
demolish 2
destroy 4
discredit 3
explode 2
rebut
disputable°
controversial 1
debatable
doubtful 1
exceptionable
marginal 2
moot 1
problematic
questionable
disputant
opponent
disputation
controversy 1
disputatious
aggressive 1
argumentative
belligerent 2
controversial 3
factious
legalistic
negative 1
pugnacious
quarrelsome
touchy 1
dispute°
argue 1
argument 1
battle 2
bicker
brawl 1
case[1] 2
cavil 2
challenge 1, 4
clash 2, 3
combat 2
conflict 2
contest 2, 3
contradict 1
controversy 1, 2
debate 1, 3
deny 1
difference 2
disagree 2

dispute *(cont.)*
disagreement 3
discredit 2
encounter 5
fall 18
feud 1, 2
fight 2, 4, 8
flap 5
fracas 2
fray[1]
friction 2
haggle
issue 4, 9
misunderstanding 2
quarrel 1, 2
query 3
question 5, 10
rivalry
row[2] 1, 3
run-in
scrap[2] 1
spar[2] 2
stand 12a
strife 1
tangle 4
tiff
tilt 4
trouble 7
variance 2
vendetta
word 9a
-in dispute
debatable
issue 8
questionable
variance 3
war 2
disputed
problematic
disputing
negative 1
disqualify°
disquiet
agitate 1
anxiety 1
care 1
concern 6
dissatisfaction 1
doubt 3
dread 2
excitement 1
fluster 1, 2
fuss 1
hurry 3
jar[2] 3
misgiving
move 4
pain 2
perturb
phobia
shake 5
shock 1
solicitude
trouble 1, 5
tumult
unrest
upset 1
worry 4
disquieted
agitated
anxious 1
nervous 1
unsettled 2
upset 8
worried
disquieting
disturbing
harrowing
painful 2
provocative 2
tense 3
trying
ugly 3
disquietude
concern 6
excitement 1
solicitude
disquisition
essay 1
exposition 3
lecture 1
memoir 1
monograph

disquisition *(cont.)*
paper 4
speech 2
talk 14
theme 2
tract[2]
disrate
degrade 1
disregard°
back 9
blink 4
break 9
brush[2] 6
close 7
discount 3
dismiss 2
disobey
excuse 1, 5
forget 3
forgive 1
ignore 1
indifference 1
jump 3
kiss 3
laugh 2b
leave[1] 10
licence 3
mind 19
miss[1] 4
neglect 1, 2, 3
negligence
non-compliance
oblivion 2
omit 2
overlook 1, 2
pass 3, 22
put 11
rule 8
scorn 3
skip 2, 4
slight 5, 8
slur 3
snap 6
trample 2
tune 5
violate 1
violation 1
waive 2
write 5
disregarded
broken 5
unsung
disregardful
disobedient 1
oblivious
promiscuous 1
disregarding
even 11
independent 8
non-compliance
violation 1
disrelish
dislike 2
distaste 1
reluctance
disrepair°
-in disrepair
blink 6
broken 7
order 13c
ramshackle
rickety
disreputable°
base[2] 2
deplorable 2
disgraceful 1
dishonourable 2
doubtful 3
fly-by-night 2
infamous 1
mangy
notorious 1
public 6
scandalous 1
seamy
shabby 4
shady 2
shameful
sleazy 2
sordid 1
unreliable
unseemly 1
unworthy 1

disrepute
degradation 2
discredit 4
disfavour 2
disgrace 1
dishonour 4
infamy 1
notoriety
scandal 2
shame 2
disrespect°
derision
dishonour 4
disregard 3
flippancy 2
freedom 7
impertinence
impudence
indignity
mouth 4
neglect 3
sacrilege 2
sauce 2
slight 5, 7
disrespectable
disreputable 1
disrespectful°
audacious 2
blasphemous
brash 2
cheeky
discourteous
familiar 3
flippant 2
forward 2
fresh 8
ill-mannered
immodest 2
impertinent
impolite
impudent
insolent
irreverent 2
offensive 2
pert 1
profane 1
rough 3
rude 1, 2
sacrilegious
tactless
disrespectfully
vain 3b
disrespectfulness
flippancy 2
sauce 2
disrobe°
divest 2
peel 2
strip[2] 2
disrupt°
break 10
disturb 1
inconvenience 3
interrupt 2
rupture 3
sabotage 3
upset 3
disrupting
inconvenient
tempestuous
disruption
disturbance 1
gap 1
havoc 2
inconvenience 1
interruption 1
mischief 2
rift 1
riot 1
tempest 2
upheaval
dissatisfaction°
disappointment 1
disapproval
discontent
displeasure 1
distaste 1
resentment
trouble 7
dissatisfied°
disappointed 1
discontented
disgruntled

dissatisfied *(cont.)*
resentful
dissatisfy
disappoint 1
displease
let[1] 4
dissatisfying
disappointing
dissect
analyse 1
decompose 1
scrutinize
dissection
analysis 1
breakdown 3
disseise
evict
disseisin
eviction
dissemble
act 8
conceal 2
cover 2
dissimulate
fake 2
game 6
let[1] 7b
pretend 3
dissembler
Pharisee
poseur
dissembling
dissimulation
evasive
hypocritical
insincere
two-faced
disseminate
broadcast 2
carry 8
circulate 2
diffuse 3
disperse 1
dissipate 1
distribute 2
emanate 2
give 15b
hand 17
issue 10
propagate 3
radiate 2
radio 2
release 2
scatter 1
sow
spread 1, 2
throw 7a
dissemination
circulation 2
distribution 2
issue 6
publication 1
spread 8
transmission 2
dissension°
antagonism 2
difference 2
disagreement 3
discord
faction 2
feud 1
fight 8
friction 2
misunderstanding 2
rivalry
strife 1
variance 2
dissent
disagree 1
disagreement 2
dispute 1
dissension
fight 8
friction 2
protest 1, 3
rebel 2
revolt 2
variance 2
dissenter
dissident 1
naysayer
nonconformist 1

dissenter *(cont.)*
rebel 4
dissenting
dissident 2
negative 1
nonconformist 2
quarrelsome
dissertation
essay 1
exposition 3
lecture 1
memoir 1
monograph
paper 4
talk 14
theme 2
tract[2]
disservice°
disadvantage 2
grievance 1
turn 34
dissever
sever 1
dissidence
fight 8
dissident°
nonconformist 1, 2
opposing
quarrelsome
schismatic
seditious
subversive 2
dissimilar°
differ 1
different 1
discordant 1
disproportionate
distinct 2
divergent
diverse
several 2
unlike 1, 3
unrelated
dissimilarity°
contrast 3
difference 1
disagreement 1
discrepancy
disparity
disproportion
diversity 1
inequality 1
odds 3
dissimulate°
act 8
game 6
let[1] 7b
dissimulating
hypocritical
phoney 1
dissimulation°
act 3
deceit 1
deception 1
disguise 4
masquerade 2
dissipate°
consume 3
diffuse 3
disperse 2
evaporate 2
exhaust 1
expend 2
fritter
lavish 4
lift 5
lose 4
pass 5
run 34b
scatter 2
spend 2
splurge 2
spread 1
waste 1
dissipated
abandoned 2
decadent 2
dissolute
epicurean 1
fast[1] 2
misspent
outrageous 3
promiscuous 2

dissipated *(cont.)*
sensual
wanton 1
dissipating
profligate 1
self-indulgent
dissipation°
evaporation 2
excess 2
extravagance 1
prodigality 1
profligacy 1
waste 5
dissociate°
distance 3
divorce 2
dissociated
estranged
dissociation
separation 2
dissolute°
abandoned 2
decadent 2
degenerate 1
epicurean 1
fast[1] 2
immoral 1
impure 4
incontinent 2
lecherous
lewd
libertine 2
loose 7
lost 7
obscene 1
outrageous 3
perverted
profligate 1
promiscuous 2
reprobate 1
self-indulgent
sensual
wanton 1
wicked 2
dissolutely
fast[1] 9
dissoluteness
dissipation 1
excess 2
impurity 3
profligacy 1
ribaldry
waste 6
dissolution°
collapse 6
dissipation 1
divorce 1
evaporation 2
ruin 1
solution 4
dissolve°
attack 5
collapse 2
die 2
disband
divorce 2
evaporate 2
melt 1, 3, 4
resolve 4
ruin 7
run 8
sever 2
dissolving
dissolution 2
solution 4
dissonance
jangle 3
noise 1
dissonant
brassy 2
discordant 2
grating 1
harsh 1
incongruous
noisy
raucous
dissuade
argue 6
choke 3
deter
discourage 2
reason 8
dissuasion
deterrent

do in (*cont.*)
kill 1
murder 3
polish 3b
remove 4
ride 5b
rout 2
doing
execution 1
performance 1
undertaking 2
doing away with
destruction 2
removal 2
doings
proceeding 2b
relation 6b
transaction 2
dolce far niente
idleness 1
indolence
lethargy 1
dolce vita
dissipation 1
doldrums
gloom 2
-in the doldrums
dejected
gloomy 2
moody 1
sorrowful 1
dole°
allowance 3
charity 3
divide 2
gift 1
give 15a
mete
parcel 4
present[2] 3
ration 1, 3
-on the dole
needy
unemployed
work 6
doleful°
broken-hearted
dark 3
dismal
dreary 1
funereal
gloomy 2
glum
heartbroken
joyless 1
mournful 1
pathetic 1
piteous
sinking 2
sombre 1
sorrowful 2
woebegone
wretched 2
dolefulness
desolation 2
dole out
allot
deal 1
dispense 1
distribute 1
divide 2
give 15b
hand 17
measure 14
mete
parcel 4
pass 20b
portion 4
present[2] 6
ration 3
serve 3
share 3
split 4
doling out
partition 2
doll
broad 9
puppet 1
dollar
-dollars
purse 2
dollar-a-year
unpaid 2
dollop
dab 2
helping
little 10
morsel 1
doll-sized
little 1
doll up
preen 2
primp
dolorous
broken-hearted
dismal
doleful
forlorn 1
mournful 1
oppressive 1
pathetic 1
piteous
sinking 2
sombre 1
tragic
woebegone
dolour
care 1
desolation 2
gloom 2
hurt 6
melancholy 2
misery 1
pain 2
regret 2
sadness
sorrow 1
woe
dolt°
clod 2
clown 2
dummy 3
fool 1
gawk 1
halfwit
silly 3
doltish
dim 2
dull 1
halfwitted
obtuse 2
opaque 3
slow 7
stolid
stupid 1
thick 6
wooden 3
doltishness
stupidity 1
domain°
class 2
department 2
dominion 2
element 2
estate 1
field 4
habitat
kingdom 2
monarchy 1
nation
province 1
realm 1
region 2
sphere 2
territory 2
universe 2
world 3
zone
dome
head 1
domestic°
civil 2
help 7
home 6, 7, 8
homely 2
interior 2
maid 2
native 2
servant 1
woman 4
domesticate
civilize 2
tame 5
domesticated
broken 4
domestic 2
pet[1] 2
tame 1
domestic servant
servant 1
domicile°
abode
dwell 1
dwelling
home 1
house 1, 8
place 6
quarter 5
residence 1
seat 5
domiciliate
domicile 2
dominance
advantage 1
clutch 2b
control 5
dominion 1
hold 26
power 2
predominance
superiority 1
supremacy 2
upper 6
dominant°
central 2
influential
main 1
major 2
mighty 1
overriding
paramount
popular 2
predominant
prevailing 1
prevalent
principal 1
rampant 2
sovereign 2
dominate°
boss 3
browbeat
command 2, 5
control 1
dwarf
enslave
excel
finger 10
loom 2, 3
monopolize
obsess
occupy 1
overawe
overshadow 1
possess 3
predominate
prevail 2
reign 2
ride 3
rule 5
string 6
subdue 1
subject 10
subjugate
triumph 3
tyrannize
dominated
possess 4
possessed
-ridden
dominating
major 2
masterful 2
obsessive
overriding
possessive 2
prevailing 2
domination°
clutch 2b
conquest 1
control 5
dominion 1
government 1
grip 2
reign 1
subjection
tyranny
domineer
boss 3
lord 3
overawe
push 7
tyrannize
domineering°
assertive
authoritarian
bossy
despotic
dictatorial 2
dogmatic
heavy-handed 2
imperative 2
masterful 2
overbearing
possessive 2
dominie
schoolteacher
teacher
dominion°
authority 1
command 7
crown 2
domain 1
grip 2
jurisdiction
might 2
monarchy 1
possession 2
power 2
predominance
province 2
region 1
rule 2
sovereignty
supremacy 2
sway 4
domino
mask 1
don
assume 2
get 39a
instructor
put 22a
teacher
wear 1
-dons
faculty 3
donate°
afford 2
bestow
contribute 1
give 1
grant 1
put 28e
sign 11
spare 8
stump 4
subscribe 2
donation°
benevolence 2
charity 3
dole 1
endowment 1
gift 1
grant 3
offering
philanthropy 2
present[2] 2
presentation 1
-donations
largesse
done
complete 2
correct 7
exhausted 2
over 6
past 1
through 5
done for
dead 1
spent 1
washed up
done in
exhausted 1
spent 1
tired 1
washed out 2
weary 1
worn 3
done with
over 6
past 1
through 5
-be done with
dismiss 2
finish 8
forsake 3
go 9
donjon
dungeon
hole 4
keep 16
Don Juan
charmer
libertine 1
philanderer
playboy
rake[2]
roué
sensualist
donkey
dolt
donkey-work
drudgery
labour 1
donnée
given 4
donnish
pedantic 1
Donnybrook
argument 1
battle 1
brawl 1
conflict 1
disorder 2
dispute 4
disturbance 2
fight 7
fracas 2
fray[1]
quarrel 1
riot 1
scrap[2] 1
scrimmage
tumult
donor°
benefactor
philanthropist
do nothing
twiddle 2
do-nothing
slack 1
slothful
Don Quixote
romantic 5
visionary 2
doodah
accessory 1
contraption
gadget
gimmick 2
thing 5
trifle 1
doodle
scrawl 2
doohickey
gadget
gimmick 2
doolally
crazy 1
doom°
condemn 2
damn 2
destine 1
destiny
fate 1, 2
jinx 3
lot 2
perdition
predestination
reckoning 3
doomed°
bound[3] 4
condemn 3
destined 1
fated 1, 2
inauspicious
predetermined 2
unfortunate 2
doomsday
-till doomsday
ever 2
for ever 1
do one's best
endeavour 1
exert 2
strive 1
do one's damnedest
exert 2
do one's part
finger 6
play 8a
serve 2
do one's utmost
strive 1
door
entrance[1] 2
entry 2
exit 1
gate 1
mouth 2
opening 2
-out of doors
abroad 3
outdoor
outside 5, 10
door-keeper
porter[2] 2
doormat
flunkey 2
inferior 4
doorstep
threshold 1
door-to-door salesman
merchant 2
doorway
gate 1
mouth 2
threshold 1
do out of
rob 3
screw 6
do over
make 38a
modernize
renew 1
renovate
doozy
killer 2
dope°
clod 2
dirt 4
dolt
drug 2, 4
fool 1
gossip 2
information
intelligence 2
jerk 5
low-down
news 1
scoop 3
silly 3
talk 17
twit[2]
dope-fiend
addict 1
do penance°
at **penance 2**
doper
addict 1
dopey
daft 1
foolish 2
groggy
scatterbrained
stupid 1
thick 6
dopiness
folly 1
doppelgänger
double 7
ghost 1
image 2
look-alike
spectre 1
dopy
daft 1
foolish 2
scatterbrained

dormancy
inertia
dormant°
abeyance
extinct 3
inactive 2
inert 3
leaden 4
potential 1
quiet 3
dorsum
back 4
dosage
dose 1
dose°
draught 2
drug 3
potion
dosh
money
purse 2
do something
finger 6
step 11
doss down
rest[1] 6
retire 3
dosser
tramp 4
dossier
file 1
journal 2
paper 2b
portrait
record 3
dot°
dapple 2
particle
pepper
point 1
speck
-on the dot°
at **dot 2**
punctual
sharp 10
time 19a
dotage
decrepitude 1
senility
-in one's dotage
senile
dotard
ruin 5
dote°
dote on°
at **dote**
adore 1
love 7
make 34b
pet[1] 5
spoil 3
do the trick°
at **trick 7**
take 11
doting
affectionate
devoted
maternal
senile
do to death
overdo 1
dotted
dapple 1
flecked
speckled
spotty 1
dotty
crazy 1,5
deranged
flighty 2
foolish 2
halfwitted
inane
insane 1
mad 1,6
off 4
preposterous
queer 4
senile
wild 9
double°
copy 1
cover 8
double (*cont.*)
duplicate 2,3
fold 1
image 2
intensify
look-alike
match 1
pair 1,2
picture 2
relief 4
reproduction 2
second[1] 8
sit 6b
stand 8
stand-in
substitute 1
twin 1
understudy 1,2
-at the double°
at **double 8**
quickly 2
soon 2
double agent
spy 1
turncoat
double-barrelled
double 3
double bind
dilemma
fix 17
double-cross°
deceit 2
deceive
sell 3
stab 2,6
double-crosser
snake 2
traitor
double-crossing
traitorous
doubled
double 1
double-dealer
hypocrite
phoney 3
traitor
double-dealing
artful 1
chicanery
crafty
deceit 1
deceitful
deception 1
designing
devious 1
dishonest
disingenuous
dissimulation
double 5
foul 7
foul play
fraud 1
fraudulent 2
hanky-panky
hypocrisy
hypocritical
insincere
intrigue 3
traitorous
trickery
tricky 1
two-faced
wily
double Dutch
nonsense 1
double entendre
ambiguity 2
epigram 1
pun
quip 1
double for
stand 8
substitute 1
understudy 2
double-ganger
see **doppel-gänger**
double-quick
rapidly 1,2
doublet
pair 1
double-talk
ambiguity 2
dodge 3
equivocate
evasion 2
gobbledegook 2
mumbo-jumbo 1
nonsense 1
doubt°
challenge 1,4
discredit 2,6
dispute 1
distrust 1,2
misgiving
mistrust 1,2
objection
perplexity 1
qualm
query 2,3
question 2,5,10
scepticism
scruple 1
suspect 1
suspense 1
suspicion 1
-beyond (a) doubt
doubtless 1
easily 2
far 3
indisputable
positively
question 4
surely 1
truly 3
undoubtedly
well[1] 7
-in doubt°
at **doubt 5**
debatable
doubtful 1
question 6b
suspicious 1,2
vague 2
-without (a) doubt
certainty 3
clearly 2
course 6
doubtless
easily 2
evidently 1
far 3
positively
presumably
question 4
seriously 3
truly 3
undoubtedly
well[1] 9
doubted
problematic
doubter
non-believer
sceptic
doubtful°
ambiguous 2
arbitrary 1
controversial 1
debatable
dicey
disputable
distrustful
far-fetched
fishy 2
implausible
improbable
incredulous
indecisive 1,2
leery
left-handed 2
marginal 2
mistrust 1
moot 1
obscure 2
precarious
problematic
queasy 1
queer 2
question 6b
questionable
rocky[2]
sceptical
shady 2
shaky 1
doubtful (*cont.*)
speculative 2
suspect 3
suspicious 1,2
tenuous 2
tremulous 1
uncertain 3
unlikely 1
vague 2
doubtfully
salt 5
doubtfulness
discredit 6
distrust 2
scepticism
doubting
distrustful
faithless 1
heathen 2
leery
sceptical
unbelieving
doubting Thomas
non-believer
sceptic
doubtless°
certain 4
easily 2
evidently 1
far 3
indeed 1
obviously
presumably
surely 1
doubtlessly
doubtless 1
easily 2
evidently 1
far 3
indeed 1
obviously
presumably
probably
question 4
surely 1
well[1] 9
douceur
perquisite
tip[3] 1
douche
flush[1] 2
wash 1
dough
cash 1
fund 2
money 1
purse 2
-in the dough
rich 1
doughboy
soldier 1
doughtiness
grit
nerve 1
prowess 2
doughty
audacious 1
gritty 2
intrepid
mighty 1
stout 2
tough 3
venturesome 1
doughy
mushy 1
do up
clean 9
fix 16b
refurbish
renovate
revamp
wrap 1
dour°
dark 3
glum
grave[2] 1
harsh 2
moody 1
po-faced
serious 1
severe 2
stern 2
dour (*cont.*)
sullen
dourly
severely 3
douse
dip 1
flush[1] 2
put 23c
quench 2
shut 4a
soak 1
steep[2] 1
submerge 1
wash 1
water 6
doused
out 14
dousing
soaking 1
dovetail
fit[1] 6
mesh 4
weave 2
do violence to°
at **violence 3**
outrage 5
dovish
peaceable 2
dowdy°
heel[1] 3
sloppy 1
dowel
peg 1
pin 1
rod 1
do well
flourish 1
get 27
do without
dispense 3a,3b
forgo 1
go 41
spare 9
down
below 1,6
blue 1
broken-hearted
dejected
desolate 3
despondent
doleful
downwards
fluff 1
forlorn 1
gloomy 2
glum
joyless 1
low[1] 2,8
lower[1] 6
nap[2]
over 10
plain 6
swallow 1
under 8
unhappy 1
down and out°
broke
destitute 1
heel[1] 3
needy
poor 1
sordid 4
down-and-out°
derelict 3
down and out 2
pauper
tramp 4
-down-and-outs
dregs 2
down at heel
disreputable 2
heel[1] 3
ragged 1
shabby 1
down at the mouth°
at **mouth 6**
downbeat
rhythm
downcast
blue 1
broken-hearted
dejected
downcast (*cont.*)
desolate 3
despondent
disappointed 1
downhearted
dreary 1
gloomy 2
heavy 6
hopeless 3
joyless 1
low[1] 8
melancholy 1
moody 1
morbid 3
mouth 6
sad 1
sorrowful 1
subdued 2
unhappy 1
woebegone
downer
dope 2
drug 2
sedative 1
tranquillizer
downfall°
breakdown 1
collapse 6
death 3
decay 3
destruction 3
doom
failure 4
fall 24,28
fate 2
finish 10
loss 5
overthrow 2
perdition
ruin 1
undoing 1
downgrade°
belittle
decline 8
degrade 1
diminish 2
disparage 1
fall 27
grade 4
hill 3
humble 4
lower[1] 1
mortify 1
peg 3
reduce 6
relegate 2
slope 2
vitiate 1
-on the downgrade°
at **downgrade 4**
downhearted°
bad 9
blue 1
broken-hearted
dejected
desolate 3
despondent
disappointed 1
doleful
gloomy 2
heartbroken
heavy 6
joyless 1
melancholy 1
miserable 1
moody 1
mournful 1
pessimistic
sad 1
unhappy 1
woebegone
wretched 2
downheartedness
depression 2
gloom 2
melancholy 2
downhill
fall 27
down in the dumps
dejected
despondent
doleful

down in the dumps (*cont.*)
sorrowful 1
down in the mouth°
at **mouth 6**
blue 1
dejected
despondent
doleful
gloomy 2
melancholy 1
moody 1
sorrowful 1
subdued 2
downland
hill 1
plain 6
down on one's luck
unfortunate 1
down payment
deposit 3
earnest 3
downplay
downgrade 2
minimize 2
whitewash
downpour°
precipitation
rain 1
storm 1
down-putting
vituperative
downright°
absolute 2
barefaced 1
categorical
dead 14
express 5
flat 4
frank 1
open 13
out-and-out
outright 2
plump[2] 6
point-blank 1
profound 4
pronounced 2
pure 5
rank[2] 2
sheer 2
solid 8
stark 4
thorough 1
thoroughly 1
total 3
unmitigated
unqualified 2
downs
hill 1
downslide
slump 1
downspout
spout 3
downstairs
below 2
down-swing
fall 26
twilight 2
down the drain°
at **drain 3**
lost 2
down-to-earth
easy 6
homespun
literal 3
philosophical 2
practical 2
rational 3
realistic 1
sensible 1
steady 6
down tools
walk 4b
down to the ground
completely 1
entirely 1
downtrodden°
base[2] 2
downturn
decline 6
depression 3
eclipse 4
fall 26
recession
slack 5
slump 1
twilight 2
downward°
downwards
downward movement
movement 6
downwards°
deeply 1
downwind
wind[1] 4
downy
fluffy 1
fuzzy 1
hairy 1
soft 8
woolly 1
do wrong
err 2
transgress 1
dowry
endowment 1
dowse
soak 1
dowsing
soaking 1
doxy
friend 3
mistress 1
squeeze 10
tart[2] 2
doyen, doyenne
elder 3
sage 2
doze°
nap[1] 1, 3
nod 3
repose 2
rest[1] 1, 6
sleep 1, 2
dozens
score 4
dozing
rest[1] 3
dozy
drowsy
sleepy 1
stupid 1
DP
emigrant
exile 2
outcast
refugee
drab°
bitch 2
colourless 2
dark 3
dingy
dowdy
dreary 2
dull 7
grey 2
jade 2
lacklustre
mousy 1
muddy 3
neutral 2
nondescript
plain 4
sober 3
tart[2] 2
tedious
drabness
tedium
uniformity 2
Draconian
brutal 1
drastic
extreme 4
harsh 2
severe 4
strong 13
swingeing
draft°
call 12a
design 2, 3, 5
draft (*cont.*)
devise 1
draw 6, 15b
drink 6
enlist 1
frame 7
induct 2
mobilize
nip[2]
note 4, 10
outline 2, 3
pattern 4
pen[1] 2
piece 4
project 3
proposal 2
protocol 2
recruit 1
rough 14, 15
scheme 1
draftee
recruit 2
drag°
carry 1
cart 2
connection 3
crawl 2
creep 2
delay 3
drain 2
draw 1
drip 3
encumbrance
fag 2
force 9
haul 1, 3
hump 3
lug
pain 3
pass 11
pill 2
plague 2
plod 1
power 2
prolong
puff 2, 5
pull 1, 22
rake[1] 8
shuffle 2
tag 5
tow
traction
trail 4, 5
tug 1, 2
wear 5
dragging
shambling
draggle
drag 4
draggle-tailed
sloppy 1
unkempt
untidy
drag into
mix 5
drag on
extend 3
prolong
dragon
monster 1
shrew
drag one's feet°
at **drag 6**
delay 3
play 14
shuffle 2
stall[2] 1
dragoon
force 7
push 4
railroad 2
drag out
draw 14a
extend 3
get 44c
lengthen
prolong
spin 5
spread 4
string 11b
trot 2
drag queen
homosexual 1
drag through the mud
disgrace 4
smear 2
drain°
consume 2
draw 3
ebb 2
empty 8
enervate
escape 3
evacuate 1
exhaust 3, 4, 5
expend 2
fatigue 2
filter 3
finish 3
milk
ooze 2
percolate
pump 3
sap[1] 3
sap[2]
secrete[2]
secretion
spout 3
strain[1] 5
tap[2] 5, 6
tire 1
undermine 1
void 7
wear 6
weary 5
drainage
escape 7
drained
beat 13
empty 1
exhausted 1
impoverished 2
pale[1] 1
peaky
prostrate 5
run-down 1
spent 1
tired 1
washed out 2
weary 1
white 2
draining
escape 7
exhaustion 1
secretion
toilsome
weary 2
dram
draught 2
drink 6
drop 2
modicum
nip[2]
shot 7
sip 2
drama°
piece 4
play 20
production 4
show 14
theatre 2, 3
dramatic°
melodramatic
poignant 3
sensational 2
stirring
theatrical 1
Thespian 1
vivid 2
dramatic art(s)
drama 2
theatre 3
dramatics
drama 3
dramatis personae
cast 2
character 5
dramatist°
playwright
scribe 2
dramatize°
magnify 1
play 17a
rub 3
set 20b
dramaturge
dramatist
playwright
scribe 2
dramaturgic(al)
dramatic 1
dramaturgy
drama 2
theatre 2, 3
drape°
drapery
hang 3
string 9
drapery°
drape 2
drastic°
extreme 4
forcible 2
heroic 3
radical 2
stiff 2
strong 13
swingeing
ultra-
draught°
air 2
breeze 1
drink 4, 6
gulp 3
nip[2]
potion
puff 1, 2
wind[1] 1
-on draught
tap[2] 4a
draughting
preparation 3
draughtsman
designer 1
piece 5
draughty
breezy 1
draw°
attract
attraction 1, 2
base[1] 5
borrow
bring 3
catch 12
charm 3
collect 2
cut 10
deadlock 1
deduce
derive 1
describe 4
design 3
determine 2
draft 3
drag 1, 2
earn 2
engage 4
entice
extract 1, 2, 3
fascination
feature 2, 5
gather 4
get 44c
gut 4
haul 1, 3
heave 1
incur
infer
interest 7
invitation 2
magnetism
make 4, 37c
mine 3
paint 4
picture 7
plot[1] 4
produce 5
profile 4
puff 2, 5
pull 1, 5, 9b, 19, 20, 22
raffle
receive 2
represent 3
rope 4
sap[1] 3
spell[2] 3
star 2
stimulant 1
draw (*cont.*)
take 5
tap[2] 5
tempt 1
temptation 2
tie 10
tow
trace 6
trail 4
tug 1
verge[2]
wrench 3
-be drawn
trail 5
draw a bead
level 10
sight 7
draw a blank
forget 1
draw a distinction
discriminate 1
draw ahead of
overhaul 1
pull 7
draw and quarter
punish 2
draw attention to
emphasize
spotlight 3
draw away
distract 1
draw 12b
gain 5
pull 7
sidetrack
draw back°
at **draw 10**
fall 8
flinch
pull 8a, 14b
retract 1
retreat 4, 5
shrink 2
start 5
withdraw 1
drawback°
catch 18
complication 2
deterrent
detriment
disadvantage 1
fly 10
hindrance 1
inconvenience 1
joker 2
liability 3
shortcoming
draw close
approach 1
halt 2
drawers
pants 1
draw even
overtake 1
pull 18c
draw forth
extract 1, 3
fetch 2
draw in°
at **draw 11**
inhale
involve 3
lure 1
pull 11a
rope 4
tempt 1
drawing°
attractive
cut 25
design 5
draft 1
figure 5
likeness 2
lot 3
lottery
picture 1
plan 2
scheme 2

drink in
devour 3
drinking-bout
spree
drinking-glass
glass 4
drinking-water
water 1
drink to°
at **drink 3**
pledge 6
toast 3
drink up
consume 1
drain 4
finish 3
drip°
drag 7
drain 6
drop 1, 5
filter 3
leak 4
percolate
sap[1] 2
scrap[1] 1
secrete[2]
secretion
silly 3
trickle 1, 2
weep 2
wet 6
drippiness
sentimentality
dripping
drip 2
secretion
soaking 2
wet 1
drippy
sentimental 2
drive°
ambition 2
campaign 1
carry 3
crash 2
crowd 4
dynamism
energy
enterprise 2
excursion 1
exert 2
exertion
flight[2] 2
force 8
herd 4
hit 2
hustle 2, 4
impetus
incite
inflame 1
initiative 2
inject 1
invasion 2
lust 2
manoeuvre 4
momentum
motivate
movement 5
offensive 5
operate 2
pilot 3
plough 2
power 8
propel
propulsion
provoke 1
pull 11a
purpose 2
push 1, 14
ram 1
ride 1, 4
roll 3
run 13, 17, 36
see 6
shame 7
sink 7
soldier 4
spin 7
spirit 2
spur 4
stimulant 1
street 1
taxi 2
thrust 1, 4
drive (*cont.*)
tour 2
trip 3
turn 4, 16b, 31
urge 1, 5
wash 2
will 1
drive at°
at **drive 6**
mean[1] 2
drive away
banish 1, 2
beat 9
chase 3
flight[2] 2
freeze 4
pack 7
pull 7
rebuff 2
repel 1
shoo 2
drive back
repel 1
repulse 1
turn 13a
drive crazy
disturb 1
exasperate 1
exercise 3
irritate
tease 1
wall 3
drive home
home 11
drive in
inject 1
drivel°
babble 3
froth 2
gab 2
gibberish
gobbledegook 1
jabber 1
jargon 2
moonshine 2
mumbo-jumbo 1
nonsense 1
prattle 1, 2
rot 4
slaver[1] 1, 2, 3
driven
possessed
driven apart
estranged
drive off
beat 9
flight[2] 2
pack 7
repel 1
drive out
banish 1, 2
cast 14
dispossess
eject 1
exile 3
expel 1
freeze 4
pump 3
driver
engineer 2
operator 1
servant 1
driverless
runaway 2
drive round the bend
madden 1
driver's seat
helm 2
-be in the driver's seat
dominate 1
govern 1
shot 9
string 6
drive up
pull 11a
drive up the wall°
at **wall 3**
disturb 1
exasperate 1
exercise 3
drive up the wall (*cont.*)
irritate
madden 1
pester
tease 1
driveway
drive 9
driving
motive 3
driving force
propulsion
drizzle
drip 1
mist 1
precipitation
rain 1, 4
shower 1
spray[1] 2
trickle 1
drizzling
wet 2
drizzly
moist 2
droll
comic 1
dry 3
farcical
fool 2
funny 1
humorous
joker 1
ludicrous
priceless 2
ridiculous
wag[2]
witty
wry 2
drollery
humour 1
wit 2
drone
buzz 1, 5
go 32f
hum 1, 4
idler
loafer
murmur 1
wastrel 2
droning
hum 4
murmur 1
drool
drivel 1
slaver[1] 1, 2
spit 1, 3
droop°
dangle 1
die 2
fade 2
flag[2] 1
sag 1, 2, 3
slouch 1, 2
weaken 2
wilt 1, 2
drooping
flabby 1
limp[2] 1
pendulous 1
slack 2
drop°
abandon 4
advantage 1
blob
collapse 3
dab 2
dash 7
deposit 1
descend 2
dip 5
discontinue
drapery
drip 1, 2
dump 1
ebb 2, 4
eliminate 1
faint 3
fall 1, 3, 11a, 22, 26, 27
flop 1
fumble 2
go 27b
jilt
lapse 3, 4
drop (*cont.*)
leave[1] 4
lower[1] 1, 2
lurch[1]
modicum
morsel 1
nip[2]
pass 20a
pendant
pitch[1] 3
plump[2] 1, 4
plunge 1, 3
reduce 5
reject 2
relinquish 1
sag 2, 3
scrap[1] 1
scrub 2
secrete[2]
secretion
set 1
shake 7
shed[2] 3, 4
shower 3
sink 2, 3, 5, 6
sip 2
slash 3
slide 3
slope 1, 2
slump 1, 2
sphere 1
start 13
stick[1] 2
subside 1
tablet 4
taper 2
taste 1
terminate
throw 8
topple 3
touch 15
trace 2
trickle 1
trifle 2
truckle
tumble 1, 2
-at the drop of a hat
immediately 1
offhand 4
willingly
drop a brick
err 1
drop away
drop 6
drop back
fall 10
pull 8b
drop behind
trail 6
drop by
come 16c
drop by drop
gradually
drop dead
fall 6
drop down
decline 5
drop 6
fall 1
flop 1
subside 1
drop in (on)°
at **drop 12**
come 16c
look 11b
pop 2
visit 1
drop-kick
kick 3
droplet
blob
bubble 1
drop 1
sphere 1
drop off
decline 3
doze 1
drop 6, 11
fall 3
flake 3a
nap[1] 1
nod 3
sleep 1
drop off (*cont.*)
slope 1
taper 2
drop-off
drop 4
fall 26
slack 5
drop out°
at **drop 13**
hide[1] 1
leave[1] 4
secede
drop-out
hippie
dropped
abandoned 1
dropping
fall 22
omission 1
secretion
-droppings
dung
filth 1
muck 1
dropsical
swollen
dross
dirt 1
garbage
refuse[2]
rubbish 1
trash 3
drove
drive 5
flock 1
host[2]
many 3
mass 2
pack 3
score 4
swarm 1
throng 1
-droves
many 3
mass 2
score 4
drown°
drench
flood 4
submerge 3
drown one's sorrows
drink 2
drowse
doze 1
nod 3
sleep 1
drowsiness
lethargy 2
torpor
drowsy°
dreamy 3
lethargic 2
sleepy 1
drub
beat 1
floor 4
lambaste 1
lather 4
overcome 1
pound[1] 4
rout 2
whip 2
drubbing
loss 5
rout 1
thrashing 1
works 36
drub into
pound[1] 4
drudge
fag 3
hack[2] 1, 2
labour 5
labourer
plod 2
robot 2
slave 2, 3
soldier 4
sweat 3
drudgery°
grind 7
job 4
drudgery (*cont.*)
labour 1
slavery 3
struggle 4
sweat 6
work 1
drug°
antidote
cure 1
doctor 4
dope 2
medicine
narcotic 2
numb 2
pill 1
prescription 2
remedy 1
spike 4
drug addict
user 2
drugged
high 9
druggist°
pharmacist
drugstore
pharmacy 1
drum
advertisement 2
din 2
patter[1] 3
pulsate
roller 1
tap[1] 1
drummer
merchant 2
pedlar
seller
drumming
pulse 1
drum out
degrade 1
dismiss 1
eject 3
expel 2
lay[1] 16a
punish 2
drum up
enlist 2
drunk°
alcoholic 2
bender
carouse 2
far 5b
high 9
loaded 5
orgy 1
soak 3
stinking 3
tight 8
under 6
drunkard
alcoholic 2
drunk 3
soak 3
drunk as a lord *etc.*
stinking 3
drunken
drunk 1
stinking 3
drunkenness°
dry°
barren 2
boring
cake 3
colourless 2
cure 3
dead 12
dreary 2
fair[1] 5
fine[1] 2
flat 5
heavy 7
humdrum
husky 2
matter-of-fact
monotonous
parch
pedantic 1
pedestrian 2
preserve 3
prosaic
scratchy 2

dry (*cont.*)
sober 1
stale 1
thirsty 1
wipe 1
wooden 2
wry 2
dry-as-dust
boring
colourless 2
heavy 7
matter-of-fact
monotonous
slow 9
stodgy
tedious
tiresome 1
dry-clean
clean 9
dry humour
salt 3
drying
evaporation 1
dry out
dry 5
parch
sober 4
wipe 1
dry-point
engraving 1, 2
dry run
rehearsal 1
trial 1
dry up
dry 5
parch
shrivel
wipe 1
DT's
shake 10
dual
double 3
dub
call 2
christen 2
designate 4
entitle 2
label 5
name 4
tag 4
term 8
title 6
dubiety
doubt 4
scepticism
suspicion 1
dubious
ambiguous 2
debatable
disputable
disreputable 1
distrustful
doubtful 1, 3
far-fetched
fishy 2
fly-by-night 2
implausible
improbable
incredulous
leery
left-handed 2
marginal 2
obscure 2
precarious
queer 2
questionable
rocky[2]
sceptical
shady 2
shaky 1
speculative 2
suspect 3
suspicious 1
tenuous 2
uncertain 3
unlikely 1
dubiousness
discredit 6
doubt 4
question 2
scepticism
suspicion 1
duchess
peer[1] 1
royal 3
duchy
realm 1
duck°
dip 1
dive 1
dodge 1, 3
elude 1
evade 1
flinch
immerse 1
nil
shirk
sidestep
stoop 1
zero 1
duck out (of)
escape 1
shirk
duck-walk
waddle
duct
main 5
pipe 1
pipeline 1
shaft 4
spout 3
vent 1
ductile
adaptable
flexible 1
plastic 1
pliable 1
tractable 2
ductility
elasticity 1
flexibility 1
dud°
duff
failure 3
flop 4
loser
misfire 2
non-event
washout
-duds
apparel
clothes
garments
gear 3
rag[1] 3
dude°
dandy 1
guy 1
dude up
primp
dudgeon
displeasure 2
due°
befitting
debt 1
desert[2]
eventual 2
just 3
outstanding 2
payable
prerogative
proper 3
share 1
unpaid 1
-dues°
custom 2
subscription 1
tax 1
toll[2] 1
tribute 2
-in due course
eventually
presently
run 48
soon 5
-past due
back 13
delinquent 13
late 1
overdue
duel
battle 1
bout 3
combat 1, 5
encounter 5
duel (*cont.*)
fight 7
match 2
duende
magnetism
duenna
companion 3
due to
for 13
owe 2
reason 5
thank 4
through 1
duff°
bottom 1
buttocks
dud 2
duffer°
mug 3
duffle bag
pack 1
duke
lord 2
peer[1] 1
royal 3
dukedom
realm 1
dulcet
lyric 3
mellow 2
melodious
musical
pretty 2
silver 4
smooth 7
sweet 3
tuneful
dull°
backward 2
bland 2
blunt 1, 3
boring
brute 1
colourless 2
cut 29b
dampen 2
dark 3
dead 10, 12, 13
deaden 1, 2
deadly 5
dense 3
depress 2
dim 1, 2, 3
dingy
dormant 1
dowdy
drab
dreary 2
drug 4
dry 2
dumb 2
everyday 3
fade 1
faint 1
feeble-minded
flat 5, 11, 12
glassy 2
gloomy 1
grey 2
hazy 2
heavy 7
hollow 6
humdrum
inert 3
insane 2
jaded 2
kill 3
lackadaisical 2
lacklustre
leaden 2, 3
lengthy
lethargic 1
lifeless 3
literal 3
matter-of-fact
mitigate
moderate 5
monotonous
mousy 1
muddy 2, 4
neutral 2
numb 2
obscure 7
obtuse 2
dull (*cont.*)
opaque 3
overcast
pedestrian 2
philistine 2
ponderous 2
prosaic
simple 4
sleepy 2
slow 7, 9
sombre 2, 3
stodgy
stolid
stupid 1, 3
tame 4
tasteless 2
tedious
thick 6
thick-skinned
threadbare 2
tiresome 1
tone 5
torpid
vacant 2
vague 6
watery 1
weak 5, 6
wooden 3
dullard
dolt
halfwit
dulling
narcotic 1
dullness
boredom
gloom 1
inertia
lethargy 1
opacity 3
simplicity 4
stupidity 1
tedium
torpor
uniformity 2
dull-witted
blind 2
dim 2
feeble-minded
foolish 2
obtuse 2
opaque 3
simple 4
slow 7
stupid 1
thick 6
weak 5
wooden 3
dull-wittedness
simplicity 4
stupidity 1
duly°
properly 2
truly 2
dumb°
backward 2
daft 1
dense 3
dim 2
dull 1
feeble-minded
foolish 2
halfwitted
inane
inarticulate 3
insane 2
mute 1
nonsensical
simple 4
slow 7
speechless 1
stupid 1
weak 5
dumb-bell
dolt
fool 1
dumbfound°
amaze
astonish
astound
daze 1
floor 5
jolt 3
nonplus
overpower 2
dumbfound
(*cont.*)
overwhelm 3
perplex
petrify 2
rock[2] 3
shock 1
stagger 2
stump 2
surprise 1
throw 4
dumbfounded°
goggle-eyed
petrified 2
speechless 2
thunderstruck
tongue-tied
unprepared 1
dumbfounding
prodigious 2
dumbness
folly 1
silence 2
dumbstruck
dumbfounded
petrified 2
speechless 2
dummy°
dolt
figurehead
model 1, 5
pawn[2]
silly 3
unreal 3
dump°
discard 1
dispose 3b
dive 3
drop 7
empty 8
hole 3
hovel
jilt
joint 2
shack
throw 5a
tip[2] 3, 4
tumble 2
unload
vent 4
-dumps
depression 2
gloom 2
-in the dumps
gloomy 2
melancholy 1
moody 1
mouth 6
dumping-ground
tip[2] 4
dumpy°
chubby
short 1
stocky
dun°
dead 10
mousy 1
dunce
clod 2
dolt
dummy 3
fool 1
halfwit
retard 2
sap[1] 2
silly 3
dunderhead
dolt
gawk 1
halfwit
dunderheaded
opaque 3
dunderpate
dolt
gawk 1
halfwit
dunderpated
opaque 3
wooden 3
dune
drift 5
mound 1
dung°
filth 1
muck 1
dungeon°
hole 4
keep 16
prison
tower 2
dunk
dip 1
duck 2
immerse 1
submerge 1
duo
couple 1
pair 1
team 2
duologue
dialogue 1
dupe°
beguile 1
betray 3
bluff[1] 1
butt[1]
chisel 2
defraud
facsimile
fool 3, 4
hoax 2
hoodwink
misinform
mislead
mug 3
outsmart
pawn[2]
plaything 2
prey 2, 3b
puppet 2
replica
rip 2b
sap[1] 2
scapegoat
score 7
string 10c
sucker
swindle 1
take 32b
tool 3
transcript 2
trap 6
trick 8
victim 2
victimize 2
-be duped
fall 13b
duplex
flat 18
duplicate°
copy 1, 4
double 1, 6, 7
echo 4
facsimile
identical 1
image 2
imitation 4
likeness 2
mimic 2
monkey 4
parallel 4
pattern 7
picture 2
quote 1
repeat 2, 3
replica
reproduce 1
reproduction 2
run 29b
second[1] 6
spit 2
tally 5
transcribe 1
transcript 2
twin 1, 2
duplicated
double 1
duplication
copy 1
echo 2
imitation 4
knock-off
repeat 3
repetition 1, 2
replica
reproduction 1

E

earnest (*cont.*)
diligent
eager
emphatic
enterprising
enthusiastic
fervent 2
genuine 2
grave[2] 1
heartfelt
hearty 2
hot 4
impassioned
instant 4
intense 2
intent 4
keen[1] 1
painful 3
passionate 1
pledge 2
poignant 3
real 3
serious 1
sober 2
solemn 1
solicitous 2
strenuous 2
strong 22
truthful
urgent 2
voracious 2
warm 4
wholehearted
-in earnest°
at **earnest** 4
earnestly
deep 10
hard 13, 15
intently
seriously 3
sincerely
warmly 3
earnest-money°
earnest 3
pledge 2
earnestness
devotion 1, 3
eagerness 1
enthusiasm 1
fervour
heat 2
industry 3
solemnity
earnings°
gain 8
net[2] 1
remuneration 1
return 9
salary
stipend
wage 1
yield 5
earshot
sound[1] 3
-within earshot
call 17
ear-splitting
high 7
loud 1
noisy
penetrating 2
piercing 1
raucous
sharp 7
shrill
thunderous
earth°
dirt 2
globe 1
ground 1
land 1, 2
mould[3]
soil[2]
world 1
-on earth
below 3
earthbound
terrestrial 1
earthenware
pottery
earthiness
ribaldry
earthling
mortal 6
terrestrial 2
earthly°
material 7
mortal 2
physical
temporal 1
terrestrial 1
worldly 1
earth-man, -woman
terrestrial 2
earthquake
quake 2
earth-shaking
fateful 1
special 2
stunning 2
earth-slip
slide 5
earthwork
rampart
earthy°
bawdy
gross 3
racy 2
sexual 2
suggestive 2
earwitness
witness 1
ease°
comfort 3
content[2] 2
decrease 1
diminish 3
expedite 2
facilitate
facility 1
familiarity 2
flag[2] 2
fluency
freedom 4
grace 1
help 2
lag 2
leisure 2
let[1] 9
liberalize 2
loose 12
mitigate
moderate 5
pave 2
quiet 5
readiness 2
reduce 2
relax 1
relaxation 1
relief 1
relieve 1
remedy 3
remit 2
rest[1] 3
salve 3
slack 3a
slake
smooth 10
soften 2, 4
sweeten 2
thread 4
time 8
wind[2] 3a
-at ease
collected
comfortable 1
disarm 2
home 4a
nonchalant
reassure
relaxed
easement
relief 1
ease off
decrease 1
diminish 3
phase 6
remit 2
slack 3a
weaken 3
wind[2] 3b
ease up
break 3
decrease 1
flag[2] 2
ease up (*cont.*)
lag 2
let[1] 9, 10
mitigate
reduce 2
relax 1, 3
remit 2
slow 15
soften 4
weaken 3
wind[2] 3a, 3b
easily°
cheap 6
freely 5
hand 13
handily 1
naturally 3
readily 2
slow 13
swimmingly
well[1] 10
easiness
ease 2
facility 1
easing
decrease 2
relaxation 2
relief 1
remission 2
east
orient 1
Easter card
card 3
eastern
orient 2
Eastertide
spring 9
easy°
accommodating 1
breeze 2
carefree
casual 5
comfortable 1, 3
cosy 1
easygoing
elementary 1
expansive 2
flexible 3
fluent
free 8
gentle 1, 3
glib
gradual
homely 2
lazy 2
lenient
light[2] 10
mellow 4
mug 3
natural 4
offhand 1
painless
pretty 1
pushover 2
runaway 3
secure 4
serene 2
simple 1
slow 1, 13
smooth 3
snap 12
snug
soft 2, 5, 13
sucker
tuneful
unhurried
vernacular 2
-on Easy Street
flush[2] 3
money 4
opulent 1
prosperous 1
rich 1
wealthy
easy as A, B, C
effortless
painless
easy as 1, 2, 3
effortless
painless
easy as pie *etc.*
easily 1
easy 1
effortless
easy as pie *etc.* (*cont.*)
painless
easy chair
chair 1
easy game
pushover 2
sucker
easygoing°
carefree
casual 5
easy 2, 4, 6
equable 1
genial
good-natured
indulgent
lax 1
lazy 2
lenient
light[2] 9
mellow 4
mild 1
nonchalant
offhand 1
outgoing 2
permissive
relaxed
serene 2
slack 1
soft 5
sweet 4
tractable 1
unhurried
uninhibited
easy prey
pushover 2
easy touch
mug 3
eat°
attack 5
board 7
consume 1
devour 1
dine
dispose 3d
feast 4
feed 2
finish 3
get 36d
gnaw 1
have 7
lap[1] 3a
polish 3c
prey 3a
swallow 1
take 13
touch 5
use 3
wash 5
eatable
edible
tender[1] 2
-eatables
fare 3
food
meat 1
provender 1
provision 4
ration 2
refreshment 1
sustenance 1
table 1
eat away
erode
gnaw 2
wash 5
whittle 2
eaten away
pitted
eaten up
possessed
eatery
café
eating away
erosion
eating-house
café
eating out of one's hand
thumb 5
eat into
etch 1
eat one's heart out
brood 4
grieve 1
long[2]
eats
food
meat 1
provender 1
refreshment 1
scoff[2] 2
sustenance 1
eat up
consume 1, 5
devour 3
finish 3
occupy 4
run 31
eau-de-Cologne
perfume 1
eavesdrop°
tap[2] 7
eavesdropping
nosy
ebb°
decay 1
decline 2, 6
decrease 1, 2
die 2
diminish 3
drain 6
dwindle
fade 2
fail 3
flag[2] 2
lag 2
recede 1
remit 2
retreat 5
taper 2
twilight 2
wane 1, 3
waste 2
-on the ebb
wane 4
ebb and flow
surge 1
wash 14
ebbing
remission 2
ebb tide
ebb 3
ebony
black 1
dusky 1
pitch-black
swarthy
ebriate
drunk 1
ebriety
drunkenness
ebullience
excitement 3
exuberance 1
fervour
inspiration 1
pep 1
sparkle 4
warmth 3
ebullient°
animated 1
bubbly 2
buoyant 2
effervescent 2
effusive
exuberant 1
gush 2
irrepressible
lyrical 2
pert 2
sunny 2
vivacious
eccentric°
abnormal 2
bizarre 1
character 6
crank 1
cranky 1
curious 3
deviant 1
erratic 2
extreme 5
fantastic 1
eccentric (*cont.*)
funny 2
insane 1
irregular 3
kinky 1
misfit
odd 1
oddity 2
off 4
offbeat
ordinary 4
original 6
outlandish
peculiar 1
quaint 1
queer 1
singular 1
step 8
strange 1
twist 11
unbalanced 2
unnatural 5
way-out 1
weirdo
whimsical 2
eccentricity°
abnormality 1
foible
folly 1
freak 3
kink 4
oddity 1, 3
peculiarity 1
quirk
singularity 2
trick 6
twist 10
ecchymosis
bruise 1
ecclesiastic
clergyman 1
clerical 1
divine 5
minister 1
pastor
pastoral 3
preacher
priest
priestly
spiritual 1
ecclesiastical
clerical 1
pastoral 3
priestly
sacred 3
solemn 2
spiritual 1
echelon
grade 1
rank[1] 1
stage 1
tier
echo°
blare 1
copy 5
follow 2
imitate 1
mimic 1
mirror 3
parallel 4
parrot 2
reflect 1
reflection 1
repeat 1
repercussion
repetition 2
resound
ring[2] 1, 3
roll 5, 15
sound[1] 4
echoing
repetition 2
resonant
ring[2] 3
éclat
applause
approval
display 5
fire 2
flair 2
panache
renown
virtuosity

efficacious
(*cont.*)
potent 2
strong 7
take 11
efficaciousness
efficiency 2
efficacy
effect 2
efficiency 1
force 4
efficiency°
facility 1
output 2
efficient°
capable 1
effective 1
effectual 1
efficacious
expeditious
experienced 1
neat 4
practical 1
professional 1, 2
streamlined 2, 3
strong 6
effigy
figure 4
idol 1
image 1
representation 4
statue
effloresce
flower 3
efflorescence
flower 1
rash[2] 1
effluence
escape 7
outburst
outpouring
stream 2
effluent
exhaust 6
filth 1
effluvium
exhalation 2
fume 3
smell 2
stench
efflux
escape 7
issue 1
outburst
outpouring
stream 2
effort°
application 3
attempt 2
bother 5
campaign 1
drive 8, 10
endeavour 2
enterprise 1
essay 2
exertion
industry 2
labour 1, 3
main 6
pain 4
pass 27
production 2
push 14
spurt 1
stand 14
strain[1] 7
struggle 4
task 2
trial 3
try 5
undertaking 1
work 1
effortless°
easy 1
fluent
light[2] 10
painless
runaway 3
smooth 3
effortlessly
easily 1
easy 7
hand 13
handily 1
effortlessly
(*cont.*)
readily 2
swimmingly
effortlessness
ease 2
facility 1
fluency
effrontery°
arrogance
assurance 4
brass
face 5
front 7
gall[1] 2
impertinence
impudence
nerve 2
presumption 1
effulgence
brilliance 1
glare 1
glory 3
glow 2
radiance 1
splendour 2
effulgent
bright 1
brilliant 1
light[1] 13
luminous 1
radiant 1
scintillating 1
effulgently
clear 17
effusion
gush 4
outburst
outpouring
stream 2
torrent
effusive°
demonstrative 1
ebullient
expansive 2
gush 2
gushy
lavish 2
lyrical 2
rhapsodic
talkative
windy 2
effusiveness
exuberance 2
warmth 3
e.g.
example 4
instance 2
like[1] 6
namely
say 15
egalitarian
democratic
egalitarianism
equality 3
egg
chap
hurry 2
motivate
prompt 3
seed 1
egghead
highbrow 1
intellectual 3
scholar 1
scholarly
-eggheads
intelligentsia
egg on
abet 1
encourage 1
energize
foment
incite
induce 1
motivate
prod 2
prompt 3
provoke 1
push 4
put 29
spur 4
urge 1, 2
egg-shaped
oval
egocentric
conceited
egoistic
misanthropic
subjective 2
egoism
self-esteem 1
egoistic°
misanthropic
selfish 1
subjective 2
egotism
arrogance
conceit 1
pride 2
self-esteem 1
snobbery
vanity 1
egotist
show-off
egotistical°
arrogant 1
boastful
cocky
conceited
haughty
inflated 1
pompous 1
presumptuous
proud 2
self-important
selfish 1
snobbish
vain 1
egregious
bad 1
flagrant
flaming
glaring 1
great 11
grievous 2
infamous 2
monstrous 2
monumental 4
outrageous 2
positive 9
prominent 1
unconscionable 2
wicked 2
egregiousness
infamy 2
egress
exit 1
issue 1
outlet 1
eiderdown
cover 13
spread 14
eidolon
phantom 1
vision 4
eighteen
blue 2
side 4
Einstein
genius 1
prodigy 1
eisegesis
note 3
ejaculate
exclaim
ejaculation
exclamation
interjection
eject°
banish 1
boot 3
cast 14
discharge 2
displace 2
dispossess
emit
empty 8
erupt 1
evict
exclude 3
exhale
exile 3
expel 1
freeze 4
hustle 4
eject (*cont.*)
isolate
overturn 2
purge 2
rid 2
spew
spit 1
spout 1
supplant
suspend 3
throw 6a, 7b
turf 4
turn 20c
vent 4
void 7
ejection°
discharge 9
eviction
exclusion 3
expulsion
purge 4
suspension 1
eke out
exist 2
elaborate°
amplify 3
beautify
busy 3
complicated
decorate 1
detailed 2
develop 1
dwell 2
embellish 1, 2
enlarge 2
exaggerate
expand 4
exquisite 1, 4
fancy 1
finicky 2
flamboyant 1
flowery
fussy 2
high 12
intricate 1
involved 2
laboured 2
linger 3
lush 3
luxuriant 3
maximize 2
ornament 2
ornate
overwrought 2
rich 4
showy
sophisticated 2
work 19e
elaborately
richly 1
elaboration°
embellishment 1
exaggeration
flourish 3
élan
animation 1
dash 6
display 5
eagerness 1
energy
finesse 1
fire 2
flair 2
initiative 2
inspiration 1
life 7
panache
pep 1
psyche
snap 11
sparkle 4
spice 2
spirit 3
style 4
verve
virtuosity
élan vital
life 7
psyche
elapse°
fly 4
go 11, 26a
intervene 2
lapse 6
pass 11
elapse (*cont.*)
passage 6
roll 2
slip[1] 5
elastic°
flexible 1
pliable 1
supple 1
yielding 1
elasticity°
flexibility 1
life 9
resilience
spring 7
stretch 4
elate
cheer 6
flush[1] 3
gladden
intoxicate 2
raise 13
elated°
blithe 1
ebullient
ecstatic
elevated 3
exalted 3
exultant
gleeful
happy 1
high 8
joyful 2
overjoyed
proud 1
radiant 2
rapt 2
rapturous
rejoice
rhapsodic
world 7
elating
exhilarating 2
elation
ecstasy 1, 2
flush[1] 6
gaiety 1
glee
happiness
hilarity
joy 1
rapture
transport 5
triumph 2
elbow
hustle 3
jab 2
jolt 2
nudge 1, 2
poke 1, 5
prod 1, 4
push 3
shoulder 7
thrust 1
-at one's elbow
available
elbow-grease
effort 1
labour 1
elbowing
hustle 5
elbow-joint
swivel 2
elbow-room
leeway
room 1
scope 2
space 1
elder°
sage 2
senior
-elders
ministry 2
elderly°
aged
ancient 3
decrepit 1
grey 3
old 1
elderly person
senior citizen
elder statesman
elder 3
eldritch
unearthly 2
weird
elect°
appoint 2
choose
decide 2
designate 2
élite 1, 2
favour 6
make 23
name 5
pick 1
pitch[1] 7
please 2
elected
elect 2
representative 2
election°
appointment 2
choice 1
option 2
selection 3
electioneer°
campaign 3
canvass 1
stump 3
elective
optional
voluntary 1
elector
vote 3
electric°
dynamic
electrical storm
storm 1
electricity°
power 9
electrified
excited 2
hot 9
live 5
electrify°
energize
exalt 3
excite 1
intoxicate 2
pump 4b
rouse 2
send 4
spark 2
stir 4
thrill 3
transfix 2
transport 3
electrifying
arresting
electric
exciting 1
intoxicating 2
rousing
sensational 1
shocking 1
thrilling
electrocute
punish 2
zap
electrocution
punishment 2
electronic eavesdropper
bug 5
tap[2] 3
eleemosynary
bountiful 1
charitable 1
generous 1
large 2
philanthropic
elegance°
charm 2
chic 2
class 3
courtesy
culture 1
finesse 3
flair 2
grace 1
refinement 1
sophistication 1
style 3, 4
subtlety 1
taste 4

embezzle (*cont.*)
take 3
embezzlement°
rip-off 2
stealing
theft
embezzler
thief 1
embitter
aggravate 2
exasperate 1
sour 6
embittered°
bitter 4
resent
resentful
sour 4
venomous 2
embitteredness
venom 2
emblazon
illustrate 2
emblem°
character 1
colour 2b
crest 2
device 3
figure 7
mark 2
seal 1
sign 4
stamp 7
standard 3
symbol
token 2
-emblems
regalia
emblematic°
characteristic 1
representative 1
stand 7a
symbolic
symptomatic
token 4
embodiment°
epitome 1
image 4
picture 4
quintessence
soul 3
-be the embodiment of
personify 1
embody°
cover 7
embrace 3
exemplify 1
express 2
flesh 6
include 1
incorporate
involve 1
personify 1
possess 2
represent 4
symbolize
typify
embodying
inclusive 2
embolden
encourage 1
fortify 2
embolism
stroke 5
embonpoint
fatness
obesity
emboss
impress 2
stamp 2
embouchure
mouth 2
mouthpiece 1
embrace°
adopt 2
caress 1,2
clasp 2,4
clinch 2
cling 2,3
clutch 2a
cuddle 2,3
fold 2
go 29a

embrace (*cont.*)
grasp 3
hold 2
hug 1,3
include 1
incorporate
involve 1
love 6
possess 2
prefer 1
press 5
ring[1] 4
squeeze 5,7
take 32c, 39c
uphold
embracing
inclusive 2
embrocate
apply 2
embrocation
lotion
ointment
salve 1
wash 13
embroider
amplify 3
blow[1] 8c
decorate 1
embellish 1,2
exaggerate
lay[1] 14
maximize 2
ornament 2
overstate
sweeten 2
trim 4
embroidered
fancy 1
pompous 2
embroidery
braid 2
embellishment 1
exaggeration
flourish 3
ornament 1
trim 5
embroil
entangle 1
implicate 1
embroiled
involved 3
embrue
suffuse
embryo
germ 2
seed 1
embryonic
potential 1
primary 2
rudimentary 2
seminal 2
undeveloped
emcee
announcer
host[1] 2
moderator
present[2] 8
emend
amend 2
edit 1
elaborate 4
fix 3
improve 1
mend 2
perfect 9
polish 2
rectify
reform 1
revise 1
emendation
amendment 1
correction 1
reform 3
revision
emerge°
appear 1
break 13, 20a
come 14b, 15a
dawn 4
derive 2
develop 4
emanate 1
issue 11

emerge (*cont.*)
light[1] 10
loom 1
materialize 1
originate 2
peer[2] 2
pour 4
proceed 2
result 2
spring 2
start 2
surface 3
emergence°
birth 2
conception 1
dawn 2
infancy 2
issue 1
start 11
emergency°
crisis 2
makeshift 1
necessity 4
need 4
pinch 8
predicament
rush 5
stopgap 2
urgency
urgent 1
emeritus
outgoing 1
emetic
nauseous
emigrant°
exile 2
emigrate°
migrate 1
move 2
stake[1] 2
émigré
emigrant
exile 2
refugee
eminence
celebrity 1
dignity 1
distinction 2
elevation 2
excellence
fame
glory 1
grandeur 2
height 3
hill 1
importance 2
mark 8
mountain 1
name 2
note 8
peak 1
pre-eminence 2
prestige
projection 1
prominence 1
quality 3
rank[1] 2
renown
rise 13
standing 6
status 1
superiority 2
worthy 3
eminent°
big 5
brilliant 3
celebrated
conspicuous 3
distinguished 1
elder 2
elevated 2
exalted 1
famous
glorious 1
grand 2
great 5
heroic 6
honourable 4
illustrious
important 2
legendary 3
lofty 2
noble 3
notable 1

eminent (*cont.*)
noted
outstanding 1
pre-eminent 2
prestigious
prominent 2
proud 3
public 6
renowned
salient
singular 2
splendid 2
star 3
sublime 1
successful 3
top 8
well-known 2
eminently°
large 4
pre-eminently
emissary
agent 1
ambassador
delegate 1
deputy
envoy
messenger
minister 2
representative 3
emission
discharge 11
ejection 1
eruption 1
exhalation 2
exhaust 6
radiation
secretion
emit°
discharge 4
eject 2
emanate 2
erupt 1
exhale
give 8,14
let[1] 6d, 8c
loose 10
ooze 2
radiate 2
secrete[2]
send 7
shed[2] 3
spew
spout 1
throw 6a, 7a
vent 4
void 7
-be emitted
pass 17
emitting
secretion
emollient
mild 3
ointment
salve 2
soothing 2
emolument
benefit 2
consideration 2
earnings
fee 2
fruit
gain 8
honorarium
perquisite
remuneration 1
salary
stipend
wage 1
-emoluments
benefit 2
emotion°
expression 4
feeling 4
passion 1
sentiment 1,2
soul 4
-emotions
feeling 5
psychology
sensibility 2
emotional°
demonstrative 1
effusive
excitable

emotional (*cont.*)
expressive 3
fervent 2
full 9
gut 6
impassioned
impulsive
intense 3
lyrical 2
maudlin
moving 1
passionate 1
pathetic 1
piteous
poignant 3
romantic 3
sensitive 2
sentimental 1,2
soulful
stirring
strong 22
tender[1] 7
touching
warm 2
emotionalism
sentimentality
emotionalistic
melodramatic
emotionally
badly 9
deeply 2
emotion-charged
stirring
emotionless
blank 4
blasé 2
cold 3
cool 3
dead 4
immovable 2
impassive
insensible 2
rocky[1] 3
stoical
straight 8
emotionlessness
emptiness 3
emotive
emotional 3
moving 1
pathetic 1
stirring
empathetic
sympathetic 1
empathize (with)
feel 8
identify 4
relate 4
respond 2
sympathize 1
understand 5
empathy
feeling 3
heart 5
identification 4
instinct
rapport
sympathy 1
understanding 2
vibes
emperor
crown 3
monarch 1
sovereign 1
emphasis°
accent 1
point 17
stress 1,2,4
tone 2
emphasize°
accent 4
bring 13a
dwell 2
feature 4
home 11
impress 3
insist 2
intensify
play 17a
point 17, 21b, 22
pump 4c
punctuate 2

emphasize (*cont.*)
rub 3
spotlight 3
stress 4
emphatic°
assertive
broad 3
categorical
dogmatic
dynamic
insistent
peremptory 3
positive 2
strong 16, 20
emphatically
positively
empire
domain 1
kingdom 1
monarchy 1
realm 1
reign 1
empirical°
experimental 2
practical 1
emplacement
placement 1
position 2
emplane
embark 1
get 38a
employ°
apply 3
assume 1
busy 4
draw 13a
embrace 2
engage 1,2
enlist 2
exercise 1
exert 1
expend 1
fall 9
handle 7
hire 1
job 6
line[1] 23b
manipulate 2
pass 5
retain 2
service 4
sign 10b
take 21, 35a
touch 9
turn 6
use 1,4
wield 1,2
work 9,15
employed
busy 1
engaged 2
used 2
work 9
employee°
hand 4
help 7
operative 2
worker
-employees
help 7
labour 2
rank[1] 5
staff 2
employer°
boss 1
head 2
master 1
employing
employment 2
mean[3] 3
employment°
application 1
calling
career 1
engagement 4
exercise 5
job 1
line[1] 7
occupation 1
office 4
place 5
placement 2
post[2] 1

employment (*cont.*)
profession 1
pursuit 3
racket 3
service 4
situation 3
trade 2
use 6
vocation
work 2
empower
authorize
delegate 2
enable 1
entitle 1
license 2
permit 1
trust 6
warrant 4
empowered
privileged 2
empress
crown 3
monarch 1
queen 1
sovereign 1
emptied
empty 1
exhausted 2
spent 2
emptiness°
blank 8
hunger 1
solitude 2
vacancy 1, 3
vanity 2
void 4, 5
waste 8
wild 10
empty°
bare 3
blank 1, 3
clean 10b
clear 25
dead 10
desert[1] 2
deserted
desolate 1
discharge 7
drain 4
dump 1
evacuate 1
exhaust 3, 4, 5
exhausted 2
flat 5
flush[1] 2
fond 2
free 3
futile
glassy 2
gut 5
hollow 1, 3, 5
hungry 1
ill-founded
impoverished 2
lifeless 4
meaningless 1
pale[1] 3
plausible 2
pointless
pound[1] 5
pour 2
pump 3
purposeless
shallow 1
stark 3
superficial 2
tip[2] 3
trackless
uninhabited
unload
vacant 1, 2
vague 6
vain 2
vent 4
void 2, 7
walk 2
weak 4
wild 2
wooden 2
empty-headed
dizzy 2
feeble-minded
foolish 2

empty-headed (*cont.*)
light[2] 8
senseless 3
stupid 1
empty-headedness
stupidity 1
emptying
discharge 11, 14
exhaustion 1
empty of°
at **empty 7**
empty talk
exaggeration
mouth 3
empyrean
celestial 1
firmament
heaven 2
seraphic
sky 1
sublime 1, 2
emulate
copy 5
echo 4
imitate 1
model 9
pattern 7
emulation
imitation 1
emulsion
combination 3
solution 3
wash 13
enable°
expedite 2
let[1] 2
license 2
permit 1
enact°
establish 1
make 6
transact
enactment
act 4
decree 1
execution 1
law 1
passage 9
enamel
glaze 1, 2
paint 2
enamour
captivate
enamoured
care 6b
infatuated
keen[1] 7
smitten 2
sweet 8
wedded
encamp
camp[1] 3
encampment
camp[1] 1
settlement 1
encapsulate
sum 2a
encapsulation
summary 1
encase
box[1] 2
case[2] 3
package 3
wrap 1
enceinte
expecting
pregnant 1
enchain
enslave
enchant°
bewitch
captivate
catch 11
charm 5
dazzle 1
enrapture
entrance[2]
fascinate
hypnotize
intoxicate 2

enchant (*cont.*)
possess 3
regale
transfix 2
transport 3
enchanted°
charmed 1, 3
delighted
ecstatic
infatuated
rapturous
smitten 2
taken
enchanted forest
fairyland
enchanté(e)
delighted
enchanted
enchanter
charmer
magician 1
sorcerer
enchanting°
catching 2
darling 4
delicious 2
delightful 2
enthralling
fetching
glamorous 1
interesting
lovable
magic 6
seductive
sexy 1
spellbinding
taking
winning 1
enchantment°
charm 2
fascination
glamour
magic 3
rapture
sorcery
spell[2] 1
enchantress
charmer
magician 1
siren 2
sorcerer
temptress
witch 1
enchase
scribe 3
enchiridion
companion 2
guide 8
manual
school-book
encipher
code 4
encircle°
bind 3
circle 3, 4
enclose 1
fence 3
garland 2
mantle 3
orbit 2
ring[1] 4
round 17
siege 2
surround 1
twine 2
encirclement
siege 1
encircling
about 7
around 5
round 20
enclose°
box[1] 3
cage 2
circle 4
clasp 4
cover 2
encircle
envelop 1
fence 3
fold 2
frame 8
package 3

enclose (*cont.*)
pen[2] 2
picket 4
stake[1] 4
surround 1
wall 5
wrap 1
enclosing
around 5
round 20
enclosure°
area 5
cage 1
fence 1
housing 2
pen[2] 1
pound[2]
ring[1] 2
run 46
stall[1] 2, 3
wall 1
encode
code 4
encoded
secret 2
encomiastic
complimentary 1
glowing 3
good 17
laudatory
lyrical 2
encomium
eulogy
praise 1
rave 3
tribute 1
encompass
beset
embrace 3
encircle
enclose 1
include 1
involve 1
ring[1] 4
surround 1
take 32c
encompassing
around 5
comprehensive
encore
repeat 3
encounter°
action 6
battle 1
bout 3
brave 3
brush[2] 3
bump 4
clash 2
combat 1
come 5a
discover 2
engage 5
engagement 5
experience 2, 4
face 14
fight 1, 7
find 1
game 2
happen 3
hit 7
light[2] 15
meet[1] 1, 6
meeting 1
skirmish 1
stand 12a
strike 14
struggle 5
stumble 3
taste 8
tilt 4
war 1
encourage°
abet 1
advise 1
animate 2
arouse 3
ask 6a
assure 2
back 2a
bear 10b
boost 5
cheer 5
confirm 3

encourage (*cont.*)
cultivate 3
favour 8
flush[1] 3
foment
fortify 2
forward 6
foster 1
fuel 4
incite
induce 1
inspire 2
motivate
nourish 3
nudge 1
pat[1] 2
patronize 3
prod 2
promote 1
prompt 3
provoke 1
pull 10
push 4
put 29
raise 7
reassure
rise 16
root[3]b
run 16
sanction 6
second[1] 9
spur 4
stimulate 1, 2
stir 4
strengthen 2
urge 2
encouragement°
boost 2
cheer 3
flush[1] 6
fuel 2
impetus
incentive
incitement 2
inducement
inspiration 2
lift 9
nudge 2
pat[1] 5
patronage 1
progress 3
promotion 1
recommenda-
tion 1
sanction 2
shot 12
spur 1
start 12
support 7
encouraging
favourable 1, 2
heart-warming 1
hopeful 2
positive 7, 8
promising
propitious
rosy 2
supportive
sympathetic 2
upbeat
encroach°
infringe 2
intrude
presume 3
tie 7b
trample 2
encroacher
intruder 1
encroachment
aggression 2
inroad 1
invasion 1
encrust
cake 3
encrustation
scale[2] 2
encrypt
code 4
encrypted
secret 2
encumber°
bog 2
burden 2
clog

encumber (*cont.*)
hamper[1]
handicap 2
hinder 1
interfere 2
load 4
lumber 3
oppress 1
overload 1
stick[1] 8
tax 4
trouble 1
weigh 6
encumbered
debt 2
heavy 13
encumbrance°
debt 1
handicap 1
hindrance 1
impediment
interference 2
liability 3
load 1
overload 2
shackle 2
tax 2
encyclopedic°
comprehensive
exhaustive
general 3
thorough 3
wide 2
encypher
code 4
end°
abolish
abolition
accomplish
aim 5
break 19a
butt[1]
cease 1
close 3, 22
collapse 2
come 15c
complete 5
completion 1
consummation 1
cut 15b
death 1, 2, 3
defeat 2
demolish 2
destination
destroy 2
destruction 2, 3
determination 2
determine 1
die 3
discontinue
dismissal 2
dispatch 3
dissolution 2
doom
drop 7
event 2
expiration
expire 1
exterminate
extremity 1
fate 2, 3
final 1
finish 1, 4, 5, 9
goal
halt 1, 2
heel[1] 1
idea 4
intent 1
intention
interrupt 2
issue 2
kill 1, 9
lapse 5
last[1] 6
let[1] 8d
lift 3
limit 1, 2, 4a
live 7
lot 2
mark 6
measure 8
motive 2
net[2] 3
object 3
objective 2

end (*cont.*)
outcome
overthrow 2
pack 6
pan 6
pass 10, 14b
passing 4
phase 6
pole[2] 1
polish 3a
purpose 1
put 16b
raise 9
rear[1] 1, 3
reason 3
remnant 1
resolution 4
result 1, 3
round 18
ruin 1, 3
run 30a
scrub 2
settle 3
sever 2
stamp 4
stanch
stay[1] 4
stop 1, 4, 6
stub 1
stump 1
stunt[2]
suppress 1
suppression
take 15
target
terminal 3
terminate
termination 1
tip[1] 1
ultimate 1
upshot
use 12
wane 2
wind[2] 4a
wrap 3a
-at an end
exhausted 2
over 6
-at the end
last[1] 5
-at the end of one's tether
beside 3
desperate 6
through 5
-at the end of the day
effect 5
eventually
finally 1
practically 1
really 3
run 48
soon 5
ultimately
-from one end to the other
through 7
throughout 2, 3
-in the end
eventually
finally 1
last[1] 5
really 3
run 48
soon 5
ultimately
-on end°
at **end 7**
upright 1
-the end°
at **end 8**
limit 4a
-till the end of time
always 2
ever 2
for ever 1
-to the end that
order 11

endanger°
adventure 3
chance 8
expose 2

endanger (*cont.*)
fire 6
hazard 3
jeopardize
lean[2] 4b
risk 2
threaten 2
venture 3

endangered°

endangerment
exposure 2
hazard 1

endear
attach 3

endearing°
lovable
winning 1

endeavour°
activity 2
attempt 1, 2
effort 2
essay 2, 3
exert 2
pass 27
pretend 2
seek 2
shot 3
strive 1
struggle 1
trial 3
try 1, 5

ended
complete 2
out 11
over 6

endemic
indigenous 1

ending
consummation 1
dissolution 2
end 2
expiration
final 1
finish 9
moribund 2
suffix 1
suppression
terminal 1
termination 1, 2
upshot

endless°
boundless
constant 2
continual
continuous 2
eternal 1, 2
everlasting
immeasurable
immortal 1
indefinite 4
indestructible
inexhaustible 1
infinite 1, 2
lengthy
non-stop 2
ongoing 1
perennial 2
permanent 1
perpetual 2
protracted
rambling 1
steady 2
tedious
timeless
universal 2
unlimited 2
vast

endlessly
cease 2
ever 2
for ever 2
night 3
non-stop 3
permanently

endlessness
eternity

endmost
extreme 3

end of the line
terminal 3

endorse°
abet 2
advocate 1
approve 1

endorse (*cont.*)
authenticate
authorize
back 2a
certify 1
confirm 1
favour 6
initial 2
OK 5
pass 7
praise 3
promote 3
ratify
recognize 3
recommend 2
seal 4
sign 7
subscribe 1
support 6
sustain 5
underwrite 2
uphold
vouch
witness 5

endorsed
official 1

endorsement°
approval
backing 1
clearance 2
indemnity 2
OK 6
passage 9
pat[1] 5
praise 1
recommendation 2
reference 3
seal 2
testimonial

endow
award 1
bless 2
clothe 2
enrich 1
fund 3
supply 1
-be endowed with
possess 1, 2

endowment°
award 3
bounty 2
foundation 3
fund 2
grant 3
present[2] 2
scholarship 2
talent 1
-endowments°
at **endowment 3**
largesse

end-piece
supplement 1

end result
outcome
resolution 4
result 1
upshot

endue
clothe 2

end up
come 13c
end 9
finish 6
pan 6
prove 3
reach 2
rest[1] 5
turn 20b
wind[2] 4a, 4b

endurable
bearable
light[2] 10
supportable 1
tolerable 1

endurance°
bearing 2
existence 2
follow-through
fortitude
gut 3b
patience 2
permanence

endurance (*cont.*)
perseverance
stamina
strength 6
tolerance 3
vigour
vitality 2

endure°
abide 1
accept 4
bear 2, 4
brook[2]
continue 2
digest 2
exist 1
experience 4
feel 5
go 15, 32a, 36a
hang 7c
hold 20a, 22c
labour 7
last[2] 1, 2
linger 1
live 7
lump[2]
meet[1] 6
persevere
persist 2
put 30
receive 4
remain 3
resist 1
see 10
serve 6
soldier 4
stand 3, 10b, 12b
stick[1] 6, 10
stomach 3
suffer 2
support 3
survive 1
sustain 3
take 6
tolerate 2
undergo
wear 4
weather 3
withstand

enduring°
abiding
bearing 2
classic 2
durable
eternal 3
have 5
indelible
inextinguishable
invariable 3
irrevocable
lasting
monumental 1
old 4
perennial 1
permanent 1
perpetual 1
stable 2
steadfast
sturdy 2

enemy°
adversary 1
antagonist
opponent
opposition 2

energetic°
active 1, 3
alive 3
ambitious 2
animated 1
arduous 2
brisk 2, 4
busy 2
dashing 1
dynamic
eager
emphatic
enterprising
enthusiastic
excited 2
exuberant 1
forceful 1
fresh 5
hard 7
hearty 3
industrious

energetic (*cont.*)
live 2
lively 1, 2
lusty 1
make 43
nifty 2
nimble 1
passionate 1
powerful 1
quick 3
racy 1
rousing
smart 5
spanking 3
spirited
sprightly
stiff 4
strenuous 2
strong 5
tireless
urgent 2
vigorous
violent 3
vital 3
vivacious
wholehearted

energetically
hard 13
hotly
madly 3
vengeance 2b
vigorously
warmly 4, 5

energize°
activate
animate 2
enliven 1
excite 1
fire 8b
fortify 2
inspire 1
kindle
liven 2
pep 2
pump 4b
quicken 3
refresh 1
spark 2
stir 4
strengthen 2
turn 18a
vitalize
wind[2] 4c

energized
eager
electric
excited 2

energizer
stimulant 2

energizing
animation 2
exciting 1
invigorating
rousing

energy°
action 1
activity 1
agency
ambition 2
animation 1
bounce 2
dash 6
drive 8
dynamism
eagerness 1
effort 1
electricity
enterprise 2
exuberance 1
fire 2
force 1
gumption 2
impetus
industry 2, 3
initiative 2
inspiration 1
intensity
life 7
lust 2
main 6
might 1
momentum
panache
pep 1
power 4, 8, 9

energy (*cont.*)
push 14
sinew 2
snap 11
soul 4
sparkle 4
spirit 2
stamina
strength 5
thrust 5
verve
vigour
violence 1
vitality 1, 2

enervate°
cripple 2
demoralize 1
depress 2
exhaust 2
fatigue 2
incapacitate
sap[2]
tire 1
waste 3
weaken 1
wear 6
weary 5

enervated
decrepit 1
exhausted 1
fatigued
feeble 1
helpless 3
impotent 1
jaded 1
lethargic 2
limp[2] 2
listless
low[1] 4
run-down 1
waste 2
weak 2

enervating
exhausting 1
killing 3
toilsome

enervation
decrepitude 1
exhaustion 2
fatigue 1
impotence 1
prostration 4

en face
face 8
opposite 1

enfeeble
destroy 4
enervate
incapacitate
waste 2, 3
weaken 1

enfeebled
broken 3
decrepit 1
delicate 3
feeble 1
helpless 3
infirm 1
pale[1] 3
waste 2

enfeeblement
impairment

enfold
embrace 1
envelop 1
fold 2
hold 2
lap[2] 3
muffle 1
roll 9
squeeze 5
wrap 1

enforce°
dispense 2
exact 3
force 7
police 3

enforcement
imposition 1

enforcer
bruiser

enfranchise
deliver 3
emancipate

enthusiastic (*cont.*)
animated 1
anxious 2
ardent
burning 2
crazy 4
devoted
eager
earnest 2
ebullient
effervescent 2
effusive
emotional 1
enterprising
excited 2
exuberant 1
fanatical
favourable 2
fervent 2
fire 5
get 39c
glowing 3
good 17
great 9
gushy
hearty 3
hot 3, 4
impassioned
intense 2
intent 5
keen[1] 1
lyrical 2
mad 6
passionate 1
pert 2
positive 7
pull 10
ready 2
rhapsodic
ripe 3b
rousing
sanguine
strenuous 2
strong 5
voracious 2
warm 4, 8
wholehearted
wild 9
willing

enthusiastically
favourably 1
happily 2
highly 1, 3
hotly
mad 5
vengeance 2b
warmly 3, 4
willingly

enthusiastic reception
rave 3

entice°
attract
catch 11
chat 3
decoy 2
induce 1
lead 9b
lure 1
pull 5
rope 4
seduce 1
solicit 2
tempt 1

enticement°
attraction 2
come-on
decoy 1
draw 16
incentive
incitement 2
inducement
invitation 2
motive 1
temptation 2

enticing
attractive
catching 2
exciting 2
flirtatious
inviting
lovely 1
seductive
temptation 1

enticing (*cont.*)
tempting 1
voluptuous 2

entire°
clear 14
complete 1, 3
dead 14
full 3, 12
gross 2
intact
one 2
overall
perfect 1
radical 2
round 5
self-contained 3
solid 10
total 2
unabridged 1
undivided 1, 2
whole 1
wholehearted

entirely°
absolutely 2
altogether
blast 4
clean 7
clear 19
cold 11
completely 1, 3
dead 18, 19
deeply 2
directly 4
downright 2
full 13, 17
head 8
hook 4
merely 2
out 7
outright 4
perfectly 1
quite 1, 4
root[1] 3
severely 1
simply 1, 2
stark 1
thoroughly 1
through 7
throughout 3
totally
utterly
vastly
very 1, 2
well[1] 11
wholly 1

entirety°
amount 3
ensemble 3
everything
integrity 2
totality
whole 4

-in its entirety
full 17

entitle°
authorize
call 2
designate 4
enable 1
license 2
name 4
tag 4
term 8
title 6
warrant 4

entitled
claim 3
deserve
earn 1
merit 3
privileged 1
rate[1] 7
welcome 3

entitlement
licence 1
title 5
warrant 1, 2

entitling
denomination 3

entity°
creature 1
existence 3
life 1
object 1

entity (*cont.*)
thing 5
unit

entombment
burial
funeral

entourage
company 2
escort 1
parade 1
retinue
suite 3
train 2

entr'acte
interlude
interval 1
rest[1] 2

entrails
gut 1
inside 2

entrain
embark 1
get 38a

entrance°
admittance
bewitch
captivate
dazzle 1
delight 1
enchant 2
enrapture
entry 1, 2, 3
fascinate
gate 1
grip 7
hypnotize
initiation 2
intoxicate 2
mouth 2
penetration 1
ravish 1
regale
threshold 1
transport 3

entranced
rapt 1
taken

entrance-hall
lobby 1

entrancement
fascination

entrancing
catching 2
enchanting
enthralling
glamorous 1
heavenly 2
intoxicating 2
inviting
magic 6
magnetic
piercing 2
provocative 1
ravishing
scintillating 2
seductive
taking

entrant
candidate
contestant
entry 5

-entrants
field 3

entrap
ambush 2
bag 6
catch 2
decoy 2
entangle 1
frame 9
hook 6
implicate 1
mesh 3
net[1] 2
seduce 1
snare 2
trap 4

entreat
appeal 1
ask 3
beg 1
beseech
bid 2
call 7a, 10a

entreat (*cont.*)
hit 8
petition 2
plead 2
pray 1
press 6
push 4
request 1
solicit 1
sue 2
urge 2

entreating
supplicant 1
supplication 2

entreaty
appeal 3
desire 4
petition 1
plea 1
prayer 1
request 2
suit 5
supplication 1

entrée
admission 1
admittance
entrance[1] 1
entry 1
mouth 2
recourse 1
road 1

entrench
establish 2
root[1] 6

entrenched°
rooted

entrepreneur
producer 2

entrepreneurial
self-made

entropy
chaos

entrust°
charge 9
commit 1
delegate 3
deposit 2
enable 1
give 1, 16
leave[1] 7
trust 6

entry°
admission 1
admittance
approach 5
entrance[1] 1, 2, 3
hall 1
lobby 1
mouth 2
passage 11
penetration 1
submission 2

entry-way
entrance[1] 2
entry 2
hall 1
lobby 1
mouth 2

entwine°
lock[1] 4
loop 2
splice 1
twine 2
twist 1
weave 1

enumerate°
count 1
detail 5
figure 8
itemize
list[1] 2
number 4
poll 3
rattle 5
recapitulate
reckon 2
record 1
recount 2
reel 2
specify
tally 2

enumeration
account 2
litany 2

enumeration (*cont.*)
reckoning 1
rehearsal 2
specification 2
tally 3

enunciate°
deliver 4
go 14
mouth 7
proclaim 1
profess 1
pronounce 1
set 18c
sound[1] 7
speak 4
vent 3
voice 4

enunciated
oral
verbal 1

enunciation
delivery 4
diction 2
expression 1
oratory
pronunciation
speech 1

enuretic
incontinent 3

envelop°
clasp 4
cover 2
enclose 1
fold 2
lap[2] 3
mantle 3
muffle 1
ring[1] 4
roll 9
shroud 1
smother 3
surround 1
swathe
wrap 1

envelope
case[2] 2
wrapper 2

enveloping
around 5

envenom
poison 3

envenomed
embittered
venomous 2

enviable°

envious°
jaundiced 2
jealous 1
resent
resentful

enviousness
envy 1

environment°
atmosphere 2
condition 4
context
element 2
habitat
medium 4
milieu
nature 2
setting
surround 2

environmental
green 3

environmentalist°
green 5

environs
environment
milieu
neighbourhood 1
outskirts
precinct 1
setting
surround 2
vicinity

envisage°
conceive 3
day-dream 2
design 1
envision

envisage (*cont.*)
expect 1
fancy 9
fantasize
foresee
form 8
imagine 1
picture 6
plan 4
see 3

envisaging
vision 3

envision°
see **envisage**

envoy°
agent 1
ambassador
delegate 1
deputy
forerunner 1
messenger
minister 2
representative 3

envy°
begrudge 1
grudge 2
resentment

enwrap
coil 1
envelop 1
fold 2
roll 9
swathe
wrap 1

eon
see **aeon**

EP
record 7

ephemeral
brief 1
fleeting
fly-by-night 1
fugitive 3
immaterial 2
meteoric 1
momentary
mortal 1
passing 1
short-lived
temporary
transient

epic
heroic 5
legend 1
legendary 1
myth 1
poetic 1
romance 3
saga
story 1

epicedium
keen[2] 2
lament 2

epicene
neuter 1

epicure°
epicurean 3
gourmet
sensualist
sybarite

epicurean°
epicure
luscious
luxurious 1
self-indulgent
sensualist
sensuous
sybarite

epidemic°
global
pestilence 1
plague 1
rampant 2
rash[2] 2
universal 1

epidermis
skin 1

epigram°
maxim
moral 3
proverb
quip 1
saw

evil-doing
outrage 1
vice 1
evil eye
jinx 1
evil intentions
design 8
evil-minded°
base[2] 4
evil 1
perverted
evil one
devil 1
evil-smelling
foul 3
rancid
smelly
evil spirit
demon 1
devil 1
imp
evince
argue 4
demonstrate 1
display 1
evidence 4
exhibit
express 2
indicate 2
manifest 2
prove 4
typify
eviscerate
gut 4
evocative
impressive
redolent 2
reminiscent
representative 1
stirring
suggestive 1
evoke°
call 9
draw 14b
elicit
extract 3
occasion 5
partake 2b
produce 2
prompt 5
raise 10
evolution°
development 2
growth 1
mutation 1
progress 3
transition 1
evolve
become 2
conceive 2
develop 1, 4
emerge 1
formulate 3
grow 2
light[1] 10
originate 1, 2
progress 6
result 2
shape 10a
spring 3
turn 20b
unfold 2
work 19d
evolvement
development 2
evolution
growth 1
evolving
evolution
mutation 1
ongoing 2
evzone
guard 3
ewer
jar[1]
jug
ex-
former 1
late 3
old 6
outgoing 1
prior 1

exacerbate
aggravate 1
compound 3
fuel 4
inflame 2
magnify 1
worsen 1
exact°
accurate 1
claim 3
command 4
correct 8
dead 17
deadly 6
definite 1
definitive 3
demand 2
detailed 1
determined 2
distinct 1
elaborate 1
even 8
explicit 1
express 5
extort
faithful 2
flat 9
force 7, 9
formal 3
impose 3
literal 1
mathematical
measured 4
meticulous
narrow 3
nice 3
particular 3
pedantic 2
perfect 5
photographic 1
precise 1, 2, 4
prescribe
proper 2
refined 3
religious 2
right 2
rigid 3
round 5
same 1
specific 1
square 3
squeeze 2
strict 1
take 12
tax 3
true 3
verbatim 1
very 3
exacting°
choosy
conscientious 2
demanding 1
exact 2
formal 1
fussy 1
hard 4
meticulous
narrow 3
nice 3
overcritical
painful 3
particular 3
perfectionist 2
precise 3
refined 2
rigid 3
scrupulous 1
selective
severe 1
squeamish 1
strait 1
strict 1
tough 4
exactingly
precisely 2
exaction
toll[2] 2
tribute 2
exactitude
precision 1
resolution 5
exactly°
completely 1
dead 20
directly 4

exactly *(cont.)*
dot 2
due 5
expressly 1
flat 16
full 14
indeed 1
just 5
letter 4
literally 1
nearly 2
outright 4
particular 6
pat[2] 1
perfectly 3
plumb 4
precisely 1, 2
purpose 4b
right 14
sharp 10
slap 6
true 5
verbatim 2
world 6
exactness
accuracy
formality 2
precision 1
resolution 5
rigour 2
exact payment
revenge 2
exaggerate°
amplify 2
blow[1] 8c
camp[2] 2
dramatize
embellish 2
inflate 3
lay[1] 14
magnify 1
make 34a
maximize 2
overdo 1
overreact
overstate
pile[1] 7
talk 8
exaggerated
camp[2] 1
dramatic 3
exalted 2
extravagant 4
heroic 4
immoderate
inflated 1
lavish 3
melodramatic
outrageous 1
pretentious 1
sensational 2
tall 3
theatrical 2
exaggerating
satirical
exaggeration°
burlesque 1
embellishment 2
romance 5
satire 1
tale 2
exalt°
adore 2
celebrate 3
dignify
enhance
exaggerate
extol
glorify 1
hallow 2
honour 6
idealize
idolize
immortalize
laud
lift 2
pedestal 2
praise 4
promote 2
sanctify 1
worship 1
exaltation
ecstasy 2
elevation 4
exaggeration

exaltation *(cont.)*
flight[1] 4
glory 1, 2
joy 1
praise 2
promotion 2
rapture
trance
transport 5
tribute 1
worship 2
exalted°
dignified
divine 2
elevated 2
eminent 1
glorified 1
grand 2
great 7
high 5
honourable 4
imperial 2
lofty 2, 3
magnificent
majestic 1
rarefied 2
regal 1
sublime 1
examination°
analysis 1
canvass 4
check 15
consideration 3
discussion
experiment 1
exploration
eye 7
inquiry 1
interpretation 2
interrogation
investigation
observance 3
observation 1
perusal
probe 3
profile 3
quiz 1
reconnaissance
research 1
review 5
scan 3
scrutiny
search 4
study 4
survey 3
test 1
trial 1, 2
view 4
examine°
analyse 2
canvass 2
check 4, 10b
consider 1
contemplate 2
discuss
experiment 3
explore 2
eye 9
frisk 2
go 30b, 34a
hunt 2
inquire 1
inspect
interview 3
investigate
look 8, 10
monitor 3
mull
observe 2
peer[2] 1
peruse
pore[1]
probe 1, 2
prove 2
pry 1
pump 2
question 9
quiz 2
ransack 1
reconnoitre
reflect 3
report 6
research 2
review 1
rummage 1

examine *(cont.)*
scan 2
scout 1
screen 8
scrutinize
search 1
sift 2
sound[3] 1
speak 10
study 3
survey 1
taste 7
test 2
traverse 4
treat 2
try 2
vet
view 7
watch 3
weigh 2
example°
case[1] 1, 4
copy 2
epitome 1
footstep 2
gauge 3
guide 6
ideal 1
illustration 1
image 4
instance 1
lead 13
lesson 3
manifestation
model 2
monument 2
pattern 5
precedent
prototype 2
sample 1
specimen
standard 1
stroke 7
warning 1
–for example°
at **example 4**
instance 2
like[1] 6
namely
say 15
exasperate°
aggravate 2
anger 2
annoy 1
displease
frustrate 2
gall[2] 4
get 17
harass
inflame 1
infuriate
irk
irritate
madden 2
pester
plague 3
provoke 3
put 23b
rankle
sour 6
tire 2
trouble 2
wall 3
wear 7
exasperated
angry 1
discontented
disgruntled
huff 1
indignant
mad 4
tired 2
umbrage
exasperating
irksome
nightmarish
painful 2
provocative 2
tiresome 2
trying
weary 2
wicked 5
exasperation
annoyance 1
displeasure 2

exasperation *(cont.)*
gall[2] 2
indignation
rage 1
umbrage
excavate°
burrow 2
deepen 1
dig 1
hollow 8
mine 3
scoop 5
sink 7
tunnel 2
undercut 1
unearth
wash 5
excavation°
burrow 1
hole 1
hollow 7
mine 1
pit[1] 1
quarry[2] 1
exceed°
cap 4
excel
far 7
lead 4
outdo
outstrip
overstep
pass 6
run 33c
shade 8
strain[1] 1
surpass
top 3
transcend
transgress 2
exceeding°
above 4
over 2
exceedingly°
awfully
degree 4b
devil 5
eminently
extreme 9
extremely
fault 7
fearfully 2
fiercely
full 15
madly 4
overly
really 4
surpassingly
terribly
vastly
very 1
excel°
better[1] 11
cap 4
exceed 1
lead 4
outdo
outstrip
overshadow 1
shine 3
surpass
top 3
transcend
excellence°
class 3
dignity 2
distinction 2
glory 3
grace 4
merit 1
nobility 1
perfection 1
pre-eminence 2
quality 3
superiority 2
supremacy 1
virtuosity
excellent°
admirable
aesthetic 1
beautiful 2
best 1
capital 6
choice 4

excellent *(cont.)*
classic 2
desirable 3
divine 2,3
estimable
exceptional 2
exemplary 2
expert 2
exquisite 1,5
fine[1] 1,5,11
first-rate
gifted
glorious 1,3,4
golden 5
good 2
gorgeous 2
grand 5
great 6,12
heavenly 2
ideal 4
imperial 2
laudable
magnificent
marvellous
masterful 1
mean[2] 6
meritorious
neat 5
nifty 3
optimum 2
outstanding 1
par 3
peerless
perfect 2,5
polished 1
pre-eminent 2
prime 2
prize[1] 5
professional 2
rare[1] 2
ripping
select 2
shine 3
splendid 3
sterling 2
superb
superior 2
superlative
supreme 4
talented
terrific 2
top 8
transcendent
unbeatable
virtuoso 2
world 8

excellently
beautifully 2
famously
well[1] 2

except°
bar 10
barring
exclude 2
exempt 1
leave[1] 10
omit 1
waive 2

excepted
exempt 2

except for°
at **except 1**
apart 4
bar 10
barring
besides 2
exclusive 4
independent 8
short 10

excepting
apart 4
bar 10
barring
besides 2
except 1
exclusive 4
short 10

exception°
disapproval
exclusion 2
exemption
liberty 3
nonconformist 1
objection
omission 1

exception *(cont.)*
phenomenon 2
protest 1
provision 2
reservation 2

-without exception
always 1
entirely 1
universally

-with the exception of
except 1

exceptionable°
inadmissible

exceptional°
abnormal 1
brilliant 2
choice 4
conspicuous 3
defective 2
different 2
eccentric 1
exceeding
excellent
extraordinary 1
extreme 1
feeble-minded
fine[1] 1
first-rate
freak 5
golden 6
great 6
irregular 3
isolated 1
mean[2] 6
neat 5
noteworthy
noticeable 2
odd 1
optimum 2
ordinary 4
outlandish
out-of-the-way 2
outstanding 1
par 3
particular 2
peculiar 1
phenomenal
prime 2
prodigious 2
psychotic 1
queer 1
rare[1] 1
remarkable 1
select 2
signal 3
singular 2
special 1
splendid 1,3
sterling 2
strange 1
striking
superb
superior 2
superlative
supernatural
terrific 2
unparalleled
unusual
virtuoso 2
world 8

exceptionally
eminently
especially 1
exceedingly
extra 6
extreme 9
extremely
highly 2
infrequently
particularly 1,2
really 4
very 1

except that°
at **except 2**

excerpt°
clip[2] 5
extract 6
passage 2
quotation 1
quote 1
selection 4

excess°
abundance
balance 7
dissipation 1
embarrassment 3
exaggeration
excessive 1
extra 2
extravagance 1
exuberance 2
flood 3
flow 6
give 18
glut 1
great 3
leftover 1,2
needless 1
prodigality 1
profit 1
profligacy 2
remainder 2
residue
rest[2] 1
satiety
superfluity
superfluous
supplementary 2
surfeit
surplus 1,2

-in excess
above 4
galore
over 2
redundant 1

excessive°
breakneck
exceeding
excess 3
exorbitant
extravagant 1
extreme 2,6
fanatical
great 3
gushy
heavy 2
high 2
immoderate
inordinate 1
intense 1
laboured 2
lavish 3
needless 1
outrageous 1
pricey
prodigal 1
profligate 2
profuse 3
prohibitive 2
redundant 1
steep[1] 2
stiff 6
superfluous
surpassing
swingeing
towering 2
ultra-
unconscionable 2
unreasonable 2
unwarranted

excessively
awfully
devil 5
exceedingly
fault 7
madly 4
overly
sky 2
unduly 1
water 3

excessiveness
extravagance 2
prodigality 1

exchange°
alternate 1
alternation
cash 2
change 1,5
dealings
discussion
give 2
intercourse 1
market 1
mix 4d,6
passage 10
reciprocate

exchange *(cont.)*
redeem 3
return 4
reverse 2
rotate 2
sale 1
sell 1
substitute 1
substitution 1
supplant
switch 2,4
trade 1,3,6
transpose
turn 43
turn-about
volley 3

-in exchange for
for 3

exchangeable
synonymous

exchange blows
fight 1
spar[2] 1

exchanged
reciprocal

exchanging
substitution 1

exchequer
purse 2
treasury

excise
custom 2
cut 16a,16b
duty 3
eliminate 3
tariff 1
tax 1
toll[2] 1
tribute 2

excision
cut 22
omission 1

excitable°
emotional 2
fiery 3
frantic
irritable
nervous 1
quick 5
quick-tempered
restless
sensitive 2
temperamental 1

excitation
excitement 1

excite°
agitate 1
animate 1,2
arouse 2
awake 2
carry 9
delight 1
electrify 2
energize
exalt 3
ferment 2
fire 8b
flurry 2
flush[1] 3
foment
fuel 4
get 16
heat 4
incite
inflame 1
inspire 1
interest 7
intoxicate 2
kindle
madden 1
motivate
move 5
pump 4b
quicken 3
rouse 2
spark 2
spur 4
stimulate 1
stir 4
thrill 3
touch 6
turn 18c
whet 2
whip 7a

excite *(cont.)*
wind[2] 4c
work 20a

excited°
agitated
animated 1
bubbly 2
burning 2
crazy 4
delirious 2
distraught
drunk 2
eager
ebullient
ecstatic
effervescent 2
elated
emotional 1
exalted 3
fervent 1
feverish
fiery 3
fire 5
frantic
heated
hectic
high 8
hot 3,4
tumultuous
uproarious 1
warm 2,8
wild 6

excitedly
mad 5
madly 3

excitedness
warmth 3

excitement°
agitation 2
alarm 2
animation 1
buzz 4
ecstasy 2
electricity
enthusiasm 1
exuberance 1
flurry 1
flush[1] 6
frenzy 1
furore 1
fuss 1
glow 3
heat 2
incitement 2
pell-mell 3
rampage 1
romance 4
rush 3
sensation 2
sparkle 4
spice 2
splash 4
stew 2
stir 6
suspense 2
sweat 7
thrill 1
tumult
twitter 4

excite the curiosity of
intrigue 1

exciting°
delightful 1,2
electric
eventful
impressive
incitement 1
interesting
intoxicating 2
juicy 2
moving 1
provocative 1
ripping
scintillating 2
sensational 1
sexy 1
steamy 3
stimulating
stirring
thrilling
wild 6

exclaim°

exclamation°
interjection

exclude°
bar 9
block 4b
disqualify
drop 9
eliminate 1
except 3
exile 3
expel 2
filter 2
forbid
freeze 4
isolate
leave[1] 10
lock[1] 8
omit 1
ostracize
outlaw 2
preclude
rule 8
scratch 3
segregate
shoulder 2
shut 5a,5b
suspend 3

excluded
isolated 2
outside 9
unwelcome 2

excluding
apart 4
bar 10
barring
besides 2
except 1
exclusive 4
independent 8
omission 1
short 10

exclusion°
exception 1
exemption
immunity 1
omission 1
segregation
suspension 1

exclusive°
élite 2
high-class 2
inside 4
native 3
one-sided 3
only 1
personal 2
private 2
rarefied 3
scoop 2
select 3
sole
special 4
story 4
undivided 2

exclusively
alone 4
custom 4
entirely 2
only 2
specially
wholly 2

exclusive of°
at **exclusive 4**
barring
besides 2
except 1
independent 8
short 10

excogitate
ponder

excogitative
meditative

excommunicate
banish 1
curse 4
ostracize
punish 2

excommunication
punishment 2

excoriate
berate
pan 5
pare 1
skin 3
strip[2] 1

excoriating
scorching 2
excorticate
shell 3
excrement
dirt 1
dung
filth 1
muck 1
soil[1] 3
excrescence
growth 4
hump 1
lump[1] 2
nub 1
pimple
prominence 3
protrusion
swelling
tumour
excrescent
prominent 3
protuberant
excreta
filth 1
secretion
excrete
defecate
discharge 4
pass 12
secrete[2]
void 7
excretion
discharge 11
secretion
excruciate
torment 1
excruciating°
acute 3
agonizing
deadly 5
exquisite 4
heart-rending
painful 1
piercing 4
poignant 1
pungent 3
stiff 2
swingeing
exculpate
excuse 1
forgive 2
justify
pardon 2
purge 3
purify 2
vindicate 1
exculpation
excuse 5
forgiveness 1
pardon 1
remission 1
excursion°
drive 7
expedition 1
flight[1] 1
journey 1
outing
pilgrimage
ride 4
run 36
spin 7
tour 1
travel 2, 3
trip 3
excursus
digression 1
excursion 2
excusable
permissible
venial
excusal
pardon 1
excusatory
mitigating
excuse°
alibi 1, 2
allowance 5
call 15
clear 21
defecate
defence 3
evasion 2

excuse (*cont.*)
except 3
exempt 1
explain 2
explanation 2
forgive 1
ground 3
immunity 1
justify
let[1] 6a
out 15
overlook 2
pardon 1, 2
plea 3
pretence 3
pretext 1
purify 2
rationalize 1
reason 4
refuge 2
remission 1
story 3
subject 3
subterfuge
urinate
vindicate 1
warrant 4
whitewash
-excuses
allowance 5
excused
exempt 2
excuse-me-for-living
passive 2
execrable
abhorrent
abominable 1
atrocious 1
awful 2
bad 1
beastly 2
damnable
deplorable 2
diabolic 2
hateful 1
hideous 2
infamous 2
infernal 2
loathsome
obnoxious
obscene 2
outrageous 2
regrettable
repugnant
repulsive
sordid 1
ugly 2
vicious 1
vile 1
wicked 2
execrate
abhor
blaspheme 1
curse 4
damn 3
detest
dislike 1
hate 1
loathe
swear 2
thunder 3
use 15
vituperate
execration
abuse 8
curse 1
dislike 2
horror 1
phobia
revulsion
execute°
accomplish
achieve 1
administer 2
bump 5
carry 12
discharge 5
dispatch 3, 4
dispense 2
effect 7
effectuate
exercise 1
fill 8
fulfil 1

execute (*cont.*)
hang 2
implement 2
kill 1
massacre 2
negotiate 2
obey 2
perfect 8
perform 1
perpetrate
punish 2
put 27a
remove 4
render 1
ride 5b
rub 6
shoot 3
slaughter 3
work 16
wreak
executed
complete 2
execution°
course 3
delivery 4
discharge 12
dispatch 7
exercise 5
fulfilment
killing 1
massacre 1
performance 1
punishment 2
removal 2
rendition 1
slaughter 2
touch 18
executioner
butcher 1
hangman
murderer
executive°
director 1
management 2
manager
responsible 3
supervisory
-executives
management 2
exegesis
explanation 1
exposition 2
gloss[2] 1
interpretation 2
note 3
paper 4
exegetic(al)
explanatory
exemplar
classic 3
epitome 1
example 2
guide 6
hero 1
ideal 1
illustration 1
instance 1
lead 13
lesson 3
model 2, 3
monument 2
nonpareil
optimum 1
paragon
pattern 1
precedent
prototype 1
quintessence
specimen
standard 1
type 3
yardstick
exemplary°
classic 2
classical 1
complete 4
faultless
good 2
meritorious
model 11
praiseworthy
proverbial 2
splendid 2
worthwhile 2

exemplification
instance 1
exemplify°
embody 2
exhibit
illustrate 1
personify 1
quote 1
reflect 2
represent 4
stand 7a
symbolize
typify
exempli gratia
example 4
namely
exempt°
excuse 2
immune
privileged 2
quit 4
exempt from°
at **exempt 1**
free 11
quit 4
exemption°
freedom 3
immunity 1
indemnity 2
liberty 3
privilege
remission 1
exequies
funeral
exercise°
action 3
coach 3
discipline 1, 6
drill 2, 4
enjoyment 2
exert 1
flex 3
leg 10
lesson 1
manoeuvre 2
operation 4
practice 2, 3
practise 1
prosecute 3
pursue 2
put 23d
rehearsal 1
rehearse 1
theme 2
train 4, 5
use 1
wield 2
work 19a
wreak
exercise book
school-book
text 4
exercise caution
beware
step 12
exercise control
control 1
dominate 1
govern 1
exert°
exercise 1
press 1
put 23d
string 5
trouble 4
wield 2
wreak
exert influence
string 5
exert pressure
press 1
exertion°
action 3
effort 1
grind 7
industry 2
labour 1
pain 4
strain[1] 7
struggle 4
work 1
exert oneself°
at **exert 2**
endeavour 1

exert oneself (*cont.*)
strain[1] 4
strive 1
struggle 1
work 7
exfoliate
flake 2
exhalation°
fume 3
reek 4
sigh 3
vapour 1
exhale°
blow[1] 1
breathe 3
emanate 2
emit
expire 3
give 14
exhaling
exhalation 1
exhaust°
bolt 7
bore[2] 2
break 6
clean 10a
consume 2
destroy 4
dissipate 3
drain 5
empty 8
enervate
evacuate 1
exhalation 2
expend 2
fag 1
fatigue 2
finish 3
fume 3
incapacitate
kill 4
overdo 2
prostrate 2
run 31, 34b
satiate 1
tax 4
tire 1
use 5
waste 3
weaken 1
wear 6
weary 5
exhausted°
beat 13
breathless 1
dead 9
drawn
empty 1
fatigued
feeble 1
give 15d
haggard
helpless 3
impoverished 2
jaded 1
leg 7
lethargic 2
limp[2] 2
lost 2
out 11
poor 3
prostrate 5
ragged 3
run 30a, 30b
run-down 1
sleepy 1
spent 1, 2
tired 1
washed out 2
weak 2
weary 1
worn 3
exhausting°
arduous 1
boring
hard 2
killing 3
laborious 1
murderous 2
oppressive 1
punishing
stiff 9
strenuous 1
tedious

exhausting (*cont.*)
toilsome
exhaustion°
drain 2
fatigue 1
lethargy 2
prostration 4
exhaustive°
comprehensive
definitive 2
detailed 1
elaborate 1
encyclopedic
full 2
intensive
intimate[1] 2
laborious 2
radical 2
sweeping 1
thorough 2, 3
unabridged 2
exhaustively
detail 4
entirely 1
length 4c
thoroughly 2
exhaust one's resources
bolt 7
exhibit°
air 7
bear 5
demonstrate 1
develop 3
display 1, 4
evidence 4
exemplify 2
exhibition
expose 1
exposition 1
express 2
fair[2]
flaunt
float 6
hold 22d
indicate 3
manifest 2
mount 5
open 23
performance 2
persevere
point 21a
present[2] 5
produce 4
reflect 2
register 8
shake 4
show 1, 6
spectacle 1
sport 5
stage 4
trot 2
wear 2
whip 6
exhibition°
demonstration 1
display 4
entertainment 2
exposition 1
fair[2]
flash 2
manifestation
ostentation
parade 2
performance 2, 5
scene 3
scholarship 2
show 13
spectacle 1
exhibitionism
ostentation
exhibitionist
daredevil 1
pompous 1
poseur
show-off
trendy 2
exhilarate
enliven 1
gladden
intoxicate 2
pep 2
raise 13

expensive (*cont.*)
rich 4
steep[1] 2
stiff 6
sumptuous
tight 9
expensively
dearly 3
experience°
accept 4
acquaintance 1
adventure 1
background 1
bear 2
efficiency 1
encounter 2
episode 1
event 1
exposure 3
face 14
fact 2
familiarity 1
feel 1, 3
find 5
fortune 3
go 36a
have 7
history 4
hit 7
incident 1
knowledge 3
lead 5
meet[1] 6
occurrence 1
patch 4
phenomenon 1
receive 4
sample 2
see 10
skill 1
stand 3
standing 7
suffer 2
sustain 3
take 23
taste 8
time 6
undergo
-experiences
fortune 3
history 3
story 6
experienced°
elder 2
expert 2
grey 4
learned
mature 1
mill 3
old 7
perfect 7
practised 1
professional 1
proficient
qualified 1
ripe 2
seasoned
skilful
sophisticated 1
strong 6
versed
veteran 2
experiential
empirical
experimental 2
experiment°
trial 1
venture 1
experimental°
avant-garde
empirical
new 8
tentative 1
trial 6
underground 3
way-out 2
experimentation
experiment 1
research 1
experiment on°
at **experiment 3**
experiment with°
at **experiment 3**
research 2
expert°
able 2
accomplished
adept 1, 2
authority 3
brilliant 4
capable 1
consultant 1, 2
dab hand
experienced 1
genius 1
gifted
great 8
handy 3
home 5
judge 3
knowing 2
knowledgeable 1
learned
master 2, 4, 7
masterful 1
neat 4
old 7
perfect 7
polished 1
practised 1
professional 1, 3
proficient
qualified 1
quick 4
sage 2
scholar 1
skilful
specialist
talented
thinker
versed
virtuoso 1, 2
wicked 7
expertise°
art 1
calling
craft 1
efficiency 1
facility 1
field 4
finesse 1
knowledge 3
proficiency
prowess 1
science 2
skill 1
speciality 1
technique 2
touch 16
understanding 3
virtuosity
expertly
handily 2
well[1] 6
expertness
craft 1
efficiency 1
expertise
facility 1
finesse 1
proficiency
readiness 2
skill 1
understanding 3
expiate
atone
cleanse 2
compensate 1
expiation
atonement
run 40
satisfaction 2
expiatory
compensatory
propitiatory 1
sacrificial 2
expiration°
death 2
end 2
exhalation 1
passing 4
expire°
die 1, 3
end 9
expire (*cont.*)
fizzle 2
fly 4
go 13, 33a
lapse 5
pass 11, 14a
perish
roll 2
run 26c, 30a
sink 4
expired
dead 7
defunct 2
expiring
dying
moribund 1
passing 1
expiry
death 2
expiration
passing 4
explain°
account 1
alibi 2
brief 6
clarify 1
clear 22
decipher 1
define 2
demonstrate 2
describe 2
excuse 3
gloss[2] 2
illuminate 2
interpret 1
justify
light[1] 12
open 23
paraphrase 2
put 10
render 6
say 4
show 1
simplify
solve
tell[1] 4
translate 3
warrant 4
explain away°
at **explain 2**
rationalize 1
explanation°
account 4
alibi 1
answer 2, 3
comment 1
defence 3
definition 2
demonstration 2
description 2
excuse 4
exposition 2
gloss[2] 1
interpretation 1
key 2, 4
light[1] 5
meaning 3
note 3
plea 3
pretext 2
rationale
reason 1
reasoning 2
solution 1
song 3b
translation 3
explanatory°
explanatory note
legend 3
expletive°
oath 2
explicate
clarify 1
clear 22
explain 1
gloss[2] 2
illuminate 2
interpret 1
paraphrase 2
simplify
solve
explication
definition 2
explanation 1
exposition 2
gloss[2] 1
interpretation 2
key 4
reasoning 2
resolution 4
solution 1
explicit°
broad 3
categorical
circumstantial 3
clear 6, 7
definite 1
direct 9
distinct 1
downright 1
emphatic
express 5
expressive 2
flat 4
formal 2
frank 1
graphic 1
honest 3
luminous 3
manifest 1
observable
outrageous 3
outspoken
patent 2
pictorial 1
point-blank 1
positive 1
precise 1
sexy 2
specific 1
straight 5
taboo 1
undisguised
undisputed
user-friendly
explicitly
completely 3
exactly 2
expressly 1
outright 4
particularly 2
perfectly 1
point-blank 3
straight 14
undoubtedly
wholly 2
explicitness
precision 2
explode°
blast 5
blow[1] 7b, 8b
boom 1
break 1
burst
crash 3
discharge 3
erupt 1
flare 3
fly 7
fragment 3
fume 1
go 31b, 39b
let[1] 6c
pop 1
rage 4
shiver[2]
storm 4
thunder 2
trip 8
exploit°
abuse 1
accomplishment 2
achievement 2
act 1
adventure 1
deed 2
develop 1
draw 13a
effort 3
feat
impose 4b
manipulate 1
milk
play 15
prey 3b
profit 4
exploit (*cont.*)
profiteer 2
stunt[1]
swindle 1
throw 5b
use 2
victimize 1
work 10, 15
exploitation
rip-off 3
exploitative
abusive 2
opportunistic
exploited
downtrodden
put-upon
exploiter
profiteer 1
exploitive
abusive 2
opportunistic
exploration°
discovery 2
examination 1
expedition 1
inquiry 1
investigation
probe 3
quest 1
reconnaissance
research 1
scrutiny
search 4
study 4
exploratory
experimental 1
tentative 1
trial 6
way-out 2
explore°
check 10b, 12a
dig 5
examine 1
hunt 2
inquire 1
investigate
look 8
plumb 5
probe 1, 2
prospect 5
ransack 1
reconnoitre
report 6
research 2
scan 2
scout 1
search 1
treat 2
explorer
pioneer 1
exploring
inquisitive 1
explosion°
blast 3
boom 3
crash 4
discharge 10
eruption 1
fit[2] 3
gale 2
outburst
paroxysm
pop 4
report 2
storm 2
tantrum
thunder 1
explosive°
bomb 1
inflammatory
live 4
temperamental 1
volatile 3
expo
exhibition
exposition 1
show 13
exponent
advocate 2
party 4
proponent
protagonist 2
supporter 1
expose°
air 7
bare 6, 7
betray 2
blab
comment 4
demonstrate 2
develop 1
dig 6
disclose 2
display 1
endanger
excavate 2
exhibit
express 2
give 12b
lay[1] 9
let[1] 7a
light[1] 9
open 23
rebut
reflect 2
reveal
show 1, 12a
slip[1] 4
subject 9
turn 25c
unearth
unveil
-be exposed
light[1] 10
exposé
exposure 1
news 1
revelation
writing 2
exposed
bare 1
bleak 3
defenceless
insecure 2
liable 3
naked 1, 4
open 2, 5, 12, 18, 19
out 4
public 4
raw 4
subject 6
unguarded 2
vulnerable
expose to°
at **expose 3**
incur
expose to danger
endanger
exposition°
comment 1
demonstration 2
display 4
exhibition
explanation 1
extravaganza
fair[2]
representation 3
scheme 1
show 13
spectacle 1
theme 2
expository
explanatory
expostulate
insist 1
exposure°
aspect 3
experience 1
jeopardy
liability 4
manifestation
peril
revelation
expound
enlarge 2
explain 1
lecture 3
rant 1
treat 2
express°
air 7
categorical
couch 2
definite 1
deliver 4
direct 9

express (*cont.*)
dispatch 2
embody 1
emphatic
entire 1
enunciate 1
evident
exhibit
explicit 1
fast[1] 1
formal 2
forward 7
give 3
imply 2
indicate 3
luminous 3
manifest 2
mean[1] 2
mouth 7
particular 1
pass 9
phrase 4
positive 1
pronounce 1
put 4
quick 1
raise 11
rapid
register 4
say 4
self-evident
set 18a
shape 8
show 1
signify 1
speak 4
special 4
specific 1
state 7
symbolize
take 24
talk 1
tell[1] 4
turn 8
vent 3
voice 4
word 10

express appreciation
thank 1

express approval
applaud 1, 2

express differently
reword

expressed
verbal 1

express gratitude
thank 1

expression°
delivery 4
diction 1
embodiment 1
face 2
front 4
idiom 2
look 14
manifestation
phrase 2
speech 1
statement
term 1
tongue 2
voice 1
word 3, 5

expressionless
blank 4
empty 5
glassy 2
vacant 2
vague 6
wooden 2

expressionlessness
emptiness 3

expressive°
dramatic 2
eloquent 1
fluent
knowing 1
meaningful 2
mobile 3

expressive (*cont.*)
pictorial 1
pregnant 2
rhetorical 1
significant 2
soulful

expressively
well[1] 3

expressiveness
diction 1
expression 4
rhetoric 1

expressly°
completely 3
custom 4
exactly 2
particularly 2
purpose 4b
specially

express one's opinion
piece 12
speak 11b
vote 4

express one's preference
vote 4

express regret(s)
apologize 1

express thanks
thank 1

expressway
road 2

expropriate
appropriate 2
confiscate
deprive
grab 2
help 5
misappropriate 1
pre-empt
requisition 3
strip[2] 4

expropriated
assumed 1

expulsion°
discharge 9
dismissal 1
ejection 1, 2
eruption 1
eviction
exclusion 3
exile 1
purge 4
removal 3
suspension 1

expunge
abolish
cancel 2
delete
eliminate 3
erase 1
obliterate 1
remove 3
rub 4
scratch 3
strike 5
wash 4

expurgate
edit 2

exquisite°
acute 3
beautiful 2
choice 4
dainty 1
delicate 2
elegant 1
excruciating
fine[1] 1, 5
gorgeous 1
heavenly 2
masterful 1
nice 4
noble 5
perfect 2
piercing 4
precious 3
rare[1] 2
rich 4
stunning 2
subtle 1
superb

exquisitely
perfectly 2
richly 1

exquisiteness
delicacy 1
elegance 2
splendour 1
subtlety 1

exsert
protrude

exsiccate
parch

exsiccation
evaporation 1

exsufflate
exhale

extant
remaining 1

extemporaneous°
impulsive
offhand 3
spontaneous 1
unpremeditated

extemporaneously
offhand 4

extemporary
extemporaneous
unpremeditated

extempore
extemporaneous
offhand 3, 4
scratch 6
spontaneous 1
unpremeditated

extemporize
improvise 1
play 12

extemporized
extemporaneous

extend°
amplify 1
continue 3, 5
drag 5
draw 14a
enlarge 1
expand 1, 3
gather 5
go 8
hold 16b, 20b, 21b
increase 1
join 4
jut
lengthen
liberalize 1
offer 3
open 24
overhang 1
pad 5
pass 2
pay 3
perpetuate
progress 6
project 5
prolong
protrude
range 6, 8
reach 1
run 12, 33c
spin 5
spread 3, 4, 5, 6
stand 9b
stick[1] 15
stretch 1
string 11a
supplement 2
tender[2] 1
traverse 2
verge[2]
widen

extendable
expansive 1

extended
ample 6
drag 5
general 3
long[1] 1, 2
open 17
protracted

extendible
expansive 1

extending
expansive 1
progression 2
spread 8

extend over
cover 6, 7
occupy 4
span 3

extensible
elastic 1
expansive 1
flexible 1

extensile
elastic 1
flexible 1

extension°
addition 3, 4
expansion 1
flex 1
growth 1
increase 3
overhang 3
progress 3
progression 2
projection 1
ramification 2
respite 2
sprawl 3
spread 8
supplement 1
swell 4

extensive°
ample 1, 2, 3, 6
broad 1, 6
comprehensive
deep 1
encyclopedic
exhaustive
expansive 3
full 2
general 1
global
good 16
great 1
immense
inclusive 1
large 3
limitless
long[1] 1, 2
open 9
panoramic
prevalent
prodigious 1
spacious
sweeping 1
thorough 2, 3
unabridged 2
unlimited 2
voluminous 1
wide 1, 2

extensively
abroad 2
amply 1
depth 6
far 4
length 4c
thoroughly 2
widely 1

extensiveness
extension 2
prevalence 1
width 2

extent°
amount 3
area 2, 4
bound[1] 1
breadth 2
deal 6
degree 2
depth 1
diversity 2
end 1
expanse
extension 2
fetch 4
gauge 4
incidence
length 1
limit 1, 2
magnitude 1
measure 1, 8
measurement 2
proportion 4
quantity

extent (*cont.*)
range 1
room 1
scope 1
size 1
space 3
span 2
spread 9, 10
stretch 5
sweep 7
vengeance 2b
width 2

–to a great extent
amply 2
deeply 2
largely
very 1
widely 2

extenuate
excuse 3
explain 2
whitewash

extenuating°
mitigating
saving 1

extenuation
excuse 4

extenuatory
saving 1

exterior°
external 1, 2
extrinsic
face 6
front 4
outside 1, 5
outward
persona
semblance 1
shell 2
superficial 1
surface 1

exterminate°
butcher 3
destroy 1
eliminate 4
end 10
extinguish 2
finish 4
kill 1
massacre 2
mow 2
murder 3
obliterate 2
purge 2
put 16d
remove 4
root[1] 7a
rout 2
slaughter 3
stamp 4
wipe 3

exterminating
massacre 1

extermination
death 3
destruction 2
end 5
finish 10
holocaust 2
killing 1
loss 7
massacre 1
murder 2
purge 4
removal 2
slaughter 2

exterminator
killer 1

external°
exterior 1, 2
extraneous 2
extrinsic
independent 7
outside 5
outward
peripheral 2
skin-deep
superficial 1, 2

externalize
embody 1

externally
ostensibly
outwardly

externals
shell 2
superficies

extinct°
antiquated
dead 1, 7
defunct 1
die 4
disappear 2
lost 4, 5
obsolete

extinction
death 3
destruction 2
doom
holocaust 2
loss 7
oblivion 1
passing 4
suppression

extinguish°
abolish
blow[1] 7a
end 10
kill 1
murder 3
nip[1] 2
put 23c
quench 2
smother 5
stamp 4
stifle 3
suppress 2
trample 3
turn 17a
wash 4

–be extinguished
go 33a

extinguished
dead 5
extinct 3
out 14

extinguishing
suppression

extirpate
abolish
bury 2
destroy 1
exterminate
obliterate 2
root[1] 7a
stamp 4
uproot 2
waste 11

extirpation
death 3
desolation 1
extraction 1

extol°
bless 1
celebrate 3
eulogize
exalt 2
glorify 2
immortalize
laud
look 12
praise 3
puff 7
worship 1

extolling
celebration 2

extort°
blackmail 2
exact 3
extract 3
force 9
gouge 2
profiteer 2
shake 6b
squeeze 2

extortion
blackmail 1
graft[2]
protection 3

extortionate
exorbitant
extravagant 3
predatory 2
pricey
prohibitive 2
steep[1] 2
unconscionable 2
unreasonable 2

fallacious (*cont.*)
unsound 4
wrong 2
fallacy°
absurdity 2
delusion 2
hole 6
illusion 1
fall all over
truckle
fall apart°
at **fall 7**
collapse 1,4
decompose 1
deteriorate 2
disintegrate
give 9
grief 3
panic 2
piece 6
separate 1
split 5
fall asleep
nod 3
fall away
ebb 1
fall 4
lag 2
fall back°
at **fall 8**
ebb 1
pull 8b
recede 1
relapse 1
retreat 4
fall back on°
at **fall 9**
draw 13a
resort 3
fall behind°
at **fall 10**
lag 1
trail 6
fall down°
at **fall 11**
collapse 1
flop 1
topple 3
trip 5
tumble 1
way 11a
fallen
lost 5,7
fallen woman
prostitute 1
slattern
tart[2] 2
fall flat°
at **fall 12**
collapse 2
fail 1
flop 3
fall for°
at **fall 13**
lap[1] 3b
swallow 2
fall from grace
sin 3
transgress 1
transgression
wrong 8a
fall guy
dupe 1
fool 3
plaything 2
prey 2
sap[1] 2
scapegoat
score 7
sucker
underdog
victim 2
fall headlong
pitch[1] 3
plunge 1
fall heir to
get 1
inherit
fallibility
frailty 2
imperfection
fallible
human 2
fall ill
get 5
sicken 1
fall in°
at **fall 14**
cave 2a
collapse 1
queue 3
sink 2
falling
downgrade 4
fall 22
falling apart
dilapidated
leg 7
shaky 2
tumbledown
falling back
relapse 3
retreat 1
falling down
shaky 2
falling off
decadent 1
decrease 2
downgrade 4
slump 1
falling out
argument 1
feud 1
misunderstand-
ing 2
row[2] 1
variance 2
falling star
star 1
falling to pieces
leg 7
rotten 2
tumbledown
fall in love
fall 13a
fall in with°
at **fall 15**
fraternize
fall off°
at **fall 16**
decline 2,3
decrease 1,6
drop 4,11
fall 3
flag[2] 2
lag 2
remit 2
slack 5
slump 1,2
suffer 4
taper 2
fall on°
at **fall 17**
lace 5a
light[2] 14
make 30b
set 21
fall on one's knees
prostrate 1
fall out°
at **fall 18**
differ 2
disagree 2
feud 2
fight 4
quarrel 2
row[2] 3
fallout
product 1
repercussion
upshot
fall over
topple 3
fall short°
at **fall 19**
default 3
fail 1
lack 2
want 2
fall through°
at **fall 20**
collapse 2
fail 1
fizzle 2
founder[2] 2
fall through (*cont.*)
miscarry
misfire 1
wrong 8b
fall to°
at **fall 21**
prostrate 1
fall together
coincide
fall to pieces
come 7
disintegrate
fall 7
go 12
rot 1
separate 1
fall upon°
at **fall 17**
assault 3
attack 1
lace 5a
light[2] 14
make 30b
pounce 1
set 21,24
tackle 4
visit 2
false°
affected 2
artificial 2
assumed 2
betray 1
bogus
bum 3
counterfeit 2
deceitful
deceptive 1,2
disingenuous
disloyal
double 5
duff
erroneous
factitious
faithless 2
fake 5
fictitious 2
forced
fraudulent 1
glossy 2
hollow 4
hypocritical
illusory
improper 1
inaccurate
incorrect
inexact
insincere
insubstantial 2
invalid[2]
lying 2
mistaken 2
mock 3
oblique 2
outward
perfidious
phoney 1
pretend 3
pretended
seeming
sham 2
slippery 2
sophistic
spurious
synthetic
theatrical 2
unnatural 4
unreal 3
unscrupulous
untrue 1,2
wily
wrong 2
false colours
mask 2
false front
masquerade 2
outside 2
falsehood°
fabrication 3
fib 1
invention 3
libel 2
lie[1] 2
misstatement 1
myth 2
falsehood (*cont.*)
story 3
tale 2
false impression
delusion 2
illusion 1
misunderstand-
ing 1
falsely
seemingly
false move
feint
misstep 1
falseness
falsity
hypocrisy
impropriety 1
infidelity 1
perfidy
false scent
misinformation
false show
masquerade 2
false step
misstep 1
mistake 2
trip 1,2
false witness
liar
perjury
falsification
fabrication 3
forgery 1
invention 3
lie[1] 2
lying 1
misstatement 1
perversion 1
pretence 2
tale 2
twist 9
falsified
factitious
fraudulent 1
unreal 3
falsifier
liar
falsify°
adulterate
camouflage 2
colour 4,6
counterfeit 4
disguise 2
distort 2
doctor 4
fabricate 3
fake 1
fib 2
fiddle 1
forge 3
garble 1
juggle
manipulate 3
misrepresent
pervert 1
rig 2
twist 2
falsity°
impropriety 1
perfidy
falter
fail 1
flag[2] 2
founder[2] 2
hang 5
hesitate 3
hobble 1
lag 2
limp[1] 1,2
pause 1
reel 1
sag 2
scruple 2
shilly-shally
stammer 1
stumble 1,2
totter
trip 5
wallow 3
wrong 8a
faltering
doddering
faint 1
faltering (*cont.*)
halting
hesitant 2
inarticulate 2
infirm 2
irresolute
limp[1] 2
sag 3
shambling
tremulous 1
weak 6
fame°
celebrity 1
distinction 2
glory 1
honour 2
kudos
laurels
lustre 2
name 2
popularity
prestige
prominence 1
renown
famed
celebrated
exalted 1
famous
glorious 1
great 5
honourable 4
illustrious
legendary 3
notable 1
noted
outstanding 1
prestigious
prominent 2
renowned
star 3
successful 3
well-known 2
familial
domestic 1
familiar°
accustomed 1
chum 1
close 15
common 1
everyday 2
experience 4
frequent 1
friend 1
friendly 1
general 2
homely 1
informal 1
intimate[1] 1,5
know 1
knowledgeable 1
old 8
ordinary 1
outgoing 2
personal 3
read 2
regular 1,7
routine 3
stale 2
standard 6
usual
vernacular 2
well-known 1
familiar face
steady 10
familiarity°
acquaintance 1
experience 1
exposure 3
fellowship 3
friendship 1
knowledge 3
understanding 3
familiarization
orientation 2
familiarize°
accustom
acquaint
orient 3
teach
familiarized
seasoned
familiarly
well[1] 13
familiar with°
at **familiar 4**
acquainted 1,2
experience 4
home 5
used 3
read 2
versed
family°
background 1
birth 3
breed 1
brood 1
clan 1,2
connection 4
descendant
domestic 1
dynasty
flesh 5
home 8
house 2
kin 1
line[1] 15
lineage 2
parentage
paternity
pedigree
people 2
race[2] 1,2
root[1] 4
sort 3
stock 2
strain[2] 1
syndicate 2
tribe
–in a family way
expecting
pregnant 1
trouble 9b
family member
relation 3
family tree
family 3
lineage 1
root[1] 4
famine°
hunger 1
famished°
hollow 3
hungry 1
ravenous 1
starved 1
famous°
big 7
brilliant 3
celebrated
distinguished 1
eminent 1
exalted 1
glorious 1
great 5
honourable 4
illustrious
immortal 3
legendary 3
lofty 2
notable 1
noted
notorious 2
outstanding 1
popular 1
prestigious
prominent 2
public 6
renowned
reputation 2
splendid 2
star 3
successful 3
well-known 2
famously°
well[1] 2
famousness
celebrity 1
fan°
addict 2
admirer 1
awake 2
bug 4
devotee
disciple 2
enthusiast
fiend 2
follower 3

fashion (*cont.*)
fabricate 1
fad
fit[1] 7
forge 1
form 4,7
frame 7
generate 4
genre
make 1
manner 1
mode[1] 1
mode[2]
model 6,7
mould[1] 4
prepare 5
rage 3
rave 4
school 2
sculpture 2
shape 6
stamp 8
style 1,2,8
tailor 2
taste 5
technique 1
thing 3
trend 2
turn 8
vein 5
vogue 1
way 1
work 13
-in fashion°
at **fashion 4**
fashionable
minute[1] 3
modern
popular 1
stylish
-in this fashion
thus 1
-out of fashion
obsolete
fashionable°
becoming
catch 13b
chic 1
contemporary 2
current 3
dapper
dashing 2
date 5
elegant 2
exclusive 2
glamorous 2
latest 2
minute[1] 3
modern
new 2
now 5
popular 1
posh
rakish
sharp 9
smart 3
snappy 2
sporty
stylish
swanky
swell 7
swinging
swish 3
trendy 1
fashionableness
style 4
vogue 2
fashionably
beautifully 1
fashion industry
rag[1] 4
fashioning
composition 4
fabrication 1
fashion plate
swell 6
fast°
abiding
bound[3] 1
close 10,15
diet[1] 3
durable
expeditious

fast (*cont.*)
express 7
firm 2
firmly 1
fleet[2]
great 10
hasty 1
immovable 1
invariable 1
loose 7
persistent 1
precipitate 3
promiscuous 2
prompt 1
quick 1
quickly 1,2
rapid
rapidly 1
rooted
secure 2
spanking 3
speedy 1,3
stable 1
stick[1] 7
swift
swiftly
tight 1
true 2
fasten°
adjust 4
anchor 3
apply 1
attach 1
bar 8
bind 1
bolt 10,11
chain 3
clamp 2
clasp 3
cling 1
clip[1] 1
close 1
connect 3
fix 1,4,9
hitch 1
join 1
knit 1
knot 3
lash[2]
link 3
nail 7
peg 4
pin 3
rope 3
secure 8
sew
shut 1
stake[1] 3
stick[1] 4
suffix 2
suspend 2
tack 5
tether 2
tie 1
tighten 1
unite 3
whip 5
fastened
attached 2
bound[3] 1
fast[1] 3
fixed 1
secure 2
shut 7
fastener
brace 3
buckle 1
catch 17
clamp 1
clasp 1
clip[1] 2
fastening
hook 1
nail 1
snap 10
fastening°
attachment 1,2
brooch
buckle 1
catch 17
clasp 1
nail 1
snap 10
splice 2
tack 2

fastening (*cont.*)
tie 8
whipping 2
fasten on
decide 2
grab 1
set 4
single 4
take 2
fasten together
clamp 2
join 1
knit 1
link 3
unite 3
fastidious°
careful 2
choosy
dainty 2
deliberate 3
delicate 5
difficult 5
discriminating
exact 2
faithful 3
finicky 1
fussy 1
gingerly 1,2
hair-splitting
meticulous
neat 1
nice 3
overcritical
particular 4
pedantic 2
perfectionist 2
precise 3
priggish
prissy
refined 2
religious 2
scrupulous 1
severe 1
squeamish 1
tasteful
well-groomed
fastidiousness
precision 2
refinement 2
severity 1
fasting
fast[2] 2
fast living
dissipation 1
fastness
security 1
stronghold
tower 2
fast one
gag[2] 2
fast-talk
defraud
fast-talking
glib
fastuous
pretentious 1
fat°
beamy
big 2
dumpy
greasy 1
gross 1
heavy 11
large 1
money 4
obese
oily 1
plump[1] 1
rich 6
rotund 3
stout 1
weighty 1
well-fed
fatal°
calamitous
deadly 1
destructive 1
disastrous 1
fated 3
fateful 2
hopeless 1
incurable 1
lethal
malignant 1

fatal (*cont.*)
mortal 3
murderous 1
poisonous 1
ruinous
severe 3
terminal 2
virulent 1
fatalism
stoicism
fatality°
casualty 2a
killing 1
-fatalities
casualty 2b
fatally
severely 5
fat cat
dignitary
fate°
chance 1
destine 1
destiny
doom
fortune 2
lot 2
luck 1
predestination
providence 2
fated°
bound[3] 4
card 12
condemn 3
destined 1
doomed 1
fatal 3
inevitable
necessary 3
predetermined 2
unavoidable
fateful°
fatal 1,2,3
fated 1,3
ominous 1
portentous 1
sinister 1
fat-head
dolt
fool 1
fat-headed
daft 1
thick 6
father°
author
clergyman 1
conceive 1
create 1
creator 1
founder[1]
generate 2
have 8
minister 1
parent 1
pastor
priest
raise 4
spawn
start 7
stock 3
fatherhood
paternity
fathering
generation 1
fatherland°
country 2
land 4
root[1] 4
fatherless
illegitimate 2
fatherly°
paternal 1
fathership
paternity
fathom°
catch 10
comprehend
figure 12b
follow 8
get 19
make 37d
penetrate 5
pierce 3
plumb 5

fathom (*cont.*)
see 2
sound[3] 1
twig[2]
fathomable
intelligible
fatidic
prophetic
fatigue°
detail 3
enervate
exhaust 2
exhaustion 2
fag 1
kill 4
lethargy 2
overdo 2
prostrate 2
tire 1
wear 6
weary 5
fatigued°
beat 13
dead 9
drawn
exhausted 1
jaded 1
lethargic 2
limp[2] 2
prostrate 5
ragged 3
run-down 1
sleepy 1
spent 1
tired 1
washed out 2
weary 1
worn 3
fatiguing
arduous 1
exhausting 1
hard 2
killing 3
laborious 1
punishing
stiff 9
tedious
tiresome 1
toilsome
trying
weary 2
fatness°
fatten
fill 10a
swell 1
fattening
rich 6
fatty
fat 2
greasy 1
oily 1
fatuitous
daft 1
foolish 2
preposterous
fatuity
folly 1
insanity 2
stupidity 1
vacancy 3
vanity 2
fatuous
daft 1
empty 5
foolish 2
inane
insane 2
mad 2
meaningless 1
mindless 1
pointless
preposterous
senseless 3
silly 1
stupid 1
unreasonable 1
vacant 2
fatuousness
folly 1
insanity 2
fat-witted
daft 1
faubourg(s)
outskirts

faucet
tap[2] 1
fault°
abuse 6
blame 1
blemish 3
bug 6
default 1
defect 2
disadvantage 1
error 1
failing 1
flaw 1
foible
frailty 2
hole 6
imperfection
lapse 1
misdeed
mistake 1
offence 1
oversight 1
peccadillo
responsibility 3
rift 2
sin 1
slip[1] 8
solecism
transgression
twist 10
vice 2
weakness 3
-at fault°
at **fault 5**
amiss 1
error 3a
guilty 1
out 12
responsible 4
-to a fault°
at **fault 7**
fault-finding°
critical 1
fretful
hair-splitting
overcritical
peevish
querulous
reproachful
faultily
badly 3
faultiness
incompetence
faultless°
absolute 1
blameless
clear 12
complete 4
correct 8
exact 1
flawless 1
immaculate 3
impeccable
incorrupt 1
infallible 1
innocent 1
irreproachable
nice 3
perfect 2,3
polished 1
pure 1
spotless 2
untarnished
watertight 2
faultlessly
exactly 1
pat[2] 1
perfectly 2,3
faultlessness
perfection 1
precision 1
purity 1
faulty°
amiss 1
defective 1
deficient 2
dicky
erroneous
false 1,5
flawed
halting
imperfect
improper 1
inaccurate

feedback
reaction 1
response
upshot
feed-bag
eat
feeder
tributary
turn-off 1
feed on°
at **feed 3**
prey 3a
feel°
atmosphere 2
believe 1
climate 2
detect 2
distinguish 3
experience 4
feeling 6
find 4
finger 11
flair 1
flavour 2
fumble 1
grip 3
grope
guess 2
handle 2
instinct
perceive 2
perception 2
seem
sense 6
surmise 1
suspect 2
sympathize 1
take 8, 23
texture
touch 1, 13, 17
feeler°
feel for°
at **feel 8**
pity 3
respond 2
sympathize 1
feeling°
air 1, 3
anticipation 2
atmosphere 2
attitude 2
aura
climate 2
emotion
estimate 4
expression 4
feel 11
fire 2
flavour 2
foreboding 1
grip 3
guess 3
heart 4
hunch 1
idea 3
impression 1
inspiration 1
instinct
love 4
mind 6, 7
misgiving
mood 1
observation 2
passion 1
perception 2
philosophy 2
position 3
posture 3
premonition
presumption 3
psychology
qualm
regard 9
sensation 1
sensible 3
sensitivity 2, 3
sentiment 1, 2
sniff 2
soul 4
spirit 7
stand 13
surmise 2
suspicion 1
sympathy 2
tender[1] 6

feeling (*cont.*)
thing 4
touch 13, 17
undercurrent 2
vein 4
view 2
way 2
-feelings°
at **feeling 5**
heart 4
psychology
sensibility 2
spirit 8, 9a
vibes
-without feeling
numb 1
feel in one's bones
feel 4
sense 6
feel one's way
orient 3
feign
act 8
affect[2] 1
assume 4
bluff[1] 2
counterfeit 5
dissimulate
fabricate 3
fake 2
fool 5
game 6
let[1] 7b
make 25
play 10
pretend 1, 3
put 22b
strike 12
feigned
affected 2
artificial 3
assumed 2
counterfeit 2
false 4
forced
glossy 2
hollow 4
mimic 5
mock 3
pretended
seeming
spurious
studied
unnatural 4
feigning
act 3
hypocritical
pretence 1
feint°
subterfuge
felicitate
compliment 3
congratulate
hail[1] 2
toast 3
felicitations
compliment 2
congratulations
toast 1
felicitous
appropriate 1
fluent
happy 2
mellow 4
opportune 1
providential
felicity
bliss
content[2] 1
festivity 1
fluency
gaiety 1
glee
happiness
joy 1
merriment
welfare
fell°
bloodthirsty
brutal 1
cut 13a
destructive 1
ferocious

fell (*cont.*)
fierce 1
floor 4
grim 2
height 3
hide[2] 1
hill 1
knock 4b
lay[1] 18c
moor[1]
mountain 1
murderous 1
prostrate 2
sanguinary 1
savage 2
skin 1
throw 3
topple 1
vicious 3
fellah
peasant
felled
prostrate 4
fellow°
accomplice
acquaintance 2
associate 2
beggar 2
boy 1
brother
bugger 2
chap
chum 1
cohort 3
companion 1
customer 2
devil 3
dude 2
equal 4
friend 2
guy 1
lad
like[1] 7
man 1
match 1
mate 1, 3
member
partner 1
punter 2
steady 9
stick[2] 2
teacher
fellow-citizen *etc.*
brother
fellow-creature
brother
fellow-criminal
accessory 2
accomplice
fellow-feeling
love 4
sympathy 2
fellow-man
brother
fellowship°
association 3
brotherhood 1
circle 2
clan 2
club 2
companionship
company 1
familiarity 2
fraternity 2
friendship 1
league 1
order 9
scholarship 2
society 1, 5
sympathy 2
union 2
fellow-traveller
sympathizer
fellow-worker
associate 2
colleague
felon°
criminal 3
miscreant 1
terrorist
transgressor

felonious
black 6
evil 2
illegal
lawless 2
miscreant 2
unlawful
villainous 1
wicked 2
wrong 1
feloniousness
guilt 1
felony
crime
job 5
misdeed
offence 1
female
feminine 1
girl 1
woman 1
feminine°
femme fatale
siren 2
temptress
fen
bog 1
flat 14b
marsh
mire 1
morass 1
swamp 1
fence°
barrier 1
compete
enclosure 2
equivocate
evade 2
jump 10
picket 4
rail[1] 1
shuffle 3
stake[1] 4
wall 1
-on the fence°
at **fence 2**
non-partisan 1
pussyfoot 2
fence in
enclose 1
keep 14b
picket 4
shut 3a
stake[1] 4
fence off
enclose 1
partition 6
stake[1] 4
fend°
fend for oneself°
at **fend 1**
shift 2
fending off
prevention
fend off°
at **fend 2**
defend 2
deflect
fence 4
forestall
head 13b
hold 18b
prevent
repel 1
repulse 2
turn 7
ward 3
fenny
muddy 1
feral
bloodthirsty
cutthroat 3
ferocious
fierce 1
ghoulish 2
grim 2
savage 1
truculent
untamed
vicious 3
wild 1
fermata
pause 2

ferment°
agitation 2
boil[1] 2
brew 1
buzz 2
disorder 2
excitement 2
passion 2
rush 3
seethe 2
sour 5
tempest 2
tumult
fermented
sour 2
ferocious°
bloodthirsty
brutal 1
cruel 2
cutthroat 3
deadly 3
fierce 1
ghoulish 2
grim 2
homicidal
mad 3
militant 1
ruthless
savage 2
scathing
torrential
truculent
untamed
vicious 3
violent 1
wild 3
ferociously
fiercely
madly 3
vengeance 2a
ferociousness
violence 1
ferocity
fury 2
severity 3, 5
violence 1, 2
ferret (about)
pry 1
root[2]
ferret out
dig 6
discover 1
scrounge 1
track 8
ferrule
tip[1] 1
ferry
ship 2
take 9
fertile°
fruitful 1, 2
golden 5
plentiful 2
pregnant 3
productive 1, 2
prolific 1, 2
rank[2] 1
rich 2, 9
vivid 3
fertile patch
oasis 1
fertile source
hotbed
fertility
fat 6
plenty 2
fertilize°
impregnate 1
fertilizer
dung
ferule
tip[1] 1
fervency
ardour
electricity
feeling 4
fervour
fire 2
glow 3
passion 1
fervent°
animated 1
ardent

fervent (*cont.*)
burning 2
deep 6
drunk 2
eager
earnest 2
emotional 1
enthusiastic
excited 2
fanatical
feverish
fire 5
heartfelt
heated
hot 3, 4
impassioned
inflammatory
intense 2
keen[1] 1
mad 6
rousing
soulful
strong 5, 22
torrid 2
voracious 2
warm 2
wholehearted
fervently
hotly
mad 5
madly 4
sincerely
warmly 3, 4
fervid
ardent
burning 2
drunk 2
eager
earnest 2
emotional 1
enthusiastic
excited 2
fanatical
fervent 1
fire 5
heartfelt
heated
hot 3, 4
impassioned
inflammatory
intense 2
keen[1] 1
mad 6
passionate 1
sanguine
strong 5
torrid 2
voracious 2
warm 2
warm-blooded 2
fervidly
hotly
madly 4
warmly 4
fervidness
heat 2
passion 1
fervour°
animation 1
ardour
dash 6
devotion 3
eagerness 1
enthusiasm 1
fanaticism 1
feeling 4
fire 2
flame 2
glow 3
heat 2
inclination 4
intensity
love 1
passion 1
soul 4
warmth 3
zealotry
Fescennine
foul 5
lascivious 2
lewd
obscene 1
outrageous 3
profane 3
prurient 2

Fescennine (*cont.*)
scurrilous
fess up
clean 8
fester°
mortify 3
rankle
rot 1
smoulder
festered
rotten 1
festering
rotten 1
ulcerous
festering spot
ulcer 2
festival°
fair[2]
feast 2
festivity 2
fête 1
gala 1
holiday 2
jamboree
party 1
revel 3
festive
gala 2
jolly 1
merry 1
special 2
festivity°
frolic 1
fun 1
gaiety 2
gala 1
jamboree
merriment
party 1
revelry
–festivities°
at **festivity 2**
celebration 3
festival 2
fête 1
gaiety 2
party 1
festoon
drape 1
flag[2] 1
garland 1,2
string 9
fetch°
bring 1,10a
call 8b
catch 6
cost 2
get 4
go 28a
make 12
retrieve 1
transport 1
fetching°
adorable
attractive
becoming
catching 2
darling 4
desirable 2
lovable
lovely 1
picturesque 1
prepossessing
pretty 1
taking
tempting 1
winning 1
fête°
celebration 3
fair[2]
feast 2
festival 1,2
gala 1
holiday 2
jamboree
party 1
rave 5
revel 3
fête champêtre
picnic 1
fetid
filthy 1
foul 3
fetid (*cont.*)
musty 1
nasty 1
offensive 3
putrid
rancid
rank[2] 4
rotten 1
smelly
sordid 3
stinking 1
stuffy 1
fetidness
smell 2
fetish°
amulet
charm 1
fixation
idol 1
image 1
partiality 2
talisman
thing 4
fetor
odour 1
reek 3
smell 2
stench
fetter
chain 2,3
enslave
hobble 2
manacle 2
shackle 1,3,4
tether 1,2
trammel 2
–fetters
bond 1
manacle 1
restraint 2
shackle 1
fettle
condition 3
fitness 2
form 5
health 1
repair 3
shape 4
trim 6
feud°
argument 1
clash 3
combat 2
conflict 2
dispute 4
fight 1,8
quarrel 1,2
rivalry
vendetta
feuding
rivalry
fever
fire 2
frenzy 1
heat 1
fevered
inflamed
feverish°
breathless 3
distraught
drunk 2
excitable
excited 1
fanatical
hectic
hurried 1
inflamed
intense 3
passionate 1
pell-mell 2
seethe 2
stormy 2
feverishly
mad 5
madly 3
pell-mell 1
suddenly 2
warmly 5
feverishness
fire 2
flame 2
glow 3
passion 1
few°
couple 2
handful 1
number 2
several 1
sparse 1
thin 7
–for a few moments
briefly 2
–in a few words
briefly 1
word 8
–with few exceptions
whole 5
few and far between
rare[1] 1
scarce
sparse 1
thin 7
fey
queer 1
whimsical 1
wry 2
FFV
élite 1
fiancé(e)°
girl 2
love 3
sweetheart
fiasco°
catastrophe 2
disappointment 1
flop 4
hash 2
loser
washout
fiat
dictate 2
order 4
precept 1
regulation 3
warrant 2
fib°
fabrication 3
falsehood
invention 3
lie[1] 1,2
myth 2
romance 5
story 3
tale 2
fibber
liar
fibbing
lying 1
fibre°
grain 4
nap[2]
string 1
thread 1
yarn 1
fibril
fibre 1
fibrous
ropy 1
stringy
tough 2
fickle°
capricious
changeable 1
faithless 2
fanciful 1
flighty 1
giddy 2
inconsistent 2
inconstant
moody 3
ticklish 1
uncertain 4
unstable 1
untrue 1
variable
volatile 2
whimsical 2
fickleness
inconstancy
fictile
plastic 1
pliable 1
suggestible
fictile (*cont.*)
supple 1
tractable 2
yielding 1
fiction
fabrication 3
falsehood
fantasy 3
fib 1
invention 3
legend 1
lie[1] 2
myth 2
pretence 1,2
romance 3,5
tale 2
writing 2
yarn 2
fictional°
fabulous 1
illusory
imaginative 2
legendary 2
non-existent
pretended
romantic 1
fictitious°
bogus
fabulous 1
false 1
ideal 5
imaginary
imaginative 2
incredible 1
mythical 2
pretended
romantic 1,2
sham 2
unreal 2
fictive
fictitious 1
imaginary
non-existent
fiddle°
cheat 2
fidget 1
finger 11
fix 12,18
fool 6
manipulate 3
massage 3
monkey 5
play 19c
potter
rig 2
swindle 1,2
take 27
tamper
tinker
toy 3
trifle 3
twiddle 1
wangle
fiddle about, around°
at **fiddle 2**
mess 4a
tamper
tinker
fiddle-de-dee
fiddlesticks
fiddle-faddle
fiddlesticks
prattle 3
stuff 4
fiddlesticks°
fidelity
attachment 3
dedication 1
duty 2
faith 3
homage
loyalty
precision 1
fidget°
fiddle 2
play 19c
squirm
trifle 3
twiddle 1
wriggle 1
–the fidgets°
at **fidget 3**
jitters
fidgetiness
fidget 3
tension 2
fidgety
agitated
edge 5
excitable
excited 1
ill 6
impatient 1
jumpy
nervous 1
overwrought 1
restless
tense 2
field°
area 3,5
discipline 5
domain 2
game 4
gamut
job 1
kingdom 2
line[1] 7
meadow
occupation 1
patch 2
practical 3
profession 1
province 3
pursuit 3
region 2
science 1
scope 1
speciality 1
sphere 3
subject 2
field-day
gala 1
field-glasses
glass 7
field of action
theatre 4
field of study
topic
field of vision
horizon
sight 2
field trip
expedition 1
fiend°
addict 2
demon 1,2
devil 2
devotee
enthusiast
fan
fanatic
freak 4
maniac 2
monster 1
ogre
sectarian 4
terror 2
fiendish°
atrocious 1
cruel 2
devilish
diabolic 1,2
dreadful 2
ferocious
ghoulish 1
grim 2
infernal 2
inhuman 2
macabre
monstrous 1
satanic 1
ungodly 1
vicious 1,3
vile 1
wicked 1
wrong 1
fiendishness
devilry 2
monstrosity 2
fierce°
acute 3
ardent
bloodthirsty
brutal 1
cutthroat 3
drastic
ferocious
fierce (*cont.*)
fiery 3
furious 2
grim 2
hot 3
intense 1
keen[1] 3
militant 1
piercing 3,4
ruthless
savage 2
scathing
severe 5
sharp 8
sore 5
stormy 2
tempestuous
torrential
truculent
tumultuous
untamed
vicious 3
violent 1
wild 3
fiercely°
madly 3
vengeance 2a
warmly 4
fierceness
fury 2
severity 3,5
violence 1,2
fieriness
heat 1
fiery°
burning 1,2
fervent 1
feverish
heated
hot 1,3
impassioned
incandescent
inflammatory
lurid 4
passionate 3
stormy 2
tempestuous
torrid 1
towering 2
fifteen minutes
quarter 2
fifth column
underground 5
fifth-columnist
spy 1
subversive 2
traitor
turncoat
underground 5
fifty-fifty
equal 2
even 5
fig
primp
fight°
action 6
argue 1
argument 1
attack 1
battle 1,2,3
box[2] 1
brawl 1,2
clash 2,3
combat 1,5,6
compete
conflict 1
contest 2
crusade 2
disagree 2
disorder 2
dispute 1,4
encounter 5
engage 5
engagement 5
fall 18
feud 2
fracas 2
fray[1]
issue 4
oppose 1
quarrel 1,2
resist 1
riot 3
run 5

fixed°
abiding
attached 2
bound[3] 1
certain 1
changeless 1
close 10
constant 3
decided 2
definite 2
determined 1, 2
durable
entrenched
eternal 3
fast[1] 3, 4
final 2
firm 2
flat 7
foregone
formal 1
glassy 2
grim 1
habitual 1
immovable 1, 2
indelible
indestructible
indisputable
inflexible
ingrained
intent 4
invariable 1, 3
irreversible
irrevocable
limited 1
obstinate
off 10
permanent 2
persistent 1
predetermined 1
purposeful
quiet 4
regular 1
rigid 4
rooted
secure 2
sedentary
set 29
specific 1
stable 2
standing 1, 3
static 1
steadfast
steady 3
stick 17
tight 1
time-honoured
unavoidable
fixed idea
fixation
obsession
fixed look
gaze 2
stare 2
fixedly
fast[1] 7
intently
searchingly
fixedness
dedication 1
finality
obstinacy
permanence
resolution 1
fixed price
quotation 2
fixing
attachment 2
determination 3
overhaul 3
regulation 1
repair 2
fix on°
at **fix 15**
decide 2
determine 3
lock[1] 7
pick 1
settle 2
single 4
understanding 3
zero 4
fixture°
date 2
regular 12
-fixtures
fitting 2
furniture 2
gear 2
plant 3
fix up°
at **fix 16**
decorate 2
fix 3
improve 1
overhaul 2
patch 6
refresh 3
refurbish
rehabilitate 2
renovate
repair 1
restore 3
revamp
tidy 4
fizz°
bubble 2, 3
fizzle 1
foam 1
froth 3
sparkle 2
fizziness
fizz 2
fizzing
effervescent 1
fizzle°
disappointment 1
fail 1
failure 3
fall 20
fiasco
fizz 1, 2
flop 4
misfire 1, 2
fizzle out°
at **fizzle 2**
collapse 2
fail 1
fall 20
misfire 1
fizzy
bubbly 1
effervescent 1
fizzy drink
pop 5
fizzy water
water 1
fjord
gulf 1
sound[4]
flabbergast
amaze
astonish
astound
daze 1
dumbfound
perplex
petrify 2
shock 1
stagger 2
stun 2
surprise 1
flabbergasted
daze 4
dumbfounded
petrified 2
thunderstruck
flabbergasting
perplexing
prodigious 2
flabbiness
fat 5
flabby°
fat 1
limp[2] 1
slack 2
soft 12
spineless 2
flaccid
flabby 1
limp[2] 1
slack 2
flack
flak
flag°
banner 1
colour 2a
decline 2
flag *(cont.)*
droop 2
ebb 2
fade 2
fail 3
go 12
lag 2
mask 2
pave 1
pennant
peter out
sag 2
sign 4
sink 4
standard 3
streamer
symbol
tab 1
tail 1
weaken 2
wilt 2
flagellate
flog 1
hit 1
scourge 3
slash 2
whip 1
flagellation
whipping 1
flagging
sag 3
flagitious
abandoned 2
atrocious 1
black 6
criminal 2
devilish
diabolic 2
dreadful 2
evil 1
evil-minded 2
flagrant
foul 4
glaring 1
grim 3
immoral 1
infamous 2
infernal 2
lawless 3
monstrous 2
scandalous 1
ungodly 1
vicious 1
flagitiousness
atrocity 1
enormity
error 2
evil 6
flagon
jar[1]
flag-pole
pole[1]
flagrant°
atrocious 1
blatant 1
disgraceful 2
dishonourable 3
flaming
glaring 1
great 11
grievous 2
gross 4
naked 3
notorious 1
open 13
outrageous 2
patent 2
prominent 1
public 5
rank[2] 2
shameless
stark 4
whopping 2
flagrante delicto
red-handed
flagrantly
openly 1
flagstaff
pole[1]
flag-waver
patriot
flag-waving
jingoism
patriotic
flail
flap 1
hide[2] 2
lash[1] 3
lather 4
slash 2
flair°
aptitude 2
craft 1
dash 6
faculty 1
genius 3
gift 2
head 4
ingenuity
knack
life 7
panache
style 4
talent 1
touch 16
verve
virtuosity
flak°
fire 3
opposition 1
static 2
flake°
chip 1
coil 1
dolt
foil[2]
scale[2] 1
shed[2] 4
sliver
flaked-out
crazy 1
flake off°
at **flake 2**
peel 1
shed[2] 4
flake out°
at **flake 3**
flaky
crazy 1
way-out 1
flam
deceit 2
defraud
hoax 1
flambeau
flare 5
flamboyance
exuberance 2
ostentation
panache
flamboyant°
brassy 1
camp[2] 1
dashing 3
dramatic 3
extravagant 4
flashy 1
grand 3
grandiose 1
jaunty 2
luxuriant 3
ornate
ostentatious
rhetorical 3
showy
swashbuckling
flamboyantly
gaily 1
flame°
beloved 2
blaze 1, 4
burn 1
fire 1
flare 1, 4
flash 1, 4
glare 1
light[1] 7
paramour
sparkle 1
sweetheart
-flames
fire 1
-in flames
fiery 1
flame-proof
incombustible
flaming°
burning 1
fiery 1
fire 5
incandescent
live 3
lurid 4
flammable°
inflammable
flan
tart[2] 1
flânerie
idleness 1
flâneur
loafer
flange
projection 1
flank°
side 1
flannel°
flatter 1
flap°
flicker 2
flop 2
flutter 1
fly 1, 9
fuss 1
lap[2] 2
lather 2
overlap 3
shake 4
shiver[1] 2
slap 2
song 3a
swing 1, 3
tab 1
wag[1] 1, 2
wave 4
-in a flap
nervous 1
panic-stricken
flapdoodle
jargon 2
prattle 3
rubbish 2
stuff 4
trash 1
flappable
nervous 1
flapping
flap 2
flutter 4
swing 3
flare°
beacon
burn 1
flame 4
flash 1, 4
flicker 1, 3
glare 1
gleam 1
light[1] 2
ruffle 1
shine 1
flare out°
at **flare 2**
flare up°
at **flare 1**
blaze 4
blow[1] 8a
bristle 3
fume 1
flare-up
blaze 2
explosion 2
outburst
paroxysm
tantrum
flaring
incandescent
flash°
bit 3
blink 2
bulletin
display 3
flare 1, 4
flashy 1
flit
garish
glance 2, 5
gleam 1
glitter 4
grandiose 1
flash *(cont.)*
instant 2
jaunty 2
minute[1] 1
moment 1
news 2
ostentatious
ray 1
second[2]
shine 1
shoot 1
sparkle 1
streak 2
trendy 1
twinkle 1, 2
twinkling 1
vulgar 1
whip 6
-in a flash
hastily 1
rapidly 2
suddenly 1
swiftly
flash-freeze
freeze 1
flashily
gaily 1
flashiness
glare 3
glitter 4
ostentation
flashing
bright 1
meteoric 2
scintillating 1
shiny
twinkle 2
flashlight
light[1] 2
flashy°
brassy 1
conspicuous 2
extravagant 4
flamboyant 2
garish
gaudy
gay 3
grandiose 1
jaunty 2
loud 2
luxuriant 3
rakish
shiny
showy
sporty
tasteless 1
tawdry
flask
bottle 1
jug
flat°
boring
broke,
dead 10, 12
downright 1
even 1
flush[2] 1
hollow 6
horizontal
lacklustre
level 1
lifeless 3
matter-of-fact
mousy 1
muddy 3
needy
pad 3
pedestrian 2
peremptory 2
place 6
plain 1
plane 1, 3
point-blank 1, 3
prosaic
puncture 1
recumbent
regular 5
room 3
small 3
smooth 1
stagnant
stale 1
still 1
stodgy

flat (*cont.*)
straight 3
supine 1
tame 4
tasteless 2
tedious
tiresome 1
uniform 2
vapid
washed out 1
watery 1
wishy-washy 2
-flats°
at **flat 14**
flatfoot
constable
police officer
flatland
plain 6
table 2
flatly
completely 3
flat 16, 17b
point-blank 3
flatmate
friend 3
flatness
uniformity 2
flat on one's back
recumbent
supine 1
flat out°
at **flat 17**
flat sheet
sheet 1
flat surface
plane 1
flatten°
devastate 1
even 13
fell
knock 6a
lay[1] 18c
level 8
press 4
raze
roll 7
rout 2
ruin 7
smooth 9
trample 1
flatter°
compliment 3
eulogize
flannel 2
get 46b
make 34b
play 18
romance 7
flatterer°
charmer
flattering°
complimentary 1
good 17
ingratiating
menial 2
obsequious
oily 2
servile
flattery°
compliment 1
flannel 1
pat[1] 5
servility
flatties
flat 14a
flat tyre
puncture 1
flatulence
bombast
hot air
rant 3
raving 3
rhetoric 2
wind[1] 3
flatulent
bombastic
pompous 2
flatus
wind[1] 3
flatware
silver 1

flaunt°
camp[2] 2
dangle 2
display 3
exhibit
flourish 2
parade 5
promenade 4
show 11
splurge 2
sport 5
trot 2
flaunting
ostentation
ostentatious
pretentious 2
flauntingly
openly 1
flavorous
savoury 1
tasty
flavour°
air 3
aroma 2
life 7
odour 2
salt 6
savour 1
season 3
seasoning
spice 1, 3
suspicion 2
tang 1, 2
taste 1
undercurrent 2
zest 1
flavourful
delicious 1
mellow 1
pungent 1
racy 3
robust 2
savoury 1
spicy 1
tasty
flavouring
flavour 1
spice 1
flavourless
flat 8
tasteless 2
vapid
watery 1
wishy-washy 2
flavour of the month
favourite 1
modern
flavoursome
savoury 1
spicy 1
tasty
flaw°
blemish 2, 3
crack 1
defect 2
disadvantage 1
drawback
error 1
failing 1
fault 1
foible
frailty 2
hole 6
impairment
imperfection
kink 3
leak 2
nick 1
rift 2
shortcoming
taint 1
twist 10
vice 2
weakness 3
flawed°
defective 1
deficient 2
erroneous
false 1, 5
faulty
imperfect
inaccurate
inadequate 1

flawed (*cont.*)
mistaken 2
poor 4
unsatisfactory
unsound 4
untenable
wanting 1
wrong 5
flawed merchandise
second[1] 7
flawless°
absolute 1
complete 4
exquisite 5
faultless
immaculate 3
impeccable
incorrupt 1
infallible 1
nice 3
perfect 2, 3
polished 1
pure 1
spotless 2
watertight 2
flawlessly
pat[2] 1
perfectly 2, 3
flawlessness
perfection 1
precision 1
purity 1
flaxen
golden 1
flaxen-haired
fair[1] 3
flay
flog 1
lambaste 2
lash[1] 4
pan 5
peel 1
pull 6
reprimand 2
skin 3
slam 3
slash 2
strip[2] 1
flea
-with a flea in one's ear
lecture 4
reprimand 2
send 8
flea-bitten
dapple 1
flèche
spire 1
tower 1
fleck
dot 1, 3
grain 3
pepper
speck
spot 1, 7
streak 1
flecked°
dapple 1
mottled
speckled
spotty 1
fledgling
immature 1
initiate 4
newcomer 2
novice
stripling
flee°
bolt 8
escape 1
flight[2] 3
flit
fly 2
forsake 1
get 31a
heel[1] 4
loose 8
make 26
pull 8b
quit 1
retreat 4
run 2

flee (*cont.*)
shun
stampede 3
take 38b
turn 22
fleece°
cheat 2
defraud
fool 4
gouge 2
hide[2] 1
pelt[2]
pile[2]
profiteer 2
rip 2b
rob 3
screw 6
skin 1
sting 4
swindle 1
fleecy
fuzzy 1
hairy 1
soft 8
woolly 1
fleeing
flight[2] 1
fugitive 2
run 49b
fleer
flout
mock 1
parody 3
fleet°
expeditious
fast[1] 1
flock 1
navy
quick 1
rapid
speedy 3
swift
fleeting°
brief 1
elusive 2
fly-by-night 1
fugitive 3
hasty 3
intangible
meteoric 1
momentary
passing 1, 2
perfunctory 1
shadowy 3
short-lived
temporary
transient
fleetingly
briefly 2
suddenly 1
temporarily 2
fleetness
speed 1
velocity
Fleet Street
press 10a
flesh°
meat 1
pulp 1
-in the flesh°
at **flesh 4**
person 2
personal 1
personally 1
flesh and blood°
at **flesh 3**
kinship 1
-one's flesh and blood°
at **flesh 5**
family 1
flesh-colour(ed)
pink[1] 2
fleshiness
fat 5
fleshly
animal 4
carnal
earthly 2
mortal 2
outward
physical
sensual

fleshly (*cont.*)
sexual 2
temporal 1
worldly 1
flesh out°
at **flesh 6**
complement 3
elaborate 4
expand 4
make 39a
pad 5
flesh-peddler
pander 3
procurer
fleshy
fat 1
obese
plump[1] 1
rotund 3
stout 1
well-fed
flex°
lead 17
flexibility°
elasticity 1, 2
give 18
play 24
resilience
spring 7
flexible°
adaptable
dutiful
easy 3
elastic 1, 2
fluid 3
lax 1
liberal 3
limp[2] 1
mobile 3
open 11
passive 2
plastic 1
pliable 1, 2
receptive 1
soft 1
submissive 1
supple 1
versatile 1, 2
willowy 1
wiry
yielding 1, 2
flexibleness
flexibility 1
flexile
flexible 1
soft 1
supple 1
yielding 1
flexuosities
meander 2
flexuous
meandering
pliable 1
soft 1
tortuous 1
flexure
bend 1
sweep 6
flibbertigibbet
gossip 3
scatterbrained
flick
browse
film 2
flash 5
flip 1
flit
movie 1
thumb 7
whisk 4
-flicks
movie 2
flicker°
blink 1, 2, 5
flare 1
flash 1, 4
flutter 2
glance 2, 5
gleam 1, 2
movement 3
ray 2
shimmer 1, 2
shine 1

flicker (*cont.*)
spark 1
sparkle 1
twinkle 1, 2
wag[1] 1, 2
flickering
faint 1
flash 1
shiny
twinkle 2
weak 6
flier
insert 2
leaflet
pilot 1
poster
promotion 5
publication 2
flight°
escape 5
exit 2
flock 1
getaway
hop 4
pass 29
retreat 1
rise 15
stampede 1
take-off 1
-in flight
aloft
run 49b
flightiness
extravagance 2
flight of fancy
romance 5
flight path
trajectory
flighty°
capricious
dizzy 2
erratic 1
fickle
frivolous 2
giddy 2
hare-brained 2
inconstant
light[2] 8
moody 3
scatterbrained
unstable 1
volatile 2
whimsical 2
wild 7
flimflam
cheat 2
deceit 2
defraud
dupe 3
fiddle 1
fleece
fraud 2, 3
hoax 1
hocus-pocus 1
hypocrite
impostor
mislead
prey 3b
swindle 1
thief 2
victimize 2
flimflammer
fraud 3
hypocrite
flimsy°
delicate 1
feeble 2
filmy 1
fine[1] 6
fragile
groundless
immaterial 1
infirm 2
insecure 3
insubstantial 1
lame 2
limp[2] 3
pale[1] 3
ramshackle
rickety
rocky[2]
shaky 1, 2
shallow 1
sleazy 1

flimsy (*cont.*)
slight 4
tenuous 2
thin 4
tinny 1
unreliable
weak 1, 4
flinch°
blink 3
cringe 1
dread 1
hate 2
jump 2
pull 8a
recoil 1
shrink 2
start 5
fling°
affair 4
carouse 2
cast 7
clap 3
dash 2
flounce 2
fly 8a
heave 2
hurl
lark 1
launch 3
lob 1
orgy 2
pitch[1] 1
precipitate 2
project 4
put 7
revel 3
send 3
shoot 2
slap 3
sling 1
spree
throw 1
toss 1, 2
trial 3
try 5
venture 1
fling back
retort 2
fling closed
slam 1
fling down
dump 1
fling to the winds
trample 2
flintiness
severity 1
flinty
hard 1
icy 2
rocky[1] 2, 3
severe 1
steely 2
stern 1
unkind
unmerciful
flip°
explode 3
flippant 2
fly 7
forward 2
fresh 8
frivolous 2
fume 1
irreverent 2
peg 6
pert 1
thumb 7
wag[1] 1, 2
flip-flop
wave 4
flip one's lid
blow[1] 8a
explode 3
flip 2
fly 7
fume 1
rage 4
rave 1
flippancy°
levity
mouth 4
flippant°
forward 2
frivolous 2
irreverent 2
pert 1
rude 2
satirical
flip side
reverse 7
flip through
browse
run 33b
scan 1
skim 2
thumb 7
flirt°
chat 3
mess 4b
philanderer
play 9b
roué
temptress
toy 4
trifle 3
flirtation
liaison 3
flirtatious°
kittenish
seductive
sexy 1
flirty
flirtatious
flit°
flutter 2
fly 1
gad
leave[1] 1
roll 2
run 1
sail 3
tear 3
whip 3
flitter
flutter 2
flivver
rattletrap
float°
buoy 1
drift 1
glide
hover 1
launch 4
poise 3
ride 2
roll 3
sail 3
soar 1
waft 1
floatable
buoyant 1
floating
buoyant 1
migrant 2
movable
floating dock
pier 1
floccose
fuzzy 1
woolly 1
flocculent
fuzzy 1
woolly 1
floccus
fuzzy 1
flock°
assembly 1
cluster 2
company 2
crowd 1, 3
flake 1
flight[1] 4
gather 2
herd 1, 3
huddle 3
many 3
mass 8
pack 3
press 7
score 4
swarm 1, 2
throng 1, 2
flocky
woolly 1
flog°
beat 1
chastise
hide[2] 2
hit 1
lambaste 1
lash[1] 3
lather 4
paddle 4
peddle
punish 2
scourge 3
sell 2
slash 2
strike 1
switch 3
whip 1
flogging
punishment 2
thrashing 1
whipping 1
works 3b
flood°
crowd 1, 3
drench
drown 1
flock 2
flow 2, 6
flush[1] 2, 5
glut 3
gush 1, 3
infest
many 3
ocean 2
outburst
outpouring
overwhelm 2
pile[1] 6
pour 1
rain 3
rash[2] 2
rinse 1, 3
rise 5
river 2
run 6
satiate 1
sea 3
shower 2
spate
spill 4
stream 2, 3, 4, 5
submerge 3
suffuse
surfeit
surge 1, 2
swamp 2
swarm 1, 2
torrent
volley 2
water 6
wave 2
floor°
amaze
astonish
astound
daze 1
devastate 2
dumbfound
fell
flatten 2
knock 4b, 6a
lay[1] 18c
level 13
overpower 2
prostrate 2
stagger 2
storey
surprise 1
throw 3
–to the floor
over 10
floored
daze 4
dumbfounded
prostrate 4
thunderstruck
flooring
floor 1
floor show
cabaret 2
floor-walker
foreman
floozie
bitch 2
jade 2
tart[2] 2
flop°
dud 1
fail 1
failure 3
fall 12, 20
fiasco
flip 1
flutter 1
loser
misfire 1, 2
pad 3
plump[2] 1, 4
strike 17a
washout
wrong 8b
flopping
flutter 4
floppy
flabby 1
limp[2] 1
slack 2
floral arrangement
spray[2]
Florence Nightingale
nurse 1
floret
flower 1
florid
brassy 1
flamboyant 1
flowery
garish
gaudy
grandiose 1
luxuriant 3
ornate
overwrought 2
rhetorical 3
rosy 1
showy
floridity
glare 3
glitter 4
floridness
flourish 3
glare 3
glitter 4
floss
fluff 1
flossy
fuzzy 1
flotilla
fleet[1]
navy
flounce°
camp[2] 2
flop 1
frill 1
fringe 1
ruffle 1
sweep 3
walk 1
flounder°
blunder 1
pitch[1] 4
reel 1
squirm
stumble 1
trip 5
wallow 3
welter 2
floundering
incompetent
flourish°
abound 1
boom 2
dangle 2
dash 6
display 3, 5
fanfare 1
flaunt
get 27
grow 1
increase 1
make 31b
ostentation
pan 6
flourish (*cont.*)
panache
place 10
prosper
root[1] 5
shake 4
shoot 4
stroke 3
succeed 3
swing 1, 3
thrive
verve
wield 1
flourishing°
expansion 1
fresh 6
fruitful 3
going 1
golden 5
hale
healthy 1
lush 1
prosperous 2
rampant 2
rank[2] 1
strong 11
successful 1
swing 3
flout°
break 9
defy 1
deride
disobey
fly 6
gibe 1
jeer 1
mock 1
rebel 2
scorn 3
snap 6
taunt 1
thumb 8
flouted
broken 5
flow°
circulate 1
circulation 1
current 5
derive 2
discharge 11
drain 6
drift 3
ebb 1
emanate 1
flood 3, 6
flush[1] 5
follow 7
fuse
glide
gush 1, 3
issue 11
movement 1
originate 2
outpouring
pass 2
passage 6
pour 1
progression 3
river 2
roll 2, 10a
run 6, 7
sail 3
shed[2] 3
spate
spout 1
stem[1] 3
stream 2, 3, 4
succession 2
surge 1, 2
swarm 2
torrent
trickle 1
wash 3, 14
well[2] 2
flower°
choice 3
develop 2
flourish 1
gem 2
grow 1
pearl
plant 1
pride 3
put 17b
sprout
flower arrangement
spray[2]
flowerbed
border 6
flower child
hippie
floweret
flower 1
floweriness
flourish 3
flowering
flourishing
growth 1
flowerpot
planter
flowery°
luxuriant 3
ornate
overwrought 2
pompous 2
flowing
circulation 1
fluent
fluid 2
graceful 1
liquid 2
loose 3
smooth 3
streamlined 1
flu
chill 2
cold 10
flub
fumble 2
mistake 1
solecism
fluctuate°
change 7
doubt 2
flicker 2
flutter 1
hesitate 2
oscillate
quaver 1
quiver 1
range 6
see-saw 2
shilly-shally
sway 1
swing 1
vary 2
vibrate
wag[1] 1
wave 4
fluctuating
chequered 2
fitful
flutter 4
hesitant 1
inconstant
indecisive 1
swing 3
unstable 1
variable
versatile 2
whimsical 2
fluctuation°
flutter 4
flux
indecision
quaver 2
swing 3
vicissitude 1
wag[1] 2
–fluctuations° *at* **fluctuation**
vicissitude 2
flue
shaft 4
vent 1
fluency°
facility 1
oratory
fluent°
eloquent 1
glib
liquid 2
smooth 3
voluble
windy 2

fluff°
blow[1] 3
blunder 2
error 1
folly 2
lapse 1
fluff up°
at **fluff 5**
whip 4
fluffy°
fuzzy 1
hairy 1
soft 8
fluid°
glib
graceful 1
juice 1
liquid 1, 2
liquor 2
sap[1] 1
solution 3
fluke°
accident 2
coincidence 3
luck 1
flukiness
vicissitude 2
fluky
incidental 1
flume
race[1] 2
flummery
gab 2
nonsense 1
flummox°
confuse 1
mystify
nonplus
puzzle 1
stagger 2
stump 2
stymie
throw 6c
flummoxed
confused 2
flunk
fail 1
flunkey°
attendant 2
fag 3
hack[2] 2
inferior 4
menial 3
yes-man
fluorescence
illumination 1
light[1] 3
fluorescent
bright 5
light[1] 13
luminous 2
flurry°
daze 3
flap 4
fluster 1, 2
fuss 1
ripple 2
ruffle 2
rush 3
stir 6
flush°
blush
colour 5
even 1, 2
glow 3, 6, 7
level 1
loaded 4
money 4
opulent 1
prosperous 1
rich 1
rinse 1
smooth 1
successful 1
suffuse
wash 1
wealthy
flushed
drunk 2
feverish
rosy 1
flushing
rinse 3
fluster°
agitate 1
confuse 1
demoralize 3
discomfit 1
distract 3
disturb 4
embarrass
excite 2
flurry 1, 2
fuss 1
irritate
mix 4b
perturb
ruffle 3
shake 5
unnerve
upset 1
wind[2] 4d
flustered
agitated
confused 2
daze 4
disconcerted
embarrassed 1
excited 1
nervous 1
unsettled 2
flute
channel 3
furrow 1, 2
groove
flutter°
bet 1
bother 6
flap 1, 2
flare 1
flicker 2
flit
flurry 1
fluster 1, 2
fly 1
fuss 2
lather 2
quaver 1
ripple 2
shake 4
shiver[1] 2, 3
thrill 2
twitter 4
wag[1] 1, 2
wave 4
fluttering
flutter 4
flux°
vicissitude 1
fly°
bolt 8
bug 1
career 2
dash 3
depart 1
escape 1
flap 3
flash 5
flee 1
flit
go 11
hasten 1
hop 2
hurry 1
leave[1] 1
lob 2
make 26
mount 3
overlap 3
pass 2, 11
pilot 3
race[1] 4
rise 7
roll 3
sail 3
scud
scurry
sharp 6
shoot 1
skim 3
soar 1
speed 3
spring 1
streak 5
tear 3
wily
-flies°
at **fly 9**
overlap 3
fly apart
explode 1
fly at
come 8
set 21
fly away°
at **fly 2**
fly-blown
filthy 1
sordid 3
fly-by
pass 29
fly-by-night°
fleeting
transient
flyer
insert 2
leaflet
pamphlet
promotion 5
publication 2
fly front
fly 9
overlap 3
flying
ecstatic
flight[1] 1
take-off 1
fly in the face of°
at **fly 6**
disobey
trample 2
fly in the ointment°
at **fly 10**
catch 18
deterrent
drawback
fly into a rage
fly 7
fly like the wind
speed 3
fly off°
at **fly 2**
take 34c
fly off the handle°
at **fly 7**
explode 3
flare 3
fume 1
rage 4
rave 1
snap 3b
storm 4
flyover
review 8
span 1
fly-past
review 8
fly the coop
escape 1
flee 1
heel[1] 4
make 26
run 2
fly to pieces
come 7
fly up
mount 3
fly-whisk
whisk 5
foam°
bubble 2, 3
ferment 1
froth 1, 3, 4
lather 1, 3
seethe 1, 2
smoulder
foam at the mouth
rage 4
seethe 2
foaming
effervescent 1
foaming at the mouth
furious 1
foamy
bubbly 1
effervescent 1
fob off
foist
wish 3
focal°
basic
pivotal
focal point
centre 1
focus 1
hub
pith 1
pivot 2
focus°
aim 1, 2, 4
apply 5
bend 4
bring 13a
centre 2
concentrate 1, 4
definition 1
direct 4
dwell 2
fasten 2
fix 4, 6
get 37
gist
go 28e
heart 3
hub
intensify
intensity
level 10
limit 6
nail 7
narrow 9
nucleus
object 2
pin 4b
pith 1
point 5
refine 3
seat 2
set 5
shed[2] 2
spotlight 2, 3
stress 4
text 3
thick 10
zero 4
-in focus°
at **focus 2**
-out of focus°
at **focus 3**
focused
diligent
focal
intensive
intent 4
focusing
aim 4
fodder
feed 4
provender 2
foe
adversary 1
antagonist
enemy
opponent
opposition 2
foetid
filthy 1
foul 3
musty 1
nasty 1
offensive 3
rancid
rank[2] 4
rotten 1
stinking 1
stuffy 1
foetor
odour 1
reek 3
smell 2
stench
foetus
child 2
fog°
blur 2
exhalation 2
film 3
fog *(cont.)*
mist 1, 2
obscurity 1
vapour 1
wet 5
-in a fog
disorientated
fogey
see **fogy**
fogged up
steamy 2
fogginess
blur 1
foggy
ambiguous 2
clammy 2
dark 5
dim 1
fuzzy 2
grey 2
hazy 1
indistinct 1
misty
moist 1
nebulous
obscure 1
remote 5
rough 10
soft 11
thick 3
vague 1
woolly 2
foghorn
siren 1
fog over°
at **fog 5**
fog up°
at **fog 5**
fogy°
ruin 5
square 9
stick-in-the-mud
-fogies
elderly 2
foible°
failing 1
fault 1
frailty 2
imperfection
sin 1
trick 6
twist 10
vice 2
weakness 3
foil°
break 4
defeat 2
disappoint 3
discomfit 2
frustrate 1
hinder 1
impede
militate 1
oppose 2
prevent
prohibit 2
spike 3
stay[1] 4
stump 2
stymie
thwart 1
foiled
disappointed 2
unsuccessful 2
foiling
prevention
foist°
impose 1
wish 3
fold°
enclosure 1
fail 4
flap 3
flop 3
go 38b
lap[2] 2, 3
pen[2] 1
ply
pucker 2
rumple
squeeze 5
stall[1] 3
stir 1
fold *(cont.)*
wall 4
wrap 1
wrinkle[1] 1, 2
folded over
double 2
folder
brochure
file 1
leaflet
pamphlet
fold in
mix 3
stir 1
folding
failure 4
folding money
bill[1] 2
money 1
note 4
fold up
fail 4
wall 4
folio
page[1] 1, 3
sheet 2
folk°
people 4
population
race[2] 1
racial
-folks
family 1
folklore
lore 1
mythology
folkloric
mythical 1
folksy
homely 1
follow°
abide 4
attend 4
catch 10
chase 2
conform 1
get 19
go 29a
grasp 2
heed 1
heel[1] 5
keep 6
lock[1] 7
make 37d
model 9
monitor 3
obey 1
observe 1
parallel 4
pattern 7
prosecute 3
pursue 1, 2
result 2
run 26a
shadow 7
spy 2
stalk[1]
string 10a
succeed 1, 2
tag 5
tail 4
take 29b
trace 4
track 4, 6
trail 6, 7
watch 3
-as follows
thus 1
follow closely
heel[1] 5
hug 2
follower°
addict 2
admirer 1
attendant 2
disciple 2
enthusiast
fan
fiend 2
hanger-on
henchman
partisan 1
satellite 2

follower (*cont.*)
student 2
supporter 1
-followers
company 2
public 9
retinue
school 2
suite 3
train 2
following
attendant 1
back 5
clientele
company 2
future 2
posterior 2
public 9
pursuit 1
retinue
second[1] 1
subsequent 1, 2
suite 3
trade 4
train 2
wake[2] 2
follow in the footsteps of
trace 4
follow on with
pursue 2
take 39b
follow through°
at **follow 10**
prosecute 2
follow-through°
follow up°
at **follow 11**
prosecute 2
pursue 2
follow-up°
outcome
result 1
sequel
follow up on°
at **follow 11**
get 39b
put 27b
folly°
absurdity 1
indiscretion 1
insanity 2
lunacy 2
madness 2
stupidity 2
vanity 2
foment°
arouse 3
excite 1
ferment 2
fire 8b
incite
inflame 1
kindle
pick 3
provoke 2
rise 16
touch 11b
fomentation
incitement 2
sedition
fomenting
incitement 1
inflammatory
fond°
affectionate
attached 3
care 6b
devoted
dote
infatuated
keen[1] 7
like[2] 1
love 8
maternal
partial 3
paternal 1
sweet 8
tender[1] 6
fondle°
caress 2
cuddle 2
feel 2

fondle (*cont.*)
handle 2
love 6
pet[1] 4
stroke 10
fondling
caress 1
fondly°
dearly 2
warmly 1
fondness
affection
affinity 2
appetite 1
attachment 3
devotion 3
eye 4
fancy 7
friendship 2
liking 1
love 1, 2
partiality 2
passion 3
penchant
regard 7
relish 1
taste 3
weakness 4
wish 5
font
fountain 1
head 6
sink 12
type 2
food°
board 3
diet[1] 1
fare 3
feed 4
fuel 3
keep 15
meal 1
meat 1
nourishment
provender 1
provision 4
ration 2
refreshment 1
scoff[2] 2
subsistence 2
sustenance 1
table 1
food and drink
sustenance 1
foodstuffs
food
provender 1
provision 4
sustenance 1
foofaraw
frill 2
row[2] 2
splash 4
fool°
beguile 1
betray 3
blind 5
bluff[1] 1, 2
bugger 2
chisel 2
clod 2
clown 1, 3
comedian
dabble 2
deceive
defraud
dolt
dummy 3
dupe 1, 3
fiddle 2
finesse 4
gawk 1
halfwit
have 12c
hoax 2
hoodwink
jerk 5
joke 4
jolly 2
lead 7
leg 8
mess 4a
misinform
mislead

fool (*cont.*)
monkey 2
mug 3
mystify
natural 12
nonsensical
outsmart
potter
put 26
retard 2
sap[1] 2
silly 3
spectacle 2
string 10c
sucker
swindle 1
take 32b
tamper
tinker
toy 3
trap 6
trick 8
twit[2]
victim 2
victimize 2
zany 2
-be fooled
fall 13b
fool about°
at **fool 6**
bugger 4a
dabble 2
idle 6
potter
tamper
tinker
fool around°
at **fool 6**
carry 11c
clown 3
dabble 2
idle 6
mess 4a, 4b
monkey 5
muck 3
play 9a, 9b
potter
tamper
tinker
fool away
idle 6
foolhardiness
desperation 1
indiscretion 1
lunacy 2
stupidity 2
foolhardy°
adventurous
audacious 1
bold 1
daredevil 2
desperate 1
foolish 1
hare-brained 1
hotheaded
ill-advised 2
imprudent
impulsive
indiscreet
mad 2
overconfident 2
precipitate 5
quixotic
rash[1]
reckless
silly 1
stupid 2
unwary
wild 7
fooling about, around
fun 2
foolish°
absurd 1
crazy 2
daft 1
dense 3
dim 2
empty 5
extravagant 2
farcical
fond 2
frivolous 2
halfwitted
hare-brained 2

foolish (*cont.*)
imprudent
inane
indiscreet
insane 2
light[2] 8
ludicrous
mad 2
meaningless 1
misguided
nonsensical
preposterous
puerile
reckless
ridiculous
senseless 3
shallow 1
silly 1
small 6
soft 6
stupid 2
thoughtless 2
unreasonable 1
unthinking 1
untoward 2
weak 5
wet 3
wild 7
zany 1
foolishly
madly 2
foolishness
absurdity 1
folly 1
hanky-panky
indiscretion 1
insanity 2
lunacy 2
madness 2
nonsense 2
prattle 3
rigmarole
stupidity 2
vanity 2
foolproof°
easy 1
faultless
flawless 2
infallible 2
sure 3
foolscap
paper 3
fool with°
at **fool 6**
dabble 2
fiddle 2
potter
toy 3
twiddle 1
foot
base[1] 1
bottom 2
foundation 1
pedestal 1
walk 1
-feet
extremity 2
-on foot
pedestrian 3
-on one's feet
standing 4
-with one foot in the grave
dying
moribund 1
footage
distance 1
measurement 2
football field
field 2
foot-boy
page[2] 1
servant 1
foot-dragging
stall[2] 2
footfall
footstep 1
step 2
tramp 5
foothill
hill 1

foothold
footing 3
hold 25
opening 2
purchase 5
footing°
balance 6
basis 1
bottom 2
ground 3
standard 4
term 7b
foot in the door
opening 2
foot it
walk 1
footle
fool 7b
potter
footlights
stage 3
foot-locker
trunk 3
footman
flunkey 1
servant 1
footmark(s)
footstep 2
trace 3
track 3
footnote
comment 1
gloss[2] 1
note 3
footpad
outlaw 1
thief 1
footpath
path 1
sidewalk
track 2
trail 1
walk 5
footprint(s)
footstep 2
outline 1
step 3
trace 3
track 3
trail 2
foot-race
race[1] 1
foot-rail
rail[1] 1
footslogger
pedestrian 1
foot-soldier
private 5
soldier 1
footstep°
step 2, 3, 6
tramp 5
-footsteps°
at **footstep 2**
trail 2
foot the bill
defray
footway
path 1
sidewalk
walk 5
foozle
bungle
fop
blade 4
dandy 1
dude 1
swell 6
foppish
mincing
rakish
for°
behalf
favour 5
over 4
part 10
towards 1, 2
-as for°
at **for 12**
concerning
-as for oneself
personally 2

-be for
lend 3
serve 2
suit 2
forage
feed 4
look 6b
provender 2
raid 2
root[2]
foray
charge 7
inroad 1
invasion 1
push 15
forbear
help 3
leave[1] 9
refrain[1] 1
sacrifice 4
forbearance
chastity
indulgence 1
mercy
patience 1
self-control 2
stoicism
temperance 1
tolerance 1
forbearing
easygoing
forgiving
indulgent
lenient
merciful
mild 1
passive 2
patient 3
temperate 1
tolerant
forbid°
ban 1
bar 9
contradict 2
deny 2
exclude 1
keep 13
obstruct 3
outlaw 2
prevent
prohibit 1
rule 8
suppress 1
taboo 3
forbiddance
exclusion 1
obstruction 2
prevention
prohibition 1
suppression
forbidden
foul 11
illegal
impure 3
inadmissible
out 13
pale[2] 3
taboo 1
unlawful
unmentionable 1
forbidding°
cool 5
dour 1
frigid 2
gaunt 2
grim 2
icy 2
inhospitable 2
obstruction 2
po-faced
prevention
severe 2
stern 2
suppression
unapproachable 1
wintry 3
forbiddingly
severely 3
force°
accent 1
action 2
agency
agent 2
blackmail 2

forgetfulness
negligence
oblivion 2
forging
production 1
forgivable
venial
forgive°
clear 21
excuse 1
let[1] 6a
overlook 2
pardon 2
purge 3
purify 2
understand 5
write 5
forgiven
clear 32
forgiveness°
excuse 5
grace 3
mercy
pardon 1
quarter 4
remission 1
forgiving°
charitable 2
human 3
lenient
merciful
mild 1
pardon 1
patient 3
forgo°
abandon 4
decline 1
dispense 3a
forfeit 2
forsake 3
give 17a
miss[1] 1
part 14
pass 22
renounce
repudiate
resist 2
sacrifice 4
shun
sign 8
spare 9
surrender 1
swear 4
throw 5b
waive 1
forgoing
resignation 1
sacrifice 1, 2
waiver
forgone
forfeit 3
forgotten
escape 4
lost 4
undone[2]
fork
diverge 1
separate 4
split 3
forkful
morsel 1
mouthful
fork out *etc.*
expend 1
give 15b
lay[1] 18b
pay 11b
shell 5
spend 1
stump 4
forlorn°
abandoned 1
broken-hearted
dejected
desolate 1, 3
desperate 6
dismal
doleful
dreary 1
gaunt 2
gloomy 2
hopeless 3
inconsolable
isolated 2
forlorn (*cont.*)
melancholy 1
miserable 1
mournful 1
pessimistic
sinking 2
tragic
unfortunate 2
unhappy 1
wistful 1
woebegone
form°
appearance 2
arrange 1
base[1] 5
beat 5
brew 3
cast 3, 9
ceremony 2
class 4
compose 1, 3
composition 2
conceive 2
condition 3
create 1
custom 1
design 2, 3, 6
devise 1
disguise 3
effect 4
erect 3
establish 1
etiquette
fabricate 1
fashion 5
figure 1
formality 1
format 1
frame 1, 3, 7
generate 4
grade 3
health 1
image 6
jell 2
last[3]
make 1, 39b
make-up 3
manner 3
materialize 1
mode[1] 1
model 6, 7
mould[1] 1, 2, 4, 6
observance 2
order 1
organization 2
organize 2
originate 1
paper 2a
phase 3
physique
procedure
propriety 2
protocol 1
repair 3
rule 3
school 2, 4
sculpture 2
semblance 1
shape 1, 2, 3, 5, 6, 8
silhouette
state 2
structure 1, 3
style 1, 5, 8
taste 5
tradition
trim 6
turn 8, 20a, 37
usage 1
version 1
work 13
-off form
off colour 1
par 5b
formal°
aloof 2
ceremonial 2
ceremonious 1
civil 3
dignified
distant 3
dress 5a
dressy 1
icy 2
impersonal 2
literary 2
formal (*cont.*)
nominal 1
official 2
outward
parliamentary
perfunctory 1
polite 1
priggish
proper 2
prudish
reserved
ritual 2
sedate 2
self-contained 2
solemn 3
state 6
stiff 7, 8
stilted
formalist
Pharisee
prig
purist
formalistic
Pharisaic
priggish
formality°
ceremonial 3
ceremony 1, 2
convention 2
courtesy
dignity 1
form 6
function 2
gesture 2
observance 2
pageant
propriety 3
protocol 1
reserve 4
rite
ritual 3
sobriety 2
-formalities°
at **formality 1**
ceremony 2
etiquette
manner 3
propriety 3
protocol 1
rigmarole
formalized
formal 2
form an opinion
mind 13
format°
design 6
form 4
get-up 2
make-up 3
mould[1] 2
organization 2
posture 2
formation°
cast 3
conception 1
creation 1
establishment 1
evolution
fabrication 1
form 1
generation 3
institution 1
line[1] 14
pattern 6
platoon
production 1
rank[1] 4
structure 1
formative
rudimentary 1
seminal 1
former°
ancient 1
bygone
foregoing
late 3
old 5, 6
outgoing 1
past 2
preceding
previous 1, 2
prior 1
sometime 1
-in former time(s)
late 5
-on a former occasion
once 1
formerly°
before 1
late 5
once 1
previously
time 12a
formidable°
arduous 1
awesome
fearsome
frightening
grim 2
important 3
impressive
mountainous 2
overwhelming 1
potent 1
powerful 2
strong 7, 9
terrible 6
formidableness
difficulty 1
forming
fabrication 1
formation 1
institution 1
production 1
formless
chaotic 1
fluid 3
rough 9
shapeless 1
formlessness
chaos
formula°
composition 3
form 4
index 4
law 3
mumbo-jumbo 2
plan 1
prescription 1
recipe 1
routine 1
spell[2] 2
theorem 2
formulaic
formal 1
formulary
formula
formulate°
compose 2
compound 1
conceive 2
construct 2
devise 1
draw 15b
form 8
frame 7
hatch 2
invent 1
line[1] 23a
originate 1
phrase 4
programme 4
scheme 4
shape 8
turn 8
work 19e
formulation
cast 3
composition 3, 4
conception 1
fabrication 1
generation 3
fornicator
libertine 1
forsake°
abandon 3
back 9
desert[1] 3
drop 7
emigrate
fail 2
forgo 1
give 17a
go 25
jilt
forsake (*cont.*)
kiss 3
lurch[1]
maroon
part 14
pass 22
quit 1
recant
relinquish 1
renounce
resign 1
run 32
scrap[1] 4
secede
spare 9
surrender 1
swear 4
throw 8
waive 1
forsaken
abandoned 1
derelict 1
deserted
desolate 1
empty 3
forlorn 2
lonely 3
lonesome 1
forsooth
truly 4
forswear
deny 3
dispense 3a
forgo 1, 2
forsake 3
lie[1] 1
pass 22
recant
relinquish 1
renounce
repudiate
retract 2
sacrifice 4
swear 4
forswearing
perjury
forte°
field 4
genius 3
gift 2
line[1] 7
resource 1
skill 2
speciality 1
sphere 3
talent 1
forth
forward 5
onwards
forthcoming°
impending
near 4
pending 2
prospective
for this
thus 2
forthright°
above-board 2
broad 5
candid 1
card 14
direct 10
explicit 2
frank 1
front 9b
honest 3
ingenuous 2
matter-of-fact
open 15
outspoken
plain 3
plump[2] 6
simple 3
straight 4
transparent 3
truthful
forthrightly
honestly 2
openly 2
outright 4
straight 14
forthrightness
candour 1
honesty 2
forthrightness (*cont.*)
simplicity 3
sincerity
forthwith
flat 17b
immediately 1
instantaneously
right 13
soon 2
summarily 1
time 17
fortification
bulwark 1
defence 2
rampart
refreshment 2
stronghold
wall 2
fortified
charmed 2
fortify°
confirm 3
defend 2
fence 3
freshen 4
harden 2
inspire 2
lace 4
nourish 3
prepare 6
refresh 1
reinforce
steel 2
strengthen 1, 2
support 1, 2
vitalize
fortifying
bracing
exhilarating 1
refreshing
support 7
tonic 2
fortissimo
loud 1
fortitude°
backbone 3
bravery
determination 1
endurance 1
grit
manhood 2
nerve 1
patience 2
pluck 1
prowess 2
self-control 1
stamina
stoicism
strength 2
fortnightly
journal 1
organ 2
periodical
publication 2
regular 2
fortress
castle 1
stronghold
tower 2
fortuitous
accidental
casual 1
circumstantial 2
coincidental
fortunate 1
haphazard 1
happy 2
incidental 1
lucky 2
random 1
unforeseen
fortuitously
random 2
fortuitousness
coincidence 3
fortuity
accident 2
coincidence 3
fluke
fortune 2
luck 1

fortunate°
benign 3
happy 2
lucky 1
opportune 1
propitious
providential
seasonable
successful 1
Fortunate Isles
heaven 1
fortunately
happily 1
well[1] 15
fortune°
accident 2
chance 1
destiny
doom
estate 2
fate 1
gamble 2
hazard 2
lot 2
luck 1,3
mint 1
money 2
packet 2
pile[1] 2
predestination
property 2
prosperity
providence 2
riches
treasure 1
welfare
-fortunes°
at **fortune 3**
luck 3
story 6
fortune-hunter
adventurer 2
fortune-hunting
time-serving
fortune-teller°
oracle 1
prophet
psychic 3
seer
fortune-telling
prophecy 1
45
record 7
forty winks
doze 2
nap[1] 3
repose 2
rest[1] 1
sleep 2
forum
conference
organ 2
voice 3
forward°
advance 2
aggressive 2
ahead 3
audacious 2
barefaced 2
before 4
benefit 3
bold 2
brash 2
brassy 1
brazen
champion 4
cheeky
contribute 2
dispatch 2
disrespectful
ease 8
encourage 2
expedite 2
familiar 3
favour 8
foment
foster 1
fresh 8
further 5
immodest 2
impertinent
impudent
intrusive
liberty 5
forward *(cont.)*
move 7
nominate
obtrusive
officious
onward
onwards
pert 1
presumptuous
promote 1
pushy
recommend 1
remit 1
send 2
shameless
speed 2
support 1
translate 4
transmit 1
transport 1
forwarder
merchant 3
forwarding
translation 4
transmission 1
forward-looking
forward 3
go-ahead 2
sanguine
forward movement *etc.*
advance 7
gain 9
headway 1
forwardness
freedom 7
impertinence
presumption 1
forwards
ahead 3
forward 4
onwards
fosse
furrow 1
fossick
dig 6
fossil
ancient 3
fogy
old 2
prehistoric 1
ruin 5
stick-in-the-mud
fossil fuel
fuel 1
fossilize
petrify 3
fossilized
ancient 3
petrified 3
foster°
arouse 3
cherish 2
cultivate 3
encourage 2
entertain 3
foment
forward 6
further 5
harbour 3
nourish 2
nurse 2,4
patronize 3
promote 1
protect 2
raise 7
fostering
furtherance
promotion 1
foster-parent
parent 1
foul°
abominable 1
abusive 1
bad 2
beastly 2
black 6
coarse 3
contaminate
contrary 3
damnable
dark 4
foul *(cont.)*
diabolic 2
dirty 1,4
disgusting
dishonourable 3
distasteful
entangle 1
evil 1,5
filthy 1
hateful 1
hideous 2
impure 1
indecent 2
infamous 2
lewd
low[1] 12
monstrous 2
nasty 1
nauseous
obnoxious
obscene 1
offensive 3
outrageous 2,3
perverted
poisonous 2
pollute 1
profane 3
prurient 2
putrid
rank[2] 2,3,4
reprobate 1
repugnant
repulsive
revolting
rotten 1
scurrilous
seamy
sexy 2
shocking 2
smelly
soil[1] 2
sordid 3
stagnant
stormy 1
strong 3
taint 2
terrible 1,4
ugly 2
vile 2
wicked 2,6
wrong 1
yucky
fouled
muddy 1
fouled up
confused 2
fouling
pollution
sacrilege 1
foul language
profanity
foul matter
filth 1
foul-mouthed
coarse 3
evil-minded 1
filthy 3
foul 5
obscene 1
outrageous 3
profane 3
scurrilous
foulness
dirt 3
evil 6
filth 2
impurity 1
ribaldry
vulgarity 2
foul odour
stench
foul play°
conspiracy
foul-smelling
foul 3
rancid
rank[2] 4
smelly
stinking 1
foul temper
temper 3
foul-tempered
waspish
foul up°
at **foul 16**
bungle
butcher 4
err 1
fluff 4
hash 3
mess 5b
foul-up
error 1
mess 3
mix-up
found°
base[1] 5
begin 2
break 17
build 2
cast 9
erect 3
establish 1
exist 3
father 6
float 2
ground 5
institute 3
launch 2
organize 2
originate 1
pioneer 2
prove 3
rest[1] 7
root[1] 6
set 23b
start 7
foundation°
base[1] 2
basis 1
bottom 2,3
derivation
establishment 1
excuse 4
fabric 2
footing 1
ground 3
groundwork
institution 1,2
keystone
origin 1
pedestal 1
preparation 1a
root[1] 1
start 15
substratum
support 8
-foundations
element 3b
-without foundation
groundless
ill-founded
foundation-stone
essence 1
founder°
author
collapse 2
creator 1
fail 1
father 3
flop 3
go 27a
miscarry
sink 1
stock 3
swamp 3
wreck 2
foundering
breakdown 1
wreck 5
founding
establishment 1
formation 2
foundation 3
institution 1
start 15
foundling°
found object
curiosity 3
foundry
mill 2
plant 2
fount
fountain 1
germ 2
fount *(cont.)*
head 6
origin 1
root[1] 1
spring 8
type 2
well[2] 1
fountain°
stream 2
well[2] 1
fountain-head
fountain 1
head 6
origin 1
parent 2
root[1] 1
seat 2
source 1
spring 8
well[2] 1
fountain-pen
pen[1] 1
four-flusher
fraud 3
impostor
swindler
Four Hundred
élite 1
nobility 3
upper 5
four-letter word
expletive 2
oath 2
profanity
four sheets to the wind
drunk 1
four-sided
square 1
four-square
ingenuous 2
simple 3
fourth
quarter 1
fourth estate
press 10a
fox
devil 4
flummox
temptress
foxed
spotty 1
foxiness
craft 2
foxy°
artful 1
astute 1
clever 2
crafty
devious 1
disingenuous
furtive 2
insincere
Machiavellian
politic 1
scheming
sharp 6
shifty
shrewd
slippery 2
sly 1
smooth 8
subtle 3
tempting 1
tricky 1
wily
foxy lady
temptress
foyer
hall 1
lobby 1
lounge 3
passage 4
fracas°
argument 1
battle 1
brawl 1
conflict 1
disorder 2
dispute 4
disturbance 2
fight 7
fray[1]
fracas *(cont.)*
incident 2
mayhem
noise 1
quarrel 1
riot 1
row[2] 1
rumpus
scrap[2] 1
scrimmage
skirmish 1
tumult
uproar
fraction
bit 4
hair 2
morsel 2
piece 3
portion 1
section 2
segment 1
shade 6
fractional
part 15
fractionation
breakdown 3
fractious
cross 6
disobedient 1
fretful
insubordinate
naughty 2
perverse 2
prickly 3
pugnacious
quarrelsome
querulous
recalcitrant
rogue 2
testy
unruly
fracture°
break 1,23b,25
crack 1,5
cranny
flaw 2
rift 2
rupture 1,3
separation 3
shatter 1
snap 1
split 7
fractured
broken 2
split 9
fracturing
separation 3
fragile°
brittle 1,2
delicate 1
feeble 1
flimsy 1
hothouse 2
infirm 1
insubstantial 1
slight 4
tender[1] 1
tenuous 1
thin 4
ticklish 2
weak 1
fragility
delicacy 2
frailty 1
weakness 1
fragment°
bit 1
break 1,23b
chip 1
clip[2] 5
crumb
crumble
dash 1
fall 7
flake 1,2
gob
grain 3
modicum
morsel 2
part 1
piece 1
portion 1
rag[1] 1
relic 2

fragment (*cont.*)
remnant 1
scrap[1] 1
segment 1, 2
shatter 1
shiver[2]
shred 1, 2
sliver
snatch 5
snip 3
splinter 1, 2
vestige
-fragments°
at **fragment 2**
litter 1
odds 5
remain 4a
rubbish 1
ruin 6
wreckage
-into fragments
piecemeal 2
fragmentary°
broken 6
incomplete
partial 1
piecemeal 3
fragmentation
separation 3
fragmented
broken 1, 6
incomplete
fragrance°
aroma 1
bouquet 2
fume 3
odour 1
perfume 1
savour 2
scent 1
smell 1
fragrant°
aromatic
redolent 1
rich 8
strong 2
sweet 2
frail°
brittle 2
decrepit 1
delicate 1, 3
doddering
feeble 1
fine[1] 6
flimsy 1
fragile
girl 1
hothouse 2
impotent 1
infirm 1
insecure 3
insubstantial 1
limp[2] 2
low[1] 4
puny 3
rickety
slight 4
soft 12
tender[1] 1
tenuous 2
thin 4
unhealthy 1
unsound 1
wan 2
weak 1, 2
frailness
delicacy 2
infirmity 1
frailty°
defect 1
delicacy 2
fault 1
foible
imperfection
impotence 1
infirmity 1
shortcoming
vice 2
weakness 1
frame°
border 4
coin 3
compose 2
conceive 2

frame (*cont.*)
construct 1
context
couch 2
create 2
design 2
devise 1
draft 3
draw 6, 15b
fabricate 1
fashion 5
father 6
forge 2
form 1, 4
hull 1
make 1, 4, 6
meditate 2
mount 6
phrase 4
physique
rack 1
raise 2
set-up 1
setting
shape 7
shell 2
stand 17
support 8
framed
fixed 4
frame of mind°
at **frame 5**
cheer 1
disposition 1
habit 2
humour 3
mentality 2
mood 1
posture 3
spirit 8
temper 1
frame of reference
context
viewpoint
framer
author
creator 1
father 3
founder[1]
framework
context
fabric 2
form 4
frame 1, 3
hull 1
organization 2
outline 2
rack 1
scenario 1
set-up 1
shell 2
structure 1
framing
fabrication 1
frame 1
franchise
charter 2, 4
enable 1
liberty 2
patent 1
permission
permit 1, 2
prerogative
privilege
suffrage
vote 2
frangible
brittle 1
crisp 1
delicate 1
flimsy 1
fragile
weak 1
frank°
above-board 2
artless 1
bluff[2] 2
blunt 2
broad 5
candid 1
direct 10
dispassionate 2
downright 1

frank (*cont.*)
expansive 2
explicit 2
forthright
front 9b
genuine 2
honest 3
ingenuous 2
level 11
natural 4
open 15
outspoken
plain 3
raw 6
round 8
simple 3
sincere
straight 4, 6
transparent 3
truthful
uninhibited
unvarnished
frankly
above-board 1
face 13
freely 1
honestly 2
openly 2
point-blank 3
shoulder 6
sincerely
true 4
frankness
candour 1
freedom 6
honesty 2
naïvety
simplicity 3
sincerity
frantic°
delirious 1
desperate 1, 6
distraught
emotional 4
excited 1
fanatical
fervent 1
feverish
furious 2
heated
hectic
hurried 1
hysterical 1
inflammatory
intense 2
lost 8
overwrought 1
raving 1
stormy 2
tempestuous
tumultuous
uncontrolled
wild 5
frantically
warmly 5
franticness
fanaticism 1
fraternal°
brotherly
friendly 1
fraternity°
body 6
brotherhood 2
circle 2
clan 2
club 2
companionship
fellowship 2
friendship 1
league 1
order 9
ring[1] 3
society 5
union 2
world 3
fraternization
fellowship 1
fraternize°
associate 1b
hang 4b
hobnob
mingle 2
mix 2
pal 2

fraternize (*cont.*)
rub 7
shoulder 4
socialize
travel 4
fratricide
murder 1
fraud°
cheat 1
craft 2
deceit 1
deception 1
fake 4
fiddle 3
forgery 1
hoax 1
impostor
operator 3
Pharisee
phoney 2
poseur
quack 1
rip-off 2
sham 1
swindle 2
swindler
trick 1
trickery
twister 1
fraudulence
deceit 1
falsity
forgery 1
fraudulent°
base[2] 5
bogus
counterfeit 1
deceitful
deceptive 2
dishonest
fake 5
false 2, 3
foul 7
glossy 2
hollow 4
mock 3
phoney 1
pious 2
quack 2
sham 2
spurious
unreal 3
fraught°
explosive 1
momentous
pregnant 2
tense 3
fray°
action 6
argument 1
battle 1
brawl 1
conflict 1
disorder 2
disturbance 2
fight 7
fracas 1
quarrel 1
riot 1
scrap[2] 1
scrimmage
skirmish 1
wear 3
frayed
ragged 1
shabby 1
threadbare 1
worn 1
fraying
erosion
wear 9
frazzle
exhaust 2
fray[2]
frazzled
exhausted 1
ragged 1
weary 1
worn 3
freak°
addict 2
demon 2
devotee
eccentric 2

freak (*cont.*)
enthusiast
exception 3
fan
fanatic
fiend 2
flip 2
maniac 2
monster 2
odd 1
oddity 2
stray 5
weirdo
freaked out
upset 10
freakish
abnormal 2
curious 3
freak 5
grotesque 1
irregular 3
kinky 1
monstrous 1
odd 1
outlandish
outré
peculiar 1
phenomenal
queer 1
unnatural 5
unusual
way-out 1
weird
freak out
explode 3
flip 2
rage 4
trip 9
freaky
deviant 1
formidable 2
freak 5
irregular 3
odd 1
offbeat
peculiar 1
way-out 1
weird
freckled
flecked
mottled
speckled
spotty 1
free°
clear 13, 15, 16, 24, 27, 32
complimentary 2
detach
detached 1
discharge 1
disengage
excuse 2
exempt 1, 2
expansive 2
extricate
fair[1] 6
familiar 3
forthcoming 3
frank 1
generous 1
get 40d
gratuitous 1
hook 5
house 7
independent 1
informal 1
ingenuous 2
jaunty 1
large 5a
lavish 2
leisure 3a, 5
let[1] 8b
liberal 1, 3
liberate 1
liberty 4
loose 1, 2, 5, 11
non-partisan 1
off 6
open 4, 8, 16
optional
out 6
outspoken
profuse 3
public 3
put 24

free (*cont.*)
quit 4
redeem 2
release 1
relieve 2
relinquish 2
rescue 1
rid
save 1
single 1
smooth 3
spare 2, 7
unimpeded
uninhibited
unmarried
unselfish
vacant 3
voluntary 1
wild 4
work 6
-for free
free 4
free and easy
Bohemian
familiar 3
free 8
informal 1
jaunty 1
nonchalant
relaxed
uninhibited
freebie
premium 2
treat 6
freebooter
pirate 1
robber
thief 3
freebooting
pillage 2
free-born
free 1
free choice
licence 1
freed
clear 15
free 2
loose 2
freedom°
exemption
immunity 1
independence 1
laissez-faire
leave[2] 1
leeway
leisure 1
liberty 1, 2, 3
licence 1
margin 3
partisan 4
pass 24
passage 8
play 24
privilege
release 3
right 9
run 39
scope 2
self-government 1
way 7
freedom fighter
guerrilla
partisan 2
rebel 3
-freedom fighters
resistance 3
underground 5
free enterprise
laissez-faire
free-flowing
loose 3
free-for-all
brawl 1
disorder 2
fight 7
fracas 1
scramble 4
scrimmage
free hand
freedom 4
free-handed
wasteful

fulfilment (*cont.*)
realization 2
satisfaction 1
fulgent
bright 1
shiny
fulgurate
flash 4
twinkle 1
fulguration
bolt 5
flash 1
twinkle 2
fulgurous
flashy 1
full°
abundant 2
active 1
ample 4, 6
brim 2
broad 2
complete 1
comprehensive
dead 16
detailed 1
entire 1, 3
eventful
flush[2] 2
generous 3
good 16
implicit 2
inclusive 1
luxuriant 1, 2
mellow 2
mobbed
outright 1
packed
perfectly 4
replete 1
rich 7
rotund 2
round 5, 7
square 5
teem 1
thick 2
thorough 3
total 2
undivided 2
unlimited 1
whole 1
-at full gallop
flat 17a
-at full length°
at **length 3**
-at full speed
double 8
flat 17a
rapidly 1
-at full tilt
blast 4
double 8
post-haste
-in full°
at **full 17**
completely 1
-in full sway
rampant 2
-in full swing°
at **swing 6**
-to the full°
at **full 18**
full blast°
at **blast 4**
full-blooded
pure-bred
full-bodied
full 7
plump[1] 1
robust 2
spicy 1
fullest
full 16
-to the fullest°
at **full 18**
length 4c
-to the fullest extent
best 9
full 18
length 3
vengeance 2b
full-flavoured
mellow 1
full-fledged
mature 1
full gallop
flat 17a
full-grown
adult 1
mature 1
full growth
maturity 1
full knowledge
daylight 2
full-length
unabridged 1
fullness
body 7
entirety 1
maturity 3
tone 2
wealth 2
-in the fullness of time
sometime 3
full of beans
energetic
racy 1
vigorous
vivacious
full of it
mistaken 1
full of life
lively 1
vital 3
full-scale
exhaustive
full score
score 5
full speed
double 8
flat 17a
rapidly 1
full stop
dot 1
period 3
full tilt
blast 4
double 8
post-haste
full-toned
rotund 2
full view
daylight 2
fully
absolutely 2
altogether
amply 2, 3, 4
blast 4
bloated
clean 7
completely 1, 3
entirely 1
full 13, 17, 18
head 8
length 3
quite 1
richly 2
severely 1
simply 1
stark 1
thoroughly 1
through 7
throughout 3
totally
utterly
well[1] 13, 14
wholly 1
wide 6
fully fledged
mature 1
fully grown
mature 1
fulminate
boil[1] 2
explode 1
lecture 4
rage 4
rail[2]
rave 1
thunder 3
fulmination
explosion 1
outburst
fulminous
foul 6
fulsome
disgusting
distasteful
effusive
excessive 2
flattering 2
foul 1
gushy
obnoxious
ornate
outrageous 3
repulsive
scandalous 1
fulsomely
sky 2
fulsomeness
disgust 2
fumarole
vent 1
fumble°
err 1
grope
hesitate 2
mistake 1
solecism
fumbling
left-handed 1
fume°
boil[1] 2
chafe 3
exhalation 2
flare 3
pet[2]
rage 4
seethe 2
simmer 2
smoulder
storm 4
-fumes°
at **fume 3**
exhaust 6
reek 4
fumigant
disinfectant
fumigate°
disinfect
purify 1
sterilize 1
fuming
angry 1
furious 1
mad 4
fun°
amusement 1
entertaining
entertainment 1
frolic 1
merriment
mirth
pastime
play 22
relaxation 1
revelry
sport 1, 2
-for fun
fun 3
-in fun°
at **fun 3**
tongue 5
fun and games
festivity 2
frolic 1
recreation
function°
act 9
action 7
activity 2
behave
business 1
capacity 3
ceremony 1
duty 1
effect 6
go 3, 32c
hold 11
job 2
live 6
manage 4
mission 1
occasion 3
office 4
operate 1
operation 1
function (*cont.*)
part 3
party 1
perform 2
place 4
position 6
post[2] 1
process 2
province 3
reception 2
role 2
run 11
serve 2, 5
take 11
use 7, 9
work 3, 11, 12
functional°
effective 1
effectual 1
operable
operation 5
positive 6
practical 1
serviceable 1
take 11
useful
functionary°
officer 1
functioning
action 7
active 2
effective 3
functional 1
operation 1, 5
serviceable 1
use 9
way 12
fund°
finance 3
get 34
hoard 1
mine 2
patronize 3
pool 2
reserve 3
set 23b
sponsor 3
store 3
subsidize
supply 4
support 4
-funds°
at **fund 2**
backing 2
capital 3
finance 2
mean[3] 4b
money 2
pool 2
purse 2
resource 2
stock 5
treasury
fundament
bottom 1, 2
bum 1
buttocks
seat 4
substratum
fundamental°
basic
cardinal
element 1
elemental
elementary 2
essential 2
first 3
foundation 2
ingrained
integral 1
intrinsic
introductory 2
main 3
natural 3
necessity 1
need 3
organic 2
preparatory 2
primary 1, 4, 5
prime 3
principle 1
radical 1
rooted
rudimentary 1
simple 2
fundamental (*cont.*)
staple 1
ultimate 3
vital 1
-fundamentals
element 3b
heart 3
rudiments
staple 3
stuff 1
fundamentalist
conservative 2, 3
narrow-minded
ultra-
fundamentally
bottom 5
essence 3
inside 6
largely
merely 1
practically 1
primarily 1
principally
principle 4
substantially
ultimately
funding
aid 3
backing 2
subsidy
support 9
funeral°
burial
wake[1] 3
funeral director
undertaker
funereal°
black 4
dismal
doleful
dreary 1
hopeless 3
mournful 1
murky
sad 2
sombre 1
sullen
sunless
tragic
fungus
mould[2]
funk
fright 1
fun-loving
playful 1
funnel
stack 4
vent 1
funniness
humour 1
funny°
comic 1
entertaining
farcical
fishy 2
hilarious
humorous
hysterical 2
ludicrous
odd 1
peculiar 1
priceless 2
queer 1
rich 10
ridiculous
strange 1
tongue 5
uproarious 2
whimsical 1
witty
zany 1
funny business
deceit 1
fiddle 3
fraud 1
hanky-panky
trickery
funny feeling
misgiving
premonition
qualm
sensation 1
funny feeling (*cont.*)
suspicion 1
funny man, woman
card 11
clown 1
comedian
joker 1
riot 2
funster
comedian
fur
hide[2] 1
pelt[2]
furbelow
flounce 1
flourish 3
frill 1
fringe 1
ornament 1
furbish
decorate 2
embellish 1
fix 16b
polish 1
furfuraceous
scaly 2
furious°
angry 1
black 7
blow[1] 8a
bristle 3
cross 7
desperate 2
dirty 5
fierce 2
flip 2
heated
indignant
mad 4
rabid 1
resentful
seethe 2
stack 5
tempestuous
tumultuous
upset 10
violent 1
warm 2
furiously
fiercely
mad 5
madly 3
vengeance 2a
warmly 5
furiousness
severity 5
furl
roll 9
swirl 2
furlough
free 14
holiday 1
leave[2] 2
furnish°
accommodate 3
administer 3
afford 3
appoint 3
award 1
bless 2
contribute 1
dispense 1
equip
fill 3
fit[1] 8
fix 16a, 16b
give 1
grant 1
lend 2
market 4
offer 2
open 25
outfit 4
present[2] 6
produce 6
provide 1
render 3, 7
replenish
sell 2
stock 9
supply 1, 2

furnished room
flat 18
furnishing
administration 3
provision 1
supply 5
-furnishings
equipment
fitting 2
furniture 1
kit
regalia
trappings
furniture°
fitting 2
stuff 2
trappings
furore°
bedlam
excitement 2
flurry 1
frenzy 1
fuss 1
hurry 3
mania 1
pandemonium
passion 2
pell-mell 3
rampage 1
scene 3
sensation 2
storm 2, 3
tempest 2
tumult
upheaval
furrow°
channel 3
cranny
crevasse
crevice
gouge 3
groove
hollow 7, 8
knit 3
line[1] 3
plough 1
pucker 1
rut 1
split 7
wrinkle[1] 1, 2
furry
fuzzy 1
soft 8
further°
abet 2
advance 2
assist 2
benefit 3
besides 1
bolster
cultivate 3
ease 8
extra 1
facilitate
far 9
foment
forward 6
foster 1
fresh 4
improve 2
increase 2
likewise 2
militate 2
moreover
new 3
precipitate 1
profit 3
promote 1
speed 2
ulterior 2
yet 3
furtherance°
progress 2, 3
promotion 1
further down
below 1
lower[1] 6
furthermore
addition 6
besides 1
further 3
likewise 2
measure 10
moreover
furthermore (*cont.*)
yet 3
furthest
outlying
outside 6
ultimate 4
furtive°
devious 1
illicit 2
mysterious 2
oblique 2
sinister 2
sly 1
sneaky
stealthy
surreptitious
furtively
back 6
private 6
secrecy 2
secret 4
secretly
sly 3
furtiveness
secrecy 1
stealth
furuncle
boil[2]
furuncular
ulcerous
fury°
anger 1
bitch 1
frenzy 1
hag
heat 2
indignation
passion 2
rage 1, 2
rampage 1
resentment
scold 2
severity 5
shrew
tantrum
temper 4
violence 1, 2
witch 2
fuse°
blend 2
combine 3
compound 2
connect 3
dissolve 1
fasten 1
fix 1
integrate
marry 2
melt 1
merge
run 8
stick[1] 4
unify
unite 1, 3
weave 2
wed 2
weld 1
fuselage
body 3
fusillade
discharge 10
fire 3
volley 1
fusion
amalgamation
merger
mixture 2
synthesis
union 1
wedding 2
fuss°
bother 2, 8
disorder 2
excitement 2
fanfare 2
fault 6
fête 2
fiddle 2
fidget 1
flap 4
flurry 1
flutter 2
fracas 1
fuss (*cont.*)
fret 1
furore 1
gush 2
hurry 3
lather 2
mother 6
niggle
racket 1
row[2] 2
rumpus
song 3a
squawk 2
stir 6
sweat 2
uproar
fuss-budget
fidget 2
perfectionist 1
fussiness
fault-finding 1
fusspot
fidget 2
perfectionist 1
fussy°
careful 2
choosy
difficult 5
discriminating
elaborate 2
fastidious
fault-finding 2
finicky 1, 2
hair-splitting
meticulous
narrow 3
niggling 2
ornate
overcritical
overwrought 2
particular 4
pedantic 2
perfectionist 2
precise 3
priggish
prissy
prudish
querulous
scrupulous 1
sedate 2
showy
squeamish 1
strait-laced
fustian
bombastic
grandiose 1
mouth 3
nonsense 1
pompous 2
raving 3
rhetoric 2
rhetorical 3
wind[1] 2
fustigate
beat 1
hit 1
fusty
close 12
musty 1
rancid
stuffy 1
futile°
bootless
fruitless
hollow 5
hopeless 4
idle 4
ineffectual 1
pointless
thankless
unprofitable 2
useless 1
vain 2
void 1
worthless 2
futilely
vain 3a
futility
emptiness 2
madness 2
vanity 2
future°
fate 3
fortune 2
future (*cont.*)
potential 1
predestination
prospect 3
prospective
sometime 2
subsequent 1
-in the future
before 3
hence 3
yet 4
futurologist
fortune-teller
fuze
compound 2
fuzz
blur 2
constable
fluff 1
officer 2
pile[2]
police 1
police officer
fuzz ball
fluff 1
police officer
fuzzily
vaguely 2
fuzzy°
dim 1
focus 3
hazy 2
imprecise
indefinite 3
indistinct 1
inexact
misty
muddy 2
nebulous
obscure 2
sketchy
soft 8, 11
vague 1
woolly 1, 2

G

gab°
babble 1
chat 1, 2
chatter 1
drivel 2
froth 2
jabber 1
jargon 2
patter[2] 2, 3
prattle 1, 2
rap 3
raving 4
talk 3
wind[1] 2
gabble
babble 1
chatter 1
drivel 2
gab 1
gibberish
go 32f
gossip 4
jabber 1
jargon 2
palaver 4
patter[2] 2, 3
prattle 1, 2
raving 4
yap 2
gabby
talkative
gabfest
chat 1
gabion
rampart
gad°
journey 3
gad about°
at **gad**
get 25b
journey 3
knock 3a
gadabout
rover
gadfly
pest
troublemaker
gadget°
apparatus
attachment 4
contraption
device 1
fixture 2
gimmick 2
implement 1
instrument 1
invention 2
machine 1
thing 5
tool 1
gaff
spar[1]
spur 2
gaffe
blunder 2
error 1
fault 2
folly 2
howler
impropriety 4
indiscretion 2
misstatement 2
misstep 2
mistake 1
peccadillo
solecism
tongue 4
gaffer
boss 1
chief 1
director 1
employer 1
foreman
leader 1
master 1
overseer
gag°
heave 4
joke 1
quip 1
regurgitate
shut 6b
silence 4
story 1
trick 2
vomit
wisecrack 1
witticism
-for a gag
fun 3
-gags
humour 2
gaga
crazy 1
decrepit 1
smitten 2
gage
gauge 1, 2, 3
hostage
measure 2, 4, 11
pace 4
pawn[1] 1
pledge 2, 5
security 3
gaging
measurement 1
gagster
joker 1
gaiety°
bliss
cheer 2
festivity 1
frolic 1
fun 1
glee
hilarity
joy 2
merriment
mirth
revelry
sparkle 4
gaieties°
at **gaiety 2**
gaily°
happily 2
gain°
accomplish
achieve 2
gain (*cont.*)
acquire
acquisition 1
advantage 2
appreciate 2
appreciation 2
benefit 1, 4
blessing 2
booty
buy 1
carry 6, 10a
conquer 2
derive 1
find 5
get 44d
good 19
grow 5
headway 2
hit 6
improve 3
improvement 2
increase 4
increment
jump 5, 9
killing 2
look 11c
make 7
money 3
net[2] 1
notch 4
obtain 2
pay 12
pick 8f
plus 3
possess 5
prevail 1
prize[1] 2
proceed 3
procure 1
profit 1, 2, 5
prosper
purchase 2
purpose 3
put 22c
realize 3
reap 2
receive 1
recovery 1
return 5, 9
revenue
rise 14
sake 1
secure 5
take 1, 40
triumph 3
usefulness
win 1, 2
yield 5
-gains
income
receipt 3
gain access to
get 30a
gain command of
take 37
gain consciousness
revive 1
gain control
prevail 1
snap 7
subdue 1
take 37
gainful°
advantageous
profitable 1
rewarding
useful
worthwhile 1
gain ground
gain 2, 3, 4, 7
headway 2
improve 3
gain mastery
prevail 1
subdue 1
gain on
overhaul 1
overtake 1
gain possession (of)
possess 5
possession 4

gain possession (of) *(cont.)*
take 1, 37
gainsay
contradict 1
deny 1
dispute 1
traverse 3
gainsaying
negative 4
gain the advantage over
upset 4
gain the upper hand over
subdue 1
gait
motion 3
rate[1] 1
walk 6
gal
girl 1
miss[2]
steady 9
woman 3
gala°
celebration 3
feast 2
fête 1
function 2
holiday 2
occasion 3
pageant
revel 3
special 2
gala day
festival 2
galavant
journey 3
gale°
blast 1
blow[1] 9
hurricane
storm 1
gal Friday
aide
second[1] 8
galilee
portico
galivant
journey 3
gall°
anger 2
arrogance
assurance 4
brass
chafe 2
effrontery
exasperate 2
face 5
fester 2
freedom 7
gnaw 3
impertinence
impudence
infuriate
jar[2] 3
molest 1
nerve 2
offend 1
plague 3
presumption 1
provoke 3
rankle
sauce 2
scandalize
spite 1
venom 2
worry 2
gall and wormwood
bitterness 1
spite 1
gallant°
attentive 2
brave 1
chivalrous
courageous
dandy 1
daredevil 2
dauntless
fearless
heroic 1
gallant *(cont.)*
intrepid
manly
philanderer
stout 2
well-bred
gallantry
chivalry
courage
prowess 2
gallery
portico
galley
kitchen
gallimaufry
assortment 2
clutter 1
confusion 5
hash 1
hotchpotch
medley
mess 2
miscellany
mishmash
mixture 1
pastiche
patchwork
pot-pourri
stew 1
galling
grating 1
painful 2
provocative 2
wicked 5
gallivant
gad
journey 3
roam
run 23
galloot
clown 2
gawk 1
hulk 2
peasant
slob
gallop
run 1
tear 3
-at a gallop
flat 17a
rapidly 1
gallows°
galoot
boor 2
clown 2
gawk 1
hulk 2
peasant
slob
galore°
galumph
bound[2] 3
plod 1
galvanize
activate
electrify 2
energize
excite 1
foment
inspire 1
intoxicate 2
kindle
motivate
pump 4b
quicken 3
rouse 2
spark 2
stimulate 1
stir 4
thrill 3
transfix 2
wake[1] 2
galvanized
excited 2
galvanizing
electric
exciting 1
sensational 1
thrilling
gam
leg 1
gambado
caper 1
frolic 2
gambit
device 2
feint
gesture 2
machination
manoeuvre 1
wile
gamble°
adventure 4
bet 2
chance 4
dare 2
fling 3
game 9
hazard 2, 3
lay[1] 4
pawn[1] 2
play 7
plunge 4
punt 1, 2
put 6
risk 1, 2
speculate 2
speculation 3
stake[2] 4
venture 1, 3
gamble on°
at **gamble 2**
gambler
better[2]
player 3
punter 1
gambling
speculation 3
gambol
bound[2] 3
caper 1, 3
cavort
dance 1
fool 7a
frisk 1
frolic 2, 3
hop 1
jump 1
lark 2
leap 2
play 1
prance
skip 1, 3
sport 4
trip 4
gambolling
sportive
game°
amusement 2
competition 2
contest 1
diversion 3
gamble 1
gritty 2
hoax 1
intrepid
joke 2
kill 8
lark 1
line[1] 7
match 2
monkey 2
plaything 1
prey 1
quarry[1]
racket 2
ready 2
running 2
scheme 3
stalwart 3
venturesome 2
wile
willing
gameness
grit
gumption 2
pluck 1
spirit 5
spunk
strength 2
game plan
path 3
scheme 1
strategy
gamesome
sportive
gamester
better[2]
player 3
punter 1
game surface
board 2
game table
board 2
gamin
guttersnipe
imp
lad
ragamuffin
gaming-table
board 2
gammon
nonsense 1
rubbish 2
trash 1
trick 8
gamp
umbrella 1
gamut°
range 2
scale[3] 1
gamy
high 10
rancid
smelly
stinking 1
gander
glance 4
peek 2
gang°
band[2] 1
cabal 2
clan 2
crew
faction 1
flock 1
group 1
junta
knot 2
machine 3
number 2
pack 3
party 2
rabble 1
ring[1] 3
set 26
shift 4
squad
team 1
union 2
gangland
underworld 1
gangling
lanky
lean[1] 1
raw-boned
skinny
spare 3
tall 2
thin 1
gangly
lean[1] 1
skinny
gang member
gangster
gangrene
mortify 3
gangrenous
ulcerous
gangster°
criminal 3
henchman
hoodlum
outlaw 1
racketeer
thug
gang up°
at **gang 3**
gannet
glutton
Ganymede
servant 1
waiter
gaol
imprison
jail 1
gaol *(cont.)*
keep 9
lock[1] 9
nick 2
prison
punish 2
put 13b
restrain 3
send 5, 9b
stir 7
-in gaol
inside 7
gaolbird
inmate
prisoner
gaoler
jailer
gaoling
punishment 2
gap°
aperture
breach 3
break 26, 27
canyon
cavity
chink
clearance 1
crack 1
delay 5
discrepancy
disparity
distance 1
gorge 1
gulf 2
hold-up 2
interlude
interruption 2
interval 3
jump 12
lapse 2
leak 2
opening 1
pass 23
ravine
rift 1
skip 4
space 3
split 7
vacancy 1
void 5
wait 4
gape°
gawk 2
gaze 1
marvel 1
ogle 2, 3
rubberneck 1
stare 1
wonder 4
gaping
open 1
gaping void
abyss
garage sale
sale 3
garb
clothe 1
costume
cover 5
dress 1
ensemble 1
garments
habit 3
outfit 2
robe 2, 3
suit 3
wear 8
garbage°
dirt 1
drivel 3
filth 1
gab 2
gibberish
gobbledegook 1
jargon 2
junk 1
moonshine 2
nonsense 1
prattle 3
refuse[2]
rubbish 1, 2
stuff 4
swill 1
trash 1, 3
garbage *(cont.)*
waste 7
garbage dump
dump 3
garble°
distort 2
misrepresent
slur 2
twist 2
garbled
disconnected 2
inarticulate 2
incoherent
garbling
twist 9
garden
flat 18
park 1
Garden of Eden
heaven 3
garden party
picnic 1
garden plot
allotment 2
garden-variety
common 1
informal 1
mediocre
mill 4
ordinary 2
gargantuan
big 2
colossal 1
enormous
gigantic
great 1
huge
large 3
massive
monstrous 3
prodigious 1
thumping 1
gargle
wash 13
gargoyle
spout 3
garish°
conspicuous 2
extravagant 4
flashy 1
gaudy
gay 3
glaring 2
loud 2
luxuriant 3
overwrought 2
showy
strong 19
tasteless 1
tawdry
garishly
gaily 1
garishness
gaiety 3
glare 3
glitter 4
garland°
ring[1] 1
garment
robe 1
-garments°
apparel
clothes
costume
ensemble 1
gear 3
habit 3
rag[1] 3
robe 2
garment-industry
rag[1] 4
garment-maker
tailor 1
garner°
gain 1
gather 1
harvest 3
heap 3
make 7
pick 2
reap 1
scrape 6

garnering
collection 1

garnish
beautify
decorate 1
decoration 1
elaborate 3
elaboration 1
embellish 1
embellishment 2
grace 6
ornament 1, 2
top 4

garnishing
ornamental

garnishment
decoration 1
elaboration 1
ornament 1

garrison
occupy 1
station 4

garrotte
choke 1
mug 5

garrulous
expansive 2
lengthy
talkative
voluble
windy 2
wordy

garter
decoration 2

gas
exhalation 2
exhaust 6
fluid 1
froth 2
fume 3
hot air
jabber 1
moonshine 2
mouth 3
nonsense 1
patter[2] 2, 3
prattle 1, 2
riot 2
talk 3
wind[1] 3

gasbag
braggart
talker 2

gasconade
bluff[1] 3
bombast
bravado
exaggeration
hot air
rant 3
rhetoric 2

gash°
cut 1, 19
flaw 2
furrow 1, 2
gouge 1, 3
hack[1] 1, 3
incision
lacerate
leak 2
nick 1
notch 1, 3
rent[2]
rip 3
scratch 1, 4
slash 1, 4
slit 1, 2
snip 2
split 7
tear 4
wound 1, 3

gash-hound
roué

gaslight
light[1] 1

gas main
main 5

gasp°
exhale
gag[1] 2
heave 3
pant 1
puff 4

gasper
fag 5

gasping
breathless 1
short-winded

gassy
effervescent 1

gastralgia
indigestion

gastronome
epicure
gourmet
sensualist
sybarite

gat
pistol
revolver

gate°
attendance 2
discharge 9
entrance[1] 2
exit 1
gross 7
mouth 2
proceed 3
receipt 3
revenue
take 40
turnout 1
yield 5

gateau
cake 1

gatecrasher
intruder 1
outsider

gatehouse
lodge 1

gatekeeper
porter[2] 2

gateway
gate 1
mouth 2

gather°
accumulate
amass
assemble 1, 2
brush[2] 4
bunch 4
bundle 2
call 4
catch 10
clump 3
cluster 3
collect 1, 2
compile
concentrate 3
crowd 3
deduce
derive 1
draw 4
enlist 2
find 7
flock 2
fold 1, 2, 4
gain 1
garner
get 50a, 50b
group 4
harvest 2
heap 3
hear 2
herd 3, 4
hoard 2
huddle 3
imagine 2
infer
learn 1
make 7
mass 7, 8
meet[1] 2
muster 1
perceive 2
pick 2, 8b
piece 13
pool 4
press 7
presume 1
pucker 1, 2
raise 5
rake[1] 1, 3, 8
rally 3
reap 1
receive 5
round 19

gather *(cont.)*
ruffle 1
scare 2
scoop 6
scrape 6
sit 2
summon 2
surmise 1
swarm 2
take 19
throng 2
understand 3, 4
wind[1] 6
wrinkle[1] 2

gatherer
collector

gathering°
accumulation 1
assembly 1
attendance 2
bunch 2
cluster 2
collection 1
company 2
convention 1
council 1
flock 1
function 2
get-together
group 1
jamboree
knot 2
meeting 2
muster 2
pack 3
party 1
press 8
rally 1
round-up 1
ruffle 1
throng 1
turnout 1

gathering-place
haunt 3

gather together
amass
band[2] 3
bundle 2
collect 1
herd 4
pack 8a
raise 5
rake[1] 1

gather up
collect 2
find 7
rake[1] 1, 3
scoop 6

gauche
awkward 1
clumsy
incompetent
inept 1
left-handed 1
plebeian 2
rude 4
tactless
tasteless 1
uncivilized 2
ungracious
unrefined 1
vulgar 1

gaucheness
vulgarity 1

gaucherie
fault 2
impropriety 4
ineptitude 1
solecism
vulgarity 1

gaudily
gaily 1

gaudiness
gaiety 3
glare 3
glitter 4

gaudy°
conspicuous 2
extravagant 4
flamboyant 2
flashy 1
garish
gay 3
loud 2

gaudy *(cont.)*
luxuriant 3
overwrought 2
shoddy
showy
tacky[2]
tasteless 1
tawdry

gauge°
calculate
calibre 1
consider 3
estimate 1, 3
estimation 3
evaluate 2
extension 2
fathom
indicator
make 21
measure 2, 4, 11, 12
norm 2
pace 4
pattern 1
plumb 5
rate[1] 6
reckon 2
regard 4
screen 8
size 3
standard 1
view 9
yardstick

gauging
measurement 1

gaunt°
emaciated
haggard
lanky
lean[1] 1
meagre 2
peaky
raw-boned
scrawny
skinny
spare 3
thin 1

gauntlet
dare 1

gaup
gape 1
gawk 2
ogle 2

gauze
filter 1

gauzy
filmy 1
fine[1] 6
flimsy 3
see-through
sheer 3
thin 5

gawk°
gape 1
ogle 2
rubberneck 1
stare 1
wonder 4

gawking
goggle-eyed

gawky
awkward 2
boorish
clumsy
rustic 2

gawp
gape 1
gawk 2
ogle 2
stare 1

gay°
blithe 1
bright 8
cheerful 1, 2
debonair 2
effeminate
frolicsome
gala 2
gleeful
hilarious
homosexual 1, 2
jaunty 1
jolly 1
joyful 1
light[2] 9

gay *(cont.)*
lively 1, 4
merry 1
perky
radiant 2
sportive
sprightly
sunny 2
swish 4
vivacious
zany 1

gay blade
swell 6

gay dog
philanderer
playboy
roué

gazabo
chap
fellow 1
guy 1
man 1

gaze°
contemplate 1
eye 10
look 13
ogle 2
regard 1
sight 2
stare 1, 2
watch 1

gazebo
chap
guy 1

gazette
journal 1
paper 1
sheet 6

GDP
turnout 2

gear°
apparatus
apparel
clothes
costume
effects
equipment
finery
furniture 1, 2
garments
good 21a
habit 3
kit
luggage
outfit 1
paraphernalia
plant 3
property 1
regalia
rig 3
robe 2
stuff 2
supply 1
tack 4
tackle 1
thing 8c
trappings
turnout 3
wear 8

-gears
movement 4

gearbox
gear 1

gearing up
preparation 2

gear-tooth
cog 1

gear up
fit[1] 8
supply 1

gee-gee
nag[2]

geezer
bugger 2
chap
fellow 1
guy 1
man 1
punter 2
ruin 5
stick[2] 2

-geezers
elderly 2

gegenschein
light[1] 1

Gehenna
hell 1

gel
coagulate
set 3
solidify 1
thicken

gelatinize
jell 1

gelatinous
thick 5

geld
fix 13
neuter 2
sterilize 2

gelid
cold 1

gelignite
explosive 2

gelt
cash 1
money 1

gem°
jewel 1, 2
pearl
pride 3
treasure 2

-gems
jewellery

gemstone
gem 1
jewel 1

gen
dope 3
fact 3
information
intelligence 2
rope 2
scoop 3
tip[3] 2
word 2

gendarme
officer 2
police officer

-gendarmes
police 1

gender
sex 1

genealogical
racial

genealogy
derivation
family 3
line[1] 15
lineage 1
origin 3
pedigree
root[1] 4
stock 2

general°
average 3
broad 4, 6
catholic
common 1, 5
epidemic 1
inclusive 1
indefinite 1
lax 2
loose 5
meagre 3
normal 1
ordinary 1
panoramic
pervasive
popular 2
prevalent
public 1
rough 10
sweeping 1
universal 1
vague 1
vulgar 3

-in general
chiefly
generally 1
large 5b
largely
mainly
ordinarily
whole 5

give someone what for
rebuke 1
scold 1
give substance
flesh 6
give testimony
testify
witness 3
give thanks
praise 4
thank 1
give the coup de grâce
finish 4
give the game away
talk 5
give the go-by
bypass 1
disregard 2
ignore 2
give the green light
approve 1
authorize
enable 3
OK 5
give the impression
feel 6
make 25
give the Judas kiss
stab 2
give the lie
explode 2
give the stamp of approval to
approve 2
give the thumbs down°
at **thumb 3**
refuse[1] 1
reject 1
give the thumbs up
OK 5
thumb 4
give the word
say 10
give thought
note 11
see 12a
give tit for tat
requite 2
retaliate
revenge 3
score 9
give trouble
play 17b
give up°
at **give 17**
abandon 1, 4
abdicate
afford 2
break 10
capitulate 1
cede
climb 5b
come 5b
concede 2
dedicate 1
deliver 2
despair 2
devote 2
discontinue
dispense 3a
drop 7
fall 5
forfeit 2
forgo 1, 2
forsake 3
give 5, 13, 16
grant 2
hand 18a
kiss 3
leave[1] 4, 7, 9
lose 3
pack 6
part 14
pass 22
pull 14d

give up (*cont.*)
quit 2
refrain[1] 2
relinquish 1, 2
render 3
renounce
resign 1
retire 2
sacrifice 3, 4
scrap[1] 4
scrub 2
shun
sign 8
spare 9
stop 1
submit 1
succumb
surrender 1, 2
swear 4
throw 9b
vacate 2
vouchsafe 1
waive 1
wallow 2
yield 1, 2
give up the ghost
die 1
pack 8b
pass 14a
give vent to°
at **vent 2**
let[1] 8c
reveal
vent 3
voice 4
give voice
voice 4
give way°
at **way 11**
bend 5
break 16c
cave 2a, 2b
cede
defer[2]
fold 3
give 9
go 12
obey 1
relent
snap 1
soften 4
succumb
surrender 2
weaken 2, 3
yield 3
giving
assignment 1
big 6
distribution 2
donation 2
presentation 1
soft-hearted
unselfish
giving ground
retreat 1
giving in
submission 1
giving off
secretion
giving out
assignment 1
distribution 2
partition 2
giving up
sacrifice 1, 2
self-denial 2
gizmo
contraption
gadget
gimmick 2
instrument 1
invention 2
machine 1
thing 5
tool 1
glabrous
hairless
smooth 4
glacial
chill 4
cold 1
freezing
frigid 1

glacial (*cont.*)
icy 1
polar 1
wintry 1, 2
glad°
cheerful 1
content[2] 3
ecstatic
elevated 3
exuberant 2
exultant
happy 1
joyful 2
pleased
proud 1
radiant 2
thankful
-be glad
rejoice
gladden°
cheer 6
comfort 1
content[2] 4
delight 1
enliven 2
feast 6
flush[1] 3
gratify
lighten[1] 2
please 1
gladdening
cheerful 2
exhilarating 2
glad eye
eye 5
leer 2
ogle 3
gladly°
happily 3
readily 1
soon 4
willingly
gladness
bliss
cheer 2
ecstasy 1
glee
happiness
joy 1
radiance 2
glad rags
apparel
clothes
dress 5a
finery
primp
gladsome
cheerful 1
Gladstone bag
bag 2
glamorous°
prestigious
romantic 3
glamour°
flair 2
magic 3
prestige
romance 4
glance°
look 13
peek 2
scan 1
sight 5
skim 2
glancing
passing 2
gland
ring[1] 1
glare°
flare 4
flash 4
flicker 3
frown 1, 3
gleam 1
light[1] 3
scowl 1, 2
shine 1
glaring°
blatant 1
fiery 2
flagrant
flashy 1
full 10

glaring (*cont.*)
garish
gaudy
great 11
gross 4
lurid 4
naked 3
obvious
open 13
positive 9
prominent 1
strong 19
glass°
drink 6
mirror 1
pane
telescope 1
-glasses°
at **glass 7**
spectacle 3
glasshouse
hothouse 1
prison
stir 7
glassware
glass 1
glassy°
glossy 1
shiny
slick 1
slippery 1
smooth 1, 2
glaze°
film 4
gloss[1] 1, 3
icing 1
polish 5
shine 4
spread 7
wash 7, 15
glazed
glassy 2
glossy 1
gleam°
beam 2
blink 2
dawn 3
flash 1, 4
flicker 3
glance 2, 5
glisten
gloss[1] 1
glow 2, 4
light[1] 3
lustre 1
particle
polish 5
radiance 1
radiate 1
ray 1
shaft 2
sheen
shimmer 1, 2
shine 1, 4
sparkle 3
twinkle 1, 2
gleaming
ablaze 2
bright 1
fiery 2
glassy 1
golden 3
luminous 1
radiant 1
scintillating 1
shiny
silver 3
spanking 1
spotless 1
twinkle 2
glean
deduce
derive 1
extract 2, 4
gain 1
gather 1
get 21
harvest 2
heap 3
pick 8b
reap 1
scrape 6
win 2

gleaning
collection 1
glee°
bliss
festivity 1
fun 1
gaiety 1
happiness
hilarity
joy 2
merriment
mirth
gleeful°
cheerful 1
ecstatic
elated
exultant
gala 2
gay 2
happy 1
joyful 1
merry 1
radiant 2
sportive
gleefully
gaily 2
happily 2
glen
hollow 7
valley
glib°
eloquent 1
flashy 2
fluent
greasy 2
offhand 2
oily 2
slick 2, 4
smooth 6
voluble
windy 2
glibness
fluency
oratory
glide°
coast 2
elapse
float 1
flow 1
plane 4
roll 2
sail 3
skim 3
slide 1
slip[1] 1
slither
snake 3
stream 4
sweep 3
glimmer
blink 2
flare 1
flash 1, 4
flicker 1, 3, 4
ghost 2
glance 2, 5
gleam 1, 2, 4
glisten
glow 4
ray 2
sheen
shimmer 1, 2
spark 1
sparkle 1
suspicion 2
vestige
glimmering
flicker 3
inkling
glimpse
glance 1, 4
peek 1, 2
perceive 1
see 1
sight 5, 8
spot 6
spy 3
glint
flash 1
flicker 1, 3
glance 2, 5
gleam 1, 3, 4
glisten
sheen

glint (*cont.*)
shimmer 1, 2
shine 1
spark 1
sparkle 1
twinkle 1, 2
glinting
shiny
glissade
glide
slide 1
glisten°
glance 2
gleam 4
radiate 1
shimmer 1
shine 1
twinkle 1
glistening
glossy 1
luminous 1
radiant 1
scintillating 1
shiny
twinkle 2
glitch
bug 6
glitter°
brilliance 1
dazzle 3
flash 1, 4
glamour
glance 2, 5
gleam 1, 4
glisten
radiate 1
shine 1
sparkle 1, 3
splendour 2
twinkle 1, 2
glittering
bright 1
brilliant 1
golden 3
radiant 1
scintillating 1
shiny
twinkle 2
glitz
glitter 4
glitzy
flashy 1
garish
gloaming
evening
night 2
twilight 1
gloat°
glory 5
glob
blob
clod 1
clump 1
global°
extensive 1
general 1
international
terrestrial 1
globally
everywhere
globate
round 3
spherical
globe°
earth 1
orb
round 10
sphere 1
world 1
globelike
round 3
spherical
globe-trot
tour 4
trip 7
globe-trotter
sightseer
traveller
globe-trotting
travel 1
globular
rotund 1
round 3

go along°
at **go 20**
get 28c
play 8a
progress 5
shape 10b
string 10a
sympathize 2
go along with°
at **go 20**
accompany 1
approve 1
enable 3
fall 15
follow 2
play 8a
second[1] 9
side 10
string 10a
sympathize 2
goal-oriented
enterprising
go amiss
miscarry
go ape
rage 4
go around°
at **go 21**
circle 3
circulate 1, 3
flank 3
get 25a
mix 2
revolve 1
roll 1
round 16, 17
turn 1, 4
go ashore
disembark
land 5
go astray
err 1
sin 3
transgress 1
wrong 8a
go at°
at **go 22**
peg 7
goat
libertine 1
monkey 2
score 7
stock 4
sucker
goatish
lascivious 1
lecherous
lewd
libertine 2
obscene 1
prurient 1
sensual
go away°
at **go 23**
abandon 2
bugger 5
depart 1
draw 12b
drop 13
evacuate 2
exit 3
flee 1
flight[2] 3
fly 2
get 28c, 44a
go 31d
leave[1] 1
melt 4
nick 5
part 12
pass 10, 14b
pull 7, 14b
push 9b
ramble 1
retire 1
run 22
shoo 1
slip[1] 6
take 34c
go awry
miscarry
gob°
blob
clod 1
gob (*cont.*)
clump 1
lump[1] 1
mouth 1
mouthful
sailor
trap 3
yap 3
-gobs
lot 5b
ocean 2
sea 3
go back°
at **go 24**
get 32a
recede 1
relapse 1
return 1
revert
turn 13b
go back and forth
swing 1
go back on°
at **back 18**
renege 2
withdraw 2
go back to°
at **go 24**
go backwards
back 2b
reverse 5
go bad
decay 2
decompose 2
go 31e
putrefy
rot 1
sour 5
spoil 4
turn 5
go bankrupt
collapse 2
fail 4
fold 3
go 38b
wall 4
gobbet
blob
gob
lump[1] 1
morsel 1
gobble
consume 1
devour 1
gorge 3
gulp 1
scoff[2] 1
take 13
gobbledegook°
cant 2
gab 2
gibberish
hocus-pocus 2
jargon 2
lingo
mumbo-jumbo 1
nonsense 1
prattle 3
rigmarole
rubbish 2
trash 1
go before
precede
go behind
follow 1
go belly up
go 38b
go berserk
flip 2
fly 7
rage 4
rampage 3
go between
intervene 2
go-between°
agent 1
broker
delegate 1
deputy
factor 2
intermediary
liaison 2
go-between (*cont.*)
mediator
messenger
negotiator
peacemaker
go beyond
exceed 1, 2
excel
far 7
overstep
pass 6
run 33c
surpass
transcend
transgress 2
goblet
glass 4
goblin°
imp
go bottoms up
turn 24
go broke
fail 4
fold 3
wall 4
gobsmacked
speechless 2
go bust
fail 4
fold 3
wall 4
go by°
at **go 26**
elapse
fly 4
get 11
lapse 6
pass 1, 11
slip[1] 5
walk 1
go-by
skip 4
go by the board
pass 10
go counter to
disobey
fly 6
traverse 3
go crazy
flip 2
fly 7
rage 4
god°
creator 2
deity
immortal 4
lord 3
God-awful
ungodly 2
God bless
farewell 3
goddess
deity
immortal 4
God-fearing
godly
holy 2
pious 1
religious 1
God-forsaken
deserted
remote 2
godless°
heathen 2
heretical
profane 1
satanic 1
ungodly 1
wicked 1
godlike°
divine 1
good 5
holy 2
immortal 2
pious 1
superhuman 1
godliness
devotion 1
piety 2
sanctity
godly°
celestial 1
devout 1
divine 1
godlike 1
good 5
holy 2
pious 1
saintly
seraphic
go down°
at **go 27**
climb 5a
decline 2, 5
descend 1
dip 2
ebb 1
fall 3
founder[2] 1
get 36a
land 5
light[2] 13
sag 2
set 2
sink 1, 2, 3, 5
submerge 2
subside 1
suffer 4
taper 1
godown
storehouse
warehouse
go downhill
deteriorate 1
seed 4
sink 4
worsen 2
wrong 8a
go down with
contract 3
God's acre
graveyard
godsend°
blessing 2
jewel 2
windfall
Godspeed
farewell 3
God's will
fate 1
God willing
possibly 1
go far°
at **far 6**
gofer
flunkey 1
menial 3
messenger
orderly 3
runner 2
slave 2
go first
lead 4
precede
go for°
at **go 28**
buy 2
come 8
favour 6
fetch 1, 3
get 4
like[2] 1
make 30b
pick 8i
regard 5
go for a burton
die 1
go for broke
wind[1] 12
go forth
issue 11
pour 4
go forward
advance 1, 3
go 19
proceed 1
progress 5
go from
depart 1
drain 6
quit 1
go from bad to worse
worsen 2
go further
gain 5
go get
get 4
goggle
gape 1
gawk 2
ogle 2, 3
protrude
rubberneck 1
stare 1, 2
wonder 4
-goggles
glass 7
goggle-box
television
goggle-eyed°
go-go
exotic 3
go great guns
flourish 1
go grey
worry 1
go head over heels
pitch[1] 4
go hell for leather
hurry 1
speed 3
go home
knock 5
go hungry
fast[2] 1
go in
enter 1
get 38b
ride 1
side 10
go in advance
precede
go in for°
at **go 29**
favour 6
going°
dying
functional 2
motion 1
moving 2
parting 2
passage 1
passing 1
swing 6
take-off 1
way 12
going after
pursuit 1
going around
current 2
going away
parting 2
going back
relapse 3
going down
downward
going downhill
downgrade 4
going forward
progress 1
going in
entrance[1] 3
entry 3
going off at a tangent
digression 2
going on
go 32e
prattle 2
progress 4
going out of use
obsolescent
going-over
examination 1
going round
current 2
goings-on
hanky-panky
proceeding 2b
goings-on (*cont.*)
transaction 2
go in search for
hunt 2
go in search of
hunt 2
pursue 3
go into°
at **go 30**
begin 2
embark 2
enter 1
examine 1
get 39b
go 29a
look 8
penetrate 1
probe 1
strike 3
study 3
treat 2
turn 16b
go into a nose-dive
slump 2
go into hiding
hide[1] 1
go into hysterics
laugh 1
go into receivership
fail 4
go kaput
wrong 8b
go lame
founder[2] 3
gold
first 7
golden 1, 2
trophy 1
gold brick
good-for-nothing 2
idler
loafer
shirk
slacker
gold-brick
idle 6
loaf[2] 1
slack 4
gold-bricking
idleness 1
gold-digging
time-serving
golden°
melodious
sweet 3
golden-ager
pensioner
senior citizen
-golden-agers
elderly 2
golden handshake
pension 1
gold medal
first 7
gold-mine
mine 2
Golgotha
graveyard
Goliath
giant 1
go like a shot *etc.*
hurry 1
rush 1
speed 3
gollop
scoff[2] 1
go mad
flip 2
fly 7
rage 4
gombo
mud
gomerel
fool 1
gone
absent 1
dead 1
drain 3

gone (*cont.*)
exhausted 2
extinct 1
hopeless 1
lost 1
out 2, 11
past 1
spent 2
spout 4
sweet 8
-be gone
go 13
leave[1] 1
gone to rack and ruin
dilapidated
tumbledown
gone to the wall
insolvent
go next
follow 1
gonfalon
banner 1
flag[1] 1
pennant
standard 3
streamer
gong
alarm 1
buoy 1
ring[2] 1
Gongorism
gibberish
Gongoristic
flowery
gonorrhoeal
venereal
goo
ooze 1
sludge
good°
agreeable 1
beneficial 1
benefit 1
benevolent
benign 1
charitable 2
chaste 1
clean 4
desirable 3
edible
estimable
ethical
exhilarating 2
favourable 2
fine[1] 1, 3, 11
generous 2
gifted
godly
golden 5
handsome 2
incorrupt 1
interest 3
just 2
kind[1]
large 2
merit 1
moral 1
nice 2, 3
nifty 4
noble 4
OK 2
opportune 1
passable 1
pious 1
pleasant 1
profit 2
proper 4
pukka 2
pure 6
purpose 3
rare[1] 2
regular 8
reputable
right 1, 10
righteous 1
sake 1
secure 3
sensational 3
solid 7
sound[2] 4, 5
special 5
sterling 2
strong 10

good (*cont.*)
sublime 1
substantial 3
talented
tenacious 4
tidy 3
tolerable 2
upright 2
use 7
versed
vintage 2
virtuous 1
welfare
well[1] 17
worth
worthwhile 2
worthy 1
-as good as
intent 3
nearly 1
stack 7b
tantamount to
virtually
-be good
behave
-be good enough to
kindly 3
-for good
dispatch 3
finally 2
for ever 1
once 3
permanently
-for good measure°
at **measure 10**
-goods°
at **good 21**
belongings
booty
capacity 2
cargo
effects
freight 2
gear 4
line[1] 16
merchandise 1
power 1
product 2
spoil 6
stock 1
stuff 2
thing 8c
truck 1
wares
-in good condition
fit[1] 3
OK 4
sound[2] 1
-in good faith
bona fide
honestly 1
-in good fettle
hale
healthy
robust 1
trim 2
vigorous
well[1] 16
-in good form
nifty 2
-in good health
healthy 1
-in good shape
fit[1] 3
pink[1] 1
sound[2] 1
well[1] 16
-in good spirits
gleeful
merry 1
-in good taste
aesthetic 1
tasteful
-in good time
soon 1
time 10, 18a, 19a
-of good cheer
cheerful 1

-on good terms
friendly 1
thick 8
good and bad
chequered 2
Good Book
Scripture
good books
favour 4
good buy°
at **buy 5**
goodbye°
farewell 1, 3
leave[1] 1
part 12
parting 2
good chance
likelihood
good character
rectitude
good deal
bargain 2
good deed
favour 2
kindness 2
good enough
adequate 3
decent 3
par 6
presentable 1
satisfactory
scratch 5
good form
decorum 1
manner 3
place 11a
propriety 2
-in good form
nifty 2
good-for-nothing°
derelict 3
miscreant 1
rascal
reprobate 2
rogue 1
scoundrel
shiftless
wastrel 2
wretch 1
good fortune
blessing 2
luck 2
success 1
good-hearted
amiable
considerate
good 6
good-natured
good-heartedness
kindness 1
good heavens
indeed 3
good-humoured
genial
good-natured
good-looking
attractive
beautiful 1
comely
exquisite 3
fair[1] 7
fine[1] 10
handsome 1
lovely 1
prepossessing
pretty 1
shapely
good Lord
indeed 3
good-luck piece
amulet
charm 1
goodly°
considerable 1
desirable 3
handsome 2
large 2
respectable 2
substantial 1
tidy 3

good manners
courtesy
decorum 1
good-natured°
amiable
bluff[2] 2
cordial
friendly 2
genial
gracious
human 3
kind[1]
likeable
mellow 4
mild 1
sympathetic 1
tender[1] 6
good-naturedly
well[1] 8
good-naturedness
kindness 1
goodness
benevolence 1
bounty 1
character 3
excellence
good 20
grace 3, 4
heart 5
honour 1
indeed 3
integrity 1
kindness 1
merit 1
nobility 1
probity
rectitude
right 10
virtue 1
good point
virtue 3
good result
success 1
goods
see **good**
Good Samaritan
humanitarian 2
philanthropist
saviour 1
good sense
discretion 1
understanding 2
good show
congratulations
good-sized
respectable 2
tidy 3
good spirits
gaiety 1
glee
merriment
-in good spirits
gleeful
merry 1
good taste
chic 2
elegance 1
good turn°
at **turn 35**
favour 2
kindness 2
good will
affection
benevolence 1
charity 1
favour 1
grace 3
humanity 3
indulgence 1
kindness 1
readiness 1
good wishes
compliment 2
greeting 3
regard 10
respect 5
toast 1
good word
recommendation 2
goody
titbit

goody-goody°
Pharisaic
pious 2
prig
priggish
prude
sanctimonious
self-righteous
strait-laced
gooey°
mushy 2
sentimental 2
slimy 1
sticky 1
tacky[1]
gooeyness
sentimentality
goof
blunder 2
err 1
error 1
fault 2
folly 2
foul 16b
lapse 1
misstep 2
mistake 1
peccadillo
goof around
idle 6
loaf[2] 1
slack 4
go off°
at **go 31**
clear 30
decay 2
decompose 2
depart 1
drop 13
explode 1
flight[2] 3
fly 2
get 40b
go 23, 33a
leave[1] 1, 2
move 2
nick 5
part 12
pop 1
pull 14b
put 21e
putrefy
ramble 1
retire 1
rot 1
scatter 2
slip[1] 6
sour 5
spoil 4
stray 2
swear 4
turn 5
wander 3
go off at a tangent
stray 2
wander 4
go off into°
at **go 31f**
go off the deep end
flip 2
fume 1
overdo 1
rage 4
goof off
idle 6
loaf[2] 1
slack 4
goof-off
good-for-nothing 2
slacker
goof up
err 1
foul 16b
goof-up
blunder 2
mistake 1
goofy
crazy 1
foolish 2
inane
mad 1
zany 1

go on°
at **go 32**
add 3
advance 3
brew 3
carry 11a
continue 1, 2, 5
extend 3
go 19
hang 7c
happen 1
hold 16a
place 14
prattle 1
proceed 1
progress 5
ramble 3
ride 1
spout 2
talk 3
goon
dolt
fool 1
gangster
henchman
hoodlum
punk 1
thug
go on a binge ***etc.***
carouse 1
dissipate 4
drink 2
paint 7
revel 2
go on about
brag
hold 16a
lecture 3
go on social security
retire 2
go on strike
walk 4b
go on the blink
play 17b
go on the lam
run 2
go on with
continue 1
proceed 1
prosecute 2
take 39b
goop
boor 2
ooze 1
goose
fool 1
silly 3
goose-egg
nil
zero 1
goose-pimples
shiver[1] 4
goose-step
walk 1
go out°
at **go 33**
date 7
depart 1
drain 6
ebb 1
exit 3
fail 3
get 25b, 44a
go 2, 31a
scene 6
slip[1] 6
socialize
step 17b
vacate 1
go out of control
drain 6
flare 3
piece 6
go out of business
close 5
fail 4
fold 3
go out of circulation
retire 2

go with (*cont.*)
go without°
at **go 41**
forgo 1
go without saying
needless 2
gown
dress 6
go wool-gathering
wander 3
go wrong°
at **wrong 8**
err 1
fail 1
miscarry
misfire 1
sin 3
slip[1] 3
transgress 1
GP
doctor 1
physician
grab°
abduct
capture 2
catch 1, 9
clasp 5
claw 3
clutch 1
get 8
grapple 1
grasp 1
hang 7a
hook 6
impress 1
intercept
jump 6
lay[1] 11
mesh 3
occupy 3
pilfer
pluck 3
seize 1
snap 4
snatch 1, 4
take 1
grab-bag
miscellany
grab some shut-eye
doze 1
rest[1] 6
retire 3
grace°
become 4
bless 2
charm 2
elegance 1
enrich 2
favour 4
finesse 3
fluency
forgiveness 2
piety 2
propriety 2
sanctity
savoir faire
taste 4
graceful°
dainty 1
delicate 2
elegant 1
exquisite 1
fluent
light[2] 5
lyric 3
neat 3
polished 2
pretty 1
shapely
sleek 2
slender 1
supple 2
tasteful
willowy 2
gracefulness
delicacy 1
grace 1
graceless
heavy-handed 1
stilted
ungraceful 2
gracious°
attentive 2
benevolent
benign 1
chivalrous
considerate
cordial
debonair 1
decent 4
fair[1] 8
gallant 2
genteel 2
gentle 1
good 6
good-natured
hospitable 1
indeed 3
kind[1]
ladylike
merciful
neighbourly
nice 1
obliging
pleasant 2
ready 2
refined 1
respectful
suave
sweet 6
well-bred
graciously
favourably 1
kindly 2
readily 1
well[1] 5
graciousness
grace 4
hospitality
kindness 1
mercy
readiness 1
gradate
blend 2
graduate 2
gradatim
gradually
gradation
grade 1
notch 2
scale[3] 1
step 5
grade°
blend 2
bracket 3
category
class 1, 4, 5
climb 6
coordinate 1
correct 5
degree 1
denomination 2
distinguish 2
divide 5
downgrade 3
graduate 2
hill 3
incline 4
mark 4, 14
notch 2
place 3, 16
quality 2
ramp
range 7
rank[1] 1, 6
rate[1] 4, 6
roll 7
score 1
screen 8
slope 2
sort 8
stage 1
stamp 8
standing 5
tabulate
gradient
downgrade 3
grade 4
hill 3
incline 4
ramp
slant 3
slope 2
grading
mark 4
gradual°
delicate 6
gentle 3
lingering 2
piecemeal 3
progressive 1
slow 1, 2
unhurried
gradually°
degree 3
piecemeal 1
step 9
graduate°
blend 2
calibrate
rank[1] 6
score 10
graduation
scale[3] 1
graft°
blackmail 1
bribe 1
implant 2, 3
line[2] 2
pay-off 3
rebate 2
union 3
grain°
bit 1
jot 2
kernel 1
modicum
morsel 2
particle
provender 2
scrap[1] 1
seed 1
shade 3
shred 1
speck
taste 1
texture
-with a grain of salt°
at **salt 5**
grainy
granular
gritty 1
lumpy
galloch
gut 1
grammar-book
school-book
grammar school
school 1
grammatically
well[1] 3
gramophone record
record 7
grand°
big 1
brave 2
dignified
distinguished 2
elegant 3
elevated 2
exalted 1
gallant 3
gorgeous 1
grandiose 2
great 1, 7, 12
heroic 4, 6
high 12
imperial 2
imposing
lofty 2, 4
luxurious 1
magnificent
majestic 1
mighty 3
monumental 1
neat 5
noble 3, 5
palatial
posh
proud 4
regal 1
royal 2
scenic
solemn 3
splendid 1
stately
statuesque
grand (*cont.*)
stunning 2
sublime 1
swanky
swell 7
grandchild
descendant
grandeur°
dignity 1
display 5
elegance 2
elevation 4
glory 3
luxury 1
nobility 1
pageant
pomp
quality 3
solemnity
splendour 1
state 3
grand finale
consummation 2
pay-off 2
grandiloquence
bluster 3
bombast
hot air
oratory
raving 3
rhetoric 2
grandiloquent
bombastic
flowery
inflated 2
ornate
pompous 2
ponderous 2
pretentious 1
rhetorical 3
stilted
grandiose°
bombastic
fancy 2
grand 3
heroic 4
inflated 1
lofty 4
majestic 2
ornate
pompous 1
pretentious 1
rhetorical 3
grandly
well[1] 4
grandstand
show 11
theatrical 2
grandstander
trendy 2
grand total
sum 1
grange
farm 1
granger
farmer
grangerize
illustrate 2
granite(-like)
hard 1
grant°
accommodation 5
admit 2, 3
afford 3
agree 3
aid 3
allow 1, 5
assign 1
award 1, 3
backing 2
benevolence 2
bestow
bounty 2
cede
concede 1, 2
confer 2
contribute 1
dole 1
donate
donation 1
endowment 1
extend 4
fund 3
grant (*cont.*)
gift 1
give 1
impart 1
largesse
patent 1
permit 1
philanthropy 2
present[2] 2, 6
recognize 2
scholarship 2
show 10
stipend
subsidy
vouchsafe 1
granted
though 1
grant-in-aid
accommodation 5
aid 3
grant 3
grant-money
aid 3
granular°
gritty 1
lumpy
granulate
grind 1
mill 5
powder 3
pulverize 1
granulated
granular
granule
grain 3
morsel 2
grapevine°
gossip 2
rumour 1
graph
chart 2
profile 3
schematic 2
grapheme
sign 4
graphic°
dramatic 2
eloquent 1
lifelike
lurid 1
photographic 1
pictorial 1
picturesque 2
plain 2
realistic 2
schematic 1
strong 15
vivid 2
grapple°
claw 3
combat 5
fight 1
lock[1] 4
grapple with°
at **grapple 2**
combat 5
deal 4
encounter 3
engage 5
fight 1
grip 5
oppose 1
tackle 3
withstand
grasp°
catch 1, 10, 13a
clasp 2, 5
cling 3
clutch 1, 2a
command 8
comprehend
digest 3
dominion 1
embrace 1
familiarity 1
fathom
figure 12b
follow 8
get 19
grab 1, 4
grapple 1
grip 1, 3, 6
hand 8
hang 7a
grasp (*cont.*)
hold 1, 19a, 24
know 1
knowledge 1
lock[1] 4
make 37d
master 7
mesh 2
obtain 1
penetrate 5
perceive 2
perception 1
pierce 3
pinch 1
purchase 5
realize 2
relate 4
see 2
seize 1
snatch 1, 4
sway 4
take 1
twig[2]
understand 1
understanding 3
uptake
grasping°
avaricious
greedy 2
mercenary 1
possessive 2
rapacious
selfish 1
sordid 2
tenacious 3
grasp the nettle
face 18b
grass°
inform 2
informer
pasture
sell 3
sneak 2
talk 5
tell[1] 11
turf 1
-out to grass
retire 2
grassland
field 1
green 4
pasture
plain 6
grass roots
people 3
grassy
green 1
grate°
gall[2] 3
grating 3
grind 1, 3
jar[2] 3
mesh 1
mill 5
net[1] 1
rake[1] 2
rankle
rasp 3, 4
scratch 1
grateful°
beholden
obliged 1
thankful
gratefulness
appreciation 1
gratitude
thank 3
grate on someone's nerves
pester
trouble 2
grater
mesh 1
rasp 2
graticule
mesh 1
gratification°
content[2] 1
delight 3
ecstasy 1
enjoyment 1
feast 3
joy 1, 3

gratification (*cont.*)
luxury 3
pleasure 1
satisfaction 1
gratified
content[2] 3
feed 3
glad 1
happy 1
joyful 2
pleased
proud 1
gratify°
content[2] 4
delight 1
distract 2
feast 6
feed 3
humour 4
indulge 1
meet[1] 5
oblige 1
pander 1
please 1
regale
satiate 2
satisfy 1, 2
serve 1
slake
suit 2
tickle
gratifying
flattering 2
heart-warming 2
lovely 2
pleasant 1
rewarding
satisfying
welcome 2
gratifyingly
nice 6
grating°
brassy 2
discordant 2
friction 1
harsh 1
mesh 1
net[1] 1
noisy
ragged 5
rasp 1
raucous
riddle[2] 3
rough 8
scratchy 2
strident
thick 7
gratis
complimentary 2
free 4, 13
gratuitous 1
house 7
voluntarily
gratitude°
appreciation 1
glory 2
thank 1, 3
gratuitous°
expletive 1
free 6
groundless
irrelevant
needless 1
non-essential 1
superfluous
unasked
unsolicited
unwarranted
voluntary 1
wanton 4
gratuitously
voluntarily
gratuity
bonus
boon
bounty 3
consideration 2
dole 1
gift 1
perquisite
present[2] 3
tip[3] 1
gravamen
burden 1
nub 2
pith 2
substance 2
grave°
acute 2
bad 11
big 4
carve 1
chisel 1
critical 3
crypt
deplorable 1
desperate 4
dignified
earnest 1
etch 1
funereal
grievous 1
heavy 3
high 6
important 1
major 2
momentous
pensive
po-faced
pressing
scribe 3
sedate 1
self-contained 1
sepulchre
serious 1, 2, 4
severe 2
solemn 1
sombre 1
staid
stern 2
subdued 2
terrible 1
tomb
weighty 2
-with one foot in the grave
dying
moribund 1
grave-clothes
shroud 2
gravedo
cold 10
gravelly
granular
gritty 1
strident
thick 7
gravely
badly 5
deeply 2
seriously 1
severely 3
graven image
image 1
statue
graveolent
foul 3
gravestone
monument 1
tablet 3
tombstone
graveyard°
gravid
expecting
pregnant 1
gravitas
dignity 1
gravity 3
gravitate
incline 3
lean[2] 3
settle 11
tend[1]
gravitating
inclined 3
gravitation
attraction 1
gravity 1
gravity°
dignity 1
emphasis
moment 3
pith 2
severity 2, 3
sobriety 2
gravity (*cont.*)
solemnity
gravy
profit 1
sauce 1
graze
brush[2] 5
feed 2
gall[2] 1
kiss 2
rake[1] 2
scrape 1, 7
scratch 1, 4
skin 5
grease
oil 1, 3
slick 5
greasepaint
make-up 1
paint 3
grease someone's palm
bribe 2
fix 11
pay 10b
greasy°
fat 2
oily 1
ratty 2
slippery 1
greasy spoon
café
great°
admirable
ample 1
big 1
bully 4
capital 6
considerable 1
dandy 2
desperate 4
divine 3
eminent 1
exceeding
excellent
extensive 2
fabulous 3
fantastic 4
fine[1] 1, 11
first-rate
glorious 3
good 2, 18
goodly
gorgeous 2
grand 1, 5
gross 1
heavenly 2
high 4, 13
high-class 1
historic
huge
illustrious
immeasurable
immortal 4
intense 1
large 1
legendary 3
long[1] 1
magnificent
marvellous
mean[2] 6
memorable
mighty 3
mortal 5
neat 5
nifty 3
notable 1
powerful 3
profound 3
proud 3
raving 2
sensational 3
spacious
spanking 1
splendid 3
striking
strong 7, 14
sublime 1
substantial 1
superb
superlative
surpassing
sweet 5
swell 8
great (*cont.*)
terrific 2
thumping 1
towering 1
vast
voluminous 1
whopping 1
world 8
-at great cost
dear 4
dearly 3
-to a great extent
amply 2
deeply 2
largely
very 1
widely 2
greatcoat
coat 1
great deal°
at **deal 6**
full 18
heap 2
lot 5a
packet 2
pile[1] 3
plenty 1
greater
better[1] 2
major 1
greater part
majority 1
mass 4
preponderance 1
greater than
above 4
over 2
greatest
arch 1
best 4
chief 2
end 8b
full 4
leading 2
main 2
maximum 1, 3
outside 6
sovereign 2
supreme 1, 2, 3
terminal 1
top 8
ultimate 2
-to the greatest extent
full 18
length 4c
-with greatest satisfaction
best 10
greatly
amply 1
awfully
badly 8
dearly 1
deeply 2
exceedingly
full 18
highly 1
materially
profoundly
vastly
very 1
widely 2
greatness
dignity 2
distinction 2
excellence
glory 3
magnitude 1
nobility 1
size 1
superiority 2
great unwashed
herd 2
hoi polloi
mob 2
populace
rabble 2
riff-raff
Great White Father
chief 1
greed°
avarice
gluttony
rapacity
greedy°
ambitious 3
avaricious
bourgeois 1
gluttonous
grasping
hoggish
hungry 2, 3
materialistic
mercenary 1
miserly
possessive 1
predatory 2
rapacious
ravenous 2
self-indulgent
selfish 1
sordid 2
thirsty 2
time-serving
venal
voracious 1
greedy-guts
glutton
Greek
classical 2
green°
callow
envious
environmentalist
field 1
fresh 3
fund 2
gullible
ignorant 3
immature 2
inexperienced
innocent 4
jealous
lawn
leafy
lush 1
money 1
naïve
new 6
park 1
premature 1
raw 3
simple 3
square 8
tender[1] 3
turf 1
unfledged
young 2
green about the gills
queasy 2
sick 1
greenbacks
money 1
green-eyed
envious
jealous 1
greengrocery
produce 7
greenhorn°
apprentice 1
fool 3
initiate 4
innocent 5
newcomer 2
novice
recruit 2
score 7
greenhouse
hothouse 1
green light
approval
go-ahead 1
pass 24
greenness
ignorance
inexperience
greensward
field 1
lawn
park 1
turf 1
green with envy
envious
jealous 1
greet°
address 4
hail[1] 1
nod 1
receive 3
salute 1
see 9
toast 3
welcome 1
greeting°
reception 1
salute 3
toast 1
welcome 4
-greetings°
at **greeting 3**
compliment 2
regard 10
respect 5
toast 1
greetings card
card 3
greeting 2
gregarious
pleasant 2
sociable
grey°
aged
ancient 3
dead 10
dingy
drab
dull 5
elderly 1
heavy 9
leaden 3
mousy 1
murky
old 1
overcast
silver 2
sombre 2
stark 3
steely 1
sunless
grey matter
head 4
intelligence 1
mind 1
grey panther
senior citizen
grid
grating 3
mesh 1
net[1] 1
network 2
gride
rasp 4
gridiron
field 2
grid-work
net[1] 1
grief°
affliction 1
anguish 2
care 1
desolation 2
distress 1
misery 1
mourning 1, 2
ordeal
pain 2
penitence
prostration 3
regret 2
sadness
sorrow 1
stress 3
trial 4
trouble 5
woe
wrench 5
grief-stricken
broken-hearted
heartbroken
inconsolable
joyless 1
mournful 1
penitent
sorrowful 1
stricken 2

group (*cont.*)
folk
front 6
gang 1
gather 2
grade 6
herd 1
huddle 1
include 2
lot 1
lump[1] 3
mass 8
mission 3
mob 1
movement 5
order 3
organization 3
organize 1
outfit 3
pack 3
parcel 3
party 2
place 16
platoon
pool 3
rally 3
range 7
ring[1] 3
school 2
sculpture 1
section 1
selection 2
separate 2
set 25, 26
shift 4
social 1
society 5
sort 1, 8
squad
stratum 2
system 1
tabulate
team 1
tribe
trust 4
type 1
groupie
addict 2
devotee
enthusiast
fan
follower 3
hanger-on
miss[2]
-groupies
retinue
grouping
arrangement 1
assortment 1
bracket 3
category
combination 1
disposition 2
distribution 3
formation 3
group 2
inclusion
lot 1
order 1
organization 2
set 25
tableau
group therapy
therapy 2
grouse
complain
complaint
gripe 1
groan 2
moan 2
murmur 2, 4
mutter 2
niggle
protest 1, 3
squawk 2, 3
grousing
gripe 2
groan 4
murmur 2
querulous
grout
-grouts
ground 4
grove
brush[1] 2
stand 19
thicket
grovel
crawl 3
cringe 2
kowtow
prostrate 1
scrape 4
truckle
grovelling°
base[2] 2
ingratiating
menial 2
obsequious
servile
servility
slimy 2
grow°
age 6
boom 2
breed 4
climb 2
come 19b
cultivate 2
develop 1, 2
fill 10a
flourish 1
form 11
gather 5
get 7, 28e
increase 1
knit 2
mount 7
originate 2
proceed 2
produce 3
progress 6
proliferate
propagate 2
prosper
put 17b
raise 3
rise 5, 10
root[1] 5
send 7
shoot 4
spread 6
spring 2
stem[1] 3
swell 1, 2
thrive
grower
producer 1
growing
evolution
flourishing
going 1
increase 5
ongoing 2
progressive 1
grow into
become 2
make 10
growl
roar 1, 3
snap 3b
snarl[1] 1, 2
growling
roar 3
grown
adult 1
big 3
mature 1
ripe 1
grown-up
adult 2
big 3
grow older
age 6
get 28e
grow on°
at **grow 5**
grow rich
prosper
growth°
accumulation 2
appreciation 2
boom 4
development 2
epidemic 2
evolution
expansion 1
growth (*cont.*)
hump 1
increase 3
leap 6
lump[1] 2
maturity 1
progress 3
proliferation
prominence 3
spread 8
tumour
grow up°
at **grow 6**
mature 4
grub
bug 1
food
meat 1
plod 2
provender 1
refreshment 1
scoff[2] 2
slave 3
sustenance 1
-off one's grub
indisposed
grubby
muddy 1
seedy 1
shabby 1
Grub Streeter
hack[2] 1
scribe 2
writer
grudge°
begrudge 1
feud 1
grievance 2
resentment
grudging
jealous 1
penurious 1
petty 2
selfish 2
shabby 2
small 4
small-minded
gruelling
arduous 1
exhausting 2
laborious 1
punishing
gruesome°
atrocious 1
awful 2
fearful 3
ghastly 1
ghoulish 2
gory
grim 3
grisly
grotesque 1
hideous 1
horrible 1
lurid 2
macabre
monstrous 1
morbid 2
sick 5
terrible 4
ugly 1
wicked 2
gruff°
abrupt 3
bluff[2] 1
brusque
cranky 2
curt
harsh 3
husky 2
irritable
po-faced
rough 8
rude 2
short 4
short-tempered
snappish 2
stern 2
tactless
temperamental 1
terse 2
thick 7
ungracious
gruffly
shortly 3
grumble
bitch 3
complain
complaint
gripe 1
groan 2, 4
moan 2
murmur 2, 4
mutter 2
peep 3
protest 1, 3
sound[1] 9
squawk 2, 3
grumbling
gripe 2
murmur 2
querulous
grump
killjoy
misery 4
grumpish
irritable
peevish
grumpy
cantankerous
cross 6
disgruntled
fretful
gruff 1
irritable
peevish
petulant
querulous
sullen
surly
temperamental 1
testy
waspish
Grundyish
priggish
Grundyism
prudery
Grundyist
prig
grunge
dirt 1
filth 1
muck 2
grungy
bedraggled
dirty 1
filthy 1, 2
shabby 1
sloppy 1
grunt
mutter 1
private 5
guano
dung
filth 1
muck 1
guarantee°
answer 7a
assurance 1
assure 1
certify 1
commit 4
confirm 2
earnest 3
engage 3
ensure 1
indemnity 2
insurance
oath 1
pawn[1] 3
pledge 1, 2
promise 1, 3
ratify
seal 2, 4
secure 6
security 3
stipulate
stipulation
undertake 2
undertaking 3
underwrite 1
verify
vouch
warrant 1, 3
warranty
word 4
guaranteed
certain 2
foolproof
sure 4
guaranty
assurance 1
guarantee 1, 2
insurance
oath 1
pawn[1] 3
pledge 1, 2
promise 1, 3
seal 2
security 3
undertaking 3
word 4
guard°
champion 4
cover 1
defence 1
defend 1
ensure 2
escort 1, 5
eye 8
harbour 2
jailer
keep 2
keeper
lookout 1, 2
mind 18
monitor 1
patrol 1, 3
picket 3
police 2
preserve 1
protect 1
protection 1
rampart
safeguard 2
save 2
screen 7
secure 7
sentinel
shelter 4
shield 1, 2
train 2
watch 2, 4, 7
watchman
-be on guard
look 9
-off guard
nap[1] 2
unawares 1
unprepared 1
unsuspecting
-on guard
alert 1
awake 4
noncommittal
observant 1
warn 1
wary
watch 8
-on one's guard
beware
step 12
vigilant
guard against
watch 4
guarded°
cautious
close 16
discreet
gingerly 2
noncommittal
prudent 1
reserved
shy 2
vigilant
guardedly
gingerly 1
jealously
guardedness
reserve 4
vigilance
guardhouse
prison
guardian°
champion 2
escort 1
guard 3
keeper
monitor 1
parent 1
guardian (*cont.*)
patron 1
protector
guardian angel
patron 1
protector
guardianship
care 3
charge 4
custody 1
hand 8
patronage 1
possession 1
protection 2
safe keeping
trust 3
guarding
patrol 2
security 4
gubbins
contraption
device 1
instrument 1
gubernatorial
executive 3
guck
ooze 1
gudgeon
pivot 1
guerdon
price 3
prize[1] 1
reward 2
guerrilla°
partisan 2, 4
-guerrillas
resistance 3
underground 5
guess°
assume 3
divine 4
estimate 1, 2, 3
estimation 3
expect 2
expectation 2
fancy 10
feel 4
gauge 2
hunch 1
idea 2
imagine 2
infer
judge 7
presume 1
presumption 3
reckon 3
say 6
shot 3
speculation 1
stab 4
surmise 1, 2
suspect 2
theorize
guessed
hypothetical
guesswork
guess 3
speculation 1
guest°
company 3
outsider
visitor
guest-house
hotel
guestimate
estimate 1, 3
guess 1, 3
guestimated
approximate 1
guff
hot air
impudence
moonshine 2
prattle 3
guffaw
laugh 1, 3
roar 2, 4
scream 2
guffawing
laughter
guidance°
advice 1
auspices

guidance (*cont.*)
conduct 2
control 4
counsel 1
direction 1
edification
government 1
instruction 2
lead 13
leadership
management 1
oversight 2
providence 2
recommenda-
tion 1
schooling
steer 3
tuition
guide°
advise 1
adviser
channel 5
coach 3
companion 2
conduct 3, 4
control 1
counsel 3, 4
direct 2
director 2
ease 7
escort 2, 4
gauge 3
govern 1
handle 3
head 11
index 1, 2
inspiration 2
instruct 1
key 2
landmark 1
lead 1
lesson 3
limit 6
manoeuvre 4
manual
mark 7
master 3
motto
mould[1] 6
navigate 2
pattern 4
pilot 2, 3
precept 1
principle 1
progenitor 2
recommend 1
regulate 2
rule 1, 6
run 17
see 11
shepherd
show 2
standard 1
steer 1
take 18
teach
teacher
template
train 4
tutor 2
vade-mecum
work 14
-be guided by
follow 2
go 26b
guidebook
guide 8
guided missile
missile
guideline
gauge 3
instruction 1
precept 1
rule 1
standard 1
guidepost
landmark 1
guiding
direction 1
influential
guiding light
guide 7
guidon
standard 3

guild
association 1
brotherhood 2
club 2
fellowship 2
fraternity 3
group 1
institute 1
league 1
order 9
ring[1] 3
society 5
guile
art 5
artifice 1
craft 2
deceit 1
dexterity 2
foul play
fraud 1
hypocrisy
intrigue 3
subtlety 2
trickery
guileful
artful 1
astute 1
clever 2
crafty
deceitful
designing
dexterous 2
disingenuous
foxy 1
fraudulent 2
sly 1
tricky 1
wily
guileless
above-board 2
artless 1
callow
candid 1
childlike
clear 12
frank 2
honourable 3
ingenuous 1
innocent 4
naïve
natural 4
open 15
plain 3
pure 3
rustic 2
simple 3
sincere
transparent 3
unaffected[1]
unguarded 3
unsophisticated 1
guilelessly
simply 3
guilelessness
honesty 2
naïvety
purity 2
simplicity 3
guillotine
behead
guilt°
blame 4
pang 2
regret 2
remorse
responsibility 3
guiltiness
guilt 1
guiltless
blameless
innocent 1
guilt-ridden
remorseful
sorry 1
guilty°
convict 1
fault 5
regretful
remorseful
responsible 4
terrible 2
guilty conscience
remorse

guinea-pig
subject 4
guise°
camouflage 1
disguise 3
front 5
image 6
mask 2
pass 16b
persona
pretence 2
pretext 1
represent 2
semblance 2
shape 5
veneer
gulch
canyon
gully
ravine
gulf°
breach 2
gap 1
rift 1
gull
butt[1]
chisel 2
dupe 1, 3
fool 3, 4
hoax 2
hoodwink
misinform
mislead
mug 3
outsmart
prey 3b
ride 5a
sap[1] 2
scapegoat
score 7
screw 6
sucker
swindle 1
take 32b
trick 8
victim 2
victimize 2
gullibility
naïvety
gullible°
green 2
innocent 4
naïve
susceptible 2
trusting
unsuspecting
gully°
canyon
gorge 1
pass 23
ravine
gulosity
gluttony
gulp°
bolt 9
consume 1
devour 1
draught 2
drink 1, 6
gasp 1, 2
gorge 3
nip[2]
scoff[2] 1
swallow 1, 5
take 13
gum
cement 1
glue 1
stick[1] 4
gumbo
mud
gumboil
ulcer 1
gumminess
tenacity 2
gummy
clammy 1
gooey 1
ropy 1
sticky 1
tacky[1]
tenacious 2

gumption°
assurance 5
bottle 2
enterprise 2
gut 3a
nerve 1
push 14
resource 1
spunk
gumshoe
detective
operative 3
sleuth
gum up
queer 5
upset 5
gun
pistol
revolver
gun down
dispatch 3
gunfighter
killer 1
gunfire
report 2
gunge
dirt 1
filth 1
muck 2
gung-ho
hot 4
gungy
bedraggled
dirty 1
filthy 1, 2
shabby 1
gunk
muck 2
ooze 1
gunky
slimy 1
gunman
cutthroat 1
gangster
terrorist
thief 1
thug
gunpowder
explosive 2
gunsel
cutthroat 1
gangster
henchman
hoodlum
killer 1
gunshot
report 2
gunslinger
gangster
gunyah
hut
gup
gossip 1
gurges
whirlpool
gurgitation
eddy 1
gurgle°
babble 1
flow 1
gurgling
gurgle 2
gurry
gut 1
rubbish 2
trash 1
guru
clergyman 1
guide 5
intellectual 4
master 3
oracle 1
sage 2
teacher
tutor 1
gush°
discharge 4
erupt 1
flow 1, 2, 5
flush[1] 5
pour 1
prattle 1

gush (*cont.*)
run 6
spew
spout 1
spurt 3
stream 4
surge 1, 2
well[2] 2
gushiness
sentimentality
gushing
effusive
gushy
outpouring
sloppy 3
sweet 7
torrent
gush over
rave 2
gushy°
sentimental 2
sloppy 3
sweet 7
gussy up
primp
gust°
blast 1
breath 1
breeze 1
puff 1
wind[1] 1
gusting
windy 1
gusto°
eagerness 1
enthusiasm 1
fervour
inspiration 1
panache
passion 1
punch[1] 3
relish 1
sparkle 4
spice 2
verve
vigour
zest 1
gusty
breezy 1
stiff 5
windy 1
gut°
bosom 3
bowels
consume 4
desolate 5
devastate 1
inside 2
instinctive 1
pot 3
sneaking 1
stomach 1
waste 11
-guts°
at **gut 1**
assurance 5
bottle 2
bowels
courage
daring 1
determination 1
enterprise 2
face 5
fortitude
gall[1] 2
grit
gumption 2
heart 2
inside 2
machismo
manhood 2
nerve 1
perseverance
pluck 1
point 5
resource 1
spirit 5
spunk
stamina
strength 2
works 2
gutless
limp[2] 3
timid

gutsiness
assurance 5
face 5
grit
gut 3a
strength 2
gutsy
brave 1
daring 2
defiant
foolhardy
game 8
gritty 2
gutter
channel 1
drain 1
fail 3
flicker 1
furrow 1
guttersnipe°
ragamuffin
guttural
gruff 2
harsh 1
strident
thick 7
guv('nor)
employer 1
head 2
guy°
beggar 2
boy 1
bugger 2
cable 1
chap
customer 2
devil 3
dude 2
fellow 1, 4
flout
lad
leg 8
love 3
man 1
mock 1
parody 3
punter 2
ridicule 2
stay[2] 1
steady 9
stick[2] 2
support 8
taunt 1
tease 1
guzzle
drink 1
gulp 1
overeat
scoff[2] 1
swallow 1, 5
swill 3
guzzler
drunk 3
gymnastics
exercise 4
gyp
defraud
fleece
fraud 2
hoax 1, 2
racket 2
rip 2b
rob 3
swindle 1, 2
gypsy
bum 2
migrant 1, 2
rover
tramp 4
traveller
vagabond 1, 2
gyrate°
revolve 1
rotate 1
shake 2
spin 1
swirl 1
turn 1
twirl 1
gyration
revolution 3
shake 8
spin 6

gyve(s)
chain 2,3
manacle 1
restraint 2
shackle 1

H

H_2O
water 1
habiliment(s)
garments
gear 3
habit 3
trappings
habit°
custom 1
garments
gear 3
institution 4
mannerism
moral 4
morality 2
observance 2
practice 1
robe 1,2
routine 1
rut 2
suit 3
tradition
trick 6
uniform 3
usage 1
way 2
-habits
moral 4
morality 2
time 9
habitable°
habitat°
element 2
environment
setting
habitation
abode
domicile 1
dwelling
home 1
housing 1
quarter 5
residence 1
shelter 3
habit-forming
hard 11
habitual°
accustomed 1
chronic 2
conventional
customary 2
everyday 2
familiar 2
fixed 3
frequent 1
general 2
incorrigible
incurable 2
mechanical 2
natural 1
non-stop 2
ordinary 1
popular 2
recurrent
regular 1,7
relentless 2
ritual 2
routine 3
set 29
standard 6
staple 2
steady 2
time-honoured
traditional
usual
habitually
daily 3
frequently 2
generally 1
non-stop 3
often
ordinarily
popularly
habituate
accustom
adapt 2
break 18b
haunt 1
orient 3
habituated
accustomed 1
seasoned
used 3
habitué°
patron 2
regular 12
steady 10
hack°
accomplish
butcher 3
cab
chop 1
cut 15a
execute 1
grade 5
jade 1
journalist
lop
mangle
mutilate 1
nag[2]
politician
scribe 2
sever 1
shape 6
slash 1
slave 2
taxi 1
writer
hackle
eager 2
infuriate
madden 1
outrage 4
hackney
cab
hack[2] 3
taxi 1
hackneyed
banal
common 6
cut 29b
hack[2] 4
pedestrian 2
prosaic
ready-made 3
routine 4
set 30
stale 2
stock 7
threadbare 2
time-worn
tired 3
usual
hack to pieces
butcher 3
had best°
at **have 10**
had better°
at **have 10**
Hadean
infernal 1
Hades
hell 1
underworld 2
hadj
pilgrimage
hadji
pilgrim
had rather
at **have 11**
and **rather 3**
haecceity
property 4
substance 2
haemorrhoids
piles
haft
handle 1
hag°
bag 4
devil 2
fury 3
jade 2
ruin 5
shrew
hag (*cont.*)
witch 2
haggard°
drawn
emaciated
gaunt 1
ghastly 2
lean[1] 1
peaky
scrawny
sunken 1
worn 2,3
haggle°
bargain 3
dicker 1,2
negotiate 1
ha-ha
barrier 1
hail°
address 4
applaud 2
call 1
flag[1] 2
glorify 2
greet 2
greeting 1
honour 6
precipitation
salute 1
storm 5
volley 1
welcome 1
hail-fellow-well-met
sociable
hailstorm
storm 1
tempest 1
hair°
bristle 1
shade 6
-by a hair's breadth
just 5
narrowly 1
hairbreadth
narrow 6
near 8
touchy 2
-by a hair-breadth
just 5
narrowly 1
hairbrush
brush[2] 1
hairdo°
hairless°
smooth 4
hairpin bend
turn 27
hair-raising
frightening
scary
sensational 1
touchy 2
hair's breadth
hair 2
shade 6
-by a hair's breadth
just 5
narrowly 1
hair-splitting°
fault-finding 1,2
fine[1] 9
legalistic
nice 4
overcritical
pedantic 2
quibble 2
hairstyle
hairdo
hair-trigger
volatile 3
hairy°
delicate 4
dicey
dodgy
harsh 1
hazardous
nice 4
parlous
precarious
hairy (*cont.*)
problematic
shaggy
sticky 2
thorny 2
touchy 2
haji
pilgrim
hajj
pilgrimage
halcyon
calm 3
fair[1] 5
golden 5
idyllic
serene 1
soft 3
tranquil
hale°
fit[1] 3
hardy 1
healthy 1
hearty 5
lusty 1
robust 1
rugged 3
sound[2] 2
stalwart 1
vigorous
well[1] 16
haleness
health 2
haler
better[1] 4
half a mo *etc.*
minute[1] 1
moment 1
second[2]
half-baked
feeble 2
half-hearted
lame 2
lukewarm 2
pale[1] 3
stupid 2
weak 4
half-bred
mixed 1
half-breed
hybrid
mongrel
half-cocked
prematurely 2
half-consciousness
trance
half-dead
moribund 1
half-grown
immature 1
half-hearted°
irresolute
limp[2] 3
lukewarm 2
pale[1] 3
wishy-washy 1
half-inch
lift 6
half-light
twilight 1
half-starved
emaciated
raw-boned
skinny
half-tone
cut 25
halfway
intermediate 1
middle 1
halfway point
middle 2
midst
halfwit°
dolt
fool 1
natural 12
silly 3
twit[2]
halfwitted°
daft 1
feeble-minded
foolish 2
halfwitted (*cont.*)
senseless 3
simple 4
stupid 1
thick 6
halfwittedness
simplicity 4
stupidity 1
hall°
castle 2
corridor
lobby 1
passage 4
residence 3
theatre 1
hallmark°
device 3
feature 1
label 1,4
mark 2
peculiarity 2
property 4
stamp 5
hallow°
adore 2
bless 1
celebrate 1
commemorate
dedicate 2
praise 4
sanctify 1
venerate
hallowed
divine 1
holy 1
precious 2
sacred 1
solemn 2
hallowing
celebration 1
dedication 3
hallucinate
dream 2
fantasize
trip 9
hallucination°
delusion 2
dream 1
fancy 6
fantasy 2
ghost 1
illusion 2
phantom 2
vision 4
hallucinatory
dreamlike
illusory
insubstantial 2
shadowy 3
hallucinogen
dope 2
drug 2
hallway
corridor
hall 1
lobby 1
passage 4
halo°
glory 4
ring[1] 1
halt°
arrest 1
cease 1
check 1
deadlock 2
delay 2
draw 15a
end 9
frustrate 1
gap 1
interlude
interrupt 2
lame 1
lull 1
moratorium
obstruct 1
paralyse 1
prevent
prevention
pull 18a
shut 2
stall[1] 1
stanch
stand 15
halt (*cont.*)
standstill
stay[1] 4,6
stem[2] 1
stop 1,6
suppress 1
suppression
tie 7c
wait 4
halter
tether 1
halting°
hesitant 2
inarticulate 2
lame 1
obstruction 2
prevention
suppression
halve
cleave
halved
split 9
ham
camp[2] 2
dramatize
theatrical 2
Thespian 1,2
ham-fisted
awkward 1
clumsy
thumb 2
hamlet
place 2
settlement 1
town
hammer
beat 5
din 2
pan 5
pound[1] 1,3,4
pulsate
ram 1
strike 1
hammer and tongs
vigorously
hammer away
peg 7
rub 3
wade 4
hammering
knock 8
pulse 1
thrashing 1
hammer out
forge 1
pound[1] 5,6
hammy
melodramatic
theatrical 2
Thespian 1
hamper°
bar 9
block 3
bog 2
check 1
clog
encumber 2
entangle 2
foil[1]
frustrate 1
handicap 2
hinder 1
hobble 2
impede
interfere 2
manacle 3
obstruct 2
prevent
prohibit 2
repress
restrain 2
stay[1] 4
stunt[2]
tie 2
hampering
prevention
preventive 1
repression 2
hamstring
frustrate 1
maim

happen°
appear 3
become 5
chance 7
come 4a, 14a
develop 4
emerge 1
exist 3
go 31c, 32b
materialize 2
occur 1
pass 13
place 14
result 2
rise 9
spring 4
transpire 2
true 6
turn 20b
unfold 2
-as it happens
instance 2
happen again
recur
happening°
adventure 1
affair 3
case[1] 1
circumstance 2
development 1
episode 1
event 1
eventuality
experience 2
fact 2
gala 1
incident 1
occasion 3
occurrence 1
phenomenon 1
progress 4
stroke 9
-happenings
thing 8b
happen on
see **happen upon**
happenstance
coincidence 3
fortune 2
luck 1
happen upon°
at **happen 3**
come 5a
encounter 1
find 1
hit 9a
light[2] 15
meet[1] 1
run 20
strike 14
stumble 3
happier
better[1] 6a
happily°
gaily 2
gladly
readily 1
soon 4
well[1] 15
willingly
happiness°
bliss
cheer 2
content[2] 1
ecstasy 1
gaiety 1
glee
heaven 3
joy 1
merriment
paradise 3
pleasure 1
radiance 2
satisfaction 1
transport 5
triumph 2
welfare
happy°
appropriate 1
blithe 1
bright 8
carefree
charmed 3
cheerful 1
happy (*cont.*)
content[2] 3
delighted
ecstatic
elated
elevated 3
enchanted
exalted 3
exhilarating 2
exuberant 2
gala 2
gay 2
glad 1, 2
gleeful
golden 4
jaunty 1
joyful 1, 2
light[2] 9
mellow 4
merry 1
opportune 1
overjoyed
pleased
propitious
proud 1
providential
radiant 2
rapt 2
ready 2
rejoice
rhapsodic
seasonable
sunny 2
vivacious
willing
world 7
happy as a sand-boy *etc.*
rhapsodic
happy-go-lucky
blithe 2
carefree
casual 5
improvident 1
light[2] 9
nonchalant
relaxed
happy hunting-ground
heaven 1
paradise 1
Happy Isles
heaven 1
happy valley
fairyland
harangue°
berate
bluster 1
hold 16a
lecture 1, 3
light[2] 14
preach 2
rant 1
sermon 1
speech 2
talk 14
tirade
haranguer
talker 1
haranguing
bluster 3
harass°
aggravate 2
annoy 2
beset
bother 1
browbeat
bug 7
bully 2
distress 3
disturb 1
exasperate 2
exercise 3
gall[2] 4
gnaw 3
grind 5
heckle
henpeck
hound
irritate
molest 1
nag[1] 1
obsess
oppress 2
harass (*cont.*)
persecute 2
pester
pick 4a, 6
plague 3
prod 3
provoke 3
push 4
rack 3
-ridden
ride 3
tease 1
torment 2
trouble 2
wear 7
worry 2
harassing
obsessive
painful 2
persecution 2
provocative 2
harassment
torment 4
harbinger°
announce 4
forerunner 1
messenger
omen
precursor 1
prognosticate 2
prophesy 2
harbour°
bear 7
creek 1
entertain 3
house 8
keep 12
lodge 4
nourish 2
nurse 4
oasis 2
port
question 5
refuge 1
shelter 4
suspect 1
umbrage
hard°
arduous 1
badly 9
bare 2
bitter 2
callous
cruel 1
demanding 1
difficult 1, 4
domineering
dour 2
dull 2
exacting
exhausting 2
firm 1
harsh 2
implacable
inflexible
laborious 1
laboured 1
lean[1] 3
merciless
obstinate
prickly 4
punishing
relentless 1
rigid 1, 2
rocky[1] 1, 3
rough 5, 7
rugged 2, 3
severe 1
solid 3
Spartan
stark 2
steely 2
stern 1
stiff 1, 9, 10
stony 2
strenuous 1
strict 2
thorny 2
toilsome
tough 1, 2, 4, 6
unkind
hard and fast
abiding
inflexible
rigid 3
hard and fast (*cont.*)
tight 3
hard as nails°
at **nail 4**
hard-boiled
callous
hard 4
realistic 1
stony 2
thick-skinned
tough 6
hard by
beside 1
hard cash
cash 1
hard cheese
tough 7
hard-cover
book 1
harden°
cake 3
fix 7
freeze 2
jell 1
set 3
solidify 1
stiffen 1
temper 6
thicken
hardened
callous
chronic 2
dead 4
dull 2
habitual 2
hard 1
incorrigible
mill 3
seasoned
stale 1
thick-skinned
tough 6
used 3
hard feelings
feud 1
grudge 1
strife 2
hard-headed
hard 6
practical 2
realistic 1
strong 16
hard-hearted
brutal 1
callous
cold-hearted
cruel 1
hard 4
heartless
inhuman 1
insensible 2
merciless
remorseless 1
ruthless
severe 1
stern 1
stony 2
unkind
unmerciful
unmoved
unsympathetic
hardihood
grit
hardily
vigorously
hardiness
grit
pluck 1
vitality 2
hard-line
puritan 2
rigid 2
hard luck
misfortune 1
sorrow 2
tough 7
trial 4
hardly°
almost
barely
ill 13
just 5
hardly (*cont.*)
little 8, 9
narrowly 1
nearly 1
rarely
scarcely 1
hardly any
few 1
little 3
hardly ever
little 7
rarely
seldom
hard money
cash 1
hardness
severity 1
hard-nosed
callous
dour 2
hard 6
positive 6
practical 2
puritan 2
realistic 1
strong 13
tough 6
ultra-
hard nut to crack
problem 2
hard of hearing
deaf 1
hard pressed
back 10
hard sell
promotion 4
hardship°
affliction 1
calamity 2
difficulty 1, 2
discomfort 1
distress 2
grievance 1
misery 3
oppression
ordeal
privation
rigour 1, 2
self-denial 2
sorrow 2
suffering
trial 4
woe
hard stuff
alcohol
drink 5
liquor 1
hard task-master
tyrant
hard times
trial 4
hard to believe
far-fetched
improbable
hard to come by
premium 4a
scarce
thin 7
tight 9
hard to imagine
improbable
hard to please
choosy
finicky 1
hard to take
bitter 2
hard up°
at **hard 17**
broke
destitute 1
embarrassed 2
hot 7
indigent
needy
penurious 2
poor 1
straitened
hardware°
hard-wearing
durable
serviceable 2
hard-wearing (*cont.*)
strong 12
hard-working
diligent
earnest 2
enterprising
industrious
laborious 3
strong 5
tireless
hardy°
daring 2
dour 2
gritty 2
hale
mighty 2
nail 4a
robust 1
rugged 3
stalwart 1
stout 2
sturdy 1
vigorous
hare
race[1] 4
run 1
hare-brained°
crazy 2
daft 1
dizzy 2
flighty 2
foolish 2
insane 2
light[2] 8
nonsensical
rash[1]
reckless
scatterbrained
senseless 3
stupid 2
harem
brothel
hark
hear 1
listen 1
hark back
reminisce
harken
listen 1
harlequin
fool 2
harlot
bitch 2
prostitute 1
slattern
tart[2] 2
wanton 5
harlotry
prostitution 1
harm°
assault 5
batter 3
blemish 2
bruise 2
curse 2
damage 1, 4
deface
detriment
disadvantage 2
discredit 5
disgrace 2
disservice
disturb 3
evil 7
flaw 3, 4
get 24
grievance 1
hurt 1, 5
ill 8
ill-treat
impair
impairment
injure 1
injury
loss 3
maim
mar 2
mischief 2
mishandle 1
mistreat
offence 2
outrage 1, 5
punish 3

harm *(cont.)*
punishment 3
ruin 9
shake 3
shoot 3
smart 8
spoil 1, 2
stab 2
strain[1] 3, 6
taint 2
tarnish
trample 2
turn 34
undermine 1
violence 3a
vitiate 1
wear 3
wound 2, 3
wrong 9
-out of harm's way
safe 1
harmattan
storm 1
harmed
disabled
flawed
harmful°
abusive 2
bad 2
dangerous 2
deadly 1
destructive 1
detrimental
disastrous 2
evil 3
fatal 2
grievous 1
hurtful 1
ill 4
injurious 1
malignant 1
mischievous 2
prejudicial
ruinous
scathing
sinister 2
traumatic
unhealthy 2
unwholesome 1
violent 2
virulent 1
harmless°
benign 4
innocent 3
inoffensive
safe 2
soft 10
harmlessness
purity 1
harmonic
tuneful
harmonious°
amicable
consistent 1
equal 2
melodious
musical
neighbourly
one 2
orderly 1
pastoral 1
piece 8
pleasant 1
pretty 2
proportional
regular 3
step 7
sweet 3
symmetrical
tasteful
unison
united 3
well-balanced 2
harmoniousness
peace 2
regularity 1
uniformity 1
union 4
harmonization
adjustment 2
harmonize
accommodate 2
accord 1

harmonize *(cont.)*
adjust 1
agree 1
chime 5a
conform 2
coordinate 2
correspond 1
go 6, 37a, 40a
match 7
square 12
sympathize 2
tally 1
harmony°
accord 2, 4
adjustment 2
agreement 2
balance 6
coincidence 2
composition 2
friendship 1
love 4
melody 2
order 2
peace 2
proportion 2
rapport
reconciliation 1
regularity 1
solidarity
symmetry
sympathy 2
tune 2
uniformity 1
union 4
-in harmony
accord 1
consistent 1
hang 11a
line[1] 19b
piece 8
step 7
unison
united 3
harness
hitch 1
rein 1, 3
tack 4
harp on
dwell 2
labour 6
linger 3
reiterate
rub 3
harpy
bitch 1
demon 1
devil 2
hag
nag[1] 2
shrew
harridan
bag 4
hag
jade 2
scold 2
shrew
witch 2
harrow
distress 3
furrow 2
plough 1
rack 3
till[1]
torment 1
harrowing°
agonizing
disastrous 1
doleful
excruciating
frightening
grim 3
gruff 2
heart-rending
horrible 1
murderous 2
nerve-racking
oppressive
painful 2
sore 5
stiff 9
terrible 4

harry
annoy 2
beset
distress 3
disturb 1
exercise 3
gall[2] 4
gnaw 3
grind 5
harass
heckle
hound
irritate
molest 1
nag[1] 1
oppress 2
overrun
persecute 2
pester
pick 6
plague 3
ride 3
torment 2
trouble 2
worry 2
harrying
persecution 2
harsh°
biting
bitter 1, 5
brassy 2
brutal 1
caustic 2
cruel 1
curt
cutting 2
discordant 2
domineering
dour 2
drastic
exacting
extreme 4
forbidding 2
full 10
garish
gaunt 2
glaring 2
grating 1
grim 2
gruff 2
hard 4, 9
heavy-handed 2
husky 2
ill 3
inclement
injurious 2
intense 1
merciless
noisy
oppressive 1
overcritical
penetrating 2
piercing 1
pungent 2
ragged 5
raucous
remorseless 1
rigid 2
rough 5, 8
rugged 2
ruthless
sarcastic
savage 2
scathing
scorching 2
severe 1, 4, 5
sharp 4, 7
Spartan
stark 2, 3
stern 1
stiff 2
strict 2
strident
strong 13
swingeing
tart[1] 1, 2
tight 3
tinny 2
tough 6
truculent
tyrannical
unflattering 1
unkind
violent 3
vituperative

harsh *(cont.)*
wintry 3
harshly
badly 6
hard 16
home 10
ill 11, 12
roughly 2
severely 2, 4
sharply 1
harshness
bitterness 1
edge 3
gall[1] 1
rigour 1, 2
sarcasm
severity 1, 4, 5
harum-scarum
rush 3
haruspex
fortune-teller
prophet
harvest°
derive 1
gain 1
gather 1
haul 4
heap 3
output 1
pick 2
raise 3
reap 1
vintage 1
hash°
chop 2
clutter 1
disorder 1
hotchpotch
mess 2
miscellany
mishmash
mixture 1
patchwork
stew 1
hash up°
at hash 3
hasp
lock[1] 1
hassle
annoy 2
bother 1, 5
browbeat
disturb 1
fluster 1
heckle
irritate
job 4
madden 3
nuisance 1
pester
plague 2
ride 3
rigmarole
scramble 4
taunt 1
trial 5
worry 2
hasta la vista
farewell 3
goodbye
hasta luego
farewell 3
goodbye
haste°
dispatch 5
expedition 2
hurry 3
indiscretion 1
press 9
rush 3
speed 1
-in haste
hastily 1
run 49a
-with all haste
fast[1] 6
hasten°
advance 4
dash 3
dispatch 4
expedite 1
flash 5
fly 3

hasten *(cont.)*
forward 8
hurry 1, 2
hustle 1, 2
leap 3
leg 5, 9a
move 12b
precipitate 1
quicken 1, 2
race[1] 4
run 1
rush 1
scramble 2
scurry
speed 3
step 16
streak 5
tear 3
trot 1
whisk 2
hastily°
briefly 2
fast[1] 6
pell-mell 1
prematurely 2
quickly 3
run 49a
short 11
shot 10
sketchily
spur 3
suddenly 2
swiftly
hastiness
haste 2
indiscretion 1
speed 1
hasty°
abrupt 1
brash 1
cursory
desperate 2
fast[1] 1
foolhardy
foolish 1
hotheaded
hurried 1
ill-advised 2
impetuous
imprudent
indiscreet
momentary
overconfident 2
passing 2
pell-mell 2
perfunctory 1
precipitate 5
premature 2
quick 2
rapid
rash[1]
rough 10
scratch 6
sketchy
snap 13
speedy 2
sudden
superficial 3
swift
unguarded 3
unthinking 1
unwary
whirlwind 2
hat
cap 1
hatch°
breed 2
brew 2, 3
brood 2
conceive 2
fabricate 2
incubate
make 39c
plot[1] 3
produce 3
scheme 4
hatchet man
cutthroat 1
killer 1
hatching
fabrication 2
hate°
abhor
aversion 2
contempt

hate *(cont.)*
despise
detest
dislike 1
ill will
loathe
loathing
rancour
resentment
spite 1
use 15
venom 2
hateful°
abhorrent
beastly 2
bitter 4
black 5
damnable
evil-minded 2
hideous 2
loathsome
lousy 1
malignant 2
obnoxious
rancorous
spiteful
ugly 2
vicious 2
virulent 2
hatless
bare 1
hat-rack
rack 1
hatred
animosity
aversion 1, 2
bitterness 2
contempt
disgust 3
dislike 2
feud 1
grudge 1
hate 3
horror 1
ill will
infamy 2
loathing
phobia
rancour
revulsion
spite 1
strife 2
vendetta
venom 2
virulence 2
hatstand
rack 1
stand 17
haughtiness
air 5
arrogance
distance 2
front 7
pride 2
side 5
snobbery
vanity 1
haughty°
aloof 2
arrogant 2
cocky
condescending
disdainful
distant 3
frigid 2
hoity-toity
lofty 4
majestic 2
overbearing
pompous 1
pretentious 2
proud 2
regal 2
scornful
self-important
snobbish
standoffish
stiff 7
supercilious
vain 1
haul°
cart 2
drag 1
draw 1
freight 2

-to the heart
home 10
-with one's heart in one's mouth
edge 5
heartache
distress 1
grief 1
misery 1
mourning 2
sorrow 1
heart and soul
completely 1
heartbreak
grief 1
sorrow 1
wrench 5
heartbreaking
heart-rending
pathetic 1
piteous
poignant 1
sad 2
touching
heartbroken°
broken-hearted
dejected
inconsolable
low[1] 8
melancholy 1
miserable 1
mournful 1
sad 1
woebegone
wretched 2
heartburn
wind[1] 3
hear tell
understand 4
wind[1] 6
hearten
assure 2
buoy 2
cheer 6
comfort 1
encourage 1
fortify 2
gladden
reassure
solace 2
strengthen 2
heartening
encouragement 1
exhilarating 2
hopeful 2
promising
upbeat
heartfelt°
deep 6
devout 3
emotional 1
fervent 2
gut 6
hearty 2
intense 2
keen[1] 3
poignant 3
profound 3
real 3
sincere
tender[1] 7
undisguised
wholehearted
heartier
better[1] 4
heartily
happily 2
hard 13
vigorously
heartiness
warmth 2
heartland
interior 7
heartless°
brutal 1
callous
cold-blooded 2
cold-hearted
cruel 1
deadly 3
grim 2
hard 4
inhuman 1
heartless (*cont.*)
merciless
remorseless 1
ruthless
sanguinary 1
stony 2
unkind
unmerciful
heartlessly
roughly 2
heartlessness
barbarity
heart 2
heart of hearts
bosom 3
breast 2
heart-rending°
harrowing
moving 1
pathetic 1
piteous
poignant 1
tender[1] 7
touching
heart's desire
passion 4
heartsick
broken-hearted
heartbroken
joyless 1
mournful 1
sad 1
sick 3
sorrowful 1
wistful 1
wretched 2
heartthrob
flame 3
passion 4
sweetheart
heart-to-heart
chat 1
heart-warming°
hearty°
bluff[2] 2
buxom 1
devout 3
enthusiastic
fit[1] 3
hale
heartfelt
pink[1] 1
robust 1
stalwart 1
vigorous
warm 3
well[1] 16
wholehearted
heat°
ardour
chafe 1
feeling 4
glow 5
inflame 1
police 1
round 13
thaw 1
warm 7
warmth 1
-in heat, on heat
randy
heated°
emotional 1
hot 1
impassioned
inflamed
warm 1,2
heatedly
warmly 5
heater
pistol
heath
flat 14b
moor[1]
plain 6
heathen°
heretical
infidel
non-believer
pagan 1,2
profane 1
heatless
cold 2
heat up°
at **heat** 4
chafe 1
hot 11
intensify
thaw 1
warm 7
heave°
fling 1
fly 8a
gag[1] 2
haul 1,3
hoist 1
hump 3
hurl
lift 1
lob 1
lug
pant 1
pitch[1] 1
put 7
sling 1
strain[1] 2
surge 1
throw 9a
toss 1,6
vomit
wave 1
heave-ho
brush-off
dismissal 1
ejection 3
expulsion
rejection
sack 3
heaven°
firmament
paradise 1,3
transport 5
Utopia
-heavens°
at **heaven** 2
atmosphere 1
firmament
sky 1
-in heaven
joyful 2
radiant 2
-in heaven's name
devil 6
-in the heavens
above 1
heavenly°
celestial 1
divine 1
glorious 3
godlike 2
holy 1
idyllic
immortal 2
seraphic
stunning 2
sublime 1
heavenly body
star 1
heavenly kingdom
paradise 1
heaven on earth
ecstasy 1
heaven 3
paradise 2
Utopia
heaven-sent
sacred 1
heavenwards
aloft
heave up
lift 1
throw 9a
heavily
deep 10
deeply 2
heaviness
fat 5
lethargy 1
weight 1
heavy°
beamy
burly
chubby
deep 2
heavy (*cont.*)
dense 1
fat 1
grievous 1
gross 1
henchman
laboured 1
large 1
leaden 1,2
lethargic 1
lifeless 3
listless
obese
oppressive 1
ponderous 1
rich 6
rotund 3
sore 5
stodgy
stout 1
strong 17
thug
weighty 1
heavy-duty
durable
strong 12
heavy-handed°
tyrannical
heavy-handedly
roughly 3
heavy-hearted
broken-hearted
dejected
desolate 3
heavy 6
joyless 1
low[1] 8
moody 1
mournful 1
pessimistic
sorrowful 1
unhappy 1
heavy-laden
sinking 2
heavy-lidded
drowsy
heavy-set
chubby
large 1
stocky
stout 1
heavy water
water 1
hebdomadal
organ 2
periodical
publication 2
regular 2
Hebe
waiter
hebetate
pointed 1
hebetude
sloth
sluggishness
hebetudinous
phlegmatic 1
slothful
hecatomb
slaughter 2
heckle°
gibe 1
pester
ride 3
heckler
pest
trouble 6
hectic°
busy 2
chaotic 2
frantic
hurried 1
tumultuous
hector
aggravate 2
beset
bother 1
browbeat
bully 2
disturb 1
exasperate 2
gall[2] 4
gnaw 3
hector (*cont.*)
grind 5
harass
heckle
henpeck
irritate
molest 1
nag[1] 1
overawe
persecute 2
pester
pick 6
prod 3
provoke 3
railroad 2
ride 3
torment 2
trouble 2
worry 2
hectoring
persecution 2
hedge
dodge 3
enclose 1
enclosure 2
equivocate
evade 2
fence 3,4
flannel 2
shrubbery
stall[2] 1,2
waffle 2
hedgerow
shrubbery
hedging
equivocal 1
reservation 1
reserve 7
shrubbery
stall[2] 2
hedonism
dissipation 1
luxury 2
hedonist
epicure
sensualist
sensuous
sybarite
voluptuous 1
hedonistic
dissolute
epicurean 1
luxurious 2
self-indulgent
sensuous
voluptuous 1
heebie-jeebies
dread 2
fidget 3
jitters
nerve 4
heed°
attend 2
attention 1
care 2
caution 2
consider 2
ear 1
follow 2
hear 1
keep 6
listen 2
mark 12
meet[1] 5
mind 16
note 7
notice 1,4
obey 1
observance 1
regard 9
respect 7
watch 3
heedful
alert 1
attentive 1
awake 4
cautious
conscientious 3
discreet
guarded
mindful
observant 2
observe 1
protective
heedful (*cont.*)
prudent 1
thoughtful 3
wakeful 2
wary
heedfulness
care 2
prudence 1
heeding
observance 1
heedless°
absent-minded
blind 3
blithe 2
careless 1
deaf 2
derelict 2
foolhardy
foolish 1
hare-brained 1
hasty 2
hotheaded
improvident 2
imprudent
inadvertent 2
inattentive
inconsiderate
indiscreet
mad 2
near-sighted 2
overconfident 2
perfunctory 1
promiscuous 1
rash[1]
reckless
regardless 1
remiss
thoughtless 2
unaware
unconscious 2
ungrateful
unguarded 1
unwary
wanton 3
heedlessly
blindly
hastily 2
heedlessness
desperation 1
disregard 3
excuse 5
indiscretion 1
neglect 3
negligence
oblivion 2
oversight 1
heel°
list[2] 1,2
lurch[2] 2
scoundrel
stinker
tilt 3
heel over
careen
list[2] 1
tilt 1
heft
pick 8a
weight 1
hefty°
big 2
brawny
burly
buxom 1
husky 1
large 1
mighty 2
stalwart 1
strong 1
sturdy 1
weighty 1
hegemony
authority 1
domination 1
dominion 1
jurisdiction
predominance
preponderance 2
reign 1
sovereignty
superiority 1
supremacy 2

hesitancy
distrust 2
reluctance
reservation 1, 2
reserve 7
hesitant°
disinclined
distrustful
doubtful 2
fearful 2
halting
indecisive 1
indefinite 5
indisposed 2
irresolute
mealy-mouthed
queasy 1
reluctant
self-conscious
slow 10
tentative 2
tremulous 1
uncertain 2
hesitantly
fearfully 1
hesitate°
blow[1] 6
delay 3
doubt 2
hang 5
pause 1
play 14
procrastinate 2
pussyfoot 2
scruple 2
shilly-shally
stall[2] 1
stammer 1
stick[1] 12
stumble 2
-without hesitating
right 13
hesitating
distrustful
doubtful 2
halting
hesitant 1
indecisive 1
irresolute
uncertain 2
hesitation
break 27
check 13
compunction 2
distrust 2
doubt 3
fear 1
indecision
interruption 2
let-up
misgiving
pang 2
pause 2
qualm
reservation 1
reserve 7
scruple 1
suspicion 1
-without hesitation
immediately 1
promptly
right 13
summarily 1
Hesperides
paradise 1
hetaera
prostitute 1
hetero
straight 11
heteroclite
unorthodox
heterodox
dissident 2
heretical
heterogeneity
diversity 2
variety 1, 2
heterogeneous
dissimilar
diverse
general 3
miscellaneous
heterogeneous (*cont.*)
promiscuous 3
varied 1
various 1
heterosexual
straight 11
het up
huff 1
hew
butcher 3
carve 1
chip 3
chop 1
cleave
cut 13a
fell
hack[1] 1
shape 6
sever 1
whittle 1
hex
enchant 1
enchantment 1
jinx 1, 3
ruffle 3
heyday
day 2
prime 4
time 4
hiatus
break 27
delay 5
gap 1
hold-up 2
interlude
interruption 2
jump 12
lapse 2
lull 1
moratorium
pause 2
respite 2
space 3
split 7
vacancy 1
wait 4
hibernal
cold 1
polar 1
wintry 1
hibernate
hide[1] 1
retire 1
hibernating
dormant 1
hibernation
inactivity 2
hiccup
set-back
hick
boor 1
clown 2
peasant
provincial 2, 3
rustic 3
hickey
gadget
gimmick 2
pimple
spot 5
hicksville
province 4
hick-town
provincial 2
hidden°
close 19
cryptic 1
dark 7
dormant 2
furtive 1
interior 3
intimate[1] 2
invisible 2
isolated 3
mysterious 2
mystical 1
obscure 3
occult 1
out-of-the-way 1
potential 1
private 1, 2
secret 1
hidden (*cont.*)
sneaking 2
subconscious 1
subtle 2
surreptitious
ulterior 1
underground 2
untold 2
vague 3
veiled
withdrawn 2
hide°
blind 6
blot 4a
blur 4
bury 4
cache 3
camouflage 2
cloak 3
conceal 1
cover 2, 14
disguise 1
eclipse 1
envelop 2
gloss[1] 4
harbour 2
hold 17b
hush 4
keep 14a
lie[2] 5
lurk
mantle 3
mask 3
obscure 6
pelt[2]
plant 8
screen 7
secrete[1]
shade 12
shroud 1
shut 5c
skin 1
smother 4
stow
submerge 3
suppress 3
veil 2
whitewash
withhold 1
hideaway°
lair 2
nest 2
nook 2
refuge 1
retreat 3
sanctum 2
hidebound°
conservative 2
extreme 4
narrow-minded
parochial
priggish
small-minded
hideous°
awful 1
damnable
diabolic 2
dreadful 2
fearful 3
frightful 2
ghastly 1
ghoulish 2
grim 3
grisly
gruesome
horrible 1
monstrous 1
outrageous 2
satanic 2
shocking 2
terrible 1, 5
ugly 1
unsightly
wicked 2
hideousness
monstrosity 2
hide-out
cover 14
hideaway
lair 2
nest 2
nook 2
refuge 1
retreat 3
sanctum 2
hiding
eclipse 3
rout 1
suppression
thrashing 1
hiding-place
cache 1
cover 14
hideaway
lair 2
sanctum 2
hie
run 1
hiemal
wintry 1
hierarchy
order 3
scale[3] 1
hieratic
clerical 1
priestly
sacred 3
hierodule
slave 1
hieroglyph
character 1
sign 4
hifalutin
disdainful
grandiose 1
haughty
mannered
ornate
overbearing
pompous 1
pretentious 2
rhetorical 3
snobbish
standoffish
supercilious
uppish
higgle
haggle
higgledy-piggledy
chaotic 1
confused 1
disorderly 1
helter-skelter 1, 2
indiscriminate 2
promiscuous 3
topsy-turvy 2
high°
buzz 4
drunk 1
elevated 2
exalted 1
excited 1
extravagant 3
fancy 4
flamboyant 2
get 39c
lofty 1
mountainous 2
off 7
powerful 3
prohibitive 2
rancid
rarefied 2
smelly
steep[1] 2
stiff 6
stinking 3
sublime 1
tall 1
tight 8
towering 1
under 6
-at a high price
dear 4
dearly 3
-in high dudgeon
furious 1
huff 1
indignant
moody 2
-in high spirits
gleeful
merry 1
-on a high
excited 1
-on high
above 1
aloft
overhead 1
-on one's high horse
arrogant 2
haughty
mannered
snobbish
uppish
high and low
everywhere
far 4
pole[2] 2
high and mighty
arrogant 2
disdainful
domineering
haughty
hoity-toity
lofty 4
overbearing
pretentious 2
proud 2
snobbish
supercilious
uppish
high as a kite
drunk 1
highbinder
thief 2
high birth
rank[1] 3
high-born
elegant 1
noble 2
upper-class 1
highboy
cabinet 1
highbrow°
intellectual 2, 3
learned
scholar 1
scholarly
-highbrows
intelligentsia
high-class°
fancy 3
genteel 2
high 5
noble 2
superior 2
upper-class 2
high dudgeon
rage 1
-in high dudgeon
furious 1
huff 1
indignant
moody 2
higher
superior 1
upper 1, 2
-of a higher order *etc.*
superior 1
higher-calibre
superior 1
higher-ranking
senior
superior 1
higher up
upper 1
highest
cardinal
full 4
grand 6
maximum 1, 3
outside 6
sovereign 2
supreme 1
top 9
ultimate 2
uppermost 1
-of the highest
water 5
highest point
maximum 2
highest-ranking
premier 2
highfalutin
disdainful
grandiose 1
haughty
mannered
ornate
overbearing
pompous 1
pretentious 2
rhetorical 3
snobbish
standoffish
supercilious
uppish
high-flown
bombastic
exalted 2
flowery
glorified 1
grandiose 1
inflated 2
ornate
pompous 2
pretentious 1
rhetorical 3
stilted
high-flying
grandiose 1
high-frequency
high 7
high-grade
fine[1] 1
first-rate
high-handed
arbitrary 2
arrogant 2
condescending
domineering
masterful 2
overbearing
scornful
strong 13
tyrannical
high-hat
mannered
pompous 1
pretentious 2
snobbish
high jinks
caper 2
clown 3
frolic 1
fun 1
revelry
high-keyed
quick-tempered
highland
hill 1
plateau 1
rise 13
high-level
important 2
highlight
accent 4
emphasize
feature 4
light[1] 8
pièce de résistance
play 17a
rinse 2
set 20b
spotlight 3
stress 4
-highlights
run-down 3
high living
dissipation 1
highly°
degree 4b
sky 2
well[1] 5
highly priced
dear 2
highly regarded
well-thought-of
highly-strung
emotional 2
excitable
intense 3
nervous 1
quick-tempered
restless

highly-strung (*cont.*)
tense 2
touchy 1
high-minded
conscientious 1
ethical
generous 2
good 5
great 7
honest 1
honourable 1
moral 1
principled
pure 6
scrupulous 2
sublime 1
upright 2
virtuous 1
high-mindedness
equity
good 20
nobility 1
right 10
virtue 1
high noon
midday
noon
high opinion
regard 7
high-pitched
high 7
piercing 1
sharp 7
shrill
high point
climax 1
feature 2
height 2
maximum 2
peak 2
top 1
zenith
-high points
run-down 3
high-powered
dynamic
energetic
high-pressure
drive 1
strong-arm
high-priced
dear 2
expensive
high 3
invaluable
precious 1
premium 4b
priceless 1
high-principled
virtuous 1
high-priority
necessary 1
pressing
rush 5
urgent 1
high-quality
choice 4
high-ranking
important 2
noble 2
high road
road 2
street 1
high school
school 1
high seas
deep 9
ocean 1
sea 1
high sign
gesture 1
word 7
high society
society 4
high-sounding
affected 3
artificial 3
extravagant 4
glorified 1
high-speed
fast[1] 1
rapid
high-spirited
effervescent 2
game 8
gay 2
jaunty 1
jolly 1
vivacious
high spirits
fun 1
gaiety 1
glee
happiness
hilarity
merriment
mirth
high spot
feature 2
high-strung
emotional 2
excitable
intense 3
restless
tense 2
touchy 1
high style
style 3
hightail
escape 1
flee 1
fly 2
hurry 1
make 26
rush 1
scramble 2
speed 3
high up
overhead 1
highway
road 2
highwayman
outlaw 1
robber
thief 1
highway robbery
rip-off 3
high, wide, and handsome
flamboyant 2
hijack
rob 1
robbery
steal 1
hijacker
thief 1
hijacking
robbery
theft
hike
boost 3
excursion 1
hitch 2
jump 9
march 3
mark 16b
ramble 1, 4
tramp 1, 3
walk 1, 7
hiker
traveller
hilarious°
comic 1
funny 1
high 8
humorous
hysterical 2
merry 1
priceless 2
rich 10
ridiculous
riot 2
uproarious 2
zany 1
hilarity°
festivity 2
gaiety 1
merriment
mirth
hill°
elevation 2
grade 4
height 3
incline 4
knoll
mound 1
peak 1
prominence 2
rise 13
slope 2
stack 1
-over the hill
elderly 1
old 1
vintage 3
hill-billy
boor 1
peasant
rustic 2, 3
hillock
hill 1
hump 1
knoll
mound 1
prominence 2
rise 13
tell[2]
hilt
handle 1
Himalayan
mountainous 1
himself
boss 1
chief 1
person 2
personally 1
hind
peasant
posterior 1
hinder°
arrest 1
bar 9
block 3
check 1
delay 2
deter
discourage 3
embargo 2
encumber 2
forbid
forestall
frustrate 1
hamper[1]
handicap 2
hobble 2
hold 14a, 22b
impede
inhibit
interfere 2
militate 1
obstruct 2
oppose 2
posterior 1
preclude
prevent
prohibit 2
repress
resist 1
restrain 2
retard 1
set 16
shackle 4
stay[1] 4
stop 2
stunt[2]
stymie
suppress 1
thwart 1
tie 2
trammel 2
hindering
obstruction 2
prevention
preventive 1
repression 2
suppression
hindmost
last[1] 1
hind part
rear[1] 1
hindquarters
bottom 1
bum 1
hindquarters (*cont.*)
buttocks
rear[1] 2
seat 4
hindrance°
bar 3
barrier 2
block 2
check 14
deterrent
difficulty 2
drawback
embargo 1
encumbrance
fly 10
handicap 1
hitch 4
hurdle 1
impediment
inconvenience 1
inhibition
interference 2
let[2]
liability 3
obstacle
obstruction 1
overload 2
prevention
preventive 3
repression 2
rub 11
set-back
shackle 2
snag 1
stumbling-block
trammel 1
hindsight
retrospect
hinge
base[1] 5
depend 1
pivot 1, 4
rest[1] 7
turn 18b
hinged
jointed
hinie
bottom 1
bum 1
buttocks
posterior 3
rear[1] 2
seat 4
tail 2
hint°
announce 2
appearance 4
aroma 2
bit 2
breath 2
breathe 4
broach
cast 6
clue 1, 2
cue 1
dab 2
dash 7
discourage 2
drive 6
evidence 3
feeler 2
feeling 2
flash 2
flavour 2
flicker 4
get 30b
ghost 2
gleam 2
grain 3
idea 2
implication 2
imply 1
impute
index 2
indicate 3
indication 1
inkling
innuendo
insinuate 1
intimate[2]
lead 14
line[1] 10
make 37e
mean[1] 2
hint (*cont.*)
mention 2
modicum
note 6
notify 2
odour 2
overtone
partake 2b
particle
point 11
pointer 2
predict
prediction
promise 4
prompt 6
reference 1
ripple 2
savour 2
say 2
scattering
scrap[1] 1
shade 3
shadow 3
shred 1
sign 3
sniff 2
spark 1
speck
steer 3
strain[2] 2
stroke 8
suggest 2
suggestion 2
suspicion 2
tang 2
taste 1
tell[1] 2
tint 1
tip[3] 2
touch 15
trace 1
vein 4
vestige
waft 2
whisper 2, 4
word 6
hinterland
country 3
interior 7
province 4
stick[2] 3
hinting
indicative of
hip°
aware 1
minute[1] 3
modern
new 2
privy 2
relate 4
smart 2
sophisticated 1
swinging
well-informed
worldly 2
hip hep
sensible 4
hippie°
Hippocrenian
poetic 2
hippodrome
stadium
theatre 1
hippy
plump[1] 1
hipster
hippie
hircine
lascivious 1
lecherous
lewd
libertine 2
sensual
hire°
charter 5
employ 1
employment 2
engage 1
enlist 2
get 1
job 6
lease 2
let[1] 3
line[1] 23b
hire (*cont.*)
rent[1] 1, 2
retain 2
sign 10b
take 4, 35a
hireling
flunkey 1
mercenary 3
puppet 2
subordinate 2
hire out°
at **hire** 3
lease 2
let[1] 3
rent[1] 1
hire purchase
-on hire purchase
time 19b
hiring
employment 2
placement 2
hirsute
hairy 1
shaggy
His Highness
crown 3
His Majesty
crown 3
hispid
hairy 1
hiss°
fizz 1, 3
jeer 2
outcry
swish 1, 2
whisper 1
hissing
fizz 3
hiss 1
outcry
historic°
former 2
landmark 3
memorable
monumental 1
significant 1
traditional
historical°
history°
account 4
background 1
chronicle 1
description 2
journal 2
memoir 2
myth 1
narrative 1
past 5
record 6
story 1
tale 1
history-making
monumental 1
histrionic
dramatic 1, 3
grand 3
grandiose 1
melodramatic
theatrical 1
Thespian 1
histrionics
drama 3
rant 3
theatre 2
hit°
arrive 1
assault 5
batter 1
belt 3
blow[2] 1
box[2] 2, 3
bum 5
bump 1, 3
catch 6
clip[2] 3, 6
dispatch 3
finger 4
get 24
impact 3
jab 2
jolt 2
kill 1

hold off (*cont.*)
hold 19c, 21a
put 21a
repel 1
suspend 1
hold on°
at **hold 19**
brace 6
hang 7a
wait 1
hold one's ground
stick[1] 14
hold one's horses
sit 8
hold one's tongue°
at **tongue 3**
hold on to
conserve 1
hang 7a
retain 1
hold out°
at **hold 20**
bear 10a
endure 2
extend 4
hang 7c
hold 16b
last[2] 1
reach 1
resist 1
tender[2] 1
withstand
hold over°
at **hold 21**
reserve 1
hold someone responsible
accuse 1
blame 2
fault 8
pin 5
thank 2
hold someone's attention
occupy 3
hold spellbound
fascinate
hold sway
command 2
control 1
govern 1
predominate
prevail 1
reign 2, 3
rule 5
hold the line
resist 1
hold the reins
string 6
hold the whip hand
govern 1
hold tight(ly)
press 5
hold to
abide 4
redeem 6
hold together
bond 4
hold true
hold 11
hold up°
at **hold 22**
bear 2, 10a
brake 2
carry 5
delay 1, 2
embargo 2
hamper[1]
hang 6
hold 11
impede
interrupt 2
pause 1
prop 1
rear[2] 3
retard 1
rob 1, 2
set 16
shake 6b

hold up (*cont.*)
stick[1] 17a
support 2, 5
suspend 1
uphold
wash 8
wear 4
hold-up°
assault 2
delay 4, 5
impediment
lapse 2
pause 2
robbery
set-back
suspension 2
wait 4
hold-up man
robber
thief 1
hold water
hold 11
wash 8
hold with°
at **hold 23**
hold your tongue
hush 1
wrap 3b
hole°
aperture
bore[1] 1
breach 3
break 26
burrow 1
cache 1
cave 1
cavity
clearance 1
excavation
fix 17
flaw 2
gap 1
hideaway
hollow 7
hovel
interval 3
jam 6
jump 12
lair 1
leak 2
opening 1
pan 3
passage 11
pierce 2
pit[1] 1
plight
pore[2]
predicament
prick 1
puncture 1, 3
rent[2]
rift 2
tear 4
tunnel 1, 2
vent 1
hole in the wall
hole 3
hole up
hide[1] 1
shelter 5
holiday°
feast 2
festival 1
gala 1
leave[2] 2
leisure 2, 5
recess 2
respite 1
rest[1] 2
sojourn 1, 2
-on holiday
leisure 3a
off 6
holiday-maker
tourist
traveller
holier-than-thou
goody-goody
Pharisaic
sanctimonious
self-righteous
smug

holiness
devotion 1
piety 2
sanctity
holing
puncture 2
holler
bawl 1
bellow 1, 2
call 1, 13
exclaim
exclamation
howl 1, 2
shout 1, 2
whoop 1, 2
yell 1, 2
hollering
din 1
hollow°
affected 2
cave 1
cavity
depression 1
empty 1, 4
excavate 1
excavation
gouge 1, 3
hole 1
hungry 1
impression 3
indentation
lair 1
meaningless 1
niche 1
pan 3
pit[1] 2
pocket 2
pointless
recess 1
slot 1
sunken 1
vacant 1
valley
wan 2
weak 4
hollow-cheeked
gaunt 1
haggard
raw-boned
skinny
thin 1
hollowed-out
sunken 1
hollow-eyed
haggard
peaky
hollowness
emptiness 1, 2
vanity 2
hollow out
bore[1] 2
dig 1
excavate 1
gouge 1
pit[1] 5
scoop 5
slot 3
undercut 1
hollowware
silver 1
holm
island
holocaust°
blaze 1
carnage
destruction 2
fire 1
holograph
paper 4
holy°
devout 1
divine 1
godlike 1
godly
heavenly 1
perfect 3
pious 1
religious 1
sacred 1
saintly
seraphic
solemn 2
spiritual 1

holy day
feast 2
festival 1
gala 1
holy expedition
pilgrimage
Holy Joe
minister 1
holy man
clergyman 1
divine 5
priest
holy of holies
sanctum 1
holy orders
ministry 1
holy place
temple
Holy Scripture(s)
Scripture
holy war
crusade 1
holy woman
priest
Holy Writ
Scripture
homage°
compliment 1
eulogy
glory 2
honour 2
memory 3
obeisance
praise 2
prostration 2
recognize 4
reverence 1
tribute 1
veneration
worship 2
home°
abode
base[1] 4
domestic 1, 3
domicile 1
dwelling
habitat
house 1
housing 1
institution 3
interior 2
outside 7
pad 3
place 6
quarter 5
residence 1
seat 5
setting
shelter 3
-at home°
at **home 4**
friendly 1
-at home in°
at **home 5**
home-brew
moonshine 3
whisky
home-coming
return 10
home ground
home 2
turf 2
home-grown
native 2
home in on
identify 1
pin 4b
set 5
zero 4
homeland
country 2
fatherland
land 4
homeless°
stray 4
homelessness
want 5
homely°
modest 2
plain 5
prosaic

homely (*cont.*)
simple 2
snug
ugly 1
undistinguished
unsightly
homeothermic
warm-blooded 1
home-owner
resident 3
Homeric
heroic 5
home rule
independence 1
self-government 1
homesick°
homespun°
homely 1
ordinary 2
provincial 2
rude 4
undistinguished
vulgar 3
homestead
dwelling
farm 1
house 1
spread 13
homeward(s)
home 9
homework
assignment 2
lesson 1
homey
homely 1, 2
homicidal°
bloodthirsty
cutthroat 3
deadly 3
fierce 1
grim 2
sanguinary 1
homicide
foul play
killing 1
murder 1
murderer
slaughter 2
homiletic
proverbial 1
homily
moral 3
oration
proverb
sermon 2
speech 2
tract[2]
hominoid
human 1
homo
homosexual 1
homoeothermic
warm-blooded 1
homoerotic
homosexual 2
homogeneity
uniformity 1
unity 2
homogeneous°
solid 4
uniform 1
homogenization
wedding 2
homogenize
standardize
wed 2
homoiothermic
warm-blooded 1
homologous
like[1] 1
matching 1
parallel 1
homologue
parallel 2
homophile
homosexual 1, 2
Homo sapiens
humanity 1
man 2
homosexual°
effeminate
swish 4

honcho
bigwig 1
boss 1
chief 1
executive 1
head 2
overseer
principal 3
hone
refine 3
sharpen
whet 1
honest°
above-board 2
artless 1
bona fide
candid 1
card 14
decent 4
direct 10
ethical
even 7
fair[1] 2
faithful 4
frank 1
free 9
front 9b
genuine 2
good 8
heartfelt
hearty 2
honourable 1, 3
incorrupt 1
ingenuous 1, 2
innocent 1
irreproachable
just 2
level 11, 15
moral 1
natural 4
noble 4
open 15
plain 3
principled
pure 6
raw 6
real 3, 4
reliable
reputable
respectable 1
responsible 2
right 1, 12
righteous 1
round 8
savoury 2
serious 3
simple 2, 3
sincere
square 4
straight 4
trustworthy
truthful
unaffected[1]
unvarnished
upright 2
virtuous 1
honestly°
fairly 2
naturally 3
quite 4
really 1
right 12
seriously 2
shoulder 6
sincerely
straight 14
true 4
truly 1, 4
honest-to-God
literal 2
solid 4
honesty°
candour 1
character 3
credit 3
freedom 6
good 20
honour 1
integrity 1
morality 1
nobility 1
principle 3
probity
purity 2
rectitude

honesty (*cont.*)
right 10
sincerity
sportsmanship
virtue 1
-in all honesty
right 12
truly 1
honey
dear 3
love 3
honeycomb
perforate
riddle[2] 1
honeyed
flattering 2
sweet 1, 7
honeyed words
pat[1] 5
honey-like
sweet 1
honey-tongued
smooth 6
honky-tonk
dive 3
gaudy
joint 2
pub
honorarium°
bonus
consideration 2
fee 2
gift 1
pay 12
price 3
wage 1
honorary°
unpaid 2
honour°
adore 1
celebrate 1, 3
character 3
chivalry
commemorate
compliment 1, 3
conscience
credit 4
dignity 2
discharge 6
distinction 2
esteem 1
eulogize
exalt 2
extol
face 4
fête 2
glorify 2
glory 1, 2
grace 7
hail[1] 2
hallow 1, 2
homage
honesty 1
immortalize
integrity 1
kudos
laud
laurels
look 12
lustre 2
memorialize
memory 3
name 2
obeisance
pay 1
plaque 3
praise 2, 3
pride 1
principle 3
prize[1] 1
probity
recognition 2
recognize 4
regard 7
renown
respect 6
revere
reverence 1
reward 2
salute 2
self-respect
sportsmanship
toast 1, 3
tribute 1

honour (*cont.*)
trophy 1
venerate
veneration
virtue 1, 2
worship 1, 2
honourable°
above-board 2
clean 4
conscientious 1
decent 4
dignified
distinguished 1
estimable
fair[1] 2
good 5, 9
heroic 2
honest 1
incorrupt 1
ingenuous 2
just 2
lofty 2, 3
meritorious
moral 1
noble 4
principled
prominent 2
proud 3
pukka 2
pure 6
reliable
reputable
right 1
righteous 1
savoury 2
scrupulous 2
square 4
straight 4
sublime 1
true 2
trustworthy
upright 2
venerable
virtuous 1
wholesome 2
worthwhile 2
honourableness
dignity 2
good 20
nobility 1
right 10
sportsmanship
honourably
honestly 1
honoured
dear 1
distinguished 1
eminent 1
estimable
exalted 1
famous
glorious 1
honourable 4
illustrious
immortal 3
lofty 2
noble 3
prestigious
privileged 1
prominent 2
proud 1, 3
renowned
time-honoured
venerable
honouring
celebration 2
hooch
alcohol
booze 1
drink 5
liquor 1
moonshine 3
spirit 9b
whisky
hood
bruiser
criminal 3
gangster
hoodlum
miscreant 1
rowdy 2
thug
hoodlum°
bruiser
criminal 3

hoodlum (*cont.*)
gangster
henchman
miscreant 1
punk 1
rowdy 2
thug
hoodoo
enchant 1
hoodwink°
beguile 1
betray 3
blind 5
bluff[1] 1
cheat 2
defraud
double-cross
dupe 3
finesse 4
flummox
fool 4
hoax 2
lead 7
mislead
outsmart
prey 3b
pull 15
put 26
swindle 1
take 32b
trick 8
victimize 2
hooey
drivel 3
moonshine 2
mumbo-jumbo 1
nonsense 1
prattle 3
rubbish 2
talk 18
trash 1
wind[1] 2
hoof
-hooves
extremity 2
hoof it
dance 1
leg 9b
run 1
walk 1
hoo-ha
fuss 1
tempest 2
uproar
hook°
attach 1
bend 1
buckle 1
catch 2, 17
clasp 1, 3
completely 1
connect 3
fasten 1
gimmick 1
hitch 1
lock[1] 1
make 27
peg 1
pilfer
pocket 4
put 27c
steal 1
take 3
wholly 1
-by hook or by crook°
at **hook 3**
somehow
-off the hook°
at **hook 5**
exempt 2
hookah
pipe 2
hook a ride
thumb 6
hooked
catch 7
fond 3
mad 6
hooker
bitch 2
catch 18
prostitute 1
provision 2

hooker (*cont.*)
slattern
tart[2] 2
wanton 5
hook, line, and sinker
completely 1
hook 4
wholly 1
hook up
fasten 1
hitch 1
put 27c
hook-up
marriage 3
hooligan
barbarian 2
bruiser
criminal 3
delinquent 1
gangster
henchman
hoodlum
killer 1
miscreant 1
punk 1
rough 13
rowdy 2
thug
tough 8
hooliganism
rowdyism
hoop
circle 1
loop 1
ring[1] 1
round 10
wheel 1
hoop-la
advertisement 2
fuss 1
promotion 4
propaganda 2
uproar
hoop-like
round 2
hooray
cheer 4
hoosegow
jail 1
prison
hoot
damn 4
hiss 2, 3
jeer 2
laugh 1
outcry
roar 2, 4
scream 2
squawk 1
whoop 1, 2
hootch
liquor 1
moonshine 3
spirit 9b
hooting
outcry
hoover
clean 9
hop°
bounce 1, 3
bound[2] 1, 3
caper 1, 3
dance 2
flit
jump 1, 8
leap 5
party 1
skip 1, 3
spring 1, 6
trip 4
-on the hop
swing 6
hope°
ambition 3
anticipation 1
aspiration
aspire
desire 1
expect 3
expectation 2
look 6c
mean[1] 1

hope (*cont.*)
objective 2
prospect 3
pull 10
seek 2
thought 3
view 5
want 1
wish 1
-beyond hope
desperate 5
hopeless 1
spout 4
-it is hoped
hopefully 2
-without hope
back 10
hope for the best
finger 3
hopeful°
ambitious 1
bright 4
desirous
expectant
optimistic
promising
rosy 2
sanguine
hopefully°
hopefulness
expectation 1
hopeless°
deplorable 1
desolate 3
desperate 5
impossible 1
incorrigible
incurable 1, 2
lost 8
pessimistic
unpromising
useless 2
wretched 3
hopelessness
despair 1
desperation 2
hophead
addict 1
hoping
desirous
desperate 3
hop it
leave[1] 1
run 1
hop over
leap 1
hop-pole
pole[1]
hop to it
race[1] 4
hop up
excite 1
horde
assembly 1
band[2] 1
crowd 1
flock 1
herd 1
host[2]
jam 5
many 3
mass 2
mob 1
number 2
pack 3
press 8
rabble 1
score 4
swarm 1
throng 1
many 3
score 4
horizon°
background 2
-on the horizon
forthcoming 1
impending
prospect 4
horizontal°
flat 1
level 2, 12
plane 3

horizontal (*cont.*)
prone 1
prostrate 3
recumbent
straight 3
horn
alarm 1
gore[2]
pipe 3
siren 1
telephone 1
hornbook
school-book
text 4
hornet's nest
problem 1
horn in
interfere 1
interrupt 1
intervene 1
intrude
horniness
lust 1
hornswoggle
perplex
horny
hot 7
lascivious 1
lecherous
lewd
libertine 2
lustful
prurient 1
randy
steamy 3
horrendous
atrocious 2
awful 2
disastrous 1
dreadful 2
fearful 3
frightful 2
ghastly 1
ghoulish 2
great 11
grim 3
grisly
gruesome
horrible 1
lurid 2
monstrous 1
outrageous 2
satanic 2
scary
terrible 4
horrible°
abominable 2
atrocious 1
awful 1, 2
beastly 2
damnable
diabolic 2
disastrous 1
dreadful 2
evil 1
fearful 3
frightful 2
ghastly 1
ghoulish 2
great 11
grim 3
gruesome
harrowing
hateful 1
loathsome
monstrous 1
nameless 3
nasty 1
nightmarish
outrageous 2
repulsive
revolting
rotten 4
satanic 2
scary
shocking 2
terrible 4, 5
tragic
unsightly
vile 1
wicked 2

horrible-looking
ugly 1
horribleness
enormity
monstrosity 2
horribly
badly 6
horrid
abhorrent
abominable 1
atrocious 2
awful 1
beastly 2
damnable
diabolic 2
dreadful 2
evil 1
frightful 2
ghastly 1
ghoulish 2
grim 3
grisly
gruesome
hateful 1
horrible 1, 2
lurid 2
monstrous 1
outrageous 2
repulsive
revolting
satanic 2
scary
shocking 2
terrible 4
vile 1
wicked 2
horridness
enormity
monstrosity 2
horrific
awful 2
fearful 3
gory
great 11
grim 3
grisly
gruesome
hideous 2
horrible 1
monstrous 1
nightmarish
rotten 4
shocking 2
horrified
panic-stricken
petrified 1
scared
horrify°
appal
dismay 1
frighten
petrify 1
revolt 3
scandalize
scare 1
shock 1
terrify
horrifying
abhorrent
atrocious 1
awesome
awful 2
disastrous 1
dreadful 2
fearful 3
formidable 1
frightening
frightful 2
ghastly 1
ghoulish 2
grisly
harrowing
hideous 2
horrible 1
lurid 2
monstrous 1
satanic 2
scary
shocking 2
terrible 4
terrifying
horripilate
bristle 2
horror°
abhor
atrocity 1
aversion 1
dismay 3
distaste 2
dread 1, 2
enormity
fear 1, 3
fright 1
loathing
monster 2
monstrosity 2
panic 1
phobia
terror 1
thing 4
horror story
romance 3
story 1
horror-stricken
panic-stricken
petrified 1
hors-d'oeuvre°
savoury 3
horse
mount 9
nag[2]
trot 4
-horses
stock 4
-on one's high horse
arrogant 2
mannered
snobbish
horse about
clown 3
frolic 3
play 9a
horse-apples
dung
horse feathers
drivel 3
gibberish
nonsense 1
prattle 3
rubbish 2
stuff 4
talk 18
trash 1
horseplay
frolic 1
fun 2
lark 1
nonsense 2
play 22
trick 2
horse-race
race[1] 1, 3
turf 3
horse sense
gumption 1
horseshit
fiddlesticks
flannel 1, 2
gab 2
moonshine 2
nonsense 1
rubbish 2
stuff 4
talk 18
trash 1
horse's mouth
source 3
horsewhip
flog 1
hit 1
lambaste 1
lash[1] 3
scourge 2, 3
slash 2
strike 1
whip 1, 8
horsewhipping
whipping 1
hortatory
advisory 1
hosanna
praise 2
rave 3
hose
pipe 1
pipeline 1
water 6
hose down
flush[1] 2
hospice
home 3
monastery
hospitable°
accommodating 1
genial
pleasant 2
receptive 1
warm 3
hospitably
kindly 2
hospital°
infirmary
institution 3
hospitality°
fellowship 3
kindness 1
hospitalize
lay[1] 19b
host°
assembly 1
entertain 2
flock 1
herd 1
landlord 1
mass 2
mob 1
number 2
press 8
profusion
score 4
stack 3
swarm 1
throng 1
waiter
-be host to
entertain 2
hostage°
captive 1
hostelry
hotel
pub
hostess
host[1] 1
landlady 1
waiter
hostile°
adversary 2
aggressive 1
belligerent 2
chilly 2
contrary 2
defiant
fierce 2
forbidding 2
gaunt 2
hard 9
icy 2
ill 3
incompatible
inhospitable 1, 2
jaundiced 2
mean[2] 5
militant 1
offensive 1
opposed
opposing
opposition 3
polar 2
pugnacious
quarrelsome
rancorous
resentful
spiteful
truculent
turn 19b
ugly 4
unsocial
venomous 2
virulent 2
warlike
hostility°
aggression 1
animosity
antagonism 1
aversion 1
bitterness 2
chill 3
hostility *(cont.)*
dislike 2
feud 1
friction 2
hate 3
horror 1
ill will
opposition 1
rancour
resentment
spite 1
strife 2
venom 2
virulence 2
-hostilities°
at **hostility 2**
fight 7
war 1
hostler
groom 1
hot°
ardent
burning 4
eager
energetic
excited
fabulous 3
fervent 1
feverish
fiery 1
inflamed
lascivious 1
lewd
minute[1] 3
modern
passionate 2
popular 1
prurient 1
pungent 1
racy 2, 3
randy
scorching 1
sharp 4
spicy 1, 2
steamy 3
strong 2
sultry 1, 2
superb
sweltering
torrid 1, 2
trendy 1
-in hot water
trouble 9a
hot air°
bluff[1] 3
bluster 3
bombast
drivel 3
exaggeration
froth 2
inaccurate
mistaken
moonshine 2
mouth 3
nonsense 1
palaver 2
patter[2] 2
prattle 3
raving 3
rhetoric 2
stuff 4
talk 18
waffle 3
wind[1] 2
hot and bothered
excited 1
hotbed°
hothouse 1
hot-blooded
excitable
feverish
fire 5
quick-tempered
temperamental 1
warm-blooded 2
hot-bloodedness
temper 3
hotchpotch°
clutter 1
confusion 5
disorder 1
hash 1
medley
hotchpotch *(cont.)*
mess 1
miscellany
mishmash
mix-up
mixture 1
muddle 4
pastiche
patchwork
pot-pourri
promiscuous 3
rummage 2
stew 1
tangle 2
welter 1
hotel°
hotelier
host[1] 1
landlord 1
proprietor 2
hotfoot
hurry 1
run 1
rush 1
scramble 2
hotheaded°
emotional 2
fervent 1
fiery 3
foolhardy
intense 3
passionate 3
precipitate 5
rash[1]
temperamental 1
hotheadedness
temper 3
hothouse°
hotly°
warmly 4
hotness
heat 1
hot pants
desire 3
short 15
hot potato
difficulty 3
hots
desire 3
hotshot
bigwig 1
dignitary
mogul
personage
somebody 2
hot-tempered
hasty 4
hotheaded
impatient 2
pugnacious
quick-tempered
sensitive 2
snappish 1
temperamental 1
testy
touchy 1
hot to trot
eager
hot under the collar
angry 1
warm 2
hot up°
at **hot 11**
heat 4
intensify
hot water
difficulty 3
embarrassment 2
hole 5
jam 6
mess 3
plight
strait 3
-in hot water
trouble 9a
Houdini
magician 1
hound°
addict 2
bother 1
chase 3
hound *(cont.)*
devotee
enthusiast
fan
fiend 2
grind 5
harass
hunt 1
persecute 2
plague 3
prod 3
push 4
stalk[1]
hour
day 2
moment 2
present[1] 4
time 3
-hours
shift 4
hourly
regular 2
house°
abode
accommodate 4
attendance 2
board 7
business 4
chamber 1
clan 1
company 4
concern 7
diet[2]
dwelling
dynasty
family 3
firm 6
home 1
lodge 1, 4
lodging
office 1
parliament 1
place 6
put 28b
quarter 5, 6
residence 1
root[1] 4
stock 2
structure 2
theatre 1
tribe
-houses
housing 1
-on the house°
at **house 7**
complimentary 2
free 4
-the House
parliament 1
housebound
sedentary
houseboy
man 3
servant 1
housebreaker
burglar
robber
thief 1
house-broken
domestic 2
tame 1
housecoat
robe 1
wrapper 1
household
domestic 1
family 1
furniture 1
home 7
house 1
traditional
train 2
vulgar 3
householder
citizen 1
landlord 2
occupant
resident 3
household goods
furniture 1

housekeeper
domestic 4
servant 1
woman 4
housemaid
maid 2
houseman
man 3
servant 1
house-moving
removal 5
house of correction
prison
house of God
sanctuary 1
temple
house of ill fame
brothel
house 6
House of Lords and House of Commons
parliament 1
house of worship
sanctuary 1
temple
house organ
organ 2
house-servant
boy 2
Houses of Parliament
parliament 1
house-train
tame 5
house-trained
domestic 2
housing°
accommodation 4
domicile 1
lodging
shelter 3
hovel°
hole 3
shack
hovel-like
sordid 4
hover°
float 1
flutter 2
fly 1
hang 1
loom 2
poise 3
soar 1
hovercraft
craft 4
hovering
poised 3
how
however 2,3
however°
nevertheless
only 4
still 8
though 2
time 13a
howl°
bellow 1
cry 4,5
gale 2
outcry
rave 1
roar 1,2,3,4
scream 1,2,3
shout 1,2
sob
storm 5
whoop 1,2
yell 1,2
howler°
blunder 2
error 1
fault 2
fluff 3
misstatement 2
misstep 2
mistake 1
howling
fabulous 3
outcry
stiff 5
stormy 1
how on earth
however 3
howsoever
however 2
hoyden
boor 2
hub°
centre 1
focus 1
heart 3
pivot 2
seat 2
hubble-bubble
pipe 2
hubbub
babble 3
bedlam
bother 8
din 1
disorder 2
disturbance 2
excitement 2
fanfare 2
flurry 1
fracas 1
furore 1
fuss 1
noise 1
pell-mell 3
racket 1
riot 1
row² 2
stir 6
tumult
uproar
hubby
husband 1
mate 2
hubris
arrogance
pride 2
hubristic
overconfident 1
huckster
merchant 2
peddle
pedlar
huddle°
cuddle 1
dialogue 2
gather 2
nestle
palaver 3,5
parley 1,2
press 7,8
word 1
Hudibrastic
satirical
hue°
colour 1
shade 2
tint 1
tone 4
hue and cry
racket 1
huff°
exhale
gasp 1
pant 1
puff 1,4
-in a huff°
at **huff 1**
indignant
huffing
short-winded
huffishness
temper 3
huffy
cross 6
indignant
moody 2
passionate 3
petulant
temperamental 1
hug°
caress 1,2
clasp 2,4
clinch 2
hug (*cont.*)
cling 3
cuddle 2,3
embrace 1,4
fold 2
hold 2
press 5
squeeze 5,7
huge°
big 1,2
colossal 1
enormous
exceeding
extensive 2
gigantic
grand 1
great 1,2,11
hefty 3
heroic 4
high 4
immeasurable
immense
jumbo
large 3
massive
mighty 3
monolithic
monstrous 3
monumental 2,4
mountainous 2
ponderous 1
princely 1
prodigious 1
spacious
substantial 2
swingeing
tall 2
thumping 1
towering 1
vast
voluminous 1
weighty 1
whopping 1
hugely
exceedingly
full 18
highly 1
vastly
very 1
hugeness
enormousness
size 1
hugger-mugger
furtive 1
stealthy
hulk°
wreck 3
hulking°
big 2
massive
stout 4
hull°
body 3
peel 1
shell 2,3
skin 4
hullabaloo
din 1
disorder 2
disturbance 2
fanfare 2
fracas 1
noise 1
outcry
racket 1
row² 2
tumult
uproar
hum°
buzz 1,5
murmur 1
reek 1,3
smell 4
human°
earthly 3
figure 3
flesh 3
individual 3
life 5
mortal 1,6
person 1
terrestrial 2
worldly 1
human being
figure 3
human 4
individual 3
life 5
man 2
mortal 6
person 1
hum and haw
pussyfoot 2
shilly-shally
shuffle 3
stammer 1
humane
benevolent
charitable 2
forgiving
generous 2
gentle 1
good 6
human 3
lenient
merciful
philanthropic
tender¹ 6
humaneness
altruism
kindness 1
mercy
humanistic
liberal 2
humanitarian°
benevolent
generous 2
human 3
kind¹
open 14
philanthropic
philanthropist
unselfish
humanitarianism
altruism
benevolence 1
charity 1
heart 5
humanity°
altruism
benevolence 1
charity 1
heart 5
kindness 1
man 2
mercy
quarter 4
world 2
-humanities
letter 3
humanize
personify 2
humankind
humanity 1
man 2
world 2
human nature
flesh 2
humanity 2
human race
humanity 1
man 2
world 2
humble°
artless 2
degrade 2
dishonour 2
downgrade 1
embarrass
hang 8
inferior 2
low¹ 7
lower¹ 4
mean² 2
meek 1
menial 1
modest 1,2
mortify 1
obscure 4
pastoral 2
peg 3
place 13
plebeian 1
prostrate 2
puncture 4
reduce 6
humble (*cont.*)
retiring
shame 6,7
simple 5
small 4
subject 10
subjugate
submissive 2
take 31b
unknown 1
unobtrusive
humbled
embarrassed 1
hang 8
prostrate 4
remorseful
shamefaced 2
humbleness
vulgarity 1
humble oneself
condescend
sink 9
stoop 2
humbling
humiliation
shameful
subjection
sublime 2
humbly
cap 3
quietly 4
humbug
cant 1
defraud
dupe 3
fake 4
fiddlesticks
flannel 1
fool 4
fraud 1,3
gobbledegook 1
hoax 1
hocus-pocus 1
hoodwink
jargon 2
mislead
moonshine 2
mumbo-jumbo 1
mystify
Pharisee
phoney 3
prattle 3
pretence 1,2
ride 5a
sham 1
stuff 4
trick 8
wind¹ 2
humbuggery
fraud 1
pretence 1
humdinger
killer 2
humdrum°
banal
boring
deadly 5
dreary 2
dull 4
hack² 4
literal 3
monotonous
ordinary 1
pedestrian 2
prosaic
repetitive
slow 9
stodgy
stupid 3
tame 4
tedious
tiresome 1
vapid
humid°
clammy 2
damp 1
moist 1
muggy
steamy 1
sticky 3
sultry 1
sweltering
torrid 1
watery 3
humidity
damp 2
wet 4,5
humiliate°
crush 5
degrade 2
devastate 2
diminish 2
disgrace 3
dishonour 2
embarrass
humble 4
libel 3
lower¹ 4
mortify 1
offend 1
patronize 1
peg 3
pull 9c
put 16e
shame 6,7
squelch 1
subjugate
take 31b
humiliated
ashamed
embarrassed 1
hang 8
remorseful
shamefaced 2
small 6
humiliating
degrading
disgraceful 1
embarrassing
provocative 2
shameful
humiliation°
degradation 2
discredit 4
disgrace 1
indignity
libel 1
patronage 3
prostration 2
remorse
shame 1
subjection
undoing 1
humility°
shame 4
humming
alive 4
murmur 1
hummock
hill 1
hump 1
knoll
mound 1
prominence 2
humongous
big 1
gigantic
immense
incredible 2
jumbo
large 3
massive
prodigious 1
vast
humorist
card 11
comedian
joker 1
wit 3
humorous°
comic 1
entertaining
farcical
funny 1
hilarious
playful 2
rich 10
ridiculous
witty
humour°
cater 2
coddle
disposition 1
frame 5
indulge 1
jolly 2
key 5
make 34b

humour (*cont.*)
mind 5
mood 1
pander 1
pet[1] 5
please 1
spirit 8
sport 2
strain[1] 9
suffer 3
temper 1
vein 4
wit 2

-out of humour
sullen

humourless
po-faced
serious 1

hump°
bulge 1
love 6
mound 1
run 1

humus
mould[3]
soil[2]

hunch°
feeling 2
hump 1, 2
intuition
premonition
sensation 1
slouch 1, 2
stoop 1, 3

100%
wholly 1

hundred(s)
many 3
number 2
score 4
umpteen

hunger°
ache 2
ambition 1
anxiety 2
appetite 2
desire 3
die 5
eagerness 1
itch 2, 4
long[2]
longing
passion 3
stomach 2
thirst 1
urge 5
want 4
wish 5
yearn
zest 2

hunger for°
at **hunger 3**
desire 1
fancy 11
hanker
lust 3
pant 2
thirst 2
want 1

hungering
hungry 2
starved 2

hunger strike
fast[2] 2

hung-over
ropy 3
rotten 5

hungriness
hunger 1

hungry°
desperate 3
eager
famished
hollow 3
ravenous 1
starved 1, 2
thirsty 2
voracious 2

hung up

-be hung up on
love 7

hunk
block 1
brick 1
clod 1
clump 1
lump[1] 1
mass 3
mouthful
piece 1
portion 1
slab
wad 1

hunker down
crouch
stoop 1

hunt°
chase 1
follow 4
prey 3a
pursue 1
pursuit 1
quest 1, 2
rummage 1
run 26a
scout 1
search 3
seek 1
stalk[1]
trace 5
track 6, 8
trail 7

hunter°

hunt for°
at **hunt 2**
angle[2]
look 6b, 11a
pursue 1
quest 2
scout 1
seek 1

hunting
chase 1
hunt 3
prowl 3
pursuit 1

hunting-lodge
lodge 1

huntress
hunter

hunt through°
at **hunt 2**
search 1

hunt up°
at **hunt 2**
pursue 1
trace 5

hurdle°
drawback
jump 1, 8, 10
leap 1, 5
obstacle
obstruction 1
stumbling-block

hurdler
runner 1

hurl°
cast 7
dash 2
deliver 5
fire 9
fling 1
fly 8a
heave 2
launch 3
lob 1
pitch[1] 1
precipitate 2
project 4
retort 2
send 3
shoot 2
slap 3
sling 1
throw 1
toss 1

hurly-burly
din 1
disturbance 2
excitement 2
furore 1
tempest 2

hurrah
cheer 4, 7
whoop 1, 2

hurray
cheer 4

hurricane°
blow[1] 9
eddy 1
storm 1
tempest 1
twister 2
whirlwind 1

hurried°
cursory
fast[1] 1
pell-mell 2
perfunctory 1
quick 2
rapid
scratch 6
sketchy
snap 13
speedy 2
superficial 3

hurriedly
briefly 2
fast[1] 6
hastily 1
pell-mell 1
quickly 3
run 49a
short 11
shot 10
sketchily
suddenly 2
swiftly

hurriedness
speed 1

hurry°
bundle 3
dash 3
dispatch 4, 5
expedite 1
flash 5
flurry 1
fly 3
forward 8
haste 2
hasten 1, 2
hustle 1
leg 5, 9a
move 12b
pelt[1] 3
precipitate 1
press 9
quicken 2
race[1] 4
run 1
rush 1, 3
scramble 2
scurry
speed 1, 3
step 16
streak 5
tear 3
trot 1
urge 1
weave 5
whip 3
whisk 2

-in a hurry
run 49a

hurry up
hasten 2
leg 9a
run 1
rush 1
step 16
weave 5

hurry-up
rush 5

hurt°
abuse 2
abused 2
ache 1
affected 5
ail 1
bruise 1, 2
cut 3
damage 1, 4
detriment
evil 7
flaw 4
get 24
grief 1
harm 1, 3
hit 4

hurt (*cont.*)
ill 8
ill-treat
injure 1, 2
injury
kill 5
lacerate
mar 2
mischief 2
mishandle 1
mistreat
offence 2
offend 1
outrage 2
pain 1, 5
pinch 2
prick 4
punish 3
rack 3
rankle
rend 3
ruin 9
shoot 3
smart 7
spite 3
stab 5
sting 2
strain[1] 3
suffer 1
taint 2
tarnish
trample 2
undermine 1
wound 1, 3, 4

hurtful°
abusive 2
bad 2
destructive 1
detrimental
evil 3
grievous 1
ill 4
injurious 1
mischievous 2
painful 1
pungent 3
sharp 5
stiff 2
traumatic

hurting
painful 1
sore 1
starved 2
tender[1] 8

hurtle°
career 2
plough 2
rattle 4
shoot 1
streak 5

hurt someone's feelings
offend 1

husband°
economize
garner
keep 3
mate 2
partner 2

husbandman
farmer

husbandry
conservation
economy 1
farming
providence 1
prudence 2
thrift

husband-to-be
fiancé

hush°
calm 1, 5
hide[1] 4
lull 2, 3
muffle 2
mute 3
pipe 7
quiet 5
quieten
silence 1, 3
still 3

hushed
faint 1
low[1] 13

hushed (*cont.*)
noiseless
quiet 1
silent 1
still 2
subdued 1
weak 7

hushed tone(s)
whisper 3

-in hushed tones
quietly 2

hush-hush
confidential
private 1
privileged 4
secret 1

hush money
pay-off 3

hush up°
at **hush 4**
hide[1] 4
hush 1
pipe 7

hush your mouth
hush 1

husk
hull 2, 3
rind
shell 3
skin 2, 4

huskiness
brawn

husky°
brawny
burly
gruff 2
hardy 1
harsh 1
hefty 2
large 1
lusty 2
mighty 2
muscular
raucous
robust 1
rough 8
stalwart 1
stout 4
strident
strong 1
sturdy 1
thick 7

hussy
flirt 3
jade 2
slattern
tart[2] 2

hustle°
drive 8
flurry 1
haste 2
hurry 1
industry 3
initiative 2
pimp 2
press 9
run 1
rush 1, 3
scramble 2
scurry
shoulder 7
solicit 2
speed 3
trot 1
urge 1
whisk 2

hustle away
bundle 3
pack 7

hustler
bitch 2
pimp 1
prostitute 1
slattern

hustling
busy 2
industrious

hut°
cabin 1
cottage
hole 3
hovel

hut (*cont.*)
lodge 1
shack
shed[1]

hutch
cage 1
pen[2] 1
shed[1]

huzzah
cheer 4
whoop 1, 2

hyacinthine
black 1

hyaena
parasite

hybrid°
cross 2
general 3
mixed 1
mongrel

hydrodynamic
streamlined 1

hydrophobic
rabid 2

hyena
parasite

hygienic°
sanitary

hymeneal
nuptial

hymn
chant 1
praise 2

hype
advertisement 2
feature 4
get 34
plug 3
promote 4
promotion 4
propaganda 2
publicize
puff 3
push 6
talk 13

hyperactive
active 3
hectic
restless

hyperbole
exaggeration
raving 3

hyperbolize
exaggerate
make 34a
overstate

hyperborean
cold 1
freezing
frigid 1
icy 1
polar 1
wintry 1

hypercritical
fastidious
fault-finding 2
hair-splitting
overcritical
particular 4
querulous
reproachful

hypercriticism
fault-finding 1

hypermetropic
far-sighted 2

hyperopic
far-sighted 2

hypersensitive
sensitive 2
temperamental 1
ticklish 3
touchy 1

hypersensitivity
sensitivity 1

hypertrophied
swollen

hypnotic
drug 2
enchanting
glassy 2
magic 6
narcotic 1, 2

hypnotic (*cont.*)
restful 1
riveting
sedative 1, 2
tiresome 1
hypnotic effect
spell[2] 3
hypnotic state
trance
hypnotize°
captivate
charm 5, 6
dazzle 1
enchant 1
entrance[2]
fascinate
fix 5
grip 7
transfix 2
transport 3
hypnotized
infatuated
rapt 1
hypnotizing
enthralling
riveting
hypochondria
vapour 2
hypocrisy°
cant 1
deceit 1
deception 1
dissimulation
falsity
perfidy
pretence 1
pretension 2
hypocrite°
impostor
Pharisee
hypocritical°
deceitful
dishonest
dishonourable 2
disingenuous
double 5
empty 4
faithless 2
goody-goody
hollow 4
insincere
lying 2
mannered
mealy-mouthed
oily 2
perfidious
Pharisaic
phoney 1
pious 2
sanctimonious
self-righteous
sleek 3
sophistic
time-serving
two-faced
untrue 1
hypothecate
pawn[1] 1
premise 2
presume 1
secure 6
hypothecator
theorist
hypothesis°
guess 3
idea 5
position 7
premise 1
presumption 3
reasoning 2
speculation 1
supposition
surmise 2
theorem 1
hypothesize
conceive 3
divine 4
guess 1
posit
premise 2
presume 1
speculate 1
suppose 2
surmise 1

hypothesize (*cont.*)
theorize
hypothesized
hypothetical
hypothesizer
theorist
hypothetical°
academic 2
alleged
assumed 3
experimental 1
groundless
pure 4
speculative 1
supposed 1
theoretical 1
unreal 2
hypothetically
supposedly
hysteria
fanaticism 1
mania 2
nerve 4
panic 1
vapour 2
zealotry
hysterical°
delirious 1
distraught
emotional 4
excitable
excited 1
frantic
funny 1
hilarious
humorous
intense 3
maniacal 1, 2
panic-stricken
priceless 2
raving 1
tumultuous
uproarious 2
wild 5
hysterically
mad 5
madly 1
hysterics
rage 2

I

iatric(al)
medicinal
ice
bump 5
chill 7
cool 9
delay 1
dispatch 3
eliminate 4
execute 3
finish 4
freeze 1
kill 1
murder 3
postpone
refrigerate
shelve
table 5
wait 2
waste 4
zap
–**on ice**
abeyance
rock[1] 3a
–**without ice**
straight 16
ice-cold
cold 1
freezing
icy 1, 2
reserved
ice-free
open 9
iceman
killer 1
ice over
freeze 2

ice-storm
storm 1
ice up
freeze 2
ice-up
freeze 5
ichor
fluid 1
sap[1] 1
iciness
chill 3
cold 9
nip[1] 4
icing°
ickiness
sentimentality
icky
revolting
sentimental 2
sweet 7
icon
figure 4
idol 1
image 1
likeness 2
statue
iconoclast
nonconformist 1
iconoclastic
heretical
nonconformist 2
ungodly 1
ictus
seizure 2
stress 1
throe
icy°
chill 4
chilly 1
cold 1, 3
cutting 1
freezing
frigid 1
glassy 1
piercing 3
polar 1
reserved
slippery 1
stony 2
tough 6
wintry 1
ID
card 10
identification 3
label 1
idea°
belief 3
conception 2
discovery 1
doctrine
eye 6
fancy 8
feeling 2
gist
image 3
impression 1
inkling
intent 1
message 3
misconception
motif
note 6
notion 1
object 3
opinion 1
perception 2
philosophy 2
picture 3
point 12
principle 2
resolution 3
significance 1
slant 1
spirit 7
suggestion 1
tenet
theme 1
thesis 1
thinking 2
thought 2
understanding 3
version 1
vision 3
wrinkle[2]

ideal°
cause 4
choice 4
classic 1
complete 4
faultless
favourite 1, 2
gem 2
goal
guide 6
heavenly 2
hero 1
idyllic
impeccable
model 2, 3, 11
nonpareil
optimum 1, 2
paragon
pattern 1
perfect 1, 2
perfection 3
platonic
quintessence
ripe 3a
romantic 1, 2
speculative 1
standard 1
tailor-made 2
theoretical 2
treasure 2
understanding 3
–**ideals°**
at **ideal 3**
moral 4
morality 1
idealist
dreamer
romantic 5
visionary 2
idealistic°
academic 2
fraternal
ideal 5
optimistic
quixotic
speculative 1
visionary 1
idealization
perfection 3
idealize°
glorify 2
idealized
idyllic
romantic 1
speculative 1
idealizer
dreamer
ideally°
principle 4
ideational
abstract 1
speculative 1
idée fixe
fetish 2
fixation
obsession
preconception
thing 4
idée reçu
conception 2
opinion 1
identical°
duplicate 1
equal 1
even 5
exact 1
homogeneous
indistinguish-
able 1
like[1] 1, 4
matching 2
one 2
piece 8
same 1
similar 1
synonymous
twin 2
uniform 1
very 3
identically
alike 2
nearly 2

identifiable
discernible 2
prominent 1
pronounced 1
visible 2
identification°
cachet 1
colour 2b
denomination 3
feeling 3
hallmark 2
label 1
landmark 1
mark 2
paper 2a
recognition 1
seal 1
specification 1
identification card
card 10
identified
determined 2
specific 2
synonymous
identifier
label 1
identify°
brand 2
call 2
characterize
define 1
describe 3
designate 1, 2
detect 2
diagnose
discover 1
distinguish 2, 3, 4
find 2
finger 5c, 12
flag[1] 3
inform 2
know 2, 4
label 4, 5
mark 11, 13
name 5, 6
notice 2
perceive 1
pin 4b
place 17
point 21a
recognize 1
savour 3
sight 8
specify
spot 6
stamp 3
sympathize 2
tag 3
tell[1] 8
identifying
denomination 3
specification 1
identify with°
at **identify 4**
link 4
relate 4
sympathize 2
identity°
colour 2b
disguise 3
equality 1
nature 1
persona
personality 1
unity 2
identity card
card 10
identification 3
identity theory
mechanism 4
ideogram
sign 4
ideology°
philosophy 2
tenet
id est
namely
idiocy
folly 1
insanity 2
stupidity 2

idiolect
idiom 1
language 1
speech 3
idiom°
dialect
expression 5
jargon 1
language 1
lingo
parlance
phrase 2
provincialism 1
speech 3
tongue 1
vernacular 3
idiomatic expression
phrase 2
idiosyncrasy
abnormality 1
character 2
characteristic 2
difference 4
eccentricity 2
feature 1
foible
freak 3
kink 4
mannerism
oddity 3
peculiarity 1
property 4
quirk
singularity 1
trait
trick 6
twist 10
warp 2
idiosyncratic
characteristic 1
deviant 1
distinctive
eccentric 1
individual 2
kinky 1
lyric 2
odd 1
offbeat
peculiar 1
special 1
subjective 1
symptomatic
idiot
bugger 2
clod 2
dolt
dummy 3
fool 1
halfwit
jerk 5
natural 12
retard 2
sap[1] 2
silly 3
twit[2]
idiot box
television
idiotic
absurd 1
crazy 2
daft 1
feeble-minded
foolish 2
inane
insane 2
mindless 1
nonsensical
preposterous
senseless 3
silly 1
stupid 2
unreasonable 1
unthinking 1
idiotically
madly 2
idle°
dawdle
empty 4
fool 7b
fruitless
hang 4a
inactive 1, 2
indolent

idle (*cont.*)
ineffective 1
inert 3
kill 7
lackadaisical 1
lazy 1
leisure 5
lethargic 1
linger 2
loaf[2] 1
lounge 1
misspent
muck 3
off 6
passive 1
rest[1] 6
shallow 1
shiftless
slack 1
slothful
stagnate
supine 2
twiddle 2
unemployed
useless 1
vacant 3
void 1
work 6
idle away°
at **idle 5**
fritter
loaf[2] 2
twiddle 2
idleness°
inactivity 1
indolence
inertia
lethargy 1
rest[1] 3
sloth
torpor
idler°
good-for-nothing 2
laggard
loafer
slacker
slouch 3
truant 1
wastrel 2
idle talk
mouth 3
idly°
vaguely 3
idol°
figure 4
hero 1
image 1
passion 4
pet[1] 1
queen 2
star 2
toast 2
idolater
heathen 1
pagan 1
idolatrous
heretical
pagan 2
profane 1
idolatry
worship 2
idolization
reverence 1
veneration
idolize°
admire 2
adore 1
dote
exalt 2
glorify 2
look 12
love 7
pedestal 2
revere
worship 1
idolized
beloved 1
precious 2
idyll
pastoral 4
romance 3
idyllic°
ideal 4
pastoral 1
idyllic (*cont.*)
picturesque 1
poetic 1
romantic 1
serene 1
i.e.
like[1] 6
namely
if
case[1] 6b
providing
supposing
-as if
like[1] 3
quasi- 1
iffy
arbitrary 1
dangerous 1
dicey
explosive 1
parlous
precarious
problematic
risky
rocky[2]
shaky 1
speculative 2
tricky 2
if not
otherwise 1
if only
providing
if possible
possibly 1
if the truth be known
indeed 2
ignis fatuus
illusion 2
ignite
awake 2
burn 2
excite 1
fire 8, 10
heat 4
inflame 1
kindle
light[1] 15
set 20a
spark 2
strike 6
touch 11a, 11b
ignition
light[1] 7
ignobility
vulgarity 1
ignoble
base[2] 2
degenerate 1
despicable
dirty 6
humble 3
low[1] 7, 12
mean[2] 2
menial 1
plebeian 2
scurvy
shabby 4
sordid 1
unrefined 1
unworthy 1
vile 1
vulgar 1
ignominious
contemptible
despicable
dirty 6
disgraceful 1
dishonourable 1
disreputable 1
foul 4
infamous 1
mangy
notorious 1
scandalous 1
shabby 4
shameful
sordid 1
vile 1
ignominy
degradation 2
discredit 4
disgrace 1
ignominy (*cont.*)
dishonour 4
humiliation
infamy 1
notoriety
scandal 2
shame 1, 2
ignoramus
barbarian 2
dolt
fool 1
gawk 1
philistine 1
sap[1] 2
silly 3
ignorance°
dark 12
ignorant°
benighted
dark 9
illiterate
unaware
uneducated
unfamiliar 2
uninformed
unsuspecting
ignore°
back 9
blink 4
break 9
brush[2] 7
bypass 1
close 7
cut 12
discount 3
dismiss 2
disobey
dispense 3b
disregard 1
excuse 1
fail 2
forget 3
forgive 1
isolate
jump 3
kiss 3
laugh 2b
leave[1] 10
mind 19
miss[1] 4
neglect 1
omit 2
overlook 1, 2
pass 3, 22
put 11
rebuff 2
rule 8
scorn 3
skip 2
slide 4
slight 5
slur 3
snap 6
trample 2
tune 5
violate 1
waive 2
write 5
ignored
broken 5
unpopular
ignoring
despite
exclusive 4
independent 8
irrespective of
spite 2
violation 1
ikon
idol 1
image 1
likeness 2
statue
ilk
description 3
mould[1] 3
sort 1
type 1
ill°
ail 2
bad 3
detriment
diseased
evil 7
ill (*cont.*)
frail 2
get 5
ghastly 3
grievance 1
hard 16
indisposed 1
infirm 1
invalid[1] 1
low[1] 4
off colour 1
par 5b
peaky
poor 7
psychotic 1
queasy 2
queer 3
ropy 3
rotten 5
run-down 1
seedy 2
sick 2
sicken
sort 6
unhealthy 1
unsound 2
unwholesome 3
weather 2
ill-advised°
foolish 1
imprudent
indiscreet
inept 2
mad 2
misguided
rash[1]
stupid 2
unhappy 3
unseemly 2
ill at ease°
at **ill 6**
agitated
awkward 3
bashful 1
confused 2
edge 5
queasy 1
worried
ill-behaved
bad 10
difficult 3
disobedient 1
ill-bred
boorish
brutal 2
ill-mannered
impolite
low[1] 3
rough 3
rude 1
ungracious
unrefined 1
ill breeding
incivility
ill-chosen
inopportune
ill-conceived
untoward 2
ill-considered
crazy 3
foolish 1
hasty 2
ill-advised 1
imprudent
indiscreet
inept 2
mad 2
rash[1]
thoughtless 2
wrong 4
ill-defined
dim 1
faint 1
fuzzy 2
general 4
imperceptible 1
imprecise
indefinite 3
indistinct 2
nebulous
shadowy 2
sketchy
vague 1, 3
weak 6
ill-defined (*cont.*)
woolly 2
ill-disposed
averse
incapable 2
illegal°
bent 3
criminal 1
crooked 1
foul 11
lawless 2
taboo 1
unauthorized
unlawful
wrong 1
illegal activity
racket 2
illegality
foul 17
illegible°
indistinct 1
illegitimate°
illegal
natural 8
unauthorized
unlawful
wrong 1
ill-equipped
unqualified 1
ill fame
infamy 1
ill-famed
infamous 1
ill-fated
doomed 2
inauspicious
poor 6
portentous 1
tragic
unfortunate 2
unhappy 2
ill-favoured
homely 3
ugly 1
ill feeling
friction 2
ill-fitting
tight 2
ill-formed
rude 4
ill fortune
grief 2
hardship
misfortune 1
ill-founded°
ill humour
temper 3
ill-humoured
disagreeable 3
disgruntled
gruff 1
irritable
moody 2
peevish
petulant
querulous
snappish 2
sulk
sullen
surly
testy
illiberal
intolerant 2
little 6
merciless
narrow-minded
near-sighted 2
parochial
selfish 2
totalitarian
illiberality
intolerance
illicit°
criminal 1
crooked 1
illegal
lawless 2
taboo 1
unauthorized
unlawful
wrong 1
illimitable
boundless
infinite 1
limitless
illiterate°
ignorant 1
uneducated
ill-judged
ill-advised 1
imprudent
indiscreet
inept 2
ill-lit
dark 1
ill luck
grief 2
misfortune 1
ill-made
misshapen
ill-making
sentimental 2
yucky
ill-mannered°
boorish
brusque
brutal 2
coarse 2
disagreeable 3
discourteous
disrespectful
ignorant 4
impolite
impudent
indecent 2
pert 1
rough 3
rude 1
uncivilized 2
unrefined 1
ill-matched
mismatched
unlike 1, 3
ill-mated
mismatched
ill-natured
bilious
cantankerous
fretful
gruff 1
nasty 4
peevish
querulous
sour 4
sullen
surly
illness°
ailment
bug 2
disease 1
disorder 3
trouble 8
illogic
lunacy 2
madness 2
illogical
absurd 2
circular 3
disconnected 2
false 5
foolish 3
impossible 2
inaccurate
inarticulate 1
incoherent
paradoxical
rambling 1
senseless 3
silly 1
unrealistic 1
unreasonable 1
unsound 4
untenable
unthinkable 2
unthinking 1
water 2
illogicality
absurdity 1
lunacy 2
madness 2
ill-omened
inauspicious
ominous 1
portentous 1

immeasurably
exceedingly
well[1] 7
immediacy
gravity 2
priority
immediate°
express 7
hasty 1
imminent
impulsive
instant 3
instinctive 2
near 4
present[1] 2
primary 3
prompt 1
quick 2
rapid
ready 5
speedy 1
spontaneous 2
sudden
unhesitating 1
urgent 1
immediately°
cold 11
demand 8
directly 2
double 8
fast[1] 8
flat 17b
hastily 1
instantaneously
nail 6
now 3
once 6a
outright 3
post-haste
promptly
quickly 3
readily 3
right 13
shortly 2
shot 10
soon 2
straight 15
summarily 1
time 17
immediateness
rapidity
immense°
big 1, 2
boundless
colossal 1
enormous
extensive 2
gigantic
grand 1
great 1, 2
huge
immeasurable
inestimable 2
infinite 1
jumbo
large 3
limitless
massive
monstrous 3
monumental 2
mountainous 2
prodigious 1
spacious
swingeing
thumping 1
unlimited 2
vast
weighty 1
whopping 1
immensely
highly 1
vastly
immensity
enormousness
extent 1
magnitude 1
mass 5
size 1
immerse°
catch 14a
dip 1
drench
drown 1
duck 2
immerse (*cont.*)
flood 4
overwhelm 2
plunge 2
sink 8
soak 1
steep[2] 1, 2
submerge 1, 3
swamp 2
immersed
absorbed
deep 4
full 6
preoccupied 2
wrap 2
immersing
soaking 1
immersion
dip 4
plunge 3
immigrant°
alien 2
arrival 2
foreigner
newcomer 1
settler
immigrate
migrate 1
imminent°
forthcoming 1
hand 9
impending
near 4
oncoming 1
pending 2
pipeline 2
potential 1
prospective
threatening
wind[1] 8
immobile
dormant 1
fixed 1
immovable 1
inactive 1
inanimate
inert 2
sedentary
stagnant
static 1
immobility
inactivity 1
inertia
immobilization
freeze 6
immobilize
fix 5
freeze 3
incapacitate
numb 2
paralyse 1
pin 4c
immobilized
crippled 2
fixed 1
inactive 1
immoderate°
epicurean 1
excessive 1
exorbitant
extravagant 1, 2
extreme 2
fanatical
inordinate 1
lavish 3
outrageous 1
prodigal 1
profligate 2
promiscuous 2
radical 3, 4
self-indulgent
towering 2
ultra-
unconscionable 2
unmitigated
unreasonable 2
unwarranted
wanton 2
immoderately
fault 7
overly
unduly 2
immoderation
excess 2
extravagance 2
gluttony
prodigality 1
immodest°
barefaced 2
bold 2
brazen
foul 5
immoral 2
improper 3
indecent 1
inflated 1
obscene 1
presumptuous
profane 3
racy 2
rank[2] 3
scandalous 1
sexy 2
shameless
suggestive 2
unchaste
unmentionable 2
immodesty
impropriety 3
indelicacy
presumption 1
ribaldry
immolate
sacrifice 3
immolated
sacrificial 1
immolation
sacrifice 1
immoral°
abandoned 2
bad 3
criminal 2
decadent 2
dissolute
evil 1
fast[1] 2
filthy 3
foul 4
ill 2
improper 3
impure 4
libertine 2
loose 7
naughty 3
obscene 1
outrageous 3
perverted
profligate 1
promiscuous 2
reprobate 1
rotten 3
satanic 1
scandalous 1
sinful
ugly 2
unchaste
unconscionable 1
ungodly 1
unscrupulous
unwholesome 2
vicious 1
vile 1
wanton 1
wicked 1
wrong 1
immorality
evil 6
impropriety 3
impurity 3
profligacy 1
sin 2
vice 1
immorally
badly 4
fast[1] 9
immortal°
celestial 1
classic 2
deathless
enduring
eternal 1
everlasting
god
grand 2
heavenly 1
legendary 3
immortal (*cont.*)
lofty 2
perennial 2
timeless
immortality
glory 1
immortalize°
commemorate
glorify 1
lift 2
perpetuate
immovable°
constant 1
fast[1] 4
firm 2, 4
fixed 1
inflexible
monolithic
obstinate
parochial
recalcitrant
resistant 2
rigid 4
secure 2
static 1
steadfast
stern 1
stick[1] 7
tenacious 1
wilful 2
immovably
fast[1] 7
firmly 1
immune°
exempt 2
free 11
privileged 2
secure 1
unaffected[2]
immunity°
exemption
freedom 3
privilege
protection 1
tolerance 3
immure
enclose 1
shut 6a
wall 5
immutability
finality
resolution 1
immutable
abiding
changeless 1
constant 3
eternal 3
final 2
fixed 2
hard 8
immovable 2
indestructible
inflexible
invariable 2
irrevocable
permanent 2
perpetual 1
resolute
stable 2
timeless
imp°
devil 4
goblin
monkey 3
rascal
impact°
brunt
effect 1, 2, 4
force 1
hit 3, 4, 10
impression 2
influence 1
punch[1] 3
shock 4
strike 3
weight 3
impair°
alloy 2
blemish 1
cripple 2
damage 4
debase 2
deface
drain 5
impair (*cont.*)
hurt 1
incapacitate
injure 1
maim
mar 2
overshadow 2
ruin 9
shake 3
strain[1] 3
undermine 1
vitiate 1
wear 3
impaired
defective 1
deficient 2
disabled
disfigured
faulty
hurt 8
invalid[2]
lame 1
under 6
wanting 1
impairment°
blemish 3
damage 1
detriment
disability 1
expense 2
injury
loss 3
sabotage 1
impale°
gore[2]
pierce 1
spike 2
stab 1
stick[1] 1
transfix 1
impalpable
disembodied
elusive 2
insubstantial 2
intangible
shadowy 3
imparity
disparity
impart°
betray 2
communicate 1
deliver 5
disclose 1
extend 4
get 26
give 3, 15c
inform 1
instil
lend 2
make 33
mention 2
recount 1
relate 2
say 4
shed[2] 2
signify 1
tell[1] 2
vouchsafe 1
-be imparted to
rub 5
impartial°
candid 2
detached 2
disinterested
dispassionate 2
equitable
even 7
fair[1] 1
fence 2
honourable 3
indifferent 2
judicial 3
just 1
liberal 3
neutral 1
non-aligned
non-partisan 2
objective 1
unprejudiced
impartiality
candour 2
chivalry
equality 3
equity
impartiality (*cont.*)
honesty 3
indifference 3
justice 1
objectivity
impartially
fairly 2
honestly 1
impassable
dense 2
impermeable
inaccessible 2
thick 3
impasse°
deadlock 1
dilemma
predicament
stalemate
impassion
fire 8b
flush[1] 3
heat 4
inflame 1
rise 16
thrill 3
touch 6
turn 18c
impassionate
tender[1] 7
impassioned°
animated 1
ardent
emotional 1
excited 2
fervent 1
heated
intense 2
keen[1] 1
lyrical 2
passionate 1
romantic 4
tempestuous
tender[1] 7
torrid 2
warm 2
impassive°
blank 4
calm 4
even 4
frigid 3
immovable 2
indifferent 1
insensible 2
listless
passive 1
rocky[1] 3
stoical
stolid
straight 8
unmoved
unsympathetic
wooden 2
impassiveness
indifference 1
impatient°
agog
anxious 2
eager
fretful
hasty 4
intolerant 1
irritable
moody 2
petulant
quick 5
quick-tempered
ratty 1
sour 4
temperamental 1
weary 3, 4
impeach°
accuse 2
incriminate
impeachment
accusation
impeccable°
flawless 1
immaculate 3
incorrupt 1
irreproachable
polished 1
pure 3

impeccably
perfectly 2
impecunious
destitute 1
hard 17
impoverished 1
indigent
needy
penurious 2
poor 1
short 8
impecuniousness
need 4
poverty 1
want 5
impedance
interference 2
prevention
impede°
bar 9
block 3
bog 2
check 1
clog
delay 2
deter
embargo 2
encumber 2
entangle 1
foil[1]
frustrate 1
hamper[1]
handicap 2
hinder 1
hobble 2
hold 22b
inhibit
intercept
interfere 2
obstruct 2
oppose 2
overload 1
preclude
prevent
prohibit 2
resist 1
restrict
retard 1
set 16
stay[1] 4
stop 2
stunt[2]
stymie
thwart 1
trammel 2
impediment°
bar 3
barrier 2
block 2
charge 1
check 14
deterrent
drawback
embargo 1
encumbrance
fly 10
handicap 1
hindrance 1
hitch 4
hurdle 1
inconvenience 1
inhibition
interference 2
let[2]
liability 3
obstacle
obstruction 1
overload 2
preventive 3
rub 11
set-back
shackle 2
snag 1
stricture 1
stumbling-block
trammel 1
wall 1
impedimenta
gear 4
luggage
paraphernalia
stuff 2
thing 8c
impeding
obstruction 2
prevention
preventive 1
impel
activate
carry 3
drive 1
force 7
hasten 2
induce 1
make 2
motivate
move 6
occasion 5
press 1
prod 2
prompt 3
propel
provoke 1
push 4
spur 4
thrust 1
urge 1
impelling
motive 3
moving 1
impend
loom 2
overhang 2
threaten 3
impending°
forthcoming 1
imminent
menacing
near 4
pending 2
prospective
threatening
wind[1] 8
impenetrability
opacity 1, 2
perplexity 2
impenetrable
dark 6
deep 2
dense 1, 2
hard 1
heavy 12
impermeable
impregnable
inaccessible 2
incomprehensible
invincible 2
monolithic
occult 2
opaque 1, 2
perplexing
proof 3
recondite
resistant 3
thick 3
tight 1
impenetrableness
perplexity 2
impenitent
unrepentant
imperative°
essential 1
exacting
indispensable 1
instant 4
necessary 1
peremptory 1
precondition
prerequisite 1
pronouncement 2
urgent 1
vital 1
imperativeness
urgency
imperceptible°
dim 1
faint 1
feeble 3
inaudible
indistinguishable 2
intangible
invisible 1
light[2] 3
sight 6a
slow 2
imperceptible (*cont.*)
weak 6
imperceptibly
degree 3
imperceptive
blind 2
dull 2
obtuse 2
imperfect°
defective 1
deficient 2
faulty
flawed
inaccurate
inadequate 1
incomplete
inferior 3
invalid[2]
partial 1
ragged 4
rough 9
rude 4
rudimentary 2
second[1] 7
sketchy
unsatisfactory
unsound 1
untrue 3
vestigial
wanting 1
wrong 5
imperfection°
blemish 3
defect 1, 2
failing 1
fault 1
flaw 1
foible
frailty 2
impairment
inferiority 3
kink 3
shortcoming
taint 1
vice 2
weakness 3
imperfectly
amiss 2
sketchily
wrong 7
imperial°
lofty 2
majestic 1
regal 1
royal 1
state 6
stately
imperil
adventure 3
chance 8
endanger
expose 2
fire 6
hazard 3
jeopardize
lean[2] 4b
overhang 2
risk 2
threaten 2
venture 3
imperilled
endangered
jealous 2
imperilment
exposure 2
imperious
arbitrary 2
arrogant 2
authoritarian
bossy
condescending
despotic
dictatorial 2
dogmatic
domineering
heavy-handed 2
imperative 2
majestic 2
masterful 2
overbearing
peremptory 3
pompous 1
positive 5
imperious (*cont.*)
prescriptive
tyrannical
imperishable
deathless
immortal 1
indestructible
inextinguishable
perennial 2
permanent 1
impermanent
fly-by-night 1
meteoric 1
momentary
passing 1
temporary
transient
impermeability
opacity 1
impermeable°
opaque 1
tight 1
impersonal°
detached 2
disinterested
mechanical 3
impersonate
act 7
copy 5
imitate 1
masquerade 3
mimic 3
monkey 4
pass 16b
personify 1
portray 2
pose 2
represent 2
impersonation
imitation 1, 2
impression 5
mockery 2
role 1
impersonator
impostor
mimic 4
impertinence°
arrogance
disrespect
effrontery
face 5
familiarity 3
flippancy 2
freedom 7
gall[1] 2
impudence
mouth 4
nerve 2
presumption 1
sauce 2
impertinent°
audacious 2
barefaced 2
bold 2
brash 2
brazen
cheeky
cool 6
discourteous
extraneous 2
flippant 2
forward 2
fresh 8
ill-mannered
immodest 2
impudent
insolent
irrelevant
irreverent 2
liberty 5
offensive 2
pert 1
presumptuous
pushy
rude 2
tactless
imperturbability
patience 1
philosophy 3
poise 2
presence 5
sang-froid
self-control 2
imperturbability (*cont.*)
stoicism
imperturbable
cold-blooded 2
collected
cool 2
equable 1
even 4
impassive
level-headed
nonchalant
passive 1
philosophical 2
phlegmatic 2
poised 1
sedate 1
self-contained 1
self-possessed
serene 1
stoical
temperate 1
impervious
blind 4
dead 4
deaf 2
frigid 2
hard 1
hermetic
impermeable
incapable 2
insensible 2
proof 3
resistant 1, 3
thick-skinned
tight 1
unaffected[2]
imperviousness
tolerance 3
impetration
supplication 1
impetuosity
desperation 1
fury 2
haste 2
heat 2
indiscretion 1
impetuous°
blind 3
brash 1
daredevil 2
dashing 1
desperate 1
foolhardy
foolish 1
hasty 2
hot 3
hotheaded
hurried 1
ill-advised 2
impatient 1
improvident 2
imprudent
impulsive
indiscreet
intense 3
pell-mell 2
precipitate 5
rapid
rash[1]
spontaneous 2
sudden
violent 3
warm-blooded 2
whirlwind 2
wild 4
impetuously
blindly
fiercely
hastily 2
madly 3
pell-mell 1
spur 3
impetus°
drive 8
incentive
momentum
power 8
propulsion
signal 2
spirit 2
stimulant 1
urge 5
impiety
sacrilege 2
sin 1, 2
impinge
infringe 2
impious°
blasphemous
diabolic 2
godless 1
heretical
irreverent 1
profane 1
sacrilegious
satanic 1
sinful
ungodly 1
wicked 1
impiousness
sacrilege 2
sin 2
impish
devilish
elfin 1
mischievous 1
naughty 1
playful 1
sly 2
wicked 5
impishness
mischief 1
implacable°
deadly 2
grim 1
hard 4
mortal 4
relentless 1
remorseless 2
stony 2
vindictive
implant°
graft[1] 1, 2
indoctrinate
instil
lock[1] 6a
plant 6
strike 11
implantation
graft[1] 1
implanted
rooted
implausible°
fantastic 3
far-fetched
fishy 2
flimsy 2
improbable
incredible 1
remote 6
unbelievable
unlikely 1
untenable
implement°
administer 2
apparatus
carry 12
device 1
dispense 2
effectuate
enforce 1
execute 1
fulfil 2
gadget
instrument 1
machine 1
organ 1
tool 1
work 16
-implements
gear 2
kit
thing 8c
implementation
employment 3
execution 1, 2
fulfilment
implicate°
denounce 1
entangle 1
impeach 1
incriminate
inform 2
involve 3
mix 5

implicated
involved 1
implication°
effect 3
hint 1
import 3
imputation
indication 1
innuendo
matter 4
meaning 2
message 3
overtone
point 7
ramification 1
significance 1
spirit 6
suggestion 2
tenor
undercurrent 2
implicative
circumstantial 1
implicit°
constructive 2
passive 3
potential 1
silent 3
tacit
unhesitating 2
implied
circumstantial 1
implicit 1
oblique 2
potential 1
silent 3
tacit
implode
shiver[2]
implore
appeal 1
ask 3
beg 1
beseech
hit 8
petition 2
plead 2
pray 1
solicit 1
sue 2
imploring
supplicant 1
imply°
clue 2
drive 6
get 30b
hint 3
import 2
impute
indicate 2,3
insinuate 1
intimate[2]
involve 2
make 37e
mean[1] 2
mention 2
partake 2b
say 7,9
suggest 2
symbolize
impolite°
abrupt 3
blunt 2
brusque
coarse 2
disagreeable 3
discourteous
disrespectful
harsh 3
ignorant 4
ill-mannered
impertinent
improper 3
impudent
offensive 2
pert 1
rough 3
rude 1
shabby 2
short 4
taboo 1
tactless
thoughtless 1
ungracious
unrefined 1
impolite *(cont.)*
unthinking 2
untoward 2
impoliteness
disrespect
impertinence
impudence
incivility
indelicacy
impolitic
foolish 1
ill-advised 1
indiscreet
inept 2
misguided
short-sighted 2
tactless
unseemly 2
wrong 4
imponderable°
intangible
import°
content[1] 3
drift 4
effect 3
force 5
impact 2
implication 3
importance 1
matter 4
meaning 1
message 3
moment 3
pith 2
point 7
sense 4
significance 1
substance 3
tenor
importance°
account 5
cachet 2
class 3
dignity 2
distinction 2
emphasis
gravity 2
import 4
interest 2
magnitude 2
mark 8
matter 4
moment 3
note 8
order 3
overrate
pith 2
position 5
precedence
premium 3
prestige
priority
prominence 1
quality 2,3
significance 2
solemnity
status 1
stress 2
superiority 2
urgency
weight 3
worth
–of importance
concern 2
matter 6
serious 2
signify 2
important°
banner 2
big 4,5
capital 5
cardinal
central 2
considerable 2
critical 2
crucial
eminent 1
essence 4
essential 1
eventful
fateful 1
functional 1
fundamental 1
grave[2] 2
great 4,5
important *(cont.)*
heavy 3
high 6,11
historic
illustrious
indispensable 1
influential
instrumental
key 6
landmark 3
leading 1
main 1
major 1,2
material 6
matter 6
meaningful 1
memorable
momentous
necessary 1
notable 1
noticeable 2
outstanding 1
pivotal
powerful 2
predominant
pressing
prestigious
principal 2
prominent 1
proud 3
rank[1] 7
responsible 3
salient
seminal 1
serious 2
signal 3
significant 1
signify 2
singular 2
solemn 3
special 2
star 3
telling 1
urgent 1
vital 2
weighty 2
importantly
highly 4
notably 2
imported
exotic 1
foreign 1
importunate
insistent
intrusive
obtrusive
officious
supplicant 1
urgent 2
importune
beg 1
beseech
besiege 3
buttonhole 1
desire 2
dun
hit 8
insist 1
instruct 2
persecute 2
persuade 1
petition 2
plead 2
pray 1
press 6
push 4
request 1
scrounge 1
solicit 1
urge 2
work 18
importunity
urgency
impose°
clap 4
dictate 1
enforce 1
entail
exact 3
fix 9
foist
inflict
lay[1] 17b
obtrude
penalize
impose *(cont.)*
prescribe
presume 3
tax 3
thrust 3
wreak
imposed upon
put-upon
impose on°
at **impose 4**
deceive
enforce 2
play 15
presume 3
put 23a
stick[1] 8
subject 9
thrust 3
tie 7b
trouble 3
impose upon°
at **impose 4**
deceive
enforce 2
lumber 3
presume 3
put 23a
take 32b
thrust 3
wish 3
wrong 9
imposing°
awesome
elevated 2
gallant 3
grand 1
grandiose 2
imperial 2
impressive
lofty 2
magnificent
majestic 1
monolithic
noble 5
prestigious
royal 2
solemn 3
splendid 1
stately
statuesque
striking
towering 1
imposingly
large 4
imposition°
impossible°
hopeless 4
impracticable 1
improbable
inconceivable
incredible 1
insufferable
paradoxical
question 7
unthinkable 2
impost
custom 2
duty 3
tariff 1
tax 1
toll[2] 1
tribute 2
impostor°
cheat 1
fake 4
fraud 3
hypocrite
phoney 3
poseur
quack 1
twister 1
imposture
deception 2
hoax 1
masquerade 2
ruse
sham 1
trick 1
trickery
impotence°
disability 2
inability
weakness 2
impotent°
defenceless
feeble 1
flabby 2
frigid 3
futile
incapable 1
ineffectual 2
prostrate 4
spineless 2
unable
useless 1
weak 3
impound
appropriate 2
cage 2
confiscate
lock[1] 9
pen[2] 2
seize 5
stake[1] 4
impounding
seizure 1
impoverish
beggar 3
ruin 10
weaken 1
impoverished°
broke
deprived
destitute 1
down and out 1
exhausted 3
hard 17
heel[1] 3
indigent
insolvent
lean[1] 2,3
needy
penurious 2
poor 1,3
sordid 4
straitened
impoverishment
loss 2
impracticable°
crazy 3
hopeless 4
impossible 1
impractical 2
quixotic
useless 1
wild 7
impractical°
academic 2
crazy 3
extravagant 2
idealistic
non-productive 2
philosophical 1
quixotic
romantic 2
speculative 1
theoretical 2
unrealistic 1
unreasonable 3
useless 1
visionary 1
wild 7
impracticality
madness 2
imprecate
blaspheme 1
swear 2
imprecation
abuse 8
curse 1
oath 2
imprecise°
approximate 1
broad 6
careless 3
erroneous
false 1
general 4
generality 1
improper 1
inaccurate
incorrect
indefinite 1,2
inexact
intangible
lax 2
loose 5
imprecise *(cont.)*
sketchy
untrue 3
vague 1
wrong 2
imprecisely
vaguely 2
imprecision
ambiguity 1
impropriety 1
impregnable°
hard 1
invincible 2
proof 3
watertight 2
impregnate°
fertilize 1
saturate
impresario
director 2
producer 2
showman
imprescriptible
inalienable
impress°
affect[1] 2
dazzle 1
engrave 2
enlist 1
etch 2
get 16
implant 1
impression 3
influence 3
plant 6
print 1
reach 6
recruit 1
register 7
signify 2
stamp 2
strike 7,10
sway 2
touch 6
impressed
affected 5
like[2] 1
strong 15
impressible
impressionable
suggestible
impression°
depression 1
effect 2,4
engraving 2
face 3
fancy 6
feeling 2
hole 1
hollow 7
hunch 1
idea 2
image 3
imitate 1
imitation 1
impact 2
indentation
mark 1,5
note 10
notion 1
observation 2
opinion 1,2
perception 2
picture 3
pretence 2
recollection
semblance 2
sensation 1
sense 5
significance 1
sound[1] 2
splash 4
step 3
strain[1] 9
view 2
–under the impression
sense 6
impressionability
frailty 2
impressionable°
plastic 2
pliable 2

impressionable (*cont.*)
sensitive 2
suggestible
susceptible 2
tender[1] 3

impressionist
mimic 4

impressive°
arresting
conspicuous 2, 3
dramatic 2
effective 2
elevated 2
extraordinary 2
forceful 2
formidable 2
grand 1
grandiose 2
hefty 3
important 2, 3
imposing
magnificent
majestic 1
monumental 1
moving 1
noble 5
persuasive
potent 2
powerful 2
prestigious
remarkable 1
royal 2
salient
scenic
significant 1
solemn 3
splendid 1, 2
stately
statuesque
striking
substantial 2
towering 1
venerable
weighty 3

impressiveness
solemnity

impress on the memory
retain 4

impress upon°
at **impress 3**
enforce 2
home 11
influence 3

imprimatur
approval
approve
consent 3
endorsement 1
sanction 1

imprint
engrave 2
etch 2
implant 1
impress 2
label 1, 4
plant 6
print 1
run 19
seal 1
stamp 2, 7
step 3

imprinted
strong 15

imprison°
cage 2
commit 2
hold 6
jail 2
keep 9
lock[1] 9
punish 2
put 13b
restrain 3
send 5, 9b
shut 6a
trap 5

imprisoned
arrest 6
captive 2
inside 7

imprisonment°
captivity
custody 2
detention
duress 2
justice 2
penalty
punishment 2

improbable°
far-fetched
fishy 2
implausible
incredible 1
off 5
paradoxical
remote 6
tall 3
unlikely 1
unthinkable 2

impromptu
candid 3
extemporaneous
offhand 3, 4
scratch 6
spontaneous 1
spur 3
stopgap 2
unpremeditated

improper°
abusive 2
amiss 1
blue 2
broad 8
bum 3
coarse 3
crude 4
disgraceful 2
dishonourable 3
foul 5
gross 3
illegitimate 3
illicit 2
immodest 1
inadmissible
inappropriate
incongruous
incorrect
indecent 1
ineligible
inept 2
liberty 5
low[1] 3
naughty 3
obscene 1
off colour 2
order 13b
outrageous 3
pale[2] 3
perverse 1
place 12
profane 3
risqué
scandalous 1
sexy 2
shameless
spicy 2
suggestive 2
tasteless 1
unacceptable
unbecoming 2
unnatural 1
unprofessional 1
unreasonable 2
unseemly 1, 2
untoward 2
unwarranted
vulgar 2
wrong 1, 3, 4, 6

improperly
amiss 3
badly 3, 4, 6
ill 12
poorly 1
turn 42b
unduly 1
vain 3b
wrong 7

impropriety°
familiarity 3
liberty 5
slip[1] 8
solecism
vulgarity 2

improve°
advance 2
amend 1
benefit 3
better[1] 10, 11
boost 5
break 3
convalesce
develop 1
dignify
elaborate 4
embellish 1
enhance
enrich 1
gain 3, 7
heal 1
help 2
increase 2
lift 2
look 11c
maximize 1
mellow 5
mend 2, 3
perfect 9
pick 8f
polish 2
profit 3
progress 6
pull 17
rally 4
recover 2
rectify
recuperate
refine 2
reform 1
remedy 4
retouch
revise 1
shape 10b
step 18a

improved
better[1] 4, 6a

improvement°
advance 7
advantage 2
amendment 1
correction 1
development 2
edification
elaboration 1
gain 9
growth 3
headway 1
progress 2
promotion 1
rally 2
recovery 1
refinement 4
reform 3
repair 2
revision
revival 3
spurt 2

improvidence
extravagance 1
indiscretion 1
prodigality 1
profligacy 2
waste 6

improvident°
extravagant 1
hare-brained 1
ill-advised 2
imprudent
indiscreet
lavish 3
prodigal 1
profligate 2
short-sighted 2
spendthrift 2
wasteful

improving
mend 5
promotion 1

improvisation
makeshift 2
stopgap 1

improvise°
formulate 2
invent 1
knock 7a
patch 6
play 12
strike 16
think 6

improvise (*cont.*)
whip 7b

improvised
extemporaneous
fictitious 2
makeshift 1
stopgap 2

imprudence
desperation 1
indiscretion 1

imprudent°
careless 2
crazy 3
daredevil 2
foolhardy
foolish 1
ill-advised 1
improvident 1
indiscreet
inept 2
mad 2
misguided
rash[1]
reckless
short-sighted 2
tactless
thoughtless 2
unguarded 3
unseemly 2
unthinking 2
untoward 2
unwary
wild 7
wrong 4

imprudently
turn 42b

impudence°
assurance 4
brass
disrespect
effrontery
face 5
familiarity 3
flippancy 2
freedom 7
gall[1] 2
impertinence
mouth 4
nerve 2
presumption 1
sauce 2

impudent°
audacious 2
barefaced 2
bold 2
brash 2
brassy 1
brazen
cheeky
cool 6
disrespectful
familiar 3
flippant 2
forward 2
fresh 8
ill-mannered
immodest 2
impertinent
insolent
irreverent 2
liberty 5
offensive 2
pert 1
presumptuous
rude 2
shameless

impugn
challenge 1
criticize 2
denounce 3
dispute 1
fault 8
impeach 2

impuissant
feeble 1

impulse
bias 3
fancy 8
impetus
incentive
incitement 2
inspiration 1
momentum
notion 2

impulse (*cont.*)
occasion 2
propulsion
spirit 7
spur 1
stimulant 1
urge 5

impulsive°
automatic 2
brash 1
capricious
daredevil 2
fanciful 1
giddy 2
hasty 2
impetuous
improvident 2
imprudent
indiscreet
intense 3
involuntary
natural 4
pell-mell 2
precipitate 5
premature 2
quick-tempered
rash[1]
reckless
short-sighted 2
spontaneous 2
sudden
unpremeditated

impulsively
hastily 2
pell-mell 1
spur 3

impulsiveness
indiscretion 1

impunity
exemption
indemnity 2

impure°
filthy 3
foul 2
immoral 1
mixed 1
obscene 1
profane 2
unchaste
unrefined 2

impurity°
-impurities°
at **impurity 2**

imputation°
accusation
aspersion
charge 6
innuendo
reflection 3
slur 1

impute°
accuse 2
attribute 2
credit 6
insinuate 1
lay[1] 7
make 37e
read 4
set 17b

in
contact 2
contemporary 2
elegant 2
fashionable
home 4b
latest 2
minute[1] 3
modern
now 5
popular 1
stylish
trendy 1

-be in
wear 1

-be in with
relate 4

inability°
disability 2
incompetence

inaccessible°
distant 3
frigid 2
out-of-the-way 1
private 2

inaccessible (*cont.*)
remote 1
standoffish
unapproachable 2

inaccuracy
error 1
impropriety 1

inaccurate°
careless 3
err 1
erroneous
false 1
imprecise
improper 1
incorrect
inexact
loose 5
mistaken 1, 2
off 3
out 12
rude 4
unrealistic 2
untrue 2
wrong 2

inaccurately
badly 3

inaction
default 1
idleness 1
inactivity 2
indolence
neglect 4

inactivate
incapacitate
paralyse 1

inactive°
dead 11
dormant 1
dull 3
extinct 3
flat 11
idle 1
inanimate
indolent
inert 1, 3
lackadaisical 1
lazy 1
leaden 4
leisure 3a
lethargic 1
passive 1
phlegmatic 1
quiet 3, 4
silent 4
sleepy 2
slothful
slow 6
supine 2
torpid
unemployed

inactivity°
idleness 1
indolence
inertia
lethargy 1
neglect 4
repose 1
rest[1] 3
slack 5
torpor

inadequacy
dearth
defect 1
imperfection
impotence 2
incompetence
inferiority 2
lack 1
poverty 2
scarcity
want 3

inadequate°
bad 1
deficient 1
disappointing
fail 1
fall 11b, 19
feeble 2
flimsy 2
hopeless 2
impotent 2
incompetent
ineffective 1

inadequate (*cont.*)
ineffectual 2
insufficient
little 3
low[1] 2
meagre 1, 3
miserable 3
pale[1] 3
par 5a
pathetic 2
poor 2, 4
ropy 2
scarce
short 6, 13
slender 3
slight 4
small 4
straitened
thin 2
unsatisfactory
wanting 1

inadequately
badly 1
poorly 1

inadequateness
scarcity

inadmissible°
pale[2] 3

inadvertence
neglect 3
negligence
oversight 1
slip[1] 8

inadvertent°
absent-minded
accidental
chance 6
thoughtless 2
unguarded 1

inadvertently
chance 5a
unawares 2

inadvisable
ill-advised 1
imprudent
unseemly 2

inadvised
inept 2

inalienable°

inamorata
beloved 2
girl 2
love 3
mistress 1
paramour
sweetheart

inamorato
beloved 2
love 3
paramour
suitor
sweetheart

inane°
absurd 1
crazy 2
empty 5
foolish 2
halfwitted
hare-brained 2
imprudent
light[2] 8
pointless
ridiculous
silly 1
stupid 2
vacant 2
worthless 2
zany 1

inanely
madly 2

inanimate°
dead 6
inactive 1
inert 2
leaden 4
lifeless 2
mechanical 3
supine 2

inanity
folly 1
insanity 2
nonsense 2

inanity (*cont.*)
stupidity 2
vacancy 3

inapplicability
impropriety 2

inapplicable°
defunct 2
extraneous 2
impracticable 2
improper 2
inadmissible
inappropriate
irrelevant

inapposite
extraneous 2
improper 2
inapplicable
inappropriate
irrelevant

inappreciable
imperceptible 2
inconsequential
indifferent 4
negligible
sparse 2

inappropriate°
early 4
extraneous 2
foreign 3
gross 3
ill-advised 1
improper 2
inadmissible
inapplicable
incongruous
inconvenient
indecent 1
ineligible
inept 2
inopportune
irrelevant
mismatched
off colour 2
outrageous 3
place 12
point 15
remote 4
step 8
unacceptable
unbecoming 1
unhappy 3
unlikely 2
unreasonable 3
unrelated
unsatisfactory
unseasonable
unseemly 2
untoward 2
unworthy 2
wide 4
wrong 4

inappropriately
amiss 3
turn 42b
unduly 1
wrong 7

inappropriate-ness
impropriety 2
inconvenience 2
ineptitude 2

inapt
extraneous 2
improper 2
inadequate 2
inapplicable
inappropriate
inept 2
irrelevant
point 15
unbecoming 1
unreasonable 3
unseemly 2
wrong 4

inaptness
impropriety 2
ineptitude 2

inarticulate°
dumb 1
incoherent
rambling 1
speechless 2
thick 7
tongue-tied

inarticulately
mumble

inartistic
camp[2] 1
rude 4
ungraceful 2

inartistically
badly 3
roughly 3

inasmuch as
considering
for 13
seeing

inattention
detachment 2
disregard 3
indifference 1
neglect 3
negligence
slight 8

inattentive°
absent-minded
careless 2
forgetful
heedless
inadvertent 2
indifferent 1
mindless 2
neglect 1
nod 4
perfunctory 1
preoccupied 2
remiss
slack 1
thoughtless 2
unguarded 1

inattentiveness
negligence

inaudible°
faint 1
imperceptible 1
noiseless
weak 7

inaudibly
quietly 1

inaugural
initial 1
introductory 1
maiden 3

inaugurate°
begin 2
break 17
commence 3
establish 1
found 1
induct 1
initiate 1
install 1
institute 4
invest 3
launch 1
lead 8
open 20
originate 1
pioneer 2

inauguration
conception 1
dawn 2
début 1
establishment 1
foundation 3
initiation 1
installation 1
launch 5
onset 2
opening 4
origin 2
outset
start 14

inauspicious°
bad 5
contrary 3
evil 4
ill 5
inopportune
ominous 1
pessimistic
portentous 1
sinister 1
threatening
tragic
unfortunate 3
unhappy 2
unlikely 3

inauspicious (*cont.*)
unpromising
unseemly 2
untoward 1

inauspiciously
ill 10

in-between
intermediate 1

inborn°
hereditary 1
indigenous 2
ingrained
inherent
instinctive 1
intrinsic
native 1
organic 2

inbred
inborn
indigenous 2
ingrained
inherent
instinctive 1
intrinsic
rooted

incalculable
boundless
immeasurable
indefinite 4
inestimable 1, 2
inexhaustible 1
infinite 1
numberless
priceless 1
untold 1
vast

–of incalculable value
invaluable

in camera
private 6

incandesce
glow 4

incandescence
flare 4
glow 1
illumination 1
light[1] 3
radiance 1

incandescent°
bright 1
brilliant 1
fiery 2
glowing 1
light[1] 13
luminous 2
radiant 1

incantation
hocus-pocus 2
mumbo-jumbo 2
spell[2] 2

incapability
inability

incapable°
helpless 4
inadequate 2
incompetent
ineffective 2
inefficient 1
powerless 1

incapacitate°
cripple 2
hurt 4
lay[1] 19b
maim
paralyse 3
sabotage 3
strike 13

incapacitated
crippled 1
decrepit 1
disabled
lame 1
powerless 2

incapacity
decrepitude 1
disability 2
inability
incompetence
weakness 2

incarcerate
commit 2
imprison
jail 2
keep 9
lock[1] 9
punish 2
put 13b
restrain 3
send 5, 9b
shut 6a

incarcerated
captive 2
inside 7

incarceration
captivity
custody 2
detention
duress 2
imprisonment
justice 2
penalty
punishment 2

incarnate
embody 1
physical

incarnation
embodiment 1
image 4
picture 4
soul 3

incautious
bold 1
careless 2
daredevil 2
foolhardy
foolish 1
hasty 2
ill-advised 2
improvident 2
imprudent
indiscreet
pell-mell 2
precipitate 5
reckless
short-sighted 2
snap 13
trusting
unguarded 1, 3
unwary

incautiously
hastily 2
pell-mell 1
spur 3

incendiary
agitator
inflammatory
rabble-rouser
terrorist
troublemaker

incense
aggravate 2
anger 2
annoy 1
enrage
exasperate 1
gall[2] 4
inflame 1
infuriate
madden 1
provoke 3

incensed
angry 1
flare 3
furious 1
indignant
mad 4
resentful
seethe 2

incensing
provocative 2

incentive°
impetus
incitement 2
inducement
inspiration 1
motive 1
premium 2
provocation 1
shot 12
spur 1
stimulant 1

inception
beginning 1, 2
conception 1
creation 1
dawn 2
first 6
generation 3
infancy 2
initiation 1
onset 2
origin 2
outset
source 1
start 10, 11, 15

incessant
constant 2
continual
continuous 2
endless 2
eternal 2
everlasting
limitless
perennial 1
perpetual 2
persistent 2
recurrent
relentless 2
repetitive
steady 2
sustained

incessantly
cease 2
end 7b
for ever 2
night 3
permanently

inch
climb 4
crawl 2
creep 1
drag 3
ease 7
edge 6
lag 1
thread 4

inch by inch
degree 3
piecemeal 1

inchmeal
degree 3
gradual
gradually
piecemeal 1, 3

inchoate
undeveloped

incidence°
occurrence 3

incident°
adventure 1
affair 3
circumstance 2
development 1
episode 1
event 1
experience 2
fact 2
happening
matter 2
occasion 1
occurrence 1
phenomenon 1
scene 3

incidental°
chance 6
circumstantial 2
extraneous 1
indirect 2
occasional 1, 2
odd 2
peripheral 1
point 15
random 1
side 8
trifling

incidentally°
offhand 5
passing 3
random 2
way 9

incinerate
burn 2

incipient
initial 1
prospective

incipient (*cont.*)
seminal 2
undeveloped

incise
carve 1
etch 1
gash 2
gouge 1
lance 2
score 10
scribe 3

incision°
cut 19
gash 1
penetration 1
slash 4
slit 2
snip 2

incisive°
acute 5
devastating 1
eloquent 1
emphatic
keen[1] 2
luminous 3
penetrating 1
poignant 2
pointed 2
pungent 2
sarcastic
scathing
strong 16
tart[1] 2
trenchant

incisiveness
edge 3
penetration 2
strength 7

incite°
abet 1
animate 2
awake 2
encourage 1
excite 1
ferment 2
fire 8b
foment
fuel 4
induce 1
inflame 1
interest 7
kindle
motivate
pick 3
precipitate 1
prod 2, 3
prompt 3
provoke 2
push 4
put 29
rise 16
rouse 2
spur 4
stimulate 1
stir 4
urge 2
whip 7a
work 20a

incitement°
agitation 2
encouragement 1
fuel 2
incentive
inducement
inspiration 1
motive 1
occasion 2
premium 2
provocation 1
sedition
signal 2
spur 1
stimulant 1

inciter
rabble-rouser

inciting
encouragement 1

incivility°
disrespect
impertinence
impudence
indelicacy

inclemency
rigour 1
severity 5

inclement°
bad 4
miserable 2
severe 5
stormy 1

inclementness
rigour 1

inclination°
affinity 2
appetite 1
attitude 2
bent 5
bias 1
cast 6
current 6
device 4
discretion 2
downgrade 3
drift 3
fancy 7
favouritism
habit 2
intent 2
leaning
liking 1
list[2] 2
love 2
mentality 2
mind 5
mood 1
notion 2
partiality 1
penchant
pleasure 2
position 3
preference 2
spirit 2, 7
stomach 2
strain[1] 9
talent 2
taste 3
tendency
tilt 3
trend 1
turn 38
vein 4
weakness 4
will 1, 2
wish 5

incline°
bend 4, 6
bias 4
bow 3
chute 2
climb 6
decline 8
descend 2
dispose 2
drop 4
favour 6
feel 9
grade 4
heel[2]
hill 3
inclination 2
influence 3
interest 8
lead 2
lean[2] 2, 3
list[2] 1
persuade 1
prefer 1
prevail 3
ramp
rise 6, 13
slant 3, 4
slope 1, 2
sway 2
tempt 2
tend[1]
tilt 1, 3
tip[2] 2
trend 3
verge[2]
weight 6
win 3

inclined°
capable 2
disposed
fit[1] 4
fond 3
given 3

inclined (*cont.*)
glad 2
liable 1
likely 4
mood 2
oblique 1
open 18
partial 2
prefer 1
prepared 3
prone 2
ready 3
tend[1]

inclining
oblique 1

inclose
enclose 1

include°
count 2
cover 7
embody 3
embrace 3
enclose 2
get 38c
have 4
hold 9
implicate 1
imply 2
incorporate
involve 1
let[1] 5
mix 5
number 4
package 3
pertain
phase 5
possess 2
reckon 2
take 32c
work 17

–be included
appear 3
figure 10

included in
under 3

including
inclusive 2
through 3

inclusion°
embodiment 2
implication 1

inclusive°
broad 6
catholic
comprehensive
detailed 1
encyclopedic
expansive 3
general 1, 3
grand 4
gross 2
overall
panoramic
radical 2
sweeping 1
unabridged 2
wide 2

inclusive of°
at **inclusive 2**
through 3

incognito°
nameless 1
pseudonym

incognizant
unaware
uninformed

incoherent°
chaotic 1
delirious 1
disconnected 2
disjointed 2
fragmentary
inarticulate 1
incongruous
rambling 1

incombustible°
non-flammable

income°
circumstance 1
earnings
fruit
gain 8
pay 12
proceed 3

income (*cont.*)
purse 2
receipt 3
remuneration 1
return 9
revenue
salary
stipend
yield 5

incoming°

incommensurate
disproportionate

incommode
inconvenience 3
trouble 3

incommodious
cramped
narrow 2

incomparability
supremacy 1

incomparable°
beautiful 2
exquisite 5
great 6
matchless
peerless
perfect 2
pre-eminent 2
rare[1] 2
star 3
sterling 2
superlative
supreme 4
top 8
transcendent
unbeatable
unique 2
unparalleled

incomparably
awfully
exceedingly
far 2, 3
highly 2
perfectly 2
pre-eminently
surpassingly

incompatibility
disagreement 1
discord
discrepancy
impropriety 2

incompatible°
conflict 4
contradictory
discordant 1
exclusive 1
improper 2
inappropriate
incongruous
mismatched
opposing
unlike 1, 3
unrelated

incompetence°
impotence 2
inability
ineptitude 1

incompetent°
artless 3
defective 2
duffer
failure 3
helpless 4
hopeless 2
impotent 2
incapable 1
ineffective 2
ineffectual 2
inefficient 1
inept 1
powerless 1
unprofessional 2
useless 2
weak 3

incompetently
poorly 1

incomplete°
deficient 1, 2
fragmentary
immature 1
imperfect
inadequate 1
nodding

incomplete (*cont.*)
partial 1
rough 9
sketchy
undone[2]
unprepared 2
vestigial
wanting 1

incompletely
partially
sketchily

incompleteness
non-completion

incompliant
disobedient 1
insubordinate

incomprehensibility
profundity 1

incomprehensible°
dark 6
deep 2
hard 3
heavy 12
illegible
imponderable
inarticulate 1
inconceivable
inexplicable
mysterious 2
obscure 2
occult 2
paradoxical
perplexing
profound 1
recondite
secret 2
unaccountable 1
unthinkable 1

incomprehensibleness
profundity 1

incomprehension
vacancy 3

incomputable
inestimable 1, 2

inconceivable°
fabulous 2
imponderable
impossible 1
improbable
incomprehensible
incredible 1
question 7
unbelievable
unheard-of 2
unlikely 1
unthinkable 1
untold 3

inconclusive°
ambiguous 2
indecisive 2
pending 2

inconclusiveness
ambiguity 1

incondite
uncivilized 2

incongruity
absurdity 1
difference 1
disagreement 1
discrepancy
disparity
disproportion
impropriety 2
inequality 1
oddity 1
paradox
solecism
twist 10
variance 1

incongruous°
absurd 2
bizarre 1
contradictory
discordant 1
disproportionate
eccentric 1
grotesque 2
improper 2

incongruous (*cont.*)
inappropriate
incompatible
ludicrous
mismatched
paradoxical
queer 1
senseless 3
unworthy 2
wrong 4

incongruousness
impropriety 2
oddity 1

inconsequence
indifference 2
triviality 1

inconsequential°
frivolous 1
immaterial 1
incidental 2
indifferent 4
insignificant
light[2] 6
little 5
meaningless 2
minor 2
negligible
niggling 2
non-essential 1
obscure 4
paltry
petty 1
point 15
poor 5
puerile
puny 1
side 8
slight 1
small 2
tiny
trifling
triviality 2

inconsequentiality
triviality 1

inconsiderable
imperceptible 2
inconsequential
insignificant
light[2] 6
little 5
minor 2
nominal 2
paltry
remote 6
side 8
trifling
unimposing

inconsiderate°
arbitrary 2
blind 3
blunt 2
careless 1
crude 4
flagrant
hasty 2
indifferent 1
insensible 2
intolerant 1
merciless
nasty 4
rough 3
selfish 2
tactless
thoughtless 1
unkind
unthinking 2

inconsistency
confusion 3
difference 1
discrepancy
disparity
disproportion
diversity 1
gap 2
hole 6
inconstancy
inequality 1
paradox
solecism
twist 10
variance 1

inconsistent°
arbitrary 1
circular 3
confused 1
contradictory
desultory
disproportionate
erratic 1
incompatible
incongruous
inconstant
mismatched
opposite 2
paradoxical
step 8
temperamental 2
unstable 1
unworthy 2
water 2
whimsical 2

inconsolable°
bad 9
broken-hearted
desolate 3
forlorn 1
hopeless 3
joyless 1
mournful 1
sorrowful 1
wretched 2

inconspicuous°
background 3
modest 2
obscure 3, 4
unobtrusive
unsung

inconspicuousness
obscurity 3

inconstancy°
fluctuation
vicissitude 2

inconstant°
capricious
changeable 1
desultory
faithless 2
fanciful 1
fickle
flighty 1
inconsistent 2
indefinite 5
infirm 2
moody 3
uncertain 4
unsettled 1
unstable 1
vague 5
variable
volatile 2

incontestable
certain 4
conspicuous 1
decided 1
hard 8
incontrovertible
indisputable
inevitable
positive 1
self-evident
solid 7
undisputed
unquestionable

incontestably
clearly 2
evidently 1
undoubtedly

incontinent°
dissolute

incontrovertibility
finality

incontrovertible°
certain 4
clear 6
conspicuous 1
decided 1
evident
final 2
hard 8
indisputable
peremptory 1
self-evident

incontrovertible (*cont.*)
solid 7
undisputed
unquestionable
watertight 2

incontrovertibly
evidently 1
necessarily
undoubtedly

inconvenience°
bother 4
discomfort 2
disturb 1
encumber 2
headache 2
nuisance 1
put 23a
trouble 1, 3, 5

inconvenienced
put-upon

inconvenient°
inopportune
miserable 2
unseemly 2

incorporate°
combine 2
cover 7
embody 3
embrace 3
flesh 6
include 1
involve 1
mix 1
package 3
phase 5
work 13

incorporating
inclusive 2

incorporation
embodiment 2
inclusion

incorporeal
disembodied
immaterial 2
insubstantial 2
intangible
spectral
spiritual 2
unearthly 1

incorrect°
abusive 2
amiss 1
careless 3
err 1
erroneous
error 3a
false 1
illegitimate 3
improper 1
inaccurate
inadmissible
inexact
invalid[2]
mistaken 1, 2
off 3
out 12
perverse 1
untrue 2
wrong 2, 3, 6

incorrectly
amiss 3
badly 3
error 3b
wrong 7

incorrectness
impropriety 1

incorrigible°
incurable 2
problem 3
rebellious 2
rogue 2
self-willed
ungovernable
wicked 2

incorrupt°
innocent 2

incorruptibility
integrity 1
rectitude

incorruptible
conscientious 1
honest 1

incorruptible (*cont.*)
honourable 1
incorrupt 1
moral 1
noble 4
trustworthy
upright 2
virtuous 1

incrassate
thicken

increase°
accumulation 2
add 4
advance 8
aggravate 1
amplify 1
appreciate 2
appreciation 2
blow[1] 8d
boom 2, 4
boost 3, 6
breed 4
build 4
compound 3
deepen 2
develop 2
development 2
double 6
enhance
enlarge 1
expand 1, 3
expansion 1
explosion 3
extend 2
extension 1
fill 10a
flare 2, 6
flourish 1
freshen 1
gain 5, 7, 9
gather 5
go 39a
grow 1, 5
growth 1
gust 2
heighten 1, 2
hot 11
improve 2
improvement 2
increment
inflame 2
inflate 2
intensify
jump 5, 9
leap 6
magnification
magnify 1
mark 16b
maximize 1
mount 7
movement 6
pick 8f
progress 3, 6
proliferate
proliferation
propagate 2
pump 4c
put 28f
raise 6
recovery 1
revival 3
rise 5, 10, 14
scale[3] 5
screw 7a
soar 2
spread 6, 8
spurt 2
step 18b
stimulate 2
stretch 2
swell 1, 2, 3, 4
thrive
whet 2
widen
worsen 1

-on the increase°
at **increase 5**

increased by
plus 1

increasing
flourishing
increase 5
progressive 1
spread 8

incredible°
awesome
colossal 2
extraordinary 2
fabulous 2
fantastic 3
far-fetched
formidable 2
implausible
improbable
inconceivable
marvellous
miraculous
phenomenal
preposterous
remarkable 1
sensational 1
sight 6b
splendid 3
superb
superhuman 1
tall 3
terrific 2
unbelievable
unthinkable 1
water 2
world 8

incredibly
pretty 3
terribly
well[1] 2

incredulity
discredit 6
distrust 2
doubt 4
scepticism
surprise 3

incredulous°
sceptical
unbelieving

incredulousness
distrust 2
scepticism

increment°
addition 3
development 2
gain 9
increase 4
jump 9
rise 14

-with an increment of
plus 1

incriminate°
accuse 2
blame 2
denounce 1
frame 9
impeach 1
implicate 2
indict
inform 2
involve 3

incrimination
accusation

incrustation
scale[2] 2
skin 2

incubate°
brood 2
hatch 1

inculcate
discipline 6
educate
implant 1
indoctrinate
instil
instruct 1
preach 2
school 4
teach

inculcation
discipline 1

inculpable
irreproachable

inculpate
impeach 1
implicate 2
incriminate
indict
involve 3
vituperate

incumbency
seat 3
tenure 1
term 3

incumbent°
behove
obligatory
occupant

-incumbents
power 10

incur°
run 16

incurable°
hopeless 1
incorrigible
invalid[1] 2
terminal 2

incursion
assault 1
attack 6
inroad 1
invasion 1
push 15
raid 1

indebted°
beholden
debt 2
obliged 1
owe 1
thankful

indebtedness
debt 1
liability 2

indecency
dirt 3
filth 3
impropriety 3
indelicacy
profligacy 1
ribaldry

indecent°
base[2] 4
bawdy
blue 2
broad 8
coarse 3
dirty 2
disgraceful 2
earthy
filthy 3
foul 5
gross 3
immodest 1
immoral 2
improper 3
lascivious 2
lewd
low[1] 3
nasty 3
naughty 3
obscene 1
off colour 2
outrageous 2, 3
pale[2] 3
pornographic
profane 3
profligate 1
promiscuous 2
prurient 2
racy 2
rank[2] 3
risqué
rude 3
scandalous 1
scurrilous
sexy 2
shameful
shameless
spicy 2
suggestive 2
ungodly 2
unmentionable 2
unseemly 1
vulgar 2
wicked 3

indecipherability
profundity 1

indecipherable
illegible
incomprehensible
occult 2
profound 1

indecision°
flux
suspense 1

indecisive°
doubtful 2
end 6
fence 2
fickle
inconclusive
indefinite 5
irresolute
spineless 2
tentative 2
uncertain 2
unstable 1
vague 5
wishy-washy 1

indecisiveness
flux
indecision

indecorous
bawdy
disrespectful
fast[1] 2
ill-mannered
immodest 1
impolite
improper 3
indecent 1
obscene 1
order 13b
outrageous 3
profane 3
rank[2] 3
risqué
scandalous 1
sexy 2
shameless
spicy 2
taboo 1
tasteless 1
unbecoming 2
unseemly 1
untoward 2
vulgar 2
wrong 4

indecorously
fast[1] 9

indecorousness
impropriety 3
incivility

indecorum
disrespect
incivility
indelicacy
liberty 5

indeed°
actually
dearly 1
even 10
fact 4
really 1, 2
substantially
truly 3, 4
well[1] 9

indefatigability
patience 2
perseverance
persistence
resolution 1
stamina

indefatigable
constant 1
diligent
energetic
enterprising
hard 7
indomitable
industrious
inexhaustible 2
laborious 2
patient 2
persevere
persistent 1
resolute
stalwart 2
steadfast
strenuous 2
strong 5
tireless
untiring

indefatigableness
follow-through

indisputably (*cont.*)
positively
undoubtedly
indissolubly
inextricably
indistinct°
ambiguous 2
dim 1
dreamy 1
dull 8
equivocal 2
faint 1
feeble 3
focus 3
fuzzy 2
hazy 2
imperceptible 2
imprecise
inarticulate 2
inaudible
indefinite 3
indistinguish-able 2
light² 3
low¹ 13
misty
nebulous
neutral 2
obscure 2
shadowy 2
shady 2
sketchy
thick 7
vague 1
weak 6,7
woolly 2
indistinctness
ambiguity 1
blur 1
indistinguish-ability
identity 1
indistinguish-able°
dim 1
identical 1
imperceptible 1
inconspicuous
indefinite 3
indistinct 1,2
neutral 2
indite
pen¹ 2
write 1
individual°
character 4
discrete
distinct 2
distinctive
eccentric 1
entity 1
fellow 1
figure 3,6
human 4
independent 9
interior 3
isolated 1
life 5
lyric 2
misfit
mortal 6
odd 1
one 1,4
particular 1
party 5
peculiar 2
person 1
personal 1,4
private 3
proper 6
punter 2
respective
separate 5
several 2
single 2,3
sole
solitary 1
solo 2
sort 4
soul 2
special 1,4
specific 1,2
subjective 1
various 2
-as an individual
personally 3
-individuals
people 1
individualism
eccentricity 1
laissez-faire
individualist°
eccentric 2
nonconformist 1,2
original 6
individualistic
independent 3,6
individual 2
liberal 2
nonconformist 2
rugged 3
individuality
diversity 1
eccentricity 1
identity 2
oddity 1
originality
singularity 1
individualize
distinguish 2
specify
individualized
personalized
individually°
apart 2
respectively
separately
singly
indoctrinate°
discipline 6
drill 2
educate
implant 1
instruct 1
school 4
teach
train 4
tutor 2
indoctrination
discipline 1
education 1
instruction 2
schooling
indolence°
idleness 1
inactivity 1
inertia
lethargy 1
rest¹ 3
sloth
torpor
indolent°
idle 3
inactive 1
inert 3
lackadaisical 1
lazy 1
lethargic 1
phlegmatic 1
remiss
shiftless
slack 1
slothful
supine 2
tardy 2
torpid
indolently
idly 1
indomitability
bravery
stamina
indomitable°
brave 1
formidable 3
impregnable
invincible 1
irresistible 1
mighty 1
stalwart 1,3
stiff 4
sturdy 2
indorse
endorse 1,2
underwrite 2
indorsement
endorsement 1
indubitable
certain 4
incontrovertible
indisputable
manifest 1
positive 1
probable
sure 4
undisputed
unquestionable
indubitably
absolutely 3
certainty 3
clearly 2
course 6
definitely
doubtless 1
downright 2
easily 2
evidently 1
far 3
likely 5
manifestly
obviously
positively
presumably
probably
question 4
quite 4
surely 1
truly 3
undoubtedly
induce°
bring 12b
cause 5,6
chat 3
decoy 2
dispose 2
drag 2
draw 14b
drive 1
get 14
give 10
have 9
influence 3
interest 8
lead 2
lure 1
make 2
motivate
occasion 5
persuade 1
press 6
prevail 3
prompt 3
provoke 1
push 4
spur 4
stir 4
strike 11
take 25
tempt 2
urge 2,3
win 3
work 18
inducement°
attraction 2
bribe 1
come-on
decoy 1
enticement 2
incentive
incitement 2
invitation 2
lift 9
lure 2
motive 1
occasion 2
persuasion 1
premium 2
pressure 4
provocation 1
shot 12
spur 1
temptation 2
inducing
persuasion 1
induct°
enlist 1
inaugurate 2
install 1
invest 3
let¹ 5
recruit 1
induction
admission 2
initiation 2
installation 1
inductive
logical 1
indulge°
baby 2
banquet 2
cater 2
coddle
dote
drink 2
favour 7
feast 4
forgive 1
humour 4
make 34b
mother 6
oblige 1
pamper
pander 1
pardon 2
pet¹ 5
regale
satisfy 2
spoil 3
suffer 3
tolerate 1
indulged
pet¹ 3
privileged 1
indulge in°
at **indulge 1**
luxuriate 1
roll 10b
savour 3
wallow 2
indulgence°
charity 2
excuse 5
fling 2
forgiveness 2
grace 3
kindness 1
luxury 2,4
mercy
office 5
pardon 1
permission
privilege
remission 1
splurge 1
tolerance 1
waste 6
indulgent°
charitable 2
easy 3
fatherly
gentle 1
gracious
kind¹
lax 1
lenient
merciful
mild 1
obliging
paternal 1
permissive
soft 5
soft-hearted
tolerant
voluptuous 1
indulgently
favourably 1
indurate
hard 4
steely 2
industrial
technical 2
industrialist
manufacturer
merchant 3
industrious°
busy 2
diligent
earnest 2
enterprising
hard 7
laborious 3
studious 1
tireless
industriously
hard 13
industry°
application 3
drive 8
exertion
labour 1
work 1
indweller
occupant
indwelling
inherent
intrinsic
native 1
inebriant
intoxicating 1
inebriate
intoxicate 1
inebriated
drunk 1
high 9
stinking 3
inebriating
alcoholic 1
inebriety
drunkenness
inedible
revolting
unpalatable
ineffable°
inexpressible
mystical 1
nameless 3
unmentionable 1
ineffaceable
indelible
ineffective°
bootless
feeble 2
flabby 2
fruitless
futile
hollow 5
impotent 2
impractical 2
incompetent
ineffectual 1
inefficient 1
invalid²
lame 2
limp² 3
low¹ 5
meaningless 2
non-productive 2
pale¹ 3
pointless
powerless 1
shiftless
spineless 2
unprofitable 2
unsuccessful 1
useless 1,2
vain 2
void 1
weak 3
wet 3
ineffectiveness
impotence 2
ineffectual°
faint-hearted 2
feeble 2
flabby 2
fruitless
futile
impotent 2
impractical 2
incompetent
ineffective 1
inefficient 1
irresponsible
limp² 3
low¹ 5
meaningless 2
non-productive 2
pale¹ 3
pointless
powerless 1
spineless 2
tame 3
unsuccessful 1
useless 1,2
void 1
wan 2
weak 3
wet 3
ineffectualness
impotence 2
inefficacious°
bootless
ineffective 1
ineffectual 1
meaningless 2
unsuccessful 1
inefficacy
impotence 2
inefficiency
incompetence
ineptitude 1
inefficient°
helpless 4
incompetent
ineffective 2
ineffectual 2
inept 1
poor 4
unprofessional 2
unprofitable 2
useless 2
inefficiently
roughly 3
inelastic
firm 1
inflexible
rigid 2
stiff 1
inelegance
indelicacy
simplicity 3
inelegant
awkward 2
broad 8
homespun
hulking
obscene 1
off colour 2
rude 4
tasteless 1
uncivilized 2
ungraceful 2
unrefined 1
vulgar 1
ineligible°
unqualified 1
unworthy 1
ineluctable
automatic 3
certain 3
destined 2
eventual 2
fatal 3
fated 3
hard 8
indispensable 2
inevitable
irresistible 2
necessary 2
sure 4
unavoidable
ineluctably
inextricably
necessarily
inept°
artless 3
awkward 1
clumsy
heavy-handed 1
helpless 4
hopeless 2
impotent 2
inadequate 2
incompetent
ineffective 2
inefficient 1
tactless
useless 2
weak 3
ineptitude°
inability
incompetence
ineptly
badly 1,3
roughly 3
ineptness
impotence 2
inability
ineptitude 1

inflame *(cont.)*
kindle
madden 1
rise 16
work 20a
inflamed°
angry 2
drunk 2
fervent 1
feverish
heated
hot 3
impassioned
raw 4
sore 1
tender[1] 8
torrid 2
inflaming
incitement 1
inflammatory
inflammable°
explosive 1
flammable
inflammation°
incitement 2
sore 7
ulcer 1
inflammatory°
seditious
inflatable
expansive 1
inflate°
blow[1] 8c, 8e
enlarge 1
exaggerate
expand 1
fill 2
increase 1
magnify 1
maximize 2
overstate
pad 5
puff 6
pump 4a
raise 6
stretch 2
swell 1
inflated°
bloated
bombastic
exalted 2
fancy 4
flowery
grandiose 1
pompous 1, 2
ponderous 2
pretentious 1
rhetorical 3
stilted
swollen
inflatedness
snobbery
inflation
exaggeration
expansion 2
increase 4
swell 4
inflection
accent 1, 3
diction 2
intonation
pronunciation
tone 2
inflexibility
formality 2
obstinacy
perseverance
persevere
resolution 1
rigour 2
severity 1
tenacity 1
inflexible°
dour 2
firm 1, 4
fixed 2
formal 1
grim 1
hard 1
hidebound
immovable 2
implacable
incorrigible
merciless
inflexible *(cont.)*
monolithic
obstinate
opinionated 1
persevere
persistent 1
perverse 3
precise 2
recalcitrant
relentless 1
resolute
rigid 2, 4
stern 1
stiff 1
stony 2
strict 2
stubborn
tenacious 1
tight 3
tough 2, 6
unkind
wilful 2
inflexibly
precisely 2
inflict°
deliver 5
enforce 1
impose 1
visit 2
wreak
infliction
imposition 1
influence°
action 2
affect[1] 3
auspices
bear 8
bias 3, 4
bring 14b
charm 5
clutch 2b
colour 4
come 16b
condition 6
connection 3
department 2
determine 4
dispose 2
domination 1
effect 2
factor 1
fascination
finger 2, 10
fix 11
get 14, 30d
grip 2
guide 3
hand 3
hold 26
impact 2
importance 2
impress 1
impression 2
incite
incitement 2
incline 2
induce 1
inspiration 2
interest 8
jurisdiction
lead 2
leadership
lobby 3
manipulate 1
mark 5
might 2
motivate
motive 1
mould[1] 6
move 6
nobility 1
part 3
persuade 1
persuasion 1
power 2
predominance
prejudice 3
preponderance 2
pressure 4, 5
prevail 3
prominence 1
prompt 3
pull 16, 21
push 4
rank[1] 2
influence *(cont.)*
reach 6
reign 1
say 12
screw 4
shape 7
speak 12b
spell[2] 3
squeeze 11
strike 7
string 5
sway 2, 4
tint 4
touch 6, 18
urge 3
weight 3
win 3
work 18
-be influenced
depend 1
possess 4
-under the influence°
at **under 6**
drunk 1
stinking 3
tight 8
influenceable
susceptible 2
influenced
affected 5
overcome 2
partial 2
influencing
incitement 1
persuasion 1
influential°
active 2
classical 1
considerable 2
dominant 1
effectual 1
great 5
important 3
leading 1
mighty 1
persuasive
potent 1
powerful 2
predominant
prevailing 2
public 6
seminal 1
strong 7
tell[1] 6
telling 1
weighty 3
influentially
highly 4
influenza
chill 2
cold 10
info
dope 3
fact 3
gossip 2
information
intelligence 2
low-down
news 1
rumour 1
scoop 3
talk 17
word 2
inform°
acquaint
advise 2
brief 6
clue 2
discipline 6
disclose 1
educate
enlighten
familiarize
fill 9c
flag[1] 2
grass 1
ground 6
help 4
instruct 1
notice 7
notify 1
picture 5
post[3] 4
inform *(cont.)*
prime 6
register 5
show 4
talk 5
teach
tell[1] 3
warn 1
wise 4
-be informed
hear 2
know 5
receive 5
understand
inform against°
at **inform 2**
denounce 2
finger 8
sell 3
shop 3
informal°
candid 3
casual 4
easy 6
familiar 3
free 8
homely 1
intimate[1] 4
offhand 1, 3
outgoing 2
scratch 6
sporty
unofficial
vernacular 2
informality
ease 4
familiarity 2
informally
offhand 4, 5
informant
informer
plant 4
source 3
spy 1
information°
advice 2
clue 1
data
direction 2
dope 3
edification
education 2
fact 3
file 1
good 21c
gossip 2
history 2, 4
illumination 2
instruction 1
intelligence 2
knowledge 2
learning
line[1] 10
literature 2
low-down
material 4
message 1
news 1, 2
notice 5
particular 5
record 4
report 1
revelation
rumour 1
science 1
steer 3
story 4
talk 17
testimony
tip[3] 2
word 2
informational
instructive
informative°
educational 2
forthcoming 3
instructive
significant 2
informatory
instructive
informed°
acquainted 2
aware 1
current 4
informed *(cont.)*
educated 1
enlightened
experienced 1
familiar 4
hip
home 5
judicious
knowing 2
knowledgeable 1
learned
level 5
privy 2
profound 2
rational 2
ripe 2
versed
wise 2, 5, 6
informer°
grass 2
plant 4
snake 2
sneak 2
spy 1
talebearer
inform on°
at **inform 2**
betray 1
familiarize
finger 8
give 12b
shop 3
turn 15c
infraction
breach 1
foul 17
infringement
invasion 1
offence 1
peccadillo
sin 1
transgression
infra dig
base[2] 2
infrastructure
base[1] 2
basis 1
infrequent
few 1
occasional 1
rare[1] 1
unwonted
infrequently°
now 4
rarely
seldom
infringe°
break 9
disobey
encroach
intrude
pirate 3
trample 12
transgress 2
violate 1
infringed
broken 5
infringement°
breach 1
foul 17
invasion 1
offence 1
plagiarism
sin 1
violation 1
infringer
pirate 2
infringing
plagiarism
violation 1
infuriate°
aggravate 2
anger 2
displease
enrage
exasperate 1
gall[2] 4
inflame 1
madden 1
outrage 4
provoke 3
wall 3
infuriated
angry 1
bristle 3
furious 1
mad 4
rabid 1
stack 5
infuriating
provocative 2
trying
infuse
brew 1
impregnate 2
insinuate 3
instil
percolate
school 4
suffuse
transfuse 2
infusion
liquor 2
solution 3
ingenious°
acute 5
artful 2
astute 1
bright 6
brilliant 4
clever 3
creative
cute 2
dexterous 2
elegant 4
exquisite 2
foxy 1
imaginative 1
master 4
neat 4
original 4
politic 1
productive 2
quick 4
resourceful
shrewd
slick 3
smart 1
subtle 3
wicked 7
witty
ingénue
innocent 5
ingenuity°
art 1
craft 1
dexterity 2
genius 2
imagination 1
originality
proficiency
prowess 1
resource 1
skill 1
talent 1
ingenuous°
above-board 2
artless 1
candid 1
careless 4
childlike
frank 2
honest 3
honourable 3
innocent 4
naïve
natural 4
plain 3
provincial 2
rustic 2
simple 3
transparent 3
unaffected[1]
unsophisticated 1
unsuspecting
ingenuously
honestly 2
simply 3
ingenuousness
candour 1
ease 4
honesty 2
naïvety
provincialism 2
simplicity 3

innate (*cont.*)
ingrained
inherent
instinctive 1
intrinsic
mother 4
native 1
organic 2
sneaking 2
innately
naturally 2
inner
central 1
interior 1, 3
spiritual 2
subconscious 1
innermost
recess 3
subconscious 1
inner person
psyche
subconscious 2
innervate
animate 1
kindle
strengthen 2
vitalize
wind[2] 4c
innervation
animation 2
encouragement 1
innings
bout 2
innkeeper
host[1] 1
landlord 1
proprietor 2
innocence
honour 4
inexperience
naïvety
provincialism 2
purity 2
virtue 2
innocent°
artless 1
blameless
callow
childlike
clean 4
clear 12, 32
excuse 1
frank 2
gullible
harmless
ignorant 3
immaculate 2
inexperienced
ingenuous 1
irreproachable
mug 3
naïve
pastoral 1
provincial 2
pure 3
respectable 3
savoury 2
simple 3
square 6
trusting
unsophisticated 1
unsuspecting
virtuous 2
white 3
young 2
innocently
simply 3
innocuous
harmless
innocent 3
inoffensive
safe 2
innocuousness
purity 1
innominate
nameless 1
innovate
break 17
innovation°
originality
innovative
avant-garde
break 17

innovative (*cont.*)
imaginative 1
offbeat
original 4
revolutionary 2
seminal 1
way-out 2
innovativeness
novelty 1
originality
innovator
pioneer 1
innuendo°
hint 1
implication 2
imputation
libel 2
overtone
reference 1
scandal 3
slur 1
suggestion 2
innumerable
frequent 1
immeasurable
inestimable 2
infinite 1
limitless
many 1
numberless
umpteen
unlimited 2
untold 1
inobservant
unaware
unguarded 1
inoculant
preventive 4
inoculate
inject 1
inoculated
immune
inoculation
immunity 2
shot 6
inoculum
preventive 4
inoffensive°
clean 4
harmless
innocent 3
mild 1
peaceable 2
in on
hip
privy 2
inoperable
duff
incurable 1
inoperative
crippled 2
defunct 2
disabled
dud 2
duff
inactive 2
ineffective 1
ineffectual 1
order 13c
out 14
void 1
inopportune°
contrary 3
early 4
improper 2
inappropriate
inconvenient
premature 2
unseasonable
unseemly 2
untoward 1
inopportunely
amiss 2
inopportune-ness
impropriety 2
inordinate°
excessive 1
exorbitant
extreme 6
great 3
immoderate

inordinate (*cont.*)
mortal 5
outrageous 1
towering 2
unconscionable 2
unreasonable 2
inordinately
awfully
overly
sky 2
unduly 1
inorganic
dead 6
inquest
inquiry 1
investigation
probe 3
inquire°
ask 1
demand 4
enquire 1
follow 11a
pry 1
query 3
see 12b
wonder 3
inquire into°
at **inquire 1**
examine 1
explore 2
go 30b
investigate
report 6
research 2
inquire of
ask 1
consult 1
refer 3
search 1
sound[3] 1
inquiring
curious 1
inquisitive 1
quizzical
inquiry°
analysis 1
examination 1, 3
experiment 1
exploration
investigation
probe 3
query 1
question 1
research 1
scrutiny
search 4
study 4
survey 3
topic
trial 2
inquisition
examination 3
inquiry 1
interrogation
investigation
trial 2
tribunal
inquisitive°
curious 1
intrusive
nosy
pry 1
wonder 3
inquisitiveness
curiosity 1
inroad°
attack 6
invasion 1
penetration 1
-inroads°
at **inroad 2**
insalubrious
injurious 1
unhealthy 2
unwholesome 1
insalutary
unwholesome 1
ins and outs
rope 2
insane°
crazy 1
delirious 1

insane (*cont.*)
deranged
distraught
disturbed 2
foolish 2
homicidal
improbable
imprudent
mad 1
maniacal 1
mind 14
off 4
preposterous
psychotic 1
queer 4
raving 1
ridiculous
senseless 3
sick 4
silly 1
stupid 2
twist 11
unbalanced 2
unreasonable 1
unsound 3
unthinking 1
violent 1
insanely
madly 1
insanitary
sordid 3
insanity°
folly 1
lunacy 1
madness 1
mania 2
stupidity 2
insatiability
greed 3
gluttony
rapacity
insatiable
gluttonous
greedy 1
hoggish
hungry 3
rapacious
ravenous 2
unquenchable
voracious 1
inscribe
dedicate 3
engrave 1
enrol 2
enter 3
etch 1
letter 5
line[1] 21
scribe 3
sign 7
stamp 2
write 1
inscribed
enrol 2
inscription
dedication 2
legend 4
title 3
inscrutability
complexity 2
mystery 2
mystique
profundity 1
inscrutable
cryptic 2
deep 2
hard 3
incomprehensible
inexplicable
mysterious 2
occult 2
profound 1
unaccountable 1
insect
bug 1
insecure°
brittle 2
disorientated
jealous 2
perilous
precarious
self-conscious
shaky 2
slight 4

insecure (*cont.*)
unstable 1
insecurity
peril
suspense 1
inseminate
fertilize 1
impregnate 1
insensate
brute 1
dead 2
insensible 1
lifeless 2
numb 1
senseless 1, 2
thick-skinned
insensibility
indifference 1
oblivion 2
stupor
insensible°
blind 4
callous
dead 2, 3
deaf 2
dull 2
indifferent 1
lifeless 2
mechanical 3
numb 1
oblivious
out 8
phlegmatic 1
senseless 1, 2
stony 2
unaware
unconscious 1
insensibly
idly 2
insensitive
barbarian 3
blind 2
brutal 1
callous
chill 6
cold 3
cold-blooded 2
cold-hearted
dead 4
deaf 2
dull 2
hard 4
inconsiderate
indifferent 1
indiscreet
inhuman 1
insensible 2
merciless
monstrous 2
oblivious
obtuse 2
phlegmatic 1
stony 2
tactless
thick 6
thick-skinned
thoughtless 1
unconscious 2
unkind
unsympathetic
wooden 3
insensitivity
heart 2
indiscretion 1
tolerance 3
insentient
insensible 1
senseless 2
inseparable
close 15
indistinct 2
indistinguish-able 1
one 2
thick 8
inseparably
inextricably
insert°
enclose 2
enter 3
get 38c
graft[1] 2
implant 3
inject 1, 2

insert (*cont.*)
insinuate 2
introduce 5
phase 5
put 19a
stick[1] 3
supplement 1
work 17
insertion
insert 2
inside°
central 1
intelligence 2
interior 1, 5
privileged 4
-insides°
at **inside 2**
bowels
core 1
gut 1
works 2
inside informa-tion
dirt 4
inside out°
at **inside 3**
detail 4
inside story
low-down
insidious
black 6
crafty
disingenuous
evil 2
loaded 3
perfidious
serpentine 1
sinister 2
sly 1
subtle 3
unscrupulous
insidiously
back 6
insidiousness
perfidy
subtlety 2
insight°
depth 3
discrimination 2
foresight 1
illumination 2
imagination 1
inspiration 1
intelligence 1
intuition
knowledge 1
light[1] 5
mind 1
penetration 2
perception 2
reason 2
understanding 2
uptake
vision 2
wisdom 1
wit 1
insightful
acute 5
astute 2
far-sighted 1
intelligent
profound 2
wise 1
insightfulness
profundity 2
insigne
character 1
colour 2b
crest 2
device 3
emblem
mark 2
plaque 2
regalia
seal 1
stamp 7
standard 3
symbol
-insignia
colour 2b
plaque 2
regalia
seal 1
symbol

insignificance
indifference 2
inferiority 1, 2
obscurity 3
triviality 1
insignificant°
empty 4
expendable
feeble 2
frivolous 1
humble 3
idle 4
immaterial 1
incidental 2
inconsequential
inconspicuous
indifferent 4
inferior 2
insubstantial 1
light[2] 4, 6
little 5
marginal 1
meaningless 2
minor 2
minute[2] 2
negligible
niggling 2
nominal 2
non-essential 1
obscure 4
pale[1] 3
paltry
petty 1
pitiful 2
poor 5
puerile
puny 1
remote 6
side 8
slender 3
slight 1
small 2, 4, 5
small-time
sparse 2
superficial 2
tenuous 2
tiny
trifling
triviality 2
unsung
venial
wee 2
worthless 1
insincere°
affected 2
artificial 3
counterfeit 2
deceitful
devious 1
disingenuous
double 5
empty 4
factitious
faithless 2
false 4
glossy 2
hollow 4
hypocritical
mannered
Pharisaic
phoney 1
strained
two-faced
unnatural 4
untrue 1
insincerity
affectation 1
cant 1
falsity
hypocrisy
insinuate°
get 30b
hint 3
implant 1
imply 1
impose 2
impute
instil
intimate[2]
libel 4
make 37e
mention 2
phase 5
plant 6
suggest 2

insinuate (*cont.*)
whisper 2
insinuation
dig 8
hint 1
implication 2
imputation
innuendo
libel 2
overtone
reference 1
scandal 3
slur 1
suggestion 2
insipid
bland 2
colourless 2
dead 12
flat 5, 8
humdrum
lacklustre
nondescript
pedestrian 2
prosaic
sickly 3
stupid 3
tame 4
tasteless 2
tedious
tiresome 1
vapid
watery 1
wishy-washy 2
insipidity
tedium
insist°
claim 3
demand 1
maintain 3
persist 1
require 1
screw 4
stipulate
swear 1
insistence
assertion 2
demand 5
expectation 3
pressure 4
stress 2
urgency
insistent°
assertive
demanding 2
dogmatic
emphatic
officious
peremptory 3
urgent 2
insist on
claim 3
demand 2
enforce 1, 2
exact 3
lay[1] 10
maintain 3
make 2
persist 1
pressure 5
protest 4
request 1
stipulate
insobriety
drunkenness
insolence
arrogance
assurance 4
brass
disrespect
effrontery
familiarity 3
flippancy 2
gall[1] 2
impertinence
impudence
mouth 4
nerve 2
presumption 1
sauce 2
side 5
insolent°
audacious 2
barefaced 2
brash 2

insolent (*cont.*)
brassy 1
brazen
cheeky
contemptuous
cool 6
discourteous
disdainful
disrespectful
familiar 3
flippant 2
forward 2
fresh 8
ill-mannered
immodest 2
impertinent
impudent
irreverent 2
offensive 2
pert 1
presumptuous
pushy
rude 2
insoluble
hard 3
mysterious 1
insolvency
failure 4
poverty 1
insolvent°
broke
destitute 1
embarrassed 2
fail 4
impoverished 1
needy
pauper
poor 1
straitened
insomniac
sleepless 1
wakeful 1
insomuch as
considering
insouciance
detachment 2
ease 4
indifference 1
torpor
insouciant
bland 1
blasé 2
blithe 2
carefree
casual 3
comfortable 2
debonair 2
half-hearted
impassive
indifferent 1
lackadaisical 2
listless
lukewarm 2
nonchalant
offhand 1
relaxed
torpid
insouciantly
gaily 2
inspect°
check 4, 10b
contemplate 1
examine 1
explore 2
eye 10
frisk 2
go 34a
inquire 1
look 1, 8
observe 2
peruse
reconnoitre
research 2
review 1
scan 2
scrutinize
search 1
study 3
survey 1
traverse 4
try 2
vet
watch 3

inspection
check 15
examination 1
exploration
inquiry 1
observance 3
observation 1
perusal
reconnaissance
research 1
review 5
scan 3
scrutiny
search 4
survey 3
view 4
inspiration°
encouragement 1
guide 6
imagination 1
impetus
incitement 2
lift 9
promotion 1
spirit 7
inspirational
moving 1
stimulating
inspire°
animate 2
call 9
draw 7
encourage 1
energize
enliven 1
exalt 3
excite 1
fire 8b
foment
generate 3
incite
induce 1
inhale
kindle
motivate
move 6
pep 2
possess 4
promote 1
prompt 5
pump 4b
raise 10
spark 2
stimulate 1
stir 4
vitalize
wake[1] 2
inspired
fire 5
imaginative 1
impassioned
possess 4
prophetic
inspiring
encouragement 1
exciting 1
imaginative 1
moving 1
rousing
stimulating
stirring
sublime 2
inspirit
animate 1, 2
assure 2
cheer 5
encourage 1
energize
enliven 1
exalt 3
excite 1
fire 8b
heat 4
inspire 1
intoxicate 2
kindle
liven 2
perk up
promote 1
pump 4b
reassure
rouse 2
spark 2
spice 4
stimulate 1

inspirit (*cont.*)
vitalize
wake[1] 2
inspirited
drunk 2
eager
inspiriting
exhilarating 2
heart-warming 1
hopeful 2
promotion 1
refreshing
rousing
stirring
inspissate
solidify 1
thicken
inspissated
thick 5
instability
fluctuation
flux
vertigo
install°
establish 2
fit[1] 8
fix 2, 8
inaugurate 2
induct 1
invest 3
let[1] 5
mount 5
seat 7
set 1
site 2
situate
station 4
installation°
admission 2
initiation 2
institution 1
-installations
fitting 2
instalment
episode 2
-in instalments
time 19b
instance°
case[1] 1, 4
example 1
exemplify 1
illustrate 1
illustration 1
manifestation
occurrence 2
pattern 5
prototype 2
quote 1
specimen
typify
-for instance°
at **instance 2**
example 4
illustration 1
like[1] 6
namely
say 15
-in all instances
universally
instant°
crack 3
flash 3
immediate 1
minute[1] 1
moment 1, 2
point 4
prepared 4
prompt 1
rapid
second[2]
snap 13
spurt 1
twinkling 1
urgent 1
-(at) this instant
immediately 1
instantaneously
now 1
-in an instant
swiftly
instantaneous
hasty 1
immediate 1

instantaneous (*cont.*)
instant 3
prompt 1
quick 2
rapid
snap 13
unhesitating 1
instantaneously°
hastily 1
immediately 1
outright 3
promptly
rapidly 2
readily 3
shot 10
suddenly 1
instantaneousness
rapidity
instanter
immediately 1
instantaneously
now 3
rapidly 2
readily 3
instantly
directly 2
immediately 1
instantaneously
now 3
once 6a
outright 3
post-haste
promptly
quickly 3
rapidly 2
readily 3
right 13
short 11
shot 10
straight 15
suddenly 1
summarily 1
instate
inaugurate 2
induct 1
install 1
invest 3
seat 7
instatement
initiation 2
installation 1
instead°
rather 2
instead of°
at **instead 2**
behalf
for 3
instigate
abet 1
excite 1
ferment 2
foment
induce 1
initiate 1
inspire 1
kindle
motivate
precipitate 1
provoke 2
put 29
raise 10
rise 16
touch 11b
instigating
incitement 1
instigation
incitement 2
provocation 1
sedition
spur 1
instigator
aggressor
rabble-rouser
troublemaker
instil°
charge 8
din 2
implant 1
indoctrinate
inject 2
insinuate 3

instil (*cont.*)
plant 6
pound[1] 4
school 4
strike 11
teach
transfuse 1
instilled
rooted
instinct°
feeling 2
intuition
perception 2
instinctive°
automatic 2
brute 1
gut 6
immediate 1
impulsive
inborn
involuntary
mechanical 2
spontaneous 2
unconscious 2
instinctively
naturally 2
instinctual
automatic 2
gut 6
inborn
instinctive 1
involuntary
spontaneous 2
institute°
bring 6
erect 3
establish 1
father 6
fix 2
found 1
inaugurate 1
initiate 1
install 1
institution 2
introduce 4
make 6
organize 2
originate 1
pioneer 2
raise 10
school 1
seminary
society 5
start 7
institution°
admission 2
company 4
establishment 1, 2
formation 2
foundation 3
generation 3
home 3
installation 1
observance 2
organization 3
school 1
seminary
tradition
institutionalize
put 13b
institutor
founder[1]
instruct°
brief 6
charge 10
coach 3
command 1
counsel 4
direct 2, 3
discipline 6
drill 2
educate
enlighten
familiarize
ground 6
guide 4
indoctrinate
initiate 3
order 14
prescribe
prime 5
require 1
school 4
show 4

instruct (*cont.*)
teach
tell[1] 5
train 4
tutor 2
-be instructed in
learn 2
instruction°
bidding 2
charge 5
command 6
counsel 1
dictate 2
direction 1
discipline 1
edification
education 1
guidance 2
illumination 2
injunction 2
knowledge 4
lecture 1
lesson 2
order 4, 7
orientation 2
precept 1
preparation 2
prescription 1
schooling
tuition
word 7
-instructions°
at **instruction 1**
direction 2
formula
manual
instructional
educational 1
instructive
instructive°
educational 2
informative
instructor°
coach 2
master 3
schoolteacher
teacher
tutor 1
instructress
mistress 2
instrument°
agent 2
apparatus
deed 3
device 1
document 1
fixture 2
gadget
implement 1
machine 1
mean[3] 4a
mechanism 1
organ 1
paper 2a
pawn[2]
thing 5
tool 1
vehicle 2
voice 3
-instruments
kit
instrumental°
influential
instrumentalist
player 4
instrumentality
agency
instrument 2
medium 5
tool 2
instrumentation
arrangement 4
insubordinate°
defiant
disobedient 1
insolent
mutinous 2
naughty 2
rebellious 1
recalcitrant
unruly
wild 4
insubordination
rebellion 2

insubstantial°
disembodied
dreamlike
empty 4
feeble 2
filmy 1
flashy 2
flimsy 1, 2
fluffy 2
fragile
insignificant
intangible
meaningless 2
nominal 2
ramshackle
shaky 2
skin-deep
sleazy 1
slight 4
subtle 2
superficial 2
tenuous 2
thin 4
insufferable°
base[2] 6
excruciating
obscene 2
unbearable
insufficiency
absence 2
dearth
defect 1
imperfection
incompetence
lack 1
need 5
poverty 2
scarcity
want 3
insufficient°
deficient 1
disappointing
fall 19
feeble 2
few 1
inadequate 1
incompetent
ineffective 1
little 3
low[1] 2
meagre 1
poor 2
scarce
short 13
slender 3
small 4
straitened
thin 2
unsatisfactory
wanting 1
insufficiently
badly 1
insular
near-sighted 2
parochial
provincial 2
sectarian 2
insularity
provincialism 2
insulate°
cushion 2
steel 2
insult°
abuse 3
cut 3, 23
dig 8
dishonour 1, 4
disparage 2
flout
indignity
injure 2
knock 10
offence 2
offend 1
outrage 3, 4
provocation 2
provoke 3
put-down
slap 5
slight 6, 7
slur 1
taunt 1, 2
wound 2, 4

insulting
abusive 1
contemptuous
derisory
derogatory
disdainful
foul 6
ill-mannered
injurious 2
insolent
irreverent 2
left-handed 2
offensive 2
outrageous 3
personal 4
rude 2
scurrilous
unflattering 2
vituperative
insuperable
invincible 1
insupportable
heavy 4
insufferable
leg 6
prohibitive 2
question 7
untenable
insuppressible
irrepressible
insurance°
assurance 2
indemnity 2
precaution 1
security 3
insure
cover 10
ensure 1, 2
underwrite 1
warrant 3
insurgence
mutiny 1
rebellion 1
sedition
insurgency
mutiny 1
rebellion 1
revolution 1
sedition
insurgent
guerrilla
inflammatory
insubordinate
mutinous 1
rebel 3
rebellious 1
revolutionary 1, 3
seditious
subversive 2
terrorist
traitorous
-insurgents
underground 5
insurrection
mutiny 1
rebellion 1
revolt 1
revolution 1
sedition
tumult
uprising
insurrectional
insubordinate
insurrectionary
mutinous 1
rebellious 1
revolutionary 1, 3
seditious
subversive 1, 2
insurrectionist
agitator
insubordinate
rabble-rouser
rebel 3
revolutionary 1, 3
seditious
subversive 2
traitorous
-insurrectionists
underground 5
insusceptibility
immunity 2

insusceptible
above 5
immune
incapable 2
intact°
complete 1
entire 2
flawless 1
full 12
maiden 2
pure 3
sound[2] 1
unabridged 1
undivided 1
unused 1
whole 1, 2
intacta
maiden 2
intaglio
engraving 1
intake
diet[1] 1
gross 7
intangible°
disembodied
dreamy 1
elusive 2
insubstantial 2
integer
number 1
integral°
intact
organic 2
integrate°
amalgamate
combine 1
coordinate 2
embody 3
incorporate
unify
integrated
organic 3
integration
amalgamation
embodiment 2
marriage 3
synthesis
integrity°
character 3
entirety 1
good 20
gut 3b
honesty 1
honour 1
moral 4
morality 1
nobility 1
principle 3
probity
purity 2
rectitude
right 10
self-respect
sportsmanship
unity 2
virtue 1
integument
film 1
skin 1
surface 1
intellect°
aptitude 3
brain 1
brilliance 2
capacity 2
genius 1
head 4
intellectual 3
intelligence 1
mastermind 2
mentality 1
mind 1, 4
prodigy 1
reason 2
soul 1
thought 6
understanding 5
intellectual°
abstract 1
brain 2
fraternal
highbrow 1, 2
learned
mental 1

intellectual
(*cont.*)
mind 4
platonic
prodigy 1
profound 2
psychic 1
psychological
scholar 1
scholarly
speculative 1
thinking 1
-intellectuals
intelligentsia
intelligence°
advice 2
aptitude 3
brain 1
brilliance 2
capacity 2
genius 2
head 4
history 2
imagination 2
information
intellect 1
judgement 1
knowledge 2
logic 3
low-down
mentality 1
message 1
mind 1
news 1
penetration 2
reason 2
rhyme 2
sense 2
spying
thought 6
understanding 5
wisdom 1
wit 1
word 2
intelligence agent
operative 4
spy 1
intelligent°
acute 5
advisable
astute 2
bright 6
brilliant 4
clever 1, 3
informed 1
judicious
keen[1] 6
knowing 2
knowledgeable 2
logical 2
nimble 2
penetrating 1
perceptive
politic 2
precocious
quick 4
rational 2
ready 6
reasonable 1
receptive 2
sage 1
sensible 1
sharp 3
shrewd
smart 1
thinking 1
well-advised
wise 1
intelligentsia°
intelligibility
clarity 2
sense 4
simplicity 1
intelligible°
clear 6
coherent 2
luminous 3
plain 2
readable 1
simple 1
intemperance
abandon 5
dissipation 1
drunkenness

intemperance (*cont.*)
excess 2
gluttony
intemperate
dissolute
epicurean 1
fast[1] 2
immoderate
inclement
inordinate 1
lavish 3
overdo
prodigal 1
self-indulgent
towering 2
uninhibited
unwarranted
wanton 2
intemperately
fast[1] 9
intemperateness
prodigality 1
intend°
aim 3
contemplate 3
design 4
destine 2
drive 6
get 30b
mean[1] 1
plan 4
propose 2
purpose 5
think 5a
intended
calculated 1
deliberate 1
destined 1
fiancé(e)
intentional
love 3
premeditated
purposeful
supposed 2
sweetheart
voluntary 2
wilful 1
intending
intent 2
intense°
acute 2, 3
ardent
bright 5
burning 2
close 14
deep 3, 4, 6, 8
earnest 1
emphatic
excruciating
exquisite 4
extreme 2
fervent 1, 2
fierce 3
fire 5
forceful 1
full 10
furious 2
heated
heavy 10
hot 3, 4, 8
industrious
intent 4
keen[1] 1, 3
lively 2
mortal 5
passionate 1
piercing 4
poignant 2
powerful 3
profound 3
pungent 3
rich 5
severe 5
sharp 8
soulful
stiff 7
strenuous 2
strong 2, 22
tense 2
torrid 2
towering 2
violent 3

intense (*cont.*)
vivid 1
warm 2
intensely
deep 10
deeply 2
fiercely
hard 13, 14
madly 4
profoundly
warmly 4
intensification
progression 2
intensified
heated
intensive
strong 4
intensify°
aggravate 1
build 4
compound 3
concentrate 2
deepen 2
enhance
gather 5
harden 2
heat 4
heighten 2
hot 11
inflame 2
mount 7
pump 4c
step 18b
worsen 1
intensity°
accent 1
animation 1
depth 4
devotion 3
electricity
energy
expression 4
feeling 4
fervour
fire 2
flame 2
force 1
heat 2
passion 1
severity 3, 5
shade 2
strength 4, 5
violence 1
vitality 1
intensive°
solid 8
intensively
depth 6
hotly
thoroughly 2
warmly 4
intent°
aim 5
attentive 1
bent 4
close 14
deep 4
design 7
determined 1
diligent
effect 3
end 3
fixed 2
hard 7
intention
motive 2
object 3
objective 2
point 6
purpose 1
pursue 3
spirit 6
tenor
view 5
will 1
–to all intents and purposes°
at intent 3
effect 5
outwardly
part 8
practically 1
probably
quasi 1

intent (*cont.*)
substantially
virtually
intention°
aim 5
aspiration
design 7
drift 4
effect 3
end 3
eye 6
import 3
intent 1
meaning 2
mind 5
motive 2
object 3
objective 2
point 6
prospect 2
purpose 1
reason 3
resolution 2
spirit 2, 6
thought 3
view 5
will 1
intentional°
calculated 2
conscious 2
deliberate 1
measured 2
premeditated
purposeful
studied
voluntary 2
wilful 1
intentionally
deliberately
purpose 4a
voluntarily
intently°
hard 13, 15
searchingly
warmly 4
inter
bury 1
interact
cooperate 1
interaction
cooperation 1
give and take
intercourse 1
language 2
volley 3
interactive
mutual 1
interbred
mixed 1
intercalate
insert 1
intercede
chime 5b
chip 4b
interfere 1
intervene 1
step 15
interceder
go-between
mediator
negotiator
peacemaker
interceding
interference 1
intercept°
ambush 2
anticipate 1
catch 9
cut 15b
forestall
head 13a
prevent
waylay 1
intercepting
prevention
interception
prevention
intercession
agency
interference 1
office 5

intercessor
advocate 3
go-between
mediator
negotiator
interchange
alternate 1
alternation
change 1, 5
exchange 1, 2
junction
mix 4d, 6
reverse 2
rotate 2
substitution 1
trade 3, 6
transpose
interchangeable
equal 1
equivalent 1
identical 1
synonymous
interchanging
substitution 1
intercolumniation
interval 3
interconnect
knit 1
interconnected
related 1
relative 1
interconnection
relation 1
intercontinental
extensive 1
international
intercourse°
language 2
relation 6b
society 1
interdependence
link 2
relation 1
interdependent
related 1
interdict
ban 1, 2
black 8
embargo 2
exclude 1
forbid
injunction 1
outlaw 2
prevent
prohibit 1
prohibition 2
restraint 1
suppress 1
taboo 2, 3
veto 1
interdicted
foul 11
illegal
pale[2] 3
taboo 1
unlawful
unmentionable 1
interdicting
prevention
prohibition 1
suppression
interdiction
ban 2
embargo 1
exclusion 1
injunction 1
prevention
prohibition 1
restraint 1
stricture 1
suppression
taboo 2
veto 2
interest°
account 3
activity 2
advantage 2
affair 1
amuse 1
appeal 2
concern 2, 5
curiosity 1

interest (*cont.*)
distract 2
divert 3
enthusiasm 1, 2
field 4
intrigue 1
lot 4
moment 3
occupy 3
part 1, 5
party 3, 5
passion 3
percentage
piece 3, 11
please 1
profit 2
pursuit 3
quota
return 9
revenue
share 1, 2
side 3
spice 2
stake[2] 2
title 5
use 7
welfare
zest 2
–interests°
at interest 3
–in the interest of
behalf
for 5, 7
interested°
concerned 1
curious 1
inquisitive 1
involved 1
keen[1] 7
receptive 1
interesting°
attractive
entertaining
eventful
fine[1] 3
juicy 2
picturesque 1
readable 2
interexchange
alternate 1
interface
surface 1
interfere°
break 18a
butt[2] 2
chime 5b
chip 4b
cut 14
disrupt 2
disturb 1
fiddle 1
finger 2
impose 2
intercept
interrupt 1
intervene 1
intrude
meddle
mess 6
monkey 5
object 4
poke 3
pry 2
snoop 1
step 15
tamper
interference°
curiosity 2
disturbance 1
hitch 4
hurdle 1
inhibition
interruption 1
objection,
static 2
–without interference
direct 7
freely 3
interfere with
destroy 3
disrupt 2
disturb 1

interfere with (*cont.*)
fiddle 1
hamper[1]
hinder 1
inhibit
intercept
interrupt 2
mess 6
molest 2
monkey 5
object 4
obstruct 2
oppose 2
preclude
restrain 2
retard 1
touch 4
upset 5
interfering
curious 2
intrusive
obtrusive
officious
interfile
file 3
shuffle 1
interim
interval 2
meanwhile 1
provisional 1
–in the interim
meanwhile 2
temporarily 1
interior°
bosom 2
bowels
inside 1, 5
interject
break 18a
inject 2
insert 1
interjection°
exclamation
interlace
braid 3
entwine
knit 1
splice 1
tangle 3
twist 1
weave 1
interlacing
mesh 1
interline
line[2] 1
interlock
mesh 4
interlope
meddle
interloper
intruder 1
outsider
interlude°
break 28
delay 5
interval 1
lull 1
recess 2
rest[1] 2
truce 1
intermeddle
meddle
tamper
intermediary°
agent 1
broker
deputy
factor 2
go-between
intermediate 1
liaison 2
mediator
messenger
peacemaker
intermediate°
intermediary
mean[3] 6
intermediation
agency
medium 5
office 5

intermediator
mouthpiece 2
peacemaker
interment
burial
funeral
interminable
continual
continuous 2
endless 2
eternal 2
everlasting
immeasurable
infinite 1
lengthy
limitless
non-stop 2
ongoing 1
persistent 2
protracted
rambling 1
sustained
unlimited 2
vast
interminably
cease 2
for ever 2
length 4b
non-stop 3
permanently
intermingle
blend 1
mingle 1
mix 1
scramble 3
stir 1
weave 2
wed 2
intermingled
promiscuous 3
intermingling
blend 3
confusion 4
mixture 1, 2
wedding 2
intermission°
break 28
gap 1
interlude
interruption 2
interval 1
lapse 2
let-up
lull 1
recess 2
respite 1
rest[1] 2
space 3
suspension 2
truce 1
wait 4
intermit
pause 1
intermittent°
broken 6
fitful
occasional 1
periodic
recurrent
spasmodic 2
sporadic
intermittently
fit[2] 4
now 4
occasionally
piecemeal 1
intermix
mingle 1
shuffle 1
unite 1
wed 2
intermixed
promiscuous 3
intermixing
wedding 2
intern
commit 2
imprison
shut 6a
internal°
civil 2
domestic 3
home 6
internal (*cont.*)
inside 4, 5
interior 1, 2
international°
extensive 1
global
internecine
destructive 1
internee
captive 1
prisoner
internment
captivity
detention
internuncio
delegate 1
go-between
interplay
connection 2
interpolate
insert 1
introduce 5
interpolation
interjection
interpose
break 18a
chip 4b
impose 2
insert 1
interfere 1
intervene 1
introduce 5
intrude
interpret°
analyse 2
decipher 2
define 2
diagnose
explain 1
figure 12b
gloss[2] 2
read 2
render 6
solve
take 19
transcribe 2
translate 1, 3
understand 1, 3
interpretation°
analysis 2
arrangement 4
aspect 2
explanation 1
exposition 2
gloss[2] 1
meaning 3
performance 3
recital 2
rendering
rendition 1
transcript 1
translation 1, 3
trot 4
twist 8
understanding 4
version 1, 2
interpretive
circumstantial 1
explanatory
interrelated
related 1
relative 1
interrogate
ask 1
consult 1
examine 2
interview 3
pump 2
question 9
quiz 2
interrogation°
examination 3
inquiry 1, 2
investigation
interrupt°
arrest 1
break 10, 18a
butt[2] 2
chime 5b
chip 4b
cut 14, 15b
discontinue
disrupt 2
interrupt (*cont.*)
disturb 1
hinder 1
impose 2
intercept
interfere 1
intervene 1
intrude
obstruct 2
pause 1
punctuate 1
short 12b
stay[1] 4
stop 5
suspend 1
interrupted
broken 6
spasmodic 2
interruption°
break 27
check 13
delay 5
disturbance 1
gap 1
hold-up 2
interlude
jump 12
lapse 2
let-up
lull 1
pause 2
respite 1
space 3
stay[1] 6
suspension 2
-without interruption
succession 5
intersect
cross 4
meet[1] 4
overlap 2
traverse 2
intersection
angle[1] 1
joint 1
junction
meeting 3
intersperse
punctuate 1
shuffle 1
interstice
interval 3
mesh 1
intertwine
braid 3
entwine
knit 1
lace 3
splice 1
tangle 3
twine 2
twist 1
weave 1
intertwist
tangle 3
interval°
clearance 1
clip[2] 5
delay 5
distance 1
gap 1
interlude
interruption 2
lapse 2
lull 1
meanwhile 1
patch 4
period 1
remove 8
respite 1
rest[1] 2
run 38
snap 9
space 3
span 2
spell[1] 1
spurt 1
term 2
time 1, 2
truce 1
wait 4
-at intervals
once 4
succession 5
time 14
intervene°
break 18a
interfere 1
intrude
meddle
mess 6
step 15
intervener
negotiator
intervening
intermediate 1
-in the intervening time
meanwhile 2
intervention
agency
interference 1
interview°
apply 6
canvass 2
poll 3
question 9
screen 8
see 9
tête-à-tête 1
word 1
interweave
entwine
knit 1
lace 3
tangle 3
twine 2
twist 1
weave 1
interweaving
mixture 2
tissue
intestinal
instinctive 1
intestines
bowels
gut 1
intimacy
association 3
familiarity 2
fellowship 1, 3
friendship 2
intercourse 2
intrigue 4
sex 2
understanding 3
intimate°
advise 2
announce 2
bosom 4
chummy
close 15
clue 2
confidential
drive 6
express 2
familiar 3
friend 1
great 10
hint 3
impart 2
imply 1
indicate 3
insinuate 1
interior 3
make 37e
mean[1] 2
mention 2
near 7
notify 2
old 8
pal 2
partake 2b
personal 2, 3, 4
predict
private 3
rumour 2
signify 1
snug
special 5
spicy 3
suggest 2
tell[1] 2
tête-à-tête 3
thick 8
intimately
confidence 3
hand 10
immediately 2
tête-à-tête 2
well[1] 13
intimateness
familiarity 2
intimation
clue 1
foreboding 2
hint 1
idea 2
implication 2
import 3
indication 1
inkling
innuendo
lead 14
note 6
notice 5
overtone
prediction
reference 1
shade 3
shadow 3
suggestion 2
threat 2
touch 15
trace 1
intime
intimate[1] 1, 2, 4
tête-à-tête 3
intimidate°
appal
browbeat
bully 2
daunt
deter
discourage 1
dismay 1
enforce 2
face 17
force 7
frighten
get 30d
horrify 1
lean[2] 4b
menace 1
overawe
pick 6
pressure 5
prey 3b
push 7
railroad 2
ride 3
ruffle 3
scare 1
threaten 1
thunder 3
tyrannize
unnerve
intimidated
afraid 1
fearful 2
intimidating
fearsome
formidable 1
frightening
menacing
scary
strong-arm
threatening
intimidation
menace 3
pressure 4
terror 1
threat 1
intimidator
bully 1
oppressor
into
deep 4
for 6
through 4
-be into
get 39c
relate 4
intolerable
beastly 2
grievous 2
heavy 4
inexcusable
insufferable
intolerable (*cont.*)
lamentable
murderous 2
obscene 2
oppressive 1
outrageous 1
repugnant
terrible 1
unbearable
intolerance°
bigotry
discrimination 1
fanaticism 2
prejudice 2
intolerant°
bigoted
discriminate 2
hidebound
inconsiderate
narrow-minded
near-sighted 2
one-sided 1
parochial
prejudiced 2
puritan 2
small-minded
intonation°
accent 3
diction 2
expression 4
pronunciation
tone 2
intone
chant 2
hum 3
sing 1
in toto
entirely 1
full 17
outright 4
wholly 1
intoxicants
liquor 1
intoxicate°
intoxicated
drunk 1
excited 2
high 9
rhapsodic
stinking 3
tight 8
intoxicating°
alcoholic 1
exciting 1
stirring
intoxication
drunkenness
high 16
intractability
obstinacy
intractable
difficult 3
disobedient 1
disorderly 2
fierce 2
grim 1
hard 4
hidebound
implacable
incorrigible
inflexible
monolithic
obstinate
parochial
persevere
perverse 3
problem 3
recalcitrant
relentless 1
resistant 2
rogue 2
self-willed
stony 2
stubborn
tough 6
ungovernable
unruly
wild 4
wilful 2
intransferable
inalienable

investigate (*cont.*)
sound[3] 1
study 3
survey 1
trace 5
traverse 4
treat 2
vet

investigating
research 1

investigation°
analysis 1
canvass 4
examination 1
experiment 1
exploration
inquiry 1
interrogation
probe 3
reconnaissance
research 1
scrutiny
study 4,5
survey 3
test 1

investigative
inquisitive 1

investigator
detective
operative 3
sleuth

investiture
admission 2
initiation 2
installation 1

investment
backing 2
finance 1
interest 4
principal 5
stake[2] 2
stock 5
subscription 1

investor
backer 2
benefactor
financier
friend 4

inveterate
chronic 1,2
habitual 2
incorrigible
incurable 2
ingrained
steady 5

inveterately
usually

invidious
cutting 2
malignant 2
spiteful

invigilator
monitor 1

invigorant
tonic 1

invigorate
animate 1
energize
enliven 1
excite 1
fortify 2
freshen 2
inspire 1
intoxicate 2
liven 2
pep 2
perk up
quicken 3
raise 13
refresh 1
rouse 2
spice 4
strengthen 2
tone 6
vitalize
wind[2] 4c

invigorated
drunk 2
energetic
fresh 5
passionate 1
perky

invigorating°
bracing
brisk 3,4
cheerful 2
exciting 1
exhilarating 1
hearty 4
intoxicating 2
refreshing
rousing
scintillating 2
spanking 2
tonic 2
vital 4

invigoration
animation 2
refreshment 2

invincible°
impregnable
indomitable

inviolable
impregnable
inalienable
sacred 2

inviolate
entire 2
intact
sacred 2

invisible°
imperceptible 1
sight 6a

invitation°
bidding 1
call 14
challenge 5
temptation 2

invite
appeal 2
ask 4,6a
attract
bear 3
bid 2
bring 2
call 4
challenge 2
incur
invitation 1
run 16
seek 3
summon 1
take 36
tempt 1

invited
welcome 3

inviting°
attractive
interesting
magnetic
pleasant 1
prepossessing
provocative 1
seductive
sexy 1
tempting 1
voluptuous 2

invocation
litany 1
prayer 2

invoice
bill[1] 1,3
charge 12
damage 2
reckoning 2

invoke
bring 6
call 7a,9
evoke
summon 2

involuntarily
protest 2

involuntary°
automatic 2
impulsive
instinctive 2
mechanical 2
spontaneous 2
unconscious 2
unpremeditated
willy-nilly 2

involuted
tortuous 1

involve°
busy 4
catch 14a
come 18c
concern 1,2
employ 3
engage 2
entail
entangle 1
go 28b
hold 4
immerse 2
implicate 1,2
imply 2
include 3
incriminate
interest 8
mesh 3
mix 5
occupy 3
regard 5

involved°
busy 1
come 18c
complicated
compound 4
concern 1
concerned 1
deep 4
elaborate 1
engaged 2
feature 5
finger 2
get 39c,52
hard 3
interested 1,2
intricate 1
involve 3
mire 3
mixed 3
part 11
participate
perplexing
profound 1
stake[2] 3
step 15
take 10,39c
thorny 2
tortuous 2
welter 2
wrap 2

involvedness
profoundity 1

involvement
complexity 2
complication 1
concern 4
experience 1
hand 3
implication 1
inclusion
interest 4
part 3
perplexity 2
profundity 1
stake[2] 2
tie 8

involving
about 11

invulnerability
immunity 1

invulnerable
immune
impregnable
invincible 2
monolithic

inward
interior 1

inwards
deeply 1
gut 1

iota
bit 2
dot 1
grain 3
jot 2
modicum
particle
scrap[1] 1
shade 3
shred 1
spark 1
speck
stroke 8

iota (*cont.*)
suggestion 2
trace 2
trifle 2

IQ
mentality 1

irascibility
temper 3

irascible
angry 1
bad 7
cantankerous
cranky 2
cross 6
edge 5
fiery 3
fretful
gruff 1
harsh 3
hasty 4
impatient 2
irritable
nasty 4
passionate 3
perverse 2
petulant
pugnacious
quarrelsome
querulous
quick 5
quick-tempered
sensitive 2
short-tempered
snappish 1
temperamental 1
testy
touchy 1
ugly 4
warm 2
waspish

irate
angry 1
cross 7
furious 1
indignant
mad 4
resentful
upset 10
warm 2

ire
anger 1
displeasure 2
fury 1
indignation
madden 1
outrage 2
rage 1
resentment

ireful
angry 1

iridescent
opalescent

Irish briar
pipe 2

Irish bull
howler

irk°
annoy 1
bug 7
displease
disturb 1
exasperate 2
gall[2] 4
get 17
gnaw 3
grate 3
inconvenience 3
infuriate
jar[2] 3
madden 2
molest 1
nag[1] 1
pall[2] 1
pester
plague 3
prod 3
provoke 3
put 23b
rankle
rasp 4
rub 8
tire 2
torment 2
trouble 2

irk (*cont.*)
worry 2

irked
indignant
resentful
sore 4
tired 2

irksome°
burdensome
grating 1
inconvenient
nerve-racking
niggling 1
painful 2
provocative 2
tiresome 2
tough 5
troublesome
trying
weary 2
wicked 5

iron
flatten 1
grim 1
press 4
rigid 2
smooth 9
steely 2

in irons
imprison
manacle 2

-irons
manacle 1,2
shackle 1

iron-fisted
strict 2

iron hand
oppressor

iron-handed
dictatorial 2
heavy-handed 2
severe 1
tyrannical

iron horse
railway

ironic(al)
derisory
dry 3
incisive 2
sarcastic
sardonic
satirical
wry 2

ironically
tongue 5

ironmonger
seller

ironmongery
hardware 1

irony
sarcasm
satire 1

irradiate
radiate 2

irrational
absurd 2
arbitrary 1
blind 3
brute 1
circular 3
delirious 1
deranged
disconnected 2
distraught
emotional 4
fantastic 2
foolish 2,3
gratuitous 2
hysterical 1
inarticulate 1
incoherent
insane 2
instinctive 2
mad 2
neurotic
nonsensical
preposterous
raving 1
senseless 3
silly 1
stupid 2
unreasonable 1
unthinking 1

irrational (*cont.*)
violent 1
wild 5,7

irrationality
absurdity 1
extravagance 2
folly 1
insanity 2
lunacy 2
stupidity 2

irrationally
blindly
fault 7
madly 2
unduly 1

irreclaimable
irretrievable 1
lost 6

irreconcilable
incompatible
opposing
opposite 2
pole[2] 3

irrecoverable
irretrievable 1
lost 1

irredeemable
incurable 2
invaluable
irretrievable 2
irreversible
reprobate 1

irrefutability
finality

irrefutable
certain 4
decided 1
final 2
flawless 2
incontrovertible
indisputable
peremptory 1
positive 1
solid 7
strong 8
undisputed
unquestionable

irrefutably
undoubtedly

irregardless
regardless 1,2

irregular°
abnormal 1,2
bizarre 2
bumpy
casual 2
changeable 1
chaotic 1
curious 3
desultory
disorderly 1
disproportionate
eccentric 1
erratic 1
exceptional 1
fitful
guerrilla
illegitimate 3
improper 1
inconsistent 2
inordinate 2
intermittent
kinky 1
lopsided 1
occasional 1
odd 2
pale[2] 3
partisan 2,4
perverse 1
queer 1
ragged 2
rambling 2
reject 4
rough 1
rugged 1
spasmodic 2
sporadic
spotty 3
uncertain 4
unorthodox
unstable 1
unwonted

-irregulars
resistance 3

irregularity
abnormality 1
break 27
cast 5
defect 1, 2
disproportion
eccentricity 1
exception 3
freak 2
impropriety 1
inconstancy
oddity 3
peculiarity 1
perversion 1
turn 27
twist 10
irregularly
fit[2] 4
infrequently
occasionally
random 2
irrelevance
indifference 2
irrelevant°
extraneous 2
extrinsic
inapplicable
inappropriate
meaningless 2
peripheral 1
point 15
remote 4
tangential
irreligious
blasphemous
heathen 2
impious
irreverent 1
profane 1
sinful
ungodly 1
wicked 1
irremediable
hopeless 1
incurable 1
irretrievable 2
lost 6
irreparable
hopeless 1
incurable 2
irretrievable 2
irrevocable
lost 6
irrepealable
irrevocable
irreplaceable
invaluable
precious 1
priceless 1
irrepressible°
effervescent 2
enthusiastic
indomitable
inextinguishable
irresistible 1
obstreperous
unquenchable
irreproachable°
blameless
faultless
spotless 2
worthwhile 2
irresistibility
magnetism
irresistible°
forceful 2
inviting
magnetic
overpowering
overwhelming 1
provocative 1
seductive
taking
tempting 1
unavoidable
irresistibly
necessarily
irresolute°
faint-hearted 2
fence 2
fickle
hesitant 1
inconstant
indecisive 1

irresolute *(cont.)*
infirm 2
spineless 2
uncertain 2
unresolved
unstable 1
vague 5
weak 3
wet 3
wishy-washy 1
irresoluteness
weakness 2
irresolution
doubt 4
indecision
suspense 1
weakness 2
irrespective of°
independent 8
irresponsibility
insanity 2
stupidity 2
irresponsible°
careless 1
derelict 2
fast[1] 2
fickle
flighty 2
fly-by-night 2
foolhardy
frivolous 2
giddy 2
imprudent
insane 2
promiscuous 1
puerile
reckless
shiftless
silly 1
stupid 2
unreliable
wanton 3
irresponsibly
fast[1] 9
irrestrainable
irrepressible
irretrievable°
hopeless 1
irreversible
irrevocable
irretrievably
inextricably
irreverence
dishonour 4
disrespect
flippancy 2
sacrilege 2
sin 2
irreverent°
blasphemous
disrespectful
flippant 2
impious
profane 1
sacrilegious
satirical
sinful
irreverently
vain 3b
violate 2
irreversibility
finality
resolution 1
irreversible°
final 2
irretrievable 2
irrevocable
resolute
irrevocable°
final 2
flat 10
inevitable
irretrievable 2
irreversible
irrevocableness
finality
irrevocably
deeply 2
finally 2
flat 16
irrigate
rinse 1
water 6

irrigation
rinse 3
irritability
anger 1
sensitivity 1
temper 3
irritable°
angry 1
bad 7
cantankerous
cranky 2
cross 6
edge 5
fiery 3
fretful
gruff 1
hasty 4
impatient 2
moody 2
passionate 3
peevish
perverse 2
petulant
prickly 3
pugnacious
quarrelsome
querulous
quick 5
quick-tempered
ratty 1
sensitive 2
short-tempered
snappish 1
temperamental 1
testy
touchy 1
warm 2
irritant
annoyance 2
bind 6
bother 7
nuisance 1
pest
thorn 2
trial 5
irritate°
aggravate 2
anger 2
annoy 1
bother 1
bug 7
chafe 2, 3
displease
disturb 1
exasperate 2
exercise 3
fret 2
gall[2] 3, 4
get 17
gnaw 3
grate 3
harass
heckle
inconvenience 3
infuriate
irk
jangle 2
jar[2] 3
madden 2
molest 1
nag[1] 1
nerve 3
offend 1
pall[2] 1
persecute 2
pester
pick 4a
plague 3
prod 3
provoke 3
put 23b
rasp 4
ride 3
rub 8
spite 3
tease 1
tire 2
torment 2
trouble 2
wall 3
wear 7
irritated
angry 1, 2
cross 6, 7
discontented

irritated *(cont.)*
disgruntled
huff 1
indignant
inflamed
mad 4
querulous
ratty 1
resentful
sick 6
sore 1, 4
tired 2
warm 2
irritating
bitter 2
grating 1
inconvenient
irksome
nerve-racking
niggling 1
painful 2
provocative 2
scratchy 1
tiresome 2
troublesome
trying
untoward 2
weary 2
wicked 5
irritation
anger 1
annoyance 1
bind 6
bother 5
chafe 4
discomfort 2
displeasure 2
dissatisfaction 2
gall[2] 2
indignation
inflammation
itch 3
nuisance 1
pain 3
persecution 2
plague 2
provocation 2
resentment
thorn 2
torment 4
trial 5
trouble 6
warmth 4
worry 3
island°
pocket 3
isle
island
Isles of the Blessed
heaven 1
paradise 1
islet
island
ism
sect 2
isolate°
dissociate
insulate 1
maroon
ostracize
segregate
shut 4b
isolated°
back 12
deserted
desolate 1
detached 1
out-of-the-way 1
parochial
particular 1
reclusive
remote 2
secluded 1
separate 5, 7
single 2
singular 3
stray 6
withdrawn 2
isolation
privacy 1
retreat 2
seclusion
segregation

isolation *(cont.)*
solitude 1
isolationist
nationalistic
isometrics
exercise 4
issuance
circulation 2
distribution 2
issue 1, 6
publication 1
issue°
affair 1
bring 13b
business 2
cause 4
child 1
circulate 2
come 15b
concern 8
derive 2
descendant
dispense 1
distribute 1
edition
emanate 1
emerge 2
emit
escape 3
event 2
exhale
exhaust 5
family 2
flow 2, 3
follow 7
give 8, 15b, 15c
grow 2
impression 4
litter 2
matter 2
measure 14
number 3
offspring
originate 2
pass 9
point 10
posterity
pour 4
print 1
proceed 2
product 1
progeny
put 17d, 23e
question 3
release 2
resolution 4
result 1
run 6
seed 3
sequel
stem[1] 3
stream 4, 5
subject 1
text 3
topic
upshot
vent 4
young 4
-at issue°
at **issue 8**
moot 1
question 6b
issuing
circulation 2
issue 6
it
limit 4a
punch[1] 3
itch°
burn 3
hanker
hunger 2
passion 3
prickle 2, 3
spoil 5
thirst 1
urge 5
wish 5
yearn
itchiness
fidget 3
prickle 2

itching
keen[1] 1
thirsty 2
itchy
eager
edge 5
excited 1
impatient 1
prickly 2
restless
scratchy 1
item°
detail 1
entry 4
fact 3
feature 2
news 4
object 1
particular 5
point 10
puff 3
story 4
thing 1, 2, 5
unit
item-by-item
detail 4
particular 3
itemization
breakdown 3
specification 2
table 3
tally 3
itemize°
detail 5
enumerate 1
list[1] 2
record 1
reel 2
specify
tabulate
tally 2
itemized
detailed 1
particular 3
itemizing
specification 2
iterate
parallel 4
reiterate
iteration
echo 1
tautology
iterative
expletive 1
frequent 1
periodic
recurrent
repetitive
ithyphallic
indecent 2
itinerant
migrant 1, 2
pedestrian 1
rambling 3
rover
travelling
vagabond 1, 2
itinerary
route 1
itsy-bitsy
little 1
minute[2] 1
tiny
wee 1
itty-bitty
little 1
minute[2] 1
tiny
wee 1
ivory
white 1
ivory-tower(ed)
academic 2
scholarly

J

jab°
dig 2, 7
jolt 2
knock 9
lunge 1, 3

nudge 1,2
poke 1,5,6
prick 3
prickle 4
prod 1,4
punch[1] 1,2
stab 1,3
stick[1] 1
thrust 2
jabber°
babble 1,3
chatter 1
drivel 2
gab 1,2
gibberish
gush 2
jargon 2
palaver 2,4
patter[2] 2,3
prattle 1,2
rattle 6
talk 3
tattle 2
waffle 1,3
yap 2
jabbering
chatter 3
patter[2] 2
prattle 2
jabberwocky
gitterish
jargon 2
mumbo-jumbo 1
nonsense 1
prattle 3
jack
flag[1] 1
pennant
streamer
jackal
flunkey 2
parasite
yes-man
jackanapes
pup
jackass
fool 1
silly 3
jacket
coat 1
cover 12
wrapper 2
Jack Ketch
hangman
jackknife
blade 2
jackpot
pool 2
pot 2
prize[1] 2
windfall
Jack Robinson
-before you can say 'Jack Robinson'
fast[1] 6
flash 3
hastily 1
immediately 1
minute[1] 1
moment 1
once 6a
post-haste
rapidly 2
shot 10
swiftly
jackstaff
pole[1]
Jack Tar
sailor
jack up
raise 6
jade°
bore[2] 2
fag 1
glut 4
nag[2]
pall[2] 1
satiate 1
tart[2] 2
jaded°
blasé 1
surfeited
jaded (*cont.*)
weary 3,4
worn 3
jag°
bender
drunk 4
orgy 1
spree
jagged°
irregular 1
ragged 2
rough 1
rugged 1
serrated
jail°
hold 6
hole 4
imprison
keep 9
lock[1] 9
nick 2
prison
punish 2
put 13b
restrain 3
run 27
send 5,9b
shut 6a
stir 7
-in jail
inside 7
jailbird
convict 2
inmate
prisoner
jailbreak
escape 5
jailer°
screw
jail-house
stir 7
jailing
punishment 2
jalopy
car 1
rattletrap
jam°
abound 2
bind 5
clog
cram 1
crowd 4,5
difficulty 3
dilemma
fill 1
fix 17
foul 13
huddle 3
load 3
mess 3
mob 1
pack 5
pile[1] 6
pinch 8
plight
plug 4
predicament
preserve 4
press 1
ram 1
seize 6
snarl[2] 2
spread 12
squeeze 4,9
stop 3
stow
strait 3
stuff 6
tangle 1,3
throng 1,2
thrust 1
tie-up 1
wedge 3
jamboree°
fête 1
revel 3
jammed
abound 2
congested
full 1
loaded 1
overcrowded
packed
populous
jammed (*cont.*)
replete 1
solid 2
thick 2
jam-packed
full 1
overcrowded
packed
populous
replete 1
solid 2
Jane Doe, Jane Roe
mass 6
people 3
jangle°
chime 2
ring[2] 1,3
jangling
discordant 2
grating 2
jangle 3
ring[2] 3
janitor
porter[2] 1
Janus-faced
insincere
perfidious
shifty
two-faced
jape
lark 1
prank
trick 2
jar°
clash 4
electrify 1
grate 3
jangle 2
jog 2
jolt 1,4
jug
rasp 4
rattle 2
rock[2] 3
shake 9
shock 1
startle
stun 2
jargon°
cant 2
dialect
gibberish
gobbledegook 1
idiom 1
language 1,3
lingo
nonsense 1
parlance
shibboleth
speech 3
talk 19
terminology
vernacular 3
jarring
bumpy
discordant 2
grating 1
hustle 5
incompatible
jangle 3
noisy
raucous
rough 8
shake 9
startling
strident
jaundice
prejudice 1,3
jaundiced°
biased
bigoted
disenchanted
intolerant 2
opinionated 2
partial 2
prejudiced 1
jaunt
excursion 1
journey 1
outing
ride 4
roam
run 36
jaunt (*cont.*)
spin 7
tour 1
trip 3
jauntily
gaily 2
jaunty°
buoyant 2
debonair 2
flamboyant 2
perk up
perky
pert 2
rakish
smart 5
sprightly
vivacious
javelin
lance 1
jaw
chat 2
chatter 1
gab 1
gossip 4
palaver 4
prattle 1
talk 3
yap 2
-jaws
bill[2]
mouth 1
jawing
palaver 2
prattle 2
jay
fool 1
Jayhawker
guerrilla
jazz
frill 2
jazzy
flashy 1
loud 2
jealous°
envious
jaundiced 2
protective
resent
resentful
jealously°
jealousy
envy 1
resentment
jeer°
deride
dig 8
flout
gibe 1,2
heckle
hiss 2,3
laugh 2a
mock 1
poke 4
ridicule 1
scoff[1]
sneer 2,3
snicker 1
taunt 1,2
twit[1]
jeer at°
at **jeer 1**
deride
gibe 1
laugh 2a
leg 8
mock 1
poke 4
ridicule 2
scoff[1]
scorn 4
sneer 2
snicker 1
taunt 1
thumb 8
twit[1]
jeering
derisory
disdainful
ridicule 1
scorn 2
sneer 3
jehad
crusade 1
Jehovah
lord 3
jejune
banal
flat 5
humdrum
immature 2
pedestrian 2
prosaic
stodgy
vapid
jell°
coagulate
set 3
solidify 1
stiffen 1
thicken
jelled
thick 5
jellied
thick 5
jelly
preserve 4
spread 12
jellyfish
weakling
jemmy
force 8
je ne sais quoi
quality 1
jeopardize°
adventure 3
chance 8
endanger
expose 2
hazard 3
pawn[1] 2
risk 2
stake[2] 4
threaten 2
venture 3
jeopardized
stake[2] 3
jeopardy°
danger 1
exposure 2
hazard 1
peril
risk 1
-in jeopardy
endanger
stake[2] 3
threaten 2
jeremiad
tirade
jerk°
bugger 2
clod 2
clown 2
dolt
fool 1
hitch 2
jar[2] 1
jiggle 1,2
jog 3
jolt 1,4
jump 2,11
pluck 3
pull 2,19
recoil 1
retard 2
shudder 1
silly 3
toss 2
tug 1,2
tweak 1,2
twit[2]
whip 6
wrench 1,4
yank 1,2
jerking
spasmodic 1
jerky
bumpy
spasmodic 1
stupid 1
jerry-build
throw 9d
jerry-built
flimsy 1
ramshackle
sleazy 1
jest
fool 5
gag[2] 1
humour 2
joke 1,4
laugh 2a
prank
put-on 1
quip 1,2
sport 2
wisecrack 1
witticism
-in jest
fun 3
tongue 5
-jests
humour 2
jester
clown 1
comedian
fool 2
joker 1
wag[2]
zany 2
jesting
banter
fun 2
nonsense 2
playful 2
raillery
jestingly
tongue 5
Jesuitic(al)
evasive
legalistic
plausible 2
sophistic
subtle 3
Jesus
lord 3
saviour 2
jet
black 1
fly 5
fountain 1
gush 1,3
plane 2
spout 1
spurt 3
stream 4
well[2] 2
jet-black
black 1,3
dark 1
dusky 1
pitch-black
swarthy
jet set
élite 1
jet-setter
sybarite
traveller
-jet-setters
élite 1
jettison
discard 1
dispose 3b
dump 2
forsake 2
junk 2
reject 3
throw 5a
jetty
dock 1
landing 3
pier 1
jeu de mots
epigram 1
jeu d'esprit
epigram 1
jewel°
gem 1
masterpiece
pride 3
treasure 2
-jewels
jewellery
jewellery°
Jezebel
wanton 5
jib
hesitate 1

jibber-jabber
babble 3
chatter 1
drivel 2
gab 2
gibberish
patter[2] 3
prattle 1
talk 3
waffle 3
jibe
agree 1
check 5
coincide
cut 23
flout
gibe 1,2
jeer 1,2
parallel 4
ridicule 1,2
shaft 3
squelch 2
stack 7a
tally 1
twit[1]
wisecrack 1,2
jibing
coincidence 2
ridicule 1
jiffy
flash 3
instant 2
minute[1] 1
moment 1
second[2]
twinkling 1
-in a jiffy
immediately 1
once 6a
presently
rapidly 2
soon 1
swiftly
jig
jerk 2
jiggle 1,2
jigger
drink 6
shot 7
spar[1]
jiggered
fatigued
jiggery-pokery
hanky-panky
hocus-pocus 1
trickery
jiggle°
jar[2] 1
jerk 2
rattle 2
shake 2,8
toss 3
wriggle 1
jihad
crusade 1
jilt°
abandon 3
desert[1] 3
drop 7
forsake 2
lurch[1]
reject 2
stand 10c
throw 8
jilted
abandoned 1
Jim Crowism
prejudice 2
segregation
jim-jams
fidget 3
jingle°
chime 2
jangle 1
piece 4
poem
ring[2] 1,2,3,4
jingling
ring[2] 3
jingo
patriot
jingoism°
jingoist(ic)
belligerent 1,3
militant 1
national 2
nationalistic
patriot
patriotic
warlike
jinx°
enchantment 1
jinxed
poor 6
unhappy 2
unsuccessful 2
jitteriness
tension 2
jitters°
dread 2
fidget 3
nerve 4
tension 2
jittery
afraid 1
agitated
fearful 2
jumpy
nervous 1
overwrought 1
panic-stricken
restless
sinking 1
tense 2
tremulous 1
jive
moonshine 2
job°
activity 2
appointment 3
assignment 2
business 2
calling
capacity 3
caper 2
career 1
duty 1
employment 1
engagement 4
function 1
game 4
labour 3
let[1] 3
line[1] 7
mission 1
occupation 1
office 4
opening 3
place 5
position 6
post[2] 1
profession 1
project 2
racket 3
responsibility 2
role 2
situation 3
slot 2
stint 1
task 1
trade 2
vocation
work 2
-out of a job
inactive 2
unemployed
jobber
dealer
merchant 3
jobbery
graft[2]
job history
résumé 2
jobless
idle 2
inactive 2
unemployed
work 6
job lot
miscellany
job out°
at **job 6**
let[1] 3
Job's comforter
misery 4
jock
player 1
jockey
manoeuvre 4
jocose
comic 1
funny 1
humorous
jolly 1
ludicrous
jocoseness
humour 1
jocosity
humour 1
jocular
comic 1
flippant 1
funny 1
humorous
jolly 1
ludicrous
witty
jocularity
flippancy 1
fun 2
humour 1
wit 2
jocularly
tongue 5
jocund
jolly 1
joyful 1
jocundity
joy 2
mirth
Joe Bloggs
people 3
jog°
jar[2] 1
jiggle 1,2
nudge 1,2
poke 1,5
refresh 2
remind
run 1,35
trot 1,3
work 19a
jogger
runner 1
joggle
jar[2] 1
jiggle 1,2
jog 3
rattle 2
shake 2,8
toss 3
john
facility 2b
toilet 1
John Barley-corn
alcohol
booze 1
liquor 1
whisky
John Doe, John Roe
mass 6
people 3
John Hancock
sign 7
John Q. Public
hoi polloi
mass 6
people 3
public 8
unwashed 2
joie de vivre
gaiety 1
join°
add 1
ally 2
amalgamate
associate 1a
attach 1,2
bracket 4
bridge 4
butt[2] 1
cement 2
close 8b
club 6
collaborate
combine 1
join (*cont.*)
connect 1,3
converge
cooperate 1
couple 3
cross 4
encounter 3
enlist 1
enrol 1
enter 5
fall 15
fasten 1
fit[1] 6
gang 3
graft[1] 2
hitch 1
integrate
knit 1,2
league 3
link 3
lock[1] 4
lump[1] 3
marry 1,2
match 5
mate 4,6
meet[1] 4
merge
mingle 1,2
mix 2
nail 7
pair 2
part 11
participate
play 2
side 10
sign 10a
sit 6a
splice 1
stick[1] 4,16a
string 8
suffix 2
tack 5
team 3
tie 1,3
twin 3
unify
unite 2
wade 3a
weave 2
wed 1,2
weld 1
join battle
engage 5
join combat
engage 5
joined
affiliated
attached 1
one 2
join forces
club 6
collaborate
cooperate 1
gang 3
hang 11a
league 3
stick[1] 16a
unite 2
join in
chime 5a
part 11
participate
play 2
sit 6a
wade 3a
joining
addition 1
amalgamation
association 2
attachment 2
connection 1
junction
meeting 3
splice 2
union 1
wedding 2
joining together
assembly 3
joint°
common 2
connection 1
dive 3
hole 3
mutual 2
pub
joint (*cont.*)
reciprocal
related 1
seam 1
segment 1
splice 2
union 3
united 1,2
weld 2
jointed°
joint effort
give and take
jointly
cooperate 1
hand 10
shoulder 5
side 6
join together
assemble 2,3
band[2] 3
club 6
connect 1
knit 1
team 3
join up
ally 2
enlist 1
enrol 1
sign 10a
team 3
joke°
amusement 1
fool 5
fun 3
gag[2] 1
giggle 3
humour 2
laugh 2a
limit 4b
mockery 3
nonsense 2
one 5
prank
put-on 1
quip 1,2
story 1
trick 2
wisecrack 1,2
witticism
-jokes
humour 2
nonsense 2
joker°
card 11
fool 2
wag[2]
wit 3
zany 2
jokesmith
comedianc
jokester
fool 2
joker 1
wag[2]
joking
banter
chaff 1
fun 2
nonsense 2
playful 2
raillery
wit 2
joking aside
indeed 1
seriously 2
jokingly
fun 3
tongue 5
jollification
festivity 1
frolic 1
jollity
festivity 1
frolic 1
fun 1
gaiety 1
glee
hilarity
joy 2
merriment
mirth
revelry
jolly°
bully 3
cajole
cheerful 1
coax
gala 2
gleeful
hilarious
humour 4
jaunty 1
joyful 1
light[2] 9
merry 1
perfectly 4
pert 2
sunny 2
very 1
jolly along°
at **jolly 2**
cajole
play 8b
jolly-boat
tender[3] 1
jollying
cajolery
jolt°
blow[2] 2
electrify 1
hit 12
jar[2] 1,4
jerk 2,4
jog 3
jump 11
kindle
rattle 4
shake 9
shock 1,3,4
stagger 2
startle
stimulate 1
stun 2
surprise 4
yank 1,2
jolting
shake 9
sight 6b
Jonah
jinx 2
jongleur
minstrel
josh
chaff 2
fool 4
ridicule 2
joshing
chaff 1
ridicule 1
jostle
hustle 3
jolt 1
mob 3
poke 1,5
push 3
shoulder 7
thrust 1
jostling
hustle 5
jot°
bit 2
dot 1
grain 3
modicum, particle
pinch 7
scrap[1] 1
shade 3
shred 1
spark 1
speck
touch 15
trace 2
trifle 2
jot down°
at **jot 1**
enter 3
note 12
pen[1] 2
put 16a
register 3
set 17a
write 4a
jot or tittle
damn 4
grain 3

jot or tittle (*cont.*)
spark 1
speck
stroke 8
suggestion 2

jotter
pad 2

jotting
item 2
note 10
notation 1

jounce
jar[2] 1
jog 3
rattle 4
shake 9

jouncing
shake 9

journal°
chronology
diary
magazine 1
memoir 1
minute[1] 2
organ 2
paper 1
periodical
publication 2
rag[1] 2
record 3
register 1
review 7
sheet 6

journalist°
correspondent
editor
reporter
scribe 2
writer

–journalists
press 10b

journey°
cruise 1, 2
drive 3, 7
errand 1
excursion 1
expedition 1
flight[1] 2
get 10, 11
hop 4
navigate 1
passage 7
pilgrimage
ride 1, 4
run 36
step 10a
tour 1, 4
travel 2, 3
trip 3, 7

journeying
step 10a

journeyman
tradesman 2

journey's end
destination

journo
scribe 2
writer

–journos
press 10b

joust (with)
combat 5
compete
encounter 3
fight 1
tilt 2, 4

jovial
gala 2
gay 2
gleeful
hilarious
jaunty 1
jolly 1
joyful 1
light[2] 9
mellow 4
merry 1

joviality
gaiety 1
glee
hilarity
joy 2

joviality (*cont.*)
merriment
mirth

joy°
bliss
cheer 2
delight 3
ecstasy 1
enjoyment 1
exuberance 1
fun 1
gaiety 1
glee
happiness
heaven 3
honour 3
paradise 3
pleasure 1
radiance 2
rapture
satisfaction 1
sparkle 4
treasure 2
triumph 2

joyful°
blithe 1
cheerful 1
delightful 1
ecstatic
elated
elevated 3
exalted 3
exuberant 1, 2
exultant
gala 2
gay 2
glad 1
gleeful
golden 4
happy 1
hilarious
jolly 1
light[2] 9
merry 1
radiant 2
rapt 2
rapturous
sunny 2
triumphal

joyfully
gaily 2
happily 2

joyfulness
exuberance 1
festivity 1
gaiety 1
glee
happiness
hilarity
joy 2
merriment
rapture

joyless°
dark 3
desolate 3
dismal
doleful
dreary 1
forlorn 1
gloomy 2
mournful 1
pessimistic
sombre 1
sunless
terrible 3
wretched 2

joyous
blithe 1
cheerful 1
elated
exalted 3
gala 2
gay 2
gleeful
golden 4
happy 1
hilarious
joyful 1
merry 1
radiant 2
rapt 2
rapturous
sunny 2

joyously
gaily 2
happily 2

joyousness
bliss
gaiety 1
glee
happiness
joy 2
mirth
rapture

joyride
run 36
spin 7

jubilant
blithe 1
cheerful 1
elated
exalted 3
exultant
gay 2
gleeful
happy 1
jaunty 1
jolly 1
joyful 1, 2
merry 1
overjoyed
radiant 2
triumphal

jubilantly
gaily 2

jubilation
festivity 1
gaiety 1
glee
happiness
hilarity
joy 2
merriment
triumph 2

jubilee
feast 2
jamboree

Judas
snake 2
traitor

Judas kiss
stab 6

judder
vibrate

judge°
authority 3
choose
consider 3
count 2
criticize 1
decide 1
determine 1
distinguish 1
esteem 2
estimate 1, 2
evaluate 2
feel 4
figure 9
find 9
gauge 2
go 26b
guess 2
hold 7
imagine 2
intermediary
make 21
measure 11
mediator
mind 13
moderate 6
moderator
officiate
pace 4
perceive 3
pronounce 2
rate[1] 6
reckon 2
regard 4
review 3
rule 7
say 6
size 3
speculate 1
take 8, 19
think 2, 5b
try 2, 4
umpire 1, 2

judge (*cont.*)
view 9
weigh 3

judged
reputed

judgelike
judicial 3

judgement°
analysis 2
belief 4
capacity 2
conscience
counsel 1
criticism 1
decision 2
decree 1
determination 2
discretion 1, 2
discrimination 2
estimate 4
estimation 1
evaluation 2
experience 3
expertise
eye 3
finding 2
guess 3
gumption 1
insight
intellect 1
logic 2
lunacy 2
measurement 1
mentality 1
mind 6
opinion 1
pronouncement 2
prudence 1
reason 2, 7
reckoning 3
resolution 3
review 4
sense 2
sentence
sentiment 2
tact
taste 4
thinking 2
understanding 4
view 2
wisdom 1
wit 1

judgemental
critical 1

judicator
judge 2

judicatory
judicial 1

judicature
chamber 1

judicial°
legal 3

judicial proceeding
trial 2

judiciary
chamber 1
judicial 1
legal 3
tribunal

judicious°
advisable
discreet
equitable
judicial 2
logical 2
moderate 1
objective 1
philosophical 2
politic 2
practical 2
provident 1
prudent 1
reasonable 1
sage 1
sane
sensible 1
sound[2] 4
tactful
wise 1, 3

judiciousness
equity
judgement 1
justice 3

judiciousness (*cont.*)
logic 3
tact
wisdom 1

jug°
jail 1
jar[1]
mug 1
prison
put 13b

–jugs
bosom 1

juggle°
manipulate 3
rig 2
twiddle 1

jugglery
hocus-pocus 3

juice°
alcohol
booze 1
liquid 1
liquor 1
sap[1] 1

juice-head
drunk 3

juicer
drunk 3
soak 3

juicy°
luscious
lush 2
mellow 1
succulent

ju-ju
talisman

Juke
boor 1

juke-joint
dive 3

jumble°
assortment 2
clutter 1
confuse 3
confusion 1
disorder 1, 4
garble 2
hash 1, 3
hotchpotch
lumber 1
medley
mess 1
miscellany
mishmash
mix 4c
mix-up
mixture 1
muddle 2, 4
patchwork
pot-pourri
rummage 2
scramble 3
shuffle 1
tangle 1, 2, 3
tumble 2
upset 3
welter 1

jumbled
chaotic 1
confused 1, 3
disjointed 2
disorderly 1
helter-skelter 1
inarticulate 1
incoherent
indiscriminate 2
promiscuous 3
rambling 1
topsy-turvy 2
untidy
upset 9

jumble sale
sale 3

jumbo°
big 1
colossal 1
gigantic
huge
immense
large 3
massive
monstrous 3

jumbo (*cont.*)
thumping 1
vast

jump°
attack 1
bound[2] 1, 3
caper 3
cavort
dive 1
flutter 3
hop 1, 3
hurdle 2
jerk 2
jolt 4
leap 1, 2, 3, 5, 6
lunge 2, 3
pile[1] 6, 8a
pounce 1, 2
prance
pull 8a
recoil 1
rush 1
skip 1, 3
spring 1, 6
start 5, 13

jump all over
rubbish 3
scold 1
upbraid

jump at°
at **jump 6**
leap 4
pounce 1

jump down some-one's throat
pitch[1] 6a
scold 1
snap 3b

jumped-up
glorified 1

jump for joy
exult

jumpiness
excitement 1
tension 2

jumping
alive 4

jump on°
at **jump 7**
pile[1] 8a, 8b
pitch[1] 6a
pounce 1
rubbish 3
scold 1
upbraid

jump over°
at **jump 3**
clear 28
hurdle 2

jumpy°
afraid 1
agitated
excitable
fearful 2
insecure 1
nervous 1
overwrought 1
panic-stricken
restless
sinking 1
tense 2
tremulous 1

junction°
contact 1
joint 1
meeting 3
seam 1
union 1, 3

juncture°
crunch 2
joint 1
junction
moment 2
pass 26
phase 2
point 4
present[1] 4
seam 1
stage 1
wedding 2
weld 2

killing°
bloodshed
carnage
destruction 2
destructive 1
dispatch 7
execution 3
finish 10
kill 9
massacre 1
murder 1, 2
murderous 2
purge 4
removal 2
slaughter 2
uproarious 2
veto 2
killjoy°
drip 3
misery 4
spoilsport
turn-off 2
kill off
dispose 3d
exterminate
extinguish 2
kill 1, 2
wipe 3
kill the fatted calf
fête 2
kill time
fool 7b
idle 6
kilometres per hour
velocity
kilter
-out of kilter
broken 7
order 13c
kimono
robe 1
wrapper 1
kin°
brother
connection 4
family 1
flesh 5
offshoot 2
people 2
race[2] 2
related 2
kind°
accommodating 1
amiable
benevolent
benign 1, 3
brand 1
breed 1
brotherly
category
character 2
charitable 2
chivalrous
class 2
considerate
decent 4
denomination 2
description 3
family 4
fatherly
flattering 1
form 3
friendly 2
genial
genre
gentle 1
good 6
good-natured
gracious
helpful
human 3
indulgent
kindly 3
large 2
lenient
line[1] 16
make 42
maternal
merciful
mild 1
model 6
mould[1] 2, 3

kind (*cont.*)
nature 4
neighbourly
nice 1
obliging
order 3
range 2
rate[1] 4
run 44
school 2
soft 5
soft-hearted
sort 1, 2, 3
stamp 8
stripe 2
style 1
sweet 4, 6
tender[1] 6
thoughtful 1
type 1
variety 3
version 1
-of a kind
equivalent 1
kind deed
favour 2
kindergarten
school 1
kindest
best 2
kind-hearted
amiable
amicable
benevolent
benign 1
considerate
friendly 2
good 6
good-natured
gracious
hearty 1
human 3
kind[1]
lenient
merciful
soft 5
soft-hearted
sweet 6
sympathetic 1
tender[1] 6
thoughtful 1
kind-heartedly
well[1] 5
kind-heartedness
charity 2
consideration 1
humanity 3
kindness 1
mercy
philanthropy 1
sensitivity 2
thought 4
kindle°
arouse 3
awake 2
burn 2
enliven 1
excite 1
fire 8
foment
heat 4
inspire 1
interest 7
light[1] 15
provoke 2
quicken 3
set 20a
spark 2
wake[1] 2
whet 2
kindliness
benevolence 1
consideration 1
fellowship 3
grace 4
heart 5
humanity 3
kindness 1
mercy
sensitivity 2
thought 4
warmth 2

kindling
fuel 1
kindly°
accommodating 1
amiable
benevolent
benign 1
charitable 2
considerate
cordial
fatherly
friendly 2
generous 2
genial
gentle 1
good 6
good-natured
gracious
human 3
indulgent
kind[1]
lenient
maternal
merciful
mild 1
neighbourly
nice 1
obliging
paternal 1
sympathetic 1
thoughtful 1
warm 3
warmly 3
well[1] 5
kindness°
benevolence 1
consideration 1
favour 2
grace 4
heart 5
humanity 3
mercy
thought 4
kind of
fairly 1
moderately
quasi- 2
rather 1
somewhat
kindred°
family 1
kin 1, 2
offshoot 2
related 2
kinetic
motive 3
kinfolk
family 1
flesh 5
kin 1
people 2
king°
bigwig 1
crown 3
monarch 1
royal 3
sovereign 1
kingdom°
domain 1
dominion 2
monarchy 1
realm 1
reign 1
king-fish
master 1
kinglike
imperial 1
royal 1
kingly
imperial 1
majestic 1
regal 1
royal 1
sovereign 3
King of Kings
saviour 2
kingpin
bigwig 1
boss 1
chief 1
director 1
executive 1
leader 1
master 1

kingpin (*cont.*)
pivot 1
King's counsel
lawyer
kingship
royalty 1
king-size
gigantic
king-sized
jumbo
king's ransom
mint 1
packet 2
kink°
foible
notion 2
oddity 3
peculiarity 1
perversion 2
quirk
snarl[2] 2
tangle 1, 3
warp 2
kinkiness
oddity 1
perversion 2
kinky°
abnormal 2
bizarre 1
curious 3
deviant 1
eccentric 1
homosexual 2
insane 1
odd 1
offbeat
outlandish
sick 5
step 8
strange 1
swish 4
unnatural 1
way-out 1
weird
kin(s)folk
family 1
flesh 5
kin 1
people 2
kinship°
affinity 1
brotherhood 1
comparison 2
fraternity 2
parallel 3
relation 1, 2
kinsman
brother
kin 1
relation 3
kinsmen
family 1
people 2
kinswoman
kin 1
relation 3
kiosk
booth 2
kip
doze 1, 2
rest[1] 6
retire 3
sack 2
kipper
preserve 3
kippered
salt 10
kirmess
fair[2]
kismet
destiny
doom
fate 1
fortune 2
lot 2
predestination
providence 2
kiss°
caress 1, 2
kiss and make up
patch 7

kisser
face 1
feature 3
mouth 1
mug 2
pan 2
kiss goodbye°
at kiss 3
exit 3
kiss of death
stab 6
kiss someone's arse
cringe 2
flatter 1
truckle
kiss someone's ass
cringe 2
flatter 1
truckle
kiss someone's feet
scrape 4
kiss the hem
scrape 4
kiss the ring
scrape 4
kit°
costume
equipment
fiddle 4
gear 4
pack 1
rig 3
set 27
stuff 2
tack 4
kitbag
pack 1
kitchen°
kitchenette
kitchen
kitchen garden
allotment 2
kitchen range
range 4
kith and kin
connection 4
flesh 5
people 2
kit out
clothe 1
equip
furnish 1
outfit 4
rig 1
supply 1
kitschy
coarse 4
kittenish°
playful 1
sportive
kitty°
pool 2
pot 2
kit up
clothe 1
equip
furnish 1
supply 1
kleptomaniac
thief 1
klutz
hulk 2
klutzy
ungraceful 1
km/hr
velocity
knack°
ability 1
art 4
dexterity 1
faculty 1
finesse 1
flair 1
genius 3
gift 2
ingenuity
instinct
power 5
proficiency

knack (*cont.*)
skill 1
talent 1
technique 2
touch 16
trick 3
knacker
fag 1
ragman
knackered
dead 9
exhausted 1
fatigued
ragged 3
spent 1
tired 1
weary 1
knapsack
pack 1
knave
adventurer 2
boy 2
criminal 3
devil 2
fraud 3
heel[1] 2
hoodlum
miscreant 1
rascal
reprobate 2
rogue 1
scoundrel
stinker
swindler
villain
wretch 1
knavery
deceit 1
deception 1
devilry 1
swindle 2
trickery
knavish
black 6
dishonest
evil 2
unscrupulous
wicked 2
knavishness
devilry 1
knead
massage 2
mould[1] 4
rub 1
work 13
kneading
massage 1
knee
punish 2
spank
-on one's knees
prostrate 1
knee-breeches
short 15
knee-deep
lousy 4
knee-high to a grasshopper
short 1
knee-jerk
automatic 2
immediate 1
spontaneous 2
kneel
bend 3
prostrate 1
worship 1
kneeling
prostration 1
knee-pants
short 15
knees-up
carouse 2
party 1
knell
keen[2] 2
lament 2
peal 1, 2
ring[2] 1, 3
toll[1] 2
knickers
pants 1

knick-knack
bauble
curiosity 3
gewgaw
novelty 2
ornament 1
plaything 1
toy 2
trifle 1
-knick-knacks
bric-à-brac
rummage 2
sundries
trash 2
knife°
blade 1,2
dagger
slash 1
slit 1
stab 1
steel 1
-before you can say 'knife'
post-haste
swiftly
knife-edged
keen[1] 2
sharp 1
knife-like
sharp 1
knight
gallant 4
hero 1
knight errant
saviour 1
knight-errantry
chivalry
knighthood
order 9
knight in shining armour
protector
saviour 1
knightly
chivalrous
knight(s) of the road
drifter
homeless 2
knit°
contract 5
entwine
furrow 3
integrate
mesh 4
splice 1
weave 1
knit one's brows
frown 1
pout 1
knob°
bump 2
control 6
hump 1
lump[1] 2
mound 1
nub 1
protrusion
knobbly
bumpy
knobby
bumpy
knock°
blow[2] 1
bump 1,3
carp
criticize 2
deride
disapprove
fault 6
flout
hit 1,2,10
jeer 1
jolt 2
pan 5
pull 6
punch[1] 1,2
rap 1,2,4
run 26b
shaft 3
sneer 2
strike 1
knock *(cont.)*
stroke 1
talk 9a
tap[1] 1,2
knock about°
at **knock 3**
manhandle
mishandle 1
pal 2
punish 3
rough 16
knockabout
boat
knock around°
at **knock 3**
manhandle
mishandle 1
pal 2
punish 3
knock back
drink 1
gulp 1
swill 3
knock down°
at **knock 4**
demolish 1
fell
flatten 2
floor 4
lay[1] 18c
level 9
overturn 1
raze
reduce 5
run 26d
strike 4
throw 3
tip[2] 1
topple 1
upset 2
knocked for six
dumbfounded
thunderstruck
knocked out
dumbfounded
exhausted 1
fatigued
prostrate 5
tired 1
unconscious 1
washed out 2
weary 1
knocked sideways
dumbfounded
knocked up
washed out 2
weary 1
knocker(s)
bosom 1
breast 1
knock for a loop
surprise 1
knock for six
knock 6b
lay[1] 18c
overwhelm 3
surprise 1
knocking
tap[1] 2
knocking down
destruction 1
knocking off
theft
knocking-shop
brothel
knock off°
at **knock 5**
accomplish
deduct
discount 1
dispatch 3
dispose 3d
execute 3
hold 22a
kill 1
lay[1] 16b
murder 3
perform 1
pinch 3
rout 2
shoot 3
swill 3
knock off *(cont.)*
take 3
zap
knock-off°
knock off one's feet, pins
overwhelm 3
knock oneself out
exert 2
knock out°
at **knock 6**
drug 4
eliminate 2
flatten 2
lay[1] 18c
stun 1
knockout°
beauty 2
good 2
stunning 1
wonder 1
knock-out drop
sedative 1
knock over
flatten 2
floor 4
hold 22a
knock 5b
overturn 1
run 26d
throw 3
tip[2] 1
topple 1
turn 21c
upset 2
knock the bottom out of
rebut
knock together
knock 7a
patch 6
throw 9d
whip 7b
knock unconscious
knock 6a
knock up°
at **knock 7**
call 6
patch 6
whip 7b
knoll°
hill 1
mound 1
ring[2] 1,3
rise 13
knop
nub 1
knot°
bunch 2
cluster 2
entangle 1
kink 1
knit 3
nub 1
snarl[2] 2,4
tangle 1,3
tie 1
knotted
gnarled
kinky 3
labyrinthine
knotty
complicated
difficult 2
gnarled
hairy 3
hard 3
intricate 1
involved 2
labyrinthine
perplexing
prickly 4
profound 1
thorny 2
tough 5
tricky 2
knout
lash[1] 1
scourge 2
whip 8
know°
appreciate 3
experience 4
feel 4
love 6
master 7
read 2
recognize 1
see 2
taste 8
tell[1] 7,9
twig[2]
understand 1
-before you know it
sometime 3
soon 1
-in the know
aware 1
current 4
enlightened
experienced 2
familiar 4
informed 2
knowledgeable 1
mill 3
privy 2
well-informed
wise 5
know-all
wise guy
know-how
ability 1
art 1
craft 1
efficiency 1
experience 3
expertise
proficiency
prowess 1
qualification 1
scholarship 1
skill 2
technique 2
understanding 3
knowing°
aware 1
deep 3,5
experienced 1
foxy 1
hip
intelligent
knowledge 1
knowledgeable 1
sophisticated 1
wise 2
knowingly
deliberately
purpose 4a
know-it-all
wise guy
knowledge°
acquaintance 1
appreciation 3
art 1
brain 1
cognizance,
command 8
conception 2
education 2
experience 1,3
expertise
exposure 3
eye 3
familiarity 1
information
intelligence 2
learn 2
learning
lore 2
perception 1
qualification 1
savoir faire
savoir vivre
scholarship 1
science 1
sophistication 1
technique 2
understanding 3
wisdom 2
knowledgeability
profundity 2
savoir faire
knowledgeability *(cont.)*
sophistication 1
knowledgeable°
acquainted 2
astute 2
aware 1
deep 3
educated 1
enlightened
experienced 1
expert 2
familiar 4
hip
home 5
informed 1
intelligent
knowing 2
learned
lettered
mature 1
mill 3
old 7
privy 2
professional 1
proficient
profound 2
qualified 1
rational 2
refined 2
smart 2
sophisticated 1
strong 6
versed
well-informed
wise 2,5
knowledgeableness
profundity 2
known
acquainted 2
current 2
public 4
reputation 2
well-known 1
know one's mind°
at **mind 12**
knuckle
-knuckles
piece 10
punish 1
rap 2
reprimand 1,2
scold 1
knuckle down
shoulder 3
turn 23c
knuckle-head
dolt
fool 1
silly 3
knuckle-headed
wooden 3
knuckle under
cave 2b
obey 1
submit 1
yield 1
KO
knock 6a
knockout 1
lay[1] 18c
kobold
goblin
kook
madman
maniac 1
oddity 2
psychotic 2
weirdo
kookiness
folly 1
oddity 1
kooky
deranged
extreme 5
insane 1
odd 1
strange 1
way-out 1
zany 1
Koran
Scripture
kosher
permissible
regular 6
kowtow°
bend 3
bow 1,5
cringe 2
prostrate 1
prostration 1
scrape 4
truckle
kowtowing
grovelling
prostration 1
kriegspiel
manoeuvre 2
kris
dagger
kudos°
applause
honour 2
mention 4
ovation
praise 1
tribute 1
kurfuffle
disorder 2
uproar
upset 3
kvetch
niggle

L

labarum
pennant
standard 3
label°
brand 1,2,3
call 2
character 1
characterize
describe 3
designate 4
entitle 2
flag[1] 3
identify 1
mark 2,11
name 1,4
stamp 3,7
style 7
tab 1
tag 1,2,3,4
tally 4
term 8
title 6
labelling
identification 1
labile
changeable 1
protean
laborious°
arduous 1
difficult 1
elaborate 2
exhausting 2
hard 2
laboured 1
methodical
painful 3
ponderous 2
punishing
rough 7
stiff 9
strenuous 1
tedious
toilsome
tough 4
laboriously
hard 13
laboriousness
difficulty 1
labour 1
sweat 6
labour°
activity 2
drudgery
dwell 2
effort 1
grind 4,7
industry 2

labour (*cont.*)
linger 3
pain 4
persist 1
plod 1,2
reiterate
slave 3
slavery 3
strain[1] 4
struggle 1,4
sweat 3,6
work 1,7
laboured°
elaborate 2
forced
laborious 4
methodical
ornate
ponderous 2
stiff 8
stilted
strained
studied
unnatural 4
labourer°
hand 4
slave 2
worker
-labourers
help 7
labour pains
labour 4
labour-saving
streamlined 2,3
labour under°
at **labour 7**
labyrinth
maze
network 2
snarl[2] 4
tangle 2
labyrinthian
labyrinthine
labyrinthine°
complicated
intricate 1
involved 2
meandering
perplexing
serpentine 2
tortuous 1
lace°
braid 2
freshen 4
punch[1] 1
tie 9
lace into°
at **lace 5**
light[2] 14
pitch[1] 6a
punch[1] 1
scold 1
lacerate°
gash 2
hack[1] 1
mangle
rend 2
slash 1
wound 3
laceration
gash 1
slash 4
sore 7
tear 4
wound 1
lace-work
lace 1
mesh 1
net[1] 1
lachrymose
low[1] 8
maudlin
miserable 1
moist 3
tearful
tragic
unhappy 1
watery 2
lacing
lace 2
lack°
absence 2
dearth

lack (*cont.*)
defect 1
famine
go 41
need 1,5
poverty 2
require 2
scarcity
shortage
want 2,3
lackadaisical°
careless 1
casual 3
half-hearted
idle 3
impassive
inactive 1
indifferent 1
lukewarm 2
shiftless
slothful
slow 1
supine 2
tardy 2
torpid
lackey
attendant 2
boy 2
fag 3
flunkey 1
hack[2] 2
inferior 4
menial 3
servant 1
slave 1
subordinate 2
lacking
absent 2
deficient 1
destitute 2
empty 7
fail 1
failing 2
fall 11b, 19
require 2
scarce
short 6
shy 3
starved 3
unsatisfactory
void 3
wanting 2
lacklustre°
colourless 2
deadly 5
dingy
drab
flat 5
lifeless 3
mousy 1
washed out 1
laconic
compact 3
concise
curt
epigrammatic
short 3
summary 2
terse 1
laconicism
brevity
laconism
brevity
lacquer
glaze 1,2
lacquey
slave 1
lacuna
break 27
delay 5
discrepancy
gap 1
hold-up 2
interlude
interruption 2
interval 3
jump 12
lapse 2
pause 2
skip 4
space 3
split 7
vacancy 1
wait 4

lad°
boy 1
bugger 2
chap
child 2
guy 1
minor 3
stripling
youth 2
ladder
run 18
laddie
child 2
minor 3
youth 2
lade
load 3
la de da
see **la-di-da**
laden
heavy 13
loaded 1
momentous
la-di-da
affected 3
genteel 1
haughty
mannered
mincing
supercilious
ladies and gentlemen
gentry
people 1
ladies' man
blade 4
charmer
dandy 1
rake[2]
roué
ladies of the press
press 10b
ladies' room
facility 2b
toilet 1
ladle
scoop 1,4
ladle off
skim 1
lady
girl 1
noble 1
peer[1] 1
woman 1,2
-ladies'
facility 2b
lavatory
toilet 1
lady-in-waiting
woman 4
lady-killer
charmer
dandy 1
flirt 3
libertine 1
philanderer
playboy
rake[2]
roué
ladylike°
courteous
decorous
feminine 1
genteel 2
nice 1
proper 3
refined 1
respectful
seemly 2
well-bred
lady-love
love 3
sweetheart
woman 2
Lady Muck
dignitary
lady of the evening
prostitute 1
slattern
tart[2] 2

lady of the house
landlady 1
lady of the night
prostitute 1
tart[2] 2
lady of the press
journalist
reporter
scribe 2
lady's maid
maid 2
servant 1
lag°
convict 2
dawdle
delay 3
drag 4
fall 10
flag[2] 2
inmate
insulate 2
linger 2
prisoner
trail 6
lag-bolt
screw 1
lager lout
rowdy 2
laggard°
idler
slack 1
slothful
slouch 3
slow 1
laggardness
sluggishness
lagging
slow 1
lagn(i)appe
perquisite
tip[3] 1
lagoon
pool 1
lag-screw
screw 1
lah-di-dah
affected 3
genteel 1
haughty
mannered
mincing
supercilious
laic(al)
civil 1
lay[2] 1
secular
temporal 1
laid-back
easygoing
free 8
lukewarm 2
nonchalant
passive 1
laid hold of
affected 4
laid low
flat 3
prostrate 3,4
stricken 1
laid off
unemployed
laid up
indisposed 1
sick 2
laid waste
desolate 2
lair°
hideaway
nest 1
laissez-aller
laissez-faire
laissez-faire°
laissez-faireism
laissez-faire
lake
pool 1
lakeshore
beach 1
lallapalooza
killer 2

lallygag
bugger 4a
drag 4
idle 6
loaf[2] 1
lallygagging
idleness 1
slow 1
lam
run 49b
lamasery
monastery
lambaste°
abuse 3
belabour
box[2] 2
club 5
criticize 2
hit 1
lash[1] 3,4
lay[1] 13
light[2] 14
pound[1] 1
punch[1] 1
rough 16
slash 2
strike 1
lambasting
thrashing 1
works 3b
lambency
glow 1
lambent
bright 1
glowing 1
shiny
lambently
clear 17
Lambeth run(s)
run 50
lamblike
passive 2
Lamb of God
saviour 2
lambrequin
drapery
lame°
cripple 2
crippled 1
deformed 2
disabled
feeble 2
helpless 1
hurt 4
incapacitate
ineffectual 2
infirm 1
maim
mutilate 1
pale[1] 3
thin 4
weak 4
lame-brain
dolt
lamella
scale[2] 1
lamellar
scaly 1
lamellate
scaly 1
lament°
bemoan
bewail
complain
grieve 1
keen[2] 1,2
moan 1,2
mourn
mourning 1
murmur 4
regret 1
repent
sigh 2
sorrow 3
weep 1
lamentable°
deplorable 1
grievous 2
miserable 3
mournful 2
pathetic 1
piteous
regrettable

lamentable (*cont.*)
sad 3
sorrowful 2
tragic
unfortunate 3
lamentably
painfully
sadly 1
lamentation°
keen[2] 2
lament 2
moan 1
mourning 1
lamenting
lamentation
lamina
flake 1
foil[2]
plate 3
scale[2] 1
sheet 4
skin 2
laminar
scaly 1
laminate
plate 6
lamination
foil[2]
plate 4
sheet 4
lam out
beat 8
depart 1
escape 1
exit 3
flee 1
flight[2] 3
fly 2
run 2
lamp
light[1] 2
lamplight
light[1] 1
lampoon°
burlesque 1,3
caricature 1,2
derision
fun 5
guy 2
laugh 2a
mimic 3
mock 2
mockery 2
parody 1,3
ridicule 2
satire 2
satirize
scoff[1]
send 9a
take 34b
take-off 2
taunt 1
lamppost
standard 4
lampshade
shade 5
lanate
hairy 1
woolly 1
lance°
penetrate 1
pierce 1
prick 3
spike 2
stab 1
lancet
lance 1
land°
bag 6
country 2
disembark
dock 2
domain 1
estate 1
farm 1
field 1
get 38d
ground 1
light[2] 13
lumber 3
nation
property 3

land (*cont.*)
reach 2
set 17c
settle 5
state 4
strike 3
territory 1
touch 10
-in the land of Nod
sleep 1
-in the land of the living
alive 1
-lands
domain 1
landed
substantial 4
landed estate
estate 1
landed gentry
gentry
landed proprietor
squire 2
landholder
proprietor 1
squire 2
landholding
spread 13
landing°
pier 1
landing-place
landing 3
pier 1
landing-stage
pier 1
landlady°
host[1] 1
landlord 2
proprietor 1
land-locked
interior 4
landlord°
host[1] 1
proprietor 1, 2
landmark°
guide 7
mark 7
seminal 1
Land of Beulah
paradise 2
landowner
landlord 2
proprietor 1
squire 2
-landowners
gentry
landscape°
prospect 1
scene 4
terrain
view 1
landslide
slide 5
lane
drive 9
road 2
street 1
walk 5
language°
dialect
diction 1
expression 6
idiom 1
lingo
parlance
phrase 3
print 3
profanity
prose
speech 1, 3
style 5
talk 19
terminology
tongue 1
vernacular 3
wording
languid
feeble 1
inactive 1
indolent

languid (*cont.*)
inert 3
lackadaisical 1
lazy 2
leaden 4
lethargic 1
listless
relaxed
slothful
supine 2
tardy 2
torpid
languidness
inactivity 1
indolence
lethargy 1
sloth
sluggishness
languish
droop 2
fade 2
fail 3
flag[2] 2
lounge 1
rest[1] 6
rot 2
sink 4
stagnate
wilt 2
languishing
frail 2
languor
fatigue 1
indolence
inertia
lethargy 1
sloth
sluggishness
stupor
torpor
languorous
fatigued
indolent
inert 3
lackadaisical 1
lazy 2
leaden 4
lethargic 1
relaxed
slothful
supine 2
torpid
laniferous
woolly 1
lank(y)°
gaunt 1
lanky
lean[1] 1
scrawny
skinny
slender 1
spare 3
tall 2
thin 1
wiry
lanose
hairy 1
woolly 1
lantern
light[1] 2
lanuginose
hairy 1
woolly 1
lanuginous
hairy 1
woolly 1
Laodicean
indifferent 1
listless
lukewarm 2
lap°
circuit 2
drink 1
flap 3
fold 4
gurgle 1
leg 3
overhaul 1
overlap 1, 3
revel 1
revolution 3
stage 1
wash 3

-in the lap of luxury
luxuriate 2
lap-dog
yes-man
lapel
lap[2] 2
lappet
flap 3
lap[2] 2
tab 1
lapse°
default 1, 3
err 2
fall 26
fault 2
indiscretion 2
interval 1
lull 1
misstep 2
offence 1
pause 2
peccadillo
relapse 1, 3
revert
sin 3
solecism
space 3
transgress 1
transgression
trip 2
wander 4
wrong 8a
lapsing
relapse 3
lapsus
lapse 1
lapsus linguae
misstatement 2
trip 2
lap up
drink 1
revel 1
larboard
left 1, 3
larcenous
lawless 2
predatory 2
larceny
embezzlement
rip-off 1
robbery
stealing
theft
lardaceous
oily 1
larder
kitchen
lardy
greasy 1
large°
ample 5
big 1, 2, 3, 8
broad 1
bulky
burly
considerable 1
extensive 2
gigantic
good 16
goodly
grand 1
great 1, 2
gross 1
handsome 2
hefty 1
huge
liberal 1
long[1] 1
massive
mighty 3
ponderous 1
roomy
spacious,
spanking 1
strong 14
substantial 1, 2
tall 2
tidy 3
voluminous 1
weighty 1
wide 3

-at large°
at **large 5**
abroad 2
free 2
loose 2
out 6
-in large measure
substantially
-in large numbers
galore
-to a large extent
substantially
widely 2
large-hearted
large 2
large-heartedness
charity 2
largely°
amply 2
chiefly
generally 2
mainly
principally
substantially
whole 5
widely 2
largeness
breadth 3
bulk 1
size 1
larger
better[1] 2
major 1
larger-than-life
heroic 4
largesse°
bonus
bounty 2
charity 3
dole 1
donation 1
gift 1
philanthropy 2
present[2] 2
largest
best 4
main 2
outside 6
largish
considerable 1
lariat
lasso 1
lark°
amusement 1
caper 2
fun 3
prank
sport 4
spree
lark about, around°
at **lark 2**
fool 7b
larrikin
gangster
hoodlum
miscreant 1
rough 13
thug
larva
bug 1
lascivious°
abandoned 2
base[2] 4
bawdy
broad 8
carnal
coarse 3
dirty 2
disgraceful 2
erotic 3
evil-minded 1
filthy 3
immodest 1
immoral 2
improper 3
impure 4
incontinent 2
indecent 2
lecherous

lascivious (*cont.*)
lewd
libertine 2
lustful
obscene 1
profligate 1
prurient 1
scandalous 1
sensual
sexy 2
unchaste
unseemly 1
vulgar 2
wanton 1
lasciviousness
desire 3
impropriety 3
impurity 3
profligacy 1
ribaldry
lash°
beat 1
connect 3
flog 1
hide[2] 2
hit 1
knot 3
lambaste 1
lather 4
punish 2
rack 4
rod 2
rope 3
scourge 2, 3
slash 2
stake[1] 3
strike 1
switch 1, 3
tie 1, 2
toss 3
whip 1, 8
lashing
punishment 2
thrashing 1
whipping 1
-lashings
heap 2
lash out
fly 8b
pitch[1] 6a
snap 3b
swipe 1
lash up
inflame 1
lass°
child 2
girl 1
maid 1
minor 3
miss[2]
woman 3
youth 2
lassie
child 2
lass
maid 1
minor 3
miss[2]
woman 3
youth 2
lassitude
exhaustion 2
fatigue 1
idleness 1
indolence
inertia
prostration 4
sluggishness
stupor
lasso°
last°
continue 2
endure 1
eventual 1
extend 3
extreme 3
final 1
former 1
go 15, 32a
hold 20a, 22c
keep 11
late 2
live 7
parting 3

last (*cont.*)
past 2
persist 2
prior 1
rear[1] 3
remain 3
resist 1
see 14b, 14c
serve 6
sit 7
stand 3, 10b, 12b
stick[1] 6
survive 1
ultimate 1, 4
wear 4
withstand
-as a last resort
always 3
-at last
eventually
finally 1
length 4a
ultimately
-at the last moment
finally 1
-in the last
soon 5
-in the last analysis
bottom 5
ultimately
-on its last legs
leg 7
shaky 2
-on one's last legs°
at **leg 7**
moribund
ragged 3
lasting°
abiding
chronic 1
durable
enduring
eternal 3
fast[1] 5
indelible
monumental 1
old 4
perennial 1
permanent 1
perpetual 1
stable 2
lasting quality
endurance 2
permanence
stability 2
lastly
finally 1
last-minute
unpremeditated
last resting-place
grave[1]
tomb
last straw
end 8a
limit 4a
last wishes
will 3
last word
craze
rage 3
rave 4
vogue 1
latch
bolt 2, 10
fastening
lock[1] 1, 3
latchkey
key 1
latch on to
grab 1
snatch 1
late°
back 13
backward 3
belated
dead 1
delinquent 3
former 1
fresh 1

late (*cont.*)
get 42d
lost 5
new 2, 7
overdue
past 2
prior 1
recent
slow 5, 12
tardy 1
-of late°
at **late 4**
lately°
just 6
late 5, 8
late-model
new 2
recent
latent
abeyance
dormant 2
implicit 1
potential 1
subconscious 1
undeveloped
later
directly 3
future 2
posterior 2
second[1] 5
subsequent 1
subsequently
upper 3
yet 4
laterally
sideways
latest°
contemporary 2
current 3
date 5
fashion 2
former 1
fresh 1
hot 5
last[1] 2
minute[1] 3
modern
new 2
prior 1
recent
scoop 3
score 6
vogue 1
lather°
bother 6
bubble 2
foam 1, 2
froth 1, 4
stew 2
sweat 7
wash 1
latibulize
hide[1] 1
Latin
classical 2
latitude
breadth 3
freedom 4
leeway
licence 1
margin 3
range 1
room 1
scope 2
space 1
latitudinarian
broad 7
liberal 2, 4
permissive
tolerant
latrine
lavatory
privy 3
toilet 1
latter
posterior 2
latterly
late 6
lattice
grating 3
mesh 1
net[1] 1
lattice-work
mesh 1
net[1] 1
laud°
applaud 2
celebrate 3
compliment 3
eulogize
extol
glorify 2
hail[1] 2
honour 6
praise 3
rave 2
laudable°
deserving
estimable
meritorious
praiseworthy
splendid 3
laudation
glory 2
kudos
ovation
tribute 1
laudative
laudatory
laudatory°
complimentary 1
favourable 2
flattering 2
glowing 3
good 17
lauded
immortal 3
laugh°
chuckle 1, 2
deride
giggle 1, 2, 3
jeer 1
joke 1
mockery 3
riot 2
roar 2
scream 2
sneer 2
snicker 1
laughable
absurd 1
crazy 2
farcical
funny 1
humorous
inane
ludicrous
nonsensical
preposterous
rich 10
ridiculous
silly 1
stupid 2
unreasonable 1
unthinkable 2
laugh at°
at **laugh 2**
deride
jeer 1
mock 1
parody 3
ridicule 2
scorn 4
sneer 2
snicker 1
laughing
laughter
laughing-stock
joke 2
monkey 2
spectacle 2
zany 2
laugh off
deride
laugh 2b
trivialize
laughter°
chuckle 2
derision
hilarity
mirth
titter 2
laugh up one's sleeve
snicker 1
launch°
begin 2
commence 1, 3
conception 1
début 1, 2
deliver 5
embark 2
fire 9
float 2
fly 8a
heave 2
inaugurate 1
initiate 1
institute 3
introduce 4
mount 5
open 20
opening 4
origin 2
originate 1
pioneer 2
pitch[1] 1
precipitate 2
presentation 3
project 4
propel
release 2
set 12a
shoot 2
shot 8
sling 1
spearhead 1
take-off 1
tender[3] 1
throw 1
toss 1
launching
conception 1
début 1
origin 2
shot 8
launder°
clean 9
wash 1
laundered
clean 2
laundering
wash 11
laundry list
list[1] 1
laurel(s)°
decoration 2
trophy 1
lav
lavatory
lavabo
sink 12
lavage
rinse 3
lavalière
pendant
lavatory°
facility 2b
privy 3
toilet 1
lave
clean 9
rinse 1
wash 1
laving
rinse 3
lavish°
abundant 2
ample 5
blow[1] 4
consume 3
effusive
extravagant 1
free 7
generous 1, 3
grand 1
high 12
improvident 1
liberal 1
lush 1
luxuriant 2
luxurious 1
magnificent
opulent 2
ornate
plentiful 1
plush
posh
princely 1, 2
lavish (*cont.*)
prodigal 1, 2
profuse 2, 3
rain 7
rich 4
shower 4
spend 2
splendid 1
sumptuous
wanton 3
wasteful
lavishly
amply 4
freely 4
richly 1
unduly 2
water 3
lavishness
extravagance 1
exuberance 2
plenty 2
prodigality 2
profligacy 2
splendour 1
waste 6
law°
act 4
book 3
code 1
decree 1
fundamental 2
generality 2
justice 2, 3
measure 7
order 4
police 1
precept 1
principle 1
regulation 2
rule 1
science 1
standard 1
-against the law
unlawful
-by law
legitimate 2
law-abiding
honest 1
orderly 2
respectable 1
solid 5
law and order
order 8
lawbreaker
criminal 3
delinquent 1
felon
offender
transgressor
lawcourt
bar 5
lawful°
effectual 2
fair[1] 2
formal 2
just 2
legal 1
legitimate 2
official 1
permissible
right 1
rightful 1
lawfulness
justice 3
order 8
lawless°
criminal 1
disorderly 2
riotous 1
rogue 2
unruly
wicked 2
lawlessness
crime
riot 1
lawmaker
politician
lawman
officer 2
lawn°
field 1
green 4
turf 1
lawsuit
case[1] 2
litigation
suit 4
trial 2
lawyer°
advocate 3
counsel 3
counsellor
mouthpiece 3
solicitor
lax°
derelict 2
easygoing
flabby 1
forgetful
indulgent
lazy 1
limp[2] 1
loose 6
nod 4
permissive
promiscuous 2
slack 1
slipshod
slothful
slow 1
soft 5
unprofessional 1
laxative
purgative 1, 2
laxity
neglect 4
negligence
oversight 1
permission
laxness
laissez-faire
neglect 4
negligence
oversight 1
lay°
amateur 2
bet 2
civil 1
clap 4
deposit 1
foist
material 7
place 15
popular 3
profane 2
put 1, 8
rest[1] 8
screw 3
secular
set 1, 8, 10
smooth 10
temporal 1
unprofessional 3
worldly 1
lay a bet
gamble 2
punt 1
lay about
pelt[1] 1
layabout
good-for-nothing 2
idler
loafer
truant 1
wastrel 2
lay a finger, hand on°
at **finger 4**
touch 4
lay an egg
fall 12
lay aside
defer[1]
dismiss 2
hoard 2
postpone
put 11, 12
salt 8
save 3
shelve
lay a stake
punt 1
lay at someone's door
blame 2
fault 8
pin 5
lay a wager
gamble 2
punt 1
lay away
accumulate
deposit 2
hoard 2
put 12
save 3
set 14b
store 1
lay bare
bare 6, 7
betray 2
excavate 2
reflect 2
strip[2] 1
unveil
lay blame
blame 2
lay by
garner
heap 3
put 12
salt 8
save 3
lay claim
profess 2
lay down
define 1
deposit 1
dictate 1
die 1
garner
plan 3
plot[1] 4
prescribe
provide 3
set 7
layer
coat 2
cover 3
film 1
foil[2]
plate 3, 4
ply
scale[2] 2
seam 2
sheet 4, 5
slice 1
spread 7
stratum 1
streak 1
tier
lay eyes on
behold
discover 2
lay finger(s) on
come 9a
finger 5
locate 2
location 2
pin 4b
lay hands on
come 9a
finger 5b
find 2
get 30a
locate 2
location 2
procure 1
snatch 1
take 1
lay hold of
affect[1] 1
attach 6
capture 2
clutch 1
come 9a
get 8
grab 1
grasp 1
snatch 1
take 1
lay in
garner
heap 3
hoard 2
lay[1] 19a
stock 10
laying on
imposition 1
laying open
exposure 1

leaning (*cont.*)
instinct
love 2
partiality 1
penchant
position 3
preference 2
prejudice 1
prone 2
recumbent
slant 3
taste 3
tendency
trend 1
turn 38
weakness 4
lean on
enforce 2
pressure 5
railroad 2
reckon 4
rely
squeeze 3
lean on the side of
lean² 3
prefer 1
lean over
heel²
list² 1
lean-to
hut
shack
shed¹
lean to(wards)
feel 9
near 10
prefer 1
leap°
bounce 1
bound² 1,3
caper 1,3
cavort
dance 1
dive 1
frisk 1
hop 1,3
hurdle 2
jump 1,4,8
lunge 2
pounce 1,2
prance
shoot 1
skip 1,3
spring 1,6
-by leaps and bounds°
at **bound² 2**
leap at°
at **leap 4**
jump 6
pounce 1
leap over
clear 28
hurdle 2
learn°
determine 2
discover 1
find 2
gather 4
get 21,30e,51f
grasp 2
hear 2
master 7
pick 8d
polish 4
receive 5
run 33d
see 4
soak 2
study 1
take 10
learn about
get 43c
scent 3
study 1
learn by heart
learn 4
memorize
learn by rote
memorize
learned°
academic 1
authoritative 2

learned (*cont.*)
deep 3
educated 1
expert 2
highbrow 2
informed 1
knowledgeable 2
lettered
literary 1,2
philosophical 1
profound 2
scholarly
smart 2
thinker
versed
well-informed
wise 2
learner°
apprentice 1
disciple 1
greenhorn
newcomer 2
novice
pupil
student 1
learning°
culture 1
education 2
illumination 2
knowledge 4
letter 3
lore 2
scholarship 1
schooling
study 5
wisdom 2
learn of°
at **learn 1**
detect 1
wind¹ 6
leary
guarded
lease°
charter 3,5
farm 4
get 1
hire 2,3,4
improve 2
let¹ 3
rent¹ 1,2
take 4
leaseholder
occupant
tenant
leash
lead 15
stake¹ 3
string 2
tether 1,2
tie 9
least
minimal
minimum 1,2
minute² 2
very 4
leather
hide² 1
whip 1
leathery
hard 1
stringy
tough 2
leave°
abandon 1,2
approval
beat 8
bequeath
break 15,24a
bugger 5
check 10a
clear 30
clearance 2
depart 1,2
deposit 1,2
desert¹ 3
disembark
drain 6
draw 12b
drop 7,13
emigrate
evacuate 2
exit 3
fly 2
forget 2

leave (*cont.*)
forsake 1,2
get 28c,31a,40b, 44a
go 2,23,31d,33b
go-ahead 1
holiday 1
liberty 2
licence 1
park 3
part 12
permission,
pile¹ 9
privilege
pull 14b,14c
push 9b
put 21e
quit 1,2
relinquish 1
resign 1
run 22
secede
set 18b
ship 3
shoo 2
slip¹ 6
split 6
stake¹ 2
start 3
step 17a
take 34c
throw 8,9b
vacate 1
walk 4a
wash 10
will 6
withdraw 5
-be left
inherit
remain 1,2
leave alone
avoid
forgo 1
lay¹ 16b
leave a mark on
get 16
hit 4
leave an impression
hit 4
leave bare
clean 10b
leave behind
forget 2
gain 5
overhaul 1
overtake 1
surpass
leave flat
desert¹ 3
leave high and dry
desert¹ 3
run 32
leave holding the baby
run 32
leave in the lurch
desert¹ 3
run 32
leave much to be desired
wanting 1
leaven
ferment 1
leave no stone unturned
pole² 2
search 2
leave of absence
holiday 1
leave² 2
leave off
cease 1
discontinue
give 17a
lay¹ 16b
quit 3
refrain¹ 2
shut 2
stop 1
take 38b

leave out
drop 9
eliminate 1
except 3
exclude 2
forgo 1
jump 3
miss¹ 4
omit 1
overlook 1
skip 2
leave-taking
exit 2
farewell 2
parting 2
leaving
exit 2
outgoing 1
parting 2
take-off 1
-leavings
dirt 1
filth 1
leftover 1
odds 5
remain 4a
rubbish 1
scrap¹ 2
waste 7
leaving aside
exclusive 4
leaving off
omission 1
leaving out
barring
omission 1
short 10
lecher
libertine 1
profligate 3
rake²
roué
sensualist
lecherous°
carnal
evil-minded 1
fast¹ 2
hot 7
immoral 2
impure 4
incontinent 2
lascivious 1
lewd
libertine 2
obscene 1
passionate 2
profligate 1
prurient 1
randy
scandalous 1
sensual
unchaste
wanton 1
lecherously
fast¹ 9
lecherousness
desire 3
impurity 3
lechery
desire 3
profligacy 1
lectern
rostrum
lecture°
address 1,3
course 5
harangue 2
hold 16a
lesson 1
oration
piece 10
preach 2
rant 1
rebuke 1,2
reprimand 1,2
scold 1
sermon 1,2
speak 12a
speech 2
talk 6,14
task 3
tell¹ 10
lecture-hall
hall 2

lecturer
instructor
speaker
talker 1
teacher
lecture-room
hall 2
ledge°
overhang 3
projection 1
ledger
register 1
leech
bloodsucker
flatterer
hanger-on
menial 4
parasite
leer°
eye 5
ogle 1,3
smirk 1,2
leeriness
suspicion 1
leery°
distrust 1
distrustful
guarded
mistrust 1
reluctant
shy 2
suspicious 2
wary
lees
deposit 4
dregs 1
ground 4
rubbish 1
sediment
leeway°
clearance 1
give 18
margin 3
play 24
room 1
scope 2
space 1
left°
abandoned 1
knock 9
liberal 2
punch¹ 2
remaining 1
undone²
unused 3
left hand
left 3
left-hand
left 1
left-handed°
awkward 1
leftist
left 2
liberal 4
progressive 3
radical 5
left over
remaining 1
leftover°
excess 3
extra 2
odd 3
outstanding 2
remaining 2
remnant 2
residual
residue
spare 1,2
surplus 2
unused 3
waste 9
-leftovers°
at **leftover 1**
difference 5
excess 1
odds 5
remain 4a
remainder 2
rest² 1
rubbish 1
scrap¹ 2
surplus 1

left-wing
left 2
left-winger
liberal 4
progressive 3
radical 5
leg°
post¹ 1
run 1
section 3
-legs
extremity 2
-not a leg to stand on°
at **leg 6**
-on one's last legs°
at **leg 7**
moribund 1
ragged 3
legacy
bequest
heritage 1
inheritance
legal°
effectual 2
formal 2
judicial 1
lawful 1
legitimate 1,2
official 1
permissible
real 1
regular 6
right 1
rightful 1
legalistic°
legalization
passage 9
sanction 1
legalize
justify
launder 2
legitimate 4
sanctify 3
sanction 5
legal papers
paper 2a
legal remedy
litigation
legal tender
cash 1
money 1
legate
agent 1
ambassador
delegate 1
deputy
envoy
messenger
minister 2
representative 3
legatee
heir
recipient
legation
mission 3
legend°
device 3
immortal 4
key 4
myth 1
romance 3
saga
story 1
title 3
legendary°
classic 2
fabulous 1
famous
fictional
grand 2
heroic 5
imaginary
mythical 1
notorious 2
superhuman 1
legerdemain
hanky-panky
hocus-pocus 3
magic 2
trick 5

leggy
tall 2
legible°
clear 5
intelligible
readable 3
legion
cohort 1
host[2]
sea 3
-legions
mass 2
number 2
score 4
legionnaire
mercenary 3
leg-iron(s)
shackle 1
legislate
enact 1
legislation
measure 7
passage 9
legislative body
house 3
legislator
politician
legislature
chamber 1
diet[2]
house 3
parliament 2
leg it°
at **leg 5**
run 1
legit
legal 2
permissible
legitimacy
justice 3
legitimate°
authentic
authoritative 1
bona fide
explain 2
fair[1] 2
genuine 1
good 8
honest 4
just 3
justify
launder 2
lawful 1
legal 2
official 1
permissible
real 1,3
regular 6
rightful 1
sanctify 3
straight 4
veritable
legitimately
truly 2
legitimatization
passage 9
sanction 1
legitimatize
explain 2
justify
launder 2
legitimate 4
sanctify 3
sanction 5
legitimization
passage 9
sanction 1
legitimize
justify
launder 2
legitimate 4
sanctify 3
sanction 5
legman
journalist
leg-pull
put-on 1
trick 2
leg up°
at **leg 4**
boost 1
hand 2
leisure°
ease 1
freedom 5
pastime
recreation
relaxation 1
rest[1] 3
spare 2
time 8
-at leisure°
at **leisure 3**
idle 2
off 6
unemployed
-at one's leisure°
at **leisure 3b**
leisured°
leisurely
easy 2,5
measured 1
slow 1,13
unhurried
leitmotif
motif
leman
love 3
lemon
dud 1
failure 3
flop 4
loser
lemonade
pop 5
lemony
sour 1
tart[1] 1
lend°
advance 6
impart 1
loan 2
provide 2
lend a hand
cooperate 2
help 1
lend an ear
listen 1
lend dimension
flesh 6
lender
factor 3
lend itself to°
at **lend 3**
lend one's name
stand 7b
lend substance
flesh 6
lend support
stand 7b
length°
bolt 4
extension 2
leg 3
measure 1
measurement 2
segment 1
stripe 1
term 2
-at length°
at **length 4**
finally 1
last[1] 7
-lengths
degree 2
extent 2
length and breadth
expanse
lengthen°
amplify 3
draw 14a
enlarge 1
expand 2
extend 2
grow 1
increase 1
pad 5
prolong
stretch 2
lengthening
extension 1
lengthy°
long[1] 2
leniency
charity 2
forgiveness 2
grace 3
humanity 3
mercy
patience 1
permission
quarter 4
lenient°
charitable 2
easy 2,3
easygoing
forgiving
gentle 1
human 3
indulgent
kind[1]
liberal 3
merciful
mild 1
patient 3
permissive
soft 5
lenis
unaccented
lenitive
mild 3
sedative 1,2
soothing 2
lenity
humanity 3
lens
glass 6
lensman
photographer
lenswoman
photographer
leper
outcast
undesirable 1
leprechaun
goblin
imp
lesbian
homosexual 1,2
lesion
ulcer 1
wound 1
lessee
occupant
tenant
lessen
belittle
bring 8b
cool 10
cushion 2
cut 8
dampen 2
deaden 2
decline 2
decrease 1
depreciate 1
detract
die 2
dilute
diminish 1
discount 2
drop 11
dull 9
dwindle
ease 6
flag[2] 2
hamper[1]
let[1] 9
lighten[2]
lower[1] 1
minimize 1
mitigate
moderate 5
modify 2
narrow 8
pale[1] 5
pare 2
recede 2
reduce 1,7
relax 2
relieve 1
remit 2
sag 2
smooth 12
soften 2,3
stem[2] 1
subside 2
lessen (*cont.*)
taper 2
trail 8
trivialize
wane 1
weaken 1
lessening
decline 6
decrease 2
ebb 4
extenuating
impairment
let-up
relaxation 2
remission 2
sag 3
slack 5
wane 3
lesser
incidental 2
inferior 2
junior
low[1] 10
minor 1
side 8
small 2
subordinate 1
subsidiary
lesson°
assignment 2
education 3
example 3
lecture 1
moral 3
parable
sermon 1,2
warning 1
-lessons
instruction 2
study 5
lessor
landlord 2
less than
below 5,8
under 5
lest
case[1] 6a
let°
allow 3
charter 5
farm 4
grant 2
hire 3
lease 2
permit 1
rent[1] 1
suffer 3
-without let or hindrance
freely 3
let be known
leak 5
let[1] 7a
pronounce 3
publish
reveal
tell[1] 2
let bygones be bygones
overlook 2
let down
betray 1
disappoint 1
disappointed 1,2
fail 2
lower[1] 2
let-down°
disappointment 1
let fall
shed[2] 2
let fly°
at **fly 8**
fling 1
heave 2
hurl
loose 13
pitch[1] 1
send 3
shoot 2
sling 1
toss 1
let go
abandon 1
discharge 1
dismiss 1
disregard 1
drop 7,8,10
emancipate
excuse 2
expel 1
finish 8
fire 9,11
fly 8a,8b
free 2,14
lay[1] 16a
let[1] 6a,8b
liberate 1
loose 10,11,12,13
overlook 2
part 14
pass 3,22
relax 1
release 1
relinquish 1,2
rescue 1
resign 1
sack 4
sacrifice 4
slack 3a
spare 7,8
surrender 1
thaw 2
vacate 2
vent 3
wreak
lethal°
cutthroat 3
deadly 1
destructive 1
evil 3
fatal 1
fateful 2
homicidal
hopeless 1
mortal 3
murderous 1
poisonous 1
terminal 2
venomous 1
virulent 1
lethargic°
dormant 1
drowsy
fatigued
idle 3
inactive 1
indolent
lackadaisical 1
lazy 1
leaden 4
listless
phlegmatic 1
slack 1
sleepy 1
slothful
stolid
supine 2
tardy 2
torpid
lethargical
lethargic 1
lethargy°
fatigue 1
idleness 1
inactivity 1
indolence
sloth
sluggishness
stupor
torpor
let have
allow 5
fly 8b
rebuke 1
scold 1
spare 8
Lethean
narcotic 1
oblivious
let in
admit 1
receive 3
take 32a
let in on
fill 9c
show 4
tip[3] 4
let know
tell[1] 3
tip[3] 4
let loose°
at **loose 10**
emancipate
finish 8
free 14
let[1] 6d,8b
loose 11
slack 3a
vent 3
let off
discharge 1,3
excuse 2
exempt 1,2
fire 10
fly 8a
forgive 2,3
free 2
hook 5
let[1] 6b
liberate 1
pardon 2
release 1
reprieve 1
spare 7
let on
reveal
let one's hair down
wind[2] 3b
let out
discharge 1
expose 1
farm 4
free 14
give 12b
hire 3
job 6
lease 2
let[1] 7a
liberate 1
pay 11c
pour 2
release 1
rent[1] 1
reveal
slip[1] 4
tell[1] 2
let pass
miss[1] 4
neglect 2
overlook 2
pass 3,22
let ride
overlook 2
let rip
fly 8a
let run
slack 3a
let slide°
at **slide 4**
neglect 2
omit 2
let slip
disclose 1
give 12b
leak 5
let[1] 7a
lose 4
make 33
miss[1] 4
reveal
tell[1] 2
letter°
character 1
line[1] 8
message 1
missive
note 2
writing 2
-letters°
at **letter 3**
literature 1
mail 1
memoir 2
writing 3

Lothario
charmer
libertine 1
philanderer
playboy
rake[2]
roué
sensualist

lotion°
ointment
salve 1
wash 13

lottery°
lot 3
raffle

louche
disreputable 1
doubtful 3

loud°
blatant 2
brassy 2
conspicuous 2
extravagant 4
flashy 1
full 11
garish
gaudy
hot 8
noisy
obstreperous
piercing 1
pushy
raucous
resonant
rowdy 1
sharp 7
sporty
strident
tasteless 1
tawdry
thunderous
urgent 2

loud-mouth
braggart

loudness
expression 4
volume 3

lough
gulf 1

lounge°
bar 6
casual 4
dawdle
idle 6
loaf[2] 1
parlour
recline
rest[1] 6
sprawl 2

lounge bar
pub

lounge lizard
flirt 3
idler
loafer
swell 6

lounging robe
robe 1
wrapper 1

lour°
frown 1, 3
glare 2, 4
pout 1
scowl 1

louring
black 4
dark 5
heavy 9
menacing
ominous 1
overcast
portentous 1
sombre 1

louse
rogue 1
scoundrel
stinker
wretch 1

louse up
botch
bungle
butcher 4
foul 16b

louse up (*cont.*)
hash 3
queer 5
ruin 9
screw 7b

lousy°
alive 4
atrocious 2
awful 1
bad 1, 4
bum 4
cheap 3
dreadful 1
inferior 3
miserable 2, 3
off colour 1
par 5a
pit[1] 4
poor 4
punk 2
replete 1
rotten 4, 5
sad 3
stinking 2
terrible 1, 2, 3
wretched 1

lousy with°
at **lousy 4**
replete 1
thick 2

lout
barbarian 2
clod 2
clown 2
gawk 1
hulk 2
peasant
rowdy 2
slob

loutish
barbarian 3
boorish
coarse 2
hulking
obtuse 2
provincial 2
rough 3
rude 1
rustic 2
uncivilized 2
unrefined 1

lovable°
adorable

love°
adore 3
affection
appetite 1
attachment 3
beloved 2
care 6b
darling 1
dear 3
delight 2
devotion 3
dote
esteem 1
fellow 4
friendship 2
heart 5
like[2] 1
liking 1
luxuriate 1
nil
paramour
partiality 2
passion 3, 4
romance 2
sweetheart
thing 4
wallow 2
warmth 2

-in love
adore 3
love 7
sweet 8

loveable
lovable

love affair°
at **love 5**
affair 4

loved
adorable
beloved 1
darling 3

loved (*cont.*)
dear 1
old 8
precious 2

love-letter°
note 2

loveliness
beauty 1

lovely°
beautiful 1
bonny
comely
cute 1
darling 4
delightful 1
exquisite 3
extraordinary 2
fair[1] 7
fine[1] 10
picturesque 1
pleasant 1
prepossessing
pretty 1
stunning 2
sweet 4

lovemaking
intercourse 2
sex 2

lover°
admirer 2
beloved 2
date 3
enthusiast
fan
fellow 4
flame 3
friend 3
gallant 5
girl 2
love 3
mistress 1
paramour
philanderer
suitor
sweetheart

love-seat
couch 1
lounge 5

love story
romance 3

lovey-dovey
romantic 4

loving
affectionate
demonstrative 1
devoted
fond 1
friendly 2
great 10
intimate[1] 1
paternal 1
tender[1] 6, 9
warm 3

lovingly
dearly 2
fondly
warmly 1
well[1] 5

low°
base[2] 1, 2
contemptible
deep 7
degenerate 1
dejected
despicable
despondent
dirty 6
disgraceful 1
dishonourable 3
disreputable 1
faint 1
filthy 2
flat 14a
foul 4
glum
grovelling
gruff 2
hollow 6
humble 3
inaudible
infamous 2
lousy 1
mangy
mean[2] 2

low (*cont.*)
melancholy 1
menial 1
obsequious
paltry
poor 2
profane 3
prurient 2
rank[2] 2
reprobate 1
rotten 4
sad 1
scurrilous
scurvy
seamy
servile
shabby 4
shameful
short 6
soft 4
sordid 1
sort 6
stinking 2
tasteless 1
vulgar 1
weak 7
wicked 2
wretched 4

-in low spirits
dejected

low blow
dig 8

low-born
humble 3
low[1] 7
plebeian 1

lowboy
cabinet 1

lowbrow
barbarian 2
philistine 1, 2
plebeian 2

low-class
common 3
plebeian 1
sleazy 2
vulgar 1

low-cost
cheap 1
inexpensive

low-cut
low[1] 11

low down
beneath 1

low-down°
dirt 4
dirty 6
dope 3
fact 3
information
intelligence 2
news 1
rotten 4
rumour 1
scoop 3
word 2

lower°
bow 3
cut 8
debase 1
decrease 1
degrade 2
depreciate 1
depress 2, 3
diminish 1
discount 1
discredit 1
downgrade 1
downwards
fall 3
frown 1, 3
glare 2, 4
humble 4
inferior 1, 2
junior
lapse 4
lour 1, 2
low[1] 10
modify 2
modulate
pare 2
peg 3
pout 1
prostitute 2

lower (*cont.*)
pull 9c
put 16e
reduce 5, 6
scale[3] 5
scowl 1
slash 3
soften 3
subordinate 1
subside 1
take 31b
vitiate 1
weaken 1

Lower chamber, House
parliament 2

lower-class
plebeian 1

lower class(es)
mass 6
mob 2
rabble 2

lower down
below 1
beneath 1

lowered
cut 28
sunken 3

lowering
black 4
dark 5
decrease 2
degrading
derogatory
dip 5
dismal
fall 26
heavy 9
lapse 3
leaden 3
menacing
ominous 1
overcast
portentous 1
prostitution 2
sombre 1

lower oneself
condescend
descend 3
scrape 4
sink 9
stoop 2

lower than
below 5, 8, 9, 10
beneath 4
subordinate 1
under 5

lower world
hell 1

lowest
floor 3
minimum 1, 2

lowest level
floor 3

low-grade
cheap 3
common 4
inferior 3
poor 4
sleazy 2

low-key
subdued 1
understated
unobtrusive

lowland(s)
flat 14b

low-life
reprobate 1, 2

lowliness
humility
inferiority 1

lowly°
base[2] 2
humble 3
inferior 2
low[1] 7
mean[2] 2
meek 1
menial 1
modest 2
obscure 4
plebeian 1
shabby 4

lowly (*cont.*)
simple 5

low-lying
low[1] 1

low point
ebb 3

low-priced
cheap 1
inexpensive

low-quality
coarse 4
inferior 3
lousy 2
unprofessional 2

low regard
disregard 3

low road
road 2

low-spirited
blue 1
dejected
desolate 3
despondent
downhearted
forlorn 1
melancholy 1
miserable 1
unhappy 1

low spirits
gloom 2

-in low spirits
dejected

low tide
ebb 3

low water
ebb 3

loyal°
brotherly
constant 1
devoted
faithful 1
fast[1] 5
great 10
noble 4
real 4
special 5
stand 5a
staunch 1
steadfast
steady 5
stick[1] 13
true 2
trustworthy
yeomanly

loyalist
patriot
patriotic
stalwart 4

loyalty°
attachment 3
dedication 1
devotion 2, 3
duty 2
faith 3
homage
piety 1

-loyalties
colour 2b

lozenge
pill 1
tablet 4

LP
record 7

l.s.d.
purse 2

L-7
square 6, 9

lubberly
clumsy
hulking
ungraceful 1

lubricant
oil 1

lubricate
oil 3
smooth 10

lubricated
slippery 1

lubricator
oil 1

lubric(i)ous
bawdy
erotic 3
hot 7
impure 4
incontinent 2
indecent 2
lascivious 1
lecherous
lewd
libertine 2
prurient 1
rude 3
sensual
lubricity
impurity 3
ribaldry
lucid
clear 6
coherent 2
distinct 1
graphic 1
intelligible
luminous 3
pictorial 1
plain 2
right 4
simple 1
sound[2] 4
vivid 1
lucidity
clarity 2
simplicity 1
Lucifer
devil 1
luck°
accident 2
adventure 4
blessing 2
chance 1
coincidence 3
fate 1
fortune 2
gamble 2
godsend
hazard 2
lot 2
place 10
windfall
-as luck would have it
incidentally 2
-in luck
fortunate 1
-out of luck
unfortunate 1
-with luck
hopefully 2
luckily
happily 1
well[1] 15
luckless
doomed 2
poor 6
unfortunate 1
unhappy 2
unsuccessful 2
luck out
place 10
lucky°
accidental
coincidental
fortunate 1
happy 2
narrow 6
opportune 1
propitious
providential
seasonable
successful 1
lucky break, stroke
fluke
lucky dip
miscellany
lucrative
fat 4
gainful
profitable 1
successful 2
lucre
fund 2
money 1

lucre (*cont.*)
purse 2
riches
lucubrate
cram 2
grind 4
mug 6
overwork 2
slave 3
study 1
Lucullan
epicurean 2
Lucullus
epicure
gourmet
ludicrous°
absurd 1
crazy 2
farcical
foolish 3
funny 1
grotesque 2
humorous
impossible 2
improbable
inane
insane 2
nonsensical
preposterous
queer 1
rich 11
ridiculous
senseless 3
silly 1
stupid 2
unreasonable 1
unthinkable 2
witty
zany 1
ludicrously
madly 2
ludicrousness
absurdity 1
humour 1
stupidity 2
luff
shiver[1] 2
lug°
carry 1
cart 2
drag 1
draw 1
gawk 1
haul 1
hump 3
pull 1
tow
luggage°
bag 2
thing 8c
lugubrious
dismal
doleful
forlorn 1
funereal
gloomy 2
glum
hopeless 3
joyless 2
melancholy 1
moody 1
morbid 3
mournful 1
sad 1, 2
sombre 1
stern 2
sullen
tragic
woebegone
lugubriously
sadly 2
lugubriousness
melancholy 2
lukewarm°
cold 3
cool 5
dead 4
half-hearted
indifferent 1
lackadaisical 2
limp[2] 3
listless
tepid 1, 2
unenthusiastic

lukewarm (*cont.*)
warm 1
lull°
break 28
calm 5
delay 5
gap 1
interlude
pause 2
plateau 2
quieten
rock[2] 1
slack 5
still 9
tranquillize
truce 1
lulling
dreamy 3
lulu
killer 2
lumber°
plod 1
stuff 2
timber 2
lumbering
shambling
luminary
celebrity 2
dignitary
hero 1
idol 2
legend 2
name 3
notable 3
personage
personality 2
somebody 2
star 2
worthy 3
luminescence
light[1] 3
luminescent
luminous 2
luminosity
flare 4
glow 1
illumination 1
light[1] 3
lustre 1
radiance 1
splendour 2
luminous°
ablaze 2
bright 1
brilliant 1
fiery 2
glowing 1
light[1] 13
radiant 1
luminously
clear 17
luminousness
glow 2
lustre 1
radiance 1
splendour 2
lummox
boor 2
clown 2
duffer
gawk 1
lump°
assemble 2
blob
block 1
bulge 1
bump 2
cake 2
clod 1
clump 1, 3
elevation 2
gob
growth 4
hump 1
loaf[1] 1
mass 3
mouthful
nub 1
pat[1] 4
peasant
piece 1
portion 1
protrusion
swelling

lump (*cont.*)
tumour
wad 1
welt 2
lumpen
rustic 2
lumpish
obtuse 2
stolid
stupid 1
lumpishness
stupidity 1
lumpy°
bumpy
gnarled
irregular 1
rough 1
lunacy°
folly 1
insanity 1, 2
madness 1, 2
mania 2
lunatic
crazy 1
delirious 1
deranged
inane
insane 1
mad 1
madman
maniac 1
maniacal 1
mental 2
psychotic 1, 2
weirdo
lunch
dine
eat
meal 1
tiffin
luncheon
meal 1
tiffin
lunch-hook
hand 1
lunch-room
café
lune
crescent 1
lunette
crescent 1
lunge°
make 30b
plough 2
snap 3b
thrust 2, 4
lunkhead
dolt
lupine
rapacious
lurch°
careen
founder[2] 3
jerk 2, 4
jolt 4
jump 11
pitch[1] 4
reel 1
rock[2] 2
stagger 1
stumble 1
toss 5
trip 5
walk 1
wallow 3
lurcher
mongrel
lurching
shambling
lure°
appeal 4
attract
attraction 2
bring 3
chat 3
come-on
decoy 1, 2
draw 4, 16
entice
enticement 2
incentive
induce 1
inducement

lure (*cont.*)
invitation 2
lead 9b
magnetism
motive 1
premium 2
pull 5, 20
rope 4
seduce 1
solicit 2
spell[2] 3
stratagem
take 20
tempt 1
temptation 2
lurid°
conspicuous 2
frightful 2
juicy 2
lascivious 2
prurient 2
pulp 4
rank[2] 3
sensational 2
luring
attractive
lurk°
ambush 2
hide[1] 1
prowl 1
sneak 1
steal 3
lurking
prowl 3
sneaking 1
luscious°
delicious 1
mellow 1
rich 6
savoury 1
succulent
tasty
tempting 2
voluptuous 2
yummy
lush°
alcoholic 2
drunk 3
flourishing
juicy 1
luxuriant 1, 2
profuse 2
prolific 1
rank[2] 1
rich 4
soak 3
splendid 1
lust°
desire 3
impurity 3
passion 3
thirst 1
lust after°
at **lust 3**
fancy 11
hanker
thirst 2
want 1
lustful°
carnal
erotic 1
fast[1] 2
hot 7
immoral 2
impure 4
incontinent 2
lascivious 1
lecherous
lewd
obscene 1
passionate 2
prurient 1
randy
romantic 4
scandalous 1
sensual
sexual 2
sultry 2
torrid 2
vulgar 2
wanton 1
lustfully
fast[1] 9

lustfulness
desire 3
eye 4
impurity 3
lust 1
ribaldry
lustily
vigorously
lustrate
purify 2
lustre°
brilliance 1
glare 1
glaze 2
gloss[1] 1
glow 1
polish 5
radiance 1
renown
sheen
shine 4
splendour 2
lustreless
dead 10
drab
lacklustre
mousy 1
lustrous°
bright 3
brilliant 1
clear 3
glossy 1
golden 3
luminous 1
opalescent
pearly
radiant 1
rich 5
scintillating 1
shiny
silky
silver 3
sleek 1
lusty°
bawdy
buxom 1
earthy
racy 2
sexy 2
stalwart 1
stout 4
suggestive 2
sultry 2
vigorous
lusus naturae
monster 2
luxe
plush
posh
luxuriance
prodigality 2
luxuriant°
abundant 2
fertile
flourishing
lush 1
overgrown
plentiful 2
prodigal 2
profuse 2
rampant 2
rank[2] 1
thick 4
luxuriate°
flourish 1
grow 1
revel 1
luxuriate in°
at **luxuriate 1**
revel 1
roll 10b
savour 3
wallow 2
luxurious°
elegant 3
epicurean 1
fancy 3
fruitful 3
grand 1
high 12
lush 3
luxuriant 1
magnificent
noble 5

luxurious (*cont.*)
opulent 2
palatial
plush
posh
princely 2
rich 4
sensuous
soft 13
splendid 1
sumptuous
swanky
swell 7
upper-class 2
voluptuous 1
luxuriously
richly 1
well[1] 4
luxuriousness
elegance 2
grandeur 1
luxury 1
prodigality 2
splendour 1
luxury°
comfort 3
delicacy 4
ease 3
elegance 2
fancy 3
frill 2
indulgence 2, 3
posh
prodigality 2
prosperity
splendour 1
style 3
-luxuries
creature 2
lycée
school 1
Lyceum
school 1
lying°
deceitful
dishonest
evasion 2
false 2
flat 2
hypocrisy
hypocritical
insincere
perjury
recumbent
supine 1
two-faced
lying down
flat 2
prone 1
prostrate 3
recumbent
supine 1
lymphatic
supine 2
lynch
hang 2
string 12
lynx-eyed
eagle-eyed
sharp-eyed
lyric°
lay[3]
poem
poetic 1
pretty 2
sweet 3
-lyrics°
at **lyric 4**
book 2
word 9b
lyrical°
lyric 1
melodious
musical
poetic 1
pretty 2
lyricist
poet
lyrist
poet

M

ma
mother 1
macabre°
frightful 2
ghastly 2
ghoulish 2
grim 3
gruesome
horrible 1
lurid 2
morbid 2
sick 5
terrible 4
unearthly 2
macadamize
pave 1
macaroni
dude 1
swell 6
mace
club 1
staff 1
Machiavellian°
calculating
designing
insincere
opportunistic
politic 1
scheming
serpentine 1
smooth 8
subtle 3
two-faced
Machiavellian-ism
diplomacy 2
machinate
cabal 3
engineer 5
manoeuvre 3
plot[1] 3
scheme 4
wangle
machination°
device 2
diplomacy 2
dodge 4
finesse 2
intrigue 3
manoeuvre 1
plot[1] 1
politics 2
scheme 3
trick 1
wile
machinator
operator 3
machine°
apparatus
car 1
device 1
engine
gadget
mechanism 1
tool 1
machine copy
duplicate 2
machine-driven
mechanical 1
machine-like
mechanical 2
machine-made
mechanical 1
machinery
apparatus
device 1, 2
gear 1
hardware 2
mechanism 2
movement 4
plant 3
works 2
machine screw
bolt 3
screw 1
machine shop
shop 2

machinist
operative 2
machismo°
bravado
bravery
manhood 1
macho°
brave 1
manly
macilent
lean[1] 1
mack
pander 3
macrocosm
universe 1
macula
spot 1
macular
spotty 1
mad°
absurd 1
angry 1
berserk
beside 3
crazy 1, 5
delirious 1
deranged
desperate 2
distraught
disturbed 2
fanatical
flighty 2
foolish 2
frantic
furious 1
hectic
homicidal
hysterical 1
improbable
imprudent
inane
indignant
insane 1
maniacal 1
mental 2
mind 14
nonsensical
off 4
pell-mell 2
preposterous
psychotic 1
queer 4
quixotic
rabid 1, 2
rampage 2
raving 1
reckless
romantic 2
senseless 3
sick 4
silly 1
stupid 2
twist 11
unbalanced 2
unreasonable 1
unsound 3
unthinking 1
upset 10
way-out 1
wild 5, 9
zany 1
mad about°
at **mad 6**
daft 3
love 7
sweet 8
madam
procurer
mad as a hatter, March hare
crazy 1
deranged
insane 1
mad 1
madcap
daredevil 2
devilish
foolhardy
hare-brained 1
hotheaded
impulsive
mad 2
rash[1]
reckless

madcap (*cont.*)
wild 6, 7
wit 3
zany 1
madden°
anger 2
annoy 1
enrage
exasperate 1
inflame 1
infuriate
outrage 4
provoke 3
wall 3
maddened
bristle 3
crazy 1
furious 1
possessed
maddening
provocative 2
trying
mad dog
terror 2
mademoiselle
girl 1
lass
maid 1
miss[2]
youth 2
made of money
opulent 1
made to meas-ure
tailor-made 1
made to order
perfect 4
tailor-made 1, 2
made-up
artificial 2
assumed 2
bum 3
false 2
fictional
fictitious 1, 2
imaginary
mythical 2
romantic 1
sham 2
unreal 2
mad for°
at **mad 6**
madhouse
bedlam
zoo 2
madly°
head 8
mad 5
madman°
maniac 1
psychotic 2
weirdo
madness°
fanaticism 2
folly 1
insanity 1
lunacy 1
mania 2
stupidity 2
madwoman
madman
maniac 1
psychotic 2
weirdo
Maecenas
friend 4
patron 1
philanthropist
sponsor 1
maelstrom
eddy 1
whirlpool
maenad
hag
shrew
maestro
director 2
genius 1
master 2
professional 3
specialist
virtuoso 1

mafficking
festivity 1
gaiety 2
obstreperous
Mafia
syndicate 2
underworld 1
Mafioso
criminal 3
gangster
racketeer
thug
magazine°
journal 1
organ 2
periodical
publication 2
rag[1] 2
review 7
storehouse
maggoty
filthy 1
sordid 3
magic°
admirable
charm 2
divine 3
enchant 1
enchantment 1
excellent
fabulous 3
fascination
glamour
hocus-pocus 3
magnetism
mumbo-jumbo 2
mystique
sorcery
spell[2] 1
superb
trick 5
world 8
magical
charmed 1
glamorous 1
magic 4, 6
miraculous
occult 2
psychic 2
supernatural
magician°
charmer
sorcerer
witch 1
magisterial
arbitrary 2
hard 4
heavy-handed 2
imperative 2
judicial 3
lofty 2
majestic 2
masterful 2
overbearing
pompous 1
magistrate
judge 1
magnanimity
benevolence 1
charity 1, 2
heart 5
humanity 3
mercy
nobility 1
philanthropy 1
self-denial 1
tolerance 1
magnanimous
benevolent
big 6
bountiful 1
charitable 1
chivalrous
forgiving
generous 1, 2
heroic 2
human 3
large 2
lenient
liberal 1
merciful
noble 4
open 14
philanthropic

magnanimous (*cont.*)
profuse 4
selfless
tolerant
unselfish
magnate
dignitary
merchant 3
mogul
personage
tycoon
magnet
lure 2
magnetic°
glamorous 1
magic 6
prepossessing
magnetism°
attraction 1
charm 2, 3
draw 16
fascination
glamour
invitation 2
magic 3
pull 20
spell[2] 3
magnification°
exaggeration
magnificence
brilliance 1
dazzle 3
display 5
glory 3
grandeur 1
luxury 1
pageantry
pomp
pre-eminence 2
splendour 1
state 3
magnificent°
beautiful 2
bright 7
brilliant 2
dazzling
fine[1] 1
gallant 3
glorious 2
gorgeous 1
grand 1
grandiose 2
imperial 2
imposing
lofty 2
luxurious 1
majestic 1
monumental 1
noble 5
palatial
princely 2
proud 4
regal 1
royal 2
splendid 1
statuesque
striking
stunning 2
sumptuous
superb
terrific 2
transcendent
magnificently
beautifully 1, 2
magnified
inflated 1
magnify°
aggravate 1
amplify 2
blow[1] 8c, 8d
deepen 2
double 6
enhance
enlarge 1
exaggerate
expand 3
heighten 2
inflate 3
intensify
maximize 1, 2
overstate

make a pretence (of) (*cont.*)
profess 2

make a run for it
flee 1
make 26

make a shambles (of)
clutter 3
complicate 2
mess 5b

make as if°
at **make 25, 37e**

make a speech
lecture 3

make a splash
place 10

make a stand
fight 2, 3
maintain 4

make as though
make 25, 37e

make a sucker of
swindle 1

make available
enlist 2
market 4
offer 2
release 2
serve 3
stock 9

make away°
at **make 26**
abduct
appropriate 2

make away with°
at **make 27**
embezzle
spirit 10
steal 1
take 3

make believe°
at **believe 3**
act 8
fake 2
fool 5
play 10
pretend 1, 3

make-believe
counterfeit 2
fancied
fanciful 2
fancy 6
fantasy 3
fictitious 2
mimic 5
mock 3
mythical 2
pretence 1, 2
pretended
sham 2
unreal 1, 2, 3

make bold
dare 2
presume 2
venture 2

make both ends meet
get 28b

make capital out of
exploit 2
profit 4

make certain
assure 1, 3
ensure 1
guarantee 2
see 5
settle 2

make clear
clarify 1
clear 22
get 26
home 11
indicate 3
put 10
show 1
solve
spell[3] 2

make concessions
allow 6
way 11b

make contact with
reach 3

make do°
at **make 29**
cope 1
fend 1
get 28b
improvise 2
manage 4
muddle 3
shift 2

make ends meet
get 28b

make enquiries
see 12b

make every effort
shoulder 3
strive 1

make excuses (for)
apologize 2
rationalize 1

make eyes at
ogle 1
watch 3

make fast (to)
bind 1
bolt 11
clamp 2
fix 1
lash[2]
moor[2]
peg 4
secure 8
tie 1

make for°
at **make 30**
come 8
occasion 5
take 38b

make fun (of)°
at **fun 5**
deride
gibe 1
guy 2
jeer 1
laugh 2a
leg 8
mimic 3
mock 1
parody 3
poke 4
pull 15
rag[2]
ridicule 2
satirize
scorn 4
send 9a
taunt 1
twit[1]

make good°
at **make 31**
compensate 1
flourish 1
follow 10
get 27, 31a
make 32a, 40
offset 1
place 10
prosper
prove 1
recoup
redeem 6
replace 3
rise 8
satisfy 4
succeed 3

make happen
effect 7
effectuate
realize 1

make haste
hasten 1
hurry 1
move 12b
rush 1
speed 3
step 16

make head(s) or tail(s) of
figure 12b
get 19
grasp 2

make headway°
at **headway 2**
go 1
look 11c
pick 8f
proceed 1
progress 5
stem[2] 2

make inquiries
follow 11a
see 12b

make inroads
encroach

make it°
at **make 32**
arrive 2
grade 5
make 31b
manage 4
mark 9
muddle 3
pan 6
prosper
reach 2
rise 8
shift 2
squeeze 6
succeed 3

make it snappy
rush 1

make it with
make 24

make it worth someone's while
reward 4

make known°
at **make 33**
advise 2
air 7
announce 1
bring 13b
circulate 2
communicate 1
declare 2
deliver 4
expose 1
express 2
give 15c
indicate 3
intimate[2]
introduce 1
leak 5
light[1] 9
mention 1
open 23
present[2] 4
proclaim 1
pronounce 3
propagate 3
publish
put 9, 17d, 18b, 23e
register 5
relate 2
reveal
rumour 2
show 1
signify 1
speak 4
spread 2
tell[1] 2
vent 3
voice 4

make light of
disregard 1
minimize 2
play 13, 19a
scoff[1]
trivialize
whitewash

make little (of)
minimize 2
write 4b

make love (to)°
at **love 6**
cuddle 2
romance 6

make manifest
show 1

make mention
mention 1
refer 1

make merry°
at **merry 2**
carouse 1
celebrate 2
dissipate 4
enjoy 3
exult
paint 7
revel 2

make mincemeat of
rout 2

make money
coin 4
pay 7
rake[1] 4

make much ado about nothing
overreact

make much of°
at **make 34**
dote
extol
gush 2
maximize 2
overstate

make no mistake
doubtless 1

make note of
mark 15a
mind 16
minute[1] 4
notice 1
register 3, 5
watch 3

make obeisance
bow 5
scrape 4

make obsolescent, obsolete
date 6

make off°
at **make 35**
embezzle
flee 1
go 2
make 26
move 2
run 2
spirit 10
steal 1
take 3

make off with°
at **make 36**
abduct
appropriate 2
nick 3
snap 4

make one's blood boil
anger 2
enrage
infuriate
madden 1
outrage 4

make one's blood run cold
horrify 1
terrify

make oneself heard
pipe 8
speak 11a

make oneself scarce
depart 1
escape 1
flee 1
push 9b

make oneself understood
communicate 3
put 10

make one's escape
flee 1
fly 2

make one's flesh crawl, creep
scare 1
terrify

make one's fortune
prosper

make one's gorge rise
sicken 2

make one's hair stand on end
frighten
horrify 1
scare 1
terrify

make one's head spin
intoxicate 2

make one's head swim
stagger 2

make one's home
occupy 2
settle 4

make one's mark°
at **mark 9**

make one's pile
prosper

make one's rounds
patrol 3

make one's skin crawl
repel 2

make one's way
fare 4
journey 3
mount 2
wade 1

make out°
at **make 37**
cuddle 2
decipher 2
distinguish 3
fare 4
fend 1
fill 9a
get 28b
love 6
make 4, 29
manage 4
notice 2
perceive 1
pet[1] 4
pick 7b
pretend 1
score 14
see 1
spot 6
tell[1] 8
understand 1
write 1

make over°
at **make 38**
bequeath
cede
deliver 2
dispose 3c
give 1
pass 18b
sign 11
trust 6
turn 3

make-over
shake-up

make overtures to
approach 3

make plain
clarify 1
clear 22
explain 1
show 1
solve
spell[3] 2

make progress
look 11c
proceed 1

make provision(s) for
prepare 1

make public°
at **public 7**
air 7
announce 1
break 2
bring 13b
give 15c
leak 5
publish
put 17d, 23e
report 4
spread 2
vent 3

maker
author
brand 1
creator
manufacturer
producer 1

make ready (for)
condition 5
poise 3
provide 5
ready 10
set 12a

make redundant
eject 3
fire 11
sack 4

make reference to
observe 4
refer 1
speak 9

make reparation(s)
amends
compensate 1
penance 2

make restitution
amends
compensate 1
make 31a
offset 1
redeem 5
replace 3
requite 2
restore 1

make room
make 41

make sense (of)
hang 11b
interpret 1
stack 7a
tie 6a
wash 8

make sheep's eyes at
ogle 1

makeshift°
excuse 6
flimsy 1, 2
rude 4
scratch 6
stopgap 1, 2
temporary

make someone eat humble pie
mortify 1

make someone pay
pay 5

make someone see red
enfuriate
enrage
madden 1

make something of oneself
rise 8

make space
make 41

make sport of°
at **sport 3**
deride
fun 5

make sport of
(*cont.*)
laugh 2a
mock 1
parody 3
poke 4
ridicule 2
satirize
taunt 1
make sternway
reverse 5
make sure
assure 1
check 4
ensure 1
guarantee 2
see 5
settle 2
make the acquaintance of
meet[1] 3
make the grade°
at **grade 5**
arrive 2
make 32a
mark 9
measure 15b
muster 3
qualify 2
rise 8
make the most of
profit 4
profiteer 2
make tracks
bugger 5
flee 1
fly 3
make 26
nick 5
speed 3
make uncomfortable
discomfit 1
trouble 1
make up°
at **make 39**
coin 3
compensate 1
compose 1, 2
compound 1
conceive 2
devise 1
discover 3
fabricate 2
fancy 9
form 9
generate 4
invent 1, 2
make 4, 31a
manufacture 2
offset 1
recoup
retrieve 3
set 9
spin 2
stage 5
think 6
turn 8
write 3
make-up°
composition 2, 5
design 6
disposition 1
fabric 2
fabrication 2
fibre 3
format 2
frame 3
nature 1
organization 2
paint 3
personality 1
psychology
set-up 1
structure 1
substance 1
temper 1
make up for°
at **make 40**
balance 3
cancel 3
compensate 1

make up for
(*cont.*)
correct 4
cover 10
make 31a
neutralize
offset 1
outweigh
redeem 5
right 19
make up one's mind°
at **mind 13**
decide 1
determine 3
resolve 1
see 8
make use of
draw 13a
embrace 2
employ 2
enjoy 2
fall 9
profit 4
take 21
tap[2] 6
touch 9
use 1, 2
work 10
make water°
at **water 4**
urinate
make way°
at **make 41**
progress 5
thread 4
walk 1
weave 4
make whoopee
carouse 1
frolic 3
paint 7
revel 2
making
assembly 3
creation 1
fabrication 1
manufacture 3
preparation 3
production 1
-makings
ingredient
stuff 1, 3
making allowance for
considering
making love
intercourse 2
sex 2
making out
sex 2
maladjusted
disturbed 2
neurotic
problem 3
maladroit
awkward 1
clumsy
heavy-handed 1
incompetent
inept 1
left-handed 1
tactless
tasteless 1
thumb 2
maladroitly
roughly 3
maladroitness
ineptitude 1
malady
ailment
bug 2
disease 1
disorder 3
illness
infirmity 2
malaise
ailment
concern 6
discontent
dissatisfaction 1
excitement 1
pang 2

malapert
pert 1
malapropism
howler
misuse 2
malapropos
improper 2
inappropriate
incongruous
inopportune
irrelevant
point 15
malarkey
drivel 3
gobbledegook 1
moonshine 2
mumbo-jumbo 1
nonsense 1
rot 4
rubbish 2
stuff 4
talk 18
trash 1
malcontent
disgruntled
killjoy
misery 4
troublemaker
male°
man 1
manly
malediction
abuse 8
curse 1
jinx 1
oath 2
malefaction
offence 1
outrage 1
malefactor
criminal 3
culprit 2
delinquent 1
felon
miscreant 1
offender
sinner
transgressor
villain
malefic
dreadful 2
evil 1
hateful 2
miscreant 2
perverted
sarcastic
maleficent
devilish
diabolic 2
dreadful 2
evil 1
infernal 2
malevolence
animosity
devilry 2
grudge 1
hostility 1
ill will
rancour
sarcasm
spite 1
venom 2
virulence 2
malevolent
cutting 2
damnable
devilish
diabolic 2
dirty 3
dreadful 2
evil 1
evil-minded 2
fiendish
hateful 2
ill 3
infernal 2
malignant 2
merciless
miscreant 2
perverted
poisonous 2
rancorous
sarcastic
sinister 2

malevolent
(*cont.*)
spiteful
venomous 2
vicious 2
virulent 2
wanton 4
malevolently
ill 12
malformation
abnormality 2
malformed
deformed 1
grotesque 1
misshapen
malfunction
play 17b
wrong 8b
malfunctioning
dud 2
faulty
mal gré
willy-nilly 1
malice
animosity
devilry 2
grudge 1
hate 3
hostility 1
ill will
rancour
resentment
sarcasm
spite 1
venom 2
virulence 2
malicious
black 6
cutting 2
damnable
diabolic 2
dirty 3
evil-minded 2
fiendish
hateful 2
hurtful 2
ill 3
infernal 2
malignant 2
mean[2] 4
mischievous 2
perverted
poisonous 2
rancorous
sarcastic
sharp 5
spiteful
venomous 2
vicious 2
virulent 2
wanton 4
maliciously
ill 12
maliciousness
sarcasm
spite 1
venom 2
virulence 2
malign
abuse 3
attack 2
blacken 2
blaspheme 2
devilish
diabolic 2
discredit 1
disparage 2
evil 3
ghoulish 1
impeach 2
libel 4
malignant 2
mischievous 2
perverted
rancorous
scurrilous
sinister 2
slander 2
unhealthy 2
venomous 2
vilify
virulent 2
vituperative
wrong 9

malignancy
tumour
virulence 1
malignant°
black 5
destructive 1
devilish
evil 3
fiendish
hateful 2
poisonous 1, 2
rancorous
sharp 5
sinister 2
venomous 2
vicious 2
virulent 2
maligning
abuse 8
foul 6
malignity
outrage 1
rancour
spite 1
venom 2
virulence 1, 2
malingerer
derelict 3
slouch 3
truant 1
wastrel 2
malingering
idleness 2
truant 2
mall
parade 3
malleability
flexibility 2
malleable
adaptable
dutiful
flexible 2
passive 2
plastic 1
pliable 1
tractable 2
malodorous
foul 3
nasty 1
offensive 3
rancid
smelly
stinking 1
maltreat
abuse 2
batter 3
grind 5
harm 3
ill-treat
injure 2
knock 3d
manhandle
mishandle 1
mistreat
molest 2
oppress 2
persecute 1
punish 3
torment 1
wrong 9
maltreated
abused 2
downtrodden
maltreatment
abuse 6
ill 9
injury
mistreatment
oppression
outrage 1
persecution 1
punishment 3
sacrilege 1
mam
mother 1
mama's boy
milksop
sissy
mamma
breast 1
mother 1
mammal
animal 1

Mammon
purse 2
mammoth
colossal 1
enormous
giant 1
gigantic
great 1
huge
immense
large 3
massive
monstrous 3
prodigious 1
thumping 1
vast
voluminous 1
weighty 1
whopping 1
man°
beggar 2
boss 1
bugger 2
chap
chief 1
date 3
director 1
dude 2
fellow 1, 4
friend 3
guy 1
hand 4
head 2
human 4
humanity 1
leader 1
love 3
mass 6
master 1
mortal 6
one 4
person 1
physician
piece 5
servant 1
soul 2
steady 9
stick[2] 2
unwashed 2
-man's
male
-men
people 1
reinforcement 3
world 2
-men's
facility 2b
lavatory
man about town
blade 4
dude 1
playboy
manacle(s)°
bond 1
chain 2
handcuffs
restraint 2
shackle 1, 3
tether 2
manage°
administer 1
afford 1
boss 2
carry 11b
chair 4
conduct 3
control 1, 3
cope 1
direct 1
discipline 7
dispense 3b
fare 4
find 8
get 9, 28b
go 41
govern 1
guide 3
handle 3, 4
head 11
hold 15b
husband 2
lead 3
make 29, 37f
manipulate 1

marred
defective 1
disfigured
flawed
hurt 8
pitted
marriage°
alliance 2
bridal
match 3
matrimonial
union 1
wed 1
wedding 1, 2
married
attached 4
matrimonial
marring
impairment
marrow
core 2
essence 1
gist
heart 3
meat 2
pith 1
pulp 1
quintessence
spirit 6
spunk
marry°
join 1
match 5
mate 4
mingle 1
pair 2
splice 1
unite 2
wed 1, 2
marrying
union 1
wedding 2
marsh°
bog 1
flat 14b
mire 1
morass 1
swamp 1
marshal
assemble 1
draw 15c
mass 8
mobilize
muster 1
rally 3
round 19
scrape 6
marshland
morass 1
marshy
muddy 1
watery 3
mart
fair[2]
martial°
aggressive 1
belligerent 1
militant 1
military 1
offensive 1
martinet
disciplinarian
tyrant
martyr
persecute 1
victim 1
martyrdom
passion 5
marvel°
admire 1
gem 2
jewel 2
magician 2
phenomenon 2
prodigy 2
sight 3
spectacle 1
wonder 1, 4
marvellous°
admirable
amazing
awesome
beautiful 2

marvellous (*cont.*)
bully 4
capital 6
dandy 2
divine 3
excellent
exquisite 5
extraordinary 2
fabulous 2, 3
fantastic 4
fine[1] 1
glorious 2
good 2
gorgeous 2
grand 5
great 12
heavenly 2
incredible 2
magnificent
majestic 1
mean[2] 6
miraculous
monumental 1
neat 5
outstanding 1
phenomenal
portentous 2
prodigious 2
remarkable 2
ripping
sensational 3
splendid 1, 2, 3
striking
stunning 2
superb
superlative
supreme 4
sweet 5
swell 8
terrific 2
transcendent
virtuoso 2
world 8
marvellously
beautifully 2
charm 4
famously
perfectly 2
well[1] 2
marvy
gorgeous 2
grand 5
great 12
marvellous
Mary Doe
people 3
masculine
macho
male
manly
masculinity
machismo
manhood 1
mash
crush 3
grind 1
pound[1] 2
press 3
pulp 2, 3
masher
flirt 3
rake[2]
roué
mash note
love letter
note 2
mask°
block 4b
blur 4
camouflage 1, 2
cloak 3
colour 6
cover 2, 15
disguise 1
face 3
front 4, 5
gloss[1] 2, 4
hide[1] 2
keep 14a
mantle 3
obscure 6
outside 2
persona

mask (*cont.*)
pretence 2
screen 7
secrete[1]
semblance 1
shade 12
shroud 1, 3
shut 5c
smother 4
veil 1, 2
veneer
masked
invisible 2
veiled
masked ball
masquerade 1
mask-like
straight 8
masochistic
sick 5
masquerade°
dress 5b
face 3
fantasy 3
pretence 2
masquerade as°
at **masquerade 3**
pass 16b
pose 2
represent 2
masquerader
poseur
mass°
accumulate
accumulation 3
amass
amount 2
body 5
bulk 1
bunch 2
clod 1
clump 1, 3
cluster 3
crowd 1
drift 5
flock 1, 2
heap 1
herd 1
huddle 1
hump 1
jam 5
lot 5b
lump[1] 1, 3
majority 1
measure 1
mob 1
mountain 2
number 2
pack 2, 3
pile[1] 1
pile-up 2
preponderance 1
profusion
proportion 4
pulp 2
sea 3
size 1
stack 1, 3
swarm 1, 2
throng 1, 2
tissue
volume 1
wad 1
weight 1, 4
welter 1
-masses
herd 2
hoi polloi
humanity 1
lot 5c
many 3
mob 2
people 3
plenty 1
populace
public 8
rabble 2
riff-raff
score 4
unwashed 2
massacre°
butcher 3
carnage
destruction 2

massacre (*cont.*)
exterminate
holocaust 2
kill 1
killing 1
mow 2
murder 2, 3
removal 2
remove 4
rout 2
slaughter 2, 3
wipe 3
massage°
rub 1, 10
stroke 10
mass destruction
killing 1
mass execution
slaughter 2
mass extermination
slaughter 2
massive°
colossal 1
enormous
extensive 2
gigantic
great 1
gross 1
heavy 1
hefty 1
huge
hulking
immense
large 3
mighty 3
monolithic
monstrous 3
monumental 2
ponderous 1
substantial 2
thumping 1
vast
voluminous 1
weighty 1
whopping 1
massiveness
mass 5
mass murder
holocaust 2
killing 1
slaughter 2
massy
heavy 1
massive
mast
pole[1]
spar[1]
master°
adept 2
back 7a
beat 2
best 11
chief 1
command 3
conquer 3
control 3
dab hand
executive 1
experienced 1
expert 1
finger 10
genius 1
gifted
govern 2
guide 5
instructor
learn 2
lord 1
magician 2
monarch 2
original 3, 5
overcome 1
overpower 1
overthrow 1
pick 8d
principal 4
professional 1, 3
skipper
sovereign 1
specialist
subdue 1
tame 5

master (*cont.*)
teacher
virtuoso 1
masterful°
able 2
adept 1
brilliant 4
capable 1
domineering
expert 2
gifted
master 4
perfect 7
polished 1
practised 1
professional 1
skilful
supreme 4
talented
virtuoso 2
wicked 7
masterfully
handily 2
masterfulness
facility 1
masterliness
facility 1
masterly
able 2
adept 1
capable 1
experienced 1
expert 2
fine[1] 4
gifted
master 4
masterful 1
perfect 7
polished 1
professional 1, 2
skilful
supreme 4
virtuoso 2
wicked 7
mastermind°
brain 2
direct 2
engineer 1, 4
genius 1
highbrow 1
intellectual 3
intelligentsia
master 2
oracle 1
originate 1
prodigy 1
tactician
thinker
masterminding
tactic 2
master of ceremonies
announcer
host[1] 2
moderator
masterpiece°
classic 4
gem 2
pièce de
résistance
work 4
master plan
strategy
master-work
classic 4
masterpiece
work 4
mastery
art 4
better[1] 8
command 8
conquest 2
control 5
craft 1
domination 1
dominion 1
execution 4
expertise
facility 1
grasp 4
grip 2
hold 26
influence 1
power 2

mastery (*cont.*)
predominance
prevalence 2
prowess 1
reign 1
rule 2
skill 1
supremacy 2
sway 4
understanding 3
victory
virtuosity
workmanship
masticate
chew 1
mill 5
munch
masturbation
abuse 7
self-abuse
mat
see **matt**
match°
balance 2, 3
bout 3
coincide
compare 2
comparison 2
competition 2
conform 2
contest 1
coordinate 1
correspond 1
duplicate 2, 3
equal 5
equalize
equivalent 2
fellow 3
fight 7
fit[1] 6
fixture 1
game 2
go 6
hang 11b
light[1] 7, 15
like[1] 7
liken
look-alike
marry 2
mate 4, 6
measure 15a
meet[1] 7
mesh 4
oppose 3
pair 2
parallel 2, 4
peer[1] 2
pit[1] 6
proportion 5
reach 5
reciprocate
reproduce 1
rival 2
running 2
square 11
struggle 5
tally 1
tie 4
tilt 4
touch 7, 11a
tournament
twin 3
-be a match for
compare 2
cope 2
rival 2
touch 7
matched
equal 2
twin 2
matched set
pair 1
matching°
coincidence 2
duplicate 1
equal 2
identical 2
kindred 1
parallel 1
twin 2
matchless°
alone 2
capital 6
excellent

matchless (*cont.*)
exquisite 5
first-rate
great 6
incomparable
leading 2
masterful 1
notable 2
peerless
perfect 2
pre-eminent 2
prime 2
rare[1] 2
sensational 3
splendid 3
star 3
sterling 2
superb
superior 2
superlative
supreme 4
surpassing
transcendent
unbeatable
unparalleled
virtuoso 2
worthwhile 2
matchlessly
pre-eminently
matchlessness
superiority 2
supremacy 1
match up
coordinate 1
couple 3
hang 11b
marry 2
match 5
mate 4, 6
pair 2
tally 1
mate°
associate 4
brother
chum 1
colleague,
companion 1
comrade
equal 4
fellow 3
friend 1
husband 1
intimate[1] 5
lay[1] 8
love 3
match 1
pair 2
pal 1
partner 1, 2
stalemate
tally 5
wife
woman 2
mater
mother 1
parent 1
materfamilias
mother 1
parent 1
material°
brute 1
cloth 1
concrete
data
earthly 2, 3
essential 1
fabric 1
fibre 2
form 3
gear 2
good 21d
important 1
live 1
matter 1
outward
paraphernalia
physical
preparation 5
real 2
secular
sensible 2
stuff 1
substance 1
substantial 1
tangible
material (*cont.*)
temporal 1
timber 3
-materials
data
gear 2
paraphernalia
stuff 5
materialism
mechanism 4
materialistic°
bourgeois 1
earthly 2
greedy 2
material 7
philistine 2
possessive 1
materialization
embodiment 1
emergence
formation 1
fruition
image 4
occurrence 2
realization 2
vision 4
materialize°
appear 1
embody 1
form 11
happen 1
jell 2
loom 1
occur 1
realize 1
surface 3
transpire 2
materially°
essence 3
substantially
matériel
equipment
gear 2
hardware 2
paraphernalia
maternal°
maternalistic
maternal
maternity°
matey
friendly 1
thick 8
mathematical°
matinal
morning 2
matinée idol
idol 2
Thespian 2
mating
intercourse 2
sex 2
matriarch
mother 1
matricide
murder 1
matrimonial°
nuptial
matrimony
marriage 1
marry 1
pair 2
wed 1
matrix
last[3]
mould[1] 1
pattern 4
stamp 6
matt(e)
flat 12
mount 6
soft 9
matted
ratty 2
shaggy
matter°
affair 1
business 2
cause 4
concern 8
data
episode 1
importance 1
matter (*cont.*)
issue 3
item 1
job 3
material 1
occurrence 1
pith 2
point 10
question 3
regard 8
respect 4
signify 2
stroke 9
stuff 1, 5
subject 1
substance 1
text 1
thing 2, 6, 8a
topic
transaction 1
weigh 5
wrong 5
-as a matter of fact
actually
fact 4
indeed 2
really 1
substantially
-in the matter of
about 11
concerning
point 16
regarding
relation 5
term 6
-matters
thing 8a
matter-of-fact°
direct 9
literal 3
mechanical 3
plump[2] 6
positive 6
practical 2
realistic 1
sensible 1
small 3
matter-of-factly
practically 2
maturate
mature 5, 6
ripen
maturation
development 2
evolution
fruition
maturity 2, 3
progress 3
mature°
adult 1
age 6
become 2
big 3
develop 2
experienced 2
flourish 1
grey 4
grow 1, 6
mellow 1, 5
payable
precocious
progress 6
ripe 1, 2
ripen
season 4
veteran 2
vintage
maturing
adolescent 2
development 2
maturity°
age 2
development 2
fruition
majority 2
matutinal
morning 2
maudlin°
drunk 1
gooey 2
mushy 2
romantic 3
sentimental 2
maudlin (*cont.*)
sickly 3
sloppy 3
stinking 3
sweet 7
tender[1] 7
maudlinism
sentimentality
maul
batter 3
knock 3d
lambaste 1
lather 4
manhandle
mishandle 1
mistreat
pound[1] 1
punish 3
mauling
mistreatment
punishment 3
thrashing 1
maunder
prattle 1
ramble 2
spout 2
maundering
prattle 2
rambling 1
mausoleum
crypt
grave[1]
monument 1
sepulchre
tomb
maven, mavin
expert 1
master 2
professional 3
virtuoso 1
maverick
independent 9
individualist
misfit
nonconformist 1, 2
oddity 2
maw
mother 1
mouth 1
mawkish
gooey 2
gushy
maudlin
mushy 2
romantic 3
sentimental 2
sickly 3
sloppy 3
tender[1] 7
mawkishness
sentimentality
max
-to the max
blast 4
world 8
maxim°
belief 3
byword
code 3
epigram 2
lesson 3
moral 3
motto
phrase 2
precept 2
principle 1
proverb
saw
tenet
truism
maximal
exhaustive
maximum 3
outside 6
maximally
blast 4
maximize°
profit 4
maximum°
climax 1
exhaustive
extreme 2, 7, 8
extremity 3
maximum (*cont.*)
full 4, 16
height 2
high 15
outside 3, 6
pinnacle
supreme 2
terminal 1
ultimate 2
-at (the) maximum
blast 4
flat 17a
maybe°
chance 5b
perhaps
possibly 1
mayhap
maybe
perhaps
possibly 1
mayhem°
destruction 1
havoc 2
injury
rumpus
Maytime
spring 9
maze°
network 2
snarl[2] 4
tangle 2
maze-like
labyrinthine
tortuous 1
mazuma
cash 1
money 1
mazy
labyrinthine
meandering
tortuous 1
MC
announcer
host[1] 2
moderator
MD
doctor 1
head 2
physician
mead
field 1
meadow
plain 6
meadow°
field 1
pasture
meadow-land
meadow
pasture
plain 6
meagre°
bare 5
diffuse 1
feeble 2
frugal 3
gaunt 1
inadequate 1
insubstantial 1
insufficient
lean[1] 1, 2
limited 2
little 3
measly
minute[2] 2
narrow 2
pale[1] 3
paltry
pathetic 2
poor 2
raw-boned
remote 6
scanty 1, 2
scarce
short 9
skinny
slender 2
small 4
spare 3, 5
sparse 1, 2
tenuous 2
thin 1
meagreness
poverty 2
meal°
spread 11
-meals
board 3
fare 3
meals
board 3
fare 3
mealy-mouthed°
obsequious
pious 2
sanctimonious
self-righteous
mean°
avaricious
average 1
base[2] 1, 2, 3
close 18
cold-hearted
common 4
contemptible
denote 2
design 4
designate 3
despicable
destine 2
dirty 3, 6
disgraceful 1
dishonourable 3
drive 6
economical 2
filthy 2
frugal 2
get 30b
grasping
greedy 3
grovelling
hateful 2
humble 3
hurtful 2
imply 2
import 2
intend
involve 2
little 6
lousy 1
low[1] 12
mangy
medium 3
menial 1
middle 1
miserable 4
miserly
narrow 7
nasty 4
near 6
norm 1
obscure 4
paltry
penurious 1
petty 2
pitiful 2
plebeian 1
poor 5
propose 2
purpose 5
refer 4
reprobate 1
rotten 4
ruthless
say 9
scurvy
selfish 2
servile
severe 1
shabby 2, 4
shameful
signify 1
simple 5
sleazy 2
small-minded
sordid 1, 3
sparing 1
spell[3] 1
stand 7a
standard 2
stinking 2
symbolize
tight 5
ugly 4
unkind
unmerciful
venomous 2

mean (*cont.*)
vicious 2
vile 1
violent 1
wicked 4
wretched 4
meander°
drift 2
mill 6
ramble 2
roam
run 4
saunter
snake 4
sprawl 1
straggle
stray 1
stroll 1, 2
turn 11, 27
twist 4, 7
wander 1, 2
wind[2] 1
meandering°
diffuse 2
digression 2
discursive
erratic 3
indirect 1
meander 2
serpentine 2
meaning°
definition 2
drift 4
effect 3
force 5
impact 2
implication 3
import 3
matter 4
message 3
point 7
rhyme 2
sense 4
significance 1
spirit 6
substance 3
tenor
meaningful°
eloquent 2
expressive 1
knowing 1
ominous 3
pregnant 2
significant 2
speak 12b
meaningfully
notably 2
meaningfulness
matter 4
meaningless°
absurd 2
empty 4
hollow 5
idle 4
nonsensical
pointless
purposeless
senseless 3
superficial 3
meaningless-ness
absurdity 1
emptiness 2
triviality 1
mean-minded
narrow-minded
meanness
avarice
greed 2
servility
severity 1
means°
agency
agent 2
asset 1
capability
capital 3
channel 4
expedient 3
form 4
formula
fortune 1
fund 2
instrument 2

means (*cont.*)
manner 1
material 4
measure 6
mechanism 3
medium 5
method 1
money 2
path 3
property 2
purse 2
recipe 2
riches
road 1
substance 5
tool 2
vehicle 2
way 1
–by all means
course 6
–by any means
possibly 2
–by means of
by 3
through 1
way 10a
mean-spirited
mean[2] 1
narrow-minded
servile
shabby 4
wretched 4
mean-spiritedness
servility
meant
destined 1
intentional
supposed 2
meantime°
interval 2
meanwhile 1, 2
–in the meantime
meanwhile 2
temporarily 1
meanwhile°
interval 2
time 16
–in the mean-while
meanwhile 2
temporarily 1
measly°
meagre 1
mean[2] 1
pathetic 2
petty 1
scanty 1
small 4
measurable
slow 2
measurably
far 3
measure°
act 4
allotment 1
beat 11
cadence
calibre 3
compare 3
content[1] 1
degree 2
depth 1
dose 1
draught 2
expedient 3
fathom
gauge 1, 3, 4
index 4
indication 2
judge 5
law 1
length 1
mark 3
melody 1
norm 2
pace 4
pattern 1
plumb 5
portion 2
proceeding 1
proof 2
quantity
rate[1] 1, 6, 8

measure (*cont.*)
ration 1
register 8
rhythm
size 2, 3
space 5
standard 1
step 4
sum 2b
survey 1, 3
tempo
time 7
touchstone
volume 2
width 1
yardstick
–measures°
at **measure 6**
preparation 1a
provisioin 3
–to (a) measure
slightly
somewhat
measured°
deliberate 2
even 3
rhythmic
measureless
boundless
immeasurable, inestimable 1, 2
inexhaustible 1
infinite 1
universal 2
unlimited 2
untold 1
vast
measurement°
length 1
measure 4
size 1
survey 3
–measurements
proportion 4
size 1
measure out°
at **measure 13**
divide 2
mete
ration 3
section 4
space 5
measure up°
at **measure 15**
grade 5
match 6
muster 3
rival 2
stack 7b
sum 2b
touch 7
measuring
measurement 1
meat°
flesh 1
gist
kernel 1
nub 2
pith 1
point 5
spirit 6
substance 2
sustenance 1
meat-head
dolt
meaty
forceful 2
mechanic
engineer 3
operative 2
mechanical°
animated 2
automatic 1, 2
impersonal 2
instinctive 2
involuntary
mobile 2
monotonous
perfunctory 1
routine 4
spontaneous 2
technical 2
tedious

mechanicalism
mechanism 4
mechanically
idly 2
rote 2b
mechanism°
agency
contraption
control 6
device 1, 2
engine
gadget
gear 1
implement 1
instrument 1, 2
machine 1
medium 5
movement 4
thing 5
tool 1
vehicle 2
works 2
mechanistic
mechanical 3
medal
decoration 2
plaque 2
trophy 1
medallion
pendant
plaque 1, 2
meddle°
butt[2] 2
fiddle 1
fool 6
interfere 1
intervene 1
mess 6
monkey 5
poke 3
potter
pry 2
snoop 1
tamper
tinker
meddler
busybody
intruder 2
snoop 2
troublemaker
meddlesome
curious 2
intrusive
nosy
obtrusive
officious
meddlesome-ness
curiosity 2
meddle with
fiddle 1
finger 2
fool 6
mess 6
molest 2
monkey 5
potter
touch 4
meddling
interference 1
intrusive
obtrusive
officious
media
press 10a
mediaeval
antiquated
medial
central 1
intermediate 1
mean[3] 6
medium 1
middle 1
median
central 1
mean[3] 6
medium 1
mediate
adjust 1
judge 6
moderate 6
negotiate 1
officiate

mediate (*cont.*)
settle 3
mediation
negotiation 1
office 5
mediator°
go-between
intermediary
judge 2
moderator
mouthpiece 2
negotiator
peacemaker
medic
doctor 1
physician
medical
medicinal
therapeutic
medical centre
hospital
institution 3
medical practi-tioner
doctor 1
physician
medicament
antidote
cure 1
drug 1
medicine
pill 1
prescription 2
remedy 1
medicate
doctor 2
dress 3
drug 3
treat 3
medication
antidote
cure 1
drug 1
medicine
pill 1
prescription 2
remedy 1
medicinal°
therapeutic
medicine°
antidote
cure 1
drug 1
pill 1
prescription 2
remedy 1
medicine man
sorcerer
medico
doctor 1
physician
medieval
antiquated
mediocre°
amateur 2
average 4
decent 3
everyday 3
fair[1] 4
hack[2] 4
indifferent 3
inferior 3
low[1] 9
moderate 3
OK 3
ordinary 2
par 5a
poor 4
prosaic
ropy 2
so so
tolerable 2
undistinguished
unworthy 1
mediocrity
inferiority 3
medium 3
meditate°
brood 3
chew 4
consider 1
contemplate 2
debate 4

meditate (*cont.*)
deliberate 4
digest 3
imagine 1
mull
muse
ponder
puzzle 2
reflect 3
revolve 3
see 8
speculate 1
think 3
wonder 3
meditating
preoccupied 1
reflection 2
reflective
thought 1
wistful 2
meditation
debate 2
reflection 2
reverie
speculation 2
thought 1
meditative°
pensive
philosophical 2
reflective
thinking 1
thoughtful 2
wistful 2
medium°
agency
channel 4
element 2
environment
go-between
liaison 2
mean[3] 1, 4a, 6
mechanism 3
mediocre
milieu
moderate 3
money 1
organ 2
psychic 3
tool 2
voice 3
medley°
assortment 2
clutter 1
composition 3
hash 1
hotchpotch
jumble 2
mess 2
miscellany
mishmash
mixture 1
pastiche
patchwork
pot-pourri
tangle 2
variety 1
meek°
bashful 1
humble 2
mild 1
modest 1
passive 2
retiring
shamefaced 1
sheepish 1
shy 1
submissive 1
tame 3
weak 3
meekly
cap 3
quietly 3
meekness
humility, submission 1
meerschaum
pipe 2
meet°
answer 5
appropriate 1
assemble 1
becoming
bout 3
brave 3

metage
measurement 1
metagrobolized
confused 2
metal goods
hardware 1
metallic
tinny 2
metamorphose
change 6,8
convert 1
make 9
resolve 4
transform
translate 2
turn 16a
metamorphosis
change 3
difference 3
mutation 1
revolution 2
transformation
transition 1
translation 2
metaphor°
image 5
prototype 2
symbol
metaphoric°
symbolic
metaphorical
metaphoric
symbolic
metaphorically
speak 6
metaphrase
translate 1
translation 1
metaphysic(al)
abstract 1
psychic 1
supernatural
metaphysics
philosophy 1
metastasis
transition 1
metastasize
spread 6
metathesize
transpose
metempsychosis
rebirth
meteoric°
precipitate 3
mete out°
at **mete**
administer 3
deal 1
dispense 1
distribute 1
divide 2
dole 3
give 15b
hand 17
measure 14
parcel 4
partition 2
pass 20b
present[2] 6
ration 3
meter
indicator
measure 11
method°
approach 7
form 4
formula
manner 1
mean[3] 4a
measure 3,6
mechanism 3
medium 5
mode[1] 1
path 3
plan 1
policy
procedure
process 1
recipe 2
road 1
routine 1
scheme 1
science 2
method (*cont.*)
system 2
tack 3
technique 1
touch 18
way 1
wrinkle[2]
methodical°
deliberate 2,3
even 3
formal 1
hard 6
orderly 1
organic 3
regular 1,6
scientific
systematic
thorough 2
tidy 2
methodically
exactly 1
thoroughly 2
methodology
method 1
mode[1] 1
procedure
system 2
meticulous°
accurate 2
careful 2
conscientious 2
diligent
elaborate 1
exact 2
faithful 3
fastidious
finicky 1
methodical
narrow 3
nice 3
painful 3
particular 4
pedantic 2
perfectionist 2
precise 2,3
religious 2
rigid 3
scientific
scrupulous 1
squeamish 1
strict 1
thorough 2
meticulously
narrowly 2
precisely 2
thoroughly 2
meticulousness
care 2
precision 2
rigour 2
métier
calling
career 1
craft 3
employment 1
field 4
job 1
mission 2
occupation 1
profession 1
speciality 1
trade 2
vocation
work 2
metonymic
metaphoric
metonymous
metaphoric
metonymy
metaphor
metre
cadence
measure 9
rhythm
tempo
time 7
metrical
even 3
poetic 1
metrical composition
poetry
rhyme 1
metrics
poetry
metrist
poet
metro
underground 4
metropolis°
city
municipality
town
metropolitan
municipal
mettle
backbone 3
bottle 2
daring 1
enterprise 2
fight 9
fortitude
grit
gumption 2
gut 3a
heart 2
nerve 1
pluck 1
prowess 2
self-control 1
spirit 2
spunk
stamina
vigour
mettled
racy 1
mettlesome
audacious 1
daring 2
enterprising
gallant 1
gritty 2
indomitable
racy 1
spirited
stalwart 3
mettlesomeness
vigour
mewl
cry 2
moan 3
snivel
sob
weep 1
Mexican foxtrot *etc.*
run 50
Mexican stand-off
deadlock 1
stalemate
mezzo-rilievo
relief 3
MIA(s)
casualty 2b
miasma
fume 3
poison 1
reek 3
miasmal
rancid
rank[2] 4
smelly
stinking 1
miasmatic(al)
rancid
rank[2] 4
smelly
stinking 1
miasmic
bad 2
poisonous 1
rancid
rank[2] 4
smelly
stinking 1
strong 3
Mickey Finn
drug 4
sedative 1
spike 4
Mickey Mouse
paltry
micro
diminutive
miniature
micro (*cont.*)
minute[2] 1
tiny
microbe°
bug 2
germ 1
microcosm
universe 2
micro-organism
germ 1
microbe
microphone
bug 5
microscope
glass 6
microscopic
diminutive
imperceptible 2
little 1
miniature
minute[2] 1
tiny
wee 1
microwavable
prepared 4
microwave-ready
prepared 4
microzoon
microbe
micturate
urinate
mid
amid
among 1
medium 1
middle 1
midday°
noon
midden
mound 2
middle°
central 1
centre 1
core 1
dead 21
heart 3
inside 1
interior 6
intermediate 1
mean[3] 1,6
medium 1,3
midst
moderate 3
thick 10
–in the middle
amid
among 1
through 2
middle class
public 8
middle-class
bourgeois 1
middleman
broker
factor 2
go-between
intermediary
mediator
negotiator
middle of nowhere
wild 10
middle-of-the-road
conservative 2
moderate 2
middle-of-the-roader
conservative 3
moderate 4
middle school
school 1
middling
adequate 2
average 4
decent 3
fair[1] 4
indifferent 3
mean[3] 6
mediocre
moderate 3
middling (*cont.*)
OK 3
par 5a
passable 1
so so
tolerable 2
undistinguished
midget
diminutive
little 1
miniature
puny 3
runt
short 1
small 1
tiny
wee 1
mid-point
centre 1
medium 3
middle 2
midst
midriff
middle 3
mid-section
middle 3
mid-sized
medium 1
midst°
bosom 2
dead 21
middle 2
thick 10
–in the midst
amid
among 1
midway
intermediate 1
middle 1
midwife°
world 5b
mien
appearance 2
aspect 2
bearing 1
carriage 2
expression 3
face 2
front 4
guise 1
look 14
manner 2
outside 2
pan 2
presence 3
semblance 1
miff
displease
disturb 1
infuriate
irk
offend 1
miffed
indignant
MI5
spy 1
might°
brawn
energy
force 1
main 6
power 4
sinew 2
stamina
strength 1
violence 1
–with might and main
vigorously
mightily
hard 13
mightiness
might 2
power 4
strength 1
violence 1
mighty°
brawny
forceful 1,2
formidable 3
important 3
impregnable
massive
mighty (*cont.*)
mountainous 2
potent 1
powerful 1
sinewy
solid 8
stalwart 1
strong 1
towering 2
mignon(ne)
petite
pretty 1
small 1
twee
undersized
migraine
headache 1
migrant°
arrival 2
immigrant
vagabond 1,2
migrate°
emigrate
range 8
stake[1] 2
migration
movement 1
migrator
migrant 1
migratory
migrant 2
rambling 3
travelling
mild°
benign 2,3
bland 1
calm 3
easy 2,3
gentle 1
harmless
humble 2
inoffensive
light[2] 4
meek 1
merciful
peaceable 2
quiet 2
smooth 5
soft 3
tame 2,3
temperate 1
tender[1] 6
mildew
mould[2]
spoil 4
mildewed
mouldy
musty 1
rotten 1
mildewy
musty 1
stuffy 1
mildly
quietly 3
mildness
humility
mile
–within a mile of
near 9
mileage
distance 1
measurement 2
miler
runner 1
miles per hour
velocity
milestone
landmark 2
milieu°
climate 2
environment
medium 4
scene 1
setting
site 1
universe 2
militancy
fight 9
militant°
belligerent 1,3
hostile 3
martial 1

militant (*cont.*)
radical 3, 4
soldier 2
zealot
militantism
zealotry
militaristic
warlike
military°
martial 2
service 8
military science
tactic 2
militate°
milk°
extort
fleece
gouge 2
profiteer 2
sap[1] 3
squeeze 2, 3
tap[2] 6
milksop°
coward
drip 3
sissy
weakling
wet 6
milky
filmy 2
white 1
mill°
factory
grind 1
plant 2
press 7
pulverize 1
works 1
mill about, around°
at **mill 6**
million
number 2
-millions
mint 1
score 4
umpteen
millionaire
tycoon
mill-race
race[1] 2
millstone
burden 1
encumbrance
load 1
weight 2
milquetoast
coward
drip 3
milksop
pushover 2
sissy
weakling
mime
monkey 4
mimetic
mimic 5
mimic°
copy 5
echo 4
follow 2
imitate 1, 2
masquerade 3
mock 2
monkey 4
parody 3
parrot 1, 2
pass 16b
pattern 7
pose 2
represent 2
satirize
take 34b
mimicking
imitation 1
mimicry
imitation 1
parody 1
minacious
menacing
sinister 1
strong-arm
minacious (*cont.*)
threatening
minaret
tower 1
minatorial
menacing
sinister 1
minatory
menacing
ominous 2
sinister 1
threatening
mince
chop 2
cut 17a
mill 5
walk 1
mincing°
affected 3
dainty 2
mealy-mouthed
mind°
beware
care 5
damn 5
dislike 1
dismiss 2
estimation 1
flair 1
follow 2
grudge 2
guard 1, 2
head 4
heed 1, 2
intellect 1
judgement 4
keep 2, 6
light[1] 11
listen 2
look 4
mark 12
mastermind 2
note 7
notice 1, 2
obey 1
opinion 1
protect 2
psyche
reach 6
reason 2
regard 9
remind
see 5
soul 1
spirit 2
stir 5
understanding 5
watch 2
wit 1
-of a mind
disposed
inclined 1
prepared 3
prone 2
-of one mind
communicate 3
united 3
-out of one's mind°
at **mind 14**
beside 3
crazy 1
deranged
disturbed 2
excited 1
frantic
insane 1
mad 1
raving 1
unbalanced 2
mind-blowing
exciting 1
formidable 2
overwhelming 2
phenomenal
prodigious 2
sensational 1
shocking 1
superb
unthinkable 1
mind-boggler
problem 2
wonder 1
mind-boggling
dazzling
exciting 1
formidable 2
inconceivable
marvellous
miraculous
overwhelming 2
phenomenal
portentous 2
prodigious 2
sensational 1
shocking 1
stunning 2
sublime 2
superb
terrific 2
unbelievable
unthinkable 1
minded
disposed
inclined 2
mood 2
minder°
bruiser
guard 3
henchman
keeper
protector
mindful°
attentive 1
guarded
mind 9
observant 1
sensible 4
thoughtful 3
mindfulness
care 2
cognizance
mindless°
blank 4
blind 3
brute 1
foolish 1
hare-brained 2
indiscreet
preposterous
senseless 3
stupid 1
unconscious 2
unreasonable 1
unthinking 1
unwary
mindlessly
blindly
mindlessness
stupidity 1
mind-reader
psychic 3
mind-set
mentality 2
mind's eye
imagination 1
mind-shattering
overwhelming 2
mine°
excavation
fund 1
pit[1] 1
quarry[2] 1, 2
tap[2] 6
tunnel 2
unearth
wealth 2
mineral water
water 1
mine-shaft
pit[1] 1
shaft 4
mingle°
associate 1b
blend 1
combine 2, 3
fraternize
hang 4b
hobnob
jumble 1
merge
mix 1
scramble 3
stir 1
unite 1
wed 2
mingling
amalgamation
blend 3
merger
mixture 1, 2
wedding 2
mingy
close 18
greedy 3
mean[2] 1
measly
miserly
paltry
penurious 1
petty 2
sparing 1
stint 4
tight 5
mini
diminutive
little 1
miniature
minute[2] 1
small 1
tiny
miniature°
diminutive
little 1
minute[2] 1
model 1, 10
slight 3
small 1
tiny
toy 5
wee 1
minify
minimize 1
minimal°
bare 5
limited 1
marginal 1
miniature
minimum 2
nominal 2
scanty 1, 2
token 5
minimize°
belittle
depreciate 2
discount 2
disparage 1
disregard 2
downgrade 2
dwarf
flout
laugh 2b
overshadow 1
play 13
reduce 7
slight 6
smooth 12
talk 9a
trivialize
underestimate
whitewash
write 4b
minimizing
derogatory
minimum°
floor 3
minimal
minion
flunkey 1
menial 3
satellite 2
minister°
ambassador
clergyman 1
delegate 1
deputy
divine 5
envoy
father 4
missionary
pastor
politician
preacher
priest
wait 3
ministerial
clerical 1
pastoral 3
priestly
minister to°
at **minister 3**
attend 3
cater 2
indulge 1
nurse 2
provide 4
serve 1
tend[2]
wait 3
ministry°
cabinet 2
cloth 2
council 2
government 2
mission 3
minnesinger
minstrel
minor°
adolescent 1
frivolous 1
incidental 2
inconsequential
indifferent 4
inferior 2
insignificant
junior
juvenile 1, 2
little 5
minute[2] 2
negligible
nominal 2
obscure 4
peripheral 1
petty 1
puny 1
secondary 1
side 8
slight 1
small 2, 5
small-time
stripling
subordinate 1
teenager
trifling
unimposing
venial
ward 2
young 1
youth 2
-to a minor extent
slightly
minority
childhood
youth 1
minor-league
minor 2
Minotaur
ogre
minstrel°
poet
singer
mint°
brand-new
coin 2
packet 2
pile[1] 2
strike 10
minus
out 5
minuscule
close 11
diminutive
imperceptible 2
little 1
lower[1] 8
miniature
minute[2] 1
nominal 2
short 1
small 1
tiny
wee 1
minute°
bit 3
close 11, 14
detailed 1
diminutive
elaborate 1
enter 3
flash 3
imperceptible 2
instant 2
minute (*cont.*)
instantaneously
little 1
memorandum
miniature
moment 1, 2
nice 3
now 1
particular 3
protocol 2
puny 2
register 5
second[2]
slight 2
small 1
tiny
wee 1
-in a minute
immediately 1
once 6a
presently
soon 1
-minutes
journal 2
notation 1
proceeding 2a
record 3
transaction 2
-to the minute
dot 2
-up to the minute
fashionable
latest 2
modern
trendy 1
minute-book
journal 2
minutely
precisely 2
minutest
minimal
minimum 2
minutia
particular 5
refinement 2
-minutiae
detail 2
minx
flirt 3
jade 2
miracle
marvel 2
phenomenon 2
prodigy 2
wonder 1
miracle drug
elixir 1
miracle-worker
magician 2
miraculous°
extraordinary 2
fabulous 2
heroic 5
magic 4
marvellous
phenomenal
portentous 2
prodigious 2
superb
superhuman 1
supernatural
miraculously
charm 4
mirage
dream 1
fancy 6
fantasy 2
hallucination
illusion 2
phantom 2
vision 4
mire°
dirt 1
muck 2
mud
ooze 1
sludge
soil[1] 3
mirror°
echo 4
follow 2
glass 2

mirror (*cont.*)
mimic 1
reflect 1
represent 3
reverse 1
mirror image
echo 2
mirror-image
symmetrical
mirror-like
glassy 1
smooth 2
symmetrical
mirth°
cheer 2
festivity 1
frolic 1
fun 1
gaiety 1
hilarity
merriment
revelry
mirthful
comic 1
gleeful
hilarious
merry 1
ridiculous
sunny 2
mirthfulness
gaiety 1
glee
merriment
mirth
mirthless
solemn 1
miry
muddy 1
mushy 1
misaddress
misdirect
misadventure
accident 1
calamity 1
casualty 1
catastrophe 2
misfortune 2
reverse 8
misadvise
misdirect
misinform
misalliance°
misallied
incongruous
mismatched
misanthrope°
man-hater
misanthropic°
unsocial
misanthropist
man-hater
misanthrope
misapplication
abuse 4
anachronism
embezzlement
misuse 1
waste 5
misapplied
abusive 2
misapply
abuse 1
embezzle
misappropriate 2
misuse 4
pervert 1
misappreciate
miscalculate
misapprehend
misconceive
misinterpret
miss[1] 3
mistake 3
misunderstand
misapprehension
illusion 1
misconception
mistake 1
misunderstanding 1
misappropriate°
embezzle
misuse 4
pilfer
steal 1
take 3
misappropriation
abuse 4
embezzlement
misuse 1
misarticulate
slur 2
misbegotten
illegitimate 2
misbehave°
carry 11c
cut 17b
err 2
play 17b
transgress 1
misbehaved
discourteous
misbehaving
bad 10
misbehaviour°
fault 4
incivility
mischief 1
transgression
misbelief
delusion 2
miscalculate°
err 1
misunderstand
slip[1] 3
underestimate
miscalculation
fallacy
misconception
mistake 1
misunderstanding 1
miscarriage°
defeat 4
failure 2
misfire 2
mockery 2
miscarry°
boomerang
fail 1
fall 20
fizzle 2
founder[2] 2
grief 3
misfire 1
wrong 8b
miscellanea
rummage 2
sundries
miscellaneous°
confused 3
divers
diverse
general 3
manifold
odd 2
promiscuous 3
sundry
varied 1
various 1
miscellany°
assortment 2
hotchpotch
mass 1
medley
mess 2
mixture 1
pastiche
pot-pourri
sundries
variety 1
mischance
accident 1
calamity 1
casualty 1
catastrophe 2
misfortune 2
mischief°
caper 2
devilry 1
evil 7
hanky-panky
mischief (*cont.*)
harm 1
hocus-pocus 1
ill 8
injury
lark 1
nonsense 2
prank
trick 2
mischief-maker
handful 2
imp
miscreant 1
monkey 3
rascal
troublemaker
mischievous°
arch 3
bad 10
devilish
disobedient 1
elfin 1
evil 3
fatal 2
hurtful 1
misbehave
miscreant 2
naughty 1
playful 1
sly 2
wicked 5
mischievously
badly 4
mischievousness
devilry 1
mischief 1
miscitation
misstatement 1
miscite
twist 2
miscompute
miscalculate
misconceive°
misinterpret
misunderstand
misconception°
delusion 2
fallacy
illusion 1
mistake 1
misunderstanding 1
misconduct
error 2
fault 4
guilt 1
misbehaviour
misdeed
mishandle 2
misconstrual
misconception
twist 9
misconstruction
misconception
misstatement 1
misunderstanding 1
stick[2] 4
twist 9
misconstrue
garble 1
misconceive
misinterpret
miss[1] 3
mistake 3
misunderstand
pervert 1
twist 2
miscount
miscalculate
miscreant°
criminal 3
delinquent 1
felon
offender
reprobate 2
rogue 1
sinner
transgressor
villain
miscreation
monster 2
misdate
anachronism
misdating
anachronism
misdeed°
crime
fault 4
offence 1
peccadillo
sin 1
transgression
-misdeeds°
at **misdeed**
misdemeanour
crime
fault 4
misbehaviour
misdeed
offence 1
sin 1
transgression
-misdemeanours
misbehaviour
misdesignated
so-called 2
misdirect°
lead 7
misinform
mislead
pervert 1
throw 6c
misdirected
misguided
misdirection
perversion 1
misdoing
misdeed
mise en scène
environment
production 3
scene 2
set 28
setting
misemploy
abuse 1
misappropriate 2
misuse 4
misemployment
abuse 4
misuse 1
waste 5
miser°
stiff 12
miserable°
bad 1
base[2] 2
bitter 3
broken-hearted
dejected
deplorable 1
desolate 3
despicable
despondent
dismal
doleful
downhearted
dreary 1
filthy 2
forlorn 1
gloomy 2
heartbroken
heavy 6
hopeless 3
ill 5
inconsolable
joyless 1
lamentable
lousy 1,2
low[1] 6,8
mangy
mean[2] 3
measly
melancholy 1
oppressive 1
paltry
par 5a
pathetic 1
piteous
poignant 1
poor 6
rotten 4
sad 1,3
scurvy
miserable (*cont.*)
sick 3
sinking 2
sordid 4
sorrowful 1
sorry 2
terrible 3
tragic
unfortunate 2
unhappy 1
vile 1
weak 4
woebegone
wretched 1,2,3
miserableness
despair 1
melancholy 2
miserably
sadly 2
miserliness
avarice
greed 2
thrift
miserly°
avaricious
cheap 4
close 18
economical 2
frugal 2
grasping
greedy 3
mean[2] 1
measly
narrow 7
near 6
penurious 1
petty 2
selfish 2
small 4
sparing 1
thrifty
tight 5
misery°
affliction 1
agony
anguish 1
calamity 2
care 1
desolation 2
despair 1
desperation 2
distress 1
evil 7
gloom 2
grief 1
hardship
hell 2,3
hurt 6
ill 8
melancholy 2
mourning 2
ordeal
pain 2
privation
prostration 3
rack 2
sadness
scourge 1
sorrow 1
suffering
torment 3
trial 4
woe
misestimate
miscalculate
misevaluate
miscalculate
misfile
mislay
misfire°
fail 1
fizzle 2
miscarry
misfit°
loser
oddity 2
misfortune°
accident 1
affliction 1
blight 2
calamity 2
catastrophe 2
curse 2
disaster
misfortune (*cont.*)
distress 2
evil 7
grief 2
hardship
harm 1
ill 8
mischief 2
misery 3
necessity 4
ordeal
picnic 3
pity 2
reverse 8
scourge 1
sorrow 2
tragedy
trial 4
undoing 2
woe
misgiving°
compunction 2
doubt 3
dread 2
foreboding 1
pang 2
qualm
scruple 1
suspicion 1
worry 4
-misgivings
distrust 2
fear 3,4
mistrust 2
misguide
betray 3
lead 7
misdirect
misinform
mislead
throw 6c
trick 8
misguided°
foolish 1
ill-advised 1
inept 2
mistaken 2
off 3
wrong 4
mishandle°
foul 16b
fumble 2
hash 3
ill-treat
screw 7b
mishap°
accident 1
calamity 1
casualty 1
catastrophe 2
disaster
hitch 4
misfortune 2
reverse 8
mishegaas
rigmarole
mishmash°
assortment 2
clutter 1
disorder 1
hash 1
hotchpotch
medley
mess 1
mix-up
mixture 1
muddle 4
pastiche
patchwork
pot-pourri
stew 1
tangle 2
welter 1
misidentify
mistake 4
mix 6
misinform°
mislead
trick 8
misinformation°
misinformed
mistaken 2

mixed breed
mongrel
mixed-up
confused 1, 2, 3
disconnected 2
disjointed 2
disorientated
inarticulate 1
incoherent
indiscriminate 2
muddy 2
topsy-turvy 2
mixed up in, with°
at **mixed 3**
involved 3
mixing
confusion 4
merger
mixture 2
solution 4
synthesis
union 1
wedding 2
mixture°
alloy 1
amalgam
amalgamation
assortment 2
blend 3
brew 4
combination 1, 3
composition 3
compound 5
confusion 5
elixir 2
hash 1
hotchpotch
hybrid
medley
mess 2
miscellany
mishmash
mix 7
pastiche
patchwork
pot-pourri
preparation 5
solution 3, 4
stew 1
synthesis
union 1
variety 1
wedding 2
mix up°
at **mix 4**
bemuse 1
complicate 1
confuse 2, 3
disorder 4
entangle 2
garble 2
hash 3
jumble 1
mistake 4
muddle 1, 2
muddy 4
mystify
ruffle 4
scramble 3
shake 5
shuffle 1
snarl[2] 1
stir 1
mix-up°
confusion 1, 3
muddle 4
tangle 2
mix with
associate 1b
fraternize
hang 4b
rub 7
shoulder 4
mizen
spar[1]
mizen-stay
stay[2] 1
mizzle
escape 1
mist 1
rain 4
mnemonic
reminder
symbolic
MO
approach 7
formula
method 1
practice 1
procedure
recipe 2
technique 1
way 1
mo
moment 1
moan°
bemoan
bewail
complain
cry 2
grieve 2
gripe 1
groan 1, 3
heave 3
keen[2] 1
murmur 4
sob
sorrow 3
weep 1
moaning
gripe 2
lament 2
lamentation
moan 1
moat
channel 1
mob°
crowd 1
flock 1, 2
gang 1
hoi polloi
host[2]
jam 5
mass 2
number 2
pack 3
populace
press 8
rabble 1
ring[1] 3
swarm 1
underworld 1
unwashed 2
mobbed°
mobile°
fluid 3
moving 2
travelling
mobile vulgus
people 3
mobility
motion 2
mobilize°
activate
enlist 2
mass 8
muster 1
raise 5
rally 3
recruit 1
summon 2
mobster
criminal 3
gangster
henchman
hoodlum
racketeer
mock°
caricature 2
deride
discredit 3
factitious
false 3
flout
gibe 1
guy 2
hiss 3
imitate 2
imitation 5
jeer 1
lampoon 2
laugh 2a
leg 8
mimic 3, 5
parody 3
mock (*cont.*)
phoney 1
poke 4
put 22e
quasi- 2
rag[2]
ridicule 2
satirize
scoff[1]
scorn 4
sham 2
snap 6
sneer 2
snicker 1
spurious
synthetic
take 34b
taunt 1
thumb 8
twit[1]
unreal 3
mockery°
burlesque 1
charade
derision
gibe 2
imitation 2
joke 3
parody 1, 2
ridicule 1
satire 1
scorn 2
sneer 3
sport 2
take-off 2
mock-heroic
burlesque 4
mocking
derisory
disdainful
irreverent 2
ridicule 1
sarcastic
sardonic
satirical
scornful
mock-pathetic
burlesque 4
mock-up
dummy 2
model 1
rough 14, 15
mod
modern
new 2
mode°
execution 4
fashion 1, 3
form 4
habit 1
manner 1
mean[3] 4a
medium 5
method 1
practice 1
procedure
rage 3
style 1, 2
taste 5
technique 1
trend 2
turn 37
vein 5
vogue 1
way 1
model°
carve 1
cast 4
classic 1, 3
classical 1
complete 4
design 5
dummy 1
epitome 1
example 2
exemplary 2
exemplify 2
fashion 5
follow 2
form 4
gauge 3
guide 6
ideal 1, 4
image 4
last[3]
model (*cont.*)
lead 13
lesson 3
likeness 2
mould[1] 4
nonpareil
norm 2
optimum 1
original 5
paragon
pattern 1, 7
perfection 3
picture 4
pose 1
precedent
principle 1
prototype 1, 2
queen 2
quintessence
representation 1, 4
sculpture 2
shape 6
specimen
standard 1
statue
template
type 3
version 1
moderate°
alloy 3
chair 4
chasten 2
conservative 2, 3
cool 10
dampen 2
deaden 2
decent 3
easy 5
fresh 7
frugal 1
gentle 1, 3
gradual
judge 6
let[1] 9
liberalize 2
light[2] 10
lower[1] 5
mild 2
mitigate
modest 3
modify 2
modulate
officiate
philosophical 2
phlegmatic 2
qualify 3
quell 2
reasonable 3
reduce 1
relax 1, 2
respectable 2
slack 3b
slow 2
soft 3
soften 2
subdue 3
subdued 1
subside 2
sweeten 2
tame 6
temper 5
temperate 1, 2
tone 5
umpire 2
weaken 1
moderately°
fairly 1
partially
pretty 3
quite 2
rather 1
somewhat
moderating
extenuating
moderation
let-up
measure 8
relaxation 2
temperance 1
-in moderation
moderately
moderator°
chair 3
judge 2
moderator (*cont.*)
mediator
negotiator
umpire 1
modern°
contemporary 2
date 5
fresh 2
latest 2
minute[1] 3
new 2
now 5
recent
streamlined 2
swinging
trendy 1
modernistic
streamlined 2
modernization
innovation 2
modernize°
improve 1
renew 1
renovate
modernized
streamlined 2
modest°
bashful 2
coy
decent 2, 5
delicate 5
homely 1
humble 1
inconspicuous
mean[2] 2
meek 1
mild 1
moderate 1, 3
ordinary 2
poor 5
pure 3
respectable 3
retiring
self-conscious
severe 6
shamefaced 1
shy 1
simple 2
small 4
so so
spare 5
timid
unobtrusive
modestly
quietly 4
severely 6
simply 4
modesty
humility
propriety 2
purity 2
severity 6
shame 4
simplicity 3
modicum°
shade 3
speck
modifiable
changeable 2
flexible 2
modification
accommodation 1
adaptation 2
alteration
change 3
difference 3
flux
mutation 1
qualification 2
reform 3
regulation 1
revision
transformation
transition 1
variant 1
variation 1
modified
prepared 2
qualified 2
modify°
accommodate 1
adapt 2
adjust 2
modify (*cont.*)
affect[1] 3
alloy 3
alter
change 6
condition 5
convert 1
correct 4
differentiate 2
doctor 4
edit 1
fake 1
fit[1] 7
impact 4
influence 3
liberalize 2
make 9
modulate
prepare 7
process 3
proportion 5
qualify 3
reduce 4
regulate 1
relax 2
reverse 4
revise 1
shape 9
square 12
tailor 2
temper 5
tone 5
transform
turn 3
vary 1
water 7
modifying
adaptation 1
mutation 1
variation 1
modish
chic 1
contemporary 2
current 3
dashing 2
elegant 2
fashionable
modern
new 2
nifty 1
smart 3
snappy 2
sporty
stylish
swell 7
modishness
chic 2
modiste
dressmaker
tailor 1
modulate°
change 6
lower[1] 5
modify 2
proportion 5
qualify 3
regulate 1
relax 2
tone 5
modulated
measured 4
modulating
variation 1
modulation
change 3
intonation
pronunciation
regulation 1
tone 2
variation 1
module
terminal 4
unit
modus loquendi
phrase 3
modus operandi
approach 7
formula
method 1
mode[1] 1
practice 1
procedure
recipe 2
system 2

modus operandi (*cont.*)
technique 1
way 1
modus scribendi
phrase 3
modus vivendi
way 2
mofette
vent 1
mogul°
merchant 3
personage
tycoon
moil
drudgery
plod 2
slave 3
slavery 3
work 7
moist°
clammy 1, 2
damp 1
humid
juicy 1
lush 2
muggy
steamy 1
sultry 1
watery 3
wet 1
moisten
dampen 1
water 6
moistened
wet 1
moistness
damp 2
moisture
damp 2
wet 4
moistureless
dry 1
mole
spy 1
molecule
crumb
grain 3
particle
scrap[1] 1
speck
molest°
annoy 2
assault 4
mishandle 1
mistreat
persecute 1
violate 3
molestation
assault 2
mistreatment
persecution 1
violation 3
moll
friend 3
girl 2
prostitute 1
squeeze 10
woman 3
mollification
euphemism
mollify
blunt 4
calm 5
cushion 2
deaden 2
disarm 2
ease 6
humour 4
hush 5
lull 3
melt 2
mitigate
moderate 5
quell 2
salve 3
silence 4
smooth 12
soften 1
still 9
sweeten 2
tame 6

mollify (*cont.*)
temper 5
water 7
mollifying
mild 3
soothing 2
mollycoddle
baby 2
cater 2
coddle
humour 4
indulge 2
milksop
pamper
pet[1] 5
sissy
spoil 3
weakling
molten
liquid 2
mom
mother 1
moment°
bit 3
crack 3
emphasis
flash 3
import 4
importance 1
instant 1, 2
interest 2
juncture 2
matter 4
minute[1] 1
note 8
occasion 1
opportunity
phase 2
pith 2
point 4
second[2]
significance 2
spurt 1
time 3
weight 3
–a moment ago
just 6
–at the moment
now 2
–for the moment
meanwhile 2
temporarily 2
time 16
–in a moment
once 6a
presently
rapidly 2
soon 1
suddenly 1
–of moment
serious 2
–the moment (that)
immediately 3
present[1] 4
momentarily
briefly 2
directly 2
instantaneously
promptly
soon 1
suddenly 1
momentary°
brief 1
fleeting
fugitive 3
hasty 3
imminent
meteoric 1
passing 1
short 7
temporary
transient
moment of truth
crunch 2
showdown
momentous°
banner 2
big 4
critical 2
crucial
eventful
fateful 1

momentous (*cont.*)
great 4
high 6
historic
important 1
landmark 3
memorable
portentous 1
pressing
serious 2
signal 3
significant 1
solemn 3
special 2
weighty 2
momentousness
gravity 2
solemnity
momentum°
impetus
power 8
propulsion
mommy
mother 1
monarch°
crown 3
king
lord 1
master 1
queen 1
sovereign 1
monarchism
monarchy 2
monarchy°
kingdom 1
realm 1
reign 1
monastery°
monastic
clergyman 2
clerical 1
isolated 2
monk
reclusive
secluded 1
severe 6
monastically
severely 6
monasticism
privacy 1
severity 6
monetary°
economic 1
financial
fiscal
money°
asset 1
backing 2
capital 3
cash 1
coin 1
deliver 7
finance 1, 2
fortune 1
fund 2
gain 8
gamble 2
mean[3] 4b
monetary
note 4
pay 12
pile[1] 2
principal 5
prosperity
purse 2
ready 8
resource 2
roll 18
stick[1] 18
tender[2] 3
till[2]
treasure 1
treasury
wealth 1
–in the money°
at **money 4**
flush[2] 3
prosperous 1
rich 1
successful 1
wealthy
–moneys
treasury

money box
register 2
moneyed
flush[2] 3
leisured
loaded 4
money 4
prosperous 1
rich 1
wealthy
money-grubbing
bourgeois 1
mean[2] 1
mercenary 1
miserly
sordid 2
moneylender
factor 3
moneymaking
economic 2
gainful
profitable 1
successful 2
money order
draft 2
money-saving
economical 1
-monger
seller
mongrel°
cross 2
general 3
hybrid
mixed 1
moni(c)ker
name 1
nickname 1
tag 2
monied
leisured
money 4
prosperous 1
monism
mechanism 4
monition
caution 1
monitor°
check 4
observe 2
police 3
regulate 2
terminal 4
track 4
monitory
advisory 1
exemplary 3
monk°
clergyman 2
monkey 1
recluse
monkey°
enrage
fiddle 2
finger 2
fool 6
imitate 1
tamper
tinker
twiddle 1
monkey about, around°
at **monkey 5**
play 9a
potter
tamper
tinker
monkey business, tricks
deceit 1
fiddle 3
fraud 1
hanky-panky
mischief 1
nonsense 2
play 22
prank
trickery
monkeyshines
mischief 1
nonsense 2
play 22
prank

monkey wrench
wrench 6
monochrome
drawing
monocracy
despotism
monarchy 2
monody
chant 1
keen[2] 2
lament 2
monogram
character 1
device 3
initial 3
seal 1
sign 4
stamp 7
symbol
monogrammed
personalized
monograph°
theme 2
tract[2]
monolithic°
totalitarian
monologue
oration
recitation 1
monomachy
fight 7
monomania
fanaticism 2
fixation
zealotry
monomaniac
crank 2
monomaniacal
fanatical
monopolize°
hold 4
occupy 3
monopoly
syndicate 1
trust 4
monotonic
monotonous
monotonous°
boring
dead 12
dreary 2
dry 2
dull 4
even 3
flat 5
heavy 7
humdrum
measured 3
pedestrian 2
prosaic
repetitive
routine 4
slow 9
stupid 3
tedious
threadbare 2
tiresome 1
monotony
boredom
tedium
uniformity 2
monsoon
downpour
storm 1
monster°
animal 2
bag 4
beast 2
demon 1
devil 2
freak 1
fright 3
giant 1
hag
massive
monstrous 3
ogre
terror 2
monstrosity°
freak 1
infamy 2
monster 2
sight 4

monstrous°
abominable 1
atrocious 1
big 2
diabolic 2
dreadful 2
enormous
fearful 3
ferocious
fiendish
flagrant
foul 4
ghoulish 2
great 1
grievous 2
grim 3
gross 4
hideous 1
horrible 2
infamous 2
large 3
misshapen
monumental 4
morbid 2
outrageous 2
prodigious 1
sadistic
satanic 2
shocking 2
terrible 4
ungodly 2
unnatural 1
vicious 1
whopping 1
monstrousness
enormity
monstrosity 2
Montezuma's revenge
run 50
monthly
journal 1
organ 2
periodical
publication 2
regular 2
sheet 6
monument°
landmark 2
attributive
memorial 2
tombstone
monumental°
colossal 1
grand 1
grandiose 2
huge
large 3
majestic 1
mighty 3
monolithic
mountainous 2
prodigious 1
thumping 1
vast
monumentally
terribly
moo
low[2]
mooch
borrow
bum 5
moocher
bloodsucker
mood°
air 1
atmosphere 2
climate 2
feeling 6
frame 5
humour 3
key 5
lie[2] 6
note 5
pet[2]
posture 3
spirit 8, 9a
strain[1] 9
style 5
temper 1
vein 4
–in the mood°
at **mood 2**
like[1] 2

moody°
cross 6
disgruntled
fickle
fretful
gloomy 2
glum
inconstant
irritable
petulant
snappish 2
sulk
sullen
temperamental 1
moolah
cash 1
money 1
moon
satellite 1
-over the moon
ecstatic
elated
exalted 3
exultant
happy 1
joyful 2
overjoyed
pleased
radiant 2
rapturous
world 7
moonbeams
moonshine 1
mooncalf
fool 1
mooning
absent-minded
moonless
black 3
overcast
moonlight
light[1] 1
moonshine 1
moonlight flit
bolt 8
bundle 3
depart 1
escape 1
flee 1
flight[2] 3
heel[1] 4
leave[1] 1
powder 2
pull 14b
moonshine°
alcohol
fiddlesticks
gab 2
gobbledegook 1
liquor 1
mumbo-jumbo 1
nonsense 1
prattle 3
rot 4
rubbish 2
trash 1
whisky
moor°
anchor 3
connect 3
dock 2
flat 14b
plain 6
swamp 1
tie 1
moored
firm 2
secure 2
mooring
anchor 1
cable 1
harbour 1
port
mooring-buoy
buoy 1
moorland
moor[1]
morass 1
plain 6
moot°
controversial 1
debatable
debate 3
moot *(cont.)*
disputable
indecisive 2
open 7
problematic
questionable
raise 8
theoretical 1
unresolved
mop
clean 9
wipe 1
mope
brood 4
grieve 1
lour 2
pout 1
sulk
moping
moody 1
mopish
moody 1
mopy
moody 1
moral°
chaste 1
clean 4
conscientious 1
equitable
ethical
faithful 4
godly
good 5
honest 1
honourable 1
incorrupt 1
just 2
lesson 3
motto
noble 4
pious 1
principled
proverb
pure 3
respectable 3
right 1
righteous 1
scrupulous 2
trustworthy
upright 2
virtuous 1
wholesome 2
-morals°
at **moral 4**
conscience
ideal 3
morality 1
principle 3
morale°
self-respect
spirit 8, 9a
moral fibre
self-control 1
moralism
proverb
moralist
puritan 1
moralistic
moral 1, 2
proverbial 1
puritan 2
strait-laced
morality°
character 3
conscience
good 20
honour 1
integrity 1
justice 3
moral 4
principle 3
probity
purity 2
rectitude
right 10
virtue 1
morality tale
parable
moralize
lecture 3
preach 2
moralizing
moral 2
morally
honestly 1
moralness
morality 1
morass°
mire 1
swamp 1
moratorium°
pause 2
postponement
suspension 2
truce 1
morbid°
ghoulish 2
macabre
sick 5
solemn 1
sombre 1
morbidity
vapour 2
mordacious
trenchant
mordaciousness
gall[1] 1
mordacity
gall[1] 1
mordant
bitter 1
caustic 1
cutting 2
devastating 1
incisive 2
keen[1] 2
penetrating 2
poignant 2
pungent 2
scathing
scorching 2
tart[1] 2
trenchant
virulent 2
more
better[1] 2
extra 7
further 1
more often than not
rule 4
whole 5
more or less
about 2
effect 5
intent 3
moderately
nearly 1
neighbourhood 2
quasi- 1
rather 1
relatively
somewhat
virtually
way 10b
moreover°
addition 6
besides 1
boot 1
further 3
likewise 2
measure 10
way 9
yet 3
mores
civilization 2
culture 2
moral 4
morality 1
time 9
more than
above 4
over 2
more than enough
plenty 1
moribund°
dying
morn
morning 1
morning°
morning star
star 1
moron
dolt
fool 1
moron *(cont.)*
halfwit
jerk 5
retard 2
twit[2]
moronic
absurd 1
crazy 2
daft 1
feeble-minded
foolish 2
halfwitted
inane
insane 2
mindless 1
nonsensical
preposterous
senseless 3
simple 4
stupid 1
thick 6
unreasonable 1
unthinking 1
weak 5
morose
blue 1
broken-hearted
dejected
despondent
disagreeable 3
dismal
dour 1
dreary 1
funereal
gloomy 2
glum
heartbroken
heavy 6
joyless 1
low[1] 8
melancholy 1
moody 1
morbid 3
sad 1
solemn 1
sombre 1
sour 4
sullen
tragic
wistful 1
morosely
sadly 2
moroseness
gloom 2
melancholy 2
morrow
morning 1
morsel°
bit 1
bite 3
chip 1
crumb
dainty 4
fragment 1
gob
grain 3
modicum
mouthful
nip[1] 3
particle
piece 1
portion 1
savoury 3
scrap[1] 1
snack 1
snatch 5
snip 3
spot 3
swallow 5
taste 2
titbit
mortal°
deadly 2
earthly 3
fatal 1
homicidal
human 1, 4
individual 3
lethal
life 5
murderous 1
person 1
physical
poisonous 1
severe 3
mortal *(cont.)*
soul 2
temporal 1
terminal 2
terrestrial 2
-mortals
man 2
people 1
mortality
flesh 2
humanity 2
mortally
severely 5
mortar
cement 1
mortgage
pawn[1] 1
pledge 5
put 28d
mortician
undertaker
mortification
confusion 6
decay 4
disappointment 2
embarrassment 1
humiliation
libel 1
pang 2
remorse
shame 1
undoing 1
wound 2
mortified
ashamed
embarrassed 1
remorseful
shamefaced 2
small 6
mortify°
crush 5
degrade 2
devastate 2
disgrace 3
dishonour 2
embarrass
fester 1
humble 4
libel 3
peg 3
place 13
put 16e
shame 6, 7
show 12c
slight 6
wound 4
mortifying
embarrassing
provocative 2
shameful
mosaic
combination 3
mosey
drift 2
meander 1
ramble 1
roam
saunter
straggle
stroll 1
wander 1
mosque
sanctuary 1
temple
mosquito
bug 1
moss
morass 1
swamp 1
most
best 4
maximum 1, 3
outside 3, 6
very 2
-at most
just 4
only 3
-for the most part°
at **part 8**
average 2
generally 1
mainly
most *(cont.)*
ordinarily
primarily 1
principally
rule 4
substantially
usually
whole 5
mostly
chiefly
generally 1
largely
mainly
part 8
primarily 1
principally
rule 4
substantially
usually
whole 5
most of all
chiefly
mainly
mot
epigram 1
maxim
pun
quip 1
mote
crumb
grain 3
particle
speck
spot 1
motel
hotel
mothball
table 5
moth-eaten
hack[2] 4
mangy
threadbare 1
time-worn
mother°
parent 1
priest
raise 4
mother country
country 2
fatherland
motherhood
maternity 1, 2
motherland
country 2
fatherland
land 4
root[1] 4
mother-lode
mine 2
motherly
maternal
mother-of-pearl
pearly
mother's boy
milksop
mother's ruin
booze 1
drink 5
liquor 1
ruin 4
whisky
mother wit
capacity 2
intelligence 1
intuition
motif°
design 6
figure 7
measure 9
note 5
pattern 2
taste 5
text 3
thread 2
tune 1
motile
moving 2
motility
motion 2
motion°
action 1
activity 1
beckon

motion (*cont.*)
circulation 1
flux
gesture 1, 3
move 11
movement 1
operation 1
play 24
resolution 3
sign 2
signal 4
step 4
stroke 2
transit 1
way 5
-in motion
moving 2
pioneer 2
raise 10
-motions
ceremony 2
rigmarole
motionless
calm 3
dead 11
dormant 1
freeze 3
immovable 1
inactive 1
inanimate
inert 2
passive 1
quiet 4
stagnant
standing 2
static 1
still 1, 7
supine 2
motionlessly
still 7
motionlessness
inactivity 1
inertia
motion picture
film 2
movie 1
production 4
-motion pictures
screen 5
motivate°
activate
animate 2
cause 6
dispose 2
drive 1
energize
excite 1
fire 8b
foment
induce 1
inflame 1
influence 3
mean[1] 1
move 6
prod 2
prompt 3
provoke 1
pump 4b
push 4
rise 16
spur 4
stir 4
motivation
end 3
impetus
incentive
incitement 2
motive 1
provocation 1
purpose 1
seed 2
shot 12
spirit 2
spur 1
motive°
cause 3
end 3
explanation 3
ground 3
provocation 1
purpose 1
reason 3
seed 2
spur 1
motive (*cont.*)
subject 3
motiveless
wanton 4
motley
confused 3
miscellaneous
miscellany
pastiche
pot-pourri
promiscuous 3
spotty 1
variegated
motor
car 1
drive 3
engine
machine 2
motor boat
boat
launch 6
motorcade
procession 1
motor car
car 1
machine 2
motor coach
coach 1
motor hotel
hotel
motorized
mobile 2
motorway
road 2
motor yacht
boat
mottle
dapple 2
pepper
splash 1
mottled°
dapple 1
speckled
spotty 1
variegated
motto°
byword
device 3
legend 4
maxim
moral 3
phrase 2
precept 2
saw
slogan
moue
mouth 5
pout 2
mould°
beat 5
cast 3, 4, 9
condition 6
decay 4
design 2
earth 2
fashion 5
fibre 3
figure 4
forge 1
form 1, 7
frame 7
generate 4
image 6
land 2
last[3]
like[1] 8
make 1
model 2, 7
nature 4
pattern 4
perfection 3
prepare 5
produce 1
prototype 1
rot 1, 3
school 4
shape 6
sort 1, 9
stamp 6, 8
tailor 2
template
work 13
mouldable
plastic 1
suggestible
moulder
decay 2
decompose 2
die 2
disintegrate
go 31e
putrefy
rot 1, 2
spoil 4
stagnate
turn 5
mouldering
mouldy
putrid
rotten 1
moulding
border 4
production 1
mouldy°
bad 6
foul 2
hack[2] 4
musty 1
off 7
prosaic
putrid
rotten 1
stale 1
stuffy 1
moult
shed[2] 4
mound°
drift 5
heap 1
height 3
hill 1, 2
hump 1
knoll
mass 1
mountain 2
pile[1] 1, 5
stack 1
tell[2]
mount°
arise 2
climb 1, 3
frame 2
get 51c
hill 1
mountain 1
perform 3
present[2] 5
produce 4
prominence 2
put 22d
rise 3, 7
scale[3] 3
set 1
slope 2
stage 4
swell 2
mountain°
heap 1
height 3
hill 2
lot 5b
mass 1, 2
peak 1
pile-up 2
profusion
stack 1
-mountains
country 3
lot 5b
plenty 1
sea 3
mountain dew
booze 1
liquor 1
mountainous°
huge
massive
mountain top
peak 1
mountebank
cheat 1
fake 4
fraud 3
hypocrite
impostor
phoney 3
mountebank (*cont.*)
rogue 1
slicker 1
swindler
thief 2
twister 1
mounting
mount 8
pedestal 1
set 28
setting
mount up
mount 7
total 5
mourn°
bemoan
bewail
grieve 1, 2
keen[2] 1
lament 1
moan 3
regret 1
sigh 2
sorrow 3
sympathize 1
weep 1
mournful°
bleak 1
dark 3
desolate 3
doleful
dreary 1
forlorn 1
funereal
heartbroken
hurt 7
joyless 1
low[1] 8
melancholy 1
miserable 1
pathetic 1
piteous
regretful
sad 1
sinking 2
sombre 1
tragic
wistful 1
woebegone
wretched 2
mournfully
sadly 2
mournfulness
melancholy 2
regret 2
mourning°
lament 2
lamentation
mouse
coward
girl 1
mouse-coloured
mousy 1
mousey
mousy 1
mousy°
timid
mouth°
effrontery
flippancy 2
impudence
trap 3
yap 3
mouthful°
bite 3
gulp 3
morsel 1
nip[2]
sip 2
swallow 5
taste 2
mouthpiece°
figurehead
lawyer
organ 2
mouthwash
wash 13
mouth-watering
delicious 1
luscious
lush 2
rich 6
mouth-watering (*cont.*)
succulent
tasty
tempting 2
yummy
mouzhik
peasant
movability
motion 2
movable°
loose 1
mobile 1, 2
-movables
furniture 1
good 21a
move°
act 1
activate
advance 3
affect[1] 2
agitate 1
animate 2
bear 1
blink 3
bowl[1]
carry 1, 3
cart 2
come 1
displace 1
dispose 1, 2
drive 1, 3
edge 6
electrify 2
emigrate
energize
evacuate 2, 3
excite 1
feint
fire 8b
flit
flow 1
gain 5
gesture 2
get 16
give 10
go 1, 2, 26a
hasten 2
haul 2
head 10
heave 1
hit 4
hum 2
impress 1
incite
induce 1
inflame 1
influence 3
inspire 1
interest 8
jump 4
lead 2
machination
make 20
manoeuvre 1
melt 2
migrate 1
misstep 1
motivate
movement 1, 2, 3
pass 2
pierce 4
play 23
proceed 1
proceeding 1
prod 2
progress 5
prompt 3
propel
provoke 1
push 1, 4, 10
range 8
reach 6
removal 4
remove 6
respond 2
rise 16
roll 2, 3
rouse 2
run 6
rush 1
sail 3
scheme 3
second[1] 10
send 4
move (*cont.*)
set 11, 18a
settle 4
shift 1, 3
ship 2
slide 2
speed 2
stake[1] 2
stall[2] 2
stand 2a
start 3, 9
step 1, 4, 5, 11, 13
stir 2, 4
stream 5
stroke 2
sue 1
sway 2
swivel 1
tactic 1
tempt 2
thrill 3
touch 6
trail 5
transfer 1, 2
transit 3
translate 4
transplant
transport 1
travel 3, 4
traverse 1
turn 2, 30
uproot 1
urge 1
verge[2]
walk 1
warm 9
wash 2
wile
work 20a
-on the move°
at **move** 13
active 1
moving 2
run 49c
swing 6
way 12
moveable
see **movable**
move about
circulate 1
mill 6
ramble 1
move across
transit 3
move against
sue 1
move ahead
gain 7
get 28d
go 1
pick 8f
proceed 1
push 10
work 20c
move along
come 6
get 28d
proceed 1
progress 5
shape 10b
move around
circulate 1
go 21a, 21c
mill 6
turn 4
move aside
dodge 1
make 41
move away
get 28c
go 2
move 2
pull 7
move back
recede 1
retreat 5
move back and forth
swing 1
move backwards
back 2b
reverse 5

moved
affected 5
agitated
overcome 2
respond 2
move down
descend 1
lower[1] 2
sink 3
move forward(s)
advance 1,3
go 1,19
headway 2
proceed 1
progress 5
push 10
move house
migrate 1
move 2
stake[1] 2
move in(to)
occupy 2
move it
fall 21
rush 1
movement°
action 1
activity 1
approach 6
cause 4
course 2
flow 5
flux
front 6
gesture 1
hustle 6
motion 1
operation 1
passage 1
play 24
progress 1
progression 1
shift 5
sign 2
step 1,10a
stir 6
stroke 2,3
tendency
touch 17
traffic 1
transit 1
translation 4
transmission 1
wave 2
way 5
move off
start 3
move on
get 28d
proceed 1
roll 2
stake[1] 2
start 3
work 20c
move onward(s)
advance 3
go 1
pass 2
progress 5
push 10
move out
evacuate 2
go 2
move 2
start 3
mover
instrument 2
move the goal-posts
cheat 2
deceive
move to and fro
sway 1
swing 1
wave 4
move up(wards)
advance 5
progress 6
promote 2
rise 10
work 20c
movie°
film 2
production 4
-movies
movie 2
screen 5
movie queen
queen 2
moving°
animate 4
animated 2
awesome
effective 2
electric
emotional 3
exciting 1
expressive 3
heart-warming 1
impressive
motion 1
motive 3
move 13a
movement 1,2
passage 1
pathetic 1
piteous
poignant 1,3
removal 4,5
sight 6b
soulful
stirring
swing 6
tender[1] 7
thrilling
touching
transit 1
translation 4
transmission 1
transport 4
way 12
moving parts
movement 4
moving picture
movie 1
production 4
moving spirit
life 7
protagonist 2
mow°
cut 4
fell
reap 1
mow down°
at **mow 2**
fell
massacre 2
moxie
bottle 2
courage
gall[1] 2
grit
gumption 2
nerve 1
pluck 1
MP
politician
representative 3
mph
velocity
Mr Average
people 3
public 8
unwashed 2
Mr Big
bigwig 1
boss 1
chief 1
dignitary
director 1
executive 1
head 2
leader 1
master 1
mogul
somebody 2
Mrs Average
people 3
public 8
Mrs Grundy
prude
Ms
miss[2]
MS, ms
paper 4
much
far 2,3
highly 1
lot 5b
materially
often
very 1
well[1] 7
-as much as possible
wide 6
much the same as
tantamount to
mucid
mouldy
mucilage
glue 1
mucilaginous
gooey 1
ropy 1
slimy 1
tenacious 2
thick 5
mucilaginousness
tenacity 2
muck°
dirt 1
dung
fiddle 2
filth 1
garbage
grime
mire 2
mud
ooze 1
sludge
soil[1] 3
tamper
tinker
muck about°
at **muck 3**
fool 7b
idle 6
tamper
tinker
mucker
intimate[1] 5
muck up°
at **muck 4**
botch
bungle
foul 16b
mess 5b
queer 5
mucky
dirty 1
filthy 1
muddy 1
slimy 1
sordid 3
yucky
mucous
slimy 1
mucronate(d)
pointed 1
mucroniform
pointed 1
mucronulate
pointed 1
mud°
dirt 1
grime
mire 2
muck 2
ooze 1
sludge
soil[1] 3
mud-caked
muddy 1
muddied
bedraggled
muddy 1
muddle°
bemuse 1
clutter 1
complicate 1
confuse 2,3
confusion 1
disorder 1,4
muddle *(cont.)*
fiasco
fluff 4
fog 4
hash 3
hole 5
intoxicate 1
jumble 1,2
mess 1
mishandle 2
mix 4b
mix-up
morass 2
perplex
problem 1
queer 5
scrape 8
screw 7b
shambles
snarl[2] 1,3
tangle 2,3
upset 3
welter 1
-in a muddle
topsy-turvy 2
muddled
confused 1,2,3
disjointed 2
disorderly 1
dizzy 2
groggy
hazy 2
helpless 2
helter-skelter 1
inarticulate 1
incoherent
inexact
mixed 2
muddy 2
rambling 1
topsy-turvy 2
upset 9
muddle-headed
confused 1
foolish 2
senseless 3
muddle-headedness
folly 1
muddler
butcher 2
muddle through°
at **muddle 3**
make 29
manage 4
muddy°
bedraggled
dirty 7
indistinct 1
mire 4
nebulous
opaque 1
sloppy 2
soil[1] 1,2
taint 2
mud-flat(s)
flat 14b
mudlark
guttersnipe
ragamuffin
mud-slide
slide 5
mud-slinging
smear 4
mud-spattered
muddy 1
muff
blow[1] 3
bungle
err 1
foul 16b
fumble 2
hash 3
mishandle 2
mistake 1
muddle 2
queer 5
muffle°
gag[1] 1
kill 3
mute 3
silence 4
smother 4
muffle *(cont.)*
soften 3
suppress 3
swathe
wrap 1
muffled
dead 13
dull 8
faint 1
hollow 6
inarticulate 2
inaudible
indistinct 1
low[1] 13
noiseless
weak 7
muffler°
muffling
suppression
mug°
attack 1
dupe 1
face 1
feature 3
fool 3
hold 22a
hoodlum
miscreant 1
pan 2
pounce 1
prey 2
punk 1
pushover 2
rob 2
rough 13
score 7
set 24
stick[1] 17a
sucker
waylay 2
mugger
assailant
gangster
robber
thief 1
thug
mugging
assault 2
hold-up 1
robbery
muggins
dolt
mug 3
sap[1] 2
muggy°
clammy 2
damp 1
humid
moist 1
steamy 1
sticky 3
stuffy 1
sultry 1
sweltering
torrid 1
mug up°
at **mug 6**
study 1
mugwump
non-partisan 3
mujik
peasant
mulch
fertilize 2
mulct
deprive
divest 1
fine[2] 1,2
forfeit 1
penalize
penalty
punish 2
rob 3
swindle 1
take 32b
mulish
inflexible
obstinate
opinionated 1
rigid 4
stubborn
wilful 2
mulishness
obstinacy
mull°
fantasize
mull over°
at **mull**
consider 1
contemplate 2
debate 4
fantasize
meditate 2
muse
ponder
puzzle 2
reflect 3
see 8
speculate 1
study 2
think 5a
weigh 2
multicolour(ed)
mottled
variegated
multifaceted
compound 4
sophisticated 2
versatile 1
multifarious
different 3
divers
manifold
many 2
miscellaneous
multifariousness
diversity 2
variety 1
multiform
compound 4
diverse
miscellaneous
protean
multiformity
diversity 2
multinational
firm 6
multiple
compound 4
multiplex
manifold
miscellaneous
multiplication
increase 3
multiplicity
diversity 2
variety 1
multiply
breed 4
compound 3
grow 1
increase 1
mount 7
proliferate
propagate 1,2
reproduce 2
multi-purpose
versatile 1
multi-storey
tall 1
multitude
assembly 1
crowd 1
flock 1
herd 1
hoi polloi
host[2]
jam 5
many 3
mass 2
mob 1
number 2
ocean 2
pack 2
people 3
plenty 1
populace
press 8
profusion
public 8
rash[2] 2
score 4
sea 3
stack 3
swarm 1
throng 1

necrologue
obituary
necrology
obituary
necromancer
magician 1
sorcerer
necromancy
magic 1
sorcery
necromantic
magic 5
necropolis
graveyard
necropsy
post-mortem 1
necrose
fester 1
mortify 3
necrosed
ulcerous
necrotic
ulcerous
need°
call 15
cry 3
dearth
demand 3, 6
expect 3
go 41
indicate 4
lack 1, 2
miss[1] 2
necessity 1, 3
poverty 2
privation
require 2
requirement 2
scarcity
stomach 2
take 16
urgency
use 13
want 2, 3, 5
wish 5
-in need
deprived
destitute 2
poor 1
starved 3
want 2
needed
demand 7
due 3
indispensable 1
mandatory
necessary 1
order 10b
vital 1
needful
desperate 3
destitute 2
indispensable 1
necessary 1
short 6
needfulness
necessity 2
need 4
neediness
necessity 3
need 4
poverty 1
privation
want 5
needle
aggravate 2
annoy 2
bother 1
exasperate 2
gall[2] 4
index 3
indicator
irk
irritate
molest 1
nag[1] 1
offend 1
pester
pick 6
pointed 1
poke 4
prickle 1
prod 3, 5
needle (*cont.*)
sharp 1
spine 2
spite 3
tease 1
torment 2
needless°
dispensable
expletive 1
extraneous 1
gratuitous 2
non-essential 1
superfluous
unnecessary
needless to say°
at **needless 2**
naturally 1
needling
incitement 1
torment 4
needy°
broke
deprived
destitute 1
impoverished 1
indigent
lean[1] 3
penurious 2
poor 1
straitened
ne'er-do-well
derelict 3
good-for-nothing 2
idler
loafer
miscreant 1, 2
rascal
reprobate 2
rogue 1
shiftless
wastrel 2
nefarious
black 6
dark 4
evil 1
flagrant
foul 4
immoral 1
lawless 3
Machiavellian
miscreant 2
monstrous 2
scheming
sinister 2
vicious 1
nefariousness
evil 6
negate
deny 1
destroy 4
disprove
disturb 5
neutralize
rebut
reverse 3
revoke
rule 8
thwart 1
negating
negative 4
negation
denial 1, 3
negative°
destructive 2
pessimistic
photograph 1
negatively
negative 5
neglect°
default 1, 3
disregard 3
fail 2
failure 1
forget 2
leave[1] 10
negligence
omission 2
omit 2
overlook 1
oversight 1
slack 4
slide 4
slight 8
waste 5
neglected
abandoned 1
derelict 1
deserted
desolate 1
disused
forlorn 2
ragged 4
ramshackle
shabby 3
undone[2]
unused 2
neglectful
careless 2
delinquent 2
derelict 2
forgetful
heedless
inattentive
promiscuous 1
remiss
slack 1
thoughtless 2
unthinking 2
neglectfulness
neglect 3, 4
negligee
wrapper 1
negligence°
default 1
neglect 4
omission 2
negligent
careless 2
delinquent 2
derelict 2
forgetful
inadvertent 2
inattentive
lax 1
loose 6
nod 4
perfunctory 2
promiscuous 1
reckless
remiss
slack 1
thoughtless 2
unprofessional 1
negligible°
frugal 3
incidental 2
inconsequential
insignificant
little 5
marginal 1
minor 2
petty 1
puny 1
remote 6
slight 1
small 2, 4, 5
tenuous 2
tiny
trifling
unimposing
negotiable
navigable 1
negotiate°
bargain 3
dicker 1
float 3
haggle
leap 1
manipulate 2
palaver 5
parley 2
settle 3
transact
negotiation°
deal 5
dicker 2
diplomacy 2
transaction 1
-negotiations
dealings
negotiator°
go-between
mediator
Negro
black 2
Negroid
black 2
neighbourhood°
area 3
district
local 1, 2
locale
part 6
place 2
precinct 2
proximity
quarter 3
resident 2
site 1
spot 2
surrounding
territory 1
turf 2
vicinity
whereabouts
-in the neighbourhood°
at **neighbourhood 2**
close 20
near 1, 9
nearby 1
round 22, 26
neighbouring°
adjoining
local 1
near 5
resident 2
surrounding
neighbourliness
familiarity 2
friendship 1
neighbourly°
brotherly
considerate
friendly 1
genial
helpful
homely 1
obliging
sociable
neither here nor there
decent 3
end 6
indifferent 4
irrelevant
limbo
wishy-washy 1
nemesis
fate 2
jinx 2
ruin 3
neologism°
neology
neologism
neonate
baby 1
child 2
neophyte
convert 3
greenhorn
initiate 4
learner
newcomer 2
novice
pupil
recruit 2
neoplasm
tumour
neoterism
neologism
nephelococcygeal
quixotic
Nephelococcygia
fairyland
forgetful
Utopia
ne plus ultra
model 3
nonpareil
peak 2
peerless
nepotism
favouritism
patronage 4
Neptune's kingdom *etc.*
deep 9
Neptune's kingdom *etc.* (*cont.*)
sea 1
nerd
jerk 5
silly 3
square 9
Neronic *etc.*
cruel 2
nerve°
arrogance
assurance 4
bottle 2
brass
confidence 2
courage
daring 1
effrontery
face 5
fortitude
freedom 7
gall[1] 2
grit
gumption 2
gut 3a
heart 2
impertinence
pluck 1
presumption 1
sauce 2
spunk
steel 2
strength 2
-nerves°
at **nerve 4**
jitters
nerve-racking°
fraught 2
hairy 2
harrowing
stormy 2
tense 3
touchy 2
nervous°
afraid 1
agitated
anxious 1
bashful 1
distraught
distrustful
disturbed 1
edge 5
emotional 2
excitable
excited 1
fearful 2
fidget 2
frantic
gingerly 2
ill 6
impatient 1
insecure 1
intense 3
jumpy
neurotic
overwrought 1
panic-stricken
queasy 1
restless
self-conscious
shy 1
sinking 1
tense 2, 3
timid
tremulous 1
upset 8
worried
nervous breakdown
breakdown 2
nervous exhaustion
shock 2
nervously
fearfully 1
gingerly 1
nervousness
alarm 2
anxiety 1
dread 2
excitement 1
fidget 3
fluster 2
horror 2
nervousness (*cont.*)
jitters
nerve 4
panic 1
phobia
solicitude
suspense 2
tension 2
unrest
vapour 2
worry 4
nervure
vein 1
nervy
daring 2
foolhardy
game 8
impertinent
nervous 1
nescient
ignorant 2
uninformed
ness
cape[1]
nest°
lair 1
nook 2
perch 2
nest egg
cache 2
fund 2
reserve 3
saving 4
nestle°
cuddle 1
huddle 3
pet[1] 4
snuggle
Nestor
sage 2
thinker
net°
catch 2
clear 13
earn 2
gain 1
get 3
harvest 3
lace 1
make 7
mesh 1
money 3
profit 1
realize 3
receive 2
revenue
snare 1
trap 4
web
win 2
yield 4
nether
inferior 1
infernal 1
nethermost regions
depth 5
nether regions
hell 1
underworld 2
nett
net[2] 1
profit 1
netting
lace 1
mesh 1
net[1] 1
nettle
aggravate 2
anger 2
annoy 1
displease
exasperate 2
gall[2] 4
get 17
gnaw 3
heckle
infuriate
irk
irritate
jar[2] 3
molest 1

non compos mentis (*cont.*)
maniacal 1
psychotic 1
unbalanced 2
non-compulsory
optional
nonconformer
nonconformist 1
nonconforming
bizarre 2
dissident 2
irregular 3
nonconformist 2
unorthodox
nonconformist°
bizarre 2
Bohemian
dissident 1, 2
eccentric 2
independent 9
individualist
irregular 3
misfit
oddity 2
original 6
rebel 4
underground 3
unorthodox
nonconformity
disagreement 1
eccentricity 1
inequality 1
licence 3
non-compliance
originality
non-consent
regret 3
non-constraining
permissive
non-cooperation
non-compliance
non-critical
secondary 1
nondescript°
non-discriminatory
indifferent 2
promiscuous 1
none°
non-ecclesiastic(al)
lay² 1
secular
temporal 1
non-effervescent
flat 8
nonentity
cog 2
failure 3
nobody 2
non-essential 2
nothing 2
zero 3
non-eradicable
indelible
non-erasable
indelible
non-essential°
accident 3
circumstantial 2
dispensable
expendable
expletive 1
extraneous 1
immaterial 1
incidental 2
insignificant
luxury 4
needless 1
peripheral 1
petty 1
redundant 1
secondary 1
triviality 2
unnecessary
nonesuch
model 3
nonpareil

nonetheless°
even 12
however 1
nevertheless
notwithstanding 1
same 3
though 2
time 13a
yet 5
non-event°
non-exclusive
general 1, 3
public 3
non-existence
absence 2
oblivion 1
non-existent°
defunct 2
fictitious 1
unreal 1
non-fatal
benign 4
non-fiction
writing 2
non-flammable°
incombustible
non-fluctuating
certain 1
non-fulfilment
default 1
disappointment 1
dissatisfaction 1
miscarriage
non-completion
non-functional
order 13c
non-functioning
disabled
dud 2
inactive 2
ineffective 1
order 13c
out 14
non-germane
irrelevant
non-glare
flat 12
non-gloss(y)
flat 12
non-gregarious
private 4
non-inclusion
omission 1
non-indulgence
sobriety 1
non-inflammable
incombustible
non-flammable
non-initiate
outsider
non-interference
freedom 4
laissez-faire
non-intervention
laissez-faire
non-kosher
profane 2
non-liability
immunity 1
non-liable
irresponsible
non-literal
metaphoric
non-malignant
benign 4
non-mandatory
optional
non-material
spiritual 2
non-member
outsider
non-militant
meek 2
non-military
civil 1
non-muscular
soft 12

non-native
alien 2
exotic 1
foreign 1
foreigner
non-natural
affected 1
non-negotiable
inalienable
non-objective
interested 2
narrow-minded
prejudiced 1
non-observance
breach 1
disregard 3
non-compliance
no-nonsense°
realistic 1
straight 6
non-operative
idle 1
nonpareil°
excellent
gem 2
ideal 2
incomparable
model 3
pearl
peerless
perfect 2
quintessence
sensational 3
splendid 3
sterling 2
superior 2
non-participant
bystander
observer
non-participating
silent 4
non-partisan°
fence 2
independent 4
indifferent 2
liberal 2
neutral 1
unprejudiced
non-payer
welsher
non-payment
default 2
non-performance
default 1
failure 1
non-completion
non-perishable
indestructible
non-physical
platonic
soft 12
nonplus°
amaze
daze 2
devastate 2
dumbfound
floor 5
flummox
fog 4
overpower 2
overwhelm 3
perplex
puzzle 1
stagger 2
stick¹ 9
stump 2
stymie
surprise 1
nonplussed
blank 5
confused 2
daze 4
dumbfounded
helpless 2
speechless 2
thunderstruck
non-poisonous
harmless
safe 2
non-prejudicial
honourable 3

non-presence
absence 1
non-private
common 5
non-productive°
infertile
non-professional
amateur 1, 2
green 2
homespun
lay² 2
popular 3
non-profit-making
unprofitable 1
non-public
private 2
non-radical
moderate 2, 4
non-radioactive
clean 5
non-reactionary
moderate 2, 4
non-realistic
abstract 2
non-recognition
ingratitude
non-reflective
flat 12
non-religious
profane 2
secular
temporal 1
worldly 1
non-representational
abstract 2
unrealistic 2
non-requisite
optional
non-resonant
dead 13
non-restricted
full 8
non-restrictive
permissive
non-retrievable
irretrievable 1
non-returnable
disposable 1
non-reversible
irreversible
non-sacred
profane 2
non-secular
spiritual 1
non-selective
promiscuous 1
nonsense°
absurdity 1
babble 3
drivel 3
fiddlesticks
flannel 1
folly 1
froth 2
fun 2
gab 2
gibberish
gobbledegook 1
hocus-pocus 2
insanity 2
jargon 2
madness 2
moonshine 2
mumbo-jumbo 1
palaver 1
prattle 3
rigmarole
romance 5
rot 4
rubbish 2
slaver¹ 3
stuff 4
stupidity 2
swill 2
talk 18
trash 1
wind¹ 2

nonsensical°
absurd 1
crazy 2
daft 1
farcical
foolish 2
inane
insane 2
ludicrous
mad 2
meaningless 1
pointless
preposterous
rich 11
ridiculous
senseless 3
silly 1
stupid 2
unreasonable 1
unthinking 1
zany 1
nonsensicalness
folly 1
non-sequential
order 13a
non sequitur
fallacy
non-sexual
platonic
non-specialist
lay² 2
unprofessional 3
non-specialized
general 2
non-specific
broad 4, 6
certain 6
general 2, 4
indefinite 1, 2
lax 2
loose 5
meagre 3
random 1
vague 1, 2, 3
non-specifically
generally 2
non-specified
certain 6
vague 1, 2
non-speculative
sound² 5
non-spiritual
earthly 2, 3
material 7
outward
secular
temporal 1
worldly 1
non-standard
bad 1
illegitimate 3
untrue 3
non-starter
failure 3
flop 4
loser
non-event
non-static
fluid 3
non-stationary
mobile 1
non-stop°
cease 2
constant 2
continual
continuous 2
endless 2
eternal 2
express 7
night 3
ongoing 1
permanently
perpetual 2
persistent 2
relentless 2
repetitive
steady 2
non-success
miscarriage
nonsuch
model 3
nonpareil

non-technical
unprofessional 3
non-toxic
harmless
safe 2
non-translucent
opaque 1
non-transparent
opaque 1
non-trivial
no-nonsense
non-U
plebeian 1
non-venomous
harmless
non-violent
mild 1
orderly 2
peaceable 2
non-virulent
benign 4
non-vital
non-essential 1
non-warring
peaceable 2
non-working
leisure 5
noodge
pest
noodle
head 1
loaf¹ 2
sap¹ 2
nook°
chamber 3
hole 1
niche 1
recess 1
-in every nook and cranny
everywhere
thoroughly 2
noon°
midday
noonday
noon
no one
nobody 1
none
noontide
noon
noontime
midday
noon
noose
loop 1
ring¹ 1
snare 1
no person
nobody 1
none
no picnic°
at picnic 3
nor'easter
blow¹ 9
norm°
average 1
example 2
gauge 3
mark 3
mean³ 1
medium 3
ordinary 3
prototype 2
standard 2
touchstone
normal°
accustomed 1
average 3
character 8
common 1
conventional
correct 7
customary 1
formal 1
frequent 1
general 2
habitual 1
medium 1
natural 1, 2
norm 1

notion (*cont.*)
philosophy 2
picture 3
point 12
principle 2
resolution 3
spirit 7
suggestion 1
surmise 2
suspicion 2
theme 1
thesis 1
thought 2
understanding 4
view 2
-notions
sundries
notional
abstract 1
ideal 5
imaginary
pure 4
speculative 1
not later than
by 4
not more than
only 3
not much cop
puny 1
not on
out 13
unthinkable 2
not oneself
par 5b
sort 6
notoriety°
attention 2
celebrity 1
fame
infamy 1
notorious°
disgraceful 2
flagrant
infamous 1
noted
public 6
reputation 2
spicy 3
notoriousness
notoriety
not quite
almost
barely
cry 8
go 32e
hardly
near 3
nearly 1
scarcely 1
not think much of
frown 2
not till hell freezes over
never 1
not to be sneezed at
tidy 3
not to say
indeed 2
not up to expectations
wanting 1
not up to par
low[1] 9
par 5a
poor 4
wanting 1
not up to scratch
par 5a
not up to snuff
ill 1
indisposed 1
par 5a, 5b
poor 4
ropy 3
sick 2
sort 6
'Not Wanted on Voyage'
trash 2
not well
ill 1
par 5b
notwithstanding°
despite
even 11, 12
face 9
for 11
however 1, 4
independent 8
irrespective of
nevertheless
rate[1] 5
regardless 1, 2
same 3
spite 2
still 6, 8
though 1, 2
time 13a
yet 5, 6
not worth a rap *etc.*
meaningless 2
not worth mentioning *etc.*
negligible
nought
naught
nil
nothing 1
tongue 3
zero 1
nourish°
cherish 2
feed 1, 3
fertilize 2
forward 6
foster 1
fuel 4
keep 2
mother 5
nurse 3
stimulate 1
strengthen 2
nourisher
mother 3
nourishing
healthy 2
hearty 4
nutritious
wholesome 1
nourishment°
diet[1] 1
food
fuel 3
meal 1
meat 1
provender 1
refreshment 1
subsistence 2
sustenance 1
nous
gumption 1
intelligence 1
sense 2
nouveau riche
parvenu 1, 2
upstart
nova
star 1
novel°
contemporary 2
different 2
fresh 2
modern
new 1
offbeat
original 4
revolutionary 2
romance 3
unfamiliar 1
writing 2
novelette
novel 2
novelist
author
scribe 2
writer
novella
novel 2
novelty°
change 2
gewgaw
innovation 1
originality
variation 2
novice°
apprentice 1
greenhorn,
initiate 4
innocent 5
learner
newcomer 2
pupil
recruit 2
noviciate, novitiate
initiate 4
novice
now°
instantaneously
just 6
minute[1] 3
present[1] 1, 3, 4
presently
trendy 1
-for now
meanwhile 2
temporarily 1
time 16
-from now on
hence 3
henceforth
nowadays°
now 2
present[1] 4
now and again°
at **now 4**
occasionally
once 4
sometimes
now and then°
at **now 4**
fit[2] 4
infrequently
occasionally
once 4
random 2
sometimes
time 14
no way
fun 4
mean[3] 5
shot 11
no way José
mean[3] 5
no-win situation
joker 2
nowise
scarcely 2
noxious
bad 2
deadly 1
destructive 1
disagreeable 2
evil 3, 5
harmful
hurtful 1
mischievous 2
nasty 1
obnoxious
offensive 3
rank[2] 4
ruinous
terrible 5
unhealthy 2
unwholesome 1
vile 2
virulent 1
wicked 6
noxiousness
virulence 1
noxious
poisonous 1
nuance
expression 4
refinement 2
sense 4
shade 3, 7
nub°
bottom 3
gist
nub (*cont.*)
heart 3
kernel 2
nucleus
pith 1
point 5
substance 2
nubility
puberty
nuclear°
fuel 1
nucleus°
centre 1
core 1
heart 3
hub
kernel 2
nub 2
pith 1
point 5
nuddy
-in the nuddy
naked 1
nude
nude°
bare 1
exotic 3
naked 1
raw 7
-in the nude
naked 1
nude
raw 7
nudge°
bother 1, 7
dig 2, 7
induce 1
jab 1, 3
jog 2
jolt 2
pest
poke 1, 5
prod 1, 4
prompt 3
push 3, 13
nudging
hustle 5
nudie show
burlesque 2
nudnik
pest
trouble 6
nudzh
pest
nugatory
frivolous 1
idle 4
immaterial 1
inconsequential
indifferent 4
insignificant
meaningless 2
negligible
niggling 2
petty 1
puny 1
small 2
unimposing
nugget
lump[1] 1
mass 3
nuisance°
annoyance 2
bore[2] 1
bother 5, 7
discomfort 2
drag 7
fag 2
gall[2] 2
handful 2
headache 2
inconvenience 1
job 4
pain 3
palaver 1
pest
pill 2
plague 2
thorn 2
torment 4
trial 5
trouble 6
null
invalid[2]
zero 1
null and void
invalid[2]
void 1
nullification
abolition
cancellation 1
recall 5
repeal 2
reversal 3
nullifidian
godless 2
heathen 1, 2
infidel
non-believer
sceptic
nullified
invalid[2]
nullify
abolish
anticipate 1
cancel 1, 3
contradict 2
correct 4
counteract
destroy 3
extinguish 2
foil[1]
forgive 3
frustrate 1
kill 3
neutralize
offset 1
quash 1
recall 3
repeal 1
reverse 3
revoke
ruin 9
set 15b
spike 3
thwart 1
undo 3
vacate 3
vitiate 3
void 6
nullifying
negative 3
nulling
reversal 3
numb°
bemuse 2
chill 5
dead 2, 4
deaden 1
drug 4
dull 2, 11
groggy
insensible 1
paralyse 2
petrify 1
senseless 2
shock 1
stun 1
thick-skinned
thunderstruck
unconscious 1
numbed
chill 5
groggy
numb 1
petrified 1
senseless 2
thick-skinned
number°
amount 2
batch 2
broad 9
character 1
count 1
edition
enumerate 2
figure 7
flock 1
group 1
incidence
include 3
involve 1
issue 5
itemize
many 3
mass 2
number (*cont.*)
pack 3
page[1] 3
piece 4
plenty 1
profusion
quantity
range 2
rash[2] 2
reckon 2
routine 2
score 1, 4
selection 2
set 25
several 1
song 1
stack 3
strong 14
suite 1
variety 1
various 1
woman 3
-numbers
many 3
mass 2
number 2
plenty 1
rash[2] 2
score 4
numbering
inclusion
numberless°
immeasurable
infinite 1
limitless
many 1
substantial 2
unlimited 2
untold 1
number one
chief 1
director 1
executive 1
leader 1
urinate
number two
defecate
second[1] 8
numbing
chill 4, 5
cold 1
dull 8
freezing
leaden 2
narcotic 1
piercing 3
polar 1
shocking 1
stunning 1
numbness
stupor
num(b)skull
dolt
dummy 3
fool 1
halfwit
silly 3
num(b)skulled
foolish 2
numen
god
numerable
finite
numeral
figure 7
number 1
numerate
figure 8
numerically
strong 14
numero uno
chief 1
director 1
executive 1
leader 1
numerous
different 3
divers
frequent 1
lot 5c
manifold
many 1
numberless

numerous (*cont.*)
strong 14
substantial 2
umpteen
various 1
-on numerous occasions
often
numismatic
monetary
nummary
monetary
nummular
monetary
nun
buoy 1
recluse
nun-buoy
buoy 1
nuncio
ambassador
delegate 1
deputy
envoy
messenger
representative 3
nuptial°
bridal
matrimonial
-nuptials
marriage 2
wedding 1
nurse°
care 4, 6a
cherish 2
forward 6
harbour 3
incubate
keeper
look 4
minder 1
mother 3, 5
nourish 1, 2
rear[2] 1
servant 1
tend[2]
treat 3
nursemaid
servant 1
nursery school
school 1
nurse's aide
orderly 3
nursing home
home 3
hospital
infirmary
sanatorium
nurture
bring 15a
cherish 2
feed 1
foster 1
grow 3
harbour 3
incubate
keep 2
maintain 2
mother 5
nourish 1, 2
nurse 2, 4
promote 1
protect 2
raise 3, 4, 7
rear[2] 1
rise 11
tend[2]
upbringing
nurturer
mother 3
nurturing
growth 1
maternal
parenting
promotion 1
nut
addict 2
character 6
crank 1
devotee
enthusiast
fan
fanatic

nut (*cont.*)
fiend 2
freak 4
head 1
kernel 1
madman
maniac 1
psychotic 2
sectarian 4
weirdo
zany 2
nutcase
character 6
crank 1
madman
weirdo
nut-meat
kernel 1
nutriment
diet[1] 1
food
fuel 3
meat 1
nourishment
refreshment 1
subsistence 2
sustenance 1
nutrimental
nutritious
nutrition
fuel 3
nourishment
nutritious°
healthy 2
square 5
wholesome 1
nutritive
nutritious
nuts
absurd 1
crazy 1, 5
curious 3
daft 3
deranged
disturbed 2
foolish 2
inane
insane 1
love 7
mad 1, 6
mental 2
psychotic 1
queer 4
sweet 8
twist 11
unbalanced 2
wild 9
nutshell
-in a nutshell
briefly 1
short 14
word 8
nutter
character 6
crank 1
madman
maniac 1
psychotic 2
weirdo
nuttiness
absurdity 1
folly 1
nutty
absurd 1
crazy 1, 5
curious 3
deranged
flighty 2
foolish 2
inane
insane 1, 2
mad 1
mental 2
nonsensical
off 4
preposterous
psychotic 1
queer 4
robust 2
senseless 3
twist 11
way-out 1
wild 9
zany 1

nuzzle
caress 1, 2
nestle
pet[1] 4
snuggle
nymph
maid 1
miss[2]
nymphet
maid 1
miss[2]
nympholepsy
ecstasy 1
nympholeptic
ecstatic

O

oaf
barbarian 2
boor 2
clod 2
clown 2
duffer
fool 1
gawk 1
hulk 2
peasant
rustic 3
slob
oafish
awkward 1
barbarian 3
boorish
clumsy
hulking
obtuse 2
provincial 2
rude 1
rustic 2
simple 4
wooden 3
oafishness
simplicity 4
OAP
pensioner
ruin 5
senior citizen
-OAP's
elderly 2
oar°
interfere 1
intervene 1
paddle 1, 2
oarsman, oars-woman
oar 2
oasis°
oath°
assurance 1
curse 1, 3
expletive 2
guarantee 1
pledge 1
promise 1
resolution 2
vow 2
word 4
obduracy
obstinacy
persevere
persistence
self-control 1
severity 1
tenacity 1
obdurate
disobedient 2
dogmatic
dour 2
firm 4
frigid 2
grim 1
hard 1, 4
immovable 2
incorrigible
inflexible
laborious 3
obstinate
opinionated 1
persevere
persistent 1

obdurate (*cont.*)
perverse 3
positive 5
relentless 1
rigid 4
severe 1
stern 1
stony 2
tenacious 1
tough 6
wilful 2
obdurateness
perseverance
severity 1
obeahism
magic 1
obedience°
deference 2
faith 3
flexibility 2
observance 1
submission 1
obedient°
broken 4
dutiful
flexible 2
good 4
observant 2
serve 2
sheepish 1
subject 8a
submissive 1
tame 1
tractable 1
yielding 2
obediently
behave
obeisance°
bow 1
deference 2
homage
prostration 2
reverence 1
obeisant
propitiatory 2
obelisk
tower 1
obese°
beamy
big 2
fat 1
gross 1
heavy 11
large 1
plump[1] 1
rotund 3
stout 1
weighty 1
well-fed
obesity°
fat 5
fatness
obey°
abide 4
comply
conform 1
follow 2
fulfil 2
heed 1
keep 6
listen 2
mark 12
mind 16
observe 1
respect 7
square 11
obeying
observance 1
obfuscate
obscure 7
obfuscated
opaque 1
obfuscation
gobbledegook 2
obit
obituary
obiter dictum
digression 1
obituary°
object°
acquisition 2
aim 5
ambition 3

object (*cont.*)
bitch 3
butt[1]
cavil 2
challenge 1
contest 3
design 7
disapprove
dispute 1
drift 4
effect 3
end 3
entity 1
exception 4
goal
groan 2
idea 4
intent 1
intention
mark 6
mind 15
motive 2
objective 2
oppose 1
point 6
protest 3
purpose 1
quarry[1]
reason 3
squawk 2
target
thing 1, 5
use 12
view 5
-for the object of
for 4
objection°
disapproval
grievance 2
gripe 2
opposition 1
protest 1
reservation 2
objectionable
disagreeable 1, 2
disgraceful 2
disgusting
dishonourable 3
distasteful
exceptionable
inadmissible
nasty 1, 2
obnoxious
obscene 2
offensive 2
outrageous 3
repugnant
repulsive
revolting
ugly 2
unacceptable
undesirable 2
unlikely 2
unsavoury
objective°
aim 5
ambition 3
aspiration
candid 2
design 7
destination
detached 2
disinterested
dispassionate 2
effect 3
end 3
equitable
factual 2
fair[1] 1
goal
idea 4
impartial
impersonal 1
indifferent 2
intent 1
intention
just 1
literal 2
mark 6
mission 1
motive 2
non-partisan 2
object 3
point 6
prey 1, 2

objective (*cont.*)
purpose 1
reason 3
sake 2
tangible
target
tolerant
unprejudiced
view 5
objectively
fairly 2
honestly 1
objectiveness
justice 1
objectivity°
candour 2
equity
honesty 3
indifference 3
justice 1
objet d'art
antique 2
curiosity 3
-objets d'art
bric-à-brac
objet de vertu
antique 2
curiosity 3
-objets de vertu
bric-à-brac
objurgate
abuse 3
berate
objurgation
abuse 8
blame 3
objurgative
foul 6
objurgatory
foul 6
oblation
offering
sacrifice 1
obligate°
bind 2
oblige 2
tie 7d
obligated
accountable
beholden
bound[3] 2
indebted
liable 2
must 1
obliged 1, 2
thankful
obligation°
appreciation 1
assignment 2
business 1
charge 1
contract 1
debt 1
duty 1
engagement 3
faith 3
guarantee 1
liability 2
must 2
office 4
place 4
project 2
resolution 2
responsibility 1
stint 1
stipulation
strain[1] 7
subscription 2
-obligations
string 7
-under (an) obligation
beholden
debt 2
thankful
-without obligation
free 4
obligatory°
imperative 1
incumbent 1
indispensable 2
mandatory

odious
abhorrent
abominable 1
damnable
diabolic 2
disagreeable 1
forbidding 1
hateful 1
hideous 2
infamous 2
loathsome
mangy
nasty 1
obnoxious
rancid
repulsive
seamy
shabby 4
ugly 2
vicious 1
odium
aversion 1
contempt
discredit 4
disgrace 1
disgust 3
hate 3
horror 1
infamy 2
loathing
revulsion
shame 2
odoriferous
fragrant
smelly
strong 3
odorous
fragrant
redolent 1
odour°
aroma 1, 2
aura
bouquet 2
flavour 1
fragrance
fume 3
perfume 1
reek 3
savour 2
scent 1
smell 1
sniff 1
stench
tang 1
touch 15
odyssey
journey 1
oecumenic(al)
international
oeillade
ogle 3
oestrus
-in oestrus
randy
oeuvre
opus
production 2
work 4
off°
absent 1
absent-minded
amiss 1
bad 6
beside 2
chase 3
distant 2
far 1
foul 2
hook 5
misguided
mistaken 1
out 12, 14
rotten 1
sick 5
soft 6
sour 2
stale 1
unpalatable
-be off
get 44a
leave[1] 1
offal
dirt 1
filth 1
offal (*cont.*)
garbage
gut 1
off and on
occasionally
sometimes
off base
cock-eyed
inaccurate
inapplicable
off beam
disorientated
erroneous
wrong 2
offbeat°
abnormal 2
bizarre 1
curious 3
deviant 1
eccentric 1
extreme 5
grotesque 2
irregular 3
kinky 1
odd 1
ordinary 4
outlandish
peculiar 1
quaint 1
queer 1
singular 1
step 8
strange 1
way-out 1
whimsical 1
wild 7
off-centre
wry 1
off colour°
blue 2
broad 8
dirty 2
foul 5
improper 3
nasty 3
naughty 3
obscene 1
par 5b
profane 3
racy 2
rank[2] 3
risqué
sexy 2
spicy 2
suggestive 2
vulgar 2
off course
erroneous
offence°
atrocity 2
crime
cut 23
dishonour 4
error 2
fault 2, 4
indignity
injury
insult 2
misdeed
offensive 4, 5
provocation 2
put-down
sin 1
slap 5
slight 7
transgression
offend°
cut 3
disgust 1
dishonour 1
displease
hurt 3
injure 2
insult 1
jar[2] 3
nauseate
offence 2
outrage 4
provoke 3
repel 2
revolt 3
scandalize
sicken 2
sin 3
offend (*cont.*)
slight 6
spite 3
transgress 1
turn 17b
wound 4
offended
bridle 3
disgusted
exception 4
mind 15
nauseated
sick 6
umbrage
offender°
criminal 3
culprit 2
delinquent 1
felon
sinner
transgressor
offending
guilty 1
offensive°
abhorrent
abominable 1
abusive 1
assault 1
attack 6
bad 4
base[2] 4
beastly 2
blue 2
campaign 1
coarse 3
crude 4
damnable
derogatory
disagreeable 1, 2
disgusting
distasteful
evil 5
filthy 3
forbidding 1
foul 1, 6
frightful 2
grating 1
gross 3
horrible 2
indecent 2
injurious 2
insolent
invasion 2
lascivious 2
lewd
loathsome
low[1] 3
militant 1
nasty 1
naughty 3
nauseous
obnoxious
obscene 1
outrageous 2, 3
personal 4
pornographic
provocative 2
push 15
pushy
rank[2] 3, 4
repellent
repugnant
repulsive
revolting
rude 2
scurrilous
smelly
sordid 3
spicy 2
suggestive 2
terrible 5
ugly 1, 2
unbecoming 2
undesirable 2
unheard-of 3
uninviting
unpalatable
unsavoury
unseemly 1
vile 2
vulgar 2
wicked 2, 3, 6
offensively
strong 23
offensiveness
indelicacy
ribaldry
offer°
afford 3
bid 1
bring 9b
carry 7, 8
communicate 1
declare 1
dedicate 1
donation 2
enter 6
exhibit
extend 4
finger 6
give 6, 7
grant 1
hand 16
hold 16b, 20b
introduce 2
lay[1] 6
nominate
open 25
overture
pass 9
pipe 8
plead 3
posit
pray 2
prefer 2
present[2] 5, 7
produce 4
profess 1
proposal 1
propose 1, 2
propound
provide 2
put 5, 17a, 18b, 28d, 28h
render 3, 7
return 6
sacrifice 1, 3
sell 2
serve 3
set 18a
stock 9
submit 2
suggest 1
table 4
tender[2] 1, 2
turn 15b
venture 2
vouchsafe 1
-on offer
sale 6
offer cause
warrant 4
offer grounds
warrant 4
offer hospitality
welcome 1
offering°
donation 1
exhibition
gift 1
motion 5
offer 5
present[2] 2
presentation 1
product 2
sacrifice 1
submission 2
tribute 2
-offerings
line[1] 16
offer justification
warrant 4
offer reason
warrant 4
offer thanks
thank 1
off form
off colour 1
par 5b
off guard
nap[1] 2
unawares 1
unprepared 1
unsuspecting
offhand°
casual 3, 5
extemporaneous
offhand (*cont.*)
flippant 1
haphazard 2
hurried 2
impetuous
impulsive
loose 5
nonchalant
oblique 2
perfunctory 1
preoccupied 2
short 4
spontaneous 1, 2
unpremeditated
offhanded
offhand 1
offhandedly
idly 2
offhand 5
offhandedness
flippancy 1
office°
appointment 3
branch 2
bureau 2
capacity 3
clerical 2
department 1
duty 1
establishment 2
function 1
ministry 3
mission 1
position 6
practice 3
room 2
study 6
-offices°
at **office 5**
office 3
office-bearer
officer 1
politician
office equipment
stationery
office-holder
functionary
incumbent 3
officer 1
servant 2
office-holding
incumbent 2
officer°
constable
functionary
police officer
office-seeker
candidate
nominee
office supplies
stationery
official°
authoritative 1
celebrant
dignitary
director 1
executive 1, 3
formal 1, 2
functionary
incumbent 3
judicial 1
officer 1
orthodox
politician
professional 1
real 1
regular 6
regulation 4
servant 2
standard 5
state 6
umpire 1
-officials
authority 4
officialdom
authority 4
bureaucracy
officialism
bureaucracy
officiant
celebrant
officiate°
celebrate 1
hold 10
preside
umpire 2
officious°
domineering
intrusive
obtrusive
overbearing
pushy
offing
background 2
-in the offing
card 12
forthcoming 1
impending
near 4
pending 2
pipeline 2
prospect 4
wind[1] 8
off limits
taboo 1
offload
discharge 7
dump 1
unload
offloading
discharge 14
off pat
pat[2] 1
off-putting
disconcerting
disgusting
distasteful
disturbing
obscene 2
repellent
repugnant
repulsive
revolting
uninviting
offscouring
trash 3
waste 7
offset°
balance 3
cancel 3
compensate 1, 2
correct 4
cover 10
foil[1]
make 31a
neutralize
oppose 3
parallel 3, 4
redeem 5
run 19
offshoot°
branch 1
derivative 2
descendant
product 1
ramification 2
shoot 5
slip[2] 2
tributary
twig[1]
off somewhere
dreamy 2
offspring°
brood 1
child 1
descendant
family 2
issue 7
lineage 2
litter 2
offshoot 2
posterity
progeny
seed 3
young 4
off target
wide 4, 5
wrong 2
off-the-wall
deranged
funny 2
insane 1
irrelevant
mad 1

off-the-wall (*cont.*)
offbeat
unusual
way-out 1
off-white
white 1
off work
off 6
oft
often
often°
always 1
frequently 1, 2
repeatedly
time 21
-as often as not
frequently 2
oftentimes
frequently 1, 2
often
ogle°
eye 5
leer 1, 2
watch 3
ogre°
demon 1
devil 2
giant 1
monster 1
ogress
bag 4
devil 2
hag
ogre
witch 2
Ogygian
ancient 2
old 2
oil°
bribe 2
flatter 1
polish 6
slick 5
oiled
drunk 1
oilskin
slicker 2
oily°
fat 2
greasy 1, 2
ingratiating
mealy-mouthed
Pharisaic
pious 2
sleek 3
slippery 1
smooth 6
wily
ointment°
lotion
salve 1
OK, okay°
acceptable 1
adequate 2
approval
approve 1
authorize
competent 1
consent 3
decent 3
enable 3
endorse 1
endorsement 1
fair[1] 4
fine[1] 1, 12
go-ahead 1
good 1
nod 6
par 6
pass 24
passable 1
permissible
place 11b
presentable 1
regular 6
safe 1, 4
sanction 3
satisfactory
thumb 4
tolerable 2
underwrite 2
well[1] 1, 17

old°
aged
ancient 1, 2, 3
antiquated
antique 1
cold 6
cut 29b
date 4
decrepit 1
doddering
early 6
elderly 1, 2
former 2
grey 3
late 3
obsolete
primitive 1
prior 1
second-hand
stale 1, 2
stock 7
time-worn
traditional
used 1
usual
-in the old days
formerly
once 1
previously
time 12a
-of old
bygone
old age
decrepitude 1
old-age pension
pension 1
old-age pensioner
elderly 2
old bag
jade 2
witch 2
old bat
bag 4
old bean
boy 3
Old Bill
officer 2
police officer
old boy°
at boy 3
father 1
old crumpet
boy 3
old days
past 6
-in the old days
formerly
once 1
previously
time 12a
old egg
boy 3
olden
ancient 1
bygone
old 5
olden days
history 6
past 6
-in olden days
once 1
previously
olden times
past 6
-in olden times
previously
older
elder 1
senior
oldest
first 2
oldest profes-sion
prostitution 1
old-fangled
old-fashioned
old-fashioned°
ancient 3
antiquated
antique 1
conventional

old-fashioned (*cont.*)
date 4
dowdy
extinct 2
mouldy
musty 2
narrow-minded
obsolete
out 9
passé
prehistoric 2
quaint 2
sedate 2
sensible 4
slow 8
square 6
stale 2
strait-laced
stuffy 2
time 15
time-worn
vintage 3
old fog(e)y
fogy
old-fog(e)yish
elderly 1
narrow-minded
slow 8
stuffy 2
vintage 3
old folks' home
home 3
old hand
adept 2
master 2
veteran 1
virtuoso 1
Old Harry
devil 1
old hat
antiquated
banal
conventional
date 4
extinct 2
hack[2] 4
history 7
musty 2
obsolete
old-fashioned
out 9
passé
threadbare 2
time 15
time-worn
oldish
elderly 1
old lady
mate 2
mother 1
parent 1
wife
woman 2
old maid°
at maid 3
miss[2]
old-maidish
priggish
prissy
prudish
strait-laced
unmarried
old-maidishness
prudery
old man
father 1
husband 1
mate 2
parent 1
old maxim
cliché
old people's home
home 3
old saw
cliché
old-time
old 2, 7
old-fashioned
vintage 3
old-timer
veteran 1

-old-timers
elderly 2
old woman
mate 2
mother 1
wife
woman 2
oleaginous
fat 2
greasy 1
oily 1
oleo
spread 12
olio
hotchpotch
medley
mess 2
miscellany
mishmash
mixture 1
patchwork
stew 1
olla podrida
clutter 1
hash 1
hotchpotch
medley
mess 2
miscellany
mishmash
mixture 1
pastiche
patchwork
pot-pourri
stew 1
Olympian
immortal 4
standoffish
omen°
foreboding 2
forerunner 2
harbinger
indication 3
sign 6
spell[3] 1
threat 2
warning 2
ominous°
evil 4
fateful 1
forbidding 2
ill 5
inauspicious
menacing
portentous 1
sinister 1
threatening
ugly 3
unpromising
wintry 3
ominously
dangerously 2
omission°
cut 22
exception 1
exclusion 2
failure 1
lapse 1
miss[1] 5
negligence
oversight 1
skip 4
omit°
cut 16a
discount 3
drop 9
eliminate 1, 2
except 3
exclude 2
forget 2
forgo 1
jump 3
leave[1] 10
miss[1] 4
neglect 2
overlook 1
pass 3, 22
skip 2
omitted
undone[2]
omitting
barring
except 1
exclusive 4

omitting (*cont.*)
omission 1
omnibus
coach 1
omnipotence
supremacy 2
omnipotent
dictatorial 1
omnipresence
prevalence 1
omnipresent
pervasive
prevalent
universal 1
omnium gath-erum
collection 2
hotchpotch
medley
miscellany
mishmash
mixture 1
pastiche
omphalos
navel
on°
card 12
about 10
above 3
ahead 3
board 5
by 3
fast[1] 8
onwards
over 1
past 3
possible 2
on-and-off
intermittent
onanism
self-abuse
once°
before 1
formerly
late 5
previously
time 12a
-at once°
at once 6
demand 8
directly 2
double 8
flat 17b
hastily 1
immediately 1
instantaneously
nail 6
now 3
outright 3
plump[2] 5
post-haste
promptly
quickly 3
rapidly 2
readily 3
right 13
shot 10
soon 2
straight 15
summarily 1
time 12b, 17
once and for all°
at once 3
definitely
finally 2
permanently
once a year
yearly 1, 3
once in a blue moon
now 4
rarely
once in a while°
at once 4
now 4
occasionally
random 2
sometimes
time 14
once more
over 9

once-over
leer 2
ogle 3
once upon a time
formerly
once 1
previously
time 12a
oncoming°
oncosts
upkeep 2
on dit
gossip 2
rumour 1
one°
exclusive 3
fellow 1
human 4
individual 3
lonely 1
single 2
somebody 1
-as one
hang 11a
shoulder 5
-at one
accord 1
one 2
-at one go
once 6b
-at one time°
at time 12
formerly
previously
-from one end to the other
through 7
throughout 2, 3
-in one go
once 6b
-in one piece
entire 2
intact
unscathed
whole 2
-of one mind
communicate 3
united 3
-to one side
apart 1
wide 5
-with one foot in the grave
dying
moribund 1
one after the other
singly
succession 5
turn 41
one and all
everyone
one and only
only 1
one and the same
equal 1
one 2
one at a time
individually
separately
singly
one behind the other
succession 5
one by one
individually
separately
singly
one day
sometime 2
soon 5
time 18b
one-horse
minor 2
one in a million
nonpareil
one-liner
joke 1
one 5
quip 1

operation (*cont.*)
leadership
management 1
manoeuvre 2
procedure
proceeding 1
process 1
running 1
touch 17
upkeep 1
usage 2
–in operation°
at **operation 5**
effective 3
force 6
progress 4
swing 6
–into operation
open 20
use 1
–operations°
at **operation 4**
campaign 1
operational
effective 3
functional 2
operable
operation 5
operative°
active 2
deputy
effective 1, 3
efficient
force 6
hold 11
motive 3
operation 5
operator 1
serviceable 1
take 11
operator°
charmer
cheat 1
devil 4
engineer 2
tactician
tycoon
user 1
operose
arduous 1
ophidian
snake 1
opiate
dope 2
drug 2
narcotic 1, 2
salve 2
sedative 1, 2
tranquillizer
opine
comment 3
opinion°
advice 1
analysis 2
attitude 2
belief 3
comment 2
conviction 2
counsel 1
doctrine
esteem 3
estimate 4
estimation 1
evaluation 2
favour 4
feeling 2
idea 3
judgement 2, 4
mind 6, 13
observation 2
outlook 1
persuasion 2
philosophy 2
piece 12
point of view 2
position 3
pronouncement 1
reckon 3
respect 1
school 3
sentiment 2
side 3
speak 11b
speculation 1
opinion (*cont.*)
stand 13
suggestion 1
tenet
thesis 1
thinking 2
understanding 4
view 2
vote 3, 4
opinionated°
assertive
dogmatic
intolerant 2
jaundiced 1
narrow-minded
near-sighted 2
parochial
partisan 3
positive 5
prejudiced 1
strong 16
ultra-
opinion piece
editorial
opinion poll
poll 2
oppidan
citizen 2
opponent°
adversary 1
antagonist
competitor
contestant
enemy
entry 5
opposition 2
rival 1
opportune°
advantageous
convenient 1
expedient 2
favourable 1
fortunate 2
golden 7
good 13
happy 2
lucky 2
propitious
providential
ripe 3a
seasonable
serve 4
suitable
timely
well-timed
opportunely
happily 1
right 16
opportunist
adventurer 2
opportunistic
opportunistic°
time-serving
opportunity°
bout 2
break 29
chance 2
go 42
leisure 1
move 10
occasion 1
opening 2, 3
option 1, 2
possibility 2
prospect 3
say 13
scope 2
season 1
shot 3
start 12
thing 7
time 5
turn 30
way 7
oppose°
combat 6
contest 3
contradict 1
contrast 1
counteract
differentiate 1
discourage 2
disobey
dispute 1
oppose (*cont.*)
exception 4
fight 2
fly 6
issue 9
jar[2] 2
militate 1
object 4
pit[1] 6
protest 3
resist 1
rival 2
take 35b
thwart 1
traverse 3
withstand
opposed°
adversary 2
averse
contrary 1
destructive 2
discordant 1
disinclined
disobedient 2
hostile 1
incompatible
opposition 3
polar 2
reluctant
resistant 1
–as opposed to
instead 2
opposing°
contrary 1
destructive 2
mixed 2
negative 4
opposed
opposite 2
opposite°
contrary 1, 4
different 1
discordant 1
face 8, 15
front 11
incompatible
mixed 2
opposed
opposing
polar 2
reverse 1, 6
unlike 1, 3
wrong 6
–at opposite extremes *etc.*
pole[2] 3
oppositely
contrary 5
opposite number
like[1] 7
opposition°
antagonism 1
antagonist
combat 3
competitor
conflict 3
disagreement 2
enemy
hostility 1
interference 2
objection
opponent
protest 1
resistance 1
rival 1
–in opposition°
at **opposition 3**
conflict 4
contrary 5
face 9
odds 4
opposed
traverse 3
oppress°
afflict
burden 2
depress 1
distress 3
encumber 1
grind 5
overload 1
overwhelm 1
overwork 1
oppress (*cont.*)
persecute 1
prey 3c
rack 3
ride 3
subjugate
tyrannize
weigh 4, 6
wrong 9
oppressed
downtrodden
straitened
oppression°
despotism
domination 2
occupation 2
overload 2
persecution 1
pressure 3
severity 1
tyranny
oppressive°
burdensome
close 12
deplorable 1
despotic
domineering
exacting
hard 4
heavy 4
heavy-handed 2
leaden 2, 3
muggy
overpowering
pungent 3
repressive
severe 1
sore 5
sticky 3
stuffy 1
sultry 1
sweltering
swingeing
totalitarian
tyrannical
unmitigated
oppressively
severely 2
oppressiveness
severity 1, 4
oppressor°
despot
dictator
tyrant
opprobrious
abusive 1
disgraceful 1
disreputable 1
infamous 2
notorious 1
scurrilous
shabby 4
vituperative
wrong 1
opprobrium
discredit 4
disgrace 1
infamy 2
notoriety
shame 2
oppugn
fight 2
opt
choose
decide 2
favour 6
pick 1
pitch[1] 7
please 2
prefer 1
select 1
take 2
vote 4
optic
eye 1
optimal
optimum 2
optimistic°
bright 4
golden 7
hopeful 1
idealistic
positive 8
promising
optimistic (*cont.*)
quixotic
rosy 2
sanguine
upbeat
optimistically
hopefully 1
optimum°
option°
alternative 2
choice 2
discretion 2
pick 9
pleasure 2
preference 1
refusal 2
selection 1
suffrage
voice 2
volition
optional°
voluntary 2
opulence
comfort 3
ease 3
fortune 1
luxury 1
prosperity
riches
style 3
wealth 1
opulent°
elegant 3
grand 1
lavish 1
lush 3
luxurious 1
magnificent
palatial
plush
posh
rich 1
soft 13
sumptuous
wealthy
opulently
well[1] 4
opus°
piece 4
production 2
work 4
oracle°
fortune-teller
prophet
sage 2
seer
oracular
ambiguous 2
infallible 1
ominous 3
prophetic
oral°
spoken 1
verbal 1
oral cavity
mouth 1
orate
hold 16a
lecture 3
mouth 7
rant 1
spout 2
oration°
address 1
harangue 1
speech 2
talk 14
orator
speaker
talker 1
oratorical
eloquent 1
rhetorical 1
oratory°
diction 2
rhetoric 2
orb°
eye 1
globe 2
round 10
sphere 1
orbicular
rotund 1
round 3
orbit°
circuit 2
circulate 1
circulation 1
course 1
jurisdiction
lap[2] 1
path 2
range 1
reach 7
revolution 3
revolve 1
roll 1
round 17
scope 1
orbiting
round 20
orb-like
round 3
orb-shaped
round 3
orchestra
band[2] 2
ensemble 2
orchestrate
arrange 2, 3
manipulate 1
negotiate 2
orchestration
arrangement 4
tactic 2
orchestrator
tactician
Orcus
underworld 2
ordain
appoint 1
assign 2
decree 2
destine 1
dictate 1
direct 3
enact 1
establish 1
invest 3
order 14
prescribe
will 5
ordained
condemn 3
doomed 1
fatal 3
fated 1
inevitable
predetermined 2
ordainment
passage 9
ordeal°
affliction 1
bind 6
experience 2
grief 2
hell 2
misery 3
nuisance 1
pain 2
torment 4
visitation 2
order°
act 4
adjustment 2
arrange 1
arrangement 1
assign 3
bid 3
bidding 2
book 4
bracket 3
brotherhood 2
call 8a, 14
caste
categorize
charge 5, 10
class 1, 5
club 2
command 1, 6
compile
condition 3
coordinate 1
course 3
decoration 2

order (*cont.*)
decree 1, 2
degree 1
demand 1, 5
denomination 1, 2
desire 2, 4
dictate 1, 2
direct 3
discipline 3
dispose 1
distribute 3
distribution 3
divide 5
draw 15c
edit 4
enact 1
establishment 3
estate 3
family 4
fellowship 2
file 3
form 1, 4
format 2
frame 3
grade 6
group 3
injunction 2
institution 4
instruct 2
instruction 1
judgement 2
law 1
line[1] 23d
make 2
method 2
neaten
organization 2
organize 1
pattern 3
place 15, 16
placement 1
precept 1
prepare 1
prescribe
progression 3
pronouncement 2
queue 1
range 5
rank[1] 6
regime
regiment
regularity 1
regulate 1
regulation 2
repair 3
require 1
requisition 1, 2
rule 1
say 10
say-so
scheme 2
script 4
send 6
sequence
settle 1
shape 4
sort 8
space 5
standing 5
structure 1
succession 2
symmetry
tabulate
tell[1] 5
tier
trim 6
type 1
variety 3
warrant 2
will 5
wish 2
word 7
–in order°
at **order 10**
adjust 4
clear 31b
correct 7
file 3
OK 2
orderly 1
place 11b
settle 1
straight 7
straighten 3
succession 5

order (*cont.*)
tidy 4
turn 41
–in order that°
at **order 11**
–in order to°
at **order 12**
–out of order°
at **order 13**
amiss 1
blink 6
broken 7
defective 1
faulty
mistaken 1
out 14
turn 42a
wrong 5
–to order
custom 4
order about, around
boss 3
tyrannize
ordered
even 3
methodical
parliamentary
regular 2, 6
scientific
sequential
symmetrical
uniform 1
ordering
arrangement 1
disposition 2
distribution 3
placement 1
orderliness
harmony 2
method 2
order 2
pattern 3
regularity 1
symmetry
orderly°
coherent 1
deliberate 3
even 3
formal 1
good 3
methodical
neat 1
order 10a
organic 3
parliamentary
regular 6
scientific
sequential
shipshape
smooth 3
straight 7
symmetrical
systematic
taut 2
tidy 1
tight 4
trim 1
uniform 1
well-balanced 2
order of the day
institution 4
prevail 2
programme 1
ordinance
act 4
decree 1
law 1
order 4
precept 1
pronouncement 2
regulation 2
rule 1
ordinarily°
average 2
frequently 2
generally 1
often
popularly
rule 4
ordinary°
accustomed 1
artless 2
average 3, 4

ordinary (*cont.*)
banal
common 1, 3
conventional
customary 1
daily 2
dead 12
decent 3
dreary 2
everyday 2
familiar 1
frequent 1
general 2
habitual 1
homely 1
humble 3
humdrum
indifferent 3
informal 1, 3
mediocre
medium 1
mill 4
moderate 3
modest 2
monotonous
natural 1, 2
nondescript
normal 1
orthodox
pedestrian 2
plain 5
popular 2
practical 2
prosaic
regular 1, 11
regulation 5
routine 3, 4
so so
standard 6
staple 2
stock 7, 8
tame 4
tolerable 2
typical 1, 2
undistinguished
unprofessional 3
usual
vernacular 2
vulgar 3
–out of the ordinary°
at **ordinary 4**
curious 3
different 2
eccentric 1
exceptional 1
exotic 2
noteworthy
obscure 5
odd 1
peculiar 1
rare[1] 1
remarkable 2
special 1
strange 1
striking
unearthly 3
unusual
ordination
initiation 2
installation 1
ordure
dirt 1
filth 1
muck 1
or else
otherwise 1
organ°
genitals
paper 1
periodical
voice 3
organic°
fundamental 1
ingrained
intrinsic
natural 10
radical 1
organism°
animal 1
creature 1
entity 1
organization 2, 3

organization°
arrangement 1
association 1
brotherhood 2
business 4
club 2
code 3
combination 2
composition 2
concern 7
design 6
disposition 2
embodiment 2
employer 2
establishment 1, 2
fabric 2
fabrication 1
fellowship 2
firm 6
form 1
format 2
formation 2, 3
foundation 3
frame 3
front 6
group 1
house 4
institute 1
institution 1
machine 3
mechanism 2
method 2
mould[1] 2
network 2
office 1
order 1, 2, 9
outfit 3
placement 1
posture 2
preparation 3
regulation 1
rhyme 2
ring[1] 3
scheme 2
sequence
set-up 1
society 3, 5
staff 2
structure 1
system 1
union 2
organize°
arrange 1, 2
categorize
compile
coordinate 1
cut 16e
design 2
dispose 1
divide 5
edit 4
embody 3
engineer 5
enlist 2
erect 3
establish 1
file 3
fix 2, 8, 16b
float 2
form 7
found 1
get 51d
grade 6
ground 5
group 3, 4
have 6
institute 3
introduce 4
launch 2
line[1] 23a
make 22
mastermind 1
mobilize
mount 5
negotiate 2
order 16
originate 1
plan 3
plot[1] 3
prepare 1
process 4
programme 4
put 27b
rally 3
range 7

organize (*cont.*)
rank[1] 6
ready 10
regiment
regulate 1
schedule 2
scheme 4
script 4
see 12a
separate 2
set 23b
settle 1
sort 8, 10a
space 5
stage 5
straighten 2
structure 3
tabulate
tidy 4
time 23
organized
careful 2
coherent 1
methodical
neat 1
order 10a
orderly 1
organic 3
pitched
scientific
sequential
straight 7
streamlined 2
systematic
tidy 2
organized crime
underworld 1
organizer
producer 2
organizing
formation 2
foundation 3
organization 1
preparation 3
orgasm
climax 3
orgasmic
ecstatic
rhapsodic
orgiastic
epicurean 1
orgy°
jag
party 1
spree
orient°
guide 1
oriental
orient 2
orientate
guide 1
orient 3
orientation°
aspect 3
attitude 2
bearing 4
exposure 4
point of view 1
posture 3
site 1
orifice
hole 2
mouth 2
opening 1
passage 11
pore[2]
vent 1
origin°
beginning 1
birth 2, 3
bottom 3
cause 1
conception 1
creation 1
dawn 2
derivation
establishment 1
extraction 3
fountain 2
germ 2
head 6
mother 2
onset 2
opening 4

origin (*cont.*)
parent 2
parentage
progenitor 2
root[1] 1
seed 2
source 1
spring 8
start 11, 15
vintage 1
–origins°
at **origin 3**
root[1] 4
original°
avant-garde
clever 3
creative
crude 1
different 2
early 5, 6
eccentric 2
elemental
fanciful 3
first 2
fresh 2
genuine 1
imaginative 1
indigenous 1
ingenious
initial 1
matchless
model 2
native 3
new 1
novel 1
oddity 2
ordinary 4
pattern 1
picturesque 1
première 3
primary 2
prime 3
primitive 1
pristine 1
progenitor 2
prototype 1
revolutionary 2
seminal 1
unused 1
way-out 2
originality°
fantasy 1
ingenuity
novelty 1
originally°
early 2
primarily 2
originate°
arise 4
begin 2, 3
breed 4
coin 3
compose 2
create 1
dawn 4
derive 2
design 2
develop 4
devise 1
discover 3
engineer 4
fabricate 2
father 6
flow 3
form 8
formulate 2
found 1
frame 7
generate 1
go 24b
grow 2
hatch 2
inaugurate 1
initiate 1
institute 4
introduce 4
invent 1
issue 11
launch 2
make 1, 39c
manufacture 1
organize 2
pioneer 2
proceed 2
produce 2

originate (*cont.*)
raise 10
rise 9
spring 3
stage 5
start 1, 2
stem[1] 3
origination
beginning 1
birth 2
composition 4
conception 1
discovery 1
establishment 1
fabrication 2
foundation 3
generation 3
initiation 1
institution 1
invention 1
manufacture 3
origin 2
production 1
originative
creative
originator
author
cause 2
creator 1
designer 1
engineer 1
father 3
founder[1]
parent 2
progenitor 2
source 2
O-ring
ring[1] 1
Orion
hunter
orison
prayer 2
ornament°
attachment 4
bauble
beautify
decorate 1
decoration 1
drape 1
elaborate 3
embellish 1
embellishment 1
enrich 2
flounce 1
frill 1
fringe 1
grace 6
illuminate 3
illustrate 2
jewel 1
motif
novelty 2
pattern 2, 8
pendant
tool 4
trim 4, 5
-ornaments
finery
jewellery
ornamental°
fancy 1
ornamentation
decoration 1
embellishment 1
flourish 3
frill 2
ornament 1
trim 5
ornamented
elaborate 2
fancy 1
flamboyant 1
flowery
ornate°
busy 3
complicated
detailed 2
elaborate 2
extravagant 4
fancy 1
flamboyant 1
flowery
fussy 2
intricate 1
ornate (*cont.*)
laboured 2
luxuriant 3
overwrought 2
pompous 2
showy
splendid 1
ornery
testy
orotund
inflated 2
pompous 2
rhetorical 3
round 7
orphan
foundling
orthodox°
conservative 2
conventional
correct 7
normal 1
proper 2
regular 6
standard 6
typical 2
orthodoxy
code 3
orts
dirt 1
leftover 1
waste 7
oscillate°
flap 1
flicker 2
fluctuate
flutter 1
pulsate
quaver 1
quiver 1
see-saw 2
shake 2
sway 1
swing 1
vibrate
wag[1] 1
wave 4
oscillating
flutter 4
pendulous 2
swing 3
oscillation
flap 2
fluctuation
flutter 4
flux
quaver 2
sway 3
swing 3
wag[1] 2
oscillatory
pendulous 2
oscitance
negligence
oscitancy
indolence
negligence
oscitant
drowsy
inattentive
sleepy 1
osculate
kiss 1
osculation
kiss 4
Ossianic
flowery
grandiose 1
ornate
ossified
petrified 3
ossify
petrify 3
ostensible
apparent 2
obvious
outward
pretended
probable
professed 1
seeming
so-called 2
specious
ostensibly°
apparently 2
evidently 2
outwardly
seemingly
surface 2
ostensive
tangible
ostensively
ostensibly
ostentation°
display 5
frill 2
glare 3
glitter 4
pose 5
pretence 1
pretension 2
show 15
swagger 3
ostentatious°
boastful
camp[2] 1
conspicuous 2
dashing 3
extravagant 4
flamboyant 2
flash 6
flashy 1
gaudy
grand 3
grandiose 1
loud 2
luxuriant 3
overwrought 2
pedantic 1
pompous 1
pretentious 1
showy
theatrical 2
vulgar 1
ostentatiously
well[1] 4
ostentatious-ness
splurge 1
ostler
groom 1
ostracism
segregation
ostracize°
banish 1
freeze 4
isolate
segregate
shoulder 2
other
alternate 4
alternative 1
different 1
further 1
second[1] 4, 5
separate 6
-in other words
like[1] 6
-on the other hand
however 1
only 4
otherwise 1
other place
hell 1
other side
enemy
opposition 2
over 3
other than
besides 2
except 1
other way around
vice versa
otherwise°
other-worldly
heavenly 1
mystical 1
supernatural
unearthly 1
weird
otiose
idle 4
inert 3
lazy 1
otiose (*cont.*)
shiftless
slack 1
oubliette
dungeon
hole 4
prison
ought
have 10
must 1
naught
nil
ounce
grain 3
modicum
Our Lord
lord 3
saviour 2
ourselves
person 2
personally 1
our times
present[1] 4
oust
banish 1
bring 8a
cast 14
discharge 2
dismiss 1
displace 2
dispossess
drop 10
eject 1
evict
exclude 3
exile 3
expel 2
fire 11
overthrow 1
overturn 2
purge 2
remove 5
supersede
supplant
topple 2
turf 4
turn 20c
oustandingly
big 10
ouster
discharge 9
ejection 2
eviction
exclusion 3
expulsion
overthrow 2
overturn 3
purge 4
removal 3
ousting
overthrow 2
overturn 3
purge 4
removal 3
out°
absent 1
chase 3
dead 3, 5
defunct 2
drunk 1
extinct 3
forward 5
free 2
insensible 1
obsolete
off 1
old-fashioned
outwards
overhang 1
passé
project 5
senseless 1
sleepy 1
unconscious 1
-be out of
depart 1
run 31
out and about
abroad 3
out-and-out°
absolute 2
bare 2
barefaced 1
dead 14
out-and-out (*cont.*)
downright 1
express 5
flagrant
flat 4
great 11
main 4
open 13
outright 2
peremptory 2
perfect 6
positive 9
profound 4
pronounced 2
proper 5
pukka 2
pure 5
radical 2
rank[2] 2
right 8
sheer 2
stark 4
sweeping 1
thorough 1
total 3
ultra-
undisguised
unmitigated
unqualified 2
utterly
out at the elbows
heel[1] 3
outback
country 3
stick[2] 3
outbalance
outweigh
outbreak
epidemic 2
eruption 1, 2
explosion 2
fit[2] 2
flash 2
outburst
rash[2] 2
spurt 1
tempest 2
trouble 7
volley 2
outburst°
blaze 2
disturbance 2
eruption 1
explosion 1, 2
fit[2] 2
flare 4
flash 2
flurry 1
frenzy 2
furore 1
gale 2
gush 4
outcry
outpouring
paroxysm
passion 2
riot 1
roar 4
round 14
spasm 2
splurge 1
storm 2
tantrum
tirade
torrent
uproar
outcast°
abandoned 1
castaway
derelict 3
down and out 2
exile 2
forlorn 2
foundling
homeless 1
lonely 3
lonesome 1
undesirable 1
-outcasts
dregs 2
rabble 2
outclass
end 11
outstrip
shade 8
shame 5a
surpass
out cold
drunk 1
out 8
senseless 1
unconscious 1
outcome°
decision 2
determination 2
effect 1
end 4
event 2
fate 3
fruit
issue 2
judgement 2
pay-off 2
product 1
purpose 3
repercussion
resolution 4
result 1
solution 2
upshot
outcrop
prominence 2
rock[1] 2
outcropping
projection 1
prominence 2
rock[1] 2
outcry°
demand 5
exclamation
noise 1
peep 3
racket 1
roar 3
storm 2
uproar
whoop 1
out-dated
mouldy
obsolete
old 2
old-fashioned
out 9
prehistoric 2
quaint 2
time 15
time-worn
outdistance
exceed 1
gain 5
outstrip
overhaul 1
overtake 1
pass 6
surpass
transcend
outdo°
beat 2
best 11
better[1] 11
cap 4
discomfit 2
end 11
exceed 1
excel
extinguish 3
lead 4
outstrip
pass 6
shade 8
shame 5a
squelch 1
surpass
top 3
transcend
whip 2
outdoor°
outside 5
outdoors
out 1
outside 10
outer
exterior 1
external 1
extrinsic

outer (*cont.*)
outlying
outward
peripheral 2
outermost
extreme 3
outlying
outer reaches
outskirts
outfall
mouth 2
outfit°
apparatus
clothe 1
clothes
complement 2
condition 5
costume
disguise 3
dress 1, 6
employer 2
ensemble 1
equip
equipment
firm 6
fit[1] 8
furnish 1
garments
gear 2
get 51e
get-up 1
house 4
paraphernalia
party 2
platoon
prepare 1
provide 1
rig 1, 3
robe 2
set 27
suit 3
supply 1
tack 4
tackle 1
turnout 3
uniform 3
outfitter
tailor 1
outfitting
provision 1
supply 5
outflank
flank 3
get 46a
outflow
drain 2
escape 7
issue 1
outburst
outpouring
spate
outflowing
outburst
spate
out for numero uno
time-serving
outfox
outsmart
prey 3b
victimize 2
outgo
drain 2
outgoing°
easy 6
expansive 2
forthcoming 3
issue 1
nice 1
pleasant 2
sociable
sunny 2
-outgoings
expenditure
expense 1
outgrowth
fruit
offshoot 3
outcome
prominence 3
ramification 2
outhouse
lavatory
privy 3
toilet 1
outing°
drive 7
excursion 1
journey 1
ride 4
run 36
spin 7
spree
tour 1
trip 3
out in the open
above-board 1
outlander
alien 2
foreigner
immigrant
newcomer 1
outsider
stranger
outlandish°
absurd 1
alien 1
bizarre 2
curious 3
eccentric 1
erratic 2
exotic 2
extraneous 2
fantastic 1
foreign 2
grotesque 2
impossible 2
kinky 1
odd 1
offbeat
ordinary 4
out-of-the-way 2
outré
peculiar 1
preposterous
prohibitive 2
quaint 1
queer 1
rich 11
ridiculous
singular 1
strange 1
unheard-of 3
unnatural 5
weird
outlandishness
oddity 1
singularity 2
outlast°
resist 1
sit 7
stand 12b
survive 2
outlaw°
ban 1
banish 1
criminal 3
deserter
exile 3
expel 2
felon
forbid
offender
prohibit 1
thief 1
veto 1
outlawed
illegal
taboo 1
unlawful
outlawing
prohibition 1
outlawry
prohibition 1
outlay°
cost 1
expenditure
expense 1
overhead 3
payment 2
price 1
upkeep 2
outlet°
drain 1
exit 1
outlet (*cont.*)
issue 1
loophole
mouth 2
passage 11
spout 3
store 4
vent 1
out like a light
out 8
outline°
abridgement 3
abstract 3
block 4a
brief 4
circuit 1
conception 3
describe 4
design 2
draft 1, 3
draw 5
drawing
epitome 2
figure 1
lay[1] 18a
line[1] 5
note 10
plan 3
plot[1] 2, 4
précis
profile 1
programme 1
project 3
projection 3
proposal 2
prospectus
protocol 2
represent 3
résumé 1
rough 14, 15
round-up 2
run-down 3
scenario 1
schedule 1, 2
scheme 1
silhouette
stake[1] 4b
story 5
summary 1
synopsis
tell[1] 4
trace 6
outlining
definition 1
projection 2
outlive
outlast
sit 7
survive 2
outlook°
aspect 3
expectation 4
exposure 4
idea 3
mentality 2
perspective 2
philosophy 2
point of view 1
position 3
posture 3
prospect 1, 2, 3
sentiment 2
thinking 2
view 1
outlying°
back 12
far-away 1
out 10
out-of-the-way 1
outward
remote 1
outlying districts
province 4
outmanipulate
outsmart
outmanoeuvre
flank 3
get 46a
outsmart
trick 8
outmoded
antiquated
antique 1
outmoded (*cont.*)
date 4
dead 7
defunct 2
extinct 2
obsolete
old 2
old-fashioned
out 9
passé
time 15
out-of-body
unearthly 1
out of it
confused 2
disorientated
forgetful
hook 5
insane 1
insensible 1
passive 1
preoccupied 2
slow 8
square 6
out-of-pocket expenses
expense 1
out-of-the-way°
inaccessible 2
isolated 3
obscure 3
outlying
outré
peculiar 1
remote 2
secluded 2
solitary 1
strange 1
unapproachable 2
withdrawn 2
out-of-towner
provincial 3
rubberneck 2
tourist
outpace
exceed 1
excel
pull 7
outperform
outstrip
shade 8
surpass
outplay
outsmart
shade 8
outpost
settlement 1
outpouring°
escape 7
flood 3
outburst
rain 3
spate
spill 4
storm 2
stream 2
torrent
volley 2
output°
harvest 1
product 1, 2
production 1, 2
turnout 2
work 4
yield 5
outrage°
anger 1
atrocity 2
disgust 1, 2
dishonour 1
enormity
grievance 1
horrify 2
indignity
infamy 2
injure 2
injury
insult 1, 2
limit 4b
offence 2
offend 1
persecute 1
persecution 1
provoke 3
outrage (*cont.*)
sacrilege 2
scandal 1
scandalize
shame 3
shock 1
slight 7
violate 3
violation 3
outraged
disgusted
outrageous°
black 6
camp[2] 1
curious 3
damnable
disgraceful 2
disgusting
dishonourable 3
excessive 1
exorbitant
extravagant 2
extreme 5, 6
fancy 4
flagrant
glaring 1
grievous 2
gross 4
hideous 2
high 2
immoderate
impossible 2
indecent 2
infamous 2
inordinate 1
monstrous 2
obscene 2
preposterous
pricey
prohibitive 2
provocative 2
rank[2] 3
rude 2
scandalous 1
shameful
shameless
shocking 2
sight 6b
spicy 3
tall 3
ultra-unconscionable 2
unearthly 3
ungodly 2
unheard-of 3
unreasonable 2
unwarranted
wanton 2
way-out 1
whopping 2
wild 7
outrageously
extremely
terribly
outrageousness
enormity
extravagance 2
outrank
exceed 1
excel
outré°
bizarre 2
camp[2] 1
curious 3
extreme 5
offbeat
outlandish
out-of-the-way 2
pale[2] 3
preposterous
queer 1
singular 1
outreach
exceed 1
reach 1
outright°
absolute 2
barefaced 1
categorical
dead 14
direct 9
downright 1
express 5
flat 4
openly 2
outright (*cont.*)
out-and-out
peremptory 2
point-blank 1, 3
positive 9
pronounced 2
pure 5
shoulder 6
stark 4
straight 5, 6, 14
total 3
unmitigated
unqualified 2
outrun
exceed 1
lead 4
pass 6
pull 7
outrush
outpouring
outsert
insert 2
outset°
beginning 1
dawn 2
first 6
onset 2
opening 4
origin 2
source 1
start 10
threshold 2
-at the outset
first 5, 8
originally
-from the outset
originally
outshine
eclipse 2
end 11
exceed 1
excel
outdo
outstrip
overshadow 1
shade 8
shame 5a
shine 3
show 12c
surpass
transcend
outshoot
prominence 3
outside°
abroad 3
bar 10
exterior 1, 2, 3
external 1, 2
extrinsic
face 6
independent 7
out 1
outdoor
outward
outwards
peripheral 2
remote 4, 6
shell 2
skin 2
superficial 1
superficies
surface 1
ulterior 2
outsider°
alien 2
exile 2
foreigner
immigrant
newcomer 1
square 9
outsized
spacious
swollen
voluminous 2
outskirts°
fringe 2
outsmart°
get 46a
prey 3b
victimize 2
outspoken°
bluff[2] 2
blunt 2
brazen

overhead°
above 1
aloft
overhead 3
upkeep 2

-overheads
overhead 3
upkeep 2

overhear
eavesdrop

overheat
glow 5

overheated
fiery 1

overindulge
overdo 1
overeat
satiate 1
stuff 8

overindulgence
dissipation 1
excess 2
orgy 2
satiety
waste 6

overindulgent
dissolute
epicurean 1
self-indulgent
wasteful

overjoyed°
ecstatic
elated
exalted 3
exuberant 2
exultant
glad 1
gleeful
happy 1
joyful 2
radiant 2
rapt 2
rapturous
rejoice
rhapsodic
world 7

overkill
excess 1

overlap°
fold 1, 4
lap[2] 2, 3

overlapped
double 2

overlay
coat 2
face 16
facing
film 1
overlap 1, 3
plaster
plate 6
scale[2] 2
skin 2
spread 7
wash 7, 15

overlie
cover 3
overlap 1

overload°
bow 4
encumber 1
glut 3, 4
lumber 3
oppress 1
overdo 2
overwork 1
swamp 2
tax 4
weigh 6

overloaded
heavy 13
loaded 1
lousy 4
packed
replete 1

over-long
lengthy
protracted
redundant 2
tedious

overlook°
blink 4
boss 2

overlook (*cont.*)
close 7
command 5
discount 3
disregard 1
dominate 2
excuse 1
face 15
forget 3
forgive 1
front 11
ignore 1
jump 3
look 3
miss[1] 4
neglect 1
omit 2
pardon 2
pass 3
rule 8
skip 2
supervise
waive 2

overlooked
unnoticed

overlooking
indulgence 1
pardon 1

overlord
dictator
oppressor
tyrant

overly°
fault 7
sky 2
unduly 1

over-modest
prudish

over-nice
dainty 2
fastidious
finicky 1
nice 4
precious 3
priggish
prissy
prudish
scrupulous 1

overnight
instant 3
meteoric 1

overnight bag
bag 2
suitcase

over-particular
querulous

overpass
span 1

over-permissive
easygoing

overplay
dramatize
exaggerate
maximize 2
meal 2

over-polite
genteel 1

overpopulated
overcrowded

over-populous
overcrowded

overpower°
best 11
daze 1
defeat 1
drown 2
entrance[2]
oppress 2
overcome 1
overthrow 1
overwhelm 1
prostrate 2
rout 2
subdue 1
subjugate
whip 2

overpowered
daze 4
overcome 2
prostrate 4

overpowering°
dazzling
devastating 2

overpowering (*cont.*)
exciting 1
irresistible 1
oppressive 1
overwhelming 1
profound 3
spellbinding
stiff 3
stunning 2
sublime 2

over-precise
fastidious
finicky 1

overpriced
expensive
extravagant 3
steep[1] 2

overprize
overrate

overprotect
mother 6

overprotected
hothouse 2

overprotective
possessive 2

overrate°
miscalculate

overrated
glorified 1

overreach
overdo 1
run 33c

overreact°
dainty 2

overrefined
dainty 2
precious 3

override
outweigh
reverse 3
vacate 3

overriding°
irresistible 1

overripe
rotten 1

overrule
predominate
quash 1
reverse 3
set 15b
vacate 3

overruling
overriding

overrun°
conquer 2
crawl 4
infest
occupy 1
overgrown
rout 2
swarm 3
teem[1]

overscrupulous
pedantic 2

overseas°
abroad 1
foreign 1

oversee°
administer 1
boss 2
chair 4
control 1
govern 1
guide 3
handle 3
head 11
manage 1
monitor 3
officiate
police 3
preside
regulate 2
rule 6
run 10
supervise
track 4

overseer°
boss 1
chief 1
director 1
executive 1
foreman
manager

overseer (*cont.*)
master 1
superintendent
supervisor

oversell
maximize 2

over-sensitivity
sensitivity 1

oversexed
hot 7

overshadow°
blind 6
dominate 2
dwarf
eclipse 2
exceed 1
excel
extinguish 3
loom 2
obscure 7
predominate
shade 8
shame 5a
show 12c
surpass
transcend

overshoot
pass 6
run 33c

oversight°
administration 1
command 7
control 4
default 1
fault 2
government 1
lapse 1
miss[1] 5
misstep 2
neglect 3
negligence
omission 2
rule 2
slip[1] 8
trip 2

oversimplified
meagre 3

oversized
jumbo
massive
spacious
swollen
unwieldy
voluminous 2

overspending
extravagance 1

overspread
cover 3
flow 4
infest
overgrown
spread 7
suffuse

overstate°
amplify 2
blow[1] 8c
dramatize
exaggerate
lay[1] 14
magnify 1
make 34a
maximize 2

overstated
inflated 1

overstatement
exaggeration

overstep°
disobey
exceed 2
far 7
infringe 1
transcend
transgress 2

over-stimulated
overwrought 1

over-stimulation
agitation 2

overstock
glut 3

overstrain
overwork 1, 3
push 5

overstrain (*cont.*)
wrench 2

overstress
exaggerate
labour 6
maximize 2
overstate

overstuff
cram 1
satiate 1

over-sufficiency
abundance
excess 1
extravagance 2

over-sufficient
abundant 1

oversupplied
fraught 1

oversupply
abundance
embarrassment 3
flood 5
glut 1, 3
profusion
superfluity, surfeit
surplus 1

overt°
bare 2
blatant 1
glaring 1
naked 3
obvious
public 4
undisguised

overtake°
catch 14b
exceed 1
gain 4
outstrip
overhaul 1

overtax
encumber 1
overdo 2
overload 1
overwhelm 1
overwork 1
push 5
strain[1] 1
stretch 3
swamp 2
weigh 6

over-the-transom
unsolicited

overthrow°
bring 8a
defeat 1, 3
demolish 2
destroy 4
dissolution 2
downfall
fall 28
floor 4
overcome 1
overturn 2, 3
put 16b
quash 1, 2
reverse 3
revolution 1
rout 1, 2
ruin 1, 7
subversion
subvert
throw 3
tip[2] 1
topple 2
undoing 1
upset 4, 11

-be overthrown
fall 5

overthrown
flat 3

overtire
exhaust 2

overtired
exhausted 1
fatigued
ragged 3

over-tolerant
easygoing

overtone°
innuendo
shade 3
undercurrent 2

overture°
approach 4
feeler 2
pass 28
preliminary 2
proposition 3

-overtures°
at **overture**
approach 4

overturn°
bring 8a
capsize
demolish 2
destroy 4
overthrow 1, 2
reverse 2, 3
set 15b
throw 3
tip[2] 1
topple 2
turn 21c, 24
upset 2

overturned
upset 6

overturning
overthrow 2
overturn 3

overuse
overwork 1

overused
common 6
stale 2
threadbare 2
time-worn
tired 3

overvalue
miscalculate
overrate

overview
outline 2
précis
scan 3

overweening
arrogant 2
egotistical
haughty
hoity-toity
lofty 4
masterful 2
overbearing
positive 5
presumptuous
scornful
self-important
uppish

overweening-ness
pride 2

overweigh
outweigh

overweight
chubby
fat 1, 5
gross 1
heavy 11
large 1
obese
plump[1] 1
rotund 3
stout 1
well-fed

overwhelm°
astound
beat 2
besiege 3
best 11
bury 5
consume 5
crush 4
defeat 1
devastate 2
devour 3
drown 2
exceed 1
flood 5
floor 4
gang 3
intoxicate 2
knock 6b
load 4

overwhelm (*cont.*)
oppress 1
overawe
overcome 1
overpower 1, 2
overrun
overtake 2
overthrow 1
pile[1] 8b
plunge 2
prostrate 2
quash 2
rock[2] 3
rout 2
shatter 3
shower 4
slaughter 4
smother 3
stagger 2
stun 2
submerge 3
swamp 2
triumph 3
whip 2
overwhelmed
broken-hearted
downtrodden
dumbfounded
loaded 1
overcome 2
prostrate 4
stricken 2
overwhelming°
awesome
colossal 2
compulsive
dazzling
exciting 1
fantastic 4
formidable 3
inconceivable
irresistible 1
oppressive 1
overpowering
overriding
profound 3
runaway 3
stiff 2
sublime 2
sweeping 2
towering 2
overwhelmingly
large 4
utterly
over with
over 6
overwork°
exhaust 4
overdo 2
strain[1] 1, 3
overworked
hack[2] 4
laborious 4
laboured 2
melodramatic
overwrought 2
threadbare 2
tired 3
overwrought°
beside 3
distraught
excited 1
flowery
frantic
laboured 2
melodramatic
neurotic
tense 2
theatrical 2
overzealous
ambitious 3
oviform
oval
ovine
passive 2
ovoid
oval
ovule
seed 1
ovum
seed 1
owe°
owed
due 1
outstanding 2
payable
unpaid 1
owing
debt 2
due 1
indebted
outstanding 2
payable
unpaid 1
owing to°
at **owe 2**
for 13
reason 5
thank 4
through 1
virtue 4
wake[2] 2
own
acknowledge 1
admit 4
allow 1
concede 1
confess
have 1
individual 2
monopolize
possess 1
private 3
proper 6
recognize 2
respective
-of one's own accord
freely 2
willingly
-of one's own free will
freely 2
voluntarily
willingly
-of one's own volition
freely 2
-on one's own
deliberately
freely 2
personally 1
proper 7
single-handed 2
solo 1
unaccompanied
unattached 2
voluntarily
willingly
-on one's own initiative *etc.*
voluntarily
owner°
boss 1
employer 1
landlord 2
master 1, 6
monarch 2
occupant
principal 3
proprietor 1, 2
user 1
ownership
possession 1
stock 5
title 5
ownership papers
paper 2a
owning
acknowledge-ment 1
own up
acknowledge 1
clean 8
concede 1
confess
ox
duffer
hulk 2
oxen
cattle
stock 4
ox-like
clumsy
stupid 1
oxymoronic
paradoxical

P

pa
father 1
pace°
clip[2] 7
march 1
measure 12, 13
rate[1] 1
regularity 2
step 6, 13
swing 5
tempo
throw 4
trot 3
velocity
walk 1
paced
deliberate 2
methodical
pacemaker
pioneer 1
pace-setter
pioneer 1
pachydermatous
thick-skinned
pacific
calm 3
gentle 1
idyllic
inactive 1
mild 1
pastoral 1
peaceable 2
quiet 2
relaxed
restful 2
serene 1
silent 1
still 1
pacification
reconciliation 1
pacificator
peacemaker
pacificatory
propitiatory 1
pacifier
dummy 4
peacemaker
pacify
calm 5
compose 4
disarm 2
ease 5
hush 5
lull 3
quell 2
satisfy 1
silence 4
still 9
tame 6
tranquillize
pacifying
propitiatory 1
satisfying
soothing 1
pack°
band[2] 1
batch 2
bundle 1, 2
case[2] 3
cram 1
crowd 1, 4, 5
fill 1
flock 1
gang 1
herd 1
host[2]
huddle 1
jam 1, 5
load 3
mob 1
package 3
packet 1
pack (*cont.*)
parcel 3
press 8
ram 1
ring[1] 3
score 4
squeeze 4
stack 3
stow
stuff 6, 7
swarm 1
throng 2
tissue
wad 1
wedge 3
wrap 1
-packs
score 4
package°
box[1] 2
bundle 1, 2
case[2] 3
pack 1, 5
packet 1
parcel 1
wrap 1
wrapper 2
package deal
package 2
pack away
eat
overeat
swallow 1
packed°
abound 2
alive 4
compact 1
dense 2
fraught
full 1
loaded 1
mobbed
overcrowded
pile 16
populous
serried
solid 2
stop 1
thick 2, 3
throng 2
packet°
bundle 1
mint 1
pack 1
package 1
parcel 1
pile[1] 2
profit 5
pack in°
at **pack 5**
pile[1] 6
stop 1
packing
wrapper 2
pack into°
at **pack 5**
pile[1] 6
throng 2
pack it in°
at **pack 6**
pack off°
at **pack 7**
bundle 3
pack of lies
moonshine 2
pack up°
at **pack 8**
stuff 9
pact°
accord 3
agreement 1
alliance 1
bargain 1
bond 2
contract 1
instrument 3
negotiation 2
protocol 2
treaty
truce 2
understanding 1
pad°
cushion 1
domicile 1
pad (*cont.*)
patch 1
place 6
sneak 1
tablet 1
wad 1
waddle
walk 1
padding
expletive 3
filling
pad 1
paddle°
oar 1
punish 2
spank
waddle
wade 2
paddle one's own canoe
shift 2
paddler
oar 2
paddling
punishment 2
paddling pool
pool 1
paddock
run 46
paddy°
explosion 2
pet[2]
rage 2
tantrum
temper 4
paddyw(h)ack
explosion 2
paddle 4
paddy
pet[2]
rage 2
spank
padlock
bar 8
close 1
lock[1] 1, 3
pad out°
at **pad 5**
padre
father 4
minister 1
priest
paean
chant 1
eulogy
praise 2
pagan°
heathen 1, 2
heretical
infidel
non-believer
profane 1
page°
messenger
runner 2
servant 1
sheet 2
pageant°
display 5
entertainment 2
extravaganza
gala 1
sight 3
pageantry°
display 5
glitter 4
glory 3
pomp
page-boy
page[2] 1
paginate
page[1] 3
pagoda
sanctuary 1
temple
tower 1
pail
bucket
pain°
ache 1, 3, 4
affliction 1
agony
pain (*cont.*)
ail 1
anguish 1
annoyance 2
bind 6
bother 7
cut 3
discomfort 2
distress 1
drag 7
evil 7
fag 2
grief 1
gripe 3
headache 2
hell 3
hurt 2, 3, 6
ill 8
inconvenience 1
job 4
kill 5
nuisance 1
offend 1
oppression
pang 1
passion 5
pest
pierce 4
pill 2
plague 2
prick 2
rack 2, 3
rankle
rend 3
smart 7, 8
stab 5
sting 2
stress 3
suffering
torment 1, 3
trial 5
twinge 1, 2
wound 2, 4
wrench 5
-pains
at **pain 4**
care 2
effort 1
endeavour 2
labour 1
pained
hurt 7
painful°
agonizing
arduous 1
bad 11
bitter 2
excruciating
grievous 1
hard 5
harrowing
heart-rending
keen[1] 3
nasty 2, 5
picnic 3
piercing 4
poignant 1
pungent 3
raw 4
severe 4
sore 1, 5
stiff 2
swingeing
tender[1] 8
thorny 2
traumatic
painfully°
hard 14
severely 4
painfulness
difficulty 1
severity 4
torment 3
pain in the arse
annoyance 2
bind 6
bother 7
headache 2
job 4
nuisance 1
pain 3
pest
picnic 3
plague 2
thorn 2

pass (*cont.*)
lapse 6
lead 5
make 6
melt 4
negotiate 3
overhaul 1
overtake 1
parade 4
permit 2
pronounce 3
ravine
resolve 3
roll 2
run 6
secrete[2]
serve 3
slip[1] 5
slip[2] 1
spend 3
squeeze 6
subside 2
sweep 5
thread 4
transfer 1
transit 3
void 7
passable°
acceptable 1
adequate 2
decent 3
fair[1] 4
good 1,3
indifferent 3
navigable 1
OK 3
open 9
ordinary 2
par 6
presentable 1
satisfactory
sort 5
so so
tolerable 2
passably
enough 3
fairly 1
moderately
passage°
approach 5
circulation 2
corridor
course 1
entrance[1] 2
entry 2
excerpt 1
extract 6
gate 1
hall 1
journey 2
motion 1
mouth 2
narrow 10
pass 23, 29
pipe 1
pipeline 1
quotation 1
road 1
run 37
selection 4
step 10a
street 1
text 2
transit 1
tunnel 1
vent 1
way 5
passageway
corridor
hall 1
mouth 2
passage 4
tunnel 1
pass around
circulate 2
distribute 1
give 15b
hand 17
rumour 2
serve 3
turn 4
pass as°
at **pass 16**
masquerade 3
pose 2
pass away°
at **pass 14**
die 1
elapse
expire 2
go 13
subside 2
pass by°
at **pass 1**
boycott 1
elapse
fly 4
go 26a
ignore 1
jump 3
neglect 1
refuse[1] 1
skip 2
passé°
antiquated
antique 1
date 4
dead 7
defunct 2
extinct 2
musty 2
obsolete
old 2
old-fashioned
out 9
prehistoric 2
time 15
time-worn
passed over
undone[2]
passenger°
arrival 2
fare 1
passenger car
car 1
passenger station
station 3
passer-by
bystander
eyewitness
onlooker
pass for°
at **pass 16**
pose 2
passing°
brief 1
cursory
death 1
fleeting
fly-by-night 1
fugitive 3
hasty 3
journey 2
loss 7
momentary
passage 1, 5, 6, 9
short-lived
succession 1
superficial 2, 3
temporary
transient
transit 1
-in passing°
at **passing 3**
offhand 5
passing fashion
obsolescent
passing on
succession 1
passing out
partition 2
pass into
enter 1
penetrate 1
perforate
passion°
appetite 2
ardour
desire 3
devotion 3
emotion
enthusiasm 1, 2
expression 4
feeling 4
fervour
fire 2
flame 2
passion (*cont.*)
flush[1] 6
frenzy 1
heat 2
inspiration 1
intensity
life 8
love 1, 2, 5b
mania 1
obsession
rage 1, 2
temper 4
thing 4
thirst 1
violence 2
warmth 3
wish 5
-passions°
at **passion 1**
spirit 2
passionate°
animated 1
ardent
burning 2
eager
earnest 2
emotional 1
enthusiastic
excited 2
fanatical
fervent 1
feverish
fiery 3
fire 5
great 9
hasty 4
heartfelt
heated
hot 3, 4
impassioned
inflammatory
intense 2
keen[1] 1
mad 6
obsessive
romantic 4
steamy 3
strong 22
sultry 2
tender[1] 7
torrid 2
towering 2
violent 3
voracious 2
warm 2
warm-blooded 2
wild 6
passionately
deeply 2
madly 4
passionless
wooden 2
passive°
blank 4
frigid 3
inactive 1
inert 3
mild 1
obedient
patient 1
phlegmatic 1
potential 1
sheepish 1
silent 4
submissive 1
supine 2
torpid
willing
passively
willingly
passiveness
inactivity 1
neglect 4
obedience
passivity
inactivity 1
inertia
neglect 4
obedience
resignation 2
submission 1
torpor
pass judgement
judge 4
passkey
key 1
pass muster°
at **muster 3**
check 10c
go 36b
pass 4
pass off°
at **pass 17**
exhale
foist
pass 16b, 19
pass on°
at **pass 18**
bequeath
communicate 1
delegate 3
die 1
give 3
go 13
hand 15a
impart 2
pass 8, 14a
pay 3
proceed 1
refer 2
relegate 3
transfer 1
transmit 1, 2
will 6
pass one over on
mislead
pass oneself off
masquerade 3
pass out°
at **pass 20**
circulate 2
collapse 3
dispense 1
distribute 1
faint 3
flake 3a
give 15b
hand 17
measure 14
mete
present[2] 6
release 2
serve 3
pass over°
at **pass 21**
boycott 1
bridge 3
cover 9
cross 5
delegate 3
discount 3
excuse 1
forgive 1
give 1
ignore 1
jump 3
miss[1] 4
omit 1
overlook 1
pass 8
range 8
refer 2
run 3
skip 2
slide 4
slur 3
transfer 1
transit 3
traverse 1
passport
permit 2
pass round
circulate 2
distribute 1
hand 17
pass scrutiny
check 10c
pass sentence
judge 4
pass the buck
delegate 3
pass through
die 1
filter 3
penetrate 1
transit 3
transmit 2
traverse 1
pass up°
at **pass 22**
disregard 1
forgo 1
miss[1] 1, 4
overlook 1
refuse[1] 1
pass water
urinate
water 4
password°
shibboleth
symbol
past°
ancient 1
by 2, 7
bygone
dead 7
former 2
history 3, 6
late 3
lost 4
outgoing 1
over 6, 7
previous 1
sometime 1
through 6
-in the past
before 1
previously
-to the past
backward 4
past due
back 13
delinquent 3
late 1
overdue
paste
cement 1, 2
glue 1, 2
hit 1
pelt[1] 1
phoney 1
plastic 3
pound[1] 1
pulp 2
punch[1] 1, 2
sham 2
spread 12
stick[1] 4
tack 5
pasteboard
card 1
pastel
mellow 3
pale[1] 2
soft 9
pasteurized
pure 2
pasticcio
patchwork
pot-pourri
pastiche°
medley
mishmash
patchwork
pot-pourri
pastille
pill 1
tablet 4
pastime°
amusement 2
diversion 3
entertainment 1
enthusiasm 2
fun 1
game 1
hobby
interest 5
plaything 1
pursuit 3
recreation
sport 1
pasting
thrashing 1
past it
elderly 1
old 1
senile
slow 8
past master
dab hand
master 2
past master (*cont.*)
professional 3
veteran 1
pastor°
clergyman 1
divine 5
father 4
minister 1
pastoral°
clerical 1
idyllic
priestly
rural 1
serene 1
pastoralism
simplicity 3
pastry
cake 1
tart[2] 1
pasturage
feed 4
pasture
pasture°
feed 2
field 1
meadow
plain 6
-out to pasture
pension 2
retire 2
pasture land
meadow
pasture
pasty°
clammy 1
ghastly 2
pale[1] 1
peaky
tart[2] 1
unwholesome 3
wan 1
white 2
pasty-faced
ghastly 2
pasty
pat°
caress 1, 2
clap 2
dab 1, 3
fondle
handle 2
pet[1] 4
stroke 6, 10
tap[1] 2
touch 14
patch°
allotment 2
doctor 3
fix 3, 16d
mend 1, 4
overhaul 2
period 1
plaque 2
plot[2]
repair 1, 2
run 38
spot 1
territory 2
time 1
tract[1]
patched
ragged 1
patchily
sketchily
patch up°
at **patch 6**
adjust 1
doctor 3
fix 3, 16d
heal 2
mend 1
overhaul 2
patch 5
renovate
repair 1
settle 3
square 13
touch 12
patchwork°
chequered 1
combination 3
pastiche

-in payment
for 3
pay no attention to
disregard 1
excuse 1
forgive 1
mind 19
neglect 1
pay no heed
disregard 1
excuse 1
pass 3, 22
put 11
slide 4
pay no mind
slide 4
pay off°
at **pay 10**
bribe 2
buy 3
pay 1, 4, 5, 7, 8a
redeem 1
score 9
pay-off°
clincher
gain 8
issue 2
kickback
outcome
ransom 2
upshot
payola
bribe 1
graft[2]
kickback
pay-off 3
rebate 2
pay old scores
score 9
pay out°
at **pay 11**
expend 1
pay 1, 5
share 3
shell 5
spend 1
stump 4
payout
gain 8
payment 2
ransom 2
pay respect(s)
hallow 2
memorialize
recognize 4
salute 2
pay suit
pursue 4
pay tribute
compliment 3
commemorate
exalt 2
extol
glorify 2
memorialize
praise 3
salute 2
toast 3
pay up
come 5b
pay 1
stump 4
PC
police officer
terminal 4
p.d.q.
double 8
fast[1] 6
hastily 1
post-haste
straight 15
summarily 1
pea-brained
senseless 3
peace°
calm 1, 2
content[2] 1
ease 1
hush 6
inactivity 1
lull 2
order 8
peace (*cont.*)
quiet 5
repose 1
serenity 1
silence 1
peaceable°
amicable
dreamy 3
mild 1
orderly 2
pastoral 1
peaceful 1
serene 1
peaceableness
peace 1
serenity 2
peaceably
happily 3
quietly 3
peaceful°
amicable
calm 3
dispassionate 1
dreamy 3
easy 2
equable 1
even 4
gentle 1
home 4a
homely 2
idyllic
inactive 1
mild 1
pastoral 1
quiet 2
relaxed
restful 2
sedate 1
self-contained 1
self-possessed
serene 1
silent 1
smooth 1
soothing 1
sound[2] 6
still 1
subdued 1
tranquil
peacefully
easy 7
quietly 3
peacefulness
calm 1
content[2] 2
ease 1
inactivity 1
lull 2
order 8
peace 1, 2
serenity 1, 2
silence 1
still 3
peace-loving
peaceable 2
peacemaker°
mediator
peacemonger
peacemaker
peace officer
officer 2
police officer
peace of mind
peace 1
quiet 5
peace-pipe
pipe 2
peacetime
peace 2
peach
disclose 1
finger 8
grass 1
inform 2
shop 3
sing 3
tell[1] 2
peaches and cream
fair[1] 3
peachy
bully 4
fine[1] 1
peacock
braggart
strut
peak°
acme
climax 1, 4
consummation 2
crag
crest 1
extreme 8
head 5
height 2, 3
high 15
maximum 1, 2
mountain 1
pinnacle
point 2
prime 4
prominence 2
spire 2
summit
tip[1] 1
top 1
vertex
zenith
peaked
pale[1] 1
peaky
pointed 1
run-down 1
sickly 2
peakish
pale[1] 1
peaky
sickly 2
peaky°
pale[1] 1
sickly 2
peal°
chime 1, 2, 3
gale 2
ring[2] 1, 3
roll 5, 15
toll[1] 1, 2
pealing
ring[2] 3
thunder 1
toll[1] 2
peanuts
nothing 3
pittance
-for peanuts
cheap 7
pearl°
gem 2
jewel 2
pearl-like
pearly
pearl of great price
gem 2
pearly°
filmy 2
grey 1
opalescent
silver 3
pear-shaped
rotund 2
round 7
smooth 7
peasant°
boor 1
clown 2
ordinary 2
rustic 2, 3
peasant-like
plebeian 1
peasantry
populace
rabble 2
pea-soup
thick 3
pea-souper
fog 1
pebbly
rocky[1] 1
stony 1
peccadillo°
fault 1
imperfection
indiscretion 2
misdeed
offence 1
peccadillo (*cont.*)
sin 1
slip[1] 8
peck
heap 2
kiss 1, 4
pack 2
peg 7
pick 4b
tap[1] 1, 2
peck at
pick 4b
pecker
bill[2]
pecking
tap[1] 2
pecking order
order 3
peckish
hungry 1
Pecksniff
Pharisee
Pecksniffian
goody-goody
Pharisaic
peculate
embezzle
misappropriate 1
steal 1
take 3
peculation
embezzlement
stealing
peculator
thief 1
peculiar°
abnormal 2
bent 2
bizarre 1
character 1
cranky 1
curious 3
deviant 1
different 2
distinct 2
distinctive
eccentric 1
erratic 2
exceptional 1
exotic 2
extraordinary 1
fanciful 3
fantastic 1
fishy 2
foreign 2
funny 2
grotesque 2
improbable
individual 2
irregular 3
kinky 1
local 2
odd 1
offbeat
ordinary 4
outlandish
out-of-the-way 2
outré
pale[2] 3
particular 1
proper 6
quaint 1
queer 1
remarkable 3
sick 5
singular 1
special 1
specific 1, 2
strange 1
symptomatic
unaccountable 1
unaccustomed 1
unearthly 3
unfamiliar 1
unnatural 1, 3
unusual
unwonted
way-out 1
weird
whimsical 1
wild 7
wrong 2
peculiarity°
character 2
characteristic 2
difference 4
eccentricity 2
exception 3
fancy 8
feature 1
foible
freak 3
mannerism
oddity 1, 2, 3
property 4
quirk
singularity 2
trait
trick 6
twist 10
peculiarly
especially 1
particularly 1
pecuniary
economic 1
financial
fiscal
monetary
pedagogic
pedantic 1
pedagogical
educational 1
pedagogue
instructor
scholar 1
schoolteacher
pedant
perfectionist 1
prig
purist
pedantic°
literary 2
pompous 2
priggish
stiff 8
stuffy 2
pedantical
pedantic 1
peddle°
market 4
sell 2
tout 1
peddler
pedlar
seller
pedestal°
base[1] 1
idealize
idolize
standard 4
worship 1
pedestrian°
banal
mediocre
ordinary 2
ponderous 2
prosaic
ready-made 3
undistinguished
pedicel
stem[1] 1
pedicular
lousy 3
pediculous
lousy 3
pedigree°
class 1
extraction 3
family 3
lineage 1
nationality 2
origin 3
parentage
root[1] 4
stock 2
strain[2] 1
tribe
pedigreed
pure-bred
pedlar°
merchant 2
peduncle
stem[1] 1
pee
go 17
urinate
water 4
peek°
glance 1, 4
peer[2] 1
pry 1
sight 5, 7
show 5
peekaboo
filmy 1
see-through
sheer 3
peel°
film 1
hull 2, 3
pare 1
rind
shed[2] 4
shell 3
skin 2, 4
strip[2] 1
peeler
police officer
peeling
peel 4
peel off°
at **peel 1**
shed[2] 4
strip[2] 2
take 34a
peep°
busybody
chirp 1, 2
glance 1, 4
peek 1, 2
peer[2] 1, 2
pipe 4
sight 5, 7
sing 2
twitter 1, 3
pee-pee
urinate
peeper
busybody
detective
snoop 2
peeping
curiosity 2
nosy
twitter 3
peer°
equal 4
equivalent 2
eye 10
fellow 2
like[1] 7
lord 2
match 1
noble 1
peek 1
pry 1
royal 3
sight 7
watch 3
peerage
rank[1] 3
royal 4
royalty 3
peerless°
alone 2
capital 6
excellent
exquisite 5
great 6
incomparable
leading 2
masterful 1
matchless
notable 2
optimum 2
perfect 2
pre-eminent 2
prime 2
rare[1] 2
sensational 3
splendid 3
star 3
sterling 2
superb
superior 2
superlative
supreme 4

peerless (*cont.*)
surpassing
top 8
transcendent
unbeatable
unique 2
unparalleled
virtuoso 2
peerlessness
pre-eminence 2
superiority 2
supremacy 1
peeve
aggravate 2
displease
disturb 1
exasperate 2
gnaw 3
infuriate
irk
irritate
pester
rub 8
sour 6
spite 3
worry 2
peeved
disgruntled
huff 1
indignant
resentful
sore 4
peevish°
bad 7
bilious
cantankerous
cranky 2
cross 6
disagreeable 3
disgruntled
edge 5
fretful
gruff 1
harsh 3
irritable
moody 2
passionate 3
perverse 2
petulant
prickly 3
quarrelsome
querulous
short-tempered
snappish 1
sour 4
sullen
surly
temperamental 1
testy
touchy 1
waspish
peevishness
temper 3
peewee
small 1
peg°
freeze 3
heave 2
hook 1
label 5
leg 1
nip²
notch 2
picket 1
pin 1
pitch¹ 1
plod 2
spike 1
tack 5
tap² 2
–off the peg°
at **peg 2**
ready-made 1
peg away°
at **peg 7**
labour 5
plod 2
wade 4
work 7
peignoir
robe 1
wrapper 1
pelagic
marine 2
oceanic
pelerine
mantle 1
pelf
fund 2
money 1
purse 2
riches
pelisse
mantle 1
pellet
pill 1
shot 2
tablet 4
pellicle
film 1
skin 2
pell-mell°
disorderly 1
helter-skelter 2
rush 3
pellucid
clear 2
distinct 1
transparent 1
pellucidity
clarity 1
pelmet
drapery
pelt°
batter 1
beat 1
belabour
hail² 1
hide² 1
patter¹ 2
pound¹ 1
skin 1
strike 1
pen°
bring 15b
cage 1, 2
enclose 1
enclosure 1
jail 1
pound²
prison
run 46
script 3
shed¹
shut 3a
siege 2
stake¹ 4
stall¹ 3
stir 7
write 1
penal°
penal institution
prison
penalize°
castigate
discipline 8
fine² 2
punish 1
penalty°
discipline 2
fine² 1
forfeit 1
penance 1
price 2
punishment 2
sanction 4
toll² 2
penance°
atonement
penalty
penitence
punishment 2
penchant°
fancy 7
habit 2
inclination 4
leaning
liking 1
partiality 2
talent 2
taste 3
weakness 4
pencil
beam 2
ray 1
shaft 2
pencil-mark
line¹ 1
pencil-pusher
writer
pencil-thin
thin 3
pendant°
pendent
pendulous 1
pending°
abeyance
open 6
prospective
unresolved
pendulous°
flabby 1
penetrable
porous
penetralia
recess 3
penetrate°
bore¹ 2
break 22
come 5c
drill 1
enter 2
fathom
get 39b
gore²
impregnate 2
infest
percolate
perforate
permeate
pierce 1, 2, 3
plumb 5
puncture 3
riddle² 2
see 14a
sink 11
stick¹ 1
suffuse
tunnel 2
understand 1
penetrating°
acute 3, 5
biting
chill 4
cutting 1
deep 3
devastating 1
good 11
hard 6
high 7
incisive 1
intimate¹ 2
keen¹ 5
luminous 3
penetration 1
pervasive
piercing 2, 3
poignant 2
pointed 2
profound 2
pungent 1, 3
raw 5
sharp 3, 7
shrill
strong 2
trenchant
penetratingly
searchingly
penetration°
depth 3
discrimination 2
inroad 1
wisdom 1
pen-friend
friend 1
peninsula
cape¹
point 8
penitence°
penance 1
remorse
repent
penitent°
apologetic
guilty 2
penitent (*cont.*)
regretful
remorseful
repent
repentant
sorry 1
penitential
sorry 1
penitentiary
jail 1
prison
stir 7
penknife
blade 2
penman
scribe 2
penmanship°
hand 7
script 1
writing 1
pen-mark
line¹ 1
pen-name
pseudonym
pennant°
banner 1
colour 2a
flag¹ 1
standard 3
streamer
symbol
penniless
broke
destitute 1
down and out 1
hard 17
indigent
insolvent
needy
penurious 2
poor 1
rock¹ 3c
short 8
stony 3
straitened
pennon
banner 1
flag¹ 1
pennant
streamer
penny-a-liner
hack² 1
scribe 2
writer
penny-ante
frivolous 1
minor 2
paltry
penny-pincher
miser
penny-pinching
avaricious
cheap 4
close 18
economical 2
frugal 2
grasping
greed 2
greedy 3
mean² 1
miserly
near 6
penurious 1
selfish 2
sparing 1
thrifty
tight 5
penny wise and pound foolish
improvident 1
wasteful
pen-pal
friend 1
pen-pusher
writer
pensile
pendulous 1
pension°
allowance 3
hotel
pensioner°
senior citizen
–pensioners
elderly 2
pension off°
at **pension 2**
–be pensioned off
retire 2
pensive°
dreamy 2
meditative
preoccupied 1
reflective
serious 1
thinking 1
thoughtful 2
wistful 2
penthouse
flat 18
shed¹
pent-up°
penurious°
avaricious
broke
cheap 4
close 18
destitute 1
economical 2
frugal 2
grasping
greedy 3
impoverished 1
indigent
lean¹ 3
mean² 1
miserly
near 6
selfish 2
sparing 1
stint 4
thrifty
tight 5
penuriousness
avarice
greed 2
thrift
penury
misery 2
necessity 3
need 4
poverty 1
privation
want 5
peon
peasant
people°
family 1
folk
humanity 1
inhabit
lineage 2
man 2, 4
one 4
populace
populate
population
public 8
race² 1
settle 6
society 2
tribe
unwashed 2
world 2
peopled
populous
pep°
animation 1
bounce 2
drive 8
dynamism
energetic
energy
enterprise 2
fire 2
initiative 2
life 7
lively 1
perky
racy
salt 2
snap 11
spice 2
vigorous
vigour
vitality 1
vivacious
peplum
flounce 1
ruffle 1
pepper°
pelt¹ 1
punctuate 1
riddle² 1
salt 2, 6
spice 2
spirit 3
zest 1
peppery
fiery 3
hot 2
passionate 3
pungent 1
spicy 1
pep pill
stimulant 2
peppy
buoyant 2
dashing 1
energetic
lively 1
perky
racy 1
rousing
vigorous
vivacious
pep talk
encouragement 2
pep up°
at **pep 2**
encourage 1
energize
enliven 1
liven 2
perk up
season 3
peradventure
maybe
perhaps
possibly 1
perambulate
promenade 3
ramble 1
roam
walk 1
perambulation
tour 2
per annum
yearly 2
perceivable
discernible 1
evident
noticeable 1
observable
perceptible
sensible 2
visible 1
perceive°
appreciate 3
behold
catch 10
comprehend
conceive 3
detect 2
discover 1
distinguish 3
divine 4
feel 1, 3, 4
figure 12b
find 3
get 19
hear 1
hit 9b
make 37a, 37d
miss¹ 3
note 11
notice 1, 2
observe 3
penetrate 5
realize 2
recognize 2
regard 2
remark 1
savour 3
scent 3
see 1, 2, 14a
sense 6
take 19
tell¹ 8
tumble 3
understand 1

perceive of°
- *at* perceive 3

percentage°
- cut 20
- interest 4, 6
- kickback
- money 3
- part 1
- piece 3, 11
- portion 2
- proportion 3
- quota
- rate[1] 3
- ration 1
- rebate 2
- royalty 2
- share 1

perceptible°
- conspicuous 1
- discernible 1
- distinct 1
- evident
- external 3
- noticeable 1
- observable
- obvious
- sensible 2
- slight 2
- slow 2
- tangible
- visible 1

perceptibly
- clear 18

perception°
- appreciation 3
- brain 1
- capacity 2
- cognizance
- depth 3
- discrimination 2
- eye 2, 3
- feeling 1
- foresight 2
- grasp 5
- grip 3
- head 4
- idea 2
- identification 1
- image 3
- insight
- intelligence 1
- intuition
- judgement 1, 4
- mind 1, 3
- notice 3
- opinion 1
- penetration 2
- realization 1
- recognition 2
- sensation 1
- sense 2
- sensitivity 3
- sight 2
- tact
- taste 4
- understanding 2, 4
- uptake
- vision 1, 3
- wisdom 1

perceptive°
- acute 5
- astute 2
- clear 9
- clever 1
- diplomatic
- discriminating
- eagle-eyed
- far-sighted 1
- hip
- incisive 1
- intelligent
- judicial 2
- judicious
- keen[1] 6
- knowing 2
- luminous 3
- nice 3
- observant 1
- penetrating 1
- politic 2
- quick 4
- quick-witted
- ready 6
- receptive 2
- shrewd

perceptive (*cont.*)
- smart 2
- sound[2] 4
- tactful
- wise 1

perceptiveness
- brain 1
- capacity 2
- discrimination 2
- head 4
- insight
- intuition
- penetration 2
- uptake
- wisdom 1

perceptual
- mental 1

perch°
- nest 1
- settle 5

perchance
- incidentally 2
- maybe
- perhaps
- possibly 1

percipience
- brain 1
- eye 3
- insight
- intelligence 1
- intuition
- judgement 1
- mind 1
- penetration 2
- reason 2
- understanding 2
- wisdom 1

percipient
- acute 5
- incisive 1
- intelligent
- judicial 2
- judicious
- keen[1] 6
- luminous 3
- penetrating 1
- perceptive
- politic 2
- shrewd
- smart 2
- sound[2] 4
- wise 1

percolate°
- filter 3
- penetrate 2
- permeate
- strain[1] 5

perdition°

peregrinate
- journey 3
- roam

peregrinating
- vagabond 2

peregrination
- journey 1
- tour 1
- trip 3

-peregrinations
- travel 2

peregrinator
- migrant 1

peremptorily
- sharply 1
- short 11
- shortly 3
- summarily 2

peremptory°
- arbitrary 2
- assertive
- dogmatic
- domineering
- emphatic
- explicit 1
- flat 4
- imperative 2
- overbearing
- positive 2
- shabby 2
- short-tempered
- summary 2

perennial°
- constant 2
- indestructible

perennial (*cont.*)
- permanent 1
- perpetual 1
- yearly 3

perennially
- yearly 1

perestroika
- reform 3

perfect°
- absolute 1
- accomplished
- clear 14
- complement 3
- complete 4, 6
- correct 8
- divine 3
- exact 1
- exquisite 3, 5
- faithful 2
- faultless
- finish 2, 7
- flawless 1
- heavenly 2
- ideal 4
- immaculate 3
- impeccable
- infallible 1
- intact
- mature 3, 6
- model 11
- optimum 2
- out-and-out
- polish 2
- polished 1
- positive 9
- precise 1
- profound 4
- proper 5
- pukka 1
- pure 1, 5
- refine 2
- regular 9
- right 2, 8
- ripen
- stark 4
- superb
- tailor-made 2
- thorough 1
- thumping 2
- total 3
- unmitigated
- unqualified 2
- very 3

-in a perfect world
- ideally 1

perfected
- mature 3
- perfect 1
- practised 2

perfect example
- gem 2
- picture 4

perfection°
- complement 1
- consummation 2
- entirety 1
- fruition
- ideal 2
- maturity 3
- optimum 1
- peak 2
- pinnacle
- precision 1
- purity 1
- refinement 4
- Utopia

perfectionist°
- meticulous
- pedantic 2

perfect likeness
- look-alike

perfectly°
- altogether
- charm 4
- completely 1
- detail 4
- downright 2
- exactly 1
- full 15
- ideally 3
- just 5
- pat[2] 1
- pukka 1
- quite 1

perfectly (*cont.*)
- supremely
- thoroughly 1
- totally
- utterly

perfect match
- look-alike

perfervid
- fanatical
- intense 2

perfidious°
- black 6
- dirty 3
- dishonest
- dishonourable 2
- disloyal
- evil 2
- faithless 2
- foul 7
- hypocritical
- insincere
- lying 2
- Machiavellian
- renegade 2
- slippery 2
- traitorous
- two-faced
- unscrupulous
- untrue 1
- villainous 1
- wily

perfidiously
- back 6

perfidiousness
- foul play
- perfidy

perfidy°
- betrayal 1
- foul play
- infidelity 1

perforate°
- bore[1] 2
- hole 7
- penetrate 1
- pierce 2
- pink[2]
- prick 3
- punch[2] 2
- puncture 3
- riddle[2] 1
- stick[1] 1

perforated
- pitted

perforating
- puncture 2

perforation
- flaw 2
- hole 2
- penetration 1
- pore[2]
- prick 1
- puncture 1, 2

perforator
- punch[2] 1

perforce
- necessarily
- willy-nilly 1

perform°
- accomplish
- act 6, 9
- appear 2
- behave
- belt 4
- bring 11
- carry 10c, 12
- celebrate 1
- commit 3
- deliver 7
- discharge 5
- enact 2
- execute 1
- feature 5
- follow 10
- fulfil 1
- function 3
- give 7
- go 3
- implement 2
- make 10
- obey 2
- operate 1
- perpetrate
- play 4, 5
- practise 2

perform (*cont.*)
- prosecute 3
- pull 12b
- put 22d
- redeem 6
- render 4
- run 11
- take 11, 26
- transact

performable
- practicable

performance°
- act 2, 3
- action 1, 7
- attraction 2
- celebration 1
- course 3
- deed 1
- delivery 4
- discharge 12
- entertainment 2
- execution 1
- exercise 5
- fulfilment
- observance 2
- operation 1
- palaver 1
- presentation 2
- proceeding 2b
- production 4
- programme 2
- recital 1
- recitation 1
- record 5
- rendition 1
- routine 2
- song 3a
- spectacle 1
- stand 15
- technique 2
- theatre 2
- undertaking 2

performance level
- touch 17

performed
- complete 2

performer°
- player 2, 4
- Thespian 2

-performers
- cast 2
- company 2

performing
- theatre 2
- Thespian 1
- undertaking 2

perfume°
- aroma 1
- bouquet 2
- fragrance
- odour 1
- savour 2
- scent 1, 4
- smell 1

perfumed
- aromatic
- fragrant
- redolent 1
- sweet 2

perfunctorily
- sketchily

perfunctory°
- careless 1
- cursory
- hasty 3
- hurried 2
- mechanical 2
- offhand 2
- promiscuous 1
- quick 2
- ritual 2
- routine 4
- sketchy
- summary 2
- superficial 3
- token 5

perhaps°
- chance 5b
- maybe
- possibly 1
- probably

periapt
- fetish 1
- talisman

pericope
- excerpt 1

peril°
- adventure 1
- danger 1
- exposure 2
- fire 6
- hazard 1
- jeopardy
- menace 2
- pitfall 2
- risk 1
- threat 1

perilous°
- awkward 4
- critical 3
- dangerous 1
- desperate 5
- dodgy
- explosive 1
- grave[2] 2
- hairy 2
- menacing
- nice 4
- parlous
- precarious
- risky
- serious 4
- tight 7
- ugly 3
- unhealthy 3

perilously
- dangerously 1

perimeter°
- belt 2
- boundary
- circuit 1
- edge 1
- fringe 2
- girth 1
- limit 2
- margin 1
- periphery 1
- rim
- side 1
- silhouette

-in perimeter
- round 25

perimetric
- peripheral 2

period°
- age 3, 5
- bout 1
- date 1
- day 2
- dot 1
- era
- eve 1
- fit[2] 2
- generation 2
- interval 1
- juncture 2
- length 2
- measurement 2
- page[1] 2
- patch 4
- phase 1
- point 1
- round 14
- run 38
- season 1
- session 2
- snap 9
- space 3
- span 2
- spell[1] 1
- streak 3
- stretch 6
- style 1
- term 2
- time 1, 2, 4
- tour 3
- world 4

-at any period
- ever 1

periodic°
- fitful
- intermittent
- occasional 1
- recurrent
- regular 2

pester (*cont.*)
provoke 3
push 4
ride 3
tease 1
torment 2
trouble 2
worry 2
pestiferous
irksome
troublesome
pestilence°
blight 1
epidemic 2
plague 1
poison 2
ulcer 2
visitation 2
pestilential
evil 5
wicked 6
pet°
baby 2
bother 6
caress 2
cuddle 2
darling 2
dear 1, 3
favoured 1
favourite 1, 2
feel 2
fondle
golden 6
idol 2
love 6
pamper
pat[1] 1
stroke 10
-in a pet
huff 1
indignant
pet-cock
tap[2] 1
peter away
fade 2
peter out°
collapse 2
decline 2
die 2
diminish 3
dissipate 2
dissolve 1
dwindle
ebb 2
end 9
fade 2
fail 3
fizzle 2
flag[2] 2
run 26c, 30b
stop 4
taper 2
trail 8
wane 1, 3, 4
Peter('s) pence
tribute 2
petiole
stem[1] 1
petite°
diminutive
little 1
short 1
slight 3
small 1
tiny
undersized
petition°
appeal 1, 3
application 4
apply 7
ask 3
besiege 3
call 7a
claim 1
desire 4
hit 8
litany 1
plea 1
plead 2
pray 1
prayer 1
put 20a
request 2
solicit 1

petition (*cont.*)
sue 2
suit 5
supplication 1
petitioner
litigant
supplicant 2
petitioning
supplicant 1
supplication 2
pet name
nickname 1
petrified°
hard 1
panic-stricken
petrify°
dismay 1
frighten
horrify 1
intimidate
shock 1
terrify
petrifying
formidable 1
frightening
terrifying
petrolatum
ointment
pettifog
quibble 1
pettifoggery
chicanery
pettifogging
fault-finding 1, 2
legalistic
narrow-minded
pettiness
triviality 1
pettish
cross 6
peevish
petulant
touchy 1
petty°
banal
frivolous 1
hair-splitting
immaterial 1
incidental 2
inconsequential
insignificant
little 5, 6
mean[2] 1
minor 2
minute[2] 2
narrow-minded
negligible
niggling 2
paltry
parochial
pathetic 2
puny 1
small 4
small-minded
small-time
trifling
unworthy 1
venial
petty detail
triviality 2
petty sin
peccadillo
petulance
temper 3
petulant°
bilious
cranky 2
cross 6
discontented
fretful
gruff 1
harsh 3
hasty 4
huff 1
irritable
moody 2
peevish
perverse 2
prickly 3
pugnacious
quarrelsome
querulous
quick 5

petulant (*cont.*)
sensitive 2
short-tempered
snappish 1
sour 4
sullen
temperamental 1
terse 2
testy
touchy 1
waspish
p'hansigar
thug
phantasm
fancy 6
ghost 1
hallucination
illusion 2
phantom 1
shade 4
vision 4
phantasma
phantom 1
phantasmagoria
illusion 2
phantasmagoric
dreamlike
shadowy 3
unreal 1
phantasmagor-ical
dreamlike
insubstantial 2
shadowy 3
unreal 1
phantasmal
ghostly 1
insubstantial 2
shadowy 3
unreal 1
phantasy
see **fantasy**
phantom°
disembodied
fancy 6
ghost 1
ghostly 1
hallucination
illusion 2
insubstantial 2
shade 4
shadowy 3
spectral
spectre 1
vision 4
Pharisaic°
hypocritical
pious 2
self-righteous
Pharisaical
hypocritical
Pharisaic
sanctimonious
self-righteous
Pharisaism
hypocrisy
Pharisee°
hypocrite
purist
Phariseeism
hypocrisy
pharmaceutical
drug 1
medicine
pill 1
remedy 1
pharmaceutics
pharmacy 2
pharmacist°
druggist
pharmacologist
pharmacist
pharmacopoeia
pharmacy 2
pharmacy°
pharos
beacon
phase°
date 1
page[1] 2
quarter 2
stage 1

phase (*cont.*)
state 2
phase in°
at **phase 5**
phase out°
at **phase 6**
Pheidippides
messenger
phenomenal°
fabulous 2
marvellous
miraculous
portentous 2
prodigious 2
rare[1] 1
raving 2
remarkable 1
sensational 3
superhuman 1
phenomenon°
development 1
happening
legend 2
marvel 2
object 1
occurrence 1
oddity 2
prodigy 2
sight 3
wonder 1
philander
flirt 1
mess 4b
play 9b
run 23
philanderer°
adventurer 2
flirt 3
heel[1] 2
libertine 1
philandering
flirtatious
libertine 2
philanthropic°
charitable 1
generous 1
kind[1]
large 2
liberal 1
unselfish
philanthropist°
benefactor
humanitarian 2
patron 1
philanthropy°
altruism
benevolence 1
bounty 1
charity 1
kindness 1
largesse
philippic
harangue 1
lecture 1
rant 3
speech 2
tirade
philistine°
barbarian 2, 3
boor 2
bourgeois 1
heathen 3
uncivilized 2
philosopher
sage 2
theorist
thinker
philosophic
philosophical 1
psychic 2
psychological
philosophical°
patient 1
phlegmatic 2
psychic 1
psychological
pure 4
thinking 1
philosophy°
idea 3
ideology
principle 2
rationale

philosophy (*cont.*)
school 3
side 3
stand 13
thinking 2
philtre
potion
phiz(og)
face 1
mug 2
phlegm
indifference 1
lethargy 1
presence 5
sang-froid
sloth
sluggishness
torpor
phlegmatic°
blasé 2
cool 2
half-hearted
impassive
indifferent 1
lackadaisical 2
lethargic 1
listless
lukewarm 2
passive 1
slothful
stoical
stolid
supine 2
tardy 2
torpid
phlegmatical
phlegmatic 1, 2
phobia°
fear 3
obsession
thing 4
Phoebus (Apollo)
sun 1
phone
buzz 7
call 3, 12b
contact 4
look 11b
ring[2] 2
telephone 1, 2
transmit 1
phone call
buzz 3
call 14
phoney°
affected 2
artificial 2, 3
assumed 2
bogus
cheat 1
counterfeit 1, 3
deceitful
deceptive 2
duff
dummy 2
factitious
fake 3, 4, 5
false 2, 3
fictitious 2
forced
forgery 2
fraud 3
fraudulent 1
genteel 1
glorified 2
glossy 2
hypocrite
imitation 5
impostor
insincere
mannered
mock 3
Pharisee
plastic 3
poseur
pretended
quack 1, 2
quasi- 2
sham 1, 2
spurious
synthetic
theatrical 2

phoney (*cont.*)
toy 6
phoneyness
hypocrisy
phonogram
sign 4
symbol
phonographer
stenographer
phonograph record
record 7
phony
see **phoney**
phosphoresce
glow 4
phosphores-cence
glow 1
illumination 1
light[1] 3
radiance 1
phosphorescent
light[1] 13
luminous 2
radiant 1
photo
photograph 1
print 2
shot 5
photocopy
copy 1
duplicate 2, 3
facsimile
replica
transcript 2
photograph°
film 5
likeness 2
picture 1
print 2
shot 5
snap 5
photographer°
photographic°
graphic 1
photographist
photographer
photojournalist
reporter
photoplay
drama 1
Photostat
facsimile
transcript 2
phrase°
couch 2
express 1
expression 5
idiom 2
passage 2
put 4
say 3
term 1
word 3, 10
phraseology
dialect
diction 1
expression 6
idiom 1
language 4
parlance
phrase 3
style 5
terminology
vernacular 3
wording
phrasing
diction 1
expression 6
idiom 2
language 4
parlance
phrase 3
print 3
style 5
terminology
tone 2
wording
phthisic
emaciated
frail 2

pig *(cont.)*
overeat
police officer
slob
pigeon
butt[1]
dupe 1
fool 3
plaything 2
sucker
pigeon-hole
compartment
delay 1
file 3
identification 2
identify 1
label 5
niche 2
organize 1
range 7
shelve
slot 2,4
table 5
tabulate
piggish
epicurean 1
gluttonous
greedy 1
hoggish
ravenous 2
sordid 2
voracious 1
piggishness
gluttony
pigheaded
disobedient 2
inflexible
obstinate
opinionated 1
perverse 3
positive 5
rigid 4
self-willed
stubborn
wilful 2
pigheadedness
obstinacy
pigment
colour 1,3
paint 1
stain 3
pigmentation
colour 1
pigmy
see **pygmy**
pignorate
pawn[1] 1
pig out
devour 1
overeat
pigpen
hovel
shambles
pigsty
hovel
shambles
pigswill
swill 1
pigtail
plug 2
queue 2
pigwash
swill 1
pike
lance 1
road 2
spike 1
staff 1
stake[1] 1
stick[2] 1
piker
stiff 12
pikestaff
staff 1
pilaster
pillar 1
pile°
accumulation 3
car 1
clump 3
crowd 3
drift 5
gather 1
pile *(cont.)*
group 2
heap 1,3
hill 2
hoard 2
load 3
lot 5b
mass 1
mint 1
mound 2
mountain 2
nap[2]
pack 2
packet 2
pier 2
pillar 1
plenty 1
post[1] 1
profusion
sea 3
stack 1,6
store 1
tissue
-piles°
heap 2
lot 5b
mass 2
mountain 2
packet 2
plenty 1
sea 3
pile it on
dramatize
exaggerate
pile up
accumulate
amass
collect 1
garner
gather 1
heap 3
hoard 2
mass 7
mount 7
salt 8
scrape 6
stack 6
stock 10
store 1
pile-up°
collision
stack 3
pilfer°
appropriate 2
embezzle
hook 7
knock 5b
liberate 2
lift 6
make 27
pinch 3
pocket 4
rip 2a
steal 1
swipe 2
take 3
pilferage
embezzlement
rip-off 1
robbery
stealing
theft
pilferer
thief 1
pilfering
embezzlement
rip-off 1
robbery
theft
pilgarlic
wretch 2
pilgrim°
pilgrimage°
journey 1
quest 1
-pilgrimages
travel 2
piling
accumulation 1
pier 2
pillar 1
post[1] 1
pill°
drip 3
tablet 4
pillage°
depredation
gut 5
loot 2
overrun
plunder 1,3
raid 2
ransack 2
rape 2,5
ravage 2
rifle 1
rob 1
robbery
spoil 6
strip[2] 5
waste 11
pillaging
depredation
predatory 2
robbery
pillar°
backbone 2
leg 2
post[1] 1
shaft 1
stake[1] 1
standard 4
support 8
pillock
fool 1
pillory
denounce 3
parody 3
punish 2
satirize
slam 3
stigmatize
pillow
cushion 1
pad 1
pillow talk
tête-à-tête 1
pill popper
addict 1
pill pusher
pharmacist
pill roller
pharmacist
pilot°
control 1
direct 2
director 2
drive 2
fly 5
govern 1
guide 2
lead 1
navigate 2
navigator
sail 1
steer 1
trial 6
pilotage
navigation
pilule
pill 1
pimp°
pander 2,3
procurer
slaver[2] 2
pimple°
spot 5b
pimpled
spotty 2
pimply
spotty 2
pin°
anchor 3
attach 1,4
bolt 2
brooch
catch 17
clasp 1,3
connect 3
fix 1,9
freeze 3
hook 1
leg 1
nail 1,7
peg 1,4,5
pin *(cont.)*
pivot 1
plaque 2
post[1] 2
put 8
spike 1
stab 1
stick[1] 1,4
tack 1,5
tang 3
transfix 1
-on pins and needles
nervous 1
sweat 2
tense 2
pincers°
pinch°
appropriate 2
arrest 2
capture 1,2
carry 10b
catch 1
dab 2
dash 7
drop 2
emergency
fix 17
get 8
grab 3
help 5
hook 6,7
hurt 2
knock 5b
lift 6
make 27
mess 3
morsel 2
nab
necessity 4
nick 3
nip[1] 1,3
pang 1
pick 8h
pilfer
pirate 3
pocket 4
predicament
prick 2,4
pull 11b
rip 2a
run 27
scrape 3,8
seize 2
smart 7
squeeze 1
steal 1
stint 4
swipe 2
take 3
taste 1
top 5
touch 15
trifle 2
tweak 1,2
twinge 1
-with a pinch of salt°
at **salt 5**
pinchbeck
base[2] 5
fake 5
fraudulent 1
plastic 3
shoddy
pinched
drawn
emaciated
gaunt 1
impoverished 1
lean[1] 1
narrow 2
needy
peaky
poor 1
short 8
skinny
thin 1
pinch-hit
sit 6b
stand 8
substitute 1
understudy 2
pinch-hitter
alternate 5
understudy 1
pinching
rip-off 1
robbery
theft
pinch pennies°
at **pinch 5**
economize
stint 4
pinchpenny
miser
pin down°
at **pin 4**
box[1] 3
finger 5a, 5c
set 5
pine
ache 2
brood 4
die 5
itch 2
yearn
pine for
desire 1
fancy 11
hanker
miss[1] 2
pant 2
sigh 2
want 1
pinguid
fat 2
greasy 1
oily 1
pinhead
dolt
fool 1
pin-headed
thick 6
pinhole
prick 1
pining
desperate 3
homesick
starved 2
pinion
shackle 3
tie 2
-pinions
restraint 2
pink°
left 2
radical 5
rosy 1
-in the pink
hale
healthy 1
pinked
notched
pinkish
pink[1] 2
rosy 1
pinko
radical 5
pink slip
dismissal 1
push 16
sack 3
pin money
allowance 3
pinnacle°
acme
crest 1
extreme 8
height 2
maximum 1,2
peak 1
perfection 3
prime 4
prominence 2
spire 2
summit
tip[1] 1
top 1
vertex
zenith
pin on°
at **pin 5**
pin one's faith on
lean[2] 4a
pin one's faith on *(cont.)*
trust 5
pin one's hopes on
lean[2] 4a
trust 5
pinpoint
designate 1
diagnose
focus 4
get 22
identify 1
locate 1
name 5
pin 4b
place 15
set 5
zero 4
pinpointing
identification 1
pinprick
prick 1
pin someone's ears back
reprimand 2
pin spotlight
spotlight 1
pint
drink 6
pintle
pivot 1
pinto
dapple 1
pint-sized
minute[2] 1
short 1
slight 3
small 1
tiny
pin up
post[1] 2
pioneer°
discover 3
early 5
institute 4
introduce 4
originate 1
settle 6
settler
spearhead 1
pioneering
avant-garde
pious°
devout 1
godly
holy 2
pure 6
religious 1
piousness
piety 2
pip
grain 1
kernel 1
pit[2]
vapour 2
pipe°
chirp 1
drain 1
main 5
peep 1,2
pipeline 1
sight 5
sing 1,2
vent 1
pipe down°
at **pipe 7**
pipedream
day-dream 1
dream 1
fancy 6
fantasy 2
pipeline°
main 5
pipe 1
-in the pipeline°
at **pipeline 2**
way 12
pipe of peace
pipe 2
pipe up°
at **pipe 8**

piping
hot 1
shrill
trim 5
pip pip
farewell 3
goodbye
piquancy
flavour 1
salt 2
savour 1
spice 2
spirit 3
tang 1
zest 1
piquant
epigrammatic
hot 2
pungent 1
racy 3
sharp 4, 5
spicy 1
strong 2
tart[1] 1
witty
pique
anger 1, 2
annoyance 1
displease
disturb 1
exasperate 2
get 17
grudge 1
infuriate
intrigue 1
irritate
madden 2
offence 3
offend 1
pester
pet[2]
provoke 3
resentment
spite 3
umbrage
warmth 4
whet 2
-in a pique
moody 2
querulous
piqued
angry 1
cross 6
discontented
huff 1
indignant
moody 2
querulous
resentful
umbrage
piracy
pillage 2
plagiarism
stealing
pirate°
cutthroat 1
help 5
outlaw 1
plunder 2
robber
steal 2
take 3
thief 3
piratical
predatory 2
pirating
plagiarism
stealing
pirouette°
gyrate
revolution 3
rotate 1
spin 1, 6
swivel 1
turn 26
piscatorial
fishy 1
piscatory
fishy 1
piscina
sink 12
piscine
fishy 1
pish and tush
fiddlesticks
gobbledegook 1
prattle 3
piss
go 17
urinate
water 4
pissed
drunk 1
far 5b
stinking 3
pissed off
discontented
furious 1
indignant
piss off
bugger 5
enrage
exasperate 2
infuriate
pissoir
toilet 1
piste
run 45
pistol°
revolver
piston°
pit°
cavity
core 3
depression 1
depth 5
excavation
grain 1
hole 1
hollow 7
indentation
mark 10
mine 1
opening 1
pan 3
pitfall 1
pocket 2
quarry[2] 1
seed 1
shaft 4
sink 13
pit against
divide 3
oppose 3
play 3
take 35b
pit-a-pat
patter[1] 2, 3
pitch°
camp[1] 3
careen
cast 1, 7
climb 6
dash 2
erect 2
field 2
fling 1
fly 8a
head 5
heave 2
hurl
incline 4
intonation
key 3
launch 3
line[1] 18
lob 1, 2
lurch[2] 1, 2
patter[2] 1
plunge 1, 3
put 7
reel 1
slant 3, 4
sling 1
slope 1, 2
speech 2
stagger 1
throw 1
tilt 1, 3
tone 2
toss 1, 5, 6
tumble 1
tune 2
wallow 3
pitch-black°
black 3
swarthy
pitch camp
camp[1] 3
pitch-dark
dark 1
pitch-black
pitched°
pitcher
jar[1]
jug
pitch in
shoulder 3
turn 23c
pitching
roll 14
pitchpole
pitch[1] 4
pitchy
sunless
piteous°
heart-rending
pathetic 1
poignant 1
sorrowful 1
tragic
pitfall°
difficulty 2
joker 2
trap 1
pith°
core 2
elixir 3
essence 1
gist
heart 3
implication 3
juice 2
kernel 2
matter 4
meat 2
nub 2
nucleus
point 5
pulp 1
quintessence
significance 1
spirit 6
substance 2
vigour
pithiness
brevity
pithy
compact 3
concise
epigrammatic
expressive 2
forceful 2
meaningful 1
short 3
significant 2
succinct
terse 1
thumbnail
pitiable°
forlorn 1
paltry
pathetic 1
piteous
poignant 1
poor 6
sad 3
sorry 2
tragic
unfortunate 2
wretched 3
pitiful°
forlorn 1
lamentable
miserable 3
paltry
pathetic 1
piteous
poignant 1
poor 6
sad 3
sorry 2
touching
tragic
wan 2
weak 4
wretched 3
pitiless
bloodthirsty
brutal 1
pitiless (*cont.*)
cold-blooded 3
cold-hearted
cruel 1
cutthroat 2
deadly 3
ferocious
ghoulish 2
grim 2
hard 4
harsh 2
heartless
implacable
inhuman 1
merciless
relentless 1
remorseless 1
ruthless
sanguinary 1
savage 2
severe 1
stony 2
strict 2
unmerciful
unsympathetic
pitilessly
roughly 2
pitilessness
severity 1
pittance°
pitted°
bumpy
irregular 1
rugged 1
pitter-patter
patter[1] 2, 3
pity°
feel 8
heart 5
mercy
quarter 4
relent
respond 2
shame 3
sympathy 1
pivot°
centre 1
depend 1
hub
pirouette 2
revolve 1, 2
rotate 1
spin 1
swivel 1, 2
turn 1
wheel 2
pivotal°
critical 2
crucial
fateful 1
grave[2] 2
key 6
landmark 3
momentous
pressing
vital 1, 2
pivoting
pirouette 1
pix
photograph 1
print 2
pixie
goblin
imp
pixilated
curious 3
pixy
see **pixie**
pixyish
whimsical 1
pizazz, pizzazz
flair 2
glitter 4
snap 11
sparkle 4
spice 2
style 4
verve
vigour
vitality 1
zest 1
placard
advertisement 1
poster
promotion 5
sign 5
placate
calm 5
disarm 2
humour 4
hush 5
mitigate
reconcile 1
satisfy 1
placater
peacemaker
placation
reconciliation 1
placative
propitiatory 1
placatory
propitiatory 1
place°
appointment 3
attach 4
base[1] 6
capacity 3
clap 3
deposit 1, 2
dispose 1
estate 3
fix 8
get 15, 22
group 4
home 1
identify 1
impose 3
insert 1
install 1
lay[1] 1
locale
locate 1
location 1
make 14
niche 2
office 4
pad 3
perch 1, 2
pitch[1] 2
plant 7
play 7
point 3
pose 1
position 5, 6, 8, 9
post[2] 1, 2
put 1, 8, 28h
quarter 3
rank[1] 1
rate[1] 4, 8
recognize 1
residence 1
rest[1] 8
role 2
run 19
scene 1
seat 1, 7
set 1, 11
site 1, 2
situate
situation 1, 3
slot 2, 4
space 1, 4
spot 2
spread 13
square 8
stage 1
stand 2a
standing 5
station 1, 2, 4
stick[1] 2
stow
take 21
true 6
void 5
whereabouts
-be placed
make 14
rest[1] 7
-in all places
everywhere
-in every place
everywhere
-in place°
at **place 11**
-in place of
behalf
for 3
instead 2
line[1] 23a
mount 5
replace 1
-out of place°
at **place 12**
awkward 3
extraneous 2
improper 2
inept 2
inopportune
irrelevant
order 13b
unbecoming 1
unseemly 2
unworthy 2
wrong 4
-to every place
everywhere
placement°
composition 2
disposition 2
imposition 1
installation 1, 2
orientation 1
position 2
setting
site 1
place of action
theatre 4
place of worship
temple
place one's faith
credit 5
place to turn
recourse 2
resort 2
place under arrest
nab
placid
calm 3
dispassionate 1
equable 1
even 4
gentle 1
home 4a
inactive 1
mild 1, 2
passive 1
pastoral 1
peaceful 1
philosophical 2
phlegmatic 2
quiet 2
sedate 1
self-contained 1
self-possessed
serene 2
silent 1
still 1
subdued 1
tranquil
placidity
calm 2
inactivity 1
peace 1
philosophy 3
self-control 2
serenity 2
placidness
calm 2
inactivity 1
peace 1
placing
composition 2
disposition 2
imposition 1
orientation 1
placement 1
position 2
plagiarism°
stealing
plagiarist
pirate 2
plagiaristic
derivative 1
plagiarize
help 5
lift 6

plagiarize (*cont.*)
pirate 3
steal 2
take 3
plagiarized
derivative 1
plagiarizer
pirate 2
plagiarizing
plagiarism
stealing
plagiary
plagiarism
plague°
affliction 2
annoy 2
blight 1,3
bother 1
disease 2
distress 3
disturb 1
dun
epidemic 2
exasperate 2
gall[2] 4
gnaw 3
grind 5
harass
haunt 2
heckle
infest
irritate
madden 3
molest 1
nag[1] 1
obsess
persecute 2
pester
pestilence 1
poison 2
prod 3
provoke 3
push 4
rack 3
rankle
rash[2] 2
ride 3
scourge 1
tantalize
tease 1
thorn 2
torment 2
trial 5
trouble 2
ulcer 2
visitation 2
worry 2
plagued
downtrodden
smitten 1
stricken 2
plaguing
provocative 2
plaid
chequered 1
plain°
apparent 1
appear 4
artless 2
bare 2,5
blank 1
bluff[2] 2
broad 2,3
candid 1
clear 6,7,8
common 1,3
conspicuous 1
definite 3
direct 9
discernible 1
distinct 1
downright 1
dry 2
easy 1
elementary 1
evident
explicit 1
express 5
fizz 4
flat 14b
graphic 1
gross 4
hard 8
homely 1,3

plain (*cont.*)
homespun
honest 3
intelligible
legible
level 1
main 4
manifest 1
meagre 3
modest 2
mousy 1
naked 3
observable
obvious
open 13
ordinary 2
overt
patent 2
perceptible
pictorial 1
plane 3
plump[2] 6
pronounced 1
prosaic
public 4
raw 6
readable 1
round 8
rustic 2
self-evident
severe 6
sheer 2
simple 1,2
sober 3
stark 2,4
straight 5,6
table 2
transparent 2
ugly 1
unadorned
unaffected[1]
undistinguished
unmitigated
unperfumed
unprofessional 3
unsightly
unsophisticated 2
unvarnished
vernacular 2
–as plain as day
transparent 2
–as plain as the nose on one's face
transparent 2
–in plain sight
naked 3
–in plain view
naked 3
–in plain words
honestly 2
–plains
flat 14b
plainchant
chant 1
plain English
honestly 2
straight 14
unprofessional 3
plain-featured
ugly 1
plain-looking
ugly 1
plainly
above-board 1
apparently 1
clearly 1
definitely
evidently 1
expressly 1
far 3
flat 14b, 17b
freely 1
honestly 2
manifestly
naturally 3
obviously
openly 2
ostensibly
outright 4
point-blank 3
severely 6
shoulder 6
simply 2,3,4,5

plainly (*cont.*)
stark 1
straight 14
well[1] 7
plainness
severity 6
simplicity 2,3
plainsong
chant 1
plain-speaking
candid 1
outspoken
plain-spoken
bluff[2] 2
blunt 2
broad 5
candid 1
direct 10
downright 1
frank 1
honest 3
outspoken
transparent 3
plaint
grievance 2
plaintiff
litigant
party 5
supplicant 2
plaintive
pathetic 1
piteous
plain vanilla
bland 2
plait
braid 1,3
entwine
queue 2
splice 1
twist 1
weave 1
–plaits
hair 1
plan°
aim 2,3,5
arrange 2
arrangement 3,5
aspiration
block 4a
brew 2
card 13
chart 3
conceive 2
conception 3
contemplate 3
cut 16e
design 1,2,4,5
devise 1
dodge 4
draft 1,3
drawing
engineer 4
enterprise 1
eye 6
figure 11b
format 1,2
frame 3
game 3
idea 1
intend
intent 1
lay[1] 18a
line[1] 9
manoeuvre 1
mastermind 1
mean[1] 1
measure 6,7
meditate 2
method 1
mind 7
organization 2
outline 2,3
path 3
pattern 3,4
plot[1] 1,3,4
point 12
policy
procedure
programme 1,4
project 1,3
projection 3
proposal 2
propose 2
prospect 2

plan (*cont.*)
prospectus
provide 5
purpose 1,5
recipe 2
resolution 3
routine 1
scenario 1
schedule 1,2
schematic 2
scheme 1,3,4
script 4
stratagem
strategy
suggestion 1
system 2
tactic 1
thought 3
vision 3
work 19e
wrinkle[2]
–plans
arrangement 5
mind 7
preparation 1b
tactic 2
plane°
craft 4
even 1
flat 1
flight[1] 3
flush[2] 1
horizontal
level 1,12,14
plain 1
regular 5
sail 3
shave 2
side 2
slide 1
smooth 1,11
stratum 1
surface 1
planet
earth 1
globe 1
world 1
planetary
erratic 3
plank°
beam 1
board 1
platform 2
–planks
lumber 2
timber 2
planking
floor 1
planned
calculated 1,2
deliberate 1
intentional
measured 2
pitched
premeditated
prepared 1
purposeful
studied
systematic
voluntary 2
planner
brain 2
engineer 1
mastermind 2
tactician
planning
arrangement 5
forethought
preparation 3
projection 3
prudence 2
thought 3
–in the planning stage(s)
work 5
plan of action
procedure
plant°
facility 2a
factory
grow 3
lock[1] 6a
mill 2
raise 3

plant (*cont.*)
root[1] 6
set 1
sow
works 1
plantation
spread 13
planted
entrenched
planter°
planting(s)
shrubbery
plaque°
chip 2
memorial 2
scale[2] 2
tablet 2
plaquette
plaque 1
tablet 2
plash
gurgle 1
lap[1] 2
wallow 1
wash 3
plashing
gurgle 2
plaster°
smear 1
splash 2
spread 7
plaster down
slick 5
plastered
drunk 1
stinking 3
plastic°
artificial 1
disposable 1
elastic 1
explosive 2
fluid 3
mobile 3
pliable 1
shoddy
soft 1
synthetic
tawdry
tractable 2
yielding 1
plasticity
elasticity 1
plastique
explosive 2
plat
parcel 2
patch 2
plot[2]
site 1
plate°
cut 24,25
figure 5
plaque 1
platter
portion 3
scale[2] 1
sheet 3
silver 1
spread 7
stamp 6
tablet 2
wash 7
plateau°
plain 6
table 2
plateful
helping
plate glass
glass 3
plate-mark
hallmark 1
platform°
float 4
pedestal 1
rostrum
stage 2
stand 18
plating
plate 4
wash 15
platitude
cliché
phrase 2

platitude (*cont.*)
proverb
saw
truism
platitudinous
banal
platonic°
fraternal
platoon°
band[2] 1
cohort 1
corps
group 1
number 2
party 2
squad
platter°
plate 1,2
portion 3
record 7
plaudit
applause
–plaudits
applause
eulogy
kudos
ovation
praise 1
rave 3
plausibility
possibility 1
presumption 2
plausible°
likely 2
logical 2
possible 1
presumptive 1
probable
ready-made 2
reasonable 2
slick 2
smooth 6,8
specious
tenable
thinkable
plausibly
seemingly
play°
act 6
appear 2
bet 2
diversion 3
drama 1
enact 2
entertainment 1
fiddle 2
fool 6
freedom 4
frisk 1
frolic 1,3
gamble 1
game 1
give 18
lark 2
leeway
margin 3
mess 4a
monkey 5
pass 16b
pastime
perform 3
performance 2
piece 4
portray 2
pose 2
pretend 3
production 4
programme 2
put 6
recreation
render 4
script 2
service 10
show 9
sit 6a
slack 6
space 1
sport 1,4
take 26
tinker
tolerance 2
toy 3,4
trifle 3
use 2

plethora
excess 1
flood 3
flow 6
heap 2
ocean 2
pile[1] 3
profusion
sea 3
superfluity
surfeit

plexure
mesh 1

plexus
mesh 1
net[1] 1
network 2

pliability
flexibility 1

pliable°
accommodating 2
adaptable
elastic 1
flexible 1
limp[2] 1
passive 2
plastic 1
sheepish 1
soft 1
supple 1
tractable 2
yielding 1

pliancy
elasticity 1
flexibility 1

pliant
accommodating 1
adaptable
bend 5
dutiful
easy 4
flexible 1
fluid 3
obedient
open 11
plastic 1
pliable 1, 2
receptive 1
soft 1
submissive 1
supple 1, 2
tame 3
willowy 1
yielding 1

pliantness
flexibility 1

pliers
pincers

plight°
difficulty 3
dilemma
lot 2
mess 3
oath 1
pawn[1] 1
quandary
scrape 8
situation 2
strait 3

plighted
engaged 1

plinth
pedestal 1

plod°
tramp 1, 3
wade 4
walk 1

plodder
hack[2] 2

plodding
methodical
rustic 2
slow 1

plonk
set 1
stick[1] 2

plook
pimple

plooky
spotty 2

plop
flop 1
plump[2] 2

plop (*cont.*)
stick[1] 2

plot°
allotment 2
aspiration
cabal 1, 3
chart 3
conceive 2
conspiracy
design 4, 8
device 2
dodge 4
engineer 5
game 3
intrigue 2, 3
machination
manoeuvre 1, 3
parcel 2
patch 2
plan 3
reservation 4
scenario 1
scheme 1, 3, 4
site 1
story 5
stratagem
tactic 1
thread 2
tract[1]
wangle
wile
wrinkle[2]

plotted
put-up

plotter
designer 2
tactician

plotting
crafty
designing
devious 1
disingenuous
forethought
foxy 1
machination
scheming
serpentine 1
sly 1
wily

plough°
cultivate 1
furrow 2
till[1]
tramp 1
work 8

plough through
search 1
wade 4

plouk
pimple

plouky
spotty 2

plow
see plough

ploy
deceit 2
device 2
dodge 4
feint
game 3
gesture 2
gimmick 1
machination
manoeuvre 1
move 9
ruse
scheme 3
stratagem
subterfuge
tactic 1
trap 2
wile
wrinkle[2]

pluck°
bottle 2
bravery
courage
daring 1
extract 1
fight 9
fleece
fool 4
grit
gumption 2

pluck (*cont.*)
gut 3a
heart 2
jerk 1
manhood 2
nerve 1
perseverance
persevere
persistence
pick 2
pull 2, 3
snap 4
snatch 1
spirit 5
spunk
strength 2
swindle 1
uproot 2

plucky
bold 1
brave 1
courageous
daring 2
dauntless
fearless
gallant 1
game 7, 8
gritty 2
hardy 2
heroic 1
indomitable
intrepid
manly
persevere
stalwart 3
stout 2
venturesome 1

plug°
advertisement 1
fill 7
foul 15
get 34
jade 1
jam 2
nag[2]
peg 7
plod 2
promote 4
publicize
puff 3, 7
punch[1] 1, 2
push 6
recommend 2
seal 3
shoot 3
stop 3
stopper
stuff 9
talk 13
tap[2] 2
tout 1
wad 1

plugged
congested
foul 9

plugging
promotion 4

plugola
bribe 1
kickback
pay-off 3
rebate 2

plug-ugly
bruiser
hoodlum

plum°

plumb°
erect 1
fathom
flush[2] 4
line[1] 19a
perpendicular 1
probe 2
regular 5
slap 6
sound[3] 1
straight 2
upright 1
very 1

plume
preen 1
primp

plummet°
descend 2
dive 1
drop 6
fall 1
pitch[1] 3
plumb 1
plump[2] 1
plunge 1, 3
slump 2
submerge 2
taper 2

plummy
choice 4
desirable 3

plump°
buxom 1
chubby
dumpy
fat 1
flop 1
full 7
heavy 11
obese
rotund 3
set 1
stout 1
well-fed

plumpness
fat 5
fatness
obesity

plunder°
booty
depredation
fleece
gut 5
loot 1, 2
overrun
pilfer
pillage 1, 2, 3
prize[1] 4
raid 2
ransack 2
rape 2, 5
ravage 2
rifle 1
rob 1
robbery
spoil 6
strip[2] 5
waste 11

plunderer
thief 1

plundering
depredation
predatory 2
rape 2
robbery

plunge°
bury 3
descend 2
dig 2
dip 1, 4
dive 1, 2
drive 4
drop 6
duck 2
fall 1, 22
flounder
hurtle
immerse 1, 2
jab 1
lunge 2, 3
pitch[1] 3, 4
plough 2
plump[2] 1
sink 1, 8
slump 1, 2
sound[3] 2
stab 1
submerge 1, 2
thrust 2
toss 5
trip 5
venture 1, 3
wade 3b

plunger
piston

plunk
deposit 1
plump[2] 2, 4, 5
set 1
stick[1] 2

plus°

plush°
elegant 3
lush 3
luxurious 1
pile[2]
princely 2
soft 13
splendid 1
sumptuous
swanky
swish 3

plushy
soft 1

plutocrat
financier

ply°
fold 1
operate 2
work 15

p.m.
evening

PM
premier 1

pneu
telegram

pneuma
psyche
spirit 1

poach
pirate 3

poacher
thief 1

poaching
stealing

pock
mark 1

pocket°
bag 1
diminutive
earn 2
get 3
hole 1
lift 6
make 7
miniature
misappropriate 1
net[2] 4
portable
pouch
purse 1
receive 2
short 2
slight 3
small 1
take 3
tiny

-out of pocket
out 5
poor 1

pocketbook
purse 1
wallet

pocketful
wad 2

pocketing
theft

pocket money
allowance 3

pocket-sized
diminutive
portable
slight 3
small 1
tiny

pocket watch
watch 6

pock-mark
mark 1, 10
pit[1] 2, 5

-pock-marks
spot 5

pock-marked
pitted
spotty 2

pocky
spotty 2

pococurante
blasé 2
casual 3
indifferent 1
lackadaisical 2

pococurante (*cont.*)
listless
nonchalant
shiftless
slothful
torpid

pococuran t(e)ism
indifference 1
sloth
sluggishness
torpor

pod
hull 2

podginess
fat 5
fatness

podgy
chubby
fat 1
heavy 11
plump[1] 1
rotund 3
well-fed

podium
platform 1
rostrum
stage 2

poem°
lay[3]
piece 4
rhyme 1
writing 2

poesy
poetry

poet°
scribe 2

poetaster
poet

poetess
poet

poetic°
imaginative 2
rhetorical 1

poetical
imaginative 2
poetic 1

poetically
well[1] 3

poetry°
rhyme 1
writing 2

po-faced°
grave[2] 1

pogrom
holocaust 2
massacre 1
slaughter 2

poignancy
salt 2
spice 2
tang 1

poignant°
deep 6
emotional 3
expressive 3
heart-rending
keen[1] 3
moving 1
pathetic 1
piteous
pungent 3
sharp 8
smart 4
tender[1] 7
touching
trenchant

poikilothermal
cold-blooded 1

poikilothermic
cold-blooded 1

point°
aim 1
angle[1] 1
argument 2
brink 2
business 2
cape[1]
degree 2
design 7
detail 1
direct 2, 4

point (*cont.*)
dot 1
end 3
fact 3
fasten 2
gist
head 5, 10
idea 4
instant 1
issue 3
item 1
juncture 2
level 10
message 3
moment 2
moral 3
nub 2
page[1] 2
pith 1
place 1
prominence 2
purpose 1
quarter 3
question 3
reason 3
regard 8
respect 4
score 11
significance 1
stage 1
subject 1
substance 2, 3
theme 1
thesis 1
thing 2
thorn 1
time 3
tip[1] 1
topic
turn 9
use 12
usefulness
way 6
-at any point
ever 1
-at this point in time
present[1] 3
-beside the point°
at **point 15**
extraneous 2
inapplicable
irrelevant
peripheral 1
tangential
-in point of°
at **point 16**
-in point of fact
actually
fact 4
-off the point
extraneous 2
tangential
-on the point of
ready 4
verge[1] 2
-points
fact 3
-to a point
partially
-to the point°
at **point 18**
brief 2
direct 9
point-blank 1
relevant
terse 1
-to this point
far 8a
point-blank°
direct 9
slap 6
straight 6, 14
point by point
detail 4
pointed°
acute 1
epigrammatic
expressive 2
fine[1] 8
keen[1] 2
lively 2
meaningful 2
pointed (*cont.*)
poignant 2
pregnant 2
sharp 1
smart 4
special 3
trenchant
pointedly
deliberately
expressly 1
pointer°
clue 1
hand 5
hint 1
index 2, 3
indicator
point 11
tip[3] 2
pointing
aim 4
direction 1
point in time
moment 2
pointless°
aimless 1
bootless
crazy 3
fruitless
hollow 5
hopeless 4
idle 4
meaningless 2
non-productive 2
point 15
purposeless
senseless 3
silly 1
unprofitable 2
useless 1
vain 2
void 1
worthless 2
pointlessness
emptiness 2
madness 2
vanity 2
point of departure
base[1] 4
basis 2
point of view°
angle[1] 2
aspect 1
attitude 2
observation 2
outlook 1
phase 4
position 3
stance
stand 13
standpoint
thinking 2
view 2
point out°
at **point 21**
designate 1
finger 12
identify 1
indicate 1
mention 1
point the finger
accuse 1
blame 1
incriminate
pin 5
point the way
direct 2
point to°
at **point 19**
blame 1
find 2
finger 5c
indicate 1
refer 1
reflect 2
register 8
spell[3] 1
point up°
at **point 22**
emphasize
point 21b
spotlight 3
poise°
assurance 5
balance 2
confidence 2
cool 8
float 1
grace 1
hover 1
presence 3
proportion 5
repose 3
restraint 3
sang-froid
savoir faire
self-confidence
self-control 2
serenity 2
sophistication 1
poised°
collected
hang 1
level-headed
ready 9a
self-confident
serene 2
steady 6
poison°
booze 1
contaminate
corrupt 4
debase 2
doctor 4
drug 4
gall[1] 1
pollute 1
prejudice 3
ruin 9
sarcasm
spike 4
ulcer 2
venom 1, 2
virulence 2
poisoning
pollution
poisonous°
bad 2
deadly 1
destructive 1
evil 3
fatal 1
harmful
malignant 1
ruinous
sarcastic
sharp 5
venomous 1, 2
virulent 1, 2
poisonousness
sarcasm
venom 2
virulence 1, 2
poke°
bag 1
dab 3
delay 3
dig 2, 7
drag 4
gore[2]
jab 1, 3
lag 1
nudge 1, 2
pierce 1
pouch
probe 1, 2
prod 1, 4
pry 2
purse 1
root[2]
sack 1
stab 1
stick[1] 1, 3, 15
thrust 2, 4
poke about
probe 1
pry 2
poke along
delay 3
drag 4
lag 1
poke around
probe 1
pry 2
poke full of holes
disprove
explode 2
poke fun°
at **poke 4**
deride
fun 5
gibe 1
guy 2
laugh 2a
mock 1
parody 3
pull 15
ridicule 2
satirize
scoff[1]
scorn 4
taunt 1
poke into
pierce 1
probe 1
pry 2
poke one's nose
interfere 1
intervene 1
meddle
pry 2
snoop 1
poke out
project 5
protrude
stick[1] 15
poker-faced
empty 5
reserved
serious 1
pok(e)y
jail 1
prison
polar°
chill 4
cold 1
freezing
frigid 1
icy 1
pole°
bar 1
post[1] 1
rod 1
shaft 1
spar[1]
staff 1
stake[1] 1
standard 4
stick[2] 1
upright 3
polecat
stinker
polemic
argument 1
debatable
debate 1
dispute 3
polemical
controversial 2
debatable
police°
authority 4
guard 1
justice 2
patrol 3
policeman
constable
detective
officer 2
police officer
-policemen
police 1
police officer°
officer 2
-police officers
police 1
police station
nick 2
policewoman
constable
officer 2
police officer
-policewomen
police 1
policing
patrol 2
policy°
experiment 2
habit 1
line[1] 9
platform 2
procedure
rule 3
stand 13
strategy
polish°
brighten 2
charm 2
civilization 1
civilize 1
clean 9
edit 1
elaborate 4
elegance 1
finesse 3
finish 7, 11
fluency
glaze 1, 2
gloss[1] 1, 3
grace 1
grind 2
mature 6
perfect 9
refine 2
refinement 1
refurbish
rub 1
savoir faire
savoir vivre
scour 1
sheen
shine 2
smooth 11
sophistication 1
style 4
taste 4
polished°
adept 1
bright 3
civil 3
courteous
cultivated
decorous
educated 2
elegant 1
expert 2
fluent
genteel 3
glossy 1
graceful 2
ladylike
lustrous
mature 3
perfect 7
pleasant 2
professional 1
refined 1
shiny
silver 3
smooth 2
sophisticated 1
spotless 1
talented
tasteful
well-bred
polish off°
at **polish 3**
accomplish
dispatch 3
dispose 3d
eliminate 4
finish 3, 4
kill 1
murder 3
perform 1
rout 2
swill 3
zap
polish up°
at **polish 2**
polite°
accommodating 1
amicable
attentive 2
ceremonious 2
chivalrous
civil 3
cordial
courteous
debonair 1
decent 2
polite (*cont.*)
decorous
diplomatic
dutiful
fair[1] 8
gallant 2
genteel 2
graceful 2
gracious
ladylike
nice 1
obliging
orderly 2
pleasant 2
polished 2
presentable 2
proper 3
refined 1
respect 7
respectful
suave
tactful
tasteful
well-bred
politely
kindly 2
properly 1
politeness
breeding 2
chivalry
civility
courtesy
decorum 1
deference 1
elegance 1
etiquette
grace 2
manner 3
propriety 2
refinement 1
respect 2
tact
taste 6
polite society
society 4
politesse
breeding 2
civility
courtesy
elegance 1
etiquette
formality 3
manner 3
propriety 2
protocol 1
refinement 1
tact
taste 6
politic°
advisable
conscientious 3
diplomatic
expedient 1
judicious
prudent 1
seemly 2
sound[2] 4
tactful
tactical
wise 3
political°
political science
politics 1
politician°
politico
politician
politics°
polity
nation
poll°
canvass 1, 2, 4
election
plebiscite
register 1
sound[3] 1
pollex
thumb 1
pollinate
fertilize 1
pollutant
impurity 2

pollute°
adulterate
alloy 2
contaminate
corrupt 4
debase 2
desecrate
dirty 7
foul 12
poison 3
profane 4
soil[1] 2
sully
taint 2
polluted
bad 2
dirty 1
drunk 1
filthy 1
foul 2
impure 1
sordid 3
stagnant
polluting
pollution
pollution°
filth 1, 2
fume 3
impurity 1, 2
Pollyannaish
optimistic
poltergeist
ghost 1
poltroon
coward
milksop
polychromatic
variegated
polychrome
variegated
polyclinic
hospital
polymath
intellectual 4
polymorphic
protean
polymorphous
protean
polytechnic
technical 2
polytheist
heathen 1
pagan 1
polytheistic
heathen 3
pagan 2
pomace
pulp 2
pomade
lotion
ointment
pomatum
ointment
pommel
batter 1
beat 1
belabour
pelt[1] 1
rough 16
strike 1
pomp°
display 5
glory 3
grandeur 1
pageantry
parade 2
splendour 1
state 3
pomposity
arrogance
hot air
rant 3
raving 3
snobbery
pompous°
affected 3
arrogant 1
bloated
bombastic
condescending
disdainful
flowery
pompous (*cont.*)
genteel 1
glorified 1
grandiose 1
inflated 2
lofty 4
majestic 2
mannered
official 2
ornate
pedantic 1
ponderous 2
pretentious 1
regal 2
self-important
snobbish
standoffish
stiff 7
stilted
stuffy 2
supercilious
windy 2
pompously
big 9
pompousness
arrogance
snobbery
ponce
pander 3
poncey
effeminate
poncho
cloak 1
wrap 4
pond
pool 1
sea 1
ponder°
balance 1
brood 3
chew 4
consider 1
contemplate 2
debate 4
deliberate 4
digest 3
imagine 1
meditate 1, 2
mull
muse
puzzle 2
reflect 3
revolve 3
see 8
speculate 1
study 2
think 5a
turn 21a
weigh 2
wonder 3
ponderable
tangible
pondering
preoccupied 1
reflection 2
reflective
speculation 2
thought 1
thoughtful 2
ponderous°
gross 1
heavy 1, 7
hulking
laborious 4
leaden 1
massive
slow 1
stodgy
weighty 1
pong
reek 1, 3
smell 2, 4
stench
pongy
high 10
stinking 1
poniard
blade 2
dagger
pontifical
clerical 1
pompous 1
positive 5
pontificate
harangue 2
lecture 3
preach 2
rant 1
spout 2
pontoon
float 5
pony
nag[2]
trot 4
pony-tail
queue 2
poof(ter)
homosexual 1
Pooh Bah
master 1
mogul
pooh-pooh
belittle
deride
dismiss 2
laugh 2b
scorn 3
trivialize
pool°
combine 1
fund 1
kitty
lottery
merge
pooled
united 1
pooling
merger
poop
bolt 7
dope 3
fact 3
fag 1
gossip 2
information
intelligence 2
rumour 1
scoop 3
score 6
word 2
pooped
dead 9
exhausted 1
fatigued
jaded 1
prostrate 5
ragged 3
sleepy 1
spent 1
tired 1
washed out 2
weary 1
worn 3
poop sheet
promotion 5
poor°
bad 1
barren 2
base[2] 3, 5
broke
bum 4
cheap 3
deprived
destitute 1
disappointing
down and out 1
exhausted 3
feeble 2
flimsy 2
frugal 3
hard 17
heel[1] 3
hopeless 2
impoverished 1
indifferent 3
indigent
inferior 3
lame 2
lean[1] 2
lousy 2
low[1] 7, 9
mangy
meagre 1, 4
mean[2] 3
mediocre
miserable 3
needy
poor (*cont.*)
pale[1] 3
par 5a
pathetic 2
penurious 2
punk 2
ragged 6
remote 6
ropy 2
shabby 2
shoddy
short 8
sleazy 1
slender 2
small 4
sordid 4
stony 3
straitened
thin 2, 4
unfortunate 2
unhappy 3
unprofessional 2
unsatisfactory
upper 7
wanting 1
weak 4, 6
worthless 3
–in poor health
unsound 2
–in poor taste
tasteless 1
unhealthy 1
unseemly 1
poor as a church-mouse
poor 1
poor bastard, bugger, ***etc.***
wretch 2
poorhouse
home 3
–in the poorhouse
needy
–on the way to the poorhouse
needy
poorly°
ail 2
amiss 2
badly 1, 2, 3
frail 2
ill 1, 10, 12
indisposed 1
off colour 1
par 5b
queer 3
ropy 3
seedy 2
sick 2
weather 2
poorly made
tinny 1
poor mouth
disparage 2
poor white (trash)
peasant
pop°
father 1
pawn[1] 1
protrude
snap 2, 8
spring 4
pop by°
at pop 2
visit 1
pope's nose
tail 1
pop in°
at pop 2
drop 12
visit 1
popinjay
dude 1
pup
pop off
die 1
pop one's clogs
die 1
pop out°
at pop 2
poppet
fluff 2
poppycock
fiddlesticks
gab 2
gibberish
gobbledegook 1
mumbo-jumbo 1
nonsense 1
prattle 3
rot 4
rubbish 2
stuff 4
talk 18
trash 1
popsy
fluff 2
girl 1, 2
woman 3
populace°
folk
hoi polloi
mob 2
people 3
population
public 8
unwashed 2
popular°
big 7
current 2
demand 7
democratic
famous
favoured 1
general 1
hot 6
national 1
noted
orthodox
plebeian 2
public 1
regular 8
social 1
successful 3
vernacular 2
vulgar 3
popular ballot
plebiscite
popularity°
celebrity 1
laurels
name 2
prevalence 1
vogue 2
popularized
popular 3
popularly°
popular vote
plebiscite
populate°
inhabit
people 5
settle 6
populated
populous
populating
settlement 2
population°
folk
people 4
public 8
unwashed 2
populous°
overcrowded
pop up
return 2
surface 3
turn 25b
porcelain
pottery
porch
portico
porcine
epicurean 1
pore°
pore over
examine 1
inspect
observe 2
read 1
scan 2
watch 3
weigh 2
porn
pornography
porno
pornographic
pornographic°
base[2] 4
blue 2
broad 8
dirty 2
erotic 3
filthy 3
gross 3
immoral 2
indecent 2
lascivious 2
lewd
low[1] 3
nasty 3
naughty 3
obscene 1
outrageous 3
prurient 2
racy 2
rank[2] 3
rough 6
rude 3
sexy 2
suggestive 2
vulgar 2
wicked 3
pornography°
dirt 3
filth 3
porous°
port°
harbour 1
left 1, 3
portable°
light[2] 1
mobile 1
movable
radio 1
portend
announce 4
bode
foreshadow
mean[1] 3
predict
prognosticate 2
prophesy 2
spell[3] 1
threaten 3
portent
foreboding 2
forerunner 2
harbinger
indication 3
omen
sign 6
significance 1
threat 2
warning 2
portentous°
fateful 1
important 1
impressive
inauspicious
momentous
ominous 3
pressing
sinister 1
threatening
unpromising
weighty 2
porter°
carrier 1
portfolio
file 1
scrapbook
portico°
portière
drapery
portion°
allotment 1
bit 4
clip[2] 5
cut 20
dole 1
dose 1
draught 2
fragment 1
helping
interest 4
leg 3

portion *(cont.)*
lot 1,4
measure 5
nip[2]
parcel 2
part 1,2,7
passage 2
pat[1] 4
percentage
piece 1,2,3,11
plate 2
proportion 3
public 10
quota
ration 1
section 1,3
segment 1
share 1
slice 2
tract[1]
unit

portliness
fat 5
fatness
obesity

portly
dumpy
fat 1
heavy 11
large 1
obese
plump[1] 1
rotund 3
stout 1
well-fed

portmanteau
bag 2
neologism
suitcase

portrait°
description 1
image 1
likeness 2
picture 1
profile 2
representation 1

portray°
act 7
characterize
describe 3
draw 5
enact 2
express 1
label 5
paint 4
picture 7
play 4
pose 2
render 1
represent 3
show 8
tell[1] 4

portrayal
description 1
history 1
narration 1
narrative 1
performance 3
portrait
relation 4
rendering
representation 1
version 1

port side
left 3

pose°
affectation 2
form 2
masquerade 2,3
model 8
pass 16b
portray 2
posit
position 1
posture 1,4
pretence 2
represent 2
show 11

posed
mannered

Poseidon's domain
deep 9
sea 1

Poseidon's kingdom
deep 9
sea 1

poser
enigma
model 4
problem 2
puzzle 4
riddle[1]

poseur°

posh°
elegant 3
fancy 3
genteel 1
grand 1
luxurious 1
palatial
plush
princely 2
refined 1
soft 13
splendid 1
sumptuous
swanky
swell 7
swish 3
upper-class 2

poshness
splendour 1

posit°
conceive 3
moot 2
pose 3
premise 2
presume 1
suppose 2

position°
angle[1] 2
appointment 3
argument 2
arrange 1
aspect 1
assignment 2
attitude 1,2
base[1] 6
bearing 4
capacity 3
caste
chair 2
character 7
conviction 2
degree 1
dignity 2
draw 15c
engagement 4
estate 3
fix 8
footing 2
fortune 1
game 4
grade 1
idea 3
importance 2
install 1
job 1
lay[1] 1
level 14
locate 1
location 1
mean[3] 4c
mind 6,7
niche 2
nobility 2
occupation 1
office 4
opening 3
order 3
orientation 1
outlook 1
perch 1,2
perspective 1,2
pitch[1] 2
place 1,3,5,8,9,15
placement 1
plant 7
point 3
point of view 1
pose 1,4
post[2] 1,2
posture 1,2,3
precedence
presumption 3
profession 1
prominence 1

position *(cont.)*
purchase 5
put 1
rank[1] 1
rate[1] 4
reputation 1
rest[1] 8
role 2
run 19
scrape 8
seat 3
sentiment 2
set 1,11
side 3
site 1,2
situate
situation 1,3
slot 2,4
sphere 2
stage 1
stance
stand 2a,13
standing 5
standpoint
state 1
station 1,2,4
tenet
term 7b
terminal 4
vacancy 2
view 2,3
viewpoint
whereabouts
work 2

-in position
place 11b
ready 9a

positioning
installation 2
orientation 1
placement 1

position statement
editorial

positive°
absolute 4
assertive
categorical
certain 5
clear 10
confident 1
constructive 1
definite 2
demonstrable
dogmatic
emphatic
explicit 1
express 5
favourable 2
firm 4
flat 4
good 17
incontrovertible
indisputable
know 3
mind 12
optimistic
peremptory 3
photograph 1
print 2
promising
purposeful
self-confident
sure 1
tell[1] 17
unquestionable
upbeat

positively°
absolutely 1,3
certainty 3
clearly 2
course 6
definitely
doubtless 1
entirely 2
exactly 2
expressly 1
fairly 3
favourably 1,2
firm 4
flat 16
indeed 1
mean[3] 2a
once 3
perfectly 1

positively *(cont.)*
quite 4
really 2
surely 1
thoroughly 1
truly 3
well[1] 7

positiveness
certainty 2
conviction 3
trust 1

posologist
pharmacist

posolutely
doubtless 1

possess°
come 16b
command 5
enjoy 2
haunt 2
have 1,4
hold 12
obsess
partake 2b
possession 4
pre-empt
seize 3

possessed°
infatuated
possess 1,4
rage 4

possessing
obsessive

possession°
acquisition 2
clutch 2b
enjoyment 2
grasp 4
hand 8
occupation 2
possess 1
seizure 1
tenancy
tenure 1
thing 1
title 5

-be the possession of
belong 3

-possessions°
at **possession 3**
acquisition 2
asset 1
belongings
effects
estate 2
fortune 1
furniture 1
good 21a
paraphernalia
property 1
resource 2
stuff 2
substance 5
thing 8c

possession-oriented
materialistic

possessive°
hoggish
protective
selfish 2

possessor
owner

possibility°
alternative 2
candidate
chance 3
eventuality
lead 14
opportunity
potential 2
probability
prospect 3
thing 7

-possibilities°
at **possibility 2**
choice 2
field 3
prospect 3

possible°
card 12
earthly 4

possible *(cont.)*
feasible
potential 1
practicable
probable
prospect 4
specious
tenable
thinkable
viable

-it is possible that
perhaps

possibly°
chance 5b
maybe
perhaps
probably
seemingly

possie
position 6

POSSLQ
friend 3
girl 2
love 3
mistress 1
paramour

possy
see **possie**

post°
appointment 3
assignment 2
base[1] 4,6
book 4
capacity 3
direct 5
dispatch 2
engagement 4
forward 7
installation 3
mail 1,2
occupation 1
office 4
pale[2] 1
paper 5
picket 1
pier 2
pillar 1
place 5,15
position 6
profession 1
put 28d
quarter 6
role 2
send 2
service 6
settlement 1
shaft 1
situation 3
stake[1] 1
standard 4
station 1,4
stick[1] 17b
transmit 1
upright 3
vacancy 2
work 2

postage
carriage 3

postal card
card 4
line[1] 8
note 2

postal order
draft 2

postal service
post[3] 1

postcard
card 4
line[1] 8
missive
note 2

postdate
anachronism

postdating
anachronism

posted
aware 1
current 4
versed

poster°
advertisement 1
promotion 5

poster *(cont.)*
sign 5

posterior°
bottom 1
bum 1
buttocks
rear[1] 2
seat 4
tail 2

-posteriors
seat 4
tail 2

posterity°
descendant
progeny

postgraduate
graduate 1

post-haste°
fast[1] 6
flat 17a
hastily 1
once 6a
quickly 2

postilion
servant 1

post-mortem°
review 6

postpone°
call 11
defer[1]
delay 1
hinder 1
hold 18a, 21a
procrastinate 1
put 21a
reserve 1
shelve
stay[1] 4
string 11b
suspend 1
table 5
waive 2

-be postponed
fire 4
hang 10
wait 2

postponed
abeyance
off 9

postponement°
delay 4
moratorium
reprieve 2
respite 2
stay[1] 6
suspension 2
waiver

postponing
suspension 2

postscript
supplement 1

postulate
conceive 3
doctrine
guess 1,3
hypothesis
law 3
pose 3
posit
position 7
premise 1,2
presume 1
principle 1
propound
reasoning 2
speculate 1
suppose 2
supposition
theorem 1
thesis 1

postulated
given 2

postulation
presumption 2
speculation 1

posture°
act 3,8
attitude 1,2
bearing 1
camp[2] 2
carriage 2
pose 2,4
position 1

practised (*cont.*)
proficient
qualified 1
seasoned
skilful
versed
veteran 2
practising
practice 2
preparation 4
practitioner
operator 1
praepostor
monitor 1
pragmatic
empirical
expedient 1
hard 6
helpful
philosophical 2
positive 6
practical 1
rational 3
realistic 1
pragmatical
philosophical 2
positive 6
prairie
flat 14b
plain 6
-prairies
flat 14b
praise°
applaud 2
applause
bless 1
bouquet 3
celebrate 3
compliment 1,3
credit 4
eulogize
eulogy
exalt 2
extol
flatter 1
glorify 2
glory 2
hail[1] 2
honour 2,6
kudos
laud
mention 4
ovation
pat[1] 2,5
puff 3,7
rave 2,3
recommend 2
recommendation 2
tribute 1
worship 1,2
-praises
eulogize
laud
praised
immortal 3
praiseful
laudatory
praisefully
highly 3
praiseworthy°
deserving
estimable
exemplary 2
famous
laudable
meritorious
splendid 3
worthy 1
praising
celebration 2
prance°
camp[2] 2
caper 3
cavort
frisk 1
leap 2
skip 1,3
strut
swagger 1,3
walk 1
prang
collision
shell 4
prank°
caper 2
frolic 2
gag[2] 2
giggle 3
lark 1
put-on 1
trick 2
-pranks
fun 2
nonsense 2
prankish
arch 3
devilish
sportive
prankster
card 11
joker 1
prat
bottom 1
buttocks
prate
chatter 1,3
drivel 2
gab 1
jabber 1
palaver 4
patter[2] 2,3
prattle 1,2
rattle 6
talk 3
tattle 2
twitter 2
waffle 1
yap 2
prating
palaver 2
prattle 2
prattle°
babble 1,3
chatter 1,3
drivel 2
gab 1,2
gibberish
gossip 1
gush 2
jabber 1
jargon 2
palaver 2,4
patter[2] 2,3
rattle 6
talk 3,18
tattle 2
twitter 2
waffle 1,3
yap 2
prattling
palaver 2
talk 18
praxis
habit 1
practice 1
tradition
pray°
appeal 1
ask 3
beg 1
bid 2
finger 3
plead 1
pull 10
solicit 1
sue 2
prayer°
appeal 3
blessing 1
devotion 1
grace 5
litany 1
suit 5
supplication 1
praying
prayer 2
supplicant 1
preach°
harangue 2
hold 16a
lecture 3
rant 1
preacher°
clergyman 3
minister 1
missionary
priest
preaching
sermon 1
preachy
pedantic 1
preamble°
foreword
preface 1
preliminary 3
prearrange
arrange 2
fix 12
programme 4
prearranged
cut 29a
deliberate 1
fixed 3,4
inside 5
predetermined 1
prepared 1
put-up
set 29
prearrangement
fix 18
provision 3
set-up 2
prebend(ary)
clergyman 1
precarious°
awkward 4
dangerous 1
delicate 4
desperate 5
explosive 1
hairy 2
hazardous
hot 10
insecure 3
nice 4
parlous
rickety
risky
serious 4
shaky 1,2
slight 4
ticklish 2
tight 7
touchy 2
precariously
dangerously 1
precaution°
foresight 1
providence 1
prudence 2
precautional
noncommittal
precautionary
noncommittal
preventive 2
precautious
noncommittal
precede°
announce 4
head 12
lead 4,10a
preface 2
precedence°
predominance
preliminary 2
priority
precedency
precedence
priority
precedent°
foregoing
instance 1
lead 13
prototype 1
precedent-setting
avant-garde
landmark 3
seminal 1
way-out 2
preceding°
before 6,8
foregoing
former 1
late 3
old 6
preliminary 1
preparatory 3
previous 1,2,4
prior 2
precept°
charge 5
doctrine
lesson 3
moral 3
motto
principle 1
rule 1
standard 1
tenet
thesis 1
preceptor
instructor
précieux
priggish
precinct°
area 3
district
limit 3
neighbourhood 1
region 1
territory 1
ward 1
zone
-precincts°
at **precinct 1**
limit 3
milieu
neighbourhood 1
vicinity
precious°
beloved 1
darling 3
dear 1,3
expensive
exquisite 5
inestimable 1
invaluable
mincing
old 8
pet[1] 3
priceless 1
priggish
prissy
rich 3,4
sweet 5,7
twee
precious stone
gem 1
-precious stones
jewellery
precipice°
bluff[2] 3
cliff
crag
precipitancy
haste 2
precipitate°
abrupt 1
brash 1
cause 6
deposit 4
dregs 1
hasty 2
hotheaded
hurried 1
impetuous
impulsive
pell-mell 2
quick 2
rapid
rash[1]
sediment
settle 11
sink 6
sludge
snap 13
spark 2
speedy 2
sudden
precipitately
hastily 1
pell-mell 1
sharply 2
summarily 2
swiftly
precipitateness
speed 1
precipitation°
rain 1,2
precipitous°
abrupt 2
sharp 2
sheer 1
precipitous (*cont.*)
speedy 2
steep[1] 1
whirlwind 2
precipitously
sharply 2
precipitousness
speed 1
précis°
abridgement 3
abstract 3
brief 4
digest 5
epitome 2
outline 2
programme 1
résumé 1
run-down 3
scenario 2
summary 1
synopsis
table 3
telescope 2
precise°
accurate 1
careful 2
circumstantial 3
close 14
correct 8
dead 17
deadly 6
definite 1
definitive 3
delicate 6
detailed 1
determined 2
distinct 1
elaborate 1
even 8
exact 1
explicit 1
express 5
factual 2
faithful 2
fine[1] 9
flat 9
formal 3
graphic 1
literal 1
mathematical
measured 4
meticulous
nail 5
narrow 3
neat 3
nice 3
particular 1,3
perfect 5
perfectionist 2
photographic 1
precious 3
proper 2
refined 2,3
religious 2
right 2
rigid 3
round 5
scientific
scrupulous 1
special 1
specific 1
square 3
strict 1
true 3
verbatim 1
very 3
precisely°
completely 1
dead 20
directly 4
dot 2
due 5
exactly 1,2
flat 16
full 14
just 5
letter 4
literally 1
nearly 2
outright 4
particular 6
pat[2] 1
perfectly 3
plumb 4
precisely (*cont.*)
purpose 4b
right 14,17
sharp 10
slap 6
verbatim 2
world 6
preciseness
accuracy
precision 1
rigour 2
precisian
perfectionist 1
prig
purist
precisianism
prudery
precision°
accuracy
definition 1
formality 2
resolution 5
rigour 2
precisionist
perfectionist 1
prig
preclude°
anticipate 1
exclude 2
forbid
forestall
hinder 2
obstruct 3
oppose 2
prevent
prohibit 2
resist 1
rule 8
save 4
suppress 1
veto 1
precluding
short 10
suppression
preclusion
exclusion 2
prevention
suppression
veto 2
preclusive
peremptory 2
precocious°
bright 6
forward 3
precocity
brilliance 2
precognition
anticipation 2
preconceived°
deliberate 1
intentional
jaundiced 1
preconception
prejudice 1
premeditated
put-up
preconception°
prejudice 1
presumption 2
preconcerted
put-up
precondition°
prerequisite 2
requirement 1
precooked
instant 5
prepared 4
precursor°
ancestor
forerunner 1
harbinger
pioneer 1
progenitor 2
stock 3
predacious
predatory 1
rapacious
voracious 1
predaciousness
rapacity
predate
precede

predatory°
ferocious
mercenary 1
rapacious
predecessor°
forerunner 1
pioneer 1
predecessor 1
progenitor 2
-predecessors
root[1] 4
predestination°
predestine
destine 1
predestined
bound[3] 4
certain 3
destined 1
doomed 1
eventual 2
fatal 3
fated 1
necessary 3
unavoidable
predetermination
preconception
predetermine
arrange 2
destine 1
fix 12
predetermined°
certain 1
cut 29a
destined 1
determined 2
fatal 3
fated 1
foregone
limited 1
measured 4
necessary 3
preconceived
set 29
specific 1
unavoidable
predicament°
bind 5
complication 2
difficulty 2, 3
dilemma
embarrassment 2
emergency
fix 17
hole 5
jam 6
mess 3
pass 26
perplexity 3
pinch 8
plight
problem 1
quandary
scrape 8
situation 2
snarl[2] 3
spot 4
strait 3
trouble 9a
predicate
pose 3
posit
premise 2
predicated
presumptive 2
predication
position 7
predict°
anticipate 2
divine 4
envisage 2
envision
forecast 1
foresee
foreshadow
prognosticate 1
project 6
prophesy 1
say 8
tell[1] 9
predictability
chance 3
regularity 1
predictable°
consistent 2
regular 1
reliable
square 6
usual
predicted
presumptive 2
prediction°
advisory 2
calculation 3
foreboding 2
forecast 2
oracle 2
prognosis
projection 4
prophecy 1, 2
tip[3] 2
predictive
ominous 3
prophetic
predilection
appetite 1
aptitude 2
bias 1
fancy 7
inclination 3, 4
leaning
like[2] 3
liking 1
love 2
partiality 1
passion 3
penchant
preference 2
prejudice 1
talent 2
tendency
thing 4
weakness 4
predispose
bias 4
incline 2
predisposed
capable 2
disposed
fond 3
incline 3
inclined 1
interested 2
open 18
partial 3
preconceived
prejudiced 1
prepared 3
prompt 2
prone 2
susceptible 1
predisposition
bent 5
bias 1
favour 4
favouritism
habit 2
inclination 3
instinct
liking 1
partiality 1
penchant
preconception
preference 2
prejudice 1
talent 2
tendency
weakness 4
wish 5
predominance°
preponderance 2
prestige
prevalence 1, 2
priority
superiority 1
predominancy
predominance
predominant°
dominant 2
influential
main 1
mighty 1
overriding
paramount
popular 2
prevailing 1
prevalent
predominant *(cont.)*
primary 1
prime 2
principal 1
rampant 2
sovereign 2
uppermost 2
predominantly
chiefly
especially 2
generally 1
mainly
primarily 1
principally
usually
whole 5
predominate°
dominate 2
loom 3
prevail 1, 2
reign 3
rule 5
predominately
primarily 1
predominating
main 1
overriding
popular 2
predominant
pre-eminence°
distinction 2
domination 1
dominion 1
emphasis
excellence
fame
importance 2
lead 12
name 2
perfection 1
precedence
predominance
prestige
priority
prominence 1
sovereignty
status 1
superiority 1
supremacy 1
pre-eminent°
arch 1
best 1, 3
capital 5
cardinal
central 2
choice 4
distinguished 1
divine 2
dominant 2
elevated 2
eminent 1
excel
famous
first 1
foremost 1
grand 2
head 9
leading 2
lofty 2
main 1
major 2
noble 3
notable 2
paramount
peerless
perfect 2
predominant
premier 2
prestigious
primary 1
prime 2
principal 1
prominent 2
shine 3
singular 2
sovereign 2
splendid 3
star 3
successful 3
supreme 3
top 8
transcendent
uppermost 2
well-known 2
pre-eminently°
chiefly
large 4
primarily 1
pre-empt°
beat 2
pre-empted
assumed 1
preen°
groom 3
primp
pre-established
foregone
predetermined 1
prefabricated
ready-made 1
preface°
foreword
preamble
preliminary 3
prefatory°
introductory 1
preliminary 1
preparatory 1
prefect
monitor 1
prefer°
choose
fancy 11
favour 6
feel 9
go 28c
have 11
lay[1] 7
lean[2] 3
like[2] 2
please 2
rather 3
select 1
side 10
yearn
preferable
right 3
select 2
preferably
better[1] 5
instead 2
rather 2
prefer charges
sue 1
preference°
appetite 1
choice 1
discretion 2
fancy 7
favour 3
favourite 1
favouritism
inclination 3
leaning
like[2] 3
liking 1, 2
love 2
partiality 1, 2
patronage 4
penchant
pick 9
pleasure 2
precedence
priority
relish 1
selection 1
taste 3
vogue 2
volition
vote 4
weakness 4
wish 5
-in preference to
before 7
instead 2
preferential°
inside 4
preferment
favouritism
promotion 2
preferred
choice 4
favoured 1
favourite 1, 2
inside 4
pet[1] 3
right 3
preferred *(cont.)*
select 2
superior 2
prefix
preface 2
preggers
expecting
pregnant 1
pregnancy
maternity 1
pregnant°
conceive 1
eloquent 2
expecting
expressive 3
meaningful 2
significant 2
trouble 9b
prehistoric°
ancient 2
early 6
old 2
primitive 1
prejudged
preconceived
prejudgement
preconception
prejudice 1
prejudice°
bent 5
bias 1, 4
bigotry
disadvantage 2
discriminate 2
discrimination 1
fanaticism 2
favour 3
favouritism
incline 2
inequality 2
injustice 1
intolerance
leaning
partiality 1
preconception
preference 2
slant 2
prejudiced°
biased
bigoted
incline 3
interested 2
intolerant 2
jaundiced 1
loaded 3
narrow-minded
near-sighted 2
one-sided 1
opinionated 2
parochial
partial 2
partisan 3
preconceived
preferential
sectarian 2
subjective 1
ultra-
prejudicial°
detrimental
hurtful 1
interested 2
loaded 3
sectarian 2
prelate
divine 5
prelatic
clerical 1
preliminary°
foregoing
introductory 1
prefatory
preparatory 1
-preliminaries
preliminary 3
prelims°
preliminary 3
prelude
foreword
preliminary 2
premature°
early 4
immature 1
previous 3
premature *(cont.)*
undeveloped
prematurely°
early 1
time 10
premeditated°
calculated 2
cool 3
deliberate 1
intentional
measured 2
studied
voluntary 2
wilful 1
premeditation
forethought
premier°
chief 2
first 1
head 9
lead 18
principal 6
premier danseur
lead 16
principal 6
première°
come 15b
début 1
première danseuse
heroine
lead 16
principal 6
premise°
hypothesis
presumption 2
thesis 1
-premises
accommodation 4
reasoning 2
premised
given 2
premiss
hypothesis
premise 1
presumption 2
thesis 1
premium°
bounty 3
extra 3
gift 1
inducement
price 3
prize[1] 1
treat 6
-at a premium°
***at* premium 4**
scarce
premonish
warn 1
premonition°
feeling 2
foreboding 2
forerunner 2
hunch 1
intuition
misgiving
omen
premonitory
ominous 3
preliminary 1
preoccupation
fixation
foible
life 8
mania 1
obsession
thing 4
preoccupied°
absent-minded
absorbed
deep 4
engaged 2
forgetful
full 6
pensive
wistful 2
preoccupy
consume 5
engage 2
obsess
occupy 3

preoccupy *(cont.)*
possess 3
preordain
destine 1
preordained
eventual 2
fatal 3
fated 1
given 1
pre-owned
used 1
prep
preparation 2
preparation°
groundwork
instruction 2
orientation 2
practice 2
preliminary 2
prescription 2
production 1
providence 1
provision 3
prudence 2
scholarship 1
schooling
tuition
wash 13
-in preparation for
preparatory 3
-preparations°
at **preparation 1**
arrangement 5
groundwork
preparative
preparatory 1
preparatory°
introductory 1
prefatory
preliminary 1
prepare°
anticipate 3
arrange 2
brace 6
break 18b
brew 2
coach 3
condition 5
cut 10,16e
draw 6,15b
edit 4
educate
get 51d
groom 4
ground 6
have 6
instruct 1
lead 10a
line[1] 23a
make 15,17
mobilize
mount 5
poise 3
practise 1
prime 5
process 3
project 3
provide 5
qualify 1
ready 10
school 4
script 3
set 8,23a
smooth 10
train 4
tutor 2
verge 1,2
whip 7b
work 20b
prepared°
bargain 4
calculated 1
competent 2
experienced 1
fit[1] 2
game 7
instant 5
order 10a
poised 2
provident 1
qualified 1
qualify 2
ready 1
prepared *(cont.)*
ripe 2,3b
seasoned
set 31
watch 4
preparedness°
prudence 2
prepare the way
lead 10a
pave 2
preparing
preparation 1a,2,4
prepay
advance 6
prepayment
advance 9
preplanned
predetermined 1
premeditated
preponderance°
balance 5
majority 1
mass 4
predominance
weight 4
preponderancy
weight 4
preponderant
overriding
predominant
preponderate
outweigh
predominate
prevail 2
prepositional phrase
phrase 1
prepositor
monitor 1
prepossessing°
seductive
taking
tempting 1
winning 1
prepossession
favouritism
obsession
preconception
preposterous°
absurd 1
crazy 2
exorbitant
extravagant 2
fantastic 3
farcical
far-fetched
foolish 3
grotesque 2
immoderate
impossible 2
inane
incredible 1
inordinate 1
ludicrous
meaningless 1
nonsensical
outrageous 1
pointless
question 7
quixotic
rich 11
ridiculous
silly 1
tall 3
unbelievable
unreasonable 1
unthinkable 2
whimsical 1
wild 7
preposterousness
extravagance 2
folly 1
madness 2
prepping
preparation 2
prepubescence
youth 1
prepubescent
young 1
prerequisite°
condition 2
necessity 1
need 3
precondition
provision 2
qualification 2
requirement 1
stipulation
want 4
-prerequisites
string 7
prerogative°
authority 1
faculty 4
jurisdiction
liberty 2
power 6
precedence
priority
privilege
right 9
presage
announce 4
bode
foreboding 2
forecast 1
foresee
foreshadow
mean[1] 3
omen
predict
prognosticate 1
prophesy 2
spell[3] 1
threat 2
threaten 3
presbyopic
far-sighted 2
presbyter
clergyman 1
prescience
foresight 2
sensation 1
prescient
far-sighted 1
prophetic
prescribe°
appoint 1
assign 2
command 1
decree 2
dictate 1
dose 2
treat 3
prescribed
formal 1
incumbent 1
regulation 4
ritual 2
prescription°
cure 1
decree 1
formula
medicine
precept 1
recipe 1
remedy 1
prescriptive°
presence°
appearance 1
attendance 1
bearing 1
carriage 2
class 3
company 1
existence 1
figure 6
-in the presence of
before 5
presence of mind°
at **presence 5**
logic 2
poise 2
prudence 1
present°
actual 2
attend 1
available
award 1
bestow
present *(cont.)*
boon
bounty 2
bring 9b
carry 8
come 19a
communicate 1
confer 2
contribute 1
current 1
deliver 4
demonstrate 2
display 2
donate
donation 1
endowment 1
enter 6
enunciate 1
exhibit
exist 3
expose 1
extend 4
feature 4
gift 1
give 1,6,7
going 2
grant 1,3
hand 9,14
hold 20b,22d
immediate 3
introduce 1,2,3
lay[1] 6
lead 10b
make 18,37e
mount 5
nominate
offer 2,4
offering
open 23,25
perform 3
pose 3
prefer 2
produce 4
profess 1
project 3
promote 3
propose 1
provide 2
purse 3
put 5,18a,18b,22d
radio 2
raise 8
read 3
recite 1
relate 2
release 2
render 3,7
represent 2
serve 3
set 7,9,18c
show 1,9
sign 11
stage 4
submit 2
suggest 1
supply 1
table 4
tender[2] 1
tip[3] 1
treat 6
voice 4
whip 6
-at present
now 1
presently
-for the present
present[1] 3
time 16
-in the present circumstances
now 2
-in the present climate
now 2
-presents
largesse
-to the present
far 8a
yet 1
presentable°
decent 2
passable 1
plausible 1
respectable 3
presentation°
attraction 2
award 3
delivery 4
demonstration 2
diction 2
display 4
endowment 2
entertainment 2
exhibition
exposition 1
manifestation
message 2
offer 6
opening 4
pageant
performance 3
production 3
programme 2
projection 2
promotion 3
proposal 1
recital 1
rendering
representation 3
show 13,14
spectacle 1
talk 14
tender[2] 2
-on presentation
demand 8
present-day
contemporary 2
current 2
modern
present[1] 1
presenter
announcer
host[1] 2
presentiment
anticipation 2
feeling 2
foreboding 2
hunch 1
intuition
premonition
sensation 1
presenting
presentation 1
projection 2
presently°
directly 3
present[1] 3
shortly 1
soon 1
preservation°
conservation
maintenance 1
protection 1
upkeep 1
preservationist
environmentalist
green 5
preservative
protective
preserve°
cherish 2
conserve 1,2
cure 3
defend 1
husband 2
insulate 1
keep 1,3,4,11
lay[1] 19a
maintain 1,2
nurse 2,4
park 1
perpetuate
protect 2
put 28c
reservation 4
reserve 1
retain 1,3
salt 7
sanctuary 3
save 2,3
secure 7
spread 12
store 2
sustain 1
uphold
-preserves°
at **preserve 4**
preserver
guardian
pre-set
predetermined 1
preside°
chair 4
hold 10
lead 3
manage 1
moderate 6
officiate
rule 6
presidency
helm 2
president
boss 1
director 1
executive 1
head 2
moderator
premier 1
principal 3
presiding officer
chair 3
moderator
press°
agitate 2
besiege 3
bid 2
crowd 1,3,4
crush 3,6
depress 3
drive 1
dun
enforce 2
express 4
flatten 1
force 7
have 9
herd 1
huddle 3
hurry 2
hustle 2
induce 1
jam 1,5
lie[2] 4
lobby 3
make 2
mob 1
oppress 1
pack 5
persuade 1
pin 4a
pinch 1
precipitate 1
pressure 3,5
purse 4
push 1,2,4,11
require 1
rise 16
screw 4
smooth 9
spur 4
squeeze 1,4,9,11
stuff 6
throng 1,2
thrust 1,3
touch 3
trample 1
urge 1,2
work 18
press card
card 6
pressed
possessed
pressing°
desperate 4
grave[2] 2
immediate 3
imperative 1
instant 4
pivotal
pressure 2,4
serious 2
sore 3
urgent 1
press into service
use 1
pressman
correspondent
journalist
reporter

press on
proceed 1
progress 5
push 10
thrust 3
press release
release 4
press suit with
pursue 4
pressure°
besiege 3
burden 1
crush 6
drive 1
duress 1
enforce 2
force 1, 2, 7
influence 1, 3
lean[2] 4b
load 1
lobby 3
make 2
oppress 1
pin 4a
press 1, 6, 9
propulsion
railroad 2
screw 4
sorrow 2
spur 1, 4
squeeze 8, 11
strain[1] 7
stress 1, 3, 5
tax 2, 4
tension 1
twist 6
urge 5
urgency
weight 2
work 18
pressure group
faction 1
lobby 2
pressurize
besiege 3
drive 1
enforce 2
force 7
influence 3
lean[2] 4b
lobby 3
make 2
oppress 1
pin 4a
press 1
pressure 5
railroad 2
screw 4
spur 4
squeeze 11
stress 5
tax 4
twist 6
work 18
presswoman
correspondent
reporter
prestidigitation
hocus-pocus 3
magic 2
prestige°
cachet 2
celebrity 1
class 3
distinction 2
glory 1
honour 2
importance 2
mark 8
name 2
nobility 1
note 8
prominence 1
pull 21
rank[1] 3
renown
superiority 2
prestigious°
exalted 1
honourable 4
influential
noble 3
prominent 2

presto
fast[1] 6
presumable
circumstantial 1
specious
presumably°
doubtless 2
probably
supposedly
presume°
assume 3
deduce
divine 4
expect 2
fancy 10
figure 9
imagine 2
imply 2
pretend 2
read 4
reckon 3
suppose 1
surmise 1
presumed
alleged
assumed 3
circumstantial 1
hypothetical
presumptive 2
probable
reputed
specious
supposed 1
presuming
familiar 3
presumptuous
presumption°
arrogance
assurance 4
effrontery
expectation 2
face 5
familiarity 3
freedom 7
impertinence
impudence
inference
liberty 5
nerve 2
preconception
probability
supposition
surmise 2
presumptive°
circumstantial 1
presumptuous°
arrogant 1
audacious 2
bold 2
brash 2
cool 6
familiar 3
forward 2
fresh 8
haughty
immodest 2
impertinent
impudent
insolent
intrusive
liberty 5
obtrusive
pert 1
presume 2
pushy
self-important
presumptuousness
arrogance
effrontery
familiarity 3
freedom 7
impertinence
impudence
liberty 5
mouth 4
nerve 2
presumption 1
snobbery
presuppose°
assume 3
involve 2
premise 2
presume 1

presuppose *(cont.)*
suppose 1
presupposed
assumed 3
given 2
presupposition°
preconception
premise 1
presumption 2
pre-tax
gross 2
pretence°
act 3
affectation 2
air 5
blind 8
camouflage 1
cant 1
cover 15
deceit 2
deception 2
delusion 1
disguise 4
dissimulation
excuse 6
face 3
fantasy 3
feint
guise 2
hocus-pocus 1
mask 2
outside 2
pose 5
pretension 1, 2
pretext 1, 2
put-on 1
ruse
semblance 2
sham 1
veneer
-pretences
pretension 1
pretend°
act 8
affect[2] 1
assume 4
believe 3
bluff[1] 2
counterfeit 2, 5
dissimulate
fake 2
fool 5
game 6
glorified 2
let[1] 7b
make 25, 28, 37e
masquerade 3
mimic 5
mock 3
overlook 2
pass 16b
play 10
pose 2
pretended
profess 2
put 22b
represent 2, 3
unreal 3
pretended°
affected 2
artificial 3
assumed 2
counterfeit 2
glossy 2
mimic 5
nominal 1
outward
phoney 1
pious 2
professed 1
quasi- 2
seeming
so-called 2
spurious
unreal 3
pretender°
fake 4
fraud 3
hypocrite
impostor
Pharisee
phoney 3
poseur
quack 1

pretender *(cont.)*
upstart
pretending
hypocritical
pretence 1
pretension 2
pretension°
affectation 2
air 5
arrogance
cant 1
ostentation
pretence 1, 3
show 15
side 5
snobbery
-pretensions°
at **pretension 1**
pretentious°
affected 3
bombast
dashing 3
exalted 2
flashy 1
genteel 1
glorified 1
grand 3
grandiose 1
haughty
inflated 2
mannered
mincing
ornate
ostentatious
overbearing
pedantic 1
Pharisaic
pompous 1
precious 3
rhetorical 3
showy
snobbish
stilted
supercilious
pretentiously
big 9
well[1] 4
pretentiousness
affectation 1
arrogance
bombast
bravado
hot air
ostentation
pretence 1
pretension 2
show 15
side 5
snobbery
preterhuman
supernatural
pretermission
disregard 3
pretermit
disregard 1
preternatural
ghostly 1
miraculous
mystical 1
occult 2
psychic 2
supernatural
unearthly 1
unnatural 5
weird
preternaturalism
mystique
pretext°
blind 8
excuse 6
front 5
loophole
plea 3
pretence 1, 2, 3
pretension 2
reason 1
refuge 2
ruse
stall[2] 2
prettify
preen 2
primp

prettiness
charm 3
pretty°
attractive
beautiful 1
bonny
comely
cute 1
fair[1] 7
fairly 1
fine[1] 10
lovely 1
moderately
picturesque 1
rather 1
scenic
silver 4
somewhat
sweet 4
pretty good
fair[1] 4
OK 3
tolerable 2
pretty kettle of fish
strait 3
pretty much
largely
pretty penny
packet 2
prevail°
abound 1
conquer 3
defeat 1
endure 1
exist 1, 3
obtain 3
outweigh
overcome 1
overpower 1
predominate
reign 3
rule 5
stand 4
stem[2] 2
surpass
triumph 3
win 1
prevailing°
current 2
dominant 2
epidemic 1
general 1
going 2
orthodox
overriding
popular 2
predominant
prevalent
principal 1
standard 6
staple 2
universal 1
prevail (up)on°
at **prevail 3**
argue 6
chat 3
entice
get 14
induce 1
interest 8
make 2
persuade 1
pressure 5
prompt 3
reason 8
urge 3
win 3
work 18
prevalence°
incidence
vogue 2
prevalency
prevalence 1
prevalent°
about 5
common 1
current 2
epidemic 1
general 1
going 2
obtain 3
orthodox
pervasive

prevalent *(cont.)*
popular 2
predominant
prevail 2
prevailing 1
rampant 2
reign 3
standard 6
universal 1
prevalently
popularly
prevaricate
equivocate
fence 4
fib 2
lie[1] 1
pussyfoot 2
shuffle 3
stall[2] 1
waffle 2
prevarication
dodge 4
evasion 2
fabrication 3
falsehood
fib 1
flannel 1
invention 3
libel 2
lie[1] 2
lying 1
myth 2
perjury
romance 5
shuffle 5
song 3b
prevaricator
liar
prevent°
anticipate 1
arrest 1
bar 9
block 3
deter
discourage 3
embargo 2
forbid
forestall
frustrate 1
hamper[1]
head 13b
hinder 2
inhibit
keep 13
militate 1
obstruct 1, 3
oppose 2
preclude
prohibit 2
resist 1
save 4
stanch
stay[1] 4
stifle 2
stop 2
suppress 1
turn 7
veto 1
preventative
preventive 1, 2, 3, 4
preventing
prevention
preventive 1
suppression
prevention°
hindrance 2
preventive 4
stay[1] 6
suppression
veto 2
preventive°
preventive measure
precaution 1
preview°
reception 2
previous°
before 6, 8
foregoing
former 1
late 3
old 6
past 2
preceding

previous (*cont.*)
prior 1, 2
previously°
before 1, 8
formerly
late 5
once 1
previous 4
prior 2
time 12a
prevision
foresight 2
prex
boss 1
prexy
boss 1
prey°
butt[1]
game 5
kill 8
quarry[1]
preying
predatory 1
prey on°
at **prey 3**
haunt 2
plunder 2
rob 2
victimize 1
weigh 4
price°
charge 2
cost 1
damage 2
expenditure
expense 1
fare 2
fee 1
hire 5
penalty
quotation 2
ransom 2
rate[1] 2
subscription 1
-without price
price 4
priceless°
expensive
inestimable 1
invaluable
precious 1
rich 3, 4
price-list
tariff 2
price tag
tag 1
pricey°
dear 2
precious 1
prick°
bore[1] 2
incite
kindle
lance 2
pink[2]
prickle 4
puncture 3
signal 2
stab 1
stick[1] 1
sting 1
twinge 1
pricking
compunction 1
incitement 1
prickle 2
prickly 2
prickle°
bristle 1, 2
itch 1, 3
prick 2, 4
smart 7
spine 2
thorn 1
prickliness
prickle 2
prickling
itch 3
prickly 2
prickly°
coarse 1
edge 5
irritable

prickly (*cont.*)
scratchy 1
snappish 1
sore 2
thorny 1, 2
ticklish 3
prick-teaser
flirt 3
prick up one's ears
listen 1
pricy
see **pricey**
pride°
arrogance
conceit 1
dignity 3
glory 5
presumption 1
self-respect
treasure 2
vanity 1
pride and joy
pride 3
treasure 2
prideful
cocky
conceited
disdainful
presumptuous
proud 2
priest°
celebrant
clergyman 1
divine 5
father 4
minister 1
pastor
priestess
priest
priesthood
cloth 2
ministry 1
priestly°
clerical 1
sacred 3
spiritual 1
prig°
prude
steal 1
priggish°
goody-goody
prudish
self-righteous
strait-laced
stuffy 2
priggishness
prudery
prim
formal 3
frigid 2
goody-goody
impersonal 2
po-faced
precise 2
priggish
prissy
prudish
puritan 2
reserved
sedate 2
staid
stiff 8
strait-laced
stuffy 2
prima ballerina
heroine
lead 16
principal 6
primacy
dominion 1
lead 12
nobility 1
precedence
preponderance 2
prestige
prevalence 2
priority
sovereignty
superiority 1
supremacy 1

prima donna
heroine
lead 16
principal 6
queen 2
star 2
vocalist
primaeval
see **primeval**
primal
elemental
prehistoric 1
primitive 1
pristine 1
rudimentary 1
primarily°
above 6
chiefly
especially 2
foremost 2
mainly
pre-eminently
principally
primary°
arch 1
basic
capital 5
cardinal
central 2
chief 3
dominant 2
elementary 2
essential 2
first 1, 3
foremost 1
fundamental 1
initial 1
introductory 2
leading 1
main 1
major 2
organic 2
original 1, 3
overriding
paramount
predominant
premier 2
preparatory 2
principal 1
radical 1
rudimentary 1
salient
seminal 1
special 6
staple 1
supreme 3
ultimate 3
primary school
school 1
primate
monkey 1
prime°
arch 1
basic
capital 5
cardinal
central 2
chief 3
choice 4
day 2
excellent
fancy 3
fine[1] 1
first 1
first-rate
foremost 1
fundamental 1
groom 4
head 9
initial 1
leading 1
main 1
major 2
master 5
optimum 2
overriding
par 3
paramount
premier 2
prepare 1
primary 1
principal 1
school 4
select 2
seminal 1

prime (*cont.*)
smooth 10
special 6
supreme 3
top 8
-past one's prime
old 1
stale 1
primed
loaded 2
ready 1
set 31
prime minister
head 2
premier 1
prime mover
author
cause 1
creator 1
machine 2
participant 1
pioneer 2
protagonist 2
primer
school-book
text 4
primeval
ancient 2
early 6
original 2
prehistoric 1
primary 2
primitive 1
pristine 1
primitive°
ancient 2
antiquated
artless 3
back 12
crude 2
early 6
elemental
heathen 3
old 5
original 2
prehistoric 1
primary 2
pristine 1
rude 4
rudimentary 2
savage 3
severe 6
uncivilized 1
wild 3
primitively
roughly 3
severely 6
primitiveness
nature 3
severity 6
primness
prudery
primogenitor
ancestor
father 2
primordial
ancient 2
early 6
elemental
old 5
original 2
prehistoric 1
primary 2
primitive 1
pristine 1
rudimentary 2
primp°
groom 3
preen 2
spruce 2
prince
king
royal 3
sovereign 1
princelike
imperial 1
princely°
imperial 1
majestic 1
regal 1
royal 1

prince of darkness
devil 1
Prince of Peace
saviour 2
princess
royal 3
sovereign 1
principal°
arch 1
basic
capital 3, 5
cardinal
central 2
chief 1, 3
director 1
dominant 2
essential 2
executive 1
first 1
fundamental 1
grand 6
head 2, 9
hero 2
high 11
lead 16, 18
leader 1
main 1
mainstay
major 2
master 1, 5, 6
overriding
paramount
premier 2
prevailing 1, 2
primary 1, 5
prominent 1
protagonist 1
radical 1
responsible 3
right 7
salient
sovereign 2
staple 1
star 2, 3
stellar 2
strategic
supreme 1
top 8
uppermost 2
principality
kingdom 1
monarchy 1
realm 1
principally°
chiefly
especially 2
generally 2
mainly
part 8
particularly 2
pre-eminently
primarily 1
principle°
base[1] 2
basis 1
belief 3
code 3
doctrine
elixir 3
essence 1
foundation 2
fundamental 2
generality 2
idea 3
integrity 1
keystone
law 3
moral 4
morality 1
motto
platform 2
point of view 2
policy
position 7
precept 1
purpose 1
rationale
rectitude
rule 1
spirit 7
standard 1
tenet
theorem 2

-in principle°
at **principle 4**
ideally 2
-on principle
principle 4
-principles°
at **principle 2**
belief 3
code 3
conscience
creed
element 3b
generality 2
honour 1
ideal 3
ideology
moral 4
morality 1
platform 2
policy
principle 2
school 3
science 1
principled
conscientious 1
equitable
ethical
honest 1
honourable 1
just 2
moral 1
noble 4
pure 6
reliable
reputable
right 1
scrupulous 2
trustworthy
upright 2
wholesome 2
prink
preen 2
primp
print°
come 15b
copy 1
engraving 2
facsimile
impress 2
impression 4
photograph 1
plate 5
reproduction 2
run 19, 29b
stamp 2
strike 10
trace 3
track 3
-prints
trace 3
track 3
printed matter
print 3
text 1
printer's error
misprint
printing
edition
impression 4
issue 5
reproduction 1
printing error
misprint
print run
edition
prior°
before 6
foregoing
former 1
old 6
past 2
preceding
preliminary 1
previous 1, 2, 4
priority°
emphasis
lead 12
precedence
rank[1] 2
priory
monastery
prise
extract 3
force 8

prison°
dungeon
hole 4
jail 1
justice 2
stir 7
tower 2
-in prison
inside 7
prison-break
escape 5
prisoner°
captive 1
convict 2
culprit 1
hostage
inmate
prissy°
priggish
prudish
pristine°
flawless 1
immaculate 2
innocent 2
primitive 1
unspoiled
unused 1
privacy°
seclusion
secrecy 1
solitude 1
-in privacy
confidence 3
private°
aloof 2
close 16
confidential
domestic 1
exclusive 2
furtive 1
hidden
inside 4
interior 3
intimate[1] 2
knowing 1
mystical 1
occult 1
outside 7
personal 2
privileged 4
rarefied 3
record 8
secluded 1, 2
seclusion
secret 1, 2, 3
sneaking 2
surreptitious
tête-à-tête 1, 3
ulterior 1
undercover
underground 2
unofficial
untold 2
withdrawn 2
-in private°
at **private 6**
personally 3
tête-à-tête 2
-privates°
at **private 7**
genitals
privateer
pirate 1
robber
thief 3
private eye
detective
operative 3
sleuth
snoop 2
privately
back 6
confidence 3
personally 3
private 6
record 8
scene 5
secrecy 2
secret 4
secretly
tête-à-tête 2
private parts°
at **private 7**
genitals
private school
school 1
private showing
preview
private soldier
private 5
privation°
hardship
loss 1
misery 2
need 4
self-denial 2
want 5
privilege°
charter 2
faculty 4
freedom 4
honour 3
immunity 1
indemnity 2
liberty 2, 3
licence 1
option 2
passage 8
power 6
precedence
prerogative
refusal 2
right 9
title 5
use 10
privileged°
élite 1, 2
favoured 2
inside 4
preferential
private 2
select 3
privy°
close 16
facility 2b
familiar 4
inside 4
intimate[1] 2
lavatory
occult 1
privileged 4
toilet 1
prize°
appreciate 1
award 2
catch 15
cherish 1
choice 4
esteem 1
force 8
gem 2
gift 1
honour 5
jewel 2
joy 3
loot 1
pearl
plaque 3
plum
premium 1
price 3
pride 3
purse 3
quarry[1]
reward 2
treasure 2, 3
trophy 1
-prizes
plunder 4
spoil 6
prized
beloved 1
dear 1
pet[1] 3
precious 1, 2
sweet 5
prizefight
bout 3
prizefighter
bruiser
pugilist
prizefighting
pugilism
prizewinner
champion 1
victor
winner
pro
bitch 2
expert 1
favour 5
for 1
master 2
professional 3
prostitute 1
slattern
probability°
chance 3
eventuality
likelihood
odds 1
presumption 2
promise 2
-in all probability
doubtless 2
likely 5
presumably
probably
well[1] 9
probable°
card 12
eventual 2
likely 1, 2, 3
plausible 1
predictable
promise 4
prospect 4
secure 4
probably°
doubtless 2
easily 3
likely 5
presumably
well[1] 9
probationary
provisional 2
trial 6
probationer
novice
probative
demonstrative 2
tentative 1
probe°
check 10b, 12a
dig 5
examination 1
examine 1
experiment 3
exploration
explore 2
fathom
feeler 2
go 30b
grope
inquire 1
inquiry 1
investigate
investigation
look 8
mine 4
penetrate 1
plumb 5
poke 3
pump 2
rake[1] 6
report 6
research 2
scrutinize
scrutiny
search 1, 4
see 12b
sift 2
sound[3] 1
test 2
treat 2
probing
inquisitive 1
piercing 2
research 1
scrutiny
probingly
depth 6
probity°
credit 3
good 20
honesty 1
honour 1
integrity 1
moral 4
nobility 1
probity *(cont.)*
principle 3
rectitude
sportsmanship
virtue 1
problem°
business 2
catch 18
challenge 6
complication 2
concern 4
difficulty 2
drawback
embarrassment 2
enigma
fly 10
handful 2
headache 2
hitch 4
issue 3, 4
job 4
lookout 3
matter 3
paradox
perplexity 3
pressure 3
puzzle 4
query 2
question 2
reverse 8
riddle[1]
rub 11
snag 1
snarl[2] 3
static 2
worry 3
-problems
pressure 3
static 2
-without a problem
swimmingly
problematic°
debatable
difficult 2
doubtful 1
hairy 3
moot 1
open 7
paradoxical
precarious
questionable
thorny 2
tight 7
unresolved
problematical
debatable
difficult 2
moot 1
problematic
questionable
unresolved
problem drinker
alcoholic 2
drunk 3
proboscis
trunk 4
procedural
parliamentary
ritual 2
procedure°
approach 7
course 3
experiment 2
form 4
formality 1
formula
job 3
line[1] 9
manner 1
mean[3] 4a
measure 6
mechanism 3
method 1
mode[1] 1
operation 3
order 5
palaver 1
path 3
plan 1
policy
practice 1
proceeding 1
procedure *(cont.)*
process 1
propriety 3
recipe 2
rigmarole
rite
road 1
rope 2
routine 1
step 4
strategy
system 2
tack 3
technique 1
way 1
proceed°
advance 3
carry 11a
continue 1, 5
derive 2
drive 3
emanate 1
emerge 2
flow 1
get 28c, 28d
go 1, 19, 32a
head 10
headway 2
hop 2
make 30a
move 1
originate 2
pass 1, 2, 18a
precede
progress 5
push 10
react 1
ride 1
shape 10a
spring 3
stem[1] 3
step 11
stream 5
sue 1
travel 3
walk 1
proceeding°
action 4
affair 3
incident 1
job 3
matter 2
measure 6
move 13c
operation 3
order 5
process 1
progress 4
suit 4
thing 6
transaction 1
way 12
-proceedings°
at **proceeding 2**
minute[1] 2
order 5
preparation 1a
programme 3
transaction 2
proceeds°
proceed 3
earnings
gain 8
income
profit 1
receipt 3
return 9
revenue
take 40
yield 5
proceed with°
at **proceed 1**
continue 1
pursue 2
wage 2
process°
action 4
course 3
mean[3] 4a
mechanism 3
method 1
organ 1
path 3
prepare 7
proceeding 1
process *(cont.)*
put 27b
screen 8
spur 2
suit 4
system 2
processed
prepared 2
procession°
line[1] 6
march 2
pageant
parade 1
queue 1
review 8
string 3
succession 2
train 3
processor
producer 1
prochronism
anachronism
proclaim°
announce 1
broadcast 2
circulate 2
declare 1, 2
decree 2
deliver 4
enunciate 2
exclaim
issue 10
maintain 3
notify 2
post[1] 2
pronounce 2, 3
propagate 3
publish
tell[1] 2
testify
vent 3
proclaiming
proclamation 2
proclamation°
announcement 1
assertion 2
circulation 2
declaration 1, 2
decree 1
issue 6
observation 2
order 4
pronouncement 1, 2
publication 1
regulation 3
revelation
statement
proclivity
appetite 1
aptitude 2
bent 5
bias 1
favouritism
flair 1
habit 2
inclination 3
love 2
penchant
preference 2
talent 2
tendency
vein 4
weakness 4
procrastinate°
dawdle
delay 3
drag 6
linger 4
play 14
stall[2] 1
tarry 1
procrastinating
stall[2] 2
procrastination
stall[2] 2
procreant
sexual 1
procreate
father 5
generate 2
propagate 1
reproduce 2

procreation
generation 1
procreative
sexual 1
procreator
parent 1
proctor
monitor 1
procumbent
prone 1
prostrate 3
supine 1
procure°
acquire
buy 1
come 9a
derive 1
draw 8
earn 2
enlist 2
find 5
gain 1
get 1
harvest 3
have 2
make 7
obtain 1
pander 2
pimp 2
possess 5
purchase 1
reap 2
secure 5
take 1
win 2
procured
derivative 1
procurement
acquisition 1
purchase 3
procurer°
pander 3
pimp 1
procuress
procurer
prod°
abet 1
dig 2
drive 1
excite 1
incentive
incite
induce 1
inflame 1
jab 1,3
jog 2
motivate
motive 1
move 6
nudge 1,2
poke 1,5
press 6
probe 2
prompt 3
push 4
refresh 2
rouse 2
spur 1,4
stick[1] 3
stimulant 1
stir 4
thrust 1,4
urge 1,2
prodding
encouragement 1
incitement 1
prodigal°
extravagant 1
high 12
improvident 1
lavish 3
misspent
profligate 2,4
rake[2]
spendthrift 1,2
wasteful
wastrel 1
prodigality°
dissipation 1
excess 2
extravagance 1
exuberance 2
plenty 2
profligacy 2
prodigality
(*cont.*)
waste 6
prodigious°
enormous
exceptional 2
formidable 2
great 1,2
heavy 2
huge
incredible 2
inestimable 2
massive
mighty 3
monstrous 3
monumental 1,2
mountainous 2
overwhelming 2
phenomenal
portentous 2
vast
virtuoso 2
voracious 1
weighty 1
whopping 1
prodigy°
virtuoso 1
wonder 1
prodromal
preliminary 1
prodrome
preliminary 3
prodromic
preliminary 1
prodromus
preliminary 3
produce°
afford 3
bear 6
breed 2
brew 2
bring 5,7,9a,9b, 10a,12a,12b,13b
cause 6
create 1,2
cultivate 2
deliver 7
effect 7
fabricate 1
form 7
gain 2
generate 1,3,4
good 21b
grind 6
grow 3
harvest 1
induce 2
lead 6
let[1] 8c
make 1,5
manufacture 1
merchandise 1
mint 2
model 7
occasion 5
originate 1
output 3
perform 3
pound[1] 6
prepare 5,7
present[2] 5,7
procure 2
product 2
provide 2
provoke 2
put 17b,22d
raise 2
realize 1,3
rear[2] 1
render 1
reproduce 2
rise 17
run 29b
spawn
spin 2
stage 4
turn 20a
wares
whip 6
work 16,20b
yield 4
-be produced
come 15b
result 2
rise 11
producer°
cause 2
manufacturer
showman
producing
production 1
product°
calculation 2
fruit
preparation 5
production 2
-products
fruit
merchandise
production°
drama 1
entertainment 2
evolution
execution 4
extravaganza
fabrication 1
formation 1
generation 1
industry 1
manufacture 3
opus
output 1
piece 4
play 20
presentation 2
programme 2
reproduction 3
show 14
turnout 2
work 4
yield 5
-in production
work 5
productive°
constructive 1
economic 2
effective 1
effectual 1
efficacious
efficient
fertile
fruitful 1,2
gainful
golden 5
helpful
persuasive
plentiful 2
positive 4,6
pregnant 3
profitable 1,2
profuse 2
prolific 1,2
rank[2] 1
rewarding
rich 2,9
streamlined 3
useful
worthwhile 1
productivity
efficiency 2
output 2
proem
foreword
preamble
preface 1
preliminary 3
profanation
prostitution 2
sacrilege 1,2
sin 1
violation 2
profane°
abusive 1
base[2] 4
blaspheme 1
blasphemous
desecrate
earthly 3
foul 5
godless 1
impious
irreverent 1
outrageous 3
pollute 2
prostitute 2
sacrilegious
scurrilous
sinful
temporal 1
profane (*cont.*)
ungodly 1
violate 2
wicked 1
worldly 1
profaning
violation 2
profanity°
curse 3
oath 2
sacrilege 2
swear 2
profess°
declare 1
maintain 3
pose 2
pretend 1
proclaim 1
protest 4
professed°
nominal 1
pretended
seeming
self-styled
so-called 1
professedly
seemingly
profession°
admission 4
art 3
business 1
calling
career 1
craft 3
declaration 1
employment 1
game 4
job 1
line[1] 7
mission 2
occupation 1
practice 3
pursuit 3
racket 3
trade 2
vocation
work 2
professional°
accomplished
clerical 2
experienced 1
expert 1
master 2
perfect 7
proficient
service 9
skilful
slick 3
specialist
professor
instructor
intellectual 4
scholar 1
schoolteacher
teacher
professorial
pedantic 1
professorship
chair 2
proffer
bid 1
communicate 1
enter 6
extend 4
hand 16
hold 16b,20b
moot 2
offer 1,3,6
prefer 2
present[2] 7
profess 1
proposal 1
propose 1
propound
put 18b
render 3,7
return 6
submit 2
suggest 1
table 4
tender[2] 1
turn 15b
venture 2
proffering
presentation 1
proficiency°
ability 1
capability
dexterity 1
efficiency 1
facility 1
finesse 1
knack
knowledge 3
prowess 1
qualification 1
readiness 2
science 2
skill 1
sort 5
technique 2
understanding 3
proficient°
able 1
accomplished
adept 1
capable 1
competent 2
efficient
experienced 1
expert 2
good 12
great 8
handy 3
home 5
learn 2
master 4
masterful 1
old 7
perfect 7
polished 1
practised 1
professional 1,2
qualified 1
skilful
talented
versed
proficiently
handily 2
well[1] 3,6
profile°
form 2
line[1] 5
outline 1,3
portrait
shape 1
silhouette
profit°
account 3
advantage 2
benefit 1,4
blessing 2
boot 4
enjoy 2
exploit 2
fruit
gain 2,8
get 44d
good 19
income
interest 3
killing 2
money 3
net[2] 1
pay 4,12
plus 3
proceed 3
prosper
purpose 3
realize 3
reap 2
receive 1
return 5,9
sake 1
take 40
use 2,7
usefulness
welfare
yield 5
-profits°
at **profit 1**
fruit
income
proceed 3
profit 1
revenue
take 40
profitability
boom 4
usefulness
profitable°
advantageous
beneficial 1
desirable 4
economic 2
fat 4
fruitful 2
gainful
good 13
helpful
liquid 4
nifty 4
opportune 1
pay 4
productive 3
rewarding
rich 9
secure 3
solvent
sound[2] 5
streamlined 3
substantial 4
successful 2
useful
worthwhile 1
profitably
right 16
profiteer°
profitless
bootless
futile
hollow 5
misspent
thankless
unprofitable 1
vain 2
profit-oriented
time-serving
profligacy°
dissipation 1
evil 6
extravagance 1
indulgence 2
prodigality 1
vice 1
waste 6
profligate°
abandoned 2
degenerate 3
dissolute
extravagant 1
fast[1] 2
improvident 1
incontinent 2
lavish 3
lecherous
libertine 1,2
loose 7
outrageous 3
perverted
prodigal 1,3
promiscuous 2
rake[2]
reprobate 1,2
scandalous 1
self-indulgent
sensual
sensualist
sinful
spendthrift 1,2
vicious 1
wanton 1
wasteful
wastrel 1
profligately
water 3
pro forma
formal 1
-pro formas
ceremony 2
profound°
abysmal 1,2
dark 6
dead 15
deep 1,2,3,6
difficult 2
great 11
heartfelt
heavy 12
intense 1
intimate[1] 2

profound (*cont.*)
keen[1] 3
poignant 3
pressing
radical 1
recondite
sage 1
scholarly
soulful
strong 7
subtle 2
profoundly°
deep 10
deeply 2
depth 6
downright 2
home 10
very 1
well[1] 13
profoundness
depth 1, 2
profundity 1
profundity°
depth 1, 2, 3, 4
profuse°
abundant 1
effusive
extravagant 1
fertile
heavy 2
improvident 1
lavish 1
luxuriant 1
many 1
opulent 3
plentiful 1
prodigal 2
prolific 1
rampant 2
rank[2] 1
rich 2
torrential
voluble
profusely
sky 2
unduly 2
profuseness
prodigality 2
profusion
profusion°
abundance
embarrassment 3
exuberance 2
flood 3
many 3
mass 2
ocean 2
plenty 2
prodigality 2
rash[2] 2
sea 3
shower 2
stack 3
superfluity
wealth 2
-in profusion
galore
prog
food
scoff[2] 2
sustenance 1
progenitive
sexual 1
progenitor°
ancestor
father 2
forerunner 1
founder[1]
parent 1
stock 3
-progenitors
family 3
progenitrix
mother 1
parent 1
progenitor 1
progeny°
brood 1
child 1
descendant
family 2
issue 7
lineage 2
offspring

progeny (*cont.*)
posterity
seed 3
young 4
prognosis°
forecast 2
prediction
prophecy 2
prognostic
omen
ominous 3
prophetic
prognosticate°
forecast 1
predict
prophesy 1
say 8
prognostication
foreboding 2
forecast 2
oracle 2
prognosis
projection 4
prophecy 1
sign 6
prognosticator
fortune-teller
oracle 1
prophet
programme°
broadcast 4
course 5
enterprise 1
method 1
plan 1
platform 2
policy
project 2
projection 3
proposal 2
prospectus
recipe 2
register 1
routine 1
schedule 1, 2
scheme 1
timetable
programmed
routine 3
progress°
advance 7
boom 2
come 6
course 2
current 6
development 2
evolution
far 6a
flow 1
gain 3, 7, 9
get 27, 28d
go 19
growth 3
headway 1, 2
improve 3
improvement 2
inroad 2
journey 2
look 11c
motion 1
move 1
movement 6
pass 2, 18a
passage 1, 6
pick 8f
proceed 1
progression 1, 2
prosper
revival 3
rise 8
shape 10b
step 18a
succeed 3
transit 1
way 5
-in progress°
at **progress 4**
way 12
progressing
move 13c
ongoing 2
onward
way 12

progression°
course 2
evolution
passage 5, 6
procession 2
progress 1
run 41
scale[3] 1
sequence
step 5
succession 2
train 3
transit 1
progressive°
avant-garde
forward 3
go-ahead 2
left 2
liberal 2, 4
ongoing 2
onward
sequential
slow 2
way-out 2
progressivist
liberal 4
prohibit°
ban 1
bar 9
choke 3
embargo 2
exclude 1
forbid
keep 13
obstruct 3
outlaw 2
preclude
prevent
rule 8
shut 5a
suppress 1
taboo 3
veto 1
prohibited
foul 11
illegal
inadmissible
out 13
pale[2] 3
taboo 1
unlawful
prohibiting
prevention
suppression
prohibition°
ban 2
embargo 1
exclusion 1
injunction 1
prevention
stop 6
suppression
taboo 2
temperance 2
veto 2
prohibitive°
prohibitory
prohibitive 1
project°
activity 2
design 5
enterprise 1
job 3
jut
operation 3
overhang 1
plan 1
precipitate 2
proposal 2
protrude
send 3
shoot 2
stand 9b
stick[1] 15
throw 1, 2
undertaking 1
projected
prospect 4
public 4
projectile°
bolt 1
missile
shell 1
shot 2

projecting
prominent 3
protuberant
projection°
angle[1] 1
bulge 1
hump 1
knob
lap[2] 2
ledge
nub 1
overhang 3
point 8
prognosis
prominence 3
protrusion
relief 3
scheme 1
spur 2
tang 3
view 3
prole
plebeian 3
-proles
hoi polloi
people 3
prolegomenon
foreword
preamble
preface 1
preliminary 3
proletarian
bourgeois 2
common 3
mean[2] 2
plebeian 1, 3
worker
proletariat
hoi polloi
low[1] 7
mass 6
mob 2
people 3
populace
public 8
rabble 2
proliferate°
abound 2
increase 1
propagate 1
spread 6
teem[1]
proliferating
increase 5
spread 8
proliferation°
growth 1
increase 3
reproduction 3
spread 8
prolific°
fertile
fruitful 1, 3
lavish 1
luxuriant 2
opulent 3
plentiful 2
productive 1
profuse 2, 3
rank[2] 1
rich 9
teem[1]
vivid 3
prolix
boring
diffuse 2
discursive
expletive 1
lengthy
ponderous 2
rambling 1
redundant 2
repetitious
rhetorical 3
talkative
windy 2
wordy
prolixity
rhetoric 2
tautology
waffle 3
prologue
foreword
preamble

prologue (*cont.*)
preface 1
preliminary 3
prolong°
continue 2, 3
drag 5
draw 14a
expand 2
extend 3
hold 21b
increase 2
keep 5
lengthen
maintain 1
spin 5
spread 4
sustain 1
prolongation
maintenance 2
prolonged
lengthy
long[1] 2
protracted
sustained
tedious
prom
dance 2
promenade°
dance 2
parade 1, 3, 4
ramble 4
stroll 1, 2
strut
turn 31
walk 1, 5
prominence°
accent 1
attention 2
cachet 2
celebrity 1
distinction 2
elevation 2
emphasis
excellence
fame
height 3
hill 1
importance 2
lump[1] 2
moment 3
mountain 1
name 2
note 8
prestige
projection 1
protrusion
quality 3
relief 3
renown
rise 13
standing 6
status 1
stress 1
superiority 2
swelling
prominent°
big 5
brilliant 3
celebrated
conspicuous 1, 2
distinguished 1
elevated 2
eminent 1
exalted 1
famous
foremost 1
glaring 1
great 5
heroic 6
historic
illustrious
important 2
legendary 3
lofty 2
marked
monumental 1
notable 1
noted
obvious
outstanding 1
patent 2
perceptible
prestigious
principal 2
pronounced 1

prominent
(*cont.*)
protuberant
proud 3
public 6
renowned
salient
shine 3
singular 2
special 6
splendid 2
stand 9a
star 3
successful 3
visible 2
well-known 2
prominently
clear 18
large 4
notably 2
ostensibly
pre-eminently
promiscuity
impurity 3
profligacy 1
promiscuous°
fast[1] 2
impure 4
indiscriminate 1
loose 7
profligate 1
unchaste
wanton 1
promiscuously
fast[1] 9
promiscuous-ness
impurity 3
promise°
assurance 1
assure 4
bode
commit 4
contract 2
engage 3
engagement 3
faith 3
guarantee 1, 2
hope 2
mean[1] 3
oath 1
obligation 2
pledge 1, 4
possibility 2
promising
prophesy 2
prospect 2
resolution 2
spell[3] 1
stipulate
stipulation
subscribe 2
subscription 2
swear 1
undertake 2
undertaking 3
vow 1, 2
warrant 3
warranty
word 4
promised
engaged 1
Promised Land
paradise 1
promising°
bright 4
favourable 1, 2
golden 7
hopeful 2
likely 3
positive 8
propitious
right 3
rosy 2
promissory note
note 4
promontory
bluff[2] 3
cape[1]
height 3
hill 1
point 8
prominence 2

promote°
abet 2
advance 2, 5
agitate 2
aid 1
assist 2
back 2a
benefit 3
boost 5
cause 6
champion 4
contribute 2
cultivate 3
develop 1
electioneer
encourage 2
exalt 1
expedite 2
facilitate
favour 8
feature 4
flog 2
foment
forward 6
foster 1
further 5
get 34
glorify 1
improve 2
laud
lift 2
lobby 3
make 30c
merchandise 2
militate 2
nourish 3
patronize 3
plug 5
profit 3
propagate 3
provoke 2
publicize
puff 7
push 6
recommend 2
rip 2a
rise 8
second[1] 9
sell 4
speed 2
sponsor 3
stand 7b
support 1
talk 13
tout 1
uphold

promoter
backer 1
enthusiast
follower 3
party 4
patron 1
proponent
sponsor 1
supporter 1

promoting
encouragement 1
promotion 3
towards 2

promotion°
advertisement 2
elevation 3
encouragement 1
furtherance
patronage 1
plug 3
progress 2, 3
propaganda 2
recommendation 2
succession 3

prompt°
activate
coach 3
cue 1, 2
dispose 2
express 7
foment
give 10
hasty 1
incite
induce 1
inspire 1
jog 2
kindle
lead 2

prompt (*cont.*)
motivate
move 6
nudge 1
occasion 5
persuade 1
prod 2, 6
produce 2
professional 2
provoke 1
punctual
push 4
put 29
quick 2
raise 10
rapid
ready 5
remind
reminder
rouse 2
speedy 1
spur 4
stimulant 1
stimulate 2
stir 4
tempt 2
timely
unhesitating 1
urge 2

–without being prompted
voluntarily

prompting
incitement 1
occasion 2
recommendation 1
spur 1
suggestion 1

–without prompting
voluntarily

promptitude
rapidity

promptly°
cold 11
directly 2
hastily 1
immediately 1
instantaneously
nail 6
now 3
once 6a
post-haste
quickly 3
rapidly 2
readily 3
right 13
soon 2, 3
straight 15
summarily 1

promptness
dispatch 5
expedition 2
rapidity
readiness 2
speed 1

promulgate
announce 1
circulate 2
communicate 1
declare 2
deliver 4
enunciate 2
issue 10
make 33
post[1] 2
proclaim 1
pronounce 3
propagate 3
publish
put 17d
report 4
spread 2

promulgating
imposition 1
proclamation 2

promulgation
circulation 2
declaration 2
decree 1
imposition 1
issue 6
proclamation 1
pronouncement 1

promulgation (*cont.*)
publication 1

prone°
disposed
flat 2
given 3
horizontal
inclined 1, 2
level 2
liable 1
lie[2] 1
prostrate 3
ready 3
subject 6
susceptible 1
tend[1]

proneness
inclination 3
penchant
tendency
weakness 4

prong
point 2
prickle 1
spike 1
spine 2
spur 2
tang 3

pronounce°
declare 2
decree 2
deliver 4
dictate 1
enunciate 1, 2
find 9
go 14
mouth 7
pass 9
proclaim 1, 2
profess 1
rule 7
say 3
sound[1] 7
speak 4
spread 2
vent 3

pronounced°
bold 3
broad 3
decided 1
definite 1
emphatic
great 3
marked
noticeable 2
obvious
oral
prominent 1
salient
strong 15
thick 9

pronouncement°
announcement 1
assertion 1
circulation 2
declaration 1, 2
dictate 2
expression 1
finding 2
observation 2
order 4
publication 1
regulation 3
revelation

pronto
hastily 1
immediately 1
instantaneously
post-haste
quickly 3
readily 3
right 13
soon 2
swiftly

pronunciamento
declaration 2
decree 1
order 4
proclamation 1
pronouncement 1

pronunciation°
accent 3
delivery 4

pronunciation (*cont.*)
dialect
diction 2
intonation

proof°
demonstration 1
evidence 1
experiment 1
good 21c
print 1
reflection 4
resist 1
resistant 3
test 1
token 2
trial 1
witness 3

proof of purchase
receipt 1

prop°
bolster
brace 1, 5
buttress
leg 2
pillar 1
post[1] 1
reinforce
reinforcement 1
rest[1] 4, 8
support 1, 2, 8
sustain 2

propaganda°
advertisement 2
literature 2
promotion 4

propagandize
indoctrinate
propagate 3
push 6

propagate°
breed 3
generate 2
grow 3
post[1] 2
produce 3
raise 3
reproduce 2

propagation
breeding 1
generation 1
reproduction 3

propagative
sexual 1

propel°
boot 3
cycle
drive 1
fire 9
fling 1
fly 8a
force 8
hit 2
hurl
project 4
push 1
ride 1
run 17
send 3
shoot 2
sling 1
throw 1
thrust 1
toss 1

propelling
motive 3

propelling force
propulsion

propensity
aptitude 2
bent 5
bias 1
flair 1
habit 2
inclination 3
instinct
penchant
talent 2
tendency

proper°
adequate 3
advisable
applicable

proper (*cont.*)
appropriate 1
become 3
becoming
befitting
behove
belong 2
ceremonious 2
character 8
civil 3
correct 6, 8
courteous
decent 1, 4
delicate 5
deserved
due 2
eligible 1
equitable
ethical
expedient 1
fair[1] 2
fit[1] 1
fitting 1
for 9
formal 1
genteel 2
genuine 1
good 3, 4, 8
honest 2, 4
honourable 2
impeccable
individual 2
intrinsic
just 3
ladylike
lawful 1
legal 2
legitimate 1, 3
likely 3
logical 2
meet[1]
moral 1
natural 9
official 1, 2
perfect 4
permissible
place 11a
polite 1
presentable 2
principled
prudish
pukka 2
pure 3
puritan 2
real 5
reason 6
reasonable 4
regular 6
relevant
respectable 1, 3
right 1, 2, 8
rightful 1
ripe 3a
safe 4
savoury 2
seasonable
sedate 2
seemly 1, 2
specific 2
square 4
strait-laced
suitable
tasteful
thorough 1
true 3
utterly
virtuous 2
well[1] 17
wholesome 2
wise 3

properly°
appropriately
behave
duly 1
fairly 2
pukka 1
right 12, 17
truly 2
utterly
well[1] 3, 14

properness
propriety 1
purity 2

propertied
bourgeois 1
substantial 4

property°
acquisition 2
asset 1
attribute 1
belongings
capital 3
characteristic 2
domain 1
effects
estate 1, 2
feature 1
flavour 2
fortune 1
good 21a
inheritance
interest 5
land 3
mark 2
mean[3] 4c
paraphernalia
peculiarity 2
point 14
possession 3
quality 1
resource 2
respect 4
spread 13
stock 5
stuff 2
substance 5
trait
wealth 1

–be the property of
belong 3

–properties
endowment 3
nature 1

property owner
proprietor 1

prophecy°
foreboding 2
forecast 2
oracle 2
prediction
prognosis
sign 6
warning 2

prophesier
seer

prophesy°
anticipate 2
envision
forecast 1
foresee
foreshadow
predict
prognosticate 1
tell[1] 9

prophet°
fortune-teller
oracle 1
psychic 3
seer

prophetess
prophet
psychic 3
seer

prophetic°
ominous 3

prophet of doom
killjoy
misery 4
naysayer

prophylactic
preventive 2, 4

propinquitous
present[1] 2

propinquity
presence 1
proximity

propitiate
atone
disarm 2
silence 4

propitiation
atonement
reconciliation 1

propitiative
propitiatory 1

propitiator
peacemaker
propitiatory°
sacrificial 2
propitious°
benign 3
bright 4
expedient 2
favourable 1
fortunate 2
golden 7
good 13
happy 2
hopeful 2
inside 4
lucky 2
opportune 1
positive 8
promising
right 3
ripe 3a
seasonable
timely
propitiously
happily 1
proponent°
advocate 2
follower 3
party 4
proportion°
composition 2
measure 5, 12
parallel 3
parity 2
percentage
piece 3
quota
rate[1] 3
ratio
scale[3] 2, 4
symmetry
-in proportion
parallel 1
symmetrical
-out of proportion
disproportionate
-proportions°
at **proportion 4**
extension 2
measure 1
size 1
proportional°
parallel 1
regular 4
relative 2
symmetrical
proportionate
equal 2
parallel 1
proportional
relative 2
symmetrical
proportioned
equal 2
proportional
proposal°
conception 3
design 5
measure 7
motion 5
offer 5, 6
overture
premise 1
project 1
projection 2, 3
recommendation 1
resolution 3
suggestion 1
supposition
tender[2] 2
-proposals
approach 4
propose°
approach 3
hold 16b
intend
introduce 2
move 7
nominate
offer 1
plan 4
posit
prefer 2

propose *(cont.)*
premise 2
project 3
propound
purpose 5
put 5, 17a, 18a, 18b
recommend 1
set 18a, 18c
submit 2
suggest 1
table 4
tender[2] 1
think 5a
proposed
nominal 1
proposer
proponent
proposition°
approach 3
chat 3
doctrine
hypothesis
law 3
motion 5
offer 6
overture
pass 28
position 7
premise 1
presumption 2
principle 1
proposal 1, 2
question 3
resolution 3
suggestion 1
supposition
tender[2] 2
theorem 1
thesis 1
-propositions
approach 4
propositional
nominal 1
propound°
announce 1
enunciate 2
hold 16b
moot 2
move 7
posit
propose 1
put 18b
recommend 1
set 9, 18a
proprietary limited company°
company 4
proprietor°
boss 1
employer 1
host[1] 1
landlady 1
landlord 1
manager
owner
principal 3
proprietorship
business 4
company 4
firm 6
possession 1
proprietress
host[1] 1
landlady 1
owner
proprietor 1
propriety°
civility
decorum 1, 2
elegance 1
etiquette
form 6
formality 3
grace 2
morality 1
purity 2
rectitude
refinement 1
right 10
shame 4
taste 6
-proprieties°
at **propriety 3**
ceremony 2

proprieties *(cont.)*
manner 3
propulsion°
thrust 5
propulsive
motive 3
prorate
scale[3] 4
prorogue
stay[1] 4
prosaic°
common 1
dead 12
dreary 2
dry 2
everyday 3
flat 5
heavy 7
humdrum
lacklustre
literal 3
matter-of-fact
monotonous
ordinary 2
pedestrian 2
philistine 2
stupid 3
tame 4
tedious
threadbare 2
undistinguished
usual
proscribe
ban 1
embargo 2
exclude 1
expel 2
forbid
outlaw 2
prevent
prohibit 1
rule 8
taboo 3
veto 1
proscribed
illegal
narrow 4
taboo 1
unlawful
proscribing
prevention
prohibition 1
proscription
ban 2
embargo 1
exclusion 1
obstruction 2
prevention
prohibition 1, 2
restraint 1
taboo 2
veto 2
prose°
prosecute°
administer 2
enforce 1
follow 11b
wage 2
prosecution
execution 1
proselyte
convert 3
disciple 1
newcomer 2
novice
proselytize
convert 2
proselytizer
missionary
prosopography
résumé 2
prospect°
aspect 3
candidate
chance 3
foresight 2
hope 2
horizon
landscape
lead 14
match 4
outlook 1, 2

prospect *(cont.)*
perspective 1
possibility 1
scene 4
thought 3
timber 3
view 1, 3, 5
-in prospect°
at **prospect 4**
impending
-prospects°
at **prospect 3**
expectation 4
prospective°
forthcoming 2
future 2
prospectus°
draft 1
programme 1
prosper°
arrive 2
boom 2
flourish 1
get 27
grow 1
make 31b, 32a
pan 6
place 10
rise 8
succeed 3
thrive
work 19d
prospering
flourishing
going 1
prosperous 2
successful 1
prosperity°
boom 4
ease 3
fat 6
fortune 1
riches
success 1
wealth 1
welfare
prosperous°
fat 3
favoured 2
flourishing
flush[2] 3
going 1
golden 5
leisured
money 4
opulent 1
rich 1
strong 11
substantial 4
successful 1
wealthy
well off
prosperously
well[1] 4
prosperousness
prosperity
prostitute°
bitch 2
slattern
tart[2] 2
wanton 5
prostitution°
sacrilege 1
prostrate°
bow 5
exhaust 2
exhausted 1
fell
flat 2
flatten 2
floor 4
helpless 3
knock 6a
kowtow
lay[1] 18c
lie[2] 1
mournful 1
overwhelm 1
prone 1
scrape 4
spent 1
supine 1

prostrated
break 16c
undone[1] 1
prostration°
bow 1
collapse 7
shock 2
prosy
tedious
protagonist°
champion 2
hero 2
lead 16
protean°
changeable 1
fluid 3
unsettled 1
variable
versatile 1, 2
protect°
bulwark 2
cap 5
care 6a
champion 4
cover 1, 10
defend 1
ensure 2
escort 5
favour 7
fence 3
guard 1
harbour 2
insulate 2
keep 2
look 4
mother 5
muffle 1
patrol 3
police 2
preserve 1
safeguard 2
save 2
screen 7
secure 7
shade 10
shelter 4
shield 2
shroud 1
steel 2
uphold
watch 2
protected
charmed 2
immune
privileged 2
sacred 2
safe 1, 3, 5
secure 1
protecting
patrol 2
preservation 2
protection°
auspices
care 3
case[2] 2
charge 4
conservation
cover 14
custody 1
defence 1
escort 1
guard 4, 5
housing 1
immunity 1, 2
indemnity 2
insurance
oversight 2
patrol 2
patronage 1
possession 1
precaution 1
preservation 2
preventive 4
providence 2
refuge 1
safeguard 1
safe keeping
safety
sanctuary 2
screen 2
security 1, 4
shade 5
shadow 2
shelter 1

protection *(cont.)*
shield 1
trust 3
umbrella 2
wall 2
protection money
protection 3
protective°
camouflage 1
fatherly
preventive 2
proof 3
protectively
jealously
protector°
champion 2
escort 1
guard 3
guardian
minder 2
patron 1
protectorate
possession 2
protectress
protector
protégé(e)°
follower 1
pro tem
provisional 1
temporarily 1
temporary
time 16
pro tempore
provisional 1
temporarily 1
temporary
time 16
protest°
bitch 3
declare 1
demonstrate 3
demonstration 3
fight 2
gripe 2
groan 2
object 4
objection
outcry
peep 3
picket 5
proclaim 1
revolt 2
squawk 2, 3
walk 4b
-under protest
at **protest 2**
protestation
outcry
peep 3
protest 1
protester, protestor
dissident 1
picket 2
protocol°
ceremony 2
civility
code 3
decorum 2
etiquette
form 6
formality 1
manner 3
policy
programme 1
propriety 2
ritual 3
prototype°
classic 3
design 5
epitome 1
example 2
model 2
original 5
paragon
pattern 1
picture 4
precedent
progenitor 2
quintessence
type 3

prototypic(al)
classic 1
original 3
protract
drag 5
draw 14a
lengthen
pad 5
prolong
spin 5
spread 4
string 11b
protracted°
lengthy
lingering 1
long[1] 2
protrude°
bulge 2
jut
overhang 1
pop 3
project 5
stand 9b
start 8
stick[1] 15
protruding
prominent 3
protuberant
protrusion°
hump 1
knob
lump[1] 2
nub 1
overhang 3
projection 1
prominence 3
swelling
protrusive
prominent 3
protuberant
protuberance
bulge 1
bump 2
hump 1
knob
lump[1] 2
nub 1
projection 1
prominence 3
protrusion
swelling
tumour
protuberant°
prominent 3
proud°
cocky
conceited
disdainful
egotistical
haughty
macho
pompous 1
presumptuous
pride 4
regal 2
swollen
vain 1
proudness
pride 1
provable
demonstrable
demonstrative 2
solid 7
prove°
argue 4
come 13b
confirm 3
demonstrate 1
establish 3
evidence 4
fall 19
happen 1
make 11
manifest 3
shake 6a
show 3
substantiate
test 2
try 2, 3
turn 20b
verify
vindicate 2
witness 3
proved
solid 7
prove guilty
convict 1
prove innocent
excuse 1
provenance
origin 1
source 1
provender°
feed 1, 4
meat 1
provide 1
provision 4
ration 2
sustenance 1
table 1
provenience
origin 1
source 1
proverb°
byword
epigram 2
maxim
moral 3
motto
phrase 2
precept 2
saw
proverbial°
byword
common 1
epigrammatic
self-evident
provide°
accommodate 3
administer 3
afford 1, 3
bless 2
care 6a
cater 1
contribute 1
cover 7
dispense 1
donate
equip
feed 1
fill 3
fit[1] 8
fix 16a
furnish 1
give 1
heap 4
invest 2
keep 2, 8
lay[1] 17a
nourish 1
offer 3
open 25
prepare 1
present[2] 6
produce 6
render 3, 7
replenish
satisfy 2
serve 3
stipulate
stock 9
supply 1, 2
provided
providing
provide for°
at **provide 4**
care 6a
cover 7
feed 1
fend 1
keep 2, 8
nourish 1
prepare 1
satisfy 2
stipulate
providence°
fate 1
foresight 1
precaution 2
prudence 2
saving 3
provident°
economical 2
far-sighted 1
frugal 1
prudent 2
saving 2
providential°
fortunate 2
lucky 2
propitious
seasonable
providentially
happily 1
provider
donor
providing°
provision 1
supply 5
province°
business 1
calling
capacity 3
district
domain 1, 2
field 4
function 1
job 2
jurisdiction
kingdom 2
possession 2
precinct 1
region 1, 2
sphere 3
territory 2
universe 2
zone
-provinces°
at **province 4**
country 3
stick[2] 3
provincial°
boor 1
clown 2
intolerant 2
local 2
native 5
ordinary 2
parochial
pastoral 2
peasant
plebeian 2
sectarian 2
square 6
uncivilized 2
provincialism°
provision°
administration 3
cater 1
donation 2
feed 1
furnish 1
keep 2
outfit 4
precaution 1
precondition
preparation 1a
prerequisite 2
ration 1
requirement 1
reservation 2
restriction 1
rig 1
stipulation
subsistence 2
supply 1, 5
term 4
-provisions°
at **provision 4**
board 3
fare 3
food
meat 1
preparation 1a
provender 1
ration 2
scoff[2] 2
string 7
sustenance 1
table 1
term 4
provisional°
circumstantial 2
qualified 2
relative 2
secondary 3
stopgap 2
temporary
tentative 1
trial 6
provisionary
provisional 1, 2
provisioning
provision 1
supply 5
proviso°
condition 2
precondition
prerequisite 2
provision 2
qualification 2
requirement 1
reservation 2
restriction 1
stipulation
term 4
-provisos
string 7
term 4
-with the proviso
providing
provisory
provisional 2
provocation°
agitation 2
challenge 5
dare 3
fuel 2
incentive
incitement 2
inducement
inspiration 2
occasion 2
resentment
score 8
seed 2
shot 12
spur 1
stimulant 1
provocative°
controversial 3
exciting 2
expressive 3
flirtatious
immodest 1
impressive
inflammatory
interesting
juicy 2
offensive 1
seductive
sexy 1
stimulating
suggestive 2
sultry 2
tender[1] 4
weighty 2
provoke°
abet 1
aggravate 2
anger 2
annoy 1
arouse 3
ask 6a
bear 3
cause 6
challenge 2
dare 1
displease
disturb 1
enrage
exasperate 2
excite 1
ferment 2
fire 8b
foment
fret 2
fuel 4
gall[2] 4
get 17
incite
incur
inflame 1
infuriate
inspire 1
interest 7
irk
irritate
kindle
madden 1
make 2
molest 1
motivate
provoke *(cont.)*
move 5, 6
nag[1] 1
occasion 5
offend 1
pester
pick 3
precipitate 1
press 6
prod 2
prompt 3, 5
put 23b
raise 10
rankle
ride 3
rise 16
rouse 2
rub 8
spark 2
spite 3
spur 4
stimulate 2
stir 4
tantalize
tease 1
tempt 3
touch 11b
trouble 2
provoked
angry 1
furious 1
huff 1
indignant
mad 4
resentful
provoker
aggressor
provoking
incitement 1
prow
stem[1] 2
prowess°
prowl°
lurk
pussyfoot 1
roam
slink
sneak 1
steal 3
straggle
walk 1, 3
wander 1
-on the prowl°
at **prowl 3**
proximal
close 9
proximate
close 9
immediate 2
present[1] 2
proximity°
presence 1
proxy°
agent 1
deputy
factor 2
representative 3
prude°
prig
prudence°
calculation 3
caution 2
discretion 1
foresight 1
judgement 1
precaution 2
providence 1
saving 3
tact
thrift
wisdom 1
prudent°
advisable
careful 1
cautious
conscientious 3
conservative 2
deliberate 3
diplomatic
discreet
economical 2
expedient 2
far-sighted 1
frugal 1
prudent *(cont.)*
guarded
judicious
measured 2
noncommittal
politic 2
provident 1, 2
rational 2
sage 1
saving 2
seemly 2
sensible 1
sound[2] 4
sparing 1
tactful
thoughtful 3
thrifty
wary
well-advised
wise 1, 3
prudential
prudent 2
prudery°
prudish°
delicate 5
po-faced
priggish
prissy
puritan 2
sedate 2
squeamish 1
strait-laced
prudishness
prudery
shame 4
prune°
diminish 1
lop
minimize 1
shorten 1
snip 1
thin 8
top 5
trim 3
prurience
desire 3
impurity 3
prurient°
carnal
dirty 2
erotic 3
hot 7
impure 4
indecent 2
lascivious 1
lecherous
lewd
libertine 2
lustful
obscene 1
pornographic
sensual
suggestive 2
wicked 3
pry°
busybody
eavesdrop
force 8
get 44c
hunt 2
meddle
poke 3
root[2]
search 1
snoop 1
squeeze 2
wrench 3
prying
curiosity 2
curious 2
inquisitive 2
intrusive
nosy
psalm
chant 1
pseud
phoney 1, 3
trendy 2
pseudo
counterfeit 2
deceptive 2
false 3
glossy 2
mannered

pull the wool over someone's eyes *(cont.)*
deceive
flannel 2
fool 4
hoodwink
mislead
put 26
take 32b
trick 8

pull through°
at **pull 17**
recover 2
recuperate
survive 1

pull together
coordinate 2
gather 3
organize 2
raise 5
round 19
solidify 2

pull to pieces
demolish 1
mess 5c
pull 6
rend 1

pull to shreds
pull 6

pull up°
at **pull 3**
draw 15a
hitch 2
raise 1
stop 5

pull up stakes
leave[1] 1
move 2

pull wires°
at **string 5**
influence 3
lobby 3
pull 16

pulp°
crush 3
pound[1] 2
reduce 4

pulpit
ministry 1
rostrum

pulpy
mushy 1

pulsate°
beat 3
pound[1] 3
resound
shake 2
surge 1
vibrate

pulsating
intermittent
pulse 1
resonant
rhythmic
spasmodic 2

pulsation
beat 11
pulse 1
stroke 4
thrill 2

pulse°
beat 11
cadence
pound[1] 3
pulsate
rhythm
stroke 4
tempo
vibrate

pulsing
pulse 1
rhythmic

pulverize°
crush 1
grind 1
mill 5
pound[1] 2
powder 3
pulp 3
rout 2
ruin 7

pulverize *(cont.)*
shatter 1
whip 2

pulverized
broken 1
fine[1] 7

pummel
batter 1
beat 1
belabour
hit 1
lambaste 1
lather 4
manhandle
pelt[1] 1
pound[1] 1
punch[1] 1
rough 16
strike 1

pump°
examine 2
heart 1
question 9
quiz 2

pump full of lead
shoot 3

pump out°
at **pump 3**
drain 4

pump up°
at **pump 4**
inflate 1
puff 6

pun°
ambiguity 2
epigram 1
gag[2] 1
joke 1, 4
quip 1
wisecrack 1, 2
witticism

punch°
assault 5
belt 3
blow[2] 1
bore[1] 2
box[2] 2, 3
clip[2] 3, 6
effect 2
finger 4
get 24
hit 1, 10
jab 2, 4
knock 9
nail 9
perforate
pierce 2
poke 2, 6
prick 3
rap 4
salt 2
spice 2
stamp 6
stick[1] 1
strike 1, 10

Punch
fool 2

punch-drunk
groggy

puncheon
keg

Punchinello
fool 2

punching
puncture 2

punch-line
clincher
pay-off 2

punch-up
brawl 1
fracas 1
fray[1]
riot 1

punchy
epigrammatic
groggy

punctilio
decorum 2
formality 2, 3
propriety 2
rigmarole
rigour 2

punctilious
careful 2
ceremonious 2
conscientious 2
deliberate 3
diligent
dutiful
elaborate 1
exact 2
faithful 3
fastidious
finicky 1
formal 1
meticulous
nice 3
pedantic 2
perfectionist 2
priggish
proper 3
reliable
religious 2
rigid 3
scrupulous 1
squeamish 1
strict 1

punctiliously
precisely 2

punctiliousness
care 2
precision 2

punctual°
prompt 1
ready 5
timely

punctually
dot 2
duly 2
promptly
sharp 10
time 19a

punctuate°
interrupt 1

puncture°
bore[1] 2
burst
disprove
enter 2
flaw 2
gore[2]
hole 2, 7
lance 2
leak 2
penetrate 1
penetration 1
perforate
pierce 1
pink[2]
prick 1, 3
punch[2] 2
rebut
riddle[2] 1
stab 1, 3
stick[1] 1
wound 1

punctured
flat 6

puncturing
penetration 1
puncture 2

pundit
expert 1
intellectual 4
sage 2
scholar 1
thinker
wag[2]
wit 3

pungency
edge 3
life 7
salt 2
spice 2
spirit 3
tang 1
zest 1

pungent°
aromatic
caustic 2
epigrammatic
hot 2
keen[1] 2
penetrating 2
pointed 2
racy 3

pungent *(cont.)*
rank[2] 4
rich 8
robust 2
sharp 4
spicy 1
strong 2
tart[1] 1

puniness
weakness 2

punish°
castigate
chasten 1
chastise
correct 3
discipline 8
flog 1
lash[1] 4
mortify 2
pay 5, 6
penalize
persecute 1
revenge 3
scourge 4
spank
whip 1

punishing°
harsh 2
killing 3
severe 4
stiff 2
swingeing

punishment°
correction 2
discipline 2
justice 2
lesson 4
pay 6
penalty
penance 1
persecution 1
rap 6
retribution
reward 3
rod 2
sanction 4
sentence
severity 4
thrashing 2
visitation 2

punitive°
harsh 2
penal
severe 1, 4
spiteful
stiff 2

punitively
dearly 3
severely 4

punitive measures
punishment 1

punitiveness
severity 4

punitory
punitive

punk°

punnet
hamper[2]

punster
joker 1
wag[2]
wit 3

punt°
adventure 4
bet 1, 2
gamble 1, 4
kick 1, 3
punter 1

punter°
backer 3
better[2]
player 3

puny°
faint-hearted 2
feeble 1
frail 2
insignificant
insubstantial 1
meagre 1
meaningless 2
measly
pale[1] 3

puny *(cont.)*
paltry
pathetic 2
petty 1
small 2
soft 12
thin 1
tiny
trifling
unimposing
unworthy 1
weak 2
wee 2

pup°

pupil°
disciple 1
follower 1
learner
protégé
scholar 2
student 1

puppet°
dupe 2
figurehead
nominal 1
pawn[2]
robot 2
tool 3

puppy
pup

purblind
blind 1

purchasable
venal

purchase°
acquire
acquisition 2
buy 1, 4
finger 5b
get 1
hold 25
obtain 1
order 15
patronize 2
pick 8e
procure 1
sale 2
shop 4
traction
use 4

-purchases
use 11

purchase order
order 7

purchaser
buyer
customer 1
patron 2
trader
user 1

-purchasers
public 9

purchasing
purchase 3
sale 2

pure°
absolute 1, 2
blank 6
celibate 2
chaste 1, 2
clean 1, 4
clear 11, 12, 14
complete 3
decent 5
devout 1
flawless 1
fresh 7
godly
good 5
holy 2
hygienic
immaculate 1, 2
impeccable
incorrupt 1
innocent 2
irreproachable
literal 2
main 4
mellow 2
mere
moral 1
naked 3
neat 2
out-and-out

pure *(cont.)*
outright 2
perfect 1
primary 5
pristine 2
refined 4
respectable 3
right 8
saintly
sheer 2
solid 4
spotless 2
stark 4
sterile 2
sterling 1
straight 9
theoretical 2
undiluted
unmitigated
unqualified 2
unvarnished
very 4
virtuous 1
white 3

pure-bred°

purely
merely 1
only 3
outright 4
perfectly 1
simply 1

pureness
purity 1

purfle
border 1, 7
fringe 1

purfling
border 1
fringe 1
trim 5

purgative°

purge°
clean 11b
cleanse 2
clear 27
disinfect
evacuate 1
flush[1] 2
pound[1] 5
purgative 1
removal 2, 3
remove 4, 5
sweep 5
void 7

purification
refinement 3

purified
clean 1
refined 4

purifier
disinfectant

purify°
clarify 2
clean 11b
cleanse 2
clear 20
disinfect
filter 2
freshen 3
fumigate
purge 1, 3
refine 1
sanctify 2
sterilize 1
strain[1] 5
wash 6

purifying
detergent 2
refinement 3

purist°
perfectionist 1
prig
priggish
puritan 1

puristic
delicate 5
priggish

puritan°
prig
prude

puritanical
narrow-minded
po-faced

put over (*cont.*)
execute 1
get 26
put 21a
sell 4
put over one's knee
punish 2
spank
put paid to
end 9
putrefacient
foul 2
putrefaction
decay 4
filth 1
rot 3
putrefactive
foul 2
putrefied
bad 6
putrid
stagnant
putrefy°
decay 2
decompose 2
fester 1
mortify 3
rot 1
spoil 4
turn 5
putrefying
mouldy
offensive 3
putrid
putresce
fester 1
mortify 3
putrescence
filth 1
rot 3
putrescent
foul 2
impure 1
mouldy
offensive 3
putrid
rotten 1
stagnant
strong 3
putrescing
rotten 1
putrid°
bad 6
evil 5
filthy 1
foul 2
impure 1
mouldy
musty 1
offensive 3
rancid
rank[2] 4
rotten 1
smelly
sordid 3
stagnant
stinking 1
strong 3
put right
correct 1
heal 2
improve 1
mend 2
rectify
remedy 4
repair 1
right 19
straighten 1
putsch
revolt 1
revolution 1
uprising
put someone's back up
infuriate
offend 1
put someone's mind at rest
reassure
satisfy 3
put someone's nose out of joint
offend 1
put someone up to something°
at **put 29**
prompt 3
put something over on°
at **put 26**
defraud
dupe 3
fool 4
hoodwink
mislead
misinform
outsmart
string 10c
trick 8
put straight
heal 2
sort 10a
straighten 1
putter
dabble 2
delay 3
fool 7b
idle 6
put the arm on
extort
squeeze 3
put the finger on°
at **finger 8**
finger 12
incriminate
inform 2
put the finishing touches on
finish 7
retouch
put the frighteners on
frighten
put the kibosh on
ruin 9
upset 5
veto 1
put the screws on°
at **screw 4**
pressure 5
squeeze 3
put the squeeze on°
at **squeeze 11**
force 7
screw 4
squeeze 3
put the wind up
frighten
put through°
at **put 27**
subject 9
work 16
putting on airs
genteel 1
snobbish
uppish
putting out
manufacture 3
production 1
publication 1
putting right
adjustment 1
putting to death
destruction 2
putting together
addition 1
assembly 3
fabrication 1
manufacture 3
organization 1
preparation 3
putting to rights
adjustment 1
put to death
dispatch 3
end 10
execute 3
kill 1
put to death (*cont.*)
murder 3
put 16d
slaughter 3
put to effect
exercise 1
exert 1
put to flight
chase 3
rout 2
put together
assemble 3
combine 2
compile
compound 1
connect 3
construct 1
draw 15b
form 7
frame 6, 7
generate 4
group 4
integrate
knock 7a
lump[1] 3
make 1
manufacture 1
marry 2
match 5
mix 1
organize 2
pair 2
piece 13
prepare 5
produce 1
put 28a
raise 2
set 23a
turn 20a
whip 7b
work 19e, 20b
put to rights
adjust 1
fix 3
make 31a
right 19
straighten 1
put to rout
rout 2
put to sea
sail 2
put to shame°
at **shame 5**
shade 8
put to sleep
kill 1
put 16d
put to the sword
execute 3
massacre 2
slaughter 3
put to the torch
fire 8
put to use
apply 3
exercise 1
exert 1
tap[2] 6
touch 9
use 1
work 15
put to work
exert 1
put two and two together
reason 7
put under arrest
nab
put under a spell
fascinate
put under contract
sign 10b
put under strain
stress 5
put under stress
stress 5
put up°
at **put 28**
accommodate 4
board 7
put up (*cont.*)
construct 1
erect 2
fabricate 1
form 7
frame 6
house 8
lodge 4
nominate
offer 2
pitch[1] 2
post[1] 2
preserve 3
propose 3
quarter 6
raise 2, 6
rear[2] 2, 3
set 23a
stick[1] 17b
stop 5
tender[2] 1
put-up°
fixed 4
put-up job
set-up 2
put-upon°
put up the shutters
close 5
put up to°
at **put 29**
prompt 3
put up with°
at **put 30**
abide 1
allow 4
bear 4, 11
brook[2]
endure 3
go 36a
lump[2]
stand 3
stomach 3
submit 1
suffer 2
support 3
sustain 3
take 6
tolerate 1
put wise°
at **wise 4**
puzzle°
bemuse 1
bewilder
confuse 1
daze 2
distract 3
elude 2
enigma
escape 4
floor 5
flummox
fluster 1
fog 4
get 18
matter 3
mix 4b
muddle 1
mystery 1
mystify
nonplus
paradox
perplex
perplexity 3
problem 2
question 2
riddle[1]
shake 5
stick[1] 9
stump 2
tangle 2
wonder 3
puzzled
confused 2
daze 4
disconcerted
groggy
lost 3
quizzical
vague 6
puzzle out°
at **puzzle 3**
puzzle over°
at **puzzle 2**
puzzler
problem 2
puzzling°
ambiguous 2
confused 1
cryptic 2
dark 6
difficult 2
disconcerting
equivocal 2
funny 2
hard 3
incomprehensible
indefinite 2
inexplicable
intricate 2
labyrinthine
mysterious 1
obscure 2
occult 2
opaque 2
paradoxical
perplexing
profound 1
queer 2
tough 5
unaccountable 1
pygmy
diminutive
little 1
miniature
puny 3
runt
tiny
undersized
pyknic
stocky
pylon
post[1] 1
pyramid
sepulchre
pyretic
feverish
pyrexic
feverish
pyrotechnics
virtuosity
Pyrrhic
hollow 5
pythoness
witch 1

Q

q.t., Q.T.
–on the q.t.
confidence 3
private 6
scene 5
secret 4
secretly
sly 3
quack°
fake 4
fraud 3
hypocrite
phoney 3
quackery
hypocrisy
quad
enclosure 1
quadrangle
enclosure 1
square 8
quadrangular
square 1
quadrature
quarter 2
quadrilateral
square 1
quaff
drain 4
drink 1
gulp 1
swill 3
take 13
quaggy
flabby 1
quagmire
bog 1
marsh
mire 1
morass 1, 2
swamp 1
quail
blink 3
cringe 1
dread 1
fear 5
flinch
start 5
tremble 1
truckle
quaint°
antiquated
bizarre 2
curious 3
eccentric 1
erratic 2
fantastic 1
odd 1
ordinary 4
outlandish
passé
peculiar 1
picturesque 1
queer 1
strange 1
twee
whimsical 1
quake°
cringe 1
fear 5
shake 1, 8
shiver[1] 1, 3
shudder 1, 2
totter
tremble 1, 2
vibrate
quaking
doddering
shake 8
tremulous 1
qualification°
capacity 3
condition 2
fitness 1
precondition
prerequisite 2
provision 2
requirement 1
reservation 2
restriction 1
specification 3
stint 2
term 4
–qualifications
at **qualification 1**
background 1
endowment 3
fitness 1
resource 1
string 7
term 4
–with qualification(s)
salt 5
qualified°
able 1
adequate 3
capable 1
competent 2
eligible 1
experienced 1
expert 2
fit[1] 2
home 5
knowing 2
likely 3
merit 3
practised 1
professional 1
proficient
provisional 2
ripe 2
skilful
strong 6
worthy 1
qualifiedly
salt 5

qualify°
adapt 1
charter 4
earn 1
enable 1
entitle 1
fence 4
grade 5
measure 15b
modify 2
narrow 8
pass 4
restrict
screen 8
water 7
whitewash
qualifying
extenuating
mitigating
saving 1
qualifyingly
salt 5
quality°
air 1,3
aspect 4
attribute 1
aura
calibre 2,3
character 2
characteristic 2
distinction 2
excellence
fancy 3
feature 1
feel 11
fibre 3
fine[1] 1
flavour 2
mark 2
merit 1
nature 1
note 5
odour 2
peculiarity 2
point 14
property 4
resource 1
respect 4
savour 2
sort 5
sound[1] 2
strain[1] 9
style 5
timber 3
timbre
tone 2
trait
vintage 2
virtue 3
worth
-qualities
endowment 3
stuff 3
qualm°
compunction 2
discredit 6
distrust 2
doubt 3
dread 2
misgiving
pang 2
phobia
protest 1
regret 2
reservation 2
scruple 1
suspicion 1
-qualms
fear 1
qualmish
sick 1
squeamish 2
quandary°
dilemma
fix 17
jam 6
matter 3
mess 3
paradox
perplexity 3
plight
predicament
problem 1
scrape 8

quandary *(cont.)*
snarl[2] 3
spot 4
quantified
measured 4
quantify
count 1
evaluate 2
quantity°
amount 2
batch 1,2
deal 6
dose 1
draught 2
entity 1
flock 1
incidence
lot 1,5c
mass 1,2
matter 5
measure 1,5
piece 1
pile[1] 3
plenty 1
portion 2
profusion
provision 4
rash[2] 2
river 2
sea 3
stack 3
sum 1
supply 4
volume 1
wad 2
-quantities
lot 5c
plenty 1
quarantine
insulate 1
isolate
quarrel°
argue 1
argument 1
battle 2
bicker
bolt 1
brawl 1,2
clash 2,3
combat 2
conflict 2
controversy 2
differ 2
difference 2
disagree 2
disagreement 3
dispute 1,2,3
encounter 5
exchange 3
fall 18
feud 1,2
fight 4,8
flap 5
fracas 2
fray[1]
jar[2] 2
misunderstand-
ing 2
pane
row[2] 1,3
run-in
scrap[2] 1
tiff
tilt 4
variance 2
vendetta
word 9a
quarrelling
faction 2
strife 1
variance 3
quarrelsome°
aggressive 1
argumentative
belligerent 2
cantankerous
factious
irritable
offensive 1
passionate 3
perverse 2
pugnacious
querulous
quick-tempered
sensitive 2

quarrelsome *(cont.)*
surly
testy
quarry°
excavation
game 5
kill 8
mine 3
object 2
pit[1] 1
prey 1
target
unearth
quarter°
accommodate 4
area 3
board 7
district
domicile 2
flank 1
house 8,9
limit 3
lodge 4
mercy
neighbourhood 1
part 6
place 2
precinct 2
province 1
put 28b
region 1
spot 2
take 32a
territory 1
tract[1]
universe 2
ward 1
zone
-quarters°
at **quarter 5**
abode
accommodation 4
condition 4
domicile 1
dwelling
home 1
house 1
housing 1
lodging
pad 3
place 6
residence 1
room 3
stall[1] 2
quarterly°
journal 1
organ 2
periodical
publication 2
regular 2
quash°
abolish
cancel 1,2
crush 4
demolish 2
hush 4
kill 6
nip[1] 2
overwhelm 1
put 16b
quell 1
repress
reverse 3
revoke
set 15b
silence 4
squelch 1
stifle 3
subdue 1
suppress 2
vacate 3
veto 1
vitiate 3
void 6
quashing
overthrow 2
suppression
veto 2
quasi-°
self-styled
quaver°
quiver 1,2
shudder 1,2
tremble 1,2

quavering
doddering
tremulous 1
quay
dock 1
landing 3
pier 1
quean
prostitute 1
queasiness
ailment
dread 2
horror 2
jitters
qualm
queasy°
delicate 5
disconcerted
disgusted
jumpy
nauseated
off colour 1
queer 3
sick 1
sinking 1
upset 7
queen°
bigwig 1
crown 3
homosexual 1
monarch 1
royal 3
sovereign 1
queenlike
imperial 1
royal 1
queenly
imperial 1
majestic 1
regal 1
royal 1
sovereign 3
statuesque
Queen's counsel
lawyer
queenship
royalty 1
queer°
abnormal 2
bizarre 1
cranky 1
curious 3
deviant 1
eccentric 1,2
erratic 2
extraordinary 1
extreme 5
fantastic 1
fishy 2
freak 5
funny 2
grotesque 2
homosexual 1,2
irregular 3
kinky 1
odd 1
offbeat
outlandish
out-of-the-way 2
peculiar 1
quaint 1
queasy 2
quizzical
ridiculous
sabotage 3
singular 1
spoil 1
strange 1
swish 4
undermine 1
unnatural 5
unusual
way-out 1
weird
whimsical 1
-in Queer Street
insolvent
poor 1
queer fish
original 6
weirdo
queerness
oddity 1
singularity 2

queer someone's pitch
sabotage 3
quell°
crush 4
master 8
overpower 1
overwhelm 1
put 16b
quash 2
repress
soften 3
squelch 1
stamp 4
stem[2] 1
subdue 1
subjugate
suppress 2
quelling
suppression
victory
quench°
extinguish 1
put 23c
satiate 2
satisfy 2
slake
suffice
suppress 2
quenched
extinct 3
quenching
suppression
quern
mill 1
querulous°
cranky 2
cross 6
fault-finding 2
fretful
gruff 1
impatient 2
overcritical
peevish
puling
quarrelsome
testy
touchy 1
waspish
query°
ask 1
enquire 1
inquiry 2
question 1,2,5,9,
10
wonder 3
querying
inquiry 1
quest°
expedition 1
hunt 2,4
investigation
pursue 3
search 3
seek 1
-in quest of
for 2
question°
ask 1
business 2
canvass 2
challenge 1,4
consult 1
contest 3
debate 3
discredit 2,6
dispute 1
distrust 1
doubt 1
enquire 1
examine 2
exception 4
fight 2
impeach 2
inquiry 2
interview 3
issue 3
matter 2,5
misgiving
mistrust 1
mystery 1
objection
point 10

question *(cont.)*
poll 3
problem 1,2
pump 2
puzzle 4
query 1,3
question 5
quiz 2
riddle[1]
sound[3] 1
stand 12a
topic
wonder 3,5
-be a question of
come 18c
-beside the question
inapplicable
-in question°
at **question 6**
debatable
questionable
-out of the question°
at **question 7**
impossible 1
unthinkable 2
-without question°
at **question 8**
easily 2
question 4
questionable°
ambiguous 2
controversial 1
debatable
disputable
disreputable 1
doubtful 1,3
equivocal 1
exceptionable
far-fetched
fishy 2
fly-by-night 2
hazardous
implausible
improbable
left-handed 2
marginal 2
moot 1
precarious
problematic
queer 2
question 6b
rocky[2]
ropy 2
shady 2
shaky 1
slippery 2
soft 7
suspect 3
suspicious 1
uncertain 3
unresolved
questioned
problematic
questioner
sceptic
questioning
controversy 1
inquiry 1
inquisitive 1
interrogation
investigation
quizzical
sceptical
question period
interview 1
queue°
file 2
line[1] 6,23c
rank[1] 4
stream 3
string 3
train 3
quibble°
cavil 1,2
dodge 3
equivocate
evade 2
exception 4
fence 4
haggle
loophole

quibble (*cont.*)
pick 4a
shuffle 3,5
waffle 2
quibbling
chicanery
evasion 2
fault-finding 1,2
gobbledegook 2
hair-splitting
legalistic
pedantic 2
quibble 2
quiche
tart[2] 1
quick°
abrupt 1
active 3
agile 1
alert 2
alive 3
animate 3,4
animated 1
astute 2
brisk 2
cursory
dexterous 1
expeditious
express 7
fast[1] 1,6
fleet[2]
hasty 1,3
hurried 1
impetuous
impulsive
intelligent
keen[1] 6
mobile 4
momentary
nifty 2
nimble 1
passing 2
penetrating 1
perceptive
precipitate 3
precocious
prompt 1,2
quickly 2,3
rapid
ready 5,6
receptive 2
rough 10
sharp 3
short 7
smart 1,5,6
snap 13
snappy 1
spanking 3
speedy 1,3
sudden
summary 2
superficial 3
swift
thumbnail
unhesitating 1
whirlwind 2
-to the quick
home 10
quicken°
arouse 3
enliven 1
excite 1
flush[1] 3
forward 8
hasten 2
heat 4
inspire 1
intensify
interest 7
pep 2
perk up
precipitate 1
raise 7
stimulate 1,2
wake[1] 2
quickened
heated
quickening
flush[1] 6
revival 2
vital 4
quickly°
briefly 2
directly 2
double 8

quickly (*cont.*)
fast[1] 6
flat 17a
hand 12
hastily 1
leap 7
post-haste
promptly
rapidly 1
readily 3
right 13
sharply 2
shot 10
soon 2,3
suddenly 1
summarily 1
swiftly
time 17
quickness
dispatch 5
expedition 2
facility 1
haste 1
intelligence 1
rapidity
readiness 2
sense 2
skill 1
speed 1
velocity
quicksand
morass 2
quick-tempered°
excitable
hasty 4
hotheaded
passionate 3
sensitive 2
snappish 1
testy
touchy 1
warm 2
quick-witted°
astute 2
bright 6
brilliant 4
clever 1
intelligent
keen[1] 6
nimble 2
perceptive
quick 4
shrewd
smart 1
wise 1
quick-wittedness
aptitude 3
penetration 2
presence 5
resource 1
sense 2
quid
plug 2
quiddity
entity 2
essence 1
existence 3
kernel 2
point 5
property 4
quintessence
substance 2
quidnunc
gossip 3
talebearer
quid pro quo
exchange 2
indemnity 1
requital 2
retribution
quids in
wealthy
quiescence
inactivity 2
lull 2
quiescent
dormant 1
inactive 1
inert 2
passive 1
peaceful 1
potential 1

quiescent (*cont.*)
quiet 3
silent 4
still 1
quiet°
calm 1,3,5
compose 4
cool 2
dead 11
dormant 1
dreamy 3
dumb 1
ease 5,6
easy 2
gag[1] 1
gentle 1
hush 1,2,5,6
inactive 1
inactivity 1
inaudible
inert 2
leisure 2
low[1] 13
lull 2,3
mild 1
mitigate
muffle 2
mum 1
mute 1,3
noiseless
off 8
order 8
passive 1
pastoral 1
peace 1
peaceful 1
quell 2
quieten
relax 4
repose 1
rest[1] 10
restful 2
reticent
secret 1
serene 1
serenity 1
settle 7,8
silence 1,3
silent 1
simmer 3
sleepy 2
slow 6
sober 3
soft 4,9
soften 3
soothing 1
stagnant
staid
still 1,2,3,7,9
subdued 1
subside 2
suppress 3
taciturn
temperate 1
tight-lipped
tone 5
tranquil
tranquillize
unobtrusive
withdrawn 1
wrap 3b
quiet(en)°
calm 5
compose 4
ease 5,6
gag[1] 1
hush 2,5
lower[1] 5
mitigate
muffle 2
mute 3
quell 2
settle 7,8
shut 6b
silence 3
soften 3
still 9
subside 2
suppress 3
tone 5
tranquillize
quiet(en) down°
at **quieten**
compose 4
pipe 7

quiet(en) down (*cont.*)
relax 4
settle 7
simmer 3
subdue 3
subside 2
quieting
soothing 1
suppression
quietly°
secret 4
secretly
silently
sly 3
still 7
-as quietly as a mouse
silently
quietness
quiet 5
silence 1
quietude
quiet 5
silence 1
quill
bristle 1
pen[1] 1
spine 2
spur 2
quilt
cover 13
spread 14
quintessence°
core 2
elixir 3
entity 2
epitome 1
essence 1
extract 5
extraction 2
gem 2
gist
heart 3
kernel 2
paragon
perfection 3
pith 1
soul 3
spirit 6
substance 2
type 3
quintessential
essential 1
fundamental 1
quip°
epigram 1
gag[2] 1
joke 1,4
pun
squelch 2
wisecrack 1,2
witticism
quirk°
eccentricity 2
exception 3
fancy 8
feature 1
fluke
foible
freak 3
kink 4
mannerism
notion 2
oddity 3
peculiarity 1
property 4
thing 4
trait
trick 6
twist 10
warp 2
quirky
capricious
cranky 1
deviant 1
eccentric 1
insane 1
kinky 1
peculiar 1
quirt
lash[1] 1
scourge 2
whip 8

quisling
snake 2
subversive 2
traitor
quit°
abandon 2
abdicate
clear 15
cut 16c
depart 1
desert[1] 4
despair 2
discontinue
drop 7
emigrate
evacuate 2
exit 3
flee 1
forsake 1
give 17a
go 31e
halt 2
knock 5
lay[1] 16b
leave[1] 1,4
pack 6,8b
pull 14d
refrain[1] 2
relinquish 1
resign 1
secede
ship 3
sign 8
stall[1] 1
stand 6
step 14a
stop 1
surrender 2
throw 9b
vacate 1
quite°
absolutely 2
altogether
clean 7
completely 1,2
cry 8
degree 4a
exactly 2
fairly 1
full 15,18
highly 2
moderately
outright 4
perfectly 1,4
pretty 3
probably,
rather 1
really 4
somewhat
thoroughly 1
very 1,2
wholly 1
quits
even 6
quittance
indemnity 1
requital 1
settlement 4
quiver°
cringe 1
fear 5
flicker 2
flutter 3,4
pulsate
quake 1
quaver 1,2
shake 1,8
shiver[1] 1,3
shudder 1,2
thrill 2
totter
tremble 1,2
vibrate
wag[1] 1,2
wave 4
wriggle 1,4
quivering
doddering
flutter 4
quaver 2
shake 8
thrill 2
tremulous 1
wriggle 4

qui vive
lookout 2
-on the qui vive
acute 5
alert 1
awake 4
current 4
disingenuous
look 9
mindful
observant 1
perceptive
sharp 3
sharp-eyed
step 12
tune 4
vigilant
wakeful 2
wary
watch 4,8
quixotic°
idealistic
impractical 1
rash[1]
romantic 2
unrealistic 1
quiz°
ask 1
examination 2
examine 2
pump 2
question 9
quizzical°
quod
jail 1
prison
stir 7
-in quod
inside 7
quoit
ring[1] 1
quondam
former 1
old 6
past 2
previous 1
prior 1
sometime 1
quorum
complement 2
quota°
allotment 1
allowance 3
complement 2
dole 1
measure 5
piece 11
portion 2
proportion 3
ration 1
share 1
stint 1
quotation°
excerpt 1
extract 6
passage 2
price 1
reference 1
selection 4
text 2
quote°
enumerate 1
excerpt 2
extract 4
mention 1
quotation 1,2
recite 1
refer 1
repeat 1
selection 4
quotidian
daily 1
diurnal
everyday 1

R

Ra
sun 1
rabbi
clergyman 1

ravage (*cont.*)
waste 11
-ravages°
at **ravage 3**
depredation
ravaged
desolate 2
stark 3
ravagement
desolation 1
destruction 1
rape 2
ravaging
depredation
rape 2
rave°
explode 3
lace 5b
party 1
rage 4
ramble 3
rampage 3
rant 2
seethe 2
spout 2
storm 4
ravel
fray[2]
snarl[2] 2
tangle 3
ravelled
ragged 1
raven
black 1
pitch-black
swarthy
ravening
famished
rapacious
ravenous 2
vicious 3
voracious 1
ravenous°
famished
gluttonous
greedy 1
hollow 3
hungry 1
predatory 2
rapacious
starved 1
thirsty 2
voracious 1
ravenousness
greed 3
hunger 1
lust 2
rapacity
thirst 1
rave-up
party 1
rave 5
revelry
ravine°
canyon
crevasse
gorge 1
gully
raving°
bluster 3
delirious 1
hysterical 1
psychotic 1
stormy 2
violent 1
wild 5
-ravings°
at **raving 3**
ravish°
dishonour 3
outrage 6
rape 4
ruin 11
seduce 2
transport 3
violate 3
ravishing°
delightful 2
devastating 2
enchanting
exciting 2
lovely 1
raving 2

ravishing (*cont.*)
stunning 2
tempting 1
voluptuous 2
ravishment
rape 1
violation 3
raw°
back 12
bleak 2
callow
chill 4
cold 1
crude 1
cutting 1
foul 5
fresh 3
green 2
gross 3
icy 1
immature 2
inclement
inexperienced
lewd
painful 1
piercing 3
primitive 2
rough 6,9
rude 4
scratchy 2
sore 1
tender[1] 3,8
unfledged
unrefined 2
-in the raw°
at **raw 7**
naked 1
raw-boned°
gaunt 1
lean[1] 1
scrawny
skinny
spare 3
rawhide
whip 8
rawness
sore 7
ray°
beam 2
flash 1
gleam 1,2
shaft 2
spine 2
raze°
consume 4
demolish 1
desolate 5
destroy 1
devastate 1
flatten 3
knock 4a
level 9
pillage 1
pull 9a
ravage 1
ruin 7
waste 11
razing
destruction 1
pillage 2
wreck 5
razor-like
keen[1] 2
razor-sharp
fine[1] 8
keen[1] 2
sharp 1
razz
gibe 1
ridicule 2
razzing
ridicule 1
razzle-dazzle
dazzle 3
glitter 4
virtuosity
razzmatazz
dazzle 3
glitter 4
moonshine 2
re
concerning
regarding

re (*cont.*)
relation 5
-in re
regarding
reach°
accomplish
achieve 2
arrive 2,3
catch 14b
communicate 2,3
contact 4
crest 4
expanse
extend 1
extension 2
fetch 4
gain 6
get 10,12,30a,47,
48b
go 8
hit 6
impress 1
jurisdiction
length 1
make 14
measure 1,15a
overtake 1
pass 8
penetrate 3
pull 11a,18c
range 1
run 12,33c
scope 1
span 3
spread 9
stretch 1,5
strike 8
string 11a
sweep 7
touch 7
width 2
-beyond reach
unapproachable 2
-out of reach
above 5
unapproachable 2
-reaches
frontier
-within easy reach
call 17
-within reach
available
convenient 2
hand 9
handy 1
near 1,9
nearby 1,2
reach a conclusion
decide 1
reach a decision
decide 1
reach-me-down
stale 2
used 1
reachable
accessible
possible 2
susceptible 2
reach out°
at **reach 1**
reacquire
get 32b
react°
acknowledge 2
behave
field 6
respond 1,2
rise 12b
reaction°
action 7
backlash
comment 2
reception 1
repercussion
reply 2
response
thing 4
reactionary°
conservative 1,3
conventional
hidebound

reactionary (*cont.*)
narrow-minded
right 6
reactivate
revive 3
reactive
responsive
sensitive 2,3
read°
carry 8
decipher 2
deliver 4
detect 2
give 7
go 34a
interpret 2
look 10
make 37d
mine 4
peruse
pore[1]
reel 2
register 8
rehearse
scan 1
study 1
take 10
understand 3
readable°
clear 5
legible
reader
oracle 1
school-book
text 4
readily°
easily 1
freely 2,5
gladly
hand 13
handily 1
pat[2] 2
promptly
soon 4
swimmingly
willingly
readiness°
devotion 3
facility 1
maturity 2,3
preparation 2
preparedness
providence 1
tendency
-in readiness°
at **readiness 3**
ready 1
reserve 8
ripe 3b
stand 5b
reading
indication 2
interpretation 2
lesson 1
narration 2
perusal
recitation 1
rendition 1
review 5
study 5,6
understanding 4
version 2
reading-stand
rostrum
read into°
at **read 4**
read the riot act
castigate
mind 10
reprimand 2
read-through
rehearsal 1
ready°
accessible
available
call 16
cash 1
condition 5
convenient 2
cut 16e
disposed
educate
expectant

ready (*cont.*)
expeditious
fit[1] 2,4
fluent
fund 2
game 7
glad 2
glib
groom 4
handy 1
line[1] 20,23a
loaded 2
mature 2,3
mellow 1
mobilize
money 1
mood 2
mount 5
order 10a
pat[2] 3
pipeline 2
place 11b
poise 3
poised 2
prepare 1,2,3,6
prepared 1,3
prime 5
process 3
prompt 1,2
purse 2
qualified 1
qualify 1,2
reserve 8
ripe 1,2,3b
school 4
season 2
set 31
smooth 10
stand 5b
tap[2] 4b
unhesitating 1
verge[1] 2
watch 4
willing
work 20b
-at the ready°
at **ready 9**
ready 7
-readies°
at **ready 8**
cash 1
fund 2
money 1
purse 2
readying
preparation 2
ready-made°
instant 5
peg 2
prepared 4
ready-mixed
instant 5
ready money
fund 2
money 1
ready reference
vade-mecum
ready to drop
tired 1
weary 1
ready-to-eat
prepared 4
ready-to-serve
instant 5
prepared 4
ready-to-wear
peg 2
ready-made 1
ready-witted
nimble 2
reaffirm
renew 4
stand 5c
real°
absolute 2
actual 1,2
authentic
bona fide
concrete
effective 3
factual 1
flesh 3
genuine 1
good 8

real (*cont.*)
hard 8
historical
honest 2
intrinsic
legitimate 1
lifelike
literal 2
live 1
material 5
materialize 2
natural 3,6
original 3
physical
pure 1
realistic 2
really 4
right 8
solid 4
sterling 1
tangible
unaffected[1]
veritable
wholehearted
-in real life
practice 4
real estate
land 3
property 3
realignment
shake-up
realistic°
actual 1
concrete
factual 1
feasible
graphic 1
hard 6
indeed 1
lifelike
natural 7
philosophical 2
photographic 1
picturesque 2
positive 6
practical 1
raw 6
sensible 1
sober 2
true 1
truthful
unflattering 1
vivid 2
realistically
practically 2
practice 4
reality°
case[1] 8
certainty 1
fact 1
given 4
object 1
substance 4
true 6
truth 1
-in reality°
at **reality 2**
actually
bottom 5
fact 4
indeed 1
really 1,3
substantially
truly 1
-in the reality
event 4
realizable
feasible
possible 2
realization°
accomplishment 1
achievement 3
appreciation 3
completion 1
consummation 1
embodiment 1
execution 1
fruition
fulfilment
perception 2
perfection 2
undertaking 2

reconcilement
reconciliation 1
resignation 2
reconcileoneself
accept 4
approve 3
bear 4
stomach 3
reconciler
peacemaker
reconciliation°
accord 2
rapprochement
resignation 2
settlement 3
understanding 1
recondite°
cryptic 2
dark 6
deep 2
difficult 2
heavy 12
hidden
incomprehensible
mysterious 2
obscure 5
occult 1
opaque 2
perplexing
profound 1
remote 3
secret 2
subtle 2
reconditeness
depth 2
opacity 2
perplexity 2
profundity 1
recondition
improve 1
overhaul 2
refresh 3
refurbish
renew 1
renovate
retouch
revamp
reconditioning
overhaul 3
reconfirm
renew 4
reconnaissance°
exploration
surveillance
reconnoitre°
explore 1
scout 1
spy 2
traverse 4
reconnoitring
reconnaissance
reconsider
better[1] 7
review 2
reconsideration
retrospect
review 6
reconstruct
modify 1
rehabilitate 2
restore 3
reconstruction
restoration 2
reconversion
restoration 2
record°
book 4
chronicle 1, 2
chronology
description 2
diary
document 1, 2
enrol 2
enter 3, 7
entry 4
file 3
get 36b
high 15
history 1, 4, 5
itemize
jot 1
journal 2

record (*cont.*)
list[1] 1, 2
lodge 6
make 16, 37c
mark 15a
memoir 1, 2
memorandum
minute[1] 2, 4
monitor 3
monument 2
narrative 1
notation 1
note 10, 12
paper 2b
poll 3
portrait
post[3] 3
present[2] 7
proceeding 2a
put 16a
register 1, 3, 4, 5
report 1
roll 13
schedule 1, 2
score 1, 11
set 17a
stamp 2
story 1
table 3
tabulate
take 31a
tale 1
tally 2, 3
tape 4
trace 1, 6
track 4
transaction 2
trophy 2
write 4a
-off the record°
at **record 8**
private 1, 6
privileged 4
unofficial
-records
memoir 2
note 10
paper 2b
proceeding 2a
transaction 2
record book
journal 2
record-breaking
record 9
recorded
go 27d
historical
recording
narration 1
record 3, 7
tape 2
recount°
chronicle 2
describe 1
detail 5
enumerate 1
narrate
recapitulate
recite 2
record 2
rehearse 2
relate 2
repeat 1
report 3
spin 2
tell[1] 1, 4
recounting
narration 1
recital 2
rehearsal 2
relation 4
story 1
recoup°
find 6
get 32b
pick 8f
recover 1
retrieve 2
recouping
recovery 2
recourse°
expedient 3
option 1
refuge 2

recover°
come 17a, 18b
convalesce
find 6
get 32b, 45b
heal 1
improve 2, 3
mend 3, 5
pick 8f
pull 13, 17
rally 4
reclaim
recoup
recuperate
redeem 1
reform 1
retrieve 2, 3
revive 1
salvage 1
save 1
snap 7
sober 4
recovered
better[1] 4
recovery°
improvement 2
rally 2
reform 3
restitution 2
revival 3
salvage 2
-beyond recovery
spout 4
recreant
disloyal
faithless 2
recreate
reproduce 1
recreation°
amusement 1, 2
diversion 3
enjoyment 1
entertainment 1
escape 6
fun 1
game 1
hobby
leisure 2
pastime
play 22
pleasure 1
relaxation 1
sport 1
recreational
leisure 4
recriminate
blame 1
task 3
recrimination°
blame 3
recrudescence
return 7
recruit°
call 12a
employ 1
enlist 1
enrol 1
initiate 4
raise 5
soldier 1
rectangle
square 7
rectangular
square 1
rectification
amendment 1
correction 1
reform 3
revision
rectify°
adjust 1
amend 2
correct 1
cure 2
fix 3
improve 1
make 31a
mend 1, 2
perfect 9
reform 1
remedy 4
revise 1

rectify (*cont.*)
right 19
straighten 1
rectilinear
square 7
rectitude°
character 3
good 20
honesty 1
honour 1
integrity 1
moral 4
morality 1
nobility 1
probity
purity 2
right 10
virtue 1
recto
page[1] 1
rector
clergyman 1
pastor
principal 4
recumbent°
flat 2
lie[2] 1
prone 1
prostrate 3
supine 1
recuperate°
come 17a
convalesce
gain 3
get 45b
heal 1
improve 3
mend 3, 5
pull 13
rally 4
recover 2
recuperation
improvement 2
rally 2
recovery 1
recur°
cycle 2
return 2
recurrence
return 7
recurrent°
eternal 2
frequent 1
periodic
perpetual 2
repetitive
recurrently
repeatedly
recurring
frequent 1
nagging
recurrent
recusant
dissident 1
rebel 4
recycle
cycle 2
red
embarrassed 1
fiery 2
inflamed
left 2
radical 5
rosy 1
tranquillizer
-in the red
debt 2
embarrassed 2
hard 17
insolvent
redact
edit 1
revise 1
redaction
revision
redactor
editor
red-blooded
hardy 1
manly
stalwart 3
redcap
porter[1]

redden
blush
colour 5
flush[1] 1
glow 7
reddish
rosy 1
redecorate
decorate 2
make 38a
modernize
refurbish
rehabilitate 2
renew 1
renovate
redeem°
atone
cancel 1
deliver 3
free 16
honour 8
improve 1
purify 2
ransom 3
reclaim
recoup
recover 1
rehabilitate 1
retrieve 3
salvage 1
save 1
spare 6
redeemer
saviour 1
redeeming
saving 1
redemption
ransom 1
recovery 2
salvage 2
redemptional
saving 1
redemptive
saving 1
redemptory
saving 1
redesign
modernize
redesigned
new 5
red-eye
booze 1
drink 5
liquor 1
red-faced
ashamed
embarrassed 1
guilty 2
shamefaced 2
red-handed°
red herring
misinformation
pretext 2
red-hot
fiery 1
hot 1
incandescent
live 3
redirect
divert 1
switch 5
red-letter
historic
special 2
red-letter day
feast 2
festival 2
gala 1
holiday 2
red-necked
narrow-minded
redness
flush[1] 4
glow 3
inflammation
rash[2] 1
redo
modernize
modify 1
reform 1
refresh 3
rehash 1, 2

redo (*cont.*)
renew 1
revamp
redolence
aroma 1
fragrance
odour 1
savour 2
scent 1
redolent°
fragrant
reminiscent
rich 8
sweet 2
redone
new 5
redouble
intensify
redoubt
bulwark 1
redoubtable
impressive
stalwart 2
strong 9
terrible 6
redound
boomerang
redress
adjust 1
amends
atone
compensate 1
correct 1
correction 1
improve 1
indemnity 1
make 40
offset 1
rectify
redeem 5
relief 1
remedy 2, 4
remuneration 2
reprisal
requital 1
requite 2
restitution 1
retribution
return 11
reward 4
right 19
sanction 4
satisfaction 2
satisfy 4
red tape
bureaucracy
palaver 1
rigmarole
reduce°
abbreviate 1
abridge
belittle
bring 8b
clip[2] 2
concentrate 2
consume 2
contract 4
cool 10
curtail
cushion 2
cut 5, 8
dampen 2
deaden 2
debase 1
decrease 1
degrade 2
demolish 1
depreciate 1
depress 2
detract
diet[1] 3
digest 4
diminish 1
discount 1
discredit 1
disparage 1
downgrade 1
dull 9
dwindle
ease 6
edit 3
erode
hamper[1]
hold 15a

reduce (*cont.*)
humble 4
lighten[2]
lower[1] 1, 3
mark 15b
militate 1
minimize 1
mitigate
moderate 5
modify 2
mortify 1
narrow 8
pare 2
pull 9c
rebate 3
relax 1, 2
relieve 1
remit 2
resolve 4
ruin 7, 10
scale[3] 5
shorten 1
slash 3
slim 3
smooth 12
soften 2
stem[2] 1
step 14b
subjugate
taper 2
temper 5
thin 8, 9
tone 5
vitiate 1
weaken 1
whittle 2
wind[2] 3a
wreck 1
-be reduced
give 15d
suffer 4
reduced
cheap 2
cut 28
limited 1
minimum 2
sale 5
small 5
straitened
-in reduced circumstances
needy
poor 1
reduce speed
brake 2
slack 3b
slow 14
reduce to nothing *etc.*
demolish 1
ruin 7, 10
wreck 1
reduction
abridgement 1
allowance 4
cut 21
decline 6
decrease 2
deduction 1
discount 4
drain 2
impairment
loss 2
rebate 1
sag 3
slack 5
slash 5
redundancy
excess 1
expletive 3
repetition 1
tautology
-redundancies
repetition 1
redundant°
circular 3
expletive 1
idle 2
needless 1
non-essential 1
repetitious
repetitive
superfluous
surplus 2

redundant (*cont.*)
unemployed
wordy
work 6
re-echo
ring[2] 1, 3
roll 5
re-echoing
ring[2] 3
re-educate
rehabilitate 1
reedy
scrawny
reek°
smell 4
stench
reeking
rancid
rank[2] 4
stinking 1
reeky
rank[2] 4
smelly
reel°
hobble 1
revolve 1
rock[2] 2
roll 12
rotate 1
spin 1, 6
stagger 1
sway 1
tape 2
turn 1
wind[2] 2
reeling
dizzy 1
doddering
giddy 1
groggy
reel off°
at **reel 2**
rattle 5
re-emergence
return 7
re-establish
rehabilitate 1
restore 2
revive 3
re-establishment
restitution 2
re-examination
review 6
revision
re-examine
review 2
ref
umpire 1
refashion
modernize
modify 1
reform 1
turn 3
refection
meal 1
refer°
apply 4
assign 4
compare 1
hint 3
observe 4
relegate 3
referee
decide 1
intermediary
judge 2, 6
mediator
moderate 6
moderator
officiate
peacemaker
umpire 1, 2
reference°
application 2
bearing 3
comment 1
connection 2
innuendo
mention 3, 5
metaphor
quotation 1

reference (*cont.*)
quote 1
regard 6
relation 1
respect 3
testimonial
touchstone
-in, with reference to
about 11
concerning
point 16
regarding
relation 5
reference book
companion 2
referendum
election
plebiscite
vote 1
referent
prototype 2
referential
metaphoric
referral
mention 5
reference 1
refer to°
at **refer 1**
borrow
concern 1
consult 2
drive 6
imply 2
intimate[2]
mean[1] 2
mention 1
observe 4
pertain
quote 1
regard 5
relate 3
speak 9
stand 7a
subject 7
tell[1] 2
touch 8
turn 23b
refill
replenish
top 7
refine°
civilize 1
concentrate 2
elaborate 4
enrich 1
filter 2
mature 6
perfect 9
polish 2
refined°
aesthetic 2
civil 3
cultivated
debonair 1
decorous
delicate 5
discriminating
educated 2
elegant 1
exquisite 1
fine[1] 9
genteel 3
graceful 2
ladylike
literary 1
mature 3
nice 1
polished 2
proper 3
respectable 1
sedate 2
self-possessed
sophisticated 1, 2
subtle 1
tasteful
well-bred
refinement°
charm 2
civilization 1
class 3
culture 1
discrimination 2
elaboration 1

refinement (*cont.*)
elegance 1
elevation 4
finesse 3
grace 1
propriety 2
sophistication 1, 2
style 4
subtlety 1
taste 4, 6
refining
refinement 3
refit
refurbish
renew 1
renovate
revamp
reflect°
consider 1
contemplate 2
debate 4
deliberate 4
disgrace 4
echo 4
follow 2
glance 2, 3
glisten
meditate 1, 2
mirror 3
mull
muse
ponder
puzzle 2
register 4
remark 2
represent 3
revolve 3
see 8
speculate 1, 3
study 2
think 3
weigh 2
reflecting
preoccupied 1
reflective
thought 1
reflection°
consideration 3
debate 2
discredit 5
echo 2
light[1] 3
mirror 2
observation 2
reminiscence
smear 4
speculation 2
thought 1
-reflections
reminiscence
reflective°
meditative
pensive
philosophical 2
preoccupied 1
thinking 1
thoughtful 2
wistful 2
reflector
mirror 1
reflex
automatic 2
immediate 1
instinctive 1
involuntary
mechanical 2
rebound 2
spontaneous 2
unconscious 2
reflexion
reflection 1
reform°
amend 1
amendment 1
improve 1
improvement 1
mend 2
modify 1
redeem 4
rehabilitate 1
remedy 4
straighten 2
turn 3

reformation
amendment 1
difference 3
reformatory
Borstal
jail 1
prison
reform school
reformer
liberal 4
progressive 3
reformist
liberal 2
progressive 2, 3
reform school
Borstal
jail 1
prison
refractoriness
obstinacy
refractory
contrary 2
defiant
difficult 3
disobedient 1
disorderly 2
factious
inflexible
insubordinate
mutinous 2
naughty 2
obstinate
perverse 3
problem 3
rebellious 2
recalcitrant
resistant 2
rogue 2
seditious
self-willed
stubborn
tenacious 1
tough 6
ungovernable
unruly
wilful 2
refrain°
avoid
cease 1
help 3
hold 18a
lay[3]
leave[1] 9
melody 1
motif
sacrifice 4
stop 1
refresh°
air 6
brush[2] 8
freshen 2
groom 3
modernize
rejuvenate
renew 1
restore 2
retouch
revive 2
top 7
vitalize
refreshed
fresh 5, 6
refresher
reminder
tonic 1
refreshing°
bracing
brisk 3
cool 1
exhilarating 1
tonic 2
refreshment°
snack 1
-refreshments°
at **refreshment 1**
snack 1
refrigerate°
chill 7
cool 9
freeze 1
preserve 3

refuge°
cover 14
hideaway
home 3
lair 2
nest 2
oasis 2
port
protection 1
recourse 2
resort 2
retreat 3
safety
sanctuary 2
security 1
shelter 1
refugee°
emigrant
fugitive 1
outcast
runaway 1
refulgence
glitter 4
glory 3
radiance 1
splendour 1, 2
refulgent
bright 1
gorgeous 1
luminous 1
radiant 1
refund
kickback
pay 1, 8a
rebate 1, 3
recoup
reimburse
repay
replace 3
refurbish°
decorate 2
fix 16b
improve 1
modernize
overhaul 2, 3
refresh 3
rehabilitate 2
renew 1
renovate
restore 3
revamp
refurbishment
restoration 2
refurnish
modernize
refresh 3
refurbish
renew 1
renovate
refusal°
denial 3
exclusion 1
non-compliance
objection
rebuff 1
regret 3
rejection
repulse 3
resistance 1
self-denial 2
refuse°
begrudge 2
boycott 1
decline 1
deny 2
deprive
dirt 1
dispense 3a
exclude 1
filth 1
garbage
hold 14b
junk 1
leftover 1
litter 1
object 4
pass 22
rebuff 2
reject 1, 2
repulse 2
resist 2
rid 2
rubbish 1
soil[1] 3

refuse (*cont.*)
spurn
swill 1
trash 3
turn 14a
waste 7
refuse heap
tip[2] 4
refuser
naysayer
refusing
negative 4
self-denial 2
refutation
denial 1
rebuttal
refute
contest 3
contradict 2
demolish 2
deny 1
destroy 4
discredit 3
disprove
explode 2
fight 2
rebut
regain
get 32b
reclaim
recoup
recover 1
redeem 1
retrieve 2,3
regain consciousness
come 18b
regain equilibrium
wind[2] 3b
regain one's health, strength
recover 2
recuperate
regal°
dignified
disdainful
distinguished 2
imperial 1,2
lofty 2
magnificent
majestic 1
plush
posh
princely 2,3
royal 1
sovereign 3
state 6
stately
statuesque
sumptuous
upper-class 2
regale°
banquet 2
feast 5
treat 4
regalia°
gear 3
habit 3
robe 2
uniform 3
regard°
abhor
admiration
admire 2
affection
appreciate 1
attachment 3
attention 1
behold
care 2
come 18c
concern 1,5
consider 3
consideration 1
contemplate 1
count 2
deference 1
dig 4
ear 1
esteem 1,2,3
estimation 2
eye 6,7,9,10

regard (*cont.*)
favour 4
feeling 3
find 4
friendship 2
gaze 1
hold 7
honour 2
interest 1
keep 6
look 1,12
love 1
name 2
note 7
notice 4
observance 1
observe 1,2
perceive 3
pertain
place 16
popularity
premium 3
prestige
put 16f
reckon 2
reference 2
relate 3
remark 1
respect 1,2,3
review 1
see 1
solicitude
take 8
think 2
thought 4
touch 8
view 7,9
watch 1
-as regards
concerning
for 12
part 10
point 16
term 6
-be regarded as
pass 16a
-in regard to
about 11
concerning
for 12
-regards°
at **regard 10**
compliment 2
greeting 3
respect 5
-without regard for
despite
-without regard to
irrespective
-with regard to
about 11
concerning
regarding
relation 5
term 6
regarded
reputed
regardful
observant 1
regard highly
admire 2
appreciate 1
esteem 1
look 12
regarding°
about 11
concerning
for 12
point 16
relation 5
term 6
regardless°
event 3
heedless
however 1,4
nevertheless
rate[1] 5
same 3
yet 5
regardless of°
at **regardless 1**
despite

regardless of (*cont.*)
irrespective of
notwithstanding 2
spite 2
regatta
game 2
regenerate
reclaim
rejuvenate
renew 1
reproduce 2
resurrect
regeneration
rebirth
renaissance
resurgence
regent
king
regicide
murder 1
regime°
diet[1] 2
government 2
set-up 1
regimen
diet[1] 2
discipline 1
form 4
regime
regiment°
standardize
regimentals
uniform 3
regimented
uniform 1
region°
area 3
belt 2
district
dominion 2
extent 3
limit 3
neighbourhood 1
part 6
place 2
precinct 1
province 1,2
quarter 3
reservation 4
territory 1
tract[1]
zone
-in the region of
neighbourhood 2
regional
local 2
parochial
provincial 1
resident 2
vernacular 1
regionalism
provincialism 1
regisseur
producer 2
register°
advise 2
apply 6
book 4
check 7
chronicle 1,2
enlist 1
enrol 1,2
enter 3,7
file 3
include 2
indicate 3
induct 2
journal 2
list[1] 1,2
lodge 6
mark 15a
notch 4
note 12
penetrate 4
poll 3,4
post[3] 3
present[2] 7
put 16a
range 2
reach 6
receipt 1
record 1,3

register (*cont.*)
reserve 2
roll 13
scale[3] 1
schedule 1,2
score 1
set 17a
show 1,6
sign 10a
sink 11
stamp 2
strike 9
table 3
tally 2,3
till[2]
write 4a
registration
entry 4
regnant
sovereign 2
regress
degenerate 2
relapse 1
revert
waste 2
wrong 8a
regressing
relapse 3
regression
relapse 3
regressive
backward 5
regressively
backwards 1
regret°
compunction 1
disappointment 2
grief 1
grieve 1
guilt 2
mourn
pang 2
penance 1
penitence
remorse
repent
-regrets°
at **regret 2**
sorrow 3
regretful°
afraid 2
apologetic
apologize 1
bad 8
guilty 2
penitent
remorseful
repentant
sorrowful 1
sorry 1
terrible 2
regretfulness
penitence
regret 2
regrettable°
deplorable 1
lamentable
piteous
unfortunate 3
regrettably
sadly 1
regular°
accustomed 1
average 3
common 1
consistent 2
constant 2
continual
conventional
customary 2
daily 2
deliberate 2
diurnal
equable 2
equal 2
even 1,3
everyday 2
fixed 3
formal 1
frequent 1
general 2
gradual
habitual 1
habitué

regular (*cont.*)
invariable 1
measured 3
methodical
natural 1,2
neat 3
non-stop 2
normal 1
orderly 1
ordinary 1
orthodox
patron 2
periodic
plane 3
recurrent
relentless 2
rhythmic
routine 3
set 29
smooth 1
solid 5
standard 6
standing 1
steady 2,10
stock 8
straight 1
strong 5
symmetrical
systematic
tranquil
typical 1
uniform 2
usual
yearly 3
regularity°
method 2
order 2
pattern 3
symmetry
uniformity 1
regularize
equalize
normalize
regularly
consistently 1
daily 3
frequently 1,2
non-stop 3
often
popularly
usually
yearly 1
regulate°
adjust 2
conduct 3
determine 4
direct 1
discipline 7
fix 3
govern 1
guide 3
manage 1
measure 12
moderate 6
modulate
normalize
peg 5
police 3
preside
regiment
restrain 2
restrict
rule 6
run 10
scale[3] 4
set 6
shape 7
time 22
tune 3
regulated
measured 1,2,4
regular 6
scientific
regulating
adjustment 1
regulation°
adjustment 1
code 1
administration 1
command 7
conduct 2
decree 1
direction 1
discipline 4
disposition 4

regulation (*cont.*)
government 1
guidance 1
law 1
leadership
order 4
policy
precept 1
regime
rule 1
-regulations
book 3
code 1
regulative
standard 5
regulatory
executive 3
standard 5
regurgitate°
bring 15d
heave 4
spew
throw 9a
vomit
rehab
rehabilitate 1
rehabilitate°
improve 1
mend 1
redeem 4
reform 1
renew 1
renovate
restore 3
revamp
straighten 2
rehabilitation
improvement 1
reform 3
restoration 2
shake-up
rehash°
paraphrase 1
reiterate
review 6
rehashing
review 6
rehearsal°
drill 4
narration 1
practice 2
recital 2
repetition 2
run-through 1
rehearse°
drill 2
go 34d
narrate
practise 1
relate 2
repeat 1
run 33d
rehearsed
practised 2
reification
embodiment 1
image 4
reify
embody 1
reign°
dominate 1
govern 1
predominate
regime
rule 5
reigning
dominant 1
sovereign 2
reimburse°
compensate 1
defray
offset 1
pay 1,8a
recoup
repay
restore 5
-be reimbursed
retrieve 3
reimbursement
allowance 2
indemnity 1
remuneration 2

reimbursement (*cont.*)
return 11
rein°
bend 1
brake 1
restraint 1
shackle 4
-reins°
at **rein 2**
bond 1
rein 3
reincarnate
resurrect
reincarnation
rebirth
reinforce°
bolster
brace 5
buttress
confirm 3
enforce 1
enhance
follow 11b
fortify 1
harden 2
heighten 2
inspire 2
intensify
patch 5
stay[2] 2
stiffen 2
strengthen 1
support 1, 2
sustain 2
reinforced
strong 12
reinforcement°
assistance
brace 1
follow-up
patch 1
refreshment 2
stay[2] 1
support 7, 8
-reinforcements°
at **reinforcement 3**
reserve 5
reinforcer
brace 1
reinforcing
support 7
rein in°
at **rein 3**
reinstate
redeem 4
rehabilitate 1
restore 4
reinstatement
restitution 2
reinterpretation
revision
reintroduce
bring 15b
resurrect
reinvigorate
quicken 3
refresh 1
rejuvenate
renew 1
restore 2
revive 3
vitalize
reiterate°
go 34d
parallel 4
parrot 2
recapitulate
renew 4
repeat 1
rub 3
reiteration
echo 1
repetition 1, 2
-reiterations
repetition 1
reiterative
expletive 1
frequent 1
reject°
back 9
banish 2

reject (*cont.*)
boycott 1
cast 11
castaway
cut 15d
decline 1
deny 2
diminish 2
discard 2
discredit 3
dismiss 2
dispense 3a
disqualify
drop 7
dump 2
eliminate 1
exclude 2
explode 2
forsake 2
freeze 4
give 17a
ignore 2
isolate
jilt
laugh 2b
leave[1] 10
outcast
pan 5
pass 22
push 8
put 16e
quash 1
rebuff 2
refuse[1] 1
renounce
repel 1
repudiate
repulse 2
rid 2
scorn 3
scrap[1] 4
shoulder 2
shun
spurn
suspend 3
throw 6b
thumb 3
turn 14a
undesirable 1
use 15
veto 1
-rejects
lumber 1
rubbish 1
scrap[1] 2
rejected
abandoned 1
deserted
lonesome 1
unpopular
unwelcome 2
rejecter
naysayer
rejection°
brush-off
denial 3
exclusion 2
non-compliance
rebuff 1
refusal 1
repulse 3
scorn 1
suspension 1
veto 2
-rejections
scrap[1] 2
rejector
naysayer
rejoice°
celebrate 2
exult
glory 5
revel 1
roll 10b
rejoicing
festivity 1
fête 1
gaiety 2
merry 1
mirth
triumph 2
rejoin
answer 4
reply 1

rejoin (*cont.*)
respond 1
retort 2
rejoinder
answer 1, 2
rebuttal
reply 2
response
retort 1
wisecrack 1
rejuvenate°
heal 1
modernize
reclaim
renew 1
restore 2, 3
resurrect
revive 3
strengthen 2
vitalize
rejuvenated
new 5
rejuvenating
exhilarating 1
invigorating
refreshing
vital 4
rejuvenation
rebirth
refreshment 2
renaissance
restoration 2
resurgence
rekindle
restore 2
relapse°
revert
set-back
relate°
apply 4
chronicle 2
combine 1
communicate 3
compare 3
connect 2
describe 1
enumerate 1
identify 2, 4
impart 2
link 4
measure 12
narrate
obtain 3
pertain
put 25a
recapitulate
recite 2
record 2
recount 1
rehearse 2
report 3
spin 2
sympathize 2
tell[1] 1
tie 6b
related°
akin
attendant 1
fellow 5
kin 2
kindred 1, 2
near 7
proportional
relative 1
relevant
relatedness
fraternity 2
relater
raconteur
relate to°
at **relate 4**
bear 8
come 18c
concern 1
go 28b
identify 4
pertain
regard 5
sympathize 2
touch 8
turn 19a
relating
narration 1

relating to
about 11
concerning
term 6
relation°
account 6
bearing 3
belonging
brother
comparison 2
connection 2
history 1
kin 1
link 2
narration 1
offshoot 2
proportion 1
recital 2
reference 2
regard 6
rehearsal 2
relevance
respect 3
tie-in
-in relation to°
at **relation 5**
term 6
-relations°
at **relation 6**
connection 4
dealings
family 1
flesh 5
kin 1
liaison 1
people 2
term 7b
truck 2
relationship°
affair 4
affinity 1
association 2, 3
bearing 3
belonging
bond 3
comparison 2
connection 2
identification 4
kinship 1, 2
liaison 1, 3
link 2
love 5a
parallel 3
proportion 1
rapport
ratio
relation 1, 2, 6b
romance 1
term 7b
tie 8
tie-in
-relationships
dealings
relative°
brother
kin 1
offshoot 2
proportional
relation 3
relevant
-relatives
connection 4
family 1
flesh 5
people 2
relatively°
part 9
partially
quite 2
somewhat
relative to°
at **relative 2**
about 11
concerning
term 6
relator
narrator
raconteur
relax°
break 3
ease 5
give 9
liberalize 2
loose 9, 12

relax (*cont.*)
mitigate
moderate 5
relent
remit 2
rest[1] 6
settle 8
sit 4
slack 3a
slow 15
soften 1, 4
temper 5
thaw 2
tranquillize
weaken 3
wind[2] 3b
relaxation°
amusement 1
diversion 3
ease 1
entertainment 1
hobby
interest 5
leisure 2
let-up
pastime
recreation
remission 2
repose 1
rest[1] 2, 3
sport 1
relaxed°
casual 3, 5
comfortable 1
cool 2
easy 2, 6
easygoing
familiar 3
free 8, 9
genial
home 4a
indulgent
informal 1
lax 1
level-headed
limp[2] 1
loose 6
nonchalant
offhand 1
restful 2
slow 1
tranquil
uninhibited
relaxing
comfortable 3
cosy 1
dreamy 3
easy 6
restful 1
sedative 2
snug
soft 3
soothing 1
relay
broadcast 1
shift 4
release°
bring 13b
carry 8
deliver 3
delivery 2
discharge 1, 8, 11
disclose 1
disengage
dismiss 1, 3
dismissal 2
drop 8
emancipate
excuse 2
exempt 1
exemption
extricate
finish 8
free 14, 15
freedom 2
give 14
immunity 1
issue 10
leak 5
let[1] 6a, 6d, 8b
liberate 1
liberation
loose 11
news 2
open 23

release (*cont.*)
outlet 1
pardon 1, 2
part 14
pay 11c
promotion 5
put 23e, 24
ransom 1, 3
record 7
redeem 2
relax 1
relief 1
relieve 2
relinquish 2
remission 1
rescue 1, 2
resign 1
save 1
secrete[2]
secretion
send 3
shed[2] 2
sign 8
slack 3a
spare 7
story 4
tell[1] 2
trip 8
vent 3, 4
-be released
get 40d, 44b
released
clear 15
exempt 2
free 2
loose 2
quit 4
releasing
liberation
release 3
relegate°
delegate 3
relent°
capitulate 2
thaw 2
weaken 3
yield 3
relentless°
constant 2
cutthroat 2
eternal 2
incurable 2
irresistible 2
laborious 2
merciless
mortal 4
nagging
non-stop 2
ongoing 1
remorseless 2
repetitive
rigid 4
ruthless
severe 1
stalwart 2
steady 2
stiff 4
torrential
unmerciful
unmitigated
relentlessly
hard 13
non-stop 3
severely 2
relentlessness
resolution 1
severity 1
relevance°
application 2
aptitude 1
bear 8
bearing 3
connection 2
reference 2
regard 6
significance 2
relevancy
application 2
bearing 3
point 7
regard 6
relevance

relevant°
applicable
apply 4
bear 8
come 18c
concern 1
fitting 1
hold 11
meaningful 1
obtain 3
pat² 3
pertinent
point 18
regard 5
relative 1
respective
significant 1
relevantly
pat² 2
reliability
credit 3
loyalty
permanence
regularity 2
responsibility 4
stability 2
strength 6
trust 2
reliable°
authentic
authoritative 2
certain 2
concrete
definitive 2
durable
dutiful
faithful 4
foolproof
good 8, 13
historical
honest 1
infallible 2
loyal
perfect 5
positive 1
pukka 2
reputable
responsible 2
ripe 2
rocky¹ 2
safe 3
secure 3
solid 5
solvent
sound² 4
staunch 1
steady 6
straight 4
sure 2, 3
true 2
trustworthy
truthful
yeomanly
reliably
honestly 1
reliance°
belief 1
confidence 1
expectation 3
faith 1
trust 1
reliant
confident 2
relative 2
relic°
fogy
keepsake
memento 1
remnant 1
vestige
relief°
aid 2
assistance
charity 3
comfort 2
entertainment 1
escape 6
freedom 3
hand 2
help 9
leisure 2
let-up
outlet 1
relaxation 2
relief (*cont.*)
remedy 2
salve 2
sculpture 1
set 20b
solace 1
substitute 2
-on relief
needy
relieve°
aid 1
assist 3
comfort 1
divest 1
dull 9
ease 6
excuse 2
free 16
help 2
lighten²
mitigate
moderate 5
put 24
raise 9
relax 1
rid 1
remedy 3
salve 3
slake
soften 2
solace 2
spell¹ 2
stand 8
still 9
substitute 1
relieved
exempt 2
free 11
relieve oneself
defecate
religion°
faith 2
ministry 1
persuasion 2
religionist
puritan 1
religiosity
devotion 1
religious°
clergyman 2
devout 1, 2
divine 1
godly
holy 1
monk
pious 1
sacred 3
solemn 2
spiritual 1
religious body, cult, ***etc.***
sect 1
religiousness
devotion 1
piety 2
relinquish°
abandon 1
abdicate
cede
concede 2
deliver 2
dispense 3a
drop 7
evacuate 2
forfeit 2
forgo 2
forsake 3
give 11, 16
kiss 3
leave¹ 7
part 14
pull 14d
quit 2
render 3
resign 1
sacrifice 4
sign 8
spare 8
surrender 1
throw 9b
vacate 2
waive 1
yield 2
relinquished
forfeit 3
relinquishment
resignation 1
sacrifice 2
surrender 3
waiver
reliquary
receptacle
relish°
appetite 1
delight 2
devour 3
eagerness 1
enjoy 1
enjoyment 1
enthusiasm 1
gloat
glory 5
gusto
hors-d'oeuvre
like² 1
love 2, 8
luxuriate 1
partiality 2
revel 1
roll 10b
salt 2
savour 3
seasoning
spice 1
stomach 2
taste 1, 3
zest 1
relisting
repetition 2
relocate
displace 1
emigrate
evacuate 3
migrate 1
move 2
remove 6
second¹ 10
shift 1
transplant
relocation
move 8
movement 1
reluctance°
aversion 1
compunction 2
qualm
reservation 1
scruple 1
reluctant°
averse
backward 1
coy
disinclined
guarded
hang 5
hate 2
indisposed 2
loath
mealy-mouthed
modest 1
scruple 2
shy 4
slow 10
tardy 2
reluctantly
protest 2
rely°
hang 7e
pivot 4
revolve 2
trust 5
rely (up)on°
at **rely**
believe 2
count 3
credit 5
depend 2
draw 13a
fall 9
figure 11a
gamble 2
go 26b, 32g
hang 7e
hope 3
lean² 4a
look 7b
reckon 4
rely (up)on (*cont.*)
store 5
swear 3
trust 5
remain°
abide 3
cling 2
continue 2
dwell 1
endure 1
exist 3
hang 7c
hold 11, 13
keep 7
last² 1
lie² 3
linger 1
live 8
persist 2
rest¹ 7, 9
rest² 2
settle 4
sit 4
stand 2b, 4
stay¹ 1, 2, 3, 5
stick¹ 5, 6, 7, 11, 19
tarry 2
-remains°
at **remain 4**
body 1
cadaver
corpse
dregs 1
embers
relic 2
remainder 1
remnant 2
residue
rest² 1
ruin 6
scrap¹ 2
sediment
vestige
wreckage
remainder°
balance 7
difference 5
heel¹ 1
leftover 1
remain 4a
remnant 2
residue
rest² 1
-as a remainder
over 8
-remainders
leftover 1
remaining°
enduring
excess 3
leftover 2
lingering 1
odd 3
outstanding 2
over 8
present¹ 2
resident 1
residual
unused 3
remain silent
tongue 3
remake
convert 1
modernize
modify 1
remand
imprison
imprisonment
put 13b
remand centre
prison
remand home
prison
remark°
behold
comment 1, 2, 3
find 3
mention 5
note 3
notice 1
observation 2
observe 4
perceive 1
remark (*cont.*)
reference 1
say 1
sight 8
remarkable°
amazing
arresting
brilliant 2
considerable 2
conspicuous 3
different 2
effective 2
excellent
exotic 2
extraordinary 1, 2
extreme 1
fantastic 1
first-rate
funny 2
great 6
marked
marvellous
memorable
miraculous
notable 2
noticeable 2
odd 1
out-of-the-way 2
outstanding 1
particular 2
phenomenal
portentous 2
prodigious 2
prominent 1
queer 1
salient
signal 3
singular 1
spanking 1
special 1
splendid 2
strange 1
striking
stunning 2
supernatural
unusual
virtuoso 2
remarkably
awfully
eminently
especially 1
exceedingly
extra 6
notably 1
perfectly 1
really 4
very 1
remark on
comment 4
note 13
observe 4
remedial
medicinal
therapeutic
remedial programme
therapy 1
remedy°
action 4
amends
antidote
atone
correct 1
correction 1
cure 1, 2
drug 1
fix 3
heal 2
help 2, 9
make 31a
medicine
mend 1
pill 1
prescription 2
preventive 4
recourse 2
rectify
reform 1
relief 1
resort 2
therapy 1
-as a remedy for
for 4
remedying
treatment 2
remember°
commemorate
finger 5a
forget 1
know 2
memorialize
memorize
mind 9
observe 5
place 17
recall 1
reckon 5b
recognize 1
recollect
reminisce
retain 4
think 4
-be remembered
go 27d
remembered
immortal 3
remembering
recall 4
retrospect
remembrance°
keepsake
memento 1
memorial 2
memory 3
mind 2
recall 4
recollection
relic 1
thought 5
toast 1
token 3
trophy 2
-remembrances
thought 5
toast 1
remembrancer
token 3
remind°
cue 2
move 6
point 21b
prompt 4
take 29a
reminder°
cue 1
keepsake
memorandum
memorial 2
notation 1
prod 6
prompt 6
remembrance 2
token 3
trophy 2
remindful
redolent 2
reminisce°
recall 1
remember 2
reminiscence°
memory 2
recollection
remembrance 1
thought 5
-reminiscences°
at **reminiscence**
memoir 2
thought 5
reminiscent°
homesick
suggestive 1
reminiscent of°
at **reminiscent**
redolent 2
suggestive 1
remiss°
careless 2
delinquent 2
derelict 2
disobedient 1
inattentive
neglect 2
slack 1
thoughtless 2
remissible
venial

remission°
excuse 5
forgiveness 1
pardon 1
relaxation 2
release 3
relief 1
reprieve 2
waiver
remissness
failure 1
neglect 4
negligence
remit°
dispatch 2
forward 7
mitigate
moderate 5
pardon 2
pay 1
relax 1
send 2
remittable
venial
remittance°
allowance 2
pay 12
stipend
subscription 1
remnant°
fragment 1
heel[1] 1
leftover 1
morsel 2
piece 1
relic 2
shadow 3
shred 1
snip 3
stub 1
trace 2
vestige
-remnants
embers
leftover 1
odds 5
remain 4a
rest[2] 1
rubbish 1
scrap[1] 2
remodel
adapt 2
alter
convert 1
improve 1
make 38a
modernize
modify 1
reform 1
refurbish
renovate
shape 9
turn 3
vary 1
remodelled
new 5
remodelling
alteration
remonstrance
objection
reprimand 1
sermon 1
remonstrate
argue 1
codemn 1
damn 1
insist 1
lecture 4
object 4
reason 8
remonstration
lecture 2
objection
reprimand 1
sermon 1
remorse°
apologize 1
compunction 1
grief 1
guilt 2
pang 2
penitence
regret 1, 2
repent

remorseful°
apologetic
apologize 1
bad 8
guilty 2
penitent
regret 1
regretful
repent
repentant
shamefaced 2
sorry 1
terrible 2
remorseless°
brutal 1
relentless 1
ruthless
sanguinary 1
unrepentant
remote°
aloof 2, 3
back 12
cold 3, 8
cool 4
cry 8
desolate 1
distant 1
extraneous 2
far 9
far-away 1
foreign 3
forgetful
frigid 2
icy 2
impassive
improbable
isolated 3
neutral 1
obscure 3
off 5
outlying
outside 8
reserved
secluded 2
sight 6a
slender 2
solitary 1
standoffish
subtle 2
ulterior 2
unaffected[2]
unapproach-
able 1, 2
unlikely 1
withdrawn 2
remotely
vaguely 1
remoteness
distance 1
reserve 4
solitude 2
remoter
ulterior 2
remotest
extreme 3
ultimate 4
remould
modify 1
removable
separable
removal°
deduction 1
ejection 2
eviction
exclusion 3
execution 3
expulsion
extraction 1
move 8
purge 4
remove°
cast 14
clear 26, 31a
cut 16a, 16b
deduct
delete
deprive
detach
dismiss 1
dispense 3b
displace 2
divest 2
drain 4
draw 8

remove (*cont.*)
eject 1
eliminate 1
empty 8
erase 2
evict
exclude 3
execute 3
expel 1
extinguish 2
extract 1
get 40c
hook 7
mine 3
move 2
phase 6
pluck 2
pull 3
purge 2
raise 9
rake[1] 5
rub 4
scrape 2
shave 1
skim 1
snatch 3
strike 4
strip[2] 4
supplant
sweep 2
take 3, 14, 34a
transfer 1
transplant
transport 1
wash 2, 4
wipe 2, 3
withdraw 3
removed
cool 4
detached 1
distant 1
indifferent 1
isolated 2
neutral 1
oblivious
perfunctory 1
remote 1
retiring
separate 7
standoffish
removing
removal 1
remunerate
compensate 3
pay 1, 8a
recoup
reimburse
reward 4
remuneration°
allowance 2
bonus
consideration 2
fee 2
honorarium
indemnity 1
pay 12
requital 1
restitution 1
run 40
salary
satisfaction 2
stipend
wage 1
remunerative
compensatory
economic 2
fat 4
gainful
productive 3
profitable 1
successful 2
worthwhile 1
renaissance°
rebirth
resurgence
revival 2
renascence
rebirth
renaissance
resurgence
revival 2
rend°
lacerate
pull 4
rip 1

rend (*cont.*)
split 1
tear 1
render°
account 1
leave[1] 5
paint 4
portray 1
return 6
transcribe 2
translate 1
render down°
at **render 8**
rendering°
execution 4
paraphrase 1
portrait
rendition 1
transcript 1
translation 1
version 2
rendezvous
appointment 1
date 2
engagement 1
meet[1] 2
meeting 1
rendition°
execution 4
paraphrase 1
recital 2
rendering
revision
translation 1
version 1, 2
renegade°
defector
deserter
disloyal
nonconformist 1, 2
outlaw 1
runaway 2
traitor
traitorous
turncoat
renege°
back 18
go 25
renew°
heal 1
proceed 1
refresh 1, 3
refurbish
rehabilitate 2
rejuvenate
repair 1
replace 1
replenish
restore 2, 3
resurrect
revive 2, 3
strengthen 1
vitalize
renewal
rally 2
rebirth
refreshment 2
renaissance
repair 2
restoration 2
resurgence
return 7
revival 1
renewed
fresh 4
new 5
renounce°
abandon 4
abdicate
break 24b
cede
climb 5b
deny 3
dispense 3a
drop 7
forfeit 2
forgo 1, 2
forsake 3
give 17a
kiss 3
leave[1] 4, 9
part 14
pass 22
quit 2

renounce (*cont.*)
recant
refrain[1] 2
reject 1
relinquish 1
repudiate
resign 1
retract 2
reverse 4
revoke
sacrifice 4
swear 4
throw 6b, 9b
vacate 2
waive 1
yield 2
renounced
forfeit 3
renouncing
self-denial 2
renovate°
decorate 2
fix 16b
improve 1
modernize
overhaul 2
reform 1
refresh 3
refurbish
rehabilitate 2
renew 1
restore 3
revamp
touch 12
renovation
overhaul 3
reform 3
repair 2
restoration 2
renown°
celebrity 1
distinction 2
fame
glory 1
kudos
laurels
lustre 2
name 2
note 8
popularity
prestige
prominence 1
superiority 2
renowned°
big 5
brilliant 3
celebrated
distinguished 1
eminent 1
famous
glorious 1
grand 2
great 5
honourable 4
illustrious
immortal 3
legendary 3
lofty 2
noble 3
notable 1
notorious 2
outstanding 1
popular 1
prestigious
prominent 2
public 6
successful 3
well-known 2
rent°
charter 5
engage 1
flaw 2
gap 1
get 1
hire 2, 3, 4, 5
hole 2
leak 2
lease 2
let[1] 3
opening 1
ragged 1
rift 2
rip 1, 3
slash 4
split 7

rent (*cont.*)
take 4
tattered
tear 4
rental
hire 5
lease 1
rent[1] 2
rent-boy
prostitute 1
renter
occupant
tenant
renunciation
denial 2
rejection
resignation 1
self-denial 1, 2
surrender 3
waiver
reoccur
recur
return 2
reoccurring
recurrent
reopen
renew 2
revive 2, 3
reorder
edit 4
reorganization
reform 3
shake-up
reorganize
edit 4
modify 1
reform 1
straighten 2
tidy 4
turn 3
vary 1
reorient
modify 1
rehabilitate 1
rep
merchant 2
representative 4
seller
repair°
amend 2
amendment 1
correct 1
cure 2
doctor 3
fix 3, 16d
go 2
heal 1, 2
improve 1
improvement 1
mend 1, 4
overhaul 2
patch 5
rectify
reform 1
refresh 3
refurbish
rehabilitate 2
remedy 4
renovate
resort 3
restoration 2
restore 3
retouch
revamp
right 19
service 2
sew
trim 6
upkeep 1
withdraw 4
-beyond repair
hopeless 1
ramshackle
rock[1] 3b
repairman
engineer 3
reparation
atonement
correction 1
damage 3
indemnity
penance 1
remuneration 2

repress (*cont.*)
curb 2
gag[1] 1
govern 2
hide[1] 4
hold 14a
hush 4
inhibit
keep 14a
master 8
oppress 2
quash 2
quell 1
quench 2
restrain 2
silence 4
smother 4
stamp 4
stifle 2
subdue 1
suppress 1, 3
swallow 4
withhold 1
repressed
inhibited
meek 2
passive 2
pent-up
sober 3
subconscious 1
subdued 1
repressing
suppression
repression°
check 14
despotism
domination 2
oppression
suppression
repressive°
oppressive 1
overbearing
prohibitive 1
reprieval
pardon 1
reprieve°
excuse 5
forgiveness 1
pardon 2
remission 1
respite 2
stay[1] 6
reprimand°
bawl 3
blame 1
call 7b
castigate
chew 3
come 11
condemn 1
correct 2
damn 1
discipline 8
dress 4
hell 4
jump 7
lambaste 2
lecture 2, 4
lesson 4
mind 10
piece 10
preach 2
rap 2
rate[2]
rebuke 1, 2
scold 1
sermon 1
slap 5
speak 12a
task 3
tell[1] 10
tongue-lashing
upbraid
vituperate
reprint
dummy 2
reprisal°
reaction 3
recrimination
requital 2
retribution
revenge 1
vengeance 1
reprise
refrain[2]
repeat 3
repetition 2
reproach
abuse 3
blame 1, 3
condemn 1
disapproval
imputation
indignity
lecture 2, 4
mind 10
rate[2]
rebuke 1, 2
reprimand 1, 2
scold 1
sermon 1
task 3
tell[1] 10
twit[1]
upbraid
vituperate
-above reproach
innocent 2
pure 6
-beyond reproach
irreproachable
reproachful°
abusive 1
bitter 5
reprobate°
abandoned 2
degenerate 1, 3
immoral 1
libertine 1, 2
miscreant 1, 2
profligate 3
sinner
reproduce°
copy 4
counterfeit 4
duplicate 3
echo 4
forge 3
mimic 2
mirror 3
pirate 3
proliferate
propagate 1
quote 1
reflect 1
render 1
repeat 2
represent 3
run 19
trace 6
transcribe 1
reproduction°
copy 1
counterfeit 3
dummy 2
duplicate 2
echo 2
facsimile
generation 1
imitation 4, 5
likeness 2
mirror 2
print 2
repeat 3
replica
representation 1, 4
transcript 2
reproductive
sexual 1
reproductive organs
genitals
reproof°
blame 3
disapproval
judgement 3
lecture 2
lesson 4
punishment 1
rebuke 2
reprimand 1
sermon 1
slap 5
tongue-lashing
reprove°
blame 1
call 7b
condemn 1
correct 2
damn 1
discipline 8
dress 4
lambaste 2
lecture 4
mind 10
punish 1
rate[2]
rebuke 1
reprimand 2
scold 1
speak 12a
task 3
tell[1] 10
upbraid
reproving
reproachful
reptile
snake 1
villain
reptilian
serpentine 1
slippery 2
republican
democratic
repudiate°
back 9, 18
break 24b
cancel 1
deny 3
dismiss 2
drop 7
exclude 2
explode 2
forsake 3
go 25
kiss 3
rebuff 2
recant
refuse[1] 1
reject 1
renege 2
renounce
retract 2
revoke
set 15b
spurn
take 30
throw 6b
vacate 3
wash 10
repudiated
invalid[2]
repudiation
abolition
denial 1
exclusion 2
expulsion
rebuff 1
rejection
repugnance
abhor
aversion 1
disgust 2
dislike 2
distaste 2
horror 1
loathing
phobia
revulsion
repugnant°
abhorrent
abominable 1
disagreeable 1
disgusting
distasteful
fearful 3
foul 1
frightful 2
grisly
gruesome
hateful 1
loathsome
nasty 1
nauseous
obnoxious
offensive 3
outrageous 3
repellent
repugnant (*cont.*)
repulsive
ugly 2
undesirable 2
unpalatable
unsavoury
vile 2
wicked 6
yucky
repulse°
defeat 1, 3
defy 2
fight 5
frustrate 1
hold 18b
offend 2
rebuff 1, 2
reject 2
repel 1
revolt 3
sicken 2
turn 13a, 17b
ward 3
repulsed
sick 6
repulsion
reaction 2
repulsive°
abhorrent
abominable 1
disagreeable 1
disgusting
distasteful
evil 5
fearful 3
forbidding 1
foul 1
frightful 2
ghastly 1
grisly
gross 5
gruesome
hateful 1
hideous 1
horrible 1
indecent 2
loathsome
mangy
monstrous 1
nameless 3
nauseous
obnoxious
obscene 1, 2
offensive 3
outrageous 3
repellent
repugnant
revolting
seamy
shocking 2
ugly 1, 2
uninviting
unsavoury
vile 2
wicked 6
repurchase
redeem 1
reputable°
estimable
good 9
honest 1
honourable 2
prominent 2
proud 3
reliable
respectable 1
righteous 1
savoury 2
well-thought-of
reputation°
blot 3
celebrity 1
distinction 2
face 4
fame
glory 1
laurels
name 2
note 8
popularity
prestige
prominence 1
record 6
renown
reputation (*cont.*)
standing 6
status 1
repute
celebrity 1
distinction 2
face 4
fame
glory 1
name 2
note 8
popularity
prestige
prominence 1
renown
reputation 1
standing 6
status 1
reputed°
pretended
supposed 1
reputedly
supposedly
request°
appeal 3
application 4
apply 7
ask 2, 6b
beg 1
bid 2
call 7a, 8a, 10a, 14
claim 1
command 1
demand 4, 5
desire 2, 4
invitation 1
order 4, 7
petition 1, 2
plea 1
plead 1, 2
pray 1
prayer 1
press 6
put 20a
requisition 1, 2
run 43
seek 3
send 6
speak 7c
sue 2
suit 5
urge 2
wish 2, 4
-in request
demand 7
-on request
demand 7, 8
requested
demand 7
Requiem
keen[2] 2
lament 2
require°
ask 2
call 8a
charge 10, 13
claim 3
command 1
demand 1, 2, 3
desire 2
direct 3
drive 1
enforce 1, 2
entail
exact 3
expect 3
force 7
have 9
indicate 4
insist 1
instruct 2
involve 2
lack 2
lay[1] 10, 17b
look 6a
make 2
need 1
obligate
oblige 2
order 14
prescribe
pressure 5
provide 3
require (*cont.*)
say 10
screw 4
speak 7c
stipulate
take 16
tell[1] 5
want 2
will 5
wish 2
required
behove
bound[3] 2
essential 1
imperative 1
incumbent 1
indispensable 1
mandatory
must 1
necessary 1
obligatory
obliged 2
order 10b
prerequisite 1
regulation 4
standard 5
staple 1
supposed 2
vital 1
requirement°
call 15
claim 1
condition 2
demand 6
desire 4
dictate 2
expectation 3
must 2
necessity 1
need 2
obligation 1, 2
order 4
precondition
prerequisite 2
provision 2
qualification 2
specification 3
standard 1
stipulation
ultimatum
want 4
-requirements
string 7
ultimatum
requisite
condition 2
essence 4
essential 1
imperative 1
indispensable 1
mandatory
must 2
necessary 1
necessity 1
need 3
obligatory
paramount
prerequisite 1, 2
requirement 1
staple 1
stipulation
vital 1
want 4
-requisites
apparatus
requisition°
claim 1
demand 4, 5
desire 4
exact 3
order 7, 15
procure 1
request 1, 2
requital°
desert[2]
gratification
indemnity 1
reprisal
restitution 1
retribution
return 11
reward 1
run 40
satisfaction 2
vengeance 1

resolve (*cont.*)
follow-through
grit
intend
loyalty
nail 10
patch 7
patience 2
perseverance
persevere
persistence
pluck 1
purpose 2, 5
resolution 1, 3
rule 7
satisfy 2
self-control 1
settle 1, 3
solve
sort 10a
spirit 2
spunk
stability 2
straighten 1
tenacity 1
will 1
work 19c
resolved
bent 4
bound³ 3
determined 1
earnest 1
enterprising
firm 4
fixed 2, 3
indomitable
inflexible
intent 5
mind 12
patient 2
persevere
persistent 1
purposeful
reconcile 4
resolute
rigid 4
steadfast
stiff 4
strong-minded
resolving
decision 1
determination 2
resonance
timbre
tone 2
vibes
-resonances
vibes
resonant°
deep 7
full 11
rich 7
rotund 2
resonate
blare 1
boom 1
peal 2
resound
ring² 1
roll 5
sound¹ 4
vibrate
resonating
ring² 3
resort°
expedient 3
nest 2
oasis 2
recourse 1
refuge 2
retreat 3
resort to°
at **resort 3**
draw 13a
fall 9
frequent 2
refer 3
take 21
turn 23
use 1
resound°
blare 1
boom 1
echo 3

resound (*cont.*)
peal 2
ring² 1
roll 5
sound¹ 4
thunder 2
resounding
deep 7
noisy
resonant
resource°
asset 2
expedient 3
finance 1
recourse 2
resort 2
stand-by 3
-resources°
at **resource 1**
asset 1
capital 3
circumstance 1
estate 2
finance 1, 2
fund 2
material 4
mean³ 4b
money 2
principal 5
property 2
purse 2
riches
saving 4
substance 5
treasury
resourceful°
agile 2
brilliant 4
clever 3
creative
enterprising
foxy 1
go-ahead 2
imaginative 1
ingenious
productive 2
shrewd
versatile 1
resourcefulness
gumption 1
ingenuity
initiative 2
originality
resource 1
resourceless
blank 5
respect°
admiration
admire 2
adore 1
appreciate 1
approve 3
civility
conform 1
consider 2
consideration 1
courtesy
deference 1
detail 1
duty 2
esteem 1, 3
estimation 2
eye 6
fear 2, 6
hallow 2
heed 1, 2
homage
honour 2, 5
keep 6
look 12
mark 12
memory 3
name 2
note 7
notice 4
obedience
obeisance
obey 1
observance 1
observe 1, 5
piety 1
prostration 2
recognize 2
reference 2
regard 3, 7, 8, 9

respect (*cont.*)
relate 3
revere
reverence 1
submit 1
tribute 1
venerate
veneration
way 6
worship 2
-in all respects
altogether
entirely 1
exactly 2
precisely 2
through 7
wholly 1
world 6
-in any respect
however 2
-in every respect
entirely 1
exactly 2
world 6
-respects°
at **respect 5**
compliment2
greeting 3
regard 10
-with respect to
about 11
concerning
point 16
regarding
relation 5
respectability
character 3
decorum 1
dignity 2
propriety 2
rectitude
shame 4
virtue 1
respectable°
clean 4
considerable 1, 2
decent 2, 3, 5
estimable
fair¹ 4
genteel 2
good 9
honourable 2
ladylike
moral 1
presentable 2
proper 3
reputable
savoury 2
straight 4
substantial 1
tidy 3
venerable
respectableness
dignity 2
respected
beloved 1
distinguished 1
elder 2
eminent 1
estimable
good 9
grand 2
honourable 4
illustrious
important 2
lofty 2
noble 3
noted
prestigious
prominent 2
proud 3
reputable
respectable 1
time-honoured
venerable
well-thought-of
respectful°
attentive 2
civil 3
courteous
dutiful
humble 2
obedient
observant 2
polite 1

respectfully
cap 3
respectfulness
courtesy
obedience
obeisance
respecting
about 11
concerning
for 12
observance 1
regarding
relation 5
respective°
proper 6
several 2
respectively°
respiration
exhalation 1
respire
breathe 2
exhale
respite°
break 28
gap 1
holiday 1
interlude
interruption 2
leisure 2
let-up
lull 1
moratorium
recess 2
repose 1
reprieve 1, 2
rest¹ 2
truce 1
wait 4
resplendence
glare 1
glow 2
radiance 1
splendour 1
resplendent
bright 1
brilliant 1
dazzling
glorious 4
golden 3
gorgeous 1
luminous 1
magnificent
radiant 1
regal 1
splendid 1
respond°
answer 4
perform 2
react 2
reply 1
retort 2
say 5
respond to°
at **respond 2**
acknowledge 2
field 6
requite 1
rise 12b
response°
acknowledge-
ment 3
answer 1
reaction 1
rebuttal
reception 1
repercussion
reply 2
retort 1
touch 17
responsibility°
accountability
answer 7a
assignment 2
blame 2, 4
business 1
capacity 3
care 3
charge 4
concern 4
debt 1
department 2
duty 1
fault 3
function 1

responsibility
(*cont.*)
guilt 1
job 2
liability 1
load 1
lookout 3
obligation 1
office 4
part 3
patch 3
place 4
province 3
rap 6
realm 2
role 2
stint 1
thing 6
undertake 1
work 3
worry 3
responsible°
accountable
answer 7a
care 4
concerned 1
conscientious 1
debt 2
dutiful
fault 5
guilty 1
indebted
liable 2
look 4
perpetrate
reliable
sound² 4
stable 3
subject 8a
trustworthy
responsive°
impressionable
interested 1
mobile 4
open 11
plastic 2
pliable 2
quick 4
receptive 1
respond 2
sensitive 2, 3
soft-hearted
susceptible 1
sympathetic 1, 2
responsiveness
sensibility 2
touch 17
rest°
abide 3
balance 7
break 28
depend 1
difference 5
doze 2
dwell 1
ease 1
found 2
gap 1
interlude
interruption 2
interval 1
lean² 1
leftover 1
leisure 2
lie² 2, 3, 4
pause 1
perch 1, 2
prop 2
put 1
quiet 5
reassure
recess 2
recline
relax 3
relaxation 1
remainder 1
remnant 2
repose 1, 4
residue
respite 1
satisfy 3
settle 5
sit 1, 4
sleep 1, 2
sojourn 1, 2

rest (*cont.*)
stop 5, 7
tarry 2
wait 4
-at rest
dormant 1
quiet 4
still 1
restart
renew 2
restate
paraphrase 2
recapitulate
rehash 1
reiterate
render 6
renew 4
repeat 1
restatement
paraphrase 1
rehash 2
repetition 2
restaurant
café
restaurateur
landlord 1
proprietor 2
restful°
cosy 1
easy 2
gentle 1
homely 2
pastoral 1
peaceful 1
quiet 2
serene 1
snug
soft 3
soothing 1
still 2
restfulness
repose 1
serenity 1
rest-home
home 3
sanatorium
resting
dormant 1
idle 2
inactive 1
leisure 3a
unemployed
resting-place
grave 1
tomb
restitution°
atonement
indemnity 1
remuneration 2
requital 1
return 8
satisfaction 2
restitutory
compensatory
restive°
edge 5
excitable
impatient 1
jumpy
restless
unsettled 2
wakeful 1
restless°
anxious 1
edge 5
excitable
impatient 1
jumpy
sleepless 1
travelling
unsettled 2
volatile 2
wakeful 1
restlessness
excitement 1
fidget 3
jitters
restock
refresh 3
renew 3
replenish

reverential
devout 2
holy 2
pious 1
solemn 2
reverie°
day-dream 1
dream 1
-in a reverie
dreamy 2
muse
pensive
reversal°
about-turn
repeal 2
reverse 8
set-back
switch 2
reverse°
about-turn
back 2b
backward 5
calamity 2
contradict 2
contrary 4
correct 4
destroy 3
disaster
misfortune 2
opposite 3
quash 1
repeal 1
repudiate
retract 2
reversal 1
set 15b
set-back
tail 3
turn 3, 13a, 21b
undo 3
void 6
wrong 6
-in reverse
backwards 1, 2
reversed
inside 3
reverse 1
topsy-turvy 1
upset 6
vice versa
reversion
relapse 3
revert°
go 24a
relapse 1
return 1
review°
analyse 2
analysis 2
breakdown 3
brush[2] 8
check 11
chew 4
criticism 3
discuss
discussion
exploration
explore 2
gloss[2] 2
go 34a, 34d
investigation
journal 1
judge 5
mull
narrate
notice 6
outline 2
perusal
peruse
polish 4
post-mortem 2
puff 3
read 1
recapitulate
recount 2
reel 2
rehearse 2
résumé 1
retrospect
round-up 2
run 33b, 33d
run-down 3
stock 6
study 4
review (*cont.*)
sum 2a
summary 1
survey 1
theme 2
traverse 4
treat 2
vet
writing 2
review article
review 4
reviewer
judge 3
scribe 2
reviewing
review 5
revile
abuse 3
attack 2
berate
blacken 2
blaspheme 2
come 11
denounce 3
lace 5b
lambaste 2
rail[2]
rebuke 1
twit[1]
vilify
vituperate
revilement
abuse 8
attack 7
rebuke 2
tongue-lashing
reviling
abuse 8
abusive 1
revise°
alter
amend 2
edit 1
mend 2
modify 1
rectify
reform 1
reword
reviser
editor
revising
revision
revision°
alteration
revisionist
progressive 2, 3
revitalization
rebirth
revival 1
revitalize
animate 1
heal 1
refresh 1
rejuvenate
renew 1
restore 2
revive 3
revitalized
new 5
revitalizing
refreshing
revival°
rally 2
rebirth
recovery 1
refreshment 2
renaissance
restoration 2
resurgence
revivalist
clergyman 3
revive°
arouse 1
awake 2
bring 14a
come 18b
freshen 2
improve 3
perk up
quicken 3
rake[1] 7b
rally 4
recover 2
revive (*cont.*)
recuperate
refresh 1
restore 2, 3
resurrect
snap 7
stir 5
vitalize
revivify
rejuvenate
reviving
tonic 2
vital 4
revocation
cancellation 1, 2
recall 5
repeal 2
reversal 3
revoke°
cancel 1
deny 2
quash 1
recall 3
recant
renege 1
repeal 1
retract 2
reverse 3
vacate 3
vitiate 3
revolt°
disgust 1
disobey
mutiny 1, 2
nauseate
offend 2
put 21d
rebel 1
rebellion 1
repel 2
revolution 1
riot 3
rise 4
shock 1
sicken 2
strike 15
trouble 7
turn 12
uprising
revolted
nauseated
sick 6
revolting°
abhorrent
disagreeable 1, 2
disgusting
disobedient 2
distasteful
fearful 3
foul 1
frightful 2
gross 5
gruesome
hateful 1
hideous 1
horrible 1
infamous 2
loathsome
lurid 2
monstrous 1
nasty 1
nauseous
obnoxious
offensive 3
outrageous 3
repellent
repugnant
repulsive
shocking 2
terrible 5
ugly 2
uninviting
unsavoury
vile 1
wicked 6
yucky
revolution°
change 3
lap[2] 1
mutiny 1
orbit 1
pirouette 1
rebellion 1
revolt 1
spin 6
revolution (*cont.*)
turn 26
twirl 2
uprising
revolutionary°
avant-garde
dissident 1
inflammatory
insubordinate
mutinous 1
progressive 2
rabble-rouser
radical 2, 3, 4
rebel 3
rebellious 1
seditious
subversive 1, 2
terrorist
underground 3
-revolutionaries
underground 5
revolutionist
rebel 3
revolutionary 3
revolutionize
reform 1
revolve°
go 35a
gyrate
muse
orbit 2
pirouette 2
pivot 3, 4
roll 1
rotate 1
spin 1
swivel 1
turn 1, 19a, 21a, 21e
twirl 1
revolver°
pistol
revolving
spin 6
revulsion°
disgust 2
distaste 2
horror 1
infamy 2
loathing
phobia
reward°
award 2
bonus
boon
bounty 3
compensate 3
consideration 2
crown 5
gratification
gratify
icing 2
indemnity 1
inducement
kickback
pay 1, 2, 8a, 12
premium 1, 2
price 3
prize[1] 1
purse 3
recognize 4
remember 4
remuneration 1
repay
requite 1
run 40
stipend
tip[3] 3
trophy 1
wage 1
-rewards
laurels
rewarding°
fruitful 2
gainful
heart-warming 2
productive 3
profitable 1, 2
worthwhile 1
reword°
modify 1
paraphrase 2
render 6
translate 3
rewording
paraphrase 1
rehash 2
translation 3
rework
modify 1
rehash 1
revise 1
reworked
threadbare 2
reworking
adaptation 2
rehash 2
revision
rewrite
edit 1
paraphrase 1, 2
revise 1
revision
reword
translate 1, 3
translation 3
rewriter
editor
scribe 2
rewriting
paraphrase 1
translation 3
Rhadamanthine
inflexible
rhapsodic°
ecstatic
effusive
glowing 3
lyric 2
lyrical 2
poetic 1
radiant 2
rapturous
rhapsodize
rave 2
rhapsody
poem
rhetoric°
diction 1
oratory
rant 3
raving 3
rhetorical°
eloquent 1
rheuminess
vapour 2
rheumy
watery 2
rhino
money 1
rhizome
root[1] 2
rhizomorph
root[1] 2
rhubarb
disagreement 3
rhyme°
jingle 3
lay[3]
one 5
poem
poetry
rhyme or reason°
at **rhyme 2**
rhymer
poet
rhymester
poet
rhythm°
beat 11
cadence
measure 9
regularity 2
tempo
time 7
rhythmic°
even 3
intermittent
measured 3
regular 2
tuneful
rhythmic(al) pattern
rhythm
riata
lasso 1
rib
fun 5
gibe 1
guy 2
leg 8
mock 1
parody 3
poke 4
pull 15
put 22e
ridicule 2
scoff[1]
taunt 1
tease 1
ribald
base[2] 4
bawdy
coarse 3
dirty 2
earthy
erotic 1
filthy 3
foul 5
gross 3
lascivious 2
lewd
low[1] 3
nasty 3
naughty 3
obscene 1
off colour 2
profane 3
prurient 2
racy 2
risqué
rude 3
sexy 2
spicy 2
suggestive 2
vulgar 2
ribaldry°
ribbing
banter
ridicule 1
ribbon
band[1] 1
braid 2
decoration 2
strip[1]
tape 1
tie 9
rich°
abound 2
abundant 2
afford 1
bountiful 2
deep 8
fat 3
favoured 2
fertile
flush[2] 3
fruitful 3
full 11
glowing 2
high 12
leisured
lively 4
loaded 4
luscious
luxuriant 1
magnificent
mellow 1, 2
money 4
noble 5
opulent 1
ornate
plush
posh
pregnant 3
privileged 3
prodigal 2
productive 1
profuse 2
prolific 1
prosperous 1
robust 2
rotund 2
round 7
sensuous
soft 13
splendid 1
substantial 4
successful 1

room°
accommodation 4
area 1
board 7
capacity 1
cell
chamber 4
clearance 1
flat 18
leeway
live 8
lodge 3
margin 3
office 3
pad 3
partition 4
place 6
play 24
scope 2
seating
slack 6
space 1,4
-rooms°
at **room 3**
accommodation 4
flat 15,18
lodging
pad 3
place 6
quarter 5
room and board
keep 15
roomer
guest
occupant
room-mate
friend 3
room temperature
lukewarm 1
roomy°
open 9
spacious
voluminous 1
wide 1
roost
nest 1
perch 1,2
settle 5
root°
applaud 1
base[1] 3
basic
cause 1
derivation
follow 9
germ 2
implant 2
parent 2
plant 6
pull 10
seed 2
source 1
spring 8
transfix
-roots
natioinality 2
parentage
pedigree
settle 4
source 1
stock 2
strain[2] 1
root and branch
completely 1
entirely 1
wholly 1
rooted°
entrenched
fixed 1,2
habitual 1
immovable 1
time-honoured
rooter
follower 3
partisan 1
root for
applaud 1
follow 9
pull 10
rooting out
purge 4
rootle
root[2]
rootlet
root[1] 2
root out
discover 1
exterminate
pull 18b
purge 2
unearth
uproot 2
rootstock
root[1] 2
root to the spot
transfix 2
root up
root[1] 7a
rope°
bond 1
cable 1
cord
lash[2]
lasso 1,2
line[1] 11
stay[2] 1
string 1
tether 1
tie 1,9
twine 1
-ropes°
at **rope 2**
bond 1
-the ropes°
at **rope 2**
rope in°
at **rope 4**
defraud
rope's end
lash[1] 1
ropy°
rotten 5
stringy
tacky[1]
thick 5
tough 2
roscoe
pistol
revolver
rose-coloured
pink[1] 2
rosy 1
Rosinante
nag[2]
rosiness
flush[1] 4
roster
list[1] 1
register 1
roll 13
rostrum°
platform 1
stage 2
rosy°
bright 4
fair[1] 3
fresh 6
golden 7
hopeful 2
pink[1] 2
promising
propitious
sanguine
sound[2] 2
rot°
contaminate
decay 2,4
decompose 2
disintegrate
fester 1
fiddlesticks
gab 2
go 31e
gobbledegook 1
jargon 2
moonshine 2
mortify 3
mumbo-jumbo 1
nonsense 1
prattle 3
putrefy
rubbish 2
spoil 4
stagnate
stuff 4
swill 2
rot (*cont.*)
trash 1
turn 5
wind[1] 2
rota
list[1] 1
register 1
roll 13
rotary
roundabout 4
rotate°
alternate 1
cycle 2
go 35a
gyrate
pivot 3
revolve 1
roll 1,8
screw 5
spin 1
swivel 1
turn 1,21e,43
twirl 1
rotating
spin 6
rotation
alternation
cycle 1
revolution 3
roll 16
spin 6
turn 26
-in rotation
alternate 2,3
turn 40
rote°
routine 3,4
-by rote°
at **rote 2**
rot-gut
alcohol
booze 1
drink 5
liquor 1
ruin 4
whisky
rotogravure
print 2
rotted
rotten 1,2
rotten°
atrocious 2
awful 1
bad 1,2,4,6
beastly 2
bum 4
damnable
dirty 3
dreadful 1
filthy 1
foul 2
impure 1
infamous 2
lousy 1
miserable 2,3
mouldy
musty 1
off 7
off colour 1
offensive 3
poor 4
poorly 2
punk 2
putrid
rancid
rank[2] 4
repulsive
revolting
sad 3
scurvy
seamy
shabby 2
sordid 1
stale 1
stinking 2
strong 3
terrible 1,2,3,5
ugly 2
unsound 1
vicious 2
wicked 6
wretched 1
rottenness
filth 2
rotter
heel[1] 2
rascal
rogue 1
scoundrel
stinker
villain
wretch 1
rotting
decay 4
mouldy
putrid
rotund°
fat 1
large 1
obese
plump[1] 1
well-fed
rotundity
fat 5
fatness
obesity
rouche
fringe 1
roué°
degenerate 3
libertine 1
philanderer
playboy
profligate 3
rake[2]
reprobate 2
sensualist
rough°
approximate 1
back 12
barbarian 3
bluff[2] 1
boisterous
broad 4
brutal 2
bumpy
coarse 1,2
crude 2,3
draft 1
earthy
foul 5,8
gritty 1
gruff 2
hard 5
harsh 1
homespun
husky 2
incomplete
irregular 1
jagged
loose 5
merciless
miscreant 1
picnic 3
primitive 2,3
ragged 1,2,4,5
raucous
regrettable
ropy 3
rotten 5
round 6
rude 4
rugged 1,2
rustic 2
scaly 1
scratch 6
scratchy 2
sexy 2
sketchy
stiff 9
strident
strong 18
surly
tactless
thick 7
thug
thumbnail
tough 3
uncivilized 2
unrefined 1
rough-and-ready
rough 9
rugged 3
rough-and-tumble
fracas 1
rough 4
roughcast
rough 9
rough handling
mistreatment
rough-hewn
coarse 1
rough 9
rude 4
sketchy
rough-house°
fracas 1
rowdyism
rumpus
rough idea
run-down 3
rough in°
at **rough 15**
roughing-up
mistreatment
roughly°
about 2
approximately
around 1,6
generally 2
say 14
sketchily
roughneck
bruiser
criminal 3
delinquent 1
hoodlum
miscreant 1
rough 4,13
tough 8
roughness
indelicacy
rough out°
at **rough 15**
block 4a
outline 3
rough sketch
draft 1
rough-spoken
blunt 2
rough 3
rough up°
at **rough 16**
manhandle
mistreat
punish 3
roulade
run 47
round°
about 1,8
around 3,4,5
beat 12
bout 1
circuit 2
circular 1
cycle 1
even 8
full 7
game 2
orbit 1
revolution 3
rotund 1,2
run 37
spell[1] 1
spherical
tour 2
turn 26,30
-rounds°
at **round 12**
patrol 2
roundabout°
circular 2
detour 1
devious 2
diffuse 2
discursive
equivocal 1
indirect 1
mealy-mouthed
meandering
oblique 2
rambling 1
redundant 2
serpentine 2
tortuous 2
rounded
even 8
full 7
obtuse 1
rounded (*cont.*)
rotund 1
round 4,6,7
well-fed
roundheels
prostitute 1
slattern
tart[2] 2
roundish
full 7
roundlet
ring[1] 1
round off°
at **round 18**
complement 3
complete 6
round-the-clock
night 3
non-stop 2,3
steady 2
round the twist°
at **twist 11**
crazy 1
insane 1
mad 1
round up°
at **round 19**
assemble 1
catch 2
herd 4
muster 1
pen[2] 2
raise 5
rally 3
seize 2
round-up°
muster 2
rouse°
activate
agitate 1
animate 2
arouse 1
awake 1,2
call 6
electrify 2
energize
enliven 1
evoke
exalt 3
excite 1
ferment 2
find 7
fire 8b
foment
freshen 2
heat 4
incite
inflame 1
inspire 1
kindle
motivate
move 5,6
pierce 4
prod 2
prompt 3
provoke 1
push 4
rally 4
refresh 2
stimulate 1
stir 4,5
summon 1
wake[1] 1
whip 7a
work 20a
roused
agitated
awake 4
excited 1
rousing°
erotic 3
exciting 1
impassioned
inflammatory
stirring
thrilling
rout°
beat 2,9
best 11
chase 3
defeat 1,3
disperse 2
flight[2] 2
floor 4

rout (*cont.*)
overcome 1
overthrow 1, 2
purge 2
reverse 8
slaughter 4
stampede 1, 2
triumph 3
upset 4, 11
whip 2

route°
beat 12
bypass 2
climb 6
course 1
direction 2
drive 9
journey 2
line[1] 9
medium 5
method 1
pass 23
passage 3
path 2
road 1
round 12
run 37
step 10a
track 2
trail 1
way 3, 4

routine°
accustomed 1
act 2
common 1
course 3
custom 1
customary 1
daily 2
discipline 3
everyday 2
familiar 2
formal 1
habit 1
habitual 1
hack[2] 4
humdrum
institution 4
mechanical 2
menial 1
method 1
methodical
monotonous
natural 1
normal 1
ordinary 1
perfunctory 1
popular 2
practice 1
procedure
programme 1
prosaic
ready-made 3
regular 1, 2
regularity 2
rite
ritual 2, 3
rope 2
rote 1
round 12
rule 3
run 37
rut 2
scenario 1
set 30
step 7
stint 1
stock 7, 8
swing 5
system 2
systematic
tedious
tedium
traditional
usage 1
usual

routinely
ordinarily

routing out
purge 4

rove
drift 2
journey 3
knock 3a
meander 1

rove (*cont.*)
migrate 2
prowl 2
ramble 1
range 8
roam
run 4
straggle
stray 1
travel 3
walk 3
wander 1

rover°
migrant 1
thief 3
tramp 4
traveller
vagabond 1

roving
indirect 1
rambling 3
stray 4
travelling
vagabond 2

row°
argue 1
argument 1
brawl 1, 2
conflict 2
din 1
dispute 4
feud 2
fight 4, 7, 8
file 2
fracas 2
fray[1]
line[1] 6
paddle 2
quarrel 1
queue 1
racket 1
range 3
rank[1] 4
riot 1
rumpus
scene 3
scrap[2] 1, 2
scrimmage
serried
stream 3
street 1
string 3
tier
tiff
trouble 7
tumult

–in a row
line[1] 19a
succession 5

row-boat
boat
tender[3] 1

rowdiness
rough-house 1
rowdyism

rowdy°
blatant 2
boisterous
disorderly 2
hoodlum
miscreant 1
obstreperous
riotous 2
rough 4, 13
tough 8
tumultuous
uproarious 1
wild 4

rowdyism°
misbehaviour
rough-house 1

rowel
prod 5

rower
oar 2

rowing-boat
boat
tender[3] 1

row on row
serried

royal°
distinguished 2
genteel 2
imperial 1, 2

royal (*cont.*)
king
majestic 1
posh
princely 2, 3
regal 1
sovereign 3
state 6
stately
sumptuous
upper-class 2

–of royal blood
princely 3

–royals°
at **royal 4**
royalty 3

royal family
royalty 1

royalism
monarchy 2

royalty°
royal 4

rozzer
police officer

rub°
chafe 1, 2
deterrent
fly 10
fray[2]
gall[2] 3
grate 1, 2
massage 1
polish 1
reduce 4
scour 1
scrape 2
scratch 2
shine 2
smear 1
spread 7
stroke 10
touch 3
wear 3
wipe 1

–the rub°
at **rub 11**

rubberiness
elasticity 1

rubberneck°
gape 1
gawk 2
sightseer
stare 1
tourist
traveller

rubbernecker
rubberneck 2
sightseer
tourist
traveller

rubber stamp
approval

rubber-stamp
approve 1
OK 5

rubbery
yielding 1

rubbing
friction 1
rub 9

rubbing away
erosion

rubbing out
destruction 2
removal 2

rubbish°
babble 3
dirt 1
drivel 3
fiddlesticks
filth 1
flannel 1
froth 2
gab 2
garbage
gibberish
gobbledegook 1
jargon 2
junk 1
leftover 1
litter 1
lumber 1
moonshine 2

rubbish (*cont.*)
mumbo-jumbo 1
nonsense 1
odds 5
pan 5
paraphernalia
prattle 3
refuse[2]
rigmarole
rot 4
scrap[1] 3
slaver[1] 3
stuff 2, 4
swill 2
talk 18
trash 1, 3
truck 1
waste 7

rubbish heap
dump 3
tip[2] 4

rubbishy
shoddy
worthless 3

rubble
leftover 1
rubbish 1
ruin 6
trash 3
wreckage

rub down
massage 2
shine 2

rub-down
massage 1
rub 10

rube
peasant

Rube Goldberg invention
contraption
gimmick 2

rub elbows (with)
hang 4b
hobnob
rub 7

rubicund
rosy 1

rub in°
at **rub 2**
apply 2

rub off°
at **rub 4**
delete
remove 3
scrape 2
scratch 3
wear 3

rub off on°
at **rub 5**

rub on°
at **rub 2**
apply 2

rub out°
at **rub 4**
blot 4b
bump 5
cancel 2
cross 3
delete
dispatch 3
eliminate 4
erase 1
execute 3
exterminate
finish 4
kill 1
murder 3
obliterate 1
polish 3b
remove 3, 4
ride 5b
scratch 3
strike 5
waste 4
zap

rub-out
destruction 2
removal 2

rubric
formula
title 3

rubricate
embellish 1
illuminate 3

rub shoulders°
at **rub 7** *and* **shoulder 4**
fraternize
hobnob
mingle 2

rub up
shine 2

rub up the wrong way°
at **exasperate 2**
rub 8
get 17
grate 3
irk
irritate
rasp 4

ruby
rosy 1

ruche
fringe 1
pucker 2
ruffle 1

ruck
pucker 1, 2
wrinkle[1] 2

ruckle
pucker 2

rucksack
pack 1

ruckus
brawl 1
disturbance 2
fight 8
fracas 1
fray[1]
noise 1
riot 1
row[2] 2
scrap[2] 1
scrimmage
tumult

ruction
noise 1
riot 1

rudder
helm 1

ruddiness
glow 3

ruddy
fresh 6
rosy 1
sound[2] 2

rude°
abrupt 3
abusive 1
animal 4
audacious 2
barbarian 3
base[2] 4
bawdy
beastly 1
blunt 2
boorish
brash 2
brassy 1
brazen
broad 8
brusque
brutal 2
cheeky
coarse 2, 3
crude 3
curt
dirty 2
disagreeable 3
discourteous
disgraceful 2
disrespectful
flippant 2
foul 5
fresh 8
gross 3
gruff 1
harsh 3
homespun
ill-mannered
impertinent
impolite
impudent
inconsiderate

rude (*cont.*)
indecent 2
insolent
irreverent 2
lewd
low[1] 3
merciless
nasty 3, 4
obscene 1
offensive 2
outrageous 3
pert 1
primitive 2
provincial 2
racy 2
rough 3, 6, 9
rugged 4
savage 3
sexy 2
shabby 2
shameless
short-tempered
suggestive 2
surly
taboo 1
tactless
terse 2
thoughtless 1
truculent
uncivilized 2
ungracious
ungrateful
unrefined 1
unseemly 1
unthinking 2
untoward 2
vulgar 2
wicked 3
wild 3

rudely
roughly 3
shortly 3

rudeness
brass
disrespect
flippancy 2
impertinence
impudence
incivility
indelicacy
mouth 4
ribaldry
vulgarity 1

rudimentary°
crude 2
elementary 1
fundamental 1
immature 1
introductory 2
preparatory 2
primary 4, 5
radical 1
rough 9
vestigial

rudiments°
element 3b
germ 2

rue
grieve 1
mourn
regret 1, 2
repent

rueful
afraid 2
apologetic
bad 8
guilty 2
hurt 7
mournful 1
penitent
piteous
regretful
remorseful
repentant
sorrowful 1
terrible 2

ruefully
painfully

ruefulness
penitence
regret 2
remorse

ruff
fringe 1
ruffle 1
ruffian
barbarian 2
bruiser
criminal 3
delinquent 1
gangster
hoodlum
miscreant 1
punk 1
rough 13
rowdy 2
thief 1
thug
tough 8
ruffianism
rough-house 1
rowdyism
ruffle°
agitate 1
chafe 3
discomfit 1
displease
disturb 4
excite 2
flounce 1
frill 1
fringe 1
gall[2] 4
gather 3
irritate
move 4
offend 1
perturb
pucker 1,2
ripple 1,3
rumple
tousle
trouble 2
unnerve
upset 1
wind[2] 4d
ruffled
agitated
disconcerted
excited 1
nervous 1
unsettled 2
ruffling
ripple 1
rugged°
burly
hard 1
hardy 1
hefty 2
husky 1
muscular
robust 1
rough 1,7
solid 6
sound[2] 3
stalwart 1
staunch 2
steely 2
strong 18
sturdy 1
tough 1
ruggedness
stamina
strength 6
ruin°
back 7b
bitch 4
blast 5,6
break 4,5
breakdown 1
bugger 3
calamity 1,2
collapse 6
consume 4,5
damage 4
dash 1
death 3
decrepitude 2
deface
desolate 5
desolation 1
destroy 1,2,4
destruction 1,3
devastate 1
devour 2
disrepair
ruin (*cont.*)
dissolution 2
disturb 5
doom
downfall
end 5,10
evil 7
expense 2
failure 4
fall 24
fate 2
flaw 3
fluff 4
foul 16b
hack[1] 1
hash 3
havoc 1
hurt 1
ill 8
impair
kill 2
loss 5
mangle
mar 1,2
mess 5b
mishandle 2
muck 4
murder 4
mutilate 2
naught
overshadow 2
overthrow 2
overturn 3
perdition
pillage 1,2
prostrate 2
pulverize 2
puncture 4
queer 5
ravage 1,3
rebut
rout 1,2
sabotage 3
screw 7b
seduce 2
shatter 2
spoil 1
stain 5
stymie
subversion
subvert
sully
taint 2
tarnish
trash 4
undermine 1
undoing 1
uproot 2
upset 5
vitiate 1
wall 4
waste 11
whip 2
wreck 1,4
wreckage
-be ruined
rot 1
wall 4
-in ruins
dilapidated
rock[1] 3b
tatter 2
tumbledown
-ruins°
at **ruin 6**
wreck 3
wreckage
ruination
calamity 2
destruction 1,3
disrepair
perdition
ruin 1
undoing 1
ruined
broke
broken 3
derelict 1
desolate 2
dilapidated
disabled
disfigured
impoverished 1
insolvent
lost 6
ruined (*cont.*)
piece 7
poor 1
prostrate 4
ramshackle
rock[1] 3b
tatter 2
tumbledown
undone[1] 1
ruining
destruction 1
ruinous°
bad 2
calamitous
disastrous 1
evil 3
fatal 2
fateful 2
ill 4
injurious 1
killing 3
unfortunate 3
violent 2
rule°
code 1,3
command 2
control 1,4
convention 2
crown 2
declare 2
decree 2
direct 1,3
direction 1
discipline 4
dominate 1
domination 1
dominion 1
enact 1
form 4
formula
fundamental 2
gauge 3
govern 1
government 1
grip 2
guidance 1
habit 1
head 11
helm 2
institution 4
instruction 1
judge 4
jurisdiction
law 1
line[1] 1,21
manage 1
measure 2,3
motto
norm 2
occupation 2
order 4
policy
power 2
practice 1
precept 1
predominate
preponderance 2
prescribe
preside
prevalence 2
principle 1
proclaim 2
regime
regulation 2
reign 1,2
rein 2
sovereignty
standard 1
supremacy 2
sway 4
theorem 2
-as a rule°
at **rule 4**
average 2
chiefly
generally 1
largely
mainly
ordinarily
usually
whole 5
-rules
book 3
code 1,3
etiquette
rule (*cont.*)
form 4
formula
rule out°
at **rule 8**
disqualify
eliminate 1
obliterate 1
preclude
prohibit 2
veto 1
ruler
crown 3
king
leader 1
lord 1
master 1
monarch 1,2
queen 1
sovereign 1
rulership
crown 2
rules and regulations
law 2
rules of conduct etc.
protocol 1
rule the roost
dominate 1
reign 2
shot 9
rule with an iron hand
dominate 1
ruling
decision 2
decree 1
dominant 1
injunction 2
judgement 2
predominant
prevailing 2
prevalent
privileged 3
regulation 2
rule 1
sentence
sovereign 2
ruling class
establishment 3
nobility 3
ruly
regular 11
rum
odd 1
peculiar 1
strange 1
rumble
boom 1,3
fight 7
find 2
murmur 1
noise 1
peal 1,2
roar 3
roll 5,15
thunder 1,2
twig[2]
rumbling
deep 7
murmur 1
noise 1
thunder 1
rumbustious
obstreperous
riotous 2
tumultuous
ruminate
brood 3
chew 4
consider 1
contemplate 2
debate 4
meditate 1
mull
muse
ponder
reflect 3
revolve 3
see 8
speculate 1
study 2
ruminate (*cont.*)
think 3
turn 21a
weigh 2
ruminating
preoccupied 1
reflective
thought 1
wistful 2
rumination
consideration 3
reflection 2
speculation 2
thought 1
ruminative
meditative
pensive
wistful 2
rummage°
rake[1] 6
ransack 1
rifle 2
root[2]
search 1
rummage sale
sale 3
rummy
alcoholic 2
drunk 3
rumour°
dirt 4
gossip 2,4
grapevine
news 1
noise 3
say 2
supposedly
tale 3
talk 16,17
transpire 1
whisper 2
-rumours
propaganda 1
rumoured
reputed
wind[1] 8
rumour-mill
gossip 3
grapevine
rumour-monger
gossip 3
talebearer
rump
bottom 1
bum 1
posterior 3
rear[1] 2
seat 4
tail 2
rumple°
crumple
crush 2
ruffle 4
tousle
wrinkle[1] 2
rumpled
unkempt
untidy
rumple up°
at **rumple**
rumpus°
din 1
disorder 2
dispute 4
disturbance 2
fracas 1
fray[1]
noise 1
racket 1
riot 1
row[2] 2
scrap[2] 1
scrimmage
storm 3
tumult
uproar
run°
administer 1
beat 12
bolt 8
boss 2
brook[1]
campaign 3
run (*cont.*)
chair 4
circulate 1
conduct 3
course 1
cover 8
crash 2
creek 2
cycle 1
dash 3,5
direct 1
discipline 7
dominate 1
drive 7
enclosure 1
exit 3
fester 1
flash 5
flow 1,5
fly 2,3,4
function 3
get 25b
go 3,5
govern 1
gush 1
handle 3
hasten 1
head 11
hold 10
hurry 1
hustle 1
impression 4
jog 1
leave[1] 1
leg 5
make 26
manage 1
manoeuvre 4
moderate 6
move 12b
officiate
operate 1,2
oversee
pass 2
passage 7
pelt[1] 3
perform 2
pilot 3
pour 1
prattle 1
preside
procession 2
rain 5
range 6
reach 5
regulate 2
reign 2
retreat 4
round 14
rule 5,6
rush 1
scramble 2
secrete[2]
sequence
shoot 1
shot 9
shun
speed 3
spell[1] 1
stampede 3
streak 3,5
stream 1,4
string 6
supervise
tear 3
tributary
trickle 1
trot 1,3
wash 3
whip 3
work 11,12
-on the run°
at **run 49**
double 8
flat 17a
move 13b
-runs°
at **run 50**
runabout
boat
launch 6
run across°
at **run 20**
bump 4
come 5a

sack (*cont.*)
gut 5
lay[1] 16a
loot 2
overrun
pillage 1,2
plunder 1,3
pocket 1
pouch
raid 2
ransack 2
rape 2,5
ravage 2
remove 5
rob 1
robbery
strip[2] 5
turf 4
turn 20c
waste 11
–the sack°
at **sack 3**
discharge 9
ejection 3
expulsion
push 16
sackcloth and ashes
mourning 3
sacking
depredation
dismissal 1
ejection 3
expulsion
pillage 2
plunder 3
rape 2
removal 3
robbery
sack out
rest[1] 6
retire 3
sack 2
sacramental
ritual 1
sacred 3
solemn 2
sacred°
divine 1
godlike 1
holy 1
solemn 2
spiritual 1
sacred calling
ministry 1
sacredness
sanctity
sacred writings
Scripture
sacrifice°
afford 2
expense 2
forgo 1
give 5
loss 1
offering
part 14
price 2
sign 8
slaughter 2
spare 9
undercut 2
vacate 2
sacrificed
sacrificial 1
sacrificial°
sacrificial lamb
victim 1
sacrilege°
pity 2
sin 1,2
violation 2
sacrilegious°
blasphemous
godless 1
impious
irreverent 1
profane 1
sinful
ungodly 1
wicked 1
sacristan
clergyman 1
sacrosanct
inalienable
sacred 2
sad°
bad 8,9
bleak 1
blue 1
broken-hearted
dark 3
dejected
deplorable 1
desolate 3
despondent
disappointing
dismal
doleful
downhearted
dreary 1
forlorn 1
funereal
gloomy 2,3
glum
heavy 5,6
hopeless 3
hurt 7
joyless 1
low[1] 8
melancholy 1
miserable 1
moody 1
morbid 3
mournful 1
mouth 6
pathetic 1
penitent
pessimistic
piteous
pity 2
poignant 1
regretful
regrettable
sadly 1
sombre 1
sorrowful 1
subdued 2
touching
tragic
unhappy 1
wistful 1
woebegone
wretched 2
sadden°
depress 1
desolate 6
get 36c
pain 5
saddened
disappointed 1
joyless 1
subdued 2
saddening
mournful 2
sad 2
saddle
burden 2
curse 6
encumber 1
govern 1
helm 2
impose 4a
load 4
lumber 3
overload 1
stick[1] 8
tax 4
saddle-horse
hack[2] 3
saddlery
tack 4
sadist
ogre
sadistic°
bloodthirsty
brutal 1
cruel 2
savage 2
sick 5
sadly°
painfully
sadness°
care 1
depression 2
desolation 2
distress 1
sadness (*cont.*)
gloom 2
grief 1
hurt 6
melancholy 2
misery 1
mourning 2
penitence
regret 2
sorrow 1
woe
wrench 5
sado-masochistic
sick 5
sad sack
loser
wretch 2
safe°
foolproof
free 11
good 8,13
harmless
immune
impregnable
innocent 3
noncommittal
reliable
secure 1,3
sound[2] 5
sure 2
unscathed
safe-blower
robber
safe-breaker
robber
safe conduct
escort 1
pass 24
passage 8
safe-cracker
robber
thief 1
safe-deposit box
safe 7
safeguard°
bulwark 1
defence 1
defend 1
ensure 2
guard 1,5
harbour 2
keep 2,12
precaution 1
preserve 1
preventive 4
protect 1,2
protection 1
save 2
secure 7
shelter 4
shield 1,2
watch 2
safeguarding
conservation
patrol 2
preservation 2
protective
security 4
safe house
refuge 1
safe keeping°
care 3
charge 4
conservation
custody 1
preservation 2
protection 1,2
safety
security 1,4
trust 3
safely
safe 6
safeness
safety
safer
better[1] 3
safety°
guard 5
indemnity 2
protection 1
sanctuary 2
security 1
safety (*cont.*)
shelter 1
safety-deposit box
safe 7
safety measure
precaution 1
safety-valve
outlet 1
sag°
dip 2
droop 1,2
fade 2
flag[2] 1
slouch 1,2
weaken 2
wilt 1,2
saga°
legend 1
myth 1
story 1
sagacious
astute 2
clever 3
deep 3
experienced 1
far-sighted 1
intelligent
knowing 2
knowledgeable 2
politic 2
profound 2
provident 1
prudent 1
sage 1
shrewd
wise 1
sagacity
brain 1
brilliance 2
depth 3
discretion 1
experience 3
foresight 1
intelligence 1
judgement 1
mind 1
profundity 2
prudence 1
sense 2
understanding 2
wisdom 1
wit 1
sage°
astute 2
authority 3
clever 3
deep 3
experienced 1
highbrow 1
intellectual 4
intelligent
judicious
knowledgeable 2
mind 4
politic 2
profound 2
provident 1
prudent 1
ripe 2
sensible 1
shrewd
thinker
wise 1
sageness
depth 3
understanding 2
wisdom 1
sagging
flabby 1
pendulous 1
sag 3
slack 2
said
according to
oral
reputed
verbal 1
saignant(e)
rare[2]
sail°
coast 2
cruise 1,2
excursion 1
sail (*cont.*)
float 1
fly 1
glide
navigate 1,2
passage 7
pitch[1] 6b
push 9a
roll 3
scold 1
skim 3
sweep 3
sailable
navigable 2
sailboat
boat
sailing
nautical
navigation
sailing-boat
boat
sailing-yacht
boat
sailor°
sail under false colours
pretend 3
sainted
godlike 1
sacred 1
saintly
saintlike
holy 2
saintliness
sanctity
saintly°
devout 1
divine 1
godlike 1
godly
good 5
heavenly 1
holy 2
pious 1
seraphic
sake°
account 3
benefit 1
–for the sake of
for 5,7
part 10
salaam
bend 3
bow 1,5
kowtow
prostration 1
scrape 4
truckle
salaaming
prostration 1
salacious
bawdy
dirty 2
erotic 3
evil-minded 1
foul 5
immoral 2
impure 4
incontinent 2
indecent 2
lascivious 1
lecherous
lewd
libertine 2
lustful
obscene 1
outrageous 3
pornographic
prurient 1
racy 2
risqué
sensual
suggestive 2
vulgar 2
wicked 3
salaciousness
desire 3
impurity 3
ribaldry
salad days
youth 1
salary°
earnings
fee 2
pay 12
remuneration 1
stipend
wage 1
sale°
–for sale°
at **sale 6**
–on sale°
at **sale 5,6**
saleable
hot 6
sale-priced
cheap 1
sales agent
seller
sales-clerk
salesperson
seller
sales event
sale 3
salesgirl
salesperson
saleslady
salesperson
seller
salesman
dealer
merchant 2
pedlar
representative 4
salesperson
seller
trader
sales marathon
sale 3
salesperson°
pedlar
seller
trader
sales receipt
receipt 1
sales slip
receipt 1
sales talk
patter[2] 1
saleswoman
pedlar
representative 4
salesperson
seller
trader
salient°
prominent 1
saline
salt 9
saliva
slaver[1] 2
spit 3
salivate
froth 4
slaver[1] 1
spit 1
sallow
colourless 1
lurid 3
pale[1] 1
pasty
peaky
wan 1
sally
charge 7
onset 1
pour 4
push 15
quip 1
raid 1
set 18b
squelch 2
witticism
salmagundi
assortment 2
medley
miscellany
mishmash
mixture 1
pot-pourri
stew 1
salmon
pink[1] 2

scam *(cont.)*
fraud 2
hoax 1
racket 2
swindle 2
scamp
devil 4
heel[1] 2
imp
miscreant 1
monkey 3
rascal
reprobate 2
rogue 1
scoundrel
scamper
flash 5
fly 3
hasten 1
hurry 1
hustle 1
run 1
rush 1
scramble 2
scurry
speed 3
trot 1
whip 3
scampish
mischievous 1
naughty 1
sly 2
wicked 5
scan°
browse
contemplate 1
dip 3
examine 1
glance 1
go 34a
inspect
look 1, 10
mine 4
monitor 3
peruse
read 1
reconnoitre
run 33b
screen 8
skim 2
study 3
survey 1, 3
traverse 4
vet
scandal°
dirt 4
discredit 4
disgrace 2
gossip 2
news 1
notoriety
shame 2
smear 4
scandalize°
disgrace 4
shame 8
smear 2
scandalmonger
gossip 3
talebearer
troublemaker
scandalous°
deplorable 2
disgraceful 2
disreputable 1
flagrant
foul 4
glaring 1
infamous 1
injurious 2
monstrous 2
notorious 1
outrageous 1
shameful
shocking 2
spicy 3
unmentionable 1
vicious 2
scanning
perusal
survey 3
scant
bare 5
insufficient

scant *(cont.)*
little 3
low[1] 2
meagre 1
measly
mere
poor 2
premium 4a
rarefied 1
scanty 1
scarce
sparse 2
thin 2, 7
scantiness
absence 2
dearth
want 3
scantling
beam 1
board 1
scanty°
bare 5
frugal 3
inadequate 1
insufficient
lean[1] 2
little 3
low[1] 2
meagre 1
measly
poor 2
premium 4a
rare[1] 1
rarefied 1
scarce
short 9
slender 2, 3
small 4
spare 5
sparse 1
thin 7
tight 9
scapegoat°
underdog
victim 1
scapegrace
rascal
rogue 1
scoundrel
scar°
blemish 1, 2, 3
blot 1
cliff
mar 1
pit[1] 5
seam 1
slash 1
spoil 2
stigmatize
taint 1
welt 2
Scaramouch(e)
braggart
coward
scarce°
deficient 1
inadequate 1
insufficient
premium 4a
rare[1] 1
scanty 1
short 9
sparse 1
thin 7
tight 9
scarcely°
almost
barely
hardly
ill 13
just 5
little 7, 8, 9
merely 2
narrowly 1
nearly 1
rarely
scarcely any
few 1
scarcely ever
rarely
scarceness
poverty 2
want 3

scarcity°
absence 2
dearth
famine
lack 1
need 5
poverty 2
rarity 2
shortage
want 3
scare°
alarm 3
appal
daunt
deter
dismay 1
fright 2
frighten
horrify 1
intimidate
lean[2] 4b
menace 1, 3
overawe
panic 2, 3
petrify 1
shake 5
shock 1
shoo 2
startle
terrify
turn 36
upset 1
wind[1] 11
scarecrow
ragamuffin
scared°
afraid 1
cowardly
faint-hearted 1
fear 5
fearful 1
nervous 1
panic-stricken
timid
tremulous 2
upset 8
scare up°
at **scare 2**
scarf
muffler
stole
scarf-pin
pin 2
scarp
bluff[2] 3
cliff
crag
height 3
rock[1] 2
scarper
bolt 8
depart 1
flee 1
flight[2] 3
fly 2
nick 5
powder 2
run 2
scarred
disfigured
hurt 8
scary°
dreadful 2
eerie
frightening
ghastly 1
ghostly 1
hairy 2
nightmarish
terrifying
scat
shoo 1
scatheless
unscathed
scathing°
caustic 2
cutting 2
pungent 2
sarcastic
scorching 2
sharp 5
tart[1] 2
truculent

scatological
bawdy
foul 5
indecent 2
obscene 1
outrageous 3
rank[2] 3
vulgar 2
scatter°
break 11
broadcast 3
diffuse 3
disband
disperse 1, 2
dissipate 1
distribute 2
litter 4
pepper
seed 5
shed[2] 2
shuffle 1
spray[1] 1
spread 1
stampede 2
strew
scatterbrained°
dizzy 2
foolish 2
frivolous 2
giddy 2
hare-brained 2
insane 2
light[2] 8
stupid 2
scattered
diffuse 1
fragmentary
loose 4
sparse 1
scattering°
dissipation 2
few 2
stampede 1
scavenge
prowl 2
scenario°
drama 1
outline 2
path 3
plan 1
plot[1] 2
scheme 1
script 2
story 5
strategy
scenarist
dramatist
playwright
scene°
episode 2
incident 2
landscape
mount 8
performance 5
place 1
prospect 1
set 28
setting
sight 3
spot 2
tableau
theatre 4
view 1
-behind the scenes°
at **scene 5**
background 3
scenery
nature 3
scene 2, 4
set 28
setting
scenic°
panoramic
picturesque 1
scent°
aroma 1
bouquet 2
detect 2
flavour 1
fragrance
misinform
mislead
odour 1

scent *(cont.)*
perfume 1, 2
savour 2
smell 1, 3
sniff 1
touch 15
track 3
trail 2
vestige
wake[2] 1
scented
redolent 1
sweet 2
sceptic°
heathen 1, 2
heretical
naysayer
non-believer
sceptical°
distrust 1
distrustful
doubtful 2
faithless 1
godless 2
heathen 2
incredulous
leery
suspicious 2
unbelieving
sceptically
salt 5
scepticism°
discredit 6
distrust 2
doubt 4
mistrust 2
query 2
suspicion 1
sceptre
staff 1
schedule°
calendar 1
list[1] 1, 2
programme 1, 4
ration 4
register 1
roll 13
routine 1
shift 4
slot 4
tariff 2
term 7a
time 22, 23
timetable
-behind schedule
tardy 1
scheduled
bound[3] 5
due 4
regular 1, 2
routine 3
set 29
schema
frame 3
scenario 1
scheme 1, 2
schematic°
scheme 2
scheme°
aspiration
cabal 1
conception 3
conspiracy
design 4, 5
device 2
devise 1
dodge 4
engineer 5
enterprise 1
finesse 2
frame 3
game 3
idea 1
intrigue 2, 3
machination
manoeuvre 1, 3
meditate 2
method 1
organization 2
path 3
plan 1
plot[1] 1, 3
policy
procedure

scheme *(cont.)*
programme 1
project 1, 3
projection 3
proposal 2
prospectus
purpose 1
racket 2
scenario 1
schematic 2
stratagem
strategy
system 2
tactic 1
thought 3
vision 3
wangle
way 1
wile
wrinkle[2]
-schemes
art 6
schemer
designer 2
tactician
scheming°
artful 1
calculating
crafty
deceitful
deep 5
designing
devious 1
disingenuous
foxy 1
Machiavellian
machination
politic 1
serpentine 1
shifty
sly 1
smooth 8
subtle 3
two-faced
wily
schism°
breach 2
break 25
faction 2
rift 1
rupture 1
separation 2, 3
split 8
variance 2
schismatic°
heretical
rebel 4
schismatical
schismatic
schizo
insane 1
psychotic 2
schizoid
insane 1
schizophrenia
insanity
schizophrenic
insane 1
psychotic 2
schlemiel
loser
sap[1] 2
victim 2
weakling
schlep
carry 1
cart 2
schlimazel
loser
schmaltz
sentimentality
schmaltziness
sentimentality
schmaltzy
melodramatic
mushy 2
sentimental 2
schmooze
talk 4
schnapps
liquor 1

self-governing
automatic 1
democratic
free 1
independent 1
unattached 1
self-government°
freedom 1
independence 1
liberty 1
self-gratification
dissipation 1
indulgence 2
self-abuse
self-gratifying
self-indulgent
self-idolatry
self-esteem 1
self-importance
arrogance
dignity 3
pride 2
self-esteem 1
snobbery
vanity 1
self-important°
cocky
conceited
egoistic
haughty
hoity-toity
inflated 1
pompous 1
proud 2
smug
snobbish
stuffy 2
uppish
vain 1
self-indulgence
dissipation 1
indulgence 2
luxury 2
self-indulgent°
decadent 2
dissolute
egoistic
epicurean 1
fast[1] 2
luxurious 2
selfish 1
time-serving
self-indulgently
fast[1] 9
self-interested
selfish 1
self-involved
conceited
selfish°
avaricious
base[2] 1
egoistic
greedy 3
hoggish
near 6
opportunistic
possessive 1
self-indulgent
small 4
small-minded
sordid 2
subjective 2
time-serving
ungrateful
selfishness
avarice
greed 2
selfless°
unselfish
selflessness
altruism
self-denial 1
self-love
conceit 1
pride 2
self-esteem 1
self-loving
selfish 1
self-made°

self-manipulation
self-abuse
self-mortification
penance 1
self-denial 2
self-pollution
abuse 7
self-abuse
self-possessed°
confident 2
cool 2
dispassionate 1
even 4
level-headed
patient 1
phlegmatic 2
poised 1
self-contained 1
serene 2
stoical
temperate 1
tranquil
self-possession
assurance 5
calm 2
philosophy 3
poise 2
presence 3, 5
repose 3
restraint 3
sang-froid
self-control 1
serenity 2
stoicism
temper 2
self-punishment
penance 1
self-regard
dignity 3
self-esteem 1
self-respect
self-regulated
unattached 1
self-regulating
automatic 1
unattached 1
self-reliance
assurance 5
confidence 2
independence 2
self-confidence
self-reliant
confident 2
independent 3
rugged 3
self-confident
self-made
self-sufficient
unattached 1
self-reproach
compunction 1
guilt 2
pang 2
penitence
regret 2
remorse
self-reproachful
penitent
self-respect°
dignity 3
face 4
pride 1
self-confidence
self-restraint
chastity
restraint 3
self-control 1, 2
self-righteous°
goody-goody
Pharisaic
pious 2
righteous 2
sanctimonious
self-rule
independence 1
liberty 1
self-government 1
self-ruling
free 1

self-sacrifice
altruism
self-denial 1
self-sacrificing
noble 4
selfless
unselfish
selfsame
equal 1
identical 1
same 1
very 3
self-satisfaction
indulgence 2
self-esteem 1
self-satisfied
comfortable 2
conceited
haughty
proud 2
self-important
self-righteous
smug
snobbish
self-seeking
egoistic
hoggish
self-important
selfish 1
time-serving
self-serving
cosy 2
egoistic
selfish 1
subjective 2
time-serving
self-soiling
incontinent 3
self-stimulation
self-abuse
self-styled°
nominal 1
professed 1
so-called 1
titular
self-sufficiency
independence 2
self-confidence
self-sufficient°
independent 3, 5
rugged 3
self-made
self-supporting
self-sufficient
self-sustained
unattached 1
self-sustaining
self-sufficient
unattached 1
self-willed°
contrary 2
defiant
masterful 2
obstinate
perverse 3
rogue 2
strong 16
wild 4
wilful 2
self-worship
vanity 1
self-worshipping
egotistical
sell°
bring 10a
carry 7
cash 2
cost 2
dispose 3c
fetch 3
flog 2
handle 5
market 4
merchandise 2
offer 2
peddle
promote 4
shift 3
stock 9
supply 1
tout 1
trade 5

sell (*cont.*)
turn 21d
–be sold on°
at **sell 5**
undercut 2
sellathon
sale 3
sell down the river
betray 1
sell 3
seller°
merchant 1
pedlar
trader
tradesman 1
selling
promotion 4
sale 1
sell out°
at **sell 3**
betray 1
grass 1
line[2] 2
prostitute 2
stab 2
sell-out
hit 11
seltzer
fizz 4
semantic
literal 2
semblance°
appearance 4
disguise 3, 4
face 3
figure 2
gloss[1] 2
guise 1, 2
image 6
mask 2
mockery 2
representation 1
semester
term 2
semi-annual
organ 2
periodical
publication 2
regular 2
semi-conscious state
trance
semi-darkness
shade 1
semi-lune
crescent 1, 2
semi-monthly
periodical
publication 2
regular 2
seminal°
rudimentary 1
seminar
conference
convention 1
course 5
seminary°
school 1
semiprecious stone
gem 1
semi-solid
stiff 10
semi-weekly
publication 2
regular 2
sempiternal
constant 2
immortal 1
perennial 2
perpetual 1
senate
cabinet 2
chamber 1
diet[2]
senator
politician
send°
cast 7
commit 2
deliver 5

send (*cont.*)
detail 6
direct 5
dispatch 2
drive 4
fling 1
forward 7
give 3
hasten 2
heave 2
hurl
launch 3
mail 2
pack 7
pitch[1] 1
post[3] 2
propel
pump 1
put 3, 7, 13b
refer 2
remit 1
ship 2
thrill 3
throw 1
toss 1
translate 4
transmit 1, 2
transport 1
write 2
send after
page[2] 2
send away
brush[2] 7
bundle 3
commit 2
discharge 1
dismiss 3
dispatch 1
disperse 2
flight[2] 2
lecture 4
pack 7
put 21b
reject 2
reprimand 2
send 5, 8, 9b
transport 2
send back
mirror 3
reflect 1
send down°
at **send 5**
imprison
jail 2
punish 2
put 13b
send for°
at **send 6**
order 15
page[2] 2
summon 1
send forth°
at **send 7**
discharge 4
eject 2
emanate 2
emit
put 17b
spew
throw 7a
vent 4
send in
file 4
sending
translation 4
transmission 1, 2
send off°
at **send 1**
brush[2] 7
bundle 3
dispatch 1
disperse 2
flight[2] 2
pack 7
send-off
farewell 2
opening 4
send on
communicate 1
forward 7
send on one's way
dispatch 1
reject 2

send out°
at **send 7**
discharge 4
dispatch 1
eject 2
emanate 2
emit
give 14
put 17b
radiate 2
vent 4
send packing
brush[2] 7
dismiss 1
eject 3
flight[2] 2
send 8
send to Coventry
ignore 2
isolate
ostracize
rebuff 2
shoulder 2
shut 4b
send to the gallows
hang 2
send to the gas chamber
punish 2
send up°
at **send 9**
caricature 2
fun 5
guy 2
imitate 2
imprison
jail 2
lampoon 2
mock 2
parody 3
poke 4
punish 2
put 13b
ridicule 2
satirize
take 34b
send-up
caricature 1
imitation 2
impression 5
lampoon 1
mockery 2
parody 1
put-on 2
satire 2
take-off 2
send up the river
imprison
jail 2
send 9b
senescence
decrepitude 1
senility
senescent
decrepit 1
elderly 1
senile
seneschal
servant 1
senile°
decrepit 1
doddering
elderly 1
senile dementia
senility
senility°
decrepitude 1
senior°
editor
elder 1, 3
first 2
head 9
senior citizen°
pensioner
–senior citizens
elderly 2
seniority
age 2
majority 2
priority

set up°
at **set 23**
arrange 1, 2
assemble 3
begin 2
break 17
build 1
construct 1, 2
design 1
dispose 1
engineer 5
erect 3
establish 1
fabricate 1
factitious
firm 5
fix 12, 16a, 16b
float 2
form 7
found 1
frame 6, 9
have 6
inaugurate 1
install 2
institute 4
introduce 4
launch 2
lay[1] 18a
line[1] 23a
locate 1
make 1, 22
mount 5
open 20
organize 2
originate 1
pioneer 2
pitch[1] 2
place 11b
pose 1
predetermined 1
programme 4
put 28a
rig 1
set 8
start 7
set-up°
arrangement 1, 2
assembly 3
composition 2
fix 18
fixed 4
format 2
formation 2
mode[1] 2
order 1
orientation 1
outfit 3
system 1
set up home
settle 4
set up house
settle 4
set upon°
at **set 24**
assault 3
attack 1
bombard 2
fall 17
firm 4
go 28d
lace 5a
make 30b
mug 5
pitch[1] 6b
raid 2
set 21
turn 19b
waylay 2
set upright
right 18
seventh heaven
heaven 3
paradise 1, 3
Utopia
-in seventh heaven
ecstatic
elated
exalted 3
exuberant 2
exultant
happy 1
joyful 2
overjoyed
pleased
seventh (*cont.*)
radiant 2
rapturous
rhapsodic
world 7
78
record 7
sever°
break 10, 19b
chop 1
cut 15a, 15c
disconnect
dissociate
divide 1
divorce 2
loosen 2
tear 1
severable
separable
several°
couple 2
different 3
divers
number 2
respective
various 1
severally
individually
respectively
separately
severance
breach 2
divorce 1
rupture 1
separation 2
severe°
acute 2, 3
authoritarian
bad 4, 11
biting
bitter 6
brutal 1
chaste 2
critical 3
cutting 1
dour 2
drastic
exact 2
exacting
excruciating
extreme 2, 4
faithful 3
fierce 3
forcible 2
grievous 1
grim 1
hard 4, 5
harsh 2
heavy 4, 10
heavy-handed 2
inclement
inflexible
inhuman 1
intense 1
joyless 2
keen[1] 3
merciless
nasty 5
oppressive 1
overcritical
piercing 4
po-faced
poignant 2
precise 2
priggish
pungent 2, 3
puritan 2
radical 2
rigid 2
rough 5
rugged 2
ruthless
scathing
scrupulous 1
serious 1, 4
sharp 5, 8
simple 2
smart 6
sore 5
Spartan
stark 2, 3
stern 1
stiff 2
strict 2
strong 13
severe (*cont.*)
swingeing
terrible 1
tight 3
tough 6
tyrannical
unkind
violent 3
severed
cut 26
severely°
badly 5, 6
deeply 2
hard 14, 16
home 10
roughly 2
seriously 1
sharply 1
simply 4
severity°
gravity 2
rigour 1, 2
simplicity 2
violence 1
sew°
connect 3
patch 5
tack 5
sewage
filth 1
muck 2
sewer
drain 1
sewerage
filth 1
sew up
finalize
patch 5
sew
sex°
intercourse 2
relation 6a
sexual 1
sexy 2
sex appeal
magnetism
sex-crazed
hot 7
sexism
intolerance
prejudice 2
sexist
intolerant 2
prejudiced 2
sexless
neuter 1
sex-mad
hot 7
sex organs
genitals
private 7
sex-oriented
racy 2
sexpot
temptress
sexton
clergyman 1
sexual°
carnal
intimate[1] 3
passionate 2
racy 2
sensual
social 2
venereal
sexual appetite
lust 1
sexual assault
rape 1
sexual congress
intercourse 2
sexual connection
intercourse 2
sexual intercourse
intercourse 2
relation 6a
screw 3
sex 2
sexuality
lust 1
sexually transmitted
social 2
venereal
sexual maturity
puberty
sexual organs
genitals
private 7
sexual partner
screw 3
sexual relations
intercourse 2
sex 2
sexual union
intercourse 2
sexy°
blue 2
erotic 1
exciting 2
foxy 2
immodest 1
provocative 1
racy 2
seductive
sexual 2
shapely
spicy 2
steamy 3
suggestive 2
sultry 2
tempting 1
torrid 2
voluptuous 2
SFA
nothing 1
shabby°
base[2] 3
cheap 3
contemptible
despicable
dilapidated
disreputable 2
dowdy
filthy 2
heel[1] 3
leg 7
lousy 2
low[1] 9
mangy
mean[2] 3
miserable 4
old 3
poor 4
ragged 1, 4, 6
sad 3
scurvy
seed 4
seedy 1
shoddy
sleazy 1
sloppy 1
sordid 1
tacky[2]
tawdry
threadbare 1
time-worn
tinny 1
wanting 1
worn 1
worthless 3
shack°
cabin 1
cottage
hole 3
hovel
hut
shed[1]
shacking up
sex 2
shackle°
chain 2, 3
enslave
hamper[1]
hobble 2
manacle 2
tether 2
trammel 1
-shackles°
at **shackle 1**
bond 1
handcuffs
manacle 1
restraint 2
shackle (*cont.*)
trammel 1
shack up with
lay[1] 8
shade°
blend 2
blind 7
colour 1
dim 4
ghost 1
gloom 1
hue
obscure 7
obscurity 1
overshadow 1
phantom 1
presence 4
shroud 1
spectre 1
suspicion 2
tint 1
tone 4
vision 4
-in the shade
extinguish 3
outstrip
-shades°
at **shade 9**
shaded
gloomy 1
leafy
shadowy 1
shades of night
night 1
shadiness
shade 1
shading
eclipse 3
expression 4
shadow°
follow 4
ghost 2
gloom 1
heel[1] 5
obscurity 1
pursue 1
run 26a
satellite 2
shade 1, 12
silhouette
spy 2
stalk[1]
suspicion 2
tag 5
tail 4
trace 4
track 6
trail 7
shadow-box
spar[2] 1
shadowiness
gloom 1
shadowing
pursuit 1
shadowy°
dark 2
dim 1
dingy
dreamy 1
dusky 2
fuzzy 2
gloomy 1
indistinct 1
intangible
misty
murky
obscure 1
occult 1
sombre 2
subtle 2
sunless
suspect 3
twilight 4
vague 1
shady°
dark 2
dishonest
disreputable 1
doubtful 3
dusky 2
fishy 2
fly-by-night 2
foul 7
fraudulent 2
shady (*cont.*)
gloomy 1
leafy
murky
obscure 1
queer 2
questionable
shadowy 1
slippery 2
sly 1
suspect 3
suspicious 1
tricky 1
twilight 4
shaft°
bar 1
beam 2
chute 2
excavation
flash 1
gleam 1
pillar 1
pit[1] 1
pole[1]
post[1] 1
ray 1
rod 1
staff 1
stalk[2]
tunnel 1
victimize 2
shafting
sex 2
shag
nap[2]
pile[2]
shagged out
prostrate 5
shagging
sex 2
shaggy°
hairy 1
ragged 1
unkempt
woolly 1
shah
sovereign 1
shake°
agitate 1, 3
cringe 1
daunt
demoralize 3
disengage
disturb 2, 4
flash 3
flicker 2
flourish 2
flurry 2
fluster 1
flutter 3
jar[2] 1
jiggle 1, 2
jog 2, 3
jolt 1, 3
minute[1] 1
moment 1
move 3
quake 1
quaver 1
quiver 1, 2
rack 4
rattle 2, 3
shatter 3
shiver[1] 1, 2, 3
shock 1
shudder 1, 2
stagger 2
stir 1
toss 2, 3
totter
tremble 1, 2
unnerve
vibrate
wag[1] 1, 2
wave 4
wriggle 1
-the shakes°
at **shake 10**
jitters
shiver 14
shake a leg°
at **leg 9**
hurry 1
rush 1

sharp-sighted
eagle-eyed
sharp-eyed
sharp-witted
acute 5
bright 6
brilliant 4
clever 1
sharp 3
shatter°
blast 5
blow[1] 8b
break 1
burst
crack 5
dash 1
devastate 2
disintegrate
fall 7
fragment 3
piece 6
pulverize 2
rout 2
ruin 7
shiver[2]
splinter 2
wreck 1
shattered
broken 1
piece 6,7
shabby 3
tatter 2
undone[1] 1
shattering
separation 3
shatter-proof
indestructible
shave°
pare 1
trim 3
whittle 1,2
shaver
boy 1
lad
youth 2
shaving
flake 1
slice 1
sliver
shawl
cape[2]
mantle 1
muffler
stole
wrap 4
sheaf
bundle 1
shear
cut 4
mow 1
nip[1] 1
shave 1
trim 3
shear off
lop
sever 1
shave 1
shears
snip 4
sheathe
cover 5
face 16
wrap 1
sheave
pulley
tackle 2
shed°
cast 13
drop 8
get 40c
hut
radiate 2
remove 1
spread 1
stall[1] 3
strip[2] 2
throw 2
shedding
radiation
resistant 3
she-devil
fury 3
shed light on°
at light[1] 12
clarify 1
illuminate 1,2
interpret 1
spotlight 3
shed tears
bewail
cry 1
grieve 2
sob
weep 1
shed weight
slim 3
sheen°
gloss[1] 1
lustre 1
polish 5
shine 4
sheep
stock 4
sheepish°
ashamed
bashful 1
coy
embarrassed 1
guilty 2
passive 2
self-conscious
shamefaced 1
shy 1
sheeplike
sheepish 1
sheer°
abrupt 2
barefaced 1
blank 6
clear 14
filmy 1
fine[1] 6
flimsy 3
implicit 2
main 4
mere
naked 3
outright 2
positive 9
precipitous 1
pure 5
rank[2] 2
see-through
sharp 2
stark 4
steep[1] 1
swerve
thin 5
thorough 1
transparent 1
ultra-
unmitigated
very 4
sheerest
very 4
sheer off
swerve
sheet°
film 1
foil[2]
mantle 2
page[1] 1
pane
paper 1
plate 3
-sheets
linen
sheet anchor
anchor 2
mainstay
sheik
flirt 3
Sheikh of Araby
sovereign 1
sheila
girl 1
shekels
money 1
purse 2
shelf
bracket 2
ledge
rest[1] 4
shallow 2
-on the shelf
abeyance
limbo
shell°
blaze 5
bomb 1,2
bombard 1
exterior 3
frame 1
hulk 1
hull 2,3
outside 1
pelt[1] 1
projectile
round 15
skin 2,4
storm 6
shellac
glaze 1,2
shellacking
rout 1
shellback
sailor
shell-game
fiddle 3
shell-game artist
thief 2
shelling
fire 3
shell out°
at shell 5
expend 1
give 15b
lay[1] 18b
pay 11b
spend 1
stump 4
shelter°
accommodate 4
accommodation 4
bulwark 2
cover 1,14
defence 1
defend 1
harbour 2
home 3
house 8
housing 1
hut
insulate 1
lodge 1,4
lodging
mother 5
preserve 1
protect 2
protection 1
quarter 5,6
refuge 1
retreat 3
safeguard 2
safety
sanctuary 2
save 2
screen 2,7
secure 7
security 1
shade 5,10
shed[1]
shield 1,2
sheltered
hothouse 2
safe 1
secure 1
snug
sheltering
protective
shelve°
defer[1]
delay 1
pension 2
postpone
procrastinate 1
put 21a
slant 4
suspend 1
table 5
shelved
abeyance
fire 4
wait 2
shenanigan
caper 2
-shenanigans
hanky-panky
lark 1
mischief 1
nonsense 2
trick 2
Sheol
hell 1
shepherd°
drive 5
escort 4
father 4
guide 1
herd 4
pilot 3
see 11
sherd
chip 1
fragment 1
morsel 2
piece 1
relic 2
scrap[1] 1
Sherlock
detective
sleuth
shibboleth°
password
symbol
shield°
cover 1
defence 1
defend 1
envelop 2
guard 1,5
harbour 2
housing 2
insulate 2
preserve 1
preventive 4
protect 1
protection 1
safeguard 2
save 2
screen 2,7
secure 7
shade 5,10
shadow 2
shelter 4
shroud 1,3
umbrella 2
veil 2
watch 2
shielded
hothouse 2
safe 1
secure 1
shielding
protective
shift°
change 3,7
deceit 2
displace 1
divert 2
dodge 1
fluctuate
get 28b
manage 4
motion 1
move 1,8
movement 1,6
passage 5
remove 2,6
second[1] 10
shuffle 1,3,5
spell[1] 1
squirm
stint 1
subterfuge
succession 1
swing 4
switch 2,4
tour 3
transfer 1
transplant
trend 3
turn 2,29,30
vary 3
weave 4
shift for (oneself)°
fend 1
manage 4
shift 2
shiftiness
gobbledegook 2
trickery
shifting
changeable 1
desultory
faithless 2
fluid 3
halting
irresolute
motion 1
removal 3
shifting spanner
wrench 6
shiftless°
idle 3
indolent
lazy 1
slack 1
slothful
shiftlessness
idleness 1
indolence
sluggishness
shifty°
crafty
deceptive 2
desultory
devious 1
disingenuous
elusive 1
evasive
faithless 2
fly-by-night 2
foxy 1
fraudulent 2
furtive 2
insincere
politic 1
serpentine 1
shady 2
shuffle 3
slippery 2
sly 1
smooth 8
sneaky
subtle 3
tricky 1
unscrupulous
wily
shillelagh
staff 1
shilling-mark
line[1] 1
shillings
purse 2
shilly-shally°
blow[1] 6
dawdle
delay 3
fence 4
hesitate 2
indecision
linger 4
oscillate
procrastinate 2
time 20
shilly-shallying
delay 6
hesitant 1
idleness 2
indecision
indecisive 1
indefinite 5
mind 11
uncertain 2
wishy-washy 1
shimmer°
blink 2
flare 1
flash 1,4
flicker 1
glance 2,5
gleam 1,4
radiance 1
radiate 1
sheen
shine 1,4
twinkle 1,2
shimmering
luminous 1
radiant 1
scintillating 1
shimmering (*cont.*)
shimmer 2
shiny
twinkle 2
shimmery
shiny
shimmy
shake 2
shimmying
wriggle 4
shin°
climb 1
shindig
dance 2
fête 1
party 1
shindy
dance 2
party 1
shine°
beam 3
brighten 2
excel
flash 4
glare 1
glaze 1,2
gleam 1,4
glisten
gloss[1] 1,3
glow 4
light[1] 3
lighten[1] 2
polish 1,5
radiance 1
radiate 1
rub 1
scour 1
shed[2] 2
sheen
shimmer 1,2
sparkle 1
splendour 2
twinkle 1,2
shined
lustrous
shine light upon
spotlight 3
shine up to
cultivate 4
flatter 1
kowtow
shingle
overlap 1
sign 5
shingled
stony 1
shingly
rocky[1] 1
scaly 1
stony 1
shininess
sheen
shining
bright 1
brilliant 1
clear 3
full 10
glassy 1
glossy 1
golden 3
light[1] 13
liquid 3
luminous 1
radiant 1
scintillating 1
silver 3
sleek 1
slick 1
twinkle 2
shinny up
climb 1
shin
shin-plasters
money 1
shin up°
at shin
climb 1
shiny°
bright 3
clear 3
glassy 1
glossy 1

shiny (*cont.*)
golden 3
luminous 1
lustrous
radiant 1
silky
silver 3
sleek 1
slick 1
smooth 2
spotless 1
ship°
board 6
boat
craft 4
dispatch 2
forward 7
send 2
translate 4
transmit 1
transport 1
vessel 2
shipload
cargo
freight 2
shipment
cargo
freight 1
load 2
passage 10
translation 4
transmission 1
transport 4
ship out°
at **ship 3**
shipper
carrier 1
shipping
carriage 3
freight 1
passage 10
traffic 1
translation 4
transmission 1
transport 4
shipshape°
neat 1
order 10a
orderly 1
straight 7
taut 2
tidy 1
trim 1
shipwreck
cast 12
hulk 1
wreck 3
shire
local 2
shirk°
duck 3
evade 1
neglect 2
slack 4
shirker
idler
loafer
slacker
truant 1
wastrel 2
shirking
evasion 1
idleness 2
truant 2
shirr
gather 3
pucker 1,2
shirring
pucker 2
shirt-pocket
portable
shirty
cross 6
shit
defecate
dung
effects
filth 1
flannel 1,2
furniture 1
gab 2
gear 4
go 17

shit (*cont.*)
paraphernalia
stinker
stuff 2
thing 8c
shithouse
privy 3
shitting green
panic-stricken
shitty
stinking 2
shivaree
noise 1
shiver°
break 1
crack 5
crumble
crush 1
dash 1
quaver 1
quiver 1,2
shake 1,8
shatter 1
shudder 1,2
totter
tremble 1,2
vibrate
shivered
broken 1
shivering
chill 5
freezing
shake 8
shiver[1] 4
tremulous 1
shlemiel
loser
sap[1] 2
victim 2
weakling
shlimazel
loser
shoal(s)
bar 4
flat 14b
many 3
score 4
shallow 2
swarm 1
shock°
appal
astonish
astonishment
astound
blow[2] 2
bolt 6
bombshell
breath 3
brunt
catastrophe 2
daze 1
devastate 2
dismay 2,3
dumbfound
electrify 1
floor 5
fright 2
frighten
horrify 2
jar[2] 1,4
jolt 3,5
misfortune 2
nonplus
outrage 2
overwhelm 3
petrify 2
revolt 3
rock[2] 3
scandalize
scare 1,3
shake 5
sicken 2
stagger 2
startle
stun 2
surprise 1,3
take 28
terrify
terror 1
turn 36
shocked
daze 4
dumbfounded
petrified 2

shocked (*cont.*)
scared
sick 6
speechless 2
thunderstruck
shocker
bolt 6
bombshell
shock 3
surprise 4
shocking°
arresting
awesome
awful 2
disgraceful 2
dramatic 2
dreadful 2
flagrant
frightening
frightful 2
ghastly 1
glaring 1
grievous 2
grisly
gruesome
hideous 2
horrible 1
lurid 1
monstrous 2
obscene 2
outrageous 1,3
rank[2] 3
scandalous 1
sensational 1
shameless
sick 5
sight 6b
startling
terrible 4
terrifying
tragic
traumatic
ungodly 2
unheard-of 3
unmentionable 2
shockingly
notably 1
shoddily
badly 1
shoddiness
inferiority 3
shoddy°
base[2] 3,5
cheap 3
coarse 4
feeble 2
gaudy
inferior 3
lousy 2
low[1] 9
plastic 3
poor 4
shabby 2
tacky[2]
tinny 1
unprofessional 2
wanting 1
shoe
boot 2
-shoes
flat 14a
shoe-brush
brush[2] 1
shoelace
lace 2
tie 9
shoestring
lace 2
pittance
shoo°
shoo away°
at **shoo 2**
shoo-fly
informer
sneak 2
shook (up)
disconcerted
shoo off°
at **shoo 2**
shoot°
bag 6
blade 3
blaze 5

shoot (*cont.*)
branch 1
career 2
deliver 5
discharge 3
film 5
fire 9
flash 5
fly 8a
get 24
graft[1] 1
hurry 1
hurtle
inject 1
launch 3
loose 13
nail 9
offshoot 1
pelt[1] 3
photograph 2
pick 5
pitch[1] 1
project 4
put 7
runner 3
scud
send 3
sling 1
slip[2] 2
snap 5
snipe
speed 3
spout 1
spurt 3
stem[1] 1
stream 4
tear 3
twig[1]
use 3
wound 3
zap
shoot down
pick 5
rebut
slam 3
squelch 1
shoot full of holes
disprove
explode 2
rebut
shooting
acute 3
discharge 10
piercing 4
shot 1
shooting-iron
pistol
revolver
shooting star
star 1
shoot off
bolt 8
shoot off one's mouth
prattle 1
shoot one's bolt°
at **bolt 7**
shoot the breeze
palaver 4
talk 4
shoot the bull
talk 4
shoot through
clear 30
escape 1
flee 1
heel[1] 4
shoot up
rocket
soar 2
spring 2
use 3
shop°
betray 1
cant 2
establishment 2
market 2
mill 2
outlet 2
plant 2
sell 3
store 4
works 1

shop assistant
salesperson
seller
shop at
patronize 2
shop for°
at **shop 4**
shop-girl
salesperson
seller
shopkeeper
dealer
merchant 1
seller
tradesman 1
shoplift
hook 7
pinch 3
rip 2a
steal 1
take 3
shoplifter
robber
thief 1
shoplifting
rip-off 1
stealing
theft
shopper
client
-shoppers
trade 4
shopping bag
bag 1
shopping list
list[1] 1
shop-talk
cant 2
terminology
shopwalker
foreman
shop-worn
hurt 8
stale 2
usual
shore
beach 1
coast 1
post[1] 1
prop 3
sea-coast
stay[2] 2
shoreline
sea-coast
shore up
bolster
brace 5
buttress
fortify 1
prop 1
reinforce
stay[2] 2
support 1,2
sustain 2
shoring (up)
reinforcement 2
shorn
bare 4
short°
abrupt 3
bluff[2] 1
blunt 2
brief 1,2,3
broke
brusque
concise
curt
deficient 1
disagreeable 3
discourteous
embarrassed 2
fleeting
fretful
gruff 1
hurried 1
impatient 2
impoverished 1
inadequate 1
indigent
lack 2
little 1,4
low[1] 1,2
momentary

short (*cont.*)
moody 2
out 5
point-blank 2
poor 1
quick 2
quick-tempered
require 2
rough 3
scanty 2
short-tempered
slight 3
small 1
snap 3b
snappish 2
succinct
summary 2
temperamental 1
terse 1,2
thumbnail
undersized
want 2
wanting 2
-at short notice
readily 3
-in short°
at **short 14**
briefly 1
word 8
-in short order
soon 2
-in short supply°
at **short 9**
premium 4a
scanty 2
scarce
sparse 1
-on a short fuse
cross 6
temperamental 1
-on a short string
excitable
snappish 1
-on a short tether
snappish 1
-on the short list for
line[1] 20
shortage°
dearth
deficit
famine
lack 1
need 5
poverty 2
scarcity
want 3
short and curlies
intimidate
short and sweet
short 5
terse 1
short-circuit
blow[1] 5,7c
thwart 1
shortcoming°
bug 6
defect 1
disadvantage 1
failing 1
fault 1
foible
hole 6
imperfection
lapse 1
omission 2
peccadillo
vice 2
weakness 3
shorten°
abbreviate 1,2
abridge
abstract 4
clip[2] 2
curtail
cut 4,5
digest 4
diminish 1
edit 3
lop
minimize 1

shrewish
short-tempered
shriek°
cry 4
gale 2
scream 1, 3
squawk 1
whoop 1, 2
shrieking
piercing 1
shrift
forgiveness 1
shrill°
brassy 2
grating 2
harsh 1
high 7
noisy
penetrating 2
piercing 1
raucous
sharp 7
strident
shrine
monument 1
sanctuary 1
sanctum 1
temple
shrink°
blink 3
contract 4
cringe 1
decline 2
decrease 1
diminish 1
draw 10
dry 5
dwindle
flinch
hang 5
melt 3, 4
minimize 1
recede 2
recoil 1
scruple 2
shrivel
start 5
stick[1] 12
therapist
waste 2
wilt 1
withdraw 1
shrinkage
loss 2
shrink from°
at **shrink 2**
abhor
draw 10
dread 1
fear 5
flinch
hang 5
hate 2
hesitate 1
loathe
pull 8a
scruple 2
shirk
shun
stick[1] 12
shrinking
decrease 2
self-conscious
withdrawn 1
shrive
purify 2
shrivel°
decrease 1
dry 5
dwindle
fade 2
parch
shrink 1
wilt 1
shrivelled (up)
emaciated
thin 1
wizened
shrivelling
decrease 2
scorching 1
shrivel up°
at **shrivel**
decrease 1
shrivel up (*cont.*)
dwindle
parch
shrink 1
wilt 1
shroud°
cloak 2, 3
cover 2
dim 4
eclipse 1
envelop 1, 2
fog 5
hide[1] 2
keep 14a
mantle 2, 3
mask 3
muffle 1
obscure 6, 7
pall[1] 1
roll 9
screen 3
secrete[1]
shade 12
submerge 3
swathe
veil 1, 2
wrap 1
shrouded
occult 1
secret 1
vague 3
shrub
plant 1
-shrubs
brush[1] 1
shrubbery
shrubbery°
shrug off
brush[2] 6
dismiss 2
laugh 2b
light[2] 12
put 11
rid 2
shrunken
emaciated
haggard
lean[1] 1
skinny
stunted
thin 1
wizened
shtick
act 2
concern 4
office 4
routine 2
shtook
trouble 9a
shuck
hull 2, 3
pare 1
peel 1
shell 3
shudder°
abhor
fear 5
loathe
quake 1
quaver 1
quiver 1, 2
shake 1, 8
shiver[1] 1, 3
thrill 2
tremble 1, 2
vibrate
shuddering
shake 8
thrill 2
tremulous 1
shuffle°
drag 3
evade 2
fidget 1
hobble 1, 3
jumble 1
tangle 3
waddle
waffle 2
walk 1
shuffle off this mortal coil
go 13
shuffling
shambling
shuffle 5
shufti
glance 4
shul
temple
shun°
avoid
boycott 1
cut 12
duck 3
flee 2
forgo 1
isolate
ostracize
reject 1
renounce
scorn 3
shirk
shoulder 2
sidestep
steer 2
swear 4
shunned
abandoned 1
forlorn 2
unpopular
shunt
sidetrack
shunted aside
abeyance
shush
hush 1, 2
pipe 7
shut 6b
silence 3
shushed
silent 1
shut°
close 1, 2, 6, 8a, 10
seal 3
secure 2
shut 4c
slam 1
unopened
shut away
close 19
separate 7
shut down°
at **shut 2**
close 5
fold 3
halt 2
shut 4a, 4c
stall[1] 1
shut-eye
doze 2
nap[1] 3
repose 2
rest[1] 1
shut in°
at **shut 3**
enclose 1
keep 14b
picket 4
restrain 3
shut 6a
siege 2
stake[1] 4
shut-in
invalid[1] 2
shut off°
at **shut 4**
block 3
close 6
reclusive
seal 3
separate 7
shut 2
silence 4
shut (one's) eyes to
overlook 2
shut out°
at **shut 5**
bar 9
exclude 1
isolate
lock[1] 8
preclude
shut 4b
shut-out
exception 2
exclusion 1
shutter(s)
blind 7
close 5
shuttle°
shut up°
at **shut 6**
bar 8
cage 2
close 8a, 10, 19
commit 2
halt 2
hush 1
imprison
keep 14b
pen[2] 2
perform 1
pipe 7
restrain 3
shut 1, 2
tongue 3
wrap 3b
shut up shop
close 5
shut your face *etc.*
hush 1
wrap 3b
shy°
backward 1
bashful 1
cast 1, 7
coy
deflect
faint-hearted 1
fearful 2
flinch
gingerly 2
hurl
inhibited
lob 1
meek 1
modest 1
mousy 2
peg 6
pull 8a
put 7
recoil 1
reticent
retiring
self-conscious
shamefaced 1
short 6
sling 1
start 5
tentative 2
throw 1
timid
toss 1, 6
tremulous 2
wanting 2
withdrawn 1
shy (away) (from)
back 3
duck 3
flinch
recoil 1
shrink 2
shun
shyly
fearfully 1
gingerly 1
shy-making
outrageous 3
shyness
humility
shame 4
shyster
mouthpiece 3
siamoise
couch 1
Siberian
cold 1
freezing
frigid 1
icy 1
polar 1
wintry 1
sibilance
fizz 3
hiss 1
sibilance (*cont.*)
rustle 2
sibilate
rustle 1
sibilation
rustle 2
sibling
brother
sibyl
fortune-teller
oracle 1
prophet
psychic 3
seer
witch 1
sibyllic
ominous 3
sibylline
prophetic
sic
letter 4
literally 1
sick°
ail 1, 2
diseased
disgusted
frail 2
ghastly 3
ghoulish 2
heave 4
ill 1
indisposed 1
infirm 1
invalid[1] 1
low[1] 4
morbid 1
nauseated
off colour 1
poorly 2
psychotic 1
queasy 2
queer 3
rotten 5
throw 9a
unhealthy 1
unsound 2
unwholesome 3
upset 7
vomit
weather 2
sick and tired (of)
disgusted
weary 3, 4
-on the sick-list
ill 1
indisposed 1
sick 2
sick-bay
hospital
infirmary
sicken°
disgust 1
glut 4
nauseate
offend 2
pall[2] 1
put 21d
relapse 2
repel 2
revolt 3
shock 1
turn 17b
sickened
disgusted
nauseated
sick 6
sickening
disagreeable 2
disgusting
foul 1
grisly
hideous 1
horrible 1
loathsome
nasty 1
nauseous
obnoxious
obscene 2
offensive 3
repellent
repugnant
repulsive
revolting
sickening (*cont.*)
sentimental 2
shocking 2
sweet 7
ugly 2
uninviting
unsavoury
vile 2
wicked 6
sickliness
infirmity 1
sickly°
colourless 1
delicate 3
feeble 1
frail 2
ill 1
indisposed 1
infirm 1
invalid[1] 1
low[1] 4
par 5b
pasty
peaky
puny 3
ropy 3
run-down 1
seedy 2
sick 2
tender[1] 1
unhealthy 1
unsound 2
unwholesome 3
wan 1
weak 2
weather 2
sick-making
disgusting
distasteful
repellent
revolting
sentimental 2
yucky
sickness
ailment
bug 2
disease 1
disgust 2
disorder 3
illness
infirmity 2
trouble 8
sick of°
at **sick 7**
disgusted
jaded 2
tired 2
side°
ally 2
angle[1] 2
arrogance
aspect 1, 4
bravado
edge 1
effrontery
flank 1
flippancy 2
impudence
indirect 2
margin 1
page[1]
part 5
party 3, 5
phase 4
point 14
shoulder 1
surface 1
sympathize 2
team 1
version 2
-from side to side
sway 1
-on all sides
around 2, 5
round 23
-on every side
about 1
-on the side
sly 3
-on the side of
favour 5
for 1

-sides°
_at_ side 1
-to one side
apart 1
wide 5
side-arm
revolver
side by side°
_at_ side 6
hand 11
shoulder 5
sidekick
chum 1
henchman
intimate[1] 5
pal 1
partner 1
satellite 2
shadow 6
sideline
hobby
-on the sidelines
stand 5b
sidelong°
oblique 2
sideways
sidelong glance
eye 5
side-note
note 3
sidereal
stellar 1
side-road
turn-off 1
side-splitting
comic 1
funny 1
hilarious
humorous
hysterical 2
priceless 2
rich 10
ridiculous
uproarious 2
sidestep°
avoid
bypass 1
dodge 1,3
duck 3
equivocate
evade 1
fence 4
get 44e
shuffle 5
sidetrack°
deflect
distract 1
diversion 2
divert 2
pervert 1
sidetracking
perversion 1
side-trip
excursion 2
side-view
profile 1
sidewalk°
walk 5
sideways°
sidelong
side with°
_at_ side 10
back 2a
favour 6
plump[2] 3
promote 3
stand 5a, 11
sympathize 2
sidle°
edge 6
sneak 1
walk 1
siege°
storm 6
siesta
doze 2
nap[1] 3
repose 2
rest[1] 1
sleep 2

sieve
filter 1
mesh 1
net[1] 1
riddle[2] 3
screen 4
sift 1
strain[1] 5
talebearer
sift°
examine 1
filter 2
investigate
pan 4
pick 1
rake[1] 5
rummage 1
screen 8
scrutinize
search 1
strain[1] 5
wash 6
sifter
net[1] 1
riddle[2] 3
sifting
scrutiny
search 4
sigh°
groan 1,3
heave 3
moan 3
whisper 1
sigh for°
_at_ sigh 2
desire 1
pant 2
sight°
eye 2
fright 3
phenomenon 2
prospect 1
scene 4
see 1
spectacle 1
spot 6
tableau
view 4
vision 1,5
wonder 1
-in sight
out 4
prospect 4
-out of sight°
_at_ sight 6
splendid 3
superb
under 8
world 8
sight for sore eyes
vision 5
sighting
aim 4
sightless
blind 1
sightsee
tour 4
trip 7
sightseer°
rubberneck 2
tourist
traveller
sign°
beacon
character 1
close 4
cue 1
cut 10
emblem
employ 1
engage 1
enter 8
evidence 3
execute 2
expression 2
figure 7
flash 2
foreboding 2
forerunner 2
gesture 3
guide 7
hallmark 1
harbinger

sign (*cont.*)
index 2
indication 1
initial 2
join 2
letter 1
line[1] 23b
make 4
manifestation
mark 2
motion 4,6
movement 3
nod 5
omen
pointer 1
reflection 4
seal 1
signal 4
signify 1
stamp 2,5,7
strain[2] 2
subscribe 2
symbol
symptom
token 2
trace 1
underwrite 2
vestige
warning 2
wave 3,5
witness 5
-signs
indication 4
notation 2
signal°
alert 4,5
announce 2,4
beacon
beckon
buoy 1
buzz 7
cue 1,2
eventful
extraordinary 1
flag[1] 2
flare 5
foreshadow
gesture 1,3
guide 7
hail[1] 1
hint 3
historic
imply 2
important 1
indication 1
marked
mean[1] 2
motion 4,6
movement 3
nod 5
note 6
noticeable 2
prod 6
prognosticate 2
remarkable 2
sign 1,2
significant 1
signify 1
singular 2
siren 1
sound[1] 6
warning 2
wave 3,5
word 7
signally
eminently
especially 1
notably 1
pre-eminently
signatory
party 5
signature
sign 7
stamp 7
touch 18
sign away°
_at_ sign 8
waive 1
signboard
sign 5
signed
personalized
signer
party 5

signet
device 3
sanction 1
seal 1
stamp 6
significance°
account 5
bearing 3
content[1] 3
distinction 2
drift 4
effect 3
emphasis
essence 1
force 4,5
gist
gravity 2
implication 3
import 4
importance 1
interest 2
magnitude 2
matter 4
meaning 2
moment 3
nobility 1
pith 2
point 7
prestige
relevance
sense 4
status 1
stress 2
substance 3
tenor
worth
-of significance
signify 2
significant°
big 4
central 2
eventful
expressive 1
fateful 1
goodly
great 3,4,11
historic
important 1
influential
instrumental
knowing 1
landmark 3
major 2
marked
material 6
meaningful 1,2
memorable
momentous
monumental 1
noticeable 2
pivotal
pregnant 2
pressing
prestigious
prominent 1
relevant
remarkable 2
respectable 2
salient
sensible 5
serious 2
signal 3
signify 2
singular 2
speak 8
special 2
substantial 1
telling 1
tidy 3
weighty 2
significantly
materially
notably 2
signification
effect 3
explanation 3
import 3
matter 4
meaning 1
point 7
significance 1
spirit 6
substance 3

signify°
argue 4
denote 1
evidence 4
express 2,3
foreshadow
imply 2
import 2
indicate 2
insinuate 1
mark 11
mean[1] 2
refer 4
say 9
speak 5
spell[3] 1
stand 7a
symbolize
vote 4
wave 5
signifying
indicative of
sign in
check 7
come 2
register 3,6
report 5
sign off°
_at_ sign 9
terminate
sign on°
_at_ sign 10
check 7
enlist 1
enrol 1
enter 5
hire 1
register 3,6
sign on the dotted line
sign 7
sign over°
_at_ sign 11
make 38b
trust 6
signpost
mark 7
sign up°
_at_ sign 10
employ 1
engage 1
enlist 1
enrol 1
enter 5
join 2
line[1] 23b
register 3
sign 10a
silage
feed 4
provender 2
silence°
dispatch 3
gag[1] 1
hide[1] 4
hush 2,6
kill 1,3
lull 2
muffle 2
mute 3
put 16e
quiet 5
quieten
shut 6b
stifle 3
still 3,9
suppress 3
-in silence
quietly 1
silencing
suppression
silent°
close 17
dumb 1
hush 1
movie 1
mum 1
mute 1,2
noiseless
quiet 1,2
reserved
reticent
secretive
still 2,7

silent (*cont.*)
tacit
taciturn
tight-lipped
tongue 3
withdrawn 1
wrap 3b
silently°
quietly 1
still 7
silent majority
hoi polloi
people 3
silent picture
movie 1
silhouette°
figure 1
form 2
line[1] 5
outline 1
profile 1
shape 1
silken
silky
sleek 1
slick 1
smooth 2,6
soft 8
thin 5
silklike
silky
silk screen
print 2
silk-stocking
genteel 2
silky°
sleek 1
slick 1
smooth 2,6
soft 8
thin 5
sill
ledge
threshold 1
sillcock
tap[2] 1
silliness
absurdity 1
folly 1
nonsense 2
vanity 2
silly°
absurd 1
childish
crazy 2
daft 1
dizzy 2
farcical
flighty 2
fool 1
foolish 2
frivolous 2
giddy 2
halfwitted
hare-brained 2
imprudent
inane
insane 2
light[2] 8
ludicrous
mad 2
meaningless 1
nonsensical
pointless
puerile
ridiculous
senseless 3
soft 6
stupid 2
thoughtless 2
unreasonable 1
unthinking 1
untoward 2
wild 7
worthless 2
zany 1
silly billy
silly 3
twit[2]
silt°
deposit 4
mud
ooze 1

silt (*cont.*)
sludge
silt over°
at **silt 2**
silt up°
at **silt 2**
silver°
change 4
coin 1
trophy 1
white 1
silver screen
movie 2
screen 5
silver-toned
silver 4
silver-tongued
eloquent 1
silver 4
smooth 7
silverware
silver 1
trophy 1
silvery
lyric 3
melodious
silver 3, 4
sweet 3
simian
monkey 1
similar°
akin
alike 1
equal 1
equivalent 1
homogeneous
identical 2
kindred 1
like[1] 1
parallel 1
piece 8
similarity
comparison 2
equality 2
kinship 2
likeness 1
parallel 3
parity 1
resemblance
uniformity 1
unity 2
similar kind *etc.*
like[1] 8
similarly
alike 2
likewise 1
similarly constituted
piece 8
similarly to°
like[1] 5
similar to
at **similar 2**
akin
equal 1
like[1] 1, 4
reminiscent
resemble
simile
image 5
metaphor
similitude
equality 2
parity 1
uniformity 1
unity 2
simmer°
boil[1] 1
brew 3
rage 4
seethe 1, 2
smoulder
stew 3
simmer down°
at **simmer 3**
simmering
hot 1
simoleons
money 1
simoniacal
venal
Simon Legree
tyrant
simon-pure
pure 1
simoom
storm 1
simpatico
friendly 1
harmonious
likeable
sympathetic 2
sympathize 2
simper
twitter 2
simpering
sentimental 2
smirk 1
simple°
artless 1, 2
bare 2, 5
chaste 2
clean 3
common 1, 3
defective 2
easy 1
effortless
elementary 1
feeble-minded
gullible
halfwitted
homely 1
homespun
humble 3
informal 1, 2, 3
ingenuous 1
innocent 4
literal 2
meagre 3
mill 4
modest 2
naïve
natural 3
neat 3
obtuse 2
obvious
ordinary 2
painless
pastoral 1
plain 2, 4
plump[2] 6
primary 5
primitive 3
pure 1, 5
rude 4
rustic 2
senile
severe 6
sheer 2
slow 7
sober 3
soft 6
stark 2
straight 5
stupid 1
transparent 3
unadorned
unaffected[1]
understated
undistinguished
unsophisticated 1, 2
unvarnished
user-friendly
vernacular 2
very 4
weak 5
-in simple English
straight 14
simple-hearted
simple 3
simple job
breeze 2
simple-minded
daft 1
foolish 2
light[2] 8
literal 2
naïve
obtuse 2
senseless 3
simple 4
stupid 1
weak 5
simple-mindedness
folly 1
simplicity 4
stupidity 1
simpleton
clod 2
dolt
dummy 3
fool 1
gawk 1
halfwit
mug 3
natural 12
sap[1] 2
silly 3
twit[2]
simplicity°
candour 1
ease 2
naïvety
nature 3
provincialism 2
severity 6
stupidity 1
simplification
explanation 1
interpretation 1
light[1] 5
simplified
meagre 3
popular 3
streamlined 3
simplify°
clarify 1
ease 8
explain 1
interpret 1
light[1] 12
simplistic
literal 2
naïve
primitive 3
simply°
alone 4
easily 1
honestly 2
just 4
merely 1, 2
naturally 3
obviously
only 3
practically 2
severely 6
straight 14
simulacrum
image 1
imitation 4
likeness 2
simulate
act 8
approximate 3
assume 4
counterfeit 5
echo 4
fake 2
imitate 1
let[1] 7b
masquerade 3
mimic 1
pattern 7
play 10
profess 2
reproduce 1
simulated
affected 2
artificial 1
assumed 2
counterfeit 2
factitious
false 3
glossy 2
imitation 5
mimic 5
mock 3
sham 2
spurious
toy 6
simulation
affectation 2
dummy 2
echo 2
imitation 4
knock-off
simulation (*cont.*)
semblance 2
simultaneity
coincidence 1
simultaneous°
current 1
simultaneously
once 6b
time 12b
sin°
blot 3
err 2
error 2
evil 6
fault 4
ill 9
misdeed
offence 1
pity 2
profligacy 1
scandal 1
transgress 1
transgression
vice 1
since
for 13
past 4
seeing
sincere°
artless 1
bona fide
candid 1
deep 6
devout 3
direct 10
earnest 1, 4
frank 1
genuine 2
heartfelt
hearty 2
honest 3
honourable 3
ingenuous 1
innocent 4
intense 2
level 15
open 15
plain 3
poignant 3
profound 3
pure 6
real 3
serious 3
simple 3
soulful
strenuous 2
true 2
truthful
unaffected[1]
undisguised
unvarnished
warm 4
wholehearted
sincerely°
dearly 1
honestly 2
profoundly
seriously 2
substantially
true 4
truly 1, 4
sincerity°
candour 1
heart 4
honesty 2
intensity
naïvety
probity
simplicity 3
soul 4
sine qua non
fundamental 2
indispensable 2
must 2
necessity 1
need 3
precondition
prerequisite 2
requirement 1
sinew°
strength 1
-sinews°
at **sinew 2**
sinewy°
muscular
robust 1
stalwart 1
stringy
strong 1
tough 2
wiry
sinful°
abandoned 2
bad 3
blasphemous
criminal 2
damnable
devilish
diabolic 2
disgraceful 1
evil 1
evil-minded 2
foul 4
godless 1
ill 2
immoral 1
impious
improper 3
impure 4
incorrigible
lawless 3
perverted
profane 1
profligate 1
reprobate 1
scandalous 1
ungodly 1
unwholesome 2
vicious 1
vile 1
wicked 1
wrong 1
sinfulness
guilt 1
impropriety 3
impurity 3
profligacy 1
sin 2
vice 1
sing°
belt 4
chant 2
clean 8
give 7
inform 2
spill 3
talk 5
singe°
burn 5
scorch
singer°
vocalist
single°
celibate 1
eligible 2
exclusive 3
individual 1
isolated 1
lonely 1
one 1
only 1
particular 1
record 7
singular 3
solitary 1
stray 6
unattached 2
unique 1
unmarried
single-foot
trot 3
single-handed°
single-handedly
single-handed 2
single-minded°
determined 1
obstinate
opinionated 1
resolute
steadfast
single-mindedness
dedication 1
determination 1
fanaticism 2
purpose 2
resolution 1
single-mindedness (*cont.*)
solidarity
zealotry
singleness
celibacy 1
solidarity
unity 2
single out°
at **single 4**
distinguish 2
favour 6
identify 1
pick 1
point 17, 21b
prefer 1
select 1
separate 2
spot 6
singling out
selection 3
singly°
apart 2
individually
respectively
separately
singsong
chant 1
sing the praises of
eulogize
extol
laud
praise 3
singular°
alone 2
curious 3
deviant 1
different 2
distinct 2
distinctive
eccentric 1
exceptional 1
exclusive 3
exotic 2
extraordinary 1
individual 2
irregular 3
isolated 1
notable 2
noteworthy
noticeable 2
odd 1
ordinary 4
outlandish
particular 1
peculiar 1
phenomenal
proper 6
quaint 1
queer 1
rare[1] 1
remarkable 1
signal 3
single 2
sole
special 1
strange 1
stray 5
superlative
unparalleled
unusual
unwonted
whimsical 1
singularity°
abnormality 1
eccentricity 1
identity 2
oddity 1
peculiarity 2
unity 2
singularly
eminently
especially 1
particularly 1
sinister°
black 5
dark 4
devilish
diabolic 2
evil 2
ghostly 1
grim 3

skill (*cont.*)
touch 16
trick 3
understanding 3
virtuosity
workmanship
-skills
ability 3
skilled
able 2
accomplished
adept 1
capable 1
clever 1
experienced 1
expert 2
gifted
good 12
great 8
handy 3
home 5
ingenious
know 1
learned
master 4
masterful 1
mean^{2} 6
old 7
perfect 7
practised 1
professional 1
proficient
qualified 1
skilful
strong 6
talented
versed
skillet
pan 1
skim°
browse
coast 2
dip 3
flit
go 34a
plane 4
read 1
run 33a
sail 3
scan 1
scud
slide 1
sweep 3
thumb 7
skim off°
at **skim 1**
skim over°
at **skim 2**
go 34a
skimp
economize
pinch 5
scrape 3
stint 4
skimpily
sketchily
skimping
thrift
thrifty
skimpy
abbreviated
deficient 1
frugal 3
inadequate 1
little 3
meagre 1
measly
poor 2
scanty 2
sketchy
small 4
spare 5
thin 2
skim through°
at **skim 2**
browse
go 34a
run 33b
thumb 7
skin°
exterior 3
face 6
facing
film 1

skin (*cont.*)
gouge 2
hide^{2} 1
hull 2, 3
outside 1
pare 1
peel 1, 4
pelt^{2}
reprimand 2
rind
rip 2b
scrape 1
sheet 5
strip^{2} 1
surface 1
-by the skin of one's teeth
hair 2
just 5
narrowly 1
skin alive
mind 10
reprimand 2
scold 1
skin-deep°
flashy 2
outward
shallow 1
superficial 1, 2
skinflint
miser
stiff 12
skinflinty
cheap 4
close 18
penurious 1
skin game
fiddle 3
skinhead
barbarian 2
gangster
rowdy 2
skinny°
emaciated
frail 2
gaunt 1
lean^{1} 1
light^{2} 2
meagre 2
raw-boned
scrawny
spare 3
thin 1
skint
broke
down and out 1
embarrassed 2
hard 17
impoverished 1
indigent
insolvent
poor 1
stony 3
skip°
caper 1, 3
cavort
dance 1
depart 1
escape 1
flee 1
flit
frisk 1
frolic 3
hop 1, 3
jump 1, 3, 4, 8
leap 1, 5
make 26
miss^{1} 1
omit 1
pass 3, 22
patter^{1} 1
prance
quit 1
run 2
skim 2
sport 4
spring 6
trip 4
skipped
undone^{2}
skipper°
director 2
lead 3
master 1

skipper (*cont.*)
navigate 2
navigator
sailor
skipping
omission 1
skip town
escape 1
flee 1
make 26
skirl
pipe 4
skirmish°
action 6
brush^{2} 3
combat 1
encounter 5
fight 1, 7
fray^{1}
incident 2
scrimmage
trouble 7
skirmishing
trouble 7
skirt
broad 9
bypass 1
equivocate
flank 3
fluff 2
get 46a
girl 1
sidestep
woman 3
skit
act 2
skitter
slither
skittish
flighty 1
jumpy
nervous 1
restless
skittishness
jitters
skive
loaf^{2} 1
shirk
slack 4
skiver
loafer
slacker
truant 1
wastrel 2
skiving
idleness 2
truant 2
skivvy
menial 3
slave 1, 3
-skivvies
underclothes
unmentionable 3
skivvying
drudgery
skol
bottom 6
skulduggery
chicanery
foul play
trickery
skulk
creep 3
lurk
prowl 1, 3
slink
sneak 1
steal 3
walk 1
skulking
furtive 1
stealthy
skulking about
prowl 3
skull
head 1
skunk
rout 2
stinker
sky°
atmosphere 1
firmament

sky (*cont.*)
heaven 2
-in the sky
above 1
overhead 1
-skies
firmament
heaven 2
sky 1
-to the skies°
at **sky 2**
skycap
porter^{1}
sky-high
towering 1
skylark
frolic 3
lark 2
skylarking
frolic 1
fun 2
play 22
sky pilot
father 4
minister 1
sky-rocket
rocket
soar 2
sky-scraping
towering 1
skyward
aloft
overhead 1
slab°
block 1
brick 1
cake 2
plank
plaque 1
plate 3
sheet 3
slice 1
tablet 2
slabber
slaver^{1} 1, 2
slack°
derelict 2
flabby 1
give 18
inattentive
inert 3
lax 1
lazy 1
leeway
limp^{2} 1
loose 3
off 8
remiss
slothful
slow 6
tardy 2
slacken
brake 2
decrease 1
diminish 3
drop 11
ebb 2
lag 2
let^{1} 9
liberalize 2
loose 12
mitigate
moderate 5
relax 1
remit 2
slack 3a
taper 2
temper 5
slackening
decrease 2
ebb 4
relaxation 2
slacken off°
at **slack 3**
pay 11c
slow 14
wind^{2} 3a
slacken up°
at **slack 3**
mitigate
reduce 2
relax 1

slacker°
derelict 3
idler
slackness
neglect 4
slack 6
slack off°
at **slack 3**
drop 11
let^{1} 10
pay 11c
slow 14
wind^{2} 3a
slack up°
at **slack 3**
slag
trash 3
slake°
quench 1
satiate 2
satisfy 2
slaked
jaded 2
slaking
refreshing
slam°
jam 3
pull 6
punch^{1} 1, 2
ram 2
run 26d
stroke 1
slammer
jail 1
prison
stir 7
slander°
abuse 3
aspersion
blacken 2
discredit 1, 5
dishonour 5
disparage 2
impeach 2
insult 1, 2
libel 2, 4
scandal 3
slur 1
smear 2, 4
stigmatize
tale 3
vilify
slanderous°
abusive 1
foul 6
injurious 2
poisonous 2
scandalous 2
vicious 2
vituperative
slang
cant 2
dialect
jargon 1
slanging-match
row^{2} 1
slant°
angle^{1} 1, 2
bias 2
colour 4
decline 3, 8
descend 2
distort 2
garble 1
inclination 2
incline 1, 4
lean^{2} 2
list^{2} 1, 2
outlook 1
phase 4
point of view 1
position 3
prejudice 3
rise 6
slope 1, 2
sway 2
tilt 1, 3
tip^{2} 2
twist 2, 8
viewpoint
weight 6
slanted
oblique 1

slanting
inclined 3
oblique 1
slap°
clap 2, 3, 5
dig 8
flap 1
full 14
hit 1
indignity
insult 2
knock 10
pelt^{1} 4
plumb 4
precisely 1
shaft 3
slam 2
spank
strike 1
taunt 2
throw 9d
whip 7b
slap-bang
pell-mell 1
slapdash
careless 2
cursory
haphazard 2
hasty 3
hurried 2
loose 5
makeshift 1
pell-mell 1, 2
slipshod
superficial 3
slap down
squelch 1
slap-happy
scatterbrained
slap in the face°
at **slap 5**
brush-off
cut 23
dig 8
indignity
insult 2
knock 10
shaft 3
taunt 2
slap on°
at **slap 6**
slap on the wrist
reprimand 1, 2
slap someone's wrist
punish 1
scold 1
slapstick
funny 1
zany 1
slap together
throw 9d
whip 7b
slash°
claw 2
cut 1, 8, 19
gash 1, 2
hack^{1} 1, 3
incision
knife 2
lacerate
lash^{1} 2
line^{1} 1
lower^{1} 1
mark 15b
pare 2
reduce 5
rent^{2}
rip 3
score 10
slit 1, 2
snip 2
split 7
streak 1, 4
stripe 1
tear 4
wound 1, 3
slat
flap 1
slap 2
slate
calendar 1
criticize 2

slate (*cont.*)
list[1] 1
pan 5
programme 1,4
pull 6
reprimand 2
roll 13
schedule 2
slam 3
slated
card 12
slating
reprimand 1
tongue-lashing
slattern°
jade 2
slatternly
dirty 1
untidy
slaughter°
bloodshed
butcher 3
carnage
destruction 2
exterminate
gore[1]
kill 1
killing 1
massacre 1,2
mow 2
murder 2,3
purge 4
removal 2
remove 4
whip 2
zap
slaughterer
butcher 1
slaughtering
massacre 1
slaughterous
sanguinary 1
slave°
attendant 2
boy 2
captive 1
flunkey 1
grind 4
hack[2] 2
labour 5
menial 3
overwork 2
plod 2
subordinate 2
sweat 3
work 7
slave-driver
master 1
oppressor
tyrant
slave-girl
slave 1
slaveling
slave 1
slaver°
drivel 1
spit 1
slavery°
bondage
captivity
drudgery
labour 1
servitude
slave ship
slaver[2] 1
slave-trade
slavery 2
slave-trader
slaver[2] 1,2
slavey
slave 1
slavish
base[2] 2
grovelling
menial 1
obsequious
servile
submissive 2
slavishness
servility
slay
dispatch 3
eliminate 4

slay (*cont.*)
execute 3
kill 1
massacre 2
murder 3
polish 3b
remove 4
rub 6
shoot 3
slaughter 3
zap
-be slain
fall 6
slayer
killer 1
murderer
slaying
destruction 2
dispatch 7
execution 3
killing 1
massacre 1
murder 1,2
removal 2
slaughter 2
sleazy°
cheap 3
mangy
seedy 1
sordid 4
tacky[2]
sleek°
glossy 1
silky
slick 1
slippery 1
smooth 2
sleep°
doze 1,2
lay[1] 8
repose 2
rest[1] 1,6
retire 3
sleep around
mess 4b
play 9b
run 23
sleeper
tie 12
sleep-inducing
monotonous
narcotic 1
restful 1
sedative 2
sleepiness
lethargy 2
torpor
sleeping
dormant 1
silent 4
sleeping-pill
sedative 1
sleepless°
wakeful 1
sleepwalking°
sleepy°
dormant 1
dreamy 3
drowsy
leaden 4
lethargic 2
slow 9
torpid
sleet
precipitation
storm 5
sleety
foul 8
sleeveless
futile
sleight of hand
dexterity 1
hocus-pocus 3
magic 2
trick 5
slender°
fine[1] 6
lean[1] 1
narrow 1
remote 6
slight 2,3
spare 3
tenuous 1

slender (*cont.*)
thin 1
trim 2
willowy 2
slenderize
reduce 3
slim 3
sleuth°
detective
operative 3
sleuth-hound
operative 3
slew
heap 2
mass 2
number 2
plenty 1
wind[2] 1
-slews
mass 2
number 2
plenty 1
slice°
cut 2
piece 2
portion 1
rend 2
section 2
segment 1
sever 1
share 2
slab
slash 4
slit 1
slicer
slice 3
slick°
devious 1
dexterous 2
disingenuous
flashy 2
fluent
foxy 1
glassy 1
glib
glossy 2
greasy 2
insincere
mealy-mouthed
resourceful
scheming
serpentine 1
shifty
sleek 1
slippery 1,2
smooth 2,6,8
sophisticated 1
subtle 3
wily
slick down°
at **slick 5**
slicker°
slickness
fluency
slick operator
devil 4
operator 3
slide°
chute 2
coast 2
deteriorate 1
glide
photograph 1
plane 4
roll 2
sag 2,3
sail 3
skim 3
slip[1] 1
slither
stream 4
worsen 2
slide by
elapse
fly 4
sliding
downward
slight°
belittle
cut 3,12,23
depreciate 2
dishonour 1,4
disregard 2

slight (*cont.*)
fail 2
faint 1
feeble 1
flimsy 1,2
fragile
frail 2
frivolous 2
immaterial 1
imperceptible 2
inconsequential
indifferent 4
indignity
injure 2
insubstantial 1
insult 1,2
light[2] 2,4,5,6
little 1
marginal 1
minor 2
minute[2] 2
neglect 1
negligible
nice 3
nodding
offence 2
offend 1
outrage 3
overlook 1
petite
petty 1
poor 5
put 16e
put-down
rebuff 1,2
remote 5,6
shallow 1
short 1
skin-deep
sleazy 1
slender 1,2,3
slur 1
small 2,5
superficial 1,2
thin 1,2,4
tiny
token 5
trifling
trivialize
undersized
wound 2,4
-to a slight extent *etc.*
slightly
slightest
jot 2
minimal
minimum 2
slighting
neglect 3
personal 4
slightly°
little 8
moderately
rather 1
somewhat
slily
sly 3
slim°
diet[1] 3
lean[1] 1
narrow 1
outside 8
reduce 3
remote 6
slender 1,2,3
slight 3
spare 3
thin 1
trim 2
willowy 2
slime
dirt 1
filth 1
grime
mire 2
muck 2
mud
ooze 1
sludge
sliminess
servility

slimy°
clammy 1
filthy 1
flattering 2
ingratiating
insincere
muddy 1
obsequious
oily 1
Pharisaic
servile
sleek 3
slippery 1
smooth 6
sordid 3
subtle 3
sling°
cast 7
fling 1
fly 8a
heave 2
hurl
launch 3
peg 6
pitch[1] 1
slap 3
string 9
throw 1
toss 1
slingshot
sling 2
slink°
creep 3
lurk
prowl 1,3
pussyfoot 1
slide 2
slither
sneak 1
walk 1
slip°
blunder 2
cutting 3
deteriorate 1
ease 7
err 1
error 1
escape 1
fault 2
fluff 3
get 38c
glide
impropriety 4
indiscretion 2
lapse 1,4
miss[1] 5
misstep 1
mistake 1
nod 4
offence 1
peccadillo
plane 4
put 22a
relapse 1
roll 2
run-around
sag 2
sail 3
shoot 5
slide 1,2
slither
sliver
slump 2
solecism
steal 3
stream 4
stumble 1,2
tongue 4
trip 1,2,5
tumble 4
worsen 2
slip away
elapse
elude 1
escape 1
fly 4
go 11
lapse 6
pass 11
sink 2
slip by
elapse
fly 4
pass 11

slip of the pen
slip[1] 8
slip of the tongue°
at **tongue 4**
misstatement 2
slip[1] 8
trip 2
slip one over on someone
defraud
mislead
outsmart
slippery°
deceptive 2
devious 1
elusive 1
foxy 1
glassy 1
greasy 2
insincere
oily 1
precarious
scheming
shady 2
shifty
slick 1
slimy 1,2
smooth 6
sneaky
tricky 1
unscrupulous
wily
slipping
downgrade 4
downward
slipping away
dying
passing 1
slip-road
turn-off 1
slipshod°
derelict 2
haphazard 2
inefficient 2
lax 1
perfunctory 2
poor 4
promiscuous 1
sleazy 1
sloppy 1
slip someone something
pay 10b
slip something over on some-one
defraud
misinform
outsmart
slip through one's fingers°
at **finger 9**
slip up
err 1
miss[1] 4
nod 4
overlook 1
slip-up
blunder 2
error 1
fault 2
lapse 1
miss[1] 5
misstep 2
peccadillo
slip[1] 8
slit°
break 26
chink
cleave
crack 1
cut 1
flaw 2
gash 1,2
hole 2
incision
lance 2
opening 1
rent[2]
slash 1,4
slot 1,3
snip 2
split 7

small (*cont.*)
slender 2
slight 1, 3
small-minded
small-time
spare 5
stunted
tight 2
tiny
toy 5
undersized
wee 1
small amount
thought 7
small-boned
petite
small change
money 1
small-clothes
pants 1
underclothes
unmentionable 3
small craft
boat
smaller
low[1] 10
minor 1
smallest
minimal
smallest room (in the house)
toilet 1
small fry
boy 1
cog 2
smallholder
farmer
smallholding
farm 1
small items
sundries
small matter
triviality 2
small-minded°
little 6
narrow-minded
overcritical
petty 2
smallness
triviality 1
small number
handful 1
small potatoes
pittance
small print
joker 2
smalls
pants 1
underclothes
unmentionable 3
small-scale
miniature
small 4
small-time
small screen
screen 5
television
small talk
chat 1
gossip 1
patter[2] 2
small-time°
frivolous 1
minor 2
petty 1
small-town
provincial 2
smarminess
servility
smarmy
flattering 2
greasy 2
ingratiating
obsequious
oily 2
Pharisaic
pious 2
sanctimonious
servile
sleek 3
slick 2
slimy 2

smarmy (*cont.*)
smooth 6
subtle 3
smart°
ache 1
advisable
brave 2
bright 6
brilliant 4
chic 1
clever 3
dapper
dashing 2
dressy 2
elegant 1
exquisite 3
fashionable
flash 6
glamorous 2
hurt 2
ingenious
intelligent
jaunty 2
keen[1] 6
minute[1] 3
neat 3
nifty 1
nimble 1, 2
penetrating 1
precocious
prick 4
prickle 3
quick 4
quick-witted
rakish
resourceful
sharp 3, 9
shrewd
snappy 1, 2
spanking 1, 3
sporty
spruce 1
stylish
subtle 3
suffer 1
swanky
swell 7
swish 3
tactical
taut 2
tight 4
trim 1
well-advised
well-groomed
wise 1
smart alec
wise guy
smart-alecky
fresh 8
smart-arse
wise guy
smart-arsed
insolent
pert 1
smarten up
decorate 1
dress 1
groom 3
perk up
spruce 2
smarting
ache 3
angry 2
pain 1
painful 1
smart 6, 8
sore 1
tender[1] 8
smartness
ingenuity
panache
style 4
smarty(-pants)
wise guy
smash
break 4
bump 3
clash 2
collide 2
collision
crack 5
crash 2, 4
crush 1
dash 1

smash (*cont.*)
demolish 1
destroy 1
hack[1] 1
hit 3, 11
impact 1
knockout 2
pile-up 1
pulverize 2
rout 2
run 26d
ruin 7
shatter 1
shiver[2]
slam 2
slaughter 4
strike 3
whip 2
wreck 1
smashed
broken 1
drunk 1
piece 7
stinking 3
smash hit
hit 11
knockout 2
smashing
admirable
beautiful 1, 2
capital 6
divine 3
excellent
extraordinary 2
fabulous 3
good 2
gorgeous 2
grand 5
great 12
heavenly 2
impact 1
marvellous
neat 5
outstanding 1
sensational 3
splendid 3
striking
superb
superlative
terrific 2
world 8
smashingly
beautifully 1, 2
smash to smithereens
shiver[2]
splinter 2
smash-up
collision
pile-up 1
smattering
scattering
tang 2
touch 15
smear°
blacken 2
blemish 3
blot 1
dirty 7
discredit 1, 4
disgrace 2, 4
dishonour 5
foul 14
libel 2, 4
mark 1, 10
mire 4
plaster
rub 2
scandal 3
shame 8
slander 2
slanderous
slur 1
soil[1] 1, 2
splash 3
spread 7
streak 1, 4
taint 2
vilify
smell°
aroma 1, 2
detect 2
distinguish 3
fragrance

smell (*cont.*)
fume 3
give 14
odour 1
perfume 1
reek 1, 3
savour 2
scent 1, 3
sniff 3
tang 1
touch 15
trail 2
smell a rat
distrust 1
smell out
scrounge 1
track 8
smelly°
foul 3
rancid
rank[2] 4
stinking 1
strong 3
smidgen
blob
dab 2
dash 7
drop 2
grain 3
jot 2
little 10
modicum
morsel 2
particle
pinch 7
shade 6
speck
spot 3
trifle 2
smile°
beam 3
lighten[1] 2
smile upon
favour 8
smiling
sunny 2
smirch
blot 1
discredit 1
disgrace 2, 4
dishonour 5
libel 2
muddy 5
scandal 3
stain 1, 5
stigma
sully
taint 2
smirk°
sneer 1
smite
assault 5
batter 1
beat 1
hit 1
lash[1] 3
move 4
poke 2
rend 3
strike 1
visit 2
smithereens
fragment 2
shiver 2
splinter 2
-in smithereens
piece 7
smitten°
infatuated
stricken 2
smock
bunch 4
shift 6
smocking
ruffle 1
smog
fog 1
fume 3
mist 1
vapour 1
smoggy
hazy 1
thick 3

smoke
cure 3
fag 5
fume 2, 3
preserve 3
puff 5
reek 2, 4
use 3
vapour 1
whisky
smoke out
discover 1
smokescreen
blind 8
cover 15
film 3
smokestack
stack 4
smoking gun
evidence 3
smoky
dingy
grey 1
opaque 1
thick 3
smooch
cuddle 2
kiss 1, 4
pet[1] 4
smoodge
cuddle 2
pet[1] 4
smooth°
bland 1
calm 3
clean 3
debonair 1
devious 1
disingenuous
ease 8
effortless
eloquent 1
even 1, 13
facilitate
flat 1
flatten 1
fluent
flush[2] 1
foxy 1
gentle 1
glassy 1
glib
glossy 1
graceful 1
greasy 2
grind 2
level 1, 8
offhand 1, 2
oily 1, 2
plain 1
plane 3
plausible 2
polish 1
press 4
quiet 2
regular 5
roll 7
rub 1, 2
shifty
silky
sleek 1
slick 1, 2, 3, 5
slippery 1
soft 4, 8
spread 7
still 1
straight 3
streamlined 1, 3
suave
tranquil
tuneful
uniform 2
wily
smooth away°
at **smooth 9**
smoothen
smooth 12
smoothie
charmer
devil 4
operator 3
smoothly
easily 1
freely 5

smoothly (*cont.*)
readily 2
swimmingly
smoothness
facility 1
fluency
polish 5
savoir faire
smooth operator
devil 4
operator 3
smooth out°
at **smooth 9**
flatten 1
level 8
roll 7
smooth over°
at **smooth 12**
gloss[1] 4
smooth-shaven
smooth 4
smooth-spoken
glib
slick 2
smooth 6
smooth talker
charmer
smooth-talking
glib
smooth the way
pave 2
smooth-tongued
glib
smorgasbord
hors-d'oeuvre
hors-d'oeuvre
mess 2
miscellany
pot-pourri
smother°
choke 1, 3
gulp 2
keep 14a
kill 3
put 23c
quench 2
rout 2
silence 4
stifle 1
suppress 2
swallow 4
smothered
dead 5
smothering
suppression
smoulder°
boil[1] 2
burn 1
fester 2
fume 1
rage 4
seethe 2
simmer 2
stew 3
smouldering
dirty 5
glowing 1
smudge
blacken 1
blot 1, 2
mark 1, 10
mire 4
smear 1, 3
splash 3
spot 1, 7
stain 4
smudged
dirty 1
smudgy
dingy
smug°
comfortable 2
conceited
goody-goody
haughty
inflated 1
proud 2
self-important
self-righteous
slick 2
snobbish

smuggle
run 14
smugness
pride 2
self-esteem 1
snobbery
smut
dirt 3
filth 3
impurity 2
mould[2]
pornography
ribaldry
smutch
stain 1,4
smuttiness
ribaldry
smutty
abusive 1
bawdy
blue 2
coarse 3
dirty 2
evil-minded 1
filthy 3
foul 5
gross 3
immodest 1
immoral 2
indecent 2
lascivious 2
lewd
low[1] 3
nasty 3
naughty 3
obscene 1
outrageous 3
pornographic
profane 3
prurient 2
racy 2
rank[2] 3
rough 6
rude 3
sexy 2
suggestive 2
vulgar 2
wicked 3
smutty language
profanity
snack°
bite 3
eat
tiffin
-snacks
refreshment 1
snack bar
café
snaffle
pilfer
pocket 4
swipe 2
snafu
bungle
confused 2
fluff 4
foul 16b
hash 2
mess 3
mix-up
muddle 4
snag°
catch 18
clutch 1
complication 2
deterrent
difficulty 2
drawback
entangle 1
fly 10
foul 13
grab 1
hindrance 1
hitch 4
hold-up 2
hook 6
hurdle 1
impediment
interference 2
joker 2
kink 3
liability 3
obstacle

snag (*cont.*)
obstruction 1
pitfall 2
rub 11
snarl[2] 3
stumbling-block
tangle 1,3
trammel 1
-snags
trammel
snail
laggard
snail-like
slow 1
snake°
coil 1
meander 1
slither
turn 11
twist 4
wind[2] 1
wriggle 2
snake-hipped
slender 1
snake in the grass
snake 2
stinker
traitor
turncoat
villain
snakelike
serpentine 2
snake-oil artist
cheat 1
snaking
serpentine 2
snap°
breeze 2
clap 5
crack 2,4
flip 1
impulsive
initiative 2
nip[1] 1
photograph 1,2
picnic 2
piece 9
pushover 1
put 7
shot 5
snarl[1] 1
split 1
snap at°
at **snap 3**
snap off°
at **snap 4**
snap one's fingers at°
at **snap 6**
disobey
snap out of it°
at **snap 7**
pull 13
rally 4
snappish°
abrupt 3
cantankerous
cranky 2
cross 6
curt
fretful
impatient 2
irritable
moody 2
passionate 3
perverse 2
petulant
quick-tempered
short 4
short-tempered
sour 4
temperamental 1
testy
touchy 1
snappy°
abrupt 1
epigrammatic
irritable
moody 2
sharp 9
smart 3
snappish 1,2

snappy (*cont.*)
spanking 1,3
spicy 1
snapshot
photograph 1
shot 5
snap 5
snap up°
at **snap 4**
snatch 1
snare°
bag 6
catch 2
foul 13
gimmick 1
hook 2,6
mesh 3
net[1] 2
temptation 2
trap 1,4
web
wile
snarl°
complicate 1
confuse 2,3
disorder 4
entangle 1,2
foul 13
knot 1
mix 4c
roar 1,3
snap 3b
tangle 1,3
snarled
confused 1
foul 10
involved 2
labyrinthine
snarling
roar 3
touchy 1
snarl up
confuse 2,3
upset 3
snarl-up
snarl[2] 3
snatch°
abduct
catch 9
clutch 1
fragment 1
grab 1,4
grapple 1
grasp 1
jump 6
kidnap
lay[1] 11
pilfer
pluck 3
pull 3
rip 2a
scrap[1] 1
seize 1
snap 3a,4
take 1
tear 2
yank 1,2
snatching
rape 3
snazzy
dapper
flash 6
loud 2
posh
sporty
stylish
swanky
sneak°
creep 3
lurk
prowl 1,3
pussyfoot 1
slink
slip[1] 6,7
steal 3
talebearer
walk 1
sneakily
back 6
private 6
secrecy 2
sly 3
sneakiness
stealth

sneaking°
private 2
stealthy
sneakingly
private 6
sneaking suspicion
premonition
sensation 1
sneak-thief
burglar
robber
thief 1
sneaky°
crafty
deceitful
devious 1
furtive 1,2
illicit 2
machiavellian
serpentine 1
sharp 6
sinister 2
slippery 2
sly 1
stealthy
surreptitious
unscrupulous
Sneaky Pete
whisky
sneer°
deride
despise
flout
gibe 1,2
jeer 1
look 5
mock 1
parody 3
put-down
scoff[1]
smirk 1,2
taunt 1,2
sneering
contemptuous
cutting 2
disdainful
scorn 2
scornful
sneer 3
sneeze°
sneeze at°
at **sneeze 2**
disregard 2
sneer 2
spurn
sneezing
sneeze 3
sneezles and wheezles
chill 2
cold 10
snicker°
giggle 1,2
laugh 1,3
titter 1,2
twitter 2
snickering
laughter
snide
scornful
sniff°
scent 3
smell 3
sneer 1,2
sob
sniff at°
at **sniff 4**
sneer 2
sniffle
snivel
-sniffles
chill 2
cold 10
sniff out
scent 3
track 8
snifter
drink 6
snigger
chuckle 1,2
giggle 1,2

snigger (*cont.*)
laugh 1,3
snicker 1,2
titter 1,2
twitter 2
sniggering
chuckle 2
laughter
snip°
clip[2] 1
cut 4
lop
nip[1] 1,3
patch 1
scrap[1] 1
shave 1
sliver
trim 3
-snips°
at **snip 4**
snipe°
snipe at°
at **snipe**
sniper
shot 4
snippet
clip[2] 5
crumb
fragment 1
modicum
patch 1
scrap[1] 1
shred 1
sliver
snatch 5
snip 3
wisp
-snippets
odds 5
snitch
disclose 1
finger 8
grass 1,2
hook 7
inform 2
informer
pilfer
pocket 4
shop 3
sing 3
sneak 2
steal 1
swipe 2
take 3
snitching
theft
snivel°
cry 2
moan 3
sob
weep 1
snivelling
grovelling
menial 2
puling
tearful
snobbery°
arrogance
pride 2
snobbish°
arrogant 2
conceited
condescending
disdainful
exclusive 2
haughty
hoity-toity
lofty 4
pompous 1
pretentious 2
proud 2
self-important
stiff 7
supercilious
uppish
snobbishness
arrogance
pride 2
snobbery
snobbism
snobbery

snooker
dilemma
dupe 3
prey 3b
stymie
victimize 2
snoop°
busybody
detective
eavesdrop
intruder 2
meddle
poke 3
pry 2
sleuth
snooper
busybody
detective
intruder 2
snoop 2
snooping
curiosity 2
curious 2
inquisitive 2
nosy
snoopy
inquisitive 2
intrusive
nosy
snootiness
snobbery
snooty
condescending
haughty
hoity-toity
lofty 4
overbearing
pompous 1
proud 2
scornful
self-important
snobbish
standoffish
stiff 7
supercilious
uppish
snooze
doze 1,2
nap[1] 1,3
repose 2
rest[1] 1,6
retire 3
sleep 1,2
snore
sleep 1
snort
drink 6
gasp 1,2
nip[2]
shot 7
snottiness
arrogance
snobbery
snotty
arrogant 2
conceited
condescending
disdainful
haughty
hoity-toity
lofty 4
overbearing
pompous 1
pretentious 2
proud 2
scornful
self-important
snobbish
uppish
snout
trunk 4
snow
dupe 3
fool 4
hoodwink
precipitation
storm 5
snowball
increase 1
proliferate
rise 10
swell 2
snowfall
precipitation

snowflake
flake 1
snow job
dupe 3
fool 4
hoax 1
snowstorm
storm 1
snow under
swamp 2
snow-white
immaculate 1
white 1
snowy
foul 8
white 1
wintry 1
snub
brush-off
cut 12,23
disregard 2
ignore 2
indignity
isolate
offend 1
ostracize
put 16e
put-down
rebuff 1,2
repulse 2,3
scorn 3
shoulder 2
slight 5,8
spurn
snubbed
unpopular
snuff
execute 3
kill 1
murder 3
shoot 3
smother 1
sniff 3
zap
-up to snuff
adequate 2
measure 15b
muster 3
par 6
presentable 1
scratch 5
snuff it
die 1
go 13
snuffle
sniff 3
snivel
sob
snuff out
execute 3
extinguish 1
kill 1
murder 3
put 23c
quench 2
shoot 3
smother 1,5
stamp 4
suppress 2
zap
snug°
compact 2
cosy 1
homely 2
intimate[1] 4
secure 1
snuggle
tight 1
snuggery
nest 2
snuggle°
cuddle 1,3
fondle
hug 1
nestle
pet[1] 4
snug harbor
home 3
so
accordingly 1
consequently
order 11
therefore
so (*cont.*)
thus 1,2
soak°
alcoholic 2
drench
drunk 3
fleece
impregnate 2
penetrate 4
permeate
saturate
steep[2] 1
sting 4
submerge 1
wash 1
water 6
soaked
bedraggled
soaking 2
wet 1
soaking°
bedraggled
flush[1] 5
wet 1
soak up°
at **soak 2**
retain 3
soap
detergent 1
foam 2
lather 3
wash 1
soap powder *etc.*
detergent 1
soapy
greasy 1
oily 1
soar°
fly 1
glide
mount 3
rise 7
rocket
skim 3
tower 3
soaring
flight[1] 1
lofty 1
tall 1
towering 1
S.O.B.
rogue 1
stinker
villain
sob°
cry 1
moan 3
weep 1
sobbing
lamentation
tearful
sober°
conservative 2
dignified
dispassionate 1
earnest 1
even 4
grave[2] 1
judicious
matter-of-fact
meaningful 1
measured 2
moderate 1
pensive
philosophical 2
rational 1
reasonable 1
sedate 1
self-contained 1
serious 1
severe 2
solemn 1
solid 5,7
sombre 1,3
staid
steady 6
straight 8
subdued 2
temperate 1,2
well-balanced 1
sobered
subdued 2
soberly
seriously 3
severely 3
well[1] 8
sober-minded
temperate 1
soberness
gravity 3
sobriety 2
solemnity
sober-sided
even 4
staid
temperate 1
sober up°
at **sober 4**
sobriety°
gravity 3
temperance 2
sobriquet
label 2
nickname 1
sob sister
scribe 2
writer
so-called°
alleged
nominal 1
pretended
professed 1
proper 7
quasi- 2
seeming
self-styled
specious
titular
soccer field
field 2
sociability
familiarity 2
fellowship 1,3
friendship 1
hospitality
sociable°
chummy
expansive 2
familiar 3
forthcoming 3
friendly 1
genial
gracious
hospitable 1
neighbourly
outgoing 2
pleasant 2
social°
dance 2
familiar 3
fête 1
neighbourly
public 2
reception 2
sociable
venereal
social climber
parvenu 1
social code
manner 3
-social codes
propriety 3
social convention
propriety 3
-social conventions
manner 3
propriety 3
social graces
manner 3
propriety 3
socialist(ic)
left 2
socialize°
associate 1b
fraternize
get 25b,50b
go 21b,33c,40b
hang 4b
hobnob
mingle 2
mix 2
rub 7
scene 6
socialize (*cont.*)
see 7
shoulder 4
steady 8
step 17b
travel 4
socially active
get 25b
social security
pension 1
societal
public 2
social 1
society°
association 1
body 6
brotherhood 2
circle 2
clan 2
club 2
combination 2
companionship
company 1
federation
fellowship 2
folk
fraternity 1,3
group 1
humanity 1
institute 1
league 1
order 9
organization 3
people 4
presence 2
public 8
ring[1] 3
sphere 2
union 2
world 2
sock
box[2] 2,3
clip[2] 3,6
get 24
hit 1,10
jab 2,4
punch[1] 1,2
rap 4
strike 1
wrap 3b
sock away
salt 8
socking great
big 1
hefty 3
socle
pedestal 1
sod
clod 1
devil 3
earth 2
ground 1
heel[1] 2
land 2
lawn
stinker
turf 1
soda
fizz 4
pop 5
water 1
sodality
fraternity 2
order 9
society 5
solidarity
soda pop
pop 5
soda water
fizz 4
pop 5
water 1
sodden
sloppy 2
soaking 2
steamy 1
wet 1
so-designated
titular
sodium chloride
salt 1
sod off
clear 30
sodomite
bugger 1
profligate 3
sodomitic(al)
unnatural 2
sofa
couch 1
lounge 5
seat 1
so far°
at **far 8**
yet 1
soft°
delicate 6
easy 4
faint 1
feminine 1
flabby 1
fluffy 1
fond 3
foolish 2
gentle 1
inaudible
limp[2] 1
low[1] 13
mellow 1,3
mushy 1
noiseless
plastic 1
silky
slack 2
smooth 5
soothing 1
tender[1] 2,5
weak 7
yielding 1
soft-cover
book 1
soft drink
fizz 4
pop 5
soften°
blunt 4
cushion 2
deaden 2
hush 3
liberalize 2
lower[1] 5
mellow 5
melt 1,2
mitigate
moderate 5
modify 2
modulate
relent
relieve 1
smooth 12
subdue 3
sweeten 2
tame 6
temper 5
thaw 2
tone 5
turn 14b
water 7
weaken 3
softened
mellow 3
soft 4
softening
mild 3
soften up°
at **soften 1**
soft-headed
weak 5
soft-hearted°
benign 1
forgiving
merciful
tender[1] 6
soft-heartedness
mercy
softie
sissy
weakling
wet 6
soft in the head°
at **soft 6**
feeble-minded
foolish 2
softly
quietly 1
whisper 1
soft mark
pushover 2
softness
expression 4
soft part
pulp 1
soft-pedal
hush 3
mute 3
soften 3
subdue 3
tone 5
soft sell
promotion 4
soft soap
cajolery
enticement 2
flannel 1
flattery
soft-soap
cajole
entice
flannel 2
flatter 1
play 18
romance 7
soft spot
liking 1
partiality 2
weakness 4
soft touch
mug 3
pushover 2
sucker
softy
sissy
weakling
wet 6
soggy
humid
moist 2
muggy
sloppy 2
watery 3
soi-disant
nominal 1
professed 1
self-styled
so-called 1
titular
soigné(e)
cultivated
debonair 1
elegant 1
polished 2
smart 3
smooth 6
sophisticated 1
soil°
blacken 2
contaminate
dirt 1,2
dirty 7
earth 2
filth 1
foul 12,14
ground 1
land 2
mire 4
mould[3]
muddy 5
pollute 1
smear 1,2
spot 7
stain 5
sully
taint 2
tarnish
soiled
bedraggled
dingy
dirty 1
filthy 2
foul 2
impure 1
muddy 1
spotty 1
soiling
pollution
soil stack
stack 4

soirée
party 1
rave 5
reception 2
so it seems
evidently 2
sojourn°
abide 2
residence 2
run 36
stay[1] 2,7
stop 5,7
tarry 2
visit 3
sojourner
rover
sojourning
visitation 1
Sol
sun 1
solace°
cheer 3,5
comfort 1,2
console
solder
attach 1
cement 1,2
connect 3
join 1
stick[1] 4
tack 5
unite 3
weld 1
soldier°
gangster
militant 3
-soldiers
force 3
rank[1] 5
reinforcement 3
soldierly
martial 2
military 1
soldier of fortune
adventurer 1
daredevil 1
mercenary 3
soldier on°
at **soldier 4**
stick[1] 14
soldiery
military 2
sold on°
at **sell 5**
sole°
exclusive 3
individual 1
lonely 1
one 1
only 1
single 2
solitary 1
solecism°
error 1
fallacy
misstatement 2
misuse 2
solely
alone 4
entirely 2
just 4
merely 2
only 2
particularly 2
proper 7
simply 1
wholly 2
solemn°
ceremonial 2
ceremonious 1
devout 2
dignified
dismal
earnest 1
formal 1,2
funereal
grave[2] 1
measured 1
official 2
po-faced
sacred 3
sedate 1

solemn (*cont.*)
self-contained 1
serious 1
sober 2
sombre 3
staid
state 6
stately
subdued 2
solemnity°
ceremony 1
dignity 1
gravity 3
rite
severity 2
sobriety 2
solemnization
celebration 1
feast 2
installation 1
rite
solemnize
celebrate 1
commemorate
keep 10
observe 5
solemnness
solemnity
solicit°
appeal 1
apply 7
approach 3
ask 3
beg 2
canvass 1
desire 2
dun
pander 2
petition 2
pimp 2
plead 2
pray 1
proposition 3
raise 12
request 1
seek 3
sue 2
solicitation
appeal 3
application 4
canvass 3
collection 1
petition 1
plea 1
request 2
suit 5
supplication 1
soliciting
supplication 2
solicitor°
advocate 3
lawyer
pander 3
solicitous°
anxious 1
attentive 2
concerned 1
considerate
good 6
paternal 1
supplicant 1
sweet 6
sympathetic 1
tender[1] 6
thoughtful 1
urgent 2
solicitously
warmly 2
solicitousness
sympathy 1
solicitude°
anxiety 1
care 2
concern 6
consideration 1
fear 4
love 4
thought 4
solid°
actual 1
close 15
compact 1
decided 1
dense 1

solid (*cont.*)
fast[1] 4
firm 1,2
fixed 1
full 1
good 8,9
hard 1
hearty 4
intact
large 1
material 5
monolithic
physical
pure 1
rocky[1] 2
safe 3
secure 2,3
solvent
sound[2] 3,5
splendid 3
square 5
stable 1
stalwart 1
staunch 2
steady 1
stiff 1,10
stocky
strong 12
sturdy 1
substantial 2,3
superb
sure 2
tangible
thick 1,2,5
watertight 2
yeomanly
-solids
dregs 1
solidarity°
fraternity 2
unity 1
solidified
hard 1
stiff 1
solidify°
cake 3
firm 5
fix 2,7,10
freeze 2
harden 1
jell 1
set 3
stiffen 1
thicken
solidity
body 7
stability 1,2
strength 6
substance 4
solidly
fast[1] 7
firmly 1
steady 7
surely 2
tight 11
solidus
line[1] 1
solitarily
alone 3
solitariness
privacy 1
solitude 1
solitary°
alone 1
deserted
desolate 1
hermit
individual 1
isolated 1
lonely 1
one 1
only 1
private 4
reclusive
secluded 1
separate 5,7
single 2,3
single-handed 1
sole
solo 2
unique 1
unsocial
withdrawn 2

solitary confinement
solitary 2
solitude°
privacy 1
retreat 2
solo°
alone 1,3
lonely 3
single-handed 1,2
solitary 1
unaccompanied
soloist
singer
vocalist
Solomon
sage 2
thinker
so long
farewell 3
goodbye
solution°
answer 3
combination 3
determination 2
explanation 3
fluid 1
interpretation 1
liquid 1
remedy 2
resolution 4
solve°
decipher 1
figure 12b
puzzle 3
resolve 2
satisfy 2
sort 10a
tackle 3
trick 7
work 19c
solvency
credit 3
solvent°
economic 2
flush[2] 3
liquid 4
strong 11
solving
resolution 4
solution 1
somatic
physical
tangible
sombre°
black 4
bleak 1
dark 3
dim 1
dismal
doleful
drab
dreary 1
dull 5
funereal
grave[2] 1
grey 2
heavy 5
leaden 3
morbid 3
mournful 1
murky
obscure 1
overcast
pall[1] 2
po-faced
sad 2
serious 1
sober 3
solemn 1
stern 2
sullen
sunless
twilight 4
sombrely
sadly 2
sombreness
gravity 3
some
divers
few 2
part 1
several 1

-at some time or other
sometime 2
soon 5
-in some measure
moderately
part 9
partially
-in some way
somehow
-to some degree
moderately
part 9
partially
quite 2
rather 1
relatively
somewhat
-to some extent
moderately
part 9
partially
quasi- 1
quite 2
rather 1
relatively
somewhat
somebody°
figure 6
human 4
legend 2
name 3
personage
personality 2
star 2
someday
sometime 2
time 18b
somehow°
hook 3
someone
human 4
somebody 1
some person
somebody 1
somersault
roll 1
somerset
roll 1
something
point 12
something like
way 10b
sometime°
past 2
previous 1
soon 5
time 18b
some time ago
once 1
previously
sometimes°
now 4
occasionally
once 4
time 14
someway
hook 3
somehow
somewhat°
degree 4a
fairly 1
moderately
part 9
partially
pretty 3
quite 2
rather 1
relatively
slightly
somewhere else
elsewhere
sommelier
servant 1
waiter
somnambulant
sleepwalking 2
somnambulation
sleepwalking 1
somnambulism
sleepwalking 1

somnolence
inactivity 1
lethargy 2
torpor
somnolent
dormant 1
drowsy
inactive 1
lethargic 2
narcotic 1
restful 1
sleepy 1
slow 9
torpid
son
child 1
descendant
issue 7
progeny
song°
air 4
chant 1
jingle 3
lay[3]
melody 1
one 5
piece 4
poem
refrain[2]
rhyme 1
strain[1] 8
tune 1
-for a song°
at **song 2**
cheap 5,6,7
song and dance°
at **song 3**
line[1] 18
moonshine 2
palaver 1
speech 2
songbird
singer
vocalist
song-like
lyric 1
song of praise
praise 2
songster
singer
sonneteer
poet
son of a bitch
rogue 1
stinker
villain
son of a gun
rogue 1
Son of God
saviour 2
sonority
tone 2
sonorous
deep 7
loud 1
rich 7
rotund 2
round 7
sonorousness
tone 2
soon°
directly 3
presently
quickly 3
shortly 1,2
sometime 2
time 18b
-as soon as
directly 5
immediately 3
once 5
verge[1] 2
-too soon
premature 2
prematurely 1
previous 3
sooner
before 7
by 4
first 4
have 11
rather 2

sooner or later°
at **soon 5**
eventually
sometime 3
time 18b
soon to
verge[1] 2
soot
dirt 1
grime
soothe
blunt 4
calm 5
charm 6
comfort 1
console
content[2] 4
deaden 2
ease 5
humour 4
hush 5
lull 3
mitigate
moderate 5
quell 2
relieve 1
remedy 3
salve 3
settle 8
silence 3
smooth 12
soften 1
solace 2
still 9
stroke 10
temper 5
tranquillize
soothing°
bland 1
dreamy 3
gentle 1
mild 3
restful 1
sedative 2
smooth 5
soft 4, 9
tender[1] 5
soothsayer
fortune-teller
oracle 1
prophet
psychic 3
seer
soothsaying
prophecy 1
sooty
black 1
dingy
dirty 1
grey 1
SOP
mode[1] 1
procedure
technique 1
sophism
fallacy
quibble 3
sophistic°
circular 3
smooth 8
sophistical
circular 3
deceptive 2
evasive
plausible 2
smooth 8
sophistic
specious
subtle 2
sophisticated°
blasé 2
chic 1
cultivated
elegant 1
enlightened
experienced 2
genteel 3
highbrow 2
knowledgeable 2
mature 1
mill 3
oily 2
polished 2
refined 1, 2, 3
sophisticated
(*cont.*)
ripe 2
steady 6
suave
well-bred
worldly 2
sophisticated-ness
charm 2
style 4
sophistication°
charm 2
civilization 1
culture 1
experience 3
panache
presence 5
refinement 1
savoir faire
savoir vivre
style 4
subtlety 1
sophistry
chicanery
deception 1
evasion 2
quibble 2
sophomoric
childish
puerile
young 3
soporific
boring
drug 2
leaden 4
monotonous
narcotic 1, 2
restful 1
sedative 1, 2
sleepy 2
slow 9
tedious
tiresome 1
soppiness
sentimentality
sopping
bedraggled
sloppy 2
soaking 2
wet 1
soppy
maudlin
romantic 3
sentimental 2
sloppy 2, 3
sweet 7
wet 1
soprano
high 7
sorcerer°
charmer
magician 1
sorceress
charmer
magician 1
siren 2
sorcerer
temptress
witch 1
sorcery°
charm 2
enchantment 1
fascination
glamour
magic 1
occult 3
sordid°
base[2] 2, 4
despicable
dirty 6
filthy 2
foul 4
grovelling
low[1] 12
mean[2] 3
nasty 3
scandalous 1
seamy
sleazy 2
sorry 2
ugly 2
vile 1
sordidness
misery 2
sore°
angry 2
chafe 2, 4
gall[2] 1
heavy 4
indignant
inflamed
inflammation
painful 1
raw 4
scratchy 2
sensitive 1
tender[1] 8
ulcer 1
soreness
ache 3
chafe 4
discomfort 2
pain 1
sensitivity 1
sore spot
gall[2] 1
sore straits°
at **sore 6**
strait 3
–in sore straits
impoverished 1
sororicide
murder 1
sorority
club 2
fellowship 2
order 9
ring[1] 3
society 5
sorrow°
care 1
desolation 2
desperation 2
distress 1
evil 7
gloom 2
grief 1
grieve 2
guilt 2
lament 1
melancholy 2
misery 1
moan 3
mourn
mourning 2
pain 5
penitence
pity 1
regret 2
remorse
sadden
sadness
woe
sorrowful°
broken-hearted
dark 3
dejected
desolate 3
despondent
doleful
forlorn 1
funereal
gloomy 2
guilty 2
heartbroken
heavy 5
hopeless 3
hurt 7
joyless 1
low[1] 8
melancholy 1
miserable 1
mournful 1, 2
mouth 6
pathetic 1
penitent
poignant 1
regretful
remorseful
sad 1
unhappy 1
wistful 1
woebegone
sorrowfulness
melancholy 2
penitence
sorrowfulness
(*cont.*)
sadness
sorrowing
mourning 1
sorry°
afraid 2
apologetic
apologize 1
bad 8
base[2] 3
disappointing
guilty 2
low[1] 6
mangy
mean[2] 3
miserable 3
paltry
pathetic 2
penitent
pitiful 2
poor 4
regretful
remorseful
repent
repentant
sad 3
scurvy
sorrowful 1
terrible 2
threadbare 1
wan 2
wretched 3
sorry for
feel 8
pity 3
regret 1
sort°
arrange 1
brand 1
breed 1
bunch 3
categorize
category
character 1, 2
class 2
denomination 2
description 3
distribute 3
divide 5
form 3
genre
grade 6
group 3
identify 1
kind[2] 1, 2
make 42
model 6
mould[1] 3
nature 4
order 3, 16
organize 1
peculiar 3
place 16
range 2, 7
rank[1] 6
rate[1] 4
run 44
screen 8
separate 1, 2
stamp 8
stripe 2
style 1
tabulate
type 1
variety 3
–of a sort
sort 5
–of sorts°
at **sort 5**
–out of sorts°
at **sort 6**
diseased
ill 1
moody 1
off colour 1
ropy 3
seedy 2
sullen
weather 2
sorted out
straight 7
sortie
action 6
assault 1
charge 7
onset 1
push 15
raid 1
sortilege
magic 1
sorcery
sorting out
interpretation 1
resolution 4
sort of°
at **sort 7**
fairly 1
moderately
quasi- 2
rather 1
somewhat
sort out°
at **sort 10**
arrange 1
fix 14, 16c
identify 1
interpret 2
order 16
organize 1
pick 1
puzzle 3
right 19
screen 8
see 12a
separate 1
settle 1
sift 1
sort 8
straighten 1
so so°
adequate 2
average 4
decent 3
fair[1] 4
indifferent 3
mediocre
OK 3
ordinary 2
passable 1
tolerable 2
undistinguished
so-styled
titular
sot
alcoholic 2
drunk 3
soak 3
Sotadean
scurrilous
so that
order 11
so to speak°
at **speak 6**
effect 5
quasi- 2
sotted
drunk 1
stinking 3
sottishness
drunkenness
sough
sigh 1
sought-after
demand 7
desirable 1
enviable
hot 6
popular 1
soul°
bosom 3
breast 2
elixir 3
essence 1
heart 5
human 4
individual 3
life 5, 7
mortal 6
person 1
psyche
spirit 1
soulful°
soulless
inanimate
soul mate
friend 3
soul-stirring
tender[1] 7
thrilling
touching
sound°
advisable
authoritative 2
blare 2
blast 2
boom 1
chime 3
cry 6
dive 1
durable
effectual 2
entire 2
fathom
flawless 2
go 14
good 8, 13
gulf 1
hale
hardy 1
hearty 5
honest 4
intact
judicious
legal 2
logical 2, 3
mouth 7
noise 1, 2
note 9
OK 4
peep 3
plausible 1
plumb 5
potent 2
practical 1
presumptive 1
rational 1
reasonable 1
reliable
right 2, 4
ring[2] 1
robust 1
roll 5
safe 1, 3
secure 2
seem
sensible 1
sigh 3
solid 3, 6, 7
solvent
stable 1
staunch 2
steady 1
strain[1] 8
strong 11
submerge 2
substantial 2, 3
toll[1] 1, 2
tone 1, 2
tough 1
well-balanced 1
whole 3
wise 1
–of sound mind
rational 1
sane
sound colour
tone 2
sounding
ring[2] 3
toll[1] 2
sound judge-ment
discretion 1
logic 2
soundless
noiseless
quiet 1
silent 1
still 2
soundlessly
quietly 1
silently
soundlessness
quiet 5
silence 1
sound like
resemble
sound[1] 5

speaker°
talker 1
speak for°
at **speak 7**
advocate 1
promote 3
stick[1] 18
speak for itself°
at **speak 8**
speak ill of
vilify
speaking
speech 1
-on speaking terms
acquainted 1
familiar 4
speak of°
at **speak 9**
refer 1
touch 8
speak on°
at **speak 10**
speak one's mind
speak 11b
speak one's piece°
at **piece 12**
speak out°
at **speak 11**
speak to°
at **speak 12**
address 3
contact 4
see 9
speak 10
talk 12
speak up°
at **speak 11**
pipe 8
speak up for
defend 3
spear
gore[2]
impale
lance 1
male
penetrate 1
pierce 1
spike 2
stab 1
stick[1] 1
transfix 1
spear-carrier
extra 5
non-essential 2
spearhead°
special°
bosom 4
cardinal
choice 4
different 2
distinct 2
exceptional 1
express 6
extraordinary 1
fancy 3
golden 6
individual 2
isolated 1
occasional 3
outstanding 1
particular 1, 2, 6
peculiar 1, 2
personal 2, 3
pet[1] 3
private 2
privileged 1
proper 6
rare[1] 2
remarkable 2
respective
select 2
signal 3
singular 1
speciality 2
specific 2
unparalleled
special attraction
feature 2
special case
exception 3
special-interest group
lobby 2
public 10
specialist°
adept 2
authority 3
consultant 1
expert 1
physician
professional 3
spécialité
pièce de résistance
speciality 2
speciality°
calling
discipline 5
domain 2
field 4
forte
line[1] 7
peculiarity 2
pièce de résistance
profession 1
pursuit 3
sphere 3
specialization
domain 2
field 4
line[1] 7
pursuit 3
speciality 1
specialize
differentiate 2
specialized
special 1
technical 1
specially°
custom 4
especially 1
expressly 2
particular 6
particularly 1
purpose 4b
special-occasion
good 15
specie
cash 1
coin 1
money 1
tender[2] 3
species
breed 1
denomination 2
description 3
family 4
form 3
genre
kind[2] 1
nature 4
sort 1, 3
stamp 8
type 1
variety 3
specific°
antidote
categorical
certain 6
circumstantial 3
concrete
definite 1
detail 1
emphatic
explicit 1
express 5, 6
individual 2
keen[1] 4
local 2
luminous 3
one 3
outspoken
particular 1, 5, 6
precise 1
pronounced 2
proper 6
remedy 1
respective
several 2
special 1
specify
specific *(cont.)*
symptomatic
-specifics
detail 2
point 10
specifically
detail 4
especially 1
exactly 2
expressly 2
namely
notably 1
particular 6
particularly 2
purpose 4b
specification°
assignment 4
reference 1
stipulation
specific to°
at **specific 2**
peculiar 2
symptomatic
specified
given 1
specific 1
specify°
assign 2
define 1
denote 1
describe 2
designate 1
detail 5, 6
enumerate 1
fix 2, 9
formulate 1
identify 1, 3
indicate 1
itemize
mark 11
mean[1] 2
name 5, 6
pin 4b
prescribe
provide 3
recount 2
refer 1
register 8
set 7
signify 1
spell[3] 2
state 7
stipulate
wish 2
specifying
specification 1
specimen°
case[1] 4
copy 2
example 1
illustration 1
pattern 5
sample 1, 3
snatch 5
type 3
specious°
affected 1
deceptive 2
glossy 2
incorrect
plausible 2
seeming
sleek 3
slick 4
sophistic
unsound 4
untenable
speciously
seemingly
speciousness
falsity
speck°
bit 2
crumb
dot 1
fragment 1
grain 3
jot 2
little 10
modicum
morsel 2
particle
point 1
scrap[1] 1
speck *(cont.)*
shade 3
shred 1
spark 1
spot 1
stain 1
touch 15
trace 2
specked
flecked
speckle
dapple 2
dot 3
pepper
spatter
speck
spot 1, 7
stain 4
speckled°
dapple 1
flecked
mottled
spotty 1
specs
glass 7
spectacle 3
spectacle°
display 5
entertainment 2
extravaganza
glitter 4
pageant
parade 2
phenomenon 2
pomp
presentation 2
prospect 1
sight 3
splendour 1
tableau
view 1
wonder 1
-spectacles°
at **spectacle 3**
glass 7
spectacular
beautiful 2
brave 2
bully 4
colossal 2
dandy 2
devastating 2
dramatic 3
entertainment 2
extravaganza
fantastic 4
glorious 2
gorgeous 2
great 12
marvellous
meteoric 2
miraculous
monumental 1
prodigious 2
scenic
sensational 1
splendid 1
stunning 2
superlative
swell 8
theatrical 2
spectacularly
beautifully 2
famously
well[1] 2
spectator°
bystander
eyewitness
observer
onlooker
witness 1
spectral°
disembodied
eerie
ghastly 2
ghostly 1
shadowy 3
supernatural
unearthly 2
unreal 1
spectre°
fear 3
fright 3
ghost 1
spectre *(cont.)*
hallucination
illusion 2
ogre
phantom 1
presence 4
shade 4
vision 4
spectrum
gamut
scale[3] 1
speculate°
conceive 3
divine 4
fantasize
gamble 1
guess 1
presume 1
punt 1
surmise 1
theorize
wonder 3
speculated
hypothetical
speculation°
adventure 2
chance 4
dream 1
gamble 3
guess 3
hypothesis
surmise 2
venture 1
speculative°
academic 2
experimental 1
groundless
hypothetical
pure 4
tentative 1
theoretical 1
uncertain 3
visionary 1
speculator
better[2]
player 3
punter 1
theorist
speculum
mirror 1
speech°
address 1
dialect
diction 2
expression 6
harangue 1
idiom 1
language 1
lecture 1
line[1] 17
lingo
message 2
oration
paper 4
parlance
pronunciation
sermon 2
talk 14, 19
tongue 1
vernacular 3
voice 1
speech habit
phrase 3
speechify
hold 16a
spout 2
speechless°
dumb 1
dumbfounded
inarticulate 3
mute 1
overcome 2
petrified 2
thunderstruck
tongue-tied
speechlessly
silently
speechlessness
silence 2
speech-maker
talker 1
speech-making
oratory
speech pattern
accent 3
dialect
intonation
pronunciation
speech 1
speed°
advance 4
career 2
clip[2] 7
course 2
dash 3
dispatch 5
expedition 2
facility 1
flash 5
forward 8
haste 1
hasten 1, 2
hurry 1
hurtle
pace 2
precipitate 1
quicken 2
race[1] 4
rapidity
rate[1] 1
rattle 4
run 1
rush 1, 3
scud
scurry
shoot 1
stimulant 2
streak 5
tear 3
tempo
urge 1
velocity
way 5
whisk 2
-at full speed
double 8
flat 17a
rapidly 1
-at speed
run 49a
-at the speed of light
rapidly 1, 2
-with all speed
fast[1] 6
quickly 2
speedboat
boat
speedily
devil 5
directly 2
fast[1] 6
flat 17a
hand 12
hastily 1
leap 7
post-haste
promptly
quickly 1, 2
rapidly 1
readily 3
right 13
shot 10
soon 2, 3
suddenly 1
summarily 1
swiftly
time 17
speediness
rapidity
speed 1
speed up°
at **speed 2**
dispatch 4
expedite 1
forward 8
hasten 2
hurry 2
pick 8g
precipitate 1
quicken 1, 2
step 16, 18b
speedwriting
stenography
speedy°
expeditious
express 7

speedy (*cont.*)
fast[1] 1
fleet[2]
hasty 1, 3
hurried 1
precipitate 3
prompt 1
quick 1
rapid
ready 5
snappy 1
swift
whirlwind 2
spell°
attack 8
bout 1
charm 2, 5
enchantment 1
fit[2] 1, 2
interlude
interval 1
jinx 1
letter 5
magic 1, 3
mumbo-jumbo 2
paroxysm
patch 4
period 1
relieve 4
round 11, 14
run 38
snap 9
space 3
span 2
spasm 2
spurt 1
streak 3
stretch 6
term 2
time 1
tour 3
turn 30
–under a spell
fascinate
spellbind
bewitch
dazzle 1
enchant 1
enrapture
entrance[2]
fascinate
fix 5
grip 7
hypnotize
ravish 1
regale
transport 3
spellbinder
talker 1
spellbinding°
absorbing
devastating 2
enchanting
enthralling
interesting
magic 6
magnetic
piercing 2
ravishing
riveting
spellbound
charmed 1
infatuated
rapt 1
spelled out
formal 2
specific 1
spell out
define 2
detail 5
enumerate 1
explain 1
interpret 1
letter 5
put 10
specify
translate 3
spelt out
formal 2
specific 1
spend°
blow[1] 4
drain 5
exhaust 1

spend (*cont.*)
expend 1
invest 2
kill 7
lavish 4
lay[1] 18b
lead 5
live 7
lose 4
pass 5
pay 11b
put 19b
run 34b
serve 6
shell 5
spendable
disposable 2
spend a penny
defecate
urinate
spender
spendthrift 1
spending
expenditure
expense 1
outlay
spendthrift°
extravagant 1
improvident 1
prodigal 1, 3
profligate 2, 4
wasteful
wastrel 1
spend time
fraternize
go 21b
hang 4b
haunt 1
mingle
pal 2
run 24
spent°
beat 13
breathless 1
dead 9
empty 1
exhausted 1, 3
haggard
helpless 3
jaded 1
limp[2] 2
listless
lost 2
prostrate 5
ragged 3
run-down 1
tired 1
washed out 2
weary 1
worn 3
spew°
eject 2
flow 2
spit 1
spout 1
spurt 3
spew forth°
at **spew**
eject 2
erupt 1
spit 1
spout 1
spew out°
at **spew**
erupt 1
pour 1
spout 1
vomit
spew up°
at **spew**
regurgitate
spout 1
throw 9a
vomit
sphacelated
ulcerous
sphere°
capacity 3
category
department 2
domain 2
element 2
field 4
globe 2

sphere (*cont.*)
jurisdiction
kingdom 2
milieu
orb
precinct 2
profession 1
province 3
range 1
reach 7
realm 3
region 2
round 10
scene 1
science 1
scope 1
speciality 1
theatre 4
universe 2
world 1, 3
zone
spheric
spherical
spherical°
rotund 1
round 3
spheroid(al)
round 3
spherical
spherule
sphere 1
spice°
dash 6
flavour 1, 3
salt 2, 6
season 3
seasoning
spirit 3
tang 1
zest 1
spiced
spicy 1
spice up°
at **spice 4**
spiciness
salt 2
spice 2
tang 1
spick and span
immaculate 1
neat 1
shipshape
spanking 1
spotless 1
tidy 1
trim 1
spicula
spine 2
spiculate
pointed 1
prickly 1
thorny 1
spicule
spine 2
spiculose
thorny 1
spiculum
spine 2
spicy°
aromatic
hot 2
juicy 2
pungent 1
racy 2, 3
risqué
sharp 4
strong 2
suggestive 2
spider
bug 1
pan 1
spider's web
web
spiel
harangue 1
line[1] 18
oration
patter[2] 1
speech 2
talk 14
spieler
speaker

spiff one's biscuits
heave 4
regurgitate
vomit
spiffy
dapper
neat 5
sporty
stylish
trim 1
well-groomed
spigot
tap[2] 1
spike°
doctor 4
freshen 4
impale
impede
lace 4
nail 1
pin 1
point 2
prickle 1
spine 2
spur 2
stab 1
stake[1] 1
stalk[2]
stick[1] 1
stymie
tang 3
thorn 1
transfix 1
spiked
jagged
pointed 1
thorny 1
spiky
pointed 1
prickly 1
spile
tap[2] 2
spill°
flow 2
leak 4
light[1] 7
run 6, 33c
shed[2] 1, 3
trickle 1, 2
tumble 4
upset 2
spill one's guts
spill 3
tell[1] 2
spill the beans°
at **spill 3**
clean 8
disclose 1
leak 5
sing 3
talk 5
tell[1] 2
spillway
race[1] 2
spin°
bowl[1]
daze 3
drive 7
eddy 2
flip 1
go 35a
gyrate
outing
pirouette 1, 2
pivot 3
revolution 3
revolve 1
ride 4
roll 8, 16
rotate 1
run 36
swirl 1, 2
swivel 1
turn 1, 21e, 26, 31
twirl 1, 2
weave 3
wheel 2
spinal column
backbone 1
spine 1
spindle
pivot 1

spindly
gaunt 1
thin 1
spindrift
spray[1] 2
spine°
backbone 1
prickle 1
prominence 2
spike 1
spur 2
thorn 1
spine-chilling
scary
spineless°
flabby 2
limp[2] 3
weak 3
wet 3
spine-tingling
ripping
sensational 1
thrilling
spinner of yarns
raconteur
spinney
clump 2
stand 19
thicket
spinning
twirl 2
spin off°
at **spin 4**
spin-off
branch 2
derivative 2
offshoot 3
product 1
spinose
thorny 1
spinous
prickly 1
thorny 1
spin out°
at **spin 5**
drag 5
draw 14a
pad 5
string 11b
–be spun out
drag 5
spinster
celibate 3
maid 3
miss[2]
unmarried
spinsterhood
celibacy 1
spinulose
thorny 1
spiny
prickly 1
thorny 1
spiracle
pore[2]
vent 1
spiral°
coil 1, 2
garland 2
rocket
screw 2
soar 2
swirl 2, 3
turn 28
twine 2
twirl 3
twist 7
wind[2] 2
spiralling
downward
spire°
tower 1
spirit°
action 1
animation 1
atmosphere 2
aura
booze 1
bottle 3
cheer 1
daring 1
dash 6

spirit (*cont.*)
devil 1
disposition 1
drift 4
dynamism
eagerness 1
energy
enterprise 2
essence 1
expression 4
exuberance 1
fervour
fight 9
fire 2
flavour 2
ghost 1
god
grit
gumption 2
gut 3a
heart 4
humour 3
inspiration 1
juice 2
lie[2] 6
life 7
manhood 2
meaning 2
mood 1
morale
nerve 1
odour 2
panache
passion 1
pep 1
phantom 1
pith 1
pluck 1
presence 4
psyche
push 14
shade 4
sniff 2
soul 1, 4
sparkle 4
spectre 1
spice 2
spunk
strain[1] 9
stuff 3
style 5
tenor
tone 3
vein 4
verve
vigour
way 2
–spirits°
at **spirit 8**
alcohol
booze 1
bottle 3
drink 5
humour 3
liquor 1
morale
whisky
spirit away°
at **spirit 10**
spirited°
alive 3
animate 3
animated 1
breezy 2
bright 8
brisk 2
dashing 1
dynamic
eager
energetic
enterprising
enthusiastic
excited 2
exuberant 1
fiery 3
frisky
frolicsome
gallant 1
game 7, 8
gritty 2
impassioned
intense 3
jaunty 1
live 2
lively 1

spirited (*cont.*)
passionate 1
perky
playful 1
quick 3
racy 1
rousing
smart 5
sportive
sprightly
stalwart 3
stirring
tireless
venturesome 1
vigorous
vital 3
vivacious
warm 2
wholehearted
spiritedly
hard 13
vigorously
spiritedness
animation 1
dynamism
eagerness 1
exuberance 1
passion 1
vitality 1
spiritless
cold 3
colourless 2
desolate 3
feeble 1
flat 5
inanimate
lackadaisical 1
leaden 4
mechanical 3
meek 2
pale[1] 3
pedestrian 2
spineless 3
supine 2
torpid
wooden 2
spirit off°
at **spirit 10**
spiritual°
celestial 1
disembodied
divine 1
heavenly 1
insubstantial 2
pious 1
platonic
psychic 1
psychological
sacred 3
spiritualist
psychic 3
spiritualistic
psychic 2
spirituality
devotion 1
spiritual-minded
religious 1
spirituous
hard 10
intoxicating 1
spit°
gore[2]
impale
pierce 1
rain 4
run 34a
slaver[1] 1, 2
spike 2
spout 1
stab 1
stick[1] 1
transfix 1
-be the spit and image of
take 29a
spite°
grudge 1
ill will
rancour
sarcasm
venom 2
virulence 2
-in spite of°
at **spite 2**
despite
even 11, 12
face 9
for 11
irrespective of
nevertheless
notwithstanding 1, 2
regardless 1
same 3
though 1
yet 5, 6
spiteful°
evil-minded 2
hateful 2
hurtful 2
jaundiced 2
malignant 2
mischievous 2
nasty 4
rancorous
resentful
sarcastic
sharp 5
ugly 4
venomous 2
vicious 2
vindictive
virulent 2
waspish
spitefulness
revenge 1
sarcasm
spite 1
venom 2
spitfire
bitch 1
fury 3
shrew
spit out
erupt 1
spew
spitting image°
at **spit 2**
double 7
image 2
look-alike
picture 2
-be the spitting image of
take 29a
spittle
slaver[1] 2
spit 3
spit up
erupt 1
spew
throw 9a
vomit
splash°
dabble 1
display 5
gurgle 1, 2
lap[1] 2
parade 2
ripple 3
slap 3
spatter
splurge 1
spot 7
stain 4
stroke 3
wade 2
wallow 1
wash 3
water 6
splash down
land 5
splashdown
landing 1
splashed
mottled
splashing
gurgle 2
splash out
spend 1
splashy
loud 2
splatter
spatter
splash 1, 3
splatter (*cont.*)
stain 4
wash 3
spleen
anger 1
bitterness 1
gall[1] 1
rancour
spite 1
venom 2
virulence 2
splendid°
admirable
beautiful 2
brave 2
bright 7
brilliant 2
capital 6
dandy 2
dazzling
divine 3
excellent
exquisite 5
fantastic 4
fine[1] 1, 11
flamboyant 2
gallant 3
glorious 2, 4
good 2
gorgeous 1
grand 1, 5
heavenly 2
imperial 2
luxurious 1
magnificent
majestic 1
marvellous
neat 5
nifty 3
noble 5
palatial
princely 2
proud 4
radiant 1
regal 1
rich 4
ripping
royal 2
sensational 3
striking
stunning 2
sublime 2
sumptuous
superb
sweet 5
swell 8
terrific 2
splendidly
beautifully 1, 2
famously
gaily 1
richly 1
well[1] 2
splendidness
splendour 1
splendiferous
dazzling
divine 3
gorgeous 1
splendid 1
splendorous
gorgeous 1
radiant 1
splendid 1
splendour°
brilliance 1
dazzle 3
display 5
elegance 2
glare 1
glitter 4
glory 3
glow 2
grandeur 1
luxury 1
pomp
radiance 1
state 3
style 3
splenetic
angry 1
cranky 2
cross 6
disagreeable 3
fretful
splenetic (*cont.*)
harsh 3
hasty 4
jaundiced 2
peevish
perverse 2
petulant
querulous
quick-tempered
rancorous
snappish 2
sullen
surly
testy
touchy 1
venomous 2
vindictive
virulent 2
waspish
splice°
entwine
graft[1] 1, 2
tie 1
twist 1
union 3
weave 2
splicing
splice 2
splinter°
break 1
chip 1
crush 1
fragment 1, 3
modicum
morsel 2
shatter 1
shiver[2]
sliver
splintered
broken 1
splinter group
faction 1
split°
breach 2, 3
break 1, 25
broken 1
cleave
crack 1
cranny
crevice
cut 15c
dash 1
depart 1
disconnected 1
disjointed 1
diverge 1
divide 1, 3, 4
division 1
divorce 1, 2
faction 2
flaw 2
flee 1
flight[2] 1, 3
fracture 2, 3
fragment 3
gap 1
gape 2
gash 1, 2
gulf 2
heel[1] 4
inform 2
leak 2
leave[1] 1
move 2
opening 1
parting 1
partition 5
rend 2
rent[2]
rift 1
rip 1, 3
roll 17
rupture 1, 3
schism
section 4
segment 2
separate 1, 4
separation 1, 2, 3
sever 1
share 3
slit 1, 2
snap 1
splinter 2
take 34c
tear 1, 4
split (*cont.*)
wedge 2
split apart°
at **split 1**
split hairs
cavil 2
quibble 1
shuffle 3
split one's sides
laugh 1
split second
minute[1] 1
second[2]
-in a split second
once 6a
suddenly 1
split-second
instant 4
splitting
division 1
parting 1
partition 1
rupture 1
secession
separation 3
splitting hairs
quibble 2
split up°
at **split 1**
disjointed 1
divide 1
divorce 2
fragment 3
part 12
partition 5
portion 4
separate 1, 2, 3, 4
throw 8
split-up
divorce 1
partition 1
separation 1
splodge
blot 1
mark 1
smear 3
spatter
splash 1, 3
spot 1
stain 1
splodged
mottled
spotty 1
splotch
see **splodge**
splurge°
orgy 2
spend 2
waste 1
splurge on°
at **splurge 2**
splutter
boil[1] 2
hesitate 3
spit 1
spoil°
baby 2
bitch 4
blemish 2
botch
bungle
cater 2
coddle
contaminate
corrupt 4
damage 4
dash 1
debase 2
decay 2
decompose 2
deface
destroy 4
deteriorate 1
devastate 1
dote
flaw 3
fluff 4
foul 16b
go 31e
hash 3
humour 4
hurt 1
impair
spoil (*cont.*)
indulge 2
mangle
mar 1
mother 6
murder 4
mutilate 2
overshadow 2
pamper
pet[1] 5
plunder 1
pollute 1
putrefy
queer 5
rot 1
ruin 8, 9
sabotage 3
sour 5
stagnate
stain 5
sully
taint 2
tarnish
turn 5
undermine 1
upset 5
vitiate 1
waste 11
wreck 1
-be spoiling for°
at **spoil 5**
-spoils°
at **spoil 6**
booty
loot 1
patronage 4
pillage 3
plunder 4
prize[1] 4
trophy 1
spoiled
bad 6
disfigured
foul 2
hothouse 2
mouldy
putrid
rancid
rotten 1
sour 2
stale 1
spoil game
foil[1]
spoiling
pollution
spoilsport°
killjoy
misery 4
spoilt
bad 6
disfigured
mouldy
musty 1
putrid
rancid
rotten 1
sour 2
spoke
foil
spoken°
oral
verbal 1
vernacular 2
spoken for°
at **speak 13**
attached 4
engaged 1
spokesperson
agent 1
delegate 1
deputy
mouthpiece 2
proponent
representative 3
voice 3
spoliate
rape 5
spoliation
desolation 1
havoc 1
plunder 3
rape 2

spondulicks
cash 1
money 1
sponge
beg 2
bloodsucker
borrow
bum 5
clean 9
drunk 3
flatterer
hanger-on
parasite
soak 2,3
wash 1
wipe 1
sponge bag
bag 2
sponge bath
wash 11
spongelike
porous
sponger
beggar 1
hanger-on
parasite
scrounge 2
spongy
mushy 1
porous
soft 1
yielding 1
sponsor°
answer 7a
back 2a
backer 1
benefactor
favour 6
patron 1
patronize 3
philanthropist
promote 3
sanction 6
second[1] 9
stand 7b
subsidize
support 4
take 39c
talk 13
underwrite 1
vouch
sponsoring
subsidy
sponsorship
auspices
backing 1,2
cooperation 2
patronage 1
protection 2
sanction 2
start 12
subsidy
spontaneous°
automatic 2
extemporaneous
free 6
gratuitous 1
immediate 1
impetuous
impulsive
independent 4
instinctive 2
involuntary
natural 2,4
optional
unasked
unpremeditated
voluntary 1
spontaneously
freely 2
pell-mell 1
voluntarily
spoof
burlesque 1,3
caricature 1
imitate 2
mock 2
mockery 2
parody 1,3
put-on 1,2
satire 2
scoff[1]
send 9a
take 34b
spoof (*cont.*)
take-off 2
spoofing
satire 1
satirical
spook
ghost 1
phantom 1
ruffle 3
scare 1
shade 4
spectre 1
spooky
eerie
frightening
ghostly 1
scary
spectral
stark 3
unearthly 2
weird
spool
roll 12
tape 2
spoon
distribute 1
kiss 1
scoop 1,4,5
spoondrift
spray[1] 2
spoonfeed
spoil 3
spoonful
little 10
morsel 1
mouthful
sip 2
spoor
footstep 2
scent 2
step 3
trace 3
track 3
trail 2
wake[2] 1
sporadic°
broken 6
casual 2
fitful
intermittent
irregular 2
occasional 1
odd 2
periodic
piecemeal 3
spasmodic 2
spotty 3
uncertain 4
sporadically
fit[2] 4
infrequently
now 4
occasionally
once 4
piecemeal 1
spore
seed 1
sporran
bag 3
purse 1
sport°
amusement 1,2
better[2]
entertainment 1
flaunt
frolic 1,3
fun 1,2
game 1
lark 2
model 8
pastime
play 1,22
recreation
toy 3
trick 2
wear 1
sporting
venturesome 2
sporting house
brothel
house 6
sportive°
frolicsome
jolly 1
kittenish
mischievous 1
playful 1
sprightly
zany 1
sportscaster
announcer
sportsman
player 1
sportsmanliness
sportsmanship
sportsmanship°
sportswoman
player 1
sporty°
jaunty 2
spot°
advertisement 1
announcement 3
blot 1,2
bruise 1
dab 2
dapple 2
detect 2
dilemma
discover 2
dot 1,3
drop 2
engagement 4
find 2
fix 17
hole 5
jam 6
little 10
locale
location 1
mark 1,10
modicum
notice 2
particle
pepper
perceive 1
perch 1
pimple
pipe 6
place 1,15
plight
plumb 4
point 3
predicament
quarter 3
scandal 3
scene 1
scrape 8
see 1
shot 7
sight 5,8
site 1
situate
situation 1
slot 2
slur 1
smear 3
soil[1] 1
speck
splash 1,3
spotlight 1
spy 3
stage 1
stain 1,4
station 1,4
stigma
tarnish
touch 15
trace 2
ulcer 2
witness 4
-on the spot
instant 3
nail 6
outright 3
put 23a
spur 3
trouble 9a
-spots°
at **spot 5**
spot announcement
advertisement 1
spotless°
clean 2
fair[1] 3
flawless 1
holy 2
immaculate 1
impeccable
incorrupt 1
innocent 2
perfect 3
pristine 2
pure 2
shipshape
unspoiled
untarnished
white 3
spotlessness
purity 1
spotlight°
emphasize
feature 4
flaunt
focus 4
play 17a
point 22
stress 4
spot of bother
brush[2] 3
disturbance 2
spot on
accurate 3
faultless
marvellous
perfect 4,5
precisely 1
right 2
true 3
spotted
dapple 1
dirty 1
flecked
mottled
speckled
spotty 1
spotty°
mottled
perfunctory 2
sparse 1
spousal
nuptial
spouse
husband 1
mate 2
partner 2
wife
woman 2
spout°
eject 2
erupt 1
flow 2
fountain 1
gush 1,3
pour 1
prattle 1
run 6
spew
stream 4
tap[2] 1
well[2] 2
-up the spout°
at **spout 4**
drain 3
pregnant 1
spouting
eruption 1
outpouring
sprain
strain[1] 6
turn 10
twist 5
wrench 2
sprawl°
recline
spread 6
trip 5
sprawling
rambling 2
spray°
bouquet 1
bunch 1
fountain 1
pepper
shower 3
spray (*cont.*)
spatter
splash 1,3
spot 7
water 6
sprayer
spray[1] 3
spread°
breadth 1
circulate 2,3
circulation 2
coat 3
communicate 1
cover 3
diffuse 1,3
disperse 1
dissipate 1,2
distribute 2
diverge 1
diversify
enlarge 1
epidemic 2
expand 1
expanse
expansion 1
extend 1
extension 1,2
feast 1
flare 2,6
flow 4
gamut
get 25a
grow 1
growth 1
increase 1,3
lay[1] 1
meal 1
measure 1
noise 3
open 17,24
permeate
plaster
progress 3,6
progression 2
proliferation
propagate 2,3
publish
put 23e
radiate 2
range 2,6
riddle[2] 2
roll 11
root[1] 5
rub 2
run 33c
scatter 1
scope 2
set 10
shed[2] 2
smear 1
splash 2
sprawl 1,3
spray[1] 1
straggle
stretch 1,5
strew
suffuse
swell 4
unfold 1
widen
spread about°
at **spread 2**
diffuse 1
distribute 2
loose 4
measure 14
publish
put 9
spread around°
at **spread 2**
diffuse 1
distribute 2
loose 4
measure 14
publish
put 9
spread-eagle(d)
flat 2
spreading
circulation 2
expansive 1
extension 1
increase 5
progression 2
rambling 2
spreading (*cont.*)
spread 8
spread out°
at **spread 1**
broad 1
diffuse 1
disperse 1,2
display 2
dissipate 1
expand 1
extend 1
flare 2
flat 2
open 17,24
rambling 2
roll 11
sparse 1
sprawl 1,2
unfold 1
spread the Gospel
preach 1
spread the Word
preach 1
spree°
bender
bout 2
carouse 2
fête 1
fling 2
frolic 2
jag
jamboree
lark 1
orgy 1,2
party 1
revel 3
revelry
splurge 1
sprig
branch 1
offshoot 1
slip[2] 2
spray[2]
twig[1]
sprightliness
exuberance 1
gaiety 1
life 7
pep 1
snap 11
spring 7
sprightly°
active 3
agile 1
alert 2
alive 3
brisk 2
debonair 2
elfin 1
energetic
exuberant 1
frolicsome
jaunty 1
light[2] 7
lively 1
nimble 1
perky
pert 2
playful 1
racy 1
spirited
sportive
vigorous
vivacious
spring°
bolt 8
bound[2] 1,3
caper 1
dash 3,5
flexibility 1
flow 2
fountain 1
grow 2
hop 1,3
issue 11
jump 1,8
leap 1,5
life 9
lunge 2
originate 2
pounce 1,2
prance
resilience
shoot 1

spring (*cont.*)
stem[1] 3
trip 4
well[2] 1,2
spring back
rebound 1
recoil 1
spring catch
snap 10
springe
snare 1
trap 1
spring for°
at **spring 5**
spring from°
at **spring 3**
derive 2
proceed 2
springiness
elasticity 1
flexibility 1
resilience
spring 7
springlike
soft 3
springtime
prime 4
spring 9
spring up°
at **spring 3**
arise 4
grow 2
rise 11
shoot 4
springy
elastic 1
flexible 1
yielding 1
sprinkle
dabble 1
dampen 1
drip 1
pepper
powder 4
punctuate 1
rain 1,4
scatter 1
shower 1,3
spatter
splash 1,3
spray[1] 1,2
strew
water 6
sprinkled
flecked
mottled
speckled
sprinkler
spray[1] 3
sprinkling
handful 1
scattering
several 1
shade 3
shower 1
spray[1] 2
sprint
dash 3,5
flash 5
fly 3
hasten 1
hustle 1
race[1] 4
run 1,3,35
rush 1
scurry
speed 3
streak 5
tear 3
sprinter
runner 1
sprite
imp
sprocket
cog 1
sprog
child 1
youth 2
sprout°
lad
offshoot 1
root[1] 5
shoot 4,5

sprout (*cont.*)
slip[2] 2
spring 2
stem[1] 3
twig[1]
-sprouts
progeny
spruce°
dapper
immaculate 1
jaunty 2
neat 1
nifty 1
rakish
sharp 9
smart 3
straight 7
taut 2
tidy 1
trim 1
well-groomed
spruce up°
at **spruce 2**
decorate 1
groom 3
neaten
preen 2
primp
refresh 3
refurbish
straighten 3
tidy 4
touch 12
sprung
free 2
spry
active 3
agile 1
alert 2
alive 3
brisk 2
dynamic
energetic
exuberant 1
fresh 5
light[2] 7
lively 1
nifty 2
nimble 1
quick 3
sprightly
vigorous
spume
bubble 2
foam 1,2
froth 1,3
spunk°
bottle 2
courage
daring 1
drive 8
grit
gumption 2
gut 3a
heart 2
nerve 1
pluck 1
spirit 5
strength 2
vigour
spunkiness
grit
spunk
spunky
defiant
gritty 2
spur°
animate 2
drive 1
encouragement 1
exalt 3
excite 1
foment
incentive
incite
induce 1
inducement
inflame 1
inspiration 1
kindle
motivate
motive 1
move 6
offshoot 1

spur (*cont.*)
point 2
premium 2
prickle 1
prod 2,5
projection 1
prominence 2,3
prompt 3
provoke 1
push 4
put 29
signal 2
spine 2
stimulant 1
stimulate 1
stir 4
urge 1,2
work 20a
-on the spur of the moment°
at **spur 3**
hastily 1
offhand 4
suddenly 2
spurious°
affected 2
assumed 2
base[2] 5
bogus
counterfeit 1
deceptive 2
erroneous
factitious
fake 5
false 1,3
fictitious 2
fraudulent 1
hollow 4
illegitimate 3
invalid[2]
phoney 1
pretended
sham 2
synthetic
unreal 3
spuriousness
falsity
spurn°
cut 12
despise
dismiss 2
flout
isolate
laugh 2b
look 5
neglect 1
pass 22
rebuff 2
refuse[1] 1
reject 1,2
renounce
repulse 2
scorn 3
shun
use 15
spurning
rejection
repulse 3
spur-of-the-moment
impetuous
impulsive
spontaneous 1
unpremeditated
-on the spur of the moment°
at **spur 3**
hastily 1
offhand 4
suddenly 2
spur on
animate 2
encourage 1
excite 1
inflame 1
provoke 1
spurring
encouragement 1
incitement 1
spurt°
dash 5
flow 2
gush 1,3
outpouring

spurt (*cont.*)
pour 1
run 6
spew
spout 1
stream 2,4
well[2] 2
sputnik
satellite 1
sputter
boil[1] 2
fizz 1
hesitate 3
spit 1
sputum
spit 3
spy°
eavesdrop
operative 4
peer[2] 1
plant 4
scout 1
see 1
sight 5,8
snoop 1,2
spyglass
glass 6
telescope 1
spying°
nosy
spy on°
at **spy 2**
bug 8
squabble
argue 1
argument 1
bicker
brawl 1,2
clash 2,3
conflict 2
controversy 2
disagree 2
fall 18
feud 1
fight 4,8
fracas 2
haggle
quarrel 1,2
row[2] 1
scrap[2] 1,2
spar[2] 2
tiff
tilt 4
squabbling
quarrelsome
strife 1
squad°
cohort 1
corps
detail 3
group 1
party 2
platoon
shift 4
side 4
squaddie
private 5
soldier 1
squadron
cohort 1
corps
fleet[1]
platoon
squad
squalid
dirty 1
filthy 2
mangy
mean[2] 3
miserable 4
seamy
seedy 1
shabby 3
sleazy 2
sordid 3
squall
bawl 2
rain 1
roar 1,3
shriek 1,2
storm 5
tempest 1
yell 1,2

squally
dirty 4
inclement
windy 1
squalor
misery 2
squama
flake 1
scale[2] 1
squamous
scaly 2
squander
blow[1] 4
burn 4
consume 3
dissipate 3
exhaust 1
fool 7b
fritter
lavish 4
lose 4
run 34b
spend 2
splurge 2
throw 5b
use 5
waste 1
squandered
lost 2
misspent
squanderer
prodigal 3
profligate 4
spendthrift 1
wastrel 1
squandering
dissipation 1
extravagance 1
loss 4
prodigal 1
prodigality 1
profligacy 2
profligate 2
spendthrift 2
waste 5,6
square°
area 5
clear 29
compensate 2
conform 2
discharge 6
enclosure 1
equal 5
equalize
equitable
even 6,7
fair[1] 1
flush[2] 1,4
fogy
formal 1
hearty 4
honest 2
honourable 2
ingenuous 1
level 15
make 31a
narrow-minded
neutralize
offset 1
rectify
settle 10
simple 3
slow 8
stick-in-the-mud
straight 3,4,10
tally 1
square-dealing
honest 2
square footage
area 2
size 1
squarely
flush[2] 4
full 14
slap 6
square peg in a round hole
misfit
oddity 2
square-shooting
honest 2
square with°
at **square 11**
conform 2

square with (*cont.*)
equal 5
repay
squaring
discharge 13
squash
crush 3
pulp 3
rout 2
squeeze 1,9
stuff 6
telescope 3
trample 1
whip 2
squashable
soft 1
squashy
muddy 1
mushy 1
slimy 1
soft 1
squat
crouch
dumpy
low[1] 1
plump[1] 1
short 1
stocky
undersized
squatter
intruder 1
outsider
squawk°
complain
complaint
protest 1,3
rasp 5
shriek 1,2
squawking
grating 2
squeak
disclose 1
grass 1
peep 1,2
scrape 5
squeeze 6
tell[1] 2
squeaker
grass 2
shave 3
squeaky
grating 2
high 7
squeal
disclose 1
finger 8
grass 1
inform 2
scream 1,3
shriek 1,2
sing 3
spill 3
talk 5
tattle 1
turn 15c
tell[1] 2
whoop 1,2
squealer
grass 2
informer
talebearer
squeamish°
dainty 2
delicate 5
fastidious
gingerly 2
nauseated
prissy
prudish
sick 1
spineless 3
squeamishly
gingerly 1
squeamishness
prudery
scruple 1
squeezable
soft 1
squeeze°
contract 4
crowd 5
crush 3

squeeze *(cont.)*
dilemma
embrace 4
express 4
fill 1
force 7
friend 3
get 38c
girl 2
gouge 2
huddle 3
hug 1, 3
jam 1, 5
load 3
nip[1] 1
pack 5
pinch 1, 2, 6
press 2, 3
pucker 1
railroad 2
ram 1
screw 4
shake 6b
stuff 6
sweat 4
thread 4
tweak 1, 2
wedge 3
work 17
squeeze by°
at **squeeze 6**
squeeze through°
at **squeeze 6**
thread 4
squeezing
pressure 2
squelch°
crush 4
demolish 2
hush 4
nip[1] 2
place 13
quash 2
quell 1
quench 2
repress
silence 4
stamp 4
suppress 2
squelching
repression 2
suppression
squelchy
muddy 1
watery 3
squib
lampoon 1, 2
squidgy
mushy 1
squiffy
drunk 1
high 9
squiggle
scrawl 1
wriggle 3
squinny
peek 1
peer[2] 1
squint
cast 5
peek 1
peer[2] 1
squire°
accompany 1
attend 4
escort 4
man 1
squirearchy
gentry
squirm°
crawl 1
creep 1
fidget 1
shake 2
struggle 3
toss 4
twist 3
wriggle 2, 4
squirming
wriggle 4

squirrel away
cache 3
hide[1] 1
hoard 2
put 12
salt 8
stack 6
squirt
flow 2
spout 1
spurt 3
stream 4
squish
trample 1
squishy
muddy 1
mushy 1
slimy 1
squush
trample 1
squushy
muddy 1
mushy 1
slimy 1
watery 3
stab°
bore[1] 2
dig 2, 7
disparage 2
drive 4
effort 2
endeavour 2
enter 2
go 42
gore[2]
impale
jab 1, 3
kink 2
knife 2
lance 2
lunge 3
pang 1
penetrate 1
pierce 1
poke 1, 5
prick 3, 4
punch[2] 2
puncture 3
rend 3
run 34a
shot 3
smart 7
spike 2
stick[1] 1
sting 1
thrust 2, 4
trial 3
try 5
twinge 1
wound 3
stabbing
acute 3
painful 1
piercing 4
puncture 2
pungent 3
stability°
anchor 2
backbone 3
balance 6
footing 3
loyalty
permanence
regularity 1
responsibility 4
sanity
strength 2, 6
stabilization
settlement 5
stabilize
assure 1
balance 2
fix 2, 10
lock[1] 6a
steady 11
stabilizer
anchor 2
stab in the back°
at **stab 2**
disparage 2
stable°
certain 1
changeless 1
conservative 2

stable *(cont.)*
durable
equable 2
even 3
fast[1] 4, 5
firm 2
fixed 1
immovable 1
invariable 1
loyal
manly
normal 2
perennial 1
permanent 1, 2
reliable
responsible 2
secure 2
solid 3, 6
stall[1] 3
steadfast
steady 1
strong 11, 21
sure 2
temperate 1
true 2
stable-boy
groom 1
stable-lad
groom 1
stableman
groom 1
stack°
heap 1
hill 2
load 3
lot 5b
mass 1
mound 2
mountain 2
pile[1] 1, 3, 5
pile-up 2
plenty 1
profusion
-stacks
lot 5b
mountain 2
pile[1] 3
plenty 1
stacked
full 7
voluptuous 2
stack up°
at **stack 6**
pile[1] 5
scrape 6
touch 7
stadium°
staff°
club 1
employee
faculty 3
help 7
man 4
pole[1]
rank[1] 5
rod 1
shaft 1
shift 4
stick[2] 1
subordinate 2
train 2
wand
staffer
subordinate 2
staff member
employee
subordinate 2
stag
unaccompanied
stage°
age 3
bring 13b
date 1
degree 1
dramatic 1
era
grade 1
infancy 2
juncture 2
leg 3
level 14
moment 2
mount 5
notch 2

stage *(cont.)*
page[1] 2
pass 26
patch 4
perform 3
phase 1
platform 1
point 3
present[2] 5
produce 4
put 22d
rostrum
round 13
section 3
show 9
stand 18
state 2
step 5
stop 8
theatre 3
theatrical 1
-be staged
show 9
-stages
infancy 2
stagecraft
drama 2
theatre 2
stage-manage
stage 5
stage name
pseudonym
stage play
drama 1
play 20
stage set
set 28
setting
stagger°
amaze
astonish
astound
breath 3
daze 1
dumbfound
electrify 1
flounder
founder[2] 3
hobble 1, 3
knock 6b
limp[1] 1, 2
lurch[2] 1, 2
overpower 2
overwhelm 1, 3
quake 1
reel 1
rock[2] 3
shock 1
stumble 1
stun 2
surprise 1
teeter
totter
trip 5
walk 1
wallow 3
staggered
breathless 2
daze 4
dumbfounded
thunderstruck
staggering
amazing
colossal 2
doddering
formidable 3
gigantic
groggy
immense
inconceivable
large 3
limp[1] 2
monumental 1
mountainous 2
overwhelming 2
phenomenal
prodigious 2
sensational 1
startling
stunning 1, 2
superb
staginess
theatre 2
virtuosity

staging
production 3
stand 18
stagnant°
dead 11
indolent
leaden 4
moribund 2
standing 2
static 1
stagnate°
stagnating
moribund 2
stagnation
sluggishness
stagy
melodramatic
theatrical 2
unnatural 4
staid°
calm 4
even 4
grave[2] 1
heavy 7
poised 1
sedate 2
sober 2
solemn 1
sombre 3
steady 6
straight 8
stuffy 2
staidness
gravity 3
poise 2
sobriety 2
solemnity
stain°
blemish 2, 3
blot 1, 2
colour 3
contaminate
defect 2
dirty 7
disgrace 2, 4
flaw 1, 4
foul 14
libel 2, 4
mar 2
mark 1, 10
notoriety
paint 1, 6
pollute 1
shame 8
slur 1
smear 1, 3
soil[1] 1
splash 3
spot 1, 7
stigma
sully
taint 1, 2
tarnish
tint 2, 3, 4
stained
bedraggled
dirty 1
filthy 2
flawed
spotty 1
staining
pollution
stainless
chaste 1
immaculate 1, 2
unspoiled
white 3
stair
step 10b
-stairs
step 10b
stake°
adventure 4
bar 1
bet 1, 2
chance 8
fund 3
gamble 1, 2, 4
hazard 3
interest 4
lay[1] 4
pale[2] 1
pawn[1] 2
picket 1

stake *(cont.)*
piece 11
play 7
post[1] 1
punt 1, 2
put 6, 28d
share 2
spike 1
staff 1
stick[2] 1
tether 2
-stakes
pool 2
prize[1] 2
stale°
bad 6
boring
close 12
cold 5, 6
common 6
cut 29b
dry 2
flat 5, 8
foul 2
hack[2] 4
lifeless 3
mouldy
musty 1, 2
old 2
old-fashioned
pedestrian 2
prosaic
rancid
rank[2] 4
ready-made 3
rotten 1
stagnant
sterile 3
stock 7
stuffy 1
threadbare 2
time-worn
tired 3
wishy-washy 2
stalemate°
deadlock 1
dilemma
draw 17
impasse
tie 10
Stalinism
tyranny
stalk°
follow 4
hunt 1
prey 3a
pursue 1
quest 2
run 26a
shadow 7
stem[1] 1
tail 4
trace 4
track 6
trail 7
trunk 1
walk 1, 3
stalker
hunter
stalking
hunt 3
prowl 3
pursuit 1
stall°
arrest 1
booth 1
cell
deadlock 2
delay 3
drag 6
excuse 6
hang 6
hesitate 1
obstruct 2
pack 8b
partition 4
pen[2] 1
play 14
procrastinate 1
retard 1
shed[1]
stand 16
tarry 1

stalling
stall[2] 2
stalwart°
bold 1
brave 1
dauntless
fit[1] 3
gritty 2
hardy 1
hearty 2
heroic 2
martial 2
persevere
powerful 1
rugged 3
soldier 2
solid 5, 6
stand-by 1
stout 4
strong 1
sturdy 2
tenacious 1
tough 3
vigorous
stalwartly
vigorously
stalwartness
bravery
grit
stamina
stamina°
backbone 3
endurance 1
follow-through
gumption 2
gut 3b
perseverance
persistence
sinew 2
strength 2, 6
tenacity 1
vigour
vitality 2
stammer°
hesitate 3
stammering
halting
hesitant 2
stamp°
brand 2
cachet 1
calibre 3
cast 4
character 1
coin 2
endorse 1
engrave 2
flavour 2
flounce 2
form 3
hallmark 1, 2
impress 2
impression 3
label 1, 4
mark 2, 13
measure 4
mould[1] 2, 3, 5
nature 4
print 1
sanction 1
seal 1
sign 4
sort 1
strike 10
trample 1
walk 1
stampede°
flight[2] 2
stamping-ground
habitat
haunt 3
home 2
territory 2
turf 2
stamping out
suppression
stamp of approval
endorsement 1
sanction 1
stamp of authenticity
hallmark 1
stamp out°
at **stamp 4**
abolish
eliminate 4
stifle 3
suppress 2
trample 3
wipe 3
stance°
act 3
attitude 1
bearing 1
carriage 2
idea 3
point of view 1
pose 4
position 1, 3
posture 1, 3
stand 13
viewpoint
stanch°
stem[2] 1
stop 2
stanchion
picket 1
post[1] 1
shaft 1
standard 4
stand°
abide 1
accept 4
act 2
allow 4
base[1] 1
bear 4
booth 1
brook[2]
campaign 3
digest 2
endure 2, 3
feel 5
get 51b
go 36a
lump[2]
objection
pedestal 1
platform 1
position 3
presumption 3
prop 2
put 1, 30
rack 1
rank[1] 7
rise 1
rostrum
run 5
set 1
side 3
stall[1] 2
stance
stand 10a
stay[1] 1
stick[1] 10
stomach 3
support 3, 5
sustain 3
take 6
tolerate 1, 2
undergo
weather 3
withstand
stand aghast
abhor
stand-alone
self-contained 3
standard°
average 1
banner 1
certain 1
classic 1
classical 1
code 3
colour 2a
common 1
conservative 2
conventional
correct 7
example 2
flag[1] 1
flat 7
formal 1
gauge 3
guide 6
habitual 1
ideal 1
standard *(cont.)*
lead 13
leg 2
mark 3
measure 3
medium 1
model 2
natural 1
nonpareil
norm 2
normal 1
ordinary 3
orthodox
par 1, 2, 4
paragon
pattern 1
pennant
perfection 3
pole[1]
popular 2
post[1] 1
precedent
principle 1
proof 2
protocol 1
prototype 2
regular 1
regulation 4
rule 3
set 30
sign 4
staff 1
standing 1
staple 2
stock 7, 8
symbol
systematic
touchstone
traditional
type 3
typical 1
uniform 1
yardstick
-standards
code 3
conscience
ideal 3
moral 4
morality 1
protocol 1
-up to standard
presentable 1
scratch 5
standard-bearer
protagonist 2
standardize°
calibrate
equalize
normalize
organize 1
regiment
standardized
systematic
standard operating procedure
mode[1] 1
procedure
technique 1
stand behind
advocate 1
back 2a
defend 3
guarantee 2
stand 5a
warrant 3
stand by°
at **stand 5**
call 16
defend 3
maintain 4
poised 2
stick[1] 11, 13, 18
support 1
uphold
wait 1
warrant 3
stand-by°
makeshift 1
stand-in
stopgap 2
substitute 2
temporary
-on stand-by
call 16
stand down°
at **stand 6**
stand fast
persevere
persist 1
stick[1] 14
stand firm
abide 4
hold 20a
persevere
persist 1
stand for°
at **stand 7**
allow 4
designate 3
embody 2
express 3
personify 1
put 30
represent 1, 4
run 5
stand 3
support 3
symbolize
tolerate 1
stand guard
patrol 3
stand in°
at **stand 8**
cover 8
fill 9b
relieve 4
sit 6b
substitute 1
understudy 2
stand-in°
alternate 5
deputy
double 7
relief 4
second[1] 8
substitute 2
understudy 1
standing°
account 5
caste
dead 11
degree 1
dignity 2
end 7a
erect 1
estate 3
face 4
footing 2
grade 1
importance 2
level 14
mark 8
name 2
note 8
par 2
place 3
position 5
prestige
prominence 1
quality 3
rank[1] 1
rate[1] 4
reputation 1
stagnant
station 2
status 1
stratum 2
term 7b
standing up
upright 1
stand in the way of
obstruct 3
stand motionless
freeze 3
stand-off
deadlock 1
impasse
stalemate
standoffish°
aloof 2, 3
cold 3
cool 5
distant 3
frigid 2
standoffish *(cont.)*
inhospitable 1
remote 7
reserved
retiring
self-contained 2
stiff 7
unapproachable 1
unsocial
withdrawn 1
standoffishness
reserve 4
stand on the sidelines
stand 5b
stand out°
at **stand 9**
project 5
protrude
shine 3
show 12b
signify 2
stick[1] 15
stand pat
hold 20a
standpoint°
angle[1] 2
aspect 1
outlook 1
perspective 1
point of view 1
side 3
slant 1
stance
stand 13
viewpoint
stand still
freeze 3
standstill°
deadlock 1
halt 1
stalemate
stop 6
stand the test of time
wash 8
stand up°
at **stand 2**
arise 1
bear 10a
bristle 2
disappoint 2
get 51b
hold 11
keep 11
last[2] 2
resist 1
rise 1
wash 8
wear 4
stand-up
upright 1
stand up for°
at **stand 11**
champion 4
defend 3
recommend 2
speak 7a
stand 5a
stick[1] 18
support 1
stand up to°
at **stand 12**
bear 4
defy 1
resist 1
tackle 3
withstand
stand up under
stand 3
stand watch
patrol 3
stand with
defend 3
stanza
passage 2
staple°
clip[1] 1
connect 3
pin 3
standard 6
stock 7, 8
staple *(cont.)*
tack 5
-staples°
at **staple 3**
merchandise 1
provision 4
star°
celebrity 2
decoration 2
dignitary
feature 4
hero 1, 2
name 3
personage
personality 2
principal 6
queen 2
somebody 2
stellar 1
success 2
Thespian 2
starboard
right 5, 11
starch
bottle 2
enterprise 2
grit
stamina
Star Chamber
tribunal
starched
formal 1
starchy
ceremonious 1
star-crossed
doomed 2
ominous 1
poor 6
portentous 1
sorry 2
tragic
unfortunate 2
unhappy 2
woebegone
stardom
celebrity 1
fame
prestige
renown
stare°
gape 1
gawk 2
gaze 1, 2
glare 2, 4
ogle 2, 3
regard 1
rubberneck 1
wonder 4
star-gaze
fantasize
star-gazer
dreamer
fortune-teller
seer
star-gazing
absent-minded
staring
glassy 2
goggle-eyed
stark°
blank 6
gaunt 2
hard 12
harsh 2
mere
naked 3
outright 2
plain 4
positive 9
severe 6
simple 2
sorry 2
unadorned
unflattering 1
unvarnished
starkers
bare 1
naked 1
nude
raw 7
starkly
clear 18
clearly 1

stay°
abide 2,3
bar 9
board 7
brace 1
check 1,2
dwell 1
endure 1
freeze 3
hang 7b
hold 13
keep 7
last[2] 1
linger 1
live 8
lodge 3
moratorium
obstruct 2
persist 2
post[1] 1
postponement
prop 1,3
put 21a
reinforce
reinforcement 1
remain 1,3
reprieve 2
residence 2
respite 2
rest[1] 7,9,10
room 4
set 16
settle 4
sit 4
sojourn 1,2
stanch
stand 2b,5b,15
stem[2] 1
stick[1] 7,11
stop 5,7
support 8
suspension 2
table 5
tarry 2
visit 3
wait 1,4
stay alive
exist 2
stay at it
peg 7
stay away from
absent 3
hang 5
wash 10
stay behind
linger 1
remain 1
staying
resident 1
visitation 1
staying power
backbone 3
endurance 1
perseverance
stamina
stay on the side-lines
stand 5b
stay put
remain 1
stay together
stick[1] 5
stay with (it)
peg 7
pursue 2
stick[1] 19
tenacious 3
stead
place 7
steadfast°
abiding
changeless 2
consistent 2
constant 1
devoted
diligent
enduring
faithful 1
fast[1] 5
firm 4
fixed 2
grim 1
heroic 2
immovable 2

steadfast *(cont.)*
indomitable
intent 4
intrepid
laborious 2
loyal
manly
noble 4
obstinate
patient 2
persevere
persist 1
persistent 1
purposeful
resolute
rigid 4
rocky[1] 2
single-minded
solid 5
special 5
stable 2
stalwart 2
staunch 1
stern 1
strong 5
sturdy 2
sure 1,2
tenacious 1
tireless
true 2
trustworthy
unhesitating 2
yeomanly
steadfastly
firmly 2
hard 13
intently
steadfastness
decision 3
determination 1
follow-through
loyalty
nerve 1
patience 2
perseverance
persistence
pluck 1
purpose 2
resolution 1
self-control 1
stability 2
tenacity 1
steadily
consistently 1
hand 12
intently
non-stop 3
step 9
surely 2
steadiness
assurance 5
balance 6
regularity 2
stability 1
steading
farm 1
steady°
balance 2
brace 5,6
brisk 3
certain 1
consistent 2
constant 2
continual
date 3
deliberate 2
determined 1
diligent
earnest 1
easy 5
enduring
equable 2
even 3,4
firm 2,3
gradual
intent 4
invariable 1
laborious 2
level 3
loyal
measured 3
moderate 1
non-stop 2
regular 2
relentless 2

steady *(cont.)*
rhythmic
rocky[1] 2
secure 2
sober 2
solid 5,6
stable 1,2
staunch 1
steadfast
stiff 5
strong 21
sure 1
sustained
sweetheart
temperate 1
tireless
tranquil
true 2
trustworthy
unhurried
untiring
steady look
gaze 2
steal°
appropriate 2
bargain 2
buy 5
creep 3
edge 6
embezzle
help 5
hook 7
knock 5b
liberate 2
lift 6
lurk
make 27
misappropriate 1
nick 3
pilfer
pinch 3
pirate 3
pocket 4
prowl 1,3
pussyfoot 1
rip 2a
roll 6
slide 2
slink
slip[1] 6
sneak 1
spirit 10
swipe 2
take 3
walk 1
steal a march on
get 46a
outsmart
steal away
escape 1
spirit 10
stealing°
embezzlement
plagiarism
rip-off 1
robbery
theft
steal off
escape 1
spirit 10
stealth°
secrecy 1
–by stealth
secret 4
steal the lime-light from
overshadow 1
stealthful
stealthy
stealthily
secrecy 2
secret 4
secretly
silently
sly 3
stealthy°
furtive 1
sly 1
surreptitious
underground 2
steam
boil[1] 1
exhalation 2
film 3

steam *(cont.)*
mist 2
press 4
reek 2,4
simmer 2
vapour 1
steamed up
angry 1
steamy 2
warm 2
steamer
ship 1
steaming
furious 1
hot 1
steamy 1
sultry 1
sweltering
torrid 1
steamy°
damp 1
humid
moist 1
muggy
sultry 1
sweltering
torrid 1
steatopygous
plump[1] 1
steed
mount 9
steel°
prepare 6
reinforce
strengthen 2
steeled
thick-skinned
steel engraving
engraving 1
steely°
cold-blooded 2
frigid 2
hard 1
icy 2
inflexible
relentless 1
rigid 2
stern 1
stony 2
steelyard
balance 4
steep°
abrupt 2
extravagant 3
high 2
impregnate 2
mountainous 2
percolate
precipitous 1
premium 4b
pricey
saturate
sheer 1
soak 1
stiff 6,9
tall 3
steeple
spire 1
tower 1
steer°
bend 4
control 1
direct 2
drive 2
ease 7
govern 1
guide 1,2
handle 4
head 10
lead 1
make 30a
navigate 2
pilot 3
regulate 2
run 17
sail 1
show 2
–steers
cattle
steerable
navigable 2

steer clear of°
at **steer 2**
avoid
duck 3
shun
sidestep
skip 2
steering
navigation
steering gear
helm 1
steersman
director 2
navigator
pilot 2
steersmanship
navigation
stein
mug 1
stellar°
stem°
base[1] 3
branch 1
derive 2
grow 2
halt 2
issue 11
offshoot 1
originate 2
proceed 2
resist 1
runner 3
shaft 1
shoot 5
spring 3
stalk[2]
stanch
stop 2
twig[1]
–from stem to stern
thoroughly 2
through 7
stem-post
stem[1] 2
stench°
fume 3
odour 1
reek 3
smell 2
stencil
pattern 4
stenographer°
stenographic
clerical 2
stenography°
stenotypist
stenographer
stenotypy
stenography
stentorian
loud 1
step°
act 1
degree 2
footstep 1
ledge
march 1
measure 6
motion 3
notch 2
pace 1
phase 1
proceeding 1
stage 1
stamp 1
tramp 5
trample 1
walk 1,6
–a step at a time
step 9
–in step°
at **step 7**
line[1] 19b
–out of step°
at **step 8**
incongruous
–steps°
at **step 10**
measure 6
provision 3
step aside
stand 6

step by step°
at **step 9**
degree 3
gradually
progressive 1
step down°
at **step 14**
get 36a, 40a
stepfather
parent 1
step forward
offer 4
step in°
at **step 15**
intervene 1
wear 1
step into the shoes of
follow 5
stepladder
step 10b
step lively
race[1] 4
run 1
stir 2
stepmother
parent 1
step off
disembark
step on it°
at **step 16**
hurry 1
move 12a
race[1] 4
run 1
rush 1
speed 3
step on someone's toes
offend 1
step on the gas
hurry 1
move 12a
race[1] 4
run 1
rush 1
speed 3
step out°
at **step 17**
disembark
paint 7
steppe
flat 14b
plain 6
table 2
–steppes
flat 14b
step up°
at **step 18**
expedite 1
forward 8
intensify
strengthen 1
swell 3
stereotype
cliché
stamp 6
stereotyped
banal
cold 5
common 6
hack[2] 4
prosaic
ready-made 3
set 30
stale 2
stock 7
threadbare 2
time-worn
tired 3
stereotypic(al)
banal
common 6
musty 2
prosaic
ready-made 3
routine 4
time-worn
tired 3
usual
sterile°
barren 1,2
clean 1

stimulating (*cont.*)
refreshing
rousing
scintillating 2
sensational 1
stirring
thrilling
tonic 2
wholesome 1
stimulation
agitation 2
buzz 4
challenge 6
encouragement 1
heat 2
impetus
incitement 1
inspiration 2
motive 1
promotion 1
refreshment 2
spice 2
spur 1
thrill 1
stimulus
encouragement 1,2
fuel 2
impetus
incentive
incitement 2
inducement
inspiration 1,2
lift 9
motive 1
occasion 2
premium 2
prod 6
prompt 6
provocation 1
shot 12
signal 2
spur 1
stimulant 1
sting°
ache 1
bite 2,4
hurt 2
prick 2,4
prickle 2,3
shaft 3
smart 7
swindle 1
stinginess
avarice
greed 2
thrift
stinging
bitter 5
gruff 1
incisive 2
keen[1] 2
painful 1
penetrating 2
poignant 2
prickly 2
provocative 2
pungent 2
raw 5
smart 6
sore 1
tart[1] 2
stingingly
home 10
stingy
avaricious
cheap 4
close 18
economical 2
frugal 2
grasping
greedy 3
mean[2] 1
measly
miserly
narrow 7
near 6
penurious 1
petty 2
possessive 1
scrape 3
selfish 2
shabby 4
small 4
stingy (*cont.*)
small-minded
sordid 2
sparing 1
stint 4
thrifty
tight 5
stink
fume 3
fuss 1
odour 1
reek 1,3
smell 2,4
stench
stinker°
rogue 1
wretch 1
stinkeroo
stinker
stinking°
foul 3
money 4
prosperous 1
rancid
rank[2] 4
rotten 4
smelly
strong 3
wealthy
stinko
drunk 1
stinkpot
stinker
stink to high heaven
rancid
reek 1
stint°
bout 2
duty 1
scrape 3
shift 4
spell[1] 1
stretch 6
task 1
term 3
turn 30
work 3
stinting
mean[2] 1
small 4
stipend°
allowance 3
earnings
fee 2
maintenance 3
pay 12
remuneration 1
wage 1
stipple
dapple 2
dot 3
pepper
stippled
flecked
mottled
speckled
stipulate°
lay[1] 10
prescribe
provide 3
say 10
set 7
specify
undertake 2
stipulation°
condition 2
precondition
provision 2
qualification 2
requirement 1
restriction 1
specification 3
term 4
ultimatum
–stipulations
string 7
term 4
ultimatum
stipulatory
provisional 2
stir°
activate
affect[1] 2
agitate 3
animate 1
arouse 1
beat 6
bother 8
breath 1
buzz 2
disturb 2
electrify 2
energize
exalt 3
excite 1
excitement 2
fanfare 2
fire 8b
flurry 1
flush[1] 3,6
fluster 1
furore 1
fuss 1
get 16
go 1
heat 4
hit 4
hum 2
hurry 3
hustle 6
impress 1
incite
inflame 1
inspire 1
jail 1
jar[2] 1
jog 2
kindle
liven 2
mix 3
motion 1
motivate
move 1,3,4,12a
movement 2
pierce 4
prison
prod 2
provoke 1
reach 6
rise 16
rouse 2
row[2] 2
ruffle 2
rumpus
send 4
sensation 2
shake 5
storm 3
thrill 3
toss 3
touch 6
tumult
wake[1] 1,2
warm 9
work 13,20a
stir one's stumps
run 1
stir 2
stirred
affected 5
agitated
excited 1
fire 5
stirring°
agitation 1,2
awesome
breath 1
dramatic 3
electric
emotional 3
exciting 1
flush[1] 6
impassioned
impressive
incitement 1
juicy 2
lively 3
move 11
movement 2,6
moving 1
pathetic 1
poignant 3
ripping
sedition
stirring (*cont.*)
sensational 1
shake 9
stimulating
stir 6
tender[1] 7
thrilling
touching
stirrup-cup
drink 5
stir up°
***at* stir 1**
agitate 1,3
arouse 1,2,3
awake 2
disturb 2
exalt 3
excite 1,2,3
ferment 2
fluster 1
foment
incite
inflame 1
infuriate
kindle
liven 2
motivate
move 3,5
pick 3
prompt 3
provoke 1
raise 10
revive 2
rise 16
rouse 2
ruffle 3
shake 5
stimulate 1
toss 2,3
whip 7a
wind[2] 4c
stitch
connect 3
kink 2
pang 1
sew
stab 5
stroke 8
tack 2,5
twinge 1
–without a stitch (on)
nude
stock°
accumulate
accumulation 3
banal
breed 1
broth
carry 7
cattle
class 1
common 1
completely 1
deal 2
equip
extraction 3
family 3
fill 5
flesh 5
fund 1
garner
gather 1
good 21b
hack[2] 4
hoard 1
kin 1
line[1] 15,16
lineage 1
liquor 2
merchandise 1
nationality 2
origin 3
outfit 4
parentage
paternity
pedestrian 2
pedigree
peg 2
popular 2
premium 3
prosaic
provide 1
provision 4,5
race[2] 1,2
stock (*cont.*)
ready-made 3
repertory
reserve 3
root[1] 4
sell 2
sort 3
stack 1,6
stale 2
standard 6
stem[1] 1
store 1,3
strain[2] 1
supply 1,4
traditional
tribe
truck 1
trunk 1
usual
wholly 1
in stock
sale 6
–stocks
provision 4
stockade
wall 2
stockbroker
broker
Stock Exchange
exchange 4
market 1
stocking
supply 5
stock-in-trade
wares
stockist
dealer
stockjobber
broker
stock market
exchange 4
stockpile
accumulate
accumulation 3
cache 2
gather 1
heap 1,3
hoard 1,2
pile[1] 1,5
provision 4,5
repertory
reserve 3
salt 8
stack 1,6
stock 1,10
store 2,3
supply 4
stockpiling
supply 5
stockroom
warehouse
stock-still
freeze 3
still 7
stock up°
***at* stock 10**
amass
furnish 1
garner
provide 1
stocky°
burly
dumpy
large 1
stodgy°
conventional
heavy 7
stuffy 2
stoic
stoical
stoical°
calm 4
impassive
patient 1
philosophical 2
phlegmatic 1
unmoved
unsympathetic
stoicism°
patience 2
philosophy 3
stole°
cape[2]
wrap 4
stolid°
dense 3
dull 1
foolish 2
impassive
indifferent 1
monolithic
obtuse 2
opaque 3
phlegmatic 1
slow 7
stoical
stupid 1
thick 6
thick-skinned
unmoved
unsympathetic
stolidity
folly 1
indifference 1
obstinacy
stupidity 1
stolidness
folly 1
stoma
mouth 1
pore[2]
stomach°
accept 4
digest 2
endure 2,3
gut 1,2
heart 2
inclination 4
indigestion
inside 2
middle 3
put 30
stand 3
support 3
take 6
taste 3
tolerate 1
stomach-ache
indigestion
stomach-churning
revolting
terrible 5
stomach-turning
nauseous
repellent
revolting
sick 1
terrible 5
stomp
plod 1
stamp 1
trample 1
stone
brick 1
gem 1
grain 1
kernel 1
pit[2]
rock[1] 1
tablet 3
–a stone's throw from
near 9
stone-blind
blind 1
stone-cold
cold 1
stoned
drunk 1
high 9
stinking 3
stone-deaf
deaf 1
stonewall
fence 4
stall[2] 1
stonewalling
stall[2] 2
stoneware
pottery

stony°
cold-blooded 2
dead 12
decided 2
frigid 2
grim 1
hard 1, 4
icy 2
immovable 2
impassive
inflexible
obstinate
rocky[1] 1, 2, 3
rugged 1
severe 1
stern 1
tough 6
unmoved
unsympathetic

stony-broke
broke
impoverished 1
indigent
needy
penurious 2
stony 3

stony-hearted
brutal 1
cold 3
cold-blooded 2
cruel 1
hard 4
inhuman 1
merciless
remorseless 1
severe 1
stern 1
stony 2
unmerciful
unmoved
unsympathetic

stooge
dupe 2
flunkey 2
fool 3
inferior 4
pawn[2]
puppet 2
pushover 2
tool 3

stool
chair 1
seat 1

stoolie
grass 2
informer
sneak 2
spill 3
spy 1
talebearer

stool-pigeon
decoy 1
grass 2
informer
sneak 2
spill 3
spy 1
talebearer

stoop°
condescend
crouch
deign
descend 3
duck 1
lower[1] 4
sink 9
slouch 1, 2
step 10b
swoop 1, 2

stoop down°
at **stoop 1**
crouch

stooping
patronage 3
stoop 3

stoop low°
at **stoop 2**

stop°
arrest 1, 3, 5
bar 9
break 19a
catch 8
cease 1
check 1, 13

stop (*cont.*)
choke 2, 3
close 5
cut 15b, 16c
deadlock 2
defeat 2
delay 2, 5
destination
destroy 3
deter
die 3
discontinue
discourage 3
dot 1
draw 15a
drop 7
embargo 2
end 9
field 5
fill 7
finger 7
finish 1
flag[1] 2
forbid
forestall
foul 15
freeze 3
frustrate 1
gag[1] 1
gap 1
give 17a
halt 1, 2
hang 7b
head 13a, 13b
help 3
hinder 2
hold 19c
impede
inhibit
intercept
interlude
interrupt 2
interruption 2
lapse 5
lay[1] 16b
leave[1] 9
let[1] 8d
let-up
lift 3
lodge 3
lull 1
nip[1] 2
nonplus
obstruct 1, 3
oppose 2
pack 6, 8b
paralyse 1
pass 14b
period 3
phase 6
plug 4
point 1
pop 2
preclude
prevent
prohibit 2
pull 18a
quit 3
refrain[1] 2
resist 1
rest[1] 5
sacrifice 4
scrub 2
seal 3
seize 3, 6
sever 2
short 12b
shut 2
sojourn 1, 2
stalemate
stall[1] 1
stanch
stand 15
standstill
stay[1] 1, 2, 4, 5, 6, 7
stem[2] 1
stick[1] 7, 9, 12
stifle 3
stump 2
stunt[2]
suppress 1
suppression
suspend 1
tarry 2
terminate
termination 1

stop (*cont.*)
thwart 1
tie 7c, 9
turn 17a
veto 1
visit 3
wait 4
whip 2
wrap 3b

stop-and-go
intermittent

stop at nothing
persevere

stop by
come 16c
visit 1

stopcock
tap[2] 1

stop dead
freeze 3
transfix 2

stopgap°
makeshift 1, 2
provisional 1
temporary

stop-go
intermittent

stop in
come 16c
drop 12
stop 5
visit 1

stop off
stop 5

stop over
sojourn 2
stop 5

stopover
sojourn 1
stand 15
stay[1] 7
stop 7
visit 3

stoppage
arrest 5
cancellation 3
check 13
deadlock 1
delay 5
embargo 1
halt 1
hold-up 2
interlude
jam 4
stay[1] 6
stop 9
termination 1
tie-up 1
veto 2
wait 4

stopped
congested
foul 9
stick[1] 7

stopper°
plug 1, 4
tap[2] 2
top 2

stopping
check 13
interruption 2
let-up
obstruction 2
prevention
stop 9
suppression
termination 1
visitation 1

stopping over
visitation 1

stopping-place
destination
stop 8

stopping up
stop 9

stopple
plug 1
stopper
tap[2] 2

stop up°
at **stop 3**
fill 7
foul 15

stop up (*cont.*)
gag[1] 1
jam 2
obstruct 1
plug 4
seal 3
stuff 9

stop work(ing)
knock 5
retire 2

store°
accumulate
accumulation 3
cache 2, 3
collection 2
deposit 2
establishment 2
fund 1
garner
heap 1
hoard 1, 2
husband 2
keep 4
lay[1] 19a
market 2
mass 1
mine 2
outlet 2
pack 8a
park 3
premium 3
put 12
repertory
reserve 3
set 14b
shop 1
stack 1, 6
stock 1, 10
storehouse
stow
supply 4
warehouse
wealth 2

-in store
impending
promise 4
prospect 4
reserve 8

-stores
provision 4

storehouse°
mine 2
thesaurus 1
warehouse

storekeeper
dealer

store owner
merchant 1

storeroom
storehouse
warehouse

store up
amass
garner
salt 8
stock 10

storey°
floor 2
level 13
tier

storied
fabulous 1
legendary 1
mythical 1

storm°
assault 3
attack 1
blow[1] 9
bluster 1
charge 14
explode 3
flounce 2
fume 1
gale 1
hail[2] 2
hurricane
make 30b
overrun
passion 2
rage 4
raid 2
rampage 3
rave 1
riot 3

storm (*cont.*)
rush 2
tantrum
tempest 1, 2
volley 2

storminess
severity 5

storming
bluster 3
invasion 2
onset 1

storm-tossed
rough 2

stormy°
boisterous
dirty 4
fierce 2
foul 8
heated
inclement
rough 2
severe 5
tempestuous
tumultuous
unruly
warm 2

stormy petrel
troublemaker

story°
account 6
composition 1
description 2
dispatch 6
dope 3
excuse 4
fabrication 3
falsehood
fib 1
history 1, 3
invention 3
joke 1
legend 1
lie[1] 2
life 6
line[1] 18
myth 1
narration 1
narrative 1
news 2
novel 2
one 5
piece 4
plot[1] 2
portrait
pretence 2
relation 4
release 4
report 1
romance 3
saga
scoop 3
score 6
song 3b
storey
tale 1, 2, 3
theme 2
version 2
word 2
yarn 2

-stories
mythology

story-book
fabulous 1
mythical 1

story-line
plot[1] 2
story 5
thread 2

storyteller
narrator
raconteur

storytelling
narrative 2

stoup
sink 12

stout°
bold 1
brave 1
brew 4
burly
dumpy
durable
fat 1
hardy 1

stout (*cont.*)
hearty 2
heavy 11
husky 1
large 1
obese
plump[1] 1
robust 1
rotund 3
sinewy
solid 3, 5, 6
stable 1
stalwart 1
staunch 2
steady 1
strong 1
sturdy 1
substantial 2
tough 1, 3
well-fed

stout-hearted
bold 1
brave 1
dauntless
gallant 1
heroic 1
intrepid
manly
martial 2
stalwart 3

stout-heartedness
pluck 1
prowess 2
spirit 5

stoutness
fat 5
fatness
pluck 1
strength 1

stove
range 4

stow°
garner
store 2

stow away
garner
keep 3
put 12
store 2

straddle
mount 4
sprawl 1

strafe
pelt[1] 1

straggle°
dawdle
drag 4
lag 1
sprawl 1
stray 1
trail 6

straggler
laggard
stray 3

straggling
rambling 2

straggly
rambling 2
ratty 2

straight°
above-board 2
blunt 2
bolt 12
candid 1
clean 3
direct 6
directly 1
due 5
erect 1
even 1
formal 1
hard 8
heal 2
honest 2
honestly 2
honourable 3
incorrupt 1
ingenuous 1
just 2
level 1, 11, 15
line[1] 19a
natural 4
neat 2

streamline
modernize
simplify
streamlined°
sleek 2
trim 2
stream of abuse
tirade
street°
drive 9
exchange 4
road 1, 2
track 2
way 3
–up someone's street°
at **street 2**
street Arab
ragamuffin
streetcar
tram
street lamp
light[1] 2
street-light
light[1] 2
street urchin
ragamuffin
streetwalker
bitch 2
prostitute 1
slattern
tart[2] 2
streetwalking
prostitution 1
streetwise
smart 2
strength°
action 2
asset 2
backbone 3
beauty 3
brawn
calibre 2
depth 4
energy
field 4
force 1, 4
forte
fortitude
gift 2
grace 4
health 2
intensity
juice 2
main 6
might 1
momentum
pillar 2
power 4
preponderance 2
pressure 1
resource 1
self-control 1
sinew 2
skill 2
speciality 1
stability 1
stamina
talent 1
tenacity 1, 2
vigour
violence 1
virtue 3
vitality 2
–in strength
strong 14
–strengths
endowment 3
strengthen°
brace 5
build 4
buttress
concentrate 2
confirm 3
deepen 2
develop 1
enhance
fortify 1
freshen 1, 4
harden 2
heighten 2
increase 2
inspire 2

strengthen (*cont.*)
intensify
lace 4
nourish 3
prepare 6
promote 1
reinforce
restore 2
spike 4
stay[2] 2
steady 11
stiffen 2
support 1, 2
sustain 2
temper 6
tighten 2
strengthening
hearty 4
magnification
promotion 1
reinforcement 2
tonic 2
wholesome 1
strength of character
backbone 3
grace 4
self-control 1
strenuous°
active 1
arduous 1, 2
difficult 1
exhausting 2
hard 2
laborious 1
murderous 2
punishing
strong 13
toilsome
tough 4
strenuously
hard 13
vigorously
stress°
accent 1, 4
beat 11
brunt
dwell 2
emphasis
emphasize
enforce 1
feature 4
heat 2
home 11
impress 3
insist 2
need 4
nerve 4
play 17a
point 17, 21b, 22
press 9
pressure 2, 3
pump 4c
punctuate 2
rub 3
spotlight 3
strain[1] 7
tension 1
tone 2
urgency
stressful
fraught 2
murderous 2
tense 3
trying
stress pattern
rhythm
stretch°
amplify 2, 3
area 3
cover 6
distance 1
draw 14a
elastic 1
elasticity 1
enlarge 1
exaggerate
exaggeration
expand 2
expanse
extend 1, 2, 3
extension 2
fetch 4
fill 2, 10a

stretch (*cont.*)
flex 2
flexibility 1
give 18
go 8
hang 2
leg 3
length 2
lengthen
liberalize 1
overstate
pad 5
period 1
prolong
puff 6
pull 4
range 1, 6
reach 1
run 12, 33c, 38
scope 2
screw 7a
sheet 5
space 3
span 1, 2, 3
sprawl 1, 3
spread 4, 5, 9
stint 1
strain[1] 1, 2, 4
streak 3
string 11a
sweep 7
tailor 2
tax 4
tense 4
term 2
time 1, 2
tract[1]
verge[2]
widen
stretchability
elasticity 1
stretch 4
stretchable
elastic 1
flexible 1
stretched
far-fetched
taut 1
tight 2
stretched out
drag 5
flat 2
prostrate 3
protracted
recumbent
stretcher
litter 3
rack 1
stretchiness
elasticity 1
stretch 4
stretching
expansion 2
expansive 1
extension 1
stretch one's legs°
at **leg 10**
stretch out
display 2
extend 1, 2
lie[2] 1
open 24
prolong
reach 1
recline
spin 5
sprawl 1, 2
spread 3, 4
unfold 1
stretchy
elastic 1
flexible 1
strew°
clutter 3
distribute 2
litter 4
scatter 1
spread 1
strewn about
loose 4
stria
groove
vein 2

striate
streak 4
striated
striped
striation
groove
streak 1
stripe 1
vein 2
stricken°
affected 4
come 12
sick 3
sicken 1
sinking 2
smitten 1
stricken by°
at **stricken 1**
strict°
authoritarian
close 14
conscientious 1
domineering
dour 2
exact 2
extreme 4
firm 4
formal 1
hard 4, 8
legalistic
literal 1
meticulous
narrow 3
nice 3
precise 1, 2
priggish
proper 7
puritan 2
religious 2
rigid 2, 3
scrupulous 1
set 29
severe 1
sharp 5
Spartan
stern 1
strait-laced
tight 3
verbatim 1
–in the strictest sense
proper 7
strictly
exactly 1
letter 4
literally 1
precisely 1, 2
severely 2
sharply 1
verbatim 2
strictly speaking
proper 7
strictness
formality 2
precision 2
rigour 2
severity 1
stricture°
impediment
inhibition
snag 1
stride
march 1
pace 1, 3
step 6, 13
throw 4
walk 1, 6
strident°
blatant 2
brassy 2
discordant 2
grating 1
harsh 1
high 7
penetrating 2
piercing 1
raucous
rough 8
sharp 7
stridor
jangle 3
stridulant
strident

stridulate
grate 2
stridulation
rasp 1
stridulous
strident
strife°
antagonism 2
combat 2
contest 2
disagreement 3
discord
dispute 4
dissension
division 5
faction 2
feud 1
friction 2
riot 1
rivalry
storm 3
struggle 5
trouble 5
unrest
war 1
strigose
hairy 1
strike°
affect[1] 1, 2
assault 1, 5
attack 1, 6
batter 1
beat 1
belt 3
box[2] 2, 3
bump 3
catch 6
chime 3
clap 2
clip[2] 3, 6
disobey
eliminate 3
finger 4
get 24
hit 1, 2, 3, 5, 10
impact 3
impress 1
jab 2
jolt 2
knock 1, 3d
lash[1] 2
lunge 1, 3
move 4
mutiny 2
nail 9
occur 2
omit 1
onset 1
overpower 2
overtake 2
penetrate 3
pierce 4
poke 2
pounce 1
pound[1] 1
punch[1] 1
push 15
ram 2
rap 1
run 26d
stroke 1
surprise 1
swipe 3
switch 3
tap[1] 1, 2
thrill 3
toll[1] 1
touch 6
walk 4b
windfall
strike back
fix 14
pay 5
retaliate
strikebreaker
blackleg
strike down°
at **strike 13**
fell
lay[1] 18c
strike dumb
jolt 3
stun 2

strike from°
at **strike 5**
obliterate 1
strike home
hit 4
strike it rich
place 10
strike off°
at **strike 5**
erase 1
obliterate 1
scratch 3
strike on°
at **strike 16**
strike out°
at **strike 5**
cancel 2
cross 3
cut 16a
delete
eliminate 3
erase 1
obliterate 1
omit 1
scratch 3
striker
picket 2
strike up°
at **strike 18**
strike up an acquaintance with
pick 8j
strike upon°
at **strike 16**
striking°
arresting
bold 3
brilliant 2
chime 2
conspicuous 2
dramatic 2
effective 2
eloquent 1
expressive 3
exquisite 3
fine[1] 10
hot 8
impact 1
majestic 1
monumental 1
moving 1
noble 5
notable 2
ordinary 4
pictorial 1
picturesque 2
prodigious 2
prominent 1
pronounced 1
raving 2
ravishing
remarkable 2
salient
scenic
sexy 1
shocking 1
signal 3
splendid 2
stately
strong 15
stunning 2
superb
telling 1
thrilling
toll[1] 2
vivid 2
strikingly
especially 1
extra 6
notably 1
particularly 1
string°
chain 1
cord
lace 2, 3
line[1] 11
procession 2
provision 2
queue 1
range 3
rope 1
row[1]
run 41

sudden°
abrupt 1,2
acute 3
dead 16
dramatic 2
immediate 1
impulsive
precipitate 4
quick 2
rapid
sharp 2,8
shocking 1
snap 13
spasmodic 1
swift
whirlwind 2
–of a sudden
plump[2] 5
suddenly°
dead 19
hastily 1
plump[2] 5
sharp 11
sharply 2
short 11
spur 3
summarily 2
swiftly
unawares 1
suddenness
speed 1
sudor
perspiration
sweat 5
suds
bubble 2
foam 1,2
froth 1
lather 1
sue°
appeal 1
besiege 3
petition 2
prosecute 1
suer
litigant
suffer°
abide 1
accept 4
ail 2
allow 3
bear 2
brook[2]
endure 2,3
experience 4
feel 5
go 36a
grieve 2
labour 7
let[1] 1
lump[2]
meet[1] 6
nail 3
pay 6
penance 2
permit 1
receive 4
stand 3,12b
stomach 3
support 3
sustain 3
sympathize 1
take 6
tolerate 1
undergo
vouchsafe 2
weather 3
withstand
sufferable
supportable 1
tolerable 1
sufferance
allowance 1
indulgence 1
patience 1
permission
tolerance 1
suffered
welcome 3
sufferer
invalid[1] 2
patient 4
victim 1
suffer from°
at **suffer 1**
catch 5
get 5
have 5
suffering°
affliction 1
agony
allowance 1
anguish 1,2
care 1
distress 1
evil 7
grief 1
hardship
hell 3
hurt 6
ill 8
misery 3
ordeal
pain 1,2
passion 5
penance 1
rack 2
self-denial 2
smart 8
sorrow 1
stress 3
torment 3
trial 4
trouble 5
worried
suffer the consequences
answer 7b
pay 6
suffer with°
at **suffer 1**
have 5
sympathize 1
suffice°
answer 5
go 35b
serve 2
trick 7
sufficiency
enough 2
fill 11
sufficient°
acceptable 1
adequate 1
ample 4
competent 1
cover 10
due 3
enough 1
equal 3
go 35b
good 16
passable 1
satisfactory
scratch 5
serve 2
suffice
sufficiently
amply 4
enough 3
fairly 1
well[1] 1
suffix°
termination 2
suffocate
choke 1
satiate 1
smother 1,2
stifle 1
suffocating
close 12
oppressive 2
stuffy 1
sultry 1
sweltering
suffrage°
vote 2
suffuse°
charge 8
impregnate 2
penetrate 2
percolate
saturate
sugar
sweeten 1
sugar-coat
sweeten 1,2
whitewash
sugar-daddy
friend 3
paramour
sugary
flattering 2
gooey 2
ingratiating
mushy 2
romantic 3
sweet 1
suggest°
advise 1
announce 2
argue 4
bid 2
breathe 4
broach
clue 2
conceive 3
counsel 4
drive 6
get 30b
hint 3
imply 1
impute
indicate 2,3
insinuate 1
intimate[2]
introduce 2
involve 2
make 37e
mean[1] 2
mention 2
moot 2
move 7
nominate
offer 3
partake 2b
predict
promise 4
propose 1,3
propound
put 18b
raise 8
recommend 1
reflect 2
rumour 2
say 2,7,9
set 18a
signify 1
symbolize
typify
urge 3
suggestibility
frailty 2
suggestible°
easy 4
impressionable
ingenuous 1
susceptible 2
suggesting
indicative of
symptomatic
suggestion°
advice 1
appearance 4
aroma 2
bit 2
breath 2
clue 1
dab 2
dash 7
evidence 3
feeler 2
flash 2
flavour 2
flicker 4
ghost 2
gleam 2
grain 3
hint 1,2
idea 1,2
implication 2
import 3
indication 1
inkling
innuendo
inspiration 2
lead 14
modicum
motion 5
note 6
suggestion (*cont.*)
occur 2
odour 2
overtone
particle
point 11
pointer 2
prediction
proposal 1
recommendation 1
resolution 3
ripple 2
savour 2
scattering
scrap[1] 1
shade 3
shadow 3
shred 1
sign 3
sniff 2
spark 1
speck
steer 3
strain[2] 2
stroke 8
suspicion 2
tang 2
taste 1
tint 1
tip[3] 2
touch 15
trace 1,2
trifle 2
undercurrent 2
vein 4
vestige
waft 2
whisper 4
word 6
suggestive°
bawdy
blue 2
eloquent 2
erotic 1
expressive 1
filthy 3
foul 5
improper 3
indecent 2
juicy 2
lewd
meaningful 2
nasty 3
obscene 1
off colour 2
pregnant 2
provocative 1
prurient 2
racy 2
risqué
sexy 1,2
significant 2
spicy 2
subliminal
symptomatic
suggestiveness
impropriety 3
suggestive of°
at **suggestive 1**
indicative of
redolent 2
reminiscent
symptomatic
sui generis
distinct 2
peculiar 1
rare[1] 2
specific 2
unique 1
suit°
accommodate 1,5
adapt 1
agree 4
answer 5
appeal 3
apply 4
become 3
case[1] 2
cut 16d
fit[1] 5
flatter 2
gear 5
lend 3
suit (*cont.*)
litigation
match 7
petition 1
plea 1
please 1
prayer 1
serve 2
sue 1
supplication 1
tailor 2
suitability
aptitude 1
fitness 1
propriety 1
qualification 1
relevance
suitable°
adequate 1,3
applicable
appropriate 1
becoming
befitting
character 8
comfortable 4
competent 1
convenient 1
correct 6,8
decent 1
deserved
due 2
eligible 1
equal 3
expedient 1
favourable 1
fit[1] 1,5
fitting 1
for 9
go 6,37a,40a
good 3
lend 3
likely 3
make 11
measure 15b
meet[2]
nifty 3
OK 2
opportune 2
order 10b
pat[2] 3
perfect 4
pertinent
place 11a
pleasant 1
presentable 1
proper 1,3,4
qualified 1
qualify 2
ready-made 2
reasonable 4
right 2
ripe 3a
safe 4
seasonable
seemly 1
serve 2
suit 2
tailor-made 2
take 38a
suitableness
aptitude 1
fitness 1
proportion 2
propriety 1
qualification 1
relevance
suitably
accordingly 2
appropriately
duly 1
pat[2] 2
properly 1,2
right 17
well[1] 14
suitcase°
bag 2
case[2] 1
grip 4
suite°
company 2
flat 15,18
retinue
train 2
suited
adequate 3
applicable
appropriate 1
befitting
calculated 1
equal 3
fit[1] 1,5
for 9
go 40a
proper 1
relevant
seemly 1
tailor-made 2
suiting
adaptation 1
suiting to a T
street 2
suitor°
admirer 2
fellow 4
gallant 5
litigant
love 3
pretender
supplicant 2
sulcation
furrow 1
sulcus
furrow 1
groove
slot 1
split 7
sulk°
brood 4
lour 2
pet[2]
pout 1
sulking
moody 1
sullen
sulky
black 7
disagreeable 3
disgruntled
fretful
glum
gruff 1
moody 1
sullen
sullage
filth 1
sullen°
disagreeable 3
disgruntled
dour 1
gloomy 2
glum
gruff 1
harsh 3
leaden 3
moody 1
perverse 2
sour 4
sulk
truculent
sullied
dirty 1
impure 1
sully°
blacken 2
blemish 2
contaminate
dirty 7
discredit 1
disgrace 4
foul 12,14
mire 4
pollute 1
smear 2
soil[1] 2
spot 7
stain 5
stigmatize
taint 2
tarnish
vilify
vitiate 1
sullying
filth 2
pollution
sultan
sovereign 1

sultry°
hot 1
humid
muggy
steamy 1
sticky 3
sweltering
torrid 1
sum°
add 2
figure 8
grand 4
matter 5
number 4
quantity
score 1
total 1
totality
-in sum
brief 5
word 8
-to sum up
brief 5
briefly 1
sum and substance
core 2
matter 1
quintessence
substance 2
summarily°
straight 15
summarization
summary 1
summarize
abbreviate 2
abridge
abstract 4
cut 5
digest 4
recapitulate
sum 2a
telescope 2
summary°
abridgement 3
abstract 3
arbitrary 2
brief 4
concise
cursory
digest 5
epitome 2
history 2
minute[1] 2
outline 2
passing 2
précis
programme 1
prompt 1
quick 2
résumé 1,2
round-up 2
run-down 3
scenario 2
speedy 2
story 5
synopsis
terse 1
-in summary
brief 5
word 8
summation
addition 2
summer-house
stand 18
summersault
roll 1
summerset
roll 1
summery
soft 3
summing-up
addition 2
summit°
acme
climax 1
crest 1
extreme 8
height 2,3
maximum 2
mountain 1
peak 1
perfection 3
summit (*cont.*)
pinnacle
spire 2
tip[1] 1
top 1
vertex
zenith
summon°
ask 4
assemble 1
beckon
buzz 7
call 4,9,12a
challenge 2
collect 2
command 3
desire 2
evoke
excite 1
fetch 2
find 7
indict
muster 1
page[2] 2
rally 3
recall 2
screw 7a
send 6
summons
bidding 1
call 14
challenge 5
indict
invitation 1
sue 1
warrant 2
summon up°
at **summon 2**
arouse 2
collect 2
evoke
excite 1
find 7
muster 1
sump
mire 1
sumptuous°
elegant 3
gorgeous 1
grand 1
lush 3
luxurious 1
magnificent
noble 5
opulent 2
palatial
plush
posh
princely 2
prodigal 2
rich 4
sensuous
splendid 1
upper-class 2
sumptuously
richly 1
well[1] 4
sumptuous meal
banquet 1
sumptuousness
elegance 2
luxury 1
prodigality 2
splendour 1
sum total
entirety 2
substance 2
sum 1
total 1
totality
volume 1
sum up°
at **sum 2**
add 2
number 4
recapitulate
reckon 1
total 4
sun°
daylight 1
-under the sun
below 3
sunbathe
sun 2
Sunday
good 15
Sunday best
finery
sunder
divide 1
rupture 3
sundering
parting 1
sundown
dusk
evening
night 2
twilight 1
sundowner
drink 6
sundries°
truck 1
sundry°
different 3
divers
manifold
many 2
miscellaneous
odd 2
several 2
various 1
sun-glasses
glass 7
shade 9
sunken°
hollow 2
underground 1
sunless°
dark 1
dull 5
grey 2
overcast
sunlight
daylight 1
light[1] 1
sunlit
clear 1
sunny 1
Sunna
sun 1
sunny°
clear 1,23
fair[1] 5
fine[1] 2
golden 3
joyful 1
light[2] 9
pleasant 3
rosy 2
vivacious
sunrise
dawn 1
light[1] 4
morning 1
sunset
dusk
evening
night 2
twilight 1
-after sunset
nightly 3
sunshine
daylight 1
sunshiny
sunny 1
sunshower
rain 1
suntan
sun 2
sun-up
dawn 1
light[1] 4
morning 1
sup
dine
eat
sip 1
super°
boss 1
capital 6
chief 1
divine 3
excellent
extra 5
super (*cont.*)
extraordinary 2
fabulous 3
foreman
gorgeous 2
grand 5
high-class 1
marvellous
outstanding 1
overseer
porter[2] 1
sensational 3
splendid 3
superb
superlative
swell 8
terrific 2
superabundance
abundance
embarrassment 3
excess 1
exuberance 2
flood 3
flow 6
glut 1
heap 2
pile[1] 3
prodigality 2
profusion
satiety
superfluity
surfeit
superabundant
abundant 1
luxuriant 2
prodigal 2
profuse 2
rank[2] 1
superfluous
superannuate
pension 2
superannuated
aged
ancient 3
decrepit 1
doddering
elderly 1
obsolete
old 1
retire 2
superannuation
decrepitude 1
pension 1
superb°
beautiful 2
best 1
brilliant 2
capital 6
complete 4
desirable 3
divine 3
excellent
expert 2
exquisite 5
fabulous 3
fine[1] 1,11
first-rate
gifted
glorious 3
good 2
gorgeous 2
grand 5
great 12
heavenly 2
magnificent
marvellous
masterful 1
nice 3
noble 5
outstanding 1
peerless
perfect 2,5
polished 1
practised 1
pre-eminent 2
princely 2
rich 4
royal 2
sensational 3
splendid 1
sterling 2
striking
stunning 2
superlative
supreme 4
superb (*cont.*)
terrific 2
top 8
transcendent
virtuoso 2
wicked 7
world 8
superbly
beautifully 2
famously
perfectly 2
pre-eminently
richly 1
well[1] 2
supercilious°
aloof 2
arrogant 2
blasé 2
disdainful
flippant 1
haughty
hoity-toity
lofty 4
majestic 2
overbearing
proud 2
scornful
snobbish
superciliousness
air 5
snobbery
supercolossal
splendid 3
supercritical
fastidious
overcritical
super-duper
gigantic
good 2
supererogation
excess 1
supererogatory
needless 1
superfluous
unnecessary
superficial°
apparent 2
cursory
exterior 1
external 3
flashy 2
flippant 1
fluffy 2
frivolous 1
glib
hasty 3
hurried 2
idle 4
light[2] 6,8
nodding
offhand 1
outward
passing 2
perfunctory 1
peripheral 1
pretentious 1
seeming
shallow 1
sketchy
skin-deep
slick 4
specious
thumbnail
token 5
topical 2
trifling
superficially
apparently 2
face 11
generally 2
offhand 5
ostensibly
outwardly
seemingly
sketchily
surface 2
superficies°
periphery 2
semblance 2
surface 1
veneer
superfluity°
abundance
embarrassment 3
excess 1
extravagance 2
exuberance 2
flood 3
frill 2
glut 1
leftover 1
profusion
satiety
surfeit
superfluous°
dispensable
excess 3
excessive 1
expletive 1
extra 2
extraneous 1
needless 1
non-essential 1
odd 3
redundant 1
surplus 2
unnecessary
waste 9
superfluousness
extravagance 2
superfluity
superhero
superhuman 2
superhuman°
divine 2
giant 1
miraculous
superimpose
plaster
superintend
administer 1
boss 2
direct 1
dispense 2
govern 1
guide 3
lead 3
manage 1
monitor 3
officiate
oversee
regulate 2
rule 6
run 10
supervise
watch 2
superintendence
administration 1
government 1
leadership
management 1
oversight 2
superintendent°
boss 1
chief 1
director 1
executive 1
foreman
head 2
manager
master 1
operator 2
overseer
porter[2] 1
principal 3
supervisor
superior°
able 2
above 5
admirable
arrogant 1
beautiful 2
best 1
better[1] 1
blasé 2
capital 6
chief 1,2
choice 4
classic 2
complete 4
desirable 3
disdainful
divine 2
dominant 1

-in support of
favour 5
for 1
part 10
supportable°
bearable
light[2] 10
tenable
tolerable 1
viable
supporter°
addict 2
admirer 1
advocate 2
auxiliary 4
backer 1, 2
benefactor
champion 2
donor
enthusiast
fan
follower 3
friend 4
help 8
henchman
partisan 1
party 4
patron 1
pillar 2
proponent
protagonist 2
second[1] 8
soldier 2
sponsor 1
stalwart 4
stand-by 1
support 8
sympathizer
-supporters
public 9
supporting
bearing 2
encouragement 1
favourable 1
instrumental
secondary 3
supportive
towards 2
supportive°
auxiliary 1
beneficial 1
favourable 1
helpful
instrumental
obliging
positive 7
pull 10
secondary 3
supplementary 2
sympathetic 1
warm 8
suppose°
assume 3
believe 1, 3
conceive 3
deduce
divine 4
expect 2
fancy 10
figure 9
guess 2
imagine 2
judge 7
make 21
premise 2
presume 1
reckon 3
surmise 1
take 19
think 1
supposed°
alleged
assumed 3
hypothetical
nominal 1
presumptive 2
quasi- 2
reputed
so-called 2
specious
supposedly°
doubtless 2
supposing°
though 1
supposition°
expectation 2
guess 3
hypothesis
premise 1
presumption 2
speculation 1
surmise 2
suppositional
assumed 3
groundless
hypothetical
speculative 1
theoretical 1
supposi(ti)tious
hypothetical
nominal 1
speculative 1
supposed 1
theoretical 1
suppositive
speculative 1
suppress°
bottle 4a
chasten 2
choke 3, 4
contain 3
control 3
crush 4
curb 2
dampen 2
demolish 2
discourage 3
gag[1] 1
govern 2
grind 5
gulp 2
hide[1] 4
hold 14a, 17b
hush 3, 4
keep 14a
kill 3, 6
lay[1] 5
master 8
mortify 1
muffle 2
mute 3
nip[1] 2
oppress 2
overcome 1
overwhelm 1
peg 3
persecute 1
put 16b
quash 2
quell 1
quench 2
repress
restrain 2
rout 2
shame 6
silence 4
smother 4
squelch 1
stamp 4
stem[2] 1
stifle 2
still 9
stop 2
subdue 1
subjugate
swallow 4
tyrannize
vitiate 3
suppressed
meek 2
sneaking 2
subconscious 1
tame 3
unobtrusive
suppressing
suppression
suppression°
cancellation 2
despotism
domination 2
oppression
overthrow 2
persecution 1
repression 1
tyranny
suppressive
prohibitive 1
repressive
suppurate
fester 1
suppurating
ulcerous
suppuration
discharge 11
suppurative
ulcerous
supramundane
supernatural
supranational
international
supremacist°
supremacy°
domination 1
dominion 1
excellence
lead 12
precedence
predominance
preponderance 2
prestige
quality 3
sovereignty
superiority 1
upper 6
victory
supreme°
absolute 3
cardinal
chief 2
divine 2
dominant 1
excellent
fine[1] 1
foremost 1
head 9
ideal 4
imperial 2
incomparable
leading 2
masterful 1
maximum 3
paramount
peerless
perfect 2
predominant
pre-eminent 2
select 2
sovereign 2
splendid 1
sublime 1
superior 2
superlative
top 8
towering 1
transcendent
ultimate 2
unbeatable
unparalleled
Supreme Being
creator 2
deity
lord 3
supremely°
pre-eminently
supremist
supremacist
supremo
boss 1
chief 1
sovereign 1
surcease
check 13
interruption 2
let-up
suppression
-without surcease
for ever 2
time 11
surcharge
extra 4
overload 2
tribute 2
sure°
absolute 4
assertive
assure 1
bound[3] 4
certain 2, 3, 4, 5
clear 10
confident 1
sure (*cont.*)
count 3
course 6
dead 17
decided 1
definite 2
deliberate 2
depend 2
destined 2
emphatic
fated 2
final 2
flat 10
foolproof
incontrovertible
indisputable
inevitable
infallible 2
know 3
mind 12
necessary 3
positive 1, 3
predictable
purposeful
reliable
rely
rocky[1] 2
safe 3
secure 4
self-confident
solid 5
stable 1
surely 1
tell[1] 7
unavoidable
undisputed
unquestionable
-for sure
certainty 3
doubtless 1
-to be sure
absolutely 3
definitely
evidently 1
fact 4
indeed 1
naturally 1
necessarily
positively
surely 1
sure-fire
foolproof
sure 3
surely°
absolutely 1
certainty 3
course 6
definitely
doubtless 1
downright 2
easily 2
evidently 1
exactly 2
indeed 1
mean[3] 2a
naturally 1
necessarily
positively
presumably
quite 4
really 1
truly 3
undoubtedly
very 2
sureness
conviction 3
faith 1
finality
trust 1
sure thing
certain 3
certainty 1
pushover 1
surety
assurance 1, 3
hostage
insurance
pawn[1] 3
pledge 2
security 2
surface°
appear 1
come 19a
emerge 1
exterior 1, 3
surface (*cont.*)
external 3
face 6, 16
facing
feel 10
finish 11
flashy 2
gloss[1] 2
loom 1
occur 1
outside 1
outward
paint 2
pave 1
periphery 2
report 5
seeming
shallow 1
sheet 5
side 2
skin-deep
superficial 1, 2
superficies
texture
token 5
turn 20e, 25a
-on the surface°
at surface 2
outwardly
-to the surface
forward 5
surface-active agent
detergent 1
surfacing
emergence
surfactant
detergent 1
surfeit°
excess 1
fill 11
flood 3
glut 1, 4
pall[2] 2
profusion
quench 1
satiate 1
satiety
sea 3
superfluity
surplus 1
surfeited°
jaded 2
surge°
flood 3, 6
flow 1, 2, 5
flush[1] 5
gust 2
jump 5, 9
leap 6
outburst
rush 4
shed[2] 3
spurt 3
stream 2, 4, 5
swell 4, 5
swirl 1
wash 3, 12, 14
wave 2
well[2] 2
surgeon
physician
surgery
infirmary
surging
wash 14
surliness
temper 3
surly°
cantankerous
cranky 2
cross 6
gruff 1
harsh 3
nasty 4
perverse 2
rough 3
short-tempered
truculent
ugly 4
ungracious
surmise°
assume 3
deduce
surmise (*cont.*)
divine 4
expect 2
expectation 2
fancy 10
guess 2, 3
imagine 2
infer
inference
judge 7
premise 1, 2
presume 1
presumption 2
speculation 1
suppose 1
supposition
suspect 2
understand 3
surmised
hypothetical
surmount
conquer 3
crest 3
crown 5
get 45a
pass 6
scale[3] 3
tip[1] 2
top 4, 6
surpass°
beat 2
best 11
better[1] 11
cap 4
eclipse 2
end 11
exceed 1
excel
lead 4
outdo
outstrip
outweigh
overstep
pass 6
run 33c
shade 8
shame 5a
shine 3
strain[1] 1
top 3
transcend
surpassing°
above 4
exceeding
incomparable
surpassingly
transcendent
surpassingly°
surplice
robe 1
surplus°
abundance
balance 7
embarrassment 3
excess 1, 3
extra 2
flood 3
glut 1
leftover 1
odd 3
profit 1
profusion
redundant 1
remainder 2
residual
residue
rest[2] 1
spare 1, 2
superfluity
superfluous
surfeit
unnecessary
-as surplus
over 8
surplusage
surplus 1
surprise°
amaze
amazement
astonish
astonishment
astound
blow[2] 2
bolt 6

swallow (*cont.*)
taste 2
tolerate 1
wash 9
swallow back°
at **swallow 4**
swallow one's words
mumble
swallow up°
at **swallow 3**
devour 1,3
swallow whole
bolt 9
lap[1] 3b
swami
master 3
swamp°
bog 1
devour 3
drown 1,2
flat 14b
flood 4
glut 3
marsh
mire 1
morass 1
overwhelm 2
submerge 3
-be swamped
crawl 4
swampy
muddy 1
mushy 1
watery 3
swan (about)
roam
meander 1
swank
splendour 1
swagger 2
swanky
swankiness
splendour 1
swanky°
dapper
elegant 3
luxurious 1
palatial
plush
posh
princely 2
sharp 9
soft 13
splendid 1
sporty
stylish
swell 7
swish 3
upper-class 2
swap
change 5
exchange 1,2
give 2
rotate 2
substitute 1
substitution 1
switch 2
trade 3,6
transpose
swapping
substitution 1
sward
field 1
green 4
lawn
turf 1
swarm°
bristle 4
cluster 2
crawl 4
crowd 1,3
flight[1] 4
flock 1,2
flood 6
gather 2
herd 1
host[2]
infest
jam 5
mill 6
mob 1
number 2

swarm (*cont.*)
pack 3
pour 4
press 7,8
rabble 1
stack 3
stream 3
teem[1]
throng 1,2
-swarms
many 3
mass 2
score 4
swarming
alive 4
lively 3
lousy 4
mobbed
overcrowded
populous
prodigal 2
solid 2
swarm 3
thick 2
swarm with°
at **swarm 3**
abound 3
teem[1]
swart
black 1
dark 8
dusky 1
swarthy
swarthy°
black 1
dark 8
dusky 1
swash
swagger 1
swashbuckler
adventurer 1
swashbuckling°
flamboyant 2
swat
hit 1,2,10
swatch
sample 1
swath°
belt 2
strip[1]
swathe°
bind 3
drape 1
envelop 1
muffle 1
roll 9
shroud 1
strip[1]
swath
wrap 1
sway°
advantage 1
affect[1] 3
bias 4
careen
command 7
control 4
convince
dangle 1
domination 1
dominion 1
get 14
government 1
guide 3
hold 26
impress 1
induce 1
influence 1,3
lobby 3
lock[1] 2
lurch[2] 1,2
might 2
oscillate
persuade 1
power 2
predominance
preponderance 2
pressure 4,5
prevail 3
prevalence 2
reach 6
reel 1
rock[2] 1,2
rule 2

sway (*cont.*)
say 12
shake 2,8
sovereignty
stagger 1
supremacy 2
swing 1,3
talk 10
teeter
totter
upper 6
urge 3
wag[1] 1,2
wave 4
win 3
swayed
affected 5
swaying
pendulous 2
swing 3
swear°
abuse 3
attest
blaspheme 1
certify 1
commit 4
curse 5
damn 3
declare 1
guarantee 2
plead 3
pledge 4
promise 3
tell[1] 7
testify
thunder 3
undertake 2
vow 1
swear by°
at **swear 3**
believe 2
rely
swear in
induct 1
invest 3
seat 7
swearing
profanity
swearing-in
installation 1
swearing off
self-denial 2
swear off°
at **swear 4**
give 17a
renounce
swear-word
curse 3
expletive 2
oath 2
profanity
sweat°
bother 6
drudgery
flap 4
hurry 3
labour 1,5
lather 2
perspiration
slave 3
squirm
stew 2
suffer 1
work 7
-in a sweat
nervous 1
sweat blood
sweat 2
worry 1
sweating
perspiration
sweat 6
sweat out°
at **sweat 2**
endure 2
sweaty
steamy 1
sweep°
brush[2] 4
carry 6
clean 9
drift 3
expanse

sweep (*cont.*)
extension 2
extent 1
flood 6
gamut
paddle 1
pass 2
purge 2
raffle
range 1
sail 3
scan 2
spread 9
stretch 5
sway 1,3
swing 4
swoop 2
trail 5
wash 2,14
whisk 1,4
sweep away°
at **sweep 2**
purge 2
sweep down
swoop 1
sweeping°
broad 4
comprehensive
exhaustive
extensive 1
general 3
panoramic
radical 2
wash 14
-sweepings
dirt 1
garbage
refuse[2]
rubbish 1
trash 3
waste 7
sweeping statement
generality 1
sweepstake(s)
lottery
raffle
sweep together
scoop 6
sweep up
scoop 6
sweet°
adorable
candy
dear 3
dessert
gooey 2
lovable
love 3
luscious
lyric 3
mellow 1,2
melodious
romantic 3
savoury 3
sentimental 2
silver 4
smooth 7
twee
winning 1
-sweets°
at **sweet 9**
sweeten°
mellow 5
sweetened
sweet 1
sweet FA, Fanny Adams
nothing 1
zero 1
sweetheart°
admirer 2
beloved 2
darling 1
dear 3
fellow 4
flame 3
friend 3
gallant 5
girl 2
love 3
squeeze 10
steady 9
swain

sweetheart (*cont.*)
woman 2
sweetie
dear 3
love 3
squeeze 10
sweetheart
woman 2
sweetie-pie
dear 3
sweetmeat(s)
candy
dainty 4
delicacy 4
sweet 9
sweetness
melody 2
sentimentality
sweet on°
at **sweet 8**
daft 3
sweet-scented
fragrant
sweet 2
sweet-smelling
fragrant
redolent 1
sweet 2
sweet-sounding
melodious
sweet 3
tuneful
sweet talk
cajolery
flannel 1
flattery
sweet-talk
cajole
entice
flannel 2
flatter 3
seduce 1
wheedle
sweet-talker
flatterer
sweet-talking
ingratiating
sweet tooth
weakness 4
swell°
blow[1] 8e
bulge 2
dandy 1
dapper
dude 1
enhance
enlarge 1
expand 1
fill 2,10a
fine[1] 1
flare 2
gorgeous 2
grow 1
increase 1
inflate 1
mound 1
mount 7
neat 5
puff 6
pump 4a
rise 5
roll 14
roller 2
sea 2
sharp 9
sporty
stretch 2
stylish
surge 1,2
swish 3
wash 14
wave 1,2
well[2] 2
swell(ed)-headed
egotistical
haughty
inflated 1
self-important
vain 1
swell-headedness
vanity 1

swelling°
bulge 1
bump 2
elevation 2
expansion 2
flare 6
growth 4
hump 1
inflammation
lump[1] 2
nub 1
pimple
prominence 3
protrusion
protuberant
sore 7
swell 4
tumour
swell out°
at **swell 1**
bulge 2
puff 6
swell up°
at **swell 1**
puff 6
sweltering°
hot 1
scorching 1
steamy 1
sticky 3
sultry 1
torrid 1
swept off one's feet
overcome 2
smitten 2
swerve°
careen
deflect
deviate 1
divert 2
dodge 1
shift 5
wind[2] 1
swift°
agile 1
expeditious
express 7
fast[1] 1
fleet[2]
hasty 1
hurried 1
immediate 1
light[2] 7
meteoric 1
nimble 1
precipitate 3
prompt 1
quick 1,3
rapid
ready 5
smart 6
spanking 3
speedy 1,3
sudden
unhesitating 1
whirlwind 2
swiftly°
fast[1] 6
flat 17a
hand 12
hastily 1
leap 7
post-haste
promptly
quickly 1,2
rapidly 1
readily 3
right 13
shot 10
soon 3
suddenly 1
summarily 1
time 17
swiftness
dispatch 5
expedition 2
facility 1
haste 1
rapidity
speed 1
velocity

swig
draught 2
drink 1,6
gulp 1,3
shot 7
sip 2
swallow 1,5
swill 3
swill°
drink 1
garbage
gulp 1,3
prattle 3
rinse 1
stuff 4
swallow 1
swiller
drunk 3
swim
dip 4
float 1
luxuriate 1
spin 3
-in the swim
swinging
swimmingly°
swimming-pool
pool 1
swindle°
beguile 1,2
cheat 2
chisel 2
clip[2] 4
deceit 2
deceive
defraud
double-cross
dupe 3
fiddle 1,3
fleece
fool 4
fraud 2
gouge 2
hoax 1,2
hocus-pocus 1
outsmart
prey 3b
racket 2
ride 5a
rip 2b
rip-off 2
rob 3
screw 6
sting 4
take 27,32b
trick 8
victimize 2
swindler°
adventurer 2
cheat 1
fraud 3
impostor
rogue 1
slicker 1
thief 2
twister 1
welsher
swindling
fraud 1
rip-off 2
swindle 2
trickery
swine
heel[1] 2
stinker
wretch 1
swing°
accomplish
cadence
dangle 1
engineer 5
execute 1
extreme 7
float 3
flop 2
flourish 2
fluctuate
fluctuation
flux
hang 1
movement 7
oscillate
rock[2] 1,2
see-saw 2
swing (*cont.*)
shake 2,8
suspend 2
sway 1,3
sweep 7
swerve
swipe 1,3
trend 3
turn 2
wangle
wave 4
wheel 2
wield 1
-swings
fluctuation
swingeing°
swinging°
flux
pendulous 2
swing 3
swinging both ways
bisexual 2
swinish
epicurean 1
gluttonous
greedy 1
ravenous 2
swipe°
make 27
pilfer
pinch 3
pocket 4
rip 2a
steal 1
stroke 1
take 3
swiping
rip-off 1
theft
swirl°
eddy 1,2
flow 1
gyrate
whirlpool
swish°
dashing 2
dressy 2
flash 6
flourish 2
homosexual 2
rustle 1,2
swanky
swishing
rustle 2
swishy
homosexual 2
swish 4
switch°
change 1,2,5
control 6
convert 2
deflect
divert 1
exchange 1,2
lash[1] 3
reversal 1
rod 2
rotate 2
see-saw 2
shift 1,5
substitute 1
substitution 1
swing 4
trade 6
transpose
turn 33
vary 2
whip 1,8
switching
substitution 1
whipping 1
switch off
shut 2,4a
turn 17a
switch on
activate
light[1] 17
start 1
turn 18a
swither
shilly-shally
swivel°
gyrate
pivot 1,3
revolve 1
turn 1
wheel 2
swizz
swindle 2
swizzle
swindle 2
swollen°
bloated
inflamed
packed
protuberant
swollen-headed
egotistical
haughty
inflated 1
self-important
vain 1
swoon
collapse 3
faint 3,4
pass 20a
swoop°
descend 4
dive 1
jump 6,7
mob 3
pounce 1,2
raid 2
waylay 1
swoosh
swish 2
swop
change 5
exchange 1,2
give 2
rotate 2
substitute 1
substitution 1
switch 2
trade 3,6
transpose
swopping
substitution 1
sword
blade 2
steel 1
sworn
mortal 4
professed 2
swot
cram 2
grind 4
hack[2] 2
labour 1,5
mug 6
polish 4
prepare 2
student 1
study 1
sweat 3
swotter
student 1
swotting
preparation 4
study 5
sweat 6
sybarite°
epicure
profligate 3
sensualist
sybaritic(al)
epicurean 1
fast[1] 2
high 12
luxurious 2
profligate 1
self-indulgent
sensuous
voluptuous 1
sybaritically
fast[1] 9
sybaritism
dissipation 1
luxury 2
profligacy 1
sycophancy
servility
sycophant
flatterer
flunkey 2
hanger-on
menial 4
satellite 2
yes-man
sycophantic
greasy 2
ingratiating
menial 2
obsequious
oily 2
servile
slick 2
slimy 2
submissive 2
time-serving
sycophantish
grovelling
obsequious
servile
sycophantism
servility
syllabus
epitome 2
programme 1
syllogistic(al)
logical 1
sylphlike
slender 1
willowy 2
sylvan
rural 1
wooded
symbol°
banner 1
character 1
colour 2b
crest 2
device 3
emblem
expression 2
figure 7
gesture 2
hallmark 1
idol 1
image 5
letter 1
mark 2
metaphor
reflection 4
seal 1
sign 1,4
stamp 7
token 2
-symbols
colour 2b
legend 3
notation 2
symbolic°
abstract 2
characteristic 1
emblematic
metaphoric
mystical 1
mythical 1
representative 1
symptomatic
token 4
symbolical
symbolism
imagery
metaphor
notation 2
symbolize°
denote 2
designate 3
embody 2
express 3
personify 1
represent 4
say 9
show 8
signify 1
speak 5
stand 7a
typify
symmetric
symmetrical
well-balanced 2
symmetrical°
equal 2
orderly 1
symmetrical
(*cont.*)
proportional
regular 3,4
well-balanced 2
symmetry°
order 2
parallel 3
proportion 2
regularity 1
uniformity 1
sympathetic°
agreeable 2
benevolent
benign 1
charitable 2
considerate
fatherly
favourable 2
feeling 7
good 6
harmonious
helpful
human 3
kind[1]
merciful
mood 2
responsive
sentimental 1
soft 5
soft-hearted
supportive
sweet 6
tender[1] 6
thoughtful 1
sympathetically
favourably 1
sympathize°
identify 4
pity 3
relate 4
respond 2
understand 5
sympathizer°
patron 1
stand-by 1
sympathize with°
at **sympathize 1**
feel 8
identify 4
respond 2
stand 5a
understand 5
sympathizing
sympathetic 1
sympathy°
affinity 1
charity 2
feeling 3
heart 5
humanity 3
identification 4
inclination 4
kindness 1
leaning
love 4
mercy
patronage 1
pity 1
rapport
regard 9
sensitivity 2
thought 4
understanding 2
unity 1
vibes
-in sympathy
sympathize 2
understand 5
-sympathies
feeling 5
symposium
conference
convention 1
symptom°
indication 1
symptomatic (of)°
at **symptomatic**
characteristic
indicative of
peculiar 2
symbolic
synagogue
sanctuary 1
temple
sync
-out of sync
wrong 7
synchronic
contemporary 1
synchronism
coincidence 1
synchronize
coincide
coordinate 2
mate 6
set 6
synchronous
contemporary 1
simultaneous
synchrony
coincidence 1
syncope
faint 4
syndicate°
association 1
combination 2
organization 3
pool 3
underworld 1
union 2
syndication
combination 2
syndicate 1
syndrome
symptom
synergetic
united 2
synergism
cooperation 1
synergistic
united 2
synergy
cooperation 1
give and take
synod
assembly 2
convention 1
council 1
synonymous°
equivalent 1
synonymy
thesaurus 2
synopsis°
abridgement 3
abstract 3
brief 4
digest 5
epitome 2
note 10
outline 2
précis
programme 1
résumé 1
round-up 2
run-down 3
scenario 2
summary 1
synopsize
abbreviate 2
abridge
abstract 4
sum 2a
syntax
phrase 3
synthesis°
compound 5
embodiment 2
mixture 2
union 1
synthesize
combine 3
embody 3
syndicate 3
synthesized
unreal 3
synthesizing
union 1
synthetic°
artificial 1
counterfeit 2
factitious
false 3
imitation 5

synthetic (*cont.*)
mock 3
phoney 1
plastic 3
sham 2
spurious
unreal 3
syphilitic
venereal
syrupy
gooey 2
mushy 2
smooth 6
sweet 7
system°
code 3
establishment 3
facility 2a
form 4
frame 3
machine 3
measure 3
mechanism 2
method 1,2
mode[1] 1
network 2
order 2
organization 2,3
pattern 3
plan 1
policy
procedure
process 1
recipe 2
regime
scheme 1
science 2
sequence
set-up 1
society 3
structure 1
technique 1
way 1
systematic°
careful 2
deliberate 3
formal 1
hard 6
measured 2
methodical
neat 1
orderly 1
organic 3
regular 2,11
scientific
sequential
tidy 2
systematically
exactly 1
systematization
embodiment 2
order 1
organization 1
systematize
arrange 1
compile
coordinate 1
embody 3
file 3
formulate 1
order 16
organize 1
regiment
sort 8
standardize
structure 3
tabulate
systematized
orderly 1
pitched
systematic
systematizing
organization 1
systemization
order 1
systemize
coordinate 1
organize 1
sort 8
systemized
orderly 1

T

T
-to a T
entirely 1
tab°
bill[1] 1
check 19
flag[1] 3
flap 3
reckoning 2
tag 1
tally 4
tang 3
table°
board 2
chart 2
counter 2
defer[1]
delay 1
legend 3
postpone
procrastinate 1
propose 1
put 21a
shelve
spread 11
stall[1] 2
stand 16
stratum 1
suspend 1
-be tabled
wait 2
-on the table
prospect 4
stake[2] 3
-on to the table
forward 5
-under the table
drunk 1
furtive 1
unlawful
tableau°
pageant
view 1
tabled
abeyance
wait 2
tableland
plateau 1
table 2
table linen(s)
linen
table of contents
index 1
précis
table 3
table salt
salt 1
tablet°
monument 1
pill 1
plaque 1
tabloid
journal 1
paper 1
publication 2
sheet 6
taboo°
ban 2
bawdy
filthy 3
forbid
ineffable 1
pornographic
prevent
prevention
profane 3
prohibit 1
prohibition 1
restraint 1
rude 3
scandalous 1
unmentionable 1
veto 1,2
wicked 3
tabooing
prevention
taboo language
profanity
tabu
see **taboo**
tabulate°
detail 5
include 2
itemize
list[1] 2
organize 1
tally 2
tabulation
bill[1] 1
chart 2
list[1] 1
table 3
tally 3
tachygrapher
stenographer
tachygraphy
stenography
tacit°
implicit 1
mute 1,2
passive 3
silent 3
taciturn°
close 17
dumb 1
impassive
mute 1
reserved
reticent
secretive
silent 2
solemn 1
stern 2
straight 8
tight-lipped
withdrawn 1
taciturnity
reserve 4
silence 2
solemnity
tack°
beat 4
connect 3
course 4
equipment
furniture 2
line[1] 9
nail 7
outfit 1
pin 3
post[1] 2
sew
stick[1] 4
technique 1
tackiness
sentimentality
tackle°
apparatus
embark 2
equipment
essay 3
fall 21
furniture 2
gear 2
go 18
grapple 2
grip 5
handle 7
hoist 2
kit
outfit 1
paraphernalia
regalia
rig 3
set 12a
stuff 2
tack 4
take 10,35c
undertake 1
tack on°
at **tack 7**
attach 1
suffix 2
tacky°
cheap 3
dowdy
flashy 1
gaudy
gooey 1
sentimental 2
tacky (*cont.*)
shabby 1
shoddy
sticky 1
tawdry
tact°
civility
dexterity 2
diplomacy 1
discretion 1
finesse 3
grace 2
prudence 1
refinement 1
savoir faire
tactful°
courteous
diplomatic
discreet
graceful 2
judicious
polite 1
politic 2
tactical
tasteful
wise 3
tactfulness
diplomacy 1
savoir faire
taste 6
tactic°
feint
game 3
line[1] 9
machination
manoeuvre 1
measure 6
point 12
policy
scheme 3
stratagem
strategy
-tactics°
at **tactic 2**
line[1] 9
machination
measure 6
policy
strategy
tactical°
strategic
wise 3
tactician°
tactile
tangible
tactless°
brash 2
direct 10
inconsiderate
indiscreet
outspoken
rude 2
thoughtless 1
unthinking 2
untoward 2
tactlessness
incivility
indiscretion 1
tad
dash 7
jot 2
pinch 7
suspicion 2
trifle 2
youth 2
tag°
brand 2
call 2
denomination 3
flag[1] 3
identify 1
label 1,4
name 1,4
stamp 3
style 7
tab 1
tack 7
tally 4
title 6
tag along°
at **tag 5**
follow 1
trail 4
tag end
rear[1] 1
tagging
denomination 3
tag sale
sale 3
tail°
buttocks
flap 3
follow 4
heel[1] 1
posterior 3
pursue 1
queue 2
rear[1] 1
seat 4
shadow 7
spy 2
stalk[1]
stub 1
tag 5
trace 4
track 6
trail 7
tailback
line[1] 6
queue 1
tail end
heel[1] 1
rear[1] 1
stub 1
tail-end
tail 2
tailing
pursuit 1
tailor°
adapt 2
dressmaker
gear 5
measure 12
style 8
suit 1
tailored
fitted
tailor-made°
fitted
tailpiece
tail 1
tail side
reverse 7
tailspin
slump 1,2
taint°
adulterate
bias 4
blacken 2
blight 3
colour 4
contaminate
corrupt 4
debase 2
discredit 1,5
disgrace 2,4
filth 2
flaw 1,4
foul 12,14
mar 2
poison 3
pollute 1
profane 4
scandal 3
shame 8
smear 3
spot 7
stain 5
stigma
tarnish
tint 4
tainted
bad 6
filthy 1
flawed
foul 2
high 10
impure 1
jaundiced 1
mixed 1
putrid
rancid
rot 1
rotten 1
tainting
pollution
take°
accept 1,4
adopt 1,2
alternate 1
appropriate 2
arrest 2
assume 1,3
bear 1
booty
borrow
bring 1
buy 2
capture 2
carry 2,3,6,10b
catch 1,3,15
cheat 2
clear 26
confiscate
deceive
defraud
draw 8,9
dupe 3
earnings
employ 3
endure 2,3
excerpt 2
figure 9
film 5
fleece
gain 8
get 3,8,11
go 36a
gross 7
haul 4
have 2
heed 1
help 5
hold 7
interpret 2
leap 4
liberate 2
lift 6
love 6
mislead
money 3
net[2] 1
nick 3
pass 5
pay 12
perform 3
photograph 2
pilfer
pinch 3
pocket 4
possess 5
possession 4
pre-empt
prize[1] 2
proceed 3
profit 1
put 30
receipt 3
receive 1
requisition 3
revenue
ride 1
rip 2a
rise 12b
run 13
screw 6
see 6
seize 1,5
shepherd
snap 4
snatch 1
spoil 6
squire 1
stand 3
steal 1,2
stomach 3
suffer 2
support 5
suppose 1
swallow 2
sweep 2
tolerate 2
touch 5,9
transfer 1
transport 1
travel 3
trick 8
true 6
understand 2,3
use 3
victimize 2
walk 2

take (*cont.*)
withstand
-be taken
fall 5
-on the take
line[2] 2
mercenary 2
time-serving
take aback°
at **take 28**
amaze
devastate 2
dismay 2
jar[2] 3
nonplus
overwhelm 3
stagger 2
startle
surprise 1
take a bath
clean 11a
take a break
stop 5
take account of°
at **account 7**
disregard 1
take a chance
gamble 2
speculate 2
take a crack at
attempt 1
essay 3
tackle 3
try 1
take a crap
go 17
take action
card 13
take a decision
decide 1
take a dekko at
glance 1
peek 1
take a dim view of
frown 2
take advantage of
enjoy 2
exploit 2
impose 4b
play 15
prey 3b
profit 4
rape 4
seize 4
throw 5b
touch 9
use 2
victimize 1
wrong 9
take a fancy to
prefer 1
shine 5
take affront at
bridle 3
take a flier on
gamble 2
take after°
at **take 29**
favour 9
resemble
take a gander at
peek 1
sight 5
take a hand in
part 11
take a holiday
get 31b
take a leak
go 17
take a liberty°
at **liberty 5**
take a load off one's feet
sit 1
take amiss°
at **amiss 4**
take a new lease on life
improve 2
take an interest in
follow 9
take an oath
promise 3
swear 1
tell[1] 7
take a nosedive
slump 2
take a part
figure 10
take apart
analyse 1
decompose 1
pull 6
separate 1
single 4
strike 4
take a picture of
photograph 2
take a plunge
speculate 2
take a rest
get 31b
rest[1] 6
take a run-out powder°
at **powder 2**
bolt 8
clear 30
depart 1
escape 1
exit 3
flee 1
flight[2] 3
fly 2
heel[1] 4
make 26
run 2
split 6
take as read
suppose 1
take a seat
sit 1
take as given
suppose 1
take a shine to°
at **shine 5**
like[2] 1
take a shot
try 1
take aside
single 4
take a stab at
endeavour 1
essay 3
take a stand
fight 2, 3
maintain 4
object 4
oppose 1
speak 11b
take a stroll
promenade 3
take a tailspin
slump 2
take a trip
hop 2
journey 3
travel 3
take a turn for the better
improve 2
rally 4
recover 2
recuperate
take a turn for the worse
worsen 2
take a vacation
get 31b
take a voyage
hop 2
take a walk
promenade 3
take away
confiscate
deduct
deprive
detract
drain 4
eliminate 2
take away (*cont.*)
empty 8
lift 4
remove 2
seize 5
snap 4
spirit 10
steal 1
strike 4
strip[2] 4
subtract 1, 2
sweep 2
take 14
wipe 2
take a whack at
essay 3
take a zizz
sleep 1
take back°
at **take 30**
recall 3
recant
recover 1
retract 2
retrieve 2
reverse 4
revoke
withdraw 2
take by surprise
pounce 1
take captive
catch 1
land 6
-be taken captive
fall 5
take care
beware
keep 2
mind 17
see 12a
step 12
take care of°
at **care 4**
attend 2, 3
care 6a
conserve 2
deal 4
fend 1
foster 2
look 4
maintain 2
manage 1, 3
meet[1] 5
mind 17, 18
mother 5
nourish 1
preserve 1
process 4
protect 2
provide 4
reckon 5a
run 10
shift 2
tend[2]
trick 7
watch 2
take charge (of)
boss 2
care 4
cover 8
head 11
keep 2
mind 18
see 12a
take cognizance of
admit 3
understand 1
take command of
lead 3
take 37
take control
take 37
possess 3
take counsel
confer 1
consult 1
take cover
hide[1] 1
take down°
at **take 31**
enter 3
jot 1
lower[1] 3
minute[1] 4
put 16e
record 1
register 3
strike 4
write 4a
take down a notch
put 16e
humble 4
take down a peg°
at **peg 3**
downgrade 1
humble 4
place 13
put 16e
squelch 1
take effect°
at **effect 6**
act 9
take 11
take exception (to)°
at **exception 4**
challenge 1
dispute 1
fault 6
issue 9
object 4
protest 3
stick[1] 12
take flight
bolt 8
flee 1
fly 1, 2
heel[1] 4
pull 8b
retreat 4
rise 7
run 2
stampede 3
take for
mistake 4
put 16f
take 8
-be taken for
pass 16a
take for a ride°
at **ride 5**
bump 5
cheat 2
deceive
defraud
dispatch 3
eliminate 4
fleece
hoodwink
kill 1
murder 3
polish 3b
sting 4
string 10c
swindle 1
take for granted
assume 3
imagine 2
presume 1
reckon 4
suppose 1
take form
form 11
loom 1
materialize 1
shape 10a
take forty winks
rest[1] 6
retire 3
take French leave
escape 1
run 2
take fright
wind[1] 7
take from
deduct
enjoy 1
subtract 1
take from (*cont.*)
take 14
take heed
beware
notice 1
step 12
take hold (of)
capture 2
catch 1, 5, 13
clasp 4
clutch 1
grasp 1
seize 1
snatch 1
take 1, 11
take home
earn 2
get 3
net[2] 4
receive 2
take-home
net[2] 2
pay 12
take in°
at **take 32**
admit 1
adopt 1
arrest 2
beguile 1
catch 10
cheat 2
comprehend
cover 7
deceive
defraud
devour 3
digest 3
dupe 3
embrace 2
follow 8
fool 4
get 19, 21
gross 6
harvest 3
hoax 2
house 8
include 1
involve 1
let[1] 5
lodge 4
make 7
mislead
net[2] 4
nick 4
outsmart
perceive 1
pick 2
put 28b
realize 3
reap 1, 2
ride 5a
run 27
scoop 6
see 2
soak 2
swindle 1
trick 8
victimize 2
view 7, 8
visit 1
watch 1
witness 4
-be taken in
fall 13b
take industrial action
walk 4b
take into account°
at **account 7**
allow 6
bargain 4
consider 2
cover 7
figure 11b
reckon 5b
regard 4
take into consideration
account 7
allow 6
consider 1, 2
considering
figure 11b
take into consideration (*cont.*)
reckon 5b
take into custody
arrest 2
nab
pick 8h
pinch 4
pull 11b
run 27
seize 2
take issue°
at **issue 9**
differ 2
protest 3
take it°
at **take 33**
believe 1
deduce
endure 2
fancy 10
imagine 2
presume 1
run 2
suppose 1
understand 4
take it as given
imagine 2
take it easy
idle 6
loaf[2] 1
loose 9
luxuriate 2
relax 3, 4
rest[1] 6
retire 3
slow 14, 15
wind[2] 3b
take it on the lam
beat 8
depart 1
escape 1
exit 3
flee 1
flight[2] 3
fly 2
powder 2
run 2
split 6
take leave of
leave[1] 1, 4
take legal action
sue 1
take liberties
presume 2, 3
taken°
assumed 1, 3
infatuated
sweet 8
taken aback
dumbfounded
thunderstruck
unprepared 1
taken advantage of
put-upon
taken for granted
assumed 3
take no account of
disregard 1, 2
take no action
sit 8
take no notice
disregard 1
overlook 2
take note (of)
account 7
mind 16
notice 1
refer 1
register 3
remark 1
watch 3
take notice (of)
mark 12
notice 1
remark 1

task°
assignment 2
business 2
concern 4
duty 1
errand 2
function 1
grind 7
job 2,3
labour 3
lesson 1
mission 1
office 4
operation 4
place 4
post[2] 1
responsibility 2
role 2
stint 1
thing 6
undertaking 1
work 3
task force
fleet[1]
taskmaster
disciplinarian
master 1
oppressor
taskmistress
disciplinarian
oppressor
tassel
pendant
taste°
aesthetic 1
affinity 2
appetite 1
art 2
bite 3
class 3
culture 1
dash 7
discrimination 2
distinguish 3
drink 6
drop 2
ear 2
experience 4
eye 3
fancy 7
fashion 1
favour 4
finesse 3
flair 2
flavour 1,2
grace 2
grain 3
hint 2
impropriety 3
inclination 3,4
indelicacy
leaning
liking 2
little 10
love 2
morsel 1
nip[2]
panache
partiality 2
penchant
pinch 7
refinement 1
relish 1
salt 2
sample 1,2
savour 1,3
sip 1,2
sophistication 1
stomach 2
style 4
suspicion 2
tang 1
touch 5,15
vestige
vogue 1
weakness 4
-to one's taste
agreeable 1
tasteful°
aesthetic 1
becoming
chic 1
decent 2
elegant 1
graceful 2
tasteful (*cont.*)
savoury 2
tastefulness
art 2
chic 2
elegance 1
grace 2
refinement 1
sophistication 1
style 4
taste 6
tasteless°
awful 1
bland 2
crude 4
flashy 1
flat 8
garish
gaudy
loud 2
philistine 2
tacky[2]
unacceptable
unbecoming 2
ungraceful 2
vapid
vulgar 1,2
watery 1
wishy-washy 2
tastelessness
indelicacy
tastemaker
aesthete
tastiness
flavour 1
tasty°
dainty 3
delicious 1
luscious
pungent 1
racy 3
savoury 1
yummy
ta-ta
farewell 3
goodbye
tatter°
patch 1
rag[1] 1
shred 1,2
-in tatters°
at **tatter 2**
-tatters°
at **tatter 1**
tattered°
disreputable 2
ragged 1
shabby 1
threadbare 1
worn 1
tatting
lace 1
tattle°
babble 2
blab
finger 8
gossip 4
grass 1
prattle 1,2
sell 3
sing 3
spill 3
tell[1] 2,11
yap 2
tattler
talebearer
tattle-tale
blabbermouth
gossip 3
informer
sneak 2
talebearer
tattling
prattle 2
telling 2
tattoo
patter[1] 3
tatty
cheap 3
gaudy
ragged 1
seedy 1
shabby 1
tatty (*cont.*)
shoddy
sleazy 1
tacky[2]
tawdry
threadbare 1
worn 1
taunt°
dare 3
deride
dig 8
flout
fun 5
get 30c
gibe 1,2
heckle
hiss 3
jeer 1,2
joke 4
laugh 2a
leg 8
mock 1
pick 6
poke 4
provocation 2
rag[2]
ridicule 1,2
scorn 4
tantalize
tease 1
twit[1]
taunting
derisory
mockery 1
ridicule 1
scorn 2
taut°
fraught 2
tense 1,2
tight 2,4
tauten
stiffen 2
tense 4
tighten 4
tautness
tension 1,2
tautological
expletive 1
needless 1
redundant 2
repetitious
tautologism
tautology
tautologous
redundant 2
tautology°
expletive 3
repetition 1
-tautologies
repetition 1
tavern
bar 6
pub
tawdriness
glare 3
vulgarity 1
tawdry°
cheap 3
coarse 4
conspicuous 2
flashy 1
garish
gaudy
loud 2
shoddy
sleazy 1
tacky[2]
tasteless 1
tinny 1
worthless 3
tax°
burden 2
charge 9
custom 2
drain 5
duty 3
encumber 1
exhaust 2
overload 1,2
push 5
stagger 2
strain[1] 1,3,7
tariff 1
tribute 2
tax (*cont.*)
try 3
wear 7
weary 5
weigh 6
-after taxes
net[2] 2
taxi°
cab
taxi-cab
cab
taxi 1
taxing
arduous 1
demanding 1
exacting
laborious 1
punishing
severe 1
strenuous 1
tough 4
trying
weary 2
taxpayer
citizen 1
subject 5
tchotchke
ornament 1
tea
brew 4
meal 1
tea break
break 28
teach°
bring 15a
condition 6
discipline 6
drill 2
educate
enlighten
familiarize
ground 6
guide 4
implant 1
indoctrinate
initiate 3
instruct 1
prepare 3
prime 5
school 4
show 4
train 4
tutor 2
-be taught
learn 2
teachable
manageable
teacher°
coach 2
instructor
master 3
scholar 1
schoolteacher
tutor 1
teaching
creed
doctrine
edification
education 1
faith 2
guidance 2
idea 3
instruction 2
lesson 2
lore 1
moral 3
preparation 2
principle 1
school 3
schooling
tenet
tuition
-teachings
idea 3
ideology
lore 1
teach someone a lesson
punish 1
teach someone her, his place
mortify 1
tea dance
dance 2
tea-leaf reader
fortune-teller
team°
ally 2
brace 4
club 6
complement 2
couple 1
crew
gang 2
group 1
pair 1,2
party 2
platoon
ring[1] 3
shift 4
side 4
squad
staff 2
tie 3
union 2
team-mate
colleague
partner 1
team spirit
spirit 9a
team up (with)°
at **team 3**
ally 2
band[2] 3
chum 3
club 6
collaborate
cooperate 1
join 2
pair 2
pool 4
side 10
tie 3
teamwork
cooperation 1
give and take
tear°
career 2
carouse 2
claw 2
drop 1
drunk 4
flash 5
flaw 2
fly 3
gap 1
hole 2
hurry 1
hurtle
lacerate
leak 2
orgy 1
pluck 3
pull 4
race[1] 4
rack 4
rend 1,2
rent[2]
rift 2
rip 1,3
run 1
scurry
shred 2
snag 2
speed 3
split 7
squeeze 2
strain[1] 3
streak 5
sweep 3
wrench 1
-in tears
tearful
tear along
run 1
tear apart
pull 4
rend 1
rip 1
split 1
tear a strip off
dress 4
rebuke 1
tell[1] 10
tear asunder
rend 1
rip 1
tear down
demolish 1
destroy 1
flatten 3
level 9
raze
tear-drop
pendant
tearful°
low[1] 8
maudlin
miserable 1
moist 3
piteous
sentimental 2
sorrowful 1
unhappy 1
watery 2
tearfulness
sentimentality
tearing down
destruction 1
wreck 5
tear into
fly 8b
pitch[1] 6a,6b
scold 1
turn 19b
tear-jerking
sentimental 2
tear off
mutilate 1
pull 12a
tear one's hair
fret 1
tearoom
café
tear out
pull 3
uproot 2
tear to pieces
rend 1
tear up
pull 3,4
shred 2
teary
maudlin
moist 3
watery 2
teary-eyed
maudlin
tease°
chaff 2
deride
flirt 1,3
fool 4,5
fun 5
get 30c
gibe 1
harass
have 12c
joke 4
laugh 2a
leg 8
mock 1
molest 1
nuisance 2
parody 3
pick 6
play 9a
poke 4
pull 15
put 22e
rag[2]
ridicule 2
scoff[1]
sport 3
tantalize
taunt 1
twit[1]
worry 2
teasing
banter
chaff 1
playful 2
provocative 1
raillery
teasingly
fun 3

teat
breast 1
tec
detective
officer 2
sleuth
technic
practice 1
technique 1, 2
technical°
technicality
detail 1
triviality 2
-technicalities
detail 2
technical writer
scribe 2
technician
engineer 3
technique°
approach 7
art 1, 3, 4
execution 4
form 4
formula
manner 1
mean[3] 4a
measure 6
mechanism 3
medium 5
method 1
mode[1] 1
path 3
practice 1
process 1
recipe 2
road 1
scheme 1
science 2
skill 1
style 5
system 2
tack 3
touch 18
trick 3
virtuosity
way 1, 2
workmanship
wrinkle[2]
technologic(al)
technical 2
tedious°
boring
colourless 2
dead 12
deadly 5
dreary 2
dry 2
dull 4
hack[2] 4
heavy 7
humdrum
irksome
lacklustre
lengthy
lifeless 3
literal 3
monotonous
pedestrian 2
ponderous 2
prosaic
repetitious
routine 4
slow 9
stodgy
stupid 3
tame 4
threadbare 2
tiresome 1
vapid
weary 2
tediousness
tedium
tedium°
boredom
uniformity 2
teed off
indignant
teem°
abound 3
bristle 4
crawl 4
flow 2
pelt[1] 2
teem (*cont.*)
pour 3, 4
rain 4
swarm 3
teeming
alive 4
fertile
fraught 1
lively 3
lousy 4
luxuriant 2
mobbed
populous
pregnant 3
prodigal 2
profuse 2
replete 1
solid 2
thick 2
torrential
wet 2
teen
adolescent 1
youth 2
-teens
childhood
puberty
teenage(d)
adolescent 2
juvenile 1
young 1
teenager°
adolescent 1
child 2
minor 3
miss[2]
stripling
youth 2
teensy-weensy
diminutive
little 1
minute[2] 1
tiny
wee 1
teeny
diminutive
little 1
minute[2] 1
small 1
tiny
wee 1
teeny-bopper
addict 2
adolescent 1
enthusiast
miss[2]
youth 2
teeny-weeny
diminutive
little 1
tiny
wee 1
tee someone off
enrage
madden 1
teeter°
see-saw 1, 2
stagger 1
totter
wallow 3
teetering
poised 3
rickety
rocky[2]
teeter-totter
shilly-shally
teetotal
sober 1
temperate 2
teetotalism
sobriety 1
temperance 2
telecast
broadcast 1, 4
programme 2
send 2
telecasting
transmission 2
telegram°
cable 2
telegraph
cable 3
send 2
telegraph (*cont.*)
transmit 1
telekinetic
psychic 2
Telemessage
telegram
telepathic
psychic 2
telepathist
psychic 3
telephone°
buzz 7
call 3, 12b
contact 4
line[1] 13
ring[2] 2
transmit 1
telephone call
call 14
teleplay
script 2
telescope°
glass 6
televise
broadcast 1
send 2
spread 2
television°
press 10a
screen 5
telex
telegram
transmit 1
tell°
advise 2
air 7
announce 1, 3
babble 2
bare 7
betray 2
bid 3
break 2
breathe 4
chronicle 2
communicate 1
describe 1
direct 3
disclose 1
express 1
fill 9c
hump 1
impart 2
indicate 3
inform 1, 2
instruct 2
let[1] 7a
mound 2
narrate
notify 1
order 14
recite 2
recount 1
rehearse 2
relate 2
rumour 2
say 4
show 4
sing 3
speak 4
spill 3
spin 2
tattle 1
-be told
hear 2
receive 5
understand 4
tell all
spill 3
tell apart
differentiate 1
distinguish 1
pick 7b
teller of tales
liar
narrator
telling°
big 4
devastating 1
effective 2
effectual 1
expressive 3
forceful 2
graphic 1
telling (*cont.*)
history 1
influential
meaningful 1
moving 1
narration 1
overpowering
persuasive
pictorial 1
pointed 2
potent 2
powerful 2
predominant
prevailing 2
recital 2
rehearsal 2
relation 4
seminal 1
solid 8
stirring
strong 7
substantial 3
weighty 3
tellingly
home 10
telling-off
lecture 2
reprimand 1
tongue-lashing
tell of
describe 1
make 33
record 2
report 3
touch 8
tell off
castigate
dress 4
lecture 4
mind 10
rebuke 1
reprimand 2
scold 1
upbraid
tell on
finger 8
inform 2
sell 3
turn 15c
tell someone a thing or two
reprimand 2
upbraid
tell someone where to go *etc.*
rebuff 2
rebuke 1
tell-tale
blabbermouth
gossip 3
meaningful 2
talebearer
tell the difference
discriminate 1
distinguish 1
tell the world
spread 2
tellurian
terrestrial 1
telluric
earthly 1
terrestrial 1
tell what's what
distinguish 1
tell who's who
distinguish 1
telly
screen 5
television
temblor
quake 2
temerarious
adventurous
bold 2
foolhardy
indiscreet
presumptuous
temerity
brass
effrontery
gall[1] 2
indiscretion 1
temerity (*cont.*)
nerve 2
presumption 1
temper°
alloy 3
chasten 2
dampen 2
disposition 1
humour 3
lie[2] 6
mind 5
mitigate
moderate 5
modify 2
modulate
mood 1
paddy
pet[2]
qualify 3
rage 2
relax 2
silence 4
smooth 12
soften 2
spirit 2, 8, 9a
subdue 3
sweeten 2
tame 6
tone 3, 5
vein 4
-in a temper
indignant
temperament
disposition 1
humour 3
mentality 2
mind 5
nature 1
personality 1
spirit 2
temper 1
way 2
temperamental°
emotional 2
intense 3
irritable
moody 2
passionate 3
quick-tempered
sensitive 2
snappish 2
sullen
surly
touchy 1
waspish
temperance°
serenity 2
sobriety 1
temperate°
conservative 2
even 4
gentle 1
mild 1, 2
moderate 1
peaceable 2
philosophical 2
phlegmatic 2
quiet 4
serene 2
sober 1
subdued 1
temperately
easy 7
moderately
temperateness
sobriety 2
tempered
proof 3
seasoned
subdued 1
used 3
tempering
extenuating
tempest°
blow[1] 9
gale 1
passion 2
storm 1
tempestuous°
boisterous
fierce 2
heated
inclement
obstreperous
tempestuous (*cont.*)
rough 2
stormy 1, 2
tumultuous
unruly
uproarious 1
violent 3
wild 4, 6
windy 1
tempestuousness
fury 2
severity 5
template°
mould[1] 1
pattern 4
temple°
sanctuary 1
templet
mould[1] 1
pattern 4
template
tempo°
beat 11
cadence
pace 2
rhythm
time 7
temporal°
earthly 3
material 7
mortal 1
outward
profane 2
secular
temporary
worldly 1
temporarily°
meanwhile 2
time 16
temporarily inactive
abeyance
temporary°
brief 1
fleeting
fly-by-night 1
makeshift 1
meteoric 1
momentary
passing 1
provisional 1
short 7
short-lived
stopgap 2
transient
temporize
delay 1
hesitate 1
linger 4
play 14
postpone
procrastinate 1
sit 8
stall[2] 1
tarry 1
tempt°
appeal 2
chat 3
decoy 2
dispose 2
entice
interest 8
lead 9b
lure 1
motivate
rope 4
seduce 1
tantalize
-be tempted
rise 12b
temptation°
come-on
enticement 1, 2
incitement 2
invitation 2
lure 2
tempt fate
endanger
fire 6
tempting°
exciting 2
inviting

tickled pink
elated
glad 1
happy 1
joyful 2
overjoyed
pleased
rejoice
tickled to death
glad 1
tickling
itch 3
ticklish°
awkward 5
critical 3
delicate 4
dicey
difficult 2
dodgy
hazardous
nice 4
parlous
precarious
prickly 4
sore 2
sticky 2
tender[1] 4
thorny 2
tight 7
touchy 2
tricky 2
ticklishness
delicacy 3
tick off
castigate
check 9
enrage
enumerate 1
flag[3] 3
madden 1
rap 2
rebuke 1
reprimand 2
scold 1
tell[1] 10
upbraid
tick over
hum 2
tidal wave
flood 3
tidbit
dainty 4
delicacy 4
savoury 3
snack 1
titbit
tiddly
tight 8
tide
flood 3
flow 6
outpouring
stream 3
torrent
wave 2
tidiness
order 2
tidings
information
intelligence 2
message 1
news 1
rumour 1
story 4
word 2
tidy°
clean 3, 9
clear 31b
considerable 1
go 34c
immaculate 1
large 2
make 15
methodical
neat 1
neaten
nice 5
order 10a
orderly 1
pick 8c
respectable 2
shipshape
sort 10a
spruce 2
tidy (*cont.*)
straight 7
straighten 3
substantial 1
taut 2
tight 4
trim 1
well-groomed
tidy sum
packet 2
pile[1] 2
tidy up°
at **tidy 4**
clear 31b
go 34c
groom 3
make 15
neaten
pick 8c
sort 10a
spruce 2
straighten 3
sweep 1
wrap 3a
tie°
association 2
attachment 1
band[1] 1, 3
bind 1
bond 3
bridge 2, 4
chain 3
connect 1, 2, 3
connection 2
draw 17
equal 5
fasten 1
fastening
fix 1
hitch 1
join 1
knit 1
knot 1, 3
lace 2
lash[2]
liaison 2
link 1, 4
loop 2
match 6
relate 1
relation 1
rope 3
shackle 3
splice 2
stake[1] 3
stalemate
stick[1] 4
swathe
tack 5
tether 1, 2
unite 3
whip 5
-ties
bond 1
kinship 1
tied
bound[3] 1
even 5
fast[1] 3
level 6
tie down°
at **tie 5**
pin 4c
tether 2
tie 2
tied up
engaged 2
related 1
tie in°
at **tie 6**
connect 2
link 4
tie-in°
connection 2
link 2
regard 6
relation 1
relevance
tie on
attach 1
tie-pin
pin 2
tier°
range 3
row[1]
stage 1
storey
tiered
serried
tie someone's tubes
sterilize 2
tie tack
pin 2
tie the knot
marry 1
wed 1
tie up°
at **tie 7**
bind 1
bundle 2
dock 2
engage 2
knit 1
link 4
moor[2]
stake[1] 3
tether 2
tie 1, 2
tie-up°
jam 4
link 2
tie 8
tie-in
tiff°
argument 1
bicker
conflict 2
controversy 2
dispute 4
fight 4
fracas 2
quarrel 1
row[2] 1, 3
scrap[2] 1
tilt 4
tiffin°
tigerish
fierce 1
tight°
avaricious
cheap 4
close 10, 11, 13
compact 2
cramped
dense 2
drunk 1
economical 2
fast[1] 4
firm 3
frugal 2
grasping
greedy 3
mean[2] 1
miserly
narrow 2, 7
penurious 1
petty 2
secure 2
selfish 2
small 4
sparing 1
strait 1
taut 1
tighten°
flex 3
pucker 1
telescope 2
tense 4
tighten down°
at **tighten 1**
tighten one's belt
economize
tighten up°
at **tighten 1**
telescope 2
tight-fisted
avaricious
cheap 4
close 18
economical 2
frugal 2
grasping
greedy 3
tight-fisted (*cont.*)
mean[2] 1
miserly
narrow 7
near 6
penurious 1
petty 2
selfish 2
small 4
sparing 1
thrifty
tight 5
tight-fistedness
avarice
greed 2
thrift
tight-lipped°
close 17
mum 1
mute 1
reticent
secretive
silent 2
taciturn
tightly°
fast[1] 7
firmly 1
tight 10
tightness
tension 1
tightrope
-on a tightrope
nervous 1
tights°
pants 1
tight spot
bind 5
snarl[2] 3
strait 3
tightwad
miser
stiff 12
tigress
scold 2
tiki
idol 1
image 1
talisman
'til
pending 1
tile
pave 1
tiler
porter[2] 2
till°
cultivate 1
farm 3
pending 1
plough 1
prior 2
register 2
work 8
till doomsday
ever 2
for ever 1
tiller
helm 1
rein 2
tillerman
navigator
till hell freezes over
for ever 1
till now
far 8a
still 4
yet 1, 2
till such time as
pending 1
till that time
still 4
till the cows come home
ever 2
for ever 1
till the end of time
always 2
ever 2
for ever 1
till the present
far 8a
till this
still 4
till this point
far 8a
tilt°
heel[2]
inclination 1, 2
incline 1
lean[2] 2
list[2] 1, 2
lurch[2] 1, 2
set 11
slant 3, 4
slope 1, 2
sway 2
tip[2] 2
war 3
-at full tilt
blast 4
double 8
post-haste
tilt at°
at **tilt 2**
tilted
oblique 1
wry 1
tilting
inclination 1
inclined 3
oblique 1
tilt 4
timber°
beam 1
board 1
lumber 2
plank
standard 4
timbered
wooded
timbre°
key 3
tone 2
time°
age 3, 5
bout 1
chance 2
crack 3
date 1
day 2
era
generation 2
get 47
instant 1
interval 1
juncture 2
leisure 1
life 4
measure 9
measurement 2
moment 2
move 10
occasion 1
opportunity
page[1] 2
patch 4
period 1
phase 2
play 14
point 4
record 5
rhythm
run 38
schedule 2
season 1
space 3
span 2
spell[1] 1
stint 1
stretch 6
tempo
term 2
turn 30
work 17
world 4
-after a time
length 4a
presently
-ahead of time°
at **time 10**
advance 10a
early 1
-at all times
always 1
ever 2
time 11
-at any time
once
-at the time
event 4
-at times°
at **time 14**
now 4
occasionally
once 4
sometimes
-behind the times°
at **time 15**
passé
slow 8
square 6
-behind time
belated
-for all time
finally 2
-for a time
temporarily 2
-for the time being°
at **time 16**
meanwhile 2
now 2
present[1] 3, 4
temporarily 1
-from time to time
now 4
occasionally
once 4
sometimes
time 14
-in one's own time
leisure 3b
-in recent time(s)
late 5
-in these times
now 2
-in time°
at **time 18**
eventually
run 48
sometime 3
soon 5
-in time past
back 16
formerly
previously
-in time to come
yet 4
-of the time
contemporary 1
-on time°
at **time 19**
dot 2
duly 2
prompt 1
punctual
-times°
at **time 9**
era
generation 2
world 4
-to this time
still 4
time after time
frequently 1
often
repeatedly
time 21
time and again°
at **time 21**
frequently 1
often
repeatedly
time and time again
time 21
time before
eve 1
time-consuming
non-productive 2

time-honoured°
classic 2
old 4
proverbial 1
regular 1
traditional
usual
timeless°
classic 2
deathless
eternal 1
everlasting
immortal 1,3
perennial 2
perpetual 1
timelessness
eternity
perpetuity
timeliness
speed 1
timely°
fortunate 2
happy 2
lucky 2
opportune 2
prompt 1
propitious
providential
punctual
quick 2
ready 5
ripe 3a
safe 4
seasonable
suitable
topical 1
well-timed
-in timely fashion
time 18a
time off
holiday 1
leave[2] 2
leisure 1
let-up
recess 2
rest[1] 2
time out
let-up
timepiece
watch 6
time-saving
streamlined 2,3
time-scarred
time-worn
time-server
flatterer
menial 4
yes-man
time-serving°
ingratiating
insincere
menial 2
servile
times gone by
past 6
timetable°
schedule 1
time to come
future 1
time was
formerly
time-wasting
bootless
idleness 2
non-productive 2
time-worn°
ancient 3
old 3
ready-made 3
timid°
afraid 1
backward 1
bashful 1
cowardly
coy
faint-hearted 1
fearful 2
gingerly 2
meek 2
modest 1
mousy 2
obedient
timid (*cont.*)
reticent
retiring
self-conscious
shamefaced 1
sheepish 1
shy 1
spineless 3
submissive 1
tame 3
tentative 2
tremulous 2
weak 3
withdrawn 1
timidity
cowardice
fear 1
humility
shame 4
submission 1
timidly
fearfully 1
gingerly 1
timing
rhythm
timorous
afraid 1
cowardly
coy
faint-hearted 1
fearful 2
gingerly 2
modest 1
mousy 2
retiring
self-conscious
shamefaced 1
shy 1,2
spineless 3
tame 3
timid
tremulous 2
weak 3
wet 3
withdrawn 1
timorously
fearfully 1
gingerly 1
timorousness
cowardice
humility
tin
receptacle
tincture
colour 1,3
elixir 2
essence 2
hue
taint 1
tint 1,2
tinder
fuel 1
tine
prickle 1
spur 2
tang 3
tinge
cast 6
colour 1,3
dab 2
dash 7
flavour 2
hint 2
hue
modicum
shade 2,3
speck
stain 3,4
suggestion 2
suspicion 2
taint 1
tang 2
thought 7
tint 1,3,4
tone 4
touch 15
trace 2
undercurrent 2
vestige
tingle
flush[1] 6
itch 1,3
prick 2
prickle 2,3
tingle (*cont.*)
shock 4
smart 7
thrill 1
tingling
itch 3
prickle 2
prickly 2
thrill 1
tiniest
minimal
minute[2] 1
tinker°
bum 2
dabble 2
fiddle 2
finger 2
flirt 2
mess 6
monkey 5
tamper
toy 3
trifle 3
tinker's cuss
damn 4
tinker's damn
damn 4
tinkle
call 14
chime 2
jingle 1,2
ring[2] 1,3,4
urinate
tinkling
jingle 2
ring[2] 3
tin Lizzie
rattletrap
tinny°
brassy 2
tawdry
worthless 3
tinpot
cheap 3
tinsel
embellishment 2
shoddy
tawdry
trash 2
tinselly
gaudy
shoddy
tawdry
tinsnips
snip 4
tint°
cast 6
colour 1,3
form 3
hue
paint 1,6
rinse 2,4
shade 2
stain 3
tone 4
tin-tack
tack 1
tintinnabulate
chime 3
jingle 1
peal 2
ring[2] 1
tintinnabulation
chime 2
jingle 2
peal 1
ring[2] 3
tiny°
close 11
diminutive
elfin 2
imperceptible 2
little 1
marginal 1
miniature
minute[2] 1
nominal 2
petite
puny 2
short 1
slight 2,3
small 1,5
tiny (*cont.*)
stunted
toy 5
undersized
wee 1
tiny-minded
wooden 3
tip°
bonus
capsize
careen
caution 3
clue 1
consideration 2
dump 1,2
end 1
gift 1
heel[2]
hint 1,3
inform 1
inkling
intimate[2]
lead 14
lean[2] 2
list[2] 1,2
note 6
peak 2
perquisite
pinnacle
point 2,11
pointer 2
present[3] 3
remember 4
slant 4
slope 1,2
spire 2
steer 3
tilt 1,3
top 4
vertex
warning 1
tip-in
insert 2
tip off
caution 3
hint 3
inform 1
intimate[2]
make 33
warn 1
tip-off
clue 1
hint 1
inkling
lead 14
note 6
tip[3] 2
tip over
capsize
overturn 1
upset 2
tippet
stole
tipple
booze 2
draught 2
drink 2
tippler
alcoholic 2
drunk 3
soak 3
tipsiness
drunkenness
tipster
tout 2
tipsy
dizzy 1
drunk 1
high 9
stinking 3
tight 8
under 6
tip the scales
outweigh
weigh 1
tiptoe
creep 3
patter[1] 1
pussyfoot 1
steal 3
walk 1
tiptop
excellent
first-rate
tiptop (*cont.*)
good 2
high-class 1
peak 2
select 2
splendid 3
superlative
tip[1] 1
tirade°
harangue 1
rant 3
speech 2
talk 14
tire°
bore[2] 2
enervate
exhaust 2
fag 1
fatigue 2
kill 4
pall[2] 1
prostrate 2
run 26c
satiate 1
slack 3b
weaken 2
wear 6
weary 4,5
tired°
banal
boring
common 6
dead 9
drawn
drowsy
exhausted 1
fatigued
flat 5
hack[2] 4
jaded 1
lethargic 2
limp[2] 2
musty 2
old-fashioned
prosaic
prostrate 5
ragged 3
run-down 1
seedy 2
sick 7
sleepy 1
spent 1
stale 2
stock 7
threadbare 2
time-worn
washed out 2
weak 2
weary 1
worn 3
tiredness
exhaustion 2
fatigue 1
lethargy 2
tired of°
***at* tired 2**
tired out
breathless 1
dead 9
prostrate 5
tired 1
washed out 2
tireless°
constant 1
diligent
energetic
enterprising
indomitable
industrious
inexhaustible 2
laborious 2
non-stop 2
patient 2
persevere
persistent 1
resolute
single-minded
stalwart 2
steadfast
strenuous 2
strong 5
studious 1
untiring
tirelessly
non-stop 3
tirelessness
perseverance
persistence
tire out
exhaust 2
fag 1
kill 4
prostrate 2
tire 1
weary 5
tiresome°
boring
dead 12
deadly 5
dreary 2
dry 2
dull 4
flat 5
humdrum
irksome
lacklustre
lifeless 3
matter-of-fact
monotonous
pedestrian 2
ponderous 2
prosaic
repetitious
routine 4
slow 9
stale 2
stodgy
stupid 3
tame 4
tedious
threadbare 2
trying
vapid
tiresomeness
tedium
tiring
arduous 1
boring
dreary 2
dry 2
exhausting 1
hard 2
killing 3
laborious 1
monotonous
punishing
stiff 9
strenuous 1
tedious
tiresome 1
toilsome
trying
weary 2
tiro
amateur 1
apprentice 1
greenhorn
initiate 4
learner
newcomer 2
novice
pupil
recruit 2
tisane
tonic 1
tissue°
flesh 1
tit
breast 1
-tits
bosom 1
titan
giant 1
titanic
colossal 1
enormous
gigantic
great 1
heroic 4
huge
immense
massive
monstrous 3
prodigious 1
thumping 1
vast
titbit°
dainty 4
delicacy 4

tone (*cont.*)
odour 2
shade 2
sound[1] 1,2
strain[1] 9
style 5
tenor
timbre
tint 1
vein 4
tone colour
timbre
tone 2
toned down
soft 4
subdued 1
tone down°
at **tone 5**
lower[1] 5
mitigate
modify 2
modulate
muffle 2
mute 3
reduce 2
relax 2
soften 3
subdue 3
tame 6
temper 5
water 7
toneless
hollow 6
neutral 2
tone of voice
tone 3
tone quality
timbre
tone 2
tone up°
at **tone 6**
tongue°
clapper
dialect
idiom 1
language 1
lap[1] 1
speech 3
tang 3
tongue in cheek°
at **tongue 5**
fun 3
tongue-in-cheek
irreverent 2
playful 2
tongue-lash
lecture 4
light[2] 14
tongue-lashing°
abuse 8
lecture 2
piece 10
rebuke 2
reprimand 1
tongue-tied°
inarticulate 3
speechless 2
tonic°
bracing
exhilarating 1
fizz 4
healthy 2
invigorating
potion
refreshing
refreshment 2
stimulant 2
wholesome 1
tonier
superior 1
tonnage
freight 2
measurement 2
weight 1
tony
genteel 2
high-class 2
too
addition 6
besides 1
boot 1
further 3

too (*cont.*)
likewise 2
moreover
overly
too bad
regrettable
tough 7
too big for one's boots
presumptuous
toodle-oo
farewell 3
goodbye
tool°
apparatus
device 1,2
dupe 2
fixture 2
gadget
implement 1
instrument 1
machine 1
organ 1
pawn[2]
plaything 2
puppet 2
robot 2
-tools
gear 2
hardware 1
kit
tackle 1
thing 8c
tool along
drive 3
too much
end 8a
limit 4a
unbearable
toot
bender
carouse 2
drunk 4
jag
orgy 1
tooter
pipe 3
tooth
cog 1
-in the teeth of
despite
toothbrush
brush[2] 1
tooth-chattering
freezing
toothed
jagged
notched
ragged 2
serrated
toothsome
dainty 3
delicious 1
luscious
pleasant 1
savoury 1
succulent
tasty
tempting 2
yummy
tootle
pipe 4
toot one's (own) trumpet
boast 2
brag
top°
acme
cap 2,4
capital 1
cover 11
crest 1,3,4
crown 5
eclipse 2
élite 2
exceed 1
excel
fill 2
first-rate
full 4
great 6
head 7,12
height 2

top (*cont.*)
lop
maximum 1,2,3
outdo
outstrip
peak 1,2,4
pinnacle
premier 2
responsible 3
spire 2
star 3
successful 3
summit
supreme 1
surface 1
surpass
tip[1] 1,2
transcend
uppermost 1
vertex
zenith
-at top speed
flat 17a
-from top to bottom
thoroughly 2
through 7
-in top form
pink[1] 1
-of top quality
water 5
-on top of
above 3
over 1
-on top of everything else
besides 1
-on top of the world°
at **world 7**
elated
happy 1
pleased
rhapsodic
-tops
high-class 1
top banana
director 1
executive 1
star 2
top dog
director 1
executive 1
top-drawer
admirable
fine[1] 1
gifted
high-class 1
talented
top 8
tope
drink 2
top edge
ridge
toper
alcoholic 2
drunk 3
soak 3
top-flight
gifted
top-grade
fine[1] 1
swell 7
top 8
water 5
Tophet
hell 1
top-hole
capital 6
excellent
neat 5
striking
topic°
affair 1
business 1
content[1] 3
issue 3
matter 2
motif
question 3
subject 1
talk 16
text 3

topic (*cont.*)
theme 1
topical°
topic of conversation
talk 16
topless
exotic 3
top-level
important 2
topmost
maximum 3
supreme 1
top 8,9
upper 1
uppermost 1
top-notch
expert 2
first-rate
gifted
neat 5
proficient
talented
top 8
top off
complement 3
fill 2
topography
terrain
top out
crest 4
peak 4
topping
capital 6
neat 5
striking
topple°
bring 8a
crash 1
demolish 1
fall 2
flop 1
founder[2] 3
overthrow 1
put 16b
rout 2
subvert
tip[2] 1
totter
trip 5
upset 2
toppled
upset 6
toppling
overthrow 2
overturn 3
top-priority
necessary 1
rush 5
top-ranking
premier 2
topsoil
mould[3]
topsy-turvy°
chaotic 1
confused 3
disorderly 1
helter-skelter 1
upset 6
top up°
at **top 7**
fill 2
replenish
tor
crag
height 3
hill 1
mound 1
mountain 1
peak 1
prominence 2
rock[1] 2
torc
ring[1] 1
torch
burn 2
fire 8
flare 5
light[1] 2
torchlight
light[1] 1

torment°
afflict
affliction 1
agony
anguish 1,3
bully 2
curse 2
distress 1,3
exasperate 2
fret 2
gnaw 3
grief 1
harass
haunt 2
hell 2,3
henpeck
hurt 2,6
kill 5
madden 3
molest 1
nag[1] 1
obsess
oppression
pain 2
persecute 1
persecution 1
pester
pick 6
plague 2,3
push 7
rack 2,3
rankle
rend 3
scourge 1,4
sorrow 1
suffering
sweat 2
tantalize
taunt 1
tease 1
thorn 2
trouble 2,5
worry 2
wound 2
tormented
agonizing
stricken 2
tormenter
nuisance 2
oppressor
trouble 6
tormenting
excruciating
obsessive
stiff 2
tormentor
nuisance 2
oppressor
trouble 6
torn
ragged 1
tattered
threadbare 1
-be torn
rip 1
tornado
blow[1] 9
eddy 1
hurricane
storm 1
tempest 1
twister 2
whirlwind 1
torpedo
bruiser
cutthroat 1
gangster
henchman
hoodlum
killer 1
shatter 2
torpid°
dormant 1
drowsy
dull 3
inactive 1
indolent
inert 3
insensible 1
leaden 4
lethargic 1
lifeless 3
phlegmatic 1
sleepy 1

torpid (*cont.*)
slothful
slow 1,9
supine 2
torpidity
indolence
sloth
torpor°
idleness 1
inactivity 1
indolence
inertia
lethargy 1
sloth
sluggishness
stupor
torque
ring[1] 1
torrent°
downpour
flood 2,3
gush 3
hail[2] 2
many 3
outpouring
rain 3
river 2
shower 2
stream 2
volley 2
-torrents
many 3
torrential°
heavy 10
torrential rain
downpour
torrid°
hot 1
scorching 1
sweltering
torridity
heat 1
torridness
heat 1
torso
body 2
trunk 2
torticollis
stoop 3
tortoise-like
slow 1
torpid
tortuosities
meander 2
tortuous°
circular 2
devious 2
indirect 1
intricate 1
involved 2
labyrinthine
meandering
rambling 1
serpentine 2
torture
agony
anguish 1,3
distort 2
distress 1,3
gnaw 3
harass
hell 2,3
hurt 6
kill 5
oppression
pain 2
persecute 1
persecution 1
picnic 3
plague 2,3
punishment 3
rack 2,3
suffering
sweat 2
tantalize
thorn 2
torment 1,2,3,4
wound 2
wrench 5
tortured
agonizing
torturer
oppressor

train (*cont.*)
succession 2
suite 3
tame 5
teach
thread 2
tutor 2
work 19a
-by train
rail[1] 2
trainable
manageable
trained
broken 4
experienced 1
expert 2
learned
pet[1] 2
practised 2
professional 1
proficient
qualified 1
seasoned
skilful
strong 6
tame 1
versed
trainee
learner
newcomer 2
novice
recruit 2
student 1
trainer
coach 2
instructor
teacher
training
background 1
discipline 1
drill 4
education 1
exercise 4
instruction 2
manoeuvre 2
orientation 2
practice 2
preparation 2
scholarship 1
schooling
tuition
upbringing
-out of training
soft 12
training ground
seminary
trainload
cargo
train of events
thread 2
train of thought
thread 2
train station
station 3
traipse
gad
roam
saunter
walk 1
trait°
attribute 1
character 2
characteristic 2
feature 1
mannerism
mark 2
peculiarity 2
point 14
property 4
quality 1
respect 4
strain[2] 2
symptom
trick 6
-traits
stamp 5
traitor°
defector
deserter
grass 2
informer
renegade 1
snake 2

traitor (*cont.*)
subversive 2
turncoat
traitorous°
dishonourable 2
disloyal
double 5
evil 2
faithless 2
foul 7
inflammatory
perfidious
renegade 2
shifty
subversive 1
villainous 1
traitorously
back 6
traitorousness
betrayal 1
infidelity 1
perfidy
trajectory°
path 2
tram°
tramcar
tram
trammel°
chain 2
encumber 2
enslave
hamper[1]
handicap 1, 2
hobble 2
interfere 2
shackle 1
trammels°
at **trammel 1**
bond 1
shackle 1
tramontane
foreign 1
remote 2
tramp°
beggar 1
bitch 2
bum 2
derelict 3
down and out 2
drifter
loafer
pauper
plod 1
ramble 4
rover
slattern
stamp 1
trample 1
traverse 1
vagabond 1
walk 1, 7
-tramps
dregs 2
homeless 2
trample°
beat 7
rout 2
stamp 1
trample down
trample 3
trample out°
at **trample 3**
trample under-foot
oppress 2
trample 3
trample (up)on°
at **trample 2**
tramp (up)on°
at **tramp 2**
trample 1
trance°
fog 2
stupor
-in a trance
absent-minded
daze 4
groggy
muse
pensive
trancelike
glassy 2

tranche
slab
tranny
radio 1
tranquil°
calm 3, 4
collected
comfortable 1
dispassionate 1
dreamy 3
easy 2
equable 1
even 4
gentle 1
home 4a
homely 2
inactive 1
level-headed
mild 1
orderly 2
passive 1
pastoral 1
peaceful 1
philosophical 2
phlegmatic 2
poised 1
quiet 2
relaxed
restful 2
sedate 1
self-contained 1
self-possessed
serene 1
settle 7
silent 1
smooth 1
sober 2
soft 3
still 1
subdued 1
temperate 1
wind[2] 3b
tranquillity
calm 1
content[2] 2
ease 1
hush 6
inactivity 1
leisure 2
lull 2
order 8
peace 1
poise 2
quiet 5
repose 1
self-control 2
serenity 1, 2
silence 1
still 3
tranquillize°
ease 5
hush 5
lull 3
mitigate
quell 2
quieten
settle 8
silence 3
tame 6
tranquillizer°
drug 2
narcotic 2
salve 2
sedative 1
tranquillizing
narcotic 1
restful 1
sedative 2
tranquilly
easy 7
transact°
float 3
negotiate 1
transact business (with)
patronize 2
trade 5
transaction°
bargain 1
business 3
deal 5
negotiation 2
operation 3
passage 10

transaction (*cont.*)
proceeding 1
sale 1, 4
truck 2
-transactions°
at **transaction 2**
dealings
minute[1] 2
proceeding 2a
record 3
transalpine
foreign 1
transatlantic
foreign 1
transcend°
exceed 1
far 7
outdo
outstrip
overstep
pass 6
run 33c
surpass
top 3
transcendence
perfection 1
predominance
transcendency
predominance
supremacy 1
transcendent°
divine 2
incomparable
predominant
supreme 4
transcendental
occult 2
transcendent
transcendently
supremely
transcribe°
copy 4
minute[1] 4
record 1
render 6
take 31a
translate 1
type 4
write 4a
transcriber
scribe 1
transcript°
copy 1
minute[1] 2
transcription
transcript 1
translation 1
transfer°
carry 2
cede
commit 1
communicate 1
delegate 3
deliver 2
devise 2
displace 1
dispose 3c
disposition 3
exchange 2
give 1, 2
hand 15a, 18a
leave[1] 6
make 38b
move 2, 8
movement 1
pass 8, 18b, 30
relegate 1, 3
removal 3, 4
remove 2, 6
second[1] 10
sell 1
shift 5
sign 11
succession 1
surrender 3
transfuse 1
transit 2
translate 4
translation 4
transmission 1
transmit 1
transplant
transport 1, 4

transfer (*cont.*)
transpose
uproot 1
will 6
-be transferred
rub 5
transferable
hereditary 1
movable
transference
disposition 3
removal 3
surrender 3
transit 2
translation 4
transmission 1
transferrable
hereditary 1
movable
transferral
removal 3
succession 1
surrender 3
transit 2
translation 4
transmission 1
transport 4
transferring
transmission 1
transfiguration
mutation 1
transformation
translation 2
transfigure
convert 1
transform
transfigurement
transformation
transfiguring
mutation 1
transfix°
fascinate
freeze 3
impale
paralyse 1
pierce 1
run 34a
seize 3
stab 1
stick[1] 1
transfixing
riveting
transform°
affect[1] 3
alter
become 1
change 6, 8
convert 1
differentiate 2
make 9
modify 1
prepare 7
process 3
rehabilitate 2
renew 1
resolve 4
sublimate
translate 2
turn 3
vary 1
transformable
changeable 2
transformation°
alteration
change 3
difference 3
mutation 1
revolution 2
transition 1
translation 2
transforming
mutation 1
transfuse°
percolate
suffuse
transgress°
blot 3
break 9
disobey
err 2
infringe 1
sin 3

transgressed
broken 5
transgression°
error 2
fault 4
ill 9
infringement
invasion 1
misdeed
offence 1
peccadillo
sin 1
slip[1] 8
vice 1
transgressor°
offender
sinner
transient°
brief 1
fleeting
fly-by-night 1
fugitive 3
meteoric 1
migrant 1, 2
mortal 1
passing 1
short 7
short-lived
temporary
vagabond 2
transistor
radio 1
transit°
journey 2
motion 1
pass 29
passage 1
-in transit
move 13a
transition°
journey 2
passage 1
transit 1
transitional
intermediate 1
passing 1
provisional 1
transitory
brief 1
elusive 2
fleeting
fly-by-night 1
fugitive 3
meteoric 1
momentary
mortal 1
passing 1
shadowy 3
short 7
short-lived
temporary
transient
translate°
decipher 1
figure 12b
gloss[2] 2
interpret 1
render 6
say 3
transcribe 2
translation°
gloss[2] 1
interpretation 1
key 4
transcript 1
trot 4
version 2
transliterate
transcribe 2
transliteration
transcript 1
translation 1
translucent
clear 2
filmy 1
liquid 3
see-through
sheer 3
thin 5
transmissible
catching 1
hereditary 1
infectious

-barking up the wrong tree
misguided
mistaken 1
-trees
timber 1
tree-covered
wooded
treeless
open 9
treenail
spike 1
tref
impure 3
profane 2
treif(a)
impure 3
profane 2
trek
excursion 1
go 1
journey 1,3
march 3
pilgrimage
ramble 1,4
run 36
tour 1,4
tramp 1,3
travel 2,3
trip 3,7
walk 1
trekking
travel 2
trellis
grating 3
mesh 1
net[1] 1
trellis-work
mesh 1
net[1] 1
tremble°
cringe 1
fear 5
flicker 2
flutter 3
quake 1
quaver 1,2
quiver 1,2
shake 1,8
shiver[1] 1,3
shudder 1,2
teeter
thrill 2
totter
vibrate
wriggle 1
trembler
quake 2
trembling
doddering
flutter 4
poised 3
quaver 2
shake 8,10
shiver[1] 3,4
thrill 2
tremulous 1
wriggle 4
tremblor
quake 2
trembly
doddering
tremendous
big 1
enormous
fantastic 4
gigantic
great 1,2
huge
immense
incredible 2
massive
mighty 3
monstrous 3
monumental 2
prodigious 1
vast
voluminous 1
whopping 1
tremendously
fearfully 2
highly 1
tremor
quake 2
quaver 2
quiver 1,2
shiver[1] 3
thrill 2
tremble 2
-tremors
shake 10
tremulous°
trench
channel 1
drain 1
excavation
furrow 1
gouge 3
pit[1] 1
trenchant°
caustic 2
concise
devastating 1
eloquent 1
epigrammatic
incisive 1
keen[1] 2
penetrating 1
pointed 2
pungent 2
sarcastic
sharp 5
smart 4
strong 7
tart[1] 2
violent 3
virulent 2
trencher
plate 1
trencherman
glutton
trend°
craze
current 6
drift 3
fad
fashion 1
mode[2]
movement 7
popularity
rave 4
style 2
swing 4
tendency
thing 3
turn 32
undercurrent 2
vogue 1
trendiness
popularity
trend-setter
pioneer 1
trendy°
chic 1
contemporary 2
current 3
date 5
exclusive 2
fashionable
glamorous 2
minute[1] 3
modern
new 2
now 5
popular 1
snappy 2
sporty
stylish
swinging
trepidation
alarm 2
dismay 3
dread 2
fear 1
fright 1
horror 2
trespass
encroach
err 2
error 2
fault 4
infringe 2
invasion 1
misdeed
offence 1
peccadillo
trespass *(cont.)*
sin 1,3
transgress 1
transgression
trespasser
intruder 1
outsider
sinner
transgressor
tress
lock[2]
-tresses
hair 1
trestle
beam 1
rack 1
rest[1] 4
tret
allowance 4
triad
trio
trial°
affliction 1
bind 6
challenge 6
contest 1
distress 2
experience 2
experiment 1
grief 2
hell 2
match 2
misery 3
nuisance 1
ordeal
pain 2
pass 27
pest
predicament
proof 2
prosecute 1
run-through 1
sample 3
sorrow 2
suffering
suit 4
tentative 1
test 1
tilt 4
visitation 2
woe
trial run
trial 1
tribade
homosexual 1
tribadic
homosexual 2
unnatural 2
tribadistic
unnatural 2
tribal
native 4
racial
tribe°
clan 1,2
folk
nationality 2
people 4
race[2] 1
tribulation
affliction 1,2
care 1
difficulty 1
grief 2
misery 3
ordeal
pain 2
sorrow 2
suffering
trial 4
trouble 5
woe
tribunal°
bar 5
tributary°
river 1
stream 1
tribute°
blackmail 1
compliment 1
credit 4
eulogy
homage
tribute *(cont.)*
laurels
memory 3
mention 4
pledge 3
praise 1
rave 3
reward 2
tax 1
toast 1
toll[2] 1
trice
flash 3
instant 2
minute[1] 1
moment 1
twinkling 1
-in a trice
once 6a
post-haste
rapidly 2
suddenly 1
swiftly
trichoid
hairy 1
trick°
artifice 2
blind 8
bluff[1] 1
catch 18
cheat 2
chisel 2
deceit 2
deceive
deception 2
decoy 2
defraud
delusion 1
device 2
dodge 4
double-cross
dupe 3
finesse 2,4
fool 4
fraud 2
gag[2] 2
game 3
gimmick 1
have 12c
hoax 1,2
hocus-pocus 1
hoodwink
machination
manoeuvre 1,3
mislead
move 9
outsmart
prank
prey 3b
put 26
put-on 1
quirk
racket 2
refuge 2
ride 5a
rip 2b
ruse
scheme 3
shuffle 5
stall[2] 2
stratagem
string 10c
stunt[1]
subterfuge
swindle 1
take 32b
trap 2,6
tricky 3
trip 6
turn 30
twist 10
victimize 2
wile
wrinkle[2]
-tricks
art 6
nonsense 2
trickery°
art 5
artifice 1
camouflage 1
chicanery
craft 2
deceit 1
deception 1
trickery *(cont.)*
evasion 2
fraud 1
hanky-panky
hocus-pocus 1
intrigue 3
machination
magic 2
racket 2
swindle 2
trickiness
artifice 1
trickle°
drain 6
drip 1,2
drop 5
filter 3
flow 1
leak 1,4
ooze 2
percolate
rain 5
run 6
secrete[2]
secretion
well[2] 2
trickling
secretion
trick out
embellish 1
primp
trickster
adventurer 2
cheat 1
devil 4
fraud 3
impostor
joker 1
phoney 3
rogue 1
swindler
thief 2
twister 1
trick up
embellish 1
primp
tricky°
arch 2
artful 1
awkward 5
crafty
deceptive 2
delicate 4
designing
devious 1
dicey
disingenuous
dodgy
elfin 1
elusive 1
evasive
foxy 1
fraudulent 2
hairy 2
hazardous
insincere
loaded 3
Machiavellian
politic 1
precarious
problematic
profound 1
scheming
serpentine 1
shady 2
shifty
slippery 2
sly 1
smooth 8
sticky 2
subtle 3
tender[1] 4
tight 7
tortuous 2
wily
tricky Dick
impostor
tried and true
constant 1
safe 3
sure 3
trifle°
bauble
dabble 2
trifle *(cont.)*
fiddle 2
fool 6
gewgaw
hair 2
lose 4
mess 4b
modicum
nothing 3
novelty 2
potter
scattering
thought 7
tinker
toy 2,3
trace 2
triviality 2
-trifles
trash 2
trifler
dilettante
trifle with°
at **trifle 3**
dabble 2
fiddle 2
flirt 2
fool 6
play 19a
potter
toy 3
trifling°
frivolous 1
idle 4
immaterial 1
incidental 2
inconsequential
indifferent 4
insignificant
light[2] 6
little 5
meagre 1
meaningless 2
minor 2
minute[2] 2
negligible
niggling 2
nominal 2
paltry
petty 1
pitiful 2
poor 5
puny 1
slender 3
slight 2
small 2,4,5
small-time
tenuous 2
tiny
unimposing
trifocals
glass 7
trig
neat 1
neaten
trim 1
trigger
activate
initiate 1
pioneer 2
precipitate 1
set 20a
spark 2
touch 11b
trip 8
triggered
immediate 1
triggerman
killer 1
trill
chirp 1,2
sing 1
twitter 1,3
trilling
twitter 3
trillions
umpteen
trilogy
trio
trim°
abbreviate 1
abridge
border 1,7
clean 3
clip[2] 1

true (*cont.*)
even 1
exact 1
express 6
factual 1, 2
faithful 1, 2, 4
flush² 1
genuine 1
great 10
historical
hold 11
intrinsic
legitimate 1
level 1
line¹ 19a
literal 2
loyal
natural 6
noble 4
official 1
original 3
perfect 5
physical
precise 1
pure 1
real 1, 2, 3, 4, 5
right 1
rightful 1
self-evident
sincere
solid 4
square 3
staunch 1
steadfast
sterling 1
straight 3
trustworthy
truthful
unmitigated
unqualified 2
veritable
virtuous 2
wash 8
wholehearted

true-blue
conservative 2
solid 5
staunch 1
strong 5
true 2

true-hearted
sincere

true-love
darling 1
dear 3
love 3

true to life
actual 1
factual 1
graphic 1
lifelike
natural 7
photographic 1
realistic 2
truthful
vivid 2

truism°
cliché
maxim
principle 1
proverb
saw

trull
bitch 2
jade 2
prostitute 1

truly°
absolutely 1
actually
bottom 5
completely 3
doubtless 1
effect 5
exactly 2
fact 4
honestly 2
indeed 1
literally 2
perfectly 1
quite 4
really 1
seriously 2
sincerely
substantially
true 4

truly (*cont.*)
truth 3
very 1

trump
discomfit 2
outdo

trumped up
bum 3
phoney 1

trumpet
bawl 1
bellow 1
blare 1
brag
declare 2
proclaim 1
puff 7
rant 1
spread 2
tell¹ 2

trump up
fabricate 3
falsify
stage 5

truncate
abbreviate 1
diminish 1
reduce 1
telescope 2

truncation
abridgement 1

truncheon
club 1
staff 1

trundle
bowl¹
roll 1

trunk°
body 2
case² 1
chest 1
stalk²
stem¹ 1

-trunks
pants 1

truss
brace 1
prop 3
shackle 3
support 8
tie 1, 2

trust°
assurance 3
belief 1
believe 2
combination 2
confidence 1
count 3
credit 1, 3, 5
depend 2
entrust
expect 2
faith 1
fellowship 2
figure 11a
hope 2, 4
lean² 4a
naïvety
obligation 1
pool 3
reckon 4
reliance
rely
responsibility 2
store 5
swear 3
syndicate 1
union 2

trusted
faithful 4
loyal
real 4
reliable
reputable
staunch 1

trustee
guardian

-trustees
board 4

trusteeship
trust 3

trustful
childlike
innocent 4
naïve
trusting

trusting°
childlike
easy 4
ingenuous 1
innocent 4
naïve
unsuspecting

trustworthiness
credit 3
honesty 1
integrity 1
loyalty
probity
responsibility 4
trust 2

trustworthy°
authentic
authoritative 2
certain 2
fair¹ 2
faithful 4
foolproof
good 8
honest 1
honourable 1
ingenuous 2
loyal
noble 4
plausible 1
real 4
reliable
reputable
responsible 2
righteous 1
solid 5
straight 4
sure 2
true 2
truthful
upright 2
virtuous 1

trusty
constant 1
faithful 4
honest 1
honourable 1
loyal
prisoner
reliable
solid 5
staunch 1
sure 2
true 2
trustworthy

truth°
case¹ 8
certainty 1
fact 1
given 4
gospel
principle 1
reality 1
right 10
rope 2
scoop 3

-in truth°
at **truth 3**
actually
bottom 5
effect 5
fact 4
substantially
truly 1, 4

truthful°
authoritative 2
candid 1
faithful 4
frank 1
honest 1
precise 1
real 3
right 2
round 8
sincere
true 1

truthfully
fact 4
honestly 1
indeed 1

truthfully (*cont.*)
true 4
truly 1

truthfulness
honesty 2
sincerity

try°
aim 2
angle²
attempt 1, 2
effort 2
endeavour 1, 2
essay 2, 3
exercise 3
exert 2
experiment 3
fling 3
go 42
pass 27
pester
pretend 2
prosecute 1
prove 2
pursue 3
sample 2
seek 2
shot 3
stab 4
strain¹ 4
strive 1
struggle 1
tackle 3
taste 7
tax 4
test 2
trial 3
undertake 1
wall 3

-without even trying
easily 1

trying°
arduous 1
awkward 5
demanding 1
difficult 4
fraught 2
nerve-racking
tight 7
tiresome 2
wicked 5

trying out
trial 1

try on
assume 2
attempt 1
flirt 2

try one's fortune on
gamble 2

try one's hand at
try 1

try one's luck
adventure 4
gamble 2

try out
apply 6
test 2
try 2

try-out
trial 1

try (some)one's patience
pester
provoke 3

tryst
appointment 1
date 2
meeting 1

tsar
dictator
monarch 1

tub
wash 11

tub-bath
wash 11

tubbiness
fat 5
obesity

tubbing
wash 11

tubby
chubby
dumpy
fat 1
heavy 11
obese
plump¹ 1
rotund 3
stout 1

tube
pipe 1
pipeline 1
roll 12
roller 1
subway 1
television
underground 4

tuber
root¹ 2
seed 1

tub-thumper
preacher
speaker
talker 1

tuchis
bottom 1
bum 1
buttocks
posterior 3

tuck
gather 3
pucker 2

tuckered out
washed out 2

tuft
cluster 1
flake 1
wisp

tug°
drag 1
draw 1
haul 1, 3
heave 1
hitch 2
jerk 1, 3
lug
pluck 4
pull 2, 19
strain¹ 2
tow
wrench 1, 4
yank 1, 2

tugging the forelock
grovelling

tuition°
edification
education 1
instruction 2
preparation 2
schooling

tumble°
collapse 1
fall 2, 22
flop 1
flounder
roll 1
slip¹ 2
spill 5
topple 3
toss 3
trip 5
wallow 1

tumbledown°
decrepit 2
derelict 1
dilapidated
leg 7
old 3
ramshackle
rickety
run-down 2
shabby 3
sordid 4
time-worn

tumbler
glass 4

tumble to°
at **tumble 3**
find 2
twig²
understand 1

tumefaction
hump 1
prominence 3

tumefy
swell 1

tumescence
bump 2
hump 1
lump¹ 2
nub 1
prominence 3
protrusion
swelling

tumescent
protuberant
swollen

tumid
protuberant
swollen

tummler
host¹ 2

tummy
stomach 1

tummy rot
run 50

tumour°
growth 4
swelling

tump
hill 1
hump 1

tumult°
bedlam
bluster 3
chaos
confusion 2
din 1
disorder 2
disturbance 2
excitement 2
flurry 1
fracas 1
furore 1
noise 1
pandemonium
pell-mell 3
racket 1
rampage 1
riot 1
row² 2
rumpus
stir 6
tempest 2
throe
trouble 7
uproar

tumultuous°
chaotic 2
disorderly 2
fierce 2
noisy
obstreperous
pell-mell 2
riotous 1
tempestuous
thunderous
unruly
unsettled 3
uproarious 1
wild 4

tumulus
hump 1
mound 2
tell²

tun
keg

tundra
flat 14b
plain 6

tune°
air 4
jingle 3
measure 9
melody 1
modulate
piece 4
refrain²
song 1
strain¹ 8
tone 6

-in tune
communicate 3
relate 4

typescript
paper 4
typewrite
type 4
Typhoid Mary
carrier 2
typhoon
blow[1] 9
eddy 1
hurricane
storm 1
tempest 1
twister 2
whirlwind 1
typical°
average 3
character 8
characteristic 1
distinctive
exemplary 1
indicative of
natural 1
normal 1
ordinary 1
peculiar 2
proverbial 2
regular 1
regulation 5
representative 1
specific 2
standard 6
symbolic
thick 9
usual
typically
average 2
generally 1
ordinarily
typification
soul 3
typify°
embody 2
exemplify 1
personify 1
represent 4
stand 7a
symbolize
typifying
indicative of
typo
misprint
typographical error
error 1
misprint
tyrannical°
absolute 3
arbitrary 2
authoritarian
bossy
despotic
dictatorial 2
domineering
exacting
hard 4
harsh 2
heavy-handed 2
imperative 2
masterful 2
merciless
oppressive 1
overbearing
peremptory 3
repressive
severe 1
strict 2
totalitarian
tyrannically
severely 2
tyrannize°
browbeat
bully 2
grind 5
intimidate
oppress 2
persecute 1
push 7
railroad 2
ride 3
subjugate
tyrannized
downtrodden
tyrannize over°
at **tyrannize**
oppress 2
tyrannous
tyrannical
tyranny°
despotism
domination 2
monarchy 2
oppression
persecution 1
severity 1
tyrant°
bully 1
despot
dictator
disciplinarian
oppressor
tyro
amateur 1
apprentice 1
greenhorn
initiate 4
learner
newcomer 2
novice
pupil
recruit 2

U

übermensch
superhuman 2
ubiquitous
pervasive
prevalent
universal 1
ubiquitously
everywhere
ubiquitousness
prevalence 1
ubiquity
prevalence 1
uglify
ruin 8
ugly°
awful 1
explosive 1
forbidding 2
frightful 2
ghastly 1
hideous 1
homely 3
monstrous 1
nasty 4
plain 5
repulsive
seamy
ungraceful 2
unsightly
wintry 3
ukase
declaration 2
decree 1
dictate 2
law 1
order 4
precept 1
pronouncement 2
regulation 3
rule 1
warrant 2
ulcer°
sore 7
ulcerate
fester 1
ulcerated
ulcerous
ulceration
ulcer 1
ulcerative
ulcerous
ulcerous°
uliginous
slimy 1
ulterior°
ultimate°
definitive 1,2
eventual 1
extreme 3
ultimate *(cont.)*
final 1
last[1] 3
net[2] 3
primary 2
supreme 2
terminal 1
ultimately°
eventually
finally 1
last[1] 7
length 4a
run 48
soon 5
ultimatum°
challenge 5
dare 3
ultra-°
ultra-conservative
narrow-minded
ultra-conventional
hidebound
ultra-modern
streamlined 2
ultramontane
remote 2
ultramundane
heavenly 1
supernatural
ululate
howl 1
moan 3
ululating
howl 2
ululation
howl 2
umbilicus
navel
umbrage°
umbral
obscure 1
umbrella°
inclusive 1
shade 5
shelter 2
sweeping 1
ump
umpire 1
umpire°
decide 1
intermediary
judge 2,6
mediator
moderator
officiate
peacemaker
umpteen°
umpy
umpire 1
unabashed°
audacious 2
barefaced 2
brazen
cool 6
downright 1
forward 2
frank 1
ingenuous 2
shameless
unabashedly
openly 1
shoulder 6
unabated
complete 1
relentless 2
unmitigated
unable°
incapable 1
incompetent
powerless 1
unabridged°
complete 1
full 12
unaccented°
unaccentuated
unaccented
unacceptable°
exceptionable
inadmissible
ineligible
unacceptable *(cont.)*
out 13
pale[2] 3
poor 4
taboo 1
unbearable
undesirable 2
unlikely 2
unsatisfactory
unthinkable 2
wrong 4
unacceptably
badly 3
unaccepted
unpopular
unwelcome 2
unaccommodating
contrary 2
difficult 3
inflexible
mean[2] 1,4
unaccompanied°
alone 1
lonely 1
solo 1,2
unaccomplished
incomplete
undone[2]
unaccountable°
inexplicable
irresponsible
strange 1
unnatural 5
unaccustomed°
practice 5
strange 2
unfamiliar 2
unused 4
unachievable
impossible 1
impracticable 1
unacknowledged
thankless
unacquainted with
unfamiliar 2
unadaptable
inflexible
rigid 4
unadmitted
sneaking 2
unadorned°
bare 2
blank 2
chaste 2
dry 2
empty 1
matter-of-fact
meagre 3
naked 3
natural 3
neat 3
plain 4
severe 6
simple 2
stark 2
understated
unadulterated
absolute 1
clean 1
immaculate 2
literal 2
naked 3
neat 2
primary 5
pure 1
sheer 2
solid 4
straight 9
true 1
undiluted
unadvertised
unheralded
unadvisable
inept 2
unadvised
inept 2
unaesthetic
tasteless 1
ungraceful 2
unaffected°
above 5
artless 2
blind 4
free 11
homely 1
immune
informal 1,3
ingenuous 1
insensible 2
naïve
natural 4
passive 1
phlegmatic 1
real 3
resistant 1
simple 3
unmoved
unsympathetic
unaffectedly
naturally 3
simply 3
unaffectedness
ease 4
simplicity 3
unaffiliated
independent 6,7
neutral 1
non-aligned
non-partisan 1
unattached 1
unrelated
unafraid
bold 1
brave 1
daring 2
dauntless
gallant 1
indomitable
intrepid
tame 2
unaggressive
meek 2
patient 1
unobtrusive
unagitated
calm 3
quiet 2
silent 1
tranquil
unagreed
open 6
unaided
naked 2
single-handed 1
unaligned
fence 2
independent 4
liberal 2
neutral 1
non-aligned
non-partisan 1
unalike
different 1
dissimilar
unlike 1
unalleviated
unmitigated
unallied
independent 6
neutral 1
non-aligned
unrelated
unallowable
inadmissible
unacceptable
unallowed
inadmissible
unalloyed
absolute 1
barefaced 1
complete 3
entire 1
implicit 2
naked 3
out-and-out
perfect 6
point-blank 1
pronounced 2
pure 1,5
rank[2] 2
regular 9
right 8
unalloyed *(cont.)*
sheer 2
solid 4
straight 9
thorough 1
total 3
undiluted
undisguised
unmitigated
unalterability
finality
resolution 1
unalterable
changeless 1
constant 3
eternal 3
final 2
firm 4
fixed 2
hard 8
immovable 2
incorrigible
indestructible
invariable 2
irreversible
irrevocable
level 3
permanent 2
resolute
rigid 2
stable 2
unavoidable
uniform 1
unaltered
invariable 3
same 2
straight 9
uniform 1
unambiguous
absolute 4
categorical
clear 6
decided 1
definite 3
definitive 3
direct 9
distinct 1
downright 1
emphatic
explicit 1
express 5
flat 4
forthright
graphic 1
honest 3
intelligible
manifest 1
outspoken
plain 2
plump[2] 6
positive 1
precise 1
pronounced 2
specific 1
straight 5
transparent 2,3
unambiguously
completely 3
entirely 2
expressly 1
honestly 2
outright 4
perfectly 1
shoulder 6
simply 5
straight 14
wholly 2
unambiguousness
clarity 2
precision 2
unambitious
meek 1
shiftless
unamiable
unsocial
unanimated
mechanical 3
phlegmatic 1
wooden 2
unanimity
accord 2
agreement 2
harmony 1

unanimity
(*cont.*)
identity 1
solidarity
union 4
unity 1
unanimous
united 3
unannounced
abrupt 1
precipitate 4
spontaneous 1
sudden
unheralded
unofficial
unanswerable
irresponsible
rhetorical 2
unanswered
unresolved
unanticipated
abrupt 1
accidental
precipitate 4
sudden
unaccustomed 1
unforeseen
unheralded
unapologetic
unrepentant
unappealing
uninviting
unappeasable
implacable
mortal 4
unappetizing
bitter 2
disgusting
uninviting
unpalatable
unsavoury
yucky
unapplied
abstract 1
unappreciated
thankless
unappreciative
ungrateful
unappreciative-ness
ingratitude
unapproach-able°
aloof 3
cold 3
cool 5
distant 3
frigid 2, 3
inaccessible 1
standoffish
unapproved
unauthorized
unapt
extraneous 2
incongruous
unbecoming 1
unreasonable 3
untoward 2
unarguable
certain 4
unarm
disarm 1
unarmed°
clean 6
unarranged
unpremeditated
unartificial
artless 1
innocent 4
natural 3
unaffected[1]
unartistic
matter-of-fact
mechanical 3
unascertainable
uncertain 1
unashamed
blatant 1
brazen
forward 2
shameless
unabashed

unashamed
(*cont.*)
unrepentant
unashamedly
openly 1
shoulder 6
unasked°
free 6
gratuitous 2
unsolicited
unwarranted
voluntary 1
unassailable
flawless 2
invincible 2
spotless 2
watertight 2
unasserted
passive 3
unassertive
passive 2
submissive 1
tame 3
unobtrusive
weak 3
unassertiveness
submission 1
unassimilable
foreign 3
unassisted
alone 1
naked 2
single-handed 1
unassociated
unrelated
unassuming
artless 2
bashful 2
childlike
coy
homely 1
humble 1
inconspicuous
informal 1
meek 1
mild 1
modest 1
retiring
simple 2
sweet 4
unaffected[1]
unobtrusive
unassumingly
quietly 4
unattached°
detached 1
disconnected 1
discrete
free 5
loose 1
single 1
unmarried
unattainable
impossible 1
impracticable 1
inaccessible 1
unattended
alone 1
solitary 1
unaccompanied
unattended to
undone[2]
unattentive
absent-minded
unattested
unfounded
unattractive
homely 3
plain 5
seamy
ugly 1
unenviable
ungraceful 2
uninviting
unlikely 2
unpalatable
unsightly
unauthentic
factitious
spurious
unrealistic 2

unauthorized°
illegal
illegitimate 3
unlawful
unofficial
unavailable
attached 4
inaccessible 1
unavailing
bootless
feeble 2
fruitless
futile
helpless 4
hollow 5
hopeless 4
idle 4
impractical 2
ineffectual 1
meaningless 2
non-productive 2
unprofitable 2
unsuccessful 1
useless 1
vain 2
void 1
worthless 2
unavoidability
necessity 2
unavoidable°
automatic 3
certain 3
destined 2
eventual 2
fatal 3
fated 3
hard 8
indispensable 2
inevitable
irresistible 2
necessary 2
sure 4
willy-nilly 2
unavoidably
inextricably
necessarily
unavowed
sneaking 2
unaware°
absent-minded
blind 4
ignorant 2
insensible 2
mindless 2
oblivious
preoccupied 2
unconscious 2
uninformed
unsuspecting
vacant 2
unawareness
ignorance
oblivion 2
vacancy 3
unawares°
nap[1] 2
unawed
unabashed
unbalanced°
crazy 1
deranged
disproportionate
disturbed 2
insane 1
lopsided 1
mad 1
mental 2
one-sided 2
psychotic 1
queer 4
sick 4
unsound 3
unbar
open 21
unbarred
open 1
unbearable°
excruciating
grievous 2
heavy 4
insufferable
irresistible 1
murderous 2
oppressive 1

unbearable
(*cont.*)
overpowering
overwhelming 1
stiff 2
terrible 1
unbeatable°
impregnable
indomitable
invincible 1
unbecoming°
dishonourable 3
dowdy
improper 3
incongruous
indecent 1
undesirable 2
unlikely 2
unprofessional 1
unseemly 1
untoward 2
unworthy 2
wrong 4
unbefitting
below 11
beneath 4
improper 2
inappropriate
unprofessional 1
unreasonable 3
unseemly 2
unbeknownst
unknown 3
unbelievable°
awesome
colossal 2
dreamlike
extraordinary 2
fabulous 2
fantastic 3
far-fetched
flimsy 2
formidable 2
good 2
implausible
improbable
inconceivable
incredible 1
marvellous
miraculous
monumental 4
phenomenal
preposterous
remarkable 1
sensational 1
splendid 3
superb
superhuman 1
tall 3
terrific 2
thin 4
unheard-of 2
unthinkable 1
water 2
weak 4
world 8
unbelievably
pretty 3
terribly
unbeliever
heathen 1
infidel
non-believer
pagan 1
unbelieving°
distrustful
faithless 1
godless 2
incredulous
profane 1
suspicious 2
unbelligerent
peaceable 2
unbemoaned
unlamented
unbend
relax 3
thaw 2
unbendable
rigid 1
stiff 1
unbending
firm 4
formal 1

unbending
(*cont.*)
grim 1
immovable 2
inflexible
merciless
monolithic
perverse 3
precise 2
recalcitrant
relentless 1
rigid 1, 2
rocky[1] 2
severe 1
stalwart 2
stiff 1
straight 1
tough 6
unkind
unbesmirched
pure 2
unbetrothed
unmarried
unbewailed
unlamented
unbiased
candid 2
detached 2
disinterested
dispassionate 2
equitable
even 7
factual 2
fair[1] 1
fence 2
honourable 3
impartial
impersonal 1
independent 4
indifferent 2
just 1
literal 2
neutral 1
non-partisan 2
objective 1
unprejudiced
unbidden
free 6
independent 4
spontaneous 2
unasked
voluntary 1
unbigoted
candid 2
equitable
liberal 3
objective 1
tolerant
unprejudiced
unbind
disengage
free 15
loosen 1
undo 2
unblemished
chaste 1
clear 4
fair[1] 3
flawless 1
immaculate 1, 2
impeccable
innocent 2
intact
pure 2
white 3
unblended
neat 2
undiluted
unblessed
unfortunate 1
unblinking
fixed 2
steady 3
unblock
clear 24
open 22
unblocked
clear 16
navigable 1
open 9
passable 2
unimpeded

unblushing
barefaced 2
shameless
unabashed
unbolt
disengage
open 21
undo 1
unbolted
open 1
unbooked
open 8
unborn
future 2
unbosom
free 16
open 23
unbound
loose 4
unbounded
boundless
endless 1
immeasurable
indefinite 4
inexhaustible 1
limitless
rampant 2
unlimited 2
vast
unbowdlerized
full 12
unabridged 1
unbreakable
indestructible
unbridled
boundless
incontinent 1
promiscuous 2
rampant 1
uninhibited
wild 4
unbroken
complete 1
continual
continuous 1
dead 14
direct 8
entire 2
even 3
flat 1
intact
non-stop 1, 2
ongoing 1
plane 3
relentless 2
savage 1
smooth 1
solid 4, 10
sound[2] 6
standing 3
steady 2
successive
undivided 1
uniform 2
untamed
whole 1
wild 1
unbuckle
disengage
loosen 1
unburden
clear 27
free 16
relieve 2
tell[1] 2
unload
unburdened
clear 32
unburnable
non-flammable
unbutton
loosen 1
undo 1
unbuttoned
undone[1] 2
uncage
free 14
uncalculated
accidental
candid 1
inadvertent 1
random 1

uncalculating
candid 1
uncalled-for
gratuitous 2
groundless
improper 2
inordinate 1
intrusive
irrelevant
misguided
needless 1
non-essential 1
order 13b
superfluous
unreasonable 2
unseemly 2
unsolicited
untoward 2
unwarranted
wanton 4
uncancellable
indelible
uncanny
eerie
ghostly 1
mysterious 1
odd 1
queer 1
strange 1
supernatural
unaccountable 3
unearthly 2
unnatural 5
weird
uncaring
blithe 2
callous
careless 1
cold 3
cold-blooded 2
cold-hearted
half-hearted
heedless
impassive
inattentive
inconsiderate
indifferent 1
lackadaisical 2
listless
phlegmatic 1
promiscuous 1
rocky[1] 3
shiftless
tepid 2
torpid
tough 6
unkind
unsympathetic
wanton 3
unceasing
constant 2
continual
continuous 2
endless 2
eternal 2
everlasting
limitless
mortal 4
non-stop 2
perennial 2
permanent 1
perpetual 1
persistent 2
relentless 2
repetitive
running 3
steady 2
sustained
unceasingly
always 2
end 7b
for ever 2
night 3
non-stop 3
time 11
uncelebrated
unsung
uncensored
full 12
unceremonious
abrupt 3
blunt 2
curt
easy 6
unceremonious (*cont.*)
familiar 3
free 8
informal 1
offhand 1
outspoken
rude 1
unceremoni-ously
freely 1
unceremoni-ousness
familiarity 2
uncertain°
ambiguous 2
anxious 1
arbitrary 1
casual 2
changeable 1
chequered 2
critical 3
debatable
dicey
disorientated
disputable
distrustful
dodgy
doubt 2
doubtful 1, 2
equivocal 2
explosive 1
fence 2
fickle
fluid 3
hairy 2
hazardous
hesitant 1
ill 6
indecisive 1
indefinite 1, 5
insecure 1, 3
irregular 2
irresolute
issue 8
mind 11
obscure 2
parlous
perilous
precarious
problematic
questionable
rocky[2]
shady 2
shaky 1
speculative 2
suspicious 2
tentative 2
ticklish 1
touchy 2
tricky 2
unreliable
unresolved
unsettled 1
vague 2, 5
variable
wishy-washy 1
uncertainty
ambiguity 1
distrust 2
doubt 3
gamble 3
hazard 2
indecision
jeopardy
misgiving
mistrust 2
peril
qualm
quandary
query 2
question 2
suspense 1
suspicion 1
–uncertainties
vicissitude 2
unchain
disengage
emancipate
free 14
release 1
unchained
free 1
loose 2
unchaining
liberation
unchallengeable
inalienable
unchallenged
undisputed
unchangeability
finality
resolution 1
uniformity 1
unchangeable
changeless 1
final 2
firm 4
fixed 2
flat 7
immovable 2
incorrigible
indestructible
inevitable
inflexible
invariable 2
irreversible
irrevocable
obstinate
parochial
permanent 2
resolute
stable 2
unavoidable
uniform 1
unchanged
constant 3
cut 29c
eternal 3
invariable 3
same 2
set 30
stable 2
static 1
sustained
timeless
uniform 1
unchanging
abiding
certain 1, 3
changeless 1, 2
consistent 2
constant 3
cut 29c
equable 2
eternal 3
even 3
firm 4
fixed 2
flat 7
formal 1
humdrum
indestructible
invariable 1
level 3
parochial
permanent 2
perpetual 1
resolute
rocky[1] 2
routine 4
same 2
set 29
stable 2
static 1
steady 2
sustained
tedious
timeless
uniform 1
unchaperoned
unaccompanied
uncharacteristic
character 9
unlike 2
unnatural 3
uncharitable
cold-hearted
intolerant 1
mean[2] 1
merciless
selfish 2
small 4
small-minded
unkind
uncharted°
new 8
trackless
uncharted (*cont.*)
unknown 2
unchaste°
impure 4
lewd
lost 7
obscene 1
promiscuous 2
sensual
wanton 1
unchastity
impurity 3
unchecked
boundless
effusive
frank 1
rampant 1, 2
runaway 2
uncontrolled
unimpeded
uninhibited
unlimited 1
wild 4
unchristian
unkind
uncircum-scribed
universal 2
uncivil
abrupt 3
barbarian 3
beastly 1
blunt 2
brusque
cheeky
coarse 2
crude 3
disagreeable 3
discourteous
disrespectful
gruff 1
harsh 3
ignorant 4
ill-mannered
impertinent
impolite
impudent
insolent
irreverent 2
offensive 2
pert 1
rough 3
rude 1, 2
short 4
surly
tactless
ungracious
unthinking 2
uncivilized°
back 12
barbarian 3
beastly 1
heathen 3
primitive 2
rough 3
rude 1
rugged 4
savage 3
tactless
unrefined 1
wild 3
unclad
bare 1
naked 1
unclarified
unrefined 2
unclasp
disengage
unclassifiable
nondescript
unclassified
nondescript
unclean
dirty 1
filthy 1
foul 2
impure 1, 3
nasty 1
profane 2
sordid 3
unwashed 1
uncleaned
unwashed 1
uncleanness
impurity 1
uncleansed
unwashed 1
unclear
ambiguous 2
cryptic 2
dim 1
doubtful 1
equivocal 2
faint 1
feeble 3
focus 3
fuzzy 2
hazy 2
imperceptible 2
inarticulate 1, 2
indefinite 2
indistinct 1
indistinguish-able 2
light[2] 3
misty
muddy 2
mysterious 2
nebulous
obscure 2
opaque 2
shadowy 2
uncertain 2
vague 1
weak 6
woolly 2
unclearly
vaguely 2
unclinched
open 6
unclog
clear 24
open 22
unclosed
open 1
unclothe
divest 2
strip[2] 2
unclothed
bare 1
naked 1
nude
raw 7
unclouded
bright 2
clear 1, 2, 7
sunny 1
uncloudy
clear 2
unclutter
clean 9
uncluttered
neat 1
open 9
simple 2
smooth 3
uncoerced
optional
uncoil
roll 11
unfold 1
uncoloured
objective 1
uncombed
unkempt
uncomely
homely 3
uncomfortable
awkward 3, 5
bashful 1
cramped
disconcerted
disturbed 1
embarrassed 1
embarrassing
ill 6
insecure 1
oppressive 2
place 12
queasy 1
rocky[1] 1
scene 3
self-conscious
shamefaced 2
small 6
squirm
uncomfortable (*cont.*)
sticky 2
strained
ugly 3
warm 5
uncommitted
end 6
fence 2
independent 6
neutral 1
non-aligned
non-partisan 1
open 8
unattached 2
unmarried
uncommon
deviant 1
distinct 2
eccentric 1
exceptional 1
extraordinary 1
extreme 1
irregular 3
notable 2
noteworthy
odd 1
ordinary 4
out-of-the-way 2
peculiar 1
phenomenal
quaint 1
queer 1
rare[1] 1
raving 2
remarkable 1
singular 1, 3
special 1
strange 1
thin 7
unaccustomed 1
unfamiliar 1
unorthodox
unusual
unwonted
uncommonly
especially 1
extra 6
extremely
notably 1
particularly 1
really 4
very 1
uncommonness
abnormality 1
eccentricity 1
rarity 2
singularity 2
uncommunicat-ive
private 4
reserved
secretive
silent 2
taciturn
tight-lipped
uncommunicat-iveness
silence 2
uncompassion-ate
hard 4
harsh 2
implacable
indifferent 1
inhuman 1
ruthless
unsympathetic
uncomplaining
submissive 1
uncompleted
rough 9
undone[2]
unprepared 2
uncompliant
inflexible
insubordinate
resistant 2
uncomplicated
artless 1
blunt 2
clean 3
easy 1
effortless

understandable (*cont.*)
distinct 1
elementary 1
evident
intelligible
legible
luminous 3
natural 9
plain 2
popular 3
readable 1
simple 1
transparent 2
unprofessional 3
user-friendly
understandably
clear 18
clearly 3
well[1] 3
understanding°
accord 2
acquaintance 1
agreement 1
appreciation 3
bargain 1
brain 1
capacity 2
charitable 2
charity 2
conception 2
contract 1
deal 5
depth 3
familiarity 1
fatherly
feeling 3
grasp 5
grip 3
heart 5
human 3
humanity 3
idea 2
illumination 2
indulgence 1
indulgent
inference
insight
intellect 1
intelligence 1
intelligent
interpretation 2
judgement 1
kind[1]
kindness 1
knowledge 1
lenient
light[1] 5
maternal
mentality 1
negotiation 2
pact
penetration 2
perception 1
picture 3
rapport
rapprochement
realization 1
reason 2
reconciliation 1
rendition 1
sensible 4
sensitivity 3
supportive
surmise 2
sympathetic 1
sympathy 1
tact
tactful
twist 8
uptake
version 2
view 2
vision 2
wisdom 1
wise 1
wit 1
–with the understanding
providing
understated°
modest 3
understood°
given 2
implicit 1
understood (*cont.*)
presumptive 2
silent 3
simple 1
tacit
virtual
understructure
foundation 1
understudy°
alternate 5
double 7
relief 4
second[1] 8
stand 8
stand-by 2
stand-in
substitute 2
undertake°
accept 3
assume 1
attack 3
attempt 1
commit 4
contract 2
endeavour 1
engage 3, 6
enter 4
essay 3
fall 21
go 18, 29a
grip 5
guarantee 2
manage 3
play 2
pledge 4
pretend 2
promise 3
pursue 2
resolve 1
see 12a
seek 2
set 12a
swear 1
take 7, 35c
try 1
wage 2
undertaker°
undertaking°
act 1
action 3
activity 2
adventure 1
affair 1
attempt 2
cause 4
design 5
enterprise 1
expedition 1
guarantee 1
house 4
job 2, 3
labour 3
mission 1
operation 3
proceeding 1
project 2
promise 1
representation 3
resolution 2
stipulation
task 1
try 5
warranty
word 4
work 3
under the counter
furtive 1
unlawful
under the influence°
at **under 6**
drunk 1
stinking 3
tight 8
under the table
drunk 1
furtive 1
unlawful
under the weather°
at **weather 2**
drunk 1
under the weather (*cont.*)
ill 1
indisposed 1
off colour 1
par 5b
poorly 2
ropy 3
seedy 2
sick 2
sort 6
stinking 3
underthings
underclothes
unmentionable 3
undertone
hint 2
murmur 1
overtone
shade 3
undercurrent 2
whisper 3
undertow
undercurrent 1
undervalue
belittle
depreciate 2
disparage 1
disregard 2
minimize 2
miscalculate
trivialize
underestimate
underwater
sunken 2
under 8
under way°
at **way 12**
pipeline 2
progress 4
swing 6
work 5
underwear
underclothes
unmentionable 3
underweight
gaunt 1
light[2] 2
skinny
thin 1
undersized
underwood
brush[1] 1
underworld°
hell 1
infernal 1
underwrite°
back 2a
finance 3
patronize 3
recommend 2
secure 6
sponsor 3
subscribe 1
subsidize
support 4
warrant 3
underwriter
backer 2
underwriting
indemnity 2
subscription 2
subsidy
undescribable
ineffable 2
undescribed
untold 2
undeserved
extravagant 2
unwarranted
undeserving
beneath 4
unworthy 1
undesigned
accidental
inadvertent 1
undesigning
simple 3
undesirable°
unacceptable
unenviable
unpopular
unwelcome 1
undesirable (*cont.*)
wrong 4
undesired
unwelcome 1
undetailed
general 4
meagre 3
thumbnail
unsophisticated 2
undetectable
imperceptible 1
invisible 1
undeterminable
uncertain 1
undetermined
indefinite 1
irresolute
moot 1
pending 2
uncertain 2
unresolved
vague 2
undeterred by
despite
undeveloped°
back 12
childish
crude 2
immature 1
imperfect
incomplete
potential 1
premature 1
primitive 3
rough 9
rudimentary 2
seminal 2
tender[1] 3
undersized
unfledged
vestigial
undeviating
consistent 2
constant 1
direct 6
firm 4
fixed 2
perpetual 1
persistent 1
relentless 1
religious 2
resolute
rigid 2, 3
staunch 1
steady 2
straight 1
strict 1
sure 1
tireless
unhesitating 2
undeviatingly
directly 1
straight 12
undevious
artless 1
undexterous
awkward 1
undies
pants 1
underclothes
unmentionable 3
undifferentiated
indistinguishable 1
monolithic
undignified
base[2] 1, 2
mean[2] 2
unprofessional 1
unrefined 1
unseemly 1
undiluted°
absolute 1
barefaced 1
implicit 2
mere
neat 2
out-and-out
rank[2] 2
straight 9
strong 4
thorough 1
undiluted (*cont.*)
unmitigated
undiminished
complete 1
entire 1
eternal 3
intact
unmitigated
undimmed
full 10
undiplomatic
blunt 2
brash 2
direct 10
indiscreet
inept 2
outspoken
tactless
thoughtless 1
unthinking 2
untoward 2
undirected
aimless 2
meaningless 2
random 1
undiscerning
indiscriminate 1
unreasonable 1
unthinking 1
undisciplined°
boisterous
disorderly 2
naughty 2
obstreperous
rogue 2
uncontrolled
unruly
wanton 2
wild 4
undisclosed
dormant 2
passive 3
private 1
sneaking 2
ulterior 1
untold 2
undiscovered
uncharted
unnoticed
undiscriminating
blind 3
indiscriminate 1
promiscuous 1
unthinking 1
undisguised°
bare 2
barefaced 1
broad 3
naked 3
noticeable 1
outright 2
pronounced 2
transparent 2
undismayed
unabashed
undisputed°
authentic
certain 4
clear 6
decided 1
undissembling
childlike
ingenuous 1
sincere
transparent 3
undistinctive
nondescript
undistinguished°
average 4
common 1
humble 3
inconspicuous
indifferent 3
mediocre
obscure 4
ordinary 2
plebeian 2
prosaic
sort 5
so so
unknown 1
undistorted
factual 2
regular 4
undistracted
undivided 2
undisturbed
calm 3
comfortable 1
cool 2
easy 2
even 4
gentle 1
impassive
level-headed
nonchalant
peaceful 1
phlegmatic 2
sedate 1
self-contained 1
self-possessed
serene 1
silent 1
smooth 1
sound[2] 6
still 1
tranquil
unmoved
undiversified
humdrum
undiverted
undivided 2
undivided°
complete 1
entire 1
intact
one 2
solid 10
undivulged
sneaking 2
untold 2
undo°
detach
disappoint 3
disconnect
disengage
free 15
loose 12
loosen 1
neutralize
open 21
remove 7
reverse 3
ruin 7
undocumented
unofficial
undogmatic
unprejudiced
undoing°
death 3
defeat 4
destruction 3
dissolution 1
downfall
fate 2
ruin 1
undomesticated
savage 1
untamed
wild 1
undone°
disappointed 2
incomplete
undoubted
certain 4
probable
undisputed
unquestionable
undoubtedly°
certainty 3
clearly 2
course 6
definitely
doubtless 1
downright 2
easily 2
evidently 1
far 3
indeed 1
likely 5
manifestly
positively
presumably
probably
question 4

unexcitable
cool 2
dispassionate 1
lackadaisical 2
nonchalant
serene 2
unexcited
cold-blooded 2
collected
cool 2
dispassionate 1
lackadaisical 2
nonchalant
quiet 4
sober 2
temperate 1
tranquil
unenthusiastic
unexcitedly
easy 7
well[1] 8
unexciting
boring
dreary 2
everyday 3
flat 5
humdrum
lacklustre
monotonous
tame 4
tedious
undistinguished
unexpected
abrupt 1
accidental
casual 1
chance 6
character 9
coincidental
freak 5
haphazard 1
odd 1
offbeat
ordinary 4
precipitate 4
shocking 1
sporadic
stray 5
sudden
unaccustomed 1
unforeseen
unheralded
unnatural 3
unusual
upset 12
unexpectedly
extra 6
nap[1] 2
plump[2] 5
short 11
spur 3
suddenly 2
swiftly
unawares 1
unexplainable
inexplicable
miraculous
occult 2
supernatural
unaccountable 1
unexplained
occult 2
unaccountable 1
vague 4
unexplicit
vague 1, 3
unexploded
live 4
unexplored
new 8
trackless
uncharted
unknown 2
unexposed
secure 1
unexpressed
dormant 2
passive 3
silent 3
sneaking 2
tacit
ulterior 1
unexpressive
blank 4
unexpurgated
unabridged 1
unextravagant
reasonable 3
unfactual
false 1
unfading
immortal 3
unfailing
certain 2
constant 1
deadly 6
foolproof
inexhaustible 2
infallible 2
invariable 1
patient 2
perennial 2
perpetual 2
purposeful
relentless 2
reliable
strong 5
sure 3
tireless
untiring
unfailingly
consistently 2
unfair
bum 4
dirty 3
dishonest
disproportionate
foul 7
jaundiced 1
lopsided 2
one-sided 1
partial 2
perverse 1
prejudiced 1
rough 11
tricky 3
unreasonable 2
unwarranted
wrong 1
unfairly
ill 12
unfairness
discrimination 1
grievance 1
inequality 2
injustice 1
prejudice 2
unfaithful
dishonourable 2
disloyal
faithless 2
fickle
perfidious
play 9b
promiscuous 2
run 23
seditious
traitorous
untrue 1
unfaithfulness
inconstancy
infidelity 1
perfidy
unfaltering
constant 1
decided 2
deliberate 2
determined 1
eternal 3
inexhaustible 2
insistent
non-stop 2
patient 2
persistent 1
purposeful
relentless 2
resolute
rocky[1] 2
stalwart 2
staunch 1
steadfast
steady 3
sturdy 2
sure 1
tenacious 1
tireless
unhesitating 2
untiring
unfalteringly
hard 13
surely 2
unfamiliar°
alien 1
exotic 2
foreign 2, 3
ignorant 2
new 4
novel 1
obscure 2, 5
odd 1
ordinary 4
outlandish
rare[1] 1
remote 3
strange 2
unaccustomed 1, 2
uncharted
unheard-of 1
unidentified
unknown 1, 2
unused 4
unwonted
unfamiliarity
ignorance
unfashionable
dowdy
old-fashioned
out 9
passé
unfasten
detach
disengage
free 15
loose 12
loosen 1
open 21
remove 7
undo 1
unfastened
detached 1
free 5
loose 1
open 1, 3
undone[1] 2
unfastening
detachment 1
unfastidious
promiscuous 1
unfathomability
perplexity 2
unfathomable
abysmal 2
abyss
bottomless
dark 6
deep 1, 2
heavy 12
immeasurable
incomprehensible
inestimable 2
infinite 1
mysterious 2
occult 2
opaque 2
perplexing
profound 1
recondite
unaccountable 1
unfathomed
abysmal 2
bottomless
unfavourable
bad 4, 5
contrary 3
destructive 2
detrimental
difficult 4
foul 8
hostile 2
ill 4, 5
inauspicious
inhospitable 2
injurious 1
inopportune
jaundiced 2
low[1] 14
miserable 2
ominous 1
portentous 1
prejudicial
sinister 1
unflattering 2
unfavourable *(cont.)*
unhappy 2
unpromising
untoward 1
unfavourably
amiss 2
badly 2, 7
ill 10, 11
unfearing
brave 1
unfeasible
impracticable 1
water 2
unfeeling
brutal 1
brute 1
callous
cold 3
cold-blooded 2
cold-hearted
dead 2, 4
dull 2
frigid 2
hard 4
harsh 2
heartless
impassive
indifferent 1
inhuman 1
insensible 2
mechanical 3
nail 4b
oblivious
obtuse 2
phlegmatic 1
rocky[1] 3
rough 5
ruthless
senseless 2
severe 1
stony 2
thick-skinned
tough 6
unkind
unmerciful
unmoved
unsympathetic
unfeigned
genuine 2
heartfelt
hearty 2
real 3
sincere
unaffected[1]
undisguised
unfeigning
ingenuous 1
unfenced
open 9
unfertile
non-productive 1
unfetter
disengage
emancipate
free 14
release 1
unfettered
free 1, 2
independent 2
large 5a
liberty 4
loose 2
wild 4
unfettering
liberation
unfilled
empty 1
hollow 1
open 10
vacant 3
void 2
unfinished
coarse 1
crude 2
deficient 1
immature 1
imperfect
incomplete
pending 2
raw 2
rough 9
rude 4
rudimentary 2
unfinished *(cont.)*
sketchy
undone[2]
unprepared 2
unrefined 2
wanting 1
unfit
decrepit 1
helpless 4
hopeless 2
impracticable 2
improper 2
inadequate 2
inappropriate
incapable 1
incompetent
incongruous
indecent 1
ineffective 2
inefficient 1
ineligible
inept 2
mismatched
powerless 1
unable
unbecoming 1
undesirable 2
unlikely 2
unqualified 1
unworthy 1, 2
unfitness
disability 2
impropriety 2
inability
ineptitude 1
unfitting
character 9
extraneous 2
improper 2
inappropriate
incongruous
inept 2
unbecoming 1
unhappy 3
unlikely 2
unprofessional 1
unseemly 2
untoward 2
wrong 4
unfixed
fluid 3
indefinite 1
mobile 1
movable
moving 2
uncertain 4
unsettled 1
vague 2
variable
unflagging
constant 1
fixed 2
incurable 2
indomitable
industrious
inexhaustible 2
laborious 3
persistent 1
relentless 2
resolute
stalwart 2
steadfast
strong 5
tireless
untiring
unflappability
patience 1
sang-froid
serenity 2
stoicism
unflappable
cool 2
dispassionate 1
equable 1
level-headed
nonchalant
poised 1
sedate 1
self-contained 1
self-possessed
serene 2
steady 6
stoical
unflattering°
unfledged°
callow
fresh 3
immature 1
inexperienced
new 6
premature 1
young 2
unflinching
dauntless
determined 1
firm 4
fixed 2
game 8
grim 1
immovable 2
indomitable
manly
rocky[1] 2
stalwart 2
staunch 1
steadfast
steady 3
sure 1
unflinchingly
intently
unfluctuating
certain 1
fixed 2
level 3
steady 2
unflustered
sober 2
unfocused
broad 6
unfold°
bare 7
dawn 4
develop 1
display 2
expand 1
explain 1
extend 1
flower 3
narrate
recount 1
roll 11
spin 2
spread 3
unfolded
open 17
unfolding
development 2
narration 1
ongoing 2
unforbearing
intolerant 1
unforced
optional
spontaneous 2
unforeseeable
casual 1
uncertain 1
unforeseen°
abrupt 1
accidental
casual 1
chance 6
coincidental
freak 5
haphazard 1
sudden
unheralded
unforgettable
historic
memorable
monumental 1
notable 2
outstanding 1
remarkable 2
unforgivable
great 11
inexcusable
monumental 4
unconscionable 2
unforgiving
implacable
merciless
relentless 1
spiteful
stern 1
unmerciful
vindictive

unformed
fluid 3
immature 1
plastic 2
rough 9
shapeless 1
unforthcoming
reserved
reticent
taciturn
tight-lipped
unsocial
unfortified
open 19
unguarded 2
unfortunate°
bad 5
contrary 3
deplorable 1
devil 3
disastrous 2
evil 4
ill 5
inauspicious
inopportune
lamentable
poor 6
regrettable
rough 11
sad 3
sorrowful 2
terrible 3
tragic
unhappy 2, 3
unseemly 2
unsuccessful 1, 2
untoward 1
woebegone
wretch 2
wretched 3
unfortunately
badly 2
ill 10
painfully
sadly 1
unfouled
untarnished
unfounded°
gratuitous 2
groundless
unsound 4
untenable
unfreeze
thaw 1
unfrequented
deserted
desolate 1
isolated 3
out-of-the-way 1
solitary 1
unfresh
stale 1
unfriendliness
chill 3
hostility 1
opposition 1
strife 2
unfriendly
aggressive 1
aloof 3
chilly 2
cold 3
contrary 2
cool 5
disagreeable 3
distant 3
dour 1
forbidding 2
frigid 2
gaunt 2
hard 9
harsh 2
hostile 2
icy 2
ill 3
impersonal 2
inhospitable 1
jaundiced 2
misanthropic
personal 4
pugnacious
shabby 2
spiteful
standoffish
unfriendly (*cont.*)
stiff 7
unapproachable 1
unsocial
wintry 3
unfrivolous
no-nonsense
unfrock
degrade 1
unfruitful
barren 2
dead 8
fruitless
idle 4
ineffective 1
infertile
lean[1] 2
meagre 4
non-productive 1
poor 3
sterile 1
unprofitable 1
unsuccessful 1
unfulfilled
dissatisfied
unfulfilment
disappointment 1
non-completion
unfurl
display 2
open 24
roll 11
spread 3
unfold 1
unfurnished
bare 3
empty 1
unfussy
promiscuous 1
ungainful
unprofitable 1
ungainliness
ineptitude 1
ungainly
awkward 1, 2
bulky
clumsy
hulking
inept 1
rustic 2
ungraceful 1
unwieldy
wooden 2
ungallant
ill-mannered
rude 1
ungenerous
little 6
mean[2] 1
penurious 1
possessive 1
selfish 2
shabby 2, 4
small 4
small-minded
ungentle
rough 5
ungentleman-like
unrefined 1
ungentlemanli-ness
incivility
ungentlemanly
broad 8
discourteous
ill-mannered
impolite
rough 3
rude 1
shabby 2
tactless
unbecoming 2
ungracious
unrefined 1
unseemly 1
untoward 2
vulgar 1
ungenuine
insincere
spurious
ungermane
inappropriate
ungiving
possessive 1
tough 6
unglorified
unsung
ungodliness
sin 2
ungodly°
godless 1
impious
irreverent 1
profane 1
satanic 1
sinful
unearthly 3
wicked 1
ungovernable°
disobedient 1
disorderly 2
incontinent 1
irresistible 1
mutinous 2
naughty 2
problem 3
rebellious 2
recalcitrant
resistant 2
rogue 2
self-willed
unruly
violent 1
wanton 2
wild 4
wilful 2
ungoverned
disorderly 2
incontinent 1
promiscuous 2
uncontrolled
wanton 2
ungraceful°
awkward 2
clumsy
heavy 8
heavy-handed 1
hulking
provincial 2
rugged 4
stilted
ungracious°
blunt 2
brusque
discourteous
ill-mannered
impolite
inconsiderate
merciless
offhand 2
rough 3
rude 1
terse 2
unrefined 1
ungrammatic-ality
misuse 2
ungrateful°
ungratefulness
ingratitude
ungratified
dissatisfied
ungregarious
private 4
ungroomed
unkempt
ungrounded
gratuitous 2
ungrown
unfledged
ungrudging
generous 1
philanthropic
profuse 1
selfless
unselfish
ungrudgingly
freely 4
readily 1
willingly
unguarded°
defenceless
insecure 2
unguarded (*cont.*)
spontaneous 2
unwary
vulnerable
-in an unguarded moment
nap[1] 2
unawares 2
unguent
lotion
oil 1
ointment
salve 1
unhallowed
impure 3
profane 2
unhampered
free 10
open 4
unimpeded
unhandy
awkward 1
clumsy
unwieldy
unhappily
painfully
sadly 1, 2
unhappiness
depression 2
desolation 2
discontent
disfavour 1
dissatisfaction 1
distress 1
grief 1
hardship
melancholy 2
misery 1
prostration 3
resentment
sadness
sorrow 1
woe
unhappy°
afraid 2
bad 9
bleak 1
blue 1
dejected
desolate 3
despondent
disappointed 1
disgruntled
dismal
dissatisfied
doleful
dreary 1
forlorn 1
funereal
gloomy 2
heartbroken
heavy 6
hopeless 3
hurt 7
joyless 1
low[1] 8
melancholy 1
miserable 1
moody 1
mournful 1
mouth 6
pessimistic
regrettable
resentful
sad 1
sombre 1
sorrowful 1
sunless
terrible 3
tragic
unfortunate 2
woebegone
wretched 2
unharmed
intact
safe 1
unscathed
whole 2
unharmonious
grating 1
harsh 1
strident
unharmonious (*cont.*)
ungraceful 2
unhealthful
unwholesome 1
unhealthy°
bad 2
delicate 3
diseased
harmful
ill 1
indisposed 1
injurious 1
low[1] 4
morbid 1
par 5b
peaky
run-down 1
sick 2
unsound 2
unwholesome 1
virulent 1
unheard
inaudible
unnoticed
unheard-of°
different 2
extraordinary 1
inconceivable
nameless 1
new 4
obscure 4
outlandish
out-of-the-way 2
phenomenal
strange 1
unaccountable 3
unearthly 3
unknown 1
unhearing
deaf 2
unheated
cold 2
cool 1
unheedful
absent-minded
deaf 2
unconscious 2
unheeding
absent-minded
inconsiderate
remiss
unconscious 2
unhelpful
shabby 2
unheralded°
unhesitant
resolute
unhesitating 1
unhesitating°
decided 2
deliberate 2
determined 1
immediate 1
non-stop 2
prompt 1, 2
resolute
unhesitatingly
cold 11
firmly 2
flat 17b
immediately 1
outright 4
plump[2] 5
promptly
readily 1
right 13
summarily 1
surely 2
willingly
unhidden
obvious
unhindered
free 10
open 4
unimpeded
unhinged
crazy 1
delirious 1
deranged
insane 1
mad 1
psychotic 1
unhinged (*cont.*)
queer 4
unbalanced 2
wild 5
unhip
square 6
unhitch
disconnect
disengage
unholster
draw 2
unholy
godless 1
impious
irreverent 1
profane 2
satanic 1
sinful
unhonoured
unsung
unhook
disconnect
disengage
loosen 1
separate 1
undo 1
unhooked
undone[1] 2
unhoped for
unforeseen
unhorse
overthrow 1
unhoused
homeless 1
unhurried°
deliberate 2
easy 2, 5
measured 1
slow 1, 3
unhurriedly
leisure 3b
slow 11
unhurt
safe 1
unscathed
whole 2
unhygienic
unwholesome 1
unidentifiable
nameless 2
unidentified°
incognito 1
nameless 1
unheard-of 1
unknown 1, 2
unsung
unification
amalgamation
embodiment 2
solidarity
synthesis
unity 3
unified
inclusive 1
one 2
united 1
uniform°
changeless 1
consistent 2
constant 3
costume
equable 2
equal 2
even 1, 2, 3
garments
gear 3
habit 3
homogeneous
invariable 1
level 1, 3
measured 3
monolithic
orderly 1
parallel 1
piece 8
plane 3
regular 2, 3, 5
robe 2
same 2
smooth 2
solid 4
steady 2
suit 3

uniform (*cont.*)
sustained
symmetrical
uniformity°
equality 1
order 2
parity 1
regularity 1
symmetry
unity 1, 2
uniformly
alike 2
consistently 1, 2
universally
unify°
combine 1
coordinate 2
embody 3
gang 3
incorporate
join 1
marry 2
solidify 2
stick[1] 16a
unite 1, 2
unifying
synthesis
unilateral
one-sided 3
unilluminated
dark 1
dusky 2
unimaginable
impossible 1
incomprehensible
inconceivable
incredible 1
unbelievable
unheard-of 2
unlikely 1
unthinkable 1
untold 3
unimaginative
banal
everyday 3
lacklustre
literal 3
little 6
matter-of-fact
mediocre
near-sighted 2
pedestrian 2
prosaic
routine 4
short-sighted 2
slow 7
small 3
small-minded
square 6
stodgy
stupid 3
tired 3
usual
unimagined
unheard-of 2
unimpaired
entire 2
flawless 1
intact
sound[2] 1
whole 2
unimpassioned
cold-blooded 2
icy 2
philosophical 2
temperate 1
wooden 2
unimpeach-ability
rectitude
unimpeachable
blameless
correct 8
faultless
flawless 2
impeccable
incorrupt 1
innocent 1
irreproachable
respectable 1
unquestionable
upright 2
unimpeded°
clear 16
free 10
open 4
unimperilled
secure 1
unimportance
indifference 2
inferiority 1, 2
obscurity 3
triviality 1
unimportant
circumstantial 2
expendable
fluffy 2
frivolous 1
humble 3
idle 4
immaterial 1
incidental 2
inconsequential
indifferent 4
inferior 2
insignificant
light[2] 6
little 5
meaningless 2
minor 2
minute[2] 2
negligible
niggling 2
non-essential 1
obscure 4
paltry
peripheral 1
petty 1
pitiful 2
point 15
punk 2
puny 1
secondary 1
shallow 1
side 8
skin-deep
small 2
small-time
superficial 2
thin 2
trifling
triviality 2
unimposing
venial
wee 2
worthless 1
unimportunate
modest 3
unimposing°
unimpressed
blasé 1
lackadaisical 2
unaffected[2]
unenthusiastic
unimpression-able
impassive
unimpressive
decent 3
undistinguished
unimposing
unincumbered
open 4
unindulgent
intolerant 1
uninfected
clean 1
pure 2
sterile 2
uninfluenced
unaffected[2]
uninformed°
benighted
ignorant 1
inexperienced
provincial 2
unaware
unfamiliar 2
uninhabitable
inhospitable 2
uninhabited°
desert[1] 2
deserted
desolate 1
empty 2, 3
uninhabited (*cont.*)
free 3
lifeless 4
lonely 2
vacant 1
wild 2
uninhibited°
abandoned 2
bawdy
direct 10
earthy
forthright
frank 1
free 9
honest 3
ingenuous 2
liberty 4, 5
open 16
outspoken
promiscuous 2
rampant 1, 2
raw 6
riotous 2
uninitiated
inexperienced
tender[1] 3
unaccustomed 2
unfamiliar 2
unused 4
young 2
uninjured
intact
safe 1
sound[2] 1
unscathed
whole 2
uninspired
colourless 2
dry 2
dull 4
indifferent 3
lackadaisical 2
mechanical 3
mediocre
ordinary 2
pale[1] 3
pedestrian 2
prosaic
shiftless
small 3
stupid 3
tame 4
uninspiring
colourless 2
dull 4
lifeless 3
pedestrian 2
prosaic
tame 4
uninstructed
uninformed
unintelligent
brute 1
opaque 3
senseless 3
slow 7
stupid 1
wooden 3
unintelligibility
obscurity 2
opacity 2
unintelligible
disconnected 2
illegible
inarticulate 1, 2
incoherent
incomprehensible
indistinct 1
inexplicable
misty
rambling 1
unaccountable 1
unintended
accidental
inadvertent 1
unintentional
accidental
chance 6
inadvertent 1
involuntary
unconscious 2
unintentionally
chance 5a
unawares 2
uninterested
casual 3
cool 4
dead 4
half-hearted
indifferent 1
lackadaisical 2
negative 2
nonchalant
offhand 1
passive 1
perfunctory 1
phlegmatic 1
stolid
supine 2
tepid 2
unenthusiastic
uninteresting
bland 2
boring
colourless 2
dead 12
dreary 2
dry 2
dull 4
flat 5
heavy 7
humdrum
irksome
lacklustre
lifeless 3
monotonous
nondescript
pedestrian 2
prosaic
routine 4
slow 9
stodgy
stupid 3
tame 4
tedious
tiresome 1
vapid
uninterrupted
constant 2
continual
continuous 1
direct 7
endless 2
entire 3
eternal 2
even 3
flat 1
non-stop 1, 2
ongoing 1
perennial 1
perpetual 2
plane 3
regular 5
repetitive
running 3
smooth 3
solid 10
sound[2] 6
steady 2
successive
uninterruptedly
end 7b
non-stop 3
succession 5
uninvestigated
unknown 2
uninvited
intruder 1
unasked
unsolicited
unwelcome 1
uninviting°
inhospitable 1, 2
uninvolved
cool 4
detached 2
disinterested
neutral 1
non-partisan 1
outside 9
passive 1
perfunctory 1
phlegmatic 1
simple 1
unsophisticated 2
union°
alliance 1
amalgamation
association 1
bond 3
brotherhood 2
club 2
combination 1, 2
connection 1
federation
fellowship 2
fraternity 3
group 1
joint 1
junction
league 1
marriage 3
match 3
meeting 3
merger
ring[1] 3
sex 2
society 5
splice 2
synthesis
wedding 2
union card
card 6
unique°
alone 2
different 2
distinct 2
distinctive
eccentric 1
exclusive 1, 3
exotic 2
extraordinary 1
freak 5
individual 2
isolated 1
kinky 1
matchless
new 1, 4
noteworthy
odd 1
optimum 2
ordinary 4
original 4
outlandish
peculiar 1, 2
peerless
picturesque 1
pre-eminent 2
priceless 1
proper 6
rare[1] 1
remarkable 2
salient
signal 3
single 2
singular 3
sole
special 1
specific 2
superlative
transcendent
unparalleled
unusual
uniquely
especially 1
notably 1
particularly
pre-eminently
uniqueness
distinction 2
eccentricity 1
identity 2
novelty 1
originality
rarity 2
singularity 1
unison°
tune 2
-in unison°
at **unison**
one 2
time 12b
unit°
cabal 2
cohort 1
corps
denomination 2
department 1
division 3
element 1
unit (*cont.*)
group 1
organ 1
outfit 3
package 2
part 7
party 2
platoon
point 13
squad
-units
fitting 2
unitary
individual 2
self-contained 3
unite°
add 1
ally 2
amalgamate
assemble 2
associate 1a
attach 1
band[2] 3
blend 2
bracket 4
bridge 4
cement 2
close 8b
combine 1, 3
compound 2
connect 1, 3
converge
cooperate 1
couple 3
embody 3
fuse
gang 3
hang 11a
hitch 1
incorporate
integrate
join 1
knit 1
league 3
link 3
lump[1] 3
marry 2
match 5
mate 4
meet[1] 4
merge
mingle 1
mix 1
package 3
pair 2
piece 13
reconcile 1
solidify 2
splice 1
stick[1] 4, 16a
tack 5
team 3
tie 1, 3
unify
weave 2
wed 1, 2
weld 1
united°
affiliated
attached 2
kindred 1
league 2
one 2
shoulder 5
uniting
addition 1
amalgamation
connection 1
union 1
unity 3
wedding 2
unity°
agreement 2
alliance 1
entirety 1
fraternity 2
harmony 1
integrity 2
morale
solidarity
sympathy 2
union 1, 4
universal°
catholic
common 5

universal (*cont.*)
encyclopedic
epidemic 1
extensive 1
general 1
global
going 2
international
normal 1
pervasive
popular 2
prevailing 1
prevalent
public 1
reign 3
standard 6
staple 2
sweeping 1
thorough 3
universality
generality 2
prevalence 1
–universalities
generality 2
universally°
everywhere
popularly
widely 1
universe°
creation 2
nature 2
world 1
university
institution 2
school 1
seminary
unjaundiced
liberal 3
objective 1
unprejudiced
unjust
foul 7
one-sided 1
rough 5, 11
tricky 3
tyrannical
unconscionable 1
unreasonable 2
unwarranted
wrong 1
unjustifiable
excessive 1
exorbitant
extravagant 2
gratuitous 2
groundless
inexcusable
leg 6
unfounded
unreasonable 2
untenable
wanton 4
unjustifiably
unduly 1
unjustified
bum 3
exorbitant
extravagant 2
gratuitous 2
groundless
ill-founded
inexcusable
unfounded
unreasonable 2
untenable
unwarranted
wanton 4
unjustly
ill 12
unjustness
injustice 1
unkempt°
disreputable 2
dowdy
filthy 2
mangy
ragged 1
ratty 2
shaggy
sloppy 1
untidy
wild 8
unkind°
bitter 5
brutal 1
cold-hearted
cruel 1
hard 4
harsh 2
heartless
hurtful 2
ill 3
inhuman 1
mean[2] 4
sharp 5
unmerciful
unkindly
badly 6
ill 3, 11, 12
inhuman 1
roughly 2
unkind
unkindness
disservice
unkink
straighten 1
unknowing
ignorant 1
unaware
unsuspecting
unknowingly
unawares 2
unknowledge-able
uninformed
unknown°
foreign 3
incognito 1
indefinite 4
mysterious 2
nameless 1
new 4, 8
nobody 2
obscure 4
occult 3
outlandish
strange 2
uncharted
unfamiliar 1
unheard-of 1
unidentified
unsung
unlace
disengage
loosen 1
undo 1
unlaced
undone[1] 2
unladylike
broad 8
discourteous
ill-mannered
impolite
rough 3
rude 1
shabby 2
tactless
unbecoming 2
ungracious
unrefined 1
unseemly 1
untoward 2
vulgar 1
unlamented°
unlatch
disengage
open 21
unlatched
open 1
unlawful°
criminal 1
crooked 1
illegal
lawless 2
taboo 1
unauthorized
wrong 1
unlearned
ignorant 1
philistine 2
uncivilized 2
unleash
disengage
loose 13
wreak
unlessened
unmitigated
unlettered
ignorant 1
illiterate
philistine 2
uneducated
unlicensed
unlawful
unlifelike
unrealistic 2
unlighted
dark 1
pitch-black
sunless
unlike°
different 1
dissimilar
unlikeable
obnoxious
unliked
unpopular
unlikely°
fantastic 3
far-fetched
fishy 2
implausible
improbable
incredible 1
off 5
outside 8
remote 3, 6
slender 2
slight 1
unthinkable 2
unlikeness
difference 1
dissimilarity
diversity 1
unlimited°
absolute 3
bottomless
boundless
clear 14
dictatorial 1
endless 1
immeasurable
implicit 2
indefinite 4
independent 5
inexhaustible 1
infinite 1
inordinate 2
limitless
sovereign 2
universal 1, 2
untold 1
vast
unlinked
unrelated
unlit
dark 1
dusky 2
obscure 1
out 14
pitch-black
sunless
unload°
discharge 7
dump 1
empty 8
foist
tip[2] 3
unloading
discharge 14
unlock
disengage
free 15
open 21
puzzle 3
undo 1
unlocked
open 1
unlooked-for
chance 6
gratuitous 2
haphazard 1
incidental 1
unforeseen
unsolicited
unloose
disengage
free 14
unloose (*cont.*)
release 1
relinquish 2
unloosing
release 3
unloved
unlamented
unpopular
unlovely
homely 3
plain 5
ugly 1
ungraceful 2
unsightly
unluckily
badly 2
ill 10
sadly 1
unlucky
accidental
bad 5
coincidental
contrary 3
disastrous 2
evil 4
ill 5
inauspicious
poor 6
regrettable
rough 11
sorrowful 2
tragic
unfortunate 1
unhappy 2
unsuccessful 2
unmaintainable
untenable
unman
discourage 1
unmanageable
difficult 3
disobedient 1
disorderly 2
heavy 2
irrepressible
irresistible 1
mutinous 2
naughty 2
obstreperous
problem 3
rebellious 2
recalcitrant
resistant 2
riotous 1
rogue 2
self-willed
ungovernable
unruly
unwieldy
wanton 2
wild 4
unmandatory
optional
unmanful
soft 12
unmanly
effeminate
feminine 2
soft 12
unmannerliness
disrespect
incivility
indelicacy
unmannerly
brusque
discourteous
disrespectful
offensive 2
pert 1
rude 1
rustic 2
uncivilized 2
ungracious
unrefined 1
unmanoeuv-rable
unwieldy
unmapped
uncharted
unmarked
unidentified
unnoticed
unscathed
unmarred
pure 2
sound[2] 1
unmarried°
celibate 1
eligible 2
maiden 2
single 1
unattached 2
unmasculine
feminine 2
unmask
bare 7
expose 1
unmasking
exposure 1
unmatched
matchless
notable 2
odd 4
peerless
perfect 2
star 3
surpassing
towering 1
unique 2
unparalleled
unmatured
unfledged
unmeasurable
imponderable
unmeet
incongruous
unmelodious
discordant 2
strident
unmentionable°
ineffable 1
nameless 3
profane 3
scandalous 1
taboo 1
unmention-ables°
at **unmention-able 3**
underclothes
unmerciful°
cold-hearted
cutthroat 2
merciless
relentless 1
remorseless 1
ruthless
savage 2
unmercifully
roughly 2
unmerited
unwarranted
unworthy 1
unmethodical
chaotic 1
desultory
indiscriminate 2
irregular 2
uncertain 4
unmindful
absent-minded
careless 2
heedless
improvident 2
inattentive
inconsiderate
oblivious
reckless
remiss
short-sighted 2
unaware
unconscious 2
unmissed
unlamented
unmistakable
apparent 1
clear 6
conspicuous 2
decided 1
direct 9
distinct 1
emphatic
evident
explicit 1
express 5
flat 4
unmistakable (*cont.*)
graphic 1
keen[1] 4
manifest 1
marked
naked 3
noticeable 1
observable
obvious
outright 1, 2
patent 2
perceptible
plain 2
plump[2] 6
pointed 2
positive 1
prominent 1
pronounced 1, 2
self-evident
strong 7
transparent 2
undisguised
undisputed
unquestionable
visible 1
unmistakably
expressly 1
manifestly
obviously
perfectly 1
positively
simply 5
undoubtedly
unmistaken
infallible 1
keen[1] 4
unmitigated°
absolute 2, 3
barefaced 1
complete 3
direct 9
implicit 2
mere
naked 3
out-and-out
outright 2
peremptory 2
perfect 6
point-blank 1
positive 9
pronounced 2
proper 5
pure 5
rank[2] 2
regular 9
right 8
sheer 2
stark 4
thorough 1
thumping 2
total 3
ultra-
undisguised
unqualified 2
wholehearted
unmitigatedly
downright 2
point-blank 3
unmixed
absolute 1
blank 6
clean 1
complete 3
entire 1
mere
naked 3
neat 2
primary 5
pronounced 2
pure 1
sheer 2
solid 4
straight 9
thorough 1
undiluted
unmitigated
unmoderated
unmitigated
unmodifiable
flat 7
invariable 2
unmodified
flat 7
invariable 3

unmodified
(*cont.*)
same 2
straight 9
unmitigated
unmollifiable
implacable
unmollified
raw 6
unmitigated
unmoral
perverted
unmotivated
shiftless
unmourned
unlamented
unmovable
firm 2
immovable 1, 2
unmoved°
blasé 2
blind 4
calm 4
cold 3
cold-blooded 2
deaf 2
dispassionate 1
grim 1
immovable 2
impassive
insensible 2
lackadaisical 2
lukewarm 2
merciless
passive 1
phlegmatic 1
relentless 1
stern 1
unaffected[2]
unsympathetic
unmoving
cold 5
dead 11
dormant 1
grim 1
inactive 1
inanimate
lifeless 2
obstinate
passive 1
quiet 4
relentless 1
sedentary
stagnant
standing 2
static 1
still 1
unmusical
discordant 2
noisy
rough 8
strident
unnamed
certain 6
nameless 1
obscure 4
unidentified
unknown 1
unnarrated
untold 2
unnatural°
abnormal 2
affected 1
artificial 1, 3
false 3
forced
genteel 1
ghostly 1
irregular 3
kinky 2
laboured 2
mannered
perversion 2
perverted
queer 1
stilted
strained
supernatural
theatrical 2
unearthly 1
unrealistic 2
weird
wooden 2
unnaturalness
oddity 1
unnecessarily
unduly 1
unnecessary°
dispensable
expendable
expletive 1
extraneous 1
needless 1
non-essential 1
peripheral 1
redundant 1
superfluous
unwarranted
unneeded
dispensable
expletive 1
extraneous 1
needless 1
non-essential 1
redundant 1
superfluous
unnecessary
unnegotiable
inalienable
unnerve°
agitate 1
alarm 3
appal
daunt
demoralize 3
discomfit 1
discourage 1
dismay 1
frighten
panic 3
perturb
rattle 3
rock[2] 3
ruffle 3
shake 5
shatter 3
throw 4
unnerved
agitated
insecure 1
panic-stricken
unsettled 2
upset 8
unnerving
disconcerting
frightening
harrowing
scary
unsettling
unnoted
unnoticed
unnoticeable
imperceptible 2
inconspicuous
obscure 3
unnoticed°
background 3
inconspicuous
obscure 3, 4
unsung
unnumbered
umpteen
untold 1
unobjectionable
innocent 3
inoffensive
unobjective
near-sighted 2
prejudiced 1
unobscured
full 10
unobservant
careless 2
heedless
inadvertent 2
inattentive
unobserved
unnoticed
unobstruct
open 22
unobstructed
clear 16
direct 7
fair[1] 6
free 10
navigable 1
unobstructed
(*cont.*)
open 4, 9
passable 2
smooth 3
unobstructedly
freely 5
unobtainable
inaccessible 1
unobtrusive°
background 3
inconspicuous
modest 1, 2
quiet 3
unobtrusively
quietly 4
unoccupied
deserted
empty 2
end 6
free 3
idle 1
inactive 2
leisure 3a, 5
lifeless 4
spare 2
unemployed
uninhabited
vacant 1, 3
void 2
unoffending
inoffensive
unofficial°
informal 2
private 1
record 8
unauthorized
unofficially
record 8
unopened°
unopinionated
liberal 3
unoppressive
easy 2
unordered
random 1
unorganized
chaotic 1
desultory
disjointed 2
disorderly 1
indiscriminate 2
order 13a
promiscuous 3
purposeless
rambling 1
random 1
slipshod
unsettled 3
unoriginal
banal
cut 29b
derivative 1
dull 4
hack[2] 4
ready-made 3
secondary 2
small 3
stale 2
tired 3
usual
unornamented
blank 2
neat 3
unadorned
unorthodox°
Bohemian
eccentric 1
erratic 2
fresh 2
heretical
kinky 1
offbeat
peculiar 1
phenomenal
quaint 1
queer 1
special 1
unaccountable 3
unusual
unwonted
way-out 2
unorthodoxy
originality
unostentatious
bashful 2
humble 1
inconspicuous
modest 2
plain 4
simple 2
unobtrusive
unostenta-tiously
quietly 4
unpacifiable
implacable
unpack
unload
unpaid°
amateur 2
delinquent 3
due 1
outstanding 2
payable
unpaired
odd 4
unpalatable°
bitter 2
disagreeable 2
distasteful
flat 8
obnoxious
obscene 2
offensive 3
repugnant
seamy
unsavoury
vapid
unparalleled°
alone 2
extraordinary 1, 2
first-rate
freak 5
incomparable
marvellous
matchless
notable 2
odd 1
peerless
phenomenal
prime 2
queer 1
rare[1] 1
star 3
supreme 4
towering 1
transcendent
unbeatable
unique 2
unpardonable
inexcusable
unconscionable 2
unparticular
indiscriminate 1
unpatriotic
disloyal
unpeopled
desert[1] 2
deserted
uninhabited
unperceivable
intangible
unperceived
invisible 2
unnoticed
unperceiving
unreasonable 1
unthinking 1
unperceptive
unreasonable 1
unthinking 1
unperfumed°
unpersuaded
unbelieving
unpersuasive
lame 2
weak 4
unperturbed
collected
cool 2
level-headed
nonchalant
passive 1
philosophical 2
unperturbed
(*cont.*)
phlegmatic 2
quiet 2
sedate 1
self-contained 1
self-possessed
serene 1
sober 2
temperate 1
tranquil
unpin
undo 1
unpinned
undone[1] 2
unpitying
ruthless
unmerciful
unsympathetic
unplanned
abrupt 1
accidental
casual 1
chance 6
extemporaneous
impetuous
impulsive
inadvertent 1
incidental 1
rambling 2
random 1
scratch 6
snap 13
spontaneous 1
unpremeditated
unpleasant
abominable 2
awful 2
awkward 5
bad 4, 5
beastly 2
bitter 2, 5
disagreeable 1
distasteful
evil 5
forbidding 2
hard 5, 9
harsh 3
horrible 2
mean[2] 5
miserable 2
nasty 2, 4
nauseous
obnoxious
painful 2
repugnant
repulsive
revolting
rough 3, 7
shabby 2
sour 3, 4
surly
terrible 3
tiresome 2
truculent
ugly 2, 4
unacceptable
uninviting
unpalatable
unsavoury
unwelcome 1
warm 5
unpleasantly
painfully
unpleasantness
exchange 3
ill 8
trouble 5
word 9a
unpleasing
disagreeable 1
distasteful
unwelcome 1
unplentiful
short 9
thin 2
unplighted
unmarried
unplug
tap[2] 6
unplumbable
bottomless
opaque 2
unpoetic
matter-of-fact
prosaic
unpointed
obtuse 1
unpolished
coarse 2
crude 2
flat 12
homespun
plebeian 2
primitive 3
provincial 2
rough 9
rude 1, 4
rugged 4
rustic 2
sketchy
uncivilized 2
unrefined 1
unpolluted
clean 1
fresh 7
innocent 2
pristine 2
pure 2
safe 2
sanitary
sterile 2
unspoiled
unpopular°
lonesome 1
unpopulated
uninhabited
wild 2
unposed
candid 3
unpractical
abstract 1
academic 2
romantic 2
speculative 1
useless 1
visionary 1
wild 7
unpractised
artless 3
practice 5
unaccustomed 2
undisciplined
unfamiliar 2
unused 4
unpraised
unsung
unprecedented
extraordinary 1
original 4
phenomenal
seminal 1
unaccustomed 1
unheard-of 2
unusual
unwonted
unpredictability
vicissitude 1, 2
unpredictable
arbitrary 1
capricious
casual 1
changeable 1
coincidental
dicey
doubtful 1
erratic 1
explosive 1
fickle
freak 5
hazardous
hot 10
impulsive
incidental 1
inconsistent 2
moody 3
precarious
rogue 2
temperamental 2
uncertain 1, 3
undisciplined
unsettled 1
unstable 1
variable
whimsical 2

unpredicted
coincidental
freak 5
unforeseen
unheralded
unprejudiced°
candid 2
detached 2
disinterested
dispassionate 2
equitable
even 7
factual 2
fair[1] 1
fence 2
generous 2
honourable 3
impartial
impersonal 1
independent 4
indifferent 2
just 1
liberal 3
literal 2
non-partisan 2
objective 1
tolerant
unpremeditated°
accidental
candid 1
casual 1
chance 6
extemporaneous
impetuous
impulsive
inadvertent 1
involuntary
natural 4
offhand 3
random 1
scratch 6
snap 13
spontaneous 1
unconscious 2
unpremeditatedly
random 2
spur 3
unprepared°
cold 7
extemporaneous
raw 1
scratch 6
spontaneous 1
undisciplined
unpremeditated
unqualified 1
unprepossessing
humble 3
ugly 1
unsightly
unpresuming
humble 1
modest 1
unobtrusive
unpretended
undisguised
unpretending
naïve
unpretentious
artless 2
coy
homely 1
humble 1
informal 1, 3
meek 1
modest 1, 2
naïve
natural 3
ordinary 2
retiring
simple 2, 3
small 4
unaffected[1]
undistinguished
unobtrusive
unpretentiously
naturally 3
quietly 4
simply 3
unpretentiousness
humility
naïvety
unpretentiousness (*cont.*)
simplicity 3
unpretty
unsightly
unpreventable
inevitable
unprincipled
abandoned 2
black 6
cutthroat 2
dishonest
dishonourable 2
evil 2
immoral 1
miscreant 2
opportunistic
perverted
profligate 1
reprobate 1, 2
rotten 3
shameful
unconscionable 1
unprofessional 1
unscrupulous
venal
vicious 1
wicked 1
unprintable
profane 3
unprocessed
crude 1
raw 2
rough 9
unrefined 2
unproductive
barren 2
bootless
dead 8
fruitless
futile
idle 4
ineffective 1
ineffectual 1
infertile
lean[1] 2
meagre 4
non-productive 1
pointless
poor 3
slow 6
sterile 1, 3
unprofitable 2
unsuccessful 1
useless 1, 2
vain 2
waste 10
worthless 2
unproductively
idly 1
unprofessional°
amateur 2
homespun
poor 4
unworthy 1
unprofessionally
poorly 1
unproficient
artless 3
ineffective 2
unprofitable°
barren 2
bootless
fruitless
futile
hollow 5
soft 7
thankless
unsuccessful 1
waste 10
worthless 2
unprofound
skin-deep
small 3
unprogressive
conservative 2
narrow-minded
short-sighted 2
slow 8
unpromised
open 8
unmarried
unpromising°
ill 5
inauspicious
ominous 1
portentous 1
unlikely 3
untoward 1
unprompted
unasked
unpronounced
silent 5
unpropitious
bad 5
contrary 3
evil 4
ill 5
ill-advised 1
inauspicious
inopportune
off 8
ominous 1
portentous 1
sinister 1
unhappy 2
unlikely 3
unpromising
untoward 1
unpropitiously
amiss 2
unprotected
defenceless
insecure 2
naked 4
open 5, 19
raw 4
unarmed
unguarded 2
vulnerable
unproved
speculative 2
theoretical 1
untried
unproven
ill-founded
speculative 2
theoretical 1
unfounded
untried
unprovoked
gratuitous 2
unwarranted
wanton 4
unpublicized
unheralded
unofficial
unpublishable
secret 1
unpublished
secret 1
untold 2
unpunctual
late 1
overdue
slow 4, 5
tardy 1
unpunctually
late 7
slow 12
unpurified
unrefined 2
unqualified°
absolute 2
blank 6
categorical
clear 14
complete 3
dead 14
decided 1
definitive 3
direct 9
enthusiastic
explicit 1
express 5
flat 4
full 8
helpless 4
hopeless 2
implicit 2
inadequate 2
inadmissible
incapable 1
incompetent
inefficient 1
unqualified (*cont.*)
ineligible
open 4
out-and-out
outright 1
peremptory 2
perfect 6
positive 1, 9
pronounced 2
pure 5
regular 9
rigid 3
sheer 2
stark 4
straight 5
thorough 1
total 3
ultra-
unable
unhesitating 2
unlimited 1
unmitigated
unworthy 1
wholehearted
unqualifiedly
absolutely 1
completely 2
dead 18
downright 2
entirely 1
outright 5
point-blank 3
positively
really 2
simply 2
stark 1
thoroughly 1
totally
utterly
wholly 1
unqualifiedness
inability
unquenchable°
greedy 1
inextinguishable
voracious 1
unquestionable°
absolute 4
certain 4
clear 6, 14
conspicuous 1
decided 1
demonstrable
flawless 2
hard 8
incontrovertible
indisputable
manifest 1
positive 1
probable
secure 4
undisputed
unquestionably
absolutely 1
certainty 3
clearly 2
definitely
doubtless 1
downright 2
easily 2
evidently 1
manifestly
positively
presumably
probably
really 2
surely 1
truly 3
undoubtedly
very 2
well[1] 7
unquestioned
certain 4
clear 14
decided 1
implicit 2
positive 1
undisputed
unquestioning
implicit 2
unquestioningly
seriously 3
unquiet
impatient 1
sinking 1
unravel
decipher 1
explain 1
extricate
fray[2]
interpret 2
penetrate 5
puzzle 3
run 18
separate 1
simplify
solve
straighten 1
unravelling
interpretation 1
resolution 4
solution 1
unreachable
inaccessible 1
unapproachable 2
unreactive
inert 1
unmoved
unsympathetic
unread
ignorant 1
philistine 2
uneducated
unreadable
illegible
unreadied
unprepared 3
unready
cold 7
premature 1
unprepared 1
unreal°
counterfeit 2
disembodied
dreamlike
extraordinary 2
fabulous 1
factitious
false 1
fancied
fanciful 2
fantastic 2
fictional
fictitious 1
ghostly 1
glossy 2
ideal 5
illusory
imaginary
incredible 1
insubstantial 2
non-existent
phoney 1
shadowy 3
sight 6b
superb
supernatural
unearthly 2
unrealistic 2
visionary 1
unrealistic°
academic 2
fancy 2
fantastic 2
far-fetched
flat 13
idealistic
impractical 1
improbable
incredible 1
quixotic
romantic 2
speculative 1
theoretical 2
unreal 1
unreasonable 3
visionary 1
unreality
fancy 6
vanity 2
unrealizable
impossible 1
quixotic
unrealistic 1
unrealized
potential 1
unreasonable°
absurd 2
excessive 1
exorbitant
extravagant 2, 3
foolish 3
groundless
immoderate
implausible
inane
inordinate 1
lavish 3
misguided
outrageous 1
rabid 1
silly 1
unconscionable 2
unearthly 3
unrealistic 1
untenable
unthinking 1
unwarranted
wild 7
unreasonableness
absurdity 1
extravagance 2
unreasonably
fault 7
unduly 1
unreasoned
absurd 2
arbitrary 1
groundless
impetuous
unreasoning
blind 3
brute 1
rabid 1
unrecallable
irrevocable
unreceptive
chilly 2
inhospitable 1
unrecognizable
incognito 1
indefinite 3
unrecognizably
incognito 2
unrecognized
incognito 1
unidentified
unknown 1
unsung
unrecounted
untold 2
unrecoverable
irretrievable 1
unrectifiable
incurable 2
irretrievable 2
unrecyclable
waste 10
unreduced
complete 1
intact
unmitigated
unrefined°
animal 4
beastly 1
broad 8
brutal 2
coarse 1, 2
common 3
crude 1, 2, 3
earthy
gross 3
homespun
impolite
impure 2
low[1] 3
ordinary 2
philistine 2
plebeian 2
primitive 2, 3
provincial 2
raw 2
risqué
rough 3, 9
rude 1, 3
rugged 4
rustic 2
sketchy

unrefined (*cont.*)
tasteless 1
uncivilized 2
ungraceful 2
unseemly 1
unsophisticated 2
untoward 2
vulgar 1
unrefinement
indelicacy
unreflected
direct 7
unreflecting
unthinking 1
unreflective
impetuous
thoughtless 2
unreformed
ultra-
unrepentant
unrefracted
direct 7
unregenerate
immoral 1
ultra-
unrepentant
wicked 2
unregretful
unrepentant
unregulated
free 10
independent 2
inordinate 2
lawless 1
open 4
unruly
unrehabilitated
unrepentant
unrehearsed
extemporaneous
spontaneous 1
unrelated°
dissimilar
extraneous 2
extrinsic
foreign 3
inapplicable
independent 2
irrelevant
isolated 1
remote 4
separate 6
tangential
unrelaxed
stiff 7, 8
unrelenting
constant 2
grim 1
implacable
insistent
laborious 2
merciless
mortal 4
nagging
persistent 2
relentless 1, 2
remorseless 2
rigid 2, 4
ruthless
stern 1
stubborn
unreliability
inconstancy
unreliable°
ambiguous 3
capricious
changeable 1
deceptive 1
dicky
dodgy
erratic 1
faithless 2
fickle
fly-by-night 2
inconsistent 2
inconstant
insecure 3
irresponsible
moody 3
precarious
questionable
rocky[2]
shady 2

unreliable
(*cont.*)
shaky 1
slippery 2
speculative 2
temperamental 2
uncertain 3, 4
unstable 1
untrue 1
unreliably
fit[2] 4
unrelieved
blank 6
dead 14
relentless 1, 2
solid 10
steady 2
unmitigated
unremarkable
mill 4
nondescript
ordinary 2
undistinguished
usual
unremarked
unnoticed
unremitting
constant 2
continual
continuous 2
endless 2
eternal 2
laborious 2
mortal 4
non-stop 2
perpetual 2
persistent 2
relentless 2
remorseless 2
repetitive
steady 2
stern 1
sustained
unremittingly
cease 2
intently
non-stop 3
unremorseful
unrepentant
unremunerative
bootless
unprofitable 1
unrepealable
irreversible
unrepentant°
ultra-
wicked 2
unrepenting
unrepentant
unreported
untold 2
unrepresentat-ive
unrealistic 2
unrepressed
uninhibited
unreprovable
irreproachable
unrequested
gratuitous 2
unasked
unsolicited
unrequired
unnecessary
unrequisite
optional
unrequited
thankless
unresearched
unknown 2
unreserved
broad 5
categorical
demonstrative 1
direct 10
downright 1
easy 6
effusive
entire 1
expansive 2
explicit 2
familiar 3
flat 4

unreserved
(*cont.*)
forthcoming 3
forthright
frank 1
friendly 2
honest 3
implicit 2
ingenuous 2
open 8, 14, 15, 16
outright 1
outspoken
peremptory 2
plain 3
point-blank 1
raw 6
shameless
undisguised
uninhibited
unqualified 2
wholehearted
unreservedly
absolutely 1
cold 11
completely 2
deeply 2
entirely 1
freely 1, 4
honestly 2
openly 1, 2
outright 5
point-blank 3
quite 1, 4
simply 2
thoroughly 1
utterly
water 3
unreservedness
candour 1
unresistant
supple 3
unresisting
passive 2
submissive 1
supple 3
unresolvable
impossible 1
unresolved°
doubtful 1
hesitant 1
inconclusive
irresolute
issue 8
moot 1
open 7
outstanding 2
uncertain 3
unresounding
dead 13
unrespectable
disreputable 1
unresponsive
aloof 3
chilly 2
cold 3
cold-blooded 2
dead 4
deaf 2
dull 2, 3
frigid 3
inert 1
lukewarm 2
negative 2
passive 1
phlegmatic 1
reserved
reticent
slow 7
stony 2
unaffected[2]
unenthusiastic
unmoved
unsympathetic
unresponsive-ness
non-compliance
unrest°
disorder 2
excitement 1
flux
fuss 1
riot 1
tempest 2
trouble 7

unrest (*cont.*)
upheaval
unrestrainable
hysterical 1
irrepressible
ungovernable
wild 4
unrestrained
abandoned 2
absolute 3
bawdy
broad 5
demonstrative 1
disorderly 2
dissolute
downright 1
effusive
epicurean 1
explicit 2
extravagant 2
familiar 3
fast[1] 2
forthright
frank 1
free 1, 9
furious 2
honest 3
hysterical 1
immoderate
immodest 1
incontinent 1
independent 2
inordinate 1
large 5a
lavish 3
liberty 4, 5
limitless
obstreperous
open 16
outrageous 3
precipitate 5
profligate 1
promiscuous 2
rampant 1, 2
raw 6
riotous 1, 2
rogue 2
towering 2
tumultuous
uncontrolled
undisciplined
undisguised
unimpeded
uninhibited
unlimited 1
unwarranted
wanton 2
wild 4
unrestrainedly
fast[1] 9
freely 1, 3
unrestraint
abandon 5
extravagance 2
freedom 6
profligacy 1
unrestricted
absolute 3
boundless
categorical
entire 1
frank 1
free 1, 10
full 8
general 1
incontinent 1
independent 2, 5
inexhaustible 1
liberty 4
limitless
open 4, 16
outright 1
public 3
unimpeded
unlimited 1
unqualified 2
wild 4
unrestrictedly
free 12
freely 3
outright 5
unreticent
outspoken
unretrievable
irretrievable 1

unrevealed
dormant 2
mystical 1
passive 3
sneaking 2
ulterior 1
unknown 2, 3
untold 2
veiled
unreversible
irreversible
unrewarding
bootless
fruitless
thankless
unrighteous
godless 1
unripe
green 2
immature 1
new 6
premature 1
unripened
green 2
unrivalled
incomparable
leading 2
peerless
perfect 2
pre-eminent 2
star 3
superb
superlative
surpassing
towering 1
transcendent
unbeatable
unique 2
unparalleled
unroll
extend 1
roll 11
spread 3
unromantic
prosaic
realistic 1
unruffled
bland 1
calm 4
collected
cool 2
deliberate 3
dispassionate 1
equable 1
even 4
gentle 1
impassive
level-headed
nonchalant
peaceful 1
philosophical 2
phlegmatic 2
poised 1
sedate 1
self-contained 1
self-possessed
serene 1
silent 1
smooth 1
sober 2
still 1
temperate 1
tranquil
unruliness
rowdyism
unruly°
bad 10
boisterous
defiant
disobedient 1
disorderly 2
insubordinate
irresponsible
lawless 1
mutinous 2
naughty 2
obstreperous
problem 3
rebellious 2
recalcitrant
resistant 2
riotous 2
rogue 2
rowdy 1

unruly (*cont.*)
self-willed
tumultuous
uncontrolled
undisciplined
ungovernable
wild 4
wilful 2
unrushed
unhurried
unsacred
profane 2
unsafe
dangerous 1
hazardous
insecure 2
perilous
unsafely
dangerously 1
unsaid
mute 2
silent 3
tacit
unsalaried
unpaid 2
unsalvageable
irretrievable 1
lost 6
waste 10
unsanctified
profane 2
unsanctioned
unauthorized
unlawful
unsanitary
sordid 3
unsatisfaction
disappointment 1
unsatisfactorily
badly 1
ill 12
poorly 1
unsatisfactory°
bad 1
deficient 2
disappointing
exceptionable
feeble 2
flimsy 2
inadequate 1
insufficient
off 8
par 5a
poor 4
ropy 2
sad 3
small 4
unacceptable
wanting 1
unsatisfiable
unquenchable
unsatisfied
disappointed 1
dissatisfied
resentful
unsatisfying
disappointing
empty 4
thin 6
wanting 1
unsavable
irretrievable 1
unsavoury°
bitter 2
disagreeable 2
disgusting
nasty 2
obnoxious
offensive 3
repugnant
repulsive
seamy
tasteless 1, 2
undesirable 2
uninviting
unpalatable
unscarred
clear 4
unscathed
unscathed°
entire 2
intact
sound[2] 1

unscathed *(cont.)*
whole 2
unscented
unperfumed
unscheduled
open 8
unscholarly
unprofessional 1
unschooled
ignorant 1
illiterate
inexperienced
primitive 3
undisciplined
uneducated
uninformed
unprofessional 2
unscramble
decipher 1
unscratched
unscathed
unscrew
loosen 1
unscripted
extemporaneous
unscrupulous°
black 6
dirty 3
dishonest
dishonourable 2
evil 2
faithless 2
foul 7
immoral 1
rotten 3
shady 2
sharp 6
sneaky
unconscionable 1
villainous 1
unseal
open 21
unsealed
open 2, 3, 6
unseasonable°
inopportune
premature 2
unseasoned
green 2
inexperienced
raw 3
unseat
bring 8a
degrade 1
displace 2
overthrow 1
overturn 2
remove 5
supplant
topple 2
unseated
standing 4
unseating
overthrow 2
overturn 3
purge 4
removal 3
unsecretive
card 14
unsecure
rickety
unsecured
loose 1
unseeable
invisible 1
sight 6a
unseemliness
impropriety 2, 3
indelicacy
ineptitude 2
liberty 5
unseemly°
base[2] 4
disgraceful 2
dishonourable 3
dowdy
gross 3
improper 2, 3
incongruous
indecent 2
inept 2
inopportune
low[1] 3

unseemly *(cont.)*
off colour 2
order 13b
outrageous 3
pale[2] 3
scandalous 1
seamy
sexy 2
spicy 2
suggestive 2
unbecoming 2
unlikely 2
unnatural 1
unprofessional 1
untoward 2
wrong 4
unseen
background 3
hidden
invisible 1
unnoticed
unselective
indiscriminate 1
promiscuous 1
unselfconscious
uninhibited
unrepentant
unselfish°
big 6
charitable 1
considerate
generous 2
large 2
lavish 2
liberal 1
open 14
profuse 4
selfless
unselfishness
altruism
benevolence 1
bounty 1
charity 1
humanity 3
self-denial 1
unsentimental
hard 4
nail 4b
realistic 1
stony 2
tough 6
unseparated
undivided 1
unserious
flippant 1
unseriousness
flippancy 1
unserviceable
out 14
useless 1
unsettle
agitate 1
concern 3
discomfit 1
dismay 2
disorder 4
displace 1
disrupt 1
disturb 2, 3, 4
flurry 2
jar[2] 3
perturb
ruffle 3
shake 5
shatter 3
shock 1
startle
throw 4
trip 6
unnerve
upset 1
unsettled°
agitated
changeable 1
controversial 1
debatable
disconcerted
disputable
doubtful 1
end 6
fluid 3
hesitant 1
homeless 1
inconclusive

unsettled *(cont.)*
inconstant
indecisive 2
indefinite 1
issue 8
moot 1
open 6, 7
outstanding 2
pending 2
precarious
problematic
rambling 1
ticklish 1
uncertain 3, 4
unpaid 1
unresolved
unstable 1
vague 5
whimsical 2
unsettling°
disconcerting
disturbing
inconvenient
startling
unshackle
emancipate
free 15
release 1
unshackled
free 1, 2
loose 2
wild 4
unshackling
liberation
unshaded
broad 2
full 10
unshakability
resolution 1
tenacity 1
unshakable
constant 1
entrenched
fast[1] 4
firm 3, 4
immovable 2
inflexible
obsessive
resolute
solid 3
sure 1
tenacious 1
unshakably
fast[1] 7
unshakeability
resolution 1
tenacity 1
unshakeable
constant 1
entrenched
fast[1] 4
firm 3, 4
immovable 2
inflexible
obsessive
resolute
solid 3
sure 1
tenacious 1
unshakeably
fast[1] 7
unshaken
firm 4
passive 1
resolute
tenacious 1
unshaky
solid 3
unshaped
rough 9
rudimentary 2
unshapely
shapeless 2
unshared
exclusive 1
unshaven
hairy 1
unsheathe
draw 2
unsheathed
naked 4
unsheltered
open 5

unshielded
vulnerable
unshiny
flat 12
unshod
bare 1
unshorn
shaggy
unshortened
full 12
unabridged 1
unshrinking
manly
outspoken
staunch 1
unshrouded
public 5
unsighted
blind 1
unsightly°
awful 1
hideous 1
ugly 1
unsigned
open 6
unskilful
amateur 2
artless 3
awkward 1
clumsy
green 2
heavy-handed 1
hopeless 2
incompetent
ineffective 2
inefficient 1
inept 1
rude 4
tactless
unprofessional 2
unskilfully
roughly 3
unskilled
amateur 2
artless 3
awkward 1
green 2
incompetent
ineffective 2
inefficient 1
inept 1
menial 1
raw 3
rude 4
unfamiliar 2
unprofessional 2
unslakable
unquenchable
unslakeable
unquenchable
unsleeping
sleepless 2
wakeful 1
unsmiling
grave[2] 1
serious 1
severe 2
solemn 1
straight 8
unsmilingly
severely 3
unsnap
undo 1
unsnapped
undone[1] 2
unsnarl
straighten 1
unsociable
aloof 2
cool 5
inhospitable 1
private 4
retiring
standoffish
sullen
unsocial
unsocial°
aloof 2
inhospitable 1
lonely 3
misanthropic
private 4

unsocial *(cont.)*
reserved
retiring
solitary 1
standoffish
unsoftened
unmitigated
unsoiled
clean 2
flawless 1
immaculate 1
untarnished
unsolicited°
free 6
gratuitous 2
independent 4
unasked
voluntary 1
unsolvable
hard 3
impossible 1
mysterious 1
unsolved
unresolved
unsophistic(al)
natural 4
unsophisticated°
artless 2
callow
childlike
clear 12
crude 4
fresh 3
green 2
gross 3
gullible
homely 1
homespun
ignorant 3
immature 2
inexperienced
ingenuous 1
innocent 4
juvenile 1
naïve
natural 4
near-sighted 2
parochial
primitive 2, 3
provincial 2
rustic 2
simple 1, 3, 4
square 6
tactless
unaffected[1]
uncivilized 2
unrefined 1
young 2
unsophistic-atedness
provincialism 2
simplicity 3
unsophistication
inexperience
vulgarity 1
unsought
gratuitous 2
intrusive
unasked
unforeseen
unpopular
unsolicited
unwelcome 1
unsound°
absurd 2
crazy 3
dicky
diseased
erroneous
explosive 1
false 1, 5
faulty
feeble 1
flawed
groundless
ill 1
ill-founded
inaccurate
indisposed 1
insecure 3
invalid[2]
morbid 1
shaky 1, 2
sophistic

unsound *(cont.)*
tender[1] 1
unfounded
unhealthy 1
untenable
wanting 1
water 2
weak 1
wrong 5
-of unsound mind
deranged
insane 1
mad 1
maniacal 1
psychotic 1
unbalanced 2
unsparing
ample 5
bountiful 1
charitable 1
cruel 1
exacting
free 7
hard 4
lavish 2
liberal 1
merciless
profuse 1, 4
relentless 1
stern 1
unmerciful
unselfish
unspeakable
atrocious 1
awful 2
bad 3
black 6
fearful 3
frightful 2
horrible 1
ineffable 1
inexpressible
nameless 3
outrageous 2
satanic 2
scandalous 1
shocking 2
taboo 1
terrible 4
unmentionable 1
untold 3
unspeakably
badly 6
unspeaking
silent 3
unspecialized
general 2
unprofessional 3
unspecifiable
nameless 2
unspecific
broad 4
general 2, 4
indefinite 1, 2
lax 2
loose 5
random 1
vague 1, 2, 3
unspecifically
generally 2
unspecified
broad 6
certain 6
indefinite 1
nameless 2
random 1
vague 1, 2
unsplit
undivided 1
unspoiled°
clean 1
flawless 1
good 7
idyllic
immaculate 2
pristine 2
unspoilt
clean 1
flawless 1
good 7
idyllic
immaculate 2
unspoiled

unspoken
implicit 1
mute 2
silent 3
tacit
unspoken for
open 8
unattached 2
vacant 3
unspontaneous
perfunctory 1
unsporting
dirty 3
unsportsmanlike
dirty 3
foul 7
tricky 3
unspotted
spotless 1
untarnished
unstable°
capricious
changeable 1
decrepit 2
erratic 1
explosive 1
fickle
fitful
flighty 1
fluid 3
foolish 2
hot 10
inconsistent 2
inconstant
infirm 2
insecure 3
mental 2
moody 3
neurotic
precarious
ramshackle
rocky²
shaky 1, 2
slight 4
tender¹ 1
ticklish 1
unbalanced 1, 2
unreliable
unsettled 1
unsound 1, 3
variable
variant 2
volatile 2
unstained
chaste 1
clean 2
innocent 2
pure 2
unspoiled
unstarched
limp² 1
soft 1
unstated
silent 3
tacit
unstatic
fluid 3
unstationary
mobile 1
moving 2
unsteadfast
fickle
inconstant
infirm 2
unsteadfastness
inconstancy
unsteadiness
fluctuation
inconstancy
unsteady
capricious
desultory
dicky
dizzy 1
doddering
faint 2
fickle
flighty 1
giddy 1
groggy
halting
inconsistent 2
unsteady (*cont.*)
inconstant
infirm 2
insecure 3
moody 3
precarious
ramshackle
rickety
rocky²
shaky 1, 2
shambling
ticklish 1
tremulous 1
unbalanced 1
uncertain 4
unsound 1
unstable 1
variable
weak 1
whimsical 2
unstiffened
limp² 1
unstilted
informal 1
unstimulating
dreary 2
unstinted
ample 5
unstinting
ample 5
bountiful 1
enthusiastic
free 7
generous 1
lavish 2
liberal 1
open 14
philanthropic
profuse 1, 4
square 5
unselfish
wholehearted
unstintingly
amply 4
freely 4
water 3
unstirred
unaffected²
unmoved
unsympathetic
unstop
clear 24
open 22
unstoppable
boundless
indomitable
invincible 1
irrepressible
irresistible 2
relentless 1, 2
remorseless 2
unstraightforward
tortuous 2
unstrained
easy 5
unstressed
unaccented
unstring
ruffle 3
unstructured
incoherent
loose 5
shapeless 1
unstuck
chaotic 2
undone¹ 2
unstudied
careless 4
extemporaneous
inadvertent 1
natural 4
offhand 3
unaffected¹
unpremeditated
unsubdued
untamed
unsubmissive
disobedient 1
recalcitrant
resistant 1
unsubstantial
disembodied
dreamlike
flimsy 1, 2
fragile
immaterial 2
insecure 3
insignificant
insubstantial 1
intangible
light² 6
meaningless 1
ramshackle
shadowy 3
shaky 2
sleazy 1
slight 4
tenuous 2
thin 2, 4
weak 1
unsubstantiated
ill-founded
shaky 1
unsubtle
broad 3
obvious
outspoken
unsuccessful°
fail 1, 11b
fruitless
futile
ineffectual 1
useless 1
vain 2
unsuccessfully
badly 2
vain 3a
unsuitability
ineptitude 2
unsuitable
impossible 1
impracticable 2
improper 2
inadequate 1
inadmissible
inapplicable
inappropriate
incongruous
indecent 1
ineligible
inept 2
inopportune
mismatched
order 13b
pale² 3
place 12
unacceptable
unbecoming 1
undesirable 2
unhappy 3
unlikely 2
unreasonable 3
unsatisfactory
unseasonable
unseemly 2
untoward 2
unworthy 2
wrong 3
unsuitableness
impropriety 2
ineptitude 1
unsuited
improper 2
inadequate 2
inadmissible
inapplicable
inappropriate
incompatible
incongruous
ineligible
inopportune
mismatched
unbecoming 1
unhappy 3
unqualified 1
unsullied
celibate 2
chaste 1
clean 1, 2
flawless 1
holy 2
immaculate 1
innocent 2
intact
unsullied (*cont.*)
pristine 2
pure 2
spotless 2
unspoiled
untarnished
virtuous 2
white 3
unsung°
nameless 1
obscure 4
unheard-of 1
unknown 1
unsupportable
heavy 4
insufferable
leg 6
unbearable
unfounded
untenable
unsupported
groundless
ill-founded
leg 6
shaky 1
unfounded
unsuppressed
runaway 2
unsuppressible
inextinguishable
irrepressible
unquenchable
unsure
casual 2
debatable
dicey
disorientated
distrustful
doubtful 2
fickle
ill 6
indefinite 5
insecure 1
irresolute
mind 11
perilous
precarious
questionable
rocky²
self-conscious
tentative 2
ticklish 1
touchy 2
tremulous 1
uncertain 1, 2, 3
unresolved
unsureness
mistrust 2
unsurpassable
incomparable
unbeatable
unsurpassed
alone 2
best 1
first-rate
incomparable
leading 2
optimum 2
peerless
pre-eminent 2
splendid 3
superlative
supreme 1
surpassing
towering 1
unique 2
unparalleled
unsusceptibility
immunity 2
unsusceptible
immune
insensible 2
thick-skinned
unsuspecting°
gullible
innocent 4
naïve
trusting
unaware
unsuspicious
gullible
innocent 4
naïve
trusting
unsuspicious (*cont.*)
unsuspecting
unsustainable
untenable
unsustained
spasmodic 2
unswerving
consistent 2
constant 1
decided 2
direct 6
faithful 1
firm 3
immovable 2
indomitable
loyal
patient 2
persistent 1
relentless 1
religious 2
resolute
rigid 3
single-minded
stalwart 2
staunch 1
steadfast
strong 5
sturdy 2
sure 1
tenacious 1
tireless
true 2
unhesitating 2
yeomanly
unswervingly
consistently 2
directly 1
straight 12
surely 2
unsymmetric(al)
irregular 1
lopsided 1
unbalanced 1
ungraceful 2
unsympathetic°
aloof 3
brutal 1
callous
chill 6
cold 3
cold-blooded 2
cold-hearted
cool 4
dead 4
dull 2
hard 4
heartless
hostile 2
impassive
implacable
inconsiderate
indifferent 1
inhuman 1
intolerant 1
merciless
nail 4b
rocky¹ 3
ruthless
severe 1
stern 1
stony 2
strict 2
tough 6
unflattering 1
unkind
unmerciful
unmoved
unsympathetically
roughly 2
unsystematic
casual 2
chaotic 1
desultory
fitful
haphazard 2
indiscriminate 2
inordinate 2
irregular 2
promiscuous 3
random 1
uncertain 4
unsystematically
fit² 4
helter-skelter 2
random 2
unsystematized
chaotic 1
indiscriminate 2
irregular 2
promiscuous 3
untactful
thoughtless 1
untoward 2
untainted
clean 2
holy 2
immaculate 2
innocent 2
intact
pure 2
unspoiled
untarnished
untaken
open 10
untalented
artless 3
untalkative
taciturn
untamed°
savage 1, 3
vicious 3
violent 1
wild 1
untangle
explain 1
extricate
simplify
solve
straighten 1
untarnished°
flawless 1
immaculate 1
pristine 2
spotless 2
untaught
ignorant 1
illiterate
primitive 3
undisciplined
uneducated
uninformed
untaxing
light² 10
untempered
unmitigated
unwarranted
wanton 2
untenable°
invalid²
leg 6
sophistic
unsound 4
weak 4
untenanted
empty 2
free 3
uninhabited
vacant 1
untested
fresh 3
green 2
novel 1
raw 3
speculative 2
theoretical 1
untried
unthankful
ungrateful
unthankfulness
ingratitude
unthinkable°
impossible 1
improbable
inconceivable
incredible 1
outrageous 2
question 7
unbelievable
unheard-of 3
unlikely 1
untold 3

unthinking°
blind 3
brute 1
careless 2
foolhardy
hasty 2
immediate 1
impetuous
improvident 2
inadvertent 1
inconsiderate
indiscreet
involuntary
mindless 2
near-sighted 2
perfunctory 1
promiscuous 1
rash[1]
remiss
spontaneous 2
thoughtless 1,2
unconscious 2
unguarded 1,3
unreasonable 1
unwary
unthinkingly
blindly
hastily 2
idly 2
rote 2b
spur 3
unthoughtful
cold-hearted
improvident 2
inconsiderate
unkind
unthinking 1
unthought of
inconceivable
unforeseen
unthreatened
secure 1
unthrifty
wasteful
unthrone
overturn 2
untidiness
disorder 1
mess 1
untidy°
bedraggled
dirty 1
disorderly 1
disreputable 2
lax 2
loose 5
shaggy
slipshod
sloppy 1
sordid 3
topsy-turvy 2
unkempt
wild 8
untie
disengage
free 15
loose 12
loosen 1
open 21
release 1
undo 1,2
untied
free 5
loose 2,4
undone[1] 2
until
pending 1
prior 2
until now
far 8a
still 4
yet 1,2
untimeliness
inconvenience 2
untimely
early 4
inappropriate
inconvenient
inopportune
premature 1,2
prematurely 1
previous 3
unseasonable
unseemly 2
untiring°
constant 1
energetic
hard 7
indomitable
industrious
inexhaustible 2
laborious 2
patient 2
persevere
persistent 1
resolute
stalwart 2
tireless
untiringly
hard 13
untold°
inestimable 1,2
numberless
unknown 3
untouchable
outcast
sacred 2
untouched
blind 4
free 11
immune
insensible 2
intact
passive 1
pristine 2
unaffected[2]
unmoved
unscathed
unsympathetic
unused 1
untoward°
amiss 1
contrary 3
ill 5
improper 3
inauspicious
inopportune
miserable 2
nasty 2
untrained
amateur 2
fresh 3
green 2
inexperienced
new 6
primitive 3
raw 3
tender[1] 3
undisciplined
unprofessional 2
unqualified 1
untrammelled
free 1
independent 2
loose 2
uncontrolled
unimpeded
wild 4
untransferable
inalienable
untransparent
opaque 1
untravelled
out-of-the-way 1
untreated
raw 2
unrefined 2
untried°
callow
fresh 3
novel 1
raw 3
untrivial
no-nonsense
untrod
trackless
untrodden
new 8
trackless
untroubled
careless 1
comfortable 1
easy 2
gentle 1
home 4a
nonchalant
peaceful 1
untroubled (*cont.*)
serene 1
silent 1
sound[2] 6
tranquil
untrue°
bum 3
disloyal
erroneous
false 1,2
fictitious 1
illusory
imaginary
improper 1
incorrect
invalid[2]
mythical 2
perfidious
traitorous
untrusting
distrustful
untrustworthy
corrupt 1
deceitful
dishonest
dishonourable 2
disloyal
disreputable 1
faithless 2
false 2
fickle
fly-by-night 2
furtive 2
hypocritical
irresponsible
jaundiced 1
shaky 1
shifty
slippery 2
speculative 2
two-faced
unreliable
unscrupulous
untrue 1
untruth
fabrication 3
falsehood
fib 1
libel 2
lie[1] 2
misstatement 1
myth 2
story 3
tale 2
untruthful
deceitful
deceptive 2
dishonest
false 1,2
insincere
lying 2
untruthfulness
falsity
lying 1
untutored
philistine 2
primitive 3
uncivilized 2
undisciplined
uninformed
unprofessional 2
untypical
character 9
odd 1
unlike 2
unusual
ununified
disjointed 2
unusable
defunct 2
dud 2
impracticable 2
useless 1
waste 10
unused°
brand-new
defunct 2
disused
empty 6
extra 2
free 3
idle 1
leftover 2
unused (*cont.*)
mouldy
obsolete
odd 3
old 3
remaining 2
surplus 2
vacant 3
void 2
waste 9
unused to°
at **unused 4**
unaccustomed 2
unfamiliar 2
unusual°
abnormal 1,2
bizarre 1
conspicuous 3
curious 3
deviant 1
different 2
distinct 2
eccentric 1
erratic 2
exceptional 1
exotic 2
extraordinary 1
extreme 1
fanciful 3
freak 5
fresh 2
funny 2
irregular 3
new 1
notable 2
noteworthy
novel 1
odd 1
offbeat
ordinary 4
original 4
outlandish
out-of-the-way 2
outré
pale[2] 3
particular 2
peculiar 1
phenomenal
picturesque 1
prodigious 2
quaint 1
queer 1
rare[1] 1
raving 2
remarkable 1
remote 3
scarce
sight 6b
signal 3
singular 1
special 1
strange 1
striking
supernatural
thin 7
unaccountable 3
unaccustomed 1
unearthly 3
unfamiliar 1
unheard-of 2
unnatural 1,3
unorthodox
unparalleled
unwonted
whimsical 1
unusually
especially 1
extra 6
extreme 9
extremely
notably 1
particularly 1
really 4
very 1
unusualness
abnormality 1
eccentricity 1
oddity 1
rarity 2
unutilized
vacant 3
void 2
unutterable
ineffable 1
inexpressible
unutterable (*cont.*)
nameless 3
satanic 2
unmentionable 1
untold 3
unuttered
silent 5
tacit
unvaried
changeless 1
equable 2
even 3
flat 7
humdrum
inflexible
invariable 3
routine 4
same 2
set 29,30
uniform 1
unvarnished°
bare 2
factual 2
hard 8
literal 2
matter-of-fact
naked 3
plain 4
raw 6
round 8
simple 2
true 1
truthful
unvarying
changeless 2
constant 2,3
equable 2
eternal 3
even 3
flat 7
homogeneous
humdrum
inflexible
invariable 1,3
level 3
perpetual 1
regular 1,5
rocky[1] 2
routine 4
same 2
set 29
static 1
steady 2
strong 21
tedious
uniform 1
unveil°
bare 6
disclose 2
display 1
expose 1
lay[1] 9
light[1] 9
open 23
release 2
unveiling
exposure 1
presentation 3
revelation
unventilated
close 12
oppressive 2
stuffy 1
unversed
green 2
unfamiliar 2
unvigilant
unguarded 1
unvirginal
impure 4
unvirtuous
impure 4
lewd
unchaste
unvisited
deserted
unvoiced
sneaking 2
tacit
unwanted
intrusive
needless 1
redundant 1
unwanted (*cont.*)
unasked
undesirable 2
unnecessary
unpopular
unwelcome 2
unwarlike
peaceable 2
unwarned
unprepared 3
unwarranted°
excessive 1
exorbitant
gratuitous 2
groundless
inordinate 1
outrageous 1
unconscionable 2
unfounded
unreasonable 2
untoward 2
unwary°
careless 2
foolish 1
gullible
improvident 2
short-sighted 2
unguarded 1
unsuspecting
unwashed°
dirty 1
filthy 2
unwasteful
economical 1
efficient
unwatchful
unguarded 1
unwatered
undiluted
unwavering
clear 11
constant 1
decided 2
determined 1
eternal 3
faithful 1
fast[1] 5
firm 3,4
fixed 2
grim 1
immovable 2
indomitable
insistent
invariable 1
laborious 3
loyal
manly
patient 2
persistent 1
resolute
rigid 3
rocky[1] 2
single-minded
stable 2
stalwart 2
staunch 1
steadfast
steady 2
strong 5
sturdy 2
sure 1
tenacious 1
tireless
true 2
unhesitating 2
yeomanly
unwaveringly
firmly 2
unwearied
constant 1
inexhaustible 2
untiring
unwearying
constant 1
inexhaustible 2
untiring
unwed
celibate 1
eligible 2
maiden 2
single 1
unmarried
unwedded
unmarried

unwelcome°
bitter 2
gratuitous 2
intruder 1
intrusive
lonesome 1
unasked
undesirable 2
unpopular
unwelcoming
chilly 2
cool 5
inhospitable 1
unwell
ail 2
diseased
frail 2
ill 1
indisposed 1
infirm 1
off colour 1
par 5b
peaky
poorly 2
queer 3
ropy 3
rotten 5
seedy 2
sick 2
sort 6
tender[1] 1
unhealthy 1
unsound 2
weather 2
unwholesome°
destructive 1
ill 5
morbid 1
peaky
seamy
unhealthy 2
virulent 1
unwieldiness
inconvenience 2
unwieldy°
bulky
clumsy
gross 1
hefty 1
hulking
inconvenient
ponderous 1
unwilling
averse
backward 1
disinclined,
fearful 2
hate 2
indisposed 2
loath
reluctant
shy 4
slow 10
unwillingly
fearfully 1
protest 2
unwillingness
aversion 1
compunction 2
reluctance
unwind
relax 3
rest[1] 6
roll 11
unfold 1
wind[2] 3b
unwise
foolish 1
ill-advised 1
imprudent
indiscreet
inept 2
mad 2
misguided
reckless
silly 1
tactless
unguarded 3
unseemly 2
unthinking 2
untoward 2
unwary
unwished for
unenviable
unwelcome 1
unwitting
accidental
ignorant 2
inadvertent 1
involuntary
spontaneous 2
unconscious 2
unthinking 1
unwittingly
unawares 2
unwonted°
sudden
unworkable
crazy 3
duff
hopeless 4
impossible 1, 2
impracticable 1
impractical 2
unrealistic 1
visionary 1
water 2
wild 7
unworked
rough 9
unworldly
inexperienced
innocent 4
naïve
parochial
unearthly 1
unsophisticated 1
unworried
carefree
careless 1
unworthy°
base[2] 2
contemptible
disgraceful 2
dishonourable 3
miserable 3
shabby 2
unprofessional 1
unsatisfactory
unwarranted
unworthy of°
at **unworthy 2**
below 11
beneath 4
inadequate 2
unwrap
open 21
undo 2
unwrapped
open 3
unwrinkled
smooth 1
unwritten
traditional
verbal 1
unwritten law
code 1
precept 1
tradition
unwrought
rough 9
unyielding
authoritarian
deaf 2
defiant
determined 1
difficult 3
dour 2
firm 1, 4
grim 1
hard 1
immovable 2
implacable
indomitable
inflexible
insistent
obstinate
patient 2
perverse 3
possessive 1
precise 2
recalcitrant
relentless 1
rigid 2
rocky[1] 2
unyielding (*cont.*)
severe 1
stalwart 2
steely 2
stern 1
stiff 1, 4
stubborn
sturdy 2
tenacious 1
tight 3
tough 6
unkind
wilful 2
unyoke
separate 1
unzip
undo 1
unzipped
undone[1] 2
up
adequate 3
aloft
awake 4
equal 3
familiar 4
forward 5
hip
home 5
informed 2
level 5
line[1] 20
mark 16b
pink[1] 1
ready 1
step 18b
vivacious
-be up to
get 52
measure 15b
-on the up and up
artless 1
frank 2
honest 1, 2
honourable 3
level 15
sincere
square 4
up above
aloft
up against it
broke
impoverished 1
needy
up ahead
ahead 1
up-anchor
leave[1] 1
up and about
awake 4
stir 2
up and down
about 3
chequered 2
Upanishad(s)
Scripture
upbeat°
positive 8
rhythm
upbraid°
abuse 3
bawl 3
berate
call 7b
condemn 1
damn 1
dress 4
lace 5b
lambaste 2
lecture 4
light[2] 14
mind 10
nag[1] 1
rail[2]
rate[2]
rebuke 1
reprimand 2
scold 1
task 3
twit[1]
vituperate
upbraiding
abuse 8
hell 4
lecture 2
rebuke 2
reprimand 1
reproachful
upbringing°
background 1
breeding 2
education 1
parenting
savoir vivre
upchuck
heave 4
regurgitate
vomit
upcoming
forthcoming 1
up-country
interior 4, 7
update
improve 1
modernize
revise 1
revision
updating
revision
up-end
overturn 1
reverse 2
stand 2a
tip[2] 1
topple 1
turn 24
upset 2
up front
before 2
upfront°
artless 1
candid 1
front 9
frank 2
honest 3
honourable 3
level 11, 15
round 8
sincere
straight 4
transparent 3
uninhibited
upgrade
dignify
enrich 1
exalt 1
glorify 1
grade 4
hill 3
improve 1
lift 2
progress 6
promote 2
promotion 2
rise 13
slope 2
upgrading
improvement 1
promotion 2
upheaval°
disorder 2
disturbance 1
explosion 2
revolution 2
subversion
tempest 2
uphill
laborious 1
stiff 9
strenuous 1
uphold°
abet 2
advocate 1
aid 1
approve 2
back 2a
bear 2, 9
bolster
carry 5
champion 4
confirm 1
defend 3
justify
maintain 1
prop 1
uphold (*cont.*)
prove 1
ratify
speak 7a
stand 5a, 11
stick[1] 6
support 1
sustain 1, 5
underwrite 1
vindicate 2
vouch
warrant 3
upholder
advocate 2
party 4
pillar 2
proponent
stalwart 4
stand-by 1
upholster
pad 4
up in arms
angry 1
furious 1
militant 2
up in the air
doubtful 1
fire 4
inconclusive
issue 8
limbo
moot 1
open 7
pending 2
uncertain 3
unresolved
vague 5
upkeep°
conservation
keep 15
maintenance 1, 3
preservation 1
subsistence 2
support 9
sustenance 2
upland
hill 1
interior 4
plateau 1
rise 13
upper 2
-uplands
interior 7
uplift
cheer 6
dignify
enliven 2
exalt 1
extol
hoist 1
improve 1
inspire 2
lift 2
raise 7, 13
rear[2] 3
reassure
uplifted
elated
elevated 1, 2
exalted 3
uplifting
edification
elevation 3
exalted 2
exhilarating 2
heart-warming 1
up-market
expensive
upon
above 3
over 1
up one side and down the other
wholly 1
upon my word
indeed 1
upper°
dope 2
drug 2
overhead 2
right 7
stimulant 2
superior 1
-on one's uppers°
at **upper 7**
broke
destitute 1
hard 17
heel[1] 3
impoverished 1
indigent
needy
poor 1
Upper chamber
parliament 2
Upper House
parliament 2
upper case°
at **upper 4**
big 8
capital 4
upper class
élite 1
gentry
upper 5
-upper classes
gentry
society 4
upper-class°
best 5
élite 2
exclusive 2
genteel 2
high-class 2
noble 2
superior 1
upper crust°
at **upper 5**
best 5
élite 1
genteel 2
gentry
high-class 2
nobility 3
society 4
upper-class 1
upper-cut
punch[1] 2
upper hand°
at **upper 6**
advantage 1
domination 1
edge 4
predominance
upper-level
superior 1
uppermost°
supreme 1
top 9
upper 1
upper strata
gentry
uppish°
haughty
hoity-toity
lofty 4
mannered
presumptuous
snobbish
supercilious
uppishness
snobbery
uppitiness
pride 2
snobbery
uppity
arrogant 2
haughty
hoity-toity
lofty 4
mannered
pompous 1
snobbish
supercilious
uppish
upraise
dignify
exalt 1
heighten 1
raise 1
rear[2] 3
upraised
elevated 1

upright°
conscientious 1
end 7a
erect 1
ethical
even 7
fair[1] 2
faithful 4
good 5
honest 1
honourable 1
incorrupt 1
just 2
leg 2
moral 1
noble 4
pale[2] 1
perpendicular 1
picket 1
pier 2
pillar 1
pole[1]
post[1] 1
principled
prop 3
pure 6
respectable 1
right 1
righteous 1
savoury 2
shaft 1
simple 3
solid 5
square 4
stake[1] 1
stand 2a
standing 4
steep
straight 2, 4
true 2
virtuous 1
wholesome 2
worthwhile 2
uprightly
honestly 1
uprightness
honesty 1
honour 1
integrity 1
morality 1
principle 3
probity
rectitude
right 10
sincerity
sportsmanship
virtue 1
uprising°
mutiny 1
rebellion 1
revolt 1
revolution 1
trouble 7
wave 2
uproar°
bedlam
din 1
disorder 2
disturbance 2
fracas 1
furore 1
fuss 1
noise 1
outcry
pandemonium
racket 1
rampage 1
riot 1
row[2] 2
rumpus
splash 4
tempest 2
tumult
uproarious°
blatant 2
chaotic 2
funny 1
hilarious
hysterical 2
noisy
obstreperous
riotous 2
rowdy 1
tempestuous
tumultuous
uproarious (*cont.*)
wild 4
uproot°
abolish
pull 3, 14a, 18b
root[1] 7a
transplant
uprooting
extraction 1
ups and downs
fluctuation
vicissitude 2
upset°
affect[1] 2
affected 5
agitate 1
agitated
ail 1
alarm 3
anguish 3
anxious 1
bad 8
beside 3
bother 3, 5
broken-hearted
capsize
concern 3
concerned 2
confuse 1
confused 2
cut 3
daunt
demoralize 3
discomfit 1
disconcerted
dismay 2
disorder 4
displease
disrupt 1
distraction 1
distraught
distress 3
disturb 1, 3, 4, 5
disturbance 1, 2
disturbed 1
division 5
embarrass
excite 2
excited 1
excitement 2
fit[1] 4
flap 4
flurry 1, 2
fluster 1, 2
frantic
fret 1
frustrate 2
fuss 1
havoc 2
heartbroken
horrify 2
horror 2
hurry 3
hurt 3
incident 2
inconvenience 1, 3
jangle 2
jar[2] 3
matter 3
mess 5c
mix 4b
move 4
nerve 3
nervous 1
overawe
overturn 1, 2
panic-stricken
perturb
piece 6
provoke 3
put 21c
rankle
rattle 3
regret 1
resentful
resentment
reverse 3
ripple 2
ruffle 3
scandalize
scene 3
set-back
shake 5
shatter 3
upset (*cont.*)
shock 1
sick 6
sicken 2
slaughter 4
sore 4
spite 3
spoil 1
startle
stir 3
stress 5
sweat 7
tense 2
tension 2
throw 3
tip[2] 1
topple 1
trouble 1, 7
tumult
turn 21c, 24
unnerve
unsettled 2
upheaval
weigh 4
worried
worry 4
upset stomach
indigestion
run 50
upsetting
deplorable 1
disconcerting
disturbing
fraught 2
harrowing
heavy 5
inconvenient
mournful 2
poignant 1
provocative 2
pungent 3
regrettable
startling
tragic
traumatic
trying
unfortunate 3
unsettling
upset 11
up shit creek
trouble 9a
upshot°
determination 2
effect 1
end 4
event 2
judgement 2
outcome
pay-off 2
product 1
ramification 1
repercussion
result 1
sequel
upside down
reverse 1
topsy-turvy 1
upset 6
upstage
show 12c
upstairs
above 2
upstairs maid
servant 1
upstanding
conscientious 1
erect 1
good 5
heroic 2
honourable 1
incorrupt 1
just 2
moral 1
righteous 1
scrupulous 2
solid 5
straight 2
upright 1, 2
virtuous 1
–be upstanding
rise 1
stand 1
upstart°
parvenu 1, 2
pup
up sticks
move 2
upsurge
epidemic 2
jump 9
outburst
revival 3
surge 2
wave 2
upswing
improvement 2
leap 6
revival 3
uptake°
uptight
edge 5
inhibited
intense 3
nervous 1
overwrought 1
priggish
puritan 2
restless
square 6
stiff 7
stuffy 2
tense 2
up to date°
at **date 5**
contemporary 2
current 3, 4
fashionable
fresh 2
informed 2
knowledgeable 1
late 2
level 5
minute[1] 3
modern
new 2
now 5
present[1] 1
recent
sporty
streamlined 2
swinging
topical 1
trendy 1
up to par°
at **par 6**
presentable 1
scratch 5
up to scratch°
at **scratch 5**
par 6
presentable 1
up to snuff
adequate 2
measure 15b
muster 3
par 6
presentable 1
scratch 5
up to the minute
fashionable
latest 2
modern
trendy 1
upturn
revival 3
upward movement
gain 9
movement 6
upward(s)
upright 4
upward(s) of
over 2
upwelling
outburst
upwind
wind[1] 10
urban
city
metropolis
municipal
urbane
bland 1
civil 3
courteous
urbane (*cont.*)
cultivated
debonair 1
elegant 1
genteel 3
graceful 2
oily 2
pleasant 2
polished 2
refined 1
slick 2
smooth 6
sophisticated 1
suave
well-bred
worldly 2
urbaneness
refinement 1
urbanity
charm 2
civility
culture 1
refinement 1
savoir faire
sophistication 1
urchin
boy 1
guttersnipe
imp
lad
ragamuffin
urge°
abet 1
advise 1
charge 10
coax
desire 4
dispose 2
drive 1
encourage 1
energize
excite 1
fancy 8
foment
further 5
hasten 2
hurry 2
impress 3
incite
induce 1
inflame 1
insist 1
lobby 3
make 2
mania 1
motivate
motive 1
persuade 1
preach 2
press 6
pressure 5
prod 2
prompt 3
push 4
put 29
reason 8
recommend 1
root 3b
spirit 2
spur 4
squeeze 11
stimulant 1
stir 4
suggest 1
thrust 1, 3
wish 5
work 18
urgency°
drive 8
edge 3
gravity 2
haste 1
hurry 3
necessity 4
press 9
pressure 3
priority
stress 2
use 13
urgent°
compulsive
demanding 2
desperate 4
grave[2] 2
immediate 3
urgent (*cont.*)
imperative 1
important 1
indispensable 1
insistent
instant 4
necessary 1
pivotal
pressing
rush 5
serious 2
sore 3
strong 20
urgently
hard 13
urging
encouragement 1
incitement 1
pressure 4
recommendation 1
spur 1
suggestion 1
urinal
toilet 1
urinate°
go 17
pass 12
void 7
water 4
urn
jar[1]
jug
uropygium
tail 1
usability
use 9
usable
disposable 2
feasible
handy 2
operable
practical 1
ready-made 2
serviceable 1
useful
user-friendly
usage°
convention 2
custom 1
diction 1
expression 6
habit 1
observance 2
phrase 3
practice 1
protocol 1
routine 1
service 5
tradition
treatment 1
use 6, 8, 9
use°
account 5
advantage 2
affect[2] 2
application 1
apply 3
assume 1
draw 13a
embrace 2
employ 2
employment 3
enjoy 2
enjoyment 2
exercise 1, 5
exert 1
exhaust 1
expend 1
exploit 2
fall 9
finish 3
function 1
go 16, 32g
good 19
handle 7
lose 4
manipulate 1, 2
occupy 4
pass 5
play 15
prey 3b
profit 2, 4
purpose 3

V

vague°
ambiguous 2
broad 6
cryptic 2
dim 1
doubtful 1
dreamy 1
equivocal 2
faint 1
fuzzy 2
general 4
generality 1
hazy 2
imperceptible 1
imprecise
inconstant
indefinite 1,2,5
indistinct 1,2
intangible
lax 2
loose 5
meagre 3
mealy-mouthed
misty
muddy 2
nebulous
neutral 2
obscure 2
occult 1
opaque 2
preoccupied 2
rough 10
shadowy 2
shapeless 1
sketchy
subtle 2
tenuous 2
uncertain 3
unresolved
weak 6
woolly 2
vaguely°
sketchily
vagueness
ambiguity 1
gobbledegook 2
mystery 2
opacity 2
vain°
boastful
bootless
cocky
conceited
egotistical
fond 2
fruitless
futile
haughty
hollow 5
hopeless 4
idle 4
ineffective 1
inflated 1
meaningless 2
ostentatious
pedantic 1
pointless
pompous 1
proud 2
self-important
snobbish
thankless
unsuccessful 1
useless 1
void 1
wind[1] 2
worthless 2
-in vain°
at **vain 3**
vainglorious
boastful
conceited
egotistical
lofty 4
ostentatious
overconfident 1
pompous 1
pretentious 1
proud 2
self-important
vain 1
vainglory
conceit 1
vanity 1
vainly
vain 3a
vainness
snobbery
vanity 2
valance
drapery
flounce 1
vale
goodbye
valley
valediction
parting 2
valedictory
oration
parting 3
Valentino
charmer
valet
man 3
servant 1
valetudinarian
ill 1
indisposed 1
invalid[1] 1,2
patient 4
valetudinary
unhealthy 1
Valhalla
heaven 1
paradise 1
valiance
prowess 2
valiant
bold 1
brave 1
courageous
dauntless
fearless
gallant 1
hardy 2
heroic 1
intrepid
manly
martial 2
stalwart 3
stout 2
superhuman 1
valid
authoritative 1,2
bona fide
certain 4
concrete
correct 8
effectual 2
factual 1
faithful 2
force 6
good 8
hold 11
honest 4
just 3
lawful 1
legitimate 1,3
logical 2
meaningful 1
official 1
persuasive
potent 2
real 1,3
right 2
rightful 1
solid 7
sound[2] 4
substantial 3
true 1
validate
authenticate
check 3
confirm 1
document 2
establish 3
execute 2
justify
legitimate 4
license 2
prove 1
ratify
recognize 3
sanction 5
seal 4
substantiate
support 6
sustain 5
validate (*cont.*)
underwrite 2
verify
vet
warrant 4
validated
authoritative 1
validation
check 15
evidence 1
proof 1
sanction 1
seal 2
warrant 1
validity
force 4
valise
bag 2
grip 4
suitcase
valley°
gully
hollow 7
ravine
Valley girl
miss[2]
valorous
bold 1
brave 1
courageous
daring 2
dauntless
fearless
gallant 1
gritty 2
hardy 2
heroic 1
intrepid
manly
martial 2
stout 2
valour
bravery
courage
daring 1
grit
nerve 1
prowess 2
spirit 5
valuable
advantageous
desirable 4
estimable
expensive
gainful
helpful
instrumental
invaluable
precious 1
priceless 1
productive 3
profitable 2
rich 3,4
significant 1
useful
worthwhile 2
valuables
asset 1
treasure 1
valuation
criticism 1
evaluation 1
judgement 5
measure 4
measurement 1
price 1
rate[1] 4
value
account 5
appreciate 1
criticize 1
denomination 2
distinction 2
esteem 1
estimate 1
evaluate 1
excellence
force 4
honour 5
importance 1
interest 3
judge 5
love 8
measure 4,11
value (*cont.*)
merit 1
premium 3
price 1,5
prize[2]
profit 2
quality 2
quotation 2
rate[1] 4
reckon 2
regard 3
respect 6
savour 3
significance 2
size 3
store 5
think 5b
treasure 3
usefulness
weigh 3,5
weight 3
worth
-values
culture 2
philosophy 2
time 9
valued
beloved 1
dear 1
estimable
old 8
precious 2
significant 1
special 5
well-thought-of
valueless
dud 2
empty 4
hollow 5
meaningless 2
trifling
worthless 1,3
valve
tap[2] 1
vamoose
depart 1
escape 1
flee 1
fly 2
leave[1] 1
make 26
run 2
vamp
charmer
flirt 3
patch 5
repair 1
seduce 1
siren 2
temptress
wanton 5
vampire
demon 1
devil 2
vampish
flirtatious
foxy 2
van
front 3
head 3
lead 11
spearhead 2
-in the van
front 8
spearhead 1
vandal
barbarian 2
punk 1
vandalism
plunder 3
vandalization
pillage 2
plunder 3
vandalize
destroy 1
mutilate 2
overrun
pillage 1
plunder 1
trash 4
vandalizing
plunder 3
vanguard
front 3
head 3
lead 11
line[1] 14
precursor 1
spearhead 2
-in the vanguard
ahead 1
before 2
front 8
spearhead 1
vanish
depart 1
die 2
disappear 1
disperse 2
dissipate 2
dissolve 1
end 9
escape 1
evaporate 2
exit 3
finger 9
flee 1
go 10
lift 5
melt 4
pass 10,14b
powder 2
roll 2
sink 5
slip[1] 5,6
vanished
extinct 1
lost 1,4
vanishing
dissipation 2
passing 1
vanishment
passing 4
vanity°
conceit 1
gewgaw
pride 2
self-esteem 1
snobbery
vanquish
back 7b
beat 2
best 11
conquer 1
crush 4
defeat 1
overcome 1
overpower 1
rout 2
slaughter 4
subdue 2
topple 2
triumph 3
upset 4
vanquished
underdog
vanquishment
conquest 1
defeat 3
rout 1
vantage point
perch 1
perspective 1
point of view 1
standpoint
viewpoint
vapid°
colourless 2
dead 10
dreary 2
flat 5
inane
lacklustre
lifeless 3
pedestrian 2
stodgy
stupid 3
tame 4
tasteless 2
tedious
wishy-washy 2
vapidity
tedium
vanity 2
vaporization
evaporation 1
vaporize
disappear 1
dissipate 2
evaporate 1
vaporizer
spray[1] 3
vaporizing
volatile 1
vaporous
intangible
vapour°
exhalation 2
film 3
fluid 1
fog 1
fume 3
mist 1
reek 4
-vapours°
at **vapour 2**
vapouring
raving 3
variability
inconstancy
vicissitude 1
variable°
capricious
changeable 1
chequered 2
erratic 1
fanciful 1
fitful
flighty 1
fluid 3
inconsistent 2
inconstant
movable
protean
uncertain 4
unsettled 1
unstable 1
variant 2
versatile 2
volatile 2
variance°
conflict 3
discrepancy
-at variance°
at **variance 3**
conflict 4
differ 2
discordant 1
odds 4
opposed
variant°
alternate 5
alternative 1,2
divergent
mutation 2
version 1
variation°
change 2,3
difference 1
diversity 1
fluctuation
mutation 1,2
shade 7
tolerance 2
twist 8
variance 1
variant 1
variety 2
version 1
vicissitude 1
-variations
fluctuation
vicissitude 2
varicoloured
variegated
varied°
different 3
divers
diverse
manifold
many 2
miscellaneous
mixed 2
odd 2
sundry
variegate
diversify

variegated°
chequered 2
divers
mottled
variegation
diversity 2
variation 2
variety°
assortment 2
brand 1
breed 1
category
change 2
denomination 2
description 3
diversity 1, 2
form 3
genre
kind[2] 1
line[1] 16
miscellany
model 6
nature 4
range 2
selection 2
several 2
shade 7
sort 1, 3
stamp 8
stock 1
style 1
type 1
variation 1, 2
various 1
version 1
vicissitude 1
various°
different 3
divers
diverse
manifold
many 2
miscellaneous
mixed 2
odd 2
several 2
sundry
varlet
boy 2
miscreant 1
stinker
wretch 1
varnish
distort 2
embellish 1
glaze 1, 2
spread 7
vary°
alter
change 7
depart 2
differ 2
diversify
fluctuate
range 6
see-saw 2
stagger 3
turn 43
varying
arbitrary 1
chequered 2
diverse
fitful
miscellaneous
mutation 1
unsettled 1
variable
variant 2
variation 1
vase
jar[1]
vasectomize
sterilize 2
vassal
satellite 2
slave 1
subject 5
subordinate 2
vassalage
bondage
servitude
slavery 1
vast°
boundless
colossal 1
enormous
extensive 1, 2
gigantic
great 1, 2
huge
immeasurable
immense
inestimable 2
infinite 1
limitless
massive
monstrous 3
monumental 1, 2
prodigious 1
spacious
substantial 2
unlimited 2
voluminous 1
vastly°
very 1
vastness
size 1
spread 9
waste 8
wild 10
vasty
boundless
vast
vatic
prophetic
vaticinal
ominous 3
vaticinate
forecast 1
predict
prophesy 1, 2
vaticination
forecast 2
prophecy 1
vaticinator
prophet
seer
vault
bound[2] 1, 3
cache 1
cellar
clear 28
crypt
firmament
grave[1]
hop 1, 3
hurdle 2
jump 1, 8
leap 1, 5
safe 7
spring 1, 6
tomb
vault of heaven
firmament
sky 1
vaunt
boast 2
brag
display 3
flourish 2
parade 5
shake 4
swagger 2
talk 8
vaunting
egotistical
ostentatious
Vaya con Dios
farewell 3
VDU
monitor 2
terminal 4
vector
carrier 2
vedette (boat)
picket 3
veer
careen
deflect
depart 2
deviate 1
dodge 1
lurch[2] 2
shift 5
sway 2
veer *(cont.)*
swerve
tack 6
trend 3
turn 2, 4
vary 3
wheel 2
wind[2] 1
vegetable
clod 2
plant 1
–vegetables
produce 7
vegetate
loaf[2] 1
lounge 1
stagnate
vegetation
growth 2
vehemence
eagerness 1
edge 3
feeling 4
fervour
fury 2
heat 2
intensity
rage 1
violence 1, 2
warmth 3
vehement
burning 2
eager
excited 2
fierce 2
heated
hot 3, 4
impassioned
intense 2
passionate 1
strong 5
tempestuous
torrential
towering 2
violent 1, 3
wild 6
vehemently
fiercely
madly 3
vengeance 2a
warmly 5
vehicle°
agent 2
car 1
machine 2
mean[3] 4a
medium 5
organ 2
tender[3] 2
tool 2
voice 3
veil°
blur 4
camouflage 2
cloak 2, 3
eclipse 1
envelop 2
film 1, 3, 4
gloss[1] 4
hide[1] 2
mantle 2, 3
mask 2, 3
obscure 6
pall[1] 1
pretence 2
pretext 1
screen 7
shade 5, 12
shadow 2
shroud 1, 3
shut 5c
submerge 3
veiled°
hidden
interior 3
invisible 2
mystical 1
obscure 1
occult 1
subtle 2
surreptitious
vague 1, 3
vein°
mine 1, 2
seam 2
significance 1
strain[1] 9
stratum 1
streak 1
style 5
tone 3
veld
plain 6
veldt
plain 6
velitation
contest 2
disagreement 3
dispute 3, 4
velleity
inclination 3
vellicate
pluck 4
wag[1] 1
vellication
wag[1] 2
velocity°
haste 1
pace 2
rate[1] 1
speed 1
way 5
velvet
–in velvet
opulent 1
on velvet
opulent 1
rich 1
velvety
sleek 1
smooth 2
soft 8
venal°
abusive 3
corrupt 1
foul 7
lawless 2
mercenary 1, 2
rotten 3
time-serving
vicious 1
venality
vice 1
vend
market 4
peddle
sell 1, 2
vendetta°
combat 2
feud 1
vending
sale 1
vendor
dealer
merchant 1
pedlar
seller
trader
tradesman 1
veneer°
face 3, 16
gloss[1] 2
semblance 1, 2
sheet 4, 5
skin 2
venerable°
aged
ancient 3
classic 2
elder 2
elderly 1
famous
grand 2
grey 3
illustrious
lofty 2
precious 2
sacred 1
time-honoured
well-established
venerate°
admire 2
adore 2
commemorate
esteem 1
venerate *(cont.)*
exalt 2
fear 6
glorify 2
hallow 2
honour 5
idolize
look 12
praise 4
respect 6
revere
worship 1
venerated
dear 1
holy 1
noble 3
precious 2
sacred 1
time-honoured
well-thought-of
veneration°
fear 2
glory 2
honour 2
piety 2
praise 2
prostration 2
regard 7
respect 2
reverence 1
worship 2
venereal°
erotic 2
social 2
venetian blind
shade 5
vengeance°
reprisal
requital 2
retribution
revenge 1
–with a vengeance°
at **vengeance 2**
vigorously
vengeful
rancorous
vindictive
vengefulness
rancour
venial°
permissible
venom°
gall[1] 1
grudge 1
ill will
poison 1
rancour
sarcasm
spite 1
virulence 2
venomous°
cutting 2
harmful
malignant 2
poisonous 1
profane 3
rancorous
sarcastic
sharp 5
spiteful
vicious 2
virulent 2
venomousness
rancour
sarcasm
virulence 1, 2
vent°
emit
evacuate 1
exhaust 5
exit 1
mouth 2
outlet 1
pore[2]
wreak
ventilate
air 6
expose 1
freshen 3
reveal
vent one's spleen
fly 8b
vent one's spleen *(cont.)*
piece 12
venture°
activity 2
adventure 2, 3
attempt 1
bet 1, 2
dare 2
effort 2
endeavour 2
enterprise 1
essay 2, 3
fling 3
gamble 1, 3
hazard 3
invest 1
jeopardize
operation 3
pawn[1] 2
presume 2
pretend 2
project 2
reckon 3
say 6
sink 10
stake[2] 4
trial 3
try 1, 5
undertaking 1
venturesome°
adventurous
audacious 1
bold 1
daring 2
dauntless
enterprising
fearless
foolhardy
intrepid
manly
rash[1]
venue
locale
veracious
faithful 4
honest 1
precise 1
right 2
sincere
true 1
truthful
veracity
honesty 2
integrity 1
veranda
portico
verandah
portico
verbal°
oral
spoken 1
verbalization
expression 1
verbalize
express 1
phrase 4
say 4
vent 3
voice 4
verbatim°
exactly 1
letter 4
literal 1
literally 1
perfectly 3
precise 1
same 2
verbal 2
verbiage
hot air
talk 18
tautology
waffle 3
verbose
diffuse 2
discursive
expletive 1
lengthy
ponderous 2
rambling 1
redundant 2
talkative
windy 2

verbose (*cont.*)
wordy
verbosity
rhetoric 2
tautology
verboten
illegal
pale[2] 3
taboo 1
unlawful
verb phrase
phrase 1
verdant
green 1
leafy
lush 1
verdict
decision 2
determination 2
finding 2
judgement 2
resolution 3
sentence
verecund
bashful 2
modest 1
shy 1
verge°
border 5
brink 2
edge 1
eve 2
margin 1
perimeter
point 9
shoulder 1
side 1
tend[1]
threshold 2
-on the verge of
almost
ready 4
verge on
approximate 2
border 8, 9
join 4
near 10
verging
inclined 3
verging on
almost
verifiable
absolute 4
actual 1
authoritative 2
demonstrable
factual 1
hard 8
historical
real 1
stack 7a
supportable 2
true 1
verification
check 15
demonstration 1
evidence 1
hallmark 1
identification 1
proof 1
seal 2
testimony
verified
actual 1
official 1
real 1
true 1
verify°
attest
authenticate
certify 1
check 3, 4, 8, 10c, 11
confirm 1
determine 2
document 2
establish 3
prove 1
ratify
seal 4
show 3
substantiate
support 6
warrant 4

verify (*cont.*)
witness 3
verily
substantially
truly 4
veritable°
absolute 2
authentic
authoritative 2
bona fide
genuine 1
real 1
veritably
fairly 3
substantially
verkrampte
reactionary 1, 2
verligte
liberal 2, 4
vermicular
serpentine 2
vermiculate
serpentine 2
vermin
rabble 2
vernacular°
cant 2
dialect
idiom 1
informal 3
jargon 1
language 1, 3
lingo
tongue 1
vulgar 3
vernal
spring 10
vernissage
opening 4
preview
reception 2
versatile°
adaptable
mobile 4
versatility
flexibility 2
verse
jingle 3
passage 2
poem
poetry
rhyme 1
text 2
versed°
adept 1
experienced 1
familiar 4
informed 2
know 1
learned
lettered
old 7
practised 2
versemaker
poet
versification
poetry
rhyme 1
versifier
poet
version°
arrangement 4
edition
issue 5
model 6
paraphrase 1
recital 2
rendering
revision
story 2
twist 8
verso
page[1] 1
reverse 7
vertebrae
spine 1
vertex°
spire 2
tip[1] 1
top 1
zenith

vertical
erect 1
perpendicular 1
picket 1
plumb 2
prop 3
sharp 2
sheer 1
standing 4
steep
straight 2
upright 1, 3
vertically
plumb 3
upright 4
vertiginous
dizzy 1
faint 2
giddy 1
queer 3
vertigo°
spin 3
verve°
animation 1
bounce 2
dash 6
eagerness 1
electricity
energy
fervour
fire 2
flair 2
heart 4
life 7
panache
passion 1
pep 1
push 14
snap 11
vigour
very°
awfully
downright 2
eminently
exceedingly
extra 6
extreme 3, 9
extremely
fearfully 2
fiercely
frightfully
full 15
highly 2
level 3
mighty 4
overly
particularly 1
perfectly 1, 4
precise 4
pretty 3
profoundly
quite 1
rather 1
really 4
same 1
supremely
terribly
Very light
beacon
very much
awfully
badly 8
dearly 1
deeply 2
quite 4
vastly
widely 2
very well
OK 1
vesica
halo
vespasienne
toilet 1
vespers
night 2
vessel°
boat
craft 4
jar[1]
receptacle
ship 1
vestal
immaculate 2
pure 3

vestibule
hall 1
lobby 1
lounge 3
passage 4
vestige°
flicker 4
gleam 2
remnant 1
shadow 3
sign 3
spark 1
step 3
strain[2] 2
trace 1
-vestiges
remain 4a
scrap[1] 2
vestigial°
rudimentary 2
vestment
clothes
costume
robe 1
-vestments
clothes
garments
gear 3
habit 3
robe 2
vest-pocket
diminutive
miniature
portable
short 2
slight 3
vesture
robe 2
vet°
examine 1
inspect
interview 4
monitor 3
screen 8
veteran°
champion 3
elder 2
experienced 2
old 7
pensioner
professional 1
proficient
ripe 2
seasoned
veto°
decline 1
denial 3
forbid
kill 6
reject 1
reverse 3
revoke
vetoing
veto 2
vetting
interview 2
vex
aggravate 2
anger 2
annoy 1
chafe 3
displease
distress 3
disturb 1
exasperate 2
exercise 3
fret 2
gall[2] 4
get 17
gnaw 3
grate 3
harass
infuriate
irk
irritate
jar[2] 3
madden 2
molest 1
nag[1] 1
offend 1
outrage 4
persecute 2
perturb
pester

vex (*cont.*)
plague 3
prey 3c
provoke 3
put 23b
rankle
rasp 4
ruffle 3
sour 6
spite 3
tease 1
torment 2
trouble 2
umbrage
wear 7
worry 1
vexation
anger 1
annoyance 1
bind 6
bother 5
discomfort 1
displeasure 2
gall[2] 2
headache 2
indignation
pain 3
persecution 2
pest
plague 2
pressure 3
thorn 2
torment 4
trouble 5
umbrage
worry 3
vexatious
burdensome
grating 1
irksome
nerve-racking
niggling 1
painful 2
provocative 2
self-willed
thorny 2
tiresome 2
troublesome
untoward 2
wicked 5
vexed
angry 1
concerned 2
cross 6
discontented
disgruntled
fretful
huff 1
indignant
smitten 1
sore 4
warm 2
vexillum
flag[1] 1
pennant
vexing
harrowing
irksome
nerve-racking
niggling 1
painful 2
provocative 2
tiresome 2
trying
untoward 2
weary 2
via
by 2
mean[3] 3
rail[1] 2
through 1
way 10a
viability
feasibility
life 1
viable°
feasible
live 1
possible 2
practicable
tenable
viands
fare 3
food

viands (*cont.*)
meat 1
provision 4
ration 2
sustenance 1
vibes°
undercurrent 2
vibrant
animated 1
brisk 4
energetic
glowing 2
mellow 2
resonant
rich 5
round 7
vibrate°
flap 1
flicker 2
flutter 3
hum 1
oscillate
pulsate
quake 1
quaver 1
quiver 1
rattle 2
shake 2
shiver[1] 2
shudder 1
swing 1
tremble 1
wag[1] 1
vibrating
pulse 1
resonant
swing 3
vibration
hum 4
pulse 1
quaver 2
shudder 2
swing 3
thrill 2
tremble 2
wag[1] 2
-vibrations
electricity
undercurrent 2
vibes
vicar
clergyman 1
minister 1
pastor
priest
vicarious°
Vicar of Bray
turncoat
vice°
clamp 1
evil 6
fault 4
perversion 2
profligacy 1
prostitution 1
sin 2
vice-president
director 1
vice-ridden
profligate 1
vice versa°
topsy-turvy 1
vicinage
neighbourhood 1
outskirts
part 6
proximity
territory 1
vicinity
vicinity°
neighbourhood 1
outskirts
part 6
place 2
presence 1
proximity
territory 1
whereabouts
-in the vicinity
near 1, 9
nearby 1
round 22, 26

vicious°
bad 3
bitter 5
black 6
bloodthirsty
cold-blooded 3
cruel 2
cutthroat 3
cutting 2
deadly 3
disreputable 1
evil 1
evil-minded 2
ferocious
foul 4
ghoulish 2
grim 2
ill 2
inhuman 1
lousy 1
malignant 2
mischievous 2
miscreant 2
monstrous 2
nasty 4
outrageous 2
poisonous 2
ruthless
savage 2
tart[1] 2
unmerciful
venomous 2
virulent 2
wanton 4
wicked 4
viciously
badly 4
fiercely
viciousness
barbarity
devilry 2
enormity
evil 6
vicissitude°
reverse 8
-vicissitudes°
at **vicissitude 2**
victim°
butt[1]
case[1] 3
casualty 2a
dupe 1
fool 3
game 5
invalid[1] 2
monkey 2
prey 2
scapegoat
score 7
sucker
underdog
victimization
persecution 1
victimize°
defraud
dupe 3
fleece
persecute 1
prey 3b
rob 3
swindle 1
victor°
champion 1
winner
-be the victor
win 1
Victorian
delicate 5
strait-laced
victorious°
defeat 1
successful 4
triumph 3
triumphant
upset 4
win 1
winning 2
victory°
achievement 2
conquest 2
first 7
prevail 1
triumph 1,3
upset 11
victory (*cont.*)
win 1,4
victual
cater 1
feed 1
keep 2
provide 1
provision 5
supply 1
victualling
provision 1
victuals
diet[1] 1
fare 3
food
meal 1
meat 1
nourishment
provender 1
provision 4
ration 2
scoff[2] 2
subsistence 2
sustenance 1
table 1
videlicet
namely
video
film 2
tape 2,4
television
video receiver
television
videotape
film 2
vidette boat
picket 3
vie°
compete
match 6
play 3
rival 2
run 5
take 35b
view°
advice 1
attitude 2
behold
belief 3
comment 2
contemplate 1
conviction 2
discover 2
esteem 2
estimate 4
estimation 1
exposure 4
eye 6,7,10
favour 4
feeling 2
find 4
gaze 1
grip 3
horizon
idea 3
judgement 4
landscape
look 1
mentality 2
mind 6
observe 2
opinion 1
outlook 1
overlook 3
perceive 3
perception 1
perspective 1
philosophy 2
place 16
point 12
point of view 2
posture 3
principle 2
prospect 1
purpose 1
reckon 2
regard 1,2,4
scene 4
school 3
see 1
sentiment 2
side 3
sight 2,7,8
slant 1
view (*cont.*)
standpoint
survey 2
take 8
tenet
thesis 1
understand 3
understanding 4
version 2
viewpoint
vision 3
witness 4
-in full view
daylight 2
-into view
forward 5
-in view
impending
out 4
prospect 4
-in view of°
at **view 6**
considering
light[1] 11
seeing
-with a view
for 2
viewable
public 4,5
viewed
reputed
viewer
eyewitness
observer
onlooker
spectator
witness 1
viewing
observation 1
viewpoint°
angle[1] 2
aspect 1
attitude 2
estimate 4
idea 3
mind 6
opinion 1
outlook 1
perspective 1
phase 4
philosophy 2
point of view 1
position 3
posture 3
principle 2
side 3
slant 1
stance
stand 13
standpoint
tenet
thinking 2
vigil
eve 1
eye 8
wake[1] 3
watch 5
vigilance°
care 2
caution 2
patrol 2
precaution 2
preparedness
prudence 1
vigilant°
alert 1
careful 1
cautious
look 9
mindful
observant 1
protective
provident 1
prudent 1
see 5
sleepless 2
wakeful 2
wary
watch 4,8
vigilantly
jealously
sharp 12
vignette
portrait
profile 2
vigorish
interest 6
profit 1
vigorous°
active 1
alive 3
ambitious 2
animated 1
arduous 2
bold 3
brisk 1
buxom 1
dashing 1
drastic
dynamic
emphatic
energetic
enterprising
enthusiastic
exuberant 1
fit[1] 3
forceful 1
fresh 5
hardy 1
healthy 1
hearty 3,5
impassioned
industrious
live 2
lively 1
lusty 1,2
make 43
nail 4a
passionate 1
perky
potent 1
powerful 1
productive 2
quick 3
racy 1
robust 1
rousing
rugged 3
smart 5
solid 8
sound[2] 2
spanking 3
spirited
stalwart 1
stiff 4
strenuous 2
strong 5,17
sturdy 2
tireless
tough 3
vital 3
warm 2
well[1] 16
vigorously°
hard 13
tightly
warmly 4,5
vigorousness
health 2
stamina
vigour°
action 1
activity 1
ambition 2
animation 1
dash 6
drive 8
dynamism
eagerness 1
energy
enterprise 2
exuberance 1
fire 2
fitness 2
force 1
gumption 2
health 2
industry 3
initiative 2
inspiration 1
intensity
juice 2
life 7
main 6
panache
passion 1
pep 1
vigour (*cont.*)
power 4
punch[1] 3
push 14
salt 2
sinew 2
snap 11
sparkle 4
spice 2
stamina
strength 5
verve
violence 1
vitality 1
warmth 3
vihara
monastery
vile°
abominable 1
abusive 1
bad 2,3
base[2] 2
beastly 2
black 6
contemptible
criminal 2
damnable
dark 4
degenerate 1
despicable
diabolic 2
dirty 6
disgraceful 1
disgusting
dishonourable 3
disreputable 1
evil 1,5
filthy 1
foul 4
frightful 2
hateful 1
hideous 2
ill 2
immoral 1
impure 4
indecent 2
infamous 2
lascivious 2
loathsome
lousy 1
low[1] 12
mean[2] 3
miserable 4
monstrous 2
nasty 1
obnoxious
obscene 1
offensive 3
outrageous 2
prurient 2
rank[2] 3
reprobate 1
repugnant
repulsive
revolting
rotten 3,4
satanic 2
scurrilous
scurvy
seamy
servile
shabby 4
shameful
sinful
sordid 1
stinking 2
terrible 1,5
ugly 2
ungodly 1
vicious 1
wicked 2
wretched 4
wrong 1
vileness
dirt 3
evil 6
filth 2
impurity 3
infamy 2
servility
vulgarity 2
vilification
abuse 8
attack 7
disgrace 2
vilification (*cont.*)
libel 1
shame 2
slander 1
smear 4
vilify°
abuse 3
attack 2
blacken 2
denounce 3
discredit 1
disgrace 4
disparage 2
impeach 2
libel 3,4
run 26b
slam 3
slander 2
smear 2
vituperate
vilifying
abusive 1
scurrilous
vilipend
depreciate 2
diminish 2
libel 4
vilify
vilipenditory
vituperative
villa
palace
residence 3
village
local 2
municipal
municipality
place 2
settlement 1
town
villager
citizen 2
villain°
criminal 3
devil 2
miscreant 1
ogre
rascal
reprobate 2
rogue 1
scoundrel
stinker
swindler
transgressor
wretch 1
villainous°
atrocious 1
bad 3
base[2] 6
black 6
criminal 2
dark 4
devilish
dirty 3
dreadful 2
evil 1
flagrant
foul 4
immoral 1
incorrigible
infamous 2
infernal 2
lawless 3
miscreant 2
monstrous 2
outrageous 2
reprobate 1
rotten 3
sinister 2
stinking 2
ungodly 1
wicked 2
wrong 1
villainously
badly 4
villainy
atrocity 2
devilry 2
evil 6
infamy 2
vice 1
villeinage
bondage

vitalize°
animate 1,2
electrify 2
enliven 1
fire 8b
freshen 2
inspire 1
pep 2
perk up
quicken 3
raise 13
refresh 1
strengthen 2
tone 6
wake[1] 2
vitalized
eager
perky
vitalizing
exhilarating 1
invigorating
refreshing
rousing
vital 4
vital part
meat 2
–vital parts
gut 1
vitals
bowels
gut 1
vitelline
cowardly
vitiate°
alloy 2
contaminate
debase 2
demoralize 2
desecrate
diminish 2
disgrace 4
dishonour 2
foul 14
hurt 1
poison 3
profane 4
taint 2
vitiated
bad 2
degenerate 1
impure 4
vitiating
ruin 2
vitiation
degradation 1
disgrace 1
impairment
pollution
ruin 2
sacrilege 1
vitriol
gall[1] 1
ill will
vitriolic
devastating 1
keen[1] 2
scathing
sharp 5
trenchant
vituperate°
denounce 3
harangue 2
rail[2]
sound[1] 9
vituperation
abuse 8
harangue 1
tongue-lashing
vituperative°
abusive 1
foul 6
profane 3
scorching 2
scurrilous
vivacious°
alert 2
alive 3
animate 3
animated 1
bright 8
bubbly 2
buoyant 2
effervescent 2
vivacious (*cont.*)
exuberant 1
gay 2
lively 1
merry 1
perky
pert 2
quick 3
racy 1
scintillating 2
spirited
sprightly
vigorous
vital 3
vivaciously
vigorously
vivaciousness
passion 1
spirit 3
verve
vitality 1
vivacity
animation 1
bounce 2
energy
exuberance 1
fire 2
hilarity
life 7
passion 1
pep 1
soul 4
sparkle 4
spirit 3
verve
vigour
vitality 1
viva voce
oral
spoken 1
verbal 1
vivid°
bold 3
bright 5
clear 5
conspicuous 2
distinct 1
dramatic 2
eloquent 1
expressive 3
full 10
gay 3
glaring 2
graphic 1
hot 8
juicy 2
keen[1] 4
lifelike
lively 2,4
lurid 1
photographic 1
pictorial 1
picturesque 2
plain 2
realistic 2
sensational 2
strong 15,19
vividness
depth 4
vivify
animate 1
enliven 1
fire 8b
inspire 1
pep 2
quicken 3
raise 13
vitalize
wake[1] 2
vivifying
exhilarating 1
invigorating
vital 4
vixen
devil 2
fury 3
hag
jade 2
shrew
viz
like[1] 6
namely
vocabulary
diction 1
language 3
phrase 3
style 5
terminology
verbal 3
vocal
oral
spoken 1
verbal 1
vocalist°
singer
vocalization
intonation
vocalize
enunciate 1
mouth 7
pronounce 1
sing 1
sound[1] 7
vocalized
oral
vocal score
score 5
vocation°
activity 2
bag 5
business 1
calling
career 1
craft 3
employment 1
job 1
line[1] 7
mission 2
occupation 1
practice 3
profession 1
pursuit 3
racket 3
trade 2
work 2
vociferate
bawl 1
exclaim
rail[2]
rant 2
vociferation
exclamation
outcry
vociferous
blatant 2
noisy
obstreperous
torrential
vociferously
warmly 5
vogue°
fad
fashion 1
furore 2
mode[2]
popularity
rage 3
rave 4
style 2
trend 2
–in vogue
current 3
fashionable
minute[1] 3
modern
obtain 3
popular 1
stylish
trendy 1
voguish
trendy 1
voice°
choice 2
enunciate 1
express 1
mouth 7
organ 2
part 3
phrase 4
pronounce 1
say 12
set 18a
sound[1] 7
speak 4
state 7
voice (*cont.*)
suffrage
take 24
tone 3
tongue 2
vent 3
voiced
oral
voiceless
dumb 1
inarticulate 3
mute 1
speechless 1
voice-over
narration 2
narrator
voicing
expression 1
void°
abolish
blank 2,8
cancel 1
defecate
discharge 4,11
emptiness 1
empty 1,8
evacuate 1
exhaust 3
forgive 3
gap 1
glassy 2
gulf 2
hollow 1
interval 3
invalid[2] 1
lapse 5
lift 4
neutralize
oblivion 1
pass 12
quash 1
repeal 1
revoke
spike 3
undo 3
vacancy 1
vacant 1
vacate 3
vitiate 3
withdraw 2
voiding
cancellation 1
discharge 11
exhaustion 1
negative 3
repeal 2
voidness
emptiness 1
void of°
at void 3
volatile°
changeable 1
emotional 2
excitable
explosive 1
fickle
flighty 1
fugitive 3
giddy 2
hasty 4
hotheaded
inconstant
intense 3
moody 3
passionate 3
precipitate 5
quick-tempered
sensitive 2
short-lived
temperamental 1
transient
unstable 1
waspish
whimsical 2
volatility
inconstancy
temper 3
volition°
discretion 2
–of one's own volition
freely 2
volitional
voluntary 2
volley°
discharge 10
fire 3
hail[2] 1,2
rain 3
round 14
volleying
volley 3
volte-face
about-turn
reversal 1
volubility
fluency
voluble°
effusive
fluent
talkative
windy 2
volume°
amount 2
batch 1
book 1
bulk 1
capacity 1
content[1] 1
extension 2
mass 2
measure 1
measurement 2
proportion 4
quantity
size 1
stack 3
turnout 2
turnover
voluminous°
bulky
extensive 2
immense
spacious
vast
voluntarily°
freely 2
willingly
voluntary°
free 6
independent 4
optional
unpaid 2
wilful 1
volunteer
enlist 1
enrol 1
offer 4
pipe 8
sign 10a
unpaid 2
venture 2
voluptuary
luxurious 2
profligate 3
rake[2]
sensualist
sybarite
voluptuous 1
wanton 5
voluptuous°
carnal
epicurean 1
erotic 1
exciting 2
full 7
luxurious 2
profligate 1
provocative 1
prurient 1
sensual
sexual 2
shapely
sultry 2
tempting 1
voluptuousness
dissipation 1
luxury 2
profligacy 1
volute
spiral 1,2
twirl 3
voluted
spiral 2
vomit°
bring 15d
eject 2
vomit (*cont.*)
erupt 1
gorge 2
heave 4
regurgitate
spew
spout 1
throw 9a
vomiting
ejection 1
eruption 1
vomit-provoking
nasty 1
nauseous
repellent
revolting
terrible 5
yucky
vomitus
gorge 2
voodoo
enchant 1
jinx 1
magic 1
ruffle 3
voracious°
famished
gluttonous
greedy 1
hoggish
hungry 1
predatory 2
rapacious
ravenous 2
thirsty 2
voraciousness
gluttony
greed 3
hunger 1
rapacity
thirst 1
voracity
gluttony
greed 3
hunger 1
lust 2
rapacity
thirst 1
vortex
eddy 1
whirlpool
votaries
school 2
votary
devotee
disciple 2
sectarian 3
vote°
elect 1
election
make 23
poll 1
say 13
suffrage
voice 2
voter
citizen 1
subject 5
vote 3
–voters
public 8
voting
election
poll 1
selection 3
voting right(s)
suffrage
vouch°
certify 1
pledge 4
voucher
check 17
receipt 1
requisition 1
vouch for°
at vouch
attest
authenticate
certify 1
guarantee 2
recommend 2
support 6

vouch for (*cont.*)
verify
warrant 3
vouchsafe°
attest
certify 1
commit 4
deign
donate
give 1
maintain 3
pledge 4
sanction 5
swear 1
testify
vow°
assurance 1
attest
commit 4
insist 2
oath 1
pledge 1, 4
profess 1
promise 1, 3
resolution 2
swear 1
undertake 2
undertaking 3
wed 1
word 4
voyage
cruise 1, 2
excursion 1
expedition 1
flight^{1} 2
go 1
hop 4
journey 1, 3
migrate 2
navigate 1
passage 7
pilgrimage
quest 1
roam
tour 1, 4
travel 3
trip 3, 7
-voyages
travel 2
voyager
passenger
tourist
traveller
vulgar°
abusive 1
barbarian 3
base^{2} 4
bawdy
blue 2
boorish
broad 8
coarse 3
common 3
conspicuous 2
crude 4
earthy
flashy 1
foul 5
garish
gaudy
gross 3
impolite
indecent 2
low^{1} 3, 12
nasty 3
naughty 3
obscene 1
plebeian 2
profane 3
prurient 2
racy 2
rank^{2} 3
rough 3, 6
rude 3
scurrilous
sexy 2
suggestive 2
tacky^{2}
tasteless 1
ungraceful 2
unrefined 1
vernacular 2
wicked 3
vulgarian
philistine 1
vulgarity°
filth 3
indelicacy
ribaldry
vulgarization
burlesque 1
vulgarize
vitiate 1
vulgar language
profanity
vulgate
vernacular 2
vulnerability
exposure 2
frailty 2
jeopardy
liability 4
peril
weakness 1
vulnerable°
defenceless
helpless 1
human 2
insecure 2
jealous 2
liable 3
perilous
sensitive 2
subject 6
susceptible 2
tender^{1} 3
unguarded 2
vulpine
devious 1
foxy 1
insincere
wily
vulturine
predatory 2
rapacious
vying
rivalry

wabble
waddle
wacky
deranged
foolish 2
inane
mad 1
preposterous
senseless 3
zany 1
wad°
clod 1
clump 1
lump^{1} 1
mint 1
pad 1, 4
pile^{1} 2
plug 2
roll 18
-wads
mint 1
wadding
filling
pad 1
waddle°
walk 1
wade°
paddle 3
wade in(to)°
at **wade 3**
wade through°
at **wade 4**
wadi
gorge 1
gully
wading pool
pool 1
wady
gorge 1
gully
wafer
flake 1
foil^{2}
waffle°
chatter 1
dodge 3
equivocate
evade 2
fence 4
fib 2
flannel 1
nonsense 1
shuffle 3
waffle on°
at **waffle 1**
waffling
equivocal 1, 2
waft°
blow^{1} 2
drift 1
float 1
sail 3
wag°
card 11
comedian
flap 1, 2
flourish 2
joker 1
wave 4
wit 3
zany 2
wage°
fee 2
salary
war 3
-wages°
at **wage 1**
earnings
fee 2
pay 12
remuneration 1
salary
wage-earner
employee
worker
-wage-earners
labour 2
wager
adventure 4
back 1
bet 1, 2
chance 8
gamble 1, 2, 4
lay^{1} 4
play 7
plunge 4
punt 1, 2
put 6
speculate 2
speculation 3
stake^{2} 1, 4
venture 3
wagerer
better^{2}
punter 1
wagering
speculation 3
wage war
war 3
waggish
arch 3
comic 1
funny 1
humorous
ludicrous
playful 2
sly 2
sportive
witty
waggishness
humour 1
nonsense 2
wit 2
waggle
flap 1, 2
shake 2, 4
swing 1, 3
waddle
wag^{1} 1, 2
wave 4
wriggle 1, 4
waggling
swing 3
wriggle 4
wagon
cart 1
stand 16
tender^{3} 2
-on the wagon
sober 1
wagon-load
cargo
waif
foundling
guttersnipe
ragamuffin
stray 3
wail
bawl 2
complain
cry 1, 4
groan 1, 3
howl 1, 2
keen^{2} 1
lament 1
moan 1, 2, 3
murmur 4
scream 1, 3
sob
wailer
siren 1
wailing
howl 2
lamentation
mourning 1
puling
wainscot
border 4
wainscot(t)ing
border 4
waist
middle 3
waistband
girth 2
wait°
dangle 3
delay 3, 4, 5
expect 1
gap 1
hang 4a, 7b, 7c
hesitate 1
hold 19c
hope 3
hover 2
interlude
interval 1
look 7a
lurk
pause 1, 2
remain 1
sit 8
space 3
stand 5b
stay^{1} 1, 5
stick^{1} 11
tarry 1
watch 4
waiter°
servant 1
waiting
attendance 3
attendant 1
delay 5
expectant
pending 1
poised 2
ready 9a
service 3
tap^{2} 4b
waiting-period
moratorium
waiting-room
lobby 1
lounge 3
wait on°
at **wait 3**
attend 3
look 4
minister 3
serve 1
tend^{2}
wait out
sit 7
waitress
servant 1
waiter
wait upon°
at **wait 3**
attend 3, 4
serve 1
waive°
abdicate
concede 2
dispense 3a
forfeit 2
forgive 3
forgo 1, 2
pass 22
relinquish 1
sign 8
waived
forfeit 3
waiver°
wake°
awake 1
evoke
excite 1
get 51a
incite
outcome
revive 1
rouse 1
track 3
trail 2
upshot
wash 12
-in the wake
subsequent 2
wakeful°
sharp-eyed
sleepless 1
vigilant
waken
arouse 1
energize
evoke
excite 1
foment
heat 4
incite
inspire 1
kindle
knock 7b
provoke 1
refresh 2
revive 1
rise 2, 16
rouse 1
stimulate 1
wake^{1} 1, 2
wakening
incitement 1
wake up
arise 1
arouse 1
awake 1, 3
call 6
come 18b
enliven 1
get 51a
knock 7b
revive 1
rise 2
rouse 1
snap 7
stimulate 1
wise 6
waking
wakeful 1
wale
welt 1, 2
whip 1
walk°
excursion 1
exit 3
file 5
leg 10
march 1, 2, 3
mill 6
motion 3
pace 3
parade 3, 4
path 1
promenade 1, 2, 3
ramble 1, 4
roam
saunter
see 6
sidewalk
stagger 1
walk (*cont.*)
step 13
stream 5
stroll 1, 2
tour 2
tramp 1, 3
traverse 1
turn 4, 16b, 31
wade 1
wander 1
walk a beat
patrol 3
walkabout
ramble 4
tour 2
walk away with
make 27
pocket 4
receive 2
steal 1
take 3
walk behind
follow 1
walker
pedestrian 1
walking
pedestrian 3
walking dictionary
prodigy 1
walking encyclop(a)edia
prodigy 1
walking on air
pleased
rhapsodic
walking papers
brush-off
discharge 9
dismissal 1
push 16
sack 3
walking-stick
stick^{2} 1
walk off the job
strike 15
walk off with
make 27
pilfer
pocket 4
receive 2
steal 1
take 3
walk of life
sphere 2
walk-on
extra 5
walk out°
at **walk 4**
exit 3
go 33c
strike 15
walk-out
strike 20
walk out on
abandon 3
desert^{1} 3
exit 3
throw 8
walk 4a
walk out with
go 40b
walk-over
picnic 2
pushover 1, 2
walk-up
flat 18
walkway
path 1
wall°
barrier 1
enclosure 2
fence 1
partition 3
rampart
screen 1
-off the wall
deranged
funny 2
insane 1
irrelevant
mad 1

wall (*cont.*)
offbeat
unusual
way-out 1
-up the wall
frantic
furious 1
wallet°
bag 3
purse 1
wall in
enclose 1
picket 4
stake[1] 4
wall off°
at **wall 5**
partition 6
screen 6
wallop
batter 1
beat 1
blow[2] 1
bump 3
clip[2] 3, 6
hit 1
jab 2, 4
pelt[1] 1, 4
punch[1] 1, 2
rough 16
shiver[1] 2
slap 1, 4
spank
strike 1
stroke 1
walloping
gigantic
massive
thumping 1
wallow°
lurch[2] 2
revel 1
toss 5
wallow in°
at **wallow 2**
luxuriate 1
revel 1
roll 10b
wallpaper
decorate 2
paper 3, 5
Wall Street
exchange 4
wall-to-wall
packed
sweeping 1
wall up°
at **wall 5**
wamble
waddle
wampum
money 1
wan°
colourless 1
deadly 4
ghastly 2
grey 1
lurid 3
pale[1] 1
pasty
peaky
sickly 2
unwholesome 3
washed out 1
white 2
wand°
rod 1
staff 1
stick[2] 1
wander°
deviate 1
diverge 2
drift 2
go 21c
journey 3
knock 3a
meander 1
migrate 2
mill 6
ramble 1, 2
range 8
roam
run 4
saunter

wander (*cont.*)
snake 4
sprawl 1
straggle
stray 1, 2
stroll 1, 2
traverse 1
walk 3
wanderer
drifter
migrant 1
rover
traveller
vagabond 1
wandering
digression 2
discursive
erratic 3
indirect 1
meandering
purposeless
rambling 3
stray 4
tortuous 1
travelling
vagabond 2
-wanderings
travel 2
wander off
ramble 1
wane°
decay 1
decline 2
decrease 1, 2
die 2
diminish 3
dwindle
ebb 2, 4
fade 2
fail 3
flag[2] 2
lag 2
peter out
recede 2
taper 2
twilight 2
wilt 2
-on the wane°
at **wane 4**
decadent 1
downgrade 4
moribund 2
obsolescent
wangle°
engineer 5
get 9
manoeuvre 3
waning
downgrade 4
moribund 2
obsolescent
twilight 2
want°
absence 2
aim 2
beggar 3
dearth
defect 1
demand 3, 6
desire 1
die 5
expect 3
expectation 3
fancy 11
feel 9
hanker
hardship
hope 4
hunger 3
itch 2
lack 1, 2
like[2] 2
long[2]
mean[1] 1
miss[1] 2
necessity 3
need 1, 5
pant 2
please 2
poverty 1, 2
privation
require 2
requirement 2
scarcity

want (*cont.*)
shortage
will 5
wish 1, 4
yearn
-in want
deprived
destitute 1
empty 7
indigent
need 1
poor 1
starved 3
want 2
wanted
demand 7
desirable 1
enviable
wanting°
absent 2
deficient 1
destitute 2
eager
empty 7
fail 1
failing 2
fall 11b, 19
imperfect
par 5a
scarce
short 6
unsatisfactory
wanton°
abandoned 2
aimless 2
capricious
dissolute
earthy
fast[1] 2
gratuitous 2
immodest 1
immoral 2
impure 4
incontinent 2
lascivious 1
lecherous
libertine 2
loose 7
lost 7
obscene 1
prodigal 1
profligate 1, 3
promiscuous 2
sensual
sensualist
shameless
slattern
tart[2] 2
trifle 3
unchaste
wantonly
fast[1] 9
wantonness
abandon 5
dissipation 1
impurity 3
prodigality 1
profligacy 1
ribaldry
war°
battle 2
combat 1, 4, 5
conflict 1
contest 2
crusade 2
encounter 5
fight 1, 7
hostility 2
-at war°
at **war 2**
militant 2
warble
chirp 1, 2
pipe 4
sing 1
siren 1
twitter 1, 3
warbling
twitter 3
war cry
cry 7
slogan

ward°
district
minor 3
protégé
warden
jailer
keeper
warder
guard 3
jailer
keeper
ward-heeler
politician
warding off
prevention
ward off°
at **ward 3**
defend 2
fend 2
forestall
head 13b
prevent
repel 1
repulse 1
wardress
guard 3
wardrobe°
clothes
garments
wardship
charge 4
warehouse°
store 2
storehouse
wares°
good 21b
stock 1
truck 1
warfare
combat 1
fight 7
hostility 2
war 1
war-game
manoeuvre 2
warhorse
veteran 1
warily
gingerly 1
jealously
salt 5
wariness
calculation 3
caution 2
distrust 2
mistrust 2
precaution 2
prudence 1
suspicion 1
warlike°
aggressive 1
belligerent 1
hostile 3
martial 1
militant 1
offensive 1
truculent
warlock
magician 1
prophet
sorcerer
witch 1
warm°
affectionate
amiable
amicable
ardent
benign 1, 2
chafe 1
cheer 5
comfortable 3
cordial
cosy 1
demonstrative 1
emotional 3
expansive 2
fatherly
fond 1
friendly 2
genial
glowing 2
good-natured
gracious

warm (*cont.*)
hearty 1, 2
heat 3, 4
homely 2
hospitable 1
impassioned
intimate[1] 1, 4
kind[1]
lukewarm 1
maternal
mellow 4
mild 2
neighbourly
nice 1
outgoing 2
rich 5
snug
sociable
soft 3
soulful
sunny 2
sweet 4
tender[1] 6
thaw 1, 2
wholehearted
warm-blooded°
warmed-over
stale 2
warm-hearted
benevolent
benign 1
friendly 2
good-natured
gracious
kind[1]
nice 1
sentimental 1
soft-hearted
sympathetic 1
tender[1] 6
warm-heartedly
warmly 2
well[1] 5
warm-heartedness
humanity 3
kindness 1
sympathy 1
warming
heart-warming 1
warming up
exercise 4
warmish
tepid 1
warmly°
fondly
highly 1, 3
hotly
well[1] 5
warmness
heat 1
warmonger
belligerent 3
warmongering
belligerent 1
jingoism
warlike
warmth°
affection
ardour
feeling 4
fellowship 3
fervour
flame 2
friendship 2
glow 3
heat 1
hospitality
humanity 3
kindness 1
love 1
radiance 2
sensitivity 2
soul 4
spirit 3
sympathy 1
warm to°
at **warm 8**
warm up
chafe 1
exercise 2
heat 3, 4
hot 11

warm up (*cont.*)
thaw 1
warm 7
work 19a
warm-up
exercise 4
practice 2
warn°
advise 1
alert 5
caution 3
flag[1] 2
intimate[2]
lean[2] 4b
lecture 4
notice 7
notify 1
speak 12a
threaten 1
tip[3] 4
wise 4
warner
hors-d'oeuvre
savoury 3
warning°
advice 1
advisory 2
alarm 1
alert 4
caution 1
exemplary 3
foreboding 2
indication 3
injunction 2
lesson 3
menace 3
notice 5
ominous 2
sign 6
siren 1
threat 1
tip[3] 2
-without warning
plump[2] 5
short 11
suddenly 2
summarily 2
warp°
buckle 2
cast 5
colour 4
corrupt 3
distort 1, 2
garble 1
poison 3
prejudice 1, 3
quirk
screw 7c
slant 5
stretch 3
twist 2
violence 3b
warpaint
make-up 1
paint 3
warpath
-on the warpath
angry 1
furious 1
warped
bent 2
biased
crooked 2
deformed 1, 3
gnarled
intolerant 2
kinky 2
lopsided 2
misshapen
mistaken 2
nonsensical
perverted
rotten 3
tortuous 2
warping
twist 9
warrant°
assure 1
bear 3
certify 1
deserve
earn 1
excuse 3

warrant *(cont.)*
indemnity 2
justify
legitimate 4
merit 3
oath 1
occasion 2
permit 2
pledge 1
power 6
promise 3
ratify
stipulate
swear 1
undertake 2
verify
word 4
warranted
deserved
foolproof
warranty°
assurance 1
guarantee 1, 2
insurance
oath 1
pledge 1
promise 1
stipulation
undertaking 3
warrant 1
word 4
warren
burrow 1
slum
warring
belligerent 1, 3
hostile 3
militant 2
warrior
champion 3
hero 1
militant 3
soldier 1
wart
growth 4
lump[1] 2
war-whoop
whoop 1
wary°
alert 1
anxious 1
beware
careful 1
cautious
discreet
distrust 1
distrustful
gingerly 2
guarded
leery
mistrust 1
noncommittal
provident 1
prudent 1
reluctant
sharp-eyed
shy 2, 4
step 12
suspicious 2
thoughtful 3
vigilant
wakeful 2
watch 8
wash°
clean 9, 11a
cleanse 1
flush[1] 2
hold 11
lap[1] 2
launder 1
pan 4
purge 1
purify 1
rinse 1, 3
ripple 3
scour 1
spread 7
submerge 1
sweep 2
tint 1, 2
wake[2] 1
wash away°
at **wash 2**
cleanse 2
wash away *(cont.)*
erode
flush[1] 2
sweep 2
wash-basin
sink 12
wash-bowl
sink 12
wash-cloths
linen
wash down°
at **wash 9**
washed
clean 2
washed out°
colourless 1
muddy 3
neutral 2
pale[1] 1, 2
peaky
washed up°
washer
ring[1] 1
washing
detergent 2
rinse 3
wash 11
washing away
erosion
washing (one's) hands (of)
through 5
wash off°
at **wash 2**
rinse 1
wash (one's) hands
defecate
urinate
wash (one's) hands of°
at **wash 10**
leave[1] 4
secede
wash out°
at **wash 2**
fade 1
flush[1] 2
purge 1
rinse 1
washout°
disappointment 1
dud 1
failure 3
flop 4
loser
reverse 8
washroom
toilet 1
wash up
clean 11a
rinse 1
wash 1
waspish°
cranky 2
cross 6
fretful
harsh 3
hasty 4
impatient 2
moody 2
peevish
perverse 2
petulant
prickly 3
querulous
quick-tempered
short-tempered
snappish 1
temperamental 1
testy
touchy 1
wassail
carouse 2
celebrate 2
wastage
loss 4
waste°
attack 5
blast 5
blow[1] 4
waste *(cont.)*
bump 5
burn 4
consume 3, 4, 5
desert[1] 1
desolation 1
devastate 1
devour 2
dirt 1
dispatch 3
dissipate 3
dissipation 1
ebb 2
eliminate 4
empty 3
execute 3
exhaust 1
exterminate
extravagance 1
finish 4
fritter
garbage
idle 5
junk 1
kill 1
lavish 4
leftover 1
lifeless 4
loaf[2] 2
lose 4
loss 4
murder 3
pass 5
prodigality 1
profligacy 2
refuse[2]
remove 4
rubbish 1
run 34b
scrap[1] 3
soil[1] 3
spend 2
spill 2
splurge 2
swill 1
throw 5b
trash 3
uninhabited
use 5
wild 2
zap
waste away°
at **waste 2**
decay 1b
dwindle
ebb 2
fade 2
flag[2] 2
fool 7b
rot 2
wasted
decrepit 1, 2
drain 3
emaciated
fatigued
gaunt 1
haggard
impoverished 2
infirm 1
lean[1] 1
limp[2] 2
lost 2
misspent
peaky
raw-boned
skinny
weak 2
wizened
wasteful°
bootless
extravagant 1
improvident 1
inefficient 2
lavish 3
non-productive 2
prodigal 1
profligate 2
spendthrift 2
wastefully
water 3
wastefulness
dissipation 1
extravagance 1
prodigality 1
profligacy 2
wastefulness *(cont.)*
waste 6
wasteland
desert[1] 1
moor[1]
waste 8
wild 10
waste matter
soil[1] 3
waste money (on)
splurge 2
waster
good-for-nothing 2
prodigal 3
profligate 4
wastrel 1
waste time
bugger 4a
dawdle
fool 7b
muck 3
stall[2] 1
twiddle 2
wasting
attack 9
decay 3
emaciated
loss 4
removal 2
waste 6
wasting away
emaciated
erosion
frail 2
wastrel°
degenerate 3
derelict 3
good-for-nothing 2
loafer
prodigal 3
profligate 4
rascal
reprobate 2
rogue 1
spendthrift 1
watch°
eye 8, 10
follow 9
guard 1, 3
look 1, 4
lookout 2
mark 12
mind 17
monitor 3
observe 2
oversee
patrol 1
police 2
regard 1
see 1
sentinel
sit 6a
spell[1] 1
spy 2
stare 1
supervise
surveillance
track 4
turn 30
view 7, 8
wake[1] 3
watchman
witness 4
-on the watch (for)°
at **watch 8**
watch 4
watchdog
monitor 1
watchman
watched for
forthcoming 2
watcher
eyewitness
observer
onlooker
spectator
witness 1
watch for°
at **watch 4**
expect 1
watchful
alert 1
anxious 1
attentive 1
awake 4
careful 1
cautious
discreet
eagle-eyed
expectant
gingerly 2
look 9
mindful
noncommittal
observant 1
protective
prudent 1
sharp-eyed
shy 4
sleepless 2
vigilant
wakeful 2
wary
watch 4, 8
watchfully
gingerly 1
jealously
sharp 12
watchfulness
caution 2
expectation 1
foresight 1
patrol 2
precaution 2
prudence 1
vigilance
watching
observance 3
observation 1
watchman°
guard 3
lookout 1
patrol 1
picket 3
porter[2] 2
sentinel
watch 7
watch one's step°
at **step 12**
watch out
beware
look 9
watch over
attend 3
care 6a
defend 1
escort 5
guard 1
keep 2
manage 1
mind 18
mother 5
oversee
patrol 3
preserve 1
protect 2
supervise
tend[2]
watch 2
watch the grass grow
loaf[2] 1
watch the sub-marine races
cuddle 2
watchword
cry 7
password
shibboleth
slogan
symbol
water°
adulterate
cut 6
degrade 3
dilute
doctor 4
thin 9
weaken 4
wet 4
-waters
deep 9
water-closet
facility 2b
lavatory
privy 3
water-colour°
watercourse
channel 1
drain 1
gully
race[1] 2
river 1
stream 1
water down°
at **water 7**
adulterate
cut 6
degrade 3
dilute
doctor 4
thin 9
weaken 4
watered down
thin 6
vapid
watery 1
wishy-washy 2
waterfall°
chute 1
fall 25
watering-hole
oasis 1
pub
watering-place
resort 1
waterless
dry 1
waterlog
saturate
waterlogged
soaking 2
Waterloo
defeat 4
water main
main 5
water-pipe
pipe 2
waterproof
tight 1
watertight 1
watershed
landmark 2
waterspout
eddy 1
spout 3
twister 2
whirlwind 1
watertight°
staunch 2
tight 1
waterway
channel 1
river 1
stream 1
watery°
fluid 2
liquid 2
sickly 3
sloppy 2
tasteless 2
thin 6
vapid
wishy-washy 2
wave°
dangle 2
deep 9
flap 1, 2
flop 2
flourish 2, 4
flutter 1, 4
motion 6
parade 5
rash[2] 2
ripple 1, 3
roll 14
roller 2
sea 2
shake 4
signal 4
snap 9
surge 1, 2
sway 1, 3
swell 5
swing 1

well (*cont.*)
healthy 1
highly 1,3,4
indeed 3
OK 4,7
pit[1] 3
properly 1,2
richly 2
right 16,17
shaft 4
spring 8
stream 4
sweat 8
swimmingly
warmly 3
whole 3
-as well
addition 5,6
besides 1,2
boot 1
likewise 2
moreover
well-adjusted
normal 2
well-balanced 1
well-advised°
better[1] 3,6a
judicious
wise 3
well-aged
ripe 1
well and truly
truly 2
well-balanced°
rational 1
sane
well-behaved
courteous
decorous
good 4
orderly 2
respectful
well-being
ease 1
fitness 2
health 2
sake 1
welfare
well-born
elegant 1
ladylike
upper-class 1
well-bred°
courteous
debonair 1
decent 5
elegant 1
gallant 2
genteel 2
ladylike
pleasant 2
polished 2
presentable 2
refined 1
well brought up
decent 5
well-bred
well-built
full 7
husky 1
mighty 2
solid 6
sound[2] 3
staunch 2
strong 12
sturdy 1
substantial 2
tough 1
voluptuous 2
well-chosen
choice 5
well-connected
important 3
well-considered
wise 3
well-constructed
solid 6
sound[2] 3
staunch 2
well-crafted
exquisite 1
well-defined
clear 5,11
definite 3
distinct 1
explicit 1
express 5
focus 2
graphic 1
hard 12
precise 1
pronounced 1
visible 2
well-disciplined
taut 2
well-disposed
agreeable 2
amiable
benevolent
charitable 2
favourable 2
friendly 1
genial
good 6
indulgent
kind[1]
neighbourly
ready 2
sympathetic 2
well-balanced 2
willing
well done
beautiful 2
congratulations
pukka 1
well-drawn
graphic 1
well-dressed
dapper
well-groomed
well-educated
knowledgeable 2
smart 2
well-informed
well-endowed
bosomy
buxom 2
voluptuous 2
well enough
OK 7
well-established°
old 4
strong 9
substantial 3
well-executed
exquisite 1
well-fed°
fat 1
well-fixed
rich 1
successful 1
well off
well forth
flow 2
stream 4
surge 1
well-fortified
impregnable
well-found
flush[2] 3
well-founded
good 8
just 3
solid 7
stable 1
strong 9
substantial 3
well-established
well-groomed°
smart 3
spruce 1
tidy 1
trim 1
well-grounded
just 3
reasonable 2
well-head
fountain 1
well[2] 1
well-heeled
fat 3
flush[2] 3
loaded 4
well-heeled (*cont.*)
money 4
opulent 1
prosperous 1
rich 1
successful 1
wealthy
well off
well in
thick 8
well-informed°
enlightened
lettered
profound 2
qualified 1
welling
outburst
wash 14
welling up
explosion 3
wave 2
well-intentioned
innocent 3
kind[1]
sympathetic 1
well-kempt
trim 1
well-kept
tidy 1
well-knit
robust 1
well-known°
big 7
celebrated
common 5
eminent 1
familiar 1
famous
great 5
illustrious
legendary 3
notable 1
noted
notorious 2
old 8
open 12
prestigious
prominent 2
proverbial 1
public 6
regular 9
renowned
stale 2
successful 3
traditional
usual
well-established
well made
pukka 1
well-made
exquisite 1
fine[1] 5
solid 6
staunch 2
well-mannered
civil 3
courteous
genteel 2
good 4
graceful 2
gracious
orderly 2
pleasant 2
polished 2
polite 1
presentable 2
refined 1
respectful
well-bred
well-meaning
charitable 2
fatherly
kind[1]
sympathetic 1
well-modulated
smooth 7
well-muscled
muscular
sturdy 1
wellnigh
almost
near 3
wellnigh (*cont.*)
nearly 1
practically 1
well off°
comfortable 2
fat 3
favoured 2
flush[2] 3
loaded 4
money 4
opulent 1
prosperous 1
rich 1
wealthy
well-ordered
coherent 1
neat 1
smooth 3
systematic
tidy 2
trim 1
well-balanced 2
well-organized
coherent 1
logical 3
neat 1
systematic
taut 2
tidy 2
tight 4
well-paid
profitable 1
well-pleased
blithe 1
well-proportioned
full 7
good 10
regular 4
shapely
statuesque
symmetrical
voluptuous 2
well-balanced 2
well provided
replete 1
rich 1
well-read
educated 1
knowledgeable 2
learned
lettered
literary 1
profound 2
smart 2
versed
well-informed
wise 2
well-reasoned
logical 3
well-received
popular 1
welcome 2
well-rounded
full 7
well-run
streamlined 3
well-shaped
full 7
well-skilled
adept 1
well-spent
fruitful 2
well-spoken
eloquent 1
fluent
well-spring
beginning 1
cause 1
fountain 1
head 6
mine 2
origin 1
parent 2
root[1] 1
source 1
spring 8
well[2] 1
well-stacked
full 7
well stocked
replete 1
rich 2
well-substantiated
strong 8
well-suited
seasonable
well supplied
flush[2] 3
full 1
replete 1
rich 2
well-supported
strong 8
well-thought-of°
good 9
honourable 4
prominent 2
reputable
well-thought-out
deliberate 3
logical 3
measured 2
reasonable 2
sensible 1
studied
wise 3
well-timed°
fortunate 2
happy 2
opportune 2
propitious
seasonable
timely
well-to-do
fat 3
flush[2] 3
leisured
loaded 4
money 4
opulent 1
prosperous 1
rich 1
substantial 4
successful 1
wealthy
well off
well turned out
dapper
elegant 1
nice 5
shapely
spruce 1
trim 1
well up
stream 4
surge 1
well-upholstered
plump[1] 1
well-versed°
home 5
proficient
seasoned
smart 2
strong 6
versed
well-informed
wise 2
well-wishing
benevolent
charitable 2
kind[1]
neighbourly
well-worn
time-worn
welsh
renege 2
welsher°
welt°
bruise 1
bump 2
welter°
hotchpotch
wallow 1
wen
elevation 2
growth 4
lump[1] 2
-wens
spot 5
wench
girl 1
maid 1
wend
go 1
walk 1
wend one's way
journey 3
weave 4
West End
stage 3
Western
romance 3
Westminster
parliament 1
wet°
bedraggled
clammy 2
drench
drip 3
feeble 2
foul 8
humid
moist 2
mushy 2
sap[1] 2
saturate
sissy
sloppy 2,3
soak 1
soaking 2
steamy 1
steep[2] 1
submerge 1
sweltering
wash 1
water 6
watery 3
wetback
migrant 1
wet behind the ears
callow
fresh 3
green 2
immature 2
inexperienced
wet blanket
drip 3
killjoy
misery 4
pall[1] 2
spoilsport
turn-off 2
wetness
perspiration
wet 4,5
wet-nurse
nurse 3
wet one's whistle
drink 1
wetting
soaking 1
wettish
damp 1
moist 1
whack
beat 1
blow[2] 1
box[2] 2,3
bump 1
clip[2] 3,6
endeavour 2
go 42
hit 1,10
jab 2,4
knock 1,9
lash[1] 3
lather 4
pelt[1] 4
punch[1] 1,2
rap 4
shot 3
slap 1,4
spank
strike 1
stroke 1
trial 3
try 5
turn 30
-out of whack
blink 6
broken 7
order 13c

whacked
fatigued
tired 1
weary 1
whacking
big 1
massive
whale
scourge 3
wham
thud
wharf
dock 1
landing 3
pier 1
what
-at what place
whereabouts 2
-in what manner
however 3
-in what place
whereabouts 2
-in what way
however 3
-to what place
whereabouts 2
whatchama-callit
contraption
gadget
gimmick 2
instrument 1
thing 5
whatever
-in whatever manner
however 2
-in whatever way
however 2
-to whatever degree
however 2
-to whatever extent
however 2
-to whatever manner
however 2
what for
piece 10
rebuke 2
what is more
further 3
indeed 2
moreover
what it takes
potential 2
power 1
punch[1] 3
whatnot
instrument 1
what of it
bully 4
what's coming to one
desert[2]
whatsit
contraption
gadget
gimmick 2
instrument 1
thing 5
what's what
rope 2
wheal
welt 2
wheedle°
beg 1
cajole
coax
drag 2
entice
flatter 3
get 14, 46b
motivate
work 18
wheedler
flatterer
wheedling
cajolery
enticement 1
wheedling (*cont.*)
flattery
ingratiating
servile
servility
wheel°
bowl[1]
circle 1
helm 1
revolution 3
revolve 1
roll 1
rotate 1
turn 1, 2
twirl 1
-wheels
car 1
wheeler-dealer
operator 3
tycoon
wheelman
navigator
pilot 2
wheel-mark
rut 1
wheelsman
pilot 2
wheeze
dodge 4
gasp 2
pant 1
puff 4
quip 1
wrinkle[2]
whelp
pup
when
directly 5
immediately 3
when all is said and done
eventually
finally 1
practically 1
run 48
sometime 3
soon 5
word 8
when convenient
leisure 3b
when it happened
event 4
when (one) pleases
will 4
when (one) thinks fit(ting)
will 4
when (one) wishes
will 4
when requested
demand 8
when required
demand 8
when the opportunity arises
sometime 2
when the world was young(er)
formerly
where
whereabouts 2
-from where one stands
personally 2
whereabouts°
address 2
position 2
scene 1
whereas
seeing
wherefore
therefore
where it hurts
home 10
where one is coming from
perspective 1
where one lives
home 10
wherewithal
capability
capital 3
finance 2
fund 2
instrument 2
mean[3] 4b
money 2
ready 8
wealth 1
whet°
grind 2
intensify
rouse 2
sharpen
whet (one's) appetite
tempt 1
whether one likes it or not
willy-nilly 1
whether or no
willy-nilly 1
whey-faced
pale[1] 1, 3
pasty
peaky
wan 1
white 2
whiff
breath 1
exhalation 2
hint 2
puff 1
scent 1
smell 1
sniff 1
touch 15
trace 2
trifle 2
vestige
waft 1, 2
whiffle
wave 4
whiffy
smelly
stinking 1
while
pending 1
period 1
space 3
term 2
though 1
time 2
-after a while
length 4a
presently
-for a while
temporarily 2
-in a while
directly 3
presently
shortly 1
while ago
previously
while away
idle 5
kill 7
lead 5
pass 5
twiddle 2
whilom
former 1
past 2
previous 1
prior 1
whim
conceit 2
device 4
extravagance 2
fancy 8
freak 3
kink 4
notion 2
quirk
wish 4, 5
-at (one's) whim
will 4
whimper
bawl 2
bewail
whimper (*cont.*)
complain
cry 2
gripe 1
groan 1, 3
moan 2
snivel
sob
weep 1
whimpering
gripe 2
puling
tearful
whimsical°
arbitrary 1
bizarre 1
capricious
cranky 1
fanciful 1
fancy 2
fickle
giddy 2
humorous
imaginative 2
kinky 1
quaint 1
whimsically
tongue 5
whimsy
fancy 8
notion 2
whim-whams
jitters
nerve 4
whine
blow[1] 2
cry 2
fret 1
gripe 1
groan 1, 3
moan 2
snivel
squawk 2
weep 1
whinge
carp
complain
gripe 1
groan 2
moan 2
snivel
weep 1
whinging
gripe 2
whining
fretful
gripe 2
puling
querulous
whip°
beat 1, 6
chastise
defeat 1
domination 1
flog 1
floor 4
hide[2] 2
hit 1
knock 6a
lambaste 1
lash[1] 1, 3
lather 4
overcome 1
paddle 4
punish 2
rout 2
scourge 2, 3
slap 2
slash 2
stir 1
strike 1
swipe 2
switch 1, 3
whisk 2, 6
whip hand
predominance
whip into shape
regiment
work 20b
whip out°
at whip 6
whipped up
fluffy 1
whippersnapper
pup
youth 2
whipping°
incitement 1
punishment 2
sedition
thrashing 1
whipping-boy
scapegoat
whip-round
collection 1
whip up°
at whip 7
fire 8b
foment
generate 3
incite
inflame 1
kindle
prepare 4
stimulate 1
stir 1
whirl
daze 3
drive 7
eddy 1, 2
fling 3
flow 1
flurry 1
go 35a, 42
gyrate
pirouette 1, 2
pivot 3
revolution 3
revolve 1
roll 16
rotate 1
spin 1, 3, 6, 7
swirl 1, 2, 3
trial 3
turn 1, 26
twirl 1, 2
twitter 4
wheel 2
whirlpool
whirligig
roundabout 3
whirling
spin 6
twirl 2
whirlpool°
eddy 1
whirlwind°
blow[1] 9
eddy 1
hurricane
passion 2
storm 1
twister 2
whirly
whirlwind 1
whirr
hum 1, 4
whirring
hum 4
whisk°
brush[2] 4
flit
shoot 1
spirit 10
sweep 1
swish 1
whip 4, 6
whisker
bristle 1
hair 2
-by a whisker
narrowly 1
whiskered
hairy 1
whiskey
booze 1
liquor 1
whisky
whisky°
booze 1
liquor 1
spirit 9b
whisper°
breath 2
breathe 4
gossip 4
whisper (*cont.*)
hint 2
hush 3
inkling
insinuate 1
murmur 3
pipe 7
rumour 2
rustle 1, 2
say 2
suggestion 2
swish 1
-in whispers
quietly 2
whispered
low[1] 13
whispering
murmur 1
rustle 2
whistle
alarm 1
blow[1] 2
flash 5
pipe 3, 4
signal 4
sing 2
siren 1
streak 5
swish 2
whit
bit 2
grain 3
jot 2
modicum
morsel 2
particle
scrap[1] 1
shred 1
spark 1
speck
trifle 2
white°
colourless 1
deadly 4
pale[1] 1
silver 2, 3
wan 1
whitecap
surge 2
wave 1
white-collar
clerical 2
white-collar worker
worker
whited sepulchre
hypocrite
Pharisee
white elephants
lumber 1
white flag
surrender 2
yield 1
white-haired
favourite 1
golden 6
whitehead
pimple
-whiteheads
spot 5
white-headed
favourite 1
golden 6
white horse
surge 2
wave 1
white-hot
fiery 1
hot 1
incandescent
live 3
white lie
fib 1
white lightning
booze 1
liquor 1
moonshine 3
whisky
white-livered
afraid 1
cowardly
faint-hearted 1

white-livered (*cont.*)
spineless 3
tame 3
white magic
magic 1
white mule
booze 1
liquor 1
moonshine 3
whisky
whiten
bleach 1
fade 1
pale[1] 4
whitener
bleach 2
white sale
sale 3
White slaver
pander 3
pimp 1
procurer
slaver[2] 2
white squall
whirlwind 1
whitewash°
gloss[1] 4
whither
whereabouts 2
whitish
pale[1] 1
white 2
whitish-grey
silver 2
whittle°
carve 1
chip 3
shave 2
whittle away at°
at **whittle 2**
whittle down°
at **whittle 2**
whiz
expert 1
flash 5
magician 2
prodigy 1
professional 3
run 1
shoot 1
streak 5
virtuoso 1
whiz-bang
first-rate
proficient
whiz-kid
prodigy 1
virtuoso 1
whizz
flash 5
prodigy 1
professional 3
run 1
streak 5
virtuoso 1
whizz-bang
first-rate
proficient
whizz-kid
prodigy 1
virtuoso 1
whizzo
expert 2
talented
whodunit
mystery 3
story 1
whole°
complete 1
ensemble 3
entire 1, 2, 3
entirety 2
flawless 1
full 3, 12
gross 2
intact
one 2
overall
perfect 1
round 6
safe 1

whole (*cont.*)
self-contained 3
solid 10
sound[2] 1
sum 1
total 1, 2
totality
unabridged 1
undivided 1, 2
unspoiled
-as a whole
large 5b
-on the whole°
at **whole 5**
chiefly
generally 1
largely
mainly
part 8
primarily 1
principally
rule 4
usually
wholehearted°
heartfelt
hearty 2
implicit 2
unhesitating 2
wholeheartedly
sincerely
vengeance 2b
wholehearted-ness
dedication 1
whole hog
wholly 1
whole kit and caboodle
everything
lot 6
whole 4
works 3a
wholeness
entirety 1
integrity 2
wholesale
broad 6
indiscriminate 2
sweeping 1
wholesaler
dealer
merchant 3
trader
whole shebang
everything
works 3a
whole shooting match
everything
works 3a
wholesome°
chaste 1
comely
edible
fresh 6
good 5, 14
hale
healthy 2
nutritious
pure 2
sanitary
savoury 2
sound[2] 4
wholesomeness
fitness 2
purity 1
whole world
everyone
wholly°
absolutely 2
altogether
clean 7
clear 19
completely 1, 3
entirely 1
flat 16
full 13, 17
head 8
hook 4
perfectly 1
quite 1, 4
root[1] 3
simply 1

wholly (*cont.*)
stark 1
thoroughly 1
through 7
throughout 3
totally
utterly
well[1] 11
whomp
box[2] 2, 3
thud
whoop°
call 13
cry 5
shout 1, 2
squawk 1
whoop-de-do(o)
propaganda 2
whoopee
fun 1
whoop it up
celebrate 2
paint 7
revel 2
whoosh
swish 2
whopper
fib 1
lie[1] 2
myth 2
yarn 2
whopping°
fabulous 3
gigantic
huge
massive
monumental 4
thumping 1
whore
bitch 2
prostitute 1
slattern
tart[2] 2
wanton 5
whoredom
prostitution 1
whore-house
brothel
house 6
whoremaster
procurer
whoremonger
libertine 1
pander 3
pimp 1
profligate 3
whoreson
wretch 1
whorl
coil 2
loop 1
spiral 1
swirl 2
twirl 3
whorled
spiral 2
whosis
gadget
gimmick 2
thing 5
why
reason 1
why and where-fore
reason 1
wicked°
abandoned 2
atrocious 1
bad 3
base[2] 2, 6
black 6
blasphemous
corrupt 2
criminal 2
damnable
dark 4
devilish
diabolic 2
disreputable 1
dreadful 2
evil 1
evil-minded 2
fiendish

wicked (*cont.*)
foul 4
godless 1
grim 3
ill 2
immoral 1
impious
improper 3
impure 4
incorrigible
infamous 2
infernal 2
lawless 3
mischievous 2
miscreant 2
monstrous 2
naughty 2
obscene 2
outrageous 2
perverted
profane 1
profligate 1
reprobate 1
risqué
rotten 3
satanic 1
scandalous 1
severe 5
sinful
sinister 2
unconscionable 1
ungodly 1
unscrupulous
unwholesome 2
vicious 1
vile 1
wanton 4
wrong 1
wickedly
badly 4
wickedness
atrocity 1
devilry 2
enormity
error 2
evil 6
harm 2
impropriety 3
impurity 3
infamy 2
profligacy 1
sin 2
vice 1
wicked one
devil 1
widdershins
backwards 1
wide°
ample 1
beamy
beside 2
broad 1
catholic
comprehensive
deep 1
extensive 1
flamboyant 2
full 5
inclusive 1
large 3
panoramic
spacious
sweeping 1
thick 1
wide awake
alert 1
awake 4
observant 1
sharp-eyed
wide berth
leeway
wide-eyed
goggle-eyed
gullible
widely°
abroad 2
amply 1
broad 6
far 4
popularly
widely known
current 2
open 12

widen°
amplify 1
enlarge 1
expand 3
extend 2
flare 2
increase 1
liberalize 1
spread 6
stretch 2
wideness
breadth 1
width 1
widening
extension 1
flare 6
spread 8
widen the gap
gain 5
wide of the mark°
at **wide 4**
misguided
mistaken 1
out 12
wide 5
wrong 2
wide open
open 9
wide-ranging
ample 2
broad 6
encyclopedic
epidemic 1
expansive 3
extensive 1
global
sweeping 1
universal 2
wide 2
widespread
catholic
current 2
diffuse 1
epidemic 1
expansive 3
extensive 1
general 1
pervasive
prevail
prevalent
rampant 2
sweeping 1
universal 1
wide 2, 3
widget
contraption
device 1
gadget
gimmick 2
widow's weeds
mourning 3
width°
breadth 1
extension 2
measure 1
measurement 2
wield°
command 2
exercise 1
exert 1
finger 10
flourish 2
govern 1
handle 7
work 10, 15
wield the sceptre
govern 1
reign 2
rule 5
wife°
mate 2
partner 2
woman 2
wife-to-be
fiancée
wig
lecture 4
rebuke 1
reprimand 2

wigging
lecture 2
rebuke 2
reprimand 1
tongue-lashing
wiggle
crawl 1
creep 1
fidget 1
get 15
jerk 2
jiggle 1, 2
shake 2, 8
struggle 3
twiddle 1
twist 3
wave 4
wriggle 1, 3, 4
wiggling
wriggle 4
wigwag
swing 1, 3
wave 4
wigwagging
swing 3
wild°
abandoned 2
bad 10
berserk
boisterous
chaotic 2
crazy 5
daredevil 2
delirious 1, 2
desert[1] 2
desperate 2
disorderly 2
distraught
emotional 4
empty 3
epicurean 1
extravagant 2
extreme 5
fast[1] 2
fierce 1, 2
flighty 1
foolhardy
foolish 3
frantic
furious 2
hare-brained 1
hectic
hotheaded
hysterical 1
impractical 1
improbable
impulsive
inarticulate 1
incoherent
insane 2
irresponsible
lewd
love 7, 8
mad 2, 3, 6
maniacal 2
marvellous
obstreperous
pell-mell 2
profligate 1
promiscuous 2
quixotic
rabid 1
rampage 2
rampant 1, 2
rash[1]
reckless
ridiculous
riotous 1, 2
rogue 2
romantic 2
runaway 2
savage 1, 3
senseless 3
shameless
stormy 1, 2
sweet 8
tempestuous
tumultuous
uncivilized 1
uncontrolled
undisciplined
ungovernable
uninhibited
untamed
uproarious 1

wild (*cont.*)
vicious 3
violent 1
wanton 1
way-out 1
windy 1
zany 1
-wilds°
at **wild 10**
waste 8
wilderness
country 3
desert[1] 1
solitude 2
waste 8
wild 10
wildly
fast[1] 9
head 8
mad 5
madly 1,3,4
pell-mell 1
vengeance 2a
wild man
savage 4
wildness
nature 3
violence 2
wild party
spree
wild woman
savage 4
wile°
artifice 2
deceit 2
deception 2
finesse 2
fraud 2
gimmick 1
machination
manoeuvre 1
ruse
scheme 3
stall[2] 2
stratagem
trap 2
trick 1
-wiles°
at **wile**
art 6
wilful°
conscious 2
cool 3
deliberate 1
disobedient 2
intentional
obstinate
overbearing
perverse 3
premeditated
recalcitrant
resistant 2
rigid 4
self-willed
strong 16
studied
undisciplined
unruly
voluntary 2
wanton 3
wilfully
deliberately
purpose 4a
wilfulness
obstinacy
wiliness
art 5
artifice 1
craft 2
will°
backbone 3
bequeath
determination 1
device 4
devise 2
discretion 2
donate
hand 15a
heart 2
leave[1] 6
mind 7
nerve 1
pass 18b
please 2

will (*cont.*)
purpose 2
self-control 1
spirit 2,5
volition
-at will°
at **will 4**
free 12
willed
hereditary 2
willful
wilful 1
willfully
deliberately
willies
dread 2
jitters
nerve 4
willing°
agreeable 2
disposed
dutiful
game 7
glad 2
inclined 1
mood 2
obliging
open 11
prepared 3
ready 2
receptive 1
tractable 1
voluntary 1
willingly°
freely 2
gladly
happily 3
readily 1
soon 4
voluntarily
willingness
devotion 3
readiness 1
williwaw
storm 1
will-o'-the-wisp
illusion 2
willowy°
flexible 1
slender 1
supple 2
will-power
backbone 3
determination 1
fortitude
gut 3b
self-control 1
spirit 2,5
strength 2
will 1
willy-nilly°
necessarily
willy-willy
whirlwind 1
wilt°
die 2
droop 1,2
dry 5
fade 2
sag 2
shrivel
wilted
stale 1
wizened
wilting
sweltering
wily°
artful 1
astute 1
clever 2
crafty
deceitful
designing
devious 1
disingenuous
foxy 1
furtive 2
insincere
knowing 1
Machiavellian
politic 1
scheming
serpentine 1

wily (*cont.*)
shifty
shrewd
sly 1
subtle 3
tricky 1
wimp
drip 3
weakling
wet 6
wimpish
meek 2
spineless 3
tame 3
win°
achieve 2
acquire
captivate
carry 6,10a
come 9b,13a
conquer 2,3
conquest 2
earn 1
find 5
first 7
gain 1
get 3
land 7
make 7,14,32a
notch 4
overcome 1
poll 4
possess 5
possession 4
prevail 1
procure 1
purchase 2
score 13
secure 5
snatch 1
succeed 3
take 1
triumph 3
upset 4
win back
recover 1
wince
blink 3
cringe 1
dread 1
flinch
jump 2
recoil 1
shrink 2
start 5
winch
hoist 1,2
wind°
air 2
blast 1
breeze 1
coil 1
draught 1
gust 1
hot air
loop 2
meander 1
pipe 3
puff 1
roll 9
snake 4
swirl 2
thread 4
turn 11
twine 2
twirl 1
twist 4
wander 2
whip 5
wrap 1
-in the wind
prospect 4
-into the wind
wind[1] 10
-off the wind
wind[1] 4
-to the wind
wind[1] 10
windbag
braggart
show-off
talker 2

wind-blown
unkempt
wild 8
wind down
diminish 3
end 9
taper 2
terminate
wane 1
winded
breathless 1
short-winded
windfall°
find 10
fluke
godsend
killing 2
prize[1] 2
windiness
rhetoric 2
wind[1] 3
winding
coil 2
indirect 1
intricate 1
labyrinthine
meander 2
meandering
serpentine 2
tortuous 1
twirl 3
whipping 2
-windings
coil 2
meander 2
winding down
wane 3,4
winding-sheet
shroud 2
winding up
finish 9
termination 1
wind instrument
pipe 3
wind-jammer
ship 1
windlass
roller 1
windless
calm 3
window
glass 3
light[1] 6
-out of the window
lost 2
window-blind
shade 5
window-card
card 8
window-dressing
ostentation
windowless
solid 10
window-pane
glass 3
light[1] 6
pane
wind-storm
gale 1
hurricane
storm 1
tempest 1
windswept
bleak 3
windy 1
wind up
accomplish
clinch 1
close 3,5
dissolve 3
end 9
excite 1
finish 5
pack 6
pep 2
phase 6
roll 9
terminate
wind[2] 2,3a

wind up (*cont.*)
wrap 3a
wind-up
completion 2
end 2
finish 9
pay-off 2
termination 1
windward
wind[1] 10
windy°
breezy 1
dirty 4
discursive
foul 8
pompous 2
ponderous 2
repetitious
rhetorical 3
voluble
wordy
wine and dine
banquet 2
feast 4,5
feed 1
fête 2
treat 4
wine bar
bar 6
winebibber
alcoholic 2
drunk 3
wine steward
servant 1
waiter
wing
addition 4
cohort 1
extension 3
fly 1
front 6
maim
movement 5
wound 3
-wings
extremity 2
wingding
fête 1
party 1
rave 5
winged
speedy 3
wing-footed
speedy 3
winging
flight[1] 1
wing it
improvise 1
play 12
wink
blink 1,5
eye 5
glisten
second[2]
signal 4
sparkle 1
twinkle 1
-in a wink
fast[1] 6
hastily 1
immediately 1
once 6a
post-haste
rapidly 2
soon 2
wink at
blink 4
disregard 1
excuse 1
ignore 1
overlook 2
winking
twinkle 2
winkle (out)
dig 6
extract 3
tease 2
wink of an eye
minute[1] 1
moment 1
second[2]
swiftly
twinkling 1

winner°
champion 1
hit 11
knockout 2
victor
winning°
ahead 2
amiable
attractive
catching 2
delightful 2
desirable 2
endearing
engaging
fetching
front 8
likeable
magnetic
persuasive
pleasant 2
prepossessing
prize[1] 5
seductive
smooth 6
successful 4
sweet 4
taking
triumphant
victory
-winnings
gain 8
prize[1] 2
winnow
derive 1
filter 2
investigate
sift 1
strain[1] 5
wino
alcoholic 2
drunk 3
win over°
at **win 3**
beat 2
best 11
bring 14b
convince
disarm 2
get 46b
overcome 1
persuade 2
prevail 3
rout 2
sell 5
slaughter 4
sway 2
winsome
amiable
comely
delightful 2
desirable 2
enchanting
endearing
engaging
fetching
inviting
likeable
lovable
magnetic
nice 1
prepossessing
pretty 1
taking
tempting 1
winning 1
wintry°
biting
bitter 6
chill 4
cold 1
freezing
frigid 1
icy 1
piercing 3
polar 1
wipe°
rub 1,9
smear 1
wiped out
exhausted 1
impoverished 1
insolvent
poor 1
prostrate 5

wiped out (*cont.*)
tired 1
wipe off°
at wipe 1
remove 3
wipe off the face of the earth
wipe 3
wipe out°
at wipe 1
blot 4b
bump 5
cross 3
delete
destroy 1
devour 2
erase 1
execute 3
exterminate
extinguish 2
mow 2
murder 3
obliterate 1, 2
remove 3, 4
rout 2
ruin 7
strike 5
sweep 2
take 15
wash 4
waste 11
wipe the floor with
rout 2
whip 2
wipe up°
at wipe 1
wiping out
destruction 1, 2
murder 2
ruin 1
wire
cable 1, 2, 3
flex 1
lead 17
line[1] 13
press 10a
stick[1] 4
telegram
terminal 5
transmit 1
wireless
radio 1
wirepuller
politician
wirepulling
politics 2
wire-tap
tap[2] 3, 7
wiry°
kinky 3
lean[1] 1
sinewy
spare 3
strong 1
tough 2
wisdom°
brain 1
depth 3
discretion 1
experience 3
foresight 1
intelligence 1
judgement 1
learning
logic 2
lore 1
mind 1
profundity 2
propriety 1
prudence 1
rhyme 2
sense 2
understanding 2, 5
wit 1
wise°
acute 5
advisable
astute 2
aware 1
clever 3
deep 3
diplomatic
expedient 2
wise (*cont.*)
experienced 1
far-sighted 1
foxy 1
grey 4
hip
informed 2
insolent
intelligent
judicious
keen[1] 6
knowing 2
knowledgeable 2
logical 2
mode[1] 1
politic 2
profound 2
provident 1
prudent 1
rational 2
reasonable 1
ripe 2
sage 1
sensible 1, 4
shrewd
sound[2] 4
well-advised
well-informed
–in this wise
thus 1
wiseacre
wise guy
wise-ass(ed)
pert 1
wisecrack°
dig 8
gag[2] 1
gibe 2
joke 1, 4
quip 1, 2
squelch 2
–wisecracks
humour 2
wise guy°
operator 3
wise-guy
pert 1
wise man
intellectual 4
sage 2
thinker
wisenheimer
wise guy
wiser
better[1] 3
wise to°
at wise 5
hip
privy 2
see 14a
sensible 4
twig[2]
wise up°
at wise 6
tumble 3
wish°
aim 2
ambition 3
aspiration
aspire
bear 7
burn 3
desire 4
discretion 2
expect 3
expectation 3
fancy 7
hope 1, 4
itch 2
like[2] 2
long[2]
longing
mean[1] 1
mind 7
please 2
pleasure 2
want 1, 4
will 1, 5
yearn
–as one wishes
will 4
–wishes
will 2
wishbone
talisman
wish for
desire 1
fancy 11
miss[1] 2
pant 2
thirst 2
want 1
wishful
desirous
visionary 2
wishing
desperate 3
eagerness 2
wishy-washy°
easygoing
equivocal 1
feeble 2
fickle
indecisive 1
indefinite 5
irresolute
lacklustre
limp[2] 3
tame 4
tasteless 2
vague 5
vapid
watery 1
weak 3
wisp°
wisp-like
insubstantial 1
wispy
fluffy 1
insubstantial 1
thin 1
wistful°
homesick
pensive
thoughtful 2
wit°
ability 2
brain 1
brilliance 2
capacity 2
comedian
genius 2
gumption 1
head 4
humour 1, 2
imagination 2
intelligence 1
joker 1
judgement 1
mentality 1
mind 1
penetration 2
salt 3
sense 2
wag[2]
–at one's wits' end
desperate 6
distraught
frantic
–to wit
like[1] 6
namely
–wits
mind 1
witch°
bag 4
devil 2
fury 3
hag
jade 2
magician 1
prophet
ruin 5
shrew
sorcerer
witchcraft
enchantment 1
fascination
glamour
magic 1, 3
occult 3
sorcery
spell[2] 1
witch-doctor
sorcerer
witchery
magic 3
spell[2] 1
with
about 10
beside 1
plus 1
–be with
join 3
take 10
withal
addition 6
nevertheless
withdraw°
absent 3
back 3
cancel 1
clear 30
climb 5b
deduct
depart 1
deprive
drain 4
draw 8, 10, 12b
drop 13
evacuate 2
exit 3
extract 1
fall 8
flight[3] 3
flinch
go 2, 23
leave[1] 1
lift 4
milk
phase 6
pluck 2
pull 3, 7, 8a, 8b, 14a, 14b, 14d
quit 2
recall 2, 3
recant
recede 1
retire 1
retract 1, 2
retreat 4
revoke
secede
shrink 2
stand 6
step 17c
take 30
tap[2] 5
turn 15a
vacate 1
vitiate 3
way 11b
withdrawal
cancellation 1
deduction 1
denial 2
drain 2
exit 2
extraction 1
recall 5, 6
retreat 1, 2
secession
withdrawing
outgoing 1
shy 1
withdrawn°
absent-minded
aloof 2
distant 3
estranged
lonely 3
neutral 1
private 4
quiet 3
remote 7
reserved
self-contained 2
separate 7
sheepish 1
shy 1
solitary 1
standoffish
unapproachable 1
unsocial
withe
twig[1]
wither
blight 3
decay 1b
wither (*cont.*)
die 2
droop 2
dry 5
fade 2
parch
rot 2
shrink 1
shrivel
waste 2
wilt 1, 2
withered
decrepit 2
emaciated
haggard
stale 1
thin 1
wizened
withering°
burning 4
decadent 1
keen[1] 2
scathing
vituperative
withershins
backwards 1
withhold°
deny 2
deprive
hold 14b
keep 14a
refuse[1] 2
reserve 1
stifle 2
stint 4
suppress 1
suspend 1
withholding
reservation 1
suppression
within
inside 8
with it
elegant 2
fashionable
hip
minute[1] 3
modern
now 5
sophisticated 1
stylish
swinging
trendy 1
worldly 2
without
destitute 2
empty 7
failing 2
free 11
lack 2
outwards
void 3
withstand°
accept 4
bear 10a
combat 6
cope 2
defy 2
endure 2
feel 5
fight 2
hold 18b
oppose 1
repel 1
resist 1
stand 3, 12a, 12b
stem[2] 2
suffer 2
support 5
sustain 3
take 6, 33a
undergo
weather 3
withy
twig[1]
witless
daft 1
feeble-minded
foolish 2
hare-brained 2
mindless 1
senseless 3
simple 4
stupid 1
witless (*cont.*)
unthinking 1
witlessness
simplicity 4
stupidity 1
witling
wise guy
witness°
bystander
evidence 4
eyewitness
look 1
monument 2
observer
onlooker
see 1
sign 7
spectator
view 8
witter
babble 1
chat 1, 2
chatter 1
drivel 2
gab 1
go 32f
gush 2
hold 16a
jabber 1
palaver 2, 4
patter[2] 3
prattle 1
ramble 3
rattle 6
spout 2
talk 3
tattle 2
waffle 1
yap 2
wittering
palaver 2
witticism°
epigram 1
gag[2] 1
joke 1
maxim
pun
quip 1
wisecrack 1
–witticisms
humour 2
wittiness
sparkle 4
wittingly
deliberately
purpose 4a
witty°
bright 6
comic 1
dry 3
entertaining
epigrammatic
funny 1
humorous
light[2] 11
ludicrous
smart 4
wry 2
wive
wed 1
wiz
virtuoso 1
wizard
dab hand
expert 1, 2
first-rate
magician 1, 2
master 2
oracle 1
prodigy 1
professional 3
proficient
sorcerer
talented
virtuoso 1
wizardry
enchantment 1
magic 1, 3
sorcery
wizen
shrivel
wizened°
emaciated

wobble
quiver 1
rock[2] 2
shake 1,8
stagger 1
swing 1,3
teeter
totter
waddle
wag[1] 1,2
wriggle 1
wobbling
infirm 2
poised 3
rocky[2]
shake 8
shaky 2
swing 3
wobbly
groggy
infirm 2
insecure 3
rage 4
rickety
rocky[2]
shaky 1,2
unbalanced 1
unsound 1
wodge
slab
woe°
affliction 1
agony
anguish 2
blight 2
care 1
desolation 2
distress 1
evil 7
gloom 2
grief 1
hurt 6
ill 8
melancholy 2
misery 1,3
mourning 2
pain 2
prostration 3
regret 2
remorse
scourge 1
sorrow 1
torment 3
trial 4
trouble 5
woebegone°
broken-hearted
dejected
desolate 3
dismal
doleful
forlorn 1
glum
heartbroken
hopeless 3
hurt 7
joyless 1
melancholy 1
miserable 1
mournful 1
sad 1
sorrowful 1
unfortunate 2
wistful 1
wretched 2
woeful
broken-hearted
deplorable 1
dismal
doleful
evil 4
forlorn 1
funereal
joyless 1
melancholy 1
miserable 1
pathetic 1
piteous
poignant 1
regrettable
remorseful
sinking 2
sorrowful 1
wistful 1
woebegone
woeful (*cont.*)
wretched 2
woefully
painfully
woefulness
distress 1
ill 8
melancholy 2
mourning 2
prostration 3
wold
plain 6
wolf
charmer
devour 1
flirt 3
gorge 3
gulp 1
libertine 1
overeat
philanderer
playboy
polish 3c
rake[2]
roué
scoff[2] 1
take 13
wolfish
rapacious
ravenous 2
wolflike
rapacious
woman°
broad 9
date 3
friend 3
girl 1
human 4
love 3
mortal 6
one 4
person 1
soul 2
steady 9
woman-hater
misanthrope
womanhood
majority 2
woman in the street
mass 6
people 3
plebeian 3
public 8
punter 2
unwashed 2
womanish
effeminate
feminine 2
womanize
play 9b
womanizer
libertine 1
philanderer
playboy
rake[2]
roué
womanlike
feminine 1
womanly
effeminate
feminine 1
woman of easy virtue
tart[2] 2
woman of God
priest
woman of ill repute
prostitute 1
slattern
tart[2] 2
woman of letters
scholar 1
woman of the cloth
minister 1
priest
woman on the Clapham omnibus
mass 6
woman on the Clapham omnibus (*cont.*)
people 3
plebeian 3
wonder°
admiration
admire 1
amazement
astonishment
gaze 1
legend 2
marvel 1,2
pearl
phenomenon 2
prodigy 2
sight 3
spectacle 1
speculate 1
surprise 3
wonder about°
at **wonder 5**
speculate 1
wonder child
prodigy 1
wonder drug
elixir 1
wonderful
admirable
amazing
awesome
beautiful 2
colossal 2
divine 3
expert 2
exquisite 5
fabulous 2,3
fantastic 4
glorious 2
good 2
gorgeous 2
grand 5
great 12
heavenly 2
heroic 5
incredible 2
marvellous
mean[2] 6
miraculous
monumental 1
neat 5
phenomenal
prodigious 2
remarkable 2
sensational 3
stunning 2
super
superb
sweet 5
terrific 2
world 8
wonderfully
beautifully 2
perfectly 2
well[1] 2
wondering
speculation 2
wonderland
fairyland
wonderment
astonishment
wonder 2
wondrous
awesome
fabulous 2
miraculous
monumental 1
portentous 2
prodigious 2
striking
wonky
feeble 1
order 13c
play 17b
wont
custom 1
formality 1
habit 1
observance 2
practice 1
procedure
routine 1
wonted
accustomed 1
customary 2
habitual 1
regular 1
set 29
usual
won't-power
self-control 1
woo
chase 2
cultivate 4
pursue 4
romance 6
run 21
see 7
take 36
wood
clump 2
lumber 2
stand 19
thicket
timber 2
wooden 1
-woods
country 3
woodcut
engraving 1
print 2
wooded°
wooden°
awkward 2
dead 4
impersonal 2
lifeless 3
stiff 7,8
stilted
stolid
wooden-headed
thick 6
wooden 3
woodland
park 1
timber 1
woodwind
pipe 3
woody
leafy
wooded
wooden 1
wooer
suitor
wool-bearing
woolly 1
wool-gathering
absent-minded
day-dream 1
inattentive
reverie
scatterbrained
thoughtful 2
woollen
woolly 1
woolly°
focus 3
fuzzy 1,2
hairy 1
imprecise
shaggy
soft 11
wooziness
vertigo
woozy
dizzy 1
faint 2
feeble 1
giddy 1
groggy
queasy 2
stinking 3
tight 8
word°
announcement 2
assurance 1
authority 2
express 1
expression 5
gossip 2
guarantee 1
information
intelligence 2
line[1] 8,10
message 1
word (*cont.*)
news 1,2
note 2
oath 1
observation 2
phrase 4
pledge 1
promise 1
puff 3
put 4
resolution 2
say-so
score 6
shape 8
tell[1] 4
term 1
verbal 3
vow 2
warning 1
-beyond words
ineffable 2
-from the word go
completely 1
first 6,8
originally
-in a word°
at **word 8**
brief 5
briefly 1
short 14
-words°
at **word 9**
book 2
language 4
line[1] 17
lyric 4
print 3
terminology
text 1
voice 1
wordbook
dictionary
glossary
word choice
diction 1
phrase 3
style 5
wording
word for word
exactly 1
letter 4
literally 1
perfectly 3
verbatim 2
word-for-word
literal 1
precise 1
same 2
verbal 2
verbatim 1
word-group
phrase 2
wordiness
rhetoric 2
tautology
waffle 3
wording°
diction 1
expression 6
language 4
parlance
phrase 3
print 3
style 5
terminology
text 1
wordless
dumb 1
mute 1
speechless 2
wordlessly
silently
word-list
glossary
Word of God
Scripture
word of honour
assurance 1
guarantee 1
oath 1
pledge 1
promise 1
word of honour (*cont.*)
resolution 2
vow 2
word 4
word-of-mouth
oral
verbal 1
wordplay
joke 1
repartee
wit 2
wordsmith
scribe 2
writer
word to the wise
warning 1
wordy°
boring
diffuse 2
discursive
expletive 1
lengthy
ponderous 2
rambling 1
redundant 2
repetitious
rhetorical 3
talkative
voluble
windy 2
work°
act 9
activity 2
assist 3
behave
book 1
business 1
calling
career 1
cultivate 1
drudgery
duty 1
edge 6
effect 6
effort 1
employment 1
engagement 4
exert 2
exertion
exploit 2
fashion 5
ferment 1
function 1,3
go 3
industry 2
insinuate 2
job 1
labour 1,5
line[1] 7
manipulate 2
mission 1
mould[1] 4
occupation 1
office 4
operate 1
opus
peg 7
perform 2
persist 1
plod 2
post[2] 1
practice 3
preparation 4
product 2
production 2
profession 1
project 2
pursue 3
pursuit 3
retire 2
run 11
serve 2,5
service 9
shoulder 3
stew 3
strive 1
stroke 7
struggle 4
study 5
sweat 6
take 11
task 1
tease 2
till[1]

yielding (*cont.*)
soft 1
submission 1
submissive 1
supple 3
surrender 3
tractable 1
yob
barbarian 2
hoodlum
slob
yobbo
barbarian 2
hoodlum
slob
yodel
sing 1
yoke
couple 1, 3
enslave
join 1
pair 1, 2
slavery 1
team 2
twin 3
yokel
boor 1
clown 2
peasant
provincial 3
rustic 3
yore
-of yore
bygone
you don't say
indeed 3
young°
adolescent 2
boyish 1
brood 1
childlike
immature 1
issue 7
juvenile 1
litter 2
little 2
new 7
offspring
progeny
seed 3
small 1
tender[1] 3
unfledged
youth 3
young boy
youth 2
younger
junior
second[1] 5
young fellow
stripling
young gentle-man
child 2
young lady
child 2
love 3
miss[2]
teenager
young man
boy 1
child 2
fellow 4
lad
love 3
stripling
teenager
youth 2
young manhood
youth 1
young people
youth 3
youngster
adolescent 1
boy 1
child 1, 2
lad
minor 3
offspring
stripling
youth 2
-youngsters
youth 3
young 'un
stripling
young woman
child 2
lass
miss[2]
young woman-hood
youth 1
yourself
person 2
personally 1
-yourselves
person 2
personally 1
youth°
adolescent 1
boy 1
child 2
childhood
guy 1
juvenile 2
lad
minor 3
prime 4
stripling
teenager
youth custody centre
Borstal
reform school
youthful
adolescent 2
boyish 1
childlike
juvenile 1
little 2
tender[1] 3
young 1
yowl
cry 4
howl 1, 2
rave 1
roar 1, 3
scream 1, 3
sob
squawk 1, 2
whoop 1, 2
yell 1, 2
yowling
howl 2
yo-yo
jerk 5
shilly-shally
yuckiness
sentimentality
yucky°
revolting
sentimental 2
yukkiness
sentimentality
yukky
sentimental 2
yucky
yummy°
delicious 1
luscious
tasty
yuppy
ambitious 3
materialistic

Z

Z
-Z's
doze 1
nap[1] 6
rest[1] 6
retire 3
sleep 1
zaftig
full 7
zany°
clown 1
comedian
fool 2
funny 1
joker 1
ludicrous
ridiculous
wit 3
zap°
dispatch 3
hit 1
shoot 3
zeal
ambition 2
appetite 1
ardour
devotion 3
drive 8
eagerness 1
enterprise 2
enthusiasm 1
exuberance 1
fanaticism 1
fervour
fight 9
flame 2
gusto
heat 2
inclination 4
inspiration 1
intensity
passion 1
push 14
sparkle 4
spirit 2
verve
warmth 3
zealot°
crank 2
enthusiast
fan
fanatic
maniac 2
partisan 1
puritan 1
radical 4
sectarian 4
supremacist
zealotry°
passion 1
zealous
ambitious 2
ardent
crazy 4
devoted
devout 3
dynamic
zealous (*cont.*)
eager
earnest 2
emotional 1
enterprising
enthusiastic
excited 2
exuberant 1
fanatical
favourable 2
fervent 2
feverish
great 9
hard 7
hearty 3
hot 3, 4
impassioned
intense 2
intent 5
keen[1] 1
mad 6
passionate 1
sanguine
solicitous 2
strenuous 2
strong 5
voracious 2
warm 2
wholehearted
willing
zealously
hard 13
hotly
jealously
warmly 4
willingly
zealousness
gusto
heat 2
passion 1
spirit 2
vigour
zees
doze 1
nap[1] 1
rest[1] 6
retire 3
sleep 1
zenith°
acme
climax 1
extreme 8
height 2
maximum 2
peak 2
pinnacle
prime 4
summit
top 1
vertex
zephyr
air 2
breath 1
breeze 1
wind[1] 1
zero°
blank 8
cog 2
naught
nil
nobody 2
non-essential 2
nothing 2
zero in (on)°
at **zero 4**
finger 5c
focus 4
pin 4b
set 5
zest°
animation 1
appetite 1
bounce 2
dash 6
eagerness 1
enjoyment 1
enthusiasm 1
exuberance 1
fight 9
flavour 1
gusto
life 7
panache
passion 1
pep 1
punch[1] 3
relish 1
salt 2
savour 1
seasoning
spice 2
spirit 2, 3
tang 1
verve
vigour
zestful
ebullient
energetic
passionate 1
racy 1
spicy 1
zestfulness
passion 1
zest 2
zestiness
salt 2
tang 1
zesty
energetic
racy 3
spicy 1
zigzag
devious 2
indirect 1
meander 1, 2
notched
ragged 2
serrated
snake 4
stagger 3
swing 1, 3
tack 6
tortuous 1
turn 11, 27
twist 4, 7
wander 2
wave 4
weave 4
wind[2] 1
wriggle 3
-zigzags
meander 2
zigzagging
swing 3
zilch
zero 1
zillions
ocean 2
zing
energy
initiative 2
life 7
pep 1
punch[1] 3
push 14
salt 2
snap 11
sparkle 4
verve
zing (*cont.*)
vigour
vitality 1
zest 1
zingy
energetic
Zion
heaven 1
paradise 1
zip
adjust 4
bounce 2
drive 8
dynamism
eagerness 1
energy
enterprise 2
fly 9
initiative 2
nil
pep 1
punch[1] 3
push 14
race[1] 4
run 1
salt 2
scurry
seal 3
shoot 1
snap 11
sparkle 4
speed 3
spice 2
streak 5
tang 1
tear 3
verve
vitality 1
whip 3
zest 1
zipper
fly 9
zippy
energetic
vivacious
zizz
doze 1, 2
nap[1] 1, 3
repose 2
rest[1] 1
sleep 2
zone°
area 3
belt 1, 2
girth 2
limit 3
precinct 2
province 1
quarter 3
region 1
territory 1
tract[1]
ward 1
zonked
weary 1
zoo°
zooid
animal 3
zoological
animal 3
zoological gar-den
zoo 1
zoom
buzz 6
career 2
flash 5
rocket
scurry
speed 3
streak 5
sweep 3
tear 3
whip 3